The Complete Internal Revenue Code

For customer service or to obtain the name
and telephone number of your local account representative,
please call 1-800-431-9025.

Additional copies of this product are available, at a fee.
Please call 1-800-950-1216 or visit our Product Store at
http://ria.thomson.com to order.

RIA

© 2011, 2010, 2009, 2008, 2007, 2006, 2005, 2004, 2003, 2002, 2001, 2000, 1999, 1998, 1997, 1996, 1995, 1994, 1993, 1992, 1991, 1990, 1989, 1988, 1987, 1986, 1985, 1984, 1983, 1982, 1981, 1980, 1979, 1978, 1977, 1976, 1975, 1974, 1973, 1972, 1971, 1970

Thomson Reuters/RIA
195 Broadway, New York, NY 10007

Copyright is not claimed in any material secured from
official U.S. Government sources.

Any gaps in the numbering of pages are intentional and are intended to allow for editorial growth and expansion.

Internal Revenue Code
as amended through June 30, 2011

	Page
Index to Code	101
Amending Acts Table	401
Table of Sections	501
Income tax	1,001
Estate tax	2,964
Gift tax	3,024
Employment taxes	3,063
Excise taxes	3,178
Alcohol, tobacco, etc., taxes	3,383
Procedure and administration	3,480

Internal Revenue Code
as amended through June 30, 2011

	Page
Index to Code	101
Amending Acts Table	401
Table of Sections	501
Income tax	1,001
Estate tax	2,961
Gift tax	3,024
Employment taxes	3,063
Excise taxes	3,178
Alcohol, tobacco, etc. taxes	3,383
Procedure and administration	3,480

Index to Internal Revenue Code

CODE SEC.

A

Abandoned spouse 7703
. child support obligations, collection of 6305
Abatements ...... 6404; 7486 (See also Refunds and credits)
. armed forces members 692
. astronauts 692
. claims for....................................... 6403
. deficiency disallowed 7486
. distilled spirits tax 5008; 5064
. erroneous written advice by IRS 6404
. estate tax claim 6404
. first-tier taxes 4962
. 501(c)(3) organizations 4962
. insolvent banks 7507
. jeopardy assessment 6861
. mathematical and clerical errors as basis 6213; 6404
. overpayments 6401
. private foundations .... 507; 4961 et seq.
. second-tier taxes 4961
. small balances 6404
Abroad, citizens living (See Income earned abroad)
Abusive tax shelters
. injunctions against promotion 7408
. list of investors 6112; 6709
. penalties for promotion 6700; 6703; 7422
. promotion of
. . injunctions against 7408
. . list of investors 6112; 6709
. . failure to maintain 6708
. . penalties 6700; 6703
. . refunds, suit for 7422
Abusive transactions
. bonds, refunding 149
Academy zone bonds (See Qualified zone academy bonds)
Accelerated cost recovery system (ACRS) .... 168 (See also Depreciation)
. additions or improvements to property .... 168(i)(6)
. agricultural structure which include work space
 .... 168(i)(13)(B)(iii)
. Alaska natural gas pipeline .... 168(i)(16)
. alternate depreciation system for certain property
. . automobiles .... 168(g)(3)(D)
. . certain real property .... 168(g)(3)(E)
. . class life determination .... 168(g)(3)
. . classes, property assigned to .... 168(g)(3)(B)
. . election to use .... 168(g)(7)
. . Executive order, imported property covered by
 .... 168(g)(1)(D)
. . . discriminatory act, countries maintaining trade restrictions or engaging in .... 168(g)(6)(A)
. . . imported property defined .... 168(g)(6)(B)
. . purpose of using alternative system .... 168(g)(2)
. . qualified technology equipment .... 168(g)(3)(C)
. . tangible property used outside U.S. .... 168(g)(1)(A)

CODE SEC.

Accelerated cost recovery system (ACRS)—Cont'd
. *alternate depreciation system for certain property — Cont'd*
. . *tangible property used outside U.S.— Cont'd*
. . . aircraft .... 168(g)(4)(A)
. . . cable, domestic corporations .... 168(g)(4)(I)
. . . communication satellite .... 168(g)(4)(H)
. . . container used in transportation .... 168(g)(4)(E)
. . . Continental Shelf, property used to transport, explore, or develop from the .... 168(g)(4)(F)
. . . energy for U.S. international property used to generate
 .... 168(g)(4)(K)
. . . motor vehicles .... 168(g)(4)(D)
. . . ocean waters, property used to transport, explore, or develop from the .... 168(g)(4)(J)
. . . possession of U.S., property used in a ...... 168(g)(4)(G)
. . . rolling stock .... 168(g)(4)(B)
. . . satellite .... 168(g)(4)(L)
. . . vessels documented under U.S. laws ...... 168(g)(4)(C)
. . tax-exempt bond financed property .... 168(g)(1)(C)
. . . allocation of bond proceeds .... 168(g)(5)(B)
. . . defined .... 168(g)(5)(A)
. . . qualified residential rental property .... 168(g)(5)(C)
. . tax-exempt entity
. . . defined .... 168(h)(2)(A)
. . . foreign person, property subject to U.S. tax and used
 .... 168(h)(2)(B)
. . . foreign person or entity .... 168(h)(2)(C)
. . . tax-exempt property subject to lease ...... 168(g)(3)(A)
. . . tax-exempt use property .... 168(g)(1)(B)
. . . defined .... 168(h)(1)(A)
. . . nonresidential real property factor .... 168(h)(1)(E)
. . . nonresidential use property .... 168(h)(1)(B)
. . . short-term lease exception .... 168(h)(1)(C)
. . . unrelated trade or business income as factor
 .... 168(h)(1)(D)
. alternative minimum tax and research credit in lieu of bonus depreciation, election .... 168(k)(4)(A)
. . allocation of bonus depreciation amounts .... 168(k)(4)(E)
. . bonus depreciation amount .... 168(k)(4)(C)
. . eligible qualified property .... 168(k)(4)(D)
. . limitations, increase in .... 168(k)(4)(B)
. . partnerships .... 168(k)(4)(G)(ii)
. . passenger aircraft .... 168(k)(4)(G)(iii)
. applicable convention .... 168(d)
. . half-year convention .... 168(d)
. . . defined .... 168(d)(4)
. . mid-month convention .... 168(d)(4)(B)
. . mid-quarter convention .... 168(d)(4)(C)
. . property place in service during last 3 month of taxable year
 .... 168(d)(3)
. . real property .... 168(d)(2)
. applicable depreciation method
. . defined .... 168(b)(1)
. . election of .... 168(b)(5)
. . 150% declining balance method .... 168(b)(2)
. . salvage value treatment .... 168(b)(4)
. . straight line method .... 168(b)(3)

101

Accelerated — Index to Code

CODE SEC.

Accelerated cost recovery system (ACRS)—Cont'd
. applicable recovery period, table .... 168(c)
. cellulose biomass ethanol plant property
.. additional allowance .... 168(l)(1)
.. alternative depreciation property .... 168(l)(4)(B)
.. alternative minimum tax, allowance against .... 168(l)(6)
.. bonus depreciation property .... 168(l)(4)(A)
.. cellulose biomass ethanol defined .... 168(l)(3)
.. defined .... 168(l)(2)
.. double benefit denial .... 168(l)(8)
.. election out .... 168(l)(4)(D)
.. recapture .... 168(l)(7)
.. special rules .... 168(l)(5)
.. tax-exempt bond-financed property .... 168(l)(4)(C)
. class life defined .... 168(i)(1)
. classification of property .... 168(e)(1)
.. fifteen-year property .... 168(e)(3)(E)
.. five-year property .... 168(e)(3)(B)
.. qualified leasehold improvement property .... 168(e)(6)
.. qualified restaurant property .... 168(e)(7)
.. race horse .... 168(e)(3)
.. railroad grading or tunnel bore defined .... 168(e)(4)
.. rent-to-own property .... 168(e)(3)
.. residential rental or nonresidential rental property .. 168(e)(2)
.. seven-year property .... 168(e)(3)(C)
.. ten-year property .... 168(e)(3)(D)
.. three-year property .... 168(e)(3)
.. twenty-year property .... 168(e)(3)(F)
.. water utility property defined .... 168(e)(5)
. consumer property .... 168(i)(14)(C)
. December 31, 2007 and before January 1, 2013, allowance for property acquired after
.. additional allowance .... 168(k)(1)
.. adjusted basis of qualified property, reduction of .... 168(k)(1)(B)
.. alternate depreciation property .... 168(k)(2)(D)
.. bonus depreciation
... election to accelerate the AMT and research credits in lieu of .... 168(k)(4)
.. depreciation deduction under 167(a) .... 168(k)(1)(A)
.. qualified leasehold improvement property .... 168(k)(3)
.. Qualified New York Liberty Zone property .... 168(k)(2)(D)(ii)
.. qualified property defined .... 168(k)(2)(A)
.. sale-leasebacks .... 168(k)(2)(E)(ii)
.. Sec. 280F, coordination with .... 168(k)(2)(F)
.. self-constructed property .... 168(k)(2)(E)(i)
.. syndication .... 168(k)(2)(E)(iii)
.. users and related parties .... 168(k)(2)(E)(iv)
. 50% bonus depreciation 168
. general asset accounts .... 168(i)(4)
. Indian reservation, property on .... 168(j)(1)
.. alternative depreciation property .... 168(j)(4)(B)
.. applicable recovery period for .... 168(j)(2)
.. December 31, 2011, property placed in service after .... 168(j)(8)
.. deductions allowed in computing minimum tax ..... 168(j)(3)
.. Indian reservation defined .... 168(j)(6)
.. nonrevenue laws, coordination with .... 168(j)(7)
.. qualified Indian reservation property defined .... 168(j)(4)(A)
.. real estate rentals .... 168(j)(5)

CODE SEC.

Accelerated cost recovery system (ACRS)—Cont'd
. *Indian reservation, property on—Cont'd*
.. reservation infrastructure investment .... 168(j)(4)(C)
. intangible drilling and development costs 57
. lease term defined .... 168(i)(3)(A)
. leasehold improvements, treatment of certain .... 168(i)(8)
. motorsport entertainment complex defined .... 168(i)(15)
. natural gas gathering line .... 168(i)(17)
. non applicable property
.. churning transactions, property placed in service in .... 168(f)(5)
.. films .... 168(f)(3)
.. methods of depreciation, certain .... 168(f)(1)
.. public utility property, certain .... 168(f)(2)
.. sound recordings .... 168(f)(4)
.. video tape .... 168(f)(3)
. normalization rules .... 168(i)(9)
. 150% declining balance method 168
. partnership, property owned by
.. non-tax exempt use .... 168(h)(6)(A)(i)
.. pass-thru entities rule, other .... 168(h)(6)(E)
.. proportional share, determination of .... 168(h)(6)(C)
.. qualified allocation defined .... 168(h)(6)(B)
.. regulations .... 168(h)(8)
.. regulations on unified allocations .... 168(h)(6)(G)
.. taxable entities, treatment of .... 168(h)(6)(F)
.. tax-exempt controlled entity defined .... 168(h)(6)(F)(iii)
.. tiered entities rule .... 168(h)(6)(E)
.. unrelated trade or business, determination of use in .... 168(h)(6)(D)
. partnership, tax-exempt use of property leased to
.. foreign entities, presumption with respect to ..... 168(h)(5)(C)
.. lease defined .... 168(h)(8)
.. partner's proportionate share .... 168(h)(5)
.. pass-thru entities rule, other .... 168(h)(5)(B)
.. tiered entities rule, other .... 168(h)(5)(B)
. pollution control facilities 291
. poultry defined as livestock .... 168(i)(13)(B)(iv)
. pre-1987 property 57
. public utility property defined .... 168(i)(10)
. qualified rent-to-own property .... 168(i)(14)(A)
. qualified restaurant property .... 168(e)(7)
. qualified retail improvement property .... 168(e)(8)
. qualified technology equipment
.. computer or peripheral equipment defined .... 168(i)(2)(B)
.. defined .... 168(i)(2)
.. high technology equipment, 5 year or less lease for .... 168(h)(3)(A)
.. high technology equipment defined .... 168(h)(3)(B)(i)
.. high technology medical equipment .... 168(i)(2)(C)
.. leaseback during first 3 month of use .... 168(h)(3)(B)(ii)
. regulations for determination of deduction .... 168(i)(5)
. related entities .... 168(h)(4)
. rent-to-own contract .... 168(i)(14)(D)
. rent-to-own dealer .... 168(i)(14)(B)
. research and experimentation defined .... 168(i)(11)
. Sec. 1245 property defined .... 168(i)(12)
. Sec. 1250 property defined .... 168(i)(12)
. Sept. 10, 2001 before Jan. 1, 2005, special allowance for property acquired after 168

Index to Code — Accounting

CODE SEC.

Accelerated cost recovery system (ACRS)—Cont'd
- single purpose agricultural or horticultural structure .... 168(i)(13)(A)
- single purpose horticultural structure .... 168(i)(13)(B)(ii)
- single purpose livestock structure .... 168(i)(13)(B)(i)
- straight-line recovery method
 - . tax preference items 57
- 3-year property 168
- transferees, treatment of certain .... 168(i)(7)
- 20-year property 168

Accelerated death benefit riders
- life insurance, treatment as 818

Acceleration of tax rate
- 10% income tax rate for 2001, acceleration of 6428

Access for disabled individuals, credit for providing (See Disabled access credit)

Accessories (See Parts and accessories)

Accident and health plans 105
- annuity contracts combined with 848
- cafeteria plans 125
- continuation coverage, group health plan (See Group health plans)
- credits against tax
 - . premium assistance 36B
 - . . definitions and rules concerning 36B
- employer contributions
 - . amounts attributable to 105
 - . employee's gross income, exclusion from 106
 - . large group plans, nonconforming 5000
- government plans, special rules for
 - . description, plan .... 105(j)(2)
 - . exclusions of amounts paid directly or indirectly to taxpayers .... 105(j)(1)
- high deductible health plans 220
- Indian tribal government, treatment as state 7871
- injuries and sickness, compensation for 104
- large group, excise tax on nonconforming plan 5000
- long-term care insurance (See Long-term care insurance)
- medical care, amounts expended for 105
- minimum essential coverage (See Health insurance coverage subhead monthly health coverage after 2013)
- premium assistance credits
 - . applicable taxpayer defined .... 36B(c)(1)
 - . coverage amount defined .... 36B(c)(2)
 - . excess advance payments .... 36B(f)(2)
 - . exchange information .... 36B(f)(3)
 - . family size defined .... 36B(d)(1)
 - . grandfathered health plan defined .... 36B(c)(3)(B)
 - . household income defined .... 36B(d)(2)
 - . individual not lawfully present .... 36B(e)(1)
 - . information requirements .... 36B(f)(3)
 - . lawful presents .... 36B(e)(2)
 - . pediatric dental coverage .... 36B(b)(3)(e)
 - . poverty line defined .... 36B(d)(3)
 - . premium assistance credit amount
  - . . additional benefits .... 36B(b)(3)(D)
  - . . adjusted monthly premiums .... 36B(b)(3)(C)
  - . . applicable percentage .... 36B(b)(3)(A)
  - . . applicable second lowest cost silver plan ..... 36B(b)(3)(B)

CODE SEC.

Accident and health plans—Cont'd
- . premium assistance credits —Cont'd
 - . . premium assistance credit amount —Cont'd
  - . . . defined .... 36B(b)(1)
  - . . . determination of .... 36B(b)(2)
  - . . qualified health plan defined .... 36B(c)(3)(A)
  - . . reconciliation of credit and advance credit .... 36B(f)(1)
  - . . regulations, prescription of .... 36B(g)
  - . . Secretarial authority .... 36B(e)(3)
- qualifying organizations 833
- retired employees
 - . medical benefits 401
 - . transfer of excess pension assets 420
- S corporation stockholders 162
- self-employed individuals 162
- . reimbursements 3401
- single-employer defined benefit pension plan funds transferred to .... 430(l)

Account numbers (See Identification numbers)

Accounting for collected taxes 7512

Accounting methods .... 446 et seq.
- accrual 446
- adjustments .... 481 et seq.
- allocations
 - . income and deductions among taxpayers 482
 - . new accounting method, under 481
 - . 3-year 481
- deferred payment sales, interest on 483
- interest, deferred payment sales 483
- limitation on tax substantial adjustments 481
- at risk limitations 465
- bankruptcy 1398
- banks, reserve for bad debts 585; 593
- books and records 446
- carryovers, acquiring corporations 381
- cash basis
 - . election, imputed interest 1274A
 - . limitation 448
- cash receipts and disbursements 446
- change in 446
 - . adjustments .... 481 et seq.
 - . computation of tax 418
 - . failure to request change 446
 - . functional currency change treated as 985
- collected taxes 7512
- completed contract method of accounting
 - . earnings and profits of corporation 312
- crop insurance proceeds 451
- dealers in personal property 453
- death of taxpayer 451
- deferred payment sales, imputed interest 1274A
- discount bonds and notes 454
- employee tips 451
- exceptions 446
- exempt organization, deferred compensation plans 457
- failure to request change 446
- farming corporations 447
- farming syndicates 464
- foreign tax credit 905

103

Accounting | Index to Code

	CODE SEC.
Accounting methods—Cont'd	
. frozen deposits	451
. installment method	453; 453B
. installment sales	453 et seq.
. inventories	471 et seq.
. life insurance companies	811
. . contiguous country branches	814
. . variable contracts	817
. LIFO inventories	472
. long-term contracts	460
. magazines, returned	458
. manufacturers excise taxes, like articles	6416
. membership dues income	456
. mine site reclamation and closing expenses	468
. more than one business	446
. nuclear power decommissioning costs	468A
. obligations issued at discount	454
. paperbacks, returned	458
. percentage of completion method	460
. permissible	446
. prepaid dues income	456
. prepaid subscription income	455
. public utilities	451
. rental agreements	467
. returned merchandise	458
. services, use of	467
. several businesses	446
. solid waste disposal site reclamation and closing expenses	468
. sound recording, returned	458
. state or local government deferred compensation plans	457
. 10% method	460
. time to report income	451 et seq.
. tips	451
Accounting periods	441 et seq.
. adjustment in deduction for personal exemption	443
. annual	441
. change	443
. insurance companies	843
. books and records	441
. calendar year (See Calendar year)	
. change in	442; 443
. . accumulated earnings tax	536
. . 52-53-week year	441
. . foreign personal holding companies	557
. . partner and partnership	706
. . personal holding company tax	546
. . REITs	857; 859
. . returns	6012
. collected taxes	7512
. computation of taxable income	441
. 52-53-week year	441
. fiscal year (See Fiscal year)	
. insurance companies	843
. partners and partnerships	444; 706; 7519
. personal service corporations	280H; 444
. REITs	859
. retention of, election	444
. returns for less than 12 months	443

	CODE SEC.
Accounting periods—Cont'd	
. S corporations	444; 7519
. . taxable year election other than required year	444
. short period (See Short tax year)	
Accounting records (See Books and records)	
Accounts receivable	
. capital asset status	1221
. partnership distribution of	735; 751
. partnership interest	736
. unrealized	751
Accrual basis	446
. charitable contributions	170
. decedent's income	451; 461
. deferred rental agreements	467
. foreign tax credit	905
. real estate mortgage investment conduits	860B; 860E
. returned merchandise	458
. short-term obligations issued on discount basis	454
Accumulated adjustments account	1368
Accumulated earnings credit	
. controlled corporations	1551; 1561
. disallowance of	1551
Accumulated earnings tax	531 et seq.
. accounting periods, change in	536
. burden of proof	534
. capital gains and losses	535 et seq.
. charitable contributions	535
. controlled group of corporations	1561
. corporations	531 et seq.
. . burden of proof	534
. . credit	1551
. . evidence of purpose to avoid	533
. . imposition of	531
. . income not placed on annual basis	536
. . reasonable needs of the business	537
. . subject to	532
. . taxable income	535
. credit	535
. dividends-paid deduction	563
. evidence of purpose to avoid income tax	533
. holding companies	535
. investment companies	535
. jeopardy assessments	534
. net operating loss deduction	535
. possession tax credit	936
. rate of tax	531
. reasonable needs of business	537
. recovery exclusions	111
. special corporate deductions	535
. U.S.-owned foreign corporations	535
Accumulated taxable income	535
Accumulation distributions	665 et seq.
. foreign estates or trusts, foreign tax credit	904
Accuracy-related penalty	
. reportable transactions	6662A
. underpayment of tax	6662

104

Index to Code — Advance

	CODE SEC.
Acetylene hazardous waste clean up	4661; 4662
Achievement awards	
. deduction, disallowance of	274
. gross income	74
Acquisitions	
. covered asset	
. . foreign income not subject to U.S. taxation by reason of	
. . . denial of foreign tax credit	901
. returns relating to	6043A
ACRS (See Accelerated cost recovery system (ACRS))	
Activities not engaged in for profit (See Not-for-profit activities)	
Acts of God	
. casualty losses (See Casualty losses)	
. disaster losses (See Disaster losses and relief)	
. fire losses (See Fire losses)	
. storm losses (See Storm losses)	
Actuarial reports, employee retirement and benefit plans	
. deferred compensation, information returns	6058
. deficiency assessment	7422
. failure to file	6692
. funding method	412
. information returns	
. . deferred compensation	6058
. . periodic report	6059
. prohibited transactions	7422
Additions to tax .... 6651 et seq. (See also Penalties)	
. bankruptcy proceedings	6658
. estate tax	2032A
. interest on	6601
. joint return after filing separate returns	6013
. Tax Court jurisdiction	6214
Adjusted basis	1016
. alternative minimum tax	56
. annuities, sale of	1021
. bargain sales to charitable organization	1011
. consenting corporation stock, recognition of gain	341
. controlled foreign corporation	961
. cooperative housing corporations	216(c)(2)
. depreciation	1245
. DISC distributions	996
. discharge of indebtedness, effect of	1017
. earnings and profits computation	1503
. enhanced oil recovery credit	43
. generation-skipping transfers	2654
. investment credit property	50
. life insurance company segregated asset accounts	817
. low-income housing credit (See Low-income housing credit sub-head eligible basis)	
. market discount bonds	1278
. mines or deposits	
. . development expenditures	616
. . exploration expenditures	617
. optional adjustment for partnership property	743; 754
. passive foreign investment companies	1293
. pollution control facilities	169
. research expenditures	1016
. S corporation stock	1367

	CODE SEC.
Adjusted basis—Cont'd	
. Sec. 1245 property upon dispositions	1245
. short-term obligations issued at discount	1283
. stock and securities	
. . acquired in distribution	307
. . controlled foreign corporations	961
. term interests	167; 1001
. undistributed partnership property	734
Adjusted current earnings (ACE)	
. alternative minimum tax	56
Adjusted gross estate	
. family owned businesses	2057
Adjusted gross income	22; 62; 67
Adjustments	
. alternative minimum tax computation	56
. basis, to (See Adjusted basis)	
. closed taxable year	1311 et seq.
. corporations	301 et seq.
. errors of prior year affecting current year	1311 et seq.
. inflation as basis (See Inflation adjustments)	
. nonconventional fuel source credit (See Nonconventional fuel source credit)	
Administrative expenses	
. estate tax	2053
. estates and trust stock redemption	303
. private foundations	4942
Administrative review of decisions, prohibition of	6406
Administrators (See Executors and administrators)	
Adopted children	
. dependents	152
. foreign-born	152
. status	
. . estate freezes	2701
. . generation-skipping transfers	2651
Adoption assistance programs	
. defined	137(c)
. exclusion	137(a)
. inflation adjustments	137(f)
. limitations	137(b)
. qualified adoption expenses	137(d)
Adoption credit	
. allowance of	23; 36C(a)
. basis adjustments	36C(g)
. eligible child defined	36C(d)(2)
. filing requirements	36C(f)
. foreign adoptions	36C(e)
. inflation adjustments	36C(h)
. limitations	36C(b)
. qualified adoption expense defined	36C(d)(1)
. regulations, prescription of	36C(i)
. special needs children	
. . $13,170 special needs credit	36C(a)(3); 137(a)(2)
Advance payments	
. black lung disability trust fund, payments to	9501
. child tax credit for 2003	6429
. earned income credit	32
. . employment taxes	3507
. . information statements	6051

105

Advance / Index to Code

CODE SEC.

Advance payments —Cont'd
. membership dues 456
. premium assistance credit
. . health plan coverage 36B
. subscriptions 455
. taxes 6513
. . interest on overpayments 6611
Advanced coal project credit .... 48A(a)
. advanced coal-based generation technology .... 48A(f)
. aggregation credits .... 48A(d)(3)
. applicability .... 48A(g)
. certification of advanced coal project program ... 48A(d)(2)
. definitions concerning .... 48A(c)
. establishment of advanced coal project program .. 48A(d)(1)
. qualified investments .... 48A(b)
. qualifying projects .... 48A(e)
. review and redistribution .... 48A(d)(4)
. subsidized property .... 48A(b)(2)
Advanced insulation 4053
Advanced mine safety equipment
. expense, election to (See Mine safety equipment)
Advanced nuclear power facilities
. credit for production from 45J
Adverse party defined 672
Advertising
. air transportation, taxes imposed 7275
. expenditures
. . broadcasting 162
. . exclusion from sale price 4216
. . foreign 162
. . political convention program 276
. . price readjustments 6416
. handbill, delivery of
. . FICA 3121
. . FUTA 3306
. . withholding tax on wages 3401
. outdoor displays, involuntary conversion 1033
Affidavits
. fraudulent 7206; 7207
. U.S. real property interest dispositions
. . affidavit that interests in corporation not U.S. real property, nonpublicly traded domestic corporation ...... 1445(b)(3)
. . false affidavit .... 1445(d)(1)
. . nonforeign affidavits, alternative procedure for .... 1445(b)(9)
Affiliated corporations
. allocation of interest 864
. basis of property acquired 1051
. built-in gains offset by preacquisition losses 384
. consolidated returns (See Consolidated returns)
. defined 338; 865; 1504
. discharge of indebtedness, basis reduction upon 1017
. dividends-paid deduction 562
. dividends-received deduction 243
. earnings and profits 312; 1552
. expatriated corporation insider, stock compensation to ... 4985
. foreign affiliates (See Foreign affiliates)
. foreign export corporations 993
. foreign tax credit 902; 904; 6038

CODE SEC.

Affiliated corporations —Cont'd
. insolvent, refunds to members 6402
. interest on acquisition indebtedness 279
. liability for tax, election as to allocation 1552
. life insurance companies 818
. liquidating distributions 336
. passive activity losses and credits 469
. period of affiliation defined 1051
. personal holding companies 542
. property acquired during affiliation, basis of .. 1051
. purchasing corporation's acquisition of assets of target affiliate .... 338 et seq.
. real estate mortgage investment conduits 860E
. S corporations 1361
. stock in, basis of 1503
. stock ownership rule 1504
. stock purchase as asset purchase .... 338 et seq.
. straddles 1092
. transportation by air, excise taxes 4282
. worthless securities 165
. worthless stock in affiliated bank 582
Affiliated groups
. air transportation 4282
. allocation, foreign corporations 864
. DISCs 1504
. domestic production activities .... 199(d)(4)
. foreign corporations 864
. golden parachute payments .... 280G(d)(5)
. insurance companies dividends paid to member of 832
. life insurance companies
. . including mutual parent and stock subsidiary, group .. 809
. . policyholder dividends 818
. refunds and credits; insolvent affiliated group 6402
. REMICs 860E
. S corporation affiliated group membership 1361
. transportation by air 4282
Affiliated service groups
. employee retirement and benefit plans 414
. pension, profit-sharing, and stock bonus plans .... 414(m)(2)
. . separate lines of business .... 414(r)(8)
AFR (See Applicable federal rates)
Age 50 or older
. catch-up contributions to pension plan (See Pension, profit-sharing, and stock bonus plans)
Age 55 or older
. health savings accounts contributions for individuals 223
. spouses, sale of principal residence 121
Age 65 or older, taxable income 63
Agents and agencies
. employment taxes 3504
. housing credit agencies
. . low-income housing projects (See Low-income housing credit)
. real estate (See Real estate dealers and agents)
. returns by 882; 6012
. withholding tax on wages 3402
. work opportunity credit 51
Agricultural activities
. domestic production activities .... 199(d)(3)

Index to Code

Agricultural activities —Cont'd
- farmers and farming (See Farmers and farming)
- small agri-biodiesel producer credit (See Small agri-biodiesel producer credit)

Agricultural chemicals security credit 450

Agricultural cooperatives
- domestic production activities deductions .... 199(d)(3)
- farmers (See Farmers cooperatives)
- organization dues .... 512(d)

Agricultural irrigation projects 90

Agricultural labor (See also Farmers and farming)
- crew leader 3121
- FICA 3121
- FUTA 3306
- withholding tax on wages 3401
- work opportunity credit 51

Agricultural organizations
- exemption 501
- unrelated business taxable income 511

Agricultural products
- crop damage (See Crop damage)
- crops (See Crops)

Agricultural structure depreciation 168

Agricultural vehicle highway use tax exemption 4483

Aiding and abetting penalty, understatement of tax liability 6701; 6703
- injunctions 7408
- refunds, suit for 7422

Air, depletion of minerals from 613

Air ambulances
- emergency medical transportation, persons by air
- - excise tax exemption .... 4262(g)
- excise tax exemption, air transportation 4261

Air force (See Armed Forces)

Air transportation (See Transportation by air)

Aircraft
- affiliated group, services furnished member, transportation taxes 4282
- charitable contributions
- - fraudulent acknowledgment 6720
- - used 170
- commercial aviation, gasoline used in 6421
- depreciation 168
- foreign, earnings from 872; 883
- foreign base company income 955
- fuel, taxes on 4041
- aircraft museums, exceptions for certain 4041
- Airport and Airway Trust Fund (See Airport and Airway Trust Fund)
- - chemicals used in production, environmental tax 4662
- - farming purposes 6416
- - refunds and credits 6421; 6427
- noncommercial, fuel for 4041; 6421; 6427
- passenger aircraft
- - alternative minimum tax and research credit in lieu of bonus depreciation, election .... 168(k)(4)(G)(iii)
- private activity bonds financing 147
- small, nonestablished lines, transportation taxes 4281

Aircraft —Cont'd
- supplies
- - manufacturers excise taxes 4221; 4222
- - motor fuels tax 4041; 6416

Aircraft museum special fuels tax 4041

Airline affiliate fringe benefits 132

Airline pilots benefits and contributions 415

Airplanes (See Aircraft)

Airport and Airway Trust Fund
- appropriation of funds .... 9502(c)
- creation .... 9502(a)
- expenditures from
- - airport and airway program .... 9502(d)(1)
- - airports, on account of certain .... 9502(d)(6)
- - exceeding fund revenues attributable to fuel used, transfers for refunds and credits .... 9502(d)(4)
- - general fund, payments into the .... 9502(d)(2)
- - sec. 34 credits .... 9502(d)(3)
- - transportation by air, refund of taxes on ...... 9502(d)(5)
- fuel tax 4091; 4093
- limitations on transfers to .... 9502(e)
- transfers to .... 9502(b)

Airports
- exempt facility bonds 142; 146
- private activity bonds 147
- rural, segments to and from .... 4261(e)(1)

Alaska
- charitable contributions by whaling captains in support of native Alaskan subsistence whaling 170
- harbor maintenance tax 4462
- Native settlement trusts 646
- natural gas 43
- transportation by air of person to, excise tax rate ... 4261(c)(3)

Alaska Native Settlement Trusts
- information statements 6039H

Alaska natural pipeline depreciation 168

Alcohol fuel credit 40
- disclosures of returns and return information to states 6103
- distilled spirits for fuel use 5181
- ethanol blenders 40
- excise tax exemption, coordination with 40
- gasoline tax 4081; 6426
- gasoline used to produce certain alcohol fuels 6427
- general business credit 38
- gross income, inclusion in 87
- small ethanol producer credit, allocation of 40
- special fuels tax 4041
- taxable purpose, not used for 6427
- unused credit 196

Alcohol mixture credit
- definition 40
- excise tax 4041; 4081; 6426
- - Airport and Airway Trust Fund 4091
- - Highway Trust Fund 4041; 4091; 9503
- gasoline used to produce, refund of taxes on 6427

Alcohol taxes .... 5001 et seq.; 5061 et seq.; 5141 et seq. (See also Liquors)
- alcohol fuel credit (See also Alcohol fuel credit)

107

Alcohol

Index to Code

CODE SEC.

Alcohol taxes—Cont'd
. beer (See Beer tax)
. bonded premises, operations on .... 5211 et seq.
.. denaturation .... 5241 et seq.
.. discontinuation of storage facilities 5236
.. production .... 5221 et seq.
.. storage .... 5231 et seq.
. books and records
.. distilled spirits plants 5207
.. occupational 5146
... retail dealers 5124
... wholesale dealers 5114
.. wholesale dealers 5432
. bottling for industrial purposes 5235
. credit allowance requirement 6423
. definitions concerning 5112
. denaturation .... 5241 et seq.
. disaster losses 5064
. distilled spirits (See Distilled spirits)
. failure to file return or pay tax 6651
. fruit-flavor concentrate plants, volatile .... 5511 et seq.
. gallonage taxes ..... 5001 et seq.; 5041 et seq.; 5051 et seq.; 5061 et seq.
. liability for occupational taxes 5143
. manufacturers of stills 5101; 5102
. method of collecting 5061
. miscellaneous general provisions .... 5551 et seq.
. miscellaneous plants and warehouses ... 5501 et seq.; 5511 et seq.
. nonbeverage domestic drawback claimants .... 5131 et seq.
. occupational taxes .. 5081; 5091 et seq.; 5101 et seq.; 5111 et seq.; 5121 et seq.; 5131 et seq.; 5141 et seq.
.. liability for 5143
.. payment of tax 5142
.. penalties 5691
.. permits 5271; 5276
.. recordkeeping and inspection 5146
.. registration 5141
.. stamps 6806
.. state laws, application of 5145
. payment of taxes 5142
. penalties, seizures and forfeitures .... 5601 et seq.; 5661 et seq.; 5671 et seq.; 5681 et seq.
. refund and drawback in case of exportation 5062
. refunds and credits 6423
. registration 5141
. retail dealers .... 5121 et seq.
. returns 6091
. territories subject to 5065
. ultimate burden 6423
. vinegar plants .... 5501 et seq.
. wholesale dealers .... 5111 et seq.
.. recordkeeping 5432
. wines (See Wines)

Aliens (See also Nonresident aliens; Resident aliens)
. defined 7701
. departure from U.S., compliance with tax laws 6851
. dependents 152
. first and last year of residency 7701
. marital deduction

CODE SEC.

Aliens (See also Nonresident aliens; Resident aliens) — Cont'd
. marital deduction — Cont'd
.. gift tax 2523
.. surviving spouse of U.S. citizen 2056
. premium assistance credit, health plan coverage
.. individuals not lawfully present 36B
. students (See Foreign students and exchange visitors)

Alimony and separate maintenance payments
. absent parent, collection of child support obligations 6103; 6305; 6402
. adjusted gross income 62
. children 71
. death 71
. deductions 215
. definition 71; 215
. dependency exemption 152
. divorce or separation instrument 71
. domestic relations order (See Domestic relations order)
. exceptions 71
. excess payments 71
. front-loaded payments 71
. gift tax 2516
. gross income 61; 71
. identifying numbers, reporting requirements 215
. joint returns 71
. trusts 215; 682

All-events test 461

Allocation
. accounting method 482
. acquisitions, tax avoidance 269A
. affiliated groups, foreign corporations 864
. asset acquisitions 1060
. basis
.. adjusted basis partnership property 743; 755
.. asset acquisitions 1060
.. charitable contributions 170
.. partnership distributions 732
.. reorganization exchanges 358
.. sports franchises, player contracts 1056
.. undistributed partnership property 734; 755
. controlled corporations 1552
. controlled foreign corporations 958
. DISC distributions 994
. distributions
.. controlled foreign corporations 958
.. DISCs 994
. foreign corporations 882
. generation-skipping transfers, tax on 2632
. income, partnership 514
. interest and principal 864; 884
.. property produced by taxpayer 263A
. partnership income 514
. prohibited, qualified securities 4979A
. research and experimental expenditures 864
. source of income 863
. stock purchase as asset purchase 338

Alternate fuel vehicle refueling property credit
. allowance .... 30C(a)

108

Index to Code — American

CODE SEC.

Alternate fuel vehicle refueling property credit —Cont'd
. basis reduction .... 30C(e)(1)
. election not to take credit .... 30C(e)(4)
. general business credit and .... 30C(d)(1)
. limitation .... 30C(b)
. outside the U.S., property used .... 30C(e)(3)
. personal credit and .... 30C(d)(2)
. qualified alternate fuel vehicle refueling property defined
   .... 30C(c)
. recapture rules .... 30C(e)(5)
. tax-exempt entity, property used by .... 30C(e)(2)

Alternate motor vehicle credits
. allowance .... 30B(a)
. fuel efficiency, increase for .... 30B(b)(2)
. general business credit, treatment as .... 30B(g)(1)
. lifetime fuel savings .... 30B(c)(4)
. new advanced lean burn technology motor vehicle credit
   .... 30B(c)
. new qualified alternative fuel motor vehicle credit .... 30B(e)(1)
. new qualified fuel cell motor vehicle credit ... 30B(b)
. new qualified hybrid motor vehicle credit ...... 30B(d)
. personal credit, treatment as .... 30B(g)(2)

Alternate valuation, estate tax .... 2032 (See also Estate tax; Valuation)
. basis, property acquired from decedent 1014

Alternative energy (A-E) property service contracts 7701

Alternative fuel credit 6426; 6427

Alternative minimum tax .... 55(a)
. adjusted basis .... 56(a)(6)
. adjusted current earnings .... 56(g)
. adjustments, corporate .... 56(c)
. adjustments, medical expenses .... 56(b)(1)
. adjustments to individuals .... 56(b)
. allowance of credit .... 53(a)
. alternative tax net operating loss deduction ... 56(d)
. arbitrage bonds 148
. bonds, tax-exempt 148
. circulation expenditures .... 56(b)(2)
. common trust funds 59
. computation 56
. controlled foreign corporation distributions .. 56
. credit for prior year's liability 53; 381
. current earnings, adjusted .... 56(c)(1)
. depreciation .... 56(a)(1)
. earned income credit 32
. energy preference deduction 56
. environmental tax 59A
. estates and trusts 59
. exemptions .... 55(d)
. experimental expenditures 56
. farm losses 58
. farmers and fishermen, coordination with income averaging for
   .... 55(c)(2)
. federally declared disasters .... 56(d)(3)
. foreign tax credit limitations 59
. housing interest .... 56(e)
. incentive stock options .... 53(f); 56(b)(3)
. insolvent taxpayers 58
. installment sales 56

CODE SEC.

Alternative minimum tax—Cont'd
. itemized deductions 56
. limitations 59
. long-term contracts .... 56(a)(3)
. long-term unused credits .... 53(e); 53(e)(3)
. Merchant marine capital construction funds .... 56(c)(2)
. mining exploration and development costs ...... 56(a)(2)
. net minimum tax defined .... 53(d)(1)
. net operating loss deduction .... 56(a)(4)
. ownership change 382
. passive activity loss disallowance 58
. phase-out of exemption amount .... 55(d)
. pollution control facilities .... 56(a)(5)
. prior year minimum tax liability .... 55(e)(5)
. qualified dwelling .... 56(e)(2)
. refundable credit .... 53(e)(2)
. regular tax .... 55(c)
. regulated investment companies 59
. REITs 59
. research expenditures .... 56(b)(2)
. Sec. 936 credit 59
. short taxable years 443
. simplified Sec. 904 election 59
. small corporations .... 55(e)
. small corporations ceased to exist .... 55(e)(2)
. tax benefit rule 59
. tax preference items .... 57; 59(e)
. taxable income .... 55(b)(2)
. tentative minimum tax .... 53(d)(1); 53(d)(2); 55(b)
. timber gain, maximum corporate tax on .... 55(b)(4)
. trust funds 59
. unearned income of minor children 59

Alternative tax
. alternative minimum tax (See Alternative minimum tax)
. capital gains and losses (See Capital gains and losses)
. shipping activities (See Ships and shipping)

Amateur athletic competitions, sponsorship
. contributions 170
. exemption 501

Ambulances
. air ambulances, excise tax exemption
. . air transportation 4261
. . emergency medical transportation .... 4262(g)
. retail excise taxes 4053

American employer 1402
. employees of foreign affiliates 406
. FICA 3121
. FUTA 3306

American Indians (See Native Americans)

American Opportunity Tax Credit 25A

American Samoa
. alien residents of 876
. corporations 881
. employment tax, overpayment 6413
. FICA 3121; 6205
. . government employees 3125
. . overpayments 6413
. income of U.S. citizens residing in 931

109

CODE SEC.

American Samoa — Cont'd
. residents, self-employment tax 1402
American vessel and aircraft 3121
Ammonia, hazardous waste clean up 4661; 4662
Amortization
. basis, adjustment to 1016
. bond premiums 171
.. adjustment to basis 1016
.. carryovers, acquiring corporation 381
.. insurance companies other than life 834
.. life insurance companies 805; 811
. corporate organizational expenditures 248
. employee retirement and benefit plans 412
. estates and trusts 642
. goodwill 197
. insurance policy acquisition expenses 848
. insurance premium and accrual of discount 811
. intangible drilling and development costs 291
. intangible property 197
. leases
.. acquisition costs 178
.. exempt property 168
. mining exploration and development costs 291
. partnership organizational expenditures 709
. pollution control facilities 169; 291
. reforestation expenditures 194
. research and experimental expenses 174
. start-up expenditures 195
. tax preference items
.. accelerated amortization, pre-1987 property 57
. taxable bond premiums 171
. tax-exempt bond premiums 171
. timber property, reforestation expenditures 1245
Amusement expense deductions 274
Annual accounting period
. computation of taxable income 441
Annual reports
. employee retirement and benefit plans 6057; 6058
.. failure to file 6652
.. penalties for failure to file 6690
. low-income housing credit .... 42(l)(2); 42(l)(3)
Annualization of income
. accumulated earnings tax 536
. estimated tax underpayments 6654; 6655
. foreign personal holding companies 557
. life insurance companies 811
. personal holding companies 546
. withholding tax on wages, computation 3402
Annuities 72
. amounts received by surviving annuitant under joint and survivor annuity contract 691
. anti-abuse rule 72
. armed force servicemen, retired 72; 101
. backup withholding 3406
. basis of property 1021
. beneficiaries, taxation 403
. charitable trusts
.. income interest 170

CODE SEC.

Annuities — Cont'd
. *charitable trusts — Cont'd*
.. lead trusts, inclusion ratio rules 2642
.. remainder interests 170; 664; 2522
. contracts 817
.. adjusted basis 1021
.. allocation, amounts not received as annuities 72
. amounts not received as annuities .... 72 et seq.
.. anti-abuse rule 72
.. death of holder 72
.. defined 1035
.. defined contribution plans 415
.. dividends 72
.. exchange of, gain or loss upon nontaxable 1035
.. 5% owners 72
.. foreign policies, excise taxes on .... 4371 et seq.
.. investment in the contract 72
.. limitations on benefit and contributions 415
.. loans 72
.. maturities 72
.. natural persons, not held by 72
.. nontaxable exchange of 1035
.. payments, deductibility of 264
.. penalties, premature distributions 72
.. personal injuries, damages 130
.. policyholder dividends 72
.. premature distributions, 10% penalty 72
.. proceeds 72
.. qualified plans 72
.. redemption 72
.. refunds 72
.. sale of, adjusted basis 1021
.. single premium payments 264
.. surrenders 72
.. 10% penalty, premature distributions 72
.. transfers without adequate consideration 72
. controlled foreign corporations, annuity contract 954
. deductions
.. contributions of employer to 404
.. estate tax 691
. defined contribution plan, employee contributions ... 72
. definition 401
. employee plans (See Employee annuities)
. estate tax 2039; 2056
. exclusion ratio 72
. exempt organizations 403
. expected returns 72
. face-amount certificates 401
. foreign personal holding company income 553
. gross income 61; 72
. individual retirement accounts 219; 408; 2039
. information returns 6041; 6047
. injuries and sickness, compensation for 104
. interest 72
. investment in the contract 72
. joint and survivor 401; 417
.. basis to survivor 1014
.. employee death benefits 101
.. estate tax deduction 691; 2056

Index to Code

CODE SEC.

Annuities—Cont'd
joint and survivor—Cont'd
. . gift tax deduction 2523
. . unfunded liability 7448
. levy on 6334
. loan treated as distribution 72
. lump-sum distributions 402
. option to receive in lieu of 72
. modified endowment contracts 72
. noncancelable accident and health insurance, combined with
  848
. nonqualified, taxability of beneficiary 403
. nonresident aliens 871
. payor's reports, recordkeeping 6704
. personal holding company income 543
. plans for employees (See Employee annuities)
. preretirement survivor annuities 401; 417
. proceeds from contracts 72
. railroad retirement benefits 72; 86
. refund feature, adjustment in investment 72
. retired servicemen 72; 101; 6334
. rollovers 72
. self-employed individuals (See Self-employed retirement plans)
. separate contracts, employee contributions under defined contribution plan 72
. Social Security benefits 86
. special trial judges; surviving spouse and children ... 7448
. spouses and dependent children of Tax Court judges ... 7448
. starting date 72
. survivor annuities 72; 401; 417
. Tax Court judges and dependents 7447; 7448
. tax-favored accounts, failure to provide reports on ... 6693
. 10% additional tax 72
. transferee rules, valuable consideration transfers ... 72
. trusts, charitable (See subhead charitable trusts)
. unrelated business taxable income 512
. valuation tables 7520
. variable, life insurance companies 817
. withholding tax 3402; 6652
. . deferred income 3405
. . information returns 6047; 6867
. . nonresident aliens and foreign corporations 1441
. . special rules 3405
Anorthosite depletion 613
Anti-cruelty organizations (See Cruelty prevention organizations)
Antimony
. depletion 613
. hazardous waste clean up 4662
. trioxide 4661; 4662
Antimony hazardous waste clean up 4661
Antique firearm defined 5845
Antitrust Act
. treble damages 162
. violations of 162; 186
Aplite, percentage depletion 613
Apostolic associations .... 501 (See also Churches; Religious organizations)
. examination of business activities 7611

CODE SEC.

Apothecaries, distilled spirits used by 5002
Appeals
. dispute resolution procedures, Treas. Dept. 7123
. lien for taxes 6326
. refunds and credit 6406
. Tax Court decisions, review of (See Tax Court subhead court review of decisions)
Appliances, energy efficient (See Energy efficient appliance credit)
Applicable asset acquisition allocation 1060
Applicable dollar threshold defined for FICA ... 3121
Applicable federal rates 7872
. below-market interest rates 7872
. debt instruments issued for property, OID rules ... 1274
. life insurance company reserves 807
Appraisals (See also Valuation)
. charitable contributions 170
. incorrect, valuation misstatements attributable to ... 6695A
Appreciated financial positions
. constructive sales 1259
Appreciated property
. charitable contribution, tax preference item 57
. controlled corporation 355
. distribution of 311; 312
. partnerships 311
. political organizations, transfers to 84
. trusts 311
Aquatic resources trust fund 9504
Arbitrage bonds
. clean renewable energy bonds .... 54(i)
. construction expenditures 148
. defined 148
. exemption 143
. interest 103
. mortgage revenue bonds .... 143(g)(1)
. natural gas, prepaid .... 148(b)(4)
. qualified tax credit bonds .... 54A(d)(4)
. qualified zone academy bonds ...... 1397E(f)(3); 1397E(g)
Arbitrage operations 1233
Archer MSA (See Medical savings accounts, Archer)
Architectural barriers to handicapped and elderly .. 190; 263
Archivist of the United States
. disclosure of returns and return information 6103
Area of chronic economic distress
. mortgage revenue bonds, targeted areas ...... 143(j)(3)
. recovery zone bonds (See Recovery zone bonds)
. recovery zone economic development bonds (See Recovery zone economic development bonds)
Armed Forces
. annuities, retired servicemen 72; 101
. association exemption from tax 501
. benefits 134
. civilian employees
. . FICA 3122
. . prisoners of war combat pay 112
. combat pay 104; 112; 3401; 7508
. combat service 7508
. . contingency operations 7508

111

Armed   Index to Code

	CODE SEC.
Armed Forces — Cont'd	
combat service — Cont'd	
.. death, estate tax	2201
.. defined	112
.. postponement of filing and claims requirements	7508
.. retirement savings	219
.. telephone calls from combat zone	4253
. compensation	112
. contingency operations	7508
. death of member	
.. benefits	101
.. combat zone service, estate tax	2201
.. income tax abatement	692
.. refunds and credits	692
.. USERRA-qualified active service	401(a)(37)
. defined	3121; 7701
. Desert Shield service	7508
. disability pay	6334
. earned income credit	32
. enlisted personnel, combat zone compensation	112
. estate tax	2201
. exempt income	112; 134
. FICA	3121; 3122
. gross income, military benefit exclusion from	134
. hospitalization	7508
. housing allowance	265
. injuries and sickness, compensation for	104; 112
. levy, disability pay exemption from	6334
. missing in action (See Missing in action)	
. moving expenses	217
. overpayment of tax, war postponements	7508
. postponement of certain tax-related deadlines	7508A
. prisoners of war, combat zone compensation	112
. receipts for wages paid	6051
. receipts for withheld taxes	6051
. reserves	162; 219
. retired serviceman's family protection plan	6334
. retirement savings, combat service	219
. sale of principal residence, exclusion of gain from	121
. spouse of service person	7508
. terrorist or noncombat zone military actions, death of member	692
. Title 11 cases	7508
. transportation tax	4262
. travel benefits	134
. veterans (See Veterans)	
. Vietnam	112
. war postponements	7508
. withholding tax on wages	3401
Arsenic, hazardous waste clean up	4661; 4662
Artists	
. capital expenditures	263A
Artwork	
. capital gain or loss	1221; 1231
. charitable bequests, estate tax	2055
. collectibles	
.. simplified employee pension plans	
... coin and bullion exception	408(m)(3)
... investments as distributions	408(m)(1)

	CODE SEC.
Artwork — Cont'd	
. individual retirement savings plan investments in	408
. loan of	
.. charitable organizations, to	2503
.. nonresidents, by	2105
. noncapital asset, as	1221
Asbestos, percentage depletion	613
Assessable penalties, rules for application of	6671 et seq.
Assessments	
. administrative review	7429
. amount	
.. not to be assessed	6201
.. reasonableness of	7429
. authority	6201
. bankruptcy and receivership	6871; 6872
. bond to stay	7485
. burden of proof as to reasonableness of	7429
. cash, unknown owner of	6867
.. income, state and gift taxes	6861
.. other taxes	6862
.. stay of collection	6863
. child, compensation of	6201
. court determination of	7429
. court procedures	
.. bond to stay collection	6863; 7485
.. prohibition of suits to restrain collections	7421
. criminal restitution	
.. certain orders of	6201
.. exceptions to restrictions on assessment	6213
.. limitation period for	6501
. deficiencies (See Deficiencies)	
. employment taxes	6201; 6205
. erroneous or illegal, abatement of	6404
. estimated tax, exemption for	6201
. excessive	
.. abatement of	6404
.. refund claims	6206
. exempt organizations	6501
. extension of 20-day period	7429
. Federal unemployment tax, exemption for	6201
. general rule	6201
. injunction (See Injunction against assessment and collection)	
. insolvent banks	7507
. jeopardy (See Jeopardy assessments)	
. judicial review	7429
. jurisdiction for determination of	7429
. limitation period (See Statute of limitations)	
. listed transactions	6501
. method of	6202; 6203
. mode and time of	6202
. ownership of cash unknown (See subhead cash, unknown owner of)	
. procedures, review of	7429
. reasonableness of	7429
. regulations as to mode or time	6202
. request for prompt	6501
. restrictions on	6213
. review of procedures	7429
. supplemental	6204

112

Index to Code — Away-from-home

CODE SEC.

Assessments —Cont'd
. taxable year, termination of 6851
. termination (See Termination assessments)
. time of 6202
. waivers, limitations on assessment 6501

Assets
. acquisition treatment as stock purchase 338
. capital (See Capital assets)

Assignments
. benefit of creditors, for
.. notice of qualification of assignee 6036
. corporate returns
.. assignee 6012
.. signatures 6062
. personal injuries liability 130

Assistant commissioner
. employee plans and organizations 7802

Assumption of indebtedness (See Indebtedness)

Astronauts
. abatement of taxes 692
. death 101; 692; 2201
. estate tax 2201
. income taxes 692

At risk limitations 465
. accounting methods 465
. enhanced oil recovery credit 43
. investment credit, computation of 49
. low-income housing credit (See Low-income housing credit)
. recourse financing exclusion from credit base .... 49(a)(1)

Athletes, professional
. contracts, transfers
.. basis for gain or loss 1056
.. depreciation recapture 1245

Athletic competition sponsorship, amateur
. contributions 170
. exemption 501

Athletic facilities 132

Attorney General, State
. disclosures to, return and return information 6104

Attorney General defined 7701

Attorneys
. government, disclosure of returns and return information 6103

Attorney's fees
. recovery 7430
. whistle blowers, relating to award to 62

Attorney's lien
. judgment or settlement, upon 6323

Attribution of ownership
. passive foreign investment companies 1298

Audit selection procedures 6103

Audits
. executive branch influences, prohibition against ... 7217

Authors, capital expenditures 263A

Auto salesmen, fringe benefits 132

Automatic contribution arrangements (See Pension, profit-sharing, and stock bonus plans)

CODE SEC.

Automobiles (See also Motor vehicles)
. alternate depreciation system for certain property .... 168(g)(3)(D)
. basis
.. gas guzzler tax, effect of 1016
.. unrecovered 280F
. depreciation 168; 280F
. disallowed deductions 280F
. excise tax 4001
.. demonstration models 4002
.. first retail sale defined for 4002
.. long-term leases 4002
.. parts and accessories 4003
. floor stock refunds 6412
. gas guzzler tax 1016; 4064; 4217; 4222
. highway use, taxes for (See Highway motor vehicle use taxes)
. investment tax credit 280F
. lien for taxes 6323
. limitation on depreciation 280F
. luxury (See Luxury automobiles)
. manufacturers excise taxes .... 4064 et seq.; 9503
. mileage allowances 170
. motor vehicle defined 4064; 6323
. parts and accessories
.. excise tax, luxury 4003
.. manufacturer's tax 4218
. passenger vehicles (See Passenger vehicles)
. personal use 280F
. price inflation adjustment 280F
. retail excise taxes .... 4051 et seq.
.. exemptions 4053; 4221
.. Highway Trust Fund 9503
. seized for taxes, transfer of title 6339
. several interest holders, treatment of 280F

Average wages, withholding 3402

Aviation fuel
. Airport and Airway Trust Fund 4091; 9502
. alcohol mixture, reduced rates for 4091
. defined 4092
. excise taxes .... 4091 et seq.
. exemption 4041; 4092
. failure to pay tax 4103
. gasoline 6421
. information reporting 4104
. liability for tax 4103
. LUST Fund 4041; 4093
. noncommercial 4041
. nontaxable use 6427
. producer defined 4093
. reduced rate; alcohol mixture 4091
. two-party exchanges 4104
. wholesale distributor defined 4093

Avoidance of tax (See Evasion or avoidance of tax)

Awards (See Prizes and awards)

Away-from-home expenses 274
. business expenses 162
. medical care 213
. state legislators 162

Away-from-home

Index to Code

CODE SEC.

B

Backup withholding 3406
. broker defined .... 3406(h)(5)
. confidentiality of information .... 3406(f)
. coordination with other sections .... 3406(h)(10)
. credits against tax 31
. determination of reportable payment ...... 3406(b)(4)
. dividends 3406; 7205
. exceptions .... 3406(g)
. failure to provide certification payee is not subject to
.. period for which withholding is in effect ... 3406(e)(4)
. governmental units .... 3406(g)(A)
. interest 3406; 7205
. joint payees .... 3406(h)(3)
. new accounts and instruments
.. interest and dividend backup withholding, applying .. 3406(d)
. notice to payee requirement .... 3406(h)(8)
. notice to Secretary requirement .... 3406(h)(9)
. notified payee underreporting .... 3406(c)
. obviously incorrect number .... 3406(h)
. original issue discount .... 3406(h)(7)
. other reportable payment defined .... 3406(b)(3)
. payor defined .... 3406(h)(4)
. period for which withholding is in effect ...... 3406(e)
. readily tradable instrument .... 3406(h)(6)
. regulations, prescription of .... 3406(i)
. reportable interest or dividend payment defined ... 3406(b)(2)
. reportable payment defined .... 3406(b)(1)
. Sec. 6041(a) or 6041A(a) reportable payments ... 3406(b)(5)
. TIN, failure to furnish or incorrect .... 3406(1)
.. obviously incorrect number .... 3406(h)(1)
.. period for which withholding is in effect ..... 3406(e)
.. 2 incorrect TINS, payee furnished .... 3406(h)(2)
. trusts and estates 643
. window payments of interest .... 3406(b)(7)
Bad debts 166
. banks and trust companies
.. building and loan associations 593
.. net operating losses deduction ...... 172(b)(1)(D); 172(g)(1)
.. reserves for 585; 593
.. securities held by banks 582
Bank holding companies, dividends received 246A
Bankruptcy 1398
. basis reduction upon discharge of indebtedness 1017
. claims for income, estate and gift taxes 6871
. defined benefit plan benefit increase when sponsor is in .. 401
. discharge of indebtedness, adjustment to basis upon 1017
. extensions 6161
. individuals, rules relating to 1399
. insolvent banks 7507
. receivers (See Receivers)
. S corporations, bankruptcy estate as 1361
. Title 11 cases 1399
. transferees and fiduciaries .... 6901 et seq.
.. notice of fiduciary relationship 6903
.. prohibition of injunctions 6904
.. provisions of special application to 6902
.. refunds and credits 6402

CODE SEC.

Bankruptcy—Cont'd
. *transferees and fiduciaries—Cont'd*
.. transferred assets 6901
Banks and trust companies .... 581 et seq.
. bad debt (See Bad debt)
. common trust funds 584; 6032
. cooperative (See Cooperative banks)
. definition of bank 581
. deposit account dividends or interest paid 461
. depositaries for taxes 5703; 6302
. deposits, levy on 6332
. dividends paid on deposits 591
. dividends received deduction 243; 246A
. federal financial assistance 597
. federal home loan banks 246
. foreign banks (See Foreign banks)
. foreign personal holding company income 954
. holding companies 246A
. individual retirement accounts 408
. insolvent banks 7507
. interest on corporate acquisition indebtedness 279
. loans, lien against tax 6323
. mutual savings banks (See Mutual savings banks)
. personal holding company status of finance companies ... 542
. portfolio stock, debt-financed 246A
. premature withdrawals, adjusted gross income 62
. reserves for losses on loans 585; 593
. S corporations, becoming 1361
. savings banks life insurance 594
. securities held by, bad debt and loss deduction on .. 582
. withdrawal accounts, dividends or interest paid 461
Barite, percentage depletion 613
Barium sulfide hazardous waste clean up 4661; 4662
Barrel-of-oil equivalent
. nonconventional fuel source credit (See Nonconventional fuel source credit)
Barriers to handicapped and elderly
. removal expenditures 44; 190; 263
Barter exchanges 6041; 6045
Basis .... 1011 et seq.
. acquisition of property
.. affiliation during 1051
.. decedent, acquired from 1014
.. gifts 1015
. adjustments (See Adjusted basis)
. affiliation, property acquired during 1051
. allocation (See Allocation)
. alternate valuation for estate tax 1014
. annuity contracts 1014; 1021
. appreciated property, political contributions of 84
. bankruptcy and receiverships 1017; 1398
. beneficiaries of trusts or estates 643
. bequests 1014
.. holding period 1223
.. pecuniary, special valuation property satisfying 1040
. charitable remainder trust distributions 664
. clean fuel vehicles, reduction of basis 179A
. corporations 362
. cost basis 612; 1012

Index to Code

Basis—Cont'd

	Code Sec.
decedent, property acquired from	1014
depreciation	167; 312; 1016; 1245
.. bankruptcy	1017
.. earnings and profits	312
devise	1014
discharge of indebtedness	1017
distributions, corporate	301
employee stock option, estate exercise of	421
foreclosed property	1038
foreign expropriation loss recoveries	1351
gifts	1014; 1015
ground rents	1055
imported property	1059A
improvements by lessee, effect of	1019
inherited property	1014
installment obligations	453B; 1038
inventories	1013; 1017
investment credit	49
involuntary conversions	1033
liabilities in excess of	357
LIFO inventories, liquidation of	473
like-kind exchanges	1031
limitation for player contracts	1056
liquidating distributions	334; 336
low-income housing credit (See Low-income housing credit subhead eligible basis)	
March 1, 1913, property acquired before	1053
mineral interests	616; 617
nontaxable exchanges	1031 et seq.
partnerships (See Partners and partnerships)	
passive activity losses and credits	469
passive foreign investment companies	1293
patronage dividends	1385
player contracts	1056; 1245
political contributions of appreciated property	84
pollution control facilities, amortization	169
qualified replacement property	1016
reacquired real property	1038
real estate mortgage investment conduits	860F
redeemable ground rents	1055
reduction	
.. debt discharge amount	108
.. refueling property	179A
reorganization exchanges	
.. assumption of liabilities	357
.. corporations	362
.. distributees	358
Revenue Acts, established by	1052
sales and exchanges	
.. exchanged basis property defined	7701
.. nontaxable	1031 et seq.
.. productive use or investment, property held for	1031
.. reorganization exchanges	357; 358; 362
.. residences	1033
.. SEC orders	1082
.. stock	1032; 1036
Sec. 1245 property	1017; 1245

Basis—Cont'd

	Code Sec.
Sec. 1250 property	1017
SEC orders	1082
sports franchises, player contracts transferred	1056
stock and securities	
.. acquired in distributions	307
.. affiliated corporations	1503
.. dispositions	306
.. extraordinary dividends, nontaxed portion	1059
.. Federal National Mortgage Association	1054
.. foreign investment company	1246
.. foreign personal holding company	551; 1014
.. nonaffiliated 10% owned corporations	864
.. nontaxable transfers	1058
.. options	421
.. reduction for extraordinary dividends	1059
.. S corporations	1367
.. small business	1244
.. stock for stock of same corporation	1036
.. stock purchase as asset purchase	338
.. wash sales	1091
substituted basis defined	7701
transferred basis property defined	7701
transfers in trust	1015
transfers of compensatory property	83
trust property	1014 et seq.
wash sales	1091

Bauxite, percentage depletion ... 613

Beer tax ... 5051 et seq.

breweries	5091; 5401 et seq.
collection of	5054; 5061
definitions	5052
determination of	5054
development, removal of beer for	5053
drawback of	5055
electronic fund transfer payments	5061
exemptions	5053
exports, refunds and drawbacks	5062
family use	5053
gallonage taxes	5051 et seq.
illegal production	5051; 5054
laboratory analysis, removal for	5053
loss or destruction of beer	5056; 5064
penalties, seizures and forfeitures	5671 et seq.; 5681 et seq.
personal use	5053
rate of tax	5051
refunds	5056; 5064
removal exemption	5053
retail dealers	5121; 5122
unfit for beverage use	5053
wholesale dealer in beer defined	5112(c)
wholesale dealers	5111 et seq.; 5432

Below-market rate loans ... 7872

Beneficiaries

employees' trust, taxability of beneficiary of	402
estates and trusts (See Estates and trusts)	
failure to pay premium to, penalty	9707

115

	CODE SEC.
Benevolent life insurance associations exemption	501
Bentonite depletion	613
Benzene	
. environmental tax for hazardous waste clean up	4661; 4662
. special fuels tax	4041
Benzol, special fuels tax	4041
Bequests (See also Devises; Inheritances)	
. basis (See Basis)	
. charitable	2055
. death taxes payable out of	2055
. employee stock options	421
. exemption	102; 663
. expatriates, imposition of tax from	2801
. holding period	1223
. income	102
. pecuniary, special valuation property satisfying	1040
. private foundation, to	508
. shrinkage in value	273
. surviving spouse	2056
Beryllium depletion	613
Betting taxes (See Wagering taxes)	
Bicycle tires and tubes	4218
Bingo games	
. exempt organizations, unrelated trade or business	513
. political organization conducting, exempt function income	527
Biodiesel fuel	38; 40A
. credit	40A(b)(2); 6426
. defined	40A(2)(1)
. general business credit	38; 196
. gross income inclusion	87
. mixture credit	40A(b)(1)
. mixture or biodiesel not used as fuel	40A(3)
. renewable diesel	40A(f)
. small agri-biodiesel producer credit (See Small agri-biodiesel producer credit)	
. taxable purpose, not used for	6427
Biomass	
. cellulosic biomass ethanol plant property (See Cellulosic biomass ethanol plant property)	
. closed-loop biomass	45
. nonconventional fuel source credit (See Nonconventional fuel source credit)	
. open-loop biomass	45
Bismuth depletion	613
Black lung benefit trusts	9501
. allowance of deduction	192
. benefit payments	9501
. Black Lung Disability Trust Fund	501; 9501
. claims	192
. contributions	192; 4953
. disqualified person defined	4951
. excess contributions	192; 4953
. excise taxes	4951 et seq.
. . bankruptcy proceedings	6871
. . excess contributions to trust	4953
. . limitation on assessment and collection	
. . . suspension period	6213

	CODE SEC.
Black lung benefit trusts—Cont'd	
. *excise taxes—Cont'd*	
. . refunds, suit for	7422
. . self-dealing	4951
. . taxable expenditures	4952
. . transfers to Black Lung Disability Trust Fund	9501
. exemption	501
. funding	192; 9501
. investments by	9602
. limitation, deduction for contributions	192
. prohibited transactions	4951 et seq.; 7422
. qualification requirements	501
. reporting requirements	9602
. self-dealing	4951
. taxable expenditures	4952; 7422
. taxes on	4951 et seq.
. time contribution deemed made	192
. trustees	9501
. . prohibited transactions, liability for taxes on	4951; 4952
. . reporting requirements	9602
Blighted area redevelopment bonds	144
Blind persons	
. blindness defined	63(f)(4)
. withholding tax on wages, exemptions	3402
Blocked foreign income, controlled foreign corporation	964
Blood collector organization	7701
Blood donor locators	
. disclosure of taxpayer identity information	6103
Blue Cross/Blue Shield organizations	833
Board and lodging (See Meals and lodging)	
Board of trade	501
Boat safety account expenditures	9504(c)
Boating Trust Fund tax transfers	9504(b)
Boats (See also Ships and shipping)	
. charitable contribution	
. . fraudulent acknowledgment of	6720
. . used	170
. Highway Trust Fund transfers to boat safety accounts	9503
. motorboat fuel taxes, transfers from Highway Trust Fund for	9503
. registry, failure to display	6718
Bodies for self-propelled mobile homes	4051
Bond premiums	
. amortization	171
. basis adjusted for	1016
. carryovers, acquiring corporation	381
. corporation, repurchase by	249
. dealers in tax-exempts	75
. insurance companies other than life	834
. life insurance companies	805; 811; 1016
. public utilities, amortization	171
. repurchase by corporation	249
. tax-exempt bonds	1016
Bonds	
. abusive transactions, advance refunding	149
. adjustments to basis	1016
. advance refunding	149

Index to Code

CODE SEC.

Bonds —Cont'd
- arbitrage (See Arbitrage bonds)
- backup withholding 3406
- bank losses on 582
- build America bonds (See Build America Bonds)
- capital gains and losses .... 1271 et seq.
- charitable contributions 170
- clean renewable energy bonds (See Clean renewable energy bonds (CREBs))
- convertible bond premium, corporate repurchase of 249
- corporate acquisition indebtedness 279
- deficiency in tax, posting where extension granted 6165
- defined
  - amortizable bond premium 171
  - state and local bond exemption, for 150
  - stripped bonds 1286
- discount (See Discount bonds and notes)
- distilled spirits plants (See Distilled spirits plants subhead bonds required)
- educational facilities (See Exempt facility bonds subhead qualified public educational facilities)
- employee retirement and benefit plans 412
- exempt, tax (See Exempt bonds)
- exempt facilities (See Exempt facility bonds)
- extension to pay tax or deficiency 6165
- federal bonds (See United States obligations; United States savings bonds)
- hedge bonds (See State and Local bonds)
- indemnity bonds (See Indemnity bonds)
- industrial development bonds (See Industrial development bonds)
- information reporting 149
- installment sales, as payments in year of sale 453
- interest
  - earnings and profits of corporation, effect on 312
  - registration-required 163
- lien for taxes, release or discharge 6324A; 6325
- local (See State and local bonds)
- market discount bonds (See Market discount bonds)
- mortgage bonds (See Mortgage bonds)
- mortgage revenue bonds (See Mortgage revenue bonds)
- new clean renewable energy bonds (See New clean renewable energy bonds)
- nonresident aliens as holder, tax on 871
- original issue discount not currently includible .... 1271 et seq.
- pooled financing bonds (See Pooled financing bonds)
- pre-1986 bond issues, advance refunding 149
- premiums (See Bond premiums)
- prior exemption 149
- private activity (See Private activity bonds)
- purchase plans, pension funds 402
- qualified energy conservation bonds (See Qualified energy conservation bonds)
- qualified Gulf Opportunity Zone bond (See Gulf Opportunity Zone)
- qualified tax credit bonds (See Qualified tax credit bonds)
- qualified veterans' mortgage bonds (See Veteran's mortgage bonds)
- recovery zone bonds (See Recovery zone bonds)
- recovery zone economic development bonds (See Recovery zone economic development bonds)

CODE SEC.

Bonds —Cont'd
- recovery zone facility bonds (See Recovery zone facility bonds)
- redemption, advance refunding 149
- redevelopment bonds (See Redevelopment bonds)
- refunding bonds 149
- registration-required (See Registration-required obligations)
- retirement or sale or exchange of debt instruments, amounts .... 1271 et seq.
- small issue (See Small issue bonds)
- state and local (See State and local bonds)
- stripped (See Stripped bonds or coupons)
- student loan bonds (See Student loan bonds)
- surety bonds (See Surety bonds)
- tax credit bonds (See Qualified tax credit bonds)
- tax-exempt (See Exempt bonds)
- tribal economic development bonds (See Tribal economic development bonds)
- United States obligations (See United States obligations)
- United States savings bonds (See United States savings bonds)
- veterans mortgage bonds (See Veterans mortgage bonds)
- volunteer fire department 147; 150
- wash sales 1091

Bonus depreciation
- ACRS
  - alternative minimum tax and research credit in lieu of bonus depreciation, election .... 168(k)(4)(A)
  - allocation of bonus depreciation amounts ..... 168(k)(4)(E)
  - bonus depreciation amount ....168(k)(4)(C)
  - eligible qualified property ....168(k)(4)(D)
  - limitations, increase in ....168(k)(4)(B)
  - partnerships .... 168(k)(4)(G)(ii)
- cellulose biomass ethanol plant property ...... 168(l)(4)(A)
- December 31, 2007 and before January 1, 2013, allowance for property acquired after
  - election to accelerate the AMT and research credits in lieu of .... 168(k)(4)
  - 50% bonus depreciation 168
- cellulosic biomass ethanol plant property
  - ACRS, bonus depreciation property .... 168(l)(4)(A)
- passenger aircraft
  - alternative minimum tax and research credit in lieu of bonus depreciation, election .... 168(k)(4)(G)(iii)
- research credit
  - alternative minimum tax and research credit in lieu of bonus depreciation, election (See Accelerated cost recovery system (ACRS))

Books and records
- accounting method 446
- alcohol taxes (See Alcohol taxes)
- aviation fuel taxes, inspection of records 4102
- beer tax 5555
- business expenses 274
- cafeteria plans 6039D
- charitable contributions 170
- cigarettes and cigars 5741
- diesel fuel taxes, inspection of records 4102
- disclosure of returns and return information 6103
- distilled spirits plants 5555
- educational assistance programs 6039D
- employee retirement and benefit plans

Books

CODE SEC.

Books and records —Cont'd
. *employee retirement and benefit plans —Cont'd*
. . limitation on benefits and contributions 415
. . examination of 6333; 7210; 7602; 7605
. . . costs and fees to witness 7610
. . . distraint proceedings 6333
. . . district court jurisdiction 7402; 7609
. . . motor fuels, nontaxable use 6427
. . . religious organizations 7611
. . . Tax Court 7456
. . . transferees 6902
. failure to produce 982; 7269
. falsifications 7206
. foreign documents, admissibility 982
. formal request for 982
. fringe benefit plans 6039D
. gasoline taxes, inspection of records 4102
. legal services plans for employees 6039D
. levy and distraint 6333
. liquor 5555; 5603
. notice requiring 6001
. petroleum product taxes, inspection of records 4102
. redemption of seized realty 6337
. regulations requiring, authority 6001
. seizure of property 6333; 6340
. summons to produce 7210; 7609
. third-party recordkeepers 7609
. tobacco products 5741
. U.S. shareholders of controlled foreign corporation 964
. wagering taxes 4403; 4423
. wine 5555
Boot
. nontaxable exchanges 1031
. reorganization exchanges . . . . 356 et seq.
Borax depletion 613
Bows and arrow excise tax 4161
Boycotts, participation in 908; 999
Branch profits tax 884
Branch transaction taxable income 987
Breach of contract damages 186
Breach of fiduciary duty 186
Breweries . . . . 5401 et seq. (See also Beer tax)
. defined 5092
. establishment of . . . . 5401 et seq.
. experimental 5417
. imported beer 5418
. occupational tax . . . . 5091 et seq.
. operations . . . . 5411 et seq.
. pilot brewing plants 5417
. procurement of beer from other breweries 5413
. records and returns 5415; 5555
. removal of beer . . . . 5412 et seq.
. revenue protecting apparatus 5552
. use of 5411
Bribes 162
. government officers and employees 7214

Index to Code

CODE SEC.

Brick and tile clay deposits 613
Brine well depletion 613
Broadcasting
. business expenses 162
. facilities, sale of 1245; 1250
Brokers
. backup withholding 3406; 6705
. information returns (See Information returns)
. personal holding company income 543
Bromine
. hazardous waste clean up 4661; 4662
. percentage depletion 613
Brother-sister controlled group
. consolidated returns 1563
. defined 1563
. employee retirement benefit plans 414
Brownfield site
. unrelated business taxable income . . . . 512(b)(19)
Brucite depletion 613
Build America Bonds
. credit against tax . . . . 54AA(a); 6431(a)
. . amount of credit . . . . 54AA(b)
. . arbitrage rules, application of . . . . 6431(c)
. . limitation based on amount of tax . . . . 54AA(c)(1)
. . payment of credit . . . . 6431(b)
. . unused, carryover of . . . . 54AA(c)(e)
. . defined . . . . 54AA(d)(1)
. . federal guarantees . . . . 54AA(d)(2)(A)
. . gross income treatment of interest . . . . 54AA(f)(1)
. . interest payment date . . . . 54AA(e); 6431(d)
. . nontreatment as, rules for . . . . 54AA(d)(2)(C)
. . qualified bonds
. . . application of credit to certain . . . . 6431(f)
. . . defined . . . . 54AA(g)(2); 6431(e)
. . . issued before 2011 . . . . 54AA(g)
. . . refundable credits . . . . 54AA(g)(1)
. . . regulations, prescription of . . . . 54AA(h)
. . . special rule for new clean renewable energy bonds
. . . . 6431(f)(2)
. . . special rule for qualified energy conservation bonds
. . . . 6431(f)(2)
. . . specified credit bonds . . . . 6431(f)(3)
. . yield, determination of . . . . 54AA(d)(2)(B)
Building and loan associations
. bad debt reserves 593
. bank status 581
. cooperative associations, taxation as . . . . 1381 et seq.
. defined 7701
. depositaries for taxes 6302
. distributions to shareholders 591; 593
. dividends paid deduction 591
. dividends' taxable year of deduction 461
. federal financial assistance 597
. organizations providing reserve funds for, and insurance of,
. . shares in 501
. passbook loans, liens for taxes 6323
. personal holding company status 542
. reacquisition of real property 1038

Index to Code — Calendar

CODE SEC.

Buildings
. demolition expenses 280B
. energy efficient commercial building deduction (See Energy efficient commercial building deduction)
. low-income housing credit (See Low-income housing credit)
. qualified green building and sustainable design projects, facility bonds for (See Exempt facility bonds)
. rehabilitation (See Rehabilitation)

Built-in gains
. change of ownership 382
. preacquisition losses offsetting 384
. recognized built-in gain 384
. S corporations, tax imposed on gains 1366; 1374

Bullion, IRA investment in 408

Burden of proof (See also Evidence)
. abusive tax shelters 6703
. accumulated earnings tax 534
. business expenses 274
. convention expenses 274
. counterclaim by Government where deficiency notice issued while refund suit pending 7422
. credible evidence and shift of burden of proof, introduction of 7491
. distilled spirits, seizure of 5614
. evasion or avoidance of tax (See Evasion or avoidance of tax)
. foreign tax credit 905
. fraud 7454
. frivolous income tax returns 6703
. tax return preparers, willful understatement of tax 7427
. transferee liability 6902; 7454
. understatement of tax liability
.. aiding and abetting 6703
.. tax return preparers 7427

Burdensome taxes by foreign country
. estate tax 2108
. income tax 896

Burial benefit insurance companies 816

Buses
. excise tax 6416
. gasoline tax refunds 6421; 6427
. highway use taxes .... 4481 et seq.
. manufacturers excise taxes 4221

Business (See Trade or business)

Business credit .... 38 et seq.
. alcohol fuels credit 40
. allowance 38
. biodiesel fuel 38
. carrybacks and carryforwards
.. corporate acquisitions 381
.. marginal oil and gas well production credit 39
.. ownership change 383
.. preacquisition losses 384
.. refunds 6511; 6611
.. tentative adjustments 6411
. child care, employer provided 38
. controlled groups 38
. current year 38
. debt discharge amounts, reduction by 108
. deductions 196

CODE SEC.

Business credit—Cont'd
. disabled access credit 44
. enhanced oil recovery credit 43
. Hurricane Katrina 38
. investment credit .... 46 et seq.
. low sulfur diesel fuels 38
. low-income housing (See Low-income housing credit)
. marginal oil and gas well production 38; 39
. mine rescue team training credit 38
. New York Liberty Zone business employee credit 38
. research credit 41
. small business, limitation of amount of tax 38
. small employer health insurance credit 38
. small employer pension plan startup costs 38
. unused 39; 196

Business expenses .... 162; 274 (See also specific items)
. disallowance of deductions 280C
. foreign personal holding companies 556
. insurance companies 834
. meals and lodging (See Meals and lodging)
. personal holding companies 545
. related taxpayers, transactions between 267
. research and experimentation, credit for 6611
. sales and exchanges, related taxpayers 267
. Sec. 179 property 179
. start-up 195
. travel (See Travel expenses)

Business gifts, deductibility of 274

Business income, exempt organization ..... 501; 511 et seq.

Business league exemption 501

Business leases
. unrelated business taxable income 514

Business meeting, deductibility of 274

Business purpose test, private activity bond 141

Business use of home 280A

Butadiene hazardous waste clean up 4661; 4662

Butane hazardous waste clean up 4661; 4662

Butyline hazardous waste clean up 4661; 4662

C

C corporation defined 1361

Cable depreciation, telephone 168

Cadillac insurance plans (See High-cost employer-sponsored health coverage)

Cadmium
. depletion 613
. hazardous waste clean up 4661; 4662

Cafeteria as a fringe benefit 132

Cafeteria plans 125
. information returns 6039D; 6652
. simple cafeteria plans (See Simple cafeteria plans)

Calcium carbonate depletion 613

Calcium chloride depletion 613

Calendar year .... 441 (See also Fiscal year; Taxable year)
. change to or from 442; 443

119

Calls   Index to Code

CODE SEC.

Calls (See Puts and calls)
Campaign contributions (See Political contributions)
Camper coaches retail excise tax 4051; 4053
Camps 119
Campus lodging 119
Cancellation of indebtedness 108
  . basis 1017
  . earnings and profits, effect on 312
  . exempt income 1017
  . farms 1017
  . financial entity return 6050P
  . gross income 61; 108
  . income from 108
  . National Health Services Corp. loan repayment 108
  . principal residence .... 108(h)
  . reaquisition of debt instrument after Dec. 31, 2008 and before Jan. 1, 2001 .... 108(i)
Candidate defined for presidential election campaign fund 9002
Capital assets
  . corporations 362
  . defined 1221
  . losses 165
  . short sales, gains and losses from 1223
Capital construction fund
  . Merchant Marine Act 7518
Capital contributions
  . basis, reorganization exchanges 362
  . business expenses 162
  . controlled corporation 367
  . discharge of indebtedness 108
  . exempt income 118
  . family partnerships 704
  . Federal National Mortgage Association, to 162
  . foreign corporations 897
  . loss carryover, ownership change 382
  . partnerships .... 704; 707; 721 et seq.
  . reorganization exchanges, basis to corporation .. 362
  . undistributed foreign personal holding company income ... 551
Capital expenditures 263; 263A
  . adjustments to basis 1016
  . circulation expenses 173
  . small issue bonds 144
Capital gains and losses ..... 1201 et seq.; 1221 et seq. (See also Gain or loss; Losses)
  . accumulated earnings tax 535
  . allocation of basis, charitable contributions ... 170
  . alternative tax
  . . corporations 1201
  . . insurance companies 831
  . . life insurance companies 801
  . . . mutual savings banks 594
  . . . mutual savings banks, life insurance business ... 594
  . . nonresident aliens 877
  . . REITs .... 857(b)(3)
  . arbitrage operations 1233
  . bonds .... 1271 et seq.
  . cancellation of lease or distributor's agreement ... 1241

CODE SEC.

Capital gains and losses—Cont'd
  . capital asset defined 1221
  . carrybacks and carryovers, capital losses (See Carrybacks and carryovers)
  . charitable contributions 170
  . coal royalties 1231; 1441
  . commodities derivative financial instrument 1221
  . constructive ownership transactions 1260
  . contributions of property 170; 724; 1250
  . controlled foreign corporation stock, sale of .. 1248
  . converted wetlands 1257
  . corporate loss 1212
  . dealers in securities 1236
  . debt instruments .... 1271 et seq.
  . deductibility 165
  . definitions 904; 1221; 1222
  . denial of treatment as 1287
  . depreciable property, gain from disposition 291; 341; 1245
  . determining, rules for .... 1221 et seq.; 1231 et seq.
  . distributor's agreement, cancellation 1241
  . employee retirement or benefit plan distributions
  . . withholding tax at source on nonresident aliens and foreign corporations 1441
  . estates and trusts 642; 643; 691
  . farmlands, erosion of 1257
  . floor specialists 1236
  . foreign corporations 545; 1212
  . foreign expropriation loss recoveries 80
  . foreign investment companies
  . . distributions 1247
  . . election to distribute income currently 1247
  . . stock 1223; 1246; 1247
  . foreign tax credit 904
  . franchises, transfers of 1253
  . government publications 1221; 1231
  . holding period of property
  . . bankrupt's assets 1398
  . . futures transactions subject to exchange 1222
  . . general rules 1223
  . . livestock 1231
  . . replacement property 1223
  . . Sec. 1250 property 1250
  . . short sales 1233
  . insurance companies other than life 832; 834
  . involuntary conversions 1223; 1231
  . iron ore royalties 1231
  . lease, cancellation of 1241
  . life insurance companies 801; 812; 818
  . limitations on losses 1211
  . livestock 1231
  . long-term 545; 642; 852; 1222; 1260
  . loss carrybacks and carryovers (See Carrybacks and carryovers)
  . market discount bonds .... 1276 et seq.
  . musical work, sale or exchange of 1221
  . net capital gain
  . . accumulated earnings tax 535
  . . defined 1222
  . . maximum tax rate 1
  . . personal holding companies 545

120

CODE SEC.

Capital gains and losses—Cont'd
. net capital losses
.. carrybacks and carryovers (See Carrybacks and carryovers)
.. defined 1222
. net income defined 1222; 4982
. net long-term 1222
. net short-term 1222
. nonresident aliens 871
. obligations .... 1271 et seq.
. options to buy and sell 1233; 1234
. ordinary income, gain from related-person sale of depreciable property treated as 1239
. original issue discount .... 1271 et seq.
. partnerships 702; 703; 724; 741
. patents 1235; 1441
. personal holding companies 543; 545
. puts and calls 1233; 1234
. reacquisition of real property 1038
. real estate 1221; 1231; 1237
. recharacterization of gain from certain financial transactions 1258
. registration-required obligations 1287
. regulated investment companies 852
. REITs .... 291; 857(b)(3)
. related-taxpayer transactions 1239
. S corporations 1366; 1374
. sales or exchanges
.. customers, property held primarily for sale to 1221; 1231
.. patents 1235
... foreign corporations, to 1249
.. related taxpayers, between 1239
.. stock in certain foreign corporations 1248
. Sec. 1245 property 1245
. Sec. 1250 property 1250
. Sec. 1256 contracts 1212; 1256
. securities futures contracts 1234B
. short sales 1233
. short-term 1222
.. obligations issued at discount .... 1281 et seq.
. small business investment company stock 1242; 1243
. special rules .... 1231 et seq.
. stocks and securities
.. losses 1244
.. when issued 1233
.. subdivided lots 1237
. termination 1234A
. 30% tax 871
. timber 631; 1201; 1231; 1441
. trade or business, property used in 1221; 1231
. trademarks and trade names, transfers of 1253
. uninsured property loss 1231
. unrelated business taxable income 512
. wash sales 1091
. withholding tax at source on nonresident aliens and foreign corporations 1441

Capitalization
. creative expenses, qualified 263A
. expenses 263A
. insurance companies policy acquisition expenses 848

CODE SEC.

Capitalization —Cont'd
. inventories 263A
Captive insurance companies 953
Carbon dioxide sequestration credit
. attributable to taxpayer .... 45Q(d)(5)
. captured, disposed of or used within the U.S., requirement that carbon dioxide be .... 45Q(d)(1)
. general rules .... 45Q(a)(1)
. inflation adjustment .... 45Q(d)(7)
. qualified carbon dioxide defined .... 45Q(b)
. qualified enhanced oil or natural gas recovery project .... 45Q(d)(4)
. qualified facility defined .... 45Q(c)
. recapture .... 45Q(d)(6)
. recycled carbon dioxide defined .... 45Q(b)(2)
. secure geological storage requirement ..... 45Q(d)(2)
. tertiary injectant defined .... 45Q(d)(3)
Cargo container depreciation 168
Caribbean
. conventions, expense of attending 274
. investment in 936
Carriers, common (See Common carriers)
Carrybacks and carryovers
. acquiring corporation .... 381 et seq.
. alcohol fuel credits 40
. bankruptcy 1398
. black lung benefit trusts, excess contributions ... 192
. business credit (See Business credit)
. capital losses
.. accumulated earnings tax 535
.. acquiring corporation 381
.. corporations 1212
.. debt discharge amounts, reduced by 108
.. foreign expropriations 1212
.. foreign investment companies 1247
.. foreign personal holding companies 1212
.. limitations 383; 384
.. preacquisition losses 384
.. regulated investment company 1212
.. REIT 1212
. charitable contributions 170
. consolidated returns, adjustments 6411
. contributions to employee retirement and benefit plans 404; 404A
. corporations
.. acquisitions .... 381 et seq.
.. capital losses 1211; 1212
.. extensions 6164
.. limitations on net operating loss deductions ... 382
. credits against tax
.. adoption expenses 23
.. bankruptcy 1398
.. deficiency assessments 6501; 6601
.. refund claims 6511; 6611
. debt discharge amounts, reduced by 108
. disabled access credit 39
. dividends, personal holding companies 564
. enhanced oil recovery credit 39
. excess credits 383; 384; 6411; 6511; 6611

121

Carrybacks

CODE SEC.

Carrybacks and carryovers —Cont'd
- expected, extension of time to pay tax 6164
- extension of time for payment by corporations 6164; 6864
- foreign tax (See Foreign tax credit)
- general business credit 38
- insurance companies 844
- interest on overpayments 6611
- investment interest 163
- life insurance companies
- . operations loss deduction 810
- loss corporations 382
- marginal oil and gas well production 39
- mortgage interest credit 25; 6709
- net operating losses
- . acquiring corporation 381
- . bankruptcy 1398
- . beneficiaries of estates or trusts 642
- . damage recoveries 186
- . debt discharge amounts, reduced by 108
- . deduction (See Net operating losses subhead deduction)
- . deficiency reduced by
- . . . interest............................ 6601
- . distributor or transferor corporation 1212
- . estates and trusts 642
- . excess credits......................... 383; 384
- . foreign tax credits 383
- . insurance companies 844
- . limitations 382; 6501
- . overpayments attributable to 6511; 6611
- . ownership change .... 382(n); 383
- . personal service corporations................ 280H
- . preacquisition losses 384
- . renegotiated government contracts 1341; 6511
- . S corporation, from C years 1374
- . tentative adjustments 6213; 6405; 6411; 6501
- operations loss of insurance companies 810; 844
- ownership change......................... 382(n)(1)
- . control in corporation .... 382(n)(3)
- . net operating loss 382; 383
- . subsequent acquisitions .... 382(n)(2)
- payment of tax extended due to 6164
- pecuniary bequest, use of appreciated carryover basis to satisfy 1040
- personal service corporations 280H
- private activity bonds, volume cap 146
- recapture of investment credit property 50
- recovery exclusion 111
- S corporations, C and S years 1371
- Sec. 1256 contracts 1212
- straddles, losses 1092
- tentative adjustments 6213; 6405; 6411; 6501; 6611
- termination of extended period for payment in case of ... 6864
- trusts and estates unused loss carryovers
- . deductions on termination 642
- unused business credits 39
- unused loss on termination of estate or trust 642

Carrying charges
- basis for gain or loss, adjustments 1016
- construction period 312

CODE SEC.

Carrying charges —Cont'd
- definition 263
- disallowance of deductions 266
- installment sales 163
- interest, adjustments 483
- straddles 263

Cartridges, excise tax 4181; 4182; 4222

Cash
- payments received in, information returns ... 6050I; 6103; 6652
- presumption of ownership, jeopardy assessments 6867
- reporting 6050I

Cash basis 446
- debt instruments 1274A
- imputed interest 1274A
- limitation on use 448
- membership dues income 456
- prepaid interest 461
- subscription income election 455

Cash equivalents
- reorganization exchanges, received in .... 356 et seq.

Cash or deferred arrangements (CODAs) 401
- catch-up contributions (See Pension, profit-sharing, and stock bonus plans)
- compensation 404
- contributions having effect of plan 404
- elective deferral limitation 401
- FICA 3121
- independent contractors 404
- limitation on elective deferral exclusion 402
- state or local governments 3121; 3306
- taxability of beneficiary 402
- unfunded deferred benefit plans 404

Cash settlement options 1234

Casual labor
- FICA 3121
- FUTA 3306
- withholding tax on wages 3401

Casual sales of personal property
- lien for taxes 6323

Casualty losses (See also Disaster losses and relief)
- adjusted gross income, estates and trusts 165
- business expenses 274
- business property 1231
- business use of home 280A
- deduction of losses 165
- distilled spirits 5008; 5064
- estate tax 165; 2054; 2106
- estates and trusts 165; 2054
- fire (See Fire losses)
- insurance claim, timely filing 165
- insurance payments for added living expenses 123
- involuntary conversion 1033; 1231
- joint returns 165
- limitation, losses of individuals 165
- living expenses, insurance compensation 123
- net casualty losses allowed 165
- nonresident aliens 873
- $100 limitation per casualty 165

Index to Code   Charitable

CODE SEC.

Casualty losses (See also Disaster losses and relief) — Cont'd
. personal casualty gains and losses 165
. reimbursement, insurance compensation 123
. REIT income from prohibited transactions
. . fire, storm, or other casualty, expenditures for restoration of .... 857(b)(6)(E)(iv)
. storm (See Storm losses)
. theft (See Theft losses)
. uninsured property loss 1231
. vacation home, rental of 280A

Catch-up contributions, pension plan (See Pension, profit-sharing, and stock bonus plans)

Celestite depletion 613

Cellulosic biomass ethanol plant property
. accelerated cost recovery system
. . additional allowance .... 168(l)(1)
. . alternative depreciation property .... 168(l)(4)(B)
. . alternative minimum tax, allowance against .... 168(l)(6)
. . bonus depreciation property .... 168(l)(4)(A)
. . cellulosic biomass ethanol defined .... 168(l)(3)
. . defined .... 168(l)(2)
. . double benefit denial .... 168(l)(8)
. . election out .... 168(l)(4)(D)
. . recapture .... 168(l)(7)
. . special rules .... 168(l)(5)
. . tax-exempt bond-financed property .... 168(l)(4)(C)
. depreciation .... 168(l)(4)(A)

Cement mixer retail excise tax 4053
Cemetery companies 170; 501; 642
Cent, fractional part 6313
Center for Medicare and Medicaid Services
. disclosure of returns and return information 6103
Central liquidity facility exemption 501
Certificates
. face-amount certificates 401
. mortgage credit (See Mortgage credit certificates)
. wage withholding exemptions 3402
. withholding exemption (See Withholding exemption certificates)

Certificates of deposit, premature withdrawal 62
Certificates of sale, seized property 6338; 6339
Certification
. authority, IRS 7622
. low-income housing credit (See Low-income housing credit)
. work opportunity credit 51

Certified historic structures
. conservation contributions 170
. rehabilitation credit 47

Certified mail, use of 6212; 7455; 7502
CERTs (See Corporate equity reduction transactions (CERTs))
Chambers of commerce exempt status 501
Change of ownership .... 382; 382(n)(1)
. business credits 383
. control in corporation .... 382(n)(3)
. net operating loss 382
. subsequent acquisitions .... 382(n)(2)

CODE SEC.

Charitable bequests
. foreign private foundations 4948
. nonresident aliens 2106
. private foundations 4943
. taxable estate 2055

Charitable contributions
. accrual basis corporations 170
. accumulated earnings tax 535
. acquiring corporation, carryovers by 381
. adjusted current earnings, computation of 56
. airplanes 170; 6720
. amateur athletic competitions, sponsorship 170
. amounts permanently set aside for 642
. annuity trusts, remainder interest 170; 664
. appraisals 170
. appreciated property 57
. bargain sales 1011
. base, contribution 170
. bonds 170
. books and records 170
. business expenses 162
. capital gains 170; 642
. carrybacks and carryovers 170; 381; 1398
. cemetery companies 170
. charitable remainder trust distributions 664
. clothing 170
. colleges 170
. computers 170
. corporations 170
. cruelty prevention organizations 170
. deductions
. . disallowance 508
. . estates and trusts 642
. . nonresident aliens 873
. . trusts claiming, returns 6034
. deductions, disallowance of 170
. defined 170
. disallowed deductions 170; 508
. disclosure of nondeductibility 6113; 6710
. documentation 170
. donor advised funds 170; 2522
. educational organizations 170
. estate tax 2055
. estates and trusts 170; 642; 663; 681; 2014; 2032; 6034
. excess, carryback and carryover of 170
. exempt use property, deduction recapture of 170
. farm, remainder interest in 170
. foreign corporations 882
. foreign personal holding companies 556
. foundations 170
. fractional gifts 170
. fraternal organizations 170
. fraudulent acknowledgments 6720
. future interests 170
. generation-skipping transfers, tax on 2642
. gift tax 2522; 2524
. gifts 170; 2522
. . deduction 2522; 2524
. . foreign private foundations 4948

123

Charitable

CODE SEC.

Charitable contributions —Cont'd
. governmental unit 170
. grantor trusts 170
. higher education institutions, to 170
. household items 170
. Indian tribal governments, treatment as state 7871
. information returns
.. sale or exchange of contributed property 6050L
. insurance companies other than life 832
. intellectual property income 170
. inventories 170
. liabilities transferred as part of contribution 170
. life insurance companies 805
. literary organizations 170
. lobbying activities 170
. medical research organizations 170
. mileage allowances 170
. nonresident aliens 873
. ordinary income 170
. partial interest in property 170
. partners and partnerships 702; 703
. percentage limitations 170
. personal holding companies 545
. personal residence, remainder interest in 170
. political campaigns 170
. pooled income funds 170; 642
. private foundations 170; 642
. prizes and awards transferred to charities 74
. prohibited transactions 170
. property
.. information returns 6050L; 6652
.. tax preference item 57
. real property, remainder interest in 170
. recapture of deduction 170
. recordkeeping 170
. rehabilitation credits 170
. remainder interests 170; 642
. research equipment 170
. sale or exchange of contributed property 6050L; 6652
. scientific property used for research 170
. split-dollar life insurance contracts 170
. sports events, tickets to 274
. stock 170
. students in taxpayer's household 170
. substantiation requirement 170
. taxidermy property 170
. travel expenses, denial of 170
. trust, property placed in 170
. unitrust, remainder interest 170; 664
. universities 170
. unrelated business income 512
. used motor vehicles, boat, and airplanes 170
. valuation
.. charitable remainder trusts 664
.. remainder interest in real property 170
. veterans organizations 170
. whaling captains in support of native Alaskan subsistence whaling 170

Index to Code

CODE SEC.

Charitable organizations and foundations 501
. bargain sales to 1011
. business income 511
. deficiency assessment .... 6211 et seq.; 7422
. exemption 501
. information returns 6033
. IRA distribution for 408
. legislative activities 501; 504
. lobbying expenditures 501; 504
.. disqualifying 4912; 6852; 7409
.. excessive, excise tax on 4911
. nondeductibility of contributions, required disclosure 6113; 6710
. political expenditures 4912; 4955; 6852; 7409
. private foundations 508; 4947; 6033
. property transfer to, for unrelated business 1245; 1250
. related taxpayers, transactions between 267
. sales or exchanges with related taxpayers 267
. transfers for public, religious and charitable use 2055
. unrelated business income, tax on .... 511 et seq.

Charitable remainder trusts 664
. contributions to 170
. disallowance of deductions, contributions to trust 170
. estate tax
.. recovery 2207B
.. transfers to trust 2055
. gift tax
.. deductions 2522
.. recovery 2207B
. husband and wife, gifts between 2523
. split-interest trusts 4947
. surviving spouse 2056
. unitrust 664

Charitable trusts
. business income 511
. contributions to 170
. generation-skipping transfers, tax on 2642; 2651
. information returns 6652
. private foundation treatment 4947
. remainder trusts (See Charitable remainder trusts)
. taxable year 644

Check, payment of tax by 6201; 6311; 6657

Chemicals
. environmental taxes
.. definitions 4662
.. hazardous waste clean up .... 4661 et seq.
.. imported substances 4671; 4672
.. imposition of 4661
.. ozone-depleting chemicals 4681; 4682

Child care, employer provided 38; 45F
Child care center exemption 501
Child care expenses
. collection of liabilities for 6305
. credit
.. employment-related expenses 21
. dependent care assistance programs (See Dependent care assistance programs)

Index to Code — Claim

CODE SEC.

Child tax credit
. advance payments for 2003 6429
. allowance 24
. qualifying child defined 24

Children
. absent parent, collection of support obligations 6103; 6305; 6402
. alimony for support of 71; 682; 6103; 6305; 6402
. compensation 73; 6201
. death of minor
.. estates and trust beneficiary, reversionary interest 673
. definition 151
. dependents 151; 152
. divorced or separated parents, of 152; 213
. earned income credit 32
. earnings 73; 3121; 3306; 6201
. employee benefit plans, payments 401
. estates and trust beneficiary
.. reversionary interest taking effect at death of minor 673
. expenses for care (See Child care expenses)
. fringe benefits 132
. levy and distraint, exemptions for support 6334
. personal exemptions 151
. qualifying child for earned income credit 32
. special needs children 23
.. $13,170 special needs adoption credit ... 36C(a)(3); 137(a)(2)
. support payments 71
. unearned income
.. alternative minimum tax 59
.. parent's income, taxed as if 1
.. tax rates 1

Children's Health Insurance Programs (CHIP)
. preexisting conditions, crediting previous coverage .... 9801(f)(3)

China clay depletion 613
Chlorine hazardous waste clean up 4661; 4662
Christian Science practitioners
. self-employment income 1402
Chromite depletion 613
Chromite hazardous waste clean up 4661; 4662
Chromium hazardous waste clean up 4661; 4662
Churches (See also Apostolic associations; Religious organizations)
. convention or association defined .... 7701(o)
. deferred compensation plans 457
. examination of, restrictions 7611
. net earning from self-employment, church employee 1402
. pension, profit-sharing, and stock bonus plans (See Pension, profit-sharing, and stock bonus plans subhead church plans)
Churning transactions 168
Cider, distilled spirit tax 5042
Cigarettes and cigars .... 5701 et seq. (See also Tobacco)
. abandoned and condemned products, disposal of 5753
. bond, requirement of 5711
. defined 5702
. export warehouse 5702
. failure to pay tax 6651
. forfeitures 5753

CODE SEC.

Cigarettes and cigars—Cont'd
. Internal Revenue enforcement officers 7214; 7608
. labels 5723; 5752
. large 5701
. marks required 5723; 5752
. notices required 5723; 5752
. packages 5723; 5752
. papers and tubes .... 5701 et seq.
.. defined 5702
.. disaster, losses caused by 5708
.. exemption from tax 5704
.. importer of 5702
.. imposition and rate of tax 5731
.. inventories 5721
.. liability for tax 5703
.. manufacturer of 5702
.. rate of tax 5701; 5731
.. reports required 5722
. penalties
.. assessment of 5703
.. civil 5761
.. criminal 5762
. permits .... 5711 et seq.
. rate of tax 5701
. records 5741
. removal, purchase, receipt, possession, or sale after 5751
. returns 5703; 6091
. small 5701
. tax credits or refunds 5705; 6423
. ultimate tax burden 6423

Circulation costs 173
. alternative minimum tax .... 56(b)(2)
. basis for gain or loss, adjustments 1016

Citizens and citizenship
. definition of citizen, FICA 3121
. departure from U.S., terminating taxable year upon 6851
. earned income 911; 912
. exempt income 912
. expatriation 877; 2107; 2501
. foreign tax credit 901
. living abroad 911
. loss of U.S. citizenship
.. information 6039F; 6039G
.. termination of U.S. citizenship defined 7701
. personal property sales by U.S. citizen 865
. premium assistance credit, health plan coverage
.. individuals not lawfully present 36B
. termination of U.S. citizenship defined 7701

Civic leagues 501
Civil actions by U.S. (See Court action)
Civil service employees
. benefit plan distributions, nonresident alien 402
. FICA 3122
. FUTA 3306

Claim of right
. computation of tax for substantial amount held under 1341
. restoration of income held under 1341; 6213; 6411
. tentative refunds under 6213; 6411

125

CODE SEC.

Claims
. abatement ... 6404
. correction of error after taxable year closed ... 1311 et seq.
. deficiencies in case of bankruptcy or receivership ... 6871
. deficiency-dividend deduction ... 547; 860
. refunds (See Refunds and credits)
. timely mailing as timely filing ... 7502

Claims Court jurisdiction
. deficiency notice issued while refund suit pending ... 7422
. exempt organizations and private foundations, qualification as ... 7428

Class lives depreciation ... 168
Classification of provisions ... 7806
Clay deposits depletion ... 613
Clean fuel vehicles ... 179A
Clean renewable energy bonds (CREBs)
. amount of bonds designated, limitation on ... 54(f)
. arbitrage ... 54(i)
. cooperative electric company ... 54(j)(1)
. credit to holders of
.. allowance ... 54(a)
.. amount of credit ... 54(b)
.. annual credit ... 54(b)(2)
.. bond defined ... 54(l)(1)
.. date, allowance ... 54(b)(4)
.. gross income inclusion ... 54(g)
.. limitations based on amount of tax ... 54(c)
.. partnerships ... 54(l)(3)
.. pass-thru entities ... 54(l)(3)
.. pooled financing bond defined ... 54(l)(2)
.. ratable principal amortization requirement ... 54(l)(4)
.. reporting requirements ... 54(l)(5)
.. S corporations ... 54(l)(3)
.. termination ... 54(m)
. expenditures ... 54(h)
. governmental body ... 54(j)(3)
. gross income inclusion ... 54(f)
. information reporting requirements ... 6049
. lenders ... 54C(d)(5); 54(j)(2)
. maturity limitations ... 54(e)
. newly issued (See New clean renewable energy bonds)
. pool bonds
.. definitions concerning ... 54(k)(1)
.. estimated taxes ... 54(k)(5)
.. ratable principal amortization ... 54(k)(6)
.. regulated investment companies, held by ... 54(k)(4)
.. reporting ... 54(k)(7)
. qualified borrower ... 54(j)(5)
. qualified issuer ... 54(j)(4)
. qualified project ... 54(d)(2)

Clergy
. FICA ... 3121
. FUTA ... 3309
. parsonage rental value ... 107; 265
. rental allowances or value of parsonage ... 107; 265
. self-employment tax ... 1402
. social security, waiver of exemption from ... 1402
. waiver of exemption from Social Security coverage ... 1402

CODE SEC.

Clergy —Cont'd
. withholding ... 3401
Clifford trusts ... 674
Clinical testing expenses
. credit for ... 280C(b)
. qualifying therapeutic discovery projects (See Qualifying therapeutic discovery projects)
. rare diseases or conditions ... 45C
Closed-loop biomass
. electricity produced from renewable resources, credit ... 45
Closed-loop biomass facilities
. electricity production credit ... 45
Closely held business property
. estate tax ... 2032A; 6166; 6601
. transfers, gain or loss ... 1040; 1223
Closely held corporations
. change in status ... 469
. equipment leasing
.. at risk limitations ... 465
. farming operations
.. accounting methods ... 447
. leasing activities, at risk amounts ... 465
. passive activity losses and credits ... 469
. real estate investments ... 856
Closing agreements ... 7121 et seq.
. determination of claim for refund ... 1313
. penalties connected with ... 7206
Clothes washers and dryers
. energy efficient appliance credits (See Energy efficient appliance credits)
Clothing, charitable contribution of ... 170
Clubs
. colleges, domestic service
.. FICA ... 3121
.. FUTA ... 3306
.. withholding tax on wages ... 3401
. dues
.. deductibility ... 274
.. prepayment ... 456
. exemption ... 501
. information returns ... 6033
. social club exemption from tax ... 501
. transactions with members, deductions incurred ... 277
Coal
. advanced coal project credit (See Advanced coal project credit)
. black lung disease (See Black lung benefit trusts)
. deduction, disposal expenditure ... 272
. definition ... 1231
. derivatives, environmental tax for hazardous waste clean up ... 4662
. disposal of ... 272; 617; 631
. imposition of tax ... 4121
. Indian coal production facility ... 45
. percentage depletion ... 291; 613
. Railroad Retirement Tax Act ... 3231
. refined coal defined ... 45
. sales and exchanges ... 631

Index to Code   Collection

CODE SEC.

Coal mines
. black lung disease (See Black lung benefit trusts)
. excise taxes 4121; 4218; 9501
. nonconventional fuel source credit (See Nonconventional fuel source credit)
. royalties
. . capital gains and losses 1231
. . expenditures connected with
. . . basis adjustments 1016
. . . self-employment earnings 1402
. . withholding tax at source on nonresident aliens and foreign corporations 1441

Coast and geodetic survey
. injuries or sickness, compensation for 104

Coast guard (See Armed forces)

Cobalt
. depletion 613
. hazardous waste clean up 4661; 4662

COBRA
. premium assistance .... 139C; 6432(a)
. . cessation of eligibility, failure to notify plan of 6720C
. . involuntary termination, qualifying event as .... 6432(e)
. . method of reimbursement .... 6432(c)
. . overstatement of reimbursement .... 6432(c)(2)
. . payment of remaining premium, reimbursement contingent on .... 6432(c)(3)
. . payroll taxes
. . . defined .... 6432(d)(1)
. . . treatment as payment of .... 6432(c)(1)
. . person
. . . defined .... 6432(d)(2)
. . . entitled to reimbursement .... 6432(b)
. . regulations, issuance of .... 6432(g)
. . reporting requirements .... 6432(f)
. . temporary extension of coverage .... 4980B(f)(5)(C)

CODAs (See Cash or deferred arrangements (CODAs))

Cohabitation, dependent 152

Coin-operated gaming devices
. disposal of 7326
. wagering tax 4402

Coin-operated telephones 4253; 4254

Coins
. coin and bullion exception to IRA definition of collectible .... 408(m)(3)
. IRA investments in 408

Collapsible corporations 341
. stock purchase as asset purchase 338

Collectibles
. simplified employee pension plans .... 408(m)(1) et seq.

Collection of foreign items 7001
. failure to obtain license 7231
. information returns 6041; 6652

Collection of taxes .... 6301 et seq.
. abatement, mathematical and clerical errors 6213; 6404
. absent parent, child support payments 6305
. accounting for 7512
. after assessments 6502
. authority 6301

CODE SEC.

Collection of taxes—Cont'd
. backup withholding 3406
. beer 5054; 5061
. bond to stay .... 7101 et seq.
. child support obligations 6305
. contingency operation, military 7508
. contracts for
. . civil damages for unauthorized collection under 7433A
. . fair debt collection practices act 6306
. . qualified tax collection contract 6306
. coordination of collection of income taxes with domestic service employment taxes 3510
. court review of decision, bond to stay assessments and 7485
. credits or refunds to persons who collected 6415
. departure from country 6851
. deposits 6302; 6656; 7808; 7809
. Desert Shield 7508
. discretionary method 6302
. distraint (See Seizure of property)
. employment taxes 3501; 6205; 6302
. excessive refund claims 6206
. expenses 212
. facilities and services 4291
. failure to collect or pay over tax 6672; 7202; 7215; 7512
. fair tax collection practices 6304
. FICA 3122; 3501
. FUTA 3501
. hospitalization due to combat related injuries 7508
. injunction (See Injunction against assessment and collection)
. insolvent banks 7507
. levying on property (See Levy)
. liability for 7501
. lien for taxes (See Lien for taxes)
. limitation period (See Statute of limitations)
. limitations 6501
. methods 6302
. mode or time of 6302
. notice and demand for tax 6303
. offenses 7215
. possessions of U.S. 7651
. prohibition of suits to restrain collections 7421
. Railroad Retirement Tax Act 3501
. receipt of payment .... 6311 et seq.
. regulations 6302
. removal of property from U.S. 6503
. seizure of property (See Seizure of property)
. services and facilities, taxes on 4291
. stamp taxes 6201; 6501
. statute of limitations (See Statute of limitations)
. stay of jeopardy assessment 6863
. suit (See Suits)
. termination of taxable year 6851
. time of 6302
. unauthorized, damages 7433
. wages, at source on .... 3401 et seq.
. waiver (See Waiver)
. war postponement 7508
. willful failure to pay over tax 7202

127

Collection   Index to Code

CODE SEC.

Collection of taxes—Cont'd
. wines 5043; 5061
. withheld on wages (See Withholding)
Collective bargaining agreements
. determination as to status as 7701
. employee benefit plans 401
. endangered or critical status multiemployer plans (See Endangered or critical status multiemployer plans)
. multiemployer plans 401
. top-heavy plans 416
Collectively bargained plans 413
. cafeteria plans 125
. contribution deduction 404
. limitations on benefits and contributions 415
. top-heavy plans 416
. voluntary employee benefit associations 505
. welfare benefit plans 419A
College club, domestic service in
. FICA 3121
. FUTA 3306
. withholding tax on wages 3401
Colleges (See Educational organizations)
Columbium depletion 613
Combat, military (See Armed Forces)
Combined heat and power system property .... 48(c)(3)
Combined reporting (See Joint returns)
Commercial buildings
. energy efficient commercial building deduction (See Energy efficient commercial building deduction)
Commercial cargo excise taxes 4462
Commercial fishing vessel crew meals 274
Commercial golf course
. financing, small issue bonds 144
Commercial inland waterway transportation, fuel tax .. 4042
Commercial transactions financing agreement defined
.... 6323
Commercial vessels excise taxes 4462
Commission
. defined for presidential election campaign fund 9002
Commissioner of Internal Revenue 7701; 7802
. assistant to, retirement plans 7802
. change of, proceedings pending before appellate court .. 7484
. employment by 7804
. powers and duties 7802
. suit for damages 7402
Commissions
. backup withholding 3406
. DISCs 994
. gross income 61
. noncash remuneration, withholding tax on wages 3402
Commodities
. dealers (See Dealers in options and commodities)
. trading in 864
Commodities derivative financial instruments
. capital assets, defined as 1221
Commodity contracts
. controlled foreign corporations 954

CODE SEC.

Commodity credit corporation
. loans 77; 1016
. transactions, information reporting 6039J
Commodity futures
. foreign personal holding company income 553
. holding period 1223
. straddles 1092
. transactions 1222; 1233
Commodity pools
. electing large partnership defined 775
Common carriers
. communications tax exemption 4253
. defined 3231
Common nontaxable exchanges .... 1031 et seq.
Common trust funds 584
. alternative minimum tax 59
. bond premiums, election to amortize 171
. defined 584
. regulated investment company status 851
. returns 6032
Common-law marriage, dependents 152
Commonly controlled businesses
. work opportunity credit 52
Communications taxes (See also Telephone and telegraph taxes)
. coin-operated services 4253
. companies in communications, exemption from toll telephone tax for 4253
. computation of tax 4254
. definitions 4251; 4252
. deposit of 6302
. exemptions 4253
. imposition of 4251
. Indian tribal government, treatment as state 7871
. international income 863
. possessions of U.S 4293
. rates 4251
. refunds and credits 6415
. satellites 168; 883
. U.S. use 4293
Communist controlled organizations
. charitable contributions 170
. employees, FICA 3121
Community assets
. renewal community capital gain 1400F
Community chest 170; 501
Community health needs assessments
. exempt entities and organizations 501
Community income 66
Community property
. annuities, estate tax 2039
. basis after death of spouse 1014
. estate tax 2032A; 2039
. gift tax 2524
. innocent spouse 6013
. laws 66
. marital deduction 2523
. nonresident aliens 879

128

Index to Code

Computers

CODE SEC.

Community property — Cont'd
. self-employment income 1402
Companion sitting placement services 3506
Compensation
. agricultural labor 51
. armed forces 112
. backup withholding 3406
. business expenses 274
. children 73
. clergy, rental value of parsonages 107
. CODAs (See Cash or deferred arrangements (CODAs))
. deduction, limitation on . . . . 280C(a)
. deferred
. . deduction for contributions of employer 404
. . employee annuities 403
. . employee stock ownership plan 409
. . employee stock purchase plans 423
. . employees of domestic subsidiaries engaged in business outside U.S. 407
. . employees of foreign affiliates 406
. . pension, profit-sharing, and stock bonus plans . . . 401 et seq.
. . state and local governments and tax-exempt organizations, plans of 457
. . stock options . . . . 421 et seq.
. . taxability of beneficiary of employees' trust 402
. defined
. . FUTA 3306
. . Railroad Retirement Tax Act 3231
. . self-employment tax 1402
. . withholding tax on wages 3401
. employee annuities 403
. employee retirement and benefit plans 414
. employee stock options 421
. employment taxes (See Employment taxes)
. excess benefit transaction tax 4958
. exempt (See Exempt income)
. expatriated corporation insider, stock compensation 4985
. foreign government employees 893
. foreign students and exchange visitors 872
. golden parachute payments, reasonable compensation . . . . 280G(b)(4)
. gross income 61
. information returns 6041; 6051; 6652
. injuries and sickness, for . . . . 104 et seq.
. international organization employees 893
. levy upon 6331; 6334
. meals and lodging (See Meals and lodging)
. Native Americans 45A
. nonresident aliens (See Nonresident aliens)
. offshore mining operations 638
. partners 707
. Peace Corps 3401; 6011
. pension, profit-sharing, and stock bonus plans
. . defined . . . . 414(s)
. . highly compensated employees . . . . 414(q)(4)
. . veterans' reemployment rights under USERRA . . . . . 414(u)(7)
. personal services (See Compensation for personal services)
. railway labor 51
. reasonable compensation, golden parachute payment . . . . 280G(b)(4)

CODE SEC.

Compensation — Cont'd
. rental value of parsonages 107
. reorganization exchanges 356
. restoration of amount held under claim of right 1341
. salary reduction agreement, employee annuities purchased under 403
. services of child 73
. Social Security taxes (See Employment taxes)
. sources within U.S. 861
. sources without U.S. 862
. third party paying or providing for 3505
. tips (See Tips)
. trust fund, vaccine-related injury 9510
. U.S. citizens or residents living abroad 911
. wages
. . defined 51; 3401
. . FICA 3121
. . FUTA 3306
. . self-employment tax 1402
. . withholding tax (See Withholding)
. work opportunity credit 51
Compensation for personal services
. business expenses 162
. exchanges of compensatory property 83
. passive activity losses and credits 469
. source of income; labor performed in the U.S. 861
. transfers of compensatory property 83
Complex estates and trusts . . . . 661 et seq.
Compressed natural gas special fuels tax 4041
Compromise of tax liability cases 7122
. administrative review 7122
. authorization 7122
. deemed acceptance not rejected within certain period . . . 7122
. disclosures 6103
. evaluation of offers, standards for 7122
. evaluation of offers-in-compromise, standards for 7122
. penalties connected with 7206
. submission of offers-in-compromise, rules for 7122
. treatment of offer, special rules for 7122
Comptroller General
. disclosure of returns and return information 6103
Computation of tax
. accounting method, change in 418
. alternative minimum tax 56
. bankruptcy 1398
. changes in rates during year 15
. communications taxes 4254
. consolidated returns 1503
. estate tax 1561; 2001; 2101
. gift tax 2502
. rate schedule 2001; 2502
. restoration of substantial amount held by taxpayer under claim of right 1341
. returns 1503; 6102
. tax not computed by taxpayer 6014
Computers
. accelerated cost recovery system (ACRS) (See Qualified technology equipment)
. alcohol taxes, payment by 5061

129

Computers

CODE SEC.

Computers —Cont'd
. depreciation 280F
. software
.. depreciation 167
.. disclosure 7213
.. royalties 543
.. summons to analyze tax related 7612
. technology and equipment
.. charitable contributions for educational purposes 170
Concealment, penalties 7206
Concrete mixer excise tax exemption 4053
Condemnation of property
. interest on awards
.. personal holding companies 543
. involuntary conversion upon 1033; 1231
. nonrecognition of gain or loss 1033
Condominium management associations
. definition 528
. returns 6012
Confidentiality
. Privacy Act of 1974, inapplicability to IRC provisions 7852
. returns, disclosure on .... 6103 et seq. (See also Disclosure of tax information)
. tax shelters 7525
. taxpayer communications 7525
Conflict-of-interest requirement
. sales or exchanges 1043
Congress persons, expenses of 162
Congressional committees
. disclosures of return and return information to 6103; 6104
Conscientious objectors
. insurance, self-employment tax 1402
Consent dividends 565; 1016
Conservation
. charitable contributions 170
. cost-sharing payments 126
. efficient appliance credit (See Energy efficient appliance credit)
. energy
.. efficient appliance credit (See Energy efficient appliance credit)
.. public utilities subsidies provided by 136
.. qualified energy conservation bonds (See Qualified energy conservation bonds)
. environmental taxes (See Environmental taxes)
. gain from disposition of Sec. 126 property 1255
. green building and sustainable design projects (See Exempt facility bonds subhead qualified green building and sustainable design projects)
. hazardous waste cleanup (See Hazardous waste cleanup)
. historic structures, conservation contributions 170
. qualified green building and sustainable design projects (See Exempt facility bonds subhead qualified green building and sustainable design projects)
. soil and water
.. assessments for depreciable property 175
.. cost-sharing program payments 194; 1255
... basis of property, increase in 126
.... gain from disposition of Sec. 126 property 1255

Index to Code

CODE SEC.

Conservation —Cont'd
. soil and water —Cont'd
.. definition 175
.. depreciable property 175
.. expenditures 175; 263
.. farmland
... expenditures 175
... gain from disposition 1252
.. limitation, deduction 175
Consolidated returns .... 1501 et seq.
. adjusted basis, special rule for determining 1503
. avoidance of tax, regulations for prevention of 1502
. carrybacks
.. adjustment, tentative 6411
.. extension of time to pay tax 6164
. computation of tax 1502; 1503
. controlled corporations .... 1561 et seq.
. dual consolidated loss 1503
. earnings and profits 1552
. estimated tax, overpayment adjustment 6425
. includible corporations 1504
. insurance companies 843; 1504
. life insurance companies 818; 1503; 1504
. limitations on assessment and collection 6503
. overpayment of estimated tax, adjustment 6425
. payment of tax 1503
. personal holding companies 542
. property acquisition by corporation during affiliation 1051
. stock ownership rule 1504
. tentative carrybacks and refund adjustments 6411
. termination as group member, reconsolidation 1504
Consolidations (See Reorganization exchanges)
Construction
. arbitrage bonds, financing 148
. contracts 460
. period, carrying charges 312
. projects, hedge bonds (See State and Local bonds)
Constructive ownership of stock 318
. controlled corporations 304; 958; 1563
. foreign personal holding companies 554
. loss carryover, ownership change 382
. partnerships 267
. personal holding companies 544
. redemption of stock 302
. REITs 856
. related taxpayers
.. sales of depreciable property 1239
.. transactions between 267
. rules for determining ownership 544
. sales and exchanges between related taxpayers ... 267; 1239
Constructive ownership transaction, gains from 1260
Constructive receipt of income
. FICA deductions as remuneration paid 3123
. FUTA deductions as remuneration paid 3307
Constructive sale price, manufacturers excise tax 4216
Constructive sales
. appreciated financial positions 1259

130

Index to Code

Controlled

	CODE SEC.
Consumer cooperatives	6044
Consumer loans	
. property as loan security, information returns	6050J; 6652
Consumer price index	1
Consumer reporting agency	6103
Containers	
. depreciation	168
. distilled spirits	5206; 5301; 5311; 5604; 5606
Contaminated sites	
. environmental remediation costs, expensing of	198
Contested liabilities	461
Contiguous country life insurance branches	814
Continental shelf areas	638
Continental U.S. defined for transportation tax	4262
Contingency operations, military	
. postponement of actions relating to tax liability	7508
Continuation coverage, group health plans (See Group health plans)	
Continuing care facilities, elderly individuals	
. imputed interest on loans to facilities	7872
. private foundations	4942
Contracts	
. annuities	72
. breach of contract	186
. collection of tax (See Collection of taxes)	
. Federal executive agencies, returns for	6050M
. first-time homebuyers	
. . binding contract exception, application of sec. 36	36(h)(2)
. long-term (See Long-term contracts)	
Contributions	
. black lung benefit trusts	192; 4953
. capital (See Capital contributions)	
. charitable (See Charitable contributions)	
. construction, to aid	118
. corporate capital, to	118
. deductibility	
. . employee trusts by employers, to	404
. employee retirement and benefit plans (See Employee retirement and benefit plans)	
. employees annuities (See Employee annuities)	
. employer contributions to accident and health plans	105; 106
. employer liability trusts	194A
. excess (See Excess contributions)	
. FUTA	3306
. partnerships (See Partners and partnerships)	
. pension, profit-sharing, and stock bonus plans (See Pension, profit-sharing, and stock bonus plans)	
. political	276
. Presidential Election Campaign Fund	6096
. qualified plans, to	404
. quid pro quo contributions	
. . disclosure	6115
. . failure to meet disclosure requirements	6114
. self-employed retirement plans (See Self-employed retirement plans)	
. State unemployment fund	3302 et seq.
. surtax exemption, transitional rules	1564

	CODE SEC.
Contributions — Cont'd	
. withdrawal liability payment funds	194A
Controlled corporations (See also Controlled foreign corporations; Controlled group of corporations)	
. accumulated earnings credit	1561
. acquisitions of, avoidance of tax	269
. capital contributions	367
. consolidated returns	1561 et seq.
. constructive ownership	304
. control defined	304
. definition of controlled entity	1239
. distribution of stock and securities	312; 355; 356
. exempt organizations	4958
. foreign (See Controlled foreign corporations)	
. life insurance company small business deduction	1561
. multiple tax benefits	1561
. redemption of stock	304
. reorganization exchanges	351; 355
. sale of property to	1239
. special rules	52
. stock	
. . acquired in transaction	304
. . transfers, voting rights retained	
. . . estate tax	2036
. transferor controlled	351
. transfers to	304; 306; 346; 1250; 2036
Controlled entity defined	1239
Controlled foreign corporations	951 et seq.
. adjustments to basis	961
. alternative minimum tax special rule	56
. banking or financing income	954
. blocked income	964
. boycotts, participation in	908; 999
. branch income	954
. commodity contracts	954
. controlled group	1563
. deductions, accounting for	954
. defined	957
. distributions	1291
. earnings and profits	952; 956; 959; 960; 964
. election of individual shareholder to be taxed at corporate rates	962
. exempt income	883; 954
. export trade corporations	970; 971
. factoring trade receivables	864
. foreign base company income	954; 970
. foreign country income	952
. foreign tax credit	960
. graduated tax rate structure, corporations	
. . shareholders, election to be taxed at corporate rates	962
. gross income	
. . exclusion of previously taxed earnings and profits	959
. . U.S. shareholders	951
. income from U.S. sources	952
. information returns	6038; 6046
. insurance branches	964
. insurance business, active conduct of	954
. insurance income	953; 954; 957
. interest	881

131

Controlled — Index to Code

CODE SEC.

Controlled foreign corporations—Cont'd
. investments
. . bank-holding company 956
. . earnings in U.S. property 956
. . export trade assets 970
. . shipping operations 955
. . U.S. property 956
. lending or finance business 954
. life insurance and annuity contracts 954
. limitations on subpart F income 952
. loans from 864
. notional principal contracts, income from 954
. oil and gas income 954
. partnership sales, look-thru rule for 954
. patents transferred to 1249
. personal service contracts 954
. pledges and guarantees 956
. portfolio debt investments 881
. receivables acquired from U.S. persons 956
. related corporations, look-thru rule for 954
. sales income 954
. Sec. 1248, amounts previously taxed under 959
. services income 954
. shipping, investment in 955
. stock
. . basis 961; 1016
. . gain on sale or exchange 1248
. . ownership rules 958
. . redemptions and liquidations 1248
. Subpart F income 951; 952; 955; 970
. taxable year 898
. taxes paid by 960; 962
. temporary dividends received deduction 965
. unearned premiums 954
. U.S. shareholders 904; 951; 957; 960; 962; 964

Controlled group of corporations
. accumulated earnings credit 1551; 1561
. acquisitions to evade or avoid tax 1551
. brother-sister group 1563
. business credit 38
. cafeteria plans 125
. certain stock excluded 1563
. children, grandchildren, parents and grandparents defined 1563
. component members defined 1563
. consolidated returns .... 1501 et seq.
. deferral of loss 267
. definition 267; 414; 1563
. depletion, oil and gas 613A
. depreciation, expensing in lieu of 179
. DISCs 995
. earnings and profits 1552
. employee .... 414(b); 1563
. employee retirement and benefit plans 412; 414; 4971
. excluded members defined 1563
. farming operations 447
. foreign corporations 1563
. fringe benefits, penalties for excess 4977
. general business credit 38

CODE SEC.

Controlled group of corporations —Cont'd
. graduated corporate rates
. . disallowance of benefits 1551
. graduated rate structure 1561
. insurance companies
. . capitalization of policy acquisition expenses 848
. . liability for tax, election as to allocation 1552
. . life insurance companies special deductions 806
. LIFO inventories
. . conformity rules 472
. . simplified dollar-value 474
. long-term contract accounting methods 460
. loss deferral 267
. multiple tax benefits, limitations 1561
. overlapping groups defined 1563
. parent-subsidiary controlled group 1563
. pension, profit-sharing, and stock bonus plans
. . application of rules to certain employees .... 414(t)
. . employees defined .... 414(b)
. preacquisition losses offsetting built-in gains 384
. reforestation expenditures 194
. regulated investment company 851
. research credit 41
. rules for determining stock ownership 1563
. sales or exchanges 267
. simplified dollar-value LIFO method 474
. special rules 1563
. stock 1563
. transactions between 267
. U.S. real property holding corporation 897
. wash sales 897
. work opportunity credit 52

Controlled substances (See Narcotic drugs)

Convention, expense of attending 274

Conversion transactions
. ordinary income into capital gain 1258

Converted wetlands 1257

Convertible bond repurchased by corporation 249

Convertible securities 554

Convertible stock disposition 306

Conveyances (See Deeds)

Convicts, work opportunity credit 51

Cooling system, exempt facility bonds 142

Co-op health insurance providers
. exemption 501

Cooperative apartments and housing corporations 216
. interest
. . disallowance of deduction 163
. . information returns 6050H
. limited equity cooperative housing 143
. mortgage revenue bonds 143
. sale of residence, gain exclusion 121
. tenant-stockholder
. . deductions
. . . adjusted basis in stock .... 216(c)(2)
. . . allowance .... 216(a)
. . . cooperative housing corporation defined ...... 216(b)(1)
. . . depreciation, property subject to .... 216(c)

Index to Code

Corporations

CODE SEC.

Cooperative apartments and housing corporations—Cont'd
. *tenant-stockholder — Cont'd*
. . *deductions —Cont'd*
. . . disallowance of deduction for payment to corporation .... 216(d)
. . . distributions by housing corporation .... 216(e)
. . . governmental-unit, stock owned by .... 216(b)(4)
. . . prior approval of occupancy .... 216(b)(5)
. . . tenant-stock holder defined .... 216(b)(2)
. . . tenant-stock holder proportionate share defined .... 216(b)(3)
. sale of residence 121

Cooperative banks
. bad debts 593
. defined 7701
. distributions to shareholders 591
. dividends paid deduction 591
. market discount bonds, interest paid to purchase or carry 1277
. organizations providing reserve funds for, and insurance of, deposits in 501
. passbook loans, liens for taxes 6323
. reacquisition of real property 1038
. returns and records 6033
. taxation .... 1381 et seq.

Cooperative electric companies
. clean renewable energy bonds (CREBs) .... 54(j)(1)
. new clean renewable energy bonds, defined for .... 54C(d)(4)
. unrelated business taxable income .... 512(b)(18)

Cooperatives
. apartments (See Cooperative apartments and housing corporations)
. banks (See Cooperative banks)
. computation of tax 1383
. educational organization's management and investment service 501
. educational programs 501
. electric companies (See Cooperative electric companies)
. eligible worked-owned (See Eligible worker-owned cooperatives (EWOCs))
. employer securities, sales to
. . dispositions, premature 4978
. . estate tax 6018
. . holding period 1223
. . nontaxable exchanges 1042
. exemption 501; 521
. farmers (See Farmers cooperatives)
. filing of returns 6072
. gains and losses, special rules for netting of 1388
. gross income of 1382
. hospital service organizations 501; 513
. housing (See Cooperative apartments and housing corporations)
. information returns 6011; 6044
. insurance companies .... 1381 et seq.
. nonpatronage distributions 1382
. patronage dividends (See Patronage dividends)
. per-unit retain allocations 1382; 1383; 1385
. pole rentals 513
. returns
. . patronage dividends, involving 6044

CODE SEC.

Cooperatives —Cont'd
. *returns —Cont'd*
. . time to file 6072
. . taxable income 1382
. . taxation of .... 1381 et seq.
. . telephone company exemption 501; 513
. . work opportunity credit, education programs 51
. . worker-owned cooperatives (See Eligible worker-owned cooperatives (EWOCs))
. . written notice of allocation 1383; 1385; 1388

Copyrights
. capital gain or loss 1221; 1231
. depreciation 167
. noncapital asset, as 1221
. royalties 543

Cordials, imported, alcohol taxes 5001
Corporate acquisition indebtedness 279
Corporate bonds (See Bonds)
Corporate distributions (See Distributions)
Corporate equity reduction interest loss
. allocable interest deduction .... 172(h)(2)
. corporate equity reduction transactions ..... 172(h)(3)
. defined .... 172(h)(1)
. ordering rules .... 172(h)(4)
. regulations concerning .... 172(h)(5)

Corporate interest
. acquisition indebtedness 279
. debt *vs.* equity 385
. related taxpayers, paid to 163
. special use valuation property 2032A
. valuation rules for certain transfers to family members ... 2701

Corporate reorganizations (See Reorganization exchanges)

Corporations
. accumulated earnings tax (See Accumulated earning tax)
. acquisitions
. . carryovers .... 381 et seq.
. . evasion or avoidance of tax 269
. . indebtedness 279
. active closely held businesses, at risk amounts 465
. adjustments .... 301 et seq.
. affiliated (See Affiliated corporations)
. alternative capital gains tax 1201
. alternative minimum tax 55; 56
. amount of tax 11
. at risk limitations 465
. avoidance of tax on shareholders .... 531 et seq.
. basis
. . stock and stock rights acquired in distribution 307
. bonds, repurchase of convertible 249
. capital gains
. . alternative tax 1201
. . disposition of depreciable realty 291; 341
. carrybacks and carryovers (See Carrybacks and carryovers)
. charitable contributions 170
. collapsible (See Collapsible corporations)
. common trust funds as 584
. consent dividends 565
. consolidated returns (See Consolidated returns)

133

Corporations — Index to Code

CODE SEC.

Corporations —Cont'd
- constructive ownership of stock 318
- contributions to capital
  - basis to corporation 362
  - exclusion from gross income 118
- controlled (See Controlled corporations)
- convertible bonds, repurchase of premium 249
- cooperative housing (See Cooperative apartments and housing corporations)
- dealing in own stock 1036
- death taxes, redemption of stock for payment of 303
- debt instruments issued by 1272
- debt *vs.* equity 385
- deductions ..... 241 et seq.
  - dividends paid
    - preferred stock of public utilities 247
  - dividends received ..... 243 et seq.
    - debt-financed portfolio stock 246A
    - foreign corporations 245
    - preferred stock 244
    - rules applying 246
  - exempt organizations (See Exempt entities and organizations)
  - organizational expenditures 248
- defined 7701
- dispositions
  - capital gains treatment 291
  - depreciable realty 291
  - stock 306
- dissolution
  - deficiency notice 6212
  - disclosure of returns and return information 6103
  - information returns 6043
  - request for prompt assessment 6501
  - transferee liability ..... 6901 et seq.
- distributions (See Distributions)
- dividends (See Dividends)
- dividends-received deduction (See also Dividends-received deductions)
- domestic
  - defined 7701
  - foreign-owned, information returns 6038A
  - stapled to foreign 269B
- earnings and profits 312
- estate freezes, special rules for ..... 2701 et seq.
- estimated tax (See Estimated income tax)
- excess credits, limitations 383; 384
- exempt (See Exempt entities and organizations)
- exemption from tax ..... 501 et seq.
- existing 80/20 companies
  - nonresident aliens 871
- export trade 970; 971
- foreign (See Foreign corporations)
- foreign tax credit (See Foreign tax credit)
- gain or loss, liquidations ..... 331 et seq.
- golden parachute payments (See Golden parachute payments)
- graduated rate structure 11; 962
- greenmail 5881
- income from sources within U.S. possessions (See Possessions of U.S.)
- installment payments of estimated tax 6315

CODE SEC.

Corporations —Cont'd
- intangible property transfers 936
- interests (See Corporate interest)
- itemized deductions ..... 161 et seq.
- life insurance 264
- limitation period for assessments 6501
- liquidation
  - basis of property received 334
  - collapsible corporations 341
  - effects on liquidating corporation ..... 336 et seq.
  - effects on recipients ..... 331 et seq.
  - employee stock options 424
  - gain or loss ..... 331 et seq.
  - partial 346
  - purchase of stock 338
  - stockholders, gain or loss to 331
  - subsidiaries (See Subsidiaries)
  - termination of taxable year by Secretary 6851
- loss corporation 382
- minimum tax on preference income (See Alternative minimum tax)
- nonrecognition of gain or loss
  - sales or exchanges, SEC ordered 1081
- notice of failure to collect and pay over taxes 7512
- officers
  - disclosure of returns and return information 6103
  - employee status
    - FICA 3121
    - withholding tax on wages 3401
  - excess benefit transaction of exempt organizations 4958
  - life insurance 264
- OID, information returns 6049
- organizational expenditures 248
- ownership change 382
- parent 337
- partnerships taxable as, limitation on assessment and collection 6164; 6501
- passive activity losses and credits 469
- personal holding (See Personal holding companies)
- personal service corporations (See Personal service corporations)
- preference items 291
- property acquired during affiliation 1051
- property use by shareholder 543
- publicly traded partnership treated as 7704
- railroad terminal 281
- rates of tax 11
- realty subdivided for sale 1237
- redemption of stock ..... 302 et seq.
- reduction in preference items 291
- related corporations, redemption of stock through 304
- related taxpayers, transactions between 267
- reorganizations (See Reorganization exchanges)
- returns (See Consolidated returns; Returns)
- S corporations (See S corporations)
- sales and exchanges
  - related taxpayers, between 267
  - subdivided realty 1237
- seasonal income, estimated tax 6655
- separate entities in bankruptcy 1399

Index to Code

CODE SEC.

Corporations —Cont'd
- shipments from U.S. 7653
- small business (See Small business corporations; S corporations)
- special deductions
  - accumulated earnings tax 535
  - foreign corporations 556
  - life insurance companies 806
  - personal holding companies, undistributed taxable income 545
- stapled entities 269B
- stock and stock rights, distribution of .... 301 et seq.
- stock for stock of same corporation, nontaxable exchanges of 1036
- stock ownership 318
- Subchapter S (See S corporations)
- subsidiaries 332; 902; 1083
- system group 1083
- tax, alternative 1201
- tax imposed 11
- taxable income, unrelated business .... 511 et seq.
- taxes paid for shareholders 164; 556
- transferor controlled, reorganization exchanges 351
- transfers to controlled corporations
  - redemption of stock, coordination with 304
- trusts taxable as, limitation on assessment and collection 6501
- used to avoid income tax on shareholders
  - improperly accumulating surplus .... 531 et seq.
- valuation rules
  - transfers of certain interests to family members 2701
- voting rights, lapsed 2704

Corundum, depletion 613
Cosmetic surgery 213
Cost basis of property 1012
Cost depletion 612
Cost-of-living adjustments
- defined benefit plans 415
- defined contribution plans 415
- employee retirement and benefit plans 404; 415
- foreign service officers and employees 912; 6011
- medical savings accounts, Archer 220
- tax rates 1

Cost-sharing conservation program 126
- gain from disposition of Sec. 126 property 126
- property acquired under, gain on sale 1255
- reforestation expenditures 194

Cotton futures, penalties relating to 7273
Counterfeit stamps 7208; 7303
Country clubs
- financing, small issue bonds 144

Coupons, stripped (See Stripped bonds and coupons)
Court action
- civil actions by U.S.
  - accounting for certain collected taxes 7512
  - administration of real estate acquired by U.S. 7506
  - authorization 7401
  - disposition of judgments and money recovered 7406
  - enforce lien or subject property to payment of tax 7403

Credits

CODE SEC.

Court action —Cont'd
- *civil actions by U.S. —Cont'd*
  - estate taxes, for 7404
  - intervention 7424
  - jurisdiction of district courts 7402
  - recovery of erroneous refunds 6602; 7405
  - sale of personal property acquired by U.S. 7505
  - time for performing certain acts postponed by reason of service in combat zone 7508
  - erroneous refund recoverable by suit 6602; 7405
  - forfeiture of property 7323
  - intervention by trustee of debtor's estate 7464
  - limitation period 6531; 6532
- Tax Court (See Tax Court)
  - taxpayer, other than 7426
- taxpayer proceedings
  - discharge of liens 7425
  - prohibition of suits to restrain assessment or collection 7421
  - refunds, civil action for 7402; 7422
  - repayments to officers or employees 7423

Court of claims (See Claims court jurisdiction)
Courts (See also specific courts)
- appeal from Tax Court .... 7481 et seq.
- assets in control of
  - limitations on assessment and collection 6503
- collection of tax in (See Suits, collection of tax by)
- review of Tax Court decisions .... 7481 et seq.
- Tax Court (See Tax Court)

Courts of review 7428; 7482; 7483
Coverdell education savings accounts
- defined 530
- education account rollover 530
- education expenses 530
- excess contributions 4973
- exemptions 530
- higher education 530
- prohibited transaction tax 4975
- tuition program, tax on 529
- U.S. savings bonds redeemed to pay 135

Covered call options 1092
Creative expenses, qualified, exemption from capitalization 263A

CREBs (See Clean renewable energy bonds; New clean renewable energy bonds)
Credit card issuers
- gasoline tax refunds and credits administration 6416

Credit unions .... 408(n)(2); 501; 6302
Credits against tax .... 21 et seq.; 6401 et seq. (See also Refunds and credit)
- adoption expenses 23
- advanced coal project credit (See Advanced coal project credit)
- advanced nuclear power facilities, credit for production from (See Advanced nuclear power facilities)
- alcohol fuels credit (See Alcohol fuels credit)
- alternative minimum tax, prior year 53; 381
- appliances, energy efficient (See Energy efficient appliance credit)
- authority to make 6402
- backup withholding 31

135

Credits

Index to Code

CODE SEC.

Credits against tax—Cont'd
- bankruptcy 1398
- biodiesel fuel credit .... 40A(b)(2); 6426
- bond holders of clean renewable energy bonds (See Clean renewable energy bonds; New clean renewable energy bonds)
- build America bonds (See Build America Bonds)
- business credit (See Business credit)
- business-related expenses .... 38 et seq.
- carrybacks and carryovers
  - . bankruptcy 1398
  - . deficiency assessment 6501; 6601
  - . refund claims 6511; 6611
- child care, employer provided 38; 45F
- child tax credit 24; 6429
- clinical testing expenses
  - . drugs .... 280C(b)
  - . orphan drugs 45C
  - . rare diseases or conditions 45C
- coal project, advanced 48A
- D.C. first-time home buyers 1400C
- decedents, in respect of 691
- dependent care credit (See Dependent care credit)
- disabled access credit (See Disabled access credit)
- disabled persons, credit for 21; 22
- disallowance of
  - . . dependent care assistance programs 129
  - . . educational assistance programs 127
- distilled spirits tax 5010
- drugs credit .... 280C(b)
- earned income credit (See Earned income credit)
- elderly, credit for 22
- electricity production credit 45
- employee stock ownership plans 404; 409
- employer provided child care 38; 45F
- employer wage, for employees who are active duty members of the uniformed services 450
- employment credit
  - . . empowerment zone 1396
  - . . Indian employment 45A
- employment-related expenses 21
- empowerment zone employment credit ... 38; 39; 1396
- energy credit 48
- enhanced oil recovery credit 43
- estate tax .... 642; 2010 et seq.; 2102
  - . . death taxes on remainders 2015
  - . . foreign death taxes 2013; 2014
  - . . gift tax 2012
  - . . nonresident aliens 2102
  - . . prior transfers, tax on 2013
  - . . recovery of taxes claimed as credit 2016
  - . . state death taxes, credit for 2011
  - . . unified credit against 2010
- estates and trusts 642; 691; 901
- estimated tax 6402; 6513
- excess credits 383; 384; 6401
- excise taxes, refundable amounts 6416
- Federal unemployment tax
  - . . additional credit allowance, conditions of ... 3303
  - . . State unemployment contributions 3302

CODE SEC.

Credits against tax—Cont'd
- foreign corporations 33; 882; 906
- foreign tax credit (See Foreign tax credit)
- fuels
  - . nonconventional sources (See Nonconventional fuel source credit)
  - . special fuels 34
- gasification project credit (See Qualifying gasification project credit)
- gasoline 34; 1366
- generation-skipping transfer (GST) tax credit for certain state taxes 2604
- gift tax purposes 2505
- health insurance premiums .... 280C(g)
- health plan coverage
  - . premium assistance credit 36B
- home mortgages, interest on 25; 163
- Indian employment credit 45A
- interest, mortgage 25; 163; 6709
- investment credit .... 46 et seq.
- limitations, credit
  - . alternative minimum tax .... 53(c)
  - . carryback of unused business credit 39
  - . dependent care 21
  - . disabled persons 22
  - . earned income 32
  - . elderly 22
  - . employment-related expenses 21
  - . general business credit 38
  - . household expenses 21
  - . mortgage credit rates 25
  - . nonconventional fuel source (See Nonconventional fuel source credit)
  - . tax liabilities, based on .... 26; 904(i)
  - . unused business credit carrybacks 39
  - . work opportunity credit 51
- limited partnerships, self-employment tax .. 1402
- low-income housing (See Low-income housing credits)
- marginal well production (See Marginal wells)
- mine rescue team training credit (See Mine rescue team training credit)
- minimum tax, prior year 53
- mortgage credit certificates 163; 6709
- mortgage interest 25; 163; 6709
- new employees 51; 52
- new energy efficient home credit (See New energy efficient home credit)
- new markets 45D
- New York Liberty Zone 1400L
- nonconventional fuel source credit (See Nonconventional fuel source credit)
- nonrefundable personal credits .... 21 et seq.
- nonresident aliens 33; 874; 906; 6401
- overpayment 6401
- partners 702
- passive activities 469
- personal credits (See Personal credits)
- possession tax credit (See Possession tax credit)
- Puerto Rico 936
- qualified electric vehicle credit 30

136

Index to Code — Customs

Credits against tax—Cont'd
- qualified ex-felon ... 51(d)(4)
- qualified IV-A recipients ... 51(d)(2)
- railroad track maintenance credit ... 45G
- reciprocal (See Reciprocal credits or exemptions)
- recovery exclusion ... 111
- refundable credits ... 31 et seq.
- regulated investment companies ... 852; 860
- rehabilitation credit ... 47
- REITs ... 860
- research and experimental expenses ... 41; 280C(c); 6411; 6511
- residential property, mortgage interest ... 25; 163; 6709
- S corporations, passthrough to shareholders ... 1366
- salaries and wages ... 280C(a)
- small employer pension plan startup costs ... 45E
- Social Security taxes ... 31
- special fuels ... 34
- special rules ... 52
- State unemployment contributions ... 3302 et seq.
- targeted group members ... 51(d)(14)
- taxable year ... 461
- tips, cash ... 45B
- trusts and estates ... 642; 691; 2010 et seq.
- unemployment tax, Federal ... 3302
- unified credit, estate and gift taxes ... 2010; 2102; 2107; 2505
- wages, taxes withheld on ... 31
- welfare-to-work credits ... 51A
- withheld taxes ... 6401
- . . nonresident aliens and foreign corporations ... 33; 1462; 1464
- . . overstatement ... 6201
- . . wages ... 31
- work opportunity credit ... 51; 52; 1400L
- zone academy bonds, holders of (See Qualified zone academy bonds)

Crematory, exemption ... 501

Crimes
- attempt to evade or defeat tax ... 7201
- documents, fraudulent ... 7207
- failure to collect or pay over taxes ... 7202
- failure to produce records ... 7269
- failure to register ... 7272
- false statements to purchasers or lessees ... 7211
- filing returns ... 7203
- forfeiture of property (See Forfeiture of property)
- fraud and false statements ... 7206
- general provisions ... 7201 et seq.
- information
- . . unauthorized disclosure ... 7213; 7216
- . . willful failure to supply ... 7203
- Internal Revenue laws, interference with ... 7212
- offenses by officers and employees ... 7214
- offenses with respect to collected taxes ... 7215
- paying taxes ... 7203
- penalties ... 7201 et seq. (See also Penalties)
- . . antitrust law violations ... 162
- . . firearms ... 5871; 5872
- . . liquors ... 5601
- . . tobacco articles ... 5762

Crimes —Cont'd
- person defined ... 7343
- possession with intent to sell in fraud of law, or to evade tax ... 7268
- relating to special taxes ... 7273
- returns
- . fraudulent ... 7207
- . . willful failure to file ... 7203
- . stamps ... 7270; 7271
- . . counterfeiting ... 7208
- . . unauthorized use or sale of ... 7209
- . statement to employees ... 7204
- . unauthorized disclosure of information ... 7213
- . civil damages ... 7431
- . return preparers ... 7216
- . wagering tax law violations ... 7262
- . withholding exemption certificates ... 7205

Criminal prosecutions
- disclosure of returns and return information ... 6103
- limitation period ... 6531

Criminal restitution
- assessments
- . . authority, certain orders ... 6201
- . . exceptions to restrictions on ... 6213
- . . limitation period for ... 6501

Critical status multiemployer plans (See Endangered or critical status multiemployer plans)

Cropland, eroded ... 1257

Crops
- damage ... 263A
- . insurance ... 451
- . . inventory costs ... 263A
- . financing cooperatives ... 501; 521
- . rental of ... 1401
- unharvested sold with land
- . . basis adjustments ... 1016
- . . capital gain or loss ... 1231

Crop-share rentals ... 1402
- FICA ... 3121

Cruelty prevention organizations
- charitable contributions ... 170
- contributions to, estate and trusts ... 642
- exemption ... 501

Cruise ships, convention held on ... 274
Cumulative wages, withholding tax on ... 3402
Cupric oxide ... 4661; 4662
Cupric sulfate ... 4661; 4662
Cuprous oxide ... 4661; 4662
Currency, foreign (See Foreign currency)
Currency, functional ... 985
Curtesy interests ... 2034; 2043
Custodial accounts, employee benefit plans ... 401; 4973
Custodial parents ... 152
Customer, employees as ... 132

Customs Service
- disclosure of returns and return information ... 6103
- duties

137

Customs

CODE SEC.

Customs Service — Cont'd
. *duties — Cont'd*
.. alcohol taxes 5061
... related persons, property imported into U.S. by 1059A
. laws 7327

D

Damages
. Antitrust Act, violation of 186
. breach of contract 186
. civil, against U.S. for
.. failure to release lien 7432
.. unauthorized collection actions 7433
.. unauthorized disclosure 7435
.. unauthorized inspection 7435
. collection of taxes, unauthorized 7433
. court review instituted merely for delay 7482
. exempt income 104
. fiduciary breach of duty 186
. information returns, fraudulent 7434
. lien for taxes, failure to release 7432
. personal injuries 104
.. assignment of liability 130
. recoveries, Antitrust Act violations 186
. suit by U.S. officers or employees 7402
. TC proceeding instituted merely for delay or with frivolous or groundless positions 6673

Day care centers
. exemption 501
. services in home, business expense deduction 280A

De minimis fringe benefits 132

Dealers in options and commodities
. backup withholding 3406
. equity options 1256
. passive investment income 1362
. recharacterization of gain from certain financial transactions 1258
. Sec. 1256 contracts 1256
. self-employment tax 1402

Dealers in personal property
. installment sales .... 453 et seq.

Dealers in securities
. backup withholding 3406
. capital gains and losses 1236
. cost of securities sold 75
. floor specialists, special rule for 1236
. gross income computation 75
. information returns 6041; 6045; 6652
. mark to market accounting 475
. municipal bonds 75; 1016
. options, special rule for 1236
. ordinary losses 1236
. partnership status 761
. personal holding companies 543
. security defined for purposes of 1236
. self-employment tax 1402
. short sales 1233
. tax-exempt securities 75

Index to Code

CODE SEC.

Dealers in securities — Cont'd
. trading for own account 864
. wash sale loss 1091

Death
. astronauts 692; 2201
. benefits (See Death benefits)
. combat zone, estate tax 2201
. decedents (See Decedents)
. disclosure, return and return information 6103
. gifts made within 3 years of, gross estate adjustments for 2035; 2104
. moving expenses 217
. passive activity losses and credits 469
. stock acquired by reason of 382
. taxes (See Death taxes)
. transfers and gifts at death, failure to file information with respect to 6716
. transfers taking effect at 2037

Death benefits
. annuities 101
. beneficiaries 101
. chronically ill persons 101
. church self-funded 7702
. employees 101
. flexible premium life insurance contract proceeds .. 101
. FUTA 3306
. gross income, exclusion from 101
. life insurance contract proceeds 101
. modified endowment contracts 7702A
. nonforfeitable rights, employees 101
. payments on death of participant 401; 402
. public safety officer killed in the lie of duty 101
. rollovers 402
. spouse's receipt of payment 402
. terrorist victims 101
. viatical settlements 101
. withholding tax on retirement or benefit plan distributions and other deferred income 3405

Death taxes (See also Estate tax; Foreign death taxes; Inheritance taxes)
. charitable bequests reduced by 2055; 2106
. credit against estate tax 2011; 2014; 2015; 2102
. deductibility 275; 2053; 2106
. foreign (See Foreign death taxes)
. redemption of stock to pay 303; 312
. refunded, estate tax redetermination 2016
. remainders, estate tax credit for 2015
. state
.. credit against Federal estate tax 2011; 2016
.. valuation of estate for federal estate tax, and .. 2058
. taxable estate, effect on 2053

Debentures (See also Bonds)
. corporate acquisition indebtedness 279
. exempt organizations 503

Debt
. bad (See Bad debts)
. cancellation (See Cancellation of indebtedness)
. discharge of (See Cancellation of indebtedness)
. indebtedness (See Indebtedness)

138

Index to Code   Deductions

CODE SEC.

Debt instruments
- bonds (See Bonds; specific bond type)
- cancellation of indebtedness
  - reacquisition of debt instrument after Dec. 31, 2008 and before Jan. 1, 2001 .... 801(i)
- cash method election, imputed interest 1274A
- deferred payment sales, imputed interest 1274A
- definition 1274A; 1275
- discharge of indebtedness, issuance in satisfaction of 108
- foreign expropriation loss recoveries 1351
- gains and losses 1271; 1276
- Indian tribal governments, treatment as state 7871
- information returns 1275; 6049
- installment obligation status 453
- interest; information returns 6049
- issue price
  - determination of, OID rules 1274
  - property, issued on sale or exchange 1274
- market discount bonds (See Market discount bonds)
- original issue discount (See Original issue discount)
- premium, purchased at 1272
- property, issue price of instruments issued for 1274
- real estate mortgage investment conduits 1272
- retirement, sale or exchange of, treatment of amounts received upon 1271
- sale or exchange 1271; 1276
- satisfied by issuance of corporation stock 108
- short-term issued at discount (See Short-term obligations issued at discount)
- special rules 1274A; 1275

Debt service
- federally guaranteed bonds 149

Debt vs. equity
- corporate interests 385

Debt-financed income, exempt organizations 514
Debt-financed portfolio stock 246A

Decedents
- accounting method 451
- armed forces members 692
- astronauts 692
- basis of property acquired from 1014
- credits against tax 691
- deductions
  - accounting methods 461
  - accrual basis 461
  - allowable to whom 691
  - business credit, unused 196
- DISC stock 1014
- employee retirement or benefit plan distributions
  - estate tax 2039
  - lump-sum 691
- employee stock options 421
- farm or business real property, transfer of 1040
- foreign investment company stock acquired from 1246
- foreign personal holding company stock 1014
- gift made within three years of death 1014; 2035; 2104
- income
  - property representing, basis 1014
  - taxable year or inclusion 451

CODE SEC.

Decedents —Cont'd
- income in respect of (See Income in respect of decedent)
- installment obligations 453B; 691
- installment sales, resales by related taxpayers 453
- interests passing from defined 2056
- medical expenses 213
- property acquired from
  - basis 1014; 1016
  - decedent dying after December 31, 2009 1022
  - holding period 1223
  - Sec. 1245 property 1245
  - Sec. 1250 property 1250
  - spousal property 1022
- property in which decedent had interest 2033
- request for prompt assessment 6501
- returns 6012; 6072; 6103
- sale of principal residence, gain on 121
- taxable year, deductions 461

Declaratory judgments
- employee retirement and benefit plans, qualification as to 7476
- exempt organizations, qualification as 7428
- gifts, value of 7477
- governmental obligations, exempt status 7478
- installment payments under Sec. 6166 7479
- private foundations, qualification as 7428

Declining-balance depreciation 168
Decommissioning costs, nuclear power plants 88; 468A
Deductions .... 164; 275 (See also specific item)
- accelerated cost recovery system 168
- accumulated taxable income computation 535
- activities not engaged in for profit 183
- adjusted gross income 62
- alimony payments 215
- allowance of 211
  - corporations 161
  - individuals 161
  - nonresident aliens 874
  - personal exemptions 151
- amortization, pollution-control facility 169
- at risk limitations 465
- bad debts 166
- barriers to the handicapped and elderly, removal expenditures 190
- black lung benefit trust, contributions to 192
- bonds
  - premiums, amortizable 171
  - repurchase by corporation 249
- business expenses 162; 274
- business use of home 280A
- carrying charges 266
- charitable contributions 170
- circulation expenditures 173
- clubs, transactions with members 277
- conservation expenditures, soil and water 175
- convertible bond, corporate repurchase of premium 249
- cooperative housing corporation tenant-stockholders, by .... 216(a)
- corporate acquisition indebtedness, interest on 279

139

Deductions

Index to Code

CODE SEC.

Deductions—Cont'd
- corporations .... 161 et seq.; 241 et seq.
- .. convertible bonds, repurchase of premiums 249
- .. dividends paid, public utility preferred stock 247
- .. dividends received .... 243 et seq.
- .. exempt organizations (See Exempt entities and organizations)
- .. organizational expenditures 248
- . damage recoveries 186
- . decedent, in respect of 691
- . deficiency dividends 547; 860
- . dental expenses 213
- . depletion allowance .... 611 et seq.
- . depreciation 167; 168
- . development expenditures 616
- . disallowance of .... 261 et seq.
- .. acquisitions made to evade or avoid income tax ...... 269 et seq.
- .. automobiles 280F
- .. business expenses 274
- .. business use of home 280A
- .. carrying charges 266
- .. coal, disposal of 272
- .. corporate acquisition indebtedness, interest on 279
- .. crops, unharvested, sale of land with 268
- .. demolition of structures 280B
- .. dependent care assistance programs 129
- .. disposal of coal or iron ore 272
- .. double deductions, trusts and estates 642
- .. educational assistance programs 127
- .. estates and trusts 2055
- .. expenses on tax-exempt income 265
- .. gifts and bequests to taxable foundation 508
- .. golden parachutes, excess payments .... 280G(b)
- .. illegal drug sales 280E
- .. interest on tax-exempt income 265
- .. iron ore, disposal of 272
- .. luxury automobiles 280F
- .. passthrough entities 67
- .. payment on insurance contracts 264
- .. personal holding companies 545
- .. political parties
- ... contributions to 276
- ... debts owed by 271
- .. related taxpayers, transactions between 267
- .. sale of land with unharvested crops 268
- .. taxes 275
- .. tax-exempt income, expenses and interest 265
- .. vacation homes, rental of 280A
- . dividends paid .... 561 et seq.; 591; 808
- . domestic production activities income (See Domestic production activities)
- . double 642; 663; 7852
- . drug dealers 280E
- . educational loan, interest on 221
- . employer securities, dividends paid on 404
- . employers contributions
- .. annuity plan 404
- .. deferred-payment plan 404
- .. employees' trusts 404

CODE SEC.

Deductions—Cont'd
employers contributions —Cont'd
- .. liability trusts 194A
- . employment taxes 3502
- . endangered species recovery expenditures 175
- . entertainment expenses 274
- . environmental protection agency sulfur regulations 179B
- . estate tax (See Estate tax)
- . expensing depreciable business assets 179
- . exploration expenditures 617
- . farmers, expenditures by 180; 1252
- . FICA 3502
- . foreign corporations 882
- . foreign personal holding company 556
- . foreign subsidiaries, payments to U.S. citizen employees 176
- . gift taxes, deductions (See Gift tax)
- . gifts, business 274
- . illegal drug sales 280E
- . individuals .... 161 et seq.; 211 et seq.
- . insurance companies other than life .... 832 et seq.
- . insurance payments 264
- . interest 163; 267
- . itemized (See Itemized deductions)
- . lease, acquisition costs 178
- . life insurance companies .... 804 eq seq.
- . limitations .... 261 et seq.
- .. business expenses 274
- .. business use of home 280A
- .. capital expenditures 263
- .. clubs, transactions with members 277
- .. coal disposal 272
- .. corporate acquisition indebtedness, interest on 279
- .. family expenses 262
- .. farming syndicates 464
- .. holders of life or terminable interest 273
- .. insurance contracts, payment on 264
- .. interest on tax-exempt income 265
- .. iron ore disposal 272
- .. life tenants 273
- .. living expenses 262
- .. personal expenses 262
- .. personal service corporations 280H
- .. related taxpayers, transaction between 267
- .. tax-exempt income, expenses and interest 265
- .. terminable interest 273
- .. vacation home rentals 280A
- . losses 165; 267
- . low sulfur diesel fuels .... 280C(d)
- . meals and lodging 274
- . medical expenses 213
- . medical savings accounts, Archer 220
- . moving expenses 217
- . nonresident aliens 873
- . partnerships 703
- . personal exemptions .... 151 et seq.; 443; 642
- . personal holding companies 545
- . political parties, contributions to 276
- . production of income, expenses for 212

140

Index to Code

Deductions—Cont'd

- qualified tuition and related expenses (See Tuition)
- Railroad Retirement Tax Act 3502
- real property deduction for taxable income .... 63(c)(7)
- recovery exclusion 111
- reforestation expenditures 194
- related taxpayers, transactions between 267
- removal of architectural or transportation barriers 190
- rentals, vacation home 280A
- research and experimental expenditures 174
- retirement savings, contributions to 219
- sales and exchanges between related taxpayers 267
- self-employment tax 1402
- soil and water conservation 175
- standard deductions (See Standard deductions)
- taxable year .... 461 et seq.
- taxes 164
- tertiary injectant expenses 193
- trade or business expenses 162
- transfers of compensatory property 83
- transportation barriers to the handicapped and elderly, removal expenditures 190
- travel expenses 274
- trusts and estates
  - accumulating income or distributing corpus 661
  - distributing current income only 651
  - in respect of decedents 691
  - unused loss and excess deductions on termination available to beneficiaries 642
- tuition and related expenses (See Tuition subhead qualified tuition programs)
- vacation home rentals 280A
- withholding tax on wages 3502

Deeds 6338; 6339
Deep-in-the-money options 1092
Deferred compensation ...... 401 et seq. (See also Annuities; Employee annuities; Pension, profit sharing, and stock bonus plans; Self-employed retirement plans)

- accounting method 457
- cafeteria plans 125
- cash or deferred arrangements (CODA) (See Cash or deferred arrangements (CODA))
- employee annuities 403
- employee benefit plan beneficiary, taxability of 402
- employee stock ownership plan .... 409; 409A(a)
- exempt organization employee plans 457
- foreign plans 404A
- gross income 409A
- information returns 6041
- plan defined 3405
- railroad Retirement Tax Act .... 3231 et seq.
- state or local government employee plans 457
- withholding tax 3405

Deferred like-kind exchanges 1031
Deferred payment sales (See also Installment sales)

- accounting method .... 453 et seq.
- imputed interest 163; 1274A
- interest 483
- original issue discount 483
- reacquisition 1038

Deficiency

Deferred rental agreements 467
Deferred tax liability, installment sale 453A
Deficiencies .... 6211 et seq.

- amount determined as 6161
- applications 6211
- assessments
  - additional after notice of deficiency 6212
  - credits against tax, carrybacks and carryovers ... 6501; 6601
  - exploration expenditures 617
  - foreign tax carrybacks 6501
  - involuntary conversions 1033
  - limitations 6501
  - Tax Court, found by 6215
- bankruptcy and receivership .... 6213; 6871 et seq.
- collection
  - adjustment under mitigation rule .... 1311 et seq.
  - extension of time 6161; 6165
  - husband and wife, joint return 6013
  - limitation 6501
  - notice and demand 6303
  - personal holding companies 547
- definition 6211
- disallowed by courts 6215; 7486
- estimated tax 6654; 6655; 6658
- executors, discharge from liability 6905
- Federal loan applicant, disclosures 6103
- foreign taxes, redetermination of 6689
- fractional dollar 7504
- interest on 6601
- estate tax
  - closely held business interest 6166
  - foreign expropriation loss recoveries 6167
  - rate 6621
- issuance of statutory notice of 6503
- mathematical or clerical errors 6213; 6404
- notice 6212
  - accumulated earnings tax 534
  - address for 6212
  - contents 7522
  - issued while refund suit pending 7422
  - jeopardy assessments 6861
  - suspension of limitations on assessment and collection 6503
  - termination assessments 6851
- overpayment credited against 6601; 6611
- restrictions 6212
- Tax Court
  - assessment of deficiency found by 6215
  - determinations 6214
  - jurisdiction 6214
  - petitions .... 6213 et seq.
- waiver of restrictions on assessment and collection 6213

Deficiency dividends

- carryovers, acquiring corporation 381
- defined 547
- personal holding companies 381; 547
- regulated investment companies 316; 381; 860
- REIT 316; 381; 860

Defined   **Index to Code**

CODE SEC.

Defined benefit plans (See also Pension, profit sharing, and stock bonus plans)
. aggregation of plans 415
. at-risk status, benefit limitations on plans in 401
. bankruptcy, benefit increase when sponsor is in 401
. benefit percentages, excess plans 401
. collectively bargained retirement plans 415
. combined with qualified cash or deferred arrangement
 . . . . 414(x) et seq.
. combining plans 415
. cost-of-living adjustments 415
. defined . . . . 414(j)
. disparity in contributions and benefits 401
. excess plans 401
. forfeitures 401
. funding standards
. . endangered or critical status, funding rules for multiple employer plans in (See Multiemployer plans)
. . single-employer, minimum funding standards (See subhead single-employer, minimum funding standards)
. Indian tribal governments contribution limitations 414
. joint and survivor annuity 401
. limitations on contributions and benefits 414; 415
. maximum excess allowance 401
. maximum offset allowance 401
. medical benefits 415
. minimum funding standards 412
. offset plans 401
. pension trusts 404
. reductions 401
. single-employer, funding based limits . . . . 436(a)
. . accelerated benefit distributions . . . . 436(d)(1); 436(d)(3)
. . alternate valuation date, Secretarial authority for plans with
 . . . . 436(k)
. . bankruptcy . . . . 436(d)(2)
. . benefits
. . . accelerated benefit distributions . . . . 436(d)(1)
. . . limited payment if percentage at least 60 percent but less
 than 80 percent . . . . 436(d)(3)
. . . liability for benefits, plan amendments increasing
 . . . . 436(c)(1); 436(g)
. . . shutdown benefits . . . . 436(b)(1); 436(g)
. . . unpredictable contingent event benefits . . . . 436(b)(3)
. . close of prohibited or cessation period, treatment after
 . . . . 436(i)(1) et seq.
. . . affected benefits . . . . 436(i)(2)
. . . operation of plan . . . . 436(i)(1)
. . contributions required to avoid benefit limitations
. . . deemed reduction of funding balances . . . . 436(f)(3)
. . . funding standard carryover balance . . . . 436(f)(2)
. . . prefunding balances . . . . 436(f)(2)
. . . security . . . . 436(f)(1); 436(f)(1) et seq.
. . defined, single employer . . . . 436(l)
. . funding target attainment percentage . . . . . . 436(j)(1) et seq.
. . . adjusted funding target attainment percentage . . . 436(j)(2)
. . . defined . . . . 436(j)(1)
. . . fully funded plans without regard to reduction for funding
 balances . . . . 436(j)(3)
. . 2008, special rules for . . . . 436(m)
. . generally . . . . 436(a)

CODE SEC.

Defined benefit plans (See also Pension, profit sharing, and stock bonus plans) —Cont'd
. single-employer, funding based limits—Cont'd
. . liability for benefits, plan amendments increasing
 . . . . 436(c)(1); 436(g)
. . new plans . . . . 436(g)
. . presumed underfunding for purposes of benefit limitations
 . . . . 436(h)(1) et seq.
. . . presumption of continued underfunding . . . . 436(h)(1)
. . . presumption of underfunding after 4th month . . . . 436(h)(3)
. . . presumption of underfunding after 10th month . . . 436(h)(2)
. . severe funding shortfalls, benefit accruals for plans with
 . . . . 436(e); 436(g)
. . shutdown benefits . . . . 436(b)(1); 436(g)
. . unpredictable contingent event benefits . . . . 436(b)(3)
. single-employer, minimum funding standards
. . actuarial assumptions and methods . . . . 430(h)(1) et seq.
. . at-risk plans . . . . 430(i)(1) et seq.
. . early deemed amortization upon attainment of funding target
 . . . . 430(c)(6)
. . funding shortfall . . . . 430(c)(4)
. . . accelerated quarterly contribution schedule for underfunded
 plans . . . . 430(j)(3)
. . funding targets . . . . 430(d)(1)
. . . at-risk plans . . . . 430(i)(1)
. . . attainment percentage . . . . 430(d)(2)
. . . early deemed amortization upon attainment of . . . 430(e)(4)
. . . interest rates for determining funding target . . . 430(h)(2)(B)
. . . target normal costs, at risk plan transition between
 . . . . 430(i)(5)
. . health benefit accounts, qualified transfers to . . . . 430(l)
. . minimum amount, at-risk plans . . . . 430(i)(3)
. . minimum required contributions
. . . election to apply balances against minimum required contribution . . . . 430(f)(3)
. . . elections, prescriptions for . . . . 430(f)(9)
. . . failure to make, lien on . . . . 430(k)(1) et seq.
. . . funding standard carryover balance . . . . 430(f)(7)
. . . investment experience, adjustments for . . . . 430(f)(8)
. . . payments . . . . 430(j)(1) et seq.
. . . reduction by prefunding balance and funding standard carryover balance . . . . 430(f)(1) et seq.
. . shortfall amortization base . . . . 430(c)(3); 430(c)(5)
. . shortfall amortization charge . . . . 430(c)(1)
. . shortfall amortization installment . . . . 430(c)(2)
. . target normal costs
. . . at-risk plans . . . . 430(i)(2); 430(i)(5)
. . . defined . . . . 430(b)
. . valuation of plan assets and liabilities . . . . . . 430(g)(1) et seq.
. . waiver amortization charge . . . . 430(e)(1) et seq.
. termination, distributions on 401
. top-heavy plans 416
. total distributions 401
. vesting standards 411

Defined contribution plans (See also Pension, profit sharing, and stock bonus plans)
. aggregation of plans 415
. annuities 72
. combining plans 415
. contribution percentages 401
. cost-of-living adjustments 415

Index to Code — Depletion

	CODE SEC.
Defined contribution plans (See also Pension, profit sharing, and stock bonus plans) — Cont'd	
. defined	414(i)
. disparity in contributions	401
. diversification requirements	401
. employee contribution treated as separate contracts	72
. employee stock ownership plans	415
. joint and survivor annuity	401
. limitations on benefits and contributions	415
. medical benefits	415
. qualification requirements	401
. top-heavy plans	415; 416
. vesting standards	411
Definitions (See specific item)	
Delegates	
. definition	7701
. disclosures by	7213
Delinquency amounts, bankruptcy	1398
Delinquency penalty	6651
Delinquent revenue officers and employees	7803
Delinquent taxes	
. Federal loan applicant, disclosure	6103
. interest on	6601
. . estate tax, closely held business interest	6166
. . foreign expropriation loss recoveries	6167
. . rate	6621
. notice	7524
Demand for payment	6155; 6303
Demolition expenses	280B
Demonstration automobiles	
. retail sales luxury tax exemption	4002
Dental expenses	213
Department of Agriculture	
. disclosure of returns and return information	6103
Department of Education	
. student address disclosed to collect defaulted loan	6103
Department of Health, Education and Welfare (See Department of Health and Human Services)	
Department of Health and Human Services	
. disclosure of returns and return information	6103
. information returns	
. . employee retirement and benefit plans	6057
. . Social Security benefits	6050F
. inspection of returns	6103
. parent locator service, collection of child support payments	6305
Department of Justice	
. disclosure of returns and return information	6103
Department of Labor	
. employee retirement and benefit plans, information to	6103
Department of the Treasury	
. appeals dispute resolution procedures	7123
. Assistant Commissioner (employee plans and organizations)	7802
. authority of	7801
. closing agreements and compromises	7121 et seq.
. Commissioner of Internal Revenue	7802
. disclosure of returns and return information	6103

	CODE SEC.
Department of the Treasury — Cont'd	
. Office of General Counsel	7801
. other personnel	7803
. penalties relating to officers	7344
. powers and duties of Secretary	7801
. seal, authorization	7514
Department store fringe benefits	132
Dependent care assistance programs	129
. receipts for employees	6051
. withholding tax on wages	3401
Dependent care credit	
. employment-related expenses	21
. medical expenses	213
. TIN on return, use of	21
Dependents	
. adopted children	152
. children, personal exemptions	151
. common-law marriages	152
. custodial parents, children of	152
. dependent care assistance programs (See Dependent care assistance programs)	
. disabled	151
. divorced or separated parents, children of (See Divorced or separated parents, children of)	
. earnings	73
. . assessment of tax	6201
. . family employment, FUTA	3306
. foreign-born	152
. foster children	152
. fringe benefits	132
. handicapped	151; 152
. husband and wife	152
. levy and distraint, exemptions for support	6334
. married	151
. meals and lodging	119
. medical expenses	105
. missing or kidnapped children	151
. missing parent, collection of support obligations	6103; 6305; 6402
. multiple support agreements	152
. nonresident aliens	152
. personal exemptions	151 et seq.
. qualifying child	152
. qualifying relative	152
. remarriage of parent, new spouse's support payments	152
. sheltered workshop income	151
. standard deduction, limitation	63
. students	151; 152
. support test, divorced or separated parents	152
. taxable income	63
. tuition deduction	222(c)(3)
. unmarried persons living together	152
. violation of local law, individuals living together in	152
Depletion	
. allowance of deduction	611; 614
. basis	
. . adjustments	1016
. . cost	612
. decedent's estate	691

143

Depletion

CODE SEC.

Depletion —Cont'd
- estates and trusts ... 642
- insurance companies other than life ... 832; 834
- natural resources ... 611 et seq.
- oil and gas wells ... 613A
- percentage ... 613
- . basis for gain or loss, adjustments ... 1016
- . limitations ... 613A
- . . reduction ... 291
- preference items ... 57; 291
- property defined ... 614

Deposit accounts
- interest paid, taxable year of deductions ... 461

Depositaries for collections (See also Government depositaries)
- banks as ... 5703; 6302
- failure to make deposit ... 6656
- locations serving as ... 5703; 6302
- requirements of ... 7808; 7809
- trust companies as ... 5703; 6302

Depreciation ... 167; 168
- accelerated cost recovery system (See Accelerated cost recovery system (ACRS))
- alternative depreciation property ... 168
- alternative minimum tax ... 56
- automobiles ... 168; 280F
- basis (See Basis)
- beneficiaries, estates and trusts ... 167
- bonus (See Bonus depreciation)
- carryovers, acquiring corporation ... 381
- computer software ... 167
- cooperative housing corporation ... 216(c)
- copyrights ... 167
- declining balance method ... 168
- deductions
- . . amortization of pollution control facilities ... 169
- . . estates and trusts ... 642
- . definitions ... 864
- earnings and profits, effect on ... 312
- estates and trusts ... 167; 642
- expensing in lieu of ... 179; 263
- farms ... 263A
- foreign corporations
- . . earnings and profits computation ... 312
- foreign personal holding company ... 556
- income forecast method interest computation ... 167
- installment sales ... 453
- insurance companies other than life ... 832; 834
- life tenant, estates and trusts ... 167
- listed property ... 280F
- look-back method interest computation ... 167
- low-income housing ... 1250
- luxury automobiles ... 280F
- mines ... 611; 616; 617
- musical works ... 167
- obsolescence ... 167
- oil and gas wells ... 611
- oil companies, major integrated ... 167
- participants and residuals ... 167

Index to Code

CODE SEC.

Depreciation—Cont'd
- personal holding company ... 545
- personal property ... 865
- pollution control facilities ... 169
- production of income, property held for ... 167
- property
- . definition ... 108
- . discharge of indebtedness ... 108; 1017
- . . gain from disposition of ... 1239; 1245
- . . inventories, election to treat as ... 1017
- . related parties, sales between ... 1239
- recapture
- . basis reductions, of ... 1017
- . . dispositions of property ... 1245; 1250
- . sports franchises, player contracts ... 1245
- straight line ... 168
- tangible property and earnings and profits ... 312
- tax-exempt use property ... 167
- term interests ... 167
- trade or business, property used in ... 167
- wear and tear ... 167

Desert shield service ... 7508
Designated local agency, work opportunity credit ... 51
Designated settlement funds ... 468B
Designee, taxpayer
- disclosure of returns and return information ... 6103

Destroyed vehicles ... 4481
Destructive devices defined ... 5845
Determination letters
- public inspection ... 6110
- request, user fee for ... 7528

Determinations
- claim for refund defined ... 1313
- defined for regulated investment companies and REITs ... 860
- international boycott ... 999

Development expenditures
- basis adjusted for ... 1016
- long-term contract, accounting methods ... 460
- mines or deposits ... 616; 1016

Devises
- basis for gain or loss ... 1014
- depreciation recapture ... 1250
- exemption ... 102
- income ... 102

Diatomaceous earth, depletion ... 613
Diesel fuel (See also Special fuels tax)
- adulterated, penalties for ... 6720A
- biodiesel (See Biodiesel fuel)
- deficit reduction rate ... 4091; 4093; 6427
- excise taxes ... 4091 et seq.
- . . alcohol mixtures, used to produce ... 4091; 6427
- . . chemicals used in production, environmental tax ... 4662
- . definitions ... 4092
- . exemptions ... 4091; 4092
- . . failure to pay ... 4103
- . . failure to register ... 6719; 7232
- . imposition of ... 4041; 4091
- . . information reporting ... 4104

144

Index to Code

Disclosure

CODE SEC.

Diesel fuel (See also Special fuels tax) — Cont'd
excise taxes — Cont'd
.. inspection of records by local officers 4102
.. penalty for taxable use 6715
.. possessions of U.S. 4293
.. registration and bond 4101
.. two-party exchanges 4104
.. U.S. use of fuel 4293
. exemption, gasoline tax 4082
. farmer, sales to 6427
. low-sulfur diesel fuels
.. adulterated, penalties for 6720A
.. credit determination 45H
.. deduction .... 280C(d)
.. general business credit 38; 196
.. mixture or biodiesel not used as fuel .... 40A(3)
.. renewable diesel .... 40A(f)(1) et seq.
.. small agri-biodiesel producer credit (See Small agri-biodiesel producer credit)

Difficulty of care, foster care payments 131

Direct sellers
. employment taxes 3508
. failure to file information returns 6652
. independent contractors, status as 3508
. information returns 6041A; 6652
. reporting payments to 6041A

Direct skips, GST tax (See Generation-skipping transfer (GST) tax)

Directors
. excess benefit transaction of exempt organizations ... 4958
. fees 1402

Dirt, depletion 613

Disability
. definition 44
. moving expenses 217
. permanent and total, defined 22
. returns 6012
. terrorist attacks, compensation 104

Disability benefits
. employee retirement and benefit plans 401; 415
. FICA 3121
. FUTA 3306
. service-connected payments, exemption from levy 6334
. veterans' disability compensation 104

Disabled access credit 38
. carryback and carryforward 39
. denial of double benefit 44
. eligible small businesses 44
. expenditures, eligible 44
. unused business credit 39

Disabled individuals
. access provided for, credit (See Disabled access credit)
. credit 22
. dependent 151
. dependent care credit 21
. employee fringe benefits 132
. foster care payments 131
. household expenses, credit for 21
. personal exemptions 151

CODE SEC.

Disabled individuals — Cont'd
. sheltered workshop income 151

Disaster losses and relief 165; 5064
. crops, payments for 451
. deduction for
.. demolition .... 165(k)
.. denial for obligation not in registered form .... 165(j)
.. preceding year, election to take deduction in ... 165(i)(1)
.. relocation .... 165(k)
. employment taxes coordination with relief payments ... 139(d)
. federally declared disasters
.. alternative tax net operating loss deduction ... 56(d)(3)
.. deduction, casualty loss .... 165(h)(3)
. Gulf Opportunity Zone (See Gulf Opportunity Zone)
. mitigation payments .... 139(g)
. Presidentially declared disasters ...... (Presidentially declared disasters)
. qualified disaster assistance property
.. adjusted basis, reduction of .... 168(n)(1)(B)
.. applicable disaster date defined .... 168(n)(3)(A)
.. defined .... 168(n)(2)
.. disaster area defined .... 168(n)(3)(C)
.. eligible taxpayer defined .... 168(n)(3)(D)
.. federally declared disaster defined .... 168(n)(3)(B)
.. 167(a) depreciation deduction allowance .... 168(n)(1)(A)
.. recapture .... 168(n)(4)
.. Sec. 179 property, election to expense
... defined .... 179(e)(2)
... dollar amount .... 179(e)(1)
... empowerment zones, coordination with ...... 179(e)(3)
... recapture .... 179(e)(4)
... renewal communities, coordination with .... 179(e)(3)
.. special allowances for .... 168(n)(1)
. qualified disaster defined .... 139(c)
. qualified disaster losses
.. net operating losses deduction
... coordination with 172(b)(2) .... 172(j)(2)
... defined .... 172(j)(1)
... election .... 172(j)(3)
... exclusion .... 172(j)(4)
. qualified disaster relief payments defined .... 139(b)
. qualified mortgage bonds
.. residence destroyed in disaster area .... 143(k)(13)
.. residences located in disaster area .... 143(k)(11)
. refunds and credits 6405
. Robert T. Stafford Disaster Relief and Emergency Assistance Act 5064; 5708
. standard deduction and deduction for .... 63(c)(8)
. terrorist actions, participants in .... 139(e)

DISC (See Domestic international sales corporations (DISCS))

Discharge of indebtedness (See Cancellation of indebtedness)

Disclaimers, estate and gift taxes 2518

Disclosure of tax information 6103
. backup withholding 3406
. executive branch influences, prohibition against .. 7217
. exempt organizations 6104
. identification numbers 6109
. material advisor

145

Disclosure

Index to Code

CODE SEC.

Disclosure of tax information—Cont'd
material advisor —Cont'd
- .. defined 6111
- .. lists, reportable transactions 6112; 6708
- .. reportable transactions 6111
- .. retention of documents 6112
- . penalties 7213
- . Privacy Act of 1974, inapplicability to IRC provisions 7852
- . private foundations 6104
- . public inspection 6110
- . quid pro quo contributions 6115; 6714
- .. failure to meet disclosure requirements 6114
- . reportable transactions 6111
- . statistical use 6103; 6108
- . Tax Court proceedings 6110; 7461
- . tax return preparers 6107; 7216
- . treaty obligations, information arising under 6105
- . treaty-based return positions 6114
- . unauthorized 7213
- .. civil damages 7431; 7435
- .. federal employees 7213
- .. return preparer, by 6713; 7216
- . wagering taxes 4424
- . written determinations 6110

Discount
- . bonds and notes (See Discount bonds and notes)
- . fringe benefit exclusion 132

Discount bonds and notes
- . accounting methods 454
- . carryovers, acquiring corporation 381
- . foreign corporations 881
- . Indian tribal governments, treatment as state 7871
- . insurance companies other than life 834
- . life insurance companies 811; 1016
- . market (See Market discount bonds)
- . non-interest bearing obligations 454
- . nonresident aliens 871
- . original issue discount (See Original issue discount)
- . short-term obligations .... 454; 852; 1281 et seq.
- . stripped bonds (See Stripped bonds or coupons)
- . tax-exempt 1288
- . U.S. savings bonds 454

Discounted unpaid losses
- . determination .... 846(a)
- . insurance company estimated income tax 847

Discrimination
- . adjusted gross income of costs for case concerning 62
- . cafeteria plans 125
- . cash or deferred arrangements (CODAs) 401
- . collectively bargained plans 413
- . dependent care assistance programs 129
- . employee benefit plans 401
- . foreign taxes 891; 896; 901; 2108
- . group-term life insurance 79
- . highly-compensated employees
- .. IRA plan discrimination in favor of 408
- ... simplified employee pension plans discrimination in favor of .... 408(k)(3)
- . long-term care insurance health status discrimination 9802

CODE SEC.

Discrimination—Cont'd
- . student loan bonds 144
- . unlawful discrimination defined 62

Diseased livestock sales 1033

Dishwashers
- . energy efficient appliance credit (See Energy efficient appliance credits)

Displays for advertising outdoors
- . involuntary conversion 1033

Disposition
- . gain or loss
- .. depreciable property 291; 341
- .. earnings and profits, effect on 312
- . geothermal deposits 291
- . investment credit 50
- . low-income housing credit (See Low-income housing credit)
- . mines 291
- . oil and gas wells 291
- . stock 306

Disqualified investment corporation distributions 355

Dissolved corporation (See Corporations, dissolution)

Distilled spirits ..... 5001 et seq. (See also Alcohol taxes; Beer tax; Liquors; Wines)
- . alcohol taxes .... 5001 et seq.; 5291; 5301; 5311 et seq.
- .. credit for wine and flavors content 5010
- .. foreign embassies, use by 5066
- .. industrial use .... 5271 et seq.
- .. plants 5081
- . attachment of tax 5001
- . bonded premises defined 5002
- . closures 5301; 5604; 5613
- . collection of tax 5007; 5061
- . containers 5206; 5301; 5311; 5604; 5606
- . credits against tax 5010
- . definition 5002
- . denaturation
- .. authority for 5241
- .. excise tax 5001
- .. materials for process 5242
- .. sale, use and recovery of 5273
- .. sale of abandoned spirits for, without tax collection 5243
- . determination of tax 5006
- . discontinuation of storage facilities 5236
- . disposal of forfeited equipment and materials 5610
- . drawbacks 5114
- .. claims 5134
- .. eligibility and rate of tax 5131
- .. fraudulent claims 5608; 7304
- .. investigation of claims 5133
- .. penalty, fraudulent claims 7304
- .. rate of drawback 5134
- .. registration and regulation 5132
- . electronic fund transfers, payments by 5061
- . exemptions 5003; 5081; 5113; 5123; 5561; 5562
- . experimental research, production and use for 5312
- . exports, refunds and drawbacks 5062
- . flavors content, credit for 5010
- . foreign official's withdrawals of 5066

Index to Code

Distributions

CODE SEC.

Distilled spirits—Cont'd
- forfeiture of tax paid distilled spirits remaining on bonded premises 5612
- fuels, use as 5181
- gallonage taxes .... 5001 et seq.
- imported 5232
- industrial uses
  - bonds 5272
  - bottling 5235
  - occupational taxes on packager of 5116
  - other laws, applicability of 5274
  - permits 5271
  - records and reports 5275
  - regulation of operations 5201
  - sale, use and recovery of denatured spirits 5273
- liability for tax 5005
- lien for taxes 5004
- losses 5006; 5008; 5064
- materials used in manufacture of, return of 5291; 5605
- nonbeverage purposes .... 5002; 5131 et seq.
- occupational taxes .... 5081 et seq.; 5116
- operations defined 5002
- payment of tax 5061
- penalties, seizures and forfeitures ... 5601 et seq.; 5681 et seq.
- plants (See Distilled spirits plants)
- processor defined 5002
- prohibited purchases by dealers 5132
- rate of tax 5001
- recordkeeping 5114
- redistillation of spirits, articles and residues 5223
- refund for loss or destruction 5008; 5064
- release of distillery before judgment 5611
- retail dealers .... 5121 et seq.
- returns and records 5555
- shipments from U.S. possessions 7652
- smuggled in U.S. 5006
- stills
  - excise taxes on manufacturers of 5101; 5102
  - registration 5179
- storage .... 5231 et seq.
- time of attachment 5001
- trademarks and brands 5604
- transfer between bonded premises 5212
- unbonded 5006
- unlawful use, penalties 5607
- wine content, credit for 5010

Distilled spirits plants .... 5171 et seq.
- bonded premises
  - defined 5002
  - production and entry of spirits 5211
  - regulations of operations 5216
  - return of spirits to 5215
  - transfer between premises 5212
  - withdrawal from premises 5213; 5214
- bonds required .... 5171 et seq.; 5173 et seq.; 5551
  - export bonds 5175
  - new or renewed bonds 5176
  - provisions relating to 5177
- commencement of operations 5221

CODE SEC.

Distilled spirits plants—Cont'd
- defined 5002
- distiller defined 5002
- enforcement officers, investigations by 5557; 5558
- establishment of 5171
- experimental operations 5312; 5554
- fuel, manufacture for use as 5181
- gauging requirements 5204; 5211
- inspection of records and premises 5203
- installation of meters, tanks, and other apparatus 5552
- location, construction, and arrangement of 5178
- occupational taxes .... 5171 et seq.; 5276
- operation of .... 5002; 5201 et seq.
- permits 5171
- pilot operations 5554
- premises
  - inspection 5203
  - requirements 5178
- processor defined 5002
- production, receipt, removal, and use of distilling materials 5222
- proprietors of, occupational tax 5081
- qualification requirements .... 5171 et seq.; 5201 et seq.
- rate of tax 5081
- records and reports 5207
- redistillation of spirits, articles and residues 5223
- registration 5171
- resumption after suspension of operations 5221
- return of spirits 5215
- returns and records 5555
- revenue protecting apparatus 5552
- signs, required 5180
- small proprietors of, occupational tax 5081
- storage .... 5231 et seq.
- supervision of premises and operations 5553
- suspension of operations 5221
- transfers between 5212
- withdrawal of spirits 5213; 5214

Distraint (See Seizure of property)

Distributions (See also Dividends; specific subject headings)
- active business requirement 355
- appreciated property 311
  - earnings and profits, effect on 312
  - nonrecognition of gain or loss 361
  - reorganization exchanges 361
- basis
  - property received in liquidations 334
  - stock and stock rights acquired in distribution 307
  - stock reduced by 1016
- complete liquidation, received in
  - basis of property 334
  - effect on liquidating corporation .... 336 et seq.
  - effect on recipients .... 331 et seq.
  - subsidiaries 332; 337
- consent dividends 565
- controlled corporation stock and securities 312; 355
- controlled foreign corporations 959; 962
- cooperative housing associations .... 216(e)
- corporations .... 301 et seq.

147

Distributions | Index to Code

CODE SEC.

Distributions (See also Dividends; specific subject headings)—Cont'd
- corporations—Cont'd
  - collapsible corporations 341
  - earnings and profits, effect on 312
  - effects on recipients
    - taxability of corporation on distribution 311
  - partial liquidations 346
  - passive foreign investment companies ..... 1291 et seq.
  - redemption of stock ..... 302 et seq.
  - taxability of corporation 311
  - creditors, transfers to 361
- death taxes, redemption of stock for payment of 303
- deferred compensation plan 409A
- DISCs ..... 992; 995 et seq.
- disposition of stock 306
- disqualified investment corporations 355
- earnings and profits 312
- effect on recipients ..... 301 et seq.
- 80% distributee, gains or losses 337
- election to recognize gain 643
- employee benefit plans ..... 72; 401 et seq.
- estate freezes 2701
- 50% or greater interest defined for 355
- foreign corporation reorganization exchanges 367
- foreign trusts 665
- gain or loss nonrecognition 361; 1081
- generation-skipping transfers, taxable distributions in 2612; 2621
- in-kind, trusts and estates 643
- life insurance companies
  - special 2005 and 2006 rules 815
- liquidation
  - basis of property 334; 336
  - effect on recipients ..... 331 et seq.
  - stockholders, gain or loss to 331
  - subsidiaries 332; 337
- partnerships ..... 702; 704; 731 et seq.
- personal holding companies 316
- proceeds of loan insured by U.S. 312
- qualified electing funds 1293; 1294
- real estate mortgage investment conduits 860C; 860F
- redemptions ..... 302 et seq.; 312
- regulated investment companies 852
- related corporations, redemption of stock through 304
- reorganization exchanges, in ..... 351 et seq.; 361; 367
- required by SEC 1081
- right to distributions defined 2701
- S corporations
  - cash, post-termination 1371
  - general rule 1368
  - restricted bank director receiving distributions 1368
- SEC orders
  - basis for gain or loss 1082
  - definitions 1083
  - depreciation recapture 1245; 1250
  - gain or loss, nonrecognition of 1081
  - obedience to ..... 1081 et seq.
- securities, controlled corporation 355

CODE SEC.

Distributions (See also Dividends; specific subject headings)—Cont'd
- stock and stock rights 305
- controlled corporation, of 355
- dispositions of certain stock 306
- earnings and profits, effect on 312
- taxability of corporation 311
- stockholders, to 305
- subsidiaries
  - parent, nonrecognition of gain by 337; 453B
- tax deferral, interest on 1291
- tax-free
  - adjustment of basis of stock 1016
  - earnings and profits, effect on 312
- trusts and estates
  - accumulating income or distributing corpus ..... 661 et seq.
  - charitable remainder trusts 664
  - current income only
    - deductions 651
    - gross income of beneficiaries 652
  - deduction for 643
  - distributable net income 643
  - foreign trusts 665
  - sixty-five day rule 663
  - treatment of excess ..... 665 et seq.

Distributive shares of partners
- self-employment tax 1402

Distributor of goods
- cancellation of agreements
  - amounts received, gain on 1241

District Courts, jurisdiction 7402
- deficiency notice issued while refund suit pending 7422
- enforce summons 7604
- exempt organizations and private foundations, qualification as 7428
- jeopardy assessments 7429
- Railroad Retirement Tax Act 3232
- third-party recordkeepers 7609
- third-party suits 7426

District directors of Internal Revenue
- change of, proceedings pending before appellate court 7484
- delinquent 7803
- suit for damages 7402

District of Columbia
- employment tax overpayment 6413
- enterprise zones/communities (See Enterprise zones/communities)
- exempt income 115
- FICA 3121
- government employees 3125; 6205
- overpayments 6413
- First-time homebuyers (See First-time homebuyers)
- FUTA 3306
- short-term obligations issued at discount ..... 1271; 1281 et seq.
- taxes 164

District of Columbia Retirement Protection Act of 1997
- disclosure of returns and return information 6103

Index to Code

Dividends-received

CODE SEC.

Districts (See Internal Revenue Districts)
Divestiture, certificate of
. conflict-of-interest requirement; property sales 1043
Dividend equivalent payments
. nonresident aliens 871
Dividends 316
. annuities 72
. apostolic association's members' pro rata shares of taxable income 501
. backup withholding 3406; 7205
. building and loan associations 591
. capital expenditures
. . payments in lieu of dividends 263
. capital gain
. . regulated investment companies 852; 854; 860
. . REITs .... 857(b)(3)(C); 860
. carryovers
. . acquiring corporation, by 381
. . personal holding companies 381; 564
. consent dividends 565; 1016
. controlled foreign corporation stock, sale, exchange or distribution 1248
. cooperative banks 591
. cooperatives
. . capital stock 521
. . patronage dividends (See Patronage dividends)
. date considered paid 563
. deduction for (See Dividends-paid deduction; Dividends-received deduction)
. deficiency (See Deficiency dividends)
. defined 316; 6042
. deposit accounts, taxable year of deduction 461
. distributions 301; 316; 959
. exclusion
. . failure to file 6652
. . regulated investment companies 852
. exemptions, RIC shareholder dividends 852
. extraordinary 1059
. failure to report 3406
. foreign corporations (See Foreign corporations)
. foreign personal holding companies 552; 553
. foreign tax credit 78; 904
. gross income 61; 78
. gross-up, foreign tax credit 78
. information returns
. . failure to file 6652
. . information at source .... 6041 et seq.
. . magnetic tape, use of 6011
. insurance companies 316; 832
. life insurance policyholders 808
. liquidating
. . dividends-paid deduction 562
. . foreign corporation involved 1248
. . foreign personal holding companies 551
. . information returns 6043
. . partial defined 346
. . terminating corporation's taxable year 6851
. mutual savings banks 591
. paid deductions (See Dividends-paid deductions)

CODE SEC.

Dividends—Cont'd
. partners 702
. passive activity losses and credits 469
. patronage (See Patronage dividends)
. payments in lieu of 263
. personal holding companies 316; 381; 543
. preferred 565; 1059
. received deduction (See Dividends-received deductions)
. regulated investment companies 265; 316; 852; 854; 855
. REIT 316; 858
. religious organization's members' pro rata shares of taxable income 501
. reorganization exchanges 356
. S corporations 1368
. self-employment income 1402
. short sales
. . payments in lieu of dividends 263
. source of distribution 316
. source of income 861
. statements to recipients 6042; 6044
. stock
. . distributable net income computation 643
. . distributions, basis 1059
. . estates and trusts 643
. . holding period 1223
. undistributed foreign personal holding company income as 551
. unrelated business taxable income 512
. withholding tax
. . backup withholding 3406; 7205
. . nonresident aliens and foreign corporations 565; 1441
Dividends-paid deductions 561
. bank deposits 591
. carryover of dividends 564
. cash to employee stock ownership plans 404
. consent dividends 565
. defined 561; 562
. eligible dividends 562
. foreign personal holding companies 556
. information returns 6042; 6652
. life insurance policyholders 808
. payment after close of taxable year 563
. personal holding companies 545; 547
. preferential dividends 562
. preferred stock, public utilities 247
. public utilities preferred stock 247
. regulated investment companies 852; 855; 860
. REITs 857; 858; 860
. return requirements
. . statement furnished by corporations 6042
Dividends-received deductions
. affiliated corporations 243
. aggregate amount of deductions 246
. cash to employee stock ownership plans 404
. controlled foreign corporations 965
. corporate deductions .... 243 et seq.
. credits against tax
. . foreign tax credit 902
. . REIT 857

149

Dividends-received

CODE SEC.

Dividends-received deductions —Cont'd
. debt-financed portfolio stock 246A
. disallowance of deductions 246
. DISCs 246
. foreign corporations 78; 243; 245
. foreign sales corporation 245
. holding periods 246
. income reduced by 469
. insurance companies other than life 834
. life insurance companies 243; 805
. limitations 246
. net operating loss 246
. 100% allowable deductions
. . debt-financed portfolio stock 246A
. passive activity losses and credits 469
. personal holding companies 545
. portfolio stock, debt-financed 246A
. possessions corporation 246
. preference dividends, 90-day rule 246
. preferred stock
. . portfolio stock, debt-financed 246A
. . public utilities 243; 244
. public utilities 243; 244
. qualifying dividends 243
. reductions
. . portfolio stock, debt-financed 246A
. regulated investment company 243; 854
. REITs 243; 857; 1373
. . restrictions applicable to
. . . Sec. (1)(h)(11) .... 857(c)(2)
. . . Sec. 243 .... 857(c)(1)
. short sales 246
. small business investment companies 243
. 20% owned corporation 243

Divorce
. alimony (See Alimony and separate maintenance payments)
. Archer medical savings account transfer after 220
. children of divorced or separated parents
. . credits 21
. . medical and dental expenses 213
. . support, collection 6305
. . support test 152
. domestic relations orders (See Domestic relations order)
. gift tax on property settlement 2516
. income of an estate or trust in case of 682
. individual retirement accounts 408
. installment obligations 453B
. instrument of, definition 71
. status of individuals 6013; 7703
. transfers incident to
. . basis for gain or loss 1015
. . employee stock options 424
. . gain or loss 1041
. . nontaxable exchanges 1041

Docks
. exempt facility bonds 142; 146

Index to Code

CODE SEC.

Documentary stamp taxes (See Stamp taxes (documentary))
Documentation defined 982
Documents
. timely mailing treatment as timely filing 7502
Dollar
. fractional 3402; 6102; 6313; 7504
. functional currency, as 985
Dolomite, depletion 613
Domestic building and loan association (See Building and loan associations)
Domestic corporations (See Corporations)
Domestic defined 7701
Domestic fraternal organizations 501
Domestic international sales corporations (DISC) .... 991 et seq. (See also Foreign sales corporations (FSCs))
. accounting period 441
. accumulated income, redemptions, corporate adjustment 996
. affiliated group member 1504
. allocation rules, distributions and losses 996
. asset transfers 995
. basis of stock owned by decedent 1014
. commissions, rentals and marginal costing 994
. controlled group 995
. decedent, stock owned by 1014
. deferred tax liability, interest 995
. definitions 992; 993
. distributions to stockholders 996
. . deemed distributions 995
. . DISC status revoked 995
. . dividends-received deduction 246
. . foreign tax credit 901
. . previously taxed income 996
. . property to corporate distributee 997
. . qualifying distributions 992
. . source 861
. . tax treatment .... 995 et seq.
. earnings and profits 995; 996
. election of status 992
. exempt shareholders 995
. film production 992; 993
. foreign investments attributable to earnings 995
. foreign tax credit 901; 904
. former DISC status 992
. gross receipts defined 993
. ineligible corporations 992
. information to shareholders 6011
. inter-company pricing rules 994
. losses 996
. military property, income from 995
. personal holding company provisions, coordination with .. 992
. possession tax credit 936
. pricing rules, inter-company 994
. producer's loans 993
. qualification requirements 992
. redemption of stock 995; 996
. related foreign export corporation 993
. requirements 992

150

Index to Code — Earned

CODE SEC.

Domestic international sales corporations (DISC)—Cont'd
. returns
.. consolidated return 1504
.. failure to file 6686
.. ineligible corporation filing as DISC 6501
.. requirement 6011
.. time for 6072
. revocation of election 992
. stockholders, taxation of .... 995 et seq.
. Subchapter C rules 997
. taxable year 441
. termination of status 992
. transitional funds uncommitted 995

Domestic production activities
. deductions
.. affiliated groups .... 199(d)(4)
.. agricultural and horticultural cooperatives ..... 199(d)(3)
.. allowance of .... 199(a)(1)
.. cost, determination of .... 199(c)(3)
.. domestic production gross receipts defined ..... 199(c)(4)
.. individuals .... 199(d)(2)
.. minimum tax, coordination with .... 199(d)(6)
.. net operating loss deduction, disallowance of ... 172(d)(7)
.. oil related qualified production activities income .... 199(d)(9)
.. pass-thru entities .... 199(d)(1)
.. Puerto Rico, activities in .... 199(d)(8)
.. qualified domestic production activities income .... 199(c)
.. qualified film .... 199(c)(6)
.. qualifying production property .... 199(c)(5)
.. regulations, prescription of .... 199(d)(10)
.. related persons .... 199(c)(7)
.. trade of business requirement .... 199(d)(5)
.. unrelated business taxable income .... 199(d)(7)
.. W-2 wages defined .... 199(b)(2)
.. wages paid limitations .... 199(1)(b)

Domestic relations orders
. definition 414
. employee benefits, assignment or alienation of 401
.. alternate payee
... defined 414
... treatment as distributee 402
.. lump-sum distributions 402
.. rollovers 402
.. surviving spouse, former spouse as 414

Domestic service
. coordination of collection of income taxes with employment taxes 3510
. FICA 3121
. FUTA 3306
. withholding tax on wages 3401

Donations (See Charitable contributions)

Donor advised funds
. charitable contributions 170; 2522
. fractional gifts 2522
. recapture of deduction 2522

Double deductions or credits 7852
. estates and trusts 642; 663
. insurance companies other than life 832; 834

CODE SEC.

Double deductions or credits—Cont'd
. life insurance companies 811; 812
. U.S. citizens or residents living abroad 911

Double taxation 7852
. debt instruments 1271; 1283

Dower interests
. estate tax 2034; 2043
. gross estate, effect on value of 2034
. insufficient consideration 2043

Drawbacks
. alcohol .... 5131 et seq.
. beer tax 5055; 5062
. fraudulent claims 5608; 7304
. penalties for fraudulently claiming 7304
. tobacco taxes 5706

Drilling rig employees, meals provided to 274

Drought
. livestock sales
.. nontaxable exchanges 1033
.. proceeds from 451

Drugs
. narcotic (See Narcotic drugs)
. prescription (See Prescription drugs)

Due dates
. Presidentially declared disaster
.. postponement of certain tax-related deadlines 7508A
. returns filed before due date
.. interest on overpayments 6611
.. limitation on assessment and collection 6501
.. limitation on refunds 6513

Dues
. agricultural and horticultural organization dues .... 512(d)
. business expenses 162
. deductibility 274
. membership organizations accounting method 456
. prepaid 456

Dumps, chemical, cleanup of, excise taxes (See Hazardous waste cleanup subhead excise taxes)

Duress, payment of tax under 7422

Dwelling unit
. public utilities, energy conservation subsidies provided by 136

Dye injection systems
. security, tampering or failure to provide 6715A

Dyed fuel
. kerosene 4082
. penalty for taxable use 6715

E

Earned income (See also Compensation)
. consolidated returns 1551; 1552
. controlled foreign corporations
.. sale or exchange of stock 1248
. defined 32
. employment taxes and 3507
. foreign corporations
.. exclusions 1248

Earned   Index to Code

CODE SEC.

Earned income (See also Compensation) — Cont'd
. information returns 6042
. limitations
.. employment-related expenses, amount creditable for 21
. self-employed individual 401
. unregistered obligations 4701
Earned income credit 32; 3507; 6012; 6051; 6201
. advance payments
.. employment taxes 3507
.. information statements 6051
.. returns 6012
. excessive 6401
. notification, IRS 3507
Earnings and profits
. accumulated
.. defined for foreign and affiliated corporations credit 902
.. tax on (See Accumulated earnings tax)
. affiliated corporations 1552
. carryovers, acquiring corporation 381
. consolidated returns 1552
.. adjusted basis for gain or loss 1503
. controlled foreign corporations 952; 956; 959; 964
. corporate acquisitions 381
. corporate distributions and adjustments 312
. foreign corporations 986; 1248
. foreign earned income .... 911 et seq
. information returns 6042
. previously taxed
.. exclusion from gross income 959
.. foreign currency gain or loss on distributions from 986
. regulated investment companies 852
. REITs .... 857(d)(1) et seq.
. restricted countries, from 911
. S corporations 1368; 1371; 1375
. U.S. citizens or residents living abroad .... 911 et seq.
Easements, irrevocable transfers of 2055
Economic activity credit, Puerto Rico 30A
Economic development
. recovery zone bonds (See Recovery zone bonds)
. recovery zone economic development bonds (See Recovery zone economic development bonds)
. tribal economic development bonds (See Tribal economic development bonds)
Economic distress, area of chronic
. mortgage revenue bonds, targeted areas .... 143(j)(3)
. recovery zone bonds (See Recovery zone bonds)
. recovery zone economic development bonds (See Recovery zone economic development bonds)
Economic performance test
. liabilities 461
. nuclear decommissioning costs 468A
Economic substance doctrine
. transactions in which the court determines relevancy of ... 7701
Economically disadvantaged persons
. work opportunity credit 51
Education expenses
. adjusted gross income 62
. Coverdell education savings accounts 530

CODE SEC.

Education expenses — Cont'd
. deduction of qualified tuition and related expenses (See Tuition)
. gift tax exclusion 2503
. higher education, savings bonds redeemed to pay 135
. reporting 6050S
. tuition (See Tuition)
Education individual retirement accounts 530
Education IRA (See Coverdell education savings accounts)
Education programs, cooperative
. work opportunity credit 51
Education tax benefits
. Gulf Opportunity Zone 1400O
Educational assistance programs 127
. books and records 6039D
. fringe benefits 132
. information returns 6039D; 6652
. railroad retirement taxes 3231
. withholding tax on wages 3401
Educational facilities
. exempt facility bonds (See Exempt facility bonds subhead qualified public educational facilities)
Educational institutions
. Coverdell education savings accounts 530
. definition 119
. higher education
.. contributions 170
.. educational loan, interest on 221
. private foundations (See Private foundations)
. zone academy bonds, credits for holders of (See Qualified zone academy bonds)
Educational loans
. defaulted
.. mailing address disclosed for collection purposes 6103
. interest 163; 221
Educational organizations
. charitable contributions 170
. communications taxes, exemption 4253
. cooperative service organization, investments of 501
. day care centers 501
. employee retirement and benefit plans 410
. employees
.. annuities 403; 415
.. excess contributions tax 4973
.. FICA 3121
.. FUTA 3306
.. meals and lodging 119
. exemption 501
. fringe benefits
.. FICA 3121
.. FUTA 3306
.. withholding tax on wages 3401
. Indian tribal government, treatment as state 7871
. lobbying activities, expenditures, excise tax 501; 4911
. manufacturers excise taxes 4221; 6416
. meals and lodging, employees 119
. research income 512
. scholarships 117
. tuition reductions 117

152

Index to Code

Employee

CODE SEC.

Educational organizations —Cont'd
tuition reductions—Cont'd
.. employees, withholding tax on wages 3401
. wines, alcohol taxes, exemptions 5042
Effectively connected income (See Nonresident aliens)
Elderly individuals (See also Federal Insurance Contributions Act (FICA); Social Security)
. architectural and transportation barriers, removal expenditures 190; 263
. credit for 22
. long-term care facilities
.. imputed interest on loans to 7872
.. private foundations 4942
. old-age, survivors, and disability insurance (OASDI) 1401
. residence sale, one-time exclusion of gain 121
. taxable income 63
Electing investment partnership returns 6031
Electing large partnerships 6240
. adjustments, partnership 6242
.. administrative adjustment requests 6251
.. judicial review of adjustment 6247
.. judicial review when administrative adjustment requests not fully allowed 6252
.. period of limitations for making 6248
.. secretarial authority 6245
. computations at partnership level 773
. consistency requirement 6241
. defined 775
. definitions concerning 6255
. oil and gas properties, rules when holding 776
. optional adjustments 774
. simplified flow-through 772
. special rules 6255
Electing small business trusts 641
Election commission (See Federal Election Commission)
Elections
. alcohol fuels credit 40
. business expenses 162
. enhanced oil recovery credit 43
. rehabilitation credit 47
. tax preference items, optional 10-year writeoff 59
. work opportunity credit 51
Electric cooperatives, taxation of .... 1381 et seq.
Electric outboard motor excise tax 4161
Electric utilities (See Public utilities)
Electric vehicles
. plug-in drive motor vehicles credit (See Plug-in electric vehicles)
. qualified electric vehicle credit 30
Electricity
. closed-loop biomass 45
. open-loop biomass 45
. production credit; renewable sources
.. closed-loop biomass facility .... 45(d)(2)
.. geothermal energy facility .... 45(d)(4)
.. hydropower facility .... 45(d)(9)
.. Indian coal production facility .... 45(d)(10)
.. landfill gas facility .... 45(d)(6)
.. marine and hydrokinetic renewable energy facility .... 45(d)(11)

CODE SEC.

Electricity —Cont'd
production credit; renewable sources —Cont'd
.. open-loop biomass facility .... 45(d)(3)
.. refined coal production facility .... 45(d)(8)
.. small irrigation power facility .... 45(d)(5)
.. solar energy facility .... 45(d)(4)
.. trash facility .... 45(d)(7)
.. wind facility .... 45(d)(1)
Electronic filing
. authorization 7502
. Information returns, promotion and encouragement for ... 6011
Electronic fund transfers, tax payments 5061
Eligible candidate
. defined for presidential election campaign fund 9002
Eligible worker-owned cooperatives (EWOCs)
. defined 1042
. liability for tax, prohibited allocation of securities 4979A
Emergency medical responders
. benefits provided to volunteer
.. double benefits denial .... 139B(b)
.. gross income, inclusion in .... 139B(a)
.. qualified payment defined .... 139B(c)(2)
.. qualified state and local tax benefit defined . 139B(c)(1)
.. qualified volunteer emergency response organization defined .... 139B(c)(3)
Emergency medical transportation
. excise tax exemption .... 4262(g)
Employee achievement awards 74
Employee annuities
. books and records, failure to keep 6704
. charitable organizations 415
. church plans 403
. computation of consideration paid by employees 72
. contracts 401
. contributions
.. corporate acquisitions 381
.. deductibility 404
.. employee 72
. Indian tribal government, treatment as state 7871
. limitations 415
. custodial accounts 403
. death benefits 101
. endowments 403
. excess contributions, exempt organizations 4973
. exempt organizations 403; 4973
. FICA 3121
. foreign affiliates 406
. FUTA 3306
. health insurance coverage 403
. home health service agency 415
. hospitals 415
. information returns 6652; 6704
. joint and survivor 417
. life insurance companies 817
. life insurance contracts 403
. limitations on benefit and contributions 415
. loans treated as distributions 72
. long-term care insurance 403

153

Employee

CODE SEC.

Employee annuities —Cont'd
. multiple distributions 402
. nonqualified, taxability of beneficiary 403
. nonresident aliens 871
. preretirement survivor annuities 417
. public schools 403
. purchased under salary reduction agreement 403
. regulated investment company custodial accounts ... 403
. rollovers 403
. self-employed individuals 403
. trustee-to-trustee transfers 403
. U.S. citizens or residents living abroad 911
. withholding tax 3401; 3405; 6652
.. foreign corporations 1441
.. information returns 6047
.. nonresident aliens 1441

Employee associations
. exemption 501; 505
.. unrelated business taxable income 512
. sales between employer and 1239
. vesting of rights, minimum standards 411

Employee benefit plans
. definitions and special rules 414

Employee discounts 132

Employee engaged in high-risk profession
. high-cost employer-sponsored health coverage .... 4980I(f)(3)

Employee retirement and benefit plans ..... 401 et seq. (See also Pension, profit-sharing, and stock bonus plans)
. accumulated funding deficiency 4971
. actuarial report requirements 6058; 6059
.. failure to file 6692
. American employer 1402
.. foreign affiliates, employees of 406
. annual information reports 6057; 6058
.. failure to file 6652; 6690
. annuities (See Employee annuities)
. beneficiaries 401; 402
. benefit limitations 415
. black lung benefit trusts (See Black lung benefit trusts)
. bond purchase plans 7207
. cafeteria plans 125
. cash or deferred compensation plans 402; 404
. change in plans 6057; 6652
. collectively bargained plans (See Collectively bargained retirement plans)
. computation of consideration paid by employees 72
. consolidation of plans 6058
. contributions
.. limitations 415
.. nondeductible, tax on 4972
. controlled group of corporations
.. minimum funding standards, failure to meet 4971
. cost-of-living adjustments, advance funding 404
. custodial accounts, excess contributions 4973
. death benefits 101
.. FUTA 3306
.. withholding tax on deferred income 3405
. deferred compensation plans 457
. deficiency assessment .... 6211 et seq.

Index to Code

CODE SEC.

Employee retirement and benefit plans—Cont'd
. defined contribution plans 404; 4975
. disabled individual defined 72
. disclosure of plans and reports 6103
. disqualified benefit defined 4976
. disqualified person 4975
. distributions 72
.. estate tax 691; 2039
.. exemption from levy 6334
.. FICA 3121
.. FUTA 3306
.. information returns 6047
.. Railroad Retirement Tax Act 3231
.. rollovers 402; 3405
.. voluntary employee contributions 3405; 6652
.. withholding tax 3401; 6047; 6652
.. written notice, rollover eligibility 402
... failure to provide 6652
. early retirement benefits 401
. employee annuities 72
. employee defined 7701
. employee funding 501
. employee stock ownership plans 4975
. enrolled actuary defined 7701
. excise and miscellaneous taxes .... 4971 et seq.
. exemption from tax 501; 6104
. false or fraudulent information returns 6690
. 5% owners, amounts received by 72
. foreign affiliates employees 406
. foreign plan, contributions to 404A
. fringe benefits, excess 4977
. funded solely by employees 501
. government plans, FICA 3121
. individual medical benefit accounts 4976
. individual retirement accounts 219
. information .... 6057 et seq.
. information returns 6047; 6050G; 6690; 7207
. investment in the contract, QDROs 72
. judicial remedies for qualification 7476
. key employees (See Key employees)
. life insurance 809; 817; 818
. life insurance contracts 72
. limitations on contributions and benefits 404; 415
. loans, excise tax on prohibited 4975
. lump-sum payments
.. estate tax 691
.. withholding tax on deferred income 3405
. medical benefits 401; 4976
. minimum funding standards .... 412; 4971 et seq.
. minimum participation requirements 410
. multiemployer plans (See Multiemployer plans)
. nonresident alien beneficiaries 871
. participant of plan
.. information to 6057; 6652; 6690; 6693
... distributions, rollover eligibility 402
.. standards 410
. penalties
.. excise taxes .... 4971 et seq.
.. failure to file registration or reports 6652

154

Index to Code

Employees

CODE SEC.

Employee retirement and benefit plans—Cont'd
. penalties —Cont'd
. . 5% owners, amounts received by 72
. prohibited transactions .... 4971 et seq.; 4975
. qualified domestic relations order, distributions or payments
.... 72
. qualified plans
. . defined 4974; 4980
. . employer reversion of assets 4980
. refunds and credit 6511; 7422
. registration of plan 6057; 6103; 6652
. returns .... 6057 et seq.
. rollovers
. . contributions
. . . failure to provide written notice of eligibility 6652
. . . written notice of eligibility 402
. . distributions
. . . eligible 3405
. . . failure to provide written notice of eligibility 6652
. rulings 7476
. Secretaries of Treasury and Labor, coordination between
.... 4975
. service requirements 401
. simple retirement accounts, reports and records 6693
. simplified pension plans 404
. subsidiaries doing business outside U.S. 407
. termination, insurance program 404
. top-heavy plans 416
. transfer of funds 6058
. UMWA benefit plans .... 9701 et seq.
. unfunded deferred benefit plans 404
. unrelated business income 511
. U.S. citizens or residents living abroad 407; 911
. voluntary employee contributions, distributions 6652
. welfare benefit plans 404; 419; 419A; 4976
. withholding tax 3405; 6652
. . information returns 6047
. . nonresident aliens and foreign corporations, withholding at
source 1441
. . wages, on 3401
. written notice, distribution rollover eligibility 402; 6652
. years of service factor 401
Employee stock options .... 421 et seq.
. definitions and special rules 424
. incentive stock options 422
. replacement property 1042
. stock purchase plans 423
. stock transfer reporting requirements 6039
Employee stock ownership plans (ESOPs) 401
. allocation of securities 4979A
. benefit limitations 415
. contributions
. . deductibility 404
. . limitations 415
. deferred compensation, gross income inclusion 409A
. defined 4975
. employer reversion of assets 4980
. employer securities
. . dispositions of 4978
. . estate tax 6018

CODE SEC.

Employee stock ownership plans (ESOPs)—Cont'd
. employer securities —Cont'd
. . holding period 1223
. . sales to plan 1042
. . nontaxable sales of stock to 1042
. . pension, profit-sharing, and stock bonus plans 410
. . prohibited allocation of securities 4979A
. . qualified plans 409
. . recapture of gain 1042
. . sales of stock to 1042
Employee stock purchase plans 423
Employee trusts (See Employee retirement and benefit plans)
Employees (See also Pension, profit-sharing and annuity plans and Trusts)
. accident and health benefits 104
. annuities (See Employee annuities)
. awards 74; 274
. backup withholding 3406
. benefit plans (See Pension, profit-sharing and annuity plans)
. conventions, expense of attending 274
. death benefits 101
. . employment taxes 3121
. . FUTA 3306
. defined 7701
. . FICA 3121
. . FUTA 3306
. . Railroad Retirement Tax Act 3231
. . self-employment tax 1402
. . withholding on wages 3401
. dependent care assistance programs 21; 219
. domestic subsidiaries engaged in business outside the U.S.
.... 407
. educational assistance programs (See Educational assistance programs)
. Federal (See Federal officers and employees)
. foreign affiliates, of 406
. fringe benefits
. . FICA 3121
. . FUTA 3306
. . qualified transportation fringe 132
. gifts to 102
. government (See Federal officers and employees)
. group legal service exclusion 120
. group-term life insurance 6052; 6652
. . definition of employee 7701
. . gross income, inclusion of costs in 79
. . withholding tax on wages 3401
. highly-compensated employees (See Highly compensated employees)
. insurance on lives of 264
. . definition of employee 7701
. . premiums 6052; 6652
. . . withholding tax on wages..................... 3401
. key employees (See Key employees)
. leased (See Leased employees)
. legal services plans (See Group legal services plans for employees)
. listed property deductions 280F
. meals and lodging 119; 274

155

Employees

Index to Code

	CODE SEC.
Employees (See also Pension, profit-sharing and annuity plans and Trusts) — Cont'd	
. moving expenses	217
. . FICA	3121
. newly hired, credit for	51; 52
. railroad retirement tax	3201 et seq.
. recreational activities, business expenses	274
. reimbursed expenses, deductions for	62
. relocation loans, imputed interest	7872
. Social Security taxes (See Employment taxes)	
. statement of wages paid	6051 et seq.
. . fraudulent statement or failure to make	6674; 7204
. . in form of group-term life insurance	6052
. stock options (See Employee stock options)	
. stock purchase plans	423
. tips	451; 6053
. tuition reductions	117
. withholding exemption certificates	3402; 7205
. withholding tax statements	6051; 6652; 6674; 7204
. work opportunity credit	51; 52
Employer identification number	6109
Employer liability trusts	
. contributions	194A
. exemption	501
Employer reversion, qualified plan assets	4980
Employer securities	
. dividends paid on, deduction	404
Employers	
. backup withholding	3406
. child care, credits for	38; 45F
. deduction for contributions to employees' trust	194A
. defined	
. . FUTA	3306
. . Railroad Retirement Tax Act	3231
. . withholding tax on wages	3401
. dependent care assistance programs	21; 219
. educational assistance programs (See Educational assistance programs)	
. employment tax liability, determination of	3509
. federal unemployment tax	3301 et seq.
. fringe benefits	3501
. . excess, penalties	4977
. . FICA	3121
. . FUTA	3306
. legal services plans (See Group legal services plans for employees)	
. railroad retirement tax	3221
. relocation loans to employees, imputed interest	7872
. reversion, qualified plan assets	4980
. sales between employees associations and	1239
. Social Security taxes	3111 et seq.
. tips, reporting of	6053
. unemployment taxes	3301 et seq.
. wage credit for active duty members of the uniformed services	45P
. withholding tax liability, determination of	3509
. work opportunity credit	51; 52
Employment	
. defined	

	CODE SEC.
Employment — Cont'd	
. defined — Cont'd	
. . FICA	3121
. . FUTA	3306
. expenses	
. . credit for	21
. . dependent care assistance programs	129
. . impairment-related work expenses	
. . . 2% floor on miscellaneous itemized deductions	67
. . incurred to enable employment	129
. . proceedings for determination of employment status	7436
Employment taxes	3101 et seq.; 3501 et seq. (See also Federal Unemployment Tax Act (FUTA))
. abatements	6413
. agents, acts to be performed by	3504
. agricultural labor defined	3121
. American employer	3121
. American vessel and aircraft defined	3121
. assessments	6205
. bankruptcy	1398; 3302; 6658
. carriers (See Railroad Retirement Tax Act)	
. collection and payment	3501 et seq.; 6302
. collection of income tax at source on wages	3401 et seq.
. concurrent employment by two or more employers	3121
. deductibility	275; 3502
. definitions	3121
. direct sellers	3508
. disaster relief payments, coordination with	139(d)
. disclosure of returns and return information	6103
. employer liability	3509
. employment defined	3121
. erroneous payments	3503
. FICA (See Federal Insurance Contributions Act (FICA))	
. fiduciaries, acts to be performed by	3504
. FUTA (See Federal Unemployment Tax Act (FUTA))	
. governmental employer, payment by	3126
. included and excluded services	3121
. insolvent bank exemption	7507
. levy of disqualified	6331(h)
. nondeductibility of taxes in computing taxable income	3502
. old-age benefit tax. (See Federal Insurance Contributions Act (FICA))	
. over and underpayments	3121
. overpayment	6413
. Peace Corps volunteer service	3121
. Railroad Retirement Tax Act (See Railroad Retirement Tax Act)	
. rate	3301
. real estate agents	3508
. refunds and credits	3503; 6413
. religious opposition to	3127
. religious order, services performed by members of	3121
. remuneration paid	3121
. retired judges, services performed by certain members of	3121
. salesmen	3508
. self-employment (See Self-employment income tax)	
. services performed	3121
. Social Security taxes	3101 et seq.
. transportation services	3121
. underpayments	6205

156

Index to Code — Endowment

CODE SEC.

Employment taxes—Cont'd
. uniformed services, service in the 3121
. wage withholding (See Withholding)
. wages defined 3121

Empowerment zones (See also Enterprise zones/communities)
. business in; partial exclusion for gain from small business stock .... 1202(a)(2)
. defined 1393
. definitions concerning 1397
. designation
.. criteria for eligibility 1392
.. procedure 1391
. employment credit 39; 1396
. offset of minimum tax 38
. qualified zone property defined 1397D
. recapture rules 1397A
. sale-leaseback rules 1397C
. special rules 1397

Endangered or critical status multiemployer plans .... 432(a)
. accumulated funding deficiency .... 432(i)(3)
. active participant defined .... 432(i)(4)
. actuarial method defined .... 432(i)(8)
. adoption period, rehabilitation
.. amendments to plan .... 432(d)(1)(B); 432(d)(2)(A); 432(f)(4)
.. benefit increases, special rules for .... 432(d)(2)(C)
.. collective bargaining agreement, acceptance of .... 432(d)(1)(A); 432(f)(4)
.. funding improvement plan, compliance with ...... 432(d)(2)
.. participation agreement, acceptance of ...... 432(d)(1)(A)
.. reduction in contributions .... 432(d)(2)(B)
.. seriously endangered status, rules for plans in .... 432(d)(1)(C)
. annual certification, actuary .... 432(b)(3)
. benefit commencement date .... 432(i)(10)
. collective bargaining agreements
.. adoption period, rehabilitation .... 432(d)(1)(A); 432(f)(4)
.. bargaining party .... 432(i)(1)
.. nonbargained employees .... 432(h)(2)
.. one or more agreements, employees covered ..... 432(h)(1)
. critical status, determination of .... 432(b)(2)
. endangered status, determination of .... 432(b)(1)
. expedited dispute resolution procedure .... 432(g)
. failure to meet minimum funding standards .... 4971(g)(1)
. failure to meet requirement for plans in endangered or critical status .... 4971(g)(3)
. funding improvement period defined .... 432(c)(4)
. funding improvement plan
.. adoption by plans in endangered status ..... 432(c)(1)
.. adoption period .... 432(c)(8)
.. default schedule, imposition of .... 432(c)(7)
.. defined .... 432(c)(3)
.. exception to adoption rule .... 432(c)(2)
.. failure to adopt, default schedule imposed .. 432(c)(7)
.. failure to comply with .... 4971(g)(2)
.. schedules, plan .... 432(c)(6)
.. seriously endangered plans more than 70% funded .... 432(c)(5)
.. updates to plan .... 432(c)(6)
. funding percentage defined .... 432(i)(2)

CODE SEC.

Endangered or critical status multiemployer plans—Cont'd
. inactive participant defined .... 432(i)(5)
. obligation to contribute .... 432(i)(7)
. operation of plan during adoption and rehabilitation period
.. amendments to plan after adoption of rehabilitation plan .... 432(f)(1)(A)
.. benefit increases after adoption of rehabilitation plan .... 432(f)(1)(B)
.. lump sums, restrictions on .... 432(f)(2)
.. plan adoption period, special rules during ..... 432(f)(4)
.. withdrawal liability determination, adjustments regarded in .... 432(f)(3)
. pay status defined .... 432(i)(6)
. plan sponsor defined .... 432(i)(9)
. rehabilitation plan
.. actions needed .... 432(e)(3)(A)(i)
.. amendments to plans after adoption of ..... 432(f)(1)(A)
.. annual standards provisions, requirement for .... 432(e)(3)(A)(i)
.. automatic employer surcharge .... 432(e)(7)
.. benefits
... adjustable benefits .... 432(e)(8)
... increases, special rules for .... 432(f)(1)(B)
... normal retirement benefits, protection of ..... 432(e)(8)(B)
... notice of reduction .... 432(e)(8)(C)
.. critical status .... 432(e)(1)
.. date of implementation .... 432(e)(3)(C)(ii)
.. default schedule, imposition of .... 432(e)(3)(C)(i)
.. defined .... 432(e)(3)
.. due date for adoption .... 432(e)(1)(A)
.. duration of schedule .... 432(e)(3)(B)(iii)
.. enforcement of automatic employer surcharge ... 432(e)(7)(B)
.. exceptions for years after process begins, adoption .... 432(e)(2)
.. failure to adopt .... 4971(g)(4)
.. failure to comply with .... 4971(g)(2)
.. future accruals, reduction limitations in rates of ..... 432(e)(6)
.. notice of automatic employer surcharge ... 432(e)(7)(D)
.. operation of plan during adoption and rehabilitation period .... 432(f)(1)
.. rehabilitation plan adoption period defined ..... 432(e)(5)
.. schedule requirements .... 432(e)(1)(B)
.. schedules .... 432(e)(3)(B)(ii)
.. ten year rehabilitation period .... 432(e)(4)
.. termination of automatic employer surcharge ... 432(e)(7)(C)
.. updates .... 432(e)(3)(B)(i)
.. withdrawal liability determinations .... 432(e)(9)

Endangered species recovery expenditures 175

Endowment contracts 72
. defined 1035; 7702
. employee annuities 403
. exchange of, gain or loss upon nontaxable 1035
. gross income 61
. individual retirement savings plans 219
. levy against 6332
. modified endowment contracts 7702A
. nontaxable exchange of 1035
. single premium payments, deductibility 264
. withholding tax 3405; 6652
.. information returns 6047

Energy

Index to Code

CODE SEC.

Energy bonds
. clean renewable energy bonds (See Clean renewable energy bonds (CREBs))
. new clean renewable energy bonds (See New clean renewable energy bonds)
. qualified energy conservation bonds (See Qualified energy conservation bonds)

Energy conservation
. public utilities subsidies provided by 136
. qualified energy conservation bonds (See Qualified energy conservation bonds)

Energy credit .... 48(a)(1)
. combined heat and power system property .... 48(c)(3)
. energy percentage .... 48(a)(2)
. energy property .... 48(a)(3)
. . qualified facility election to treat as .... 48(a)(5)
. . Sec. 45 credit 48
. fuel cell property .... 48(c)(1)
. investment credit 46; 49
. microturbine property .... 48(c)(2)
. nonconventional fuel source credit (See Nonconventional fuel source credit)
. progress expenditure rules .... 48(b)
. property financed by subsidized energy financing or industrial development bonds .... 48(a)(4)
. qualified fuel cell property defined .... 48(c)(1)
. qualified microturbine property .... 48(c)(2)
. qualified small wind energy property .... 48(c)(4)

Energy efficient appliance credit
. allowance .... 45M(a)
. applicable amount .... 45M(b)
. clothes washer defined .... 45M(f)(3)
. conservation standard, 2001 energy .... 45M(f)(7)
. controlled groups .... 45M(g)(2)
. dishwasher defined .... 45M(f)(2)
. EF defined .... 45M(f)(5)
. eligible production .... 45M(c)
. energy efficient appliance defined .... 45M(f)
. foreign corporations .... 45M(g)(2)(B)
. limitations .... 45M(e)
. produced defined .... 45M(f)(6)
. refrigerators .... 45M(c)(2); 45M(f)(4)
. 2001 energy conservation standard defined .... 45M(f)(7)
. verification .... 45M(g)(3)

Energy efficient commercial building deduction
. allowance .... 179D(a)
. basis reduction .... 179D(e)
. calculation .... 179D(d)(2)
. certification .... 179D(d)(6)
. energy efficient commercial building defined ..... 179D(c)(1)
. lighting system, interim rules for .... 179D(f)
. maximum amount of deduction .... 179D(b)
. notice to owner .... 179D(d)(5)
. partial allowances .... 179D(d)(1)
. public property, deduction allocation for .... 179D(d)(4)
. regulations, promulgation of .... 179D(g)
. standard 90.1-2001 defined .... 179D(c)(2)
. termination of .... 179D(h)

CODE SEC.

Energy efficient homes
. new energy efficient home credit (See New energy efficient home credit)

Energy grants and financing information returns 6050D

Energy property
. depreciation 168
. nonbusiness energy property credit (See Nonbusiness energy property credit)

Energy research consortium .... 41(f)(6)
Energy resources, disc exportation 993
Enhanced oil recovery credit 29; 38; 43
. carryback and carryforward 39
. phase out 29
. unused business credits 39; 196

Enrolled actuary defined 7701
Enterprise zone business
. defined 1397C
. expensing 1397A
. qualified zone property defined 1397D

Enterprise zone facility bonds, tax-exempt 1394
Enterprise zones/communities (See also Empowerment zones)
. carryover, corporate acquisition 381
. defined 1393
. definitions concerning 1397
. designation
. . criteria for eligibility 1392
. . procedure 1391
. District of Columbia
. . establishment 1400
. . first-time home buyers 1400; 1400C
. . renewal community business property 1400F
. . tax-exempt bonds 1400A; 1400B
. Indian reservation, within 1393
. qualified zone property defined 1397D
. regulations, prescription of 1397F
. sale-leaseback rules 1397C
. special rules 1397

Entertainment expenses 274
Entity defined 269B
Entry of premises
. examination of taxable objects 7342; 7606

Environment, conservation or preservation
. conservation (See Conservation)
. hazardous waste cleanup (See Hazardous waste cleanup)
. private activity bonds (See Private activity bonds)
. public utilities (See Public utilities, energy conservation subsidies provided by)
. qualified energy conservation bonds (See Qualified energy conservation bonds)
. taxes (See Environmental taxes)

Environmental Protection Agency
. sulfur regulations, capital costs deduction 179B

Environmental remediation costs, expensing of ...... 198(a)
. coordination with other provisions .... 198(f)
. December 31, 2009, expenditures paid or incurred after .... 198(h)
. depreciable property .... 198(b)(2)

Index to Code

Estate

CODE SEC.

Environmental remediation costs, expensing of—Cont'd
. hazardous substance defined .... 198(d)
. national priorities listed sites, exclusion of .... 198(c)(2)
. qualified contaminated site defined .... 198(c)
. qualified environmental remediation expenditure defined
.... 198(b)(1)
. recapture of deduction on sale .... 198(e)
Environmental taxes .... 59A (See also Hazardous waste cleanup, excise taxes)
. chemicals 4661
.. definitions and special rules 4662; 4682
.. ozone-depleting .... 4681 et seq.
. deductibility 164
. fuels 4662
. imported substances, certain 4672
. ozone-depleting chemicals 4681; 4682
. petroleum 4611; 4612
. termination 59A
Equipment leasing 465
Equity option defined 1256
Equity reduction
. corporate equity reduction interest loss (See Corporate equity reduction interest loss)
Equity structure shift 382
Erosion
. cropland 1257
. losses 1257
. prevention costs 175
Errors
. adjustments and corrections .... 1311 et seq.
. correction of errors .... 1311 et seq.
. de minimis error, waiver of 42
. employment taxes 3503
. income, reporting
.. mitigation rule .... 1311 et seq.
. mathematical or clerical errors
.. abatements 6213
.. returns 6201
. payment of tax, correction of errors .... 1311 et seq.
. refunds and credits
.. erroneous claim for
... civil penalties .... 6676(a)
... excessive amounts .... 6676(b)
... noneconomic substance transactions ..... 6676(c)
... other penalties, coordination with .... 6676(c)
.. interest, recoverable by suit 6602
.. mitigation of effect of limitations and other provisions ... 1311 et seq.
.. recovery 6514
.. suit to recover 6532; 7405
. returns, mathematical or clerical error on 6201
. Treasury settlement procedure correction 1311
. underpayments due to IRS error 6404
ESOPs (See Employee stock ownership plans)
Estate freezes
. family .... 2701 et seq.
.. member of family defined for purposes of 2701; 2704
. rights and restrictions
.. certain disregarded 2703

CODE SEC.

Estate freezes —Cont'd
. rights and restrictions —Cont'd
.. lapsing, treatment of 2704
.. trusts, transfers of certain interests in 2702
. valuation rules, special .... 2701 et seq.
Estate tax .... 641 et seq.; 2001 et seq. (See also Death taxes; Inheritance taxes)
. abatement claims 6404
. additions to tax 2032A
. administration expenses 2053; 2106
. administrators (See Executors and administrators)
. allocation among beneficiaries .... 2205 et seq.
. alternate valuation 2032
.. basis for gain or loss 1014
. amounts deemed distributed in preceding years 667
. annuities 2039; 2056
. armed forces, death in combat zone 2201
. art works 2055
. assessment, request for prompt 2204
. astronaut 2201
. authority to bring civil action for 7404
. bankruptcy and receiverships 6871
. basic estate tax defined 2011
. bond for payment of tax 2032A; 6863
. burdensome tax by foreign country 2108
. casualty gains and losses 165; 2054
. charitable bequests 2055; 2106
.. alternate valuation 2032
. charitable deductions 2055
. claims against estate 2053; 2106
. claims in bankruptcy and receivership 6871
. closely held business interest 1014; 1016; 1040; 2032A; 6601
.. extension of time to pay 6166
.. lien for taxes 6324A
. collection by suit 7404
. computation of tax
.. general rules 2001
.. gift tax and 2502
.. nonresident aliens 2101
. contribution to person paying .... 2205 et seq.
. credits against tax (See Credits against tax)
. curtesy interests 2034; 2043
. death of members of Armed Forces in or due to combat
.... 2201
. deductions .... 275; 642; 691; 2053 et seq.; 2106
. disallowance 2055
.. Indian tribal governments, treatment as State 7871
. deferred under Sec. 6166
.. lien for taxes 6324A
. deficiency .... 6211 et seq.
.. closely held business interest 6166
.. interest on 6601
.. lien for tax deferred under Sec. 6166 .... 6324A
.. payment, extension 6161
. definition 665
. disclaimed legacies passing to charities 2106
. disclaimers 2046; 2518
. dower interests 2034; 2043
. employee retirement or benefit plan distributions 2039

159

Estate | Index to Code

CODE SEC.

Estate tax—Cont'd
- employee stock options 421
- employee stock ownership plans 6018
- exchanges, special use valuation property 2032A
- executors (See Executors and administrators)
- exemption 2201
- expatriation to avoid 2107
- extensions 6161; 6163; 6503
- . closely held business interests 6166; 6324; 6324A; 6601
- . . future interests 6163
- . interest on underpayment 6601
- . partnerships, interest in 6166
- . . suspension of limitations on assessment and collection 6503
- . failure to file return or pay tax 6651
- farms 1014; 1016; 1040; 2032A; 6324B
- foreign country, burdensome tax by 2108
- foreign death taxes 2014; 2016
- generation-skipping transfers 691; 2013
- gift tax credit 2012
- gifts between husband and wife 2012
- gifts within three years of death 2035; 2104
- gross estate (See Gross estate)
- holding company stock 6166
- imposition of tax 641; 2101
- indebtedness in respect of property 2053
- installment payments 6161; 6166; 6601
- . . closely held business interest, lien for taxes 6324A
- . involuntary conversions 2032A
- . jeopardy assessment 6861; 6863
- . joint interests 2040
- . liability for payment .... 2002; 2205 et seq.
- . . discharge of executor or fiduciary 2204
- . . employee stock ownership plans 6018
- . . fiduciaries .... 2204; 6901 et seq.
- . . transferees .... 6324; 6901 et seq.
- . lien for 6324
- . . release or discharge 6325
- . . special valuation property 6324B
- . . tax deferred under Sec. 6166 .... 6324A
- . life estate
- . . dispositions 2519
- . . marital deductions 2523
- . life insurance
- . . beneficiaries, liability of 2206
- . . marital deduction 2056
- . . proceeds, valuation 2042
- . life interest retained by grantor 2036; 2207B
- . marital deduction
- . . alternate valuation 2032
- . . bequest to surviving spouse 2056
- . . gross estate, effect on 2044
- . . nonresident alien with citizen spouse 2106
- . . recovery 2207A
- . marital rights 2043
- . medical expenses 213
- . mortgages 2053
- . nonresidents .... 2101 et seq.
- . . bank deposits 2105

CODE SEC.

Estate tax—Cont'd
. *nonresidents—Cont'd*
- . . computation of tax 2101
- . . credits against tax 2102
- . . debt obligations 2103
- . . expatriation to avoid tax 2107
- . . gross estate defined 2103
- . . possessions of U.S., residents of 2209
- . . proceeds of life insurance 2105
- . . property within U.S. 2104
- . . property without U.S. 2105
- . . returns 6018
- . . revocable transfers 2104
- . . stock in corporations 2104
- . . tax imposed 2101
- . . taxable estate 2106
- . . transfers in contemplation of death 2104
- . . works of art on loan 2105
- . omission from gross income 6501
- . optional valuation, gain or loss basis 1014
- . overpayments .... 6511 et seq.
- . payment .... 2205 et seq.
- . . extension (See subhead extensions)
- . . interest on delinquency 6601
- . . liability for 2002
- . . receipts 6314
- . penalties
- . . failure to produce records 7269
- . . Tax Court added 6214
- . possessions of U.S., residents of 2208; 2209
- . powers of appointment 2037
- . . charitable bequests 2055; 2106
- . . gross estate inclusion 2037; 2041; 2207
- . . marital deduction 2056
- . . nonresidents 2106
- . . recipient of property over which decedent had power 2207
- . . valuation 2041
- . prior interests 2045
- . prior transfers, credit for 2013
- . proceeds of life insurance 2042
- . . nonresidents 2105
- . property previously taxed 2013; 2102
- . QTIP property 2056
- . qualified domestic trust 2056A
- . qualified domestic trust distributions 2210
- . rate 2001
- . . gift tax and 2502
- . . nonresident aliens 2101
- . real property 6324A; 6324B
- . recovery of taxes claimed as credit 2016
- . recovery rights 2207A; 2207B
- . redemption of stock to pay 303; 312
- . reimbursement for payment of 2205
- . remaindermen, claims against estate, deductibility 2053
- . remainders 2015
- . . payment 6163
- . request for prompt assessment 2204
- . residents of possession of U.S.
- . . considered citizens 2208

160

Index to Code

CODE SEC.

Estate tax—Cont'd
. *residents of possession of U.S. —Cont'd*
. . . not considered citizens 2209
. . returns 6018
. . . account numbers 6109
. . . false or fraudulent 6501
. . . fiduciaries and receivers, by 6012
. . . place to file 6091
. . . time to file 6075
. . reversionary interests
. . . credit for death taxes on 2015
. . . gross estate, effect on 2037
. . . payment 6163
. . revocable transfers
. . . gross estate, effect on 2038
. . . nonresidents 2104
. . sale of property for unpaid tax 7404
. . special use valuation property 1014; 1016; 2032A
. . state death taxes 2011; 2016
. . . valuation of estate 2058
. . statute of limitations
. . . additional tax qualified use real property 2032A
. . . assessment and collection .... 6501 et seq.
. . . claim for refund 6511
. . . death taxes on remainders, credit for 2015
. . . foreign death taxes, credit for 2014
. . . prior transfers, credit for tax on 2013
. . . refunds and credits .... 6511 et seq.
. . . state death taxes, credit for 2011
. . stock transfers, voting rights retained 2036
. . taxable estate (See Taxable estate)
. . tenancy by the entirety 2040
. . transferees and fiduciaries .... 6901 et seq.
. . . liability for tax 6324
. . . notice of fiduciary relationship 6903
. . . prohibition of injunctions 6904
. . . provisions of special application to transferees 6902
. . . transferred assets 6901
. . transfers
. . . death, effective at or after 2037
. . . gifts made within 3 years of death 2035
. . . insufficient consideration 2043
. . . life estates, dispositions 2519
. . . nonresidents 2104
. . . previously taxed 2013; 2102
. . . retained life estate 2036
. . . recovery, right of 2207B
. . . revocable 2038; 2104
. . . within three years of death 2035; 2104
. . unified computation with gift tax 2001
. . unified credit against 2010; 2102
. . valuation 2031
. . . alternate 2032
. . . farm or closely-held business real property 2032A
. . . furnishing statement on request 7517
. . . interest passing to surviving spouse 2056
. . . IRS statement to executor 7517
. . war postponements 7508

CODE SEC.

Estates and trusts ..... 641 et seq. (See also Bequests; Death taxes; Devises; Estate tax; Generation-skipping transfer (GST) tax; Generation-skipping transfers; Gift tax; Inheritances; Inheritance taxes)
. accumulating income or distributing corpus
. . deductions 661
. . exclusions 663
. . gross income of beneficiaries 662
. accumulation distributions .... 665 eq seq.
. adjusted gross income 67
. adjustments in barred years, mitigation rule ..... 1311 et seq.
. administration expenses 303; 2053; 2106
. administrative powers 675
. adverse party 672
. alimony or separate maintenance payments 215; 682
. alternative minimum tax 59
. amortization deductions 642
. . reforestation expenditures 194
. appreciated property, distribution of 311
. backup withholding 643
. bankrupt's estate 1398
. . gross income requirement for return 6012
. . separate taxable entities 1399
. . trustees, intervention on behalf of 7464
. basis 1016
. beneficial enjoyment, power to control 674; 676
. beneficiaries .... 641 et seq.
. . account numbers 6109
. . adjusted gross income 62
. . adjustments in barred years, mitigation rule .... 1311 et seq.
. . amortization deductions 642
. . basis 643
. . charitable remainder trusts 664
. . complex trusts 662
. . credits against tax 642; 901
. . defined 643
. . depletion 611
. . depreciation 167
. . estate tax allocation .... 2205 et seq.
. . estate tax returns 6018
. . estimated tax, payment of 643
. . foreign corporations 875
. . foreign tax credit 901
. . foreign taxes deemed paid by 667
. . gross income
. . . trusts accumulating income or distributing corpus 662
. . . trusts distributing current income only 652
. . holding period of property passing to 1223
. . individual retirement savings plans
. . . limitations and restrictions 219
. . information returns by fiduciary 6034A
. . lien for taxes 6324
. . . agreement, written by parties 6324A
. . life insurance proceeds, estate tax 2042; 2206
. . nonresident aliens 875
. . . accumulation distributions 667
. . real estate, reacquisition upon indebtedness for 1038
. . refunds of excess distributions 666
. . REITs 857

161

Estates

CODE SEC.

Estates and trusts—Cont'd
. *beneficiaries—Cont'd*
. . returns 6018; 6034A
. . reversionary interest taking effect at death of minor 673
. . simple trusts 652
. . tax year of estate or trust different 652; 662
. . transferee liability 6324
. . U.S. beneficiary of foreign trust 667; 679
. . wife 682
. borrowing from corpus or income 675
. business credit (See Business credit)
. capital gains and losses 643; 691
. . contributions out of 642
. casualty gains and losses 165; 2054
. charitable bequests 642; 663; 681
. charitable deduction claims 6034
. charitable remainder trusts 664
. charitable trusts 170
. . unrelated business income tax 511
. Clifford type trusts 674
. closely held business property transfers
. . gain or loss 1040; 1223
. common trust fund (See Common trust funds)
. complex .... 661 et seq.
. computation of income and tax 641
. constructive ownership of stock 318
. contributions by 642
. credits against tax 642; 667; 901
. . grantor, attributable to 671
. death benefits 101
. decedents 691
. deductions .... 642 (See also specific subhead)
. . accumulating income or distributing corpus 661; 663
. . charitable, limitations on 681
. . distributions 643
. . double deductions, disallowance 663
. . grantor, attributable to 671
. . income in respect of decedent 691
. . limitations 651; 681
. . personal exemptions 643
. . trusts distributing current income only 651
. definitions 643; 665; 672
. depletion 611; 642
. depreciation 642
. . expensing in lieu of 179
. . life tenants and beneficiaries 167
. discharge of indebtedness
. . Title 11 cases 108
. disclosure of returns and return information 6103
. distributable net income 643
. distributions
. . corpus, of .... 661 et seq.; 674
. . current income only
. . . deductions 651
. . . inclusion of amounts in gross income of beneficiaries .. 652
. . deductions 643; 661; 663
. . first 65 days of taxable year 663
. . dividends 643
. divorce, income in case of

CODE SEC.

Estates and trusts—Cont'd
. *divorce, income in case of —Cont'd*
. . former spouse 215
. . wife considered beneficiary 682
. double deductions 642; 663
. election to recognize gain on distributions 643
. electricity production credit 45
. employee retirement and benefit plans (See Employee retirement and benefit plans)
. employee stock options exercised after death 421
. employees 404
. . information returns 6047
. estimated taxes 643; 6654
. excess distributions by .... 665 eq seq.
. exchange fund, as 683
. exchanged property, basis for gain or loss 1040
. executors, notice of qualification 6036
. exemption from tax .... 501 et seq.
. farm property transfers, gain or loss 1040; 1223
. fiduciaries
. . definition 7701
. . returns of 6012
. . transferee liability .... 6901 et seq.
. foreign (See Foreign estates and trusts)
. foreign corporations
. . beneficiaries, as 875; 897
. . distributions to 667
. foreign grantor 671
. foreign personal holding company stock held by 551; 554
. foreign tax credit 642; 667; 901
. freezing of estates (See Estate freezes)
. funeral expenses 303
. general business credit 38
. generation-skipping transfers 667; 691
. grantors and others treated as substantial owners ..... 671 et seq.
. hazardous substance superfund 9507
. holders of life or terminable interest 273
. income
. . accumulation .... 661 et seq.
. . benefit of grantor 677
. . bequest or gift exclusion 663
. . currently distributable 651; 652
. . defined 643
. . distributable 643
. . foreign personal holding company receiving 553
. . grantor, attributable to 671
. . gross income 61
. . obligations of support, for 677; 678
. . personal holding company income 543
. . powers over 674
. . properly paid or credited .... 661 et seq.
. . spouse of grantor, benefit to 677
. . taxability 641
. information returns 6034A; 6047; 6048; 6677
. in-kind distributions 643
. inland waterways trust fund 9506
. installment payments under Sec. 6166 7479
. interest
. . distributable net income defined 643

Index to Code — Estimated

CODE SEC.

Estates and trusts—Cont'd
. *interest —Cont'd*
. . qualified residence interest 163
. leaking underground storage tank 9508
. life tenants
. . depreciation 167
. . reforestation expenditures 194
. low-income housing credit 42
. management of trust funds 9602
. medical expenses paid after death 213
. miscellaneous itemized deductions, 2% floor 67
. multiple 643; 667
. net operating losses 642
. nonadverse party defined 672
. nonresident (See Foreign estates and trusts)
. nonresident alien beneficiaries 667; 875; 897
. oil spill liability 4611; 9509
. passive activity losses and credits 469
. payment of tax 641
. pension trusts (See Employee retirement and benefit plans)
. permanently set aside amounts, charitable purposes 642; 663
. perpetual care fund distributions 642
. personal exemption 642; 643
. personal holding company stock owned by 544
. pooled income funds 642
. . transfers to 683
. property distributions 643
. publicity of information required from 6104
. qualified domestic trust, estate tax 2056; 2056A
. rates of tax 2502
. real estate, reacquisition upon indebtedness for 1038
. real estate investment trusts (See Real estate investment trusts)
. redemption of stock to pay death taxes 303
. reforestation expenditures 194
. refunds and credits of excess distributions 666
. related or subordinate party defined 672
. remainder interest to charity 642; 2522
. remainderman, reforestation expenditures 194
. rental activities 469
. returns 6012; 6034A
. . disclosure 6103
. reversionary interests 673
. revocable 676
. revocable trust treatment as part of estate 645
. S corporation shareholders 1361
. Sec. 1256 contracts 1212
. separate shares as separate trusts 663
. simple 651; 652
. small business stock losses 1244
. special use valuation property
. . farm real property 1040
. . transfers, gain or loss 1040; 1223
. spouse, for benefit of 677
. stock bonus trusts (See Employee retirement and benefit plans)
. stock ownership 318
. straddles, gain or loss 1092
. subordinate party 672
. substantial owners .... 671 et seq.

CODE SEC.

Estates and trusts—Cont'd
. *substantial owners—Cont'd*
. . person other than grantor treated as substantial owner .. 678
. . swap funds 683
. . tax rates 1
. . taxable year 644
. . . beneficiary having different year 652; 662
. . termination of, unused loss carryovers and excess deductions 642
. Title 11 cases
. . debt discharge amounts, reduction of tax attributes by ... 108
. transfers in trust, basis of property 1015
. 2% floor on miscellaneous itemized deductions 67
. undistributed net income 665
. unrelated trade or business 511; 513
. U.S. real property interest dispositions, withholding
. . disposition of interest in trusts, or estates, rules relating to .... 1445(e)(5)
. . taxable distributions by domestic or foreign trust or estate .... 1445(e)(4)
. vaccine injury compensation trust fund 9510
. work opportunity credit 51

Estimated income tax
. acceleration of 10% income tax rate for 2001 and 6428
. assessments 6201
. coordination of collection of income taxes with domestic service employment taxes 3510
. corporations
. . adjustments, overpayment 6425
. . assessment 6201
. . credits against 6402; 6513
. . defined 7701
. . excessive adjustment 6655
. . failure to pay 6601; 6651; 6655
. . installment payments 6315; 6655
. . overpayment of tax 6425
. . overstatement of amount paid 6201
. . payment 6315
. . underpayment of tax 6622; 6655; 6658
. credit against 6402; 6513
. estates and trusts 643; 6654
. exempt organizations 6655
. individuals
. . assessment 6201
. . bankruptcy proceedings 6658
. . credits against 6402; 6513
. . date of payment for refund limitation 6513
. . defined 7701
. . failure to pay 6601; 6651; 6654
. . no tax liability for preceding year 6654
. . overpayment of income tax credited to 6513
. . overstatement of amount paid as 6201
. . payment 6315
. . penalties 6654
. . short taxable years 6654
. . underpayments 6622; 6654
. insurance companies
. . discounted unpaid losses 847
. payment 6315
. . beneficiary, by 643

CODE SEC.

Estimated income tax —Cont'd
. return, willful failure to file 7203
. stock purchase as asset purchase 338
Estimated wages
. withholding tax on wages computation 3402
Ethanol
. blender credit 40
. cellulosic biomass ethanol plant property 168
. producer credit 40
. small producer credit, allocation of 40
. special fuels tax 4041
Ethylene hazardous waste clean up 4661; 4662
Evasion or avoidance of tax
. accumulating earnings 533
. acquisitions to effect 269; 357; 1551
. allowance of deductions 269
. assumption of liabilities 357
. burden of proof
. . expatriation 877
. . judicial proceedings 7454
. . reorganizations, assumption of liabilities 357
. conduit arrangements in multiple-party transactions 7701
. controlled group of corporations, acquisitions to avoid tax by 1551
. corporations used to avoid income tax on shareholders .... 531 et seq.
. expatriation for purpose of 877; 2107; 2501
. installment sales 453
. limitations on assessment and collection 6501
. limitations on prosecution for 6531
. liquidations after qualified stock purchases 269
. penalties 6672; 7201
. personal service corporations 269A
. possession with intent of 7268
. reinsurance contracts, related taxpayers 845
. rental agreements 467
. reorganization exchanges 357
. sales 7341
. stapled entities 269B
. stock, disposition of 306
. transfers to foreign entities
. . U.S. real property interests 897
Evergreen trees timber status 631
Evidence
. avoidance of income tax 533
. burden of proof (See Burden of proof)
. credible evidence and shift of burden of proof, introduction of 7491
. foreign expropriation losses
. . indebtedness, special rule for evidences of 1351
. Tax Court
. . disclosure 7461
. . fraud cases 7454
. . rules 7453
EWOCs (See Eligible worker-owned cooperatives)
Examination and inspection .... 7601 et seq. (See also Public inspection)
. authority, IRS officer 7608
. books and witnesses (See Books and records)

CODE SEC.

Examination and inspection—Cont'd
. canvass of districts for taxable persons and objects 7601
. churches, restrictions on examination of 7611
. entry of premises for purposes of 7606
. expenses of detection and punishment of frauds 7623
. foreign documentation, admissibility of 982
. Internal Revenue Districts 7621
. restrictions on examination 7605; 7611
. returns .... 6103 et seq.; 7431
. summons
. . enforcement 7604
. . service 7603
. . third-party summonses 7609
. time and place of 7605
. witnesses (See Witnesses subhead examination)
. written determinations 6110
Excess benefit transaction tax 4958
Excess contributions 4979
. Archer MSA 4973
. black lung benefit trusts 4953
. Coverdell education savings account 4973
. health savings accounts 4973
. individual retirement savings plans 219; 4973
. regulated investment company stock, custodial accounts 4973
. Roth IRA 4973
. Sec. 403(b) annuities 4973
Excess distributions by employee retirement or benefit plans (See specific plan)
Excess interest
. life insurance companies, defined for 809
. net operating losses deduction .... 172(b)(1)(E)
. REITs .... 857(b)(7)(A); 857(b)(7)(D)
Excess noncash income, REITs .... 857(e)(1) et seq.
Excess profits tax
. deductibility 164; 275
. foreign (See Foreign taxes)
Excessive employee remuneration
. business expenses 162
Exchange funds 683
Exchange programs, nonresident aliens 871
Exchange students and visitors (See Foreign students and exchange visitors)
Exchanged basis property defined 7701
Exchanges, health (See State health insurance exchanges)
Exchanges of property (See also Sales or exchanges)
. compensatory property 83
. conflict-of-interest requirements 1043
. gain or loss
. . productive use or investment, property held for 1031
. . stock for property, exchange of 1032
. . stock for stock exchange 1032
. held for productive use or investment 1031
. livestock, different sex 1031
. nontaxable .... 1031 et seq.
. . annuity contracts 1035
. . conflict-of-interest requirements, sales to comply with 1043
. . divorce, transfers incident to 1041

Index to Code — Executors

Exchanges of property (See also Sales or exchanges) — Cont'd
. *nontaxable — Cont'd*
. . endowment contracts 1035
. . ESOPs or cooperatives, stock sales to 1042
. . farm or business real property 1040
. . insurance policies 1035
. . involuntary conversions 1033
. . productive use or investment, property held for 1031
. . reacquisition of real property 1038
. . securities transferred under certain agreements 1058
. . spouses, transfers between 1041
. . stock for property, exchange of 1032
. . stock for stock of same corporation 1036
. . U.S. obligations 1037
. not solely in-kind 1031
. redemption of stock 302
. SEC orders, under .... 1081 et seq.
. stocks and securities
. . property, exchange of stock for 1032
. . SEC orders 1081
. . stock for stock of same corporation, exchange of ... 1032

Excise tax registration information
. disclosure of returns and return information 6103

Excise taxes .... 4041 et seq. (See also specific items)
. accounting for collected taxes 7215; 7512
. air transportation .... 4261 et seq.
. alcohol (See Alcohol taxes)
. assessment and collection, limitations on 6501
. bankruptcy and receiverships 6871
. Black lung benefits .... 4951 et seq.
. coal 4121
. continuation coverage 4980B
. definitions 4462
. distilled spirits, gallonage taxes on .... 5001 et seq.
. employee retirement and benefit plans .... 4971 et seq.
. employment taxes 3221; 3301
. environmental taxes .... 4611 et seq.
. excess fringe benefits 4977
. exemption
. . alcohol fuels credit, coordination with 40
. . demonstration automobiles 4002
. . exemption certificates 4253
. facilities and services (See Facilities and services excise tax)
. failure to pay 4103
. FICA taxes, status as 3111
. firearms 4181; 4182
. foreign insurance companies, policies issued by ...... 4371 et seq.
. FUTA 3301
. gallonage taxes on distilled spirits .... 5001 et seq.
. golden parachute payments, excess 4999
. harbor maintenance 4461; 4462
. hazardous waste cleanup, excise taxes for ...... 4611 et seq.
. health care continuation coverage requirements, failure to satisfy 4980B
. income tax credit
. . average cost of carrying excise tax 5011
. Indian tribal government, treatment as state 7871
. information reporting 4104

Excise taxes — Cont'd
. insurance companies, policies issued by foreign ...... 4371 et seq.
. jeopardy assessment 6862
. liability of person collecting 7501
. lobbying expenses of public charities
. . disqualified 4912
. . excessive 4911
. luxury automobiles 4001
. luxury excise taxes (See Luxury tax)
. manufacturers (See also Manufacturers excise taxes)
. miscellaneous rules
. . alcohol and tobacco tax, allowance conditions 6423
. . gasoline tax, excessive claims 6675
. . sales and services taxes 6416
. omission from gross income 6501
. overpayments 6416
. ozone-depleting chemicals 4681; 4682
. passenger vehicles 4001
. pension, profit sharing and annuity plans ..... 4971 et seq.
. political expenditures by charitable organizations ... 4955
. private foundations .... 4940 et seq.
. Railroad Retirement Act tax, status as 3221
. refunds and credits .... 6415 et seq.
. registered-required obligations, failure to register ... 4701
. regulated investment companies, undistributed income ... 4982
. REITs, undistributed income 4981
. retail excise taxes (See Retail excise taxes)
. returns, sufficiency for limitations statute 6501
. services and facilities .... 4251 et seq.
. ships, passengers on covered voyages 4471; 4472
. sporting equipment 4161
. taxable substance defined 4672
. tires (See Tires)
. tobacco (See Tobacco taxes)
. transportation by air .... 4261 et seq.
. two-party exchanges 4104
. unregistered obligations 4701
. wagering 6419

Exclusions
. gift tax purposes 2503; 2504
. gross income (See Gross income exclusions)
. income tax purposes (See Exempt income)
. self-employment tax purposes 1402
. small business stock, partial exclusion for gain from ... 1202

Executive branch officials
. trade or business expense deduction 162

Executive orders
. alternate depreciation system for imported property covered by .... 168(g)(1)(D)
. . discriminatory act, countries maintaining trade restrictions or engaging in .... 168(g)(6)(A)
. . imported property defined .... 168(g)(6)(B)

Executors and administrators (See also Estates and trusts; Fiduciaries; Trustees; Trusts)
. assessment, suspension of period 6872
. books and records, failure to produce 7269
. defined 2203; 7701
. discharge

165

CODE SEC.

Executors and administrators (See also Estates and trusts; Fiduciaries; Trustees; Trusts) —Cont'd
. discharge —Cont'd
. . notice 6903
. . personal liability, from 2204
. . . income and gift tax, decedents 6905
. estate tax
. . definition 2203
. . discharge from personal liability 2204
. . liability for payment of tax 2002
. . returns 6018
. fiduciary status 7701
. gift tax returns, good faith reliance on 2204
. liability .... 6901 et seq.
. . estate tax 2002
. . personal liability, discharge of 2204; 6905
. life insurance proceeds, estate tax 2042
. notice
. . qualifications, of 6036
. . . recovery of taxes claimed as credit 2016
. returns 6018
. termination notice 6903
. war postponements, estate tax 7508

Exempt bonds
. amortization of premiums 171
. bond premiums 1016
. D. C. Enterprise Zone 1400A; 1400B
. definition 150
. enterprise zone 1394
. facility bonds (See Exempt facility bonds)
. New York Liberty zone 1400L
. prior exemption 149
. registration 149
. requirements 149

Exempt entities and organizations ..... 501 et seq. (See also specific organizations)
. accumulated earnings tax 532
. acquisition indebtedness 514
. ACRS
. . alternate depreciation system for certain property
. . . foreign person, property subject to U.S. tax and used .... 168(h)(2)(B)
. . . foreign person or entity .... 168(h)(2)(C)
. . . tax exempt entity defined .... 168(h)(2)(A)
. . partnership, property owned by
. . . tax-exempt controlled entity defined ...... 168(h)(6)(F)(iii)
. . partnership, tax-exempt use of property leased to
. . . foreign entities, presumption with respect to .. 168(h)(5)(C)
. . . pass-thru entities rule, other .... 168(h)(5)(B)
. . . tiered entities rule, other .... 168(h)(5)(B)
. advertising 513
. alternate fuel vehicle refueling property credit ...... 30C(e)(2)
. annual returns 6033
. . public inspections 6104
. application for exemption, disclosure of 6014; 6104
. artwork lent to 2503
. assessment and collection 6501
. bingo 513
. business income .... 501; 511 et seq.
. community health needs assessments 501

CODE SEC.

Exempt entities and organizations—Cont'd
. consolidated returns 1504
. controlled group of corporations 1563
. controlled organizations, UBTI 512
. convention and trade show activities 513
. cooperative hospital service organizations 501; 513
. debt-financed income 514
. deferred compensation plans 457
. deficiency assessment .... 6211 et seq.; 7422
. denial of exemption 504
. depreciation deduction, used or leased property 168
. disclosure
. . application for exemption 6014; 6104
. . fundraising solicitations, nondeductibility ... 6113; 6710
. . information returns 6104
. . returns 6104
. dividends-received deduction 246
. employee annuities, nonqualified 403
. entertainment activities 513
. excess benefit transactions 4958
. exempt status, application for 6104
. fairs 513
. feeder organizations 502
. FICA 3121
. foreign (See Foreign exempt organizations)
. foreign countries and U.S. possessions, taxes of 515
. foreign personal holding company status 552
. foreign tax credit 515
. fundraising solicitations, disclosure of nondeductibility ... 6113; 6710
. FUTA 3303; 3306; 3309
. homeowners associations 528
. information or services, sale of
. . failure to disclose availability from Federal government 6711
. information returns
. . clubs 6033
. . contributed property, sale or exchange 6050L; 6652
. . cooperative banks 6033
. . disclosure 6104
. . dissolution 6043
. . foundations 6033
. . inspection of annual return 6104
. . liquidation, dissolution, termination or contraction .. 6043
. . political organizations 6033
. insolvent banks 7507
. inspection of annual return 6104
. investment credit property 50
. judicial remedies for qualification 7428
. leases
. . depreciation deduction 168
. . property used by, limitation on allowable deductions on 470
. legislative activities 501; 504
. . excess expenditures, excise tax 4911
. limitation on allowable deductions for property used by ... 470
. liquidations 6043
. list of 501
. loan of art to, nontaxable transfers 2503
. lobbying activities 501

Index to Code — Exempt

CODE SEC.

Exempt entities and organizations—Cont'd
. *lobbying activities—Cont'd*
.. disqualifying expenditures 4912
.. excess expenditures, excise tax 4911
.. loss of exemption 504
. loss of exemption 503
. basis of property 1016
. limitations on assessment and collection 6501
. lobbying activities 504
. notification of exempt status to IRS 508
. partners and partnerships, ACRS (See subhead ACRS)
. personal holding company status 542
. previously exempt organizations 168
. private foundations (See Private foundations)
. prohibited transactions 503
. property transfers to, unrelated business 1245; 1250
. public inspection
.. annual returns 6104
.. exempt status, application for 6104
.. penalties 6685
.. publicity of information required from 6104
. publishing business of 513
. related taxpayers, transactions between 267
. requirements for exemption 503; 505
. returns 6033
.. disclosure 6104
.. inspection of annual information returns 6104
.. liquidation, dissolution, termination or contraction, on .. 6043
.. taxable corporations, limitations on assessment and collection purposes 6501
.. time to file 6072
. sales or exchanges with related taxpayers 267
. shipowners' protection and indemnity associations ... 526
. special rule for loans 503
. tax shelters, entering into prohibited 4965
. terrorist organization, suspension of exempt status to ... 501
. trade show activities 513
. trusts benefiting certain owner-employees 503
. unrelated business income (See Unrelated business taxable income; Unrelated trade or business)
. unrelated debt-financed income 514
. veterans associations 501
. work opportunity credit 51

Exempt exchanges (See Exchanges, nontaxable)

Exempt facility bonds 142; 146
. defined .... 142(a)
. electric energy or gas, local furnishing of
.. outside local area, electric energy transmitted .... 142(f)(2)
.. environmental enhancements of hydroelectric generating facilities
... defined .... 142(j)(1)
... proceeds, use of .... 142(j)(2)
.. governmentally owned .... 142(b)(1)
. high-speed intercity rail facilities
.. defined .... 142(i)(1)
.. nongovernmental owners, election by .... 142(i)(2)
.. proceeds, use of .... 142(i)(3)
. local district heating or cooling system ...... 142(g)
. office space limitations .... 142(b)(2)
. private facility exception .... 142(c)(2)

CODE SEC.

Exempt facility bonds—Cont'd
. qualified green building and sustainable design projects
.. aggregate face amount of tax-exempt financing .... 142(l)(7)
.. Brownfield redevelopment .... 142(l)(4)(A)(ii)
.. current refunding bonds .... 142(l)(9)
.. defined .... 142(l)(1)
.. limited designation of .... 142(l)(3)
.. local government defined .... 142(l)(6)(B)
.. minimum conservation and technology innovations .... 142(l)(2)(B)
.. more than one project in a state .... 142(l)(2)(B)
.. net benefit of tax-exempt financing .... 142(l)(6)(C)
.. prohibited facilities .... 142(l)(4)(A)(vi)
.. rural state .... 142(l)(6)(A)
.. Sept. 30, 2009, bond issued after .... 142(l)(8)
.. size .... 142(l)(4)(A)(iv)
.. state and local support .... 142(l)(4)(A)(iii)
.. tax benefit, use of .... 142(l)(4)(A)(v)
... certification of .... 142(l)(5)
.. U.S. Green Building Council's LEED certification, determination of .... 142(l)(4)(A)(i)
. qualified hazardous waste facilities .... 142(h)
. qualified public educational facilities
.. allocation of annual aggregate face amount of tax-exempt financing .... 142(k)(5)(B)
.. annual aggregate face amount of tax-exempt financing, determination of .... 142(k)(5)
.. carryforward of unused limitation .... 142(k)(5)(B)(ii)
.. defined .... 142(k)(1)
.. elementary school .... 142(k)(4)
.. public schools .... 142(k)(4)
.. public-private partnership agreements .... 142(k)(2)
.. school facility defined for .... 142(k)(3)
.. secondary school .... 142(k)(4)
. qualified residential project .... 142(d)(1)
.. applicable income limit .... 142(d)(5)
.. area median gross income .... 142(d)(2)(B)
.. certification to Secretary .... 142(d)(7)
.. current income determinations .... 142(d)(3)
.. deep rent skewing .... 142(d)(4)
.. defined .... 142(d)(2)
.. high cost housing area .... 142(d)(6)
.. HUD hold harmless policy .... 142(d)(2)(E)
.. qualified building .... 142(d)(2)(B)(iii)
.. qualified military instillation .... 142(d)(2)(B)(iv)
.. single-room occupancy units .... 142(d)(2)(D)
.. special rules .... 142(d)(2)
.. students .... 142(d)(2)(C)
. special rules .... 142(b)
. storage and training facility, treatment of ... 142(c)(1)
. termination of future financing .... 142(f)(3)
. termination of tax-exempt financing, election for ... 142(f)(4)
. water, facilities for the furnishing of
.. defined .... 142(e)

Exempt income .... 101 et seq.
. accident and health benefits 105; 106
. adjustments of prior errors, mitigation rule .. 1311 et seq.
. armed forces 112; 265
. cafeteria plans 125
. clergyman's dwelling 107; 265

Exempt

Code Sec.

Exempt income—Cont'd
- combat pay ... 112
- conservation cost-sharing payments ... 126
- contributions to capital ... 118
- cost-of-living allowances ... 6011
- death benefits ... 101
- dependent care assistance program benefits ... 129
- discharge of indebtedness ... 108; 1017
- distributions by corporations ... 312
- dividends ... 1016
- education expenses, redeemed U.S. savings bond ... 135
- expenses ... 265
- fellowships
  - . FICA ... 3121
  - . FUTA ... 3306
- FICA
  - . fringe benefits ... 3121
  - . instrumentalities of the U.S. ... 3112
  - . scholarships and fellowships ... 3121
  - . tuition reduction ... 3121
- financial institution interest ... 265
- foreign service employees ... 6011
- foreign students and exchange visitors ... 1441; 3121
- foster care payments ... 131
- fringe benefits ... 132
  - . excess, penalties ... 4977
  - . FICA ... 3121
  - . FUTA ... 3306
- FUTA
  - . fellowships ... 3306
  - . fringe benefits ... 3306
  - . tuition reduction ... 3306
- gifts ... 102
- income earned abroad by U.S. citizens or residents ... 6012
- inheritances ... 102
- injuries and sickness, compensation for ... 104 et seq.
- interest ... 265
  - . basis adjusted for ... 1016
  - . government obligations ... 103
  - . Indian tribal government, treatment as state ... 7871
  - . original issue discount ... 1288
  - . stripped bonds or coupons ... 1286
  - . tax preference items ... 57
- legal services plans, contributions and value of ... 120
- lessee, improvements by ... 109
- life insurance proceeds ... 101
- meals and lodging ... 119
- military benefits ... 134
- military housing ... 265
- municipalities ... 115
- obligations ... 265
- parsonage, expenses and interest ... 265
- passive foreign investment company qualifying electing fund ... 1283
- Peace Corps, filing of return ... 6011
- political committees ... 6012
- possessions of U.S. ... 115
- post allowances ... 6011
- principal residence sale, gain from ... 121

Code Sec.

Exempt income—Cont'd
- recovery of tax benefit items ... 111; 1398
- redeemed savings bonds for education expenses ... 135
- regulated investment companies ... 265
- scholarships ... 117
  - . FICA ... 3121
  - . FUTA ... 3306
- shipowners' associations ... 526
- small issue bonds ... 265
- state ... 115
- tuition
  - . educational organization employee reduction
    - . FICA ... 3121
    - . FUTA ... 3306
  - . qualified state program ... 529
- uniformed services ... 122
- U.S. savings bond redemption for education expenses ... 135
- withholding tax on wages ... 3401
- workmen's compensation ... 3306

Exempt securities (See also Exempt income)
- basis ... 1016
- bonds (See Exempt bonds)
- dealers, bond premiums ... 75; 1016
- facility bond (See Exempt facility bonds)
- registration-required ... 149
- stripped bonds or coupons ... 1286

Exempt use property (See Tax-exempt use property)

Exemption certificates, withholding (See Withholding exemption certificates)

Exemptions (See also Exempt income)
- charitable remainder trusts ... 664
- common trust funds ... 584
- communications taxes ... 4253
- dividends
  - . regulated investment company shareholders ... 852
- domestic goods purchased for U.S. ... 7510
- education individual retirement accounts ... 530
- entities (See Exempt entities and organizations)
- estate tax purposes ... 2201
- farmers' cooperatives ... 521
- federal officers and employees stationed abroad ... 912
- firearm taxes ... 5851 et seq.
- foreign central banks of issue ... 895
- foreign corporations ... 883
- foreign government employees ... 893
- foreign states consular officers and employees ... 7511
- generation-skipping transfer tax ... 2631; 2632
- highway motor vehicle use taxes ... 4483
- insolvent banks ... 7507
- interest
  - . estates and trusts, distributable net income computation ... 643
  - . insurance companies other than life ... 834
  - . life insurance companies ... 805; 812
  - . international organizations ... 892; 893
  - . levy, from ... 6334
- manufacturers excise taxes ... 4221 et seq.
- nonresident aliens ... 872
- organizations (See Exempt entities and organizations)

168

Index to Code — Facility

CODE SEC.

Exemptions (See also Exempt income) —Cont'd
. Peace Corps 912
. personal income tax .... 151 et seq.
.. nonresident aliens 873
.. trusts and estates 642
. Puerto Rican source income 933
. qualified state tuition programs 529
. regulated investment company shareholder dividends 852
. REITs 857
. shipments to U.S. possessions 7653
. state tuition programs 529
. treaty obligations 894
. U.S. citizens or residents living abroad .... 911 et seq.
. wages, FUTA 3306
. withholding tax on wages 3401; 3402
.. failure to supply information 7205
Ex-felon, work opportunity credit 51
Expatriated corporations and entities
. domestic corporation, inverted corporation treatment as 7874
. inversion gains 7874
. stock compensation to insider 4985
Expatriation to avoid tax 2501
. alternative tax 877
. gross estate, determination of 2107
. rate of tax 2107
. special rules of source 877
Expenditure report
. defined for presidential election campaign fund 9002
Expenses (See also specific items)
. business expenses (See Business expenses)
. capitalization 263A
. family 262
. inventory costs, inclusion in 263A
. living (See Living expenses)
. nondeductible .... 261 et seq.
. personal 262
. related taxpayers, transactions between 267
. taxable estate 2053
. tax-exempt income 265
Expensing depreciable business assets 179
. capital expenditures 263
. elections, irrevocable 179
. in lieu of depreciation 263
. limitation reductions 179
. Sec. 179 property, election to expense (See Section 179 property)
. sports utility vehicles 179
Experimental expenditures
. alternative minimum tax 56
. basis adjustments 1016
. credit 41; 6411; 6511; 6611
Exploration expenditures
. at risk limitations 465
. deduction for 617
. oil and gas wells 465
. partners and partnerships 703
. research and experiments 174

CODE SEC.

Exports
. assets defined 993
. liquors to U.S. possessions 5002
. promotion expenses defined 971; 994
. receipts 993; 995
. refund to exporter or shipper 6416
. trade corporations 970; 971
. transportation taxes 4272
Expropriation losses (See Foreign expropriation losses)
Extensions 6161
. air transportation of persons .... 4261(j)
. air transportation of property .... 4271(d)
. Airport and Airway Trust Fund, limitations on transfers to
.. prior obligations exception .... 9502(e)
. amount determined as deficiency 6161
. assessments 6901
. aviation fuel, tax rates .... 4081(d)
. bonds 1294; 6165
.. payment of extended deficiency with 6165
. corporations expecting carrybacks 6164; 6864
. estate taxes (See Estate tax)
. federal unemployment tax 6601
. filing returns 6081
. gift tax
.. interest 6601
.. pay deficiency 6161
.. returns 6075
. interest 6601
.. estate tax, closely held business interests 6166
.. foreign expropriation loss recoveries 6167
. payment of tax .... 6161 et seq.
. recovery of foreign expropriation losses 6167
. undistributed earnings 1294
Extortion by federal employee 7214
Extraordinary dividends 1059
Extraterritorial income 114

F

Face-amount certificates 401
Facilities
. business expenses 274
. entertainment 274
. exempt securities, financed with 142
. private activity bonds, financed with
.. change in use of facility 150
. small issue bonds 144
Facilities and services excise taxes ... 4251 et seq. (See also specific tax)
. collection 6302
. communications (See Communications taxes)
. exemptions for U.S. and possessions 4293
. special provisions 4293
. transportation by air (See Transportation by air)
Facility bonds
. exempt facility bonds (See Exempt facility bonds)
. recovery zone facility bonds (See Recovery zone facility bonds)

169

CODE SEC.

Factoring trade receivables
. related taxpayers 864
Failure to file or pay tax (See Returns subhead failure to file)
Fair market value
. employer reversion 4980
. extraordinary dividends 1059
. foreign expropriation losses recoveries, basis 1351
False or fraudulent returns 7207
. assistance in preparation 7206
. information returns 7434
. joint returns 6013
. limitations on assessment and collection 6501
. limitations on prosecution 6531
. Secretary making return where 6020
Family (See also Children; Dependents; Estates and trusts; Generation-skipping transfers; Parents; Related taxpayers)
. compensation to members
. . excess benefit transaction tax of exempt organizations 4958
. . FUTA 3306
. constructive ownership of stock 318
. economically disadvantaged, work opportunity credit 51
. estate freezes (See Estate freezes)
. exclusion for family owned business 2057
. expenses 262
. farming operations accounting methods 447
. foreign personal holding company stock held by 554
. medical savings accounts coverage, Archer 220
. oil and gas depletion allowance 613A
. partnerships 704
. personal holding company stock owned by 544
. premium assistance credit, health plan coverage
. . terms relating to 36B
. S corporations 1366
. sales and exchanges 267
. stock ownership 318
. transactions between 267
Fannie Mae (See Federal National Mortgage Association)
Farmers and farming
. accounting methods, corporate 447; 448
. acquisition financed with private activity bonds 147
. agricultural labor (See Agricultural labor)
. agricultural structures, depreciation recapture 1245
. alternative minimum tax
. . income averaging, coordination with .... 55(c)(2)
. . losses denied 58
. at risk amounts 465
. averaging farm income 1301
. basis of property, adjustments 1016
. capital expenditures .... 263 et seq.
. conservation expenditures 175
. cooperatives (See Agricultural cooperatives; Farmers cooperatives)
. corporation accounting methods 447; 448
. crop damage (See Crop damage)
. crops (See Crops)
. definitions
. . farm 2032A; 6420
. . farm land 1252

CODE SEC.

Farmers and farming — Cont'd
. definitions — Cont'd
. . farming 464
. . FICA 3121
. . FUTA 3306
. depreciation 144; 263A
. development expense deductions, recapture 1252
. diesel fuel or kerosene sold to 6427
. discharge of indebtedness 108; 1017
. dispositions, recapture on expensed amount 263A
. elected farm income 1301
. equipment, retail excise taxes 4053
. erosion
. . loss from 1257
. . prevention costs 175
. estate and trust farm property transfers 1040; 1223
. estate tax 1014; 1016; 1040; 2032A; 6324B
. estimated tax 6654
. expenses 180; 268
. farm land defined 1252
. fertilizers (See Fertilizers)
. gasoline used for farming purposes 34; 4041; 6206; 6416; 6421; 6427
. . refunds and credits 6420; 6675
. highway use tax, exemption 4483
. installment sales 453A
. inventory costs .... 263A et seq.
. land acquisition financed with private activity bonds 147
. land disposition 1252; 1257
. livestock (See Livestock)
. losses
. . alternative minimum tax 58
. . net operating losses deduction
. . . coordination with 172(b)(2) .... 172(i)(2)
. . . election .... 172(i)(3)
. . . farming loss defined .... 172(i)(1)
. material participation in farming activity 469
. new employees, credit for hiring 51
. ordinary income, capital gains treated as 1252
. personal service corporations
. . alternative minimum tax on losses 58
. preproductive period 263A
. private activity bonds
. . first-time farmer land acquisitions 147
. recapture
. . conservation expenses 1252
. . dispositions 263A
. remainder interest, charitable contribution 170
. sales of farm land, gain from
. . converted wetlands 1257
. . general rules 1252
. . highly erodible croplands 1257
. . unharvested crop, with 268
. self-employment tax 1402
. small issue bond depreciation 144
. soil and water conservation 175; 1252
. special use valuation 1040
. syndicates 461; 464
. tax shelter farm activity 58

Index to Code — Federal

CODE SEC.

Farmers and farming — Cont'd
- transfers of property 1040; 1223
- valuation
  - property 2032A
  - special use, real property 1040
- work opportunity credit 51

Farmers cooperatives .... 1381 et seq.
- crop financing 501; 521
- dividends-received deduction 246
- exemption from tax 521
- FICA 3121
- FUTA 3306
- patronage dividends (See Patronage dividends)
- per-unit retain allocations 1382; 1388
- tax subjectivity to .... 1381 et seq.

FASIT (See Financial asset securitization investment trust)

FCC (See Federal Communications Commission)

FDIC (See Federal Deposit Insurance Corporation (FDIC))

FEC (See Federal Election Commission)

Federal agencies
- debts owed to, offset of tax overpayments 6402

Federal bonds (See United States obligations; United States Savings bonds)

Federal Communications Commission (FCC)
- sales or exchanges to effectuate policies of
  - depreciation recapture 1245; 1250

Federal credit unions
- central liquidity facility, exemption 501

Federal Deposit Insurance Corporation (FDIC)
- federal financial assistance 597
- overpayment of tax 6413

Federal Election Commission
- audits of expenses 9007
- certification of payments to candidates 9005; 9036
- defined for presidential election campaign fund 9002
- false or fraudulent statements to 9012; 9042
- judicial proceedings of 9010; 9011; 9040; 9041
- kickbacks and illegal payments for campaign expenses 9042
- reports to Congress 9009; 9039

Federal employees (See Federal officers and employees)

Federal financial assistance defined 597

Federal government appointees
- disclosure of returns and return information 6103

Federal guarantees
- generally (See Guarantees)
- mortgage bonds (See Mortgage bonds)
- state bonds (See State and local bonds)

Federal Home Loan Mortgage Corporation
- bonds; guarantee 149
- dividends received deduction 246

Federal Housing Administration
- bonds; guarantee 149
- loans; private activity bonds 147

Federal income tax (See Income tax)

Federal instrumentalities (See Instrumentalities of U.S.)

Federal Insurance Contributions Act (FICA) .... 3101 et seq.; 3121 (See also Withholding)

CODE SEC.

Federal Insurance Contributions Act (FICA) — Cont'd
- additional tax 3102
- adjustments 6413
- agents 3504
- American Samoa 3121; 3125; 6205; 6413
- applicable dollar threshold defined for 3121
- assessment and collection of tax .... 6205; 6501 et seq.
- church exemption 3127
- collection and payment 3501; 6302
- companion sitting placement services 3506
- constructive receipt, deductions as remuneration paid 3123
- credits against tax 31
- deductibility 3502
- deduction from wages 3102
- deductions as constructive payments 3123
- deferred compensation 3127
- District of Columbia 3125; 6205; 6413
- earned income credit, advance payments 3507
- employee tax paid by employer, FUTA 3306
- erroneous payments 3503
- estimate of revenue reduction 3124
- excise tax on employer 3111
- exemption for 2010 hires .... 3111(d)(1)
- foreign wages 3101; 3111
- government employees
  - federal employees 3122
  - Guam and American Samoa 3125
  - refunds 6413
- Guam 3125; 6205; 6413
- hospital insurance tax 3111; 3122; 6051
- identification of taxpayers subject to 6011
- indemnification of employer 3102
- information returns 6652
- insolvent banks 7507
- instrumentalities of U.S. 3112; 3122
- liability for tax 3102; 3504; 3505; 3509
- Medicare qualified government employment 3127
- mitigation of statute of limitation effect 6521
- overpayments 6413
- Peace Corps 3122
- rate of tax, employers 3111
- receipts for employees 6051; 6652; 6674; 7204
- refunds and credits .... 3503; 6413; 6511 et seq.
- religious organizations 3127
- revenue reduction, estimate 3124
- state and local government employees refunds 6413
- tax on employees
  - deductions of tax from wages 3102
  - rate of tax 3101
- tax on employers
  - instrumentalities of U.S. 3112
  - rate of tax 3111
- third-party liability 3505
- tips 45B; 3102
- underpayments 6205
- U.S. postal service 7509
- withholding tax on wages 3102

Federal irrigation subsidies
- gross income inclusion 90

Federal

	CODE SEC.
Federal loans	
. tax delinquency of applicants, disclosure of	6103
Federal National Mortgage Association	
. basis of stock	1054
. capital contributions	162
Federal officers and employees	
. bribes	162
. business expenses	162
. compensation, information returns	6041
. disability pay	104
. disclosure of returns and return information	7213
. employment taxes	6413
. exemption for certain allowances	912
. Foreign Service (See Foreign Service officers and employees)	
. hospital insurance, FICA	3121
. illegal payments	162
. kickbacks	162
. military actions in noncombat zones, abatement of tax	692
. nonresident alien employee benefit plan distributions	402
. offenses by	7213; 7214; 7344
. possessions of U.S., income from	931
. repayments to	7423
. suit for damages	7402
. terrorist actions, victims of	
.. abatement of tax	692
.. compensation for	104
. third-party action against	7426
. unauthorized inspection of returns by	7213A
Federal Pell Grants	
. disclosure of returns and return information	6103
Federal procurement	
. imposition of tax on	5000C
Federal programs and federally assisted programs	
. refunds disregarded in administration of	6409
Federal Savings and Loan Insurance Company	
. federal financial assistance	597
Federal subsidies	
. irrigation projects, illegal	90
. prescription drug plans	139A
Federal thrift savings fund	
. nondiscrimination requirements, employee retirement and savings plans	7701
. tax court judge election to contribute to	7447(j)
Federal Trade Commission	
. disclosure of returns and return information	6103
Federal Unemployment Tax Act (FUTA)	3301 et seq.
. additional credits allowance, conditions of	3303
. adjustments	6205
. applicability of State law	3305
. approval of state laws	3304; 3305
.. judicial review	3310
. assessment	6201
. bankruptcy	3302
. banks	3305
. certification of state laws	3304
.. judicial review	3310
. collection and payment	3501

	CODE SEC.
Federal Unemployment Tax Act (FUTA)—Cont'd	
. companion sitting placement services	3506
. constructive receipt, deductions as remuneration paid	3307
. credits against tax	3302; 3303
.. judicial review	3310
. deductions as constructive payments	3307
. excise tax status	3301
. exempt organizations	3303; 3306; 3309
. extension of time for payment	6601
. failure to pay, interest	6601
. guaranteed employment account	3303
. Indian tribes	3309
. insolvent banks	7507
. instrumentalities of U.S.	3305; 3308
. interstate commerce	3305
. judicial review	3310
. levy against benefits, exemption	6334
. nonprofit organizations or governmental entities, state coverage	3309
. overpayments	6413
. payment of	6157; 6317; 6513; 6601
. pooled account	3303
. rate of tax	3301
. refunds and credits	3302; 6413
. religious organizations	3309
. reserve account defined	3303
. ships officers and crews	3305
. state and local government employees	3309
. state laws and	3304 et seq.
. state unemployment contributions	3302 et seq.; 3309
. successor employer	3302
. time for payment	6157
. timely payment	6513
. voluntary contributions	3303
Federally assisted buildings	
. low income housing credit (See Low-income housing credit)	
Federally declared disasters (See Disaster losses and relief; Presidentially declared disasters)	
Federally guaranteed bonds	
. state and local (See State and local bonds)	
Federally subsidized debt	
. recapture from mortgage bond activity (See Mortgage bonds)	
Feed equipment retail excise tax	4053
Feeder organizations	502
Fees	
. backup withholding	3406
. copies of returns	6103
. gross income	61
. recovery of legal and accounting fees, tax cases	7430
Feldspar, percentage depletion	613
Fellowships (See Scholarships and fellowships)	
Fertilizers	
. chemicals used in production of	4662
. equipment, retail excise taxes	4053
. expenditures for	180; 263
. fuel used in application, taxes on	6416

Index to Code — Firearms

CODE SEC.

FHA (See Federal Housing Administration)
FICA (See Federal Insurance Contributions Act (FICA))
Fiduciaries .... 6901 et seq. (See also Estates and trusts; Executors and administrators; Trustees; Trusts)
. breach of duty, damages for 186
. defined 4975; 7701
. discharge, notice of 6903
. employment taxes 3504
. information returns 6034A
. lien for taxes 6324
. pension, profit sharing and annuity plans 4975
. personal liability............................. 2204; 6324
. qualification, notice of 6036
. refunds and credit 6402
. related taxpayers transactions 267
. relationship, notice of 6903
. request for prompt assessment 6501
. returns 6012; 6034A
. rights and obligations 6903
. termination notice 6903
. withholding tax on wages 3402
Field service personnel
. D.C., orders for duty in 7804
. post of duty, designation of 7803
50% or greater interest
. defined for corporate distributions and adjustments 355
52-53-week year
. election for computation of taxable income 441
Filing of tax return, failure (See Returns subhead failure to file or pay tax)
Film, motion picture (See Motion picture film)
Finance companies (See Banks and trust companies)
Financed property depreciation 168
Financial asset defined for constructive ownership 1260
Financial asset securitization investment trusts
. definitions 860L
. gain recognition on contribution to 860I
. high-yield interest transfers to disqualified holders 860K
. offset of non-FASIT losses 860J
. prohibited transactions tax 860L
. regular interest treatment 860H
. securities dealers 860K
. special rules 860L
. taxation of 860H
Financial institutions .... 581 et seq.
. bad debt reserves computation methods 593
. banks (See Bank and trust companies)
. bond, guarantees 149
. business credit (See Business credit)
. cancellation of indebtedness, return relating to 6050P
. definition .... 265; 1471(d)(5)
. deposits or accounts
.. dividends or interest paid 461
.. federally insured 149
. exempt interest, pro rata allocation of interest expense to
.... 265(b)(1)
.. aggregation of issuers .... 265(b)(3)(E)
.. allocation, determination of .... 265(b)(2)

CODE SEC.

Financial institutions—Cont'd
. exempt interest, pro rata allocation of interest expense to—Cont'd
.. composite issue treatment .... 265(b)(3)(F)
.. deduction allowance .... 265(b)(1)
.. financial institution define .... 265(b)(5)
.. limitation on amount of obligations which may be designated
.... 265(b)(3)(D)
.. qualified small users defined .... 265(b)(3)(C)
.. qualified tax-exempt obligation defined ..... 265(b)(3)(B)
.. special rules
... coordination with Sec. 263A and indebted disallowances
.... 265(b)(6)
... 2009 or 2010, obligations issued during .... 265(b)(3)(G)
.. tax-exempt obligation exception .... 265(b)(3)
. 2009 or 2010, obligations issued during
.. de minimis exception .... 265(b)(7)
.. special rules .... 265(b)(3)(G)
. federally guaranteed bonds 149
. foreign (See Foreign financial institutions)
. foreign banks (See Foreign banks)
. foreign transfers, returns with withholdings on .... 6011(e)(4)
. frozen deposits 451
. insolvent 165
. interest expense allocation to exempt interest 265
. loans, federally guaranteed 149
. market discount bonds, interest paid to purchase or carry
.... 1277
. mutual savings banks (See Mutual savings banks)
. preference items
.. bad debt reserves 57
.. reductions 291
. real estate mortgage investment conduits 860E
. REITs 856
. savings and loan associations, building and loan association status 7701
. trust companies (See Banks and trust companies)
. withdrawal accounts, dividends or interest paid 461
Financial transactions
. recharacterization of gain 1258
Financing agreements
. lien for taxes 6323
Fines (See Penalties)
Fire departments
. employee benefit plans 401
. volunteer (See Volunteer fire departments)
Fire losses 165
. deduction from gross estate 2054; 2106
Firearms .... 5801 et seq.; 5841 et seq.
. antique firearm 5845
. application, use of information on 5847
. authority of IRS enforcement officers to carry 7608
. definitions 5845
. disposal of 7326
. excise taxes
.. exemptions 4182
.. imposition of 4181
.. rate of tax 4181
.. registration, exempt sales 4222
. exemptions from tax .... 4182; 5851 et seq.

173

Firearms Index to Code

CODE SEC.

Firearms—Cont'd
. failure to file return or pay tax 6651
. forfeitures 5872
. identification, manufacturer 5842
. importation 5844
. liquor violations 5685
. make defined 5845
. manufacturing tax 5821; 5822
. National Firearms Act, citing 5849
. occupational taxes .... 5801 et seq.
. other laws, applicability of 5846
. penalties and forfeitures .... 5871 et seq.
. pistols and revolvers 4181; 4182; 4222
. prohibited acts 5861
. records concerning manufacture 5843
. registration of 5802; 5841
. returns 6091
. tax on making .... 5821 et seq.
. transfer tax .... 5811 et seq.
. . exemption .... 5851 et seq.
. unserviceable firearm 5845

Firefighters
. volunteer (See Volunteer firefighters)

First responders
. emergency medical responders (See Emergency medical responders)
. mine rescue team training credit (See Mine rescue team training credit)
. volunteer emergency response organizations (See Volunteer emergency response organizations)
. volunteer firefighters (See Volunteer firefighters)

First-time homebuyers
. binding contract exception, application of sec. 36 ..... 36(h)(2)
. defined .... 36(c)(1)
. District of Columbia 1400C
. . allocation of dollar limitations .... 1400C(e)(1)
. . carryforward on unused credit
. . . years in which all personal credits allowed against regular and alternate minimum tax .... 1400C(d)(1)
. . . years other than in which all personal credits allowed against regular and alternate minimum tax ... 1400C(d)(2)
. . enterprise zones/communities 1400; 1400C
. . national first-time homebuyers credit, coordination with .... 1400C(e)(4)
. . purchase defined .... 1400C(e)(2)
. . purchase price defined .... 1400C(e)(3)
. election to treat purchase in prior year .... 36(f)
. principle residence
. . binding contract exception, application of sec. 36 ... 36(h)(2)
. . defined .... 36(c)(2)
. . prior year, election to treat purchase in ..... 36(g)
. . purchase defined .... 36(c)(3)
. . purchase price defined .... 36(c)(4)
. refundable credit for 10% of purchase price
. . dollar limitations .... 36(b)(1)
. . information reporting .... 36(e)(1)
. . modified adjusted gross income, limitations based on .... 36(b)(2)
. . . recapture .... 36(f)(1)
. . related person defined .... 36(c)(5)

CODE SEC.

Fiscal year .... 441 (See also Calendar year; Taxable year)
. change to or from 442; 443
. defined 441; 7701
. election not to have, required payments 7519
. employee retirement and benefit plan
. . minimum funding standards 412
. partnerships, other than required 7519
. returns, time to file 6072
. S corporations, other than required 7519
. taxable income computation 441

Fish, reporting purchases of 6050R

Fishermen
. alternate minimum tax coordination with income averaging .... 55(c)(2)
. backup withholding 3406
. boat operators 3406; 6050A
. estimated tax 6654
. FICA 3121
. FUTA 3306
. information returns 6050A
. self-employed retirement plans 401
. withholding tax on wages 3401

Fishing equipment, sport
. Aquatic Resources Trust Fund 9504
. defined 4162
. excise taxes
. . definitions 4162
. . imposition of 4161
. . parts or accessories sold with 4161
. . sonar device 4162
. Sport Fish Restoration Account .... 9504(b)(1)

Fishing-rights-related income of Indians (See Native Americans)

Flake graphite depletion 613

Flavor content
. alcohol used in preparation, drawback of 5111
. distilled spirits tax, credits against 5010

Flexible premium life insurance contracts 101

Flexible spending arrangements
. cafeteria plans, qualified benefit limitations ..... 125(i)
. information returns 6041
. termination to fund HSA 106

Flood, livestock sale after
. nontaxable exchanges 1033
. proceeds from 451

Floor specialists 1236

Floor stock taxes 6412

Fluorspar depletion 613

FNLMC (See Federal Home Loan Mortgage Corporation)

FNMA (See Federal National Mortgage Association)

Food and beverage facilities
. exempt facility bonds 142

Food products
. alcohol used in, drawback of 5111
. U.S. possessions, shipments from 7652

Index to Code — Foreign

	Code Sec.
Football league exemption, professional	501
Foreclosures	
. definition of foreclosure property	856
. depreciation recapture	1250
. disposition of foreclosure property	1250
. property as loan security, information returns	6050J; 6652
. reacquisition by mortgagee	1038
. real estate mortgage investment conduits	860G
. recovery zone bonds (See Recovery zone bonds)	
. recovery zone facility bonds (See Recovery zone facility bonds)	
. REITs	856(e); 857
. returns on foreclosure property	6050J
Foreign adoptions, credit	36C(e)
Foreign affiliates	
. earnings and profits	312
. employee benefit plans	406
. employee retirement and benefit plans	406
. FICA	3121
. information returns	6038
. sale of stock	865
Foreign banks	
. foreign personal holding company status	552
. income on U.S. obligations or deposits	861; 882; 895
Foreign base company income	954
. export trade corporation income	970
Foreign central banks of issue	
. income from bankers acceptances	861
. income from U.S. obligations	895
Foreign conventions, expense of attending	274
Foreign corporations	881 et seq.
. acquisition of	279
. affiliated groups	864
. aircraft, income from	883
. allocation of interest on worldwide basis	864
. American Samoa	881
. beneficiaries of estates or trusts	875
. books and records, Tax Court examination	7456
. branch profits tax	884
. branch transactions, taxable income computation of	987
. capital contributions	367
. . U.S. real property interests	897
. charitable contributions	882
. collapsible corporations	
. . consenting corporation, sale of stock of	341
. communications satellite system	883
. consent dividends	565
. consolidated returns	1504
. controlled (See Controlled foreign corporations)	
. . credits	882; 902; 906; 6401
. deductions	882
. deferred payments	864
. defined	7701
. distributions	667
. . assessment and collection, limitation period	6501
. . U.S. real property interests	897
. dividend equivalent amount for purposes of branch profits tax	884
. dividends paid	

	Code Sec.
Foreign corporations—Cont'd	
. *dividends paid*—Cont'd	
. . accumulated earnings tax	535
. . deduction	565
. . information returns	6041; 6652
. . source of income	535; 861
. . withholding tax at source on nonresident aliens	1441
. dividends received	
. . deduction	243; 245
. . gross income of domestic corporation, inclusion in	78
. . source of income	906
. domestic corporation	
. . dividends paid to	78
. . treatment as	897; 906
. . U.S. real property investments	897
. doubling of rates	891
. earnings and profits	312; 986; 1248
. effectively connected income	
. . defined	864
. . foreign tax credit	906
. . gross transportation income	887
. . real property income	882; 897
. elections	
. . domestic corporation treatment	897
. . real property income treated as effectively connected	882
. financial institutions	864
. foreign business requirement	861
. foreign personal holding (See Foreign personal holding companies)	
. foreign tax credit (See Foreign tax credit)	
. gains or loss, reorganization exchange	367
. gross income	882
. . exclusions	883
. . transportation income, taxation	887
. Guam corporation	881; 1442
. income not connected with U.S. business	864; 881
. income taxes translated into U.S. dollars	986
. information returns	
. . acquisition of stock	6046
. . control by U.S. person	6038
. . distributions	6038B
. . dividends	6041; 6652
. . failure to file	6679
. . foreign-owned U.S. corporation, failure to file	6038A
. . organization or reorganization	6046
. . transfers by U.S. persons	6038B
. . . assessment and collection, limitation period	6501
. . U.S. real property investments	6039C; 6652
. . U.S. trade or business, engaged in	6038C
. insurance business within U.S.	842
. insurance companies (See Foreign insurance companies)	
. intangible property transfers	367
. interest	
. . allocable to effectively connected income	884
. . bonds, information returns	6041; 6652
. . U.S. obligations	882
. interest expense	864
. less developed country corporations	955
. loss carryovers, change of ownership	382

175

Foreign Index to Code

CODE SEC.

Foreign corporations—Cont'd
. noncontrolled Sec. 902 corporations 904
. nonrecognition provisions for exchanges of real property interests 897
. Northern Mariana Islands 881
. organization or reorganization, failure to file returns 6679
. original issue discount 881
. ownership 897
. partnerships
.. reorganization exchanges 367
.. U.S., members of 875
. passive foreign investment companies (PFICs) .. 1291 et seq.
. patents transferred to, gain on sales or exchanges 1249
. personal holding companies (See Foreign personal holding companies)
. portfolio debt investments 881
. possession tax credit 882
. qualified resident of foreign country status 884
. railroad rolling stock, income from lease of 883
. rate of tax 896
. real estate mortgage investment conduit interests 860G
. real property income 882
.. U.S. property investments (See subhead U.S. real property investments)
. reciprocal discriminatory taxes 891
. REIT interests 897
. reorganization exchanges 367
. reorganization involving 6046
. repeal of tax on portfolio debt investments 881
. research and experimental expenditures 864
. returns 882
.. failure to report personal holding company tax 6683
.. filing, time for 6072
.. formation or reorganizations 6046
.. information returns (See subhead information returns)
.. personal holding company, failure to file 6683
. securities, reorganization exchange 367
. shareholders 897
. ships, earnings from 883
. stapled to U.S. corporation 269B
. stock, gain on sale or exchange 367; 751; 1248
. tax credit 6038
. tax year 898
. taxation of 881; 882
. trade or business, U.S. 864
. transfers to 367
.. assessment and collection, limitation period 6501
.. information returns 6038B
.. recognition of gain on U.S. real property interest 897
. treaty provisions, effect of 894
. U.S. net equity defined 884
. U.S. owners
.. accumulated earnings tax 535
.. foreign tax credit 904
. U.S. real property interests
.. dispositions, withholding
... affidavit that interests in corporation not U.S. real property, nonpublicly traded domestic corporation ...... 1445(b)(3)
... exemptions .... 1445(b)(1)

CODE SEC.

Foreign corporations—Cont'd
. U.S. real property interests —Cont'd
.. dispositions, withholding —Cont'd
... foreign person defined .... 1445(f)(3)
... general rule .... 1445(a)
... qualified substitute defined .... 1445(f)(6)
... qualifying statement, transferee receives .... 1445(b)(4)
... residence where amount realized does not exceed $300,000 .... 1445(b)(5)
... stock regularly traded on established securities market .... 1445(b)(6)
... transferee defined .... 1445(f)(2)
... transferor defined .... 1445(f)(1)
... transferor's maximum tax liability defined ...... 1445(f)(4)
... transferor's unsatisfied withholding liability defined .... 1445(f)(5)
. U.S. real property investments
.. disposition of 861; 862; 897; 1445
.. information returns 6039C; 6652
.. wash sale transactions .... 1445(b)(8)
. U.S. trade or business, information returns 6038C
. Virgin Islands 881; 934
. withholding of tax
.. general rule 1442
.. withholding at source credit 33; 6401
Foreign Corrupt Practices Act
. illegal payments to foreign governments 162
Foreign countries
. contiguous country subsidiaries, consolidated returns ... 1504
. discriminatory taxes by 2108
. expropriations (See Foreign expropriation losses)
. moving expenses 217
. reciprocal credits or exemptions 4221
. self-employment tax, exemption 1401
. taxes of (See Foreign taxes)
Foreign currency
. appropriate exchange rate defined 989
. blocked
.. controlled foreign corporations 964
.. contracts 1256
.. income taxes translated into U.S. dollars 986
.. payment in 6316
.. information returns 6050I; 6652
.. straddles 1092
.. transactions .... 985 et seq.
.. branch transactions 987
.. definitions 988; 989
.. earnings and profits of foreign corporation, determination 986
.. functional currency 985
.. gain or loss 988
.. partners and partnerships 988
.. regulations 989
.. REITs .... 856(n)
.. Sec. 988 988
Foreign death taxes
. credit 2014; 2016
. deduction 2053
. taxable estate, effect on 2053

Index to Code   Foreign

CODE SEC.

Foreign deferred compensation plans 404A
Foreign documents, admissibility of 982
Foreign earned income (See Income earned abroad)
Foreign employers
. defined 872
. personal services performed for 864
Foreign entities
. defined for withholding .... 1473(5)
. investment credit property 50
. nonfinancial, withholdable payments to
. . beneficial owner of payment, institution is ...... 1474(b)(2)
. . confidentiality of information .... 1474(c)
. . credits and refunds .... 1474(b)
. . exceptions .... 1472(c)
. . generally .... 1472(a)
. . liability for withheld tax .... 1474(a)
. . nonfinancial foreign entity defined .... 1472(d)
. . substantial United States owners identification requirement
     .... 1474(b)(3)
. . waiver of withholding .... 1472(b)
. specified United States person .... 1473(3)
. substantial United States owner .... 1473(2)
. United States foreign entity defined .... 1471(d)(3)
. withholdable payments to defined .... 1473(1)
. withholding agent defined .... 1473(4)
Foreign estates and trusts
. accumulation distribution 667
. . foreign tax credit 904
. . interest charge on 668
. beneficiaries
. . taxability, employee retirement and benefit plans ... 402
. . taxes deemed paid by beneficiary 667
. . U.S. beneficiaries 667; 679
. books and records, Tax Court examination 7456
. defined 7701
. distributions 665
. employee retirement and benefit plans
. . beneficiaries, taxability of 402
. . contributions to, deductibility 404; 404A
. foreign personal holding company stock held by 551
. foreign tax credit 667
. income 643
. information returns 6039C; 6048; 6677
. preceding taxable year defined 665
. private foundations 1443; 4948
. recognition of gain on transfers to 684
. taxes deemed paid by beneficiary 667
. taxes imposed on trust defined 665
. transfer to, tax on 679
. U.S. beneficiaries 667; 679
. U.S. real property holding organizations 897
Foreign exempt organizations 878
. unrelated business taxable income 512; 1443
Foreign expropriation losses 1212
. defined 1351
. indebtedness, special rule for evidences of 1351
. recoveries 1351
. . extension of time to pay tax 6167; 6503

CODE SEC.

Foreign expropriation losses—Cont'd
. recoveries—Cont'd
. . gross income 80
. . suspension of limitation period 6503
Foreign financial assets
. information in respect to
. . applicable entities .... 6038D(f)
. . continued failure to disclose, penalties for ... 6038D(d)(2)
. . exceeds dollar threshold, presumption asset ... 6038D(e)
. . failure to disclose, penalties for .... 6038D(d)(1)
. . generally .... 6038D(a)
. . reasonable cause exception .... 6038D(g)
. . regulations, prescribed .... 6038D(h)
. . required information .... 6038D(c)
. . specified foreign assets defined .... 6038D(b)
Foreign financial institutions
. affiliated groups .... 1471(e)(1); 1471(e)(2)
. defined .... 1471(d)(4)
. expanded affiliated groups .... 1471(e)(2)
. financial account defined .... 1471(d)(2)
. financial institution defined .... 1471(d)(5)
. foreign entity defined .... 1473(5)
. pass-thru payments defined .... 1471(d)(7)
. recalcitrant account holders
. . defined .... 1471(d)(6)
. . elections by .... 1471(b)(3)
. specified United States person .... 1473(3)
. substantial United States owner .... 1473(2)
. United States foreign entity defined .... 1471(d)(3)
. withholdable payments to
. . defined .... 1473(1)
. . exceptions .... 1471(f)
. . generally .... 1471(a)
. . nonparticipating institutions, elections by ... 1471(b)(3)
. . recalcitrant account holders, elections by ... 1471(b)(3)
. . reporting requirements .... 1471(b)(1)
. . requirement, institutions deemed meeting .... 1471(b)(2)
. . 30% deduction and withholding requirement ...... 1471(a)
. United States accounts
. . defined .... 1471(d)(1)
. . election to be subject to same reporting and U.S. financial
     institution .... 1471(c)(2)
. . information required to be reported .... 1471(c)(1)
. . qualified intermediary reporting requirements ... 1471(c)(3)
. withholding agent defined .... 1473(4)
Foreign governments
. communications satellite system 883
. compensation of employees 893
. credits against tax 901
. depreciation deduction, used or leased property 168
. disclosure of returns and return information 6103
. discriminatory reciprocal tax 891; 896
. distilled spirits for government or family use 5066
. employees of
. . compensation 893
. . FICA 3121
. . FUTA 3306
. . withholding tax on wages 3401
. exempt organizations 515

177

Foreign   **Index to Code**

CODE SEC.

Foreign governments —Cont'd
- income 892
- obligation interest, information returns 6041; 6652
- tax discrimination by 891; 896; 901; 2108
- taxes of (See Foreign taxes)
- wines for government or family use 5362

Foreign insurance companies 842
- controlled foreign corporations 953; 957; 964
- defined for excise tax purposes 4372
- election for treatment as domestic corporation 953
- excise taxes on policies issued by .... 4270; 4371 et seq.
- . . definitions 4372
- . . exemptions 4373
- . . liability for tax 4374
- foreign tax credit 841
- income 953
- U.S. risks insured, source of income 861; 862

Foreign investment companies
- capital gains and losses
- . . carrybacks 1212
- . . current distributions 1247
- defined 1246
- distribute income currently, election to 1247
- distributions 1247
- earnings and profits 312
- foreign tax credit 1247
- information with respect to 1246
- passive .... 551; 1291 et seq.
- stock
- . . capital gains and losses .... 1246 et seq.
- . . gain or loss 1246; 1247; 1293
- . . holding period 1223
- . U.S. shareholders 951

Foreign items, collection of
- failure to obtain license 7231
- information returns 6041
- license 7001

Foreign moving expenses 217

Foreign mutual insurance companies (See Foreign insurance companies)

Foreign partnerships
- defined 7701
- foreign personal holding company stock held by 551
- information returns 6039C; 6046A
- . . failure to file 6679
- U.S. real property holding organizations 897
- withholding tax
- . . distributions from U.S. partners 1446
- . . foreign partners 1446

Foreign personal holding companies .... 545; 551 et seq.
- accumulated earnings tax 532
- bond premiums, election to amortize 171
- decedent, basis of stock acquired from 1014
- defined 552
- dividends paid deduction 562; 563
- exceptions 552
- foreign corporations, stock held by 551
- gross income 555

CODE SEC.

Foreign personal holding companies—Cont'd
- income
- . . banking or financing income 954
- . . factoring trade receivables 864
- . . foreign base company income 954
- . . not placed on annual basis 557
- . . related persons 954
- . . rents and royalties 553
- . . taxed to U.S. shareholders 551
- . . undistributed 556
- information returns 6035; 6046
- limitations on gross income 553
- personal holding company tax 542
- returns
- . . formation of company 6046
- . . officers, directors and shareholders 558; 6035
- stock ownership 554
- tax subjectivity to 542; 545
- taxable year 898
- undistributed income 556
- U.S. shareholders 551; 951
- . . information returns 6035

Foreign persons
- defined 881
- depreciation deduction, used or leased property 168
- gift received from, notice of large 6039F
- holding U.S. real property investments, returns 6039C
- investment credit property 50
- related taxpayers, transactions between 267
- transfers by U.S. persons to 6038B

Foreign sale and leasing income
- defined 941

Foreign sales corporations (FSCS)
- accounting period 441
- books and records 6011
- controlled foreign corporations 951
- dividends received deduction 245
- foreign tax credit 901; 904; 906
- information to shareholders 6011
- possession tax credit 936
- preference items, reduction 291
- returns 6011
- . . failure to file 6686
- . . time to file 6072
- taxable year 441

Foreign service officers and employees
- disability annuities 104
- returns, allowances 6011
- sale of principal residence, exclusion of gain from 121

Foreign students and exchange visitors
- compensation 872; 1441
- FICA 3121
- FUTA 3306
- nonresident alien individual treatment 871
- withholding tax at source on nonresident aliens corporations 1441

Foreign subsidiaries
- contiguous country corporations, consolidated returns 1504

Index to Code — **Foreign**

CODE SEC.

Foreign subsidiaries — Cont'd
. credit for taxes 960
. dividends received deduction 245
. exclusions from gross income 959
. foreign tax credit 902
. information returns 6038
. payments to U.S. citizen employees
. . domestic corporation deductions 176
Foreign tax credit .... 27; 901 et seq.; 960
. adjustments on payment of accrued taxes 905
. affiliated corporations 902; 904
. alternative minimum tax 59
. boycotts, participation in 908
. capital gains 904
. carrybacks and carryovers 904
. . debt discharge amounts, reductions by 108
. . deficiency assessment 6501
. . foreign oil or gas income 907
. . interest on refund caused by 6611
. . limitation 383
. . oil and gas income 907
. citizens of U.S. 901
. controlled foreign corporations 904; 960
. corporate minimum tax 901
. corporate stockholder in foreign corporations ... 902
. corporations 901; 902
. covered asset acquisitions
. . foreign income not subject to U.S. taxation by reason of
. . . denial of credit 901
. decedent's estate 691
. denial with respect to certain foreign countries 901
. determination, foreign currency transactions 986
. DISC dividends 901; 904
. discriminatory policies of foreign governments 901
. dividends 904
. . income to domestic corporation 78
. . received from foreign corporations 245
. . domestic corporations 901
. employee retirement or benefit plan distributions 901
. estate tax purposes 2014; 2016
. estates and trusts 642; 667; 901
. . foreign accumulation distributions 904
. exempt organizations having business income 515
. failure to file notice of redetermination 6689
. financial services income 904
. foreign corporations 882; 901; 904; 906
. foreign expropriation loss recoveries 901; 1351
. foreign insurance companies 841
. foreign investment companies 1247
. foreign sales corporations 901; 904; 906
. gross-up of deemed foreign paid taxes 78
. in lieu taxes 903
. individual retirement savings plans 901
. information returns, failure to file
. . foreign subsidiaries 6038
. insurance companies 841
. interest income 904
. life insurance companies, U.S. 841
. . contiguous country branches 814

CODE SEC.

Foreign tax credit — Cont'd
. limitations 383; 904
. losses 904
. lump-sum distributions 402
. mineral income 901
. nonresident aliens 874; 901; 906
. oil and gas companies 901; 907
. overall foreign losses 904
. ownership change 383
. partnerships 702; 901
. passive foreign investment company distributions 1291
. passive income 904
. personal exemptions 904
. proof of 905
. Puerto Rico residents 901
. railroad rolling stock leased for foreign use 861
. recovery exclusion 111
. refunds resulting from 6511
. regulated investment companies 853; 855
. related income taken into account
. . suspension of taxes and credits until 909
. resident aliens 901
. section 956 inclusions, limitation with respect to 960
. shipping income 904
. South Africa 901
. stock purchase as asset purchase 338
. taxable income for purposes of 904
. taxes in lieu of income taxes 903
. taxes of foreign countries and possessions of U.S. 901
. time to take 905
. unrelated business taxable income 515
. U.S. owned foreign corporations 904
. U.S. shareholders in controlled foreign corporation 960
. war profits 903
. year in which taken 905
Foreign taxes
. accrual 905
. burdensome 896
. carrybacks
. . limitation period for assessments 6501
. . refund of income tax caused by 6611
. contested taxable year of deduction 461
. credit (See Foreign tax credit)
. deductibility 164; 275; 905; 960
. . estate tax 2053
. deficiency due to redetermination 6689
. definitions 902
. discriminatory 891; 896; 2108
. estate tax deductibility 2053
. estates and trusts, accumulation distributions 667
. interest on 905
. life insurance companies, U.S.
. . contiguous country branches 814
. partnerships 702; 703
. redetermination of 6689
. refunds 905; 2016
. U.S. dollars, translated into 986
Foreign trade income
. applicable foreign corporation 943

179

Foreign

CODE SEC.

Foreign trade income —Cont'd
. defined 941
. domestic corporation, election to be treated as 943
. extraterritorial income, gross income 114
. foreign sales corporations
. . controlled foreign corporations 951
. . exemptions 951
. . foreign tax credit 901; 904; 906
. gross receipts, foreign trading 942
. property in short supply 943
. qualifying foreign trade income 941
. qualifying foreign trade property 942; 943
. shared partnership, allocation of qualifying foreign trade income
    from 943
. source rule 943
. withholding taxes 943
Foreign travel expenses 274
Foreign trusts (See Foreign estates and trusts)
Foreign-based documentation defined 982
Forests
. reforestation expenditures (See Reforestation expenditures)
Forfeiture of property ...... 7301 et seq.; 7321 et seq.; 7341 et seq.
. authority to seize property 7321
. counterfeit stamps 7303
. customs laws, applicable 7327
. delivery to U.S. marshal 7322
. disposal of 7326
. disposition of perishable goods 7324
. employee retirement and benefit plans 401
. . matching contributions 411
. fraudulent bonds, permits and entries 7303
. judicial action to enforce 7323
. lien for taxes 6323
. penalty for fraudulently claiming drawback 7304
. personal property value at $2,500 or less 7325
. property subject to 5615
. retired judges of TC 7447
. seizure for taxes, authority for 7321
. stamping, marking and branding seized goods 6807
. suits by U.S. for 7401
. violation of Internal Revenue laws, used in 7302
Forward contracts, foreign currency 988
Foster children
. dependents 152
. payments for care, exemption 131
Foundations, private (See Private foundations)
401(k) plans (See Cash or deferred arrangements (CODAs))
Fractional dollar
. computation of returns 6102
. credits and refunds 7504
. fractional cent 6313
. withholding tax on wages 3402
Fractional year (See Short tax year)
Franchises
. amortization 197
. expenditures 1016
. small issue bonds 144

Index to Code

CODE SEC.

Franchises —Cont'd
. sports, player contracts
. . basis for gain or loss 1056
. . depreciation recapture 1245
. transfers of
. . basis for gain or loss 1056
. . definitions 1253
. . depreciation recapture 1245
Fraternal organizations
. charitable contributions 170
. exemption 501
Fraud (See also Crimes)
. acknowledgments of charitable contribution 6720
. affidavits, fraudulent 7206; 7207
. burden of proof 7454
. criminal prosecutions 6531
. deficiency dividend deduction 547; 860
. drawbacks, fraudulent claims 7304
. evasion of tax (See Evasion or avoidance of tax)
. expenses of detection and punishment of 7623
. failure to pay taxes 6663
. limitation on prosecution 6531
. penalty (See Penalties)
. possession with intent to sell in fraud of law 7268
. refund based on, recovery 6532
. returns (See False or fraudulent returns)
. reward to informers 7623
. statement or failure to furnish statements to employees .. 6674
Free choice vouchers
. health care benefits .... 139D[sic E]
. large employer health coverage
. . premium tax credits or cost-sharing reductions, offering
    .... 4980H(b)(3)
Freelancer creative expenses 263A
Freezing estate tax (See Estate freezes)
Fringe benefits .... 132; 3402 (See also Cafeteria plans; Educational assistance programs)
. books and records 6039D
. educational organizations
. . FICA 3121
. . FUTA 3306
. . withholding tax on wages 3401
. employment taxes, collection and payment of 3501
. excess, penalties 4977
. excess benefit transaction 4958
. exclusions from gross income 132
. FICA 3121; 3501
. FUTA 3306; 3501
. gross income 61
. inflation adjustment 132
. information returns 6039D; 6652
. legal services plans for employees (See Legal services plans for employees)
. moving expenses 132
. qualified transportation fringe 132
. returns 6039D
. S corporations 1372
. withholding tax on wages 3401; 3501
. . highway motor vehicle use 3402

Index to Code   Gain

CODE SEC.

Frivolous returns 6702
Frivolous tax court proceedings 6673
Frozen deposits, financial institutions 451
Fruit bearing trees and vines, depreciation 168
Fruit growers association exemption 521
Fruit-flavored concentrates
. alcohol taxes 5001
. plants 5511
FSCs (See Foreign sales corporations (FSCs))
Fuel cell property, energy credit .... 48(c)(1)
Fuels
. adulterated, penalties for 6720A
. Airport and Airway Trust Fund 4091
. alcohol fuels credit 40
. aviation fuel (See Aviation fuel)
. biodiesel (See Biodiesel fuel)
. butane used as, environmental tax 4662
. chemicals used in production, environmental tax .. 4662
. diesel (See Diesel fuel)
. environmental tax 4662
. excise taxes (See also Special fuels tax)
.. commercial transportation, fuel used in 4042
.. diesel and aviation fuels .... 4091 et seq.
.. imposition of 4041
.. information reporting 4104
.. inland waterways, fuel used in 4042
.. liability for tax 4103
.. refunds and credits 6427
. exempt use, refunds and credits 6427; 6675
. Highway Trust Fund .... 4041; 4091 et seq.
. LUST Trust Fund (See Leaking Underground Storage Tank Trust Fund)
. methane used as, environmental tax 4662
. new qualified alternative fuel motor vehicle credit (See Alternate motor vehicle credits)
. nonconventional source credit (See Nonconventional fuel source credit)
. off-highway business use of fuel
.. LUST tax rate 4041
.. special fuels tax 4041
. special fuels 34; 40
. special fuels tax (See Special fuels tax)
. underground storage tanks (See Leaking Underground Storage Tank Trust Fund)
Fugitives from justice
. disclosure of tax information 6103
Fullers earth depletion 613
Functional currency
. branch transactions 987
. defined 985
Fund
. charitable contributions 170
. defined for presidential election campaign fund .. 9002
Funded welfare benefit plans 419; 419A; 4976
Funding assets, qualified
. personal injury damages 130

CODE SEC.

Funding standards, defined benefit plans
. endangered or critical status, funding rules for multiple employer plans in (See Multiemployer plans)
. single-employer, minimum funding standards (See Defined benefit plans subhead single-employer, minimum funding standards)
Fundraising, exempt organization
. disclosure of nondeductibility 6113
. failure to disclose nondeductibility 6710
Funeral benefit insurance companies 816
Funeral expenses
. gross estate deductions 2053; 2106
. stock redemption to pay 303
Funeral trusts
. qualified funeral trust defined 685
. recognition of gain on transfers to 685
FUTA (See Federal Unemployment Tax Act (FUTA))
Future interests, contributions of 170
Futures 1222; 1233
. capital gains and losses
.. securities futures contracts 1234B
. foreign personal holding company income 553
. holding period 1223
. regulated futures contracts. (See Section 1256 contracts)
. straddles 1092
.. interest and carrying charges 263

G

Gain or loss (See also Capital gains and losses; Casualty losses; Losses)
. additional consideration received, reorganization exchanges 356
. adjusted basis for determining 1011; 1016
. affiliation, property acquired during 1051
. amount realized 1001
. annuities, sales of 1021
. appreciated property, distribution of 311
. assumption of liability, reorganization exchanges .. 357
. at risk limitations 465
. basis (See Basis)
. built-in gains (See Built-in gains)
. capital (See Capital gains and losses)
. casualty (See Casualty losses)
. coal 631
. collapsible corporation 341
. computation of 1001
. condemnation of property 1033; 1231
. constructive ownership transactions 1260
. controlled corporations 355
. cooperatives, special rules for netting of gains and losses 1388
. corporate distributions 311
. crop unharvested sold with land 1231
. dealers in securities 1236
. determination of amount 1001
. discharge of indebtedness 1017
. disposition of stock 306
. dispositions of depreciable realty 1001; 1250
. distributions, corporate 311

181

Gain — Index to Code

CODE SEC.

Gain or loss (See also Capital gains and losses; Casualty losses; Losses) —Cont'd
- earnings and profits adjustments 312
- ESOPs 409
- exchange of property
  - productive use of investment, property held for 1031
  - stock for property 1032
  - stock for stock 1036
- farm land 1252; 1257
- foreign corporations
  - reorganization exchanges 367
  - stock of 1248
- foreign currency transactions 988
- foreign expropriation losses 1351
- foreign investment company stock 1246; 1247
- highly erodible croplands, dispositions of 1257
- improvements by lessee 1019
- installment obligations 453B
- installment sales ..... 453 et seq.; 1001
  - repossession of property 1038
- insurance policies, exchanges of 1035
- involuntary conversions (See Involuntary conversions)
- iron ore 631; 1231
- life interests, sale of 1001
- liquidating distributions
  - basis 334
  - parent corporation 337; 453B
  - recognition ..... 331 et seq.
  - stockholders, effect on 331
  - subsidiaries 332; 337
- loans, property subject to 7701
- low-income housing, sale and reinvestment in 1250
- market discount bonds 1276
- mineral interest 617
- minerals, sale of 1254
- natural resources 631
- nonrecognition 361; 7701
- obligations ..... 1271 et seq.
- oil, gas, or geothermal property sales 1254
- options to buy or sell 1233; 1234
- partnerships
  - contributions to 721
  - disposition of distributed property 735
  - distributions 731
  - precontribution gain, distributions by partnerships to contributing partner 737
  - sale or exchange 741
- passive activities 469
- patents 1235; 1249
- property, distribution of 311
- puts and calls 1233; 1234
- real estate mortgage investment conduits 860B; 860F
- real property
  - reacquisition 1038
  - subdivided for sale, real estate 1237
  - recognition of 1001
- related taxpayers, transactions between 267
- reorganization exchanges ..... 351 et seq.
- repossession of property 1038

CODE SEC.

Gain or loss (See also Capital gains and losses; Casualty losses; Losses) —Cont'd
- S corporations
  - built-in gains, tax imposed on 1366; 1374
  - recapture of overall foreign loss 1373
- sale or disposition of property
  - earnings and profits, effect on 312
  - Sec. 126 property, gain from disposition of 1255
- sale or exchanges
  - related taxpayers 267
  - residence, exclusion of gain on 121
  - SEC, orders of 1081; 1082
  - timber, coal or iron ore 631
- Sec. 126 property dispositions 1255
- securities held by financial institutions 582
- ships, transfers of 1061
- short sales 1233
- small business stock
  - 50% exclusion for gain 1202
  - partial exclusion for gain 1202
    - empowerment zone businesses ..... 1202(a)(2)
    - special rules for 2009 and certain periods in 2010 ..... 1202(a)(3)
  - rollover of gain to another qualified small business stock 1202
- stock and stock rights
  - collapsible corporation stock purchase as asset purchase 338
  - disposition of stock 306
  - distribution of 311
  - reorganization exchanges, stock and securities 354
  - small business stock partial gain exclusion 1202
  - stock for property exchanges 1032
  - stock purchase as asset purchase 338
  - stockholder liquidating distributions 331
  - straddles 1092; 1234A
  - target affiliate stock purchase 338
  - term interest defined 1001
- timber 631; 1231
- treasury stock 1032
- wash sales 1091
- wetland dispositions 1257

Gallonage taxes ..... 5001 et seq.; 5061 et seq.
- beer (See Beer tax)
- collection, method of 5061
- distilled spirits (See Distilled spirits)
- exportation, refund and drawback in case of 5062
- foreign embassies and legations, spirits for use of 5066
- liquors (See Liquors)
- losses from disaster, vandalism, or malicious mischief 5064
- refund and drawback in case of exportation 5062
- territorial extent of law 5065
- wines (See Wines)

Gambling (See also Wagering taxes)
- backup withholding 3406
- losses 165
- nonresident aliens 871
- tax on ..... 4401 et seq.
- withholding 3402
  - nonresident aliens 1441

Index to Code

Generation-skipping

CODE SEC.

Gambling facilities
. private activity bonds financing 147
Gaming devices
. occupational taxes 6806
. wagering tax 4402
Garnet depletion 613
Gas guzzler tax
. definitions 1016
. imposition of 4064
. leases of automobiles subject to 4217
. registration, exempt sales 4222
Gas utilities (See Public utilities)
Gas wells (See Marginal wells; Oil and gas wells)
Gasification project credit (See Qualifying gasification project credit)
Gasohol
. excise tax 4041; 4081
. gasoline used to produce, refund of tax on 6427
. noncommercial aviation, used in 6427
Gasoline tax .... 4081 et seq.
. alcohol mixed with gasoline 6426
. blender, treatment of removal or subsequent sale by .. 4081(b)
. bulk transfer, pipeline .... 4081(a)(1)(A)
. buses 6421
. credit against income tax 34
. . S corporations, passthrough to shareholder 1366
. deep-draft vessel, operator entering by .... 4081(a)(1)(B)
. definitions 4082; 4083
. deposit of 6302
. diesel fuel defined 4083
. excessive claims 6206; 6421; 6675
. exemption, bulk transfer .... 4081(a)(1)(B)
. failure to register 7232
. false statements in registration application 7232
. farming purposes 4041; 6206; 6416; 6421; 6427
. . refunds and credits 6420; 6675
. farms, gasoline used on 6206; 6420
. floor stocks, refunds 6412
. further manufacture, use in 4221; 6416
. gasoline defined 4083
. government-owned highway vehicles 6206; 6421
. Highway Trust Fund 9503
. imposition of .... 4081(a)
. information reporting 4104
. kerosene, aviation grade .... 4081(a)(4)
. nonfuel purposes 4218
. nonhighway uses 4041; 6206; 6421
. nonresident aliens 874
. off-highway business use 6421
. penalties 7232
. petroleum and petroleum products .... 4081 et seq.; 4102
. . excessive claims with respect to use of 6675
. producer or importer, use by 4218
. refueler trucks, tankers, and tank wagons treated as terminal .... 4081(a)(3)
. refunds and credits
. . administration 6416
. . aviation purposes 6421

CODE SEC.

Gasoline tax—Cont'd
. *refunds and credits —Cont'd*
. . excessive claims 6206; 6675
. . farming purposes 6420; 6675
. . floor stocks 6412
. . fuels not used for taxable purposes 6427
. . imposition of tax .... 4081(e)
. . railroad train purposes 6421
. . S corporations, passthrough to shareholder 1366
. . removal, entry, or sale .... 4081(a)(1); 4082
. . termination 4081
. . transit systems, local 6206; 6675
. . two-party exchanges 4104
Gems
. individual retirement savings plans, investments 408
General business credit (See Business credit)
General counsel, Treasury Department 7801
General sales tax deductibility 164
Generation-skipping transfer (GST) tax .... 2601 et seq. (See also Generation-skipping transfers)
. adjusted basis 2654
. adopted child 2651
. amount of tax 2602
. basis for gain or loss 2654
. charitable deductions 2642
. charitable trusts 2651
. credit for certain state taxes 2604
. death, allocation after 2642
. deductions 164; 691; 2622
. definitions .... 2611; 2613; 2651 et seq.
. direct skips
. . defined 2612
. . exemption, allocation 2632
. . nontaxable gifts 2642
. . payment of tax 6166
. . taxable amount in case of 2623
. . valuation elections 2624
. distributions 667; 2612; 2621
. estate tax 691
. expense deduction 2622
. generation assignment 2651
. gifts 2642
. gift-splitting 2652
. grandchildren, special rule for transfer to 2612
. imposition of 2601
. inclusion ratio 2642; 2653
. information returns 2662
. inter vivos allocations 2642
. interest in property defined 2652
. liability for payment 2603
. lineal descendants 2651
. marital status 2651
. multiple skips 2653
. nonskip person defined 2613
. personal liability for payment 2603
. pour-over trust 2653
. qualified terminable interest property 2642; 2652
. rate of tax 2602; 2641
. returns 2662

183

Generation-skipping

CODE SEC.

Generation-skipping transfer (GST) tax—Cont'd
- . skip person defined 2613
- . source of tax 2603
- . state taxes, credit for 2604
- . taxable distributions
- . . amount, taxable 2621
- . . defined 2612
- . taxable termination
- . . amount, taxable 2622
- . . defined 2612
- . . valuation elections 2624
- . termination 2664
- . transfer defined 2611
- . transferor defined 2652
- . trust defined 2652
- . trustee
- . . defined 2652
- . . personal liability, limitation on 2654
- . valuation 2624; 2642

Generation-skipping transfers .... 2601 et seq. (See also Generation-skipping transfer (GST) tax)
- . administration 2661
- . allocation of exemption
- . . general rule 2631
- . . inflation adjustment 2631
- . . irrevocability 2631
- . . lifetime direct skips, deemed allocation to ... 2632
- . . special rules 2632
- . . unused GST exemption 2632
- . definitions .... 2611; 2613; 2651 et seq.
- . direct skips
- . . defined 2612
- . . exemption, allocation 2632
- . . nontaxable gifts 2642
- . . payment of tax 6166
- . . taxable amount in case of 2623
- . . valuation elections 2624
- . inclusion ratio 2642
- . information returns 2662
- . liability for tax 2603
- . multiple skips 2653
- . non-skip person 2613
- . rate of tax 2641
- . redemption of stock 303
- . returns 2662
- . skip person defined 2613
- . special rules for 2654
- . state taxes 2604
- . tax imposed .... 2601 et seq.
- . taxable distributions
- . . defined 2612
- . . taxable amount in case of 2621
- . taxable termination
- . . defined 2612
- . . taxable amount in case of 2622
- . termination 2664
- . valuation 2624

Index to Code

CODE SEC.

Geopressurized brine
- . nonconventional fuel source credit (See Nonconventional fuel source credit)
- . percentage depletion 613A

Geothermal deposits
- . defined 613
- . dispositions 291
- . exploration expenditures, at risk amounts 465
- . intangible drilling and development costs
- . . earnings and profits computation 312

Geothermal energy defined 45

Geothermal energy facility
- . electricity produced from renewable sources; credit .... 45(d)(4)

Geothermal resources
- . deposit defined 613
- . operating mineral interests defined 614
- . percentage depletion 613
- . property defined 614
- . sale of property, gain from 1254

Geothermal wells 263

Gift tax .... 2501 et seq.
- . abatement claims 6404
- . alimony 2516
- . art, loan of 2503
- . assessment and collection .... 6213 et seq.; 6501
- . bankruptcy and receiverships .... 6161; 6871 et seq.
- . basis for gain or loss 1015
- . charitable and similar gifts 2522
- . claims in bankruptcy and receivership proceedings ... 6871
- . computation 2001; 2502; 2504
- . credit against 2505
- . deductibility 275
- . deductions
- . . charitable and similar gifts 2522
- . . extent of 2524
- . . Indian tribal government, treatment as state ... 7871
- . . marital 2523
- . . spouse, gift to 2523
- . deficiency .... 6211 et seq.
- . disclaimers 2518
- . disclosure of returns and return information ... 6103
- . divorce settlement 2516
- . donee's liability 6324
- . donor, paid by 2502
- . educational expense exclusions 2503
- . estate tax credit 2012; 2013; 2102
- . exclusions 2503; 2504
- . executors and administrators (See Executors and administrators)
- . expatriation to avoid 2501
- . extensions 6075
- . . deficiency payments 6161
- . . interest 6601
- . failure to file return 6651
- . failure to pay 6651
- . fiduciary's liability .... 6901 et seq.
- . husband and wife
- . . adjustments 2001

184

Index to Code   Golden

	CODE SEC.
Gift tax—Cont'd	
husband and wife —Cont'd	
. . deductions	2524
. . divorce settlements	2516
. . joint and several liability	2513
. . spouse, gift to	2523
. . third party gifts	2513
. imposition	2501
. interest	
. . underpayment, nonpayment, or extensions of time to pay tax	6601
. jeopardy assessments	6861; 6863
. joint and survivor annuities	2523
. liability	2501 et seq.
. lien for	6324
. . release or discharge	6325
. life estates, dispositions	2519
. limitation period (See subhead statute of limitations)	
. marital deduction	
. . alien spouse of U.S. citizen donor	2523
. . extent of	2524
. . recovery	2207A
. medical expenses, certain exclusions for	2503
. nonresident aliens (See Nonresident aliens subhead gift tax)	
. omission from gross income	6501
. overpayments	6511 et seq.
. possessions of U.S., residents of	2501
. powers of appointment	
. . creation and lapse of	2514
. . defined	2514
. . general rules	2514
. . marital deduction	2523; 2524
. private foundations, remainder and income interests transfers	2522
. qualified terminable interest property	2523; 2524
. rate	2502
. refunds and credits	6511 et seq.
. schedule	2502
. recovery rights	2207A; 2207B
. returns	6019
. . false or fraudulent limitation on assessment and collection	6501
. . generation-skipping transfers	2642
. . qualified charitable transfers	6019
. . tenancy by the entirety	6019
. . time to file	6075
. statute of limitations	
. . appeal to Tax Court	6213
. . assessment and collection	6501 et seq.
. . . bankruptcy and receiverships	6872
. . refunds and credits	6511 et seq.
. taxable gifts	
. . defined	2503
. . direct skips, GST tax	2612; 2623; 2624; 2632
. . exclusions	2503; 2504
. . preceding years and quarters	2504
. tenancy by the entirety	
. . marital deduction	2523; 2524
. . returns	6019
. terminable interest property	2523; 2524

	CODE SEC.
Gift tax—Cont'd	
. three years of death, gifts made within	2035
. transferees	6324; 6901 et seq.
. . disclaimers	2518
. transfers	2511 et seq.
. . benefit of minors	2503
. . intangible property	2501
. tuition program, qualified	529
. unified computation with estate tax	2001
. unified credit against	2107; 2505
. valuation of gifts	
. . credit for gift tax	2012
. . furnishing statement on request	7517
. . general rules	2512
. . IRS statement to donor	7517
. . preceding calendar periods, gifts for	2504
. war postponements	7508
Gifts (See also Bequests; Contributions; Devises; Gift tax)	
. basis of property received	1015
. below-market rate loans	7872
. beneficiaries	102
. business	274
. charitable (See Charitable contributions)	
. death transfers and gifts, failure to file information with respect to	6716
. declaratory judgments relating to value of	7477
. depreciation recapture	1250
. employee	102
. exemption	102; 663
. expenses	274
. foreign person, large gift from	6039F
. from expatriates, imposition of tax	2801
. gain or loss, basis for	1015
. generation-skipping transfer tax	2642
. gross income, exclusion from	102
. holding period	1223
. husband and wife	274
. husband and wife to third party	1015; 2513
. income	102
. loans	7872
. partnership interest	704
. partnerships	274
. passive activity losses and credits	469
. private foundations, to taxable	508
. reorganization exchanges	356
. Sec. 1245 property	1245
. Sec. 1250 property	1250
. stock, of	382
. taxable defined	2503
Gilsonite depletion	613
GO Zone (See Gulf Opportunity Zone)	
Golden parachute payments	280G(a)
. affiliated groups	280G(d)(5)
. base amount defined	280G(b)(3)
. base period	
. . annualized includible compensation for	280G(d)(1)
. . defined	280G(d)(2)
. defined	280G(b)(2)
. disqualified individuals	280G(c)

185

	CODE SEC.
Golden parachute payments—Cont'd	
. excess	280G(b); 4999
. parachute payment defined	280G(b)(2)
. present value	280G(d)(4)
. property transfers	280G(d)(3)
. qualified plan payments, exemption	280G(b)(6)
. reasonable compensation	280G(b)(4)
. regulations, prescription of	280G(f)
. small business exemption	280G(b)(5)
. troubled asset relief programs, employers participating in	280G(e)
Golf course, small issue bond financing	144
Goodwill	
. amortization	197
. partners and partnerships	736
. sale of	865
Government, property used by	
. limitation on allowable deductions	470
Government contracts	
. carrybacks, net operating loss	1341; 6511
. exempt organization's income from	512
. renegotiated	
. . claim of right	1341
. . net operating loss carrybacks	1341; 6511
. repayments pursuant to price redetermination	1341
Government corporations (See Instrumentalities of U.S.)	
Government depositaries	7808 (See also Depositaries for collection)
. failure to make payment of taxes to	6656; 7215; 7512
. overstatement of tax paid to	6656
. payment of tax to	5703; 6302
Government employees (See Federal officers and employees)	
Government employer	
. return and payment by, FICA rules	3126
. withholding tax on wages, return and payment	3404
Government National Mortgage Association	
. bond guarantee	149
Government obligations	
. federal (See United States obligations)	
. municipalities (See State and local bonds)	
. state and local bonds (See State and local bonds)	
. United States savings bonds (See United States savings bonds)	
Government pensions and annuities	401
Government plans	
. accident and health plans	
. . description, plan	105(j)(2)
. . exclusions of amounts paid directly or indirectly to taxpayers	105(j)(1)
. definition	414
. distributions for	
. . health and long-term care insurance	402
. Indian tribal governments	414
. pensions and annuities	401
. vesting standards	411
Government publications	
. capital gains and losses	1221; 1231

	CODE SEC.
Governmental units	
. arbitrage bonds	148
. bonds, financed with	
. . change in use of facility	150
. charitable contributions	170
. cooperative housing corporations	216(b)(4)
. definition	150
. investment credit property	50
. private activity bonds	
. . change in use of facility	150
. . volume cap	146
. return relating to cancellation of indebtedness	6050P
Government-owned highway vehicles	
. gasoline for	6206; 6421
Graduated tax rate structure, corporations	11
. controlled foreign corporations	
. . shareholders, election to be taxed at corporate rates	962
. controlled group of corporations	1561
. . disallowance of benefits	1551
. disclosure of returns and return information	6103
Grandchildren	
. generation-skipping transfer tax	2612
Granite depletion	613
Grantor of trust	671 et seq.
. sale or exchange with fiduciary	267
Grantor trusts	
. income interest, charitable contributions	170
Graphic illustration requirements	
. instruction booklets	7523
Graphite depletion	613
Grass roots lobbying expenditures	501; 4911
Gratuities (See Tips)	
Green building and sustainable design projects	
. exempt facility bonds (See Exempt facility bonds subhead qualified green building and sustainable design projects)	
Green cards applicants	6039E
Greenhouses depreciation recapture	1245
Greenmail	5881
Gross estate	2031 et seq.
. annuities	2039
. defined	2031; 2103
. disclaimers	2046; 2518
. estate tax	2031 et seq.
. alternate valuation	2032
. annuities	2039
. death, transfers taking effect at	2037
. defined	2031
. dower or curtesy interests	2034
. farm or closely-held business real property	2032A
. gifts made within 3 years of death	2035
. individual retirement accounts	2039
. insufficient consideration, transfers for	2043
. joint interests	2040
. marital deduction	2044
. nonresidents	2103
. powers of appointment	2041
. prior interests	2045

Index to Code

Gross estate—Cont'd
estate tax—Cont'd
- proceeds of life insurance ... 2042
- property in which decedent had interest ... 2033
- retained life estate, transfers with ... 2036
  - recovery, right of ... 2207B
- revocable transfers ... 2038
- valuation of unlisted stock and securities ... 2031
- family owned business exclusion ... 2057
- gifts made within 3 years of, adjustments for ... 2035
- insufficient consideration, transfers with ... 2043
- joint interests ... 2040
- life insurance proceeds ... 2042
- marital deduction ... 2044
- nonresident aliens ... 2103 et seq.
- prior interests ... 2045
- retained life estate, transfers with ... 2036
- taxable estate (See Taxable estate)
- valuation
  - alternate ... 2032
  - farm property ... 2032A
  - inclusions in value of ... 2031 et seq.
  - qualified real property ... 2032A
  - special rules ... 2032
  - stock and securities, unlisted ... 2031

Gross income (See also specific item)
- accounting methods
  - taxable year of inclusion ... 451 et seq.
- adjusted (See Adjusted gross income)
- adoption assistance programs ... 137
- alcohol fuel credit ... 87
- alimony and separate maintenance payments ... 71
- annuities ... 72
- appreciated property, political contributions ... 84
- biodiesel fuels credit ... 87
- child, services of ... 73
- commodity credit loans ... 77
- compensatory property, transfers of ... 83
- controlled foreign corporations ... 951; 959
- cooperatives ... 1382
- dealers in tax-exempt securities ... 75
- decedents ... 691
- deferred compensation plan ... 409A
- definitions ... 61; 543; 6501
- discount on short-term obligations ... 1281
- dividends from foreign corporations ... 78
- divorce ... 682
- exclusions (See Gross income exclusions)
- extraterritorial income ... 114
- farmers' cooperatives ... 1382
- foreign corporations ... 882
- foreign personal holding companies ... 551; 552; 555
- group-term life insurance purchased for employees, costs of ... 79
- illegal Federal irrigation subsidies ... 90
- income in respect of decedents ... 691
- insurance companies
  - life ... 803; 807
  - mortgage guaranty insurance companies ... 832

Gross income (See also specific item) —Cont'd
insurance companies —Cont'd
- other than life ... 543; 831
- special loss discount account amounts ... 847
- interest, state and local bond ... 103
- life insurance companies ... 803; 807
- mortgage guaranty insurance companies ... 832
- moving expenses, reimbursements for ... 82
- nonresident aliens ... 872
- nuclear decommissioning costs ... 88
- omission from gross income ... 6501
- ordinary gross income defined ... 543
- original issue discount ... 1272
- partners ... 702
- personal holding company adjusted gross income requirement ... 542
- political contributions ... 84
- prepaid dues income ... 456
- prepaid subscription income ... 455
- prizes and awards ... 74
- proceeds from annuity, endowment and life insurance contracts ... 72
- property
  - appreciated property ... 84
  - payment for services rendered, transfers of property in ... 83
- public utilities, energy conservation subsidies provided by ... 136
- railroad retirement, tier 1 benefits ... 86
- regulated investment company
  - failure to satisfy gross income test ... 851
- renewal community capital gain ... 1400F
- report, time to ... 451 et seq.
- requirement for return ... 6012
- securities, restored value of ... 80
- self-employed income ... 1402
- Social Security benefits ... 86
- sources within U.S. ... 861
- sources without U.S. ... 862
- taxable year of inclusion ... 451 et seq.
  - installment sales ... 453 et seq.
  - obligations issued at discount ... 454
  - prepaid dues income ... 456
  - prepaid subscription income ... 455
- transportation income, taxation ... 887
- trust, beneficiaries of
  - accumulating income or distributing corpus ... 662
  - distributing current income only ... 652
- unemployment compensation ... 85
- wife, divorced ... 682

Gross income exclusions ... 101 et seq. (See also Exempt income)
- accident and health benefits ... 105; 106
- combat pay, armed forces ... 112
- conservation cost-sharing payments ... 126
- contribution to capital of corporation ... 118
- controlled foreign corporations ... 959
- death benefits ... 101
- dependent care assistance program benefits ... 129
- discharge of indebtedness, income from ... 108
- educational assistance programs ... 127

Gross   Index to Code

CODE SEC.

Gross income exclusions—Cont'd
. foreign corporations 883
. foster care payments 131
. fringe benefits 132
. gain on sale of principal residence 121
. gifts and inheritances 102
. group legal services plans 120
. improvements by lessee on lessor's property .. 109
. injuries and sickness, compensation for ..... 104 et seq.
. leases, improvements by lessee 109
. living expenses, casualty loss insurance compensation ... 123
. meals and lodging 119
. military benefits 134
. municipalities, income of 115
. nonresident aliens 871; 872
. personal injuries
.. compensation .... 104 et seq.
.. liability assignments 130
. previously taxed earnings and profits 959
. recovery of tax benefit items 111
. retirement pay, uniformed services 122
. returned merchandise 458
. savings bonds redeemed for education expenses ... 135
. scholarships 117
. state and local bonds, interest on 103
. states, income of 115
. tuition reductions 117
. uniformed services reduced retirement pay ... 122
. U.S. citizens or residents living abroad ... 911; 912

Gross receipts
. construction contracts, determination of 460
. domestic production activities income (See Domestic production activities)
. family corporations 447
. foreign trading gross receipt 942
. limitation 448

Gross-up dividends, foreign tax credit 78

Ground rents
. basis rules 1055
. interest, redeemable ground rents 163
. mortgages, treatment as 1055
. redeemable 163; 1055

Groundless tax court proceedings 6673
Group, partnership status 7701
Group health plans
. continuation coverage .... 4980B(f)(1)
.. applicable premium defined .... 4980B(f)(4)
.. cessation of eligibility for COBRA premium assistance, failure to notify plan of 6720C
.. COBRA, temporary extension of ..... 4980B(f)(5)(C)
.. covered employees .... 4980B(f)(7)
.. defined .... 4980B(f)(2)
.. election period .... 4980B(f)(5)
.. notice requirements .... 4980B(f)(6)
.. optional extension of required period ... 4980B(f)(8)
.. other beneficiaries, election and ..... 4980B(f)(5)(B)
.. period of coverage .... 4980B(f)(2)(B)
.. premium requirements .... 4980B(f)(2)(C)
.. qualifying events .... 4980B(f)(3)

CODE SEC.

Group health plans —Cont'd
. definitions concerning 9832
. exceptions 9831
. failure to meet requirements 4980D
. market reforms 9815
. mental health benefit limitations 9812
. mothers and newborns 9811
. supplemental benefits 9831
. trade or business expense deduction 162

Group legal services plans 120
. books and records 6039D
. exemption 501
. FICA 3121
. FUTA 3306
. information returns 6039D
. railroad retirement taxes 3231
. unrelated business taxable income 512

Group-term life insurance
. benefits taxable 3102; 3202
. definition of employee 7701
. information returns 6052; 6652
. nondiscrimination requirements 79
. withholding tax on wages 3401

GST tax (See Generation-skipping transfer (GST) tax)

Guam
. alien residents 876
. citizens residing in, income of 931
. coordination with U.S. tax 7654
. corporations 881; 1442
. employment tax overpayments 6413
. FICA 3121; 6205
.. government employees 3125
.. overpayments 6413
. residents, self-employment tax 1402
. Revised Organic Act 7651
. taxes, coordination with U.S. individual taxes ... 7654
.. information, failure to furnish 6688
. withholding tax at source
.. nonresident aliens and foreign corporations ... 1442

Guarantees
. controlled foreign corporations 956
. federally guaranteed bonds 149
. lien for taxes against pledges 6323
. life insurance company reserves
.. guarantees beyond end of contract year 811
. multiemployer plans
.. average guaranteed benefits 418C
. partners and partnership payments ... 267; 707; 736

Guardians
. fiduciary status 7701
. income collected by 641
. returns 6012; 6103

Gulf Opportunity Zone
. August 28, 2005, special allowances for property acquired on or after .... 1400N(d)
. certain property, tax benefits not available to
.. property described .... 1400N(p)(3)
.. qualified GO Zone casualty losses defined for ... 1400N(p)(2)

188

Index to Code

Gulf

CODE SEC.

Gulf Opportunity Zone —Cont'd
. certain property, tax benefits not available to —Cont'd
... qualified GO Zone property defined for .... 1400N(p)(1)
. charitable contributions
... temporary suspension of limitations on .... 1400S(a)(1)
.... excess contributions .... 1400S(a)(2)
.... itemized deductions exception .... 1400S(a)(3)
.... qualified contributions defined .... 1400S(a)(4)
. definitions concerning 1400N
. earned income determination, special rule for .... 1400S(d)(1)
.. applicable date defined for .... 1400S(d)(3)
.. earned income defined for .... 1400S(d)(4)
.. qualified individual defined for .... 1400S(d)(2)
. education tax benefits 1400O
. employee retention credits
.. Hurricane Katrina .... 1400R(a)
.. Hurricane Rita .... 1400R(b)
.. Hurricane Wilma .... 1400R(c)
. expensing for certain demolition and cleanup costs
   .... 1400N(f)(1)
.. qualified GO Zone cleanup cost .... 1400N(f)(2)
. expensing for environmental remediation costs, extension of
   .... 1400N(g)(1)
. gulf tax credit bond holders
.. allowance of credit .... 1400N(l)(1)
.. amount of credit .... 1400N(l)(2)
.. defined, Gulf tax credit bond .... 1400N(l)(4)
.. gross income inclusions .... 1400N(l)(6)
.. limitations, credit .... 1400N(l)(3)
.. qualified bonds .... 1400N(l)(5)
.. special rules .... 1400N(l)(7)
. housing tax benefits
.. employer credits for housing employees affected by Hurricane Katrina .... 1400P(b)
.. employer provided housing for individuals affected by Hurricane Katrina, exclusion of .... 1400P(a)
.. qualified employee defined .... 1400P(c)
.. qualified employer defined .... 1400P(d)
. Hurricane Katrina disaster area defined .... 1400N(2)
. Hurricane Rita disaster area defined .... 1400N(4)
. Hurricane Wilma disaster area defined .... 1400N(6)
. low-income housing credit
.. additional dollar amounts for GO Zone .... 1400N(c)(1)
.. additional dollar amounts for Texas and Florida
   .... 1400N(c)(2)
.. community development block grants not taken into account in determining if building is federally subsidized
   .... 1400N(c)(6)
.. difficult development areas .... 1400N(c)(3)
.. income tests .... 1400N(c)(4)
. mortgage revenue bonds, special rules 1400T
. net operating loss attributable to GO Zone losses
   .... 1400N(k)(1)
.. qualified Gulf Opportunity Zone casualty loss defined
   .... 1400N(k)(3)
.. qualified Gulf Opportunity Zone loss defined ... 1400N(k)(2)
.. special rules .... 1400N(k)(4)
. new markets tax credit to investment in community development entities serving, application of .... 1400N(m)
. personal casualty losses, suspension of certain limitations on
   .... 1400S(b)

CODE SEC.

Gulf Opportunity Zone —Cont'd
. public utility casualty losses, special rules for
.. elections .... 1400N(j)(5)
.. general disaster loss, coordination with ...... 1400N(j)(4)
.. Gulf Opportunity Zone public utility casualty loss defined
   .... 1400N(j)(2)
.. involuntary conversions, reduction in gains for ... 1400N(j)(3)
. public utility property disaster losses .... 1400N(o)(1)
.. eligible public utility property loss .... 1400N(o)(2)
.. limitation waivers .... 1400N(o)(3)
. qualified Gulf Opportunity Zone bond
.. advance refunding .... 1400N(b)(1)
.. Alabama counties included .... 1400N(a)(8)
.. counties included .... 1400N(a)(8)
.. defined .... 1400N(a)(2)
.. exempt facility bond treatment .... 1400N(a)(1)
.. limitations .... 1400N(a)(3)
.. repairs and reconstruction .... 1400N(a)(7)
.. separate issue treatment .... 1400N(a)(6)
.. special rules .... 1400N(a)(5)
. qualified project costs defined .... 1400N(a)(4)
. rehabilitation credit, increase in .... 1400N(h)
. residential rental project
.. treatment of presentations regarding income eligibility
   .... 1400N(n)
. retirement funds use
.. amendments, plan .... 1400Q(d)
.. home purchases, withdrawals for
... qualified distributions .... 1400Q(b)(2)
... recontributions .... 1400Q(b)(1)
.. loans from qualified plans
... increase in loan limits .... 1400Q(c)(1)
... qualified individuals .... 1400Q(c)(3)
... repayment delays .... 1400Q(c)(2)
.. rules, special 1400Q
.. withdrawals, tax favored .... 1400Q(a)
... aggregate distribution amounts .... 1400Q(a)(2)
... definitions concerning .... 1400Q(a)(4)
... repayments, distribution .... 1400Q(a)(3)
... special rules .... 1400Q(a)(6)
... 3-year income inclusion spread .... 1400Q(a)(5)
. Rita GO Zone defined .... 1400N(3)
. Sec. 179 expensing, increase in .... 1400N(e)(1)
.. empowerment zones and renewal communities, coordination with .... 1400N(e)(3)
.. extensions for certain property .... 1400N(e)(2)
.. qualified Sec. 179 GO Zone property .... 1400N(e)(5)
.. recapture .... 1400N(e)(4)
. Sec. 7508A, exercise of authority under .... 1400S(c)
. secretarial authority to make adjustments regarding taxpayer and dependency status .... 1400S(e)
. timber producers, small
.. certain entities, inapplicability of rules to ..... 1400N(i)(3)
.. definitions concerning .... 1400N(i)(5)
.. expensing, increased .... 1400N(i)(1)
.. 5-year NOL carryback of losses .... 1400N(i)(2)
.. large timber producers, inapplicability of rules to
   .... 1400N(i)(4)
. Wilma GO zone defined .... 1400N(5)

189

Guns

Guns (See Firearms)
Gym as fringe benefit 132

H

Handbills, delivery
. FICA 3121
. FUTA 3306
. withholding tax on wages 3401
Hand-carried returns 6091
Handguns (See Firearms)
Handicapped individuals
. architectural and transportation barriers, removal expenditures
  .... 190; 263
. dependent 151; 152
. dependent care credit 21
. foster care payments 131
. household expenses credit 21
. personal exemptions 151
. sheltered workshop income 151
Harbors
. maintenance tax 4461; 4462
. maintenance trust fund 9505
Hardship camp meal and lodging exemption 119
Hawaii
. harbor maintenance tax 4462
. transportation by air of person to, excise tax rate ... 4261(c)(3)
Hazardous substances
. environmental remediation costs, expensing of .... 198(d)
. superfund 4611; 9507
Hazardous waste cleanup
. disposal facility exempt facility bonds 142
. excise taxes
. . chemicals 4661; 4662
. . environmental 4661; 4662
. . petroleum and petroleum products 4611; 4612
Head of household
. definition 2
. rate of tax 1
Health and Human Services, Department of (See Department of Health and Human Services)
Health benefit accounts
. single-employer defined benefit pension plan funds transferred
  to .... 430(l)
Health clubs
. private activity bonds financing 147
Health insurance coverage
. defined 9832
. employee annuities 403
. government plan distributions for 402
. group health plans continuation coverage (See Group health plans)
. large employers
. . generally (See Large employer health coverage)
. . reporting (See subhead reporting, large employer health coverage)
. market reforms 9815
. monthly health coverage after 2013
. . administration .... 5000A(g)(1)

Index to Code

Health insurance coverage —Cont'd
. *monthly health coverage after 2013 —Cont'd*
. . applicable individual .... 5000A(d)(1)
. . eligible employer-sponsored plan .... 5000A(f)(2)
. . excepted benefits not treated as minimum essential coverage
  .... 5000A(f)(3)
. . exemptions .... 5000A(e)
. . failure to maintain, penalty for .... 5000A(b)(3); 5000A(c)(1)
. . family size defined for .... 5000A(c)(4)
. . household income defined for .... 5000A(c)(4)
. . incarcerated individuals .... 5000A(d)(4)
. . individuals, requirement for .... 5000A(a)
. . individuals not lawfully present .... 5000A(d)(3)
. . minimum essential coverage .... 5000A(f)(1)
. . modified adjusted gross income defined for ... 5000A(c)(4)
. . religious exemption .... 5000A(d)(2)
. . residing outside U.S., individuals .... 5000A(f)(4)
. . share responsibility payments .... 5000A(b)(1)
. . special rules .... 5000A(g)(2)
. reporting
. . employer provided coverage, information concerning
  .... 6055(b)(2)
. . form and manner of return .... 6055(b)(1)
. . government units, coverage provided by .... 6055(d)
. . minimum essential coverage .... 6055(e)
. . statements generally .... 6055(c)(1)
. . time for furnishing statement .... 6055(c)(2)
. reporting, large employer health coverage
. . coordination with other requirements .... 6056(d)
. . form and manner of return .... 6056(b)
. . generally .... 6056(a)
. . government units, coverage provided by .... 6056(e)
. . offering employer .... 6056(f)(1)
. . statements to be furnished to individuals ..... 6056(c)
. . time for furnishing statements .... 6056(c)(2)
Health insurance credits
. Archer MSA distributions 35
. earned income 32
. health savings account distributions 35
. individuals 35
. advance payment of credit 7527
. returns relating to credit 6050T
. medical expenses 213
. qualified health insurance 35
. qualifying family member 35
. small employer (See Small employer health insurance credits)
. state based coverage 35
Health insurance issuer defined 9832
Health insurance premiums
. assistance credits (See Accident and health plans subhead premium assistance credits)
. credits against tax .... 280C(g)
Health insurance providers
. trade or business expenses, special rules for ..... 162(m)(6)
Health maintenance organization defined 9832
Health plans (See Accident and health plans)
Health savings accounts
. adjusted gross income 62

Index to Code — High-speed

CODE SEC.

Health savings accounts —Cont'd
. comparable contributions, failure of employer to make 4980G
. compensation as contribution 3231
. contributions 3231
. coordination with other contributions 223
. cost-of-living adjustments 223
. deductions, allowable 223
. defined 223
. dependents 223
. distributions, tax treatment for 223
. employer contributions 106
. excess contributions 4973
. 55 or older, contributions for individuals 223
. health insurance credits 35
. information returns 6041
. IRA distribution for 408
. Medicare eligible individuals 223
. prohibited transactions, excise tax 4975
. qualified medical expenses 223

Hearse retail excise tax 4053

Heating systems
. combined heat and power system property
. . energy credit .... 48(c)(3)
. exempt facility bonds 142

Hedge bonds (See State and local bonds)

Hedges .... 988 (See also Futures)
. capital assets, hedging transaction defined for purposes of
  1221
. capital expenditures 263
. interest and carrying charges 263
. losses, limitation 1256
. marked to market reporting 1256
. regulated investments 851
. short sales, gains and losses 1233

Heirs
. disclosure of returns and return information .. 6103

Helicopters
. fuel for mining, oil exploration or timber use 4041; 4261; 6427
. transportation of persons by
. . excise tax exemption .... 4261(f)

High technology equipment
. depreciation deduction, used or leased property 168

High-cost employer-sponsored health coverage
. aggregation rules .... 4980I(f)(9)
. applicable employer-sponsored coverage
. . cost determinations .... 4980I(d)(2)
. . defined .... 4980I(d)(1)
. applicable share
. . calculation of tax .... 4980I(c)(4)
. . coverage provider .... 4980I(c)(3)
. calculation of tax
. . applicable share .... 4980I(c)(4)
. . coverage determination .... 4980I(f)(1)
. . coverage provider
. . . applicable share .... 4980I(c)(3)
. . . liability to pay tax .... 4980I(c)(2)
. denial of regulations .... 4980I(f)(10)

CODE SEC.

High-cost employer-sponsored health coverage —Cont'd
. employee defined .... 4980I(d)(3)
. employee engaged in high-risk profession ...... 4980I(f)(3)
. excess benefit
. . annual limitations .... 4980I(b)(3)
. . defined .... 4980I(b)(1)
. . monthly excess amount, determination of ...... 4980I(b)(2)
. . penalty for failure to properly calculate .... 4980I(c)
. excise tax on 4980I
. former employees .... 4980I(d)(3)
. group health plan defined .... 4980I(f)(4)
. health insurance coverage defined .... 4980I(f)(5)
. health insurance issuer defined .... 4980I(f)(5)
. liability to pay tax
. . coverage provider .... 4980I(c)(2)
. . generally .... 4980I(c)(1)
. person that administers the plan benefits ...... 4980I(f)(6)
. plan sponsor .... 4980I(f)(7)
. primary insured individuals .... 4980I(d)(3)
. qualified retiree defined .... 4980I(f)(2)
. regulations, prescription of .... 4980I(g)
. surviving spouses .... 4980I(d)(3)
. taxable period defined .... 4980I(f)(8)

High-cost housing
. exempt facility bonds 142

Higher education expenses
. adjusted gross income 62
. qualified expenses defined for qualified tuition ...... 529(e)(3)
. savings bonds redeemed to pay 135
. scholarships and fellowships 135
. veterans 135

Highly-compensated employees
. accident and health plans 105
. cafeteria plans 125
. definition 105
. employee benefit plans
. . matching and employee contributions 401
. fringe benefits 132
. IRA plan discrimination in favor of 408
. pension, profit-sharing, and stock bonus plans ... 410; 411; 414
. . compensation defined .... 414(q)(4)
. . coordination with other provisions ..... 414(q)(7)
. . defined .... 414(q)
. . excluded employees defined .... 414(q)(5)
. . 5% owner .... 414(q)(2)
. . former employees defined .... 414(q)(6)
. . nonresident alien .... 414(q)(8)
. . percentage defined, separate lines of business .... 414(r)(4)
. . pre-ERISA rules, excluded employees under ...... 414(q)(9)
. . top-paid group .... 414(q)(3)
. self-insured medical expense reimbursement plan 105
. tuition reduction 117

High-risk youth work opportunity credit 51

High-speed intercity rail facilities
. exempt facility bonds
. . defined .... 142(i)(1)
. . nongovernmental owners, election by .... 142(i)(2)
. . proceeds, use of .... 142(i)(3)

191

High-speed   Index to Code

CODE SEC.

High-speed intercity rail facilities —Cont'd
exempt facility bonds —Cont'd
. . volume cap 146
. private activity bonds 147
Highway motor vehicle use taxes .... 4481 et seq.
. definitions 4482
. exemptions 4483
. Indian tribal government, treatment as state 7871
. installment payments 6156
. rate of tax 4482
. taxable gross weight defined 4482
Highway Trust Fund 9503
. diesel fuel and special motors fuel tax 4041
. expenditures 4483
. federal-aid highway program 9503
. floor stock refunds 9503
. gasoline mixed with alcohol at refinery 4081
. highway motor vehicle use tax transfers to 4483
. Mass Transit Account 9503
. rate of tax 4091
. revenue deposits of taxes on alcohol mixtures 9503
. small engine fuel taxes 9503
. transfers for small-engine fuel taxes 9503
Highway vehicles
. gasoline tax, government-owned vehicles 6206; 6421
. highway vehicle use tax, installment payment of 6156
. mobile machinery treatment as 7701
High-yield discount obligations 163
Historic structures
. conservation contributions 170
. rehabilitation credit 47
Hobby activity losses 183
Holding companies
. accumulated earnings tax 533; 535
. banks
. . dividends received deduction 246A
. . portfolio stock, debt-financed 246A
. definitions 1083
. exemption 501
. business income 511
. personal (See Personal holding companies; Foreign personal holding companies)
. stock, estate tax 6166
. United States real property holding corporation defined ... 897
Holding period of property
. capital gains and losses 1223
. compensatory property, transfers of 83
Holidays, legal
. last day of performance falling on 7503
. . petition to Tax Court 6213
Home (See Residential property)
Home equity indebtedness 163
Home health service agency
. employees annuities 415
Home improvement
. defined 25
. loans, mortgage revenue bonds 143

CODE SEC.

Home workers, FICA 3121
Homeowners associations
. defined 528
. exemption 528
. . returns 6012
Hope and Lifetime Learning Credits 25A
Hope Scholarship Credit 25A
Horse racing
. depreciation of horses 168
. losses 183
Horticultural activities
. domestic production activities .... 199(d)(3)
Horticultural organizations
. domestic production activities deductions for cooperatives
  .... 199(d)(3)
. exemption 501
. unrelated business taxable income 511
Horticultural structures
. depreciation 168
. . recapture 1245
Hospital bond exemption 145
Hospital insurance
. FICA
. . federal employees 3121; 3122
. . information statements 6051
. Railroad Retirement Tax Act 3201; 3221
. self-employment, rate of tax .... 1401(b)
. withholding tax statements 6051
Hospital insurance tax
. application of 6413
. federal employment taxes 3121
. FICA 3101; 3111
. self-employed 1401; 1402
Hospital service organizations
. exemption 501
. unrelated trade or business 513
Hospitalization
. combat zone injuries, postponement of tax 7508
. employee retirement and benefit plans 401
Hospitals
. communications taxes 4253
. cooperative service organizations 501; 513
. employees annuities 415
. failures by hospital organizations, tax on 4959
. FUTA 3306
. legislation, expenditures to influence 501
. medical expenses 213
House trailers
. retail excise tax 4053
Household expenses credit
. employment-related expenses 21
Household items, charitable contribution of 170
House-hunting costs 217
Housing bonds
. federally guaranteed 149
. mortgage credit certificates (See Mortgage credit certificates)

192

Index to Code   Income

CODE SEC.	CODE SEC.

Housing credit agencies
. low-income housing credit (See Low-income housing credit)
Housing expenses
. U.S. citizens or residents living abroad 911
Housing interest
. alternative minimum tax 56
Housing programs
. federally guaranteed bonds 149
Housing projects
. exempt facility bonds 142
. 501(c)(3) bonds 145
. low-income housing credit (See Low-income housing credit)
. private activity bonds 147
. . change in use of facility 150
Humane societies (See Cruelty prevention organizations)
Hurricane Katrina
. business credit .... 38(b)
. Gulf Opportunity Zone (See Gulf Opportunity Zone)
Hurricane Rita
. Gulf Opportunity Zone (See Gulf Opportunity Zone)
Hurricane Wilma
. Gulf Opportunity Zone (See Gulf Opportunity Zone)
Husbands and wives (See Spouses)
Hydrochloric acid hazardous waste clean up 4661; 4662
Hydroelectric generation facilities
. environmental enhancements 142
Hydrogen fluoride hazardous waste clean up 4661; 4662
Hydropower facility
. electricity produced from renewable sources; credit ... 45(d)(9)

I

Identification numbers
. adoption expenses 23
. alimony payments 215
. child's return, providing parent PIN on 1
. defined 7701
. dependent care credit 21
. employer 6109
. failure to supply, backup withholding 3406
. incorrectly supplied, backup withholding 3406
. specified information reporting requirement defined 6724
. tax shelters 6111; 6707
Identified straddles 1092
Idling reduction device
. retail excise taxes 4053
Illegal drug sales (See also Narcotic drugs)
. expenses, deductions and credits 280E
Illegal payments
. business expenses 162
. denial of deductions 162
. government officers and employees 162
. Medicare and Medicaid 162
Illness (See Disability)
Immunization programs, excise tax ...... 4131 et seq.; 9510
Impairment related work expenses
. definition 67

Impairment related work expenses —Cont'd
. 2% floor on miscellaneous itemized deductions 67
Imported property
. basis limitation 1059A
. chemicals substances derived from 4671; 4672
. depreciation 168
. transfer price 1059A
. wines 5364
Importer defined 5845
Improvements
. construction costs 263
. deductibility 263
. depreciation deduction 168
. depreciation recapture 1250
. leasehold, depreciation deduction 168
. lessee (See Lessee and lessor)
Imputed interest, deferred payments 163; 1274A
Incentive stock options
. alternative minimum tax .... 56(b)(3)
. . underpayments, interest and penalties .... 53(f)
. defined 422
Includes and including defined 7701
Income
. accumulated (See Accumulation distributions)
. adjusted gross income (See Adjusted gross income)
. allocation of basis, charitable contributions 170
. annualizing (See Annualization of income)
. annuities
. . proceeds of endowment 72
. . proceeds of life insurance contracts 72
. charitable contributions 170
. community income (See Community income)
. deferred (See Deferred compensation)
. definitions
. . estates and trusts 643
. . export trade income 971
. . foreign income 904; 907
. double taxation 7852
. effectively connected with U.S. 864
. errors in reporting, mitigation rule .... 1311 et seq.
. exclusions (See Exempt income)
. expenses for production of 212; 274
. foreign central banks of issues 895
. foreign personal holding companies 551; 553
. foreign trusts 643
. gifts and inheritances 102
. gross income (See Gross income)
. high-taxed income defined 904
. Indian tribal governments, fishing rights treaty 7873
. interest on property placed in trust 170
. international communications, from 863
. international organizations 892
. nonresident aliens 871
. ocean activity, from 863
. ordinary (See Ordinary income)
. partnerships 702; 703
. personal holding companies 543
. . not placed on annual basis 546

193

Income | Index to Code

CODE SEC.

Income —Cont'd
. *personal holding companies—Cont'd*
.. undistributed income 545
. premium assistance credit, health plan coverage
.. terms relating to 36B
. production
.. expenses 212; 274
.. gift expenses 274
.. seminars, expenses for 274
. restoration of amount held under claim of right 1341
. sources .... 861 et seq.
.. definitions 864
.. determination 863
.. effectively connected 864
.. partly within and partly without U.S. 863
.. personal property sales 865
.. special rule for determining 863
.. unregistered obligations 4701
.. within U.S. 861; 864
... expatriation to avoid tax 877
... gross transportation income 887
.. without U.S. .... 862; 864; 901 et seq.
... controlled foreign corporations .... 951 et seq
... currency transactions .... 985 eq seq.
... documentation 982
... earned income .... 911et seq.
... exemptions 912
... export trade corporations .... 970 eq seq.
... foreign tax credit .... 901et seq.
... possessions of U.S. .... 931 et seq.
... S corporations 1373
. space or ocean activity 863
. taxable income (See Taxable income)
. transportation income 863; 887
. trusts and estates
.. benefit of grantor or spouse 677
.. definition 643
.. distributable net income 643
. withholding from wages (See Withholding)
Income earned abroad .... 911 et seq.
. FICA 3101; 3111
. foreign service officers and employees, allowances 6011
. self-employment tax 1402
. Social security taxes 3101; 3111
Income in respect of decedent 61; 691; 753
Income percentage defined 143
Income tax (See also particular items relating to income tax)
. avoidance of (See Evasion or avoidance of tax)
. coordination of collection of income taxes with domestic service employment taxes 3510
. credits against (See Credits against tax)
. deductions (See Deductions)
. estimated (See Estimated income tax)
. foreign (See Foreign taxes)
. self-employed individuals (See Self-employment income tax)
. statistics, publication of 6108
Income tax return preparers (See Preparers of returns)
Incompetent persons
. dependent care assistance programs 129

CODE SEC.

Incompetent persons —Cont'd
. dependent care expenses 21
. disclosure of returns and return information 6103
. foster care payments 131
Inconsistent position
. erroneous actions 1311
Indebtedness
. assumption
.. corporate acquisitions 279; 381
.. exchange of productive-use or investment property 1031
.. insurance contracts 805
.. partners and partnerships 752
.. SEC distributions and exchanges 1081
. at risk amounts 465
. bad debts (See Bad debts)
. controlled corporation, reorganization exchanges 351
. corporate acquisitions 279
. discharge (See Cancellation of indebtedness)
. foreign expropriation losses 1351
. insurance contracts
.. amounts paid or accrued 264
. nonresidents, estate tax and 2104; 2105
. real property reacquisition 1038
. retirement 1017
. subsidiary, to parent 337
. taxable estate 2053
. taxpayer defined 108
. U.S., as offsets against tax overpayments 6402
. worthless, treatment prior to reacquisition of real property as 1038
Indemnity bonds
. defined 4372
. distilled spirits plant (See Distilled spirits plants)
. foreign insurance company, excise tax on bond issued by 4371
. general rules 7101
. multiple versus single bond 7102
Indemnity reinsurance
. gross income computation 803
Independent contractors (See also Self-employed individuals)
. direct sellers 3508
. information returns 6041A
. real estate agents 3508
Indexing for inflation
. rates of tax 1
Indian coal production facility
. electricity produced from renewable sources ...... 45(d)(10)
Indians, American (See Native Americans)
Individual medical benefit accounts 4976
Individual retirement account (IRA) plans
. account requirements 408
.. accumulations, excise tax on 4974
.. excessive contributions, penalties 4973
. accumulations, excise tax on 4974
. active participants, reduced limitations 219
. age 70 1/2 requirement for beneficiaries 219
. allowance of deductions 219

Index to Code — Industrial

	CODE SEC.
Individual retirement account (IRA) plans —Cont'd	
. annuities	219; 408
. . contract, borrowing on	408(e)(3)
. application as to qualification	6104
. armed forces reserves	219
. bank defined for	408(n)
. beneficiary 70 1/2 age requirement	219
. bullion, investment in	408
. charitable purpose, distributions for	408
. coins, investment in	408
. collectibles, investments in	408
. combat zone, armed forces members in	219
. common investment funds, commingling with	408(e)(6)
. common trust funds, commingling with	408(e)(6)
. community property	408
. compensation	219
. contributions	
. . designated nondeductible contributions	408(o)(4)
. . elective deferrals and	25B
. . limits	408(o)(2)
. . nondeductible	408
. . time of	408(o)(3)
. corporation status as bank	408(n)(3)
. custodial accounts	408(h)
. . excess contributions	4973
. deduction of contributions	219
. deemed IRAs	408(q)(1)
. . qualified employer plans	408(q)(2); 408(q)(3)
. . voluntary employee contributions	408(q)(3)(B)
. defined	408(a); 7701
. distributions	
. . charitable	408(d)(8)
. . collectibles, investments in	408
. . contributions returned before return due date	408(d)(4)
. . divorce, transfers incident to	408(d)(6)
. . excess contributions	408(d)(5)
. . gross income	408(d)(1)
. . health savings account funding	408(d)(9)
. . inherited IRAs	402
. . minimum, failure to make	4974
. . rollover contributions	408(d)(3)
. . Sec. 72, special rules for	408(d)(2)
. . simplified employee pensions	408(d)(7)
. . tax treatment	408
. . withholding tax on deferred income	3405
. divorce, transfers incident to	408
. education	530
. election not to deduct contributions	219
. elective deferrals	25B
. employer contributions	219
. employer payments	219
. employers and certain associations of employers, accounts established by	408(c)
. employers and employee association establishment	408
. endowment contracts	219; 4973
. . purchase of	408(e)(5)
. estate tax	2039
. excess contributions	219; 408
. . penalties	4973

	CODE SEC.
Individual retirement account (IRA) plans —Cont'd	
. excise taxes	4973; 4974; 4975
. exemption	
. . losses, employee prohibited transaction	408(e)(2)
. . rules for	408(e)(1)
. firefighters, volunteer	219
. health savings account funding, distributions for	408
. highly compensated, discrimination in favor of	408
. husband and wife	219
. individual retirement annuity defined	408(b)
. information returns	6047; 6058
. inherited IRAs	408
. . distributions	402
. . limitations and restrictions	219
. insured credit union status as bank	408(n)(2)
. investments, collectibles	408
. limitations and restrictions, deductions for contributions	219
. maximum amount of deduction	219
. minimum distributable amount, failure to make	4974
. nondeductible contributions	408
. partial rollovers	408
. pledging of accounts as security	408
. prohibited transactions	408; 4975
. publicity of information required from	6104
. qualified contributions	219
. recontributed amounts	219
. reporting by plan administrator	219
. reports	408(i)
. rollover contributions	219; 408
. Roth IRA	408A
. salary reduction arrangements	408
. security, pledging account as	408(e)(4)
. simple retirement accounts (See Simple retirement accounts)	
. simplified employee pensions (See Simplified employee pension plans)	
. time contribution deemed made	219
. transfers to other plans	6058
. withholding tax	6652
. . deferred income, on	3405
. . information returns	6047
Individual taxpayers (See also Unmarried individuals)	
. bankruptcy cases, rules relating to	1398; 1399
. charitable contributions	170
. election to be taxed at corporate tax rate	962
. health insurance cost credits	35
. . advance payment of credit	7527
. . returns related to credit	6050T
. hedging transactions	988
. itemized deductions	63; 161 et seq.
. losses, limitations on deductions	165
. retirement account	408
. returns, excused from filing	6012
. standard deduction	7703
. tax rates	1
. tax tables	3
. taxable income	63
Indoor tanning services (See Tanning services, indoor)	
Industrial development bonds	
. energy credit financing	48

Industrial

CODE SEC.

Industrial development bonds —Cont'd
. hydroelectric generation facilities, environmental enhancements 142
. Indian tribal government, treatment as state 7871
Industrial parks, exempt facility bonds 142
Inflation adjustments
. adoption assistance programs .... 137(f)
. adoption credit .... 36C(h)
. automobiles 280F
. carbon dioxide sequestration credit .... 45Q(d)(7)
. earned income credit 32
. electricity production credit 45
. enhanced oil recovery credit 43
. itemized deductions, limitations 68
. marriage penalty phaseout 1
. personal exemptions 151
. property acquired from decedent dying after December 31, 2009 1022
. rate of tax 1
. standard deduction 63
. taxable income 63
Information
. Alaska Native Settlement Trusts 6039H
. death transfers and gifts, failure to file information with respect to 6716
. loss of U.S. citizenship 6039F; 6039G
. original issue discount 6706
. persons filing income tax returns, concerning 6103
. sale of, exempt organizations
. . failure to disclose availability from Federal government, penalty 6711
. unauthorized disclosure 7213
Information returns .... 6031 et seq.
. abandoned property as loan security 6050J; 6652
. actuarial report 6059
. banks, common trust funds 6032
. beneficiaries, estate and trust 6034A
. brokers 6041; 6041A; 6042; 6045
. . failure to file 6652
. . failure to provide notice to payor 6705
. cafeteria plans 6039D; 6652
. cash payments received 6050I; 6652
. . disclosure to Federal agencies 6103
. charitable contributions, estates and trusts 6034
. clean renewable energy bonds 6049
. collection of foreign items 6041
. common trust funds 6032
. compensation 6041; 6051; 6652
. compliance, failure to comply 6723
. comply, failure to 6723
. consumer cooperatives 6044
. corporate dissolution or liquidation 6043
. creation or transfers to certain foreign trusts 6048
. damages for fraudulent returns 7434
. dealers 6041; 6045
. debt instruments 1275; 6049
. . original issue discount 6706
. deferred compensation plans 6058; 6103
. defined 6724

Index to Code

CODE SEC.

Information returns —Cont'd
. direct sellers 6041A
. disclosure
. . SSI or RRA benefits, withholding 6103
. dissolution of corporation 6043
. dividends .... 6041 et seq.; 6652
. donated property, exempt organizations 6050L
. educational assistance programs 6039D; 6652
. electronic filing, promotion of 6011
. employee retirement and benefit plans 6652
. . fringe benefit plans 6039D; 6652
. employee stock options 6039
. employees' trust and annuity plans 6047; 7207
. employment taxes 6051
. estates or trusts 6034A
. executors or receivers, notice of qualification 6036
. exempt organizations (See Exempt entities and organizations)
. failure to file 6652; 6695; 6721; 6724
. . foreign persons, transfers to 6038B
. . foreign subsidiaries 6038
. . foreign trusts .... 6677 et seq.
. . foreign-owned U.S. corporations 6038A
. . penalties 6652
. failure to include correct information 6723
. FICA 6051
. fiduciaries to beneficiaries 6034A
. first-time homebuyers
. . refundable credit for 10% of purchase price ..... 36(e)(1)
. fishermen 6050A
. fishing boat operators 6050A
. foreclosed property as loan security 6050J; 6652
. foreign corporations (See Foreign corporations)
. foreign currency payments received 6050I; 6652
. foreign financial asset (See Foreign financial assets)
. foreign partnerships 6046A
. foreign personal holding companies 551; 6035
. foreign sales corporations 6686
. foreign trusts 6048; 6677
. fringe benefit plans 6039D; 6652
. generation-skipping transfers 2662
. group legal services plans for employees 6039D
. group-term life insurance 6052; 6652
. identifying numbers (See Identification numbers)
. income, estate, and gift taxes 6011
. independent contractors, payments to 6041A
. individual retirement account or annuity 6047
. individual retirement savings plans 408
. inspection 6104
. interest
. . cooperative housing corporations 6050H
. . debt instruments 6049
. . magnetic tape, use of 6011
. . mortgage credit certificates 6709
. . mortgage interest received in trade or business from individual 6050H
. . real estate mortgage investment conduits 6049
. legal services plans for employees 6039D
. life insurance contracts, employer-owned 6039I
. liquidation of corporation 6043

Index to Code — Installment

CODE SEC.

Information returns—Cont'd
- mortgage credit certificates ... 25; 6709
- original issue discount ... 6049
- partnership income ... 6031
- patronage dividends
  - amounts subject to reporting ... 6044
  - consumer cooperatives ... 6044
  - magnetic tape, use of ... 6011
  - payments of ... 6044
  - penalties ... 6652
  - requirement of reporting ... 6044
- pension plans ... 6047; 6058; 6059; 6163
- periodic actuarial report ... 6059
- persons ... 6041
- political organizations ... 6033
- preparers of returns ... 6060; 6695
- private foundations ... 6033; 6652
- property as loan security, abandonment or foreclosure ... 6050J; 6652
- property interests ... 6039C
- Railroad Retirement Tax Act benefits ... 6050G
- recipient to furnish name and address ... 6041
- retirement savings ... 6047
- return preparers ... 6060; 6107; 6694; 7427
- royalties ... 6050N
- S corporations ... 6037
- Sec. 912 allowances ... 6011
- self-employed retirement plans ... 6047; 7207
- sick pay ... 6051
- $600 or more, payments of ... 6041
- Social Security benefits ... 6050F
- specified information reporting requirement defined ... 6724
- split-interest trusts ... 6034(a)
- statement to employees ... 6039; 6041; 6052
  - fraudulent or failure to furnish ... 6674
- states, payments of refunds and credits ... 6050E
- stock options ... 6039
- tax return preparers ... 6060; 6695; 6696
- tax-favored accounts, failure to provide reports on ... 6693
- $10, payments aggregating less than ... 6652
- termination ... 6043
- tips ... 6053
- transfer of stock ... 6039; 6652
- treaty-based return positions, disclosure of ... 6114
  - failure to disclose ... 6712
- trusts, claiming charitable deductions ... 6034
- trusts and annuity plans ... 6047
- unemployment benefits ... 6050B
- U.S. real property interests ... 6039C
  - penalty for failure to file ... 6652
- verification ... 6201
- wages paid employees ... 6051; 6052
  - receipts for employees ... 6051
  - reporting of tips ... 6053; 6652
  - statement furnished employees ... 6052
- willful failure to supply ... 7203
- with respect to U.S. real property interests
  - penalty for failure to file ... 6652
- withholding tax

CODE SEC.

Information returns—Cont'd
- *withholding tax—Cont'd*
  - employee retirement and benefit plans distributions ... 6047
  - statements ... 6051; 6652

Informers, rewards to ... 7214; 7623

Inhalers, metered-dose ... 4682

Inheritance taxes (See also Death taxes; Estate tax; Foreign death taxes)
- charitable bequests reduced by ... 2055; 2106
- credit against estate tax ... 2011; 2014; 2015
  - nonresident aliens ... 2102
- deductibility ... 275
  - estate tax purposes ... 2053; 2106
- redemption of stock to pay ... 303; 312
- refunded, estate tax redetermination ... 2016

Inheritances (See also Bequests; Devises; Estates and trusts)
- basis for gain or loss ... 1014; 1223
- depreciation recapture ... 1250
- employee stock options ... 421
- exemption ... 102
- income ... 102
- individual retirement savings plans ... 219; 408
- S corporation stock ... 1361
  - adjustment to basis ... 1367(b)(4)
- shrinkage in value ... 273

Injunction against assessment and collection ... 7421
- deficiencies ... 6213
- 501(c)(3) organizations
  - political campaign expenses, prohibited ... 7409
  - third parties ... 7426

Injuries, personal (See Personal injury and sickness)

Inland waterway commercial transportation
- fuel tax ... 4042

Inland Waterways Trust Fund ... 9506

Innocent spouse
- liability ... 66; 6013
- relief, partner's spouse claiming ... 6230

Insolvency
- alternative minimum tax ... 58
- bankruptcy (See Bankruptcy)
- banks, exemption ... 7507
- defined ... 418E
- multiemployer plans ... 418E
- ownership change ... 382
- receivers (See Receivers)

Inspection (See Examination and inspection; Public inspection)

Installation charges, telephone ... 4253

Installment accounts, sales of ... 4216; 6416

Installment method of accounting ... 453 et seq.

Installment obligations
- basis ... 453B; 1038
- carryovers, acquiring corporation ... 381
- decedents ... 691
- husband and wife ... 453B
- repossessions, gain or loss on realty ... 1038

Installment

	CODE SEC.
Installment payment of tax	6315
. agreements for	6159
. carrybacks, expected	6164
. declaratory judgments	
. . estate eligibility with respect to installment payments under Sec. 6166	6159
. . Sec. 6166, eligibility of estate under	7479
. failure to make	6601
. . estate tax, closely held business interest	6166
. . estimated tax by corporations	6655
. . foreign expropriation loss recoveries	6167
. foreign expropriation loss recoveries	6167
. highway vehicle use tax	6156
. interest on underpayment, nonpayment or extensions	6601
. . estate tax, closely held business interests	6166
. . foreign expropriation loss recoveries	6167
. overpayment	6403
Installment sales	453; 453A
. alternative minimum tax	56
. bad debts	1038
. carrying charges	163
. deferred tax liability	453A
. earnings and profits of corporation, adjustment for	312
. gain or loss	1001
. . repossession of property	1038
. imputed interest	163; 1274A
. interest	163; 469
. manufacturer's excise taxes	4216; 6416
. reacquisition	1038
Instruction booklets	
. graphic illustration requirements	7523
Instrumentalities of U.S.	
. depreciation deduction, used or leased property	168
. disclosure of returns and return information	6103
. employee retirement or benefit plan benefits	414
. employment taxes	3112
. exempt income	115; 501
. federally guaranteed bonds	149
. FICA	3112; 3308
. FUTA	3306
. occupational taxes, alcohol	4906; 5143
. Social security taxes	3112
. wagering and occupational tax	4906; 5143
Insufficient consideration, transfers for	
. gross estate, effect on	2043
Insulation	
. advanced insulation, retail excise tax	4053
Insulin	
. reimbursements	106(f)
Insurance	
. accident and health plans, amounts received	105
. casualty losses, living expenses compensation	123
. conscientious objections to	1402
. contracts, payment on	264
. crop damage	451
. designated settlement funds, transfers of amounts to	468B
. estate tax (See Estate tax subhead life insurance)	
. exemption	

Index to Code

	CODE SEC.
Insurance —Cont'd	
. exemption —Cont'd	
. . casualty loss reimbursements	123
. . commercial type insurance	501
. foreign insurers, policies issued by	4371 et seq.
. indebtedness	
. . amounts paid or accrued	264
. life (See Life insurance)	
. minimum funding standards	412
. payments	
. . deductibility	264
. . limitations on deductions	264
. . nondeductibility	264
. reinsurance transactions, amortization of	197
. stamp taxes	7270
Insurance agents, FUTA	3306
Insurance companies	801 et seq. (See also Foreign insurance companies; Life insurance companies)
. accounting period	843
. adjustments to contracts	848
. alternative tax	831
. amortization of bond premium or discount	834
. attorney-in-fact	835
. Blue Cross/Blue Shield	833
. bond purchases	832
. business expenses	834
. capital gains and losses	834
. capitalization of policy acquisition expenses	848
. carryovers	
. . acquiring corporation, by	381
. . losses	844
. ceding commissions	848
. consolidated returns (See Consolidated returns)	
. contract as qualified pension plan	401
. controlled group of corporations	1563
. cooperative association, taxed as	1381 et seq.
. corporation status	7701
. deductions	805; 832 et seq.; 848
. depletion	834
. definitions	832
. depreciation	834
. discounted unpaid losses	
. . estimated tax payments	847
. distributions to shareholders	
. . 2005 and 2006 rules	815
. dividends	316
. . affiliated group members, paid to	832
. . double deductions	832; 834
. election	
. . foreign company treated as domestic	953
. . reciprocal	835
. expenses incurred defined	832
. foreign (See Foreign insurance companies)	
. foreign tax credit	841
. government obligations	832
. gross income defined	832
. gross investment income defined	834
. guaranteed renewable contracts	848
. imposition of tax	831

Index to Code

CODE SEC.

Insurance companies—Cont'd
. interest 834
. interinsurers 832
. investment expenses 834
. investment income
.. defined 832
.. determination of taxable 834
. lease guaranty insurance 832
. life insurance companies (See Life insurance companies)
. liquidation or termination of business 847
. loss carryover 844
. losses incurred defined 832
. mortgage guaranty insurance 832
. mutual 835
. net operating losses 831; 834
. net premiums 834; 848
. operations loss deduction (See Operations loss deduction)
. other than life or mutual .... 831 et seq.
.. gross income 543
.. personal holding company income 543
. policy acquisition expenses, capitalization of 848
. policyholder dividends 832; 834
. premiums earned defined 832
. qualified foreign contracts 848
. real estate expenses 834
. reciprocal underwriters' election 835
. reinsurance agreements 848
. REITs 856
. small companies, alternative tax 831
. specified insurance contract defined 848
. stock insurance companies 833
. successor, carryovers 381
. tax imposed 11
. taxable income 832
. taxation of .... 1381 et seq.
. title insurance 832
. underwriting income defined 832
Insurance policies
. exchanges 1031; 1035
. foreign, excise taxes on .... 4371 et seq.; 7270
. levy against 6332
. lien for taxes, priority 6323
Insurance premiums
. adjustment defined 809
. amortization of 811
. deductibility 264
. earned on insurance contracts during taxable year 832
. group-term life (See Group-term life insurance)
. insurance company gross income 803
. medical expenses 213
. net premiums defined 834; 848
. title insurance 832
Insurance programs
. federally guaranteed bonds 149
Intangible drilling and development costs
. alternative minimum tax 56
. amortization 291
. capital expenditures 263; 263A

CODE SEC.

Intangible drilling and development costs —Cont'd
. earnings and profits computation 312
. inventory costs 263A
. outside U.S. 263
. preference items 57
. reduction in deductions 291
. straight line recovery, tax preference item ... 57
. tax preferences 291
.. excess costs .... 57(a)(1)(B)
.. independent producer exception ..... 57(a)(1)(E)
.. net income .... 57(a)(1)(C)
.. oil, gas, and geothermal properties .. 57(a)(1)(A)
. straight line recovery of intangibles
... defined .... 57(b)(1)
... election of .... 57(b)(2)
Intangible property
. amortization 197
. . disposition of 1245
. foreign corporations, reorganization exchanges 367
. gift transfers, gift tax 2501; 2511
. sale of 865
. Sec. 197 intangible, disposition of
. capital gains and losses 1245
. transfers of 367; 936
Intellectual property
. charitable contributions of income from 170
. copyrights (See Copyrights)
. patents (See Patents)
Intelligence community
. sale of principal residence, exclusion of gain from 121
Intercity rail facilities, high-speed (See High-speed intercity rail facilities)
Interest
. abatement, underpayments due to IRS error 6404
. accumulation distributions 668
. allocation 864
. annuities 72
. Applicable Federal Rate 1274; 7872
. backup withholding 3406; 7205
. bank accounts (See Banks and trust companies)
. below-market rate loans 7872
. business expenses 274
. business use of home 280A
. compounded daily 6622
. cooperative housing corporation 216
. . information returns 6050H
. corporate acquisition indebtedness 279
. corporate interest paid to related taxpayers .. 163
. credit, home mortgages 25
. death benefits 101
. deductions 163; 691
. deferrals
.. market discount bonds 1277
.. short-term obligations 1282
. deferred payment sales 483
. deferred tax amount 1291
. defined 6049
. delinquent payment of taxes 6601; 6621
.. estate tax, closely held business interests 6166

199

CODE SEC.

Interest —Cont'd
. delinquent payment of taxes—Cont'd
.. foreign expropriation loss recoveries 6167
. DISCs, deferred tax liability 995
. distributions by corporations 1291
. educational loans 163; 221
. erroneous refund recoveries 6602; 6621
. estimated tax underpaid 6654; 6655
. exempt income 265
. export financing interest defined 904
. extension of time to pay tax 6601
.. estate tax, closely held business interests 6166
.. foreign expropriation loss recoveries 6167
. failure of Secretary to contact taxpayer
.. suspension of interest and penalties 6404
. failure to report, backup withholding 3406
. foreign 904
.. backup withholding 3406; 7205
.. nonresident aliens and foreign corporations, withholding at source 1441
. foreign corporation income 881
. foreign estates and trusts, accumulation distributions 668
. foreign government 892
. foreign personal holding company income 552; 553
. foreign tax credit 904; 905
. gain or loss on foreign currency transactions treated as ... 988
. gift loans 7872
. governmental obligations
.. declaratory judgments 7478
. gross income 61
. ground rents, redeemable 163
. high-yield discount obligations 163
. home mortgages 25
. imputed 163; 1274A
. information returns 6041; 6049; 6050H; 6652
.. debt instruments 6049
.. magnetic tape 6011
.. real estate mortgage investment conduits 6049
. installment purchases 163; 453A
. installment sales 469
. insurance companies other than life 834
. investment, property held for 163
. investment indebtedness 163
. itemized deductions 163
. jeopardy assessments 6601
. life insurance
.. indebtedness, interest paid on 264
. life insurance companies 812
.. excess interest 809
.. partially exempt 812
.. payments of 805
.. reserves 807
. market discount bonds
.. constant rate, election of 1276
.. deferred interest deduction 1277
.. net direct interest expense 1277
. mortgage credit certificates 163
. mortgages, residential property 25; 163
. nonpayment of tax 6601; 6621

CODE SEC.

Interest —Cont'd
. notice requirement 6631
. obligations, tax-exempt 265
. original issue discount 163
.. current reporting 1272
.. ratable daily portion 1272
. overpayments, on
.. payment of estimated tax 6611
.. rates, determination of 6621
. paid
.. information returns 6049
.. purchase or carry, to
... market discount bonds 1277
... short-term obligations issued at discount 1282
.. taxable year of deduction 461
. penalties 6601
. personal holding companies 543
. personal interest deduction disallowance 163
. points, deduction 461
. prepaid, taxable year of deduction 461
. real estate mortgage investment conduits 860G
. refunds and credits
.. administrative review 6406
.. erroneous refunds recovered 6602; 6621
.. overpayment credited against deficiency 6601; 6611
. registration-required obligations 163
. regulated investment companies 265
. REITs .... 856(f)
. related taxpayers
.. corporate interest paid to 163
.. transactions between 267
. required interest amount defined for tax lien purposes .. 6324A
. residence, qualified 163
. sales or exchanges between related taxpayers 267
. seizure of property, wrongful
.. money received by U.S. 6343; 6621
. short sales 265
. short-term obligations 1282
. small issue bonds 265
. source of income 861; 862
. stamp taxes underpaid 6601
. state and local bonds 103
. statements to recipients 6048
. straddles 263
. tax-exempt obligations 265
. trusts and estates 643
. underpayment of tax 6601; 6622
.. deposits made to suspend interest 6603
.. erroneous refund recoverable by suit 6602
.. estate tax, closely held business interests 6166
.. foreign expropriation loss recoveries 6167
.. increase in rate for large corporate underpayments 6621
.. rates, determination of 6621
. unregistered obligations 4701
. U.S. obligations (See United States obligations)
. vacation home, rental of 280A
. wrongful levy recovery 6343; 6621
Interest expense
. definition 265

Index to Code

CODE SEC.

Interest expense —Cont'd
. financial institution
. . allocation to exempt interest 265
Interest-free loans 7872
Interinsurers 832; 835
Internal Revenue Code
. basis established by 1052
. construction 7806
. definition 7701
. reference in other laws to 7852
. repeal, effect 7851
Internal Revenue Districts . . . . 7621 et seq.
. canvass for taxable persons and objects 7601
. expenses of detection and punishment of frauds 7623
Internal Revenue laws
. administration of, attempts to interfere with 7212
. application of . . . . 7801 et seq.; 7851 et seq.
. construction of title 7806
. deposit of collections 7808; 7809
. enforcement of . . . . 7601 et seq.
. interference with administration of 7212
. personnel, other 7803
. rules in effect upon enactment of title 7807
. Treasury Department authority 7801
. violation of, property used in 7302
Internal Revenue Service
. Assistant Commissioner (employer plans and organizations)
. . . . 7802
. authority (See Taxpayer bill of rights)
. Chief Counsel . . . . 7803(b)
. Commissioner . . . . 7802; 7803(a)(1)
. construction of title 7806
. depositaries, collection 7808
. employee plans and exempt organizations 7802
. erroneous written advice by 6404
. estate and gift tax valuation, statements supporting 7517
. executive branch influences, prohibition against 7217
. field service 7803
. law enforcement agencies, reimbursements to 7624
. Office of the Taxpayer Advocate . . . . 7803(c)
. officers and employees 7803
. . appointment and supervision 7803
. . authority 7608; 7622
. . delinquent 7804
. . interviews by 7521
. . offenses by 7214; 7215
. Oversight Board
. . disclosure of returns and return information 6103
. rules and regulations 7805; 7807
. training courses 7516
International organizations
. branch profits tax 884
. communications taxes 863; 4253
. compensation of employees 893
. defined 7701
. depreciation deduction, used or leased property 168
. employees
. . exemptions 893

Investment

CODE SEC.

International organizations —Cont'd
. employees —Cont'd
. . FICA 3121
. . withholding tax on wages 3401
. income 892
Intracoastal waterway commercial transportation
. fuel tax 4042
Inventories
. accounting methods . . . . 471 et seq.
. basis
. . election to reduce 1017
. . general rules 1013
. capitalization 263A
. carryovers, acquiring corporation 381
. charitable contributions 170
. costs 263A
. depreciable property, election to treat as 1017
. farms 263A
. imported property, transfer price of 1059A
. inventory property defined 865
. LIFO 472
. . earnings and profits, adjustments to 312
. . liquidation 473
. . S corporation conversion from C corporation, recapture upon
. . . . 1363
. . small businesses 474
. partners and partnerships
. . contribution 724
. . distributions 735; 751
. . substantial appreciation 751
. . transfer of interest, information returns 6050K; 6652
. property basis 1013
. sale of property 865
. small businesses 474
. source of income from 861; 862
Investment companies (See also Real estate investment trusts; Regulated investment companies)
. accumulated earnings tax 533; 535
. foreign (See Foreign investment companies)
. regulated investment companies (See Regulated investment companies)
. reorganization exchanges 351
. small business (See Small business investment companies)
Investment credit
. amount of 46
. at-risk rules 49
. automobiles 280F
. basis adjustments 50
. computation . . . . 46 et seq.
. energy 46; 48; 49
. exempt organizations, property used by 50
. gasification 46
. general business credit 38
. listed property 280F
. lodging, property used for 50
. low-income housing (See Low-income housing credits)
. luxury automobiles 280F
. nonrecourse financing 49
. outside U.S., property located 50

Investment

	CODE SEC.
Investment credit —Cont'd	
. partnerships	50
. recapture	50
. recovery exclusion	111
. reforestation	46
. rehabilitation	46; 47
. S corporations	50; 1371
. unused credit	196
Investment expenses	212
. insurance companies	834
Investment income	
. foreign insurance companies	842
. insurance companies other than life	832; 834
. life insurance companies	812
. net capital gain	1
. net investment income (See Net investment income)	
. qualified possession source investment income defined	936
Investment indebtedness	
. interest	163
Investment interest	163
. foreign corporations	881
. nonresident aliens	871; 1441
Investment property	
. alternative minimum tax bonds	148
. arbitrage bonds	148
. defined	148
. exchange of, nontaxable	1031
. involuntary conversions	1033
. options	1236
Involuntary conversions	
. basis of property acquired through	1033
. capital gains and losses	1231
. carryover basis property	1016
. carryover by acquiring corporation	381
. condemnation of real property held for use or investment	1033
. depreciation recapture	1250
. environmental contamination of livestock	1033
. FCC ordered sales or exchanges	1245; 1250
. gain or loss	1033; 1231
. general rule	1033
. holding period	1223
. installment sales, second dispositions	453
. investment property	1033
. Presidentially declared disasters	1033
. residence sale, exclusion of gain	121
. similar property, conversion into	1033
. special use valuation property	2032A
Involuntary termination	
. moving expenses	217
. work opportunity credit	51
IRAs (See Individual retirement account (IRA) plans)	
Iron ore	
. deductions, disposal expenditure	272
. disposal of	272
. . retained interest	617; 631
. percentage depletion reduction	291
. royalties	

Index to Code

	CODE SEC.
Iron ore —Cont'd	
. *royalties —Cont'd*	
. . capital gains and losses	1231
. . expenditures connected with	
. . . basis adjustments	1016
. . self-employment earnings	1402
. . sales and exchanges	631
Irrigation companies	
. exemption	501
. small irrigation power defined	45
Irrigation projects	
. federal irrigation water defined	90
. federal subsidies, illegal	90
Isonipecaine (See Narcotic drugs)	
Itemized deductions (See also Deductions)	
. alternative minimum tax	56
. corporations	161 et seq.
. defined	63
. disallowed	261 et seq.
. election to itemize	63
. indirect deductions, disallowance	67
. individuals	161 et seq.; 211 et seq.
. limitations	68; 261 et seq.
. miscellaneous, 2% floor on	67

J

Jeopardy	
. termination of taxable year	6851; 6852
Jeopardy assessments	6213; 6861 et seq.; 7429 (See also Assessments; Termination assessments)
. accumulated earnings tax	534
. administrative review	7429
. burden of proof	7429
. interest	6601
. judicial review	7429
. jurisdiction for determination	7429
. large amount of cash, no identification of owner of	6867
. reasonableness of	7429
. restrictions	6213
. review of	7429
. time for filing petition	6213
Jobs credit, new employees	51; 52
Joint and survivor annuities (See Annuities)	
Joint committee on taxation	
. authorization	8001
. chairman	8003
. inspection of returns	6103; 8023
. organization and membership	8001 et seq.
. payment of expenses	8005
. powers and duties	8021 et seq.
. . hearings and sessions	8021
. . investigations	8022
. . simplification of tax, investigation of methods for	8022
. reports	
. . credits and refunds	6405
. . Finance; Ways and Means; Congress	8002
. staff	8004
. vice chairman	8003

Index to Code — Leaking

CODE SEC.

Joint returns . . . . 6013 (See also Returns; Spouses)
. alimony or separate maintenance payments 71
. casualty gains and losses 165
. computation of tax by IRS, election 6014
. credit for the elderly and disabled 22
. deficiency notice 6212
. defined 7701
. disclosure 6103
. imposition of tax 1
. rate of tax 1
. relief from joint and several liability 6015
. self-employment tax 6017
. tax rates 1
Joint stock company corporate status 7701
Joint tenants
. employee stock options 424
. estate tax 2040
Joint venture partnership status 761; 7701
Jointly-held property gain on sale 121
Judges, FICA 3121
Judgment creditor tax lien 6323
Judgments
. disposition of, suits by U.S. 7406
. interest on, personal holding company 543
Judicial and administrative tax proceedings
. disclosure of returns and return information 6103
Judicial proceedings . . . . 7401 et seq.
. employment status determination 7436
. limitation periods . . . . 6531 et seq.
Judicial review
. assessments 7429
. credits against tax, FUTA rules 3310
. jeopardy assessments 7429
. partnership administrative adjustments 6226; 6228
. Presidential election campaign fund 9011
. Presidential primary matching payment account 9041
Jury duty pay 62
Justice Department (See Department of Justice)

K

Katrina, Hurricane
. Gulf Opportunity Zone (See Gulf Opportunity Zone)
Keogh plans (See Self-employed retirement plans)
Kerosene
. aviation grade, gasoline tax . . . . 4081(a)(4)
. excise tax 4041
. exemption, gasoline tax 4082
. farmer, sales to 6427
Key employees
. cafeteria plans 125
. definition 79; 416
. employee retirement and benefit plans 410; 414
. group-term life insurance 79
. top-heavy plans 416
. welfare benefit funds 419A

CODE SEC.

Kickbacks 162
Kiddie tax 1
Kidnapped children, personal exemption 151
Kyanite depletion 613

L

Labor Department (See Department of Labor)
Labor disputes
. work opportunity credit 51
Labor organizations (See also Unions)
. collective bargaining agreements, determination as to status as 7701
. exemption 501
. unrelated business taxable income 511
Land
. acquisition, private activity bond financed 147
. clearing of 1252
. farm land dispositions 1252; 1257
Landfill gas facility
. electricity produced from renewable sources . . . . 45(d)(6)
Large employer health coverage
. applicable large employer . . . . 4980H(c)(2)
. applicable payment amount defined . . . . 4980H(c)(1)
. applicable premium tax credit and cost sharing reduction defined . . . . 4980H(c)(3)
. coordination with credits . . . . 4980H(d)(3)
. denial of deduction . . . . 275; 4980H(c)(7)
. full-time employee defined . . . . 4980H(c)(4)
. inflation adjustment . . . . 4980H(c)(5)
. not offering health coverage, employer . . . . 4980H(a)
. payments upon notice . . . . 4980H(d)(1)
. premium tax credits or cost-sharing reductions, offering
. . free choice vouchers . . . . 4980H(b)(3)
. . generally . . . . 4980H(b)(1)
. . limitations . . . . 4980H(b)(2)
. reporting requirements (See Health insurance coverage subhead reporting)
. time for payment . . . . 4980H(d)(2)
Last-in, first-out inventories (See LIFO inventories)
Laterite depletion 613
Law enforcement agencies, state and local
. drug-related activities investigation costs 7624; 7809
Lead depletion 613
Lead oxide
. hazardous waste clean up 4661; 4662
Leaking Underground Storage Tank Trust Fund (LUST)
. commercial transportation on inland waterways 4042
. creation of fund . . . . 9508(a)
. expenditures . . . . 9508(c)
. financing rate . . . . 4081(c)(3); 6430
. nonhighway use gasoline 6421
. nontaxable use of fuels 6427
. off-highway business use 4041
. rate of tax 4091
. taxes to fund 4041
. transfers . . . . 9508(b); 9508(e)
. U.S. liability limitations . . . . 9508(d)

Leasebacks

	Code Sec.
Leasebacks (See Sale leasebacks)	
Leased employees	
. pension, profit-sharing, and stock bonus plans	414(n)(1)
. . defined	414(n)(2)
. . requirements	414(n)(3)
. . safe harbor	414(n)(5)
. . special rules	414(n)(6)
. . time when first considered leased	414(n)(4)
. retirement and benefit plans	414
Leasehold improvement property depreciation	168
Leases (See also Lessees and lessors)	
. acquisition costs, amortization	178
. amortization of acquisition costs	178
. basis of property	1019
. bonuses, depletion	613; 613A
. business	514
. cancellation of	1241
. definition	168
. depletion allowance	611
. depreciation, improvements to leasehold	168
. disqualified lease	168
. equipment, at risk amounts	465
. exempt entities and organizations	
. . depreciation deduction	168
. . property used by, limitation on allowable deductions on	470
. . realty	514
. exempt property, amortization	168
. false statements about tax	7211
. foreign person or entity	168
. foreign sales and leasing income	941
. government, deduction limitations on property used by	470
. high technology equipment	168
. improvements by lessee on lessor's property	109; 1019
. instrumentalities of U.S.	168
. international organizations	168
. listed property	280F
. long-term automobile leases	4002
. manufacturers excise taxes	4216; 4217
. mineral interests	636
. motor vehicle	4002; 7701
. moving expenses	217
. nonresidential real property	168
. partners and partnerships	168
. possessions of U.S.	168
. railroads, foreign use	
. . income from within U.S.	861
. realty acquired by U.S	7506
. realty by exempt organization	514
. related taxpayers	168
. sales status of automobile lease	4002
. service contracts	7701
. short-term leases	168
. . construction allowances	110
. technological equipment	168
. term defined	168
. unrelated trade or business	168; 514
. U.S.	168

Index to Code

	Code Sec.
Legacies (See also Bequests)	
. taxes, deductibility	275
Legal fees, recovery of	7430
Legal holiday (See Holidays, legal)	
Legal services plans for employees	120
. books and records	6039D
. exemption	501
. FICA	3121
. FUTA	3306
. group legal services plan	120
. information returns	6039D
. railroad retirement taxes	3231
Legislation	
. business expenses	162
. contributions to influence	170
. expenditures to influence	
. . excise tax on excessive	4911
. . Indian tribal government	7871
. . public charities	501
Legislators business expenses	162
Lepidolite depletion	613
Lessees and lessors (See also Leases)	
. accounting method, rental amounts	467
. deferred rental agreements	467
. depreciation recapture	1250
. exempt income	109
. expensing depreciable business assets	179
. improvements by lessee	
. . basis, effect on	1019
. . exempt income	109
. listed property	280F
. noncorporate expensing	179
. renewal option	467
Letter rulings	
. user fee for request	7528
Letters	
. capital asset status	1221; 1231
Levy	6331 et seq. (See also Seizure of Property)
. application of proceeds	6342
. authority of Secretary or delegate	6331
. authority to release levy and return property	6343
. books and records	6333
. certificate of sale	6338; 6339
. child support payments exemption	6334
. civil action to subject property to payment of taxes	7403
. collection after assessment	6502
. date when levy is considered made	6502
. deed to real property	6338
. defined	7701
. employment taxes, disqualified	6331(h)
. enforcement	6332
. exempt from levy, property	6334
. exempt property	6334
. expenses of levy and sale	6341
. hearing, right to	6330(b)
. honoring levy	6332
. notice of sale or seizure	6335
. notice requirement	6330(a)

Index to Code

Lien

	CODE SEC.
Levy—Cont'd	
. penalty for violation	6332
. perishable goods, sale of	6336
. records of sale	6340
. redemption of property	6337
. review of procedures	7429
. salary and wages	6331
. sale of perishable goods	6336
. sale of seized property	6331; 6335; 6336
. summons, levy on date of	6331
. surrender of property	6332
. uneconomical levies	6331
. wages and salary	6334
. wrongful	6343
Liabilities	
. all-events test	461
. assumed (See Indebtedness subhead assumption)	
. contested liabilities	
. . taxable year of deduction	461
. distributed property, gain or loss	336
. earnings and profits	312
. economic performance test	461
. executors	6905
. partnerships	752
. personal injury liability, assignment of	130
. recurring items	461
. reorganization exchanges, assumption in	357; 358
. stock purchase as asset purchase	338
. transferees	
. . notice of fiduciary relationship	6903
. . provisions of special application to	6902
. . transferred assets	6901
Liability for tax	
. alcohol tax	5005; 5041; 5143
. alternative minimum tax, prior year	53
. aviation fuel taxes	4103
. backup withholding	3406
. beneficiaries of estates and trusts	2205 et seq.
. black lung benefit trusts, excise taxes	4951; 4952
. cigars and cigarettes, excise taxes	5703
. collection and withholding	7501
. controlled group of corporations	1552
. credit limitation based on	26; 904(i)
. definition	26
. diesel fuel tax	4103
. distilled spirits	5005
. employment taxes	3505; 3509
. environmental taxes	4611; 4661; 4681
. estate tax	2002; 2205 et seq.
. executors	2204; 6905
. facilities and services taxes	4291
. FICA	3102; 3504; 3505
. fiduciaries	2204
. firearms excise taxes	5801; 5811; 5821
. foreign insurance policies, excise taxes	4374
. fuels taxes	4103
. gallonage tax	5005; 5041
. gasoline tax	4103
. generation-skipping transfer tax	2603

	CODE SEC.
Liability for tax — Cont'd	
. gift tax	2501 et seq.
. harbor maintenance tax	4461
. highway motor vehicle use tax	4481
. manufacturers excise taxes	4219; 4221
. occupational taxes	4902 et seq.; 5091 et seq.
. overpayment where no tax liability exists	6401
. petroleum and petroleum products, excise taxes on	4103
. private foundations	6684
. Railroad Retirement Tax Act	3202; 3505
. recipient of property over which decedent had power of appointment	2207
. satisfied or unenforceable, release of lien	6325
. ship, excise tax on travel by	4471
. special rules for taxable years 2000 through 2011	26
. tobacco products, excise taxes	5703
. transferees	
. . notice of fiduciary relationship	6903
. . provisions of special application to	6902
. . transferred assets	6901
. understatements (See Understatement of tax liability)	
. wagering taxes	4401; 4411; 4901 et seq.
. water transportation, excise taxes for	4471
. wines	5041; 5043
. withholding tax	1461; 3402 et seq.; 3504; 3505
. workers' cooperatives	
. . prohibited allocation of securities	4979A
Liberty Zone (See New York Liberty Zone)	
Licenses	
. cancellation payment	1241
. collection of foreign items	7001; 7231
Lien for taxes	
. additional property requirements	6324A
. administrative appeal	6326
. alcohol taxes	5004
. bond for lien, partial substitution of	6324A
. certificate of discharge or release	6325; 6326
. check dishonored	6311
. civil actions	
. . persons other than taxpayer	6532; 7426
. . U.S. to enforce, by	7403
. definitions	6324A
. discharge	6325; 6326; 7425
. distilled spirits taxes	5004
. enforcement	7403
. estate and gift taxes	6324; 6324B
. exceptions	6323
. fair hearing, right to	6320(b)
. filing	
. . defined	6323
. . requirements	6324A
. gift tax, disposition	2519
. indexing requirements	6323
. intervention by U.S.	7424
. invalidity, without notice	6323
. national filing system	6323
. nonattachment of lien	6325
. notice	6320(a); 6323
. period of	6322; 6324A; 6324B

205

Lien | Index to Code

CODE SEC.

Lien for taxes — Cont'd
. priority 6323
. receivership 7403
. redemption of property by U.S. 7425
. refiling of notice 6323
. release or discharge 6325; 6326; 7425; 7432
. Sec. 6324 lien, in lieu of 6324A
. security substituted 6324B
. subordination 6325
. subrogation 6323
. validity 6323

Life estates
. gift tax on disposition
.. power of appointment in donee spouse 2523

Life expectancy, employee benefit plan 401

Life insurance
. beneficiaries, liability of 2206
. companies (See Life insurance companies)
. contracts (See Life insurance contracts)
. employees 264
. estate tax (See Estate tax subhead life insurance)
. exchanges of policies
.. defined for purposes of exchange 1035
.. long-term care insurance policies or riders ... 1035
.. nontaxable 1035
. group-term (See Group-term life insurance)
. interest paid 264
. officers of corporation 264
. premiums
.. deductibility 264
.. withholding tax on wages 3401
. proceeds (See Life insurance proceeds)
. self-employed retirement plans
.. allocation of contributions 404
.. single premium payments 264
.. withholding tax, information returns 6047

Life insurance companies .... 801 et seq.
. accelerated death benefit riders 818
. accounting methods 811; 814; 816
. adjustments in reserves for policy loans 816
. adjustments to basis 1016
. affiliated groups including mutual parent and stock subsidiary 809
. AFR on reserves 807
. allocations 818
. alternative tax for mutual savings bank conducting life insurance business 594
. amortization of bond premium or discount 805; 811; 1016
. annual statement defined 809
. annualizing income 811
. assessment company reserves 816
. assumption of liabilities by another 805
. average equity base defined 809
. average mutual earnings rate defined 809
. base period earnings rate defined 809
. benevolent, exemption 501
. capital gains and losses 801; 812; 818
. carrybacks and carryovers 381; 810
. charitable contributions 805

CODE SEC.

Life insurance companies — Cont'd
. commissioners' standard tables for computing reserves ... 807
. company's share
.. definition 812
.. investment income 812
. consolidated returns 818; 1503; 1504
. contiguous country branches 814
. contracts (See Life insurance contracts)
. controlled groups 806; 1563
. current stock earnings rate defined 809
. death benefits 805
. debt instruments
.. original issue discount, current reporting 1272
. deductions 804
.. increase in reserves treated as 807
.. mutual companies, reduction for 809
.. operations loss 810
.. policyholder dividends 808
.. reserves 807
.. small companies, for 806
. deficiency reserves 816
. definitions 808; 809; 816; 818
. differential earnings 809
. distributions to shareholders 801; 815
. dividends received deduction 243; 805
. dividends to policyholders (See subhead policyholder dividends)
. domestic 814
. double deductions 811; 812
. elections
.. allocations 818
.. contiguous country branches 814
.. operations loss carryback 809
. employee retirement and benefit plans 809; 817; 818
. equity base 809
. equity percentage defined 809
. excess equity base defined 809
. exemption 501
. experience-rated refunds defined 809
. foreign branches of U.S. 807
. foreign expropriation loss recoveries 80; 1351
. foreign tax credit 814; 841
. fresh-start adjustment for policyholder dividends ... 809
. gain or loss from operations 809; 810
. gross income
.. decrease in reserves treated as 807
.. defined 803
.. exclusions 812
.. investment income 812
. group life insurance contract defined 848
. guaranteed renewable contracts 816
. high surplus mutual life insurance companies ... 809
. imposition of tax 801
. imputed earnings rate defined 809
. installment obligations 453B
. interest
.. deduction 805
.. excess interest defined 809
.. partially exempt 812

Index to Code

CODE SEC.

Life insurance companies—Cont'd
. *interest —Cont'd*
. . policy interest defined 812
. investment advisers 817
. investments
. . income 812
. . . U.S. obligations 817
. look-through rules 817
. losses, carryovers 1503
. modified guaranteed contracts 817A
. mutual life insurance companies 808; 809; 814
. mutual savings banks life insurance departments as 594
. net investment income 812
. net operating loss deduction 805
. new company defined 810
. nonadmitted financial assets defined 809
. nondiversified contracts 816
. noninsurance business items excluded 806; 812
. offset dividend defined 810
. operations loss deduction 805; 810
. ordering rule for distributions to shareholders 815
. pension plans 817; 818
. personal holding company status 542
. policyholder
. . share, definition 812
. . surplus accounts 815
. policyholder dividends 808
. . affiliated group members 818
. . . deduction for 805; 809
. . . exclusion 813
. . gross income computation 803
. . investment income 812
. . . reimbursable 805
. . surplus and capital adjusted for 809
. premiums
. . adjustment defined 809
. . gross income computation 803
. prevailing state assumed interest rate on reserves 807
. property used in trade or business defined 818
. recomputed differential earnings amount 809
. reserves 807
. . amounts not involving life, accident or health contingencies
   816
. . contracts issued before 1/1/85 809
. . . deduction 805; 809
. . deficiency reserves 816
. . defined 816
. . double counting 811; 812
. . gross income computation 803
. . guarantees beyond end of contract year 811
. . nonlife reserves 807
. . required by law 816
. . statutory reserves exceeding tax reserves 809
. . total reserves defined 816
. returns, consolidated 818; 1503; 1504
. safe harbor for diversification 817
. sale of property, gain or loss 818
. savings banks life insurance 594
. segregated asset accounts 817

Lignite

CODE SEC.

Life insurance companies—Cont'd
. shareholders surplus account 815
. short taxable years 811
. small companies 806
. special deductions 806
. statement gain or loss from operations defined 809
. stock earnings rate defined 809
. stock life insurance companies 809
. substandard risk 807
. supplemental benefits 807
. surplus and capital, increase in 809
. tax imposed 11
. tax reserve method 807
. taxable income
. . defined 801
. . short taxable years 811
. . small companies 806
. termination and adjustment of reserves 807
. variable contracts 817
Life insurance contracts 72; 818
. amounts not received as annuities . . . . 72 et seq.
. annuity contracts 817; 818
. controlled foreign corporations 954
. defined 1035; 7702
. employee annuities 72; 403
. employer-owned
. . information returns 6039I
. flexible premium contracts 101
. gross income 61
. proceeds (See Life insurance proceeds)
. qualified plans 401
. variable contracts 817
Life insurance proceeds
. death benefits 101
. flexible premium contracts 101
. gross estate inclusion 2042
. gross income inclusion 72
. nonresidents, estate tax and proceeds on life of 2105
. withholding tax on deferred income 3405
Life tenants
. adjusted gross income 62
. amortization, pollution control facilities 169
. depletion for 611
. depreciation 167
. estates and trusts, depreciation 167
. interest, sale of 1001
. pollution control facilities, amortization 169
. reforestation expenditures 194
. sale or transfer 1001
. shrinkage of interest 273
Lifetime Learning Credit 25A
LIFO inventories (See Inventories)
Light duty trucks
. retailers excise taxes 4051
Lignite
. depletion 613
. excise tax exemption 4121

Like-kind

Like-kind exchanges
. basis for gain or loss 1031
. depreciation, recapture 1245; 1250
. gain or loss 1031
. installment sales 453
. replacements 1033
. sale of principal residence, exclusion of gain from 121
Limestone depletion 613
Limitation period (See Statute of limitations)
Limitations, credit (See Credits against tax)
Limousine retail excise tax 4001
Liquidations
. asset transfers, distributions treated as 336
. basis of property received 334
. collapsible corporation 341
. complete 346
.. basis of property received 334
.. distributions received in .... 331 et seq.
.. liability, distributed property subject to 336
.. liquidating corporation, effect on .... 336 et seq.
.. recipients, effect on .... 331 et seq.
.. subsidiaries (See Subsidiaries subhead liquidations)
. controlled foreign corporation stock
.. redemptions and liquidations 1248
. corporations .... 331 et seq.
.. basis of property received 334
.. collapsible corporations 341
.. employee stock options 424
.. gain or loss .... 331 et seq.
.. liquidating corporation, effect on .... 336 et seq.
.. partial 346
.. purchase of stock 338
.. recipients, effect on .... 331 et seq.
.. stockholders, gain or loss to 331
.. subsidiaries (See Subsidiaries)
.. termination of taxable year by Secretary 6851
. definitions 346
. distributions
.. basis 732
.. personal holding companies 562
. employee stock options 424
. evasion or avoidance of tax 269
. exempt organizations 6043
. foreign corporation reorganization exchanges 367
. gain or loss .... 331 et seq.
. information returns 6043
. installment method used by stockholder 453
. LIFO inventories 473
. liquidating corporation, effect on .... 336 et seq.
. partial liquidation 302; 346
. periodic liquidation, exception
.. REIT stock held 6 months or less, loss on sale of
 .... 857(b)(8)(C)
.. purchase of stock 338
. real estate mortgage investment conduits 860F
. recipients, effect on .... 331 et seq.
. redemption of stock 306
. REIT .... 856; 857(b)(8)(C)

Index to Code

Liquidations —Cont'd
. return regarding corporate dissolution or 6043
. rights, lapsed 2704
. stock and securities
.. options 424
.. qualified stock purchases, tax evasion or avoidance 269
.. redemptions 306
.. REIT stock held for 6 month or less, loss on sale of
 .... 857(b)(8)(C)
. stockholders
.. gain or loss to 331
.. installment method, use of 453
.. receipt of obligations, treatment of 453
. subsidiaries (See Subsidiaries)
. termination of taxable year by Secretary 6851
Liquors .... 5001 et seq. (See also Alcohol taxes; Beer tax; Distilled spirits; Wines)
. administrative procedures 5560
. bonded warehouses
.. distilled spirits .... 5171 et seq.
.. facilities 5178
.. wines .... 5351 et seq.
. bonds 5551
. books and records 5555; 5603
. drawbacks .... 5062; 5131 et seq.
. exports 5062; 5175; 5608
. gallonage taxes .... 5001 et seq.
. imported, alcohol taxes 5001; 5007
. individual retirement savings plans, investments 408
. loss or destruction 5064
. miscellaneous general provisions .... 5551 et seq.
. occupational taxes .... 5091 et seq.
.. imposition and rate of tax 5081
.. nonpayment, penalties 5691
.. permits 5271; 5276
. penalties, seizures and forfeitures ... 5601 et seq.; 5681 et seq.
. prohibited purchases 5117
. retail dealers 5121; 5122
. returns and payment of tax 5061
. revenue protecting apparatus 5552
. state stores 5113; 5114; 5123
. wholesale dealer occupational tax ...... 5111 et seq.; 5691
Listed option defined 1256
Listed property
. limitation on deductions 280F
Listed transaction assessments 6501
Literary organizations
. charitable contributions 170
. exemptions 501
Literary works 1221; 1231
Lithium depletion 613
Litigation
. disclosure of returns and return information 6103
Livestock
. defined 1231
. diseased 1033
. drought sales 451; 1033
. environmental contamination 1033

Index to Code

Long-term

	CODE SEC.
Livestock —Cont'd	
. exchange of different sex animals	1031
. involuntary conversions	1033
. poultry defined as	168(i)(13)(B)(iv)
. replacement with other farm property	1033
. sale of	451; 1033; 1231
Living apart, husband and wife	7703
. childcare expenses	
. . collection of support obligations	6305
. community income	66
. definition	2
. employment-related expenses, credit for	21
. individual retirement accounts	219
. marital status determination	7703
. retirement savings	219
Living expenses	262
. Congressmen	162
. family	262
. insurance compensation for casualty loss	123
Living together	
. dependent status	152
Loans	
. annuities	72
. below-market rate	7872
. Commodity Credit Corporation	77; 1016
. continuing care facilities	7872
. defined for mutual savings banks	593
. DISCs, producer's loans	993
. educational purposes (See Educational loans; Student loans)	
. employee relocation, imputed interest	7872
. employee retirement and benefit plans	4975
. employee stock ownership plans	4975
. exempt organizations	503
. federal	
. . disclosure of applicant's tax delinquency	6103
. FHA insured	
. . private activity bonds, financed with	147
. financial institution, federally guaranteed loan to	149
. gift	7872
. government-insured, distribution of proceeds	312
. home improvement, mortgage revenue bonds	143
. information returns	
. . property as security, abandonment or foreclosure	6050J; 6652
. insured by U.S.	
. . distribution of proceeds	312
. interest-free	7872
. lien against taxes	6323
. low interest	7872
. personal use	1272; 1275
. pooled financing bonds (See Pooled financing bonds)	
. private activity bonds, financed with (See Private activity bonds)	
. proceeds, distribution of	312
. production payments of mineral interests as	636
. property subject to, gain or loss	7701
. qualified electing fund	1294
. rehabilitation, mortgage revenue bonds	143
. repayment, arbitrage bonds	148

	CODE SEC.
Loans —Cont'd	
. reserves for losses on	585; 593
. student (See Student loans)	
Lobbying	
. contributions	170
. expenses	
. . activities	501
. . business	162
. . charitable organizations	4911; 4912; 6852; 7409
. . definitions	4911
. . disqualified	4912
. . excessive, excise tax	4911
. . Indian tribal government	7871
. . status of organization	504
. grass roots lobbying expenditures	501; 4911
. loss of exemption due to, status after	504
. organizations, generally	501
Local benefit tax deductibility	164
Local bonds	
. exemption requirements	141 et seq.
. interest	103
Local taxes (See State and local taxes)	
Local telephone service	4251 et seq.
Lodges (See Fraternal organizations)	
Lodging (See Meals and lodging)	
Logging industry highway use tax exemption	4483
Long-term automobile lease	4002
Long-term capital gains and losses (See Capital gains and losses)	
Long-term care benefits, reporting	6050Q
Long-term care insurance	
. chronically ill individuals	7702B(c)(2)
. consumer protection provisions	7702B(g)
. defined	7702B(b)
. employee annuities	403
. government plan distributions for	402
. health status, discrimination based on	9802
. issuer qualifications	4980C
. licensed health care practitioner	7702B(c)(4)
. life insurance or annuity contract coverage	7702B(e)
. Medicare	7702B(b)(2)
. multiemployer plans	9803
. personal care services	7702B(c)(3)
. preexisting conditions	9801
. qualified long-term care services defined	7702B
. renewability in multiemployer plans	9803
. state maintained plans	7702B(f)
. treatment as accident and health care contract	7702B
Long-term contracts	460
. accounting methods	460
. alternative minimum tax computation	56
. capital expenditures	263A
. inventory costs	263A
Long-term family assistance recipients	
. incentives for employing	51A
. work opportunity credit	51

209

Long-term   Index to Code

	Code Sec.
Long-term real property defined	110
Lookback method, computation of interest	460
Loss corporation	382
Losses (See also Gain or loss)	
. alternative minimum tax loss denial	58
. business losses	164; 165
. capital (See Capital gains and losses)	
. casualty (See Casualty losses)	
. dealers in securities	1236
. deductions	
. . amount of	165
. . estate tax	2054; 2106
. . wash sales	1091
. disaster (See Disaster losses and relief)	
. discounted unpaid	847
. distilled spirits	5006; 5008; 5064
. exchanges	1001
. federally declared disasters	165
. financial institutions, insolvent	165
. fire (See Fire losses)	
. foreign currency	988
. foreign expropriations (See Foreign expropriation losses)	
. gambling	165
. insurance company carryovers	844
. late-year	
. . regulated investment companies	852
. limitation, losses of individuals	165
. malicious mischief	5064
. net operating loss (See Net operating losses)	
. nonresident aliens	873; 897
. ordering rules, DISC	996
. ordinary defined	65
. overall foreign loss defined	904
. partner's distributive share	704
. real estate mortgage investment conduits	860C
. recapture of foreign	904
. registration-required bonds	165
. regulated investment company stock held less than 6 months	852
. rehabilitation of rental	1250
. REIT shares held less than 6 months	857
. repossessions	1038
. S corporation passthrough to shareholders	1366
. separate limitation losses	904
. shipwreck	165
. small business investment companies	
. . loss of company	1243
. . loss of stock	1242
. small business stock	1244
. storm (See Storm losses)	
. straddles	1092; 1234A
. taxable estates	2054
. theft (See Theft losses)	
. transactions entered into for profit	164; 165
. uninsured property	1231
. unpaid	847
. unregistered obligations	4701
. vandalism	5064
. wagering	165

	Code Sec.
Losses (See also Gain or loss) —Cont'd	
. wash sales of stock	1091
. worthless securities	165
Lot sales	1237
Lottery taxes (See Wagering taxes)	
Low-income allowance	6012
Low-income communities	
. new markets; credits against tax	45D
Low-income housing credit	42
. aggregate credit allowed, limitation on	
. . agency allocation in excess of limits	42(h)(7)(B)
. . allocated to building, credit exceeding amount	42(h)(1)
. . commitment to low-income housing requirement, long-term	42(h)(6)
. . housing credit agency defined	42(h)(8)(A)
. . housing credit dollar amount for agencies	42(h)(3)
. . location of building	42(h)(7)(A)
. . nonprofit organizations, ceiling set-aside for project involving qualified	42(h)(5)
. . percentage and maximum qualified basis, agency specified	42(h)(7)(D)
. . possession status as state	42(h)(8)(B)
. . reduction of credit if dollar amount is less that allowed credit without regard to placed in service	42(h)(7)(C)
. . taxable years ending during or after allocation year	42(h)(2)
. . tax-exempt bonds, buildings financed by	42(h)(4)
. annual reports	
. . housing credit agencies	42(l)(3)
. . Secretary, to the	42(l)(2)
. at-risk rules	
. . failure to fully repay	42(k)(4)
. . present value of financing	42(k)(3)
. . qualified basis, use in determining	42(k)(1)
. . qualified person, special rules for determining	42(k)(1)
. building with four or fewer units	42(i)(3)
. certification with respect to first year of credit period	42(l)(1)
. compliance period defined	42(i)(1)
. credit period defined	42(f)(1)
. disposition of property	42(f)(4)
. eligible basis	
. . adjusted basis, determination of	42(d)(4)
. . disproportionate standards for units	42(d)(3)
. . new buildings, 70% present value credit	42(d)(1)
. . other buildings, 30% present value credit	42(d)(2)
. estates and trusts, application to	42(i)(6)
. existing building defined	42(i)(5)
. federally or state-assisted building	42(d)(6)
. . acquisition of building before end of prior compliance period	42(d)(7)
. federally subsidized, determination of whether building is	42(i)(2)
. first year of credit period	
. . certification with respect to first year of credit period	42(l)(1)
. . determination of applicable percentage with respect to increase in qualified basis	42(f)(3)
. . special rule for	42(f)(2)
. first year of credit period, special rule for	42(f)(2)
. general business credit	38

Index to Code

Low-income housing credit—Cont'd

	Code Sec.
housing credit agencies	
..annual report from	42(l)(3)
..defined	42(h)(8)(A)
..housing credit dollar amount	42(h)(3)
..housing credit dollar amount allocation to project exceeding amount considered feasible	42(m)(2)
..percentage and maximum qualified basis, agency specified	42(h)(7)(D)
..plans for allocation of credit among projects	42(m)(1)
..responsibilities	42(m)(1)
.low-income housing grants, coordination with	42(i)(8)
.low-income unit defined	42(i)(3)
.new building defined	42(i)(4)
.new buildings, 70% present value credit	
..determination of	42(b)(1)
..eligible basis	42(d)(1)
..temporary minimum credit rate for non-federally subsidized new buildings	42(b)(1)
.other buildings, 30% present value credit	
..determination of	42(b)(1)
..eligible basis	42(d)(1)
...existing buildings	42(d)(2)
..temporary minimum credit rate for non-federally subsidized new buildings	42(b)(1)
.owner-occupied buildings	42(i)(5)
.partnerships	267
.qualified basis determination	42(c)(1)
.qualified low-income building	42(c)(2)
.qualified low-income housing project	
..date, requirement	42(g)(3)
..de minimis equity contribution, special rule	42(g)(6)
..de minimis errors and recertifications, waiver of	42(g)(8)
..defined	42(g)(1)
..election to treat building not part of project after compliance period	42(g)(5)
..gross-rent defined	42(g)(4)
..rent-restricted units define	42(g)(2)
..scattered site projects	42(g)(7)
.recapture	42(j)(1)
..accelerated portion of credit	42(j)(3)
..additional credit	42(j)(4)(C)
..amount, determination of	42(j)(2)
..casualty loss	42(j)(4)(E)
..credits against tax	42(j)(4)(D)
..de minimis changes in floor space	42(j)(4)(F)
..disposition of building which continues in qualified use	42(j)(6)
..husband and wife partnership	42(j)(5)(C)
..partnership treated as taxpayer	42(j)(5)
..qualified basis into account, taking	42(j)(4)(B)
..tax benefit rule	42(j)(4)(A)
.regulations, prescribed	42(n)
.rehabilitation credit	
..existing building credit not to begin before allowance of	42(f)(5)
.rehabilitation expenditures	
..defined	42(e)(2)
..minimum expenditures	42(e)(4)
..separate new building status	42(e)(1)

Low-income housing credit—Cont'd
rehabilitation expenditures—Cont'd

	Code Sec.
..special rules	42(e)(4)
.right of first refusal to acquire property, tenant	42(i)(7)
.rural projects	42(i)(8)
.single-room occupancy	42(i)(3)
.students and low-income building status	42(i)(3)
.transitional housing	42(i)(3)

Low-income housing grants
.low-income housing credit coordinated with	42(i)(8)

Low-income taxpayer clinics
.funds for, appropriated	7526

Low-sulfur diesel fuels
.adulterated, penalties for	6720A
.credit determination	45H
.deduction	280C(d)
.general business credit	38; 196
.unused business credits	196

Lump-sum distributions and payments
.annuity in lieu of lump-sum distribution, option to receive	72
.railroad retirement benefits, tier 1	86
.retirement plans, adjusted gross income	62
.Social Security benefits	86

LUST (See Leaking Underground Storage Tank Trust Fund)

Luxury automobiles
.depreciation	280F
.excise tax	4001
..first retail sale defined for	4002
..parts and accessories	4003

Luxury tax
	4001 et seq. (See also Excise taxes)
.limousines	4001
.luxury automobiles	4001; 4003
.passenger vehicles	4001

M

Machine guns (See also Firearms)
.defined	5845
.excise tax exemption	4182

Machine-readable returns ... 6011

Magazine vendors
.FICA	3121
.FUTA	3306
.withholding tax on wages	3401

Magazines
.circulation expenses	173
.prepaid subscriptions	455
.returned, accounting methods	458

Magnesite depletion ... 613
Magnesium chloride depletion ... 613

Magnetic tapes
.alcohol tax payment by	5061
.returns on	6011
..partnership	6724

Mail and mailing (See also Postal service, U.S.)
.certified mail, use of	6212; 7455; 7502
.electronic filing and	7502
.filing and paying, mailing treated as	7502

Mail Index to Code

CODE SEC.

Mail and mailing (See also Postal service, U.S.) —Cont'd
. levies on mail 6334
. registered mail, use of 6212; 7502
. timely mailing treated as timely filing 7502
Major integrated oil company depreciation 167
Major party
. defined for presidential election campaign fund 9002
Making work pay credit
. allowance .... 36A(a)
. earned income defined .... 36A(d)(2)
. eligible individual defined .... 36A(d)(1)
. modified gross income
.. defined .... 36A(b)(2)
.. limitations .... 36A(b)
. reduction for certain other payments .... 36A(c)
. termination of .... 36A(e)
Malicious mischief losses 5064
Manganese depletion 613
Manufactured housing
. low-income housing credit 25
Manufacturers
. defined 4221; 5845
. disclosure of operations by Federal employees 7213
. excise taxes (See Manufacturers excise taxes)
. long-term contracts, accounting methods 460
Manufacturers excise taxes .... 4064 et seq.
. accounting procedures for like articles 6416
. aircraft supplies 4221
. automotive and related items .... 4064 et seq.; 9503
. bankruptcy and receiverships, sale of installment accounts
 4216
. buses 4221; 6416
. coal 4121
. collection 6302
. conditional sales 4216
. consignment sales 4216
. constructive sale price 4216
. credit on returns 6416
. exemptions .... 4221 et seq.
. exports 4221; 4222; 6416
. firearms 4181; 4182; 4222
. fishing equipment 4161; 4162; 9504
. floor stock taxes 6412
. further manufacture special rules 4223
. gas guzzler tax 4064; 4217
. gasoline .... 4081 et seq.; 6420; 6421; 6426; 9503
. Highway Trust Fund 9503
. information reporting 4104
. installment sales 4216; 6416
. leases 4216; 4217
. liability for tax 4219; 4221
. motor vehicles, Highway Trust Fund 9503
. Native Americans
.. crafts 4225
.. exemptions 4225; 7871
.. tribal government, treatment as state 7871
.. petroleum products 6426
.. possessions of U.S. 4293

CODE SEC.

Manufacturers excise taxes—Cont'd
. price
.. defined 4216
.. readjustments 6416
. reciprocal exemptions, foreign countries 4221
. recreational equipment .... 4161 et seq.; 6302
. refunds and credits 6416
.. buses 6421
.. farm-use gasoline 6206; 6420; 6421; 6675
.. gasoline 6675
.. local transit systems gasoline 6206
.. nonhighway use gasoline or special fuels 1366; 6206; 6421; 6675
. registration 4222
. repossessions 6416
. resales 4221; 4223; 6416
. returned articles 6416
. sales by other than manufacturer or importer 4219
. sales for further manufacture 4221; 4223; 6416
. sales price 4216
. sonar device 4162
. special provisions applicable to .... 4216 et seq.
. special rules relating to further manufacture 4223
. sporting goods 4161; 4162; 9504
. state and local government exemption 4221; 4222; 6416
. supplies for vessels or aircraft 4221; 4222
. tax-free sales 4221; 4222
. tires .... 4071 et seq.; 4221; 9503
. U.S. use 4293
. use by manufacturer or importer, as sale 4218
. use in further manufacture .... 4221 et seq.
. vaccine 4131; 4132
. vessel supplies 4221; 4222
Manufacturing equipment
. semiconductor, depreciation 168
Manufacturing facility
. exempt facility bonds 142
. private activity bonds 144
Marble depletion 613
March 1, 1913, basis 1053
Marginal wells
. credit for producing oil and gas from
.. amount .... 45I(b)(1)
.. nonconventional sources exclusion .... 45I(d)(3)
.. operating interest .... 45I(d)(2)
.. production attributable to taxpayer .... 45I(d)(1)
.. qualified crude oil and natural gas production .... 45I(c)(1)
.. reduction as oil and gas prices increase .... 45I(b)(2)
. marginal oil and gas production 45I; 613A
.. carrybacks of unused credits, 5-year 39
Marijuana
. Bureau of Customs authority 7607
Marine and hydrokinetic renewable energy facility
. electricity produced from renewable sources credit ... 45(d)(11)
Marine Corps (See Armed forces)
Marital deduction
. estate tax
.. alien surviving spouse of U.S. citizen 2056

212

Index to Code

Medical

	CODE SEC.
Marital deduction —Cont'd	
. estate tax —Cont'd	
. . alternate valuation	2032
. . disallowance of deduction	2056
. . gross estate, effect of deduction on	2044
. . nonresident alien decedent with citizen spouse	2106
. . nonresident alien surviving spouses	2056
. . qualified domestic trust	2056
. . recovery	2207A
. . survivor annuities	2056
. . taxable estate	2056
. gift tax	
. . alien surviving spouse of U.S. citizen	2523
. . extent of deduction	2524
. . recovery	2207A
. . noncitizen spouse	2056; 2523
Marital status	
. determination date	7703
. . generation-skipping transfers, tax on	2651
. . joint returns	6013
. . withholding tax on wages	3402
. disabled persons, credit for	22
. elderly, credit for	22
. employment-related expenses credit	21
. residential property sales	121
. taxable income	63
Mark to market	
. marketable stock election	1296
. Sec. 1256 contracts	1256
. securities dealers	475
Market discount bonds	1276 et seq.
. accrued market discount	1276
. basis adjustment	1278
. constant interest rate accrual of discount	1276
. current inclusion of market discount	1278
. definitions	1278
. interest deduction deferral	1277
. interest paid to purchase or carry	1277
. market discount defined	1278
. net direct interest expense	1277
. ordinary income	1276
. original issue discount	1276; 1278
. ratable accrual of discount	1276
. reorganization	1278
. special rules	1278
Marriage penalty	
. elimination, 15% bracket	1
. phaseout	1
Married filing separately	
. joint return after filing separate returns, additions to tax	6013
. Sec. 179 property election to expense	179(b)(4)
. standard deduction, when spouse itemized	63(c)(6)(a)
. tuition deduction	222(d)(4)
Married persons (See Spouses)	
Mass transit	
. exempt facility bonds	142
. FICA	3121
. high-speed intercity rail facilities (See High-speed intercity rail facilities)	

	CODE SEC.
Mass transit —Cont'd	
. Highway Trust Fund, Mass Transit Account	9503
Master limited partnerships (See Publicly traded partnerships)	
Matching funds	
. low income taxpayer clinics	7526
Matching taxable years	
. related taxpayers, transactions between	267
Material advisors, reportable transactions	6111
. lists of	6112
. retention of information	6112
Material interest	
. disclosure of returns and return information	6103
Material participation	
. defined	469
. family owned businesses	2057
. passive activity losses and credits	469
Maternity or paternity leaves	
. employee retirement and benefit plans	
. . breaks in service requirements	410; 411
Maximum capital gains tax (See Capital gains and losses)	
Meals and lodging	
. business expenses	162; 274
. camps, foreign	119
. campus lodging	119
. educational organizations, employees	119
. 80% deduction limitation	274
. employees	274
. employer's convenience	119
. exception, exclusion from gross income	119
. exclusion from gross income	119
. expense deductions	170
. FICA	3121
. fixed charges	119
. FUTA	3306
. medical expense	213
. moving expenses	217
. rent, campus lodging	119
. substantiation of expenses	274
. temporary quarters	217
Mechanical dye injection systems	
. security, tampering or failure to provide	6715A
Mechanic's lien priority over tax lien	6323
Medicaid	
. bribes and kickbacks	162
. preexisting conditions, crediting previous coverage	9801(f)(3)
Medical benefit accounts	415; 4976
Medical care defined	213
Medical devices, manufacturers' sales of	
. 2.3%-of-sales-price excise tax on	4191(a)
. . exemption from	4191(b)(2)
. . taxable medical device defined	4191(b)
Medical expenses	213
. accident and health plans, amounts received under	105
. employee retirement and benefit plans	401
. gift tax exclusion	2503
. health savings accounts, qualified for	223

213

Medical | Index to Code

CODE SEC.

Medical expenses—Cont'd
. injuries or sickness, compensation for 104
. medical savings accounts, Archer 220
. partnerships 703
. qualified retirement plans 72
. reimbursements, withholding tax on wage 3401
. special rule for 2013, 2014, 2015 and 2016 . . . . 213(f)
. travel away from home 213

Medical research organizations (See also Research organizations)
. charitable contributions 170
. legislation, expenditures to influence 501

Medical savings accounts, Archer
. adjusted gross income 62
. contribution defined 3231
. cost-of-living adjustments 220
. death of account holder 220
. deductions 220
. distributions, tax treatment of . . . . 220(f)(4)
. divorce 220
. employer contributions 106
. excess contributions 4973
. failure to make comparable contribution, employer 4980E
. family coverage 220
. high deductible health plans 220
. prohibited transactions, excise tax 4975
. qualified medical expenses defined . . . . 220(d)(2)
. rollover contributions 220
. small employers 220
. trustees, reporting by 220

Medicare
. bribes and kickbacks 162
. federal employees, eligibility 3121
. health savings accounts 223
. part B premium subsidy adjustment
. . disclosure of returns and return information 6103

Medicare Advantage MSA 138

Medicines
. alcohol used in preparation, drawback of 5111
. expenses 213
. prescription drugs (See Prescription drugs)
. U.S. possession, shipments from 7652

Membership organizations
. dues
. . deductibility 274
. . prepaid, income 456
. transactions with members, deductions incurred 277

Memoranda
. capital asset status 1221; 1231
. noncapital asset status 1221

Mental health benefit
. limitations, group health plans 9812
. parity for . . . . 9812(a)

Merchandise returned, accounting for 458

Merchant Marine Act
. capital construction fund 7518
. personal holding company income 543

CODE SEC.

Mercury
. depletion 613
. environmental tax for hazardous waste clean up . . 4661; 4662

Mergers (See also Reorganization exchanges)
. employee stock options 424
. partnerships 708
. private foundations, excess business holding 4943
. returns relating to 6043A

Metal mines depletion 613

Methane hazardous waste clean up 4661; 4662

Methanol, special fuels tax 4041

Mica depletion 613

Microturbine property energy credit . . . . 48(c)(2)

Mileage allowances
. charitable contributions 170

Military and naval forces (See also Armed forces)
. defined 7701

Military benefits (See Armed forces)

Mine rescue team training credit
. amount of credit . . . . 45N(a)
. business credit . . . . 38(b)
. deduction . . . . 280C(e)
. eligible employer . . . . 45N(c)
. qualified mine rescue team employee . . . . 45N(b)
. termination . . . . 45N(e)
. wages defined . . . . 45N(d)

Mine safety equipment
. election to expense . . . . 179A(b)
. election to expense advanced
. . advanced mine safety equipment property defined . . 179E(d)
. . comprehensive atmospheric monitoring devices
. . . . 179E(d)(5)
. . coordination with Sec. 179 . . . . 179E(e)
. . December 31, 2011, property placed in service after
. . . . 179E(g)
. . electronic location and location devices . . . . 179E(d)(2)
. . emergency communication technology . . . . 179E(d)(1)
. . emergency oxygen-generating, self-rescue devices
. . . . 179E(d)(3)
. . irrevocability of election . . . . 179E(b)(2)
. . oxygen supplies, prepositioned . . . . 179E(d)(4)
. . qualified advanced mine safety equipment property defined
. . . . 179E(c)(1)
. . reporting requirement . . . . 179E(f)
. . treatment, expense . . . . 179E(a)
. expense treatment . . . . 179A(a)
. qualified advanced mine safety equipment property . . . 179A(c)
. reporting election to expense . . . . 179A(f)
. Sec. 179, Sec. 179E coordination with . . . . 179A(e)
. termination of election to expense . . . . 179A(g)

Mines and mining
. accounting method
. . reclamation and closing costs 468
. aggregation of properties for depletion purposes 614
. alternative minimum tax
. . exploration and development costs 56
. basis for gain or loss, adjustment 1016
. black lung (See Black lung benefit trusts)

Index to Code — Mortgage

	CODE SEC.
Mines and mining — Cont'd	
. capital expenditures	263; 263A
. carryovers by acquiring corporation	381
. carved-out production payments	636
. chemicals used in refining, environmental tax	4662
. coal or iron ore disposal	
. . deductions	272
. . expenditures, basis adjustments	1016
. continental shelf areas	638
. definitions	611; 613; 617
. depletion allowance	611
. development expenditures	263; 381; 616; 1016
. dispositions	291; 617
. exploration expenditures	
. . alternative minimum tax	56
. . amortization	291
. . deduction elections	617
. . deductions	174
. . partners and partnerships	703
. . recapture	617
. . reduction in deductions	291
. foreign	
. . development expenditures	616
. . exploration expenditures	617
. foreign tax credit	901
. gain from sale	1254
. gross income from property defined	613
. helicopter fuel	4041; 4261; 6427
. intangible drilling and development costs (See Intangible drilling and development costs)	
. inventory costs	263A
. mineral production payments	636
. nonoperating mineral interests defined	614
. operating interests as separate properties elections	614
. operating mineral interests defined	614
. ores or minerals, extraction of	613
. percentage depletion	381; 613
. personal holding company income	543
. pooling arrangements	614
. production payments	636
. property defined	614; 617; 636
. reclamation and closing costs	468
. retained production payments	636
. royalties, personal holding company income	543
. sale or exchange, gain or loss on	631
. single interest treated as more than one property, election	614
. treatment processes as mining	613
. UMWA benefit and pension plans	9701 et seq.
. unitization or pooling arrangements	614
Minimum essential coverage (See Health insurance coverage subhead monthly health coverage after 2013)	
Minimum funding standards	
. pension, profit-sharing, and stock bonus plans (See Pension, profit sharing and stock bonus plans)	
Minimum participation standards	
. pension, profit-sharing, and stock bonus plans (See Pension, profit sharing and stock bonus plans)	

	CODE SEC.
Ministers of the gospel (See Clergy)	
Minor party	
. defined for presidential election campaign fund	9002
Minors (See Children)	
Miscellaneous itemized deductions	67
Misrepresentation of tax	7211
Missing children, personal exemption	151
Missing in action	
. abatement of tax	692
. combat pay	112
. joint returns	6013
. postponement of actions relating to tax liability	7508
. surviving spouse, deceased spouse missing in action	2
Missionaries, estate tax	2202
Mistakes and errors (See Errors)	
Mitigation of effect of limitations and other provisions	1311 et seq.
. amount and method of adjustment	1314
. circumstances of adjustment	1312
. definitions	1313
. Federal Insurance Contributions Act	6521
. self-employment tax	6521
Mixed straddles	
. marked to market reporting, election out	1256
Mixture fuel credit	6427
Mobile homes	
. bodies for self-propelled mobile homes	
. . retailers excise tax exemption	4051
. retail excise taxes	4053
Mobile machinery	
. highway use tax, exemption	4483
. retail excise tax exemption	4053
Modified adjusted gross income	
. railroad retirement benefits, tier 1	86
. savings bonds redeemed to pay for education expenses	135
. Social Security benefits	86
Modified endowment contracts	72; 7702A
Modified guaranteed contract special rules	817A
Mollusk shells depletion	613
Money orders	
. payment of tax or stamps by	6201; 6311; 6657
Money purchase pension plans	
. cash or deferred arrangements	401
. distributions, rollovers	402
Moneys recovered, disposition of	7406
Monthly health coverage after 2013 (See Health insurance coverage)	
Mortgage bonds	143
. change in use of residence	150
. exemption requirements	143
. family income limits	
. . issuer's statement to mortgagor	143
. federally guaranteed bonds	149
. federally subsidized debt, recapture of	
. . adjusted qualifying income	143(m)(5)(A)
. . amount, recapture	143(m)(4)
. . basis adjustment	143(m)(8)

215

Mortgage

Index to Code

CODE SEC.

Mortgage bonds—Cont'd
. *federally subsidized debt, recapture of —Cont'd*
. . disposition by reason of death .... 143(m)(2)(A)
. . disposition more than 9 year after testing date
.... 143(m)(2)(B)
. . disposition of interest in residence .... 143(m)(1)
. . dispositions other than sales, exchanges and involuntary conversions .... 143(m)(6)(B)
. . federally subsidized amount with respect to debt
.... 143(m)(4)(B)
. . federally subsidized indebtedness defined ..... 143(m)(3)(A)
. . holding period percentage .... 143(m)(4)(C)
. . home improvement loan exception .... 143(m)(3)(B)
. . income percentage defined .... 143(m)(4)(E)
. . involuntary conversions resulting from casualties
.... 143(m)(6)(C)
. . limitation of recapture amount based on gain realized
.... 143(m)(6)
. . modified adjusted gross income .... 143(m)(5)(B)
. . regulations, prescribed .... 143(m)(8)(D)
. . spouse or former spouse, transfer to ..... 143(m)(8)(C)
. . testing date defined .... 143(m)(4)(D)
. . written statement required for potential recapture
.... 143(m)(7)
. mortgage guaranty insurance company purchases 832
. qualified mortgage bonds
. . acquisition cost defined .... 143(k)(3)
. . actuarial basis determinations .... 143(k)(6)
. . arbitrage .... 143(g)
. . definition .... 143; 143(a)(1)
. . disaster area, residence destroyed in .... 143(k)(13)
. . disaster area, residences located in ..... 143(k)(11)
. . income requirements .... 143(f)(1)
. . . family income determination .... 143(f)(2)
. . . high house cost to income adjustments ... 143(f)(5)
. . . median family income .... 143(f)(4)
. . . targeted area residences .... 143(f)(3)
. . limited equity cooperative housing .... 143(k)(9)
. . mortgage defined .... 143(k)(1)
. . new mortgage requirement .... 143(i)
. . qualified home improvement loan defined .... 143(k)(4)
. . qualified mortgage issue define .... 143(a)(2)
. . qualified rehabilitation loan defined ..... 143(k)(5)
. . recapture of portion of federal subsidy .... 143(m)(1)
. . . adjusted qualifying income .... 143(m)(5)
. . . amount, recapture .... 143(m)(4)
. . . basis adjustment .... 143(m)(8)
. . . exceptions to general rules .... 143(m)(2)
. . . federally-subsidized indebtedness .... 143(m)(3)
. . . inform mortgagor of federally-subsidized amount and family income, issuer to .... 143(m)(7)
. . . limitations based on gain realized ...... 143(m)(6)
. . . modified adjusted gross income .... 143(m)(5)
. . . regulations, prescribed .... 143(m)(8)
. . . spouses, transfers to .... 143(m)(8)
. . . two or more people hold interest in residence ... 143(m)(8)
. . resale price control programs .... 143(k)(10)
. . residence requirement .... 143(c)(1)
. . . bonds issued after date of enactment of 3-year requirement
.... 143(d)(2)

CODE SEC.

Mortgage bonds—Cont'd
. *qualified mortgage bonds —Cont'd*
. . *residence requirement—Cont'd*
. . . mortgagor's interest in residence being financed
.... 143(d)(3)
. . . targeted area residences .... 143(c)(2)
. . . 3-year .... 143(d)
. . single-family and owner-occupied residence
. . . 2 to 4 units .... 143(k)(7)
. . statistical area defined .... 143(k)(2)
. . subprime financing .... 143(k)(12)
. . subsidy lien programs .... 143(k)(10)
. . targeted area residences
. . . area of chronic economic distress .... 143(j)(3)
. . . defined .... 143(j)(1)
. . . qualified census tract .... 143(j)(2)
. . targeted areas
. . . portion of loan required to be place in ..... 143(h)
. . veteran's mortgage bonds defined .... 143(b)
. qualified veterans' mortgage bonds (See Veterans mortgage bonds)
. recapture of federally-subsidized indebtedness 143
. refunding issues 146
. residency requirement 150
. revenue bonds (See Mortgage revenue bonds)
. subsidy bonds
. . Indian tribal government, treatment as state 7871
. . mortgage credit certificates 143
. . recapture of federally-subsidized indebtedness 143
. veterans (See Veteran mortgage bonds)
. volume cap 146

Mortgage credit certificates
. credit against tax 25
. interest deduction reduction 163
. penalties 6709
. private activity bonds 146
. recapture of federally-subsidized indebtedness 143

Mortgage revenue bonds 143
. acquisition cost defined .... 143(k)(3)
. actuarial basis, determination of .... 143(k)(6)
. arbitrage .... 143(g)(1)
. . effective rate of mortgage interest .... 143(g)(2)(B)
. . mortgage interest rate excess bond yield by 1.125%
.... 143(g)(2)
. . owner-financing, used to reduce cost of .... 143(g)(3)
. . yield on the issue .... 143(g)(2)(C)
. assumption of mortgage .... 143(i)(2)
. bridge loans .... 143(i)(1)(B)(ii)
. change in use of residence 150
. construction period loans .... 143(i)(1)(B)(i)
. contract for deed agreements .... 143(i)(1)(C)
. cooperative housing
. . defined .... 143(k)(8)(C)
. . indebtedness to corporation .... 143(k)(8)(A)(ii)
. . limited equity cooperative housing
. . . defined .... 143(k)(9)(C)
. . . election, effect of .... 143(k)(9)(E)
. . . election, irrevocability of .... 143(k)(9)(E)
. . . qualified cooperative housing defined ..... 143(k)(9)(D)
. . . residential rental property status .... 143(k)(9)(A)

216

Index to Code — Motor

CODE SEC.

Mortgage revenue bonds—Cont'd
. *cooperative housing —Cont'd*
. . *limited equity cooperative housing —Cont'd*
. . . termination date, bonds subject to . . . . 143(k)(9)(B)
. . . ownership treatment . . . . 143(k)(8)(A)(i)
. . targeted area requirement, adjustment to . . . . . . 143(k)(8)(B)
. inapplicable rules 147
. income requirement . . . . 143(f)(1)
. . family income determination . . . . 143(f)(2)
. . family size as basis for adjustments . . . . 143(f)(6)
. . high housing cost areas . . . . 143(f)(5)(C)
. . housing costs to income, adjustments based on . . . 143(f)(5)
. . median family income . . . . 143(f)(4)
. . price ratios . . . . 143(f)(5)(D)
. . targeted area residences . . . . 143(f)(3)
. interest in residence being financed, mortgagor's . . . 143(d)(3)
. mortgage bond 143
. mortgage defined . . . . 143(k)(1)
. new mortgage requirement . . . . 143(i)(1)
. owner-occupied defined . . . . 143(k)(7)
. pooled financing 148
. purchase price requirement . . . . 143(e)(1)
. . average area purchase price defined . . . . 143(e)(2)
. . average purchase price defined . . . . 143(e)(2)
. . new residence, average area purchase price . . . . . . 143(e)(3)
. . old residence, average area purchase price . . . . 143(e)(3)
. . qualified home improvement loans exception . . . . . 143(e)(6)
. . targeted area residences . . . . 143(e)(5)
. . two to four family residences, special rules for . . . . 143(e)(4)
. qualified home improvement loan . . . . 143(k)(4)
. qualified mortgage issue defined . . . . 143(a)(2)
. qualified mortgage revenue bonds defined . . . . 143(a)(1)
. qualified rehabilitation
. . defined . . . . 143(k)(5)
. . new mortgage exception . . . . 143(i)(1)(B)(iii)
. qualified rehabilitation loan defined . . . . 143(k)(5)
. qualified veterans' mortgage bond defined . . . . 143(b)
. residence requirements . . . . 143(c)
. residency requirement 150
. restrictions on issuance costs 147
. single-family defined . . . . 143(k)(7)
. small, restriction on issuance costs 147
. statistical area defined . . . . 143(k)(2)
. targeted areas
. . area of chronic economic distress . . . . 143(j)(3)
. . defined . . . . 143(j)(1)
. . portion of loan placed in, requirement that
. . . limitations . . . . 143(h)(2)
. . . purchase price requirement . . . . 143(e)(5)
. . qualified census tract . . . . 143(j)(2)
. three-year requirement . . . . 143(d); 143(d)(2)
. veterans' mortgage bond 143

Mortgages
. bonds (See Mortgage bonds)
. credit against tax 163; 6709
. credit certificates (See Mortgage credit certificates)
. credit on interest 25; 143
. definition 143
. estate tax, deduction 2053

CODE SEC.

Mortgages —Cont'd
. ground rents 163; 1055
. interest
. . credit 25; 163; 6709
. . governmental unit, information returns 6050H
. . information returns 6050H; 6652
. . insurance premiums, returns relating to 6050H
. . qualified residence interest 163
. . redeemable ground rents 163
. . reporting by recipient 6050H
. mortgagees
. . foreclosures and repossessions, loss by 1038
. . lien for taxes as against 6323
. points, deduction 461
. pools 7701
. production payments of mineral interests 636
. REITs 856
. residential property, credit on interest 25; 143; 163
. revenue bonds (See Mortgage revenue bonds)
. veteran revenue bonds (See Veterans revenue bonds)

Moses depletion 613

Mothers and newborns
. group health plans 9811

Motion picture film
. deduction of expenses not chargeable to capital account . . 181
. depreciation 168
. domestic production activities deductions . . . . 199(c)(6)
. expenses of investor, deduction limitation 465
. film and television production
. . DISC 992; 993
. . domestic production activities deductions . . . . 199(c)(6)
. . expense, election to . . . . 181(a)(1)
. . . amortization deductions, allowance of . . . . 181(b)
. . . December 31, 2011, productions commencing after
. . . . 181(f)
. . . dollar limitations . . . . 181(a)(2)
. . . other deductions, allowance of . . . . 181(b)
. . . production defined . . . . 181(d)(2)
. . . qualified compensation defined . . . . 181(d)(3)
. . . qualified film or television production defined . . . . 181(d)(1)
. . . television series, special rule for . . . . 181(d)(2)(B)
. rentals
. . personal holding company income 543

Motor fuels
. chemicals used in production, environmental tax 4662
. special motor fuel tax (See Special fuels tax)
. tax, imposition of 4041

Motor vehicles (See also Automobiles)
. alternate motor vehicle credits . . . . . . (Alternate motor vehicle credits)
. charitable contributions
. . fraudulent acknowledgment of 6720
. . used 170
. clean fuel vehicles 179A
. defined 4064; 6323
. depreciation 168
. expensing depreciable business assets 179
. highway use taxes (See Highway motor vehicle use taxes)
. installment payments 6156

217

CODE SEC.

Motor vehicles (See also Automobiles) —Cont'd
. lien for taxes 6323
. luxury automobiles (See Luxury automobiles)
. new qualified alternative fuel motor vehicle credit (See Alternate motor vehicle credits)
. new qualified hybrid motor vehicle credit .... 30B(d)
. new qualified hybrid motor vehicle defined .... 30B(d)(3)
. new qualified plug-in drive motor vehicles credit (See Plug-in electric vehicles)
. operating leases 7701
. plug-in electric vehicles (See Plug-in electric vehicles)
. qualified electric vehicle credit 30
. qualified plug-in drive motor vehicles credit (See Plug-in electric vehicles)
. retail excise tax
.. exemptions 4053; 4221
.. heavy trucks 4051
.. Highway Trust Fund 9503
.. trailers 4051
. retrofitted clean fuel vehicles 179A
. seized for taxes, transfer of title 6339
. standard deduction and sales tax .... 63(c)(9)
. stolen or destroyed vehicles, highway motor vehicle use tax 4481
. tax on use .... 4481 et seq.

Motorboat fuel taxes
. Highway Trust Fund transfers 4483

Motorsport entertainment complex depreciation 168

Movies (See Motion picture film)

Moving expenses 217
. conditions for allowance, exceptions 217
. FICA 3121
. fringe benefits 132
. reimbursement inclusion in gross income 82
. withholding tax on wages 3401

MSA (See Medical savings accounts, Archer)

Multiemployer plans ..... 413; 418 et seq. (See also Pension, profit-sharing, and stock bonus plans)
. accrued benefits, adjustments 418D
. accumulated funding deficiency, waiver 418B
. active participants 418C
. actuarial assumptions 418B
. adjustments 418D
. allocation of assets 418
. base plan year 418
. cash-flow amount exceeding vested benefit charge 418B
. collective bargaining units 401
. consolidation of plans 4975
. contribution base units 418B
. current contribution base 418B
. definition 414
. employer contributions
.. rate increases requirement 418B
.. vesting standards 411
. employer liability trusts 194A; 501
. endangered or critical status, funding rules for plans in (See Endangered or critical status multiemployer plans)
. funding requirements 418A; 418B
. guaranteed benefits, average 418C
. inactive participants 418D

CODE SEC.

Multiemployer plans—Cont'd
. increases in benefits, reorganization 418D
. information returns 6039D
. insolvency 418E
. mergers 414; 418C; 4975
. minimum contribution requirement 418B; 418C
. minimum funding standards .... 412; 431(a)
.. actuarial assumptions, reasonability of .... 431(c)(3)
.. annual valuation .... 431(c)(7)
.. changes in benefits or wages .... 431(c)(4)
.. determinations made under funding method .... 431(c)(1)
.. extension of amortization .... 431(d)
.. full funding .... 431(c)(5); 431(c)(6)
.. funding standard account .... 431(b)
.. valuation of assets .... 431(c)(2)
. nonannuity payments 418
. notice of reorganization 418A
. notice requirements 418E
. overburden credit 418C
. pay status participant 418C
. person in pay status 418
. qualification requirements 401
. qualified plans, employer reversion of assets 4980
. reduction in benefits 418; 418D
. reorganization
.. accumulated funding deficiency 418B
.. first year 418C
.. increase in benefits 418D
.. index .... 418 et seq.
.. minimum funding standards 418B
.. notice of 418A
. restoration of benefits 418D
. retroactive payments 418D
. retroactive plan amendments 418B
. suspension of benefit payments 418E
. terminated plans 412; 418
. transfers between 4975
. unfunded vested benefits 418
. valuation contribution base 418B
. vested benefit charge 418; 418B
. vesting standards 411
. withdrawal liability 418; 4975

Multinational forces
. death of U.S. member, abatement of tax 692

Multiple support of dependents 152

Multiple trusts 643; 667

Multiple-party transactions
. conduit arrangements 7701

Municipal solid waste defined 45

Municipalities
. bonds (See State and local bonds)
. communications taxes 4253
. employees
.. employment tax refunds 6413
.. self-employment tax refunds 6511
. exempt income 115
. officers and employees of
.. deferred compensation 457

Index to Code

Municipalities —Cont'd
	CODE SEC.
. public utilities, depreciation	168
. research for, exempt organization's income from	512
. taxes	164

Museums, special fuels tax for aircraft ... 4041

Musical compositions ... 1231
. depreciation ... 167
. sale or exchange of ... 1221

Mutual ditch or irrigation companies ... 501

Mutual funds
. real estate investment trusts (See Real estate investment trusts)
. regulated investment company (See Regulated investment companies)

Mutual insurance companies
. controlled foreign corporations ... 953
. funds, exemption ... 501
. life insurance companies (See Mutual life insurance companies)
. other than life, marine, fire or flood
. . adjustments to basis ... 1016
. . consolidated returns ... 1504
. . exemption ... 501
. policyholder dividends
. . deduction ... 808
. . taxable investment income ... 834

Mutual life insurance companies ... 808; 809; 814

Mutual or cooperative electric companies ... 512(b)(18)

Mutual savings banks ... 591 et seq.
. alternative tax on life insurance business ... 594
. bad debts ... 593
. cooperative associations ... 1381 et seq.
. distributions to shareholders ... 591; 593
. dividends paid deduction ... 243; 591
. dividends received deduction ... 243
. federal financial assistance ... 597
. life insurance business alternative tax ... 594
. market discount bonds, interest paid to purchase or carry ... 1277
. organizations providing reserve funds for, and insurance of, deposits in ... 501
. passbook loans, liens for taxes ... 6323
. reacquisition of real property ... 1038
. returns ... 6033
. tax imposed ... 11

Mutual Security Act per diem payments ... 1441

Mutual telephone company exemptions ... 501; 513

N

Naphtha fuels tax ... 4041
Napthalene hazardous waste cleanup ... 4661
Narcotic drugs
. illegal sales, deductions and credits ... 280E
. reimbursement of state and local law enforcement agencies for costs of investigating illegal activities ... 7624; 7809

Native

	CODE SEC.

National banks (See Banks and trust companies)
National credit union central liquidity facility ... 501
National defense exemptions ... 5561
National Health Services Corporation ... 108
National Institute for Occupational Safety and Health
. disclosure of returns and return information ... 6103
National Recreational Trails Trust Fund ... 9503

Native Americans
. charitable contributions by whaling captains in support of native Alaskan subsistence whaling ... 170
. economic development bonds (See Tribal economic development bonds)
. employment credit ... 45A
. enterprise zones/communities within reservation ... 1393
. fishing rights-related income ... 7873
. . self-employment tax ... 1402
. . Social Security tax ... 3121
. . FUTA ... 3306; 3309
. health care benefits
. . accident or health insurance defined ... 139D(c)(4)
. . accident or health plan defined ... 139D(c)(4)
. . dependent defined ... 139D(c)(5)
. . double benefits, denial of ... 139D(d)
. . free choice vouchers ... 139D[E]
. . generally ... 139D(a)
. . Indian tribe defined for ... 139D(c)(1)
. . medical care defined for ... 139D(c)(3)
. . qualified Indian health care benefits defined ... 139D(b)
. . tribal organization defined for ... 139D(c)(2)
. Indian coal production facility ... 45
. Indian tribal governments
. . defined ... 7701
. . defined benefit plan, limitations on contributions and benefits ... 414
. . fishing rights treaty ... 7873
. . government plans ... 414
. . qualified energy conservation bonds
. . . population, determination of ... 54D(h)(1)
. . . treatment as qualified bond ... 54D(h)(2)
. . state, status as ... 7871
. manufacturers excise taxes
. . crafts and manufactures, exemptions for ... 4225
. . exemptions from ... 4225; 7871
. private activity bonds ... 7871
. reservation property
. . accelerated cost recovery system (ACRS) ... 168(j)(1)
. . alternative depreciation property ... 168(j)(4)(B)
. . applicable recovery period for ... 168(j)(2)
. . December 31, 2011, property placed in service after ... 168(j)(8)
. . deductions allowed in computing minimum tax ... 168(j)(3)
. . Indian reservation defined ... 168(j)(6)
. . nonrevenue laws, coordination with ... 168(j)(7)
. . qualified Indian reservation property defined ... 168(j)(4)(A)
. . real estate rentals ... 168(j)(5)
. . reservation infrastructure investment ... 168(j)(4)(C)
. . enterprise zones/communities within ... 1393
. trade or business expense deduction ... 162

219

Native

	Code Sec.
Native settlement trusts, Alaska	646
Natural gas	
. Alaska natural gas defined	43
. Arbitrage; prepaid natural gas safe harbor	148(b)(4)
. compressed	4041
. defined	613A
. depletion percentage	613A
. environmental tax	4611; 4612
. gathering line depreciation	168
. hazardous waste cleanup, excise tax for	4611; 4612
. nonconventional fuel source credit (See Nonconventional fuel source credit)	
Natural resources . . . . 611 et seq. (See also specific type)	
. continental shelf areas	638
. cost depletion, basis	612
. deductions	611 et seq.
. depletion allowance	611 et seq.
. development expenditures	616
. DISC exportations	993
. exploration	
. . depreciable property	168
. . . expenditures	617
. mineral production payments	636
. percentage depletion	613
. property defined	614
. sales and exchanges	631
Naval forces (See also Armed forces)	
. defined	7701
Negligence penalties	6013
Nephelite syenite depletion	613
Net capital gain (See also Capital gains and losses)	
. defined	1222
. investment income	1
. maximum tax rates	1
. tax rates	1
Net capital losses (See also Capital gains and losses)	
. defined	1222
Net earnings from self-employment defined	1402
Net investment income	
. active interests in partnerships and S corporations	1411(c)(4)
. defined	1411(c)(1)
. estates and trusts	1411(a)(2)
. individuals	1411(a)(1)
. investment of working capital	1411(c)(3)
. modified adjusted gross income	1411(d)
. nonresident aliens	1411(e)(1)
. qualified plan distribution exceptions	1411(c)(5)
. self-employed individuals	1411(a)(1)
. special rules	1411(c)(6)
. threshold amounts	1411(b)(1)
. trades and business to which tax applies	1411(c)(2)
Net long-term capital gains and losses	1222
Net operating losses	
. carrybacks and carryovers (See Carrybacks and carryovers)	
. commercial banks, bad debt losses	172(b)(1)(D)
. compensable injuries, attributable to	186
. corporation subject to income tax of foreign country	1503

Index to Code

	Code Sec.
Net operating losses —Cont'd	
. debt discharge amounts reducing NOL	108
. deductions	
. . accumulated earnings tax	535
. . allowance	172(a)
. . alternative minimum tax	56
. . amount	172(b)(2)
. . carrybacks and carryovers	
. . . amount of	172(b)(2)
. . . bad debt losses, commercial banks	172(b)(1)(D)
. . . waive, election to	172(b)(3)
. . . years to which loss may be carried	172(b)(1)
. . commercial banks	
. . . bad debt losses	172(g)(1)
. . . coordination with 172(b)(2)	172(g)(2)
. . common trust funds	584
. . computation of	172(c)(7)
. . corporate equity reduction interest loss	
. . . allocable interest deduction	172(h)(2)
. . . corporate equity reduction transactions	172(h)(3)
. . . defined	172(h)(1)
. . . ordering rules	172(h)(4)
. . . regulations concerning	172(h)(5)
. . disallowance	172(d)
. . dividends received	172(d)(5)
. . election to waive	172(b)(3)
. . excess interest loss	172(b)(1)(E)
. . farming losses	
. . . coordination with 172(b)(2)	172(i)(2)
. . . defined	172(i)(1)
. . . election	172(i)(3)
. . foreign oil and gas income	907
. . foreign personal holding companies	556
. . insurance companies other than life	831; 834
. . life insurance companies	805
. . manufacturing deduction under sec. 199	172(d)(7)
. . modifications	
. . . capital gains and losses of taxpayers other than corporations	172(d)(2)
. . . dividends received	172(d)(5)
. . . nonbusiness deduction of taxpayers other than corporations	172(d)(4)
. . . personal exemptions, deduction for	172(d)(3)
. . nonbusiness deductions of taxpayers other than corporations	172(d)(4)
. . other than corporations, taxpayers	172(d)(2)
. . partnerships	703
. . personal exemptions	172(d)(3)
. . personal holding companies	545
. . qualified disaster losses	
. . . coordination with 172(b)(2)	172(j)(2)
. . . defined	172(j)(1)
. . . election	172(j)(3)
. . . exclusion	172(j)(4)
. . REITs	172(b)(1)(B); 172(d)(6)
. . self-employment tax purposes	1402
. . small business investment company stock	1242
. . small business stock	1244
. . specified liability loss	
. . . defined	172(f)(1)

Index to Code

Nonconventional

CODE SEC.

Net operating losses — Cont'd
. deductions — Cont'd
.. specified liability loss — Cont'd
... election of .... 172(f)(6)
... limitations .... 172(f)(2)
... nuclear power plants .... 172(f)(3)
... product liability .... 172(f)(4)
.. trusts and estates 642
.. waiver .... 172(b)(3)
. defined .... 172(c)
. dividends-received deduction
.. effect on 246
. exempt organizations having business income 512
Net proceeds defined 150
Net Sec. 1256 contract gains and losses 1212
Net short-term capital gain defined 1222
New clean renewable energy bonds
. clean renewable energy bond lender defined .... 54C(d)(5)
. cooperative electric company defined .... 54C(d)(4)
. credit for qualified bonds allowed to issuer
.. special rules .... 6431(f)(2)
.. specified tax credit bond .... 6431(f)(3)
. defined .... 54C(a)
. governmental body defined .... 54C(d)(3)
. limitations on amount of bonds designated .... 54C(c)(1)
.. allocation, method of .... 54C(c)(3)
... governmental bodies, allocation among .... 54C(c)(3)(B)
... national limitations .... 54C(c)(2)
... public power provider allocations .... 54C(c)(3)(A)
. public power provider
.. defined .... 54C(d)(2)
.. limitations on amount of bonds designated, allocation
   .... 54C(c)(3)(A)
. qualified lender defined .... 54C(d)(6)
. qualified renewable energy facility defined ...... 54C(d)(1)
. reduced credit amounts .... 54C(b)
New employees, credit for hiring 51; 52
New energy efficient home credit
. allowance .... 45L(a)
. basis adjustment .... 45L(e)
. certification .... 45L(d)
. eligible contractor defined .... 45L(b)(1)
. energy saving requirement .... 45L(c)(1)
. general business credit, unused 196
. investment credit, coordination with .... 45L(f)
. qualified new energy efficient home defined ...... 45L(b)(2)
. termination of credit .... 45L(g)
New loss corporation 382
New markets
. credits against tax 45D
. national limitation on amount of investments designated
   .... 45D(f)
New party
. defined for presidential election campaign fund .. 9002
New qualified alternative fuel motor vehicle credit (See Alternate motor vehicle credits)
New York Liberty Zone
. benefits, tax 1400L
. business employee credit, special 38

CODE SEC.

New York Liberty Zone — Cont'd
. small business tax, limitations on amount of .... 38(c)
News services 4253
Newsboys
. FICA 3121
. FUTA 3306
. withholding tax on wages 3401
Newspaper vendors
. FICA 3121
. withholding tax on wages 3401
Newspapers
. circulation expenditures 173; 1016
. FUTA 3306
. subscriptions, prepaid 455
Nickel
. depletion 613
. hazardous waste clean up 4661; 4662
Nitric acid, hazardous waste clean up 4661; 4662
No-additional-cost services fringe benefit exclusion ... 132
NOLs (See Net operating losses)
Nonadverse party defined 672
Nonbusiness casualty losses (See Casualty losses)
Nonbusiness debts 166
Nonbusiness energy property credit
. allowance 25C
. basis adjustments 25C
. joint ownership of energy items .... 25C; 25C(e)(2)
. limitations .... 25C(b)
. property placed in service after Dec. 31, 2007 and before Jan. 1, 2009 .... 25C(g)(1)
. property placed in service after Dec. 31, 2011 ... 25C(g)(2)
. qualified energy efficiency improvements .... 25C; 25C(c)
. residential energy property expenditures .... 25C(d)
.. advanced main air circulating fan .... 25C(d)(5)
.. biomass fuel .... 25C(d)(6)
.. energy-efficient building property .... 25C(d)(3)
.. qualified energy property .... 25C(d)(2)
.. qualified natural gas, propane, or oil furnace or hot water boiler .... 25C(d)(4)
Nonbusiness expenses 212; 703
Noncash remuneration, wage withholdings
. retail commission salesmen 3402
Nonconventional fuel source credit
. allowance .... 45K9a)
. limitations and adjustments
.. barrel defined .... 45K(d)(6)
.. barrel-of-oil equivalent .... 45K(d)(5)
.. biomass defined .... 45K(c)(3)
.. energy credit, credit reduced for .... 45K(b)(4)
.. enhanced oil recovery credit, credit reduced for . 45K(b)(5)
.. extension for certain facilities .... 45K(f)(1)
.. extension for coke or coke gas producing facilities . 45K(g)
.. geopressured brine, Devonian shale, coal seam or a tight formation .... 45K(d)(4)
.. geopressured brine, gas from .... 45K(c)(2)
.. grants, tax-exempt bonds and subsidized energy financing reduction .... 45K(b)(3)
.. inflation adjustment factor and reference price . 45K(d)(2)

221

Nonconventional   Index to Code

CODE SEC.

Nonconventional fuel source credit —Cont'd
limitations and adjustments —Cont'd
.. pass-thru, estates and trust .... 45K(d)(8)
.. phaseout adjustment limitation .... 45K(b)(2)
.. phaseout of credit .... 45K(b)(1)
.. production attributable to the taxpayer .... 45K(d)(3)
.. qualified fuels .... 45K(e)
.. qualified fuels defined .... 45K(c)
.. related persons .... 45K(d)(7)
.. special rules .... 45K(d)
.. U.S. production requirement .... 45K(d)(1)
Nondeductible items .... 261 et seq.
Nondiscrimination rules (See Discrimination)
Nonequity options defined 1256
Nonfinancial foreign entities (See Foreign entities)
Nongovernment obligations, short-term 1271
Nonoperating mineral interest defined 614
Nonpatronage distributions, cooperatives 1382
Nonprofit organizations
. exempt organizations (See Exempt entities and organizations)
. low-income housing project, qualified (See Low-income housing credit)
Nonqualified deferred compensation
. tax indifferent parties, from certain .... 457A(a)
.. compensation, determination of .... 457A(c)(1)
... interest determination .... 457A(c)(2)
.. comprehensive foreign income tax .... 457A(d)(2)
.. effectively connected income .... 457A(d)(4)
.. nonqualified deferred compensation plans .... 457A(d)(3)
.. nonqualified entity .... 457A(b)
.. regulations, prescription of .... 457A(e)
.. substantial risk of forfeiture .... 457A(d)(1)
Nonrecognition transaction defined 7701
Nonrecourse financing
. investment credit 49
. partnership debt discharge 108
Nonresident aliens ..... 871 et seq. (See also Aliens; Resident aliens)
. aircraft, income derived from 872
. alternative minimum tax 877
. American Samoa 876
. annuities under qualified plans 871
. beneficiary of estate or trust 875
. books and records, Tax Court examination 7456
. capital gains and losses 871
. charitable and similar gifts 873; 2522
. community income 879
. compensation
.. exchange students and visitors 872
.. FICA 3121
.. FUTA 3306
.. withholding tax 1441
. consent dividends 565
. continental shelf areas, working in 1441
. contributions 873
. credits 874; 901; 906; 6401
. deductions and credits 873; 874
. deferred payment sales 483; 864

CODE SEC.

Nonresident aliens—Cont'd
. deficiency notice, petition to Tax Court 6213
. defined 7701
. departure from U.S., compliance with tax laws ... 6851
. dependents 152
. disabled, credit for 22
. distributions to
.. information returns 6038B
.. U.S. real property interests 897
. dividend equivalent payments 871
. dividends paid deduction 565
. divorce, transfers of property upon 1041
. doubling of rates 891
. effectively connected income
.. defined 864
.. foreign tax credit 906
.. graduated rate of tax 871
.. gross transportation income 891
.. real property income 897
. elderly, credit for 22
. elections
.. community income 879
.. real property income treated as effectively connected ... 871
. employee benefit plans 401
.. beneficiaries 402; 404A; 414; 871
.. distributions 402
. estate tax .... 2101 et seq.
.. art works 2105
.. bank deposits 2105
.. charitable bequests 2106
.. computation 2101
.. credits against 2102
.. debt obligations 2104; 2105
.. deductions 2106
.. expatriation to avoid 2107
.. gifts 2101; 2104
.. gross estate defined 2103
.. life insurance 2105
.. marital deduction 2106
.. possessions of U.S., residents of 2102; 2209
.. property within U.S. 2104
.. property without U.S. 2105
.. returns 6018
.. revocable transfers 2104
.. stock 2104
.. taxable estate 2106
.. unified credit against 2102
. estimated tax 6654
. exchange students (See Foreign students and exchange visitors)
. exclusions 871
. exempt income 872
. existing 80/20 companies 871
. expatriation
.. to acquire status as 877
.. to avoid tax 2107
. federal officers and employees
.. employee benefit plans distributions 402
. first and last year of residency 7701

222

Index to Code

Nonresident aliens—Cont'd
CODE SEC.
- foreign educational, charitable and certain other exempt organizations 878
- foreign government employees 893
- foreign students and exchange visitors (See Foreign students and exchange visitors)
- foreign tax credit 874; 901; 906
- gambling winnings 871; 1441
- gift tax
  - . charitable gifts 2522; 2524
  - . deductions 2522; 2524
  - . liability for 2501
  - . possessions of U.S., residents of 2501
  - . transfers 2511
- gross income 872; 887
- Guam 876
- husband and wife
  - . community income 879
  - . joint returns 6013
  - . noncitizen spouse, disallowance of marital deduction 2056; 2523
  - . nontaxable gifts between 1041
- income connected with U.S. business
  - . real property income 861; 897; 1445; 6039C; 6652
- income not connected with U.S. business 864; 871
- interest received 163; 1441
- international organization employees 893
- losses 873; 897
- Northern Mariana Islands 876
- notional principal contract 871
- original issue discount 163; 871; 1441
- partnership members 875
- pension, profit-sharing, and stock bonus plans
  - . beneficiaries 414
  - . highly compensated employee .... 414(q)(8)
- per diem payments under Mutual Security Act 1441
- personal exemptions 873
- personal property, sale of 865
- petition to TC 6213
- portfolio debt investments 871; 1441
- Puerto Rico 876; 1441
- qualified tuition and related expenses, deduction of 222
- rate of tax 896
- real estate mortgage investment conduit, holders of interest in 860G
- real property income 871
- U.S. property investments
  - . . disposition of 861; 897; 1445
  - . . information returns 6039C; 6652
  - . . wash sale transactions .... 1445(b)(8)
- regulated investment companies 871
- REIT interests 897
- retaliatory taxes
  - . . disclosure of returns 6103
  - . . estate tax returns 6018
  - . . joint 6013
  - . . time to file 6072
  - . . U.S. real property investments 6039C; 6652
- returns 874
- S corporation shareholders 1361

Nonresident aliens—Cont'd
CODE SEC.
- scholarships and fellowships 1441
- self-employment tax 1402
- ships operated by 872
- Social Security benefits 871
- students (See Foreign students and exchange visitors)
- tax rates 2
- taxability 871
- temporarily in U.S. 871
  - . definition 864
  - . exchange students (See Foreign students and exchange visitors)
- FICA 3121
- FUTA 3306
- . income from sources without U.S. 861
- time for filing returns 6072
- treaty provisions, effect of 894
- tuition deduction .... 222(d)(5)
- U.S. business 864; 871
- U.S. real property 897
- wages paid to
  - . FICA 3121
  - . FUTA 3306
  - . withholding tax at source 1441; 6013
  - . withholding tax on wages 3401
- withholding of tax 874
  - . U.S. real property interest dispositions .... 1445(a)
- withholding of tax at source 33; 1441; 3402; 6013

Nonresident foreign corporations (See Foreign corporations)

Nonresidential real property 168

Non-tax debts owed U.S., offsets against taxes overpaid
- disclosure of returns and return information 6103

Nontaxable exchanges (See Exchanges of property)

Nontaxable income (See Exempt income)

Nontrade expenses (See Nonbusiness expenses)

Northern Mariana Islands
- alien residents 876
- corporations 881
- income of citizens residing in 931

Northwest Power Act bond guarantees 149

Notes, discount (See Discount bonds and notes)

Not-for-profit activities 183
- residential property, rental of 280A

Notice
- administrative proceeding
  - . partners and partnerships 6223
- books and records 6001
- COBRA premium assistance
  - . cessation of eligibility, failure to notify plan of 6720C
- deficiency (See Deficiencies)
- delinquency 7524
- employee retirement and benefit plans
  - . distributions, rollover eligibility 402; 6652
  - . domestic relations orders 414
- exempt organizations, application for status as 508
- failure of Secretary to contact taxpayer
  - . . suspension of interest and penalties 6404
- foreign taxes, redetermination 6689

223

CODE SEC.

Notice —Cont'd
. gift received from foreign person 6039F
. group health plans continuation coverage .... 4980B(f)(6)
. judicial proceedings
.. S corporation shareholder 6423
. levy
.. opportunity for hearing .... 6330(b)
.. wages for unpaid taxes 6331
. lien for taxes .... 6320(a); 6323
. new technology to provide, use of 4980F
. payment of tax 6155; 6303
. pension benefit accrual reduction 4980F
. refilling, lien for taxes 6323
. returns 6001
. sale of seized property 6335
. seizure of property 6331; 6335
. Tax Court decisions, review 7483
. tobacco products 5723
Notional principal contracts
. controlled foreign corporations income from 954
Nuclear power plants
. advanced nuclear power facilities 45J
. decommissioning costs 468A
.. gross income inclusion 88
. net operating loss deduction .... 172(f)(3)

O

OASDI (See Old Age, Survivors, and Disability insurance (OASDI))
Oaths
. authority to administer 7622
. Tax Court 7456
Obligations ... 1271 et seq. (See also Bonds; Debt instruments)
. corporate acquisition indebtedness 279
. high-yield obligations 163
. installment, gain or loss on 453B
. installment sales 453
. issued at discount 454
. non-interest-bearing, issued at discount 454
. not in registered form 1287
. original issue discount (See Original issue discount)
. qualified tax exempt 265
. registration-required (See Registration-required obligations)
. short-term 163
. short-term issued at discount .... 454; 1281 et seq.
.. deferral of interest deduction 1282
.. definitions and special rules 1283
.. exempt obligations 1288
.. regulated investment companies 852
. rules covering .... 1281 et seq.
. United States (See United States obligation)
Obligatory disbursement agreement defined 6323
Obsolescence depreciation deduction 167
Occupational taxes .... 4901 et seq.; 6806
. alcohol and distilled spirits .... 5081; 5091 et seq; 5276
.. inspection of records or premises 5146
.. liability for 5143
.. payment 5142

CODE SEC.

Occupational taxes—Cont'd
alcohol and distilled spirits—Cont'd
.. penalties 5691
.. permits 5271; 5276
... exemptions 5276
.. retail dealers .... 5121 et seq.
. federal agencies or instrumentalities 4907
. firearms .... 5801 et seq.
. liability for .... 4902 et seq.
.. death of taxpayer 4905
.. location, change of 4905
.. multiple locations, business with 4903
.. partners 4902
.. same ownership and location, different businesses of .. 4904
. liquor .... 5081; 5091 et seq.
.. permits 5271; 5276
. payment of 4901
. penalties 7273
. posting stamps 6806
. small producers of distilled spirits, tax exemption 5081
. stamps 6806
. state laws, application of 4906
. suspension 5148
. tobacco products 5731
.. carrying on business 5732
.. liability provisions 5733
.. state law, application of 5734
. wagering .... 4411 et seq.; 4901 et seq.
.. penalties 7262
Ocean activity income 863
Oceanic equipment depreciation 168
Odds requirement
. withholding tax on wagering income 3402
Offers-in-compromise
. disclosure of returns and return information 6103
Off-highway business use of fuel
. LUST tax rate 4041
. special fuels tax 4041
Off-highway vehicle defined 7701
Office buildings
. exempt facility bonds 142
Officers of corporations
. disclosure of returns and return information 6103
. employee status
.. FICA 3121
.. withholding tax on wages 3401
. excess benefit transaction of exempt organizations 4958
. life insurance 264
Offsets against overpayment of tax 6103; 6402
Offsetting positions, straddles 1092
OID (See Original issue discount)
Oil and gas (See also Oil and gas wells)
. allowance of deduction for depletion 611
. average daily production 613A
. continental shelf, source of income 638
. controlled foreign corporation income 954
. daily depletable natural gas quantity 613A
. definitions 613A

Index to Code

Original

CODE SEC.
Oil and gas (See also Oil and gas wells) —Cont'd
. denial of percentage depletion 613
. depletion .... 611 et seq.
. development expenditures 616
. domestic production activities
.. oil related qualified production activities income .... 199(d)(9)
. enhanced oil recovery credit 29; 43
. environmental tax 4611; 4612
. exploration expenditures 617
. foreign income 907
. foreign tax credit 901; 907
. gasification project credit (See Qualifying gasification project credit)
. hazardous waste cleanup, excise tax for 4611; 4612
. helicopters, fuel for 4041; 4261; 6427
. independent producers 613A
. marginal property production (See Marginal wells)
. nonconventional fuel source credit (See Nonconventional fuel source credit)
. nonoperating interests defined 614
. oil spill liability trust fund 4611; 9509
. partnerships, depletion 613A; 703
. percentage depletion 613; 613A
. personal holding companies 543
. property defined 614
. royalties 543; 613A
. S corporations 613A
. small producers, depletion 613A
. submerged coastal lands 638
. windfall profit tax, prior law (See Windfall profit tax, domestic crude oil)
Oil and gas trust funds
. LUST Trust Fund (See Leaking Underground Storage Tank Trust Fund)
. oil spill liability (See Oil spill liability trust fund)
Oil and gas wells
. at risk amounts 465
. capital expenditures 263; 263A
. dispositions 291
. drilling and development costs 263; 465
. environmental tax 4611; 4612
. expenditures in taxable year of deduction 461
. exploration expenditures 174; 465
. gain from sale 1254
. hazardous waste cleanup excise tax 4611; 4612
. helicopter fuel 4041; 4261; 6427
. hydrocarbon injectant 193
. intangible drilling and development costs
.. earnings and profits computation 312
. integrated oil company 291
.. depreciation 167
. interest in
.. gain from sale 1254
.. passive activity losses and credits 469
.. inventory costs 263A
. marginal oil and gas well production credit, 5-year carryback 39
. sale, gain from 1254
. tax shelters 461
. tertiary recovery projects, injectant expenses 193; 263

CODE SEC.
Oil spill liability trust fund 4611; 9509
Old loss corporation 382
Old-age, survivors, and disability insurance (OASDI) (See also Federal Insurance Contributions Act (FICA); Social Security)
. general rules 1401
Old-age benefit taxes (See Employment taxes)
Older individuals (See Elderly individuals)
Olivine depletion 613
On-the-job training payments
. work opportunity credit 51
Open-loop biomass
. electricity produced from renewable resources, credit 45
Operating mineral interest defined 614
Operating net loss (See Net operating losses)
Operations loss deduction
. insurance companies
.. allowance of deduction .... 844(a)
.. carrybacks and carryovers .... 844(b)
.. computation of loss from operations .... 844(c)
.. new company defined .... 844(e)
.. offset defined .... 844(d)
.. subtitles A and F, application of .... 844(f)
. life insurance companies 805; 810
. net operating loss (See Net operating losses)
Opinion letter request, user fee 7528
Optional adjustment to basis of partnership property ... 734; 743; 754; 755
Optional valuation, estate tax 1014; 2032
Options
. cash settlement options 1234
. dealers in (See Dealers in options and commodities)
. employee stock (See Employee stock options)
. failure to exercise 1233; 1234
. identification as held for investment purposes 1236
. sale or exchange of
.. capital gains and losses 1233; 1234
.. corporation dealing in own stock 1032
. stock (See Stock options)
Ordinary income
. allocation of basis, charitable contributions 170
. charitable contributions 170
. defined 64
. loss defined 65
Ordinary loss defined 65
Organizational expenditures
. corporations 248
. partnerships 709
Original issue discount .... 163; 1271 et seq.
. amount, determination 1273
. cash method election for smaller transactions 1274A
. constant interest rate 1272
. current reporting 1272
. daily portions 163; 1272
. deferred payment sales 483; 1274A
. definitions 1274A; 1275
. determination of amount 1273

225

	CODE SEC.
Original issue discount—Cont'd	
. exceptions	163
. exempt interest obligations	1288
. foreign corporations	881
. gross income inclusion	1272
. high-yield obligations	163
. information reporting requirements	6049; 6706
. interest	163; 483
. investment units	1273
. issue price	
. . defined	1273
. . determination of	1274
. . property, issued on sale or exchange	1274
. market discount bonds with	1276; 1278
. nonresident aliens	871; 1441
. ratable daily portion	1272
. real estate mortgage investment conduits	1272
. reaquisition of debt instrument after Dec. 31, 2008 and before Jan. 1, 2001	108(i)(2)
. related foreign person, held by	163
. rules for	1271 et seq.
. sale-leasebacks	1274
. short-term	163; 1281 et seq.
. special rules	1274A; 1275
. stripped bonds or coupons	1286
. tax-exempt obligations, treatment of	1288
. U.S. obligations, exchange of	1037
Orphan drugs	
. clinical testing	45C
. credit	280C(b)
Other terms, definition	7701
Outdoor advertising display, involuntary conversion	1033
Out-of-pocket expenses, charitable contribution of	170
Outstanding lien	
. disclosure of returns and return information	6103
Overlapping pay periods withholdings	3402
Overpayment of tax	6401 et seq. (See also Refunds and credits)
. abatements, credits, refunds	6401
. advance payments, interest on	6611
. after 12/31/2012	6414
. American Samoa	
. . employment tax	6413
. . FICA	6413
. amounts treated as	6401
. armed forces, war postponement	7508
. before 1/1/2013	6414
. carrybacks and carryovers	
. . interest on overpayments	6611
. . net operating losses attributable to overpayments	6511; 6611
. child support	
. . past due payment offsets	6103; 6402
. . state government seizure for	6402
. consolidated returns estimated tax overpayment adjustments	6425
. credits against tax	
. . estimated tax, against	6402; 6513
. . payment, treatment as	7422

	CODE SEC.
Overpayment of tax—Cont'd	
. *credits against tax —Cont'd*	
. . taxes due, against	6402
. . underpayment, against	6601; 6611
. debts owed U.S., non-tax, offsets	6402 et seq.
. deficiencies, overpayment credited against	6601; 6611
. District of Columbia	
. . employment tax	6413
. . FICA	6413
. due dates, interests on returns filed before	6611
. employment taxes	6413
. estate tax	6511 et seq.
. estimated income tax	
. . consolidated return adjustments	6425
. . corporations	
. . . adjustments for overpayment	6425
. . . excessive adjustment	6655
. . credit against	6402; 6513
. . individuals, income tax credited to	6513
. excise taxes	6416
. FDIC	6413
. federal agencies, debts owed to	
. . offset of tax overpayments	6402
. FUTA	6413
. gift tax	6511 et seq.
. Guam	6413
. indebtedness	
. . U.S., as offsets against tax overpayments	6402
. installment payment of tax	6403
. interest	
. . deficiency, credited against	6601; 6611
. . estimated tax payments	6611
. . rate determination	6621
. liability for tax does not exist, when	6401
. offsets against	6103; 6402
. personal credit, excessive	6401
. Railroad Retirement Tax Act	6413
. refunds and credits	6401
. . amounts treated as overpayments	6401
. . credited against taxes due	6402; 6601; 6611
. . determined by TC	6512
. . limitation period, interest on overpayments	6611
. returns filed before due date	
. . interest on overpayments	6611
. Social Security benefits	
. . OASDI overpayments	6402
. state governments	
. . overpayments seized for child support	6402
. statute of limitations	
. . assessment and collection, amounts treated as overpayments	6401
. Tax Court finding of	6512
. Tax Intercept Programs (TIPs)	6402
. underpayment of tax, credits against	6601; 6611
. U.S., debts owed to	
. . non-tax, offsets against tax overpayments	6402
. war postponements	7508
. withholding	
. . refunds and credits, interest on overpayments	6611

Index to Code

	Code Sec.
Owner-employee benefit plans	401

Owners
. dependent care assistance programs ... 129
. educational assistance programs ... 127

Ownership, change in (See Change in ownership)

Ownership of property defined ... 150

Ownership of stock (See Stock and securities subhead ownership rule)

Ozone-depleting chemicals, excise taxes on
. definitions and special rules ... 4682
. imported taxable product ... 4682
. rate of tax ... 4681

P

Paid or accrued defined ... 7701

Parachute payments (See Golden parachute payments)

Parent corporations
. 80% distributee ... 337
. employee stock options ... 424
. information returns, foreign subsidiaries ... 6038
. liquidating distributions of subsidiary ... 337
. subsidiary, indebtedness of ... 337

Parents
. employee's, fringe benefits ... 132
. employment by children
. . FUTA ... 3306

Parent-subsidiary controlled group defined ... 1563

Pari-mutuel pools ... 3402; 4402

Parking ... 132

Parsonage
. exempt income ... 265
. rental value ... 107

Partial interest in property, charitable contribution ... 170

Participation standards (See Pension, profit sharing and annuity plans)

Partners and partnerships ... 701 et seq.; 6221 et seq.
. accelerated cost recovery system (ACRS)
. . property owned by partnership
. . . non-tax exempt use ... 168(h)(6)(A)(i)
. . . pass-thru entities rule, other ... 168(h)(6)(E)
. . . proportional share, determination of ... 168(h)(6)(C)
. . . qualified allocation defined ... 168(h)(6)(B)
. . . regulations ... 168(h)(8)
. . . regulations on unified allocations ... 168(h)(6)(G)
. . . taxable entities, treatment of ... 168(h)(6)(F)
. . . tax-exempt controlled entity defined ... 168(h)(6)(F)(iii)
. . . tiered entities rule ... 168(h)(6)(E)
. . . unrelated trade or business, determination of use in ... 168(h)(6)(D)
. . tax-exempt use of property leased to partnership
. . . foreign entities, presumption with respect to ... 168(h)(5)(C)
. . . lease defined ... 168(h)(8)
. . . partner's proportionate share ... 168(h)(5)
. . . pass-thru entities rule, other ... 168(h)(5)(B)
. . . tiered entities rule, other ... 168(h)(5)(B)
. accounting periods ... 444; 7519
. administrative adjustment

Partners and partnerships—Cont'd
. *administrative adjustment —Cont'd*
. . judicial review where request in not allowed in full ... 6228
. . request for ... 6227
. administrative proceedings
. . assessments after ... 6225
. . notice ... 6223
. . participation, partner right to ... 6224
. admission of new partner ... 706
. agreement
. . definition ... 761
. . distributive share, effect on ... 704
. appreciated property, distribution of ... 311
. assessments
. . period of limitations for making ... 6229
. . procedures ... 6221 et seq.
. asset allocation ... 1060
. assumption of liabilities between ... 752
. at risk limitations ... 465
. audit and judicial review procedure, unified ... 6221 et seq.
. bankruptcy ... 1398; 1399
. basis
. . allocation of ... 755
. . contributed property ... 723
. . distributed property ... 732
. . distributee partner's interest ... 733
. . optional adjustment ... 734; 743; 754; 755
. . partner's interest ... 705; 722; 733; 742
. . depreciable property, reduction of ... 1017
. property
. . allocation rules ... 755
. . contributed ... 723
. . manner of electing optional adjustment to ... 754
. . Sec. 754 election ... 743
. . substantial basis reduction ... 734
. . substantial built-in loss ... 743
. . transferee partner's interest ... 742
. . transfers of interests ... 742; 743
. . undistributed property, adjustment to basis of ... 734
. cancellation of indebtedness
. . debt instrument reaquisition after Dec. 31, 2008 and before Jan. 1, 2001 ... 108(i)(6)
. capital contributions ... 721 et seq.
. . assumption of liabilities ... 752
. . depreciation recapture ... 1250
. . distributive shares ... 704
. . family members ... 704
. . increase in partner's liabilities ... 752
. capital gains and losses ... 702; 703
. . loss property, contribution ... 724
. charitable contributions ... 702; 703
. closing of taxable year ... 706
. collapsible partnership ... 751
. community assets ... 1400F
. computation of tax ... 703
. computational adjustment ... 6231
. consolidations ... 708
. constructive ownership of stock ... 267; 318
. continuation of ... 708

227

Partners — Index to Code

Partners and partnerships—Cont'd | CODE SEC.
- contributions to .... 721 et seq.
- basis
  - interest 722
  - property 723
  - capital loss property 724
  - character of gain or loss 724
  - gain or loss 721
  - inventory items 724
  - nonrecognition of gain or loss 721
  - partner's distributive share 704
  - property, basis of 723
  - unrealized receivables 724
- controlled partnership, sales or exchanges 707
- corporation status determination, limitation on assessment and collection 6501
- corporation treated as (See S corporations)
- corporations, transactions with 267
- credits allowed partners 702; 901
- death of partner
  - closing of taxable year 706
  - optional adjustment to basis 743
  - payments to successor in interest 736; 753
  - self-employment tax 1402
- declaratory judgment relating to treatment of non-partnership items 6234
- deductions 703
- definitions 761; 6231; 7701
- depreciation
  - expensing in lieu of 179
  - recapture 1245; 1250
  - used or leased property, deduction 168
- determination of tax liability .... 701 et seq.
- discharge of indebtedness 108
- distributions .... 311; 731 et seq.
  - assumption of liabilities 752
  - basis
    - distributed property other than money 732
    - distributee partner's interest 733
    - undistributed partnership property 734
  - decrease in partner's liabilities 752
  - depreciation recapture 1245; 1250
  - foreign partner, withholdings on distribution to ... 1446
  - gross income 61
  - holding period 735
  - recognition of gain or loss 731; 735
  - sale or exchange 735; 751; 761
  - special partnership basis to transferee 732
- distributive shares 704
  - change in partnership interest 706
  - character of items 702
  - family partnerships 704
  - limitation on allowance of losses 704
  - retired or deceased partner 736
  - self-employment tax 1402
- dividends received 702
- division of partnership 708
- domestic defined 7701
- electing investment partnerships 6031

Partners and partnerships—Cont'd | CODE SEC.
- electing large partnerships (See Electing large partnerships)
- elections of, computation of tax 703
- employee achievement awards 274
- employee retirement and benefit plans 414
- estate freezes, special rules for .... 2701 et seq.
- exchanges of interest, returns for 6050K
- exploration expenditures 617; 703
- extensions on returns 6233
- failure to file return .... 6698(a)
  - deficiency procedure, application of ..... 6698(d)
  - penalty, amount per month .... 6698(b)
  - penalty assessment .... 6698(c)
- family 704
- farming accounting methods 447
- foreign (See Foreign partnerships)
- foreign corporations as members 875
- reorganization exchanges
  - sale of interest 897
- foreign currency transactions 988
- foreign partners, withholding tax on payments to ... 1446
- foreign personal holding company stock held by .. 551; 554
- foreign tax credit 901
- foreign taxes 702; 703
- foreign trade income, allocation of 943
- gain, precontribution
  - distributions by partnerships to contributing partner 737
- gifts as business expense 274
- good will 736
- gross income 702
- guaranteed payments 267; 707; 736
- income
  - computation 703
  - partner, of 702
  - taxability 706
- income in respect of decedent 753
- indirect partner defined 6231
- information returns 6031; 6050K; 6652
  - signature 6063
- innocent spouse relief, partner's spouse claiming 6230
- insurance company as member
  - gross income 834
- interest in
  - bankrupt partner 1398
  - basis 705; 722; 733; 742
  - depreciable property 1017
  - changes in, distributive shares 706
  - determination of basis 705
  - estate tax
    - extension of time to pay 6166
    - special use valuation property 2032A
  - exchange of
    - nontaxable exchange 1031
  - gift 704
  - holding period 735
  - liquidation
    - basis of distributed property 732
    - closing of partnership year 706
    - defined 761

228

Index to Code

Partners

CODE SEC.

Partners and partnerships—Cont'd
- interest in —Cont'd
  - liquidation —Cont'd
    - loss recognition 731
    - retirement or death 736
  - ownership of capital or profits interest 707
  - payments to retiring partner or deceased partner's successor 736
  - sale or exchange . . . . 741 et seq.; 751
    - basis of distributed property 732
    - closing taxable year 706
    - expenses 709
    - foreign investors 897
    - liabilities 752
  - transfer of
    - information returns 6050K; 6652
    - valuation rules for certain transfers to family members 2701
- inventory items
  - contribution 724
  - distribution 735; 751
  - transfer of interest, information returns 6050K; 6652
- investment credit 50
- itemized deductions 703
- large partnership (See Electing large partnership)
- liabilities
  - assumption of liabilities between 752
  - occupational taxes 4902
  - partner's share of 752
  - property subject to liability 752
  - treatment of certain 752
- liability for tax . . . . 701 et seq.
- life insurance company, installment obligations 453B
- limited
  - passive activity losses and credits 469
  - self-employment tax 1402
- liquidation of partner's interest
  - basis of distribution 732
  - close of tax year 706
  - defined 761
  - retirement or death 736
- liquidation rights, lapsed 2704
- losses, distributive shares 704
- low-income housing 267
- mergers 708
- mining exploration expenditures 617
- net operating loss 703
- nonbusiness expenses 703
- nonpartnership items
  - declaratory judgment relating to treatment 6234
  - defined 6231
- nonrecourse financing 465
- nonresident alien members 875
- notice of failure to collect and pay over taxes 7512
- sale of interest 897
- withholding at source on nonresident aliens and foreign corporations 1441
- notice of administrative proceeding 6223
- notice partner defined 6231
- oil and gas depletion allowance 613A; 703

CODE SEC.

Partners and partnerships—Cont'd
- organizational expenses 709
- over sheltered returns 6234
- partners
  - defined 761; 6231
  - income and credits 702
  - income in respect of decedent 753
  - liabilities of 752
  - not acting in capacity as 707
  - subject to tax 701
  - taxable year 706
- passive activity losses and credits 469
- pass-thru partner defined 6231
- payment to retiring partner or deceased partner's successor 736
- period of limitations for making assessments 6229
- personal exemptions 703
- personal holding company stock owned by 544
- personal property sales 865
- persons, as 7701
- possessions of U.S., taxes of 702; 703
- precontribution gain, distributions by partnerships to contributing partner 737
- private activity bonds 147
- property transfers between 707
- publicly traded partnerships
  - corporation, treated as 7704
  - passive activity losses and credits 469
  - unrelated business taxable income 512
- qualified tax credit bonds, credit for holders of . . . 54A(g)
- reforestation expenditures 194
- refunds and credits 6511; 7422
- reorganization exchanges 367
- retiring partner, payments to 736
- returns . . . . 6031; 6221 et seq.
  - corporation return, limitations on assessment and collection purposes 6501
  - disclosure 6103
  - inconsistent partner and partnership returns 6222
  - magnetic filing . . . . 6724(e)
  - signature 6063
- sales and exchanges with corporations 267
- self-employment income
  - distributive shares 1402
  - partner's taxable year ending as result of death . . 1402
- service partnerships
  - electing large partnership defined 775
  - services, performance by partner for partnership . . 707
- simplified flow-through 722
- small ethanol producer credit 40
- stock ownership 318
  - nondeductible losses 267
- straddles, gain or loss 1092
- syndication fees 709
- tax matters partners defined 6231
- tax year 706
- taxability . . . . 701 et seq.
- taxable years
  - election other than required 444
  - other than required; payment of tax 7519

Partners   **Index to Code**

CODE SEC.

Partners and partnerships—Cont'd
. taxable years —Cont'd
. . self-employment tax 1402
. . taxation at partnership level .... 6221 et seq.
. . termination 708
. . transactions between 707
. . transferred liabilities 752
. . transfers of interests in .... 741 et seq.
. . . adjustment to basis of property 743
. . . applicable asset acquisitions 1060
. . . basis of transferee partner's interest 742
. . . gain or loss on 741
. . . sale or exchange 751; 6050K
. . undistributed partnership property 734
. . unified audit procedures .... 6221 et seq.
. . unincorporated organization as 761
. . unrealized receivables
. . . contribution 724
. . . distribution 735; 751
. . . retirement or death 736
. . . transfer of interest, information returns 6050K; 6652
. . unrelated business income 512; 513
. . . information returns 6031
. . valuation rules
. . . transfers of certain interests to family members 2701
. . voting rights, lapsed 2704
. . withholding
. . . foreign partners, payments to 1446
. . . U.S. real property interest dispositions
. . . . disposition of interest in partnership, rules relating to
.... 1445(e)(5)
. . . . taxable distributions by domestic or foreign partnership
.... 1445(e)(4)
. . work opportunity credit 52
. . wrongly labeled entity, returns 6233
Parts and accessories
. automobiles
. . excise tax, luxury 4003
. . manufacturer's tax 4218
. sport fishing equipment excise tax 4161
Passbook loans
. lien for taxes 6323
Passenger aircraft
. alternative minimum tax and research credit in lieu of bonus depreciation, election .... 168(k)(4)(G)(iii)
Passenger vehicle excise taxes 4001
. first retail sale defined for 4002
. parts and accessories 4003
Passive activity losses and credits 469
. alternative minimum tax 58
. income, publicly traded partnerships 7704
Passive foreign investment companies (PFICs) ...... 1291 et seq.
. accumulated earnings tax 532
. attribution of ownership
. . changing businesses .... 1298(b)(3)
. . corporations .... 1298(a)(2)
. . determination .... 1298(b)(1)
. . dispositions .... 1298(b)(6)

CODE SEC.

Passive foreign investment companies (PFICs)—Cont'd
. attribution of ownership —Cont'd
. . intangibles .... 1298(e)
. . leased property .... 1298(d)
. . options .... 1298(a)(4)
. . other entity, stock held by .... 1298(b)(5)
. . partnerships .... 1298(a)(3)
. . pooled income fund .... 1298(c)
. . research expenditures .... 1298(e)(1)
. . separate interests .... 1298(b)(4)
. . start-up year, corporations not treated as PFIC during
.... 1298(b)(2)
. . subpart F inclusions .... 1298(b)(8)
. . successive application .... 1298(a)(5)
. . U.S. persons .... 1298(a)(1)
. basis for gain or loss 1293
. definition .... 1297(a)
. foreign tax credit 904; 1291
. interest on tax deferral 1291
. measuring assets .... 1297(e)
. options, holders of .... 1297(d)(4)
. passive income .... 1297(b)
. personal holding company status 542
. qualified electing funds
. . exempt income 1293
. . extensions, election for 1294
. . gain, election for recognition of 1291
. . general rule 1295
. . income from 1293
. twenty-five% owned corporations .... 1297(c)
. undistributed earnings 1294
. U.S. shareholders 951
. U.S. shareholders of CFCs .... 1297(d)(1)
Passive income, foreign tax credit 904
Passive investment income
. commodity futures 1362
. gross receipts, in excess of 1375
. S corporations
. . defined 1362
. . excess, passthrough of tax 1366
. . tax imposed upon excess of 1366; 1375
Passport applicants 6039E
Passthrough entities (See also Partners and partnerships; S corporations)
. constructive ownership transactions, defined for 1260
. domestic production activities .... 199(d)(1)
. indirect deductions, disallowance of 67
. lookback method 460
. nonconventional fuel source credit; estates and trusts
.... 45K(d)(8)
. partners and partnerships
. . pass-thru partner defined 6231
. . sales and exchanges between 267
. rate of tax 1
. redemption of stock 302
. related taxpayers 267
. research credit 41
. S corporations 1366
. sales and exchanges between 267

230

Index to Code   Payment

CODE SEC.

Passthrough entities (See also Partners and partnerships; S corporations) —Cont'd
. small agri-biodiesel producer credit . . . . 40A(e)(3)
. small ethanol producer credit 40
. transactions between 267
. 2% floor on miscellaneous itemized deductions 67
Pass-thru partner defined 6231
Patents
. applications, related party transactions 1239
. capital gains and losses from sale of 1235; 1239
. controlled foreign corporations, transfers to 1249
. damages for infringement 186
. deferred payment sales, interest 483
. depreciable property, applications treated as 1239
. holder of defined 1235
. infringement, damages received 186
. related persons, transfers between 1235
. sale or exchange 1235
. . gain on 1249
. . withholding tax at source on nonresident aliens and foreign corporations 1441
Paternity leave (See Maternity or paternity leaves)
Patient-centered outcomes research trust fund
. creation . . . . 9511(a)
. expenditures from fund
. . Patient-Centered Outcomes Research Institutes . . . . 9511(d)(1)
. . transfers of funds . . . . 9511(d)(2)
. net revenues defined . . . . 9511(e)
. termination after Sept. 30, 2019 . . . . 9511(f)
. transfers to fund
. . appropriation . . . . 9511(a)(1)
. . limitations on . . . . 9511(a)(3)
. . . Social Security sec. 1183, under . . . . 9511(a)(2)
. trustees . . . . 9511(c)
Patronage dividends . . . . 1381 et seq.
. allocation, cooperative association 1388
. backup withholding 3406
. basis to patron 1385
. consent by distributee 1388
. defined 1388
. exclusion 1385
. gross income of patron, amounts includible in 1382; 1385
. information returns (See Information returns)
. qualified check as part of defined 1388
. statement to recipients 6044
. tax treatment by patrons 1385
. taxability 1385
. taxable income of cooperatives, effect on 1382
. withholding tax 3406
. withholding tax, backup 3406
. written notice of allocation 1388
Pay period defined
. FICA 3121
. FUTA 3306
Pay-as-you-go tax . . . . 3401 et seq.
Payee statement
. defined 6724
. failure to furnish 6722

CODE SEC.

Payee statement —Cont'd
. failure to include correct information 6723
Payment cards and third party network transactions
. settlement, returns relating to . . . . 6050W(a)
. . de minimis payment by third party exception . . . . . 6050W(e)
. . intermediaries . . . . 6050W(b)(4)
. . merchant acquiring entity . . . . 6050W(b)(2)
. . participant payee . . . . 6050W(d)(1)
. . payment card defined . . . . 6050W(d)(2)
. . payment settlement entity . . . . 6050W(b)(1)
. . regulations, prescription of . . . . 6050W(g)
. . statements to be furnished . . . . 6050W(f)
. . third party payment network . . . . 6050W(d)(3)
. . third party settlement organization defined . . . . . 6050W(b)(3)
Payment of tax . . . . 6151 et seq. (See also Deficiencies; Overpayment of tax; Underpayment of tax)
. advance 6513
. . interest on overpayments 6611
. airline tickets tax 6302
. bad check 6657
. bankruptcy and receivership 1398; 6161
. check 6201; 6311
. commercially acceptable means, by 6311
. communications tax 6302
. computation of tax not by taxpayer 6151
. consolidated returns 1503
. corporations 1503
. correction of errors . . . . 1311 et seq.
. date considered paid 6513
. date fixed for 6151
. departure from country 6851
. Desert Shield 7508
. electronic fund transfers 5061
. employment taxes 3501
. estate tax (See Estate tax payment)
. estates and trusts 641
. estimated income tax 6315; 6425
. extensions (See Extensions)
. facilities and services taxes 4291
. failure to make 6654; 6672; 7202; 7203
. federal unemployment 3501; 6157; 6317
. FICA 3501
. foreign currency 6316
. foreign insurance companies, excise taxes 4374
. foreign insurance policies 4374
. fraction of cent 6313
. gasoline taxes 6302
. government depositaries 5703; 6302
. . failure to deposit 6656; 7215; 7512
. . overstatements 6656
. hospitalization due to combat related injuries 7508
. installments (See Installment payment of tax)
. interest on delinquency 6601; 6621
. . estate tax, closely held business interests 6166
. . . foreign expropriation loss recoveries 6167
. interest on underpayment, nonpayment, or extensions of time 6601
. manufacturers' excise taxes 6302
. money order 6201; 6311

Payment

Payment of tax—Cont'd   CODE SEC.
- notice and demand 6155; 6303
- occupational taxes .... 4901 et seq.; 5142
- place for 6151
- Presidential Election Campaign Fund participation 6096
- receipt for taxes 6314
- stamp tax 6311
- taxable year other than required, partnerships or S corporations 7519
- termination of taxable year 6851
- time for 6151
- .. undistributed earnings 1294
- timely mailing 7502
- tobacco products 5703
- wagering taxes 4411; 4901
- war postponements 7508
- wines 5043; 5061
- withheld taxes on wages 1461; 3403; 6302
- .. government employer 3404
- .. nonresident aliens and foreign corporations 1461; 1463

Payroll period
- defined 3401
- overlapping 3402

PBGC (See Pension Benefit Guaranty Corporation (PBGC)

Peace Corps allowances 912
- FICA 3121; 3122
- principal residence sale, gain on .... 121(d)(12)
- withholding tax on wages 3401; 6051

Peat depletion 613

Pecuniary bequests
- appreciated carryover basis to satisfy, use of 1040

Pediatric dental coverage
- premium assistance credits .... 36B(b)(3)(e)

Penalties .... 6651 et seq.; 7201 et seq. (See also Levy)
- abatement, errors by IRS 6404
- abusive tax shelters, promotion 6700; 6703
- .. refunds, suit for 7422
- accuracy-related penalty 6662; 6662A
- additions treated as tax 6665
- aiding and abetting understatements of tax liability 6701; 6703
- .. injunctions 7408
- .. refund suits 7422
- air transportation, statement of taxes imposed 7275
- assessable .... 6671 et seq.
- .. additions treated as tax 6665
- .. attempts to evade or defeat tax 6672
- .. compliance, failure 6723
- .. definitions 6664
- .. failure to collect and pay over tax 6672
- .. failure to file returns or pay tax (See Returns subhead failure to file)
- .. failure to make deposit of taxes 6656
- .. failure to produce records 7269
- .. failure to register 7272
- .. instituting proceeding before Tax Court merely for delay 6673
- .. rules for application 6671
- .. simple retirement account

Index to Code

        CODE SEC.

Penalties—Cont'd
- assessable—Cont'd
- .. simple retirement account —Cont'd
- ... trustee and issuer penalties 6693
- .. waiver, definitions 6724
- bad checks for payments 6657
- beer, unlawful production or removal of 5674
- brokers' failure to provide notice to payor 6705
- business expenses 162
- coordination with Title 11 6658
- court review instituted merely for delay 7482
- criminal .... 7201 et seq.
- defined 6751
- definitions 6664
- delay, Tax Court procedures instituted for purposes of ... 6673
- diesel fuel taxable use 6715
- disclosure
- .. availability of service or information from Federal government 6711
- .. returns and return information 7213; 7213A
- dyed fuel taxable use 6715
- employee stock ownership plans
- .. employer securities, premature dispositions 4978
- estimated tax 6651; 6654; 6655
- evasion of tax 6672; 7201
- excessive refund claims 6206; 6675
- exempt organizations
- .. failure to disclose nondeductibility in fundraising solicitations 6710
- .. sale of information or services
- ... failure to disclose availability from Federal Government 6711
- failure of Secretary to contact taxpayer
- .. suspension of interest and penalties 6404
- failure to account for tax 6672; 7512
- failure to collect or pay over tax 6672; 7202; 7215
- failure to deposit taxes 6656; 7215
- failure to disclose treaty-based return positions 6712
- failure to file information returns (See Information returns subhead failure to file)
- failure to file interest and dividend returns or statements 6724
- failure to file return (See Returns subhead failure to file)
- failure to furnish information
- .. U.S.-Guam taxes, concerning 6688
- failure to furnish notice of foreign tax redetermination 6689
- failure to furnish payee statements 6722
- failure to furnish statement as to tips 6652
- failure to furnish withholding tax statement .. 6652; 6674; 7204
- failure to include correct information 6723
- failure to keep records 7203
- failure to pay estimated taxes 6651
- failure to pay tax 6651; 6658; 6672; 7202; 7203
- failure to produce books 7269
- failure to provide notices as to rollover eligibility of employee retirement or benefit plan distributions 6652
- failure to register bonds and obligations 4701
- failure to report tips 6652
- failure to supply information 7203; 7205
- failure to surrender property subject to levy 6332; 6621
- failure to withhold tax

Index to Code

Penalties—Cont'd
failure to withhold tax —Cont'd
- nonresident aliens and foreign corporations, tax paid by recipient ... 1463
- wages ... 3402
- fines, business expenses ... 162
- firearms violations ... 5871; 5872
- foreign corporation failure to file personal holding co. return ... 6683
- forfeitures (See Forfeitures of property)
- fraud ... 7204 et seq.
- - backup withholding ... 7205
- - joint return, liability of whom ... 6013
- - joint return after filing separate returns ... 6013
- - tip statement ... 6674
- - withholding allowances ... 6682
- - withholding exemption certificates ... 7205
- - withholding tax statements ... 6674; 7204
- fringe benefits, excess ... 4977
- frivolous returns filed ... 6702; 6703
- gasoline taxes ... 6675; 7232
- golden parachute agreements ... 4999
- greenmail payments ... 5881
- insurance policies ... 7270
- interest on ... 6601
- liens for taxes (See Liens for taxes)
- liquor taxes ... 5601 et seq.
- misrepresentation of tax ... 7211
- mortgage credit certificates ... 6709
- negligence
- - joint return after filing separate returns ... 6013
- nondeductibility of contributions, failure to disclose ... 6710
- occupational taxes ... 5691
- original issue discount, information requirements ... 6706
- overstatement of taxes to government depositaries ... 6656
- payee statements, failure to furnish correct ... 6722
- payment ... 6671; 6724
- pension plans ... 6652; 6690; 6692; 6693
- possession with intent to sell in fraud of law or to evade tax ... 7268
- preparers of returns (See Preparers of returns)
- Presidential Election Campaign Fund ... 9012
- Presidential Primary Matching Payment Account ... 9042
- private foundations ... 6652; 6684
- - returns, failure to file or make public ... 6652
- procedural requirements ... 6751
- refusal to permit entry or examination ... 7342
- regulated investment companies, prior law ... 6697
- REITs ... 857
- - prior law ... 6697
- sales to evade tax ... 7341
- special taxes, offenses relating to ... 7273
- stamp tax, failure to pay ... 6653
- stamps ... 7208; 7209; 7271
- suits by U.S. ... 7401
- summons disregarded ... 7210
- Tax Court proceeding instituted merely for delay or with frivolous or groundless positions ... 6673
- tax return preparers (See Preparer of returns)
- tax shelters

Penalties—Cont'd
tax shelters —Cont'd
- - information ... 6707; 6708
- - promoters ... 6703
- tobacco products ... 5761 et seq.
- - assessments ... 5703
- - civil ... 5761
- - criminal ... 5762
- - forfeitures ... 5763
- Treasury Department officers ... 7344
- treaty-based return positions, failure to disclose ... 6712
- trust fund recovery penalty ... 6672
- understatement of tax ... 6662
- - aiding and abetting ... 6701; 6703
- - injunctions ... 7408
- - refunds, suit for ... 7422
- valuation misstatements ... 6662
- valuation overstatements ... 6662
- violation of statutes
- - business expenses ... 162
- - failure to pay ... 7262
- wagering taxes ... 4424; 4906
- welfare benefit plans ... 4976
- withholding allowances, false information ... 6682
- withholding exemption certificates ... 7205
- withholding tax on wages ... 6658; 6674; 7204

Pension, profit-sharing, and stock bonus plans
... 401 et seq.; 4971 et seq.; 6057 et seq. (See also Employee retirement and benefit plans)
- accrued benefits
- - amendment decreasing ... 411
- - defined benefit plans ... 411
- - vesting standards ... 411
- accumulations in IRA or annuities, excise tax on ... 4974
- acquisitions ... 401; 410
- actuarial assumptions, specification requirement ... 401
- actuarial report ... 6059
- - penalties ... 6692
- - prior to merger ... 6058
- administrator of plan ... 414
- affiliated service groups ... 414(m)(2)
- - separate lines of business ... 414(r)(8)
- age requirements ... 410
- aggregation rules ... 410
- alienation of benefits ... 401
- allocation of accrued benefits ... 411
- alternate payees ... 402
- alternative minimum funding standards ... 412
- amendments to plan ... 401; 411
- - retroactive, minimum funding standards ... 412
- American employer, employees of foreign affiliates ... 406
- annual registration statement ... 6057
- - disclosure ... 6103
- - penalties ... 6652
- annuities (See Employee annuities)
- annuity contracts ... 816
- application, participation standards ... 410
- assignment of benefits ... 401
- association plans, medical benefit reserve ... 419A

233

Pension, profit-sharing, and stock bonus plans—Cont'd

	CODE SEC.
. automatic contribution arrangements	414(w)(1)
. . applicable employer plan defined	414(w)(5)
. . combined plans	414(x)(5)
. . defined	414(w)(3)
. . notice requirements	414(w)(4)
. . permissible withdrawal	414(w)(2)
. average benefit percentage test	410
. backup withholding	3406
. beneficiary	401; 402
. benefits	
. . accrual reduction notice requirement	4980F
. . limitations	415
. bond purchase plan rollover	402
. bonds, valuation	412
. books and records	
. . limitation on benefits and contributions	415
. breaks in service	410; 411
. cash or deferred arrangements	401; 402
. . combined with	414(x) et seq.
. catch-up contributions for individuals age 50 or over	414(v)(1)
. . applicable employer plan defined	414(v)(6)(A)
. . contributions	414(v)(3)
. . elective deferral defined	414(v)(6)(B)
. . eligible participant defined	414(v)(5)
. . limitations on additional deferrals	414(v)(2)
. . nondiscrimination rules	414(v)(4)
. . Sec. 457 plan exception	414(v)(6)(C)
. children, distributions to	401
. church plans	410; 411; 415
. . associated with church	414(e)(3)(D)
. . chaplains	414(e)(5)
. . correction of failure to meet plan requirements	414(e)(4)
. . deferred compensation plans	457
. . defined	414(e); 414(e)(1)
. . employee annuities	
. . . taxability of beneficiary	403
. . employer status	414(e)(3)(C)
. . group-term life insurance	79
. . limitation on contributions and benefits	415
. . minimum participation standards	410
. . ministers, self-employed	414(e)(5)
. . separation from plan	414(e)(3)(E)
. . vesting standards	411
. collective bargaining agreement	401
. collectively bargained plans (See Collectively bargained plans)	
. combined plans	414(x)(1)
. . applicable defined contribution plan defined	414(x)(7)
. . automatic contribution arrangements	414(x)(5)
. . coordination with other requirements	414(x)(6)
. . eligible plans	414(x)(2)
. . nondiscrimination requirements	414(x)(3)
. . top-heavy rules, satisfaction of	414(x)(4)
. compensation	
. . defined	414; 414(s)
. . highly compensated employees	414(q)(4)
. . veterans' reemployment rights under USERRA	414(u)(7)
. consolidation of plans	401; 414

Pension, profit-sharing, and stock bonus plans—Cont'd

	CODE SEC.
. contracts	401
. contributions	
. . automatic (See subhead automatic contribution arrangements)	
. . carryovers, acquiring corporation	381
. . catch-up (See subhead catch-up contributions for individuals age 50 or over)	
. . corporate acquisitions	381
. . deductibility	404
. . disabled participants	415
. . employees	411; 501
. . employer (See subhead employer contributions)	
. . employer liability payments as	404
. . failure to make	412
. . foreign affiliates	406
. . foreign personal holding companies	556
. . limitations	415
. . matching (See subhead matching contributions)	
. . nondeductible, tax on	4972
. . quarterly	412
. . tax treatment	414(h)
. . time deemed made	412
. . voluntary	411
. controlled group of corporations	
. . application of rules to certain employees	414(t)
. . employees defined	414(b)
. . minimum funding standards	412
. cost-of-living adjustments	415
. credit or refund	6511
. custodial accounts	401
. death of participant, payments on	401; 402
. declaratory judgments on qualification	7476
. deduction for contributions of an employer	404
. deferrals, elective	
. . limitation on exclusion	402
. deferred compensation plans, disclosure of information as to	6103
. deficiencies	6213; 6214; 6501
. defined benefit plans	401; 411; 412; 414
. . combined with qualified cash or deferred arrangement	414(x) et seq.
. . defined	414(j)
. defined contribution plans	401; 411; 414(i)
. designated beneficiary	401
. determinations, profit-sharing plans	401
. disclosure of information	6103
. discriminatory benefits or contributions	411
. disparity in contributions and benefits	401
. dispositions	401; 410
. disqualified person defined	4975
. distributions	
. . beginning date	401
. . lump-sum	402
. . mandatory	411
. . nonexempt plans	402
. . requirements	401
. . restrictions, mandatory distributions	411
. . rollover, direct transfer of	401
. . taxation	402

Index to Code   Pension

CODE SEC.

Pension, profit-sharing, and stock bonus plans—Cont'd
. distributions —Cont'd
.. termination, on 401; 411
.. working retirement, during 401
. domestic relations order
.. alternate payees, treatment as distributee 402
.. assignment or alienation of employee benefits 401
.. definition 414
. domestic subsidiaries engaged in business outside the U.S., employees of 407
. educational organizations 410
. elective deferral limitations 401; 402
. eligibility to participate 401
. employee contributions
.. accrued benefits 411
.. nondiscrimination test 401
.. vesting standards 411
. employee stock ownership plans (See Employee stock ownership plan (ESOPs))
. employer contributions
.. accrued benefits 411
.. elective deferral 401
.. matching contributions 401
.. qualified nonelective contributions 401
.. vesting standards 411
. excess contributions or benefits 401; 4973; 4979
. excess pension assets, transfers to retiree health accounts 420
. excise taxes .... 4971 et seq.
. excludable employees 401; 410
. exemption from tax 501
. experience gains and losses 412
. failure to meet minimum funding standards, tax on ... 4971
. fiduciary defined 4975
. foreign affiliates, employees of 406
. foreign deferred compensation plans 404A
. foreign situs trust beneficiary taxability 402
. foreign tax credit limitations
.. lump-sum distributions 402
. forfeitures 401
.. matching contributions 411
.. vesting standards 411
. fringe benefits, excess 4977
. funded welfare benefit plans 419
.. qualified asset account 419A
.. taxes 4976
. funding method 412
. funding standard account 412
. governmental plan .... 401; 411; 414(d)
. gross income 61
. highly compensated employees (See Highly compensated employees)
. incidental death benefit distribution 401
. income recaptured under qualified plan termination ... 6511
. individual medical benefit accounts 415
. individual retirement accounts (See Individual retirement accounts)
. individual retirement annuity
.. accumulations, excise tax on 4974
.. excess contributions, tax on 4973

CODE SEC.

Pension, profit-sharing, and stock bonus plans—Cont'd
. individual retirement annuity —Cont'd
.. information returns 6047
.. penalties 6693
.. publicity of information required from 6104
. individual statement to participant 6057; 6690
. information returns 6047; 6058; 6059
. injuries and sickness, compensation for 104
. insurance contracts 401; 412
. joint and survivor annuity 401
. key employees, top-heavy plans 416
. labor unions 415
. leased employees (See Leased employees)
. levy on 6334
. liens
.. failure to make required contributions 412
. life expectancy 401
. life insurance companies 817; 818
. limitations
.. benefits 415
.. contributions 415
.. refunds or credits 6511
. line of business
.. exception to minimum coverage requirements 410
. loan, prohibited transaction 4975
. lump-sum distributions 402
. matching contributions
.. definition 401
.. forfeitures 411
.. nondiscrimination test 401
. maternity leaves 410; 411
. maximum age conditions 410
. medical benefit accounts 415
. mergers and consolidations .... 401; 414(l)(1)
.. actuarial statement prior to 6058
.. allocation in plan spin-off .... 414(l)(2)
. military death benefits 401
. minimum age 410
. minimum coverage requirements 410
. minimum funding standards 412
.. tax on failure to meet standards 4971
. minimum participation requirements 401; 410
. money purchase pension plans 401
. more than one employer plans 413
. multiemployer plans .... 401; 418 et seq.
.. common control .... 414(f)(2)
.. defined .... 414(f)(1)
.. election .... 414(f)(6)
.. minimum funding standards 412
.. special election .... 414(f)(5)
.. termination of plan .... 414(f)(3)
.. transitional rules .... 414(f)(4)
. multiple distributions 402
. net unrealized appreciation 402
. nondeductible contributions, tax on 4972
. nondiscrimination requirements 401
. nonexempt plans
.. distributions, taxation 402
.. minimum coverage requirements, failure to meet ... 402

235

Pension   **Index to Code**

CODE SEC.

Pension, profit-sharing, and stock bonus plans—Cont'd
. nonexempt plans—Cont'd
. . taxability of beneficiaries 402
. nonresident aliens 871
. . beneficiaries 401; 402
. . highly compensated employee .... 414(q)(8)
. normal retirement benefit 411
. notice
. . pension benefit accrual reduction 4980F
. owner-employee, benefiting 401
. participant, individual statement to 6057
. participation standards 410
. . year of participation 411
. partnership employee defined .... 414(c)
. payors' reports, recordkeeping 6047; 6704
. penalties
. . actuarial report 6692
. . individual statement to participant 6690
. . lump-sum distributions 402
. . notification of change of status 6652
. . periodic report of actuary 6692
. . registration statement 6652
. . reports on individual retirement accounts or annuities ... 6693
. periodic report of actuary 6059
. permitted disparity in contributions and benefits 401
. plan administrator defined .... 414(g)
. plan administrator registration statement 6057
. plan year changes, approval 412
. post-1992 distributions 402
. pre-1993 distributions 402
. predecessor employer, service for .... 414(a)
. preretirement survivor annuity 401
. prohibited allocations of qualified securities 4979A
. prohibited transactions, tax on 4975
. public safety employees, qualified 401
. publicity of information required from 6104
. qualification requirements 401
. qualified asset accounts 419A
. qualified domestic relations orders (See Qualified domestic relations orders)
. qualified employer plan defined 4972
. qualified retirement plan defined 4974
. railroad retirement benefits, tier 1 86
. refunds and credits 6511; 7422
. registration statement, annual 6057
. . disclosure 6103
. . penalties 6652
. requirements 401
. retired employees 401
. retiree health accounts, transfers of excess pension assets to 420
. retirement age, normal 411
. retirement bond excess contributions tax 4973
. retroactive changes 401
. retroactive plan amendments 411
. reversion of assets to employer 4980
. rollovers
. . bonds 402
. . optional direct transfer 401
. . written explanation of eligible distributions 402

CODE SEC.

Pension, profit-sharing, and stock bonus plans—Cont'd
. seasonal employees 411
. securities, distributions in 401
. security, underfunding 401
. self-employed (See Self-employed retirement plans)
. separate accounting, vesting standards 411
. separate lines of business (See Separate lines of business)
. service conditions 410
. service organizations .... 414(m)(3)
. service requirements 410; 411
. several employer plans 413
. simplified employee pensions (See Simplified employee pension plans)
. small employer startup costs credits 45E
. small plan minimum funding standards 412
. Social Security benefits 86
. . permitted disparity 401
. sole proprietorship 414
. status, notification of change of 6057; 6652
. surviving spouse, distributions 401; 417
. suspension of benefits, vesting standards 411
. Tax Court judges 7447
. . dependents 7448
. taxability of beneficiary 402
. termination
. . benefits upon, discriminatory effects 411
. . distributions on 401
. time of participation 410
. top-heavy plans 401; 416
. total distributions 401
. transfer of plan assets to another plan 414
. trustee-to-trustee transfers 402
. UMWA pension plans .... 9701 et seq.
. underfunding, security required 401
. union-negotiated 401
. U.S. citizens or residents living abroad 911
. valuation of assets 412
. vesting of retirement benefits 401; 411
. lump-sum distributions
. . . potential future vesting 402
. . potential future vesting 402
. . rollovers 402
. veterans' reemployment rights under USERRA
. . compensation .... 414(u)(7)
. . contributions, treatment of .... 414(u)(1)
. . death or disability resulting from active military service .... 401(a)(37); 414(u)(9)
. . differential wage payments .... 414(u)(12)
. . elective deferrals .... 414(u)(2)
. . individual account plan defined .... 414(u)(6)
. . loan repayments .... 414(u)(4)
. . plans not subject to title 38 .... 414(u)(10)
. . qualified military service defined .... 414(u)(5)
. . retroactive adjustments .... 414(u)(3)
. . USERRA requirements .... 414(u)(8)
. voluntary employee contributions 411
. withdrawals 401
. vesting standards 411
. withholding tax on deferred income 3405

236

Index to Code

Personal

CODE SEC.

Pension, profit-sharing, and stock bonus plans—Cont'd
. years of service 410
. . nonforfeiture percentage 411
. . vesting standards 411
Pension Benefit Guaranty Corporation (PBGC)
. inspection of returns 6103
. multiemployer plans, financial assistance ... 412
. pension recipients, health insurance costs of ... 35
. . advance payment of credit 7527
. . returns related to credit 6050T
Percentage depletion 613
. limitation 613A
. mines and mining
. . carryovers, acquiring corporation 381
. . oil and gas wells, limitation 613A
. reduction 291
. refiner exclusion 613A
Percentage method withholding 3402
Percentage of completion method
. long-term contracts 460
Performing artists
. adjusted gross income 62
Perfumes
. alcohol used in, drawback of 5111
. imported
. . alcohol taxes 5001
. . U.S. possession, shipments from 7652
Period of affiliation defined 1051
Period of limitations (See Statute of limitations)
Periodical circulation expenditures 173
Periods, effective
. mortgage credit certificates 25
Perishable goods 6336; 7324
Perjury 7206
Perlite depletion 613
Person defined 5690; 7343; 7701
Personal credits 21
. alternate motor vehicle credits treatment as ... 30B(g)(2)
. D.C. first-time home buyer carryforward on unused credit
. . years in which all personal credits allowed against regular and alternate minimum tax .... 1400C(d)(1)
. . years other than in which all personal credits allowed against regular and alternate minimum tax .... 1400C(d)(2)
. excessive, overpayments of tax 6401
Personal exemptions .... 151 et seq.
. children 151
. custodial parents 152
. dependents .... 151 et seq.
. disabled dependents 151
. disallowance 151
. estates and trusts 642; 643
. exemption amount 151
. foreign tax credit 904
. handicapped dependents 151
. husband and wife 151
. inflation adjustments 151
. kidnapped children 151
. married dependents 151

CODE SEC.

Personal exemptions—Cont'd
. missing children 151
. nationals of U.S. 873
. nonresident aliens 873
. partnerships 703
. phaseout 151
. self-employment tax 1402
. sheltered workshop income 151
. short-period returns 443
. students 151
. taxpayer and spouse 151
Personal expenses ... 262 (See also specific kinds of expense)
Personal holding companies .... 541 et seq.
. accounting period, change in 546
. accumulated earnings tax 532
. affiliated corporations 542
. assessment and collection 6501
. carryovers by acquiring corporation 381
. consolidated returns 542
. deduction for deficiency dividends 547
. deficiency dividends 547
. . corporate acquisitions 381
. definitions 542; 543
. distributions 316
. dividend carryover 381
. dividend income 542
. dividends 316
. dividends paid deduction .... 561 et seq.
. exceptions 542
. failure to file return 6683
. foreign corporation failure to file return .. 6683
. gross income 543
. income 543
. . not placed on annual basis 546
. . undistributed 545
. lending or finance company 542
. lien for taxes, priority 6323
. limitations on assessment and collection .. 6501
. rate of tax 541
. recovery of tax benefit items 111
. stock ownership 544
. taxes imposed 541
. undistributed income 545
Personal injury and sickness (See also Disability)
. accident and health benefits 104
. compensation 104; 130
. liability assignments 130
Personal interest 163
Personal property
. capital expenditures 263A
. dealer dispositions, installment sales 453
. depreciation 865
. exchange of 865
. future interests, charitable contributions . 170
. gain or loss 1234A
. installment sales .... 453 et seq.
. inventory costs 263A
. lien for taxes 6323; 6334

237

Personal | Index to Code

CODE SEC.

Personal property — Cont'd
- sale of 865; 7505
- source of income on sale or exchange 861; 862
- straddles 1092
  - interest and carrying charges 263
  - termination 1234A
- taxes, deductibility 164

Personal service contracts
- controlled foreign corporations 954
- foreign employers 864
- foreign personal holding company income 553
- personal holding company income 543

Personal service corporations
- accounting methods 448
- accounting periods 280H; 444
- change in status 469
- deferral period 280H
- defined 269A; 280H; 448
- distributions by 1016
- electing alternative taxable years 444
- employee-owner 269A; 280H
- evasion or avoidance of tax 269A
- farm loss, AMT 58
- graduated rates 11
- passive activity losses and credits 469
- taxable year 441
  - alternative taxable year election 280H
  - electing alternative taxable year, election 444

Personal services, compensation for (See Compensation for personal services)

Personal tax credits (See also specific credit)
- employment-related expenses 21
- foreign tax credit 904
- nonrefundable .... 21 et seq.

Personal use property
- automobiles 280F
- beer tax 5053
- capital expenditures 263A
- installment sales 453A
- inventory costs 263A
- tobacco 5761
- wines 5042

Per-unit retain allocations 1382; 1383; 1385; 1388

Petitions, Tax Court (See Tax Court)

Petroleum and petroleum products
- aviation fuel (See Aviation fuel)
- environmental taxes .... 4611 et seq.
- excise taxes .... 4081 et seq.; 6426
  - bonds and liens 4101
  - environmental taxes 4611; 4612
  - failure to register 6719; 7232
  - information reporting 4101; 4104
  - inspection of records 4102
  - registration, exempt sales 4222
  - registration and bond 4101
  - special fuels 4041
  - refunds and credits 6427
  - two-party exchanges 4104

CODE SEC.

Petroleum and petroleum products — Cont'd
- fuels
  - aviation (See Aviation)
  - biodiesel (See Biodiesel fuels)
  - diesel (See Diesel fuels; Special fuels tax)
  - generally (See Fuels)
  - special fuels tax (See Special fuels tax)
- gasoline tax (See Gasoline tax)
- mixtures not used as fuel 6426
- registration and bond, failure to comply 7232
- storage facility depreciation recapture 1245

PFICs (See Passive foreign investment companies)

Philippines government employee compensation 893

Phosphate rock percentage depletion 613

Phosphorus hazardous waste clean up 4661; 4662

Photographers capital expenditures 263A

Piggyback trailers and semitrailers
- retailers excise tax 4051

Pipe tobacco excise tax 5702

Pistols and revolvers (See also Firearms)
- excise taxes
  - exemptions 4182
  - imposition of tax 4181
  - rate of tax 4181
  - registration 4222

Plan administrator (See Pension, profit sharing and annuity plans)

Platinum depletion 613

Player contracts
- basis for gain or loss 1056
- capital gains and losses from dispositions of 1245
- depreciation recapture 1245
- sale of franchise, transfer upon 1056

Pledges and guarantees (See Guarantees)

Plug-in electric vehicles
- credits against tax 30
- new qualified plug-in drive motor vehicles credit
  - air quality and motor vehicle safety standards, interaction with .... 30D(f)(7)
  - allowance of credit .... 30D(a)
  - basis reduction .... 30D(f)(1)
  - battery capacity defined .... 30D(d)(4)
  - double benefits .... 30D(f)(2)
  - election not to take credit .... 30D(f)(6)
  - limitations
    - number of vehicles eligible for credit ... 30D(e)
    - per vehicle .... 30D(b)
  - manufacturer defined .... 30D(d)(3)
  - motor vehicle defined .... 30D(d)(2)
  - new qualified plug-in drive motor vehicles defined .... 30D(d)(1)
  - outside the U.S., property used .... 30D(f)(4)
  - recapture .... 30D(f)(5)
  - tax-exempt entities, use by .... 30D(f)(3)

Points on mortgage 461

Pole rentals
- unrelated trade or business 513

Index to Code

Possessions

CODE SEC.

Police department employee benefit plan 401
Policyholder dividends 808
. gross income computation 803
. taxable investment income 834
Political campaigns
. authorized committee defined 9032
. candidate defined 9002; 9032
. contributions to .... 9001 et seq.
. expense limitation 9035
. 501(c) organizations 6852; 7409
. kickbacks and illegal payments 9012; 9042
. principal campaign committee 527
Political candidates
. defined 9032
. defined for presidential election campaign fund 9002
. newsletter funds 527
. proceeds inuring to or for use of 276
Political committee
. defined for presidential election campaign fund 9002
Political contributions
. appreciated property 84
. campaigns, to .... 9001 et seq.
. charitable organizations 4912; 4955; 6852; 7409
. deduction 170
. defined 9032
. 501(c) organizations 4955
. Indian tribal government, treatment as state 7871
. Presidential Election Campaign Fund .... 9001 et seq.
. tax payment, from 6096
Political organizations
. appreciated property, contributions of 84
.. basis 84
... gross income, inclusion in 84
. bingo games, income from 527
. campaign committees 527
. definitions 84; 527
. information returns 6033
. nondeductibility of contributions, required disclosure 6113; 6710
. principal campaign committees 527
. returns 6012
. taxable income defined 527
. taxation 527
. transfer of money or property, gift tax 2501
. transfer of property to 84
Political parties 271; 276
Political subdivisions (See Municipalities)
Pollution control facilities (See also Environmental taxes)
. accelerated cost recovery deduction 291
. alternative minimum tax 56
. amortization 169
. sulfuric acid produced by, environment tax 4662
Pooled financing bonds
. arbitrage bonds 148
. 501(c)(3) organization 147
. state and local .... 149(f)(1)
.. cost of issuance payment requirement .... 149(f)(3)
.. defined .... 149(f)(6)

CODE SEC.

Pooled financing bonds —Cont'd
. state and local—Cont'd
.. loan defined .... 149(f)(7)
.. reasonable expectation requirements .... 149(f)(2)
.. redemption requirement .... 149(f)(5)
.. written loan commitment requirement .... 149(f)(4)
. student loan bonds 148
Pooled income funds
. charitable contributions 170
. charitable remainder
.. gift tax 2522
. defined 642
. FUTA 3303
. remainder interest, charitable contribution 170
. transfers to 683
Pools, wagering, tax on (See Wagering taxes)
Port use tax (See Harbor maintenance tax)
Portfolio debt investments
. foreign corporations 881
. nonresident aliens 871; 1441
Portfolio stock debt-financed
. dividends-received deduction 246A
Possession tax credits 27; 901; 904
. accumulated earnings tax 936
. consolidated returns 1504
. DISC 936
. foreign corporations 882
. foreign sales corporations (FSCs) 936
. Puerto Rico 936
Possessions corporations (See also Possession tax credit)
. withholding of tax, exemption from 1442
Possessions of U.S. .... 7651 et seq.
. administration 7651
. assessment and collection of taxes in 7651
. banks receiving interest on U.S. obligations 882
. coal 4121
. corporations
.. depreciable property 168
.. organized in possession, U.S. shareholders of 957
. credits against tax (See Possessions tax credits)
. defined 931; 936
. depreciable property 168
. depreciation deduction, used or leased property 168
. dividends received deduction 246
. estate tax 2208; 2209
. exempt income 115
. factoring trade receivables 864
. federally guaranteed bonds 149
. foreign country
.. status 2014
.. treatment as 872
. foreign tax credit 901
. governmental employees returns 3125
. gross transportation income 891
. harbor maintenance tax 4462
. imposition of gift taxes 2501
. income from .... 861; 904; 931 et seq.
.. Puerto Rico 933

239

CODE SEC.

Possessions of U.S. — Cont'd
. *income from — Cont'd*
. . Virgin Islands 932; 934
. liquors shipped to 5002
. private activity bonds
. . volume cap 146
. residence and source rules 937
. residents
. . estate tax 2102; 2208; 2209
. . gift tax 2501
. . income, sources of 931
. Sec. 936 credit 901; 904; 936
. . consolidated returns 1504
. . shipments from U.S. 7653
. . shipments to U.S. 7652
. . short-term obligations issued at discount .... 454; 1271; 1281 et seq.
. tax credit (See Possessions tax credit)
. taxes of 515
. . contested 461
. . credit (See Possessions tax credit)
. . deductibility 164
. . partnerships 702; 703
. transportation between U.S. and, source of income ... 863
. vaccines shipped to, excise tax 4132
. withholding tax on wages 3401
Post allowances 912; 6011
Postal service, U.S. (See also Mail and mailing)
. expenditures incurred by 7509
. postmarks as timely filing 7502
. rural mail carriers
. . reimbursement of business expenses 162
. sale of revenue stamps at post office 6802
Potash depletion 613
Poverty areas
. enterprise zones/communities (See Enterprise zones/communities)
. mortgage revenue bonds, targeted areas .... 143(j)(3)
. recovery zone bonds (See Recovery zone bonds)
. recovery zone facility bonds (See Recovery zone facility bonds)
Poverty line
. defined for health plan premium assistance credits .... 36B(d)(3)
Powers of appointment
. basis of property 1014
. charitable bequests
. . nonresident aliens 2055; 2106
. . . taxable estate 2055
. estate tax (See Estate tax)
. gift tax (See Gift tax)
. grantor of trust 672
. gross estate, effect on 2041; 2106
. life estate with powers in donee spouse, gift tax and ... 2523
. nonresident aliens 2055; 2106
Predecessor corporations
. change of ownership 382
. preacquisition losses offsetting built-in gains 384
Preexisting conditions
. crediting previous coverage
. . affiliation period .... 9801(c)(2)(C)

CODE SEC.

Preexisting conditions — Cont'd
. *crediting previous coverage — Cont'd*
. . breaks in coverage .... 9801(c)(2)
. . creditable coverage defined .... 9801(c)(1)
. . Medicaid and CHIP, special rules .... 9801(f)(3)
. . method of crediting .... 9801(c)(3)
. . period of, establishing .... 9801(c)(4)
. . periods before enrollment date .... 9801(c)(2)
. . TAA-eligible individuals .... 9801(c)(2)(D)
. long-term care insurance 9801
Preference dividends
. dividends-received deduction 246
Preferences items (See Tax preferences)
Preferential and preferred dividends
. defined 565
. dividends-paid deduction 562
Preferred items
. capital expenditures 263A
. inventory costs 263A
Preferred stock
. defined 247
. dividends received deduction
. . portfolio stock, debt-financed 246A
. public utilities
. . dividends received deductions 243; 244
Premium assistance credit
. health plan coverage 36B
. . definitions and rules concerning 36B
Premiums
. bond (See Bond premiums)
. insurance (See Insurance premiums)
Prepaid dues income 456
Prepaid subscription income 455
Preparers of returns
. adjudication and decrees .... 7407(b)(1)
. assessable penalties with respect to the preparation of returns for other persons 6695
. claim for refund defined .... 6696(e)(2)
. confidentiality 7524
. copies of returns 6107; 6695
. defined 7701
. disclosure of returns or return information ... 6107; 7216
. . improper 6713
. . state agencies regulating preparers 6103
. extension of period of collection where preparer pays 15% of penalty .... 6694(c)
. identification numbers 6109; 6695
. income tax return preparer defined 7701
. information returns 6060; 6695
. injunction against 7407
. list of taxpayers 6107
. lists of clients 6107
. penalties on .... 6694 et seq.; 6712; 6713; 7216
. recordkeeping requirements 6107; 6695
. return defined .... 6696(e)(1)
. rules concerning 6696
. understatement of liability 6694; 7427
. . defined .... 6694(e)

Index to Code

CODE SEC.

Preparers of returns — Cont'd
. *understatement of liability — Cont'd*
.. determination of liability for penalty .... 6694(c)(2)
.. unreasonable position, due to .... 6694(a)(1)
.. willful or reckless conduct, due to .... 6694(b)(1)

Preretirement survivor annuities 401; 417

Prescription drugs
. clinical testing expenses, credit for .... 280C(b)
. dealer's deductions 280E
. federal subsidies for 139A
. medical expenses 213
. narcotics (See Narcotic drugs)
. reimbursements for .... 106(f)

President of U.S.
. disclosure of returns and return information 6103
. Executive orders (See Executive orders)

Presidential appointees
. disclosure of returns and return information 6103

Presidential election campaign fund .... 9001 et seq.
. audit of candidate's expenses 9007
. authorized committee defined 9002
. candidate defined 9002
. candidate's expenses, report of 9009
. Commission defined 9002
. Congress, reports to 9009
. contributions to 6096
. criminal penalties 9012
. definitions 9002
. effective date 9013
. eligibility for payments .... 9003 et seq.
.. certification by Commission 9005
.. condition for 9003
.. entitlement of eligible candidates to payments 9004
.. establishment of campaign fund .... 9006(a)
.. expenditures from personal funds .... 9004(d)
.. limitations .... 9004(b)
.. payments from fund .... 9006(b)
.. payments to candidates 9006
.. restrictions .... 9004(c)
. eligible candidate defined 9002
. expenditure limitations, penalties for violation ... 9012
. expenditure report defined 9002
. Federal Election Commission (See Federal Election Commission)
. fund defined 9002
. judicial proceedings, participation by Commission in ... 9010
. judicial review 9011
. kickbacks and illegal payments for campaign expenses ... 9012
. major party defined 9002
. minor party defined 9002
. new party defined 9002
. nominating conventions, payments for 9008
. operational procedure 9006
. payments to candidates 9006
. penalties for violation of use 9012
. political committee defined 9002
. presidential election defined 9002
. presidential nominating conventions, payments for ... 9008

CODE SEC.

Presidential election campaign fund — Cont'd
. primary matching payment account (See Presidential Primary Matching Payment Account)
. qualified campaign expense defined 9002
. regulations 9009
. repayments to, excessive 9007; 9008
. reports to Congress 9009

Presidential Primary Matching Payment Account ... 9031 et seq.
. administration and regulation .... 9036 et seq.
. audit of expenses 9038; 9039
. campaign expenses 9032
.. limitations 9035
. certification by Commission 9036
. Congress, reports to 9039
. criminal penalties 9042
. definitions 9032
. eligibility for payments 9033; 9034
.. candidates, payments to 9037
.. termination of payments 9033
. expense limitation, qualified 9035
. Federal Election Commission (See Federal Election Commission)
. judicial proceedings, participation by commission ... 9040
. judicial review 9041
. matching payment period defined 9032
. payments to candidates, eligible 9036; 9037
. penalties, violation of expenditure rules 9042
. primary election defined 9032
. regulations 9038
. repayments 9038
. violation of expenditure rules 9042

Presidentially declared disasters
. Gulf Opportunity Zone (See Gulf Opportunity Zone)
. involuntary conversions .... 1033(h)
. postponement of certain tax-related deadlines ... 7508A

Price indexes
. U.S. government, LIFO inventories 472

Prices
. exclusion from excise tax, representation of 7261
. manufacturer's tax 4216

Principal campaign committees 527

Principal residence
. cancellation of indebtedness
.. basis reduction .... 108(h)(1)
.. defined .... 108(h)(5)
.. discharges not related to taxpayer's financial condition .... 108(h)(3)
.. ordering rules .... 108(h)(4)
.. qualified principal residence indebtedness define ... 108(h)(2)
. defined .... 25; 36(c)(2)
. first-time homebuyers
.. defined .... 36(c)(2)
.. election to treat purchase in prior year .... 36(g)
. levy against 6334
. sale of principal residence, exclusion of gain on ... 121(a)
.. deceased spouse, property of .... 121(d)(2)
.. decedent, property acquired by .... 121(d)(11)
.. depreciation, gain attributable to .... 121(d)(6)

241

CODE SEC.

Principal residence —Cont'd
sale of principal residence, exclusion of gain on—Cont'd
.. expatriates .... 121(e)
.. foreign services .... 121(d)(9)
.. former spouse, property of .... 121(d)(3)
.. intelligence community .... 121(d)(9)
.. involuntary conversions .... 121(d)(5)
.. joint returns .... 121(d)(1)
.. like-kind exchanges .... 121(d)(10)
.. limitations .... 121(b)
.. nonqualified use, gain allocated to .... 121(b)(4)
.. out-of-residence care, use during .... 121(d)(7)
.. Peace Corps, service in .... 121(d)(12)
.. remainder interests, sale of .... 121(d)(8)
.. requirements, taxpayer failure to meet ..... 121(c)
.. rollovers, residence acquired in .... 121(g)
.. tenant-stockholder in cooperative housing corporation
   .... 121(d)(4)
.. uniformed services .... 121(d)(9)

Prior years
. adjustments for errors affecting .... 1311 et seq.
. credit for minimum tax liability 53

Privacy (See also Confidentiality; Disclosure of tax information)
. Privacy Act of 1974, inapplicability to IRC provisions 7852

Private activity bonds
. advance refunding 146; 149
. aircraft 147
. airports 147
. average maturity 146
. buildings, rehabilitated 147
. business purpose tests 141
. business use test 141
. economic life 147
. electric and natural gas supply contracts 141
. environmental land, acquisition of 147
. exempt facility bonds 142
. exempt interest 57
. exemption requirements .... 141 et seq.
. existing property, acquisition of 147
. facilities 146; 150
. farmland, acquisition of 147
. FHA insured loans 147
. fire department, volunteer 147; 150
. 5% test, business use test 141
. gambling establishments 147
. government use 141
. governmental units
.. change in use of facility 150
.. volume cap 146
. health clubs 147
. high-speed intercity rail facility 146; 147
. highway or surface freight transfers facilities .... 142(m)
. housing projects
.. change in use 150
.. existing property 147
. hydroelectric generation facilities, environmental enhancements
   142
. Indian tribal governments 7871

CODE SEC.

Private activity bonds —Cont'd
. interest
.. deduction, denial of 150
.. gross income, inclusion in 103
.. land acquisition 147
. limitations
.. land acquisition 147
.. loan financing 141
.. maturity exceeding 120% of economic life .. 147
.. averages, determination of 147
. mortgage activity bonds 143
. mortgage bonds, volume cap 146
. mortgage credit certificates, volume cap 146
. mortgage revenue bonds (See Mortgage revenue bonds)
. nongovernmental output property
.. definition 141
.. exceptions 141
.. joint action agencies 141
. nonpurpose investment loans, financing 141
. nonqualified amount
.. $15 million, in excess of 141
. output facilities, lower limitation 141
. partners and partnerships
.. related persons, as 147
.. substantial user requirement 147
. pooled financing
.. 501(c)(3) organization 147
. private business use defined 141
. public approval requirement 147
. qualified bond 141
. qualified energy conservation bonds
.. allocation restrictions .... 54D(e)(3)
.. qualified conservation purpose .... 54D(f)(2)
. redevelopment bonds 144
. refunding bonds 149
.. advance refunding 146
. registration as basis for tax exempt status .... 149(a)(1)
.. book entries .... 149(a)(3)(A)
.. nominees .... 149(a)(3)(B)
.. registration required bond defined .... 149(a)(2)
. rehabilitation
.. existing property 147
.. expenditures 147
. related persons
.. substantial user of facility 147
. requirements
.. applicable 147
.. exemption .... 141 et seq.
. residential rental property, financing of 149
. restrictions on issuance costs 147
. S corporations
.. related persons, as 147
.. substantial user requirement 147
. scholarship funding bond 147
.. volume cap 146
. security or payment test 141
. skyboxes 147
. small issue bonds 144; 265
. student loan bonds 144; 146; 147

Index to Code   Private

CODE SEC.

Private activity bonds — Cont'd
. substantial user requirement 147
. tax assessment loans, financing 141
. tax preferences
.. interest on .... 57(a)(5)(A)
.. Sept. 1, 1986, issued before .... 57(a)(5)(A)(v)
. tests, business 141
. user of facility substantial 147
. veterans mortgage bonds (See Veterans mortgage bonds)
. volume cap 146
. volunteer fire department issues 147; 150

Private communication service 4252

Private foundations .... 507 et seq.; 4940 et seq.
. abatements of taxes .... 507; 4961 et seq.
.. definitions 4963
.. first-tier taxes 4962
.. second-tier taxes 4961
. administrative expenses 4942
. aggregate tax benefit 507
. assessment and collection
.. suspension period 6503
.. termination of status 6501
. capital gains and losses 4940
. charitable contributions 170; 642
. charitable trust as 4947
. credit or refund 6511; 7422
. deficiencies 6213; 6214; 6501
. deficiency assessment .... 6211 et seq.
.. petition to Tax Court 6213
. definitions 509; 4946
. disqualified persons 4946
.. excess business holding 4943
. distributions
.. failure to make 4942
.. prior year adjustments 4942
.. qualifying 4942
. employees
.. FICA 3121
. excess business holdings 4943
.. computation of 4943
.. funds for, accumulated earnings tax 537
. excise taxes .... 4940 et seq.; 4961 et seq.
.. business holdings, excessive 4943
.. definitions 4946
.. distribution of income, failure to make 4942
.. exempt foundations .... 4940 et seq.
.. foreign organizations, applied tax and exemption denial of
 4948
.. investment income, based on 4940
.. investments jeopardizing charitable purpose 4944
.. nonexempt trusts, application of taxes to certain ... 4947
.. self-dealing 4941
.. taxable expenditures, on 4945
. first tier excise taxes, abatement 4962
. 501(c)(3) organizations (See Section 501(c)(3) organizations)
. foreign 1443; 4948
. foundation managers 4946; 7454
. functionally related business defined 4942
. grants 4942; 4945

CODE SEC.

Private foundations—Cont'd
. gross investment income 4940
. imposition of tax 507
. information returns 6033; 6652
.. liquidation, dissolution, termination or contraction, on .. 6043
. investment income 509
.. excise tax on 4940
. investment jeopardizing charitable purpose 4944
. jeopardizing investments 4944
. judicial remedies for qualification 7428
. knowingly prohibited transactions 4944; 4945
. legislative influence .... 4945 et seq.
. liability on transfer of assets 507
. limitation on assessment 6501
. liquidation, dissolution, termination or contraction ... 6043
. long-term care facilities 4942
. manager defined 4946
. minimum investment returns 4942
. nonexempt, tax on 4940
. notification of exempt status to IRS 50; 507
. operating
.. audit tax, exempt 4940
.. defined 4942
. penalties 6652; 6684
. present holdings 4943
. program-related investments 4944
. prohibited transactions .... 4941 et seq.; 4961 et seq.
.. bankruptcy proceedings, claim for tax 6871
.. burden of proof 7454
.. Indian tribal government, treatment as state 7871
.. liability for tax 6684
.. petition to TC 7422
.. self-dealing 4941
. publicity of information 6104
. redemption, excess business holding 537
. refund suits 7422
. returns
.. failure to file or make public 6652
.. public inspection 6104
. second tier excise taxes, abatement 4961
. self-dealing 4941
. set-aside amounts for specific projects 4942
. speculative investments 4944
. split interest trusts 4947
. substantial contributors 507; 4946
. successor organizations 4940
. taxable expenditures tax 4945
.. abatement .... 4961 et seq.
. termination of status 507
.. assessment and collection 6501
.. status after 509
. transfer or operation as, public charity 507
. trust or will acquisitions .... 4943 et seq.
. trusts treated as 4947
. type III supporting organization
.. excess business holding 4943
. undistributed income, tax on 4942
. unrelated business income 511
. value of assets 507

243

CODE SEC.

Prizes and awards .... 74 (See also Scholarships and fellowships)
. backup withholding 3406
. bad debt deduction
.. political organizations, debts owed by 271
. common trust funds
.. information returns 6032
. employees............................... 74; 274
. exceptions, inclusion in gross income 74
. gross income, inclusion in 74
. levy against 6332
. passbook loans, liens for taxes 6323
. scholarships 117
. transferred to charities 74
. withholding tax on interest and dividends 3406
Procedure and administration .... 6001 et seq.
Produced
. defined 864
Product liability losses
. reserves, accumulated earnings tax 537
Production of income
. depreciation of property held for 167
. expenses 212
Production of records (See Books and records)
Production payments of mineral interests 636
Productive-use property
. exchange of 1031
. involuntary conversions 1033
Productivity awards 274
Professional football league exemption 501
Professionals
. collectively bargained plans 413
. tools of trade, exemption from levy 6334
Profit, activity not for (See Not-for profit activities)
Profits (See Earnings and profits)
Profit-sharing plans (See Pension, profit-sharing and stock bonus plans)
Prohibited transactions
. exempt organizations 503
.. tax shelter, entering into prohibited 4965
. 100% tax on 860F
. REIT income from
.. certain sales not to constitute prohibited transaction
  .... 857(b)(6)(C); 857(b)(6)(D)
.. fire, storm, or other casualty, expenditures for restoration of
  .... 857(b)(6)(E)(iv)
.. holding periods of foreclosed property .... 857(b)(6)(E)
.. imposition of tax .... 857(b)(6)(A)
.. net income derived from prohibited transaction
  .... 857(b)(6)(B)
Proof
. burden of proof (See Burden of proof)
. evidence (See Evidence)
Propaganda organizations 501
Property (See also Exchanges of property; Personal property; Residential property)
. adjustments to basis
.. controlled foreign corporations 961

CODE SEC.

Property (See also Exchanges of property; Personal property; Residential property) —Cont'd
. air transportation of .... 4271 et seq.
. basis rules
.. adjusted 1011; 1016
.. cost basis 1012
.. decedent, property acquired from 1014
.. gifts, property acquired by 1015
.. improvements to property by lessee 1019
.. inventory, property included in 1013
.. transfers in trust, property acquired by 1015
. capital expenditures 263; 263A
. capital gains and losses 1231
. civil action to clear title to 7402
. compensatory, transfers 83
. condemnation (See Condemnation of property)
. contributions of
.. political organizations 84
.. sale or exchange
... information returns 6050L; 6652
. corporate distributions 311
. debt instruments (See also Debt instruments)
.. issuance on sale or exchange
... cash method election, imputed interest 1274A
... issue price 1274
. deferred rental agreements 467
. defined 317
. depletion purposes 614; 617
. export property 971; 993
. U.S. property 956
. depreciable, gain from disposition of 1239; 1245; 1250
. discharge of property subject to lien 6325
. disclaimers 2046; 2518
. disposition of foreign property 904
. distributions, corporate 301; 311
. donated, dispositions of 6050L
. exchanged basis defined 7701
. exchanges (See Exchanges of property)
. existing, private activity bonds 147
. foreign personal holding company, use by shareholder ... 553
. forfeiture (See Forfeiture of property)
. gain or loss 1001
.. acquired during affiliation 1051
.. adjustment to basis 1016
.. distribution, on 311
.. productive use or investment, property held for 1031
.. stock for property, exchange of 1032
.. stock for stock of same corporation, exchange of 1036
. holding period 1223
. imported into U.S. from related persons 1059A
. improvements, deductibility 263
. income-producing, expenses 212
. inventory costs, inclusion in 263A
. investment, held for 163
. involuntary conversions 1033; 1231
. levying on property (See Levy)
. location outside U.S.
.. limitations on assessment and collection 6503
. long useful life 263A

Index to Code

Puerto

CODE SEC.

Property (See also Exchanges of property; Personal property; Residential property) —Cont'd
. March 1, 1913, acquisitions before 1053
. marital deduction 2044
. oil, gas or geothermal 1254
. ownership defined 150
. partner and partnership, transfers between 707
. payment for use of 467
. personal holding company, use by shareholder 543
. personal property (See Personal property)
. private activity bonds
.. existing property, acquisition of 147
. production expenditures 263A
. production period 263A
. real (See Real property; Residential property)
. real estate dealers (See Real estate dealers and agents)
. restoration, capital expenditures 263
. seizure for taxes .... 6331 et seq.; 6863; 7505 (See also Levy; Seizure of property)
. settlements, gift tax 2516
. substituted basis defined 7701
. taxes
.. cost basis exclusion 1012
.. deductibility 164
... estate tax purposes 2053; 2106
... purchaser and seller 1001; 1012
. trade or business, used in 1231
. transferred basis defined 7701
. transfers
.. between spouses 1041
.. private foundations, excess business holdings 4943
. uninsured, casualty loss 1231
Proprietorships
. employee retirement and benefit plans 401; 414
. work opportunity credit 52
Propylene hazardous waste clean up 4661; 4662
Prosecutions by U.S., limitation on 6531
Protest, payment of tax under 7422
Public assistance payments levy exemption 6334
Public educational facilities
. exempt facility bonds (See Exempt facility bonds subhead qualified public educational facilities)
Public health service
. injuries or sickness, compensation for 104
Public inspection (See also Examination and inspection)
. exempt organizations
.. annual returns and applications for exemptions 6104
. exempt organizations, penalty 6685
. written determinations 6110
Public power provider
. new clean renewable energy bonds
.. defined .... 54C(d)(2)
.. limitations on amount of bonds designated, allocation .... 54C(c)(3)(A)
Public safety testing organization exemption 501
Public schools (See also Educational institutions)
. employee annuities 403

CODE SEC.

Public tender offer defined 5881
Public transit (See Transit systems, local)
Public transportation
. FICA 3121
. Highway Trust Fund, Mass Transit Account 9503
Public utilities
. accounting method 451
. definition 168; 247; 7701
. depreciation 168
. dividends paid, preferred stock 247
. dividends-received deduction 243; 244
. electric facility exempt facility bonds 142
. energy conservation subsidies provided by 136
.. double benefit, denial of 136
.. dwelling unit defined 136
. exempt income 115
. gas utility, exempt facility bonds 142
. gross income
.. energy conservation subsidies provided by 136
. nuclear power plant decommissioning costs 468A
. preferred stock 244
.. dividends paid 247
. regulated public utilities defined 7701
. repayments of previously reported income 1341
. taxable year, inclusion in gross income 451
. wastewater treatment plant, depreciation 168
Publication and statistical studies of income 6103; 6108
Publicity
. determination letters 6110
. disclosure of tax information (See Disclosure of tax information)
. exempt organizations and certain trusts 6104
. information furnished by exempt organizations and trusts 6104
. refunds and credit 6405
. returns .... 6103 et seq.
. rulings 6110
. Tax Court proceedings 7461
. written determinations 6110
Publicly traded partnerships
. corporation, treated as 7704
. passive activity losses and credits 469
. unrelated business taxable income 512
Publishers circulation expenditures 173
Puerto Rico
. alcohol taxes 5001; 5064
. alien residents 876; 1441
. Commonwealth status 7701
. distilled spirits imported from, excise taxes ... 5001; 5064; 5314
. domestic production activities in .... 199(d)(8)
. economic activity credit 30A
. environmental taxes on shipments from 4612; 4662
. FUTA 3306
. income from sources within 933
.. credit against tax 936
. possession of U.S. status .... 7651 et seq.; 7701
. possession tax credit 936
. residents of
.. aliens 876

245

CODE SEC.

Puerto Rico —Cont'd
. residents of —Cont'd
. . foreign tax credit 901
. . self-employment tax 1402
. . stock sales 865
. . withholding at source on nonresident aliens and foreign corporations 1441
. . withholding on wages 3401
. . shipments from U.S. 7653
. . shipments to U.S. 7652
. . vaccines shipped to, excise tax 4132
. . withholding tax on wages 3401
Pumice depletion 613
Purchaser, lien for taxes against 6323
Puts and calls 1233; 1234
Pyrophyllite depletion 613

Q

QEFs (See Qualified electing funds)
QSSTs (See Qualified Subchapter S trusts (QSSTs))
QTIP (See Qualified terminable interest property (QTIP))
Qualified 501(c)(3) bond 145
Qualified blood collector organization defined 7701
Qualified business unit
. foreign currency transactions 989
Qualified campaign expense
. defined for presidential election campaign fund 9002
Qualified clean fuel vehicles 179A
Qualified covered call options 1092
Qualified disaster assistance property (See Disaster loss and relief)
Qualified disclaimers 2518
Qualified domestic relations orders (QDROs) . . . 72; 401 (See also Domestic relations orders)
. pension, profit-sharing, and stock bonus plans
. . after earliest retirement date, payments made . . . . . 414(p)(4)
. . alternate payee defined . . . . 414(p)(8)
. . amount, form of benefits, altered . . . . 414(p)(3)
. . defined . . . . 414(p)(1)
. . distribution requirements, waiver of . . . . 414(p)(10)
. . facts, specification of . . . . 414(p)(2)
. . former spouse as surviving spouse, treatment of . . . 414(p)(5)
. . orders, plan procedures with respect to . . . . 414(p)(6)
. . other plans . . . . 414(p)(11)
. . period during which determination is being made . . . 414(p)(7)
. . Sec. 401(a)(13), non application of . . . . 414(p)(9)
. . Sec. 457 plan payments . . . . 414(p)(12)
Qualified domestic trust (QDT) 2056A
. distributions 2210
Qualified economic development purpose
. defined for recovery zone facility bonds . . . . 1400U-2(c)(2)
Qualified electing funds (See also Passive foreign investment companies (PFICs))
. current taxation of income from 1293
. defined 1295
. distributions 1294
. extensions, election for 1294

CODE SEC.

Qualified electing funds (See also Passive foreign investment companies (PFICs)) —Cont'd
. gain, election for recognition of 1291
. general rule 1295
. loans to shareholder, treatment of 1294
. treatment of . . . . 1293 et seq.
Qualified electric vehicle credit 30
Qualified employer plans . . 72 (See also Employee retirement and benefit plans)
Qualified energy conservation bonds
. allocations . . . . 54D(e)(1)
. . issuers . . . . 54D(e)(3)
. . large local governments . . . . 54D(e)(2)
. . private activity bond restrictions . . . . 54D(e)(3)
. credit for qualified bonds allowed to issuer
. . special rules . . . . 6431(f)(2)
. . specified tax credit bond . . . . 6431(f)(3)
. defined . . . . 54D(a)
. Indian tribal governments
. . population, determination of . . . . 54D(h)(1)
. . treatment as qualified bond . . . . 54D(h)(2)
. limitation on amount of bonds designated . . . . 54D(c)
. national . . . . 54D(d)
. population
. . county, determination of . . . . 54D(g)(2)
. . Indian tribal governments, determination for . . . . . . 54D(h)(1)
. . state or local, determination of . . . . 54D(g)(1)
. private activity bonds
. . allocation restrictions . . . . 54D(e)(3)
. . qualified conservation purpose . . . . 54D(f)(2)
. qualified conservation purpose
. . defined . . . . 54D(f)(1)
. . private activity bonds . . . . 54D(f)(2)
. reduced credit amount . . . . 54D(b)
Qualified ex-felon
. defined for work opportunity credits . . . . 51(d)(4)
Qualified export asset defined 993
Qualified export receipt defined 993
Qualified funding assets
. personal injury damages 130
Qualified green building and sustainable design projects
. exempt facility bonds (See Exempt facility bonds)
Qualified Gulf Opportunity Zone bond (See Gulf Opportunity Zone)
Qualified hospitalization
. defined for postponements by war 7508
Qualified IV-A recipients
. defined for work opportunity credits . . . . 51(d)(2)
Qualified mortgage bonds (See Mortgage bonds)
Qualified plan award 274
Qualified public educational facilities
. exempt facility bonds (See Exempt facility bonds)
Qualified redevelopment bonds . . . . 144; 2701 (See also Redevelopment bonds)
Qualified refueling property deduction 179A
Qualified renewable energy facility
. new clean renewable energy bonds, defined for . . . . . 54C(d)(1)

Index to Code — Qualified

	CODE SEC.
Qualified replacement mortgage	
. real estate mortgage investment conduits	
. . defined	860G
Qualified replacement property	
. basis for gain or loss, adjustments	1016
Qualified residence interest	163
Qualified residential project	
. exempt facility bonds (See Exempt facility bonds)	
Qualified retail improvement property	
. ACRS depreciation	168(e)(8)
Qualified retirement plans	72; 4971 et seq.; 6057 et seq.
(See also Employee retirement and benefit plans)	
. vesting (See Vesting of retirement benefits)	
Qualified school construction bonds	
. credit for qualified bonds allowed to issuer	
. . specified tax credit bond	6431(f)(3)
. defined	54F(a)
. limitation, allocation of	
. . 40% allocation among largest school districts	54F(d)(2)
. . Indian schools, for	54F(d)(4)
. . possessions, to certain	54F(d)(3)
. . states, among	54F(d)(1)
. limitations	
. . amount of bonds designated, on	54F(b)
. . national limitation on amount of bonds designated	54F(c)
. . unused, carryover of	54F(e)
Qualified small issue bonds	144; 265
Qualified smart electric grid systems	168
Qualified smart electric meters	168
Qualified student loan bonds	144
Qualified Subchapter S trusts (QSSTs)	1361
Qualified tax collection contracts	6306
Qualified tax credit bonds	
. arbitrage	54A(d)(4)
. available project proceeds defined	54A(e)(4)
. bond defined	54A(e)(2)
. credit to holders of	
. . allowance	54A(a)
. . annual credit, determination of	54A(b)(2)
. . conflicts of interest prohibitions, financial	54A(d)(6)
. . credit allowance date	54A(e)(1)
. . credit rate	54A(b)(3)
. . expenditures, special rules	54A(d)(2)
. . interest, credit treated as	54A(f)
. . issuance and redemption, special rules for	54A(b)(4)
. . limitations based on amount of tax	54A(c)(1)
. . maturity limitations	54A(d)(5)
. . partnerships	54A(g)
. . regulated investment companies	54A(g); 54A(h)
. . REITs	54A(h)
. . S corporations	54A(g)
. . stripped	54A(i)
. . unused credit, carryover of	54A(c)(2)
. defined	54A(d)(1)
. regulated investment company shareholders	
. . allowance of credits	853A(a)(1)
. . applicable date defined	853A(e)(1)(B)
. . election, effect of	853A(b)(1)

	CODE SEC.
Qualified tax credit bonds —Cont'd	
. regulated investment company shareholders —Cont'd	
. . allowance of credits—Cont'd	
. . . manner of making election	853A(d)
. . . regulations, prescription of	853A(f)
. . . statements to shareholders	853A(c)
. . . stripped tax credit bonds	853A(e)(2)
. . . tax credit bond defined	853A(e)(1)(A)
. reporting	54A(d)(3)
. state defined	54A(e)(3)
Qualified tax-exempt obligation	265
Qualified technology equipment	
. accelerated cost recovery system (ACRS)	
. . alternate depreciation system for certain property	168(g)(3)(C)
. . computer or peripheral equipment defined	168(i)(2)(B)
. . defined	168(i)(2)
. . high technology equipment, 5 year or less lease for	168(h)(3)(A)
. . high technology equipment defined	168(h)(3)(B)(i)
. . high technology medical equipment	168(i)(2)(C)
. . leasebacks during first 3 month of use	168(h)(3)(B)(ii)
Qualified terminable interest property (QTIP)	
. defined	2056
. extent of deductions	2524
. generation-skipping transfers, tax on	2652
. gift to spouse	2523
. inclusion ratio	2642
. marital deduction	2044
. taxable estate	2056
Qualified total distributions (QTD)	
. withholding tax on deferred income	3405
Qualified transportation fringe	132
Qualified tuition and related expenses (See Tuition)	
Qualified veterans' mortgage bonds (See Veterans mortgage bonds)	
Qualified zone academy bonds	
. arbitrage	1397E(f)(3); 1397E(g)
. bond defined	1397E(i)(2)
. credit allowance date	1397E(i)(1)
. credit for qualified bonds allowed to issuer	
. . specified tax credit bond	6431(f)(3)
. credit to holders of	
. . allowance	1397E(a)
. . amount of credit	1397E(b)
. . determination of amount of credit	1397E(b)(2)
. . gross income inclusion	1397E(j)
. . limitation based on amount of tax	1397E(c)
. . limitations	1397E(b)(2)
. . nonrefundable bondholder credit, treatment as	1397E(k)
. . private business contribution requirement	1397E(d)(2)
. . S corporations	1397E(l)
. . term requirement	1397E(d)(2)
. defined	54E; 1397E(d)(1)
. educational institution credit for holding	1397E
. educational opportunity, contribution of	54E(d)(4)(D)
. eligible local education agency	54E(d)(2)
. equipment, contribution of	54E(d)(4)(A)
. expenditures	1397E(f)(1)

CODE SEC.

Qualified zone academy bonds — Cont'd
. *expenditures—Cont'd*
.. failure to spend required amount of bond proceeds within 5
... years .... 1397E(f)(3)
.. period of extension .... 1397E(f)(2)
. internships, contribution of .... 54E(d)(4)(D)
. limitation on amount of bonds designated .... 54E(c)
.. allocation of .... 1397E(e)(2)
.. carryover of unused limitation .... 54E(c)(4); 1397E(e)(4)
.. designation subject to limitation amount .... 1397E(e)(3)
.. national .... 54E(c)(1); 1397E(e)(1)
.. subjectivity .... 54E(c)(3)
. mentors .... 54E(d)(4)(C)
. private business contribution requirements .... 54E(b)
. qualified contribution defined .... 54E(d)(4)
. qualified purpose defined .... 54E(d)(3); 1397E(d)(5)
. qualified zone academy defined .... 1397E(d)(4)
. S corporations .... 1397E(l)
. services, contribution of .... 54E(d)(4)(C)
. state defined .... 1397E(i)(3)
. Tax Extenders and Alternative Minimum Tax Relief Act of 2008,
... obligations issued after enactment of .... 1397E(m)
. technical assistance, contribution of .... 54E(d)(4)(B)

Qualifying advanced energy project credit .... 48C(a)
. certification of program .... 48C(d)(2)
. disclosure of applicants and amount of credit .... 48C(d)(5)
. double benefits .... 48C(e)
. eligible property defined .... 48C(c)(2)
. establishment of program .... 48C(d)(1)
. qualified investment .... 48C(b)(1)
.. limitations .... 48C(b)(3)
. qualifying advanced energy project .... 48C(c)(1)
. review and redistribution of credits .... 48C(d)(4)
. selection criteria for project .... 48C(d)(3)

Qualifying gasification project credit .... 48B(a)
. definitions concerning .... 48B(c)
. qualified investment .... 48B(b)(1)
. qualifying gasification project program .... 48B(d)(1)
.. denial of double benefits .... 48B(e)
.. period of issuance .... 48B(d)(2)
.. selection criteria .... 48B(d)(3)
. subsidized property .... 48B(b)(2)

Qualifying therapeutic discovery project credit
. basis adjustments .... 48D(e)(1)
. capitalization rather than deduction of expenses .... 280C(g)(2)
. certification .... 48D(d)(2)
. controlled groups .... 280C(g)(3)
. denial of .... 48D(f)(1)
. Department of Treasury grants, coordination with .... 48D(f)
. disclosure of allocations .... 48D(d)(4)
. double benefit, denial of .... 48D(e)(2)
. eligible taxpayer defined .... 48D(c)(2)
. establishment .... 48D(d)(1)
. facility maintenance expenses defined .... 48D(c)(3)
. generally .... 48D; 280C(g)(1)
. grants, treatment of .... 48D(f)(3)
. qualified investment
.. exclusions .... 48D(b)(3)
.. generally .... 48D(b)(1)

CODE SEC.

Qualifying therapeutic discovery project credit — Cont'd
. *qualified investment —Cont'd*
.. limitation .... 48D(b)(2)
.. progress expenditures .... 48D(b)(4)
. qualifying therapeutic discovery project defined .... 48D(c)(1)
. recapture of credit .... 48D(f)(2)
. selection criteria .... 48D(d)(3)

Quartz crystals depletion 613
Quick refunds 6411; 6425
Quid pro quo contributions
. disclosure 6114; 6115; 6714

R

Racing, horse (See Horse racing)
Racquet sports facility, small issue bonds financing 144
Radio broadcasting properties (See Broadcasting)
Rail facilities, high-speed intercity (See High-speed intercity rail facilities)
Rail trailers and vans 4053
Railroad Retirement Tax Act .... 3201 et seq.
. adjustments 6205; 6413
. annuities 72; 86
. assessment and collection of tax 6205
. benefits, tier 1 .... 72; 86; 6050G
. coal mines 3231
. court jurisdiction 3232
. deductibility of taxes 275; 3502
. deduction of tax from compensation 3202
. deferred compensation .... 3231 et seq.
. definitions 3231
. employee benefit plan distributions 3231
. employee representatives
.. deductibility of taxes 275
.. determination of compensation 3212
.. imposition of tax 3211
.. rate of tax 3211
. employees
.. deduction from compensation 3202
.. rate of tax 3201
.. taxes paid by employer 3231
. employers 3221
. erroneous payments 3503
. excise tax on employer 3221
. FICA 3121
. FUTA 3306
. general provisions .... 3231 et seq.
. hospital insurance 3201; 3221
. indemnification of employer 3202
. information returns 6050F; 6050G
. liability for tax 3202
. more than one employer 3231
. overpayments 6413
. permitted disparity in contributions and benefits .. 401
. rate of tax
.. employee representatives 3211
.. employees 3201
.. employers 3221
.. individuals hired in 2010 .... 3221(c)(1)

Index to Code   Real

CODE SEC.

Railroad Retirement Tax Act—Cont'd
rate of tax —Cont'd
. . Tier 1 tax 3201; 3211; 3221
. . Tier 2 tax 3201; 3211; 3221
. refunds and credits 3503
. tier 1 benefits 72; 86
. tier 2 taxes treated as contributions 72
. tips 3202; 3231
. underpayments 6205

Railroad Unemployment Insurance Act
. repayment tax 105; 3321; 3322

Railroads
. applicable convention, depreciation 168
. capital expenditures 263
. depreciation 168
. employees, withholding tax statements 6051
. employment taxes (See Railroad Retirement Tax Act)
. exempt facility bonds 142; 146
. grading or tunnel bore, depreciation 168; 1245
. intercity facilities, high-speed
. . exempt facility bonds, volume cap 146
. . private activity bonds 147
. labor, work opportunity credit 51
. leaking underground storage tank trust tax on gasoline used in trains 6421
. new employees, credit for hiring 51
. reorganization exchanges 354; 1250
. replacement of track 263
. rolling stock
. . capital expenditures 263
. . depreciation 168
. . leased for foreign use 861
. . rentals by foreign corporations, income exemption 883
. . straight line depreciation 168
. terminal corporations 281
. track depreciation 168
. track maintenance credit 38; 45G
. work opportunity credit 51

Rare diseases or conditions
. clinical testing expenses 45C

Rates, credit
. employment tax 3301
. mortgage interest 25

Rates of tax
. acceleration of 10% income tax rate for 2001 6428
. accumulated earnings tax 531
. alternative minimum tax 55
. capital gain
. . net capital gain 1
. change during taxable year 15
. children, unearned income 1
. corporation, election by individual to be taxed as 962
. . estate tax 2001
. corporations 11
. effect of changes 15
. election by individuals to be taxed as corporation 962
. . estate tax 2001
. environmental tax 59A
. estates and trusts 1

CODE SEC.

Rates of tax —Cont'd
. FICA 3101
. FUTA 3301
. generation-skipping transfer (GST) tax 2602; 2641
. gift tax 2502
. heads of household 1
. highest rate, change during taxable year 15
. husbands and wives 1
. income tax 1
. indexing for inflation 1
. individual electing to be taxed as corporation 962
. . estate tax 2001
. inflation adjustment 1
. joint returns 1
. Kiddie tax 1
. life insurance companies 801
. long-term exempt rates
. . net operating loss carryforwards 382
. maximum rates
. . net capital gains 1
. net operating loss carryforwards
. . long-term exempt rates 382
. personal holding company tax 541
. railroad retirement 3201; 3211; 3221
. reductions after 2000 1
. reductions after 2001 1
. repeal of tax 15
. schedule of 2001; 2502
. self employment income 1401
. separate returns 1
. social security 3101; 3111
. spouses 1
. surviving spouse 1
. 10% income tax rate for 2001, acceleration of 6428
. unemployment tax 3301
. unmarried individuals 1

Reacquisitions of real property 1038
Readjustment of tax between years .... 1311 et seq.
Real estate board exemption 501
Real estate dealers and agents
. dispositions, installment sales 453
. employment taxes 3508
. independent contractors, status as 3508
. qualified, defined 3508
. separate charge for filing information return 6045

Real estate investment trusts (REITs) .... 856 et seq.
. accounting period 857; 859
. adjustment defined 860
. alternative minimum tax 59
. . adjusted current earnings exception .... 56(g)(6)
. alternative tax, capital gains .... 857(b)(3)
. beneficial ownership 856; 857
. beneficiaries, taxation of 857
. capital gains .... 857(b)(3)
. . alternative tax .... 857(b)(3)
. . capital gain dividend defined .... 857(b)(3)(C)
. . dividends 291; 857; 860
. . net operation loss, coordination with .... 857(b)(3)(E)

249

Real estate investment trusts (REITs)—Cont'd
capital gains—Cont'd
- shareholder dividends .... 857(b)(3)(B)
- undistributed .... 857(b)(3)(D)
- capital gains and losses 857; 1212
- carryovers, acquiring corporation 381
- claim for deficiency dividend deduction 860
- closely held
  - determinations .... 856; 856(h)
  - requirement that entity not be treated as .... 856(k)
- compliance with regulations 857
- consolidated returns 1504
- constructive ownership 856
- credits and refunds 860
- deficiency assessments .... 6211 et seq.; 7422
- deficiency dividends 316; 381; 858; 860
- prior law 6697
- defined 856
- determinations .... 856(b); 860
- discharge of indebtedness 108
- dividends 316; 857; 858
- dividends paid deduction 562; 857; 860
- dividends received, restrictions applicable to
  - Sec. (1)(h)(11) .... 857(c)(2)
  - Sec. 243 .... 857(c)(1)
- dividends received deduction 243; 857
- earning and profits
  - defined .... 857(d)(1)
  - subsection(a)(2)(B) requirements, distributions to meet .... 857(d)(3)
  - undistributed income, coordination with tax on ..... 857(d)(2)
- earnings and profits 857
- elections 856
- environmental tax 59A
- excess interest .... 857(b)(7)(A); 857(b)(7)(D)
- excess noncash income .... 857(e)(1)
  - defined 857
  - determination of amount .... 857(e)(2)
- excise tax on undistributed income 4981
- failure to meet certain requirements
  - 75% of gross income of trust .... 857(b)(5)(B)
  - 95% of gross income of trust .... 857(b)(5)(A)
- financial institutions 856
- foreclosure property .... 856(e); 857; 857(b)(4)
- foreign currency transactions .... 856(n)
- fraud, deficiency dividend deduction 860
- gross income requirement 856; 857
- imposition of tax .... 857(b)(1)
- interest .... 856(f)
- limitations on status .... 856(c)
- loss on sale or exchange of stock held 6 months or less .... 857(b)(8)(A)
  - holding period, determination of .... 857(b)(8)(B)
  - periodic liquidation, exception .... 857(b)(8)(C)
- method of taxation .... 857(b)
- net operating loss
  - capital gains coordination with .... 857(b)(3)(E)
- non-REIT year defined .... 857(a)(b)
- notice to shareholders; dividends 857; 858
- ownership ascertainment

Real estate investment trusts (REITs)—Cont'd
ownership ascertainment —Cont'd
- failure to comply with requirements .... 857(f)(2)
- require to comply with regulations for .... 857(f)(1)
- penalties 857; 6871
- prior law 6697
- prohibited transactions, income from
  - certain sales not to constitute prohibited transaction .... 857(b)(6)(C); 857(b)(6)(D)
  - fire, storm, or other casualty, expenditures for restoration of .... 857(b)(6)(E)(iv)
  - holding periods of foreclosed property .... 857(b)(6)(E)
  - imposition of tax .... 857(b)(6)(A)
  - net income derived from prohibited transaction .... 857(b)(6)(B)
- qualification requirements 856
- qualified investment entity defined 860
- qualified tax credit bonds, credit for holders of .... 54A(g)
- real estate mortgage investment conduit, interest in 860E
- redetermined deductions .... 857(b)(7)(A); 857(b)(7)(C)
- redetermined rents, income from ... 857(b)(7)(A); 857(b)(7)(B)
- rents from real estate defined .... 856(d)
- safe harbor in applying subsection (c)(4) .... 856(m)
- shared appreciated mortgages, treatment of .... 856(j)
- shareholders, number of 856
- stapled entities 269B
- statute of limitations on deficiency dividends 860
- stay of collection on deficiency dividends 860
- stock held for six months or less, loss on 857
- subsidiaries .... 856; 856(l)
- tax imposed 11
- taxable income 4981
- taxable mortgage pool 7701
- taxation .... 857(a)(1)
- termination of election .... 856(g)
- termination of status 856
- undistributed income 857; 4981
- U.S. real property interest dispositions 897
- withholding
  - distributions by REIT .... 1445(e)(6)
- wholly owned subsidiaries, treatment of .... 856(i)

Real estate mortgage investment conduits (REMICs) . . 860A et seq.
- accrual basis 860B; 860E
- affiliated groups 860E
- alternative minimum tax
  - adjusted current earnings exception .... 56(g)(6)
- basis 860C; 860F
- cash flow investment defined 860G
- contributions after start-up date 860F
- daily portion of income or loss 860C
- definitions 860D; 860G
- distributions 860C; 860F
- election of status 860D
- excess inclusion, residual interests 860E
- foreclosure defined 860F
- foreign corporation holder of interest in 860G
- gain or loss 860B; 860F
- information returns 6049
- interest

Index to Code

CODE SEC.

Real estate mortgage investment conduits (REMICs)— Cont'd
. interest —Cont'd
.. gain 860B
.. information returns 6049
.. taxation of 860E
. liquidation 860F
. loss, determination of 860C
. net income, determination of 860F
. net operating loss 860E
. nonresident aliens holders of interest in 860G
. original issue discount 1272
. permitted investments defined 860G
. prohibited transactions 860E; 860F
. qualified mortgage defined 860G
. qualified replacement mortgage defined 860G
. qualified reserve asset defined 860G
. regular interests
.. definition 860G
.. taxation of 860B
. REIT interests in 860E
. residual interests
.. definition 860F
... income in excess of daily accruals on 860E
.. partnerships 774
.. taxation of 860C
. subsidiaries 860E
. taxable income 860C
. taxation of 860A
. termination of status 860D
. transfers 860E; 860F
. unrelated business tax 860E
. variable insurance contracts 860
. waiver of tax 860E
. wash sales 860F

Real property
. acquired by U.S., administration of property .. 7506
. administration of real estate acquired by U.S. .. 7506
. agents (See Real estate dealers and agents)
. brokers (See Real estate dealers and agents)
. building and loan associations, reacquisition of real property 1038
. capital contributions
.. foreign corporations, U.S. real property interests 897
. capital expenditures 263A
. capital gains and losses 1221; 1231
.. reacquisition of real property 1038
. closely-held business real property or farm, valuation of 2032A
. condemnation 1033
. conservation contributions 170
. construction or improvement financing agreement defined 6323
. controlled group of corporations, U.S. real property holding corporation 897
. cooperative banks, reacquisition of real property 1038
. deeds 6338
. definitions 897
. depreciation 168; 1250
. distributions, U.S. real property interests

CODE SEC.

Real property —Cont'd
. distributions, U.S. real property interests —Cont'd
.. foreign corporations 897
.. nonresident aliens 897
. effectively connected income
.. foreign corporation real property income 882; 897
.. nonresident aliens 897
.. real property income treated as 871
. estate tax 6324A; 6324B
.. additional tax qualified use real property
... statute of limitations 2032A
.. farm or closely-held business real property .. 2032A
.. qualified use property 2032A; 6324; 6324B
. estates and trusts
.. publicly traded partnerships 7704
.. special use farm real property valuation ... 1040
.. transfers
... farms 1040
... gain or loss 1040
... holding period 1223
. evasion or avoidance of tax
.. transfers to foreign entities
... U.S. real property interests 897
. exchange of property, nontaxable
.. real property reacquisition 1038
. exempt facility bonds (See Exempt facility bonds)
. farm property
.. closely-held business real property or farm valuation 2032A
.. dispositions, farm land 1252; 1257
.. estate tax
... farm or closely-held business real property .. 2032A
... special use valuation 1040
... transfer of farm or business real property .. 1040
. foreign corporations 882; 897; 1445; 6039C; 6652
.. capital contributions
... U.S. real property interests 897
.. distributions
... U.S. real property interests 897
.. domestic corporation, treatment as
... U.S. real property investments 897
.. effectively connected income 897
.. information returns
... U.S. real property investments ... 6039C; 6652
.. real property income 882
... effectively connected, election 882
.. real property income, U.S. property investments
... disposition of 861; 862; 897; 1445
... information returns 6039C; 6652
... wash sale transactions .... 1445(b)(8)
.. transfers to
... recognition of gain 897
.. withholding of tax
... U.S. real property interest dispositions .. 1445(a)
. foreign estates and trusts
.. U.S. real property holding organizations 897
. foreign investments in real property
.. Virgin Islands 862
... information returns 6039C

251

Real Index to Code

CODE SEC.

Real property — Cont'd
- foreign partnerships
  - U.S. real property holding organizations 897
- foreign persons
  - holding U.S. real property investments, returns ... 6039C
- gain or loss
  - reacquisition of real property 1038
- gift purpose, valuation for 2032A
- green building and sustainable design projects
  - exempt facility bonds (See Exempt facility bonds subhead qualified green building and sustainable design projects)
- gross estate 2031
  - valuation, qualified real property 2032A
- held for use or investment, condemnation 1033
- holding companies
  - U.S. real property holding corporation defined 897
- income
  - effectively connected income (See subhead effectively connected income)
  - foreign corporations (See subhead foreign corporations)
  - nonresident aliens 871
- income connected with U.S. business
  - nonresident aliens 861; 897; 1445; 6039C; 6652
- indebtedness
  - real property reacquisition 1038
- information returns
  - foreign corporations
    - U.S. real property investments 6039C; 6652
  - foreign investments in real property
    - Virgin Islands 6039C
  - nonresident aliens
    - U.S. property investments 6652
    - passive activity losses and credits 6039C
    - U.S. real property interests 6039C
    - penalty for failure to file 6652
- installment sales .... 453 et seq.; 1038
- insurance company expenses 834
- inventory costs 263A
- involuntary conversions
  - condemnation of real property held for use or investment 1033
- land
  - acquisition, private activity bond financed 147
  - clearing of 1252
  - farm land dispositions 1252; 1257
- leases (See Leases)
- levy, deed to real property 6338
- lien for taxes, priority 6323
- long-term 110
- low-income housing (See Low-income housing)
- low-income housing credit (See Low income housing credit)
- mutual savings banks, reacquisition of real property ... 1038
- nonresident aliens
  - distributions to, U.S. real property interests 897
  - effectively connected income, real property income .. 897
  - income 871; 897; 1445; 6652
  - income connected with U.S. business .. 1445; 6039C; 6652
  - real property income 861; 897
  - information returns
  - U.S. property investments 6652

CODE SEC.

Real property — Cont'd
nonresident aliens — Cont'd
- real property income 871
  - effectively connected, treatment as 871
- retaliatory taxes
  - U.S. real property investments 6039C
- U.S. property investments
  - disposition of 861; 1445
  - information returns 6652
  - U.S. real property 897
- withholding of tax
  - U.S. real property interest dispositions .... 1445(a)
- nonresidential 168
- outdoor displays 1033
- passive activity losses and credits
  - information returns 6039C
- property seized for taxes
  - certificate of sale 6338
  - expenses of levy and sale 6341
  - general rules 6335
  - legal effects 6339
  - notice of sale 6335
  - perishable goods 6336
  - records of sale 6340
  - redemption of 6337
  - sale, deeds 6338; 6339
- qualified real property defined 2032A; 6324B
- reacquisition 1038
  - basis 1038
  - gain or loss 1038
  - indebtedness 1038
  - mutual savings banks 1038
  - worthless, treatment prior to reacquisition of real property as 1038
- redemption 7810
- rental activities
  - passive activity losses and credits 469
- repossession 1038
- residential property (See Residence; Residential property)
- retaliatory taxes, nonresident aliens
  - U.S. real property investments 6039C
- revolving fund for redemption of real property 7810
- sales or exchanges
  - nontaxable exchanges
    - U.S. real property interests 897
  - publicly traded partnership 7704
  - seized property, sale of
    - deeds 6338; 6339
    - redemption 6337
    - subdivided for sale 1237
- source of income from disposition 861; 862
- special use valuation 2032A
  - farm real property 1040
- stock and securities
  - U.S. real property interest, treatment as 897
- straight line depreciation 168
- subdivided for sale 1237
- taxes
  - construction period carrying charges 312

252

Index to Code

CODE SEC.

Real property —Cont'd
. *taxes —Cont'd*
. . cooperative housing corporations 216
. . deductibility 164; 275; 2053; 2106
. . deduction for taxable income . . . . 63(c)(7)
. . exclusion from cost basis 1012
. . insurance companies 834
. . priority, federal tax 6323
. . purchaser and seller 164; 1001; 1012
. . sales 164
. transfers to foreign corporation
. . recognition of gain
. . . U.S. real property interests 897
. transfers to foreign entities
. . evasion or avoidance of tax
. . . U.S. real property interests 897
. U. S. property investments, disposition of
. . nonresident aliens 861; 1445
. U. S. real property, nonresident alien 897
. U. S. real property holding corporation defined 897
. U. S. real property interests
. . defined 897
. . information returns 6039C
. . . penalty for failure to file 6652
. . nonresident aliens, distributions 897
. . wash sale transactions . . . . 1445(b)(8)
. . withholding of tax 1445
. valuation
. . charitable contributions, remainder interest in real property
. . . . 170
. . closely-held business real property or farm 2032A
. . estate and gift purposes 2032A
. . farm or closely-held business real property 2032A
. . farmers and farming, special use 1040
. . gross estate
. . . qualified real property 2032A
. . retired or disabled decedents 2032A
. . surviving spouse 2032A
. Virgin Islands
. . foreign investments in real property 862; 6039C
. wash sales 897
. withholding of tax
. . foreign corporations
. . . U.S. real property interest dispositions . . . . 1445(a)
. . nonresident aliens
. . . U.S. real property interest dispositions . . . . 1445(a)
. . qualifying statement, transferee receives . . . . 1445(b)(4)
. . residence where amount realized does not exceed $300,000
. . . . 1445(b)(5)
. . stock regularly traded on established securities market
. . . . 1445(b)(6)
. . U.S. real property interest dispositions by foreign persons
. . . affidavit that interests in corporation not U.S. real property,
. . . . nonpublicly traded domestic corporation . . . . . . 1445(b)(3)
. . . exemptions . . . . 1445(b)(1)
. . . foreign person defined . . . . 1445(f)(3)
. . . general rule . . . . 1445(a)
. . . qualified substitute defined . . . . 1445(f)(6)
. . . qualifying statement, transferee receives . . . . . . 1445(b)(4)

CODE SEC.

Real property —Cont'd
. *withholding of tax —Cont'd*
. . *U.S. real property interest dispositions by foreign persons — Cont'd*
. . . residence where amount realized does not exceed $300,000
. . . . 1445(b)(5)
. . . stock regularly traded on established securities market
. . . . 1445(b)(6)
. . . transferee defined . . . . 1445(f)(2)
. . . transferor defined . . . . 1445(f)(1)
. . . transferor's maximum tax liability defined . . . . . 1445(f)(4)
. . . transferor's unsatisfied withholding liability defined
. . . . 1445(f)(5)
. worthless, treatment prior to reacquisition of real property as
. . . . 1038

Rebates
. defined 6211
. Medicaid and Medicare 162
. recovery, for individuals (2008) 6428

Recapitalization
. depreciation 1245
. private foundations, excess business holdings 4943
. small business stock 1244

Recapture
. alternate fuel vehicle refueling property credit . . . . 30C(e)(5)
. athletes, professional
. . contracts; depreciation recapture 1245
. carbon dioxide sequestration credit . . . . 45Q(d)(6)
. cellulose biomass ethanol plant property, ACRS . . . . . 168(l)(7)
. clean fuel vehicle, deduction for 179A
. deferred rental agreements 467
. depreciation
. . basis reductions 1017
. . broadcasting facilities, sale of 1245; 1250
. . dispositions 1245; 1250
. . expensing in lieu of 179
. . installment sales 453
. . listed property 280F
. . Sec. 1245 property 1017
. . Sec. 1250 property 1017
. devises; depreciation recapture 1250
. donor advised funds; recapture of deduction 2522
. employee retirement and benefit plans, amounts paid by
. . . . 6511
. empowerment zones recapture rules 1397A
. environmental remediation cost, expensing
. . recapture of deduction on sale . . . . 198(e)
. ESOPs, recapture of gain 1042
. exploration expense deduction 617
. farm land
. . conservation expenses 1252
. . dispositions 1252
. . . expensed amounts 263A
. . sale 1252
. federally-subsidized indebtedness
. . mortgage credit certificates 25
. first-time homebuyers
. . refundable credit for 10% of purchase price . . . . . . 36(f)(1)
. foreclosures, depreciation recapture 1250
. foreign losses 904

253

Recapture — Cont'd

	Code Sec.
Recapture —Cont'd	
. foreign oil and gas losses	907
. investment credit property	50
. involuntary conversions, trade or business property	1231
. losses; at risk amounts	465
. low-income housing credit (See Low-income housing credit)	
. mortgage credit certificates, federally-subsidized indebtedness (See Mortgage credit certificates)	
. mortgage revenue bonds, federally-subsidized indebtedness (See Mortgage bonds)	
. net ordinary loss, trade or business property	1231
. pollution control facilities	291
. qualified disaster assistance property	
. . Sec. 179 property, election to expense	179(e)(4)
. qualified disaster assistance Sec. 179 property	179(e)(4)
. S corporations, overall foreign loss	1373
. trade or business property, net ordinary losses on	1231
Receipts for payment of tax	6314
. employment taxes	6051
. government depositaries	5703; 6302
. withholding tax statements	6051; 6652; 6674; 7204
Receivers	
. assessment, suspension of period	6872
. bankruptcy	
. . notice of qualification	6036
. . returns	6012
. disclosure of returns and return information	6103
. fiduciary status	7701
. notice of qualification	6036
. returns by	6012; 6062
. unpaid claims following proceeding, payment of	6873
Reciprocal credits or exemptions	
. foreign countries	883; 893; 901; 4221
Reciprocal underwriters	
. deduction, limitations, election	835
Reclamation laws, property sold pursuant to	1033
Recognition of gain or loss	1001
Recordings, sound (See Sound recordings)	
Records (See Books and records)	
Recourse financing	
. at risk limitations; exclusion from credit base	49(a)(1)
Recovery	
. damages	
. . Antitrust Act violations	186
. estate and gift taxes	2207A; 2207B
. exclusions, bankruptcy	1398
. exempt income	111
. foreign expropriation losses	6167 (See also Foreign expropriation losses)
. marital deduction	2207A
. period; depreciable property	168
. prior taxes	111
. rebates for individuals, 2008	6428
. tax benefit items	111; 381
. tertiary injectants	193
Recovery zone bonds	
. allocation	
. . minimum	1400U-1(a)(1)(B)

	Code Sec.
Recovery zone bonds —Cont'd	
. allocation —Cont'd	
. . national limitation	1400U-1(a)(1)(A)
. . state, by	1400U-1(a)(3)
. . 2008 state employment decline	1400U-1(a)(2)
. national limitations	
. . allocation of national limitation	1400U-1(a)(1)(A)
. recovery zone defined	1400U-1(b)
Recovery zone economic development bonds	
. defined	1400U-2(b)(1)
. limitation on amount of bonds designated by issuer	1400U-2(b)(2)
. qualified bond treatment	1400U-2(a)(1)
. qualified economic development purpose defined	1400U-2(c)(2)
Recovery zone facility bonds	1400U-3(a)
. allocation of national limitation	1400U-1(a)(1)(A)
. defined	1400U-3(b)(1)
. limitation on amount of bonds designated by issuer	1400U-3(b)(2)
. qualified business defined	1400U-3(c)(2)
. recovery zone property defined	1400U-3(c)
. sale-leaseback	1400U-3(c)(3)
. substantial renovations	1400U-3(c)(3)
Recreational equipment tax	4161 et seq.
. collection, mode or time of	6302
Recreational expenses and facilities	274
Red Cross communications taxes	4253
Redemption	
. distributions	
. . earnings and profits, adjustment for	312
. ground rents	163; 1055
. seized property, for taxes	6337; 7810
. stock (See Redemption of stock)	
. unused stamps	6805
Redemption of stock	302 et seq.
. abnormal, regulated investment company series fund	851
. administration expenses of estate payments, for	303
. complete liquidation, in	
. . exception to realization as ordinary income	306
. constructive ownership	302; 304
. controlled corporations	304
. death tax payment, for	303
. definition	317
. DISCs	996
. disproportionate substantially	302
. distributions	302 et seq.
. effect on recipients	302 et seq.
. estate tax payment, for	303
. exchanges, treatment as	302
. expenses	162
. foreign corporations	1248
. funeral expense payments, for	303
. generation-skipping transfers	303
. intragroup transactions	304
. liquidation	302; 306
. loss carryovers, change of ownership	382
. noncorporate shareholder	302
. not essentially equivalent to dividend	302

Index to Code — Refunds

Redemption of stock—Cont'd
. partial liquidation, in 302
. pass-thru entities 302
. private foundations, excess business holdings 4943
. pro rata 302
. qualified trade or business 302
. related corporations, through use of 304
. reserves for, accumulated earnings tax 537
. Sec. 303 redemption needs 536
. stockholder's interest, termination 302
. subsidiaries 304
. termination 302
. transfers to controlled corporation, coordination with 304
. unit investment trust interests 852

Redevelopment bonds 144

Referendums as business expense 162

Refinancings, small issue bond 144

Refined coal production facility
. electricity produced from renewable sources; credit .... 45(d)(8)

Refinery property expense election .... 179C(b)
. Clean Air Act waiver .... 179C(c)(3)
. cooperative owner, election to allocate deduction to ... 179C(g)
. ineligible refiner property .... 179C(f)
. production capacity .... 179C(e)
. qualified refinery defined .... 179C(d)
. qualified refinery property .... 179C(c)
. reporting .... 179C(h)
. sale-leasebacks .... 179C(c)(2)
. treatment .... 179C(a)

Reforestation expenditures 194
. adjusted gross income 62
. amortization 1245
. investment credit 46

Reformable interest, charitable contribution 170

Refractory and fire clay depletion 613

Refrigerators
. energy efficient appliance credit (See Energy efficient appliance credits)

Refueling property deduction 179A

Refunds and credits ... 6401 et seq. (See also Credits against tax)
. administrative review of decisions 6406
. alcohol taxes 5008; 5044; 5056; 5062; 5064; 6423
. amounts treated as overpayments 6401
. armed forces, deceased members 692
. astronauts 692
. authority to make 6402
. bad debts 6511
. beer tax 5056; 5062; 5064
. black lung benefit trusts 7422
. business credit (See Business credit)
. capital loss carrybacks 6511; 6611
. check accepted, effect on claim for additional amount ... 6611
. cigars and cigarettes, excise taxes .... 5705 et seq.
. civil action for refunds 7422
. . court review of disallowed amounts 7486
. . recovery of erroneous refunds 6602; 7405
. claim of right adjustments 6213; 6411

Refunds and credits—Cont'd
. communications taxes 6415
. credit treated as payment 7423
. date of allowance 6407
. deficiency discovered on claim 6501
. Desert Shield 7508
. determination as mitigation of error 1313
. disaster loss 6405
. disclosure of information to locate persons entitled to 6103
. distilled spirits tax 5008; 5062
. earned income
. . advance payments 3507; 6012; 6051
. . overstatement 6201
. employee retirement and benefit plans 6511
. employment taxes 3503; 6413
. environmental taxes 4662
. erroneous
. . interest, recoverable by suit 6602
. . mitigation of effect of limitations and other provisions ... 1311 et seq.
. . recovery 6514
. . suit to recover 6532; 7405
. erroneous claim for refund or credit
. . civil penalties .... 6676(a)
. . excessive amounts .... 6676(b)
. . noneconomic substance transactions .... 6676(c)
. . other penalties, coordination with .... 6676(c)
. excess distributions by trusts 666
. excessive claims, gasoline 6206; 6675
. excessive credits 6401
. excessive tax withheld
. . nonresident aliens and foreign corporations 1464
. excise taxes .... 6415 et seq.
. expense of securing 212; 7430
. experimentation expenses, credit for 6511
. federal programs and federally assisted programs
. . refunds disregarded in administration of 6409
. floor stocks 6412
. foreign corporations 882
. foreign death tax credit adjustments 2016
. foreign tax credit adjustments 905; 6511
. fractional dollar 7504
. fuels, exempt use 6427; 6675
. gasoline tax ... 1366; 4081(e); 6206; 6416; 6420 et seq.; 6427; 6675
. hazardous waste cleanup, excise tax on 4662
. insolvent affiliated group members 6402
. insolvent banks 7507
. installment payments of tax 6403
. interest on (See Interest)
. limit on amount 6511
. limitation period .. 6511 et seq. (See also Statute of limitations)
. . after period of limitation 6514; 7405
. . extension by agreement 6511
. . filing claims 6511
. . income recaptured under qualified plan termination 6511
. . income taxes 6511
. . interest on overpayments 6611
. . judicial proceedings 6532

Refunds

CODE SEC.

Refunds and credits—Cont'd
limitation period—Cont'd
.. limitation on allowance 6511
.. petition to Tax Court, in case of 6512
.. time return filed and tax paid 6513
. manufacturers excise taxes 6416
. motor fuel tax 6427
. net operating loss carrybacks 6511
. nonresident aliens 874
. overcollection of tax 6415
. overpayments 6401
.. credited against taxes due 6402; 6601; 6611
.. determined by TC 6512
. partners and partnerships 6511; 7422
. pension plans 6511; 7422
. persons who collected certain taxes 6415
. private foundations 6511; 7422
. publicity 6405
. reconsideration after mailing of notice of disallowance 6532
. recovery 6602
. reductions, review of 6402
. regulated investment companies, undistributed capital gain 852
. reports of 6405
. research expenses, credit for 6511
. retailers excise taxes 6416
. sales and services, taxes on 6416
. self-employment tax, state and municipal employees 6511
. Social Security tax 31
. special fuels tax 6206; 6427
. state and local income taxes 2604; 6050E
. state escheat laws, applicability 6408
. statute of limitations (See Statute of limitations)
. suits for refund 6532; 7422
. Tax Court jurisdiction 6512
. tentative, claim of right adjustments 6213; 6411
. tentative carrybacks 6405; 6411; 6611
. tobacco taxes .... 5705 et seq.; 6423
. toxic waste cleanup, excise taxes for 4662
. transferees and fiduciaries 6901
. transportation taxes 4263; 6415
. unclaimed, state escheat laws 6408
. wagering taxes 6419
. waiver of limitation on assessment 6511
. waiver of notice of disallowance of claim 6532
. war postponement 7508
. withholding tax .... 1464 (See also Withholding)
.. nonresident aliens, withholding at source 6414
.. wages, on 6414
. worthless securities 6511
Registered mail, use of 6212; 7502
Registration
. aircraft, fuel for 4041
. firearms 5802; 5841
. gas guzzler tax, exemptions 4222
. manufacturer's tax 4222
. obligations (See Registration-required obligations)
. penalty for failure to register 7272
. persons paying special taxes 7011

Index to Code

CODE SEC.

Registration—Cont'd
. persons required to register 4412; 7011; 7272
. retail excise taxes, exemptions 4222
. special tax 7011
. stills 5179
. tax shelters 6111; 6707
. tax-exempt bonds 149
. vessels
.. registry, failure to display 6718
. wagering taxes 4412
Registration-required obligations
. book entries 149; 163
. capital gains or losses 1287
. definitions 163; 165; 4701
. exceptions, denial of deduction for losses 165
. excise tax for obligations not in registered form .. 4701
. failure to register 4701
. interest 163; 312
. loss deduction 165
. nominees 149
. registered form defined 4701
Regulated futures contracts
. defined 1256
. marked to market 1256
Regulated investment companies (RICs) ...... 851 et seq.
. adjustment defined 860
. aggregate dividends 854
. alternative minimum tax 59
.. adjusted current earnings exception .... 56(g)(6)
. capital gains 852
.. dividends 852; 854; 860
. capital loss carrybacks and carryovers 1212
. capital to development companies 851
. carryovers, acquiring corporation 381
. claim for deficiency dividend deduction 860
. consolidated returns 1504
. credits and refunds 860
. custodial accounts
.. employee annuities 403
.. excess contributions 4973
. deficiency dividends 381; 860
.. prior law 6697
. definitions 851; 862
. determinations 851; 860
. distributions 852
. dividends
.. deficiency 316; 860
.. exclusion 852
.. exempt-interest 265
.. paid after close of year 855
. dividends received deduction 243; 854
. earnings and profits 852
. environmental tax 59A
. excise tax on undistributed income 4982
. exempt income 265
. foreign tax credit 855
.. allowed to shareholders, election of credit 853
. fraud in connection with deficiency dividend deduction 860
. furnishing capital to development corporations ... 851

256

Index to Code

	CODE SEC.
Regulated investment companies (RICs)—Cont'd	
. gross income test, failure to satisfy	851
. hedging transactions	851
. interest	265
. late-year losses	852
. limitations applicable to dividends	854
. load charges	852
. loss on sale of stock held less than 6 months	852
. nonrecognition transactions defined	852
. nonresident aliens	871
. non-RIC year distributions	852
. owned by nonresident of the U.S., stock	2105
. penalties, prior law	6697
. publicly traded partnerships qualifying as, income	7704
. qualification requirements	851
. qualified investment entity defined	860
. qualified tax credit bonds (See Qualified tax credit bonds)	
. redemption of shares	852
. reinvestment right defined	852
. series funds	851
. shareholders	
. . qualified tax credit bonds, allowance of credits (See Qualified tax credit bonds)	
. short-term obligations issued at discount	852
. stapled entities	269B
. statements to shareholders	
. . distributions	852
. . foreign taxes	853
. . undistributed capital gains	852
. statute of limitations on deficiency dividends	860
. stay of collection on deficiency dividends	860
. tax imposed	11
. taxable income	4982
. taxation of	852
. tenant service income	853
. 2% floor on miscellaneous itemized deductions	67
. undistributed income	
. . capital gains	852
. . excise tax	4982
. unit investment trusts	851; 852
. U.S. real property interest dispositions	
. . withholding	
. . . distributions by regulated investment company	1445(e)(6)
Regulated public utilities (See also Public utilities)	
. defined	7701
Regulations, authority for	7805
Rehabilitation	
. charitable contributions	170
. credits (See Rehabilitation credit)	
. existing property	147
. loans	
. . mortgage revenue bonds	143
. . withholding tax on wages	3401
. low-income housing credits (See Low-income housing credit)	
. private activity bonds	147
. residential property	
. . defined	25
. . rentals	145

	CODE SEC.
Rehabilitation credit	
. certified historic structure defined	47(c)(3)
. charitable contributions	170
. election	47(d)(5)
. expenditures	
. . progress expenditures under subsection(d), coordination with	47(b)(2)
. . taken in account in taxable year	47(b)(1)
. general rule	47(a)
. investment credit	46
. progress expenditures	47(d)(1)
. . application of subsection	47(d)(2)
. . borrowing by the taxpayer for person rehabilitating property	47(d)(3)(B)
. . component parts, property in	47(d)(3)(A)
. . coordination with rehabilitation credit	47(b)(2)
. . non self-rehabilitated buildings, limitations on	47(d)(3)(C)
. . percentage of completion, determining	47(d)(3)(D)
. . self-rehabilitated properties	47(d)(1)
. . special rules	47(d)(3)
. qualified rehabilitation building	47(c)(1)
. qualified rehabilitation expenditure	47(c)(2)
. self-rehabilitated buildings	
. . defined	47(d)(4)
. . non self-rehabilitated buildings, limitations on	47(d)(3)(C)
Rehires, work opportunity credit	51
Reimbursements	
. employees	
. . adjusted gross income	62
. . entertainment expenses	274
. . expenses exceeding	162
. . insulin	106(f)
. . living expenses, insurance compensation for casualty loss	123
. moving expenses	
. . gross income, inclusion in	82
. . prescription drugs	106(f)
Reinsurance agreements	845; 848; 4371 et seq.
REITs (See Real estate investment trusts (REITs))	
Related corporations	
. collapsible corporations	341
. interest	163
. redemption of stock through	304
Related persons	
. customs Service duties	
. . property imported into U.S. by related person	1059A
. defined for first-time homebuyers	36(c)(2)
. domestic production activities deductions	199(c)(7)
. foreign personal holding company income	954
. nonconventional fuel source credit, limitations and adjustments	45K(d)(7)
. patent transfers between	1235
. private activity bonds	
. . partners and partnerships as related persons	147
. . S corporations as related persons	147
. . substantial user of facility	147
. property imported into U.S. from related persons	1059A
Related taxpayers	
. adjustments in barred years, mitigation rule	1311 et seq.

Related   **Index to Code**

CODE SEC.

Related taxpayers —Cont'd
. boycott participation 999
. constructive ownership of stock 267
. corporate interest paid to 163
. defined 904; 954; 1313; 5881
. dependent care assistance programs 129
. depreciation deduction 168
. disallowance of deductions 267
. distributions to, gain or loss 336
. electricity production credit 45
. expenses from sales or exchanges 267
. factoring trade receivables 864
. foreign personal holding company income 552; 954
. foreign persons, OID 163
. gains
. . previously disallowed losses 267
. . sales or exchanges 1239
. import of property to U.S. by, basis limitation 1059A
. indebtedness, acquisition of 108
. installment sales 453
. insurance income 953
. interest from sales or exchanges 267
. limitation on deductions 267
. losses from sales or exchanges 267
. matching taxable years 267
. nonconventional fuel source credit . . . . 45K(d)(7)
. nontaxable exchanges 1031
. oil and gas depletion allowance 613A
. original issue discount 163
. partnerships 267
. pass-thru entities 267
. patents transferred to 1235
. payments to
. . employment-related services, for 21
. . interest on home mortgages 25
. payor's deduction with payee's reporting of income, matching
. . . . 267
. private activity bonds
. . substantial user of facility 147
. qualified clean fuel vehicles, deduction for 179A
. qualified refueling property, deduction for 179A
. reinsurance contracts, tax avoidance effect 845
. related or subordinate party defined 672
. residential property, rental of 280A
. sales and exchanges 267
. shipping operations, foreign base company income 955
. small issue bonds 144
. stock ownership 267
. straddles 1092
. transactions between 267
. work opportunity credit 51
Religious orders (See also Apostolic association; Churches; Religious organizations)
. FICA 3121
. FUTA 3309
. withholding tax on wages 3401
Religious organizations (See also Apostolic association; Churches; Religious orders)
. business income 511

CODE SEC.

Religious organizations (See also Apostolic association; Churches; Religious orders) —Cont'd
. charitable contributions 170
. conscientious objections to insurance 1402
. educational organizations operated by 512
. examination of business activities 7611
. exemption 501; 504
. FICA 3121; 3127
. FUTA 3306; 3309
. lobbying activities 501; 504; 4911
. private foundations (See Private foundations)
. retirement income accounts 415
. self-employment income of members of 1402
. withholding tax on wages 3401
Religious purposes
. transfers, estate tax 2055
Remainder interests
. amortization, pollution control facility 169
. charitable contributions 170; 642; 2522
. claims against estate, deductibility 2053
. credit for death taxes on 2015
. depletion 611
. depreciation 167
. estate tax, payment of 6163
. pollution control facilities, amortization 169
. reforestation expenditures 194
. sale of, gain or loss 1001
Remarriage, dependent support 152
REMICs (See Real estate mortgage investment conduits (REMICs))
Removal of architectural barriers to handicapped and elderly
. . . . 190; 263
Renegotiated government contracts
. claim of right 1341
. net operating loss carrybacks 1341; 6511
Renewable diesel
. biodiesel, treatment as . . . . 40A(f)(1)
. defined . . . . 40A(f)(3)
. exception to biodiesel credit . . . . 40A(f)(3)
Renewable electricity production credit 45
Renewal community
. capital gain, gross income status 1400F
. designation 1400E
. economic growth requirements 1400E
. empowerment zones, coordination with 1400E
. expansion of 1400E
Rent expense
. business expenses 162
. campus lodging 119
. personal holding companies 543
Rental income
. adjusted gross income 62
. aircraft, income from foreign 872
. allowance, clergy 107
. clergy allowance 107
. DISCs 994
. foreign personal holding company income 553
. gross income 61

Index to Code

CODE SEC.

Rental income —Cont'd
. ground rents (See Ground rents)
. husband and wife 469
. information returns 6041
. parsonages, rental value of 107
. passive activity losses and credits 469
. personal holding company income 543
. redeemable ground rents (See Ground rents)
. REITs .... 856(d)
. ships, income from foreign 872
. source of income 861; 862
. unrelated business taxable income 512
. withholding tax at source on nonresident aliens and foreign corporations 1441

Rental property
. accounting method 467
. crop rentals 1401
. defined 856
. exempt facility bonds 142
. low income housing credits (See Low-income housing credits)
. motor vehicles 7701
. passive activity losses and credits 469
. projects
. . change in use 150
. . exempt facility bonds 142
. . private activity bonds 150
. REITs
. . rents from real estate defined .... 856(d)
. residential 168
. . classification 168
. . depreciation 168
. . disallowance of expenses 280A
. . exempt facility bonds 142
. . 501(c)(3) bonds 145
. . straight line depreciation 168
. terminal rental adjustment clause 7701
. use of, accounting method 467
. vacation homes 280A

Rent-to-own property, depreciation 168

Reorganization exchanges .... 351 et seq.
. additional consideration received 356
. allocations on distribution of stock and securities ... 312
. assumption of liability 357; 358
. basis (See Basis)
. boot .... 356 et seq.
. cash equivalents, receipt of .... 356 et seq.
. control defined 368
. controlled corporations 351; 355
. corporations, effect on .... 361 et seq.
. definitions 368
. depreciation 1250
. distributee, basis to 358
. . nonrecognition property 358
. distributions
. . . controlled corporation 312; 355
. . . nonrecognition of gain or loss 361
. effect of .... 361 et seq.
. employee stock options 424
. foreign corporations 367; 6046

Requests

CODE SEC.

Reorganization exchanges—Cont'd
. gain or loss
. . additional consideration received 356
. . nonrecognition
. . . corporation, effect on 361
. in-kind, exchanges not solely 361
. liabilities, assumption of 357
. market discount bonds 1278
. money or other property, for .... 356 et seq.
. multiemployer plans .... 418 et seq.
. nonrecognition of gain or loss
. . corporation, effect on 361
. ownership change 382
. party to 368
. private foundations, excess business holdings ... 4943
. railroads 354
. regulated investment companies
. . deficiency dividends 381
. REITs, deficiency dividends 381
. security holders, effect on .... 354 et seq.
. small business stock involved 1244
. stock and securities 306; 354
. stock options 424
. stockholders, effect on .... 354 et seq.

Repayments
. federal officers and employees, proceedings by taxpayers 7423
. income held under claim of right 1341

Repeal of 1939 code 7851

Repeal of taxes, change of rate 15

Replacement funds, arbitrage bonds 148

Replacement mortgage
. real estate mortgage investment conduits defined 860G

Replacement property
. holding period 1223
. stock or securities 1042

Reportable transactions
. accuracy-related penalty applied to 6662A
. failure to furnish information concerning 6707
. failure to furnish information with return ... 6707A
. . amount of penalty .... 6707A(b)
. . coordination with other penalties .... 6707A(f)
. . imposition of penalty .... 6707A(a)
. . listed transaction defined .... 6707A(c)(2)
. . reportable transaction defined .... 6707A(c)(1)
. . rescind penalty, authority to .... 6707A(d)
. . SEC, penalty reported to .... 6707A(e)
. failure to maintain lists 6708
. material advisors 6111
. understatement, reasonable cause for 6664

Repossession
. manufacturers excise taxes 6416
. real property 1038

Reproduction of returns and other documents ... 7513

Requests
. letter rulings, opinion letters and determination letters
. . user fees 7528
. prompt assessment 6501

259

CODE SEC.

Requisitioned property 1033; 1231
Res judicata 7422
Research and experimental activities
. alternative minimum tax .... 56(b)(2)
. alternative simplified credit, election of 41
. amortization of expenditures 174
. basis adjustments, expenditures 1016
. capital expenditures 263; 263A
. costs 41
. credit .... 41; 280C(c); 6411; 6511
. deductions for expenditures 174
. definition 168
. disallowance of deductions .... 280C(c)(1)
. drugs, orphan 28
. energy research consortium .... 41; 41(f)(6)
. equipment, charitable contribution 170
. expenditures 41; 174; 263; 263A; 864
. exploration 174
. foreign corporation expenditures 864
. general business credit 38
. increasing research activity, credit for 41
. in-house research expenses 41
. inventory costs 263A
. land acquisition or improvement 174
. long-term contracts 460
. passive activity losses and credits 469
. property, acquisition or improvement 174
. reduced credit for costs, election of .... 280C(c)(3)
. Sec. 1245 property, depreciation 168
. unused credit 196
Research credit
. alternative minimum tax and research credit in lieu of bonus depreciation, election (See Accelerated cost recovery system (ACRS))
Research organizations
. medical (See Medical research organizations)
. payments to, credit for 41; 6411; 6511
. wines, alcohol taxes, exemptions 5042
Research scholarships 117
Reservation property, Native American (See Native Americans)
Reserves
. APR, life insurance companies 807
. arbitrage bonds 148
. bad debts 585; 593
. . financial institutions 57
. banks
. . bad debts 57
. . distribution to shareholders 593
. . losses on loans 585; 593
. commissioners' standard tables, life insurance reserves ... 807
. computation, life insurance companies 807
. cooperative associations, effect on exemption 501; 521
. decrease treated as gross income, life insurance companies 807
. financial institutions, bad debts 57
. foreign branches of U.S. life insurance companies 807
. increase treated as deduction, life insurance companies .. 807
. life insurance companies 807

CODE SEC.

Reserves —Cont'd
. *life insurance companies—Cont'd*
. . deduction 805; 809; 817
. . defined 816
. . double counting 811; 812
. . gross income computation 803
. . guarantees beyond end of taxable year 811
. . total reserves defined 816
. . variable contracts 817
. losses on loans 585; 593
Residence and source rules
. possessions of U.S. 937
Residences (See also Residential property)
. charitable contributions 170
. home construction contracts 460
. information as to place of, return requirements 6039E
. lawful permanent residence 7701
. personal residence, charitable contribution of remainder interest 170
. principal (See Principal residence)
. remainder interest in personal residence, charitable contribution 170
. sale or exchange
. . moving expenses 217
Resident aliens (See also Aliens; Nonresident aliens)
. defined 865; 7701
. earned income .... 911 et seq.
. estate tax, credit for foreign death taxes 2014
. exempt income 912
. first and last year of residency 7701
. foreign tax credit 901
. living abroad .... 911 et seq.
. personal property, sale of 865
Residential energy efficient property credit
. allocation .... 25D(e)(7)
. allowance .... 25D(a)
. basis adjustments .... 25D(f)
. building construction, expenditures part of ..... 25D(e)(8)
. carryforward of unused credit .... 25D(c)
. condominiums .... 25D(e)(6)
. cooperative housing corporation, tenant-stockholder in .... 25D(e)(5)
. fuel cell expenditure limitations .... 25D(e)(4)
. joint occupancy, dollar amount .... 25D(e)(4)
. labor costs .... 25D(e)(1)
. limitations .... 25D(b)
. original installation, expenditures made at ..... 25D(e)(8)
. solar panels .... 25D(e)(2)
. swimming pools used as storage .... 25D(e)(3)
. termination .... 25D(g)
Residential lot installment sales 453; 453A
Residential projects
. exempt facility bonds (See Exempt facility bonds subhead qualified residential project)
Residential property
. acquisition indebtedness 163
. basis 1016; 1033
. business use 280A
. capital gains and losses 1223

Index to Code — Retirement

CODE SEC.

Residential property —Cont'd
. cooperatives (See Cooperative apartments and housing corporations)
. credit, interest on mortgages 25
. day care services 280A
. demolition due to natural disaster 165
. disaster losses 165
. exempt facility bond, rental project 142
. family rental units financed with qualified 501(c)(3) bonds 145
. gain from sale or exchange
.. one-time exclusion 121; 1250; 6012
.. reacquisition 1038
.. holding period 1223
. home equity indebtedness 163
. income from sale 6012
. interest on mortgage
.. credit 25
.. disallowance of deduction 163
.. involuntary conversions 1033
. lien for taxes
.. exemption 6334
.. priority 6323
. limitation on deductions, business use 280A
. management associations 528; 6012
. mortgage credit certificates 25; 163; 6709
. partly residential, gain on sale of 121
. pre-Oct. 13, 1987 indebtedness 163
. principal place of business or trade 280A
. principal residence
.. defined 25
.. rental of 280A
.. sale of principal residence, gain on 121
. projects
.. change in use 150
.. exempt facility bonds 142
.. private activity bonds 150
. qualified residences 163
. reacquisition of real property 1038
. relocation due to natural disaster 165
. rentals
.. applicable convention 168
.. classification 168
.. depreciation 168
.. disallowance of expenses 280A
.. exempt facility bonds 142
.. 501(c)(3) bonds 145
.. private activity bonds 149; 150
.. straight line depreciation 168
. rollover of gain on sale 1250
. S corporations, use by 280A
. sale of principal residence, gain on 121
. separate structure for business use 280A
. small issue bonds 144
. storage use 280A
. U.S. citizens or residents living abroad, housing costs exclusion 911
. vacation homes, rental of 280A

CODE SEC.

Restaurant property
. ACRS depreciation
.. qualified restaurant property .... 168(e)(7)
.. depreciation 168
Restoration of property, capital expenditures 263
Restraining assessment or collection 6213; 7421
Restricted bank director stock
. defined 1361
. S corporation distributions, director receiving 1368
Retail commission salesmen
. noncash remuneration, withholding tax on wages 3402
Retail excise taxes .... 4001 et seq. (See also Excise taxes)
. credit on returns 6416
. dealers in beer and liquor .... 5121 et seq.
. diesel fuel 4041
. exemptions 4221
. Highway Trust Fund 9503
. luxury items .... 4001 et seq.
. passenger vehicles 4001
.. first retail sale defined for 4002
.. parts and accessories 4003
. penalties 7261
. refunds and credits 6416
. representation that tax is excluded from price 7261
. special fuels 4041; 4042
. taxicabs, exception 4001
. trucks and trailers .... 4051 et seq.; 9503
.. exemptions 4053
Retail facility, exempt facility bond 142
Retail improvement property
. qualified retail improvement property, ACRS depreciation .... 168(e)(8)
Retailers
. oil and gas depletion allowance 613A
Retaliatory taxes 2108
Retired serviceman's family protection plan
. annuities 72
. death benefits 101
. exemption form levy 6334
Retirees
. accident and health plans 401
. fringe benefits 132
. material participation in farming activity 469
. returning to U.S. 217
. transfer of excess pension assets, retired employees .. 420
. vesting of benefits (See Vesting of retirement benefits)
. welfare benefit plans 419A
Retirement age defined 415
Retirement pay (See also Pension, profit-sharing, and stock bonus plans)
. uniformed services 122
Retirement plans
. 401(k) plans (See Cash or deferred arrangements (CODAs))
. pension, profit-sharing, and stock bonus plans (See Pension, profit-sharing, and stock bonus plans)
. qualified retirement plans (See Qualified retirement plans)
. self-employed retirement plans (See Self-employed retirement plans)

Retirement

CODE SEC.

Retirement savings
. adjusted gross income 62
. deduction allowance 219
. individual retirement accounts 219
. information returns 6047

Retroactive regulations or rulings 7805

Return preparers (See Preparers of returns)

Returns .... 6001 et seq. (See also Information returns)
. accounting period, change in 443; 6012
. acquisitions 6043A
. age 65 or over 6012
. agent 882; 6012
. alcohol taxes 5555; 6091
. audit of
. . selection procedures, disclosure 6103
. bankruptcy and receiverships
. . bankrupt's estate 6012
. . corporations 6012
. breweries 5415
. cash received 6050I
. computations by treasury 6014; 6151
. condominium management association 6012
. confidentiality and disclosure 6103; 6104
. consolidated (See Consolidated returns)
. contracts from Federal executive agencies 6050M
. copies 6103
. corporations
. . corporate dissolution or liquidation 6043
. . . extensions 6081
. . information .... 6041 et seq.; 6652
. . partnership return as, limitations on assessment and collection purposes 6501
. . place to file 6091
. . signing of 6062
. . time for filing 6072
. . trust return as, limitations on assessment and collection purposes 6501
. credits taken on 6415
. . health insurance costs 6050T
. debt cancellation, financial entity 6050A
. deferred compensation plans 6103
. defined for disclosure purposes 6103
. delinquency penalty 6013; 6651
. DISC 6011; 6072; 6501
. disclosure of .... 6103 et seq. (See also Disclosure of tax information)
. disclosure of information, unauthorized 7213; 7216; 7431; 7435
. donated property dispositions 6050L
. early 6513
. energy grants and financing 6050D
. estate tax (See Estate tax)
. estates 6012; 6034A
. estimated tax (See Estimated income tax)
. executed by Secretary 6020; 6501
. executors 6012
. exempt entities (See Exempt entities and organizations)
. failure to file
. . additional penalties 6696

Index to Code

CODE SEC.

Returns—Cont'd
. *failure to file —Cont'd*
. . additions to tax 6651
. . assessment and collection limitations 6501
. . deficiency dividend deduction 547
. . DISC 6686
. . execution by Secretary 6020
. . foreign corporation 6679
. . . personal holding company income, with .. 6683
. . foreign sales corporations 6686
. . foreign trusts 6677
. . information returns 6652; 6695
. . limitations on assessment and collection ... 6724
. . organization or reorganization of foreign corporations and as to acquisition of their stock 6679
. . penalties 6651; 6652; 6677; 6721
. . pension plans
. . . actuarial report 6692
. . . annuities, reports on 6693
. . . individual statement to participant 6690
. . . notification of change of status 6652
. . . registration statement 6652
. . . simple retirement account, reports on 6693
. . personal holding companies 6683
. . preparation by Secretary 6020
. . tax-exempt organizations 6685
. . willful failure to file 7203
. failure to furnish information with return 6707A
. . amount of penalty .... 6707A(b)
. . coordination with other penalties .... 6707A(f)
. . imposition of penalty .... 6707A(a)
. . listed transaction defined .... 6707A(c)(2)
. . reportable transaction defined .... 6707A(c)(1)
. . rescind penalty, authority to .... 6707A(d)
. . SEC, penalty reported to .... 6707A(e)
. false or fraudulent
. . assessment and collection limitations 6501
. . damages 7434
. . fines 7207
. . information returns 7434
. . joint return 6013
. . preparation assistance 7206
. . prosecution limitations 6531
. . Secretary making return 6020
. Federal executive agencies 6050M
. fiduciary 6012; 6034A
. filed before due date
. . assessment and collection limitation 6501
. . overpayment interest 6611
. . refund limitation 6513
. filing requirements 6011; 6012; 7203
. . state and local laws requiring federal returns 6103
. financial entity return relating to debt cancellation 6050A
. financial institutions, foreign transfers by .... 6011(e)(4)
. firearms 6091
. fiscal year (See Fiscal year)
. fisherman 6050A
. foreclosure and abandonment of security 6050J
. foreign corporations (See Foreign corporations)

Index to Code — **Revenue**

CODE SEC.
Returns—Cont'd
. foreign personal holding companies 6035
. foreign sales corporations 6011; 6072; 6686
. foreign trusts 6677
. fractional year (See Short taxable year)
. frivolous, filing of 6702; 6703
. general requirements 6011
. generation skipping transfers 2662
. gift tax 2204; 6018; 6019; 6075
. GST tax 2662
. Guam income involved, information 6688
. guardians 6012
. hand-carried 6091
. health insurance cost credits 6050T
. homeowners associations 6012
. hospitalization due to combat related injuries 7508
. husband and wife
. . joint returns (See Joint returns)
. . spouses (See Spouses)
. identification numbers (See Identification numbers)
. income tax .... 6012 et seq.
. . joint returns (See Joint returns)
. . listing by Secretary of taxable objects owned by nonresidents of Internal Revenue districts 6021
. . persons required to make 6012
. . prepared for or executed by Secretary 6020
. . self-employment tax returns 6017
. . tax not computed by taxpayer 6014
. individuals excused from filing 6012
. information (See Information returns)
. inspection ..... 6103; 6103 et seq. (See also Disclosure of tax information)
. . failure to file or pay 6651
. . participating firms withholding tax 6651
. joint (See Joint returns)
. machine-readable 6011
. magnetic tapes 6011
. mathematical or clerical errors 6201; 6213; 6404
. mergers 6043A
. mortgage interest received 6050H
. nonresident aliens 874
. notice or regulation requiring records, statements and special returns 6001
. oversheltered returns defined 6234
. partnerships 6031
. . corporations, limitations on assessment and collection purposes 6501
. . entities filing, extension 6233
. . exchanges 6050K
. . late filing penalties 6698
. . magnetic filing 6724
. . signatures 6063
. payee statements, failure to furnish 6722
. penalties (See Penalties)
. period covered by 443; 6101
. persons required to make 6012
. place for filing 6091
. political organizations 6012
. possessions of U.S., governmental employees in ... 3125
. prepared by Secretary 6020

CODE SEC.
Returns—Cont'd
. preparers of (See Preparers of returns)
. private foundations 6033
. property acquired during affiliation 1051
. publicity .... 6103 et seq.
. . exempt organization information 6104
. . individual retirement savings plans 6104
. receivers 6012; 6062
. reproduction of 7513
. . persons required to file 6012
. . records, statements and special returns 6001
. requirements 6011
. return information, disclosure of 6103; 7213
. royalties, payments of 6050N
. S corporations 6037; 6233
. sale of residence, one-time exclusion of gain 6012
. self-employment tax 6017
. separate (See Separate returns)
. short period (See Short tax year)
. signatures on .... 6061 et seq.
. . corporation returns 6062
. . partnership returns 6063
. . presumed authentic 6064
. special, notice or regulations requiring 6001
. state and local income tax refunds 6050E
. statements required 6001
. straddles 1092
. tax not computed by taxpayer 6014
. time deemed filed
. . limitations on assessment and collection 6501
. . refund limitations 6513
. time for filing .... 6071 et seq.
. . cooperative associations 6072
. . estate and gift taxes 6075
. . extension 6081
. . general rules 6072
. . nonresident alien individuals and foreign corporations returns and other documents 6071
. . timely mailing as timely filing 7502
. time for performance of acts where last day falls on Saturday, Sunday or legal holiday 7503
. timely mailing as timely filing 7502
. tobacco 6091
. Treasury computing 6014
. trustee in bankruptcy, signature 6062
. trusts 6012; 6034A; 6501
. unauthorized inspection of 7213A
. understatements of tax liability, aiding and abetting .. 6701; 6703; 7408; 7422
. U.S. citizens residing abroad 6012
. verification 6065
. Virgin Islands income 932
. wage earners 6014
. waiver, definitions 6724
. withholding of tax .... 1461 et seq.
Revenue Acts, basis established by 1052
Revenue agents or officers
. authority of 7608
. delinquent 7803

263

CODE SEC.

Revenue agents or officers —Cont'd
. entry of premises 7606
. interest in tobacco or liquor production 7214
. oaths administered by 7622
. returns prepared by, assessments and collection 6404
. suit for damages 7402
. unlawful acts of 7214; 7344

Reverse mortgage
. real estate mortgage investment conduits defined 860G

Reversionary interests
. defined 2037
. estate tax
. . credit for death taxes 2015
. . extension of time for payment 6163
. . gross estate, effect on 2037
. . payment 6163
. . grantor as owner 673
. . gross estate, inclusion in 2037
. . valuation 2037

Revised Organic Act
. Guam 7651
. Virgin Islands 7651

Revocable transfers
. estate tax 2038
. . nonresidents 2104
. . gross estate inclusion 2038

Revocable trusts 645; 676; 1014
Revolvers (See Firearms; Pistols and revolvers)
Revolving credit sales 453
Revolving fund for redemption of real property 7810
Rewards to informers 7214; 7623
RICs (See Regulated investment companies (RICs))
Rifle defined .... 5845 (See also Firearms)
Rights, stock (See Stock and stock rights)
Rita, Hurricane
. Gulf Opportunity Zone (See Gulf Opportunity Zone)
Robert T. Stafford Disaster Relief and Emergency Assistance Act 5064; 5708
Rock asphalt depletion 613
Rolling stock (See Railroads)
Rollovers
. contribution, Archer MSAs 220
. education IRA 530
. residential property, gain on sale 1250
. retirement plans 402
. . annuities 72
. . employee annuities 403
. . individual retirement accounts 408
. . limitations and restrictions 219
. . optional direct transfer 401
. . partial rollovers, IRA 408
. . top-heavy plan contributions 416
. . Roth IRA 408A
. securities gain into special small business investment company 1044
. small business stock
. . gain into another qualified small business stock 1045

CODE SEC.

Rollovers —Cont'd
. *small business stock —Cont'd*
. . gain into specialized small business investment, publicly traded securities 1244

Roth IRA
. aggregation rules 408A
. contributions .... 408A(c); 408A(e)
. defined .... 408A(b)
. distributions .... 402A; 408A(d)
. elective deferrals 402A
. excess contributions 4973
. qualified rollover contributions defined .... 408A(e)
. qualified Roth contribution program defined 402A
. rollovers
. . contributions .... 408A(c)(6)
. . IRA other than a Roth IRA, from .... 408A(d)(3)
. . qualified rollover contributions defined .... 408A(e)

Rounding to nearest dollar 6102; 7504
Royalties
. adjusted gross income 62
. backup withholding 3406
. business computer software 543
. coal mines (See Coal mines)
. deductions attributable to, personal holding company 543
. foreign personal holding company income 553
. gross income 61
. information returns 6050N
. iron ore (See Iron ore)
. personal holding company income 543
. REITs 856
. returns 6050N
. source of income 861; 862
. unrelated business taxable income 512

Rubber defined 4072
Rulings
. authority for 7805
. employee retirement and benefit plans 7476
. in effect upon enactment of Internal Revenue title 7807
. public inspection 6110

Rum shipped from U.S. possession 7652
Rural airports
. segments to and from .... 4261(e)(1)

Rural areas
. enterprise zones/communities (See Enterprise zones/communities)

Rural cooperative plan 401
Rural electric cooperatives, taxation of ..... 1381 et seq.
Rural mail carriers
. reimbursement of business expenses 162

Rutile, depletion 613
Ryukyu Islands
. U.S. Savings bonds of resident 872

S

S corporations .... 1361 et seq
. accounting periods 444; 7519
. accumulated adjustment accounts 1368

Index to Code

S

CODE SEC.

S corporations—Cont'd
- affiliated group membership 1361
- alternative minimum tax, adjusted current earnings ... 56(g)(6)
- bank requirement to change from reserve method of accounting to become 1361
- bankruptcy estate 1361
- basis of S corporation stock 1016
  - adjustments to .... 1367 et seq.
    - decrease in .... 1367(a)(2)
    - income items .... 1367(b)
    - increase in .... 1367(a)(1)
  - indebtedness, adjustments to .... 1367(b)(2)
  - inherited stock .... 1367(b)(4)
  - Sec. 165(g) and 166(d), coordination with .... 1367(b)(3)
- built-in gains, tax imposed on 1366; 1374
- C corporations
  - defined 1361
  - earnings and profits 1362; 1371; 1375
  - years and S years 1371
- capital gains and losses 1366; 1374
- carrybacks and carryovers, C and S years 1371
- computation of taxable income
  - corporation 1363
  - shareholders 1366
- consent of shareholders to election 1362
- coordination with subchapter C 1371; 1375
- credits against tax 1366
- deductions 1366
- definitions 1361; 1363; 1377
- discharge of indebtedness 108
- distributions
  - cash, post-termination 1371
  - definitions 1368
  - general rule 1368
  - restricted bank director receiving 1368
  - undistributed taxable income 1379
- dividends 1368
- earnings and profits 1368; 1371; 1375
- electing small business trust 1361
- election
  - after termination 1362
  - effect on corporation of 1363
  - eligibility for 1361; 1362
  - parties who may make 1362; 1363
  - shareholder consent to 1362
  - time made 1362
- employee retirement and benefit plans
  - simplified pension plans 404
- estates and trusts as shareholders 1361
- excess net passive income 1366; 1375
- expensing in lieu of depreciation 179
- failure to file return .... 6699(a)
  - deficiency procedure, application of .... 6699(d)
  - penalty, amount per month .... 6699(b)
  - penalty assessment .... 6699(c)
- failure to meet requirements, termination 1362
- family groups 1366
- family members treatment as 1 shareholder 1361
- foreign income 1373

CODE SEC.

S corporations—Cont'd
- fringe benefits for employees 1372
- gross income of shareholders 1366
- gross receipts 1362; 1375
- husband-wife shareholders 1361
- inadvertent termination 1362
- ineligibility 1361; 1362
- information returns 6037
- inheritance, shares acquired through 1361
- installment obligations, liquidation distribution 453B
- investment credit 50; 1371
- LIFO inventories, recapture of benefits 1363
- losses 1366
- nonresident alien shareholder 1361
- notice and participation in administrative of judicial proceedings 6423
- number of shareholders 1361
- oil and gas depletion allowance 613A
- partnership rules for fringe benefit purposes 1372
- passive investment income 1362; 1366; 1375
- passthrough to shareholders 1366
- private activity bonds 147
- pro rata shares 1366
  - defined 1377
  - termination of election 1362
- qualified subchapter S trusts (QSSTs) 1361
- qualified tax credit bonds, credit for holders of .... 54A(g)
- recapture of overall foreign loss 1373
- reelection 1362
- reforestation expenditures 194
- related taxpayers, transactions with 267
- residential property, rental of 280A
- restricted bank director stock 1361
- returns
  - copies to shareholders 6037
  - extension for filing 6233
  - general rules 6037
- revocation of election 1362
- S period 1368
- shareholders 1361
  - accident or health insurance 162
  - basis adjustments to stock 1367
  - consent to election 1362
  - corporations returns, copies 6037
  - estates and trusts as 1361
  - oil and gas depletion allowance 613A
  - passthrough to 1366
  - pro rata shares 1366
    - defined 1377
    - termination of election 1362
  - residential property, rental of 280A
  - returns 6037; 6233
  - simplified pension plans 404
  - tax treatment of .... 1366 et seq.
  - taxable income determination 1366
  - two% 1372
- short taxable year on termination 1362
- small business corporation, ceasing to be 1362
- small ethanol producer credit 40

265

S

	Code Sec.
S corporations—Cont'd	
. special rules	1377
. stock requirement	1361
. straight debts, stock requirement	1361
. Subchapter S trusts	1361
. subsidiary, wholly owned	1361
. taxable year	
. . election of other than required year	444
. . general rule	1378
. . other than required, payment of tax	7519
. . required payments, election not to have	7519
. taxation of	6233
. termination of election	1362
. . post-termination transition period	1377
. transitional rules on enactment	1379
. trusts as shareholders	1361
. two% shareholders	1372
. wrongly labeled entity, returns	6233
Safety achievement awards	274
Safety equipment, advanced mine	
. expense, election to (See Mine safety equipment)	
Sagger clay depletion	613
Sailors (See Armed forces)	
Salary (See Compensation)	
Salary reduction arrangements	
. employee annuities purchased under	403
. IRA plan, election for	408
. Railroad Retirement Tax Act	3231 et seq.
. simplified employee pension plans	408(k)(6)
Sale leasebacks	
. deferred rental agreements	467
. disqualified	467
. enterprise zones/communities	
. . sale-leaseback rules, special	1397C
. imputed interest	1274
. recapture, prior understated inclusions	467
Sales or exchanges	
. adjusted gross income, losses	62
. amount realized	1001
. annuity contracts	
. . basis, effect on	1021
. . defined for purpose of exchange	1035
. . nontaxable exchange	1035
. basis (See Basis for gain or loss)	
. capital gain or loss (See Capital gains and losses)	
. collapsible corporations	341
. conflict-of-interest requirements	1043
. constructive sales	
. . appreciated financial positions	1259
. crops, unharvested, sold with land	268
. debt instruments	1271
. defined	865
. DISC assets	995
. distraint proceedings	6336; 7505
. distributions in complete liquidation	331
. endowment contracts	
. . defined for purposes of exchange	1035
. . nontaxable exchange	1035

	Code Sec.
Sales or exchanges — Cont'd	
. evasion of tax, penalty for	7341
. false statements to purchasers relating to tax	7211
. farm land	1252; 1257
. FCC orders	1245; 1250
. futures	1223
. gain or loss	1001
. . earnings and profits, effect on	312
. . residences	1001
. . SEC orders, in obedience to	1081 et seq.
. goodwill	865
. installment sales	453 et seq.
. insurance policies	1035
. intangible property	865
. inventory property	865
. investment property	1031
. involuntary conversion of property (See Involuntary conversions)	
. land with unharvested crop	268; 1016; 1231
. leasebacks, imputed interest	1274
. life tenant and remaindermen	1001
. like-kind exchanges	
. . depreciation recapture	1245; 1250
. . property held for productive use or investment, exchange of	1031
. livestock	1231
. losses, adjusted gross income	62
. natural resources	631
. nonresident aliens	
. . personal property	865
. . withholding tax at source on foreign corporations and	1441
. nontaxable exchanges	1031 et seq.
. . depreciation recapture	1250
. . holding period	1223
. . market discount	1276
. . U.S. real property interests	897
. not solely in-kind	1031
. partnerships	707
. . controlled partnerships	706
. . distributed property	735
. . guaranteed payments	707
. . interest in	741; 751; 752; 761; 1031
. . partner not acting in capacity as partner	707
. patents	1235; 1249
. personal property	
. . acquired by U.S.	7505
. . lien for tax	6323
. . source rules	865
. productive-use property	1031
. property seized for taxes	
. . certificate of sale	6338; 6339
. . expenses of levy and sale	6341
. . notice of sale	6335
. . perishable goods	6336
. . personal property acquired by U.S.	7505
. . proceeds of sale	6342
. . records of sale	6340
. . redemption of	6337
. . stay pending Tax Court decision	6863

Index to Code Section

CODE SEC.

Sales or exchanges —Cont'd
. radio broadcasting stations (See Broadcasting)
. real estate mortgage investment conduits 860F
. real property 164
. realty acquired by U.S. 7506
. related taxpayers 267; 453; 1239
. reorganization .... 351 et seq.
.. effect on corporation .... 361 et seq.
.. effect on stock and security holders .... 354 et seq.
. residences
.. foreign service, members of 121
.. gain on sale 121
.. uniformed services, members of 121
. resident alien personal property 865
. SEC orders .... 1081 et seq.
.. depreciation recapture 1245; 1250
.. holding period 1223
. short sales 1233
. solely in-kind 1031; 1250
. source of income 861; 862
. special use valuation property 2032A
. stock options .... 421 et seq.
. stock or securities
.. exchanged under SEC orders 1081
.. foreign corporations 1248
.. property, for 1032
.. same corporation, for stock of 1036
. term interests 1001
. timber, coal or iron ore 631
. treasury stock for property 1032
. unrelated business taxable income 512
. wash sales 1091
. when issued stocks and securities 1233
Sales price defined for excise tax 4216
Sales tax deductibility 164
Salespersons
. automobile, fringe benefit 132
. employee status 7701
. independent contractor status 3508
. information returns 6041A; 6652
. noncash remuneration, withholding on wages 3402
. retail commission salesmen 3402
Salvage value depreciation 168
Sand and gravel deposits depletion 613
Satellite depreciation 168
Saturday
. last day of performance 7503
. petition Tax Court, last day to 6213
Savings accounts
. medical (See Medical savings accounts, Archer)
. premature withdrawals 62
Savings and loan associations (See also Banks and trust companies)
. building and loan association status 7701
Savings banks (See Banks and trust companies; Mutual savings banks)

CODE SEC.

Savings bonds, U.S. (See United States savings bonds)
SCHIP (See State Child Health Insurance Programs (SCHIP)
Scholarships and fellowships
. definition 117
. dependent status, effect on 152
. exempt income 117
. FICA 3121
. foreign students and exchange visitors 1441
. funding bonds
.. declaratory judgment as to exempt status 7478
.. defined 150
.. Indian tribal government, treatment as state 7871
.. private activity bonds 147
.. public approval 147
.. state or local bond, treatment as 150
.. volume cap 146
. higher education expenses 135
. Indian tribal government, treatment as state 7871
. limitations, exempt income 117
. private activity bonds 147
. qualified 117
. research work as condition 117
. teaching as condition 117
. tuition and related expenses 117
. withholding tax
.. nonresident aliens and foreign corporations, at source on 1441
.. wages 3401
Schools (See Educational organizations)
Scientific equipment, charitable contributions 170
Scientific organizations
. charitable contributions 170
. exemption .... 501(c)
. wines, alcohol taxes 5042
Scientific property, charitable contribution 170
Scoria depletion 613
Sea water, depletion of minerals from 613
Seals, authority to prescribe or modify 7444; 7514
Seaplane transport excise tax .... 4261(i)
Search warrants 7608
Seasonal employee retirement and benefit plans
. service requirements 410
. vesting rights 411
Secrecy of returns .... 6103 et seq.
Secretary of Labor
. state law approval 3304
Secretary of the Treasury
. definition 7701
. powers and duties 7801
Section 126 property, disposition of 1255
Section 179 property
. advanced mine safety equipment, election to expense advanced
.. coordination with Sec. 179 .... 179E(e)
. controlled groups
.. defined .... 179(d)(7)
.. dollar limitations .... 179(d)(6)

Section		Index to Code

	CODE SEC.
Section 179 property —Cont'd	
. cost defined	179(d)(3)
. defined	179; 179(c)(2)
. election to expense	179(c)(1)
. . dollar limitations	179(b)(1); 179(d)(6)
. . inflation adjustments	179(b)(5)
. . limitation, reduction in	179(b)(2)
. . married individuals filing separately	179(b)(4)
. . passenger vehicles	179(b)(6)
. . trade or business, income from	179(b)(3)
. . treatment as expense generally	179(a)
. . 2008 and 2009, increase in limitation for	179(b)(7)
. estates and trusts	179(d)(4)
. noncorporate lessors	179(d)(5)
. partnerships	179(d)(8)
. purchase defined	179(d)(2)
. qualified disaster assistance property	
. . defined	179(e)(2)
. . dollar amount	179(e)(1)
. . empowerment zones, coordination with	179(e)(3)
. . recapture	179(e)(4)
. . renewal communities, coordination with	179(e)(3)
. S corporations	179(d)(8)
Section 501(c)(3) organizations	
. abatements	4962
. application for recognition	508
. family rental unit, 501(c)(3) bond financed	145
. gift or bequest to	508
. governing instruments	508
. housing projects, 501(c)(3) bonds	145
. organized after Oct. 9, 1969	508
. pooled financing bonds	147
. presumption of status as	508
. private activity bonds	147
. prohibited political campaign expenses	7409
. qualified 501(c)(3) bond	145
. residential rental property, 501(c)(3) bonds	145
. unrelated business taxable income	512(a)(3)
Section 956 inclusions	
. limitation with respect to	
. . foreign tax credit	960
Section 1256 contracts	
. capital gains and losses	1212; 1256
. carrybacks and carryovers	1212
. dealers in options and commodities	1256
. estates and trusts	1212
. mark to market	1256
Securities and Exchange Commission	
. exchanges in obedience to orders of	1081 et seq.
. . basis for determining gain or loss	1082
. . definitions	1083
. . nonrecognition of gain or loss	1081
. . tax-free exchanges	1081 et seq.
. . . depreciation recapture	1245; 1250
. . . holding period	1223
Securities futures contracts	
. capital gains and losses	1234B

	CODE SEC.
Security interests	163
Security requirements	
. dye injection systems	6715A
Seed equipment retail excise tax	4053
Seizure of property	6331 et seq. (See also Levy)
. appraisals	6334
. authorization	6331; 7608
. automobiles, transfer of title	6339
. books and records	6333; 6340
. certificate of sale	6338; 6339
. civil damages for failure to release lien	7432
. collection of taxes	6331 et seq.
. date levy made	6502
. deed to realty sold	6338; 6339
. enforcement of levy	6332
. exemption from levy	6334
. expense of levy and sale	6341
. forcible rescue of seized property	7212
. forfeitable property	7301 et seq.
. gain or loss	1033; 1231
. injunction	6213
. interest on money received by U.S. on wrongful seizure	6343; 6621
. involuntary conversion (See Involuntary conversions)	
. levy and distraint	6331; 6502; 6503
. liability	6332
. limitation period	6502; 6503
. loss due to	1212; 6331
. mail	6334
. nonapplication of levy	6331
. notice	
. . loss due to seizure	6331
. . sale	6335
. . seizure	6331; 6335
. perishable goods	6336
. proceeds of levy	6342; 7426
. property subject to seizure and sale	6331
. recovery	7426
. redemption of property	6337
. release of levy	6343
. return of property	6343; 6532
. salaries or wages, levy on	6331; 6334
. sale of seized property	6331; 6335; 6336; 6863; 7426; 7505
. stamping, marking and branding seized goods	6807
. stay of sale pending TC or District Court decision	6863
. substituted sales proceeds	7426
. successive seizures	6331
. surrender of property	6332
. taxes, for	6331 et seq.
. third party rights	7426
. uneconomical levy	6331
. U.S. as party defendant	7426
. wrongful	
. . interest on money received by U.S.	6343; 6621
. . limitation on assessment and collection	6503
. . third party suits	7426
Self-dealing	
. black lung benefit trusts	4951

Index to Code — Services

CODE SEC.

Self-dealing —Cont'd
. private foundations 4941
Self-employed individuals (See also Independent contractors; Self-employment income tax)
. accident and health plans 105; 162
. definition 217; 401
. earned income 401
. medical deductions 162
. moving expenses 217
. retirement plans (See Self-employed retirement plans)
. top-heavy plans 416
. treatment as employee 401; 1402
Self-employed retirement plans 401
. adjusted gross income 62
. contributions to
.. deductibility 404
.. insurance protection, allocation 404
.. nondeductible 4972
. death benefits 101
. employee annuities 403
. fishermen 401
. information returns 6047; 7207
. life insurance 404
. medical benefit accounts 415
. owner-employee information requirements ... 6047; 7207
. simplified pension plans 219; 404
. taxability of beneficiaries 402
Self-employment Contributions Act of 1954 1403
Self-employment income tax .... 1401 et seq.
. deductions 164
. definitions 1402
. exclusions 7873
. failure to file return and pay tax 6651
. husband and wife 6017
. Indian fishing rights-related income 7873
. limitation period 6521
. mitigation of effect of statute of limitations 6521
. one-half, deductions 164
. rate 1401
. refunds by state and municipal employees 6511
. returns 6017
. trade or business, attributable to 164
Self-insured health plans
. applicable self-insured health plan defined ..... 4376(c)
. health care spending increases in, adjustment for .. 4376(d)
. imposition of fees .... 4376(a)
. liability for fees .... 4376(b)
. plan sponsor liability for fees .... 4376(b)(2)
. termination of fees after Sept. 30, 2019 ..... 4376(e)
Self-insured medical reimbursement plan 105
Semiconductor manufacturing equipment 168
Seminar income 274
Senate finance committee inspection of returns 6103
Senior citizens (See Elderly individuals)
Separability clause 7852
Separate lines of business
. pension, profit-sharing, and stock bonus plans .. 401; 414(r)(1)
.. affiliated service groups .... 414(r)(8)

CODE SEC.

Separate lines of business —Cont'd
. *pension, profit-sharing, and stock bonus plans—Cont'd*
.. allocation of benefits to line of business .... 414(r)(5)
.. 50 employee requirement .... 414(r)(2)
.. headquarters personnel .... 414(r)(6)
.. highly compensated employee percentage defined
   .... 414(r)(4)
.. operating units .... 414(r)(7)
.. safe harbor .... 414(r)(3)
Separate maintenance payments (See Alimony and separate maintenance payments)
Separate returns
. computation of tax by IRS, election 6014
. general business credit 38
. individual retirement accounts 219
. joint return filed after 6013
. married filing separately (See Married filing separately)
. rates of tax 1
. rental activities 469
. retirement savings 219
. tax rates 1
. unused zero-bracket amount 6012
Separation, marital (See also Divorce)
. instrument of, definition 71
. payments (See Alimony and separate maintenance payments)
. stock acquired by 382
September 11, 2001 terrorism
. New York Liberty Zone 1400L
Servants
. FICA 3121
. FUTA 3306
. withholding tax on wages 3401
Service contract treated as lease 7701
Service of summons (See Summons)
Service partnerships
. electing large partnership defined 775
Servicemen (See Armed forces)
Services
. accounting methods 467
. children, of
.. assessment of tax 6201
.. FUTA 3306
. deferred rental agreements 467
. employment-related service identifying information 21
. excess benefit transactions of exempt organizations 4958
. excise taxes (See Facilities and services excise taxes)
. not in course of employer's trade or business
.. FICA 3121
.. FUTA 3306
.. withholding tax on wages 3401
. personal service contracts (See Personal service contracts)
. personal service corporations (See Personal service corporations)
. personal services, compensation for (See Compensation for personal services)
. self-employment tax 1402
. use of services, payments for 467
Services and facilities excise taxes (See Facilities and services excise taxes)

269

Settlement Index to Code

CODE SEC.

Settlement fund income 468B
Settlement procedures (See Treasury settlement procedures)
Settlement trusts, Alaska 646
Sewer depreciation 168
Shale
. depletion 613
. nonconventional fuel source credit (See Nonconventional fuel source credit)
Share-crops (See Crop-share rentals)
Shared equity financing agreements
. vacation homes 280A
Shareholders (See Stockholders)
Shares of stock (See Stock and securities)
Shells
. depletion 613
. excise tax 4181; 4182; 4222
Sheltered workshop income 151
Ships and shipping (See also Boats)
. alternative tax on shipping activities 1352
.. allocation of credits 1359
.. allocation of income and deduction to qualifying shipping activities .... 1355(g)(3)
.. bareboard charters .... 1355(b)(2)
.. definitions concerning 1355
.. depreciation 1357
.. disposition of qualifying vessel 1359
.. electing corporation .... 1355(a)(1)
.. electing group; controlled group .... 1355(a)(2)
.. election 1354
.. Great Lakes domestic shipping .... 1355(g)
.. interest 1357
.. notional shipping income 1353
.. operating a vessel .... 1355(b)(1)
.. partnership, activities carried on .... 1355(d)
.. qualified zone domestic trade .... 1355(g)(4)
.. qualifying activities 1356
.. qualifying vessel .... 1355(a)(4)
.. qualifying vessel operator .... 1355(a)(3)
.. regular tax, items not subject to 1357
.. revocation, election by 1354
.. shipping activity requirement .... 1355(c)
.. temporarily ceasing to operate a qualifying vessel ... 1355(e)
.. temporarily ceasing to operate a qualifying vessel in U.S. domestic trade .... 1355(f)
.. temporarily operating vessels in U.S. domestic trade, effect of .... 1355(g)(2)
.. termination, election by 1354
.. transactions not at arm's length 1359
. depreciation 168
. excise taxes 4471; 4472
. fuel tax 4042
. income 872; 883; 904; 955
. investment credit, Merchant Marine Act funds 7518
. meals for crew 274
. nonrecognition transfers to Maritime Administration 1061
. notional shipping income 1353
. owners of ships, protection and indemnity association 526
. registry, failure to display 6718

CODE SEC.

Ships and shipping (See also Boats) —Cont'd
. seized for violations 5608; 5688
. shipments from and to the U.S. .... 7652 et seq.
. shipwreck losses 165
. supplies
.. manufacturers excise taxes 4221; 4222
.. motor fuels tax 4041
... refunds and credits 6416
Shopping news, delivery
. FICA 3121
. FUTA 3306
. withholding tax on wages 3401
Short period returns (See Short tax year)
Short sales
. capital expenditures 263
. capital gains and losses 1233
. dividends, payments in lieu of 263
. dividends-received deduction 246
. exempt income 265
. interest 265; 1277
. investment interest 163
. market discount bonds 1277
. payments in lieu
.. dividends, of 263
.. transferred securities 6045
. wash sales 1091
Short tax year 441
. affiliated corporations 1501
. employee retirement and benefit plan
.. minimum funding standards 412
. environmental tax 59A
. estimated income tax, individuals 6654
. life insurance companies 811
. minimum tax 443
. research credit 41
. S corporations, termination of election 1362
. tax preferences 443
Short-term bonds
. veterans mortgage bonds 143
Short-term capital gains and losses (See Capital gains and losses)
Short-term leases
. construction allowances 110
. deductions 168
Short-term obligations issued at discount ..... 1281 et seq.
. acquisition discount 1283
. basis for gain or loss, adjustments 1283
. constant interest rate accrual of discount ... 1283
. current income inclusion 1281
. defined 1283
. exempt interest obligations 1288
. interest paid to purchase or carry 1282
. nongovernment 1271
. ratable accrual of discount 1283
Shotgun defined .... 5845 (See also Firearms)
Sick pay
. information returns 6051
. withholding tax on wages 3402

270

Index to Code

Small

	Code Sec.
Sickness (See **Personal injury and sickness**)	
Signatures on returns	6061 et seq.
Silver depletion	613
Simple cafeteria plans	
. small businesses	
.. compensation	125(j)(7)
.. contribution requirements	125(j)(3)
.. defined	125(j)(2)
.. eligible employer	125(j)(5)
.. generally	125(j)(1)
.. minimum eligibility and participation requirements	125(j)(4)
.. nondiscrimination requirement	125(j)(6)
Simple retirement accounts	
. acquisitions, rules for	408(p)(10)
. administration requirements	408(p)(5)
. compensation defined	408(p)(6)(A)
. defined	408(p)(1)
. designated financial institution	408(p)(7)
. dispositions, rules for	408(p)(10)
. distributions	408(d)(7)
. employee defined	408(p)(6)(B)
. matching contributions	408(p)(9)
. participation requirements	408(p)(4)
. penalties	6693
. qualified salary reduction arrangements defined	408(p)(2)
. reports and records	6693
. transition periods, rules for	408(p)(10)
. vesting requirements	408(p)(3)
. year defined	408(p)(6)(C)
Simple trusts	651; 652
Simplified employee pension plans	404; 408; 408(k)(1)
. collectibles	
.. coin and bullion exception	408(m)(3)
.. defined	408(m)(2)
.. distributions	408(m)
.. investments as distributions	408(m)(1)
. compensation defined	408(k)(7)
. contributions	
.. written allocation formula requirement	408(k)(5)
. cost-of-living adjustments	408(k)(8)
. distributions	408(d)(7); 408(m)
. employee defined	408(k)(7)
. employer contributions	219
. employer defined	408(k)(7)
. highly compensated, discrimination in favor of	408(k)(3)
. IRA plans	408
. limitations	
.. benefits and contributions	415
.. maximum, increase	408
. owner-employer defined	408(k)(7)
. participation requirements	408(k)(2)
. reports and records	408; 408(l)(1); 408(l)(2); 6693
. salary reduction arrangements	408(k)(6)
. simple retirement account reports	408(l)(2)
. special rules	408
. taxability of beneficiaries	402
. top-heavy plans	416
. withdrawals	408(k)(4)

	Code Sec.
Simplified employee pension plans—Cont'd	
. year defined	408(k)(7)
Single persons (See **Individual taxpayers**; **Unmarried individuals**)	
Single premium insurance contracts	
. payments, deductibility of	264
Single purpose agricultural or horticultural structure	168
Single-employer defined benefit pension plans (See **Defined benefit plans**)	
Skip person defined	2613
Skyboxes	
. disallowance of expenses	274
. private activity bonds financing	147
Skydiving excise tax	4261(h)
Slate depletion	613
SLOB (See **Separate lines of business**)	
Small agri-biodiesel producer credit	
. aggregation rule	40A(e)(2)
. agri-biodiesel defined	40A(d)(2)
. allocation	40A(e)(4)
.. cooperative patrons	40A(e)(6)
. allowance	40A(b)(5)
. eligible agri-biodiesel producer defined	40A(e)(1)
. pass-thru entities	40A(e)(3)
. regulations, prescription of	40A(e)(5)
Small aircraft of nonestablished line	
. transportation taxes	4281
Small Business Administration (SBA)	
. review of new regulations	7805
Small business corporations (See also **S corporations**; **Small business investment companies**; **Small business stock**)	
. defined	1244; 1361
. golden parachute payments	280G(b)(5)
. revocation of election	1362
Small business investment companies (See also **Small business stock**)	
. dividends received deduction	243; 246A
. losses	1242; 1243; 1244
. personal holding company status	542
. rollover of publicly traded securities gain into specialized company	1044
. stock	1242; 1244
Small business stock	
. partial exclusion for gain	
.. empowerment zone businesses	1202(a)(2)
.. special rules for 2009 and certain periods in 2010	1202(a)(3)
. rollover of gain into another qualified small business stock	1045
. rollover of gain into specialized small business investment, publicly traded securities	1244
.. 50% exclusion from gain	1202
.. partial exclusion from gain	1202
Small businesses	
. disabled access credit	44
. simple cafeteria plans (See **Simple cafeteria plans**)	
. simplified dollar-value LIFO method	474

271

Small

	Code Sec.
Small claims before TC	7463
Small employer health insurance credits	
. aggregation rules	45R(e)(5)
. amount of credit	45R(b)
. average annual wage defined	45R(d)(3)
. average wage as basis for phaseout of credit	45R(c)
. calendar years 2010, 2011, 2012, and 2013, application in	45R(g)
. contribution arrangement defined	45R(d)(4)
. credit period defined	45R(e)(2)
. deductions, disallowed	280C(h)
. eligible small employer defined	45R(d)
. employee defined	45R(e)(1)
. full-time equivalent employees	45R(d)(2)
. general business credit	38
. generally	45R
. insurance definitions	45R(h)
. nonelective contribution defined	45R(e)(3)
. number of employees as basis for phaseout of credit	45R(c)
. phaseout of credit	45R(c)
. regulations, prescription of	45R(i)
. seasonal workers	45R(d)(5)
. tax-exempt eligible small employers	45R(f)
. unused credit	196
. wages defined	45R(e)(4)
Small employer pension plans	
. general business credit	38
. startup costs	45E
Small employers	
. medical savings accounts, Archer	220
Small engine fuel taxes	
. Highway Trust Fund	9503
. Highway Trust Fund transfers	4483
Small ethanol producer credit	40
Small irrigation power defined	45
Small irrigation power facility	
. electricity produced from renewable sources; credit	45(d)(5)
Small issue bonds	144; 150; 265
Small tax balance abatement	6404
Small tax case procedure	7463
Small wind energy property credit	48(c)(4)
Smart electric grid system depreciation	168
Smart electric meter depreciation	168
Soapstone depletion	613
Social clubs (See Clubs)	
Social Security	
. benefits	86; 401
. . conscientious objections to	1402
. . information returns	6050F
. . OASDI overpayments	6402
. . retirement age defined	415
. . source of income	861
. . taxability, nonresident aliens	871
. . top-heavy retirement plans	416
. number as identifying number	6103; 6109
. returns	6050F

	Code Sec.
Social Security —Cont'd	
. taxes (See Federal Insurance Contributions Act (FICA); Employment)	
. work opportunity credit	51
Social welfare organization exemption	501
Sod depletion	613
Sodium chloride deposit depletion	613
Sodium dichromate	4661; 4662
Sodium hydroxide	4661; 4662
Software (See Computers)	
Soil	
. depletion	613
. erosion (See Erosion)	
Soil conservation (See Conservation subhead Soil and water)	
Solar energy facility	
. electricity produced from renewable sources; credit	45(d)(4)
Solar energy use to produce electricity	45
Soldiers and sailors (See Armed forces)	
Sole proprietorships	
. employee retirement and benefit plans	401; 414
Solid waste disposal facilities	
. exempt facility bonds	146
. municipal solid waste defined	45
. reclamation and closing costs	468
. service contracts	7701
Sonar devices, sport fishing	4162
Sound recordings	
. depreciation	168
. returned, accounting method	458
Source of income (See Income)	
South Africa, Republic of	
. foreign tax credit, denial of	901
Space activity income	863
Spacecraft depreciation	168
Special fuels tax	4041; 4042
. credits against tax	34
. Highway Trust Fund	9503
. Indian tribal government, treatment as state	7871
. nonresident aliens	874
. possessions of U.S.	4293
. refunds and credits	6206; 6427
. S corporations	1366
. U.S. use	4293
Special needs children	
. adoption credit	23
. . $13,170 special needs credit	36C(a)(3); 137(a)(2)
Special trial judges	
. annuities for surviving spouse and children	7448
. appointment	7443A(a)
. authority to make court decision	7443A(c)
. proceedings which may be assigned to	7443A(b)
Special use valuation property	
. farm real property	1040
. holding period	1223
Specified federal procurement payment	
. imposition of tax on	5000C

Index to Code

CODE SEC.

Specified health insurance policy
. accident and health coverage defined . . . . 4377(a)(1)
. defined . . . . 4375(c)(1)
. exempt governmental programs
. . defined . . . . 4377(b)(3)
. . treatment . . . . 4377(b)(2)
. exemption from definition of . . . . 4375(c)(2)
. fees
. . imposed . . . . 4375(a)
. . tax treatment . . . . 4377(c)
. government entities . . . . 4377(b)(1)
. increases in health care spending, adjustments for . . . . 4375(d)
. insurance policy defined . . . . 4377(a)(2)
. liability for fees . . . . 4375(b)
. possession of the U.S. . . . . 4377(d)
. prepaid health coverage arrangements . . . . 4375(c)(3)
. termination of fees after Sept. 30, 2019 . . . . 4375(e)
. United Stated defined . . . . 4377(a)(3)
Specified information reporting requirement
. defined 6724
Specified policy acquisition expenses defined 848
Spin offs, split offs, split ups 1551
Split-interest trusts . . . . 4947; 6034(a)
Spodumene depletion 613
Sport Fish Restoration Account
. transfers of taxes to . . . . 9504(b)(1)
Sporting goods, excise taxes
. definitions 4162
. imposition of tax 4161
. resales, treatment of certain 4162
Sports franchises, player contracts
. basis for gain or loss 1056
. depreciation recapture 1245
Sports utility vehicles
. expensing depreciable business assets 179
Spouses
. abandoned 7703
. . child support obligations, collection of 6305
. age 55 or over
. . sale of principal residence 121
. alimony (See Alimony and separate maintenance payments)
. bequests to surviving spouse
. . estate tax 2056
. . community property 2523
. credit for the elderly and the disabled 22
. defined 7701
. dependent care assistance programs 129
. dependents 21; 151; 152
. disabled
. . credit for 22
. . dependent care credit 21
. earned income credit 32
. education paid with redeemed savings bonds 135
. elderly, credit for 22
. employment-related expenses credit 21
. family employment, FICA 3121
. fringe benefits 132
. general business credit 38

Spouses

CODE SEC.

Spouses —Cont'd
. gifts
. . between spouses
. . . basis for gain or loss 1015
. . . estate tax 2001; 2012
. . . general rules 1041
. . . marital deduction 2523; 2524
. . . nonresident alien spouse 1041
. . expense deduction 274
. . gift-splitting, GST tax 2652
. . third party, to 1015; 2513
. handicapped, dependent care credit 21
. husband and wife defined 7701
. individual retirement accounts 219
. innocent spouse liability 66; 6013
. installment obligations 453B
. joint interests 2040
. joint returns (See Joint returns)
. jointly held property, gain on sale of 121
. living apart (See Living apart, husband and wife)
. marital deduction (See Marital deduction)
. marital status (See Marital status)
. mentally incapable spouse, dependent care credit 21
. moving expenses
. . new principal place of work, same location 217
. nonresident aliens
. . community income 879
. . joint returns 6013
. . noncitizen spouse, disallowance of marital deduction . . 2056; 2523
. nontaxable transfers between 1041
. partnerships 704
. passive activity losses and credits 469
. performing artists 62
. personal exemptions 151
. property settlements 2516
. qualified domestic trusts 2056A
. rental activities 469
. residence, gain on sale of 121
. returns
. . excused from filing 6012
. . joint (See Joint returns)
. . separate (See Separate returns)
. S corporation shareholders 1361
. sale of principal residence, gain on 121
. sale or exchange of residence 1250
. self-employment tax 1402; 6017
. separate maintenance payments (See Alimony and separate maintenance payments)
. separate returns (See Separate returns)
. standard deduction 7703
. straddles 1092
. student spouse, dependent care credit 21
. surviving spouse (See Surviving spouse)
. transfers between
. . gain or loss 1015; 1041
. . gift tax 2516
. . incident to divorce (See Divorce subhead transfers incident to)
. withholding tax on wages 3402

Stamp

Index to Code

	CODE SEC.
Stamp taxes (documentary)	
. affixing stamps	6804
. . failure to attach or cancel stamps	7271
. assessments and collection	6201; 6501
. bad check or money order in payment	6657
. cancellation of stamps	6804
. check or money order in payment	6201; 6311
. evasion of tax	6653
. failure to pay	6653
. interest on underpayments	6601
. nonpayment	6653
. payment	6311
. penalties for failure to pay	6653
. receipts	6314
. refunds and credits	6511
. unpaid, assessment	6201
Stamps (See also Stamp taxes (documentary))	
. accounting and safeguarding	6803
. affixing	6804
. . failure to attach or cancel	7271
. attachment and cancellation	6804
. authority for establishment, alteration, distribution	6801
. counterfeiting	7208; 7303
. forfeitures	7303
. individual retirement savings plans, investments	408
. mutilation or removal	7208
. occupational taxes	6806
. . alcohol	5142
. offenses relating to	7208; 7271
. payment by check or money order for	6201; 6311; 6657
. penalties relating to	6653; 7208; 7209; 7271
. posting occupational tax stamps	6806
. redemption of	6805
. reuse of	7208
. sale of	6802
. special provisions	6808
. stamping, marking and branding seized goods	6807
. supply and distribution	6802
. trafficking in	7208
. unauthorized use or sale	7209
Standard deduction	63(c)(1)
. additional	63(c)(3)
. adjustments for inflation	63(c)(4)
. basic	63(c)(2)
. common trusts	63(c)(6)(D)
. defined	63(c)(1)
. dependent limitation on	63(c)(5)
. disaster loss deduction	63(c)(8)
. estates and trusts	63(c)(6)(D); 1398
. ineligible individuals	63(c)(6)
. married filing separately	63(c)(6); 63(c)(6)(a)
. motor vehicle sales tax	63(c)(9)
. nonresident individuals	63(c)(6)
. partnership	63(c)(6)(D)
. Sec. 443(a)(1) returns	63(c)(6)(C)
Stapled entities	269B
Startup costs and expenditures	195
. indebtedness	2036

	CODE SEC.
Startup costs and expenditures—Cont'd	
. research credit	41
. small employer pension plans	45E
State agency disclosure of return	6103
State and local bonds	7478
. advance refunding	
. . abusive transactions, prohibition of	149(d)(4)
. . redemptions	149(d)(3)(B)
. . refunding bond defined	149(d)(3)
. . special rules	149(d)(6)
. amortizable premium	1016
. basis	1016
. dealers, income of	75
. exemption requirements	141 et seq.
. federally guaranteed bond	
. . exemption derived from Sec. 149(2)	149(c)
. . federally guaranteed defined	149(b)(2)
. . federally insured deposit or account defined	149(b)(4)
. . insurance programs	149(b)(3)
. . non exempt status of	149(b)(1)
. hedge bonds	149(g)(1)
. . construction period in excess of 5 years	149(g)(4)(A)
. . defined	149(g)(3)
. . expectation, rules for determining	149(g)(4)(B)
. . expectation as to when proceeds will be spent	149(g)(2)
. . regulations	149(g)(5)
. hospital bonds	145
. housing bonds, federally guaranteed	149
. information reporting	149(e)
. insurance on	832
. interest	103; 7478
. pooled financing bonds	149(f)(1)
. . cost of issuance payment requirement	149(f)(3)
. . defined	149(f)(6)
. . loan defined	149(f)(7)
. . reasonable expectation requirements	149(f)(2)
. . redemption requirement	149(f)(5)
. . written loan commitment requirement	149(f)(4)
. scholarship funding bonds	150
. short-term, issued at discount	1271; 1281 et seq.
. volunteer fire department bonds	150
State and local government plans	
. limitations on benefits and contributions	415
State and local governments	
. charitable contributions to	170
. CODAs	401
. deferred compensation plans	457
. defined, state	7701
. disability benefits	105
. exempt income	115
. Federal returns	
. . disclosure	6103
. . examination, gasoline products excise tax	4102
. Indian tribal governments, treatment as	7871
. law enforcement agency reimbursements	
. . illegal drug-related activities investigation costs	7624; 7809
. overpayments seized for child support	6402
. sales to	

274

Index to Code

Stock

CODE SEC.

State and local governments — Cont'd
. *sales to — Cont'd*
. . manufacturers excise taxes 4221; 4222
. . . refunds and credits 6416
. unemployment benefits
. . exemption from levy 6334
. unemployment contributions .... 3302 et seq.; 3309

State and local taxes
. death (See Death taxes; Inheritance taxes; State death taxes)
. deductibility 164
. federal collection (See Federal collection of state individual income taxes)
. generation-skipping transfers 2604
. refunds and credits, information returns 6050E
. returns, copies filed with federal returns 6103

State Child Health Insurance Programs (SCHIP)
. health insurance cost credits 35
. . advance payment of credit 7527
. . returns related to credit 6050T

State communications taxes 4253

State death taxes
. credit against Federal estate tax 2011; 2016
. valuation of estate for federal estate tax, and ... 2058

State employees
. deferred compensation plans
. . FUTA 3306
. employment tax refunds 6413
. FUTA 3306
. self-employment tax refunds 6511
. unauthorized disclosure of information 7213

State health insurance exchanges
. health plan information for premium assistance credits
.... 36B(f)(3)

State laws
. alcohol, occupational taxes 5145
. approval by Secretary of Labor 3304
. escheat, abandoned property 6408
. wagering taxes 4422; 4906

State legislator traveling expense 162

State lotteries and sweepstakes 3402; 4402

State obligations
. insurance on 832
. short-term, issued at discount .... 454; 1271; 1281 et seq

Statements
. fraudulent 7207
. timely mailing treated as timely filing 7502

Statistics of income, publication and study of ... 6103; 6108

Status determination date 7703

Statute of limitations
. adjustment, prior years for error in current year .. 1311 et seq.
. assessment and collection .... 6501 et seq.
. . amounts treated as overpayments 6401
. . bankruptcy and receiverships 6503
. . court proceedings 6531; 6532
. . credits against tax, carrybacks and carryovers .. 6501
. . excessive refund claims 6206
. . excise taxes 6501
. . involuntary conversions 1033

CODE SEC.

Statute of limitations — Cont'd
. *assessment and collection—Cont'd*
. . suspension (See subhead suspension)
. . time return deemed filed 6501
. . . transferees 6901
. capital losses 1211
. court proceedings .... 6531 et seq.
. deficiency dividends 547
. judicial proceedings .... 6531 et seq.
. levy and distraint 6502
. mitigation of effect of .... 1311 et seq.
. . related taxes 6521
. petition to TC 6213
. private foundation's distributions 6501
. refunds and credits .... 6511 et seq.
. . farm-use gasoline 6420
. . joint return after filing separate returns 6013
. . time return deemed filed 6513
. . withheld taxes 6513
. repeals by 1954 Code, effect 7851
. suspension 6503
. . assessment and collection 6503
. . bankruptcy and receiverships 6872
. . deficiency dividends 547; 860
. . foreign documentation, admissibility of 982
. . foreign expropriation loss recoveries 6503
. waiver (See Waiver)

Stills
. excise taxes on manufacturers of 5101; 5102
. registration 5179
. unregistered 5601; 5609; 5615

Stock and securities (See also Bonds)
. allocation of basis 307
. arbitrage operations 1233
. asset acquisitions, stock purchases 338
. basis (See Basis)
. charitable contributions 170
. common stock 305
. consent stock defined 565
. constructive ownership 318; 382
. . related taxpayers, transactions between 267
. controlled corporations 1563
. . redemption of stock 304
. controlled foreign corporations
. . adjustments to basis 961
. . determining ownership of 958
. convertible 306
. . personal holding companies 544
. . preferred 305
. cooperative housing corporations 216
. corporate distributions and adjustments 318
. . disallowance of deduction 163
. dealers in (See Dealers in securities)
. death taxes, redemption to pay for 303
. debt, discharge of 108
. debt versus equity 385
. defined 1083; 7701
. definitions 1083
. . dealer purposes 1236

275

Stock — Index to Code

CODE SEC.

Stock and securities (See also Bonds) —Cont'd
. definitions—Cont'd
.. Securities and Exchange Commission ordered sales or exchanges 1083
.. security 165; 6323
. discharge of indebtedness 108
.. election for treatment as depreciable property upon 1017
. DISCs, dispositions 995; 996
. dispositions 306
. distributions .... 301 et seq.
.. disposition of certain stock 306
.. earnings and profits, effect on 312
.. redemptions .... 302 et seq.
.. SEC orders, under 1081
.. taxability of corporation 311
. electing funds, pro rata share 1293
. employee options (See Employee stock options)
. employee stock ownership plans (ESOPs), nontaxable sales of stock to 1042
. employee stock purchase plans 423
. exchange of
.. employee stock options 424
.. property, for 1032
.. reorganization (See Reorganizations)
.. stock of same corporation 1036
. excluded 1563
. expatriated corporation insider, stock compensation to ... 4985
. Federal National Mortgage Association stock, basis of ... 1054
. financial institutions, held by 582
. foreign corporations
.. capital gains and losses 1248
.. earnings and profits, determination of 1248
.. failure to file returns as to acquisition of their stock 6679
.. reorganization exchanges 367
. foreign investment companies
.. gain on 1246
.. loss on sale or exchange 1247
. foreign personal holding companies .... 551 et seq.
.. income taxes to U.S. shareholders 551
.. ownership of stock 554
. gain or loss on
.. banks 582
.. foreign personal holding company income 553
.. nontaxable exchanges 1032; 1036
.. rollover of gain into specialized small business investment company 1044
. government (See United States obligations)
. greenmail payments 5881
. holding period 1223
. inherited
.. S corporation stock basis adjustments .... 1367(b)(4)
. lien for taxes 6323
. loans 1058
.. exempt organization income 512; 514
. losses
.. sale or exchange of stock held 6 months or less, REIT .... 857(b)(8)(A)
... holding period, determination of .... 857(b)(8)(B)
... periodic liquidation, exception .... 857(b)(8)(C)
.. worthless securities 165

CODE SEC.

Stock and securities (See also Bonds) —Cont'd
. March 1, 1913 value 1053
. marketable
.. defined 1296
.. installment sales 453
.. marked to market election 1296
. options (See Stock options)
. ownership rule 318; 544
.. affiliated corporations 1504
.. change of ownership 382
.. consolidated returns 1563
.. controlled foreign corporations 958; 1563
.. foreign corporations 883
.. foreign personal holding companies 552; 554
.. operating rules 382
.. personal holding companies 542; 544
.. REITs 856
.. related taxpayers, transactions between 267
. preferred stock 247; 305
.. dividend basis rules 1059
.. public utilities 243; 244
. prohibited allocation of 4979A
. purchases
.. asset acquisition, as 338
.. distribution in redemption of stock, treatment as 304
. puts and calls 1233; 1234
. redemption (See Redemption of stock)
. REITs (REITs)
.. loss on sale or exchange of stock held 6 months or less .... 857(b)(8)(A)
... holding period, determination of .... 857(b)(8)(B)
... periodic liquidation, exception .... 857(b)(8)(C)
. reorganization exchanges .... 351 et seq.
.. basis to corporation 362
.. controlled corporations 355
.. foreign corporations 367
.. receipt of additional consideration 356
.. stockholders, effect on 354
. replacement property, as 1042
. rollover of gain into specialized small business investment company 1044
. S corporations, basis adjustments 1016; 1367
. sales or exchanges
.. affiliated corporations 865
.. cooperatives, to 1042
.. employee stock ownership plans (ESOPs), to 1042
.. expatriates 877
.. foreign corporations 1248
.. property for stock and securities 1032
.. Puerto Rico residents 865
.. SEC orders, under 1081
.. stock for stock of same corporation 1036
. securities defined 1083; 6323
. seized for taxes, transfer of stock 6339
. shareholder defined 7701
. short sales (See Short sales)
. small business corporations 1244
. small business investment companies 1242
. stapled 269B

Index to Code — Storm

	CODE SEC.
Stock and securities (See also Bonds) —Cont'd	
. stripped stock	305
. tax-exempt securities (See Exempt securities)	
. trading in	864
. transfers	
. . gift tax	2511
. . information returns	6039; 6652
. . under certain agreements	1058
. . voting rights retained, estate tax	2036
. U.S. real property interest, treatment as	897
. valuation	1053; 2032; 2032A
. . unlisted	2031
. warrants by corporation to acquire own stock	1032
. wash sales	1091
. when issued basis	1233
. worthless	
. . affiliated corporation	165
. . bad debts	166
. . bank affiliate	582
. . capital loss	165
. . losses	165
. . ownership change	382
. . political parties	271
. . refund limitations	6511
Stock bonus plans (See Pension, profit-sharing and stock bonus plans)	
Stock bonus trusts (See Employee retirement and benefit plans)	
Stock life insurance companies	
. contiguous country branches	814
. distributions to shareholders	815
. mutual life insurance companies owning	809
Stock options	421 et seq.
. capital gains and losses	1233
. consolidated returns	1563
. constructive ownership	318
. corporation dealing in own stock	1032
. dealers in securities, special option rule for	1236
. employee stock purchase plans	423
. employment taxes	3231
. foreign personal holding company stock held by	554
. general rules	421
. incentive stock options	422
. . alternative minimum tax	56
. information returns	6039
. investment purposes, held for	1236
. ownership rule	318
. personal holding company, stock ownership rules	544
Stockholders	
. banks, reserves	
. . distribution to shareholders	593
. business meeting expenses	274
. charitable contributions	170
. controlled foreign corporations	
. . U.S. shareholders	904; 951; 957; 962
. corporate rate, election to be taxed at	962
. defined	7701
. dependent care assistance programs	129
. DISCs	995 eq seq.

	CODE SEC.
Stockholders —Cont'd	
. distributions	301 et seq.
. educational assistance programs	127
. employee stock options, approvals	424
. employee stock ownership plans (ESOPs)	409
. evasion or avoidance of taxing, corporations for purposes of	531 et seq.
. export trade corporations, U.S. stockholders	970
. extraordinary dividends, effect on basis	1059
. foreign corporations	897
. foreign insurance companies	953
. foreign personal holding companies	
. . income, taxed to U.S. shareholders	551
. . returns	6035
. gains or loss, corporate liquidation	331
. improperly accumulating surplus	
. . tax avoidance, used for shareholder	531 et seq.
. installment method, liquidations	453
. life insurance companies	
. . shareholder's surplus account	815
. liquidations	453
. . gains or losses	331
. personal holding companies	
. . pro rata share	1293
. . use of corporation property	543
. pro rata share, elections	1293
. property use by shareholder	543; 553
. regulated investment companies	
. . foreign tax credit	853
. . taxation of company and shareholders	852
. rents paid to corporation	543; 553
. reorganization exchanges, effect of	354 et seq.
. reserves for losses on loans, distribution	593
. S corporations	1361 et seq.; 1366 et seq.
. . accident or health insurance	162
. . fringe benefits	1372
. . pass-thru of items to shareholder	1366
. . residential property, rental of	280A
. . two% shareholders	1372
. sale or exchange with corporation	267
. taxes paid by corporation	164
. . foreign personal holding companies	556
. transactions with corporation	267
. 20% stockholder, distributions to	301
. U.S. shareholder defined	951; 953; 957
Stolen vehicles	4481
Stone quarries, percentage depletion	613
Storage facilities	1245
. carbon dioxide sequestration credit	
. . secure geological storage requirement	45Q(d)(2)
. distilled spirits	5231 et seq.
. . discontinuation of storage facilities	5236
. exempt facility bonds	142(c)(1)
. petroleum depreciation recapture	1245
. residential property, storage use	280A
. swimming pools used as storage	25D(e)(3)
Storm losses	165
. deduction from gross estate	2054; 2106

	CODE SEC.
Straddles	1092
. capital expenditures	263
. gains and losses	1234A
. holding period	1223
. short sales	1233
. special rules	1092
Straight line depreciation	168
Strikes	
. wages during, work opportunity credit	51
Stripped bonds or coupons	1286
. nonresident aliens	871
Stripped stock	305
Structure, demolition of	280B
Structured settlement factoring transactions	
. defined	5891
. factoring discount defined	5891
. imposition of tax on	5891
. responsible administrative authority	5891
. structured settlement defined	5891
Student loan bonds	144 (See also Scholarships and fellowships subhead funding bonds)
. arbitrage	148
. inapplicable rules	147
. pooled financing	148
. refunding issues	146
. volume cap	146
Student loan marketing association	
. guarantee to finance student loans	149
Student loans	
. defaulted, disclosure of mailing address for collection purposes	6103
. discharge of indebtedness	108
. disclosure	6103
. Federal Pell Grants	
. . disclosure of returns and return information	6103
. interest	163
. private activity bonds	144
Students	
. care and maintenance costs, charitable contributions for	170
. definition	151
. dependent care credit	21
. dependents	151; 152
. fellowships (See Scholarships and fellowships)	
. FICA	3121
. foreign (See Foreign students and exchange visitors)	
. FUTA	3306
. loans (See Student loans; Student loan bonds; Scholarships and fellowships)	
. personal exemptions	151
. scholarships and fellowships (See Scholarships and fellowships)	
. special support test	152
. spouse, dependent care credit	21
. summer camp employment, Federal unemployment taxes	3306

	CODE SEC.
Subchapter S corporations (See S corporations)	
Subchapter S trusts	1361
Subdivided lots	1237
Subordinate party defined	672
Subpart F income	
. controlled foreign corporations	951; 955; 970
. . limitations on subpart F income	952
. export trade corporations	970
. PFICs	
. . attribution of ownership subpart F inclusions	1298(b)(8)
. withdrawal of previously excluded, from qualified investments	955
Subpoenas	
. service of	7608
. Tax Court	7456
. . transferees	6902
Subrogation, lien for taxes	6323
Subscription income, prepaid	455
Subsidiaries	
. basis, liquidating distributions	334
. consolidated returns (See Consolidated returns)	
. defined	424
. domestic subsidiaries engaged in businesses outside U.S.	
. . employee retirement and benefit plans	407
. employee stock options granted by	424
. foreign (See Foreign subsidiaries)	
. gains and losses	
. . complete liquidation	332; 337
. . liquidating distributions	336
. indebtedness to parent	337
. liquidations	
. . basis of property received	334
. . . depreciation	1250
. . complete	332; 334; 337
. . gain or loss on property received	336
. . installment obligations	453B
. . limitation on recognition of loss	336
. . parent, gain on liquidating distributions	337
. majority-owned defined	1083
. real estate mortgage investment conduits	860E
. redemption of stock through use of	304
. REITs	
. . taxable	856(l)
. . wholly owned subsidiaries, treatment of	856(i)
Subsidies	
. energy conservation provided by public utility	136
. energy financing programs	
. . nonconventional fuel source credit (See Nonconventional fuel source credit)	
. federal subsidies	
. . irrigation projects, illegal	90
. . prescription drug plans	139A
. mortgage subsidy bonds (See Mortgage bonds subhead mortgage bonds)	
Subsistence allowance	
. nonresident aliens under Mutual Security Act	1441

Index to Code — Tables

	CODE SEC.
Substantial owners, trusts	671 et seq.
Substantial presence test, aliens	7701
Substantiation of expenses	274
Substitute rubber as rubber	4072
Substituted basis	1016
. property defined	7701
Succession tax deductibility	275
Successor corporations	
. carryovers	381
. change of ownership	382
. preacquisition losses offsetting built-in gains	384
Successor employers	
. FUTA	3302
. work opportunity credit	51
Suits	
. collection of tax by	7401 et seq.
.. injunction	6213; 7421
.. limitation period	6501 et seq.
. recovery, tax	6532; 7422
.. expenses	7430
. recovery of erroneous refunds	6532; 7405
. recovery of seized property	7426
. restraining assessment and collection of tax	6213; 7421
. third parties	7426
. U.S., by	7401 et seq.
Sulfur	
. depletion	613
. environmental protection agency sulfur regulations, capital costs deduction	179B
Sulfuric acid	4661; 4662
Summer camps	
. student employee, FUTA tax	3306
Summer youth employee	
. work opportunity credit	51
Summons	
. authority to issue	7602
. computer software, to analyze tax related	7612
. enforcement of	7402; 7604
. failure to obey	7210
. service of	7210; 7603; 7604; 7608
. third-party recordkeepers	7609
Sunday	
. last day of performance falling on	7503
.. petition to Tax Court	6213
Supplemental unemployment benefit plans	
. adjusted gross income repayments	62
. withholding tax on wages	3402
Supplemental unemployment compensation benefit trusts	
. exemption	501; 505; 512
Supplies for vessels or aircraft	
. defined	4221
. manufacturers excise taxes	4221; 4222
. motor fuels tax	4041; 6416
Support of dependents	152
Supreme Court of the U.S.	
. review of decisions of courts of appeals	7482

	CODE SEC.
Surety bonds (See also Bonds)	
. distilled spirits plants (See Distilled spirits plants subhead bonds required)	
. estate tax, payment of	2032A; 6863
. false or fraudulent posting by taxpayer	7206
. indemnity (See Indemnity bonds)	
. posting by taxpayer	7101 et seq.; 7206
. required to be posted	7101; 7102
. stay of collection	
.. Tax Court decisions, review	7485
. tobacco products	5711 et seq.
. wine cellars and warehouses (See Wines)	
Surety companies	
. personal holding company status	542
Surplus	
. accumulations to avoid tax (See Accumulated earnings tax)	
Surviving spouse	
. bequests to, estate tax	2056
. charitable remainder trusts	2056
. community property, basis for gain or loss	1014
. deceased spouse missing in action	2
. defined	2
. employee benefit plans, distributions	401; 417
.. estate tax	2039
.. former spouse, domestic relations orders	414
. fringe benefits	132
. head-of-household status	2
. joint interests	2040
. material participation in farming activity	469
. property acquired from decedent dying after December 31, 2009	1022
. qualified terminable interest property (QTIP)	2056
. rates of tax	1
. returns	6013
. rollovers, receipt of distribution	402
Survivor annuities (See Annuities)	
Suspense accounts	
. books and sound recordings	458
Suspension	
. foreign taxes and credits	
.. related income taken into account, until	909
. limitation statute (See Statute of limitations)	
Sustainable design projects	
. exempt facility bonds (See Exempt facility bonds subhead qualified green building and sustainable design projects)	
Swap funds	683
Sweepstakes and lotteries, state-conducted	4402
. withholding tax	3402
Syndicates	
. hedging transactions, marked to market reporting	1256
. partnership, as	761; 7701
.. fees, amortization	709
Synthetic rubber as rubber	4072
System group defined	1083

T

Tables

Tables

Index to Code

CODE SEC.

Tables — Cont'd
- earned income credit ... 32
- imposition of tax table tax ... 3
- indexing for inflation ... 1
- individuals ... 3
- tax rates ... 1
- valuation, for annuities, other interests ... 7520
- withholding tax on wages ... 3402

Talc depletion ... 613

Tangible property
- capital expenditures ... 263A
- charitable contribution future interests ... 170
- depreciation effect on earnings and profits ... 312
- handicapped and elderly ... 263
- inventory costs ... 263A
- used outside U.S., alternate depreciation for certain property ... 168(g)(1)(A)
- . . aircraft ... 168(g)(4)(A)
- . . cable, domestic corporations ... 168(g)(4)(I)
- . . communication satellite ... 168(g)(4)(H)
- . . container used in transportation ... 168(g)(4)(E)
- . . Continental Shelf, property used to transport, explore, or develop from the ... 168(g)(4)(F)
- . . energy for U.S. international property used to generate ... 168(g)(4)(K)
- . . motor vehicles ... 168(g)(4)(D)
- . . ocean waters, property used to transport, explore, or develop from the ... 168(g)(4)(J)
- . . possession of U.S., property used in a ... 168(g)(4)(G)
- . . rolling stock ... 168(g)(4)(B)
- . . satellite ... 168(g)(4)(L)
- . . vessels documented under U.S. laws ... 168(g)(4)(C)

Tanning services, indoor
- collection of tax ... 5000B(c)(2)
- defined ... 5000B(b)(1)
- excise tax on ... 5000B(a)
- payment of tax on ... 5000B(c)(1)
- phototherapy service exclusion ... 5000B(b)(2)
- secondary liability of tax on ... 5000B(c)(3)

Targeted area residences ... 143

Targeted jobs credit ... 51; 52
- empowerment zone employment credit coordination with ... 1396
- general business credit ... 38
- unused credit ... 196

Tax benefit rule
- alternative minimum tax ... 59
- recoveries ... 111; 381; 1398

Tax conventions
- disclosure of returns and return information ... 6103

Tax Court ... 7441 et seq.
- appeal from decision of ... 7481 et seq.
- assessment of deficiency ... 6215
- bond on appeal from ... 7485
- burden of proof ... 7454
- . . accumulated earnings tax ... 534
- contempt powers ... 7456
- court review of decisions ... 7481 et seq.
- . . affirmation of decision ... 7481

CODE SEC.

Tax Court — Cont'd
court review of decisions — Cont'd
- . . bond to stay assessment and collection ... 7485
- . . change of incumbent in office ... 7484
- . . courts of review ... 7482
- . . date of finality of decision ... 7481
- . . dismissal of appeal ... 7481
- . . modification of decision ... 7481
- . . nonreviewable decisions ... 7481
- . . notice of appeal ... 7483
- . . petition for review ... 7483; 7485
- . . refund, credit, or abatement of amounts disallowed ... 7486
- . . rehearing ... 7481
- . . reversal of decision ... 7481
- . . reviewable decisions ... 7481
- decisions ... 7459
- . . final date ... 6214; 7481
- . . res judicata ... 7422
- . . review by courts ... 7481 et seq.
- declaratory judgments ... 7428; 7476
- deficiencies disallowed by ... 6215
- deficiencies found by, assessment ... 6215
- definition ... 7701
- delay, procedures instituted for purposes of ... 6673
- depositions ... 7456
- determinations by ... 6214
- disclosure of proceedings ... 6110; 7461
- disposition of fees ... 7473
- divisions ... 7444; 7460
- employee retirement and benefit plans, judgment as to qualification ... 7476
- employees ... 7471
- evidence
- . disclosure ... 7461
- . fraud cases ... 7454
- . rules ... 7453
- expenditures ... 7472
- fees
- . disposition ... 7473
- . filing petition ... 7451
- . practice before ... 7475
- . transcript of record ... 7458; 7474
- . witnesses ... 7457
- findings of fact ... 7459
- foreign entity's records, production of ... 7456
- fraud cases ... 7454
- hearings ... 7458; 7460
- . rehearing ... 7481
- . time and place ... 7446
- interlocutory orders ... 7482
- jeopardy assessment ... 6213
- judges ... 7441; 7443
- . annuities for dependents ... 7448
- . coordination with civil service benefits ... 7447
- . disability ... 7447
- . recalling of retired ... 7447(c)
- . retirement ... 7447
- . thrift savings plans ... 7447(j)
- . waiver of civil service benefits ... 7448

Index to Code

Tax

Tax Court—Cont'd

- jurisdiction 7442
- . deficiency, increase of 6214
- . exempt organizations and private foundations 7428
- . interest and penalties 6214
- . jeopardy assessment 6861
- . other years and quarters, over 6214
- . overpayments 6512
- legal fees 7430
- limitations in case of petition to 6512
- mailing time as timely filing 7502
- membership 7441; 7443
- miscellaneous provisions .... 7471 et seq.
- notice of appeal 7483
- oaths, administration of 7456
- offices 7445
- organization and jurisdiction .... 7441 et seq.
- . establishment of jurisdiction 7442
- . membership 7441; 7443
- . particulars of organization 7444
- . retirement of judges 7447; 7448
- . special trial judges 7443A
- . status 7441
- . times and places of sessions 7446
- overpayment determined by 6512
- penalty for delay 7430
- personnel 7471
- petition to
- . abatement of assessment 6213
- . bankruptcy and receiverships 6213; 6871
- . deficiency, redetermination 6213
- . deficiency notice issued while refund suit pending ... 7422
- . dismissal, effect 7459
- . failure to file, assessment and collection of tax ... 6213
- . fee for filing 7451
- . instituted merely for delay or with frivolous or groundless positions 6673
- . refunds and credits affected by 6512
- . small tax cases 7463
- powers 7456
- practice fee 7475
- procedure .... 7451 et seq.
- . burden of proof in fraud and transferee cases 7454
- . fee for filing petition 7451
- . hearings 7458
- . judges, retirement 7447
- . procurement of testimony 7456
- . provision of special application to divisions 7460
- . provision of special application to transferees ... 7465
- . reports and decisions 7459; 7462
- . representation of parties 7452
- . rules of practice, procedure and evidence 7453
- . service of process 7455
- . witness fees 7457
- proceedings instituted merely for delay or with frivolous or groundless positions 6673
- production of records of petitioner 7456
- publicity of proceedings 7461
- quorum 7444

Tax Court—Cont'd

- reports 7459; 7460; 7462
- representation of parties 7452
- res judicata 7422
- restrictions on assessment 6213
- review of decisions by courts .... 7422; 7481 et seq.
- rules of practice 7453
- seal of 7444
- service of process 7455
- small claims 7463
- small tax cases 7463
- special trial judges 7443A; 7456
- status 7441
- subpoenas by 7456
- . transferees 6902
- time and places of sessions 7446
- time for filing petition 6213
- transcript of record 7458; 7474
- transferee proceeding 6902
- travel and subsistence, expenditures 7471
- witnesses 7456; 7457

Tax credit (See Credits against tax; Refunds and credits)

Tax credit bonds
- qualified tax credit bonds (See Qualified tax credit bonds)

Tax credit employee stock ownership plans (See Employee stock ownership plans)

Tax deferral, interest on 1291

Tax Extenders and Alternative Minimum Tax Relief Act of 2008
- qualified zone academy bonds obligations issued after enactment of .... 1397E(m)

Tax home
- U.S. citizens or residents living abroad 911

Tax intercept programs (TIPs) 6402

Tax liability (See Liability for tax)

Tax matters partner 6231

Tax practitioner confidentiality 7524

Tax preferences
- accelerated depreciation or amortization on property place in service before January 1, 1987 .... 57(a)(6)
- alternative minimum tax 55; 57
- . optional 10-year writeoff .... 59(e)
- appreciated property charitable deduction 57
- corporations 291
- depletion 57
- depreciable realty, disposition of 291
- exempt-interest dividends .... 57(a)(5)(B)
- financial institutions 291
- . bad debt reserves 57
- foreign sales corporation 291
- housing bond exception .... 57(a)(5)(C)(iii)
- intangible drilling costs 291
- . excess costs .... 57(a)(1)(B)
- . independent producer exception .... 57(a)(1)(E)
- . net income .... 57(a)(1)(C)
- . oil, gas, and geothermal properties .... 57(a)(1)(A)
- . straight line recovery of intangibles
- . . defined .... 57(b)(1)
- . . election of .... 57(b)(2)

Tax | Index to Code

CODE SEC.

Tax preferences —Cont'd
- interest, tax-exempt ... 57
- pre-1987 property, accelerated depreciated or amortized ... 57
- private activity bonds
  - interest on ... 57(a)(5)(A)
  - Sept. 1, 1986, issued before ... 57(a)(5)(A)(v)
  - qualified 501(c)(3) bond exception ... 57(a)(5)(C)(ii)
  - refunding bonds ... 57(a)(5)(C)(iv)
- REITs ... 291
- short years ... 443
- small business sale, exclusion for gain on ... 57(a)(7)
- specified private activity bonds ... 57(a)(5)(C); 57(a)(5)(C)(i)

Tax rates (See Rates of tax)

Tax return preparers (See Preparers of returns)

Tax returns (See Returns)

Tax shelters (See also Passive income)
- abusive (See Abusive tax shelters)
- confidentiality ... 7525
- defined ... 448; 461
- exempt entity entering into prohibited shelter ... 4965
- farm activity ... 58
- farming syndicates ... 461
- identifying numbers ... 6111
  - failure to provide ... 6707
- oil and gas wells ... 461
- registration requirements ... 6111; 6707
- reporting ... 6707
  - maintaining lists of investors ... 6708
  - penalties ... 6707; 6708
- taxable year deductions ... 461

Tax straddles (See Straddles)

Taxable bonds (See also Bonds)
- amortization of premiums ... 171

Taxable estate (See also Estates and trusts; Estate tax)
- administration expenses ... 2053
- bequests to surviving spouse ... 2056
- casualty losses ... 2054
- charitable remainder trusts ... 2056
- charitable transfers ... 2055
- claims against estate ... 2053
- death taxes, state and foreign ... 2053
- defined ... 2051; 2106
- expenses ... 2053
- funeral expenses ... 2053
- general rules ... 2051 et seq.
- gross estate, deductions from ... 2051 et seq.
- indebtedness ... 2053
- life estates ... 2056
- losses ... 2054
- nonresident aliens ... 2106
- nonresidents ... 2106
- public use transfers ... 2055
- qualified domestic trusts ... 2056A
- religious use transfers ... 2055
- taxes ... 2053
- theft losses ... 2054

CODE SEC.

Taxable gift defined ... 2503

Taxable income (See also Gross income, specific subject headings)
- accumulated taxable income ... 535
- additional standard deduction ... 63(c)(3)
- adjustments to
  - accumulated earnings tax ... 535
  - foreign personal holding companies ... 556
- age 65 or over ... 63
- alternative minimum tax ... 55
- basic standard deduction ... 63(c)(2)
  - limitations on, dependent ... 63(c)(5)
- blind ... 63
- common trust funds ... 584
- cooperatives ... 1382
- corporate ... 11
- defined ... 63(a)
- dependents ... 63
- elderly ... 63
- foreign corporations ... 882
- foreign tax credit purposes ... 904
- indexing for inflation ... 1
- individuals ... 3
- inflation adjustments ... 63
- installment sales ... 453 et seq.
- insurance companies other than life ... 832; 834
- investment income, insurance companies ... 834
- itemized deductions ... 63
- life insurance companies ... 801
- marital status ... 63
- nondeductibility of taxes in computing ... 3502
- partnerships ... 703
- period for computation ... 441
- personal holding company, adjustments ... 545
- real estate mortgage investment conduits ... 860C
- real property tax deduction ... 63(c)(7)
- regulated investment companies ... 852
- REITs ... 857(a)(1); 4981; 4982
- S corporations ... 1363
- single taxpayers, aged or blind ... 63
- sources within U.S. ... 861
- sources without U.S. ... 862
- standard deduction ... 63
- tax rates ... 1
- tax tables, individuals ... 3
- terminal railroad corporations ... 281
- unrelated business ... 511 et seq.

Taxable mortgage pools ... 7701

Taxable transportation defined
- persons ... 4262
- property ... 4272

Taxable year (See also Calendar year; Fiscal year; Short tax year)
- accounting periods ... 441
- at risk limitations ... 465
- bankrupt's ... 1398
- change in ... 442; 706
- changes in rates during ... 15
- close of ... 706; 6851

Index to Code

CODE SEC.

Taxable year (See also Calendar year; Fiscal year; Short tax year) —Cont'd
. common trust fund and participants 584
. deductions taken . . . . 461 et seq.
. definition 441; 7701
. designated settlement funds 468B
. earned income credit 32
. election not to have required tax year 7519
. election other than required year 444
. estates and trusts 644; 652; 662
. fiscal year 441
. foreign corporations 898
. foreign personal holding companies 898
. inclusion of gross income items . . . . 451 et seq.
. nuclear decommissioning costs 468A
. obligations issued at discount 454
. partners and partnerships 706
.. other than required, election 444
.. payment of tax 7519
. passive activity losses and credits 469
. personal service corporations 280H; 441; 444
. rate change during 15
. reclamation and closing costs, mining and solid waste disposal facilities 468
. rents 467
. research credit 41
. S corporations 1378
.. election of other than required year 444
.. other than required, payment of tax 7519
. termination of, income tax in jeopardy 6851

Tax-exempt bond financed property, ACRS
. allocation of bond proceeds . . . . 168(g)(5)(B)
. alternate depreciation system for certain property . . . . 168(g)(1)(C)
. defined . . . . 168(g)(5)(A)
. qualified residential rental property . . . . 168(g)(5)(C)

Tax-exempt bonds generally (See Exempt bonds)

Tax-exempt entity (See Exempt entities; Exempt organizations)

Tax-exempt income (See Exempt income)

Tax-exempt organizations (See Exempt entities and organizations)

Tax-exempt securities (See Exempt securities)

Tax-exempt use property
. alternate depreciation system, ACRS . . . . 168(g)(1)(B)
.. defined . . . . 168(h)(1)(A)
.. nonresidential real property . . . . 168(h)(1)(E)
.. nonresidential use property . . . . 168(h)(1)(B)
.. short-term lease exception . . . . 168(h)(1)(C)
.. unrelated trade or business income as factor . . . 168(h)(1)(D)
. charitable contribution; recapture of deduction 170
. depreciation deduction 167; 168

Tax-free exchanges (See Exchanges of property subhead nontaxable)

Tax-free interest (See Exempt income)

Taxicab retail excise tax 4001

Taxidermy property, charitable contribution 170

Taxpayer bill of rights
. assistance orders to remedy hardships caused by IRS . . . 7811

CODE SEC.

Taxpayer bill of rights —Cont'd
. Assistant Commissioner for Taxpayer Services 7802
. civil damages against U.S. for
.. failure to release lien 7432
.. unauthorized collection actions 7433
. installment payment of tax, agreements for 6159
. IRS written advice, reliance on 6404
. legal and accounting fees, recovery of 7430
. levies
.. advance notice 6331
.. duration of, on wages and salaries 6331
.. exemptions 6334
.. jeopardy levy procedures, review of 7429
.. levies on appearance date of summons 6331
.. release of 6343
.. request for sale of seized property 6335
.. surrender of bank accounts 6332
.. uneconomical levies 6331
. liens, right to appeal 6327
. preparer penalty 6712
. refunds and credits, right to appeal reduction of 6402
. review of new regulations by SBA 7805
. safeguards for IRS interviews 7520
. Tax Court jurisdiction
.. enforcing refunds 6512
.. estate tax decisions, modifying 7481
.. interest determinations 7481
.. restraining premature assessments 6213; 7482
.. sales of seized property, review of 6863
. tax due, deficiency, and other notices, explanation requirement 7521
. time limits on temporary regulations 7805

Taxpayer communications, confidentiality of 7525

Taxpayer identification numbers (TIN) (See Identification numbers)

Taxpayers
. assistance orders 7811
. confidentiality of returns 6103
. defined 1313; 7701
. disclosure of information on 6103
. examination of, restrictions 7605
. identifying numbers (See Identification numbers)
. interviews by IRS officers and employees 7521
. reports by 999
. transactions between related 1313

Teachers annuities 403

Teachers retirement fund associations 501

Teaching
. scholarships 117
. tuition reductions 117

Technology equipment
. accelerated cost recovery system (ACRS) (See Qualified technology equipment)
. depreciation deduction, used or leased property 168

Telephone and telegraph taxes (See also Communications taxes)
. coin-operated toll telephone service 4254
. computation of 4254
. definitions 4251; 4252

283

Telephone

CODE SEC.

Telephone and telegraph taxes (See also Communications taxes) —Cont'd
. exemptions 4253
. imposition of 4251
. local service 4252
. parties subject to 4251
. possessions of U.S. 4293
. private communication service 4252
. refunds and credits 6415
. teletypewriter exchange service 4252
. toll telephone service 4252; 4254
. U.S. use 4293

Telephone companies, mutual or cooperative
. exemption 501; 513
. pole rentals 513
. taxation as cooperative association . . . . . . 1381 et seq.

Telephones
. depreciation 168
. expenses 262

Teletypewriter exchange services 4251; 4252

Television
. broadcast (See Broadcasting)
. production (See See Motion picture film, subhead film and television production)

Temporary dividends-received deductions
. controlled foreign corporations 965

Tenancy by the entirety
. estate tax
. . gross estate inclusion 2040
. . valuation 2040
. gift tax 2523; 2524
. returns 6019

Tenant low-income housing credit (See Low-income housing credit)

Tenant-stockholders, cooperative housing associations
. . . . 216

Tentative carryback adjustment 6213; 6405; 6411; 6611
. limitation on assessment 6501

Tentative refunds 6213

Term interests
. adjusted basis 1001
. basis adjustments 167
. defined 1001
. depreciation deduction 167
. sale or exchange, gain or loss 1001

Terminable interest property (See also Qualified terminable interest property (QTIP))
. estate tax 2056
. gift tax 2523; 2524
. shrinkage 273

Terminal railroad corporations 281

Termination assessments . . . . . . 6601; 6851; 6852 (See also Assessments)
. aliens, imminent departure of 6851
. authority for making 6851
. charitable organizations, political expenditures of . . 6852
. citizens of U.S., imminent departure of . . . 6851
. collected amounts, treatment of 6851; 6852
. computation of tax 6851

Index to Code

CODE SEC.

Termination assessments—Cont'd
. definitions 6852
. injunction (See Injunction against assessment and collection)
. interest 6601
. jeopardy assessments (See Jeopardy assessments)
. notice of deficiency 6851
. special rules 6852
. taxable year 6851

Termination of employment
. empowerment zone employment credit, special rules related to 1396
. Indian employment credit, early termination and . . . 45A
. involuntary termination
. . CETA employee, work opportunity credit 51
. . moving expenses 217

Terrorist actions
. participants
. . disaster relief payment . . . . 139(e)
. . disclosure of tax information to appropriate officials . . 6103
. victims
. . abatement of tax 692
. . civilian employees 692
. . death benefits 101
. . disability payments 104
. New York Liberty Zone
. . September 10, 2001, allowances for property acquired after 1400L
. . . tax benefits 1400L
. . postponement of certain tax-related deadlines . . . 7508A
. . specified terrorist victim defined 692
. . tax rate 2201

Terrorist organization, exempt status 501

Tertiary injectants
. allowance of deductions for expenses 193
. capital expenditures 263
. carbon dioxide sequestration credit . . . . . . 45Q(d)(3)
. hydrocarbon injectants 193
. recovery method 193

Testing for public safety, organizations devoted to . . 501

Theft losses 165; 1231
. estate tax 2054; 2106
. involuntary conversions 1033

Therapeutic discovery projects
. qualifying (See Qualifying therapeutic discovery projects)

Thernardite mine depletion 613

Third parties
. books and records, third-party recordkeepers . . . 7609
. compensation, third party paying or providing for . . 3505
. disclosure of written determinations involving . . . 6110
. District Courts, jurisdiction
. . third-party recordkeepers 7609
. . third-party suits 7426
. employment taxes where wages paid by . . 3505
. federal officers and employees, third-party action against 7426
. FICA, third-party liability 3505
. husband and wife gifts to third party
. . gift tax transfers 2513
. injunction against assessment and collection . . 7426

284

Index to Code

Tobacco

CODE SEC.

Third parties —Cont'd
. recordkeepers, summonses issued to 7609
. seizure of property 7426
. sick pay paid by, information returns 6051
. spouse gifts to 1015
. suits by 7426
. summons 7609
. withholding liability 3505

Third party network transactions (See Payment cards and third party network transactions)

Thorium depletion 613

Thrift savings fund (See Federal thrift savings fund)

Throwback rule .... 665 et seq.

Ticket as entertainment expense 274

Tile clay deposit depletion 613

Timber and timberland
. capital expenditures 263A
. capital gains and losses 1231
. . depreciable property, dispositions of 1245
. . withholding tax at source on nonresident aliens and foreign corporations 1441
. cutting as sale or exchange 631
. depletion 611
. economic interest retained 631
. gains and losses on disposition 631
. helicopter fuel 4041; 4261; 6427
. inventory costs 263A
. reforestation expenditures 194
. self-employment income 1402
. tax rate, special 1201

Time and dates
. due dates (See Due dates)
. effective dates (See Effective dates)

Timely mailing as timely filing and paying 7502

Timeshares, installment sales 453; 453A

Tin depletion 613

Tips
. accounting method 451
. failure to file information returns 6652; 6674
. false or fraudulent statements 6674
. FICA 45B; 3102; 3121
. FUTA 3306
. Railroad Retirement Tax Act 3202; 3231
. reporting of 6041; 6053; 6652
. statements by employers 6053
. taxable year or inclusion 451
. withholding tax 3401; 3402; 6051

Tires, excise taxes .... 4071 et seq.; 9503
. buses 4221
. definitions 4072
. exemption from tax 4073
. floor stocks refunds 6412
. heavy truck and trailer retail excise tax credit against ... 4051
. Highway Trust Fund 9503
. imported articles 4071
. imposition of tax 4071
. internal wire fastenings 4073
. manufacturer or importer, sale treatment of use by 4218

CODE SEC.

Tires, excise taxes—Cont'd
. rate of tax 4071
. retail sales by manufacturer 4071
. sold on or with autos 4218; 4221; 6416
. termination of tax 4071
. use by manufacturer 4218; 6416

Titanium depletion 613

Title 11 cases (See Bankruptcy; Receivers)

Tobacco .... 5701 et seq.; 5751 et seq.
. abandoned and condemned products, disposal of 5753
. bond requirement 5711
. business in more than one location 5733
. chewing 5701
. cigarettes and cigars (See Cigarettes and cigars)
. conditions to allowance in case of 6423
. credits or refunds 5705; 6423
. dealers, imposition on 5731
. death or change of location 5733
. defined 5702
. delivery sales 5761
. disaster, losses caused by 5708
. drawback of 5706
. exemption from 5704
. exported and returned 5704
. failure to file return or pay tax 6651
. forfeitures 5753; 5763
. importation of previously exported products 5754
. importers 5702; 5741
. imposition 5731
. Internal Revenue enforcement officers
. . authority of 7608
. . unlawful interest of 7214
. inventories 5721
. labels 5723; 5752
. liability for 5703
. manufacturers .... 5701; 5711 et seq.; 5721 et seq.; 5741
. marks required 5723; 5752
. notice requirements 5723
. occupational taxes 5731
. packages 5723; 5752
. payment of tax 5732
. penalties
. . assessment of 5703
. . civil 5761
. . criminal 5762
. permits .... 5711 et seq.
. personal use quantities 5761
. pipe tobacco 5702
. rate 5731
. records to be maintained 5741
. refunds and credits .... 5705 et seq.; 6423
. removal, purchase, receipt, possession, or sale after ... 5751
. reports required 5722
. returns 5703; 6091
. smokeless 5701
. snuff 5701
. state laws, application of 5734
. ultimate burden for tax 6423

285

Toll

Index to Code

	CODE SEC.
Toll telephone service	4251 et seq.
Toluene hazardous waste clean up	4661; 4662
Top-heavy plans	401; 415; 416
Tractors	
. manufacturers excise tax	
. . Highway Trust Fund	9503
. retail excise tax	4051 et seq.
. . exemptions	4221
. . Highway Trust Fund	9503
Trade adjustment allowance	
. health insurance costs of eligible recipient	35
. . advance payment of credits	7527
. . returns related to credit	6050T
Trade or business	
. adjusted gross income	62
. collapsible corporations	
. . property used in	341
. commonly controlled businesses	
. . work opportunity credit	52
. community business property	1400F
. defined	7701
. . feeder organizations	502
. . income from U.S. sources	864
. . self-employment tax purposes	1402
. depreciation	167
. employee deductions	62
. exempt organizations	511 et seq.
. expenses (See Business expenses)	
. feeder organization	502
. foreign corporations	881 et seq.
. gross income from	61
. life insurance company gross income from noninsurance	812
. losses	
. . at risk amounts	465
. . limitation on deductions	165
. . nonresident aliens	871 et seq.
. . passive activity losses and credits	469
. property used in	
. . capital gains and losses	1231
. . defined	1231
. . depreciation	167
. . depreciation recapture	1245; 1250
. . exchange of	1031
. . expensing of depreciable assets	179
. . involuntary conversions	1033
. qualified business unit defined	989
. reasonable needs	537
. research and experimental expenditures	41; 174; 469
. self-employment income	1402
. start-up expenditures	41; 195
. tools of trade, exemption from levy	6334
. within U.S.	864
. . distributions to foreign partners, withholding tax on	1446
. work opportunity credit	51; 52
Trademarks and trade names	
. expenditures	1016
. liquors	5604

	CODE SEC.
Trademarks and trade names —Cont'd	
. tobacco products	5752
. transfers of	1253
Traders in commodities	
. mark to market accounting	475
Trailers	
. floor stocks refunds	9503
. highway use tax (See Highway motor vehicle use taxes)	
. retail excise taxes	4051 et seq.
. . definitions	4052
. . exemptions	4053; 4221
. . Highway Trust Fund	9503
. . imposition of tax	4051
. . special rules	4052
Training and training aids	7516
Training facility, exempt facility bond	142
Trans-Alaska pipeline liability fund	4612
Transferees	6901 et seq.
. burden of proof	7454
. examination of transferor's records	6902; 7602
. refunds and credits	6901
. Tax Court proceedings	6902
Transferred basis property defined	7701
Transfers (See also Exchanges of property; Sales or exchanges)	
. allocation rules for asset acquisitions	1060
. amortization	197
. bankruptcy, between debtor and estate	1398
. compensatory property	83
. controlled by transferor, to corporation	351
. corporation controlled by transferor, to	
. . basis to corporations	362
. death, failure to file information with respect to transfers at	6716
. estate tax (See Estate tax, transfers)	
. foreign entities, to	6038B
. foreign estates and trusts, recognition of gain on transfers to	684
. franchise gains and losses	1253
. generation-skipping (See Generation-skipping transfers)	
. gift tax	2511 et seq.
. . benefit of minors, for	2503
. . husband and wife gifts to third party	2513
. . powers of appointment	2514
. . property settlements	2516
. . valuation of gifts	2512
. gross estate	
. . death, effective upon	2037
. . insufficient consideration	2043
. . retained life estate	2036
. . . recovery, right of	2207B
. . revocable	2038
. imported property, between related persons	1059A
. player contracts transferred upon sale of sports franchise, basis limitation for	1056
. prior, estate tax credit for tax on	2013
. property in payment for services rendered	83
. spouses, property transfers between	1041
. trademarks and trade names, gains and losses	1253

Index to Code

Treaties

CODE SEC.

Transfers (See also Exchanges of property; Sales or exchanges) —Cont'd
. trust, basis of property acquired by transfers in 1015
Transit pass 132
Transit systems, local
. gasoline taxes 6206; 6675
. high-speed intercity rail facilities (See High-speed intercity rail facilities)
Transit-type buses, highway use tax 4483
Transportation by air
. Airport and Airway Trust Fund
. . refund of taxes on transfers by air . . . . 9502(d)(5)
. helicopter exemption . . . . 4261(f)
. nonestablished lines, small aircraft on 4281
. parents of employee 132
. persons . . . . 4261 et seq.
. . affiliated groups 4282
. . Alaska excise tax rate . . . . 4261(c)(3)
. . domestic segments . . . . 4261(b)(1)
. . emergency medical transportation exemption . . . . . . 4262(g)
. . excess baggage 4272
. . excise taxes . . . . 4261 et seq.
. . exemption from tax 4262; 4263
. . . emergency medical transportation . . . . 4262(g)
. . . helicopters . . . . 4261(f)
. . . seaplanes . . . . 4261(i)
. . . skydiving . . . . 4261(h)
. . Hawaii excise tax rate . . . . 4261(c)(3)
. . helicopter exemption . . . . 4262(f)
. . inflation adjustments . . . . 4262(e)(4)
. . international air transportation . . . . . 4261(c); 4262; 4263
. . layover or waiting time 4262
. . nonestablished lines 4281
. . Oct. 1, 1999, transportation before . . . . 4262(e)(5)
. . outside the U.S., amounts paid . . . . 4262(e)(2)
. . payment of tax 4261; 4263
. . reduced rate air transportation . . . . 4262(e)(3)
. . refunds and credits 6415
. . . deduction of tax 4263
. . rural airports, segments to and from . . . . 4261(e)(1)
. . seaplane exemption . . . . 4262(i)
. . servicemen on leave 4262
. . small aircraft on nonestablished lines 4281
. . special rules 4263
. . taxable transportation 4262
. . tickets or advertising stating taxes imposed 7275
. property
. . affiliated groups, within 4282
. . by whom paid . . . . 4271(b)(1)
. . determination of amount . . . . 4271(c)
. . excess baggage 4272
. . exports 4272
. . layover or waiting time 4272
. . nonestablished lines 4281
. . outside the U.S., payments made . . . . 4271(b)(2)
. . payment of tax . . . . 4271(b)(1)
. . refunds and credits 6415
. . small aircraft on nonestablished lines 4281
. . taxable items 4272

CODE SEC.

Transportation by air —Cont'd
. property —Cont'd
. . taxable transportation 4272
. . seaplane exemption . . . . 4261(i)
. . skydiving exemption . . . . 4261(h)
. . small aircraft on nonestablished lines 4281
. . special provisions relating to 4281; 4282
. . tickets and advertising, offenses 7275
Transportation by water, excise taxes (See Ships and shipping subhead excise taxes)
Transportation income, source of 863; 872; 887
Trash containers
. retail excise tax exemption 4053
. retailers excise tax exemption 4051
. truck mounted 4053; 4222
Trash facility
. electricity produced from renewable sources; credit . . . 45(d)(7)
Travel expenses
. business expenses 162
. deduction 170; 274
. denial of charitable contribution 170
. educational purposes 274
. foreign travel 274
. house-hunting costs 217
. legislative bodies, appearances before 162
. legislator travel away from home 162
. luxury water transportation 274
. medical expense 213
. military 134
. moving expense 217
. state legislators 162
. substantiation 274
. Tax Court members 7443
Treasury bonds (See United States obligations)
Treasury Department (See Department of the Treasury)
Treasury settlement procedures (See also Assessments; Examination and inspection)
. amount and method of adjustment 1314
. assessments . . . . 6201 et seq.
. authority to prescribe or modify seals 7514
. carryback adjustments 6411
. circumstances of adjustment 1312
. correction of error 1311
. credits and refunds . . . . 6401 et seq.
. examination and inspection . . . . 7601 et seq.
. jeopardy assessment (See Jeopardy assessment)
. limitation period (See Limitation period)
. notice and demand for tax 6303
. Post Office, expenditure incurred by 7509
. prohibition of administrative review of decisions 6406
. refunds and credits of withheld tax 1464
. supplying training and training aids 7516
. time for performance of acts where last days fall on Saturday, Sunday or legal holidays 7503
. timely mailing treated as timely filing 7502
Treasury stock sold or exchanged 1032
Treaties
. branch profits tax, coordination with 884
. disclosure

287

Treaties

Treaties — Cont'd
disclosure — Cont'd
. . . returns and return information 6103
. . . tax convention information 6105
. . dividends received from foreign corporations, coordination with 245
. . income exempt under 894
. . . stapled entities 269B
. . obligations of 7852
. . treaty-based return positions 6114
. . . disclosure of 6114
. . . failure to disclose 6712
. . U.S. owned foreign corporations 904

Treble damages, bribes 162

Tree or vine bearing fruit or nuts
. depreciation 168

Tribal economic development bonds
. defined .... 7871(f)(3)(A)
. exempt status .... 7871(f)(2)
. gaming, buildings used for .... 7871(f)(3)(B)(i)
. limitations
. . allocation of .... 7871(f)(1)(A)
. . amount bonds designated .... 7871(f)(3)(C)
. . national .... 7871(f)(1)(B)
. outside reservation, facility located .... 7871(f)(3)(B)(ii)

Tribal governments of American Indians (See Native Americans)

Tripoli depletion 613

Trona depletion 613

Troubled assets relief programs
. business expenses 162
. golden parachute payments, employers participating in .... 280G(e)

Trucks
. depreciation 168
. heavy trucks and trailers, retail excise taxes .... 4051 et seq.
. highway use tax (See Highway motor vehicle use taxes)
. manufacturers excise tax
. . Highway Trust Fund 9503
. retail excise taxes .... 4001; 4051 et seq.
. . exemptions 4053; 4221; 4222
. . heavy trucks and trailers .... 4051 et seq.
. . Highway Trust Fund 9503
. . . imposition of tax 4051

Trust companies (See Banks and trust companies)

Trust fund recovery penalty 6672

Trust funds
. Airport and Airway Trust Fund 4091; 4092; 4093; 9502
. alternative minimum tax 59
. aquatic resources 9504
. black lung disability 9500; 9501
. boat safety account 9504
. harbor maintenance 9505
. hazardous substance superfund 9507
. hazardous waste cleanup, excise taxes for 4611; 4612; 4661; 4662
. Highway Trust Fund .... 4091 et seq.; 9503
. inland waterways 9506
. investments by 9602

Trust funds — Cont'd
. LUST Trust Fund 4041; 4091; 6421; 6427
. . excise tax rate .... 4081(a)(2)(B)
. . financing rate .... 4081(d)(3)
. management of 9602
. reporting requirements 9602
. sport fish restoration account .... 9504(b)(1)
. Trans-Alaska pipeline liability trust fund 4612
. transfers from Treasury to 9601
. trustee reporting requirements 9602
. trustees, reporting requirements 9602
. Vaccine Injury Compensation Trust Fund 4131; 9510
. withheld or collected taxes 7501; 7512

Trust territory of the Pacific islands
. U.S. savings bonds of residents 872

Trustees (See also Estates and trusts; Executors and administrators; Fiduciaries; Trusts)
. defined 2652
. disclosure of returns and return information 6103
. excess benefit transaction of exempt organizations 4958
. generation-skipping transfers, tax on 2652

Trusts .... 641 et seq. (See also Estates and trusts; Trustees; Trust funds)
. Alaska Native Settlement Trusts 646; 6039H
. alimony 215
. basis of property 1014; 1015
. Black Lung Disability Trust Fund (See Black Lung Disability Trust Fund)
. charitable remainder trusts
. . gift tax 2522
. common trust fund (See Common trust funds)
. contributions
. . information returns 6034
. corporation status determination, limitation on assessment and collection 6501
. defined 2652
. employees (See Employee retirement and benefit plans)
. estate freeze rules 2702
. foreign (See Foreign estates and trusts)
. generation-skipping, tax on .... 2601 et seq. (See also Generation-skipping transfer (GST) tax; Generation-skipping transfers)
. pour-over trust 2653
. . trust defined 2652
. gift tax 2511
. income
. . alimony and separate maintenance payments 215
. . taxability 61
. information returns
. . Alaska Native Settlement Trusts 6039H
. . charitable contributions 6652
. . contributions 6034
. interest in
. . estate tax, special use valuation property 2032A
. limitations on assessment and collection 6501
. nonexempt, private foundation restrictions 4947
. notice of failure to collect and pay over taxes 7512
. pension (See Employee retirement and benefit plans)
. person, status as 7701
. pooled income fund gift tax 2522

Index to Code — Undistributed

CODE SEC.

Trusts — Cont'd
. profit-sharing (See Employee retirement and benefit plans)
. REITs (See Real estate investment trusts)
. related taxpayers, transactions between 267
. returns 6012; 6034A
. revocable 676; 1014
. S corporation shareholders 1361
. self-employed retirement (See Self-employed individuals)
. small business stock losses 1244
. split interest 4947
. stock ownership rule, nondeductible losses 267
. stock-bonus (See Employee retirement and benefit plans)
. straddles, gain or loss 1092
. SUB (See Supplemental unemployment compensation benefit trusts)
. tax trusts 7512
. valuation rules
. . transfers of interest 2702
Tubes and tires (See Tires, excise tax)
Tuition
. deduction
. . allowance .... 222(a)
. . December 31, 2011, taxable years beginning after .... 222(e)
. . dependents .... 222(c)(3)
. . dollar limitations .... 222(b)
. . double benefits .... 222(c)(1)
. . identification requirements .... 222(d)(2)
. . married individuals filing separately .... 222(d)(4)
. . nonresident aliens .... 222(d)(5)
. . other education incentives, coordination with ...... 222(c)(2)
. . qualified tuition and related expenses defined ..... 222(d)(1)
. . taxable year of deduction limitations .... 222(d)(3)
. exemption of qualified state program 529
. qualified higher education expenses defined for qualified tuition programs .... 529(e)(3)
. qualified tuition programs
. . designated beneficiary defined .... 529(e)(1)
. . eligible educational institution defined .... 529(e)(5)
. . member of the family defined .... 529(e)(2)
. . qualified higher education expenses defined ...... 529(e)(3)
. . qualified tuition and related expenses defined .... 222(d)(1)
. reduction
. . educational organizations, employees of 117
. . exempt income 117
. . fringe benefits 3401
. . . FICA 3121
. . highly-compensated employees 117
. . reporting 6050S
. U.S. savings bonds redeemed to pay 135
Tungsten depletion 613
Turf depletion 613
2% of AGI floor
. miscellaneous itemized deductions 67
Type III supporting organizations
. excess business holding 4943

U

Ultimate purchaser

CODE SEC.

Ultimate purchaser — Cont'd
. defined 6416
Ultimate vendor defined 6416
UMWA (See United Mine Workers of America (UMWA))
Undercover operations of IRS enforcement officers ... 7608
Underground storage tank trust fund
. LUST (See Leaking underground storage tank trust fund)
Underpayment of tax .... 6601 (See also Deficiencies)
. accuracy-related penalty 6662
. AMT, incentive stock options .... 53(f)
. deposits made to suspend interest 6603
. employment taxes 6201; 6205
. errors, underpayments due to IRS
. . interest abatement 6404
. estate tax, extensions
. . interest on underpayment 6601
. estimated income tax
. . corporations 6622; 6658
. . individuals 6622; 6654
. estimated tax
. . annualization of income 6654; 6655
. . corporations 6655
. FICA 6205
. gift tax, interest 6601
. incentive stock options, AMT
. . interest and penalties .... 56(f)
. interest 6601; 6622
. . abatement, underpayments due to IRS error 6404
. . deposits made to suspend interest 6603
. . erroneous refund recoverable by suit 6602
. . estate tax, closely held business interests 6166
. . foreign expropriation loss recoveries 6167
. . increase in rate for large corporate underpayments 6621
. . installment payment of tax 6601
. . . estate tax, closely held business interests 6166
. . . foreign expropriation loss recoveries 6167
. . rates, determination of 6621
. . stamp taxes (documentary) 6601
. overpayment of tax credits against 6601; 6611
. Railroad Retirement Tax Act 6205
. reasonable cause 6664
. stamp taxes (documentary)
. . interest on underpayments 6601
Understatement of income, backup withholding 3406
Understatement of tax liability, aiding and abetting 6701; 6703; 7408; 7422
Underwriting income
. definition 832
. source of 861; 862
Undiscounted unpaid loss determination .... 846(b)
Undistributed income
. charitable remainder trusts 664
. foreign personal holding companies 556
. net income defined 665
. personal holding companies 545
. private foundations 4942
. regulated investment companies 852
. REITs 857

289

Unearned income, children

	CODE SEC.
alternative minimum tax	59
exemption amount, limitations	59
parental minimum tax, limitations	59
parent's income, taxed as if	1
tax rates	1
unused parental minimum tax exemption	59

Unemployment, areas of high
- recovery zone bonds (See Recovery zone bonds)
- recovery zone facility bonds (See Recovery zone facility bonds)

Unemployment benefits (See also Employment taxes; Federal Unemployment Tax Act (FUTA))

adjusted gross income, repayments	62
definition	85
exemption from levy	6334
gross income, inclusion in	85
information returns	6050B
state	3309

Unemployment insurance gross income inclusion ... 6050B

Unemployment taxes (See Employment taxes; Federal Unemployment Tax Act (FUTA))

Unified audit procedure, partnership .... 6221 et seq.

Unified credit

estate tax, against	2010; 2102; 2107
family owned business interests	2057
gift tax, against	2107; 2505

Uniformed services (See also Armed Forces)

exempt income	122
sale of principal residence	121

Unincorporated organizations

election of exclusion as partnership	761
partnership status	7701

Unions (See also Labor organizations)

collectively bargained plans	413
employee benefit plans	401
employee retirement and benefit plans	
. limitations on benefits and contributions	415
. exemption	501

Unit investment trusts 851
- foreign investment company status 1246
- possessions of U.S. (See Possessions of United States)
- redemption by 852

United Mine Workers of America (UMWA)

- benefit and pension plans
- . assignment of beneficiaries 9706
- . benefits, plan 9703
- . civil enforcement 9721
- . definitions 9701
- . individual employer plans, continued obligations of ... 9711
- . liability of operators 9704
- . 1992 UMWA benefit plan, establishment and coverage of 9712
- . pending claims 9708
- . premium, failure to pay 9707
- . sham transactions 9722
- . transfer of assets 9705
- combined benefits fund
- . board of trustees, appointment of .... 9702(b)(1)

United Mine Workers of America (UMWA) —Cont'd
combined benefits fund —Cont'd

	CODE SEC.
establishment	9702(a)(1)
plan year	9702(c)
retirement benefit plan, merger of	9702(a)(2)
successor trustees, appointment of	9702(b)(2)
treatment of plan	9702(a)(3)

United States

- aliens, marital deduction
- . surviving spouse of U.S. citizen 2056
- archivist of the U.S. 6103
- charitable contributions to 170
- citizenship; termination of U.S. citizenship 7701
- Civil actions by U.S. (See Court action)
- Continental U.S. defined 4262
- debts owed to, non-tax, offsets against tax overpayments 6402
- defined 993; 4262; 7701
- depreciation deduction, use or leased property ... 168
- disclosure of returns and return information ... 6103
- domestic goods purchased for 7510
- employees (See Federal officers and employees)
- instrumentalities of (See Instrumentalities of U.S.)
- property defined 956
- prosecutions by, limitation on 6531
- real property
- . acquired by 6338; 7506
- . foreign investments in ... 861; 862; 897; 1445; 6039C; 6652
- . wash sale transactions .... 1445(b)(8)
- . interests
- . . defined 897
- . . information returns 6039C
- . . . penalty for failure to file 6652
- . . nonresident aliens, distributions 897
- . . wash sale transactions .... 1445(b)(8)
- . . withholding of tax 1445
- . nonresident aliens 897
- . stock and securities
- . . U.S. real property interest, treatment as 897
- . U.S. property investments, disposition of
- . . . nonresident aliens 861; 1445
- . . U.S. real property holding corporation defined ... 897
- . real property holding companies
- . . U.S. real property holding corporation defined ... 897
- . real property holding organizations 897
- shipments from and to the U.S. .... 7652 et seq.
- sources of income within (See Income subhead sources)
- stockholders
- . U.S. shareholder defined 951; 953; 957
- suits by .... 7401 et seq.
- termination of U.S. citizenship defined 7701

United States employment service, work opportunity credit
.... 51

United States obligations

deposited in lieu of surety	7101
exchanges of	1037
exemption	
. declaratory judgment as to	7478
. federally guaranteed bonds	149

Index to Code   Valuation

CODE SEC.

United States obligations — Cont'd
. foreign central banks of issue income from 895
. income derived by foreign central bank of issue from 895
. interest
. . declaratory judgment as to 7478
. . estates and trusts, distributable net income computation 643
. . personal holding companies 543
. interest received by banks organized in possessions 882
. life insurance company investments 817
. nontaxable exchanges 1037
. OID rules . . . . 1037; 1271; 1281 et seq.
. savings bonds (See United States savings bonds)
. short-term, issued at discount . . . . 454; 1271; 1281 et seq.
United States person defined 7701
United States possessions (See Possessions of U.S.)
United States savings bonds
. defined 135
. discount 454
. education expenses, redemption proceeds 135
. exemption 135
. residents of Ryuku Islands and Trust Territory of the Pacific Islands 872
. retained after maturity or exchanged 454
. tuition and fees, redeemed to pay 135
United States Tax Court (See Tax Court)
Unitized property depletion 614
Unitrust
. charitable contributions 170
. charitable remainders 664; 2522
. remainder interest, charitable contribution 170
Universities (See Educational organizations)
Unmarried individuals (See also Individual taxpayers)
. defined 7703
. living together, dependents' status 152
. tax rates 1
Unrealized receivables 724; 735; 736; 751
Unrelated business taxable income 501
. agricultural organization dues . . . . 512(d)
. amounts derived from . . . . 512(b)(17)
. Brownfield site, sale or exchange of . . . . 512(b)(19)
. controlled entities . . . . 512(b)(13)
. controlled group of corporations 1563
. debt-financed income 514
. debt-financed property 514
. defined . . . . 512(a)(1)
. domestic production activities deduction . . . . 199(d)(7)
. exempt organizations . . . . 511 et seq.
. 501(c) organizations and definition of . . . . . 512(a)(3); 512(a)(4)
. foreign organizations and definition of . . . . 512(a)(2)
. foreign tax credit 515
. horticultural organization dues . . . . 512(d)
. mutual or cooperative electric companies . . . . 512(b)(18)
. partnerships . . . . 512(c)
. payments with respect to securities loans . . . . 512(a)(5)
. S corporations . . . . 512(e)

CODE SEC.

Unrelated debt-financed income property 514
Unrelated taxpayers defined 971
Unrelated trade or business
. defined 513
. exempt entities and organizations . . . . 511 et seq.
. property used by or leased to 168
. taxable income 512
. taxes of foreign countries and U.S. possessions 515
. unrelated debt-financed income 514
. Sec. 1250 property, transfers 1250
Unused business credits
. carryback and carryforward 39
. deduction 196
Uranium depletion 613
Urban enterprise zones/communities (See Enterprise zones/communities)
U.S. (See United States)
Use in further manufacture 6416
Use of property by exempt entity (See Tax-exempt use property)
Use taxes
. highway (See Highway motor vehicle use taxes)
. motor vehicles (See Highway motor vehicle use taxes)
User fees, payment of 7528
Utilities (See Public utilities)

V

Vacation home rentals
. exceptions, disallowance of deduction for expenses 280A
Vaccine, excise tax on 4131; 4132
Vaccine injury compensation trust fund 4131; 9510
Valuation
. annuities, other interests, tables for 7520
. applicable retained interest 2701
. appraisals, incorrect
. . substantial and gross valuation misstatements attributable to 6695A
. charitable remainder trust distribution, valuing 664
. closely-held business real property or farm 2032A
. employee retirement and benefit plans, assets 412
. estate and gift purposes
. . alternate valuation 2032
. . estate freezes, special rules for (See Estate freezes)
. . farm property 2032A
. . gift tax 2512
. . gross estate . . . . 2031 et seq.
. . IRS statements supporting 7517
. . preceding calendar periods, gifts from 2504
. . real property 2032A
. . reductions 2012
. fair market value (See Fair market value)
. farm or closely-held business real property 2032A
. generation-skipping transfers, tax on 2624; 2642
. gifts, declaratory judgments relating to value of certain . . . 7477
. gross estate
. . alternate valuation 2032
. . farm property 2032A

291

CODE SEC.

Valuation —Cont'd
gross estate —Cont'd
... inclusions in value of .... 2031 et seq.
... qualified real property 2032A
.... special rules 2032
.... stock and securities, unlisted 2031
.. loss carryovers, change of ownership 382
.. property acquired from decedent dying after December 31, 2009 1022
.. remainder interest in real property, charitable contribution of 170
.. retained interest 2701
.. reversionary interest 2037
.. rules
... transfer of interests in trusts 2702
... transfers of certain corporate or partnership interests to family members 2701
.. seized property 6334
.. stock 1053
.. tables 7520

Vanadium depletion 613
Vandalism loss 5064
Vans, retail excise tax 4001
VEBAs (See Voluntary employees beneficiary associations (VEBAs))
Vehicles
. alternate motor vehicle credits (See Alternate motor vehicle credits)
. automobiles (See Automobiles)
. charitable contributions of used 170
. clean fuel vehicles 179A
. electric 30
. highway motor vehicle use taxes (See Highway motor vehicle use taxes)
. luxury automobiles (See Luxury automobiles)
. motor vehicles (See motor vehicles)
. new qualified alternative fuel motor vehicle credit (See Alternate motor vehicle credits)
. nonpersonal use 274
. off-highway vehicles 7701
. passenger vehicles .... 4001 et seq
. qualified electric vehicle credit 30
. retrofitted vehicles 179A
. stolen or destroyed vehicles, highway motor vehicle use tax 4481
. stolen vehicles 4481
. trailers (See Trailers)
. trucks (See Trucks)

Venue, review of TC decision 7482
Vermiculite depletion 613
Vessels (See Boats; Ships and shipping)
Vesting of retirement benefits (See Pension, profit-sharing, and stock bonus plans)
Veterans
. disability compensation 104
. higher education expenses 135
. mortgage bonds (See Veterans mortgage bonds)
. unemployed; credits against tax .... 51(d)(14)
. Vietnam war, work opportunity credit 51
. work opportunity credit 51

CODE SEC.

Veterans Administration
. guarantee bonds 149
Veterans mortgage bonds 143
. change in use of residence 150
. federally guaranteed bonds 149
. qualified veterans' mortgage bonds
.. Alaska, state veteran limit .... 143(l)(3)(B)(ii)
.. financing provided to veteran requirement ..... 143(l)(1)
.. June 22, 1984 effective date of state program ..... 143(l)(2)
.. Oregon, state veteran limit .... 143(l)(3)(B)(ii)
.. qualified veteran defined .... 143(l)(4)
.. refunding .... 143(l)(3)(C)
.. short-term bonds .... 143(l)(5)
.. state program be in effect before June 22, 1984, requirement that .... 143(l)(2)
.. state veteran limit .... 143(l)(3)(B)
.. veterans to whom financing may be provided ...... 143(l)(1)
.. volume limitation .... 143(l)(3)
.. Wisconsin, state veteran limit .... 143(l)(3)(B)(ii)
. residency requirement 150
. restrictions on issuance costs 147
. volume cap 146
Veterans organizations
. charitable contributions 170
. exemption 501
. insurance income, unrelated business taxable income 512
Veterans' reemployment rights under USERRA
. pension, profit-sharing, and stock bonus plans
.. compensation .... 414(u)(7)
.. contributions, treatment of .... 414(u)(1)
.. death or disability resulting from active military service .... 414(u)(9)
.. differential wage payments .... 414(u)(12)
.. elective deferrals .... 414(u)(2)
.. individual account plan defined .... 414(u)(6)
.. loan repayments .... 414(u)(4)
.. plans not subject to title 38 .... 414(u)(10)
.. qualified military service defined .... 414(u)(5)
.. retroactive adjustments .... 414(u)(3)
.. USERRA requirements .... 414(u)(8)
Viatical settlements 101
Video tapes (See Motion picture films)
Vietnam war
. missing in action 112; 692
. veterans, work opportunity credit 51
Vinegar plants
. alcohol taxes .... 5501 et seq.
. unlawful production and removal 5615
Virgin Islands
. corporations 881
.. withholding tax at source on nonresident aliens and foreign corporations 1444
. distilled spirits imported from, excise taxes 5314
. foreign investments in real property 862
. information returns 6039C
. FUTA 3306
. income taxes 934
.. coordination with U.S. 932

Index to Code

Virgin Islands —Cont'd
income taxes—Cont'd
- withholding 1444
- possession of U.S. .... 7651 et seq.
- reduction of tax liability 934
- residents of
  - self-employment tax 1402
  - tax liability 932
- Revised Organic Act 7651
- shipments from U.S. 7653
- shipments to U.S. 7652
  - environmental taxes 4612; 4662
- U.S. citizens and residents
  - income from, withholding tax at source on nonresident aliens and foreign corporations 1444
  - tax liability of 932; 934
- withholding tax at source on nonresident aliens and foreign corporations 1444

Vocational rehabilitation referral, work opportunity credit
.... 51

Volatile fruit-flavor concentrate plants 5511; 5512

Volume cap, private activity bonds 146

Voluntary deductible employee contributions 6652

Voluntary employee beneficiary associations (VEBAs)
.... 501; 505
- unrelated business taxable income 512

Voluntary withholding agreements 3402

Volunteer emergency response organizations
- benefits provided to
  - double benefits denial .... 139B(b)
  - gross income, inclusion in .... 139B(a)
  - qualified payment defined .... 139B(c)(2)
  - qualified state and local tax benefit defined ...... 139B(c)(1)
  - qualified volunteer emergency response organization defined .... 139B(c)(3)

Volunteer fire departments
- bond issues 147; 150
- definition 150
- private activity bonds 147; 150
- retirement plans 219

Volunteer firefighters
- benefits provided to
  - double benefits denial .... 139B(b)
  - gross income, inclusion in .... 139B(a)
  - qualified payment defined .... 139B(c)(2)
  - qualified state and local tax benefit defined ...... 139B(c)(1)
  - qualified volunteer emergency response organization defined .... 139B(c)(3)
- IRA plans 219

Voting rights, retention of 2036

W

Wage bracket withholding 3402
Wage earners returns 6014
Wagering losses 165
Wagering taxes .... 4401 et seq.; 6419
- books and records 4403; 4423
- definitions 4421

Wagering taxes—Cont'd
- disclosure of information 4424
- exemptions 4402
- failure to pay tax 7262
- Federal laws, applicability of 4422
- imposition of 4401; 4411
- inspection of books 4423
- laid-off wagers 6419
- liability for .... 4401; 4411; 4901 et seq.
- lotteries 3402; 4421
- miscellaneous provisions .... 4421 et seq.
- occupational tax .... 4411 et seq.; 4901 et seq.
  - applicable provisions 4413
  - imposition of 4411
  - penalties 7262
  - registration 4412
  - stamps 6806
- penalties, state or federal laws 4422; 4906
- record requirements 4403
- refunds and credits 6419
- registration 4412
- returns, disclosure of 4424
- stamps 6806
- state laws, applicability of 4422
- state-conducted lotteries and sweepstakes 3402
- territorial extent 4404
- wager defined 4421
- wagering income, on
  - nonresident aliens 871; 1441
  - withholding tax at source 1441; 3402
- withholding tax 1441; 3402

Wages (See Compensation)

Waiver
- bona fide residence requirements, foreign income exclusion purposes 911
- civil service benefits by TC judges 7448
- dependency exemption claim 152
- exemption from Social Security coverage
  - clergymen and Christian Science practitioners 1402
- limitations on assessment and collection ... 6501; 6502; 6724
  - refund and credit limitation extended by 6511
- notice of disallowance of refund claim 6532
- reasonable cause 6724
- refund limitation extended by 6511
- restrictions on assessment and collection of deficiency ... 6213; 6601
- right to deduction under Sec. 2053 or 2054 642
- Social Security benefits by conscientious objectors to insurance 1402
- stay of collection of jeopardy assessment 6863
- termination of taxable year 6851

War (See also Vietnam war)
- hospitalization due to combat related injuries 7508
- injuries or sickness, compensation for 104
- postponements in tax requirements 7508
- suspension of limitations because of 7508

War profits tax
- deductibility 164; 275
- foreign tax credit, tax in lieu of income 903

	Code Sec.
Wash sales	860F
. basis rules	1091
. holding period	1223
. losses from, deduction disallowance	1091
. real property	897
. short sales	1091
. U.S. real property, foreign taxpayer disposition of	1445(b)(8)
Washers and dryers	
. energy efficient appliance credit (See Energy efficient appliance credits)	
Waste disposal facilities	
. exempt facility bonds	146
. reclamation and closing costs	468
. service contracts	7701
Wastewater treatment plant depreciation	168
Water conservation expenditures (See Conservation subhead Soil and water)	
Water facilities	
. facilities for the furnishing of water defined for exempt facility bonds	142(e)
. treatment facility service contract	7701
Water utility property	
. depreciation	168
. exempt facility bonds	142
Weapon defined	5845 (See also Firearms)
Wear and tear depreciation deduction	167
Weather-related condition, livestock sales	
. nontaxable exchanges	1033
. proceeds from	451
Welfare benefit plans	419; 419A
. disqualified benefit defined	4976
. excise taxes	4976
. sales between employer and	1239
. unfunded deferred benefit plans	404
Welfare-to-work credits	
. long-term family assistance recipients, incentives for employing	51A
Wetlands, converted	1257
Whaling captains	
. charitable contribution in support of native Alaskan subsistence whaling	170
Wharves, exempt facility bonds	142; 146
When issued basis, securities	1233
Whistleblowers	
. attorney fees relating to award to	
. . adjusted gross income	62
. rewards to	7623(b)
Wholesale dealers, liquor	
. occupational taxes	5111 et seq.; 5691
Wills	
. charitable set-asides under	642
. powers exercisable under	674
Wilma, Hurricane	
. Gulf Opportunity Zone (See Gulf Opportunity Zone)	
Wind energy property credit	48(c)(4)
Wind facility	
. electricity produced from renewable sources; credit	45(d)(1)

	Code Sec.
Windfall profit tax, domestic crude oil	
. repeal of	6050C
Wines	5041 et seq.
. agricultural	5387
. ameliorated	5384
. bonded and tax paid premises	
. . applications	5356
. . bonds, provisions relating to	5354; 5355
. . establishment	5351 et seq.
. . exemption for	5391 et seq.
. . operations	5361 et seq.
. . premises	5357
. . tax paid wine bottling house	5352
. books and records	5367; 5555
. bulk, imported	5364
. cellar treatment and classification	5381 et seq.
. classification of	5381 et seq.
. collection of tax	5043; 5061
. credit	
. . small domestic producers	5041
. . wine content and for flavor content	5010
. definitions	5392
. designation of	5388
. distilled spirits tax	5001; 5041
. exemption from tax	5042; 5391
. experimental use	5042
. exports	5062; 5362
. family use	5042; 5362
. foreign government or family use	5362
. gallonage taxes	5041 et seq.
. gauging	5368
. imported bulk	5364
. imposition of tax	5041
. industrial use	5362
. insurance coverage	5371
. inventories	5369
. loss or destruction	5064; 5370
. marking	5368
. natural fruit and berry wines, sweetening limitations for	5384
. payment of tax	5043
. penalties and forfeitures	5661 et seq.; 5681 et seq.
. personal use	5042
. proprietor of wine cellar	5081
. rate of tax	5041; 5041 et seq.
. refunds	5044; 5062; 5064
. research purposes	5042
. returns	5555
. revenue protecting apparatus	5552
. sales by creditors, fiduciaries and officers of court	5113
. sampling	5372
. small producers, credit for	5041
. special natural	5386
. specially sweetened	5385
. spirits	5373
. sweetening limitations for natural fruit and berry wines	5384
. tolerances	5041
. unfit for beverage use	5044; 5362

Index to Code — Withholding

	CODE SEC.
Withdrawal accounts, interest paid	461
Withdrawal liability payment funds	194A; 501
Withdrawals	
. black lung benefit trusts, excess contributions	4953
. employee benefit plans	401
. Merchant Marine Act contracts	7518
Withholding	3401 et seq.
. accounting for withheld taxes after notification	7215; 7512
. additional exemptions	3402
. additional withholding	3402
. adjustments	6205; 6413
. agents	3402; 3504; 7701
. aliens	3401
. allowances	3402
. . false or fraudulent claims	6682
. annualized wages	3402
. annuities, from	3402; 3405
. assessment and collection	6205; 6501
. average wages	3402
. backup withholding (See Backup withholding)	
. bankruptcy and receiverships	6658
. certificate of nontaxability	3402; 6682; 7205
. changes in withholding	3402
. clergymen	3401
. collection and payment	3501
. companion sitting placement services	3506
. computation methods	3402
. credits	31; 1464; 6413; 6414
. . interest on overpayments	6611
. . overstated credits	6201
. cumulative wages, based on	3402
. date of payment for refund limitation	6513
. decreases	3402
. deductibility of tax	275; 3402; 3502
. deferred income	3405; 6652
. definitions	3401
. dependent care assistance programs	3401
. earned income credit, advance payments	3507; 6051
. educational assistance programs	3401
. employee defined	3401
. employee with no tax liability	3402
. employer defined	3401
. excessive	6413
. exempt organizations, foreign	1443
. exemption certificates (See Withholding exemption certificates)	
. exemptions claimed	3401; 3402; 7205
. failure to pay withheld taxes	6658; 7215; 7512
. failure to supply information	7205
. failure to withhold	3402
. fiduciaries	3402
. fishermen	3401
. foreign corporations	33; 1442
. . nonresident aliens and foreign corporations (See subhead nonresident aliens and foreign corporations)	
. . U.S. real property interest dispositions	1445(a)
. . . affidavit that interests in corporation not U.S. real property, nonpublicly traded domestic corporation	1445(b)(3)
. . . distributions by foreign corporation	1445(e)(2)
. . . exemptions	1445(b)(1)

	CODE SEC.
Withholding—Cont'd	
. *foreign corporations—Cont'd*	
. . *U.S. real property interest dispositions—Cont'd*	
. . . false affidavit	1445(d)(1)
. . . general rule	1445(a)
. . . limitations on amount required to be withheld	1445(c)
. . . nonforeign affidavits, alternative procedure for	1445(b)(9)
. . . notice, failure to furnish	1445(d)(2)
. . . qualifying statement, transferee receives	1445(b)(4)
. . . residence where amount realized does not exceed $300,000	1445(b)(5)
. . . stock regularly traded on established securities market	1445(b)(6)
. . . wash sales	1445(b)(8)
. foreign governments, employees	3401
. foreign partners, tax on payments to	1446
. foreign tax-exempt organizations	1443
. fringe benefits	3401; 3402
. gambling winnings	3402
. golden parachute agreements	4999
. government employer	3404
. graduated rates	3402
. group-term life insurance	3401
. highway motor vehicle use	3402
. identification of taxpayers subject to	6011
. included and excluded wages	3401; 3402
. income tax collected at source	3402
. increase in amounts	3402
. information statements to employees	6051
. international organizations, employees	3401
. liability for	1461; 3402; 3403; 3504; 3505; 3509; 7501
. life insurance premiums paid by employer	3401
. marital status, determination and disclosure	3402
. medical expenses, reimbursement of	3401
. methods	3402
. moving expense reimbursement	3401
. newsboys	3401
. newspaper vendors	3401
. no tax liability	3402
. noncash remuneration, retail commission salesmen	3402
. nonresident aliens and foreign corporations	
. . application of withholding provisions	1461 et seq.
. . branch profits tax, coordination with	884
. . consent dividends	565
. . credit against tax	6401
. . failure to withhold	1463
. . gambling winnings	1441
. . Guam	1442
. . income subject to	1441; 1442
. . interest	881
. . payment	1461
. . personal exemptions	874
. . refunds and credits	1462; 1464; 6414
. . tax paid by recipient	1463
. . Virgin Islands	1442; 1444
. nonresident citizens	3401
. notice of failure to collect and pay over tax	7512
. overlapping pay periods	3402
. payment of tax withheld	
. . government depositaries	6302; 6656; 7215; 7512

295

Withholding | **Index to Code**

CODE SEC.

Withholding—Cont'd
payment of tax withheld —Cont'd
.. governmental employer 3404
.. liability for 3403
. payments other than wages 3402
. payroll periods
.. defined 3401
.. overlapping 3402
. Peace Corps 3401
. penalties 6658; 6674; 7204; 7215
. pensions 3405
. percentage method 3402
. possessions of U.S. 3401
. rates 3402
. receipts for employees 6051; 6652; 6674; 7204
. refunds 6413; 6414
.. interest on overpayments 6611
.. overstated credits 6201
. religious organizations 3401
. retirement or benefit plan distributions 3405; 6652
. returns of tax withheld 3404
.. identification of taxpayers 6011
. rounding off wage payments 3402
. scholarships and fellowships 3401
. sick pay 3402
. statement to employees 6051; 6652; 6674; 7204
. supplemental unemployment benefits, from 3402
. tables 3402
. tax as credit to recipient of income 1462
. tax on dispositions 4978
. tax paid by recipient 1463; 3402
. third party, liability 3505
. tips 3401; 3402
. trust fund, withheld taxes as 7512
. underpayments 6205
. U.S. real property interest dispositions by foreign persons, withholding tax on
.. exemptions .... 1445(b)(1)
.. general rule .... 1445(a)
. voluntary withholding agreements 3402
. wage bracket withholding 3402
. wages, withholding from .... 3401 et seq.
.. backup withholding 3406
.. definitions 3401
.. income tax collected at source 3402
.. liability for tax 3403
.. pensions, annuities, and other deferred income, special rules for 3405
.. return and payment by governmental employer 3404
.. wages paid for another 3402; 3504
. withheld taxes as trust fund 7501; 7512
Withholding exemption certificates
. false or fraudulent 6682; 7205

CODE SEC.

Withholding exemption certificates —Cont'd
. furnish, procedure to 3402
. more than one employer 3402
Withholdings
. foreign transfers, financial institution returns with withholdings on .... 6011(e)(4)
Witnesses 7210; 7602
. costs and fees 7610
. examination of .... 7602 et seq.
.. district court jurisdiction 7402
.. transferees 6902
. failure to testify 7210
. Tax Court 7456; 7457
Wives (See Spouses)
Work opportunity credit 51
Work supplementation payments 51
Worker-owned cooperatives
. eligible worker-owned cooperates (See Eligible worker-owned cooperatives (EWOCs))
. employer securities
.. dispositions of 4978
.. prohibited allocations 4979A
Workers' compensation
. exempt income 104
. FUTA 3306
. information returns 6050F
. levy on 6334
. Social Security benefits substituted for 86
Workers cooperatives
. worker-owned cooperative (See Worker-owned cooperatives; Eligible worker-owned cooperatives (EWOCs))
Working condition fringe benefits 132
Worthless stock (See Stock and securities)
Written determinations
. defined for public inspection 6110

X

Xylene hazardous waste clean up 4661; 4662

Y

Year, taxable (See Taxable year)
Youth, work opportunity credit 51

Z

Zinc chloride hazardous waste clean up 4661
Zinc sulfate hazardous waste clean up 4661
Zone academy bonds (See Qualified zone academy bonds)

296

Amending Acts

Additions and amendments to the Internal Revenue Code of 1954, enacted on August 16, 1954, and the Internal Revenue Code of 1986, enacted on October 22, 1986, are made by Public Laws. Some Public Laws bear special titles, such as "Revenue Act", "Reform Act", "Technical Changes Act", or "Technical Amendments Act" of a stated year. Others bear no title. The table below lists, in order of enactment, the Public Laws that have amended the Internal Revenue Code since August 16, 1954. Each entry contains the P.L. number, the enactment date, the title or subject, and the location of the reprint in either the Cumulative Bulletin or the Statute Books.

Finding List for Amending Acts

Public Law No.	Date	Title or Subject	Reprint
\multicolumn{4}{c}{**Statutes Enacted by the 83rd Congress — 2nd Session**}
729	8-31-54	Filling oral prescriptions for certain drugs	1954-2 CB 599
746	8-31-54	Amending Railroad Retirement Act, etc.	1954-2 CB 602
761	9-1-54	Social Security Amendments of 1954	1954-2 CB 603
764	9-1-54	Extending and amending Renegotiation Act of 1951	1955-1 CB 620
767	9-1-54	Extending unemployment compensation program	1954-2 CB 612
\multicolumn{4}{c}{**Statutes Enacted by the 84th Congress — 1st Session**}
1	1-20-55	Amending Code Sec. 7237	1955-1 CB 619
9	3-2-55	Amending Code Sec. 7443(c)	1955-2 CB 747
18	3-30-55	Tax Rate Extension Act of 1955	1955-1 CB 619
66	6-8-55	Continuing suspension of duties and import taxes on metal scrap	1955-2 CB 747
74	6-15-55	Repealing Code Secs. 452 and 462	1955-2 CB 748
91	6-21-55	Continuing suspension of certain import duties on copper	1955-2 CB 749
196	8-1-55	Revising Philippines trade agreement	1955-2 CB 750
216	8-3-55	Extending Renegotiation Act of 1951	1955-2 CB 754
285	8-9-55	Amending International Settlement Act of 1949	1955-2 CB 756
299	8-9-55	Extending retirement income tax credit to members of Armed Forces	1955-2 CB 758
303	8-9-55	Extending period for claiming floor tax refunds	1955-2 CB 758
306	8-9-55	Amending Code Sec. 3402	1955-2 CB 759
310	8-9-55	Amending Sec. 345 of the Revenue Act of 1951	1955-2 CB 759
317	8-9-55	Providing for maximum manufacturers' excise tax on leases of certain automobile utility trailers	1955-2 CB 760
319	8-9-55	Amending Agricultural Act of 1949	1955-2 CB 761
321	8-9-55	Amending Code Sec. 3401	1955-2 CB 761
323	8-9-55	Providing for bonding certain civilian officers and employees	1955-2 CB 763
333	8-9-55	Providing personal exemption with respect to certain dependents in the Philippines	1955-2 CB 764
354	8-11-55	Exempting admissions to certain athletic events	1955-2 CB 765
355	8-11-55	Amending Code with respect to cutting oils tax	1955-2 CB 765
363	8-11-55	Providing for refund of credit of taxes on distilled spirits and wines lost in hurricane	1955-2 CB 766
366	8-11-55	Providing for tax treatment of damages for patent infringements	1955-2 CB 767
367	8-11-55	Removing excise tax from certain radio and television equipment	1955-2 CB 768
370	8-11-55	Amending Sec. 223 of the Revenue Act of 1950	1955-2 CB 770
379	8-12-55	Repealing excise tax on motorcycles	1955-2 CB 770
383	8-12-55	Amending Railroad Retirement Act, etc.	1955-2 CB 770
384	8-12-55	Amending tax treatment on amounts recovered held by another under claim of right	1955-2 CB 771
385	8-12-55	Amending Code Secs. 542(a)(2) and 1233	1955-2 CB 772
\multicolumn{4}{c}{**Statutes Enacted by the 84th Congress — 2nd Session**}
396	1-28-56	Providing for carryover of unused pension trust deductions in certain cases	1956-1 CB 852
397	1-28-56	Providing for claims limitation period by certain transferees and fiduciaries	1956-1 CB 852
398	1-28-56	Amending Code Sec. 37	1956-1 CB 853
399	1-28-56	Providing credits to corporation for computing alternative tax	1956-1 CB 853
400	1-28-56	Providing for documentary stamp tax on certain obligations paid for in installments	1956-1 CB 854
408	2-15-56	Relating to unlimited deduction for charitable contributions	1956-1 CB 854
414	2-20-56	Amending Sec. 208(b) of the Technical Changes Act of 1953	1956-1 CB 855
417	2-20-56	Providing credit against estate tax	1956-1 CB 857
429	3-13-56	Life Insurance Company Tax Act for 1955	1956-1 CB 858
458	3-29-56	Tax Rate Extension Act of 1956	1956-1 CB 869

Amending Acts

Public Law No.	Date	Title or Subject	Reprint
466	4-2-56	Relieving farmers of tax on certain farm fuels	1956-1 CB 870
495	4-27-56	Amending Code Sec. 1237	1956-1 CB 874
511	5-9-56	Providing for treatment of distributions made under bank holding company act	1956-1 CB 875
545	5-29-56	Amending Sugar Act of 1948	1956-1 CB 887
627	6-29-56	Providing additional revenue from taxes on motor fuels, tires, etc.	1956-2 CB 1150
628	6-29-56	Relating to tax treatment of certain railroad reorganizations	1956-2 CB 1164
629	6-29-56	Relating to trademark and trade name expenditures, etc.	1956-2 CB 1165
700	7-11-56	Amending Code Secs. 852(b)(3) and 5217(c)	1956-2 CB 1169
723	7-16-56	Continuing suspension of import taxes on metal scrap, etc.	1956-2 CB 1169
726	7-18-56	Mutual Security Act of 1956	1956-2 CB 1170
728	7-18-56	Narcotic Control Act of 1956	1956-2 CB 1171
784	7-24-56	Providing 1955 formula for taxing life insurance companies	1956-2 CB 1179
796	7-25-56	Exempting certain foreign travel from transition tax	1956-2 CB 1180
870	8-1-56	Extending and amending Renegotiation Act of 1951	1956-2 CB 1182
880	8-1-56	Social Security Amendments of 1956	1956-2 CB 1188
881	8-1-56	Servicemen's and Veterans' Survivor Benefits Act	1956-2 CB 1196
896	8-1-56	Implementing Organic Act of Guam	1956-2 CB 1204
901	8-1-56	Amending provisions relating to estate tax	1956-2 CB 1205
1010	8-6-56	Providing for exemption from admissions tax	1956-2 CB 1205
1011	8-6-56	Allowing charitable deductions for certain bequests	1956-2 CB 1206
1015	8-7-56	Extending exemption for tax on transportation of persons	1956-2 CB 1207
1022	8-7-56	Providing for deduction of contributions to medical research organizations	1956-2 CB 1207

Statutes Enacted by the 85th Congress — 1st Session

Public Law No.	Date	Title or Subject	Reprint
85-12	3-29-57	Tax Rate Extension Act of 1957	1957-1 CB 666
85-56	6-17-57	Veterans' Benefits Act of 1957	1957-2 CB 1055
85-74	6-29-57	Exempting furlough travel of service personnel from transportation tax	1957-2 CB 1057
85-165	8-26-57	Amending Internal Revenue Code to provide relief for amounts received for breach of contract and to restrict issuance of rapid amortization of emergency facilities	1957-2 CB 1058
85-235	8-30-57	Suspending tax on processing of coconut oil temporarily	1957-2 CB 1061
85-239	8-30-57	Extending time for ministers to elect coverage under Social Security program	1957-2 CB 1061
85-300	9-7-57	Providing tax exemption for certain bonds	1958-1 CB 626

Statutes Enacted by the 85th Congress — 2nd Session

Public Law No.	Date	Title or Subject	Reprint
85-318	2-11-58	Amending 1939 Code Sec. 812(e)(1)(D)	1958-1 CB 627
85-319	2-11-58	Amending Sec. 223 of the Revenue Act of 1950	1958-1 CB 628
85-320	2-11-58	Providing basis of shares acquired by exercise of restricted stock options after death of employee	1958-1 CB 628
85-321	2-11-58	Relating to administration of certain collected taxes	1958-1 CB 629
85-323	2-11-58	Preventing unjust enrichment by precluding refunds of alcohol and tobacco taxes to persons who have not borne ultimate burden of tax	1958-1 CB 630
85-345	3-17-58	Extending 1955 formula for taxing life insurance companies	1958-1 CB 632
85-367	4-7-58	Amending definition of unrelated business taxable income	1958-1 CB 633
85-380	4-16-58	Extending exemption to admissions for certain musical, dramatic and athletic events	1958-1 CB 633
85-475	6-30-58	Tax Rate Extension Act of 1958	1958-3 CB 73
85-517	7-11-58	Extension of authority of distilled spirits transfers	1958-3 CB 75
85-595	8-6-58	Defining place at which certain income tax offenses take place	1958-3 CB 75
85-605	8-8-58	Allotting lands in Fort Belknap Indian Reservation	1958-3 CB 76
85-612	8-8-58	Benefitting Lummi Indian Tribe	1958-3 CB 76
85-671	8-18-58	Providing taxability of certain Indian land and income	1958-3 CB 77
85-688	8-20-58	Amending Organic Act of Guam	1958-3 CB 78
85-731	8-23-58	Providing for acquisition of Klamath Indian lands	1958-3 CB 80
85-758	8-25-58	Conveying certain lands to Makah Indians	1958-3 CB 82
85-791	8-28-58	Abbreviating records for review	1958-3 CB 83
85-840	8-28-58	Social Security Amendments of 1958	1958-3 CB 85
85-859	9-2-58	Excise Tax Technical Changes Act of 1958	1958-3 CB 92
85-866	9-2-58	Technical Amendments Act of 1958 Retirement-Straight Line Adjustment Act of 1958 Small Business Tax Revision Act of 1958	1958-3 CB 254
85-878	9-2-58	Reimbursing Pine Ridge Sioux Tribe	1958-3 CB 334
85-881	9-2-58	Amending certain Internal Revenue Code Secs	1958-3 CB 334
85-915	9-2-58	Rehabilitating Indians of Standing Rock Sioux Reservation	1958-3 CB 335
85-916	9-2-58	Providing payments to Indians of Crow Creek Sioux Reservation	1958-3 CB 336
85-920	9-2-58	Relating to venue of tax refund suits	1958-3 CB 337
85-923	9-2-58	Providing Payments to Indians of Lower Brule Sioux Reservation	1958-3 CB 338

Amending Acts

Public Law No.	Date	Title or Subject	Reprint
	**Statutes Enacted by the 86th Congress—1st Session**		
86-28	5-19-59	Amending Railroad Retirement Act, etc.	1959-2 CB 652
86-37	5-29-59	Suspending tax on processing palm oil, etc.	1959-2 CB 654
86-69	6-25-59	Life Insurance Company Income Act of 1959	1959-2 CB 654
86-70	6-25-59	Alaskan Omnibus Act	1959-2 CB 678
86-75	6-30-59	Tax Rate Extension Act of 1959	1959-2 CB 679
86-89	7-15-59	Extension of 1951 Renegotiation Act	1959-2 CB 680
86-94	7-17-59	Providing payments to Potawatomi	1959-2 CB 682
86-95	7-17-59	Providing payments to Couer D'Alene Tribe	1959-2 CB 683
86-97	7-17-59	Providing per capita distribution of funds to Quapaw Tribe	1959-2 CB 684
86-125	7-31-59	Exempting from income tax certain payments to Indians	1959-2 CB 684
86-141	8-7-59	Amending Code Sec 2038	1959-2 CB 685
86-168	8-18-59	Farm Credit Act of 1959	1959-2 CB 685
86-175	8-21-59	Providing Federal Estate Tax deduction for certain transfers to charities subjected to foreign death taxes	1959-2 CB 686
86-245	9-9-59	Transferring funds to Ute Mountain Tribe	1959-2 CB 688
86-246	9-9-59	Providing per capita distribution of funds to Siletz Indians	1959-2 CB 688
86-280	9-16-59	Extending period for filing claims for credit or refund of overpayments of income taxes from renegotiation of government contracts	1959-2 CB 689
86-319	9-21-59	Exempting from the admissions tax certain athletic games	1959-2 CB 690
86-322	9-21-59	Providing a division of tribal assets of the Catawba Indians	1959-2 CB 691
86-330	9-21-59	Providing payments to the Kiowa, Comanche, and Apache tribes	1959-2 CB 693
86-339	9-21-59	Providing equalization of allotments on the Ague Caliente Reservation	1959-2 CB 694
86-342	9-21-59	Federal-Aid Highway Act of 1959	1959-2 CB 697
86-344	9-21-59	Amending certain excise tax laws	1959-2 CB 700
86-346	9-22-59	Permitting interest rate increases of series E and H savings bonds, and amending certain provisions relating to exchanges of government securities	1959-2 CB 703
86-368	9-22-59	Providing a Chief Counsel for the Internal Revenue Service	1959-2 CB 705
86-376	9-23-59	Providing for a personal exemption for children placed for adoption and clarifying certain provisions relating to the election of small business corporations	1959-2 CB 707
	**Statutes Enacted by the 86th Congress—2nd Session**		
86-413	4-8-60	Amending Code Sec 4021 to delete "Aromatic cachous"	1960-1 CB 786
86-416	4-8-60	Relating to tax on issuance of shares or certificates of regulated investment companies	1960-1 CB 786
86-418	4-8-60	Exempting bicycle tires and tubes used in manufacture of new bicycles	1960-1 CB 786
86-422	4-8-60	Reducing cabaret tax to 10%	1960-1 CB 788
86-428	4-22-60	Exempting certain non-profit corporations	1960-1 CB 789
86-429	4-22-60	Narcotics Manufacturing Act of 1960	1960-1 CB 789
86-432	4-22-60	Continuing suspension of tax on certain oils	1960-1 CB 792
86-435	4-22-60	Treatment of corporate royalties—personal holding company tax	1960-1 CB 792
86-437	4-22-60	Excluding certain payments to non-resident aliens from gross income	1960-1 CB 794
86-440	4-22-60	Tax of 1 cent per pound on laminated tires	1960-1 CB 795
86-459	5-13-60	Providing method of paying tax by dealers having reserve income	1960-1 CB 795
86-470	5-14-60	Procedure for assessing certain tax additions, and other purposes	1960-1 CB 800
86-478	6-1-60	Relating to the tax on firearms	1960-1 CB 801
86-496	6-8-60	Providing for nontaxability of certain discharge of indebtedness of railroads	1960-2 CB 680
86-564	6-30-60	Public Debt and Tax Rate Extension Act of 1960	1960-2 CB 681
86-592	7-6-60	Amending Sugar Act of 1948	1960-2 CB 685
86-594	7-6-60	Amending Code Sec. 615(c) relating to deduction of exploration expenditures	1960-2 CB 685
86-624	7-12-60	Hawaii Omnibus Act	1960-2 CB 686
86-631	7-12-60	Amending 11 U.S.C. 1078 Bankruptcy Act	1960-2 CB 687
86-667	7-14-60	Amending unemployment trusts tax provisions	1960-2 CB 687
86-707	9-6-60	Amending Code Sec. 912	1960-2 CB 690
86-723	9-8-60	Amending Foreign Service Act	1960-2 CB 691
86-733	9-8-60	Amending Menominee Termination Act	1960-2 CB 691
86-761	9-13-60	Conveying land to Potawatomi Indians	1960-2 CB 692
86-778	9-13-60	Social Security Amendments of 1960	1960-2 CB 693
86-779	9-14-60	Amending Code Sec. 5701 and other sections of the Internal Revenue Code of 1954	1960-2 CB 709
86-780	9-14-60	Amending foreign tax credit overall limitation	1960-2 CB 720
86-781	9-14-60	Relating to treatment of local advertising to fix manufacturers' sales price	1960-2 CB 726
86-791	9-14-60	Conveying land to Cheyenne and Arapaho Indians	1960-2 CB 730

Amending Acts

Public Law No.	Date	Title or Subject	Reprint
	**Statutes Enacted by the 87th Congress—1st Session**		
87-4	3-22-61	Prescribes time for Joint Committee to file renegotiation report	1961-1 CB 854
87-6	3-24-61	Temporary Extended Unemployment Compensation Act of 1961	1961-1 CB 854
87-15	3-31-61	Amending Sugar Act of 1954	1961-1 CB 855
87-24	4-24-61	Providing Funds to Nez Perce Tribe	1960-1 CB 856
87-29	5-4-61	Exempting income derived by a foreign central bank	1960-2 CB 307
87-59	6-27-61	Qualification of Union Fund Code Sec. 401(a)	1961-2 CB 308
87-61	6-29-61	Federal-Aid Highway Act of 1961	1961-2 CB 309
87-64	6-30-61	Social Security Amendments of 1961	1961-2 CB 315
87-72	6-30-61	Tax Rate Extension Act of 1961	1961-2 CB 317
87-109	7-26-61	Prepaid dues of certain membership organizations as gross income	1961-2 CB 318
87-205	9-6-61	Providing funds to Potawatomi Tribe	1961-2 CB 320
87-235	9-14-61	Disposition of funds of the Omaha Tribe of Indians	1961-2 CB 320
87-256	9-21-61	Mutual Educational and Cultural Exchange Act of 1961	1961-2 CB 322
87-262	9-21-61	Defining employment in certain hospitals transferred	1961-2 CB 333
87-293	9-22-61	Peace Corps Act	1961-2 CB 336
87-298	9-26-61	Authorizing use of funds of Colville Tribe	1961-2 CB 338
87-312	9-26-61	Determining gross income manufacture of clay products	1961-2 CB 339
87-321	9-26-61	Amending unemployment tax credit; percentage depletion	1961-2 CB 341
87-370	10-4-61	Annuities for public school teachers and Tax Court judges' dependents	1961-2 CB 344
87-397	10-5-61	Taxpayer account numbers	1961-2 CB 348
	**Statutes Enacted by the 87th Congress—2nd Session**		
87-403	2-2-62	Distributors of stock pursuant to an order enforcing the antitrust laws	1962-1 CB 370
87-426	3-31-62	Treatment of casualty losses in disaster areas	1962-1 CB 374
87-456	5-24-62	Tariff Classification Act of 1962	1962-3 CB 57
87-508	6-28-62	Tax Rate Extension Act of 1962	1962-3 CB 58
87-520	7-3-62	Extension of the Renegotiation Act of 1951	1962-3 CB 64
87-535	7-13-62	Sugar Act Amendments of 1962	1962-3 CB 65
87-629	9-5-62	Division of tribal assets of Ponca Tribe	1962-3 CB 65
87-682	9-25-62	Estimated income tax treatment extended to fishermen	1962-3 CB 68
87-710	9-27-62	Providing a seven-year net operating loss carryover for certain regulated transportation corporations	1961-3 CB 69
87-722	9-28-62	Amending law concerning Currency Comptroller	1962-3 CB 70
87-734	10-3-62	Division of assets Lower Brule Sioux Tribe	1962-3 CB 71
87-735	10-3-62	Division of assets of Crow Creek Sioux Tribe	1962-3 CB 78
87-768	10-9-62	Relating to personal holding company tax on consumer finance companies	1962-3 CB 85
87-770	10-9-62	Relating to definition of "advertising" for excise tax purposes	1962-3 CB 86
87-775	10-9-62	Division of tribal assets of Cherokee Nation	1962-3 CB 86
87-790	10-10-62	Relating to tax on life insurance companies	1962-3 CB 88
87-792	10-10-62	Self employed Individuals Tax Retirement Act of 1962	1962-3 CB 89
87-794	10-11-62	Trade Expansion Act of 1962	1962-3 CB 107
87-834	10-15-62	Revenue Act of 1962	1962-3 CB 111
87-846	10-22-62	Amending 1948 War Claims Act	
87-858	10-23-62	Relating to manufacturers excise tax, charitable contributions, and life insurance companies taxes	1962-3 CB 206
87-859	10-23-62	Suspending the tax on palm and coconut oils	1962-3 CB 210
87-863	10-23-62	Increasing the amounts allowable on medical and dental expense deductions	1962-3 CB 210
87-870	10-23-62	Income tax treatment of terminal railroad corporations	1962-3 CB 213
87-876	10-24-62	Relating to limitation on retirement income	1962-3 CB 217
	**Statutes Enacted by the 88th Congress—1st Session**		
88-4	4-2-63	Child Care expenses for deserted wives	1963-1 CB 412
88-9	4-10-63	Tax treatment of redeemable ground rents	1963-1 CB 412
88-31	5-29-63	Federal unemployment rate change	1963-1 CB 414
88-36	6-4-63	Silver bullion transfer tax repeal	1963-2 CB 696
88-52	6-29-63	Tax Extension Act of 1963	1963-2 CB 697
88-133	10-5-63	Amending Railroad Retirement Tax Act, etc	1963-2 CB 698
88-153	10-17-63	Deductibility of accrual vacation pay	1963-2 CB 699
88-173	11-7-63	Amending Federal Unemployment Tax Act, etc	1963-2 CB 699
88-180	11-16-63	Implementing Organic Act of Guam	1963-2 CB 701
88-231	12-23-63	Division of tribal assets of Kootenai Tribe	1964-1 (Part 2) CB 5

Amending Acts

Public Law No.	Date	Title or Subject	Reprint
	**Statutes Enacted by the 88th Congress — 2nd Session**		
88-272	2-26-64	Revenue Act of 1964	1964-1 (Part 2) CB 6
88-300	4-29-64	American-Mexican Chamizal Convention Act of 1964	1964-1 (Part 2) CB 110
88-339	6-30-64	Extension of Renegotiation Act of 1951	1964-2 CB 593
88-342	6-30-64	Preventing double tax on tobacco	1964-2 CB 593
88-348	6-30-64	Excise Tax Rate Extension Act of 1964	1964-2 CB 594
88-380	7-17-64	Unrelated business taxable income	1964-2 CB 596
88-412	8-10-64	Division of assets of Lower Pend D'Oreille or Kailspel Indians	1964-2 CB 597
88-421	8-11-64	Division of assets of Potawatomi Indians	1964-2 CB 597
88-428	8-14-64	Amending Missing Persons Act	1964-2 CB 600
88-457	8-20-64	Division of assets of Shawnee Indians	1964-2 CB 602
88-461	8-20-64	Division of Assets of Cherokees	1964-2 CB 603
88-464	8-20-64	Division of assets of certain Oregon Indians	1964-2 CB 603
88-474	8-21-64	Division of judgement assets of Pawnee Indians	1964-2 CB 604
88-484	8-22-64	Collapsible corporations and inclusion of rents in personal holding company income	1964-2 CB 605
88-506	8-30-64	Division of assets of Tillamook Indians	1964-2 CB 607
88-528	8-31-64	Patronage refunds to be paid in cash	1962-2 CB 608
88-533	8-31-64	Division of Asset of members of Seneca Nation	1964-2 CB 608
88-539	8-31-64	Amending law relating to total contract price personalty sold on installment	1964-2 CB 610
88-551	8-31-64	Division of funds of Confederated Tribes of Colville Reservation	1964-2 CB 611
88-554	8-31-64	Continuing rule relating to deductibility of accrued vacation pay	1964-2 CB 612
88-559	9-1-64	Division of funds of Cheyene Tribe	1964-2 CB 615
88-563	9-2-64	Interest Equalization Tax Act	1964-2 CB 615
88-570	9-2-64	Amending law relating to reacquisitions of realty and to installment obligations	1964-2 CB 647
88-571	9-2-64	Amending law relating to life insurance company tax inequities	1964-2 CB 649
88-611	10-2-64	Exemption of gifts to Commerce Dept	1964-2 CB 655
88-650	10-13-64	Amending certain self-employment tax	1964-2 CB 656
88-653	10-13-64	Amending fruit-flavor concentrates provisions	1964-2 CB 658
88-663	10-13-64	Division of assets of Chippewas	1964-2 CB 659
	**Statutes Enacted by the 89th Congress — 1st Session**		
89-28	5-27-65	Disposition of judgement funds of Quinaielt Tribe	1965-2 CB 568
89-44	6-21-65	Excise Tax Reduction Act of 1965	1965-2 CB 568
89-97	7-30-65	Social Security Amendments of 1965	1965-2 CB 601
89-130	8-19-65	Disposition of judgement funds of Tlingit and Haida Indians of Alaska	1965-2 CB 619
89-134	8-24-65	Peace Corps Act	1965-2 CB 621
89-184	9-15-65	Amending the Federal Firearms Act	1965-2 CB 621
89-209	9-29-65	National Foundation on the Arts and the Humanities Act of 1965	1965-2 CB 622
89-212	9-29-65	Amending the Railroad Retirement Act of 1937 and the Railroad Retirement Tax Act	1965-2 CB 623
89-224	10-1-65	Disposition of tribal assets of Klamath, Modoc, and Yakooskin Indians	1965-2 CB 626
89-243	10-9-65	Interest Equalization Tax Extension Act Of 1965	1965-2 CB 627
89-331	11-8-65	Sugar Act Amendments of 1965	1965-2 CB 639
89-332	11-8-65	To provide for the right persons to be represented in matters before Federal Agencies	1965-2 CB 640
	**Statutes Enacted by the 89th Congress — 2nd Session**		
89-352	2-2-66	To expand exemption of credit unions	1966-1 CB 375
89-354	2-2-66	Fixing new method of Tax Court Judges retired pay	1966-1 CB 376
89-359	3-7-66	To amend certain estate tax provisions of the Internal Revenue Code of 1939	1966-1 CB 376
89-365	3-8-66	Tax treatment of amounts paid to certain members of uniformed services and their survivors	1966-1 CB 377
89-368	3-15-66	Tax Adjustment Act of 1966	1966-1 CB 379
89-384	4-8-66	To provide recovery of losses from foreign expropriation, etc	1966-1 CB 414
89-389	4-14-66	To amend subchapter S of the 1954 Code	1966-1 CB 419
89-429	5-24-66	To promote private financing of credit needs	1966-2 CB 593
89-480	6-30-66	To extend the Renegotiation Act of 1951	1966-2 CB 594
89-493	7-5-66	To transfer certain duties of U.S. District Court to other agencies	1966-2 CB 594
89-495	7-5-66	To amend the Bankruptcy Act	1966-2 CB 595
89-496	7-5-66	Limiting the priority and nondeductibility of taxes in bankruptcy	1966-2 CB 598
89-523	8-1-66	Amending excise taxes on tires and tubes	1966-2 CB 599
89-570	9-12-66	Treatment of exploration expenditures in the case of mining	1966-2 CB 600
89-621	10-4-66	Treatment of disclaimers in computing marital deduction for estate tax purposes	1966-2 CB 604
89-642	10-11-66	Child Nutrition Act of 1966	1966-2 CB 606

Amending Acts

Public Law No.	Date	Title or Subject	Reprint
89-655	10-14-66	Disposition of Quileute tribal funds	1966-2 CB 606
89-656	10-14-66	Disposition of Nooksack tribal funds	1966-2 CB 608
89-659	10-14-66	Disposition of Miami tribal funds	1966-2 CB 609
89-660	10-14-66	Disposition of Dumanish tribal funds	1966-2 CB 611
89-661	10-14-66	Disposition of Otoe and Missouria tribal funds	1966-2 CB 612
89-663	10-14-66	Disposition of Skokomis tribal funds	1966-2 CB 612
89-670	10-15-66	Exemption of gifts to Department of Transportation	1966-2 CB 613
89-692	10-15-66	Continues rules on accrued vacation pay	1966-2 CB 614
89-699	10-30-66	Amends various railroad retirement provisions	1966-2 CB 614
89-700	10-30-66	Amends other railroad retirement provisions	1966-2 CB 615
89-713	11-2-66	Promotes savings under IRS data processing	1966-2 CB 617
89-717	11-2-66	Disposition of Omaha tribal funds	1966-2 CB 622
89-719	11-2-66	Federal Tax Lien Act of 1966	1966-2 CB 623
89-721	11-2-66	Interest on tax refunds	1966-2 CB 643
89-722	11-2-66	Reserve deduction for certain guaranteed debts	1966-2 CB 645
89-739	11-2-66	Increase excludible combat pay	1966-2 CB 647
89-774	11-6-66	Amending the Washington Metropolitan Area Transit Regulation Compact	1966-2 CB 647
89-793	11-8-66	Narcotic Addict Rehabilitation Act of 1966	1966-2 CB 648
89-800	11-8-66	Suspends investment credits and accelerated depreciation	1966-2 CB 649
89-809	11-13-66	Tax treatment of foreign investments in United States ("Foreign Investors Tax Act of 1966")	1966-2 CB 656

Statutes Enacted by the 90th Congress — 1st Session

90-11	4-22-67	Disposition of Salish and Kootenai tribal funds	1967-1 CB 427
90-26	6-13-67	To restore the investment credit and the allowance of accelerated depreciation	1967-2 CB 481
90-59	7-31-67	Interest Equalization Tax Extension Act of 1967	1967-2 CB 482
90-60	8-1-67	Disposition of Ute Indian tribal funds	1967-2 CB 499
90-63	8-11-67	Disposition of Otawa tribal funds	1967-2 CB 500
90-73	8-29-67	Technical amendments to interest equalization tax	1967-2 CB 501
90-78	8-31-67	Dependency exemption for children of divorced parents	1967-2 CB 502
90-80	8-31-67	Disposition of Sac and Fox Tribal funds	1967-2 CB 503
90-93	9-27-67	Disposition of Emigrant New York Indian tribal funds	1967-2 CB 504
90-94	9-27-64	Disposition of Minnesota Chippewa tribal funds	1967-2 CB 505
90-114	10-24-67	Disposition of Chelais tribal funds	1967-2 CB 506
90-117	10-31-67	Disposition of Cheyene-Arapaho tribal funds	1967-2 CB 507
90-199	12-14-67	Disposition of Iowa Tribes of Kansas and Nebraska of Oklahoma tribal funds	1968-1 CB 639
90-209	12-18-67	To establish the National Park Foundation	1968-1 CB 639
90-225	12-27-67	Tax treatment of certain distributions pursuant to Bank Holding Company Act	1968-1 CB 640
90-237	1-2-68	To amend the Subversive Activities Control Act of 1950	1968-1 CB 643
90-240	1-2-68	Duty-free status of certain gifts by members of the Armed Forces and for other purposes	1968-1 CB 644
90-248	1-2-68	Social Security Act of 1967	1968-1 CB 648

Statutes Enacted by the 90th Congress — 2nd Session

90-266	3-12-68	To authorize the consolidation and use of funds arising form judgement in favor of the Apache Tribe of the Mescalero Reservation and each of its constituent groups	1968-1 CB 657
90-278	3-30-68	Disposition of Yakima tribal funds	1968-1 CB 657
90-279	3-30-68	Disposition of Chilocco Indian school lands	1968-1 CB 658
90-285	4-12-68	To continue temporarily the excise tax rates on automobiles and communication services	1968-1 CB 659
90-310	5-18-68	To convey certain federally owned lands to the Cheyenne and Arapaho Tribes of Oklahoma	1968-1 CB 661
90-355	6-10-68	To authorize purchase, sale and exchange of lands on Spokane Indian Reservation	1968-2 CB 709
90-337	6-10-68	Distribution of Spokane tribal funds	1968-2 CB 710
90-346	6-18-68	Advertising in a convention program of a national political convention [Repealed by PL93-625, I-3-75]	1968-2 CB 711
90-364	6-28-68	Revenue and Expenditure Control Act of 1968	1968-2 CB 715
90-448	8-1-68	Housing and Urban Development Act of 1968	1968-2 CB 734
90-504	9-21-68	Disposition of tribal funds of Creek Nation of Indians	1968-2 CB 737
90-506	9-21-68	Disposition of tribal funds of Creek Nation of Indians	1968-2 CB 738
90-507	9-21-68	Disposition of California tribal funds	1968-2 CB 739
90-508	9-21-68	Disposition of Funds of Delaware Nation of Indians	1968-2 CB 741
90-527	9-28-68	Disposition of Kiowa, Comanche, and Apache tribal funds	1968-2 CB 742
90-529	9-28-68	Disposition of Quechan tribal funds	1968-2 CB 743
90-530	9-28-68	Disposition of Muchleshoot tribal funds	1968-2 CB 743
90-531	9-28-68	Disposition of funds of confederated tribes of Colville Reservation	1968-2 CB 746
90-537	9-30-68	Colorado River Basin Project Act	1968-2 CB 745
90-584	10-17-68	Disposition of Southern Paiute tribal funds	1968-2 CB 746

Amending Acts

Public Law No.	Date	Title or Subject	Reprint
90-607	10-21-68	To provide an effective date for a 1966 law change	1968-2 CB 748
90-615	10-21-68	To continue existing suspension of duties on certain alumina and bauxite	1968-2 CB 748
90-618	10-22-68	Gun Control Act of 1968	1968-2 CB 749
90-619	10-22-68	To facilitate the production of wine	1968-2 CB 768
90-621	10-22-68	Treatment of certain statutory mergers of corporations	1968-2 CB 769
90-622	10-22-68	Treatment of income from operation of communications satellite	1968-2 CB 770
90-624	10-22-68	Amending the Railroad Retirement Tax Act	1968-2 CB 771
90-630	10-22-68	Amending certain provisions relating to distilled spirits	1968-2 CB 772
90-634	10-24-68	Renegotiation Amendments Act of 1968	1968-2 CB 775

Statutes Enacted by the 91st Congress — 1st Session

91-36	6-30-69	To continue for one month the existing rates of withholding of income tax	1969-3 CB 1
91-50	8-2-69	To continue the existing interest equalization tax	1969-3 CB 1
91-53	8-7-69	Surcharge extension and collection of Federal unemployment tax	1969-3 CB 1
91-65	8-25-69	To continue the existing interest equalization tax	1969-3 CB 4
91-75	9-29-69	Disposition of Salish and Kootenai tribal funds	1969-3 CB 5
91-128	11-26-69	Interest Equalization Tax Extension Act of 1969	1969-3 CB 5
91-130	12-1-69	To amend the Second Liberty Bond Act	1969-3 CB 9
91-160	12-24-69	To organize and hold a diplomatic conference and to negotiate a Patent Cooperation Treaty	83 Stat. 443
91-172	12-30-69	Tax Reform Act of 1969	1969-3 CB 10

Statutes Enacted by the 91st Congress — 2nd Session

91-215	3-17-70	To amend the Railroad Retirement Tax Act	1970-1 CB 360
91-235	4-24-70	To provide that individuals illegally detained in North Korea be treated as serving in combat zone	1970-1 CB 360
91-258	5-21-70	Airport and Airway Revenue Act of 1970	1970-1 CB 361
91-259	5-21-70	Disposition of Umatilla Indian tribal funds	1970-2 CB 343
91-264	5-22-70	To further the economic advancement of Hopi Indian tribe	1970-2 CB 344
91-283	6-19-70	Disposition of Sioux and tribal funds	1970-2 CB 345
91-290	6-25-70	Extending the period of restriction on Quapaw Indian Lands	84 Stat. 325
91-335	7-13-70	Disposition of tribal funds of Tlingit and Haida Indians of Alaska	1970-2 CB 347
91-346	7-20-70	To amend the National Foundation on the Arts and Humanities Act of 1965	84 Stat. 443
91-351	7-24-70	Emergency Home Finance Act of 1970	1970-2 CB 347
91-364	7-30-70	Disposition of tribal funds of Weas, Piankashaws, Peorias and Kaskaskias	1970-2 CB 347
91-373	8-10-70	Employment Security Amendments of 1970	1970-2 CB 348
91-400	9-16-70	Disposition of judgment funds of Hualapai tribe	1970-2 CB 361
91-401	9-16-70	Disposition of judgment funds of Potawatomi Indians	1970-2 CB 361
91-404	9-19-70	Disposition of Sac and Fox tribal funds	1970-2 CB 361
91-413	9-25-70	Disposition of Yakima tribal funds	1970-2 CB 361
91-417	9-25-70	Disposition of Chemehuevi tribal funds	1970-2 CB 362
91-420	9-25-70	Disposition of tribal funds of Confederated bands of Ute Indians	1970-2 CB 362
91-452	10-15-70	Control of organized crime in U.S.	1970-2 CB 363
91-469	10-21-70	To amend the Merchant Marine Act, 1936	1970-2 CB 372
91-478	10-21-70	To convey certain federally owned land to the Cherokee Tribe of Oklahoma	84 Stat. 1074
91-513	10-27-70	Comprehensive Drug Abuse Prevention and Control Act of 1970	1970-2 CB 376
91-518	10-30-70	Rail Passenger Service Act of 1970	1970-2 CB 381
91-575	12-24-70	Consenting to the Susquehanna River Basin Compact	1971-1 CB 529
91-598	12-30-70	Securities Investor Protection Act of 1970	1971-1 CB 530
91-605	12-31-70	Federal-Aid Highway Act of 1970	1971-1 CB 531
91-606	12-31-70	Disaster Relief Act of 1970	1971-1 CB 532
91-614	12-31-70	Excise, Estate and Gift Tax Adjustment Act of 1970	1971-1 CB 533
91-617	12-30-70	To provide interest on certain insured loans sold out of Agricultural Credit Insurance Fund	1971-1 CB 539
91-618	12-31-70	Clarifying exemption from income taxation of cemetery corporations	1971-1 CB 539
91-642	12-31-70	To extend the period for filing certain manufacturers claims for floor stocks refunds	1971-1 CB 539
91-646	1-2-71	Uniform Relocation Assistance and Real Property Acquisition Policies Act of 1970	1971-1 CB 540
91-659	1-8-71	To amend '54 Code relating to distilled spirits	1971-1 CB 542
91-673	1-12-71	To amend provisions of '54 Code relating to beer	1971-1 CB 544
91-675	1-12-71	To amend Sec. 905 of the '69 Tax Reform Act	1971-1 CB 545
91-676	1-12-71	To allow leasing of aircraft for temporary use outside the U.S. with recapture of investment credit	1971-1 CB 545
91-677	1-12-71	Treatment of losses sustained though confiscation of property by Cuban government	1971-1 CB 546
91-678	1-12-71	To provide floor stocks refunds in case of cement mixers	1971-1 CB 547
91-679	1-12-71	Relating to joint income tax returns by husband and wife	1971-1 CB 547
91-680	1-12-71	To extend the application of Code Sec. 2789 from citrus groves to almond groves	1971-1 CB 548

Amending Acts

Public Law No.	Date	Title or Subject	Reprint
91-681	1-12-71	To amend 1954 Code Sec. 367 relating to foreign corporations	1971-1 CB 548
91-683	1-12-71	To amend Code Sec. 1372 relating to passive investment income	1971-1 CB 549
91-684	1-12-71	To amend 1954 Code Secs. 902(b) and (c) to reduce the 50-percent requirement to 10-percent between first and second levels and to include third level foreign corporations in the tax credit structure if the 10-percent test is met	1971-1 CB 550
91-686	1-12-71	Relating to the income tax treatment of certain sales of real property by a corporation	1971-1 CB 550
91-687	1-12-71	To provide for treatment of losses on worthless securities	1971-1 CB 551
91-688	1-12-71	Relating to consolidated returns of life insurance companies	1971-1 CB 552
91-691	1-12-71	Relating to period of qualification of certain union-negotiated pension plans	1971-1 CB 552
91-693	1-12-71	Relating to certain statutory mergers	1971-1 CB 553

Statutes Enacted by the 92nd Congress — 1st Session

Public Law No.	Date	Title or Subject	Reprint
92-5	3-17-71	To increase the public debt limit	1971-1 CB 553
92-9	4-1-71	Interest Equalization Act of 1971	1971-1 CB 554
92-12	5-7-71	To amend the Rural Electrification Act of 1936, as amended	1971-2 CB 491
92-29	6-23-71	Disposition of funds of the Iowa Tribe of Oklahoma, Kansas and Nebraska Indians	1971-2 CB 491
92-30	6-23-71	Disposition of funds of the Snohomish, Upper Skagit, Snoquamic and Skykomish tribal funds	1971-2 CB 492
92-41	7-1-71	Amending the Renegotiation Act of 1951	1971-2 CB 492
92-59	7-29-71	Disposition of the funds of the Pembina Band of Chippewa Indians	1971-2 CB 494
92-138	10-14-71	Sugar Act Amendments of 1971	1971-2 CB 495
92-164	11-23-71	Disposition of funds of the Pueblo of Laguna Indians	1972-1 CB 442
92-178	12-10-71	Revenue Act of 1971	1972-1 CB 443
92-181	12-10-71	Farm Credit Act of 1971	1972-2 CB 663
92-203	12-18-71	Alaska Native Claims Settlement Act	1972-1 CB 490
92-206	12-18-71	Apportionment of Shoshone tribal funds	1972-1 CB 495

Statutes Enacted by the 92nd Congress — 2nd Session

Public Law No.	Date	Title or Subject	Reprint
92-244	3-9-72	Disposition of funds of the Confederated Tribes of the Colville Reservation	1972-1 CB 496
92-253	3-17-72	Disposition of funds of the Salish and Kootenai Tribes	1972-1 CB 497
92-254	3-18-72	Disposition of funds of the Blackfeet and Gros Ventre Tribes	1972-1 CB 497
92-258	3-22-72	To amend the Older Americans Act of 1965	86 Stat. 88
92-279	4-26-72	Income tax exclusion for Vietnam prisoners of war	1972-1 CB 498
92-295	5-16-72	Disposition of funds of the Jicarilla Apache Tribe	1972-2 CB 669
92-309	6-2-72	Disposition of funds of the Miami Tribe of Oklahoma and the Miami Indians of Indiana	1972-2 CB 669
92-310	6-6-72	To provide that the Federal Government shall assume the risks of its fidelity losses	1972-2 CB 670
92-329	6-30-72	To extend the emergency unemployment compensation program	1972-2 CB 671
92-336	7-1-72	To increase Social Security benefits	1972-2 CB 672
92-349	7-13-72	To amend the National Transportation Act of 1969	1972-2 CB 674
92-418	8-29-72	Exempt status of veterans' organizations	1972-2 CB 675
92-419	8-30-72	Rural Development Act of 1972	1972-2 CB 676
92-438	9-29-72	Disposition of funds of Havasupai Tribe	1972-2 CB 678
92-442	9-29-72	Disposition of funds of Shoshone-Bannock tribal funds	1972-2 CB 678
92-456	10-3-72	Disposition of funds of Delaware Tribe	1972-2 CB 678
92-461	10-6-72	Disposition of Yavapai Apache tribal funds	1972-2 CB 679
92-462	10-6-72	Disposition of Pueblo de Acoma tribal funds	1972-2 CB 680
92-467	10-6-72	Disposition of Kickapoo tribal funds	1972-2 CB 680
92-468	10-6-72	Disposition of Yankton Sioux tribal funds	1972-2 CB 681
92-500	10-18-72	Federal Water Pollution Control Act Amendments of 1972	1972-2 CB 681
92-512	10-20-72	State and Local Assistance Act of 1972	1972-2 CB 684
92-526	10-21-72	Relating to the Administrative Conference of the U.S.	1972-2 CB 701
92-552	10-25-72	Authorizing the City of Clinton Bridge Commission to convey its bridge structures and other assets to the State of Iowa	1973-1 CB 707
92-555	10-25-72	Disposition of trial funds of Mississippi Sioux Indians	1973-1 CB 708
92-557	10-25-72	Disposition of tribal funds of the Assiniboine Indians	1973-1 CB 709
92-558	10-25-72	To provide funds for certain wildlife restoration projects	1972-2 CB 701
92-578	10-27-72	Pennsylvania Avenue Development Corporation Act of 1972	1973-1 CB 710
92-580	10-27-72	Personal exemption in the case of American Samoans	1972-2 CB 703
92-586	10-27-72	Disposition of tribal funds of the Osage Indians	1973-1 CB 711
92-603	10-30-72	Social Security Amendments of 1972	1972-2 CB 703
92-606	10-31-72	Coordination of U.S. and Guam individual income taxes	1972-2 CB 709

Amending Acts

Public Law No.	Date	Title or Subject	Reprint
	**Statutes Enacted by the 93rd Congress — 1st Session**
93-17	4-10-73	Interest Equalization Tax Extension Act of 1973	1973-1 CB 712
93-29	5-3-73	"Older Americans Comprehensive Services Amendments of 1973"	1973-2 CB 437
93-53	7-1-73	Income tax treatment of payments to Presidential Election Campaign Fund	1973-2 CB 438
93-66	7-9-73	To extend the Renegotiation Act of 1951	1973-1 CB 439
93-69	7-10-73	To amend the Railroad Retirement Act of 1937 and the Railroad Retirement Tax Act	1973-2 CB 440
93-113	10-1-73	Domestic Volunteer Service Act of 1973	1973-2 CB 441
93-116	10-1-73	To amend the Merchant Marine Act, 1936	87 Stat. 421
93-129	10-19-73	Board for International Broadcasting Act of 1973	87 Stat. 456
93-133	10-19-73	National Foundation on the Arts and Humanities Amendments of 1973	87 Stat. 461
93-134	10-19-73	Disposition of funds of Indian claims	1973-2 CB 445
93-161	11-27-73	To amend the International Organizations Immunities Act	1974-1 CB 377
93-197	12-22-73	Menominee Restoration Act	1974-1 CB 377
93-198	12-24-73	District of Columbia Self-Government and Governmental Reorganization Act	1974-1 CB 378
93-203	12-28-73	Comprehensive Employment and Training Act of 1973	1974-1 CB 379
93-224	12-29-73	Federal Financing Bank Act of 1973	1974-1 CB 379
93-233	12-31-73	To increase Social Security benefits	1974-1 CB 380
	**Statutes Enacted by the 93rd Congress — 2nd Session**
93-236	1-2-74	Regional Rail Reorganization Act of 1973	1974-1 CB 383
93-286	5-21-74	To amend PL 90-335 relating to the purchase, sale and exchange of certain lands on the Spokane Indian Reservation	1974-2 CB 414
93-288	5-22-74	Disaster Relief Act of 1974	1974-2 CB 414
93-310	6-8-74	To amend Code Sec. 501 relating to exemption from tax on corporations, etc.	1974-2 CB 415
93-313	6-8-74	To delay for six months the taking effect of certain measures to provide additional funds for certain wildlife restoration projects	1974-2 CB 417
93-329	6-30-74	To extend the Renegotiation Act of 1951	1974-2 CB 417
93-355	7-25-74	To provide exemption for Legal Services Corp	1974-2 CB 417
93-368	8-7-74	Exempting from duty certain equipment and repairs for vessels, etc.	1974-2 CB 418
93-383	8-22-74	Housing and Community Development Act of 1974	1974-2 CB 418
93-387	8-24-74	Council on Wage and Price Stability Act	1974-2 CB 420
93-406	9-2-74	Employee Retirement Income Security Act of 1974 (ERISA)	1974-3 CB 1
93-443	10-15-74	Federal Election Campaign Act Amendments of 1974	1974-2 CB 421
93-445	10-16-74	To amend the Railroad Retirement Act of 1937	1974-2 CB 440
93-480	10-26-74	Treatment of life insurance company dividends for personal holding company consolidated return purposes	1974-2 CB 442
93-482	10-26-74	Accounts receivables of related DISCs and low income housing	1974-2 CB 444
93-483	10-26-74	Armed Forces Scholarships, Insurance Company guarantees and premature withdrawals from term accounts	1974-2 CB 447
93-490	10-26-74	Application of moving expense provisions to members of U.S. military services, etc.	1974-2 CB 451
93-496	10-28-74	To amend the Rail Passenger Service Act of 1970	88 Stat. 1526
93-497	10-29-74	Basis adjustment for property received in liquidation prior to 7-1-57	1974-2 CB 455
93-499	10-29-74	Wagering tax amendments	1974-2 CB 456
93-531	12-22-74	Providing for final settlement of the conflicting rights and interests of the Hopi and Navajo Tribes	1975-1 CB 425
93-597	1-2-75	Tax treatment of members of the Armed Forces of the United States and civilian employees who are prisoners of war or missing in action	1975-1 CB 495
93-618	1-3-75	Trade Act of 1974	1975-1 CB 501
93-625	1-3-75	To amend the tariff schedules of the U.S., etc.	1975-1 CB 510
96-644	1-4-75	Headstart, Economic Opportunity, and Community Partnership Act of 1974	1975-1 CB 542
93-647	1-4-75	Social Services Amendments of 1974	1975-1 CB 543
	**Statutes Enacted by the 94th Congress — 1st Session**
94-12	3-29-75	Tax Reduction Act of 1975	1975-1 CB 545
94-45	6-30-75	Emergency Compensation and Special Unemployment Assistance Extension Act of 1975	1975-2 CB 513
94-46	6-30-75	To amend PL 93-647	1975-2 CB 526
94-81	8-9-75	Treatment of Condemnation proceeds from forest lands held in trust for the Klamath Indian Tribe, etc.	1975-2 CB 526
94-92	8-9-75	To amend the Railroad Unemployment Insurance Act	1975-2 CB 528
94-93	8-9-75	Amendments to the Railroad Retirement Tax Act	1975-2 CB 528
94-114	10-17-75	Treatment of certain submarginal land held in trust for certain Indian tribes	1975-2 CB 529
94-118	10-20-75	Japan-United States Friendship Act	89 Stat. 603
94-129	11-13-75	Gifts or devises to the National Arboretum	1975-2 CB 531

Amending Acts

Public Law No.	Date	Title or Subject	Reprint
94-164	12-23-75	Revenue Adjustment Act of 1975	1976-1 CB 486
94-168	12-23-75	Metric Conversion Act of 1975	1976-1 CB 502
94-182	12-31-75	To amend the Social Security Act	1976-1 CB 490
94-185	12-31-75	To extend the Renegotiation Act of 1951	1976-1 CB 502
94-189	12-31-75	Disposition of Sac and Fox Tribes fund	1976-1 CB 502
94-202	1-2-76	To amend the Social Security Act	1976-1 CB 503
94-204	1-2-76	To amend the Alaska Native Claims Settlement Act	89 Stat. 1145

Statutes Enacted by the 94th Congress—2nd Session

Public Law No.	Date	Title or Subject	Reprint
94-236	3-19-76	Application of certain provisions of the '54 Code to specified transactions by certain public employee retirement systems created by the State of New York or any of its political subdivisions	1976-1 CB 507
94-241	3-24-76	To approve the "Covenant to Establish a Commonwealth of the Northern Mariana Islands in Political Union with the U.S.A."	1976-1 CB 513
94-253	3-31-76	Tax treatment for exchanges under the final system plan for ConRail	1976-1 CB 520
94-267	4-15-76	To permit tax-free rollovers of distribution from employee retirement plans in the event of plan termination	1976-1 CB 527
94-273	4-21-76	Fiscal Year Adjustment Act	1976-2 CB 517
94-274	4-21-76	Fiscal Year Transition Act	1976-2 CB 518
94-280	5-5-76	Authorizing appropriations for the construction of certain highways in accordance with Title 23 of the U.S. Code	1976-2 CB 518
94-283	5-11-76	Federal Election Campaign Act Amendments of 1976	1976-2 CB 522
94-331	6-30-76	To amend '54 Code Sec 815	1976-2 CB 28
94-396	9-3-76	To amend '54 Code Sec 512(b)(5)	1976-2 CB 531
94-401	9-7-76	To facilitate and encourage the implementation by States of child day care services programs	1976-2 CB 533
94-414	9-17-76	To amend Code Sec. 584 relating to common trust funds; treatment of affiliated banks	1976-2 CB 535
94-444	10-1-76	Emergency Jobs Programs Extension Act of 1976	90 Stat. 1476
94-452	10-2-76	Bank Holding Company Tax Act of 1976	1976-2 CB 536
94-455	10-4-76	Tax Reform Act of 1976	1976-3 (Vol. 1) CB 1
94-514	10-15-76	Interest deduction on certain corporate indebtedness	1976-2 CB 551
94-528	10-17-76	To provide for a distribution deduction for certain cemetery perpetual care fund, etc.	1976-2 CB 553
94-529	10-17-76	To amend Code Sec. 5051 (relating to the Federal excise tax on beer)	90 Stat. 2485
94-530	10-17-76	Exempting from fuel tax certain aircraft museums	1976-2 CB 555
94-540	10-18-76	To provide for the disposition of funds for the Grand River Band of Ottowa Indians	1976-2 CB 557
94-547	10-18-76	To amend the Railroad Retirement Act of 1974	1976-2 CB 558
94-553	10-19-76	General revision of the Copyright Law	90 Stat. 2541
94-559	10-19-76	The Civil Rights Attorney's Fees Awards Act of 1976	90 Stat. 2641
94-563	10-19-76	To amend chapter 21 of the Internal Revenue Code and title II of the Social Security Act	1976-2 CB 558
94-566	10-20-76	Unemployment Compensation Amendments of 1976	1976-2 CB 564
94-568	10-20-76	To provide for tax treatment of social clubs and certain other membership organizations, and for other purposes	1976-2 CB 596
94-569	10-20-76	To permit the authorization of means other than stamp on containers of distilled spirits as evidence of tax payment, and for other purposes	1976-2 CB 603

Statutes Enacted by the 95th Congress—1st Session

Public Law No.	Date	Title or Subject	Reprint
95-19	4-12-77	Emergency Unemployment Compensation Extension Act of 1977	1977-1 CB 437
95-30	5-23-77	Tax Reduction and Simplification Act of 1977	1977-1 CB 451
95-125	10-7-77	To amend the Accounting and Auditing Act of 1950, to provide for the audit, by the Comptroller General, of the IRS and of the Bureau of Alcohol Tobacco, and Firearms	91 Stat. 1104
95-147	10-28-77	To authorize the Secretary to invest public money, and for other purposes	1978-1 CB 455
95-170	11-12-77	To suspend until July 1, 1978, the rate of duty on mattress blanks of latex rubber, etc.	1978-1 CB 456
95-171	11-12-77	To extend certain Social Security Act provisions, etc.	1978-1 CB 457
95-172	11-12-77	To extend for an additional temporary period the existing suspension of duties on certain classifications of years of silk, etc.	1978-1 CB 459
95-176	11-14-77	To amend certain provisions of the '54 Code relating to distilled spirits, etc.	91 Stat. 1363
95-195	11-18-77	Siletz Indian Tribe Restoration Act	91 Stat. 1415
95-210	12-13-77	To amend Titles XVIII and XIX of the Social Security Act, etc.	1978-1 CB 461
95-216	12-20-77	Social Security amendments of 1977	1978-1 CB 462

Amending Acts

Public Law No.	Date	Title or Subject	Reprint
	**Statutes Enacted by the 95th Congress—2nd Session**
95-227	2-10-78	The Black Lung Benefits Revenue Act of 1977	1978-1 CB 494
95-239	3-1-78	The Black Lung Benefits Reform Act of 1977	92 Stat. 95
95-258	4-7-78	Relating to the year for including in income certain payments under the Agricultural Act of 1949 received in 1978 but attributable to 1977, and to extend for one year the existing treatment of State legislators' travel expenses away from home	1978-1 CB 505
95-339	8-8-78	New York City Loan Guarantee Act of 1978	1978-2 CB 353
95-345	8-15-78	To amend the '54 Code with respect to the treatment of mutual or cooperative telephone company income, etc.	1978-2 CB 356
95-423	10-6-78	To amend '54 Code Sec. 5064	92 Stat. 935
95-427	10-7-78	To prohibit the issuance of Regs on the taxation of fringe benefits, etc.	1978-2 CB 363
95-458	10-14-78	To amend the '54 Code with respect to excise tax on certain trucks, buses, tractors, etc., home production of beer and wine, refunds of taxes on gasoline and special fuels to aerial applicators, and partial rollovers of lump sum distributions	1978-2 CB 367
95-472	10-17-78	To amend Code Sec. 7447 with respect to the revocation of an election to receive retired pay as a judge of the Tax Court	1978-2 CB 373
95-473	10-17-78	To revise, codify, and enact without substantive change the Interstate Commerce Act and related laws	1978-2 CB 377
95-479	10-18-78	Veterans' Disability Compensation and Survivors' Benefits Act of 1978	1978-2 CB 377
95-488	10-20-78	To amend the '54 Code to insure that the deduction for contributions to a black lung benefit trust be allowed for any such contributions which are made for the purpose of satisfying unfunded future liability, etc.	1978-2 CB 378
95-496	10-21-78	To amend certain laws relating to the Osage Tribe of Oklahoma, etc.	1978-2 CB 381
95-497	10-21-78	Relating to the application of certain provisions of the '54 Code to specified transactions by certain public employee retirement systems created by the State of New York or any of its political subdivisions	1978-2 CB 382
95-498	10-21-78	To declare that the U.S. holds in trust for the Pueblo of Santa Ana certain public domain lands	1978-2 CB 392
95-499	10-21-78	To declare that the U.S. holds in trust for the Pueblo of Zio certain public domain land	1978-2 CB 393
95-502	10-21-78	To amend the '54 Code to provide that income from the conducting of certain bingo games by certain tax-exempt organizations will not be subject to tax, etc.	1978-2 CB 393
95-565	11-1-78	U.S. Railway Association Amendments Act of 1978	1978-2 CB 399
95-599	11-6-78	Highway Revenue Act of 1978	1978-2 CB 403
95-600	11-6-78	Revenue Act of 1978	1978-3 CB 1
95-602	11-6-78	Rehabilitation, Comprehensive Services, and Developmental Disabilities Amendments of 1978	1978-2 CB 415
95-615	11-8-78	Tax Treatment Extension Act of 1977 (Foreign Earned Income)	1978-2 CB 415
95-616	11-8-78	Fish and Wildlife Improvement Act of 1978	1978-2 CB 435
95-618	11-9-78	Energy Tax Act of 1978	1978-3 CB 1
95-628	11-10-78	To revise miscellaneous timing requirements of the revenue laws, etc.	1978-2 CB 435
	**Statutes Enacted by the 96th Congress—1st Session**
96-8	4-10-79	Taiwan Relations Act	1979-1 CB 459
96-39	7-26-79	Trade Agreements Act of 1979	93 Stat. 144
96-72	9-29-79	Export Administration Act of 1979	1979-2 CB 473
96-74	9-29-79	Treasury Department Appropriations Act of 1980	1979-2 CB 473
96-84	10-10-79	To amend the Unemployment Compensation Amendments of 1976 with respect to the National Commission on Unemployment Compensation	1979-2 CB 474
96-167	12-29-79	To continue through May 31, 1981, the existing prohibition on the issuance of fringe benefit regulations, etc.	1980-1 CB 483
96-178	1-2-80	To extend for one year the provision of law relating to the business expenses of State legislators	1980-1 CB 494
	**Statutes Enacted by the 96th Congress—2nd Session**
96-187	1-8-80	Federal Election Campaign Act Amendments for 1979	93 Stat. 1339
96-222	4-1-80	Technical Corrections Act of 1979	1980-1 CB 499
96-223	4-2-80	Crude Oil Windfall Profit Tax Act of 1980	1980-3 CB 1
96-249	5-26-80	Food Stamp Act Amendments of 1980	1980-2 CB 414
96-265	6-9-80	Social Security Disability Amendments of 1980	1980-2 CB 418
96-272	6-17-80	Adoption Assistance and Child Welfare Act of 1980	1980-2 CB 419
96-283	6-28-80	Deep Seabed Hard Mineral Resources Act	1980-2 CB 422
96-294	6-30-80	Energy Security Act	1980-2 CB 428
96-298	7-1-80	To provide a three-month extension of the Taxes which are transferred to the Airport and Airway Trust fund	1980-2 CB 431
96-304	7-8-80	To make supplemental appropriations for the fiscal year ending 9-30-80, rescinding certain budget authority, etc.	1980-2 CB 433

Amending Acts

Public Law No.	Date	Title or Subject	Reprint
96-318	8-1-80	Delaware Tribe of Indians judgement funds	94 Stat. 968
96-320	8-3-80	Ocean Thermal Energy Conversion Act of 1980 (To amend the '36 Merchant Marine Act)	1980-2 CB 433
96-330	8-26-80	Veteran's Administration Health-Care Amendments of 1980	1980-2 CB 435
96-364	9-26-80	Multiemployer Pension Plan Amendments Act of 1980	1980-2 CB 437
96-369	10-1-80	Continuing Appropriations, 1981	1980-2 CB 479
96-417	10-10-80	Customs Court Act of 1980	94 Stat. 1727
96-439	10-14-80	To authorize three additional judges for the Tax Court and to remove the age limitation on appointments to the Tax Court	94 Stat. 1878
96-449	10-14-80	Hostage Relief Act of 1980	1980-2 CB 479
96-451	10-14-80	Reforestation; Federal Boat Safety Act	1980-2 CB 485
96-454	10-15-80	Household Goods Transportation Act of 1980	94 Stat. 2011
96-465	10-17-80	Foreign Service Act of 1980	94 Stat. 2071
96-471	10-19-80	Installment Sales Revision Act of 1980	1980-2 CB 489
96-481	10-21-80	Equal Access to Justice Act	94 Stat. 2321
96-499	12-5-80	Omnibus Reconciliation Act of 1980	1980-2 CB 509
96-510	12-11-80	Comprehensive Environmental Response, Compensation, and Liability Act of 1980	1980-2 CB 589
96-536	12-16-80	Continuing appropriations for fiscal year '81	1980-2 CB 596
96-541	12-17-80	Tax Treatment Extension Act of 1980	1980-2 CB 596
96-589	12-24-80	Bankruptcy Tax Act of 1980	1980-2 CB 607
96-595	12-24-80	To amend the '54 Code with respect to net operating loss carryovers of taxpayers who cease to be REITs, etc.	1980-2 CB 647
96-596	12-24-80	To amend the '54 Code with respect to the determination of second tier taxes, etc.	1980-2 CB 653
96-598	12-24-80	Excise tax refunds in the case of certain uses of tread rubber, etc.	1980-2 CB 661
96-601	12-24-80	To simplify certain provisions of the '54 Code	1980-2 CB 666
96-603	12-28-80	To amend the '54 Code to simplify private foundation return and reporting requirements, etc.	1980-2 CB 684
96-605	12-28-80	Miscellaneous Revenue Act of 1980	1980-2 CB 702
96-608	12-28-80	To amend the '54 Code to waive in certain cases the residency requirements for deductions or exclusions of individuals living abroad, to allow the tax-free rollover of certain distributions from money purchase pension plans, etc.	1980-2 CB 37
96-611	12-28-80	To amend title XVIII of the Social Security Act	1980-2 CB 728
96-613	12-28-80	To make certain miscellaneous changes in the tax laws	1980-2 CB 737

Statutes Enacted by the 97th Congress — 1st Session

97-34	8-13-81	Economic Recovery Tax Act of 1981	1981-2 CB 256
97-35	8-13-81	Omnibus Budget Reconciliation Act of 1981	1981-2 CB 528
97-51	10-1-81	Continuing appropriations for fiscal year 1982	1982-1 CB 306
97-92	12-15-81	Further continuing appropriations for fiscal year 1982	1982-1 CB 306
97-119	12-29-81	To provide a temporary increase in the tax imposed on Producers of Coal, etc.	1982-1 CB 307
97-123	12-29-81	To amend the '81 Omnibus Reconciliation Act to restore minimum benefits under the Social Security Act	1982-1 CB 314

Statutes Enacted by the 97th Congress — 2nd Session

97-164	4-2-82	Federal Courts Improvement Act of 1982	1982-1 CB 316
97-216	7-18-82	To make supplemental appropriations for the fiscal year ending Sept. 30, 1982, etc.	1982-2 CB 461
97-248	9-3-82	Tax Equity and Fiscal Responsibility Act of 1982 (TEFRA)	1982-2 CB 462
97-258	9-13-82	To amend title 31, U.S.C., money and finance	96 Stat. 877
97-261	9-20-82	Bus Regulatory Reform Act of 1982	96 Stat. 1102
97-354	10-19-82	Subchapter S Revision Act of 1982	1982-2 CB 702
97-362	10-25-82	Miscellaneous Revenue Act of 1982	1983-1 CB 367
97-365	10-25-82	Debt Collection Act of 1982	1983-1 CB 390
97-402	12-31-82	To provide for the use and distribution of Clallam judgement funds	96 Stat. 2020
97-403	12-31-82	To provide for the use and distribution of funds awarded to the Pembina Chippewa Indians	96 Stat. 2022
97-408	1-3-83	To provide for the use and distribution of funds awarded to the Blackfeet and Gros Ventre Tribes, Assiniboine, and Papago Indians	96 Stat. 2035
97-414	1-4-83	Orphans Drug Act	1983-1 CB 403
97-424	1-6-83	Highway Revenue Act of 1982	1983-1 CB 405
97-436	1-8-83	To provide for the distribution of Warm Springs judgement funds awarded in docket numbered 198 before the Indian Claims Commission, and for other purposes	96 Stat. 2283
97-448	1-12-83	Technical Corrections Act of 1982	1983-1 CB 451
97-449	1-12-83	To revise, codify, and enact without substantive change certain general and permanent laws related to transportation as subtitle I and chapter 31 of subtitle II of title 49, United States Code, "Transportation"	96 Stat. 2413
97-452	1-12-83	To codify laws relating to money and finance	96 Stat. 2467
97-455	1-12-83	To reduce the rate of certain taxes paid to the Virgin Island on Virgin Islands' source income	1983-1 CB 507

Amending Acts

Public Law No.	Date	Title or Subject	Reprint
97-473	1-14-83	To amend the Code for tax treatment of periodic payments for personal injury, etc.	1983-1 CB 510

Statutes Enacted by the 98th Congress—1st Session

98-4	3-11-83	Payment-in-Kind Tax Treatment Act of 1983	1983-2 CB 296
98-21	4-20-83	Social Security Amendments of 1983	97 Stat. 65
98-63	7-30-83	Supplemental Appropriations Act, 1983	1983-2 CB 351
98-67	8-5-83	Interest and Dividend Tax Compliance Act of 1983	97 Stat. 369
98-76	8-12-83	Railroad Retirement Solvency Act of 1983	1983-2 CB 375
98-118	10-11-83	To extend the Federal Supplemental Compensation Act of 1982	1983-2 CB 401
98-123	10-13-83	To provide for tax exempt distribution of judgement funds to members of the Red Lake Band of Chippewa Indians	1983-2 CB 401
98-124	10-13-83	To provide for tax exempt distribution of judgement funds to members of the Assiniboine Tribe	1983-2 CB 402
98-134	10-18-83	Mashantucket Pequot Indian Claims Settlement Act	1984-1 CB 310
98-135	10-24-83	Federal Supplemental Compensation Amendments of 1983	1984-1 CB 311
98-213	12-8-83	To authorize capital improvement projects on Guam	97 Stat. 1459

Statutes Enacted by the 98th Congress—2nd Session

98-216	2-14-84	To amend laws related to money and finance	98 Stat. 3
98-259	4-10-84	To exempt from Federal income taxes certain military and civilian employees of the U.S. dying as a result of injuries sustained overseas.	1984-1 CB 313
98-355	7-11-84	To increase the Federal contribution for the Quadrennial Political Party Presidential National Nominating Conventions	98 Stat. 394
98-369	7-18-84	Deficit Reduction Act of 1984 [Tax Reform Act of 1984]	1984-3 CB 1
98-378	8-16-84	Child Support Enforcement Amendments of 1984	1984-2 CB 429
98-397	8-23-84	Retirement Equity Act of 1984	98 Stat. 1426
98-408	8-28-84	To convey certain lands to the Zuni Indian Tribe for religious purposes	1984-2 CB 462
98-432	9-28-84	Shoalwater Bay Indian Tribe—Dexter-by-the-Sea Claim Settlement Act	1984-2 CB 463
98-443	10-4-84	Civil Aeronautics Board Sunset Act of 1984	1985-1 CB 410
98-454	10-5-84	To enhance the economic development of Guam, the Virgin Islands, American Samoa, the Northern Mariana Islands, etc.	1985-1 CB 410
98-473	10-12-84	Making continuing appropriations for the fiscal year 1985, etc.	98 Stat. 1837
98-573	10-30-84	Trade and Tariff Act of 1984	87 Stat. 2948
98-601	10-30-84	To amend the Tax Equity and Fiscal Responsibility Act of 1982	1985-1 CB 411
98-611	10-31-84	To extend for two years the exclusion from gross income for educational assistance programs	1985-1 CB 413
98-612	10-31-84	To extend for one year the exclusion from gross income for group legal services plans	1985-1 CB 416
98-620	11-8-84	To amend Title 28, U.S.C., with respect to the places where court shall be held in certain judicial districts, and for other purposes	98 Stat. 3335

Statutes Enacted by the 99th Congress—1st Session

99-44	5-24-85	To amend the '54 Code to repeal the contemporaneous recordkeeping requirements added by the 1984 TRA, and for other purposes	1985-2 CB 350
99-92	8-16-85	Nurse Education Amendments of 1985	99 Stat. 393
99-107	9-30-85	Emergency Extension Act of 1985	1985-2 CB 366
99-121	10-11-85	To amend the '54 Code to simplify the imputed interest rules of Code Secs. 1274 and 483, etc.	1985-2 CB 367
99-155	11-14-85	To temporarily increase the limit on public debt and to restore the investment of the Social Security Trust Funds and other trust funds	99 Stat. 814
99-181	12-13-85	To extend until 12-18-85, the application of certain tobacco excise taxes, etc.	99 Stat. 1172
99-189	12-18-85	To extend until 12-20-85, the application of certain tobacco excise taxes, etc.	99 Stat. 1184
99-190	12-19-85	To make further continuing appropriations for the fiscal year 1986, etc.	99 Stat. 1185
99-201	12-23-85	To extend until 3-15-86, the application of certain tobacco excise taxes, etc.	99 Stat. 1665
99-221	12-26-85	Cherokee Leasing Act	99 Stat. 1735
99-234	1-2-86	Federal Civilian Employee Contractor Travel Expenses Act of 1985	99 Stat. 1755
99-239	1-14-86	Compact of Free Association Act of 1985	99 Stat. 1770

Statutes Enacted by the 99th Congress—2nd Session

99-272	4-7-86	Consolidated Omnibus Budget Reconciliation Act of 1985	1986-2 CB 298
99-308	5-19-86	Firearms Owners' Protection Act	100 Stat. 449
99-386	8-22-86	Congressional Reports Elimination Act of 1986	100 Stat. 821
99-335	6-6-86	Federal Employees' Retirement System Act of 1986	99 Stat. 514
99-346	6-30-86	Saginaw Chippewa Indian Tribe of Michigan Distribution of Judgement Funds Act	1987-2 CB 337
99-398	8-28-86	Klamath Indian Tribe Restoration Act	99 Stat. 849
99-499	10-17-86	Superfund Amendments and Reauthorization Act of 1986	1987-1 CB 373
99-509	10-21-86	Omnibus Budget Reconciliation Act of 1986	99 Stat. 1874

Amending Acts

Public Law No.	Date	Title or Subject	Reprint
99-514	10-22-86	Tax Reform Act of 1986	1986-3 CB 1
99-595	10-31-86	To extend the exclusion from Federal unemployment tax wages paid to certain alien farmworkers	1987-1 CB 393
99-640	11-10-86	Coast Guard Authorization Act of 1986	99 Stat. 3545
99-662	11-17-86	Water Resources Development Act of 1986	1986-2 CB 364

Statutes Enacted by the 100th Congress — 1st Session

100-17	4-2-87	Surface Transportation and Uniform Relocation Assistance Act of 1987	101 Stat. 132
100-202	12-22-87	To make further continuing appropriations for the '88 fiscal year, and for other purposes	101 Stat. 1329
100-203	12-22-87	Omnibus Budget Reconciliation Act of 1987	1987-3 CB-1
100-223	12-30-87	Airport and Airway Safety and Capacity Expansion Act of 1987	101 Stat. 1486

Statutes Enacted by the 100th Congress — 2nd Session

100-360	7-1-88	Medicare Catastrophic Coverage Act of 1988	1989-1 CB 355
100-418	8-23-88	Omnibus Trade and Competitiveness Act of 1988	102 Stat. 1107
100-448	9-28-88	Coast Guard Authorization Act of 1988	102 Stat. 1836
100-485	10-13-88	Family Support Act of 1988	1989-2 CB 338
100-647	11-10-88	Technical and Miscellaneous Revenue Act of 1988 (TAMRA)	1988-3 CB 1
100-690	11-18-88	Anti-Drug Abuse Act of 1988	1989-2 CB 347
100-707	11-23-88	Disaster Relief and Emergency Assistance Amendments of 1988	102 Stat. 4689

Statutes Enacted by the 101st Congress — 1st Session

101-73	8-9-89	Financial Institutions Reform, Recovery, and Enforcement Act of 1989	1989-2 CB 349
101-140	11-8-89	Repeal of Code Sec. 89 Non-discrimination Rules	1990-1 CB 207
101-179	11-28-89	Support for East European Democracy (SEED) Act of 1989	103 Stat. 1298
101-194	11-30-89	Ethics Reform Act of 1989	1990-1 CB 209
101-221	12-12-89	Steel Trade Liberalization Program Implementation Act	103 Stat. 1886
101-234	12-13-89	Medicare Catastrophic Coverage Repeal Act of 1989	103 Stat. 1979
101-239	12-19-89	Omnibus Budget Reconciliation Act of 1989	1990-1 CB 210

Statutes Enacted by the 101st Congress — 2nd Session

101-280	5-4-90	Technical Corrections to the Ethics Reform Act of 1989	104 Stat. 149
101-380	8-18-90	Oil Pollution Act of 1990	104 Stat. 484
101-382	8-20-90	Customs and Trade Act of 1990	104 Stat. 629
101-508	11-5-90	Omnibus Budget Reconciliation Act of 1990	1991-2 CB 481
101-509	11-5-90	Treasury, Postal Service and General Government Appropriations Act of 1991	104 Stat. 3066
101-604	11-16-90	Aviation Security Improvement Act of 1990	104 Stat. 3066
101-624	11-28-90	Food, Agriculture, Conservation, and Trade Act of 1990	1991-1 CB 306
101-647	11-29-90	Crime Control Act of 1990	1992-1 CB 485
101-649	11-29-90	Immigration Act of 1990	104 Stat. 4978

Statutes Enacted by the 102nd Congress — 1st Session

102-2	1-30-91	Armed Forces Taxes	1991-1 CB 307
102-40	5-7-91	Department of Veterans Affairs Health-Care Personnel Act of 1991	105 Stat. 187
102-54	6-13-91	Veterans programs for housing and memorial affairs	105 Stat. 267
102-90	8-14-91	Appropriations for the Legislative Branch for the fiscal year ending 9-30-92	1992-2 CB 330
102-107	8-17-91	Emergency Unemployment Compensation Act of 1991	105 Stat. 541
102-164	11-15-91	Emergency Unemployment Compensation Act of 1991	1992-2 CB 330
102-227	12-11-91	Tax Extension Act of 1991	1992-2 CB 333
102-240	12-18-91	Surface Transportation Revenue Act of 1991	1992-2 CB 335

Statutes Enacted by the 102nd Congress — 2nd Session

102-244	2-7-92	Extension of Unemployment Benefits	1992-2 CB 337
102-318	7-3-92	Unemployment Compensation Amendments of 1992	1992-2 CB 339
102-393	10-6-92	Appropriations for the Treasury Department, U.S. Postal Service, Executive Office of President, etc. for the fiscal year ending September 30, 1993	106 Stat. 1729
102-486	10-24-92	Energy Policy Act of 1992	1993-1 CB 246
102-568	10-29-92	Veterans' Benefits Act of 1992	106 Stat. 4320
102-581	10-31-92	Airport and Airway Safety, Capacity, Noise Improvement, and Intermodal Transportation Act of 1992	106 Stat. 4872

Amending Acts

Public Law No.	Date	Title or Subject	Reprint
		Statutes Enacted by the 103rd Congress — 1st Session	
103-66	8-10-93	Omnibus Budget Reconciliation Act of 1993	1993-3 CB 1
103-149	11-23-93	South African Democratic Transition Support Act of 1993	107 Stat. 1503
103-178	12-3-93	Intelligence Authorization Act for Fiscal Year 1994	107 Stat. 2024
103-182	12-8-93	North American Free Trade Agreement Implementation Act	107 Stat. 2057
		Statutes Enacted by the 103rd Congress — 2nd Session	
103-260	5-26-94	Airport Improvement Program Temporary Extension Act of 1994	108 Stat. 698
103-272	7-5-94	Codification of Certain U.S. Transportation Laws as Title 49, United States Code	108 Stat. 745
103-296	8-15-94	Social Security Independence and Program Improvements Act of 1994	1994-1 CB 543
103-305	8-23-94	Federal Aviation Administration Authorization Act of 1994	108 Stat. 1569
103-322	9-13-94	Violent Crime Control and Law Enforcement Act of 1994	108 Stat. 1799
103-337	10-5-94	National Defense Authorization Act for Fiscal Year 1995	108 Stat. 2663
103-387	10-22-94	Social Security Domestic Employment Reform Act of 1994	108 Stat. 4071
103-429	10-31-94	To codify without substantive change recent laws related to transportation and to improve the United States Code	108 Stat. 4377
103-465	12-8-94	Uruguay Round Agreements Act	1995-1 CB 230
		Statutes Enacted by the 104th Congress — 1st Session	
104-7	4-11-95	Self-Employed Health Insurance Act	109 Stat. 93
104-88	12-29-95	ICC Termination Act of 1995	109 Stat. 803
		Statutes Enacted by the 104th Congress — 2nd Session	
104-117	3-20-96	To provide that members of the Armed Forces performing services for the peacekeeping efforts in Bosnia and Herzegovina, Croatia, and Macedonia shall be entitled to tax benefits in the same manner as if such services were performed in a combat zone	1996-3 CB 1
104-134	4-26-96	Omnibus Consolidated Rescissions and Appropriations Act of 1996	1996-3 CB 17
104-168	7-30-96	Taxpayer Bill of Rights	1996-3 CB 19
104-188	8-20-96	Small Business Job Protection Act of 1996	1996-3 CB 155
104-191	8-21-96	Health Insurance Portability and Accountability Act of 1996	1996-3 CB 1111
104-193	8-22-96	Personal Responsibility and Work Opportunity Reconciliation Act of 1996	1996-3 CB 1179
104-201	9-23-96	National Defense Authorization Act for Fiscal Year 1997	110 Stat. 2422
104-264	10-9-96	Federal Aviation Reauthorization Act of 1996	110 Stat. 3213
104-316	10-19-96	General Accounting Office Act of 1996	110 Stat. 3826
		Statutes Enacted by the 105th Congress — 1st Session	
105-2	2-28-97	Airport and Airway Trust Fund Tax Reinstatement Act of 1997	1997-1 CB 315
105-33	8-5-97	Balanced Budget Act of 1997	111 Stat. 251
105-34	8-5-97	Taxpayer Relief Act of 1997	111 Stat. 788
105-35	8-5-97	Taxpayer Browsing Protection Act	1997-2 CB 278
105-61	10-10-97	Appropriations for the Treasury Dept., the U.S. Postal Service, the Executive Office of the President, and certain Independent Agencies, for the fiscal year ending 9-30-98, and for other purposes	111 Stat. 1272
105-65	10-27-97	Departments of Veterans Affairs and Housing and Urban Development, and Independent Agencies Appropriations Act, 1998	111 Stat. 1344
105-78	11-13-97	Appropriations for the Depts. of Labor, Health and Human Services, and Education, and related agencies for the fiscal year ending 9-30-98, and for other purposes	111 Stat. 1467
105-102	11-20-97	To codify without substantive change laws related to transportation and to improve the United States Code	111 Stat. 2204
105-115	11-21-97	Food and Drug Administration Modernization Act of 1997	111 Stat. 2326
105-130	12-1-97	Surface Transportation Extension Act of 1997	111 Stat. 2552
		Statutes Enacted by the 105th Congress — 2nd Session	
105-178	6-9-98	Transportation and Equity Act for the 21st Century	112 Stat. 107
105-206	7-22-98	IRS Restructuring and Reform Act of 1998	112 Stat. 685
105-277	10-21-98	Tax and Trade Relief Extension Act of 1998	112 Stat. 2681
105-306	10-28-98	Noncitizen Benefit Clarification and Other Technical Amendments Act of 1998	112 Stat. 2926

Amending Acts

Public Law No.	Date	Title or Subject	Reprint
	**Statutes Enacted by the 106th Congress — 1st Session**		
106-21	4-19-99	To extend the tax benefits available with respect to services performed in a combat zone to services performed in the Federal Republic of Yugoslavia (Serbia/Montenegro) and certain other areas	113 Stat. 34
106-36	6-25-99	Miscellaneous Trade and Technical Corrections Act of 1999	113 Stat. 127
106-78	10-22-99	Agriculture, Rural Development, Food and Drug Administration, and Related Agencies Appropriations Act, 2000	113 Stat. 1135
106-170	12-17-99	Ticket to Work and Work Incentives Improvement Act of 1999	113 Stat. 1860
	**Statutes Enacted by the 106th Congress — 2nd Session**		
106-181	4-5-00	Wendell H. Ford Aviation and Investment Reform Act for the 21st Century	114 Stat. 196
106-200	5-18-00	Trade and Development Act of 2000	114 Stat. 251
106-230	7-1-00	To require Code Sec. 527 organizations to disclose their political activities	114 Stat. 477
106-408	11-1-00	Fish and Wildlife Programs Improvement and National Wildlife Refuge System Centennial Act of 2000	114 Stat. 1775
106-476	11-9-00	Tariff Suspension and Trade Act of 2000	114 Stat. 2101
106-519	11-15-00	FSC Repeal and Extraterritorial Income Exclusion Act of 2000	114 Stat. 2423
106-554	12-21-00	Consolidated Appropriations Act, 2001	114 Stat. 2763
106-573	12-28-00	Installment Tax Correction Act of 2000	114 Stat. 3061
	**Statutes Enacted by the 107th Congress — 1st Session**		
107-15	6-5-01	Fallen Hero Survivor Benefit Fairness Act of 2001	115 Stat. 37
107-16	6-7-01	Economic Growth and Tax Relief Reconciliation Act of 2001	115 Stat. 38
107-22	7-26-01	To rename the education individual retirement accounts as the Coverdell education savings accounts	115 Stat. 196
107-67	11-12-01	Treasury and General Government Appropriations Act, 2002	115 Stat. 514
107-71	11-19-01	Aviation and Transportation Security Act	115 Stat. 597
107-90	12-21-01	Railroad Retirement and Survivors' Improvement Act of 2001	115 Stat. 878
107-110	1-8-02	No Child Left Behind Act of 2001	115 Stat. 1425
107-116	1-10-02	Departments of Labor, Health and Human Services, and Education, and Related Agencies Appropriations Act, 2002	115 Stat. 2177
107-131	1-16-02	To simplify the reporting requirements relating to higher education tuition and related expenses	115 Stat. 2410
107-134	1-23-02	Victims of Terrorism Tax Relief Act of 2001	115 Stat. 2427
	**Statutes Enacted by the 107th Congress — 2nd Session**		
107-147	3-9-02	Job Creation and Worker Assistance Act of 2002	116 Stat. 21
107-181	5-20-02	Clergy Housing Allowance Clarification Act of 2002	116 Stat. 583
107-210	8-6-02	Trade Act of 2002	116 Stat. 933
107-217	8-21-02	To revise, codify, and enact without substantive change certain general and permanent laws, related to public buildings, property, and works, as title 40, United States Code, "Public Buildings, Property, and Works"	116 Stat. 1062
107-276	11-2-02	To amend section 527 of the Internal Revenue Code of 1986 to eliminate notification and return requirements for State and local party committees and candidate committees	116 Stat. 1929
107-296	11-25-02	Homeland Security Act of 2002	116 Stat. 2135
107-330	12-6-02	Veterans Benefits Act of 2002	116 Stat. 2820
107-358	12-17-02	Holocaust Restitution Tax Fairness Act of 2002	116 Stat. 3015
	**Statutes Enacted by the 108th Congress — 1st Session**		
108-27	5-28-03	Jobs and Growth Tax Relief Reconciliation Act of 2003	117 Stat. 752
108-81	9-25-03	Museum and Library Services Act of 2003	117 Stat. 991
108-88	9-30-03	Surface Transportation Extension Act of 2003	117 Stat. 1110
108-89	10-1-03	To extend the Temporary Assistance for Needy Families block grant program, and certain tax and trade programs, and for other purposes	117 Stat. 1131
108-121	11-11-03	Military Family Tax Relief Act of 2003	117 Stat. 1335
108-173	12-8-03	Medicare Prescription Drug, Improvement, and Modernization Act of 2003	117 Stat. 2066
108-176	12-12-03	Vision 100 — Century of Aviation Reauthorization Act	117 Stat. 2490
108-178	12-15-03	To improve the United States Code	117 Stat. 2637
108-189	12-19-03	Servicemembers Civil Relief Act	117 Stat. 2835

Amending Acts

Public Law No.	Date	Title or Subject	Reprint
	**Statutes Enacted by the 108th Congress — 2nd Session**		
108-202	2-29-04	Surface Transportation Extension Act of 2004	118 Stat. 478
108-203	3-2-04	Social Security Protection Act of 2004	118 Stat. 493
108-218	4-10-04	Pension Funding Equity Act of 2004	118 Stat. 596
108-224	4-30-04	Surface Transportation Extension Act of 2004, Part II	118 Stat. 627
108-263	6-30-04	Surface Transportation Extension Act of 2004, Part III	118 Stat. 698
108-280	7-30-04	Surface Transportation Extension Act of 2004, Part IV	118 Stat. 876
108-310	9-30-04	Surface Transportation Extension Act of 2004, Part V	118 Stat. 1144
108-311	10-4-04	Working Families Tax Relief Act of 2004	118 Stat. 1166
108-357	10-22-04	American Jobs Creation Act of 2004	118 Stat. 1418
108-375	10-28-04	Ronald W. Reagan Defense Authorization Act for Fiscal Year 2005	118 Stat. 1811
108-429	12-3-04	Miscellaneous Trade and Technical Corrections Act of 2004	118 Stat. 2434
108-476	12-21-04	To treat certain arrangements maintained by the YMCA Retirement Fund as church plans for the purposes of certain provisions of the Internal Revenue Code of 1986, and for other purposes	118 Stat. 3901
108-493	12-23-04	To amend the Internal Revenue Code of 1986 to modify the taxation of arrow components	118 Stat. 3984
	**Statutes Enacted by the 109th Congress — 1st Session**		
109-1	1-7-05	To accelerate the income tax benefits for charitable cash contributions for the relief of victims of the Indian Ocean tsunami	119 Stat. 3
109-6	3-31-05	To amend the Internal Revenue Code of 1986 to extend the Leaking Underground Storage Tank Trust Fund financing rate	119 Stat. 20
109-7	4-15-05	To amend the Internal Revenue Code of 1986 to provide for the proper tax treatment of certain disaster mitigation payments	119 Stat. 21
109-14	5-31-05	Surface Transportation Extension Act of 2005	119 Stat. 324
109-20	7-1-05	Surface Transportation Extension Act of 2005, Part II	119 Stat. 346
109-35	7-20-05	Surface Transportation Extension Act of 2005, Part III	119 Stat. 379
109-37	7-22-05	Surface Transportation Extension Act of 2005, Part IV	119 Stat. 394
109-40	7-28-05	Surface Transportation Extension Act of 2005, Part V	119 Stat. 410
109-42	7-30-05	Surface Transportation Extension Act of 2005, Part VI	119 Stat. 435
109-58	8-8-05	Energy Tax Incentives Act of 2005 [title XIII of the Energy Policy Act of 2005]	119 Stat. 594
109-59	8-10-05	Safe, Accountable, Flexible, Efficient Transportation Act: A Legacy for Users [Transportation Act of 2005]	119 Stat. 1144
109-73	9-23-05	Katrina Emergency Tax Relief Act of 2005	119 Stat. 2016
109-74	9-29-05	Sportfishing and Recreational Boating Safety Amendments Act of 2005	119 Stat. 2030
109-135	12-21-05	Gulf Opportunity Zone Act of 2005	119 Stat. 2577
109-151	12-30-05	To amend title I of ERISA, title XXVII of the Public Health Service Act, and the Internal Revenue Code to extend by one year provisions requiring parity in the application of certain limits to mental health benefits	119 Stat. 2886
	**Statutes Enacted by the 109th Congress — 2nd Session**		
109-171	2-8-06	Deficit Reduction Act of 2005	120 Stat. 4
109-222	5-17-06	Tax Increase Prevention and Reconciliation Act of 2005	120 Stat. 345
109-227	5-29-06	Heroes Earned Retirement Opportunities Act	120 Stat. 385
109-241	7-12-06	Coast Guard and Maritime Transportation Act of 2006	120 Stat. 516
109-280	8-17-06	Pension Protection Act of 2006	120 Stat. 780
109-432	12-20-06	Tax Relief and Health Care Act of 2006	120 Stat. 2922
	**Statutes Enacted by the 110th Congress — 1st Session**		
110-28	5-25-07	Small Business and Work Opportunity Tax Act of 2007	121 Stat. 112
110-42	6-30-07	Andean Trade Preference Act	121 Stat. 235
110-52	8-1-07	Approving the renewal of import restrictions contained in the Burmese Freedom and Democracy Act of 2003	121 Stat. 982
110-138	12-14-07	United States-Peru Trade Promotion Agreement Implementation Act	121 Stat. 1455
110-140	12-19-07	Energy Independence and Security Act of 2007	121 Stat. 1492
110-141	12-19-07	To exclude from gross income payments from the Hokie Spirit Memorial Fund to the victims of the tragic event, loss of life and limb, at Virginia Polytechnic Institute & State University	121 Stat. 1802
110-142	12-20-07	Mortgage Forgiveness Debt Relief Act of 2007	121 Stat. 1803
110-161	12-26-07	Consolidated Appropriations Act, 2008	121 Stat. 1844
110-166	12-26-07	Tax Increase Prevention Act of 2007	121 Stat. 2461
110-172	12-29-07	Tax Technical Corrections Act of 2007	121 Stat. 2473

Amending Acts

Public Law No.	Date	Title or Subject	Reprint
	**Statutes Enacted by the 110th Congress — 2nd Session**		
110-185	2-13-08	Economic Stimulus Act of 2008	122 Stat. 613
110-190	2-28-08	Airport and Airway Extension Act of 2008	122 Stat. 643
110-233	5-21-08	Genetic Information Nondiscrimination Act of 2008	122 Stat. 881
110-234	5-22-08	Food, Conservation, and Energy Act of 2008	122 Stat. 923
110-244	6-6-08	SAFETEA-LU Technical Corrections Act of 2008	122 Stat. 1572
110-245	6-17-08	Heroes Earnings Assistance and Relief Tax Act of 2008	122 Stat. 1624
110-246	5-22-08	Food, Conservation, and Energy Act of 2008	122 Stat. 1651
110-253	6-30-08	Federal Aviation Administration Extension Act of 2008	122 Stat. 2417
110-289	7-30-08	Housing Assistance Tax Act of 2008	122 Stat. 2654
110-317	8-29-08	Hubbard Act	122 Stat. 3526
110-318	9-15-08	To amend the Internal Revenue Code of 1986 to restore the Highway Trust Fund balance	122 Stat. 3532
110-328	9-30-08	SSI Extension for Elderly and Disabled Refugees Act	122 Stat. 3567
110-330	9-30-08	Federal Aviation Administration Extension Act of 2008, Part II	122 Stat. 3717
110-343	10-3-08	Emergency Economic Stabilization Act of 2008	122 Stat. 3765
110-351	10-7-08	Fostering Connections to Success and Increasing Adoptions Act of 2008	122 Stat. 3949
110-381	10-9-08	Michelle's Law	122 Stat. 4081
110-428	10-15-08	Inmate Tax Fraud Prevention Act of 2008	122 Stat. 4839
110-458	12-23-08	Worker, Retiree, and Employer Recovery Act of 2008	122 Stat. 5092
	**Statutes Enacted by the 111th Congress — 1st Session**		
111-3	2-4-09	Children's Health Insurance Program Reauthorization Act of 2009	123 Stat. 524
111-5	2-17-09	American Recovery and Reinvestment Act of 2009	123 Stat. 115
111-12	3-30-09	Federal Aviation Administration Extension Act of 2009	123 Stat. 1457
111-46	8-7-09	To restore sums to the Highway Trust Fund and for other purposes.	123 Stat. 1970
111-69	10-1-09	Fiscal Year 2010 Federal Aviation Administration Extension Act	123 Stat. 2054
111-92	11-06-09	Worker, Homeownership, and Business Assistance Act of 2009	123 Stat. 2984
111-116	12-16-09	Fiscal Year 2010 Federal Aviation Administration Extension Act, Part II	123 Stat. 3031
111-118	12-19-09	Making appropriations for the Department of Defense for the fiscal year ending September 30, 2010, and for other purposes.	123 Stat. 3409
111-124	12-28-09	To extend the Generalized System of Preferences and the Andean Trade Preference Act, and for other purposes.	123 Stat. 3484
	**Statutes Enacted by the 111th Congress — 2nd Session**		
111-126	1-22-10	To accelerate the income tax benefits for charitable cash contributions for the relief of victims of the earthquake in Haiti.	124 Stat. 3
111-144	3-2-10	Temporary Extension Act of 2010	124 Stat. 42
111-147	3-18-10	Hiring Incentives to Restore Employment Act	124 Stat. 71
111-148	3-23-10	Patient Protection and Affordable Care Act	124 Stat. 119
111-152	3-30-10	Health Care and Education Reconciliation Act of 2010	124 Stat. 1029
111-153	3-31-10	Federal Aviation Administration Extension Act of 2010	124 Stat. 1084
111-161	4-30-10	Airport and Airway Extension Act of 2010	124 Stat. 1126
111-171	5-24-10	Haiti Economic Lift Program Act of 2010	124 Stat. 1194
111-173	5-27-10	To clarify the health care provided by the Secretary of Veterans Affairs that constitutes minimum essential coverage.	124 Stat. 1215
111-192	6-25-10	Preservation of Access to Care for Medicare Beneficiaries and Pension Relief Act of 2010	124 Stat. 1280
111-197	7-2-10	Airport and Airway Extension Act of 2010, Part II	124 Stat. 1353
111-198	7-2-10	Homebuyer Assistance and Improvement Act of 2010	124 Stat. 1356
111-203	7-21-10	Dodd-Frank Wall Street Reform and Consumer Protection Act	124 Stat. 1376
111-216	8-1-10	Airline Safety and Federal Aviation Administration Extension Act of 2010	124 Stat. 2348
111-226	8-10-10	FAA Air Transportation Modernization and Safety Improvement Act	124 Stat. 2389
111-237	8-16-10	Firearms Excise Tax Improvement Act of 2010	124 Stat. 2497
111-240	9-27-10	Small Business Jobs Act of 2010	124 Stat. 2504
111-249	9-30-10	Airport and Airway Extension Act of 2010, Part III	124 Stat. 2627
111-274	10-13-10	Plain Writing Act of 2010	124 Stat. 2862
111-291	12-8-10	Claims Resolution Act of 2010	124 Stat. 3064
111-309	12-15-10	Medicare and Medicaid Extenders Act of 2010	124 Stat. 3285
111-312	12-17-10	Tax Relief, Unemployment Insurance Reauthorization, and Job Creation Act of 2010	124 Stat. 3296
111-322	12-22-10	Continuing Appropriations and Surface Transportation Extensions Act, 2011	124 Stat. 3518
111-325	12-22-10	Regulated Investment Company Modernization Act of 2010	124 Stat. 3537
111-329	12-22-10	Airport and Airway Extension Act of 2010, Part IV	124 Stat. 3566
111-344	12-29-10	Omnibus Trade Act of 2010	124 Stat. 3611
111-347	1-2-11	James Zadroga 9/11 Health and Compensation Act of 2010	124 Stat. 3623

Amending Acts

Public Law No.	Date	Title or Subject	Reprint
112-5	3-4-11	Surface Transportation Extension Act of 2011	125 Stat. 14
112-7	3-31-11	Airport and Airway Extension Act of 2011	125 Stat. 31
112-8	4-9-11	Further Additional Continuing Appropriations Amendments, 2011	125 Stat. 34
112-9	4-14-11	Comprehensive 1099 Taxpayer Protection and Repayment of Exchange Subsidy Overpayments Act of 2011	125 Stat. 36
112-10	4-15-11	Department of Defense and Full-Year Continuing Appropriations Act, 2011	125 Stat. 38
112-16	5-31-11	Airport and Airway Extension Act of 2011, Part II	125 Stat. 218
112-21	6-29-11	Airport and Airway Extension Act of 2011, Part III	125 Stat. 233

Amending Acts

Public Law No.	Date	Title or Subject	Repeat
112-5	3-4-11	Surface Transportation Extension Act of 2011	125 Stat. 14
112-7	3-31-11	Airport and Airway Extension Act of 2011	125 Stat. 31
112-8	4-9-11	Further Additional Continuing Appropriations Amendments, 2011	125 Stat. 34
112-9	4-14-11	Comprehensive 1099 Taxpayer Protection and Repayment of Exchange Subsidy Overpayments Act of 2011	125 Stat. 36
112-10	4-15-11	Department of Defense and Full-Year Continuing Appropriations Act, 2011	125 Stat. 38
112-16	5-31-11	Airport and Airway Extension Act of 2011, Part II	125 Stat. 218
112-21	6-29-11	Airport and Airway Extension Act of 2011, Part III	125 Stat. 233

TABLE OF CODE SECTIONS
Internal Revenue Code
(as amended)

SUBTITLE A — INCOME TAXES
Chapter 1. Normal Taxes and Surtaxes
Subchapter A. Determination of Tax Liability
PART I. TAX ON INDIVIDUALS

Sec.	
1	Tax imposed
2	Definitions and special rules
3	Tax tables for individuals
4	Repealed [Rules for optional tax]
5	Cross references relating to tax on individuals

PART II. TAX ON CORPORATIONS

11	Tax imposed
12	Cross references relating to tax on corporations

PART III. CHANGES IN RATES DURING A TAXABLE YEAR

15	Effect of changes

PART IV. CREDITS AGAINST TAX

Subpart A. Nonrefundable personal credits

21	Expenses for household and dependent care services necessary for gainful employment
22	Credit for the elderly and the permanently and totally disabled
23	Adoption expenses
23	Repealed [Residential energy credit]
24	Child tax credit
24	Repealed [Contributions to candidates for public office]
25	Interest on certain home mortgages
25A	Hope and Lifetime Learning credits
25B	Elective deferrals and IRA contributions by certain individuals
25C	Nonbusiness energy property
25D	Residential energy efficient property
26	Limitation based on tax liability; definition of tax liability

Subpart B. Other credits

27	Taxes of foreign countries and possessions of the United States; possession tax credit
30	Certain plug-in electric vehicles
30A	Puerto Rico economic activity credit
30B	Alternative motor vehicle credit
30C	Alternative fuel vehicle refueling property credit
30D	New qualified plug-in electric drive motor vehicles

Subpart C. Refundable credits

31	Tax withheld on wages
32	Earned income
33	Tax withheld at source on nonresident aliens and foreign corporations
34	Certain uses of gasoline and special fuels
35	Health insurance costs of eligible individuals
36	First-time homebuyer credit
36A	Making work pay credit
36B	Refundable credit for coverage under a qualified health plan
36C	Adoption expenses
37	Overpayments of tax
36	Repealed [Credits not allowed to individuals taking standard deduction]

Subpart D. Business related credits

38	General business credit
38	Repealed [Investment in certain depreciable property]
39	Carryback and carryforward of unused credits

Sec.	
40	Alcohol, etc., used as fuel
40	Repealed [Expenses of work incentive programs]
40A	Biodiesel and renewable diesel used as fuel
41	Credit for increasing research activities
41	Repealed [Employee stock ownership credit]
42	Low-income housing credit
43	Enhanced oil recovery credit
44	Expenditures to provide access to disabled individuals
44	Repealed [Purchase of new principal residence]
44B	Repealed [Credit for employment of certain new employees]
45	Electricity produced from certain renewable resources, etc.
45A	Indian employment credit
45B	Credit for portion of employer social security taxes paid with respect to employee cash tips
45C	Clinical testing expenses for certain drugs for rare diseases or conditions
45D	New markets tax credit
45E	Small employer pension plan startup costs
45F	Employer-provided child care credit
45G	Railroad track maintenance credit
45H	Credit for production of low sulfur diesel fuel
45I	Credit for producing oil and gas from marginal wells
45J	Credit for production from advanced nuclear power facilities
45K	Credit for producing fuel from a nonconventional source
45L	New energy efficient home credit
45M	Energy efficient appliance credit
45N	Mine rescue team training credit
45O	Agricultural chemicals security credit
45P	Employer wage credit for employees who are active duty members of the uniformed services
45Q	Credit for carbon dioxide sequestration
45R	Employee health insurance expenses of small employers

Subpart E. Rules for computing investment credit

46	Amount of credit
47	Rehabilitation credit
48	Energy credit
48A	Qualifying advanced coal project credit
48B	Qualifying gasification project credit
48C	Qualifying advanced energy project credit
48D	Qualifying therapeutic discovery project credit
49	At-risk rules
50	Other special rules
50	Repealed [Restoration of credit]

Subpart C. Repealed [Rules for Computing Credit for Expenses of Work Incentive Programs]

50A	Repealed [Amount of credit]
50B	Repealed [Definitions; special rules]

Subpart F. Rules for computing work opportunity credit

51	Amount of credit
51A	Repealed [Temporary incentives for employing long-term family assistance recipients]
52	Special rules

Subpart G. Credit against regular tax for prior year minimum tax liability

53	Credit for prior year minimum tax liability
53	Repealed [Limitation based on amount of tax]

Subpart H. Nonrefundable Credit to Holders of Clean Renewable Energy Bonds

Table of Code Sections

Sec.	
54	Credit to holders of clean renewable energy bonds

Subpart I. Qualified tax credit bonds

Sec.	
54A	Credit to holders of qualified tax credit bonds
54B	Qualified forestry conservation bonds
54C	New clean renewable energy bonds
54D	Qualified energy conservation bonds
54E	Qualified zone academy bonds
54F	Qualified school construction bonds

Subpart J. Build America Bonds

54AA	Build America bonds

PART VI. ALTERNATIVE MINIMUM TAX

55	Alternative minimum tax imposed
56	Adjustments in computing alternative minimum taxable income
57	Items of tax preference
58	Denial of certain losses
59	Other definitions and special rules

PART VII. ENVIRONMENTAL TAX

59A	Environmental tax

PART VIII. REPEALED [SUPPLEMENTAL MEDICARE PREMIUM]

59B	Repealed [Supplemental medicare premium]

Subchapter B. Computation of Taxable Income

PART I. DEFINITION OF GROSS INCOME, ADJUSTED GROSS INCOME, TAXABLE INCOME, ETC.

61	Gross income defined
62	Adjusted gross income defined
63	Taxable income defined
64	Ordinary income defined
65	Ordinary loss defined
66	Treatment of community income
67	2-percent floor on miscellaneous itemized deductions
68	Overall limitation on itemized deductions

PART II. ITEMS SPECIFICALLY INCLUDED IN GROSS INCOME

71	Alimony and separate maintenance payments
72	Annuities; certain proceeds of endowment and life insurance contracts
73	Services of child
74	Prizes and awards
75	Dealers in tax-exempt securities
76	Repealed [Mortgages made or obligations issued by joint-stock land banks]
77	Commodity credit loans
78	Dividends received from certain foreign corporations by domestic corporations choosing foreign tax credit
79	Group-term life insurance purchased for employees
80	Restoration of value of certain securities
81	Repealed [Increase in vacation pay suspense account]
82	Reimbursement for expenses of moving
83	Property transferred in connection with performance of services
84	Transfer of appreciated property to political organization
85	Unemployment compensation
86	Social security and tier 1 railroad retirement benefits
87	Alcohol and biodiesel fuels credits
88	Certain amounts with respect to nuclear decommissioning costs
89	Repealed [Benefits provided under certain employee benefit plans]
90	Illegal federal irrigation subsidies

PART III. ITEMS SPECIFICALLY EXCLUDED FROM GROSS INCOME

101	Certain death benefits
102	Gifts and inheritances
103	Interest on State and local bonds
103A	Repealed [Mortgage subsidy bonds]
104	Compensation for injuries or sickness
105	Amounts received under accident and health plans
106	Contributions by employer to accident and health plans
107	Rental value of parsonages
108	Income from discharge of indebtedness
109	Improvements by lessee on lessor's property
110	Qualified lessee construction allowances for short-term leases
110	Repealed [Income taxes paid by lessee corporation]
111	Recovery of tax benefit items
112	Certain combat zone compensation of members of the Armed Forces
113	Repealed [Mustering-out payments for members of the Armed Forces]
114	Repealed [Extraterritorial income]
114	Repealed [Sports programs conducted for the American National Red Cross]
115	Income of States, municipalities, etc.
116	Repealed [Partial exclusion of dividends received by individuals]
117	Qualified scholarships
118	Contributions to the capital of a corporation
119	Meals or lodging furnished for the convenience of the employer
120	Amounts received under qualified group legal services plans
121	Exclusion of gain from sale of principal residence
122	Certain reduced uniformed services retirement pay
123	Amounts received under insurance contracts for certain living expenses
124	Repealed [Qualified transportation provided by employer]
125	Cafeteria plans
126	Certain cost-sharing payments
127	Educational assistance programs
128	Repealed [Interest on certain savings certificates]
129	Dependent care assistance programs
130	Certain personal injury liability assignments
131	Certain foster care payments
132	Certain fringe benefits
133	Repealed [Interest on certain loans used to acquire employer securities]
134	Certain military benefits
135	Income from United States savings bonds used to pay higher education tuition and fees
136	Energy conservation subsidies provided by public utilities
137	Adoption assistance programs
138	Medicare Advantage MSA
139	Disaster relief payments
139A	Federal subsidies for prescription drug plans
139B	Benefits provided to volunteer firefighters and emergency medical responders
139C	COBRA premium assistance
139D	Indian Health Care Benefits
139D	Repealed [sic 139E. Free choice vouchers]
140	Cross references to other Acts

PART IV. TAX EXEMPTION REQUIREMENTS FOR STATE AND LOCAL BONDS

Subpart A. Private activity bonds

141	Private activity bond; qualified bond
142	Exempt facility bond
143	Mortgage revenue bonds: qualified mortgage bond and qualified veterans' mortgage bond
144	Qualified small issue bond; qualified student loan bond; qualified redevelopment bond
145	Qualified 501(c)(3) bond
146	Volume cap
147	Other requirements applicable to certain private activity bonds

Table of Code Sections

Sec.	
	Subpart B. Requirements applicable to all State and local bonds
148	Arbitrage
149	Bonds must be registered to be tax exempt; other requirements
	Subpart C. Definitions and special rules
150	Definitions and special rules
	PART V. DEDUCTIONS FOR PERSONAL EXEMPTIONS
151	Allowance of deductions for personal exemptions
152	Dependent defined
153	Cross references
153	Repealed [Determination of marital status]
	PART VI. ITEMIZED DEDUCTIONS FOR INDIVIDUALS AND CORPORATIONS
161	Allowance of deductions
162	Trade or business expenses
163	Interest
164	Taxes
165	Losses
166	Bad debts
167	Depreciation
168	Accelerated cost recovery system
168	Repealed [Amortization of emergency facilities]
169	Amortization of pollution control facilities
170	Charitable, etc., contributions and gifts
171	Amortizable bond premium
172	Net operating loss deduction
173	Circulation expenditures
174	Research and experimental expenditures
175	Soil and water conservation expenditures; endangered species recovery expenditures
176	Payments with respect to employees of certain foreign corporations
177	Repealed [Trademark and trade name expenditures]
178	Amortization of cost of acquiring a lease
179	Election to expense certain depreciable business assets
179A	Deduction for clean-fuel vehicles and certain refueling property
179B	Deduction for capital costs incurred in complying with Environmental Protection Agency sulfur regulations
179C	Election to expense certain refineries
179D	Energy efficient commercial buildings deduction
179E	Election to expense advance mine safety equipment
180	Expenditures by farmers for fertilizer, etc.
181	Treatment of certain qualified film and television productions
181	Repealed [Deduction for certain unused investment credit]
182	Repealed [Expenditures by farmers for clearing land]
183	Activities not engaged in for profit
184	Repealed [Amortization of certain railroad rolling stock]
185	Repealed [Amortization of railroad grading and tunnel bores]
186	Recoveries of damages for antitrust violations, etc.
187	Repealed [Amortization of certain coal mine safety equipment]
188	Repealed [Amortization of certain expenditures for child care facilities]
189	Repealed [Amortization of real property construction period interest and taxes]
190	Expenditures to remove architectural and transportation barriers to the handicapped and elderly
191	Repealed [Amortization of certain rehabilitation expenditures for certified historic structures]
192	Contributions to black lung benefit trust
193	Tertiary injectants
194	Treatment of reforestation expenditures
194A	Contributions to employer liability trusts
195	Start-up expenditures

Sec.	
196	Deduction for certain unused business credits
197	Amortization of goodwill and certain other intangibles
198	Expensing of environmental remediation costs
198A	Expensing of qualified disaster expenses
199	Income attributable to domestic production activities
	PART VII. ADDITIONAL ITEMIZED DEDUCTIONS FOR INDIVIDUALS
211	Allowance of deductions
212	Expenses for production of income
213	Medical, dental, etc., expenses
214	Repealed [Expenses for household and dependent care services necessary for gainful employment]
215	Alimony, etc., payments
216	Deduction of taxes, interest, and business depreciation by cooperative housing corporation tenant-stockholder
217	Moving expenses
218	Repealed [Contributions to candidates for public office]
219	Retirement savings
220	Archer MSAs
220	Repealed [Jury duty pay remitted to employer]
220	Repealed [Retirement savings for certain married individuals]
221	Interest on education loans
221	Repealed [Deduction for two-earner married couples]
222	Qualified tuition and related expenses
222	Repealed [Adoption expenses]
223	Health savings accounts
224	Cross reference
	PART VIII. SPECIAL DEDUCTIONS FOR CORPORATIONS
241	Allowance of special deductions
242	Repealed [Partially tax-exempt interest]
243	Dividends received by corporations
244	Dividends received on certain preferred stock
245	Dividends received from certain foreign corporations
246	Rules applying to deductions for dividends received
246A	Dividends received deduction reduced where portfolio stock is debt financed
247	Dividends paid on certain preferred stock of public utilities
248	Organizational expenditures
249	Limitation on deduction of bond premium on repurchase
250	Repealed [Certain payments to the national railroad passenger corporation]
	PART IX. ITEMS NOT DEDUCTIBLE
261	General rule for disallowance of deductions
262	Personal, living, and family expenses
263	Capital expenditures
263A	Capitalization and inclusion in inventory costs of certain expenses
264	Certain amounts paid in connection with insurance contracts
265	Expenses and interest relating to tax-exempt income
266	Carrying charges
267	Losses, expenses, and interest with respect to transactions between related taxpayers
268	Sale of land with unharvested crop
269	Acquisitions made to evade or avoid income tax
269A	Personal service corporations formed or availed of to avoid or evade income tax
269B	Stapled entities
270	Repealed [Limitation on deductions allowable to individuals in certain cases]
271	Debts owed by political parties, etc.
272	Disposal of coal or domestic iron ore
273	Holders of life or terminable interest
274	Disallowance of certain entertainment, etc., expenses
275	Certain taxes
276	Certain indirect contributions to political parties
277	Deductions incurred by certain membership organizations in transactions with members

Table of Code Sections

Sec.	
278	Repealed [Capital expenditures incurred in planting and developing citrus and almond groves; certain capital expenditures of farming syndicates]
279	Interest on indebtedness incurred by corporation to acquire stock or assets of another corporation
280	Repealed [Certain expenditures incurred in production of films, books, records, or similar property]
280A	Disallowance or certain expenses in connection with business use of home, rental of vacation homes, etc.
280B	Demolition of structures
280C	Certain expenses for which credits are allowable
280D	Repealed [Portion of chapter 45 taxes for which credit or refund is allowable under section 6429]
280E	Expenditures in connection with the illegal sale of drugs
280F	Limitation on depreciation for luxury automobiles; limitation where certain property used for personal purposes
280G	Golden parachute payments
280H	Limitation on certain amounts paid to employee-owners by personal service corporations electing alternative taxable years

PART X. TERMINAL RAILROAD CORPORATIONS AND THEIR SHAREHOLDERS

281	Terminal railroad corporations and their shareholders

PART XI. SPECIAL RULES RELATING TO CORPORATE PREFERENCE ITEMS

291	Special rules relating to corporate preference items

Subchapter C. Corporate Distributions and Adjustments

PART I. DISTRIBUTIONS BY CORPORATIONS

Subpart A. Effects on recipients

301	Distributions of property
302	Distributions in redemption of stock
303	Distributions in redemption of stock to pay death taxes
304	Redemption through use of related corporations
305	Distributions of stock and stock rights
306	Dispositions of certain stock
307	Basis of stock and stock rights acquired in distributions

Subpart B. Effects on corporation

311	Taxability of corporation on distribution
312	Effect on earnings and profits

Subpart C. Definitions; constructive ownership of stock

316	Dividend defined
317	Other definitions
318	Constructive ownership of stock

PART II. CORPORATE LIQUIDATIONS

Subpart A. Effects on recipients

331	Gain or loss to shareholders in corporate liquidations
332	Complete liquidations of subsidiaries
333	Repealed [Election as to recognition of gain in certain liquidations]
334	Basis of property received in liquidations

Subpart B. Effects on corporation

336	Gain or loss recognized on property distributed in complete liquidation
337	Nonrecognition for property distributed to parent in complete liquidation of subsidiary
338	Certain stock purchases treated as asset acquisitions

Subpart C. Repealed [Collapsible corporations]

341	Repealed [Collapsible corporations]
342	Repealed [Liquidation of certain foreign personal holding companies]

Subpart D. Definition and special rule

346	Definition and special rule

PART III. CORPORATE ORGANIZATIONS AND REORGANIZATIONS

Subpart A. Corporate organizations

351	Transfer to corporation controlled by transferor

Subpart B. Effects on shareholders and security holders

354	Exchanges of stock and securities in certain reorganizations
355	Distribution of stock and securities of a controlled corporation
356	Receipt of additional consideration
357	Assumption of liability
358	Basis to distributees

Subpart C. Effects on corporations

361	Nonrecognition of gain or loss to corporations; treatment of distributions
362	Basis to corporations
363	Repealed [Effect on earnings and profits]

Subpart D. Special rule; definitions

367	Foreign corporations
368	Definitions relating to corporate reorganizations

PART IV. REPEALED [INSOLVENCY REORGANIZATIONS]

370	Repealed [Termination of part]
371	Repealed [Reorganization in certain receivership and bankruptcy proceedings]
372	Repealed [Basis in connection with certain receivership and bankruptcy proceedings]
373	Repealed [Loss not recognized in certain railroad reorganizations]
374	Repealed [Gain or loss not recognized in certain railroad reorganizations]

PART V. CARRYOVERS

381	Carryovers in certain corporate acquisitions
382	Limitation on net operating loss carryforwards and certain built-in losses following ownership change
383	Special limitations on certain excess credits, etc.
384	Limitation on use of preacquisition losses to offset built-in gains

PART VI. TREATMENT OF CERTAIN CORPORATE INTERESTS AS STOCK OR INDEBTEDNESS

385	Treatment of certain interests in corporations as stock or indebtedness

PART VII. REPEALED [MISCELLANEOUS CORPORATE PROVISIONS]

386	Repealed [Transfers of partnership and trust interests by corporations]

Subchapter D. Deferred Compensation, Etc.

PART I. PENSION, PROFIT-SHARING, STOCK BONUS PLANS, ETC.

Subpart A. General rules

401	Qualified pension, profit-sharing, and stock bonus plans
402	Taxability of beneficiary of employees' trust
402A	Optional treatment of elective deferrals as Roth contributions
403	Taxation of employee annuities
404	Deduction for contributions of an employer to an employees' trust or annuity plan and compensation under a deferred-payment plan
404A	Deduction for certain foreign deferred compensation plans
405	Repealed [Qualified bond purchase plans]
406	Employees of foreign affiliates covered by section 3121(l) agreements
407	Certain employees of domestic subsidiaries engaged in business outside the United States
408	Individual retirement accounts
408A	Roth IRAs
409	Qualifications for tax credit employee stock ownership plans
409	Repealed [Retirement bonds]

Sec.	
409A	Inclusion in gross income of deferred compensation under nonqualified deferred compensation plans

Subpart B. Special rules

410	Minimum participation standards
411	Minimum vesting standards
412	Minimum funding standards
413	Collectively bargained plans, etc.
414	Definitions and special rules
415	Limitations on benefits and contributions under qualified plans
416	Special rules for top-heavy plans
417	Definitions and special rules for purposes of minimum survivor annuity requirements

Subpart C. Special rules for multiemployer plans

418	Reorganization status
418A	Notice of reorganization and funding requirements
418B	Minimum contribution requirement
418C	Overburden credit against minimum contribution requirement
418D	Adjustments in accrued benefits
418E	Insolvent plans

Subpart D. Treatment of welfare benefit funds

419	Treatment of funded welfare benefit plans
419A	Qualified asset account; limitation on additions to account

Subpart E. Treatment of transfers to retiree health accounts

420	Transfers of excess pension assets to retiree health accounts

PART II. CERTAIN STOCK OPTIONS

421	General rules
422	Incentive stock options
422	Repealed [Qualified stock options]
423	Employee stock purchase plans
424	Definitions and special rules
424	Repealed [Restricted stock options]

PART III. RULES RELATING TO MINIMUM FUNDING STANDARDS AND BENEFIT LIMITATIONS

Subpart A. Minimum funding standards for pension plans

430	Minimum funding standards for single-employer defined benefit pension plans.
431	Minimum funding standards for multiemployer plans
432	Additional funding rules for multiemployer plans in endangered status or critical status

Subpart B. Benefit limitations under single-employer plans

436	Funding-based limits on benefits and benefit accruals under single-employer plans

Subchapter E. Accounting Periods and Methods of Accounting

PART I. ACCOUNTING PERIODS

441	Period for computation of taxable income
442	Change of annual accounting period
443	Returns for a period of less than 12 months
444	Election of taxable year other than required taxable year

PART II. METHODS OF ACCOUNTING

Subpart A. Methods of accounting in general

446	General rule for methods of accounting
447	Method of accounting for corporations engaged in farming
448	Limitation on use of cash method of accounting

Subpart B. Taxable year for which items of gross income included

451	General rule for taxable year of inclusion
452	Repealed [Prepaid income]
453	Installment method
453A	Special rules for nondealers
453B	Gain or loss on disposition of installment obligations
453C	Repealed [Certain indebtedness treated as payments on installment obligations]
454	Obligations issued at discount
455	Prepaid subscription income
456	Prepaid dues income of certain membership organizations
457	Deferred compensation plans of State and local governments and tax-exempt organizations
457A	Nonqualified deferred compensation from certain tax indifferent parties
458	Magazines, paperbacks, and records returned after the close of the taxable year
460	Special rules for long-term contracts

Subpart C. Taxable year for which deductions taken

461	General rule for taxable year of deduction
462	Repealed [Reserves for estimated expenses, etc.]
463	Repealed [Accrual of vacation pay]
464	Limitations on deductions for certain farming [expenses]
465	Deductions limited to amount at risk
466	Repealed [Qualified discount coupons redeemed after close of taxable year]
467	Certain payments for the use of property or services
468	Special rules for mining and solid waste reclamation and closing costs
468A	Special rules for nuclear decommissioning costs
468B	Special rules for designated settlement funds
469	Passive activity losses and credits limited
470	Limitation on deductions allocable to property used by governments or other tax-exempt entities

Subpart D. Inventories

471	General rule for inventories
472	Last-in, first-out inventories
473	Qualified liquidations of LIFO inventories
474	Simplified dollar-value LIFO method for certain small businesses
475	Mark to market accounting method for dealers in securities

PART III. ADJUSTMENTS

481	Adjustments required by changes in method of accounting
482	Allocation of income and deductions among taxpayers
483	Interest on certain deferred payments

Subchapter F. Exempt Organizations

PART I. GENERAL RULE

501	Exemption from tax on corporations, certain trusts, etc.
502	Feeder organizations
503	Requirements for exemption
504	Status after organization ceases to qualify for exemption under section 501(c)(3) because of substantial lobbying or because of political activities
505	Additional requirements for organizations described in paragraph (9), (17), or (20) of section 501(c)

PART II. PRIVATE FOUNDATIONS

507	Termination of private foundation status
508	Special rules with respect to section 501(c)(3) organizations
509	Private foundation defined

PART III. TAXATION OF BUSINESS INCOME OF CERTAIN EXEMPT ORGANIZATIONS

511	Imposition of tax on unrelated business income of charitable, etc., organizations
512	Unrelated business taxable income
513	Unrelated trade or business
514	Unrelated debt-financed income
515	Taxes of foreign countries and possessions of the United States

PART IV. FARMERS' COOPERATIVES

521	Exemption of farmers' cooperatives from tax
522	Repealed [Tax on farmers' cooperatives]

PART V. SHIPOWNERS' PROTECTION AND INDEMNITY ASSOCIATIONS

526	Shipowners' protection and indemnity associations

Sec.	
	PART VI. POLITICAL ORGANIZATIONS
527	Political organizations
	PART VII. CERTAIN HOMEOWNERS ASSOCIATIONS
528	Certain homeowners associations
	PART VIII. HIGHER EDUCATION SAVINGS ENTITIES
529	Qualified tuition programs
530	Coverdell education savings accounts
	Subchapter G. Corporations Used to Avoid Income Tax on Shareholders
	PART I. CORPORATIONS IMPROPERLY ACCUMULATING SURPLUS
531	Imposition of accumulated earnings tax
532	Corporations subject to accumulated earnings tax
533	Evidence of purpose to avoid income tax
534	Burden of proof
535	Accumulated taxable income
536	Income not placed on annual basis
537	Reasonable needs of the business
	PART II. PERSONAL HOLDING COMPANIES
541	Imposition of personal holding company tax
542	Definition of personal holding company
543	Personal holding company income
544	Rules for determining stock ownership
545	Undistributed personal holding company income
546	Income not placed on annual basis
547	Deduction for deficiency dividends
	PART III. REPEALED [FOREIGN PERSONAL HOLDING COMPANIES]
551	Repealed [Foreign personal holding company income taxed to United States shareholders]
552	Repealed [Definition of foreign personal holding company]
553	Repealed [Foreign personal holding company income]
554	Repealed [Stock ownership]
555	Repealed [Gross income of foreign personal holding companies]
556	Repealed [Undistributed foreign personal holding company income]
557	Repealed [Income not placed on annual basis]
558	Repealed [Returns of officers, directors, and shareholders of foreign personal holding companies]
	PART IV. DEDUCTION FOR DIVIDENDS PAID
561	Definition of deduction for dividends paid
562	Rules applicable in determining dividends eligible for dividends paid deduction
563	Rules relating to dividends paid after close of taxable year
564	Dividend carryover
565	Consent dividends
	Subchapter H. Banking Institutions
	PART I. RULES OF GENERAL APPLICATION TO BANKING INSTITUTIONS
581	Definition of bank
582	Bad debts, losses, and gains with respect to securities held by financial institutions
583	Repealed [Deductions of dividends paid on certain preferred stock]
584	Common trust funds
585	Reserves for losses on loans of banks
586	Repealed [Reserves for losses on loans of small business investment companies, etc.]
	PART II. MUTUAL SAVINGS BANKS, ETC.
591	Deduction for dividends paid on deposits
592	Repealed [Deduction for repayment of certain loans]
593	Reserves for losses on loans
594	Alternative tax for mutual savings banks conducting life insurance business
595	Repealed [Foreclosure on property securing loans]
596	Repealed [Limitation on dividends received deduction]

Sec.	
597	Treatment of transactions in which federal financial assistance provided
	PART III. REPEALED [BANK AFFILIATES]
601	Repealed [Special deduction for bank affiliates]
	Subchapter I. Natural Resources
	PART I. DEDUCTIONS
611	Allowance of deduction for depletion
612	Basis for cost depletion
613	Percentage depletion
613A	Limitations on percentage depletion in case of oil and gas wells
614	Definition of property
615	Repealed [Pre-1970 exploration expenditures]
616	Development expenditures
617	Deduction and recapture of certain mining exploration expenditures
	PART II. REPEALED [EXCLUSIONS FROM GROSS INCOME]
621	Repealed [Payments to encourage exploration, development, and mining for defense purposes]
	PART III. SALES AND EXCHANGES
631	Gain or loss in the case of timber, coal, or domestic iron ore
632	Repealed [Sale of oil or gas properties]
	PART IV. MINERAL PRODUCTION PAYMENTS
636	Income tax treatment of mineral production payments
	PART V. CONTINENTAL SHELF AREAS
638	Continental shelf areas
	Subchapter J. Estates, Trusts, Beneficiaries, and Decedents
	PART I. ESTATES, TRUSTS, AND BENEFICIARIES
	Subpart A. General rules for taxation of estates and trusts
641	Imposition of tax
642	Special rules for credits and deductions
643	Definitions applicable to subparts A, B, C, and D
644	Taxable year of trusts
644	Repealed [Special rule for gain on property transferred to trust at less than fair market value]
645	Certain revocable trusts treated as part of estate
646	Tax treatment of electing Alaska Native Settlement Trusts
	Subpart B. Trusts which distribute current income only
651	Deduction for trusts distributing current income only
652	Inclusion of amounts in gross income of beneficiaries of trusts distributing current income only
	Subpart C. Estates and trusts which may accumulate income or which distribute corpus
661	Deduction for estates and trusts accumulating income or distributing corpus
662	Inclusion of amounts in gross income of beneficiaries of estates and trusts accumulating income or distributing corpus
663	Special rules applicable to sections 661 and 662
664	Charitable remainder trusts
	Subpart D. Treatment of excess distributions by trusts
665	Definitions applicable to subpart D
666	Accumulation distribution allocated to preceding years
667	Treatment of amounts deemed distributed by trust in preceding years
668	Interest charge on accumulation distributions from foreign trusts
669	Repealed [Treatment of capital gain deemed distributed in preceding years]
	Subpart E. Grantors and others treated as substantial owners
671	Trust income, deductions, and credits attributable to grantors and others as substantial owners
672	Definitions and rules

Sec.	
673	Reversionary interests
674	Power to control beneficial enjoyment
675	Administrative powers
676	Power to revoke
677	Income for benefit of grantor
678	Person other than grantor treated as substantial owner
679	Foreign trusts having one or more United States beneficiaries

Subpart F. Miscellaneous

681	Limitation on charitable deduction
682	Income of an estate or trust in case of divorce, etc.
683	Use of trust as an exchange fund
684	Recognition of gain on certain transfers to certain foreign trusts and estates
684	Recognition of gain on certain transfers to certain foreign trusts and estates and nonresident aliens
685	Treatment of funeral trusts

PART II. INCOME IN RESPECT OF DECEDENTS

691	Recipients of income in respect of decedents
692	Income taxes of members of Armed Forces, astronauts, and victims of certain terrorist attacks on death

Subchapter K. Partners and Partnerships

PART I. DETERMINATION OF TAX LIABILITY

701	Partners, not partnership, subject to tax
702	Income and credits of partner
703	Partnership computations
704	Partner's distributive share
705	Determination of basis of partner's interest
706	Taxable years of partner and partnership
707	Transactions between partner and partnership
708	Continuation of partnership
709	Treatment of organization and syndication fees

PART II. CONTRIBUTIONS, DISTRIBUTIONS, AND TRANSFERS

Subpart A. Contributions to a partnership

721	Nonrecognition of gain or loss on contribution
722	Basis of contributing partner's interest
723	Basis of property contributed to partnership
724	Character of gain or loss on contributed unrealized receivables, inventory items, and capital loss property

Subpart B. Distributions by a partnership

731	Extent of recognition of gain or loss on distribution
732	Basis of distributed property other than money
733	Basis of distributee partner's interest
734	Adjustment to basis of undistributed partnership property where section 754 election or substantial basis reduction
735	Character of gain or loss on disposition of distributed property
736	Payments to a retiring partner or a deceased partner's successor in interest
737	Recognition of precontribution gain in case of certain distributions to contributing partner

Subpart C. Transfers of interests in a partnership

741	Recognition and character of gain or loss on sale or exchange
742	Basis of transferee partner's interest
743	Special rules where section 754 election or substantial built-in loss

Subpart D. Provisions common to other subparts

751	Unrealized receivables and inventory items
752	Treatment of certain liabilities
753	Partner receiving income in respect of decedent
754	Manner of electing optional adjustment to basis of partnership property
755	Rules for allocation of basis

Sec.	

PART III. DEFINITIONS

761	Terms defined

PART IV. SPECIAL RULES FOR ELECTING LARGE PARTNERSHIPS

771	Application of subchapter to electing large partnerships
772	Simplified flow-through
773	Computations at partnership level
774	Other modifications
775	Electing large partnership defined
776	Special rules for partnerships holding oil and gas properties
777	Regulations

PART IV. REPEALED [EFFECTIVE DATE FOR SUBCHAPTER]

Subchapter L. Insurance Companies

PART I. LIFE INSURANCE COMPANIES

Subpart A. Tax imposed

801	Tax imposed

Subpart B. Life insurance gross income

803	Life insurance gross income

Subpart C. Life insurance deductions

804	Life insurance deductions
805	General deductions
806	Small life insurance company deduction
807	Rules for certain reserves
808	Policyholder dividends deduction
809	Repealed [Reduction in certain deductions of mutual life insurance companies]
810	Operations loss deduction

Subpart D. Accounting, allocation, and foreign provisions

811	Accounting provisions
812	Definition of company's share and policyholders' share
813	Repealed [Foreign life insurance companies]
814	Contiguous country branches of domestic life insurance companies
815	Distributions to shareholders from pre-1984 policyholders surplus account

Subpart E. Definitions and special rules

816	Life insurance company defined
817	Treatment of variable contracts
817A	Special rules for modified guaranteed contracts
818	Other definitions and special rules

PART II. REPEALED [MUTUAL INSURANCE COMPANIES (OTHER THAN LIFE AND CERTAIN MARINE INSURANCE COMPANIES AND OTHER THAN FIRE OR FLOOD INSURANCE COMPANIES WHICH OPERATE ON BASIS OF PERPETUAL POLICIES OR PREMIUM DEPOSITS)]

821	Repealed [Tax on mutual insurance companies to which part II applies]
823	Repealed [Determination of statutory underwriting income or loss]
824	Repealed [Adjustments to provide protection against losses]
825	Repealed [Unused loss deduction]

PART II. OTHER INSURANCE COMPANIES

831	Tax on insurance companies other than life insurance companies
832	Insurance company taxable income
833	Treatment of Blue Cross and Blue Shield organizations, etc.
834	Determination of taxable investment income
835	Election by reciprocal

PART III. PROVISIONS OF GENERAL APPLICATION

841	Credit for foreign taxes
842	Foreign companies carrying on insurance business
843	Annual accounting period
844	Special loss carryover rules
845	Certain reinsurance agreements
846	Discounted unpaid losses defined
847	Special estimated tax payments
848	Capitalization of certain policy acquisition expenses

Table of Code Sections

Sec.

Subchapter M. Regulated Investment Companies and Real Estate Investment Trusts

Part I. Regulated Investment Companies
- 851 Definition of regulated investment company
- 852 Taxation of regulated investment companies and their shareholders
- 853 Foreign tax credit allowed to shareholders
- 853A Credits from tax credit bonds allowed to shareholders
- 854 Limitations applicable to dividends received from regulated investment company
- 855 Dividends paid by regulated investment company after close of taxable year

Part II. Real Estate Investment Trusts
- 856 Definition of real estate investment trust
- 857 Taxation of real estate investment trusts and their beneficiaries
- 858 Dividends paid by real estate investment trust after close of taxable year
- 859 Adoption of annual accounting period
- 859 Repealed [Deduction for deficiency dividends]

Part III. Provisions Which Apply to Both Regulated Investment Companies and Real Estate Investment Trusts
- 860 Deduction for deficiency dividends

Part IV. Real Estate Mortgage Investment Conduits
- 860A Taxation of REMIC's
- 860B Taxation of holders of regular interests
- 860C Taxation of residual interests
- 860D REMIC defined
- 860E Treatment of income in excess of daily accruals on residual interests
- 860F Other rules
- 860G Other definitions and special rules

Part V. Repealed [Financial Asset Securitization Investment Trusts]
- 860H Repealed [Taxation of a FASIT; other general rules]
- 860I Repealed [Gain recognition on contributions to a FASIT and in other cases]
- 860J Repealed [Non-FASIT losses not to offset certain FASIT inclusions]
- 860K Repealed [Treatment of transfers of high-yield interests to disqualified holders]
- 860L Repealed [Definitions and other special rules]

Subchapter N. Tax Based on Income from Sources Within or Without the United States

Part I. Determination of Sources of Income
- 861 Income from sources within the United States
- 862 Income from sources without the United States
- 863 Special rules for determining source
- 864 Definitions and special rules
- 865 Source rules for personal property sales

Part II. Nonresident Aliens and Foreign Corporations

Subpart A. Nonresident alien individuals
- 871 Tax on nonresident alien individuals
- 872 Gross income
- 873 Deductions
- 874 Allowance of deductions and credits
- 875 Partnerships; beneficiaries of estates and trusts
- 876 Alien residents of Puerto Rico, Guam, American Samoa, or the Northern Mariana Islands
- 877 Expatriation to avoid tax
- 878 Foreign educational, charitable, and certain other exempt organizations
- 879 Tax treatment of certain community income in the case of nonresident alien individuals

Sec.

Subpart B. Foreign corporations
- 881 Tax on income of foreign corporations not connected with United States business
- 882 Tax on income of foreign corporations connected with United States business
- 883 Exclusions from gross income
- 884 Branch profits tax
- 885 Cross references

Subpart C. Tax on gross transportation income
- 887 Imposition of tax on gross transportation income of nonresident aliens and foreign corporations

Subpart D. Miscellaneous provisions
- 891 Doubling of rates of tax on citizens and corporations of certain foreign countries
- 892 Income of foreign governments and of international organizations
- 893 Compensation of employees of foreign governments or international organizations
- 894 Income affected by treaty
- 895 Income derived by a foreign central bank of issue from obligations of the United States or from bank deposits
- 896 Adjustment of tax on nationals, residents, and corporations of certain foreign countries
- 897 Disposition of investment in United States real property
- 898 Taxable year of certain foreign corporations

Part III. Income from Sources Without the United States

Subpart A. Foreign tax credit
- 901 Taxes of foreign countries and of possessions of United States
- 902 Deemed paid credit where domestic corporation owns 10 percent or more of voting stock of foreign corporation
- 903 Credit for taxes in lieu of income, etc., taxes
- 904 Limitation on credit
- 905 Applicable rules
- 906 Nonresident alien individuals and foreign corporations
- 907 Special rules in case of foreign oil and gas income
- 908 Reduction of credit for participation in or cooperation with an international boycott
- 909 Suspension of taxes and credits until related income taken into account

Subpart B. Earned income of citizens or residents of United States
- 911 Citizens or residents of the United States living abroad
- 912 Exemption for certain allowances
- 913 Repealed [Deduction for certain expenses of living abroad]

Subpart C. Repealed [Taxation of foreign sales corporations]
- 921 Repealed [Exempt foreign trade income excluded from gross income]
- 922 Repealed [FSC defined]
- 923 Repealed [Exempt foreign trade income]
- 924 Repealed [Foreign trading gross receipts]
- 925 Repealed [Transfer pricing rules]
- 926 Repealed [Distributions to shareholders]
- 927 Repealed [Other definitions and special rules]

Subpart D. Possessions of the United States
- 931 Income from sources within Guam, American Samoa, or the Northern Mariana Islands
- 932 Coordination of United States and Virgin Islands income taxes
- 933 Income from sources within Puerto Rico
- 934 Limitation on reduction in income tax liability incurred to the Virgin Islands
- 934A Repealed [Income tax rate on Virgin Islands source income]
- 935 Repealed [Coordination of United States and Guam individual income taxes]
- 936 Puerto Rico and possession tax credit
- 937 Residence and source rules involving possessions

Table of Code Sections

Sec.

Subpart E. Repealed [Qualifying foreign trade income]
941 Repealed [Qualifying foreign trade income]
942 Repealed [Foreign trading gross receipts]
943 Repealed [Other definitions and special rules]

Subpart E. Repealed [China Trade Act corporations]
941 Repealed [Special deduction for China Trade Act corporations]
942 Repealed [Disallowance of foreign tax credit]
943 Repealed [Exclusion of dividends to residents of Formosa or Hong Kong]

Subpart F. Controlled foreign corporations
951 Amounts included in gross income of United States shareholders
952 Subpart F income defined
953 Insurance income
954 Foreign base company income
955 Withdrawal of previously excluded subpart F income from qualified investment
956 Investment of earnings in United States property
956A Repealed [Earnings invested in excess passive assets]
957 Controlled foreign corporations; United States persons
958 Rules for determining stock ownership
959 Exclusion from gross income of previously taxed earnings and profits
960 Special rules for foreign tax credit
961 Adjustments to basis of stock in controlled foreign corporations and of other property
962 Election by individuals to be subject to tax at corporate rates
963 Repealed [Receipt of minimum distributions by domestic corporations]
964 Miscellaneous provisions
965 Temporary dividends received deduction

Subpart G. Export trade corporations
970 Reduction of subpart F income of export trade corporations
971 Definitions
972 Repealed [Consolidation of group of export trade corporations]

Subpart H. Repealed [Income of certain nonresident United States citizens subject to foreign community property laws]

Subpart I. Admissibility of documentation maintained in foreign countries
982 Admissibility of documentation maintained in foreign countries

Subpart J. Foreign currency transactions
985 Functional currency
986 Determination of foreign taxes and foreign corporation's earnings and profits
987 Branch transactions
988 Treatment of certain foreign currency transactions
989 Other definitions and special rules

PART IV. DOMESTIC INTERNATIONAL SALES CORPORATIONS

Subpart A. Treatment of qualifying corporations
991 Taxation of a domestic international sales corporation
992 Requirements of a domestic international sales corporation
993 Definitions
994 Inter-company pricing rules

Subpart B. Treatment of distributions to shareholders
995 Taxation of DISC income to shareholders
996 Rules for allocation in the case of distributions and losses
997 Special subchapter C rules

PART V. INTERNATIONAL BOYCOTT DETERMINATIONS
999 Reports by taxpayers; determinations

Sec.

Subchapter O. Gain or Loss on Disposition of Property

PART I. DETERMINATION OF AMOUNT OF AND RECOGNITION OF GAIN OR LOSS
1001 Determination of amount of and recognition of gain or loss
1002 Repealed [Recognition of gain or loss]

PART II. BASIS RULES OF GENERAL APPLICATION
1011 Adjusted basis for determining gain or loss
1012 Basis of property—cost
1013 Basis of property included in inventory
1014 Basis of property acquired from a decedent
1015 Basis of property acquired by gifts and transfers in trust
1016 Adjustments to basis
1017 Discharge of indebtedness
1018 Repealed [Adjustment of capital structure before September 22, 1938]
1019 Property on which lessee has made improvements
1020 Repealed [Election in respect of depreciation, etc., allowed before 1952]
1021 Sale of annuities
1022 Treatment of property acquired from a decedent dying after December 31, 2009
1022 Repealed [Increase in basis with respect to certain foreign personal holding company stock or securities]
1023 Cross references

PART III. COMMON NONTAXABLE EXCHANGES
1031 Exchange of property held for productive use or investment
1032 Exchange of stock for property
1033 Involuntary conversions
1034 Repealed [Rollover of gain on sale of principal residence]
1035 Certain exchanges of insurance policies
1036 Stock for stock of same corporation
1037 Certain exchanges of United States obligations
1038 Certain reacquisitions of real property
1039 Repealed [Certain sales of low-income housing projects]
1040 Transfer of certain farm, etc., real property
1040 Use of appreciated carryover basis property to satisfy pecuniary bequest
1041 Transfers of property between spouses or incident to divorce
1042 Sales of stock to employee stock ownership plans or certain cooperatives
1043 Sale of property to comply with conflict-of-interest requirements
1044 Rollover of publicly traded securities gain into specialized small business investment companies
1045 Rollover of gain from qualified small business stock to another qualified small business stock

PART IV. SPECIAL RULES
1051 Property acquired during affiliation
1052 Basis established by the Revenue Act of 1932 or 1934 or by the Internal Revenue Code of 1939
1053 Property acquired before March 1, 1913
1054 Certain stock of Federal National Mortgage Association
1055 Redeemable ground rents
1056 Repealed [Basis limitation for player contracts transferred in connection with the sale of a franchise]
1057 Repealed [Election to treat transfer to foreign trust, etc., as taxable exchange]
1058 Transfers of securities under certain agreements
1059 Corporate shareholder's basis in stock reduced by nontaxed portion of extraordinary dividends
1059A Limitation on taxpayer's basis or inventory cost in property imported from related persons
1060 Special allocation rules for certain asset acquisitions
1061 Cross references

509

Table of Code Sections

Sec.	
	PART V. REPEALED [CHANGES TO EFFECTUATE F.C.C. POLICY]
1071	Repealed [Gain from sale or exchange to effectuate policies of F.C.C.]
	PART VI. REPEALED [EXCHANGES IN OBEDIENCE TO S.E.C. ORDERS]
1081	Repealed [Nonrecognition of gain or loss on exchanges or distributions in obedience to orders of S.E.C.]
1082	Repealed [Basis for determining gain or loss]
1083	Repealed [Definitions]
	PART VII. WASH SALES; STRADDLES
1091	Loss from wash sales of stock or securities
1092	Straddles
	PART VIII. REPEALED [DISTRIBUTIONS PURSUANT TO BANK HOLDING COMPANY ACT]
1101	Repealed [Distributions pursuant to Bank Holding Company Act]
1102	Repealed [Special rules]
1103	Repealed [Definitions]
	PART IX. REPEALED

Subchapter P. Capital Gains and Losses

	PART I. TREATMENT OF CAPITAL GAINS
1201	Alternative tax for corporations
1202	Partial exclusion for gain from certain small business stock
1202	Repealed [Deduction for capital gains]
	PART II. TREATMENT OF CAPITAL LOSSES
1211	Limitation on capital losses
1212	Capital loss carrybacks and carryovers
	PART III. GENERAL RULES FOR DETERMINING CAPITAL GAINS AND LOSSES
1221	Capital asset defined
1222	Other terms relating to capital gains and losses
1223	Holding period of property
	PART IV. SPECIAL RULES FOR DETERMINING CAPITAL GAINS AND LOSSES
1231	Property used in the trade or business and involuntary conversions
1232	Repealed [Bonds and other evidence of indebtedness]
1232A	Repealed [Original issue discount]
1232B	Repealed [Tax treatment of stripped bonds]
1233	Gains and losses from short sales
1234	Options to buy or sell
1234A	Gains or losses from certain terminations
1234B	Gains or losses from securities futures contracts
1235	Sale or exchange of patents
1236	Dealers in securities
1237	Real property subdivided for sale
1238	Repealed [Amortization in excess of depreciation]
1239	Gain from sale of depreciable property between certain related taxpayers
1240	Repealed [Taxability to employee of termination payments]
1241	Cancellation of lease or distributor's agreement
1242	Losses on small business investment company stock
1243	Loss of small business investment company
1244	Losses on small business stock
1245	Gain from dispositions of certain depreciable property
1246	Repealed [Gain on foreign investment company stock]
1247	Repealed [Election by foreign investment companies to distribute income currently]
1248	Gain from certain sales or exchanges of stock in certain foreign corporations
1249	Gain from certain sales or exchanges of patents, etc., to foreign corporations
1250	Gain from dispositions of certain depreciable realty
1251	Repealed [Gain from disposition of property used in farming where farm losses offset nonfarm income]
1252	Gain from disposition of farm land
1253	Transfers of franchises, trademarks, and trade names
1254	Gain from disposition of interest in oil, gas, geothermal, or other mineral properties
1255	Gain from disposition of section 126 property
1256	Section 1256 contracts marked to market
1257	Disposition of converted wetlands or highly erodible croplands
1258	Recharacterization of gain from certain financial transactions
1259	Constructive sales treatment for appreciated financial positions
1260	Gains from constructive ownership transactions
	PART V. SPECIAL RULES FOR BONDS AND OTHER DEBT INSTRUMENTS
	Subpart A. Original issue discount
1271	Treatment of amounts received on retirement or sale or exchange of debt instruments
1272	Current inclusion in income of original issue discount
1273	Determination of amount of original issue discount
1274	Determination of issue price in the case of certain debt instruments issued for property
1274A	Special rules for certain transactions where stated principal amount does not exceed $2,800,000.
1275	Other definitions and special rules
	Subpart B. Market discount on bonds
1276	Disposition gain representing accrued market discount treated as ordinary income
1277	Deferral of interest deduction allocable to accrued market discount
1278	Definitions and special rules
	Subpart C. Discount on short-term obligations
1281	Current inclusion in income of discount on certain short-term obligations
1282	Deferral of interest deduction allocable to accrued discount
1283	Definitions and special rules
	Subpart D. Miscellaneous provisions
1286	Tax treatment of stripped bonds
1287	Denial of capital gain treatment for gains on certain obligations not in registered form
1288	Treatment of original issue discount on tax-exempt obligations
	PART VI. TREATMENT OF CERTAIN PASSIVE FOREIGN INVESTMENT COMPANIES
	Subpart A. Interest on tax deferral
1291	Interest on tax deferral
	Subpart B. Treatment of qualified electing funds
1293	Current taxation of income from qualified electing funds
1294	Election to extend time for payment of tax on undistributed earnings
1295	Qualified electing fund
	Subpart C. Election of mark to market for marketable stock
1296	Election of mark to market for marketable stock
	Subpart D. General provisions
1297	Passive foreign investment company
1298	Special rules

Subchapter Q. Readjustment of Tax Between Years and Special Limitations

	PART I. REPEALED [INCOME AVERAGING]
1301	Repealed [Limitation on tax]
1302	Repealed [Definition of averageable income; related definitions]
1303	Repealed [Eligible individuals]
1304	Repealed [Special rules]
1305	Repealed [Regulations]

Sec.	
	PART I. INCOME AVERAGING
1301	Averaging of farm income
	PART II. MITIGATION OF EFFECT OF LIMITATIONS AND OTHER PROVISIONS
1311	Correction of error
1312	Circumstances of adjustment
1313	Definitions
1314	Amount and method of adjustment
1315	Repealed [Effective date]
	PART III. REPEALED
	PART IV. REPEALED
	PART V. CLAIM OF RIGHT
1341	Computation of tax where taxpayer restores substantial amount held under claim of right
1342	Repealed [Computation of tax where taxpayer recovers substantial amount held by another under claim of right]
	PART VI. REPEALED [MAXIMUM RATE ON PERSONAL SERVICE INCOME]
1346	Repealed [Recovery of unconstitutional Federal taxes]
1347	Repealed [Claims against United States involving acquisition of property] secno d='1348' rep='y'>Repealed [50-percent maximum rate on personal service income]
	PART VII. RECOVERIES OF FOREIGN EXPROPRIATION LOSSES
1351	Treatment of recoveries of foreign expropriation losses
	Subchapter R. Election to Determine Corporate Tax on Certain International Shipping Activities Using Per Ton Rate
1352	Alternative tax on qualifying shipping activities
1353	Notional shipping income
1354	Alternative tax election; revocation; termination
1355	Definitions and special rules
1356	Qualifying shipping activities
1357	Items not subject to regular tax; depreciation; interest
1358	Allocation of credits, income, and deductions
1359	Disposition of qualifying vessels
	Subchapter S. Tax Treatment of S Corporations and Their Shareholders
	PART I. IN GENERAL
1361	S corporation defined
1362	Election; revocation; termination
1363	Effect of election on corporation
	PART II. TAX TREATMENT OF SHAREHOLDERS
1366	Pass-thru of items to shareholders
1367	Adjustments to basis of stock of shareholders, etc.
1368	Distributions
	PART III. SPECIAL RULES
1371	Coordination with subchapter C
1372	Partnership rules to apply for fringe benefit purposes
1373	Foreign income
1374	Tax imposed on certain built-in gains
1375	Tax imposed when passive investment income of corporation having accumulated earnings and profits exceeds 25 percent of gross receipts
	PART IV. DEFINITIONS; MISCELLANEOUS
1377	Definitions and special rule
1378	Taxable year of S corporation
1379	Transitional rules on enactment
	Subchapter T. Cooperatives and Their Patrons
	PART I. TAX TREATMENT OF COOPERATIVES
1381	Organizations to which part applies
1382	Taxable income of cooperatives
1383	Computation of tax where cooperative redeems nonqualified written notices of allocation or nonqualified per-unit retain certificates

Sec.	
	PART II. TAX TREATMENT BY PATRONS OF PATRONAGE DIVIDENDS AND PER-UNIT RETAIN ALLOCATIONS
1385	Amounts includible in patron's gross income
	PART III. DEFINITIONS, SPECIAL RULES
1388	Definitions; special rules
	Subchapter U. Repealed [General Stock Ownership Corporations]
1391	Repealed [Definitions]
1392	Repealed [Election by GSOC]
1393	Repealed [GSOC taxable income taxed to shareholders]
1394	Repealed [Rules applicable to distributions of an electing GSOC]
1395	Repealed [Adjustments to basis of stock of shareholders]
1396	Repealed [Minimum distribution]
1397	Repealed [Special rules applicable to an electing GSOC]
	Subchapter U. Designation and Treatment of Empowerment Zones, Enterprise Communities, and Rural Development Investment Areas
	PART I. DESIGNATION
1391	Designation procedure
1392	Eligibility criteria
1393	Definitions and special rules
	PART II. TAX-EXEMPT FACILITY BONDS FOR EMPOWERMENT ZONES AND ENTERPRISE COMMUNITIES
1394	Tax-exempt enterprise zone facility bonds
	PART III. ADDITIONAL INCENTIVES FOR EMPOWERMENT ZONES
	Subpart A. Empowerment zone employment credit
1396	Empowerment zone employment credit
1397	Other definitions and special rules
	Subpart B. Additional expensing
1397A	Increase in expensing under section 179
	Subpart C. Nonrecognition of gain on rollover of empowerment zone investments
1397B	Nonrecognition of gain on rollover of empowerment zone investments
	Subpart D. General provisions
1397C	Enterprise zone business defined
1397D	Qualified zone property defined
	PART IV. INCENTIVES FOR EDUCATION ZONES
1397E	Credit to holders of qualified zone academy bonds
	PART V. REGULATIONS
1397F	Regulations
	Subchapter V. Title 11 Cases
1398	Rules relating to individuals' title 11 cases
1399	No separate taxable entities for partnerships, corporations, etc.
	Subchapter W. District of Columbia Enterprise Zone
1400	Establishment of DC Zone
1400A	Tax-exempt economic development bonds
1400B	Zero percent capital gains rate
1400C	First-time homebuyer credit for District of Columbia
	Subchapter X. Renewal Communities
	PART I. DESIGNATION
1400E	Designation of renewal communities
	PART II. RENEWAL COMMUNITY CAPITAL GAIN; RENEWAL COMMUNITY BUSINESS
1400F	Renewal community capital gain
1400G	Renewal community business defined
	PART III. ADDITIONAL INCENTIVES
1400H	Renewal community employment credit
1400I	Commercial revitalization deduction
1400J	Increase in expensing under section 179

Table of Code Sections

Sec.	
	Subchapter Y. Short-Term Regional Benefits
	PART I. TAX BENEFITS FOR NEW YORK LIBERTY ZONE
1400L	Tax benefits for New York Liberty Zone
	PART II. TAX BENEFITS FOR GO ZONES
1400M	Definitions
1400N	Tax benefits for Gulf Opportunity Zone
1400O	Education tax benefits
1400P	Housing tax benefits
1400Q	Special rules for use of retirement funds
1400R	Employment relief
1400S	Additional tax relief provisions
1400T	Special rules for mortgage revenue bonds
	PART III
1400U-1	Allocation of recovery zone bonds
1400U-2	Recovery zone economic development bonds
1400U-3	Recovery zone facility bonds
	Chapter 2. Tax on Self-Employment Income
1401	Rate of tax
1402	Definitions
1403	Miscellaneous provisions
	Chapter 2A. Unearned Income Medicare Contribution
1411	Imposition of tax
	Chapter 3. Withholding of Tax on Nonresident Aliens and Foreign Corporations
	Subchapter A. Nonresident Aliens and Foreign Corporations
1441	Withholding of tax on nonresident aliens
1442	Withholding of tax on foreign corporations
1443	Foreign tax-exempt organizations
1444	Withholding on Virgin Islands source income
1445	Withholding of tax on dispositions of United States real property interests
1446	Withholding tax on foreign partners' share of effectively connected income
	Subchapter B. Repealed [Tax-Free Covenant Bonds]
1451	Repealed [Tax-free covenant bonds]
	Subchapter B. Application of Withholding Provisions
1461	Liability for withheld tax
1462	Withheld tax as credit to recipient of income
1463	Tax paid by recipient of income
1464	Refunds and credits with respect to withheld tax
1465	Repealed [Definition of withholding agent]
	Chapter 4. Repealed [Rules Applicable to Recovery of Excessive Profits on Government Contracts]
	Subchapter A. Repealed [Recovery of Excessive Profits on Government Contracts]
1471	Repealed [Recovery of excessive profits on government contracts]
	Chapter 4. Taxes to Enforce Reporting on Certain Foreign Accounts
1471	Withholdable payments to foreign financial institutions
1472	Withholdable payments to other foreign entities
1473	Definitions
1474	Special rules
	Subchapter B. Repealed [Mitigation of Effect of Renegotiation of Government Contracts]
1481	Repealed [Mitigation of effect of renegotiation of government contracts]
1482	Repealed [Readjustment for repayments made pursuant to price redeterminations]
	Chapter 5. Repealed [Tax on Transfers to Avoid Income Tax]
1491	Repealed [Imposition of tax]
1492	Repealed [Nontaxable transfers]
1493	Repealed [Definition of foreign trust]
1494	Repealed [Payment and collection]
	Chapter 6. Consolidated Returns
	Subchapter A. Returns and Payment of Tax
1501	Privilege to file consolidated returns
1502	Regulations
1503	Computation and payment of tax
1504	Definitions
1505	Cross references
	Subchapter B. Related Rules
	PART I. IN GENERAL
1551	Disallowance of the benefits of the graduated corporate rates and accumulated earnings credit
1552	Earnings and profits
	PART II. CERTAIN CONTROLLED CORPORATIONS
1561	Limitations on certain multiple tax benefits in the case of certain controlled corporations
1562	Repealed [Privilege of groups to elect multiple surtax exemptions]
1563	Definitions and special rules
1564	Repealed [Transitional rules in the case of certain controlled corporations]
	SUBTITLE B — ESTATE AND GIFT TAXES
	Chapter 11. Estate Tax
	Subchapter A. Estates of Citizens or Residents
	PART I. TAX IMPOSED
2001	Imposition and rate of tax
2002	Liability for payment
	PART II. CREDITS AGAINST TAX
2010	Unified credit against estate tax
2011	Credit for State death taxes
2012	Credit for gift tax
2013	Credit for tax on prior transfers
2014	Credit for foreign death taxes
2015	Credit for death taxes on remainders
2016	Recovery of taxes claimed as credit
	PART III. GROSS ESTATE
2031	Definition of gross estate
2032	Alternate valuation
2032A	Valuation of certain farm, etc., real property
2033	Property in which the decedent had an interest
2034	Dower or curtesy interests
2035	Adjustments for certain gifts made within 3 years of decedent's death
2036	Transfers with retained life estate
2037	Transfers taking effect at death
2038	Revocable transfers
2039	Annuities
2040	Joint interests
2041	Powers of appointment
2042	Proceeds of life insurance
2043	Transfers for insufficient consideration
2044	Certain property for which marital deduction was previously allowed
2045	Prior interests
2046	Disclaimers
	PART IV. TAXABLE ESTATE
2051	Definition of taxable estate
2052	Repealed [Exemption]
2053	Expenses, indebtedness, and taxes
2054	Losses
2055	Transfers for public, charitable, and religious uses
2056	Bequests, etc., to surviving spouse
2056A	Qualified domestic trust

Table of Code Sections

Sec.	
2057	Family-owned business interests
2057	Repealed [Sales of employer securities to employee stock ownership plans or worker-owned cooperatives]
2057	Repealed [Bequests, etc., to certain minor children]
2058	State death taxes

Subchapter B. Estates of Nonresidents Not Citizens

2101	Tax imposed
2102	Credits against tax
2103	Definition of gross estate
2104	Property within the United States
2105	Property without the United States
2106	Taxable estate
2107	Expatriation to avoid tax
2108	Application of pre-1967 estate tax provisions

Subchapter C. Miscellaneous

2201	Combat zone-related deaths of members of the Armed Forces, deaths of astronauts, and deaths of victims of certain terrorist attacks
2202	Repealed [Missionaries in foreign service]
2203	Definition of executor
2204	Discharge of fiduciary from personal liability
2205	Reimbursement out of estate
2206	Liability of life insurance beneficiaries
2207	Liability of recipient of property over which decedent had power of appointment
2207A	Right of recovery in the case of certain marital deduction property
2207B	Right of recovery where decedent retained interest
2208	Certain residents of possessions considered citizens of the United States
2209	Certain residents of possessions considered nonresidents not citizens of the United States
2210	Termination
2210	Repealed [Liability for payment in case of transfer of employer securities to an employee stock ownership plan or a worker-owned cooperative]

Chapter 12. Gift Tax

Subchapter A. Determination of Tax Liability

2501	Imposition of tax
2502	Rate of tax
2503	Taxable gifts
2504	Taxable gifts for preceding calendar periods
2505	Unified credit against gift tax

Subchapter B. Transfers

2511	Transfers in general
2512	Valuation of gifts
2513	Gift by husband or wife to third party
2514	Powers of appointment
2515	Treatment of generation-skipping transfer tax
2515	Repealed [Tenancies by the entirety in real property]
2515A	Repealed [Tenancies by the entirety in personal property]
2516	Certain property settlements
2517	Repealed [Certain annuities under qualified plans]
2518	Disclaimers
2519	Dispositions of certain life estates

Subchapter C. Deductions

2521	Repealed [Specific exemption]
2522	Charitable and similar gifts
2523	Gift to spouse
2524	Extent of deductions

Chapter 13. Tax on Certain Generation-Skipping Transfers

Subchapter A. Tax Imposed

2601	Tax imposed
2602	Amount of tax
2603	Liability for tax
2604	Credit for certain State taxes

Subchapter B. Generation-Skipping Transfers

Sec.	
2611	Generation-skipping transfer defined
2612	Taxable termination; taxable distribution; direct skip
2613	Skip person and non-skip person defined

Subchapter C. Taxable Amount

2621	Taxable amount in case of taxable distribution
2622	Taxable amount in case of taxable termination
2623	Taxable amount in case of direct skip
2624	Valuation

Subchapter D. GST Exemption

2631	GST exemption
2632	Special rules for allocation of GST exemption

Subchapter E. Applicable Rate; Inclusion Ratio

2641	Applicable rate
2642	Inclusion ratio

Subchapter F. Other Definitions and Special Rules

2651	Generation assignment
2652	Other definitions
2653	Taxation of multiple skips
2654	Special rules

Subchapter G. Administration

2661	Administration
2662	Return requirements
2663	Regulations
2664	Termination

Chapter 14. Special Valuation Rules

2701	Special valuation rules in case of transfers of certain interests in corporations or partnerships
2702	Special valuation rules in case of transfers of interests in trusts
2703	Certain rights and restrictions disregarded
2704	Treatment of certain lapsing rights and restrictions

Chapter 15. Gifts and Bequests From Expatriates

2801	Imposition of tax

SUBTITLE C—EMPLOYMENT TAXES AND COLLECTION OF INCOME TAX

Chapter 21. Federal Insurance Contributions Act

Subchapter A. Tax on Employees

3101	Rate of tax
3102	Deduction of tax from wages

Subchapter B. Tax on Employers

3111	Rate of tax
3112	Instrumentalities of the United States
3113	Repealed [District of Columbia credit unions]

Subchapter C. General Provisions

3121	Definitions
3122	Federal service
3123	Deductions as constructive payments
3124	Estimate of revenue reduction
3125	Returns in the case of governmental employees in States, Guam, American Samoa, and the District of Columbia
3126	Return and payment by governmental employer
3127	Exemption for employers and their employees where both are members of religious faiths opposed to participation in Social Security Act programs
3128	Short title

Chapter 22. Railroad Retirement Tax Act

Subchapter A. Tax on Employees

3201	Rate of tax
3202	Deduction of tax from compensation

Subchapter B. Tax on Employee Representatives

3211	Rate of tax
3212	Determination of compensation

Table of Code Sections

Sec.
Subchapter C. Tax on Employers
3221 Rate of tax

Subchapter D. General Provisions
3231 Definitions
3232 Court jurisdiction
3233 Short title

Subchapter E. Tier 2 Tax Rate Determination
3241 Determination of tier 2 tax rate based on average account benefits ratio

Chapter 23. Federal Unemployment Tax Act
3301 Rate of tax
3302 Credits against tax
3303 Conditions of additional credit allowance
3304 Approval of State laws
3305 Applicability of State law
3306 Definitions
3307 Deductions as constructive payments
3308 Instrumentalities of the United States
3309 State law coverage of services performed for nonprofit organizations or governmental entities
3310 Judicial review
3311 Short title

Chapter 23A. Railroad Unemployment Repayment Tax
3321 Imposition of tax
3322 Definitions

Chapter 24. Collection of Income Tax at Source
Subchapter A. Withholding from Wages
3401 Definitions
3402 Income tax collected at source
3403 Liability for tax
3404 Return and payment by governmental employer
3405 Special rules for pensions, annuities, and certain other deferred income
3406 Backup withholding

Subchapter B. Repealed [Withholding From Interest and Dividends]
3451 Repealed [Income tax collected at source on interest, dividends, and patronage dividends]
3452 Repealed [Exemptions from withholding]
3453 Repealed [Payor defined]
3454 Repealed [Definitions of interest, dividend, and patronage dividend]
3455 Repealed [Other definitions and special rules]
3456 Repealed [Administrative provisions]

Chapter 25. General Provisions Relating to Employment Taxes and Collection of Income Taxes at Source
3501 Collection and payment of taxes
3502 Nondeductibility of taxes in computing taxable income
3503 Erroneous payments
3504 Acts to be performed by agents
3505 Liability of third parties paying or providing for wages
3506 Individuals providing companion sitting placement services
3507 Advance payment of earned income credit
3508 Treatment of real estate agents and direct sellers
3509 Determination of employer's liability for certain employment taxes
3510 Coordination of collection of domestic service employment taxes with collection of income taxes
3510 Repealed [Credit for increased social security employee taxes and railroad retirement tier 1 employee taxes imposed during 1984]

SUBTITLE D — MISCELLANEOUS EXCISE TAXES
Chapter 31. Retail Excise Taxes
Subchapter A. Luxury Passenger Vehicles
4001 Imposition of tax

Sec.
4002 1st retail sale; uses, etc. treated as sales; determination of price
4003 Special rules

Subchapter B. Special Fuels
4041 Imposition of tax
4042 Tax on fuel used in commercial transportation on inland waterways

Subchapter C. Heavy Trucks and Trailers
4051 Imposition of tax on heavy trucks and trailers sold at retail
4052 Definitions and special rules
4053 Exemptions

Chapter 32. Manufacturers Excise Taxes
Subchapter A. Automotive and Related Items
Part I. Gas Guzzlers
4061 Repealed [Imposition of tax]
4062 Repealed [Articles classified as parts]
4063 Repealed [Exemptions]
4064 Gas guzzler tax

Part II. Tires
4071 Imposition of tax
4072 Definitions
4073 Exemptions

Part III. Petroleum Products
Subpart A. Motor and aviation fuels
4081 Imposition of tax
4082 Exemptions for diesel fuel and kerosene
4083 Definitions; special rule; administrative authority
4084 Cross references

Subpart B. Repealed [Aviation fuel]
4091 Repealed [Imposition of tax]
4092 Repealed [Exemptions]
4093 Repealed [Definitions]

Subpart B. Repealed [Lubricating oil]
4091 Repealed [Imposition of tax]
4092 Repealed [Definitions]
4093 Repealed [Exemptions]
4094 Repealed [Cross reference]

Subpart B. Special provisions applicable to fuels tax
4101 Registration and bond
4102 Inspection of records by local officers
4103 Certain additional persons liable for tax where willful failure to pay
4104 Information reporting for persons claiming certain tax benefits
4105 Two-party exchanges

Subchapter B. Coal
4121 Imposition of tax

Subchapter C. Certain Vaccines
4131 Imposition of tax
4132 Definitions and special rules

Subchapter D. Recreational Equipment
Part I. Sporting Goods
4161 Imposition of tax
4162 Definitions; treatment of certain resales

Part III. Firearms
4181 Imposition of tax
4182 Exemptions

Subchapter E. Medical Devices
4191 Medical devices

Subchapter F. Special Provisions Applicable to Manufacturers Tax
4216 Definition of price
4217 Leases

Sec.	
4218	Use by manufacturer or importer considered sale
4219	Application of tax in case of sales by other than manufacturer or importer

Subchapter G. Exemptions, Registration, Etc.

4221	Certain tax-free sales
4222	Registration
4223	Special rules relating to further manufacture
4225	Exemption of articles manufactured or produced by Indians
4227	Cross references

Chapter 33. Facilities and Services
Subchapter B. Communications

4251	Imposition of tax
4252	Definitions
4253	Exemptions
4254	Computation of tax

Subchapter C. Transportation by Air
PART I. PERSONS

4261	Imposition of tax
4262	Definition of taxable transportation
4263	Special rules

PART II. PROPERTY

4271	Imposition of tax
4272	Definition of taxable transportation, etc.

PART III. SPECIAL PROVISIONS APPLICABLE TO TAXES ON TRANSPORTATION BY AIR

4281	Small aircraft on nonestablished lines
4281	Repealed [Imposition of tax]
4282	Transportation by air for other members of affiliated group
4282	Repealed [Definition of fair charge]
4283	Repealed [Reduction in aviation-related taxes in certain cases]
4283	Repealed [Exemption for oil transported within premises of a plant]

Subchapter E. Special Provisions Applicable to Services and Facilities Taxes

4291	Cases where persons receiving payment must collect tax
4292	Repealed [State and local governmental exemption]
4293	Exemption for United States and possessions
4294	Repealed [Exemption for nonprofit educational organizations]

Chapter 34. Policies Issued by Foreign Insurers

4371	Imposition of tax
4372	Definitions
4373	Exemptions
4374	Liability for tax

Subchapter B. Insured and Self-Insured Health Plans

4375	Health insurance
4376	Self-insured health plans
4377	Definitions and special rules

Chapter 35. Taxes on Wagering
Subchapter A. Tax on Wagers

4401	Imposition of tax
4402	Exemptions
4403	Record requirements
4404	Territorial extent
4405	Cross references

Subchapter B. Occupational Tax

4411	Imposition of tax
4412	Registration
4413	Certain provisions made applicable
4414	Cross references

Subchapter C. Miscellaneous Provisions

4421	Definitions
4422	Applicability of Federal and State laws
4423	Inspection of books
4424	Disclosure of wagering tax information

Chapter 36. Certain Other Excise Taxes
Subchapter A. Harbor Maintenance Tax

4461	Imposition of tax
4462	Definitions and special rules

Subchapter B. Transportation by Water

4471	Imposition of tax
4472	Definitions

Subchapter D. Tax on Use of Certain Vehicles

4481	Imposition of tax
4482	Definitions
4483	Exemptions
4484	Cross references

Subchapter E. Repealed [Tax on Use of Civil Aircraft]

4491	Repealed [Imposition of tax]
4492	Repealed [Definitions]
4493	Repealed [Special rules]
4494	Repealed [Cross reference]

Subchapter F. Repealed [Tax on Removal of Hard Mineral Resources from Deep Seabed]

4495	Repealed [Imposition of tax]
4496	Repealed [Definitions]
4497	Repealed [Imputed value]
4498	Repealed [Termination]

Chapter 37. Repealed [Sugar]

4501	Repealed [Imposition of tax]
4502	Repealed [Definitions]
4503	Repealed [Exemptions for sugar manufactured for home consumption]

Chapter 38. Environmental Taxes
Subchapter A. Tax on Petroleum

4611	Imposition of tax
4612	Definitions and special rules

Subchapter B. Tax on Certain Chemicals

4661	Imposition of tax
4662	Definitions and special rules

Subchapter C. Tax on Certain Imported Substances

4671	Imposition of tax
4672	Definitions and special rules

Subchapter C. Repealed [Tax on Hazardous Wastes]

4681	Repealed [Imposition of tax]
4682	Repealed [Definitions and special rules]

Subchapter D. Ozone-Depleting Chemicals, Etc.

4681	Imposition of tax
4682	Definitions and special rules

Chapter 39. Registration-Required Obligations

4701	Tax on issuer of registration-required obligation not in registered form

Chapter 40. General Provisions Relating to Occupational Taxes

4901	Payment of tax
4902	Liability of partners
4903	Liability in case of business in more than one location
4904	Liability in case of different businesses of same ownership and location
4905	Liability in case of death or change of location
4906	Application of State laws
4907	Federal agencies or instrumentalities

Chapter 41. Public Charities

4911	Tax on excess expenditures to influence legislation
4912	Tax on disqualifying lobbying expenditures of certain organizations

Table of Code Sections

Sec.

Chapter 42. Private Foundations and Certain Other Tax-Exempt Organizations

Subchapter A. Private Foundations

Sec.	
4940	Excise tax based on investment income
4941	Taxes on self-dealing
4942	Taxes on failure to distribute income
4943	Taxes on excess business holdings
4944	Taxes on investments which jeopardize charitable purpose
4945	Taxes on taxable expenditures
4946	Definitions and special rules
4947	Application of taxes to certain nonexempt trusts
4948	Application of taxes and denial of exemption with respect to certain foreign organizations

Subchapter B. Black Lung Benefit Trusts

4951	Taxes on self-dealing
4952	Taxes on taxable expenditures
4953	Tax on excess contributions to black lung benefit trusts

Subchapter C. Political Expenditures of Section 501(c)(3) Organizations

4955	Taxes on political expenditures of section 501(c)(3) organizations

Subchapter D. Failure by Certain Charitable Organizations to Meet Certain Qualification Requirements

4958	Taxes on excess benefit transactions
4959	Taxes on failures by hospital organizations

Subchapter E. Abatement of First and Second Tier Taxes in Certain Cases

4961	Abatement of second tier taxes where there is correction
4962	Abatement of first tier taxes in certain cases
4963	Definitions

Subchapter F. Tax Shelter Transactions

4965	Excise tax on certain tax-exempt entities entering into prohibited tax shelter transactions

Subchapter G. Donor advised funds

4966	Taxes on taxable distributions
4967	Taxes on prohibited benefits

Chapter 43. Qualified Pension, Etc., Plans

4971	Taxes on failure to meet minimum funding standards
4972	Tax on nondeductible contributions to qualified employer plans
4972	Repealed [Tax on excess contributions for self-employed individuals]
4973	Tax on excess contributions to certain tax-favored accounts and annuities
4974	Excise tax on certain accumulations in qualified retirement plans
4975	Tax on prohibited transactions
4976	Taxes with respect to funded welfare benefit plans
4977	Tax on certain fringe benefits provided by an employer
4978	Tax on certain dispositions by employee stock ownership plans and certain cooperatives
4978A	Repealed [Tax on certain dispositions of employer securities to which section 2057 applied]
4978B	Repealed [Tax on disposition of employer securities to which section 133 applied]
4979	Tax on certain excess contributions
4979A	Tax on certain prohibited allocations of qualified securities
4980	Tax on reversion of qualified plan assets to employer
4980A	Repealed [Tax on excess distributions from qualified retirement plans]
4980B	Failure to satisfy continuation coverage requirements of group health plans
4980C	Requirements for issuers of qualified long-term care insurance contracts
4980D	Failure to meet certain group health plan requirements

Sec.

4980E	Failure of employer to make comparable Archer MSA contributions
4980F	Failure of applicable plans reducing benefit accruals to satisfy notice requirements
4980G	Failure of employer to make comparable health savings account contributions
4980H	Shared responsibility for employers regarding health coverage
4980I	Excise tax on high cost employer-sponsored health coverage

Chapter 44. Qualified Investment Entities

4981	Excise tax on undistributed income of real estate investment trusts
4982	Excise tax on undistributed income of regulated investment companies

Chapter 45. Provisions Relating to Expatriated Entities

4985	Stock compensation of insiders in expatriated corporations

Chapter 46. Golden Parachute Payments

4999	Golden parachute payments

Chapter 47. Certain Group Health Plans

5000	Certain group health plans

Chapter 48. Maintenance of minimum essential coverage

5000A	Requirement to maintain minimum essential coverage

Chapter 49. Cosmetic services

5000B	Imposition of tax on indoor tanning services

Chapter 50. Foreign procurement

5000C	Imposition of tax on certain foreign procurement

SUBTITLE E — ALCOHOL, TOBACCO, AND CERTAIN OTHER EXCISE TAXES

Chapter 51. Distilled Spirits, Wines, and Beer

Subchapter A. Gallonage and Occupational Taxes

PART I. GALLONAGE TAXES

Subpart A. Distilled spirits

5001	Imposition, rate, and attachment of tax
5002	Definitions
5003	Cross references to exemptions, etc.
5004	Lien for tax
5005	Persons liable for tax
5006	Determination of tax
5007	Collection of tax on distilled spirits
5008	Abatement, remission, refund, and allowance for loss or destruction of distilled spirits
5009	Repealed [Drawback]
5010	Credit for wine content and for flavors content
5011	Income tax credit for average cost of carrying excise tax

Subpart B. Repealed [Rectification]

5021	Repealed [Imposition and rate of tax]
5022	Repealed [Tax on cordials and liqueurs containing wine]
5023	Repealed [Tax on blending of beverage rums or brandies]
5024	Repealed [Definitions]
5025	Repealed [Exemption from rectification tax]
5026	Repealed [Determination and collection of rectification tax]

Subpart C. Wines

5041	Imposition and rate of tax
5042	Exemption from tax
5043	Collection of taxes on wines
5044	Refund of tax on wine
5045	Cross references

Subpart D. Beer

5051	Imposition and rate of tax
5052	Definitions
5053	Exemptions
5054	Determination and collection of tax on beer
5055	Drawback of tax
5056	Refund and credit of tax, or relief from liability

Table of Code Sections

Sec.
- 5061 Method of collecting tax
- 5062 Refund and drawback in case of exportation
- 5063 Repealed [Floor stocks tax refunds on distilled spirits, wines, cordials, and beer]
- 5064 Losses resulting from disaster, vandalism, or malicious mischief
- 5065 Territorial extent of law
- 5066 Distilled spirits for use of foreign embassies, legations, etc.
- 5067 Cross reference

Part II. Miscellaneous Provisions

Subpart A. Repealed [Proprietors of distilled spirits plants, bonded wine cellars, etc.]
- 5081 Repealed [Imposition and rate of tax]

Subpart B. Repealed [Brewer]
- 5091 Repealed [Imposition and rate of tax]
- 5092 Repealed [Definition of brewer]
- 5093 Repealed [Cross references]

Subpart A. Manufacturers of stills
- 5101 Notice of manufacture of still; notice of set up of still
- 5102 Definition of manufacturer of stills
- 5103 Repealed [Exemptions]
- 5105 Repealed [Notice of manufacture of and permit to set up still.]
- 5106 Repealed [Export]

Subpart B. Nonbeverage domestic drawback claimants
- 5111 Eligibility
- 5111 Repealed [Imposition and rate of tax]
- 5112 Registration and regulation
- 5112 Repealed [Definitions]
- 5113 Investigation of claims
- 5113 Repealed [Exemptions]
- 5114 Drawback
- 5115 Repealed [Sign required on premises]
- 5117 Repealed [Prohibited purchases by dealers]

Subpart C. Recordkeeping and registration by dealers
- 5121 Repealed [Imposition and rate of tax]
- 5121 Recordkeeping by wholesale dealers
- 5122 Repealed [Definitions]
- 5122 Recordkeeping by retail dealers
- 5123 Repealed [Exemptions]
- 5123 Preservation and inspection of records, and entry of premises for inspection
- 5124 Repealed [Records]
- 5124 Registration by dealers
- 5125 Repealed [Cross references]

Subpart D. Other provisions
- 5131 Eligibility and rate of tax
- 5132 Registration and regulation

Subpart G. Repealed [General provisions]
- 5141 Repealed [Registration]
- 5147 Repealed [Application of subpart]
- 5148 Repealed [Suspension of occupational tax]
- 5149 Repealed [Cross references]

Subchapter B. Qualification Requirements for Distilled Spirits Plants
- 5171 Establishment
- 5172 Application
- 5173 Bonds
- 5174 Repealed [Withdrawal bonds]
- 5175 Export bonds
- 5176 New or renewed bonds
- 5177 Other provisions relating to bonds
- 5178 Premises of distilled spirits plants
- 5179 Registration of stills
- 5180 Signs
- 5181 Distilled spirits for fuel use
- 5182 Cross references

Subchapter C. Operation of Distilled Spirits Plants

Part I. General Provisions
- 5201 Regulation of operations
- 5202 Supervision of operations
- 5203 Entry and examination of premises
- 5204 Gauging
- 5205 Repealed [Stamps]
- 5206 Containers
- 5207 Records and reports

Part II. Operations on Bonded Premises

Subpart A. General
- 5211 Production and entry of distilled spirits
- 5212 Transfer of distilled spirits between bonded premises
- 5213 Withdrawal of distilled spirits from bonded premises on determination of tax
- 5214 Withdrawal of distilled spirits from bonded premises free of tax or without payment of tax
- 5215 Return of tax determined distilled spirits to bonded premises
- 5216 Regulation of operations

Subpart B. Production
- 5221 Commencement, suspension, and resumption of operations
- 5222 Production, receipt, removal, and use of distilling materials
- 5223 Redistillation of spirits, articles, and residues

Subpart C. Storage
- 5231 Entry for deposit
- 5232 Imported distilled spirits
- 5233 Repealed [Bottling of distilled spirits in bond]
- 5234 Repealed [Mingling and blending of distilled spirits]
- 5235 Bottling of alcohol for industrial purposes
- 5236 Discontinuance of storage facilities and transfer of distilled spirits

Subpart D. Denaturation
- 5241 Authority to denature
- 5242 Denaturing materials
- 5243 Sale of abandoned spirits for denaturation without collection of tax
- 5244 Cross references

Subchapter D. Industrial Use of Distilled Spirits
- 5271 Permits
- 5272 Bonds
- 5273 Sale, use, and recovery of denatured distilled spirits
- 5274 Applicability of other laws
- 5275 Records and reports
- 5276 Repealed [Occupational tax]

Subchapter E. General Provisions Relating to Distilled Spirits

Part I. Return of Materials Used in the Manufacture or Recovery of Distilled Spirits
- 5291 General

Part II. Regulation of Traffic in Containers of Distilled Spirits
- 5301 General

Part III. Miscellaneous Provisions
- 5311 Detention of containers
- 5312 Production and use of distilled spirits for experimental research
- 5313 Withdrawal of distilled spirits from customs custody free of tax for use of the United States
- 5314 Special applicability of certain provisions

Table of Code Sections

Sec.

Subchapter F. Bonded and Taxpaid Wine Premises
Part I. Establishment
5351	Bonded wine cellar
5352	Taxpaid wine bottling house
5353	Bonded wine warehouse
5354	Bond
5355	General provisions relating to bonds
5356	Application
5357	Premises

Part II. Operations
5361	Bonded wine cellar operations
5362	Removals of wine from bonded wine cellars
5363	Taxpaid wine bottling house operations
5364	Wine imported in bulk
5364	Repealed [Standard wine premises]
5365	Segregation of operations
5366	Supervision
5367	Records
5368	Gauging and marking
5369	Inventories
5370	Losses
5371	Insurance coverage, etc.
5372	Sampling
5373	Wine spirits

Part III. Cellar Treatment and Classification of Wine
5381	Natural wine
5382	Cellar treatment of natural wine
5383	Amelioration and sweetening limitations for natural grape wines
5384	Amelioration and sweetening limitations for natural fruit and berry wines
5385	Specially sweetened natural wines
5386	Special natural wines
5387	Agricultural wines
5388	Designation of wines

Part IV. General
5391	Exemption from distilled spirits taxes
5392	Definitions

Subchapter G. Breweries
Part I. Establishment
5401	Qualifying documents
5402	Definitions
5403	Cross references

Part II. Operations
5411	Use of brewery
5412	Removal of beer in containers or by pipeline
5413	Brewers procuring beer from other brewers
5414	Removals from one brewery to another belonging to the same brewer
5415	Records and returns
5416	Definitions of package and packaging
5417	Pilot brewing plants
5418	Beer imported in bulk

Subchapter H. Miscellaneous Plants and Warehouses
Part I. Vinegar Plants
5501	Establishment
5502	Qualification
5503	Construction and equipment
5504	Operation
5505	Applicability of provisions of this chapter

Part II. Volatile Fruit-Flavor Concentrate Plants
5511	Establishment and operation
5512	Control of products after manufacture

Part III. Repealed [Manufacturing Bonded Warehouses]
5521	Repealed [Establishment and operation]

Sec.

5522	Repealed [Withdrawal of distilled spirits to manufacturing bonded warehouses]
5523	Repealed [Special provisions relating to distilled spirits and wines rectified in manufacturing bonded warehouses]

Subchapter I. Miscellaneous General Provisions
5551	General provisions relating to bonds
5552	Installation of meters, tanks, and other apparatus
5553	Supervision of premises and operations
5554	Pilot operations
5555	Records, statements, and returns
5556	Regulations
5557	Officers and agents authorized to investigate, issue search warrants, and prosecute for violations
5558	Authority of enforcement officers
5559	Determinations
5560	Other provisions applicable
5561	Exemptions to meet the requirements of the national defense
5562	Exemptions from certain requirements in cases of disaster

Subchapter J. Penalties, Seizures, and Forfeitures Relating to Liquors
Part I. Penalty, Seizure, and Forfeiture Provisions Applicable to Distilling, Rectifying, and Distilled and Rectified Products
5601	Criminal penalties
5602	Penalty for tax fraud by distiller
5603	Penalty relating to records, returns, and reports
5604	Penalties relating to marks, brands, and containers
5605	Penalty relating to return of materials used in the manufacture of distilled spirits, or from which distilled spirits may be recovered
5606	Penalty relating to containers of distilled spirits
5607	Penalty and forfeiture for unlawful use, recovery, or concealment of denatured distilled spirits, or articles
5608	Penalty and forfeiture for fraudulent claims for export drawback or unlawful relanding
5609	Destruction of unregistered stills, distilling apparatus, equipment, and materials
5610	Disposal of forfeited equipment and material for distilling
5611	Release of distillery before judgment
5612	Forfeiture of taxpaid distilled spirits remaining on bonded premises
5613	Forfeiture of distilled spirits not closed, marked, or branded as required by law
5614	Burden of proof in cases of seizure of spirits
5615	Property subject to forfeiture

Part II. Penalty and Forfeiture Provisions Applicable to Wine and Wine Production
5661	Penalty and forfeiture for violation of laws and regulations relating to wine
5662	Penalty for alteration of wine labels
5663	Cross reference

Part III. Penalty, Seizure, and Forfeiture Provisions Applicable to Beer and Brewing
5671	Penalty and forfeiture for evasion of beer tax and fraudulent noncompliance with requirements
5672	Penalty for failure of brewer to comply with requirements and to keep records and file returns
5673	Forfeiture for flagrant and willful removal of beer without tax payment
5674	Penalty for unlawful production or removal of beer
5675	Penalty for intentional removal or defacement of brewer's marks and brands

Part IV. Penalty, Seizure, and Forfeiture Provisions Common to Liquors
5681	Penalty relating to signs

Sec.	
5682	Penalty for breaking locks or gaining access
5683	Penalty and forfeiture for removal of liquors under improper brands
5684	Penalties relating to the payment and collection of liquor taxes
5685	Penalty and forfeiture relating to possession of devices for emitting gas, smoke, etc., explosives and firearms, when violating liquor laws
5686	Penalty for having, possessing, or using liquor or property intended to be used in violating provisions of this chapter
5687	Penalty for offenses not specifically covered
5688	Disposition and release of seized property
5690	Definition of the term "person"

PART V. REPEALED [PENALTIES APPLICABLE TO OCCUPATIONAL TAXES]

5691	Repealed [Penalties for nonpayment of special taxes]
5692	Repealed [Penalties relating to posting of special tax stamps]

Chapter 52. Tobacco Products and Cigarette Papers and Tubes

Subchapter A. Definitions; Rate and Payment of Tax; Exemption From Tax; and Refund and Drawback of Tax

5701	Rate of tax
5702	Definitions
5703	Liability for tax and method of payment
5704	Exemption from tax
5705	Credit, refund, or allowance of tax
5706	Drawback of tax
5707	Repealed [Floor stocks refund on cigarettes]
5708	Losses caused by disaster

Subchapter B. Qualification Requirements for Manufacturers and Importers of Tobacco Products and Cigarette Papers and Tubes, and Export Warehouse Proprietors

5711	Bond
5712	Application for permit
5713	Permit

Subchapter C. Operations by Manufacturers and Importers of Tobacco Products and Cigarette Papers and Tubes, and Export Warehouse Proprietors

5721	Inventories
5722	Reports
5723	Packages, marks, labels, and notices

Subchapter D. Occupational Tax

5731	Imposition and rate of tax
5732	Payment of tax
5733	Provisions relating to liability for occupational taxes
5734	Application of State laws

Subchapter E. Records of Manufacturers and Importers of Tobacco Products and Cigarette Papers and Tubes, and Export Warehouse Proprietors

5741	Records to be maintained

Subchapter F. General Provisions

5751	Purchase, receipt, possession, or sale of tobacco products and cigarette papers and tubes, after removal
5752	Restrictions relating to marks, labels, notices, and packages
5753	Disposal of forfeited, condemned, and abandoned tobacco products, and cigarette papers and tubes
5754	Restriction on importation of previously exported tobacco products

Subchapter G. Penalties and Forfeitures

5761	Civil penalties
5762	Criminal penalties
5763	Forfeitures

Chapter 53. Machine Guns, Destructive Devices, and Certain Other Firearms

Sec.	

Subchapter A. Taxes

PART I. SPECIAL (OCCUPATIONAL) TAXES

5801	Imposition of tax
5802	Registration of importers, manufacturers, and dealers

PART II. TAX ON TRANSFERRING FIREARMS

5811	Transfer tax
5812	Transfers

PART III. TAX ON MAKING FIREARMS

5821	Making tax
5822	Making

Subchapter B. General Provisions and Exemptions

PART I. GENERAL PROVISIONS

5841	Registration of firearms
5842	Identification of firearms
5843	Records and returns
5844	Importation
5845	Definitions
5846	Other laws applicable
5847	Effect on other laws
5848	Restrictive use of information
5849	Citation of chapter

PART II. EXEMPTIONS

5851	Special (occupational) tax exemption
5852	General transfer and making tax exemption
5853	Transfer and making tax exemption available to certain governmental entities
5854	Exportation of firearms exempt from transfer tax

Subchapter C. Prohibited Acts

5861	Prohibited acts

Subchapter D. Penalties and Forfeitures

5871	Penalties
5872	Forfeitures

Chapter 54. Greenmail

5881	Greenmail

Chapter 55. Structured Settlement Factoring Transactions

5891	Structured settlement factoring transactions

SUBTITLE F—PROCEDURE AND ADMINISTRATION

Chapter 61. Information and Returns

Subchapter A. Returns and Records

PART I. RECORDS, STATEMENTS, AND SPECIAL RETURNS

6001	Notice or regulations requiring records, statements, and special returns

PART II. TAX RETURNS OR STATEMENTS

Subpart A. General requirement

6011	General requirement of return, statement, or list

Subpart B. Income tax returns

6012	Persons required to make returns of income
6013	Joint returns of income tax by husband and wife
6014	Income tax return—tax not computed by taxpayer
6015	Relief from joint and several liability on joint return
6015	Repealed [Declaration of estimated income tax by individuals]
6017	Self-employment tax returns
6017A	Repealed [Place of residence]

Subpart C. Returns relating to transfers during life or at death

6018	Estate tax returns
6018	Returns relating to large transfers at death
6019	Gift tax returns

Subpart D. Miscellaneous provisions

6020	Returns prepared for or executed by Secretary
6021	Listing by Secretary of taxable objects owned by nonresidents of internal revenue districts

Table of Code Sections

Part III. Information Returns

Subpart A. Information concerning persons subject to special provisions

Sec.	
6031	Return of partnership income
6032	Returns of banks with respect to common trust funds
6033	Returns by exempt organizations
6034	Returns by certain trusts
6034A	Information to beneficiaries of estates and trusts
6035	Repealed [Returns of officers, directors, and shareholders of foreign personal holding companies]
6036	Notice of qualification as executor or receiver
6037	Return of S corporation
6038	Information reporting with respect to certain foreign corporations and partnerships
6038A	Information with respect to certain foreign-owned corporations
6038B	Notice of certain transfers to foreign persons
6038C	Information with respect to foreign corporations engaged in U.S. business
6038D	Information with respect to foreign financial assets
6039	Returns required in connection with certain options
6039A	Repealed [Information regarding carryover basis property acquired from a decedent]
6039B	Repealed [Return of general stock ownership corporation]
6039C	Returns with respect to foreign persons holding direct investments in United States real property interests
6039D	Returns and records with respect to certain fringe benefit plans
6039D	Repealed [Returns and records with respect to certain fringe benefits plans]
6039E	Information concerning resident status
6039F	Notice of large gifts received from foreign persons
6039G	Information on individuals losing United States citizenship
6039H	Information with respect to Alaska Native Settlement Trusts and sponsoring Native Corporations
6039I	Returns and records with respect to employer-owned life insurance contracts
6039J	Information reporting with respect to commodity credit corporation transactions
6040	Cross references

Subpart B. Information concerning transactions with other persons

Sec.	
6041	Information at source
6041A	Returns regarding payments of remuneration for services and direct sales
6042	Returns regarding payments of dividends, and corporate earnings and profits
6043	Liquidating, etc., transactions
6043A	Returns relating to taxable mergers and acquisitions
6044	Returns regarding payments of patronage dividends
6045	Returns of brokers
6045A	Information required in connection with transfers of covered securities to brokers
6045B	Returns relating to actions affecting basis of specified securities
6046	Returns as to organization or reorganization of foreign corporations and as to acquisitions of their stock
6046A	Returns as to interests in foreign partnerships
6047	Information relating to certain trusts and annuity plans
6048	Information with respect to certain foreign trusts
6049	Returns regarding payments of interest
6050	Repealed [Returns relating to certain transfers to exempt organizations]
6050A	Reporting requirements of certain fishing boat operators
6050B	Returns relating to unemployment compensation
6050C	Repealed [Information regarding windfall profit tax on domestic crude oil]
6050D	Returns relating to energy grants and financing
6050E	State and local income tax refunds
6050F	Returns relating to social security benefits
6050G	Returns relating to certain railroad retirement benefits
6050H	Returns relating to mortgage interest received in trade or business from individuals
6050I	Returns relating to cash received in trade or business, etc.
6050J	Returns relating to foreclosures and abandonments of security
6050K	Returns relating to exchanges of certain partnership interests
6050L	Returns relating to certain donated property
6050M	Returns relating to persons receiving contracts from Federal executive agencies
6050N	Returns regarding payment of royalties
6050P	Returns relating to the cancellation of indebtedness by certain entities
6050Q	Certain long-term care benefits
6050R	Returns relating to certain purchases of fish
6050S	Returns relating to higher education tuition and related expenses
6050T	Returns relating to credit for health insurance costs of eligible individuals
6050U	Charges or payments for qualified long-term care insurance contracts under combined arrangements
6050V	Returns relating to applicable insurance contracts in which certain exempt organizations hold interests
6050W	Returns relating to payments made in settlement of payment card and third party network transactions

Subpart C. Information regarding wages paid employees

Sec.	
6051	Receipts for employees
6052	Returns regarding payment of wages in the form of group-term life insurance
6053	Reporting of tips

Subpart D. Information Regarding Health Insurance Coverage

Sec.	
6055	Reporting of health insurance coverage
6056	Certain employers required to report on health insurance coverage.

Subpart D. Repealed [Information concerning private foundations]

Sec.	
6056	Repealed [Annual reports by private foundations]

Subpart E. Registration of and information concerning pension, etc., plans

Sec.	
6057	Annual registration, etc.
6058	Information required in connection with certain plans of deferred compensation
6059	Periodic report of actuary

Subpart F. Information concerning income tax return preparers

Sec.	
6060	Information returns of tax return preparers

Part IV. Signing and Verifying of Returns and Other Documents

Sec.	
6061	Signing of returns and other documents
6062	Signing of corporation returns
6063	Signing of partnership returns
6064	Signature presumed authentic
6065	Verification of returns

Part V. Time for Filing Returns and Other Documents

Sec.	
6071	Time for filing returns and other documents
6072	Time for filing income tax returns
6073	Repealed [Time for filing declarations of estimated income tax by individuals]
6075	Time for filing estate and gift tax returns
6076	Repealed [Time for filing return of windfall profit tax]

Part VI. Extension of Time for Filing Returns

Sec.	
6081	Extension of time for filing returns

Part VII. Place for Filing Returns or Other Documents

Sec.	
6091	Place for filing returns or other documents

Sec.	
	PART VIII. DESIGNATION OF INCOME TAX PAYMENTS TO PRESIDENTIAL ELECTION CAMPAIGN FUND
6096	Designation by individuals

Subchapter B. Miscellaneous Provisions

Sec.	
6101	Period covered by returns or other documents
6102	Computations on returns or other documents
6103	Confidentiality and disclosure of returns and return information
6104	Publicity of information required from certain exempt organizations and certain trusts
6105	Confidentiality of information arising under treaty obligations
6106	Repealed [Publicity of unemployment tax returns]
6107	Tax return preparer must furnish copy of return to taxpayer and must retain a copy or list
6108	Statistical publications and studies
6109	Identifying numbers
6110	Public inspection of written determinations
6111	Disclosure of reportable transactions
6112	Material advisors of reportable transactions must keep lists of advisees, etc.
6113	Disclosure of nondeductibility of contributions
6114	Treaty-based return positions
6115	Disclosure related to quid pro quo contributions
6116	Cross reference

Chapter 62. Time and Place for Paying Tax
Subchapter A. Place and Due Date for Payment of Tax

6151	Time and place for paying tax shown on returns
6152	Repealed [Installment payments]
6153	Repealed [Installment payments of estimated income tax by individuals]
6154	Repealed [Installment payment of estimated income tax by corporations]
6155	Payment on notice and demand
6156	Repealed [Installment payments of tax on use of highway motor vehicles]
6157	Payment of Federal unemployment tax on quarterly or other time period basis
6158	Repealed [Installment payment of tax attributable to divestitures pursuant to Bank Holding Company Act amendments of 1970]
6159	Agreements for payment of tax liability in installments

Subchapter B. Extensions of Time for Payment

6161	Extension of time for paying tax
6163	Extension of time for payment of estate tax on value of reversionary or remainder interest in property
6164	Extension of time for payment of taxes by corporations expecting carrybacks
6165	Bonds where time to pay tax or deficiency has been extended
6166	Extension of time for payment of estate tax where estate consists largely of interest in closely held business
6166A	Repealed [Extension of time for payment of estate tax where estate consists largely of interest in closely held business]
6167	Extension of time for payment of tax attributable to recovery of foreign expropriation losses

Chapter 63. Assessment
Subchapter A. In General

6201	Assessment authority
6202	Establishment by regulations of mode or time of assessment
6203	Method of assessment
6204	Supplemental assessments
6205	Special rules applicable to certain employment taxes
6206	Special rules applicable to excessive claims under certain sections
6207	Cross references

Subchapter B. Deficiency Procedures in the Case of Income, Estate, Gift, and Certain Excise Taxes

6211	Definition of a deficiency
6212	Notice of deficiency
6213	Restrictions applicable to deficiencies; petition to Tax Court
6214	Determinations by Tax Court
6215	Assessment of deficiency found by Tax Court
6216	Cross references

Subchapter C. Tax Treatment of Partnership Items

6221	Tax treatment determined at partnership level
6222	Partner's return must be consistent with partnership return or Secretary notified of inconsistency
6223	Notice to partners of proceedings
6224	Participation in administrative proceedings; waivers; agreements
6225	Assessments made only after partnership level proceedings are completed
6226	Judicial review of final partnership administrative adjustments
6227	Administrative adjustment requests
6228	Judicial review where administrative adjustment request is not allowed in full
6229	Period of limitations for making assessments
6230	Additional administrative provisions
6231	Definitions and special rules
6232	Repealed [Extension of subchapter to windfall profit tax]
6233	Extension to entities filing partnership returns, etc.
6234	Declaratory judgment relating to treatment of items other than partnership items with respect to an oversheltered return

Subchapter D. Treatment of Electing Large Partnerships
PART I. TREATMENT OF PARTNERSHIP ITEMS AND ADJUSTMENTS

6240	Application of subchapter
6241	Partner's return must be consistent with partnership return
6242	Procedures for taking partnership adjustments into account

PART II. PARTNERSHIP LEVEL ADJUSTMENTS
Subpart A. Adjustments by Secretary

6245	Secretarial authority
6246	Restrictions on partnership adjustments
6247	Judicial review of partnership adjustment
6248	Period of limitations for making adjustments

Subpart B. Claims for adjustments by partnership

6251	Administrative adjustment requests
6252	Judicial review where administrative adjustment request is not allowed in full

PART III. DEFINITIONS AND SPECIAL RULES

6255	Definitions and special rules

Chapter 64. Collection
Subchapter A. General Provisions

6301	Collection authority
6302	Mode or time of collection
6303	Notice and demand for tax
6304	Fair tax collection practices
6305	Collection of certain liability
6306	Qualified tax collection contracts

Subchapter B. Receipt of Payment

6311	Payment of tax by commercially acceptable means
6313	Fractional parts of a cent
6314	Receipt for taxes
6315	Payments of estimated income tax
6316	Payment by foreign currency
6317	Payments of Federal unemployment tax for calendar quarter

Table of Code Sections

Sec.

Subchapter C. Lien for Taxes
Part I. Due Process of Liens
6320   Notice and opportunity for hearing upon filing of notice of lien

Part II. Liens
6321   Lien for taxes
6322   Period of lien
6323   Validity and priority against certain persons
6324   Special liens for estate and gift taxes
6324A   Special lien for estate tax deferred under section 6166
6324B   Special lien for additional estate tax attributable to farm, etc., valuation
6325   Release of lien or discharge of property
6326   Administrative appeal of liens
6327   Cross references

Subchapter D. Seizure of Property for Collection of Taxes
Part I. Due Process for Collections
6330   Notice and opportunity for hearing before levy

Part II. Levy
6331   Levy and distraint
6332   Surrender of property subject to levy
6333   Production of books
6334   Property exempt from levy
6335   Sale of seized property
6336   Sale of perishable goods
6337   Redemption of property
6338   Certificate of sale; deed of real property
6339   Legal effect of certificate of sale of personal property and deed of real property
6340   Records of sale
6341   Expense of levy and sale
6342   Application of proceeds of levy
6343   Authority to release levy and return property
6344   Cross references

Subchapter E. Repealed [Collection of State Individual Income Taxes]
6361   Repealed [General rules]
6362   Repealed [Qualified State individual income taxes]
6363   Repealed [State agreements; other procedures]
6364   Repealed [Regulations]
6365   Repealed [Definitions and special rules]

Chapter 65. Abatements, Credits, and Refunds
Subchapter A. Procedure in General
6401   Amounts treated as overpayments
6402   Authority to make credits or refunds
6403   Overpayment of installment
6404   Abatements
6405   Reports of refunds and credits
6406   Prohibition of administrative review of decisions
6407   Date of allowance of refund or credit
6408   State escheat laws not to apply
6409   Refunds disregarded in the administration of federal programs and federally assisted programs

Subchapter B. Rules of Special Application
6411   Tentative carryback and refund adjustments
6412   Floor stocks refunds
6413   Special rules applicable to certain employment taxes
6414   Income tax withheld
6414   Income tax withheld
6415   Credits or refunds to persons who collected certain taxes
6416   Certain taxes on sales and services
6418   Repealed [Sugar]
6419   Excise tax on wagering
6420   Gasoline used on farms

Sec.

6421   Gasoline used for certain nonhighway purposes, used by local transit systems, or sold for certain exempt purposes
6422   Cross references
6423   Conditions to allowance in the case of alcohol and tobacco taxes
6424   Repealed [Lubricating oil used for certain nontaxable purposes]
6425   Adjustment of overpayment of estimated income tax by corporation
6426   Credit for alcohol fuel, biodiesel, and alternative fuel mixtures
6426   Repealed [Refund of aircraft use tax where plane transports for hire in foreign air commerce]
6427   Fuels not used for taxable purposes
6428   2008 Recovery rebates for individuals
6428   Repealed [1981 rate reduction tax credit]
6429   Advance payment of portion of increased child credit for 2003
6429   Repealed [Credit and refund of Chapter 45 taxes paid by royalty owners]
6430   Treatment of tax imposed at Leaking Underground Storage Tank Trust Fund financing rate
6430   Repealed [Credit or refund of windfall profit taxes to certain trust beneficiaries]
6431   Credit for qualified bonds allowed to issuer
6432   COBRA premium assistance

Chapter 66. Limitations
Subchapter A. Limitations on Assessment and Collection
6501   Limitations on assessment and collection
6502   Collection after assessment
6503   Suspension of running of period of limitation
6504   Cross references

Subchapter B. Limitations on Credit or Refund
6511   Limitations on credit or refund
6512   Limitations in case of petition to Tax Court
6513   Time return deemed filed and tax considered paid
6514   Credits or refunds after period of limitation
6515   Cross references

Subchapter C. Mitigation of Effect of Period of Limitations
6521   Mitigation of effect of limitation in case of related taxes under different chapters

Subchapter D. Periods of Limitation in Judicial Proceedings
6531   Periods of limitation on criminal prosecutions
6532   Periods of limitation on suits
6533   Cross references

Chapter 67. Interest
Subchapter A. Interest on Underpayments
6601   Interest on underpayment, nonpayment, or extensions of time for payment, of tax
6602   Interest on erroneous refund recoverable by suit
6603   Deposits made to suspend running of interest on potential underpayments, etc.

Subchapter B. Interest on Overpayments
6611   Interest on overpayments
6612   Cross references

Subchapter C. Determination of Interest Rate; Compounding of Interest
6621   Determination of rate of interest
6622   Interest compounded daily

Subchapter D. Notice Requirements
6631   Notice requirements

Chapter 68. Additions to the Tax, Additional Amounts, and Assessable Penalties

Table of Code Sections

Subchapter A. Additions to the Tax and Additional Amounts

Part I. General Provisions

Sec.	
6651	Failure to file tax return or to pay tax
6652	Failure to file certain information returns, registration statements, etc.
6653	Failure to pay stamp tax
6654	Failure by individual to pay estimated income tax
6655	Failure by corporation to pay estimated income tax
6656	Failure to make deposit of taxes
6657	Bad checks
6658	Coordination with title 11
6658	Repealed [Addition to tax in case of jeopardy]
6659	Repealed [Addition to tax in the case of valuation overstatements for purposes of the income tax]
6659A	Repealed [Addition to tax in case of overstatements of pension liabilities]
6660	Repealed [Addition to tax in the case of valuation understatement for purposes of estate or gift taxes]
6661	Repealed [Substantial understatement of liability]
6662	Repealed [Applicable rules]

Part II. Accuracy-Related and Fraud Penalties

Sec.	
6662	Imposition of accuracy-related penalty on underpayments
6662A	Imposition of accuracy-related penalty on understatements with respect to reportable transactions
6663	Imposition of fraud penalty
6664	Definitions and special rules

Part III. Applicable Rules

Sec.	
6665	Applicable rules

Subchapter B. Assessable Penalties

Part I. General Provisions

Sec.	
6671	Rules for application of assessable penalties
6672	Failure to collect and pay over tax, or attempt to evade or defeat tax
6673	Sanctions and costs awarded by courts
6674	Fraudulent statement or failure to furnish statement to employee
6675	Excessive claims with respect to the use of certain fuels
6676	Erroneous claim for refund or credit
6677	Failure to file information returns with respect to certain foreign trusts
6678	Repealed [Failure to furnish certain statements]
6679	Failure to file returns, etc., with respect to foreign corporations or foreign partnerships
6682	False information with respect to withholding
6683	Repealed [Failure of foreign corporation to file return of personal holding company tax]
6684	Assessable penalties with respect to liability for tax under chapter 42
6685	Assessable penalty with respect to public inspection requirements for certain tax-exempt organizations
6686	Failure to file returns or supply information by DISC or FSC
6687	Repealed [Failure to supply information with respect to place of residence]
6688	Assessable penalties with respect to information required to be furnished under section 7654
6689	Failure to file notice of redetermination of foreign tax
6690	Fraudulent statement or failure to furnish statement to plan participant
6692	Failure to file actuarial report
6693	Failure to provide reports on certain tax-favored accounts or annuities; penalties relating to designated nondeductible contributions
6694	Understatement of taxpayer's liability by tax return preparer
6695	Other assessable penalties with respect to the preparation of income tax returns for other persons
6695A	Substantial and gross valuation misstatements attributable to incorrect appraisals
6696	Rules applicable with respect to sections 6694, 6695, and 6695A
6697	Repealed [Assessable penalties with respect to liability for tax of regulated investment companies]
6698	Failure to file partnership return
6698A	Repealed [Failure to file information with respect to carryover basis property]
6699	Failure to file S corporation return
6699	Repealed [Assessable penalties relating to tax credit employee stock ownership plan]
6700	Promoting abusive tax shelters, etc.
6701	Penalties for aiding and abetting understatement of tax liability
6702	Frivolous tax submissions
6703	Rules applicable to penalties under sections 6700, 6701, and 6702
6704	Failure to keep records necessary to meet reporting requirements under section 6047(d)
6705	Failure by broker to provide notice to payors
6706	Original issue discount information requirements
6707	Failure to furnish information regarding reportable transactions
6707A	Penalty for failure to include reportable transaction information with return
6708	Failure to maintain lists of advisees with respect to reportable transactions
6709	Penalties with respect to mortgage credit certificates
6710	Failure to disclose that contributions are nondeductible
6711	Failure by tax-exempt organization to disclose that certain information or service available from Federal government
6712	Failure to disclose treaty-based return positions
6713	Disclosure or use of information by preparers of returns
6714	Failure to meet disclosure requirements applicable to quid pro quo contributions
6715	Dyed fuel sold for use or used in taxable use
6715A	Tampering with or failing to maintain security requirements for mechanical dye injection systems
6716	Failure to file information with respect to certain transfers at death and gifts
6717	Refusal of entry
6718	Failure to display tax registration on vessels
6719	Failure to register or reregister
6720	Fraudulent acknowledgments with respect to donations of motor vehicles, boats, and airplanes
6720A	Penalty with respect to certain adulterated fuels
6720B	Fraudulent identification of exempt use property
6720C	Penalty for failure to notify health plan of cessation of eligibility for COBRA premium assistance

Part II. Failure to Comply with Certain Information Reporting Requirements

Sec.	
6721	Failure to file correct information returns
6722	Failure to furnish correct payee statements
6723	Failure to comply with other information reporting requirements
6724	Waiver; definitions and special rules
6725	Failure to report information under section 4101

Subchapter C. Procedural Requirements

Sec.	
6751	Procedural requirements

Chapter 69. General Provisions Relating to Stamps

Sec.	
6801	Authority for establishment, alteration, and distribution
6802	Supply and distribution
6803	Accounting and safeguarding
6804	Attachment and cancellation
6805	Redemption of stamps

Table of Code Sections

Sec.	
6806	Occupational tax stamps
6807	Stamping, marking, and branding seized goods
6808	Special provisions relating to stamps

Chapter 70. Jeopardy, Receiverships, Etc.

Subchapter A. Jeopardy

Part I. Termination of Taxable Year

6851	Termination assessments of income tax
6852	Termination assessments in case of flagrant political expenditures of section 501(c)(3) organizations

Part II. Jeopardy Assessments

6861	Jeopardy assessments of income, estate, gift, and certain excise taxes
6862	Jeopardy assessment of taxes other than income, estate, gift, and certain excise taxes
6863	Stay of collection of jeopardy assessments
6864	Termination of extended period for payment in case of carryback

Part III. Special Rules With Respect to Certain Cash

6867	Presumptions where owner of large amount of cash is not identified

Subchapter B. Receiverships, Etc.

6871	Claims for income, estate, gift, and certain excise taxes in receivership proceedings, etc.
6872	Suspension of period on assessment
6873	Unpaid claims

Chapter 71. Transferees and Fiduciaries

6901	Transferred assets
6902	Provisions of special application to transferees
6903	Notice of fiduciary relationship
6904	Prohibition of injunctions
6905	Discharge of executor from personal liability for decedent's income and gift taxes

Chapter 72. Licensing and Registration

Subchapter A. Licensing

7001	Collection of foreign items

Subchapter B. Registration

7011	Registration—persons paying a special tax
7012	Cross references

Chapter 73. Bonds

7101	Form of bonds
7102	Single bond in lieu of multiple bonds
7103	Cross references—other provisions for bonds

Chapter 74. Closing Agreements and Compromises

7121	Closing agreements
7122	Compromises
7123	Appeals dispute resolution procedures
7124	Cross references

Chapter 75. Crimes, Other Offenses, and Forfeitures

Subchapter A. Crimes

Part I. General Provisions

7201	Attempt to evade or defeat tax
7202	Willful failure to collect or pay over tax
7203	Willful failure to file return, supply information, or pay tax
7204	Fraudulent statement or failure to make statement to employees
7205	Fraudulent withholding exemption certificate or failure to supply information
7206	Fraud and false statements
7207	Fraudulent returns, statements, or other documents
7208	Offenses relating to stamps
7209	Unauthorized use or sale of stamps
7210	Failure to obey summons
7211	False statements to purchasers or lessees relating to tax
7212	Attempts to interfere with administration of internal revenue laws
7213	Unauthorized disclosure of information
7213A	Unauthorized inspection of returns or return information
7214	Offenses by officers and employees of the United States
7215	Offenses with respect to collected taxes
7216	Disclosure or use of information by preparers of returns
7217	Prohibition on executive branch influence over taxpayer audits and other investigations
7217	Repealed [Civil damages for unauthorized disclosure of returns and return information]

Part II. Penalties Applicable to Certain Taxes

7231	Failure to obtain license for collection of foreign items
7232	Failure to register or reregister under section 4101, false representations of registration status, etc.
7240	Repealed [Officials investing or speculating in sugar]
7241	Repealed [Willful failure to furnish certain information regarding windfall profit tax on domestic crude oil]

Subchapter B. Other Offenses

7261	Representation that retailers' excise tax is excluded from price of article
7262	Violation of occupational tax laws relating to wagering—failure to pay special tax
7268	Possession with intent to sell in fraud of law or to evade tax
7269	Failure to produce records
7270	Insurance policies
7271	Penalties for offenses relating to stamps
7272	Penalty for failure to register or reregister
7273	Penalties for offenses relating to special taxes
7275	Penalty for offenses relating to certain airline tickets and advertising

Subchapter C. Forfeitures

Part I. Property Subject to Forfeiture

7301	Property subject to tax
7302	Property used in violation of internal revenue laws
7303	Other property subject to forfeiture
7304	Penalty for fraudulently claiming drawback

Part II. Provisions Common to Forfeitures

7321	Authority to seize property subject to forfeiture
7322	Delivery of seized personal property to United States marshal
7323	Judicial action to enforce forfeiture
7324	Special disposition of perishable goods
7325	Personal property valued at $100,000 or less
7326	Disposal of forfeited or abandoned property in special cases
7327	Customs laws applicable
7328	Cross references

Subchapter D. Miscellaneous Penalty and Forfeiture Provisions

7341	Penalty for sales to evade tax
7342	Penalty for refusal to permit entry or examination
7343	Definition of term "person"
7344	Extended application of penalties relating to officers of the Treasury Department

Chapter 76. Judicial Proceedings

Subchapter A. Civil Actions by the United States

7401	Authorization
7402	Jurisdiction of district courts
7403	Action to enforce lien or to subject property to payment of tax
7404	Authority to bring civil action for estate taxes
7405	Action for recovery of erroneous refunds
7406	Disposition of judgments and moneys recovered
7407	Action to enjoin income tax return preparers
7408	Actions to enjoin specified conduct related to tax shelters and reportable transactions

Table of Code Sections

Sec.	
7409	Action to enjoin flagrant political expenditures of section 501(c)(3) organizations
7410	Cross references

Subchapter B. Proceedings by Taxpayers and Third Parties

7421	Prohibition of suits to restrain assessment or collection
7422	Civil actions for refund
7423	Repayments to officers or employees
7424	Intervention
7425	Discharge of liens
7426	Civil actions by persons other than taxpayers
7427	Income tax return preparers
7428	Declaratory judgments relating to status and classification of organizations under section 501(c)(3), etc.
7429	Review of jeopardy levy or assessment procedures
7430	Awarding of costs and certain fees
7431	Civil damages for unauthorized inspection or disclosure of returns and return information
7432	Civil damages for failure to release lien
7433	Civil damages for certain unauthorized collection actions
7433A	Civil damages for certain unauthorized collection actions by persons performing services under qualified tax collection contracts
7434	Civil damages for fraudulent filing of information returns
7435	Civil damages for unauthorized enticement of information disclosure
7436	Proceedings for determination of employment status
7437	Cross references

Subchapter C. The Tax Court

PART I. ORGANIZATION AND JURISDICTION

7441	Status
7442	Jurisdiction
7443	Membership
7443A	Special trial judges
7443B	Repealed [Recall of special trial judges of the Tax Court]
7444	Organization
7445	Offices
7446	Times and places of sessions
7447	Retirement
7448	Annuities to surviving spouses and dependent children of judges and special trial judges

PART II. PROCEDURE

7451	Fee for filing petition
7452	Representation of parties
7453	Rules of practice, procedure, and evidence
7454	Burden of proof in fraud, foundation manager, and transferee cases
7455	Service of process
7456	Administration of oaths and procurement of testimony
7457	Witness fees
7458	Hearings
7459	Reports and decisions
7460	Provisions of special application to divisions
7461	Publicity of proceedings
7462	Publication of reports
7463	Disputes involving $50,000 or less
7464	Intervention by trustee of debtor's estate
7465	Provisions of special application to transferees

PART III. MISCELLANEOUS PROVISIONS

7471	Employees
7472	Expenditures
7473	Disposition of fees
7474	Fee for transcript of record
7475	Practice fee

PART IV. DECLARATORY JUDGMENTS

7476	Declaratory judgments relating to qualification of certain retirement plans

Sec.	
7477	Declaratory judgments relating to value of certain gifts
7477	Repealed [Declaratory judgments relating to transfers of property from the United States]
7478	Declaratory judgments relating to status of certain governmental obligations
7479	Declaratory judgments relating to eligibility of estate with respect to installment payments under section 6166

Subchapter D. Court Review of Tax Court Decisions

7481	Date when Tax Court decision becomes final
7482	Courts of review
7483	Notice of appeal
7484	Change of incumbent in office
7485	Bond to stay assessment and collection
7486	Refund, credit, or abatement of amounts disallowed
7487	Cross references

Subchapter E. Burden of Proof

7491	Burden of proof

Subchapter E. Repealed [Miscellaneous Provisions]

Chapter 77. Miscellaneous Provisions

7501	Liability for taxes withheld or collected
7502	Timely mailing treated as timely filing and paying
7503	Time for performance of acts where last day falls on Saturday, Sunday, or legal holiday
7504	Fractional parts of a dollar
7505	Sale of personal property acquired by the United States
7506	Administration of real estate acquired by the United States
7507	Exemption of insolvent banks from tax
7508	Time for performing certain acts postponed by reason of service in combat zone or contingency operation
7508A	Authority to postpone certain deadlines by reason of Presidentially declared disaster or terroristic or military actions
7509	Expenditures incurred by the United States Postal Service
7510	Exemption from tax of domestic goods purchased for the United States
7511	Repealed [Exemption of consular officers and employees of foreign states from payment of internal revenue taxes on imported articles]
7512	Separate accounting for certain collected taxes, etc.
7513	Reproduction of returns and other documents
7514	Authority to prescribe or modify seals
7515	Repealed [Special statistical studies and compilations and other services on request]
7516	Supplying training and training aids on request
7517	Furnishing on request of statement explaining estate or gift evaluation
7518	Tax incentives relating to merchant marine capital constructions funds
7519	Required payments for entities electing not to have required taxable year
7520	Valuation tables
7521	Procedures involving taxpayer interviews
7522	Content of tax due, deficiency, and other notices
7523	Graphic presentation of major categories of federal outlays and income
7524	Annual notice of tax delinquency
7525	Confidentiality privileges relating to taxpayer communications
7526	Low income taxpayer clinics
7527	Advance payment of credit for health insurance costs of eligible individuals
7528	Internal Revenue Service user fees

Chapter 78. Discovery of Liability and Enforcement of Title

Subchapter A. Examination and Inspection

7601	Canvass of districts for taxable persons and objects
7602	Examination of books and witnesses

525

Table of Code Sections

Sec.	
7603	Service of summons
7604	Enforcement of summons
7605	Time and place of examination
7606	Entry of premises for examination of taxable objects
7607	Repealed [Additional authority for Bureau of Customs]
7608	Authority of internal revenue enforcement officers
7609	Special procedures for third-party summonses
7610	Fees and costs for witnesses
7611	Restrictions on church tax inquiries and examinations
7612	Special procedures for summonses for computer software
7613	Cross references

Subchapter B. General Powers and Duties

7621	Internal revenue districts
7622	Authority to administer oaths and certify
7623	Expenses of detection of underpayments and fraud, etc.
7624	Reimbursement to State and local law enforcement agencies

Subchapter C. Repealed [Supervision of Operations of Certain Manufacturers]

7641	Repealed [Supervision of operations of certain manufacturers]

Subchapter D. Possessions

7651	Administration and collection of taxes in possessions
7652	Shipments to the United States
7653	Shipments from the United States
7654	Coordination of United States and certain possession individual income taxes
7655	Cross references

Chapter 79. Definitions

7701	Definitions
7702	Life insurance contract defined
7702A	Modified endowment contract defined
7702B	Treatment of qualified long-term care insurance
7703	Determination of marital status
7704	Certain publicly traded partnerships treated as corporations

Chapter 80. General Rules

Subchapter A. Application of Internal Revenue Laws

7801	Authority of Department of the Treasury
7802	Internal Revenue Service Oversight Board
7803	Commissioner of Internal Revenue; other officials
7804	Other personnel
7805	Rules and regulations
7806	Construction of title
7807	Rules in effect upon enactment of this title
7808	Depositaries for collections
7809	Deposit of collections
7810	Revolving fund for redemption of real property
7811	Taxpayer Assistance Orders

Subchapter B. Effective Date and Related Provisions

7851	Applicability of revenue laws
7852	Other applicable rules

Subchapter C. Provisions Affecting More than One Subtitle

7871	Indian tribal governments treated as States for certain purposes
7872	Treatment of loans with below-market interest rates
7873	Income derived by Indians from exercise of fishing rights
7874	Rules relating to expatriated entities and their foreign parents

SUBTITLE G—THE JOINT COMMITTEE ON TAXATION

Chapter 91. Organization and Membership of the Joint Committee

8001	Authorization
8002	Membership
8003	Election of chairman and vice chairman
8004	Appointment and compensation of staff
8005	Payment of expenses

Chapter 92. Powers and Duties of the Joint Committee

8021	Powers
8022	Duties
8023	Additional powers to obtain data

SUBTITLE H—FINANCING OF PRESIDENTIAL ELECTION CAMPAIGNS

Chapter 95. Presidential Election Campaign Fund

9001	Short title
9002	Definitions
9003	Condition for eligibility for payments
9004	Entitlement of eligible candidates to payments
9005	Certification by Commission
9006	Payments to eligible candidates
9007	Examinations and audits; repayments
9008	Payments for presidential nominating conventions
9009	Reports to Congress; regulations
9010	Participation by Commission in judicial proceedings
9011	Judicial review
9012	Criminal penalties
9013	Effective date of chapter

Chapter 96. Presidential Primary Matching Payment Account

9031	Short title
9032	Definitions
9033	Eligibility for payments
9034	Entitlement of eligible candidates to payments
9035	Qualified campaign expense limitations
9036	Certification by Commission
9037	Payments to eligible candidates
9038	Examinations and audits; repayments
9039	Reports to Congress; regulations
9040	Participation by Commission in judicial proceedings
9041	Judicial review
9042	Criminal penalties

SUBTITLE I—TRUST FUND CODE

9500	Short title

Chapter 98. Trust Fund Code

Subchapter A. Establishment of Trust Funds

9501	Black Lung Disability Trust Fund
9502	Airport and Airway Trust Fund
9503	Highway Trust Fund
9504	Sport Fish Restoration and Boating Trust Fund
9505	Harbor Maintenance Trust Fund
9506	Inland Waterways Trust Fund
9507	Hazardous Substance Superfund
9508	Leaking Underground Storage Tank Trust Fund
9509	Oil Spill Liability Trust Fund
9510	Vaccine Injury Compensation Trust Fund
9511	Patient-centered outcomes research trust fund
9511	Repealed [National Recreational Trails Trust Fund]

Subchapter B. General Provisions

9601	Transfer of amounts
9602	Management of trust funds

SUBTITLE J—COAL INDUSTRY HEALTH BENEFITS

Chapter 99. Coal Industry Health Benefits

Subchapter A. Definitions of General Applicability

9701	Definitions of general applicability

Subchapter B. Combined Benefit Fund

PART I. ESTABLISHMENT AND BENEFITS

9702	Establishment of the United Mine Workers of America Combined Benefit Fund
9703	Plan benefits

PART II. FINANCING

9704	Liability of assigned operators
9705	Transfers

Sec.	
9706	Assignment of eligible beneficiaries

Part III. Enforcement
Sec.	
9707	Failure to pay premium

Part IV. Other Provisions
Sec.	
9708	Effect on pending claims or obligations

Subchapter C. Health Benefits of Certain Miners

Part I. Individual Employer Plans
Sec.	
9711	Continued obligations of individual employer plans

Part II. 1992 UMWA Benefit Plan
Sec.	
9712	Establishment and coverage of 1992 UMWA Benefit Plan

Subchapter D. Other Provisions
Sec.	
9721	Civil enforcement
9722	Sham transactions

SUBTITLE K—GROUP HEALTH PLAN REQUIREMENTS

Chapter 100. Group Health Plan Requirements

Subchapter A. Requirements Relating to Portability, Access, and Renewability

Sec.	
9801	Increased portability through limitation on pre-existing condition exclusions
9802	Prohibiting discrimination against individual participants and beneficiaries based on health status
9803	Guaranteed renewability in multiemployer plans and certain multiple employer welfare arrangements

Subchapter B. Other Requirements
Sec.	
9811	Standards relating to benefits for mothers and newborns
9812	Parity in mental health and substance use disorder benefits
9813	Coverage of dependent students on medically necessary leave of absence
9815	Additional market reforms

Subchapter C. General Provisions
Sec.	
9831	General exceptions
9832	Definitions
9833	Regulations
9834	Enforcement

TITLE 26.—INTERNAL REVENUE CODE

(Act Aug. 16, 1954, ch. 736, 68A Stat. 3 as amended)

An Act to revise the internal revenue laws of the United States.

Be it enacted by the Senate and House of Representatives of the United States of America in Congress assembled, That

(a) Citation.

(1) The provisions of this Act set forth under the heading "Internal Revenue Title" may be cited as the "Internal Revenue Code of 1954". [Note: Sec. 2(a), P.L. 99-514, 10/22/86, provided "The Internal Revenue Title enacted August 16, 1954, as heretofore, hereby, or hereafter amended may be cited as the 'Internal Revenue Code of 1986'."]

(2) The Internal Revenue Code enacted on February 10, 1939, as amended, may be cited as the "Internal Revenue Code of 1939".

(b) Publication.

This Act shall be published as volume 68A of the United States Statutes at Large, with a comprehensive table of contents and an appendix; but without an index or marginal references. The date of enactment, bill number, public law number, and chapter number, shall be printed as a headnote.

(c) Cross reference.

For saving provisions, effective date provisions, and other related provisions, see chapter 80 (sec. 7801 and following) of the Internal Revenue Code of 1954.

(d) Enactment of Internal Revenue Title into law.

The Internal Revenue Title referred to in subsection (a)(1) is as follows: ....

INTERNAL REVENUE TITLE

A. Income taxes Secs. 1–1564.

B. Estate and gift taxes Secs. 2001–2704.

C. Employment taxes and collection of income tax at source. Secs. 3103–3510.

D. Miscellaneous excise taxes Secs. 4001–5000.

E. Alcohol, tobacco, and certain other excise taxes Secs. 5001–5881.

F. Procedure and administration Secs. 6001–7873.

G. The Joint Committee on Taxation Secs. 8001–8023.

H. Financing of Presidential Election Campaign. Secs. 9001–9042.

I. Trust Fund Code. Secs. 9500–9602.

J. Coal Industry Health Benefits. Secs. 9701–9722.

K. Group Health Plan Requirements. Secs. 9801–9833.

In **1997**, P.L. 105-34, Sec. 1531(b)(3), amended item for Subtitle K.
Prior to amendment, item for Subtitle K read as follows:
"Group Health Plan Portability, Access, and Renewability Requirements."
In **1996**, P.L. 104-191, Sec. 401(b), added item K.
In **1992**, added item J.
In **1982**, P.L. 97-248, Sec. 307(b)(1), amended item C.
Prior to amendment, item C read as follows:
"C. Employment taxes Secs. 3101–3504."
—P.L. 97-119, Sec. 103(c)(2), added item I.
In **1976**, P.L. 94-455, Sec. 1907(b)(2), amended item G.
Prior to amendment, item G read as follows:
"G. The Joint Committee on Internal Revenue Taxation."

Subtitle A.—Income Taxes

Chapter

1. Normal taxes and surtaxes.
2. Tax on self-employment income.
2A. Unearned income Medicare contribution.
3. Withholding of tax on nonresident aliens and foreign corporations.
4. Taxes To Enforce Reporting on Certain Foreign Accounts
4. Repealed. [Rules applicable to recovery of excessive profits on government contracts.]
5. Repealed. [Tax on transfers to avoid income tax.]
6. Consolidated returns.

In **2010**, P.L. 111-152, Sec. 1402(a)(3), Added the item for Chapter 2A
—P.L. 111-148, Sec. 501(c)(8), Added the item for Chapter 4
In **1997**, P.L. 105-34, Sec. 1131(c)(4)[(d)(4)], deleted the item for Chapter 5.
Prior to deletion, the item for Chapter 5 read as follows:
"Tax on transfers to avoid income tax."
In **1990**, P.L. 101-508, Sec. 11801(b)(11), deleted the item for Chapter 4.
Prior to deletion, the item for Chapter 4 read as follows:
"4. Rules applicable to recovery of excessive profits on government contracts."
In **1984**, P.L. 98-369, Sec. 474(r)(29)(D), deleted "and tax-free covenant bonds" after "corporations" in the item for Chapter 3.

CHAPTER 1.—NORMAL TAXES AND SURTAXES

Subchapter

A. Determination of tax liability.
B. Computation of taxable income.
C. Corporate distributions and adjustments.
D. Deferred compensation, etc.
E. Accounting periods and methods of accounting.
F. Exempt organizations.
G. Corporations used to avoid income tax on shareholders.
H. Banking institutions.
I. Natural resources.
J. Estates, trusts, beneficiaries, and decedents.
K. Partners and partnerships.
L. Insurance companies.
M. Regulated investment companies and real estate investment trusts.
N. Tax based on income from sources within or without the United States.
O. Gain or loss on disposition of property.
P. Capital gains and losses.
Q. Readjustment of tax between years and special limitations.
R. Election to determine corporate tax on certain international shipping activities using per ton rate.
S. Tax treatment of S corporations and their shareholders.
T. Cooperatives and their patrons.
U. Designation and treatment of empowerment zones, enterprise communities, and rural development investment areas.
V. Title 11 cases.
W. District of Columbia Enterprise Zone.
X. Renewal communities.

1,001

Chapter 1

Y. Short-term regional benefits

In 2005, P.L. 109-135, Sec. 101(b)(4), amended item for Subchapter Y.
Prior to amendment, Subchapter Y read as follows:
"Y. New York Liberty Zone benefits."
In 2004, P.L. 108-357, Sec. 248(b)(2), added item for Subchapter R.
In 2002, P.L. 107-147, Sec. 301(c), added item for Subchapter Y.
In 1997, P.L. 105-34, Sec. 701(c), added item for Subchapter W.
In 1993, P.L. 103-66, Sec. 13301(b), added the item for Subchapter U.
In 1986, P.L. 99-514, Sec. 1303(c)(1), deleted the item for Subchapter U.
Prior to deletion, the item for Subchapter U read as follows:
"U. General stock ownership corporations."
In 1982, P.L. 97-354, Sec. 5(b), amended Subchapter S.
Prior to amendment, Subchapter S read as follows:
"S. Election of certain small business corporations as to taxable status."
In 1978, P.L. 95-600, Sec. 601(c)(1), added Subchapter U.
In 1962, P.L. 87-834, Sec. 17(b)(4), added subchapter T.
In 1960, P.L. 86-779, Sec. 10(c), added "and real estate investment trusts." to the item for Subchapter M.
In 1958, P.L. 85-866, Sec. 64(d)(1), added subchapter S.

Subchapter A.—Determination of Tax Liability

Part
    I. Tax on individuals.
    II. Tax on corporations.
    III. Changes in rates during a taxable year.
    IV. Credits against tax.
    V. Repealed. [Tax surcharge.]
    VI. Minimum tax for tax preferences.
    VII. Environment tax.
    VIII. [Supplemental medicare premium. Repealed.]

In 1989, P.L. 101-234, Sec. 102(a), repealed as if not enacted Sec. 111(a) of P.L. 100-360, which added Part VIII to Subchapter A of Chapter 1, see below.
In 1988, P.L. 100-360, Sec. 111(a), [repealed as if not enacted by Sec. 102(a) of P.L. 101-234, see above] added Part VIII to Subchapter A of Chapter I.
Prior to repeal, Part VIII read as follows:
"Part VIII. Supplemental medicare premium."
In 1986, P.L. 99-499, Sec. 516(b)(5), added Part VII.
In 1976, P.L. 94-455, Sec. 1901(b)(2), repealed Part V.
Prior to repeal, the heading for Part V read as follows:
"Part V. Tax surcharge."
In 1969, P.L. 91-172, Sec. 301(b)(1), added Part VI.
In 1968, P.L. 90-364, Sec. 102(d), added Part V.

PART I.—TAX ON INDIVIDUALS

Sec.
1. Tax imposed.
2. Definitions and special rules.
3. Tax tables for individuals having taxable income of less than $20,000. [Tax tables for individuals.]
4. Repealed [Rules for optional tax.]
5. Cross references relating to tax on individuals.

In 1977, P.L. 95-30, Sec. 101(b), amended Code Sec. 3. The heading was changed, but Congress did not change the item for 3 on the list of Code Secs. for Part I.
In 1976, P.L. 94-455, Sec. 501(c)(1), amended item 3 and repealed item 4.
Prior to amendment, item 3 read as follows:
"3. Optional tax tables for individuals."
Prior to repeal, item 4 read as follows:
"4. Rules for optional tax."
In 1969, P.L. 91-172, Sec. 803(d)(9), amended items 2 and 3.
Prior to repeal, items 2 and 3 read as follows:
"2. Tax in case of joint return or return of surviving spouse."
"3. Optional tax if adjusted gross income is less than $5,000."

Sec. 1. Tax imposed.

(a) Married individuals filing joint returns and surviving spouses.

There is hereby imposed on the taxable income of—

(1) every married individual (as defined in section 7703) who makes a single return jointly with his spouse under section 6013, and
(2) every surviving spouse (as defined in section 2(a)), a tax determined in accordance with the following table:

If taxable income is:	The tax is:
Not over $36,900	15% of taxable income.
Over $36,900 but not over $89,150	$5,535, plus 28% of the excess over $36,900.
Over $89,150 but not over $140,000.	$20,165, plus 31% of the excess over $89,150.
Over $140,000 but not over $250,000.	$35,928.50, plus 36% of the excess over $140,000.
Over $250,000	$75,528.50, plus 39.6% of the excess over $250,000.

(b) Heads of households.

There is hereby imposed on the taxable income of every head of a household (as defined in section 2(b)) a tax determined in accordance with the following table:

If taxable income is:	The tax is:
Not over $29,600	15% of taxable income.
Over $29,600 but not over $76,400	$4,440, plus 28% of the excess over $29,600.
Over $76,400 but not over $127,500	$17,544, plus 31% of the excess over $76,400.
Over $127,500 but not over $250,000.	$33,385, plus 36% of the excess over $127,500.
Over $250,000	$77,485, plus 39.6% of the excess over $250,000.

(c) Unmarried individuals (other than surviving spouses and heads of households).

There is hereby imposed on the taxable income of every individual (other than a surviving spouse as defined in section 2(a) or the head of a household as defined in section 2(b)) who is not a married individual (as defined in section 7703) a tax determined in accordance with the following table:

If taxable income is:	The tax is:
Not over $22,100	15% of taxable income.
Over $22,100 but not over $53,500	$3,315, plus 28% of the excess over $22,100.
Over $53,500 but not over $115,000	$12,107, plus 31% of the excess over $53,500.
Over $115,000 but not over $250,000.	$31,172, plus 36% of the excess over $115,000.
Over $250,000	$79,772, plus 39.6% of the excess over $250,000.

(d) Married individuals filing separate returns.

There is hereby imposed on the taxable income of every married individual (as defined in section 7703) who does not make a single return jointly with his spouse under section 6013, a tax determined in accordance with the following table:

Tax rates

Code Sec. 1(f)(7)(B)

If taxable income is:	The tax is:
Not over $18,450	15% of taxable income.
Over $18,450 but not over $44,575	$2,767.50, plus 28% of the excess over $18,450.
Over $44,575 but not over $70,000	$10,082.50, plus 31% of the excess over $44,575.
Over $70,000 but not over $125,000.	$17,964.25, plus 36% of the excess over $70,000.
Over $125,000	$37,764.25, plus 39.6% of the excess over $125,000.

(e) Estates and trusts.
There is hereby imposed on the taxable income of—
(1) every estate, and
(2) every trust,
taxable under this subsection a tax determined in accordance with the following table:

If taxable income is:	The tax is:
Not over $1,500	15% of taxable income.
Over $1,500 but not over $3,500	$225, plus 28% of the excess over $1,500.
Over $3,500 but not over $5,500	$785, plus 31% of the excess over $3,500.
Over $5,500 but not over $7,500.	$1,405, plus 36% of the excess over $5,500.
Over $7,500	$2,125, plus 39.6% of the excess over $7,500.

• *Caution:* The heading for Code Sec. 1(f), following, was amended by P.L. 107-16, the Economic Growth and Tax Relief Reconciliation Act of 2001 (EGTRRA). These provisions generally sunset for tax years beginning after 12/31/2012. For specific sunset provisions, see Sec. 901, P.L. 107-16 (as amended) reproduced in history notes for this Code Sec.

(f) Phaseout of marriage penalty in 15-percent bracket; adjustments in tax tables so that inflation will not result in tax increases.
(1) In general. Not later than December 15 of 1993, and each subsequent calendar year, the Secretary shall prescribe tables which shall apply in lieu of the tables contained in subsections (a), (b), (c), (d), and (e) with respect to taxable years beginning in the succeeding calendar year.
(2) Method of prescribing tables. The table which under paragraph (1) is to apply in lieu of the table contained in subsection (a), (b), (c), (d), or (e), as the case may be, with respect to taxable years beginning in any calendar year shall be prescribed—

• *Caution:* Code Sec. 1(f)(2)(A), following, was amended by P.L. 107-16, the Economic Growth and Tax Relief Reconciliation Act of 2001 (EGTRRA). These provisions generally sunset for tax years beginning after 12/31/2012. For specific sunset provisions, see Sec. 901,

P.L. 107-16 (as amended) reproduced in history notes for this Code Sec.

(A) except as provided in paragraph (8), by increasing the minimum and maximum dollar amounts for each rate bracket for which a tax is imposed under such table by the cost-of-living adjustment for such calendar year,
(B) by not changing the rate applicable to any rate bracket as adjusted under subparagraph (A), and
(C) by adjusting the amounts setting forth the tax to the extent necessary to reflect the adjustments in the rate brackets.
(3) Cost-of-living adjustment. For purposes of paragraph (2), the cost-of-living adjustment for any calendar year is the percentage (if any) by which—
(A) the CPI for the preceding calendar year, exceeds
(B) the CPI for the calendar year 1992.
(4) CPI for any calendar year. For purposes of paragraph (3), the CPI for any calendar year is the average of the Consumer Price Index as of the close of the 12-month period ending on August 31 of such calendar year.
(5) Consumer price index. For purposes of paragraph (4), the term "Consumer Price Index" means the last Consumer Price Index for all-urban consumers published by the Department of Labor. For purposes of the preceding sentence, the revision of the Consumer Price Index which is most consistent with the Consumer Price Index for calendar year 1986 shall be used.
(6) Rounding.
(A) In general. If any increase determined under paragraph (2)(A), section 63(c)(4), section 68(b)(2) or section 151(d)(4) is not a multiple of $50, such increase shall be rounded to the next lowest multiple of $50.

• *Caution:* Code Sec. 1(f)(6)(B), following, was amended by P.L. 107-16, the Economic Growth and Tax Relief Reconciliation Act of 2001 (EGTRRA). These provisions generally sunset for tax years beginning after 12/31/2012. For specific sunset provisions, see Sec. 901, P.L. 107-16 (as amended) reproduced in history notes for this Code Sec.

(B) Table for married individuals filing separately. In the case of a married individual filing a separate return, subparagraph (A) (other than with respect to sections 63(c)(4) and 151(d)(4)(A)) shall be applied by substituting "$25" for "$50" each place it appears.
(7) Special rule for certain brackets.
(A) Calendar year 1994. In prescribing the tables under paragraph (1) which apply with respect to taxable years beginning in calendar year 1994, the Secretary shall make no adjustment to the dollar amounts at which the 36 percent rate bracket begins or at which the 39.6 percent rate begins under any table contained in subsection (a), (b), (c), (d), or (e).
(B) Later calendar years. In prescribing tables under paragraph (1) which apply with respect to taxable years beginning in a calendar year after 1994, the cost-of-living adjustment used in making adjustments to the dollar amounts referred to in subparagraph (A) shall be determined under paragraph (3) by substituting "1993" for "1992."

1,003

Code Sec. 1(f)(7)(B) — Tax rates

> • **Caution:** Code Sec. 1(f)(8), following, was added by P.L. 107-16, the Economic Growth and Tax Relief Reconciliation Act of 2001 (EGTRRA), and further amended by P.L. 108-27 and P.L. 108-311. These provisions generally sunset for tax years beginning after 12/31/2012. For specific sunset provisions, see Sec. 901, P.L. 107-16 and Sec. 303, P.L. 108-27 (as amended) reproduced in history notes for this Code Sec.

(8) Elimination of marriage penalty in 15-percent bracket. With respect to taxable years beginning after December 31, 2003, in prescribing the tables under paragraph (1)—

(A) the maximum taxable income in the 15-percent rate bracket in the table contained in subsection (a) (and the minimum taxable income in the next higher taxable income bracket in such table) shall be 200 percent of the maximum taxable income in the 15-percent rate bracket in the table contained in subsection (c) (after any other adjustment under this subsection), and

(B) the comparable taxable income amounts in the table contained in subsection (d) shall be ½ of the amounts determined under subparagraph (A).

(g) Certain unearned income of children taxed as if parent's income.

(1) In general. In the case of any child to whom this subsection applies, the tax imposed by this section shall be equal to the greater of—

(A) the tax imposed by this section without regard to this subsection, or

(B) the sum of—

(i) the tax which would be imposed by this section if the taxable income of such child for the taxable year were reduced by the net unearned income of such child, plus

(ii) such child's share of the allocable parental tax.

(2) Child to whom subsection applies. This subsection shall apply to any child for any taxable year if—

(A) such child—

(i) has not attained age 18 before the close of the taxable year, or

(ii)(I) has attained age 18 before the close of the taxable year and meets the age requirements of section 152(c)(3) (determined without regard to subparagraph (B) thereof), and

(II) whose earned income (as defined in section 911(d)(2)) for such taxable year does not exceed one-half of the amount of the individual's support (within the meaning of section 152(c)(1)(D) after the application of section 152(f)(5) (without regard to subparagraph (A) thereof)) for such taxable year.

(B) either parent of such child is alive at the close of the taxable year, and

(C) such child does not file a joint return for the taxable year.

(3) Allocable parental tax. For purposes of this subsection—

(A) In general. The term "allocable parental tax" means the excess of—

(i) the tax which would be imposed by this section on the parent's taxable income if such income included the net unearned income of all children of the parent to whom this subsection applies, over

(ii) the tax imposed by this section on the parent without regard to this subsection.

For purposes of clause (i), net unearned income of all children of the parent shall not be taken into account in computing any exclusion, deduction, or credit of the parent.

(B) Child's share. A child's share of any allocable parental tax of a parent shall be equal to an amount which bears the same ratio to the total allocable parental tax as the child's net unearned income bears to the aggregate net unearned income of all children of such parent to whom this subsection applies.

(C) Special rule where parent has different taxable year. Except as provided in regulations, if the parent does not have the same taxable year as the child, the allocable parental tax shall be determined on the basis of the taxable year of the parent ending in the child's taxable year.

(4) Net unearned income. For purposes of this subsection—

(A) In general. The term "net unearned income" means the excess of—

(i) the portion of the adjusted gross income for the taxable year which is not attributable to earned income (as defined in section 911(d)(2)), over

(ii) the sum of—

(I) the amount in effect for the taxable year under section 63(c)(5)(A) (relating to limitation on standard deduction in the case of certain dependents), plus

(II) the greater of the amount described in subclause (I) or, if the child itemizes his deductions for the taxable year, the amount of the itemized deductions allowed by this chapter for the taxable year which are directly connected with the production of the portion of adjusted gross income referred to in clause (i).

(B) Limitation based on taxable income. The amount of the net unearned income for any taxable year shall not exceed the individual's taxable income for such taxable year.

(C) Treatment of distributions from qualified disability trusts. For purposes of this subsection, in the case of any child who is a beneficiary of a qualified disability trust (as defined in section 642(b)(2)(C)(ii)), any amount included in the income of such child under sections 652 and 662 during a taxable year shall be considered earned income of such child for such taxable year.

(5) Special rules for determining parent to whom subsection applies. For purposes of this subsection, the parent whose taxable income shall be taken into account shall be—

(A) in the case of parents who are not married (within the meaning of section 7703), the custodial parent (within the meaning of section 152(e)) of the child, and

(B) in the case of married individuals filing separately, the individual with the greater taxable income.

(6) Providing of parent's TIN. The parent of any child to whom this subsection applies for any taxable year shall provide the TIN of such parent to such child and such child shall include such TIN on the child's return of tax imposed by this section for such taxable year.

(7) Election to claim certain unearned income of child on parent's return.

(A) In general. If—

1,004

Tax rates

(i) any child to whom this subsection applies has gross income for the taxable year only from interest and dividends (including Alaska Permanent Fund dividends),
(ii) such gross income is more than the amount described in paragraph (4)(A)(ii)(I) and less than 10 times the amount so described,
(iii) no estimated tax payments for such year are made in the name and TIN of such child, and no amount has been deducted and withheld under section 3406, and
(iv) the parent of such child (as determined under paragraph (5)) elects the application of subparagraph (B),

such child shall be treated (other than for purposes of this paragraph) as having no gross income for such year and shall not be required to file a return under section 6012.

(B) Income included on parent's return. In the case of a parent making the election under this paragraph—
(i) the gross income of each child to whom such election applies (to the extent the gross income of such child exceeds twice the amount described in paragraph (4)(A)(ii)(I)) shall be included in such parent's gross income for the taxable year,
(ii) the tax imposed by this section for such year with respect to such parent shall be the amount equal to the sum of—
(I) the amount determined under this section after the application of clause (i), plus

> • *Caution:* Code Sec. 1(g)(7)(B)(ii)(II), following, was amended by P.L. 107-16, the Economic Growth and Tax Relief Reconciliation Act of 2001 (EGTRRA). These provisions generally sunset for tax years beginning after 12/31/2012. For specific sunset provisions, see Sec. 901, P.L. 107-16 (as amended) reproduced in history notes for this Code Sec.

(II) for each such child, 10 percent of the lessor amount described in paragraph (4)(A)(ii)(I) or the excess of the gross income of such child over the amount so described, and
(iii) any interest which is an item of tax preference under section 57(a)(5) of the child shall be treated as an item of tax preference of such parent (and not of such child).

(C) Regulations. The Secretary shall prescribe such regulations as may be necessary or appropriate to carry out the purposes of this paragraph.

(h) Maximum capital gains rate.
(1) In general. If a taxpayer has a net capital gain for any taxable year, the tax imposed by this section for such taxable year shall not exceed the sum of—
(A) a tax computed at the rates and in the same manner as if this subsection had not been enacted on the greater of—
(i) taxable income reduced by the net capital gain; or
(ii) the lesser of—

> • *Caution:* Code Sec. 1(h)(1)(A)(ii)(I), following, was amended by P.L. 107-16, the Economic Growth and Tax Relief Reconciliation Act of 2001 (EGTRRA). These provisions generally sunset for tax years beginning after 12/31/2012. For specific sunset provisions, see Sec. 901, P.L. 107-16 (as amended) reproduced in history notes for this Code Sec.

(I) the amount of taxable income taxed at a rate below 25 percent; or
(II) taxable income reduced by the adjusted net capital gain,

> • *Caution:* Code Sec. 1(h)(1)(B), following, was amended by P.L. 108-27. These provisions generally sunset for tax years beginning after 12/31/2012. For specific sunset provisions, see Sec. 303, P.L. 108-27 reproduced in history notes for this Code Sec.

(B) 5 percent (0 percent in the case of taxable years beginning after 2007) of so much of the adjusted net capital gain (or, if less, taxable income) as does not exceed the excess (if any) of—

> • *Caution:* Code Sec. 1(h)(1)(B)(i), following, was amended by P.L. 107-16, the Economic Growth and Tax Relief Reconciliation Act of 2001 (EGTRRA). These provisions generally sunset for tax years beginning after 12/31/2012. For specific sunset provisions, see Sec. 901, P.L. 107-16 (as amended) reproduced in history notes for this Code Sec.

(i) the amount of taxable income which would (without regard to this paragraph) be taxed at a rate below 25 percent, over
(ii) the taxable income reduced by the adjusted net capital gain;

> • *Caution:* Code Sec. 1(h)(1)(C), following, was amended by P.L. 108-27. These provisions generally sunset for tax years beginning after 12/31/2012. For specific sunset provisions, see Sec. 303, P.L. 108-27 reproduced in history notes for this Code Sec.

(C) 15 percent of the adjusted net capital gain (or, if less, taxable income) in excess of the amount on which a tax is determined under subparagraph (B);
(D) 25 percent of the excess (if any) of—
(i) the unrecaptured section 1250 gain (or, if less, the net capital gain (determined without regard to paragraph (11))), over
(ii) the excess (if any) of—
(I) the sum of the amount on which tax is determined under subparagraph (A) plus the net capital gain, over

(II) taxable income; and
(E) 28 percent of the amount of taxable income in excess of the sum of the amounts on which tax is determined under the preceding subparagraphs of this paragraph.

> • **Caution:** Code Sec. 1(h)(2)-(11), following, was amended by P.L. 108-27. These provisions generally sunset for tax years beginning after 12/31/2012. For specific sunset provisions, see Sec. 303, P.L. 108-27 reproduced in history notes for this Code Sec.

(2) Net capital gain taken into account as investment income. For purposes of this subsection, the net capital gain for any taxable year shall be reduced (but not below zero) by the amount which the taxpayer takes into account as investment income under section 163(d)(4)(B)(iii).

(3) Adjusted net capital gain. For purposes of this subsection, the term "adjusted net capital gain" means the sum of—
(A) net capital gain (determined without regard to paragraph (11)) reduced (but not below zero) by the sum of—
  (i) unrecaptured section 1250 gain, and
  (ii) 28-percent rate gain, plus
(B) qualified dividend income (as defined in paragraph (11)).

(4) 28 percent rate gain. For purposes of this subsection, the term "28-percent rate gain" means the excess (if any) of—
(A) the sum of—
  (i) collectibles gain; and
  (ii) section 1202 gain, over
(B) the sum of—
  (i) collectibles loss;
  (ii) the net short-term capital loss; and
  (iii) the amount of long-term capital loss carried under section 1212(b)(1)(B) to the taxable year.

(5) Collectibles gain and loss. For purposes of this subsection—
(A) In general. The terms "collectibles gain" and "collectibles loss" mean gain or loss (respectively) from the sale or exchange of a collectible (as defined in section 408(m) without regard to paragraph (3) thereof) which is a capital asset held for more than 1 year but only to the extent such gain is taken into account in computing gross income and such loss is taken into account in computing taxable income.
(B) Partnerships, etc. For purposes of subparagraph (A), any gain from the sale of an interest in a partnership, S corporation, or trust which is attributable to unrealized appreciation in the value of collectibles shall be treated as gain from the sale or exchange of a collectible. Rules similar to the rules of section 751 shall apply for purposes of the preceding sentence.

(6) Unrecaptured section 1250 gain. For purposes of this subsection—
(A) In general. The term "unrecaptured section 1250 gain" means the excess (if any) of—
  (i) the amount of long-term capital gain (not otherwise treated as ordinary income) which would be treated as ordinary income if section 1250(b)(1) included all depreciation and the applicable percentage under section 1250(a) were 100 percent, over
  (ii) the excess (if any) of—
    (I) the amount described in paragraph (4)(B); over
    (II) the amount described in paragraph (4)(A).
(B) Limitation with respect to section 1231 property. The amount described in subparagraph (A)(i) from sales, exchanges, and conversions described in section 1231(a)(3)(A) for any taxable year shall not exceed the net section 1231 gain (as defined in section 1231(c)(3)) for such year.

(7) Section 1202 gain. For purposes of this subsection, the term "section 1202 gain" means the excess of—
(A) the gain which would be excluded from gross income under section 1202 but for the percentage limitation in section 1202(a), over
(B) the gain excluded from gross income under section 1202.

(8) Coordination with recapture of net ordinary losses under section 1231. If any amount is treated as ordinary income under section 1231(c), such amount shall be allocated among the separate categories of net section 1231 gain (as defined in section 1231(c)(3)) in such manner as the Secretary may by forms or regulations prescribe.

(9) Regulations. The Secretary may prescribe such regulations as are appropriate (including regulations requiring reporting) to apply this subsection in the case of sales and exchanges by pass-thru entities and of interests in such entities.

(10) Pass-thru entity defined. For purposes of this subsection, the term "pass-thru entity" means—
(A) a regulated investment company;
(B) a real estate investment trust;
(C) an S corporation;
(D) a partnership;
(E) an estate or trust;
(F) a common trust fund; and
(G) a qualified electing fund (as defined in section 1295).

(11) Dividends taxed as net capital gain.
(A) In general. For purposes of this subsection, the term "net capital gain" means net capital gain (determined without regard to this paragraph) increased by qualified dividend income.
(B) Qualified dividend income. For purposes of this paragraph—
  (i) In general. The term "qualified dividend income" means dividends received during the taxable year from—
    (I) domestic corporations, and
    (II) qualified foreign corporations.
  (ii) Certain dividends excluded. Such term shall not include—
    (I) any dividend from a corporation which for the taxable year of the corporation in which the distribution is made, or the preceding taxable year, is a corporation exempt from tax under section 501 or 521,
    (II) any amount allowed as a deduction under section 591 (relating to deduction for dividends paid by mutual savings banks, etc.), and
    (III) any dividend described in section 404(k).
  (iii) Coordination with section 246(c). Such term shall not include any dividend on any share of stock—

Tax rates   Code Sec. 1

(I) with respect to which the holding period requirements of section 246(c) are not met (determined by substituting in section 246(c) "60 days" for "45 days" each place it appears and by substituting "121-day period" for "91-day period"), or

(II) to the extent that the taxpayer is under an obligation (whether pursuant to a short sale or otherwise) to make related payments with respect to positions in substantially similar or related property.

(C) Qualified foreign corporations.

(i) In general. Except as otherwise provided in this paragraph, the term "qualified foreign corporation" means any foreign corporation if—

(I) such corporation is incorporated in a possession of the United States, or

(II) such corporation is eligible for benefits of a comprehensive income tax treaty with the United States which the Secretary determines is satisfactory for purposes of this paragraph and which includes an exchange of information program.

(ii) Dividends on stock readily tradable on United States securities market. A foreign corporation not otherwise treated as a qualified foreign corporation under clause (i) shall be so treated with respect to any dividend paid by such corporation if the stock with respect to which such dividend is paid is readily tradable on an established securities market in the United States.

(iii) Exclusion of dividends of certain foreign corporations. Such term shall not include any foreign corporation which for the taxable year of the corporation in which the dividend was paid, or the preceding taxable year, is a passive foreign investment company (as defined in section 1297).

(iv) Coordination with foreign tax credit limitation. Rules similar to the rules of section 904(b)(2)(B) shall apply with respect to the dividend rate differential under this paragraph.

(D) Special rules.

(i) Amounts taken into account as investment income. Qualified dividend income shall not include any amount which the taxpayer takes into account as investment income under section 163(d)(4)(B).

(ii) Extraordinary dividends. If a taxpayer to whom this section applies receives, with respect to any share of stock, qualified dividend income from 1 or more dividends which are extraordinary dividends (within the meaning of section 1059(c)), any loss on the sale or exchange of such share shall, to the extent of such dividends, be treated as long-term capital loss.

(iii) Treatment of dividends from regulated investment companies and real estate investment trusts. A dividend received from a regulated investment company or a real estate investment trust shall be subject to the limitations prescribed in sections 854 and 857.

• **Caution:** Code Sec. 1(h)(13) was repealed by P.L. 107-16. These provisions generally sunset for tax years beginning after 12/31/2012. For specific sunset provisions, see Sec. 901, P.L. 107-16 (as amended) reproduced in history notes for this Code Sec.

• **Caution:** Code Sec. 1(i), following, was added by P.L. 107-16, the Economic Growth and Tax Relief Reconciliation Act of 2001 (EGTRRA) and amended by P.L. 108-27 and 108-311. These provisions generally sunset for tax years beginning after 12/31/2012. For specific sunset provisions, see Sec. 901, P.L. 107-16 and Sec. 303, P.L. 108-27 (as amended) reproduced in history notes for this Code Sec.

(i) Rate reductions after 2000.

(1) 10-percent rate bracket.

(A) In general. In the case of taxable years beginning after December 31, 2000—

(i) the rate of tax under subsections (a), (b), (c), and (d) on taxable income not over the initial bracket amount shall be 10 percent, and

(ii) the 15 percent rate of tax shall apply only to taxable income over the initial bracket amount but not over the maximum dollar amount for the 15-percent rate bracket.

(B) Initial bracket amount. For purposes of this paragraph, the initial bracket amount is—

(i) $14,000 in the case of subsection (a),

(ii) $10,000 in the case of subsection (b), and

(iii) ½ the amount applicable under clause (i) (after adjustment, if any, under subparagraph (C)) in the case of subsections (c) and (d).

(C) Inflation adjustment. In prescribing the tables under subsection (f) which apply with respect to taxable years beginning in calendar years after 2003—

(i) the cost-of-living adjustment shall be determined under subsection (f)(3) by substituting "2002" for "1992" in subparagraph (B) thereof, and

(ii) the adjustments under clause (i) shall not apply to the amount referred to in subparagraph (B)(iii).

If any amount after adjustment under the preceding sentence is not a multiple of $50, such amount shall be rounded to the next lowest multiple of $50.

(2) Reductions in rates after June 30, 2001. In the case of taxable years beginning in a calendar year after 2000, the corresponding percentage specified for such calendar year in the following table shall be substituted for the otherwise applicable tax rate in the tables under subsections (a), (b), (c), (d), and (e).

In the case of taxable years beginning during calendar year:	The corresponding percentages shall be substituted for the following percentages:				
	28%	31%	36%	39.6%
2001	27.5%	30.5%	35.5%	39.1%
2002	27.0%	30.0%	35.0%	38.6%
2003 and thereafter . .	25.0%	28.0%	33.0%	35.0%

(3) Adjustment of tables. The Secretary shall adjust the tables prescribed under subsection (f) to carry out this subsection.

In 2010, P.L. 111-312, Sec. 101(a)(1), substituted "December 31, 2012" for "December 31, 2010" both places it appears in Sec. 901, P.L. 107-16, see below, effective as if included in the enactment of P.L. 107-16, EGTRRA, 6/7/2001.

—P.L. 111-312, Sec. 102(a), substituted "December 31, 2012" for "December 31, 2010" in Sec. 303, P.L. 108-27, see below, effective as if included in the enactment of P.L. 108-27, 5/28/2003.

In 2008, P.L. 110-343, Sec. 702DivC, Sec. 702, P.L. 110-343, relating to tax relief for areas damaged by 2008 Midwestern storms, reads as follows:

"Sec. 702. Temporary tax relief for areas damaged by 2008 Midwestern severe storms, tornados, and flooding.

"(a) In general. Subject to the modifications described in this section, the following provisions of or relating to the Internal Revenue Code of 1986 shall apply to any Midwestern disaster area in addition to the areas to which such provisions otherwise apply:

"(1) GO Zone benefits.

"(A) Section 1400N (relating to tax benefits) other than subsections (b), (d), (e), (i), (j), (m), and (o) thereof.

"(B) Section 1400O (relating to education tax benefits).

"(C) Section 1400P (relating to housing tax benefits).

"(D) Section 1400Q (relating to special rules for use of retirement funds).

"(E) Section 1400R(a) (relating to employee retention credit for employers).

"(F) Section 1400S (relating to additional tax relief) other than subsection (d) thereof.

"(G) Section 1400T (relating to special rules for mortgage revenue bonds).

"(2) Other benefits included in Katrina Emergency Tax Relief Act of 2005. Sections 302, 303, 304, 401, and 405 of the Katrina Emergency Tax Relief Act of 2005.

"(b) Midwestern disaster area.

"(1) In general. For purposes of this section and for applying the substitutions described in subsections (d) and (e), the term 'Midwestern disaster area' means an area—

"(A) with respect to which a major disaster has been declared by the President on or after May 20, 2008, and before August 1, 2008, under section 401 of the Robert T. Stafford Disaster Relief and Emergency Assistance Act by reason of severe storms, tornados, or flooding occurring in any of the States of Arkansas, Illinois, Indiana, Iowa, Kansas, Michigan, Minnesota, Missouri, Nebraska, and Wisconsin, and

"(B) determined by the President to warrant individual or individual and public assistance from the Federal Government under such Act with respect to damages attributable to such severe storms, tornados, or flooding.

"(2) Certain benefits available to areas eligible only for public assistance. For purposes of applying this section to benefits under the following provisions, paragraph (1) shall be applied without regard to subparagraph (B):

"(A) Sections 1400Q, 1400S(b), and 1400S(d) of the Internal Revenue Code of 1986.

"(B) Sections 302, 401, and 405 of the Katrina Emergency Tax Relief Act of 2005.

"(c) References.

"(1) Area. Any reference in such provisions to the Hurricane Katrina disaster area or the Gulf Opportunity Zone shall be treated as a reference to any Midwestern disaster area and any reference to the Hurricane Katrina disaster area or the Gulf Opportunity Zone within a State shall be treated as a reference to all Midwestern disaster areas within the State.

"(2) Items attributable to disaster. Any reference in such provisions to any loss, damage, or other item attributable to Hurricane Katrina shall be treated as a reference to any loss, damage, or other item attributable to the severe storms, tornados, or flooding giving rise to any Presidential declaration described in subsection (b)(1)(A).

"(3) Applicable disaster date. For purposes of applying the substitutions described in subsections (d) and (e), the term 'applicable disaster date' means, with respect to any Midwestern disaster area, the date on which the severe storms, tornados, or flooding giving rise to the Presidential declaration described in subsection (b)(1)(A) occurred.
* * * * * * * * * *

"(e) Modifications to Katrina Emergency Tax Relief Act of 2005. The following provisions of the Katrina Emergency Tax Relief Act of 2005 shall be applied with the following modifications:

"(1) Additional exemption for housing displaced individual. Section 302—

"(A) by substituting '2008 or 2009' for '2005 or 2006' in subsection (a) thereof,

"(B) by substituting 'Midwestern displaced individual' for 'Hurricane Katrina displaced individual' each place it appears, and

"(C) by treating an area as a core disaster area for purposes of applying subsection (c) thereof if the area is a Midwestern disaster area without regard to subsection (b)(2) of this section (relating to areas eligible only for public assistance).
* * * * * * * * * *

"(4) Exclusion of certain cancellation of indebtedness income. Section 401—

"(A) by treating an individual whose principal place of abode on the applicable disaster date was in a Midwestern disaster area (determined without regard to subsection (b)(2) of this section) as an individual described in subsection (b)(1) thereof, and by treating an individual whose principal place of abode on the applicable disaster date was in a Midwestern disaster area solely by reason of subsection (b)(2) of this section as an individual described in subsection (b)(2) thereof,

"(B) by substituting 'the applicable disaster date' for 'August 28, 2005' both places it appears, and

"(C) by substituting 'January 1, 2010' for 'January 1, 2007' in subsection (e).
* * * * * * * * * *

—P.L. 110-185, Sec. 101(f)(2), struck out subpara. (i)(1)(D)
Prior to deletion, subpara. (i)(1)(D) read as follows:

"(D) Coordination with acceleration of 10 percent rate bracket benefit for 2001. This paragraph shall not apply to any taxable year to which section 6428 applies."

In **2007**, P.L. 110-141, Sec. 1, of this Act, reads as follows:

"Sec. 1. Exclusion from income for payments from the Hokie Spirit Memorial Fund. For purposes of the Internal Revenue Code of 1986, gross income shall not include any amount received from the Virginia Polytechnic Institute & State University, out of amounts transferred from the Hokie Spirit Memorial Fund established by the Virginia Tech Foundation, an organization organized and operated as described in section 501(c)(3) of the Internal Revenue Code of 1986, if such amount is paid on account of the tragic event on April 16, 2007, at such university."

—P.L. 110-28, Sec. 8241(a), amended subpara. (g)(2)(A)... Sec. 8241(b), deleted "minor" after "income of" in the heading of subsec. (g), effective for tax. yrs. begin after 5/25/2007.
Prior to amendment subpara. (g)(2)(A) read as follows:

"(A) such child has not attained age 18 before the close of the taxable year,"

In **2006**, P.L. 109-222, Sec. 102, substituted "December 31, 2010" for "December 31, 2008" in Sec. 303 of P.L. 108-27 [see below], effective 5/17/2006.

—P.L. 109-222, Sec. 510(a), substituted "age 18" for "age 14" in subpara. (g)(2)(A)... Sec. 510(b), added subpara. (g)(4)(C)... Sec. 510(c), deleted "and" at the end of subpara. (g)(2)(A), substituted ", and" for the period at the end of subpara. (g)(2)(B), and added subpara. (g)(2)(C), effective for tax. yrs. begin. after 12/31/2005.

In **2005**, P.L. 109-135, Sec. 201(b)(4)(A), repealed Sec. 104 of P.L. 109-73 [see below].

—P.L. 109-73, Sec. 104, of this Act [prior to repeal by Sec. 201(b)(4)(A) of P.L. 109-135, see above], read as follows:

"Sec. 104. Provisions relating to plan amendments.

"(a) In general. If this section applies to any amendment to any plan or annuity contract, such plan or contract shall be treated as being operated in accordance with the terms of the plan during the period described in subsection (b)(2)(A).

"(b) Amendments to which section applies.

"(1) In general. This section shall apply to any amendment to any plan or annuity contract which is made—

"(A) pursuant to any amendment made by this title, or pursuant to any regulation issued by the Secretary of the Treasury or the Secretary of Labor under this title, and

"(B) on or before the last day of the first plan year beginning on or after January 1, 2007, or such later date as the Secretary of the Treasury may prescribe.
In the case of a governmental plan (as defined in section 414(d) of the Internal Revenue Code of 1986), subparagraph (B) shall be applied by substituting the date which is 2 years after the date otherwise applied under subparagraph (B).

"(2) Conditions. This section shall not apply to any amendment unless—

"(A) during the period—

"(i) beginning on the date the legislative or regulatory amendment described in paragraph (1)(A) takes effect (or in the case of a plan or contract amendment not required by such legislative or regulatory amendment, the effective date specified by the plan), and

"(ii) ending on the date described in paragraph (1)(B) (or, if earlier, the date the plan or contract amendment is adopted),
the plan or contract is operated as if such plan or contract amendment were in effect; and

"(B) such plan or contract amendment applies retroactively for such period."
—P.L. 109-73, Sec. 302, of this Act, reads as follows:

"Sec. 302. Additional exemption for housing Hurricane Katrina displaced individuals.

"(a) In general. In the case of taxable years of a natural person beginning in 2005 or 2006, for purposes of the Internal Revenue Code of 1986, taxable income shall be reduced by $500 for each Hurricane Katrina displaced individual of the taxpayer for the taxable year.

"(b) Limitations.

"(1) Dollar limitation. The reduction under subsection (a) shall not exceed $2,000, reduced by the amount of the reduction under this section for all prior taxable years.

"(2) Individuals taken into account only once. An individual shall not be taken into account under subsection (a) if such individual was taken into account under such subsection by the taxpayer for any prior taxable year.

"(3) Identifying information required. An individual shall not be taken into account under subsection (a) for a taxable year unless the taxpayer identification number of such individual is included on the return of the taxpayer for such taxable year.

"(c) Hurricane Katrina displaced individual. For purposes of this section, the term 'Hurricane Katrina displaced individual' means, with respect to any taxpayer for any taxable year, any natural person if—

"(1) such person's principal place of abode on August 28, 2005, was in the Hurricane Katrina disaster area,

"(2)(A) in the case of such an abode located in the core disaster area, such person is displaced from such abode, or

"(B) in the case of such an abode located outside of the core disaster area, such person is displaced from such abode, and

"(i) such abode was damaged by Hurricane Katrina, or

"(ii) such person was evacuated from such abode by reason of Hurricane Katrina, and

"(3) such person is provided housing free of charge by the taxpayer in the principal residence of the taxpayer for a period of 60 consecutive days which ends in such taxable year.
Such term shall not include the spouse or any dependent of the taxpayer.

"(d) Compensation for housing. No deduction shall be allowed under this section if the taxpayer receives any rent or other amount (from any source) in connection with the providing of such housing."
—P.L. 109-73, Sec. 401, of this Act, reads as follows:

"Sec. 401. Exclusions of certain cancellations of indebtedness by reason of Hurricane Katrina.

Tax rates

"(a) In general. For purposes of the Internal Revenue Code of 1986, gross income shall not include any amount which (but for this section) would be includible in gross income by reason of the discharge (in whole or in part) of indebtedness of a natural person described in subsection (b) by an applicable entity (as defined in section 6050P(c)(1) of such Code).

"(b) Persons described. A natural person is described in this subsection if the principal place of abode of such person on August 25, 2005, was located—

"(1) in the core disaster area, or

"(2) in the Hurricane Katrina disaster area (but outside the core disaster area) and such person suffered economic loss by reason of Hurricane Katrina.

"(c) Exceptions.

"(1) Business indebtedness. Subsection (a) shall not apply to any indebtedness incurred in connection with a trade or business.

"(2) Real property outside core disaster area. Subsection (a) shall not apply to any discharge of indebtedness to the extent that real property constituting security for such indebtedness is located outside of the Hurricane Katrina disaster area.

"(d) Denial of double benefit. For purposes of the Internal Revenue Code of 1986, the amount excluded from gross income under subsection (a) shall be treated in the same manner as an amount excluded under section 108(a) of such Code.

"(e) Effective date. This section shall apply to discharges made on or after August 25, 2005, and before January 1, 2007."

In 2004, P.L. 108-357, Sec. 413(c)(1)(A), added "and" at the end of subpara. (h)(10)(F), deleted subpara. (h)(10)(G), and redesignated subpara. (h)(10)(H) as (h)(10)(G) . . . Sec. 413(c)(1)(B), deleted "a foreign personal holding company (as defined in section 552), a foreign investment company (as defined in section 1246(b)), or" after "preceding taxable year, is" in clause (h)(11)(C)(iii), effective for tax. yrs. of foreign corporations begin. after 12/31/2004, and for tax. yrs. of United States shareholders with or within which such tax. yrs. of foreign corporations end.

Prior to deletion, subpara. (h)(10)(G) read as follows:

"(G) a foreign investment company which is described in section 1246(b)(1) and for which an election is in effect under section 1247; and"

— P.L. 108-311, Sec. 101(c), amended para. (f)(8) . . . Sec. 101(d)(1), deleted "($12,000 in the case of taxable years beginning after December 31, 2004, and before January 1, 2008)" after "$14,000" in subpara. (i)(1)(B) . . . Sec. 101(d)(2), amended subpara. (i)(1)(C), effective for tax. yrs. begin. after 12/31/2003.

— P.L. 108-311, Sec. 105, of this Act, provides:

"SEC. 105. APPLICATION OF EGTRRA SUNSET TO THIS TITLE. Each amendment made by this title [Secs. 101-104] shall be subject to title IX of the Economic Growth and Tax Relief Reconciliation Act of 2001 [Sec. 901 of P.L. 107-16] to the same extent and in the same manner as the provision of such Act to which such amendment relates. [see below]"

Prior to amendment, para. (f)(8) read as follows:

"(8) Phaseout of marriage penalty in 15-percent bracket.

"(A) In general. With respect to taxable years beginning after December 31, 2002, in prescribing the tables under paragraph (1)—

"(i) the maximum taxable income in the 15-percent rate bracket in the table contained in subsection (a) (and the minimum taxable income in the next higher taxable income bracket in such table) shall be the applicable percentage of the maximum taxable income in the 15-percent rate bracket in the table contained in subsection (c) (after any other adjustment under this subsection), and

"(ii) the comparable taxable income amounts in the table contained in subsection (d) shall be ½ of the amounts determined under clause (i).

"(B) Applicable percentage. For purposes of subparagraph (A), the applicable percentage shall be determined in accordance with the following table:

For taxable years beginning in calendar year—	The applicable percentage is—
2003 and 2004	200
2005	180
2006	187
2007	193
2008 and thereafter	200.

"(C) Rounding. If any amount determined under subparagraph (A)(i) is not a multiple of $50, such amount shall be rounded to the next lowest multiple of $50."

Prior to amendment, subpara. (i)(1)(C) read as follows:

"(C) Inflation adjustment. In prescribing the tables under subsection (f) which apply with respect to taxable years beginning in calendar years after 2000—

"(i) except as provided in clause (ii), the Secretary shall make no adjustment to the initial bracket amounts for any taxable year beginning before January 1, 2009,

"(ii) there shall be an adjustment under subsection (f) of such amounts which shall apply only to taxable years beginning in 2004, and such adjustment shall be determined under subsection (f)(3) by substituting '2002' for '1992' in subparagraph (B) thereof,

"(iii) the cost-of-living adjustment used in making adjustments to the initial bracket amounts for any taxable year beginning after December 31, 2008, shall be determined under subsection (f)(3) by substituting '2007' for '1992' in subparagraph (B) thereof, and

"(iv) the adjustments under clauses (ii) and (iii) shall not apply to the amount referred to in subparagraph (B)(iii).

"If any amount after adjustment under the preceding sentence is not a multiple of $50, such amount shall be rounded to the next lowest multiple of $50."

— P.L. 108-311, Sec. 402(a)(1), added "(determined without regard to paragraph (11))" after "net capital gain" in clause (h)(1)(D)(i) . . . Sec. 402(a)(2)(A), substituted "section 246(c)" for "section 246(c)(1)" in subclause (h)(11)(B)(iii)(I) . . . Sec. 402(a)(2)(B), substituted "121-day period" for "120-day period" in subclause (h)(11)(B)(iii)(I) . . . Sec. 402(a)(2)(C), substituted "91-day period" for "90-day period" in subclause (h)(11)(B)(iii)(I) . . . Sec. 402(a)(3), substituted "a taxpayer to whom this section applies" for "an individual" in clause (h)(11)(D)(ii), effective for tax. yrs. begin. after 12/31/2002, except as provided in Sec. 302(f)(2) of P.L. 108-27 [as amended by Sec. 402(a)(6) of P.L. 108-311, reproduced below].

— P.L. 108-311, Sec. 402(a)(6), of this Act [which amended Sec. 302(f)(2) of P.L. 108-27, see below], provides:

"(2) Pass-thru entities. In the case of a pass-thru entity described in subparagraph (A), (B), (C), (D), (E), or (F) of section 1(h)(10) of the Internal Revenue Code of 1986, as amended by this Act, the amendments made by this section shall apply to taxable years ending after December 31, 2002; except that dividends received by such an entity on or before such date shall not be treated as qualified dividend income (as defined in section 1(h)(11)(B) of such Code, as added by this Act)."

— P.L. 108-311, Sec. 408(a)(1), substituted "10 percent" for "10 percent." in subclause (g)(7)(B)(ii)(II) . . . Sec. 408(a)(2)(A), substituted "(4)(B)" for "(5)(B)" in subclause (h)(6)(A)(ii)(I) . . . Sec. 408(a)(2)(B), substituted "(4)(A)" for "(5)(A)" in subclause (h)(6)(A)(ii)(II), enacted 10/4/2004.

In 2003, P.L. 108-27, Sec. 102(a), added the item for 2003 and 2004 of the table in subpara. (f)(8)(B) . . . Sec. 102(b)(1), substituted "2002" for "2004" in subpara. (f)(8)(A) . . . Sec. 102(b)(2), substituted "2002" for "2004" in Sec. 302(c) of P.L. 107-16 [see below], effective for tax. yrs. begin. after 12/31/2002.

— P.L. 108-27, Sec. 103(b), substituted "2002" for "2004" in Sec. 301(d) of P.L. 107-16 [see below], effective for tax. yrs. begin. after 12/31/2002.

— P.L. 108-27, Sec. 104(a), substituted "($12,000 in the case of taxable years beginning after December 31, 2004, and before January 1, 2008)" for "($12,000 in the case of taxable years beginning before January 1, 2008)" in clause (i)(1)(B)(i) . . . Sec. 104(b), amended subpara. (i)(1)(C), effective for tax. yrs. begin. after 12/31/2002. Sec. 104(c)(2) of this Act reads as follows:

"(2) Tables for 2003. The Secretary of the Treasury shall modify each table which has been prescribed under section 1(f) of the Internal Revenue Code of 1986 for taxable years beginning in 2003 and which relates to the amendment made by subsection (a) to reflect such amendment."

Prior to amendment, subpara. (i)(1)(C) read as follows:

"(C) Inflation adjustment. In prescribing the tables under subsection (f) which apply with respect to taxable years beginning in calendar years after 2000—

"(i) the Secretary shall make no adjustment to the initial bracket amount for any taxable year beginning before January 1, 2009,

"(ii) the cost-of-living adjustment used in making adjustments to the initial bracket amount for any taxable year beginning after December 31, 2008, shall be determined under subsection (f)(3) by substituting '2007' for '1992' in subparagraph (B) thereof, and

"(iii) such adjustment shall not apply to the amount referred to in subparagraph (B)(iii).

If any amount after adjustment under the preceding sentence is not a multiple of $50, such amount shall be rounded to the next lowest multiple of $50."

— P.L. 108-27, Sec. 105(a), amended the table in para. (i)(2), effective for tax. yrs. begin. after 12/31/2002.

Prior to amendment, the table in para. (i)(2) read as follows:

"In the case of taxable years beginning during calendar year:	The corresponding percentages shall be substituted for the following percentages:			
	28%	31%	36%	39.6%
2001	27.5%	30.5%	35.5%	39.1%
2002 and 2003	27.0%	30.0%	35.0%	38.6%
2004 and 2005	26.0%	29.0%	34.0%	37.6%
2006 and thereafter	25.0%	28.0%	33.0%	35.0%"

— P.L. 108-27, Sec. 107, of this Act, reads as follows:

"SEC. 107. APPLICATION OF EGTRRA SUNSET TO THIS TITLE. Each amendment made by this title [Secs. 101-106] shall be subject to title IX of the Economic Growth and Tax Relief Reconciliation Act of 2001 to the same extent and in the same manner as the provision of such Act to which such amendment relates."

— P.L. 108-27, Sec. 301(a)(1), substituted "5 percent (0 percent in the case of taxable years beginning after 2007)" for "10 percent" in subpara. (h)(1)(B) . . . Sec. 301(a)(2)(A), substituted "15 percent" for "20 percent" in subpara. (h)(1)(C) . . . Sec. 301(b)(1)(A), deleted paras. (h)(2) and (9) . . . Sec. 301(b)(1)(B), redesignated paras. (h)(3)-(8) as (h)(2)-(7) . . . Sec. 301(b)(1)(C), redesignated paras. (h)(10)-(12) as paras. (h)(8)-(10), effective for tax. yrs. end. on or after 5/6/2003.

Prior to deletion, para. (h)(2) read as follows:

"(2) Reduced capital gain rates for qualified 5-year gain.

"(A) Reduction in 10-percent rate. In the case of any taxable year beginning after December 31, 2000, the rate under paragraph (1)(B) shall be 8 percent with respect to so much of the amount to which the 10-percent rate would otherwise apply as does not exceed qualified 5-year gain, and 10 percent with respect to the remainder of such amount.

"(B) Reduction in 20-percent rate. The rate under paragraph (1)(C) shall be 18 percent with respect to so much of the amount to which the 20-percent rate would otherwise apply as does not exceed the lesser of—

"(i) the excess of qualified 5-year gain over the amount of such gain taken into account under subparagraph (A) of this paragraph; or "(ii) the amount of qualified 5-year gain (determined by taking into account only property the holding period for which begins after December 31, 2000), and 20 percent with respect to the remainder of such amount. For purposes of determining under the preceding sentence whether the holding period of property begins after December 31, 2000, the holding period of property acquired pursuant to the exercise of an option (or other right or obligation to acquire property) shall include the period such option (or other right or obligation) was held."

Prior to deletion, para. (h)(9) read as follows:

"(9) Qualified 5-year gain. For purposes of this subsection, the term 'qualified 5-year gain' means the aggregate long-term capital gain from property held for more than 5 years. The determination under the preceding sentence shall be made without regard to collectibles gain, gain described in paragraph (7)(A)(i), and section 1202 gain."

—P.L. 108-27, Sec. 301(c), of this Act, reads as follows:

"(c) Transitional rules for taxable years which include May 6, 2003. For purposes of applying section 1(h) of the Internal Revenue Code of 1986 in the case of a taxable year which includes May 6, 2003—

"(1) The amount of tax determined under subparagraph (B) of section 1(h)(1) of such Code shall be the sum of—

"(A) 5 percent of the lesser of—

"(i) the net capital gain determined by taking into account only gain or loss properly taken into account for the portion of the taxable year on or after May 6, 2003 (determined without regard to collectibles gain or loss, gain described in section 1(h)(6)(A)(i) of such Code, and section 1202 gain), or

"(ii) the amount on which a tax is determined under such subparagraph (without regard to this subsection),

"(B) 8 percent of the lesser of—

"(i) the qualified 5-year gain (as defined in section 1(h)(9) of the Internal Revenue Code of 1986, as in effect on the day before the date of the enactment of this Act) properly taken into account for the portion of the taxable year before May 6, 2003, or

"(ii) the excess (if any) of—

"(I) the amount on which a tax is determined under such subparagraph (without regard to this subsection), over

"(II) the amount on which a tax is determined under subparagraph (A), plus

"(C) 10 percent of the excess (if any) of—

"(i) the amount on which a tax is determined under such subparagraph (without regard to this subsection), over

"(ii) the sum of the amounts on which a tax is determined under subparagraphs (A) and (B).

"(2) The amount of tax determined under subparagraph (C) of section (1)(h)(1) of such Code shall be the sum of—

"(A) 15 percent of the lesser of—

"(i) the excess (if any) of the amount of net capital gain determined under subparagraph (A)(i) of paragraph (1) of this subsection over the amount on which a tax is determined under subparagraph (A) of paragraph (1) of this subsection, or

"(ii) the amount on which a tax is determined under such subparagraph (C) (without regard to this subsection), plus

"(B) 20 percent of the excess (if any) of—

"(i) the amount on which a tax is determined under such subparagraph (C) (without regard to this subsection), over

"(ii) the amount on which a tax is determined under subparagraph (A) of this paragraph.

"(3) For purposes of applying section 55(b)(3) of such Code, rules similar to the rules of paragraphs (1) and (2) of this subsection shall apply.

"(4) In applying this subsection with respect to any pass-thru entity, the determination of when gains and losses are properly taken into account shall be made at the entity level.

"(5) For purposes of applying section 1(h)(11) of such Code, as added by section 302 of this Act, to this subsection, dividends which are qualified dividend income shall be treated as gain properly taken into account for the portion of the taxable year on or after May 6, 2003.

"(6) Terms used in this subsection which are also used in section 1(h) of such Code shall have the respective meanings that such terms have in such section."

—P.L. 108-27, Sec. 302(a), added para. (h)(11) . . . Sec. 302(e)(1), amended para. (h)(3) [as redesignated by Sec. 301(b)(1)(B), of this Act, see above], effective for tax. yrs. begin. after 12/31/2002. Sec. 302(f)(2), of this Act [prior to amendment by Sec. 402(a)(6) of P.L. 108-311, see above], reads as follows:

"(2) Regulated investment companies and real estate investment trusts. In the case of a regulated investment company or a real estate investment trust, the amendments made by this section shall apply to taxable years ending after December 31, 2002; except that dividends received by such a company or trust on or before such date shall not be treated as qualified dividend income (as defined in section 1(h)(11)(B) of the Internal Revenue Code of 1986, as added by this Act)."

Prior to amendment, para. (h)(3) [as redesignated by Sec. 301(b)(1)(B), of this Act, see above] read as follows:

"(3) Adjusted net capital gain. For purposes of this subsection, the term 'adjusted net capital gain' means net capital gain reduced (but not below zero) by the sum of—

"(A) unrecaptured section 1250 gain; and

"(B) 28 percent rate gain."

—P.L. 108-27, Sec. 303, of this Act [as amended by Sec. 102, P.L. 109-222, and Sec. 102(a), P.L. 111-312, see above], reads as follows:

"Sec. 303. Sunset of title. All provisions of, and amendments made by, this title [Secs. 301 and 302] shall not apply to taxable years beginning after December 31, 2012, and the Internal Revenue Code of 1986 shall be applied and administered to such years as if such provisions and amendments had never been enacted."

In 2002, P.L. 107-358, Sec. 2, added subsec. (c) in Sec. 901 of P.L. 107-16 [see below], effective 12/17/2002.

—P.L. 107-147, Sec. 414(a)(1), substituted "included in gross income" for "recognized" in Sec. 311(e)(2)(A) of P.L. 105-34, see below . . . Sec. 414(a)(2), added Sec. 311(e)(5) of P.L. 105-34 [see below], effective for tax. yrs. end. after 5/6/97.

In 2001, P.L. 107-16, Sec. 101(a), added subsec. (i) . . . Sec. 101(c)(1), substituted "10 percent" for "15 percent" in subclause (g)(7)(B)(ii)(II) . . . Sec. 101(c)(2)(A), substituted "25 percent" for "28 percent" in subclause (h)(1)(A)(ii)(I) and clause (h)(1)(B)(i) . . . Sec. 101(c)(2)(B), deleted para. (h)(13), effective for tax. yrs. begin. after 12/31/2000.

Prior to deletion, para. (h)(13) read as follows:

"(13) Special rules.

"(A) Determination of 28-percent rate gain. In applying paragraph (5)—

"(i) the amount determined under subparagraph (A) of paragraph (5) shall include long-term capital gain (not otherwise described in such subparagraph)—

"(I) which is properly taken into account for the portion of the taxable year before May 7, 1997; or

"(II) from property held not more than 18 months which is properly taken into account for the portion of the taxable year after July 28, 1997, and before January 1, 1998;

"(ii) the amount determined under subparagraph (B) of paragraph (5) shall include long-term capital loss (not otherwise described in such subparagraph)—

"(I) which is properly taken into account for the portion of the taxable year before May 7, 1997; or

"(II) from property held not more than 18 months which is properly taken into account for the portion of the taxable year after July 28, 1997, and before January 1, 1998; and

"(iii) subparagraph (B) of paragraph (5) (as in effect immediately before the enactment of this clause shall apply to amounts properly taken income account before January 1, 1998.

"(B) Determination of unrecaptured section 1250 gain. The amount determined under paragraph (7)(A)(i) shall not include gain—

"(i) which is properly taken into account for the portion of the taxable year before May 7, 1997; or

"(ii) from property held not more than 18 months which is properly taken into account for the portion of the taxable year after July 28, 1997, and before January 1, 1998.

"(C) Special rules for pass-thru entities. In applying this paragraph with respect to any pass-thru entity, the determination of when gains and loss are properly taken into account shall be made at the entity level.

"(D) Charitable remainder trusts. Subparagraphs (A) and (B)(ii) shall not apply to any capital gain distribution made by a trust described in section 664."

—P.L. 107-16, Sec. 301(c)(1), substituted "(other than with respect to sections 63(c)(4) and 151(d)(4)(A))" shall be applied" for "(other than with respect to subsection (c)(4) of section 63 (as it applies to subsections (c)(5)(A) and (f) of such section) and section 151(d)(4)(A)] shall be applied" in subpara. (f)(6)(B), effective [as amended by Sec. 103(b) of P.L. 108-27, see above] for tax. yrs. begin. after 12/31/2002.

—P.L. 107-16, Sec. 302(a), added para. (f)(8) . . . Sec. 302(b)(1), added "except as provided in paragraph (8)," before "by increasing" in subpara. (f)(2)(A) . . . Sec. 302(b)(2), added "Phaseout of marriage penalty in 15-percent bracket;" before "Adjustments" in the heading of subsec. (f), effective [as amended by Sec. 102(b)(2) of P.L. 108-27, see above] for tax. yrs. begin. after 12/31/2002.

—P.L. 107-16, Sec. 803, of this Act provides:

"Sec. 803. No federal income tax on restitution received by victims of the Nazi regime or their heirs or estates.

"(a) In general. For purposes of the Internal Revenue Code of 1986, any excludable restitution payments received by an eligible individual (or the individual's heirs or estate) and any excludable interest—

"(1) shall not be included in gross income; and

"(2) shall not be taken into account for purposes of applying any provision of which takes into account excludable income in computing adjusted gross income, including section 86 of such Code (relating to taxation of Social Security benefits). For purposes of , the basis of any property received by an eligible individual (or the individual's heirs or estate) as part of an excludable restitution payment shall be the fair market value of such property as of the time of the receipt.

"(b) Eligible individual. For purposes of this section, the term 'eligible individual' means a person who was persecuted on the basis of race, religion, physical or mental disability, or sexual orientation by Nazi Germany, any other Axis regime, or any other Nazi-controlled or Nazi-allied country.

"(c) Excludable restitution payment. For purposes of this section, the term 'excludable restitution payment' means any payment or distribution to an individual (or the individual's heirs or estate) which—

"(1) is payable by reason of the individual's status as an eligible individual, including any amount payable by any foreign country, the United States of America, or any other foreign or domestic entity, or a fund established by any such country or entity, any amount payable as a result of a final resolution of a legal action, and any amount payable under a law providing for payments or restitution of property;

"(2) constitutes the direct or indirect return of, or compensation or reparation for, assets stolen or hidden from, or otherwise lost to, the individual before, during, or immediately after World War II by reason of the individual's status as an eligible individual, including any proceeds of insurance under policies issued on eligible individuals by European insurance companies immediately before and during World War II; or

"(3) consists of interest which is payable as part of any payment or distribution described in paragraph (1) or (2).

Tax rates — Code Sec. 1

"(d) Excludable interest. For purposes of this section, the term 'excludable interest' means any interest earned by—

"(1) escrow accounts or settlement funds established pursuant to the settlement of the action entitled 'In re: Holocaust Victim Assets Litigation,' (E.D.N.Y.) C.A. No. 96-4849;

"(2) funds to benefit eligible individuals or their heirs created by the International Commission on Holocaust Insurance Claims as a result of the Agreement between the Government of the United States of America and the Government of the Federal Republic of Germany concerning the Foundation 'Remembrance, Responsibility, and Future,' dated July 17, 2000, or

"(3) similar funds subject to the administration of the United States courts created to provide excludable restitution payments to eligible individuals (or eligible individuals' heirs or estates).

"(e) Effective date.

"(1) In general. This section shall apply to any amount received on or after January 1, 2000.

"(2) No inference. Nothing in this Act shall be construed to create any inference with respect to the proper tax treatment of any amount received before January 1, 2000. ".

—P.L. 107-16, Sec. 901, of this Act [as amended by Sec. 2 of P.L. 107-358, and Sec. 101(a)(1), P.L. 111-312, see above], reads as follows:

"Sec. 901. Sunset of provisions of Act.

"(a) In general. All provisions of, and amendments made by, this Act shall not apply—

"(1) to taxable, plan, or limitation years beginning after December 31, 2012, or

"(2) in the case of title V, to estates of decedents dying, gifts made, or generation skipping transfers, after December 31, 2012.

"(b) Application of certain laws. The Internal Revenue Code of 1986 and the Employee Retirement Income Security Act of 1974 shall be applied and administered to years, estates, gifts, and transfers described in subsection (a) as if the provisions and amendments described in subsection (a) had never been enacted.

"(c) Exception. Subsection (a) shall not apply to section 803 (relating to no federal income tax on restitution received by victims of the Nazi regime or their heirs or estates)."

In 2000, P.L. 106-554, Sec. 1(a)(7), [which enacted into law Sec. 117(b)(1) of P.L. 106-554] amended para. (h)(8), effective for stock acquired after 12/21/2000. Prior to amendment, para. (h)(8) read as follows:

"(8) Section 1202 gain. For purposes of this subsection, the term 'section 1202 gain' means an amount equal to the gain excluded from gross income under section 1202(a)."

—P.L. 106-554, Sec. 1(a)(7), which enacted into law Sec. 314(c) of P.L. 106-554 added "Such an election shall not apply to any asset which is disposed of (in a transaction in which gain or loss is recognized in whole or in part) before the close of the 1-year period beginning on the date that the asset would have been treated as sold under such election." at the end of Sec. 311(e)(3) of P.L. 105-34, see below.

In 1998, P.L. 105-277, Sec. 4002(i)(1), substituted "paragraph (7)(A)(i)" for "paragraph (7)(A)" in subpara. (h)(13)(B), effective for taxable years ending after December 31, 1997.

—P.L. 105-277, Sec. 4002(i)(2), of this Act, reads as follows:

"(2)(A) Subparagraphs (A)(i)(II), (A)(ii)(II), and (B)(ii) of section 1(h)(13) of the 1986 Code shall not apply to any distribution after December 31, 1997, by a regulated investment company or a real estate investment trust with respect to—

"(i) gains and losses recognized directly by such company or trust, and

"(ii) amounts properly taken into account by such company or trust by reason of holding (directly or indirectly) an interest in another such company or trust to the extent that such subparagraphs did not apply to such other company or trust with respect to such amounts.

"(B) Subparagraph (A) shall not apply to any distribution which is treated under section 852(b)(7) or 857(b)(8) of the 1986 Code as received on December 31, 1997.

"(C) For purposes of subparagraph (A), any amount which is includible in gross income of its shareholders under section 852(b)(3)(D) or 857(b)(3)(D) of the 1986 Code after December 31, 1997, shall be treated as distributed after such date.

"(D)(i) For purposes of subparagraph (A), in the case of a qualified partnership with respect to which a regulated investment company meets the holding requirement of clause (iii)—

"(I) the subparagraphs referred to in subparagraph (A) shall not apply to gains and losses recognized directly by such partnership for purposes of determining such company's distributive share of such gains and losses, and

"(II) such company's distributive share of such gains and losses (as so determined) shall be treated as recognized directly by such company.

The preceding sentence shall apply only if the qualified partnership provides the company with written documentation of such distributive share as so determined.

"(ii) For purposes of clause (i), the term 'qualified partnership' means, with respect to a regulated investment company, any partnership if—

"(I) the partnership is an investment company registered under the Investment Company Act of 1940,

"(II) the regulated investment company is permitted to invest in such partnership by reason of section 12(d)(1)(E) of such Act or an exemptive order of the Securities and Exchange Commission under such section, and

"(III) the regulated investment company and the partnership have the same taxable year.

"(iii) A regulated investment company meets the holding requirement of this clause with respect to a qualified partnership if (as of January 1, 1998)—

"(I) the value of the interests of the regulated investment company in such partnership is 35 percent or more of the value of such company's total assets, or

"(II) the value of the interests of the regulated investment company in such partnership and all other qualified partnerships is 90 percent or more of the value of such company's total assets."

—P.L. 105-277, Sec. 4002(i)(3), added subpara. (h)(13)(D), effective for tax. yrs. end. after 12/31/97.

—P.L. 105-277, Sec. 4003(b), of this Act, reads as follows:

"(b) Provision related to section 311 of 1997 Act. In the case of any capital gain distribution made after 1997 by a trust to which section 664 of the 1986 Code applies with respect to amounts properly taken into account by such trust during 1997, paragraphs (5)(A)(i)(I), (5)(A)(ii)(I), and (13)(A) of section 1(h) of the 1986 Code (as in effect for taxable years ending on December 31, 1997) shall not apply."

—P.L. 105-206, Sec. 5001(a)(1), amended para. (h)(5) . . . Sec. 5001(a)(2), substituted "1 year" for "18 months" in subpara. (h)(6)(A) . . . Sec. 5001(a)(3), amended clauses (h)(7)(A)(i) and (ii) . . . Sec. 5001(a)(4), amended all of para. (h)(13) that preceded subpara. (h)(13)(C), effective for tax. yrs. end. after 12/31/97.

Prior to amendment, para. (h)(5) read as follows:

"(5) 28-percent rate gain. For purposes of this subsection—

"(A) In general. The term '28-percent rate gain' means the excess (if any) of—

"(i) the sum of—

"(I) the aggregate long-term capital gain from property held for more than 1 year but not more than 18 months,

"(II) collectibles gain; and

"(III) section 1202 gain, over

"(ii) the sum of—

"(I) the aggregate long-term capital loss (not described in subclause (IV)) from property referred to in clause (i)(I);

"(II) collectibles loss;

"(III) the net short-term capital loss; and

"(IV) the amount of long-term capital loss carried under section 1212(b)(1)(B) to the taxable year.

"(B) Special rules.

"(i) Short sale gains and holding periods. Rules similar to the rules of section 1233(b) shall apply where the substantially identical property has been held more than 1 year but not more than 18 months; except that, for purposes of such rules—

"(I) section 1233(b)(1) shall be applied by substituting '18 months' for '1 year' each place it appears; and

"(II) the holding period of such property shall be treated as being 1 year on the day before the earlier of the date of the closing of the short sale or the date such property is disposed of.

"(ii) Long-term losses. Section 1233(d) shall be applied separately by substituting '18 months' for '1 year' each place it appears.

"(iii) Options. A rule similar to the rule of section 1092(f) shall apply where the stock was held for more than 18 months.

"(iv) Section 1256 contracts. Amounts treated as long-term capital gain or loss under section 1256(a)(3) shall be treated as attributable to property held for more than 18 months."

Prior to amendment, clauses (h)(7)(A)(i) and (ii) read as follows:

"(i) the amount of long-term capital gain (not otherwise treated as ordinary income) which would be treated as ordinary income if—

"(I) section 1250(b)(1) included all depreciation and the applicable percentage under section 1250(a) were 100 percent, and

"(II) only gain from the property held for more than 18 months were taken into account, over

"(ii) the excess (if any) of—

"(I) the amount described in paragraph (5)(A)(ii), over

"(II) the amount described in paragraph (5)(A)(i)."

Prior to amendment, all of para. (h)(13) that preceded subpara. (h)(13)(C) read as follows:

"(13) Special rules for periods during 1997.

"(A) Determination of 28-percent rate gain. In applying paragraph (5)—

"(i) the amount determined under subclause (I) of paragraph (5)(A)(i) shall include long-term capital gain (not otherwise described in paragraph (5)(A)(i)) which is properly taken into account for the portion of the taxable year before May 7, 1997;

"(ii) the amounts determined under subclause (I) of paragraph (5)(A)(ii) shall include long-term capital loss (not otherwise described in paragraph (5)(A)(ii)) which is properly taken into account for the portion of the taxable year before May 7, 1997; and

"(iii) clauses (i)(I) and (ii)(I) of paragraph (5)(A) shall be applied by not taking into account any gain and loss on property held for more than 1 year but not more than 18 months which is properly taken into account for the portion of the taxable year after May 6, 1997, and before July 29, 1997.

"(B) Other special rules.

"(i) Determination of unrecaptured section 1250 gain not to include pre-May 7, 1997 gain. The amount determined under paragraph (7)(A)(i) shall not include gain properly takin into account for the portion of the taxable year before May 7, 1997.

"(ii) Other transitional rules for 18-month holding period. Paragraphs (6)(A) and (7)(A)(i)(II) shall be applied by substituting '1 year' for '18 months' with respect to gain properly taken into account for the portion of the taxable year after May 6, 1997, and before July 29, 1997."

—P.L. 105-206, Sec. 6005(d)(1), amended subsec. (h), effective for tax yrs. end. after 5/6/97.

Prior to amendment, subsec. (h) read as follows:

1,011

Code Sec. 1   **Tax rates**

"(h) Maximum capital gains rate.
"(1) If a taxpayer has a net capital gain for any taxable year, the tax imposed by this section for such taxable year shall not exceed the sum of—
"(A) a tax computed at the rates and in the same manner as if this subsection had not been enacted on the greater of—
"(i) taxable income reduced by the net capital gain, or
"(ii) the lesser of—
"(I) the amount of taxable income taxed at a rate below 28 percent, or
"(II) taxable income reduced by the adjusted net capital gain, plus
"(B) 25 percent of the excess (if any) of—
"(i) the unrecaptured section 1250 gain (or, if less, the net capital gain), over
"(ii) the excess (if any) of—
"(I) the sum of the amount on which tax is determined under subparagraph (A) plus the net capital gain, over
"(II) taxable income, plus
"(C) 28 percent of the amount of taxable income in excess of the sum of—
"(i) the adjusted net capital gain, plus
"(ii) the sum of the amounts on which tax is determined under subparagraphs (A) and (B), plus
"(D) 10 percent of so much of the taxpayer's adjusted net capital gain (or, if less, taxable income) as does not exceed the excess (if any) of—
"(i) the amount of taxable income which would (without regard to this paragraph) be taxed at a rate below 28 percent, over
"(ii) the taxable income reduced by the adjusted net capital gain, plus
"(E) 20 percent of the taxpayer's adjusted net capital gain (or, if less, taxable income) in excess of the amount on which a tax is determined under subparagraph (D).
"(2) Reduced capital gain rates for qualified 5-year gain.
"(A) Reduction in 10-percent rate. In the case of any taxable year beginning after December 31, 2000, the rate under paragraph (1)(D) shall be 8 percent with respect to so much of the amount to which the 10-percent rate would otherwise apply as does not exceed qualified 5-year gain, and 10 percent with respect to the remainder of such amount.
"(B) Reduction in 20-percent rate. The rate under paragraph (1)(E) shall be 18 percent with respect to so much of the amount to which the 20-percent rate would otherwise apply as does not exceed the lesser of—
"(i) the excess of qualified 5-year gain over the amount of such gain taken into account under subparagraph (A) of this paragraph, or
"(ii) the amount of qualified 5-year gain (determined by taking into account only property the holding period for which begins after December 31, 2000, and 20 percent with respect to the remainder of such amount. For purposes of determining under the preceding sentence whether the holding period of property begins after December 31, 2000, the holding period of property acquired pursuant to the exercise of an option (or other right or obligation to acquire property) shall include the period such option (or other right or obligation) was held.
"(3) Net capital gain taken into account as investment income. For purposes of this subsection, the net capital gain for any taxable year shall be reduced (but not below zero) by the amount which the taxpayer takes into account as investment income under section 163(d)(4)(B)(iii).
"(4) Adjusted net capital gain. For purposes of this subsection, the term 'adjusted net capital gain' means net capital gain determined without regard to—
"(A) collectibles gain,
"(B) unrecaptured section 1250 gain,
"(C) section 1202 gain, and
"(D) mid-term gain.
"(5) Collectibles gain. For purposes of this subsection—
"(A) In general. The term 'collectibles gain' means gain from the sale or exchange of a collectible (as defined in section 408(m) without regard to paragraph (3) thereof) which is a capital asset held for more than 1 year but only to the extent such gain is taken into account in computing gross income.
"(B) Partnerships, etc. For purposes of subparagraph (A), any gain from the sale of an interest in a partnership, S corporation, or trust which is attributable to unrealized appreciation in the value of collectibles shall be treated as gain from the sale or exchange of a collectible. Rules similar to the rules of section 751 shall apply for purposes of the preceding sentence.
"(6) Unrecaptured section 1250 gain. For purposes of this subsection—
"(A) In general. The term 'unrecaptured section 1250 gain' means the amount of long-term capital gain which would be treated as ordinary income if—
"(i) section 1250(b)(1) included all depreciation and the applicable percentage under section 1250(a) were 100 percent, and
"(ii) in the case of gain properly taken into account after July 28, 1997, only gain from section 1250 property held for more than 18 months were taken into account.
"(B) Limitation with respect to section 1231 property. The amount of unrecaptured section 1250 gain from sales, exchanges, and conversions described in section 1231(a)(3)(A) for any taxable year shall not exceed the excess of the net section 1231 gain (as defined in section 1231(c)(3)) for such year over the amount treated as ordinary income under section 1231(c)(1) for such year.
"(C) Pre-May 7, 1997, gain. In the case of a taxable year which includes May 7, 1997, subparagraph (A) shall be applied by taking into account only the gain properly taken into account for the portion of the taxable year after May 6, 1997.
"(7) Section 1202 gain. For purposes of this subsection, the term 'section 1202 gain' means an amount equal to the gain excluded from gross income under section 1202(a).
"(8) Mid-term gain. For purposes of this subsection, the term 'mid-term gain' means the amount which would be adjusted net capital gain for the taxable year if—

"(A) adjusted net capital gain were determined by taking into account only the gain or loss properly taken into account after July 28, 1997, from property held for more than 1 year but not more than 18 months, and
"(B) paragraph (3) and section 1212 did not apply.
"(9) Qualified 5-year gain. For purposes of this subsection, the term 'qualified 5-year gain' means the amount of long-term capital gain which would be computed for the taxable year if only gains from the sale or exchange of property held by the taxpayer for more than 5 years were taken into account. The determination under the preceding sentence shall be made without regard to collectibles gain, unrecaptured section 1250 gain (determined without regard to subparagraph (B) of paragraph (6)), section 1202 gain, or mid-term gain.
"(10) Pre-effective date gain.
"(A) In general. In the case of a taxable year which includes May 7, 1997, gains and losses properly taken into account for the portion of the taxable year before May 7, 1997, shall be taken into account in determining mid-term gain as if such gains and losses were described in paragraph (8)(A).
"(B) Special rules for pass-thru entities. In applying subparagraph (A) with respect to any pass-thru entity, the determination of when gains and loss are properly taken into account shall be made at the entity level.
"(C) Pass-thru entity defined. For purposes of subparagraph (B), the term 'pass-thru entity' means—
"(i) a regulated investment company,
"(ii) a real estate investment trust,
"(iii) an S corporation,
"(iv) a partnership,
"(v) an estate or trust, and
"(vi) a common trust fund.
"(11) Treatment of pass-thru entities. The Secretary may prescribe such regulations as are appropriate (including regulations requiring reporting) to apply this subsection in the case of sales and exchanges by pass-thru entities (as defined in paragraph (10)(C)) and of interests in such entities."
—P.L. 105-206, Sec. 6007(f)(1), deleted subpara. (g)(3)(C) and redesignated subpara. (g)(3)(D) as (g)(3)(C), effective for sales or exchanges after 8/5/97. Prior to deletion, subpara. (g)(3)(C) read as follows:
"(C) Coordination with section 644. If tax is imposed under section 644(a)(1) with respect to the sale or exchange of any property of which the parent was the transferor, for purposes of applying subparagraph (A) to the taxable year of the parent in which such sale or exchange occurs—
"(i) taxable income of the parent shall be increased by the amount treated as included in gross income under section 644(a)(2)(A)(i), and
"(ii) the amount described in subparagraph (A)(ii) shall be increased by the amount of the excess referred to in section 644(a)(2)(A)."
In 1997, P.L. 105-34, Sec. 311(a), amended subsec. (h), effective for tax. yrs. end. after 5/6/97. Sec. 311(e) of this Act [as amended by Sec. 314(c), HR5662, enacted into law by P.L. 106-554, and Secs. 414(a)(1) and (2) of P.L. 107-147, see above] provides:
"(e) Election to recognize gain on assets held on January 1, 2001. For purposes of the Internal Revenue Code of 1986—
"(1) In general. A taxpayer other than a corporation may elect to treat—
"(A) any readily tradable stock (which is a capital asset) held by such taxpayer on January 1, 2001, and not sold before the next business day after such date, as having been sold on such next business day for an amount equal to its closing market price on such next business day (and as having been reacquired on such next business day for an amount equal to such closing market price), and
"(B) any other capital asset or property used in the trade or business (as defined in section 1231(b) of the Internal Revenue Code of 1986) held by the taxpayer on January 1, 2001, as having been sold on such date for an amount equal to its fair market value on such date (and as having been reacquired on such date for an amount equal to such fair market value).
"(2) Treatment of gain or loss.
"(A) Any gain resulting from an election under paragraph (1) shall be treated as received or accrued on the date the asset is treated as sold under paragraph (1) and shall be included in gross income notwithstanding any provision of the Internal Revenue Code of 1986.
"(B) Any loss resulting from an election under paragraph (1) shall not be allowed for any taxable year.
"(3) Election. An election under paragraph (1) shall be made in such manner as the Secretary of the Treasury or his delegate may prescribe and shall specify the assets for which such election is made. Such an election, once made with respect to any asset, shall be irrevocable. Such an election shall not apply to any asset which is disposed of (in a transaction in which gain or loss is recognized in whole or in part) before the close of the 1-year period beginning on the date that the asset would have been treated as sold under such election.
"(4) Readily tradable stock. For purposes of this subsection, the term 'readily tradable stock' means any stock which, as of January 1, 2001, is readily tradable on an established securities market or otherwise."
"(5) Disposition of interest in passive activity. Section 469(g)(1)(A) of the Internal Revenue Code of 1986 shall not apply by reason of an election made under paragraph (1)."
Prior to amendment, subsec. (h) read as follows:
"(h) If a taxpayer has a net capital gain for any taxable year, then the tax imposed by this section shall not exceed the sum of—
"(1) a tax computed at the rates and in the same manner as if this subsection had not been enacted on the greater of—
"(A) taxable income reduced by the amount of the net capital gain, or
"(B) the amount of taxable income taxed at a rate below 28 percent, plus

Tax rates   Code Sec. 1

"(2) a tax of 28 percent of the amount of taxable income in excess of the amount determined under paragraph (1).

For purposes of the preceding sentence, the net capital gain for any taxable year shall be reduced (but not below zero) by the amount which the taxpayer elects to take into account as investment income for the taxable year under section 163(d)(4)(B)(iii)."

In 1996, P.L. 104-188, Sec. 1704(m)(1), amended clause (g)(7)(A)(ii) ... Sec. 1704(m)(2)(A), substituted "twice the amount described in paragraph (4)(A)(ii)(I)" for "$1,000" in clause (g)(7)(B)(i) ... Sec. 1704(m)(2)(B), amended subclause (g)(7)(B)(ii)(II), effective for tax. yrs. begin. after 12/31/95.

Prior to amendment, clause (g)(7)(A)(ii) read as follows:

"(ii) such gross income is more than $500 and less than $5,000,"

Prior to amendment, subclause (g)(7)(B)(ii)(II) read as follows:

"(II) for each such child, the lesser of $75 or 15 percent of the excess of the gross income of such child over $500, and"

In 1993, P.L. 103-66, Sec. 13201(a), amended subsecs. (a) through (e) ... Sec. 13201(b)(3)(A)(i), substituted "1993" for "1990" in para. (f)(1) ... Sec. 13201(b)(3)(A)(ii), substituted "1992" for "1989" in subpara. (f)(3)(B) ... Sec. 13201(b)(3)(B), added para. (f)(7), effective for tax. yrs. begin. after 12/31/92.

Prior to amendment, subsecs. (a) through (e) read as follows:

"(a) Married individuals filing joint returns and surviving spouses. There is hereby imposed on the taxable income of—

"(1) every married individual (as defined in section 7703) who makes a single return jointly with his spouse under section 6013, and

"(2) every surviving spouse (as defined in section 2(a)), a tax determined in accordance with the following table:

If taxable income is:	The tax is:
Not over $32,450	15% of taxable income.
Over $32,450 but not over $78,400	$4,867.50, plus 28% of the excess over $32,450.
Over $78,400	$17,733.50, plus 31% of the excess over $78,400.

"(b) Heads of households. There is hereby imposed on the taxable income of every head of a household (as defined in section 2(b)) a tax determined in accordance with the following table:

If taxable income is:	The tax is:
Not over $26,050	15% of taxable income.
Over $26,050 but not over $67,200	$3,907.50, plus 28% of the excess over $26,500.
Over $67,200	$15,429.50, plus 31% of the excess over $67,200.

"(c) Unmarried individuals (other than surviving spouses and heads of households). There is hereby imposed on the taxable income of every individual (other than a surviving spouse as defined in section 2(a) or the head of a household as defined in section 2(b)) who is not a married individual (as defined in section 7703) a tax determined in accordance with the following table:

If taxable income is:	The tax is:
Not over $19,450	15% of taxable income.
Over $19,450 but not over $47,050	$2,917.50, plus 28% of the excess over $19,450.
Over $47,050	$10,645.50, plus 31% of the excess over $47,050.

"(d) Married individuals filing separate returns. There is hereby imposed on the taxable income of every married individual (as defined in section 7703) who does not make a single return jointly with his spouse under section 6013, a tax determined in accordance with the following table:

If taxable income is:	The tax is:
Not over $16,225	15% of taxable income.
Over $16,225 but not over $39,200	$2,433.75, plus 28% of the excess over $16,225.
Over $39,200	$8,866.75, plus 31% of the excess over $39,200.

"(e) Estates and trusts. There is hereby imposed on the taxable income of—

"(1) every estate, and

"(2) every trust,

taxable under this subsection a tax determined in accordance with the following table:

If taxable income is:	The tax is:
Not over $3,300	15% of taxable income.
Over $3,300 but not over $9,900	$495, plus 28% of the excess over $3,300.
Over $9,900	$2,343, plus 31% of the excess over $9,900.

—P.L. 103-66, Sec. 13202(a)(1), substituted

"Over $140,000 but not over $250,000	$35,928.50, plus 36% of the excess over $140,000.
Over $250,000	$75,528.50, plus 39.6% of the excess over $250,000."

for

"Over $140,000	$35,928.50, plus 36% of the excess over $140,000."

in subsec. (a) [as amended by Sec. 13201(a) of this Act, see above]

—P.L. 103-66, Sec. 13202(a)(2), substituted

"Over $127,500 but not over $250,000	$33,385, plus 36% of the excess over $127,500.
Over $250,000	$77,485, plus 39.6% of the excess over $250,000."

for

"Over $127,500	$33,385, plus 36% of the excess over $127,500."

in subsec. (b) [as amended by Sec. 13201(a) of this Act, see above]

—P.L. 103-66, Sec. 13202(a)(3), substituted

"Over $115,000 but not over $250,000	$31,172, plus 36% of the excess over $115,000.
Over $250,000	$79,772, plus 39.6% of the excess over $250,000."

for

"Over $115,000	$31,172, plus 36% of the excess over $115,000."

in subsec. (c) [as amended by Sec. 13201(a) of this Act, see above]

—P.L. 103-66, Sec. 13202(a)(4), substituted

"Over $70,000 but not over $125,000	$17,964.25, plus 36% of the excess over $70,000.
Over $125,000	$37,764.25, plus 39.6% of the excess over $125,000."

for

"Over $70,000	$17,964.25, plus 36% of the excess over $70,000."

in subsec. (d) [as amended by Sec. 13201(a) of this Act, see above]

—P.L. 103-66, Sec. 13202(a)(5), substituted

"Over $5,500 but not over $7,500	$1,405, plus 36% of the excess over $5,500.
Over $7,500	$2,125, plus 39.6% of the excess over $7,500."

for

"Over $5,500	$1,405, plus 36% of the excess over $5,500."

in subsec. (e) [as amended by Sec. 13201(a) of this Act, see above], effective for tax. yrs. begin. after 12/31/92.

—P.L. 103-66, Sec. 13206(d)(2), added the sentence at the end of subsec. (h), effective for tax. yrs. begin. after 12/31/92.

In 1990, P.L. 101-604, Sec. 211(c), of this Act provides:

"(c) Income tax benefit for victims of Lockerbie Terrorism.

"(1) In general. Subject to paragraph (2), in the case of any individual whose death was a direct result of the Pan American Airways Flight 103 terrorist disaster over Lockerbie, Scotland, on December 21, 1988, any tax imposed by subtitle A of the Internal Revenue Code of 1986 shall not apply—

"(A) with respect to the taxable year which includes December 21, 1988, and

"(B) with respect to the prior taxable year.

"(2) Limitation. In no case may the tax benefit pursuant to paragraph (1) for any taxable year, for any individual, exceed an amount equal to 28 percent of the annual rate of basic pay at Level V of the Executive Schedule of the United States as of December 21, 1988."

—P.L. 101-508, Sec. 11101(a), amended subsecs. (a) through (e) ... Sec. 11101(b)(1), deleted subsec. (g) ... Sec. 11101(b)(2), deleted "subsection (g)(4)," after "paragraph (2)(A)," in subpara. (f)(6)(A) ... Sec. 11101(c), amended subsec. (j) ... Sec. 11101(d)(1)(A)(i), substituted "1990" for "1988" in para. (f)(1) ... Sec. 11101(d)(1)(A)(ii), substituted "1989" for "1987" in subpara. (f)(3)(B) ... Sec. 11101(d)(2), deleted subsec. (h) and redesignated subsec. (i) and subsec (j) [as amended by Sec. 11101(c) of this Act, see above] as subsecs. (g) and (h) ... Sec. 11103(c), added "section 68(b)(2)" after "section 63(c)(4)," in subpara. (f)(6)(A) ... Sec. 11104(b)(1), substituted "section 151(d)(4)(A)" for "section 151(d)(3)" in subpara. (f)(6)(A) ... Sec. 11104(b)(2), substituted "section 151(d)(4)(A)" for "section 151(d)(3)" in subpara. (f)(6)(B), effective for tax. yrs. begin. after 12/31/90.

Prior to amendment, subsecs. (a) through (e) read as follows:

"(a) Married individuals filing joint returns and surviving spouses. There is hereby imposed on the taxable income of—

"(1) every married individual (as defined in section 7703) who makes a single return jointly with his spouse under section 6013, and

"(2) every surviving spouse (as defined in section 2(a)), a tax determined in accordance with the following table:

1,013

Code Sec. 1 — Tax rates

"If taxable income is:	The tax is:
Not over $29,750	15% of taxable income.
Over $29,750	$4,462.50, plus 28% of the excess over $29,750.

"(b) Heads of households. There is hereby imposed on the taxable income of every head of a household (as defined in section 2(b)) a tax determined in accordance with the following table:

"If taxable income is:	The tax is:
Not over $23,900	15% of taxable income.
Over $23,900	$3,585, plus 28% of the excess over $23,900.

"(c) Unmarried individuals (other than surviving spouses and heads of households). There is hereby imposed on the taxable income of every individual (other than a surviving spouse as defined in section 2(a) or the head of a household as defined in section 2(b)) who is not a married individual (as defined in section 7703) a tax determined in accordance with the following table:

"If taxable income is:	The tax is:
Not over $17,850	15% of taxable income.
Over $17,850	$2,677.50, plus 28% of the excess over $17,850.

"(d) Married individuals filing separate returns. There is hereby imposed on the taxable income of every married individual (as defined in section 7703) who does not make a single return jointly with his spouse under section 6013, a tax determined in accordance with the following table:

"If taxable income is:	The tax is:
Not over $14,875	15% of taxable income.
Over $14,875	$2,231.25, plus 28% of the excess over $14,875.

"(e) Estates and trusts. There is hereby imposed on the taxable income of—
"(1) every estate, and
"(2) every trust,
taxable under this subsection a tax determined in accordance with the following table:

"If taxable income is:	The tax is:
Not over $5,000	15% of taxable income.
Over $5,000	$750, plus 28% of the excess over $5,000."

Prior to deletion, subsec. (g) read as follows:
"(g) Phaseout of 15-percent rate and personal exemptions.
"(1) In general. The amount of tax imposed by this section (determined without regard to this subsection) shall be increased by 5 percent of the excess (if any) of—
"(A) taxable income, over
"(B) the applicable dollar amount.
"(2) Limitation. The increase determined under paragraph (1) with respect to any taxpayer for any taxable year shall not exceed the sum of—
"(A) 13 percent of the maximum amount of taxable income to which the 15-percent rate applies under the table contained in subsection (a), (b), (c), or (e) (whichever applies), and
"(B) 28 percent of the deductions for personal exemptions allowable to the taxpayer for the taxable year under section 151.
In the case of any individual taxable under subsection (d), subparagraph (A) shall apply as if such individual were taxable under subsection (a) and subparagraph (B) shall be applied as if a deduction for a personal exemption were allowable under section 151 to such individual for such individual's spouse.
"(3) Applicable dollar amount. For purposes of paragraph (1), the applicable dollar amount shall be determined under the following table:

"In the case of a taxpayer to which the following subsection of this section applies:	The applicable dollar amount is:
Subsection (a)	$71,900
Subsection (b)	61,650
Subsection (c)	43,150
Subsection (d)	35,950
Subsection (e)	13,000.

"(4) Adjustment for inflation. In the case of any taxable year beginning in a calendar year after 1988, each dollar amount contained in paragraph (3) shall be increased by an amount equal to—
"(A) such dollar amount, multiplied by
"(B) the cost-of-living adjustment determined under subsection (f)(3) for the calendar year in which the taxable year begins."
Prior to deletion, subsec. (h) read as follows:
"(h) Tax schedules for taxable years beginning in 1987.
"In the case of any taxable year beginning in 1987—
"(1) subsection (g) shall not apply, and
"(2) the following tables shall apply in lieu of the tables set forth in subsections (a), (b), (c), (d), and (e):

"(A) Married individuals filing joint returns and surviving spouses. The table to apply for purposes of subsection (a) is as follows:

"If taxable income is:	The tax is:
Not over $3,000	11% of taxable income.
Over $3,000 but not over $28,000	$330, plus 15% of the excess over $3,000.
Over $28,000 but not over $45,000	$4,080, plus 28% of the excess over $28,000.
Over $45,000 but not over $90,000	$8,840, plus 35% of the excess over $45,000.
Over $90,000	$24,590, plus 38.5% of the excess over $90,000.

"(B) Heads of households. The table to apply for purposes of subsection (b) is as follows:

"If taxable income is:	The tax is:
Not over $2,500	11% of taxable income.
Over $2,500 but not over $23,000	$275, plus 15% of the excess over $2,500.
Over $23,000 but not over $38,000	$3,350, plus 28% of the excess over $23,000.
Over $38,000 but not over $80,000	$7,550, plus 35% of the excess over $38,000.
Over $80,000	$22,250, plus 38.5% of the excess over $80,000.

"(C) Unmarried individuals other than surviving spouses and heads of households. The table to apply for purposes of subsection (c) is as follows:

"If taxable income is:	The tax is:
Not over $1,800	11% of taxable income.
Over $1,800 but not over $16,800	$198, plus 15% of the excess over $1,800.
Over $16,800 but not over $27,000	$2,448, plus 28% of the excess over $16,800.
Over $27,000 but not over $54,000	$5,304, plus 35% of the excess over $27,000.
Over $54,000	$14,754, plus 38.5% of the excess over $54,000.

"(D) Married individuals filing separate returns. The table to apply for purposes of subsection (d) is as follows:

"If taxable income is:	The tax is:
Not over $1,500	11% of taxable income.
Over $1,500 but not over $14,000	$165, plus 15% of the excess over $1,500.
Over $14,000 but not over $22,500	$2,040, plus 28% of the excess over $14,000.
Over $22,500 but not over $45,000	$4,420, plus 35% of the excess over $22,500.
Over $45,000	$12,295, plus 38.5% of the excess over $45,000.

"(E) Estates and trusts. The table to apply for purposes of subsection (e) is as follows:

"If taxable income is:	The tax is:
Not over $500	11% of taxable income.
Over $500 but not over $4,700	$55, plus 15% of the excess over $500.
Over $4,700 but not over $7,550	$685, plus 28% of the excess over $4,700.
Over $7,550 but not over $15,150	$1,483, plus 35% of the excess over $7,550.
Over $15,150	$4,143, plus 38.5% of the excess over $15,150."

Prior to amendment, subsec. (j) read as follows:
"(j) Maximum capital gains rate.
"(1) In general. If a taxpayer has a net capital gain for any taxable year to which this subsection applies, then the tax imposed by this section shall not exceed the sum of—
"(A) a tax computed at the rates and in the same manner as if this subsection had not been enacted on the greater of—
"(i) the taxable income reduced by the amount of net capital gain, or
"(ii) the amount of taxable income taxed at a rate below 28 percent, plus
"(B) a tax of 28 percent of the amount of taxable income in excess of the amount determined under subparagraph (A), plus
"(C) the amount of increase determined under subsection (g).
"(2) Years to which subsection applies. This subsection shall apply to—
"(A) any taxable year beginning in 1987, and
"(B) any taxable year beginning after 1987 if the highest rate of tax set forth in subsection (a), (b), (c), (d), or (e) (whichever applies) for such taxable year exceeds 28 percent."
In 1989, P.L. 101-239, Sec. 7811(j)(1), redesignated subpara. (i)(3)(C) [as, added by Sec. 1014(e)(7) of P.L. 100-647, see below] as (i)(3)(D), effective for tax. yrs. begin. after 12/31/86.

Tax rates — Code Sec. 1

—P.L. 101-239, Sec. 7816(b), added "(other than for purposes of this paragraph)" after "shall be treated" in subpara. (i)(7)(A), effective for tax. yrs. begin. after 12/31/88.

—P.L. 101-239, Sec. 7831(a), substituted "(other than with respect to subsection (c)(4) of section 63 (as it applies to subsections (c)(5)(A) and (f) of such section) and section 151(d)(3))" for "(other than with respect to section 63(c)(4))" in subpara. (f)(6)(B), effective for tax. yrs. begin. after 12/31/86.

In 1988, P.L. 100-647, Sec. 1001(a)(3), added "and subparagraph (B) shall be applied as if a deduction for a personal exemption were allowable under section 151 to such individual for such individual's spouse." before the period in the last sentence of para. (g)(2), effective for tax. yrs. begin. after 12/31/86.

—P.L. 100-647, Sec. 1003(b)(1), deleted Sec. 302(c) of P.L. 99-514 [see below], transitional rules for changes made by Sec. 302(a) P.L. 99-514.

Prior to deletion, Sec. 302(c) of P.L. 99-514 read as follows:

"(c) Transitional rule. The tax under section 1 of the Internal Revenue Code of 1986 on the long-term capital gain on rights to royalties paid under leases and assignments binding on September 25, 1985, by a limited partnership formed on March 1, 1977, which on October 30, 1979, assigned leases and which assignment was amended on April 27, 1981, shall not exceed 20 percent."

—P.L. 100-647, Sec. 1014(e)(1), added subpara. (i)(3)(C)...Sec. 1014(e)(2), substituted "any exclusion, deduction, or credit" for "any deduction or credit" in the last sentence of subpara. (i)(3)(A)...Sec. 1014(e)(3)(A), substituted "adjusted gross income for the taxable year which is not attributable to earned income" for "gross income for the taxable year which is not earned income" in clause (i)(4)(A)(i)...Sec. 1014(e)(3)(B), substituted "his deductions" for "his deduction" in subclause (i)(4)(A)(ii)(II)...Sec. 1014(e)(3)(C), substituted "the itemized deductions allowed" for "the deductions allowed" in subclause (i)(4)(A)(ii)(II)...Sec. 1014(e)(3)(D), substituted "adjusted gross income" for "gross income" in subclause (i)(4)(A)(ii)(II)...Sec. 1014(e)(6), substituted "custodial parent within the meaning of section 152(e))" for "custodial parent" in subpara. (i)(5)(A)...Sec. 1014(e)(7), added subpara. (i)(3)(C)[D], effective for tax. yrs. begin. after 12/31/86.

—P.L. 100-647, Sec. 6006(a), added para. (i)(7), effective for tax. yrs. begin. after 12/31/88.

In 1986, P.L. 99-514, Sec. 101(a), amended Code Sec. 1, effective for tax. yrs. begin. after 12/31/86.

Prior to amendment, Code Sec. 1 read as follows:

"(a) Married individuals filing joint returns and surviving spouses. There is hereby imposed on the taxable income of every married individual (as defined in section 143) who makes a single return jointly with his spouse under section 6013, and every surviving spouse (as defined in section 2(a)), a tax determined in accordance with the following tables:

"(1) For taxable years beginning in 1982.

"If taxable income is:	The tax is:
Not over $3,400	No tax.
Over $3,400 but not over $5,500	12% of the excess over $3,400.
Over $5,500 but not over $7,600	$252, plus 14% of the excess over $5,500.
Over $7,600 but not over $11,900	$546, plus 16% of the excess over $7,600.
Over $11,900 but not over $16,000	$1,234, plus 19% of the excess over $11,900.
Over $16,000 but not over $20,200	$2,013, plus 22% of the excess over $16,000.
Over $20,200 but not over $24,600	$2,937, plus 25% of the excess over $20,200.
Over $24,600 but not over $29,900	$4,037, plus 29% of the excess over $24,600.
Over $29,900 but not over $35,200	$5,574, plus 33% of the excess over $29,900.
Over $35,200 but not over $45,800	$7,323, plus 39% of the excess over $35,200.
Over $45,800 but not over $60,000	$11,457, plus 44% of the excess over $45,800.
Over $60,000 but not over $85,600	$17,705, plus 49% of the excess over $60,000.
Over $85,600	$30,249, plus 50% of the excess over $85,600.

"(2) For taxable years beginning in 1983.

"If taxable income is:	The tax is:
Not over $3,400	No tax.
Over $3,400 but not over $5,500	11% of the excess over $3,400.
Over $5,500 but not over $7,600	$231, plus 13% of the excess over $5,500.
Over $7,600 but not over $11,900	$504, plus 15% of the excess over $7,600.
Over $11,900 but not over $16,000	$1,149, plus 17% of the excess over $11,900.
Over $16,000 but not over $20,200	$1,846, plus 19% of the excess over $16,000.
Over $20,200 but not over $24,600	$2,644, plus 23% of the excess over $20,200.
Over $24,600 but not over $29,900	$3,656, plus 26% of the excess over $24,600.
Over $29,900 but not over $35,200	$5,034, plus 30% of the excess over $29,900.
Over $35,200 but not over $45,800	$6,624, plus 35% of the excess over $35,200.
Over $45,800 but not over $60,000	$10,334, plus 40% of the excess over $45,800.
Over $60,000 but not over $85,600	$16,014, plus 44% of the excess over $60,000.
Over $85,600 but not over $109,400	$27,278, plus 48% of the excess over $85,600.
Over $109,400	$38,702, plus 50% of the excess over $109,400.

"(3) For taxable years beginning after 1983.

"If taxable income is:	The tax is:
Not over $3,400	No tax.
Over $3,400 but not over $5,500	11% of the excess over $3,400.
Over $5,500 but not over $7,600	$231, plus 12% of the excess over $5,500.
Over $7,600 but not over $11,900	$483, plus 14% of the excess over $7,600.
Over $11,900 but not over $16,000	$1,085, plus 16% of the excess over $11,900.
Over $16,000 but not over $20,200	$1,741, plus 18% of the excess over $16,000.
Over $20,200 but not over $24,600	$2,497, plus 22% of the excess over $20,200.
Over $24,600 but not over $29,900	$3,465, plus 25% of the excess over $24,600.
Over $29,900 but not over $35,200	$4,790, plus 28% of the excess over $29,900.
Over $35,200 but not over $45,800	$6,274, plus 33% of the excess over $35,200.
Over $45,800 but not over $60,000	$9,772, plus 38% of the excess over $45,800.
Over $60,000 but not over $85,600	$15,168, plus 42% of the excess over $60,000.
Over $85,600 but not over $109,400	$25,920, plus 45% of the excess over $85,600.
Over $109,400 but not over $162,400	$36,630, plus 49% of the excess over $109,400.
Over $162,400	$62,600, plus 50% of the excess over $162,400.

"(b) Heads of households. There is hereby imposed on the taxable income of every individual who is the head of a household (as defined in section 2(b)) a tax determined in accordance with the following tables:

"(1) For taxable years beginning in 1982.

"If taxable income is:	The tax is:
Not over $2,300	No tax.
Over $2,300 but not over $4,400	12% of the excess over $2,300.
Over $4,400 but not over $6,500	$252, plus 14% of the excess over $4,400.
Over $6,500 but not over $8,700	$546, plus 16% of the excess over $6,500.
Over $8,700 but not over $11,800	$898, plus 20% of the excess over $8,700.
Over $11,800 but not over $15,000	$1,518, plus 22% of the excess over $11,800.
Over $15,000 but not over $18,200	$2,222, plus 23% of the excess over $15,000.
Over $18,200 but not over $23,500	$2,958, plus 28% of the excess over $18,200.
Over $23,500 but not over $28,800	$4,442, plus 32% of the excess over $23,500.
Over $28,800 but not over $34,100	$6,138, plus 38% of the excess over $28,800.
Over $34,100 but not over $44,700	$8,152, plus 41% of the excess over $34,100.
Over $44,700 but not over $60,600	$12,498, plus 49% of the excess over $44,700.
Over $60,600	$20,289, plus 50% of the excess over $60,600.

"(2) For taxable years beginning in 1983.

"If taxable income is:	The tax is:
Not over $2,300	No tax.
Over $2,300 but not over $4,400	11% of the excess over $2,300.
Over $4,400 but not over $6,500	$231, plus 13% of the excess over $4,400.
Over $6,500 but not over $8,700	$504, plus 15% of the excess over $6,500.
Over $8,700 but not over $11,800	$834, plus 18% of the excess over $8,700.

Code Sec. 1 — Tax rates

"If taxable income is:	The tax is:
Over $11,800 but not over $15,000	$1,392, plus 19% of the excess over $11,800.
Over $15,000 but not over $18,200	$2,000, plus 21% of the excess over $15,000.
Over $18,200 but not over $23,500	$2,672, plus 25% of the excess over $18,200.
Over $23,500 but not over $28,800	$3,997, plus 29% of the excess over $23,500.
Over $28,800 but not over $34,100	$5,534, plus 34% of the excess over $28,800.
Over $34,100 but not over $44,700	$7,336, plus 37% of the excess over $34,100.
Over $44,700 but not over $60,600	$11,258, plus 44% of the excess over $44,700.
Over $60,600 but not over $81,800	$18,254, plus 48% of the excess over $60,600.
Over $81,800	$28,430, plus 50% of the excess over $81,800.

"(3) For taxable years beginning after 1983.

"If taxable income is:	The tax is:
Not over $2,300	No tax.
Over $2,300 but not over $4,400	11% of the excess over $2,300.
Over $4,400 but not over $6,500	$231, plus 12% of the excess over $4,400.
Over $6,500 but not over $8,700	$483, plus 14% of the excess over $6,500.
Over $8,700 but not over $11,800	$791, plus 17% of the excess over $8,700.
Over $11,800 but not over $15,000	$1,318, plus 18% of the excess over $11,800.
Over $15,000 but not over $18,200	$1,894, plus 20% of the excess over $15,000.
Over $18,200 but not over $23,500	$2,534, plus 24% of the excess over $18,200.
Over $23,500 but not over $28,800	$3,806, plus 28% of the excess over $23,500.
Over $28,800 but not over $34,100	$5,290, plus 32% of the excess over $28,800.
Over $34,100 but not over $44,700	$6,986, plus 35% of the excess over $34,100.
Over $44,700 but not over $60,600	$10,696, plus 42% of the excess over $44,700.
Over $60,600 but not over $81,800	$17,374, plus 45% of the excess over $60,600.
Over $81,800 but not over $108,300	$26,914, plus 48% of the excess over $81,800.
Over $108,300	$39,634, plus 50% of the excess over $108,300.

"(c) Unmarried individuals (other than surviving spouses and heads of households). There is hereby imposed on the taxable income of every individual (other than a surviving spouse as defined in section 2(a) or the head of a household as defined in section 2(b)) who is not a married individual (as defined in section 143) a tax determined in accordance with the following tables:

"(1) For taxable years beginning in 1982.

"If taxable income is:	The tax is:
Not over $2,300	No tax.
Over $2,300 but not over $3,400	12% of the excess over $2,300.
Over $3,400 but not over $4,400	$132, plus 14% of the excess over $3,400.
Over $4,400 but not over $6,500	$272, plus 16% of the excess over $4,400.
Over $6,500 but not over $8,500	$608, plus 17% of the excess over $6,500.
Over $8,500 but not over $10,800	$948, plus 19% of the excess over $8,500.
Over $10,800 but not over $12,900	$1,385, plus 22% of the excess over $10,800.
Over $12,900 but not over $15,000	$1,847, plus 23% of the excess over $12,900.
Over $15,000 but not over $18,200	$2,330, plus 27% of the excess over $15,000.
Over $18,200 but not over $23,500	$3,194, plus 31% of the excess over $18,200.
Over $23,500 but not over $28,800	$4,837, plus 35% of the excess over $23,500.
Over $28,800 but not over $34,100	$6,692, plus 40% of the excess over $28,800.
Over $34,100 but not over $41,500	$8,812, plus 44% of the excess over $34,100.
Over $41,500	$12,068, plus 50% of the excess over $41,500.

"(2) For taxable years beginning in 1983.

"If taxable income is:	The tax is:
Not over $2,300	No tax.
Over $2,300 but not over $3,400	11% of the excess over $2,300.
Over $3,400 but not over $4,400	$121, plus 13% of the excess over $3,400.
Over $4,400 but not over $8,500	$251, plus 15% of the excess over $4,400.
Over $8,500 but not over $10,800	$866, plus 17% of the excess over $8,500.
Over $10,800 but not over $12,900	$1,257, plus 19% of the excess over $10,800.
Over $12,900 but not over $15,000	$1,656, plus 21% of the excess over $12,900.
Over $15,000 but not over $18,200	$2,097, plus 24% of the excess over $15,000.
Over $18,200 but not over $23,500	$2,865, plus 28% of the excess over $18,200.
Over $23,500 but not over $28,800	$4,349, plus 32% of the excess over $23,500.
Over $28,800 but not over $34,100	$6,045, plus 36% of the excess over $28,800.
Over $34,100 but not over $41,500	$7,953, plus 40% of the excess over $34,100.
Over $41,500 but not over $55,300	$10,913, plus 45% of the excess over $41,500.
Over $55,300	$17,123, plus 50% of the excess over $55,300.

"(3) For taxable years beginning after 1983.

"If taxable income is:	The tax is:
Not over $2,300	No tax.
Over $2,300 but not over $3,400	11% of the excess over $2,300.
Over $3,400 but not over $4,400	$121, plus 12% of the excess over $3,400.
Over $4,400 but not over $6,500	$241, plus 14% of the excess over $4,400.
Over $6,500 but not over $8,500	$535, plus 15% of the excess over $6,500.
Over $8,500 but not over $10,800	$835, plus 16% of the excess over $8,500.
Over $10,800 but not over $12,900	$1,203, plus 18% of the excess over $10,800.
Over $12,900 but not over $15,000	$1,581, plus 20% of the excess over $12,900.
Over $15,000 but not over $18,200	$2,001, plus 23% of the excess over $15,000.
Over $18,200 but not over $23,500	$2,737, plus 26% of the excess over $18,200.
Over $23,500 but not over $28,800	$4,115, plus 30% of the excess over $23,500.
Over $28,800 but not over $34,100	$5,705, plus 34% of the excess over $28,800.
Over $34,100 but not over $41,500	$7,507, plus 38% of the excess over $34,100.
Over $41,500 but not over $55,300	$10,319, plus 42% of the excess over $41,500.
Over $55,300 but not over $81,800	$16,115, plus 48% of the excess over $55,300.
Over $81,800	$28,835, plus 50% of the excess over $81,800.

"(d) Married individuals filing separate returns. There is hereby imposed on the taxable income of every married individual (as defined in section 143) who does not make a single return jointly with his spouse under section 6013 a tax determined in accordance with the following tables:

"(1) For taxable years beginning in 1982.

"If taxable income is:	The tax is:
Not over $1,700	No tax.
Over $1,700 but not over $2,750	12% of the excess over $1,700.
Over $2,750 but not over $3,800	$126, plus 14% of the excess over $2,750.
Over $3,800 but not over $5,950	$273, plus 16% of the excess over $3,800.
Over $5,950 but not over $8,000	$617, plus 19% of the excess over $5,950.
Over $8,000 but not over $10,100	$1,006.50, plus 22% of the excess over $8,000.
Over $10,100 but not over $12,300	$1,468.50, plus 25% of the excess over $10,100.
Over $12,300 but not over $14,950	$2,018.50, plus 29% of the excess over $12,300.
Over $14,950 but not over $17,600	$2,787, plus 33% of the excess over $14,950.

Tax rates

Code Sec. 1

"If taxable income is:	The tax is:
Over $17,600 but not over $22,900	$3,661.50, plus 39% of the excess over $17,600.
Over $22,900 but not over $30,000	$5,728.50, plus 44% of the excess over $22,900.
Over $30,000 but not over $42,800	$8,852.50, plus 49% of the excess over $30,000.
Over $42,800	$15,124.50, plus 50% of the excess over $42,800.

"(2) For taxable years beginning in 1983.

"If taxable income is:	The tax is:
Not over $1,700	No tax.
Over $1,700 but not over $2,750	11% of the excess over $1,700.
Over $2,750 but not over $3,800	$115.50, plus 13% of the excess over $2,750.
Over $3,800 but not over $5,950	$252, plus 15% of the excess over $3,800.
Over $5,950 but not over $8,000	$574.50, plus 17% of the excess over $5,950.
Over $8,000 but not over $10,100	$923, plus 19% of the excess over $8,000.
Over $10,100 but not over $12,300	$1,322, plus 23% of the excess over $10,100.
Over $12,300 but not over $14,950	$1,828, plus 26% of the excess over $12,300.
Over $14,950 but not over $17,600	$2,517, plus 30% of the excess over $14,950.
Over $17,600 but not over $22,900	$3,312, plus 35% of the excess over $17,600.
Over $22,900 but not over $30,000	$5,167, plus 40% of the excess over $22,900.
Over $30,000 but not over $42,800	$8,007, plus 44% of the excess over $30,000.
Over $42,800 but not over $54,700	$13,639, plus 48% of the excess over $42,800.
Over $54,700	$19,351, plus 50% of the excess over $54,700.

"(3) For taxable years beginning after 1983.

"If taxable income is:	The tax is:
Not over $1,700	No tax.
Over $1,700 but not over $2,750	11% of the excess over $1,700.
Over $2,750 but not over $3,800	$115.50, plus 12% of the excess over $2,750.
Over $3,800 but not over $5,950	$241.50, plus 14% of the excess over $3,800.
Over $5,950 but not over $8,000	$542.50, plus 16% of the excess over $5,950.
Over $8,000 but not over $10,100	$870.50, plus 18% of the excess over $8,000.
Over $10,100 but not over $12,300	$1,248.50, plus 22% of the excess over $10,100.
Over $12,300 but not over $14,950	$1,732.50, plus 25% of the excess over $12,300.
Over $14,950 but not over $17,600	$2,395, plus 28% of the excess over $14,950.
Over $17,600 but not over $22,900	$3,137, plus 33% of the excess over $17,600.
Over $22,900 but not over $30,000	$4,886, plus 38% of the excess over $22,900.
Over $30,000 but not over $42,800	$7,584, plus 42% of the excess over $30,000.
Over $42,800 but not over $54,700	$12,960, plus 45% of the excess over $42,800.
Over $54,700 but not over $81,200	$18,315, plus 49% of the excess over $54,700.
Over $81,200	$31,300, plus 50% of the excess over $81,200.

"(e) Estates and trusts. There is hereby imposed on the taxable income of every estate and trust taxable under this subsection a tax determined in accordance with the following tables:
"(1) For taxable years beginning in 1982.

"If taxable income is:	The tax is:
Not over $1,050	12% of taxable income.
Over $1,050 but not over $2,100	$126, plus 14% of the excess over $1,050.
Over $2,100 but not over $4,250	$273, plus 16% of the excess over $2,100.
Over $4,250 but not over $6,300	$617, plus 19% of the excess over $4,250.
Over $6,300 but not over $8,400	$1,006.50, plus 22% of the excess over $6,300.
Over $8,400 but not over $10,600	$1,468.50, plus 25% of the excess over $8,400.
Over $10,600 but not over $13,250	$2,018.50, plus 29% of the excess over $10,600.
Over $13,250 but not over $15,900	$2,787, plus 33% of the excess over $13,250.
Over $15,900 but not over $21,200	$3,661.50, plus 39% of the excess over $15,900.
Over $21,200 but not over $28,300	$5,728.50, plus 44% of the excess over $21,200.
Over $28,300 but not over $41,100	$8,852.50, plus 49% of the excess over $28,300.
Over $41,100	$15,124.50, plus 50% of the excess over $41,100.

"(2) For taxable years beginning in 1983.

"If taxable income is:	The tax is:
Not over $1,050	11% of taxable income.
Over $1,050 but not over $2,100	$115.50, plus 13% of the excess over $1,050.
Over $2,100 but not over $4,250	$252, plus 15% of the excess over $2,100.
Over $4,250 but not over $6,300	$574.50, plus 17% of the excess over $4,250.
Over $6,300 but not over $8,400	$923, plus 19% of the excess over $6,300.
Over $8,400 but not over $10,600	$1,322, plus 23% of the excess over $8,400.
Over $10,600 but not over $13,250	$1,828, plus 26% of the excess over $10,600.
Over $13,250 but not over $15,900	$2,517, plus 30% of the excess over $13,250.
Over $15,900 but not over $21,200	$3,312, plus 35% of the excess over $15,900.
Over $21,200 but not over $28,300	$5,167, plus 40% of the excess over $21,200.
Over $28,300 but not over $41,100	$8,007, plus 44% of the excess over $28,300.
Over $41,100 but not over $53,000	$13,639, plus 48% of the excess over $41,100.
Over $53,000	$19,351, plus 50% of the excess over $53,000.

"(3) For taxable years beginning after 1983.

"If taxable income is:	The tax is:
Not over $1,050	11% of taxable income.
Over $1,050 but not over $2,100	$115.50, plus 12% of the excess over $1,050.
Over 2,100 but not over $4,250	$241.50, plus 14% of the excess over $2,100.
Over $4,250 but not over $6,300	$542.50, plus 16% of the excess over $4,250.
Over $6,300 but not over $8,400	$870.50, plus 18% of the excess over $6,300.
Over $8,400 but not over $10,600	$1,248.50, plus 22% of the excess over $8,400.
Over $10,600 but not over $13,250	$1,732.50, plus 25% of the excess over $10,600.
Over $13,250 but not over $15,900	$2,395, plus 28% of the excess over $13,250.
Over $15,900 but not over $21,200	$3,137, plus 33% of the excess over $15,900.
Over $21,200 but not over $28,300	$4,886, plus 38% of the excess over $21,200.
Over $28,300 but not over $41,100	$7,584, plus 42% of the excess over $28,300.
Over $41,100 but not over $53,000	$12,960, plus 45% of the excess over $41,100.
Over $53,000 but not over $79,500	$18,315, plus 49% of the excess over $53,000.
Over $79,500	$31,300, plus 50% of the excess over $79,500.

"(f) Adjustments in tax tables so that inflation will not result in tax increases.
"(1) In general. Not later than December 15 of 1984 and each subsequent calendar year, the Secretary shall prescribe tables which shall apply in lieu of the tables contained in paragraph (3) of subsections (a), (b), (c), (d), and (e) with respect to taxable years beginning in the succeeding calendar year.
"(2) Method of prescribing tables. The table which under paragraph (1) is to apply in lieu of the table contained in paragraph (3) of subsection (a), (b), (c), (d), or (e), as the case may be, with respect to taxable years beginning in any calendar year shall be prescribed
"(A) by increasing
"(i) the maximum dollar amount on which no tax is imposed under such table, and
"(ii) the minimum and maximum dollar amounts for each rate bracket for which a tax is imposed under such table,
by the cost-of-living adjustment for such calendar year,
"(B) by not changing the rate applicable to any rate bracket as adjusted under subparagraph (A)(ii), and

Code Sec. 1 — Tax rates

"(C) by adjusting the amounts setting forth the tax to the extent necessary to reflect the adjustments in the rate brackets.

"If any increase determined under subparagraph (A) is not a multiple of $10, such increase shall be rounded to the nearest multiple of $10 (or if such increase is a multiple of $5, such increase shall be increased to the next highest multiple of $10).

"(3) Cost-of-living adjustment. For purposes of paragraph (2), the cost-of-living adjustment for any calendar year is the percentage (if any) by which

"(A) the CPI for the preceding calendar year, exceeds

"(B) the CPI for the calendar year 1983.

"(4) CPI for any calendar year. For purposes of paragraph (3), the CPI for any calendar year is the average of the Consumer Price Index as of the close of the 12-month period ending on September 30 of such calendar year.

"(5) Consumer price index. For purposes of paragraph (4), the term 'Consumer Price Index' means the last Consumer Price Index for all-urban consumers published by the Department of Labor."

—P.L. 99-514, Sec. 302(a), added subsec. (j), effective for tax. yrs. begin. after 12/31/86 [amended by Sec. 1003(b)(1) of P.L. 100-647, see above].

—P.L. 99-514, Sec. 406, of this Act provides:

"Sec. 406. Retention of capital gains treatment for sales of dairy cattle under milk production termination program. The amendments made by subtitles A and B of title III shall not apply to any gain from the sale of dairy cattle under a valid contract with the United States Department of Agriculture under the milk production termination program to the extent such gain is properly taken into account under the taxpayer's method of accounting after January 1, 1987, and before September 1, 1987."

—P.L. 99-514, Sec. 1411(a), added subsec. (i), effective for tax. yrs. begin. after 12/31/86.

In 1983, P.L. 97-448, Sec. 101(a)(3), of this Act provides:

"(3) Elimination of 50-cent rounding error. If any figure in any table—

"(A) which is set forth in section 1 of the Internal Revenue Code of 1954 (as amended by section 101 of the Economic Recovery Tax Act of 1981), and

"(B) which applies to married individuals filing separately or to estates and trusts,

differs by not more than 50 cents from the correct amount under the formula used in constructing such table, such figure is hereby corrected to the correct amount."

In 1981, P.L. 97-34, Sec. 101(a), amended Code Sec. 1, effective for tax. yrs. begin. after 12/31/81.

Prior to amendment, Code Sec. 1 read as follows:

"Sec. 1. Tax imposed.

"(a) Married individuals filing joint returns and surviving spouses. There is hereby imposed on the taxable income of—

"(1) every married individual (as defined in section 143) who makes a single return jointly with his spouse under section 6013, and

"(2) every surviving spouse (as defined in section 2(a)),

a tax determined in accordance with the following table:

"If taxable income is:	The tax is:
Not over $3,400	No tax.
Over $3,400 but not over $5,500	14% of excess over $3,400.
Over $5,500 but not over $7,600	$294, plus 16% of excess over $5,500.
Over $7,600 but not over $11,900	$630, plus 18% of excess over $7,600.
Over $11,900 but not over $16,000	$1,404, plus 21% of excess over $11,900.
Over $16,000 but not over $20,200	$2,265, plus 24% of excess over $16,000.
Over $20,200 but not over $24,600	$3,273, plus 28% of excess over $20,200.
Over $24,600 but not over $29,900	$4,505, plus 32% of excess over $24,600.
Over $29,900 but not over $35,200	$6,201, plus 37% of excess over $29,900.
Over $35,200 but not over $45,800	$8,162, plus 43% of excess over $35,200.
Over $45,800 but not over $60,000	$12,720, plus 49% of excess over $45,800.
Over $60,000 but not over $85,600	$19,678, plus 54% of excess over $60,000.
Over $85,600 but not over $109,400	$33,502, plus 59% of excess over $85,600.
Over $109,400 but not over $162,400	$47,544, plus 64% of excess over $109,400.
Over $162,400 but not over $215,400	$81,464, plus 68% of excess over $162,400.
Over $215,400	$117,504, plus 70% of excess over $215,400.

"(b) Heads of households. There is hereby imposed on the taxable income of every individual who is the head of a household (as defined in section 2(b)) a tax determined in accordance with the following table:

"If taxable income is:	The tax is:
Not over $2,300	No tax.
Over $2,300 but not over $4,400	14% of excess over $2,300.
Over $4,400 but not over $6,500	$294, plus 16% of excess over $4,400.
Over $6,500 but not over $8,700	$630, plus 18% of excess over $6,500.
Over $8,700 but not over $11,800	$1,026, plus 22% of excess over $8,700.
Over $11,800 but not over $15,000	$1,708, plus 24% of excess over $11,800.
Over $15,000 but not over $18,200	$2,476, plus 26% of excess over $15,000.
Over $18,200 but not over $23,500	$3,308, plus 31% of excess over $18,200.
Over $23,500 but not over $28,800	$4,951, plus 36% of excess over $23,500.
Over $28,800 but not over $34,100	$6,859, plus 42% of excess over $28,800.
Over $34,100 but not over $44,700	$9,085, plus 46% of excess over $34,100.
Over $44,700 but not over $60,600	$13,961, plus 54% of excess over $44,700.
Over $60,600 but not over $81,800	$22,547, plus 59% of excess over $60,600.
Over $81,800 but not over $108,300	$35,055, plus 63% of excess over $81,800
Over $108,300 but not over $161,300	$51,750, plus 68% of excess over $108,300
Over $161,300	$87,790, plus 70% of excess over $161,300.

"(c) Unmarried individuals (other than surviving spouses and heads of households). There is hereby imposed on the taxable income of every individual (other than a surviving spouse as defined in section 2(a) or the head of a household as defined in section 2(b)) who is not a married individual (as defined in section 143) a tax determined in accordance with the following table:

"If taxable income is:	The tax is:
Not over $2,300	No tax.
Over $2,300 but not over $3,400	14% of excess over $2,300.
Over 3,400 but not over $4,400	$154, plus 16% of excess over $3,400.
Over $4,400 but not over $6,500	$314, plus 18% of excess over $4,400.
Over $6,500 but not over $8,500	$692, plus 19% of excess over $6,500.
Over $8,500 but not over $10,800	$1,072, plus 21% of excess over $3,500.
Over $10,800 but not over $12,900	$1,555, plus 24% of excess over $10,800.
Over $12,900 but not over $15,000	$2,059, plus 26% of excess over $12,900.
Over $15,000 but not over $18,200	$2,605, plus 30% of excess over $15,000.
Over $18,200 but not over $23,500	$3,565, plus 34% of excess over $18,200.
Over $23,500 but not over $28,800	$5,367, plus 39% of excess over $23,500.
Over $28,800 but not over $34,100	$7,434, plus 44% of excess over $28,800.
Over $34,100 but not over $41,500	$9,766, plus 49% of excess over $34,100.
Over $41,500 but not over $55,300	$13,392, plus 55% of excess over $41,500.
Over $55,300 but not over $81,800	$20,982, plus 63% of excess over $55,300.
Over $81,800 but not over $108,300	$37,677, plus 68% of excess over $81,800.
Over $108,300	$55,697, plus 70% of excess over $108,300.

"(d) Married individuals filing separate returns. There is hereby imposed on the taxable income of every married individual (as defined in section 143) who does not make a single return jointly with his spouse under section 6013 a tax determined in accordance with the following table:

"If taxable income is:	The tax is:
Not over $1,700	No tax.
Over $1,700 but not over $2,750	14% of excess over $1,700.
Over $2,750 but not over $3,800	$147, plus 16% of excess over $2,750.
Over $3,800 but not over $5,950	$315, plus 18% of excess over $3,800.
Over $5,950 but not over $8,000	$702, plus 21% of excess over $5,950.
Over $8,000 but not over $10,100	$1,132.50, plus 24% of excess over $8,000.
Over $10,100 but not over $12,300	$1,636.50, plus 28% of excess over $10,100.

Tax rates Code Sec. 1

Over $12,300 but not over $14,950	$2,252.50, plus 32% of excess over $12,300.
Over $14,950 but not over $17,600	$3,100.50, plus 37% of excess over $14,950.
Over $17,600 but not over $22,900	$4,081, plus 43% of excess over $17,600.
Over $22,900 but not over $30,000	$6,360, plus 49% of excess over $22,900.
Over $30,000 but not over $42,800	$9,839, plus 54% of excess over $30,000.
Over $42,800 but not over $54,700	$16,751, plus 59% of excess over $42,800.
Over $54,700 but not over $81,200	$23,772, plus 64% of excess over $54,700.
Over $81,200 but not over $107,700	$40,732, plus 68% of excess over $81,200.
Over $107,700	$58,752, plus 70% of excess over $107,700.

"(e) Estates and trusts. There is hereby imposed on the taxable income of every estate and trust taxable under this subsection a tax determined in accordance with the following table:

"If taxable income is:	The tax is:
Not over $1,050	14% of taxable income.
Over $1,050 but not over $2,100	$147, plus 16% of excess over $1,050.
Over $2,100 but not over $4,250	$315, plus 18% of excess over $2,100.
Over $4,250 but not over $6,300	$702, plus 21% of excess over $4,250.
Over $6,300 but not over $8,400	$1,132.50 plus 24% of excess over $6,300.
Over $8,400 but not over $10,600	$1,636.50, plus 28% of excess over $8,400.
Over $10,600 but not over $13,250	$2,252.50, plus 32% of excess over $10,600.
Over $13,250 but not over $15,900	$3,100.50, plus 37% of excess over $13,250.
Over $15,900 but not over $21,200	$4,081, plus 43% of excess over $15,900.
Over $21,200 but not over $28,300	$6,360, plus 49% of excess over $21,200.
Over $28,300 but not over $41,100	$9,839, plus 54% of excess over $28,300.
Over $41,100 but not over $53,000	$16,751, plus 59% of excess over $41,100.
Over $53,000 but not over $79,500	$23,772, plus 64% of excess over $53,000.
Over $79,500 but not over $106,000	$40,732, plus 68% of excess over $79,500.
Over $106,000	$58,752, plus 70% of excess over $106,000."

—P.L. 97-34, Sec. 104(a), added subsec. (f), effective for tax. yrs. begin. after 12/31/84.

In 1980, P.L. 96-449, Sec. 201, 202 and 205, provides:

"Sec. 201. Compensation excluded from gross income. For purposes of the Internal Revenue Code of 1954, the gross income of an individual who was at any time an American hostage does not include compensation from the United States received for any month during any part of which such individual was—

"(1) in captive status, or

"(2) hospitalized as a result of such individual's captive status.

"Sec. 202. Income taxes of hostages where death results from captive status.

"(a) General rule. In the case of an individual who was at any time an American hostage and who dies as a result of injury or disease or physical or mental disability incurred or aggravated while such individual was in captive status—

"(1) any tax imposed by subtitle A of the Internal Revenue Code of 1954 shall not apply with respect to—

"(A) the taxable year in which falls the date of such individual's death, or

"(B) any prior taxable year ending on or after the first day such individual was in captive status, and

"(2) any tax imposed under such subtitle A for taxable years preceding those specified in paragraph (1) which is unpaid at the date of such individual's death (including interest, additions to the tax, and additional amounts)—

"(A) shall not be assessed,

"(B) if assessed, the assessment shall be abated, and

"(C) if collected, shall be credited or refunded as an overpayment.

"(b) Death must occur within 2 years of cessation of captive status. This section shall not apply unless the death of the individual occurs within 2 years after such individual ceases to be in captive status.

"Sec. 205. Definitions and special rules.

"(a) American hostage. For the purposes of this title, the term 'American hostage' means any individual who, while—

"(1) in the civil service or the uniformed services of the United States, or

"(2) a citizen or resident alien of the United States rendering personal service to the United States abroad similar to the service of a civil officer or employee of the United States (as determined by the Secretary of State),

is placed in a captive status during the hostage period.

"(b) Hostage period. For purposes of this title, the term 'hostage period' means the period beginning on November 4, 1979, and ending on whichever of the following dates is the earlier:

"(1) the date the President specifies, by Executive order, as the date on which all citizens and resident aliens of the United States who were placed in a captive status due to the seizure of the United States Embassy in Iran have been returned to the United States or otherwise accounted for, or

"(2) December 31, 1981.

"(c) Captive status. For purposes of this title—

"(1) In general. The term 'captive status' means a missing status arising because of a hostile action abroad—

"(A) which is directed against the United States during the hostage period, and

"(B) which is identified by the Secretary of State in the Federal Register.

"(2) Missing status defined. The term 'missing status'—

"(A) in the case of employees, has the meaning given it in section 5561(5) of title 5, United States Code,

"(B) in the case of members of the uniformed services, has the meaning given it in section 551(2) of title 37, United States Code, and

"(C) in the case of other individuals, has a similar meaning as that provided under such sections, as determined by the Secretary of State.

For purposes of the preceding sentence, the term 'employee' has the meaning given to such term by section 5561(2) of title 5, United States Code.

"(d) Hospitalized as a result of captive status.

"(1) In general. For purposes of this title, an individual shall be treated as hospitalized as a result of captive status if such individual is hospitalized as a result of injury or disease or physical or mental disability incurred or aggravated while such individual was in captive status.

"(2) 2-year limit. Hospitalization shall be taken into account for purposes of paragraph (1) only if it is hospitalization—

"(A) occurring on or before the day which is 2 years after the date on which the individual's captive status ends (or, if earlier, the date on which the hostage period ends), or

"(B) which is part of a continuous period of hospitalization which began on or before the day determined under subparagraph (A).

"(e) Civil service; uniformed services. For purposes of this section, the terms 'civil service' and 'uniformed services' have the meanings given to such terms by section 2101 of title 5, United States Code.

"(f) Application of title to all Tehran hostages. In the case of any citizen or resident alien of the United States who is determined by the Secretary of State to have been held hostage in Tehran at any time during November 1979, for purposes of this title—

"(1) such individual shall be treated as an American hostage whether or not such individual meets the requirements of paragraph (1) or (2) of subsection (a), and

"(2) if such individual was not in the civil service or the uniformed services of the United States—

"(A) section 201 shall be applied by substituting 'earned income (as defined in section 911(b) of the Internal Revenue Code of 1954) attributable to' for 'compensation from the United States received for', and

"(B) the amount excluded from gross income under section 201 for any month shall not exceed the monthly equivalent of the annual rate of basic pay payable for level V of the Executive Schedule.

"(g) Application of title to individual held captive in Colombia. For purposes of this title, Richard Starr of Edmonds, Washington, who, as a Peace Corps volunteer, was held captive in Colombia, shall be treated as an American hostage who was in captive status beginning November 4, 1979, and ending on February 10, 1980.

"(h) Special rules.

"(1) Compensation. For purposes of this title, the term 'compensation' shall not include any amount received as an annuity or as retirement pay.

"(2) Wage withholding. Any amount excluded from gross income under section 201 shall not be treated as wages for purposes of chapter 24 of the Internal Revenue Code of 1954."

In 1978, P.L. 95-600, Sec. 101(a), amended Code Sec. 1, effective for tax. yrs. begin. after 12/31/78.

Prior to amendment, Code Sec. 1 read as follows:

"Sec. 1. Tax imposed.

"(a) Married individuals filing joint returns and surviving spouses. There is hereby imposed on the taxable income of—

"(1) every married individual (as defined in section 143) who makes a single return jointly with his spouse under section 6013, and

"(2) every surviving spouse (as defined in section 2(a)), tax determined in accordance with the following table:

"If the taxable income is:	The tax is:
Not over $3,200	No tax.
Over $3,200 but not over $4,200	14% of the excess over $3,200.
Over $4,200 but not over $5,200	$140, plus 15% of excess over $4,200.
Over $5,200 but not over $6,200	$290, plus 16% of excess over $5,200.
Over $6,200 but not over $7,200	$450, plus 17% of excess over $6,200.
Over $7,200 but not over $11,200	$620, plus 19% of excess over $7,200.

1,019

Code Sec. 1 — Tax rates

If the taxable income is:	The tax is:
Over $11,200 but not over $15,200.	$1,380, plus 22% of excess over $11,200.
Over $15,200 but not over $19,200.	$2,260, plus 25% of excess over $15,200.
Over $19,200 but not over $23,200.	$3,260, plus 28% of excess over $19,200.
Over $23,200 but not over $27,200.	$4,380, plus 32% of excess over $23,200.
Over $27,200 but not over $31,200.	$5,660, plus 36% of excess over $27,200.
Over $31,200 but not over $35,200.	$7,100, plus 39% of excess over $31,200.
Over $35,200 but not over $39,200.	$8,660, plus 42% of excess over $35,200.
Over $39,200 but not over $43,200.	$10,340, plus 45% of excess over $39,200.
Over $43,200 but not over $47,200.	$12,140, plus 48% of excess over $43,200.
Over $47,200 but not over $55,200.	$14,060, plus 50% of excess over $47,200.
Over $55,200 but not over $67,200.	$18,060, plus 53% of excess over $55,200.
Over $67,200 but not over $79,200.	$24,420, plus 55% of excess over $67,200.
Over $79,200 but not over $91,200.	$31,020, plus 58% of excess over $79,200.
Over $91,200 but not over $103,200.	$37,980, plus 60% of excess over $91,200.
Over $103,200 but not over $123,200.	$45,180, plus 62% of excess over $103,200.
Over $123,200 but not over $143,200.	$57,580, plus 64% of excess over $123,200.
Over $143,200 but not over $163,200.	$70,380, plus 66% of excess over $143,200.
Over $163,200 but not over $183,200.	$83,580, plus 68% of excess over $163,200.
Over $183,200 but not over $203,200.	$97,180, plus 69% of excess over $183,200.
Over $203,200.	$110,980, plus 70% of excess over $203,200.

"(b) Heads of households. There is hereby imposed on the taxable income of every individual who is the head of a household (as defined in section 2(b)) a tax determined in accordance with the following table:

If the taxable income is:	The tax is:
Not over $2,200	No tax.
Over $2,200 but not over $3,200.	14% of the excess over $2,200.
Over $3,200 but not over $4,200.	$140, plus 16% of excess over $3,200.
Over $4,200 but not over $6,200.	$300, plus 18% of excess over $4,200.
Over $6,200 but not over $8,200.	$660, plus 19% of excess over $6,200.
Over $8,200 but not over $10,200.	$1,040, plus 22% of excess over $8,200.
Over $10,200 but not over $12,200.	$1,480, plus 23% of excess over $10,200.
Over $12,200 but not over $14,200.	$1,940, plus 25% of excess over $12,200.
Over $14,200 but not over $16,200.	$2,440, plus 27% of excess over $14,200.
Over $16,200 but not over $18,200.	$2,980, plus 28% of excess over $16,200.
Over $18,200 but not over $20,200.	$3,540, plus 31% of excess over $18,200.
Over $20,200 but not over $22,200.	$4,160, plus 32% of excess over $20,200.
Over $22,200 but not over $24,200.	$4,800, plus 35% of excess over $22,200.
Over $24,200 but not over $26,200.	$5,500, plus 36% of excess over $24,200.
Over $26,200 but not over $28,200.	$6,220, plus 38% of excess over $26,200.
Over $28,200 but not over $30,200.	$6,980, plus 41% of excess over $28,200.
Over $30,200 but not over $34,200.	$7,800, plus 42% of excess over $30,200.
Over $34,200 but not over $38,200.	$9,480, plus 45% of excess over $34,200.
Over $38,200 but not over $40,200.	$11,280, plus 48% of excess over $38,200.
Over $40,200 but not over $42,200.	$12,240, plus 51% of excess over $40,200.
Over $42,200 but not over $46,200.	$13,260, plus 52% of excess over $42,200.
Over $46,200 but not over $52,200.	$15,340, plus 55% of excess over $46,200.
Over $52,200 but not over $54,200.	$18,640, plus 56% of excess over $52,200.
Over $54,200 but not over $66,200.	$19,760, plus 58% of excess over $54,200.
Over $66,200 but not over $72,200.	$26,720, plus 59% of excess over $66,200.
Over $72,200 but not over $78,200.	$30,260, plus 61% of excess over $72,200.
Over $78,200 but not over $82,200.	$33,920, plus 62% of excess over $78,200.
Over $82,200 but not over $90,200.	$36,400, plus 63% of excess over $82,200.
Over $90,200 but not over $102,200.	$41,440, plus 64% of excess over $90,200.
Over $102,200 but not over $122,200.	$49,120, plus 66% of excess over $102,200.
Over $122,200 but not over $142,200.	$62,320, plus 67% of excess over $122,200.
Over $142,200 but not over $162,200.	$75,720, plus 68% of excess over $142,200.
Over $162,200 but not over $182,200.	$89,320, plus 69% of excess over $162,200.
Over $182,200.	$103,120, plus 70% of excess over $182,200.

"(c) Unmarried individuals (other than surviving spouses and heads of households. There is hereby imposed on the taxable income of every individual (other than a surviving spouse as defined in section 2(a) or the head of a household as defined in section 2(b)) who is not a married individual (as defined in section 143) a tax determined in accordance with the following table:

If the taxable income is:	The tax is:
Not over $2,200	No tax.
Over $2,200 but not over $2,700.	14% of the excess over $2,200.
Over $2,700 but not over $3,200.	$70, plus 15% of excess over $2,700.
Over $3,200 but not over $3,700.	$145, plus 16% of excess over $3,200.
Over $3,700 but not over $4,200.	$225, plus 17% of excess over $3,700.
Over $4,200 but not over $6,200.	$310, plus 19% of excess over $4,200.
Over $6,200 but not over $8,200.	$690, plus 21% of excess over $6,200.
Over $8,200 but not over $10,200.	$1,110, plus 24% of excess over $8,200.
Over $10,200 but not over $12,200.	$1,590, plus 25% of excess over $10,200.
Over $12,200 but not over $14,200.	$2,090, plus 27% of excess over $12,200.
Over $14,200 but not over $16,200.	$2,630, plus 29% of excess over $14,200.
Over $16,200 but not over $18,200.	$3,210, plus 31% of excess over $16,200.
Over $18,200 but not over $20,200.	$3,830, plus 34% of excess over $18,200.
Over $20,200 but not over $22,200.	$4,510, plus 36% of excess over $20,200.
Over $22,200 but not over $24,200.	$5,230, plus 38% of excess over $22,200.
Over $24,200 but not over $28,200.	$5,990, plus 40% of excess over $24,200.
Over $28,200 but not over $34,200.	$7,590, plus 45% of excess over $28,200.
Over $34,200 but not over $40,200.	$10,290, plus 50% of excess over $34,200.
Over $40,200 but not over $46,200.	$13,290, plus 55% of excess over $40,200.
Over $46,200 but not over $52,200.	$16,590, plus 60% of excess over $46,200.
Over $52,200 but not over $62,200.	$20,190, plus 62% of excess over $52,200.
Over $62,200 but not over $72,200.	$26,390, plus 64% of excess over $62,200.
Over $72,200 but not over $82,200.	$32,790, plus 66% of excess over $72,200.
Over $82,200 but not over $92,200.	$39,390, plus 68% of excess over $82,200.
Over $92,200 but not over $102,200.	$46,190, plus 69% of excess over $92,200.
Over $102,200.	$53,090, plus 70% of excess over $102,200.

"(d) Married individuals filing separate returns. There is hereby imposed on the taxable income of every married individual (as defined in section 143) who does not make a single return jointly with his spouse under section 6013 a tax determined in accordance with the following table:

Tax rates
Code Sec. 2(a)(3)

"If the taxable income is:	The tax is:
Not over $1,600	No tax.
Over $1,600 but not over $2,100.	14% of the excess over $1,600.
Over $2,100 but not over $2,600.	$70, plus 15% of excess over $2,100.
Over $2,600 but not over $3,100.	$145, plus 16% of excess over $2,600.
Over $3,100 but not over $3,600.	$225, plus 17% of excess over $3,100.
Over $3,600 but not over $5,600.	$310, plus 19% of excess over $3,600.
Over $5,600 but not over $7,600.	$690, plus, 22% of excess over $5,600.
Over $7,600 but not over $9,600.	$1,130, plus 25% of excess over $7,600.
Over $9,600 but not over $11,600.	$1,630, plus 28% of excess over $9,600.
Over $11,600 but not over $13,600.	$2,190, plus 32% of excess over $11,600.
Over $13,600 but not over $15,600.	$2,830, plus 36% of excess over $13,600.
Over $15,600 but not over $17,600.	$3,550, plus 39% of excess over $15,600.
Over $17,600 but not over $19,600.	$4,330, plus 42% of excess over $17,600.
Over $19,600 but not over $21,600.	$5,170, plus 45% of excess over $19,600.
Over $21,600 but not over $23,600.	$6,070, plus 48% of excess over $21,600.
Over $23,600 but not over $27,600.	$7,030, plus 50% of excess over $23,600.
Over $27,600 but not over $33,600.	$9,030, plus 53% of excess over $27,600.
Over $33,600 but not over $39,600.	$12,210, plus 55% of excess over $33,600.
Over $39,600 but not over $45,600.	$15,510, plus 58% of excess over $39,600.
Over $45,600 but not over $51,600.	$18,990, plus 60% of excess over $45,600.
Over $51,600 but not over $61,600.	$22,590, plus 62% of excess over $51,600.
Over $61,600 but not over $71,600.	$28,790, plus 64% of excess over $61,600.
Over $71,600 but not over $81,600.	$35,190, plus 66% of excess over $71,600.
Over $81,600 but not over $91,600.	$41,790, plus 68% of excess over $81,600.
Over $91,600 but not over $101,600.	$48,590, plus 69% of excess over $91,600.
Over $101,600	$55,490, plus 70% of excess over $101,600.

"(e) Estates and trusts. There is hereby imposed on the taxable income of every estate and trust taxable under this subsection a tax determined in accordance with the following table:

"If the taxable income is:	The tax is:
Not over $500	14% of the taxable income.
Over $500 but not over $1,000.	$70, plus 15% of excess over $500.
Over $1,000 but not over $1,500.	$145, plus 16% of excess over $1,000.
Over $1,500 but not over $2,000.	$225, plus 17% of excess over $1,500.
Over $2,000 but not over $4,000.	$310, plus 19% of excess over $2,000.
Over $4,000 but not over $6,000.	$690, plus 22% of excess over $4,000.
Over $6,000 but not over $8,000.	$1,130, plus 25% of excess over $6,000.
Over $8,000 but not over $10,000.	$1,630, plus 28% of excess over $8,000.
Over $10,000 but not over $12,000.	$2,190, plus 32% of excess over $10,000.
Over $12,000 but not over $14,000.	$2,830, plus 36% of excess over $12,000.
Over $14,000 but not over $16,000.	$3,550, plus 39% of excess over $14,000.
Over $16,000 but not over $18,000.	$4,330, plus 42% of excess over $16,000.
Over $18,000 but not over $20,000.	$5,170, plus 45% of excess over $18,000.
Over $20,000 but not over $22,000.	$6,070, plus 48% of excess over $20,000.
Over $22,000 but not over $26,000.	$7,030, plus 50% of excess over $22,000.
Over $26,000 but not over $32,000.	$9,030, plus 53% of excess over $26,000.
Over $32,000 but not over $38,000.	$12,210, plus 55% of excess over $32,000.
Over $38,000 but not over $44,000.	$15,510, plus 58% of excess over $38,000.
Over $44,000 but not over $50,000.	$18,990, plus 60% of excess over $44,000.
Over $50,000 but not over $60,000.	$22,590, plus 62% of excess over $50,000.
Over $60,000 but not over $70,000.	$28,790, plus 64% of excess over $60,000.
Over $70,000 but not over $80,000.	$35,190, plus 66% of excess over $70,000.
Over $80,000 but not over $90,000.	$41,790, plus 68% of excess over $80,000.
Over $90,000 but not over $100,000.	$48,590, plus 69% of excess over $90,000.
Over $100,000	$55,490, plus 70% of excess over $100,000."

In 1977, P.L. 95-30, Sec. 101(a), amended Code Sec. 1, effective for tax. yrs. begin. after 12/31/76. Code Sec. 1 prior to amendment not reproduced.

In 1969, P.L. 91-172, Sec. 803(a), amended Code Sec. 1, effective for tax. yrs. begin. after 12/31/70. Code Sec. 1 prior to amendment not reproduced.

In 1966, P.L. 89-809, Sec. 103(a)(2), redesignated subsec. (d) as (e), and added subsec. (d), effective for tax. yrs. begin. after 12/31/66.

In 1964, P.L. 88-272, Sec. 111(a), amended subsec. (a) . . . Sec. 111(b), amended para. (b)(1), effective for tax. yrs. begin. after 12/31/63.

Prior to amendment, text portion of subsec. (a) read as follows [Tables not reproduced]:

"(a) Rates of tax on individuals. A tax is hereby imposed for each taxable year on the taxable income of every individual other than a head of a household to whom subsection (b) applies. The amount of the tax shall be determined in accordance with the following table:"

Prior to amendment, text portion of para. (b)(1) read as follows [Tables not reproduced]:

"(1) Rates of tax. A tax is hereby imposed for each taxable year on the taxable income of every individual who is the head of a household. The amount of the tax shall be determined in accordance with the following table:"

Sec. 2. Definitions and special rules.
(a) Definition of surviving spouse.

(1) In general. For purposes of section 1, the term "surviving spouse" means a taxpayer—

(A) whose spouse died during either of his two taxable years immediately preceding the taxable year, and

(B) who maintains as his home a household which constitutes for the taxable year the principal place of abode (as a member of such household) of a dependent (i) who (within the meaning of section 152, determined without regard to subsections (b)(1), (b)(2), and (d)(1)(B) thereof) is a son, stepson, daughter, or stepdaughter of the taxpayer, and (ii) with respect to whom the taxpayer is entitled to a deduction for the taxable year under section 151.

For purposes of this paragraph, an individual shall be considered as maintaining a household only if over half of the cost of maintaining the household during the taxable year is furnished by such individual.

(2) Limitations. Notwithstanding paragraph (1), for purposes of section 1 a taxpayer shall not be considered to be a surviving spouse—

(A) if the taxpayer has remarried at any time before the close of the taxable year, or

(B) unless, for the taxpayer's taxable year during which his spouse died, a joint return could have been made under the provisions of section 6013 (without regard to subsection (a)(3) thereof).

(3) Special rule where deceased spouse was in missing status. If an individual was in a missing status (within the meaning of section 6013(f)(3)) as a result of service in a combat zone (as determined for purposes of section 112) and if such individual remains in such status until the date referred to in subparagraph (A) or (B), then, for purposes of paragraph (1)(A), the date on which such individual died shall be treated as the earlier of the date determined

under subparagraph (A) or the date determined under subparagraph (B):
  (A) the date on which the determination is made under section 556 of title 37 of the United States Code or under section 5566 of title 5 of such Code (whichever is applicable) that such individual died while in such missing status, or
  (B) except in the case of the combat zone designated for purposes of the Vietnam conflict, the date which is 2 years after the date designated under section 112 as the date of termination of combatant activities in that zone.

(b) Definition of head of household.
  (1) In general. For purposes of this subtitle, an individual shall be considered a head of a household if, and only if, such individual is not married at the close of his taxable year, is not a surviving spouse (as defined in subsection (a)), and either—
    (A) maintains as his home a household which constitutes for more than one-half of such taxable year the principal place of abode, as a member of such household, of—
      (i) a qualifying child of the individual (as defined in section 152(c), determined without regard to section 152(e)), but not if such child—
        (I) is married at the close of the taxpayer's taxable year, and
        (II) is not a dependent of such individual by reason of section 152(b)(2) or 152(b)(3), or both, or
      (ii) any other person who is a dependent of the taxpayer, if the taxpayer is entitled to a deduction for the taxable year for such person under section 151, or
    (B) maintains a household which constitutes for such taxable year the principal place of abode of the father or mother of the taxpayer, if the taxpayer is entitled to a deduction for the taxable year for such father or mother under section 151.
For purposes of this paragraph, an individual shall be considered as maintaining a household only if over half of the cost of maintaining the household during the taxable year is furnished by such individual.
  (2) Determination of status. For purposes of this subsection—
    (A) an individual who is legally separated from his spouse under a decree of divorce or of separate maintenance shall not be considered as married;
    (B) a taxpayer shall be considered as not married at the close of his taxable year if at any time during the taxable year his spouse is a nonresident alien; and
    (C) a taxpayer shall be considered as married at the close of his taxable year if his spouse (other than a spouse described in subparagraph (B)) died during the taxable year.
  (3) Limitations. Notwithstanding paragraph (1), for purposes of this subtitle a taxpayer shall not be considered to be a head of a household—
    (A) if at any time during the taxable year he is a nonresident alien; or
    (B) by reason of an individual who would not be a dependent for the taxable year but for—
      (i) subparagraph (H) of section 152(d)(2), or
      (ii) paragraph (3) of section 152(d).

(c) Certain married individuals living apart.
For purposes of this part, an individual shall be treated as not married at the close of the taxable year if such individual is so treated under the provisions of section 7703(b).

(d) Nonresident aliens.
In the case of a nonresident alien individual, the taxes imposed by sections 1 and 55 shall apply only as provided by section 871 or 877.

(e) Cross reference.
For definition of taxable income, see section 63.

In **2005,** P.L. 109-135, Sec. 412(a), substituted "subparagraph (B)" for "subparagraph (C)" in subpara. (b)(2)(C), effective 12/21/2005.
In **2004,** P.L. 108-311, Sec. 202(a), amended clause (b)(1)(A)(i) . . . Sec. 202(b)(1), deleted subpara. (b)(2)(A) and redesignated subparas. (b)(2)(B)-(D) as subparas. (b)(2)(A)-(C) . . . Sec. 202(b)(2), amended clauses (b)(3)(B)(i) and (ii) . . . Sec. 207(1), added ", determined without regard to subsections (b)(1), (b)(2), and (d)(1)(B) thereof" after "section 152" in clause (a)(1)(B)(i), effective for tax. yrs. begin. after 12/31/2004.
Prior to amendment, clause (b)(1)(A)(i) read as follows:
"(i) a son, stepson, daughter, or stepdaughter of the taxpayer, or a descendant of a son or daughter of the taxpayer, but if such son, stepson, daughter, stepdaughter, or descendant is married at the close of the taxpayer's taxable year, only if the taxpayer is entitled to a deduction for the taxable year for such person under section 151 (or would be so entitled but for paragraph (2) or (4) of section 152(e)), or"
Prior to deletion, subpara. (b)(2)(A) read as follows:
"(A) a legally adopted child of a person shall be considered a child of such person by blood;"
Prior to amendment, clauses (b)(3)(B)(i) and (ii) read as follows:
"(i) paragraph (9) of section 152(a), or
"(ii) subsection (c) of section 152."
In **1999,** P.L. 106-21, Sec. 1(a)(1), (b) and (d)(1), of this Act provides:
"SEC. 1. AVAILABILITY OF CERTAIN TAX BENEFITS FOR SERVICES AS PART OF OPERATION ALLIED FORCE.
"(a) General rule. For purposes of the following provisions of the Internal Revenue Code of 1986, a qualified hazardous duty area shall be treated in the same manner as if it were a combat zone (as determined under section 112 of such Code):
"(1) Section 2(a)(3) (relating to special rule where deceased spouse was in missing status).
* * *
"(b) Qualified hazardous duty area. For purposes of this section, the term 'qualified hazardous duty area' means any area of the Federal Republic of Yugoslavia (Serbia/Montenegro), Albania, the Adriatic Sea, and the northern Ionian Sea (above the 39th parallel) during the period (which includes the date of the enactment of this Act) that any member of the Armed Forces of the United States is entitled to special pay under section 310 of title 37, United States Code (relating to special pay: duty subject to hostile fire or imminent danger) for services performed in such area.
* * *
"(d) Effective dates.
"(1) In general. Except as provided in paragraph (2), this section shall take effect on March 24, 1999."
In **1996,** P.L. 104-117, Sec. 1(a)(1) and (b), of this Act, regarding treatment of certain individuals performing services in certain hazardous duty areas, effective 11/21/95, provides:
"(a) General rule. For purposes of the following provisions of the Internal Revenue Code of 1986, a qualified hazardous duty area shall be treated in the same manner as if it were a combat zone (as determined under section 112 of such Code):
"(1) Section 2(a)(3) (relating to special rule where deceased spouse was in missing status).
* * *
"(b) Qualified hazardous duty area. For purposes of this section, the term 'qualified hazardous duty area' means Bosnia and Herzegovina, Croatia, or Macedonia, if as of the date of the enactment [3/20/96] of this section any member of the Armed Forces of the United States is entitled to special pay under section 310 of title 37, United States Code (relating to special pay; duty subject to hostile fire or imminent danger) for services performed in such country. Such term includes any such country only during the period such entitlement is in effect. Solely for purposes of applying section 7508 of the Internal Revenue Code of 1986, in the case of an individual who is performing services as part of Operation Joint Endeavor outside the United States while deployed away from such individual's permanent duty station, the term 'qualified hazardous duty area' includes, during the period for which such entitlement is in effect, any area in which such services are performed."
In **1988,** P.L. 100-647, Sec. 1007(g)(13)(A), substituted "the taxes imposed by sections 1 and 55" for "the tax imposed by section 1" in subsec. (d), effective for tax. yrs. begin. after 12/31/86.
In **1986,** P.L. 99-514, Sec. 1301(j)(10), substituted "section 7703(b)" for "section 143(b)" in subsec. (c), effective for all bonds issued after 8/15/86.
—P.L. 99-514, Sec. 1708(a)(1), amended subpara. (a)(3)(B), effective for tax. yrs. begin. after 12/31/82.
Prior to amendment, subpara. (a)(3)(B) read as follows:
"(B) the date which is—
"(i) December 31, 1982, in the case of service in the combat zone designated for purposes of the Vietnam conflict, or

Tax rates   Code Sec. 3

"(ii) 2 years after the date designated under section 112 as the date of termination of combatant activities in that zone, in the case of any combat zone other than that referred to in clause (i)."

In 1984, P.L. 98-369, Sec. 423(c)(2)(A), substituted "which constitutes for more than one-half of such taxable year" for "which constitutes for such taxable year" in subpara. (b)(1)(A) . . . Sec. 423(c)(2)(B), substituted "under section 151 (or would be so entitled but for paragraph (2) or (4) of section 152(e))" for "under section 151 " in clause (b)(1)(A)(i), effective for tax. yrs. begin. after 12/31/84.

In 1983, P.L. 97-448, Sec. 307(a), substituted "December 31, 1982" for "January 2, 1978" in clause (a)(3)(B)(i), effective 1/12/83.

In 1976, P.L. 94-569, Sec. 3(a), amended subpara. (a)(3)(B), effective 10/20/76. Prior to amendment, subpara. (a)(3)(B) read as follows:

"(B) the date which is 2 years after—

"(i) the date of the enactment of this paragraph, in the case of service in the combat zone designated for purposes of the Vietnam conflict, or

"(ii) the date designated under section 112 as the date of termination of combatant activities in that zone, in the case of any combat zone other than that referred to in clause (i)."

—P.L. 94-455, Sec. 1901(b)(9), deleted clause (b)(3)(B)(ii), added "or" to the end of clause (b)(3)(B)(i), and redesignated clause (b)(3)(B)(iii) as clause (b)(3)(B)(ii) . . . Sec. 1901(a)(1), amended subsec. (c), effective for tax. yrs. begin. after 12/31/76.

Prior to deletion, clause (b)(3)(B)(ii) read as follows:

"(ii) paragraph (10) of section 152(a), or"

Prior to amendment, subsec. (c) read as follows:

"(c) Certain married individuals living apart. For purposes of this part, an individual who, under section 143(b), is not to be considered as married shall not be considered as married."

In 1975, P.L. 93-597, Sec. 3(b), added para. (a)(3), effective for tax. yrs. end. on or after 2/28/61.

In 1969, P.L. 91-172, Sec. 803(b), amended Code Sec. 2, effective for tax. yrs. begin. after 12/31/70, except that new subsec. (c) is effective for tax. yrs. begin. after 12/31/69.

Prior to amendment, Code Sec. 2 read as follows:

"SEC. 2. TAX IN CASE OF JOINT RETURN OR RETURN OF SURVIVING SPOUSE.

"(a) Rate of tax. In the case of a joint return of a husband and wife under section 6013, the tax imposed by section 1 shall be twice the tax which would be imposed if the taxable income were cut in half. For purposes of this subsection, section 3, and section 141, a return of a surviving spouse (as defined in subsection (b) shall be treated as a joint return of a husband and wife under section 6013.

"(b) Definition of surviving spouse.

"(1) In general. For purposes of subsection (a), the term 'surviving spouse' means a taxpayer—

"(A) whose spouse died during either of his two taxable years immediately preceding the taxable year, and

"(B) who maintains as his home a household which constitutes for the taxable year the principal place of abode (as a member of such household) of a dependent (i) who (within the meaning of section 152) is a son, stepson, daughter, or stepdaughter of the taxpayer, and

"(ii) with respect to whom the taxpayer is entitled to a deduction for the taxable year under section 151.

"(2) Limitations. Notwithstanding paragraph (1) for purposes of subsection (a) a taxpayer shall not be considered to be a surviving spouse—

"(A) if the taxpayer has remarried at any time before the close of the taxable year, or

"(B) unless, for the taxpayer's taxable year during which his spouse died, a joint return could have been made under the provisions of section 6013 (without regard to subsection (a)(3) thereof) or under the corresponding provisions of the Internal Revenue Code of 1939.

"(c) Certain married individuals living apart. For purposes of this part, an individual who, under section 143(b), is not to be considered as married shall not be considered as married."

In 1964, P.L. 88-272, Sec. 112(b), substituted ", section 3, and section 141" for "and section 3" in the second sentence of subsec. (a), effective for tax. yrs. begin. after 12/31/63.

Sec. 3. Tax tables for individuals.

(a) Imposition of tax table tax.

(1) In general. In lieu of the tax imposed by section 1, there is hereby imposed for each taxable year on the taxable income of every individual—

(A) who does not itemize his deductions for the taxable year, and

(B) whose taxable income for such taxable year does not exceed the ceiling amount,

a tax determined under tables, applicable to such taxable year, which shall be prescribed by the Secretary and which shall be in such form as he determines appropriate. In the table so prescribed, the amounts of the tax shall be computed on the basis of the rates prescribed by section 1.

(2) Ceiling amount defined. For purposes of paragraph (1), the term "ceiling amount" means, with respect to any taxpayer, the amount (not less than $20,000) determined by the Secretary for the tax rate category in which such taxpayer falls.

(3) Authority to prescribe tables for taxpayers who itemize deductions. The Secretary may provide that this section shall apply also for any taxable year to individuals who itemize their deductions. Any tables prescribed under the preceding sentence shall be on the basis of taxable income.

(b) Section inapplicable to certain individuals.

This section shall not apply to—

(1) an individual making a return under section 443(a)(1) for a period of less than 12 months on account of a change in annual accounting period, and

(2) an estate or trust.

(c) Tax treated as imposed by section 1.

For purposes of this title, the tax imposed by this section shall be treated as tax imposed by section 1.

(d) Taxable income.

Whenever it is necessary to determine the taxable income of an individual to whom this section applies, the taxable income shall be determined under section 63.

(e) Cross reference.

For computation of tax by Secretary, see section 6014.

In 1986, P.L. 99-514, Sec. 102(b), amended subsec. (a) . . . Sec. 141(b)(1), deleted para. (b)(1), and redesignated paras. (b)(2) and (b)(3) as (b)(1) and (b)(2), effective for tax. yrs. begin. after 12/31/86.

Prior to amendment, subsec. (a) read as follows:

"(a) Imposition of tax table tax.

"(1) In general. In lieu of the tax imposed by section 1, there is hereby imposed for each taxable year on the tax table income of every individual whose tax table income for such year does not exceed the ceiling amount, a tax determined under tables, applicable to such taxable year, which shall be prescribed by the Secretary and which shall be in such form as he determines appropriate. In the tables so prescribed, the amounts of tax shall be computed on the basis of the rates prescribed by section 1.

"(2) Ceiling amount defined. For purposes of paragraph (1), the term 'ceiling amount' means, with respect to any taxpayer, the amount (not less than $20,000) determined by the Secretary for the tax rate category in which such taxpayer falls.

"(3) Certain taxpayers with large number of exemptions. The Secretary may exclude from the application of this section taxpayers in any tax rate category having more than the number of exemptions for that category determined by the Secretary.

"(4) Tax table income defined. For purposes of this section, the term 'tax table income' means adjusted gross income—

"(A) reduced by the sum of

"(i) the excess itemized deductions, and

"(ii) the direct charitable deduction, and

"(B) increased (in the case of an individual to whom section 63(e) applies) by the unused zero bracket amount.

"(5) Section may be applied on the basis of taxable income. The Secretary may provide that this section shall be applied for any taxable year on the basis of taxable income in lieu of tax table income."

Prior to deletion, para. (b)(1) read as follows:

"(1) an individual to whom section 1301 (relating to income averaging) applies for the taxable year,"

In 1981, P.L. 97-34, Sec. 101(b)(2)(B), added "and which shall be in such form as he determines appropriate" after "Secretary" in para. (a)(1) . . . Sec. 101(b)(2)(C), added para. (a)(5), effective 8/13/81.

—P.L. 97-34, Sec. 101(c)(2)(A), amended para. (b)(1), effective for tax. yrs. begin. after 12/31/81.

Prior to amendment, para. (b)(1) read as follows:

"(1) an individual to whom—

"(A) section 1301 (relating to income averaging), or

"(B) section 1348 (relating to maximum rate on personal service income), applies for the taxable year,"

—P.L. 97-34, Sec. 121(c)(3), amended subpara. (a)(4)(A), effective for contributions made after 12/31/81, in tax. yrs. begin. after 12/31/81.

Prior to amendment, subpara. (a)(4)(A) read as follows:

"(A) reduced by the excess itemized deductions, and"

In 1980, P.L. 96-222, Sec. 108(a)(1)(A), redesignated Sec. 202(f) as Sec. 202(g) and added new Sec. 202(f) to P.L. 95-615 [see below].

—P.L. 96-222, Sec. 108(a)(1)(E), redesignated subparas. (b)(1)(B) and (b)(1)(C) as subparas. (b)(1)(A) and (b)(1)(B), effective for tax. yrs. begin. after 12/31/78.

—P.L. 95-615, Sec. 202(f), [as added by Sec. 108(a)(1)(A), see above], deleted subpara. (b)(1)(A), effective for tax. yrs. begin. after 12/31/77.

Prior to deletion, subpara. (b)(1)(A) read as follows:

1,023

"(A) section 911 (relating to earned income from sources without the United States),—
In 1978, P.L. 95-600, Sec. 401(b)(1), deleted subpara. (b)(1)(B) and redesignated subparas. (b)(1)(C) and (b)(1)(D) as subparas. (b)(1)(B) and (b)(1)(C), effective for tax. yrs. begin. after 12/31/78.
Prior to deletion, subpara. (b)(1)(B) read as follows:
"(B) section 1201 (relating to alternative capital gains tax)."
In 1977, P.L. 95-30, Sec. 101(b), amended Code Sec. 3, effective for tax. yrs. begin. after 12/31/76.
Prior to amendment, Code Sec. 3 read as follows:
"SEC. 3. TAX TABLES FOR INDIVIDUALS HAVING TAXABLE INCOME OF LESS THAN $20,000.
"(a) General rule.
"In lieu of the tax imposed by section 1, there is hereby imposed for each taxable year on the taxable income of every individual whose taxable income for such year does not exceed $20,000 a tax determined under tables, applicable to such taxable year, which shall be prescribed by the Secretary. In the tables so prescribed, the amounts of tax shall be computed on the basis of the rates prescribed by section 1.
"(b) Tax treated as imposed by section 1.
"For purposes of this title, the tax imposed by this section shall be treated as tax imposed by section 1."
In 1976, P.L. 94-455, Sec. 501(a), amended Code Sec. 3, effective for tax. yrs. begin. after 12/31/75.
Prior to amendment, Code Sec. 3 read as follows:
"SEC. 3. OPTIONAL TAX TABLES FOR INDIVIDUALS.
"In lieu of the tax imposed by section 1, there is hereby imposed for each taxable year beginning after December 31, 1969, on the taxable income of every individual whose adjusted gross income for such year is less than $10,000 and who has elected for such year to pay the tax imposed by this section, a tax determined under tables, applicable to such taxable year, which shall be prescribed by the Secretary or his delegate. In the tables so prescribed, the amounts of tax shall be computed on the basis of the taxable income computed by taking the standard deduction and on the basis of the rates prescribed by section 1."
In 1975, P.L. 94-164, Sec. 2(e), extended the effective date for the amendment made by Sec. 201(c) of P.L. 94-12 [see below], to include tax. yrs. end. after 12/31/74 and before 1/1/77.
—P.L. 94-12, Sec. 201(c), substituted "$15,000" for "$10,000" in Code Sec. 3, effective [as amended by Sec. 2(e) of P.L. 94-164, see above] for tax. yrs. end. after 12/31/74 and before 1/1/77.
In 1969, P.L. 91-172, Sec. 803(c), amended Code Sec. 3, effective for tax. yrs. begin. after 12/31/69.
Prior to amendment, Code Sec. 3 read as follows:
"SEC. 3. OPTIONAL TAX IF ADJUSTED GROSS INCOME IS LESS THAN $5,000.
"(a) Taxable years beginning in 1964.
"In lieu of the tax imposed by section 1, there is hereby imposed for each taxable year beginning on or after January 1, 1964, and before January 1, 1965, on the taxable income of every individual whose adjusted gross income for such year is less than $5,000 and who has elected for such year to pay the tax imposed by this section, a tax as follows:
"(b) Taxable years beginning after December 31, 1964.
"In lieu of the tax imposed by section 1, there is hereby imposed for each taxable year beginning after December 31, 1964, on the taxable income of every individual whose adjusted gross income for such year is less than $5,000 and who has elected for such year to pay the tax imposed by this section a tax as follows: [Tables not reproduced]."
In 1964, P.L. 88-272, Sec. 301(a), amended Code Sec. 3, effective for tax. yrs. begin. after 12/31/63.
Prior to amendment, Code Sec. 3 read as follows:
"SEC. 3. OPTIONAL TAX IF ADJUSTED GROSS INCOME IS LESS THAN $5,000.
"In lieu of the tax imposed by section 1, there is hereby imposed for each taxable year, on the taxable income of each individual whose adjusted gross income for such year is less than $5,000 and who has elected for such year to pay the tax imposed by this section, the tax shown in the table. (Table not reproduced)"

Sec. 4. Repealed.

In 1976, P.L. 94-455, Sec. 501(b)(1), repealed Code Sec. 4, effective for tax. yrs. begin. after 12/31/75.
Prior to repeal, Code Sec. 4 read as follows:
"SEC. 4. RULES FOR OPTIONAL TAX.
"(a) Number of exemptions. For purposes of the tables prescribed by the Secretary or his delegate pursuant to section 3, the term 'number of exemptions' means the number of exemptions allowed under section 151 as deductions in computing taxable income.
"(b) Manner of election. The election referred to in section 3 shall be made in the manner provided in regulations prescribed by the Secretary or his delegate.
"(c) Husband or wife filing separate return.
"(1) A husband or wife may not elect to pay the optional tax imposed by section 3 if the tax of the other spouse is determined under section 1 on the basis of taxable income computed without regard to the standard deduction.
"(2) Except as otherwise provided in this subsection, in the case of a husband or wife filing a separate return the tax imposed by section 3 shall be the lesser of the tax shown in—

"(A) the table prescribed under section 3 applicable in the case of married persons filing separate returns which applies the percentage standard deduction, or
"(B) the table prescribed under section 3 applicable in the case of married persons filing separate returns which applies the low income allowance.
"(3) The table referred to in paragraph (2)(B) shall not apply in the case of a husband or wife filing a separate return if the tax of the other spouse is determined with regard to the percentage standard deduction; except that an individual described in section 141(d)(2) may elect (under regulations prescribed by the Secretary or his delegate) to pay the tax shown in the table referred to in paragraph (2)(B) in lieu of the tax shown in the table referred to in paragraph (2)(A). For purposes of this title, an election under the preceding sentence shall be treated as an election made under section 141(d)(2).
"(4) For purposes of this subsection, determination of marital status shall be made under section 143.
"(d) Certain other taxpayers ineligible. Section 3 shall not apply to—
"(1) a nonresident alien individual;
"(2) a citizen of the United States entitled to the benefits of section 931 (relating to income from sources within possessions of the United States);
"(3) an individual making a return under section 443(a)(1) for a period of less than 12 months on account of a change in his accounting period;
"(4) an estate or trust; or
"(5) an individual if the amount of the standard deduction otherwise allowable to such individual is reduced under section 141(e).
"(e) Taxable income computed with standard deduction. Whenever it is necessary to determine the taxable income of a taxpayer who made the election referred to in section 3, the taxable income shall be determined under section 63(b) (relating to definition of taxable income for individuals electing standard deduction).
"(f) Cross references.
"(1) For other applicable rules (including rules as to the change of an election under section 3), see section 144.
"(2) For disallowance of certain credits against tax, see section 36.
"(3) For rule that optional tax is not to apply if individual chooses the benefits of income averaging, see section 1304(b).
"(4) For computation of tax by Secretary or his delegate, see section 6014."
In 1971, P.L. 92-178, Sec. 301(b), struck out "or" at the end of para. (d)(3), substituted "; or" for the period at the end of para. (d)(4), and added para. (d)(5), effective for tax. yrs. begin. after 12/31/71.
In 1969, P.L. 91-172, Sec. 802(c)(1), amended subsec. (a) . . . Sec. 802(c)(2), amended subsec. (c) . . . Sec. 802(c)(3), amended para. (f)(4), effective for tax. yrs. begin. after 12/31/69.
Prior to amendment, subsec. (a) read as follows:
"(a) Number of exemptions. For purposes of the tables in section 3, the term 'number of exemptions' means the number of the exemptions allowed under section 151 as deductions in computing taxable income."
Prior to amendment, subsec. (c) read as follows:
"(c) Husband or wife filing separate return.
"(1) A husband or wife may not elect to pay the optional tax imposed by section 3 if the tax of the other spouse is determined under section 1 on the basis of taxable income computed without regard to the standard deduction.
"(2) Except as otherwise provided in this subsection, in the case of a husband or wife filing a separate return the tax imposed by section 3 shall be—
"(A) for taxable years beginning in 1964, the lesser of the tax shown in Table IV or Table V of section 3(a), and
"(B) for taxable years beginning after December 31, 1964, the lesser of the tax shown in Table IV or Table V of section 3(b).
"(3) Neither Table V of section 3(a) nor Table V of section 3(b) shall apply in the case of a husband or wife filing a separate return if the tax of the other spouse is determined with regard to the 10-percent standard deduction; except that an individual described in section 141(d)(2) may elect (under regulations prescribed by the Secretary or his delegate)—
"(A) to pay the tax shown in Table V of section 3(a) in lieu of the tax shown in Table IV of section 3(a), and
"(B) to pay the tax shown in Table V of section 3(b) in lieu of the tax shown in Table IV of section 3(b).
For purposes of this title, an election under the preceding sentence shall be treated as an election made under section 141(d)(2).
"(4) For purposes of this subsection, determination of marital status shall be made under section 143."
Prior to amendment, para. (f)(4) read as follows:
"(4) For nonapplicability of Table V in section 3(a) and Table V in section 3(b) in case where tax is not computed by taxpayer, see section 6014(a)."
In 1964, P.L. 88-272, Sec. 232(f)(1), added para. (f)(3) . . . Sec. 301(b)(1), amended subsec. (c) . . . Sec. 301(b)(3)(A), substituted "tables" for "table" in subsec. (a) . . . Sec. 301(b)(3)(B), added para. (f)(4), effective for tax. yrs. begin. after 12/31/63.
Prior to amendment, subsec. (c) read as follows:
"(c) Husband or wife filing separate return.
"A husband or wife may not elect to pay the optional tax imposed by section 3 if the tax of the other spouse is determined under section 1 on the basis of taxable income computed without regard to the standard deduction. For purposes of the preceding sentence, determination of marital status shall be made under section 143."

Tax rates   Code Sec. 11

Sec. 5. Cross references relating to tax on individuals.
(a) Other rates of tax on individuals, etc.
   (1) For rates of tax on nonresident aliens, see section 871.
   (2) For doubling of tax on citizens of certain foreign countries, see section 891.
   (3) For rate of withholding in the case of nonresident aliens, see section 1441.
   (4) For alternative minimum tax, see section 55.
(b) Special limitations on tax.
   (1) For limitation on tax in case of income of members of Armed Forces, astronauts, and victims of certain terrorist attacks on death, see section 692.
   (2) For computation of tax where taxpayer restores substantial amount held under claim of right, see section 1341.

In 2003, P.L. 108-121, Sec. 110(a)(2)(A), added ", astronauts," after "Forces" in para. (b)(1), effective for any astronaut whose death occurs after 12/31/2002.
In 2002, P.L. 107-134, Sec. 101(b)(1), added "and victims of certain terrorist attacks" after "Armed Forces" in para. (b)(1), effective for tax. yrs. end. before, on, or after 9/11/2001. Sec. 101(d)(2) of this Act, provides:
  "(2) Waiver of limitations. If refund or credit of any overpayment of tax resulting from the amendments made by this section is prevented at any time before the close of the 1-year period beginning on the date of the enactment of this Act by the operation of any law or rule of law (including res judicata), such refund or credit may nevertheless be made or allowed if claim therefor is filed before the close of such period."
In 1986, P.L. 99-514, Sec. 141(b)(2), deleted para. (b)(2), and redesignated paras. (b)(3) as para. (b)(2) . . . Sec. 701(e)(4)(A), amended para. (a)(4), effective for tax. yrs. begin. after 12/31/86.
Prior to deletion, para. (b)(2) read as follows:
  "(2) For limitation on tax where an individual chooses the benefits of income averaging, see section 1301."
Prior to amendment, para. (a)(4) read as follows:
  "(4) For minimum tax for taxpayers other than corporations, see section 55."
In 1983, P.L. 97-448, Sec. 306(a)(1)(A)(i), redesignated the second Sec. 201(c) of P.L. 97-248 as Sec. 201(d) of P.L. 97-248 [see below].
In 1982, P.L. 97-248, Sec. 201(d)(4), [as redesignated by Sec. 306(a)(1)(A)(i) of P.L. 97-448, see above], substituted "section 55" for "sections 55 and 56" in para. (a)(4), effective for tax. yrs. begin. after 12/31/82.
In 1980, P.L. 96-222, Sec. 104(a)(4)(H)(vii), substituted "sections 55 and 56" for "section 55" in para. (a)(4), effective for tax. yrs. begin. after 12/31/78.
In 1978, P.L. 95-600, Sec. 401(b)(2), deleted para. (a)(3) and redesignated paras. (a)(4) and (a)(5) as paras. (a)(3) and (a)(4), effective for tax. yrs. begin. after 12/31/78.
Prior to deletion, para. (a)(3) read as follows:
  "(3) For alternative tax in case of capital gain, see section 1201(b)."
—P.L. 95-600, Sec. 421(e)(1), amended para. (a)(4) [as redesignated by Sec. 401(b)(2) of this Act, see above], effective for tax. yrs. begin. after 12/31/78.
Prior to amendment, para. (a)(4) read as follows:
  "(4) For minimum tax for tax preferences, see section 56."
In 1976, P.L. 94-455, Sec. 1901(b)(22)(B), deleted para. (b)(1) . . . Sec. 1951(c)(3)(A), deleted para. (b)(5), and redesignated paras. (b)(2), (b)(3) and (b)(4) as paras. (b)(1), (b)(2) and (b)(3), effective for tax. yrs. begin. after 12/31/76.
Prior to deletion, para. (b)(1) read as follows:
  "(1) For limitation on tax attributable to sales of oil or gas properties, see section 632."
Prior to deletion, para. (b)(5) read as follows:
  "(5) For limitation on tax attributable to claims against the United States involving acquisitions of property, see section 1347."
In 1969, P.L. 91-172, Sec. 301(b)(2), added para. (a)(5), effective for tax. yrs. end. after 12/31/69.
—P.L. 91-172, Sec. 803(d)(6), substituted "tax" for "surtax" in paras. (b)(1) and (b)(5), effective for tax. yrs. begin. after 12/31/70.
In 1964, P.L. 88-272, Sec. 232(f)(2), amended subsec. (b), effective for tax. yrs. begin after 12/31/63.
Prior to amendment, subsec. (b) read as follows:
"(b) Special limitations on tax.
  "(1) For limitation on tax attributable to receipt of lump sum under annuity, endowment, or life insurance contract, see section 72(e)(3).
  "(2) For limitation on surtax attributable to sales of oil or gas properties, see section 632.
  "(3) For limitation on tax in case of income of members of Armed Forces on death, see section 692.
  "(4) For limitation on tax with respect to compensation for long-term services, see section 1301.
  "(5) For limitation on tax with respect to income from artistic work or inventions, see section 1302.
  "(6) For limitation on tax in case of back pay, see section 1303."

"(7) For computation of tax where taxpayer restores substantial amount held under claim of right, see section 1341.
"(8) For limitation on surtax attributable to claims against the United States involving acquisitions of property, see section 1347."

PART II.—TAX ON CORPORATIONS

Sec.
11. Tax imposed.
12. Cross references relating to tax on corporations.

Sec. 11. Tax imposed.
(a) Corporations in general.
A tax is hereby imposed for each taxable year on the taxable income of every corporation.
(b) Amount of tax.
   (1) In general. The amount of the tax imposed by subsection (a) shall be the sum of—
      (A) 15 percent of so much of the taxable income as does not exceed $50,000,
      (B) 25 percent of so much of the taxable income as exceeds $50,000 but does not exceed $75,000,
      (C) 34 percent of so much of the taxable income as exceeds $75,000 but does not exceed $10,000,000, and
      (D) 35 percent of so much of the taxable income as exceeds $10,000,000.
   In the case of a corporation which has taxable income in excess of $100,000 for any taxable year, the amount of tax determined under the preceding sentence for such taxable year shall be increased by the lesser of (i) 5 percent of such excess, or (ii) $11,750. In the case of a corporation which has taxable income in excess of $15,000,000, the amount of the tax determined under the foregoing provisions of this paragraph shall be increased by an additional amount equal to the lesser of (i) 3 percent of such excess, or (ii) $100,000.
   (2) Certain personal service corporations not eligible for graduated rates. Notwithstanding paragraph (1), the amount of the tax imposed by subsection (a) on the taxable income of a qualified personal service corporation (as defined in section 448(d)(2)) shall be equal to 35 percent of the taxable income.
(c) Exceptions.
Subsection (a) shall not apply to a corporation subject to a tax imposed by—
   (1) section 594 (relating to mutual savings banks conducting life insurance business),
   (2) subchapter L (sec. 801 and following, relating to insurance companies), or
   (3) subchapter M (sec. 851 and following, relating to regulated investment companies and real estate investment trusts).
(d) Foreign corporations.
In the case of a foreign corporation, the taxes imposed by subsection (a) and section 55 shall apply only as provided by section 882.

In 1993, P.L. 103-66, Sec. 13221(a)(1), deleted "and" at the end of subpara. (b)(1)(B) . . . Sec. 13221(a)(2), amended subpara. (b)(1)(C) and added subpara. (b)(1)(D) . . . Sec. 13221(a)(3), added a new sentence at the end of para. (b)(1) . . . Sec. 13221(b), substituted "35 percent" for "34 percent" in para. (b)(2), effective for tax. yrs. begin. on or after 1/1/93.
Prior to amendment, subpara. (b)(1)(C) read as follows:
  "(C) 34 percent of so much of the taxable income as exceeds $75,000."
In 1988, P.L. 100-647, Sec. 1007(g)(13)(B), substituted "the taxes imposed by subsection (a) and section 55" for "the tax imposed by subsection (a)" in subsec. (d), effective for tax. yrs. begin. after 12/31/86.
In 1987, P.L. 100-203, Sec. 10224(a), amended subsec. (b), effective for tax. yrs. begin. after 12/31/87.
Prior to amendment, subsec. (b) read as follows:
"(b) Amount of tax.
  The amount of tax imposed by subsection (a) shall be the sum of—
  "(1) 15 percent of so much of the taxable income as does not exceed $50,000,

1,025

"(2) 25 percent of so much of the taxable income as exceeds $50,000 but does not exceed $75,000, and
"(3) 34 percent of so much of the taxable income as exceeds $75,000.
In the case of a corporation which has taxable income in excess of $100,000 for any taxable year, the amount of tax determined under the preceding sentence for such taxable year shall be increased by the lesser of (A) 5 percent of such excess, or (B) $11,750."

In 1986, P.L. 99-514, Sec. 601(a), amended subsec. (b), effective for tax. yrs. begin. on or after 7/1/87. Sec. 601(b)(2) of this Act provides the following:
"(2) Cross reference.— For treatment of taxable years which include July 1, 1987, see section 15 of the Internal Revenue Code of 1986."
Prior to amendment, subsec. (b) read as follows:
"(b) Amount of tax.
"The amount of the tax imposed by subsection (a) shall be the sum of—
"(1) 15 percent (16 percent for taxable years beginning in 1982) of so much of the taxable income as does not exceed $25,000;
"(2) 18 percent (19 percent for taxable years beginning in 1982) of so much of the taxable income as exceeds $25,000 but does not exceed $50,000;
"(3) 30 percent of so much of the taxable income as exceeds $50,000 but does not exceed $75,000;
"(4) 40 percent of so much of the taxable income as exceeds $75,000 but does not exceed $100,000; plus
"(5) 46 percent of so much of the taxable income as exceeds $100,000.
In the case of a corporation with taxable income in excess of $1,000,000 for any taxable year, the amount of tax determined under the preceding sentence for such taxable year shall be increased by the lesser of (A) 5 percent of such excess, or (B) $20,250."

In 1984, P.L. 98-369, Sec. 66(a), added the sentence at the end of subsec. (b), effective for tax. yrs. begin. after 12/31/83. Sec. 66(c)(2) also provides:
"(2) Amendments not treated as changed in rate of tax.— The amendments made by this subsection shall not be treated as a change in a rate of tax for purposes of section 21 of the Internal Revenue Code of 1954."

In 1981, P.L. 97-34, Sec. 231(a)(1), substituted "15 percent (16 percent for taxable years beginning in 1982)" for "17 percent" in para. (b)(1) . . . Sec. 231(a)(2), substituted "18 percent (19 percent for taxable years beginning in 1982)" for "20 percent" in para. (b)(2), effective for tax. yrs. begin. after 12/31/81.

In 1978, P.L. 95-600, Sec. 301(a), amended Code Sec. 11, effective for tax. yrs. begin. after 12/31/78.
Prior to amendment, Code Sec. 11 read as follows:
"Sec. 11. Tax imposed.
"(a) Corporations in general.
"A tax is hereby imposed for each taxable year on the taxable income of every corporation. The tax shall consist of a normal tax computed under subsection (b) and a surtax computed under subsection (c).
"(b) Normal tax.
"The normal tax is equal to—
"(1) in the case of a taxable year ending after December 31, 1978, 22 percent of the taxable income, and
"(2) in the case of a taxable year ending after December 31, 1974, and before January 1, 1979, the sum of—
"(A) 20 percent of so much of the taxable income as does not exceed $25,000, plus
"(B) 22 percent of so much of the taxable income as exceeds $25,000.
"(c) Surtax.
"The surtax is 26 percent of the amount by which the taxable income exceeds the surtax exemption for the taxable year.
"(d) Surtax exemption.
"For purposes of this subtitle, the surtax exemption for any taxable year is—
"(1) $25,000 in the case of a taxable year ending after December 31, 1978, or
"(2) $50,000 in the case of a taxable year ending after December 31, 1974, and before January 1, 1979,
except that, with respect to a corporation to which section 1561 (relating to certain multiple tax benefits in the case of certain controlled corporations) applies for the taxable year, the surtax exemption for the taxable year is the amount determined under such section.
"(e) Exceptions.
"Subsection (a) shall not apply to a corporation subject to a tax imposed by—
"(1) section 594 (relating to mutual savings banks conducting life insurance business),
"(2) subchapter L (sec. 801 and following, relating to insurance companies), or
"(3) subchapter M (sec. 851 and following, relating to regulated investment companies and real estate investment trusts).
"(f) Foreign corporations.
"In the case of a foreign corporation, the tax imposed by subsection (a) shall apply only as provided by section 882."

In 1977, P.L. 95-30, Sec. 201(1), substituted "December 31, 1978" for "December 31, 1977" and "January 1, 1979" for "January 1, 1978" in subsec. (b) . . . Sec. 201(2), substituted "December 31, 1978" for "December 31, 1977" and "January 1, 1979" for "January 1, 1978" in subsec. (d), effective for tax. yrs. begin. after 12/31/76, and to credit carrybacks from such years.

In 1976, P.L. 94-455, Sec. 901(a), amended subsecs. (a), (b), (c) and (d) effective 12/23/75.
Prior to amendment, subsecs. (a), (b), (c) and (d) read as follows:
"(a) Corporations in general.

"A tax is hereby imposed for each taxable year on the taxable income of every corporation. The tax shall consist of a normal tax computed under subsection (b) and a surtax computed under subsection (c).
"(b) Normal tax.
"(1) General rule. The normal tax is equal to—
"(A) in the case of a taxable year ending after December 31, 1976, 22 percent of the taxable income, and
"(B) in the case of a taxable year ending after December 31, 1974, and before January 1, 1977, the sum of—
"(i) 20 percent of so much of the taxable income as does not exceed $25,000, plus
"(ii) 22 percent of so much of the taxable income as exceeds $25,000.
"(2) Six-month application of general rule.—
"(A) Calendar year taxpayers. Notwithstanding the provisions of paragraph (1), in the case of a taxpayer who has as his taxable year the calendar year 1976, the normal tax for such taxable year is equal to the sum of—
"(i) 21 percent of so much of the taxable income as does not exceed $25,000, plus
"(ii) 22 percent of so much of the taxable income as exceeds $25,000.
"(B) Fiscal year taxpayers. Notwithstanding the provisions of paragraph (1), in the case of a taxpayer whose taxable year is not the calendar year, effective on July 1, 1976, paragraph (1) shall cease to apply and the normal tax shall be 22 percent.
"(c) Surtax.
"(1) General rule. The surtax is 26 percent of the amount by which the taxable income exceeds the surtax exemption for the taxable year.
"(2) Special rule for 1976 for calendar year taxpayers. Notwithstanding the provisions of paragraph (1), in the case of a taxpayer who has as his taxable year the calendar year 1976, the surtax for such taxable year is—
"(A) 13 percent of the amount by which the taxable income exceeds the $25,000 surtax exemption (as in effect under subsection (d)(2)) but does not exceed $50,000, plus
"(B) 26 percent of the amount by which the taxable income exceeds $50,000.
"(d) Surtax Exemption.
"(1) General rule. For purposes of this subtitle, the surtax exemption for any taxable year is $50,000, except that, with respect to a corporation to which section 1561 or 1564 (relating to surtax exemptions in case of certain controlled corporations) applies for the taxable year, the surtax exemption for the taxable year is the amount determined under such section.
"(2) Six-month application of general rule. Notwithstanding the provisions of paragraph (1)—
"(A) Calendar year taxpayers. In the case of a taxpayer who has as his taxable year the calendar year 1976, the provisions of paragraph (1) shall be applied for such taxable year by substituting the amount '$25,000' for the amount '$50,000' appearing therein.
"(B) Fiscal year taxpayers. In the case of a taxpayer whose taxable year is not the calendar year, effective on July 1, 1976, paragraph (1) shall be applied by substituting the amount '$25,000' for the amount '$50,000' appearing therein, and such substitution shall be treated, for purposes of section 21, as a change in a rate of tax."

In 1975, P.L. 94-164, Sec. 4(a), [which erroneously indicated it was amending subsec. (a)], amended subsec. (b), effective date of enactment (12/23/75).
Prior to amendment, subsec. (b) read as follows:
"(b) Normal tax.
"The normal tax is equal to—
"(1) in the case of a taxable year ending before January 1, 1975, or after December 31, 1975, 22 percent of the taxable income, and
"(2) in the case of a taxable year ending after December 31, 1974, and before January 1, 1976, the sum of—
"(A) 20 percent of so much of the taxable income as does not exceed $25,000, plus
"(B) 22 percent of so much of the taxable income as exceeds $25,000."
—P.L. 94-164, Sec. 4(b), amended subsec. (c), effective for tax. yrs. begin. after 12/31/75.
Prior to amendment, subsec. (c) read as follows:
"(c) Surtax.
"The surtax is equal to the following percentage of the amount by which the taxable income exceeds the surtax exemption for the taxable year:
"(1) 22 percent, in the case of a taxable year beginning before January 1, 1964.
"(2) 28 percent, in the case of a taxable year beginning after December 31, 1963, and before January 1, 1965, and
"(3) 26 percent, in the case of a taxable year beginning after December 31, 1964."
—P.L. 94-164, Sec. 4(c), amended subsec. (d), effective for tax. yrs. begin. after 12/31/75 and before 1/1/77.
Prior to amendment, subsec. (d) read as follows:
"(d) Surtax exemption.
"For purposes of this subtitle, the surtax exemption for any taxable year is $50,000, except that, with respect to a corporation to which section 1561 or 1564 (relating to surtax exemptions in case of certain controlled corporations) applies for the taxable year, the surtax exemption for the taxable year is the amount determined under such section."
—P.L. 94-12, Sec. 303(a), amended subsec. (b), effective for tax. yrs. end. after 12/31/74.
Prior to amendment, subsec. (b) read as follows:
"(b) Normal tax.
"The normal tax is equal to the following percentage of the taxable income:

Tax credits   Code Sec. 15(b)(2)

"(1) 30 percent, in the case of a taxable year beginning before January 1, 1964, and

"(2) 22 percent in the case of a taxable year beginning after December 31, 1963."

—P.L. 94-12, Sec. 303(b), substituted "$50,000" for "$25,000" in subsec. (d), effective for tax. yrs. end. after 12/31/74 and before 1/1/76.

In 1969, P.L. 91-172, Sec. 401(b)(2)(B), substituted "section 1561 or 1564" for "section 1561" in subsec. (d), effective for tax. yrs. begin. after 12/31/69.

In 1966, P.L. 89-809, Sec. 104, deleted para. (e)(4) and added subsec. (f), effective for tax. yrs. begin. after 1966.

Prior to deletion, para. (e)(4) read as follows:

"(4) section 881(a) (relating to foreign corporations not engaged in business in United States)."

In 1964, P.L. 88-272, Sec. 121, amended Code Sec. 11, effective for tax. yrs. begin. after 12/31/63 except for purposes of Code Sec. 21.

Prior to amendment, Code Sec. 11 read as follows:

"Code Sec. 11. Tax imposed.

"(a) Corporations in general.

"A tax is hereby imposed for each taxable year on the taxable income of every corporation. The tax shall consist of a normal tax computed under subsection (b) and a surtax computed under subsection (c).

"(b) Normal tax.

"(1) Taxable years beginning before July 1, 1964. In the case of a taxable year beginning before July 1, 1964, the normal tax is equal to 30 percent of the taxable income.

"(2) Taxable years ending after June 30, 1964. In the case of a taxable year beginning after June 30, 1964, the normal tax is equal to 25 percent of the taxable income.

"(c) Surtax.

"The surtax is equal to 22 percent of the amount by which the taxable income (computed without regard to the deduction, if any, provided in section 242 for partially tax-exempt interest) exceeds $25,000.

"(d) Exceptions.

"Subsection (a) shall not apply to a corporations subject to a tax imposed by—

"(1) section 594 (relating to mutual savings banks conducting life insurance business),

"(2) subchapter L (sec. 801 and following, relating to insurance companies),

"(3) subchapter M (sec. 951 and following, relating to regulated investment companies and real estate investment trusts),

"(4) section 881(a) (relating to foreign corporations not engaged in business in United States)."

In 1963, P.L. 88-52, Sec. 2(1), substituted "July 1, 1964" for "July 1, 1963" in the heading of para. (b)(1) . . . Sec. 2(2), substituted "July 1, 1964" for "July 1, 1963" in subsec. (b) . . . Sec. 2(3), substituted "June 30, 1964" for "June 30, 1963" in the heading of para. (b)(2) . . . Sec. 2(4), substituted "June 30, 1964" for "June 30, 1963" in subsec. (b), effective 6/29/63.

In 1962, P.L. 87-508, Sec. 2(1), substituted "July 1, 1963" for "July 1, 1962" in the heading of para. (b)(1) . . . Sec. 2(2), substituted "July 1, 1963" for "July 1, 1962" in subsec. (b) . . . Sec. 2(3), substituted "June 30, 1963" for "June 30, 1962" in the heading of para. (b)(2) . . . Sec. 2(4), substituted "June 30, 1963" for "June 30, 1962" in subsec. (b), effective 6/28/62.

In 1961, P.L. 87-72, Sec. 2(1), substituted "July 1, 1962" for "July 1, 1961" in the heading of para. (b)(1) . . . Sec. 2(2), substituted "July 1, 1962" for "July 1, 1961" in subsec. (b) . . . Sec. 2(3), substituted "June 30, 1962" for "June 30, 1961" in the heading of para. (b)(2) . . . Sec. 2(4), substituted "June 30, 1962" for "June 30, 1961" in subsec. (b), effective 6/30/61.

In 1960, P.L. 86-779, Sec. 10(d), added "and real estate investment trusts" after "regulated investment companies" in para. (d)(3), effective for tax. yrs. of real estate investment trusts begin. after 12/31/60.

—P.L. 86-564, Sec. 2(1), substituted "July 1, 1961" for "July 1, 1960" in the heading of para. (b)(1) . . . Sec. 2(2), substituted "July 1, 1961" for "July 1, 1960" in subsec. (b) . . . Sec. 2(3), substituted "June 30, 1961" for "June 30, 1960" in the heading of para. (b)(2) . . . Sec. 2(4), substituted "June 30, 1961" for "June 30, 1960" in subsec. (b), effective 6/30/60.

In 1959, P.L. 86-75, Sec. 2(1), substituted "July 1, 1960" for "July 1, 1959" in the heading of para. (b)(1) . . . Sec. 2(2), substituted "July 1, 1960" for "July 1, 1959" in subsec. (b) . . . Sec. 2(3), substituted "June 30, 1960" for "June 30, 1959" in the heading of para. (b)(2) . . . Sec. 2(4), substituted "June 30, 1960" for "June 30, 1959" in subsec. (b), effective 6/30/59.

In 1958, P.L. 85-475, Sec. 2(1), substituted "July 1, 1959" for "July 1, 1958" in the heading of para. (b)(1) . . . Sec. 2(2), substituted "July 1, 1959" for "July 1, 1958" in subsec. (b) . . . Sec. 2(3), substituted "June 30, 1959" for "June 30, 1958" in the heading of para. (b)(2) . . . Sec. 2(4), substituted "June 30, 1959" for "June 30, 1958" in subsec. (b), effective 6/30/58.

In 1957, P.L. 85-12, Sec. 2(1), substituted "July 1, 1958" for "April 1, 1957" in the heading of para. (b)(1) . . . Sec. 2(2), substituted "July 1, 1958" for "April 1, 1957" in subsec. (b) . . . Sec. 2(3), substituted "June 30, 1958" for "March 31, 1957" in the heading of para. (b)(2) . . . Sec. 2(4), substituted "June 30, 1958" for "March 31, 1957" in subsec. (b), effective 3/29/57.

In 1956, P.L. 458, Sec. 2(1), substituted "April 1, 1957" for "April 1, 1956" in the heading of para. (b)(1) . . . Sec. 2(2), substituted "April 1, 1957" for "April 1, 1956" in subsec. (b) . . . Sec. 2(3), substituted "March 31, 1957" for "March 31, 1956" in the heading of para. (b)(2) . . . Sec. 2(4), substituted "March 31, 1957" for "March 31, 1956" in subsec. (b), effective 3/29/56.

In 1955, P.L. 18, Sec. 2(1), substituted "April 1, 1956" for "April 1, 1955" in the heading of para. (b)(1) . . . Sec. 2(2), substituted "April 1, 1956" for "April 1, 1955" in subsec. (b) . . . Sec. 2(3), substituted "March 31, 1956" for "March 31, 1955" in the heading of para. (b)(2) . . . Sec. 2(4), substituted "March 31, 1956" for "March 31, 1955" in subsec. (b), effective 3/30/55.

Sec. 12. Cross references relating to tax on corporations.

(1) For tax on the unrelated business income of certain charitable and other corporations exempt from tax under this chapter, see section 511.

(2) For accumulated earnings tax and personal holding company tax, see parts I and II of subchapter G (sec. 531 and following).

(3) For doubling of tax on corporations of certain foreign countries, see section 891.

(4) For alternative tax in case of capital gains, see section 1201(a).

(5) For rate of withholding in case of foreign corporations, see section 1442.

(6) For limitation on benefits of graduated rate schedule provided in section 11(b), see section 1551.

(7) For alternative minimum tax, see section 55.

In 1986, P.L. 99-514, Sec. 701(e)(4)(B), amended para. (7), effective for tax. yrs. begin. after 12/31/86.

Prior to amendment, para. (7) read as follows:

"(7) For minimum tax for tax preferences, see section 56."

In 1984, P.L. 98-369, Sec. 474(r)(29)(E), deleted para. (6) and redesignated paras. (7) and (8) as paras. (6) and (7), effective as provided in Sec. 475(b) of this Act, which reads as follows:

"(b) Tax-Free Covenant Bonds.

The amendments made by subsections (j) and (r)(29) of section 474 shall not apply with respect to obligations issued before January 1, 1984."

Prior to deletion, para. (6) read as follows:

"(6) For withholding of tax on tax-free covenant bonds, see section 1451."

In 1978, P.L. 95-600, Sec. 301(b)(1), amended para. (7), effective for tax. yrs. begin. after 12/31/78.

Prior to amendment, para. (7) read as follows:

"(7) For limitation on the $25,000 exemption from surtax provided in section 11(c) see section 1551."

In 1975, P.L. 94-12, Sec. 303(c)(2), substituted "$50,000" for "$25,000" in para. (7), effective for tax. yrs. end. after 12/31/74 and before 1/1/76.

In 1969, P.L. 91-172, Sec. 301(b)(3), added para. (8), effective for tax. yrs. end. after 12/31/69.

In 1964, P.L. 88-272, Sec. 234(b)(4), deleted para. (8), effective for tax. yrs. begin. after 12/31/63.

Prior to deletion, para. (8) read as follows:

"(8) For additional tax for corporations filing consolidated returns, see section 1503."

PART III.—CHANGES IN RATES DURING A TAXABLE YEAR

Sec.

15. Effect of changes.

In 1984, P.L. 98-369, Sec. 474(b)(3), redesignated item 21 as 15.

Sec. 15. Effect of changes.

(a) General rule.

If any rate of tax imposed by this chapter changes, and if the taxable year includes the effective date of the change (unless that date is the first day of the taxable year), then—

(1) tentative taxes shall be computed by applying the rate for the period before the effective date of the change, and the rate for the period on and after such date, to the taxable income for the entire taxable year; and

(2) the tax for such taxable year shall be the sum of that proportion of each tentative tax which the number of days in each period bears to the number of days in the entire taxable year.

(b) Repeal of tax.

For purposes of subsection (a)—

(1) if a tax is repealed, the repeal shall be considered a change of rate; and

(2) the rate for the period after the repeal shall be zero.

(c) Effective date of change.
For purposes of subsections (a) and (b)—
(1) if the rate changes for taxable years "beginning after" or "ending after" a certain date, the following day shall be considered the effective date of the change; and
(2) if a rate changes for taxable years "beginning on or after" a certain date, that date shall be considered the effective date of the change.

(d) Section not to apply to inflation adjustments.
This section shall not apply to any change in rates under subsection (f) of section 1 (relating to adjustments in tax tables so that inflation will not result in tax increases).

(e) References to highest rate.
If the change referred to in subsection (a) involves a change in the highest rate of tax imposed by section 1 or 11(b), any reference in this chapter to such highest rate (other than in a provision imposing a tax by reference to such rate) shall be treated as a reference to the weighted average of the highest rates before and after the change determined on the basis of the respective portions of the taxable year before the date of the change and on or after the date of the change.

⎡ • **Caution:** Code Sec. 15(f), following, was amended by P.L. 107-16, EGTRRA. These provisions generally sunset for tax years beginning after 12/31/2012. For specific sunset provisions, see Sec. 901, P.L. 107-16 (as amended) reproduced in history notes for this Code Sec. ⎦

(f) Rate reductions enacted by Economic Growth and Tax Relief Reconciliation Act of 2001.
This section shall not apply to any change in rates under subsection (i) of section 1 (relating to rate reductions after 2000).

In 2010, P.L. 111-312, Sec. 101(a), substituted "December 31, 2012" for "December 31, 2010" both places it appeared in Sec. 901, P.L. 107-16, see below, effective as if included in the enactment of P.L. 107-16, EGTRRA, 6/7/2001 [see below].

In 2002, P.L. 107-358, Sec. 2, added subsec. (c) in Sec. 901 of P.L. 107-16 [see below], effective 12/17/2002.

In 2001, P.L. 107-16, Sec. 101(c)(3), added subsec. (f), effective for tax. yrs. begin. after 12/31/2000.

—P.L. 107-16, Sec. 901, of this Act [as amended by Sec. 2, P.L. 107-358, and Sec. 101(a)(1), P.L. 111-312, see above], reads as follows:

"SEC. 901. SUNSET OF PROVISIONS OF ACT.

"(a) In general. All provisions of, and amendments made by, this Act shall not apply—

"(1) to taxable, plan, or limitation years beginning after December 31, 2012, or

"(2) in the case of title V, to estates of decedents dying, gifts made, or generation skipping transfers, after December 31, 2012.

"(b) Application of certain laws. The Internal Revenue Code of 1986 and the Employee Retirement Income Security Act of 1974 shall be applied and administered to years, estates, gifts, and transfers described in subsection (a) as if the provisions and amendments described in subsection (a) had never been enacted.

"(c) Exception. Subsection (a) shall not apply to section 803 (relating to no federal income tax on restitution received by victims of the Nazi regime or their heirs or estates)."

In 1997, P.L. 105-34, Sec. 1(c), of this Act, relating to Code Sec. 15, provides:

"(c) Section 15 Not To Apply.—No amendment made by this Act shall be treated as a change in a rate of tax for purposes of section 15 of the Internal Revenue Code of 1986."

In 1993, P.L. 103-66, Sec. 13001(c), of this Act provides:

"(c) Section 15 not to apply. Except in the case of the amendments made by section 13221 (relating to corporate rate increase), no amendment made by this chapter shall be treated as a change in a rate of tax for purposes of section 15 of the Internal Revenue Code of 1986."

In 1988, P.L. 100-647, Sec. 1006(a), added subsec. (e), effective for tax. yrs. begin. on or after 7/10/87.

In 1986, P.L. 99-514, Sec. 3(b), provides:

"(b) Coordination with section 15.

"(1) In general—Except as provided in paragraph (2), for purposes of section 15 of the Internal Revenue Code of 1986, no amendment or repeal made by this Act shall be treated as a change in the rate of a tax imposed by chapter 1 of such Code.

"(2) Exception—Paragraph (1) shall not apply to the amendment made by section 601 relating to corporate rate reductions)."

—P.L. 99-514, Sec. 101(b), amended subsec. (d), effective for tax. yrs. begin. after 12/31/86.

Prior to amendment, subsec. (d) read as follows:

"(d) Section not to apply to section 1 rate changes made by economic recovery tax act of 1981.

"This section shall not apply to any change in rates under section 1 attributable to the amendments made by section 101 of the Economic Recovery Tax Act of 1981 or subsection (f) of section 1 (relating to adjustments in tax tables so that inflation will not result in tax increases)."

In 1984, P.L. 98-369, Sec. 474(b)(1), redesignated Code Sec. 21 as Code Sec. 15, effective for tax. yrs. begin. after 12/31/83, and for carrybacks from tax. yrs. begin. after 12/31/83.

In 1983, P.L. 97-448, Sec. 101(a)(1), amended Sec. 101(f)(1) of P.L. 97-34 [the effective date for changes made by Sec. 101(d)(3), see below] by adding before the period "; except that the amendment made by paragraph (3) of subsection (d) shall apply to taxable years ending after December 31, 1981".

In 1981, P.L. 97-34, Sec. 101(d)(3), amended subsec. (d) and deleted subsecs. (e) and (f), effective [as amended by Sec. 101(a)(1) of P.L. 97-448, see above] for tax. yrs. end. after 12/31/81.

Prior to amendment, subsec. (d) read as follows:

"(d) Change in surtax exemption.

"In applying subsection (a) to a taxable year of a taxpayer which is not a calendar year, the change made by section 303(b) of the Tax Reduction Act of 1975 in the surtax exemption and any change under section 11(d) in the surtax exemption shall be treated as a change in a rate of tax."

Prior to deletion, subsecs. (e) and (f) read as follows:

"(e) Changes made by Tax Reduction and Simplification Act of 1977.

"In applying subsection (a) to a taxable year of an individual which is not a calendar year, the amendments made by sections 101 and 102 of the Tax Reduction and Simplification Act of 1977 shall not be treated as changes in a rate of tax.

"(f) Changes made by Revenue Act of 1978.

"In applying subsection (a) to a taxable year which is not a calendar year—

"(1) the amendments made by sections 101, 102, and 301 of the Revenue Act of 1978 (and no other amendments made by such Act), and

"(2) the expiration of section 42 (relating to general tax credit),

shall be treated as a change in a rate of tax."

In 1978, P.L. 95-600, Sec. 106, added subsec. (f), effective 11/6/78.

In 1977, P.L. 95-30, Sec. 101(d)(2)(A), deleted subsecs. (d) and (e)...Sec. 102(d)(2)(B), redesignated subsec. (f) as subsec. (d)...Sec. 102(d)(2)(C), added subsec. (e), effective for tax. yrs. begin. after 12/31/76.

Prior to deletion, subsecs. (d) and (e) read as follows:

"(d) Changes made by Tax Reform Act of 1969 in case of individuals.

"In applying subsection (a) to a taxable year of an individual which is not a calendar year, each change made by the Tax Reform Act of 1969 in part I or in the application of part IV or V of subchapter B for purposes of the determination of taxable income shall be treated as a change in a rate of tax.

"(e) Changes made by Revenue Act of 1971.

"In applying subsection (a) to a taxable year of an individual which is not a calendar year, each change made by the Revenue Act of 1971 in section 141 (relating to the standard deduction) and section 151 (relating to personal exemptions) shall be treated as a change in a rate of tax."

In 1976, P.L. 94-455, Sec. 901(c)(2), amended subsec. (f), effective for tax. yrs. end. after '75. For purposes of Code Sec. 21, Sec. 301(f) of the Act provides that amendments made by Sec. 301 of the Act with respect to the minimum tax shall not be treated as a change in a rate of tax.

Prior to amendment, subsec. (f) read as follows:

"(f) Change in Surtax Exemption.

"In applying subsection (a) to a taxable year of a taxpayer which is not a calendar year, the change made by section 303(b) of the Tax Reduction Act of 1975 and the change made by section 3(c) of the Revenue Adjustment Act of 1975 in section 11(d) (relating to corporate surtax exemption) shall be treated as a change in a rate of tax."

In 1975, P.L. 94-164, Sec. 4(d)(2)(A), substituted "Change" for "Increase" in the caption of subsec. (f)...Sec. 4(d)(2)(B), added "and the change made by section 3(c) of the Revenue Adjustment Act of 1975" after "Tax Reduction Act of 1975" in subsec. (f), effective for tax. yrs. begin. after 12/31/75.

—P.L. 94-12, Sec. 305(b)(2), added subsec. (f), effective 3/29/75.

In 1971, P.L. 92-178, Sec. 205, added subsec. (e), effective 11/23/71.

In 1969, P.L. 91-172, Sec. 803(e), amended subsec. (d), effective 12/30/69.

Prior to amendment, subsec. (d) read as follows:

"(d) Changes made by Revenue Act of 1964.

"(1) Individuals. In applying subsection (a) to the taxable year of an individual beginning in 1963 and ending in 1964—

"(A) the rate of tax for the period on and after January 1, 1964, shall be applied to the taxable income determined as if part IV of subchapter B (relating to standard deduction for individuals), as amended by the Revenue Act of 1964, applied to taxable years ending after December 31, 1963, and

"(B) section 4 (relating to rules for optional tax), as amended by such Act, shall be applied to taxable years ending after December 31, 1963.

Tax credits — Subpart A

In applying subsection (a) to a taxable year of an individual beginning in 1963 and ending in 1964, or beginning in 1964 and ending in 1965, the change in the tax imposed under section 3 shall be treated as a change in a rate of tax.

"(2) Corporations. In applying subsection (a) to a taxable year of a corporation beginning in 1963 and ending in 1964, if—

"(A) the surtax exemption of such corporation for such taxable year is less than $25,000 by reason of the application of section 1561 (relating to surtax exemptions in case of certain controlled corporations), or

"(B) an additional tax is imposed on the taxable income of such corporation for such taxable year by section 1562(b) (relating to additional tax in case of component members of controlled groups which elect multiple surtax exemptions),

the change in the surtax exemption, or the imposition of such additional tax, shall be treated as a change in a rate of tax taking effect on January 1, 1964."

In 1964, P.L. 88-272, Sec. 132, amended subsec. (d), effective for tax. yrs. begin. after 12/31/63.

Prior to amendment, subsec. (d) read as follows:

"(d) Taxable Years Beginning Before January 1, 1954, and Ending After December 31, 1953.

"In the case of a taxable year beginning before January 1, 1954, and ending after December 31, 1953—

"(1) subsection (a) of this section does not apply; and

"(2) in the application of subsection (j) of section 108 of the Internal Revenue Code of 1939, the provisions of such code referred to in such subsection shall be considered as continuing in effect as if this subtitle had not been enacted."

PART IV.—CREDITS AGAINST TAX

Subpart
A. Nonrefundable personal credits.
B. Foreign tax credit, etc.
C. Refundable credits.
D. Business-related credits.
E. Rules for computing investment credit.
F. Rules for computing targeted jobs credit.
G. Credit against regular tax for prior year minimum tax liability.
H. Nonrefundable credit to holders of clean renewable energy bonds.
I. Qualified tax credit bonds.
J. Build America Bonds.

In 2009, P.L. 111-5, Sec. 1531(c)(6), added item for Subpart J, effective for obligations issued after 2/17/2009.

In 2008, P.L. 110-234, Sec. 15316(c)(5), deleted the item for Subpart H and added a new item for Subpart H and I, effective for obligations issued after 5/22/2008.

In 2005, P.L. 109-58, Sec. 1303(c)(1), added the item for Subpart H, effective for bonds issued after 12/31/2005.

In 1990, P.L. 101-508, Sec. 11813(b)(26), amended the item for Subpart E.

Prior to amendment, the item for Subpart E read as follows:

"E. Rules for computing credit for investment in certain depreciable property."

In 1986, P.L. 99-514, Sec. 701(b), added Subpart G.

In 1984, P.L. 98-369, Sec. 471(a), amended items A through D . . . Sec. 474(n)(3), added items E and F.

Prior to amendment, items A through D read as follows:
"A. Credits allowable.
"B. Rules for computing credit for investment in certain depreciable property.
"C. Rules for computing credit for expenses of work incentive programs.
"D. Rules for computing credit for employment of certain new employees."

In 1977, P.L. 95-30, Sec. 202(d)(1)(B), added the item for Subpart D.
In 1971, P.L. 92-178, Sec. 601(c)(2), added Subpart C.
In 1962, P.L. 87-834, Sec. 2(g)(1), added Subparts A and B.

SUBPART A.—NONREFUNDABLE PERSONAL CREDITS

Sec.
21. Expenses for household and dependent care services necessary for gainful employment.
22. Credit for the elderly and the permanently and totally disabled.
23. Adoption expenses.
23. Repealed. [Residential energy credit.]
24. Child tax credit.
24. Repealed. [Contributions to candidates for public office.]
25. Interest on certain home mortgages.
25A. Hope and Lifetime Learning credits.
25B. Elective deferrals and IRA contributions by certain individuals.
25C. Nonbusiness energy property.
25D. Residential energy efficient property.
26. Limitation based on tax liability; definition of tax liability.

In 2005, P.L. 109-58, Sec. 1333(b)(2), added item 25C.
—P.L. 109-58, Sec. 1335(b)(5), added item 25D.
In 2001, P.L. 107-16, Sec. 618(c), added item 25B.
In 1998, P.L. 105-206, Sec. 6004(a)(1), amended item 25A.
Prior to amendment, item 25A read as follows:
"25A. Higher education tuition and related expenses."
In 1997, P.L. 105-34, Sec. 101(d)(3), added item 24. . . . Sec. 201(e), added item 25A.
In 1996, P.L. 104-188, Sec. 1807(c)(6), added item 23.
In 1990, P.L. 101-508, Sec. 11801(b)(1), deleted item 23.
Prior to deletion, item 23 read as follows:
"23. Residential energy credit."
In 1986, P.L. 99-514, Sec. 112(b)(5), deleted item 24.
Prior to deletion, item 24 read as follows:
"24. Contributions to candidates for public office."
In 1984, P.L. 98-369, Sec. 471(b), amended subpart A . . . Sec. 472, added Code Sec. 25 . . . Sec. 612(f), redesignated item 25 as 26 and added new item 25.
Prior to amendment, subpart A and items 31 through 45 read as follows:
"SUBPART A — CREDITS ALLOWABLE
"Sec.
"31. Tax withheld on wages, interest, dividends, and patronage dividends.
"32. Tax withheld at source on nonresident aliens and foreign corporations and on tax-free covenant bonds.
"33. Taxes of foreign countries and possessions of the United States.
"35. Repealed.
"36. Repealed.
"37. Credit for the elderly and the permanently and totally disabled.
"38. Investment in certain depreciable property.
"39. Certain uses of gasoline and special fuels.
"40. Expenses of work incentive programs.
"41. Contributions to candidates for public office.
"42. General tax credit.
"43. Credit for certain earned income.
"44. Credit for purchase of new principal residence.
"44A. Expenses for household and dependent care services necessary for gainful employment.
"44B. Credit for employment of certain new employees.
"44C. Residential energy credit.
"44D. Credit for producing fuel from a nonconventional source.
"44E. Alcohol used as fuel.
"44F. Credit for increasing research activities.
"44G. Employee stock ownership credit.
"45. Overpayment of tax."
In 1983, P.L. 98-21, Sec. 122(c)(7), amended item 37.
Prior to amendment, item 37 read as follows:
"37. Credit for the elderly."
—P.L. 97-424, Sec. 515(b)(6)(D), substituted "and special fuels" for "special fuels, and lubricating oil" in item 39.
In 1982, P.L. 97-248, Sec. 307(b)(3), amended item 31.
Prior amendment, item 31 read as follows:
"31. Tax withheld on wages."
In 1981, P.L. 97-34, Sec. 221(c)(2), added item 44F . . . Sec. 331(e)(2), added item 44G.
In 1980, P.L. 96-223, Sec. 231(b), added item 44D . . . Sec. 232(b)(3)(B), added item 44E.
In 1978, P.L. 95-618, Sec. 101(b)(1), added item 44C.
In 1977, P.L. 95-30, Sec. 101(e)(1), deleted the item for Code Sec. 36.
Prior to amendment, item 36 read as follows:
"36. Credits not allowed to individuals taking standard deduction."
—P.L. 95-30, Sec. 202(d)(1)(A), added the item for Code Sec. 44B.
In 1976, P.L. 94-455, Sec. 401(a)(2)(D), amended item 42.
Prior to amendment, item 42 read as follows:
"42. Taxable income credit."
—P.L. 94-455, Sec. 501(c)(2), deleted "paying optional tax or" after "individuals" in item 36.
—P.L. 94-455, Sec. 503(b)(5), amended item 37.
Prior to amendment, item 37 read as follows:
"37. Retirement income."
—P.L. 94-455, Sec. 504(a)(2), added item 44A.
—P.L. 94-455, Sec. 1901(b)(1)(Z), repealed item 35.
In 1975, P.L. 94-164, Sec. 3(a)(2), amended item 42.
Prior to amendment, item 42 read as follows:
"42. Credit for personal exemptions."
—P.L. 94-12, Sec. 203(b)(1), redesignated item 42 as 43 and added new item 42.

1,029

—P.L. 94-12, Sec. 204(c), redesignated item 43 as 44 and added new item 43.
—P.L. 94-12, Sec. 208(d)(1), redesignated item 44 as 45 and added new item 44.
In 1971, P.L. 92-178, Sec. 601(c)(2), added the heading of subpart C and items 40 and 41, and redesignated former item 40 as 42.
In 1965, P.L. 89-44, Sec. 809(d)(1), added item 39 and redesignated former item 39 as 40.
In 1964, P.L. 88-272, Sec. 201(d)(1), repealed item 34 which had dealt with the dividends received credit.
In 1962, P.L. 87-834, Sec. 2(g)(1), (2), added the headings of subparts A and B and item 38, and redesignated former item 38 as 39.

Sec. 21. Expenses for household and dependent care services necessary for gainful employment.

(a) Allowance of credit.

(1) In general. In the case of an individual for which there are 1 or more qualifying individuals (as defined in subsection (b)(1)) with respect to such individual, there shall be allowed as a credit against the tax imposed by this chapter for the taxable year an amount equal to the applicable percentage of the employment-related expenses (as defined in subsection (b)(2)) paid by such individual during the taxable year.

> • **Caution:** Code Sec. 21(a)(2), following, was amended by P.L. 107-16, EGTRRA. These provisions generally sunset for tax years beginning after 12/31/2012. For specific sunset provisions, see Sec. 901, P.L. 107-16 (as amended) reproduced in history notes for this Code Sec.

(2) Applicable percentage defined. For purposes of paragraph (1), the term "applicable percentage" means 35 percent reduced (but not below 20 percent) by 1 percentage point for each $2,000 (or fraction thereof) by which the taxpayer's adjusted gross income for the taxable year exceeds $15,000.

(b) Definitions of qualifying individual and employment-related expenses.

For purposes of this section—

(1) Qualifying individual. The term "qualifying individual" means—

(A) a dependent of the taxpayer (as defined in section 152(a)(1)) who has not attained age 13,

(B) a dependent of the taxpayer (as defined in section 152, determined without regard to subsections (b)(1), (b)(2), and (d)(1)(B)) who is physically or mentally incapable of caring for himself or herself and who has the same principal place of abode as the taxpayer for more than one-half of such taxable year, or

(C) the spouse of the taxpayer, if the spouse is physically or mentally incapable of caring for himself or herself and who has the same principal place of abode as the taxpayer for more than one-half of such taxable year.

(2) Employment-related expenses.

(A) In general. The term "employment-related expenses" means amounts paid for the following expenses, but only if such expenses are incurred to enable the taxpayer to be gainfully employed for any period for which there are 1 or more qualifying individuals with respect to the taxpayer:

(i) expenses for household services, and

(ii) expenses for the care of a qualifying individual.

Such term shall not include any amount paid for services outside the taxpayer's household at a camp where the qualifying individual stays overnight.

(B) Exception. Employment-related expenses described in subparagraph (A) which are incurred for services outside the taxpayer's household shall be taken into account only if incurred for the care of—

(i) a qualifying individual described in paragraph (1)(A), or

(ii) a qualifying individual (not described in paragraph (1)(A)) who regularly spends at least 8 hours each day in the taxpayer's household.

(C) Dependent care centers. Employment-related expenses described in subparagraph (A) which are incurred for services provided outside the taxpayer's household by a dependent care center (as defined in subparagraph (D)) shall be taken into account only if—

(i) such center complies with all applicable laws and regulations of a State or unit of local government, and

(ii) the requirements of subparagraph (B) are met.

(D) Dependent care center defined. For purposes of this paragraph, the term "dependent care center" means any facility which—

(i) provides care for more than six individuals (other than individuals who reside at the facility), and

(ii) receives a fee, payment, or grant for providing services for any of the individuals (regardless of whether such facility is operated for profit).

> • **Caution:** Code Sec. 21(c)(1)-(2), following, were amended by P.L. 107-16, EGTRRA. These provisions generally sunset for tax years beginning after 12/31/2012. For specific sunset provisions, see Sec. 901, P.L. 107-16 (as amended) reproduced in history notes for this Code Sec.

(c) Dollar limit on amount creditable.

The amount of the employment-related expenses incurred during any taxable year which may be taken into account under subsection (a) shall not exceed—

(1) $3,000 if there is 1 qualifying individual with respect to the taxpayer for such taxable year, or

(2) $6,000 if there are 2 or more qualifying individuals with respect to the taxpayer for such taxable year.

The amount determined under paragraph (1) or (2) (whichever is applicable) shall be reduced by the aggregate amount excludable from gross income under section 129 for the taxable year.

(d) Earned income limitation.

(1) In general. Except as otherwise provided in this subsection, the amount of the employment-related expenses incurred during any taxable year which may be taken into account under subsection (a) shall not exceed—

(A) in the case of an individual who is not married at the close of such year, such individual's earned income for such year, or

(B) in the case of an individual who is married at the close of such year, the lesser of such individual's earned income or the earned income of his spouse for such year.

(2) Special rule for spouse who is a student or incapable of caring for himself. In the case of a spouse who is a student or a qualifying individual described in subsection (b)(1)(C), for purposes of paragraph (1), such spouse shall be deemed for each month during which such spouse is a full-time student at an educational institution, or is such a qualifying individual, to be gainfully employed and to have earned income of not less than—

(A) $250 if subsection (c)(1) applies for the taxable year, or
(B) $500 if subsection (c)(2) applies for the taxable year.

In the case of any husband and wife, this paragraph shall apply with respect to only one spouse for any one month.

(e) Special rules.

For purposes of this section—

(1) Place of abode. An individual shall not be treated as having the same principal place of abode of the taxpayer if at any time during the taxable year of the taxpayer the relationship between the individual and the taxpayer is in violation of local law.

(2) Married couples must file joint return. If the taxpayer is married at the close of the taxable year, the credit shall be allowed under subsection (a) only if the taxpayer and his spouse file a joint return for the taxable year.

(3) Marital status. An individual legally separated from his spouse under a decree of divorce or of separate maintenance shall not be considered as married.

(4) Certain married individuals living apart. If—
(A) an individual who is married and who files a separate return—
(i) maintains as his home a household which constitutes for more than one-half of the taxable year the principal place of abode of a qualifying individual, and
(ii) furnishes over half of the cost of maintaining such household during the taxable year, and
(B) during the last 6 months of such taxable year such individual's spouse is not a member of such household, such individual shall not be considered as married.

(5) Special dependency test in case of divorced parents, etc. If—
(A) section 152(e) applies to any child with respect to any calendar year, and
(B) such child is under the age of 13 or is physically or mentally incapable of caring for himself,

in the case of any taxable year beginning in such calendar year, such child shall be treated as a qualifying individual described in subparagraph (A) or (B) of subsection (b)(1) (whichever is appropriate) with respect to the custodial parent (as defined in section 152(e)(4)(A)), and shall not be treated as a qualifying individual with respect to the noncustodial parent.

(6) Payments to related individuals. No credit shall be allowed under subsection (a) for any amount paid by the taxpayer to an individual—
(A) with respect to whom, for the taxable year, a deduction under section 151(c) (relating to deduction for personal exemptions for dependents) is allowable either to the taxpayer or his spouse, or
(B) who is a child of the taxpayer (within the meaning of section 152(f)(1)) who has not attained the age of 19 at the close of the taxable year.

For purposes of this paragraph, the term "taxable year" means the taxable year of the taxpayer in which the service is performed.

(7) Student. The term "student" means an individual who during each of 5 calendar months during the taxable year is a full-time student at an educational organization.

(8) Educational organization. The term "educational organization" means an educational organization described in section 170(b)(1)(A)(ii).

(9) Identifying information required with respect to service provider. No credit shall be allowed under subsection (a) for any amount paid to any person unless—
(A) the name, address, and taxpayer identification number of such person are included on the return claiming the credit, or
(B) if such person is an organization described in section 501(c)(3) and exempt from tax under section 501(a), the name and address of such person are included on the return claiming the credit.

In the case of a failure to provide the information required under the preceding sentence, the preceding sentence shall not apply if it is shown that the taxpayer exercised due diligence in attempting to provide the information so required.

(10) Identifying information required with respect to qualifying individuals. No credit shall be allowed under this section with respect to any qualifying individual unless the TIN of such individual is included on the return claiming the credit.

(f) Regulations.

The Secretary shall prescribe such regulations as may be necessary to carry out the purposes of this section.

In 2010, P.L. 111-312, Sec. 101(a)(1), substituted "December 31, 2012" for "December 31, 2010" both places it appeared in Sec. 901, P.L. 107-16, effective as if included in the enactment of P.L. 107-16, EGTRRA, 6/7/2001 [see below].

In 2007, P.L. 110-172, Sec. 11(a)(1), substituted "section 152(e)(4)(A)" for "section 152(e)(3)(A)" in para. (e)(5), enacted 12/29/2007.

In 2005, P.L. 109-135, Sec. 404(b), added "(as defined in section 152, determined without regard to subsections (b)(1), (b)(2), and (d)(1)(B))" after "dependent of the taxpayer" in subpara. (b)(1)(B), effective for tax. yrs. begin. after 12/31/2004 as if included in the amendments made by Sec. 201 of the Working Families Tax Relief Act of 2004, P.L. 108-311.

In 2004, P.L. 108-311, Sec. 203(a), substituted "In the case of an individual for which there are 1 or more qualifying individuals (as defined in subsection (b)(1)) with respect to such individual" for "In the case of an individual who maintains a household which includes as a member one or more qualifying individuals (as defined in subsection (b)(1))" in para. (a)(1) . . . Sec. 203(b), amended para. (b)(1) . . . Sec. 203(c), amended para. (e)(1) . . . Sec. 207(2)(A), deleted "paragraph (2) or (4) of" before "section 152(e)" in subpara. (e)(5)(A) . . . Sec. 207(2)(B), substituted "as defined in section 152(e)(3)(A)" for "within the meaning of section 152(e)(1)" in the matter following subpara. (e)(5)(B) . . . Sec. 207(3), substituted "section 152(f)(1)" for "section 151(c)(3)" in subpara. (e)(6)(B), effective for tax. yrs. begin. after 12/31/2004.

Prior to amendment, para. (b)(1) read as follows:
"(1) Qualifying individual. The term "qualifying individual" means—
"(A) a dependent of the taxpayer who is under the age of 13 and with respect to whom the taxpayer is entitled to a deduction under section 151(c),
"(B) a dependent of the taxpayer who is physically or mentally incapable of caring for himself, or
"(C) the spouse of the taxpayer, if he is physically or mentally incapable of caring for himself."

Prior to amendment, para. (e)(1) read as follows:
"(1) Maintaining household. An individual shall be treated as maintaining the household for any period only if over half the cost of maintaining a household for such period is furnished by such individual (or, if such individual is married during such period, is furnished by such individual and his spouse)."

In 2002, P.L. 107-358, Sec. 2, added subsec. (c) in Sec. 901 of P.L. 107-16 [see below], effective 12/17/2002.

—P.L. 107-147, Sec. 418(b)(1), substituted "$250" for "$200" in subpara. (d)(2)(A) . . . Sec. 418(b)(2), substituted "$500" for "$400" in subpara. (d)(2)(B), effective for tax. yrs. begin. after 12/31/2002.

In 2001, P.L. 107-16, Sec. 204(a)(1), substituted "$3,000" for "$2,400" in para. (c)(1) . . . Sec. 204(a)(2), substituted "$6,000" for "$4,800" in para. (c)(2) . . . Sec. 204(b)(1), substituted "35 percent" for "30 percent" in para. (a)(2) . . . Sec. 204(b)(2), substituted "$15,000" for "$10,000" in para. (a)(2), effective for tax. yrs. begin. after 12/31/2002.

—P.L. 107-16, Sec. 901, of this Act [as amended by Sec. 2 of P.L. 107-358, and Sec. 101(a)(1), P.L. 111-312, see above], reads as follows:
"SEC. 901. SUNSET OF PROVISIONS OF ACT.
"(a) In general. All provisions of, and amendments made by, this Act shall not apply—
"(1) to taxable, plan, or limitation years beginning after December 31, 2012, or
"(2) in the case of title V, to estates of decedents dying, gifts made, or generation skipping transfers, after December 31, 2012.
"(b) Application of certain laws. The Internal Revenue Code of 1986 and the Employee Retirement Income Security Act of 1974 shall be applied and adminis-

tered to years, estates, gifts, and transfers described in subsection (a) as if the provisions and amendments described in subsection (a) had never been enacted.

"(c) Exception. Subsection (a) shall not apply to section 803 (relating to no federal income tax on restitution received by victims of the Nazi regime or their heirs or estates)."

In **1996**, P.L. 104-188, Sec. 1615(b), added para. (e)(10), effective as provided in Sec. 1615(d), of this Act, which reads as follows:

"(d) Effective date.

"(1) In general. The amendments made by this section shall apply with respect to returns the due date of which (without regard to extensions) is on or after the 30th day after the date of the enactment of this Act.

"(2) Special rule for 1995 and 1996. In the case of returns for taxable years beginning in 1995 or 1996, a taxpayer shall not be required by the amendments made by this section to provide a taxpayer identification number for a child who is born after October 31, 1995, in the case of a taxable year beginning in 1995 or November 30, 1996, in the case of a taxable year beginning in 1996."

In **1988**, P.L. 100-647, Sec. 2004(a), added Sec. 10101(b)(2) of P.L. 100-203, special rules for changes made by Sec. 10101(a) of P.L. 100-203 [see below].

—P.L. 100-485, Sec. 703(a), substituted "age of 13" for "age of 15" in subparas. (b)(1)(A) and (e)(5)(B)... Sec. 703(b), added the last sentence of subsec. (c)... Sec. 703(c)(1), added para. (e)(9), effective for tax. yrs. begin. after 12/31/88.

In **1987**, P.L. 100-203, Sec. 10101(a), added the last sentence of subpara. (b)(2)(A), effective for expenses paid in tax. yrs. begin. after 12/31/87. Sec. 10101(b)(2) of this Act [as added by Sec. 2004(a) of P.L. 100-647, see above] provides:

"(2) Special rule for cafeteria plans. For purposes of section 125 of the Internal Revenue Code of 1986, a plan shall not be treated as failing to be a cafeteria plan solely because under the plan a participant elected before January 1, 1988, to receive reimbursement under the plan for dependent care assistance for periods after December 31, 1987, and such assistance included reimbursement for expenses at a camp where the dependent stays overnight."

In **1986**, P.L. 99-514, Sec. 104(b)(1)(A), substituted "section 151(c)" for "section 151(e)" in subparas. (b)(1)(A) and (e)(6)(A)... Sec. 104(b)(1)(B), substituted "section 151(c)(3)" for "section 151(e)(3)" in subpara. (e)(6)(B), effective for tax. yrs. begin. after 12/31/86.

In **1984**, P.L. 98-369, Sec. 423(c)(4), amended para. (f)(5) [(e)(5) after redesignation by Sec. 474(c)(1) of this Act, see below], effective for tax. yrs. begin. after 12/31/84.

Prior to amendment, para. (e)(5) read as follows:

"(5) Special dependency test in case of divorced parents, etc. If—

"(A) a child (as defined in section 151(e)(3)) who is under the age of 15 or who is physically or mentally incapable of caring for himself receives over half of his support during the calendar year from his parents who are divorced or legally separated under a decree of divorce or separate maintenance or who are separated under a written separation agreement, and

"(B) such child is in the custody of one or both of his parents for more than one-half of the calendar year,

in the case of any taxable year beginning in such calendar year such child shall be treated as being a qualifying individual described in subparagraph (A) or (B) of subsection (b)(1), as the case may be, with respect to that parent who has custody for a longer period during such calendar year than the other parent, and shall not be treated as being a qualifying individual with respect to such other parent."

—P.L. 98-369, Sec. 471(c), redesignated Code Sec. 44A as Code Sec. 21... Sec. 474(c)(1), deleted subsec. (b) and redesignated subsecs. (c), (d), (e), (f) and (g) as subsecs. (b), (c), (d), (e) and (f),... Sec. 474(c)(2), substituted "subsection (b)(1)" for "subsection (c)(1)" in subsec. (a)... Sec. 474(c)(3), substituted "subsection (b)(2)" for "subsection (c)(2)" in subsec. (a)... Sec. 474(c)(4), substituted "subsection (b)(1)(C)" for "subsection (c)(1)(C)" in para. (d)(2) [as redesignated]... Sec. 474(c)(5), substituted "subsection (c)(1)" for "subsection (d)(1)" in subpara. (d)(2)(A) [as redesignated]... Sec. 474(c)(6), substituted "subsection (c)(2)" for "subsection (d)(2)" in subpara. (d)(2)(B) [as redesignated] ... Sec. 474(c)(7), substituted "subsection (b)(1)" for "subsection (c)(1)" in para. (e)(5) [as redesignated], effective for tax. yrs. begin. after 12/31/83 and for carrybacks from tax. yrs. begin. after 12/31/83.

Prior to deletion, subsec. (b) read as follows

"(b) Application with other credits. The credit allowed by subsection (a) shall not exceed the amount of the tax imposed by this chapter for the taxable year reduced by the sum of the credits allowable under—

"(1) section 33 (relating to foreign tax credit),

"(2) section 37 (relating to credit for the elderly and the permanently and totally disabled),

"(3) section 38 (relating to investment in certain depreciable property),

"(4) section 40 (relating to expenses of work incentive programs),

"(5) section 41 (relating to contributions to candidates for public office,

"(6) section 42 (relating to general tax credit), and

"(7) section 44 (relating to purchase of new principal residence)."

In **1983**, P.L. 98-21, Sec. 122(c)(1), substituted "relating to credit for the elderly and the permanently and totally disabled" for "relating to credit for the elderly" in para. (b)(2), effective for tax. yrs. begin. after 12/31/83.

In **1981**, P.L. 97-34, Sec. 124(a), amended subsec. (a), effective for tax. yrs. begin. after 12/31/81.

Prior to amendment, subsec. (a) read as follows:

"(a) Allowance of credit. In the case of an individual who maintains a household which includes as a member one or more qualifying individuals (as defined in subsection (c)(1)), there shall be allowed as a credit against the tax imposed by this chapter for the taxable year an amount equal to 20 percent of the employment-related expenses (as defined in subsection (c)(2)) paid by such individual during the taxable year."

—P.L. 97-34, Sec. 124(b)(1), substituted "$2,400" for "$2,000" and "$4,800" for "$4,000" in subsec. (d)... Sec. 124(b)(2), substituted "$200" for "$166" and "$400" for "$333" in para. (e)(2), effective for tax. yrs. begin after 12/31/81.

—P.L. 97-34, Sec. 124(c), amended subpara. (c)(2)(B)... Sec. 124(d), added new subpara. (c)(2)(C) and (D), effective for tax. yrs. begin. after 12/31/81.

Prior to amendment, subpara. (c)(2)(B) read as follows:

"(B) Exception. Employment-related expenses described in subparagraph (A) which are incurred for services outside the taxpayer's household shall be taken into account only if incurred for the care of a qualifying individual described in paragraph (1)(A)."

In **1978**, P.L. 95-600, Sec. 121(a), amended para. (f)(6), effective for tax. yrs. begin. after 12/31/78.

Prior to amendment, para. (f)(6) read as follows:

"(6) Payments to related individuals.

"(A) In general, Except as provided in subparagraph (B), no credit shall be allowed under subsection (a) for any amount paid by the taxpayer to an individual bearing a relationship to the taxpayer described in paragraphs (1) through (8) of section 152(a) (relating to definition of dependent) or to a dependent described in paragraph (9) of such section.

"(B) Exception. Subparagraph (A) shall not apply to any amount paid by the taxpayer to an individual with respect to whom, for the taxable year of the taxpayer in which the service is performed, neither the taxpayer nor his spouse is entitled to a deduction under section 151(e) (relating to deduction for personal exemptions for dependents), but only if the service with respect to which such amount is paid constitutes employment within the meaning of section 3121(b)."

In **1976**, P.L. 94-455, Sec. 504(a)(1), added Code Sec. 44A, effective for tax. yrs. begin. after 12/31/75.

Sec. 22. Credit for the elderly and the permanently and totally disabled.

(a) General rule.

In the case of a qualified individual, there shall be allowed as a credit against the tax imposed by this chapter for the taxable year an amount equal to 15 percent of such individual's section 22 amount for such taxable year.

(b) Qualified individual.

For purposes of this section, the term "qualified individual" means any individual—

(1) who has attained age 65 before the close of the taxable year, or

(2) who retired on disability before the close of the taxable year and who, when he retired, was permanently and totally disabled.

(c) Section 22 amount.

For purposes of subsection (a)—

(1) In general. An individual's section 22 amount for the taxable year shall be the applicable initial amount determined under paragraph (2), reduced as provided in paragraph (3) and in subsection (d).

(2) Initial amount

(A) In general. Except as provided in subparagraph (B), the initial amount shall be—

(i) $5,000 in the case of a single individual, or a joint return where only one spouse is a qualified individual,

(ii) $7,500 in the case of a joint return where both spouses are qualified individuals, or

(iii) $3,750 in the case of a married individual filing a separate return.

(B) Limitation in case of individuals who have not attained age 65.

(i) In general. In the case of a qualified individual who has not attained age 65 before the close of the taxable year, except as provided in clause (ii), the initial amount shall not exceed the disability income for the taxable year.

(ii) Special rules in case of joint return. In the case of a joint return where both spouses are qualified individuals and at least one spouse has not attained age 65 before the close of the taxable year—

Tax credits
Code Sec. 22

(I) if both spouses have not attained age 65 before the close of the taxable year, the initial amount shall not exceed the sum of such spouses' disability income, or

(II) if one spouse has attained age 65 before the close of the taxable year, the initial amount shall not exceed the sum of $5,000 plus the disability income for the taxable year of the spouse who has not attained age 65 before the close of the taxable year.

(iii) *Disability income.* For purposes of this subparagraph, the term "disability income" means the aggregate amount includable in the gross income of the individual for the taxable year under section 72 or 105(a) to the extent such amount constitutes wages (or payments in lieu of wages) for the period during which the individual is absent from work on account of permanent and total disability.

(3) Reduction.

(A) *In general.* The reduction under this paragraph is an amount equal to the sum of the amounts received by the individual (or, in the case of a joint return, by either spouse) as a pension or annuity or as a disability benefit—

(i) which is excluded from gross income and payable under—

(I) title II of the Social Security Act,

(II) the Railroad Retirement Act of 1974, or

(III) a law administered by the Veterans' Administration, or

(ii) which is excluded from gross income under any provision of law not contained in this title.

No reduction shall be made under clause (i)(III) for any amount described in section 104(a)(4).

(B) *Treatment of certain workmen's compensation benefits.* For purposes of subparagraph (A), any amount treated as a social security benefit under section 86(d)(3) shall be treated as a disability benefit received under title II of the Social Security Act.

(d) Adjusted gross income limitation.

If the adjusted gross income of the taxpayer exceeds—

(1) $7,500 in the case of a single individual,

(2) $10,000 in the case of a joint return, or

(3) $5,000 in the case of a married individual filing a separate return,

the section 22 amount shall be reduced by one-half of the excess of the adjusted gross income over $7,500, $10,000, or $5,000, as the case may be.

(e) Definitions and special rules.

For purposes of this section—

(1) Married couple must file joint return. Except in the case of a husband and wife who live apart at all times during the taxable year, if the taxpayer is married at the close of the taxable year, the credit provided by this section shall be allowed only if the taxpayer and his spouse file a joint return for the taxable year.

(2) Marital status. Marital status shall be determined under section 7703.

(3) Permanent and total disability defined. An individual is permanently and totally disabled if he is unable to engage in any substantial gainful activity by reason of any medically determinable physical or mental impairment which can be expected to result in death or which has lasted or can be expected to last for a continuous period of not less than 12 months. An individual shall not be considered to be permanently and totally disabled unless he furnishes proof of the existence thereof in such form and manner, and at such times, as the Secretary may require.

(f) Nonresident alien ineligible for credit.

No credit shall be allowed under this section to any nonresident alien.

In 1986, P.L. 99-514, Sec. 1301(j)(8), substituted "section 7703" for "section 143" in para. (e)(2), effective for bonds issued after 8/15/86.

In 1984, P.L. 98-369, Sec. 471(c)(1), redesignated Code Sec. 37 as Code Sec. 22 ... Sec. 474(d)(1), substituted "section 22 amount" for "section 37 amount" each place it appeared in Code Sec. 22 ... Sec. 474(d)(2), substituted "Section 22" for "Section 37" in the heading of subsec. (c) ... Sec. 474(d)(3), amended subsec. (d), effective for tax. yrs. begin. after 12/31/83 and for carrybacks from tax. yrs. begin. after 12/31/83.

Prior to amendment, subsec. (d) read as follows:

"(d) Limitations.

"(1) Adjusted gross income limitation. If the adjusted gross income of the taxpayer exceeds—

"(A) $7,500 in the case of a single individual,

"(B) $10,000 in the case of a joint return, or

"(C) $5,000 in the case of a married individual filing a separate return,

the section 22 amount shall be reduced by one-half of the excess of the adjusted gross income over $7,500, $10,000, or $5,000, as the case may be.

"(2) Limitation based on amount of tax. The amount of the credit allowed by this section for the taxable year shall not exceed the amount of the tax imposed by this chapter for such taxable year."

In 1983, P.L. 98-21, Sec. 122(a), amended Code Sec. 37, effective for tax yrs. begin. after 12/31/83. Sec. 122(d)(2) of this Act provides:

"(2) Transitional rule. If an individual's annuity starting date was deferred under section 105(d)(6) of the Internal Revenue Code of 1954 (as in effect on the day before the date of the enactment of this section), such deferral shall end on the first day of such individual's first taxable year beginning after December 31, 1983."

Prior to amendment, Code Sec. 37 read as follows:

"SEC. 37. CREDIT FOR THE ELDERLY.

"(a) General rule. In the case of an individual who has attained age 65 before the close of the taxable year, there shall be allowed as a credit against the tax imposed by this chapter for the taxable year an amount equal to 15 percent of such individual's section 37 amount for such taxable year.

"(b) Section 37 amount. For purposes of subsection (a)—

"(1) In general. An individual's section 37 amount for the taxable year is the applicable initial amount determined under paragraph (2), reduced as provided in paragraph (3) and in subsection (c).

"(2) Initial amount. The initial amount is—

"(A) $2,500 in the case of a single individual,

"(B) $2,500 in the case of a joint return where only one spouse is eligible for the credit under subsection (a),

"(C) $3,750 in the case of a joint return where both spouses are eligible for the credit under subsection (a), or

"(D) $1,875 in the case of a married individual filing a separate return.

"(3) Reduction. The reduction under this paragraph is an amount equal to the sum of the amounts received by the individual (or, in the case of a joint return, by either spouse) as a pension or annuity—

"(A) under title II of the Social Security Act,

"(B) under the Railroad Retirement Act of 1935 or 1937, or

"(C) otherwise excluded from gross income.

No reduction shall be made under this paragraph for any amount excluded from gross income under section 72 (relating to annuities), 101 (relating to life insurance proceeds), 104 (relating to compensation for injuries or sickness), 105 (relating to amounts received under accident and health plans), 120 (relating to amounts received under qualified group legal services plans), 402 (relating to taxability of beneficiary of employees' trust), 403 (relating to taxation of employee annuities), or 405 (relating to qualified bond purchase plans).

"(c) Limitations.

"(1) Adjusted gross income limitation. If the adjusted gross income of the taxpayer exceeds—

"(A) $7,500 in the case of a single individual

"(B) $10,000 in the case of a joint return, or

"(C) $5,000 in the case of a married individual filing a separate return,

the section 37 amount shall be reduced by one-half of the excess of the adjusted gross income over $7,500, $10,000, or $5,000, as the case may be.

"(2) Limitation based on amount of tax. The amount of the credit allowed by this section for the taxable year shall not exceed the amount of the tax imposed by this chapter for such taxable year.

"(d) Definitions and special rules. For purposes of this section—

"(1) Married couple must file joint return. Except in the case of a husband and wife who live apart at all times during the taxable year, if the taxpayer is married at the close of the taxable year, the credit provided by this section shall be allowed only if the taxpayer and his spouse file a joint return for the taxable year.

"(2) Marital status. Marital status shall be determined under section 143.

"(3) Joint return. The term 'joint return' means the joint return of a husband and wife made under section 6013.

"(e) Election of prior law with respect to public retirement system income.

"(1) In general. In the case of a taxpayer who has not attained age 65 before the close of the taxable year (other than a married individual whose spouse has attained age 65 before the close of the taxable year), his credit (if any) under this section shall be determined under this subsection.

"(2) One spouse age 65 or over. In the case of a married individual who has not attained age 65 before the close of the taxable year (and whose gross income includes income described in paragraph (4)(B)) but whose spouse has attained such age, this paragraph shall apply for the taxable year only if both spouses elect, at such time and in such manner as the Secretary shall by regulations prescribe, to have this paragraph apply. If this paragraph applies for the taxable year, the credit (if any) of each spouse under this section shall be determined under this subsection.

"(3) Computation of credit. In the case of an individual whose credit under this section for the taxable year is determined under this subsection, there shall be allowed as a credit against the tax imposed by this chapter for the taxable year an amount equal to 15 percent of the amount received by such individual as retirement income (as defined in paragraph (4) and as limited by paragraph (5)).

"(4) Retirement income. For purposes of this subsection, the term 'retirement income' means—

"(A) in the case of an individual who has attained age 65 before the close of the taxable year, income from—

"(i) pensions and annuities (including, in the case of an individual who is, or has been, an employee within the meaning of section 401(c)(1), distributions by a trust described in section 401(a) which is exempt from tax under section 501(a)),

"(ii) interest,

"(iii) rents,

"(iv) dividends,

"(v) bonds described in section 405(b)(1) which are received under a qualified bond purchase plan described in section 405(a) or in a distribution from a trust described in section 401(a) which is exempt from tax under section 501(a), or retirement bonds described in section 409, and

"(vi) an individual retirement account described in section 408(a) or an individual retirement annuity described in section 408(b), or

"(B) in the case of an individual who has not attained age 65 before the close of the taxable year, and who performed the services giving rise to the pension or annuity (or is the spouse of the individual who performed the services) income from pensions and annuities under a public retirement system (as defined in paragraph (9)(A)),

to the extent included in gross income without reference to this subsection, but only to the extent such income does not represent compensation for personal services rendered during the taxable year.

"(5) Limitation on retirement income. For purposes of this subsection, the amount of retirement income shall not exceed $2,500 less—

"(A) the reduction provided by subsection (b)(3), and

"(B) in the case of any individual who has not attained age 72 before the close of the taxable year—

"(i) if such individual has not attained age 62 before the close of the taxable year, any amount of earned income (as defined in paragraph (9)(B)) in excess of $900 received by such individual in the taxable year, or

"(ii) if such individual has attained age 62 before the close of the taxable year, the sum of one-half the amount of earned income received by such individual in the taxable year in excess of $1,200 but not in excess of $1,700, and the amount of earned income so received in excess of $1,700.

"(6) Limitation in case of married individuals. In the case of a joint return, paragraph (5) shall be applied by substituting '$3,750' for '$2,500'. The $3,750 provided by the preceding sentence shall be divided between the spouses in such amounts as may be agreed on by them, except that not more than $2,500 may be assigned to either spouse.

"(7) Limitation in the case of separate returns. In the case of a married individual filing a separate return, paragraph (5) shall be applied by substituting '$1,875' for '$2,500'.

"(8) Community property laws not applicable. In the case of a joint return, this subsection shall be applied without regard to community property laws.

"(9) Definitions. For purposes of this subsection—

"(A) Public retirement system defined. The term 'public retirement system' means a pension, annuity, retirement, or similar fund or system established by the United States, a State, a possession of the United States, any political subdivision of any of the foregoing, or the District of Columbia.

"(B) Earned income. The term 'earned income' has the meaning assigned to such term by section 911(d)(2), except that such term does not include any amount received as a pension or annuity.

"(f) Nonresident alien ineligible for credit. "No credit shall be allowed under this section to any nonresident alien."

In **1981**, P.L. 97-34, Sec. 111(b)(4), substituted "section 911(d)(2)" for "section 911(b)" in subpara. (e)(9)(B), effective for tax. yrs. begin. after 12/31/81.

In **1980**, P.L. 96-222, Sec. 107(a)(1)(E)(i), corrected Sec. 701(a)(3) of P.L. 95-600, to amend subsec. (e) instead of subsec. (c) [see below].

In **1978**, P.L. 95-600, Sec. 701(a)(1), substituted "who has not attained age 65 before the close of the taxable year (and whose gross income includes income described in paragraph (4)(B))" for "who has not attained age 65 before the close of the taxable year" in para. (e)(2) . . . Sec. 701(a)(2), added "and who performed the services giving rise to the pension or annuity (or is the spouse of the individual who performed the services)" after "before the close of the taxable year" in subpara. (e)(4)(B), effective for tax. yrs. begin. after 12/31/75.

—P.L. 95-600, Sec. 701(a)(3)(A), redesignated para. (c)(8) [sic (e)(8), see Sec. 107(a)(1)(E)(i) of P.L. 96-222 above] as para. (c)(9) [sic (e)(9), see above] and added new para. (c)(8) [sic (e)(8), see above] . . . Sec. 701(a)(3)(B), substituted "paragraph (9)(A)" for "paragraph (8)(A)" in subpara. (c)(4)(B) [sic (e)(4)(B), see above] . . . Sec. 701(a)(3)(C), substituted "paragraph (9)(B)" for "paragraph (8)(B)" in subpara. (c)(5)(B) [sic (e)(5)(B), see above], effective for tax. yrs. begin. after 12/31/77.

—P.L. 95-600, Sec. 703(j)(11), deleted Sec. 1901(c)(1) of P.L. 94-455 [see below], effective 11/6/78.

In **1977**, P.L. 95-30, Sec. 403, provides the following:

"Sec. 403. Election of Former Retirement Income Credit Provisions for 1976.

"A taxpayer may elect (at such time and in such manner as the Secretary of the Treasury or his delegate shall prescribe) to determine the amount of his credit under section 37 of the Internal Revenue Code of 1954 for his first taxable year beginning in 1976 under the provisions of such section as they existed before the amendment made by section 503 of the Tax Reform Act of 1976."

In **1976**, P.L. 94-455, Sec. 1901(c)(1), deleted "a Territory," in subsec. (f), effective for tax. yrs. begin. after 12/31/76. [This amendment deleted by Sec. 703(j)(11) of P.L. 95-600, see above]

—P.L. 94-455, Sec. 503(a), amended Code Sec. 37, effective for tax. yrs. begin. after 12/31/75.

Prior to amendment, Code Sec. 37 read as follows:

"Sec. 37. Retirement income.

"(a) General rule. In the case of an individual who has received earned income before the beginning of the taxable year, there shall be allowed as a credit against the tax imposed by this chapter for the taxable year an amount equal to 17 percent, in the case of a taxable year beginning in 1964, or 15 percent, in the case of a taxable year beginning after December 31, 1964, of the amount received by such individual as retirement income (as defined in subsection (c) and as limited by subsection (d)); but this credit shall not exceed such tax reduced by the credits allowable under section 32(2) (relating to tax withheld at source on tax-free covenant bonds), section 33 (relating to foreign tax credit), and section 35 (relating to partially tax exempt interest).

"(b) Individual who has received earned income. For purposes of subsection (a), an individual shall be considered to have received earned income if he has received, in each of any 10 calendar years before the taxable year, earned income (as defined in subsection (g)) in excess of $600. A widow or widower whose spouse had received such earned income shall be considered to have received earned income.

"(c) Retirement income. For purposes of subsection (a), the term 'retirement income' means—

"(1) in the case of an individual who has attained the age of 65 before the close of the taxable year, income from—

"(A) pensions and annuities (including in the case of an individual who is, or has been, an employee within the meaning of section 401(c)(1), distributions by a trust described in section 401(a) which is exempt from tax under section 501(a)),

"(B) interest,

"(C) rents,

"(D) dividends,

"(E) bonds described in section 405(b)(1) which are received under a qualified bond purchase plan described in section 405(a) or in a distribution from a trust described in section 401(a) which is exempt from tax under section 501(a), or retirement bonds described in section 409, and

"(F) an individual retirement account described in section 408(a) or an individual retirement annuity described in section 408(b), or

"(2) in the case of an individual who has not attained the age of 65 before the close of the taxable year, income from pensions and annuities under a public retirement system (as defined in subsection (f)),

to the extent included in gross income without reference to this section, but only to the extent such income does not represent compensation for personal services rendered during the taxable year.

"(d) Limitation on retirement income. For purposes of subsection (a), the amount of retirement income shall not exceed $1,524 less—

"(1) in the case of any individual, any amount received by the individual as a pension or annuity—

"(A) under title II of the Social Security Act,

"(B) under the Railroad Retirement Acts of 1935 or 1937, or

"(C) otherwise excluded from gross income, and

"(2) in the case of any individual who has not attained age 72 before the close of the taxable year—

"(A) if such individual has not attained age 62 before the close of the taxable year, any amount of earned income (as defined in subsection (g)) in excess of $900 received by such individual in the taxable year, or

"(B) if such individual has attained age 62 before the close of the taxable year, the sum of (i) one-half the amount of earned income received by such individual in the taxable year in excess of $1,200 but not in excess of $1,700, and (ii) the amount of earned income so received in excess of $1,700.

"(e) Rule for application for subsection (d)(1). Subsection (d)(1) shall not apply to any amount excluded from gross income under section 72 (relating to annuities), 101 (relating to life insurance proceeds), 104 (relating to compensation for injuries or sickness), 105 (relating to amounts received under accident and health plans), 402 (relating to taxability of beneficiary of employees' trust), or 403 (relating to taxation of employee annuities).

"(f) Public retirement system defined. For purposes of subsection (c)(2), the term 'public retirement system' means a pension, annuity, retirement, or similar fund or system established by the United States, a State, a Territory, a possession of the United States, any political subdivision of any of the foregoing, or the District of Columbia.

Tax credits Code Sec. 23(b)(2)(B)

"(g) Earned income defined. For purposes of subsections (b) and (d)(2), the term 'earned income' has the meaning assigned to such term in section 911(b), except that such term does not include any amount received as a pension or annuity.

"(h) Nonresident alien ineligible for credit. No credit shall be allowed under subsection (a) to any nonresident alien.

"(i) Special rules for certain married couples.

"(1) Election. A husband and wife who make a joint return for the taxable year and both of whom have attained the age of 65 before the close of the taxable year may elect (at such time and in such manner as the Secretary or his delegate by regulations prescribes) to determine the amount of the credit allowed by subsection (a) by applying the provisions of paragraph (2).

"(2) Special rules. If an election is made under paragraph (1) for the taxable year, for purposes of subsection (a)—

"(A) if either spouse is an individual who has received earned income within the meaning of subsection (b), the other spouse shall be considered to be an individual who has received earned income within the meaning of such subsection; and

"(B) subsection (d) shall be considered as providing that the amount of the combined retirement income of both spouses shall not exceed $2,286, less the sum of the amounts specified in paragraphs (1) and (2) of subsection (d) for each spouse.

"(j) Cross reference. For disallowance of credit where tax is computed by Secretary or his delegate, see section 6014(a)."

In **1974**, P.L. 93-406, Sec. 2002(g)(1)(A), deleted "and" at the end of subpara. (c)(1)(D) . . . Sec. 2002(g)(1)(B), added "retirement bonds described in section 409, and" at the end of subpara. (c)(1)(E) . . . Sec. 2002(g)(1)(C), added subpara. (c)(1)(F), effective 1/1/75.

In **1964**, P.L. 88-272, Sec. 113(a), substituted "an amount equal to 17 percent, in the case of a taxable year beginning in 1964, or 15 percent, in the case of a taxable year beginning after December 31, 1964, of the amount received by such individual as retirement income (as defined in subsection (c) and as limited by subsection (d));" for "an amount equal to the amount received by such individual as retirement income (as defined in subsection (c) and as limited by subsection (d)), multiplied by the rate provided in section 1 for the first $2,000 of taxable income;" in subsec. (a), effective for tax. yrs. begin. after 12/31/63.

—P.L. 88-272, Sec. 201(d)(3), deleted "section 34 (relating to credit for dividends received by individuals)," in subsec. (a), effective for dividends received after 12/31/64 in tax. yrs. end. after 12/31/64.

—P.L. 88-272, Sec. 202(a), redesignated subsec. (i) as subsec. (j) and added new subsec. (i), effective for tax. yrs. begin. after 12/31/63.

In **1962**, P.L. 87-792, Sec. 7(a)(1), amended subpara. (c)(1)(A) . . . Sec. 7(a)(2), deleted "and" at the end of subpara. (c)(1)(C), substituted "and" for "or" at the end of subpara. (c)(1)(D) and added subpara. (c)(1)(E), effective for tax. yrs. begin. after 12/31/62.

Prior to amendment, subpara. (c)(1)(A) read as follows:

"(A) pension and annuities,"

—P.L. 87-876, Sec. 1, amended subsec. (d), effective for tax. yrs. end. after 10/24/62.

Prior to amendment, subsec. (d) read as follows:

"(d) Limitation on retirement income. For purposes of subsection (a) the amount of retirement income shall not exceed $1,200 less—

"(1) in the case of any individual, any amount received by the individual as a pension or annuity—

"(A) under title II of the Social Security Act,

"(B) under the Railroad Retirement Acts of 1935 or 1937, or

"(C) otherwise excluded from gross income, and

"(2) in the case of any individual who has not attained the age of 72 before the close of the taxable year, any amount of earned income (as defined in subsection (g))—

"(A) in excess of $900 received by the individual in the taxable year if such individual has not attained the age of 65 before the close of the taxable year, or

"(B) in excess of $1,200 received by the individual in the taxable year if such individual has attained the age of 65 before the close of the taxable year."

In **1956**, P.L. 398, Sec. 1, amended para. (d)(2), effective for tax. yrs, begin. after 12/31/55.

Prior to amendment, para. (d)(2) read as follows:

"(2) in the case of any individual who has not attained the age of 75 before the close of the taxable year, any amount of earned income (as defined in subsection (g)) in excess of $900 received by the individual in the taxable year."

In **1955**, P.L. 299, Sec. 1, deleted "; except that such term does not include a fund or system established by the United States for members of the Armed Forces of the United States" in subsec. (f), effective for tax. yrs. begin. after 12/31/54.

Sec. 23. Adoption expenses.

• **Caution:** Code Sec. 23, was redesignated as Code Sec. 36C and further amended by Sec. 10909, P.L. 111-148. As provided in Sec. 10909(c), P.L. 111-148 as amended by Sec. 101(b)(1), P.L. 111-312, these amendments will read as if never enacted, effective for tax. yrs. begin. after 12/31/2011. Following is Code Sec. 23 as it will read for tax. yrs. begin. after 12/31/2011. See Code Sec. 36C for how it reads for tax years beginning before 1/1/2012.

(a) Allowance of credit.

• **Caution:** Code Sec. 23(a)(1)-(2), following, was amended by P.L. 107-16, the Economic Growth and Tax Relief Reconciliation Act of 2001 (EGTRRA). These provisions generally sunset for tax years beginning after 12/31/2012. For specific sunset provisions, see Sec. 901, P.L. 107-16 (as amended) reproduced in history notes for this Code Sec.

(1) In general. In the case of an individual, there shall be allowed as a credit against the tax imposed by this chapter the amount of the qualified adoption expenses paid or incurred by the taxpayer.

(2) Year credit allowed. The credit under paragraph (1) with respect to any expense shall be allowed—

(A) in the case of any expense paid or incurred before the taxable year in which such adoption becomes final, for the taxable year following the taxable year during which such expense is paid or incurred, and

(B) in the case of an expense paid or incurred during or after the taxable year in which such adoption becomes final, for the taxable year in which such expense is paid or incurred.

(3) $10,000 credit for adoption of child with special needs regardless of expenses. In the case of an adoption of a child with special needs which becomes final during a taxable year, the taxpayer shall be treated as having paid during such year qualified adoption expenses with respect to such adoption in an amount equal to the excess (if any) of $10,000 over the aggregate qualified adoption expenses actually paid or incurred by the taxpayer with respect to such adoption during such taxable year and all prior taxable years.

• **Caution:** Paras. (b)(1) and (b)(2), following, were amended by P.L. 107-16, EGTRRA. These provisions generally sunset for tax years beginning after 12/31/2012. For specific sunset provisions, see Sec. 901, P.L. 107-16 (as amended) reproduced in history notes for this Code Sec.

(b) Limitations.

(1) Dollar limitation. The aggregate amount of qualified adoption expenses which may be taken into account under subsection (a) for all taxable years with respect to the adoption of a child by the taxpayer shall not exceed $10,000.

(2) Income limitation.

(A) In general. The amount allowable as a credit under subsection (a) for any taxable year (determined without regard to subsection (c)) shall be reduced (but not below zero) by an amount which bears the same ratio to the amount so allowable (determined without regard to this paragraph but with regard to paragraph (1)) as—

(i) the amount (if any) by which the taxpayer's adjusted gross income exceeds $150,000, bears to

(ii) $40,000.

(B) Determination of adjusted gross income. For purposes of subparagraph (A), adjusted gross income shall be determined without regard to sections 911, 931, and 933.

(3) Denial of double benefit.
(A) In general. No credit shall be allowed under subsection (a) for any expense for which a deduction or credit is allowed under any other provision of this chapter.
(B) Grants. No credit shall be allowed under subsection (a) for any expense to the extent that funds for such expense are received under any Federal, State, or local program.

> • *Caution:* Code Sec. 23(b)(4), added by P.L. 107-16 and amended by P.L. 109-135, following, is not effective for tax. yrs. begin. during 2002, 2003, 2004, or 2005 as provided by Sec. 601(b)(2) of P.L. 107-147 and Sec. 312(b)(2) of P.L. 108-311. For sunset provisions, see Sec. 901 of P.L. 107-16 and Sec. 402(i)(3)(H) of P.L. 109-135 reproduced in the history of this Code Sec.

(4) Limitation based on amount of tax. In the case of a taxable year to which section 26(a)(2) does not apply, the credit allowed under subsection (a) for any taxable year shall not exceed the excess of—
(A) the sum of the regular tax liability (as defined in section 26(b)) plus the tax imposed by section 55, over
(B) the sum of the credits allowable under this subpart (other than this section and section 25D) and section 27 for the taxable year.

> • *Caution:* Code Sec. 23(c), following, was amended by P.L. 109-135. For sunset provisions, see Sec. 901, P.L. 107-16 and Sec. 402(i)(3)(H), P.L. 109-135, reproduced in history notes for this Code Sec.

(c) Carryforwards of unused credit.
(1) Rule for years in which all personal credits allowed against regular and alternative minimum tax. In the case of a taxable year to which section 26(a)(2) applies, if the credit allowable under subsection (a) for any taxable year exceeds the limitation imposed by section 26(a)(2) for such taxable year reduced by the sum of the credits allowable under this subpart (other than this section and sections 25D and 1400C), such excess shall be carried to the succeeding taxable year and added to the credit allowable under subsection (a) for such taxable year.
(2) Rule for other years. In the case of a taxable year to which section 26(a)(2) does not apply, if the credit allowable under subsection (a) for any taxable year exceeds the limitation imposed by subsection (b)(4) for such taxable year, such excess shall be carried to the succeeding taxable year and added to the credit allowable under subsection (a) for such taxable year.
(3) Limitation. No credit may be carried forward under this subsection to any taxable year following the fifth taxable year after the taxable year in which the credit arose. For purposes of the preceding sentence, credits shall be treated as used on a first-in first-out basis.

(d) Definitions.
For purposes of this section—
(1) Qualified adoption expenses. The term "qualified adoption expenses" means reasonable and necessary adoption fees, court costs, attorney fees, and other expenses—
(A) which are directly related to, and the principal purpose of which is for, the legal adoption of an eligible child by the taxpayer,
(B) which are not incurred in violation of State or Federal law or in carrying out any surrogate parenting arrangement,
(C) which are not expenses in connection with the adoption by an individual of a child who is the child of such individual's spouse, and
(D) which are not reimbursed under an employer program or otherwise.
(2) Eligible child. The term "eligible child" means any individual who—
(A) has not attained age 18, or
(B) is physically or mentally incapable of caring for himself.
(3) Child with special needs. The term "child with special needs" means any child if—
(A) a State has determined that the child cannot or should not be returned to the home of his parents,
(B) such State has determined that there exists with respect to the child a specific factor or condition (such as his ethnic background, age, or membership in a minority or sibling group, or the presence of factors such as medical conditions or physical, mental, or emotional handicaps) because of which it is reasonable to conclude that such child cannot be placed with adoptive parents without providing adoption assistance, and
(C) such child is a citizen or resident of the United States (as defined in section 217(h)(3)).

(e) Special rules for foreign adoptions.
In the case of an adoption of a child who is not a citizen or resident of the United States (as defined in section 217(h)(3))—
(1) subsection (a) shall not apply to any qualified adoption expense with respect to such adoption unless such adoption becomes final, and
(2) any such expense which is paid or incurred before the taxable year in which such adoption becomes final shall be taken into account under this section as if such expense were paid or incurred during such year.

(f) Filing requirements.
(1) Married couples must file joint returns. Rules similar to the rules of paragraphs (2), (3), and (4) of section 21(e) shall apply for purposes of this section.
(2) Taxpayer must include TIN.
(A) In general. No credit shall be allowed under this section with respect to any eligible child unless the taxpayer includes (if known) the name, age, and TIN of such child on the return of tax for the taxable year.
(B) Other methods. The Secretary may, in lieu of the information referred to in subparagraph (A), require other information meeting the purposes of subparagraph (A), including identification of an agent assisting with the adoption.

(g) Basis adjustments.
For purposes of this subtitle, if a credit is allowed under this section for any expenditure with respect to any property, the increase in the basis of such property which would (but for this subsection) result from such expenditure shall be reduced by the amount of the credit so allowed.

> • *Caution:* Code Sec. 23(h), following, was added by P.L. 107-16, EGTRRA. These provisions generally sunset for tax years beginning after 12/31/2012. For specific sun-

Tax credits   Code Sec. 23

set provisions, see Sec. 901, P.L. 107-16 (as amended) reproduced in history notes for this Code Sec.

(h) Adjustments for inflation.

In the case of a taxable year beginning after December 31, 2002, each of the dollar amounts in subsection (a)(3) and paragraphs (1) and (2)(A)(i) of subsection (b) shall be increased by an amount equal to—

(1) such dollar amount, multiplied by

(2) the cost-of-living adjustment determined under section 1(f)(3) for the calendar year in which the taxable year begins, determined by substituting "calendar year 2001" for "calendar year 1992" in subparagraph (B) thereof.

If any amount as increased under the preceding sentence is not a multiple of $10, such amount shall be rounded to the nearest multiple of $10.

• **Caution:** Code Sec. 23(i), following, was redesignated from Code Sec. 23(h) by P.L. 107-16, EGTRRA. These provisions generally sunset for tax years beginning after 12/31/2012. For specific sunset provisions, see Sec. 901, P.L. 107-16 (as amended) reproduced in history notes for this Code Sec.

(i) Regulations.

The Secretary shall prescribe such regulations as may be appropriate to carry out this section and section 137, including regulations which treat unmarried individuals who pay or incur qualified adoption expenses with respect to the same child as 1 taxpayer for purposes of applying the dollar amounts in subsections (a)(3) and (b)(1) of this section and in section 137(b)(1).

In 2010, P.L. 111-312, Sec. 101(a)(1), substituted "December 31, 2012" for "December 31, 2010" both places it appeared in Sec. 901, P.L. 107-16 [see below], effective as if included in the enactment of P.L. 107-16, EGTRRA, 6/7/2001.
—P.L. 111-312, Sec. 101(b)(1), amended Sec. 10909(c), P.L. 111-148 [see below].
Prior to amendment, Sec. 10909(c) of P.L. 111-148, read as follows:
"(c) Application and Extension of EGTRRA Sunset. Notwithstanding section 901 of the Economic Growth and Tax Relief Reconciliation Act of 2001, such section shall apply to the amendments made by this section and the amendments made by section 202 of such Act by substituting 'December 31, 2011' for 'December 31, 2010' in subsection (a)(1) thereof."
—P.L. 111-312, Sec. 101(b)(2), substituted "Except as provided in subsection (c), the amendments" for "The amendments" in Sec. 10909(d), P.L. 111-148 (the effective date section for amendments made by Sec. 10909, P.L. 111-148, see below).
Prior to amendment, Sec. 10909(d) of P.L. 111-148, read as follows:
"(d) Effective date. The amendments made by this section shall apply to taxable years beginning after December 31, 2009."
—P.L. 111-148, Sec. 10909(a)(1)(A), substituted "$13,170" for "$10,000" in para. (b)(1)
—P.L. 111-148, Sec. 10909(a)(1)(C), amended subsec. (h)
—P.L. 111-148, Sec. 10909(a)(1)(B)(i), substituted "$13,170" for "$10,000" in para. (a)(3)
—P.L. 111-148, Sec. 10909(a)(1)(B)(ii), substituted "$13,170" for "$10,000" in the heading to para. (a)(3)
—P.L. 111-148, Sec. 10909(b)(1)(A), redesignated Code Sec. 23, [as amended by Sec. 10909(a) of this Act, see above], as Code Sec. 36C
—P.L. 111-148, Sec. 10909(b)(2)(I)(i), deleted para. (b)(4)
—P.L. 111-148, Sec. 10909(b)(2)(I)(ii), deleted subsec. (c), effective for tax. yrs. begin. after 12/31/2009, except as provided in Sec. 10909(c) of this Act, see below, which provides that these amendments will be applied as if never enacted effective for taxable years beginning after December 31, 2011.
Prior to redesignation Code Sec. 23 read as follows:
"Code Sec. 23 Adoption expenses.
"Paras. (a)(1) and (a)(2), following, was amended by P.L. 107-16, the Economic Growth and Tax Relief Reconciliation Act of 2001 (EGTRRA). For sunset provisions, see Sec. 901, P.L. 107-16 reproduced in history notes for this Code Sec.
"(a) Allowance of credit.
"(1) In general.

"In the case of an individual, there shall be allowed as a credit against the tax imposed by this chapter the amount of the qualified adoption expenses paid or incurred by the taxpayer.
"(2) Year credit allowed.
"The credit under paragraph (1) with respect to any expense shall be allowed—
"(A) in the case of any expense paid or incurred before the taxable year in which such adoption becomes final, for the taxable year following the taxable year during which such expense is paid or incurred, and
"(B) in the case of an expense paid or incurred during or after the taxable year in which such adoption becomes final, for the taxable year in which such expense is paid or incurred.
"(3) $10,000 credit for adoption of child with special needs regardless of expenses.
"In the case of an adoption of a child with special needs which becomes final during a taxable year, the taxpayer shall be treated as having paid during such year qualified adoption expenses with respect to such adoption in an amount equal to the excess (if any) of $10,000 over the aggregate qualified adoption expenses actually paid or incurred by the taxpayer with respect to such adoption during such taxable year and all prior taxable years.
"Paras. (b)(1) and (b)(2), following, were amended by P.L. 107-16, the Economic Growth and Tax Relief Reconciliation Act of 2001 (EGTRRA). For sunset provisions, see Sec. 901, P.L. 107-16 reproduced in history notes for this Code Sec.
"(b) Limitations.
"(1) Dollar limitation.
"The aggregate amount of qualified adoption expenses which may be taken into account under subsection (a) for all taxable years with respect to the adoption of a child by the taxpayer shall not exceed $10,000.
"(2) Income limitation.
"(A) In general. The amount allowable as a credit under subsection (a) for any taxable year (determined without regard to subsection (c)) shall be reduced (but not below zero) by an amount which bears the same ratio to the amount so allowable (determined without regard to this paragraph but with regard to paragraph (1)) as—
"(i) the amount (if any) by which the taxpayer's adjusted gross income exceeds $150,000, bears to
"(ii) $40,000.
"(B) Determination of adjusted gross income. For purposes of subparagraph (A), adjusted gross income shall be determined without regard to sections 911, 931, and 933.
"(3) Denial of double benefit.
"(A) In general. No credit shall be allowed under subsection (a) for any expense for which a deduction or credit is allowed under any other provision of this chapter.
"(B) Grants. No credit shall be allowed under subsection (a) for any expense to the extent that funds for such expense are received under any Federal, State, or local program.
"Para. (b)(4), added by P.L. 107-16 and amended by P.L. 109-135, following, is not effective for tax. yrs. begin. during 2002, 2003, 2004, or 2005 as provided by Sec. 601(b)(2) of P.L. 107-147 and Sec. 312(b)(2) of P.L. 108-311. For sunset provisions, see Sec. 901 of P.L. 107-16 and Sec. 402(i)(3)(H) of P.L. 109-135 reproduced in the history of this Code Sec.
"(4) Limitation based on amount of tax.
"In the case of a taxable year to which section 26(a)(2) does not apply, the credit allowed under subsection (a) for any taxable year shall not exceed the excess of—
"(A) the sum of the regular tax liability (as defined in section 26(b)) plus the tax imposed by section 55, over
"(B) the sum of the credits allowable under this subpart (other than this section and section 25D) and section 27 for the taxable year.
" Subsec. (c)), following, was amended by P.L. 109-135. For sunset provisions, see Sec. 901, P.L. 107-16 and Sec. 402(i)(3)(H), P.L. 109-135, reproduced in history notes for this Code Sec.
"(c) Carryforwards of unused credit.
"(1) Rule for years in which all personal credits allowed against regular and alternative minimum tax.
"In the case of a taxable year to which section 26(a)(2) applies, if the credit allowable under subsection (a) for any taxable year exceeds the limitation imposed by section 26(a)(2) for such taxable year reduced by the sum of the credits allowable under this subpart (other than this section and sections 25D and 1400C), such excess shall be carried to the succeeding taxable year and added to the credit allowable under subsection (a) for such taxable year.
"(2) Rule for other years.
"In the case of a taxable year to which section 26(a)(2) does not apply, if the credit allowable under subsection (a) for any taxable year exceeds the limitation imposed by subsection (b)(4) for such taxable year, such excess shall be carried to the succeeding taxable year and added to the credit allowable under subsection (a) for such taxable year.
"(3) Limitation.
"No credit may be carried forward under this subsection to any taxable year following the fifth taxable year after the taxable year in which the credit arose. For purposes of the preceding sentence, credits shall be treated as used on a first-in first-out basis.
"(d) Definitions.
"For purposes of this section—
"(1) Qualified adoption expenses.

1,037

"The term 'qualified adoption expenses' means reasonable and necessary adoption fees, court costs, attorney fees, and other expenses—

"(A) which are directly related to, and the principal purpose of which is for, the legal adoption of an eligible child by the taxpayer,

"(B) which are not incurred in violation of State or Federal law or in carrying out any surrogate parenting arrangement,

"(C) which are not expenses in connection with the adoption by an individual of a child who is the child of such individual's spouse, and

"(D) which are not reimbursed under an employer program or otherwise.

"(2) Eligible child. The term 'eligible child' means any individual who—

"(A) has not attained age 18, or

"(B) is physically or mentally incapable of caring for himself.

"(3) Child with special needs.

"The term 'child with special needs' means any child if—

"(A) a State has determined that the child cannot or should not be returned to the home of his parents,

"(B) such State has determined that there exists with respect to the child a specific factor or condition (such as his ethnic background, age, or membership in a minority or sibling group, or the presence of factors such as medical conditions or physical, mental, or emotional handicaps) because of which it is reasonable to conclude that such child cannot be placed with adoptive parents without providing adoption assistance, and

"(C) such child is a citizen or resident of the United States (as defined in section 217(h)(3)).

"(e) Special rules for foreign adoptions.

"In the case of an adoption of a child who is not a citizen or resident of the United States (as defined in section 217(h)(3))—

"(1) subsection (a) shall not apply to any qualified adoption expense with respect to such adoption unless such adoption becomes final, and

"(2) any such expense which is paid or incurred before the taxable year in which such adoption becomes final shall be taken into account under this section as if such expense were paid or incurred during such year.

"(f) Filing requirements.

"(1) Married couples must file joint returns.

"Rules similar to the rules of paragraphs (2), (3), and (4) of section 21(e) shall apply for purposes of this section.

"(2) Taxpayer must include TIN.

"(A) In general. No credit shall be allowed under this section with respect to any eligible child unless the taxpayer includes (if known) the name, age, and TIN of such child on the return of tax for the taxable year.

"(B) Other methods. The Secretary may, in lieu of the information referred to in subparagraph (A), require other information meeting the purposes of subparagraph (A), including identification of an agent assisting with the adoption.

"(g) Basis adjustments.

"For purposes of this subtitle, if a credit is allowed under this section for any expenditure with respect to any property, the increase in the basis of such property which would (but for this subsection) result from such expenditure shall be reduced by the amount of the credit so allowed.

"Subsec. (h), following, was added by P.L. 107-16, the Economic Growth and Tax Relief Reconciliation Act of 2001 (EGTRRA). For sunset provisions, see Sec. 901, P.L. 107-16 reproduced in history notes for this Code Sec.

"(h) Adjustments for inflation. In the case of a taxable year beginning after December 31, 2002, each of the dollar amounts in subsection (a)(3) and paragraphs (1) and (2)(A)(i) of subsection (b) shall be increased by an amount equal to—

"(1) such dollar amount, multiplied by

"(2) the cost-of-living adjustment determined under section 1(f)(3) for the calendar year in which the taxable year begins, determined by substituting 'calendar year 2001' for 'calendar year 1992' in subparagraph (B) thereof.

"If any amount as increased under the preceding sentence is not a multiple of $10, such amount shall be rounded to the nearest multiple of $10.

"Subsec. (i), following, was redesignated from subsec. (h) by P.L. 107-16, the Economic Growth and Tax Relief Reconciliation Act of 2001 (EGTRRA). For sunset provisions, see Sec. 901, P.L. 107-16 reproduced in history notes for this Code Sec.

"(i) Regulations.

"The Secretary shall prescribe such regulations as may be appropriate to carry out this section and section 137, including regulations which treat unmarried individuals who pay or incur qualified adoption expenses with respect to the same child as 1 taxpayer for purposes of applying the dollar amounts in subsections (a)(3) and (b)(1) of this section and in section 137(b)(1)."

—P.L. 111-148, Sec. 10909(c), of this Act, relating to the application and extension of EGTRRA sunset provisions, [as amended by Sec. 101(b)(1), P.L. 111-312 see above], reads as follows:

"(c) Sunset provision. Each provision of law amended by this section is amended to read as such provision would read if this section had never been enacted. The amendments made by the preceding sentence shall apply to taxable years beginning after December 31, 2011."

—P.L. 111-148, Sec. 10909(d), of this Act, [as amended by Sec. 101(b)(2), P.L. 111-312, see above] reads as follows:

"(d) Effective date. Except as provided in subsection (c) [Sec. 10909(c) of this Act], the amendments made by this section shall apply to taxable years beginning after December 31, 2009."

In 2008, P.L. 110-343, Sec. 106(e)(2)(A), inserted "and section 25D" after "this section" in subpara. (b)(4)(B), effective for tax. yrs. begin. after 12/31/2007. The amendments made by subparagraphs (A) and (B) of subsection (e)(2) shall be subject to title IX of the Economic Growth and Tax Relief Reconciliation Act of 2001 in the same manner as the provisions of such Act to which such amendments relate.

In 2005, P.L. 109-135, Sec. 402(i)(3)(A)(i), substituted "In the case of a taxable year to which section 26(a)(2) does not apply, the credit" for "The credit" in the matter preceding subpara. (b)(4)(A) . . . Sec. 402(i)(3)(A)(ii), amended subsec. (c), effective for tax. yrs. begin. after 12/31/2005.

Prior to amendment, subsec. (c) read as follows:

"(c) Carryforwards of unused credit. If the credit allowable under subsection (a) for any taxable year exceeds the limitation imposed by subsection (b)(4) for such taxable year, such excess shall be carried to the succeeding taxable year and added to the credit allowable under subsection (a) for such taxable year. No credit may be carried forward under this subsection to any taxable year following the fifth taxable year after the taxable year in which the credit arose. For purposes of the preceding sentence, credits shall be treated as used on a first-in first-out basis."

—P.L. 109-135, Sec. 402(i)(3)(H), of this Act, provides:

"(H) Application of EGTRRA Sunset. The amendments made by this paragraph (and each part thereof) shall be subject to title IX of the Economic Growth and Tax Relief Reconciliation Act of 2001 [P.L. 107-16] in the same manner as the provisions of such Act to which such amendment (or part thereof) relates."

—P.L. 109-135, Sec. 402(i)(4), repealed Sec. 1335(b)(1) of P.L. 109-58 [see below], effective for property placed in service after 12/31/2005, in tax. yrs. end. after 12/31/2005.

—P.L. 109-58, Sec. 1335(b)(1), [prior to repeal by Sec. 402(i)(4) of P.L. 109-135, see above] substituted "this section, section 25D, and section 1400C" for "this section and section 1400C" in subsec. (c), effective for property placed in service after 12/31/2005, in tax. yrs. end. after 12/31/2005. Note: This amendment cannot be applied to subsec. (c) as it reads on 1/1/2006.

In 2004, P.L. 108-311, Sec. 312(b)(2), of this Act, provides:

"(2) The amendments made by sections 201(b), 202(f), and 618(b) of the Economic Growth and Tax Relief Reconciliation Act of 2001 [P.L. 107-16] shall not apply to taxable years beginning during 2004 or 2005."

In 2002, P.L. 107-358, Sec. 2, added subsec. (c) in Sec. 901 of P.L. 107-16 [see below], effective 12/17/2002.

—P.L. 107-147, Sec. 411(c)(1)(A), amended para. (a)(1) . . . Sec. 411(c)(1)(B), added para. (a)(3), effective for tax. yrs. begin. after 12/31/2002.

Prior to amendment, para. (a)(1) read as follows:

"(1) In general. In the case of an individual, there shall be allowed as a credit against the tax imposed by this chapter—

"(A) in the case of an adoption of a child other than a child with special needs, the amount of the qualified adoption expenses paid or incurred by the taxpayer, and

"(B) in the case of an adoption of a child with special needs, $10,000."

—P.L. 107-147, Sec. 411(c)(1)(C), deleted "In the case of the adoption of a child with special needs, the credit allowed under paragraph (1) shall be allowed for the taxable year in which the adoption becomes final." after "is paid or incurred." in para. (a)(2) . . . Sec. 411(c)(1)(D), substituted "subsection (a)" for "subsection (a)(1)(A)" in para. (b)(1), effective for tax. yrs. begin. after 12/31/2001.

—P.L. 107-147, Sec. 411(c)(1)(E), substituted "the dollar amounts in subsections (a)(3) and (b)(1)" for "the dollar limitation in subsection (b)(1)" in subsec. (i), effective for tax. yrs. begin. after 12/31/2002.

—P.L. 107-147, Sec. 411(c)(1)(F), of this Act, provides:

"(F) Expenses paid or incurred during any taxable year beginning before January 1, 2002, may be taken into account in determining the credit under section 23 of the Internal Revenue Code of 1986 only to the extent the aggregate of such expenses does not exceed the applicable limitation under section 23(b)(1) of such Code as in effect on the day before the date of the enactment of the Economic Growth and Tax Relief Reconciliation Act of 2001."

—P.L. 107-147, Sec. 418(a)(1)(A), substituted "subsection (a)(3)" for "subsection (a)(1)(B)" in subsec. (h) . . . Sec. 418(a)(1)(B), added a flush sentence at the end of subsec. (h), effective for tax. yrs. begin. after 12/31/2001.

—P.L. 107-147, Sec. 601(b)(2), of this Act, provides:

"(2) The amendments made by sections 201(b), 202(f), and 618(b) of the Economic Growth and Tax Relief Reconciliation Act of 2001 shall not apply to taxable years beginning during 2002 and 2003."

In 2001, P.L. 107-16, Sec. 201(b)(2)(E), substituted "and sections 24 and 1400C" for "and section 1400C" in subsec. (c) [prior to amendment by Sec. 202(f)(2)(A)(i)-(ii), see below], effective for tax. yrs. begin. after 12/31/2001. For special provisions, see Sec. 601(b)(2) of P.L. 107-147 and Sec. 312(b)(2) of P.L. 108-311, above.

—P.L. 107-16, Sec. 202(a)(1), amended para. (a)(1), effective for tax. yrs. begin. after 12/31/2002.

Prior to amendment, para. (a)(1) read as follows:

"(1) In general. In the case of an individual, there shall be allowed as a credit against the tax imposed by this chapter the amount of the qualified adoption expenses paid or incurred by the taxpayer."

—P.L. 107-16, Sec. 202(b)(1)(A)(i), substituted "$10,000" for "$5,000" in para. (b)(1) . . . Sec. 202(b)(1)(A)(ii), deleted "($6,000, in the case of a child with special needs)" after "shall not exceed $5,000" in para. (b)(1) . . . Sec. 202(b)(1)(A)(iii), substituted "subsection (a)(1)(A)" for "subsection (a)" in para. (b)(1) . . . Sec. 202(b)(2)(A), substituted "$150,000" for "$75,000" in clause (b)(2)(A)(i) . . . Sec. 202(c), added a flush sentence at the end of para. (a)(2) . . . Sec. 202(d)(1), amended para. (d)(2) . . . Sec. 202(e)(1), redesignated subsec. (h) as subsec. (i), and added new subsec. (h) . . . Sec. 202(f)(1), added para. (b)(4) . . . Sec. 202(f)(2)(A)(i), substituted "subsection (b)(4)" for "section 26(a)" in subsec. (c) [as amended by Sec. 201(b)(2)(E) of this Act, see above] . . . Sec. 202(f)(2)(A)(ii), deleted "reduced by the sum of the credits allowable under this

Tax credits   Code Sec. 23

subpart (other than this section and sections 24 and 1400C)" before ", such excess shall be carried" in subsec. (c) [as amended by Sec. 201(b)(2)(E) of this Act, see above], effective for tax. yrs. begin. after 12/31/2001. For special provisions, see Sec. 601(b)(2) of P.L. 107-147 and Sec. 312(b)(2) of P.L. 108-311, above. Prior to amendment, para. (d)(2) read as follows:

"(2) Eligible child. The term 'eligible child' means any individual—

"(A) who—

"(i) has not attained age 18, or

"(ii) is physically or mentally incapable of caring for himself, and

"(B) in the case of a qualified adoption expenses paid or incurred after December 31, 2001, who is a child with special needs."

—P.L. 107-16, Sec. 901, of this Act [as amended by Sec. 2 of P.L. 107-358, and Sec. 101(a)(1), P.L. 111-312, see above], reads as follows:

"SEC. 901. SUNSET OF PROVISIONS OF ACT.

"(a) In general. All provisions of, and amendments made by, this Act shall not apply—

"(1) to taxable, plan, or limitation years beginning after December 31, 2012, or

"(2) in the case of title V, to estates of decedents dying, gifts made, or generation skipping transfers, after December 31, 2012.

"(b) Application of certain laws. The Internal Revenue Code of 1986 and the Employee Retirement Income Security Act of 1974 shall be applied and administered to years, estates, gifts, and transfers described in subsection (a) as if the provisions and amendments described in subsection (a) had never been enacted.

"(c) Exception. Subsection (a) shall not apply to section 803 (relating to no federal income tax on restitution received by victims of the Nazi regime or their heirs or estates)."

In 1998, P.L. 105-206, Sec. 6008(d)(6), added "and section 1400C" after "other than this section" in subsec. (c), effective 8/5/97.

—P.L. 105-206, Sec. 6018(f)(1), added "(determined without regard to subsection (c))" after "for any taxable year" in subpara. (b)(2)(A), effective for tax. yrs. begin. after 12/31/96.

In 1997, P.L. 105-34, Sec. 1601(h)(2)(A), amended para. (a)(2)... Sec. 1601(h)(2)(B), substituted "determined without regard to sections 911, 931, and 933." for "determined—" and clauses (b)(2)(B)(i) and (ii), effective for tax. yrs. begin. after 12/31/96.

Prior to amendment, para. (a)(2) read as follows:

"(2) Year credit allowed. The credit under paragraph (1) with respect to any expense shall be allowed—

"(A) for the taxable year following the taxable year during which such expense is paid or incurred, or

"(B) in the case of an expense which is paid or incurred during the taxable year in which the adoption becomes final, for such taxable year."

Prior to deletion, clauses (b)(2)(B)(i) and (ii) read as follows:

"determined—

"(i) without regard to sections 911, 931, and 933, and

"(ii) after the application of sections 86, 135, 137, 219, and 469."

In 1996, P.L. 104-188, Sec. 1807(a), added Code Sec. 23, effective for tax. yrs. begin. after 12/31/96.

Sec. 23.   Repealed.

In 1990, P.L. 101-508, Sec. 11801(a)(1), repealed Code Sec. 23, effective 11/5/90, except as provided in Sec. 11821(b) of this Act, which reads as follows: "(b) Savings provision. If—

"(1) any provision amended or repealed by this part applied to—

"(A) any transaction occurring before the date of the enactment of this Act [11/5/90],

"(B) any property acquired before such date of enactment, [11/5/90], or

"(C) any item of income, loss, deduction, or credit taken into account before such date of enactment, [11/5/90], and

"(2) the treatment of such transaction, property, or item under such provision would (without regard to the amendments made by this part) affect liability for tax for periods ending after such date of enactment [11/5/90],

nothing in the amendments made by this part shall be construed to affect the treatment of such transaction, property, or item for purposes of determining liability for tax for periods ending after such date of enactment. [11/5/90]."

Prior to repeal, Code Sec. 23 read as follows:

"SEC. 23. RESIDENTIAL ENERGY CREDIT.

"(a) General rule. In the case of an individual, there shall be allowed as a credit against the tax imposed by this chapter for the taxable year an amount equal to the sum of—

"(1) the qualified energy conservation expenditures, plus

"(2) the qualified renewable energy source expenditures.

"(b) Qualified expenditures. For purposes of subsection (a)—

"(1) Energy conservation. In the case of any dwelling unit, the qualified energy conservation expenditures are 15 percent of so much of the energy conservation expenditures made by the taxpayer during the taxable year with respect to such unit as does not exceed $2,000.

"(2) Renewable energy source. In the case of any dwelling unit, the qualified renewable energy source expenditures are 40 percent of so much of the renewable energy source expenditures made by the taxpayer during the taxable year with respect to such unit as does not exceed $10,000.

"(3) Prior expenditures by taxpayer on same residence taken into account. If for any prior year a credit was allowed to the taxpayer under this section with respect to any dwelling unit by reason of energy conservation expenditures or renewable energy source expenditures, paragraph (1) or (2) (whichever is appropriate) shall be applied for the taxable year with respect to such dwelling unit by reducing each dollar amount contained in such paragraph by the prior year expenditures taken into account under such paragraph.

"(4) Minimum dollar amount. No credit shall be allowed under this section with respect to any return for any taxable year if the amount which would (but for this paragraph) be allowed with respect to such return is less than $10.

"(5) Carryforward of unused credit.

"(A) In general. If the credit allowable under subsection (a) for any taxable year exceeds the limitation imposed by section 26(a) for such taxable year reduced by the sum of the credits allowable under this subpart (other than this section and section 25), such excess shall be carried to the succeeding taxable year and added to the credit allowable under subsection (a) for such succeeding taxable year.

"(B) No carryforward to taxable years beginning after December 31, 1987. No amount may be carried under subparagraph (A) to any taxable year beginning after December 31, 1987.

"(c) Definitions and special rules. For purposes of this section—

"(1) Energy conservation expenditures. The term 'energy conservation expenditure' means an expenditure made on or after April 20, 1977, by the taxpayer for insulation or any other energy-conserving component (or for the original installation of such insulation or other component) installed in or on a dwelling unit—

"(A) which is located in the United States,

"(B) which is used by the taxpayer as his principal residence, and

"(C) the construction of which was substantially completed before April 20, 1977.

"(2) Renewable energy source expenditure.

"(A) In general. The term 'renewable energy source expenditure' means an expenditure made on or after April 20, 1977, by the taxpayer for renewable energy source property installed in connection with a dwelling unit—

"(i) which is located in the United States, and

"(ii) which is used by the taxpayer as his principal residence.

"(B) Certain labor and other costs included. The term 'renewable energy source expenditure' includes—

"(i) expenditures for labor costs properly allocable to the onsite preparation, assembly, or original installation of renewable energy source property, and

"(ii) expenditures for an onsite well drilled for any geothermal deposit (as defined in section 613(e)(3)), but only if the taxpayer has not elected under section 263(c) to deduct any portion of such expenditures.

"(C) Swimming pool, etc., used as storage medium. The term 'renewable energy source expenditure' does not include any expenditure properly allocable to a swimming pool used as an energy storage medium or to any other energy storage medium which has a primary function other than the function of such storage.

"(D) Certain solar panels. No solar panel installed as a roof (or portion thereof) shall fail to be treated as renewable energy source property solely because it constitutes a structural component of the dwelling on which it is installed.

"(3) Insulation. The term 'insulation' means any item—

"(A) which is specifically and primarily designed to reduce when installed in or on a dwelling (or water heater) the heat loss or gain of such dwelling (or water heater),

"(B) the original use of which begins with the taxpayer,

"(C) which can reasonably be expected to remain in operation for at least 3 years, and

"(D) which meets the performance and quality standards (if any) which—

"(i) have been prescribed by the Secretary by regulations, and

"(ii) are in effect at the time of the acquisition of the item.

"(4) Other energy-conserving component. The term 'other energy-conserving component' means any item (other than insulation)—

"(A) which is—

"(i) a furnace replacement burner designed to achieve a reduction in the amount of fuel consumed as a result of increased combustion efficiency,

"(ii) a device for modifying flue openings designed to increase the efficiency of operation of the heating system,

"(iii) an electrical or mechanical furnace ignition system, which replaces a gas pilot light,

"(iv) a storm or thermal window or door for the exterior of the dwelling,

"(v) an automatic energy-saving setback thermostat,

"(vi) caulking or weatherstripping of an exterior door or window,

"(vii) a meter which displays the cost of energy usage, or

"(viii) an item of the kind which the Secretary specifies by regulations as increasing the energy efficiency of the dwelling,

"(B) the original use of which begins with the taxpayer,

"(C) which can reasonably be expected to remain in operation for at least 3 years, and

"(D) which meets the performance and quality standards (if any) which—

"(i) have been prescribed by the Secretary by regulations, and

"(ii) are in effect at the time of the acquisition of the item.

"(5) Renewable energy source property. The term 'renewable energy source property' means property—

"(A) which, when installed in connection with a dwelling, transmits or uses—

"(i) solar energy, energy derived from the geothermal deposits (as defined in section 613(e)(3)), or any other form of renewable energy which the Secretary specifies by regulations, for the purpose of heating or cooling such dwelling or providing hot water or electricity for use within such dwelling, or

"(ii) wind energy for nonbusiness residential purposes,

"(B) the original use of which begins with the taxpayer,

"(C) which can reasonably be expected to remain in operation for at least 5 years, and

"(D) which meets the performance and quality standards (if any) which—
"(i) have been prescribed by the Secretary by regulations, and
"(ii) are in effect at the time of the acquisition of the property.
"(6) Regulations.
"(A) Criteria: certification procedures. The Secretary shall by regulations—
"(i) establish the criteria which are to be used in (I) prescribing performance and quality standards under paragraphs (3), (4), and (5), or (II) specifying any item under paragraph (4)(A)(viii) or any form of renewable energy under paragraph (5)(A)(i), and
"(ii) establish a procedure under which a manufacturer of an item may request the Secretary to certify that the item will be treated, for purposes of this section, as insulation, an energy-conserving component, or renewable energy source property.
"(B) Consultation. Performance and quality standards regulations and other regulations shall be prescribed by the Secretary under paragraphs (3), (4), and (5) and under this paragraph only after consultation with the Secretary of Energy, the Secretary of Housing and Urban Development, and other appropriate Federal officers.
"(C) Action on requests.
"(i) In general. The Secretary shall make a final determination with respect to any request filed under subparagraph (A)(ii) for specifying an item under paragraph (4)(A)(viii) or for specifying a form of renewable energy under paragraph (5)(A)(i) within 1 year after the filing of the request, together with any information required to be filed with such request under subparagraph (A)(ii).
"(ii) Reports. Each month the Secretary shall publish a report of any request which has been denied during the preceding month and the reasons for the denial.
"(D) Effective date.
"(i) In general. In the case of any item or energy source specified under paragraph (4)(A)(viii) or (5)(A)(i), the credit allowed by subsection (a) shall apply with respect to expenditures which are made on or after the date on which final notice of such specification is published in the Federal Register.
"(ii) Expenditures taken into account in following taxable years. The Secretary may prescribe by regulations that expenditures made on or after the date referred to in clause (i) and before the close of the taxable year in which such date occurs shall be taken into account in the following taxable year.
"(7) When expenditures made; amount of expenditures.
"(A) In general. Except as provided in subparagraph (B), an expenditure with respect to an item shall be treated as made when original installation of the item is completed.
"(B) Renewable energy source expenditures. In the case of renewable energy source expenditures in connection with the construction or reconstruction of a dwelling, such expenditures shall be treated as made when the original use of the constructed or reconstructed dwelling by the taxpayer begins.
"(C) Amount. The amount of any expenditure shall be the cost thereof.
"(D) Allocation in certain cases. If less than 80 percent of the use of an item is for nonbusiness residential purposes, only that portion of the expenditures for such item which is properly allocable to use for nonbusiness residential purposes shall be taken into account. For purposes of this subparagraph, use for a swimming pool shall be treated as use which is not for residential purposes.
"(8) Principal residence. The determination of whether or not a dwelling unit is a taxpayer's principal residence shall be made under principles similar to those applicable to section 1034, except that—
"(A) no ownership requirement shall be imposed, and
"(B) the period for which a dwelling is treated as the principal residence of the taxpayer shall include the 30-day period ending on the first day on which it would (but for this subparagraph) be treated as his principal residence.
"(9) Limitations on secretarial authority.
"(A) In general. The Secretary shall not specify any item under paragraph (4)(A)(viii) or any form of renewable energy under paragraph (5)(A)(i) unless the Secretary determines that—
"(i) there will be a reduction in oil or natural gas consumption as a result of such specification, and such reduction is sufficient to justify any resulting decrease in Federal revenues,
"(ii) such specification will not result in an increased use of any item which is known to be, or reasonably suspected to be, environmentally hazardous or a threat to public health or safety, and
"(iii) available Federal subsidies do not make such specification unnecessary or inappropriate (in the light of the most advantageous allocation of economic resources).
"(B) Factors taken into account. In making any determination under subparagraph (A)(i), the Secretary (after consultation with the Secretary of Energy)—
"(i) shall make an estimate of the amount by which the specification will reduce oil and natural gas consumption, and
"(ii) shall determine whether such specification compares favorably, on the basis of the reduction in oil and natural gas consumption per dollar of cost to the Federal Government (including revenue loss), with other Federal programs in existence or being proposed.
"(C) Factors taken into account in making estimates. In making any estimate under subparagraph (B)(i), the Secretary shall take into account (among other factors)—
"(i) the extent to which the use of any item will be increased as a result of the specification,
"(ii) whether sufficient capacity is available to increase production to meet any increase in demand caused by such specification,
"(iii) the amount of oil and natural gas used directly or indirectly in the manufacture of such item and other items necessary for its use, and
"(iv) the estimated useful life of such item.
"(10) Property financed by subsidized energy financing.

"(A) Reduction of qualified expenditures. For purposes of determining the amount of energy conservation or renewable energy source expenditures made by any individual with respect to any dwelling unit, there shall not be taken into account expenditures which are made from subsidized energy financing.
"(B) Dollar limits reduced. Paragraph (1) or (2) of subsection (b) (whichever is appropriate) shall be applied with respect to such dwelling unit for any taxable year of such taxpayer by reducing each dollar amount contained in such paragraph (reduced as provided in subsection (b)(3)) by an amount equal to the sum of—
"(i) the amount of the expenditures which were made by the taxpayer during such taxable year or any prior taxable year with respect to such dwelling unit and which were not taken into account by reason of subparagraph (A), and
"(ii) the amount of any Federal, State, or local grant received by the taxpayer during such taxable year or any prior taxable year which was used to make energy conservation or renewable energy source expenditures with respect to the dwelling unit and which was not included in the gross income of such taxpayer.
"(C) Subsidized energy financing. For purposes of this paragraph, the term 'subsidized energy financing' means financing provided under a Federal, State, or local program a principal purpose of which is to provide subsidized financing for projects designed to conserve or produce energy.
"(d) Special rules. For purposes of this section—
"(1) Dollar amounts in case of joint occupancy. In the case of any dwelling unit which is jointly occupied and used during any calendar year as a principal residence by 2 or more individuals—
"(A) the amount of the credit allowable under subsection (a) by reason of energy conservation expenditures or by reason of renewable energy source expenditures (as the case may be) made during such calendar year by any of such individuals with respect to such dwelling unit shall be determined by treating all of such individuals as one taxpayer whose taxable year is such calendar year; and
"(B) there shall be allowable with respect to such expenditures to each of such individuals a credit under subsection (a) for the taxable year in which such calendar year ends in an amount which bears the same ratio to the amount determined under subparagraph (A) as the amount of such expenditures made by such individual during such calendar year bears to the aggregate of such expenditures made by all of such individuals during such calendar year.
"(2) Tenant-stockholder in cooperative housing corporation. In the case of an individual who is a tenant-stockholder (as defined in section 216) in a cooperative housing corporation (as defined in such section), such individual shall be treated as having made his tenant-stockholder's proportionate share (as defined in section 216(b)(3)) of any expenditures of such corporation.
"(3) Condominiums.
"(A) In general. In the case of an individual who is a member of a condominium management association with respect to a condominium which he owns, such individual shall be treated as having made his proportionate share of any expenditures of such association.
"(B) Condominium management association. For purposes of this paragraph, the term 'condominium management association', means an organization which meets the requirements of paragraph (1) of section 528(c) (other than subparagraph (E) thereof) with respect to a condominium project substantially all of the units of which are used as residences.
"(4) Joint ownership of energy items.
"(A) In general. Any expenditure otherwise qualifying as an energy conservation expenditure or a renewable energy source expenditure shall not be treated as failing to so qualify merely because such expenditure was made with respect to 2 or more dwelling units.
"(B) Limits applied separately. In the case of any expenditure described in subparagraph (A), the amount of the credit allowable under subsection (a) shall (subject to paragraph (1)) be computed separately with respect to the amount of the expenditure made by each individual.
"(5) 1977 expenditures allowed for 1978.
"(A) No credit for taxable years beginning before 1978. No credit shall be allowed under this section for any taxable year beginning before January 1, 1978.
"(B) 1977 expenditures allowed for 1978. In the case of the taxpayer's first taxable year beginning after December 31, 1977, this section shall be applied by taking into account the period beginning April 20, 1977, and ending on the last day of such first taxable year.
"(e) Basis adjustments. For purposes of this subtitle, if a credit is allowed under this section for any expenditure with respect to any property, the increase in the basis of such property which would (but for this subsection) result from such expenditure shall be reduced by the amount of the credit so allowed.
"(f) Termination. This section shall not apply to expenditures made after December 31, 1985."

In 1984, P.L. 98-369, Sec. 471(c)(1), redesignated Code Sec. 44C as Code Sec. 23 . . . Sec. 474(e), deleted paras. (b)(5) and (b)(6) and added new para. (b)(5), effective for tax. yrs. begin. after 12/31/83 and to carrybacks from tax. yrs. begin. after 12/31/83.
Prior to amendment, paras. (b)(5) and (b)(6) read as follows:
"(5) Application with other credits. The credit allowed by subsection (a) shall not exceed the tax imposed by this chapter for the taxable year, reduced by the sum of the credits allowable under a section of this subpart having a lower number or letter designation than this section, other than credits allowable by sections 31, 39, and 43.
"(6) Carryover of unused credit.
"(A) In general. If the credit allowable under subsection (a) for any taxable year exceeds the limitation imposed by paragraph (5) for such taxable year, such excess shall be carried to the succeeding taxable year and added to the credit allowable under subsection (a) for such succeeding taxable year.

Tax credits Code Sec. 24(d)(1)(B)

"(B) No carryover to taxable years beginning after December 31, 1987. No amount may be carried under subparagraph (A) to any taxable year beginning after December 31, 1987."

—P.L. 98-369, Sec. 612(e)(2), substituted "section 26(a)" for "section 25(a)" and "(other than this section and section 25)" for "(other than this section)" in para. (b)(5) as amended by Sec. 474(e) of this Act), effective for interest paid or accrued after 12/31/84, on indebtedness incurred after 12/31/84 and to elections under Code Sec. 25(c)(2)(A)(ii) (as added by this Act) for calendar years after 1983.

—P.L. 98-369, Sec. 632, provided various exceptions to the amendments made by Title VI of this Act. See note following Code Sec. 103A.

In 1980, P.L. 96-294, Sec. 506, 509, 515, provide that a taxpayer cannot claim a credit under Code Sec. 44C with respect to financial assistance which was obtained from the Solar Energy and Energy Conservation Bank.

—P.L. 96-223, Sec. 201(a), redesignated para. (d)(4) as para. (d)(5) and added new para. (d)(4), effective 4/2/80. . . Sec. 201(b)(1), added para. (c)(9), . . . Sec. 201(b)(2), added subparas. (c)(6)(C) and (D).

—P.L. 96-223, Sec. 202(a), amended para. (b)(2), effective for tax. yrs. begin. after 12/31/79.

Prior to amendment, para. (b)(2) read as follows:

"(2) Renewable energy source. In the case of any dwelling unit, the qualified renewable energy source expenditures are the following percentages of the renewable energy source expenditures made by the taxpayer during the taxable year with respect to such unit:

"(A) 30 percent of so much of such expenditures as does not exceed $2,000 plus

"(B) 20 percent of so much of such expenditures as exceeds $2,000 but does not exceed $10,000."

—P.L. 96-223, Sec. 202(b), substituted "providing hot water or electricity" for "providing hot water" in clause (c)(5)(A)(i) . . . Sec. 202(c), amended subpara. (c)(2)(B) . . . Sec. 202(d), added subpara. (c)(2)(D), effective for expenditures made after 12/31/79, in tax. yrs. end. after 12/31/79.

Prior to amendment, subpara. (c)(2)(B) read as follows:

"(B) Certain labor costs included. The term 'renewable energy source expenditure' includes expenditures for labor costs properly allocable to the onsite preparation, assembly, or original installation of renewable energy source property."

—P.L. 96-223, Sec. 203(a)(1), added para. (c)(10), effective for tax. yrs. begin. after 12/31/80, but only with respect to financing or grants made after 12/31/80.

In 1978, P.L. 95-618, Sec. 101(a), added Code Sec. 44C, effective for tax. yrs. end. on or after 4/20/77.

Sec. 24. Child tax credit.

⌐ • **Caution:** Code Sec. 24, following, was amended by P.L. 107-16, EGTRRA. These provisions generally sunset for tax years beginning after 12/31/2012. For specific sunset provisions, see Sec. 901, P.L. 107-16 (as amended) reproduced in history notes for this Code Sec. Code Sec. 24 was further amended by Sec. 10909, P.L. 111-148. As provided in Sec. 10909(c), P.L. 111-148, as amended by Sec. 101(b)(1), P.L. 111-312, the amendments made by Sec. 10909(b)(2)(A) will apply as if never enacted, effective for tax years beginning after 12/31/2011. ⌐

(a) Allowance of credit.
There shall be allowed as a credit against the tax imposed by this chapter for the taxable year with respect to each qualifying child of the taxpayer for which the taxpayer is allowed a deduction under section 151 an amount equal to $1,000.

(b) Limitations.

(1) Limitation based on adjusted gross income. The amount of the credit allowable under subsection (a) shall be reduced (but not below zero) by $50 for each $1,000 (or fraction thereof) by which the taxpayer's modified adjusted gross income exceeds the threshold amount. For purposes of the preceding sentence, the term "modified adjusted gross income" means adjusted gross income increased by any amount excluded from gross income under section 911, 931, or 933.

(2) Threshold amount. For purposes of paragraph (1), the term "threshold amount" means—

(A) $110,000 in the case of a joint return,

(B) $75,000 in the case of an individual who is not married, and

(C) $55,000 in the case of a married individual filing a separate return.

For purposes of this paragraph, marital status shall be determined under section 7703.

(3) Limitation based on amount of tax. In the case of a taxable year to which section 26(a)(2) does not apply, the credit allowed under subsection (a) for any taxable year shall not exceed the excess of—

(A) the sum of the regular tax liability (as defined in section 26(b)) plus the tax imposed by section 55, over

⌐ • **Caution:** Code Sec. 24(b)(3)(B), following, reflects amendments made by Sec. 10909, P.L. 111-148. As provided in Sec. 10909(c), P.L. 111-148 as amended by Sec. 101(b)(1), P.L. 111-312, Code Sec. 24(b)(3)(B) will read as if those amendments had never been enacted, effective for tax. yrs. begin. after 12/31/2011. For Code Sec. 24(b)(3)(B) as it will read for tax. yrs. begin. after 12/31/2011, see below. ⌐

(B) the sum of the credits allowable under this subpart (other than this section and sections 25A(i), 25B, 25D, 30, 30B, and 30D) and section 27 for the taxable year.

⌐ • **Caution:** Code Sec. 24(b)(3)(B), following, is effective for tax. yrs. begin. after 12/31/2011, and reflects the sunset of the amendments made by Sec. 10909, P.L. 111-148. For details of those amendments, effective date and sunset provisions, see the history for this Code Sec. For Code Sec. 24(b)(3)(B), effective for tax. yrs. begin. before 1/1/2012, see above. ⌐

(B) the sum of the credits allowable under this subpart (other than 23, this section and sections 25A(i), 25B, 25D, 30, 30B, and 30D) and section 27 for the taxable year.

(c) Qualifying child.
For purposes of this section—

(1) In general. The term "qualifying child" means a qualifying child of the taxpayer (as defined in section 152(c)) who has not attained age 17.

(2) Exception for certain noncitizens. The term "qualifying child" shall not include any individual who would not be a dependent if subparagraph (A) of section 152(b)(3) were applied without regard to all that follows "resident of the United States".

(d) Portion of credit refundable.

(1) In general. The aggregate credits allowed to a taxpayer under subpart C shall be increased by the lesser of—

(A) the credit which would be allowed under this section without regard to this subsection and the limitation under section 26(a)(2) or subsection (b)(3), as the case may be, or

(B) the amount by which the aggregate amount of credits allowed by this subpart (determined without regard to this subsection) would increase if the limitation im-

1,041

posed by section 26(a)(2) or subsection (b)(3), as the case may be, were increased by the greater of—

(i) 15 percent of so much of the taxpayer's earned income (within the meaning of section 32) which is taken into account in computing taxable income for the taxable year as exceeds $10,000, or

(ii) in the case of a taxpayer with 3 or more qualifying children, the excess (if any) of—

(I) the taxpayer's social security taxes for the taxable year, over

(II) the credit allowed under section 32 for the taxable year.

The amount of the credit allowed under this subsection shall not be treated as a credit allowed under this subpart and shall reduce the amount of credit otherwise allowable under subsection (a) without regard to section 26(a)(2) or subsection (b)(3), as the case may be. For purposes of subparagraph (B), any amount excluded from gross income by reason of section 112 shall be treated as earned income which is taken into account in computing taxable income for the taxable year.

(2) Social security taxes. For purposes of paragraph (1)—

(A) In general. The term "social security taxes" means, with respect to any taxpayer for any taxable year—

(i) the amount of the taxes imposed by sections 3101 and 3201(a) on amounts received by the taxpayer during the calendar year in which the taxable year begins,

(ii) 50 percent of the taxes imposed by section 1401 on the self-employment income of the taxpayer for the taxable year, and

(iii) 50 percent of the taxes imposed by section 3211(a) on amounts received by the taxpayer during the calendar year in which the taxable year begins.

(B) Coordination with special refund of social security taxes. The term "social security taxes" shall not include any taxes to the extent the taxpayer is entitled to a special refund of such taxes under section 6413(c).

(C) Special rule. Any amounts paid pursuant to an agreement under section 3121(l) (relating to agreements entered into by American employers with respect to foreign affiliates) which are equivalent to the taxes referred to in subparagraph (A)(i) shall be treated as taxes referred to in such subparagraph.

(3) Inflation adjustment. In the case of any taxable year beginning in a calendar year after 2001, the $10,000 amount contained in paragraph (1)(B) shall be increased by an amount equal to—

(A) such dollar amount, multiplied by

(B) the cost-of-living adjustment determined under section 1(f)(3) for the calendar year in which the taxable year begins, determined by substituting "calendar year 2000" for "calendar year 1992" in subparagraph (B) thereof.

Any increase determined under the preceding sentence shall be rounded to the nearest multiple of $50.

(4) Special rule for 2009, 2010, 2011, and 2012. Notwithstanding paragraph (3), in the case of any taxable year beginning in 2009, 2010, 2011, or 2012, the dollar amount in effect for such taxable year under paragraph (1)(B)(i) shall be $3,000.

(e) Identification requirement.

No credit shall be allowed under this section to a taxpayer with respect to any qualifying child unless the taxpayer includes the name and taxpayer identification number of such qualifying child on the return of tax for the taxable year.

(f) Taxable year must be full taxable year.

Except in the case of a taxable year closed by reason of the death of the taxpayer, no credit shall be allowable under this section in the case of a taxable year covering a period of less than 12 months.

In 2010, P.L. 111-312, Sec. 101(a)(1), substituted "December 31, 2012" for "December 31, 2010" both places it appeared in Sec. 901, P.L. 107-16 [see below], effective as if included in the enactment of P.L. 107-16, EGTRRA, 6/7/2001.

—P.L. 111-312, Sec. 101(b)(1), amended Sec. 10909(c), P.L. 111-148.
Prior to amendment, Sec. 10909(c), P.L. 111-148, read as follows:

"(c) Application and Extension of EGTRRA Sunset. Notwithstanding section 901 of the Economic Growth and Tax Relief Reconciliation Act of 2001, such section shall apply to the amendments made by this section and the amendments mad by section 202 of such Act by substituting 'December 31, 2011' for 'December 31, 2010' in subsection (a)(1) thereof."

—P.L. 111-312, Sec. 101(b)(2), substituted "Except as provided in subsection (c), the amendments" for "The amendments" in Sec. 10909(d) of P.L. 111-148 (the effective date section for amendments made by Sec. 10909 of P.L. 111-148) [see below].

Prior to amendment, Sec. 10909(d) of P.L. 111-148, read as follows:

"(d) Effective date. The amendments made by this section shall apply to taxable years beginning after December 31, 2009."

—P.L. 111-312, Sec. 103(b)(1), substituted "2009, 2010, 2011, and 2012" for "2009 and 2010" in the heading of para. (d)(4)... Sec. 103(b)(2), substituted ", 2010, 2011, or 2012" for "or 2010" in para. (d)(4), effective for tax. yrs. begin. after 12/31/2010.

—P.L. 111-148, Sec. 10909(b)(2)(A), deleted "23," in subpara. (b)(3)(B), effective for tax. yrs. begin. after 12/31/2009, except as provided in Sec. 10909(c), see below.

—P.L. 111-148, Sec. 10909(c), of this Act, relating to the application and extension of the EGTRRA sunset, [as amended by Sec. 101(b)(1) of P.L. 111-312, see above] provides:

"(c) Application and Extension of EGTRRA Sunset. Notwithstanding section 901 of the Economic Growth and Tax Relief Reconciliation Act of 2001, such section shall apply to the amendments made by this section and the amendments made by section 202 of such Act by substituting 'December 31, 2011' for 'December 31, 2010' in subsection (a)(1) thereof."

—P.L. 111-148, Sec. 10909(d), [as amended by Sec. 101(b)(2), P.L. 111-312, see above] reads as follows:

"(d) Effective date. Except as provided in subsection (c) [Sec. 10909(c) of P.L. 111-148], the amendments made by this section shall apply to taxable years beginning after December 31, 2009."

In 2009, P.L. 111-5, Sec. 1003(a), amended para. (d)(4), effective for tax. yrs. begin. after 12/31/2008.
Prior to amendment, para. (d)(4) read as follows:

"(4) Special rule for 2008. Notwithstanding paragraph (3), in the case of any taxable year beginning in 2008, the dollar amount in effect for such taxable year under paragraph (1)(B)(i) shall be $8,500."

—P.L. 111-5, Sec. 1004(b)(1), added "25A(i)," after "23," in subpara. (b)(3)(B), effective for tax. yrs. begin. after 12/31/2008.

—P.L. 111-5, Sec. 1004(e), provides:

"(e) Application of EGTRRA sunset. The amendment made by subsection (b)(1) shall be subject to title IX of the Economic Growth and Tax Relief Reconciliation Act of 2001 in the same manner as the provision of such Act to which such amendment relates."

—P.L. 111-5, Sec. 1142(b)(1)(A), added "30", after "25D," in subpara. (b)(3)(B) [as amended by Sec. 1004(b)(1) of this Act, see above], effective for vehicles acquired after 2/17/2009.

—P.L. 111-5, Sec. 1142(e), provides:

"(e) Application of EGTRRA sunset. The amendment made by subsection (b)(1)(A) shall be subject to title IX of the Economic Growth and Tax Relief Reconciliation Act of 2001 in the same manner as the provision of such Act to which such amendment relates."

—P.L. 111-5, Sec. 1144(b)(1)(A), added "30B", after "30", in subpara. (b)(3)(B) [as amended by Secs. 1004(b)(1) and 1142(b)(1)(A) of this Act, see above], effective for tax. yrs. begin. after 12/31/2008.

—P.L. 111-5, Sec. 1144(d), provides:

"(d) Application of EGTRRA sunset. The amendment made by subsection (b)(1)(A) shall be subject to title IX of the Economic Growth and Tax Relief Reconciliation Act of 2001 in the same manner as the provision of such Act to which such amendment relates."

In 2008, P.L. 110-351, Sec. 501(c)(1), added "for which the taxpayer is allowed a deduction under section 151" after "of the taxpayer" in subsec. (a), effective for tax. yrs. begin. after 12/31/2008.

—P.L. 110-343, Sec. 106(e)(2)(B)DivB, substituted ", 25B, and 25D" for "and 25B" in subpara. (b)(3)(B), effective for tax. yrs. begin. after 12/31/2007. The amendments made by subparagraphs (A) and (B) of subsection (e)(2) shall be subject to title IX of the Economic Growth and Tax Relief Reconciliation Act of 2001 in the same manner as the provisions of such Act to which such amendments relate.

—P.L. 110-343, Sec. 205(d)(1)(A)DivB, substituted "25D, and 30D" for "and 25D" in subpara. (b)(3)(B) (as amend), effective for tax. yrs. begin. after 12/31/2008.

—P.L. 110-343, Sec. 205(f)DivB, of this Act, reads as follows:

Tax credits Code Sec. 24

"(f) Application of egtrra sunset.

"The amendment made by subsection (d)(1)(A) shall be subject to title IX of the Economic Growth and Tax Relief Reconciliation Act of 2001 in the same manner as the provision of such Act to which such amendment relates."

—P.L. 110-343, Sec. 501(a)DivC, added para. (d)(4), effective for tax. yrs. begin. after 12/31/2007.

In 2007, P.L. 110-172, Sec. 11(c)(1)(A), substituted "the greater of" for "the excess (if any) of" in clause (d)(1)(B)(i). . . . Sec. 11(c)(1)(B), substituted "section 32" for "section" in subclause (d)(1)(B)(ii)(II), effective for tax. yrs. begin. after 12/31/2005.

In 2006, P.L. 109-280, Sec. 811, of this Act [relating to Sec. 901 of P.L. 107-16, see below], provides:

"SEC. 811. PENSIONS AND INDIVIDUAL RETIREMENT ARRANGEMENT PROVISIONS OF ECONOMIC GROWTH AND TAX RELIEF RECONCILIATION ACT OF 2001 MADE PERMANENT.

"Title IX of the Economic Growth and Tax Relief Reconciliation Act of 2001 shall not apply to the provisions of, and amendments made by, subtitles A through F of title VI of such Act (relating to pension and individual retirement arrangement provisions)."

In 2005, P.L. 109-135, Sec. 201(b)(4)(B), repealed Sec. 406 of P.L. 109-73 [see below], effective 12/21/2005.

—P.L. 109-135, Sec. 402(i)(3)(B)(i), substituted "In the case of a taxable year to which section 26(a)(2) does not apply, the credit" for "The credit" in the matter preceding subpara. (b)(3)(A) . . . Sec. 402(i)(3)(B)(ii), amended para. (d)(1), effective for tax. yrs. begin. after 12/31/2005.

Prior to amendment, para. (d)(1) read as follows:

"(1) In general. The aggregate credits allowed to a taxpayer under subpart C shall be increased by the lesser of—

"(A) the credit which would be allowed under this section without regard to this subsection and the limitation under subsection (b)(3), or

"(B) the amount by which the aggregate amount of credits allowed by this subpart (determined without regard to this subsection) would increase if the limitation imposed by subsection (b)(3) were increased by the greater of—

"(i) 15 percent of so much of the taxpayer's earned income (within the meaning of section 32) which is taken into account in computing taxable income for the taxable year as exceeds $10,000, or

"(ii) in the case of a taxpayer with 3 or more qualifying children, the excess (if any) of—

"(I) the taxpayer's social security taxes for the taxable year, over

"(II) the credit allowed under section 32 for the taxable year.

The amount of the credit allowed under this subsection shall not be treated as a credit allowed under this subpart and shall reduce the amount of credit otherwise allowable under subsection (a) without regard to subsection (b)(3). For purposes of subparagraph (B), any amount excluded from gross income by reason of section 112 shall be treated as earned income which is taken into account in computing taxable income for the taxable year."

—P.L. 109-135, Sec. 402(i)(3)(H), of this Act, reads as follows:

"(H) Application of EGTRRA Sunset. The amendments made by this paragraph (and each part thereof) shall be subject to title IX of the Economic Growth and Tax Relief Reconciliation Act of 2001 [Sec. 901 of P.L. 107-16] in the same manner as the provisions of such Act to which such amendment (or part thereof) relates."

—P.L. 109-73, Sec. 406, [prior to repeal by Sec. 201(b)(4)(B) of P.L. 109-135, see above] read as follows:

"SEC. 406. SPECIAL RULE FOR DETERMINING EARNED INCOME.

"(a) In general. In the case of a qualified individual, if the earned income of the taxpayer for the taxable year which includes August 25, 2005, is less than the earned income of the taxpayer for the preceding taxable year, the credits allowed under sections 24(d) and 32 of the Internal Revenue Code of 1986 may, at the election of the taxpayer, be determined by substituting—

"(1) such earned income for the preceding taxable year, for

"(2) such earned income for the taxable year which includes August 25, 2005.

"(b) Qualified individual. For purposes of this section, the term 'qualified individual' means any individual whose principal place of abode on August 25, 2005, was located—

"(1) in the core disaster area, or

"(2) in the Hurricane Katrina disaster area (but outside the core disaster area) and such individual was displaced from such principal place of abode by reason of Hurricane Katrina.

"(c) Earned income. For purposes of this section, the term 'earned income' has the meaning given such term under section 32(c) of such Code.

"(d) Special rules.

"(1) Application to joint returns. For purposes of subsection (a), in the case of a joint return for a taxable year which includes August 25, 2005—

"(A) such subsection shall apply if either spouse is a qualified individual, and

"(B) the earned income of the taxpayer for the preceding taxable year shall be the sum of the earned income of each spouse for such preceding taxable year.

"(2) Uniform application of election. Any election made under subsection (a) shall apply with respect to both section 24(d) and section 32 of such Code.

"(3) Errors treated as mathematical error. For purposes of section 6213 of such Code, an incorrect use on a return of earned income pursuant to subsection (a) shall be treated as a mathematical or clerical error.

"(4) No effect on determination of gross income, etc. Except as otherwise provided in this section, the Internal Revenue Code of 1986 shall be applied without regard to any substitution under subsection (a)."

In 2004, P.L. 108-311, Sec. 101(a), amended subsec. (a), effective for tax. yrs. begin. after 12/31/2003.

Prior to amendment, subsec. (a) read as follows:

"(a) Allowance of credit.

"(1) In general. There shall be allowed as a credit against the tax imposed by this chapter for the taxable year with respect to each qualifying child of the taxpayer an amount equal to the per child amount.

"(2) Per child amount. For purposes of paragraph (1), the per child amount shall be determined as follows:

In the case of any taxable year beginning in—	The per child amount is—
2003 or 2004	$ 1,000
2005, 2006, 2007, or 2008	700
2009	800
2010 or thereafter	1,000."

—P.L. 108-311, Sec. 102(a), deleted "(10 percent in the case of taxable years beginning before January 1, 2005)" after "15 percent" in clause (d)(1)(B)(i), effective for tax. yrs. begin. after 12/31/2003.

—P.L. 108-311, Sec. 104(a), added "For purposes of subparagraph (B), any amount excluded from gross income by reason of section 112 shall be treated as earned income which is taken into account in computing taxable income for the taxable year." at the end of para. (d)(1), effective for tax. yrs. begin. after 12/31/2003.

—P.L. 108-311, Sec. 105, of this Act, reads as follows:

"SEC. 105. APPLICATION OF EGTRRA SUNSET TO THIS TITLE. Each amendment made by this title [Secs. 101-104] shall be subject to title IX of the Economic Growth and Tax Relief Reconciliation Act of 2001 [Sec. 901 of P.L. 107-16] to the same extent and in the same manner as the provision of such Act to which such amendment relates."

—P.L. 108-311, Sec. 204(a), amended para. (c)(1) . . . Sec. 204(b), substituted "subparagraph (A) of section 152(B)(3)" for "the first sentence of section 152(b)(3)" in para. (c)(2), effective for tax. yrs. begin. after 12/31/2004.

Prior to amendment, para. (c)(1) read as follows:

"(1) In general. The term 'qualifying child' means any individual if—

"(A) the taxpayer is allowed a deduction under section 151 with respect to such individual for the taxable year,

"(B) such individual has not attained the age of 17 as of the close of the calendar year in which the taxable year of the taxpayer begins, and

"(C) such individual bears a relationship to the taxpayer described in section 32(c)(3)(B)."

—P.L. 108-311, Sec. 312(b)(2), reads as follows:

"(2) The amendments made by sections 201(b), 202(f), and 618(b) of the Economic Growth and Tax Relief Reconciliation Act of 2001 shall not apply to taxable years beginning during 2004 or 2005."

—P.L. 108-311, Sec. 408(b)(4), substituted "Section 24(d)(2)(A)(iii)" for "Section 24(d)(3)(A)(iii)" in Sec. 204(e)(1) of P.L. 107-90 [see below].

In 2003, P.L. 108-27, Sec. 101(a), amended the table in para. (a)(2), effective for tax. yrs. begin. after 12/31/2002.

Prior to amendment, the table in para. (a)(2) read as follows:

In the case of any taxable year beginning in—	The per child amount is—
2001, 2002, 2003, or 2004	600
2005, 2006, 2007, or 2008	700
2009	800
2010 or thereafter	1,000."

—P.L. 108-27, Sec. 107, of this Act, reads as follows:

"SEC. 107. APPLICATION OF EGTRRA SUNSET TO THIS TITLE. Each amendment made by this title [Secs. 101-106] shall be subject to title IX of the Economic Growth and Tax Relief Reconciliation Act of 2001 to the same extent and in the same manner as the provision of such Act to which such amendment relates."

In 2002, P.L. 107-358, Sec. 2, added subsec. (c) in Sec. 901 of P.L. 107-16 [see below], effective 12/17/2002.

—P.L. 107-147, Sec. 411(b), substituted "aggregate amount of credits allowed by this subpart" for "amount of credit allowed by this section" in subpara. (d)(1)(B), effective for tax. yrs. begin. after 12/31/2001.

—P.L. 107-147, Sec. 601(b)(2), of this Act, provides:

"(2) The amendments made by sections 201(b), 202(f), and 618(b) of the Economic Growth and Tax Relief Reconciliation Act of 2001 shall not apply to taxable years beginning during 2002 and 2003."

In 2001, P.L. 107-90, Sec. 204(e)(1), substituted "section 3211(a)" for "section 3211(a)(1)" in clause (d)(3)(A)(iii) [as clarified by Sec. 408(b)(4) of P.L. 108-311, see above], effective for calendar yrs. begin. after 12/31/2001.

—P.L. 107-16, Sec. 201(a), amended subsec. (a), effective for tax. yrs. begin. after 12/31/2000.

Prior to amendment, subsec. (a) read as follows:

"(a) Allowance of credit.

"There shall be allowed as a credit against the tax imposed by this chapter for the taxable year with respect to each qualifying child of the taxpayer an amount equal to $500 ($400 in the case of taxable years beginning in 1998)."

—P.L. 107-16, Sec. 201(b)(1), added para. (b)(3) . . . Sec. 201(b)(2)(A), substituted "Limitations." for "Limitation based on adjusted gross income." in the heading of subsec. (b) . . . Sec. 201(b)(2)(B), substituted "Limitation based on adjusted gross income." for "In general." in the heading of para. (b)(1) . . . Sec.

1,043

201(b)(2)(C)(i), substituted "subsection (b)(3)" for "section 26(a)" each place it appeared in subsec. (d) [as amended by Sec. 201(c)(1) of this Act, see below] . . . Sec. 201(b)(2)(C)(ii), substituted "amount of credit allowed by this section" for "aggregate amount of credits allowed by this subpart" [this amendment cannot be made. Subpara. (d)(1)(B) already contains the language "amount of credit allowed by this section" in subpara. (d)(1)(B) [as amended by Sec. 201(c)(1) of this Act, see below], effective for tax. yrs. begin. after 12/31/2001. For special provision, see Sec. 601(b)(2) of P.L. 107-147, above. For special provision, see Sec. 312(b)(2) of P.L. 108-311, see above.

—P.L. 107-16, Sec. 201(c)(1), substituted "Portion of credit refundable" for "Additional credit for families with 3 or more children" in the heading of subsec. (d) and amended para. (d)(1) . . . Sec. 201(c)(2), added para. (d)(4) . . . Sec. 201(d)(1), deleted para. (d)(2) . . . Sec. 201(d)(2), redesignated para. (d)(3) as (d)(2) and (d)(4) [as added by Sec. 201(c)(2) of this Act, see above] as (d)(3), effective for tax. yrs. begin. after 12/31/2000.

Prior to amendment, para. (d)(1) read as follows:

"(1) In general. In the case of a taxpayer with three or more qualifying children for any taxable year, the aggregate credits allowed under subpart C shall be increased by the lesser of—

"(A) the credit which would be allowed under this section without regard to this subsection and the limitation under section 26(a); or

"(B) the amount by which the aggregate amount of credits allowed by this subpart (without regard to this subsection) would increase if the limitation imposed by section 26(a) were increased by the excess (if any) of—

"(i) the taxpayer's Social Security taxes for the taxable year, over

"(ii) the credit allowed under section 32 (determined without regard to subsection (n)) for the taxable year.

The amount of the credit allowed under this subsection shall not be treated as a credit allowed under this subpart and shall reduce the amount of credit otherwise allowable under subsection (a) without regard to section 26(a)."

Prior to deletion, para. (d)(2) read as follows:

"(2) Reduction of credit to taxpayer subject to alternative minimum tax. For taxable years beginning after December 31, 2001, the credit determined under this subsection for the taxable year shall be reduced by the excess (if any) of—

"(A) the amount of tax imposed by section 55 (relating to alternative minimum tax) with respect to such taxpayer for such taxable year, over

"(B) the amount of the reduction under section 32(h) with respect to such taxpayer for such taxable year."

—P.L. 107-16, Sec. 202(f)(2)(B), substituted "this section and section 23" for "this section" in subpara. (b)(3)(B), effective for tax. yrs. begin. after 12/31/2001. For special provision, see Sec. 601(b)(2) of P.L. 107-147 , above. For special provision, see Sec. 312(b)(2) of P.L. 108-311, see above.

—P.L. 107-16, Sec. 203, of this Act, reads as follows:

"SEC. 203. REFUNDS DISREGARDED IN THE ADMINISTRATION OF FEDERAL PROGRAMS AND FEDERALLY ASSISTED PROGRAMS. Any payment considered to have been made to any individual by reason of section 24 of the Internal Revenue Code of 1986, as amended by section 201, shall not be taken into account as income and shall not be taken into account as resources for the month of receipt and the following month, for purposes of determining the eligibility of such individual or any other individual for benefits or assistance, or the amount or extent of benefits or assistance, under any Federal program or under any State or local program financed in whole or in part with Federal funds."

—P.L. 107-16, Sec. 618(b)(2)(A), substituted "sections 23 and 25B" for "section 23" in subpara. (b)(3)(B) [as amended by Sec. 202(f)(2)(B) of this Act, see above], effective for tax. yrs. begin. after 12/31/2001. For special provision, see Sec. 601(b)(2) of P.L. 107-147, above. For special provision, see Sec. 312(b)(2) of P.L. 108-311, see above.

—P.L. 107-16, Sec. 901, of this Act [as amended by Sec. 2 of P.L. 107-358, and Sec. 101(a)(1), P.L. 111-312, see above, and as related to Sec. 811 of P.L. 109-280, see above], reads as follows:

"Sec. 901. Sunset of provisions of Act.

"(a) In general. All provisions of, and amendments made by, this Act shall not apply—

"(1) to taxable, plan, or limitation years beginning after December 31, 2012, or

"(2) in the case of title V, to estates of decedents dying, gifts made, or generation skipping transfers, after December 31, 2012.

"(b) Application of certain laws. The Internal Revenue Code of 1986 and the Employee Retirement Income Security Act of 1974 shall be applied and administered to years, estates, gifts, and transfers described in subsection (a) as if the provisions and amendments described in subsection (a) had never been enacted.

"(c) Exception. Subsection (a) shall not apply to section 803 (relating to no federal income tax on restitution received by victims of the Nazi regime or their heirs or estates)."

In 1999, P.L. 106-170, Sec. 501(b)(1), substituted "2001" for "1998" in para. (d)(2), effective for tax. yrs. begin. after 12/31/98.

In 1998, P.L. 105-277, Sec. 2001(b), substituted "For taxable years beginning after December 31, 1998, the credit" for "The credit" in para. (d)(2), effective for tax. yrs. begin. after 12/31/97.

—P.L. 105-206, Sec. 6003(a)(1)(A), deleted paras. (d)(3) and (4) . . . Sec. 6003(a)(1)(B), redesignated para. (d)(5) as (d)(3) . . . Sec. 6003(a)(1)(C), amended paras. (d)(1) and (2) . . . Sec. 6003(a)(2), substituted "paragraph (I)" for "paragraph (3)" in para. (d)(3) [as redesignated by Sec. 6003(a)(1)(B) of this Act, see above] effective for tax. yrs. begin. after 12/31/97.

Prior to amendment, paras. (d)(1) and (2) read as follows:

"(1) In general. In the case of a taxpayer with 3 or more qualifying children for any taxable year, the amount of the credit allowed under this section shall be equal to the greater of—

"(A) the amount of the credit allowed under this section (without regard to this subsection and after application of the limitation under section 26), or

"(B) the alternative credit amount determined under paragraph (2).

"(2) Credit amount. For purposes of this subsection, the alternative credit which would be allowed under this section if the limitation under paragraph (3) were applied in lieu of the limitation under section 26."

Prior to deletion, paras. (d)(3) and (4) read as follows:

"(3) Limitation. The limitation under this paragraph for any taxable year is the limitation under section 26 (without regard to this subsection)—

"(A) increased by the taxpayer's social security taxes for such taxable year, and

"(B) reduced by the sum of—

"(i) the credits allowed under this part other than under subpart C or this section, and

"(ii) the credit allowed under section 32 without regard to subsection (m) thereof.

"(4) Unused credit to be refundable. If the amount of the credit under paragraph (1)(B) exceeds the amount of the credit under paragraph (1)(A), such excess shall be treated as a credit to which subpart C applies. The rule of section 32(h) shall apply to such excess."

In 1997, P.L. 105-34, Sec. 101(a), added Code Sec. 24, effective for tax. yrs. begin. after 12/31/97.

Sec. 24. Repealed.

In 1986, P.L. 99-514, Sec. 112(a), repealed Code Sec. 24, effective for tax. yrs. begin. after 12/31/86.

Prior to repeal, Code Sec. 24 read as follows:

"Sec. 24. Contributions to candidates for public office.

"(a) General rule. In the case of an individual, there shall be allowed, subject to the limitations of subsection (b), as a credit against the tax imposed by this chapter for the taxable year, an amount equal to one-half of all political contributions and all newsletter fund contributions, payment of which is made by the taxpayer within the taxable year.

"(b) Limitations.

"(1) Maximum credit. The credit allowed by subsection (a) for a taxable year shall not exceed $50 ($100 in the case of a joint return under section 6013).

"(2) Verification. The credit allowed by subsection (a) shall be allowed, with respect to any political contribution or newsletter fund contribution, only if such contribution is verified in such manner as the Secretary shall prescribe by regulations.

"(c) Definitions. For purposes of this section—

"(1) Political contribution. The term 'political contribution' means a contribution or gift of money to—

"(A) an individual who is a candidate for nomination or election to any Federal, State, or local elective public office in any primary, general, or special election, for use by such individual to further his candidacy for nomination or election to such office;

"(B) any committee, association, or organization (whether or not incorporated) organized and operated exclusively for the purpose of influencing, or attempting to influence, the nomination or election of one or more individuals who are candidates for nomination or election to any Federal, State, or local elective public office, for use by such committee, association, or organization to further the candidacy of such individual or individuals for nomination or election to such office;

"(C) the national committee of a national political party;

"(D) the State committee of a national political party as designated by the national committee of such party; or

"(E) a local committee of a national political party as designated by the State Committee of such party designated under subparagraph (D).

"(2) Candidate. The term 'candidate' means, with respect to any Federal, State, or local elective public office, an individual who—

"(A) publicly announces before the close of the calendar year following the calendar year in which the contribution or gift is made that he is a candidate for nomination or election to such office; and

"(B) meets the qualifications prescribed by law to hold such office.

"(3) National political party. The term 'national political party' means—

"(A) in the case of contributions made during a taxable year of the taxpayer in which the electors of President and Vice President are chosen, a political party presenting candidates or electors for such offices on the official election ballot of ten or more States, or

"(B) in the case of contributions made during any other taxable year of the taxpayer, a political party which met the qualifications described in subparagraph (A) in the last preceding election of a President and Vice President.

"(4) State and local. The term 'State' means the various States and the District of Columbia; and the term 'local' means a political subdivision or part thereof, or two or more political subdivisions or parts thereof, of a State.

"(5) Newsletter fund contribution. The term 'newsletter fund contribution' means a contribution or gift of money to a fund established and maintained by an individual who holds, has been elected to, or is a candidate for nomination or election to, any Federal, State, or local elective public office for use by such individual exclusively for the preparation and circulation of a newsletter.

"(d) Cross references.

"(1) For disallowance of credits to estates and trusts, see section 642(a)(2).

"(2) For treatment of Indian tribal governments as States (and the political subdivisions of Indian tribal governments as political subdivisions of States), see section 7871."

In 1984, P.L. 98-369, Sec. 471(c)(1), redesignated Code Sec. 41 as Code Sec. 24 ... Sec. 474(f), deleted para. (b)(2) and redesignated para. (b)(3) as para. (b)(2), effective for tax. yrs. begin. after 12/31/83 and to carrybacks from tax. yrs. begin. after 12/31/83.

Prior to deletion, para. (b)(2) read as follows:

"(2) Application with other credits. The credit allowed by subsection (a) shall not exceed the amount of the tax imposed by this chapter for the taxable year reduced by the sum of the credits allowable under section 33 (relating to foreign tax credit), section 37 (relating to credit for the elderly and the permanently and totally disabled), and section 38 (relating to investment in certain depreciable property)."

In 1983, P.L. 98-21, Sec. 122(c)(1), substituted "relating to credit for the elderly and the permanently and totally disabled" for "relating to credit for the elderly" in para. (b)(2), effective for tax. yrs. begin. after 12/31/83.

— P.L. 97-473, Sec. 202(b)(1), amended subsec. (d), effective for tax. yrs. begin. after 12/31/82 and before 1/1/85.

Prior to amendment, subsec. (d) read as follows:

"(d) Cross references. For disallowance of credits to estates and trusts, see section 642(a)(2)."

In 1978, P.L. 95-600, Sec. 113(c), substituted "$50" for "$25" and "$100" for "$50" in para. (b)(1), effective for contributions payments made after 12/31/78, in tax. yrs. begin. after 12/31/78.

In 1976, P.L. 94-455, Sec. 503(b)(4), substituted "credit for the elderly" for "retirement income" in para. (b)(2), effective for tax. yrs. begin. after 12/31/75.

— P.L. 94-455, Sec. 1901(b)(1)(B), deleted "section 35 (relating to partially tax-exempt interest)," after "section 33 (relating to foreign tax credit)," in para. (b)(2), effective for tax. yrs. begin. after 12/31/76.

— P.L. 94-455, Sec. 1901(b)(1)(H)(ii), substituted "section 642(a)(2)" for "section 642(a)(3)" in subsec. (d), effective for tax. yrs. begin. after 12/31/76.

— P.L. 94-455, Sec. 1906(b)(13)(A), substituted "Secretary" for "Secretary or his delegate" in para. (a)(3), effective for tax. yrs. begin. after 12/31/76.

In 1975, P.L. 93-625, Sec. 11(a), added "and all newsletter fund contributions" after "all political contributions" in subsec. (a) ... Sec. 11(b)(1), substituted "political contribution or newsletter fund contribution" for "political contribution" the first place it appeared in para. (b)(3) ... Sec. 11(b)(2), substituted "contribution" for "political contribution" the second place it appeared in para. (b)(3) ... Sec. 11(c), added para. (c)(5) ... Sec. 11(e), substituted "publicly announces before the close of the calendar year following the calendar year in which the contribution or gift is made" for "has publicly announced" in subpara. (c)(2)(A) ... Sec. 12(a), amended para. (b)(1), effective for contribution payments made after 12/31/74 in tax. yrs. begin. after 12/31/74.

Prior to amendment, para. (b)(1) read as follows:

"(1) Maximum credit. The credit allowed by subsection (a) for a taxable year shall be limited to $12.50 ($25 in the case of a joint return under section 6013)."

In 1971, P.L. 92-178, Sec. 701(a), added Code Sec. 41, effective for tax. yrs. end. after 12/31/71, but only with respect to political contributions, payment of which is made after 12/31/71.

Sec. 25. Interest on certain home mortgages.

(a) Allowance of credit.

(1) In general. There shall be allowed as a credit against the tax imposed by this chapter for the taxable year an amount equal to the product of—

(A) the certificate credit rate, and

(B) the interest paid or accrued by the taxpayer during the taxable year on the remaining principal of the certified indebtedness amount.

(2) Limitation where credit rate exceeds 20 percent.

(A) In general. If the certificate credit rate exceeds 20 percent, the amount of the credit allowed to the taxpayer under paragraph (1) for any taxable year shall not exceed $2,000.

(B) Special rule where 2 or more persons hold interests in residence. If 2 or more persons hold interests in any residence, the limitation of subparagraph (A) shall be allocated among such persons in proportion to their respective interests in the residence.

(b) Certificate credit rate; certified indebtedness amount.

For purposes of this section—

(1) Certificate credit rate. The term "certificate credit rate" means the rate of the credit allowable by this section which is specified in the mortgage credit certificate.

(2) Certified indebtedness amount. The term "certified indebtedness amount" means the amount of indebtedness which is—

(A) incurred by the taxpayer—

(i) to acquire the principal residence of the taxpayer,

(ii) as a qualified home improvement loan (as defined in section 143(k)(4)) with respect to such residence, or

(iii) as a qualified rehabilitation loan (as defined in section 143(k)(5)) with respect to such residence, and

(B) specified in the mortgage credit certificate.

(c) Mortgage credit certificate; qualified mortgage credit certificate program.

For purposes of this section—

(1) Mortgage credit certificate. The term "mortgage credit certificate" means any certificate which—

(A) is issued under a qualified mortgage credit certificate program by the State or political subdivision having the authority to issue a qualified mortgage bond to provide financing on the principal residence of the taxpayer,

(B) is issued to the taxpayer in connection with the acquisition, qualified rehabilitation, or qualified home improvement of the taxpayer's principal residence,

(C) specifies—

(i) the certificate credit rate, and

(ii) the certified indebtedness amount, and

(D) is in such form as the Secretary may prescribe.

(2) Qualified mortgage credit certificate program.

(A) In general. The term "qualified mortgage credit certificate program" means any program—

(i) which is established by a State or political subdivision thereof for any calendar year for which it is authorized to issue qualified mortgage bonds,

(ii) under which the issuing authority elects (in such manner and form as the Secretary may prescribe) not to issue an amount of private activity bonds which it may otherwise issue during such calendar year under section 146,

(iii) under which the indebtedness certified by mortgage credit certificates meets the requirements of the following subsections of section 143 (as modified by subparagraph (B) of this paragraph):

(I) subsection (c) (relating to residence requirements),

(II) subsection (d) (relating to 3-year requirement),

(III) subsection (e) (relating to purchase price requirement),

(IV) subsection (f) (relating to income requirements),

(V) subsection (h) (relating to portion of loans required to be placed in targeted areas), and

(VI) paragraph (1) of subsection (i) (relating to other requirements),

(iv) under which no mortgage credit certificate may be issued with respect to any residence any of the financing of which is provided from the proceeds of a qualified mortgage bond or a qualified veterans' mortgage bond,

(v) except to the extent provided in regulations, which is not limited to indebtedness incurred from particular lenders,

(vi) except to the extent provided in regulations, which provides that a mortgage credit certificate is not transferrable, and

(vii) if the issuing authority allocates a block of mortgage credit certificates for use in connection with a particular development, which requires the developer to furnish to the issuing authority and the homebuyer a certificate that the price for the residence is no higher than it would be without the use of a mortgage credit certificate.

Under regulations, rules similar to the rules of subparagraphs (B) and (C) of section 143(a)(2) shall apply to the requirements of this subparagraph.

(B) Modifications of section 143. Under regulations prescribed by the Secretary, in applying section 143 for purposes of subclauses (II), (IV), and (V) of subparagraph (A)(iii)—

(i) each qualified mortgage certificate credit program shall be treated as a separate issue,

(ii) the product determined by multiplying—

(I) the certified indebtedness amount of each mortgage credit certificate issued under such program, by

(II) the certificate credit rate specified in such certificate,

shall be treated as proceeds of such issue and the sum of such products shall be treated as the total proceeds of such issue, and

(iii) paragraph (1) of section 143(d) shall be applied by substituting "100 percent" for "95 percent or more".

Clause (iii) shall not apply if the issuing authority submits a plan to the Secretary for administering the 95-percent requirement of section 143(d)(1) and the Secretary is satisfied that such requirement will be met under such plan.

(d) Determination of certificate credit rate.

For purposes of this section—

(1) **In general.** The certificate credit rate specified in any mortgage credit certificate shall not be less than 10 percent or more than 50 percent.

(2) **Aggregate limit on certificate credit rates.**

(A) In general. In the case of each qualified mortgage credit certificate program, the sum of the products determined by multiplying—

(i) the certified indebtedness amount of each mortgage credit certificate issued under such program, by

(ii) the certificate credit rate with respect to such certificate,

shall not exceed 25 percent of the nonissued bond amount.

(B) Nonissued bond amount. For purposes of subparagraph (A), the term "nonissued bond amount" means, with respect to any qualified mortgage credit certificate program, the amount of qualified mortgage bonds which the issuing authority is otherwise authorized to issue and elects not to issue under subsection (c)(2)(A)(ii).

(e) **Special rules and definitions.**

For purposes of this section—

(1) **Carryforward of unused credit.**

(A) In general. If the credit allowable under subsection (a) for any taxable year exceeds the applicable tax limit for such taxable year, such excess shall be a carryover to each of the 3 succeeding taxable years and, subject to the limitations of subparagraph (B), shall be added to the credit allowable by subsection (a) for such succeeding taxable year.

(B) Limitation. The amount of the unused credit which may be taken into account under subparagraph (A) for any taxable year shall not exceed the amount (if any) by which the applicable tax limit for such taxable year exceeds the sum of—

(i) the credit allowable under subsection (a) for such taxable year determined without regard to this paragraph, and

(ii) the amounts which, by reason of this paragraph, are carried to such taxable year and are attributable to taxable years before the unused credit year.

• *Caution:* Code Sec. 25(e)(1)(C), following, reflects amendments made by Sec. 10909, P.L. 111-148. As provided in Sec. 10909(c), P.L. 111-148 as amended by Sec. 101(b)(1), P.L. 111-312, Code Sec. 25(e)(1)(C) will read as if those amendments had never been enacted, effective for tax. yrs. begin. after 12/31/2011. For Code Sec. 25(e)(1)(C) as it will read for tax. yrs. begin. after 12/31/2011, see below.

(C) Applicable tax limit. For purposes of this paragraph, the term "applicable tax limit" means—

(i) in the case of a taxable year to which section 26(a)(2) applies, the limitation imposed by section 26(a)(2) for the taxable year reduced by the sum of the credits allowable under this subpart (other than this section and 25D, and 1400C), and

(ii) in the case of a taxable year to which section 26(a)(2) does not apply, the limitation imposed by section 26(a)(1) for the taxable year reduced by the sum of the credits allowable under this subpart (other than this section and sections 24, 25A(i), 25B, 25D, 30, 30B, 30D, and 1400C).

• *Caution:* Code Sec. 25(e)(1)(C), following, is effective for tax. yrs. begin. after 12/31/2011, and reflects the sunset of the amendments made by Sec. 10909, P.L. 111-148. For details of those amendments, effective date and sunset provisions, see the history for this Code Sec. For Code Sec. 25(e)(1)(C), effective for tax. yrs. begin. before 1/1/2012, see above.

(C) Applicable tax limit. For purposes of this paragraph, the term "applicable tax limit" means—

(i) in the case of a taxable year to which section 26(a)(2) applies, the limitation imposed by section 26(a)(2) for the taxable year reduced by the sum of the credits allowable under this subpart (other than this section and 23, 25D, and 1400C), and

(ii) in the case of a taxable year to which section 26(a)(2) does not apply, the limitation imposed by section 26(a)(1) for the taxable year reduced by the sum of the credits allowable under this subpart (other than this section and sections 23, 24, 25A(i), 25B, 25D, 30, 30B, 30D, and 1400C).

(2) **Indebtedness not treated as certified where certain requirements not in fact met.** Subsection (a) shall not apply to any indebtedness if all the requirements of subsections (c)(1), (d), (e), (f), and (i) of section 143 and clauses (iv), (v), and (vii) of subsection (c)(2)(A), were not in fact met with respect to such indebtedness. Except to the extent provided in regulations, the requirements described in the preceding sentence shall be treated as met if

Tax credits Code Sec. 25(g)(2)

there is a certification, under penalty of perjury, that such requirements are met.

(3) Period for which certificate in effect.

(A) In general. Except as provided in subparagraph (B), a mortgage credit certificate shall be treated as in effect with respect to interest attributable to the period—

(i) beginning on the date such certificate is issued, and

(ii) ending on the earlier of the date on which—

(I) the certificate is revoked by the issuing authority, or

(II) the residence to which such certificate relates ceases to be the principal residence of the individual to whom the certificate relates.

(B) Certificate invalid unless indebtedness incurred within certain period. A certificate shall not apply to any indebtedness which is incurred after the close of the second calendar year following the calendar year for which the issuing authority made the applicable election under subsection (c)(2)(A)(ii).

(C) Notice to secretary when certificate revoked. Any issuing authority which revokes any mortgage credit certificate shall notify the Secretary of such revocation at such time and in such manner as the Secretary shall prescribe by regulations.

(4) Reissuance of mortgage credit certificates. The Secretary may prescribe regulations which allow the administrator of a mortgage credit certificate program to reissue a mortgage credit certificate specifying a certified mortgage indebtedness that replaces the outstanding balance of the certified mortgage indebtedness specified on the original certificate to any taxpayer to whom the original certificate was issued, under such terms and conditions as the Secretary determines are necessary to ensure that the amount of the credit allowable under subsection (a) with respect to such reissued certificate is equal to or less than the amount of credit which would be allowable under subsection (a) with respect to the original certificate for any taxable year ending after such reissuance.

(5) Public notice that certificates will be issued. At least 90 days before any mortgage credit certificate is to be issued after a qualified mortgage credit certificate program, the issuing authority shall provide reasonable public notice of—

(A) the eligibility requirements for such certificate,

(B) the methods by which such certificates are to be issued, and

(C) such other information as the Secretary may require.

(6) Interest paid or accrued to related persons. No credit shall be allowed under subsection (a) for any interest paid or accrued to a person who is a related person to the taxpayer (within the meaning of section 144(a)(3)(A)).

(7) Principal residence. The term "principal residence" has the same meaning as when used in section 121.

(8) Qualified rehabilitation and home improvement.

(A) Qualified rehabilitation. The term "qualified rehabilitation" has the meaning given such term by section 143(k)(5)(B).

(B) Qualified home improvement. The term "qualified home improvement" means an alteration, repair, or improvement described in section 143(k)(4).

(9) Qualified mortgage bond. The term "qualified mortgage bond" has the meaning given such term by section 143(a)(1).

(10) Manufactured housing. For purposes of this section, the term "single family residence" includes any manufactured home which has a minimum of 400 square feet of living space and a minimum width in excess of 102 inches and which is of a kind customarily used at a fixed location. Nothing in the preceding sentence shall be construed as providing that such a home will be taken into account in making determinations under section 143.

(f) Reduction in aggregate amount of qualified mortgage bonds which may be issued where certain requirements not met.

(1) In general. If for any calendar year any mortgage credit certificate program which satisfies procedural requirements with respect to volume limitations prescribed by the Secretary fails to meet the requirements of paragraph (2) of subsection (d), such requirements shall be treated as satisfied with respect to any certified indebtedness of such program, but the applicable State ceiling under subsection (d) of section 146 for the State in which such program operates shall be reduced by 1.25 times the correction amount with respect to such failure. Such reduction shall be applied to such State ceiling for the calendar year following the calendar year in which the Secretary determines the correction amount with respect to such failure.

(2) Correction amount.

(A) In general. For purposes of paragraph (1), the term "correction amount" means an amount equal to the excess credit amount divided by 0.25.

(B) Excess credit amount.

(i) In general. For purposes of subparagraph (A)(ii), the term "excess credit amount" means the excess of—

(I) the credit amount for any mortgage credit certificate program, over

(II) the amount which would have been the credit amount for such program had such program met the requirements of paragraph (2) of subsection (d).

(ii) Credit amount. For purposes of clause (i), the term "credit amount" means the sum of the products determined under clauses (i) and (ii) of subsection (d)(2)(A).

(3) Special rule for states having constitutional home rule cities. In the case of a State having one or more constitutional home rule cities (within the meaning of section 146(d)(3)(C)), the reduction in the State ceiling by reason of paragraph (1) shall be allocated to the constitutional home rule city, or to the portion of the State not within such city, whichever caused the reduction.

(4) Exception where certification program. The provisions of this subsection shall not apply in any case in which there is a certification program which is designed to ensure that the requirements of this section are met and which meets such requirements as the Secretary may by regulations prescribe.

(5) Waiver. The Secretary may waive the application of paragraph (1) in any case in which he determines that the failure is due to reasonable cause.

(g) Reporting requirements.

Each person who makes a loan which is a certified indebtedness amount under any mortgage credit certificate shall file a report with the Secretary containing—

(1) the name, address, and social security account number of the individual to which the certificate was issued,

(2) the certificate's issuer, date of issue, certified indebtedness amount, and certificate credit rate, and

1,047

(3) such other information as the Secretary may require by regulations.

Each person who issues a mortgage credit certificate shall file a report showing such information as the Secretary shall by regulations prescribe. Any such report shall be filed at such time and in such manner as the Secretary may require by regulations.

(h) **Regulations; contracts.**

(1) **Regulations.** The Secretary shall prescribe such regulations as may be necessary to carry out the purposes of this section, including regulations which may require recipients of mortgage credit certificates to pay a reasonable processing fee to defray the expenses incurred in administering the program.

(2) **Contracts.** The Secretary is authorized to enter into contracts with any person to provide services in connection with the administration of this section.

(i) **Recapture of portion of federal subsidy from use of mortgage credit certificates.**

For provisions increasing the tax imposed by this chapter to recapture a portion of the Federal subsidy from the use of mortgage credit certificates, see section 143(m).

In 2010, P.L. 111-312, Sec. 101(a)(1), substituted "December 31, 2012" for "December 31, 2010" both places it appeared in Sec. 901 of P.L. 107-16, effective as if included in the enactment of P.L. 107-16, EGTRRA, 6/7/2001 [see below].

—P.L. 111-312, Sec. 101(b)(1), amended Sec. 10909(c) of P.L. 111-148.

Prior to amendment, Sec. 10909(c) of P.L. 111-148 read as follows:

"(c) Application and Extension of EGTRRA Sunset. Notwithstanding section 901 of the Economic Growth and Tax Relief Reconciliation Act of 2001, such section shall apply to the amendments made by this section and the amendments made by section 202 of such Act by substituting 'December 31, 2011' for 'December 31, 2010' in subsection (a)(1) thereof."

—P.L. 111-312, Sec. 101(b)(2), substituted "Except as provided in subsection (c), the amendments" for "The amendments" in Sec. 10909(d) of P.L. 111-148 (the effective date section for amendments made by Sec. 10909 of P.L. 111-148) [see below].

Prior to amendment, Sec. 10909(d) of P.L. 111-148 read as follows:

"(d) Effective date. The amendments made by this section shall apply to taxable years beginning after December 31, 2009."

—P.L. 111-148, Sec. 10909(b)(2)(B), deleted "23," both places it appeared in subpara. (e)(1)(C), effective for tax. yrs. begin. after 12/31/2009, except as provided in Sec. 10909(c) of this Act, see below.

—P.L. 111-148, Sec. 10909(c), of this Act, relating to the application and extension of the EGTRRA sunset provisions [as amended by Sec. 101(b)(1) of P.L. 111-312, see above], provides:

"(c) Sunset provision. Each provision of law amended by this section is amended to read as such provision would read if this section had never been enacted. The amendments made by the preceding sentence shall apply to taxable years beginning after December 31, 2011."

—P.L. 111-148, Sec. 10909(d), [as amended by Sec. 101(b)(2), P.L. 111-312, see above] reads as follows:

"(d) Effective date. Except as provided in subsection (c) [Sec. 10909(c) of P.L. 111-148], the amendments made by this section shall apply to taxable years beginning after December 31, 2009."

In 2009, P.L. 111-5, Sec. 1004(b)(2), added "25A(i)," after "24," in clause (e)(1)(C)(ii), effective for tax. yrs. begin. after 12/31/2008.

—P.L. 111-5, Sec. 1142(b)(1)(B), added "30," after "25D," in clause (e)(1)(C)(ii) [as amended by Sec. 1004(b)(2) of this Act, see above], effective for vehicles acquired after 2/17/2009.

—P.L. 111-5, Sec. 1144(b)(1)(B), added "30B," after "30," in clause (e)(1)(C)(ii) [as amended by Secs. 1004(b)(2) and 1142(b)(1)(B) of this Act, see above], effective for tax. yrs. begin. after 12/31/2008.

In 2008, P.L. 110-343, Sec. 205(d)(1)(B)DivB, added "30D," after "25D," in clause (e)(1)(C)(ii), effective for tax. yrs. begin. after 12/31/2008.

In 2006, P.L. 109-280, Sec. 811, of this Act [relating to Sec. 901 of P.L. 107-16, see below], provides:

"Sec. 811. Pensions and individual retirement arrangement provisions of Economic Growth and Tax Relief Reconciliation Act of 2001 made permanent.

"Title IX of the Economic Growth and Tax Relief Reconciliation Act of 2001 shall not apply to the provisions of, or amendments made by, subtitles A through F of title VI of such Act (relating to pension and individual retirement arrangement provisions)."

In 2005, P.L. 109-135, Sec. 402(i)(3)(C), amended subpara. (e)(1)(C), effective for tax. yrs. begin. after 12/31/2005.

Prior to amendment, subpara. (e)(1)(C) read as follows:

"(C) Applicable tax limit. For purposes of this paragraph, the term 'applicable tax limit' means the limitation imposed by section 26(a) for the taxable year reduced by the sum of the credits allowable under this subpart (other than this section and sections 23, 24, 25B, and 1400C."

—P.L. 109-135, Sec. 402(i)(4), repealed Sec. 1335(b)(2) of P.L. 109-58 [see below], effective for property placed in service after 12/31/2005, in tax. yrs. end. after 12/31/2005 as if included in Sec. 1335 of the Energy Policy Act of 2005, P.L. 109-58.

—P.L. 109-58, Sec. 1335(b)(2), [prior to repeal by Sec. 402(i)(4) P.L. 109-135, see above] substituted "other than this section, section 23, section 25D, and section 1400C" for "this section and sections 23 and 1400C" in subpara. (e)(1)(C), effective for property placed in service after 12/31/2005, in tax. yrs. end. after 12/31/2005. Note: This amendment cannot be applied to subpara. (e)(1)(C) as it reads on 1/1/2006.

In 2004, P.L. 108-311, Sec. 312(b)(2), of this Act, provides:

"(2) The amendments made by sections 201(b), 202(f), and 618(b) of the Economic Growth and Tax Relief Reconciliation Act of 2001 [P.L. 107-16] shall not apply to taxable years beginning during 2004 or 2005."

In 2002, P.L. 107-358, Sec. 2, added subsec. (c) in Sec. 901 of P.L. 107-16 [see below], effective 12/17/2002.

—P.L. 107-147, Sec. 601(b)(2), of this Act, provides:

"(2) The amendments made by sections 201(b), 202(f), and 618(b) of the Economic Growth and Tax Relief Reconciliation Act of 2001 shall not apply to taxable years beginning during 2002 and 2003."

In 2001, P.L. 107-16, Sec. 201(b)(2)(F), added ", 24," after "sections 23" in subpara. (e)(1)(C), effective for tax. yrs. begin. after 12/31/2001. For special provisions, see Secs. 601(b)(2) of P.L. 107-147 and Sec. 312(b)(2) of P.L. 108-311, above.

—P.L. 107-16, Sec. 618(b)(2)(B), added "25B," after "24," in subpara. (e)(1)(C) [as amended by Sec. 201(b)(2)(F) of this Act, see above], effective for tax. yrs. begin. after 12/31/2001. For special provisions, see Sec. 601(b)(2) of P.L. 107-147 and Sec. 312(b)(2) of P.L. 108-311, above.

—P.L. 107-16, Sec. 901, of this Act [as amended by Sec. 2, P.L. 107-358 and Sec. 101(a)(1), P.L. 111-312, and as related to Sec. 811 of P.L. 109-280, see above], reads as follows:

"SEC. 901. SUNSET OF PROVISIONS OF ACT.

"(a) In general. All provisions of, and amendments made by, this Act shall not apply—

"(1) to taxable, plan, or limitation years beginning after December 31, 2012, or

"(2) in the case of title V, to estates of decedents dying, gifts made, or generation skipping transfers, after December 31, 2012.

"(b) Application of certain laws. The Internal Revenue Code of 1986 and the Employee Retirement Income Security Act of 1974 shall be applied and administered to years, estates, gifts, and transfers described in subsection (a) as if the provisions and amendments described in subsection (a) had never been enacted.

"(c) Exception. Subsection (a) shall not apply to section 803 (relating to no federal income tax on restitution received by victims of the Nazi regime or their heirs or estates)."

In 1998, P.L. 105-206, Sec. 6005(e)(3), added "on or" before "before" each place it appears in Sec. 312(d)(2) [sic (e)(2)] of P.L. 105-34, 08/05/97, see below.

—P.L. 105-206, Sec. 6008(d)(7), substituted "sections 23 and 1400C" for "section 23" in subpara. (e)(1)(C), effective 8/5/97.

In 1997, P.L. 105-34, Sec. 312(d)(1), substituted "section 121" for "section 1034" in para. (e)(7), effective for sales and exchanges after 5/6/97, except as provided in Secs. 312(d)(2)-(4) [sic (e)(2)-(4)] of this Act, [as amended by Sec. 6005(e)(3), 105-206, see above] which read as follows:

"(2) Sales on or before date of enactment [8/5/97]. At the election of the taxpayer, the amendments made by this section shall not apply to any sale or exchange on or before the date of the enactment of this Act.

"(3) Certain sales within 2 years after date of enactment [8/5/97]. Section 121 of the Internal Revenue Code of 1986 (as amended by this section) shall be applied without regard to subsection (c)(2)(B) thereof in the case of any sale or exchange of property during the 2-year period beginning on the date of the enactment [8/5/97] of this Act if the taxpayer held such property on the date of the enactment [8/5/97] of this Act and fails to meet the ownership and use requirements of subsection (a) thereof with respect to such property.

"(4) Binding contracts. At the election of the taxpayer, the amendments made by this section shall not apply to a sale or exchange after the date of the enactment of this Act, if—

"(A) such sale or exchange is pursuant to a contract which was binding on such date, or

"(B) without regard to such amendments, gain would not be recognized under section 1034 of the Internal Revenue Code of 1986 (as in effect on the day before the date of the enactment [8/5/97] of this Act) on such sale or exchange by reason of a new residence acquired on or before such date or with respect to the acquisition of which by the taxpayer a binding contract was in effect on such date.

This paragraph shall not apply to any sale or exchange by an individual if the treatment provided by section 877(a)(1) of the Internal Revenue Code of 1986 applies to such individual."

In 1996, P.L. 104-188, Sec. 1807(c)(1), added "and section 23" after "this section" in subpara. (e)(1)(C), effective for tax. yrs. begin. after 12/31/96.

In 1993, P.L. 103-66, Sec. 13141(b), repealed subsec. (h) and redesignated subsecs. (i) and (j) as subsecs. (h) and (i), effective for elections for periods after 6/30/92.

Prior to repeal, subsec (h) read as follows:

"(h) Termination. No election may be made under subsection (c)(2)(A)(ii) for any period after June 30, 1992."

In 1991, P.L. 102-227, Sec. 108(b), substituted "June 30, 1992" for "December 31, 1991" in subsec. (h), effective for elections for periods after 12/31/91.

Tax credits

In 1990, P.L. 101-508, Sec. 11408(b), substituted "December 31, 1991" for "September 30, 1990" in subsec. (h), effective for elections for periods after 9/30/90.

In 1989, P.L. 101-239, Sec. 7104(b), substituted "for any period after September 30, 1990" for "for any calendar year after 1989", in subsec. (h), effective 12/19/89.

In 1988, P.L. 100-647, Sec. 1013(a)(25), amended Sec. 1301(f)(2)(C)(ii) of P.L. 99-514 to substitute "private activity bonds which it may otherwise issue during such calendar year under section 146," for "of qualified mortgage bonds which it may otherwise issue during such calendar year under section 103," instead of substituting "section 103" for "section 103A" in clause (c)(2)(A)(ii), see below, effective for certificates issued with respect to non-issued bond amounts elected after 8/15/86.

—P.L. 100-647, Sec. 1013(a)(26), substituted "1988" for "1987" in subsec. (h), effective for certificates issued with respect to non-issued bond amounts elected after 8/15/86.

—P.L. 100-647, Sec. 1013(b)(2), amended para. 1311(b)(2) of P.L. 99-514 [reproduced below], the effective date for amendments made by Sec. 1301(f) of P.L. 99-514, by adding "with respect to non-issued bond amounts elected" after "issued", see below.

—P.L. 100-647, Sec. 4005(a)(2), substituted "1989" for "1988" in subsec. (h) [as amended by Sec. 1013(a)(26) of this Act], effective for bonds issued, and non-issued bond amounts elected, after 12/31/88.

—P.L. 100-647, Sec. 4005(g)(7), added subsec. (j), effective for financing provided, and mortgage credit certificates issued, after 12/31/90, except as provided in Sec. 4005(h)(3)(B) of this Act reproduced in note following Code Sec. 143.

In 1986, P.L. 99-514, Sec. 1301(f)(1)(A), substituted "25 percent" for "20 percent" in subpara. (d)(2)(A)... Sec. 1301(f)(1)(B), substituted "0.25" for "0.20" in subpara. (f)(2)(A), effective for nonissued bond amounts elected after 8/15/86.

—P.L. 99-514, Sec. 1301(f)(2)(A), substituted "section 143(k)(4)" for "section 103A(1)(6)" in clause (b)(2)(A)(ii)... Sec. 1301(f)(2)(B), substituted "section 143(k)(5)" for "section 103A(1)(7)" in clause (b)(2)(A)(iii)... Sec. 1301(f)(2)(C)(i), substituted "section 143" for "section 103A" each place it appeared in clause (c)(2)(A)(iii) and twice in subpara. (c)(2)(B)... Sec. 1301(f)(2)(C)(ii), [as amended by Sec. 1013(a)(25) of P.L. 100-647, see above], substituted "private activity bonds which it may otherwise issue during such calendar year under section 146" for "of qualified mortgage bonds which it may otherwise issue during such calendar year under section 103", in clause (c)(2)(A)(ii)... Sec. 1301(f)(2)(D), deleted subclauses (c)(2)(A)(iii)(I)-(V) and added new subclauses (c)(2)(iii)(I)-(VI)... Sec. 1301(f)(2)(E), substituted "section 143(a)(2)" for "section 103A(c)(2)" in the last sentence of subpara. (c)(2)(A) [as added by Sec. 1862(b) of this Act, see below]... Sec. 1301(f)(2)(F)(i), substituted "subclauses (II), (IV), and (V)" for "subclauses (II) and (IV)" in subpara. (c)(2)(B)... Sec. 1301(f)(2)(F)(ii), amended clause (c)(2)(B)(iii) and the last sentence of subpara. (c)(2)(B)... Sec. 1301(f)(2)(G), deleted para. (d)(3)... Sec. 1301(f)(2)(H), substituted "subsections (c)(1), (d), (e), (f), and (i) of section 143" for "subsection (d)(1), (e), (f), and (j) of section 103A" in para. (e)(2)... Sec. 1301(f)(2)(I), substituted "section 144(a)(3)(A)" for "section 103(b)(6)(C)(i)" in para. (e)(6)... Sec. 1301(f)(2)(J), substituted "section 143(k)(5)(B)" for "section 103A(l)(7)(B)" in subpara. (e)(8)(A)... Sec. 1301(f)(2)(K), substituted "section 143(k)(4)" for "section 103A(l)(6)" in subpara. (e)(8)(B)... Sec. 1301(f)(2)(L), substituted "section 143(a)(1)" for "section 103A(c)(1)" in para. (e)(9)... Sec. 1301(f)(2)(M), substituted "section 143" for "section 103A" in para. (e)(10)... Sec. 1301(f)(2)(N), substituted "subsection (d) of section 146" for "paragraph (4) of section 103A(g)" in para. (f)(1)... Sec. 1301(f)(2)(O), substituted "section 146(d)(3)(C)" for "section 103A(g)(5)(C)" in para. (f)(3), effective for certificates issued with respect to non-issued bond amounts elected after 8/15/86 [as amended by Sec. 1013(b)(2) of P.L. 100-647, see above].

Prior to deletion, subclauses (c)(2)(A)(iii)(I)-(V) read as follows:

"(I) subsection (d) (relating to residence requirements),

"(II) subsection (e) (relating to 3-year requirement),

"(III) subsection (f) (relating to purchase price requirement),

"(IV) subsection (h) (relating to portion of loans required to be placed in targeted areas), and

"(V) subsection (j), other than paragraph (2) thereof (relating to other requirements),"

Prior to amendment, clause (c)(2)(B)(iii) and the last sentence of subpara. (c)(2)(B) read as follows:

"(iii) paragraph (1) of section 103A(e) shall be applied by substituting '100 percent' for '90 percent or more.'

Clause (iii) shall not apply if the issuing authority submits a plan to the Secretary for administering the 90-percent requirement of section 103A(e)(1) and the Secretary is satisfied that such requirement will be met under such plan."

Prior to deletion, para. (d)(3) read as follows:

"(3) Additional limit in certain cases. In the case of a qualified mortgage credit certificate program in a State which

"(A) has a State ceiling (as defined in section 103A(g)(4)) for the year an election is made that exceeds 20 percent of the average annual aggregate principal amount of mortgages executed during the immediately preceding 3 calendar years for single family owner-occupied residences located within the jurisdiction of such State, or

"(B) issued qualified mortgage bonds in an aggregate amount less than $150,000,000 for calendar year 1983,

the certificate credit rate for any mortgage credit certificate shall not exceed 20 percent unless the issuing authority submits a plan to the Secretary to ensure that the weighted average of the certificate credit rates in such mortgage credit certificate program does not exceed 20 percent and the Secretary approves such plan."

—P.L. 99-514, Sec. 1862(a), substituted "subsection (j), other than paragraph (2) thereof" for "paragraph (1) of subsection (j)" in subclause (c)(2)(A)(iii)(V) [before amendment by Sec. 1301(f)(2)(D) of this Act, see above]... Sec. 1862(b), added the last (flush) sentence to subpara. (c)(2)(A)... Sec. 1862(c), amended subpara. (e)(1)(B)... Sec. 1862(d)(1), substituted "paid or accrued" for "paid or incurred" in subpara. (a)(1)(B), effective for interest paid or accrued after 12/31/84, on indebtedness incurred after 12/31/84, and for elections under Code Sec. 25(c)(2)(A)(ii) for calendar years after 1983.

Prior to amendment, subpara. (e)(1)(B) read as follows:

"(B) Limitation. The amount of the unused credit which may be taken into account under subparagraph (A) for any taxable year shall not exceed the amount by which the applicable tax limit for such taxable year exceeds the sum of the amounts which, by reason of this paragraph, are carried to such taxable year and are attributable to taxable years before the unused credit year."

—P.L. 99-514, Sec. 1899A(1), substituted "ensure" for "insure" in para. (f)(4), effective 10/22/86.

In 1984, P.L. 98-369, Sec. 612(a), added Code Sec. 25, for interest paid or accrued after 12/31/84, on indebtedness incurred after 12/31/84 and to elections under Code Sec. 25(c)(2)(A)(ii) (as added by this Act) for calendar yrs. after 1983.

—P.L. 98-369, Sec. 632, provided various exceptions to the amendments made by Title VI of this Act. See note following Code Sec. 103A.

Sec. 25A. Hope and Lifetime Learning Credits.

(a) Allowance of credit.

In the case of an individual, there shall be allowed as a credit against the tax imposed by this chapter for the taxable year the amount equal to the sum of—

(1) the Hope Scholarship Credit, plus

(2) the Lifetime Learning Credit.

(b) Hope Scholarship Credit.

(1) Per student credit. In the case of any eligible student for whom an election is in effect under this section for any taxable year, the Hope Scholarship Credit is an amount equal to the sum of—

(A) 100 percent of so much of the qualified tuition and related expenses paid by the taxpayer during the taxable year (for education furnished to the eligible student during any academic period beginning in such taxable year) as does not exceed $1,000, plus

(B) 50 percent of such expenses so paid as exceeds $1,000 but does not exceed the applicable limit.

(2) Limitations applicable to Hope Scholarship Credit.

(A) Credit allowed only for 2 taxable years. An election to have this section apply with respect to any eligible student for purposes of the Hope Scholarship Credit under subsection (a)(1) may not be made for any taxable year if such an election (by the taxpayer or any other individual) is in effect with respect to such student for any 2 prior taxable years.

(B) Credit allowed for year only if individual is at least ½ time student for portion of year. The Hope Scholarship Credit under subsection (a)(1) shall not be allowed for a taxable year with respect to the qualified tuition and related expenses of an individual unless such individual is an eligible student for at least one academic period which begins during such year.

(C) Credit allowed only for first 2 years of postsecondary education. The Hope Scholarship Credit under subsection (a)(1) shall not be allowed for a taxable year with respect to the qualified tuition and related expenses of an eligible student if the student has completed (before the beginning of such taxable year) the first 2 years of postsecondary education at an eligible educational institution.

(D) Denial of credit if student convicted of a felony drug offense. The Hope Scholarship Credit under subsection (a)(1) shall not be allowed for qualified tuition and related expenses for the enrollment or attendance of a student for any academic period if such student has been convicted of a Federal or State felony offense consisting of the possession or distribution of a controlled substance before the end of the taxable year with or within which such period ends.

(3) Eligible student. For purposes of this subsection, the term "eligible student" means, with respect to any academic period, a student who—

(A) meets the requirements of section 484(a)(1) of the Higher Education Act of 1965 (20 U.S.C. 1091(a)(1)), as in effect on the date of the enactment of this section, and

(B) is carrying at least ½ the normal full-time work load for the course of study the student is pursuing.

(4) Applicable limit. For purposes of paragraph (1)(B), the applicable limit for any taxable year is an amount equal to 2 times the dollar amount in effect under paragraph (1)(A) for such taxable year.

(c) Lifetime Learning Credit.

(1) Per taxpayer credit. The Lifetime Learning Credit for any taxpayer for any taxable year is an amount equal to 20 percent of so much of the qualified tuition and related expenses paid by the taxpayer during the taxable year (for education furnished during any academic period beginning in such taxable year) as does not exceed $10,000 ($5,000 in the case of taxable years beginning before January 1, 2003).

(2) Special rules for determining expenses.

(A) Coordination with Hope Scholarship. The qualified tuition and related expenses with respect to an individual who is an eligible student for whom a Hope Scholarship Credit under subsection (a)(1) is allowed for the taxable year shall not be taken into account under this subsection.

(B) Expenses eligible for Lifetime Learning Credit. For purposes of paragraph (1), qualified tuition and related expenses shall include expenses described in subsection (f)(1) with respect to any course of instruction at an eligible educational institution to acquire or improve job skills of the individual.

(d) Limitation based on modified adjusted gross income.

(1) In general. The amount which would (but for this subsection) be taken into account under subsection (a) for the taxable year shall be reduced (but not below zero) by the amount determined under paragraph (2).

(2) Amount of reduction. The amount determined under this paragraph is the amount which bears the same ratio to the amount which would be so taken into account as—

(A) the excess of—

(i) the taxpayer's modified adjusted gross income for such taxable year, over

(ii) $40,000 ($80,000 in the case of a joint return), bears to

(B) $10,000 ($20,000 in the case of a joint return).

(3) Modified adjusted gross income. The term "modified adjusted gross income" means the adjusted gross income of the taxpayer for the taxable year increased by any amount excluded from gross income under section 911, 931, or 933.

• *Caution:* Code Sec. 25A(e), following, was amended by P.L. 107-16, EGTRRA. These provisions generally sunset for tax years beginning after 12/31/2012. For specific sunset provisions, see Sec. 901, P.L. 107-16 (as amended), reproduced in history notes for this Code Sec.

(e) Election not to have section apply.

A taxpayer may elect not to have this section apply with respect to the qualified tuition and related expenses of an individual for any taxable year.

• *Caution:* Code Sec. 25A(e), following, reflects the sunset of the amendments made by P.L. 107-16, EGTRRA. These provisions generally sunset for tax years beginning after 12/31/2012. For specific sunset provisions, see Sec. 901, P.L. 107-16 (as amended) reproduced in history notes for this Code Sec.

(e) Election to have section apply.

(1) In general. No credit shall be allowed under subsection (a) for a taxable year with respect to the qualified tuition and related expenses of an individual unless the taxpayer elects to have this section apply with respect to such individual for such year.

(2) Coordination with exclusions. An election under this subsection shall not take effect with respect to an individual for any taxable year if any portion of any distribution during such taxable year from an education individual retirement account is excluded from gross income under section 530(d)(2).

(f) Definitions.

For purposes of this section—

(1) Qualified tuition and related expenses.

(A) In general. The term "qualified tuition and related expenses" means tuition and fees required for the enrollment or attendance of—

(i) the taxpayer,

(ii) the taxpayer's spouse, or

(iii) any dependent of the taxpayer with respect to whom the taxpayer is allowed a deduction under section 151,

at an eligible educational institution for courses of instruction of such individual at such institution.

(B) Exception for education involving sports, etc. Such term does not include expenses with respect to any course or other education involving sports, games, or hobbies, unless such course or other education is part of the individual's degree program.

(C) Exception for nonacademic fees. Such term does not include student activity fees, athletic fees, insurance expenses, or other expenses unrelated to an individual's academic course of instruction.

(2) Eligible educational institution. The term "eligible educational institution" means an institution—

(A) which is described in section 481 of the Higher Education Act of 1965 (20 U.S.C. 1088), as in effect on the date of the enactment of this section, and

(B) which is eligible to participate in a program under title IV of such Act.

(g) Special rules.

(1) Identification requirement. No credit shall be allowed under subsection (a) to a taxpayer with respect to the qualified tuition and related expenses of an individual unless the taxpayer includes the name and taxpayer identification number of such individual on the return of tax for the taxable year.

(2) Adjustment for certain scholarships, etc. The amount of qualified tuition and related expenses otherwise taken into account under subsection (a) with respect to an individual for an academic period shall be reduced (before the application of subsections (b), (c) and (d)) by the sum

Tax credits Code Sec. 25A(i)(5)(B)

of any amounts paid for the benefit of such individual which are allocable to such period as—
 (A) a qualified scholarship which is excludable from gross income under section 117,
 (B) an educational assistance allowance under chapter 30, 31, 32, 34, or 35 of title 38, United States Code, or under chapter 1606 of title 10, United States Code, and
 (C) a payment (other than a gift, bequest, devise, or inheritance within the meaning of section 102(a)) for such individual's educational expenses, or attributable to such individual's enrollment at an eligible educational institution, which is excludable from gross income under any law of the United States.

(3) Treatment of expenses paid by dependent. If a deduction under section 151 with respect to an individual is allowed to another taxpayer for a taxable year beginning in the calendar year in which such individual's taxable year begins—
 (A) no credit shall be allowed under subsection (a) to such individual for such individual's taxable year, and
 (B) qualified tuition and related expenses paid by such individual during such individual's taxable year shall be treated for purposes of this section as paid by such other taxpayer.

(4) Treatment of certain prepayments. If qualified tuition and related expenses are paid by the taxpayer during a taxable year for an academic period which begins during the first 3 months following such taxable year, such academic period shall be treated for purposes of this section as beginning during such taxable year.

(5) Denial of double benefit. No credit shall be allowed under this section for any expense for which a deduction is allowed under any other provision of this chapter.

(6) No credit for married individuals filing separate returns. If the taxpayer is a married individual (within the meaning of section 7703), this section shall apply only if the taxpayer and the taxpayer's spouse file a joint return for the taxable year.

(7) Nonresident aliens. If the taxpayer is a nonresident alien individual for any portion of the taxable year, this section shall apply only if such individual is treated as a resident alien of the United States for purposes of this chapter by reason of an election under subsection (g) or (h) of section 6013.

(h) Inflation adjustments.
(1) Dollar limitation on amount of credit.
 (A) In general. In the case of a taxable year beginning after 2001, each of the $1,000 amounts under subsection (b)(1) shall be increased by an amount equal to—
  (i) such dollar amount, multiplied by
  (ii) the cost-of-living adjustment determined under section 1(f)(3) for the calendar year in which the taxable year begins, determined by substituting "calendar year 2000" for "calendar year 1992" in subparagraph (B) thereof.
 (B) Rounding. If any amount as adjusted under subparagraph (A) is not a multiple of $100, such amount shall be rounded to the next lowest multiple of $100.

(2) Income limits.
 (A) In general. In the case of a taxable year beginning after 2001, the $40,000 and $80,000 amounts in subsection (d)(2) shall each be increased by an amount equal to—
  (i) such dollar amount, multiplied by
  (ii) the cost-of-living adjustment determined under section 1(f)(3) for the calendar year in which the taxable year begins, determined by substituting "calendar year 2000" for "calendar year 1992" in subparagraph (B) thereof.
 (B) Rounding. If any amount as adjusted under subparagraph (A) is not a multiple of $1,000, such amount shall be rounded to the next lowest multiple of $1,000.

(i) American opportunity tax credit.
In the case of any taxable year beginning in 2009, 2010, 2011, or 2012—
(1) Increase in credit. The Hope Scholarship Credit shall be an amount equal to the sum of—
 (A) 100 percent of so much of the qualified tuition and related expenses paid by the taxpayer during the taxable year (for education furnished to the eligible student during any academic period beginning in such taxable year) as does not exceed $2,000, plus
 (B) 25 percent of such expenses so paid as exceeds $2,000 but does not exceed $4,000.

(2) Credit allowed for first 4 years of post-secondary education. Subparagraphs (A) and (C) of subsection (b)(2) shall be applied by substituting "4" for "2".

(3) Qualified tuition and related expenses to include required course materials. Subsection (f)(1)(A) shall be applied by substituting "tuition, fees, and course materials" for "tuition and fees".

(4) Increase in AGI limits for Hope Scholarship Credit. In lieu of applying subsection (d) with respect to the Hope Scholarship Credit, such credit (determined without regard to this paragraph) shall be reduced (but not below zero) by the amount which bears the same ratio to such credit (as so determined) as—
 (A) the excess of—
  (i) the taxpayer's modified adjusted gross income (as defined in subsection (d)(3)) for such taxable year, over
  (ii) $80,000 ($160,000 in the case of a joint return), bears to
 (B) $10,000 ($20,000 in the case of a joint return).

(5) Credit allowed against alternative minimum tax. In the case of a taxable year to which section 26(a)(2) does not apply, so much of the credit allowed under subsection (a) as is attributable to the Hope Scholarship Credit shall not exceed the excess of—
 (A) the sum of the regular tax liability (as defined in section 26(b)) plus the tax imposed by section 55, over

⌐ • *Caution:* Code Sec. 25A(i)(5)(B), following, reflects amendments made by Sec. 10909 of P.L. 111-148. As provided in Sec. 10909(c), P.L. 111-148, as amended by Sec. 101(b)(1) P.L. 111-312, Code Sec. 25A(i)(5)(B), will read as if those amendments had never enacted, effective for tax. yrs. begin. after 12/31/2011. For Code Sec. 25A(i)(5)(B), as it will read for tax. yrs. begin. after 12/31/2011, see below. ⌐

 (B) the sum of the credits allowable under this subpart (other than this subsection and sections 25D and 30D) and section 27 for the taxable year.

⌐ • *Caution:* Code Sec. 25A(i)(5)(B), following, is effective for tax. yrs. begin. after 12/31/2011, and reflects the sunset of the amendments made by Sec. 10909(b)(2)(C), P.L. 111-148. For details of those amendments, effective date, and sunset provisions, see the history for this Code Sec. For Code Sec. 25A(i)(5)(B), effective for tax. yrs. begin. before 1/1/2012, see above.

(B) the sum of the credits allowable under this subpart (other than this subsection and sections 23, 25D, and 30D) and section 27 for the taxable year.

Any reference in this section or section 24, 25, 26, 25B, 904, or 1400C to a credit allowable under this subsection shall be treated as a reference to so much of the credit allowable under subsection (a) as is attributable to the Hope Scholarship Credit.

(6) Portion of credit made refundable. 40 percent of so much of the credit allowed under subsection (a) as is attributable to the Hope Scholarship Credit (determined after application of paragraph (4) and without regard to this paragraph and section 26(a)(2) or paragraph (5), as the case may be) shall be treated as a credit allowable under subpart C (and not allowed under subsection (a)). The preceding sentence shall not apply to any taxpayer for any taxable year if such taxpayer is a child to whom subsection (g) of section 1 applies for such taxable year.

(7) Coordination with midwestern disaster area benefits. In the case of a taxpayer with respect to whom section 702(a)(1)(B) of the Heartland Disaster Tax Relief Act of 2008 applies for any taxable year, such taxpayer may elect to waive the application of this subsection to such taxpayer for such taxable year.

(j) Regulations.

The Secretary may prescribe such regulations as may be necessary or appropriate to carry out this section, including regulations providing for a recapture of the credit allowed under this section in cases where there is a refund in a subsequent taxable year of any amount which was taken into account in determining the amount of such credit.

In 2010, P.L. 111-312, Sec. 101(a)(1), substituted "December 31, 2012" for "December 31, 2010" both places it appeared in Sec. 901, P.L. 107-16, effective as if included in the enactment of P.L. 107-16, EGTRRA, 6/7/2001.

—P.L. 111-312, Sec. 101(b)(1), amended Sec. 10909(c), P.L. 111-148 [see below].

Prior to amendment, Sec. 10909(c) of P.L. 111-148 read as follows:

"(c) Application and Extension of EGTRRA Sunset. Notwithstanding section 901 of the Economic Growth and Tax Relief Reconciliation Act of 2001, such section shall apply to the amendments made by this section and the amendments made by section 202 of such Act by substituting 'December 31, 2011' for 'December 31, 2010' in subsection (a)(1) thereof."

—P.L. 111-312, Sec. 101(b)(2), substituted "Except as provided in subsection (c), the amendments" for "The amendments" in Sec. 10909(d), P.L. 111-148 [see below] (the effective date section for amendments made by Sec. 10909, P.L. 111-148).

Prior to amendment, Sec. 10909(d), P.L. 111-148, read as follows:

"(d) Effective date. The amendments made by this section shall apply to taxable years beginning after December 31, 2009."

—P.L. 111-312, Sec. 103(a)(1), substituted ", 2010, 2011, or 2012" for "or 2010" in subsec. (i), effective for tax. yrs. begin. after 12/31/2010.

—P.L. 111-312, Sec. 103(a)(2), substituted ", 2010, 2011, and 2012" for "and 2010" each place it appeared in Sec. 1004(c)(1), Div. B of P.L. 111-5 [see below].

—P.L. 111-148, Sec. 10909(b)(2)(C), substituted "25D" for "23, 25D," in subpara. (i)(5)(B), effective for tax. yrs. begin. after 12/31/2009, except as provided in Sec. 10909(c), see below.

—P.L. 111-148, Sec. 10909(c), relating to the application and extension of the EGTRRA sunset provisions [as amended by Sec. 101(b)(1), P.L. 111-312 see above], reads as follows:

"(c) Sunset provision. Each provision of law amended by this section is amended to read as such provision would read if this section had never been enacted. The amendments made by the preceding sentence shall apply to taxable years beginning after December 31, 2011."

—P.L. 111-148, Sec. 10909(d), of this Act, [as amended by Sec. 101(b)(2) of P.L. 111-312, see above] reads as follows:

"(d) Effective date. Except as provided in subsection (c) [of Sec. 10909, see below], the amendments made by this section shall apply to taxable years beginning after December 31, 2009."

In 2009, P.L. 111-5, Sec. 1004(a), redesignated subsec. (i) as subsec. (j) and added subsec. (i), effective for tax. yrs. begin. after 12/31/2008.

—P.L. 111-5, Sec. 1004(c), and (f) [as amended by Sec. 103(a)(2) of P.L. 111-312, see above] provides:

"(c) Treatment of possessions.

"(1) Payments to possessions.

"(A) Mirror code possession. The Secretary of the Treasury shall pay to each possession of the United States with a mirror code tax system amounts equal to the loss to that possession by reason of the application of section 25A(i)(6) of the Internal Revenue Code of 1986 (as added by this section) with respect to taxable years beginning in 2009, 2010, 2011, and 2012. Such amounts shall be determined by the Secretary of the Treasury based on information provided by the government of the respective possession.

"(B) Other possessions. The Secretary of the Treasury shall pay to each possession of the United States which does not have a mirror code tax system amounts estimated by the Secretary of the Treasury as being equal to the aggregate benefits that would have been provided to residents of such possession by reason of the application of section 25A(i)(6) of such Code (as so added) for taxable years beginning in 2009, 2010, 2011, and 2012 if a mirror code tax system had been in effect in such possession. The preceding sentence shall not apply with respect to any possession of the United States unless such possession has a plan, which has been approved by the Secretary of the Treasury, under which such possession will promptly distribute such payments to the residents of such possession.

"(2) Coordination with credit allowed against United States income taxes. Section 25A(i)(6) of such Code (as added by this section) shall not apply to a bona fide resident of any possession of the United States.

"(3) Definitions and special rules.

"(A) Possession of the United States. For purposes of this subsection, the term 'possession of the United States' includes the Commonwealth of Puerto Rico and the Commonwealth of the Northern Mariana Islands.

"(B) Mirror code tax system. For purposes of this subsection, the term 'mirror code tax system' means, with respect to any possession of the United States, the income tax system of such possession if the income tax liability of the residents of such possession under such system is determined by reference to the income tax laws of the United States as if such possession were the United States.

"(C) Treatment of payments. For purposes of section 1324(b)(2) of title 31, United States Code, the payments under this subsection shall be treated in the same manner as a refund due from the credit allowed under section 25A of the Internal Revenue Code of 1986 by reason of subsection (i)(6) of such section (as added by this section).

* * * * * * *

"(f) Treasury studies regarding education incentives.

"(1) Study regarding coordination with non-tax student financial assistance. The Secretary of the Treasury and the Secretary of Education, or their delegates, shall—

"(A) study how to coordinate the credit allowed under section 25A of the Internal Revenue Code of 1986 with the Federal Pell Grant program under section 401 of the Higher Education Act of 1965 to maximize their effectiveness at promoting college affordability, and

"(B) examine ways to expedite the delivery 2 of the tax credit.

"(2) Study regarding inclusion of community service requirements.The Secretary of the Treasury and the Secretary of Education, or their delegates, shall study the feasibility of requiring including community service as a condition of taking their tuition and related expenses into account under section 25A of the Internal Revenue Code of 1986.

"(3) Report. Not later than 1 year after the date of the enactment of this Act, the Secretary of the Treasury, or the Secretary's delegate, shall report to Congress on the results of the studies conducted under this paragraph."

In 2002, P.L. 107-358, Sec. 2, added subsec. (c) in Sec. 901 of P.L. 107-16 [see below], effective 12/17/2002.

In 2001, P.L. 107-16, Sec. 401(g)(2)(A), amended subsec. (e), effective for tax. yrs. begin. after 12/31/2001.

Prior to amendment, subsec. (e) read as follows:

"(e) Election to have section apply.

"(1) In general. No credit shall be allowed under subsection (a) for a taxable year with respect to the qualified tuition and related expenses of an individual unless the taxpayer elects to have this section apply with respect to such individual for such year.

"(2) Coordination with exclusions. An election under this subsection shall not take effect with respect to an individual for any taxable year if any portion of any distribution during such taxable year from an education individual retirement account is excluded from gross income under section 530(d)(2)."

—P.L. 107-16, Sec. 901, of this Act [as amended by Sec. 2 of P.L. 107-358, and Sec. 101(a)(1) of P.L. 111-312, see above], reads as follows:

"SEC. 901. SUNSET OF PROVISIONS OF ACT.

"(a) In general. All provisions of, and amendments made by, this Act shall not apply—

"(1) to taxable, plan, or limitation years beginning after December 31, 2012, or

"(2) in the case of title V, to estates of decedents dying, gifts made, or generation skipping transfers, after December 31, 2012.

"(b) Application of certain laws. The Internal Revenue Code of 1986 and the Employee Retirement Income Security Act of 1974 shall be applied and administered to years, estates, gifts, and transfers described in subsection (a) as if the provisions and amendments described in subsection (a) had never been enacted.

"(c) Exception. Subsection (a) shall not apply to section 803 (relating to no federal income tax on restitution received by victims of the Nazi regime or their heirs or estates)."

Tax credits   Code Sec. 25B(g)(1)

In 1997, P.L. 105-34, Sec. 201(a), added Code Sec. 25A, effective for expenses paid after 12/31/97 (in tax. yrs. end. after 12/31/97), for education furnished in academic periods begin. after 12/31/97, except for Sec. 25A(a)(2), which is effective for expenses paid after 6/30/98 (in tax. yrs. end. after 6/30/98), for education furnished in academic periods begin. after 6/30/98.

Sec. 25B. Elective deferrals and IRA contributions by certain individuals.

(a) Allowance of credit.

In the case of an eligible individual, there shall be allowed as a credit against the tax imposed by this subtitle for the taxable year an amount equal to the applicable percentage of so much of the qualified retirement savings contributions of the eligible individual for the taxable year as do not exceed $2,000.

(b) Applicable percentage.

For purposes of this section—

(1) Joint returns. In the case of a joint return, the applicable percentage is—

(A) if the adjusted gross income of the taxpayer is not over $30,000, 50 percent,

(B) if the adjusted gross income of the taxpayer is over $30,000 but not over $32,500, 20 percent,

(C) if the adjusted gross income of the taxpayer is over $32,500 but not over $50,000, 10 percent, and

(D) if the adjusted gross income of the taxpayer is over $50,000, zero percent.

(2) Other returns. In the case of—

(A) a head of household, the applicable percentage shall be determined under paragraph (1) except that such paragraph shall be applied by substituting for each dollar amount therein (as adjusted under paragraph (3)) a dollar amount equal to 75 percent of such dollar amount, and

(B) any taxpayer not described in paragraph (1) or subparagraph (A), the applicable percentage shall be determined under paragraph (1) except that such paragraph shall be applied by substituting for each dollar amount therein (as adjusted under paragraph (3)) a dollar amount equal to 50 percent of such dollar amount.

(3) Inflation adjustment. In the case of any taxable year beginning in a calendar year after 2006, each of the dollar amounts in paragraph (1) shall be increased by an amount equal to—

(A) such dollar amount, multiplied by

(B) the cost-of-living adjustment determined under section 1(f)(3) for the calendar year in which the taxable year begins, determined by substituting "calendar year 2005" for "calendar year 1992" in subparagraph (B) thereof.

Any increase determined under the preceding sentence shall be rounded to the nearest multiple of $500.

(c) Eligible individual.

For purposes of this section—

(1) In general. The term "eligible individual" means any individual if such individual has attained the age of 18 as of the close of the taxable year.

(2) Dependents and full-time students not eligible. The term "eligible individual" shall not include—

(A) any individual with respect to whom a deduction under section 151 is allowed to another taxpayer for a taxable year beginning in the calendar year in which such individual's taxable year begins, and

(B) any individual who is a student (as defined in section 152(f)(2)).

(d) Qualified retirement savings contributions.

For purposes of this section—

(1) In general. The term "qualified retirement savings contributions" means, with respect to any taxable year, the sum of—

(A) the amount of the qualified retirement contributions (as defined in section 219(e)) made by the eligible individual,

(B) the amount of—

(i) any elective deferrals (as defined in section 402(g)(3)) of such individual, and

(ii) any elective deferral of compensation by such individual under an eligible deferred compensation plan (as defined in section 457(b)) of an eligible employer described in section 457(e)(1)(A), and

(C) the amount of voluntary employee contributions by such individual to any qualified retirement plan (as defined in section 4974(c)).

(2) Reduction for certain distributions.

(A) In general. The qualified retirement savings contributions determined under paragraph (1) shall be reduced (but not below zero) by the aggregate distributions received by the individual during the testing period from any entity of a type to which contributions under paragraph (1) may be made. The preceding sentence shall not apply to the portion of any distribution which is not includible in gross income by reason of a trustee-to-trustee transfer or a rollover distribution.

(B) Testing period. For purposes of subparagraph (A), the testing period, with respect to a taxable year, is the period which includes—

(i) such taxable year,

(ii) the 2 preceding taxable years, and

(iii) the period after such taxable year and before the due date (including extensions) for filing the return of tax for such taxable year.

(C) Excepted distributions. There shall not be taken into account under subparagraph (A)—

(i) any distribution referred to in section 72(p), 401(k)(8), 401(m)(6), 402(g)(2), 404(k), or 408(d)(4), and

(ii) any distribution to which section 408A(d)(3) applies.

(D) Treatment of distributions received by spouse of individual. For purposes of determining distributions received by an individual under subparagraph (A) for any taxable year, any distribution received by the spouse of such individual shall be treated as received by such individual if such individual and spouse file a joint return for such taxable year and for the taxable year during which the spouse receives the distribution.

(e) Adjusted gross income.

For purposes of this section, adjusted gross income shall be determined without regard to sections 911, 931, and 933.

(f) Investment in the contract.

Notwithstanding any other provision of law, a qualified retirement savings contribution shall not fail to be included in determining the investment in the contract for purposes of section 72 by reason of the credit under this section.

(g) Limitation based on amount of tax.

In the case of a taxable year to which section 26(a)(2) does not apply, the credit allowed under subsection (a) for the taxable year shall not exceed the excess of—

(1) the sum of the regular tax liability (as defined in section 26(b)) plus the tax imposed by section 55, over

Code Sec. 25B(g)(1) — Tax credits

- **Caution:** Code Sec. 25B(g)(2), following, reflects amendments made by Sec. 10909, P.L. 111-148. As provided in Sec. 10909(c), P.L. 111-148 as amended by Sec. 101(b)(1), P.L. 111-312, Code Sec. 25B(g)(2) will read as if those amendments had never been enacted, effective for tax. yrs. begin. after 12/31/2011. For Code Sec. 25B(g)(2) as it will read for tax. yrs. begin. after 12/31/2011, see below.

(2) the sum of the credits allowable under this subpart (other than this section and 25A(i), 25D, 30, 30B, and 30D) and section 27 for the taxable year.

- **Caution:** Code Sec. 25B(g)(2), following, is effective for tax. yrs. begin. after 12/31/2011, and reflects the sunset of the amendments made by Sec. 10909, P.L. 111-148. For details of those amendments, effective date and sunset provisions, see the history for this Code Sec. For Code Sec. 25B(g)(2), effective for tax. yrs. begin. before 1/1/2012, see above.

(2) the sum of the credits allowable under this subpart (other than this section and 23, 25A(i), 25D, 30, 30B, and 30D) and section 27 for the taxable year.

In 2010, P.L. 111-312, Sec. 101(a)(1), substituted "December 31, 2012" for "December 31, 2010" both places it appeared in Sec. 901 of P.L. 107-16, EGTRRA, 6/7/2001 [see below]
—P.L. 111-312, Sec. 101(b)(1), amended Sec. 10909(c) of P.L. 111-148 [see below]
Prior to amendment, Sec. 10909(c) of P.L. 111-148 read as follows:
"(c) Application and Extension of EGTRRA Sunset. Notwithstanding section 901 of the Economic Growth and Tax Relief Reconciliation Act of 2001, such section shall apply to the amendments made by this section and the amendments made by section 202 of such Act by substituting 'December 31, 2011' for 'December 31, 2010' in subsection (a)(1) thereof."
—P.L. 111-312, Sec. 101(b)(2), substituted "Except as provided in subsection (c), the amendments" for "The amendments" in Sec. 10909(d) of P.L. 111-148 [the effective date section for amendments made by Sec. 10909, P.L. 111-148, see below]

Prior to amendment, Sec. 10909(d) of P.L. 111-148 read as follows:
"(d) Effective Date. The amendments made by this section shall apply to taxable years beginning after December 31, 2009."
—P.L. 111-148, Sec. 10909(b)(2)(D), deleted "23," in para. (g)(2), effective for tax. yrs. begin. after 12/31/2009, except as provided in Sec. 10909(c) of this Act, see below.
—P.L. 111-148, Sec. 10909(c), of this Act, relating to the application and extension of the EGTRRA sunset, [as amended by Sec. 101(b)(1) of P.L. 111-312, see above] provides:
"(c) Sunset provision. Each provision of law amended by this section is amended to read as such provision would read if this section had never been enacted. The amendments made by the preceding sentence shall apply to taxable years beginning after December 31, 2011."
—P.L. 111-148, Sec. 10909(d), of this Act [as amended by Sec. 101(b)(2) of P.L. 111-312, see above] reads as follows:
"(d) Effective Date. Except as provided in subsection (c), the amendments made by this section shall apply to taxable years beginning after December 31, 2009."

In 2009, P.L. 111-5, Sec. 1004(b)(4), added "25A(i)," after "23," in para. (g)(2), effective for tax. yrs. begin. after 12/31/2008.
—P.L. 111-5, Sec. 1142(b)(1)(C), added "30," after "25D," in para. (g)(2) [as amended by Sec. 1004(b)(4) of this Act, see above], effective for vehicles acquired after 2/17/2009.
—P.L. 111-5, Sec. 1144(b)(1)(C), added "30B," after "30," in para. (g)(2) [as amended by Secs. 1004(b)(4) and 1142(b)(1)(C) of this Act, see above], effective for tax. yrs. begin. after 12/31/2008.

In 2008, P.L. 110-343, Sec. 106(e)(2)(C), substituted "sections 23 and 25D" for "section 23", in para. (g)(2), effective for tax. yrs. begin. after 12/31/2007. The amendments made by subparagraphs (A) and (B) of subsection (e)(2) shall be subject to title IX of the Economic Growth and Tax Relief Reconciliation Act of 2001 in the same manner as the provisions of such Act to which such amendments relate.
—P.L. 110-343, Sec. 205(d)(1)(C) Div B, substituted ", 25D, and 30D" for "and 25D", in para. (g)(2), effective for tax. yrs. begin. after 12/31/2008.

In 2006, P.L. 109-280, Sec. 811, of this Act [relating to Sec. 901 of P.L. 107-16, see below], provides:
"Sec. 811. Pensions and individual retirement arrangement provisions of Economic Growth and Tax Relief Reconciliation Act of 2001 made permanent.
"Title IX of the Economic Growth and Tax Relief Reconciliation Act of 2001 shall not apply to the provisions of, and amendments made by, subtitles A through F of title VI of such Act (relating to pension and individual retirement arrangement provisions)."
—P.L. 109-280, Sec. 812, deleted subsec. (h), enacted 8/17/2006.
Prior to repeal, subsec. (h) read as follows:
"(h) Termination. This section shall not apply to taxable years beginning after December 31, 2006."
—P.L. 109-280, Sec. 833(a), amended subsec. (b), effective for tax. yrs. begin. after 2006.
Prior to amendment, subsec. (b) read as follows:
"(b) Applicable percentage. For purposes of this section, the applicable percentage is the percentage determined in accordance with the following table:

Adjusted Gross Income						
Joint return		Head of a household		All other cases		Applicable percentage
Over	Not over	Over	Not over	Over	Not over	
	$30,000		$22,500		$15,000	50
30,000	32,500	22,500	24,375	15,000	16,250	20
32,500	50,000	24,375	37,500	16,250	25,000	10
50,000		37,500		25,000		0

In 2005, P.L. 109-135, Sec. 402(i)(3)(D), substituted 'In the case of a taxable year to which section 26(a)(2) does not apply, the credit' for 'The credit' in the matter preceding para. (g)(1), effective for tax. yrs. begin. after 12/31/2005.
—P.L. 109-135, Sec. 402(i)(3)(H), of this Act, provides:
"(H) Application of EGTRRA sunset. The amendments made by this paragraph (and each part thereof) shall be subject to title IX of the Economic Growth and Tax Relief Reconciliation Act of 2001 [Sec. 901 of P.L. 107-16] in the same manner as the provisions of such Act to which such amendment (or part thereof) relates."
In 2004, P.L. 108-311, Sec. 207(4), substituted "152(f)(2)" for "151(c)(4)" in subpara. (c)(2)(B), effective for tax. yrs. begin. after 12/31/2004.
—P.L. 108-311, Sec. 312(b)(2), of this Act, provides:
"(2) The amendments made by sections 201(b), 202(f), and 618(b) of the Economic Growth and Tax Relief Reconciliation Act of 2001 [P.L. 107-16] shall not apply to taxable years beginning during 2004 or 2005."
In 2002, P.L. 107-358, Sec. 2, added subsec. (c) in Sec. 901 of P.L. 107-16 [see below], effective 12/17/2002.
—P.L. 107-147, Sec. 411(m), amended subpara. (d)(2)(A), effective for tax. yrs. begin. after 12/31/2001.
Prior to amendment, subpara. (d)(2)(A) read as follows:
"(A) In general. The qualified retirement savings contributions determined under paragraph (1) shall be reduced (but not below zero) by the sum of—

"(i) any distribution from a qualified retirement plan (as defined in section 4974(c)), or from an eligible deferred compensation plan (as defined in section 457(b)), received by the individual during the testing period which is includible in gross income, and
"(ii) any distribution from a Roth IRA or a Roth account received by the individual during the testing period which is not a qualified rollover contribution (as defined in section 408A(e)) to a Roth IRA or a rollover under section 402(c)(8)(B) to a Roth account."
—P.L. 107-147, Sec. 417(1), redesignated subsec. (g), related to "Termination" (added by Sec. 618(a) of P.L. 107-16) as subsec. (h).
—P.L. 107-147, Sec. 601(b)(2), of this Act, provides:
"(2) The amendments made by sections 201(b), 202(f), and 618(b) of the Economic Growth and Tax Relief Reconciliation Act of 2001 [P.L. 107-16] shall not apply to taxable years beginning during 2002 and 2003."
In 2001, P.L. 107-16, Sec. 618(a), added Code Sec. 25B [subsec. (g) relating to "Termination" as added by Sec. 618(a), is redesignated as subsec. (h) by Sec. 417(1) of P.L. 107-147, see above] . . . Sec. 618(b)(1), added subsec. (g), relating to "Limitation based on amount of tax", effective for tax. yrs. begin. after 12/31/2001. For special provisions relating to the amendments made by Sec. 618(b) of this Act, see Sec. 601(b)(2) of P.L. 107-147 and Sec. 312(b)(2) of P.L. 108-311, reproduced above.

—P.L. 107-16, Sec. 901, of this Act [as amended by Sec. 2 of P.L. 107-358 and Sec. 101(a)(1) of P.L. 111-312, and as related to Sec. 811 of P.L. 109-280], reads as follows:

"Sec. 901. Sunset of provisions of Act.
"(a) In general. All provisions of, and amendments made by, this Act shall not apply—
"(1) to taxable, plan, or limitation years beginning after December 31, 2012, or
"(2) in the case of title V, to estates of decedents dying, gifts made, or generation skipping transfers, after December 31, 2012.
"(b) Application of certain laws. The Internal Revenue Code of 1986 and the Employee Retirement Income Security Act of 1974 shall be applied and administered to years, estates, gifts, and transfers described in subsection (a) as if the provisions and amendments described in subsection (a) had never been enacted.
"(c) Exception. Subsection (a) shall not apply to section 803 (relating to no federal income tax on restitution received by victims of the Nazi regime or their heirs or estates)."

Sec. 25C. Nonbusiness energy property.
(a) Allowance of credit.
In the case of an individual, there shall be allowed as a credit against the tax imposed by this chapter for the taxable year an amount equal to the sum of—

(1) 10 percent of the amount paid or incurred by the taxpayer for qualified energy efficiency improvements installed during such taxable year, and

(2) the amount of the residential energy property expenditures paid or incurred by the taxpayer during such taxable year.

(b) Limitations.

(1) **Lifetime limitation.** The credit allowed under this section with respect to any taxpayer for any taxable year shall not exceed the excess (if any) of $500 over the aggregate credits allowed under this section with respect to such taxpayer for all prior taxable years ending after December 31, 2005.

(2) **Windows.** In the case of amounts paid or incurred for components described in subsection (c)(2)(B) by any taxpayer for any taxable year, the credit allowed under this section with respect to such amounts for such year shall not exceed the excess (if any) of $200 over the aggregate credits allowed under this section with respect to such amounts for all prior taxable years ending after December 31, 2005.

(3) **Limitation on residential energy property expenditures.** The amount of the credit allowed under this section by reason of subsection (a)(2) shall not exceed—

(A) $50 for any advanced main air circulating fan,

(B) $150 for any qualified natural gas, propane, or oil furnace or hot water boiler, and

(C) $300 for any item of energy-efficient building property.

(c) Qualified energy efficiency improvements.
For purposes of this section—

(1) **In general.** The term "qualified energy efficiency improvements" means any energy efficient building envelope component which meets the prescriptive criteria for such component established by the 2009 International Energy Conservation Code, as such Code (including supplements) is in effect on the date of the enactment of the American Recovery and Reinvestment Tax Act of 2009 (or, in the case of an exterior window, a skylight, an exterior door, a metal roof with appropriate pigmented coatings, or an asphalt roof with appropriate cooling granules, which meet the Energy Star program requirements), if—

(A) such component is installed in or on a dwelling unit located in the United States and owned and used by the taxpayer as the taxpayer's principal residence (within the meaning of section 121),

(B) the original use of such component commences with the taxpayer, and

(C) such component reasonably can be expected to remain in use for at least 5 years.

(2) **Building envelope component.** The term "building envelope component" means—

(A) any insulation material or system which is specifically and primarily designed to reduce the heat loss or gain of a dwelling unit when installed in or on such dwelling unit,

(B) exterior windows (including skylights),

(C) exterior doors, and

(D) any metal roof or asphalt roof installed on a dwelling unit, but only if such roof has appropriate pigmented coatings or cooling granules which are specifically and primarily designed to reduce the heat gain of such dwelling unit.

(3) **Manufactured homes included.** The term "dwelling unit" includes a manufactured home which conforms to Federal Manufactured Home Construction and Safety Standards (part 3280 of title 24, Code of Federal Regulations).

(4) **Repealed.**

(d) Residential energy property expenditures.
For purposes of this section—

(1) **In general.** The term "residential energy property expenditures" means expenditures made by the taxpayer for qualified energy property which is—

(A) installed on or in connection with a dwelling unit located in the United States and owned and used by the taxpayer as the taxpayer's principal residence (within the meaning of section 121), and

(B) originally placed in service by the taxpayer.

Such term includes expenditures for labor costs properly allocable to the onsite preparation, assembly, or original installation of the property.

(2) **Qualified energy property.**

(A) In general. The term "qualified energy property" means—

(i) energy-efficient building property,

(ii) a qualified natural gas, propane, or oil furnace or hot water boiler, or

(iii) an advanced main air circulating fan.

(B) Performance and quality standards. Property described under subparagraph (A) shall meet the performance and quality standards, and the certification requirements (if any), which—

(i) have been prescribed by the Secretary by regulations (after consultation with the Secretary of Energy or the Administrator of the Environmental Protection Agency, as appropriate), and

(ii) are in effect at the time of the acquisition of the property, or at the time of the completion of the construction, reconstruction, or erection of the property, as the case may be.

(C) Requirements and standards for air conditioners and heat pumps. The standards and requirements prescribed by the Secretary under subparagraph (B) with respect to the energy efficiency ratio (EER) for central air conditioners and electric heat pumps—

(i) shall require measurements to be based on published data which is tested by manufacturers at 95 degrees Fahrenheit, and

(ii) may be based on the certified data of the Air Conditioning and Refrigeration Institute that are prepared in partnership with the Consortium for Energy Efficiency.

(3) Energy-efficient building property. The term "energy-efficient building property" means—

(A) an electric heat pump water heater which yields an energy factor of at least 2.0 in the standard Department of Energy test procedure,

(B) an electric heat pump which achieves the highest efficiency tier established by the Consortium for Energy Efficiency, as in effect on January 1, 2009.

(C) a central air conditioner which achieves the highest efficiency tier established by the Consortium for Energy Efficiency, as in effect on January 1, 2009,

(D) a natural gas, propane, or oil water heater which has either an energy factor of at least 0.82 or a thermal efficiency of at least 90 percent.

(E) a stove which uses the burning of biomass fuel to heat a dwelling unit located in the United States and used as a residence by the taxpayer, or to heat water for use in such a dwelling unit, and which has a thermal efficiency rating of at least 75 percent.

(4) Qualified natural gas, propane, or oil furnace or hot water boiler. The term "qualified natural gas, propane, or oil furnace or hot water boiler" means a natural gas, propane, or oil furnace or hot water boiler which achieves an annual fuel utilization efficiency rate of not less than 95.

(5) Advanced main air circulating fan. The term "advanced main air circulating fan" means a fan used in a natural gas, propane, or oil furnace and which has an annual electricity use of no more than 2 percent of the total annual energy use of the furnace (as determined in the standard Department of Energy test procedures).

(6) Biomass fuel. The term "biomass fuel" means any plant-derived fuel available on a renewable or recurring basis, including agricultural crops and trees, wood and wood waste and residues (including wood pellets), plants (including aquatic plants), grasses, residues, and fibers.

(e) Special rules.

For purposes of this section—

(1) Application of rules. Rules similar to the rules under paragraphs (4), (5), (6), (7), and (8) of section 25D(e) shall apply.

(2) Joint ownership of energy items.

(A) In general. Any expenditure otherwise qualifying as an expenditure under this section shall not be treated as failing to so qualify merely because such expenditure was made with respect to 2 or more dwelling units.

(B) Limits applied separately. In the case of any expenditure described in subparagraph (A), the amount of the credit allowable under subsection (a) shall (subject to paragraph (1)) be computed separately with respect to the amount of the expenditure made for each dwelling unit.

(3) Property financed by subsidized energy financing. For purposes of determining the amount of expenditures made by any individual with respect to any property, there shall not be taken into account expenditures which are made from subsidized energy financing (as defined in section 48(a)(4)(C)).

(f) Basis adjustments.

For purposes of this subtitle, if a credit is allowed under this section for any expenditure with respect to any property, the increase in the basis of such property which would (but for this subsection) result from such expenditure shall be reduced by the amount of the credit so allowed.

(g) Termination.

This section shall not apply with respect to any property placed in service—

(1) after December 31, 2007, and before January 1, 2009, or

(2) after December 31, 2011.

In 2010, P.L. 111-312, Sec. 710(a), substituted "2011" for "2010" in para. (g)(2) . . . Sec. 710(b)(1), amended subsecs. (a) and (b) . . . Sec. 710(b)(2)(A), substituted "2009 International Energy Conservation Code, as such Code (including supplements) is in effect on the date of the enactment of the American Recovery and Reinvestment Tax Act of 2009" for "2000 International Energy Conservation Code, as such Code (including supplements) is in effect on the date of the enactment of this section" in para. (c)(1) . . . Sec. 710(b)(2)(B), deleted ", as measured using a lower heating value" before the period at the end of subpara. (d)(3)(E) . . . Sec. 710(b)(2)(C)(i), amended para. (d)(4) . . . Sec. 710(b)(2)(C)(ii), amended clause (d)(2)(A)(ii) . . . Sec. 710(b)(2)(D)(i), deleted para. (c)(4) . . . Sec. 710(b)(2)(D)(ii), added "an exterior window, a skylight, an exterior door," after "in the case of" in para. (c)(1) . . . Sec. 710(b)(2)(E), deleted "and meets the prescriptive criteria for such material or system established by the 2009 International Energy Conservation Code, as such Code (including supplements) is in effect on the date of the enactment of the American Recovery and Reinvestment Tax Act of 2009" before the period at the end of subpara. (c)(1) . . . Sec. 710(b)(3), added para. (e)(3), effective for property placed in service after 12/31/2010.

Prior to amendment, subsecs. (a) and (b) read as follows:

"(a) Allowance of credit. In the case of an individual, there shall be allowed as a credit against the tax imposed by this chapter for the taxable year an amount equal to 30 percent of the sum of—

"(1) the amount paid or incurred by the taxpayer during such taxable year for qualified energy efficiency improvements, and

"(2) the amount of the residential energy property expenditures paid or incurred by the taxpayer during such taxable year.

"(b) Limitation. The aggregate amount of the credits allowed under this section for taxable years beginning in 2009 and 2010 with respect to any taxpayer shall not exceed $1,500."

Prior to deletion, para. (c)(4) read as follows:

"(4) Qualifications for exterior windows, doors, and skylights. Such term shall not include any component described in subparagraph (B) or (C) of paragraph (2) unless such component is equal to or below a U factor of 0.30 and SHGC of 0.30."

Prior to amendment, clause (d)(2)(A)(ii) read as follows:

"(ii) any qualified natural gas furnace, qualified propane furnace, qualified oil furnace, qualified natural gas hot water boiler, qualified propane hot water boiler, or qualified oil hot water boiler, or"

Prior to amendment, para. (d)(4) read as follows:

"(4) Qualified natural gas, propane, and oil furnaces and hot water boilers.

"(A) Qualified natural gas furnace. The term 'qualified natural gas furnace' means any natural gas furnace which achieves an annual fuel utilization efficiency rate of not less than 95.

"(B) Qualified natural gas hot water boiler. The term 'qualified natural gas hot water boiler' means any natural gas hot water boiler which achieves an annual fuel utilization efficiency rate of not less than 95.

"(C) Qualified propane furnace. The term 'qualified propane furnace' means any propane furnace which achieves an annual fuel utilization efficiency rate of not less than 95.

"(D) Qualified propane hot water boiler. The term 'qualified propane hot water boiler' means any propane hot water boiler which achieves an annual fuel utilization efficiency rate of not less than 90.

"(E) Qualified oil furnaces. The term 'qualified oil furnace' means any oil furnace which achieves an annual fuel utilization efficiency rate of not less than 90.

"(F) Qualified oil hot water boiler. The term 'qualified oil hot water boiler' means any oil hot water boiler which achieves an annual fuel utilization efficiency rate of not less than 90."

In 2009, P.L. 111-5, Sec. 1103(b)(2)(A), substituted "and (8)" for "(8), and (9) in para. (e)(1), effective for tax. yrs. begin. after 12/31/2008.

—P.L. 111-5, Sec. 1121(a), amended subsecs. (a) and (b), effective for tax. yrs. begin. after 12/31/2008.

Prior to amendment, subsecs. (a) and (b) read as follows:

"(a) Allowance of credit. In the case of an individual, there shall be allowed as a credit against the tax imposed by this chapter for the taxable year an amount equal to the sum of—

"(1) 10 percent of the amount paid or incurred by the taxpayer for qualified energy efficiency improvements installed during such taxable year, and

"(2) the amount of the residential energy property expenditures paid or incurred by the taxpayer during such taxable year.

"(b) Limitations.

"(1) Lifetime limitation. The credit allowed under this section with respect to any taxpayer for any taxable year shall not exceed the excess (if any) of $500 over the aggregate credits allowed under this section with respect to such taxpayer for all prior taxable years.

"(2) Windows. In the case of amounts paid or incurred for components described in subsection (c)(2)(B) by any taxpayer for any taxable year, the credit allowed under this section with respect to such amounts for such year shall not exceed the excess (if any) of $200 over the aggregate credits allowed under this section with respect to such amounts for all prior taxable years.

"(3) Limitation on residential energy property expenditures. The amount of the credit allowed under this section by reason of subsection (a)(2) shall not exceed—

"(A) $50 for any advanced main air circulating fan,

"(B) $150 for any qualified natural gas, propane, or oil furnace or hot water boiler, and
"(C) $300 for any item of energy-efficient building property."
—P.L. 111-5, Sec. 1121(b)(1), amended subpara. (d)(3)(B)... Sec. 1121(b)(2), substituted "2009" for "2006" subpara. (d)(3)(C)... Sec. 1121(b)(3), amended subpara. (d)(3)(D), effective for property placed in service after 2/17/2009.
Prior to amendment, subpara. (d)(3)(B) read as follows:
"(B) an electric heat pump which has a heating seasonal performance factor (HSPF) of at least 9, a seasonal energy efficiency ratio (SEER) of at least 15, and an energy efficiency ratio (EER) of at least 13,"
Prior to amendment, subpara. (d)(3)(D) read as follows:
"(D) a natural gas, propane, or oil water heater which has an energy factor of at least 0.80 or a thermal efficiency of at least 90 percent, and"
—P.L. 111-5, Sec. 1121(b)(4), added ", as measured using a lower heating value" after "75 percent" in subpara. (d)(3)(E), effective for tax. yrs. begin. after 12/31/2008.
—P.L. 111-5, Sec. 1121(c)(1), amended para. (d)(4)... Sec. 1121(c)(2), amended clause (d)(2)(A)(ii), effective for property placed in service after 2/17/2009.
Prior to amendment, para. (d)(4) read as follows:
"(4) Qualified natural gas, propane, or oil furnace or hot water boiler. The term 'qualified natural gas, propane, or oil furnace or hot water boiler' means a natural gas, propane, or oil furnace or hot water boiler which achieves an annual fuel utilization efficiency rate of not less than 95."
Prior to amendment, clause (d)(2)(A)(ii) read as follows:
"(ii) a qualified natural gas, propane, or oil furnace or hot water boiler, or
—P.L. 111-5, Sec. 1121(d)(1), added para. (c)(4)... Sec. 1121(d)(2), added 'and meets the prescriptive criteria for such material or system established by the 2009 International Energy Conservation Code, as such Code (including supplements) is in effect on the date of the enactment of the American Recovery and Reinvestment Tax Act of 2009' after 'such dwelling unit' in subpara. (c)(2)(A), effective for property placed in service after 2/17/2009.
—P.L. 111-5, Sec. 1121(e), substituted 'December 31, 2010' for 'December 31, 2009' in para. (g)(2), effective for tax. yrs. begin. after 12/31/2008.
In 2008, P.L. 110-343, Sec. 302(a)DivB, substituted 'placed in service—' for 'placed in service after December 31, 2007' in subsec. (g) and added paras. (g)(1)-(2)... Sec. 302(b)(1)(A)DivB, deleted 'and' at the end of subpara. (d)(3)(D)... Sec. 302(b)(1)(B)DivB, substituted ', and' for the period at the end of subpara. (d)(3)(E)... Sec. 302(b)(1)(C)DivB, added subpara. (d)(3)(F)... Sec. 302(b)(2)DivB, added para. (d)(6)... Sec. 302(c)DivB, added 'or a thermal efficiency of at least 90 percent' after '0.80' in subpara. (d)(3)(E)... Sec. 302(d)(1)DivB, deleted subpara. (d)(3)(C), and redesignated subparas. (d)(3)(D)-(F) as (C)-(E) [as amended by Sec. 302(b)-(c)DivB of this Act, see above]... Sec. 302(d)(2)DivB, amended subpara. (d)(2)(C), effective for expenditures made after 12/31/2008.
Prior to amendment, subpara. (d)(2)(C) read as follows:
"(C) Requirements for standards. The standards and requirements prescribed by the Secretary under subparagraph (B)—
"(i) in the case of the energy efficiency ratio (EER) for central air conditioners and electric heat pumps—
"(I) shall require manufacturers to be based on published data which is tested by manufacturers at 95 degrees Fahrenheit, and
"(I) may be based on the certified data of the Air Conditioning and Refrigeration Institute that are prepared in partnership with the Consortium for Energy Efficiency, and
"(ii) in the case of geothermal heat pumps—
"(I) shall be based on testing under the conditions of ARI/ISO Standard 13256—1 for Water Source Heat Pumps or ARI 870 for Direct Expansion GeoExchange Heat Pumps (DX), as appropriate, and
"(II) shall include evidence that water heating services have been provided through a desuperheater or integrated water heating system connected to the storage water heater tank."
Prior to deletion, subpara. (d)(3)(C) read as follows:
"(C) a geothermal heat pump which—
"(i) in the case of a closed loop product, has an energy efficiency ratio (EER) of at least 14.1 and a heating coefficient of performance (COP) of at least 3.3,
"(ii) in the case of an open loop product, has an energy efficiency ratio (EER) of at least 16.2 and a heating coefficient of performance (COP) of at least 3.6, and
"(iii) in the case of a direct expansion (DX) product, has an energy efficiency ratio (EER) of at least 15 and a heating coefficient of performance (COP) of at least 3.5,"
—P.L. 110-343, Sec. 302(e)(1)DivB, added ", or an asphalt roof with appropriate cooling granules," before "which meet the Energy Star program requirements" in para. (c)(1)... Sec. 302(e)(2)(A)DivB, added "or asphalt roof" after "metal roof" in subpara. (c)(2)(D)... Sec. 302(e)(2)(B)DivB, added "or cooling granules" after "pigmented coatings" in subpara. (c)(2)(D), effective for property placed in service after 2/17/2009.
In 2007, P.L. 110-172, Sec. 11(a)(2), substituted "part 3280" for "section 3280" in para. (c)(3), enacted 12/29/2007.
In 2005, P.L. 109-135, Sec. 412(b), substituted "subsection (c)(2)(B)" for "subsection (c)(3)(B)" in para. (b)(2), effective 12/21/2005.
—P.L. 109-58, Sec. 1333(a), added Code Sec. 25C, effective for property placed in service after 12/31/2005.

Sec. 25D. Residential energy efficient property.
(a) Allowance of credit.
In the case of an individual, there shall be allowed as a credit against the tax imposed by this chapter for the taxable year an amount equal to the sum of—
(1) 30 percent of the qualified solar electric property expenditures made by the taxpayer during such year,
(2) 30 percent of the qualified solar water heating property expenditures made by the taxpayer during such year,
(3) 30 percent of the qualified fuel cell property expenditures made by the taxpayer during such year,
(4) 30 percent of the qualified small wind energy property expenditures made by the taxpayer during such year, and
(5) 30 percent of the qualified geothermal heat pump property expenditures made by the tax payer during such year.
(b) Limitations.
(1) Maximum credit for fuel cells. In the case of any qualified fuel cell property expenditure, the credit allowed under subsection (a) (determined without regard to subsection (c)) for any taxable year shall not exceed $500 with respect to each half kilowatt of capacity of the qualified fuel cell property (as defined in section 48(c)(1)) to which such expenditure relates.
(2) Certification of solar water heating property. No credit shall be allowed under this section for an item of property described in subsection (d)(1) unless such property is certified for performance by the non-profit Solar Rating Certification Corporation or a comparable entity endorsed by the government of the State in which such property is installed.
(c) Limitation based on amount of tax; carryforward of unused credit.
(1) Limitation based on amount of tax. In the case of a taxable year to which section 26(a)(2) does not apply, the credit allowed under subsection (a) for the taxable year shall not exceed the excess of—
(A) the sum of the regular tax liability (as defined in section 26(b)) plus the tax imposed by section 55, over
(B) the sum of the credits allowable under this subpart (other than this section) and section 27 for the taxable year.
(2) Carryforward of unused credit.
(A) Rule for years in which all personal credits allowed against regular and alternative minimum tax. In the case of a taxable year to which section 26(a)(2) applies, if the credit allowable under subsection (a) exceeds the limitation imposed by section 26(a)(2) for such taxable year reduced by the sum of the credits allowable under this subpart (other than this section), such excess shall be carried to the succeeding taxable year and added to the credit allowable under subsection (a) for such succeeding taxable year.
(B) Rule for other years. In the case of a taxable year to which section 26(a)(2) does not apply, if the credit allowable under subsection (a) exceeds the limitation imposed by paragraph (1) for such taxable year, such excess shall be carried to the succeeding taxable year and added to the credit allowable under subsection (a) for such succeeding taxable year.
(d) Definitions.
For purposes of this section—
(1) Qualified solar water heating property expenditure. The term "qualified solar water heating property expenditure" means an expenditure for property to heat water for use in a dwelling unit located in the United States and used as a residence by the taxpayer if at least half of the

energy used by such property for such purpose is derived from the sun.

(2) Qualified solar electric property expenditure. The term "qualified solar electric property expenditure" means an expenditure for property which uses solar energy to generate electricity for use in a dwelling unit located in the United States and used as a residence by the taxpayer.

(3) Qualified fuel cell property expenditure. The term "qualified fuel cell property expenditure" means an expenditure for qualified fuel cell property (as defined in section 48(c)(1)) installed on or in connection with a dwelling unit located in the United States and used as a principal residence (within the meaning of section 121) by the taxpayer.

(4) Qualified small wind energy property expenditure. The term "qualified small wind energy property expenditure" means an expenditure for property which uses a wind turbine to generate electricity for use in connection with a dwelling unit located in the United States and used as a residence by the taxpayer.

(5) Qualified geothermal heat pump property expenditure.

(A) In general. The term "qualified geothermal heat pump property expenditure" means an expenditure for qualified geothermal heat pump property installed on or in connection with a dwelling unit located in the United States and used as a residence by the taxpayer.

(B) Qualified geothermal heat pump property. The term "qualified geothermal heat pump property" means any equipment which—

(i) uses the ground or ground water as a thermal energy source to heat the dwelling unit referred to in subparagraph (A) or as a thermal energy sink to cool such dwelling unit, and

(ii) meets the requirements of the Energy Star program which are in effect at the time that the expenditure for such equipment is made.

(e) Special rules.

For purposes of this section—

(1) Labor costs. Expenditures for labor costs properly allocable to the onsite preparation, assembly, or original installation of the property described in subsection (d) and for piping or wiring to interconnect such property to the dwelling unit shall be taken into account for purposes of this section.

(2) Solar panels. No expenditure relating to a solar panel or other property installed as a roof (or portion thereof) shall fail to be treated as property described in paragraph (1) or (2) of subsection (d) solely because it constitutes a structural component of the structure on which it is installed.

(3) Swimming pools, etc., used as storage medium. Expenditures which are properly allocable to a swimming pool, hot tub, or any other energy storage medium which has a function other than the function of such storage shall not be taken into account for purposes of this section.

(4) Fuel cell expenditure limitations in case of joint occupancy. In the case of any dwelling unit with respect to which qualified fuel cell property expenditures are made and which is jointly occupied and used during any calendar year as a residence by two or more individuals, the following rules shall apply:

(A) Maximum expenditures for fuel cells. The maximum amount of such expenditures which may be taken into account under subsection (a) by all such individuals with respect to such dwelling unit during such calendar year shall be $1,667 in the case of each half kilowatt of capacity of qualified fuel cell property (as defined in section 48(c)(1)) with respect to which such expenditures relate.

(B) Allocation of expenditures. The expenditures allocated to any individual for the taxable year in which such calendar year ends shall be an amount equal to the lesser of—

(i) the amount of expenditures made by such individual with respect to such dwelling during such calendar year, or

(ii) the maximum amount of such expenditures set forth in subparagraph (A) multiplied by a fraction—

(I) the numerator of which is the amount of such expenditures with respect to such dwelling made by such individual during such calendar year, and

(II) the denominator of which is the total expenditures made by all such individuals with respect to such dwelling during such calendar year.

(5) Tenant–stockholder in cooperative housing corporation. In the case of an individual who is a tenant-stockholder (as defined in section 216) in a cooperative housing corporation (as defined in such section), such individual shall be treated as having made his tenant-stockholder's proportionate share (as defined in section 216(b)(3)) of any expenditures of such corporation.

(6) Condominiums.

(A) In general. In the case of an individual who is a member of a condominium management association with respect to a condominium which the individual owns, such individual shall be treated as having made the individual's proportionate share of any expenditures of such association.

(B) Condominium management association. For purposes of this paragraph, the term "condominium management association" means an organization which meets the requirements of paragraph (1) of section 528(c) (other than subparagraph (E) thereof) with respect to a condominium project substantially all of the units of which are used as residences.

(7) Allocation in certain cases. If less than 80 percent of the use of an item is for nonbusiness purposes, only that portion of the expenditures for such item which is properly allocable to use for nonbusiness purposes shall be taken into account.

(8) When expenditure made; amount of expenditure.

(A) In general. Except as provided in subparagraph (B), an expenditure with respect to an item shall be treated as made when the original installation of the item is completed.

(B) Expenditures part of building construction. In the case of an expenditure in connection with the construction or reconstruction of a structure, such expenditure shall be treated as made when the original use of the constructed or reconstructed structure by the taxpayer begins.

(f) Basis adjustments.

For purposes of this subtitle, if a credit is allowed under this section for any expenditure with respect to any property, the increase in the basis of such property which would (but for this subsection) result from such expenditure shall be reduced by the amount of the credit so allowed.

(g) Termination.

The credit allowed under this section shall not apply to property placed in service after December 31, 2016.

Tax credits

In 2009, P.L. 111-5, Sec. 1103(b)(2)(B), deleted para. (e)(9), effective for tax. yrs. begin. after 12/31/2008.

Prior to deletion, para. (e)(9) read as follows:

"(9) Property financed by subsidized energy financing. For purposes of determining the amount of expenditures made by any individual with respect to any dwelling unit, there shall not be taken into account expenditures which are made from subsidized energy financing (as defined in section 48(a)(4)(C))."

—P.L. 111-5, Sec. 1122(a)(1), amended para. (b)(1) . . . Sec. 1122(a)(2)(A), amended the opening paragraph of para. (e)(4) and subpara. (e)(4)(A) . . . Sec. 1122(a)(2)(B), deleted subpara. (e)(4)(C), effective for tax. yrs. begin. after 12/31/2008.

Prior to amendment, para. (b)(1) read as follows:

"(1) Maximum credit. The credit allowed under subsection (a) (determined without regard to subsection (c)) for any taxable year shall not exceed—

"(A) $2,000 with respect to any qualified solar water heating property expenditures,

"(B) $500 with respect to each half kilowatt of capacity of qualified fuel cell property (as defined in section 48(c)(1)) for which qualified fuel cell property expenditures are made

"(C) $500 with respect to each half kilowatt of capacity (not to exceed $4,000) of wind turbines for which qualified small wind energy property expenditures are made, and

"(D) $2,000 with respect to any qualified geothermal heat pump property expenditures."

Prior to amendment, para. (e)(4) opening para., and subpara. (e)(4)(A) read as follows:

"(4) Dollar amounts in case of joint occupancy. In the case of any dwelling unit which is jointly occupied and used during any calendar year as a residence by 2 or more individuals the following rules shall apply:

"(A) Maximum expenditures. The maximum amount of expenditures which may be taken into account under subsection (a) by all such individuals with respect to such dwelling unit during such calendar year shall be—

"(i) $6,667 in the case of any qualified solar water heating property expenditures,

"(ii) $1,667 in the case of each half kilowatt of capacity of qualified fuel cell property (as defined in section 48(c)(1)) for which qualified fuel cell property expenditures are made

"(iii) $1,667 in the case of each half kilowatt of capacity (not to exceed $13,333) of wind turbines for which qualified small wind energy property expenditures are made, and

"(iv) $6,667 in the case of any qualified geothermal heat pump property expenditures."

Prior to deletion, subpara. (e)(4)(C) read as follows:

"(C) Subparagraphs (A) and (B) shall be applied separately with respect to expenditures described in paragraphs (1), (2), and (3) of subsection (d)."

In 2008, P.L. 110-343, Sec. 106(a)DivB, substituted "December 31, 2016" for "December 31, 2008" in subsec. (g), effective for tax. yrs. begin. after 12/31/2007

—P.L. 110-343, Sec. 106(b)(1)(A)DivB, deleted subpara. (A) [as amended by Sec. 106(c) and Sec. 106(d) of this Act, see below] . . . Sec. 106(b)(1)(B)DivB, redesignated subpara. (B)-(E) as subpara. (A)-(D) [as amended by Sec. 106(c) and Sec. 106(d) of this Act, see below] . . . Sec. 106(b)(2)(A)DivB, deleted clause (i) [as amended by Sec. 106(c) and Sec. 106(d) of this Act, see below] . . . Sec. 106(b)(2)(B)DivB, redesignated clause (ii)-(v) as clause (i)-(iv) [as amended by Sec. 106(c) and Sec. 106(d) of this Act, see below], effective for tax. yrs. begin. after 12/31/2008

—P.L. 110-343, Sec. 106(c)(1)DivB, substituted "and" at the end of para. (a)(2), substituted ", and" for the period at the end of para. (a)(3), and added para. (a)(4) . . . Sec. 106(c)(2)DivB, deleted "and" at the end of subpara. (b)(1)(B), substituted ", and" for the period at the end of para. (b)(1)(C), and added para. (b)(1)(D) . . . Sec. 106(c)(3)(A)DivB, added para. (d)(4) . . . Sec. 106(c)(4)DivB, deleted "and" at the end of clause. (e)(4)(A)(ii), substituted ", and" for the period at the end of clause (e)(4)(A)(iii), and added clause (e)(4)(A)(iv) . . . Sec. 106(d)(1)DivB, deleted "and" at the end of para. (a)(3), substituted ", and" for the period at the end of para. (a)(4), and added para. (a)(5) [as amended by Sec. 106(c) of this Act, see above] . . . Sec. 106(d)(2)DivB, deleted "and" at the end of subpara. (b)(1)(C), substituted ", and" for the period at the end of subpara. (b)(1)(D), and added subpara. (b)(1)(E) [as amended by Sec. 106(c) of this Act, see above] . . . Sec. 106(d)(3)DivB, added para. (d)(5) [as amended by Sec. 106(c) of this Act, see above] . . . Sec. 106(d)(4)DivB, deleted "and" at the end of clause (e)(4)(A)(iii), substituted ", and" for the period at the end of clause (e)(4)(A)(iv), and added clause (e)(4)(A)(v) [as amended by Sec. 106(c) of this Act, see above] . . . Sec. 106(e)(1)DivB, amended subsec. (c), effective for tax. yrs. begin. after 12/31/2007.

In 2006, P.L. 109-432, Sec. 206(a), substituted "December 31, 2008" for "December 31, 2007" in subsec. (g). . . . Sec. 206(b)(1), substituted "qualified solar electric property expenditures" for "qualified photovoltaic property expenditures" in para. (a)(1), subpara. (b)(1)(A) and clause (e)(4)(A)(i). . . . Sec. 206(b)(2)(A), substituted "qualified solar electric property expenditure" for "qualified photovoltaic property expenditure" in para. (d)(2). . . . Sec. 206(b)(2)(B), substituted "Qualified solar electric property expenditure" for "Qualified photovoltaic property expenditure" in the heading of para. (d)(2), enacted 12/20/2006.

In 2005, P.L. 109-135, Sec. 402(i)(1), added "(determined without regard to subsection (c))" after "subsection (a)" in para. (b)(1) . . . Sec. 402(i)(2), amended subparas. (e)(4)(A) and (B), effective for property placed in service after 12/31/2005, in tax. yrs. end. after 12/31/2005 as if included in Sec. 1335 of the Energy Policy Act of 2005, P.L. 109-58.

Prior to amendment, subparas. (e)(4)(A) and (B) read as follows:

"(A) The amount of the credit allowable, under subsection (a) by reason of expenditures (as the case may be) made during such calendar year by any of such individuals with respect to such dwelling unit shall be determined by treating all of such individuals as 1 taxpayer whose taxable year is such calendar year.

"(B) There shall be allowable, with respect to such expenditures to each of such individuals, a credit under subsection (a) for the taxable year in which such calendar year ends in an amount which bears the same ratio to the amount determined under subparagraph (A) as the amount of such expenditures made by such individual during such calendar year bears to the aggregate of such expenditures made by all of such individuals during such calendar year."

—P.L. 109-135, Sec. 402(i)(3)(E), amended subsec. (c), effective for tax. yrs. begin. after 12/31/2005.

Prior to amendment, subsec. (c) read as follows:

"(c) Carryforward of unused credit. If the credit allowable under subsection (a) exceeds the limitation imposed by section 26(a) for such taxable year reduced by the sum of the credits allowable under this subpart (other than this section), such excess shall be carried to the succeeding taxable year and added to the credit allowable under subsection (a) for such succeeding taxable year."

—P.L. 109-135, Sec. 402(i)(3)(H), of this Act, provides:

"(H) Application of EGTRRA Sunset. The amendments made by this paragraph (and each part thereof) shall be subject to title IX of the Economic Growth and Tax Relief Reconciliation Act of 2001 [Sec. 901 of P.L. 107-16] in the same manner as the provisions of such Act to which such amendment (or part thereof) relates."

—P.L. 109-58, Sec. 1335(a), added Code Sec. 25D, effective for property placed in service after 12/31/2005, in tax. yrs. end. after 12/31/2005.

Sec. 26. Limitation based on tax liability; definition of tax liability.

(a) Limitation based on amount of tax.

• **Caution:** Code Sec. 26(a)(1), following, was amended by P.L. 107-16, the Economic Growth and Tax Relief Reconciliation Act of 2001. These provisions generally sunset for tax years beginning after 12/31/2012. For specific sunset provisions, see Sec. 901, P.L. 107-16, as amended, reproduced in notes following this Code Sec. Code Sec. 26(a)(1), was further amended by Sec. 10909, P.L. 111-148. As provided in Sec. 10909(c), P.L. 111-148 as amended by P.L. 111-312, Code Sec. 26(a)(1) will read as if those amendments had never been enacted, effective for tax. yrs. begin. after 12/31/2011. For Code Sec. 26(a)(1) as it will read for tax. yrs. begin. after 12/31/2011, see below:

(1) In general. The aggregate amount of credits allowed by this subpart (other than 24, 25A(i), 25B, 25D, 30, 30B, and 30D) for the taxable year shall not exceed the excess (if any) of—

(A) the taxpayer's regular tax liability for the taxable year, over

(B) the tentative minimum tax for the taxable year (determined without regard to the alternative minimum tax foreign tax credit).

For purposes of subparagraph (B), the taxpayer's tentative minimum tax for any taxable year beginning during 1999 shall be treated as being zero.

• **Caution:** Code Sec. 26(a)(1), following, is effective for tax. yrs. begin. after 12/31/2011, and reflects the sunset of the amendments made by Sec. 10909, P.L. 111-148. For details of those amendments, effective date and sunset provisions, see the history for this Code Sec. For Code Sec. 26(a)(1), effective for tax. yrs. begin. before 1/1/2012, see above.

(1) In general. The aggregate amount of credits allowed by this subpart (other than 23, 24, 25A(i), 25B, 25D, 30, 30B, and 30D) for the taxable year shall not exceed the excess (if any) of—
  (A) the taxpayer's regular tax liability for the taxable year, over
  (B) the tentative minimum tax for the taxable year (determined without regard to the alternative minimum tax foreign tax credit).
For purposes of subparagraph (B), the taxpayer's tentative minimum tax for any taxable year beginning during 1999 shall be treated as being zero.

(2) Special rule for taxable years 2000 through 2011. For purposes of any taxable year beginning during 2000, 2001, 2002, 2003, 2004, 2005, 2006, 2007, 2008, or 2009, 2010, or 2011 the aggregate amount of credits allowed by this subpart for the taxable year shall not exceed the sum of—
  (A) the taxpayer's regular tax liability for the taxable year reduced by the foreign tax credit allowable under section 27(a), and
  (B) the tax imposed by section 55(a) for the taxable year.

(b) Regular tax liability.
For purposes of this part—
(1) In general. The term "regular tax liability" means the tax imposed by this chapter for the taxable year.
(2) Exception for certain taxes. For purposes of paragraph (1), any tax imposed by any of the following provisions shall not be treated as tax imposed by this chapter:
  (A) section 55 (relating to minimum tax),
  (B) section 59A (relating to environmental tax),
  (C) subsection (m)(5)(B), (q), (t), or (v) of section 72 (relating to additional taxes on certain distributions),
  (D) section 143(m) (relating to recapture of proration of Federal subsidy from use of mortgage bonds and mortgage credit certificates),
  (E) section 530(d)(4) (relating to additional tax on certain distributions from Coverdell education savings accounts),
  (F) section 531 (relating to accumulated earnings tax),
  (G) section 541 (relating to personal holding company tax),
  (H) section 1351(d)(1) (relating to recoveries of foreign expropriation losses),
  (I) section 1374 (relating to tax on certain built-in gains of S corporations),
  (J) section 1375 (relating to tax imposed when passive investment income of corporation having subchapter C earnings and profits exceeds 25 percent of gross receipts),
  (K) subparagraph (A) of section 7518(g)(6) (relating to nonqualified withdrawals from capital construction funds taxed at highest marginal rate),
  (L) sections 871(a) and 881 (relating to certain income of nonresident aliens and foreign corporations),
  (M) section 860E(e) (relating to taxes with respect to certain residual interests),
  (N) section 884 (relating to branch profits tax),
  (O) sections 453(l)(3) and 453A(c) (relating to interest on certain deferred tax liabilities),
  (P) section 860K (relating to treatment of transfers of high-yield interests to disqualified holders),
  (Q) section 220(f)(4) (relating to additional tax on Archer MSA distributions not used for qualified medical expenses),
  (R) section 138(c)(2) (relating to penalty for distributions from Medicare Advantage MSA not used for qualified medical expenses if minimum balance not maintained),
  (S) sections 106(e)(3)(A)(ii), 223(b)(8)(B)(i)(II), and 408(d)(9)(D)(i)(II) (relating to certain failures to maintain high deductible health plan coverage),
  (T) section 170(o)(3)(B) (relating to recapture of certain deductions for fractional gifts),
  (U) section 223(f)(4) (relating to additional tax on health savings account distributions not used for qualified medical expenses),
  (V) subsections (a)(1)(B)(i) and (b)(4)(A) of section 409A (relating to interest and additional tax with respect to certain deferred compensation),
  (W) section 36(f) (relating to recapture of homebuyer credit), and
  (X) section 457A(c)(1)(B) (relating to determinability of amounts of compensation).

(c) Tentative minimum tax.
For purposes of this part, the term "tentative minimum tax" means the amount determined under section 55(b)(1).

In 2010, P.L. 111-312, Sec. 101(a)(1), substituted "December 31, 2012" for "December 31, 2010" both places it appeared in Sec. 901, P.L. 107-16, [see below], effective as if included in the enactment of P.L. 107-16, EGTRRA, 6/7/2001.
—P.L. 111-312, Sec. 101(b)(1), amended Sec. 10909(c), P.L. 111-148.
Prior to amendment, Sec. 10909(c), P.L. 111-148 read as follows:
  "(c) Application and Extension of EGTRRA Sunset. Notwithstanding section 901 of the Economic Growth and Tax Relief Reconciliation Act of 2001, such section shall apply to the amendments made by this section and the amendments mad by section 202 of such Act by substituting 'December 31, 2011' for 'December 31, 2010' in subsection (a)(1) therof."
—P.L. 111-312, Sec. 101(b)(2), substituted "Except as provided in subsection (c), the amendments" for "the amendments" in Sec. 10909(d), P.L. 111-148 (the effective date section for amendments made by Sec. 10909, P.L. 111-148)
Prior to amendment, Sec. 10909(d), P.L. 111-148, read as follows:
  "(d) Effective Date. The amendments made by this section shall apply to taxable years beginning after December 31, 2009."
—P.L. 111-312, Sec. 202(a)(1), substituted "2009, 2010, or 2011" for "or 2009" in para. (a)(2) ... Sec. 202(a)(2), substituted "2011" for "2009" in the heading of para. (a)(2), effective for tax. yrs. begin. after 12/31/2009.
—P.L. 111-148, Sec. 10909(b)(2)(E), deleted "23," in para. (a)(1), effective as provided in Sec. 10909(d) of this Act, [as amended by Sec. 101(b)(2), 111-312, see above] which reads as follows:
  "(d) Effective Date. Except as provided in subsection (c) (see below), the amendments made by this section shall apply to taxable years beginning after December 31, 2009.
—P.L. 111-148, Sec. 10909(c), of this Act, [as amended by Sec. 101(b)(1), P.L. 111-312, 12/17/2010, see above] provides:
  "(c) Sunset provision. Each provision of law amended by this section [Sec. 10909] is amended to read as such provision would read if this section had never been enacted. The amendments made by the preceding sentence shall apply to taxable years beginning after 12/31/2011."
In 2009, P.L. 111-5, Sec. 1004(b)(3), added "25A(i)," after "24," in para. (a)(1), effective for tax. yrs. begin. after 12/31/2008.
—P.L. 111-5, Sec. 1011(a)(1), substituted "2009" for "2008" in the heading of para. (a)(2) ... Sec. 1011(a)(2), substituted "2008, or 2009" for "or 2008" in para. (a)(2), effective for tax. yrs. begin. after 12/31/2008.
—P.L. 111-5, Sec. 1142(b)(1)(D), added "30," after "25D," in para. (a)(1) [as amended by Sec. 1004(b)(3) of this Act, see above]; effective for vehicles acquired after 2/17/2009.
—P.L. 111-5, Sec. 1144(b)(1)(D), added "30B," after "30," in para. (a)(1) [as amended by Secs. 1004(b)(3) and 1142(b)(1)(D) of this Act, see above], effective for tax. yrs. begin. after 12/31/2008.
In 2008, P.L. 110-343, Sec. 106(e)(2)(D)DivB, substituted "25B, and 25D" for "and 25B", in para. (a)(1), effective for tax. yrs. begin. after 12/31/2007. Sec. 106(f)(3) Div. B, relating to the EGTRRA Sunset provides:
  "(3) Application of EGTRRA Sunset. The amendments made by subparagraphs (A) and (B) of subsection (e)(2) shall be subject to title IX of the Economic Growth and Tax Relief Reconciliation Act of 2001 in the same manner as the provisions of such Act to which such amendments relate."
—P.L. 110-343, Sec. 205(d)(1)(D)DivB, substituted "25D, and 30D" for "and 25D", in para. (a)(1) [as amended by Sec. 106(e)(2)(D) Div. B of this Act, see above], effective for tax. yrs. begin. after 12/31/2008.
—P.L. 110-343, Sec. 101(a)(1)DivC, substituted "2007, or 2008" for "or 2007" in para. (a)(2) ... Sec. 101(a)(2)DivC, substituted "2008" for "2007" in the heading of para. (a)(2), effective for tax. yrs. begin. after 12/31/2007.
—P.L. 110-343, Sec. 801(b)DivC, deleted "and" at the end of subpara. (b)(2)(V), substituted ", and" for the period at the end of subpara. (b)(2)(W), and

added subpara. (b)(2)(X), effective for amounts deferred which are attributable to services performed after 12/31/2008. Sec. 802(b)(2)-(5)DivC of this Act provides:

"(2) Application to existing deferrals. In the case of any amount deferred to which the amendments made by this section do not apply solely by reason of the fact that the amount is attributable to services performed before January 1, 2009, to the extent such amount is not includible in gross income in a taxable year beginning before 2018, such amounts shall be includible in gross income in the later of—

"(A) the last taxable year beginning before 2018, or

"(B) the taxable year in which there is no substantial risk of forfeiture of the rights to such compensation (determined in the same manner as determined for purposes of section 457A of the Internal Revenue Code of 1986, as added by this section).

"(3) Accelerated payments. No later than 120 days after the date of the enactment of this Act, the Secretary shall issue guidance providing a limited period of time during which a nonqualified deferred compensation arrangement attributable to services performed on or before December 31, 2008, may, without violating the requirements of section 409A(a) of the Internal Revenue Code of 1986, be amended to conform the date of distribution to the date the amounts are required to be included in income.

"(4) Certain back-to-back arrangements. If the taxpayer is also a service recipient and maintains one or more nonqualified deferred compensation arrangements for its service providers under which any amount is attributable to services performed on or before December 31, 2008, the guidance issued under paragraph (4) shall permit such arrangements to be amended to conform the dates of distribution under such arrangement to the date amounts are required to be included in the income of such taxpayer under this subsection.

"(5) Accelerated payment not treated as material modification. Any amendment to a nonqualified deferred compensation arrangement made pursuant to paragraph (4) or (5) shall not be treated as a material modification of the arrangement for purposes of section 409A of the Internal Revenue Code of 1986."

—P.L. 110-289, Sec. 3011(b)(1), deleted "and" at the end of subpara. (b)(2)(U), substituted ", and" for the period at the end of subpara. (b)(2)(V), and added subpara. (b)(2)(W), effective for residences purchased on or after 4/9/2008, in tax. yrs. end. on or after such date.

In 2007, P.L. 110-172, Sec. 11(a)(3), redesignated subparas. (b)(2)(S) and (b)(2)(T) as subparas. (b)(2)(U) and (b)(2)(V), and added subparas. (b)(2)(S) and subpara. (b)(2)(T), enacted 12/29/2007.

—P.L. 110-166, Sec. 3(a)(1), substituted "2006, or 2007" for "or 2006" in para. (a)(2) . . . Sec. 3(a)(2), substituted "2007" for "2006" in the heading of para. (a)(2), effective for tax. yrs. begin. after 12/31/2006.

In 2006, P.L. 109-280, Sec. 811, of this Act [relating to Sec. 901 of P.L. 107-16, see below], provides:

"SEC. 811. PENSIONS AND INDIVIDUAL RETIREMENT ARRANGEMENT PROVISIONS OF ECONOMIC GROWTH AND TAX RELIEF RECONCILIATION ACT OF 2001 MADE PERMANENT.

"Title IX of the Economic Growth and Tax Relief Reconciliation Act of 2001 shall not apply to the provisions of, and amendments made by, subtitles A through F of title VI of such Act (relating to pension and individual retirement arrangement provisions)."

—P.L. 109-222, Sec. 302(a)(1), substituted "2006" for "2005" in the heading of para. (a)(2) . . . Sec. 302(a)(2), substituted "2005, or 2006" for "or 2005" in para. (a)(2), effective for tax. yrs. begin. after 12/31/2005.

In 2005, P.L. 109-135, Sec. 403(hh)(1), deleted "and" at the end of subpara. (b)(2)(R), substituted ", and" for the period at the end of subpara. (b)(2)(S), and added subpara. (b)(2)(T), effective for amounts deferred after 12/31/2004 as if included in Sec. 885 of the American Jobs Creation Act of 2004, P.L. 108-357, except as provided in Sec. 885(d)(2) and (3) of P.L. 108-357, which read as follows:

"(2) Special rules.

"(A) Earnings. The amendments made by this section shall apply to earnings on deferred compensation only to the extent that such amendments apply to such compensation.

"(B) Material modifications. For purposes of this subsection, amounts deferred in taxable years beginning before January 1, 2005, shall be treated as amounts deferred in a taxable year beginning on or after such date if the plan under which the deferral is made is materially modified after October 3, 2004, unless such modification is pursuant to the guidance issued under subsection (f).

"(3) Exception for nonelective deferred compensation. The amendments made by this section shall not apply to any nonelective deferred compensation to which section 457 of the Internal Revenue Code of 1986 does not apply by reason of section 457(e)(12) of such Code, but only if such compensation is provided under a nonqualified deferred compensation plan—

"(A) which was in existence on May 1, 2004,

"(B) which was providing nonelective deferred compensation described in such section 457(e)(12) on such date, and

"(C) which is established or maintained by an organization incorporated on July 2, 1974.

"If, after May 1, 2004, a plan described in the preceding sentence adopts a plan amendment which provides a material change in the classes of individuals eligible to participate in the plan, this paragraph shall not apply to any nonelective deferred compensation provided under the plan on or after the date of the adoption of the amendment."

—P.L. 109-135, Sec. 403(hh)(4), substituted "January 1, 2005" for "December 31, 2004" the first place it appeared in Sec. 885(f), see below.

Sec. 885(e) and (f) [as amended by Sec. 403(hh)(4) of P.L. 109-135, see above] of P.L. 108-357, provide:

"(e) Guidance relating to change of ownership or control. Not later than 90 days after the date of the enactment of this Act, the Secretary of the Treasury shall issue guidance on what constitutes a change in ownership or effective control for purposes of section 409A of the Internal Revenue Code of 1986, as added by this section.

"(f) Guidance relating to termination of certain existing arrangements. Not later than 60 days after the date of the enactment of this Act, the Secretary of the Treasury shall issue guidance providing a limited period during which a nonqualified deferred compensation plan adopted before January 1, 2005, may, without violating the requirements of paragraphs (2), (3), and (4) of section 409A(a) of the Internal Revenue Code of 1986 (as added by this section), be amended—

"(1) to provide that a participant may terminate participation in the plan, or cancel an outstanding deferral election with regard to amounts deferred after December 31, 2004, but only if amounts subject to the termination or cancellation are includible in income of the participant as earned (or, if later, when no longer subject to substantial risk of forfeiture), and

"(2) to conform to the requirements of such section 409A with regard to amounts deferred after December 31, 2004."

—P.L. 109-135, Sec. 412(c), substituted "section 530(d)(4)" for "section 530(d)(3)" in subpara. (b)(2)(E), effective 12/21/2005.

In 2004, P.L. 108-311, Sec. 312(a)(1), substituted "rule for taxable years 2000 through 2005." for "rule for 2000, 2001, 2002, and 2003." in the heading of para. (a)(2) . . . Sec. 312(a)(2), substituted "2003, 2004, or 2005" for "or 2003" in para. (a)(2), effective for tax. yrs. begin. after 12/31/2003.

—P.L. 108-311, Sec. 312(b)(2), of this Act, provides:

"(2) The amendments made by sections 201(b), 202(f), and 618(b) of the Economic Growth and Tax Relief Reconciliation Act of 2001 [P.L. 107-16] shall not apply to taxable years beginning during 2004 or 2005."

—P.L. 108-311, Sec. 401(a)(1), deleted "and" at the end of subpara. (b)(2)(Q), substituted ", and" for the period at the end of subpara. (b)(2)(R), and added subpara. (b)(2)(S), effective for tax. yrs. begin. after 12/31/2003 as if included in Sec. 1201 of the Medicare Prescription Drug, Improvement, and Modernization Act of 2003, P.L. 108-173.

—P.L. 108-311, Sec. 408(a)(5)(A), substituted "Medicare Advantage MSA" for "Medicare+Choice MSA" in subpara. (b)(2)(R), effective 10/4/2004.

In 2002, P.L. 107-358, Sec. 2, added subsec. (c) in Sec. 901 of P.L. 107-16 [see below], effective 12/17/2002.

—P.L. 107-147, Sec. 415(a), deleted "and" at the end of subpara. (b)(2)(P), substituted ", and" for the period at the end of subpara. (b)(2)(Q), and added subpara. (b)(2)(R), effective for tax. yrs. begin. after 12/31/98.

—P.L. 107-147, Sec. 601(a)(1), substituted "rule for 2000, 2001, 2002, and 2003." for "rule for 2000 and 2001." in the heading of para. (a)(2) . . . Sec. 601(a)(2), substituted "during 2000, 2001, 2002, or 2003," for "during 2000 or 2001," in para. (a)(2), effective for tax. yrs. begin. after 12/31/2001.

—P.L. 107-147, Sec. 601(b)(2), of this Act, provides:

"(2) The amendments made by sections 201(b), 202(f), and 618(b) of the Economic Growth and Tax Relief Reconciliation Act of 2001 shall not apply to taxable years beginning during 2002 and 2003."

In 2001, P.L. 107-22, Sec. 1(b)(2)(A), substituted "Coverdell education savings" for "education individual retirement" in subpara. (b)(2)(E), effective 7/26/2001.

—P.L. 107-16, Sec. 201(b)(2)(D), added "(other than section 24)" after "this subpart" in para. (a)(1), effective for tax. yrs. begin. after 12/31/2001. For special provision, see Sec. 601(b)(2) of P.L. 107-147, above. For special provision, see Sec. 312(b)(2) of P.L. 108-311, above.

—P.L. 107-16, Sec. 202(f)(2)(C), substituted "sections 23 and 24" for "section 24" in para. (a)(1) [as amended by Sec. 201(b)(2)(D) of this Act, see above], effective for tax. yrs. begin. after 12/31/2001. For special provision, see Sec. 601(b)(2) of P.L. 107-147, above. For special provision, see Sec. 312(b)(2) of P.L. 108-311, above.

—P.L. 107-16, Sec. 618(b)(2)(C), substituted ", 24, and 25B" for "and 24" in para. (a)(1) [as amended by Secs. 201(b)(2)(D) and 202(f)(2)(C) of this Act, see above], effective for tax. yrs. begin. after 12/31/2001. For special provision, see Sec. 601(b)(2) of P.L. 107-147, above. For special provision, see Sec. 312(b)(2) of P.L. 108-311, above.

—P.L. 107-16, Sec. 901, of this Act [as amended by Sec. 2, P.L. 107-358 and Sec. 101(a)(1), P.L. 111-312, and as related to Sec. 811 of P.L. 109-280, see above], reads as follows:

"Sec. 901. Sunset of provisions of Act.

"(a) In general. All provisions of, and amendments made by, this Act shall not apply—

"(1) to taxable, plan, or limitation years beginning after December 31, 2012, or

"(2) in the case of title V, to estates of decedents dying, gifts made, or generation skipping transfers, after December 31, 2012.

"(b) Application of certain laws. The Internal Revenue Code of 1986 and the Employee Retirement Income Security Act of 1974 shall be applied and administered to years, estates, gifts, and transfers described in subsection (a) as if the provisions and amendments described in subsection (a) had never been enacted.

"(c) Exception. Subsection (a) shall not apply to section 803 (relating to no federal income tax on restitution received by victims of the Nazi regime or their heirs or estates)."

In 2000, P.L. 106-554, Sec. 1(a)(7), [which enacted into law Sec. 202(a)(1) of P.L. 106-554] substituted "Archer MSA" for "medical savings account" in subpara. (b)(2)(Q), effective 12/21/2000.

In 1999, P.L. 106-170, Sec. 501(a), amended subsec. (a), effective for tax. yrs. begin. after 12/31/98.

Prior to amendment, subsec. (a) read as follows:

"(a) Limitation based on amount of tax. The aggregate amount of credits allowed by this subpart for the taxable year shall not exceed the excess (if any) of—

"(1) the taxpayer's regular tax liability for the taxable year, over

"(2) the tentative minimum tax for the taxable year (determined without regard to the alternative minimum tax foreign tax credit).

For purposes of paragraph (2), the taxpayer's tentative minimum tax for any taxable year beginning during 1998 shall be treated as being zero."

In 1998, P.L. 105-277, Sec. 2001(a), added a flush sentence at the end of subsec. (a), effective for tax. yrs. begin. after 12/31/97.

In 1997, P.L. 105-34, Sec. 213(e)(1), redesignated subparas. (b)(2)(E)-(P) as subparas. (b)(2)(F)-(Q) and added new subpara. (b)(2)(E), effective for tax. yrs. begin. after 12/31/97.

— P.L. 105-34, Sec. 1602(a)(1), deleted "and" at the end of subpara. (b)(2)(N), substituted ", and" for the period at the end of subpara. (b)(2)(O), and added subpara. (b)(2)(P), effective for tax. yrs. begin. after 12/31/96.

In 1996, P.L. 104-188, Sec. 1621(b)(1), deleted "and" at the end of subpara. (b)(2)(M), substituted ", and" for the period at the end of subpara. (b)(2)(N), and added subpara. (b)(2)(O), effective 9/1/97.

In 1989, P.L. 101-239, Sec. 7811(c)(1), amended subparas. (b)(2)(C) and (D) . . . Sec. 7811(c)(2), deleted subparas. (b)(2)(K), (L), (L)[sic (M)], (M)[sic (N)] and added new subparas. (b)(2)(K), (L), and (M), effective as provided in Sec. 1006(t)(16)(D)(ii)-(iv) of P.L. 100-647 reproduced in note following Code Sec. 860E.

Prior to amendment, subparas. (b)(2)(C) and (D) read as follows:

"(C) subsection (m)(5)(B), (q), or (v) of section 72 (relating to additional tax on certain distributions),

"(D) section 72(t) (relating to 10-percent additional tax on early distributions from qualified retirement plans)."

Prior to amendment, subparas. (b)(2)(K), (L), (L) [sic (M)] and (M) [sic (N)] read as follows:

"(K) sections 871(a) and 881 (relating to certain income of nonresident aliens and foreign corporations),

"(L) section 860E(e) (relating to taxes with respect to certain residual interests),

"(L) [sic (M)] Section 884 (relating to branch profits tax),

"(M) [sic (N)] section 143(m) (relating to recapture of portion of federal subsidy from use of mortgage bonds and mortgage credit certificates)."

— P.L. 101-239, Sec. 7821(a)(4)(A), deleted "and" at the end of subpara. (b)(2)(L) (as amended by Sec. 7811(c)(2) of this Act), substituted "and" for the period at the end of subpara. (b)(2)(M) (as amended by Sec. 7811(c)(2) of this Act), and added new subpara. (b)(2)(N), effective for dispositions in tax. yrs. begin. after 12/31/87, except as provided in Sec. 10202(e)(2), (3), (5) of P.L. 100-203 reproduced in note following Code Sec. 453.

In 1988, P.L. 100-647, Sec. 1006(t)(16)(C), deleted "and" at the end of subpara. (b)(2)(J), substituted ", and" for the period at the end of subpara. (b)(2)(K) and added subpara. (b)(2)(L), effective as provided in Sec. 1006(t)(16)(D)(ii)-(iv) of this Act reproduced in note following Code Sec. 860E.

— P.L. 100-647, Sec. 1007(g)(1), substituted ")." for the comma at the end of para. (b)(2)(K), effective for tax. yrs. begin. after 12/31/86.

— P.L. 100-647, Sec. 1011A(c)(10)(A), deleted ", (o)(2)," after "(m)(5)(B)" in subpara. (b)(2)(C) . . . Sec. 1011A(c)(10)(B), substituted "72(t) (relating to 10-percent additional tax on early distributions from qualified retirement plans)" for "408(f) (relating to additional tax on income from certain retirement accounts)" in subpara. (b)(2)(D), effective for tax. yrs. begin. after 12/31/86, except as provided in Secs. 1123(e)(3) and (4) of P.L. 99-514 [reproduced in the note following Code Sec. 72].

— P.L. 100-647, Sec. 1012(q)(8), deleted "and" at the end of subpara. (b)(2)(J) [sic (K)], deleted the period at the end of (b)(2)(K) [sic (L)] and added subpara. (b)(2)(L) [sic (M)], effective for tax. yrs. begin. after 12/31/86.

— P.L. 100-647, Sec. 4005(g)(4), deleted "and" at the end of subpara. (b)(2)(K) [sic (L)] (as added by this Act), substituted "and" for the period at the end of subpara. (b)(2)(L) [sic (M)] as added by this Act) and added subpara. (b)(2)(M) [sic (N)], effective for financing provided and mortgage certificates issued after 12/31/90, except as provided in Sec. 4005(h)(3)(B) of this Act reproduced in note following Code Sec. 143

— P.L. 100-647, Sec. 5012(b)(2), substituted "(q), or (v)" for "or (q)" in subpara. (b)(2)(C), effective for contracts entered into on or after 6/21/88. For special rules see Sec. 5012(e)(2)-(4) of this Act reproduced in note following Code Sec. 7702A.

In 1986, P.L. 99-514, Sec. 261(c), deleted "and" at the end of subpara. (b)(2)(G), substituted ", and" for the period at the end of subpara. (b)(2)(H), and added subpara. (b)(2)(I) [before amendment by Sec. 516(b)(1)(A) of P.L. 99-499, see below], effective for tax. yrs. begin. after 12/31/86.

— P.L. 99-514, Sec. 632(c)(1), substituted "certain built-in gains" for "certain capital gains" in subpara. (b)(2)(G), effective for tax. yrs. begin. after 12/31/86, but only in cases where the first tax. yr. for which the corporation is an S corporation is pursuant to an election made after 12/31/86.

— P.L. 99-514, Sec. 701(c)(1)(A), amended subsec. (a) . . . Sec. 701(c)(1)(B)(i), substituted "this part" for "this section" in the matter preceding para. (b)(1) . . . Sec. 701(c)(1)(B)(ii), substituted "regular tax liability" for "tax liability" in para. (b)(1) . . . Sec. 701(c)(1)(B)(iii), amended subpara. (b)(2) . . . Sec. 701(c)(1)(B)(iv), deleted "and" at the end of subpara. (b)(2)(H), substituted ", and" for the period at the end of subpara. (b)(2)(I), and added subpara. (b)(2)(J) [before amendment by Sec. 516(b)(1)(A) of P.L. 99-499, see below] . . . Sec. 701(c)(1)(B)(v), substituted "Regular tax liability" for "Tax liability" in the heading of subsec. (b) . . . Sec. 701(c)(1)(C), amended subsec. (c), effective for tax. yrs. begin. after 12/31/86. For special rules, see Sec. 701(f)(2) of this Act reproduced in note following Code Sec. 56.

Prior to amendment, subsec. (a) read as follows:

"(a) Limitation based on amount of tax. The aggregate amount of credits allowed by this subpart for the taxable year shall not exceed the taxpayer's tax liability for such taxable year."

Prior to amendment, subpara. (b)(2)(A) read as follows:

"(A) section 56 (relating to corporate minimum tax),"

Prior to amendment, subsec. (c) read as follows:

"(c) Similar rule for alternative minimum tax for taxpayers other than corporations. For treatment of tax imposed by section 55 as not imposed by this chapter, see section 55(c)."

— P.L. 99-499, Sec. 516(b)(1)(A), redesignated subparas. (b)(2)(B)-(J) [as in effect after the amendments made by Secs. 261(c) and 701(c)(1)(B)(iv) of P.L. 99-514, see above] as (b)(2)(C)-(K), and added new subpara. (b)(2)(B), effective for tax. yrs. begin. after 12/31/86.

In 1984, P.L. 98-369, Sec. 472, added Code Sec. 25 (redesignated Code Sec. 26, by Sec. 612(a) of this Act see below), effective for tax yrs. begin. after 12/31/83 and to carrybacks from tax. yrs. begin. after 12/31/83.

— P.L. 98-369, Sec. 491(f)(5), provides:

"(5) Treatment of tax imposed under section 409(c). For purposes of section 26(b) of the Internal Revenue Code of 1954 (as amended by this Act), any tax imposed by section 409(c) of such Code (as in effect before its repeal by this section) shall be treated as a tax imposed by section 408(f) of such Code."

— P.L. 98-369, Sec. 612(a), redesignated Code Sec. 25 [as added by Sec. 472 of this Act, see above] as Code Sec. 26, effective for interest paid or accrued after 12/31/84, on indebtedness incurred after 12/31/84 and to elections under Code Sec. 25(c)(2)(A)(ii) [as added by this Act] for calendar years after 1983.

— P.L. 98-369, Sec. 632, provided various exceptions to the amendments made by Title VI of this Act. See note following Code Sec. 103A.

SUBPART B. — OTHER CREDITS

Sec.
27. Taxes of foreign countries and possessions of the United States; possession tax credit.
30. Credit for qualified electric vehicles.
30A. Puerto Rico economic activity credit.
30B. Alternative motor vehicle credit.
30C. Alternative fuel vehicle refueling property credit.
30D. New qualified plug-in electric drive motor vehicles.

In 2008, P.L. 110-343, Sec. 205(d)(4), added item 30D.
In 2005, P.L. 109-135, Sec. 412(e), amended item 30C.
Prior to amendment, item 30C read as follows:
"30C. Clean-fuel vehicle refueling property credit."
— P.L. 109-58, Sec. 1322(a)(3)(K), deleted item 29.
Prior to deletion item 29 read as follows:
"29. Credit for producing fuel from a nonconventional source."
— P.L. 109-58, Sec. 1341(b)(5), added item 30B.
— P.L. 109-58, Sec. 1342(b)(5), added item 30C.
In 1997, P.L. 105-34, Sec. 1601(f)(1)(B), substituted "Puerto Rico" for "Puerto Rican" in the heading of item 30A.
In 1996, P.L. 104-188, Sec. 1205(a)(3)(A), deleted item 28 . . . Sec. 1601(b)(2)(E), added item 30A . . . Sec. 1601(b)(2)(F)(i), amended the heading of subpart B.
Prior to deletion, item 28 read as follows:
"Sec. 28 Clinical testing expenses for certain drugs for rare diseases or conditions."
Prior to amendment, the heading of subpart B read as follows:
"Subpart B. Foreign Tax Credit, Etc."
In 1992, P.L. 102-486, Sec. 1913(b)(2)(A), added item 30.
In 1986, P.L. 99-514, Sec. 231(d)(3)(J), deleted item 30.
Prior to deletion item 30 read as follows:
"30. Credit for increasing research activities."
In 1984, P.L. 98-369, Sec. 471(b), added Subpart B as part of amendments made to Part IV.

Sec. 27. Taxes of foreign countries and possessions of the United States; possession tax credit.

(a) Foreign tax credit.

The amount of taxes imposed by foreign countries and possessions of the United States shall be allowed as a credit against the tax imposed by this chapter to the extent provided in section 901.

(b) Section 936 credit.

In the case of a domestic corporation, the amount provided by section 936 (relating to Puerto Rico and possession tax credit) shall be allowed as a credit against the tax imposed by this chapter.

In 1984, P.L. 98-369, Sec. 471(c)(1), redesignated Code Sec. 33 as Code Sec. 27, effective for tax. yrs. begin. after 12/31/83 and to carrybacks from tax. yrs. begin. after 12/31/83.
In 1976, P.L. 94-455, Sec. 1051(a), amended Code Sec. 33, effective for tax. yrs. begin. after 12/31/75.
Prior to amendment, Code Sec. 33 read as follows:
"SEC. 33. TAXES OF FOREIGN COUNTRIES AND POSSESSIONS OF THE UNITED STATES.
"The amount of taxes imposed by foreign countries and possessions of the United States shall be allowed as a credit against the tax imposed by this chapter to the extent provided in section 901."

Sec. 30. Certain plug-in electric vehicles.
(a) Allowance of credit.
There shall be allowed as a credit against the tax imposed by this chapter for the taxable year an amount equal to 10 percent of the cost of any qualified plug-in electric vehicle placed in service by the taxpayer during the taxable year.
(b) Per vehicle dollar limitation.
The amount of the credit allowed under subsection (a) with respect to any vehicle shall not exceed $2,500.
(c) Application with other credits.
(1) Business credit treated as part of general business credit. So much of the credit which would be allowed under subsection (a) for any taxable year (determined without regard to this subsection) that is attributable to property of a character subject to an allowance for depreciation shall be treated as a credit listed in section 38(b) for such taxable year (and not allowed under subsection (a)).
(2) Personal credit.
(A) In general. For purposes of this title, the credit allowed under subsection (a) for any taxable year (determined after application of paragraph (1)) shall be treated as a credit allowable under subpart A for such taxable year.
(B) Limitation based on amount of tax. In the case of a taxable year to which section 26(a)(2) does not apply, the credit allowed under subsection (a) for any taxable year (determined after application of paragraph (1)) shall not exceed the excess of—
(i) the sum of the regular tax liability (as defined in section 26(b)) plus the tax imposed by section 55, over

> • **Caution:** Code Sec. 30(c)(2)(B)(ii), following, reflects amendments made by Sec. 10909(b)(2)(F), P.L. 111-148, 3/23/2010. As provided in Sec. 10909(c), P.L. 111-148 as amended by Sec. 101(b)(1), P.L. 111-312, Code Sec. 30(c)(2)(B)(ii) will read as if those amendments had never been enacted, effective for tax. yrs. begin. after 12/31/2011. For Code Sec. 30(c)(2)(B)(ii) as it will read for tax. yrs. begin. after 12/31/2011, see below.

(ii) the sum of the credits allowable under subpart A (other than this section and 25D and 30D) and section 27 for the taxable year.

> • **Caution:** Code Sec. 30(c)(2)(B)(ii), following, is effective for tax. yrs. begin. after 12/31/2011, and reflects the sunset of the amendments made by Sec. 10909, P.L. 111-148. For details of those amendments, effective date and sunset provisions, see the history for this Code Sec. For Code Sec. 30(c)(2)(B)(ii), effective for tax. yrs. begin. before 1/1/2012, see above.

(ii) the sum of the credits allowable under subpart A (other than this section and 23, 25D, and 30D) and section 27 for the taxable year.
(d) Qualified plug-in electric vehicle.
For purposes of this section—
(1) In general. The term "qualified plug-in electric vehicle" means a specified vehicle—
(A) the original use of which commences with the taxpayer,
(B) which is acquired for use or lease by the taxpayer and not for resale,
(C) which is made by a manufacturer,
(D) which is manufactured primarily for use on public streets, roads, and highways,
(E) which has a gross vehicle weight rating of less than 14,000 pounds, and
(F) which is propelled to a significant extent by an electric motor which draws electricity from a battery which—
(i) has a capacity of not less than 4 kilowatt hours (2.5 kilowatt hours in the case of a vehicle with 2 or 3 wheels), and
(ii) is capable of being recharged from an external source of electricity.
(2) Specified vehicle. The term "specified vehicle" means any vehicle which—
(A) is a low speed vehicle within the meaning of section 571.3 of title 49, Code of Federal Regulations (as in effect on the date of the enactment of the American Recovery and Reinvestment Tax Act of 2009), or
(B) has 2 or 3 wheels.
(3) Manufacturer. The term "manufacturer" has the meaning given such term in regulations prescribed by the Administrator of the Environmental Protection Agency for purposes of the administration of title II of the Clean Air Act (42 U.S.C. 7521 et seq.).
(4) Battery capacity. The term "capacity" means, with respect to any battery, the quantity of electricity which the battery is capable of storing, expressed in kilowatt hours, as measured from a 100 percent state of charge to a 0 percent state of charge.
(e) Special rules.
(1) Basis reduction. For purposes of this subtitle, the basis of any property for which a credit is allowable under subsection (a) shall be reduced by the amount of such credit so allowed.
(2) No double benefit. The amount of any deduction or other credit allowable under this chapter for a new qualified plug-in electric drive motor vehicle shall be reduced by the amount of credit allowable under subsection (a) for such vehicle.
(3) Property used by tax-exempt entity. In the case of a vehicle the use of which is described in paragraph (3) or (4) of section 50(b) and which is not subject to a lease, the person who sold such vehicle to the person or entity using such vehicle shall be treated as the taxpayer that placed such vehicle in service, but only if such person clearly discloses to such person or entity in a document the amount of any credit allowable under subsection (a) with respect to such vehicle (determined without regard to subsection (c)).

(4) Property used outside United States not qualified. No credit shall be allowable under subsection (a) with respect to any property referred to in section 50(b)(1).

(5) Recapture. The Secretary shall, by regulations, provide for recapturing the benefit of any credit allowable under subsection (a) with respect to any property which ceases to be property eligible for such credit.

(6) Election not to take credit. No credit shall be allowed under subsection (a) for any vehicle if the taxpayer elects to not have this section apply to such vehicle.

(f) Termination.

This section shall not apply to any vehicle acquired after December 31, 2011.

In 2010, P.L. P.L. 111-312, Sec. 101(b)(1), amended subsec. (c) of Sec. 10909, P.L. 111-148 [see below]. Prior to amendment, Sec. 10909(c) read as follows:
"(c) Application and Extension of EGTRRA Sunset. Notwithstanding section 901 of the Economic Growth and Tax Relief Reconciliation Act of 2001, such section shall apply to the amendments made by this section and the amendments made by section 202 of such Act by substituting 'December 31, 2011' for 'December 31, 2010' in subsection (a)(1) thereof."
—P.L. 111-312, Sec. 101(b)(2), substituted "Except as provided in subsection (c), the amendments" for "the amendments" in Sec. 10909(d), P.L. 111-148, (the effective date section for amendments made by Sec. 10909, P.L. 111-148), see below.
Prior to amendment, Sec. 10909(d), P.L. 111-148, read as follows:
"(d) Effective Date. The amendments made by this section shall apply to taxable years beginning after December 31, 2009."
—P.L. 111-148, Sec. 10909(b)(2)(F), substituted "25D" for "23, 25D," in clause (c)(2)(B)(ii), effective for tax. yrs. begin. after 12/31/2009, except as provided in Sec. 10909(c), see below.
—P.L. 111-148, Sec. 10909(c), of this Act, relating to the EGTRRA sunset provisions, as amended by Sec. 101(b)(1), P.L. 111-312, reads as follows:
"(c) Sunset provision. Each provision of law amended by this section is amended to read as such provision would read if this section had never been enacted. The amendments made by the preceding sentence shall apply to taxable years beginning after December 31, 2011."
—P.L. 111-148, Sec. 10909(d), of this Act, relating to the EGTRRA sunset provisions, as amended by Sec. 101(b)(2), P.L. 111-312, reads as follows:
"(d) Effective date. Except as provided in subsection (c) [Sec. 10909(c), P.L. 111-148], the amendments made by this section shall apply to taxable years beginning after December 31, 2009."
In 2009, P.L. 111-5, Sec. 1142(a), amended Code Sec. 30, effective for vehicles acquired after 2/17/2009.
Prior to amendment, Code Sec. 30 read as follows:
"Sec. 30. CREDIT FOR QUALIFIED ELECTRIC VEHICLES.
"(a) Allowance of credit. There shall be allowed as a credit against the tax imposed by this chapter for the taxable year an amount equal to 10 percent of the cost of any qualified electric vehicle placed in service by the taxpayer during the taxable year.
"(b) Limitations.
"(1) Limitation per vehicle. The amount of the credit allowed under subsection (a) for any vehicle shall not exceed $4,000.
"(2) Phaseout. In the case of any qualified electric vehicle placed in service after December 31, 2005, the credit otherwise allowable under subsection (a) (determined after the application of paragraph (1)) shall be reduced by 75 percent.
"(3) Application with other credits. The credit allowed by subsection (a) for any taxable year shall not exceed the excess (if any) of—
"(A) the regular tax for the taxable year reduced by the sum of the credits allowable under subpart A and section 27, over—
"(B) the tentative minimum tax for the taxable year.
"(c) Qualified electric vehicle. For purposes of this section—
"(1) In general. The term 'qualified electric vehicle' means any motor vehicle—
"(A) which is powered primarily by an electric motor drawing current from rechargeable batteries, fuel cells, or other portable sources of electrical current,
"(B) the original use of which commences with the taxpayer, and
"(C) which is acquired for use by the taxpayer and not for resale.
"(2) Motor vehicle. For purposes of paragraph (1), the term 'motor vehicle' means any vehicle which is manufactured primarily for use on public streets, roads, and highways (not including a vehicle operated exclusively on a rail or rails) and which has at least 4 wheels.
"(d) Special rules.
"(1) Basis reduction. The basis of any property for which a credit is allowable under subsection (a) shall be reduced by the amount of such credit (determined without regard to subsection (b)(3)).
"(2) Recapture. The Secretary shall, by regulations, provide for recapturing the benefit of any credit allowable under subsection (a) with respect to any property which ceases to be property eligible for such credit.
"(3) Property used outside United States, etc., not qualified. No credit shall be allowed under subsection (a) with respect to any property referred to in section 50(b) or with respect to the portion of the cost of any property taken into account under section 179.

"(4) Election to not take credit. No credit shall be allowed under section (a) for any vehicle if the taxpayer elects to not have this section apply to such vehicle.
"(e) Termination. This section shall not apply to any property placed in service after December 31, 2006."
In 2005, P.L. 109-58, Sec. 1322(a)(3)(A), substituted "section 27" for "sections 27 and 29" in subpara. (b)(3)(A), effective for credits determined under the Internal Revenue Code of 1986 for tax. yrs. end. after 12/31/2005.
In 2004, P.L. 108-311, Sec. 318(a), amended para. (b)(2), effective for property placed in service after 12/31/2003.
Prior to amendment, para. (b)(2) read as follows:
"(2) Phaseout. In the case of any qualified electric vehicle placed in service after December 31, 2003, the credit otherwise allowable under subsection (a) (determined after the application of paragraph (1)) shall be reduced by—
"(A) 25 percent in the case of property placed in service in calendar year 2004,
"(B) 50 percent in the case of property placed in service in calendar year 2005, and
"(C) 75 percent in the case of property placed in service in calendar year 2006."
In 2002, P.L. 107-147, Sec. 602(a)(1)(A), substituted "December 31, 2003," for "December 31, 2001," in para. (b)(2) . . . Sec. 602(a)(1)(B), substituted "2004" for "2002" in subpara. (b)(2)(A), "2005" for "2003" in subpara. (b)(2)(B), and "2006" for "2004" in subpara. (b)(2)(C) . . . Sec. 602(a)(2), substituted "December 31, 2006" for "December 31, 2004" in subsec. (e), effective for property placed in service after 12/31/2001.
In 1996, P.L. 104-188, Sec. 1205(d)(4), substituted "sections 27 and 29" for "sections 27, 28, and 29" in subpara. (b)(3)(A), effective for amounts paid or incurred in tax. yrs. end. after 6/30/96.
—P.L. 104-188, Sec. 1704(j)(4)(A)(i), added "(determined without regard to section (b)(3))" before the period at the end of para. (d)(1) . . . Sec. 1704(j)(4)(A)(ii), added para. (d)(4), effective 8/20/96.
In 1992, P.L. 102-486, Sec. 1913(b)(1), added Code Sec. 30, effective for property placed in service after 6/30/93.

Sec. 30A.   Puerto Rico economic activity credit.

(a) Allowance of credit.

(1) In general. Except as otherwise provided in this section, if the conditions of both paragraph (1) and paragraph (2) of subsection (b) are satisfied with respect to a qualified domestic corporation, there shall be allowed as a credit against the tax imposed by this chapter an amount equal to the portion of the tax which is attributable to the taxable income, from sources without the United States, from—

(A) the active conduct of a trade or business within Puerto Rico, or

(B) the sale or exchange of substantially all of the assets used by the taxpayer in the active conduct of such trade or business.

In the case of any taxable year beginning after December 31, 2001, the aggregate amount of taxable income taken into account under the preceding sentence (and in applying subsection (d)) shall not exceed the adjusted base period income of such corporation, as determined in the same manner as under section 936(j).

(2) Qualified domestic corporation. For purposes of paragraph (1), the term "qualified domestic corporation" means a domestic corporation—

(A) which is an existing credit claimant with respect to Puerto Rico, and

(B) with respect to which section 936(a)(4)(B) does not apply for the taxable year.

(3) Separate application. For purposes of determining—

(A) whether a taxpayer is an existing credit claimant with respect to Puerto Rico, and

(B) the amount of the credit allowed under this section,

this section (and so much of section 936 as relates to this section) shall be applied separately with respect to Puerto Rico.

(b) Conditions which must be satisfied.

The conditions referred to in subsection (a) are—

(1) 3-year period. If 80 percent or more of the gross income of the qualified domestic corporation for the 3-year period immediately preceding the close of the taxable year (or for such part of such period immediately preceding the close of such taxable year as may be applicable) was derived from sources within a possession (determined without regard to section 904(f)).

(2) Trade or business. If 75 percent or more of the gross income of the qualified domestic corporation for such period or such part thereof was derived from the active conduct of a trade or business within a possession.

(c) Credit not allowed against certain taxes.

The credit provided by subsection (a) shall not be allowed against the tax imposed by—

(1) section 59A (relating to environmental tax),

(2) section 531 (relating to the tax on accumulated earnings),

(3) section 541 (relating to personal holding company tax), or

(4) section 1351 (relating to recoveries of foreign expropriation losses).

(d) Limitations on credit for active business income.

The amount of the credit determined under subsection (a) for any taxable year shall not exceed the sum of the following amounts:

(1) 60 percent of the sum of—

(A) the aggregate amount of the qualified domestic corporation's qualified possession wages for such taxable year, plus

(B) the allocable employee fringe benefit expenses of the qualified domestic corporation for such taxable year.

(2) The sum of—

(A) 15 percent of the depreciation allowances for the taxable year with respect to short-life qualified tangible property,

(B) 40 percent of the depreciation allowances for the taxable year with respect to medium-life qualified tangible property, and

(C) 65 percent of the depreciation allowances for the taxable year with respect to long-life qualified tangible property.

(3) If the qualified domestic corporation does not have an election to use the method described in section 936(h)(5)(C)(ii)(relating to profit split) in effect for the taxable year, the amount of the qualified possession income taxes for the taxable year allocable to nonsheltered income.

(e) Administrative provisions.

For purposes of this title—

(1) the provisions of section 936 (including any applicable election thereunder) shall apply in the same manner as if the credit under this section were a credit under section 936(a)(1)(A) for a domestic corporation to which section 936(a)(4)(A) applies,

(2) the credit under this section shall be treated in the same manner as the credit under section 936, and

(3) a corporation to which this section applies shall be treated in the same manner as if it were a corporation electing the application of section 936.

(f) Denial of double benefit.

Any wages or other expenses taken into account in determining the credit under this section may not be taken into account in determining the credit under section 41.

(g) Definitions.

For purposes of this section, any term used in this section which is also used in section 936 shall have the same meaning given such term by section 936.

(h) Application of section.

This section shall apply to taxable years beginning after December 31, 1995, and before January 1, 2006.

In 2010, P.L. 111-312, Sec. 756(a)(1), substituted "first 6 taxable years" for "first 4 taxable years" in Sec. 119(d), P.L. 109-432, Div. A [see below]... Sec. 756(a)(2), substituted "January 1, 2012" for "January 1, 2010" in Sec. 119(d), P.L. 109-432, Div. A [see below] effective for tax. yrs. begin. after 12/31/2009.

In 2008, P.L. 110-343, Sec. 309(a)(1)DivA, substituted "first 4 taxable years" for "first two taxable years" in Sec. 119(d), P.L. 109-432, reproduced below... Sec. 309(a)(2)DivA, substituted "January 1, 2010" for "January 1, 2008" in Sec. 119(d), P.L. 109-432, reproduced below.

In 2006, P.L. 109-432, Sec. 119DivA, of this Act, as amended by Sec. 309(a)(1), Div. A, P.L. 110-343, and Sec. 756(a)(1)-(2), P.L. 111-312 [see above] provides:

"Sec. 119. American Samoa economic development credit.

"(a) In General. For purposes of section 30A of the Internal Revenue Code of 1986, a domestic corporation shall be treated as a qualified domestic corporation to which such section applies if such corporation-

"(1) is an existing credit claimant with respect to American Samoa, and

"(2) elected the application of section 936 of the Internal Revenue Code of 1986 for its last taxable year beginning before January 1, 2006.

"(b) Special rules for application of section. The following rules shall apply in applying section 30A of the Internal Revenue Code of 1986 for purposes of this section:

"(1) Amount of credit. Notwithstanding section 30A(a)(1) of such Code, the amount of the credit determined under section 30A(a)(1) of such Code for any taxable year shall be the amount determined under section 30A(d) of such Code, except that section 30A(d) shall be applied without regard to paragraph (3) thereof.

"(2) Separate application. In applying section 30A(a)(3) of such Code in the case of a corporation treated as a qualified domestic corporation by reason of this section, section 30A of such Code (and so much of section 936 of such Code as relates to such section 30A) shall be applied separately with respect to American Samoa.

"(3) Foreign tax credit allowed. Notwithstanding section 30A(e) of such Code, the provisions of section 936(c) of such Code shall not apply with respect to the credit allowed by reason of this section.

"(c) Definitions. For purposes of this section, any term which is used in this section which is also used in section 30A or 936 of such Code shall have the same meaning given such term by such section 30A or 936.

"(d) Application of section. Notwithstanding section 30A(h) or section 936(j) of such Code, this section (and so much of section 30A and section 936 of such Code as relates to this section) shall apply to the first 6 taxable years of a corporation to which subsection (a) applies which begin after December 31, 2005, and before January 1, 2012."

In 2000, P.L. 106-554, Sec. 1(a)(7), [which enacted into law Sec. 311(a)(2) of P.L. 106-554] redesignated subsecs. (f) and (g) as subsecs. (g) and (h) and added subsec. (f), effective for amounts paid or incurred after 6/30/99.

In 1997, P.L. 105-34, Sec. 1601(f)(1)(A), amended the heading of Code Sec. 30A, effective for tax. yrs. begin. after 12/31/95. Secs. 1601(c)(2) and (c)(3), of P.L. 104-188, provide special rules, reproduced below.

Prior to amendment, heading read as follows:

"SEC. 30A. PUERTO RICAN ECONOMIC ACTIVITY CREDIT."

In 1996, P.L. 104-188, Sec. 1601(b)(1), added Code Sec. 30A, effective for tax. yrs. begin. after 12/31/95. Secs. 1601(c)(2) and (c)(3), of this Act, provide:

"(2) Special rule for qualified possession source investment income. The amendments made by this section shall not apply to qualified possession source investment income received or accrued before July 1, 1996, without regard to the taxable year in which received or accrued.

"(3) Special transition rule for payment of estimated tax installments. In determining the amount of any installment due under section 6655 of the Internal Revenue Code of 1986 after the date of the enactment of this Act and before October 1, 1996, only 1/2 of any increase in tax (for the taxable year for which such installment is made) by reason of the amendments made by subsections (a) and (b) shall be taken into account. Any reduction in such installment by reason of the preceding sentence shall be recaptured by increasing the next required installment for such year by the amount of such reduction."

Sec. 30B. Alternative motor vehicle credit.

(a) Allowance of credit.

There shall be allowed as a credit against the tax imposed by this chapter for the taxable year an amount equal to the sum of—

(1) the new qualified fuel cell motor vehicle credit determined under subsection (b),

(2) the new advanced lean burn technology motor vehicle credit determined under subsection (c),

(3) the new qualified hybrid motor vehicle credit determined under subsection (d),

(4) the new qualified alternative fuel motor vehicle credit determined under subsection (e), and

(5) the plug-in conversion credit determined under subsection (i).

(b) New qualified fuel cell motor vehicle credit.
   (1) In general. For purposes of subsection (a), the new qualified fuel cell motor vehicle credit determined under this subsection with respect to a new qualified fuel cell motor vehicle placed in service by the taxpayer during the taxable year is—
   (A) $8,000 ($4,000 in the case of a vehicle placed in service after December 31, 2009), if such vehicle has a gross vehicle weight rating of not more than 8,500 pounds,
   (B) $10,000, if such vehicle has a gross vehicle weight rating of more than 8,500 pounds but not more than 14,000 pounds,
   (C) $20,000, if such vehicle has a gross vehicle weight rating of more than 14,000 pounds but not more than 26,000 pounds, and
   (D) $40,000, if such vehicle has a gross vehicle weight rating of more than 26,000 pounds.
   (2) Increase for fuel efficiency.
   (A) In general. The amount determined under paragraph (1)(A) with respect to a new qualified fuel cell motor vehicle which is a passenger automobile or light truck shall be increased by—
   (i) $1,000, if such vehicle achieves at least 150 percent but less than 175 percent of the 2002 model year city fuel economy,
   (ii) $1,500, if such vehicle achieves at least 175 percent but less than 200 percent of the 2002 model year city fuel economy,
   (iii) $2,000, if such vehicle achieves at least 200 percent but less than 225 percent of the 2002 model year city fuel economy,
   (iv) $2,500, if such vehicle achieves at least 225 percent but less than 250 percent of the 2002 model year city fuel economy,
   (v) $3,000, if such vehicle achieves at least 250 percent but less than 275 percent of the 2002 model year city fuel economy,
   (vi) $3,500, if such vehicle achieves at least 275 percent but less than 300 percent of the 2002 model year city fuel economy, and
   (vii) $4,000, if such vehicle achieves at least 300 percent of the 2002 model year city fuel economy.
   (B) 2002 Model year city fuel economy. For purposes of subparagraph (A), the 2002 model year city fuel economy with respect to a vehicle shall be determined in accordance with the following tables:
   (i) In the case of a passenger automobile:

If vehicle inertia weight class is:	The 2002 model year city fuel economy is:
1,500 or 1,750 lbs	45.2 mpg
2,000 lbs	39.6 mpg
2,250 lbs	35.2 mpg
2,500 lbs	31.7 mpg
2,750 lbs	28.8 mpg
3,000 lbs	26.4 mpg
3,500 lbs	22.6 mpg
4,000 lbs	19.8 mpg
4,500 lbs	17.6 mpg
5,000 lbs	15.9 mpg
5,500 lbs	14.4 mpg
6,000 lbs	13.2 mpg
6,500 lbs	12.2 mpg
7,000 to 8,500 lbs	11.3 mpg

(ii) In the case of a light truck:

If vehicle inertia weight class is:	The 2002 model year city fuel economy is:
1,500 or 1,750 lbs	39.4 mpg
2,000 lbs	35.2 mpg
2,250 lbs	31.8 mpg
2,500 lbs	29.0 mpg
2,750 lbs	26.8 mpg
3,000 lbs	24.9 mpg
3,500 lbs	21.8 mpg
4,000 lbs	19.4 mpg
4,500 lbs	17.6 mpg
5,000 lbs	16.1 mpg
5,500 lbs	14.8 mpg
6,000 lbs	13.7 mpg
6,500 lbs	12.8 mpg
7,000 to 8,500 lbs	12.1 mpg

(C) Vehicle inertia weight class. For purposes of subparagraph (B), the term "vehicle inertia weight class" has the same meaning as when defined in regulations prescribed by the Administrator of the Environmental

Protection Agency for purposes of the administration of title II of the Clean Air Act (42 U.S.C. 7521 et seq.).

(3) New qualified fuel cell motor vehicle. For purposes of this subsection, the term "new qualified fuel cell motor vehicle" means a motor vehicle—

(A) which is propelled by power derived from 1 or more cells which convert chemical energy directly into electricity by combining oxygen with hydrogen fuel which is stored on board the vehicle in any form and may or may not require reformation prior to use,

(B) which, in the case of a passenger automobile or light truck, has received on or after the date of the enactment of this section a certificate that such vehicle meets or exceeds the Bin 5 Tier II emission level established in regulations prescribed by the Administrator of the Environmental Protection Agency under section 202(i) of the Clean Air Act for that make and model year vehicle,

(C) the original use of which commences with the taxpayer,

(D) which is acquired for use or lease by the taxpayer and not for resale, and

(E) which is made by a manufacturer.

(c) New advanced lean burn technology motor vehicle credit.

(1) In general. For purposes of subsection (a), the new advanced lean burn technology motor vehicle credit determined under this subsection for the taxable year is the credit amount determined under paragraph (2) with respect to a new advanced lean burn technology motor vehicle placed in service by the taxpayer during the taxable year.

(2) Credit amount.

(A) Fuel economy.

(i) In general. The credit amount determined under this paragraph shall be determined in accordance with the following table:

In the case of a vehicle which achieves a fuel economy (expressed as a percentage of the 2002 model year city fuel economy) of—	The credit amount is—
At least 125 percent but less than 150 percent	$400
At least 150 percent but less than 175 percent	$800
At least 175 percent but less than 200 percent	$1,200
At least 200 percent but less than 225 percent	$1,600
At least 225 percent but less than 250 percent	$2,000
At least 250 percent	$2,400

(ii) 2002 Model year city fuel economy. For purposes of clause (i), the 2002 model year city fuel economy with respect to a vehicle shall be determined on a gasoline gallon equivalent basis as determined by the Administrator of the Environmental Protection Agency using the tables provided in subsection (b)(2)(B) with respect to such vehicle.

(B) Conservation credit.

The amount determined under subparagraph (A) with respect to a new advanced lean burn technology motor vehicle shall be increased by the conservation credit amount determined in accordance with the following table:

In the case of a vehicle which achieves a lifetime fuel savings (expressed in gallons of gasoline) of—	The conservation credit amount is—
At least 1,200 but less than 1,800	$250
At least 1,800 but less than 2,400	$500
At least 2,400 but less than 3,000	$750
At least 3,000	$1,000

(3) New advanced lean burn technology motor vehicle. For purposes of this subsection, the term "new advanced lean burn technology motor vehicle" means a passenger automobile or a light truck—

(A) with an internal combustion engine which—

(i) is designed to operate primarily using more air than is necessary for complete combustion of the fuel,

(ii) incorporates direct injection,

(iii) achieves at least 125 percent of the 2002 model year city fuel economy,

(iv) for 2004 and later model vehicles, has received a certificate that such vehicle meets or exceeds—

(I) in the case of a vehicle having a gross vehicle weight rating of 6,000 pounds or less, the Bin 5 Tier II emission standard established in regulations prescribed by the Administrator of the Environmental Protection Agency under section 202(i) of the Clean Air Act for that make and model year vehicle, and

(II) in the case of a vehicle having a gross vehicle weight rating of more than 6,000 pounds but not more than 8,500 pounds, the Bin 8 Tier II emission standard which is so established.

(B) the original use of which commences with the taxpayer,

(C) which is acquired for use or lease by the taxpayer and not for resale, and

(D) which is made by a manufacturer.

(4) Lifetime fuel savings. For purposes of this subsection, the term "lifetime fuel savings" means, in the case of any new advanced lean burn technology motor vehicle, an amount equal to the excess (if any) of—

(A) 120,000 divided by the 2002 model year city fuel economy for the vehicle inertia weight class, over

(B) 120,000 divided by the city fuel economy for such vehicle.

(d) New qualified hybrid motor vehicle credit.

(1) In general. For purposes of subsection (a), the new qualified hybrid motor vehicle credit determined under this subsection for the taxable year is the credit amount determined under paragraph (2) with respect to a new qualified hybrid motor vehicle placed in service by the taxpayer during the taxable year.

(2) Credit amount.

(A) Credit amount for passenger automobiles and light trucks. In the case of a new qualified hybrid motor vehicle which is a passenger automobile or light truck and which has a gross vehicle weight rating of not more than 8,500 pounds, the amount determined under this paragraph is the sum of the amounts determined under clauses (i) and (ii).

(i) Fuel economy. The amount determined under this clause is the amount which would be determined under subsection (c)(2)(A) if such vehicle were a vehicle referred to in such subsection.

(ii) Conservation credit. The amount determined under this clause is the amount which would be determined under subsection (c)(2)(B) if such vehicle were a vehicle referred to in such subsection.

(B) Credit amount for other motor vehicles.

(i) In general. In the case of any new qualified hybrid motor vehicle to which subparagraph (A) does not apply, the amount determined under this paragraph is the amount equal to the applicable percentage of the qualified incremental hybrid cost of the vehicle as certified under clause (v).

(ii) Applicable percentage. For purposes of clause (i), the applicable percentage is—

(I) 20 percent if the vehicle achieves an increase in city fuel economy relative to a comparable vehicle of at least 30 percent but less than 40 percent,

(II) 30 percent if the vehicle achieves such an increase of at least 40 percent but less than 50 percent, and

(III) 40 percent if the vehicle achieves such an increase of at least 50 percent.

(iii) Qualified incremental hybrid cost. For purposes of this subparagraph, the qualified incremental hybrid cost of any vehicle is equal to the amount of the excess of the manufacturer's suggested retail price for such vehicle over such price for a comparable vehicle, to the extent such amount does not exceed—

(I) $7,500, if such vehicle has a gross vehicle weight rating of not more than 14,000 pounds,

(II) $15,000, if such vehicle has a gross vehicle weight rating of more than 14,000 pounds but not more than 26,000 pounds, and

(III) $30,000, if such vehicle has a gross vehicle weight rating of more than 26,000 pounds.

(iv) Comparable vehicle. For purposes of this subparagraph, the term "comparable vehicle" means, with respect to any new qualified hybrid motor vehicle, any vehicle which is powered solely by a gasoline or diesel internal combustion engine and which is comparable in weight, size, and use to such vehicle.

(v) Certification. A certification described in clause (i) shall be made by the manufacturer and shall be determined in accordance with guidance prescribed by the Secretary. Such guidance shall specify procedures and methods for calculating fuel economy savings and incremental hybrid costs.

(3) New qualified hybrid motor vehicle. For purposes of this subsection—

(A) In general. The term "new qualified hybrid motor vehicle" means a motor vehicle—

(i) which draws propulsion energy from onboard sources of stored energy which are both—

(I) an internal combustion or heat engine using consumable fuel, and

(II) a rechargeable energy storage system,

(ii) which, in the case of a vehicle to which paragraph (2)(A) applies, has received a certificate of conformity under the Clean Air Act and meets or exceeds the equivalent qualifying California low emission vehicle standard under section 243(e)(2) of the Clean Air Act for that make and model year, and

(I) in the case of a vehicle having a gross vehicle weight rating of 6,000 pounds or less, the Bin 5 Tier II emission standard established in regulations prescribed by the Administrator of the Environmental Protection Agency under section 202(i) of the Clean Air Act for that make and model year vehicle, and

(II) in the case of a vehicle having a gross vehicle weight rating of more than 6,000 pounds but not more than 8,500 pounds, the Bin 8 Tier II emission standard which is so established,

(iii) which has a maximum available power of at least—

(I) 4 percent in the case of a vehicle to which paragraph (2)(A) applies,

(II) 10 percent in the case of a vehicle which has a gross vehicle weight rating of more than 8,500 pounds and not more than 14,000 pounds, and

(III) 15 percent in the case of a vehicle in excess of 14,000 pounds,

(iv) which, in the case of a vehicle to which paragraph (2)(B) applies, has an internal combustion or heat engine which has received a certificate of conformity under the Clean Air Act as meeting the emission standards set in the regulations prescribed by the Administrator of the Environmental Protection Agency for 2004 through 2007 model year diesel heavy duty engines or ottocycle heavy duty engines, as applicable,

(v) the original use of which commences with the taxpayer,

(vi) which is acquired for use or lease by the taxpayer and not for resale, and

(vii) which is made by a manufacturer.

Such term shall not include any vehicle which is not a passenger automobile or light truck if such vehicle has a gross vehicle weight rating of less than 8,500 pounds.

(B) Consumable fuel. For purposes of subparagraph (A)(i)(I), the term "consumable fuel" means any solid, liquid, or gaseous matter which releases energy when consumed by an auxiliary power unit.

(C) Maximum available power.

(i) Certain passenger automobiles and light trucks. In the case of a vehicle to which paragraph (2)(A) applies, the term "maximum available power" means the maximum power available from the rechargeable energy storage system, during a standard 10 second pulse power or equivalent test, divided by such maximum power and the SAE net power of the heat engine.

(ii) Other motor vehicles. In the case of a vehicle to which paragraph (2)(B) applies, the term "maximum available power" means the maximum power available from the rechargeable energy storage system, during a standard 10 second pulse power or equivalent

Tax credits

Code Sec. 30B(f)(2)

test, divided by the vehicle's total traction power. For purposes of the preceding sentence, the term "total traction power" means the sum of the peak power from the rechargeable energy storage system and the heat engine peak power of the vehicle, except that if such storage system is the sole means by which the vehicle can be driven, the total traction power is the peak power of such storage system.

(D) Exclusion of plug-in vehicles. Any vehicle with respect to which a credit is allowable under section 30D (determined without regard to subsection (c) thereof) shall not be taken into account under this section.

(e) New qualified alternative fuel motor vehicle credit.

(1) Allowance of credit. Except as provided in paragraph (5), the new qualified alternative fuel motor vehicle credit determined under this subsection is an amount equal to the applicable percentage of the incremental cost of any new qualified alternative fuel motor vehicle placed in service by the taxpayer during the taxable year.

(2) Applicable percentage. For purposes of paragraph (1), the applicable percentage with respect to any new qualified alternative fuel motor vehicle is—

(A) 50 percent, plus

(B) 30 percent, if such vehicle—

(i) has received a certificate of conformity under the Clean Air Act and meets or exceeds the most stringent standard available for certification under the Clean Air Act for that make and model year vehicle (other than a zero emission standard), or

(ii) has received an order certifying the vehicle as meeting the same requirements as vehicles which may be sold or leased in California and meets or exceeds the most stringent standard available for certification under the State laws of California (enacted in accordance with a waiver granted under section 209(b) of the Clean Air Act) for that make and model year vehicle (other than a zero emission standard).

For purposes of the preceding sentence, in the case of any new qualified alternative fuel motor vehicle which weighs more than 14,000 pounds gross vehicle weight rating, the most stringent standard available shall be such standard available for certification on the date of the enactment of the Energy Tax Incentives Act of 2005.

(3) Incremental cost. For purposes of this subsection, the incremental cost of any new qualified alternative fuel motor vehicle is equal to the amount of the excess of the manufacturer's suggested retail price for such vehicle over such price for a gasoline or diesel fuel motor vehicle of the same model, to the extent such amount does not exceed—

(A) $5,000, if such vehicle has a gross vehicle weight rating of not more than 8,500 pounds,

(B) $10,000, if such vehicle has a gross vehicle weight rating of more than 8,500 pounds but not more than 14,000 pounds,

(C) $25,000, if such vehicle has a gross vehicle weight rating of more than 14,000 pounds but not more than 26,000 pounds, and

(D) $40,000, if such vehicle has a gross vehicle weight rating of more than 26,000 pounds.

(4) New qualified alternative fuel motor vehicle. For purposes of this subsection—

(A) In general. The term "new qualified alternative fuel motor vehicle" means any motor vehicle—

(i) which is only capable of operating on an alternative fuel,

(ii) the original use of which commences with the taxpayer,

(iii) which is acquired by the taxpayer for use or lease, but not for resale, and

(iv) which is made by a manufacturer.

(B) Alternative fuel. The term "alternative fuel" means compressed natural gas, liquefied natural gas, liquefied petroleum gas, hydrogen, and any liquid at least 85 percent of the volume of which consists of methanol.

(5) Credit for mixed-fuel vehicles.

(A) In general. In the case of a mixed-fuel vehicle placed in service by the taxpayer during the taxable year, the credit determined under this subsection is an amount equal to—

(i) in the case of a 75/25 mixed-fuel vehicle, 70 percent of the credit which would have been allowed under this subsection if such vehicle was a qualified alternative fuel motor vehicle, and

(ii) in the case of a 90/10 mixed-fuel vehicle, 90 percent of the credit which would have been allowed under this subsection if such vehicle was a qualified alternative fuel motor vehicle.

(B) Mixed-fuel vehicle. For purposes of this subsection, the term "mixed-fuel vehicle" means any motor vehicle described in subparagraph (C) or (D) of paragraph (3), which—

(i) is certified by the manufacturer as being able to perform efficiently in normal operation on a combination of an alternative fuel and a petroleum-based fuel,

(ii) either—

(I) has received a certificate of conformity under the Clean Air Act, or

(II) has received an order certifying the vehicle as meeting the same requirements as vehicles which may be sold or leased in California and meets or exceeds the low emission vehicle standard under section 88.105–94 of title 40, Code of Federal Regulations, for that make and model year vehicle,

(iii) the original use of which commences with the taxpayer,

(iv) which is acquired by the taxpayer for use or lease, but not for resale, and

(v) which is made by a manufacturer.

(C) 75/25 Mixed-fuel vehicle. For purposes of this subsection, the term "75/25 mixed-fuel vehicle" means a mixed-fuel vehicle which operates using at least 75 percent alternative fuel and not more than 25 percent petroleum-based fuel.

(D) 90/10 Mixed-fuel vehicle. For purposes of this subsection, the term "90/10 mixed-fuel vehicle" means a mixed-fuel vehicle which operates using at least 90 percent alternative fuel and not more than 10 percent petroleum-based fuel.

(f) Limitation on number of new qualified hybrid and advanced lean-burn technology vehicles eligible for credit.

(1) In general. In the case of a qualified vehicle sold during the phaseout period, only the applicable percentage of the credit otherwise allowable under subsection (c) or (d) shall be allowed.

(2) Phaseout period. For purposes of this subsection, the phaseout period is the period beginning with the second calendar quarter following the calendar quarter which in-

Code Sec. 30B(f)(2) **Tax credits**

cludes the first date on which the number of qualified vehicles manufactured by the manufacturer of the vehicle referred to in paragraph (1) sold for use in the United States after December 31, 2005, is at least 60,000.

(3) Applicable percentage. For purposes of paragraph (1), the applicable percentage is—

(A) 50 percent for the first 2 calendar quarters of the phaseout period,

(B) 25 percent for the 3d and 4th calendar quarters of the phaseout period, and

(C) 0 percent for each calendar quarter thereafter.

(4) Controlled groups.

(A) In general. For purposes of this subsection, all persons treated as a single employer under subsection (a) or (b) of section 52 or subsection (m) or (o) of section 414 shall be treated as a single manufacturer.

(B) Inclusion of foreign corporations. For purposes of subparagraph (A), in applying subsections (a) and (b) of section 52 to this section, section 1563 shall be applied without regard to subsection (b)(2)(C) thereof.

(5) Qualified vehicle. For purposes of this subsection, the term "qualified vehicle" means any new qualified hybrid motor vehicle (described in subsection (d)(2)(A)) and any new advanced lean burn technology motor vehicle.

(g) Application with other credits.

(1) Business credit treated as part of general business credit. So much of the credit which would be allowed under subsection (a) for any taxable year (determined without regard to this subsection) that is attributable to property of a character subject to an allowance for depreciation shall be treated as a credit listed in section 38(b) for such taxable year (and not allowed under subsection (a)).

(2) Personal credit.

(A) In general. For purposes of this title, the credit allowed under subsection (a) for any taxable year (determined after application of paragraph (1)) shall be treated as a credit allowable under subpart A for such taxable year.

(B) Limitation based on amount of tax. In the case of a taxable year to which section 26(a)(2) does not apply, the credit allowed under subsection (a) for any taxable year (determined after application of paragraph (1)) shall not exceed the excess of—

(i) the sum of the regular tax liability (as defined in section 26(b)) plus the tax imposed by section 55, over

⌐ • *Caution:* Code Sec. 30B(g)(2)(B)(ii), following, reflects amendments made by Sec. 10909, P.L. 111-312. As provided in Sec. 10909(c), P.L. 111-148 as amended by Sec. 101(b)(1), P.L. 111-312, Code Sec. 30B(g)(2)(B)(ii) will read as if those amendments had never been enacted, effective for tax. yrs. begin. after 12/31/2011. For Code Sec. 30B(g)(2)(B)(ii) as it will read for tax. yrs. begin. after 12/31/2011, see below. ⌐

(ii) the sum of the credits allowable under subpart A (other than this section and 25D, 30, and 30D) and section 27 for the taxable year.

⌐ • *Caution:* Code Sec. 30B(g)(2)(B)(ii), following, is effective for tax. yrs. begin. after 12/31/2011, and reflects the sunset of the amendments made by Sec. 10909(b)(2)(G), P.L. 111-148. For details of those amendments, effective date and sunset provisions, see the history for this Code Sec. For Code Sec. 30B(g)(2)(B)(ii) as it will read for tax. yrs. begin. before 1/1/2012, see above. ⌐

(ii) the sum of the credits allowable under subpart A (other than this section and 23, 25D, 30, and 30D) and section 27 for the taxable year.

(h) Other definitions and special rules.

For purposes of this section—

(1) Motor vehicle. The term "motor vehicle" means any vehicle which is manufactured primarily for use on public streets, roads, and highways (not including a vehicle operated exclusively on a rail or rails) and which has at least 4 wheels.

(2) City fuel economy. The city fuel economy with respect to any vehicle shall be measured in a manner which is substantially similar to the manner city fuel economy is measured in accordance with procedures under part 600 of subchapter Q of chapter I of title 40, Code of Federal Regulations, as in effect on the date of the enactment of this section.

(3) Other terms. The terms "automobile", "passenger automobile", "medium duty passenger vehicle", "light truck", and "manufacturer" have the meanings given such terms in regulations prescribed by the Administrator of the Environmental Protection Agency for purposes of the administration of title II of the Clean Air Act (42 U.S.C. 7521 et seq.).

(4) Reduction in basis. For purposes of this subtitle, the basis of any property for which a credit is allowable under subsection (a) shall be reduced by the amount of such credit so allowed (determined without regard to subsection (g)).

(5) No double benefit. The amount of any deduction or other credit allowable under this chapter—

(A) for any incremental cost taken into account in computing the amount of the credit determined under subsection (e) shall be reduced by the amount of such credit attributable to such cost, and

(B) with respect to a vehicle described under subsection (b) or (c), shall be reduced by the amount of credit allowed under subsection (a) for such vehicle for the taxable year.

(6) Property used by tax-exempt entity. In the case of a vehicle whose use is described in paragraph (3) or (4) of section 50(b) and which is not subject to a lease, the person who sold such vehicle to the person or entity using such vehicle shall be treated as the taxpayer that placed such vehicle in service, but only if such person clearly discloses to such person or entity in a document the amount of any credit allowable under subsection (a) with respect to such vehicle (determined without regard to subsection (g)). For purposes of subsection (g), property to which this paragraph applies shall be treated as of a character subject to an allowance for depreciation.

(7) Property used outside United States, etc., not qualified. No credit shall be allowable under subsection (a) with respect to any property referred to in section 50(b)(1) or with respect to the portion of the cost of any property taken into account under section 179.

Tax credits　　　　　　　　　　　　　　　　　　　　　　　　　　　　　　　　　　　Code Sec. 30C(b)

(8) Recapture. The Secretary shall, by regulations, provide for recapturing the benefit of any credit allowable under subsection (a) with respect to any property which ceases to be property eligible for such credit (including recapture in the case of a lease period of less than the economic life of a vehicle)., except that no benefit shall be recaptured if such property ceases to be eligible for such credit by reason of conversion to a qualified plug-in electric drive motor vehicle.

(9) Election to not take credit. No credit shall be allowed under subsection (a) for any vehicle if the taxpayer elects to not have this section apply to such vehicle.

(10) Interaction with air quality and motor vehicle safety standards. Unless otherwise provided in this section, a motor vehicle shall not be considered eligible for a credit under this section unless such vehicle is in compliance with—

　(A) the applicable provisions of the Clean Air Act for the applicable make and model year of the vehicle (or applicable air quality provisions of State law in the case of a State which has adopted such provision under a waiver under section 209(b) of the Clean Air Act), and

　(B) the motor vehicle safety provisions of sections 30101 through 30169 of title 49, United States Code.

(i) Plug-in conversion credit.

(1) In general. For purposes of subsection (a), the plug-in conversion credit determined under this subsection with respect to any motor vehicle which is converted to a qualified plug-in electric drive motor vehicle is 10 percent of so much of the cost of the converting such vehicle as does not exceed $40,000.

(2) Qualified plug-in electric drive motor vehicle. For purposes of this subsection, the term "qualified plug-in electric drive motor vehicle" means any new qualified plug-in electric drive motor vehicle (as defined in section 30D, determined without regard to whether such vehicle is made by a manufacturer or whether the original use of such vehicle commences with the taxpayer).

(3) Credit allowed in addition to other credits. The credit allowed under this subsection shall be allowed with respect to a motor vehicle notwithstanding whether a credit has been allowed with respect to such motor vehicle under this section (other than this subsection) in any preceding taxable year.

(4) Termination. This subsection shall not apply to conversions made after December 31, 2011.

(j) Regulations.

(1) In general. Except as provided in paragraph (2), the Secretary shall promulgate such regulations as necessary to carry out the provisions of this section.

(2) Coordination in prescription of certain regulations. The Secretary of the Treasury, in coordination with the Secretary of Transportation and the Administrator of the Environmental Protection Agency, shall prescribe such regulations as necessary to determine whether a motor vehicle meets the requirements to be eligible for a credit under this section.

(k) Termination.

This section shall not apply to any property purchased after—

　(1) in the case of a new qualified fuel cell motor vehicle (as described in subsection (b)), December 31, 2014,

　(2) in the case of a new advanced lean burn technology motor vehicle (as described in subsection (c)) or a new qualified hybrid motor vehicle (as described in subsection (d)(2)(A)), December 31, 2010,

　(3) in the case of a new qualified hybrid motor vehicle (as described in subsection (d)(2)(B)), December 31, 2009, and

　(4) in the case of a new qualified alternative fuel vehicle (as described in subsection (e)), December 31, 2010.

In 2010, P.L. 111-312, Sec. 101(b)(1), amended Sec. 10909(c) of P.L. 111-148 [see below]

Prior to amendment, Sec. 10909(c) read as follows:

"(c) Application and Extension of EGTRRA Sunset. Notwithstanding section 901 of the Economic Growth and Tax Relief Reconciliation Act of 2001, such section shall apply to the amendments made by this section and the amendments made by section 202 of such Act by substituting 'December 31, 2011' for 'December 31, 2010' in subsection (a)(1) thereof."

—P.L. 111-312, Sec. 101(b)(2), substituted "Except as provided in subsection (c), the amendments" for "the amendments" in Sec. 10909(d), P.L. 111-148, (the effective date section for amendments made by Sec. 10909, P.L. 111-148), see below.

Prior to amendment, Sec. 10909(d), P.L. 111-148, read as follows:

"(d) Effective Date. The amendments made by this section shall apply to taxable years beginning after December 31, 2009."

—P.L. 111-148, Sec. 10909(b)(2)(G), deleted "23," in clause (g)(2)(B)(ii), effective for tax. yrs. begin. after 12/31/2009, except as provided in Sec. 10909(c), see below.

—P.L. 111-148, Sec. 10909(c), of this Act, relating to the application and extension of the EGTRRA sunset, provides:

"(c) Sunset provision. Each provision of law amended by this section is amended to read as such provision would read if this section had never been enacted. The amendments made by the preceding sentence shall apply to taxable years beginning after December 31, 2011."

—P.L. 111-148, Sec. 10909(d), of this Act, as amended by Sec. 101(b)(2), P.L. 111-312 [see above] reads as follows:

"(d) Effective date. Except as provided in subsection (c), [Sec. 10909(c), P.L. 111-148], the amendments made by this section shall apply to taxable years beginning after December 31, 2009."

In 2009, P.L. 111-5, Sec. 1141(b)(1), substituted "subsection (c) thereof" for "subsection (d) thereof" in subpara. (d)(3)(D), effective for vehicles acquired after 12/31/2009.

—P.L. 111-5, Sec. 1142(b)(2), amended para. (h)(1), effective for vehicles acquired after 2/17/2009.

Prior to amendment, para. (h)(1) read as follows:

"(1) Motor vehicle. The term 'motor vehicle' has the meaning given such term by section 30(c)(2)."

—P.L. 111-5, Sec. 1143(a), redesignated subsecs. (i) and (j) as (j) and (k) respectively, and added subsec. (i) . . . Sec. 1143(b), deleted "and" at the end of paragraph (a)(3), substituted ", and" for the period at the end of para. (a)(4), and added para. (a)(5) . . . Sec. 1143(c), added ", except that no benefit shall be recaptured if such property ceases to be eligible for such credit by reason of conversion to a qualified plugin electric drive motor vehicle." at the end of para. (h)(8), effective for property placed in service after 2/17/2009.

—P.L. 111-5, Sec. 1144(a), amended para. (g)(2), effective for tax. yrs. begin. after 12/31/2008.

Prior to amendment, para. (g)(2) read as follows:

"(2) Personal credit. The credit allowed under subsection (a) (after the application of paragraph (1)) for any taxable year shall not exceed the excess (if any) of—

"(A) the regular tax liability (as defined in section 26(b)) reduced by the sum of the credits allowable under subpart A and sections 27 and 30, over

"(B) the tentative minimum tax for the taxable year."

In 2008, P.L. 110-343, Sec. 205(b)DivB, added subpara. (d)(3)(D), effective for tax. yrs. begin. after 1231/2008.

In 2005, P.L. 109-135, Sec. 402(j), added "For purposes of subsection (g), property to which this paragraph applies shall be treated as of a character subject to an allowance for depreciation." at the end of para. (h)(6), effective for property placed in service after 12/31/2005, in tax. yrs. end. after 12/31/2005 as if included in Sec. 1341 of the Energy Policy Act of 2005, P.L. 109-58.

—P.L. 109-135, Sec. 412(d), substituted "regular tax liability (as defined in section 26(b))" for "regular tax" in subpara. (g)(2)(A), effective 12/21/2005.

—P.L. 109-58, Sec. 1341(a), added Code Sec. 30B, effective for property placed in service after 12/31/2005, in tax. yrs. end. after 12/31/2005.

Sec. 30C. Alternative fuel vehicle refueling property credit.

(a) Credit allowed.

There shall be allowed as a credit against the tax imposed by this chapter for the taxable year an amount equal to 30 percent of the cost of any qualified alternative fuel vehicle refueling property placed in service by the taxpayer during the taxable year.

(b) Limitation.

The credit allowed under subsection (a) with respect to all qualified alternative fuel vehicle refueling property placed in service by the taxpayer during the taxable year at a location shall not exceed—

(1) $30,000 in the case of a property of a character subject to an allowance for depreciation, and

(2) $1,000 in any other case.

(c) Qualified alternative fuel vehicle refueling property.

For purposes of this section, the term "qualified alternative fuel vehicle refueling property" has the same meaning as the term "qualified clean-fuel vehicle refueling property" would have under section 179A if—

(1) paragraph (1) of section 179A(d) did not apply to property installed on property which is used as the principal residence (within the meaning of section 121) of the taxpayer, and

(2) only the following were treated as clean-burning fuels for purposes of section 179A(d):

(A) Any fuel at least 85 percent of the volume of which consists of one or more of the following: ethanol, natural gas, compressed natural gas, liquefied natural gas, liquefied petroleum gas, or hydrogen.

(B) Any mixture—

(i) which consists of two or more of the following: biodiesel (as defined in section 40A(d)(1)), diesel fuel (as defined in section 4083(a)(3)), or kerosene, and

(ii) at least 20 percent of the volume of which consists of biodiesel (as so defined) determined without regard to any kerosene in such mixture.

(C) Electricity.

(d) Application with other credits.

(1) Business credit treated as part of general business credit. So much of the credit which would be allowed under subsection (a) for any taxable year (determined without regard to this subsection) that is attributable to property of a character subject to an allowance for depreciation shall be treated as a credit listed in section 38(b) for such taxable year (and not allowed under subsection (a)).

(2) Personal credit. The credit allowed under subsection (a) (after the application of paragraph (1)) for any taxable year shall not exceed the excess (if any) of—

(A) the regular tax liability (as defined in section 26(b)) reduced by the sum of the credits allowable under subpart A and section 27, over

(B) the tentative minimum tax for the taxable year.

(e) Special rules.

For purposes of this section—

(1) Basis reduction. The basis of any property shall be reduced by the portion of the cost of such property taken into account under subsection (a).

(2) Property used by tax-exempt entity. In the case of any qualified alternative fuel vehicle refueling property the use of which is described in paragraph (3) or (4) of section 50(b) and which is not subject to a lease, the person who sold such property to the person or entity using such property shall be treated as the taxpayer that placed such property in service, but only if such person clearly discloses to such person or entity in a document the amount of any credit allowable under subsection (a) with respect to such property (determined without regard to subsection (d)). For purposes of subsection (d), property to which this paragraph applies shall be treated as of a character subject to an allowance for depreciation.

(3) Property used outside United States not qualified. No credit shall be allowable under subsection (a) with respect to any property referred to in section 50(b)(1) or

with respect to the portion of the cost of any property taken into account under section 179.

(4) Election not to take credit. No credit shall be allowed under subsection (a) for any property if the taxpayer elects not to have this section apply to such property.

(5) Recapture rules. Rules similar to the rules of section 179A(e)(4) shall apply.

(6) Special rule for property placed in service during 2009 and 2010. In the case of property placed in service in taxable years beginning after December 31, 2008, and before January 1, 2011—

(A) in the case of any such property which does not relate to hydrogen—

(i) subsection (a) shall be applied by substituting "50 percent" for "30 percent",

(ii) subsection (b)(1) shall be applied by substituting "$50,000" for "$30,000", and

(iii) subsection (b)(2) shall be applied by substituting "$2,000" for "$1,000", and

(B) in the case of any such property which relates to hydrogen, subsection (b)(1) shall be applied by substituting "$200,000" for "$30,000".

(f) Regulations.

The Secretary shall prescribe such regulations as necessary to carry out the provisions of this section.

(g) Termination.

This section shall not apply to any property placed in service—

(1) in the case of property relating to hydrogen, after December 31, 2014, and

(2) in the case of any other property, after December 31, 2011.

In 2010, P.L. 111-312, Sec. 711(a), substituted "December 31, 2011." for "December 31, 2010" in para. (g)(2), effective for property placed in service after 12/31/2010.

In 2009, P.L. 111-5, Sec. 1123(a), added para. (e)(6), effective for tax. yrs. begin. after 12/31/2008.

—P.L. 111-5, Sec. 1142(b)(3), deleted ", 30," after "sections 27" in subpara. (d)(2)(A), effective for vehicles acquired after 2/17/2009.

—P.L. 111-5, Sec. 1144(b)(2), substituted "section 27" for "sections 27 and 30B" in subpara. (d)(2)(A) [as amended by Sec. 1142(b)(3) of this Act, see above], effective for tax. yrs. begin. after 12/31/2008.

In 2008, P.L. 110-343, Sec. 207(a)DivB, substituted "December 31, 2010" for "December 31, 2009" in para. (g)(2)... Sec. 207(b)DivB, added subpara. (c)(2)(C), effective for property placed in service after 10/3/2008, in tax. yrs. ending after such date.

In 2007, P.L. 110-172, Sec. 6(b)(1), substituted "(b) Limitation. The credit allowed under subsection (a) with respect to all qualified alternative fuel vehicle refueling property placed in service by the taxpayer during the taxable year at a location shall not exceed—" for "(b) Limitation. The credit allowed under subsection (a) with respect to any alternative fuel vehicle refueling property shall not exceed—" in subsec. (b)... Sec. 6(b)(2), amended subsec. (c), effective for property placed in service after 12/31/2005, in tax. yrs. end. after 12/31/2005. Prior to amendment, subsec. (c) read as follows:

"(c) Qualified alternative fuel vehicle refueling property.

"(1) In general. Except as provided in paragraph (2), the term 'qualified alternative fuel vehicle refueling property' has the meaning given to such term by section 179A(d), but only with respect to any fuel—

"(A) at least 85 percent of the volume of which consists of 1 or more of the following: ethanol, natural gas, compressed natural gas, liquefied natural gas, liquefied petroleum gas, or hydrogen, or

"(B) any mixture of biodiesel (as defined in section 40A(d)(1)) and diesel fuel (as defined in section 4083(a)(3)), determined without regard to any use of kerosene and containing at least 20 percent biodiesel.

"(2) Residential property. In the case of any property installed on property which is used as the principal residence (within the meaning of section 121) of the taxpayer, paragraph (1) of section 179A(d) shall not apply."

In 2005, P.L. 109-135, Sec. 402(k), added "For purposes of subsection (d), property to which this paragraph applies shall be treated as of a character subject to an allowance for depreciation." at the end of para. (e)(2), effective for property placed in service after 12/31/2005, in tax. yrs. end. after 12/31/2005 as if included in Sec. 1342 of the Energy Policy Act of 2005, P.L. 109-58.

—P.L. 109-135, Sec. 412(d), substituted "regular tax liability (as defined in section 26(b))" for "regular tax" in subpara. (d)(2)(A), effective 12/21/2005.

Tax credits

—P.L. 109-58, Sec. 1342(a), added Code Sec. 30C, effective for property placed in service after 12/31/2005, in tax. yrs. end. after 12/31/2005.

Sec. 30D. New qualified plug-in electric drive motor vehicles.

(a) Allowance of credit.

There shall be allowed as a credit against the tax imposed by this chapter for the taxable year an amount equal to the sum of the credit amounts determined under subsection (b) with respect to each new qualified plug-in electric drive motor vehicle placed in service by the taxpayer during the taxable year.

(b) Per vehicle dollar limitation.

(1) **In general.** The amount determined under this subsection with respect to any new qualified plug-in electric drive motor vehicle is the sum of the amounts determined under paragraphs (2) and (3) with respect to such vehicle.

(2) **Base amount.** The amount determined under this paragraph is $2,500.

(3) **Battery capacity.** In the case of a vehicle which draws propulsion energy from a battery with not less than 5 kilowatt hours of capacity, the amount determined under this paragraph is $417, plus $417 for each kilowatt hour of capacity in excess of 5 kilowatt hours. The amount determined under this paragraph shall not exceed $5,000.

(c) Application with other credits.

(1) **Business credit treated as part of general business credit.** So much of the credit which would be allowed under subsection (a) for any taxable year (determined without regard to this subsection) that is attributable to property of a character subject to an allowance for depreciation shall be treated as a credit listed in section 38(b) for such taxable year (and not allowed under subsection (a)).

(2) **Personal credit.**

(A) In general. For purposes of this title, the credit allowed under subsection (a) for any taxable year (determined after application of paragraph (1)) shall be treated as a credit allowable under subpart A for such taxable year.

(B) Limitation based on amount of tax. In the case of a taxable year to which section 26(a)(2) does not apply, the credit allowed under subsection (a) for any taxable year (determined after application of paragraph (1)) shall not exceed the excess of—

(i) the sum of the regular tax liability (as defined in section 26(b)) plus the tax imposed by section 55, over

⌐ • **Caution:** Code Sec. 30D(c)(2)(B)(ii), following, reflects amendments made by Sec. 10909, P.L. 111-148. As provided in Sec. 10909(c), P.L. 111-148 as amended by Sec. 101(b)(1), P.L. 111-312, Code Sec. 30D(c)(2)(B)(ii) will read as if those amendments had never been enacted, effective for tax. yrs. begin. after 12/31/2011. For Code Sec. 30D(c)(2)(B)(ii) as it will read for tax. yrs. begin. after 12/31/2011, see below. ⌐

(ii) the sum of the credits allowable under subpart A (other than this section and section 25D) and section 27 for the taxable year.

⌐ • **Caution:** Code Sec. 30D(c)(2)(B)(ii), following, is effective for tax. yrs. begin. after 12/31/2011, and reflects the sunset of the amendments made by Sec. 10909, P.L. 111-148. For details of those amendments, effective date and sunset provisions, see the history for this Code Sec. For Code Sec. 30D(c)(2)(B)(ii), effective for tax. yrs. begin. before 1/1/2012, see above. ⌐

(ii) the sum of the credits allowable under subpart A (other than this section and sections 23 and 25D) and section 27 for the taxable year.

(d) New qualified plug-in electric drive motor vehicle. For purposes of this section—

(1) **In general.** The term "new qualified plug-in electric drive motor vehicle" means a motor vehicle—

(A) the original use of which commences with the taxpayer,

(B) which is acquired for use or lease by the taxpayer and not for resale,

(C) which is made by a manufacturer,

(D) which is treated as a motor vehicle for purposes of title II of the Clean Air Act,

(E) which has a gross vehicle weight rating of less than 14,000 pounds, and

(F) which is propelled to a significant extent by an electric motor which draws electricity from a battery which—

(i) has a capacity of not less than 4 kilowatt hours, and

(ii) is capable of being recharged from an external source of electricity.

(2) **Motor vehicle.** The term "motor vehicle" means any vehicle which is manufactured primarily for use on public streets, roads, and highways (not including a vehicle operated exclusively on a rail or rails) and which has at least 4 wheels.

(3) **Manufacturer.** The term "manufacturer" has the meaning given such term in regulations prescribed by the Administrator of the Environmental Protection Agency for purposes of the administration of title II of the Clean Air Act (42 U.S.C. 7521 et seq.).

(4) **Battery capacity.** The term "capacity" means, with respect to any battery, the quantity of electricity which the battery is capable of storing, expressed in kilowatt hours, as measured from a 100 percent state of charge to a 0 percent state of charge.

(e) Limitation on number of new qualified plug-in electric drive motor vehicles eligible for credit.

(1) **In general.** In the case of a new qualified plug-in electric drive motor vehicle sold during the phaseout period, only the applicable percentage of the credit otherwise allowable under subsection (a) shall be allowed.

(2) **Phaseout period.** For purposes of this subsection, the phaseout period is the period beginning with the second calendar quarter following the calendar quarter which includes the first date on which the number of new qualified plug-in electric drive motor vehicles manufactured by the manufacturer of the vehicle referred to in paragraph (1) sold for use in the United States after December 31, 2009, is at least 200,000.

(3) **Applicable percentage.** For purposes of paragraph (1), the applicable percentage is—

(A) 50 percent for the first 2 calendar quarters of the phaseout period,

(B) 25 percent for the 3d and 4th calendar quarters of the phaseout period, and

(C) 0 percent for each calendar quarter thereafter.

(4) **Controlled groups.** Rules similar to the rules of section 30B(f)(4) shall apply for purposes of this subsection.

(f) Special rules.

(1) **Basis reduction.** For purposes of this subtitle, the basis of any property for which a credit is allowable under subsection (a) shall be reduced by the amount of such credit so allowed.

(2) **No double benefit.** The amount of any deduction or other credit allowable under this chapter for a new qualified plug-in electric drive motor vehicle shall be reduced by the amount of credit allowed under subsection (a) for such vehicle.

(3) **Property used by tax-exempt entity.** In the case of a vehicle the use of which is described in paragraph (3) or (4) of section 50(b) and which is not subject to a lease, the person who sold such vehicle to the person or entity using such vehicle shall be treated as the taxpayer that placed such vehicle in service, but only if such person clearly discloses to such person or entity in a document the amount of any credit allowable under subsection (a) with respect to such vehicle (determined without regard to subsection (c)).

(4) **Property used outside united states not qualified.** No credit shall be allowable under subsection (a) with respect to any property referred to in section 50(b)(1).

(5) **Recapture.** The Secretary shall, by regulations, provide for recapturing the benefit of any credit allowable under subsection (a) with respect to any property which ceases to be property eligible for such credit.

(6) **Election not to take credit.** No credit shall be allowed under subsection (a) for any vehicle if the taxpayer elects to not have this section apply to such vehicle.

(7) **Interaction with air quality and motor vehicle safety standards.** A motor vehicle shall not be considered eligible for a credit under this section unless such vehicle is in compliance with—

(A) the applicable provisions of the Clean Air Act for the applicable make and model year of the vehicle (or applicable air quality provisions of State law in the case of a State which has adopted such provision under a waiver under section 209(b) of the Clean Air Act), and

(B) the motor vehicle safety provisions of sections 30101 through 30169 of title 49, United States Code.

In 2010, P.L. 111-312, Sec. 101(b)(1), amended Sec. 10909(c) of P.L. 111-148 [see below]

Prior to amendment, Sec. 10909(c) read as follows:

"(c) Application and Extension of EGTRRA Sunset. Notwithstanding section 901 of the Economic Growth and Tax Relief Reconciliation Act of 2001, such section shall apply to the amendments made by this section and the amendments made by section 202 of such Act by substituting 'December 31, 2011' for 'December 31, 2010' in subsection (a)(1) thereof."

—P.L. 111-312, Sec. 101(b)(2), substituted "Except as provided in subsection (c), the amendments" for "the amendments" in Sec. 10909(d), P.L. 111-148, (the effective date section for amendments made by Sec. 10909, P.L. 111-148), see below.

Prior to amendment, Sec. 10909(d), P.L. 111-148, read as follows:

"(d) Effective Date. The amendments made by this section shall apply to taxable years beginning after December 31, 2009."

—P.L. 111-148, Sec. 10909(b)(2)(H), substituted "section" for "sections 23 and" in clause (c)(2)(B)(ii), effective for tax. yrs. begin. after 12/31/2009, except as provided in Sec. 10909(c), see below.

—P.L. 111-148, Sec. 10909(c), of this Act, relating to the application and extension of the EGTRRA sunset, [as amended by Sec. 101(b)(1) of P.L. 111-312, see above] provides:

"(c) Sunset provision. Each provision of law amended by this section is amended to read as such provision would read if this section had never been enacted. The amendments made by the preceding sentence shall apply to taxable years beginning after December 31, 2011."

—P.L. 111-148, Sec. 10909(d), of this Act, as amended by Sec. 101(b)(2), P.L. 111-312 [see above] reads as follows:

"(d) Effective date. Except as provided in subsection (c), [Sec. 10909(c), P.L. 111-148], the amendments made by this section shall apply to taxable years beginning after December 31, 2009."

In 2009, P.L. 111-5, Sec. 1141(a), amended Code Sec. 30D, effective for vehicles acquired after 12/31/2009.

Prior to amendment, Code Sec. 30D read as follows:

"SEC. 30D. NEW QUALIFIED PLUG-IN ELECTRIC DRIVE MOTOR VEHICLES.

"(a) Allowance of credit.

"(1) In general. There shall be allowed as a credit against the tax imposed by this chapter for the taxable year an amount equal to the applicable amount with respect to each new qualified plug-in electric drive motor vehicle placed in service by the taxpayer during the taxable year.

"(2) Applicable amount. For purposes of paragraph (1), the applicable amount is sum of—

"(A) $2,500, plus

"(B) $417 for each kilowatt hour of traction battery capacity in excess of 4 kilowatt hours.

"(b) Limitations.

"(1) Limitation based on weight. The amount of the credit allowed under subsection (a) by reason of subsection (a)(2) shall not exceed—

"(A) $7,500, in the case of any new qualified plug-in electric drive motor vehicle with a gross vehicle weight rating of not more than 10,000 pounds,

"(B) $10,000, in the case of any new qualified plug-in electric drive motor vehicle with a gross vehicle weight rating of more than 10,000 pounds but not more than 14,000 pounds,

"(C) $12,500, in the case of any new qualified plug-in electric drive motor vehicle with a gross vehicle weight rating of more than 14,000 pounds but not more than 26,000 pounds, and

"(D) $15,000, in the case of any new qualified plug-in electric drive motor vehicle with a gross vehicle weight rating of more than 26,000 pounds.

"(2) Limitation on number of passenger vehicles and light trucks eligible for credit.

"(A) In general. In the case of a new qualified plug-in electric drive motor vehicle sold during the phaseout period, only the applicable percentage of the credit otherwise allowable under subsection (a) shall be allowed.

"(B) Phaseout period. For purposes of this subsection, the phaseout period is the period beginning with the second calendar quarter following the calendar quarter which includes the first date on which the total number of such new qualified plug-in electric drive motor vehicles sold for use in the United States after December 31, 2008, is at least 250,000.

"(C) Applicable percentage. For purposes of subparagraph (A), the applicable percentage is—

"(i) 50 percent for the first 2 calendar quarters of the phaseout period,

"(ii) 25 percent for the 3d and 4th calendar quarters of the phaseout period, and

"(iii) 0 percent for each calendar quarter thereafter.

"(D) Controlled groups. Rules similar to the rules of section 30B(f)(4) shall apply for purposes of this subsection.

"(c) New qualified plug-in electric drive motor vehicle. For purposes of this section, the term 'new qualified plug-in electric drive motor vehicle' means a motor vehicle—

"(1) which draws propulsion using a traction battery with at least 4 kilowatt hours of capacity,

"(2) which uses an offboard source of energy to recharge such battery,

"(3) which, in the case of a passenger vehicle or light truck which has a gross vehicle weight rating of not more than 8,500 pounds, has received a certificate of conformity under the Clean Air Act and meets or exceeds the equivalent qualifying California low emission vehicle standard under section 243(e)(2) of the Clean Air Act for that make and model year, and

"(A) in the case of a vehicle having a gross vehicle weight rating of 6,000 pounds or less, the Bin 5 Tier II emission standard established in regulations prescribed by the Administrator of the Environmental Protection Agency under section 202(i) of the Clean Air Act for that make and model year vehicle, and

"(B) in the case of a vehicle having a gross vehicle weight rating of more than 6,000 pounds but not more than 8,500 pounds, the Bin 8 Tier II emission standard which is so established,

"(4) the original use of which commences with the taxpayer,

"(5) which is acquired for use or lease by the taxpayer and not for resale, and

"(6) which is made by a manufacturer.

"(d) Application with other credits.

"(1) Business credit treated as part of general business credit. So much of the credit which would be allowed under subsection (a) for any taxable year (determined without regard to this subsection) that is attributable to property of a character subject to an allowance for depreciation shall be treated as a credit listed in section 38(b) for such taxable year (and not allowed under subsection (a)).

"(2) Personal credit.

"(A) In general. For purposes of this title, the credit allowed under subsection (a) for any taxable year (determined after application of paragraph (1)) shall be treated as a credit allowable under subpart A for such taxable year.

"(B) Limitation based on amount of tax. In the case of a taxable year to which section 26(a)(2) does not apply, the credit allowed under subsection (a) for any taxable year (determined after application of paragraph (1)) shall not exceed the excess of—

"(i) the sum of the regular tax liability (as defined in section 26(b)) plus the tax imposed by section 55, over

Tax credits — Code Sec. 31

"(ii) the sum of the credits allowable under subpart A (other than this section and sections 23 and 25D) and section 27 for the taxable year.

"(e) Other definitions and special rules. For purposes of this section—

"(1) Motor vehicle. The term 'motor vehicle' has the meaning given such term by section 30(c)(2).

"(2) Other terms. The terms 'passenger automobile', 'light truck', and 'manufacturer' have the meanings given such terms in regulations prescribed by the Administrator of the Environmental Protection Agency for purposes of the administration of title II of the Clean Air Act (42 U.S.C. 7521 et seq.).

"(3) Traction battery capacity. Traction battery capacity shall be measured in kilowatt hours from a 100 percent state of charge to a zero percent state of charge.

"(4) Reduction in basis. For purposes of this subtitle, the basis of any property for which a credit is allowable under subsection (a) shall be reduced by the amount of such credit so allowed.

"(5) No double benefit. The amount of any deduction or other credit allowable under this chapter for a new qualified plug-in electric drive motor vehicle shall be reduced by the amount of credit allowed under subsection (a) for such vehicle for the taxable year.

"(6) Property used by tax-exempt entity. In the case of a vehicle the use of which is described in paragraph (3) or (4) of section 50(b) and which is not subject to a lease, the person who sold such vehicle to the person or entity using such vehicle shall be treated as the taxpayer that placed such vehicle in service, but only if such person clearly discloses to such person or entity in a document the amount of any credit allowable under subsection (a) with respect to such vehicle (determined without regard to subsection (b)(2)).

"(7) Property used outside United States, etc., not qualified. No credit shall be allowable under subsection (a) with respect to any property referred to in section 50(b)(1) or with respect to the portion of the cost of any property taken into account under section 179.

"(8) Recapture. The Secretary shall, by regulations, provide for recapturing the benefit of any credit allowable under subsection (a) with respect to any property which ceases to be property eligible for such credit (including recapture in the case of a lease period of less than the economic life of a vehicle).

"(9) Election to not take credit. No credit shall be allowed under subsection (a) for any vehicle if the taxpayer elects not to have this section apply to such vehicle.

"(10) Interaction with air quality and motor vehicle safety standards. Unless otherwise provided in this section, a motor vehicle shall not be considered eligible for a credit under this section unless such vehicle is in compliance with—

"(A) the applicable provisions of the Clean Air Act for the applicable make and model year of the vehicle (or applicable air quality provisions of State law in the case of a State which has adopted such provision under a waiver under section 209(b) of the Clean Air Act), and

"(B) the motor vehicle safety provisions of sections 30101 through 30169 of title 49, United States Code.

"(f) Regulations.

"(1) In general. Except as provided in paragraph (2), the Secretary shall promulgate such regulations as necessary to carry out the provisions of this section.

"(2) Coordination in prescription of certain regulations. The Secretary of the Treasury, in coordination with the Secretary of Transportation and the Administrator of the Environmental Protection Agency, shall prescribe such regulations as necessary to determine whether a motor vehicle meets the requirements to be eligible for a credit under this section.

"(g) Termination. This section shall not apply to property purchased after December 31, 2014."

—P.L. 111-5, Sec. 1142(d), of this Act, provides:

"(d) Transitional rule. In the case of a vehicle acquired after the date of the enactment of this Act and before January 1, 2010, no credit shall be allowed under section 30 of the Internal Revenue Code of 1986, as added by this section, if credit is allowable under section 30D of such Code with respect to such vehicle."

In **2008**, P.L. 110-343, Sec. 205(a)DivB, added Code Sec. 30D, effective for tax. yrs. begin. after 12/31/2008.

Subpart C.—Refundable Credits

Sec.
31. Tax withheld on wages.
32. Earned income.
33. Tax withheld at source on nonresident aliens and foreign corporations.
34. Certain uses of gasoline and special fuels.
35. Health insurance costs of eligible individuals.
36. First-time homebuyer credit.
36. Repealed. [Credits not allowed to individuals taking standard deduction.]
36A. Making work pay credit.
36B. Refundable credit for coverage under a qualified health plan. [effective for tax. yrs. end. after 12/31/2013]
36C. Adoption expenses.
37. Overpayments of tax.

In **2009**, P.L. 111-5, Sec. 1001(a), added item 36A.
In **2008**, P.L. 110-289, Sec. 3011(b)(4), redesignated item 36 as item 37 and added new item 36.
In **2002**, P.L. 107-210, Sec. 201(c)(2), redesignated item 35 as item 36 and added new item 35.
In **1984**, P.L. 98-369, Sec. 471(b), added Subpart C as part of amendments made to Part IV.

Sec. 31. Tax withheld on wages.

(a) Wage withholding for income tax purposes.

(1) In general. The amount withheld as tax under chapter 24 shall be allowed to the recipient of the income as a credit against the tax imposed by this subtitle.

(2) Year of credit. The amount so withheld during any calendar year shall be allowed as a credit for the taxable year beginning in such calendar year. If more than one taxable year begins in a calendar year, such amount shall be allowed as a credit for the last taxable year so beginning.

(b) Credit for special refunds of social security tax.

(1) In general. The Secretary may prescribe regulations providing for the crediting against the tax imposed by this subtitle of the amount determined by the taxpayer or the Secretary to be allowable under section 6413(c) as a special refund of tax imposed on wages. The amount allowed as a credit under such regulations shall, for purposes of this subtitle, be considered an amount withheld at source as tax under section 3402.

(2) Year of credit. Any amount to which paragraph (1) applies shall be allowed as a credit for the taxable year beginning in the calendar year during which the wages were received. If more than one taxable year begins in the calendar year, such amount shall be allowed as a credit for the last taxable year so beginning.

(c) Special rule for backup withholding.

Any credit allowed by subsection (a) for any amount withheld under section 3406 shall be allowed for the taxable year of the recipient of the income in which the income is received.

In **1984**, P.L. 98-369, Sec. 714(j)(2), substituted "as tax under chapter 24" for "under section 3402 as tax on the wages of any individual" in para. (a)(1), effective generally for payments or other distributions made after 12/31/82.
In **1983**, P.L. 98-67, Sec. 104(d)(2), added subsec. (c), effective for payments made after 12/31/83.
—P.L. 98-67, Sec. 102(a), repealed as if not enacted amendments to Code Sec. 31 by P.L. 97-248.
In **1982**, P.L. 97-248, Sec. 302(a), [repealed as if not enacted by Sec. 102(a) of P.L. 98-67, see above] amended Code Sec. 31, effective for payments of interest, dividends and patronage dividends paid or credited after 6/30/83.
Prior to amendment, Code Sec. 31 read as follows:
"Sec. 31. Tax withheld on wages.
"(a) Wage withholding for income tax purposes.
"(1) In general. The amount withheld under section 3402 as tax on the wages of any individual shall be allowed to the recipient of the income as a credit against the tax imposed by this subtitle.
"(2) Year of credit. The amount so withheld during any calendar year shall be allowed as a credit for the taxable year beginning in such calendar year. If more than one taxable year begins in a calendar year, such amount shall be allowed as a credit for the last taxable year so beginning.
"(b) Credit for special refunds of social security tax.
"(1) In general. The Secretary may prescribe regulations providing for the crediting against the tax imposed by this subtitle of the amount determined by the taxpayer or the Secretary to be allowable under section 6413(c) as a special refund of tax imposed on wages. The amount allowed as a credit under such regulations shall, for purposes of this subtitle, be considered an amount withheld at source as tax under section 3402.
"(2) Year of credit. Any amount to which paragraph (1) applies shall be allowed as a credit for the taxable year beginning in the calendar year during which the wages were received. If more than one taxable year begins in the calendar year, such amount shall be allowed as a credit for the last taxable year so beginning."
In **1976**, P.L. 94-455, Sec. 1906(b)(13)(A), substituted "Secretary" for "Secretary or his delegate" in para. (b)(1)... Sec. 1906(b)(13)(D), deleted "(or his dele-

Sec. 32. Earned income.

> • **Caution:** Code Sec. 32, following, was amended by P.L. 107-16, EGTRRA. These provisions will generally sunset for tax years beginning after 12/31/2012. For specific sunset provisions, see Sec. 901, P.L. 107-16 (as amended) reproduced in history notes for this Code Sec.

(a) Allowance of credit.
(1) **In general.** In the case of an eligible individual, there shall be allowed as a credit against the tax imposed by this subtitle for the taxable year an amount equal to the credit percentage of so much of the taxpayer's earned income for the taxable year as does not exceed the earned income amount.
(2) **Limitation.** The amount of the credit allowable to a taxpayer under paragraph (1) for any taxable year shall not exceed the excess (if any) of—
(A) the credit percentage of the earned income amount, over
(B) the phaseout percentage of so much of the adjusted gross income (or, if greater, the earned income) of the taxpayer for the taxable year as exceeds the phaseout amount.

(b) Percentages and amounts.
For purposes of subsection (a)—
(1) **Percentages.** The credit percentage and the phaseout percentage shall be determined as follows:
(A) **In general.** In the case of taxable years beginning after 1995:

In the case of an eligible individual with:	The credit percentage is:	The phaseout percentage is:
1 qualifying child	34	15.98
2 or more qualifying children	40	21.06
No qualifying children	7.65	7.65

(B) **Transitional percentages for 1995.** In the case of taxable years beginning in 1995:

In the case of an eligible individual with:	The credit percentage is:	The phaseout percentage is:
1 qualifying child	34	15.98
2 or more qualifying children	36	20.22
No qualifying children	7.65	7.65

(C) **Transitional percentages for 1994.** In the case of a taxable year beginning in 1994:

In the case of an eligible individual with:	The credit percentage is:	The phaseout percentage is:
1 qualifying child	26.3	15.98
2 or more qualifying children	30	17.68
No qualifying children	7.65	7.65

(2) **Amounts.**
(A) **In general.** Subject to subparagraph (B), the earned income amount and the phaseout amount shall be determined as follows:

In the case of an eligible individual with:	The earned income amount is:	The phaseout amount is:
1 qualifying child	$6,330	$11,610
2 or more qualifying children	$8,890	$11,610
No qualifying children	$4,220	$ 5,280

(B) **Joint returns.** In the case of a joint return filed by an eligible individual and such individual's spouse, the phaseout amount determined under subparagraph (A) shall be increased by—
(i) $1,000 in the case of taxable years beginning in 2002, 2003, and 2004,
(ii) $2,000 in the case of taxable years beginning in 2005, 2006, and 2007, and
(iii) $3,000 in the case of taxable years beginning after 2007.
(3) **Special rules for 2009, 2010, 2011, and 2012.** In the case of any taxable year beginning in 2009, 2010, 2011, or 2012—
(A) **Increased credit percentage for 3 or more qualifying children.** In the case of a taxpayer with 3 or more qualifying children, the credit percentage is 45 percent.
(B) **Reduction of marriage penalty.**
(i) **In general.** The dollar amount in effect under paragraph (2)(B) shall be $5,000.
(ii) **Inflation adjustment.** In the case of any taxable year beginning in 2010, the $5,000 amount in clause (i) shall be increased by an amount equal to—
(I) such dollar amount, multiplied by
(II) the cost of living adjustment determined under section 1(f)(3) for the calendar year in which the taxable year begins determined by substituting "calendar year 2008" for "calendar year 1992" in subparagraph (B) thereof.
(iii) **Rounding.** Subparagraph (A) of subsection (j)(2) shall apply after taking into account any increase under clause (ii).

(c) Definitions and special rules.
For purposes of this section—
(1) **Eligible individual.**
(A) **In general.** The term "eligible individual" means—
(i) any individual who has a qualifying child for the taxable year, or
(ii) any other individual who does not have a qualifying child for the taxable year, if—
(I) such individual's principal place of abode is in the United States for more than one-half of such taxable year,
(II) such individual (or, if the individual is married, either the individual or the individual's spouse) has attained age 25 but not attained age 65 before the close of the taxable year, and
(III) such individual is not a dependent for whom a deduction is allowable under section 151 to another taxpayer for any taxable year beginning in the same calendar year as such taxable year.
For purposes of the preceding sentence, marital status shall be determined under section 7703.
(B) **Qualifying child ineligible.** If an individual is the qualifying child of a taxpayer for any taxable year of such taxpayer beginning in a calendar year, such individual shall not be treated as an eligible individual for any taxable year of such individual beginning in such calendar year.

(C) **Exception for individual claiming benefits under section 911.** The term "eligible individual" does not include any individual who claims the benefits of section 911 (relating to citizens or residents living abroad) for the taxable year.

(D) **Limitation on eligibility of nonresident aliens.** The term "eligible individual" shall not include any individual who is a nonresident alien individual for any portion of the taxable year unless such individual is treated for such taxable year as a resident of the United States for purposes of this chapter by reason of an election under subsection (g) or (h) of section 6013.

(E) **Identification number requirement.** No credit shall be allowed under this section to an eligible individual who does not include on the return of tax for the taxable year—

(i) such individual's taxpayer identification number, and

(ii) if the individual is married (within the meaning of section 7703), the taxpayer identification number of such individual's spouse.

(F) **Individuals who do not include TIN, etc., of any qualifying child.** No credit shall be allowed under this section to any eligible individual who has one or more qualifying children if no qualifying child of such individual is taken into account under subsection (b) by reason of paragraph (3)(D).

(2) Earned income.

(A) The term "earned income" means—

(i) wages, salaries, tips, and other employee compensation, but only if such amounts are includible in gross income for the taxable year, plus

(ii) the amount of the taxpayer's net earnings from self-employment for the taxable year (within the meaning of section 1402(a)), but such net earnings shall be determined with regard to the deduction allowed to the taxpayer by section 164(f).

(B) For purposes of subparagraph (A)—

(i) the earned income of an individual shall be computed without regard to any community property laws,

(ii) no amount received as a pension or annuity shall be taken into account,

(iii) no amount to which section 871(a) applies (relating to income of nonresident alien individuals not connected with United States business) shall be taken into account,

(iv) no amount received for services provided by an individual while the individual is an inmate at a penal institution shall be taken into account,

(v) no amount described in subparagraph (A) received for service performed in work activities as defined in paragraph (4) or (7) of section 407(d) of the Social Security Act to which the taxpayer is assigned under any State program under part A of title IV of such Act shall be taken into account, but only to the extent such amount is subsidized under such State program, and

(vi) a taxpayer may elect to treat amounts excluded from gross income by reason of section 112 as earned income.

(3) Qualifying child.

(A) **In general.** The term "qualifying child" means a qualifying child of the taxpayer (as defined in section 152(c), determined without regard to paragraph (1)(D) thereof and section 152(e)).

(B) **Married individual.** The term "qualifying child" shall not include an individual who is married as of the close of the taxpayer's taxable year unless the taxpayer is entitled to a deduction under section 151 for such taxable year with respect to such individual (or would be so entitled but for section 152(e)).

(C) **Place of abode.** For purposes of subparagraph (A), the requirements of section 152(c)(1)(B) shall be met only if the principal place of abode is in the United States.

(D) **Identification requirements.**

(i) **In general.** A qualifying child shall not be taken into account under subsection (b) unless the taxpayer includes the name, age, and TIN of the qualifying child on the return of tax for the taxable year.

(ii) **Other methods.** The Secretary may prescribe other methods for providing the information described in clause (i).

(4) Treatment of military personnel stationed outside the United States. For purposes of paragraphs (1)(A)(ii)(I) and (3)(C), the principal place of abode of a member of the Armed Forces of the United States shall be treated as in the United States during any period during which such member is stationed outside the United States while serving on extended active duty with the Armed Forces of the United States. For purposes of the preceding sentence, the term "extended active duty" means any period of active duty pursuant to a call or order to such duty for a period in excess of 90 days or for an indefinite period.

(d) Married individuals.

In the case of an individual who is married (within the meaning of section 7703), this section shall apply only if a joint return is filed for the taxable year under section 6013.

(e) Taxable year must be full taxable year.

Except in the case of a taxable year closed by reason of the death of the taxpayer, no credit shall be allowable under this section in the case of a taxable year covering a period of less than 12 months.

(f) Amount of credit to be determined under tables.

(1) In general. The amount of the credit allowed by this section shall be determined under tables prescribed by the Secretary.

(2) Requirements for tables. The tables prescribed under paragraph (1) shall reflect the provisions of subsections (a) and (b) and shall have income brackets of not greater than $50 each—

(A) for earned income between $0 and the amount of earned income at which the credit is phased out under subsection (b), and

(B) for adjusted gross income between the dollar amount at which the phaseout begins under subsection (b) and the amount of adjusted gross income at which the credit is phased out under subsection (b).

(g) Repealed.

(h) Repealed.

(i) Denial of credit for individuals having excessive investment income.

(1) In general. No credit shall be allowed under subsection (a) for the taxable year if the aggregate amount of disqualified income of the taxpayer for the taxable year exceeds $2,200.

(2) Disqualified income. For purposes of paragraph (1), the term "disqualified income" means—

(A) interest or dividends to the extent includible in gross income for the taxable year,

(B) interest received or accrued during the taxable year which is exempt from tax imposed by this chapter,
(C) the excess (if any) of—
   (i) gross income from rents or royalties not derived in the ordinary course of a trade or business, over
   (ii) the sum of—
      (I) the deductions (other than interest) which are clearly and directly allocable to such gross income, plus
      (II) interest deductions properly allocable to such gross income,
(D) the capital gain net income (as defined in section 1222) of the taxpayer for such taxable year, and
(E) the excess (if any) of—
   (i) the aggregate income from all passive activities for the taxable year (determined without regard to any amount included in earned income under subsection (c)(2) or described in a preceding subparagraph), over
   (ii) the aggregate losses from all passive activities for the taxable year (as so determined).

For purposes of subparagraph (E), the term "passive activity" has the meaning given such term by section 469.

(j) Inflation adjustments.
(1) In general. In the case of any taxable year beginning after 1996, each of the dollar amounts in subsections (b)(2) and (i)(1) shall be increased by an amount equal to—
(A) such dollar amount, multiplied by
(B) the cost-of-living adjustment determined under section 1(f)(3) for the calendar year in which the taxable year begins, determined—
   (i) in the case of amounts in subsections (b)(2)(A) and (i)(1), by substituting "calendar year 1995" for "calendar year 1992" in subparagraph (B) thereof, and
   (ii) in the case of the $3,000 amount in subsection (b)(2)(B)(iii), by substituting "calendar year 2007" for "calendar year 1992" in subparagraph (B) of such section 1.

(2) Rounding.
(A) In general. If any dollar amount in subsection (b)(2)(A) (after being increased under subparagraph (B) thereof), after being increased under paragraph (1), is not a multiple of $10, such dollar amount shall be rounded to the nearest multiple of $10.
(B) Disqualified income threshold amount. If the dollar amount in subsection (i)(1), after being increased under paragraph (1), is not a multiple of $50, such amount shall be rounded to the next lowest multiple of $50.

(k) Restrictions on taxpayers who improperly claimed credit in prior year.
(1) Taxpayers making prior fraudulent or reckless claims.
(A) In general. No credit shall be allowed under this section for any taxable year in the disallowance period.
(B) Disallowance period. For purposes of paragraph (1), the disallowance period is—
   (i) the period of 10 taxable years after the most recent taxable year for which there was a final determination that the taxpayer's claim of credit under this section was due to fraud, and
   (ii) the period of 2 taxable years after the most recent taxable year for which there was a final determination that the taxpayer's claim of credit under this section was due to reckless or intentional disregard of rules and regulations (but not due to fraud).

(2) Taxpayers making improper prior claims. In the case of a taxpayer who is denied credit under this section for any taxable year as a result of the deficiency procedures under subchapter B of chapter 63, no credit shall be allowed under this section for any subsequent taxable year unless the taxpayer provides such information as the Secretary may require to demonstrate eligibility for such credit.

(l) Coordination with certain means-tested programs.
For purposes of—
(1) the United States Housing Act of 1937,
(2) title V of the Housing Act of 1949,
(3) section 101 of the Housing and Urban Development Act of 1965,
(4) sections 221(d)(3), 235, and 236 of the National Housing Act, and
(5) the Food and Nutrition Act of 2008,
any refund made to an individual (or the spouse of an individual) by reason of this section, and any payment made to such individual (or such spouse) by an employer under section 3507, shall not be treated as income (and shall not be taken into account in determining resources for the month of its receipt and the following month).

(m) Identification numbers.
Solely for purposes of subsections (c)(1)(E) and (c)(3)(D), a taxpayer identification number means a social security number issued to an individual by the Social Security Administration (other than a social security number issued pursuant to clause (II) (or that portion of clause (III) that relates to clause (II)) of section 205(c)(2)(B)(i) of the Social Security Act).

In 2010, P.L. 111-312, Sec. 101(a)(1), substituted "December 31, 2012" for "December 31, 2010" both places it appeared in Sec. 901 of P.L. 107-16, effective as if included in the enactment of P.L. 107-16, EGTRRA, 6/7/2001 [see below]
—P.L. 111-312, Sec. 103(c)(1), substituted "2009, 2010, 2011, and 2012" for "2009 and 2010" in the heading of para. (b)(3) . . . Sec. 103(c)(2), substituted ", 2010, 2011, or 2012" for "or 2010" in para. (b)(3), effective for tax. yrs. begin. after 12/31/2010.
—P.L. 111-226, Sec. 219(a)(2), deleted subsec. (g), effective for tax. yrs. begin. after 12/31/2010.
Prior to deletion, subsec. (g) read as follows:
"(g) Coordination with advance payments of earned income credit.
"(1) Recapture of excess advance payments.
"If any payment is made to the individual by an employer under section 3507 during any calendar year, then the tax imposed by this chapter for the individual's last taxable year beginning in such calendar year shall be increased by the aggregate amount of such payments.
"(2) Reconciliation of payments advanced and credit allowed.
"Any increase in tax under paragraph (1) shall not be treated as tax imposed by this chapter for purposes of determining the amount of any credit (other than the credit allowed by subsection (a)) allowable under this part."
In 2009, P.L. 111-5, Sec. 1002(a), added para. (b)(3), effective for tax. yrs. begin. after 12/31/2008.
In 2008, P.L. 110-246, Sec. 4002(b)(1)(B), substituted "Food and Nutrition Act of 2008" for "Food Stamp Act of 1977" in para. (l)(5), enacted 5/22/2008. [Ed. Note: May 22, 2008 was the date of enactment for H.R. 2419 (PL 110-234), which was repealed by (2008 Farm Act § 4(a)) (PL 110-246, 6/18/2008), in connection with the reenactment of the Farm Bill to correct a technical deficiency in its original passage.]
—P.L. 110-245, Sec. 102(a), amended clause (c)(2)(B)(vi), effective for tax. yrs. end. after 12/31/2007.
Prior to amendment, clause (c)(2)(B)(vi) read as follows:
"(vi) in the case of any taxable year ending—
"(I) after the date of the enactment of this clause, and
"(II) before January 1, 2008,
"a taxpayer may elect to treat amounts excluded from gross income by reason of section 112 as earned income."
—P.L. 110-245, Sec. 102(c), of this Act provides:
"(c) Sunset not applicable. Section 105 of the Working Families Tax Relief Act of 2004 [P.L. 108-311 see below] [relating to application of EGTRRA sunset to this title] shall not apply to section 104(b) of such Act"

Tax credits — Code Sec. 32

In 2006, P.L. 109-432, Sec. 106(a), substituted "2008" for "2007" after "before January 1," in subclause (c)(2)(B)(vi)(II) effective for tax. yrs. begin. after 12/31/2006.

In 2005, P.L. 109-135, Sec. 302(a), substituted "January 1, 2007" for "January 1, 2006" in subclause (c)(2)(B)(vi)(II), effective for tax. yrs. begin. after 12/31/2005.

— P.L. 109-73, Sec. 406, of this Act, reads as follows:

"SEC. 406. SPECIAL RULE FOR DETERMINING EARNED INCOME.

"(a) In general. In the case of a qualified individual, if the earned income of the taxpayer for the taxable year which includes August 25, 2005, is less than the earned income of the taxpayer for the preceding taxable year, the credits allowed under sections 24(d) and 32 of the Internal Revenue Code of 1986 may, at the election of the taxpayer, be determined by substituting—

"(1) such earned income for the preceding taxable year, for

"(2) such earned income for the taxable year which includes August 25, 2005.

"(b) Qualified individual. For purposes of this section, the term 'qualified individual' means any individual whose principal place of abode on August 25, 2005, was located—

"(1) in the core disaster area, or

"(2) in the Hurricane Katrina disaster area (but outside the core disaster area) and such individual was displaced from such principal place of abode by reason of Hurricane Katrina.

"(c) Earned income. For purposes of this section, the term 'earned income' has the meaning given such term under section 32(c) of such Code.

"(d) Special rules.

"(1) Application to joint returns. For purposes of subsection (a), in the case of a joint return for a taxable year which includes August 25, 2005—

"(A) such subsection shall apply if either spouse is a qualified individual, and

"(B) the earned income of the taxpayer for the preceding taxable year shall be the sum of the earned income of each spouse for such preceding taxable year.

"(2) Uniform application of election. Any election made under subsection (a) shall apply with respect to both section 24(d) and section 32 of such Code.

"(3) Errors treated as mathematical error. For purposes of section 6213 of such Code, an incorrect use on a return of earned income pursuant to subsection (a) shall be treated as a mathematical or clerical error.

"(4) No effect on determination of gross income, etc. Except as otherwise provided in this section, the Internal Revenue Code of 1986 shall be applied without regard to any substitution under subsection (a)."

In 2004, P.L. 108-311, Sec. 104(b)(1), deleted "and" at the end of clause (c)(2)(B)(iv) . . . Sec. 104(b)(2), substituted ", and" for the period at the end of clause (c)(2)(B)(v) . . . Sec. 104(b)(3), added clause (c)(2)(B)(vi), effective for tax. yrs. end. after 10/4/2004. Sec. 102(c), P.L. 110-245, see above, provides that amendments made by Sec. 104(b), P.L. 108-311 shall not be subject to Sec. 105, P.L. 108-311, following:

— P.L. 108-311, Sec. 105, of this Act, reads as follows:

"SEC. 105. APPLICATION OF EGTRRA SUNSET TO THIS TITLE. Each amendment made by this title [Secs. 101-104] shall be subject to title IX of the Economic Growth and Tax Relief Reconciliation Act of 2001 [Sec. 901 of P.L. 107-16] to the same extent and in the same manner as the provision of such Act to which such amendment relates."

— P.L. 108-311, Sec. 205(a), amended para. (c)(3) . . . Sec. 205(b)(1), deleted subpara. (c)(1)(C), and redesignated subparas. (c)(1)(D)-(G) as (c)(1)(C)-(F) . . . Sec. 205(b)(2), substituted "(3)(C)" for "(3)(E)" in para. (c)(4) . . . Sec. 205(b)(3), substituted "subsections (c)(1)(E)" for "subsections (c)(1)(F)" in subsec. (m), effective for tax. yrs. begin. after 12/31/2004.

Prior to deletion, subpara. (c)(1)(C) read as follows:

"(C) 2 or more claiming qualifying child.

"(i) In general. Except as provided in clause (ii), if (but for this paragraph) an individual may be claimed, and is claimed, as a qualifying child by 2 or more taxpayers for a taxable year beginning in the same calendar year, such individual shall be treated as the qualifying child of the taxpayer who is—

"(I) a parent of the individual, or

"(II) if subclause (I) does not apply, the taxpayer with the highest adjusted gross income for such taxable year.

"(ii) More than 1 claiming credit. If the parents claiming the credit with respect to any qualifying child do not file a joint return together, such child shall be treated as the qualifying child of—

"(I) the parent with whom the child resided for the longest period of time during the taxable year, or

"(II) if the child resides with both parents for the same amount of time during such taxable year, the parent with the highest adjusted gross income."

Prior to amendment, para. (c)(3) read as follows:

"(3) Qualifying child.

"(A) In general. The term 'qualifying child' means, with respect to any taxpayer for any taxable year, an individual—

"(i) who bears a relationship to the taxpayer described in subparagraph (B),

"(ii) who has the same principal place of abode as the taxpayer for more than one-half of such taxable year, and

"(iii) who meets the age requirements of subparagraph (C).

"(B) Relationship test.

"(i) In general. An individual bears a relationship to the taxpayer described in this subparagraph if such individual is—

"(I) a son, daughter, stepson, or stepdaughter, or a descendant of any such individual,

"(II) a brother, sister, stepbrother, or stepsister, or a descendant of any such individual, who the taxpayer cares for as the taxpayer's own child, or

"(III) an eligible foster child of the taxpayer.

"(ii) Married children. Clause (i) shall not apply to any individual who is married as of the close of the taxpayer's taxable year unless the taxpayer is entitled to a deduction under section 151 for such taxable year with respect to such individual (or would be so entitled but for paragraph (2) or (4) of section 152(e)).

"(iii) Eligible foster child. For purposes of clause (i), the term 'eligible foster child' means an individual not described in subclause (I) or (II) of clause (i) who—

"(I) is placed with the taxpayer by an authorized placement agency, and

"(II) the taxpayer cares for as the taxpayer's own child.

"(iv) Adoption. For purposes of this subparagraph, a child who is legally adopted, or who is placed with the taxpayer by an authorized placement agency for adoption by the taxpayer, shall be treated as a child by blood.

"(C) Age requirements. An individual meets the requirements of this subparagraph if such individual—

"(i) has not attained the age of 19 as of the close of the calendar year in which the taxable year of the taxpayer begins,

"(ii) is a student (as defined in section 151(c)(4)) who has not attained the age of 24 as of the close of such calendar year, or

"(iii) is permanently and totally disabled (as defined in section 22(e)(3)) at any time during the taxable year.

"(D) Identification requirements.

"(i) In general. A qualifying child shall not be taken into account under subsection (b) unless the taxpayer includes the name, age, and TIN of the qualifying child on the return of tax for the taxable year.

"(ii) Other methods. The Secretary may prescribe other methods for providing the information described in clause (i).

"(E) Abode must be in the United States. The requirements of subparagraph (A)(ii) shall be met only if the principal place of abode is in the United States."

In 2002, P.L. 107-358, Sec. 2, added subsec. (c) in Sec. 901 of P.L. 107-16 [see below], effective 12/17/2002.

— P.L. 107-147, Sec. 416(a)(1), substituted "part" for "subpart" in para. (g)(2), effective for tax. yrs. begin. after 12/31/83, and for carrybacks from such years.

In 2001, P.L. 107-16, Sec. 201(c)(3), deleted subsec. (n), effective for tax. yrs. begin. after 12/31/2000.

Prior to deletion, subsec. (n) read as follows:

"(n) Supplemental child credit.

"(1) In general. In the case of a taxpayer with respect to whom a credit is allowed under section 24(a) for the taxable year, the credit otherwise allowable under this section shall be increased by the lesser of—

"(A) the excess of—

"(i) the credits allowed under subpart A (determined after the application of section 26 and without regard to this subsection), over

"(ii) the credits which would be allowed under subpart A after the application of section 26, determined without regard to section 24 and this subsection; or

"(B) the excess of—

"(i) the sum of the credits allowed under this part (determined without regard to sections 31, 33, and 34 and this subsection), over

"(ii) the sum of the regular tax and the Social Security taxes (as defined in section 24(d)).

The credit determined under this subsection shall be allowed without regard to any other provision of this section , including subsection (d).

"(2) Coordination with other credits. The amount of the credit under this subsection shall reduce the amount of the credits otherwise allowable under subpart A for the taxable year (determined after the application of section 26), but the amount of the credit under this subsection (and such reduction) shall not be taken into account in determining the amount of any other credit allowable under this part."

— P.L. 107-16, Sec. 303(a)(1)(A), substituted "Amounts. (A) In general. Subject to subparagraph (B), the earned" for "Amounts. The earned" in para. (b)(2) . . . Sec. 303(a)(1)(B), added subpara. (b)(2)(B) . . . Sec. 303(a)(2), amended subpara. (j)(1)(B) . . . Sec. 303(a)(3), substituted "subsection (b)(2)(A) (after being increased under subparagraph (B) thereof)" for "subsection (b)(2)" in subpara. (j)(2)(A) . . . Sec. 303(b), added ", but only if such amounts are includible in gross income for the taxable year" after "other employee compensation" in clause (c)(2)(A)(i) . . . Sec. 303(c), deleted subsec. (h) . . . Sec. 303(d)(1), deleted "modified" after "much of the" in subpara. (a)(2)(B) . . . Sec. 303(d)(2)(A), deleted para. (c)(5) . . . Sec. 303(d)(2)(B), deleted "modified" before "adjusted" each place it appeared in subpara. (f)(2)(B) . . . Sec. 303(e)(1), amended clause (c)(3)(B)(i) . . . Sec. 303(e)(2)(A), amended clause (c)(3)(B)(iii) . . . Sec. 303(e)(2)(B), deleted "except as provided in subparagraph (B)(iii)," before "who" in clause (c)(3)(A)(ii) . . . Sec. 303(f), amended subpara. (c)(1)(C) . . . Sec. 303(h), substituted "subparagraph (A)(ii)" for "subparagraphs (A)(ii) and (B)(iii)(II)" in subpara. (c)(3)(E), effective for tax. yrs. begin. after 12/31/2001.

Prior to amendment, subpara. (j)(1)(B) read as follows:

"(B) the cost-of-living adjustment determined under section 1(f)(3) for the calendar year in which the taxable year begins, determined by substituting 'calendar year 1995' for 'calendar year 1992' in subparagraph (B) thereof."

Prior to deletion, subsec. (h) read as follows:

"(h) Reduction of credit to taxpayers subject to alternative minimum tax. The credit allowed under this section for the taxable year shall be reduced by the amount of tax imposed by section 55 (relating to alternative minimum tax) with respect to such taxpayer for such taxable year."

Prior to deletion, para. (c)(5) read as follows:

"(5) Modified adjusted gross income.

"(A) In general. The term 'modified adjusted gross income' means adjusted gross income determined without regard to the amounts described in subparagraph (B) and increased by the amounts described in subparagraph (C).

1,079

"(B) Certain amounts disregarded. An amount is described in this subparagraph if it is—

"(i) the amount of losses from sales or exchanges of capital assets in excess of gains from such sales or exchanges to the extent such amount does not exceed the amount under section 1211(b)(1),

"(ii) the net loss from estates and trusts,

"(iii) the excess (if any) of amounts described in subsection (i)(2)(C)(ii) over the amounts described in subsection (i)(2)(C)(i) (relating to nonbusiness rents and royalties); or

"(iv) 75 percent of the net loss from the carrying on of trades or businesses, computed separately with respect to—

"(I) trades or businesses (other than farming) conducted as sole proprietorships,

"(II) trades or businesses of farming conducted as sole proprietorships, and

"(III) other trades or businesses.

For purposes of clause (iv), there shall not be taken into account items which are attributable to a trade or business which consists of the performance of services by the taxpayer as an employee.

"(C) Certain amounts included. An amount is described in this subparagraph if it is—

"(i) interest received or accrued during the taxable year which is exempt from tax imposed by this chapter; or

"(ii) amounts received as a pension or annuity, and any distributions or payments received from an individual retirement plan, by the taxpayer during the taxable year to the extent not included in gross income.

Clause (ii) shall not include any amount which is not includible in gross income by reason of a trustee-to-trustee transfer or a rollover distribution."

Prior to amendment, clause (c)(3)(B)(i) read as follows:

"(i) In general. An individual bears a relationship to the taxpayer described in this subparagraph if such individual is—

"(I) a son or daughter of the taxpayer, or a descendant of either,

"(II) a stepson or stepdaughter of the taxpayer, or

"(III) an eligible foster child of the taxpayer."

Prior to amendment, clause (c)(3)(B)(iii) read as follows:

"(iii) Eligible foster child. For purposes of clause (i)(III), the term 'eligible foster child' means an individual not described in clause (i)(I) or (II) who—

"(I) is a brother, sister, stepbrother, or stepsister of the taxpayer (or a descendant of any such relative) or is placed with the taxpayer by an authorized placement agency,

"(II) the taxpayer cares for as the taxpayer's own child, and

"(III) has the same principal place of abode as the taxpayer for the taxpayer's entire taxable year."

Prior to amendment, subpara. (c)(1)(C) read as follows:

"(C) 2 or more eligible individuals. If 2 or more individuals would (but for this subparagraph and after application of subparagraph (B)) be treated as eligible individuals with respect to the same qualifying child for taxable years beginning in the same calendar year, only the individual with the highest modified adjusted gross income for such taxable years shall be treated as an eligible individual with respect to such qualifying child."

—P.L. 107-16, Sec. 901, of this Act [as amended by Sec. 2 of P.L. 107-358, and Sec. 101(a)(1) of P.L. 111-312, see above], reads as follows:

"SEC. 901. SUNSET OF PROVISIONS OF ACT.

"(a) In general. All provisions of, and amendments made by, this Act shall not apply—

"(1) to taxable, plan, or limitation years beginning after December 31, 2012, or

"(2) in the case of title V, to estates of decedents dying, gifts made, or generation skipping transfers, after December 31, 2012.

"(b) Application of certain laws. The Internal Revenue Code of 1986 and the Employee Retirement Income Security Act of 1974 shall be applied and administered to years, estates, gifts, and transfers described in subsection (a) as if the provisions and amendments described in subsection (a) had never been enacted.

"(c) Exception. Subsection (a) shall not apply to section 803 (relating to no federal income tax on restitution received by victims of the Nazi regime or their heirs or estates)."

In 1999, P.L. 106-170, Sec. 412(a), redesignated subclause (c)(3)(B)(iii)(I) and (II) as (II) and (III) and added subclause (c)(3)(B)(iii)(I), effective for tax. yrs. begin. after 12/31/99.

In 1998, P.L. 105-206, Sec. 6003(b)(1), redesignated subsec. (m) [sic (n)] as subsec. (n) and amended newly redesignated subsec. (n), effective for tax. yrs. begin. after 12/31/97.

Prior to amendment, subsec. (n) read as follows:

"(n) Supplemental child credit.

"(1) In general. In the case of a taxpayer with respect to whom a credit is allowed under section 24 for the taxable year, there shall be allowed as a credit under this section an amount equal to the supplemental child credit (if any) determined for such taxpayer for such taxable year under paragraph (2). Such credit shall be in addition to the credit allowed under subsection (a).

"(2) Supplemental child credit. For purposes of this subsection, the supplemental child credit is an amount equal to the excess (if any) of—

"(A) the amount determined under section 24(d)(1)(A), over

"(B) the amount determined under section 24(d)(1)(B).

The amounts referred to in subparagraphs (A) and (B) shall be determined as if section 24(d) applied to all taxpayers.

"(3) Coordination with section 24. The amount of the credit under section 24 shall be reduced by the amount of the credit allowed under this subsection."

—P.L. 105-206, Sec. 6005(e)(3), added "on or" before "before" each place it appears in Sec. 312(d)(2) [sic (e)(2)] of P.L. 105-34, 8/5/1997, see below.

—P.L. 105-206, Sec. 6010(p)(1)(A), added "and increased by the amounts described in subparagraph (C)" before the period at the end of subpara. (c)(5)(A) . . . Sec. 6010(p)(1)(B), added "or" at the end of clause (c)(5)(B)(iii) . . . Sec. 6010(p)(1)(C), deleted subclause (c)(5)(B)(iv)(III) through the end of subpara. (c)(5)(B) and added new subclause (c)(5)(B)(iv)(III) and subpara. (c)(5)(C) . . . Sec. 6010(p)(2), added "shall be taken into account" before ", but only" in clause (c)(2)(B)(v), effective for tax. yrs. begin. after 12/31/97.

Prior to deletion, subclause (c)(5)(B)(iv)(III) thru the end of subpara. (c)(5)(B) read as follows:

"(III) other trades or businesses

"(v) interest received or accrued during the taxable year which is exempt from tax imposed by this chapter, and

"(vi) amounts received as a pension or annuity, and any distributions or payments received from an individual retirement plan, by the taxpayer during the taxable year to the extent not included in gross income.

For purposes of clause (iv), there shall not be taken into account items which are attributable to a trade or business which consists of the performance of services by the taxpayer as an employee. Clause (vi) shall not include any amount which is not includible in gross income by reason of section 402(c), 403(a)(4), 403(b), 408(d)(3), (4), or (5), or 457(e)(10)."

—P.L. 105-206, Sec. 6021(a), substituted "No credit shall be allowed under this section to an eligible individual who does not include on the return of tax for the taxable year—" for "The term 'eligible individual' does not include any individual who does not include on the return of tax for the taxable year—" in subpara. (c)(1)(F), effective for returns the due date for which (without regard to extensions) is more than 30 days after 8/22/96.

—P.L. 105-206, Sec. 6021(b)(1), amended clause (c)(3)(D)(i) . . . Sec. 6021(b)(2), added subpara. (c)(1)(G) . . . Sec. 6021(b)(3), added "and" at the end of clause (c)(3)(A)(ii), substituted a period for ", and" at the end of clause (c)(3)(A)(iii) and deleted clause (c)(3)(A)(iv), effective for tax. yrs. begin. after 12/31/90.

Prior to deletion, clause (c)(3)(A)(iv) read as follows:

"(iv) with respect to whom the taxpayer meets the identification requirements of subparagraph (D)."

Prior to amendment, clause (c)(3)(D)(i) read as follows:

"(i) In general. The requirements of this subparagraph are met if the taxpayer includes the name, age, and TIN of each qualifying child (without regard to this subparagraph) on the return of tax for the taxable year."

In 1997, P.L. 105-34, Sec. 101(b), added subsec. (m) [sic (n)], effective for tax. yrs. begin. after 12/31/97.

—P.L. 105-34, Sec. 312(d)(2), deleted "(as defined in section 1034(h)(3))" after "active duty" in para. (c)(4) and added a sentence at the end of para. (c)(4), effective for sales and exchanges after 5/6/97, except as provided in Secs. 312(d)(2)-(4) [sic (e)(2)-(4)] of this Act, [as amended by Sec. 6005(e)(3), 105-206, see above] which read as follows:

"(2) Sales on or before date of enactment [8/5/97]. At the election of the taxpayer, the amendments made by this section shall not apply to any sale or exchange on or before the date of the enactment of this Act.

"(3) Certain sales within 2 years after date of enactment. Section 121 of the Internal Revenue Code of 1986 (as amended by this section) shall be applied without regard to subsection (c)(2)(B) thereof in the case of any sale or exchange of property during the 2-year period beginning on the date of the enactment of this Act if the taxpayer held such property on the date of the enactment of this Act and fails to meet the ownership and use requirements of subsection (a) thereof with respect to such property.

"(4) Binding contracts. At the election of the taxpayer, the amendments made by this section shall not apply to a sale or exchange after the date of the enactment of this Act, if—

"(A) such sale or exchange is pursuant to a contract which was binding on such date, or

"(B) without regard to such amendments, gain would not be recognized under section 1034 of the Internal Revenue Code of 1986 (as in effect on the day before the date of the enactment [8/5/97] of this Act) on such sale or exchange by reason of a new residence acquired on or before such date or with respect to the acquisition of which by the taxpayer a binding contract was in effect on such date. This paragraph shall not apply to any sale or exchange by an individual if the treatment provided by section 877(a)(1) of the Internal Revenue Code of 1986 applies to such individual."

—P.L. 105-34, Sec. 1085(a)(1), redesignated subsecs. (k) and (l) as subsecs. (l) and (m) and added a new subsec. (k), effective for tax. yrs. begin. after 12/31/96.

—P.L. 105-34, Sec. 1085(b), substituted "75 percent" for "50 percent" in clause (c)(5)(B)(iv) . . . Sec. 1085(c), deleted "and" at the end of clause (c)(2)(B)(iii), substituted ", and" for the period at the end of clause (c)(2)(B)(iv), and added clause (c)(2)(B)(v) . . . Sec. 1085(d)(1), deleted "and" at the end of clause (c)(5)(B)(iii) . . . Sec. 1085(d)(2), deleted the period at the end of subclause (c)(5)(B)(iv)(III) . . . Sec. 1085(d)(3), added clauses (c)(5)(B)(v) and (vi) . . . Sec. 1085(d)(4), added a sentence at the end of subpara. (c)(5)(B), effective for tax. yrs. begin. after 12/31/97.

In 1996, P.L. 104-193, Sec. 451(a), added subpara. (c)(1)(F) . . . Sec. 451(b), added subsec. (l), effective for returns the due date for which (without regard to extensions) is more than 30 days after 8/22/96.

—P.L. 104-193, Sec. 909(a)(1), substituted "$2,200" for "$2,350" in para. (i)(1) . . . Sec. 909(a)(2), amended subsec. (j) . . . Sec. 909(a)(3), amended para. (b)(2) . . . Sec. 909(b), deleted "and" at the end of subpara. (i)(2)(B), substituted a comma for the period at the end of subpara. (i)(2)(C) and added subparas. (i)(2)(D) and (E), effective for tax. yrs. begin. after 12/31/95. Sec. 909(c)(2) of this Act provides:

Tax credits Code Sec. 32

"(2) Advance payment of individuals. In the case of any individual who on or before June 26, 1996, has in effect an earned income eligibility certificate for the individual's taxable year beginning in 1996, the amendments made by this section shall apply to taxable years beginning after December 31, 1996."

Prior to amendment, para. (b)(2) read as follows:

"(2) Amounts. The earned income amount and the phaseout amount shall be determined as follows:

"(A) In general. In the case of taxable years beginning after 1994:

In the case of an eligible individual with:	The earned income amount is:	The phaseout amount is:
1 qualifying child	$6,000	$11,000
2 or more qualifying children	$8,425	$11,000
No qualifying children	$4,000	$ 5,000

"(B) Transitional amounts. In the case of a taxable year beginning in 1994:

In the case of an eligible individual with:	The earned income amount is:	The phaseout amount is:
1 qualifying child	$7,750	$11,000
2 or more qualifying children	$8,425	$11,000
No qualifying children	$4,000	$5,000"

Prior to amendment, subsec. (j) read as follows:

"(j) Inflation adjustments.

"(1) In general. In the case of any taxable year beginning after 1994, each dollar amount contained in subsection (b)(2)(A) shall be increased by an amount equal to—

"(A) such dollar amount, multiplied by

"(B) the cost-of-living adjustment determined under section 1(f)(3), for the calendar year in which the taxable year begins, by substituting 'calendar year 1993' for 'calendar year 1992'

"(2) Rounding. If any dollar amount after being increased under paragraph (1) is not a multiple of $10, such dollar amount shall be rounded to the nearest multiple of $10 (or, if such dollar amount is a multiple of $5, such dollar amount shall be increased to the next higher multiple of $10.)"

—P.L. 104-193, Sec. 910(a), substituted "modified adjusted gross income" for "adjusted gross income" each place it appeared in subparas. (a)(2)(B), (c)(1)(C) and (f)(2)(B)... Sec. 910(b), added para. (c)(5), effective for tax. yrs. begin. after 12/31/95. Sec. 910(c)(2) of this Act, which reads as follows:

"(2) Advance payment individuals. In the case of any individual who on or before June 26, 1996, has in effect an earned income eligibility certificate for the individual's taxable year beginning in 1996, the amendments made by this section shall apply to taxable years beginning after December 31, 1996."

In 1995, P.L. 104-7, Sec. 4(a), redesignated subsecs. (i) and (j) as subsecs. (j) and (k) and added new subsec. (i), effective for tax. yrs. begin. after 12/31/95.

In 1994, P.L. 103-465, Sec. 721(a), added para. (c)(4), effective for tax. yrs. begin. after 12/31/94.

—P.L. 103-465, Sec. 722(a), added subpara. (c)(1)(E), effective for tax. yrs. begin. after 12/31/94.

—P.L. 103-465, Sec. 723(a), deleted "and" at the end of clause (c)(2)(B)(ii), substituted ", and" for the period at the end of clause (c)(2)(B)(iii), and added clause (c)(2)(B)(iv), effective for tax. yrs. begin. after 12/31/93.

—P.L. 103-465, Sec. 742(a), amended clause (c)(3)(D)(i), effective for returns for tax. yrs. begin. after 12/31/94, except as provided in Sec. 742(c)(2) of this Act, which reads as follows:

"(2) Exception. The amendments made by this section shall not apply to—

"(A) returns for taxable years beginning in 1995 with respect to individuals who are born after October 31, 1995, and

"(B) returns for taxable years beginning in 1996 with respect to individuals who are born after November 30, 1996."

Prior to amendment, clause (c)(3)(D)(i) read as follows:

"(i) In general. The requirements of this subparagraph are met if—

"(I) The taxpayer includes the name and age of each qualifying child (without regard to this subparagraph) on the return of tax for the taxable year, and

"(II) in the case of an individual who has attained the age of 1 year before the close of the taxpayer's taxable year, the taxpayer includes the taxpayer identification number of such individual on such return of tax for such taxable year."

In 1993, P.L. 103-66, Sec. 13131(a), amended subsecs. (a) and (b)... Sec. 13131(b), amended subpara. (c)(1)(A)... Sec. 13131(c)(1), deleted paras. (i)(1) and (2), and added new para. (i)(1)... Sec. 13131(c)(2), redesignated para. (i)(3) as (i)(2)... Sec. 13131(d)(1)(A), substituted "clause (i)" for "clause (i) or (ii)" in clause (c)(3)(D)(iii) [before redesignation]... Sec. 13131(d)(1)(B), deleted clause (c)(3)(D)(ii)... Sec. 13131(d)(1)(C), redesignated clause (c)(3)(D)(iii) as (c)(3)(D)(ii), effective for tax. yrs. begin. after 12/31/93.

Prior to amendment, subsecs. (a) and (b) read as follows:

"(a) Allowance of credit. In the case of an eligible individual, there shall be allowed as a credit against the tax imposed by this subtitle for the taxable year an amount equal to the sum of—

"(1) the basic earned income credit, and

"(2) the health insurance credit.

"(b) Computation of credit. For purposes of this section—

"(1) Basic earned income credit.

"(A) In general. The term 'basic earned income credit' means an amount equal to the credit percentage of so much of the taxpayer's earned income for the taxable year as does not exceed $5,714.

"(B) Limitation. The amount of the basic earned income credit allowable to a taxpayer for any taxable year shall not exceed the excess (if any) of—

"(i) the credit percentage of $5,714, over

"(ii) the phaseout percentage of so much of the adjusted gross income (or, if greater the earned income) of the taxpayer for the taxable year as exceeds $9,000.

"(C) Percentages. For purposes of this paragraph—

"(i) In general. Except as provided in clause (ii), the percentages shall be determined as follows:

In the case of an eligible individual with:	The credit percentage is:	The phaseout percentage is:
1 qualifying child	23	16.43
2 or more qualifying children	25	17.86

"(ii) Transition percentages.

"(I) For taxable years beginning in 1991, the percentages are:

In the case of an eligible individual with:	The credit percentage is:	The phaseout percentage is:
1 qualifying child	16.7	11.93
2 or more qualifying children	17.3	12.36

"(II) For taxable years beginning in 1992, the percentages are:

In the case of an eligible individual with:	The credit percentage is:	The phaseout percentage is:
1 qualifying child	17.6	12.57
2 or more qualifying children	18.4	13.14

"(III) For taxable years beginning in 1993, the percentages are:

In the case of an eligible individual with:	The credit percentage is:	The phaseout percentage is:
1 qualifying child	18.5	13.21
2 or more qualifying children	19.5	13.93

"(D) Supplemental young child credit. In the case of a taxpayer with a qualifying child who has not attained age 1 as of the close of the calendar year in which or with which the taxable year of the taxpayer ends—

"(i) the credit percentage shall be increased by 5 percentage points, and

"(ii) the phaseout percentage shall be increased by 3.57 percentage points.

If the taxpayer elects to take a child into account under this subparagraph, such child shall not be treated as a qualifying individual under section 21.

"(2) Health insurance credit.

"(A) In general. The term 'health insurance credit' means an amount determined in the same manner as the basic earned income credit except that—

"(i) the credit percentage shall be equal to 6 percent, and

"(ii) the phaseout percentage shall be equal to 4.285 percent.

"(B) Limitation based on health insurance costs. The amount of the health insurance credit determined under subparagraph (A) for any taxable year shall not exceed the amounts paid by the taxpayer during the taxable year for insurance coverage—

"(i) which constitutes medical care (within the meaning of section 213(d)(1)(C)), and

"(ii) which includes at least 1 qualifying child.

For purposes of this subparagraph, the rules of section 213(d)(6) shall apply.

"(C) Subsidized expenses. A taxpayer may not take into account under subparagraph (B) any amount to the extent that—

"(i) such amount is paid, reimbursed, or subsidized by the Federal Government, a State or local government, or any agency or instrumentality thereof; and

"(ii) the payment, reimbursement, or subsidy of such amount is not includible in the gross income of the recipient."

Prior to amendment, subpara. (c)(1)(A) read as follows:

"(A) In general. The term 'eligible individual' means any individual who has a qualifying child for the taxable year."

Prior to deletion, paras. (i)(1) and (2) read as follows:

"(1) In general. In the case of any taxable year beginning after the applicable calendar year, each dollar amount referred to in paragraph (2)(B) shall be increased by an amount equal to—

"(A) such dollar amount, multiplied by

"(B) the cost-of-living adjustment determined under section 1(f)(3), for the calendar year in which the taxable year begins, by substituting 'calendar year 1984' for 'calendar year 1989' in subparagraph (B) thereof.

"(2) Definitions, etc. For purposes of paragraph (1)—

"(A) Applicable calendar year. The term 'applicable calendar year' means—

"(i) 1986 in the case of the dollar amounts referred to in clause (i) of subparagraph (B), and

"(ii) 1987 in the case of the dollar amount referred to in clause (ii) of subparagraph (B).

"(B) Dollar amounts. The dollar amounts referred to in this subparagraph are—

"(i) the $5,714 dollar amounts contained in subsection (b)(1), and

"(ii) the $9,000 amount contained in subsection (b)(1)(B)(ii)."

Prior to deletion, clause (c)(3)(D)(ii) read as follows:

"(ii) Insurance policy number. In the case of any taxpayer with respect to which the health insurance credit is allowed under subsection (a)(2), the Secretary may require a taxpayer to include an insurance policy number or other adequate evidence of insurance in addition to any information required to be included in clause (i)."

1,081

Code Sec. 32 — Tax credits

In 1990, P.L. 101-508, Sec. 11101(d)(1)(B), substituted "1989" for "1987" in subpara. (i)(1)(B), effective for tax. yrs. begin. after 12/31/90.
—P.L. 101-508, Sec. 11111(a), amended subsecs. (a), (b) and (c)... Sec. 11111(b), added subsec. (j)... Sec. 11111(e)(1), deleted "or (ii)" after "clause (i)" in clause (i)(2)(A)(i)... Sec. 11111(e)(2), substituted "clause (ii)" for "clause (iii)" in clause (i)(2)(A)(ii)... Sec. 11111(e)(3), amended subpara. (i)(2)(B), effective for tax. yrs. begin. after 12/31/90.
Prior to amendment, subsecs. (a)-(c) read as follows:
"(a) Allowance of credit. In the case of an eligible individual, there is allowed as a credit against the tax imposed by this subtitle for the taxable year an amount equal to 14 percent of so much of the earned income for the taxable year as does not exceed $5,714.
"(b) Limitation. The amount of the credit allowable to a taxpayer under subsection (a) for any taxable year shall not exceed the excess (if any) of—
"(1) the maximum credit allowable under subsection (a) to any taxpayer, over
"(2) 10 percent of so much of the adjusted gross income (or, if greater, the earned income) of the taxpayer for the taxable year as exceeds $9,000.
In the case of any taxable year beginning in 1987, paragraph (2) shall be applied by substituting '$6,500' for '$9,000'.
"(c) Definitions. For purposes of this section—
"(1) Eligible individual.
"(A) In general. The term 'eligible individual' means an individual who, for the taxable year—
"(i) is married (within the meaning of section 7703) and is entitled to a deduction under section 151 for a child (within the meaning of section 151(c)(3)) or would be so entitled but for paragraph (2) or (4) of section 152(e).
"(ii) is a surviving spouse (as determined under section 2(a)), or
"(iii) is a head of a household (as determined under subsection (b) of section 2 without regard to subparagraphs (A)(ii) and (B) of paragraph (1) of such subsection).
"(B) Child must reside with taxpayer in the United States. An individual shall be treated as satisfying clause (i) of subparagraph (A) only if the child has the same principal place of abode as the individual for more than one-half of the taxable year and such abode is in the United States. An individual shall be treated as satisfying clause (ii) or (iii) of subparagraph (A) only if the household in question is in the United States.
"(C) Individual who claims benefits of section 911 not eligible individual. The term 'eligible individual' does not include an individual who, for the taxable year, claims the benefits of section 911 (relating to citizens or residents of the United States living abroad).
"(2) Earned income.
"(A) The term 'earned income' means—
"(i) wages, salaries, tips, and other employee compensation, plus
"(ii) the amount of the taxpayer's net earnings from self-employment for the taxable year (within the meaning of section 1402(a)), but such net earnings shall be determined with regard to the deduction allowed to the taxpayer by section 164(f).
"(B) For purposes of subparagraph (A)—
"(i) the earned income of an individual shall be computed without regard to any community property laws,
"(ii) no amount received as a pension or annuity shall be taken into account, and
"(iii) no amount to which section 871(a) applies (relating to income of nonresident alien individuals not connected with United States business) shall be taken into account."
Prior to amendment, subpara. (i)(2)(B) read as follows:
"(B) Dollar amounts. The dollar amounts referred to in this subparagraph are—
"(i) the $5,714 amount contained in subsection (a),
"(ii) the $6,500 amount contained in the last sentence of subsection (b), and
"(iii) the $9,000 amount contained in subsection (b)(2)."
—P.L. 101-508, Sec. 11116, of this Act, provides the following:
"SEC. 11116. COORDINATION WITH REFUND PROVISION.
"For purposes of section 1324(b)(2) of title 31 of the United States Code, section 32 of the Internal Revenue Code of 1986 (as amended by this Act) shall be considered to be a credit provision of the Internal Revenue Code of 1954 enacted before January 1, 1978."

In 1988, P.L. 100-647, Sec. 1001(c), amended para. (i)(3)... Sec. 1007(g)(12), deleted "for taxpayers other than corporations" after "alternative minimum tax" in subsec. (h), effective for tax. yrs. begin. after 12/31/86.
Prior to amendment, para. (i)(3) read as follows:
"(3) Rounding. If any increase determined under paragraph (1) is not a multiple of $10, such increase shall be rounded to the nearest multiple of $10 (or, if such increase is a multiple of $5, such increase shall be increased to the next higher multiple of $10)."

In 1986, P.L. 99-514, Sec. 104(b)(1)(B), substituted "section 151(c)(3)" for "section 151(e)(3)" in clause (c)(1)(A)(i)... Sec. 111(a)(1), substituted "14 percent" for "11 percent" in subsec. (a)... Sec. 111(a)(2), substituted "$5,714" for "$5,000" in subsec. (a)... Sec. 111(b), amended subsec. (b)... Sec. 111(c), added subsec. (i)... Sec. 111(d)(1), amended subparas. (f)(2)(A) and (B), effective for tax. yrs. begin. after 12/31/86.
Prior to amendment, subsec. (b) read as follows:
"(b) Limitation. The amount of the credit allowable to a taxpayer under subsection (a) for any taxable year shall not exceed the excess (if any) of—
"(1) $550, over
"(2) 12⅔ percent of so much of the adjusted gross income (or, if greater, the earned income) of the taxpayer for the taxable year as exceeds $6,500."
Prior to amendment, subparas. (f)(2)(A) and (f)(2)(B) read as follows:

"(A) for earned income between $0 and $11,000, and
"(B) for adjusted gross income between $6,500 and $11,000."
—P.L. 99-514, Sec. 1272(d)(4), amended subpara. (c)(1)(C), effective for tax. yrs. begin. after 12/31/86, except as provided in Sec. 1277(b) of the Act, which reads as follows:
"(b) Special rule for Guam, American Samoa, and the Northern Mariana Islands. The amendments made by this subtitle shall apply with respect to Guam, American Samoa, or the Northern Mariana Islands (and to residents thereof and corporations created or organized therein) only if (and so long as) an implementing agreement under section 1271 is in effect between the United States and such possession."
Prior to amendment, subpara. (c)(1)(C) read as follows:
"(C) Individual who claims benefits of section 911, or 931 not eligible individual. The term 'eligible individual' does not include an individual who, for the taxable year, claims the benefits of—
"(i) section 911 (relating to citizens or residents of the United States living abroad),
"(ii) section 931 (relating to income from sources within possessions of the United States)."
—P.L. 99-514, Sec. 1301(j)(8), substituted "section 7703" for "section 143" in subsecs. (c) and (d), effective for bonds issued after 8/15/86.

In 1984, P.L. 98-369, Sec. 423(c)(3)(A), added "or would be so entitled but for paragraph (2) or (4) of section 152(e)" before the period at the end of clause (c)(1)(A)(i)... Sec. 423(c)(3)(B), substituted "the child has the same principal place of abode as the individual for more than one-half of the taxable year" for "the child has the same principal place of abode as the individual" in subpara. (c)(1)(B), effective for tax. yrs. begin. after 12/31/84.
—P.L. 98-369, Sec. 471(c)(1), redesignated Code Sec. 43 as Code Sec. 32, effective for tax. yrs. begin. after 12/31/83 and to carrybacks from tax. yrs. begin. after 12/31/83.
—P.L. 98-369, Sec. 1042(a), substituted "11 percent" for "10 percent" in subsec. (a)... Sec. 1042(b), amended para. (b)(2)... Sec. 1042(c), added subsec. (h)... Sec. 1042(d)(1), substituted "$550" for "$500" in para. (b)(1)... Sec. 1042(d)(2), amended subparas. (f)(2)(A) and (B), effective for tax. yrs. begin. after 12/31/84.
Prior to amendment, para. (b)(2) read as follows:
"(2) 12.5 percent of so much of the adjusted gross income (or, if greater, the earned income) of the taxpayer for the taxable year as exceeds $6,000."
Prior to amendment, subparas. (f)(2)(A) and (f)(2)(B) read as follows:
"(A) for earned income between $0 and $10,000, and
"(B) for adjusted gross income between $6,000 and $10,000."

In 1983, P.L. 98-21, Sec. 124(c)(4)(B), added ", but such net earnings shall be determined with regard to the deduction allowed to the taxpayer by section 164(f)" before the period in clause (c)(2)(A)(ii), effective for tax. yrs. begin. after 12/31/89.

In 1981, P.L. 97-34, Sec. 111(b)(2), substituted "relating to citizens or residents of the United States living abroad" for "relating to income earned by individuals in certain camps outside the United States" in clause (c)(1)(C)(i), effective for tax. yrs. begin. after 12/31/81.
—P.L. 97-34, Sec. 112(b)(3), deleted "913," before "or 931" in subpara. (c)(1)(C), deleted clause (c)(1)(C)(ii) and redesignated clause (c)(1)(C)(iii) as clause (c)(1)(C)(ii), effective for tax. yrs. begin. after 12/31/81.
Prior to amendment, clause (c)(1)(C)(ii) read as follows:
"(ii) section 913 (relating to deduction for certain expenses of living abroad), or".

In 1980, P.L. 96-222, Sec. 101(a)(1), amended subpara. (c)(1)(C), effective for tax. yrs. begin. after 13/31/77.
Prior to amendment, subpara. (c)(1)(C) read as follows:
"(C) Individual entitled to exclude income under section 911 not eligible individual. The term 'eligible individual' does not include an individual who, for the taxable year, is entitled to exclude any amount from gross income under section 911 (relating to income earned by employees in certain camps) or section 931 (relating to income from sources within the possessions of the United States)."
—P.L. 96-222, Sec. 101(a)(2)(E), redesignated subsec. (h) as subsec. (g), effective for tax. yrs. begin. after 12/31/78.
—P.L. 96-222, Sec. 108(a)(1)(A), redesignated Sec. 202(f) of P.L. 95-600 as Sec. 202(g) [see below].

In 1978, P.L. 95-615, Sec. 202(f)(5), substituted "relating to income earned by employees in certain camps" for "relating to earned from sources without the United States" in subpara. (c)(1)(B) [sic (C)], effective for tax. yrs. begin. after '77.
—P.L. 95-600, Sec. 103(a), amended Sec. 209(b) of P.L. 94-12 [as amended by Sec. 2(f) of P.L. 94-164, Sec. 401(c)(1)(A) of P.L. 94-455 and Sec. 103(b) of P.L. 95-30] which provided the effective date for changes made by Sec. 204(a) of P.L. 94-12, so that the amendments are effective for tax. yrs. begin. after 12/31/74, rather than effective for tax. yrs. begin. after 12/31/74 and before 1/1/79.
—P.L. 95-600, Sec. 103(b), amended Sec. 401(e) of P.L. 94-455 [as amended by Sec. 103(c) of P.L. 95-30], which provides the effective date for changes made by Sec. 401(c) of P.L. 94-455, so that the changes are effective for tax. yrs. begin. after 12/31/75, rather than effective for tax. yrs. end. after 12/31/75 and ceasing to be applicable for tax. yrs. end. after 12/31/78.
—P.L. 95-600, Sec. 104(a)(1), substituted "subtitle" for "chapter" in subsec. (a)... Sec. 104(a)(2), substituted "$5,000" for "$4,000" in subsec. (a)... Sec. 104(a), amended subsec. (b)... Sec. 104(c), added subsec. (f)... Sec. 104(d), deleted clause (c)(2)(B)(i) and redesignated clauses (c)(2)(B)(ii) through (iv) as clauses (c)(2)(B)(i) through (iii)... Sec. 104(e), amended para. (c)(1), effective for tax. yrs. begin. after 12/31/78.

1,082

Tax credits   Code Sec. 34

Prior to amendment, subsec. (b) read as follows:

"(b) Limitation. The amount of the credit allowable to a taxpayer under subsection (a) for any taxable year shall be reduced (but not below zero) by an amount equal to 10 percent of so much of the adjusted gross income (or, if greater, the earned income) of the taxpayer for the taxable year as exceeds $4,000."

Prior to amendment, para. (c)(1) read as follows:

"(1) Eligible individual. The term 'eligible individual' means an individual who, for the taxable year—

"(A) maintains a household (within the meaning of section 44A(f)(1)) in the United States which is the principal place of abode of that individual and—

"(i) a child of that individual if such child meets the requirements of section 151(e)(1)(B) (relating to additional exemptions for dependents), or

"(ii) a child of that individual who is disabled (within the meaning of section 72(m)(7)) and with respect to whom that individual is entitled to claim a deduction under section 151; and

"(B) is not entitled to exclude any amount from gross income under section 911 (relating to earned income from sources without the United States) or section 931 (relating to income from sources within the possessions of the United States)."

Prior to amendment, clause (c)(2)(B)(i) read as follows:

"(i) except as provided in clause (ii), any amount shall be taken into account only if such amount is includible in the gross income of the taxpayer for the taxable year,"

—P.L. 95-600, Sec. 105(a), added subsec. (h), effective for tax. yrs. begin. after 12/31/78.

In **1977**, P.L. 95-600, Sec. 105(f)(1), added ", and any payment made by an employer under section 3507 of such code (relating to advance payment of earned income credit)" before "shall not be taken into account" in Sec. 2(d) of P.L. 94-164 . . . Sec. 105(f)(2), added "in any year ending before 1990" after "shall not be taken into account" in Sec. 2(d) of P.L. 94-164, see below.

—P.L. 95-30, Sec. 103(b), amended Sec. 209(b) of P.L. 94-12 [as amended by Sec. 2(f) of P.L. 94-164, and Sec. 401(c)(1)(A) of P.L. 94-455] which provides the effective date for changes made by Sec. 204(a) of P.L. 94-12 , so that the amendments are effective for tax. yrs. begin. after 12/31/74 and before 1/1/79, rather than effective for tax. yrs. begin after 12/31/74 and before 1/1/78.

—P.L. 95-30, Sec. 103(c), amended Sec. 401(e) of P.L. 94-455 which provides the effective date for changes made by Sec. 401(c) of P.L. 94-455, so that the amendments are effective for tax. yrs. ending after 12/31/75 and ceasing to be effective for tax. yrs. ending after 12/31/78, rather than effective for tax. yrs. end. after 12/31/75 and ceasing to be effective for tax. yrs. end. after 12/31/77, see below.

In **1976**, P.L. 94-455, Sec. 401(c)(1)(B), amended subsecs. (a) and (b) . . . Sec. 401(c)(2), amended subpara. (c)(1)(A), effective for tax. yrs. end. after 12/31/75 [as amended by Sec. 103(c) of P.L. 95-30 and Sec. 103(b) of P.L. 95-600, see above].

Prior to amendment, subsecs. (a) and (b) read as follows:

"(a) Allowance of credit.

"(1) General rule. In the case of an eligible individual, there shall be allowed as a credit against the tax imposed by this chapter for the taxable year an amount equal to 10 percent of so much of the earned income for the taxable year as does not exceed $4,000.

"(2) Application of 6-month rule. Notwithstanding the provisions of paragraph (1), the term '5 percent' shall be substituted for the term '10 percent' where it appears in that paragraph.

"(b) Limitation.

"(1) General rule. The amount of the credit allowable to a taxpayer under subsection (a) for any taxable year shall be reduced (but not below zero) by an amount equal to 10 percent of so much of the adjusted gross income (or, if greater, the earned income) of the taxpayer for the taxable year as exceeds $4,000.

"(2) Application of 6-month rule. Notwithstanding the provisions of paragraph (1), the term '5 percent' shall be substituted for the term '10 percent' where it appears in that paragraph."

Prior to amendment, subpara. (c)(1)(A) read as follows:

"(A) maintains a household (within the meaning of section 214(b)(3)) in the United States which is the principal place of abode of that individual and of a child of that individual with respect to whom he is entitled to claim a deduction under section 151(e)(1)(B) (relating to additional exemption for dependents), and"

—P.L. 94-455, Sec. 401(c)(1)(A), amended Sec. 209(b) of P.L. 94-12 [as amended by Sec. 2(f) of P.L. 94-164], which provides the effective date for changes made by Sec. 204(a) of P.L. 94-12, so that the amendments are effective for tax. yrs. begin. after 12/31/74 and before 1/1/78, rather than effective for tax. yrs. begin. after 12/31/74 and before 1/1/77.

—P.L. 94-455, Sec. 402(a), amended Sec. 2(d) of 94-164, by deleting "which begins prior to July 1, 1976," after "or any month thereafter", see below.

—P.L. 94-455, Sec. 402(b), amended Sec. 2(g) of P.L. 94-164, which provides the effective date for amendments made by Sec. 2(c) of P.L. 94-164 so that the amendments are effective for tax. yrs. end. after 12/31/75 and before 1/1/77, rather than effective for tax. yrs. end. after 12/31/75 and before 1/1/77, see below.

In **1975**, P.L. 94-164, Sec. 2(c), amended subsecs. (a) and (b), effective for tax. yrs. end. after 12/31/75 and before 1/1/78 [as amended by Sec. 402(b) of P.L. 94-455, see above].

—P.L. 94-164, Sec. 2(d), [as amended by Sec. 402(a) of P.L. 94-455 and Sec. 105(f) of P.L. 95-600, see above] provides:

"(d) Disregard of refund.—Any refund of Federal income taxes made to any individual by reason of section 43 of the Internal Revenue Code of 1954 (relating to earned income credit) shall not be taken into account in any year ending before 1990, and any payment made by an employer under section 3507 of such Code (relating to advance payment of earned income credit) as income or receipts for purposes of determining the eligibility, for the month in which such refund is made or any month thereafter of such individual or any other individual for benefits or assistance, or the amount or extent of benefits or assistance, under any Federal program or under any State or local program financed in whole or in part with Federal funds, but only if such individual (or the family unit of which he is a member) is a recipient of benefits or assistance under such a program for the month before the month in which said refund is made."

Prior to amendment, subsecs. (a) and (b) read as follows:

"(a) Allowance of credit. In the case of an eligible individual, there shall be allowed as a credit against the tax imposed by this chapter for the taxable year an amount equal to 10 percent of so much of the earned income for the taxable year as does not exceed $4,000.

"(b) Limitation. The amount of the credit allowable to a taxpayer under subsection (a) for any taxable year shall be reduced (but not below zero) by an amount equal to 10 percent of so much of the adjusted gross income (or, if greater, the earned income) of the taxpayer for the taxable year as exceeds $4,000."

—P.L. 94-164, Sec. 2(f), amended Sec. 209(b) of P.L. 94-12, which provides the effective date for changes made by Sec. 204(a) of P.L. 94-12, so that the amendments are effective for tax. yrs. begin. after 12/31/74 and before 1/1/77, rather than effective for tax. yrs. begin. after 12/31/74 and before 1/1/76.

—P.L. 94-12, Sec. 204(a), redesignated Code Sec. 43 [as redesignated by Sec. 203(a) of the Act] as Code Sec. 44 and added new Code Sec. 43, effective for tax. yrs. begin. after 12/31/74 [as amended by Sec. 2(f) of P.L. 94-164, Sec. 401(c)(1)(A) of P.L. 94-455, Sec. 103(b) of P.L. 95-30 and Sec. 103(a) of P.L. 95-600, see above].

Sec. 33. Tax withheld at source on nonresident aliens and foreign corporations.

There shall be allowed as a credit against the tax imposed by this subtitle the amount of tax withheld at source under subchapter A of chapter 3 (relating to withholding of tax on nonresident aliens and on foreign corporations).

In **1984**, P.L. 98-369, Sec. 471(c)(1), redesignated Code Sec. 32 as Code Sec. 33, effective for tax. yrs. begin. after 12/31/83 and to carrybacks from tax. yrs. begin. after 12/31/83.

—P.L. 98-369, Sec. 474(j), amended Code Sec. 33 [as redesignated by Sec. 471(c) of this Act, see above], effective as provided in Sec. 475(b) of this Act which reads as follows:

"(b) Tax-Free Covenant Bonds. The amendments made by subsections (j) and (r)(29) of section 474 shall not apply with respect to obligations issued before January 1, 1984."

Prior to amendment, Code Sec. 33 read as follows:

"SEC. 33. TAX WITHHELD AT SOURCE ON NONRESIDENT ALIENS AND FOREIGN CORPORATIONS AND ON TAX-FREE COVENANT BONDS.

"There shall be allowed as credits against the tax imposed by this chapter—

"(1) the amount of tax withheld at source under subchapter A of chapter 3 (relating to withholding of tax on nonresident aliens and on foreign corporations), and

"(2) the amount of tax withheld at source under subchapter B of chapter 3 (relating to interest on tax-free covenant bonds)."

Sec. 34. Certain uses of gasoline and special fuels.
(a) General rule.

There shall be allowed as a credit against the tax imposed by this subtitle for the taxable year an amount equal to the sum of the amounts payable to the taxpayer—

(1) under section 6420 (determined without regard to section 6420(g)),

(2) under section 6421 (determined without regard to section 6421(i)), and

(3) under section 6427 (determined without regard to section 6427(k)).

(b) Exception.

Credit shall not be allowed under subsection (a) for any amount payable under section 6421 or 6427, if a claim for such amount is timely filed and, under section 6421(i) or 6427(k), is payable under such section.

In **2007**, P.L. 110-172, Sec. 11(a)(4)(A), deleted "with respect to gasoline used during the taxable year on a farm for farming purposes" after "section 6420" in para. (a)(1) . . . Sec. 11(a)(4)(B), deleted "with respect to gasoline used during the taxable year (A) otherwise than as a fuel in a highway vehicle or (B) in vehicles while engaged in furnishing certain public passenger land transportation service after 'section 6421' in para. (a)(2) . . . Sec. 11(a)(4)(C), deleted 'with respect to fuels used for nontaxable purposes or resold during the taxable year" after 'section 6427' in para. (a)(3), enacted 12/29/2007.

In **1998**, P.L. 105-206, Sec. 6023(24)(B), substituted 'section 6421(i)' for 'section 6421(j)' in subsec. (b), effective 7/22/98.

1,083

In **1996,** P.L. 104-188, Sec. 1606(b)(1), amended para. (a)(3), effective for vehicles purchased after 8/20/96.
Prior to amendment, para. (a)(3) read as follows:
"(3) under section 6427—
"(A) with respect to fuels used for nontaxable purposes or resold, or
"(B) with respect to any qualified diesel-powered highway vehicle purchased (or deemed purchased under section 6427(g)(6)),
during the taxable year (determined without regard to section 6427(k))."
In **1988,** P.L. 100-647, Sec. 1017(c)(2), substituted "section 6421(j) or 6427(k)" for "section 6421(i) or 6427(j)" in subsec. (b), effective for gasoline removed (as defined in '86 Code Sec. 4082) after 12/31/87.
In **1986,** P.L. 99-514, Sec. 1703(e)(2)(F), substituted "section 6427(k)" for "section 6427(j)" in subpara. (a)(3)(B) [as amended by Sec. 1877(a) of this Act, see below], effective for gasoline removed (as defined in Code Sec. 4082) after 12/31/87.
—P.L. 99-514, Sec. 1877(a), amended para. (a)(3) [before amendment by Sec. 1703(e)(2)(F) of this Act, see above], effective 8/1/84.
Prior to amendment, para. (a)(3) read as follows:
"(3) under section 6427 with respect to fuels used for non-taxable purposes or resold during the taxable year (determined without regard to section 6427(j))."
In **1984,** P.L. 98-369, Sec. 471(c), redesignated Code Sec. 39 as Code Sec. 34, effective for tax. yrs. begin. after 12/31/83 and for carrybacks from tax. yrs. begin. after 12/31/83.
—P.L. 98-369, Sec. 911(d)(2)(A), substituted "6427(j)" for "6427(i)" in para (a)(4) [sic (a)(3)] and subsec. (b) [as redesignated by Sec. 471(c)(1) of the Act, see above], effective 8/1/84.
In **1983,** P.L. 97-424, Sec. 515(b)(6)(A), added "and" at the end of para. (a)(2), deleted para. (a)(3) and redesignated para. (a)(4) as para. (a)(3) . . . Sec. 515(b)(6)(B)(i), substituted "section 6421 or 6427" for "section 6421, 6424, or 6427" . . . Sec. 515(b)(6)(B)(ii), substituted "section 6421(i) or 6424(j)" for "section 6421(i), 6424(f), or 6427(i)" in subsec. (b) . . . Sec. 515(b)(6)(C), substituted "and special fuels" for ", special fuels, and lubricating oil" in the heading of Code Sec. 39, effective for articles sold after 1/6/83.
Prior to deletion, para. (a)(3) read as follows:
"(3) under section 6424 with respect to lubricating oil used during the taxable year for certain nontaxable purposes (determined without regard to section 6424(f)), and"
In **1980,** P.L. 96-223, Sec. 232(d)(4)(A), substituted "section 6427(i)" for "section 6427(h)" in para. (a)(4) and subsec. (b), effective 1/1/79.
In **1978,** P.L. 95-618, Sec. 233(b)(2)(C), substituted "for certain nontaxable purposes" for "otherwise than in a highway motor vehicle" in para. (a)(3), effective on the first day of the first calendar month which begins more than 10 days after 11/9/79.
—P.L. 95-599, Sec. 505(c)(1), substituted "6427(h)" for "6427(g)" in para. (a)(4) and subsec. (b), effective 1/1/79.
In **1976,** P.L. 94-530, Sec. 1(c)(1), substituted "section 6427(g)" for "section 6427(f)" in para. (a)(4) and subsec. (c) [presumably (b)], for tax. yrs. begin. 10/1/76.
—P.L. 94-455, Sec. 1901(a)(3), amended subsec. (b) and deleted subsec. (c), effective for tax. yrs. begin. after 12/31/76.
Prior to amendment, subsec. (b) read as follows:
"(b) Transitional rules. For purposes of paragraphs (1) and (2) of subsection (a), a taxpayer's first taxable year beginning after June 30, 1965, shall include the period after June 30, 1965, and before the beginning of such first taxable year. For purposes of paragraph (3) of subsection (a), a taxpayer's first taxable year beginning after December 31, 1965, shall include the period after December 31, 1965 and before the beginning of such first taxable year."
Prior to deletion, subsec. (c) read as follows:
"(c) Exception. Credit shall not be allowed under subsection (a) for any amount payable under section 6421, 6424, or 6427, if a claim for such amount is timely filed, and under section 6421(i), 6424(g), or 6427(g) is payable, under such section."
—P.L. 94-455, Sec. 1906(b)(8), substituted "section 6420(g)" for "section 6420(h)" in para. (a)(1) . . . Sec. 1906(b)(9), substituted "section 6424(f)" for "6424(g)" in para. (a)(3), effective for tax. yrs. begin. after 12/31/76.
In **1970,** P.L. 91-258, Sec. 207(c)(1), added ", special fuels," after "gasoline" in the heading of Code Sec. 39 . . . Sec. 207(c)(2), deleted "and" at the end of para. (a)(2) and substituted ", and" for the period at the end of para. (a)(3) and added para. (a)(4) . . . Sec. 207(c)(3), substituted "6421, 6424, or 6427" for "6421 or 6424" in subsec. (c) . . . Sec. 207(c)(4), substituted "6421(i), 6424(g), or 6427(f)" for "6421(i) or 6424(g)" in subsec. (c), effective for tax. yrs. end. after 6/30/70.
In **1965,** P.L. 89-44, Sec. 809(c), redesignated Code Sec. 39 as 40 and added new Code Sec. 39, effective for tax. yrs. begin. on or after 7/1/65.

Sec. 35. Health insurance costs of eligible individuals.
(a) In general.

In the case of an individual, there shall be allowed as a credit against the tax imposed by subtitle A an amount equal to 65 percent (80 percent in the case of eligible coverage months beginning before February 13, 2011) of the amount paid by the taxpayer for coverage of the taxpayer and qualifying family members under qualified health insurance for eligible coverage months beginning in the taxable year.

(b) Eligible coverage month.

For purposes of this section—

(1) In general. The term "eligible coverage month" means any month if—

(A) as of the first day of such month, the taxpayer—

(i) is an eligible individual,

(ii) is covered by qualified health insurance, the premium for which is paid by the taxpayer,

(iii) does not have other specified coverage, and

(iv) is not imprisoned under Federal, State, or local authority, and

(B) such month begins more than 90 days after the date of the enactment of the Trade Act of 2002 [90 days after 8/6/2002].

(2) Joint returns. In the case of a joint return, the requirements of paragraph (1)(A) shall be treated as met with respect to any month if at least 1 spouse satisfies such requirements.

(c) Eligible individual.

For purposes of this section—

(1) In general. The term "eligible individual" means—

(A) an eligible TAA recipient,

(B) an eligible alternative TAA recipient, and

(C) an eligible PBGC pension recipient.

(2) Eligible TAA recipient.

(A) In general. Except as provided in subparagraph (B), the term "eligible TAA recipient" means, with respect to any month, any individual who is receiving for any day of such month a trade readjustment allowance under chapter 2 of title II of the Trade Act of 1974 or who would be eligible to receive such allowance if section 231 of such Act were applied without regard to subsection (a)(3)(B) of such section. An individual shall continue to be treated as an eligible TAA recipient during the first month that such individual would otherwise cease to be an eligible TAA recipient by reason of the preceding sentence.

(B) Special rule. In the case of any eligible coverage month beginning after the date of the enactment of this paragraph and before February 13, 2011, the term "eligible TAA recipient" means, with respect to any month, any individual who—

(i) is receiving for any day of such month a trade readjustment allowance under chapter 2 of title II of the Trade Act of 1974,

(ii) would be eligible to receive such allowance except that such individual is in a break in training provided under a training program approved under section 236 of such Act that exceeds the period specified in section 233(e) of such Act, but is within the period for receiving such allowances provided under section 233(a) of such Act, or

(iii) is receiving unemployment compensation (as defined in section 85(b)) for any day of such month and who would be eligible to receive such allowance for such month if section 231 of such Act were applied without regard to subsections (a)(3)(B) and (a)(5) thereof.

An individual shall continue to be treated as an eligible TAA recipient during the first month that such individual would otherwise cease to be an eligible TAA recipient by reason of the preceding sentence.

(3) Eligible alternative TAA recipient. The term "eligible alternative TAA recipient" means, with respect to any month, any individual who—

(A) is a worker described in section 246(a)(3)(B) of the Trade Act of 1974 who is participating in the program established under section 246(a)(1) of such Act, and
(B) is receiving a benefit for such month under section 246(a)(2) of such Act.

An individual shall continue to be treated as an eligible alternative TAA recipient during the first month that such individual would otherwise cease to be an eligible alternative TAA recipient by reason of the preceding sentence.

(4) Eligible PBGC pension recipient. The term "eligible PBGC pension recipient" means, with respect to any month, any individual who—
(A) has attained age 55 as of the first day of such month, and
(B) is receiving a benefit for such month any portion of which is paid by the Pension Benefit Guaranty Corporation under title IV of the Employee Retirement Income Security Act of 1974.

(d) Qualifying family member.
For purposes of this section—
(1) In general. The term "qualifying family member" means—
(A) the taxpayer's spouse, and
(B) any dependent of the taxpayer with respect to whom the taxpayer is entitled to a deduction under section 151(c).

Such term does not include any individual who has other specified coverage.

(2) Special dependency test in case of divorced parents, etc. If section 152(e) applies to any child with respect to any calendar year, in the case of any taxable year beginning in such calendar year, such child shall be treated as described in paragraph (1)(B) with respect to the custodial parent (as defined in section 152(e)(4)(A)) and not with respect to the noncustodial parent.

(e) Qualified health insurance.
For purposes of this section—
(1) In general. The term "qualified health insurance" means any of the following:
(A) Coverage under a COBRA continuation provision (as defined in section 9832(d)(1)).
(B) State-based continuation coverage provided by the State under a State law that requires such coverage.
(C) Coverage offered through a qualified State high risk pool (as defined in section 2744(c)(2) of the Public Health Service Act).
(D) Coverage under a health insurance program offered for State employees.
(E) Coverage under a State-based health insurance program that is comparable to the health insurance program offered for State employees.
(F) Coverage through an arrangement entered into by a State and—
(i) a group health plan (including such a plan which is a multiemployer plan as defined in section 3(37) of the Employee Retirement Income Security Act of 1974),
(ii) an issuer of health insurance coverage,
(iii) an administrator, or
(iv) an employer.
(G) Coverage offered through a State arrangement with a private sector health care coverage purchasing pool.
(H) Coverage under a State-operated health plan that does not receive any Federal financial participation.
(I) Coverage under a group health plan that is available through the employment of the eligible individual's spouse.
(J) In the case of any eligible individual and such individual's qualifying family members, coverage under individual health insurance if the eligible individual was covered under individual health insurance during the entire 30-day period that ends on the date that such individual became separated from the employment which qualified such individual for—
(i) in the case of an eligible TAA recipient, the allowance described in subsection (c)(2),
(ii) in the case of an eligible alternative TAA recipient, the benefit described in subsection (c)(3)(B), or
(iii) in the case of any eligible PBGC pension recipient, the benefit described in subsection (c)(4)(B).

For purposes of this subparagraph, the term "individual health insurance" means any insurance which constitutes medical care offered to individuals other than in connection with a group health plan and does not include Federal or State-based health insurance coverage.
(K) In the case of eligible coverage months beginning before February 13, 2012, coverage under an employee benefit plan funded by a voluntary employees' beneficiary association (as defined in section 501(c)(9)) established pursuant to an order of a bankruptcy court, or by agreement with an authorized representative, as provided in section 1114 of title 11, United States Code.

(2) Requirements for State-based coverage.
(A) In general. The term "qualified health insurance" does not include any coverage described in subparagraphs (B) through (H) of paragraph (1) unless the State involved has elected to have such coverage treated as qualified health insurance under this section and such coverage meets the following requirements:
(i) Guaranteed issue. Each qualifying individual is guaranteed enrollment if the individual pays the premium for enrollment or provides a qualified health insurance costs credit eligibility certificate described in section 7527 and pays the remainder of such premium.
(ii) No imposition of pre-existing condition exclusion. No pre-existing condition limitations are imposed with respect to any qualifying individual.
(iii) Nondiscriminatory premium. The total premium (as determined without regard to any subsidies) with respect to a qualifying individual may not be greater than the total premium (as so determined) for a similarly situated individual who is not a qualifying individual.
(iv) Same benefits. Benefits under the coverage are the same as (or substantially similar to) the benefits provided to similarly situated individuals who are not qualifying individuals.
(B) Qualifying individual. For purposes of this paragraph, the term "qualifying individual" means—
(i) an eligible individual for whom, as of the date on which the individual seeks to enroll in the coverage described in subparagraphs (B) through (H) of paragraph (1), the aggregate of the periods of creditable coverage (as defined in section 9801(c)) is 3 months or longer and who, with respect to any month, meets the requirements of clauses (iii) and (iv) of subsection (b)(1)(A); and
(ii) the qualifying family members of such eligible individual.

(3) Exception. The term "qualified health insurance" shall not include—
   (A) a flexible spending or similar arrangement, and
   (B) any insurance if substantially all of its coverage is of excepted benefits described in section 9832(c).

(f) Other specified coverage.
For purposes of this section, an individual has other specified coverage for any month if, as of the first day of such month—
   (1) Subsidized coverage.
      (A) In general. Such individual is covered under any insurance which constitutes medical care (except insurance substantially all of the coverage of which is of excepted benefits described in section 9832(c)) under any health plan maintained by any employer (or former employer) of the taxpayer or the taxpayer's spouse and at least 50 percent of the cost of such coverage (determined under section 4980B) is paid or incurred by the employer.
      (B) Eligible alternative TAA recipients. In the case of an eligible alternative TAA recipient, such individual is either—
         (i) eligible for coverage under any qualified health insurance (other than insurance described in subparagraph (A), (B), or (F) of subsection (e)(1)) under which at least 50 percent of the cost of coverage (determined under section 4980B(f)(4)) is paid or incurred by an employer (or former employer) of the taxpayer or the taxpayer's spouse, or
         (ii) covered under any such qualified health insurance under which any portion of the cost of coverage (as so determined) is paid or incurred by an employer (or former employer) of the taxpayer or the taxpayer's spouse.
      (C) Treatment of cafeteria plans. For purposes of subparagraphs (A) and (B), the cost of coverage shall be treated as paid or incurred by an employer to the extent the coverage is in lieu of a right to receive cash or other qualified benefits under a cafeteria plan (as defined in section 125(d)).
   (2) Coverage under medicare, medicaid, or SCHIP. Such individual—
      (A) is entitled to benefits under part A of title XVIII of the Social Security Act or is enrolled under part B of such title, or
      (B) is enrolled in the program under title XIX or XXI of such Act (other than under section 1928 of such Act).
   (3) Certain other coverage. Such individual—
      (A) is enrolled in a health benefits plan under chapter 89 of title 5, United States Code, or
      (B) is entitled to receive benefits under chapter 55 of title 10, United States Code.

(g) Special rules.
   (1) Coordination with advance payments of credit. With respect to any taxable year, the amount which would (but for this subsection) be allowed as a credit to the taxpayer under subsection (a) shall be reduced (but not below zero) by the aggregate amount paid on behalf of such taxpayer under section 7527 for months beginning in such taxable year.
   (2) Coordination with other deductions. Amounts taken into account under subsection (a) shall not be taken into account in determining any deduction allowed under section 162(l) or 213.
   (3) Medical and health savings accounts. Amounts distributed from an Archer MSA (as defined in section 220(d)) or from a health savings account (as defined in section 223(d)) shall not be taken into account under subsection (a).
   (4) Denial of credit to dependents. No credit shall be allowed under this section to any individual with respect to whom a deduction under section 151 is allowable to another taxpayer for a taxable year beginning in the calendar year in which such individual's taxable year begins.
   (5) Both spouses eligible individuals. The spouse of the taxpayer shall not be treated as a qualifying family member for purposes of subsection (a), if—
      (A) the taxpayer is married at the close of the taxable year,
      (B) the taxpayer and the taxpayer's spouse are both eligible individuals during the taxable year, and
      (C) the taxpayer files a separate return for the taxable year.
   (6) Marital status; certain married individuals living apart. Rules similar to the rules of paragraphs (3) and (4) of section 21(e) shall apply for purposes of this section.
   (7) Insurance which covers other individuals. For purposes of this section, rules similar to the rules of section 213(d)(6) shall apply with respect to any contract for qualified health insurance under which amounts are payable for coverage of an individual other than the taxpayer and qualifying family members.
   (8) Treatment of payments. For purposes of this section—
      (A) Payments by Secretary. Payments made by the Secretary on behalf of any individual under section 7527 (relating to advance payment of credit for health insurance costs of eligible individuals) shall be treated as having been made by the taxpayer on the first day of the month for which such payment was made.
      (B) Payments by taxpayer. Payments made by the taxpayer for eligible coverage months shall be treated as having been made by the taxpayer on the first day of the month for which such payment was made.

> • *Caution:* Code Sec. 35(g)(9), following, was added by Sec. 1899E(a) of P.L. 111-5, the American Recovery and Reinvestment Act of 2009, 2/17/2009, effective for months begin. after 12/31/2009. For Code Sec. 35(g)(9) as added by Sec. 3001(a)(14)(A) of such Act, see below.

   (9) Continued qualification of family members after certain events. In the case of eligible coverage months beginning before February 13, 2011—
      (A) Medicare eligibility. In the case of any month which would be an eligible coverage month with respect to an eligible individual but for subsection (f)(2)(A), such month shall be treated as an eligible coverage month with respect to such eligible individual solely for purposes of determining the amount of the credit under this section with respect to any qualifying family members of such individual (and any advance payment of such credit under section 7527). This subparagraph shall only apply with respect to the first 24 months after such eligible individual is first entitled to the benefits described in subsection (f)(2)(A).
      (B) Divorce. In the case of the finalization of a divorce between an eligible individual and such individual's spouse, such spouse shall be treated as an eligible individual for purposes of this section and section 7527 for

Tax credits Code Sec. 35

a period of 24 months beginning with the date of such finalization, except that the only qualifying family members who may be taken into account with respect to such spouse are those individuals who were qualifying family members immediately before such finalization.

(C) Death. In the case of the death of an eligible individual—

(i) any spouse of such individual (determined at the time of such death) shall be treated as an eligible individual for purposes of this section and section 7527 for a period of 24 months beginning with the date of such death, except that the only qualifying family members who may be taken into account with respect to such spouse are those individuals who were qualifying family members immediately before such death, and

(ii) any individual who was a qualifying family member of the decedent immediately before such death (or, in the case of an individual to whom paragraph (4) applies, the taxpayer to whom the deduction under section 151 is allowable) shall be treated as an eligible individual for purposes of this section and section 7527 for a period of 24 months beginning with the date of such death, except that in determining the amount of such credit only such qualifying family member may be taken into account.

> • *Caution:* Code Sec. 35(g)(9), following, was added by Sec. 3001(a)(14)(A) of P.L. 111-5, the American Recovery and Reinvestment Act of 2009, 2/17/2009, effective for tax. yrs. end. after 2/17/2009. For Code Sec. 35(g)(9) as added by Sec. 1899E(a) of such Act, see above.

(9) **COBRA premium assistance.** In the case of an assistance eligible individual who receives premium reduction for COBRA continuation coverage under section 3001(a) of title III of division B of the American Recovery and Reinvestment Act of 2009 for any month during the taxable year, such individual shall not be treated as an eligible individual, a certified individual, or a qualifying family member for purposes of this section or section 7527 with respect to such month.

(10) **Regulations.** The Secretary may prescribe such regulations and other guidance as may be necessary or appropriate to carry out this section, section 6050T, and section 7527.

In 2010, P.L. 111-344, Sec. 111(a), substituted "February 13, 2011" for "January 1, 2011" in subsec. (a), effective for coverage months begin. after 12/31/2010.... Sec. 113(a), substituted "February 13, 2011" for "January 1, 2011" in subpara. (c)(2)(B), effective for coverage months begin. after 12/31/2010.... Sec. 115(a), substituted "February 13, 2011" for "January 1, 2011" in para. (g)(9), effective for months begin. after 12/31/2010.... Sec. 117(a), substituted "February 13, 2012" for "January 1, 2011" in subpara. (e)(1)(K), effective for coverage months begin. after 12/31/2010.

—P.L. 111-144, Sec. 3(b)(5)(A), substituted "section 3001(a) of title III of division B of the American Recovery and Reinvestment Act of 2009" for "section 3001(a) of title III of division B of the American Recovery and Reinvestment Act of 2009" in para. (g)(9) (added by Sec. 3001(a)(14)(A) of P.L. 111-5), effective for tax. yrs. end. after 2/17/2009.

In 2009, P.L. 111-5, Sec. 1899A(a)(1), added "(80 percent in the case of eligible coverage months beginning before January 1, 2011)" after "65 percent" in subsec. (a), effective for coverage months beginning on or after the first day of the first month begin. 60 days after 2/17/2009.

—P.L. 111-5, Sec. 1899C(a), amended para. (c)(2), effective for coverage months begin. after 2/17/2009

Prior to amendment, para. (c)(2) read as follows:

"(2) Eligible TAA recipient. The term 'eligible TAA recipient' means, with respect to any month, any individual who is receiving for any day of such month a trade readjustment allowance under chapter 2 of title II of the Trade Act of 1974 or who would be eligible to receive such allowance if section 231 of such Act were applied without regard to subsection (a)(3)(B) of such section. An individual shall continue to be treated as an eligible TAA recipient during the first month that such individual would otherwise cease to be an eligible TAA recipient by reason of the preceding sentence."

—P.L. 111-5, Sec. 1899E(a), redesignated para. (g)(9) as para. (g)(10), and added para. (g)(9), effective for months begin. after 12/31/2009.

—P.L. 111-5, Sec. 1899G(a), added subpara. (e)(1)(K), effective for months begin. after 2/17/2009.

—P.L. 111-5, Sec. 1899I, of this Act, provides:

"SEC. 1899I. SURVEY AND REPORT ON ENHANCED HEALTH COVERAGE TAX CREDIT PROGRAM.

"(a) Survey.

" (1) In general. The Secretary of the Treasury shall conduct a biennial survey of eligible individuals (as defined in section 35(c) of the Internal Revenue Code of 1986) relating to the health coverage tax credit under section 35 of the Internal Revenue Code of 1986 (hereinafter in this section referred to as the 'health coverage tax credit').

"(2) Information obtained. The survey conducted under subsection (a) shall obtain the following information:

" HCTC participants. In the case of eligible individuals receiving the health coverage tax credit (including individuals participating in the health coverage tax credit program under section 7527 of such Code, hereinafter in this section referred to as the 'HCTC program')—

"(i) demographic information of such individuals, including income and education levels,

"(ii) satisfaction of such individuals with the enrollment process in the HCTC program,

"(iii) satisfaction of such individuals with available health coverage options under the credit, including level of premiums, benefits, deductibles, cost-sharing requirements, and the adequacy of provider networks, and

"(iv) any other information that the Secretary determines is appropriate.

"(B) Non-HCTC participants. In the case of eligible individuals not receiving the health coverage tax credit—

"(i) demographic information of each individual, including income and education levels,

"(ii) whether the individual was aware of the health coverage tax credit or the HCTC program,

"(iii) the reasons the individual has not enrolled in the HCTC program, including whether such reasons include the burden of the process of enrollment and the affordability of coverage,

"(iv) whether the individual has health insurance coverage, and, if so, the source of such coverage, and

"(v) any other information that the Secretary determines is appropriate.

"(3) Report. Not later than December 31 of each year in which a survey is conducted under paragraph (1) (beginning in 2010), the Secretary of the Treasury shall report to the Committee on Finance and the Committee on Health, Education, Labor, and Pensions of the Senate and the Committee on Ways and Means, the Committee on Education and Labor, and the Committee on Energy and Commerce of the House of Representatives the findings of the most recent survey conducted under paragraph (1).

"(b) Report. Not later than October 1 of each year (beginning in 2010), the Secretary of the Treasury (after consultation with the Secretary of Health and Human Services, and, in the case of the information required under paragraph (7), the Secretary of Labor) shall report to the Committee on Finance and the Committee on Health, Education, Labor, and Pensions of the Senate and the Committee on Ways and Means, the Committee on Education and Labor, and the Committee on Energy and Commerce of the House of Representatives the following information with respect to the most recent taxable year ending before such date:

"(1) In each State and nationally—

"(A) the total number of eligible individuals (as defined in section 35(c) of the Internal Revenue Code of 1986) and the number of eligible individuals receiving the health coverage tax credit,

"(B) the total number of such eligible individuals who receive an advance payment of the health coverage tax credit through the HCTC program, (C) the average length of the time period of the participation of eligible individuals in the HCTC program, and

"(D) the total number of participating eligible individuals in the HCTC program who are enrolled in each category of coverage as described in section 35(e)(1) of such Code, with respect to each category of eligible individuals described in section 35(c)(1) of such Code.

"(2) In each State and nationally, an analysis of—

"(A) the range of monthly health insurance premiums, for self-only coverage and for family coverage, for individuals receiving the health coverage tax credit, and

"(B) the average and median monthly health insurance premiums, for self-only coverage and for family coverage, for individuals receiving the health coverage tax credit, with respect to each category of coverage as described in section 35(e)(1) of such Code.

"(3) In each State and nationally, an analysis of the following information with respect to the health insurance coverage of individuals receiving the health coverage tax credit who are enrolled in coverage described in subparagraphs (B) through (H) of section 35(e)(1) of such Code:

"(A) Deductible amounts.

"(B) Other out-of-pocket cost-sharing amounts.

1,087

"(C) A description of any annual or lifetime limits on coverage or any other significant limits on coverage services, or benefits.

"The information required under this paragraph shall be reported with respect to each category of coverage described in such subparagraphs.

"(4) In each State and nationally, the gender and average age of eligible individuals (as defined in section 35(c) of such Code) who receive the health coverage tax credit, in each category of coverage described in section 35(e)(1) of such Code, with respect to each category of eligible individuals described in such section.

"(5) The steps taken by the Secretary of the Treasury to increase the participation rates in the HCTC program among eligible individuals, including outreach and enrollment activities.

"(6) The cost of administering the HCTC program by function, including the cost of subcontractors, and recommendations on ways to reduce administrative costs, including recommended statutory changes.

"(7) The number of States applying for and receiving national emergency grants under section 173(f) of the Workforce Investment Act of 1998 (29 U.S.C. 2918(f)), the activities funded by such grants on a State-by-State basis, and the time necessary for application approval of such grants."

—P.L. 111-5, Sec. 1899L, of this Act, provides:

"SEC. 1899L. GAO STUDY AND REPORT.

"(a) Study. The Comptroller General of the United States shall conduct a study regarding the health insurance tax credit allowed under section 35 of the Internal Revenue Code of 1986.

"(b) Report. Not later than March 1, 2010, the Comptroller General shall submit a report to Congress regarding the results of the study conducted under subsection (a). Such report shall include an analysis of—

"(1) the administrative costs —

"(A) of the Federal Government with respect to such credit and the advance payment of such credit under section 7527 of such Code, and

"(B) of providers of qualified health insurance with respect to providing such insurance to eligible individuals and their qualifying family members,

"(2) the health status and relative risk status of eligible individuals and qualifying family members covered under such insurance,

"(3) participation in such credit and the advance payment of such credit by eligible individuals and their qualifying family members, including the reasons why such individuals did or did not participate and the effect of the amendments made by this part on such participation, and

"(4) the extent to which eligible individuals and their qualifying family members —

"(A) obtained health insurance other than qualifying health insurance, or

"(B) went without health insurance coverage.

"(c) Access to records. For purposes of conducting the study required under this section, the Comptroller General and any of his duly authorized representatives shall have access to, and the right to examine and copy, all documents, records, and other recorded information—

"(1) within the possession or control of providers of qualified health insurance, and

"(2) determined by the Comptroller General (or any such representative) to be relevant to the study.

"The Comptroller General shall not disclose the identity of any provider of qualified health insurance or any eligible individual in making any information obtained under this section available to the public.

"(d) Definitions. Any term which is defined in section 35 of the Internal Revenue Code of 1986 shall have the same meaning when used in this section."

—P.L. 111-5, Sec. 3001(a)(14)(A), added para. (g)(9), effective for tax. yrs. end. after 2/17/2009. [Editor's note: Sec. 3001(a)(14)(A) of this Act also redesignated para. (g)(9) as para. (g)(10), however, this amendment was previously made by Sec. 1899E(a) of this Act, see above.]

In **2007**, P.L. 110-172, Sec. 11(a)(5)(A), deleted "paragraph (2) or (4) before "of section 152(e)" in para. (d)(2) . . . Sec. 11(a)(5)(B), substituted "(as defined in section 152(e)(4)(A))" for "(within the meaning of section 152(e)(1))" in para. (d)(2), enacted 12/29/2007.

In **2004**, P.L. 108-311, Sec. 401(a)(2), amended para. (g)(3), effective for tax. yrs. begin. after 12/31/2003 as if included in Sec. 1201 of the Medicare Prescription Drug, Improvement, and Modernization Act of 2003, P.L. 108-173.

Prior to amendment, para. (g)(3) read as follows:

"(3) MSA distributions. Amounts distributed from an Archer MSA (as defined in section 220(d)) shall not be taken into account under subsection (a)."

In **2002**, P.L. 107-210, Sec. 201(a), added Code Sec. 35, effective for tax. yrs. begin. after 12/31/2001.

Sec. 36. First-time homebuyer credit.
(a) Allowance of credit.

In the case of an individual who is a first-time homebuyer of a principal residence in the United States during a taxable year, there shall be allowed as a credit against the tax imposed by this subtitle for such taxable year an amount equal to 10 percent of the purchase price of the residence.

(b) Limitations.
(1) Dollar limitation.

(A) In general. Except as otherwise provided in this paragraph, the credit allowed under subsection (a) shall not exceed $8,000.

(B) Married individuals filing separately. In the case of a married individual filing a separate return, subparagraph (A) shall be applied by substituting "$4,000" for "$8,000".

(C) Other individuals. If two or more individuals who are not married purchase a principal residence, the amount of the credit allowed under subsection (a) shall be allocated among such individuals in such manner as the Secretary may prescribe, except that the total amount of the credits allowed to all such individuals shall not exceed $8,000.

(D) Special rule for long-time residents of same principal residence. In the case of a taxpayer to whom a credit under subsection (a) is allowed by reason of subsection (c)(6), subparagraphs (A), (B), and (C) shall be applied by substituting "$6,500" for "$8,000" and "$3,250" for "$4,000".

(2) Limitation based on modified adjusted gross income.

(A) In general. The amount allowable as a credit under subsection (a) (determined without regard to this paragraph) for the taxable year shall be reduced (but not below zero) by the amount which bears the same ratio to the amount which is so allowable as—

(i) the excess (if any) of—

(I) the taxpayer's modified adjusted gross income for such taxable year, over

(II) $125,000 ($225,000 in the case of a joint return), bears to

(ii) $20,000.

(B) Modified adjusted gross income. For purposes of subparagraph (A), the term "modified adjusted gross income" means the adjusted gross income of the taxpayer for the taxable year increased by any amount excluded from gross income under section 911, 931, or 933.

(3) Limitation based on purchase price.
No credit shall be allowed under subsection (a) for the purchase of any residence if the purchase price of such residence exceeds $800,000.

(4) Age limitation.
No credit shall be allowed under subsection (a) with respect to the purchase of any residence unless the taxpayer has attained age 18 as of the date of such purchase. In the case of any taxpayer who is married (within the meaning of section 7703), the taxpayer shall be treated as meeting the age requirement of the preceding sentence if the taxpayer or the taxpayer's spouse meets such age requirement.

(c) Definitions.
For purposes of this section—

(1) First-time homebuyer.
The term "first-time homebuyer" means any individual if such individual (and if married, such individual's spouse) had no present ownership interest in a principal residence during the 3-year period ending on the date of the purchase of the principal residence to which this section applies.

(2) Principal residence.
The term "principal residence" has the same meaning as when used in section 121.

(3) Purchase.

(A) In general. The term "purchase" means any acquisition, but only if—

(i) the property is not acquired from a person related to the person acquiring such property (or, if married, such individual's spouse), and

(ii) the basis of the property in the hands of the person acquiring such property is not determined—

(I) in whole or in part by reference to the adjusted basis of such property in the hands of the person from whom acquired, or

(II) under section 1014(a) (relating to property acquired from a decedent).

(B) Construction. A residence which is constructed by the taxpayer shall be treated as purchased by the taxpayer on the date the taxpayer first occupies such residence.

(4) Purchase price. The term "purchase price" means the adjusted basis of the principal residence on the date such residence is purchased.

(5) Related persons. A person shall be treated as related to another person if the relationship between such persons would result in the disallowance of losses under section 267 or 707(b) (but, in applying section 267(b) and (c) for purposes of this section, paragraph (4) of section 267(c) shall be treated as providing that the family of an individual shall include only his spouse, ancestors, and lineal descendants).

(6) Exception for long-time residents of same principal residence. In the case of an individual (and, if married, such individual's spouse) who has owned and used the same residence as such individual's principal residence for any 5-consecutive-year period during the 8-year period ending on the date of the purchase of a subsequent principal residence, such individual shall be treated as a first-time homebuyer for purposes of this section with respect to the purchase of such subsequent residence.

(d) Exceptions.

No credit under subsection (a) shall be allowed to any taxpayer for any taxable year with respect to the purchase of a residence if—

(1) the taxpayer is a nonresident alien,

(2) the taxpayer disposes of such residence (or such residence ceases to be the principal residence of the taxpayer (and, if married, the taxpayer's spouse)) before the close of such taxable year,

(3) a deduction under section 151 with respect to such taxpayer is allowable to another taxpayer for such taxable year, or

(4) the taxpayer fails to attach to the return of tax for such taxable year a properly executed copy of the settlement statement used to complete such purchase.

(e) Reporting.

If the Secretary requires information reporting under section 6045 by a person described in subsection (e)(2) thereof to verify the eligibility of taxpayers for the credit allowable by this section, the exception provided by section 6045(e) shall not apply.

(f) Recapture of credit.

(1) In general. Except as otherwise provided in this subsection, if a credit under subsection (a) is allowed to a taxpayer, the tax imposed by this chapter shall be increased by 6 ⅔ percent of the amount of such credit for each taxable year in the recapture period.

(2) Acceleration of recapture. If a taxpayer disposes of the principal residence with respect to which a credit was allowed under subsection (a)(or such residence ceases to be the principal residence of the taxpayer (and, if married, the taxpayer's spouse)) before the end of the recapture period—

(A) the tax imposed by this chapter for the taxable year of such disposition or cessation shall be increased by the excess of the amount of the credit allowed over the amounts of tax imposed by paragraph (1) for preceding taxable years, and

(B) paragraph (1) shall not apply with respect to such credit for such taxable year or any subsequent taxable year.

(3) Limitation based on gain. In the case of the sale of the principal residence to a person who is not related to the taxpayer, the increase in tax determined under paragraph (2) shall not exceed the amount of gain (if any) on such sale. Solely for purposes of the preceding sentence, the adjusted basis of such residence shall be reduced by the amount of the credit allowed under subsection (a) to the extent not previously recaptured under paragraph (1).

(4) Exceptions.

(A) Death of taxpayer. Paragraphs (1) and (2) shall not apply to any taxable year ending after the date of the taxpayer's death.

(B) Involuntary conversion. Paragraph (2) shall not apply in the case of a residence which is compulsorily or involuntarily converted (within the meaning of section 1033(a)) if the taxpayer acquires a new principal residence during the 2-year period beginning on the date of the disposition or cessation referred to in paragraph (2). Paragraph (2)shall apply to such new principal residence during the recapture period in the same manner as if such new principal residence were the converted residence.

(C) Transfers between spouses or incident to divorce. In the case of a transfer of a residence to which section 1041(a) applies—

(i) paragraph (2) shall not apply to such transfer, and

(ii) in the case of taxable years ending after such transfer, paragraphs (1) and (2) shall apply to the transferee in the same manner as if such transferee were the transferor (and shall not apply to the transferor).

(D) Waiver of recapture for purchases in 2009 and 2010. In the case of any credit allowed with respect to the purchase of a principal residence after December 31, 2008—

(i) paragraph (1) shall not apply, and

(ii) paragraph (2) shall apply only if the disposition or cessation described in paragraph (2) with respect to such residence occurs during the 36-month period beginning on the date of the purchase of such residence by the taxpayer.

(E) Special rule for members of the armed forces, etc.

(i) In general. In the case of the disposition of a principal residence by an individual (or a cessation referred to in paragraph (2)) after December 31, 2008, in connection with Government orders received by such individual, or such individual's spouse, for qualified official extended duty service—

(I) paragraph (2) and subsection (d)(2) shall not apply to such disposition (or cessation), and

(II) if such residence was acquired before January 1, 2009, paragraph (1) shall not apply to the taxable year in which such disposition (or cessation) occurs or any subsequent taxable year.

(ii) Qualified official extended duty service. For purposes of this section, the term "qualified official extended duty service" means service on qualified official extended duty as—

(I) a member of the uniformed services,

(II) a member of the Foreign Service of the United States, or

(III) an employee of the intelligence community.

(iii) Definitions. Any term used in this subparagraph which is also used in paragraph (9) of section 121(d) shall have the same meaning as when used in such paragraph.

(5) Joint returns. In the case of a credit allowed under subsection (a) with respect to a joint return, half of such credit shall be treated as having been allowed to each individual filing such return for purposes of this subsection.

(6) Return requirement. If the tax imposed by this chapter for the taxable year is increased under this subsection, the taxpayer shall, notwithstanding section 6012, be required to file a return with respect to the taxes imposed under this subtitle.

(7) Recapture period. For purposes of this subsection, the term "recapture period" means the 15 taxable years beginning with the second taxable year following the taxable year in which the purchase of the principal residence for which a credit is allowed under subsection (a) was made.

(g) Election to treat purchase in prior year.

In the case of a purchase of a principal residence after December 31, 2008, a taxpayer may elect to treat such purchase as made on December 31 of the calendar year preceding such purchase for purposes of this section (other than subsections (b)(4), (c), (f)(4)(D), and (h)).

(h) Application of section.

(1) In general. This section shall only apply to a principal residence purchased by the taxpayer on or after April 9, 2008, and before May 1, 2010.

(2) Exception in case of binding contract. In the case of any taxpayer who enters into a written binding contract before May 1, 2010, to close on the purchase of a principal residence before July 1, 2010, and who purchases such residence before October 1, 2010, paragraph (1) shall be applied by substituting "October 1, 2010" for "May 1, 2010".

(3) Special rule for individuals on qualified official extended duty outside the United States. In the case of any individual who serves on qualified official extended duty service (as defined in section 121(d)(9)(C)(i)) outside the United States for at least 90 days during the period beginning after December 31, 2008, and ending before May 1, 2010, and, if married, such individual's spouse—

(A) paragraphs (1) and (2) shall each be applied by substituting "May 1, 2011" for "May 1, 2010", and

(B) paragraph (2) shall be applied by substituting "July 1, 2011" for "July 1, 2010", and for "October 1, 2010".

In 2010, P.L. 111-198, Sec. 2(a), substituted "and who purchases such residence before October 1, 2010, paragraph (1) shall be applied by substituting 'October 1, 2010'" for "paragraph (1) shall be applied by substituting 'July 1, 2010'" in para. (h)(2)... Sec. 2(b), added ", and for 'October 1, 2010'" after "for 'July 1, 2010'" in subpara. (h)(3)(B), effective for residences purchased after 6/30/2010.

In 2009, P.L. 111-92, Sec. 11(a)(1)(A), substituted "May 1, 2010" for "December 1, 2009" in subsec. (h)... Sec. 11(a)(1)(B), substituted "section. (1) In general. This section" for "section. This section" in subsec. (h)... Sec. 11(a)(1)(C), added para. (h)(2)... Sec. 11(a)(2)(A), deleted ", and before December 1, 2009" after "December 31, 2008" in subpara. (f)(4)(D)... Sec. 11(a)(2)(B), added "and 2010" after "2009" in the heading of subpara. (f)(4)(D)... Sec. 11(a)(3), amended subsec. (g), effective for residences purchased after 11/30/2009.

Prior to amendment, subsec. (g) read as follows:

"(g) Election to treat purchase in prior year. In the case of a purchase of a principal residence after December 31, 2008, and before December 1, 2009, a taxpayer may elect to treat such purchase as made on December 31, 2008, for purposes of this section (other than subsections (c) and (f)(4)(D))."

—P.L. 111-92, Sec. 11(b), added para. (c)(6)... Sec. 11(c)(1), added subpara. (b)(1)(D)... Sec. 11(c)(2), substituted "$125,000 ($225,000" for "$75,000 ($150,000" in subclause (b)(2)(A)(i)(II)... Sec. 11(d), added para. (b)(3), effective for residences purchased after 11/6/2009.

—P.L. 111-92, Sec. 11(e), added subpara. (f)(4)(E), effective for dispositions and cessations after 12/31/2008.

—P.L. 111-92, Sec. 11(f)(1), added para. (h)(3), effective for residences purchased after 11/30/2009.

—P.L. 111-92, Sec. 11(g), deleted "or" at the end of para. (d)(1), substituted ", or" for the period at the end of para. (d)(2), and added para. (d)(3), effective for residences purchased after 11/6/2009.

—P.L. 111-92, Sec. 12(a)(1), added para. (b)(4)... Sec. 12(a)(2), added "(b)(4)" before "(c)" in subsec. (g), effective for purchases after 11/6/2009.

—P.L. 111-92, Sec. 12(b), deleted "or" at the end of para. (d)(2), substituted ", or" for the period at the end of para. (d)(3) and added para. (d)(4), effective for returns for tax. yrs. end. after 11/6/2009.

—P.L. 111-92, Sec. 12(c), added "(or, if married, such individuals spouse)" after "person acquiring such property" in clause (c)(3)(A)(i), effective for purchases after 11/6/2009.

—P.L. 111-5, Sec. 1006(a)(1), substituted "December 1, 2009" for "July 1, 2009" in subsec. (h)... Sec. 1006(a)(2), substituted "December 1, 2009" for "July 1, 2009" in subsec. (g)... Sec. 1006(b)(1), substituted "$8,000" for "$7,500" each place it appears in subsec. (b)... Sec. 1006(b)(2), substituted "$4,000" for "$3,500" in subpara. (b)(1)(B)... Sec. 1006(c)(1), added subpara. (f)(4)(D)... Sec. 1006(c)(2), substituted "subsections (c) and (f)(4)(D)" for "subsection (c)" in subsec. (g)... Sec. 1006(d)(2), repealed para. (d)(1)... Sec. 1006(e), repealed para. (d)(2) and redesignated paras. (d)(3) and (4) as paras. (d)(1) and (2), effective for residences purchased after 12/31/2008.

Prior to repeal, paras. (d)(1) and (2) read as follows:

"(1) a credit under section 1400C (relating to first-time homebuyer in the District of Columbia) is allowable to the taxpayer (or the taxpayer's spouse) for such taxable year or any prior taxable year,

"(2) the residence is financed by the proceeds of a qualified mortgage issue the interest on which is exempt from tax under section 103"

In 2008, P.L. 110-289, Sec. 3011(a), redesignated Code Sec. 36 as Code Sec. 37 and added new Code Sec. 36, effective for residences purchased on or after 4/9/2008, in tax. yrs. end. on or after such date.

In 2002, P.L. 107-210, Sec. 201(a), redesignated Code Sec. 35 as Code Sec. 36, effective for tax. yrs. begin. after 12/31/2001.

In 1984, P.L. 98-369, Sec. 471(c)(1), redesignated Code Sec. 45 as Code Sec. 35, effective for tax. yrs. begin. after 12/31/83, and to carrybacks from tax. yrs. begin. after 12/31/83.

In 1975, P.L. 94-12, Sec. 203(a), redesignated Code Sec. 42 as Code Sec. 43, effective for tax. yrs. end. after 12/31/74 and before 12/31/75.

—P.L. 94-12, Sec. 204(a), redesignated Code Sec. 43 [as redesignated by Sec 203(a), see above] as Code Sec. 44, effective for tax. yrs. begin. after 12/31/74 and before 1/1/76.

—P.L. 94-12, Sec. 208(a), redesignated Code Sec. 44 [as redesignated by Sec 204(a), see above] as Code Sec. 45, effective 3/29/75.

In 1971, P.L. 92-178, Sec. 601(a), redesignated Code Sec. 40 as Code Sec. 42, effective for tax. yrs. begin. after 12/31/71.

In 1965, P.L. 89-44, Sec. 809(c), redesignated Code Sec. 39 as Code Sec. 40, effective for tax. yrs. begin. on or after 7/1/65.

In 1962, P.L. 87-834, Sec. 2(a), redesignated Code Sec. 38 as Code Sec. 39, effective for tax. yrs. end. after 12/31/61.

Sec. 36. Repealed.

In 1978, P.L. 95-615, Sec. 4(a), extended the effective date of the amendments made by Sec. 1011(c) of P.L. 94-455 [as amended by Sec. 95-30, Sec. 302 see below] to tax. yrs. begin. after 12/31/77.

In 1977, P.L. 95-30, Sec. 101(d)(3), repealed Code Sec. 36, effective for tax. yrs. begin. after 12/31/76.

Prior to amendment, Code Sec. 36 read as follows:

"SEC. 36. CREDITS NOT ALLOWED TO INDIVIDUALS TAKING STANDARD DEDUCTION.

"If an individual elects under section 144 to take the standard deduction, the credits provided by section 32 shall not be allowed."

—P.L. 95-30, Sec. 302, extended the effective date of the amendments made by Sec. 1011 of P.L. 94-455[see below] to tax. yrs. begin. after 12/31/76.

In 1976, P.L. 94-455, Sec. 501(b)(2)(A), deleted "paying optional tax or" in the heading of Code Sec. 36... Sec. 501(b)(2)(B), deleted "elects to pay the optional tax imposed by section 3, or if he" in Code Sec. 36, effective for tax. yrs. begin. after 12/31/75.

—P.L. 94-455, Sec. 1011(c), substituted "sections 32 and" for "sections 32, 33, and" in Code Sec. 36, effective [as amended by Sec. 302 of P.L. 95-30 and Sec. 4(a) of P.L. 95-615, see above] for tax. yrs. begin. after 12/31/77.

—P.L. 94-455, Sec. 1901(b)(1)(A), substituted "section 32" for "sections 32 and 35" in Code Sec. 36, effective for tax. yrs. begin. after 12/31/76.

Sec. 36A. Making work pay credit.
(a) Allowance of credit.

In the case of an eligible individual, there shall be allowed as a credit against the tax imposed by this subtitle for the taxable year an amount equal to the lesser of—

(1) 6.2 percent of earned income of the taxpayer, or

(2) $400 ($800 in the case of a joint return).

Tax credits
Code Sec. 36A

(b) Limitation based on modified adjusted gross income.
(1) In general. The amount allowable as a credit under subsection (a) (determined without regard to this paragraph and subsection (c)) for the taxable year shall be reduced (but not below zero) by 2 percent of so much of the taxpayer's modified adjusted gross income as exceeds $75,000 ($150,000 in the case of a joint return).
(2) Modified adjusted gross income. For purposes of subparagraph (A), the term "modified adjusted gross income" means the adjusted gross income of the taxpayer for the taxable year increased by any amount excluded from gross income under section 911, 931, or 933.
(c) Reduction for certain other payments.
The credit allowed under subsection (a) for any taxable year shall be reduced by the amount of any payments received by the taxpayer during such taxable year under section 2201, or any credit allowed to the taxpayer under section 2202, of the American Recovery and Reinvestment Tax Act of 2009.
(d) Definitions and special rules.
For purposes of this section—
(1) Eligible individual.
(A) In general. The term "eligible individual" means any individual other than—
(i) any nonresident alien individual,
(ii) any individual with respect to whom a deduction under section 151 is allowable to another taxpayer for a taxable year beginning in the calendar year in which the individual's taxable year begins, and
(iii) an estate or trust.
(B) Identification number requirement. Such term shall not include any individual who does not include on the return of tax for the taxable year—
(i) such individual's social security account number, and
(ii) in the case of a joint return, the social security account number of one of the taxpayers on such return.
For purposes of the preceding sentence, the social security account number shall not include a TIN issued by the Internal Revenue Service.
(2) Earned income. The term "earned income" has the meaning given such term by section 32(c)(2), except that such term shall not include net earnings from self-employment which are not taken into account in computing taxable income. For purposes of the preceding sentence, any amount excluded from gross income by reason of section 112 shall be treated as earned income which is taken into account in computing taxable income for the taxable year.
(e) Termination.
This section shall not apply to taxable years beginning after December 31, 2010.

In 2009, P.L. 111-5, Sec. 1001(a), added Code Sec. 36A, effective for tax. yrs. begin. after 12/31/2008.
—P.L. 111-5, Sec. 1001(b), and (c) provides:
"(b) Treatment of possessions.
"(1) Payments to possessions.
"(A) Mirror code possession. The Secretary of the Treasury shall pay to each possession of the United States with a mirror code tax system amounts equal to the loss to that possession by reason of the amendments made by this section with respect to taxable years beginning in 2009 and 2010. Such amounts shall be determined by the Secretary of the Treasury based on information provided by the government of the respective possession.
"(B) Other possessions. The Secretary of the Treasury shall pay to each possession of the United States which does not have a mirror code tax system amounts estimated by the Secretary of the Treasury as being equal to the aggregate benefits that would have been provided to residents of such possession by reason of the amendments made by this section for taxable years beginning in 2009 and 2010 if a mirror code tax system had been in effect in such possession. The preceding sentence shall not apply with respect to any possession of the United States unless such possession has a plan, which has been approved by the Secretary of the Treasury, under which such possession will promptly distribute such payments to the residents of such possession.
"(2) Coordination with credit allowed against United States income taxes. No credit shall be allowed against United States income taxes for any taxable year under section 36A of the Internal Revenue Code of 1986 (as added by this section) to any person—
"(A) to whom a credit is allowed against taxes imposed by the possession by reason of the amendments made by this section for such taxable year, or
"(B) who is eligible for a payment under a plan described in paragraph (1)(B) with respect to such taxable year.
"(3) Definitions and special rules.
"(A) Possession of the United States. For purposes of this subsection, the term 'possession of the United States' includes the Commonwealth of Puerto Rico and the Commonwealth of the Northern Mariana Islands.
"(B) Mirror code tax system. For purposes of this subsection, the term 'mirror code tax system' means, with respect to any possession of the United States, the income tax system of such possession if the income tax liability of the residents of such possession under such system is determined by reference to the income tax laws of the United States as if such possession were the United States.
"(C) Treatment of payments. For purposes of section 1324(b)(2) of title 31, United States Code, the payments under this subsection shall be treated in the same manner as a refund due from the credit allowed under section 36A of the Internal Revenue Code of 1986 (as added by this section).
"(c) Refunds disregarded in the administration of federal programs and federally assisted programs. Any credit or refund allowed or made to any individual by reason of section 36A of the Internal Revenue Code of 1986 (as added by this section) or by reason of subsection (b) of this section shall not be taken into account as income and shall not be taken into account as resources for the month of receipt and the following 2 months, for purposes of determining the eligibility of such individual or any other individual for benefits or assistance, or the amount or extent of benefits or assistance, under any Federal program or under any State or local program financed in whole or in part with Federal funds."
—P.L. 111-5, Sec. 2201, reads as follows:
Sec. 2201. Economic recovery payment to recipients of Social Security, Supplemental Security Income, Railroad Retirement Benefits, and Veterans Disability Compensation or Pension Benefits.
(a) Authority to make payments.
"(1) Eligibility.
"(A) In general. Subject to paragraph (5)(B), the Secretary of the Treasury shall disburse a $250 payment to each individual who, for any month during the 3-month period ending with the month which ends prior to the month that includes the date of the enactment of this Act, is entitled to a benefit payment described in clause (i), (ii), or (iii) of subparagraph (B) or is eligible for a SSI cash benefit described in subparagraph (C).
"(B) Benefit payment described. For purposes of subparagraph (A):
"(i) Title II benefit. A benefit payment described in this clause is a monthly insurance benefit payable (without regard to sections 202(j)(1) and 223(b) of the Social Security Act (42 U.S.C. 402(j)(1), 423(b)) under -
"(I) section 202(a) of such Act (42 U.S.C. 402(a));
"(II) section 202(b) of such Act (42 U.S.C. 402(b));
"(III) section 202(c) of such Act (42 U.S.C. 402(c));
"(IV) section 202(d)(1)(B)(ii) of such Act (42 U.S.C. 402(d)(1)(B)(ii));
"(V) section 202(e) of such Act (42 U.S.C. 402(e));
"(VI) section 202(f) of such Act (42 U.S.C. 402(f));
"(VII) section 202(g) of such Act (42 U.S.C. 402(g));
"(VIII) section 202(h) of such Act (42 U.S.C. 402(h));
"(IX) section 223(a) of such Act (42 U.S.C. 423(a));
"(X) section 227 of such Act (42 U.S.C. 427); or
"(XI) section 228 of such Act (42 U.S.C. 428).
"(ii) Railroad retirement benefit. A benefit payment described in this clause is a monthly annuity or pension payment payable (without regard to section 5(a)(ii) of the Railroad Retirement Act of 1974 (45 U.S.C. 231d(a)(ii))) under —
"(I) section 2(a)(1) of such Act (45 U.S.C. 231a(a)(1));
"(II) section 2(c) of such Act (45 U.S.C. 231a(c));
"(III) section 2(d)(1)(i) of such Act (45 U.S.C. 231a(d)(1)(i));
"(IV) section 2(d)(1)(ii) of such Act (45 U.S.C. 231a(d)(1)(ii));
"(V) section 2(d)(1)(iii)(C) of such Act to an adult disabled child (45 U.S.C. 231a(d)(1)(iii)(C));
"(VI) section 2(d)(1)(iv) of such Act (45 U.S.C. 231a(d)(1)(iv));
"(VII) section 2(d)(1)(v) of such Act (45 U.S.C. 231a(d)(1)(v)); or
"(VIII) section 7(b)(2) of such Act (45 U.S.C. 231f(b)(2)) with respect to any of the benefit payments described in clause (i) of this subparagraph.
"(iii) Veterans benefit. A benefit payment described in this clause is a compensation or pension payment payable under —
"(I) section 1110, 1117, 1121, 1131, 1141, or 1151 of title 38, United States Code;
"(II) section 1310, 1312, 1313, 1315, 1316, or 1318 of title 38, United States Code;
"(III) section 1513, 1521, 1533, 1536, 1537, 1541, 1542, or 1562 of title 38, United States Code; or
"(IV) section 1805, 1815, or 1821 of title 38, United States Code, to a veteran, surviving spouse, child, or parent as described in paragraph (2), (3), (4)(A)(ii), or (5) of section 101, title 38, United States Code, who received that benefit during any month within the 3 month period ending with the month which ends prior to the month that includes the date of the enactment of this Act.

"(A) SSI cash benefit described. A SSI cash benefit described in this subparagraph is a cash benefit payable under section 1611 (other than under subsection (e)(1)(B) of such section) or 1619(a) of the Social Security Act (42 U.S.C. 1382, 1382h).

"(2) Requirement. A payment shall be made under paragraph (1) only to individuals who reside in 1 of the 50 States, the District of Columbia, Puerto Rico, Guam, the United States Virgin Islands, American Samoa, or the Northern Mariana Islands. For purposes of the preceding sentence, the determination of the individual's residence shall be based on the current address of record under a program specified in paragraph (1).

"(3) No double payments. An individual shall be paid only 1 payment under this section, regardless of whether the individual is entitled to, or eligible for, more than 1 benefit or cash payment described in paragraph (1).

"(4) Limitation. A payment under this section shall not be made —

"(A) in the case of an individual entitled to a benefit specified in paragraph (1)(B)(i) or paragraph (1)(B)(ii)(VIII) if, for the most recent month of such individual's entitlement in the 3-month period described in paragraph (1), such individual's benefit under such paragraph was not payable by reason of subsection (x) or (y) of section 202 the Social Security Act (42 U.S.C. 402) or section 1129A of such Act (42 U.S.C. 1320a-8a);

"(B) in the case of an individual entitled to a benefit specified in paragraph (1)(B)(iii) if, for the most recent month of such individual's entitlement in the 3 month period described in paragraph (1), such individual's benefit under such paragraph was not payable, or was reduced, by reason of section 1505, 5313, or 5313B of title 38, United States Code;

"(C) in the case of an individual entitled to a benefit specified in paragraph (1)(C) if, for such most recent month, such individual's benefit under such paragraph was not payable by reason of subsection (e)(1)(A) or (e)(4) of section 1611 (42 U.S.C. 1382) or section 1129A of such Act (42 U.S.C. 1320a-8a); or

"(D) in the case of any individual whose date of death occurs before the date on which the individual is certified under subsection (b) to receive a payment under this section.

"(5) Timing and manner of payments.

"(A) In general. The Secretary of the Treasury shall commence disbursing payments under this section at the earliest practicable date but in no event later than 120 days after the date of enactment of this Act. The Secretary of the Treasury may disburse any payment electronically to an individual in such manner as if such payment was a benefit payment or cash benefit to such individual under the applicable program described in subparagraph (B) or (C) of paragraph (1).

"(B) Deadline. No payments shall be disbursed under this section after December 31, 2010, regardless of any determinations of entitlement to, or eligibility for, such payments made after such date.

"(b) Identification of recipients. The Commissioner of Social Security, the Railroad Retirement Board, and the Secretary of Veterans Affairs shall certify the individuals entitled to receive payments under this section and provide the Secretary of the Treasury with the information needed to disburse such payments. A certification of an individual shall be unaffected by any subsequent determination or redetermination of the individual's entitlement to, or eligibility for, a benefit specified in subparagraph (B) or (C) of subsection (a)(1).

"(c) Treatment of payments.

"(1) Payment to be disregarded for purposes of all federal and federally assisted programs. A payment under subsection (a) shall not be regarded as income and shall not be regarded as a resource for the month of receipt and the following 9 months, for purposes of determining the eligibility of the recipient (or the recipient's spouse or family) for benefits or assistance, or the amount or extent of benefits or assistance, under any Federal program or under any State or local program financed in whole or in part with Federal funds.

"(2) Payment not considered income for purposes of taxation. A payment under subsection (a) shall not be considered as gross income for purposes of the Internal Revenue Code of 1986.

"(3) Payments protected from assignment. The provisions of sections 207 and 1631(d)(1) of the Social Security Act (42 U.S.C. 407, 1383(d)(1)), section 14(a) of the Railroad Retirement Act of 1974 (45 U.S.C. 231m(a)), and section 5301 of title 38, United States Code, shall apply to any payment made under subsection (a) as if such payment was a benefit payment or cash benefit to such individual under the applicable program described in subparagraph (B) or (C) of subsection (a)(1).

"(4) Payments subject to offset. Notwithstanding paragraph (3), for purposes of section 3716 of title 31, United States Code, any payment made under this section shall not be considered a benefit payment or cash benefit made under the applicable program described in subparagraph (B) or (C) of subsection (a)(1) and all amounts paid shall be subject to offset to collect delinquent debts.

"(d) Payment to representative payees and fiduciaries.

"(1) In general. In any case in which an individual who is entitled to a payment under subsection (a) and whose benefit payment or cash benefit described in paragraph (1) of that subsection is paid to a representative payee or fiduciary, the payment under subsection (a) shall be made to the individual's representative payee or fiduciary and the entire payment shall be used only for the benefit of the individual who is entitled to the payment.

"(2) Applicability.

"(A) Payment on the basis of a title II or SSI benefit. Section 1129(a)(3) of the Social Security Act (42 U.S.C. 1320a-8(a)(3)) shall apply to any payment made on the basis of an entitlement to a benefit specified in paragraph (1)(B)(i) or (1)(C) of subsection (a) in the same manner as such section applies to a payment under title II or XVI of such Act.

"(B) Payment on the basis of a railroad retirement benefit. Section 13 of the Railroad Retirement Act (45 U.S.C. 2311) shall apply to any payment made on the basis of an entitlement to a benefit specified in paragraph (1)(B)(ii) of subsection (a) in the same manner as such section applies to a payment under such Act.

"(C) Payment on the basis of a veterans benefit. Sections 5502, 6106, and 6108 of title 38, United States Code, shall apply to any payment made on the basis of an entitlement to a benefit specified in paragraph (1)(B)(iii) of subsection (a) in the same manner as those sections apply to a payment under that title.

"(e) Appropriation. Out of any sums in the Treasury of the United States not otherwise appropriated, the following sums are appropriated for the period of fiscal years 2009 through 2011, to remain available until expended, to carry out this section:

"(1) For the Secretary of the Treasury, $131,000,000 for administrative costs incurred in carrying out this section, section 2202, section 36A of the Internal Revenue Code of 1986 (as added by this Act), and other provisions of this Act or the amendments made by this Act relating to the Internal Revenue Code of 1986.

"(2) For the Commissioner of Social Security-

"(A) such sums as may be necessary for payments to individuals certified by the Commissioner of Social Security as entitled to receive a payment under this section; and

"(B) $90,000,000 for the Social Security Administration's Limitation on Administrative Expenses for costs incurred in carrying out this section.

"(3) For the Railroad Retirement Board-

"(A) such sums as may be necessary for payments to individuals certified by the Railroad Retirement Board as entitled to receive a payment under this section; and

"(B) $1,400,000 to the Railroad Retirement Board's Limitation on Administration for administrative costs incurred in carrying out this section.

"(4) (A) For the Secretary of Veterans Affairs-

"(i) such sums as may be necessary for the Compensation and Pensions account, for payments to individuals certified by the Secretary of Veterans Affairs as entitled to receive a payment under this section; and

"(ii) $100,000 for the Information Systems Technology account and $7,100,000 for the General Operating Expenses account for administrative costs incurred in carrying out this section.

"(B) The Department of Veterans Affairs Compensation and Pensions account shall hereinafter be available for payments authorized under subsection (a)(1)(A) to individuals entitled to a benefit payment described in subsection (a)(1)(B)(iii). "

... Sec. 2202, reads as follows:

"Sec. 2202. Special credit for certain government retirees.

"(a) In general. In the case of an eligible individual, there shall be allowed as a credit against the tax imposed by subtitle A of the Internal Revenue Code of 1986 for the first taxable year beginning in 2009 an amount equal $250 ($500 in the case of a joint return where both spouses are eligible individuals).

"(b) Eligible individual. For purposes of this section —

"(1) In general. The term 'eligible individual' means any individual -

"(A) who receives during the first taxable year beginning in 2009 any amount as a pension or annuity for service performed in the employ of the United States or any State, or any instrumentality thereof, which is not considered employment for purposes of chapter 21 of the Internal Revenue Code of 1986, and

"(B) who does not receive a payment under section 2201 during such taxable year.

"(2) Identification number requirement. Such term shall not include any individual who does not include on the return of tax for the taxable year-

"(A) such individual's social security account number, and

"(B) in the case of a joint return, the social security account number of one of the taxpayers on such return.

"For purposes of the preceding sentence, the social security account number shall not include a TIN (as defined in section 7701(a)(41) of the Internal Revenue Code of 1986) issued by the Internal Revenue Service. Any omission of a correct social security account number required under this subparagraph shall be treated as a mathematical or clerical error for purposes of applying section 6213(g)(2) of such Code to such omission.

"(c) Treatment of credit.

"(1) Refundable credit.

"(A) In general. The credit allowed by subsection (a) shall be treated as allowed by subpart C of part IV of subchapter A of chapter 1 of the Internal Revenue Code of 1986.

"(B) Appropriations. For purposes of section 1324(b)(2) of title 31, United States Code, the credit allowed by subsection (a) shall be treated in the same manner a refund from the credit allowed under section 36A of the Internal Revenue Code of 1986 (as added by this Act).

"(2) Deficiency rules. For purposes of section 6211(b)(4)(A) of the Internal Revenue Code of 1986, the credit allowable by subsection (a) shall be treated in the same manner as the credit allowable under section 36A of the Internal Revenue Code of 1986 (as added by this Act).

"(d) Refunds disregarded in the administration of federal programs and federally assisted programs. Any credit or refund allowed or made to any individual by reason of this section shall not be taken into account as income and shall not be taken into account as resources for the month of receipt and the following 2 months, for purposes of determining the eligibility of such individual or any other individual for benefits or assistance, or the amount or extent of benefits or assistance, under any Federal program or under any State or local program financed in whole or in part with Federal funds. "

Tax credits

> *Caution:* Code Sec. 36B, following, is effective for tax. yrs. end. after 12/31/2013.

Sec. 36B. Refundable credit for coverage under a qualified health plan.

(a) In general.

In the case of an applicable taxpayer, there shall be allowed as a credit against the tax imposed by this subtitle for any taxable year an amount equal to the premium assistance credit amount of the taxpayer for the taxable year.

(b) Premium assistance credit amount.

For purposes of this section—

(1) In general. The term "premium assistance credit amount" means, with respect to any taxable year, the sum of the premium assistance amounts determined under paragraph (2) with respect to all coverage months of the taxpayer occurring during the taxable year.

(2) Premium assistance amount. The premium assistance amount determined under this subsection with respect to any coverage month is the amount equal to the lesser of—

(A) the monthly premiums for such month for 1 or more qualified health plans offered in the individual market within a State which cover the taxpayer, the taxpayer's spouse, or any dependent (as defined in section 152) of the taxpayer and which were enrolled in through an Exchange established by the State under 1311 of the Patient Protection and Affordable Care Act, or

(B) the excess (if any) of—

(i) the adjusted monthly premium for such month for the applicable second lowest cost silver plan with respect to the taxpayer, over

(ii) an amount equal to 1/12 of the product of the applicable percentage and the taxpayer's household income for the taxable year.

(3) Other terms and rules relating to premium assistance amounts. For purposes of paragraph (2)—

(A) Applicable percentage.

(i) In general. Except as provided in clause (ii), the applicable percentage for any taxable year shall be the percentage such that the applicable percentage for any taxpayer whose household income is within an income tier specified in the following table shall increase, on a sliding scale in a linear manner, from the initial premium percentage to the final premium percentage specified in such table for such income tier:

In the case of household income (expressed as a percent of poverty line) within the following income tier:	The initial premium percentage is-	The final premium percentage is-
Up to 133%	2.0%	2.0%
133% up to 150%	3.0%	4.0%
150% up to 200%	4.0%	6.3%
200% up to 250%	6.3%	8.05%
250% up to 300%	8.05%	9.5%
300% up to 400%	9.5%	9.5%

(ii) Indexing.

(I) In general. Subject to subclause (II), in the case of taxable years beginning in any calendar year after 2014, the initial and final applicable percentages under clause (i) (as in effect for the preceding calendar year after application of this clause) shall be adjusted to reflect the excess of the rate of premium growth for the preceding calendar year over the rate of income growth for the preceding calendar year.

(II) Additional adjustment. Except as provided in subclause (III), in the case of any calendar year after 2018, the percentages described in subclause (I) shall, in addition to the adjustment under subclause (I), be adjusted to reflect the excess (if any) of the rate of premium growth estimated under subclause (I) for the preceding calendar year over the rate of growth in the consumer price index for the preceding calendar year.

(III) Failsafe. Subclause (II) shall apply for any calendar year only if the aggregate amount of premium tax credits under this section and cost-sharing reductions under section 1402 of the Patient Protection and Affordable Care Act for the preceding calendar year exceeds an amount equal to 0.504 percent of the gross domestic product for the preceding calendar year.

(iii) [Repealed.]

(B) Applicable second lowest cost silver plan. The applicable second lowest cost silver plan with respect to any applicable taxpayer is the second lowest cost silver plan of the individual market in the rating area in which the taxpayer resides which—

(i) is offered through the same Exchange through which the qualified health plans taken into account under paragraph (2)(A) were offered, and

(ii) provides—

(I) self-only coverage in the case of an applicable taxpayer—

(aa) whose tax for the taxable year is determined under section 1(c) (relating to unmarried individuals other than surviving spouses and heads of households) and who is not allowed a deduction under section 151 for the taxable year with respect to a dependent, or

(bb) who is not described in item (aa) but who purchases only self-only coverage, and

(II) family coverage in the case of any other applicable taxpayer.

If a taxpayer files a joint return and no credit is allowed under this section with respect to 1 of the spouses by reason of subsection (e), the taxpayer shall be treated as described in clause (ii)(I) unless a deduction is allowed under section 151 for the taxable year with respect to a dependent other than either spouse and subsection (e) does not apply to the dependent.

(C) Adjusted monthly premium. The adjusted monthly premium for an applicable second lowest cost silver plan is the monthly premium which would have been charged (for the rating area with respect to which the premiums under paragraph (2)(A) were determined) for the plan if each individual covered under a qualified health plan taken into account under paragraph (2)(A) were covered by such silver plan and the premium was adjusted only for the age of each such individual in the manner allowed under section 2701 of the Public Health Service Act. In the case of a State participating in the wellness discount demonstration project under section 2705(d) of the Public Health Service Act, the adjusted monthly premium shall be determined without regard to any premium discount or rebate under such project.

(D) Additional benefits. If—

(i) a qualified health plan under section 1302(b)(5) of the Patient Protection and Affordable Care Act offers benefits in addition to the essential health benefits required to be provided by the plan, or

(ii) a State requires a qualified health plan under section 1311(d)(3)(B) of such Act to cover benefits in addition to the essential health benefits required to be provided by the plan,

the portion of the premium for the plan properly allocable (under rules prescribed by the Secretary of Health and Human Services) to such additional benefits shall not be taken into account in determining either the monthly premium or the adjusted monthly premium under paragraph (2).

(E) Special rule for pediatric dental coverage. For purposes of determining the amount of any monthly premium, if an individual enrolls in both a qualified health plan and a plan described in section 1311(d)(2)(B)(ii)(I) of the Patient Protection and Affordable Care Act for any plan year, the portion of the premium for the plan described in such section that (under regulations prescribed by the Secretary) is properly allocable to pediatric dental benefits which are included in the essential health benefits required to be provided by a qualified health plan under section 1302(b)(1)(J) of such Act shall be treated as a premium payable for a qualified health plan.

(c) **Definition and rules relating to applicable taxpayers, coverage months, and qualified health plan.**

For purposes of this section—

(1) **Applicable taxpayer.**

(A) In general. The term "applicable taxpayer" means, with respect to any taxable year, a taxpayer whose household income for the taxable year equals or exceeds 100 percent but does not exceed 400 percent of an amount equal to the poverty line for a family of the size involved.

(B) Special rule for certain individuals lawfully present in the United States.

If—

(i) a taxpayer has a household income which is not greater than 100 percent of an amount equal to the poverty line for a family of the size involved, and

(ii) the taxpayer is an alien lawfully present in the United States, but is not eligible for the medicaid program under title XIX of the Social Security Act by reason of such alien status,

the taxpayer shall, for purposes of the credit under this section, be treated as an applicable taxpayer with a household income which is equal to 100 percent of the poverty line for a family of the size involved.

(C) Married couples must file joint return. If the taxpayer is married (within the meaning of section 7703) at the close of the taxable year, the taxpayer shall be treated as an applicable taxpayer only if the taxpayer and the taxpayer's spouse file a joint return for the taxable year.

(D) Denial of credit to dependents. No credit shall be allowed under this section to any individual with respect to whom a deduction under section 151 is allowable to another taxpayer for a taxable year beginning in the calendar year in which such individual's taxable year begins.

(2) **Coverage month.** For purposes of this subsection—

(A) In general. The term "coverage month" means, with respect to an applicable taxpayer, any month if—

(i) as of the first day of such month the taxpayer, the taxpayer's spouse, or any dependent of the taxpayer is covered by a qualified health plan described in subsection (b)(2)(A) that was enrolled in through an Exchange established by the State under section 1311 of the Patient Protection and Affordable Care Act, and

(ii) the premium for coverage under such plan for such month is paid by the taxpayer (or through advance payment of the credit under subsection (a) under section 1412 of the Patient Protection and Affordable Care Act).

(B) Exception for minimum essential coverage.

(i) In general. The term "coverage month" shall not include any month with respect to an individual if for such month the individual is eligible for minimum essential coverage other than eligibility for coverage described in section 5000A(f)(1)(C) (relating to coverage in the individual market).

(ii) Minimum essential coverage. The term "minimum essential coverage" has the meaning given such term by section 5000A(f).

(C) Special rule for employer-sponsored minimum essential coverage. For purposes of subparagraph (B)—

(i) Coverage must be affordable. Except as provided in clause (iii), an employee shall not be treated as eligible for minimum essential coverage if such coverage—

(I) consists of an eligible employer-sponsored plan (as defined in section 5000A(f)(2)), and

(II) the employee's required contribution (within the meaning of section 5000A(e)(1)(B)) with respect to the plan exceeds 9.5 percent of the applicable taxpayer's household income.

This clause shall also apply to an individual who is eligible to enroll in the plan by reason of a relationship the individual bears to the employee.

(ii) Coverage must provide minimum value. Except as provided in clause (iii), an employee shall not be treated as eligible for minimum essential coverage if such coverage consists of an eligible employer-sponsored plan (as defined in section 5000A(f)(2)) and the plan's share of the total allowed costs of benefits provided under the plan is less than 60 percent of such costs.

(iii) Employee or family must not be covered under employer plan. Clauses (i) and (ii) shall not apply if the employee (or any individual described in the last sentence of clause (i)) is covered under the eligible employer-sponsored plan or the grandfathered health plan.

(iv) Indexing. In the case of plan years beginning in any calendar year after 2014, the Secretary shall adjust the 9.5 percent under clause (i)(II) in the same manner as the percentages are adjusted under subsection (b)(3)(A)(ii).

(D) Repealed.

(3) Definitions and other rules.

(A) Qualified health plan. The term "qualified health plan" has the meaning given such term by section 1301(a) of the Patient Protection and Affordable Care Act, except that such term shall not include a qualified health plan which is a catastrophic plan described in section 1302(e) of such Act.

(B) Grandfathered health plan. The term "grandfathered health plan" has the meaning given such term by section 1251 of the Patient Protection and Affordable Care Act.

(d) Terms relating to income and families.

For purposes of this section—

(1) Family size. The family size involved with respect to any taxpayer shall be equal to the number of individuals for whom the taxpayer is allowed a deduction under section 151 (relating to allowance of deduction for personal exemptions) for the taxable year.

(2) Household income.

(A) Household income. The term "household income" means, with respect to any taxpayer, an amount equal to the sum of—

(i) the modified adjusted gross income of the taxpayer, plus

(ii) the aggregate modified adjusted gross incomes of all other individuals who—

(I) were taken into account in determining the taxpayer's family size under paragraph (1), and

(II) were required to file a return of tax imposed by section 1 for the taxable year.

(B) Modified adjusted gross income. The term "modified adjusted gross income" means adjusted gross income increased by—

(i) any amount excluded from gross income under section 911, and

(ii) any amount of interest received or accrued by the taxpayer during the taxable year which is exempt from tax.

(3) Poverty line.

(A) In general. The term "poverty line" has the meaning given that term in section 2110(c)(5) of the Social Security Act (42 U.S.C. 1397jj(c)(5)).

(B) Poverty line used. In the case of any qualified health plan offered through an Exchange for coverage during a taxable year beginning in a calendar year, the poverty line used shall be the most recently published poverty line as of the 1st day of the regular enrollment period for coverage during such calendar year.

(e) Rules for individuals not lawfully present.

(1) In general. If 1 or more individuals for whom a taxpayer is allowed a deduction under section 151 (relating to allowance of deduction for personal exemptions) for the taxable year (including the taxpayer or his spouse) are individuals who are not lawfully present—

(A) the aggregate amount of premiums otherwise taken into account under clauses (i) and (ii) of subsection (b)(2)(A) shall be reduced by the portion (if any) of such premiums which is attributable to such individuals, and

(B) for purposes of applying this section, the determination as to what percentage a taxpayer's household income bears to the poverty level for a family of the size involved shall be made under one of the following methods:

(i) A method under which—

(I) the taxpayer's family size is determined by not taking such individuals into account, and

(II) the taxpayer's household income is equal to the product of the taxpayer's household income (determined without regard to this subsection) and a fraction—

(aa) the numerator of which is the poverty line for the taxpayer's family size determined after application of subclause (I), and

(bb) the denominator of which is the poverty line for the taxpayer's family size determined without regard to subclause (I).

(ii) A comparable method reaching the same result as the method under clause (i).

(2) Lawfully present. For purposes of this section, an individual shall be treated as lawfully present only if the individual is, and is reasonably expected to be for the entire period of enrollment for which the credit under this section is being claimed, a citizen or national of the United States or an alien lawfully present in the United States.

(3) Secretarial authority. The Secretary of Health and Human Services, in consultation with the Secretary, shall prescribe rules setting forth the methods by which calculations of family size and household income are made for purposes of this subsection. Such rules shall be designed to ensure that the least burden is placed on individuals enrolling in qualified health plans through an Exchange and taxpayers eligible for the credit allowable under this section.

(f) Reconciliation of credit and advance credit.

(1) In general. The amount of the credit allowed under this section for any taxable year shall be reduced (but not below zero) by the amount of any advance payment of such credit under section 1412 of the Patient Protection and Affordable Care Act.

(2) Excess advance payments.

(A) In general. If the advance payments to a taxpayer under section 1412 of the Patient Protection and Affordable Care Act for a taxable year exceed the credit allowed by this section (determined without regard to paragraph (1)), the tax imposed by this chapter for the taxable year shall be increased by the amount of such excess.

(B) Limitation on increase.

(i) In general. In the case of a taxpayer whose household income is less than 400 percent of the poverty line for the size of the family involved for the taxable year, the amount of the increase under subparagraph (A) shall in no event exceed the applicable dollar amount determined in accordance with the following table (one-half of such amount in the case of a taxpayer whose tax is determined under section 1(c) for the taxable year):

If the household income (expressed as a percent of poverty line) is:	The applicable dollar amount is:
Less than 200%	$600
At least 200% but less than 300%	$1,500
At least 300% but less than 400%	$2,500

(ii) Indexing of amount. In the case of any calendar year beginning after 2014, each of the dollar amounts in the table contained under clause (i) shall be increased by an amount equal to—

(I) such dollar amount, multiplied by

(II) the cost-of-living adjustment determined under section 1(f)(3) for the calendar year, determined by substituting "calendar year 2013" for "calendar year 1992" in subparagraph (B) thereof.

If the amount of any increase under clause (i) is not a multiple of $50, such increase shall be rounded to the next lowest multiple of $50.

(3) Information requirement. Each Exchange (or any person carrying out 1 or more responsibilities of an Exchange under section 1311(f)(3) or 1321(c) of the Patient Protection and Affordable Care Act) shall provide the following information to the Secretary and to the taxpayer with respect to any health plan provided through the Exchange:

(A) The level of coverage described in section 1302(d) of the Patient Protection and Affordable Care Act and the period such coverage was in effect.

(B) The total premium for the coverage without regard to the credit under this section or cost-sharing reductions under section 1402 of such Act.

(C) The aggregate amount of any advance payment of such credit or reductions under section 1412 of such Act.

(D) The name, address, and TIN of the primary insured and the name and TIN of each other individual obtaining coverage under the policy.

(E) Any information provided to the Exchange, including any change of circumstances, necessary to determine eligibility for, and the amount of, such credit.

(F) Information necessary to determine whether a taxpayer has received excess advance payments.

(g) Regulations.

The Secretary shall prescribe such regulations as may be necessary to carry out the provisions of this section, including regulations which provide for—

(1) the coordination of the credit allowed under this section with the program for advance payment of the credit under section 1412 of the Patient Protection and Affordable Care Act, and

(2) the application of subsection (f) where the filing status of the taxpayer for a taxable year is different from such status used for determining the advance payment of the credit.

In **2011,** P.L. 112-10, Sec. 1858(b)(1), deleted subpara. (c)(2)(D), effective for tax. yrs. begin. after 12/31/2013, as if included in the provisions of Sec. 10108(h) of P.L. 111-148 [see below].

Prior to deletion, subpara. (c)(2)(D), read as follows:

"(D) Exception for individual receiving free choice vouchers. The term 'coverage month' shall not include any month in which such individual has a free choice voucher provided under section 10108 of the Patient Protection and Affordable Care Act."

—P.L. 112-9, Sec. 4(a), amended clause (f)(2)(B)(i), effective for tax. yrs. ending after 12/31/2013.

Prior to amendment clause (f)(2)(B)(i), read as follows:

"(i) In general.

"In the case of a taxpayer whose household income is less than 500 percent of the poverty line for the size of the family involved for the taxable year, the amount of the increase under subparagraph (A) shall in no event exceed the applicable dollar amount determined in accordance with the following table (one-half of such amount in the case of a taxpayer whose tax is determined under section 1(c) for the taxable year):

In **2010,** P.L. 111-309, Sec. 208(a), amended subpara. (f)(2)(B) heading and clause (f)(2)(B)(i).

Prior to amendment, the heading of subpara. (f)(2)(B) and clause (f)(2)(B)(i), read as follows:

"(B) Limitation on increase where income less than 400 percent of poverty line.

"(i) In general. In the case of an applicable taxpayer whose household income is less than 400 percent of the poverty line for the size of the family involved for the taxable year, the amount of the increase under subparagraph (A) shall in no event exceed $400 ($250 in the case of a taxpayer whose tax is determined under section 1(c) for the taxable year)."

—P.L. 111-309, Sec. 208(b), added "in the table contained" after "each of the dollar amounts" in clause (f)(2)(B)(ii), effective for tax. yrs. begin. after 12/31/2013.

—P.L. 111-152, Sec. 1001(a)(1)(A), substituted "for any taxable year shall be the percentage such that the applicable percentage for any taxpayer whose household income is within an income tier specified in the following table shall increase, on a sliding scale in a linear manner, from the initial premium percentage to the final premium percentage specified in such table for such income tier:

for "with respect to any taxpayer for any taxable year is equal to 2.8 percent, increased by the number of percentage points (not greater than 7) which bears the same ratio to 7 percentage points as—(I) the taxpayer's household income for the taxable year in excess of 100 percent of the poverty line for a family of the size involved, bears to (II) an amount equal to 200 percent of the poverty line for a family of the size involved" in clause (b)(3)(A)(i)

—P.L. 111-152, Sec. 1001(a)(1)(B), deleted clauses (b)(3)(A)(ii)-(iii) and added clause (b)(3)(A)(ii)

Prior to deletion, clauses (b)(3)(A)(ii)-(iii) [see asterisk below, for prior amendment by Sec. 10105(a) of P.L. 111-148 to clause (b)(3)(A)(iii)] read as follows:

"(ii) Special rule for taxpayers under 133 percent of poverty line. If a taxpayer's household income for the taxable year *equals or exceeds 100 percent, but not more than 133 percent, of the poverty line for a family of the size involved, the taxpayer's applicable percentage shall be 2 percent.

"(iii) Indexing. In the case of taxable years beginning in any calendar year after 2014, the Secretary shall adjust the initial and final applicable percentages under clause (i), and the 2 percent under clause (ii), for the calendar year to reflect the excess of the rate of premium growth between the preceding calendar year and 2013 over the rate of income growth for such period."

—P.L. 111-152, Sec. 1001(a)(2)(A), substituted "9.5 percent" for "9.8 percent" in sbcl. (c)(2)(C)(i)(II) and clause (c)(2)(C)(iv)... Sec. 1001(a)(2)(B), substituted "(b)(3)(A)(ii)" for "(b)(3)(A)(iii)" in clause (c)(2)(C)(iv) [as amended by Sec. 10105(c) of P.L. 111-148, see below]

—P.L. 111-152, Sec. 1001(b)(1)(A), substituted "94" for "90" in Sec. 1402(c)(1)(B)(i)(I) of P.L. 111-148 [see below]... Sec. 1001(b)(1)(B)(i), substituted "87" for "80" in Sec. 1402(c)(1)(B)(i)(II) of P.L. 111-148 [see below]... Sec. 1001(b)(1)(B)(ii), deleted "and" at the end of Sec. 1402(c)(1)(B)(i)(II) of P.L. 111-148 [see below]... Sec. 1001(b)(1)(C), deleted sbcl. (III) of 1402(c)(1)(B)(i) and added sbcls. (III)-(IV) to Sec. 1402(c)(1)(B)(i) of P.L. 111-148 [see below]... Sec. 1001(b)(2)(A)(i), substituted "94" for "90" in Sec. 1402(c)(2)(A) of P.L. 111-148 [see below]... Sec. 1001(b)(2)(A)(ii), deleted "and" at the end of Sec. 1402(c)(2)(A) of P.L. 111-148 [see below]... Sec. 1001(b)(2)(B)(i), substituted "87" for "80" in Sec. 1402(c)(2)(B) of P.L. 111-148 [see below]... Sec. 1001(b)(2)(B)(ii), substituted "; and" for the period at the end of Sec. 1402(c)(2)(B) of P.L. 111-148 [see below]... Sec. 1001(b)(2)(C), added subpara. (C) to Sec. 1402(c)(2) of P.L. 111-148 [see below]

Prior to repeal, sbcl. (c)(1)(B)(i)(III) of P.L. 111-148 [see below], read as follows:

"(III) 70 percent in the case of an eligible insured described in clause (ii) or (iii) of subparagraph (A)."

—P.L. 111-152, Sec. 1004(a)(1)(A), substituted "modified adjusted gross" for "modified gross" in clause (d)(2)(A)(i)–(ii)... Sec. 1004(a)(2)(A), amended subpara. (d)(2)(B)

Prior to amendment, subpara. (d)(2)(B) read as follows:

"(B) Modified gross income. The term 'modified gross income' means gross income—

"(i) decreased by the amount of any deduction allowable under paragraph (1), (3), (4), or (10) of section 62(a),

"(ii) increased by the amount of interest received or accrued during the taxable year which is exempt from tax imposed by this chapter, and

"(iii) determined without regard to sections 911, 931, and 933."

—P.L. 111-152, Sec. 1004(c), added para. (f)(3), effective for tax. yrs. end. after 12/31/2013, as if included in the provisions of Sec. 1401(e) of P.L. 111-148.

—P.L. 111-148, Sec. 1401(a), added Code Sec. 36B, effective for tax. yrs. end. after 12/31/2013.

—P.L. 111-148, Sec. 1401(c), of this Act, provides:

"(c) Study on affordable coverage.

"(1) Study and report.

"(A) In general. Not later than 5 years after the date of the enactment of this Act, the Comptroller General shall conduct a study on the affordability of health insurance coverage, including—

"(i) the impact of the tax credit for qualified health insurance coverage of individuals under section 36B of the Internal Revenue Code of 1986 and the tax credit for employee health insurance expenses of small employers under section 45R of such Code on maintaining and expanding the health insurance coverage of individuals;

"(ii) the availability of affordable health benefits plans, including a study of whether the percentage of household income used for purposes of section 36B(c)(2)(C) of the Internal Revenue Code of 1986 (as added by this section) is the appropriate level for determining whether employer-provided coverage is affordable for an employee and whether such level may be lowered without significantly increasing the costs to the Federal Government and reducing employer provided coverage; and

"(iii) the ability of individuals to maintain essential health benefits coverage (as defined in section 5000A(f) of the Internal Revenue Code of 1986).

"(B) Report. The Comptroller General shall submit to the appropriate committees of Congress a report on the study conducted under subparagraph (A), together with legislative recommendations relating to the matters studied under such subparagraph.

"(2) Appropriate committees of congress. In this subsection, the term 'appropriate committees of Congress' means the Committee on Ways and Means, the Committee on Education and Labor, and the Committee on Energy and Commerce of the House of Representatives and the Committee on Finance and the Committee on Health, Education, Labor and Pensions of the Senate."

—P.L. 111-148, Sec. 1402, of this Act [as amended by Sec. 1001(b) of P.L. 111-152, see above] provides:

"SEC. 1402. REDUCED COST-SHARING FOR INDIVIDUALS ENROLLING IN QUALIFIED HEALTH PLANS.

"(a) In general. In the case of an eligible insured enrolled in a qualified health plan—

"(1) the Secretary shall notify the issuer of the plan of such eligibility; and

"(2) the issuer shall reduce the cost-sharing under the plan at the level and in the manner specified in subsection (c).

"(b) Eligible insured. In this section, the term 'eligible insured' means an individual—

"(1) who enrolls in a qualified health plan in the silver level of coverage in the individual market offered through an Exchange; and

"(2) whose household income exceeds 100 percent but does not exceed 400 percent of the poverty line for a family of the size involved.

"In the case of an individual described in section 36B(c)(1)(B) of the Internal Revenue Code of 1986, the individual shall be treated as having household income equal to 100 percent for purposes of applying this section.

"(c) Determination of reduction in cost-sharing.

"(1) Reduction in out-of-pocket limit.

"(A) In general. The reduction in cost-sharing under this subsection shall first be achieved by reducing the applicable out-of pocket limit under section 1302(c)(1) in the case of—

"(i) an eligible insured whose household income is more than 100 percent but not more than 200 percent of the poverty line for a family of the size involved, by two-thirds;

"(ii) an eligible insured whose household income is more than 200 percent but not more than 300 percent of the poverty line for a family of the size involved, by one-half; and

"(iii) an eligible insured whose house-hold income is more than 300 percent but not more than 400 percent of the poverty line for a family of the size involved, by one-third.

"(B) Coordination with actuarial value limits.

"(i) In general. The Secretary shall ensure the reduction under this paragraph shall not result in an increase in the plans share of the total allowed costs of benefits provided under the plan above—

"(I) 94 percent in the case of an eligible insured described in paragraph (2)(A);

"(II) 87 percent in the case of an eligible insured described in paragraph (2)(B);

"(III) 73 percent in the case of an eligible insured whose household income is more than 200 percent but not more than 250 percent of the poverty line for a family of the size involved; and

"(IV) 70 percent in the case of an eligible insured whose household income is more than 250 percent but not more than 400 percent of the poverty line for a family of the size involved.

"(ii) Adjustment. The Secretary shall adjust the out-of pocket limits under paragraph (1) if necessary to ensure that such limits do not cause the respective actuarial values to exceed the levels specified in clause (i).

"(2) Additional reduction for lower income insureds. The Secretary shall establish procedures under which the issuer of a qualified health plan to which this section applies shall further reduce cost sharing under the plan in a manner sufficient to—

"(A) in the case of an eligible insured whose household income is not less than 100 percent but not more than 150 percent of the poverty line for a family of the size involved, increase the plan's share of the total allowed costs of benefits provided under the plan to 94 percent of such costs;

"(B) in the case of an eligible insured whose household income is more than 150 percent but not more than 200 percent of the poverty line for a family of the size involved, increase the plan's share of the total allowed costs of benefits provided under the plan to 87 percent of such costs; and

"(C) in the case of an eligible insured whose household income is more than 200 percent but not more than 250 percent of the poverty line for a family of the size involved, increase the plan's share of the total allowed costs of benefits provided under the plan to 73 percent of such costs.

"(3) Methods for reducing cost-sharing.

"(A) In general. An issuer of a qualified health plan making reductions under this subsection shall notify the Secretary of such reductions and the Secretary shall make periodic and timely payments to the issuer equal to the value of the reductions.

"(B) Capitated payments. The Secretary may establish a capitated payment system to carry out the payment of cost-sharing reductions under this section. Any such system shall take into account the value of the reductions and make appropriate risk adjustments to such payments.

"(4) Additional benefits. If a qualified health plan under section 1302(b)(5) offers benefits in addition to the essential health benefits required to be provided by the plan, or a State requires a qualified health plan under section 1311(d)(3)(B) to cover benefits in addition to the essential health benefits required to be provided by the plan, the reductions in cost-sharing under this section shall not apply to such additional benefits.

"(5) Special rule for pediatric dental plans. If an individual enrolls in both a qualified health plan and a plan described in section 1311(d)(2)(B)(ii)(I) for any plan year, subsection (a) shall not apply to that portion of any reduction in cost-sharing under subsection (c) that (under regulations prescribed by the Secretary) is properly allocable to pediatric dental benefits which are included in the essential health benefits required to be provided by a qualified health plan under section 1302(b)(1)(J).

"(d) Special rules for indians.

"(1) Indians under 300 percent of poverty. If an individual enrolled in any qualified health plan in the individual market through an Exchange is an Indian (as defined in section 4(d) of the Indian Self-Determination and Education Assistance Act (25 U.S.C. 450b(d))) whose household income is not more than 300 percent of the poverty line for a family of the size involved, then, for purposes of this section—

"(A) such individual shall be treated as an eligible insured; and

"(B) the issuer of the plan shall eliminate any cost-sharing under the plan.

"(2) Items or services furnished through indian health providers. If an Indian (as so defined) enrolled in a qualified health plan is furnished an item or service directly by the Indian Health Service, an Indian Tribe, Tribal Organization, or Urban Indian Organization or through referral under contract health services—

"(A) no cost-sharing under the plan shall be imposed under the plan for such item or service; and

"(B) the issuer of the plan shall not reduce the payment to any such entity for such item or service by the amount of any cost-sharing that would be due from the Indian but for subparagraph (A).

"(3) Payment. The Secretary shall pay to the issuer of a qualified health plan the amount necessary to reflect the increase in actuarial value of the plan required by reason of this subsection.

"(e) Rules for individuals not lawfully present.

"(1) In general. If an individual who is an eligible insured is not lawfully present—

"(A) no cost-sharing reduction under this section shall apply with respect to the individual; and

"(B) for purposes of applying this section, the determination as to what percentage a taxpayer's household income bears to the poverty level for a family of the size involved shall be made under one of the following methods:

"(i) A method under which—

"(I) the taxpayer's family size is determined by not taking such individuals into account, and

"(II) the taxpayer's household income is equal to the product of the taxpayer's household income (determined without regard to this subsection) and a fraction—

"(aa) the numerator of which is the poverty line for the taxpayer's family size determined after application of subclause (I), and

"(bb) the denominator of which is the poverty line for the taxpayer's family size determined without regard to subclause (I).

"(ii) A comparable method reaching the same result as the method under clause (i).

"(2) Lawfully present. For purposes of this section, an individual shall be treated as lawfully present only if the individual is, and is reasonably expected to be for the entire period of enrollment for which the cost-sharing reduction under this section is being claimed, a citizen or national of the United States or an alien lawfully present in the United States.

"(3) Secretarial authority. The Secretary, in consultation with the Secretary of the Treasury, shall prescribe rules setting forth the methods by which calculations of family size and household income are made for purposes of this subsection. Such rules shall be designed to ensure that the least burden is placed on individuals enrolling in qualified health plans through an Exchange and taxpayers eligible for the credit allowable under this section.

"(f) Definitions and special rules. In this section:

"(1) In general. Any term used in this section which is also used in section 36B of the Internal Revenue Code of 1986 shall have the meaning given such term by such section.

"(2) Limitations on reduction. No cost-sharing reduction shall be allowed under this section with respect to coverage for any month unless the month is a coverage month with respect to which a credit is allowed to the insured (or an applicable taxpayer on behalf of the insured) under section 36B of such Code.

"(3) Data used for eligibility. Any determination under this section shall be made on the basis of the taxable year for which the advance determination is made under section 1412 and not the taxable year for which the credit under section 36B of such Code is allowed."

—P.L. 111-148, Sec. 1415, of this Act, provides:

"SEC. 1415. PREMIUM TAX CREDIT AND COST-SHARING REDUCTION PAYMENTS DISREGARDED FOR FEDERAL AND FEDERALLY-ASSISTED PROGRAMS.

"For purposes of determining the eligibility of any individual for benefits or assistance, or the amount or extent of benefits or assistance, under any Federal program or under any State or local program financed in whole or in part with Federal funds—

"(1) any credit or refund allowed or made to any individual by reason of section 36B of the Internal Revenue Code of 1986 (as added by section 1401) shall not be taken into account as income and shall not be taken into account as resources for the month of receipt and the following 2 months; and

"(2) any cost-sharing reduction payment or advance payment of the credit allowed under such section 36B that is made under section 1402 or 1412 shall be treated as made to the qualified health plan in which an individual is enrolled and not to that individual."

—P.L. 111-148, Sec. 10105(a), substituted "equals or exceeds" for "is in excess of" in clause (b)(3)(A)(ii) [as added by Sec. 1401(a) of this Act, see above] . . . Sec. 10105(b), added "equals or" before 'exceeds" in subpara. (c)(1)(A) [as added by Sec. 1401(a) of this Act, see above] . . . Sec. 10105(c), substituted "subsection (b)(3)(A)(iii)' for 'subsection (b)(3)(A)(ii)" in clause (c)(2)(C)(iv) [as added by Sec. 1401(a) of this Act, see above], generally effective after 12/31/2013.

—P.L. 111-148, Sec. 10108(h)(1), added subpara. (c)(2)(D), effective for tax. yrs. begin. after 12/31/2013.

Sec. 36C. Adoption expenses.

⌐ • **Caution:** Code Sec. 23, was redesignated as Code Sec. 36C and further amended by Sec. 10909, P.L. 111-148. As provided in Sec. 10909(c), P.L. 111-148 as amended by Sec. 101(b)(1), P.L. 111-312, these amendments will read as if never enacted, effective for tax. yrs. begin. after 12/31/2011. For the Code as it will read for tax. yrs. begin. after 12/31/2011, see Code Sec. 23. ⌐

(a) Allowance of credit.

⌐ • **Caution:** Code Sec. 36C(a)(1)-(2), following, were amended by P.L. 107-16 EGTRRA. These provisions generally sunset for tax years beginning after 12/31/2012. For specific sunset provisions, see Sec. 901, P.L. 107-16 (as amended) reproduced in history notes for this Code Sec. ⌐

(1) In general. In the case of an individual, there shall be allowed as a credit against the tax imposed by this chapter the amount of the qualified adoption expenses paid or incurred by the taxpayer.

(2) Year credit allowed. The credit under paragraph (1) with respect to any expense shall be allowed—

(A) in the case of any expense paid or incurred before the taxable year in which such adoption becomes final, for the taxable year following the taxable year during which such expense is paid or incurred, and

(B) in the case of an expense paid or incurred during or after the taxable year in which such adoption becomes final, for the taxable year in which such expense is paid or incurred.

⌐ • **Caution:** Code Sec. 36C(a)(3), following, reflects amendments made by Sec. 10909, P.L. 111-148. As provided in Sec. 10909(c), P.L. 111-148 as amended by Sec. 101(b)(1), P.L. 111-312, Code Sec. 36C(a)(3) will read as if those amendments had never been enacted, effective for tax. yrs. begin. after 12/31/2011. For Code Sec. 36C(a)(3), as it will read for tax. yrs. begin. after 12/31/2011, see below. ⌐

(3) $13,170 credit for adoption of child with special needs regardless of expenses. In the case of an adoption of a child with special needs which becomes final during a taxable year, the taxpayer shall be treated as having paid during such year qualified adoption expenses with respect to such adoption in an amount equal to the excess (if any) of $13,170 over the aggregate qualified adoption expenses actually paid or incurred by the taxpayer with respect to such adoption during such taxable year and all prior taxable years.

⌐ • **Caution:** Code Sec. 36C(a)(3), following, is effective for tax. yrs. begin. after 12/31/2011, and reflects the sunset of the amendments made by Sec. 10909(a)(1)(A), P.L. 111-148. For details of those amendments, effective date, and sunset provisions, see the history for this Code Sec. For Code Sec. 36C(a)(3), effective for tax. yrs. begin. before 1/1/2012, see above. ⌐

(3) $10,000 credit for adoption of child with special needs regardless of expenses. In the case of an adoption of a child with special needs which becomes final during a taxable year, the taxpayer shall be treated as having paid during such year qualified adoption expenses with respect to such adoption in an amount equal to the excess (if any) of $10,000 over the aggregate qualified adoption expenses actually paid or incurred by the taxpayer with respect to such adoption during such taxable year and all prior taxable years.

⌐ • **Caution:** Code Sec. 36C(b)(1)-(2), following, were amended by P.L. 107-16 EGTRRA. These provisions generally sunset for tax years beginning after 12/31/2012. For specific sunset provisions, see Sec. 901, P.L. 107-16 (as amended) reproduced in history notes for this Code Sec. ⌐

(b) Limitations.

⌐ • **Caution:** Code Sec. 36C(b)(1), following, reflects amendments made by Sec. 10909(a)(1)(A), P.L. 111-148. As provided in Sec. 10909(c), P.L. 111-148, as amended by Sec. 101(b)(1), P.L. 111-312, Code Sec. 36C(b)(1) will read as if those amendments had never been enacted, effective for tax. yrs. begin. after 12/31/2011. For Code Sec. 36C(b)(1), as it will read for tax. yrs. begin. after 12/31/2011, see below. ⌐

(1) Dollar limitation. The aggregate amount of qualified adoption expenses which may be taken into account under subsection (a) for all taxable years with respect to the adoption of a child by the taxpayer shall not exceed $13,170.

⌐ • **Caution:** Code Sec. 36C(b)(1), following, is effective for tax. yrs. begin. after 12/31/2011, and reflects the sunset of the amendments made by Sec. 10909(a)(1)(A), P.L. 111-148. For details of those amendments, effective date and sunset provisions, see the history for this Code Sec. For

Tax credits Code Sec. 36C(d)(3)

Code Sec. 36C(b)(1), effective for tax. yrs. begin. before 1/1/2012, see above.

(1) Dollar limitation. The aggregate amount of qualified adoption expenses which may be taken into account under subsection (a) for all taxable years with respect to the adoption of a child by the taxpayer shall not exceed $10,000.

(2) Income limitation.
(A) In general. The amount allowable as a credit under subsection (a) for any taxable year (determined without regard to subsection (c)) shall be reduced (but not below zero) by an amount which bears the same ratio to the amount so allowable (determined without regard to this paragraph but with regard to paragraph (1)) as—
  (i) the amount (if any) by which the taxpayer's adjusted gross income exceeds $150,000, bears to
  (ii) $40,000.
(B) Determination of adjusted gross income. For purposes of subparagraph (A), adjusted gross income shall be determined without regard to sections 911, 931, and 933.

(3) Denial of double benefit.
(A) In general. No credit shall be allowed under subsection (a) for any expense for which a deduction or credit is allowed under any other provision of this chapter.
(B) Grants. No credit shall be allowed under subsection (a) for any expense to the extent that funds for such expense are received under any Federal, State, or local program.

• **Caution:** Code Sec. 36C(b)(4), following, reflects amendments made by Sec. 10909(a)(1)(A), P.L. 111-148. As provided in Sec. 10909(c), P.L. 111-148, as amended by Sec. 101(b)(1), P.L. 111-312, Code Sec. 36C(b)(4) will read as if those amendments had never been enacted, effective for tax. yrs. begin. after 12/31/2011. For Code Sec. 36(b)(4), as it will read for tax. yrs. begin. after 12/31/2011, see below.

(4) Repealed.

• **Caution:** Code Sec. 36C(b)(4), following, is effective for tax. yrs. begin. after 12/31/2011, and reflects the sunset of the amendments made by Sec. 10909(a)(1)(A), P.L. 111-148. For details of those amendments, effective date, and sunset provisions, see the history for this Code Sec. For Code Sec. 36C(b)(4), effective for tax. yrs. begin. before 1/1/2012, see above.

(4) Limitation based on amount of tax. In the case of a taxable year to which section 26(a)(2) does not apply, the credit allowed under subsection (a) for any taxable year shall not exceed the excess of—
(A) the sum of the regular tax liability (as defined in section 26(b)) plus the tax imposed by section 55, over
(B) the sum of the credits allowable under this subpart (other than this section and section 25D) and section 27 for the taxable year.

• **Caution:** Code Sec. 36C(c), following, reflects amendments made by Sec. 10909(a)(1)(A), P.L. 111-148. As provided in Sec. 10909(c), P.L. 111-148, as amended by Sec. 101(b)(1), P.L. 111-312, Code Sec. 36C(c) will read as if those amendments had never been enacted, effective for tax. yrs. begin. after 12/31/2011. For Code Sec. 36C(c), as it will read for tax. yrs. begin. after 12/31/2011, see below.

(c) Repealed.

• **Caution:** Code Sec. 36C(c), following, is effective for tax. yrs. begin. after 12/31/2011, and reflects the sunset of the amendments made by Sec. 10909(a)(1)(A), P.L. 111-148. For details of those amendments, effective date, and sunset provisions, see the history for this Code Sec. For Code Sec. 36C(c), effective for tax. yrs. begin. before 1/1/2012, see above.

(c) Carryforwards of unused credit.
(1) Rule for years in which all personal credits allowed against regular and alternative minimum tax. In the case of a taxable year to which section 26(a)(2) applies, if the credit allowable under subsection (a) for any taxable year exceeds the limitation imposed by section 26(a)(2) for such taxable year reduced by the sum of the credits allowable under this subpart (other than this section and sections 25D and 1400C), such excess shall be carried to the succeeding taxable year and added to the credit allowable under subsection (a) for such taxable year.
(2) Rule for other years. In the case of a taxable year to which section 26(a)(2) does not apply, if the credit allowable under subsection (a) for any taxable year exceeds the limitation imposed by subsection (b)(4) for such taxable year, such excess shall be carried to the succeeding taxable year and added to the credit allowable under subsection (a) for such taxable year.
(3) Limitation. No credit may be carried forward under this subsection to any taxable year following the fifth taxable year after the taxable year in which the credit arose. For purposes of the preceding sentence, credits shall be treated as used on a first-in first-out basis.

(d) Definitions.
For purposes of this section—
(1) Qualified adoption expenses. The term "qualified adoption expenses" means reasonable and necessary adoption fees, court costs, attorney fees, and other expenses—
(A) which are directly related to, and the principal purpose of which is for, the legal adoption of an eligible child by the taxpayer,
(B) which are not incurred in violation of State or Federal law or in carrying out any surrogate parenting arrangement,
(C) which are not expenses in connection with the adoption by an individual of a child who is the child of such individual's spouse, and
(D) which are not reimbursed under an employer program or otherwise.
(2) Eligible child. The term "eligible child" means any individual who—
(A) has not attained age 18, or
(B) is physically or mentally incapable of caring for himself.
(3) Child with special needs. The term "child with special needs" means any child if—

1,099

Code Sec. 36C(d)(3)(A)   **Tax credits**

(A) a State has determined that the child cannot or should not be returned to the home of his parents,

(B) such State has determined that there exists with respect to the child a specific factor or condition (such as his ethnic background, age, or membership in a minority or sibling group, or the presence of factors such as medical conditions or physical, mental, or emotional handicaps) because of which it is reasonable to conclude that such child cannot be placed with adoptive parents without providing adoption assistance, and

(C) such child is a citizen or resident of the United States (as defined in section 217(h)(3)).

(e) Special rules for foreign adoptions.

In the case of an adoption of a child who is not a citizen or resident of the United States (as defined in section 217(h)(3))—

(1) subsection (a) shall not apply to any qualified adoption expense with respect to such adoption unless such adoption becomes final, and

(2) any such expense which is paid or incurred before the taxable year in which such adoption becomes final shall be taken into account under this section as if such expense were paid or incurred during such year.

(f) Filing requirements.

(1) Married couples must file joint returns. Rules similar to the rules of paragraphs (2), (3), and (4) of section 21(e) shall apply for purposes of this section.

(2) Taxpayer must include TIN.

(A) In general. No credit shall be allowed under this section with respect to any eligible child unless the taxpayer includes (if known) the name, age, and TIN of such child on the return of tax for the taxable year.

(B) Other methods. The Secretary may, in lieu of the information referred to in subparagraph (A), require other information meeting the purposes of subparagraph (A), including identification of an agent assisting with the adoption.

(g) Basis adjustments.

For purposes of this subtitle, if a credit is allowed under this section for any expenditure with respect to any property, the increase in the basis of such property which would (but for this subsection) result from such expenditure shall be reduced by the amount of the credit so allowed.

> • *Caution:* Code Sec. 36C(h), following, was added by P.L. 107-16, EGTRRA. These provisions generally sunset for tax years beginning after 12/31/2012. For specific sunset provisions, see Sec. 901, P.L. 107-16 (as amended) in notes following this Code Sec. Code Sec. 36C(h), was further amended by Sec. 10909, P.L. 111-148. As provided in Sec. 10909(c), P.L. 111-148, as amended by P.L. 111-312, Code Sec. 36C(h) will read as if those amendments had never been enacted, effective for tax. yrs. begin. after 12/31/2011. For Code Sec. 36C(h) as it will read for tax. yrs. begin. after 12/31/2011, see below.

(h) Adjustments for inflation.

(1) Dollar limitations. In the case of a taxable year beginning after December 31, 2010, each of the dollar amounts in subsections (a)(3) and (b)(1) shall be increased by an amount equal to—

(A) such dollar amount, multiplied by

(B) the cost-of-living adjustment determined under section 1(f)(3) for the calendar year in which the taxable year begins, determined by substituting "calendar year 2009" for "calendar year 1992" in subparagraph (B) thereof.

If any amount as increased under the preceding sentence is not a multiple of $10, such amount shall be rounded to the nearest multiple of $10.

(2) Income limitation. In the case of a taxable year beginning after December 31, 2002, the dollar amount in subsection (b)(2)(A)(i) shall be increased by an amount equal to—

(A) such dollar amount, multiplied by

(B) the cost-of-living adjustment determined under section 1(f)(3) for the calendar year in which the taxable year begins, determined by substituting "calendar year 2001" for "calendar year 1992" in subparagraph (B) thereof.

If any amount as increased under the preceding sentence is not a multiple of $10, such amount shall be rounded to the nearest multiple of $10.

> • *Caution:* Code Sec. 36C(h), following, is effective for tax. yrs. begin. after 12/31/2011, and reflects the sunset of the amendment made by Sec. 10909(a)(1)(C), P.L. 111-148. For details of those amendments, effective date and sunset provisions, see the history following this Code Sec. For Code Sec. 36C(h), effective for tax. yrs. begin. before 1/1/2012, see above.

(h) Adjustments for inflation.

In the case of a taxable year beginning after December 31, 2002, each of the dollar amounts in subsection (a)(3) and paragraphs (1) and (2)(A)(i) of subsection (b) shall be increased by an amount equal to—

(1) such dollar amount, multiplied by

(2) the cost-of-living adjustment determined under section 1(f)(3) for the calendar year in which the taxable year begins, determined by substituting "calendar year 2001" for "calendar year 1992" in subparagraph (B) thereof.

If any amount as increased under the preceding sentence is not a multiple of $10, such amount shall be rounded to the nearest multiple of $10.

> • *Caution:* Code Sec. 36C(i), following, was redesignated from Code Sec. 36C(h) by Sec. 202(e)(1), P.L. 107-16, EGTRRA. These provisions generally sunset for tax years beginning after 12/31/2012. For specific sunset provisions, see Sec. 901, P.L. 107-16 (as amended) reproduced in history notes for this Code Sec.

(i) Regulations.

The Secretary shall prescribe such regulations as may be appropriate to carry out this section and section 137, including regulations which treat unmarried individuals who pay or incur qualified adoption expenses with respect to the same child as 1 taxpayer for purposes of applying the dollar amounts in subsections (a)(3) and (b)(1) of this section and in section 137(b)(1).

In 2010, P.L. 111-312, Sec. 101(a)(1), substituted "December 31, 2012" for "December 31, 2010," both places it appeared in Sec. 901, P.L. 107-16 [see below], effective as if included in the enactment of P.L. 107-16, EGTRRA, 6/7/2001.

—P.L. 111-312, Sec. 101(b)(1), amended Sec. 10909(c), P.L. 111-148 [see below].

Prior to amendment, Sec. 10909(c) of P.L. 111-148, read as follows:

Tax credits Code Sec. 36C

"(c) Application and Extension of EGTRRA Sunset. Notwithstanding section 901 of the Economic Growth and Tax Relief Reconciliation Act of 2001, such section shall apply to the amendments made by this section and the amendments made by section 202 of such Act by substituting 'December 31, 2011' for 'December 31, 2010' in subsection (a)(1) thereof."

—P.L. 111-312, Sec. 101(b)(2), substituted "Except as provided in subsection (c), the amendments" for "The amendments" in Sec. 10909(d), P.L. 111-148 (the effective date section for amendments made by Sec. 10909, P.L. 111-148, see below).

Prior to amendment, Sec. 10909(d) of P.L. 111-148, read as follows:

"(d) Effective date. The amendments made by this section shall apply to taxable years beginning after December 31, 2009."

—P.L. 111-148, Sec. 10909(a)(1)(A), substituted "$13,170" for "$10,000" in para. (b)(1)

—P.L. 111-148, Sec. 10909(a)(1)(C), amended subsec. (h)

—P.L. 111-148, Sec. 10909(a)(1)(B)(i), substituted "$13,170" for "$10,000" in para. (a)(3)

—P.L. 111-148, Sec. 10909(a)(1)(B)(ii), substituted "$13,170" for "$10,000" in the heading to para. (a)(3)

—P.L. 111-148, Sec. 10909(b)(1)(A), redesignated Code Sec. 23, [as amended by Sec. 10909(a) of this Act, see above], as Code Sec. 36C

—P.L. 111-148, Sec. 10909(b)(2)(I)(i), deleted para. (b)(4)

—P.L. 111-148, Sec. 10909(b)(2)(I)(ii), deleted subsec. (c), effective for tax. yrs. begin. after 12/31/2009, except as provided in Sec. 10909(c) of this Act, see below, effective for taxable years beginning after December 31, 2011.

Prior to redesignation Code Sec. 23 read as follows:

"Code Sec. 23 Adoption expenses.

"Paras. (a)(1) and (a)(2), following, was amended by P.L. 107-16, the Economic Growth and Tax Relief Reconciliation Act of 2001 (EGTRRA). For sunset provisions, see Sec. 901, P.L. 107-16 reproduced in history notes for this Code Sec.

"(a) Allowance of credit.

"(1) In general.

"In the case of an individual, there shall be allowed as a credit against the tax imposed by this chapter the amount of the qualified adoption expenses paid or incurred by the taxpayer.

"(2) Year credit allowed.

"The credit under paragraph (1) with respect to any expense shall be allowed—

"(A) in the case of any expense paid or incurred before the taxable year in which such adoption becomes final, for the taxable year following the taxable year during which such expense is paid or incurred, and

"(B) in the case of an expense paid or incurred during or after the taxable year in which such adoption becomes final, for the taxable year in which such expense is paid or incurred.

"(3) $10,000 credit for adoption of child with special needs regardless of expenses.

"In the case of an adoption of a child with special needs which becomes final during a taxable year, the taxpayer shall be treated as having paid during such year qualified adoption expenses with respect to such adoption in an amount equal to the excess (if any) of $10,000 over the aggregate qualified adoption expenses actually paid or incurred by the taxpayer with respect to such adoption during such taxable year and all prior taxable years.

"Paras. (b)(1) and (b)(2), following, were amended by P.L. 107-16, the Economic Growth and Tax Relief Reconciliation Act of 2001 (EGTRRA). For sunset provisions, see Sec. 901, P.L. 107-16 reproduced in history notes for this Code Sec.

"(b) Limitations.

"(1) Dollar limitation.

"The aggregate amount of qualified adoption expenses which may be taken into account under subsection (a) for all taxable years with respect to the adoption of a child by the taxpayer shall not exceed $10,000.

"(2) Income limitation.

"(A) In general. The amount allowable as a credit under subsection (a) for any taxable year (determined without regard to subsection (c)) shall be reduced (but not below zero) by an amount which bears the same ratio to the amount so allowable (determined without regard to this paragraph but with regard to paragraph (1)) as—

"(i) the amount (if any) by which the taxpayer's adjusted gross income exceeds $150,000, bears to

"(ii) $40,000.

"(B) Determination of adjusted gross income. For purposes of subparagraph (A), adjusted gross income shall be determined without regard to sections 911, 931, and 933.

"(3) Denial of double benefit.

"(A) In general. No credit shall be allowed under subsection (a) for any expense for which a deduction or credit is allowed under any other provision of this chapter.

"(B) Grants. No credit shall be allowed under subsection (a) for any expense to the extent that funds for such expense are received under any Federal, State, or local program.

"Para. (b)(4), added by P.L. 107-16 and amended by P.L. 109-135, following, is not effective for tax. yrs. begin. during 2002, 2003, 2004, or 2005 as provided by Sec. 601(b)(2) of P.L. 107-147 and Sec. 312(b)(2) of P.L. 108-311. For sunset provisions, see Sec. 901 of P.L. 107-16 and Sec. 402(i)(3)(H) of P.L. 109-135 reproduced in the history of this Code Sec.

"(4) Limitation based on amount of tax.

"In the case of a taxable year to which section 26(a)(2) does not apply, the credit allowed under subsection (a) for any taxable year shall not exceed the excess of—

"(A) the sum of the regular tax liability (as defined in section 26(b)) plus the tax imposed by section 55, over

"(B) the sum of the credits allowable under this subpart (other than this section and section 25D) and section 27 for the taxable year.

" Subsec. (c)), following, was amended by P.L. 109-135. For sunset provisions, see Sec. 901, P.L. 107-16 and Sec. 402(i)(3)(H), P.L. 109-135, reproduced in history notes for this Code Sec.

"(c) Carryforwards of unused credit.

"(1) Rule for years in which all personal credits allowed against regular and alternative minimum tax.

"In the case of a taxable year to which section 26(a)(2) applies, if the credit allowable under subsection (a) for any taxable year exceeds the limitation imposed by section 26(a)(2) for such taxable year reduced by the sum of the credits allowable under this subpart (other than this section and sections 25D and 1400C), such excess shall be carried to the succeeding taxable year and added to the credit allowable under subsection (a) for such taxable year.

"(2) Rule for other years.

"In the case of a taxable year to which section 26(a)(2) does not apply, if the credit allowable under subsection (a) for any taxable year exceeds the limitation imposed by subsection (b)(4) for such taxable year, such excess shall be carried to the succeeding taxable year and added to the credit allowable under subsection (a) for such taxable year.

"(3) Limitation.

"No credit may be carried forward under this subsection to any taxable year following the fifth taxable year after the taxable year in which the credit arose. For purposes of the preceding sentence, credits shall be treated as used on a first-in first-out basis.

"(d) Definitions.

"For purposes of this section—

"(1) Qualified adoption expenses.

"The term 'qualified adoption expenses' means reasonable and necessary adoption fees, court costs, attorney fees, and other expenses—

"(A) which are directly related to, and the principal purpose of which is for, the legal adoption of an eligible child by the taxpayer,

"(B) which are not incurred in violation of State or Federal law or in carrying out any surrogate parenting arrangement,

"(C) which are not expenses in connection with the adoption by an individual of a child who is the child of such individual's spouse, and

"(D) which are not reimbursed under an employer program or otherwise.

"(2) Eligible child. The term 'eligible child' means any individual who—

"(A) has not attained age 18, or

"(B) is physically or mentally incapable of caring for himself.

"(3) Child with special needs.

"The term 'child with special needs' means any child if—

"(A) a State has determined that the child cannot or should not be returned to the home of his parents,

"(B) such State has determined that there exists with respect to the child a specific factor or condition (such as his ethnic background, age, or membership in a minority or sibling group, or the presence of factors such as medical conditions or physical, mental, or emotional handicaps) because of which it is reasonable to conclude that such child cannot be placed with adoptive parents without providing adoption assistance, and

"(C) such child is a citizen or resident of the United States (as defined in section 217(h)(3)).

"(e) Special rules for foreign adoptions.

"In the case of an adoption of a child who is not a citizen or resident of the United States (as defined in section 217(h)(3))—

"(1) subsection (a) shall not apply to any qualified adoption expense with respect to such adoption unless such adoption becomes final, and

"(2) any such expense which is paid or incurred before the taxable year in which such adoption becomes final shall be taken into account under this section as if such expense were paid or incurred during such year.

"(f) Filing requirements.

"(1) Married couples must file joint returns.

"Rules similar to the rules of paragraphs (2), (3), and (4) of section 21(e) shall apply for purposes of this section.

"(2) Taxpayer must include TIN.

"(A) In general. No credit shall be allowed under this section with respect to any eligible child unless the taxpayer includes (if known) the name, age, and TIN of such child on the return of tax for the taxable year.

"(B) Other methods. The Secretary may, in lieu of the information referred to in subparagraph (A), require other information meeting the purposes of subparagraph (A), including identification of an agent assisting with the adoption.

"(g) Basis adjustments.

"For purposes of this subtitle, if a credit is allowed under this section for any expenditure with respect to any property, the increase in the basis of such property which would (but for this subsection) result from such expenditure shall be reduced by the amount of the credit so allowed.

"Subsec. (h), following, was added by P.L. 107-16, the Economic Growth and Tax Relief Reconciliation Act of 2001 (EGTRRA). For sunset provisions, see Sec. 901, P.L. 107-16 reproduced in history notes for this Code Sec.

"(h) Adjustments for inflation. In the case of a taxable year beginning after December 31, 2002, each of the dollar amounts in subsection (a)(3) and paragraphs (1) and (2)(A)(i) of subsection (b) shall be increased by an amount equal to—

1,101

"(1) such dollar amount, multiplied by

"(2) the cost-of-living adjustment determined under section 1(f)(3) for the calendar year in which the taxable year begins, determined by substituting 'calendar year 2001' for 'calendar year 1992' in subparagraph (B) thereof.

"If any amount as increased under the preceding sentence is not a multiple of $10, such amount shall be rounded to the nearest multiple of $10.

"Subsec. (i), following, was redesignated from subsec. (h) by P.L. 107-16, the Economic Growth and Tax Relief Reconciliation Act of 2001 (EGTRRA). For sunset provisions, see Sec. 901, P.L. 107-16 reproduced in history notes for this Code Sec.

"(i) Regulations.

"The Secretary shall prescribe such regulations as may be appropriate to carry out this section and section 137, including regulations which treat unmarried individuals who pay or incur qualified adoption expenses with respect to the same child as 1 taxpayer for purposes of applying the dollar amounts in subsections (a)(3) and (b)(1) of this section and in section 137(b)(1)."

—P.L. 111-148, Sec. 10909(c), of this Act, relating to the application and extension of EGTRRA sunset provisions, [as amended by Sec. 101(b)(1), P.L. 111-312 see above], reads as follows:

"(c) Sunset provision. Each provision of law amended by this section is amended to read as such provision would read if this section had never been enacted. The amendments made by the preceding sentence shall apply to taxable years beginning after December 31, 2011."

—P.L. 111-148, Sec. 10909(d), of this Act, [as amended by Sec. 101(b)(2), P.L. 111-312, see above] reads as follows:

"(d) Effective date. Except as provided in subsection (c) [Sec. 10909(c) of this Act], the amendments made by this section shall apply to taxable years beginning after December 31, 2009."

In 2008, P.L. 110-343, Sec. 106(e)(2)(A), inserted "and section 25D" after "this section" in subpara. (b)(4)(B), effective for tax. yrs. begin. after 12/31/2007. The amendments made by subparagraphs (A) and (B) of subsection (e)(2) shall be subject to title IX of the Economic Growth and Tax Relief Reconciliation Act of 2001 in the same manner as the provisions of such Act to which such amendments relate.

In 2005, P.L. 109-135, Sec. 402(i)(3)(A)(i), substituted "In the case of a taxable year to which section 26(a)(2) does not apply, the credit" for "The credit" in the matter preceding subpara. (b)(4)(A) ... Sec. 402(i)(3)(A)(ii), amended subsec. (c), effective for tax. yrs. begin. after 12/31/2005.

Prior to amendment, subsec. (c) read as follows:

"(c) Carryforwards of unused credit. If the credit allowable under subsection (a) for any taxable year exceeds the limitation imposed by subsection (b)(4) for such taxable year, such excess shall be carried to the succeeding taxable year and added to the credit allowable under subsection (a) for such taxable year. No credit may be carried forward under this subsection to any taxable year following the fifth taxable year after the taxable year in which the credit arose. For purposes of the preceding sentence, credits shall be treated as used on a first-in first-out basis."

—P.L. 109-135, Sec. 402(i)(3)(H), of this Act, provides:

"(H) Application of EGTRRA Sunset. The amendments made by this paragraph (and each part thereof) shall be subject to title IX of the Economic Growth and Tax Relief Reconciliation Act of 2001 [P.L. 107-16] in the same manner as the provisions of such Act to which such amendment (or part thereof) relates."

—P.L. 109-135, Sec. 402(i)(4), repealed Sec. 1335(b)(1) of P.L. 109-58 [see below], effective for property placed in service after 12/31/2005, in tax. yrs. end. after 12/31/2005.

—P.L. 109-58, Sec. 1335(b)(1), [prior to repeal by Sec. 402(i)(4) of P.L. 109-135, see above] substituted "this section, section 25D, and section 1400C" for "this section and section 1400C" in subsec. (c), effective for property placed in service after 12/31/2005, in tax. yrs. end. after 12/31/2005. Note: This amendment cannot be applied to subsec. (c) as it reads on 1/1/2006.

In 2004, P.L. 108-311, Sec. 312(b)(2), of this Act, provides:

"(2) The amendments made by sections 201(b), 202(f), and 618(b) of the Economic Growth and Tax Relief Reconciliation Act of 2001 [P.L. 107-16] shall not apply to taxable years beginning during 2004 or 2005."

In 2002, P.L. 107-358, Sec. 2, added subsec. (c) in Sec. 901 of P.L. 107-16 [see below], effective 12/17/2002.

—P.L. 107-147, Sec. 411(c)(1)(A), amended para. (a)(1) ... Sec. 411(c)(1)(B), added para. (a)(3), effective for tax. yrs. begin. after 12/31/2002.

Prior to amendment, para. (a)(1) read as follows:

"(1) In general. In the case of an individual, there shall be allowed as a credit against the tax imposed by this chapter—

"(A) in the case of an adoption of a child other than a child with special needs, the amount of the qualified adoption expenses paid or incurred by the taxpayer, and

"(B) in the case of an adoption of a child with special needs, $10,000."

—P.L. 107-147, Sec. 411(c)(1)(C), deleted "In the case of the adoption of a child with special needs, the credit allowed under paragraph (1) shall be allowed for the taxable year in which the adoption becomes final." after "is paid or incurred." in para. (a)(2) ... Sec. 411(c)(1)(D), substituted "subsection (a)" for "subsection (a)(1)(A)" in para. (b)(1), effective for tax. yrs. begin. after 12/31/2001.

—P.L. 107-147, Sec. 411(c)(1)(E), substituted "the dollar amounts in subsections (a)(3) and (b)(1)" for "the dollar limitation in subsection (b)(1)" in subsec. (i), effective for tax. yrs. begin. after 12/31/2002.

—P.L. 107-147, Sec. 411(c)(1)(F), of this Act, provides:

"(F) Expenses paid or incurred during any taxable year beginning before January 1, 2002, may be taken into account in determining the credit under section 23 of the Internal Revenue Code of 1986 only to the extent the aggregate of such expenses does not exceed the applicable limitation under section 23(b)(1) of such Code as in effect on the day before the date of the enactment of the Economic Growth and Tax Relief Reconciliation Act of 2001."

—P.L. 107-147, Sec. 418(a)(1)(A), substituted "subsection (a)(3)" for "subsection (a)(1)(B)" in subsec. (h) ... Sec. 418(a)(1)(B), added a flush sentence at the end of subsec. (h), effective for tax. yrs. begin. after 12/31/2001.

—P.L. 107-147, Sec. 601(b)(2), of this Act, provides:

"(2) The amendments made by sections 201(b), 202(f), and 618(b) of the Economic Growth and Tax Relief Reconciliation Act of 2001 shall not apply to taxable years beginning during 2002 and 2003."

In 2001, P.L. 107-16, Sec. 201(b)(2)(E), substituted "and sections 24 and 1400C" for "and section 1400C" in subsec. (c) [prior to amendment by Sec. 202(f)(2)(A)(i)-(ii), see below], effective for tax. yrs. begin. after 12/31/2001. For special provisions, see Sec. 601(b)(2) of P.L. 107-147 and Sec. 312(b)(2) of P.L. 108-311, above.

—P.L. 107-16, Sec. 202(a)(1), amended para. (a)(1), effective for tax. yrs. begin. after 12/31/2002.

Prior to amendment, para. (a)(1) read as follows:

"(1) In general. In the case of an individual, there shall be allowed as a credit against the tax imposed by this chapter the amount of the qualified adoption expenses paid or incurred by the taxpayer."

—P.L. 107-16, Sec. 202(b)(1)(A)(i), substituted "$10,000" for "$5,000" in para. (b)(1) ... Sec. 202(b)(1)(A)(ii), deleted "($6,000, in the case of a child with special needs)" after "shall not exceed $5,000" in para. (b)(1) ... Sec. 202(b)(1)(A)(iii), substituted "subsection (a)(1)(A)" for "subsection (a)" in para. (b)(1) ... Sec. 202(b)(2)(A), substituted "$150,000" for "$75,000" in clause (b)(2)(A)(i) ... Sec. 202(c), added a flush sentence at the end of para. (a)(2) ... Sec. 202(d)(1), amended para. (d)(2) ... Sec. 202(e)(1), redesignated subsec. (h) as subsec. (i), and added new subsec. (h) ... Sec. 202(f)(1), added para. (b)(4) ... Sec. 202(f)(2)(A)(i), substituted "subsection (b)(4)" for "section 26(a)" in subsec. (c) [as amended by Sec. 201(b)(2)(E) of this Act, see above] ... Sec. 202(f)(2)(A)(ii), deleted "reduced by the sum of the credits allowable under this subpart (other than this section and sections 24 and 1400C)" before ", such excess shall be carried" in subsec. (c) [as amended by Sec. 201(b)(2)(E) of this Act, see above], effective for tax. yrs. begin. after 12/31/2001. For special provisions, see Sec. 601(b)(2) of P.L. 107-147 and Sec. 312(b)(2) of P.L. 108-311, above.

Prior to amendment, para. (d)(2) read as follows:

"(2) Eligible child. The term 'eligible child' means any individual—

"(A) who—

"(i) has not attained age 18, or

"(ii) is physically or mentally incapable of caring for himself, and

"(B) in the case of a qualified adoption expenses paid or incurred after December 31, 2001, who is a child with special needs."

—P.L. 107-16, Sec. 901, of this Act [as amended by Sec. 2 of P.L. 107-358, and Sec. 101(a)(1), P.L. 111-312, see above], reads as follows:

"Sec. 901. Sunset of provisions of Act.

"(a) In general. All provisions of, and amendments made by, this Act shall not apply—

"(1) to taxable, plan, or limitation years beginning after December 31, 2012, or

"(2) in the case of title V, to estates of decedents dying, gifts made, or generation skipping transfers, after December 31, 2012.

"(b) Application of certain laws. The Internal Revenue Code of 1986 and the Employee Retirement Income Security Act of 1974 shall be applied and administered to years, estates, gifts, and transfers described in subsection (a) as if the provisions and amendments described in subsection (a) had never been enacted.

"(c) Exception. Subsection (a) shall not apply to section 803 (relating to no federal income tax on restitution received by victims of the Nazi regime or their heirs or estates)."

In 1998, P.L. 105-206, Sec. 6008(d)(6), added "and section 1400C" after "other than this section" in subsec. (c), effective 8/5/97.

—P.L. 105-206, Sec. 6018(f)(1), added "(determined without regard to subsection (c))" after "for any taxable year" in subpara. (b)(2)(A), effective for tax. yrs. begin. after 12/31/96.

In 1997, P.L. 105-34, Sec. 1601(h)(2)(A), amended para. (a)(2) ... Sec. 1601(h)(2)(B), substituted "determined without regard to sections 911, 931, and 933." for "determined—" and clauses (b)(2)(B)(i) and (ii), effective for tax. yrs. begin. after 12/31/96.

Prior to amendment, para. (a)(2) read as follows:

"(2) Year credit allowed. The credit under paragraph (1) with respect to any expense shall be allowed—

"(A) for the taxable year following the taxable year during which such expense is paid or incurred, or

"(B) in the case of an expense which is paid or incurred during the taxable year in which the adoption becomes final, for such taxable year."

Prior to deletion, clauses (b)(2)(B)(i) and (ii) read as follows:

"determined—

"(i) without regard to sections 911, 931, and 933, and

"(ii) after the application of sections 86, 135, 137, 219, and 469."

In 1996, P.L. 104-188, Sec. 1807(a), added Code Sec. 23, effective for tax. yrs. begin. after 12/31/96.

Sec. 37. Overpayments of tax.

For credit against the tax imposed by this subtitle for overpayments of tax, see section 6401.

Tax credits Code Sec. 38(b)(14)

In 2008, P.L. 110-289, Sec. 3011(a), redesignated Code Sec. 36 as Code Sec. 37, effective for residences purchased on or after 4/9/2008, in tax. yrs. end. on or after such date.

SUBPART D.—BUSINESS RELATED CREDITS

Sec.
38. General business credit.
38. Repealed. [Investment in certain depreciable property.]
39. Carryback and carryforward of unused credits.
40. Alcohol, etc., used as fuel.
40. Repealed. [Expenses of work incentive programs.]
40A. Biodiesel and renewable diesel used as fuel.
41. Credit for increasing research activities.
41. Repealed. [Employee stock ownership credit.]
42. Low-income housing credit.
43. Enhanced oil recovery credit.
44. Expenditures to provide access to disabled individuals.
44. Repealed. [Purchase of new principal residence.]
44B. Repealed. [Credit for employment of certain new employees.]
45. Electricity produced from certain renewable resources, etc.
45A. Indian employment credit.
45B. Credit for portion of employer social security taxes paid with respect to employee cash tips.
45C. Clinical testing expenses for certain drugs for rare diseases or conditions
45D. New markets tax credit.
45E. Small employer pension plan startup costs.
45F. Employer-provided child care credit.
45G. Railroad track maintenance credit.
45H. Credit for production of low sulfur diesel fuel.
45I. Credit for producing oil and gas from marginal wells.
45J. Credit for production from advanced nuclear power facilities.
45K. Credit for producing fuel from a nonconventional source.
45L. New energy efficient home credit.
45M. Energy efficient appliance credit.
45N. Mine rescue team training credit.
45O. Agricultural chemicals security credit.
45P. Employer wage credit for employees who are active duty members of the uniformed services.
45Q. Credit for carbon dioxide sequestration.
45R. Employee health insurance expenses of small employers.

In 2010, P.L. 111-148, Sec. 1421(e), added item 45R
In 2008, P.L. 110-343, Sec. 107(a)DivB, added item 45Q, effective carbon dioxide captured after 10/3/2008.
— P.L. 110-234, Sec. 15321(b)(3)(B), amended item 40.
Prior to amendment, item 40 read as follows:
"40. Alcohol used as fuel."
— P.L. 110-234, Sec. 15343(d), added item 45O.
— P.L. 110-245, Sec. 111(d), added item 45P.
In 2005, P.L. 109-58, Sec. 1306(c), added item 45J.
— P.L. 109-58, Sec. 1322(a)(3)(L), added item 45K.
— P.L. 109-58, Sec. 1332(e), added item 45L.
— P.L. 109-58, Sec. 1334(c), added item 45M.
— P.L. 109-58, Sec. 1346(b)(2), amended item 40A.
Prior to amendment, item 40A read as follows:
"40A. Biodiesel used as fuel."
In 2004, P.L. 108-357, Sec. 245(d), added item 45G. . . . Sec. 302(c)(3), added item 40A. . . . Sec. 339(e) sic [(f)], added item 45H. . . . Sec. 341(d), added item 45I. . . . Sec. 710(b)(3)(B), added ", etc" before the period at the end of item 45.

In 2001, P.L. 107-16, Sec. 205(b)(2), added item 45F. . . . Sec. 619(c)(3), added item 45E.
In 2000, P.L. 106-554, Sec. 1(a)(7) [which enacted into law Sec. 121(d) of H.R. 5662], added item 45D.
In 1996, P.L. 104-188, Sec. 1205(a)(3)(B), added item 45C.
In 1993, P.L. 103-66, Sec. 13222(e), added item 45A. . . . Sec. 13443(c), added item 45B.
In 1992, P.L. 102-486, Sec. 1914(d), added item 45.
In 1990, P.L. 101-508, Sec. 11511(c)(1), added item 43 . . . Sec. 11611(d), added item 44.
In 1986, P.L. 99-514, Sec. 231(d)(3)(K), added item 41 . . . Sec. 252(d), added item 42 . . . Sec. 1171(a), repealed old Code Sec. 41. This Act did not amend the table of Code Sections for Subpart D of Part IV, but presumably Congress intended to do so.
Prior to repeal, the heading of Code Sec. 41 read as follows:
"Sec. 41 Employee stock ownership credit."
In 1984, P.L. 98-369, Sec. 471(b), added Subpart D as part of amendments made to Part IV.

Sec. 38. General business credit.
(a) Allowance of credit.

There shall be allowed as a credit against the tax imposed by this chapter for the taxable year an amount equal to the sum of—

(1) the business credit carryforwards carried to such taxable year,
(2) the amount of the current year business credit, plus
(3) the business credit carrybacks carried to such taxable year.

(b) Current year business credit.

For purposes of this subpart, the amount of the current year business credit is the sum of the following credits determined for the taxable year:

(1) the investment credit determined under section 46,
(2) the work opportunity credit determined under section 51(a),
(3) the alcohol fuels credit determined under section 40(a),
(4) the research credit determined under section 41(a),
(5) the low-income housing credit determined under section 42(a),
(6) the enhanced oil recovery credit under section 43(a),
(7) in the case of an eligible small business (as defined in section 44(b)), the disabled access credit determined under section 44(a),
(8) the renewable electricity production credit under section 45(a),
(9) the empowerment zone employment credit determined under section 1396(a),
(10) the Indian employment credit as determined under section 45A(a),
(11) the employer social security credit determined under section 45B(a),
(12) the orphan drug credit determined under section 45C(a),

> • **Caution:** Code Sec. 38(b)(13), (14) and (15), following, were amended by P.L. 107-16, EGTRRA. These provisions generally sunset for tax years beginning after 12/31/2012. For specific sunset provisions, see Sec. 901, P.L. 107-16 (as amended) reproduced in history notes for this Code Sec.

(13) the new markets tax credit determined under section 45D(a),
(14) in the case of an eligible employer (as defined in section 45E(c)), the small employer pension plan startup cost credit determined under section 45E(a),

(15) the employer-provided child care credit determined under section 45F(a),
(16) the railroad track maintenance credit determined under section 45G(a),
(17) the biodiesel fuels credit determined under section 40A(a),
(18) the low sulfur diesel fuel production credit determined under section 45H(a),
(19) the marginal oil and gas well production credit determined under section 45I(a),
(20) the distilled spirits credit determined under section 5011(a),
(21) the advanced nuclear power facility production credit determined under section 45J(a),
(22) the nonconventional source production credit determined under section 45K(a),
(23) the new energy efficient home credit determined under section 45L(a),
(24) the energy efficient appliance credit determined under section 45M(a),
(25) the portion of the alternative motor vehicle credit to which section 30B(g)(1) applies,
(26) the portion of the alternative fuel vehicle refueling property credit to which section 30C(d)(1) applies,
(27) the Hurricane Katrina housing credit determined under section 1400P(b),
(28) the Hurricane Katrina employee retention credit determined under section 1400R(a),
(29) the Hurricane Rita employee retention credit determined under section 1400R(b),
(30) the Hurricane Wilma employee retention credit determined under section 1400R(c),
(31) the mine rescue team training credit determined under section 45N(a),
(32) in the case of an eligible agricultural business (as defined in section 45O(e)), the agricultural chemicals security credit determined under section 45O(a),
(33) the differential wage payment credit determined under section 45P(a),
(34) the carbon dioxide sequestration credit determined under section 45Q(a)
(35) the portion of the new qualified plug-in electric drive motor vehicle credit to which section 30D(c)(1) applies, plus
(36) the small employer health insurance credit determined under section 45R.

(c) Limitation based on amount of tax.

(1) In general. The credit allowed under subsection (a) for any taxable year shall not exceed the excess (if any) of the taxpayer's net income tax over the greater of—

(A) the tentative minimum tax for the taxable year, or

(B) 25 percent of so much of the taxpayer's net regular tax liability as exceeds $25,000.

For purposes of the preceding sentence, the term "net income tax" means the sum of the regular tax liability and the tax imposed by section 55, reduced by the credits allowable under subparts A and B of this part, and the term "net regular tax liability" means the regular tax liability reduced by the sum of the credits allowable under subparts A and B of this part.

(2) Empowerment zone employment credit may offset 25 percent of minimum tax.

(A) In general. In the case of the empowerment zone employment credit credit—

(i) this section and section 39 shall be applied separately with respect to such credit, and

(ii) for purposes of applying paragraph (1) to such credit—

(I) 75 percent of the tentative minimum tax shall be substituted for the tentative minimum tax under subparagraph (A) thereof, and

(II) the limitation under paragraph (1) (as modified by subclause (I)) shall be reduced by the credit allowed under subsection (a) for the taxable year (other than the empowerment zone employment credit, the New York Liberty Zone business employee credit, the eligible small business credits, and the specified credits).

(B) Empowerment zone employment credit. For purposes of this paragraph, the term "empowerment zone employment credit" means the portion of the credit under subsection (a) which is attributable to the credit determined under section 1396 (relating to empowerment zone employment credit).

(3) Special rules for New York Liberty Zone business employee credit.

(A) In general. In the case of the New York Liberty Zone business employee credit—

(i) this section and section 39 shall be applied separately with respect to such credit, and

(ii) in applying paragraph (1) to such credit—

(I) the tentative minimum tax shall be treated as being zero, and

(II) the limitation under paragraph (1) (as modified by subclause (I)) shall be reduced by the credit allowed under subsection (a) for the taxable year (other than the New York Liberty Zone business employee credit , the eligible small business credits, and the specified credits).

(B) New York Liberty Zone business employee credit. For purposes of this subsection, the term "New York Liberty Zone business employee credit" means the portion of work opportunity credit under section 51 determined under section 1400L(a).

(4) Special rules for specified credits.

(A) In general. In the case of specified credits—

(i) this section and section 39 shall be applied separately with respect to such credits, and

(ii) in applying paragraph (1) to such credits—

(I) the tentative minimum tax shall be treated as being zero, and

(II) the limitation under paragraph (1) (as modified by subclause (I)) shall be reduced by the credit allowed under subsection (a) for the taxable year (other than the eligible small business credits and the specified credits).

(B) Specified credits. For purposes of this subsection, the term "specified credits" means—

(i) for taxable years beginning after December 31, 2004, the credit determined under section 40,

(ii) the credit determined under section 42 to the extent attributable to buildings placed in service after December 31, 2007,

(iii) the credit determined under section 45 to the extent that such credit is attributable to electricity or refined coal produced—

(I) at a facility which is originally placed in service after the date of the enactment of this paragraph, and

(II) during the 4-year period beginning on the date that such facility was originally placed in service,

(iv) the credit determined under section 45B,

(v) the credit determined under section 45G,
(vi) the credit determined under section 45R,
(vii) the credit determined under section 46 to the extent that such credit is attributable to the energy credit determined under section 48,
(viii) the credit determined under section 46 to the extent that such credit is attributable to the rehabilitation credit under section 47, but only with respect to qualified rehabilitation expenditures properly taken into account for periods after December 31, 2007, and
(ix) the credit determined under section 51.

(5) Special rules for eligible small business credits in 2010.
(A) In general. In the case of eligible small business credits determined in taxable years beginning in 2010—
(i) this section and section 39 shall be applied separately with respect to such credits, and
(ii) in applying paragraph (1) to such credits—
(I) the tentative minimum tax shall be treated as being zero, and
(II) the limitation under paragraph (1) (as modified by subclause (I)) shall be reduced by the credit allowed under subsection (a) for the taxable year (other than the eligible small business credits).
(B) Eligible small business credits. For purposes of this subsection, the term "eligible small business credits" means the sum of the credits listed in subsection (b) which are determined for the taxable year with respect to an eligible small business. Such credits shall not be taken into account under paragraph (2), (3), or (4).
(C) Eligible small business. For purposes of this subsection, the term "eligible small business" means, with respect to any taxable year—
(i) a corporation the stock of which is not publicly traded,
(ii) a partnership, or
(iii) a sole proprietorship.
if the average annual gross receipts of such corporation, partnership, or sole proprietorship for the 3-taxable-year period preceding such taxable year does not exceed $50,000,000. For purposes of applying the test under the preceding sentence, rules similar to the rules of paragraphs (2) and (3) of section 448(c) shall apply.
(D) Treatment of partners and S corporation shareholders. Credits determined with respect to a partnership or S corporation shall not be treated as eligible small business credits by any partner or shareholder unless such partner or shareholder meets the gross receipts test under subparagraph (C) for the taxable year in which such credits are treated as current year business credits.

(6) Special rules.
(A) Married individuals. In the case of a husband or wife who files a separate return, the amount specified under subparagraph (B) of paragraph (1) shall be $12,500 in lieu of $25,000. This subparagraph shall not apply if the spouse of the taxpayer has no business credit carryforward or carryback to, and has no current year business credit for, the taxable year of such spouse which ends within or with the taxpayer's taxable year.
(B) Controlled groups. In the case of a controlled group, the $25,000 amount specified under subparagraph (B) of paragraph (1) shall be reduced for each component member of such group by apportioning $25,000 among the component members of such group in such manner as the Secretary shall by regulations prescribe. For purposes of the preceding sentence, the term "controlled group" has the meaning given to such term by section 1563(a).
(C) Limitations with respect to certain persons. In the case of a person described in subparagraph (A) or (B) of section 46(e)(1) (as in effect on the day before the date of the enactment of the Revenue Reconciliation Act of 1990), the $25,000 amount specified under subparagraph (B) of paragraph (1) shall equal such person's ratable share (as determined under section 46(e)(2) (as so in effect)) of such amount.
(D) Estates and trusts. In the case of an estate or trust, the $25,000 amount specified under subparagraph (B) of paragraph (1) shall be reduced to an amount which bears the same ratio to $25,000 as the portion of the income of the estate or trust which is not allocated to beneficiaries bears to the total income of the estate or trust.

(d) Ordering rules.
For purposes of any provision of this title where it is necessary to ascertain the extent to which the credits determined under any section referred to in subsection (b) are used in a taxable year or as a carryback or carryforward—
(1) In general. The order in which such credits are used shall be determined on the basis of the order in which they are listed in subsection (b) as of the close of the taxable year in which the credit is used.
(2) Components of investment credit. The order in which the credits listed in section 46 are used shall be determined on the basis of the order in which such credits are listed in section 46 as of the close of the taxable year in which the credit is used.
(3) Credits no longer listed. For purposes of this subsection—
(A) the credit allowable by section 40, as in effect on the day before the date of the enactment of the Tax Reform Act of 1984, (relating to expenses of work incentive programs) and the credit allowable by section 41(a), as in effect on the day before the date of the enactment of the Tax Reform Act of 1986, (relating to employee stock ownership credit) shall be treated as referred to in that order after the last paragraph of subsection (b), and
(B) the credit determined under section 46—
(i) to the extent attributable to the employee plan percentage (as defined in section 46(a)(2)(E) as in effect on the day before the date of the enactment of the Tax Reform Act of 1984) shall be treated as a credit listed after paragraph (1) of section 46, and
(ii) to the extent attributable to the regular percentage (as defined in section 46(b)(1) as in effect on the day before the date of the enactment of the Revenue Reconciliation Act of 1990) shall be treated as the first credit listed in section 46.

In **2010,** P.L. 111-312, Sec. 101(a)(1), substituted "December 31, 2012" for "December 31, 2010" both places it appeared in Sec. 901, P.L. 107-16 [see below], effective as if included in the enactment of P.L. 107-16, EGTRRA, 6/7/2001.
—P.L. 111-240, Sec. 2013(a), redesignated para. (c)(5) as para. (c)(6) and added para. (c)(5), effective for credits determined in tax. yrs. begin. after 12/31/2009, and to carrybacks of such credits.
—P.L. 111-240, Sec. 2013(c)(1), added "the eligible small business credits," after "the New York Liberty Zone business employee credit," in sbcl. (c)(2)(A)(ii)(II); . . . Sec. 2013(c)(2), added ", the eligible small business credits," after "the New York Liberty Zone business employee credit" in sbcl. (c)(3)(A)(ii)(II); . . . Sec. 2013(c)(3), added "the eligible small business credits and" before "the specified credits" in sbcl. (c)(4)(A)(ii)(II), effective 9/27/2010.
—P.L. 111-148, Sec. 1421(b), deleted "plus" at the end of para. (b)(34), substituted ", plus" for the period at the end of para. (b)(35) and added para. (b)(36), effective for amounts paid or incurred in tax. yrs. begin. after 12/31/2009 [as

amended by Sec. 10105(e)(4) of this Act, see below].... Sec. 1421(c), redesignated clauses (c)(4)(B)(vi)-(viii) as (vii)-(ix) and added clause (c)(4)(B)(vi), effective for credits determined under Section 45R in tax. yrs. begin. after 12/31/2009, and to carrybacks of such credits [as amended by Sec. 10105(e)(4) of this Act, see below].

—P.L. 111-148, Sec. 10105(e)(4), substituted "2009" for "2010" both places it appeared in Sec. 1421(f) [the effective date provided for the amendments of Code Sec. 38, by Sec. 1421(b)-(c) of this Act, see above].

—P.L. 111-147, Sec. 102, of this Act provides:

"SEC. 102. BUSINESS CREDIT FOR RETENTION OF CERTAIN NEWLY HIRED INDIVIDUALS IN 2010.

"(a) In General- In the case of any taxable year ending after the date of the enactment of this Act, the current year business credit determined under section 38(b) of the Internal Revenue Code of 1986 for such taxable year shall be increased, with respect to each retained worker with respect to which subsection (b)(2) is first satisfied during such taxable year, by the lesser of—

"(1) $1,000, and

"(2) 6.2 percent of the wages (as defined in section 3401(a)) paid by the taxpayer to such retained worker during the 52 consecutive week period referred to in subsection (b)(2)."

* * * * * *

"(d) Treatment of Possessions-
* * *

"(2) COORDINATION WITH CREDIT ALLOWED AGAINST UNITED STATES INCOME TAXES- No increase in the credit determined under section 38(b) of the Internal Revenue Code of 1986 against United States income taxes for any taxable year determined under subsection (a) shall be taken into account with respect to any person—

"(A) to whom a credit is allowed against taxes imposed by the possession by reason of this section for such taxable year, or

"(B) who is eligible for a payment under a plan described in paragraph (1)(B) with respect to such taxable year."

In 2009, P.L. 111-5, Sec. 1141(b)(2), substituted "30D(c)(1)" for "30D(d)(1)" in para. (b)(35), effective for vehicles acquired after 12/31/2009.

In 2008, P.L. 110-343, Sec. 103(b)(1)DivB, redesignated clauses (c)(4)(B)(v)-(vi) [sic] as (vi)-(vii) and added clause (c)(4)(B)(v) . . . Sec. 103(b)(2)DivB, substituted "section 46 to the extent that such credit is attributable to the rehabilitation credit under section 47, but only with respect to" for "section 47 to the extent attributable to" in clause (c)(4)(B)(vi) [as redesignated by Sec. 103(b)(1)DivB, of this Act, see above], effective for credits determined under Code Sec. 46 in tax. yrs. begin. after 10/3/2008, and to carrybacks of such credits.

—P.L. 110-343, Sec. 115(b)DivB, deleted "plus" at the end of para. (b)(32), substituted ", plus" for the period at the end of para. (b)(33) and added para. (b)(34), effective for carbon dioxide captured after 10/3/2008..

—P.L. 110-343, Sec. 205(c)DivB, deleted "plus" at the end of para. (b)(33) [as amended by Sec. 115(b)DivB, of this Act, see above], substituted "plus" for the period at the end of para. (b)(34) [as added by Sec. 115(b)DivB, of this Act, see above] and added para. (b)(35), effective for tax. yrs. begin. after 12/31/2008.

—P.L. 110-343, Sec. 316(b)(1)DivC, redesignated clauses (c)(4)(B)(v)-(viii) [as amended by Sec. 103(b)(1)-(2)DivB, of this Act, see above] as (vi)-(viii) and added clause (c)(4)(B)(v), effective for credits determined under Code Sec. 45G in tax. yrs. begin. after 12/31/2007, and for carrybacks of such credits.

—P.L. 110-289, Sec. 3022(b), redesignated clauses (c)(4)(B)(ii)-(iv) as (iii)-(v) and added clause (c)(4)(B)(ii), effective for credits determined under Code Sec. 42 to the extent attributable to buildings placed in service after 12/31/2007.

—P.L. 110-289, Sec. 3022(c), deleted "and" at the end of clause (c)(4)(B)(iv), redesignated clause (c)(4)(B)(v) as (vi) and added clause (c)(4)(B)(v), effective for credits determined under Code Sec. 47 to the extent attributable to qualified rehabilitation expenditures properly taken into account for periods after 12/31/2007.

—P.L. 110-246, Sec. 4, Repeals the duplicative enactment and provides effective date provisions of the Act entitled "An Act to provide for the continuation of agricultural programs through fiscal year 2012, and for other purposes" Sec. 4, P.L. 110-246 reads as follows:

"Sec. 4. Repeal of duplicative enactment.

"(a) In General- The Act entitled 'An Act to provide for the continuation of agricultural programs through fiscal year 2012, and for other purposes' (H.R. 2419 of the 110th Congress), and the amendments made by that Act, are repealed, effective on the date of enactment of that Act.

"(b) Effective Date- Except as otherwise provided in this Act, this Act and the amendments made by this Act shall take effect on the earlier of—

"(1) the date of enactment of this Act; or

"(2) the date of the enactment of the Act entitled 'An Act to provide for the continuation of agricultural programs through fiscal year 2012, and for other purposes' (H.R. 2419 of the 110th Congress)."

—P.L. 110-246, Sec. 15343(b), deleted "plus" at the end of para. (b)(30), substituted ", plus" for the period at the end of para. (b)(31), and added para. (b)(32), effective for amounts paid or incurred after 5/22/2008. [Ed. Note: May 22, 2008 was the date of enactment for H.R. 2419 (PL 110-234), which was repealed by (2008 Farm Act § 4(a)) (PL 110-246, 6/18/2008), in connection with the reenactment of the farm bill to correct a technical deficiency in its original passage.]

—P.L. 110-245, Sec. 111(b), deleted "plus" at the end of para. (b)(31), substituted ", plus" for "." at the end of para. (b)(32), and added para. (b)(33) effective for amounts paid after 6/17/2008.

In 2007, P.L. 110-172, Sec. 11(a)(6), was enacted to correctly reflect the amendments made to subsec. (b) by P.L. 109-58, P.L. 109-59, and P.L. 109-432 by removing and inserting "and" and "plus" in the proper place.

—P.L. 110-28, Sec. 8214(a), deleted "and" at the end of clause (c)(4)(B)(i), added "," at the end of clause (c)(4)(B)(ii), and added clauses (c)(4)(B)(iii) and (iv) effective for credits determined under Code Secs. 45B and 51 of the Internal Revenue Code of 1986 in tax. yrs. begin. after 12/31/06, and to carrybacks of such credits.

In 2006, P.L. 109-432, Sec. 405(b), deleted "and" at the end of para. (b)(29), substituted ", plus" for the period at the end of para. (b)(30), and added para. (b)(31), effective for tax. yrs. begin. after 12/31/2005.

—P.L. 109-280, Sec. 811, of this Act [relating to Sec. 901 of P.L. 107-16, see below], provides:

"SEC. 811. PENSIONS AND INDIVIDUAL RETIREMENT ARRANGEMENT PROVISIONS OF ECONOMIC GROWTH AND TAX RELIEF RECONCILIATION ACT OF 2001 MADE PERMANENT.

"Title IX of the Economic Growth and Tax Relief Reconciliation Act of 2001 shall not apply to the provisions of, and amendments made by, subtitles A through F of title VI of such Act (relating to pension and individual retirement arrangement provisions)."

In 2005, P.L. 109-135, Sec. 103(b)(1), deleted "and" at the end of para. (b)(25), substituted ", and" for the period at the end of para. (b)(26), and added para. (b)(27), effective 12/21/2005.

—P.L. 109-135, Sec. 201(b)(1), deleted "and" at the end of para. (b)(26) [as amended by Sec. 103(b)(1) of this Act, see above], deleted the period at the end of para. (b)(27) [as added by Sec. 103(b)(1) of this Act, see above], and added paras. (b)(28)-(30), effective 12/21/2005.

—P.L. 109-135, Sec. 204(b)(4)(B), repealed Sec. 202 of P.L. 109-73, effective 12/21/2005.

Prior to repeal, Sec. 202 of P.L. 109-73 read as follows:

"SEC. 202. EMPLOYEE RETENTION CREDIT FOR EMPLOYERS AFFECTED BY HURRICANE KATRINA.

"(a) In general. In the case of an eligible employer, there shall be allowed as a credit against the tax imposed by chapter 1 of the Internal Revenue Code of 1986 for the taxable year an amount equal to 40 percent of the qualified wages with respect to each eligible employee of such employer for such taxable year. For purposes of the preceding sentence, the amount of qualified wages which may be taken into account with respect to any individual shall not exceed $6,000.

"(b) Definitions. For purposes of this section—

"(1) Eligible employer. The term 'eligible employer' means any employer—

"(A) which conducted an active trade or business on August 28, 2005, in a core disaster area, and

"(B) with respect to whom the trade or business described in subparagraph (A) is inoperable on any day after August 28, 2005, and before January 1, 2006, as a result of damage sustained by reason of Hurricane Katrina.

"(2) Eligible employee. The term 'eligible employee' means with respect to an eligible employer an employee whose principal place of employment on August 28, 2005, with such eligible employer was in a core disaster area.

"(3) Qualified wages. The term 'qualified wages' means wages (as defined in section 51(c)(1) of such Code, but without regard to section 3306(b)(2)(B) of such Code) paid or incurred by an eligible employer with respect to an eligible employee on any day after August 28, 2005, and before January 1, 2006, which occurs during the period—

"(A) beginning on the date on which the trade or business described in paragraph (1) first became inoperable at the principal place of employment of the employee immediately before Hurricane Katrina, and

"(B) ending on the date on which such trade or business has resumed significant operations at such principal place of employment.

Such term shall include wages paid without regard to whether the employee performs no services, performs services at a different place of employment than such principal place of employment, or performs services at such principal place of employment before significant operations have resumed.

"(c) Credit not allowed for large businesses. The term 'eligible employer' shall not include any trade or business for any taxable year if such trade or business employed an average of more than 200 employees on business days during the taxable year.

"(d) Certain rules to apply. For purposes of this section, rules similar to the rules of sections 51(i)(1), 52, and 280C(a) of such Code shall apply.

"(e) Employee not taken into account more than once. An employee shall not be treated as an eligible employee for purposes of this section for any period with respect to any employer if such employer is allowed a credit under section 51 of such Code with respect to such employee for such period.

"(f) Credit to be part of general business credit. The credit allowed under this section shall be added to the current year business credit under section 38(b) of such Code and shall be treated as a credit allowed under subpart D of part IV of subchapter A of chapter 1 of such Code."

—P.L. 109-135, Sec. 412(f)(1), substituted ", the New York Liberty Zone business employee credit, and the specified credits" for "or the New York Liberty Zone business employee credit or the specified credits" in subclause (c)(2)(A)(ii)(II) . . . Sec. 412(f)(2), substituted "and the specified credits" for "or the specified credits" in subclause (c)(3)(A)(ii)(II) . . . Sec. 412(f)(3)(A), substituted "means" for "includes" in subpara. (c)(4)(B) . . . Sec. 412(f)(3)(B), added "and" at the end of clause (c)(4)(B)(i), effective 12/21/2005.

—P.L. 109-59, Sec. 11126(b), deleted "plus" at the end of para. (b)(18), substituted ", plus" for the period at the end of para. (b)(19), and added para. (b)(20), effective for tax. yrs. begin. after 9/30/2005.

—P.L. 109-59, Sec. 11151(d)(2), of this Act, provides:

"(d) Amendment related to section 1306 of the Energy Policy Act of 2005.
* * *

"(2) If the Energy Policy Act of 2005 is enacted before the date of the enactment of this Act, for purposes of executing any amendments made by the Energy Policy Act of 2005 to section 38(b) of the Internal Revenue Code of 1986, the amendments made by section 11126(b) of this Act shall be treated as having been executed before such amendments made by the Energy Policy Act of 2005."

— P.L. 109-58, Sec. 1306(b), deleted "plus" at the end of para. (b)(19) [as amended by Sec. 11126(b) of P.L. 109-59, see above], substituted ", plus" for the period at the end of para. (b)(20) [as added by Sec. 11126(b) of P.L. 109-59, see above], and added para. (b)(21), effective for production in tax. yrs. begin. after 8/8/2005.

— P.L. 109-58, Sec. 1322(a)(2), deleted "plus" at the end of para. (b)(20) [as added by Sec. 11126(b) of P.L. 109-59 and amended by Sec. 1306(b) of P.L. 109-58, see above], substituted ", plus" for the period at the end of para. (b)(21) [as added by Sec. 1306(b) of P.L. 109-58, see above], and added para. (b)(22), effective for credits determined under the Internal Revenue Code of 1986 for tax. yrs. end. after 12/31/2005.

— P.L. 109-58, Sec. 1332(b), deleted "plus" at the end of para. (b)(21) [as added by Sec. 1306(b) of P.L. 109-58 and amended by Sec. 1322(a)(2) of P.L. 109-58, see above], substituted ", plus" for the period at the end of para. (b)(22) [as added by Sec. 1322(a)(2) of P.L. 109-58, see above], and added para. (b)(23), effective for qualified new energy efficient homes acquired after 12/31/2005, in tax. yrs. end. after 12/31/2005.

— P.L. 109-58, Sec. 1334(b), deleted "plus" at the end of para. (b)(22) [as added by Sec. 1322(a)(2) of P.L. 109-58 and amended by Sec. 1332(b) of P.L. 109-58, see above], substituted ", plus" for the period at the end of para. (b)(23) [as added by Sec. 1332(b) of P.L. 109-58, see above], and added para. (b)(24), effective for appliances produced after 12/31/2005.

— P.L. 109-58, Sec. 1341(b)(1), deleted ", plus" at the end of para. (b)(23) [as added by Sec. 1332(b) of P.L. 109-58 and amended by Sec. 1334(b) of P.L. 109-58, see above], substituted ", and" for the period at the end of para. (b)(24) [as added by Sec. 1334(b) of P.L. 109-58, see above], and added para. (b)(25), effective for property placed in service after 12/31/2005, in tax. yrs. end. after 12/31/2005.

Note: The word "plus" should be substituted for the word "and" in the amendment described above in order to make subsequent amendments to subsec. (b). This assessment reflects the probable intent of Congress.

— P.L. 109-58, Sec. 1342(b)(1), deleted ", and" [sic "plus", see above] at the end of para. (b)(24) [as added by Sec. 1334(b) of P.L. 109-58 and amended by Sec. 1341(b)(1) of P.L. 109-58, see above], substituted ", and" for the period at the end of para. (b)(25) [as added by Sec. 1341(b)(1) of P.L. 109-58, see above], and added para. (b)(26), effective for property placed in service after 12/31/2005, in tax. yrs. end. after 12/31/2005.

In 2004, P.L. 108-357, Sec. 245(c)(1), deleted "plus" at the end of para. (b)(14), substituted ", plus" for the period at the end of para. (b)(15), and added para. (b)(16), effective for tax. yrs. begin. after 12/31/2004.

— P.L. 108-357, Sec. 302(b), deleted "plus" at the end of para. (b)(15) [as amended by Sec. 245(c)(1) of this Act, see above], substituted ", plus" for the period at the end of para. (b)(16) [as added by Sec. 245(c)(1) of this Act, see above], and added para. (b)(17), effective for fuel produced, and sold or used, after 12/31/2004, in tax. yrs. end. after 12/31/2004.

— P.L. 108-357, Sec. 339(b), deleted "plus" at the end of para. (b)(16) [as added by Sec. 245(c)(1) of this Act and amended by Sec. 302(b) of this Act, see above], substituted ", plus" for the period at the end of para. (b)(17) [as added by Sec. 302(b) of this Act, see above], and added para. (b)(18), effective for expenses paid or incurred after 12/31/2002, in tax. yrs. end. after 12/31/2002.

— P.L. 108-357, Sec. 341(b), deleted "plus" at the end of para. (b)(17) [as added by Sec. 302(b) of this Act and amended by Sec. 339(b) of this Act, see above], substituted ", plus" for the period at the end of para. (b)(18) [as added by Sec. 339(b) of this Act, see above], and added para. (b)(19), effective for production in tax. yrs. begin. after 12/31/2004.

— P.L. 108-357, Sec. 711(a), redesignated para. (c)(4) as (c)(5) and added para. (c)(4) . . . Sec. 711(b), deleted "or the specified credits" after "employee credit" in subclause (c)(2)(A)(ii)(II) and subclause (c)(3)(A)(ii)(II), effective for tax. yrs. end. after 10/22/2004.

In 2002, P.L. 107-358, Sec. 2, added subsec. (c) in Sec. 901 of P.L. 107-16 [see below], effective 12/17/2002.

— P.L. 107-147, Sec. 301(b)(1), redesignated para. (c)(3) as (4) and added para. (c)(3) . . . Sec. 301(b)(2), added "or the New York Liberty Zone business employee credit" after "employment credit" in subclause (c)(2)(A)(ii)(II), effective for tax. yrs. end. after 12/31/2001.

— P.L. 107-147, Sec. 411(d)(2), substituted "45F(a)" for "45F" in para. (b)(15), effective for tax. yrs. begin. after 12/31/2001.

— P.L. 107-147, Sec. 411(n)(2), substituted "first effective" for "established" in Sec. 619(b) of P.L. 107-16, which provides the effective date for amendments made by Sec. 619 of P.L. 107-16 [see below].

In 2001, P.L. 107-16, Sec. 205(b)(1), deleted "plus" at the end of para. (b)(13) substituted ", plus" for the period at the end of para. (b)(14) [as amended by Sec. 619(b) of this Act, see below], and added para. (b)(15), effective for tax. yrs. begin. after 12/31/2001.

— P.L. 107-16, Sec. 619(b), deleted "plus" at the end of para. (b)(12), substituted ", plus" for the period at the end of para. (b)(13), and added para. (b)(14), effective [as amended by Sec. 411(n)(2) of P.L. 107-147, see above] for costs paid or incurred in tax. yrs. begin. after 12/31/2001, with respect to qualified employer plans first effective after 12/31/2001.

— P.L. 107-16, Sec. 901, of this Act [as amended by Sec. 2, P.L. 107-358 and Sec. 101(a)(1), P.L. 111-312, and as related to Sec. 811 of P.L. 109-280, see above], reads as follows:

"SEC. 901. SUNSET OF PROVISIONS OF ACT.

"(a) In general. All provisions of, and amendments made by, this Act shall not apply—

"(1) to taxable, plan, or limitation years beginning after December 31, 2012, or

"(2) in the case of title V, to estates of decedents dying, gifts made, or generation skipping transfers, after December 31, 2012.

"(b) Application of certain laws. The Internal Revenue Code of 1986 and the Employee Retirement Income Security Act of 1974 shall be applied and administered to years, estates, gifts, and transfers described in subsection (a) as if the provisions and amendments described in subsection (a) had never been enacted.

"(c) Exception. Subsection (a) shall not apply to section 803 (relating to no federal income tax on restitution received by victims of the Nazi regime or their heirs or estates)."

In 2000, P.L. 106-554, Sec. 1(a)(7), [which enacted into law Sec. 121(b)(1) of P.L. 106-554] deleted "plus" at the end of para. (b)(11), substituted ", plus" for the period at the end of para. (b)(12), and added para. (b)(13), effective for investments made after 12/31/2000.

In 1996, P.L. 104-188, Sec. 1112(a)(12), added ", with respect to services performed before, on, or after such date" after "1993" in subsec. (d) of Sec. 13443 of P.L. 103-66, the effective date for changes made by Sec. 13443(b), see below.

— P.L. 104-188, Sec. 1201(e)(1), substituted "work opportunity credit" for "targeted jobs credit" in para. (b)(2), effective for individuals who begin work for the employer after 9/30/96.

— P.L. 104-188, Sec. 1205(a)(2), deleted "plus" at the end of para. (b)(10), substituted ", plus" for the period at the end of para. (b)(11), and added para. (b)(12), effective for amounts paid or incurred in tax. yrs. end. after 6/30/96.

— P.L. 104-188, Sec. 1702(e)(4), added "and without regard to the deduction under section 56(h)" before the period in subpara. (c)(2)(C) as in effect before the date of enactment of P.L. 101-508, see below, effective for property placed in service after 12/31/90, except as provided in Sec. 11813(c)(2) of this Act, reproduced in note following Code Sec. 46.

— P.L. 104-188, Sec. 1703(n)(13), substituted "section 1393(a)(2)" for "section 1393(a)(3)" in Sec. 13111(e)(2) of P.L. 103-66, see below.

In 1993, P.L. 103-66, Sec. 13302(a)(1), deleted "plus" from the end of para. (b)(7), substituted ", and" for the period at the end of para. (b)(8) and added para. (b)(9) . . . Sec. 13302(c)(1), redesignated para. (c)(2) as para. (c)(3) and added new para. (c)(2), effective 8/10/93.

— P.L. 103-66, Sec. 13311, of this Act [as amended by Sec. 1703(n)(13) of P.L. 104-188, see above], provides:

"SEC. 13311. CREDIT FOR CONTRIBUTIONS TO CERTAIN COMMUNITY DEVELOPMENT CORPORATIONS.

"(a) In general. For purposes of section 38 of the Internal Revenue Code of 1986, the current year business credit shall include the credit determined under this section.

"(b) Determination of credit. The credit determined under this section for each taxable year in the credit period with respect to any qualified CDC contribution made by the taxpayer is an amount equal to 5 percent of such contribution.

"(c) Credit period. For purposes of this section, the credit period with respect to any qualified CDC contribution is the period of 10 taxable years beginning with the taxable year during which such contribution was made.

"(d) Qualified CDC contribution. For purposes of this section—

"(1) In general. The term 'qualified CDC contribution' means any transfer of cash—

"(A) which is made to a selected community development corporation during the 5-year period beginning on the date such corporation was selected for purposes of this section,

"(B) the amount of which is available for use by such corporation for at least 10 years,

"(C) which is to be used by such corporation for qualified low-income assistance within its operational area, and

"(D) which is designated by such corporation for purposes of this section.

"(2) Limitations on amount designated. The aggregate amount of contributions to a selected community development corporation which may be designated by such corporation shall not exceed $2,000,000.

"(e) Selected community development corporations.

"(1) In general. For purposes of this section, the term 'selected community development corporation' means any corporation—

"(A) which is described in section 501(c)(3) of such Code and exempt from tax under section 501(a) of such Code,

"(B) the principal purposes of which include promoting employment of, and business opportunities for, low-income individuals who are residents of the operational area, and

"(C) which is selected by the Secretary of Housing and Urban Development for purposes of this section.

"(2) Only 20 corporations may be selected. The Secretary of Housing and Urban Development may select 20 corporations for purposes of this section, subject to the availability of eligible corporations. Such selections may be made only before July 1, 1994. At least 8 of the operational areas of the corporations selected must be rural areas (as defined by section 1393(a)(2) of such Code).

"(3) Operational areas must have certain characteristics. A corporation may be selected for purposes of this section only its operational area meets the following criteria:

"(A) The area meets the size requirements under section 1392(a)(3).

"(B) The unemployment rate (as determined by the appropriate available data) is not less than the national unemployment rate.

"(C) The median family income of residents of such area does not exceed 80 percent of the median gross income of residents of the jurisdiction of the local government which includes such area.

"(f) Qualified low-income assistance. For purposes of this section, the term 'qualified low-income assistance' means assistance—

"(1) which is designed to provide employment of, and business opportunities for, low-income individuals who are residents of the operational area of the community development corporation, and

"(2) which is approved by the Secretary of Housing and Urban Development."

—P.L. 103-66, Sec. 13322(a), deleted "plus" [sic and] from the end of para. (b)(8), substituted ", plus" for the period at the end of para. (b)(9), and added para. (b)(10), effective for wages paid or incurred after 12/31/93.

—P.L. 103-66, Sec. 13443(b)(1), deleted "plus" from the end of para. (b)(9), substituted ", plus" for the period at the end of para. (b)(10), and added para. (b)(11), effective [as amended by Sec. 1112(a)(2) of P.L. 104-188, see above] for taxes paid after 12/31/93, with respect to services performed before, on, or after such date.

In 1992, P.L. 102-486, Sec. 1914(b), deleted "plus" at the end of para. (b)(6), substituted ", plus" for the period at the end of para. (b)(7), and added para. (b)(8), effective for tax. yrs. end. after 12/31/92.

In 1990, P.L. 101-508, Sec. 11511(b)(1), deleted "plus" at the end of para. (b)(4), substituted ", plus" for the period at the end of para. (b)(5), and added para. (b)(6), effective for costs paid or incurred in tax. yrs. begin. after 12/31/90 except as provided in Sec. 11511(d)(2) of this Act, which reads as follows:

"(2) Special rule for significant expansion of projects. For purposes of section 43(c)(2)(A)(iii) of the Internal Revenue Code of 1986 (as added by subsection (a)), any significant expansion after December 31, 1990, of a project begun before January 1, 1991, shall be treated as a project with respect to which the first injection commences after December 31, 1990."

—P.L. 101-508, Sec. 11611(b)(1), deleted "plus" in para. (b)(5) [as amended by Sec. 11511(b)(1) of this Act, see above], substituted ", plus" for the period at the end of para. (b)(6), and added para. (b)(7), effective for expenditures paid or incurred after 11/5/90.

—P.L. 101-508, Sec. 11813(b)(2)(A), substituted "section 46" for "section 46(a)" in para. (b)(1)... Sec. 11813(b)(2)(B), deleted para. (c)(2), and redesignated para. (c)(3) as para. (c)(2)... Sec. 11813(b)(2)(C)(i), added "(as in effect on the day before the date of the enactment [11/5/90] of the Revenue Reconciliation Act of 1990)" after "46(e)(1)" in subpara. (c)(2)(C) [as redesignated by Sec. 11813(b)(2)(B) of this Act (see above)]... Sec. 11813(b)(2)(C)(ii), added "(as so in effect)" after "46(e)(2)" in subpara. (c)(2)(C) [as redesignated by Sec. 11813(b)(2)(B) of this Act (see above)]... Sec. 11813(b)(2)(D)(i), substituted "any provision" for "sections 46(f), 47(a), 196(a), and any other provision" in subsec. (d)... Sec. 11813(b)(2)(D)(ii), amended para. (d)(2)... Sec. 11813(b)(2)(D)(iii), amended subpara. (d)(3)(B), effective for property placed in service after 12/30/90, except as provided in Sec. 11813(c)(2) of this Act, reproduced in note following Code Sec. 38.

Prior to deletion, para. (c)(2) [as amended by Sec. 1702(e)(4) of P.L. 104-188, see above] read as follows:

"(2) Regular investment tax credit may offset 25 percent of minimum tax.

"(A) In general. In the case of a C corporation, the amount determined under paragraph (1)(A) shall be reduced by the lesser of—

"(i) the portion of the regular investment tax credit not used against the normal limitation, or

"(ii) 25 percent of the taxpayer's tentative minimum tax for the taxable year.

"(B) Portion of regular investment tax credit not used against normal limit. For purposes of subparagraph (A), the portion of the regular investment tax credit for any taxable year not used against the normal limitation is the excess (if any) of—

"(i) the portion of the credit under subsection (a) which is attributable to the application of the regular percentage under section 46, over

"(ii) the limitation of paragraph (1) (without regard to this paragraph) reduced by the portion of the credit under subsection (a) which is not so attributable.

"(C) Limitation. In no event shall this paragraph permit the allowance of a credit which would result in a net chapter 1 tax less than an amount equal to 10 percent of the amount determined under section 55(b)(1)(A) without regard to the alternative tax net operating loss deduction and without regard to the deduction under section 56(h). For purposes of the preceding sentence, the term 'net chapter 1 tax' means the sum of the regular tax liability for the taxable year and the tax imposed by section 55 for the taxable year, reduced by the sum of the credits allowable under this part for the taxable year (other than under section 34) and without regard to the deduction under section 56(h)."

Prior to amendment, para. (d)(2) read as follows:

"(2) Components of investment credit. The order in which credits attributable to a percentage referred to in section 46(a) are used shall be determined on the basis of the order in which such percentages are listed in section 46(a) as of the close of the taxable year in which the credit is used."

Prior to amendment, subpara. (d)(3)(B) read as follows:

"(B) the employee plan percentage (as defined in section 46(a)(2)(E), as in effect on the day before the date of the enactment of the Tax Reform Act of 1984) shall be treated as referred to after section 46(a)(2)."

In 1988, P.L. 100-647, Sec. 1002(e)(8)(A), amended subsec. (d), effective for tax. yrs. begin. after 12/31/83 and to carrybacks from tax. yrs. begin. after 12/31/83.

Prior to amendment subsec. (d) read as follows:

"(d) Special rules for certain regulated companies. In the case of any taxpayer to which section 46(f) applies, for purposes of sections 46(f), 47(a), and 196(a) and any other provision of this title where it is necessary to ascertain the extent to which the credits determined under section 40(a), 41(a), 42(a), 46(a), or 51(a) are used in a taxable year or as a carryback or carryforward, the order in which such credits are used shall be determined on the basis of the order in which they are listed in subsection (b)."

—P.L. 100-647, Sec. 1007(f)(2), amended Sec. 701(f)(6)(B) of P.L. 99-514 [reproduced below] by amending the last sentence, see below.

Prior to amendment the last sentence of Sec. 701(f)(6)(B) of P.L. 99-514 read as follows:

"The aggregate amount of investment tax credits with respect to such unit shall be described in this subparagraph."

—P.L. 100-647, Sec. 1007(f)(3), added Sec. 701(f)(7) of P.L. 99-514, [reproduced below], see below.

—P.L. 100-647, Sec. 1007(g)(2)(A), amended paras. (c)(1)-(3)... Sec. 1007(g)(2)(B), redesignated para. (c)(4) as (c)(3) and substituted "subparagraph (B) of paragraph (1)" for "subparagraphs (A) and (B) of paragraph (1)" each place it appeared in para. (c)(3), effective for tax. yrs. begin. before 12/31/86.

Prior to amendment, paras. (c)(1)-(3) read as follows:

"(c) Limitation based on amount of tax.

"(1) In general. The credit allowed under subsection (a) for any taxable year shall not exceed the lesser of—

"(A) the allowable portion of the taxpayer's net regular tax liability for the taxable year, or

"(B) the excess (if any) of the taxpayer's net regular tax liability for the taxable year over the tentative minimum tax for the taxable year.

"(2) Allowable portion of net regular tax liability. For purposes of this subsection, the allowable portion of the taxpayer's net regular tax liability for the taxable year is the sum of—

"(A) so much of the taxpayer's net regular tax liability for the taxable year as does not exceed $25,000, plus

"(B) 75 percent of so much of the taxpayer's net regular tax liability for the taxable year as exceeds $25,000.

For purposes of the preceding sentence, the term 'net regular tax liability' means the regular tax liability reduced by the sum of the credits allowable under subparts A and B of this part.

"(3) Regular investment tax credit may offset 25 percent of minimum tax. In the case of any C corporation, to the extent the credit under subsection (a) is attributable to the application of the regular percentage under section 46, the limitation of paragraph (1) shall be the greater of—

"(A) the lesser of—

"(i) the allowable portion of the taxpayer's net regular tax liability for the taxable year, or

"(ii) the excess (if any) of the taxpayer's net regular tax liability for the taxable year over 75 percent of the tentative minimum tax for the taxable year, or

"(B) 25 percent of the taxpayer's tentative minimum tax for the year.

In no event shall this paragraph permit the allowance of a credit which (in combination with the alternative tax net operating loss deduction and the alternative minimum tax foreign tax credit) would reduced the tax payable under section 55 below and amount equal to 10 percent of the amount which would be determined under section 55(b) without regard to the alternative tax net operating loss deduction and the alternative minimum tax foreign tax credit."

In 1986, P.L. 99-514, Sec. 221(a), substituted "75 percent" for "85 percent" in subpara. (c)(1)(B)... Sec. 231(d)(1), deleted "plus" at the end of para. (b)(2), substituted ", plus" for the period at the end of para. (b)(3), and added para. (b)(4) [after amendment by Sec. 1171(b)(1) of this Act, see below]... Sec. 231(d)(3)(B), added "41(a)," after "40(a)," in subsec. (d) [after amendment by Sec. 1171(b)(2) of this Act, see below], effective for tax. yrs. begin. after 12/31/85.

—P.L. 99-514, Sec. 252(b)(1), deleted "plus" at the end of para. (b)(3), substituted ", plus" for the period at the end of para. (b)(4), and added para. (b)(5) [after amendment by Sec. 1171(b)(1) of this Act, see below, and by Sec. 231(d)(1) of this Act, see above]... Sec. 252(b)(2), added "42(a)," before "46(a)" in subsec. (d), effective for buildings placed in service after 12/31/86, in tax. yrs. end. after 12/31/86.

—P.L. 99-514, Sec. 701(c)(4), redesignated para. (c)(3) and (c)(4), deleted paras. (c)(1) [as amended by Sec. 221(a) of this Act, see above] and (c)(2), and added new paras. (c)(1)-(3), effective for tax. yrs. begin. after 12/31/86.

Prior to deletion, paras. (c)(1) and (c)(2) read as follows:

"(1) In general. The credit allowed under subsection (a) for any taxable year shall not exceed the sum of

"(A) so much of the taxpayer's net tax liability for the taxable year as does not exceed $25,000, plus

"(B) 75 percent of so much of the taxpayer's net tax liability for the taxable year as exceeds $25,000.

"(2) Net tax liability. For purposes of paragraph (1), the term 'net tax liability' means the tax liability (as defined in section 26(b)), reduced by the sum of the credits allowable under subparts A and B of this part."

—P.L. 99-514, Sec. 701(f)(6), [as amended by Sec. 1007(f)(2) of P.L. 100-647, see above] and (f)(7) of this Act provides:

"(6) Certain public utility.

"(A) In the case of investment tax credits described in subparagraph (B) or (C), subsection 38(c)(3)(A)(ii) of the Internal Revenue Code of 1986 shall be applied by substituting '25 percent' for '75 percent', and section 38(c)(3)(B) of the Internal Revenue Code of 1986 shall be applied by substituting '75 percent' for '25 percent'.

"(B) If, on September 25, 1985, a regulated electric utility owned an undivided interest, within the range of 1,111 and 1,149, in the 'maximum dependable capacity, net, megawatts electric' of an electric generating unit located in Illinois or Mississippi for which a binding written contract was in effect on December 31, 1980, then any investment tax credit with respect to such unit shall be described in this subparagraph. The aggregate amount of investment tax credits with respect to the unit in Mississippi allowed solely by reason of being described in this subparagraph shall not exceed $11,000,000.

"(C) If, on September 25, 1985, a regulated electric utility owned an undivided interest, within the range of 1,104 and 1,111, in the 'maximum dependable capacity, net, megawatts electric' of an electric generating unit located in Louisiana for which a binding written contract was in effect on December 31, 1980, then any investment tax credit of such electric utility shall be described in this subparagraph. The aggregate amount of investment tax credits allowed solely by reason of being described by this subparagraph shall not exceed $20,000,000."

"(7) Agreement vessel depreciation adjustment.

"(A) For purposes of part VI of subchapter A of chapter 1 of the Internal Revenue Code of 1986, in the case of a qualified taxpayer, alternative minimum taxable income for the taxable year shall be reduced by an amount equal to the agreement vessel depreciation adjustment.

"(B) For purposes of this paragraph, the agreement vessel depreciation adjustment shall be an amount equal to the depreciation deduction that would have been allowable for such year under section 167 of such Code with respect to agreement vessels placed in service before January 1, 1987, if the basis of such vessels had not been reduced under section 607 of the Merchant Marine Act of 1936, as amended, and if depreciation with respect to such vessel had been computed using the 25-year straight-line method. The aggregate amount by which basis of a qualified taxpayer is treated as not reduced by reason of this subparagraph shall not exceed $100,000,000.

"(C) For purposes of this paragraph, the term 'qualified taxpayer' means a parent corporation incorporated in the State of Delaware on December 1, 1972, and engaged in water transportation, and includes any other corporation which is a member of the affiliated group of which the parent corporation is the common parent. No taxpayer shall be treated as a qualified corporation for any taxable year beginning after December 31, 1991."

—P.L. 99-514, Sec. 1171(b)(1), deleted para. (b)(4), added "plus" at the end of para. (b)(2), and substituted a period for ", plus" at the end of para. (b)(3) [before amendment by Secs. 231(d)(1) and 252(b)(1) of this Act, see above] ... Sec. 1171(b)(2), substituted "and 196(a)" for "196(a), and 404(i)" and deleted "41(a)" in subsec. (d) [before amendment by Sec. 231(d)(3)(B) of this Act, see above], effective for compensation paid or accrued after 12/31/86, in tax. yrs. end. after 12/31/86.

Prior to deletion, para. (b)(4) read as follows:

"(4) the employee stock ownership credit determined under section 41(a)."

In **1984**, P.L. 98-369, Sec. 473, added Code Sec. 38, effective for tax. yrs. begin. after 12/31/83 and for carrybacks from tax. yrs. begin. after 12/31/83

—P.L. 98-369, Sec. 612(e)(1), substituted "section 26(b)" for "section 25(b)" in para. (c)(2), effective for interest paid or accrued after 12/31/84, on indebtedness incurred after 12/31/84.

See. 612(g)(2), of this Act provides:

"(2) Elections. The amendments made by this section shall apply to elections under section 25(c)(2)(A)(ii) of the Internal Revenue Code of 1954 (as added by this section) for calendar years after 1983."

—P.L. 98-369, Sec. 632, provided various exceptions to the amendments made by Title VI of this Act. See note following Code Sec. 103A.

Sec. 38. Repealed.

In **1984**, P.L. 98-369, Sec. 450, amended Sec. 101(c)(1) of P.L. 92-178 (reproduced below) by adding "and" at the end of Sec. 101(c)(1)(A), by substituting a period for ", and" in Sec. 101(c)(1)(B) and by deleting Sec. 101(c)(1)(C).

Prior to deletion, Sec. 101(c)(1)(C) of P.L. 92-178 read as follows:

"(C) a taxpayer shall use the same method of accounting for such credit in all such reports made by him, unless the Secretary of the Treasury or his delegate consents to a change to another method."

—P.L. 98-369, Sec. 474(m)(1), repealed Code Sec. 38, effective for tax. yrs. begin. after 12/31/83 and for carrybacks from tax. yrs. begin after 12/31/83.

Prior to repeal, Code Sec. 38 read as follows:

"SEC. 38. INVESTMENT IN CERTAIN DEPRECIABLE PROPERTY.

"(a) General rule. There shall be allowed, as a credit against the tax imposed by this chapter, the amount determined under subpart B of this part.

"(b) Regulations. The Secretary shall prescribe such regulations as may be necessary to carry out the purposes of this section and subpart B."

In **1980**, P.L. 96-294, Sec. 506, 509, 515, provide that a taxpayer cannot claim a credit under Code Sec. 38 with respect to an expenditure for which financial assistance was obtained from the Solar Energy and Energy Conservation Bank.

In **1976**, P.L. 94-455, Sec. 1906(b)(13)(A), substituted "Secretary" for "Secretary or his delegate" in subsec (b), effective for tax. yrs. begin. after '76.

In **1971**, P.L. 92-178, Sec. 101(c), enacted 12/10/71, provided as follows:

"(1) In general. It was the intent of the Congress in enacting, in the Revenue Act of 1962, the investment credit allowed by section 38 of the Internal Revenue Code of 1954, and it is the intent of the Congress in restoring that credit in this Act, to provide an incentive for modernization and growth of private industry. Accordingly, notwithstanding any other provision of law, on and after the date of the enactment of this Act—

"(A) no taxpayer shall be required to use, for purposes of financial reports subject to the jurisdiction of any Federal agency or reports made to any Federal agency, any particular method of accounting for the credit allowed by such section 38, and

"(B) a taxpayer shall disclose, in any such report, the method of accounting for such credit used by him for purposes of such report.

"(2) Exceptions. Paragraph (1) shall not apply to taxpayers who are subject to the provisions of section 46(c) of the Internal Revenue Code of 1954 (as added by section 105(c) of this Act) or to section 203(e) of the Revenue Act of 1964 (as modified by section 105(e) of this Act)."

In **1964**, P.L. 88-272, Sec. 203(e), provided that:

"(e) Treatment of investment credit by federal regulatory agencies. It was the intent of the Congress in providing an investment credit under section 38 of the Internal Revenue Code of 1954, and it is the intent of the Congress in repealing the reduction in basis required by section 48(g) of such Code, to provide an incentive for modernization and growth of private industry (including that portion thereof which is regulated). Accordingly, Congress does not intend that any agency or instrumentality of the United States having jurisdiction with respect to a taxpayer shall, without the consent of the taxpayer, use—

"(1) in the case of public utility property (as defined in section 46(c)(3)(B) of the Internal Revenue Code of 1954), more than a proportionate part (determined with reference to the average useful life of the property with respect to which the credit was allowed) of the credit against tax allowed for any taxable year by section 38 of such Code, or

"(2) in the case of any other property, any credit against tax allowed by section 38 of such Code,

to reduce such taxpayer's Federal income taxes for the purpose of establishing the cost of service of the taxpayer or to accomplish a similar result by any other method."

In **1962**, P.L. 87-834, Sec. 2, added Code Sec. 38, effective for tax. yrs. end. after 1961.

Sec. 39. Carryback and carryforward of unused credits.

(a) In general.

(1) 1-year carryback and 20-year carryforward. If the sum of the business credit carryforwards to the taxable year plus the amount of the current year business credit for the taxable year exceeds the amount of the limitation imposed by subsection (c) of section 38 for such taxable year (hereinafter in this section referred to as the "unused credit year"), such excess (to the extent attributable to the amount of the current year business credit) shall be—

(A) a business credit carryback to the taxable year preceding the unused credit year, and

(B) a business credit carryforward to each of the 20 taxable years following the unused credit year,

and, subject to the limitations imposed by subsections (b) and (c), shall be taken into account under the provisions of section 38(a) in the manner provided in section 38(a).

(2) Amount carried to each year.

(A) Entire amount carried to first year. The entire amount of the unused credit for an unused credit year shall be carried to the earliest of the 21 taxable years to which (by reason of paragraph (1)) such credit may be carried.

(B) Amount carried to other 20 years. The amount of the unused credit for the unused credit year shall be carried to each of the other 20 taxable years to the extent that such unused credit may not be taken into account under section 38(a) for a prior taxable year because of the limitations of subsections (b) and (c).

(3) 5-year carryback for marginal oil and gas well production credit. Notwithstanding subsection (d), in the case of the marginal oil and gas well production credit—

(A) this section shall be applied separately from the business credit (other than the marginal oil and gas well production credit) or the eligible small business credits,

(B) paragraph (1) shall be applied by substituting "each of the 5 taxable years" for "the taxable year" in subparagraph (A) thereof, and

(C) paragraph (2) shall be applied—

(i) by substituting "25 taxable years" for "21 taxable years" in subparagraph (A) thereof, and

(ii) by substituting "24 taxable years" for "20 taxable years" in subparagraph (B) thereof.

1,109

(4) 5-year carryback for eligible small business credits.
(A) In general. Notwithstanding subsection (d), in the case of eligible small business credits determined in the first taxable year of the taxpayer beginning in 2010—
(i) paragraph (1) shall be applied by substituting "each of the 5 taxable years" for "the taxable year" in subparagraph (A)thereof, and
(ii) paragraph (2) shall be applied—
(I) by substituting "25 taxable years" for "21 taxable years" in subparagraph (A) thereof, and
(II) by substituting "24 taxable years" for "20 taxable years" in subparagraph (B) thereof.

(B) Eligible small business credits. For purposes of this subsection, the term "eligible small business credits" has the meaning given such term by section 38(c)(5)(B).

(b) Limitation on carrybacks.
The amount of the unused credit which may be taken into account under section 38(a)(3) for any preceding taxable year shall not exceed the amount by which the limitation imposed by section 38(c) for such taxable year exceeds the sum of—
(1) the amounts determined under paragraphs (1) and (2) of section 38(a) for such taxable year, plus
(2) the amounts which (by reason of this section) are carried back to such taxable year and are attributable to taxable years preceding the unused credit year.

(c) Limitation on carryforwards.
The amount of the unused credit which may be taken into account under section 38(a)(1) for any succeeding taxable year shall not exceed the amount by which the limitation imposed by section 38(c) for such taxable year exceeds the sum of the amounts which, by reason of this section, are carried to such taxable year and are attributable to taxable years preceding the unused credit year.

(d) Transitional rule.
No portion of the unused business credit for any taxable year which is attributable to a credit specified in section 38(b) or any portion thereof may be carried back to any taxable year before the first taxable year for which such specified credit or such portion is allowable (without regard to subsection (a)).

In 2010, P.L. 111-312, Sec. 101(a)(1), substituted "December 31, 2012" for "December 31, 2010" both places it appeared in Sec. 901, P.L. 107-16 [see below], effective as if included in the enactment of P.L. 107-16, EGTRRA, 6/7/2001.

—P.L. 111-240, Sec. 2012(a), added para. (a)(4) . . . Sec. 2012(b), added "or the eligible small business credits" after "credit)", effective for credits determined in tax. yrs. begin. after 12/31/2009.

In 2006, P.L. 109-280, Sec. 811, of this Act [relating to Sec. 901 of P.L. 107-16, see below], provides:

"SEC. 811. PENSIONS AND INDIVIDUAL RETIREMENT ARRANGEMENT PROVISIONS OF ECONOMIC GROWTH AND TAX RELIEF RECONCILIATION ACT OF 2001 MADE PERMANENT.

"Title IX of the Economic Growth and Tax Relief Reconciliation Act of 2001 shall not apply to the provisions of, and amendments made by, subtitles A through F of title VI of such Act (relating to pension and individual retirement arrangement provisions)."

In 2005, P.L. 109-135, Sec. 412(g)(1), substituted "the taxable year" for "each of the 1 taxable years" in subpara. (a)(1)(A), . . . Sec. 412(g)(2), amended subpara. (a)(3)(B), effective 12/21/2005.

Prior to amendment, subpara. (a)(3)(B) read as follows:

"(B) paragraph (1) shall be applied by substituting '5 taxable years' for '1 taxable years' in subparagraph (A) thereof, and"

In 2004, P.L. 108-357, Sec. 245(b)(1), amended subsec. (d), effective for tax. yrs. end. after 12/31/2003.

Prior to amendment, subsec. (d) reads as follows:

"*(d) Transitional rules.*

"(1) No carryback of enhanced oil recovery credit before 1991. No portion of the unused business credit for any taxable year which is attributable to the credit determined under section 43(a) (relating to enhanced oil recovery credit) may be carried to a taxable year beginning before January 1, 1991.

"(2) No carryback of section 44 credit before enactment. No portion of the unused business credit for any taxable year which is attributable to the disabled access credit determined under section 44 may be carried to a taxable year ending before the date of the enactment of section 44.

"(3) No carryback of renewable electricity production credit before effective date. No portion of the unused business credit for any taxable year which is attributable to the credit determined under section 45 (relating to electricity produced from certain renewable resources) may be carried back to any taxable year ending before January 1, 1993 (before January 1, 1994, to the extent such credit is attributable to wind as a qualified energy resource).

"(4) Empowerment zone employment credit. No portion of the unused business credit which is attributable to the credit determined under section 1396 (relating to empowerment zone employment credit) may be carried to any taxable year ending before January 1, 1994.

"(5) No carryback of section 45A credit before enactment. No portion of the unused business credit for any taxable year which is attributable to the Indian employment credit determined under section 45A may be carried to a taxable year ending before the date of the enactment of section 45A.

"(6) No carryback of section 45B credit before enactment. No portion of the unused business credit for any taxable year which is attributable to the employer social security credit determined under section 45B may be carried back to a taxable year ending before the date of the enactment of section 45B.

"(7) No carryback of section 45C credit before July 1, 1996. No portion of the unused business credit for any taxable year which is attributable to the orphan drug credit determined under section 45C may be carried back to the taxable year ending before July 1, 1996.

"(8) No carryback of DC Zone credits before effective date. No portion of the unused business credit for any taxable year which is attributable to the credits allowable under subchapter U by reason of section 1400 may be carried back to a taxable year ending before the date of the enactment of section 1400.

"(9) No carryback of new markets tax credit before January 1, 2001. No portion of the unused business credit for any taxable year which is attributable to the credit under section 45D may be carried to a taxable year ending before January 1, 2001.

"(10) No carryback of small employer pension plan startup cost credit before January 1, 2002. No portion of the unused business credit for any taxable year which is attributable to the small employer pension plan startup cost credit determined under section 45E may be carried back to a taxable year beginning before January 1, 2002."

—P.L. 108-357, Sec. 341(c), added para. (a)(3), effective for production in tax. yrs. begin. after 12/31/2004.

In 2002, P.L. 107-358, Sec. 2, added subsec. (c) in Sec. 901 of P.L. 107-16 [see below], effective 12/17/2002.

—P.L. 107-147, Sec. 411(n)(2), substituted "first effective" for "established" in Sec. 619(d) of P.L. 107-16, see below.

In 2001, P.L. 107-16, Sec. 619(c)(1), added para. (d)(10), effective for costs paid or incurred in tax. yrs. begin. after 12/31/2001, with respect to qualified employer plans first effective after 12/31/2001.

—P.L. 107-16, Sec. 901, of this Act [as amended by Sec. 2, PL. 107-358 and Sec. 101(a)(1), P.L. 111-312, and as related to Sec. 811 of P.L. 109-280, see above], reads as follows:

"Sec. 901. Sunset of provisions of Act.

"(a) In general. All provisions of, and amendments made by, this Act shall not apply—

"(1) to taxable, plan, or limitation years beginning after December 31, 2012, or

"(2) in the case of title V, to estates of decedents dying, gifts made, or generation skipping transfers, after December 31, 2012.

"(b) Application of certain laws. The Internal Revenue Code of 1986 and the Employee Retirement Income Security Act of 1974 shall be applied and administered to years, estates, gifts, and transfers described in subsection (a) as if the provisions and amendments described in subsection (a) had never been enacted.

"(c) Exception. Subsection (a) shall not apply to section 803 (relating to no federal income tax on restitution received by victims of the Nazi regime or their heirs or estates)."

In 2000, P.L. 106-554, Sec. 1(a)(7), [which enacted into law Sec. 121(b)(2) of P.L. 106-554] added para. (d)(9), effective for investments made after 12/31/2000.

In 1998, P.L. 105-206, Sec. 6010(n)(1), substituted "20" for "21" in Sec. 1083(a)(2) of P.L. 105-34, see below . . . Sec. 6010(n)(2), substituted "21" for "22" in Sec. 1083(a)(2) of P.L. 105-34, see below, effective for credits arising in tax. yrs. begin. after 12/31/97.

In 1997, P.L. 105-34, Sec. 701(b)(1), added para. (d)(8), effective 8/5/97.

—P.L. 105-34, Sec. 1083(a)(1), substituted "1" for "3" and substituted "20" for "15" each place either appeared in para. (a)(1) . . . Sec. 1083(a)(2), substituted "21" for "18" and substituted "20" for "17" each place either appeared in para. (a)(2), effective for credits arising in tax. yrs. begin. after 12/31/97 [amended by Sec. 6010(n)(1) and (2) of 105-206, see above].

In 1996, P.L. 104-188, Sec. 1112(a)(2), added ", with respect to services performed before, on, or after such date" after "1993" in Sec. 13443(d) of P.L. 103-66, the effective date for changes made by Sec. 13443(b)(2) of P.L. 103-66, see below.

—P.L. 104-188, Sec. 1205(c), added para. (d)(7), effective for amounts paid or incurred in tax. yrs. end. after 6/30/96.

—P.L. 104-188, Sec. 1703(n)(1)(A), substituted "45A" for "45" in the heading of para. (d)(5), effective for wages paid or incurred after 12/31/93.

—P.L. 104-188, Sec. 1703(n)(1)(B), substituted "45B" for "45" in the heading of para. (d)(6), effective for taxes paid after 12/31/93 with respect to services performed before, on, or after such date.

In 1993, P.L. 103-66, Sec. 13302(a)(2), added para. (d)(4), effective 8/10/93.

—P.L. 103-66, Sec. 13322(d), added para. (d)(5), effective for wages paid or incurred after 12/31/93.
—P.L. 103-66, Sec. 13443(b)(2), added para. (d)(6), effective [as amended by Sec. 1112(a)(2) of P.L. 104-188, see above] for taxes paid after 12/31/93, with respect to services performed before, on, or after such date.

In 1992, P.L. 102-486, Sec. 1914(c), redesignated paras. (d)(5) [as added by Sec. 11511(b)(2) of P.L. 101-508] and (d)(6) [sic (5), as added by P.L. 101-508, Sec. 11611(b)(2)] as paras. (d)(1) and (d)(2), and added para. (d)(3), effective for tax. yrs. ending after 12/31/92.

In 1990, P.L. 101-508, Sec. 11511(b)(2), added para. (d)(5), effective for costs paid or incurred in tax yrs. begin. after 12/31/90, except as provided in Sec. 11511(d)(2) of this Act, which reads as follows:

"(2) Special rule for significant expansion of projects. For purposes of section 43(c)(2)(A)(iii) of the Internal Revenue Code of 1986 (as added by subsection (a)), any significant expansion after December 31, 1990, of a project begun before January 1, 1991, shall be treated as a project with respect to which the first injection commences after December 31, 1990."

—P.L. 101-508, Sec. 11611(b)(2), added para. (d)(5) [sic (6)], effective for expenditures paid or incurred after 11/5/90.

—P.L. 101-508, Sec. 11801(a)(2), repealed paras. (d)(1)-(d)(4), effective 11/5/90, except as provided in Sec. 11821(b) of this Act, which reads as follows:

"(b) Savings provision. If—

"(1) any provision amended or repealed by this applied to—

"(A) any transaction occurring before the date of the enactment of this Act [11/5/90],

"(B) any property acquired before such date of enactment [11/5/90], or

"(C) any item of income, loss, deduction, or credit taken into account before, such date of enactment [11/5/90], and

"(2) the treatment of such transaction, property, or item under such provision would (without regard to the amendments made by this part) affect liability for tax for periods ending after such date of enactment [11/5/90],
nothing in the amendments made by this part shall be construed to affect the treatment of such transaction, property, or item for purposes of determining liability for tax for periods ending after such date of enactment [11/5/90]."

Prior to repeal, paras. (d)(1)-(d)(4) reads as follows:

"(1) Carryforwards.

"(A) In general. Any carryforward from an unused credit year under section 46, 50A, 53, 44E, or 44G (as in effect before the enactment of the Tax Reform Act of 1984) which has not expired before the beginning of the first taxable year beginning after December 31, 1983, shall be aggregated with other such carryforwards from unused credit year and shall be a business credit carryforward to each taxable year beginning after December 31, 1983, which is 1 of the first 15 taxable years after such unused credit year.

"(B) Amount carried forward. The amount carried forward under subparagraph (A) to any taxable year shall be properly reduced for any amount allowable as a credit with respect to such carryforward for any taxable year before the year to which it is being carried.

"(2) Carrybacks. In determining the amount allowable as a credit for any taxable year beginning before January 1, 1984, as the result of the carryback of a general business tax credit from a taxable year beginning after December 31, 1983—

"(A) paragraph (1) of subsection (b) shall be applied as if it read as follows:

'(1) the sum of the credits allowable for such taxable year under sections 38, 40, 44B, 44E, and 44G (as in effect before enactment of the Tax Reform Act of 1984), plus', and

"(B) for purposes of section 38(c) the net tax liability for such taxable year shall be the tax liability (as defined in section 26(b)) reduced by the sum of the credits allowable for such taxable year under sections 33, 37, 41, 44A, 44C, 44D, 44F, and 44H (as so in effect).

"(3) Similar rules and research credit. Rules similar to the rules of paragraphs (1) and (2) shall apply to the credit allowable under section 30 (as in effect before the date of the enactment of the Tax Reform Act of 1986) except that—

"(A) 'December 31, 1985' shall be substituted for 'December 31, 1983' each place it appears, and

"(B) 'January 1, 1986' shall be substituted for 'January 1, 1984'.

"(4) No carryback of low-income housing credit before 1987. No portion of the unused business credit for any taxable year which is attributable to the credit determined under section 42 (relating to low-income housing credit) may be carried back to a taxable year ending before January 1, 1987."

In 1988, P.L. 100-647, Sec. 1002(l)(26), added para. (d)(4), effective for buildings placed in service after 12/31/86 in tax. yrs. end. after 12/31/86, except as provided in Secs. 252(e)(2) and (f) of P.L. 99-514, reproduced in note following Code Sec. 42.

In 1986, P.L. 99-514, Sec. 231(d)(3)(C)(i), added para. (d)(3), effective for tax. yrs. begin. after 12/31/85.

—P.L. 99-514, Sec. 1846(1), substituted "or 44G (as in effect before the enactment of the Tax Reform Act of 1984)" for "or 44G" in subpara. (d)(1)(A) . . . Sec. 1846(2), substituted "as defined in section 26(b)" for "as so defined in section 25(b)" in para. (d)(2), effective for tax. yrs. begin. after 12/31/83, and for carrybacks from tax. yrs. begin. after 12/31/83.

In 1984, P.L. 98-369, Sec. 473, added Code Sec. 39, effective for tax. yrs. begin. after 12/31/83, and to carrybacks from tax. yrs. begin. after 12/31/83.

Sec. 40. Alcohol, etc., used as fuel.

(a) General rule.

For purposes of section 38, the alcohol fuels credit determined under this section for the taxable year is an amount equal to the sum of—

(1) the alcohol mixture credit,

(2) the alcohol credit,

(3) in the case of an eligible small ethanol producer, the small ethanol producer credit, plus

(4) the cellulosic biofuel producer credit.

(b) Definition of alcohol mixture credit, alcohol credit, and small ethanol producer credit.

For purposes of this section, and except as provided in subsection (h)—

(1) Alcohol mixture credit.

(A) In general. The alcohol mixture credit of any taxpayer for any taxable year is 60 cents for each gallon of alcohol used by the taxpayer in the production of a qualified mixture.

(B) Qualified mixture. The term "qualified mixture" means a mixture of alcohol and gasoline or of alcohol and a special fuel which—

(i) is sold by the taxpayer producing such mixture to any person for use as a fuel, or

(ii) is used as a fuel by the taxpayer producing such mixture.

(C) Sale or use must be in trade or business, etc. Alcohol used in the production of a qualified mixture shall be taken into account—

(i) only if the sale or use described in subparagraph (B) is in a trade or business of the taxpayer, and

(ii) for the taxable year in which such sale or use occurs.

(D) Casual off-farm production not eligible. No credit shall be allowed under this section with respect to any casual off-farm production of a qualified mixture.

(2) Alcohol credit.

(A) In general. The alcohol credit of any taxpayer for any taxable year is 60 cents for each gallon of alcohol which is not in a mixture with gasoline or a special fuel (other than any denaturant) and which during the taxable year—

(i) is used by the taxpayer as a fuel in a trade or business, or

(ii) is sold by the taxpayer at retail to a person and placed in the fuel tank of such person's vehicle.

(B) User credit not to apply to alcohol sold at retail. No credit shall be allowed under subparagraph (A)(i) with respect to any alcohol which was sold in a retail sale described in subparagraph (A)(ii).

(3) Smaller credit for lower proof alcohol. In the case of any alcohol with a proof which is at least 150 but less than 190, paragraphs (1)(A) and (2)(A) shall be applied by substituting "45 cents" for "60 cents".

(4) Small ethanol producer credit.

(A) In general. The small ethanol producer credit of any eligible small ethanol producer for any taxable year is 10 cents for each gallon of qualified ethanol fuel production of such producer.

(B) Qualified ethanol fuel production. For purposes of this paragraph, the term "qualified ethanol fuel production" means any alcohol which is ethanol which is produced by an eligible small ethanol producer, and which during the taxable year—

(i) is sold by such producer to another person—

(I) for use by such other person in the production of a qualified mixture in such other person's trade or business (other than casual off-farm production),
(II) for use by such other person as a fuel in a trade or business, or
(III) who sells such ethanol at retail to another person and places such ethanol in the fuel tank of such other person, or

(ii) is used or sold by such producer for any purpose described in clause (i).

(C) Limitation. The qualified ethanol fuel production of any producer for any taxable year shall not exceed 15,000,000 gallons (determined without regard to any qualified cellulosic biofuel production).

(D) Additional distillation excluded. The qualified ethanol fuel production of any producer for any taxable year shall not include any alcohol which is purchased by the producer and with respect to which such producer increases the proof of the alcohol by additional distillation.

(5) Adding of denaturants not treated as mixture. The adding of any denaturant to alcohol shall not be treated as the production of a mixture.

(6) Cellulosic biofuel producer credit.

(A) In general. The cellulosic biofuel producer credit of any taxpayer is an amount equal to the applicable amount for each gallon of qualified cellulosic biofuel production.

(B) Applicable amount. For purposes of subparagraph (A), the applicable amount means $1.01, except that such amount shall, in the case of cellulosic biofuel which is alcohol, be reduced by the sum of—

(i) the amount of the credit in effect for such alcohol under subsection (b)(1) (without regard to subsection (b)(3)) at the time of the qualified cellulosic biofuel production, plus

(ii) in the case of ethanol, the amount of the credit in effect under subsection (b)(4) at the time of such production.

(C) Qualified cellulosic biofuel production. For purposes of this section, the term "qualified cellulosic biofuel production" means any cellulosic biofuel which is produced by the taxpayer, and which during the taxable year—

(i) is sold by the taxpayer to another person—
(I) for use by such other person in the production of a qualified cellulosic biofuel mixture in such other person's trade or business (other than casual off-farm production),
(II) for use by such other person as a fuel in a trade or business, or
(III) who sells such cellulosic biofuel at retail to another person and places such cellulosic biofuel in the fuel tank of such other person, or

(ii) is used or sold by the taxpayer for any purpose described in clause (i).

The qualified cellulosic biofuel production of any taxpayer for any taxable year shall not include any alcohol which is purchased by the taxpayer and with respect to which such producer increases the proof of the alcohol by additional distillation.

(D) Qualified cellulosic biofuel mixture. For purposes of this paragraph, the term "qualified cellulosic biofuel mixture" means a mixture of cellulosic biofuel and gasoline or of cellulosic biofuel and a special fuel which—

(i) is sold by the person producing such mixture to any person for use as a fuel, or
(ii) is used as a fuel by the person producing such mixture.

(E) Cellulosic biofuel. For purposes of this paragraph—
(i) In general. The term "cellulosic biofuel" means any liquid fuel which—
(I) is produced from any lignocellulosic or hemicellulosic matter that is available on a renewable or recurring basis, and
(II) meets the registration requirements for fuels and fuel additives established by the Environmental Protection Agency under section 211 of the Clean Air Act (42 U.S.C. 7545).

(ii) Exclusion of low-proof alcohol. Such term shall not include any alcohol with a proof of less than 150. The determination of the proof of any alcohol shall be made without regard to any added denaturants.

(iii) Exclusion of certain fuels. The term "cellulosic biofuel" shall not include any fuel if—
(I) more than 4 percent of such fuel (determined by weight) is any combination of water and sediment
(II) the ash content of such fuel is more than 1 percent (determined by weight), or
(III) such fuel has an acid number greater than 25.

(F) Allocation of cellulosic biofuel producer credit to patrons of cooperative. Rules similar to the rules under subsection (g)(6) shall apply for purposes of this paragraph.

(G) Registration requirement. No credit shall be determined under this paragraph with respect to any taxpayer unless such taxpayer is registered with the Secretary as a producer of cellulosic biofuel under section 4101.

(H) Application of paragraph. This paragraph shall apply with respect to qualified cellulosic biofuel production after December 31, 2008, and before January 1, 2013.

(c) Coordination with exemption from excise tax.

The amount of the credit determined under this section with respect to any alcohol shall, under regulations prescribed by the Secretary, be properly reduced to take into account any benefit provided with respect to such alcohol solely by reason of the application of section 4041(b)(2), section 6426, or section 6427(e).

(d) Definitions and special rules.

For purposes of this section—

(1) Alcohol defined.

(A) In general. The term "alcohol" includes methanol and ethanol but does not include—
(i) alcohol produced from petroleum, natural gas, or coal (including peat), or
(ii) alcohol with a proof of less than 150.

(B) Determination of proof. The determination of the proof of any alcohol shall be made without regard to any added denaturants.

(2) Special fuel defined. The term "special fuel" includes any liquid fuel (other than gasoline) which is suitable for use in an internal combustion engine.

(3) Mixture or alcohol not used as a fuel, etc.

(A) Mixtures. If—
(i) any credit was determined under this section with respect to alcohol used in the production of any qualified mixture, and
(ii) any person—
(I) separates the alcohol from the mixture, or

Tax credits   Code Sec. 40(g)(6)(A)(i)

(II) without separation, uses the mixture other than as a fuel,

then there is hereby imposed on such person a tax equal to 60 cents a gallon (45 cents in the case of alcohol with a proof less than 190) for each gallon of alcohol in such mixture.

(B) Alcohol. If—

(i) any credit was determined under this section with respect to the retail sale of any alcohol, and

(ii) any person mixes such alcohol or uses such alcohol other than as a fuel,

then there is hereby imposed on such person a tax equal to 60 cents a gallon (45 cents in the case of alcohol with a proof less than 190) for each gallon of such alcohol.

(C) Small ethanol producer credit. If—

(i) any credit was determined under subsection (a)(3), and

(ii) any person does not use such fuel for a purpose described in subsection (b)(4)(B),

then there is hereby imposed on such person a tax equal to 10 cents a gallon for each gallon of such alcohol.

(D) Cellulosic biofuel producer credit. If—

(i) any credit is allowed under subsection (a)(4), and

(ii) any person does not use such fuel for a purpose described in subsection (b)(6)(C),

then there is hereby imposed on such person a tax equal to the applicable amount (as defined in subsection (b)(6)(B)) for each gallon of such cellulosic biofuel.

(E) Applicable laws. All provisions of law, including penalties, shall, insofar as applicable and not inconsistent with this section, apply in respect of any tax imposed under subparagraph (A), (B), (C), or (D) as if such tax were imposed by section 4081 and not by this chapter.

(4) Volume of alcohol. For purposes of determining under subsection (a) the number of gallons of alcohol with respect to which a credit is allowable under subsection (a), the volume of alcohol shall include the volume of any denaturant (including gasoline) which is added under any formulas approved by the Secretary to the extent that such denaturants do not exceed 2 percent of the volume of such alcohol (including denaturants).

(5) Pass-thru in the case of estates and trusts. Under regulations prescribed by the Secretary, rules similar to the rules of subsection (d) of section 52 shall apply.

(6) Special rule for cellulosic biofuel producer credit. No cellulosic biofuel producer credit shall be determined under subsection (a) with respect to any cellulosic biofuel unless such cellulosic biofuel is produced in the United States and used as a fuel in the United States. For purposes of this subsection, the term "United States" includes any possession of the United States.

(7) Limitation to alcohol with connection to the United States. No credit shall be determined under this section with respect to any alcohol which is produced outside the United States for use as a fuel outside the United States. For purposes of this paragraph, the term "United States" includes any possession of the United States.

(e) Termination.

(1) In general. This section shall not apply to any sale or use—

(A) for any period after December 31, 2011, or

(B) for any period before January 1, 2012, during which the rates of tax under section 4081(a)(2)(A) are 4.3 cents per gallon.

(2) No carryovers to certain years after expiration. If this section ceases to apply for any period by reason of paragraph (1) or subsection (b)(6)(H), no amount attributable to any sale or use before the first day of such period may be carried under section 39 by reason of this section (treating the amount allowed by reason of this section as the first amount allowed by this subpart) to any taxable year beginning after the 3-taxable-year period beginning with the taxable year in which such first day occurs.

(3) Exception for cellulosic biofuel producer credit. Paragraph (1) shall not apply to the portion of the credit allowed under this section by reason of subsection (a)(4).

(f) Election to have alcohol fuels credit not apply.

(1) In general. A taxpayer may elect to have this section not apply for any taxable year.

(2) Time for making election. An election under paragraph (1) for any taxable year may be made (or revoked) at any time before the expiration of the 3-year period beginning on the last date prescribed by law for filing the return for such taxable year (determined without regard to extensions).

(3) Manner of making election. An election under paragraph (1) (or revocation thereof) shall be made in such manner as the Secretary may by regulations prescribe.

(g) Definitions and special rules for eligible small ethanol producer credit.

For purposes of this section—

(1) Eligible small ethanol producer. The term "eligible small ethanol producer" means a person who, at all times during the taxable year, has a productive capacity for alcohol (as defined in subsection (d)(1)(A) without regard to clauses (i) and (ii)) not in excess of 60,000,000 gallons.

(2) Aggregation rule. For purposes of the 15,000,000 gallon limitation under subsection (b)(4)(C) and the 60,000,000 gallon limitation under paragraph (1), all members of the same controlled group of corporations (within the meaning of section 267(f)) and all persons under common control (within the meaning of section 52(b) but determined by treating an interest of more than 50 percent as a controlling interest) shall be treated as 1 person.

(3) Partnership, S corporations, and other pass-thru entities. In the case of a partnership, trust, S corporation, or other pass-thru entity, the limitations contained in subsection (b)(4)(C) and paragraph (1) shall be applied at the entity level and at the partner or similar level.

(4) Allocation. For purposes of this subsection, in the case of a facility in which more than 1 person has an interest, productive capacity shall be allocated among such persons in such manner as the Secretary may prescribe.

(5) Regulations. The Secretary may prescribe such regulations as may be necessary—

(A) to prevent the credit provided for in subsection (a)(3) from directly or indirectly benefiting any person with a direct or indirect productive capacity of more than 60,000,000 gallons of alcohol during the taxable year, or

(B) to prevent any person from directly or indirectly benefiting with respect to more than 15,000,000 gallons during the taxable year.

(6) Allocation of small ethanol producer credit to patrons of cooperative.

(A) Election to allocate.

(i) In general. In the case of a cooperative organization described in section 1381(a), any portion of the credit determined under subsection (a)(3) for the taxable year may, at the election of the organization, be apportioned pro rata among patrons of the organization on the basis of the quantity or value of business done with or for such patrons for the taxable year.

(ii) Form and effect of election. An election under clause (i) for any taxable year shall be made on a timely filed return for such year. Such election, once made, shall be irrevocable for such taxable year. Such election shall not take effect unless the organization designates the apportionment as such in a written notice mailed to its patrons during the payment period described in section 1382(d).

(B) Treatment of organizations and patrons.

(i) Organizations. The amount of the credit not apportioned to patrons pursuant to subparagraph (A) shall be included in the amount determined under subsection (a)(3) for the taxable year of the organization.

(ii) Patrons. The amount of the credit apportioned to patrons pursuant to subparagraph (A) shall be included in the amount determined under such subsection for the first taxable year of each patron ending on or after the last day of the payment period (as defined in section 1382(d)) for the taxable year of the organization or, if earlier, for the taxable year of each patron ending on or after the date on which the patron receives notice from the cooperative of the apportionment.

(iii) Special rules for decrease in credits for taxable year. If the amount of the credit of the organization determined under such subsection for a taxable year is less than the amount of such credit shown on the return of the organization for such year, an amount equal to the excess of—

(I) such reduction, over

(II) the amount not apportioned to such patrons under subparagraph (A) for the taxable year,

shall be treated as an increase in tax imposed by this chapter on the organization. Such increase shall not be treated as tax imposed by this chapter for purposes of determining the amount of any credit under this chapter or for purposes of section 55.

(h) Reduced credit for ethanol blenders.

(1) In general. In the case of any alcohol mixture credit or alcohol credit with respect to any sale or use of alcohol which is ethanol during calendar years 2001 through 2011—

(A) subsections (b)(1)(A) and (b)(2)(A) shall be applied by substituting "the blender amount" for "60 cents",

(B) subsection (b)(3) shall be applied by substituting "the low-proof blender amount" for "45 cents" and "the blender amount" for "60 cents", and

(C) subparagraphs (A) and (B) of subsection (d)(3) shall be applied by substituting "the blender amount" for "60 cents" and "the low-proof blender amount" for "45 cents".

(2) Amounts. For purposes of paragraph (1), the blender amount and the low-proof blender amount shall be determined in accordance with the following table:

In the case of any sale or use during calendar year:	The blender amount is:	The low-proof blender amount is:
2001 or 2002	53 cents	39.26 cents
2003 or 2004	52 cents	38.52 cents
2005, 2006, 2007, or 2008	51 cents	37.78 cents
2009 through 2011	45 cents	33.33 cents.

(3) Reduction delayed until annual production or importation of 7,500,000,000 gallons.

(A) In general. In the case of any calendar year beginning after 2008, if the Secretary makes a determination described in subparagraph (B) with respect to all preceding calendar years beginning after 2007, the last row in the table in paragraph (2) shall be applied by substituting "51 cents" for "45 cents".

(B) Determination. A determination described in this subparagraph with respect to any calendar year is a determination, in consultation with the Administrator of the Environmental Protection Agency, that an amount less than 7,500,000,000 gallons of ethanol (including cellulosic ethanol) has been produced in or imported into the United States in such year.

In 2010, P.L. 111-312, Sec. 708(a)(1)(A), substituted "December 31, 2011" for "December 31, 2010" in subpara. (e)(1)(A) ... Sec. 708(a)(1)(B), substituted "January 1, 2012" for "January 1, 2011" in subpara. (e)(1)(B) ... Sec. 708(a)(2), substituted "2011" for "2010" after "2001 through" in subsec. (h) and the table in subsec. (h), effective for periods after 12/31/2010.

—P.L. 111-240, Sec. 2121(a)(1), deleted "or" at the end of subclause (b)(6)(E)(iii)(I) ... Sec. 2121(a)(2), substituted ", or" for the period at the end of subclause (b)(6)(E)(iii)(II) ... Sec. 2121(a)(3), added subclause (b)((6)(E)(iii)(III) ... Sec. 2121(a)(4), substituted "certain" for "unprocessed" in the clause (b)(6)(E)(iii), effective for fuels sold or used on or after 1/1/2010.

—P.L. 111-152, Sec. 1408(a), added clause (b)(6)(E)(iii), effective for fuels sold or used on or after 1/1/2010.

In 2008, P.L. 110-343, Sec. 203(a)DivB, added para. (d)(7), effective for claims for credit or payment made on or after May 15, 2008.

—P.L. 110-246, Sec. 4, Repeals the duplicative enactment and provides effective date provisions of the Act entitled "An Act to provide for the continuation of agricultural programs through fiscal year 2012, and for other purposes" Sec. 4, P.L. 110-246 reads as follows:

"Sec. 4. Repeal of duplicative enactment.

"(a) In General- The Act entitled 'An Act to provide for the continuation of agricultural programs through fiscal year 2012, and for other purposes' (H.R. 2419 of the 110th Congress), and the amendments made by that Act, are repealed, effective on the date of enactment of that Act.

"(b) Effective Date- Except as otherwise provided in this Act, this Act and the amendments made by this Act shall take effect on the earlier of--

"(1) the date of enactment of this Act; or

"(2) the date of the enactment of the Act entitled 'An Act to provide for the continuation of agricultural programs through fiscal year 2012, and for other purposes' (H.R. 2419 of the 110th Congress)." ... Sec. 15321(a), deleted "plus" at the end of para. (a)(1), deleted "plus" at the end of para. (a)(2), substituted ", plus" for the period at the end of para. (a)(3), and added at the end para. (a)(4) ... Sec. 15321(e), added "(determined without regard to any qualified cellulosic biofuel production)" after "15,000,000 gallons" in subpara. (b)(4)(C) ... Sec. 15321(b)(1), added para. (b)(6) ... Sec. 15321(b)(2)(A), inserted "or subsection (b)(6)(H)" after "by reason of paragraph (1)" in para. (e)(2) ... Sec. 15321(b)(2)(B), added para. (e)(3) ... Sec. 15321(b)(3)(B), added ", etc.," after "Alcohol" in the heading of Code Sec. 40 ... Sec. 15321(c)(1), redesignated subpara. (d)(3)(D) as (E) and added new subpara. (d)(3)(D) ... Sec. 15321(c)(2)(A), substituted "Small ethanol producer" for "Producer" in the heading of subpara. (d)(3)(C) ... Sec. 15321(c)(2)(B), substituted "(C), or (D)" for "or (C)" in subpara. (d)(3)(E) ... Sec. 15321(d), added para. (d)(6), effective for fuel produced after 12/31/2008.

—P.L. 110-246, Sec. 15331(a)(1)(A), substituted ", 2006, 2007, or 2008" for "through 2010" in the first column of the table in para. (h)(2) ... Sec. 15331(a)(1)(B), deleted the period at the end of the third row of the table in para. (h)(2) ... Sec. 15331(a)(1)(C), added a new row at the end of the table in para. (h)(2) ... Sec. 15331(a)(2), added para. (h)(3), effective 5/22/2008.

—P.L. 110-246, Sec. 15332(a), substituted "2 percent" for "5 percent" in para (d)(4), effective for fuel sold or used after 12/31/2008. [Ed. Note: May 22, 2008

Tax credits
Code Sec. 40

was the date of enactment for H.R. 2419 (PL 110-234), which was repealed by (2008 Farm Act § 4(a)) (PL 110-246, 6/18/2008), in connection with the reenactment of the farm bill to correct a technical deficiency in its original passage.]

In 2005, P.L. 109-58, Sec. 1347(a), substituted "60,000,000" for "30,000,000" each place it appeared in subsec. (g)... Sec. 1347(b), added "Such election shall not take effect unless the organization designates the apportionment as such in a written notice mailed to its patrons during the payment period described in section 1382(d)." at the end of clause (g)(6)(A)(ii), effective for tax. yrs. end. after 8/8/2005.

In 2004, P.L. 108-357, Sec. 301(c)(1), substituted "section 4041(b)(2), section 6426, or section 6427(e)" for "subsection (b)(2), (k), or (m) of section 4041, section 4081(c), or section 4091(c)" in subsec. (c)... Sec. 301(c)(2), amended para. (d)(4), effective for fuel sold or used after 12/31/2004.

Prior to amendment, para. (d)(4) read as follows:

"(4) Volume of alcohol. For purposes of determining—

"(A) under subsection (a) the number of gallons of alcohol with respect to which a credit is allowable under subsection (a), or

"(B) under section 4041(k) or 4081(c) the percentage of any mixture which consists of alcohol,

the volume of alcohol shall include the volume of any denaturant (including gasoline) which is added under any formulas approved by the Secretary to the extent that such denaturants do not exceed 5 percent of the volume of such alcohol (including denaturants)."

—P.L. 108-357, Sec. 301(c)(3)(A), substituted "2010" for "2007" in subpara. (e)(1)(A)... Sec. 301(c)(3)(B), substituted "2011" for "2008" in subpara. (e)(1)(B)... Sec. 301(c)(4)(A), substituted "2010" for "2007" in para. (h)(1)... Sec. 301(c)(4)(B), substituted "through 2010" for ", 2006, or 2007" in the table in para. (h)(2), effective 10/22/2004.

—P.L. 108-357, Sec. 313(a), added para. (g)(6), effective for tax. yrs. end. after 10/22/2004.

In 1998, P.L. 105-178, Sec. 9003(a)(3)(A), substituted "December 31, 2007" for "December 31, 2000" in subpara. (e)(1)(A)... Sec. 9003(a)(3)(B), substituted "January 1, 2008" for "January 1, 2001" in para. (e)(1), effective 6/9/98.

—P.L. 105-178, Sec. 9003(b)(1), amended subsec. (h), effective 1/1/2001.

Prior to amendment, subsec. (h) read as follows:

"(h) Reduced credit for ethanol blenders. In the case of any alcohol mixture credit or alcohol credit with respect to any alcohol which is ethanol—

"(1) subsections (b)(1)(A) and (b)(2)(A) shall be applied by substituting '54 cents' for '60 cents';

"(2) subsection (b)(3) shall be applied by substituting '40 cents' for '45 cents' and '54 cents' for '60 cents'; and

"(3) subparagraphs (A) and (B) of subsection (d)(3) shall be applied by substituting '54 cents' for '60 cents' and '40 cents' for '45 cents'."

In 1996, P.L. 104-188, Sec. 1703(j), amended subpara. (e)(1)(B), effective 10/1/93.

Prior to amendment, subpara. (e)(1)(B) read as follows:

"(B) for any period before January 1, 2001, during which the Highway Trust Fund financing rate under section 4081(a)(2) is not in effect."

In 1990, P.L. 101-508, Sec. 11502(a)(1), substituted ", plus" for the period at the end of para. (a)(2)... Sec. 11502(a)(2), added para. (a)(3)... Sec. 11502(b)(1), redesignated para. (b)(4) as para. (b)(5)... Sec. 11502(b)(2), added new para. (b)(4)... Sec. 11502(b)(3), substituted ", alcohol credit, and small ethanol producer credit" for "and alcohol credit" in the heading of subsec. (b)... Sec. 11502(c), added subsec. (g)... Sec. 11502(d)(1), redesignated subpara. (d)(3)(C) as subpara. (d)(3)(D) and added new subpara. (d)(3)(C)... Sec. 11502(d)(2), substituted "subparagraph (A), (B), or (C)" for "subparagraph (A) or (B)" in subpara. (d)(3)(D) (as redesignated by Sec. 11502(d)(1) of this Act)... Sec. 11502(e)(1), added subsec. (h)... Sec. 11502(e)(2), added ", and except as provided in subsec. (h)" after "this section" in matter preceding para. (b)(1)... Sec. 11502(f), amended subsec. (e), effective for alcohol produced, and sold or used, in tax. yrs. begin. after 12/31/90.

Prior to amendment, subsec. (e) read as follows:

"(e) Termination.

"(1) In general. This section shall not apply to any sale or use after December 31, 1992.

"(2) No carryovers to years after 1994. No amount may be carried under section 39 by reason of this section (treating the amount allowed by reason of this section as the first amount allowed by this subpart) to any taxable year beginning after December 31, 1994."

In 1987, P.L. 100-203, Sec. 10502(d)(1), substituted ", section 4081(c), or section 4091(c)" for "or section 4081(c)" in subsec. (c), effective for sales after 3/31/88.

In 1984, P.L. 98-369, Sec. 471(c)(1), redesignated Code Sec. 44E as Code Sec. 40... Sec. 474(k)(1), amended subsec. (a)... Sec. 474(k)(2), substituted "the credit determined under this section" for "the credit allowable under this section" in subsec. (c)... Sec. 474(k)(3), substituted "credit was determined" for "credit was allowable" each place it appeared in para. (d)(3)... Sec. 474(k)(4), deleted subsec. (e) and redesignated subsec. (f) as subsec. (e)... Sec. 474(k)(5), amended para. (e)(2) (as redesignated by Sec. 474(k)(4))... Sec. 474(k)(6), added subsec. (f), effective for tax. yrs. begin. after 12/31/83 and to carrybacks from tax. yrs. begin. after 12/31/83.

Prior to amendment, subsec. (a) read as follows:

"(a) General rule. There shall be allowed as a credit against the tax imposed by this chapter for the taxable year an amount equal to the sum of—

"(1) the alcohol mixture credit, plus

"(2) the alcohol credit."

Prior to deletion, subsec. (e) read as follows:

"(e) Limitation based on amount of tax.

"(1) In general. The amount of the credit allowed by this section for the taxable year shall not exceed the tax imposed by this chapter for the taxable year, reduced by the sum of the credits allowed under a section of this subpart having a lower number designation than this section, other than credits allowable by sections 31, 39, and 43. For purposes of the preceding sentence, the term 'tax imposed by this chapter' shall not include any tax treated as not imposed by this chapter under the last sentence of section 53(a).

"(2) Carryover of unused credit.

"(A) In general. If the amount of the credit determined under subsection (a) for any taxable year exceeds the limitation provided by paragraph (1) for such taxable year (hereinafter in this paragraph referred to as the 'unused credit year'), such excess shall be an alcohol fuel credit carryover to each of the 15 taxable years following the unused credit year, and shall be added to the amount allowable as credit under subsection (a) for such years. The entire amount of the unused credit for an unused credit year shall be carried to the earliest of the 15 taxable years to which (by reason of the preceding sentence) such credit may be carried, and then to each of the other 14 taxable years to the extent that, because of the limitation contained in subparagraph (B), such unused credit may not be added for a prior taxable year to which such unused credit may be carried.

"(B) Limitation. The amount of the unused credit which may be added under subparagraph (A) for any succeeding taxable year shall not exceed the amount by which the limitation provided by paragraph (1) for such succeeding taxable year exceeds the sum of—

"(i) the credit allowable under subsection (a) for such taxable year, and

"(ii) the amounts which, by reason of this paragraph, are added to the amount allowable for such taxable year and which are attributable to taxable years preceding the unused credit year."

Prior to amendment, para. (e)(2) read as follows:

"(2) No carryovers to years after 1994. No amount may be carried under subsection (e)(2) to any taxable year beginning after December 31, 1994."

—P.L. 98-369, Sec. 912(c), substituted "60 cents" for "50 cents" and "45 cents" for "37.5 cents" each place it appeared in Code Sec. 40... Sec. 912(f), substituted "coal (including peat)" for "coal" in clause (d)(1)(A)(i), effective 1/1/85.

—P.L. 98-369, Sec. 913(b), substituted "(b)(2), (k), or (m)" for "(b)(2) or (k)" in subsec. (c), effective 8/1/84.

In 1983, P.L. 97-448, Sec. 102(d)(2), added para. (c)(3) to Sec. 209 of P.L. 97-34, the effective date for amendments made by Sec. 207(c)(3) of P.L. 97-34, see below.

—P.L. 97-448, Sec. 202(e), added Sec. 232(h)(4) to P.L. 96-223, which provided a special effective date for Code Sec. 44E(d)(4)(B), see below.

—P.L. 97-424, Sec. 511(b)(2), substituted "subsection (b)(2) or (k) of section 4041 or section 4081(c)" for "section 4041(k) or 4081(c)" in subsec. (c)... Sec. 511(d)(3)(A), substituted "50 cents" for "40 cents" each place it appeared in Code Sec. 44E... Sec. 511(d)(3)(B), substituted "37.5 cents" for "30 cents" each place it appeared in Code Sec. 44E, effective 4/1/83.

In 1982, P.L. 97-354, Sec. 5(a)(2), amended para. (d)(5), effective for tax. yrs. begin. after 12/31/82.

Prior to amendment, para. (d)(5) read as follows:

"(5) Pass-through in the case of Subchapter S corporations, etc. Under regulations prescribed by the Secretary, rules similar to the rules of subsections (d) and (e) of section 52 shall apply."

In 1981, P.L. 97-34, Sec. 207(c)(3), substituted "15" for "7" each place it appeared in subpara. (e)(2)(A) and substituted "14" for "6" in subpara. (e)(2)(A), effective for unused credit yrs. end. after 9/30/80. Sec. 209(c)(3) of this Act provides:

"(3) Carryover must have been alive in 1981. The amendments made by subsections (a), (b), and (c) of section 207 [P.L. 97-34] shall not apply to any amount which, under the law in effect on the day before the date of the enactment of this Act, could not be carried to a taxable year ending in 1981."

In 1980, P.L. 96-223, Sec. 232(b)(1), added Code Sec. 44E, effective for sales or uses after 9/30/80, in tax. yrs. end. after 9/30/80, except as provided in Sec. 232(h)(4) [as added by Sec. 202(e) of P.L. 97-448, see above] which reads as follows:

"(4) Addition of denaturants. Notwithstanding paragraph (1), the provisions of section 44E(d)(4)(B) of such Code, as added by this section, shall take effect on April 2, 1980."

Sec. 40. Repealed.

In 1984, P.L. 98-369, Sec. 474(m)(1), repealed Code Sec. 40, effective for tax. yrs. begin. after 12/31/83 and for carrybacks from tax. yrs. begin. after 12/31/83.

Prior to repeal, Code Sec. 40 read as follows:

"SEC. 40. EXPENSES OF WORK INCENTIVE PROGRAMS.

"(a) General rule. There shall be allowed, as a credit against the tax imposed by this chapter, the amount determined under subpart C of this part.

"(b) Regulations. The Secretary shall prescribe such regulations as may be necessary to carry out the purposes of this section and subpart C."

In 1976, P.L. 94-455, Sec. 1906(b)(13)(A), substituted "Secretary" for "Secretary or his delegate" in subsec. (b), effective for tax. yrs. begin. after '76.

In 1971, P.L. 92-178, Sec. 601(a), added Code Sec. 40, effective for tax. yrs. begin. after 12/31/71.

Code Sec. 40A — Tax credits

Sec. 40A. Biodiesel and renewable diesel used as fuel.
(a) General rule.
For purposes of section 38, the biodiesel fuels credit determined under this section for the taxable year is an amount equal to the sum of—
  (1) the biodiesel mixture credit, plus
  (2) the biodiesel credit, plus
  (3) in the case of an eligible small agri-biodiesel producer, the small agri-biodiesel producer credit.
(b) Definition of biodiesel mixture credit, biodiesel credit, and small agri-biodiesel producer credit.
For purposes of this section—
(1) Biodiesel mixture credit.
  (A) In general. The biodiesel mixture credit of any taxpayer for any taxable year is $1.00 for each gallon of biodiesel used by the taxpayer in the production of a qualified biodiesel mixture.
  (B) Qualified biodiesel mixture. The term "qualified biodiesel mixture" means a mixture of biodiesel and diesel fuel (as defined in section 4083(a)(3)), determined without regard to any use of kerosene, which—
    (i) is sold by the taxpayer producing such mixture to any person for use as a fuel, or
    (ii) is used as a fuel by the taxpayer producing such mixture.
  (C) Sale or use must be in trade or business, etc. Biodiesel used in the production of a qualified biodiesel mixture shall be taken into account—
    (i) only if the sale or use described in subparagraph
    (B) is in a trade or business of the taxpayer, and
    (ii) for the taxable year in which such sale or use occurs.
  (D) Casual off-farm production not eligible. No credit shall be allowed under this section with respect to any casual off-farm production of a qualified biodiesel mixture.
(2) Biodiesel credit.
  (A) In general. The biodiesel credit of any taxpayer for any taxable year is $1.00 for each gallon of biodiesel which is not in a mixture with diesel fuel and which during the taxable year—
    (i) is used by the taxpayer as a fuel in a trade or business, or
    (ii) is sold by the taxpayer at retail to a person and placed in the fuel tank of such person's vehicle.
  (B) User credit not to apply to biodiesel sold at retail. No credit shall be allowed under subparagraph (A)(i) with respect to any biodiesel which was sold in a retail sale described in subparagraph (A)(ii).
(3) Certification for biodiesel. No credit shall be allowed under paragraph (1) or (2) of subsection (a) unless the taxpayer obtains a certification (in such form and manner as prescribed by the Secretary) from the producer or importer of the biodiesel which identifies the product produced and the percentage of biodiesel and agri-biodiesel in the product.
(4) Small agri-biodiesel producer credit.
  (A) In general. The small agri-biodiesel producer credit of any eligible small agri-biodiesel producer for any taxable year is 10 cents for each gallon of qualified agri-biodiesel production of such producer.
  (B) Qualified agri-biodiesel production. For purposes of this paragraph, the term "qualified agri-biodiesel production" means any agri-biodiesel which is produced by an eligible small agri-biodiesel producer, and which during the taxable year—
    (i) is sold by such producer to another person—
      (I) for use by such other person in the production of a qualified biodiesel mixture in such other person's trade or business (other than casual off-farm production),
      (II) for use by such other person as a fuel in a trade or business, or
      (III) who sells such agri-biodiesel at retail to another person and places such agri-biodiesel in the fuel tank of such other person, or
    (ii) is used or sold by such producer for any purpose described in clause (i).
  (C) Limitation. The qualified agri-biodiesel production of any producer for any taxable year shall not exceed 15,000,000 gallons.
(c) Coordination with credit against excise tax.
The amount of the credit determined under this section with respect to any biodiesel shall be properly reduced to take into account any benefit provided with respect to such biodiesel solely by reason of the application of section 6426 or 6427(e).
(d) Definitions and special rules.
For purposes of this section—
(1) Biodiesel. The term "biodiesel" means the monoalkyl esters of long chain fatty acids derived from plant or animal matter which meet—
  (A) the registration requirements for fuels and fuel additives established by the Environmental Protection Agency under section 211 of the Clean Air Act (42 U.S.C. 7545), and
  (B) the requirements of the American Society of Testing and Materials D6751.
Such term shall not include any liquid with respect to which a credit may be determined under section 40.
(2) Agri-biodiesel. The term "agri-biodiesel" means biodiesel derived solely from virgin oils, including esters derived from virgin vegetable oils from corn, soybeans, sunflower seeds, cottonseeds, canola, crambe, rapeseeds, safflowers, flaxseeds, rice bran, mustard seeds, and camelina, and from animal fats.
(3) Mixture or biodiesel not used as a fuel, etc.
  (A) Mixtures. If—
    (i) any credit was determined under this section with respect to biodiesel used in the production of any qualified biodiesel mixture, and
    (ii) any person—
      (I) separates the biodiesel from the mixture, or
      (II) without separation, uses the mixture other than as a fuel,
  then there is hereby imposed on such person a tax equal to the product of the rate applicable under subsection (b)(1)(A) and the number of gallons of such biodiesel in such mixture.
  (B) Biodiesel. If—
    (i) any credit was determined under this section with respect to the retail sale of any biodiesel, and
    (ii) any person mixes such biodiesel or uses such biodiesel other than as a fuel,
  then there is hereby imposed on such person a tax equal to the product of the rate applicable under subsection (b)(2)(A) and the number of gallons of such biodiesel.
  (C) Producer credit. If—
    (i) any credit was determined under subsection (a)(3), and
    (ii) any person does not use such fuel for a purpose described in subsection (b)(4)(B), then there is hereby

imposed on such person a tax equal to 10 cents a gallon for each gallon of such agri-biodiesel.

(D) **Applicable laws.** All provisions of law, including penalties, shall, insofar as applicable and not inconsistent with this section, apply in respect of any tax imposed under subparagraph (A) or (B) as if such tax were imposed by section 4081 and not by this chapter.

(4) Pass-thru in the case of estates and trusts. Under regulations prescribed by the Secretary, rules similar to the rules of subsection (d) of section 52 shall apply.

(5) Limitation to biodiesel with connection to the United States. No credit shall be determined under this section with respect to any biodiesel which is produced outside the United States for use as a fuel outside the United States. For purposes of this paragraph, the term "United States" includes any possession of the United States.

(e) Definitions and special rules for small agri-biodiesel producer credit.

For purposes of this section—

(1) Eligible small agri-biodiesel producer. The term "eligible small agri-biodiesel producer" means a person who, at all times during the taxable year, has a productive capacity for agri-biodiesel not in excess of 60,000,000 gallons.

(2) Aggregation rule. For purposes of the 15,000,000 gallon limitation under subsection (b)(4)(C) and the 60,000,000 gallon limitation under paragraph (1), all members of the same controlled group of corporations (within the meaning of section 267(f)) and all persons under common control (within the meaning of section 52(b) but determined by treating an interest of more than 50 percent as a controlling interest) shall be treated as 1 person.

(3) Partnership, S corporation, and other pass-thru entities. In the case of a partnership, trust, S corporation, or other pass-thru entity, the limitations contained in subsection (b)(4)(C) and paragraph (1) shall be applied at the entity level and at the partner or similar level.

(4) Allocation. For purposes of this subsection, in the case of a facility in which more than 1 person has an interest, productive capacity shall be allocated among such persons in such manner as the Secretary may prescribe.

(5) Regulations. The Secretary may prescribe such regulations as may be necessary—

(A) to prevent the credit provided for in subsection (a)(3) from directly or indirectly benefiting any person with a direct or indirect productive capacity of more than 60,000,000 gallons of agri-biodiesel during the taxable year, or

(B) to prevent any person from directly or indirectly benefiting with respect to more than 15,000,000 gallons during the taxable year.

(6) Allocation of small agri-biodiesel credit to patrons of cooperative.

(A) Election to allocate.

(i) In general. In the case of a cooperative organization described in section 1381(a), any portion of the credit determined under subsection (a)(3) for the taxable year may, at the election of the organization, be apportioned pro rata among patrons of the organization on the basis of the quantity or value of business done with or for such patrons for the taxable year.

(ii) Form and effect of election. An election under clause (i) for any taxable year shall be made on a timely filed return for such year. Such election, once made, shall be irrevocable for such taxable year. Such election shall not take effect unless the organization designates the apportionment as such in a written notice mailed to its patrons during the payment period described in section 1382(d).

(B) Treatment of organizations and patrons.

(i) Organizations. The amount of the credit not apportioned to patrons pursuant to subparagraph (A) shall be included in the amount determined under subsection (a)(3) for the taxable year of the organization.

(ii) Patrons. The amount of the credit apportioned to patrons pursuant to subparagraph (A) shall be included in the amount determined under such subsection for the first taxable year of each patron ending on or after the last day of the payment period (as defined in section 1382(d)) for the taxable year of the organization or, if earlier, for the taxable year of each patron ending on or after the date on which the patron receives notice from the cooperative of the apportionment.

(iii) Special rules for decrease in credits for taxable year. If the amount of the credit of the organization determined under such subsection for a taxable year is less than the amount of such credit shown on the return of the organization for such year, an amount equal to the excess of—

(I) such reduction, over

(II) the amount not apportioned to such patrons under subparagraph (A) for the taxable year, shall be treated as an increase in tax imposed by this chapter on the organization. Such increase shall not be treated as tax imposed by this chapter for purposes of determining the amount of any credit under this chapter or for purposes of section 55.

(f) Renewable diesel.

For purposes of this title—

(1) Treatment in the same manner as biodiesel. Except as provided in paragraph (2), renewable diesel shall be treated in the same manner as biodiesel.

(2) Exception. Subsection (b)(4) shall not apply with respect to renewable diesel.

(3) Renewable diesel defined. The term "renewable diesel" means liquid fuel derived from biomass which meets—

(A) the registration requirements for fuels and fuel additives established by the Environmental Protection Agency under section 211 of the Clean Air Act (42 U.S.C. 7545), and

(B) the requirements of the American Society of Testing and Materials D975 or D396, or other equivalent standard approved by the Secretary.

Such term shall not include any liquid with respect to which a credit may be determined under section 40. Such term does not include any fuel derived from coprocessing biomass with a feedstock which is not biomass. For purposes of this paragraph, the term "biomass" has the meaning given such term by section 45K(c)(3).

(4) Certain aviation fuel.

(A) In general. Except as provided in the last 3 sentences of paragraph (3), the term "renewable diesel" shall include fuel derived from biomass which meets the requirements of a Department of Defense specification for military jet fuel or an American Society of Testing and Materials specification for aviation turbine fuel.

(B) Application of mixture credits. In the case of fuel which is treated as renewable diesel solely by reason of subparagraph (A), subsection (b)(1) and section 6426(c) shall be applied with respect to such fuel by treating kerosene as though it were diesel fuel.

(g) Termination.

This section shall not apply to any sale or use after December 31, 2011.

In 2010, P.L. 111-312, Sec. 701(a), substituted "December 31, 2011" for "December 31, 2009" in subsec. (g), effective for fuel sold or used after 12/31/2009.
In 2008, P.L. 110-343, Sec. 202(b)(1)DivB, substituted "$1.00" for "50 cents" in subpara. (b)(1)(A) ... Sec. 202(b)(1)DivB, substituted "$1.00" for "50 cents" in subpara. (b)(2)(A) ... Sec. 202(b)(3)(A)DivB, repealed para. (b)(3) ... Sec. 202(b)(3)(A)DivB, redesignated para. (b)(4)-(5) as para. (b)(3)-(4) ... Sec. 202(f)DivB, substituted "mustard seeds, and camelina" for "and mustard seeds" in para. (d)(2) ... Sec. 202(b)(3)(D)DivB, substituted "subsection (b)(4)(B)" for "subsection (b)(5)(B)" in clause (d)(3)(C)(ii), effective for fuel produced, and sold or used after 12/31/2008.
—P.L. 110-343, Sec. 203(b)DivB, added para. (d)(5), effective for claims for credit or payment made on or after 5/15/2008.
—P.L. 110-343, Sec. 202(b)(3)(C)DivB, substituted "subsection (b)(4)(C)" for "subsection (b)(5)(C)" in para. (e)(2) ... Sec. 202(b)(3)(C)DivB, substituted "subsection (b)(4)(C)" for "subsection (b)(5)(C)" in para. (e)(3) ... Sec. 202(b)(3)(B)DivB, amended para. (f)(2) ... Sec. 202(c)(1)DivB, substituted "liquid fuel" for "diesel fuel" in para. (f)(3) ... Sec. 202(c)(2)DivB, deleted "using a thermal depolymerization process" in para. (f)(3) ... Sec. 202(c)(3)DivB, added ", or other equivalent standard approved by the Secretary" after "D396" in para. (f)(3), effective for fuel produced, and sold or used after 12/31/2008.
—P.L. 110-343, Sec. 202(d)(1)DivB, added "Such term does not include any fuel derived from coprocessing biomass with a feedstock which is not biomass. For purposes of this paragraph, the term 'biomass' has the meaning given such term by section 45K(c)(3)." at the end of para. (f)(3) ... Sec. 202(d)(2)DivB, deleted "as defined in section 45K(c)(3))" in para. (f)(3), effective or fuel produced, and sold or used after 10/3/2008.
—P.L. 110-343, Sec. 202(e)DivB, added para. (f)(4) ... Sec. 202(a)DivB, substituted "December 31, 2009" for "December 31, 2008" in subsec. (g), effective or fuel produced, and sold or used after 12/31/2008.
—P.L. 110-246, Sec. 4, Repeals the duplicative enactment and provides effective date provisions of the Act entitled "An Act to provide for the continuation of agricultural programs through fiscal year 2012, and for other purposes" Sec. 4, P.L. 110-246 reads as follows:
"Sec. 4. Repeal of duplicative enactment.
"(a) In General- The Act entitled 'An Act to provide for the continuation of agricultural programs through fiscal year 2012, and for other purposes' (H.R. 2419 of the 110th Congress), and the amendments made by that Act, are repealed, effective on the date of enactment of that Act.
"(b) Effective Date- Except as otherwise provided in this Act, this Act and the amendments made by this Act shall take effect on the earlier of--
"(1) the date of enactment of this Act; or
"(2) the date of the enactment of the Act entitled 'An Act to provide for the continuation of agricultural programs through fiscal year 2012, and for other purposes' (H.R. 2419 of the 110th Congress)."
—P.L. 110-246, Sec. 15321(f)(1), added the sentence at the end of para. (d)(1) ... P.L. 15321(f)(2), added the sentence at the end of para. (f)(3), effective for fuel produced after 12/31/2008. [Ed. Note: May 22, 2008 was the date of enactment for H.R. 2419 (PL 110-234), which was repealed by (2008 Farm Act § 4(a)) (PL 110-246, 6/18/2008), in connection with the reenactment of the farm bill to correct a technical deficiency in its original passage.]
In 2005, P.L. 109-135, Sec. 412(h), deleted "(determined without regard to the last sentence of subsection (d)(2))" after "agri-biodiesel" in subpara. (b)(5)(B), effective 12/21/2005.
—P.L. 109-58, Sec. 1344(a), substituted "2008" for "2006" in subsec. (e) [prior to redesignation by Secs. 1345(c) and 1346(a) of this Act, see below], effective 8/8/2005.
—P.L. 109-58, Sec. 1345(a), amended subsec. (a) ... Sec. 1345(b), added para. (b)(5) ... Sec. 1345(c), redesignated subsec. (e) as (f) and added subsec. (e) ... Sec. 1345(d)(1), substituted "paragraph (1) or (2) of subsection (a)" for "this section" in para. (b)(4) ... Sec. 1345(d)(2), substituted ", biodiesel credit, and small agri-biodiesel producer credit" for "and biodiesel credit" in the heading of subsec. (b) ... Sec. 1345(d)(3), redesignated subpara. (d)(3)(C) as (d)(3)(D) and added subpara. (d)(3)(C), effective for tax. yrs. end. after 8/8/2005.
Prior to amendment, subsec. (a) read as follows:
"(a) General rule. For purposes of section 38, the biodiesel fuels credit determined under this section for the taxable year is an amount equal to the sum of—
"(1) the biodiesel mixture credit, plus
"(2) the biodiesel credit."
—P.L. 109-58, Sec. 1346(a), redesignated subsec. (f) [as redesignated by Sec. 1345(c) of this Act, see above] as (g) and added subsec. (f), effective for fuel sold or used after 12/31/2005.
—P.L. 109-58, Sec. 1346(b)(1), added "and renewable diesel" after "biodiesel" in the heading of Code Sec. 40A, enacted 8/8/2005.

In 2004, P.L. 108-357, Sec. 302(a), added Code Sec. 40A, effective for fuel produced, and sold or used, after 12/31/2004, in tax. yrs. end. after 12/31/2004.

Sec. 41. Credit for increasing research activities.
(a) General rule.

For purposes of section 38, the research credit determined under this section for the taxable year shall be an amount equal to the sum of—

(1) 20 percent of the excess (if any) of—

(A) the qualified research expenses for the taxable year, over

(B) the base amount,

(2) 20 percent of the basic research payments determined under subsection (e)(1)(A), and

(3) 20 percent of the amounts paid or incurred by the taxpayer in carrying on any trade or business of the taxpayer during the taxable year (including as contributions) to an energy research consortium for energy research.

(b) Qualified research expenses.

For purposes of this section—

(1) Qualified research expenses. The term "qualified research expenses" means the sum of the following amounts which are paid or incurred by the taxpayer during the taxable year in carrying on any trade or business of the taxpayer—

(A) in-house research expenses, and

(B) contract research expenses.

(2) In-house research expenses.

(A) In general. The term "in-house research expenses" means—

(i) any wages paid or incurred to an employee for qualified services performed by such employee,

(ii) any amount paid or incurred for supplies used in the conduct of qualified research, and

(iii) under regulations prescribed by the Secretary, any amount paid or incurred to another person for the right to use computers in the conduct of qualified research.

Clause (iii) shall not apply to any amount to the extent that the taxpayer (or any person with whom the taxpayer must aggregate expenditures under subsection (f)(1)) receives or accrues any amount from any other person for the right to use substantially identical personal property.

(B) Qualified services. The term "qualified services" means services consisting of—

(i) engaging in qualified research, or

(ii) engaging in the direct supervision or direct support of research activities which constitute qualified research.

If substantially all of the services performed by an individual for the taxpayer during the taxable year consists of services meeting the requirements of clause (i) or (ii), the term "qualified services" means all of the services performed by such individual for the taxpayer during the taxable year.

(C) Supplies. The term "supplies" means any tangible property other than—

(i) land or improvements to land, and

(ii) property of a character subject to the allowance for depreciation.

(D) Wages.

(i) In general. The term "wages" has the meaning given such term by section 3401(a).

(ii) Self-employed individuals and owner-employees. In the case of an employee (within the meaning of section 401(c)(1)), the term "wages" includes the earned income (as defined in section 401(c)(2)) of such employee.

(iii) Exclusion for wages to which work opportunity credit applies. The term "wages" shall not include any amount taken into account in determining the work opportunity credit under section 51(a).

(3) Contract research expenses.

(A) In general. The term "contract research expenses" means 65 percent of any amount paid or incurred by the taxpayer to any person (other than an employee of the taxpayer) for qualified research.

(B) Prepaid amounts. If any contract research expenses paid or incurred during any taxable year are attributable to qualified research to be conducted after the close of such taxable year, such amount shall be treated as paid or incurred during the period during which the qualified research is conducted.

(C) Amounts paid to certain research consortia.

(i) In general. Subparagraph (A) shall be applied by substituting "75 percent" for "65 percent" with respect to amounts paid or incurred by the taxpayer to a qualified research consortium for qualified research on behalf of the taxpayer and 1 or more unrelated taxpayers. For purposes of the preceding sentence, all persons treated as a single employer under subsection (a) or (b) of section 52 shall be treated as related taxpayers.

(ii) Qualified research consortium. The term "qualified research consortium" means any organization which—

(I) is described in section 501(c)(3) or 501(c)(6) and is exempt from tax under section 501(a),

(II) is organized and operated primarily to conduct scientific research, and

(III) is not a private foundation.

(D) Amounts paid to eligible small businesses, universities, and Federal laboratories.

(i) In general. In the case of amounts paid by the taxpayer to—

(I) an eligible small business,

(II) an institution of higher education (as defined in section 3304(f)), or

(III) an organization which is a Federal laboratory, for qualified research which is energy research, subparagraph (A) shall be applied by substituting "100 percent" for "65 percent".

(ii) Eligible small business. For purposes of this subparagraph, the term "eligible small business" means a small business with respect to which the taxpayer does not own (within the meaning of section 318) 50 percent or more of—

(I) in the case of a corporation, the outstanding stock of the corporation (either by vote or value), and

(II) in the case of a small business which is not a corporation, the capital and profits interests of the small business.

(iii) Small business. For purposes of this subparagraph—

(I) In general. The term "small business" means, with respect to any calendar year, any person if the annual average number of employees employed by such person during either of the 2 preceding calendar years was 500 or fewer. For purposes of the preceding sentence, a preceding calendar year may be taken into account only if the person was in existence throughout the year.

(II) Startups, controlled groups, and predecessors. Rules similar to the rules of subparagraphs (B) and (D) of section 220(c)(4) shall apply for purposes of this clause.

(iv) Federal laboratory. For purposes of this subparagraph, the term "Federal laboratory" has the meaning given such term by section 4(6) of the Stevenson-Wydler Technology Innovation Act of 1980 (15 U.S.C. 3703(6)), as in effect on the date of the enactment of the Energy Tax Incentives Act of 2005.

(4) Trade or business requirement disregarded for in-house research expenses of certain startup ventures. In the case of in-house research expenses, a taxpayer shall be treated as meeting the trade or business requirement of paragraph (1) if, at the time such in-house research expenses are paid or incurred, the principal purpose of the taxpayer in making such expenditures is to use the results of the research in the active conduct of a future trade or business—

(A) of the taxpayer, or

(B) of 1 or more other persons who with the taxpayer are treated as a single taxpayer under subsection (f)(1).

(c) Base amount.

(1) In general. The term "base amount" means the product of—

(A) the fixed-base percentage, and

(B) the average annual gross receipts of the taxpayer for the 4 taxable years preceding the taxable year for which the credit is being determined (hereinafter in this subsection referred to as the "credit year").

(2) Minimum base amount. In no event shall the base amount be less than 50 percent of the qualified research expenses for the credit year.

(3) Fixed-base percentage.

(A) In general. Except as otherwise provided in this paragraph, the fixed-base percentage is the percentage which the aggregate qualified research expenses of the taxpayer for taxable years beginning after December 31, 1983, and before January 1, 1989, is of the aggregate gross receipts of the taxpayer for such taxable years.

(B) Start-up companies.

(i) Taxpayers to which subparagraph applies. The fixed-base percentage shall be determined under this subparagraph if—

(I) the first taxable year in which a taxpayer had both gross receipts and qualified research expenses begins after December 31, 1983, or

(II) there are fewer than 3 taxable years beginning after December 31, 1983, and before January 1, 1989, in which the taxpayer had both gross receipts and qualified research expenses.

(ii) Fixed-base percentage. In a case to which this subparagraph applies, the fixed-base percentage is—

(I) 3 percent for each of the taxpayer's 1st 5 taxable years beginning after December 31, 1993, for which the taxpayer has qualified research expenses,

(II) in the case of the taxpayer's 6th such taxable year, $\frac{1}{6}$ of the percentage which the aggregate qualified research expenses of the taxpayer for the 4th and 5th such taxable years is of the aggregate gross receipts of the taxpayer for such years,

(III) in the case of the taxpayer's 7th such taxable year, $\frac{1}{3}$ of the percentage which the aggregate qualified research expenses of the taxpayer for the

5th and 6th such taxable years is of the aggregate gross receipts of the taxpayer for such years,

(IV) in the case of the taxpayer's 8th such taxable year, ½ of the percentage which the aggregate qualified research expenses of the taxpayer for the 5th, 6th, and 7th such taxable years is of the aggregate gross receipts of the taxpayer for such years,

(V) in the case of the taxpayer's 9th such taxable year, ⅔ of the percentage which the aggregate qualified research expenses of the taxpayer for the 5th, 6th, 7th, and 8th such taxable years is of the aggregate gross receipts of the taxpayer for such years,

(VI) in the case of the taxpayer's 10th such taxable year, ⅚ of the percentage which the aggregate qualified research expenses of the taxpayer for the 5th, 6th, 7th, 8th, and 9th such taxable years is of the aggregate gross receipts of the taxpayer for such years, and

(VII) for taxable years thereafter, the percentage which the aggregate qualified research expenses for any 5 taxable years selected by the taxpayer from among the 5th through the 10th such taxable years is of the aggregate gross receipts of the taxpayer for such selected years.

(iii) Treatment of de minimis amounts of gross receipts and qualified research expenses. The Secretary may prescribe regulations providing that de minimis amounts of gross receipts and qualified research expenses shall be disregarded under clauses (i) and (ii).

(C) Maximum fixed-base percentage. In no event shall the fixed-base percentage exceed 16 percent.

(D) Rounding. The percentages determined under subparagraphs (A) and (B)(ii) shall be rounded to the nearest 1/100th of 1 percent.

(4) Election of alternative incremental credit.

(A) In general. At the election of the taxpayer, the credit determined under subsection (a)(1) shall be equal to the sum of—

(i) 3 percent of so much of the qualified research expenses for the taxable year as exceeds 1 percent of the average described in subsection (c)(1)(B) but does not exceed 1.5 percent of such average,

(ii) 4 percent of so much of such expenses as exceeds 1.5 percent of such average but does not exceed 2 percent of such average, and

(iii) 5 percent of so much of such expenses as exceeds 2 percent of such average.

(B) Election. An election under this paragraph shall apply to the taxable year for which made and all succeeding taxable years unless revoked with the consent of the Secretary.

(5) Election of alternative simplified credit.

(A) In general. At the election of the taxpayer, the credit determined under subsection (a)(1) shall be equal to 14 percent (12 percent in the case of taxable years ending before January 1, 2009) of so much of the qualified research expenses for the taxable year as exceeds 50 percent of the average qualified research expenses for the 3 taxable years preceding the taxable year for which the credit is being determined.

(B) Special rule in case of no qualified research expenses in any of 3 preceding taxable years.

(i) Taxpayers to which subparagraph applies. The credit under this paragraph shall be determined under this subparagraph if the taxpayer has no qualified research expenses in any one of the 3 taxable years preceding the taxable year for which the credit is being determined.

(ii) Credit rate. The credit determined under this subparagraph shall be equal to 6 percent of the qualified research expenses for the taxable year.

(C) Election. An election under this paragraph shall apply to the taxable year for which made and all succeeding taxable years unless revoked with the consent of the Secretary. An election under this paragraph may not be made for any taxable year to which an election under paragraph (4) applies.

(6) Consistent treatment of expenses required.

(A) In general. Notwithstanding whether the period for filing a claim for credit or refund has expired for any taxable year taken into account in determining the fixed-base percentage, the qualified research expenses taken into account in computing such percentage shall be determined on a basis consistent with the determination of qualified research expenses for the credit year.

(B) Prevention of distortions. The Secretary may prescribe regulations to prevent distortions in calculating a taxpayer's qualified research expenses or gross receipts caused by a change in accounting methods used by such taxpayer between the current year and a year taken into account in computing such taxpayer's fixed-base percentage.

(7) Gross receipts. For purposes of this subsection, gross receipts for any taxable year shall be reduced by returns and allowances made during the taxable year. In the case of a foreign corporation, there shall be taken into account only gross receipts which are effectively connected with the conduct of a trade or business within the United States, the Commonwealth of Puerto Rico, or any possession of the United States.

(d) Qualified research defined.

For purposes of this section—

(1) In general. The term "qualified research" means research—

(A) with respect to which expenditures may be treated as expenses under section 174,

(B) which is undertaken for the purpose of discovering information—

(i) which is technological in nature, and

(ii) the application of which is intended to be useful in the development of a new or improved business component of the taxpayer, and

(C) substantially all of the activities of which constitute elements of a process of experimentation for a purpose described in paragraph (3).

Such term does not include any activity described in paragraph (4).

(2) Tests to be applied separately to each business component. For purposes of this subsection—

(A) In general. Paragraph (1) shall be applied separately with respect to each business component of the taxpayer.

(B) Business component defined. The term "business component" means any product, process, computer software, technique, formula, or invention which is to be—

(i) held for sale, lease, or license, or

(ii) used by the taxpayer in a trade or business of the taxpayer.

(C) Special rule for production processes. Any plant process, machinery, or technique for commercial pro-

Tax credits Code Sec. 41(e)(5)(B)

duction of a business component shall be treated as a separate business component (and not as part of the business component being produced).

(3) Purposes for which research may qualify for credit. For purposes of paragraph (1)(C)—

(A) In general. Research shall be treated as conducted for a purpose described in this paragraph if it relates to—

(i) a new or improved function,

(ii) performance, or

(iii) reliability or quality.

(B) Certain purposes not qualified. Research shall in no event be treated as conducted for a purpose described in this paragraph if it relates to style, taste, cosmetic, or seasonal design factors.

(4) Activities for which credit not allowed. The term "qualified research" shall not include any of the following:

(A) Research after commercial production. Any research conducted after the beginning of commercial production of the business component.

(B) Adaptation of existing business components. Any research related to the adaptation of an existing business component to a particular customer's requirement or need.

(C) Duplication of existing business component. Any research related to the reproduction of an existing business component (in whole or in part) from a physical examination of the business component itself or from plans, blueprints, detailed specifications, or publicly available information with respect to such business component.

(D) Surveys, studies, etc. Any—

(i) efficiency survey,

(ii) activity relating to management function or technique,

(iii) market research, testing, or development (including advertising or promotions),

(iv) routine data collection, or

(v) routine or ordinary testing or inspection for quality control.

(E) Computer software. Except to the extent provided in regulations, any research with respect to computer software which is developed by (or for the benefit of) the taxpayer primarily for internal use by the taxpayer, other than for use in—

(i) an activity which constitutes qualified research (determined with regard to this subparagraph), or

(ii) a production process with respect to which the requirements of paragraph (1) are met.

(F) Foreign research. Any research conducted outside the United States, the Commonwealth of Puerto Rico, or any possession of the United States.

(G) Social sciences, etc. Any research in the social sciences, arts, or humanities.

(H) Funded research. Any research to the extent funded by any grant, contract, or otherwise by another person (or governmental entity).

(e) Credit allowable with respect to certain payments to qualified organizations for basic research.

For purposes of this section—

(1) In general. In the case of any taxpayer who makes basic research payments for any taxable year—

(A) the amount of basic research payments taken into account under subsection (a)(2) shall be equal to the excess of—

(i) such basic research payments, over

(ii) the qualified organization base period amount, and

(B) that portion of such basic research payments which does not exceed the qualified organization base period amount shall be treated as contract research expenses for purposes of subsection (a)(1).

(2) Basic research payments defined. For purposes of this subsection—

(A) In general. The term "basic research payment" means, with respect to any taxable year, any amount paid in cash during such taxable year by a corporation to any qualified organization for basic research but only if—

(i) such payment is pursuant to a written agreement between such corporation and such qualified organization, and

(ii) such basic research is to be performed by such qualified organization.

(B) Exception to requirement that research be performed by the organization. In the case of a qualified organization described in subparagraph (C) or (D) of paragraph (6), clause (ii) of subparagraph (A) shall not apply.

(3) Qualified organization base period amount. For purposes of this subsection, the term "qualified organization base period amount" means an amount equal to the sum of—

(A) the minimum basic research amount, plus

(B) the maintenance-of-effort amount.

(4) Minimum basic research amount. For purposes of this subsection—

(A) In general. The term "minimum basic research amount" means an amount equal to the greater of—

(i) 1 percent of the average of the sum of amounts paid or incurred during the base period for—

(I) any in-house research expenses, and

(II) any contract research expenses, or

(ii) the amounts treated as contract research expenses during the base period by reason of this subsection (as in effect during the base period).

(B) Floor amount. Except in the case of a taxpayer which was in existence during a taxable year (other than a short taxable year) in the base period, the minimum basic research amount for any base period shall not be less than 50 percent of the basic research payments for the taxable year for which a determination is being made under this subsection.

(5) Maintenance-of-effort amount. For purposes of this subsection—

(A) In general. The term "maintenance-of-effort amount" means, with respect to any taxable year, an amount equal to the excess (if any) of—

(i) an amount equal to—

(I) the average of the nondesignated university contributions paid by the taxpayer during the base period, multiplied by

(II) the cost-of-living adjustment for the calendar year in which such taxable year begins, over

(ii) the amount of nondesignated university contributions paid by the taxpayer during such taxable year.

(B) Nondesignated university contributions. For purposes of this paragraph, the term "nondesignated university contribution" means any amount paid by a taxpayer to any qualified organization described in paragraph (6)(A)—

1,121

(i) for which a deduction was allowable under section 170, and
(ii) which was not taken into account—
(I) in computing the amount of the credit under this section (as in effect during the base period) during any taxable year in the base period, or
(II) as a basic research payment for purposes of this section.
(C) Cost-of-living adjustment defined.
(i) In general. The cost-of-living adjustment for any calendar year is the cost-of-living adjustment for such calendar year determined under section 1(f)(3), by substituting "calendar year 1987" for "calendar year 1992" in subparagraph (B) thereof.
(ii) Special rule where base period ends in a calendar year other than 1983 or 1984. If the base period of any taxpayer does not end in 1983 or 1984, section 1(f)(3)(B) shall, for purposes of this paragraph, be applied by substituting the calendar year in which such base period ends for 1992. Such substitution shall be in lieu of the substitution under clause (i).

(6) Qualified organization. For purposes of this subsection, the term "qualified organization" means any of the following organizations:
(A) Educational institutions. Any educational organization which—
(i) is an institution of higher education (within the meaning of section 3304(f)), and
(ii) is described in section 170(b)(1)(A)(ii).
(B) Certain scientific research organizations. Any organization not described in subparagraph (A) which—
(i) is described in section 501(c)(3) and is exempt from tax under section 501(a),
(ii) is organized and operated primarily to conduct scientific research, and
(iii) is not a private foundation.
(C) Scientific tax-exempt organizations. Any organization which—
(i) is described in —
(I) section 501(c)(3) (other than a private foundation), or
(II) section 501(c)(6),
(ii) is exempt from tax under section 501(a),
(iii) is organized and operated primarily to promote scientific research by qualified organizations described in subparagraph (A) pursuant to written research agreements, and
(iv) currently expends—
(I) substantially all of its funds, or
(II) substantially all of the basic research payments received by it,
for grants to, or contracts for basic research with, an organization described in subparagraph (A).
(D) Certain grant organizations. Any organization not described in subparagraph (B) or (C) which—
(i) is described in section 501(c)(3) and is exempt from tax under section 501(a) (other than a private foundation),
(ii) is established and maintained by an organization established before July 10, 1981, which meets the requirements of clause (i),
(iii) is organized and operated exclusively for the purpose of making grants to organizations described in subparagraph (A) pursuant to written research agreements for purposes of basic research, and

(iv) makes an election, revocable only with the consent of the Secretary, to be treated as a private foundation for purposes of this title (other than section 4940, relating to excise tax based on investment income).

(7) Definitions and special rules. For purposes of this subsection—
(A) Basic research. The term "basic research" means any original investigation for the advancement of scientific knowledge not having a specific commercial objective, except that such term shall not include—
(i) basic research conducted outside of the United States, and
(ii) basic research in the social sciences, arts, or humanities.
(B) Base period. The term "base period" means the 3-taxable-year period ending with the taxable year immediately preceding the 1st taxable year of the taxpayer beginning after December 31, 1983.
(C) Exclusion from incremental credit calculation. For purposes of determining the amount of credit allowable under subsection (a)(1) for any taxable year, the amount of the basic research payments taken into account under subsection (a)(2)—
(i) shall not be treated as qualified research expenses under subsection (a)(1)(A), and
(ii) shall not be included in the computation of base amount under subsection (a)(1)(B).
(D) Trade or business qualification. For purposes of applying subsection (b)(1) to this subsection, any basic research payments shall be treated as an amount paid in carrying on a trade or business of the taxpayer in the taxable year in which it is paid (without regard to the provisions of subsection (b)(3)(B)).
(E) Certain corporations not eligible. The term "corporation" shall not include—
(i) an S corporation,
(ii) a personal holding company (as defined in section 542), or
(iii) a service organization (as defined in section 414(m)(3)).

(f) Special rules.
For purposes of this section—
(1) Aggregation of expenditures.
(A) Controlled group of corporations. In determining the amount of the credit under this section—
(i) all members of the same controlled group of corporations shall be treated as a single taxpayer, and
(ii) the credit (if any) allowable by this section to each such member shall be its proportionate shares of the qualified research expenses, basic research payments, and amounts paid or incurred to energy research consortiums, giving rise to the credit.
(B) Common control. Under regulations prescribed by the Secretary, in determining the amount of the credit under this section—
(i) all trades or businesses (whether or not incorporated) which are under common control shall be treated as a single taxpayer, and
(ii) the credit (if any) allowable by this section to each such person shall be its proportionate shares of the qualified research expenses, basic research payments, and amounts paid or incurred to energy research consortiums, giving rise to the credit.

The regulations prescribed under this subparagraph shall be based on principles similar to the principles which apply in the case of subparagraph (A).

(2) Allocations.

(A) Pass-thru in the case of estates and trusts. Under regulations prescribed by the Secretary, rules similar to the rules of subsection (d) of section 52 shall apply.

(B) Allocation in the case of partnerships. In the case of partnerships, the credit shall be allocated among partners under regulations prescribed by the Secretary.

(3) Adjustments for certain acquisitions, etc. Under regulations prescribed by the Secretary—

(A) Acquisitions. If, after December 31, 1983, a taxpayer acquires the major portion of a trade or business of another person (hereinafter in this paragraph referred to as the "predecessor") or the major portion of a separate unit of a trade or business of a predecessor, then, for purposes of applying this section for any taxable year ending after such acquisition, the amount of qualified research expenses paid or incurred by the taxpayer during periods before such acquisition shall be increased by so much of such expenses paid or incurred by the predecessor with respect to the acquired trade or business as is attributable to the portion of such trade or business or separate unit acquired by the taxpayer, and the gross receipts of the taxpayer for such periods shall be increased by so much of the gross receipts of such predecessor with respect to the acquired trade or business as is attributable to such portion.

(B) Dispositions. If, after December 31, 1983—

(i) a taxpayer disposes of the major portion of any trade or business or the major portion of a separate unit of a trade or business in a transaction to which subparagraph (A) applies, and

(ii) the taxpayer furnished the acquiring person such information as is necessary for the application of subparagraph (A),

then, for purposes of applying this section for any taxable year ending after such disposition, the amount of qualified research expenses paid or incurred by the taxpayer during periods before such disposition shall be decreased by so much of such expenses as is attributable to the portion of such trade or business or separate unit disposed of by the taxpayer, and the gross receipts of the taxpayer for such periods shall be decreased by so much of the gross receipts as is attributable to such portion.

(C) Certain reimbursements taken into account in determining fixed-base percentage. If during any of the 3 taxable years following the taxable year in which a disposition to which subparagraph (B) applies occurs, the disposing taxpayer (or a person with whom the taxpayer is required to aggregate expenditures under paragraph (1)) reimburses the acquiring person (or a person required to so aggregate expenditures with such person) for research on behalf of the taxpayer, then the amount of qualified research expenses of the taxpayer for the taxable years taken into account in computing the fixed-based percentage shall be increased by the lesser of—

(i) the amount of the decrease under subparagraph (B) which is allocable to taxable years so taken into account, or

(ii) the product of the number of taxable years so taken into account, multiplied by the amount of the reimbursement described in this subparagraph.

(4) Short taxable years. In the case of any short taxable year, qualified research expenses and gross receipts shall be annualized in such circumstances and under such methods as the Secretary may prescribe by regulation.

(5) Controlled group of corporations. The term "controlled group of corporations" has the same meaning given to such term by section 1563(a), except that—

(A) "more than 50 percent" shall be substituted for "at least 80 percent" each place it appears in section 1563(a)(1), and

(B) the determination shall be made without regard to subsections (a)(4) and (e)(3)(C) of section 1563.

(6) Energy research consortium.

(A) In general. The term "energy research consortium" means any organization—

(i) which is—

(I) described in section 501(c)(3) and is exempt from tax under section 501(a) and is organized and operated primarily to conduct energy research, or

(II) organized and operated primarily to conduct energy research in the public interest (within the meaning of section 501(c)(3)),

(ii) which is not a private foundation,

(iii) to which at least 5 unrelated persons paid or incurred during the calendar year in which the taxable year of the organization begins amounts (including as contributions) to such organization for energy research, and

(iv) to which no single person paid or incurred (including as contributions) during such calendar year an amount equal to more than 50 percent of the total amounts received by such organization during such calendar year for energy research.

(B) Treatment of persons. All persons treated as a single employer under subsection (a) or (b) of section 52 shall be treated as related persons for purposes of subparagraph (A)(iii) and as a single person for purposes of subparagraph (A)(iv).

(C) Foreign research. For purposes of subsection (a)(3), amounts paid or incurred for any energy research conducted outside the United States, the Commonwealth of Puerto Rico, or any possession of the United States shall not be taken into account.

(D) Denial of double benefit. Any amount taken into account under subsection (a)(3) shall not be taken into account under paragraph (1) or (2) of subsection (a).

(E) Energy research. The term "energy research" does not include any research which is not qualified research.

(g) Special rule for pass-thru of credit.

In the case of an individual who—

(1) owns an interest in an unincorporated trade or business,

(2) is a partner in a partnership,

(3) is a beneficiary of an estate or trust, or

(4) is a shareholder in an S corporation,

the amount determined under subsection (a) for any taxable year shall not exceed an amount (separately computed with respect to such person's interest in such trade or business or entity) equal to the amount of tax attributable to that portion of a person's taxable income which is allocable or apportionable to the person's interest in such trade or business or entity. If the amount determined under subsection (a) for any taxable year exceeds the limitation of the preceding sentence, such amount may be carried to other taxable years under the rules of section 39; except that the limitation of the preceding sentence shall be taken into account in lieu of the limitation of section 38(c) in applying section 39.

(h) Termination.

(1) **In general.** This section shall not apply to any amount paid or incurred—

(A) after June 30, 1995, and before July 1, 1996, or

(B) after December 31, 2011.

(2) **Termination of alternative incremental credit.** No election under subsection (c)(4) shall apply to taxable years beginning after December 31, 2008.

(3) **Computation for taxable year in which credit terminates.** In the case of any taxable year with respect to which this section applies to a number of days which is less than the total number of days in such taxable year—

(A) the amount determined under subsection (c)(1)(B) with respect to such taxable year shall be the amount which bears the same ratio to such amount (determined without regard to this paragraph) as the number of days in such taxable year to which this section applies bears to the total number of days in such taxable year, and

(B) for purposes of subsection (c)(5), the average qualified research expenses for the preceding 3 taxable years shall be the amount which bears the same ratio to such average qualified research expenses (determined without regard to this paragraph) as the number of days in such taxable year to which this section applies bears to the total number of days in such taxable year.

In 2010, P.L. 111-312, Sec. 731(a), substituted "December 31, 2011" for "December 31, 2009" in subpara. (h)(1)(B), effective for amounts paid or incurred after 12/31/2009.

In 2008, P.L. 110-343, Sec. 301(a)(1)DivC, substituted "December 31, 2009" for "December 31, 2007" in subpara. (h)(1)(B), effective for amounts paid or incurred after 12/31/2007.

—P.L. 110-343, Sec. 301(b)DivC, redesignated para. (h)(2) as para. (h)(3), and added a new para. (h)(2)

—P.L. 110-343, Sec. 301(c)DivC, substituted "14 percent (12 percent in the case of taxable years ending before January 1, 2009)" for "12 percent" in subpara. (c)(5)(A)

—P.L. 110-343, Sec. 301(d)DivC, amended para. (h)(3) [sic (2)], effective for tax. yrs. begin. after 12/31/2007.

Prior to amendment, subpara. (h)(3) [sic (2)] read as follows:

"(2) Computation of base amount.

In the case of any taxable year with respect to which this section applies to a number of days which is less than the total number of days in such taxable year, the base amount with respect to such taxable year shall be the amount which bears the same ratio to the base amount for such year (determined without regard to this paragraph) as the number of days in such taxable year to which this section applies bears to the total number of days in such taxable year."

In 2007, P.L. 110-172, Sec. 6(c)(1), added "for energy research" before the period at the end of para. (a)(3) . . . Sec. 6(c)(2), added subpara. (f)(6)(E), effective for amounts paid or incurred after 8/8/2005 in tax. yrs. end. after 8/8/2005.

—P.L. 110-172, Sec. 11(e)(2), substituted "qualified research expenses, basic research payments, and amounts paid or incurred to energy research consortiums," for "qualified research expenses and basic research payments" in clauses (f)(1)(A)(ii) and (f)(1)(B)(ii), effective for amounts paid or incurred after 8/8/2005, in tax. yrs. end. after 8/8/2005.

In 2006, P.L. 109-432, Sec. 104(a)(1), substituted "2007" for "2005" in subpara. (h)(1)(B), effective for amounts paid or incurred after 12/31/2005.

—P.L. 109-432, Sec. 104(b)(1)(A), substituted "3 percent" for "2.65 percent" in clause (c)(4)(A)(i) . . . Sec. 104(b)(1)(B), substituted "4 percent" for "3.2 percent" in clause (c)(4)(A)(ii) . . . Sec. 104(b)(1)(C), substituted "5 percent" for "3.75 percent" in clause. (c)(4)(A)(iii), effective for tax. yrs. end. after 12/31/2006, except as provided in Sec. 104(b)(3), of this Act which reads as follows:

"(3) Transition rule.

"(A) In general. In the case of a specified transitional taxable year for which an election under section 41(c)(4) of the Internal Revenue Code of 1986 applies, the credit determined under section 41(a)(1) of such Code shall be equal to the sum of—

"(i) the applicable 2006 percentage multiplied by the amount determined under section 41(c)(4)(A) of such Code (as in effect for taxable years ending on December 31, 2006), plus

"(ii) the applicable 2007 percentage multiplied by the amount determined under section 41(c)(4)(A) of such Code (as in effect for taxable years ending on January 1, 2007).

"(B) Definitions. For purposes of subparagraph (A)—

"(i) Specified transitional taxable year. The term 'specified transitional taxable year' means any taxable year which ends after December 31, 2006, and which includes such date.

"(ii) Applicable 2006 percentage. The term 'applicable 2006 percentage' means the number of days in the specified transitional taxable year before January 1, 2007, divided by the number of days in such taxable year.

"(iii) Applicable 2007 percentage. The term 'applicable 2007 percentage' means the number of days in the specified transitional taxable year after December 31, 2006, divided by the number of days in such taxable year."

—P.L. 109-432, Sec. 104(c)(1), redesignated paras. (c)(5) and (c)(6) as paras. (c)(6) and (c)(7), and added a new para. (c)(5), effective for tax. yrs. end. after 12/31/2006.

—P.L. 109-432, Sec. 104(c)(2), of this Act provides:

"(2) Transition rule for deemed revocation of election of alternative incremental credit. In the case of an election under section 41(c)(4) of the Internal Revenue Code of 1986 which applies to the taxable year which includes January 1, 2007, such election shall be treated as revoked with the consent of the Secretary of the Treasury if the taxpayer makes an election under section 41(c)(5) of such Code (as added by this subsection) for such year."

—P.L. 109-432, Sec. 104(c)(4), of this Act provides:

"(4) Transition rule for noncalendar taxable years.

"(A) In general. In the case of a specified transitional taxable year for which an election under section 41(c)(5) of the Internal Revenue Code of 1986 (as added by this subsection) applies, the credit determined under section 41(a)(1) of such Code shall be equal to the sum of—

"(i) the applicable 2006 percentage multiplied by the amount determined under section 41(a)(1) of such Code (as in effect for taxable years ending on December 31, 2006), plus

"(ii) the applicable 2007 percentage multiplied by the amount determined under section 41(c)(5) of such Code (as in effect for taxable years ending on January 1, 2007).

"(B) Definitions and special rules. For purposes of subparagraph (A)-

"(i) Definitions. Terms used in this paragraph which are also used in subsection (b)(3) shall have the respective meanings given such terms in such subsection.

"(ii) Dual elections permitted.

"Elections under paragraphs (4) and (5) of section 41(c) of such Code may both apply for the specified transitional taxable year.

"(iii) Deferral of deemed revocation. Any election under section 41(c)(4) of the Internal Revenue Code of 1986 treated as revoked under paragraph (2) shall be treated as revoked for the taxable year after the specified transitional taxable year."

—P.L. 109-432, Sec. 123, of this Act provides:

"Sec. 123. Special rule for elections under expired provisions.

"(a) Research credit elections. In the case of any taxable year ending after December 31, 2005, and before the date of the enactment of this Act, any election under section 41(c)(4) or section 280C(c)(3)(C) of the Internal Revenue Code of 1986 shall be treated as having been timely made for such taxable year if such election is made not later than the later of April 15, 2007, or such time as the Secretary of the Treasury, or his designee, may specify. Such election shall be made in the manner prescribed by such Secretary or designee.

"(b) Other elections. Except as otherwise provided by such Secretary or designee, a rule similar to the rule of subsection (a) shall apply with respect to elections under any other expired provision of the Internal Revenue Code of 1986 the applicability of which is extended by reason of the amendments made by this title."

In 2005, P.L. 109-135, Sec. 402(l)(1), added subparas. (f)(6)(C) and (D) . . . Sec. 402(l)(2), deleted "(other than an energy research consortium)" before "which" in clause (b)(3)(C)(ii), effective for amounts paid or incurred after 8/8/2005, in tax. yrs. end. after 8/8/2005 as if included in Sec. 1351 of the Energy Tax Incentives Act of 2005, P.L. 109-58.

—P.L. 109-58, Sec. 1351(a)(1), deleted "and" at the end of para. (a)(1), substituted ", and" for the period at the end of para. (a)(2), and added para. (a)(3) . . . Sec. 1351(a)(2), added para. (f)(6) . . . Sec. 1351(a)(3), added "(other than an energy research consortium)" after "organization" in subpara. (b)(3)(C) . . . Sec. 1351(b), added subpara. (b)(3)(D), effective for amounts paid or incurred after 8/8/2005, in tax. yrs. end. after 8/8/2005.

In 2004, P.L. 108-311, Sec. 301(a)(1), substituted "December 31, 2005" for "June 30, 2004" in subpara. (h)(1)(B), effective for amounts paid or incurred after 6/30/2004.

In 1999, P.L. 106-170, Sec. 502(a)(1)(A), substituted "June 30, 2004" for "June 30, 1999" in subpara. (h)(1)(A) . . . Sec. 502(a)(1)(B), deleted "Notwithstanding the preceding sentence, in the case of a taxpayer making an election under subsection (c)(4) for its first taxable year beginning after June 30, 1996, and before July 1, 1997, this section shall apply to amounts paid or incurred during the 36-month period beginning with the first month of such year. The 36 months referred to in the preceding sentence shall be reduced by the number of full months after June 1996 (and before the first month of such first taxable year) during which the taxpayer paid or incurred any amount which is taken into account in determining the credit under this section." at the end of para. (h)(1), effective for amounts paid or incurred after 6/30/99.

—P.L. 106-170, Sec. 502(b)(1)(A), substituted "2.65 percent" for "1.65 percent" in subpara. (c)(4)(A) . . . Sec. 502(b)(1)(B), substituted "3.2 percent" for "2.2 percent" in subpara. (c)(4)(A) . . . Sec. 502(b)(1)(C), substituted "3.75 percent" for "2.75 percent" in subpara. (c)(4)(A), effective for tax. yrs. begin. after 6/30/99.

—P.L. 106-170, Sec. 502(c)(1), added ", the Commonwealth of Puerto Rico, or any possession of the United States" after "United States" each place it appeared in para. (c)(6) and subpara. (d)(4)(F), effective for amounts paid or incurred after 6/30/99.

—P.L. 106-170, Sec. 502(d), of this Act, reads as follows:
"(d) Special rule.
"(1) In general. For purposes of the Internal Revenue Code of 1986, the credit determined under section 41 of such Code which is otherwise allowable under such Code—
"(A) shall not be taken into account prior to October 1, 2000, to the extent such credit is attributable to the first suspension period, and
"(B) shall not be taken into account prior to October 1, 2001, to the extent such credit is attributable to the second suspension period.
On or after the earliest date that an amount of credit may be taken into account, such amount may be taken into account through the filing of an amended return, an application for expedited refund, an adjustment of estimated taxes, or other means allowed by such Code.
"(2) Suspension periods. For purposes of this subsection—
"(A) the first suspension period is the period beginning on July 1, 1999, and ending on September 30, 2000, and
"(B) the second suspension period is the period beginning on October 1, 2000, and ending on September 30, 2001.
"(3) Expedited refunds.
"(A) In general. If there is an overpayment of tax with respect to a taxable year by reason of paragraph (1), the taxpayer may file an application for a tentative refund of such overpayment. Such application shall be in such manner and form, and contain such information, as the Secretary may prescribe.
"(B) Deadline for applications. Subparagraph (A) shall apply only to an application filed before the date which is 1 year after the close of the suspension period to which the application relates.
"(C) Allowance of adjustments. Not later than 90 days after the date on which an application is filed under this paragraph, the Secretary shall—
"(i) review the application,
"(ii) determine the amount of the overpayment, and
"(iii) apply, credit, or refund such overpayment, in a manner similar to the manner provided in section 6411(b) of such Code.
"(D) Consolidated returns. The provisions of section 6411(c) of such Code shall apply to an adjustment under this paragraph in such manner as the Secretary may provide.
"(4) Credit attributable to suspension period.
"(A) In general. For purposes of this subsection, in the case of a taxable year which includes a portion of the suspension period, the amount of credit determined under section 41 of such Code for such taxable year which is attributable to such period is the amount which bears the same ratio to the amount of credit determined under such section 41 for such taxable year as the number of months in the suspension period which are during such taxable year bears to the number of months in such taxable year.
"(B) Waiver of estimated tax penalties. No addition to tax shall be made under section 6654 or 6655 of such Code for any period before July 1, 1999, with respect to any underpayment of tax imposed by such Code to the extent such underpayment was created or increased by reason of subparagraph (A).
"(5) Secretary. For purposes of this subsection, the term 'Secretary' means the Secretary of the Treasury (or such Secretary's delegate)."
In 1998, P.L. 105-277, Sec. 1001(a)(1), substituted "June 30, 1999" for "June 30, 1998" in para. (h)(1) . . . Sec. 1001(a)(2), substituted "36-month" for "24-month" in para. (h)(1) . . . Sec. 1001(a)(3), substituted "36 months" for "24 months" in para. (h)(1), effective for amounts paid or incurred after 6/30/98.
In 1997, P.L. 105-34, Sec. 601(a)(1), substituted "June 30, 1998" for "May 31, 1997" in para. (h)(1) . . . Sec. 601(a)(2), substituted "during the 24-month period beginning with the first month of such year. The 24 months referred to in the preceding sentence shall be reduced by the number of full months after June 1996 (and before the first month of such first taxable year) during which the taxpayer paid or incurred any amount which is taken into account in determining the credit under this section." for "during the first 11 months of such taxable year" in the last sentence of para. (h)(1) . . . Sec. 601(b)(1), amended subpara. (c)(4)(B), effective for amounts paid or incurred after 5/31/97.
Prior to amendment, subpara. (c)(4)(B) read as follows:
"(B) Election. An election under this paragraph may be made only for the first taxable year of the taxpayer beginning after June 30, 1996. Such an election shall apply to the taxable year for which made and all succeeding taxable years unless revoked with the consent of the Secretary."
In 1996, P.L. 104-188, Sec. 1201(e)(1), substituted "work opportunity credit" for "targeted jobs credit" in clause (b)(1)(D)(iii) . . . Sec. 1201(e)(4), substituted "work opportunity credit" for "targeted jobs credit" in the heading of clause (b)(1)(D)(iii), effective for individuals who begin work for the employer after 9/30/96.
—P.L. 104-188, Sec. 1204(a), amended subsec. (h) . . . Sec. 1204(b), amended clause (c)(3)(B)(i), effective for tax. yrs. end. after 6/30/96. Sec. 1204(f)(3) provides:
"(3) Estimated tax. The amendments made by this section shall not be taken into account under section 6654 or 6655 of the Internal Revenue Code of 1986 (relating to failure to pay estimated tax) in determining the amount of any installment required to be paid for a taxable year beginning in 1997."
Prior to amendment, subsec. (h) read as follows:
"(h) Termination.
"(1) In general. This section shall not apply to any amount paid or incurred after June 30, 1995.
"(2) Computation of base amount. In the case of any taxable year which begins before July 1, 1995, and ends after June 30, 1995, the base amount with respect to such taxable year shall be the amount which bears the same ratio to the base amount for such year (determined without regard to this paragraph) as the number of days in such taxable year before July 1, 1995, bears to the total number of days in such taxable year."
Prior to amendment, clause (c)(3)(B)(i) read as follows:
"(i) Taxpayers to which subparagraph applies. The fixed-base percentage shall be determined under this subparagraph if there are fewer than 3 taxable years beginning after December 31, 1983, and before January 1, 1989, in which the taxpayer had both gross receipts and qualified research expenses."
—P.L. 104-188, Sec. 1204(c), redesignated paras. (c)(4) and (5) as paras. (c)(5) and (6), and added a new para. (c)(4) . . . Sec. 1204(d), added subpara. (b)(3)(C), effective for tax. yrs. begin. after 6/30/96. For special rules regarding estimated tax, see Sec. 1204(f)(3) reproduced above.
—P.L. 104-188, Sec. 1702(d)(1), changed the effective date of amendments made by Sec. 11402(b)(1) of P.L. 101-508, see below from "effective for tax. yrs. begin. after 12/31/89" to "effective for tax. yrs. end. after 12/31/89".
In 1993, P.L. 103-66, Sec. 13111(a)(1)(A), substituted "June 30, 1995" for "June 30, 1992" each place it appeared in subsec. (h) . . . Sec. 13111(a)(1)(B), substituted "July 1, 1995" for "July 1, 1992" each place it appeared in subsec. (h), effective for tax. yrs. end. after 6/30/92.
—P.L. 103-66, Sec. 13112(a), amended clause (c)(3)(B)(ii) . . . Sec. 13112(b)(1), substituted "clauses (i) and (ii)" for "clause (i)" in clause (c)(3)(B)(iii) . . . Sec. 13112(b)(2), substituted "subparagraphs (A) and (B)(ii)" for "subparagraph (A)" in subpara. (c)(3)(D), effective for tax. yrs. begin. after 12/31/93.
Prior to amendment, clause (c)(3)(B)(ii) read as follows:
"(ii) Fixed-base percentage. In a case to which this subparagraph applies, the fixed-base percentage is 3 percent."
—P.L. 103-66, Sec. 13201(b)(3)(C), substituted "1992" for "1989" each place it appeared in subpara. (e)(5)(C), effective for tax. yrs. begin. after 12/31/92.
In 1991, P.L. 102-227, Sec. 102(a)(1), substituted "June 30, 1992" for "December 31, 1991" each place it appeared in subsec. (h) . . . Sec. 102(a)(2), substituted "July 1, 1992" for "January 1, 1992" each place it appeared in subsec. (h), effective for tax. yrs. end. after 12/31/91.
In 1990, P.L. 101-508, Sec. 11101(d)(1)(C)(i), added ", by substituting 'calendar year 1987' for 'calendar year 1989' in subparagraph (B) thereof" before the period at the end of clause (e)(5)(C)(i) . . . Sec. 11101(d)(1)(C)(ii), substituted "1989" for "1987" in clause (e)(5)(C)(ii). . . . Sec. 11101(d)(1)(C)(iii), added the last sentence of clause (e)(5)(C)(ii), effective for tax. yrs. begin. after 12/31/90.
—P.L. 101-508, Sec. 11402(a)(1), substituted "December 31, 1991" for "December 31, 1990" each place it appeared in subsec. (h) . . . Sec. 11402(a)(2), substituted "January 1, 1992" for "January 1, 1991" each place it appeared in subsec. (h), effective for tax. yrs. begin. after 12/31/89.
—P.L. 101-508, Sec. 11402(b)(1), deleted Sec. 7110(a)(2) of P.L. 101-239, effective [as amended by Sec. 1702(d)(1) of P.L. 104-188, see above.] for tax. years. end. after 12/31/89
Prior to deletion, Sec. 7110(a)(2) of P.L. 101-239, regarding special rules, read as follows:
"(2) Special rules.
"(A) In the case of any taxable year which begins before October 1, 1990, and ends after September 30, 1990, the amount treated as the qualified research expenses for such taxable year for purposes of section 41 of the Internal Revenue Code of 1986 shall be the amount which bears the same ratio in the amount which would have been determined for such taxable year without regard to this subparagraph as the number of days in such taxable year before October 1, 1990, bears to the total number of days in such taxable year before January 1, 1991.
"(B) In the case of a taxable year described in subparagraph (A), paragraph (2) of section 41(b) of such Code, as so redesignated, shall be applied by substituting 'October 1, 1990' for 'January 1, 1991' each place it appears and by substituting 'September 30, 1990' for 'December 31, 1990'."
In 1989, P.L. 101-239, Sec. 7110(a)(1)(A), substituted "December 31, 1990" for "December 31, 1989" each place it appeared in subsec. (h) as redesignated by Sec. 7814(e)(2)(C) of this Act, see below . . . Sec. 7110(a)(1)(B), substituted "January 1, 1991" for "January 1, 1990" each place it appeared in subsec. (h) as redesignated by Sec. 7814(e)(2)(C) of this Act, see below, effective 12/19/89.
—P.L. 101-239, Sec. 7110(a)(2), regarding special rules applying to the extension and modification of research credit [as repealed in Sec. 11402(b)(1) of P.L. 101-508] see above.
—P.L. 101-239, Sec. 7110(b)(1), amended subsec. (c) . . . Sec. 7110(b)(2)(A), substituted "(B) the base amount, and" for "(B) the base period research expenses, and" in subpara. (a)(1)(B) . . . Sec. 7110(b)(2)(B), substituted "base amount" for "base period research expenses" in clause (e)(7)(C)(ii) . . . Sec. 7110(b)(2)(C), substituted "proportionate shares of the qualified research expenses and basic research payments" for "proportionate share of the increase in qualified research expenses" each place it appeared in para. (f)(1) . . . Sec. 7110(b)(2)(D)(i), substituted "December 31, 1983" for "June 30, 1980" in subpara. (f)(3)(A) . . . Sec. 7110(b)(2)(D)(ii), added ", and the gross receipts of the taxpayer for such periods shall be increased by so much of the gross receipts of such predecessor with respect to the acquired trade or business as is attributable to such portion" before the period in subpara. (f)(3)(A) . . . Sec. 7110(b)(2)(E)(i), substituted "December 31, 1983" for "June 30, 1980" in subpara. (f)(3)(B) . . . Sec. 7110(b)(2)(E)(ii), added ", and the gross receipts of the taxpayer for such periods shall be decreased by so much of the gross receipts as is attributable to such portion" before the period in subpara. (f)(3)(B) . . . Sec. 7110(b)(2)(F), amended subpara. (f)(3)(C) . . . Sec. 7110(b)(2)(G), added "and gross receipts" after "qualified research expenses" in para. (f)(4) . . . Sec. 7110(b)(2)(H)(i), substituted "base amount" for "base period expenses" in the heading of para. (h)(2) as redesignated by Sec. 7814(e)(2)(C) of this Act, see below . . . Sec. 7110(b)(2)(H)(ii), substituted "the base amount with respect to such taxable year shall be the amount which bears the same ratio to the base amount for such year (determined without regard

to this paragraph)" for "any amount for any base period with respect to such taxable year shall be the amount which bears the same ratio to such amount for such base period" in para. (h)(2) as redesignated by Sec. 7814(e)(2)(C) of this Act, see below . . . Sec. 7110(b), [(c)], added para. (b)(4), effective for tax. yrs. begin. after 12/31/89.

Prior to amendment, subsec. (c) read as follows:

"(c) Base period research expenses. For purposes of this section—

"(1) In general. The term 'base period research expenses' means the average of the qualified research expenses for each year in the base period.

"(2) Base period.

"(A) In general. For purposes of this subsection, the term 'base period' means the 3 taxable years immediately preceding the taxable year for which the determination is being made (hereinafter in this subsection referred to as the 'determination year').

"(B) Transitional rules. Subparagraph (A) shall be applied—

"(i) by substituting 'first taxable year' for '3 taxable years' in the case of the first determination year ending after June 30, 1981, and

"(ii) by substituting '2' for '3' in the case of the second determination year ending after June 30, 1981."

"(3) Minimum base period research expenses. In no event shall the base period research expenses be less than 50 percent of the qualified research expenses for the determination year."

Prior to amendment, subpara. (f)(3)(C) read as follows:

"(C) Increase in base period. If during any of the 3 taxable years following the taxable year in which a disposition to which subparagraph (B) applies occurs, the disposing taxpayer (or a person with whom the taxpayer is required to aggregate expenditures under paragraph (1)) reimburses the acquiring person (or a person required to so aggregate expenditures with such person) for research on behalf of the taxpayer, then the amount of qualified research expenses of the taxpayer for the base period for such taxable year shall be increased by the lesser of—

"(i) the amount of the decrease under subparagraph (B) which is allocable to such base period, or

"(ii) the product of the number of years in the base period, multiplied by the amount of the reimbursement described in this subparagraph."

—P.L. 101-239, Sec. 7814(e)(2)(C), deleted subsec. (h) and redesignated subsec. (i) as subsec. (h), effective for tax. yrs. begin. after 12/31/88.

Prior to deletion, subsec. (h) read as follows:

"(h) Election to have research credit not apply.

"(1) In general. A taxpayer may elect to have this section not apply for any taxable year.

"(2) Time for making election. An election under paragraph (1) for any taxable year may be made (or revoked) at any time before the expiration of the 3-year period beginning on the last day prescribed by law for filing the return for such taxable year (determined without regard to extensions)."

"(3) Manner of making election. An election under paragraph (1) (or revocation thereof) shall be made in such manner as the Secretary may by regulations prescribe."

In 1988, P.L. 100-647, Sec. 1002(h)(1), added the last sentence to subsec. (g), effective for tax. yrs. begin. after 12/31/85.

—P.L. 100-647, Sec. 4007(a)(1), substituted "December 31, 1989" for "December 31, 1988" each place it appeared in subsec. (h) . . . Sec. 4007(a)(2), substituted "January 1, 1990" for "January 1, 1989" each place it appeared in subsec. (h), effective 11/10/88. Sec. 4007(b) of this Act provides:

"(b) GAO Study.

"(1) In general. The Comptroller General of the United States shall conduct a study of the credit provided by section 41 of the 1986 Code.

"(2) Report. The report of the study under paragraph (1) shall be submitted not later than December 31, 1989, to the Committee on Ways and Means of the House of Representatives and the Committee on Finance of the Senate."

—P.L. 100-647, Sec. 4008(b)(1), redesignated subsec. (h) as subsec. (i) and added a new subsec. (h), effective for tax. yrs. begin. after 12/31/88.

In 1986, P.L. 99-514, Sec. 231(a)(1), added subsec. (h), effective for tax. yrs. end. after 12/31/85.

—P.L. 99-514, Sec. 231(a)(2)(A), amended Sec. 221(d)(1) of P.L. 97-34, which provides the general effective date for the amendments made by Sec. 221(a) of P.L. 97-34, see below, so that the amendments are effective for amounts paid or incurred after 6/30/81, rather than effective for amounts paid or incurred after 6/30/81 and before 1/1/86.

—P.L. 99-514, Sec. 231(a)(2)(B), amended Sec. 221(d)(2) of P.L. 97-34, see below, by deleting the last sentence which read "A similar rule shall apply in the case of a Taxpayer's first taxable year ending after December 31, 1985."

—P.L. 99-514, Sec. 231(b), amended subsec. (d) . . . Sec. 231(c)(1), amended subsec. (a), effective for tax. yrs. begin. after 12/31/85, except for the provisions of para. (a)(2) [as added by this section], which are effective for tax. yrs. begin. after 12/31/86.

Prior to amendment, subsec. (d) read as follows:

"(d) Qualified research. For purposes of this section the term 'qualified research' has the same meaning as the term research or experimental has under section 174, except that such term shall not include—

"(1) qualified research conducted outside the United States,

"(2) qualified research in the social sciences or humanities, and

"(3) qualified research to the extent funded by any grant, contract, or otherwise by another person (or any governmental entity)."

Prior to amendment, subsec. (a) read as follows:

"(a) General rule. There shall be allowed as a credit against the tax imposed by this chapter for the taxable year an amount equal to 25 percent of the excess (if any) of—

"(1) the qualified research expenses for the taxable year, over

"(2) the base period research expenses."

—P.L. 99-514, Sec. 231(c)(2), amended subsec. (e), effective for tax. yrs. begin. after 12/31/86.

Prior to amendment, subsec. (e) read as follows:

"(e) Credit available with respect to certain basic research by colleges, universities, and certain research organizations.

"(1) In general. 65 percent of any amount paid or incurred by a corporation (as such term is defined in section 170(e)(4)(D)) to any qualified organization for basic research to be performed by such organization shall be treated as contract research expenses. The preceding sentence shall apply only if the amount is paid or incurred pursuant to a written research agreement between the corporation and the qualified organization.

"(2) Qualified organization. For purposes of this subsection, the term 'qualified organization' means—

"(A) any educational organization which is described in section 170(b)(1)(A)(ii) and which is an institution of higher education (as defined in section 3304(f)), and

"(B) any other organization which—

"(i) is described in section 501(c)(3) and exempt from tax under section 501(a),

"(ii) is organized and operated primarily to conduct scientific research, and

"(iii) is not a private foundation.

"(3) Basic research. The term 'basic research' means any original investigation for the advancement of scientific knowledge not having a specific commercial objective, except that such term shall not include—

"(A) basic research conducted outside the United States, and

"(B) basic research in the social sciences or humanities.

"(4) Special rules for grants to certain funds.

"(A) In general. For purposes of this subsection, a qualified fund shall be treated as a qualified organization and the requirements of paragraph (1) that the basic research be performed by the qualified organization shall not apply.

"(B) Qualified fund. For purposes of subparagraph (A), the term 'qualified fund' means any organization which—

"(i) is described in section 501(c)(3) and exempt from tax under section 501(a) and is not a private foundation,

"(ii) is established and maintained by an organization established before July 10, 1981, which meets the requirements of clause (i),

"(iii) is organized and operated exclusively for purposes of making grants pursuant to written research agreements to organizations described in paragraph (2)(A) for purposes of basic research, and

"(iv) makes an election under this paragraph.

"(C) Effect of election.

"(i) In general. Any organization which makes an election under this paragraph shall be treated as a private foundation for purposes of this title (other than section 4940, relating to excise tax based on investment income).

"(ii) Election revocable only with consent. An election under this paragraph, once made, may be revoked only with the consent of the Secretary."

—P.L. 99-514, Sec. 231(d)(2), redesignated Code Sec. 30 as Code Sec. 41 . . . Sec. 231(d)(3)(C)(ii), amended subsec. (g) . . . Sec. 231(e), amended clause (b)(2)(A)(iii), effective for tax. yrs. begin. after 12/31/85.

Prior to amendment, subsec. (g) read as follows:

"(g) Limitation based on amount of tax.

"(1) Liability for tax.

"(A) In general. Except as provided in subparagraph (B), the credit allowed by subsection (a) for any taxable year shall not exceed the taxpayer's tax liability for the taxable year (as defined in section 26(b)), reduced by the sum of the credits allowable under subpart A and sections 27, 28, and 29.

"(B) Special rule for passthrough of credit. In the case of an individual who—

"(i) owns an interest in an unincorporated trade or business,

"(ii) is a partner in a partnership,

"(iii) is a beneficiary of an estate or trust, or

"(iv) is a shareholder in an S corporation, the credit allowed by subsection (a) for any taxable year shall not exceed the lesser of the amount determined under subparagraph (A) for the taxable year or an amount (separately computed with respect to such person's interest in such trade or business or entity) equal to the amount of tax attributable to that portion of a person's taxable income which is allocable or apportionable to the person's interest in such trade or business or entity.

"(2) Carryback and carryover of unused credit.

"(A) Allowance of credit. If the amount of the credit determined under this section for any taxable years exceeds the limitation provided by paragraph (1) for such taxable year (hereinafter in this paragraph referred to as the 'unused credit year'), such excess shall be—

"(i) a research credit carryback to each of the 3 taxable years preceding the unused credit year, and

"(ii) a research credit carryover to each of the 15 taxable years following the unused credit year, and shall be added to the amount allowable as a credit by this section for such years. If any portion of such excess is a carryback to a taxable year beginning before July 1, 1981, this section shall be deemed to have been in effect for such taxable year for purposes of allowing such carryback as a credit under this section. The entire amount of the unused credit for an unused credit year shall be carried to the earliest of the 18 taxable years to which (by reason of clauses (i) and (ii)) such credit may be carried, and then to each of the other 17 taxable years to the extent that, because of the limitation contained in subparagraph (B), such unused credit may not be added for a prior taxable year to which such unused credit may be carried.

"(B) Limitation. The amount of the unused credit which may be added under subparagraph (A) for any preceding or succeeding taxable year shall not exceed

Tax credits Code Sec. 41

the amount by which the limitation provided by paragraph (1) for such taxable year exceeds the sum of—
"(i) the credit allowable under this section for such taxable year, and
"(ii) the amounts which, by reason of this paragraph, are added to the amount allowable for such taxable year and which are attributable to taxable years preceding the unused credit year."
Prior to amendment, clause (b)(2)(A)(iii) read as follows:
"(iii) any amount paid or incurred to another person for the right to use personal property in the conduct of qualified research."
—P.L. 99-514, Sec. 1847(b)(1), substituted "targeted jobs credit" for "new jobs or win credit" in clause (b)(2)(D)(iii), effective for tax. yrs. begin. after 12/31/83 and for carrybacks from tax. yrs. begin. after 12/31/83.

In **1984,** P.L. 98-369, Sec. 471(c)(1), redesignated Code Sec. 44F as Code Sec. 30 . . . Sec. 474(i)(1)(A), substituted "in determining the targeted jobs credit under section 51(a)" for "in computing the credit under section 40 or 44B" in clause (b)(2)(D)(iii) . . . Sec. 474(i)(1)(B), amended subpara. (g)(1)(A), effective for tax. yrs. begin. after 12/31/83 and for carrybacks from tax. yrs. begin. after 12/31/83. Sec. 474(i)(2) of the Act provides as follows:
"(2) New section 30 treated as continuation of old section 44F. For purposes of determining—
"(A) whether any excess credit under old section 44F for a taxable year beginning before January 1, 1984, is allowable as a carryover under new section 30, and
"(B) the period during which new section 30 is in effect, new section 30 shall be treated as a continuation of old section 44F (and shall apply only to the extent old section 44F would have applied)."
Prior to amendment, subpara. (g)(1)(A) read as follows:
"(A) In general. Except as provided in subparagraph (B), the credit allowed by subsection (a) for any taxable year shall not exceed the amount of the tax imposed by this chapter reduced by the sum of the credits allowable under a section of this part having a lower number or letter designation than this section, other than the credits allowable by sections 31, 39, and 43. For purposes of the preceding sentence, the term 'tax imposed by this chapter' shall not include any tax treated as not imposed by this chapter under the last sentence of section 53(a)."
—P.L. 98-369, Sec. 612(e)(1), substituted "section 26(b)" for "section 25(b)" in subpara. (g)(1)(A), effective for interest paid or accrued after 12/31/84, on indebtedness incurred after 12/31/84.
—P.L. 98-369, Sec. 632, provided various exceptions to the amendments made by Title VI of this Act. See note following Code Sec. 103A.

In **1983,** P.L. 97-448, Sec. 102(h)(2), added the last sentence to subpara. (b)(2)(A), effective only with respect to amounts paid or incurred after 3/31/82.

In **1982,** P.L. 97-354, Sec. 5(a)(3)(A), amended subpara. (f)(2)(A) . . . Sec. 5(a)(3)(B), substituted "an S corporation" for "an electing small business corporation (within the meaning of section 1371(b))" in clause (g)(1)(B)(iv), effective for tax. yrs. begin. after 12/31/82.
Prior to amendment, subpara. (f)(2)(A) read as follows:
"(A) Passthrough in the case of Subchapter S corporations, etc. Under regulations prescribed by the Secretary, rules similar to the rules of subsections (d) and (e) of section 52 shall apply."

In **1981,** P.L. 97-34, Sec. 221(a), added Code Sec. 44F, effective for amounts paid or incurred after 6/30/81 [as amended by Sec. 231(a)(2)(A) of P.L. 99-514 see above]. Sec. 221(d)(2) of this Act [as amended by Sec. 231(a)(2)(B) of P.L. 99-514, see above] provides:
"(2) Transitional rule.
"(A) In general. If, with respect to the first taxable year to which the amendments made by this section apply and which ends in 1981 or 1982, the taxpayer may only take into account qualified research expenses paid or incurred during a portion of such taxable year, the amount of the qualified research expenses taken into account for the base period of such taxable year shall be the amount which bears the same ratio to the total qualified research expenses for such base period as the number of months in such portion of such taxable year bears to the total number of months in such taxable year.
"(B) Definitions. For purposes of the preceding sentence, the terms 'qualified research expenses' and 'base period' have the meanings given to such terms by section 44F of the Internal Revenue Code of 1954 (as added by this section)."

Sec. 41. Repealed.

In **1986,** P.L. 99-514, Sec. 1171(a), repealed Code Sec. 41, effective for compensation paid or accrued after 12/31/86, in tax. yrs. end. after 12/31/86. Sec. 1177(a) of this Act provides:
"(a) Section 1171. The amendments made by section 1171 shall not apply in the case of a tax credit employee stock ownership plan if—
"(1) such plan was favorably approved on September 23, 1983, by employees, and
"(2) not later than January 11, 1984, the employer of such employees was 100 percent owned by such plan."
Prior to repeal, Code Sec. 41 read as follows:
"SEC. 41. EMPLOYEE STOCK OWNERSHIP CREDIT.
"(a) General rule.
"(1) Amount of credit. In the case of a corporation which elects to have this section apply for the taxable year and which meets the requirements of subsection (c)(1), for purposes of section 38, the amount of the employee stock ownership credit determined under this section for the taxable year is an amount equal to the amount of the credit determined under paragraph (2) for such taxable year.
"(2) Determination of amount.

"(A) In general. The amount of the credit determined under this paragraph for the taxable year shall be equal to the lesser of—
"(i) the aggregate value of employer securities transferred by the corporation for the taxable year to a tax credit employee stock ownership plan maintained by the corporation, or
"(ii) the applicable percentage of the amount of the aggregate compensation (within the meaning of section 415(c)(3)) paid or accrued during the taxable year to all employees under a tax credit employee stock ownership plan.
"(B) Applicable percentage. For purposes of applying subparagraph (A)(ii), the applicable percentage shall be determined in accordance with the following table:

"For aggregate compensation paid or accrued during a portion of the taxable year occurring in calendar year:	The applicable percentage is:
1983, 1984, 1985, 1986, or 1987	0.5
1988 or thereafter	0.

"(b) Certain regulated companies. No credit attributable to compensation taken into account for the ratemaking purposes involved shall be determined under this section with respect to a taxpayer if
"(1) the taxpayer's cost of service for ratemaking purposes or in its regulated books of account is reduced by reason of any portion of such credit which results from the transfer of employer securities or cash to a tax credit employee stock ownership plan which meets the requirements of section 409;
"(2) the base to which the taxpayer's rate of return for ratemaking purposes is applied is reduced by reason of any portion of such credit which results from a transfer described in paragraph (1) to such employee stock ownership plan; or
"(3) any portion of the amount of such credit which results from a transfer described in paragraph (1) to such employee stock ownership plan is treated for ratemaking purposes in any way other than as though it had been contributed by the taxpayer's common shareholders.
Under regulations prescribed by the Secretary, rules similar to the rules of paragraphs (4) and (7) of section 46(f) shall apply for purposes of the preceding sentence.
"(c) Definitions and special rules.
"(1) Requirements for corporation. A corporation meets the requirements of this paragraph if it—
"(A) establishes a plan—
"(i) which meets the requirements of section 409, and
"(ii) under which no more than one-third of the employer contributions for the taxable year are allocated to the group of employees consisting of—
"(I) officers,
"(II) shareholders owning more than 10 percent of the employer's stock (within the meaning of section 415(c)(6)(B)(iv)), or
"(III) employees described in section 415(c)(6)(B)(iii), and
"(B) agrees, as a condition for the allowance of the credit allowed by this subsection—
"(i) to make transfers of employer securities to a tax credit employee stock ownership plan maintained by the corporation having an aggregate value of not more than the applicable percentage for the taxable year (determined under subsection (a)(2)) of the amount of the aggregate compensation (within the meaning of section 415(c)(3)) paid or accrued by the corporation during the taxable year, and
"(ii) to make such transfers at the times prescribed in paragraph (2).
"(2) Times for making transfers. The transfers required under paragraph (1)(B) shall be made not later than 30 days after the due date (including extensions) for filing the return for the taxable year.
"(3) Adjustments to credit. If the credit determined under this section is reduced by a final determination, the employer may reduce the amount required to be transferred to the tax credit employee stock ownership plan under paragraph (1)(B) for the taxable year in which the final determination occurs or any succeeding taxable year by an amount equal to such reduction to the extent such reduction is not taken into account in any deduction allowed under section 404(i)(2).
"(4) Certain contributions of cash treated as contributions of employer securities. For purposes of this section, a transfer of cash shall be treated as a transfer of employer securities if the cash is, under the tax credit employee stock ownership plan, used within 30 days to purchase employer securities.
"(5) Disallowance of deduction. Except as provided in section 404(i), no deduction shall be allowed under section 162, 212, or 404 for amounts required to be transferred to a tax credit employee stock ownership plan under this section.
"(6) Employer securities. For purposes of this section, the term 'employer securities' has the meaning given such term in section 409(l).
"(7) Value. For purposes of this section, the term 'value' means—
"(A) in the case of securities listed on a national exchange, the average of closing prices of such securities for the 20 consecutive trading days immediately preceding the date on which the securities are contributed to the plan, or
"(B) in the case of securities not listed on a national exchange, the fair market value as determined in good faith and in accordance with regulations prescribed by the Secretary."

In **1984,** P.L. 98-369, Sec. 14, amended the table in subpara. (a)(2)(B), effective for tax. yrs. end. after 12/31/83. Sec. 18(b) of the Act provides:
"(b) Special rule for section 14. The amendment made by section 14 shall not apply in the case of a tax credit employee stock ownership plan if—
"(1) such plan was favorably approved on September 23, 1983, by employees, and
"(2) not later than January 11, 1984, the employer of such employees was 100 percent owned by such plan."

Code Sec. 41 — Tax credits

Prior to amendment, the table in subpara. (a)(2)(B) read as follows:

"For aggregate compensation paid or accrued during a portion of the taxable year occurring in calendar year	The applicable percentage is:
1983	0.5
1984	0.5
1985	0.75
1986	0.75
1987	0.75
1988 or thereafter	0."

—P.L. 98-369, Sec. 471(c)(1), redesignated Code Sec. 44G as Code Sec. 41 ... Sec. 474(l)(1), amended para. (a)(1) ... Sec. 474(l)(2), amended subsec. (b) ... Sec. 474(l)(3), substituted "the credit determined under this section" for "the credit allowed under this section" in para. (c)(3), effective for tax. yrs. begin. after 12/31/83 and to carrybacks from such years.

Prior to amendment, para. (a)(1) read as follows:

"(1) Credit allowed. In the case of a corporation which elects to have this section apply for the taxable year and which meets the requirements of subsection (c)(1), there is allowed as a credit against the tax imposed by this chapter for the taxable year an amount equal to the amount of the credit determined under paragraph (2) for such taxable year."

Prior to amendment, subsec. (b) read as follows:

"(b) Limitation based on amount of tax.

"(1) Liability for tax.

"(A) In general. The credit allowed by subsection (a) for any taxable year shall not exceed an amount equal to the sum of—

"(i) so much of the liability for tax for the taxable year as does not exceed $25,000, plus

"(ii) 90 percent of so much of the liability for tax for the taxable year as exceeds $25,000.

"(B) Liability for tax defined. For purposes of this paragraph, the term 'liability for tax' means the tax imposed by this chapter for the taxable year, reduced by the sum of the credits allowed under a section of this subpart having a lower number designation than this section, other than credits allowable by sections 31, 39, and 43. For purposes of the preceding sentence, the term 'tax imposed by this chapter' shall not include any tax treated as not imposed by this chapter under the last sentence of section 53(a).

"(C) Controlled groups. In the case of a controlled group of corporations, the $25,000 amount specified in subparagraph (A) shall be reduced for each component member of such group by apportioning $25,000 among the component members of such group in such manner as the Secretary shall by regulations prescribe. For purposes of the preceding sentence, the term 'controlled group of corporations' has the meaning assigned to such term by section 1563(a) (determined without regard to subsections (a)(4) and (e)(3)(C) of such section).

"(2) Carryback and carryover of unused credit.

"(A) Allowance of credit. If the amount of the credit determined under this section for any taxable year exceeds the limitation provided under paragraph (1)(A) for such taxable year (hereinafter in this paragraph referred to as the 'unused credit year'), such excess shall be—

"(i) an employee stock ownership credit carryback to each of the 3 taxable years preceding the unused credit year, and

"(ii) an employee stock ownership credit carryover to each of the 15 taxable years following the unused credit year,

and shall be added to the amount allowable as a credit by this section for such years. If any portion of such excess is a carryback to a taxable year ending before January 1, 1983, this section shall be deemed to have been in effect for such taxable year for purposes of allowing such carryback as a credit under this section. The entire amount of the unused credit for an unused credit year shall be carried to the earliest of the 18 taxable years to which (by reason of clauses (i) and (ii)) such credit may be carried, and then to each of the other 17 taxable years to the extent that, because of the limitation contained in subparagraph (B), such unused credit may not be added for a prior taxable year to which such unused credit may be carried.

"(B) Limitation. The amount of the unused credit which may be added under subparagraph (A) for any preceding or succeeding taxable year shall not exceed the amount by which the limitation provided under paragraph (1)(A) for such taxable year exceeds the sum of—

"(i) the credit allowable under this section for such taxable year, and

"(ii) the amounts which, by reason of this paragraph, are added to the amount allowable for such taxable year and which are attributable to taxable years preceding the unused credit year.

"(3) Certain regulated companies. No credit attributable to compensation taken into account for the ratemaking purposes involved shall be allowed under this section to a taxpayer if—

"(A) the taxpayer's cost of service for ratemaking purposes or in its regulated books of account is reduced by reason of any portion of such credit which results from the transfer of employer securities or cash to a tax credit employee stock ownership plan which meets the requirements of section 409A;

"(B) the base to which the taxpayer's rate of return for ratemaking purposes is applied is reduced by reason of any portion of such credit which results from a transfer described in subparagraph (A) to such employee stock ownership plan; or

"(C) any portion of the amount of such credit which results from a transfer described in subparagraph (A) to such employee stock ownership plan is treated for ratemaking purposes in any way other than as though it had been contributed by the taxpayer's common shareholders.

Under regulations prescribed by the Secretary, rules similar to the rules of paragraphs (4) and (7) of section 46(f) shall apply for purposes of the preceding sentence."

—P.L. 98-369, Sec. 491(e)(2), substituted "section 409" for "section 409A" in clause (c)(1)(A)(i) ... Sec. 491(e)(3), substituted "section 409(l)" for "section 409A(l)", effective 1/1/84.

In 1983, P.L. 97-448, Sec. 103(g)(1)(A), substituted "No credit attributable to compensation taken into account for the ratemaking purposes involved" for "No credit" in para. (b)(3) ... Sec. 103(g)(1)(B), added the last sentence to para. (b)(3), effective for aggregate compensation (within the meaning of Code Sec. 415(c)(3)), paid or accrued after 12/31/82 in tax. yrs. end. after 12/31/82.

In 1981, P.L. 97-34, Sec. 331(a), added Code Sec. 44G, effective for aggregate compensation (within the meaning of Code Sec. 415(c)(3)), paid or accrued after 12/31/82, in tax. yrs. end. after 12/31/82.

Sec. 42. Low-income housing credit.

(a) In general.

For purposes of section 38, the amount of the low-income housing credit determined under this section for any taxable year in the credit period shall be an amount equal to—

(1) the applicable percentage of

(2) the qualified basis of each qualified low-income building.

(b) Applicable percentage: 70 percent present value credit for certain new buildings; 30 percent present value credit for certain other buildings.

(1) Determination of applicable percentage.

(A [sic]) For purposes of this section, the term "applicable percentage" means, with respect to any building, the appropriate percentage prescribed by the Secretary for the earlier of—

(i) the month in which such building is placed in service, or

(ii) at the election of the taxpayer—

(I) the month in which the taxpayer and the housing credit agency enter into an agreement with respect to such building (which is binding on such agency, the taxpayer, and all successors in interest) as to the housing credit dollar amount to be allocated to such building, or

(II) in the case of any building to which subsection (h)(4)(B) applies, the month in which the tax-exempt obligations are issued.

A month may be elected under clause (ii) only if the election is made not later than the 5th day after the close of such month. Such an election, once made, shall be irrevocable.

(B) Method of prescribing percentages. The percentages prescribed by the Secretary for any month shall be percentages which will yield over a 10-year period amounts of credit under subsection (a) which have a present value equal to—

(i) 70 percent of the qualified basis of a new building which is not federally subsidized for the taxable year, and

(ii) 30 percent of the qualified basis of a building not described in clause (i).

(C) Method of discounting. The present value under subparagraph (B) shall be determined—

(i) as of the last day of the 1st year of the 10-year period referred to in subparagraph (B),

(ii) by using a discount rate equal to 72 percent of the average of the annual Federal mid-term rate and the annual Federal long-term rate applicable under section 1274(d)(1) to the month applicable under clause (i) or (ii) of subparagraph (A) and compounded annually, and

(iii) by assuming that the credit allowable under this section for any year is received on the last day of such year.

Tax credits Code Sec. 42(d)(2)(D)(i)(IV)

(2) Temporary minimum credit rate for non-federally subsidized new buildings. In the case of any new building—

(A) which is placed in service by the taxpayer after the date of the enactment of this paragraph and before December 31, 2013, and

(B) which is not federally subsidized for the taxable year,

the applicable percentage shall not be less than 9 percent.

(3) Cross references.

(A) For treatment of certain rehabilitation expenditures as separate new buildings, see subsection (e).

(B) For determination of applicable percentage for increases in qualified basis after the 1st year of the credit period, see subsection (f)(3).

(C) For authority of housing credit agency to limit applicable percentage and qualified basis which may be taken into account under this section with respect to any building, see subsection (h)(7).

(c) Qualified basis; qualified low-income building.

For purposes of this section—

(1) Qualified basis.

(A) Determination. The qualified basis of any qualified low-income building for any taxable year is an amount equal to—

(i) the applicable fraction (determined as of the close of such taxable year) of

(ii) the eligible basis of such building (determined under subsection (d)(5)).

(B) Applicable fraction. For purposes of subparagraph (A), the term "applicable fraction" means the smaller of the unit fraction or the floor space fraction.

(C) Unit fraction. For purposes of subparagraph (B), the term "unit fraction" means the fraction—

(i) the numerator of which is the number of low-income units in the building, and

(ii) the denominator of which is the number of residential rental units (whether or not occupied) in such building.

(D) Floor space fraction. For purposes of subparagraph (B), the term "floor space fraction" means the fraction—

(i) the numerator of which is the total floor space of the low-income units in such building, and

(ii) the denominator of which is the total floor space of the residential rental units (whether or not occupied) in such building.

(E) Qualified basis to include portion of building used to provide supportive services for homeless. In the case of a qualified low-income building described in subsection (i)(3)(B)(iii), the qualified basis of such building for any taxable year shall be increased by the lesser of—

(i) so much of the eligible basis of such building as is used throughout the year to provide supportive services designed to assist tenants in locating and retaining permanent housing, or

(ii) 20 percent of the qualified basis of such building (determined without regard to this subparagraph).

(2) Qualified low-income building. The term "qualified low-income building" means any building—

(A) which is part of a qualified low-income housing project at all times during the period—

(i) beginning on the 1st day in the compliance period on which such building is part of such a project, and

(ii) ending on the last day of the compliance period with respect to such building, and

(B) to which the amendments made by section 201(a) of the Tax Reform Act of 1986 apply.

(d) Eligible basis.

For purposes of this section—

(1) New buildings. The eligible basis of a new building is its adjusted basis as of the close of the 1st taxable year of the credit period.

(2) Existing buildings.

(A) In general. The eligible basis of an existing building is—

(i) in the case of a building which meets the requirements of subparagraph (B), its adjusted basis as of the close of the 1st taxable year of the credit period, and

(ii) zero in any other case.

(B) Requirements. A building meets the requirements of this subparagraph if—

(i) the building is acquired by purchase (as defined in section 179(d)(2)),

(ii) there is a period of at least 10 years between the date of its acquisition by the taxpayer and the date the building was last placed in service,

(iii) the building was not previously placed in service by the taxpayer or by any person who was a related person with respect to the taxpayer as of the time previously placed in service, and

(iv) except as provided in subsection (f)(5), a credit is allowable under subsection (a) by reason of subsection (e) with respect to the building.

(C) Adjusted basis. For purposes of subparagraph (A), the adjusted basis of any building shall not include so much of the basis of such building as is determined by reference to the basis of other property held at any time by the person acquiring the building.

(D) Special rules for subparagraph (B).

(i) Special rules for certain transfers. For purposes of determining under subparagraph (B)(ii) when a building was last placed in service, there shall not be taken into account any placement in service—

(I) in connection with the acquisition of the building in a transaction in which the basis of the building in the hands of the person acquiring it is determined in whole or in part by reference to the adjusted basis of such building in the hands of the person from whom acquired,

(II) by a person whose basis in such building is determined under section 1014(a) (relating to property acquired from a decedent),

(III) by any governmental unit or qualified nonprofit organization (as defined in subsection (h)(5)) if the requirements of subparagraph (B)(ii) are met with respect to the placement in service by such unit or organization and all the income from such property is exempt from Federal income taxation,

(IV) by any person who acquired such building by foreclosure (or by instrument in lieu of foreclosure) of any purchase-money security interest held by such person if the requirements of subparagraph (B)(ii) are met with respect to the placement in service by such person and such building is resold within 12 months after the date such building is placed in service by such person after such foreclosure, or

1,129

(V) of a single-family residence by any individual who owned and used such residence for no other purpose than as his principal residence.

(ii) Related person. For purposes of subparagraph (B)(iii), a person (hereinafter in this subclause referred to as the "related person") is related to any person if the related person bears a relationship to such person specified in section 267(b) or 707(b)(1), or the related person and such person are engaged in trades or businesses under common control (within the meaning of subsections (a) and (b) of section 52).

(3) Eligible basis reduced where disproportionate standards for units.

(A) In general. Except as provided in subparagraph (B), the eligible basis of any building shall be reduced by an amount equal to the portion of the adjusted basis of the building which is attributable to residential rental units in the building which are not low-income units and which are above the average quality standard of the low-income units in the building.

(B) Exception where taxpayer elects to exclude excess costs.

(i) In general. Subparagraph (A) shall not apply with respect to a residential rental unit in a building which is not a low-income unit if—

(I) the excess described in clause (ii) with respect to such unit is not greater than 15 percent of the cost described in clause (ii)(II), and

(II) the taxpayer elects to exclude from the eligible basis of such building the excess described in clause (ii) with respect to such unit.

(ii) Excess. The excess described in this clause with respect to any unit is the excess of—

(I) the cost of such unit, over

(II) the amount which would be the cost of such unit if the average cost per square foot of low-income units in the building were substituted for the cost per square foot of such unit.

The Secretary may by regulation provide for the determination of the excess under this clause on a basis other than square foot costs.

(4) Special rules relating to determination of adjusted basis. For purposes of this subsection—

(A) In general. Except as provided in subparagraphs (B) and (C), the adjusted basis of any building shall be determined without regard to the adjusted basis of any property which is not residential rental property.

(B) Basis of property in common areas, etc., included. The adjusted basis of any building shall be determined by taking into account the adjusted basis of property (of a character subject to the allowance for depreciation) used in common areas or provided as comparable amenities to all residential rental units in such building.

(C) Inclusion of basis of property used to provide services for certain nontenants.

(i) In general. The adjusted basis of any building located in a qualified census tract (as defined in paragraph (5)(C)) shall be determined by taking into account the adjusted basis of property (of a character subject to the allowance for depreciation and not otherwise taken into account) used throughout the taxable year in providing any community service facility.

(ii) Limitation. The increase in the adjusted basis of any building which is taken into account by reason of clause (i) shall not exceed the sum of—

(I) 25 percent of so much of the eligible basis of the qualified low-income housing project of which it is a part as does not exceed $15,000,000, plus

(II) 10 percent of so much of the eligible basis of such project as is not taken into account under subclause (I).

For purposes of the preceding sentence, all community service facilities which are part of the same qualified low-income housing project shall be treated as one facility.

(iii) Community service facility. For purposes of this subparagraph, the term "community service facility" means any facility designed to serve primarily individuals whose income is 60 percent or less of area median income (within the meaning of subsection (g)(1)(B)).

(D) No reduction for depreciation. The adjusted basis of any building shall be determined without regard to paragraphs (2) and (3) of section 1016(a).

(5) Special rules for determining eligible basis.

(A) Federal grants not taken into account in determining eligible basis. The eligible basis of a building shall not include any costs financed with the proceeds of a federally funded grant.

(B) Increase in credit for buildings in high cost areas.

(i) In general. In the case of any building located in a qualified census tract or difficult development area which is designated for purposes of this subparagraph—

(I) in the case of a new building, the eligible basis of such building shall be 130 percent of such basis determined without regard to this subparagraph, and

(II) in the case of an existing building, the rehabilitation expenditures taken into account under subsection (e) shall be 130 percent of such expenditures determined without regard to this subparagraph.

(ii) Qualified census tract.

(I) In general. The term "qualified census tract" means any census tract which is designated by the Secretary of Housing and Urban Development and, for the most recent year for which census data are available on household income in such tract, either in which 50 percent or more of the households have an income which is less than 60 percent of the area median gross income for such year or which has a poverty rate of at least 25 percent. If the Secretary of Housing and Urban Development determines that sufficient data for any period are not available to apply this clause on the basis of census tracts, such Secretary shall apply this clause for such period on the basis of enumeration districts.

(II) Limit on MSA's designated. The portion of a metropolitan statistical area which may be designated for purposes of this subparagraph shall not exceed an area having 20 percent of the population of such metropolitan statistical area.

(III) Determination of areas. For purposes of this clause, each metropolitan statistical area shall be treated as a separate area and all nonmetropolitan areas in a State shall be treated as 1 area.

(iii) Difficult development areas.

(I) In general. The term "difficult development areas" means any area designated by the Secretary of Housing and Urban Development as an area which has high construction, land, and utility costs relative to area median gross income.

(II) Limit on areas designated. The portions of metropolitan statistical areas which may be designated for purposes of this subparagraph shall not exceed an aggregate area having 20 percent of the population of such metropolitan statistical areas. A comparable rule shall apply to nonmetropolitan areas.

(iv) Special rules and definitions. For purposes of this subparagraph—

(I) population shall be determined on the basis of the most recent decennial census for which data are available,

(II) area median gross income shall be determined in accordance with subsection (g)(4),

(III) the term "metropolitan statistical area" has the same meaning as when used in section 143(k)(2)(B), and

(IV) the term "nonmetropolitan area" means any county (or portion thereof) which is not within a metropolitan statistical area.

(v) Buildings designated by State housing credit agency. Any building which is designated by the State housing credit agency as requiring the increase in credit under this subparagraph in order for such building to be financially feasible as part of a qualified low-income housing project shall be treated for purposes of this subparagraph as located in a difficult development area which is designated for purposes of this subparagraph. The preceding sentence shall not apply to any building if paragraph (1) of subsection (h) does not apply to any portion of the eligible basis of such building by reason of paragraph (4) of such subsection.

(6) Credit allowable for certain buildings acquired during 10-year period described in paragraph (2)(B)(ii).

(A) In general. Paragraph (2)(B)(ii) shall not apply to any federally- or State-assisted building.

(B) Buildings acquired from insured depository institutions in default. On application by the taxpayer, the Secretary may waive paragraph (2)(B)(ii) with respect to any building acquired from an insured depository institution in default (as defined in section 3 of the Federal Deposit Insurance Act) or from a receiver or conservator of such an institution.

(C) Federally- or State-assisted building. For purposes of this paragraph—

(i) Federally-assisted building. The term "federally-assisted building" means any building which is substantially assisted, financed, or operated under section 8 of the United States Housing Act of 1937, section 221(d)(3), 221(d)(4), or 236 of the National Housing Act, section 515 of the Housing Act of 1949, or any other housing program administered by the Department of Housing and Urban Development or by the Rural Housing Service of the Department of Agriculture.

(ii) State-assisted building. The term "State-assisted building" means any building which is substantially assisted, financed, or operated under any State law similar in purposes to any of the laws referred to in clause (i).

(7) Acquisition of building before end of prior compliance period.

(A) In general. Under regulations prescribed by the Secretary, in the case of a building described in subparagraph (B) (or interest therein) which is acquired by the taxpayer—

(i) paragraph (2)(B) shall not apply, but

(ii) the credit allowable by reason of subsection (a) to the taxpayer for any period after such acquisition shall be equal to the amount of credit which would have been allowable under subsection (a) for such period to the prior owner referred to in subparagraph (B) had such owner not disposed of the building.

(B) Description of building. A building is described in this subparagraph if—

(i) a credit was allowed by reason of subsection (a) to any prior owner of such building, and

(ii) the taxpayer acquired such building before the end of the compliance period for such building with respect to such prior owner (determined without regard to any disposition by such prior owner).

(e) Rehabilitation expenditures treated as separate new building.

(1) In general. Rehabilitation expenditures paid or incurred by the taxpayer with respect to any building shall be treated for purposes of this section as a separate new building.

(2) Rehabilitation expenditures. For purposes of paragraph (1)—

(A) In general. The term "rehabilitation expenditures" means amounts chargeable to capital account and incurred for property (or additions or improvements to property) of a character subject to the allowance for depreciation in connection with the rehabilitation of a building.

(B) Cost of acquisition, etc, not included. Such term does not include the cost of acquiring any building (or interest therein) or any amount not permitted to be taken into account under paragraph (3) or (4) of subsection (d).

(3) Minimum expenditures to qualify.

(A) In general. Paragraph (1) shall apply to rehabilitation expenditures with respect to any building only if—

(i) the expenditures are allocable to 1 or more low-income units or substantially benefit such units, and

(ii) the amount of such expenditures during any 24-month period meets the requirements of whichever of the following subclauses requires the greater amount of such expenditures:

(I) The requirement of this subclause is met if such amount is not less than 20 percent of the adjusted basis of the building (determined as of the 1st day of such period and without regard to paragraphs (2) and (3) of section 1016(a)).

(II) The requirement of this subclause is met if the qualified basis attributable to such amount, when divided by the number of low-income units in the building, is $6,000 or more.

(B) Exception from 10 percent rehabilitation. In the case of a building acquired by the taxpayer from a governmental unit, at the election of the taxpayer, subparagraph (A)(ii)(I) shall not apply and the credit under this section for such rehabilitation expenditures shall be determined using the percentage applicable under subsection (b)(2)(B)(ii).

(C) Date of determination. The determination under subparagraph (A) shall be made as of the close of the 1st taxable year in the credit period with respect to such expenditures.

(D) **Inflation adjustment.** In the case of any expenditures which are treated under paragraph (4) as placed in service during any calendar year after 2009, the $6,000 amount in subparagraph (A)(ii)(II) shall be increased by an amount equal to—
  (i) such dollar amount, multiplied by
  (ii) the cost-of-living adjustment determined under section 1(f)(3) for such calendar year by substituting "calendar year 2008" for "calendar year 1992" in subparagraph (B) thereof.
Any increase under the preceding sentence which is not a multiple of $100 shall be rounded to the nearest multiple of $100.

(4) **Special rules.** For purposes of applying this section with respect to expenditures which are treated as a separate building by reason of this subsection—
  (A) such expenditures shall be treated as placed in service at the close of the 24-month period referred to in paragraph (3)(A), and
  (B) the applicable fraction under subsection (c)(1) shall be the applicable fraction for the building (without regard to paragraph (1)) with respect to which the expenditures were incurred.
Nothing in subsection (d)(2) shall prevent a credit from being allowed by reason of this subsection.

(5) **No double counting.** Rehabilitation expenditures may, at the election of the taxpayer, be taken into account under this subsection or subsection (d)(2)(A)(i) but not under both such subsections.

(6) **Regulations to apply subsection with respect to group of units in building.** The Secretary may prescribe regulations, consistent with the purposes of this subsection, treating a group of units with respect to which rehabilitation expenditures are incurred as a separate new building.

(f) **Definition and special rules relating to credit period.**

(1) **Credit period defined.** For purposes of this section, the term "credit period" means, with respect to any building, the period of 10 taxable years beginning with—
  (A) the taxable year in which the building is placed in service, or
  (B) at the election of the taxpayer, the succeeding taxable year,
but only if the building is a qualified low-income building as of the close of the 1st year of such period. The election under subparagraph (B), once made, shall be irrevocable.

(2) **Special rule for 1st year of credit period.**
  (A) In general. The credit allowable under subsection (a) with respect to any building for the 1st taxable year of the credit period shall be determined by substituting for the applicable fraction under subsection (c)(1) the fraction—
    (i) the numerator of which is the sum of the applicable fractions determined under subsection (c)(1) as of the close of each full month of such year during which such building was in service, and
    (ii) the denominator of which is 12.
  (B) Disallowed 1st year credit allowed in 11th year. Any reduction by reason of subparagraph (A) in the credit allowable (without regard to subparagraph (A)) for the 1st taxable year of the credit period shall be allowable under subsection (a) for the 1st taxable year following the credit period.

(3) **Determination of applicable percentage with respect to increases in qualified basis after 1st year of credit period.**
  (A) In general. In the case of any building which was a qualified low-income building as of the close of the 1st year of the credit period, if—
    (i) as of the close of any taxable year in the compliance period (after the 1st year of the credit period) the qualified basis of such building exceeds
    (ii) the qualified basis of such building as of the close of the 1st year of the credit period,
  the applicable percentage which shall apply under subsection (a) for the taxable year to such excess shall be the percentage equal to ⅔ of the applicable percentage which (after the application of subsection (h)) would but for this paragraph apply to such basis.
  (B) 1st year computation applies. A rule similar to the rule of paragraph (2)(A) shall apply to any increase in qualified basis to which subparagraph (A) applies for the 1st year of such increase.

(4) **Dispositions of property.** If a building (or an interest therein) is disposed of during any year for which credit is allowable under subsection (a), such credit shall be allocated between the parties on the basis of the number of days during such year the building (or interest) was held by each. In any such case, proper adjustments shall be made in the application of subsection (j).

(5) **Credit period for existing buildings not to begin before rehabilitation credit allowed.**
  (A) In general. The credit period for an existing building shall not begin before the 1st taxable year of the credit period for rehabilitation expenditures with respect to the building.
  (B) Acquisition credit allowed for certain buildings not allowed a rehabilitation credit.
    (i) In general. In the case of a building described in clause (ii)—
      (I) subsection (d)(2)(B)(iv) shall not apply, and
      (II) the credit period for such building shall not begin before the taxable year which would be the 1st taxable year of the credit period for rehabilitation expenditures with respect to the building under the modifications described in clause (ii)(II).
    (ii) Building described. A building is described in this clause if—
      (I) a waiver is granted under subsection (d)(6)(C) with respect to the acquisition of the building, and
      (II) a credit would be allowed for rehabilitation expenditures with respect to such building if subsection (e)(3)(A)(ii)(I) did not apply and if the dollar amount in effect under subsection (e)(3)(A)(ii)(II) were two-thirds of such amount.

(g) **Qualified low-income housing project.**
For purposes of this section—

(1) **In general.** The term "qualified low-income housing project" means any project for residential rental property if the project meets the requirements of subparagraph (A) or (B) whichever is elected by the taxpayer:
  (A) 20-50 test. The project meets the requirements of this subparagraph if 20 percent or more of the residential units in such project are both rent-restricted and occupied by individuals whose income is 50 percent or less of area median gross income.
  (B) 40-60 test. The project meets the requirements of this subparagraph if 40 percent or more of the residential units in such project are both rent-restricted and occupied by individuals whose income is 60 percent or less of area median gross income.
Any election under this paragraph, once made, shall be irrevocable. For purposes of this paragraph, any property

shall not be treated as failing to be residential rental property merely because part of the building in which such property is located is used for purposes other than residential rental purposes.

(2) Rent-restricted units.

(A) In general. For purposes of paragraph (1), a residential unit is rent-restricted if the gross rent with respect to such unit does not exceed 30 percent of the imputed income limitation applicable to such unit. For purposes of the preceding sentence, the amount of the income limitation under paragraph (1) applicable for any period shall not be less than such limitation applicable for the earliest period the building (which contains the unit) was included in the determination of whether the project is a qualified low-income housing project.

(B) Gross rent. For purposes of subparagraph (A), gross rent—

(i) does not include any payment under section 8 of the United States Housing Act of 1937 or any comparable rental assistance program (with respect to such unit or occupants thereof),

(ii) includes any utility allowance determined by the Secretary after taking into account such determinations under section 8 of the United States Housing Act of 1937,

(iii) does not include any fee for a supportive service which is paid to the owner of the unit (on the basis of the low-income status of the tenant of the unit) by any governmental program of assistance (or by an organization described in section 501(c)(3) and exempt from tax under section 501(a)) if such program (or organization) provides assistance for rent and the amount of assistance provided for rent is not separable from the amount of assistance provided for supportive services, and

(iv) does not include any rental payment to the owner of the unit to the extent such owner pays an equivalent amount to the Farmers' Home Administration under section 515 of the Housing Act of 1949.

For purposes of clause (iii), the term "supportive service" means any service provided under a planned program of services designed to enable residents of a residential rental property to remain independent and avoid placement in a hospital, nursing home, or intermediate care facility for the mentally or physically handicapped. In the case of a single-room occupancy unit or a building described in subsection (i)(3)(B)(iii), such term includes any service provided to assist tenants in locating and retaining permanent housing.

(C) Imputed income limitation applicable to unit. For purposes of this paragraph, the imputed income limitation applicable to a unit is the income limitation which would apply under paragraph (1) to individuals occupying the unit if the number of individuals occupying the unit were as follows:

(i) In the case of a unit which does not have a separate bedroom, 1 individual.

(ii) In the case of a unit which has 1 or more separate bedrooms, 1.5 individuals for each separate bedroom.

In the case of a project with respect to which a credit is allowable by reason of this section and for which financing is provided by a bond described in section 142(a)(7), the imputed income limitation shall apply in lieu of the otherwise applicable income limitation for purposes of applying section 142(d)(4)(B)(ii).

(D) Treatment of units occupied by individuals whose incomes rise above limit.

(i) In general. Except as provided in clause (ii), notwithstanding an increase in the income of the occupants of a low-income unit above the income limitation applicable under paragraph (1), such unit shall continue to be treated as a low-income unit if the income of such occupants initially met such income limitation and such unit continues to be rent-restricted.

(ii) Next available unit must be rented to low-income tenant if income rises above 140 percent of income limit. If the income of the occupants of the unit increases above 140 percent of the income limitation applicable under paragraph (1), clause (i) shall cease to apply to such unit if any residential rental unit in the building (of a size comparable to, or smaller than, such unit) is occupied by a new resident whose income exceeds such income limitation. In the case of a project described in section 142(d)(4)(B), the preceding sentence shall be applied by substituting "170 percent" for "140 percent" and by substituting "any low-income unit in the building is occupied by a new resident whose income exceeds 40 percent of area median gross income" for "any residential unit in the building (of a size comparable to, or smaller than, such unit) is occupied by a new resident whose income exceeds such income limitation".

(E) Units where federal rental assistance is reduced as tenant's income increases. If the gross rent with respect to a residential unit exceeds the limitation under subparagraph (A) by reason of the fact that the income of the occupants thereof exceeds the income limitation applicable under paragraph (1), such unit shall, nevertheless, be treated as a rent-restricted unit for purposes of paragraph (1) if—

(i) a Federal rental assistance payment described in subparagraph (B)(i) is made with respect to such unit or its occupants, and

(ii) the sum of such payment and the gross rent with respect to such unit does not exceed the sum of the amount of such payment which would be made and the gross rent which would be payable with respect to such unit if—

(I) the income of the occupants thereof did not exceed the income limitation applicable under paragraph (1), and

(II) such units were rent-restricted within the meaning of subparagraph (A).

The preceding sentence shall apply to any unit only if the result described in clause (ii) is required by Federal statute as of the date of the enactment of this subparagraph and as of the date the Federal rental assistance payment is made.

(3) Date for meeting requirements.

(A) In general. Except as otherwise provided in this paragraph, a building shall be treated as a qualified low-income building only if the project (of which such building is a part) meets the requirements of paragraph (1) not later than the close of the 1st year of the credit period for such building.

(B) Buildings which rely on later buildings for qualification.

(i) In general. In determining whether a building (hereinafter in this subparagraph referred to as the "prior building") is a qualified low-income building, the taxpayer may take into account 1 or more additional buildings placed in service during the 12-month period described in subparagraph (A) with respect to the prior building only if the taxpayer elects to apply clause (ii) with respect to each additional building taken into account.

(ii) Treatment of elected buildings. In the case of a building which the taxpayer elects to take into account under clause (i), the period under subparagraph (A) for such building shall end at the close of the 12-month period applicable to the prior building.

(iii) Date prior building is treated as placed in service. For purposes of determining the credit period and the compliance period for the prior building, the prior building shall be treated for purposes of this section as placed in service on the most recent date any additional building elected by the taxpayer (with respect to such prior building) was placed in service.

(C) Special rule. A building—
(i) other than the 1st building placed in service as part of a project, and
(ii) other than a building which is placed in service during the 12-month period described in subparagraph (A) with respect to a prior building which becomes a qualified low-income building,

shall in no event be treated as a qualified low-income building unless the project is a qualified low-income housing project (without regard to such building) on the date such building is placed in service.

(D) Projects with more than 1 building must be identified. For purposes of this section, a project shall be treated as consisting of only 1 building unless, before the close of the 1st calendar year in the project period (as defined in subsection (h)(1)(F)(ii)), each building which is (or will be) part of such project is identified in such form and manner as the Secretary may provide.

(4) Certain rules made applicable. Paragraphs (2) (other than subparagraph (A) thereof), (3), (4), (5), (6), and (7) of section 142(d), and section 6652(j), shall apply for purposes of determining whether any project is a qualified low-income housing project and whether any unit is a low-income unit; except that, in applying such provisions for such purposes, the term "gross rent" shall have the meaning given such term by paragraph (2)(B) of this subsection.

(5) Election to treat building after compliance period as not part of a project. For purposes of this section, the taxpayer may elect to treat any building as not part of a qualified low-income housing project for any period beginning after the compliance period for such building.

(6) Special rule where de minimis equity contribution. Property shall not be treated as failing to be residential rental property for purposes of this section merely because the occupant of a residential unit in the project pays (on a voluntary basis) to the lessor a de minimis amount to be held toward the purchase by such occupant of a residential unit in such project if—

(A) all amounts so paid are refunded to the occupant on the cessation of his occupancy of a unit in the project, and
(B) the purchase of the unit is not permitted until after the close of the compliance period with respect to the building in which the unit is located.

Any amount paid to the lessor as described in the preceding sentence shall be included in gross rent under paragraph (2) for purposes of determining whether the unit is rent-restricted.

(7) Scattered site projects. Buildings which would (but for their lack of proximity) be treated as a project for purposes of this section shall be so treated if all of the dwelling units in each of the buildings are rent-restricted (within the meaning of paragraph (2)) residential rental units.

(8) Waiver of certain de minimis errors and recertifications. On application by the taxpayer, the Secretary may waive—

(A) any recapture under subsection (j) in the case of any de minimis error in complying with paragraph (1), or
(B) any annual recertification of tenant income for purposes of this subsection, if the entire building is occupied by low-income tenants.

(9) Clarification of general public use requirement. A project does not fail to meet the general public use requirement solely because of occupancy restrictions or preferences that favor tenants—

(A) with special needs,
(B) who are members of a specified group under a Federal program or State program or policy that supports housing for such a specified group, or
(C) who are involved in artistic or literary activities.

(h) Limitation on aggregate credit allowable with respect to projects located in a state.

(1) Credit may not exceed credit amount allocated to building.

(A) In general. The amount of the credit determined under this section for any taxable year with respect to any building shall not exceed the housing credit dollar amount allocated to such building under this subsection.

(B) Time for making allocation. Except in the case of an allocation which meets the requirements of subparagraph (C), (D), (E), or (F) an allocation shall be taken into account under subparagraph (A) only if it is made not later than the close of the calendar year in which the building is placed in service.

(C) Exception where binding commitment. An allocation meets the requirements of this subparagraph if there is a binding commitment (not later than the close of the calendar year in which the building is placed in service) by the housing credit agency to allocate a specified housing credit dollar amount to such building beginning in a specified later taxable year.

(D) Exception where increase in qualified basis.
(i) In general. An allocation meets the requirements of this subparagraph if such allocation is made not later than the close of the calendar year in which ends the taxable year to which it will 1st apply but only to the extent the amount of such allocation does not exceed the limitation under clause (ii).

(ii) Limitation. The limitation under this clause is the amount of credit allowable under this section (without regard to this subsection) for a taxable year with respect to an increase in the qualified basis of the building equal to the excess of—

(I) the qualified basis of such building as of the close of the 1st taxable year to which such allocation will apply, over
(II) the qualified basis of such building as of the close of the 1st taxable year to which the most recent prior housing credit allocation with respect to such building applied.

(iii) Housing credit dollar amount reduced by full allocation. Notwithstanding clause (i), the full amount of the allocation shall be taken into account under paragraph (2).

(E) Exception where 10 percent of cost incurred.

(i) In general. An allocation meets the requirements of this subparagraph if such allocation is made with respect to a qualified building which is placed in service not later than the close of the second calendar year following the calendar year in which the allocation is made.

(ii) Qualified building. For purposes of clause (i), the term "qualified building" means any building which is part of a project if the taxpayer's basis in such project (as of the date which is 1 year after the date that the allocation was made) is more than 10 percent of the taxpayer's reasonably expected basis in such project (as of the close of the second calendar year referred to in clause (i)). Such term does not include any existing building unless a credit is allowable under subsection (e) for rehabilitation expenditures paid or incurred by the taxpayer with respect to such building for a taxable year ending during the second calendar year referred to in clause (i) or the prior taxable year.

(F) Allocation of credit on a project basis.

(i) In general. In the case of a project which includes (or will include) more than 1 building, an allocation meets the requirements of this subparagraph if—

(I) the allocation is made to the project for a calendar year during the project period,

(II) the allocation only applies to buildings placed in service during or after the calendar year for which the allocation is made, and

(III) the portion of such allocation which is allocated to any building in such project is specified not later than the close of the calendar year in which the building is placed in service.

(ii) Project period. For purposes of clause (i), the term "project period" means the period—

(I) beginning with the 1st calendar year for which an allocation may be made for the 1st building placed in service as part of such project, and

(II) ending with the calendar year the last building is placed in service as part of such project.

(2) Allocated credit amount to apply to all taxable years ending during or after credit allocation year. Any housing credit dollar amount allocated to any building for any calendar year—

(A) shall apply to such building for all taxable years in the compliance period ending during or after such calendar year, and

(B) shall reduce the aggregate housing credit dollar amount of the allocating agency only for such calendar year.

(3) Housing credit dollar amount for agencies.

(A) In general. The aggregate housing credit dollar amount which a housing credit agency may allocate for any calendar year is the portion of the State housing credit ceiling allocated under this paragraph for such calendar year to such agency.

(B) State ceiling initially allocated to state housing credit agencies. Except as provided in subparagraphs (D) and (E), the State housing credit ceiling for each calendar year shall be allocated to the housing credit agency of such State. If there is more than 1 housing credit agency of a State, all such agencies shall be treated as a single agency.

(C) State housing credit ceiling. The State housing credit ceiling applicable to any State for any calendar year shall be an amount equal to the sum of—

(i) the unused State housing credit ceiling (if any) of such State for the preceding calendar year,

(ii) the greater of—

(I) $1.75 ($1.50 for 2001) multiplied by the State population, or

(II) $2,000,000,

(iii) the amount of State housing credit ceiling returned in the calendar year, plus

(iv) the amount (if any) allocated under subparagraph (D) to such State by the Secretary.

For purposes of clause (i), the unused State housing credit ceiling for any calendar year is the excess (if any) of the sum of the amounts described in clauses (ii) through (iv) over the aggregate housing credit dollar amount allocated for such year. For purposes of clause (iii), the amount of State housing credit ceiling returned in the calendar year equals the housing credit dollar amount previously allocated within the State to any project which fails to meet the 10 percent test under paragraph (1)(E)(ii) on a date after the close of the calendar year in which the allocation was made or which does not become a qualified low-income housing project within the period required by this section or the terms of the allocation or to any project with respect to which an allocation is cancelled by mutual consent of the housing credit agency and the allocation recipient.

(D) Unused housing credit carryovers allocated among certain states.

(i) In general. The unused housing credit carryover of a State for any calendar year shall be assigned to the Secretary for allocation among qualified States for the succeeding calendar year.

(ii) Unused housing credit carryover. For purposes of this subparagraph, the unused housing credit carryover of a State for any calendar year is the excess (if any) of—

(I) the unused State housing credit ceiling for the year preceding such year, over

(II) the aggregate housing credit dollar amount allocated for such year.

(iii) Formula for allocation of unused housing credit carryovers among qualified states. The amount allocated under this subparagraph to a qualified State for any calendar year shall be the amount determined by the Secretary to bear the same ratio to the aggregate unused housing credit carryovers of all States for the preceding calendar year as such State's population for the calendar year bears to the population of all qualified States for the calendar year. For purposes of the preceding sentence, population shall be determined in accordance with section 146(j).

(iv) Qualified State. For purposes of this subparagraph, the term "qualified State" means, with respect to a calendar year, any State—

(I) which allocated its entire State housing credit ceiling for the preceding calendar year, and

(II) for which a request is made (not later than May 1 of the calendar year) to receive an allocation under clause (iii).

(E) Special rule for states with constitutional home rule cities. For purposes of this subsection—

(i) In general. The aggregate housing credit dollar amount for any constitutional home rule city for any calendar year shall be an amount which bears the

same ratio to the State housing credit ceiling for such calendar year as—
(I) the population of such city, bears to
(II) the population of the entire State.

(ii) Coordination with other allocations. In the case of any State which contains 1 or more constitutional home rule cities, for purposes of applying this paragraph with respect to housing credit agencies in such State other than constitutional home rule cities, the State housing credit ceiling for any calendar year shall be reduced by the aggregate housing credit dollar amounts determined for such year for all constitutional home rule cities in such State.

(iii) Constitutional home rule city. For purposes of this paragraph, the term "constitutional home rule city" has the meaning given such term by section 146(d)(3)(C).

(F) State may provide for different allocation. Rules similar to the rules of section 146(e) (other than paragraph (2)(B) thereof) shall apply for purposes of this paragraph.

(G) Population. For purposes of this paragraph, population shall be determined in accordance with section 146(j).

(H) Cost-of-living adjustment.
(i) In general. In the case of a calendar year after 2002, the $2,000,000 and $1.75 amounts in subparagraph (C) shall each be increased by an amount equal to—
(I) such dollar amount, multiplied by
(II) the cost-of-living adjustment determined under section 1(f)(3) for such calendar year by substituting "calendar year 2001" for "calendar year 1992" in subparagraph (B) thereof.

(ii) Rounding.
(I) In the case of the $2,000,000 amount, any increase under clause (i) which is not a multiple of $5,000 shall be rounded to the next lowest multiple of $5,000.
(II) In the case of the $1.75 amount, any increase under clause (i) which is not a multiple of 5 cents shall be rounded to the next lowest multiple of 5 cents.

(I) Increase in State housing credit ceiling for 2008 and 2009. In the case of calendar years 2008 and 2009—
(i) the dollar amount in effect under subparagraph (C)(ii)(I) for such calendar year (after any increase under subparagraph (H)) shall be increased by $0.20, and
(ii) the dollar amount in effect under subparagraph (C)(ii)(II) for such calendar year (after any increase under subparagraph (H)) shall be increased by an amount equal to 10 percent of such dollar amount (rounded to the next lowest multiple of $5,000).

(4) Credit for buildings financed by tax-exempt bonds subject to volume cap not taken into account.
(A) In general. Paragraph (1) shall not apply to the portion of any credit allowable under subsection (a) which is attributable to eligible basis financed by any obligation the interest on which is exempt from tax under section 103 if —
(i) such obligation is taken into account under section 146, and
(ii) principal payments on such financing are applied within a reasonable period to redeem obligations the proceeds of which were used to provide such financing or such financing is refunded as described in section 146(i)(6).

(B) Special rule where 50 percent or more of building is financed with tax-exempt bonds subject to volume cap. For purposes of subparagraph (A), if 50 percent or more of the aggregate basis of any building and the land on which the building is located is financed by any obligation described in subparagraph (A), paragraph (1) shall not apply to any portion of the credit allowable under subsection (a) with respect to such building.

(5) Portion of state ceiling set-aside for certain projects involving qualified nonprofit organizations.
(A) In general. Not more than 90 percent of the State housing credit ceiling for any State for any calendar year shall be allocated to projects other than qualified low-income housing projects described in subparagraph (B).

(B) Projects involving qualified nonprofit organizations. For purposes of subparagraph (A), a qualified low-income housing project is described in this subparagraph if a qualified nonprofit organization is to own an interest in the project (directly or through a partnership) and materially participate (within the meaning of section 469(h)) in the development and operation of the project throughout the compliance period.

(C) Qualified nonprofit organization. For purposes of this paragraph, the term "qualified nonprofit organization" means any organization if—
(i) such organization is described in paragraph (3) or (4) of section 501(c) and is exempt from tax under section 501(a),
(ii) such organization is determined by the State housing credit agency not to be affiliated with or controlled by a for-profit organization; and
(iii) 1 of the exempt purposes of such organization includes the fostering of low-income housing.

(D) Treatment of certain subsidiaries.
(i) In general. For purposes of this paragraph, a qualified nonprofit organization shall be treated as satisfying the ownership and material participation test of subparagraph (B) if any qualified corporation in which such organization holds stock satisfies such test.
(ii) Qualified corporation. For purposes of clause (i), the term "qualified corporation" means any corporation if 100 percent of the stock of such corporation is held by 1 or more qualified nonprofit organizations at all times during the period such corporation is in existence.

(E) State may not override set-aside. Nothing in subparagraph (F) of paragraph (3) shall be construed to permit a State not to comply with subparagraph (A) of this paragraph.

(6) Buildings eligible for credit only if minimum long-term commitment to low-income housing.
(A) In general. No credit shall be allowed by reason of this section with respect to any building for the taxable year unless an extended low-income housing commitment is in effect as of the end of such taxable year.

(B) Extended low-income housing commitment. For purposes of this paragraph, the term "extended low-income housing commitment" means any agreement between the taxpayer and the housing credit agency—
(i) which requires that the applicable fraction (as defined in subsection (c)(1)) for the building for each taxable year in the extended use period will not be less than the applicable fraction specified in such

agreement and which prohibits the actions described in subclauses (I) and (II) of subparagraph (E)(ii),

(ii) which allows individuals who meet the income limitation applicable to the building under subsection (g) (whether prospective, present, or former occupants of the building) the right to enforce in any State court the requirement and prohibitions of clause (i),

(iii) which prohibits the disposition to any person of any portion of the building to which such agreement applies unless all of the building to which such agreement applies is disposed of to such person,

(iv) which prohibits the refusal to lease to a holder of a voucher or certificate of eligibility under section 8 of the United States Housing Act of 1937 because of the status of the prospective tenant as such a holder,

(v) which is binding on all successors of the taxpayer, and

(vi) which, with respect to the property, is recorded pursuant to State law as a restrictive covenant.

(C) Allocation of credit may not exceed amount necessary to support commitment.

(i) In general. The housing credit dollar amount allocated to any building may not exceed the amount necessary to support the applicable fraction specified in the extended low-income housing commitment for such building, including any increase in such fraction pursuant to the application of subsection (f)(3) if such increase is reflected in an amended low-income housing commitment.

(ii) Buildings financed by tax-exempt bonds. If paragraph (4) applies to any building the amount of credit allowed in any taxable year may not exceed the amount necessary to support the applicable fraction specified in the extended low-income housing commitment for such building. Such commitment may be amended to increase such fraction.

(D) Extended use period. For purposes of this paragraph, the term "extended use period" means the period—

(i) beginning on the 1st day in the compliance period on which such building is part of a qualified low-income housing project, and

(ii) ending on the later of—

(I) the date specified by such agency in such agreement, or

(II) the date which is 15 years after the close of the compliance period.

(E) Exceptions if foreclosure or if no buyer willing to maintain low-income status.

(i) In general. The extended use period for any building shall terminate—

(I) on the date the building is acquired by foreclosure (or instrument in lieu of foreclosure) unless the Secretary determines that such acquisition is part of an arrangement with the taxpayer a purpose of which is to terminate such period, or

(II) on the last day of the period specified in subparagraph (I) if the housing credit agency is unable to present during such period a qualified contract for the acquisition of the low-income portion of the building by any person who will continue to operate such portion as a qualified low-income building.

Subclause (II) shall not apply to the extent more stringent requirements are provided in the agreement or in State law.

(ii) Eviction, etc. of existing low-income tenants not permitted. The termination of an extended use period under clause (i) shall not be construed to permit before the close of the 3-year period following such termination—

(I) the eviction or the termination of tenancy (other than for good cause) of an existing tenant of any low-income unit, or

(II) any increase in the gross rent with respect to such unit not otherwise permitted under this section.

(F) Qualified contract. For purposes of subparagraph (E), the term "qualified contract" means a bona fide contract to acquire (within a reasonable period after the contract is entered into) the non low-income portion of the building for fair market value and the low-income portion of the building for an amount not less than the applicable fraction (specified in the extended low-income housing commitment) of—

(i) the sum of—

(I) the outstanding indebtedness secured by, or with respect to, the building,

(II) the adjusted investor equity in the building, plus

(III) other capital contributions not reflected in the amounts described in subclause (I) or (II), reduced by

(ii) cash distributions from (or available for distribution from) the project.

The Secretary shall prescribe such regulations as may be necessary or appropriate to carry out this paragraph, including regulations to prevent the manipulation of the amount determined under the preceding sentence.

(G) Adjusted investor equity.

(i) In general. For purposes of subparagraph (E), the term "adjusted investor equity" means, with respect to any calendar year, the aggregate amount of cash taxpayers invested with respect to the project increased by the amount equal to—

(I) such amount, multiplied by

(II) the cost-of-living adjustment for such calendar year, determined under section 1(f)(3) by substituting the base calendar year for "calendar year 1987".

An amount shall be taken into account as an investment in the project only to the extent there was an obligation to invest such amount as of the beginning of the credit period and to the extent such amount is reflected in the adjusted basis of the project.

(ii) Cost-of-living increases in excess of 5 percent not taken into account. Under regulations prescribed by the Secretary, if the CPI for any calendar year (as defined in section 1(f)(4)) exceeds the CPI for the preceding calendar year by more than 5 percent, the CPI for the base calendar year shall be increased such that such excess shall never be taken into account under clause (i).

(iii) Base calendar year. For purposes of this subparagraph, the term "base calendar year" means the calendar year with or within which the 1st taxable year of the credit period ends.

(H) Low-income portion. For purposes of this paragraph, the low-income portion of a building is the portion of such building equal to the applicable fraction specified in the extended low-income housing commitment for the building.

(I) Period for finding buyer. The period referred to in this subparagraph is the 1-year period beginning on the date (after the 14th year of the compliance period) the taxpayer submits a written request to the housing credit agency to find a person to acquire the taxpayer's interest in the low-income portion of the building.

(J) Effect of noncompliance. If, during a taxable year, there is a determination that an extended low-income housing agreement was not in effect as of the beginning of such year, such determination shall not apply to any period before such year and subparagraph (A) shall be applied without regard to such determination if the failure is corrected within 1 year from the date of the determination.

(K) Projects which consist of more than 1 building. The application of this paragraph to projects which consist of more than 1 building shall be made under regulations prescribed by the Secretary.

(7) Special rules.

(A) Building must be located within jurisdiction of credit agency. A housing credit agency may allocate its aggregate housing credit dollar amount only to buildings located in the jurisdiction of the governmental unit of which such agency is a part.

(B) Agency allocations in excess of limit. If the aggregate housing credit dollar amounts allocated by a housing credit agency for any calendar year exceed the portion of the State housing credit ceiling allocated to such agency for such calendar year, the housing credit dollar amounts so allocated shall be reduced (to the extent of such excess) for buildings in the reverse of the order in which the allocations of such amounts were made.

(C) Credit reduced if allocated credit dollar amount is less than credit which would be allowable without regard to placed in service convention, etc.

(i) In general. The amount of the credit determined under this section with respect to any building shall not exceed the clause (ii) percentage of the amount of the credit which would (but for this subparagraph) be determined under this section with respect to such building.

(ii) Determination of percentage. For purposes of clause (i), the clause (ii) percentage with respect to any building is the percentage which—

(I) the housing credit dollar amount allocated to such building bears to

(II) the credit amount determined in accordance with clause (iii).

(iii) Determination of credit amount. The credit amount determined in accordance with this clause is the amount of the credit which would (but for this subparagraph) be determined under this section with respect to the building if—

(I) this section were applied without regard to paragraphs (2)(A) and (3)(B) of subsection (f), and

(II) subsection (f)(3)(A) were applied without regard to "the percentage equal to $\frac{2}{3}$ of".

(D) Housing credit agency to specify applicable percentage and maximum qualified basis. In allocating a housing credit dollar amount to any building, the housing credit agency shall specify the applicable percentage and the maximum qualified basis which may be taken into account under this section with respect to such building. The applicable percentage and maximum qualified basis so specified shall not exceed the applicable percentage and qualified basis determined under this section without regard to this subsection.

(8) Other definitions. For purposes of this subsection—

(A) Housing credit agency. The term "housing credit agency" means any agency authorized to carry out this subsection.

(B) Possessions treated as states. The term "State" includes a possession of the United States.

(i) Definitions and special rules.

For purposes of this section—

(1) Compliance period. The term "compliance period" means, with respect to any building, the period of 15 taxable years beginning with the 1st taxable year of the credit period with respect thereto.

(2) Determination of whether building is federally subsidized.

(A) In general. Except as otherwise provided in this paragraph, for purposes of subsection (b)(1), a new building shall be treated as federally subsidized for any taxable year if, at any time during such taxable year or any prior taxable year, there is or was outstanding any obligation the interest on which is exempt from tax under section 103 the proceeds of which are or were used (directly or indirectly) with respect to such building or the operation thereof.

(B) Election to reduce eligible basis by proceeds of obligations. A tax-exempt obligation shall not be taken into account under subparagraph (A) if the taxpayer elects to exclude from the eligible basis of the building for purposes of subsection (d) the proceeds of such obligation.

(C) Special rule for subsidized construction financing. Subparagraph (A) shall not apply to any tax-exempt obligation used to provide construction financing for any building if—

(i) such obligation (when issued) identified the building for which the proceeds of such obligation would be used, and

(ii) such obligation is redeemed before such building is placed in service.

(3) Low-income unit.

(A) In general. The term "low-income unit" means any unit in a building if—

(i) such unit is rent-restricted (as defined in subsection (g)(2)), and

(ii) the individuals occupying such unit meet the income limitation applicable under subsection (g)(1) to the project of which such building is a part.

(B) Exceptions.

(i) In general. A unit shall not be treated as a low-income unit unless the unit is suitable for occupancy and used other than on a transient basis.

(ii) Suitability for occupancy. For purposes of clause (i), the suitability of a unit for occupancy shall be determined under regulations prescribed by the Secretary taking into account local health, safety, and building codes.

(iii) Transitional housing for homeless. For purposes of clause (i), a unit shall be considered to be used other than on a transient basis if the unit contains sleeping accommodations and kitchen and bathroom facilities and is located in a building—

(I) which is used exclusively to facilitate the transition of homeless individuals (within the meaning of section 103 of the Stewart B. McKinney Homeless Assistance Act (42 U.S.C. 11302), as in effect on the date of the enactment of this clause) to independent living within 24 months, and

(II) in which a governmental entity or qualified nonprofit organization (as defined in subsection (h)(5)) provides such individuals with temporary housing and supportive services designed to assist such individuals in locating and retaining permanent housing.

(iv) Single-room occupancy units. For purposes of clause (i), a single-room occupancy unit shall not be treated as used on a transient basis merely because it is rented on a month-by-month basis.

(C) Special rule for buildings having 4 or fewer units. In the case of any building which has 4 or fewer residential rental units, no unit in such building shall be treated as a low-income unit if the units in such building are owned by—

(i) any individual who occupies a residential unit in such building, or

(ii) any person who is related (as defined in subsection (d)(2)(D)(iii)) to such individual.

(D) Certain students not to disqualify unit. A unit shall not fail to be treated as a low-income unit merely because it is occupied—

(i) by an individual who is—

(I) a student and receiving assistance under title IV of the Social Security Act,

(II) a student who was previously under the care and placement responsibility of the State agency responsible for administering a plan under part B or part E of title IV of the Social Security Act, or

(III) enrolled in a job training program receiving assistance under the Job Training Partnership Act or under other similar Federal, State, or local laws, or

(ii) entirely by full-time students if such students are—

(I) single parents and their children and such parents are not dependents (as defined in section 152, determined without regard to subsections (b)(1), (b)(2), and (d)(1)(B) thereof) of another individual and such children are not dependents (as so defined) of another individual other than a parent of such children, or. [sic ,]

(II) married and file a joint return.

(E) Owner-occupied buildings having 4 or fewer units eligible for credit where development plan.

(i) In general. Subparagraph (C) shall not apply to the acquisition or rehabilitation of a building pursuant to a development plan of action sponsored by a State or local government or a qualified nonprofit organization (as defined in subsection (h)(5)(C)).

(ii) Limitation on credit. In the case of a building to which clause (i) applies, the applicable fraction shall not exceed 80 percent of the unit fraction.

(iii) Certain unrented units treated as owner-occupied. In the case of a building to which clause (i) applies, any unit which is not rented for 90 days or more shall be treated as occupied by the owner of the building as of the 1st day it is not rented.

(4) New building. The term "new building" means a building the original use of which begins with the taxpayer.

(5) Existing building. The term "existing building" means any building which is not a new building.

(6) Application to estates and trusts. In the case of an estate or trust, the amount of the credit determined under subsection (a) and any increase in tax under subsection (j) shall be apportioned between the estate or trust and the beneficiaries on the basis of the income of the estate or trust allocable to each.

(7) Impact of tenant's right of 1st refusal to acquire property.

(A) In general. No Federal income tax benefit shall fail to be allowable to the taxpayer with respect to any qualified low-income building merely by reason of a right of 1st refusal held by the tenants (in cooperative form or otherwise) or resident management corporation of such building or by a qualified nonprofit organization (as defined in subsection (h)(5)(C)) or government agency to purchase the property after the close of the compliance period for a price which is not less than the minimum purchase price determined under subparagraph (B).

(B) Minimum purchase price. For purposes of subparagraph (A), the minimum purchase price under this subparagraph is an amount equal to the sum of—

(i) the principal amount of outstanding indebtedness secured by the building (other than indebtedness incurred within the 5-year period ending on the date of the sale to the tenants), and

(ii) all Federal, State, and local taxes attributable to such sale.

Except in the case of Federal income taxes, there shall not be taken into account under clause (ii) any additional tax attributable to the application of clause (ii).

(8) Treatment of rural projects. For purposes of this section, in the case of any project for residential rental property located in a rural area (as defined in section 520 of the Housing Act of 1949), any income limitation measured by reference to area median gross income shall be measured by reference to the greater of area median gross income or national non-metropolitan median income. The preceding sentence shall not apply with respect to any building if paragraph (1) of section 42(h) does not apply by reason of paragraph (4) thereof to any portion of the credit determined under this section with respect to such building.

(9) Coordination with low-income housing grants.

(A) Reduction in state housing credit ceiling for low-income housing grants received in 2009. For purposes of this section, the amounts described in clauses (i) through (iv) of subsection (h)(3)(C) with respect to any State for 2009 shall each be reduced by so much of such amount as is taken into account in determining the amount of any grant to such State under section 1602 of the American Recovery and Reinvestment Tax Act of 2009.

(B) Special rule for basis. Basis of a qualified low-income building shall not be reduced by the amount of any grant described in subparagraph (A).

(j) Recapture of credit.

(1) In general. If—

(A) as of the close of any taxable year in the compliance period, the amount of the qualified basis of any building with respect to the taxpayer is less than

(B) the amount of such basis as of the close of the preceding taxable year,

then the taxpayer's tax under this chapter for the taxable year shall be increased by the credit recapture amount.

(2) Credit recapture amount. For purposes of paragraph (1), the credit recapture amount is an amount equal to the sum of—

(A) the aggregate decrease in the credits allowed to the taxpayer under section 38 for all prior taxable years which would have resulted if the accelerated portion of the credit allowable by reason of this section were not allowed for all prior taxable years with respect to the excess of the amount described in paragraph (1)(B) over the amount described in paragraph (1)(A), plus

(B) interest at the overpayment rate established under section 6621 on the amount determined under subparagraph (A) for each prior taxable year for the period beginning on the due date for filing the return for the prior taxable year involved.

No deduction shall be allowed under this chapter for interest described in subparagraph (B).

(3) Accelerated portion of credit. For purposes of paragraph (2), the accelerated portion of the credit for the prior taxable years with respect to any amount of basis is the excess of—

(A) the aggregate credit allowed by reason of this section (without regard to this subsection) for such years with respect to such basis, over

(B) the aggregate credit which would be allowable by reason of this section for such years with respect to such basis if the aggregate credit which would (but for this subsection) have been allowable for the entire compliance period were allowable ratably over 15 years.

(4) Special rules.

(A) Tax benefit rule. The tax for the taxable year shall be increased under paragraph (1) only with respect to credits allowed by reason of this section which were used to reduce tax liability. In the case of credits not so used to reduce tax liability, the carryforwards and carrybacks under section 39 shall be appropriately adjusted.

(B) Only basis for which credit allowed taken into account. Qualified basis shall be taken into account under paragraph (1)(B) only to the extent such basis was taken into account in determining the credit under subsection (a) for the preceding taxable year referred to in such paragraph.

(C) No recapture of additional credit allowable by reason of subsection (f)(3). Paragraph (1) shall apply to a decrease in qualified basis only to the extent such decrease exceeds the amount of qualified basis with respect to which a credit was allowable for the taxable year referred to in paragraph (1)(B) by reason of subsection (f)(3).

(D) No credits against tax. Any increase in tax under this subsection shall not be treated as a tax imposed by this chapter for purposes of determining the amount of any credit under this chapter.

(E) No recapture by reason of casualty loss. The increase in tax under this subsection shall not apply to a reduction in qualified basis by reason of a casualty loss to the extent such loss is restored by reconstruction or replacement within a reasonable period established by the Secretary.

(F) No recapture where de minimis changes in floor space. The Secretary may provide that the increase in tax under this subsection shall not apply with respect to any building if—

(i) such increase results from a de minimis change in the floor space fraction under subsection (c)(1), and

(ii) the building is a qualified low-income building after such change.

(5) Certain partnerships treated as the taxpayer.

(A) In general. For purposes of applying this subsection to a partnership to which this paragraph applies—

(i) such partnership shall be treated as the taxpayer to which the credit allowable under subsection (a) was allowed,

(ii) the amount of such credit allowed shall be treated as the amount which would have been allowed to the partnership were such credit allowable to such partnership,

(iii) paragraph (4)(A) shall not apply, and

(iv) the amount of the increase in tax under this subsection for any taxable year shall be allocated among the partners of such partnership in the same manner as such partnership's taxable income for such year is allocated among such partners.

(B) Partnerships to which paragraph applies. This paragraph shall apply to any partnership which has 35 or more partners unless the partnership elects not to have this paragraph apply.

(C) Special rules.

(i) Husband and wife treated as 1 partner. For purposes of subparagraph (B)(i), a husband and wife (and their estates) shall be treated as 1 partner.

(ii) Election irrevocable. Any election under subparagraph (B), once made, shall be irrevocable.

(6) No recapture on disposition of building which continues in qualified use.

(A) In general. The increase in tax under this subsection shall not apply solely by reason of the disposition of a building (or an interest therein) if it is reasonably expected that such building will continue to be operated as a qualified low-income building for the remaining compliance period with respect to such building.

(B) Statute of limitations. If a building (or an interest therein) is disposed of during any taxable year and there is any reduction in the qualified basis of such building which results in an increase in tax under this subsection for such taxable or any subsequent taxable year, then—

(i) the statutory period for the assessment of any deficiency with respect to such increase in tax shall not expire before the expiration of 3 years from the date the Secretary is notified by the taxpayer (in such manner as the Secretary may prescribe) of such reduction in qualified basis, and

(ii) such deficiency may be assessed before the expiration of such 3-year period notwithstanding the provisions of any other law or rule of law which would otherwise prevent such assessment.

(k) Application of at-risk rules.

For purposes of this section—

(1) In general. Except as otherwise provided in this subsection, rules similar to the rules of section 49(a)(1) (other than subparagraphs (D)(ii)(II) and (D)(iv)(I) thereof), section 49(a)(2), and section 49(b)(1) shall apply in determining the qualified basis of any building in the same manner as such sections apply in determining the credit base of property.

(2) Special rules for determining qualified person. For purposes of paragraph (1)—

(A) In general. If the requirements of subparagraphs (B), (C), and (D) are met with respect to any financing borrowed from a qualified nonprofit organization (as defined in subsection (h)(5)), the determination of whether such financing is qualified commercial financing with respect to any qualified low-income building shall be made without regard to whether such organization—

(i) is actively and regularly engaged in the business of lending money, or

(ii) is a person described in section 49(a)(1)(D)(iv)(II).

(B) Financing secured by property. The requirements of this subparagraph are met with respect to any financing if such financing is secured by the qualified low-income building, except that this subparagraph shall not apply in the case of a federally assisted building described in subsection (d)(6)(B) if—

(i) a security interest in such building is not permitted by a Federal agency holding or insuring the mortgage secured by such building, and

(ii) the proceeds from the financing (if any) are applied to acquire or improve such building.

(C) Portion of building attributable to financing. The requirements of this subparagraph are met with respect to any financing for any taxable year in the compliance period if, as of the close of such taxable year, not more than 60 percent of the eligible basis of the qualified low-income building is attributable to such financing (reduced by the principal and interest of any governmental financing which is part of a wrap-around mortgage involving such financing).

(D) Repayment of principal and interest. The requirements of this subparagraph are met with respect to any financing if such financing is fully repaid on or before the earliest of—

(i) the date on which such financing matures,

(ii) the 90th day after the close of the compliance period with respect to the qualified low-income building, or

(iii) the date of its refinancing or the sale of the building to which such financing relates.

In the case of a qualified nonprofit organization which is not described in section 49(a)(1)(D)(iv)(II) with respect to a building, clause (ii) of this subparagraph shall be applied as if the date described therein were the 90th day after the earlier of the date the building ceases to be a qualified low-income building or the date which is 15 years after the close of a compliance period with respect thereto.

(3) Present value of financing. If the rate of interest on any financing described in paragraph (2)(A) is less than the rate which is 1 percentage point below the applicable Federal rate as of the time such financing is incurred, then the qualified basis (to which such financing relates) of the qualified low-income building shall be the present value of the amount of such financing, using as the discount rate such applicable Federal rate. For purposes of the preceding sentence, the rate of interest on any financing shall be determined by treating interest to the extent of government subsidies as not payable.

(4) Failure to fully repay.

(A) In general. To the extent that the requirements of paragraph (2)(D) are not met, then the taxpayer's tax under this chapter for the taxable year in which such failure occurs shall be increased by an amount equal to the applicable portion of the credit under this section with respect to such building, increased by an amount of interest for the period—

(i) beginning with the due date for the filing of the return of tax imposed by chapter 1 for the 1st taxable year for which such credit was allowable, and

(ii) ending with the due date for the taxable year in which such failure occurs,

determined by using the underpayment rate and method under section 6621.

(B) Applicable portion. For purposes of subparagraph (A), the term "applicable portion" means the aggregate decrease in the credits allowed to a taxpayer under section 38 for all prior taxable years which would have resulted if the eligible basis of the building were reduced by the amount of financing which does not meet requirements of paragraph (2)(D).

(C) Certain rules to apply. Rules similar to the rules of subparagraphs (A) and (D) of subsection (j)(4) shall apply for purposes of this subsection.

(l) Certifications and other reports to secretary.

(1) Certification with respect to 1st year of credit period. Following the close of the 1st taxable year in the credit period with respect to any qualified low-income building, the taxpayer shall certify to the Secretary (at such time and in such form and in such manner as the Secretary prescribes)—

(A) the taxable year, and calendar year, in which such building was placed in service,

(B) the adjusted basis and eligible basis of such building as of the close of the 1st year of the credit period,

(C) the maximum applicable percentage and qualified basis permitted to be taken into account by the appropriate housing credit agency under subsection (h),

(D) the election made under subsection (g) with respect to the qualified low-income housing project of which such building is a part, and

(E) such other information as the Secretary may require.

In the case of a failure to make the certification required by the preceding sentence on the date prescribed therefor, unless it is shown that such failure is due to reasonable cause and not to willful neglect, no credit shall be allowable by reason of subsection (a) with respect to such building for any taxable year ending before such certification is made.

(2) Annual reports to the Secretary. The Secretary may require taxpayers to submit an information return (at such time and in such form and manner as the Secretary prescribes) for each taxable year setting forth—

(A) the qualified basis for the taxable year of each qualified low-income building of the taxpayer,

(B) the information described in paragraph (1)(C) for the taxable year, and

(C) such other information as the Secretary may require.

The penalty under section 6652(j) shall apply to any failure to submit the return required by the Secretary under the preceding sentence on the date prescribed therefor.

(3) Annual reports from housing credit agencies. Each agency which allocates any housing credit amount to any building for any calendar year shall submit to the Secretary (at such time and in such manner as the Secretary shall prescribe) an annual report specifying—

(A) the amount of housing credit amount allocated to each building for such year,

(B) sufficient information to identify each such building and the taxpayer with respect thereto, and

(C) such other information as the Secretary may require.

The penalty under section 6652(j) shall apply to any failure to submit the report required by the preceding sentence on the date prescribed therefor.

(m) Responsibilities of housing credit agencies.
  (1) Plans for allocation of credit among projects.
    (A) In general. Notwithstanding any other provision of this section, the housing credit dollar amount with respect to any building shall be zero unless—
      (i) such amount was allocated pursuant to a qualified allocation plan of the housing credit agency which is approved by the governmental unit (in accordance with rules similar to the rules of section 147(f)(2) (other than subparagraph (B)(ii) thereof)) of which such agency is a part,
      (ii) such agency notifies the chief executive officer (or the equivalent) of the local jurisdiction within which the building is located of such project and provides such individual a reasonable opportunity to comment on the project,
      (iii) a comprehensive market study of the housing needs of low-income individuals in the area to be served by the project is conducted before the credit allocation is made and at the developer's expense by a disinterested party who is approved by such agency, and
      (iv) a written explanation is available to the general public for any allocation of a housing credit dollar amount which is not made in accordance with established priorities and selection criteria of the housing credit agency.
    (B) Qualified allocation plan. For purposes of this paragraph, the term "qualified allocation plan" means any plan—
      (i) which sets forth selection criteria to be used to determine housing priorities of the housing credit agency which are appropriate to local conditions,
      (ii) which also gives preference in allocating housing credit dollar amounts among selected projects to—
        (I) projects serving the lowest income tenants,
        (II) projects obligated to serve qualified tenants for the longest periods, and
        (III) projects which are located in qualified census tracts (as defined in subsection (d)(5)(C)) and the development of which contributes to a concerted community revitalization plan, and
      (iii) which provides a procedure that the agency (or an agent or other private contractor of such agency) will follow in monitoring for noncompliance with the provisions of this section and in notifying the Internal Revenue Service of such noncompliance which such agency becomes aware of and in monitoring for noncompliance with habitability standards through regular site visits.
    (C) Certain selection criteria must be used. The selection criteria set forth in a qualified allocation plan must include—
      (i) project location,
      (ii) housing needs characteristics,
      (iii) project characteristics, including whether the project includes the use of existing housing as part of a community revitalization plan,
      (iv) sponsor characteristics,
      (v) tenant populations with special housing needs,
      (vi) public housing waiting lists,
      (vii) tenant populations of individuals with children,
      (viii) projects intended for eventual tenant ownership,
      (ix) the energy efficiency of the project, and
      (x) the historic nature of the project.
    (D) Application to bond financed projects. Subsection (h)(4) shall not apply to any project unless the project satisfies the requirements for allocation of a housing credit dollar amount under the qualified allocation plan applicable to the area in which the project is located.
  (2) Credit allocated to building not to exceed amount necessary to assure project feasibility.
    (A) In general. The housing credit dollar amount allocated to a project shall not exceed the amount the housing credit agency determines is necessary for the financial feasibility of the project and its viability as a qualified low-income housing project throughout the credit period.
    (B) Agency evaluation. In making the determination under subparagraph (A), the housing credit agency shall consider—
      (i) the sources and uses of funds and the total financing planned for the project,
      (ii) any proceeds or receipts expected to be generated by reason of tax benefits,
      (iii) the percentage of the housing credit dollar amount used for project costs other than the cost of intermediaries, and
      (iv) the reasonableness of the developmental and operational costs of the project.
    Clause (iii) shall not be applied so as to impede the development of projects in hard-to-develop areas. Such a determination shall not be construed to be a representation or warranty as to the feasibility or viability of the project.
    (C) Determination made-when credit amount applied for and when building placed in service.
      (i) In general. A determination under subparagraph (A) shall be made as of each of the following times:
        (I) The application for the housing credit dollar amount.
        (II) The allocation of the housing credit dollar amount.
        (III) The date the building is placed in service.
      (ii) Certification as to amount of other subsidies. Prior to each determination under clause (i), the taxpayer shall certify to the housing credit agency the full extent of all Federal, State, and local subsidies which apply (or which the taxpayer expects to apply) with respect to the building.
    (D) Application to bond financed projects. Subsection (h)(4) shall not apply to any project unless the governmental unit which issued the bonds (or on behalf of which the bonds were issued) makes a determination under rules similar to the rules of subparagraphs (A) and (B).

(n) Regulations.
The Secretary shall prescribe such regulations as may be necessary or appropriate to carry out the purposes of this section, including regulations—
  (1) dealing with—
    (A) projects which include more than 1 building or only a portion of a building,
    (B) buildings which are placed in service in portions,
  (2) providing for the application of this section to short taxable years,
  (3) preventing the avoidance of the rules of this section, and
  (4) providing the opportunity for housing credit agencies to correct administrative errors and omissions with respect to allocations and record keeping within a reasonable pe-

riod after their discovery, taking into account the availability of regulations and other administrative guidance from the Secretary.

In 2009, P.L. 111-5, Sec. 1404, added para. (i)(9), enacted 2/17/2009. . . . Sec. 1602, of this Act, reads as follows:

"Sec. 1602. Grants to states for low-income housing projects in lieu of low-income housing credit allocations for 2009.

"(a) In general. The Secretary of the Treasury shall make a grant to the housing credit agency of each State in an amount equal to such State's low-income housing grant election amount.

"(b) Low-income housing grant election amount. For purposes of this section, the term 'low-income housing grant election amount' means, with respect to any State, such amount as the State may elect which does not exceed 85 percent of the product of—

"(1) the sum of—

"(A) 100 percent of the State housing credit ceiling for 2009 which is attributable to amounts described in clauses (i) and (iii) of section 42(h)(3)(C) of the Internal Revenue Code of 1986, and

"(B) 40 percent of the State housing credit ceiling for 2009 which is attributable to amounts described in clauses (ii) and (iv) of such section, multiplied by

"(2) 10.

"(c) Subawards for low-income buildings.

"(1) In general. A State housing credit agency receiving a grant under this section shall use such grant to make subawards to finance the construction or acquisition and rehabilitation of qualified low-income buildings. A subaward under this section may be made to finance a qualified low-income building with or without an allocation under section 42 of the Internal Revenue Code of 1986, except that a State housing credit agency may make subawards to finance qualified low-income buildings without an allocation only if it makes a determination that such use will increase the total funds available to the State to build and rehabilitate affordable housing. In complying with such determination requirement, a State housing credit agency shall establish a process in which applicants that are allocated credits are required to demonstrate good faith efforts to obtain investment commitments for such credits before the agency makes such subawards.

"(2) Subawards subject to same requirements as low-income housing credit allocations. Any such subaward with respect to any qualified low-income housing building shall be made in the same manner and shall be subject to the same limitations (including rent, income, and use restrictions on such building) as an allocation of housing credit dollar amount allocated by such State housing credit agency under section 42 of the Internal Revenue Code of 1986, except that such subawards shall not be limited by, or otherwise affect (except as provided in subsection (h)(3)(J) of such section), the State housing credit ceiling applicable to such agency.

"(3) Compliance and asset management. The State housing credit agency shall perform asset management functions to ensure compliance with section 42 of the Internal Revenue Code of 1986 and the long-term viability of buildings funded by any subaward under this section. The State housing credit agency may collect reasonable fees from a subaward recipient to cover expenses associated with the performance of its duties under this paragraph. The State housing credit agency may retain an agent or other private contractor to satisfy the requirements of this paragraph.

"(4) Recapture. The State housing credit agency shall impose conditions or restrictions, including a requirement providing for recapture, on any subaward made under this section so as to assure that the building with respect to which such subaward is made remains a qualified low-income building during the compliance period. Any such recapture shall be payable to the Secretary of the Treasury for deposit in the general fund of the Treasury and may be enforced by means of liens or such other methods as the Secretary of the Treasury determines appropriate.

"(d) Return of unused grant funds. Any grant funds not used to make subawards under this section before January 1, 2011, shall be returned to the Secretary of the Treasury on such date. Any subawards returned to the State housing credit agency on or after such date shall be promptly returned to the Secretary of the Treasury. Any amounts returned to the Secretary of the Treasury under this subsection shall be deposited in the general fund of the Treasury.

"(e) Definitions. Any term used in this section which is also used in section 42 of the Internal Revenue Code of 1986 shall have the same meaning for purposes of this section as when used in such section 42. Any reference in this section to the Secretary of the Treasury shall be treated as including the Secretary's delegate.

"(f) Appropriations. There is hereby appropriated to the Secretary of the Treasury such sums as may be necessary to carry out this section."

In 2008, P.L. 110-289, Sec. 3001, added subpara. (h)(3)(I), enacted 7/30/2008.

—P.L. 110-289, Sec. 3002(a)(1), deleted para. (b)(1), redesignated para. (b)(2) as (1) and added para. (b)(2) . . . Sec. 3002(a)(2)(A), substituted "(1) Determination of applicable percentage. For purposes of this section, the term 'applicable percentage' means, with respect to any building, the appropriate" for "For purposes of this section—

"(1) Buildings placed in service after 1987.

"(A) In general. In the case of any qualified low-income building placed in service by the taxpayer after 1987, the term 'applicable percentage' means the appropriate"

in subsec. (b) [as amended by Sec. 3002(a)(1) of this Act, see above] . . . Sec. 3002(a)(2)(B), substituted "a new building which is not federally subsidized for the taxable year" for "a building described in paragraph (1)(A)" in clause (b)(1)(B)(i) [as redesignated by Sec. 3002(a)(1) of this Act, see above] . . . Sec. 3002(a)(2)(C), substituted "a building not described in clause (i)" for "a building described in paragraph (1)(B)" in clause (b)(1)(B)(ii) [as redesignated by Sec. 3002(a)(1) of this Act, see above] . . . Sec. 3002(b)(1), deleted ", or any below market Federal loan," after "section 103" in subpara. (i)(2)(A) . . . Sec. 3002(b)(2)(A)(i), deleted "balance of loan or" after "basis by" in the heading of subpara. (i)(2)(B) . . . Sec. 3002(b)(2)(A)(ii), deleted "loan or" before "tax-exempt obligation" in subpara. (i)(2)(B) . . . Sec. 3002(b)(2)(A)(iii), substituted "subsection (d) the proceeds of such obligation." for "subsection (d)—

"(i) in the case of a loan, the principal amount of such loan, and

"(ii) in the case of a tax-exempt obligation, the proceeds of such obligation.'"

in subpara. (i)(2)(B) . . . Sec. 3002(b)(2)(B)(i), deleted "or below market Federal loan" after "tax-exempt obligation" in subpara. (i)(2)(C) . . . Sec. 3002(b)(2)(B)(ii)(I), substituted "(when issued)" for "or loan (when issued or made)" in clause (i)(2)(C)(i) . . . Sec. 3002(b)(2)(B)(ii)(II), substituted "the proceeds of such obligation" for "the proceeds of such obligation or loan" in clause (i)(2)(C)(i) . . . Sec. 3002(b)(2)(B)(iii), deleted ", and such loan is repaid," after "is redeemed" in clause (i)(2)(C)(ii) . . . Sec. 3002(b)(2)(C), deleted subparas. (i)(2)(D)-(E), effective for buildings placed in service after 7/30/2008.

Prior to deletion, para. (b)(1) read as follows:

"(1) Building placed in service during 1987. In the case of any qualified low-income building placed in service by the taxpayer during 1987, the term 'applicable percentage' means—

"(A) 9 percent for new buildings which are not federally subsidized for the taxable year, or

"(B) 4 percent for—

"(i) new buildings which are federally subsidized for the taxable year, and

"(ii) existing buildings."

Prior to deletion, subparas. (i)(2)(D)-(E) read as follows:

"(D) Below market federal loan. For purposes of this paragraph, the term 'below market Federal loan' means any loan funded in whole or in part with Federal funds if the interest rate payable on such loan is less than the applicable Federal rate in effect under section 1274(d)(1) (as of the date on which the loan was made). Such term shall not include any loan which would be a below market Federal loan solely by reason of assistance provided under section 106, 107, or 108 of the Housing and Community Development Act of 1974 (as in effect on the date of the enactment of this sentence).

"(E) Buildings receiving home assistance or Native American Housing assistance.

"(i) In general. Assistance provided under the HOME Investment Partnerships Act (as in effect on the date of the enactment of this subparagraph or the Native American Housing Assistance and Self-Determination Act of 1996 (25 U.S.C. 4101 et seq.) (as in effect on October 1, 1997) with respect to any building shall not be taken into account under subparagraph (D) if 40 percent or more of the residential units in the building are occupied by individuals whose income is 50 percent or less of area median gross income. Subsection (d)(5)(C) shall not apply to any building to which the preceding sentence applies.

"(ii) Special rule for certain high-cost housing areas. In the case of a building located in a city described in section 142(d)(6), clause (i) shall be applied by substituting '25 percent' for '40 percent'."

—P.L. 110-289, Sec. 3003(a), added subpara. (d)(5)(C)(v) . . . Sec. 3003(b)(1)(A), substituted "20 percent" for "10 percent" in subclause (e)(3)(A)(ii)(I) . . . Sec. 3003(b)(1)(B), substituted "$6,000" for "$3,000" in subclause (e)(3)(A)(ii)(II) . . . Sec. 3003(b)(2), added subpara. (e)(3)(D) . . . Sec. 3003(b)(3), substituted "if the dollar amount in effect under subsection (e)(3)(A)(ii)(II) were applied by substituting '$2,000' for '$3,000'." in subclause (f)(5)(B)(ii)(II) . . . Sec. 3003(c), amended clause (d)(4)(C)(ii) . . . Sec. 3003(d), amended subpara. (d)(5)(A) . . . Sec. 3003(e)(1), deleted introductory matter of clause (d)(2)(D)(iii) and subclause (d)(2)(D)(iii)(I) . . . Sec. 3003(e)(2), redesignated subclause (d)(2)(D)(iii)(II) as clause (d)(2)(D)(iii) . . . Sec. 3003(e)(3), deleted "For purposes of the preceding sentence, in applying section 267(b) or 707(b)(1), '10 percent' shall be substituted for '50 percent'." at the end of clause (d)(2)(D)(iii) [as redesignated by Sec. 3003(e)(2) of this Act, see above] . . . Sec. 3003(f), amended para. (d)(6) . . . Sec. 3003(g)(1), amended clause (d)(2)(B)(ii) . . . Sec. 3003(g)(2), deleted clause (d)(2)(D)(i) and redesignated clauses (d)(2)(D)(ii)-(iii) as (d)(2)(D)(i)-(ii) [as amended by Sec. 3003(e) of this Act, see above] . . . Sec. 3003(g)(3), deleted subpara. (d)(5)(B) and redesignated subpara. (d)(5)(C) as (B), effective as provided by Sec. 3003(h), of this Act, which reads as follows:

"(h) Effective date.

"(1) In general. Except as otherwise provided in paragraph (2), the amendments made by this subsection shall apply to buildings placed in service after the date of the enactment of this Act.

"(2) Rehabilitation requirements.

"(A) In general. The amendments made by subsection (b) shall apply to buildings with respect to which housing credit dollar amounts are allocated after the date of the enactment of this Act.

"(B) Buildings not subject to allocation limits. To the extent paragraph (1) of section 42(h) of the Internal Revenue Code of 1986 does not apply to any building by reason of paragraph (4) thereof, the amendments made by subsection (b) shall apply buildings financed with bonds issued pursuant to allocations made after the date of the enactment of this Act."

Prior to amendment, clause (d)(2)(B)(ii) read as follows:

"(ii) there is a period of at least 10 years between the date of its acquisition by the taxpayer and the later of—

"(I) the date the building was last placed in service, or

"(II) the date of the most recent nonqualified substantial improvement of the building,"

Prior to deletion, clause (d)(2)(D)(i) read as follows:

"(i) Nonqualified substantial improvement. For purposes of subparagraph (B)(ii)—

"(I) In general. The term 'nonqualified substantial improvement' means any substantial improvement if section 167(k) (as in effect on the day before the date of enactment of the Revenue Reconciliation Act of 1990 [11/5/90]) was elected with respect to such improvement or section 168 (as in effect on the day before the date of the enactment of the Tax Reform Act of 1986) applied to such improvement.

"(II) Date of substantial improvement. The date of a substantial improvement is the last day of the 24-month period referred to in subclause (III).

"(III) Substantial improvement. The term 'substantial improvement' means the improvements added to capital account with respect to the building during any 24-month period, but only if the sum of the amounts added to such account during such period equals or exceeds 25 percent of the adjusted basis of the building (determined without paragraphs (2) and (3) of section 1016(a)) as of the 1st day of such period."

Prior to deletion, introductory matter of clause (d)(2)(D)(iii) and subclause (d)(2)(D)(iii)(I) read as follows:

"(iii) Related person, etc.

"(I) Application of section 179. For purposes of subparagraph (B)(i), section 179(d) shall be applied by substituting '10 percent' for '50 percent' in section 267(b) and 707(b) and in section 179(d)(7)."

Prior to amendment, clause (d)(4)(C)(ii) read as follows:

"(ii) Limitation. The increase in the adjusted basis of any building which is taken into account by reason of clause (i) shall not exceed 10 percent of the eligible basis of the qualified low-income housing project of which it is a part. For purposes of the preceding sentence, all community service facilities which are part of the same qualified low-income housing project shall be treated as one facility."

Prior to amendment, subpara. (d)(5)(A) read as follows:

"(A) Eligible basis reduced by federal grants. If, during any taxable year of the compliance period, a grant is made with respect to any building or the operation thereof and any portion of such grant is funded with Federal funds (whether or not includible in gross income), the eligible basis of such building for such taxable year and all succeeding taxable years shall be reduced by the portion of such grant which is so funded."

Prior to deletion, subpara. (d)(5)(B) read as follows:

"(B) Eligible basis not to include expenditures where section 167(k) elected. The eligible basis of any building shall not include any portion of its adjusted basis which is attributable to amounts with respect to which an election is made under section 167(k) (as in effect on the day before the date of enactment of the Revenue Reconciliation Act of 1990 [11/5/90])."

Prior to amendment, para. (d)(6) read as follows:

"(6) Credit allowable for certain federally-assisted buildings acquired during 10-year period described in paragraph (2)(B)(ii).

"(A) In general. On application by the taxpayer, the Secretary (after consultation with the appropriate Federal official) may waive paragraph (2)(B)(ii) with respect to any federally-assisted building if the Secretary determines that such waiver is necessary—

"(i) to avert an assignment of the mortgage secured by property in the project (of which such building is a part) to the Department of Housing and Urban Development or the Farmers Home Administration, or

"(ii) to avert a claim against a Federal mortgage insurance fund (or such Department or Administration) with respect to a mortgage which is so secured.

The preceding sentence shall not apply to any building described in paragraph (7)(B).

"(B) Federally-assisted building. For purposes of subparagraph (A), the term 'federally-assisted building' means any building which is substantially assisted, financed, or operated under—

"(i) section 8 of the United States Housing Act of 1937,

"(ii) section 221(d)(3) or 236 of the National Housing Act, or

"(iii) section 515 of the Housing Act of 1949,

as such Acts are in effect on the date of the enactment of the Tax Reform Act of 1986.

"(C) Low-income buildings where mortgage may be prepaid. A waiver may be granted under subparagraph (A) (without regard to any clause thereof) with respect to a federally-assisted building described in clause (ii) or (iii) of subparagraph (B) if—

"(i) the mortgage on such building is eligible for prepayment under subtitle B of the Emergency Low Income Housing Preservation Act of 1987 or under section 502(c) of the Housing Act of 1949 at any time within 1 year after the date of the application for such a waiver,

"(ii) the appropriate Federal official certifies to the Secretary that it is reasonable to expect that, if the waiver is not granted, such building will cease complying with its low-income occupancy requirements, and

"(iii) the eligibility to prepay such mortgage without the approval of the appropriate Federal official is waived by all persons who are so eligible and such waiver is binding on all successors of such persons.

"(D) Buildings acquired from insured depository institutions in default. A waiver may be granted under subparagraph (A) (without regard to any clause thereof) with respect to any building acquired from an insured depository institution in default (as defined in section 3 of the Federal Deposit Insurance Act) or from a receiver or conservator of such an institution.

"(E) Appropriate federal official. For purposes of subparagraph (A), the term 'appropriate Federal official' means—

"(i) the Secretary of Housing and Urban Development in the case of any building described in subparagraph (B) by reason of clause (i) or (ii) thereof, and

"(ii) the Secretary of Agriculture in the case of any building described in subparagraph (B) by reason of clause (iii) thereof."

—P.L. 110-289, Sec. 3004(a), deleted "Such term does not include any building with respect to which moderate rehabilitation assistance is provided, at any time during the compliance period, under section 8(e)(2) of the United States Housing Act of 1937 (other than assistance under the Stewart B. McKinney Homeless Assistance Act (as in effect on the date of the enactment of this sentence))." at the end of para. (c)(2)... Sec. 3004(b), substituted "(as of the date which is 1 year after the date that the allocation was made)" for "(as of the later of the date which is 6 months after the date that the allocation was made or the close of the calendar year in which the allocation is made)" in clause (h)(1)(E)(ii)... Sec. 3004(c), amended para. (j)(6)... Sec. 3004(d), deleted "and" at the end of clause (m)(1)(C)(vii), substituted a comma for the period at the end of clause (m)(1)(C)(viii) and added clauses (m)(1)(C)(ix)-(x)... Sec. 3004(e), deleted "or" at the end of subclause (i)(3)(D)(i)(I), redesignated subclause (i)(3)(D)(i)(II) as subclause (i)(3)(D)(i)(III) and added subclause (i)(3)(D)(i)(II)... Sec. 3004(f), added para. (i)(8)... Sec. 3004(g), added para. (g)(9), effective as provided by Sec. 3004(i), of this Act, which reads as follows:

"(i) Effective date.

"(1) In general. Except as otherwise provided in this subsection, the amendments made by this section shall apply to buildings placed in service after the date of the enactment of this Act.

"(2) Repeal of bonding requirement on disposition of building. The amendment made by subsection (c) shall apply to—

"(A) interests in buildings disposed after the date of the enactment of this Act, and

"(B) interests in buildings disposed of on or before such date if—

"(i) it is reasonably expected that such building will continue to be operated as a qualified low-income building (within the meaning of section 42 of the Internal Revenue Code of 1986) for the remaining compliance period (within the meaning of such section) with respect to such building, and

"(ii) the taxpayer elects the application of this subparagraph with respect to such disposition.

"(3) Energy efficiency and historic nature taken into account in making allocations. The amendments made by subsection (d) shall apply to allocations made after December 31, 2008.

"(4) Continued eligibility for students who received foster care assistance. The amendments made by subsection (e) shall apply to determinations made after the date of the enactment of this Act.

"(5) Treatment of rural projects. The amendment made by subsection (f) shall apply to determinations made after the date of the enactment of this Act.

"(6) Clarification of general public use requirement. The amendment made by subsection (g) shall apply to buildings placed in service before, on, or after the date of the enactment of this Act."

Prior to amendment, para. (j)(6) read as follows:

"(6) No recapture on disposition of building (or interest therein) where bond posted. In the case of a disposition of a building or an interest therein the taxpayer shall be discharged from liability for any additional tax under this subsection by reason of such disposition if—

"(A) the taxpayer furnishes to the Secretary a bond in an amount satisfactory to the Secretary and for the period required by the Secretary, and

"(B) it is reasonably expected that such building will continue to be operated as a qualified low-income building for the remaining compliance period with respect to such building."

—P.L. 110-289, Sec. 3004(h), of this Act, reads as follows:

"(h) GAO study regarding modifications to low-income housing tax credit. Not later than December 31, 2012, the Comptroller General of the United States shall submit to Congress a report which analyzes the implementation of the modifications made by this subtitle to the low-income housing tax credit under section 42 of the Internal Revenue Code of 1986. Such report shall include an analysis of the distribution of credit allocations before and after the effective date of such modifications."

—P.L. 110-289, Sec. 3007(b), added "or such financing is refunded as described in section 146(i)(6)" before the period a the end of clause (h)(4)(A)(ii), effective for repayments of loans received after 7/30/2008.

In 2007, P.L. 110-142, Sec. 6(a), amended subclause (i)(3)(D)(ii)(I), effective for housing credit amounts allocated before, on, or after 12/20/2007, and buildings placed in service before, on, or after 12/20/2007 to the extent paragraph (i) of section 42(h) of the Internal Revenue Code of 1986 does not apply to any building by reason of paragraph (4) thereof.

Prior to amendment, subclause (i)(3)(D)(ii)(I), read as follows:

"(I) single parents and their children and such parents and children are not dependents (as defined in section 152, determined without regard to subsections (b)(1), (b)(2), and (d)(1)(B) thereof) of another individual, or"

In 2004, P.L. 108-311, Sec. 207(8), added ", determined without regard to subsections (b)(1), (b)(2), and (d)(1)(B) thereof" after "section 152" in subclause (i)(3)(D)(ii)(I), effective for tax. yrs. begin. after 12/31/2004.

—P.L. 108-311, Sec. 408(a)(3), substituted "section 179(d)(7)" for "section 179(b)(7)" in subclause (d)(2)(D)(iii)(I), enacted 10/4/2004.

In 2002, P.L. 107-147, Sec. 417(2), substituted "the amounts described in clauses (ii) through (iv) over the aggregate housing credit dollar amount allocated for such year," for "the amounts described in clauses (i) [(ii)] through (iv) over the aggregate housing credit dollar amount allocated for such year." in subpara. (h)(3)(C)... Sec. 417(3), deleted the second "and" at the end of subclause (m)(1)(B)(ii)(II) and added "and" at the end of subclause (m)(1)(B)(ii)(III), effective 3/9/2002.

In 2000, P.L. 106-554, Sec. 1(a)(7), [which enacted into law Sec. 131(a) of P.L. 106-554] amended clauses (h)(3)(C)(i) and (ii)... Sec. 1(a)(7) [which enacted into law Sec. 131(b) of P.L. 106-554, added subpara. (h)(3)(H)... Sec. 1(a)(7) [which enacted into law Sec. 131(c)(1)(A) of P.L. 106-554], substituted "clause (i)" for "clause (ii)" in subpara. (h)(3)(C)... Sec. 1(a)(7) [which enacted into law Sec. 131(c)(1)(B) of P.L. 106-554], substituted "clauses (ii)" for "clauses (i)" in subpara. (h)(3)(C)... Sec. 1(a)(7) [which enacted into law Sec. 131(c)(2)(A) of P.L. 106-554], substituted "subparagraph (C)(i)" for "subparagraph (C)(ii)" in clause (h)(3)(D)(ii)... Sec. 1(a)(7), [which enacted into law Sec. 131(c)(2)(B) of P.L. 106-554] substituted "clauses (ii)" for "clauses (i)" in subclause (h)(3)(D)(ii)(II), effective for calendar yrs. after 2000.

Prior to amendment, clauses (h)(3)(C)(i) and (ii) read as follows:

"(i) $1.25 [$.9375 for calendar year 1990] multiplied by the State population,

"(ii) the unused State housing credit ceiling (if any) of such State for the preceding calendar year,"

—P.L. 106-554, Sec. 1(a)(7), [which enacted into law Sec. 132(a)(1) of P.L. 106-554] added ", including whether the project includes the use of existing housing as part of a community revitalization plan" after "characteristics" in clause (m)(1)(C)(iii)... Sec. 1(a)(7), [which enacted into law Sec. 132(a)(2) of P.L. 106-554] deleted clauses (m)(1)(C)(v)–(vii) and added clauses (m)(1)(C)(v)–(viii)... Sec. 1(a)(7) [which enacted into law Sec. 132(b) of P.L. 106-554], deleted "and" at the end of subclause (m)(1)(B)(ii)(I), added "and" at the end of subclause (m)(1)(B)(ii)(II), and added subclause (m)(1)(B)(ii)(III)... Sec. 1(a)(7), [which enacted into law Sec. 133(a) of P.L. 106-554] deleted "and" at the end of clause (m)(1)(A)(i), substituted a comma for the period at the end of clause (m)(1)(A)(ii), and added clauses (m)(1)(A)(iii) and (iv)... Sec. 1(a)(7), [which enacted into law Sec. 133(b) of P.L. 106-554] added "and in monitoring for noncompliance with habitability standards through regular site visits" before "becomes aware of" at the end of clause (m)(1)(B)(iii)... Sec. 1(a)(7), [which enacted into law Sec. 134(a)(1) of P.L. 106-554] substituted "subparagraphs (B) and (C)" for "subparagraph (B)" in subpara. (d)(4)(A)... Sec. 1(a)(7), [which enacted into law Sec. 134(a)(2) of P.L. 106-554] redesignated subpara. (d)(4)(C) as (d)(4)(D)... Sec. 1(a)(7), [which enacted into law Sec. 134(a)(3) of P.L. 106-554] added subpara. (d)(4)(C)... Sec. 1(a)(7), [which enacted into law Sec. 134(b)(1) of P.L. 106-554] added "or the Native American Housing Assistance and Self-Determination Act of 1996 (25 U.S.C. 4101 et seq.) (as in effect on October 1, 1997)" after "this subparagraph" in clause (i)(2)(E)(i)... Sec. 1(a)(7), [which enacted into law Sec. 134(b)(2) of P.L. 106-554] added "or Native American Housing Assistance" after "home assistance" in the heading of subpara. (i)(2)(E)... Sec. 1(a)(7), [which enacted into law Sec. 135(a)(1) of P.L. 106-554] substituted "(as of the later of the date which is 6 months after the date that the allocation was made or" for "(as of" the first place it appeared in clause (h)(1)(E)(ii)... Sec. 1(a)(7), [which enacted into law Sec. 135(a)(2) of P.L. 106-554] substituted "project which fails to meet the 10 percent test under paragraph (1)(E)(ii) on a date after the close of the calendar year in which the allocation was made or which" for "project which" in subpara. (h)(3)(C)... Sec. 1(a)(7), [which enacted into law Sec. 135(b)(1) of P.L. 106-554] added "either" before "in which 50 percent" in subclause (d)(5)(C)(ii)(I)... Sec. 1(a)(7), [which enacted into law Sec. 135(b)(2) of P.L. 106-554] added "either" before "in which 50 percent" in subclause (d)(5)(C)(ii)(I)... Sec. 1(a)(7), [which enacted into law Sec. 136(a) of P.L. 106-554] amended clause (h)(3)(D)(ii)... Sec. 1(a)(7), [which enacted into law Sec. 136(b) of P.L. 106-554] substituted "clauses (i) through (iv)" for "clauses (i) and (iii)" in subpara. (h)(3)(C), effective as provided in Sec. 137(1) and (2) of this Act which reads as follows:

"(1) housing credit dollar amounts allocated after 12/31/2000. Sec. 137(2) of this Act provides:

"(2) buildings placed in service after such date to the extent paragraph (1) of section 42(h) of the Internal Revenue Code of 1986 does not apply to any building by reason of paragraph (4) thereof, but only with respect to bonds issued after such date."

Prior to amendment, clause (h)(3)(D)(ii) read as follows:

"(ii) Unused housing credit carryover. For purposes of this subparagraph, the unused housing credit carryover of a State for any calendar year is the excess (if any) of the unused State housing credit ceiling for such year (as defined in subparagraph (C)(ii)) over the excess (if any) of—

"(I) the aggregate housing credit dollar amount allocated for such year, over

"(II) the sum of the amounts described in clauses (i) and (iii) of subparagraph (C)."

Prior to deletion, clauses (m)(1)(C)(v)–(vii) read as follows:

"(v) participation of local tax-exempt organizations,

"(vi) tenant populations with special housing needs, and

"(vii) public housing waiting lists."

—P.L. 106-400, Sec. 2, of this Act, reads as follows:

"Sec. 2. References. Any reference in any law, regulation, document, paper, or other record of the United States to the Stewart B. McKinney Homeless Assistance Act shall be deemed to be a reference to the 'McKinney-Vento Homeless Assistance Act'."

In 1998, P.L. 105-206, Sec. 6004(g)(5), substituted "this chapter" for "subpart A, B, D, or G of this part" in subpara. (j)(4)(D), effective for obligations issued after 12/31/97.

In 1996, P.L. 104-188, Sec. 1702(g)(5)(A), repealed as if not enacted Sec. 11701(a)(11) of P.L. 101-508, which added "but only with respect to bonds issued after such date" before the period in Sec. 7108(r)(2) of P.L. 101-239, see below, except as provided in Sec. 1702(g)(5)(B) of this Act, which reads as follows:

"(B) Subparagraph (A) shall not apply to any building if the owner of such building establishes to the satisfaction of the Secretary of the Treasury or his delegate that such owner reasonably relied on the amendment made by such paragraph (11)."

—P.L. 104-188, Sec. 1703(b)(1), amended Sec. 13142(b)(6)(B) of P.L. 103-66, see below... Sec. 1703(b)(2), substituted "paragraph (5)" for "paragraph (2)" in Sec. 13142(b)(6)(C) of P.L. 103-66, see below

Prior to amendment, Sec. 13142(b)(6)(B) of P.L. 103-66, read as follows:

"(B) Waiver authority and prohibited discrimination. The amendments made by paragraphs (3) and (4) shall take effect on the date of the enactment of this Act."

—P.L. 104-188, Sec. 1704(t)(53), amended Sec. 11812(b)(3) of P.L. 101-508, to not execute the amendment to the heading of subpara. 42(d)(5)(B), see below... Sec. 1704(t)(64), deleted "of 1988" after "Assistance Act" in the last sentence of para. (c)(2), effective date of enactment.

In 1993, P.L. 103-66, Sec. 13142(a)(1), deleted subsec. (o), effective for periods end. after 6/30/92.

Prior to deletion, subsec. (o) read as follows:

"(o) Termination.

"(1) In general. Except as provided in paragraph (2)—

"(A) clause (i) of subsection (h)(3)(C) shall not apply to any amount allocated after June 30, 1992, and

"(B) subsection (h)(4) shall not apply to any building placed in service after June 30, 1992.

"(2) Exception for bond-financed buildings in progress. For purposes of paragraph (1)(B), a building shall be treated as placed in service before July 1, 1992 if—

"(A) the bonds with respect to such building are issued before July 1, 1992,

"(B) the taxpayer's basis in the project (of which the building is a part) as of June 30, 1992, is more than 10 percent of the taxpayer's reasonably expected basis in such project as of June 30, 1994, and

"(C) such building is placed in service before July 1, 1994."

—P.L. 103-66, Sec. 13142(b)(1)(A), deleted "and" at the end of clause (m)(2)(B)(ii)... Sec. 13142(b)(1)(B), substituted ", and" for the period at the end of clause (m)(2)(B)(iii)... Sec. 13142(b)(1)(C), added clause (m)(2)(B)(iv)... Sec. 13142(b)(5), added subpara. (i)(2)(E), effective as provided in Sec. 13142(b)(6)(A)-(C) [amended by Sec. 1703(b)(1) and (2), P.L. 104-188, see above] of this Act, which read as follows:

"(A) In general. Except as provided in subparagraphs (B) and (C), the amendments made by this subsection shall apply to—

"(i) determinations under section 42 of the Internal Revenue Code of 1986 with respect to housing credit dollar amounts allocated from State housing credit ceilings after June 30, 1992, or

"(ii) buildings placed in service after June 30, 1992, to the extent paragraph (1) of section 42(h) of such Code does not apply to any building by reason of paragraph (4) thereof, but only with respect to bonds issued after such date.

"(B) Full-time students, waiver authority, and prohibited discrimination. The amendments made by paragraphs (2), (3), and (4) shall take effect on the date of the enactment of this Act.

"(C) Home assistance. The amendment made by paragraph (5) shall apply to periods after the date of the enactment of this Act."

—P.L. 103-66, Sec. 13142(b)(2), amended subpara. (i)(3)(D), effective for periods after 8/10/93.

Prior to amendment, subpara. (i)(3)(D) read as follows:

"(D) Certain students not to disqualify unit. A unit shall not fail to be treated as a low-income unit merely because it is occupied by an individual who is—

"(i) a student and receiving assistance under title IV of the Social Security Act, or

"(ii) enrolled in a job training program receiving assistance under the Job Training Partnership Act or under other similar Federal, State, or local laws."

—P.L. 103-66, Sec. 13142(b)(3), added para. (g)(8)... Sec. 13142(b)(4), redesignated clauses (h)(6)(B)(iv) and (v) as clauses (h)(6)(B)(v) and (vi) and added new clause (h)(6)(B)(iv), effective 8/10/93.

In 1991, P.L. 102-227, Sec. 107(a)(1)(A), deleted ", for any calendar year after 1991" after "paragraph (2)" in para. (o)(1)... Sec. 107(a)(1)(B), added "to any amount allocated after June 30, 1992" before the comma in subpara. (o)(1)(A)... Sec. 107(a)(1)(C), substituted "June 30, 1992" for "1991" in subpara. (o)(1)(B)... Sec. 107(a)(2)(A), substituted "July 1, 1992" for "1992" each place it appeared in para. (o)(2)... Sec. 107(a)(2)(B), substituted "June 30, 1992" for "December 31, 1991" in subpara. (o)(2)(B)... Sec. 107(a)(2)(C), substituted "June 30, 1994" for "December 31, 1993" in subpara. (o)(2)(B)... Sec. 107(a)(2)(D), substituted "July 1, 1994" for "January 1, 1994" in subpara. (o)(2)(C), effective for calendar yrs. after 1991.

In 1990, P.L. 101-508, Sec. 11407(a)(1)(A), substituted "1991" for "1990" each place it appeared in para. (o)(1)... Sec. 11407(a)(1)(B), amended para. (o)(2)... Sec. 11407(a)(2), deleted Sec. 7108(a)(2) of P.L. 101-239, effective for calendar years after 1989.

Prior to amendment, para. (o)(2) read as follows:

"(2) Exception for bond-financed buildings in progress. For purposes of paragraph (1)(B), a building shall be treated as placed in service before 1990 if—

"(A) the bonds with respect to such building are issued before 1990,

"(B) such building is constructed, reconstructed, or rehabilitated by the taxpayer,

"(C) more than 10 percent of the reasonably anticipated cost of such construction, reconstruction, or rehabilitation has been incurred as of January 1, 1990, and some of such cost is incurred on or after such date, and

"(D) such building is placed in service before January 1, 1992."

Prior to deletion, Sec. 7108(a)(2) of P.L. 101-239 read as follows:

"(2) Special rule. In the case of calendar year 1990, section 42(h)(3)(C)(i) of the Internal Revenue Code of 1986 (as amended by subsection (b)(1) [Sec. 7108(b)(1)]) shall be applied by substituting '$.9375' for '$1.25'."

—P.L. 101-508, Sec. 11407(b)(1), substituted "the tenants (in cooperative form or otherwise) or resident management corporation of such building or by a qualified nonprofit organization (as defined in subsection (h)(5)(C)) or government

Code Sec. 42 Tax credits

agency" for "the tenants of such building" in para. (i)(7) (as redesignated by Sec. 11701(a)(10) of this Act), effective 11/5/90.

—P.L. 101-508, Sec. 11407(b)(2), amended clause (m)(1)(B)(iv) (before redesignated as clause (m)(1)(B)(iii) by Sec. 11407(b)(7)(B) of this Act), effective 1/1/92 for buildings placed in service before, on, or after 1/1/92.

Prior to amendment, clause (m)(1)(B)(iv) (before redesignated as clause (m)(1)(B)(iii) by Sec. 11407(b)(7)(B) of this Act) read as follows:

"(iv) which provides a procedure that the agency will follow in notifying the Internal Revenue Service of noncompliance with the provisions of this section which such agency becomes aware of."

—P.L. 101-508, Sec. 11407(b)(3), deleted "and" at the end of clause (g)(2)(B)(ii), substituted ", and" for the period at the end of (g)(2)(B)(iii), and added clause (g)(2)(B)(iv) . . . Sec. 11407(b)(4), added the last sentence to subclause (d)(5)(C)(ii)(I) . . . Sec. 11407(b)(5)(A), added "(other than assistance under the Stewart B. McKinney Homeless Assistance Act of 1988 (as in effect on the date of the enactment of this sentence))" before the period in the last sentence of para. (c)(2) (as amended by Sec. 11701(a)(1)(A)), effective as provided in Sec. 11407(b)(10)(A) of this Act, see below.

—P.L. 101-508, Sec. 11407(b)(6), amended subpara. (i)(3)(D), effective 11/5/90.

Prior to amendment, subpara. (i)(3)(D) read as follows:

"(D) Students in government-supported job training programs not to disqualify unit. A unit shall not fail to be treated as a low-income unit merely because it is occupied by an individual who is enrolled in a job training program receiving assistance under the Job Training Partnership Act or under other similar Federal, State, or local laws."

—P.L. 101-508, Sec. 11407(b)(7)(A), deleted "and" at the end of clause (m)(2)(B)(i), substituted ", and" for the period at the end of clause (m)(2)(B)(ii), added clause (m)(2)(B)(iii), and added "Clause (iii) shall not be applied so as to impede the development of projects in hard-to-develop areas." following clause (m)(2)(B)(iii). . . . Sec. 11407(b)(7)(B), deleted clause (m)(1)(B)(ii) and redesignated clauses (m)(1)(B)(iii) and (m)(1)(B)(iv) [as amended by Sec. 11407(b)(2) of this Act] as clauses (m)(1)(B)(ii) and (m)(1)(B)(iii), effective as provided in Sec. 11407(b)(10)(A) of this Act, which reads as follows:

"(A) In general. Except as otherwise provided in this paragraph, the amendments made by this subsection shall apply to—

"(i) determinations under section 42 of the Internal Revenue Code of 1986 with respect to housing credit dollar amounts allocated from State housing credit ceilings for calendar years after 1990, or

"(ii) buildings placed in service after December 31, 1990, to the extent paragraph (1) of section 42(h) of such Code does not apply to any building by reason of paragraph (4) thereof, but only with respect to bonds issued after such date."

Prior to deletion, clause (m)(1)(B)(ii) read as follows:

"(ii) which gives the highest priority to those projects as to which the highest percentage of the housing credit dollar amount is to be used for project costs other than the cost of intermediaries unless granting such priority would impede the development of projects in hard-to-develop areas,"

—P.L. 101-508, Sec. 11407(b)(8), deleted "or" at the end of subclause (d)(2)(D)(ii)(III), substituted ", or" for the period at the end of subclause (d)(2)(D)(ii)(IV), and added subclause (d)(2)(D)(ii)(V) . . . Sec. 11407(b)(9)(A), added "own an interest in the project (directly or through a partnership) and" after "nonprofit organization is to" in subpara. (h)(5)(B) . . . Sec. 11407(b)(9)(B), deleted "and" at the end of clause (h)(5)(C)(i), redesignated clause (h)(5)(C)(ii) as (h)(5)(C)(iii) and added new clause (h)(5)(C)(ii) . . . Sec. 11407(b)(9)(C), added "ownership and" before "material participation" in clause (h)(5)(D)(i), effective 11/5/90.

—P.L. 101-508, Sec. 11407(c), of this Act, provides:

"(c) Election to accelerate credit into 1990.

"(1) In general. At the election of an individual, the credit determined under section 42 of the Internal Revenue Code of 1986 for the taxpayer's first taxable year ending on or after October 25, 1990, shall be 150 percent of the amount which would (but for this paragraph) be so allowable with respect to investments held by such individual on or before October 25, 1990.

"(2) Reduction in aggregate credit to reflect increased 1990 credit. The aggregate credit allowable to any person under section 42 of such Code with respect to any investment for taxable years after the first taxable year referred to in paragraph (1) shall be reduced on a pro rata basis by the amount of the increased credit allowable by reason of paragraph (1) with respect to such first taxable year. The preceding sentence shall not be construed to affect whether any taxable year is part of the credit, compliance, or extended use periods.

"(3) Election. The election under paragraph (1) shall be made at the time and in the manner prescribed by the Secretary of the Treasury or his delegate, and, once made, shall be irrevocable. In the case of a partnership, such election shall be made by the partnership."

—P.L. 101-508, Sec. 11701(a)(1)(A), added the last sentence of para. (c)(2) . . . Sec. 11701(a)(1)(B), deleted the last sentence of para. (b)(1), effective as provided in Sec. 7108(r)(1) and (2) [sic (s)(1) and (2)] of P.L. 101-239, see below.

Prior to deletion, the last sentence of para. (b)(1) read as follows:

"A building shall not be treated as described in subparagraph (B) if, at any time during the credit period, moderate rehabilitation assistance is provided with respect to such building under section 8(e)(2) of the United States Housing Act of 1937."

—P.L. 101-508, Sec. 11701(a)(2)(A), added "which is designated by the Secretary of Housing and Urban Development and, for the most recent year for which census data are available on household income in such tract," after "census tract" in subclause (d)(5)(C)(ii)(I) . . . Sec. 11701(a)(2)(B), added "for such year" after "median gross income" in subclause (d)(5)(C)(ii)(I) (before amended by Sec. 11407(b)(4) of this Act, see above), effective for buildings placed in service after 12/31/86, except as provided in Sec. 252(e)(2) and (3) of P.L. 99-514, reproduced below.

—P.L. 101-508, Sec. 11701(a)(3)(A), added "and such unit continues to be rent-restricted" before the period at the end of clause (g)(2)(D)(i), effective as provided in Sec. 7108(r)(1) and (2) [sic (s)(1) and (2)] of P.L. 101-239, reproduced below.

—P.L. 101-508, Sec. 11701(a)(3)(B), of this Act, provides the following:

"(B) In the case of a building to which (but for this subparagraph) the amendment made by subparagraph (A) [Sec. 11701(a)(3)(A) of this Act] does not apply, such amendment shall apply to—

"(i) determinations of qualified basis for taxable years beginning after the date of the enactment of this Act [11/5/90], and

"(ii) determinations of qualified basis for taxable years beginning on or before such date except that determinations for such taxable years shall be made without regard to any reduction in gross rent after August 3, 1990, for any period before August 4, 1990."

—P.L. 101-508, Sec. 11701(a)(4), added the last sentence of clause (g)(2)(D)(ii) . . . Sec. 11701(a)(5)(A), substituted "the 1st year of the credit period for such building" for "the 12-month period beginning on the date the building is placed in service" in subpara. (g)(3)(A), effective as provided in Sec. 7108(r)(1) and (2) [sic (s)(1) and (2)] of P.L. 101-239, reproduced below.

—P.L. 101-508, Sec. 11701(a)(5)(B), of this Act, provides the following:

"(B) In the case of a building to which the amendment made by subparagraph (A) [Sec. 11701(a)(5)(A) of this Act] does not apply, the period specified in section 42(g)(3)(A) of the Internal Revenue Code of 1986 (as in effect before the amendment made by subparagraph (A)) shall not expire before the close of the taxable year following the taxable year in which the building is placed in service."

—P.L. 101-508, Sec. 11701(a)(6)(A), substituted "the sum of the amounts described in clauses (i) and (iii)" for "the amount described in clause (i)" in the second sentence of subpara. (h)(3)(C) . . . Sec. 11701(a)(6)(B), substituted "the sum of the amounts described in clauses (i) and (iii)" for "the amount described in clause (i)" in subclause (h)(3)(D)(ii)(II), effective as provided in Sec. 7108(r)(3) [sic (s)(3)] of P.L. 101-239, reproduced below.

—P.L. 101-508, Sec. 11701(a)(7)(A), added "and which prohibits the actions described in subclauses (I) and (II) of subparagraph (E)(ii)" before the comma in clause (h)(6)(B)(i) . . . Sec. 11701(a)(7)(B), substituted "requirement and prohibitions" for "requirement" in clause (h)(6)(B)(ii). . . . Sec. 11701(a)(8)(A), redesignated clauses (h)(6)(B)(iii) and (h)(6)(B)(iv) as clauses (h)(6)(B)(iv) and (h)(6)(B)(v) and added new clause (h)(6)(B)(iii) . . . Sec. 11701(a)(8)(B), deleted subpara. (h)(6)(J) and redesignated subparas. (h)(6)(K) and (h)(6)(L) as subparas. (h)(6)(J) and (h)(6)(K) . . . Sec. 11701(a)(8)(C), added "not otherwise permitted under this section" before the period in subclause (h)(6)(E)(ii)(II) . . . Sec. 11701(a)(8)(D), added "the nonlow-income portion of the building for fair market value and" before "the low-income portion" in subpara. (h)(6)(F) . . . Sec. 11701(a)(9), added "unless the Secretary determines that such acquisition is part of an arrangement with the taxpayer a purpose of which is to terminate such period" before the comma in subclause (h)(6)(E)(i)(I) . . . Sec. 11701(a)(10), redesignated para. (i)(8) [sic (7)] as para. (i)(7), effective as provided in Sec. 7108(r)(1) and (2) [sic (s)(1) and (2)] of P.L. 101-239, reproduced below.

Prior to deletion, subpara. (h)(6)(J) read as follows:

"(J) Sales of less than low-income portion of buildings. In the case of a sale or exchange of only a portion of the low-income portion of the building, only the same portion (as the portion sold or exchanged) of the amount determined under subparagraph (F) shall be taken into account thereunder."

—P.L. 101-508, Sec. 11701(a)(11), amended Sec. 7108(r)(2) [sic (s)(2)] of P.L. 101-239, reproduced below, part of the effective date for changes made by Sec. 7108 of P.L. 101-239, by adding "but only with respect to bonds issued after such date" before the period, see below. [repealed as if not enacted by Sec. 1702(g)(5)(B) of P.L. 104-188, see above]

—P.L. 101-508, Sec. 11701(a)(12), amended Sec. 7108(r)(6) [sic (s)(6)] of P.L. 101-239, reproduced below, part of the effective date for amendments made by Sec. 7108 of P.L. 101-239, by adding "after" after "issued", see below.

—P.L. 101-508, Sec. 11812(b)(3), [as amended by Sec. 1704(t)(53) of P.L. 104-188, see above] substituted "section 167(k) (as in effect on the day before the date of enactment of the Revenue Reconciliation Act of 1990)" for "section 167(k)" in subclause (d)(2)(D)(i)(I) and subpara. (d)(5)(B), effective for property placed in service after 11/5/90 except as provided in Sec. 11812(c)(2) and (c)(3) of this Act, which read as follows:

"(2) Exception. The amendments made by this section shall not apply to any property to which section 168 of the Internal Revenue Code of 1986 does not apply by reason of subsection (f)(5) thereof.

"(3) Exception for previously grandfather expenditures. The amendments made by this section shall not apply to rehabilitation expenditures described in section 252(f)(5) of the Tax Reform Act of 1986 (as added by section 1002(l)(31) of the Technical and Miscellaneous Revenue Act of 1988)."

—P.L. 101-508, Sec. 11813(b)(3)(A)(i)-(iii), substituted "49(a)(1)" for "46(c)(8)", "49(a)(2)" for "46(c)(9)" and "49(b)(1)" for "47(d)(1)" in para. (k)(1) . . . Sec. 11813(b)(3)(B), substituted "49(a)(1)(D)(iv)(II)" for "46(c)(8)(D)(iv)(II)" in clause (k)(2)(A)(ii) and subpara. (k)(2)(D), effective for property placed in service after 12/31/90 except as provided in Sec. 11813(c)(2) of this Act, which reads as follows:

"(2) Exceptions. The amendments made by this section shall not apply to—

"(A) any transition property (as defined in section 49(e) of the Internal Revenue Code of 1986 (as in effect on the day before the date of the enactment of this Act [11/5/90]),

"(B) any property with respect to which qualified progress expenditures were previously taken into account under section 46(d) of such Code (as so in effect), and

Tax credits Code Sec. 42

"(C) any property described in section 46(b)(2)(C) of such Code (as so in effect)."

In 1989, P.L. 101-239, Sec. 7108(a)(1), amended subsec. (n), effective as provided in Sec. 7108(r)(1) and (2) [as amended by Sec. 11701(a)(11) of P.L. 101-508, see above] [sic (s)(1) and (2)] of this Act which reads as follows:

"(1) In general. Except as otherwise provided in this subsection, the amendments made by this section shall apply to determinations under section 42 of the Internal Revenue Code of 1986 with respect to housing credit dollar amounts allocated from State housing credit ceilings for calendar years after 1989.

"(2) Buildings not subject to allocation limits. Except as otherwise provided in this subsection, to the extent paragraph (1) of section 42(h) of such Code does not apply to any building by reason of paragraph (4) thereof, the amendments made by this section shall apply to buildings placed in service after December 31, 1989 but only with respect to bonds issued after such date."

Prior to amendment, subsec. (n) read as follows:

"(n) Termination. The State housing credit ceiling under subsection (h) shall be zero for any calendar year after 1989 and subsection (h)(4) shall not apply to any building placed in service after 1989."

—P.L. 101-239, Sec. 7108(a)(2), [as repealed by Sec. 11407(a)(2) of P.L. 101-508, see above]

—P.L. 101-239, Sec. 7108(b)(1), redesignated subparas. (h)(3)(D), (E), and (F) as (h)(3)(E), (F), and (G), deleted subpara. (h)(3)(C), and added new subparas. (h)(3)(C) and (D) . . . Sec. 7108(b)(2)(A), substituted "subparagraph (F)" for "subparagraph (E)" in subpara. (h)(5)(E) . . . Sec. 7108(b)(2)(B), deleted subpara. (h)(6)(B) and redesignated subparas. (h)(6)(C), (D), and (E) as subparas. (h)(6)(B), (C), and (D), effective as provided in Sec. 7108(r)(3) [sic (s)(3)] of this Act which reads as follows:

"(3) 1-year carryover of unused credit authority, etc. The amendments made by subsection (b) shall apply to calendar years after 1989, but clauses (ii), (iii), and (iv) of section 42(h)(3)(C) of such Code (as added by this section) shall be applied without regard to allocations for 1989 or any preceding year."

Prior to amendment, subpara. (h)(3)(C) read as follows:

"(C) State housing credit ceiling. The State housing credit ceiling applicable to any State for any calendar year shall be an amount equal to $1.25 multiplied by the State population."

Prior to deletion, subpara. (h)(6)(B) read as follows:

"(B) Housing credit dollar amount may not be carried over, etc.

"(i) No carryover. The portion of the aggregate housing credit dollar amount of any housing credit agency which is not allocated for any calendar year may not be carried over to any other calendar year."

—P.L. 101-239, Sec. 7108(c)(1), redesignated paras. (h)(6) and (7) as paras. (h)(7) and (8) and added new para. (h)(6) . . . Sec. 7108(c)(2), substituted "subsection (h)(7)" for "subsection (h)(6))" in subpara. (b)(3)(C) . . . Sec. 7108(d)(1), deleted "and" from the end of clause (d)(2)(B)(ii), substituted ", and" for the period at the end of clause (d)(2)(B)(iii), and added clause (d)(2)(B)(iv) . . . Sec. 7108(d)(2), added para. (f)(5) . . . Sec. 7108(d)(3), redesignated subpara. (e)(3)(B) as (e)(3)(C) and amended so much of para. (e)(3) as preceded (e)(3)(B) (before redesignation) . . . Sec. 7108(e)(1)(A), redesignated subpara. (g)(2)(C) as subpara. (g)(2)(E), and added new subparas. (g)(2)(C) and (D) . . . Sec. 7108(e)(1)(B), substituted "the imputed income limitation applicable to such unit" for "the income limitation under paragraph (1) applicable to individuals occupying such unit" in subpara. (g)(2)(A) . . . Sec. 7108(e)(2), added the last sentence of subpara. (g)(2)(A), effective as provided in Sec. 7108(r)(1) and (2) [sic (s)(1) and (2)] of this Act reproduced above.

Prior to amendment, the portion of para. (e)(3) that preceded subpara. (e)(3)(B) (before redesignation) read as follows:

"(3) Average of rehabilitation expenditures must be $2,000 or more.

"(A) In general. Paragraph (1) shall apply to rehabilitation expenditures with respect to any building only if the qualified basis attributable to such expenditures incurred during any 24-month period, when divided by the low-income units in the building, is $2,000 or more."

—P.L. 101-239, Sec. 7108(f), redesignated subpara. (d)(6)(C) as subpara. (d)(6)(E) and added new subparas. (d)(6)(C) and (D), effective 12/19/89.

—P.L. 101-239, Sec. 7108(g), added para. (d)(5)(D), effective as provided in Sec. 7108(r)(1) and (2) [sic (s)(1) and (2)] of this Act reproduced above.

—P.L. 101-239, Sec. 7108(h)(1), added the last sentence of subpara. (i)(3)(B), effective for buildings placed in service after 12/31/86, in tax. yrs. end. after 12/31/86, except as provided in Sec. 252(e)(2) and (f) of P.L. 99-514 reproduced below.

—P.L. 101-239, Sec. 7108(h)(2)(A)-(C), deleted "and" at the end of clause (g)(2)(B)(i), substituted ", and" for the period at the end of clause (g)(2)(B)(ii) and added clause (g)(2)(B)(iii) and the last sentence of subpara. (g)(2)(B) . . . Sec. 7108(h)(3), added para. (g)(7) . . . Sec. 7108(h)(4), added subpara. (i)(3)(E) . . . Sec. 7108(h)(5), added the last sentence of para. (b)(1) . . . Sec. 7108(i)(1), amended subpara. (i)(3)(B) . . . Sec. 7108(i)(2), added subpara. (c)(1)(E) . . . Sec. 7108(j), substituted "50 percent" for "70 percent" each place it appeared in subpara. (h)(4)(B) . . . Sec. 7108(k), added the last sentence of subpara. (i)(2)(D), effective as provided in Sec. 7108(r)(1) and (2) [sic (s)(1) and (2)] of this Act reproduced above.

Prior to amendment, subpara. (i)(3)(B) [as amended by Sec. 7108(h)(1) and Sec. 7831(c)(1) of this Act] read as follows:

"(B) Exceptions. A unit shall not be treated as a low-income unit unless the unit is suitable for occupancy (as determined under regulations prescribed by the Secretary taking into account local health, safety, and building codes) and used other than on a transient basis. For purposes of the preceding sentence, a single-room occupancy unit shall not be treated as used on a transient basis merely because it is rented on a month-by-month basis."

—P.L. 101-239, Sec. 7108(l)(1), added "as of the close of the 1st taxable year of the credit period" before the period at the end of para. (d)(1) . . . Sec. 7108(l)(2), amended clause (d)(2)(A)(i) . . . Sec. 7108(l)(3)(A), substituted "Adjusted basis" for "Acquisition cost" in the heading of subpara. (d)(2)(C) and substituted "adjusted basis" for "cost" in subpara. (d)(2)(C) . . . Sec. 7108(l)(3)(B), deleted subpara. (d)(5)(A) and redesignated subparas. (d)(5)(B), (C), and (D) [as added by Sec. 7108(g) of this Act] as subparas. (d)(5)(A), (B), and (C), and substituted "(5) Special rules for determining eligible basis." for "(5) Eligible basis determined when building placed in service." in the heading of para. (d)(5) . . . Sec. 7108(l)(3)(C), substituted "subsection (d)(2)(A)(i)" for "subsection (d)(2)(A)(i)(II)" in para. (e)(5), effective for buildings placed in service after 12/31/86, in tax. yrs. end. after 12/31/86, except as provided in Sec. 252(e)(2) and (f) of P.L. 99-514, reproduced below.

Prior to amendment, clause (d)(2)(A)(i) read as follows:

"(i) in the case of a building which meets the requirements of subparagraph (B), the sum of—

"(I) the portion of its adjusted basis attributable to its acquisition cost, plus

"(II) amounts chargeable to capital account and incurred by the taxpayer (before the close of the 1st taxable year of the credit period for such building) for property (or additions or improvements to property) of a character subject to the allowance for depreciation, and"

Prior to deletion, subpara. (d)(5)(A) read as follows:

"(A) In general. Except as provided in subparagraphs (B) and (C), the eligible basis of any building for the entire compliance period for such building shall be its eligible basis on the date such building is placed in service (increased, in the case of an existing building which meets the requirements of paragraph (2)(B), by the amounts described in paragraph (2)(A)(i)(II))."

—P.L. 101-239, Sec. 7108(m)(1), added subpara. (h)(1)(F) . . . Sec. 7108(m)(2), substituted "(E), or (F)" for "or (E)", in subpara. (h)(1)(B) . . . Sec. 7108(m)(3), added subpara. (g)(3)(D) . . . Sec. 7108(n)(2), deleted "(other than section 142(d)(4)(B)(iii))" after "such provisions", in para. (g)(4), effective as provided in Sec. 7108(r)(1) and (2) [sic (s)(1) and (2)] of this Act, reproduced above.

—P.L. 101-239, Sec. 7108(o), redesignated subsecs. (m) and (n) [as amended by Sec. 7108(a)(1) of this Act] as subsecs. (n) and (o), and added new subsec. (m), effective as provided in Sec. 7108(r)(1) and (2) [sic (s)(1) and (2)] of this Act, reproduced above and as provided in Sec. 7108(r)(6) [as amended by Sec. 11701(a)(12) of P.L. 101-508, see above] [sic (s)(6)] of this Act which reads as follows:

"(6) Certain rules which apply to bonds. Paragraphs (1)(D) and (2)(D) of section 42(m) of such Code, as added by this section, shall apply to obligations issued after December 31, 1989."

—P.L. 101-239, Sec. 7108(o), [sic (p)], added the last sentence to subpara. (k)(2)(D), effective as provided in Sec. 7108(r)(1) and (2) [sic (s)(1) and (2)] of this Act reproduced above.

—P.L. 101-239, Sec. 7108(p), [sic (q)], substituted "Following" for "Not later than the 90th day following" and added "at such time and" before "in such form" in para. (l)(1), effective for tax. yrs. end. on or after 12/31/89.

—P.L. 101-239, Sec. 7108(q), [sic (r)], added para. (i)(8) [sic (i)(7)], effective as provided in Sec. 7108(r)(1) and (2) [sic (s)(1) and (2)] of this Act reproduced above.

—P.L. 101-239, Sec. 7108(r)(8), [sic (s)(8)] provides:

"(8) Guidance on difficult development areas and posting of bond to avoid recapture. Not later than 180 days after the date of the enactment of this Act—

"(A) the Secretary of Housing and Urban Development shall publish initial guidance on the designation of difficult development areas under section 42(d)(5)(C) of such Code, as added by this section, and

"(B) the Secretary of the Treasury shall publish initial guidance under section 42(j)(6) of such Code (relating to no recapture on disposition of building (or interest therein) where bond posted)."

—P.L. 101-239, Sec. 7811(a)(1), added "section" before "167(k)" in the heading of subpara. (d)(5)(C) [before amendment by Sec. 7108(l)(3)(B) of this Act] . . . Sec. 7811(a)(2), substituted "clause (i)" for "clause (ii)" in clause (h)(5)(D)(ii) . . . Sec. 7831(c)(1), added "(as determined under regulations prescribed by the Secretary taking into account local health, safety, and building codes)" after "suitable for occupancy" in subpara. (i)(3)(B) . . . Sec. 7831(c)(2), added subpara. (i)(3)(D) . . . Sec. 7831(c)(3), added para. (i)(6) . . . Sec. 7831(c)(4), added para. (f)(4) . . . Sec. 7831(c)(5), deleted "and" at the end of para. (m)(2) [before amendment by Sec. 7108(o) of this Act], substituted ", and" for the period at the end of para. (m)(3), and added para. (m)(4) . . . Sec. 7831(c)(6), added "(or interest therein)" after "described in subparagraph (B)", in subpara. (d)(7)(A), effective for buildings placed in service after 12/31/86, in tax. yrs. end. after 12/31/86, except as provided in Sec. 252(e)(2) and (f) of P.L. 99-514 reproduced below.

—P.L. 101-239, Sec. 7841(d)(13), substituted "Farmers Home Administration" for "Farmers' Home Administration", in clause (d)(6)(A)(i) . . . Sec. 7841(d)(14), substituted "subsection (a)" for "subsection (a)" in clause (d)(7)(A)(ii) . . . Sec. 7841(d)(15), substituted "capital account" for "capital account" in subpara. (e)(2)(A), effective 12/19/89.

In 1988, P.L. 100-647, Sec. 1002(l)(1)(A), amended subpara. (b)(2)(A) . . . Sec. 1002(l)(1)(B), substituted "the month applicable under clause (i) or (ii) of subparagraph (A)" for "the month in which the building was placed in service" in clause (b)(2)(C)(ii) . . . Sec. 1002(l)(2)(A), amended subpara. (c)(2)(A) . . . Sec. 1002(l)(2)(B), amended para. (f)(1) . . . Sec. 1002(l)(3), amended clause (d)(2)(D)(ii) . . . Sec. 1002(l)(4), amended para. (d)(3) . . . Sec. 1002(l)(5), added "(increased, in the case of an existing building which meets the requirements of paragraph (2)(B), by the amounts described in paragraph (2)(A)(i)(II)) " after "placed in service" in subpara. (d)(5)(A) . . . Sec. 1002(l)(6)(A), added subpara. (d)(5)(C) . . . Sec. 1002(l)(6)(B), substituted "subparagraphs (B) and (C)" for "subparagraph (B)" in subpara. (d)(5)(A) . . . Sec. 1002(l)(7), added "or" to the end of clause (d)(6)(A)(i), substituted a period for ", or" at the end of clause (d)(6)(A)(ii), and deleted clause (d)(6)(A)(iii)... Sec. 1002(l)(8), deleted "of 1934" after "National Housing Act" in clause (d)(6)(B)(ii)... Sec. 1002(l)(9)(A), amended para. (f)(3)... Sec. 1002(l)(9)(B), amended para. (b)(3)... Sec. 1002(l)(10), substituted "rental assistance" for "Federal rental assistance" in clause (g)(2)(B)(i)... Sec. 1002(l)(11), added subpara. (g)(2)(C)... Sec. 1002(l)(12), amended para. (g)(3)... Sec. 1002(l)(13), added "; except that, in applying such provisions (other than section 142(d)(4)(B)(iii)) for such purposes the term 'gross rent' shall have the meaning given such term by paragraph (2)(B) of this subsection" after "low-income unit" in para. (g)(4)... Sec. 1002(l)(14)(A), amended para. (h)(1)... Sec. 1002(l)(14)(B), deleted clause (h)(6)(B)(ii)... Sec. 1002(l)(15), amended subpara. (h)(4)(A)... Sec. 1002(l)(16), redesignated subpara. (h)(5)(D) as (h)(5)(E) and added new subpara. (h)(5)(D)... Sec. 1002(l)(17), amended subpara. (h)(6)(D)... Sec. 1002(l)(18), added subpara. (h)(6)(E)... Sec. 1002(l)(19)(A), added "or any prior taxable year" after "such taxable year", substituted "there is or was outstanding" for "there is outstanding", and substituted "are or were used" for "are used" in subpara. (i)(2)(A)... Sec. 1002(l)(19)(B), amended subpara. (i)(2)(B)... Sec. 1002(l)(19)(C), redesignated subpara. (i)(2)(C) as (i)(2)(D) and added new subpara. (i)(2)(C)... Sec. 1002(l)(19)(D), substituted "this paragraph" for "subparagraph (A)" in subpara. (i)(2)(D) [as redesignated by Sec. 1002(l)(19)(C) of this Act]... Sec. 1002(l)(20), added subpara. (j)(4)(F)... Sec. 1002(l)(21), amended clause (j)(5)(B)(i)... Sec. 1002(l)(22)(A), added "(or interest therein)" after "building" in the heading of para. (j)(6)... Sec. 1002(l)(22)(B), added "or an interest therein" after "disposition of a building" in para. (j)(6)... Sec. 1002(l)(23), amended subpara. (k)(2)(B)... Sec. 1002(l)(24)(A), redesignated para. (l)(2) as (l)(3) and added new para. (l)(2)... Sec. 1002(l)(24)(B), substituted "certifications and other reports to secretary" for "certifications to secretary" in the heading of subsec. (l)... Sec. 1002(l)(25), added ", and except for any building described in paragraph (2)(B), subsection (h)(4) shall not apply to any building placed in service after 1989" before the period at the end of para. (n)(1)... Sec. 1002(l)(32), added para. (g)(6), effective for buildings placed in service after 12/31/86, in tax. yrs. end. after 12/31/86, except as provided in Secs. 252(e)(2) and (f) of P.L. 99-514 [as amended by this Act, reproduced below].

Prior to amendment, para. (b)(2) read as follows:

"(2) Buildings placed in service after 1987.

"(A) In general. In the case of any qualified low-income building placed in service by the taxpayer after 1987, the term 'applicable percentage' means the appropriate percentage prescribed by the Secretary for the month in which such building is placed in service.

"(B) Method of prescribing percentages. The percentages prescribed by the Secretary for any month shall be percentages which will yield over a 10-year period amounts of credit under subsection (a) which have a present value equal to—

"(i) 70 percent to the qualified basis of a building described in paragraph (1)(A), and

"(ii) 30 percent of the qualified basis of a building described in paragraph (1)(B).

"(C) Method of discounting. The present value under subparagraph (B) shall be determined—

"(i) as of the last day of the 1st year of the 10-year period referred to in subparagraph (B),

"(ii) by using a discount rate equal to 72 percent of the average of the annual Federal mid-term rate and the annual Federal long-term rate applicable under section 1274(d)(1) to the month in which the building was placed in service and compounded annually, and

"(iii) by assuming that the credit allowable under this section for any year is received on the last day of such year."

Prior to amendment, subpara. (c)(2)(A) read as follows:

"(A) which at all times during the compliance period with respect to such building is part of a qualified low-income housing project, and"

Prior to amendment, para. (f)(1) read as follows:

"(1) Credit period defined. For purposes of this section, the term 'credit period' means, with respect to any building, the period of 10 taxable years beginning with the taxable year in which the building is placed in service or, at the election of the taxpayer, the succeeding taxable year. Such an election, once made, shall be irrevocable."

Prior to amendment, clause (d)(2)(D)(ii) read as follows:

"(ii) Special rule for nontaxable exchanges. For purposes of determining under subparagraph (B)(ii) when a building was last placed in service, there shall be not taken into account any placement in service in connection with the acquisition of the building in a transaction in which the basis of the building in the hands of the person acquiring it is determined in whole or in part by reference to the adjusted basis of such building in the hands of the person from whom acquired."

Prior to amendment, para. (d)(3) read as follows:

"(3) Eligible basis reduced where disproportionate standards for units. The eligible basis of any building shall be reduced by an amount equal to the portion of the adjusted basis of the building which is attributable to residential rental units in the building which are not low-income units and which are above the average quality standard of the low-income units in the building."

Prior to deletion, clause (d)(6)(A)(iii) read as follows:

"(iii) to the extent provided in regulations, by reason of other circumstances of financial distress."

Prior to amendment, para. (f)(3) read as follows:

"(3) Special rule where increase in qualified basis after 1st year of credit period.

"(A) Credit increased. If—

"(i) as of the close of any taxable year in the compliance period (after the 1st year of the credit period) the qualified basis of any building exceeds

"(ii) the qualified basis of such building as of the close of the 1st year of the credit period,

the credit allowable under subsection (a) for the taxable year (determined without regard to this paragraph) shall be increased by an amount equal to the product of such excess and the percentage equal to ⅔ of the applicable percentage for such building.

"(B) 1st year computation applies. A rule similar to the rule of paragraph (2)(A) shall apply to the additional credit allowable by reason of this paragraph for the 1st year in which such additional credit is allowable."

Prior to amendment, para. (b)(3) read as follows:

"(3) Cross reference. For treatment of certain rehabilitation expenditures as separate new buildings, see subsection (e)."

Prior to amendment, para. (g)(3) read as follows:

"(3) Date for meeting requirements.

"(A) Projects consisting of 1 building. In the case of a project which does not have any other building in service, such project shall not be treated as meeting the requirements of paragraph (1) unless it meets such requirements not later than the date which is 12 months after the date such project is placed in service.

"(B) Projects consisting of more than 1 building. In the case of a project which has a building in service when a later building is placed in service as part of such project, such project shall not be treated as meeting the requirements of paragraph (1) with respect to such later building unless—

"(i) such project meets such requirements without regard to such later building on the date such later building is placed in service, and

"(ii) such project meets such requirements with regard to such later building not later than the date which is 12 months after the date such later building is placed in service."

Prior to amendment, para. (h)(1) read as follows:

"(1) Credit may not exceed credit amount allocated to building. No credit shall be allowed by reason of this section for any taxable year with respect to any building in excess of the housing credit dollar amount allocated to such building under this subsection. An allocation shall be taken into account under the preceding sentence only if it occurs not later than the earlier of—

"(A) the 60th day after the close of the taxable year, or

"(B) the close of the calendar year in which such taxable year ends."

Prior to deletion, clause (h)(6)(B)(ii) read as follows:

"(ii) Allocation may not be earlier than year in which building placed in service. A housing credit agency may allocate its housing credit dollar amount for any calendar year only to buildings placed in service before the close of such calendar year."

Prior to amendment, subpara. (h)(4)(A) read as follows:

"(A) In general. Paragraph (1) shall not apply to the portion of any credit allowable under subsection (a) which is attributable to eligible basis financed by any obligation the interest on which is exempt from tax under section 103 and which is taken into account under section 146."

Prior to amendment, subpara. (h)(6)(D) read as follows:

"(D) Credit allowable determined without regard to averaging convention, etc. For purposes of this subsection, the credit allowable under subsection (a) with respect to any building shall be determined—

"(i) without regard to paragraphs (2)(A) and (3)(B) of subsection (f), and

"(ii) by applying subsection (f)(3)(A) without regard to the 'percentage equal to ⅔ of'."

Prior to amendment, subpara. (i)(2)(B) read as follows:

"(B) Election to reduce eligible basis by outstanding balance of loan. A loan shall not be taken into account under subparagraph (A) if the taxpayer elects to exclude an amount equal to the outstanding balance of such loan from the eligible basis of the building for purposes of subsection (d)."

Prior to amendment, clause (j)(5)(B)(i) read as follows:

"(i) which has 35 or more partners each of whom is a natural person or an estate, and"

— P.L. 100-647, Sec. 1002(l)(28), amended Sec. 252(f) of P.L. 99-514 [reproduced below] part of the effective date for changes made by Sec. 252(a) of P.L. 99-514 by deleting "and" at the end of Sec. 252(f)(1)(A)(i) of P.L. 99-514, substituting a comma for the period at the end of Sec. 252(f)(1)(A)(ii) of P.L. 99-514, and adding Sec. 252(f)(1)(A)(iii) and (iv) of P.L. 99-514 [see below]... Sec. 1002(l)(29), amended Sec. 252(f)(1)(E) of P.L. 99-514 by substituting "maximum present value of additional credits" for "maximum annual additional credit" see below... Sec. 1002(l)(30), amended Sec. 252(f)(2)(E) of P.L. 99-514 by adding the last sentence, see below... Sec. 1002(l)(31), amended Sec. 252 of P.L. 99-514 by adding Sec. 252(f)(5) [reproduced below]

— P.L. 100-647, Sec. 1007(g)(3)(B), substituted "D, or G" for "or D" in subpara. (j)(4)(D), effective for tax. yrs. begin. after 12/31/86.

— P.L. 100-647, Sec. 4003(a), added subpara. (h)(1)(E)... Sec. 4003(b)(1), substituted "(C), (D), or (E)" for "(C) or (D)" in subpara. (h)(1)(B) (as amended by Sec. 1002(l)(14)(A) of this Act)... Sec. 4003(b)(3), amended subsec. (n), [as amended by Sec. 1002(l)(25) of this Act, see above], effective for amounts allocated in calendar years after 1987.

Prior to amendment, subsec. (n), [as amended by Sec. 1002(l)(25) of this Act, see above], read as follows:

"(n) Termination.

"(1) In general. Except as provided in paragraph (2), the State housing credit ceiling under subsection (h) shall be zero for any calendar year after 1989, and, except for any building described in paragraph (2)(B), subsection (h)(4) shall not apply to any building placed in service after 1989.

"(2) Carryover of 1989 limit for certain projects in progress.

"(A) In general. The aggregate housing credit amount of any agency for 1989 which is not allocated for 1989 shall be treated for purposes of applying this sec-

Tax credits Code Sec. 42

tion to any building described in subparagraph (B) as the housing credit amount of such agency for 1990.

"(B) Description. A building is described in this subparagraph if—

"(i) such building is constructed, reconstructed, or rehabilitated by the taxpayer,

"(ii) more than 10 percent of the reasonably anticipated cost of such construction, reconstruction, or rehabilitation has been incurred as of January 1, 1989, and

"(iii) such building is placed in service before January 1, 1991.

"(C) Certain rule not to apply. Subsection (h)(6)(B)(i) shall not apply for purposes of this paragraph."

—P.L. 100-647, Sec. 4004(a), amended subpara. (j)(5)(B), as amended by Sec. 1002(l)(21) of this Act, generally effective for buildings placed in service after 12/31/86, in tax. yrs. end. after 12/31/86, except as provided in Secs. 252(e)(2) and (f) of P.L. 99-514 [as amended by Sec. 1002 of this Act, reproduced below]. Sec. 4004(b)(2) provides the following:

"(2) Period for election. The period for electing not to have section 42(j)(5) of the 1986 Code apply to any partnership shall not expire before the date which is 6 months after the date of the enactment of this Act."

Prior to amendment, subpara. (j)(5)(B), as amended by Sec. 1002(l)(21) of this Act, read as follows:

"(B) Partnerships to which paragraph applies. This paragraph shall apply to any partnership—

"(i) more than ½ the capital interests, and more than ½ the profit interests, in which are owned by a group of 35 or more partners each of whom is a natural person or an estate, and

"(ii) which elects the application of this paragraph."

In 1986, P.L. 99-514, Sec. 252(a), added Code Sec. 42, effective for buildings placed in service after 12/31/86 in tax yrs. end. after 12/31/86, except as provided in Secs. 252(e)(2) and (f) of this Act [as amended by Sec. 1002 of P.L. 100-647, see above] which reads as follows:

"(2) Special rule for rehabilitation expenditures. Subsection (e) of section 42 of the Internal Revenue Code of 1986 (as added by this section) shall apply for purposes of paragraph (1).

"(f) Transitional rules.

"(1) Limitation to non-ACRS buildings not to apply to certain buildings, etc.

"(A) In general. In the case of a building which is part of a project described in subparagraph (B)—

"(i) section 42(c)(2)(B) of the Internal Revenue Code of 1986 (as added by this section) shall not apply,

"(ii) such building shall be treated as not federally subsidized for purposes of section 42(b)(1)(A) of such Code,

"(iii) the eligible basis of such building shall be treated, for purposes of section 42(h)(4)(A) of such Code, as if it were financed by an obligation the interest on which is exempt from tax under section 103 of such Code and which is taken into account under section 146 of such Code, and

"(iv) the amendments made by section 803 shall not apply.

"(B) Project described. A project is described in this subparagraph if—

"(i) an urban development action grant application with respect to such project was submitted on September 13, 1984,

"(ii) a zoning commission map amendment related to such project was granted on July 17, 1985, and

"(iii) the number assigned to such project by the Federal Housing Administration is 023-36602.

"(C) Additional units eligible for credit. In the case of a building to which subparagraph (A) applies and which is part of a project which meets the requirements of subparagraph (D), for each low-income unit in such building which is occupied by individuals whose income is 30 percent or less of area median gross income, one additional unit (not otherwise a low-income unit) in such building shall be treated as a low-income unit for purposes of such section 42.

"(D) Project described. A project is described in this subparagraph if—

"(i) rents charged for units in such project are restricted by State regulations,

"(ii) the annual cash flow of such project is restricted by State law,

"(iii) the project is located on land owned by or ground leased from a public housing authority,

"(iv) construction of such project begins on or before December 31, 1986, and units within such project are placed in service on or before June 1, 1990, and

"(v) for a 20-year period, 20 percent or more of the residential units in such project are occupied by individuals whose income is 50 percent or less of area median gross income.

"(E) Maximum additional credit. The maximum present value of additional credits allowable under section 42 of such Code by reason of subparagraph (C) shall not exceed 25 percent of the eligible basis of the building.

"(2) Additional allocation of housing credit ceiling.

"(A) In general. There is hereby allocated to each housing credit agency described in subparagraph (B) an additional housing credit dollar amount determined in accordance with the following table:

"For calendar year:	The additional allocation is:
"1987	$ 3,900,000
"1988	$ 7,600,000
"1989	$ 1,300,000

"(B) Housing credit agencies described. The housing credit agencies described in this subparagraph are:

"(i) A corporate governmental agency constituted as a public benefit corporation and established in 1971 under the provisions of Article XII of the Private Housing Finance Law of the State.

"(ii) A city department established on December 20, 1979, pursuant to chapter XVIII of a municipal code of such city for the purpose of supervising and coordinating the formation and execution of projects and programs affecting housing within such city.

"(iii) The State housing finance agency referred to in subparagraph (C), but only with respect to projects described in subparagraph (C).

"(C) Project described. A project is described in this subparagraph if such project is a qualified low-income housing project which—

"(i) receives financing from a State housing finance agency from the proceeds of bonds issued pursuant to chapter 708 of the Acts of 1966 of such State pursuant to loan commitments from such agency made between May 8, 1984, and July 8, 1986, and

"(ii) is subject to subsidy commitments issued pursuant to a program established under chapter 574 of the Acts of 1983 of such State having award dates from such agency between May 31, 1984, and June 11, 1985.

"(D) Special rules.

"(i) Any building—

(I) which is allocated any housing credit dollar amount by a housing credit agency described in clause (iii) of subparagraph (B), and

(II) which is placed in service after June 30, 1986, and before January 1, 1987, shall be treated for purposes of the amendments made by this section as placed in service on January 1, 1987.

"(ii) Section 42(c)(2)(B) of the Internal Revenue Code of 1986 shall not apply to any building which is allocated any housing credit dollar amount by any agency described in subparagraph (B).

"(E) All units treated as low income units in certain cases. In the case of any building—

"(i) which is allocated any housing credit dollar amount by any agency described in subparagraph (B), and

"(ii) which after the application of subparagraph (D)(ii) is a qualified low-income building at all times during any taxable year,

such building shall be treated as described in section 42(b)(1)(B) of such Code and having an applicable fraction for such year of 1. The preceding sentence shall apply to any building only to the extent of the portion of the additional housing credit dollar amount (allocated to such agency under subparagraph (A)) allocated to such building.

"(3) Certain projects placed in service before 1987.

"(A) In general. In the case of a building which is part of a project described in subparagraph (B)—

"(i) section 42(c)(2)(B) of such Code shall not apply,

"(ii) such building shall be treated as placed in service during the first calendar year after 1986 and before 1990 in which such building is a qualified low-income building (determined after the application of clause (i)), and

"(iii) for purposes of section 42(h) of such Code, such building shall be treated as having allocated to it a housing credit dollar amount equal to the dollar amount appearing in the clause of subparagraph (B) in which such building is described.

"(B) Project described. A project is described in this subparagraph if the code number assigned to such project by the Farmers' Home Administration appears in the following table:

"The code number is:	"The housing credit dollar amount is:
(i) 49284553664	$ 16,000
(ii) 4927742022446	$ 22,000
(iii) 49270742276087	$ 64,000
(iv) 490270742387293	$ 48,000
(v) 4927074218234	$ 32,000
(vi) 49270742274019	$ 36,000
(vii) 51460742345074	$53,000.

"(C) Determination of adjusted basis. The adjusted basis of any building to which this paragraph applies for purposes of section 42 of such Code shall be its adjusted basis as of the close of the taxable year ending before the first taxable year of the credit period for such building.

"(D) Certain rules to apply. Rules similar to the rules of subparagraph (E) of paragraph (2) shall apply for purposes of this paragraph.

"(4) Definitions. For purposes of this subsection, terms used in such subsection which are also used in section 42 of the Internal Revenue Code of 1986 (as added by this section) shall have the meanings given such terms by such section 42.

"(5) Transitional rule. In the case of any rehabilitation expenditures incurred with respect to units located in the neighborhood strategy area within the community development block grant program in Ft. Wayne, Indiana—

"(A) the amendments made by this section shall not apply, and

"(B) paragraph (1) of section 167(k) of the Internal Revenue Code of 1986, shall be applied as if it did not contain the phrase 'and before January 1, 1987'. The number of units to which the preceding sentence applies shall not exceed 150."

—P.L. 99-509, Sec. 8072(a), substituted "subparagraphs (D)(ii)(II) and (D)(iv)(I)" for "subparagraph (D)(iv)(I)" in para. (k)(1), effective for buildings placed in service after 12/31/86 in tax. yrs. end. after 12/31/86.

Prior to 1/1/79, Code Sec. 42 read as follows:

SEC. 42. GENERAL TAX CREDIT. [EFFECTIVE FOR TAX YEARS ENDING AFTER 12/3175 AND BEFORE 1/1/79]

"(a) Allowance of credit.

"In the case of an individual, there shall be allowed as a credit against the tax imposed by section 1, or against the tax imposed in lieu of the tax imposed by section 1, for the taxable year an amount equal to the greater of—

"(1) 2 percent of so much of the taxpayer's taxable income for the taxable year (reduced by the zero bracket amount) as does not exceed $9,000; or

"(2) $35 multiplied by each exemption for which the taxpayer is entitled to a deduction for the taxable year under section 151.

"(b) Application with other credits.

"The credit allowed by subsection (a) shall not exceed the amount of the tax imposed by section 1, or the amount of the tax imposed in lieu of the tax imposed by section 1, for the taxable year. In determining the credits allowed under—

"(1) section 33 (relating to foreign tax credit),

"(2) section 37 (relating to credit for the elderly credit [sic]),

"(3) section 38 (relating to investment in certain depreciable property),

"(4) section 40 (relating to expenses of work incentive programs), and

"(5) section 41 (relating to contributions to candidates for public office),

the tax imposed by this chapter shall (before any other reductions) be reduced by the credit allowed by this section.

"(c) Special rule for married individuals filing separate returns.

"(1) In general. In the case of a married individual who files a separate return for the taxable year, the amount of the credit allowable under subsection (a) for the taxable year shall be the amount determined under paragraph (2) of subsection (a).

"(2) Marital status. For purposes of this subsection, the determination of marital status shall be made under section 143.

"(d) Certain persons not eligible.

"This section shall not apply to any estate or trust, nor shall it apply to any nonresident alien individual.

"(e) Income tax tables to reflect credit.

"The tables prescribed by the Secretary under section 3 shall reflect the credit allowed by this section."

In 1977, P.L. 95-30, Sec. 101(c)(1), amended subsec. (a) . . . Sec. 101(c)(2), added subsec. (e) . . . Sec. 101(c)(3), amended subsec. (c) . . . Sec. 101(c)(4), substituted "by section 1, or the amount of the tax imposed in lieu of the tax imposed by section 1," for "by this chapter" in subsec. (b), effective for tax. yrs. begin. after 12/31/76.

Prior to amendment, subsec. (a) read as follows:

"(a) Allowance of credit.

"In the case of an individual, there shall be allowed as a credit against the tax imposed by this chapter for the taxable year an amount equal to the greater of—

"(1) 2 percent of so much of the taxpayer's taxable income for the taxable year as does not exceed $9,000; or

"(2) $35 multiplied by each exemption for which the taxpayer is entitled to a deduction for the taxable year under subsection (b) or (e) of section 151."

Prior to amendment, subsec. (c) read as follows:

"(c) Special rule for married individuals filing separate returns.

"(1) In general. Notwithstanding subsection (a), in the case of a married individual who files a separate return for the taxable year, the amount of the credit allowable under subsection (a) for the taxable year shall be equal to either—

"(A) the amount determined under paragraph (1) of subsection (a); or

"(B) if this subparagraph applies to the individual for the taxable year, the amount determined under paragraph (2) of subsection (a).

For purposes of the preceding sentence, paragraph (1) of subsection (a) shall be applied by substituting '$4,500' for '$9,000'.

"(2) Application of paragraph (1)(B). Subparagraph (B) of paragraph (1) shall apply to any taxpayer for any taxable year if—

"(A) such taxpayer elects to have such subparagraph apply for such taxable year, and

"(B) the spouse of such taxpayer elects to have such subparagraph apply for any taxable year corresponding, for purposes of section 142(a), to the taxable year of the taxpayer.

Any such election shall be made at such time, and in such manner, as the Secretary shall by regulations prescribe.

"(3) Marital status. For purposes of this subsection, the determination of marital status shall be made under section 143."

—P.L. 95-30, Sec. 103(a), amended Sec. 3(b) of P.L. 94-164 [as amended by Sec. 401(a)(1) of P.L. 94-455, see below], which provided the effective date for the amendment made by Sec. 3(a)(1) of P.L. 94-164. Prior to amendment, the effective date was for tax. yrs. end. after 12/31/75, and before 1/1/78.

In 1976, P.L. 94-455, Sec. 401(a)(1), amended Sec. 3(b) of P.L. 94-164 [see below], which provided the effective date for the amendment made by Sec. 3(a)(1) of P.L. 94-164. Prior to amendment, the effective date was for tax. yrs. end. after 12/31/77 and before 1/1/77.

—P.L. 94-455, Sec. 401(a)(2)(A), amended the heading of Code Sec. 42 and amended subsec. (a), effective tax. yrs. end. after 12/31/75 and before 1/1/78.

Prior to amendment the heading of Code Sec. 42 and subsec. (a) read as follows:

"SEC. 42. TAXABLE INCOME CREDIT.

"(a) Allowance of credit.

"(1) In general. In the case of an individual, there shall be allowed as a credit against the tax imposed by this chapter for the taxable year an amount equal to the greater of—

"(A) 2 percent of so much of the taxpayer's taxable income for the taxable year as does not exceed $9,000; or

"(B) $35 multiplied by each exemption for which the taxpayer is entitled to a deduction for the taxable year under subsection (b) or (e) of section 151.

"(2) Application of six-month rule. Notwithstanding the provisions of paragraph (1) of this subsection, the percentage '1 percent' shall be substituted for '2 percent' in subparagraph (A) of such paragraph, and the amount '$17.50' shall be substituted for the amount '$35' in subparagraph (B) of such paragraph."

—P.L. 94-455, Sec. 401(a)(2)(B), amended para. (c)(1), for tax. yrs. end. after 12/31/75.

Prior to amendment para. (c)(1) read as follows:

"(1) In general. Notwithstanding subsection (a), in the case of a married individual who files a separate return for the taxable year, the amount of the credit allowable under subsection (a) for the taxable year shall be equal to either—

"(A) the amount determined under paragraph (A) of subsection (a); or

"(B) if this subparagraph applies to the individual for the taxable year, the amount determined under paragraph (1)(B) of subsection (a).

For purposes of the preceding sentence, paragraph (1) of subsection (a) shall be applied by substituting '$4,500' for '$9,000'."

—P.L. 94-455, Sec. 503(b)(4), substituted "credit for the elderly" for "retirement income" in para. (b)(2), effective for tax. yrs. begin. after 12/31/75.

—P.L. 94-455, Sec. 1906(b)(13)(A), substituted "Secretary" for "Secretary or his delegate" in subsec. (c), effective for tax. yrs. begin. after 12/31/76.

In 1975, P.L. 94-164, Sec. 2(e), amended Sec. 209(a) of P.L. 94-12 [see below], which provided the effective date for the amendment made by Sec. 203(a) of P.L. 94-12. Prior to amendment, the effective date was for tax. yrs. end. after 12/31/74 and before 1/1/76.

—P.L. 94-164, Sec. 3(a)(1), amended Code Sec. 42, effective for tax. yrs. end. after 12/31/75 and before 1/1/79 [as amended by Sec. 103(a) of P.L. 95-30 and Sec. 401(a)(1) of P.L. 94-455, see above].

Prior to amendment, Code Sec. 42 read as follows:

"SEC. 42. CREDIT FOR PERSONAL EXEMPTIONS.

"(a) General rule. In the case of an individual, there shall be allowed as a credit against the tax imposed by this chapter for the taxable year $30, multiplied by each exemption for which the taxpayer is entitled for the taxable year under subsection (b) or (c) of section 151.

"(b) Application with other credits. The credit allowed by subsection (a) shall not exceed the amount of the tax imposed by this chapter for the taxable year. In determining the credits allowed under—

"(1) section 33 (relating to foreign tax credit),

"(2) section 37 (relating to retirement income),

"(3) section 38 (relating to investment in certain depreciable property),

"(4) section 40 (relating to expenses of work incentive programs), and

"(5) section 41 (relating to contributions to candidates for public office),

the tax imposed by this chapter shall (before any other reductions) be reduced by the credit allowed by this section."

—P.L. 94-12, Sec. 203(a), redesignated Code Sec. 42 as Code Sec. 43 and added new Code Sec. 42, effective for tax. yrs. end. after 12/31/74 and before 1/1/77 [as amended by Sec. 2(e) of P.L. 94-164, see above].

Sec. 43. Enhanced oil recovery credit.

(a) General rule.

For purposes of section 38, the enhanced oil recovery credit for any taxable year is an amount equal to 15 percent of the taxpayer's qualified enhanced oil recovery costs for such taxable year.

(b) Phase-out of credit as crude oil prices increase.

(1) In general. The amount of the credit determined under subsection (a) for any taxable year shall be reduced by an amount which bears the same ratio to the amount of such credit (determined without regard to this paragraph) as—

(A) the amount by which the reference price for the calendar year preceding the calendar year in which the taxable year begins exceeds $28, bears to

(B) $6.

(2) Reference price. For purposes of this subsection, the term "reference price" means, with respect to any calendar year, the reference price determined for such calendar year under section 45K(d)(2)(C).

(3) Inflation adjustment.

(A) In general. In the case of any taxable year beginning in a calendar year after 1991, there shall be substituted for the $28 amount under paragraph (1)(A) an amount equal to the product of—

(i) $28, multiplied by

(ii) the inflation adjustment factor for such calendar year.

(B) Inflation adjustment factor. The term "inflation adjustment factor" means, with respect to any calendar year, a fraction the numerator of which is the GNP implicit price deflator for the preceding calendar year and the denominator of which is the GNP implicit price deflator for 1990. For purposes of the preceding sentence, the term "GNP implicit price deflator" means the first revision of the GNP implicit price deflator for the gross national product as computed and published by the Secretary of Commerce. Not later than April 1 of any calendar year, the Secretary shall publish the inflation adjustment factor for the preceding calendar year.

(c) Qualified enhanced oil recovery costs.

For purposes of this section—

(1) In general. The term "qualified enhanced oil recovery costs" means any of the following:

(A) Any amount paid or incurred during the taxable year for tangible property—

(i) which is an integral part of a qualified enhanced oil recovery project, and

(ii) with respect to which depreciation (or amortization in lieu of depreciation) is allowable under this chapter.

(B) Any intangible drilling and development costs—

(i) which are paid or incurred in connection with a qualified enhanced oil recovery project, and

(ii) with respect to which the taxpayer may make an election under section 263(c) for the taxable year.

(C) Any qualified tertiary injectant expenses (as defined in section 193(b)) which are paid or incurred in connection with a qualified enhanced oil recovery project and for which a deduction is allowable for the taxable year.

(D) Any amount which is paid or incurred during the taxable year to construct a gas treatment plant which—

(i) is located in the area of the United States (within the meaning of section 638(1)) lying north of 64 degrees North latitude,

(ii) prepares Alaska natural gas for transportation through a pipeline with a capacity of at least 2,000,000,000,000 Btu of natural gas per day, and

(iii) produces carbon dioxide which is injected into hydrocarbon-bearing geological formations.

(2) Qualified enhanced oil recovery project. For purposes of this subsection—

(A) In general. The term "qualified enhanced oil recovery project" means any project—

(i) which involves the application (in accordance with sound engineering principles) of 1 or more tertiary recovery methods (as defined in section 193(b)(3)) which can reasonably be expected to result in more than an insignificant increase in the amount of crude oil which will ultimately be recovered,

(ii) which is located within the United States (within the meaning of section 638(1)), and

(iii) with respect to which the first injection of liquids, gases, or other matter commences after December 31, 1990.

(B) Certification. A project shall not be treated as a qualified enhanced oil recovery project unless the operator submits to the Secretary (at such times and in such manner as the Secretary provides) a certification from a petroleum engineer that the project meets (and continues to meet) the requirements of subparagraph (A).

(3) At-risk limitation. For purposes of determining qualified enhanced oil recovery costs, rules similar to the rules of section 49(a)(1), section 49(a)(2), and section 49(b) shall apply.

(4) Special rule for certain gas displacement projects. For purposes of this section, immiscible non-hydrocarbon gas displacement shall be treated as a tertiary recovery method under section 193(b)(3).

(5) Alaska natural gas. For purposes of paragraph (1)(D)—

(A) In general. The term "Alaska natural gas" means natural gas entering the Alaska natural gas pipeline (as defined in section 168(i)(16) (determined without regard to subparagraph (B) thereof)) which is produced from a well—

(i) located in the area of the State of Alaska lying north of 64 degrees North latitude, determined by excluding the area of the Alaska National Wildlife Refuge (including the continental shelf thereof within the meaning of section 638(1)), and

(ii) pursuant to the applicable State and Federal pollution prevention, control, and permit requirements from such area (including the continental shelf thereof within the meaning of section 638(1)).

(B) Natural gas. The term "natural gas" has the meaning given such term by section 613A(e)(2).

(d) Other rules.

(1) Disallowance of deduction. Any deduction allowable under this chapter for any costs taken into account in computing the amount of the credit determined under subsection (a) shall be reduced by the amount of such credit attributable to such costs.

(2) Basis adjustments. For purposes of this subtitle, if a credit is determined under this section for any expenditure with respect to any property, the increase in the basis of such property which would (but for this subsection) result from such expenditure shall be reduced by the amount of the credit so allowed.

(e) Election to have credit not apply.

(1) In general. A taxpayer may elect to have this section not apply for any taxable year.

(2) Time for making election. An election under paragraph (1) for any taxable year may be made (or revoked) at any time before the expiration of the 3-year period beginning on the last date prescribed by law for filing the return for such taxable year (determined without regard to extensions).

(3) Manner of making election. An election under paragraph (1) (or revocation thereof) shall be made in such manner as the Secretary may by regulations prescribe.

In 2005, P.L. 109-135, Sec. 412(i), amended para. (c)(5), effective 12/21/2005. Prior to amendment, para. (c)(5) read as follows:

"(5) Alaska natural gas. For purposes of paragraph (1)(D)—

"(1) In general. The term 'Alaska natural gas' means natural gas entering the Alaska natural gas pipeline (as defined in section 168(i)(16) (determined without regard to subparagraph (B) therof) which is produced from a well—

"(A) located in the area of the State of Alaska lying north of 64 degrees North latitude, determined by excluding the area of the Alaska National Wildlife Refuge (including the continental shelf thereof within the meaning of section 638(1)), and

"(B) pursuant to the applicable State and Federal pollution prevention, control, and permit requirements from such area (including the continental shelf thereof within the meaning of section 638(1)).

"(2) Natural gas. The term 'natural gas' has the meaning given such term by section 613A(e)(2)."

—P.L. 109-58, Sec. 1322(a)(3)(B), substituted "section 45K(d)(2)(C)" for "section 29(d)(2)(C)" in para. (b)(2), effective for credits determined under the Internal Revenue Code of 1986 for tax. yrs. end. after 12/31/2005.

In 2004, P.L. 108-357, Sec. 707(a), added subpara. (c)(1)(D) . . . Sec. 707(b), added para. (c)(5), effective for costs paid or incurred in tax. yrs. begin. after 12/31/2004.

In 2000, P.L. 106-554, Sec. 1(a)(7), [which enacted into law by Sec. 317(a)(1) of P.L. 106-554] added "(as defined in section 193(b))" after "injectant expenses" in subpara. (c)(1)(C) . . . Sec. 1(a)(7) , [which enacted into law by Sec. 317(a)(2) of P.L. 106-554] deleted "under section 193" after "allowable under" in subpara. (c)(1)(C), effective for costs paid or incurred in tax. yrs. begin. after 12/31/90.

In 1990, P.L. 101-508, Sec. 11511(a), added Code Sec. 43, effective for costs paid or incurred in tax. yrs. begin. after 12/31/90 except as provided in Sec. 11511(d)(2) of this Act, which reads as follows:

"(2) Special rule for significant expansion of projects.—For purposes of section 43(c)(2)(A)(iii) of the Internal Revenue Code of 1986 (as added by subsection (a)[sec. 11511(a)]), any significant expansion after December 31, 1990, of a project begun before January 1, 1991, shall be treated as a project with respect to which the first injection commences after December 31, 1990."

Sec. 44. Expenditures to provide access to disabled individuals.

(a) General rule.

For purposes of section 38, in the case of an eligible small business, the amount of the disabled access credit determined under this section for any taxable year shall be an amount equal to 50 percent of so much of the eligible access expenditures for the taxable year as exceed $250 but do not exceed $10,250.

(b) Eligible small business.

For purposes of this section, the term "eligible small business" means any person if—

(1) either—

(A) the gross receipts of such person for the preceding taxable year did not exceed $1,000,000, or

(B) in the case of a person to which subparagraph (A) does not apply, such person employed not more than 30 full-time employees during the preceding taxable year, and

(2) such person elects the application of this section for the taxable year.

For purposes of paragraph (1)(B), an employee shall be considered full-time if such employee is employed at least 30 hours per week for 20 or more calendar weeks in the taxable year.

(c) Eligible access expenditures.

For purposes of this section—

(1) **In general.** The term "eligible access expenditures" means amounts paid or incurred by an eligible small business for the purpose of enabling such eligible small business to comply with applicable requirements under the Americans With Disabilities Act of 1990 (as in effect on the date of the enactment of this section).

(2) **Certain expenditures included.** The term "eligible access expenditures" includes amounts paid or incurred—

(A) for the purpose of removing architectural, communication, physical, or transportation barriers which prevent a business from being accessible to, or usable by, individuals with disabilities,

(B) to provide qualified interpreters or other effective methods of making aurally delivered materials available to individuals with hearing impairments,

(C) to provide qualified readers, taped texts, and other effective methods of making visually delivered materials available to individuals with visual impairments,

(D) to acquire or modify equipment or devices for individuals with disabilities, or

(E) to provide other similar services, modifications, materials, or equipment.

(3) **Expenditures must be reasonable.** Amounts paid or incurred for the purposes described in paragraph (2) shall include only expenditures which are reasonable and shall not include expenditures which are unnecessary to accomplish such purposes.

(4) **Expenses in connection with new construction are not eligible.** The term "eligible access expenditures" shall not include amounts described in paragraph (2)(A) which are paid or incurred in connection with any facility first placed in service after the date of the enactment of this section.

(5) **Expenditures must meet standards.** The term "eligible access expenditures" shall not include any amount unless the taxpayer establishes, to the satisfaction of the Secretary, that the resulting removal of any barrier (or the provision of any services, modifications, materials, or equipment) meets the standards promulgated by the Secretary with the concurrence of the Architectural and Transportation Barriers Compliance Board and set forth in regulations prescribed by the Secretary.

(d) Definition of disability; special rules.

For purposes of this section—

(1) **Disability.** The term "disability" has the same meaning as when used in the Americans With Disabilities Act of 1990 (as in effect on the date of the enactment of this section).

(2) **Controlled groups.**

(A) In general. All members of the same controlled group of corporations (within the meaning of section 52(a)) and all persons under common control (within the meaning of section 52(b)) shall be treated as 1 person for purposes of this section.

(B) Dollar limitation. The Secretary shall apportion the dollar limitation under subsection (a) among the members of any group described in subparagraph (A) in such manner as the Secretary shall by regulations prescribe.

(3) **Partnerships and S corporations.** In the case of a partnership, the limitation under subsection (a) shall apply with respect to the partnership and each partner. A similar rule shall apply in the case of an S corporation and its shareholders.

(4) **Short years.** The Secretary shall prescribe such adjustments as may be appropriate for purposes of paragraph (1) of subsection (b) if the preceding taxable year is a taxable year of less than 12 months.

(5) **Gross receipts.** Gross receipts for any taxable year shall be reduced by returns and allowances made during such year.

(6) **Treatment of predecessors.** The reference to any person in paragraph (1) of subsection (b) shall be treated as including a reference to any predecessor.

(7) **Denial of double benefit.** In the case of the amount of the credit determined under this section—

(A) no deduction or credit shall be allowed for such amount under any other provision of this chapter, and

(B) no increase in the adjusted basis of any property shall result from such amount.

(e) Regulations.

The Secretary shall prescribe regulations necessary to carry out the purposes of this section.

In **1990**, P.L. 101-508, Sec. 11611(a), added Code Sec. 44, effective for expenditures paid or incurred after 11/5/90.

Sec. 44. Repealed.

In **1984**, P.L. 98-369, Sec. 474(m)(1), repealed Code Sec. 44, effective for tax. yrs. begin. after 12/31/83 and for carrybacks from tax. yrs. begin. after 12/31/83. Prior to repeal, Code Sec. 44 read as follows:

"Sec. 44. Purchase of new principal residence.

"(a) General rule. In the case of an individual there is allowed, as a credit against the tax imposed by this chapter for the taxable year, an amount equal to 5 percent of the purchase price of a new principal residence purchased or constructed by the taxpayer.

"(b) Limitations.

"(1) Maximum credit. The credit allowed under subsection (a) may not exceed $2,000.

"(2) Limitation to one residence. The credit under this section shall be allowed with respect to only one residence of the taxpayer.

"(3) Married individuals. In the case of a husband and wife who file a joint return under section 6013, the amount specified under paragraph (1) shall apply to the joint return. In the case of a married individual filing a separate return, paragraph (1) shall be applied by substituting '$1,000' for '$2,000.'

Tax credits Code Sec. 44B

"(4) Certain other taxpayers. In the case of individuals to whom paragraph (3) does not apply who together purchase the same new principal residence for use as their principal residence, the amount of the credit allowed under subsection (a) shall be allocated among such individuals as prescribed by the Secretary, but the sum of the amounts allowed to such individuals shall not exceed $2,000 with respect to that residence.

"(5) Application with other credits. The credit allowed by subsection (a) shall not exceed the amount of the tax imposed by this chapter for the taxable year, reduced by the sum of the credits allowable under sections 33, 37, 38, 40, 41, and 42.

"(c) Definitions. For purposes of this section—

"(1) New principal residence. The term 'new principal residence' means a principal residence (within the meaning of section 1034), the original use of which commences with the taxpayer, and includes, without being limited to, a single family structure, a residential unit in a condominium or cooperative housing project, and a mobile home.

"(2) Purchase price. The term 'purchase price' means the adjusted basis of the new principal residence on the date of the acquisition thereof.

"(3) Purchase. The term 'purchase' means any acquisition of property, but only if—

"(A) the property is not acquired from a person whose relationship to the person acquiring it would result in the disallowance of losses under section 267 or 707(b) (but, in applying section 267(b) and (c) for purposes of this section, paragraph (4) of section 267(c) shall be treated as providing that the family of an individual shall include only his spouse, ancestors, and lineal descendants), and

"(B) the basis of the property in the hands of the person acquiring it is not determined—

"(i) in whole or in part by reference to the adjusted basis of such property in the hands of the person from whom acquired, or

"(ii) under section 1014(a) (relating to property acquired from a decedent).

"(d) Recapture for certain dispositions.

"(1) In general. Except as provided in paragraphs (2) and (3), if the taxpayer disposes of property with respect to the purchase of which a credit was allowed under subsection (a) at any time within 36 months after the date on which he acquired it (or, in the case of construction by the taxpayer, on the day on which he first occupied it) as his principal residence, then the tax imposed under this chapter for the taxable year in which terminates the replacement period under paragraph (2) with respect to the disposition is increased by an amount equal to the amount allowed as a credit for the purchase of such property.

"(2) Acquisition of new residence. If, in connection with a disposition described in paragraph (1) and within the applicable period prescribed in section 1034, the taxpayer purchases or constructs a new principal residence, then the provisions of paragraph (1) shall not apply and the tax imposed by this chapter for the taxable year following the taxable year during which disposition occurs is increased by an amount which bears the same ratio to the amount allowed as a credit for the purchase of the old residence as (A) the adjusted sales price of the old residence (within the meaning of section 1034), reduced (but not below zero) by the taxpayer's cost of purchasing the new residence (within the meaning of such section) bears to (B) the adjusted sales price of the old residence.

"(3) Death of owner; casualty loss; involuntary conversion; etc. The provisions of paragraph (1) do not apply to—

"(A) a disposition of a residence made on account of the death of any individual having a legal or equitable interest therein occurring during the 36 month period to which reference is made under such paragraph,

"(B) a disposition of the old residence if it is substantially or completely destroyed by a casualty described in section 165(c)(3) or compulsorily and involuntarily converted (within the meaning of section 1033(a)), or

"(C) a disposition pursuant to a settlement in a divorce or legal separation proceeding where the other spouse retains the residence as principal residence.

"(e) Property to which section applies.

"(1) In general. The provisions of this section apply to a new principal residence—

"(A) the construction of which began before March 26, 1975,

"(B) which is acquired and occupied by the taxpayer after March 12, 1975, and before January 1, 1977, and

"(C) if not constructed by the taxpayer, which was acquired by the taxpayer under a binding contract entered into by the taxpayer before January 1, 1976.

"(2) Self-constructed property begun before March 13, 1975. In the case of property the construction of which was begun by the taxpayer before March 13, 1975, only that portion of the basis of such property properly allocable to construction after March 12, 1975, shall be taken into account in determining the amount of the credit allowable under subsection (a).

"(3) Binding contract. For purposes of this subsection, a contract for the purchase of a residence which is conditioned upon the purchaser's obtaining a loan for the purchase of the residence (including conditions as to the amount or interest rate of such loan) is not considered non-binding on account of that condition.

"(4) Certification must be attached to return. This section does not apply to any residence (other than a residence constructed by the taxpayer) unless there is attached to the return of tax on which the credit is claimed a written certification (which may be in any form) signed by the seller of such residence that—

"(A) construction of the residence began before March 26, 1975, and

"(B) the purchase price of the residence is the lowest price at which the residence was offered for sale after February 28, 1975.

For purposes of this paragraph, a written certification filed by a taxpayer is sufficient whether or not it is on a form prescribed by the Secretary so long as such certification is signed by the seller and contains the information required under this paragraph."

In **1976**, P.L. 94-455, Sec. 1906(b)(13)(A), substituted "Secretary" for "Secretary or his delegate" in paras. (b)(4) and (e)(4), effective for tax. yrs. begin. after 12/31/76

In **1975**, P.L. 94-45, Sec. 401(a), amended para. (e)(4), effective 6/30/75.

Prior to amendment, para. (e)(4) read as follows:

"(4) Certification must be attached to return. This section shall not apply to any residence (other than a residence constructed by the taxpayer) unless there is attached to the return of tax on which the credit is claimed a certification by the seller, in accordance with regulations prescribed by the Secretary or his delegate, that the purchase price is the lowest price at which the residence was ever offered for sale."

—P.L. 94-12, Sec. 208(a), added Code Sec. 44 effective 3/29/75. Sec. 208(b) and (c) of this Act provides:

"(b) Suits to recover amounts of price increases. If—

"(1) any person certifies under section 44(e) (4) of the Internal Revenue Code of 1954 that the price for which a residence was sold is the lowest price at which the residence was ever offered for sale, and

"(2) the price for which the residence was sold exceeded the lowest price at which the residence was ever offered for sale,

such person shall be liable to the purchaser of such residence in an amount equal to three times the amount of such excess. The United States district courts shall have jurisdiction of suits to recover such amounts without regard to any other provision of law. In any suit brought under this subsection in which judgment is entered for the purchaser, he shall also be entitled to recover a reasonable attorney's fee.

"(c) Denial of deduction. Notwithstanding the provisions of section 162 or 212 of the Internal Revenue Code of 1954, no deduction shall be allowed in computing taxable income for two-thirds of any amount paid or incurred on a judgment entered against any person in a suit brought under subsection (b)."

Sec. 44B. Repealed.

In **1984**, P.L. 98-369, Sec. 474(m)(1), repealed Code Sec. 44B, effective for tax. yrs. begin. after 12/31/83 and for carrybacks from tax. yrs. begin. after 12/31/83. Prior to repeal, Code Sec. 44B read as follows:

"SEC. 44B. CREDIT FOR EMPLOYMENT OF CERTAIN NEW EMPLOYEES.

"(a) General rule. At the election of the taxpayer, there shall be allowed as a credit against the tax imposed by this chapter the amount determined under subpart D of this part.

"(b) Regulations. The Secretary shall prescribe such regulations as may be necessary to carry out the purposes of this section and subpart D.

"(c) Election.

"(1) Time for making election. An election under subsection (a) for any taxable year may be made (or revoked) at any time before the expiration of the 3-year period beginning on the last date prescribed by law for filing the return for such taxable year (determined without regard to extensions).

"(2) Manner of making election. Any election under subsection (a) (or revocation thereof) shall be made in such manner as the Secretary may by regulations prescribe."

In **1980**, P.L. 96-222, Sec. 103(a)(6)(B), added para. (d)(5) to Sec. 321 of P.L. 95-600, the effective date for changes made by Sec. 321 of P.L. 95-600 [see below] . . . Sec. 103(a)(6)(C), added ", for purposes of applying the amendments made by this section" after "newly targeted group" in Sec. 321(d)(2)(A) of P.L. 95-600 [reproduced below] . . . Sec. 103(a)(6)(D), amended Sec. 321(d)(3) of P.L. 95-600 [reproduced below] . . . Sec. 103(a)(6)(G)(i), substituted "of the taxpayer" for "at the taxpayer" in subsec. (a) . . . Sec. 103(a)(6)(G)(ii), substituted "may by" for "may be" in para. (c)(2) . . . Sec. 103(a)(6)(G)(xi), amended Sec. 321(d)(2)(B)(i) & (ii) of P.L. 95-600 [reproduced below] effective for amounts paid or incurred after 12/31/78 in tax. yrs. end. after 12/31/78.

Prior to amendment, Sec. 321(d)(3) of P.L. 95-600 read as follows:

"(3) Transitional rule. In the case of a taxable year which begins in 1978 and ends after December 31, 1978, the amount of the credit allowable by section 44B of the Internal Revenue Code of 1954 (determined without regard to section 53 of such Code) shall be the sum of—

"(A) the amount of the credit which would be so allowable without regard to the amendments made by this section, plus

"(B) the amount which would be so allowable by reason of the amendments made by this section."

Prior to amendment, Sec. 321(d)(2)(B)(i) & (ii) of P.L. 95-600 read as follows:

"(i) such individual meets the requirements of subparagraph (A), (C), (D), (E), (F), or (G) of section 51(d)(1) of such Code, and

"(ii) in the case of an individual meeting the requirements of subparagraph (A) of such section 51(d)(1), a credit was not claimed for such individual by the taxpayer for a taxable year beginning before January 1, 1979."

In **1978**, P.L. 95-600, Sec. 321(b)(1)(A), substituted "at the election at the taxpayer, there shall be allowed" for "There shall be allowed" in subsec. (a) . . . Sec. 321(b)(1)(B), added subsec. (c), effective [as amended by Sec. 103(a)(6)(B) of P.L. 96-222, see above]. for tax. yrs. begin. after 12/31/76. Sec. 321(d)(2) and (d)(3) of this Act [as amended by Sec. 103(a) of P.L. 96-22, see above] provides:

"(2) Special rules for newly targeted groups.

"(A) Individual must be hired after September 26, 1978. In the case of a member of a newly targeted group, for purposes of applying the amendments made by this section—

"(i) such individual shall be taken into account for purposes of the credit allowable by section 44B of the Internal Revenue Code of 1954 only if such individual is first hired by the employer after September 26, 1978, and

1,153

"(ii) such individual shall be treated for the purposes of such credit as having first begun work for the employer not earlier than January 1, 1979.

"(B) Member of newly targeted group defined. For purposes of subparagraph (A), an individual is a member of a newly targeted group if—

"(i) such individual meets the requirements of paragraph (1) of section 51(d) of such Code, and

"(ii) in the case of an individual meeting the requirements of subparagraph (A) of such paragraph (1), a credit was not claimed for such individual by the taxpayer for a taxable year beginning before January 1, 1979."

"(3) Transitional rule. In the case of a taxable year which begins in 1978 and ends after December 31, 1978, the amount of the credit determined under section 51 of the Internal Revenue Code of 1954 shall be the sum of—

"(A) the amount of the credit which would be so determined without regard to the amendments made by this section, plus

"(B) the amount of the credit which would be so determined by reason of the amendments made by this section."

In 1977, P.L. 95-30, Sec. 202(a), added Code Sec. 44B, effective for tax. yrs. begin. after 12/31/76 and to credit carrybacks from 12/31/76.

Sec. 45. Electricity produced from certain renewable resources, etc.

(a) General rule.

For purposes of section 38, the renewable electricity production credit for any taxable year is an amount equal to the product of—

(1) 1.5 cents, multiplied by

(2) the kilowatt hours of electricity—

(A) produced by the taxpayer—

(i) from qualified energy resources, and

(ii) at a qualified facility during the 10-year period beginning on the date the facility was originally placed in service, and

(B) sold by the taxpayer to an unrelated person during the taxable year.

(b) Limitations and adjustments.

(1) Phaseout of credit. The amount of the credit determined under subsection (a) shall be reduced by an amount which bears the same ratio to the amount of the credit (determined without regard to this paragraph) as—

(A) the amount by which the reference price for the calendar year in which the sale occurs exceeds 8 cents, bears to

(B) 3 cents.

(2) Credit and phaseout adjustment based on inflation. The 1.5 cent amount in subsection (a), the 8 cent amount in paragraph (1), the $4.375 amount in subsection (e)(8)(A), the $3 amount in subsection (e)(8)(D)(ii)(I), and in subsection (e)(8)(B)(i) the reference price of fuel used as a feedstock (within the meaning of section (c)(7)(A)) in 2002 shall each be adjusted by multiplying such amount by the inflation adjustment factor for the calendar year in which the sale occurs. If any amount as increased under the preceding sentence is not a multiple of 0.1 cent, such amount shall be rounded to the nearest multiple of 0.1 cent.

(3) Credit reduced for grants, tax-exempt bonds, subsidized energy financing, and other credits. The amount of the credit determined under subsection (a) with respect to any project for any taxable year (determined after the application of paragraphs (1) and (2)) shall be reduced by the amount which is the product of the amount so determined for such year and the lesser of 1/2 or a fraction—

(A) the numerator of which is the sum, for the taxable year and all prior taxable years, of—

(i) grants provided by the United States, a State, or a political subdivision of a State for use in connection with the project,

(ii) proceeds of an issue of State or local government obligations used to provide financing for the project the interest on which is exempt from tax under section 103,

(iii) the aggregate amount of subsidized energy financing provided (directly or indirectly) under a Federal, State, or local program provided in connection with the project, and

(iv) the amount of any other credit allowable with respect to any property which is part of the project, and

(B) the denominator of which is the aggregate amount of additions to the capital account for the project for the taxable year and all prior taxable years.

The amounts under the preceding sentence for any taxable year shall be determined as of the close of the taxable year. This paragraph shall not apply with respect to any facility described in subsection (d)(2)(A)(ii).

(4) Credit rate and period for electricity produced and sold from certain facilities.

(A) Credit rate. In the case of electricity produced and sold in any calendar year after 2003 at any qualified facility described in paragraph (3), (5), (6), (7), (9), or (11) of subsection (d), the amount in effect under subsection (a)(1) for such calendar year (determined before the application of the last sentence of paragraph (2) of this subsection) shall be reduced by one-half.

(B) Credit period.

(i) In general. Except as provided in clause (ii) or clause (iii), in the case of any facility described in paragraph (3), (4), (5), (6), or (7) of subsection (d), the 5-year period beginning on the date the facility was originally placed in service shall be substituted for the 10-year period in subsection (a)(2)(A)(ii).

(ii) Certain open-loop biomass facilities. In the case of any facility described in subsection (d)(3)(A)(ii) placed in service before the date of the enactment of this paragraph, the 5-year period beginning on January 1, 2005, shall be substituted for the 10-year period in subsection (a)(2)(A)(ii).

(iii) Termination. Clause (i) shall not apply to any facility placed in service after the date of the enactment of this clause.

(c) Resources.

For purposes of this section—

(1) In general. The term "qualified energy resources" means—

(A) wind,

(B) closed-loop biomass,

(C) open-loop biomass,

(D) geothermal energy,

(E) solar energy,

(F) small irrigation power,

(G) municipal solid waste,

(H) qualified hydropower production, and

(I) marine and hydrokinetic renewable energy.

(2) Closed-loop biomass. The term "closed-loop biomass" means any organic material from a plant which is planted exclusively for purposes of being used at a qualified facility to produce electricity.

(3) Open-loop biomass.

(A) In general. The term "open-loop biomass" means—

(i) any agricultural livestock waste nutrients, or

(ii) any solid, nonhazardous, cellulosic waste material or any lignin material which is derived from—

(I) any of the following forest-related resources: mill and harvesting residues, precommercial thinnings, slash, and brush,

(II) solid wood waste materials, including waste pallets, crates, dunnage, manufacturing and construction wood wastes (other than pressure-treated, chemically-treated, or painted wood wastes), and landscape or right-of-way tree trimmings, but not including municipal solid waste, gas derived from the biodegradation of solid waste, or paper which is commonly recycled, or

(III) agriculture sources, including orchard tree crops, vineyard, grain, legumes, sugar, and other crop by-products or residues.

Such term shall not include closed-loop biomass or biomass burned in conjunction with fossil fuel (cofiring) beyond such fossil fuel required for startup and flame stabilization.

(B) Agricultural livestock waste nutrients.

(i) In general. The term "agricultural livestock waste nutrients" means agricultural livestock manure and litter, including wood shavings, straw, rice hulls, and other bedding material for the disposition of manure.

(ii) Agricultural livestock. The term "agricultural livestock" includes bovine, swine, poultry, and sheep.

(4) **Geothermal energy.** The term "geothermal energy" means energy derived from a geothermal deposit (within the meaning of section 613(e)(2)).

(5) **Small irrigation power.** The term "small irrigation power" means power—

(A) generated without any dam or impoundment of water through an irrigation system canal or ditch, and

(B) the nameplate capacity rating of which is not less than 150 kilowatts but is less than 5 megawatts.

(6) **Municipal solid waste.** The term "municipal solid waste" has the meaning given the term "solid waste" under section 2(27) of the Solid Waste Disposal Act (42 U.S.C. 6903).

(7) **Refined coal.**

(A) In general. The term "refined coal" means a fuel—
(i) which—

(I) is a liquid, gaseous, or solid fuel produced from coal (including lignite) or high carbon fly ash, including such fuel used as a feedstock,

(II) is sold by the taxpayer with the reasonable expectation that it will be used for purpose of producing steam, and

(III) is certified by the taxpayer as resulting (when used in the production of steam) in a qualified emission reduction.

(IV) Repealed

(ii) which is steel industry fuel.

(B) Qualified emission reduction. The term "qualified emission reduction" means a reduction of at least 20 percent of the emissions of nitrogen oxide and at least 40 percent of the emissions of either sulfur dioxide or mercury released when burning the refined coal (excluding any dilution caused by materials combined or added during the production process), as compared to the emissions released when burning the feedstock coal or comparable coal predominantly available in the marketplace as of January 1, 2003.

(C) Steel industry fuel.

(i) In general. The term "steel industry fuel" means a fuel which—

(I) is produced through a process of liquefying coal waste sludge and distributing it on coal, and

(II) is used as a feedstock for the manufacture of coke.

(ii) Coal waste sludge. The term "coal waste sludge" means the tar decanter sludge and related byproducts of the coking process, including such materials that have been stored in ground, in tanks and in lagoons, that have been treated as hazardous wastes under applicable Federal environmental rules absent liquefaction and processing with coal into a feedstock for the manufacture of coke.

(8) **Qualified hydropower production.**

(A) In general. The term "qualified hydropower production" means—

(i) in the case of any hydroelectric dam which was placed in service on or before the date of the enactment of this paragraph, the incremental hydropower production for the taxable year, and

(ii) in the case of any nonhydroelectric dam described in subparagraph (C), the hydropower production from the facility for the taxable year.

(B) Determination of incremental hydropower production.

(i) In general. For purposes of subparagraph (A), incremental hydropower production for any taxable year shall be equal to the percentage of average annual hydropower production at the facility attributable to the efficiency improvements or additions of capacity placed in service after the date of the enactment of this paragraph, determined by using the same water flow information used to determine an historic average annual hydropower production baseline for such facility. Such percentage and baseline shall be certified by the Federal Energy Regulatory Commission.

(ii) Operational changes disregarded. For purposes of clause (i), the determination of incremental hydropower production shall not be based on any operational changes at such facility not directly associated with the efficiency improvements or additions of capacity.

(C) Nonhydroelectric dam. For purposes of subparagraph (A), a facility is described in this subparagraph if—

(i) the hydroelectric project installed on the nonhydroelectric dam is licensed by the Federal Energy Regulatory Commission and meets all other applicable environmental, licensing, and regulatory requirements,

(ii) the nonhydroelectric dam was placed in service before the date of the enactment of this paragraph and operated for flood control, navigation, or water supply purposes and did not produce hydroelectric power on the date of the enactment of this paragraph, and

(iii) the hydroelectric project is operated so that the water surface elevation at any given location and time that would have occurred in the absence of the hydroelectric project is maintained, subject to any license requirements imposed under applicable law that change the water surface elevation for the purpose of improving environmental quality of the affected waterway.

The Secretary, in consultation with the Federal Energy Regulatory Commission, shall certify if a hydroelectric project licensed at a nonhydroelectric dam meets the criteria in clause (iii). Nothing in this section shall affect the standards under which the Federal Energy Regulatory Commission issues licenses for and regulates hydropower projects under part I of the Federal Power Act.

(9) Indian coal.
(A) In general. The term "Indian coal" means coal which is produced from coal reserves which, on June 14, 2005—
(i) were owned by an Indian tribe, or
(ii) were held in trust by the United States for the benefit of an Indian tribe or its members.
(B) Indian tribe. For purposes of this paragraph, the term "Indian tribe" has the meaning given such term by section 7871(c)(3)(E)(ii).

(10) Marine and hydrokinetic renewable energy.
(A) In general. The term "marine and hydrokinetic renewable energy" means energy derived from—
(i) waves, tides, and currents in oceans, estuaries, and tidal areas,
(ii) free flowing water in rivers, lakes, and streams,
(iii) free flowing water in an irrigation system, canal, or other man-made channel, including projects that utilize non-mechanical structures to accelerate the flow of water for electric power production purposes, or
(iv) differentials in ocean temperature (ocean thermal energy conversion).
(B) Exceptions. Such term shall not include any energy which is derived from any source which utilizes a dam, diversionary structure (except as provided in subparagraph (A)(iii)), or impoundment for electric power production purposes.

(d) Qualified facilities.
For purposes of this section—

(1) Wind facility. In the case of a facility using wind to produce electricity, the term "qualified facility" means any facility owned by the taxpayer which is originally placed in service after December 31, 1993, and before January 1, 2013. Such term shall not include any facility with respect to which any qualified small wind energy property expenditure (as defined in subsection (d)(4) of section 25D) is taken into account in determining the credit under such section.

(2) Closed-loop biomass facility.
(A) In general. In the case of a facility using closed-loop biomass to produce electricity, the term "qualified facility" means any facility—
(i) owned by the taxpayer which is originally placed in service after December 31, 1992, and before January 1, 2014, or
(ii) owned by the taxpayer which before January 1, 2014, is originally placed in service and modified to use closed-loop biomass to co-fire with coal, with other biomass, or with both, but only if the modification is approved under the Biomass Power for Rural Development Programs or is part of a pilot project of the Commodity Credit Corporation as described in 65 Fed. Reg. 63052.
(B) Expansion of facility. Such term shall include a new unit placed in service after the date of the enactment of this subparagraph in connection with a facility described in subparagraph (A)(i), but only to the extent of the increased amount of electricity produced at the facility by reason of such new unit.
(C) Special rules. In the case of a qualified facility described in subparagraph (A)(ii)—
(i) the 10-year period referred to in subsection (a) shall be treated as beginning no earlier than the date of the enactment of this clause, and

(ii) if the owner of such facility is not the producer of the electricity, the person eligible for the credit allowable under subsection (a) shall be the lessee or the operator of such facility.

(3) Open-loop biomass facilities.
(A) In general. In the case of a facility using open-loop biomass to produce electricity, the term "qualified facility" means any facility owned by the taxpayer which—
(i) in the case of a facility using agricultural livestock waste nutrients—
(I) is originally placed in service after the date of the enactment of this subclause and before January 1, 2014, and
(II) the nameplate capacity rating of which is not less than 150 kilowatts, and
(ii) in the case of any other facility, is originally placed in service before January 1, 2014.
(B) Expansion of facility. Such term shall include a new unit placed in service after the date of the enactment of this subparagraph in connection with a facility described in subparagraph (A), but only to the extent of the increased amount of electricity produced at the facility by reason of such new unit.
(C) Credit eligibility. In the case of any facility described in subparagraph (A), if the owner of such facility is not the producer of the electricity, the person eligible for the credit allowable under subsection (a) shall be the lessee or the operator of such facility.

(4) Geothermal or solar energy facility. In the case of a facility using geothermal or solar energy to produce electricity, the term "qualified facility" means any facility owned by the taxpayer which is originally placed in service after the date of the enactment of this paragraph and before January 1, 2014 (January 1, 2006, in the case of a facility using solar energy). Such term shall not include any property described in section 48(a)(3) the basis of which is taken into account by the taxpayer for purposes of determining the energy credit under section 48.

(5) Small irrigation power facility. In the case of a facility using small irrigation power to produce electricity, the term "qualified facility" means any facility owned by the taxpayer which is originally placed in service after the date of the enactment of this paragraph and before October 3, 2008.

(6) Landfill gas facilities. In the case of a facility producing electricity from gas derived from the biodegradation of municipal solid waste, the term "qualified facility" means any facility owned by the taxpayer which is originally placed in service after the date of the enactment of this paragraph and before January 1, 2014.

(7) Trash facilities. In the case of a facility (other than a facility described in paragraph (6)) which uses municipal solid waste to produce electricity, the term "qualified facility" means any facility owned by the taxpayer which is originally placed in service after the date of the enactment of this paragraph and before January 1, 2014. Such term shall include a new unit placed in service in connection with a facility placed in service on or before the date of the enactment of this paragraph, but only to the extent of the increased amount of electricity produced at the facility by reason of such new unit.

(8) Refined coal production facility. In the case of a facility that produces refined coal, the term "refined coal production facility" means—
(A) with respect to a facility producing steel industry fuel, any facility (or any modification to a facility) which is placed in service before January 1, 2010, and

Tax credits   Code Sec. 45(e)(8)(A)

(B) with respect to any other facility producing refined coal, any facility placed in service after the date of the enactment of the American Jobs Creation Act of 2004 and before January 1, 2012.

(9) Qualified hydropower facility. In the case of a facility producing qualified hydroelectric production described in subsection (c)(8), the term "qualified facility" means—

(A) in the case of any facility producing incremental hydropower production, such facility but only to the extent of its incremental hydropower production attributable to efficiency improvements or additions to capacity described in subsection (c)(8)(B) placed in service after the date of the enactment of this paragraph and before January 1, 2014, and

(B) any other facility placed in service after the date of the enactment of this paragraph and before January 1, 2014.

(C) Credit period. In the case of a qualified facility described in subparagraph (A), the 10-year period referred to in subsection (a) shall be treated as beginning on the date the efficiency improvements or additions to capacity are placed in service.

(10) Indian coal production facility. In the case of a facility that produces Indian coal, the term "Indian coal production facility" means a facility which is placed in service before January 1, 2009.

(11) Marine and hydrokinetic renewable energy facilities. In the case of a facility producing electricity from marine and hydrokinetic renewable energy, the term "qualified facility" means any facility owned by the taxpayer—

(A) which has a nameplate capacity rating of at least 150 kilowatts, and

(B) which is originally placed in service on or after the date of the enactment of this paragraph and before January 1, 2014.

(e) Definitions and special rules.

For purposes of this section—

(1) Only production in the United States taken into account. Sales shall be taken into account under this section only with respect to electricity the production of which is within—

(A) the United States (within the meaning of section 638(1)), or

(B) a possession of the United States (within the meaning of section 638(2)).

(2) Computation of inflation adjustment factor and reference price.

(A) In general. The Secretary shall, not later than April 1 of each calendar year, determine and publish in the Federal Register the inflation adjustment factor and the reference price for such calendar year in accordance with this paragraph.

(B) Inflation adjustment factor. The term "inflation adjustment factor" means, with respect to a calendar year, a fraction the numerator of which is the GDP implicit price deflator for the preceding calendar year and the denominator of which is the GDP implicit price deflator for the calendar year 1992. The term "GDP implicit price deflator" means the most recent revision of the implicit price deflator for the gross domestic product as computed and published by the Department of Commerce before March 15 of the calendar year.

(C) Reference price. The term "reference price" means, with respect to a calendar year, the Secretary's determination of the annual average contract price per kilowatt hour of electricity generated from the same qualified energy resource and sold in the previous year in the United States. For purposes of the preceding sentence, only contracts entered into after December 31, 1989, shall be taken into account.

(3) Production attributable to the taxpayer. In the case of a facility in which more than 1 person has an ownership interest, except to the extent provided in regulations prescribed by the Secretary, production from the facility shall be allocated among such persons in proportion to their respective ownership interests in the gross sales from such facility.

(4) Related persons. Persons shall be treated as related to each other if such persons would be treated as a single employer under the regulations prescribed under section 52(b). In the case of a corporation which is a member of an affiliated group of corporations filing a consolidated return, such corporation shall be treated as selling electricity to an unrelated person if such electricity is sold to such a person by another member of such group.

(5) Pass-thru in the case of estates and trusts. Under regulations prescribed by the Secretary, rules similar to the rules of subsection (d) of section 52 shall apply.

(6) Repealed.

(7) Credit not to apply to electricity sold to utilities under certain contracts.

(A) In general. The credit determined under subsection (a) shall not apply to electricity—

(i) produced at a qualified facility described in subsection (d)(1) which is originally placed in service after June 30, 1999, and

(ii) sold to a utility pursuant to a contract originally entered into before January 1, 1987 (whether or not amended or restated after that date).

(B) Exception. Subparagraph (A) shall not apply if—

(i) the prices for energy and capacity from such facility are established pursuant to an amendment to the contract referred to in subparagraph (A)(ii),

(ii) such amendment provides that the prices set forth in the contract which exceed avoided cost prices determined at the time of delivery shall apply only to annual quantities of electricity (prorated for partial years) which do not exceed the greater of—

(I) the average annual quantity of electricity sold to the utility under the contract during calendar years 1994, 1995, 1996, 1997, and 1998, or

(II) the estimate of the annual electricity production set forth in the contract, or, if there is no such estimate, the greatest annual quantity of electricity sold to the utility under the contract in any of the calendar years 1996, 1997, or 1998, and

(iii) such amendment provides that energy and capacity in excess of the limitation in clause (ii) may be—

(I) sold to the utility only at prices that do not exceed avoided cost prices determined at the time of delivery, or

(II) sold to a third party subject to a mutually agreed upon advance notice to the utility.

For purposes of this subparagraph, avoided cost prices shall be determined as provided for in 18 CFR 292.304(d)(1) or any successor regulation.

(8) Refined coal production facilities.

(A) Determination of credit amount. In the case of a producer of refined coal, the credit determined under this section (without regard to this paragraph) for any taxable year shall be increased by an amount equal to $4.375 per ton of qualified refined coal—

(i) produced by the taxpayer at a refined coal production facility during the 10-year period beginning on the date the facility was originally placed in service, and

(ii) sold by the taxpayer—

(I) to an unrelated person, and

(II) during such 10-year period and such taxable year.

(B) Phaseout of credit. The amount of the increase determined under subparagraph (A) shall be reduced by an amount which bears the same ratio to the amount of the increase (determined without regard to this subparagraph) as—

(i) the amount by which the reference price of fuel used as a feedstock (within the meaning of subsection (c)(7)(A)) for the calendar year in which the sale occurs exceeds an amount equal to 1.7 multiplied by the reference price for such fuel in 2002, bears to

(ii) $8.75.

(C) Application of rules. Rules similar to the rules of the subsection (b)(3) and paragraphs (1) through (5) of this subsection shall apply for purposes of determining the amount of any increase under this paragraph.

(D) Special rule for steel industry fuel.

(i) In general. In the case of a taxpayer who produces steel industry fuel—

(I) this paragraph shall be applied separately with respect to steel industry fuel and other refined coal, and

(II) in applying this paragraph to steel industry fuel, the modifications in clause (ii) shall apply.

(ii) Modifications.

(I) Credit amount. Subparagraph (A) shall be applied by substituting "$2 per barrel-of-oil equivalent" for "$4.375 per ton".

(II) Credit period. In lieu of the 10-year period referred to in clauses (i) and (ii)(II) of subparagraph (A), the credit period shall be the period beginning on the later of the date such facility was originally placed in service, the date the modifications described in clause (iii) were placed in service, or October 1, 2008, and ending on the later of December 31, 2009, or the date which is 1 year after the date such facility or the modifications described in clause (iii) were placed in service.

(III) No phaseout. Subparagraph (B) shall not apply.

(iii) Modifications. The modifications described in this clause are modifications to an existing facility which allow such facility to produce steel industry fuel.

(iv) Barrel-of-oil equivalent. For purposes of this subparagraph, a barrel-of-oil equivalent is the amount of steel industry fuel that has a Btu content of 5,800,000 Btus.

(9) Coordination with credit for producing fuel from a nonconventional source.

(A) In general. The term "qualified facility" shall not include any facility which produces electricity from gas derived from the biodegradation of municipal solid waste if such biodegradation occurred in a facility (within the meaning of section 45K) the production from which is allowed as a credit under section 45K for the taxable year or any prior taxable year.

(B) Refined coal facilities.

(i) In general. The term "refined coal production facility" shall not include any facility the production from which is allowed as a credit under section 45K for the taxable year or any prior taxable year (or under section 29, as in effect on the day before the date of enactment of the Energy Tax Incentives Act of 2005, for any prior taxable year).

(ii) Exception for steel industry coal. In the case of a facility producing steel industry fuel, clause (i) shall not apply to so much of the refined coal produced at such facility as is steel industry fuel.

(10) Indian coal production facilities.

(A) Determination of credit amount. In the case of a producer of Indian coal, the credit determined under this section (without regard to this paragraph) for any taxable year shall be increased by an amount equal to the applicable dollar amount per ton of Indian coal—

(i) produced by the taxpayer at an Indian coal production facility during the 7-year period beginning on January 1, 2006, and

(ii) sold by the taxpayer—

(I) to an unrelated person, and

(II) during such 7-year period and such taxable year.

(B) Applicable dollar amount.

(i) In general. The term "applicable dollar amount" for any taxable year beginning in a calendar year means—

(I) $1.50 in the case of calendar years 2006 through 2009, and

(II) $2.00 in the case of calendar years beginning after 2009.

(ii) Inflation adjustment. In the case of any calendar year after 2006, each of the dollar amounts under clause (i) shall be equal to the product of such dollar amount and the inflation adjustment factor determined under paragraph (2)(B) for the calendar year, except that such paragraph shall be applied by substituting "2005" for "1992".

(C) Application of rules. Rules similar to the rules of the subsection (b)(3) and paragraphs (1), (3), (4), and (5) of this subsection shall apply for purposes of determining the amount of any increase under this paragraph.

(D) Treatment as specified credit. The increase in the credit determined under subsection (a) by reason of this paragraph with respect to any facility shall be treated as a specified credit for purposes of section 38(c)(4)(A) during the 4-year period beginning on the later of January 1, 2006, or the date on which such facility is placed in service by the taxpayer.

(11) Allocation of credit to patrons of agricultural cooperative.

(A) Election to allocate.

(i) In general. In the case of an eligible cooperative organization, any portion of the credit determined under subsection (a) for the taxable year may, at the election of the organization, be apportioned among patrons of the organization on the basis of the amount of business done by the patrons during the taxable year.

(ii) Form and effect of election. An election under clause (i) for any taxable year shall be made on a timely filed return for such year. Such election, once made, shall be irrevocable for such taxable year. Such election shall not take effect unless the organization designates the apportionment as such in a written notice mailed to its patrons during the payment period described in section 1382(d).

(B) Treatment of organizations and patrons. The amount of the credit apportioned to any patrons under subparagraph (A)—

(i) shall not be included in the amount determined under subsection (a) with respect to the organization for the taxable year, and

(ii) shall be included in the amount determined under subsection (a) for the first taxable year of each patron ending on or after the last day of the payment period (as defined in section 1382(d)) for the taxable year of the organization or, if earlier, for the taxable year of each patron ending on or after the date on which the patron receives notice from the cooperative of the apportionment.

(C) Special rules for decrease in credits for taxable year. If the amount of the credit of a cooperative organization determined under subsection (a) for a taxable year is less than the amount of such credit shown on the return of the cooperative organization for such year, an amount equal to the excess of—

(i) such reduction, over

(ii) the amount not apportioned to such patrons under subparagraph (A) for the taxable year,

shall be treated as an increase in tax imposed by this chapter on the organization. Such increase shall not be treated as tax imposed by this chapter for purposes of determining the amount of any credit under this chapter.

(D) Eligible cooperative defined. For purposes of this section the term "eligible cooperative" means a cooperative organization described in section 1381(a) which is owned more than 50 percent by agricultural producers or by entities owned by agricultural producers. For this purpose an entity owned by an agricultural producer is one that is more than 50 percent owned by agricultural producers.

In 2010, P.L. 111-312, Sec. 702(a), substituted "January 1, 2012" for "January 1, 2010" in subpara. (d)(8)(B), effective for facilities placed in service after 12/31/2009.

——P.L. 111-312, Sec. 707(a)(1), substituted "2009, 2010, or 2011" for "2009 or 2010" in Sec. 1603(a)(1), Div. B of P.L. 111-5 [see below] effective 2/17/2009.

——P.L. 111-312, Sec. 707(a)(2)(A), substituted "after 2011" for "after 2010" in Sec. 1603(a)(2), Div. B of P.L. 111-5 [see below] effective 2/17/2009.

——P.L. 111-312, Sec. 707(a)(2)(B), substituted "2009, 2010, or 2011" for "2009 or 2010" in Sec. 1603(a)(2), Div. B of P.L. 111-5 [see below] effective 2/17/2009.

——P.L. 111-312, Sec. 707(b), substituted "2012" for "2011" in Sec. 1603(j), Div. B of P.L. 111-5 [see below] effective 2/17/2009.

In 2009, P.L. 111-5, Sec. 1101(a)(1), substituted "2013" for "2010" in para. (d)(1).... Sec. 1101(a)(2), substituted "2014" for "2011" each place it appears in paras. (d)(2)-(4), (d)(6)-(7), and (d)(9).... Sec. 1101(a)(3), substituted "2014" for "2012" in subpara. (d)(11)(B), effective for property placed in service after 2/17/2009.

——P.L. 111-5, Sec. 1101(b), substituted "and before October 3, 2008" for "and before the date of the enactment of paragraph (11)" in para. (d)(5), effective for electricity produced and sold after 10/3/2008, in tax. yrs. ending after 10/3/2008 (as stated in Sec. 102 Div. B of P.L. 110-343).

——P.L. 111-5, Sec. 1603, of this Act, as amended by Sec. 707(a)-(b) of P.L. 111-312, see above, reads as follows:

"Sec. 1603. Grants for specified energy property in lieu of tax credits.

"(a) In general. Upon application, the Secretary of the Treasury shall, subject to the requirements of this section, provide a grant to each person who places in service specified energy property to reimburse such person for a portion of the expense of such property as provided in subsection (b). No grant shall be made under this section with respect to any property unless such property—

"(1) is placed in service during 2009, 2010, or 2011, or

"(2) is placed in service after 2011 and before the credit termination date with respect to such property, but only if the construction of such property began during 2009, 2010, or 2011.

"(b) Grant amount.

"(1) In general. The amount of the grant under subsection (a) with respect to any specified energy property shall be the applicable percentage of the basis of such property.

"(2) Applicable percentage. For purposes of paragraph (1), the term 'applicable percentage' means—

"(A) 30 percent in the case of any property described in paragraphs (1) through (4) of subsection (d), and

"(B) 10 percent in the case of any other property.

"(3) Dollar limitations. In the case of property described in paragraph (2), (6), or (7) of subsection (d), the amount of any grant under this section with respect to such property shall not exceed the limitation described in section 48(c)(1)(B), 48(c)(2)(B), or 48(c)(3)(B) of the Internal Revenue Code of 1986, respectively, with respect to such property.

"(c) Time for payment of grant. The Secretary of the Treasury shall make payment of any grant under subsection (a) during the 60-day period beginning on the later of—

"(1) the date of the application for such grant, or

"(2) the date the specified energy property for which the grant is being made is placed in service.

"(d) Specified energy property. For purposes of this section, the term 'specified energy property' means any of the following:

"(1) Qualified facilities.— Any qualified property (as defined in section 48(a)(5)(D) of the Internal Revenue Code of 1986) which is part of a qualified facility (within the meaning of section 45 of such Code) described in paragraph (1), (2), (3), (4), (6), (7), (9), or (11) of section 45(d) of such Code.

"(2) Qualified fuel cell property. Any qualified fuel cell property (as defined in section 48(c)(1) of such Code).

"(3) Solar property. Any property described in clause (i) or (ii) of section 48(a)(3)(A) of such Code.

"(4) Qualified small wind energy property. Any qualified small wind energy property (as defined in section 48(c)(4) of such Code).

"(5) Geothermal property. Any property described in clause (iii) of section 48(a)(3)(A) of such Code.

"(6) Qualified microturbine property. Any qualified microturbine property (as defined in section 48(c)(2) of such Code).

"(7) Combined heat and power system property. Any combined heat and power system property (as defined in section 48(c)(3) of such Code).

"(8) Geothermal heat pump property. Any property described in clause (vii) of section 48(a)(3)(A) of such Code.

"Such term shall not include any property unless depreciation (or amortization in lieu of depreciation) is allowable with respect to such property.

"(e) Credit termination date. For purposes of this section, the term "credit termination date" means

"(1) in the case of any specified energy property which is part of a facility described in paragraph (1) of section 45(d) of the Internal Revenue Code of 1986, January 1, 2013,

"(2) in the case of any specified energy property which is part of a facility described in paragraph (2), (3), (4), (6), (7), (9), or (11) of section 45(d) of such Code, January 1, 2014, and

"(3) in the case of any specified energy property described in section 48 of such Code, January 1, 2017.

"In the case of any property which is described in paragraph (3) and also in another paragraph of this subsection, paragraph (3) shall apply with respect to such property.

"(f) Application of certain rules. In making grants under this section, the Secretary of the Treasury shall apply rules similar to the rules of section 50 of the Internal Revenue Code of 1986. In applying such rules, if the property is disposed of, or otherwise ceases to be specified energy property, the Secretary of the Treasury shall provide for the recapture of the appropriate percentage of the grant amount in such manner as the Secretary of the Treasury determines appropriate.

"(g) Exception for certain non-taxpayers. The Secretary of the Treasury shall not make any grant under this section to

"(1) any Federal, State, or local government (or any political subdivision, agency, or instrumentality thereof),

"(2) any organization described in section 501(c) of the Internal Revenue Code of 1986 and exempt from tax under section 501(a) of such Code,

"(3) any entity referred to in paragraph (4) of section 54(j) of such Code, or

"(4) any partnership or other pass-thru entity any partner (or other holder of an equity or profits interest) of which is described in paragraph (1), (2) or (3).

"(h) Definitions. Terms used in this section which are also used in section 45 or 48 of the Internal Revenue Code of 1986 shall have the same meaning for purposes of this section as when used in such section 45 or 48. Any reference in this section to the Secretary of the Treasury shall be treated as including the Secretary's delegate.

"(i) Appropriations. There is hereby appropriated to the Secretary of the Treasury such sums as may be necessary to carry out this section.

"(j) Termination. The Secretary of the Treasury shall not make any grant to any person under this section unless the application of such person for such grant is received before October 1, 2012."

In 2008, P.L. 110-343, Sec. 101(a)(1)DivB, substituted "January 1, 2010" for "January 1, 2009" in paras. (d)(1) and (8).... Sec. 101(a)(2)(A)DivB, substituted "January 1, 2011" for "January 1, 2009" in clauses (d)(2)(A)(i) and (ii)... Sec. 101(a)(2)(B)DivB, substituted "January 1, 2011" for "January 1, 2009" in subclause (d)(3)(A)(i)(I) and clause (b)(3)(A)(ii)... Sec. 101(a)(2)(C)DivB, substituted "January 1, 2011" for "January 1, 2009" in para. (d)(4).... Sec. 101(a)(2)(D)DivB, substituted "January 1, 2011" for "January 1, 2009" in para. (d)(5).... Sec. 101(a)(2)(E)DivB, substituted "January 1, 2011" for "January 1, 2009" in para. (d)(6).... Sec. 101(a)(2)(F)DivB, substituted "January 1, 2011" for "January 1, 2009" in para. (d)(7)... Sec. 101(a)(2)(G)DivB, substituted "January

1, 2011" for "January 1, 2009" in subparas. (d)(9)(A) and (B), effective for property originally placed in service after 12/31/2008.

—P.L. 110-343, Sec. 101(b)(1)(A)DivB, deleted subclause (c)(7)(A)(i)(IV) [as amended by Sec. 108(a)(1) of this Act, see below] . . . Sec. 101(b)(1)(B)DivB, added "and" at the end of subclause (c)(7)(A)(i)(II) [as amended by Sec. 108(a)(1) of this Act, see below] . . . Sec. 101(b)(1)(C)DivB, substituted a period for ", and" at the end of subclause (c)(7)(A)(i)(III) [as amended by Sec. 108(a)(1) of this Act, see below] . . . Sec. 101(b)(2)DivB, added "at least 40 percent of the emissions of" after "nitrogen oxide and" in subpara. (c)(7)(B), effective for coal produced and sold from facilities placed in service after 12/31/2008.

Prior to deletion, subclause (c)(7)(A)(i)(IV) [as amended by Sec. 108(a)(1) of this Act, see below] read as follows:

"(IV) is produced in such a manner as to result in an increase of at least 50 percent in the market value of the refined coal (excluding any increase caused by materials combined or added during the production process), as compared to the value of the feedstock coal, or"

—P.L. 110-343, Sec. 101(c)(1)DivB, substituted "facility (other than a facility described in paragraph (6)) which uses" for "facility which burns" in para. (d)(7) . . . Sec. 101(c)(2)DivB, deleted "combustion" after "Trash" in the heading of para. (d)(7), effective for electricity produced and sold after 10/3/2008.

—P.L. 110-343, Sec. 101(d)(1)DivB, redesignated subpara. (d)(3)(B) as (C) and added subpara. (d)(3)(B) . . . Sec. 101(d)(2)DivB, redesignated subpara. (d)(2)(B) as (C) and added subpara. (d)(2)(B), effective for property placed in service after 10/3/2008.

—P.L. 110-343, Sec. 101(e)DivB, amended subpara. (c)(8)(C), effective for property originally placed in service after 12/31/2008.

Prior to amendment, subpara. (c)(8)(C) read as follows:

"(C) Nonhydroelectric dam. For purposes of subparagraph (A), a facility is described in this subparagraph if—

"(i) the facility is licensed by the Federal Energy Regulatory Commission and meets all other applicable environmental, licensing, and regulatory requirements,

"(ii) the facility was placed in service before the date of the enactment of this paragraph and did not produce hydroelectric power on the date of the enactment of this paragraph, and

"(iii) turbines or other generating devices are to be added to the facility after such date to produce hydroelectric power, but only if there is not any enlargement of the diversion structure, or construction or enlargement of a bypass channel, or the impoundment or any withholding of any additional water from the natural stream channel."

—P.L. 110-343, Sec. 102(a)DivB, deleted "and" at the end of subpara. (c)(1)(G), substituted ", and" for the period at the end of subpara. (c)(1)(H) and added subpara. (c)(1)(I) . . . Sec. 102(b)DivB, added para. (c)(10) . . . Sec. 102(c)DivB, added para. (d)(11) . . . Sec. 102(d)DivB, substituted "(9), or (11)" for "or (9)" in subpara. (b)(4)(A) . . . Sec. 102(e)DivB, substituted "the date of the enactment of paragraph (11)" for "January 1, 2012" [sic 2011] in para. (d)(5) [as amended by Sec. 101(a)(2)(D) of this Act, see above], effective for electricity produced and sold after 10/3/2008 in tax. years end. after 10/3/2008.

—P.L. 110-343, Sec. 106(c)(3)(B)DivB, added a sentence at the end of para. (d)(1), effective for tax. yrs. begin. after 12/31/2007. Sec. 106(f)(3) of this Act reads as follows:

"(3) Application of EGTRRA sunset. The amendments made by subparagraphs (A) and (B) of subsection (e)(2) shall be subject to title IX of the Economic Growth and Tax Relief Reconciliation Act of 2001 in the same manner as the provisions of such Act to which such amendments relate."

—P.L. 110-343, Sec. 108(a)(1)DivB, amended subpara. (c)(7)(A) . . . Sec. 108(a)(2)DivB, added subpara. (c)(7)(C) . . . Sec. 108(b)(1)DivB, added subpara. (e)(8)(D) . . . Sec. 108(b)(2)DivB, added "the $3 amount in subsection (e)(8)(D)(ii)(I)," after "subsection (e)(8)(A)," in para. (b)(2) . . . Sec. 108(c)DivB, amended para. (d)(8) [as amended by Sec. 101(a)(1) of this Act, see above] . . . Sec. 108(d)(1)(A)DivB, substituted "(i) In general. The term" for "The term" in subpara. (e)(9)(B) . . . Sec. 108(d)(1)(B)DivB, added clause (e)(9)(B)(ii), effective for fuel produced and sold after 9/30/2008.

Prior to amendment, subpara. (c)(7)(A) read as follows:

"(A) In general. The term 'refined coal' means a fuel which—

"(i) is a liquid, gaseous, or solid fuel produced from coal (including lignite) or high carbon fly ash, including such fuel used as a feedstock,

"(ii) is sold by the taxpayer with the reasonable expectation that it will be used for purpose of producing steam,

"(iii) is certified by the taxpayer as resulting (when used in the production of steam) in a qualified emission reduction, and

"(iv) is produced in such a manner as to result in an increase of at least 50 percent in the market value of the refined coal (excluding any increase caused by materials combined or added during the production process), as compared to the value of the feedstock coal."

Prior to amendment, para. (d)(8) [as amended by Sec. 101(a)(1) of this Act, see above] read as follows:

"(8) Refined coal production facility. In the case of a facility that produces refined coal, the term 'refined coal production facility' means a facility which is placed in service after the date of the enactment of this paragraph and before January 1, 2010."

In 2007, P.L. 110-172, Sec. 7(b)(1), deleted "which is segregated from other waste materials and" after "any lignin material" in clause (c)(3)(A)(ii) . . . Sec. 7(b)(2), added "and" at the end of clause (d)(2)(B)(i), deleted clause (d)(2)(B)(ii) and redesignated clause (d)(2)(B)(iii) as (ii), effective for electricity produced and sold after 10/22/2004, in tax. yrs. end. after 10/22/2004. For special rule, see Sec. 710(g)(2) and (4) of P.L. 108-357, reproduced below.

Prior to deletion, clause (d)(2)(B)(ii) read as follows:

"(ii) the amount of the credit determined under subsection (a) with respect to the facility shall be an amount equal to the amount determined without regard to this clause multiplied by the ratio of the thermal content of the closed-loop biomass used in such facility to the thermal content of all fuels used in such facility, and"

—P.L. 110-172, Sec. 9(a), substituted "originally placed in service" for "placed in service by the taxpayer" in clause (e)(7)(A)(i), effective 12/17/99.

In 2006, P.L. 109-432, Sec. 201, substituted "January 1, 2009" for "January 1, 2008" each place it appeared in subsec. (d), enacted 12/20/2006.

In 2005, P.L. 109-135, Sec. 402(b), substituted "lignin material" for "nonhazardous lignin waste material" in clause (c)(3)(A)(ii), effective for electricity produced and sold after 10/22/2004, in tax. yrs. end. after 10/22/2004 as if included in Sec. 1301 of the Energy Tax Incentives Act of 2005, P.L. 109-58.

—P.L. 109-135, Sec. 403(t), deleted "synthetic" after "or solid" in clause (c)(7)(A)(i), effective for electricity produced and sold after 10/22/2004, in tax. yrs. end. after 10/22/2004 as if included in Sec. 710 of the American Jobs Creation Act of 2004, P.L. 108-357. For special rule, see Sec. 710(g)(4) of P.L. 108-357, reproduced below.

—P.L. 109-135, Sec. 412(j)(1), substituted "In the case of a facility that produces refined coal, the term" for "The term" in para. (d)(8) . . . Sec. 412(j)(2), substituted "In the case of a facility that produces Indian coal, the term" for "The term" in para. (d)(10), effective 12/21/2005.

—P.L. 109-58, Sec. 1301(a)(1), substituted "January 1, 2008" for "January 1, 2006" each place it appeared in paras. (d)(1)-(3) and paras. (d)(5)-(7) . . . Sec. 1301(a)(2), substituted "January 1, 2008 (January 1, 2006, in the case of a facility using solar energy)" for "January 1, 2006" in para. (d)(4) . . . Sec. 1301(b)(1), added "or clause (iii)' after "clause (ii)" in clause (b)(4)(B)(i) . . . Sec. 1301(b)(2), added clause (b)(4)(B)(iii) . . . Sec. 1301(c)(1), deleted "and" at the end of subpara. (c)(1)(F), substituted ", and" for the period at the end of subpara. (c)(1)(G), and added subpara. (c)(1)(H) . . . Sec. 1301(c)(2), substituted "(7), or (9)" for "or (7)" in subpara. (b)(4)(A) . . . Sec. 1301(c)(3), added para. (c)(8) . . . Sec. 1301(c)(4), added para. (d)(9) . . . Sec. 1301(d)(1), added para. (e)(10) . . . Sec. 1301(d)(2), added para. (c)(9) . . . Sec. 1301(d)(3), added para. (d)(10) . . . Sec. 1301(d)(4), substituted "Resources" for "Qualified energy resources and refined coal" in the heading of subsec. (c), effective 8/8/2005.

—P.L. 109-58, Sec. 1301(e), added "Such term shall include a new unit placed in service in connection with a facility placed in service on or before the date of the enactment of this paragraph, but only to the extent of the increased amount of electricity produced at the facility by reason of such new unit." at the end of para. (d)(7) . . . Sec. 1301(f)(1), substituted "January 1, 2005," for "the date of the enactment of this Act" in clause (b)(4)(B)(ii) . . . Sec. 1301(f)(2), added "or any nonhazardous lignin waste material" after "cellulosic waste material" in clause (c)(3)(A)(ii) . . . Sec. 1301(f)(3), deleted para. (e)(6) . . . Sec. 1301(f)(4)(A), amended para. (e)(9) . . . Sec. 1301(f)(4)(B), deleted "and (9)" after "through (5)" in subpara. (e)(8)(C), effective for electricity produced and sold after 10/22/2004, in tax. yrs. end. after 10/22/2004 as if included in the amendments made by section 710 of the American Jobs Creation Act of 2004, P.L. 108-357 [see below].

Prior to deletion, para. (e)(6) read as follows:

"(6) Credit eligibility in the case of government-owned facilities using poultry waste. In the case of a facility using poultry waste to produce electricity and owned by a governmental unit, the person eligible for the credit under subsection (a) is the lessee or the operator of such facility."

Prior to amendment, para. (e)(9) read as follows:

"(9) Coordination with credit for producing fuel from a nonconventional source. The term "qualified facility" shall not include any facility the production from which is allowed as a credit under section 29 for the taxable year or any prior taxable year."

—P.L. 109-58, Sec. 1301(f)(6), substituted "January 1, 2005" for "January 1, 2004" in Sec. 710(g)(4) of P.L. 108-357, see below.

—P.L. 109-58, Sec. 1302(a), added para. (e)(11), effective for tax. yrs. of cooperative organizations end. after 8/8/2005.

—P.L. 109-58, Sec. 1322(a)(3)(C)(i), substituted "section 45K" for "section 29" each place it appeared in para. (e)(9) [as amended by Sec. 1301(f)(4)(A) of this Act, see above] . . . Sec. 1322(a)(3)(C)(ii), added "(or under section 29, as in effect on the day before the date of enactment of the Energy Tax Incentives Act of 2005, for any prior taxable year)" at the end of para. (e)(9) [as amended by Secs. 1301(f)(4)(A) and 1322(a)(3)(C)(i) of this Act, see above], effective for credits determined under the Internal Revenue Code of 1986 for tax. yrs. end. after 12/31/2005.

In 2004, P.L. 108-357, Sec. 710(a), amended subsec. (c), effective for electricity produced and sold after 10/22/2004, in tax. yrs. end. after 10/22/2004. Sec. 710(g)(4) of this Act [as amended by Sec. 1301(f)(6) of P.L. 109-58, see above], provides:

"(4) Nonapplication of amendments to preeffective date poultry waste facilities. The amendments made by this section shall not apply with respect to any poultry waste facility (within the meaning of section 45(c)(3)(C), as in effect on the day before the date of the enactment of this Act) placed in service before January 1, 2005."

Prior to amendment, subsec. (c) read as follows:

"*(c) Definitions.* For purposes of this section—

"(1) Qualified energy resources. The term 'qualified energy resources' means—

"(A) wind,

"(B) closed-loop biomass, and

"(C) poultry waste.

"(2) Closed-loop biomass. The term 'closed-loop biomass' means any organic material from a plant which is planted exclusively for purposes of being used at a qualified facility to produce electricity.

"(3) Qualified facility.

"(A) Wind facility. In the case of a facility using wind to produce electricity, the term 'qualified facility' means any facility owned by the taxpayer which is originally placed in service after December 31, 1993, and before January 1, 2006.

"(B) Closed-loop biomass facility. In the case of a facility using closed-loop biomass to produce electricity, the term 'qualified facility' means any facility owned by the taxpayer which is originally placed in service after December 31, 1992, and before January 1, 2006.

"(C) Poultry waste facility. In the case of a facility using poultry waste to produce electricity, the term 'qualified facility' means any facility of the taxpayer which is originally placed in service after December 31, 1999, and before January 1, 2006.

"(4) Poultry waste. The term 'poultry waste' means poultry manure and litter, including wood shavings, straw, rice hulls, and other bedding material for the disposition of manure."

—P.L. 108-357, Sec. 710(b)(1), redesignated subsec. (d) as (e) and added subsec. (d), effective for electricity produced and sold after 12/31/2004, in tax. yrs. end. after 12/31/2004. Sec. 710(g)(2) of this Act, provides:

"(2) Certain biomass facilities. With respect to any facility described in section 45(d)(3)(A)(ii) of the Internal Revenue Code of 1986, as added by subsection (b)(1), which is placed in service before the date of the enactment of this Act, the amendments made by this section shall apply to electricity produced and sold after December 31, 2004, in taxable years ending after such date."

—P.L. 108-357, Sec. 710(b)(2), added para. (e)(8), effective for refined coal produced and sold after 10/22/2004.

—P.L. 108-357, Sec. 710(b)(3)(A), substituted "subsection (d)(1)" for "subsection (c)(3)(A)" in clause (e)(7)(A)(i) [as redesignated by Sec. 710(b)(1) of this Act, see above] . . . Sec. 710(b)(3)(B), added ", etc" before the period at the end of the heading of Code Sec. 45 . . . Sec. 710(b)(3)(C), substituted "The 1.5 cent amount in subsection (a), the 8 cent amount in paragraph (1), the $4.375 cent amount in subsection (e)(8)(A), and in subsection (e)(8)(B)(i) the reference price of fuel used as a feedstock (within the meaning of subsection (c)(7)(A)) in 2002" for "The 1.5 cent amount in subsection (a) and the 8 cent amount in paragraph (1)" in para. (b)(2), effective for electricity produced and sold after 10/22/2004, in tax. yrs. end. after 10/22/2004. Sec. 710(g)(4) of this Act [as amended by Sec. 1301(f)(6) of P.L. 109-58, see above], provides:

"(4) Nonapplication of amendments to preeffective date poultry waste facilities. The amendments made by this section shall not apply with respect to any poultry waste facility (within the meaning of section 45(c)(3)(C), as in effect on the day before the date of the enactment of this Act) placed in service before January 1, 2005."

—P.L. 108-357, Sec. 710(c), added para. (b)(4), effective for electricity produced and sold after 12/31/2004, in tax. yrs. end. after 12/31/2004.

—P.L. 108-357, Sec. 710(d), added para. (e)(9) [as redesignated by Sec. 710(b)(1) of this Act, see above] . . . Sec. 710(f)(1), added "the lesser of 1/2 or" before "a fraction" in para. (b)(3) . . . Sec. 710(f)(2), added a sentence at the end of para. (b)(3), effective for electricity produced and sold after 10/22/2004, in tax. yrs. end. after 10/22/2004. Sec. 710(g)(4) of this Act [as amended by Sec. 1301(f)(6) of P.L. 109-58, see above], provides:

"(4) Nonapplication of amendments to preeffective date poultry waste facilities. The amendments made by this section shall not apply with respect to any poultry waste facility (within the meaning of section 45(c)(3)(C), as in effect on the day before the date of the enactment of this Act) placed in service before January 1, 2005."

—P.L. 108-311, Sec. 313(a), substituted "January 1, 2006" for "January 1, 2004" in subparas. (c)(3)(A)-(C), effective for facilities placed in service after 12/31/2003.

In **2002**, P.L. 107-147, Sec. 603(a), substituted "2004" for "2002" in subparas. (c)(3)(A)-(C), effective for facilities placed in service after 12/31/2001.

In **2000**, P.L. 106-554, Sec. 1(a)(7), [which enacted into law Sec. 319(1) of P.L. 106-554] substituted "subsection (c)(3)(A)" for "paragraph (3)(A)" in clause (d)(7)(A)(i), effective 12/21/2000.

In **1999**, P.L. 106-170, Sec. 507(a), amended para. (c)(3) . . . Sec. 507(b)(1), deleted "and" at the end of subpara. (c)(1)(A), substituted ", and" for the period at the end of subpara. (c)(1)(B) and added subpara. (c)(1)(C) . . . Sec. 507(b)(2), added para. (c)(4) . . . Sec. 507(c), added paras. (d)(6) and (7), effective 12/17/99. Prior to amendment, para. (c)(3) read as follows:

"(3) Qualified facility. The term 'qualified facility' means any facility owned by the taxpayer which is originally placed in service after December 31, 1993 (December 31, 1992, in the case of a facility using closed-loop biomass to produce electricity), and before July 1, 1999."

In **1992**, P.L. 102-486, Sec. 1914(a), added Code Sec. 45, effective for tax. yrs. end. after 12/31/92.

Sec. 45A. Indian employment credit.
(a) Amount of credit.

For purposes of section 38, the amount of the Indian employment credit determined under this section with respect to any employer for any taxable year is an amount equal to 20 percent of the excess (if any) of—

(1) the sum of—

(A) the qualified wages paid or incurred during such taxable year, plus

(B) qualified employee health insurance costs paid or incurred during such taxable year, over

(2) the sum of the qualified wages and qualified employee health insurance costs (determined as if this section were in effect) which were paid or incurred by the employer (or any predecessor) during calendar year 1993.

(b) Qualified wages; qualified employee health insurance costs.

For purposes of this section—

(1) Qualified wages.

(A) In general. The term "qualified wages" means any wages paid or incurred by an employer for services performed by an employee while such employee is a qualified employee.

(B) Coordination with work opportunity credit. The term "qualified wages" shall not include wages attributable to service rendered during the 1-year period beginning with the day the individual begins work for the employer if any portion of such wages is taken into account in determining the credit under section 51.

(2) Qualified employee health insurance costs.

(A) In general. The term "qualified employee health insurance costs" means any amount paid or incurred by an employer for health insurance to the extent such amount is attributable to coverage provided to any employee while such employee is a qualified employee.

(B) Exception for amounts paid under salary reduction arrangements. No amount paid or incurred for health insurance pursuant to a salary reduction arrangement shall be taken into account under subparagraph (A).

(3) Limitation. The aggregate amount of qualified wages and qualified employee health insurance costs taken into account with respect to any employee for any taxable year (and for the base period under subsection (a)(2)) shall not exceed $20,000.

(c) Qualified employee.

For purposes of this section—

(1) In general. Except as otherwise provided in this subsection, the term "qualified employee" means, with respect to any period, any employee of an employer if—

(A) the employee is an enrolled member of an Indian tribe or the spouse of an enrolled member of an Indian tribe,

(B) substantially all of the services performed during such period by such employee for such employer are performed within an Indian reservation, and

(C) the principal place of abode of such employee while performing such services is on or near the reservation in which the services are performed.

(2) Individuals receiving wages in excess of $30,000 not eligible. An employee shall not be treated as a qualified employee for any taxable year of the employer if the total amount of the wages paid or incurred by such employer to such employee during such taxable year (whether or not for services within an Indian reservation) exceeds the amount determined at an annual rate of $30,000.

(3) Inflation adjustment. The Secretary shall adjust the $30,000 amount under paragraph (2) for years beginning after 1994 at the same time and in the same manner as under section 415(d), except that the base period taken into account for purposes of such adjustment shall be the calendar quarter beginning October 1, 1993.

(4) Employment must be trade or business employment. An employee shall be treated as a qualified employee for any taxable year of the employer only if more than 50 percent of the wages paid or incurred by the employer to such employee during such taxable year are for services performed in a trade or business of the employer. Any determination as to whether the preceding sentence applies with respect to any employee for any taxable year shall be made without regard to subsection (e)(2).

(5) Certain employees not eligible. The term "qualified employee" shall not include—

(A) any individual described in subparagraph (A), (B), or (C) of section 51(i)(1),

(B) any 5-percent owner (as defined in section 416(i)(1)(B)), and

(C) any individual if the services performed by such individual for the employer involve the conduct of class I, II, or III gaming as defined in section 4 of the Indian Gaming Regulatory Act (25 U.S.C. 2703), or are performed in a building housing such gaming activity.

(6) Indian tribe defined. The term "Indian tribe" means any Indian tribe, band, nation, pueblo, or other organized group or community, including any Alaska Native village or regional or village corporation, as defined in, or established pursuant to, the Alaska Native Claims Settlement Act (43 U.S.C. 1601 et seq.) which is recognized as eligible for the special programs and services provided by the United States to Indians because of their status as Indians.

(7) Indian reservation defined. The term "Indian reservation" has the meaning given such term by section 168(j)(6).

(d) Early termination of employment by employer.

(1) In general. If the employment of any employee is terminated by the taxpayer before the day 1 year after the day on which such employee began work for the employer—

(A) no wages (or qualified employee health insurance costs) with respect to such employee shall be taken into account under subsection (a) for the taxable year in which such employment is terminated, and

(B) the tax under this chapter for the taxable year in which such employment is terminated shall be increased by the aggregate credits (if any) allowed under section 38(a) for prior taxable years by reason of wages (or qualified employee health insurance costs) taken into account with respect to such employee.

(2) Carrybacks and carryovers adjusted. In the case of any termination of employment to which paragraph (1) applies, the carrybacks and carryovers under section 39 shall be properly adjusted.

(3) Subsection not to apply in certain cases.

(A) In general. Paragraph (1) shall not apply to—

(i) a termination of employment of an employee who voluntarily leaves the employment of the taxpayer,

(ii) a termination of employment of an individual who before the close of the period referred to in paragraph (1) becomes disabled to perform the services of such employment unless such disability is removed before the close of such period and the taxpayer fails to offer reemployment to such individual, or

(iii) a termination of employment of an individual if it is determined under the applicable State unemployment compensation law that the termination was due to the misconduct of such individual.

(B) Changes in form of business. For purposes of paragraph (1), the employment relationship between the taxpayer and an employee shall not be treated as terminated—

(i) by a transaction to which section 381(a) applies if the employee continues to be employed by the acquiring corporation, or

(ii) by reason of a mere change in the form of conducting the trade or business of the taxpayer if the employee continues to be employed in such trade or business and the taxpayer retains a substantial interest in such trade or business.

(4) Special rule. Any increase in a tax under paragraph (1) shall not be treated as a tax imposed by this chapter for purposes of—

(A) determining the amount of any credit allowable under this chapter, and

(B) determining the amount of the tax imposed by section 55.

(e) Other definitions and special rules.

For purposes of this section—

(1) Wages. The term "wages" has the same meaning given to such term in section 51.

(2) Controlled groups.

(A) All employers treated as a single employer under section (a) or (b) of section 52 shall be treated as a single employer for purposes of this section.

(B) The credit (if any) determined under this section with respect to each such employer shall be its proportionate share of the wages and qualified employee health insurance costs giving rise to such credit.

(3) Certain other rules made applicable. Rules similar to the rules of section 51(k) and subsections (c), (d), and (e) of section 52 shall apply.

(4) Coordination with nonrevenue laws. Any reference in this section to a provision not contained in this title shall be treated for purposes of this section as a reference to such provision as in effect on the date of the enactment of this paragraph.

(5) Special rule for short taxable years. For any taxable year having less than 12 months, the amount determined under subsection (a)(2) shall be multiplied by a fraction, the numerator of which is the number of days in the taxable year and the denominator of which is 365.

(f) Termination.

This section shall not apply to taxable years beginning after December 31, 2011.

In 2010, P.L. 111-312, Sec. 732(a), substituted "December 31, 2011" for "December 31, 2009" in subsec. (f), effective for tax. yrs. begin. after 12/31/2009.

In 2008, P.L. 110-343, Sec. 314(a)DivB, substituted "December 31, 2009" for "December 31, 2007" in subsec. (f), effective tax. yrs. begin. after 12/31/2007.

In 2006, P.L. 109-432, Sec. 111(a), substituted "2007" for "2005" in subsec. (f), effective for tax. yrs. begin. after 12/31/2005.

In 2004, P.L. 108-311, Sec. 315, substituted "December 31, 2005" for "December 31, 2004" in subsec. (f), effective 10/4/2004.

—P.L. 108-311, Sec. 404(b)(1), added ", except that the base period taken into account for purposes of such adjustment shall be the calendar quarter beginning October 1, 1993" before the period at the end of para. (c)(3), effective for yrs. begin. after 12/31/2001 as if included in Sec. 611 of the Economic Growth and Tax Relief Reconciliation Act of 2001, P.L. 107-16.

In 2002, P.L. 107-147, Sec. 613(a), substituted "December 31, 2004" for "December 31, 2003" in subsec. (f), effective 3/9/2002.

In 1998, P.L. 105-206, Sec. 6023(1), substituted "work opportunity credit" for "targeted jobs credit" in the heading of subpara. (b)(1)(B), effective 7/22/98. [Note, this amendment was previously made by Sec. 1201(e)(1) of P.L. 104-188, see below]

In 1996, P.L. 104-188, Sec. 1201(e)(1), substituted "work opportunity credit" for "targeted jobs credit" in subpara. (b)(1)(B), effective for individuals who begin work for the employer after 9/30/96.

In 1993, P.L. 103-66, Sec. 13322(b), added Code Sec. 45A, effective for wages paid or incurred after 12/31/93.

Sec. 45B. Credit for portion of employer social security taxes paid with respect to employee cash tips.

(a) General rule.

For purposes of section 38, the employer social security credit determined under this section for the taxable year is an amount equal to the excess employer social security tax paid or incurred by the taxpayer during the taxable year.

Tax credits

(b) Excess employer social security tax.
For purposes of this section—
(1) In general. The term "excess employer social security tax" means any tax paid by an employer under section 3111 with respect to tips received by an employee during any month, to the extent such tips—
  (A) are deemed to have been paid by the employer to the employee pursuant to section 3121(q) (without regard to whether such tips are reported under section 6053), and
  (B) exceed the amount by which the wages (excluding tips) paid by the employer to the employee during such month are less than the total amount which would be payable (with respect to such employment) at the minimum wage rate applicable to such individual under section 6(a)(1) of the Fair Labor Standards Act of 1938 (as in effect on January 1, 2007, and determined without regard to section 3(m) of such Act).
(2) Only tips received for food or beverages taken into account. In applying paragraph (1), there shall be taken into account only tips received from customers in connection with the providing, delivering, or serving of food or beverages for consumption if the tipping of employees delivering or serving food or beverages by customers is customary.
(c) Denial of double benefit.
No deduction shall be allowed under this chapter for any amount taken into account in determining the credit under this section.
(d) Election not to claim credit.
This section shall not apply to a taxpayer for any taxable year if such taxpayer elects to have this section not apply for such taxable year.

In 2007, P.L. 110-28, Sec. 8213(a), added "as in effect on January 1, 2007, and" before "determined without regard to" in subpara. (b)(1)(B), effective for tips received for services performed 12/31/2006.
In 1996, P.L. 104-188, Sec. 1112(a)(1), added "(without regard to whether such tips are reported under section 6053)" after "section 3121(q)" in subpara. (b)(1)(A), effective for taxes paid after 12/31/93, with respect to services performed before, on, or after such date. [as amended by Sec. 1112(a)(2) of P.L. 104-188 of 8/20/96, see below]
—P.L. 104-188, Sec. 1112(a)(2), added ", with respect to services performed before, on, or after such date" after "1993" in Sec. 13443(d) of P.L. 103-66, the effective date for amendments made by Sec. 13443(a) of P.L. 103-66, see below.
—P.L. 104-188, Sec. 1112(b)(1), amended para. (b)(2), effective for tips received for services performed after 12/31/96.
Prior to amendment, para. (b)(2) read as follows:
"(2) Only tips received at food and beverage establishments taken into account. In applying paragraph (1), there shall be taken into account only tips received from customers in connection with the provision of food or beverages for consumption on the premises of an establishment with respect to which the tipping of employees serving food or beverages by customers is customary."
In 1993, P.L. 103-66, Sec. 13443(a), added Code Sec. 45B, effective for taxes paid after 12/31/93, with respect to services performed before, on, or after such date. [as amended by Sec. 1112(a)(2) of P.L. 104-188 of 8/20/96, see above]

Sec. 45C. Clinical testing expenses for certain drugs for rare diseases or conditions.
(a) General rule.
For purposes of section 38, the credit determined under this section for the taxable year is an amount equal to 50 percent of the qualified clinical testing expenses for the taxable year.
(b) Qualified clinical testing expenses.
For purposes of this section—
(1) Qualified clinical testing expenses.
  (A) In general. Except as otherwise provided in this paragraph, the term "qualified clinical testing expenses" means the amounts which are paid or incurred by the taxpayer during the taxable year which would be described in subsection (b) of section 41 if such subsection were applied with the modifications set forth in subparagraph (B).
  (B) Modifications. For purposes of subparagraph (A), subsection (b) of section 41 shall be applied—
    (i) by substituting "clinical testing" for "qualified research" each place it appears in paragraphs (2) and (3) of such subsection, and
    (ii) by substituting "100 percent" for "65 percent" in paragraph (3)(A) of such subsection.
  (C) Exclusion for amounts funded by grants, etc. The term "qualified clinical testing expenses" shall not include any amount to the extent such amount is funded by any grant, contract, or otherwise by another person (or any governmental entity).
  (D) Special rule. For purposes of this paragraph, section 41 shall be deemed to remain in effect for periods after June 30, 1995, and before July 1, 1996, and periods after December 31, 2011.
(2) Clinical testing.
  (A) In general. The term "clinical testing" means any human clinical testing—
    (i) which is carried out under an exemption for a drug being tested for a rare disease or condition under section 505(i) of the Federal Food, Drug, and Cosmetic Act (or regulations issued under such section),
    (ii) which occurs—
      (I) after the date such drug is designated under section 526 of such Act, and
      (II) before the date on which an application with respect to such drug is approved under section 505(b) of such Act or, if the drug is a biological product, before the date on which a license for such drug is issued under section 351 of the Public Health Service Act; and
    (iii) which is conducted by or on behalf of the taxpayer to whom the designation under such section 526 applies.
  (B) Testing must be related to use for rare disease or condition. Human clinical testing shall be taken into account under subparagraph (A) only to the extent such testing is related to the use of a drug for the rare disease or condition for which it was designated under section 526 of the Federal Food, Drug, and Cosmetic Act.
(c) Coordination with credit for increasing research expenditures.
(1) In general. Except as provided in paragraph (2), any qualified clinical testing expenses for a taxable year to which an election under this section applies shall not be taken into account for purposes of determining the credit allowable under section 41 for such taxable year.
(2) Expenses included in determining base period research expenses. Any qualified clinical testing expenses for any taxable year which are qualified research expenses (within the meaning of section 41(b)) shall be taken into account in determining base period research expenses for purposes of applying section 41 to subsequent taxable years.
(d) Definition and special rules.
(1) Rare disease or condition. For purposes of this section, the term "rare disease or condition" means any disease or condition which—
  (A) affects less than 200,000 persons in the United States, or
  (B) affects more than 200,000 persons in the United States but for which there is no reasonable expectation that the cost of developing and making available in the

United States a drug for such disease or condition will be recovered from sales in the United States of such drug.

Determinations under the preceding sentence with respect to any drug shall be made on the basis of the facts and circumstances as of the date such drug is designated under section 526 of the Federal Food, Drug, and Cosmetic Act.

(2) Special limitations on foreign testing.

(A) In general. No credit shall be allowed under this section with respect to any clinical testing conducted outside the United States unless—

(i) such testing is conducted outside the United States because there is an insufficient testing population in the United States, and

(ii) such testing is conducted by a United States person or by any other person who is not related to the taxpayer to whom the designation under section 526 of the Federal Food, Drug, and Cosmetic Act applies.

(B) Special limitation for corporations to which section 936 applies. No credit shall be allowed under this section with respect to any clinical testing conducted by a corporation to which an election under section 936 applies.

(3) Certain rules made applicable. Rules similar to the rules of paragraphs (1) and (2) of section 41(f) shall apply for purposes of this section.

(4) Election. This section shall apply to any taxpayer for any taxable year only if such taxpayer elects (at such time and in such manner as the Secretary may by regulations prescribe) to have this section apply for such taxable year.

In 2010, P.L. 111-312, Sec. 731(b), substituted "December 31, 2011" for "December 31, 2009" in subpara. (b)(1)(D), effective for amounts paid or incurred after 12/31/2009.

In 2008, P.L. 110-343, Sec. 301(a)(2)DivC, substituted "after December 31, 2009" for "after December 31, 2007" in subpara. (b)(1)(D), effective for amounts paid or incurred after 12/31/2007.

In 2006, P.L. 109-432, Sec. 104(a)(2), substituted "2007" for "2005" in subpara. (b)(1)(D), effective for amounts paid or incurred after 12/31/2005.

In 2004, P.L. 108-311, Sec. 301(a)(2), substituted "December 31, 2005" for "June 30, 2004" in subpara. (b)(1)(D), effective for amounts paid or incurred after 6/30/2004.

In 1999, P.L. 106-170, Sec. 502(a)(2), substituted "June 30, 2004" for "June 30, 1999" in subpara. (b)(1)(D), effective for amounts paid or incurred after 6/30/99.

In 1998, P.L. 105-277, Sec. 1001(b), substituted "June 30, 1999" for "June 30, 1998" in subpara. (b)(1)(D), effective for amounts paid or incurred after 6/30/98.

In 1997, P.L. 105-115, Sec. 125(b)(2)(O), deleted "or 507" after "section 505(b)" in subclause (b)(2)(A)(ii)(II), effective 11/21/97.

—P.L. 105-34, Sec. 601(b)(2), substituted "June 30, 1998" for "May 31, 1997" in para. (b)(1), effective for amounts paid or incurred after 5/31/97.

—P.L. 105-34, Sec. 604(a), deleted subsec. (e), effective for amounts paid or incurred after 5/31/97.

Prior to deletion, subsec. (e) read as follows:

"(e) Termination. This section shall not apply to any amount paid or incurred—

"(1) after December 31, 1994, and before July 1, 1996, or

"(2) after May 31, 1997."

In 1996, P.L. 104-188, Sec. 1204(e), added ", and before July 1, 1996, and periods after May 31, 1997" after "June 30, 1995" in subpara. (b)(1)(D), effective for tax. yrs. end. after 6/30/96. Sec. 1204(f)(3) of this Act provides:

"(3) Estimated tax. The amendments made by this section shall not be taken into account under section 6654 or 6655 of the Internal Revenue Code of 1986 (relating to failure to pay estimated tax) in determining the amount of any installment required to be paid for a taxable year beginning in 1997."

—P.L. 104-188, Sec. 1205(a)(1), redesignated Code Sec. 28 as Code Sec. 45C ... Sec. 1205(b), amended subsec. (e) ... Sec. 1205(b)(1), substituted "For purposes of section 38, the credit determined under this section for the taxable year is" for "There shall be allowed as a credit against the tax imposed by this chapter for the taxable year" in subsec. (a) ... Sec. 1205(d)(2), deleted para. (d)(2) and redesignated paras. (d)(3)-(5) as (d)(2)-(4), effective for amounts paid or incurred in tax. yrs. end. after 6/30/96.

Prior to amendment, subsec. (e) read as follows:

"(e) Termination. This section shall not apply to any amount paid or incurred after December 31, 1994."

Prior to deletion, para. (d)(2) read as follows:

"(2) Limitation based on amount of tax. The credit allowed by this section for any taxable year shall not exceed the excess (if any) of—

"(A) the regular tax (reduced by the sum of the credits allowable under subpart A and section 27), over

"(B) the tentative minimum tax for the taxable year."

In 1993, P.L. 103-66, Sec. 13111(a)(2), substituted "June 30, 1995" for "June 30, 1992" in subpara. (b)(1)(D) ... Sec. 13111(b), substituted "December 31, 1994" for "June 30, 1992" in subsec. (e), effective for tax. yrs. end. after 6/30/92.

In 1991, P.L. 102-227, Sec. 102(b), substituted "June 30, 1992" for "December 31, 1991" in subpara. (b)(1)(D) ... Sec. 111(a), substituted "June 30, 1992" for "December 31, 1991" in subsec. (e), effective for tax. yrs. end. after 12/31/91.

In 1990, P.L. 101-508, Sec. 11402(b)(2), substituted "December 31, 1991" for "December 31, 1990" in subpara. (b)(1)(D), effective for tax. yrs. begin. after 12/31/89.

—P.L. 101-508, Sec. 11411, substituted "December 31, 1991" for "December 31, 1990" in subsec. (e), effective 11/5/90.

In 1989, P.L. 101-239, Sec. 7110(a)(3), substituted "December 31, 1990" for "December 31, 1989" in subpara. (b)(1)(D), effective 12/19/89.

In 1988, P.L. 100-647, Sec. 1018(q)(1), amended subclause (b)(2)(A)(ii)(II), effective for amounts paid or incurred after 12/31/82 in tax. yrs. end. after 12/31/82. Prior to amendment, subclause (b)(2)(A)(ii)(II) read as follows:

"(II) before the date on which an application with respect to such drug is approved under section 505(b) of such Act or, if the drug is a biological product, before the date on which a license for such drug is issued under section 351 of the Public Health Services Act,"

—P.L. 100-647, Sec. 4008(c)(1), substituted "1989" for "1988" in para. (b)(1), effective for tax. yrs. begin. after 12/31/88.

In 1986, P.L. 99-514, Sec. 231(d)(3)(A)(i), substituted "section 41" for "section 30" each place it appeared in subsecs. (b) and (c) ... Sec. 231(d)(3)(A)(ii), substituted "section 41(b)" for "section 30(b)" in para. (c)(2) ... Sec. 231(d)(3)(A)(iii), substituted "section 41(f)" for "section 30(f)" in para. (d)(4) ... Sec. 231(d)(3)(A)(iv), substituted "1988" for "1985" in subpara. (b)(1)(D), effective for tax. yrs. begin. after 12/31/85.

—P.L. 99-514, Sec. 232, substituted "1990" for "1987" in subsec. (e), effective 10/22/86.

—P.L. 99-514, Sec. 701(c)(2), amended para. (d)(2), effective for tax. yrs. begin. after 12/31/86.

Prior to amendment, para. (d)(2) read as follows:

"(2) Limitation based on amount of tax. The credit allowed by this section for any taxable year shall not exceed the taxpayer's tax liability for the taxable year (as defined in section 26(b)), reduced by the sum of the credits allowable under subpart A and section 27."

—P.L. 99-514, Sec. 1879(b)(1)(A), amended subpara. (d)(3)(B), effective as provided in Secs. 1277(c)(1) and 1277(d) of this Act, which read as follows:

"(c) Special rules for the Virgin Islands.

"(1) In general. The amendments made by section 1275(c) shall apply with respect to the Virgin Islands (and residents thereof and corporations created or organized therein) only if (and so long as) an implementing agreement is in effect between the United States and the Virgin Islands with respect to the establishment of rules under which the evasion or avoidance of United States income tax shall not be permitted or facilitated by such possession. Any such implementing agreement shall be executed on behalf of the United States by the Secretary of the Treasury, after consultation with the Secretary of the Interior.[...]

"(d) Report on implementing agreements. If, during the 1-year period beginning on the date of the enactment of this Act, any implementing agreement described in subsection (b) or (c) is not executed, the Secretary of the Treasury or his delegate shall report to the Committee on Finance of the United States Senate, the Committee on Ways and Means, and the Committee on Interior and Insular Affairs of the House of Representatives with respect to—

"(1) the status of such negotiations, and

"(2) the reason why such agreement has not been executed."

Prior to amendment, subpara. (d)(3)(B) read as follows:

"(B) Special limitation for corporations to which section 934(b) or 936 applies. No credit shall be allowed under this section with respect to any clinical testing conducted by a corporation to which section 934(b) applies or to which an election under section 936 applies."

—P.L. 99-514, Sec. 1879(b)(1)(A), substituted "the date such drug" for "the date of such drug" in subclause (b)(2)(A)(ii)(I) ... Sec. 1879(b)(1)(B), substituted "of such Act or, if the drug is a biological product, before the date on which a license for such drug is issued under section 351 of the Public Health Services Act" for "of such Act" in subclause (b)(2)(A)(ii)(II) ... Sec. 1879(b)(2), amended para. (d)(1), effective for amounts paid or incurred after 12/31/82 in tax. yrs. end. after 12/31/82.

Prior to amendment, para. (d)(1) read as follows:

"(1) Rare disease or condition. For purposes of this section, the term 'rare disease or condition' means any disease or condition which occurs so infrequently in the United States that there is no reasonable expectation that the cost of developing and making available in the United States a drug for such disease or condition will be recovered from sales in the United States of such drug. Determinations under the preceding sentence with respect to any drug shall be made on the basis of the facts and circumstances as of the date such drug is designated under section 526 of the Federal Food, Drug, and Cosmetic Act."

In 1984, P.L. 98-369, Sec. 471(c)(1), redesignated Code Sec. 44H as Code Sec. 28 ... Sec. 474(g)(1)(A), substituted "section 30" for "section 44F" each place it appeared in Code Sec. 28 ... Sec. 474(g)(1)(B), substituted "section 30(b)" for "section 44F(b)" in para. (c)(2) ... Sec. 474(g)(1)(C), substituted "section 30(f)" for "section 44F(f)" in para. (d)(4) ... Sec. 474(g)(2), amended para. (d)(2), effective for tax. yrs. begin. after 12/31/83 and to carrybacks from tax. yrs. begin. after 12/31/83.

Tax credits Code Sec. 45D(d)(2)(A)(ii)

Prior to amendment, para. (d)(2) read as follows:

"(2) Limitation based on amount of tax. The credit allowed by this section for any taxable year shall not exceed the amount of the tax imposed by this chapter for the taxable year reduced by the sum of the credits allowable under a section of this subpart having a lower number or letter designation than this section, other than the credits allowable by sections 31, 39, and 43. For purposes of the preceding sentence, the term 'tax imposed by this chapter' shall not include any tax treated as not imposed by this chapter under the last sentence of section 53(a)."

—P.L. 98-369, Sec. 612(e)(1), substituted "section 26(b)" for "section 25(b)" in para. (d)(2) (as amended by Sec. 474(g)(2) of this Act), effective for interest paid or accrued after 12/31/84, on indebtedness incurred after 12/31/84 and to elections under Code Sec. 25(c)(2)(A)(ii) (as added by this Act) for calendar years after 1983.

—P.L. 98-369, Sec. 632, provided various exceptions to the amendments made by Title VI of this Act. See note following Code Sec. 103A.

In 1983, P.L. 97-414, Sec. 4(a), added Code Sec. 44H, effective for amounts paid or incurred after 12/31/82, in tax. yrs. end. after 12/31/82.

Sec. 45D. New markets tax credit.
(a) Allowance of credit.
(1) In general. For purposes of section 38, in the case of a taxpayer who holds a qualified equity investment on a credit allowance date of such investment which occurs during the taxable year, the new markets tax credit determined under this section for such taxable year is an amount equal to the applicable percentage of the amount paid to the qualified community development entity for such investment at its original issue.
(2) Applicable percentage. For purposes of paragraph (1), the applicable percentage is—
(A) 5 percent with respect to the first 3 credit allowance dates, and
(B) 6 percent with respect to the remainder of the credit allowance dates.
(3) Credit allowance date. For purposes of paragraph (1), the term "credit allowance date" means, with respect to any qualified equity investment—
(A) the date on which such investment is initially made, and
(B) each of the 6 anniversary dates of such date thereafter.
(b) Qualified equity investment.
For purposes of this section—
(1) In general. The term "qualified equity investment" means any equity investment in a qualified community development entity if—
(A) such investment is acquired by the taxpayer at its original issue (directly or through an underwriter) solely in exchange for cash,
(B) substantially all of such cash is used by the qualified community development entity to make qualified low-income community investments, and
(C) such investment is designated for purposes of this section by the qualified community development entity.
Such term shall not include any equity investment issued by a qualified community development entity more than 5 years after the date that such entity receives an allocation under subsection (f). Any allocation not used within such 5-year period may be reallocated by the Secretary under subsection (f).
(2) Limitation. The maximum amount of equity investments issued by a qualified community development entity which may be designated under paragraph (1)(C) by such entity shall not exceed the portion of the limitation amount allocated under subsection (f) to such entity.
(3) Safe harbor for determining use of cash. The requirement of paragraph (1)(B) shall be treated as met if at least 85 percent of the aggregate gross assets of the qualified community development entity are invested in qualified low-income community investments.

(4) Treatment of subsequent purchasers. The term "qualified equity investment" includes any equity investment which would (but for paragraph (1)(A)) be a qualified equity investment in the hands of the taxpayer if such investment was a qualified equity investment in the hands of a prior holder.
(5) Redemptions. A rule similar to the rule of section 1202(c)(3) shall apply for purposes of this subsection.
(6) Equity investment. The term "equity investment" means—
(A) any stock (other than nonqualified preferred stock as defined in section 351(g)(2)) in an entity which is a corporation, and
(B) any capital interest in an entity which is a partnership.
(c) Qualified community development entity.
For purposes of this section—
(1) In general. The term "qualified community development entity" means any domestic corporation or partnership if—
(A) the primary mission of the entity is serving, or providing investment capital for, low-income communities or low-income persons,
(B) the entity maintains accountability to residents of low-income communities through their representation on any governing board of the entity or on any advisory board to the entity, and
(C) the entity is certified by the Secretary for purposes of this section as being a qualified community development entity.
(2) Special rules for certain organizations. The requirements of paragraph (1) shall be treated as met by—
(A) any specialized small business investment company (as defined in section 1044(c)(3)), and
(B) any community development financial institution (as defined in section 103 of the Community Development Banking and Financial Institutions Act of 1994 (12 U.S.C. 4702)).
(d) Qualified low-income community investments.
For purposes of this section—
(1) In general. The term "qualified low-income community investment" means—
(A) any capital or equity investment in, or loan to, any qualified active low-income community business,
(B) the purchase from another community development entity of any loan made by such entity which is a qualified low-income community investment,
(C) financial counseling and other services specified in regulations prescribed by the Secretary to businesses located in, and residents of, low-income communities, and
(D) any equity investment in, or loan to, any qualified community development entity.
(2) Qualified active low-income community business.
(A) In general. For purposes of paragraph (1), the term "qualified active low-income community business" means, with respect to any taxable year, any corporation (including a non-profit corporation) or partnership if for such year—
(i) at least 50 percent of the total gross income of such entity is derived from the active conduct of a qualified business within any low-income community,
(ii) a substantial portion of the use of the tangible property of such entity (whether owned or leased) is within any low-income community,

1,165

(iii) a substantial portion of the services performed for such entity by its employees are performed in any low-income community,

(iv) less than 5 percent of the average of the aggregate unadjusted bases of the property of such entity is attributable to collectibles (as defined in section 408(m)(2)) other than collectibles that are held primarily for sale to customers in the ordinary course of such business, and

(v) less than 5 percent of the average of the aggregate unadjusted bases of the property of such entity is attributable to nonqualified financial property (as defined in section 1397C(e)).

(B) **Proprietorship.** Such term shall include any business carried on by an individual as a proprietor if such business would meet the requirements of subparagraph (A) were it incorporated.

(C) **Portions of business may be qualified active low-income community business.** The term "qualified active low-income community business" includes any trades or businesses which would qualify as a qualified active low-income community business if such trades or businesses were separately incorporated.

(3) Qualified business. For purposes of this subsection, the term "qualified business" has the meaning given to such term by section 1397C(d); except that—

(A) in lieu of applying paragraph (2)(B) thereof, the rental to others of real property located in any low-income community shall be treated as a qualified business if there are substantial improvements located on such property, and

(B) paragraph (3) thereof shall not apply.

(e) Low-income community.

For purposes of this section—

(1) In general. The term "low-income community" means any population census tract if—

(A) the poverty rate for such tract is at least 20 percent, or

(B)(i) in the case of a tract not located within a metropolitan area, the median family income for such tract does not exceed 80 percent of statewide median family income, or

(ii) in the case of a tract located within a metropolitan area, the median family income for such tract does not exceed 80 percent of the greater of statewide median family income or the metropolitan area median family income.

Subparagraph (B) shall be applied using possessionwide median family income in the case of census tracts located within a possession of the United States.

(2) Targeted populations. The Secretary shall prescribe regulations under which 1 or more targeted populations (within the meaning of section 103(20) of the Riegle Community Development and Regulatory Improvement Act of 1994 (12 U.S.C. 4702(20))) may be treated as low-income communities. Such regulations shall include procedures for determining which entities are qualified active low-income community businesses with respect to such populations.

(3) Areas not within census tracts. In the case of an area which is not tracted for population census tracts, the equivalent county divisions (as defined by the Bureau of the Census for purposes of defining poverty areas) shall be used for purposes of determining poverty rates and median family income.

(4) Tracts with low population. A population census tract with a population of less than 2,000 shall be treated as a low-income community for purposes of this section if such tract—

(A) is within an empowerment zone the designation of which is in effect under section 1391, and

(B) is contiguous to 1 or more low-income communities (determined without regard to this paragraph).

(5) Modification of income requirement for census tracts within high migration rural counties.

(A) **In general.** In the case of a population census tract located within a high migration rural county, paragraph (1)(B)(i) shall be applied by substituting "85 percent" for "80 percent".

(B) **High migration rural county.** For purposes of this paragraph, the term "high migration rural county" means any county which, during the 20-year period ending with the year in which the most recent census was conducted, has a net out-migration of inhabitants from the county of at least 10 percent of the population of the county at the beginning of such period.

(f) National limitation on amount of investments designated.

(1) In general. There is a new markets tax credit limitation for each calendar year. Such limitation is—

(A) $1,000,000,000 for 2001,

(B) $1,500,000,000 for 2002 and 2003,

(C) $2,000,000,000 for 2004 and 2005,

(D) $3,500,000,000 for 2006 and 2007,

(E) $5,000,000,000 for 2008,

(F) $5,000,000,000 for 2009

(G) $3,500,000,000 for 2010 and 2011.

(2) Allocation of limitation. The limitation under paragraph (1) shall be allocated by the Secretary among qualified community development entities selected by the Secretary. In making allocations under the preceding sentence, the Secretary shall give priority to any entity—

(A) with a record of having successfully provided capital or technical assistance to disadvantaged businesses or communities, or

(B) which intends to satisfy the requirement under subsection (b)(1)(B) by making qualified low-income community investments in 1 or more businesses in which persons unrelated to such entity (within the meaning of section 267(b) or 707(b)(1)) hold the majority equity interest.

(3) Carryover of unused limitation. If the new markets tax credit limitation for any calendar year exceeds the aggregate amount allocated under paragraph (2) for such year, such limitation for the succeeding calendar year shall be increased by the amount of such excess. No amount may be carried under the preceding sentence to any calendar year after 2016.

(g) Recapture of credit in certain cases.

(1) In general. If, at any time during the 7-year period beginning on the date of the original issue of a qualified equity investment in a qualified community development entity, there is a recapture event with respect to such investment, then the tax imposed by this chapter for the taxable year in which such event occurs shall be increased by the credit recapture amount.

(2) Credit recapture amount. For purposes of paragraph (1), the credit recapture amount is an amount equal to the sum of—

(A) the aggregate decrease in the credits allowed to the taxpayer under section 38 for all prior taxable years which would have resulted if no credit had been determined under this section with respect to such investment, plus

(B) interest at the underpayment rate established under section 6621 on the amount determined under subparagraph (A) for each prior taxable year for the period beginning on the due date for filing the return for the prior taxable year involved.

No deduction shall be allowed under this chapter for interest described in subparagraph (B).

(3) Recapture event. For purposes of paragraph (1), there is a recapture event with respect to an equity investment in a qualified community development entity if—

(A) such entity ceases to be a qualified community development entity,

(B) the proceeds of the investment cease to be used as required of subsection (b)(1)(B), or

(C) such investment is redeemed by such entity.

(4) Special rules.

(A) Tax benefit rule. The tax for the taxable year shall be increased under paragraph (1) only with respect to credits allowed by reason of this section which were used to reduce tax liability. In the case of credits not so used to reduce tax liability, the carryforwards and carrybacks under section 39 shall be appropriately adjusted.

(B) No credits against tax. Any increase in tax under this subsection shall not be treated as a tax imposed by this chapter for purposes of determining the amount of any credit under this chapter or for purposes of section 55.

(h) Basis reduction.

The basis of any qualified equity investment shall be reduced by the amount of any credit determined under this section with respect to such investment. This subsection shall not apply for purposes of sections 1202, 1400B, and 1400F.

(i) Regulations.

The Secretary shall prescribe such regulations as may be appropriate to carry out this section, including regulations—

(1) which limit the credit for investments which are directly or indirectly subsidized by other Federal tax benefits (including the credit under section 42 and the exclusion from gross income under section 103),

(2) which prevent the abuse of the purposes of this section,

(3) which provide rules for determining whether the requirement of subsection (b)(1)(B) is treated as met,

(4) which impose appropriate reporting requirements,

(5) which apply the provisions of this section to newly formed entities, and

(6) which ensure that non-metropolitan counties receive a proportional allocation of qualified equity investments.

In 2010, P.L. 111-312, Sec. 733(a)(1), deleted "and" at the end of subpara. (f)(1)(E) ... Sec. 733(a)(2), deleted "." at the end of subpara. (f)(1)(F) ... Sec. 733(a)(3), added subpara. (f)(1)(G) ... Sec. 733(b), substituted "2016" for "2014" in para. (f)(3), effective for calendar yrs. begin. after 2009.
In 2009, P.L. 111-5, Sec. 1403(a)(1), deleted "and" at the end of subpara. (f)(1)(C) ... Sec. 1403(a)(2), substituted "and 2007" for ", 2007, 2008, and 2009." in subpara. (f)(1)(D) ... Sec. 1403(a)(3), added subparas. (f)(1)(E)-(F), enacted 2/17/2009.
—P.L. 111-5, Sec. 1403(b), of this Act, reads as follows:
(b) Special rule for allocation of increased 2008 limitation. The amount of the increase in the new markets tax credit limitation for calendar year 2008 by reason of the amendments made by subsection (a) shall be allocated in accordance with section 45D(f)(2) of the Internal Revenue Code of 1986 to qualified community development entities (as defined in section 45D(c) of such Code) which—
(1) submitted an allocation application with respect to calendar year 2008, and
(2)(A) did not receive an allocation for such calendar year, or
(B) received an allocation for such calendar year in an amount less than the amount requested in the allocation application.

In 2008, P.L. 110-343, Sec. 302, substituted "2008, and 2009" for "and 2008", effective 10/3/2008.
In 2006, P.L. 109-432, Sec. 102(a), substituted ", 2007, and 2008" for "and 2007" in subpara. (f)(1)(D) ... Sec. 102(b), deleted "and" at the end of para. (i)(4), substituted ", and " for the period at the end of para. (i)(5) and added para. (i)(6), effective 12/20/2006.
In 2004, P.L. 108-357, Sec. 221(a), amended para. (e)(2), effective for designations made by the Secretary of the Treasury after 10/22/2004.
Prior to amendment, para. (e)(2) read as follows:
"(2) Targeted areas. The Secretary may designate any area within any census tract as a low-income community if—
"(A) the boundary of such area is continuous,
"(B) the area would satisfy the requirements of paragraph (1) if it were a census tract, and
"(C) an inadequate access to investment capital exists in such area."
—P.L. 108-357, Sec. 221(b), added para. (e)(4), effective for investments made after 10/22/2004.
—P.L. 108-357, Sec. 223(a), added para. (e)(5), effective for investments made after 12/31/2000 as if included in Sec. 121(a) of the Community Renewal Tax Relief Act of 2000, P.L. 106-554 [P.L. 106-554].
In 2000, P.L. 106-554, Sec. 1(a)(7), [which enacted into law Sec. 121(a) of P.L. 106-554] added Code Sec. 45D, effective for investments made after 12/31/2000.
—P.L. 106-554, Sec. 1(a)(7), [which enacted into law Sec. 121(f)–(g) of P.L. 106-554] of this Act, reads as follows:
"(f) Guidance on allocation of national limitation. Not later than 120 days after the date of the enactment of this Act, the Secretary of the Treasury or the Secretary's delegate shall issue guidance which specifies—
"(1) how entities shall apply for an allocation under section 45D(f)(2) of the Internal Revenue Code of 1986, as added by this section;
"(2) the competitive procedure through which such allocations are made; and
"(3) the actions that such Secretary or delegate shall take to ensure that such allocations are properly made to appropriate entities.
"(g) Audit and report. Not later than January 31 of 2004, 2007, and 2010, the Comptroller General of the United States shall, pursuant to an audit of the new markets tax credit program established under section 45D of the Internal Revenue Code of 1986 (as added by subsection (a)), report to Congress on such program, including all qualified community development entities that receive an allocation under the new markets credit under such section."

• *Caution:* Code Sec. 45E, following, was added by Sec. 619(a), P.L. 107-16, the Economic Growth and Tax Relief Reconciliation Act of 2001 (EGTRRA). These provisions generally sunset for tax years beginning after 12/31/2012. For specific sunset provisions see Sec. 901, P.L. 107-16 (as amended) reproduced in history notes for this Code Sec.

Sec. 45E. Small employer pension plan startup costs.
(a) General rule.

For purposes of section 38, in the case of an eligible employer, the small employer pension plan startup cost credit determined under this section for any taxable year is an amount equal to 50 percent of the qualified startup costs paid or incurred by the taxpayer during the taxable year.

(b) Dollar limitation.

The amount of the credit determined under this section for any taxable year shall not exceed—

(1) $500 for the first credit year and each of the 2 taxable years immediately following the first credit year, and

(2) zero for any other taxable year.

(c) Eligible employer.

For purposes of this section—

(1) In general. The term "eligible employer" has the meaning given such term by section 408(p)(2)(C)(i).

(2) Requirement for new qualified employer plans. Such term shall not include an employer if, during the 3-taxable year period immediately preceding the 1st taxable year for which the credit under this section is otherwise allowable for a qualified employer plan of the employer, the employer or any member of any controlled group including the employer (or any predecessor of either) established or maintained a qualified employer plan with respect to which contributions were made, or benefits were accrued, for substantially the same employees as are in the qualified employer plan.

(d) Other definitions.
For purposes of this section—

(1) Qualified startup costs.

(A) In general. The term "qualified startup costs" means any ordinary and necessary expenses of an eligible employer which are paid or incurred in connection with—

(i) the establishment or administration of an eligible employer plan, or

(ii) the retirement-related education of employees with respect to such plan.

(B) Plan must have at least 1 participant. Such term shall not include any expense in connection with a plan that does not have at least 1 employee eligible to participate who is not a highly compensated employee.

(2) Eligible employer plan. The term "eligible employer plan" means a qualified employer plan within the meaning of section 4972(d).

(3) First credit year. The term "first credit year" means—

(A) the taxable year which includes the date that the eligible employer plan to which such costs relate becomes effective, or

(B) at the election of the eligible employer, the taxable year preceding the taxable year referred to in subparagraph (A).

(e) Special rules.
For purposes of this section—

(1) Aggregation rules. All persons treated as a single employer under subsection (a) or (b) of section 52, or subsection (m) or (o) of section 414, shall be treated as one person. All eligible employer plans shall be treated as 1 eligible employer plan.

(2) Disallowance of deduction. No deduction shall be allowed for that portion of the qualified startup costs paid or incurred for the taxable year which is equal to the credit determined under subsection (a).

(3) Election not to claim credit. This section shall not apply to a taxpayer for any taxable year if such taxpayer elects to have this section not apply for such taxable year.

In 2010, P.L. 111-312, Sec. 101(a)(1), substituted "December 31, 2012" for "December 31, 2010" both places it appeared in Sec. 901, P.L. 107-16 [see below], effective as if included in the enactment of P.L. 107-16, EGTRRA, 6/7/2001.

In 2006, P.L. 109-280, Sec. 811, of this Act [relating to Sec. 901 of P.L. 107-16, see below], provides:

"SEC. 811. PENSIONS AND INDIVIDUAL RETIREMENT ARRANGEMENT PROVISIONS OF ECONOMIC GROWTH AND TAX RELIEF RECONCILIATION ACT OF 2001 MADE PERMANENT.

"Title IX of the Economic Growth and Tax Relief Reconciliation Act of 2001 shall not apply to the provisions of, and amendments made by, subtitles A through F of title VI of such Act (relating to pension and individual retirement arrangement provisions)."

In 2002, P.L. 107-358, Sec. 2, added subsec. (c) in Sec. 901 of P.L. 107-16 [see below], effective 12/17/2002.

—P.L. 107-147, Sec. 411(n)(1), substituted "(m)" for "(n)" in para. (e)(1), effective for costs paid or incurred in tax. yrs. begin. after 12/31/2001, with respect to qualified employer plans first effective after 12/31/2001.

—P.L. 107-147, Sec. 411(n)(2), substituted "first effective" for "established" in Sec. 619(d) of P.L. 107-16, which provides the effective dates for amendments made by Sec. 619 of P.L. 107-16, see below.

In 2001, P.L. 107-16, Sec. 619(a), added Code Sec. 45E, effective for costs paid or incurred in tax. yrs. begin. after 12/31/2001, with respect to qualified employer plans first effective after 12/31/2001. [effective date amended by Sec. 411(n)(2) of P.L. 107-147, see above]

—P.L. 107-16, Sec. 901, of this Act [as amended by Sec. 2, P.L. 107-358 and Sec. 101(a)(1), P.L. 111-312, and as related to Sec. 811 of P.L. 109-280, see above], reads as follows:

"Sec. 901. Sunset of provisions of Act.

"(a) In general. All provisions of, and amendments made by, this Act shall not apply—

"(1) to taxable, plan, or limitation years beginning after December 31, 2012 or

"(2) in the case of title V, to estates of decedents dying, gifts made, or generation skipping transfers, after December 31, 2012.

"(b) Application of certain laws. The Internal Revenue Code of 1986 and the Employee Retirement Income Security Act of 1974 shall be applied and administered to years, estates, gifts, and transfers described in subsection (a) as if the provisions and amendments described in subsection (a) had never been enacted.

"(c) Exception. Subsection (a) shall not apply to section 803 (relating to no federal income tax on restitution received by victims of the Nazi regime or their heirs or estates)."

• **Caution:** Code Sec. 45F, following, was added by Sec. 205(a), P.L. 107-16, the Economic Growth and Tax Relief Reconciliation Act of 2001 (EGTRRA). These provisions generally sunset for tax years beginning after 12/31/2012. For specific sunset provisions see Sec. 901, P.L. 107-16 (as amended) reproduced in history notes for this Code Sec.

Sec. 45F. Employer-provided child care credit.

(a) In general.

For purposes of section 38, the employer-provided child care credit determined under this section for the taxable year is an amount equal to the sum of—

(1) 25 percent of the qualified child care expenditures, and

(2) 10 percent of the qualified child care resource and referral expenditures,

of the taxpayer for such taxable year.

(b) Dollar limitation.

The credit allowable under subsection (a) for any taxable year shall not exceed $150,000.

(c) Definitions.

For purposes of this section—

(1) Qualified child care expenditure.

(A) In general. The term "qualified child care expenditure" means any amount paid or incurred—

(i) to acquire, construct, rehabilitate, or expand property—

(I) which is to be used as part of a qualified child care facility of the taxpayer,

(II) with respect to which a deduction for depreciation (or amortization in lieu of depreciation) is allowable, and

(III) which does not constitute part of the principal residence (within the meaning of section 121) of the taxpayer or any employee of the taxpayer,

(ii) for the operating costs of a qualified child care facility of the taxpayer, including costs related to the training of employees, to scholarship programs, and to the providing of increased compensation to employees with higher levels of child care training, or

(iii) under a contract with a qualified child care facility to provide child care services to employees of the taxpayer.

(B) Fair market value. The term "qualified child care expenditures" shall not include expenses in excess of the fair market value of such care.

(2) Qualified child care facility.

(A) In general. The term "qualified child care facility" means a facility—

(i) the principal use of which is to provide child care assistance, and

(ii) which meets the requirements of all applicable laws and regulations of the State or local government in which it is located, including the licensing of the facility as a child care facility.

Clause (i) shall not apply to a facility which is the principal residence (within the meaning of section 121) of the operator of the facility.

(B) Special rules with respect to a taxpayer. A facility shall not be treated as a qualified child care facility with respect to a taxpayer unless—

(i) enrollment in the facility is open to employees of the taxpayer during the taxable year,

(ii) if the facility is the principal trade or business of the taxpayer, at least 30 percent of the enrollees of such facility are dependents of employees of the taxpayer, and

(iii) the use of such facility (or the eligibility to use such facility) does not discriminate in favor of employees of the taxpayer who are highly compensated employees (within the meaning of section 414(q)).

(3) Qualified child care resource and referral expenditure.

(A) In general. The term "qualified child care resource and referral expenditure" means any amount paid or incurred under a contract to provide child care resource and referral services to an employee of the taxpayer.

(B) Nondiscrimination. The services shall not be treated as qualified unless the provision of such services (or the eligibility to use such services) does not discriminate in favor of employees of the taxpayer who are highly compensated employees (within the meaning of section 414(q)).

(d) Recapture of acquisition and construction credit.

(1) In general. If, as of the close of any taxable year, there is a recapture event with respect to any qualified child care facility of the taxpayer, then the tax of the taxpayer under this chapter for such taxable year shall be increased by an amount equal to the product of—

(A) the applicable recapture percentage, and

(B) the aggregate decrease in the credits allowed under section 38 for all prior taxable years which would have resulted if the qualified child care expenditures of the taxpayer described in subsection (c)(1)(A) with respect to such facility had been zero.

(2) Applicable recapture percentage.

(A) In general. For purposes of this subsection, the applicable recapture percentage shall be determined from the following table:

If the recapture event occurs in:	The applicable recapture percentage is:
Years 1-3	100
Year 4	85
Year 5	70
Year 6	55
Year 7	40
Year 8	25
Years 9 and 10	10
Years 11 and thereafter	0.

(B) Years. For purposes of subparagraph (A), year 1 shall begin on the first day of the taxable year in which the qualified child care facility is placed in service by the taxpayer.

(3) Recapture event defined. For purposes of this subsection, the term "recapture event" means—

(A) Cessation of operation. The cessation of the operation of the facility as a qualified child care facility.

(B) Change in ownership.

(i) In general. Except as provided in clause (ii), the disposition of a taxpayer's interest in a qualified child care facility with respect to which the credit described in subsection (a) was allowable.

(ii) Agreement to assume recapture liability. Clause (i) shall not apply if the person acquiring such interest in the facility agrees in writing to assume the recapture liability of the person disposing of such interest in effect immediately before such disposition. In the event of such an assumption, the person acquiring the interest in the facility shall be treated as the taxpayer for purposes of assessing any recapture liability (computed as if there had been no change in ownership).

(4) Special rules.

(A) Tax benefit rule. The tax for the taxable year shall be increased under paragraph (1) only with respect to credits allowed by reason of this section which were used to reduce tax liability. In the case of credits not so used to reduce tax liability, the carryforwards and carrybacks under section 39 shall be appropriately adjusted.

(B) No credits against tax. Any increase in tax under this subsection shall not be treated as a tax imposed by this chapter for purposes of determining the amount of any credit under this chapter or for purposes of section 55.

(C) No recapture by reason of casualty loss. The increase in tax under this subsection shall not apply to a cessation of operation of the facility as a qualified child care facility by reason of a casualty loss to the extent such loss is restored by reconstruction or replacement within a reasonable period established by the Secretary.

(e) Special rules.

For purposes of this section—

(1) Aggregation rules. All persons which are treated as a single employer under subsections (a) and (b) of section 52 shall be treated as a single taxpayer.

(2) Pass-thru in the case of estates and trusts. Under regulations prescribed by the Secretary, rules similar to the rules of subsection (d) of section 52 shall apply.

(3) Allocation in the case of partnerships. In the case of partnerships, the credit shall be allocated among partners under regulations prescribed by the Secretary.

(f) No double benefit.

(1) Reduction in basis. For purposes of this subtitle—

(A) In general. If a credit is determined under this section with respect to any property by reason of expenditures described in subsection (c)(1)(A), the basis of such property shall be reduced by the amount of the credit so determined.

(B) Certain dispositions. If, during any taxable year, there is a recapture amount determined with respect to any property the basis of which was reduced under subparagraph (A), the basis of such property (immediately before the event resulting in such recapture) shall be increased by an amount equal to such recapture amount. For purposes of the preceding sentence, the term "recapture amount" means any increase in tax (or adjustment in carrybacks or carryovers) determined under subsection (d).

(2) Other deductions and credits. No deduction or credit shall be allowed under any other provision of this chapter with respect to the amount of the credit determined under this section.

Code Sec. 45F   **Tax credits**

In 2010, P.L. 111-312, Sec. 101(a)(1), substituted "December 31, 2012" for "December 31, 2010" both places it appeared in Sec. 901, P.L. 107-16 [see below], effective as if included in the enactment of P.L. 107-16, EGTRRA, 6/7/2001.

In 2002, P.L. 107-358, Sec. 2, added subsec. (c) in Sec. 901, P.L. 107-16 and Sec. 101(a)(1), 111-312 [see below], effective 12/17/2002.

—P.L. 107-147, Sec. 411(d)(1), substituted "this chapter or for purposes of section 55" for "subpart A, B, or D of this part" in subpara. (d)(4)(B), effective for tax. yrs. begin. after 12/31/2001.

In 2001, P.L. 107-16, Sec. 205(a), added Code Sec. 45F, effective for tax. yrs. begin. after 12/31/2001.

—P.L. 107-16, Sec. 901, of this Act [as amended by Sec. 2, P.L. 107-358, and Sec. 101(a)(1), P.L. 111-312, see above], reads as follows:

"SEC. 901. SUNSET OF PROVISIONS OF ACT.

"(a) In general. All provisions of, and amendments made by, this Act shall not apply—

"(1) to taxable, plan, or limitation years beginning after December 31, 2012, or

"(2) in the case of title V, to estates of decedents dying, gifts made, or generation skipping transfers, after December 31, 2012.

"(b) Application of certain laws. The Internal Revenue Code of 1986 and the Employee Retirement Income Security Act of 1974 shall be applied and administered to years, estates, gifts, and transfers described in subsection (a) as if the provisions and amendments described in subsection (a) had never been enacted.

"(c) Exception. Subsection (a) shall not apply to section 803 (relating to no federal income tax on restitution received by victims of the Nazi regime or their heirs or estates)."

Sec. 45G.   Railroad track maintenance credit.

(a) General rule.

For purposes of section 38, the railroad track maintenance credit determined under this section for the taxable year is an amount equal to 50 percent of the qualified railroad track maintenance expenditures paid or incurred by an eligible taxpayer during the taxable year.

(b) Limitation.

(1) **In general.** The credit allowed under subsection (a) for any taxable year shall not exceed the product of—

(A) $3,500, multiplied by

(B) the sum of—

(i) the number of miles of railroad track owned or leased by the eligible taxpayer as of the close of the taxable year, and

(ii) the number of miles of railroad track assigned for purposes of this subsection to the eligible taxpayer by a Class II or Class III railroad which owns or leases such railroad track as of the close of the taxable year.

(2) **Assignments.** With respect to any assignment of a mile of railroad track under paragraph (1)(B)(ii)—

(A) such assignment may be made only once per taxable year of the Class II or Class III railroad and shall be treated as made as of the close of such taxable year,

(B) such mile may not be taken into account under this section by such railroad for such taxable year, and

(C) such assignment shall be taken into account for the taxable year of the assignee which includes the date that such assignment is treated as effective.

(c) Eligible taxpayer.

For purposes of this section, the term "eligible taxpayer" means—

(1) any Class II or Class III railroad, and

(2) any person who transports property using the rail facilities of a Class II or Class III railroad or who furnishes railroad-related property or services to a Class II or Class III railroad, but only with respect to miles of railroad track assigned to such person by such Class II or Class III railroad for purposes of subsection (b).

(d) Qualified railroad track maintenance expenditures.

For purposes of this section, the term "qualified railroad track maintenance expenditures" means gross expenditures (whether or not otherwise chargeable to capital account) for maintaining railroad track (including roadbed, bridges, and related track structures) owned or leased as of January 1, 2005, by a Class II or Class III railroad (determined without regard to any consideration for such expenditures given by the Class II or Class III railroad which made the assignment of such track).

(e) Other definitions and special rules.

(1) **Class II or Class III railroad.** For purposes of this section, the terms "Class II railroad" and "Class III railroad" have the respective meanings given such terms by the Surface Transportation Board.

(2) **Controlled groups.** Rules similar to the rules of paragraph (1) of section 41(f) shall apply for purposes of this section.

(3) **Basis adjustment.** For purposes of this subtitle, if a credit is allowed under this section with respect to any railroad track, the basis of such track shall be reduced by the amount of the credit so allowed.

(f) Application of section.

This section shall apply to qualified railroad track maintenance expenditures paid or incurred during taxable years beginning after December 31, 2004, and before January 1, 2012.

In 2010, P.L. 111-312, Sec. 734(a), substituted "January 1, 2012" for "January 1, 2010" in subsec. (f), effective for expenditures paid or incurred in tax. yrs. begin. after 12/31/2009.

In 2008, P.L. 110-343, Sec. 316(a)DivC, substituted "January 1, 2010" for "January 1, 2008" in subsec. (f), effective for expenditures paid or incurred during tax. yrs. begin. after 12/31/2007.

In 2006, P.L. 109-432, Sec. 423(a)(1), added "gross" after "means" in subsec. (d) . . . Sec. 423(a)(2), added "(determined without regard to any consideration for such expenditures given by the Class II or Class III railroad which made the assignment of such track)" after "Class II or Class III railroad" in subsec. (d), effective for tax. yrs. begin. after 12/31/2004.

In 2005, P.L. 109-135, Sec. 403(f)(1), amended subsec. (b) . . . Sec. 403(f)(2), amended para. (c)(2), effective for tax. yrs. begin. after 12/31/2004 as if included in Sec. 245 of the American Jobs Creation Act of 2004, P.L. 108-357.

Prior to amendment, subsec. (b) read as follows:

"(b) Limitation. The credit allowed under subsection (a) for any taxable year shall not exceed the product of—

"(1) $3,500, and

"(2) the number of miles of railroad track owned or leased by the eligible taxpayer as of the close of the taxable year.

A mile of railroad track may be taken into account by a person other than the owner only if such mile is assigned to such person by the owner for purposes of this subsection. Any mile which is so assigned may not be taken into account by the owner for purposes of this subsection."

Prior to amendment, para. (c)(2) read as follows:

"(2) any person who transports property using the rail facilities of a person described in paragraph (1) or who furnishes railroad-related property or services to such a person."

In 2004, P.L. 108-357, Sec. 245(a), added Code Sec. 45G, effective for tax. yrs. begin. after 12/31/2004.

Sec. 45H.   Credit for production of low sulfur diesel fuel.

(a) In general.

For purposes of section 38, the amount of the low sulfur diesel fuel production credit determined under this section with respect to any facility of a small business refiner is an amount equal to 5 cents for each gallon of low sulfur diesel fuel produced during the taxable year by such small business refiner at such facility.

(b) Maximum credit.

(1) **In general.** The aggregate credit determined under subsection (a) for any taxable year with respect to any facility shall not exceed—

(A) 25 percent of the qualified costs incurred by the small business refiner with respect to such facility, reduced by

(B) the aggregate credits determined under this section for all prior taxable years with respect to such facility.

(2) **Reduced percentage.** In the case of a small business refiner with average daily domestic refinery runs for the

1-year period ending on December 31, 2002, in excess of 155,000 barrels, the number of percentage points described in paragraph (1) shall be reduced (not below zero) by the product of such number (before the application of this paragraph) and the ratio of such excess to 50,000 barrels.

(c) Definitions and special rule.
For purposes of this section—

(1) Small business refiner. The term "small business refiner" means, with respect to any taxable year, a refiner of crude oil—

(A) with respect to which not more than 1,500 individuals are engaged in the refinery operations of the business on any day during such taxable year, and

(B) the average daily domestic refinery run or average retained production of which for all facilities of the taxpayer for the 1-year period ending on December 31, 2002, did not exceed 205,000 barrels.

(2) Qualified costs. The term "qualified costs" means, with respect to any facility, those costs paid or incurred during the applicable period for compliance with the applicable EPA regulations with respect to such facility, including expenditures for the construction of new process operation units or the dismantling and reconstruction of existing process units to be used in the production of low sulfur diesel fuel, associated adjacent or offsite equipment (including tankage, catalyst, and power supply), engineering, construction period interest, and sitework.

(3) Applicable EPA regulations. The term "applicable EPA regulations" means the Highway Diesel Fuel Sulfur Control Requirements of the Environmental Protection Agency.

(4) Applicable period. The term "applicable period" means, with respect to any facility, the period beginning on January 1, 2003, and ending on the earlier of the date which is 1 year after the date on which the taxpayer must comply with the applicable EPA regulations with respect to such facility or December 31, 2009.

(5) Low sulfur diesel fuel. The term "low sulfur diesel fuel" means diesel fuel with a sulfur content of 15 parts per million or less.

(d) Special rule for determination of refinery runs.
For purposes this section and section 179B(b), in the calculation of average daily domestic refinery run or retained production, only refineries which on April 1, 2003, were refineries of the refiner or a related person (within the meaning of section 613A(d)(3)), shall be taken into account.

(e) Certification.

(1) Required. No credit shall be allowed unless, not later than the date which is 30 months after the first day of the first taxable year in which the low sulfur diesel fuel production credit is determined with respect to a facility, the small business refiner obtains certification from the Secretary, after consultation with the Administrator of the Environmental Protection Agency, that the taxpayer's qualified costs with respect to such facility will result in compliance with the applicable EPA regulations.

(2) Contents of application. An application for certification shall include relevant information regarding unit capacities and operating characteristics sufficient for the Secretary, after consultation with the Administrator of the Environmental Protection Agency, to determine that such qualified costs are necessary for compliance with the applicable EPA regulations.

(3) Review period. Any application shall be reviewed and notice of certification, if applicable, shall be made within 60 days of receipt of such application. In the event the Secretary does not notify the taxpayer of the results of such certification within such period, the taxpayer may presume the certification to be issued until so notified.

(4) Statute of limitations. With respect to the credit allowed under this section—

(A) the statutory period for the assessment of any deficiency attributable to such credit shall not expire before the end of the 3-year period ending on the date that the review period described in paragraph (3) ends with respect to the taxpayer, and

(B) such deficiency may be assessed before the expiration of such 3-year period notwithstanding the provisions of any other law or rule of law which would otherwise prevent such assessment.

(f) Cooperative organizations.

(1) Apportionment of credit.

(A) In general. In the case of a cooperative organization described in section 1381(a), any portion of the credit determined under subsection (a) for the taxable year may, at the election of the organization, be apportioned among patrons eligible to share in patronage dividends on the basis of the quantity or value of business done with or for such patrons for the taxable year.

(B) Form and effect of election. An election under subparagraph (A) for any taxable year shall be made on a timely filed return for such year. Such election, once made, shall be irrevocable for such taxable year.

(2) Treatment of organizations and patrons.

(A) Organizations. The amount of the credit not apportioned to patrons pursuant to paragraph (1) shall be included in the amount determined under subsection (a) for the taxable year of the organization.

(B) Patrons. The amount of the credit apportioned to patrons pursuant to paragraph (1) shall be included in the amount determined under subsection (a) for the first taxable year of each patron ending on or after the last day of the payment period (as defined in section 1382(d)) for the taxable year of the organization or, if earlier, the taxable year of each patron ending on or after the date on which the patron receives notice from the cooperative of the apportionment.

(3) Special rule. If the amount of a credit which has been apportioned to any patron under this subsection is decreased for any reason—

(A) such amount shall not increase the tax imposed on such patron, and

(B) the tax imposed by this chapter on such organization shall be increased by such amount.

The increase under subparagraph (B) shall not be treated as tax imposed by this chapter for purposes of determining the amount of any credit under this chapter or for purposes of section 55.

(g) Election to not take credit.
No credit shall be determined under subsection (a) for the taxable year if the taxpayer elects not to have subsection (a) apply to such taxable year.

In 2007, P.L. 110-172, Sec. 7(a)(1)(A), deleted subsec. (d) and redesignated subsecs. (e)-(g) as (d)-(f) . . . Sec. 7(a)(2)(A), added subsec. (g) . . . Sec. 7(a)(3)(A), substituted "qualified costs" for "qualified capital costs" in subpara. (b)(1)(A), para. (c)(2), para. (e)(1) [as redesignated by Sec. 7(a)(1)(A) of this Act, see above] and para. (e)(2) [as redesignated by Sec. 7(a)(1)(A) of this Act, see above] . . . Sec. 7(a)(3)(B), deleted "capital" after "Qualified" in the heading of para. (d)(2), effective for expenses paid or incurred after 12/31/2002, in tax. yrs. end. after 12/31/2002.

Prior to deletion, subsec. (d) read as follows:

"*(d) Reduction in basis.* For purposes of this subtitle, if a credit is determined under this section for any expenditure with respect to any property, the increase in basis of such property which would (but for this subsection) result from such expenditure shall be reduced by the amount of the credit so determined."

In 2004, P.L. 108-357, Sec. 339(a), added Code Sec. 45H, effective for expenses paid or incurred after 12/31/2002, in tax. yrs. end. after 12/31/2002.

Sec. 45I. Credit for producing oil and gas from marginal wells.

(a) General rule.

For purposes of section 38, the marginal well production credit for any taxable year is an amount equal to the product of—

(1) the credit amount, and

(2) the qualified crude oil production and the qualified natural gas production which is attributable to the taxpayer.

(b) Credit amount.

For purposes of this section—

(1) In general. The credit amount is—

(A) $3 per barrel of qualified crude oil production, and

(B) 50 cents per 1,000 cubic feet of qualified natural gas production.

(2) Reduction as oil and gas prices increase.

(A) In general. The $3 and 50 cents amounts under paragraph (1) shall each be reduced (but not below zero) by an amount which bears the same ratio to such amount (determined without regard to this paragraph) as—

(i) the excess (if any) of the applicable reference price over $15 ($1.67 for qualified natural gas production), bears to

(ii) $3 ($0.33 for qualified natural gas production).

The applicable reference price for a taxable year is the reference price of the calendar year preceding the calendar year in which the taxable year begins.

(B) Inflation adjustment. In the case of any taxable year beginning in a calendar year after 2005, each of the dollar amounts contained in subparagraph (A) shall be increased to an amount equal to such dollar amount multiplied by the inflation adjustment factor for such calendar year (determined under section 43(b)(3)(B) by substituting "2004" for "1990").

(C) Reference price. For purposes of this paragraph, the term "reference price" means, with respect to any calendar year—

(i) in the case of qualified crude oil production, the reference price determined under section 45K(d)(2)(C), and

(ii) in the case of qualified natural gas production, the Secretary's estimate of the annual average wellhead price per 1,000 cubic feet for all domestic natural gas.

(c) Qualified crude oil and natural gas production.

For purposes of this section—

(1) In general. The terms "qualified crude oil production" and "qualified natural gas production" mean domestic crude oil or natural gas which is produced from a qualified marginal well.

(2) Limitation on amount of production which may qualify.

(A) In general. Crude oil or natural gas produced during any taxable year from any well shall not be treated as qualified crude oil production or qualified natural gas production to the extent production from the well during the taxable year exceeds 1,095 barrels or barrel-of-oil equivalents (as defined in section 45K(d)(5)).

(B) Proportionate reductions.

(i) Short taxable years. In the case of a short taxable year, the limitations under this paragraph shall be proportionately reduced to reflect the ratio which the number of days in such taxable year bears to 365.

(ii) Wells not in production entire year. In the case of a well which is not capable of production during each day of a taxable year, the limitations under this paragraph applicable to the well shall be proportionately reduced to reflect the ratio which the number of days of production bears to the total number of days in the taxable year.

(3) Definitions.

(A) Qualified marginal well. The term "qualified marginal well" means a domestic well—

(i) the production from which during the taxable year is treated as marginal production under section 613A(c)(6), or

(ii) which, during the taxable year—

(I) has average daily production of not more than 25 barrel-of-oil equivalents (as so defined), and

(II) produces water at a rate not less than 95 percent of total well effluent.

(B) Crude oil, etc. The terms "crude oil", "natural gas", "domestic", and "barrel" have the meanings given such terms by section 613A(e).

(d) Other rules.

(1) Production attributable to the taxpayer. In the case of a qualified marginal well in which there is more than one owner of operating interests in the well and the crude oil or natural gas production exceeds the limitation under subsection (c)(2), qualifying crude oil production or qualifying natural gas production attributable to the taxpayer shall be determined on the basis of the ratio which taxpayer's revenue interest in the production bears to the aggregate of the revenue interests of all operating interest owners in the production.

(2) Operating interest required. Any credit under this section may be claimed only on production which is attributable to the holder of an operating interest.

(3) Production from nonconventional sources excluded. In the case of production from a qualified marginal well which is eligible for the credit allowed under section 45K for the taxable year, no credit shall be allowable under this section unless the taxpayer elects not to claim the credit under section 45K with respect to the well.

In 2005, P.L. 109-135, Sec. 412(k), substituted "qualified crude oil production" for "qualified credit oil production" in para. (a)(2), effective 12/21/2005.

—P.L. 109-58, Sec. 1322(a)(3)(B), substituted "section 45K(d)(2)(C)" for "section 29(d)(2)(C)" in clause (b)(2)(C)(i) . . . Sec. 1322(a)(3)(D)(i), substituted "section 45K(d)(5))" for "section 29(d)(5))" in subpara. (c)(2)(A) . . . Sec. 1322(a)(3)(D)(ii), substituted "section 45K" for "section 29" each place it appeared in para. (d)(3), effective for credits determined under the Internal Revenue Code of 1986 for tax. yrs. end. after 12/31/2005.

In 2004, P.L. 108-357, Sec. 341(a), added Code Sec. 45I, effective for production in tax. yrs. begin. after 12/31/2004.

Sec. 45J. Credit for production from advanced nuclear power facilities.

(a) General rule.

For purposes of section 38, the advanced nuclear power facility production credit of any taxpayer for any taxable year is equal to the product of—

(1) 1.8 cents, multiplied by

(2) the kilowatt hours of electricity—

(A) produced by the taxpayer at an advanced nuclear power facility during the 8-year period beginning on the date the facility was originally placed in service, and

(B) sold by the taxpayer to an unrelated person during the taxable year.

(b) National limitation.

(1) In general. The amount of credit which would (but for this subsection and subsection (c)) be allowed with respect to any facility for any taxable year shall not exceed the amount which bears the same ratio to such amount of credit as—

(A) the national megawatt capacity limitation allocated to the facility, bears to

(B) the total megawatt nameplate capacity of such facility.

(2) Amount of national limitation. The aggregate amount of national megawatt capacity limitation allocated by the Secretary under paragraph (3) shall not exceed 6,000 megawatts.

(3) Allocation of limitation. The Secretary shall allocate the national megawatt capacity limitation in such manner as the Secretary may prescribe.

(4) Regulations. Not later than 6 months after the date of the enactment of this section, the Secretary shall prescribe such regulations as may be necessary or appropriate to carry out the purposes of this subsection. Such regulations shall provide a certification process under which the Secretary, after consultation with the Secretary of Energy, shall approve and allocate the national megawatt capacity limitation.

(c) Other limitations.

(1) Annual limitation. The amount of the credit allowable under subsection (a) (after the application of subsection (b)) for any taxable year with respect to any facility shall not exceed an amount which bears the same ratio to $125,000,000 as—

(A) the national megawatt capacity limitation allocated under subsection (b) to the facility, bears to

(B) 1,000.

(2) Phaseout of credit.

(A) In general. The amount of the credit determined under subsection (a) shall be reduced by an amount which bears the same ratio to the amount of the credit (determined without regard to this paragraph) as—

(i) the amount by which the reference price (as defined in section 45(e)(2)(C)) for the calendar year in which the sale occurs exceeds 8 cents, bears to

(ii) 3 cents.

(B) Phaseout adjustment based on inflation. The 8 cent amount in subparagraph (A) shall be adjusted by multiplying such amount by the inflation adjustment factor (as defined in section 45(e)(2)(B)) for the calendar year in which the sale occurs. If any amount as increased under the preceding sentence is not a multiple of 0.1 cent, such amount shall be rounded to the nearest multiple of 0.1 cent.

(d) Advanced nuclear power facility.

For purposes of this section—

(1) In general. The term "advanced nuclear power facility" means any advanced nuclear facility—

(A) which is owned by the taxpayer and which uses nuclear energy to produce electricity, and

(B) which is placed in service after the date of the enactment of this paragraph and before January 1, 2021.

(2) Advanced nuclear facility. For purposes of paragraph (1), the term "advanced nuclear facility" means any nuclear facility the reactor design for which is approved after December 31, 1993, by the Nuclear Regulatory Commission (and such design or a substantially similar design of comparable capacity was not approved on or before such date).

(e) Other rules to apply.

Rules similar to the rules of paragraphs (1), (3), (4), and (5) of section 45(e) shall apply for purposes of this section.

In 2007, P.L. 110-172, Sec. 6(a), amended para. (b)(2), effective for production in tax. yrs. begin. after 8/8/2005.
Prior to amendment, para. (b)(2) read as follows:
"(2) Amount of national limitation. The national megawatt capacity limitation shall be 6,000 megawatts."

In 2005, P.L. 109-135, Sec. 402(d)(1), amended para. (c)(2) . . . Sec. 402(d)(2), deleted "(2)," before "(3)" in subsec. (e), effective for production in tax. yrs. begin. after 8/8/2005 as if included in Sec. 1306 of the Energy Tax Incentives Act of 2005, P.L. 109-58.
Prior to amendment, para. (c)(2) read as follows:
"(2) Other limitations. Rules similar to the rules of section 45(b)(1) shall apply for purposes of this section."

—P.L. 109-58, Sec. 1306(a), added Code Sec. 45J, effective for production in tax. yrs. begin. after 8/8/2005.

Sec. 45K. Credit for producing fuel from a nonconventional source.

(a) Allowance of credit.

For purposes of section 38, the nonconventional source production credit determined under this section for the taxable year is an amount equal to—

(1) $3, multiplied by

(2) the barrel-of-oil equivalent of qualified fuels—

(A) sold by the taxpayer to an unrelated person during the taxable year, and

(B) the production of which is attributable to the taxpayer.

(b) Limitations and adjustments.

(1) Phaseout of credit. The amount of the credit allowable under subsection (a) shall be reduced by an amount which bears the same ratio to the amount of the credit (determined without regard to this paragraph) as—

(A) the amount by which the reference price for the calendar year in which the sale occurs exceeds $23.50, bears to

(B) $6.

(2) Credit and phaseout adjustment based on inflation. The $3 amount in subsection (a) and the $23.50 and $6 amounts in paragraph (1) shall each be adjusted by multiplying such amount by the inflation adjustment factor for the calendar year in which the sale occurs. In the case of gas from a tight formation, the $3 amount in subsection (a) shall not be adjusted.

(3) Credit reduced for grants, tax-exempt bonds, and subsidized energy financing.

(A) In general. The amount of the credit allowable under subsection (a) with respect to any project for any taxable year (determined after the application of paragraphs (1) and (2)) shall be reduced by the amount which is the product of the amount so determined for such year and a fraction—

(i) the numerator of which is the sum, for the taxable year and all prior taxable years, of—

(I) grants provided by the United States, a State, or a political subdivision of a State for use in connection with the project,

(II) proceeds of any issue of State or local government obligations used to provide financing for the project the interest on which is exempt from tax under section 103, and

(III) the aggregate amount of subsidized energy financing (within the meaning of section 48(a)(4)(C)) provided in connection with the project, and

(ii) the denominator of which is the aggregate amount of additions to the capital account for the project for the taxable year and all prior taxable years.

(B) Amounts determined at close of year. The amounts under subparagraph (A) for any taxable year shall be determined as of the close of the taxable year.

(4) Credit reduced for energy credit. The amount allowable as a credit under subsection (a) with respect to any project for any taxable year (determined after the application of paragraphs (1), (2), and (3)) shall be reduced by the excess of—

(A) the aggregate amount allowed under section 38 for the taxable year or any prior taxable year by reason of the energy percentage with respect to property used in the project, over

(B) the aggregate amount recaptured with respect to the amount described in subparagraph (A)—

(i) under section 49(b) or 50(a) for the taxable year or any prior taxable year, or

(ii) under this paragraph for any prior taxable year.

The amount recaptured under section 49(b) or 50(a) with respect to any property shall be appropriately reduced to take into account any reduction in the credit allowed by this section by reason of the preceding sentence.

(5) Credit reduced for enhanced oil recovery credit. The amount allowable as a credit under subsection (a) with respect to any project for any taxable year (determined after application of paragraphs (1), (2), (3), and (4)) shall be reduced by the excess (if any) of—

(A) the aggregate amount allowed under section 38 for the taxable year and any prior taxable year by reason of any enhanced oil recovery credit determined under section 43 with respect to such project, over

(B) the aggregate amount recaptured with respect to the amount described in subparagraph (A) under this paragraph for any prior taxable year.

(6) Repealed.

(c) Definition of qualified fuels.

For purposes of this section—

(1) In general. The term "qualified fuels" means—

(A) oil produced from shale and tar sands,

(B) gas produced from—

(i) geopressured brine, Devonian shale, coal seams, or a tight formation, or

(ii) biomass,

and

(C) liquid, gaseous, or solid synthetic fuels produced from coal (including lignite), including such fuels when used as feedstocks.

(2) Gas from geopressured brine, etc.

(A) In general. Except as provided in subparagraph (B), the determination of whether any gas is produced from geopressured brine, Devonian shale, coal seams, or a tight formation shall be made in accordance with section 503 of the Natural Gas Policy Act of 1978 (as in effect before the repeal of such section).

(B) Special rules for gas from tight formations. The term "gas produced from a tight formation" shall only include gas from a tight formation—

(i) which, as of April 20, 1977, was committed or dedicated to interstate commerce (as defined in section 2(18) of the Natural Gas Policy Act of 1978, as in effect on the date of the enactment of this clause), or

(ii) which is produced from a well drilled after such date of enactment [11/5/90].

(3) Biomass. The term "biomass" means any organic material other than—

(A) oil and natural gas (or any product thereof), and

(B) coal (including lignite) or any product thereof.

(d) Other definitions and special rules.

For purposes of this section—

(1) Only production within the United States taken into account. Sales shall be taken into account under this section only with respect to qualified fuels the production of which is within—

(A) the United States (within the meaning of section 638(1)), or

(B) a possession of the United states (within the meaning of section 638(2)).

(2) Computation of inflation adjustment factor and reference price.

(A) In general. The Secretary shall, not later than April 1 of each calendar year, determine and publish in the Federal Register the inflation adjustment factor and the reference price for the preceding calendar year in accordance with this paragraph.

(B) Inflation adjustment factor. The term "inflation adjustment factor" means, with respect to a calendar year, a fraction the numerator of which is the GNP implicit price deflator for the calendar year and the denominator of which is the GNP implicit price deflator for calendar year 1979. The term "GNP implicit price deflator" means the first revision of the implicit price deflator for the gross national product as computed and published by the Department of Commerce.

(C) Reference price. The term "reference price" means with respect to a calendar year the Secretary's estimate of the annual average wellhead price per barrel for all domestic crude oil the price of which is not subject to regulation by the United States.

(3) Production attributable to the taxpayer. In the case of a property or facility in which more than 1 person has an interest, except to the extent provided in regulations prescribed by the Secretary, production from the property or facility (as the case may be) shall be allocated among such persons in proportion to their respective interests in the gross sales from such property or facility.

(4) Gas from geopressured brine, Devonian shale, coal seams, or a tight formation. The amount of the credit allowable under subsection (a) shall be determined without regard to any production attributable to a property from which gas from Devonian shale, coal seams, geopressured brine, or a tight formation was produced in marketable quantities before January 1, 1980.

(5) Barrel-of-oil equivalent. The term "barrel-of-oil equivalent" with respect to any fuel means that amount of such fuel which has a Btu content of 5.8 million; except that in the case of qualified fuels described in subparagraph (C) of subsection (c)(1), the Btu content shall be determined without regard to any material from a source not described in such subparagraph.

(6) Barrel defined. The term "barrel" means 42 United States gallons.

(7) Related persons. Persons shall be treated as related to each other if such persons would be treated as a single employer under the regulations prescribed under section 52(b). In the case of a corporation which is a member of an affiliated group of corporations filing a consolidated return, such corporation shall be treated as selling qualified fuels to an unrelated person if such fuels are sold to such a person by another member of such group.

(8) **Pass-thru in the case of estates and trusts.** Under regulations prescribed by the Secretary, rules similar to the rules of subsection (d) of section 52 shall apply.

(e) **Application of section.**

This section shall apply with respect to qualified fuels—

(1) which are—

(A) produced from a well drilled after December 31, 1979, and before January 1, 1993, or

(B) produced in a facility placed in service after December 31, 1979, and before January 1, 1993, and

(2) which are sold before January 1, 2003.

(f) **Extension for certain facilities.**

(1) **In general.** In the case of a facility for producing qualified fuels described in subparagraph (B)(ii) or (C) of subsection (c)(1)—

(A) for purposes of subsection (e)(1)(B), such facility shall be treated as being placed in service before January 1, 1993, if such facility is placed in service before July 1, 1998, pursuant to a binding written contract in effect before January 1, 1997, and

(B) if such facility is originally placed in service after December 31, 1992, paragraph (2) of subsection (e) shall be applied with respect to such facility by substituting "January 1, 2008" for "January 1, 2003."

(2) **Special rule.** Paragraph (1) shall not apply to any facility which produces coke or coke gas unless the original use of the facility commences with the taxpayer.

(g) **Extension for facilities producing coke or coke gas.** Notwithstanding subsection (e)—

(1) **In general.** In the case of a facility for producing coke or coke gas (other than from petroleum based products) which was placed in service before January 1, 1993, or after June 30, 1998, and before January 1, 2010, this section shall apply with respect to coke and coke gas produced in such facility and sold during the period—

(A) beginning on the later of January 1, 2006, or the date that such facility is placed in service, and

(B) ending on the date which is 4 years after the date such period began.

(2) **Special rules.** In determining the amount of credit allowable under this section solely by reason of this subsection—

(A) **Daily limit.** The amount of qualified fuels sold during any taxable year which may be taken into account by reason of this subsection with respect to any facility shall not exceed an average barrel-of-oil equivalent of 4,000 barrels per day. Days before the date the facility is placed in service shall not be taken into account in determining such average.

(B) **Extension period to commence with unadjusted credit amount.** For purposes of applying subsection (b)(2) to the $3 amount in subsection (a), in the case of fuels sold after 2005, subsection (d)(2)(B) shall be applied by substituting "2004" for "1979".

(C) **Denial of double benefit.** This subsection shall not apply to any facility producing qualified fuels for which a credit was allowed under this section for the taxable year or any preceding taxable year by reason of subsection (f).

(D) **Nonapplication of phaseout.** Subsection (b)(1) shall not apply.

(E) **Coordination with section 45.** No credit shall be allowed with respect to any qualified fuel which is steel industry fuel (as defined in section 45(c)(7)) if a credit is allowed to the taxpayer for such fuel under section 45.

In 2008, P.L. 110-343, Sec. 108(d)(2)DivB, added subpara. (g)(2)(E), effective for fuel produced and sold after 9/30/2008.

In 2006, P.L. 109-432, Sec. 211(a), added subpara. (g)(2)(D) . . . Sec. 211(b), added "(other than from petroleum based products)" after "coke or coke gas" in para. (g)(1), effective for fuel produced and sold after 12/31/2005, in tax. yrs. end. after 12/31/2005.

In 2005, P.L. 109-135, Sec. 402(g), deleted "if the taxpayer elects to have this section apply," before "the nonconventional" in subsec. (a), effective for credits determined under the Internal Revenue Code of 1986 for tax. yrs. end. after 12/31/2005 as if included in Sec. 1322 of the Energy Tax Incentives Act of 2005, P.L. 109-58.

—P.L. 109-135, Sec. 412(l)(1), substituted "subsection (e)" for "subsection (f)" in the matter preceding para. (g)(1) . . . Sec. 412(l)(2), substituted "subsection (f)" for "subsection (g)" in subpara. (g)(2)(C), effective 12/21/2005.

—P.L. 109-58, Sec. 1321(a), added subsec. (h), effective for fuel produced and sold after 12/31/2005, in tax. yrs. end. after 12/31/2005.

—P.L. 109-58, Sec. 1322(a)(1), redesignated Code Sec. 29 as Code Sec. 45K . . . Sec. 1322(a)(3)(E), substituted "For purposes of section 38, if the taxpayer elects to have this section apply, the nonconventional source production credit determined under this section for the taxable year is" for "There shall be allowed as a credit against the tax imposed by this chapter for the taxable year" in subsec. (a) . . . Sec. 1322(a)(3)(F), deleted para. (b)(6), effective for credits determined under the Internal Revenue Code of 1986 for tax. yrs. end. after 12/31/2005.

Prior to deletion, para. (b)(6) read as follows:

"(6) Application with other credits. The credit allowed by subsection (a) for any taxable year shall not exceed the excess (if any) of—

"(A) the regular tax for the taxable year reduced by the sum of the credits allowable under subpart A and section 27, over

"(B) the tentative minimum tax for the taxable year."

—P.L. 109-58, Sec. 1322(b)(1)(A), added "(as in effect before the repeal of such section)" after "1978" in subpara. (c)(2)(A) [prior to redesignation by Sec. 1322(a)(1) of this Act, see above] . . . Sec. 1322(b)(1)(B), deleted subsec. (e), and redesignated subsecs. (f)-(h) [subsec. (h) as added by Sec. 1321(a) of this Act, see above] as subsecs. (e)-(g) . . . Sec. 1322(b)(2)(A), substituted "subsection (e)(1)(B)" for "subsection (f)(1)(B)" in subpara. (g)(1)(A) [prior to redesignation by Sec. 1322(a)(1) and (b)(1)(B) of this Act, see above] . . . Sec. 1322(b)(2)(B), substituted "subsection (e)" for "subsection (f)" in subpara. (g)(1)(B) [prior to redesignation by Sec. 1322(a)(1) and (b)(1)(B) of this Act, see above], effective 8/8/2005.

Prior to deletion, subsec. (e), read as follows:

"(e) Application with the Natural Gas Policy Act of 1978.

"(1) No credit if section 107 of the natural gas policy act of 1978 is utilized. Subsection (a) shall apply with respect to any natural gas described in subsection (c)(1)(B)(i) which is sold during the taxable year only if such natural gas is sold at a lawful price which is determined without regard to the provisions of section 107 of the Natural Gas Policy Act of 1978 and subtitle B of title I of such Act.

"(2) Treatment of this section. For purposes of section 107(d) of the Natural Gas Policy Act of 1978, this section shall not be treated as allowing any credit, exemption, deduction, or comparable adjustment applicable to the computation of any Federal tax."

In 1996, P.L. 104-188, Sec. 1205(d)(3), substituted "section 27" for "sections 27 and 28" in subpara. (b)(6)(A), effective for amounts paid or incurred in tax. yrs. end. after 6/30/96.

—P.L. 104-188, Sec. 1207(a), substituted "July 1, 1998" for "January 1, 1997" and substituted "January 1, 1997" for "January 1, 1996" in subpara. (g)(1)(A), effective 8/20/96.

In 1992, P.L. 102-486, Sec. 1918, added subsec (g), effective 10/24/92.

In 1990, P.L. 101-508, Sec. 11501(a)(1), substituted "1993" for "1991" in clauses (f)(1)(A)(i) and (f)(1)(A)(ii) . . . Sec. 11501(a)(2), substituted "2003" for "2001" in subpara. (f)(1)(B), effective 11/5/90.

—P.L. 101-508, Sec. 11501(b)(1), amended subpara. (c)(2)(B), effective for gas produced after 12/31/90.

Prior to amendment, subpara. (c)(2)(B) read as follows:

"(B) Special rules for gas from tight formations. The term 'gas produced from a tight formation' shall only include—

"(i) gas the price of which is regulated by the United States, and

"(ii) gas for which the maximum lawful price applicable under the Natural Gas Policy Act of 1978 is at least 150 percent of the then applicable price under section 103 of such Act."

—P.L. 101-508, Sec. 11501(c)(1), redesignated para. (b)(5) as para. (b)(6), and added new para. (b)(5), effective for tax. yrs. beginning after 12/31/90.

—P.L. 101-508, Sec. 11813(b)(1)(A), substituted "section 48(a)(4)(C)" for "section 48(1)(11)(C)" in subclause (b)(3)(A)(i)(III) . . . Sec. 11813(b)(1)(B), substituted "section 49(b) or 50(a)" for "section 47" each place it appeared in para. (b)(4) . . . Sec. 11813(b)(1)(C), amended para. (c)(3), effective for property placed in service after 12/31/90, except as provided in Sec. 11813(c)(2) of this Act, reproduced in note following Code Sec. 46.

Prior to amendment, para. (c)(3) read as follows:

"(3) Biomass. The term 'biomass' means any organic material which is an alternate substance (as defined in section 48(1)(3)(B)) other than coal (including lignite) or any product of such coal."

—P.L. 101-508, Sec. 11816(a), added "and" at the end of subpara. (c)(1)(B), substituted a period for the comma at the end of subpara. (c)(1)(C), and deleted subparas. (c)(1)(D) and (c)(1)(E)...Sec. 11816(b)(1), deleted paras. (c)(4) and (c)(5)...Sec. 11816(b)(2), amended para. (d)(4)...Sec. 11816(b)(3), deleted para. (d)(5) and redesignated paras. (d)(6)-(d)(9) as (d)(5)-(d)(8)...Sec. 11816(b)(4), substituted "subparagraph (C)" for "subparagraph (C), (D), or (E)" in para. (d)(5) [as redesignated]...Sec. 11816(b)(5), amended subsec. (f), effective 11/5/90, except as provided in Sec. 11821(b) of this Act which reads as follows:

"(b) Savings provision. If—

"(1) any provision amended or repealed by this part applied to—

"(A) any transaction occurring before 11/5/90,

"(B) any property acquired before 11/5/90, or

"(C) any item of income, loss, deduction, or credit taken into account before 11/5/90, and

"(2) the treatment of such transaction, property, or item under such provision would (without regard to the amendments made by this part) affect liability for tax for periods ending after 11/5/90,

nothing in the amendments made by this part shall be construed to affect the treatment of such transaction, property, or item for purposes of determining liability for tax for periods ending after 11/5/90."

Prior to deletion, subparas. (c)(1)(D) and (c)(1)(E) read as follows:

"(D) qualifying processed wood fuels, and

"(E) steam produced from solid agricultural byproducts (not including timber byproducts)."

Prior to deletion, paras. (c)(4) and (c)(5) read as follows:

"(4) Qualifying processed wood fuel.

"(A) In general. The term 'qualifying processed wood fuel' means any processed solid wood fuel (other than charcoal, fireplace products, or a product used for ornamental or recreational purposes) which has a Btu content per unit of volume or weight, determined without regard to any nonwood elements, which is at least 40 percent greater per unit of volume or weight than the Btu content of the wood from which it is produced (determined immediately before the processing).

"(B) Election. A taxpayer shall elect, at such time and in such manner as the Secretary by regulations may prescribe, as to whether Btu content per unit shall be determined for purposes of this paragraph on a volume or weight basis. Any such election—

"(i) shall apply to all production from a facility; and

"(ii) shall be effective for the taxable year with respect to which it is made and for all subsequent taxable years and, once made, may be revoked only with the consent of the Secretary.

"(5) Agricultural byproduct steam. Steam produced from solid agricultural byproducts which is used by the taxpayer in his trade or business shall be treated as having been sold by the taxpayer to an unrelated person on the date on which it is used."

Prior to amendment, subsec. (f) [as amended by Sec. 11501(a)(1) and (2) of this Act, see above] read as follows:

"(f) Application of section.

"(1) In general. Except as provided in paragraph (2), this section shall apply with respect to qualified fuels—

"(A) which are—

"(i) produced from a well drilled after December 31, 1979, and before January 1, 1993, or

"(ii) produced in a facility placed in service after December 31, 1979, and before January 1, 1993; and

"(B) which are sold after December 31, 1979, and before January 1, 2003.

"(2) Special rules applicable to qualified processed wood and solid agricultural byproduct steam.

"(A) Credit allowed only for certain production. In the case of qualifying processed wood fuel and steam from solid agricultural byproducts, this section shall apply only with respect to—

"(i) qualifying processed wood fuel produced in facilities placed in service after December 31, 1979, and before January 1, 1982, which is sold before the later of—

"(I) October 1, 1983, or

"(II) the date which is 3 years after the date on which the facility is placed in service; and

"(ii) steam produced in facilities placed in service after December 31, 1979, from solid agricultural byproducts which is sold before January 1, 1985.

"(B) Expanded production of steam treated as new facility production. For purposes of this subsection and subsection (d)(5), in the case of a facility for the production of steam from solid agricultural byproducts which was placed in service before January 1, 1980, any production of steam attributable to an expansion of the capacity of the facility to produce such steam through placing additional or replacement equipment in service after December 31, 1979, shall be treated as if it were produced by a facility placed in service on the date on which such equipment is placed in service."

Prior to amendment, para. (d)(4) read as follows:

"(4) Special rules applicable to gas from geopressured brine, Devonian shale, coal seams, or a tight formation.

"(A) Credit allowed only for a new production. The amount of the credit allowable under subsection(a) shall be determined without regard to any production attributable to a property from which gas from Devonian shale, coal seams, geopressured brine, or a tight formation was produced in marketable quantities before January 1, 1980.

"(B) Reference price and application of phaseout for Devonian shale.

"(i) Reference price for Devonian shale. For purposes of this section, the term 'reference price' for gas from Devonian shale sold during calendar years 1980, 1981, and 1982 shall be the average wellhead price per thousand cubic feet for such year of high cost natural gas (as defined in section 107(c)(2), (3), and (4) of the Natural Gas Policy Act of 1978 and determined under section 503 of that Act) as estimated by the Secretary after consultation with the Federal Energy Regulatory Commission.

"(ii) Different phaseout to apply for 1980, 1981, and 1982. For purposes of applying paragraphs (1) and (2) of subsection (b) with respect to sales during calendar years 1980, 1981, and 1982 of gas from Devonian shale, '$4.05' shall be substituted for '$23.50' and '$1.03' shall be substituted for '$6.00'."

Prior to deletion, para. (d)(5) read as follows:

"(5) Phaseout does not apply for first 3 years of production from facility producing qualifying processed wood or steam from solid agricultural byproducts. In the case of a facility for the production of—

"(A) qualifying processed wood fuel, or

"(B) or steam from solid agricultural byproducts,

paragraph (1) of subsection (b) shall not apply with respect to the amount of the credit allowable under subsection (a) for fuels sold during the 3-year period beginning on the date the facility is placed in service."

In 1988, P.L. 100-647, Sec. 6302, substituted "January 1, 1991" for "January 1, 1990" in clauses (f)(1)(A)(i) and (ii), effective 11/10/88 [date of enactment].

In 1986, P.L. 99-514, Sec. 701(e)(3), amended para. (b)(5), effective for tax yrs. begin. after 12/31/86.

Prior to amendment, para. (b)(5) read as follows:

"(5) Application with other credits. The credit allowed by subsection (a) for a taxable year shall not exceed the taxpayer's tax liability for the taxable year (as defined in section 26(b)), reduced by the sum of the credits allowable under subpart A and sections 27 and 28."

—P.L. 99-514, Sec. 1879(c)(1), added the last sentence to para. (d)(8), effective for tax. yrs. end. after 12/31/79.

In 1984, P.L. 98-369, Sec. 471(c)(1), redesignated Code Sec. 44D as Code Sec. 29...Sec. 474(h), amended para. (b)(5), effective for tax. yrs. begin. after 12/31/83 and to carry backs from tax. yrs. begin. after 12/31/83.

Prior to amendment, para. (b)(5) read as follows:

"(5) Application with other credits. The credit allowed by subsection (a) for a taxable year shall not exceed the tax imposed by this chapter for such taxable year, reduced by the sum of the credits allowable under a section of this subpart having a lower number or letter designation than this section, other than the credits allowable by sections 31, 39, and 43. For purposes of the preceding sentence, the term 'tax imposed by this chapter' shall not include any tax treated as not imposed by this chapter under the last sentence of section 53(a)."

—P.L. 98-369, Sec. 612(e)(1), substituted "section 26(b)" for "section 25(b)" in para. (b)(5), effective for interest paid or accrued after 12/31/84, on indebtedness incurred after 12/31/84 and to elections under Code Sec. 25(c)(2)(A)(ii) [as added by this Act] for calendar years after 1983.

—P.L. 98-369, Sec. 632, provided various exceptions to the amendments made by Title VI of this Act. See note following Code Sec. 103A.

—P.L. 98-369, Sec. 722(d)(1), substituted "in which the sale occurs" for "in which the taxable year begins" in subpara. (b)(1)(A)...Sec. 722(d)(2), substituted "in which the sale occurs" for "in which a taxable year begins" in para. (b)(2), effective for tax. yrs. end. after 12/31/79.

In 1983, P.L. 97-448, Sec. 202(a), substituted "December 31, 1979" for "December 3, 1979" each place it appeared in subsec. (f), effective for tax. yrs. end. after 12/31/79.

In 1982, P.L. 97-354, Sec. 5(a)(1), amended para. (d)(9), effective for tax. yrs. begin. after 12/3/82.

Prior to amendment, para. (d)(9) read as follows:

"(9) Pass-through in the case of Subchapter S corporations, etc. Under regulations prescribed by the Secretary, rules similar to the rules of subsections (d) and (e) of section 52 shall apply."

In 1981, P.L. 97-34, Sec. 611(a), amended subsec. (e), effective for tax. yrs. end. after 12/31/79.

Prior to amendment, subsec. (e) read as follows:

"(e) Credit not allowable if taxpayer makes election under Natural Gas Policy Act of 1978. If the taxpayer makes an election under section 107(d) of the Natural Gas Policy Act of 1978 to have subsections (a) and (b) of section 107 of that Act, and subtitle B of title I of that Act, apply with respect to gas described in subsection (c)(1)(B)(i) produced from any well on a property, then the credit allowable by subsection (a) shall not be allowed with respect to any gas produced on that property."

In 1980, P.L. 96-223, Sec. 231(a), added Code Sec. 44D, effective for tax yrs. end. after 12/31/79.

Sec. 45L. New energy efficient home credit.
(a) Allowance of credit.

(1) In general. For purposes of section 38, in the case of an eligible contractor, the new energy efficient home credit for the taxable year is the applicable amount for each qualified new energy efficient home which is—

(A) constructed by the eligible contractor, and

(B) acquired by a person from such eligible contractor for use as a residence during the taxable year.

(2) Applicable amount. For purposes of paragraph (1), the applicable amount is an amount equal to—

Tax credits

Code Sec. 45M(b)(1)(D)

(A) in the case of a dwelling unit described in paragraph (1) or (2) of subsection (c), $2,000, and

(B) in the case of a dwelling unit described in paragraph (3) of subsection (c), $1,000.

(b) Definitions.

For purposes of this section—

(1) Eligible contractor. The term "eligible contractor" means—

(A) the person who constructed the qualified new energy efficient home, or

(B) in the case of a qualified new energy efficient home which is a manufactured home, the manufactured home producer of such home.

(2) Qualified new energy efficient home. The term "qualified new energy efficient home" means a dwelling unit—

(A) located in the United States,

(B) the construction of which is substantially completed after the date of the enactment of this section, and

(C) which meets the energy saving requirements of subsection (c).

(3) Construction. The term "construction" includes substantial reconstruction and rehabilitation.

(4) Acquire. The term "acquire" includes purchase.

(c) Energy saving requirements.

A dwelling unit meets the energy saving requirements of this subsection if such unit is—

(1) certified—

(A) to have a level of annual heating and cooling energy consumption which is at least 50 percent below the annual level of heating and cooling energy consumption of a comparable dwelling unit—

(i) which is constructed in accordance with the standards of chapter 4 of the 2003 International Energy Conservation Code, as such Code (including supplements) is in effect on the date of the enactment of this section, and

(ii) for which the heating and cooling equipment efficiencies correspond to the minimum allowed under the regulations established by the Department of Energy pursuant to the National Appliance Energy Conservation Act of 1987 and in effect at the time of completion of construction, and

(B) to have building envelope component improvements account for at least 1/5 of such 50 percent,

(2) a manufactured home which conforms to Federal Manufactured Home Construction and Safety Standards (part 3280 of title 24, Code of Federal Regulations) and which meets the requirements of paragraph (1), or

(3) a manufactured home which conforms to Federal Manufactured Home Construction and Safety Standards (part 3280 of title 24, Code of Federal Regulations) and which—

(A) meets the requirements of paragraph (1) applied by substituting "30 percent" for "50 percent" both places it appears therein and by substituting "1/3" for "1/5" in subparagraph (B) thereof, or

(B) meets the requirements established by the Administrator of the Environmental Protection Agency under the Energy Star Labeled Homes program.

(d) Certification.

(1) Method of certification. A certification described in subsection (c) shall be made in accordance with guidance prescribed by the Secretary, after consultation with the Secretary of Energy. Such guidance shall specify procedures and methods for calculating energy and cost savings.

(2) Form. Any certification described in subsection (c) shall be made in writing in a manner which specifies in readily verifiable fashion the energy efficient building envelope components and energy efficient heating or cooling equipment installed and their respective rated energy efficiency performance.

(e) Basis adjustment.

For purposes of this subtitle, if a credit is allowed under this section in connection with any expenditure for any property, the increase in the basis of such property which would (but for this subsection) result from such expenditure shall be reduced by the amount of the credit so determined.

(f) Coordination with investment credit.

For purposes of this section, expenditures taken into account under section 47 or 48(a) shall not be taken into account under this section.

(g) Termination.

This section shall not apply to any qualified new energy efficient home acquired after December 31, 2011.

In **2010**, P.L. 111-312, Sec. 703(a), substituted "December 31, 2011" for "December 31, 2009" in subsec. (g), effective for homes acquired after 12/31/2009.

In **2008**, P.L. 110-343, Sec. 304DivB, substituted "December 31, 2009" for "December 31, 2008" in subsec. (g), enacted 10/3/2008.

In **2007**, P.L. 110-172, Sec. 11(a)(7), substituted "part 3280" for "section 3280" in para. (c)(2) and (c)(3), enacted 12/29/2007.

In **2006**, P.L. 109-432, Sec. 205, substituted "December 31, 2008" for "December 31, 2007" in subsec. (g), enacted 12/20/2006.

In **2005**, P.L. 109-58, Sec. 1332(a), added Code Sec. 45L, effective for qualified new energy efficient homes acquired after 12/31/2005, in tax. yrs. end. after 12/31/2005.

Sec. 45M. Energy efficient appliance credit.

(a) General rule.

(1) In general. For purposes of section 38, the energy efficient appliance credit determined under this section for any taxable year is an amount equal to the sum of the credit amounts determined under paragraph (2) for each type of qualified energy efficient appliance produced by the taxpayer during the calendar year ending with or within the taxable year.

(2) Credit amounts. The credit amount determined for any type of qualified energy efficient appliance is—

(A) the applicable amount determined under subsection (b) with respect to such type, multiplied by

(B) the eligible production for such type.

(b) Applicable amount.

For purposes of subsection (a)—

(1) Dishwashers. The applicable amount is—

(A) $45 in the case of a dishwasher which is manufactured in calendar year 2008 or 2009 and which uses no more than 324 kilowatt hours per year and 5.8 gallons per cycle,

(B) $75 in the case of a dishwasher which is manufactured in calendar year 2008, 2009, or 2010 and which uses no more than 307 kilowatt hours per year and 5.0 gallons per cycle (5.5 gallons per cycle for dishwashers designed for greater than 12 place settings),

(C) $25 in the case of a dishwasher which is manufactured in calendar year 2011 and which uses no more than 307 kilowatt hours per year and 5.0 gallons per cycle (5.5 gallons per cycle for dishwashers designed for greater than 12 place settings),

(D) $50 in the case of a dishwasher which is manufactured in calendar year 2011 and which uses no more than 295 kilowatt hours per year and 4.25 gallons per cycle (4.75 gallons per cycle for dishwashers designed for greater than 12 place settings), and

(E) $75 in the case of a dishwasher which is manufactured in calendar year 2011 and which uses no more than 280 kilowatt hours per year and 4 gallons per cycle (4.5 gallons per cycle for dishwashers designed for greater than 12 place settings).

(2) Clothes washers. The applicable amount is—

(A) $75 in the case of a residential top-loading clothes washer manufactured in calendar year 2008 which meets or exceeds a 1.72 modified energy factor and does not exceed a 8.0 water consumption factor,

(B) $125 in the case of a residential top-loading clothes washer manufactured in calendar year 2008 or 2009 which meets or exceeds a 1.8 modified energy factor and does not exceed a 7.5 water consumption factor,

(C) $150 in the case of a residential or commercial clothes washer manufactured in calendar year 2008, 2009, or 2010 which meets or exceeds 2.0 modified energy factor and does not exceed a 6.0 water consumption factor,

(D) $250 in the case of a residential or commercial clothes washer manufactured in calendar year 2008, 2009, or 2010 which meets or exceeds 2.2 modified energy factor and does not exceed a 4.5 water consumption factor,

(E) $175 in the case of a top-loading clothes washer manufactured in calendar year 2011 which meets or exceeds a 2.2 modified energy factor and does not exceed a 4.5 water consumption factor, and

(F) $225 in the case of a clothes washer manufactured in calendar year 2011—

  (i) which is a top-loading clothes washer and which meets or exceeds a 2.4 modified energy factor and does not exceed a 4.2 water consumption factor, or

  (ii) which is a front-loading clothes washer and which meets or exceeds a 2.8 modified energy factor and does not exceed a 3.5 water consumption factor.

(3) Refrigerators. The applicable amount is—

(A) $50 in the case of a refrigerator which is manufactured in calendar year 2008, and consumes at least 20 percent but not more than 22.9 percent less kilowatt hours per year than the 2001 energy conservation standards,

(B) $75 in the case of a refrigerator which is manufactured in calendar year 2008 or 2009, and consumes at least 23 percent but no more than 24.9 percent less kilowatt hours per year than the 2001 energy conservation standards,

(C) $100 in the case of a refrigerator which is manufactured in calendar year 2008, 2009, or 2010, and consumes at least 25 percent but not more than 29.9 percent less kilowatt hours per year than the 2001 energy conservation standards,

(D) $200 in the case of a refrigerator manufactured in calendar year 2008, 2009, or 2010 and which consumes at least 30 percent less energy than the 2001 energy conservation standards,

(E) $150 in the case of a refrigerator manufactured in calendar year 2011 which consumes at least 30 percent less energy than the 2001 energy conservation standards, and

(F) $200 in the case of a refrigerator manufactured in calendar year 2011 which consumes at least 35 percent less energy than the 2001 energy conservation standards.

(c) Eligible production.

The eligible production in a calendar year with respect to each type of energy efficient appliance is the excess of—

(1) the number of appliances of such type which are produced by the taxpayer in the United States during such calendar year, over

(2) the average number of appliances of such type which were produced by the taxpayer (or any predecessor) in the United States during the preceding 2-calendar year period.

(2) Repealed.

(d) Types of energy efficient appliance.

For purposes of this section, the types of energy efficient appliances are—

(1) dishwashers described in subsection (b)(1),

(2) clothes washers described in subsection (b)(2), and

(3) refrigerators described in subsection (b)(3).

(e) Limitations.

(1) Aggregate credit amount allowed. The aggregate amount of credit allowed under subsection (a) with respect to a taxpayer for any taxable year shall not exceed $25,000,000 reduced by the amount of the credit allowed under subsection (a) to the taxpayer (or any predecessor) for all prior taxable years beginning after December 31, 2010.

(2) Amount allowed for certain refrigerators and clothes washers. Refrigerators described in subsection (b)(3)(F) and clothes washers described in subsection (b)(2)(F) shall not be taken into account under paragraph (1).

(3) Limitation based on gross receipts. The credit allowed under subsection (a) with respect to a taxpayer for the taxable year shall not exceed an amount equal to 4 percent of the average annual gross receipts of the taxpayer for the 3 taxable years preceding the taxable year in which the credit is determined.

(4) Gross receipts. For purposes of this subsection, the rules of paragraphs (2) and (3) of section 448(c) shall apply.

(f) Definitions.

For purposes of this section—

(1) Qualified energy efficient appliance. The term "qualified energy efficient appliance" means—

  (A) any dishwasher described in subsection (b)(1),

  (B) any clothes washer described in subsection (b)(2), and

  (C) any refrigerator described in subsection (b)(3).

(2) Dishwasher. The term "dishwasher" means a residential dishwasher subject to the energy conservation standards established by the Department of Energy.

(3) Clothes washer. The term "clothes washer" means a residential model clothes washer, including a commercial residential style coin operated washer.

(4) Top-loading clothes washer. The term "top-loading clothes washer" means a clothes washer which has the clothes container compartment access located on the top of the machine and which operates on a vertical axis.

(5) Refrigerator. The term "refrigerator" means a residential model automatic defrost refrigerator-freezer which has an internal volume of at least 16.5 cubic feet.

(6) Modified energy factor. The term "modified energy factor" means the modified energy factor established by the Department of Energy for compliance with the Federal energy conservation standard.

(7) Produced. The term "produced" includes manufactured.

(8) 2001 energy conservation standard. The term "2001 energy conservation standard" means the energy conservation standards promulgated by the Department of Energy and effective July 1, 2001.

(9) Gallons per cycle. The term "gallons per cycle" means, with respect to a dishwasher, the amount of water, expressed in gallons, required to complete a normal cycle of a dishwasher.

(10) Water consumption factor. The term "water consumption factor" means, with respect to a clothes washer, the quotient of the total weighted per-cycle water consumption divided by the cubic foot (or liter) capacity of the clothes washer.

(g) Special rules.

For purposes of this section—

(1) In general. Rules similar to the rules of subsections (c), (d), and (e) of section 52 shall apply.

(2) Controlled group.

(A) In general. All persons treated as a single employer under subsection (a) or (b) of section 52 or subsection (m) or (o) of section 414 shall be treated as a single producer.

(B) Inclusion of foreign corporations. For purposes of subparagraph (A), in applying subsections (a) and (b) of section 52 to this section, section 1563 shall be applied without regard to subsection (b)(2)(C) thereof.

(3) Verification. No amount shall be allowed as a credit under subsection (a) with respect to which the taxpayer has not submitted such information or certification as the Secretary, in consultation with the Secretary of Energy, determines necessary.

In 2010, P.L. 111-312, Sec. 709(a), deleted "and" at the end of subpara. (b)(1)(A), substituted a comma for the period at the end of subpara. (b)(1)(B) and added subparas. (b)(1)(C)-(E) . . . Sec. 709(b), deleted "and" at the end of subpara. (b)(2)(C), substituted a comma for the period at the end of subpara. (b)(2)(D), and added subparas. (b)(2)(E)-(F) . . . Sec. 709(c), deleted "and" at the end of subpara. (b)(3)(C), substituted a comma for the period at the end of subpara. (b)(3)(D) and added subparas. (b)(3)(E)-(F), effective for appliances produced after 12/31/2010. —P.L. 111-312, Sec. 709(d)(1)(A), substituted "$25,000,000" for "$75,000,000" in para. (e)(1) . . . Sec. 709(d)(1)(B), substituted "December 31, 2010" for "December 31, 2007" in para. (e)(1) . . . Sec. 709(d)(2)(A), substituted "subsection (b)(3)(F)" for "subsection (b)(3)(D)" in para. (e)(2) . . . Sec. 709(d)(2)(B), substituted "subsection (b)(2)(F)" for "subsection (b)(2)(D)" in para. (e)(2) . . . Sec. 709(d)(3), substituted "4 percent" for "2 percent" in para. (e)(3), effective for tax. yrs. begin. after 12/31/2010.

In 2008, P.L. 110-343, Sec. 305(a)DivB, amended subsec. (b) . . . Sec. 305(b)(1)(A)DivB, repealed para. (c)(2) . . . Sec. 305(b)(1)(B) and (C)DivB, substituted "The eligible" and moving the text of such subsection in line with the subsection heading for "(1) In general' and all that follows through "the eligible" and inserting . . . Sec. 305(b)(1)(D)DivB, redesignating subparas. (c)(1)(A) and (B) as paras. (c)(1) and (2), respectively, and by moving such paragraphs 2 ems to the left. . . . Sec. 305(b)(2)DivB, substituted "2-calendar year" for "3-calendar year". in para. (c)(2) [as amended] . . . Sec. 305(c)DivB, amended subsec. (d) . . . Sec. 305(d)(1)DivB, amended para. (e)(1) . . . Sec. 305(d)(2)DivB, amended para. (e)(2) . . . Sec. 305(e)(1)DivB, amended para. (f)(1) . . . Sec. 305(e)(2)DivB, amended para. (e)(2) . . . Sec. 305(e)(2)DivB, added "commercial" before "residential' the second place it appears in para. (f)(3) . . . Sec. 305(e)(3)DivB, redesignated para. (f)(4)-(7) as (f)(5)-(8), added new para. (f)(4) . . . Sec. 305(e)(4)DivB, amended para. (f)(6) . . . Sec. 305(e)(5)DivB, added para. (f)(9) and (10), effective for appliances produced after 12/31/2007.

Prior to repeal para. (c)(2) read as follows:

"(2) Special rule for refrigerators. The eligible production in a calendar year with respect to each type of refrigerator described in subsection (b)(1)(C) is the excess of—

"(A) the number of appliances of such type which are produced by the taxpayer in the United States during such calendar year, over

"(B) 110 percent of the average number of appliances of such type which were produced by the taxpayer (or any predecessor) in the United States during the preceding 3-calendar year period."

Prior to repeal para. (d) read as follows:

"(d) Types of energy efficient appliance. For purposes of this section, the types of energy efficient appliances are—

"(1) dishwashers described in subsection (b)(1)(A),

"(2) clothes washers described in subsection (b)(1)(B),

"(3) refrigerators described in subsection (b)(1)(C)(i),

"(4) refrigerators described in subsection (b)(1)(C)(ii), and

"(1) refrigerators described in subsection (b)(1)(C)(iii)."

Prior to repeal para. (e)(1) read as follows:

"(1) Aggregate credit amount allowed. The aggregate amount of credit allowed under subsection (a) with respect to a taxpayer for any taxable year shall not exceed $75,000,000 reduced by the amount of the credit allowed under subsection (a) to the taxpayer (or any predecessor) for all prior taxable years."

Prior to repeal para. (e)(2) read as follows:

"(2) Amount allowed for 15 percent savings refrigerators. In the case of refrigerators described in subsection (b)(1)(C)(i), the aggregate amount of the credit allowed under subsection (a) with respect to a taxpayer for any taxable year shall not exceed $20,000,000."

Prior to repeal para. (f)(1) read as follows:

"(1) Qualified energy efficient appliance. The term 'qualified energy efficient appliance' means—

"(A) any dishwasher described in subsection (b)(1)(A),

"(B) any clothes washer described in subsection (b)(1)(B), and

"(C) any refrigerator described in subsection (b)(1)(C)."

Prior to amendment para. (f)(6), as [amended] read as follows:

"(5) EF. The term 'EF' means the energy factor established by the Department of Energy for compliance with the Federal energy conservation standards."

In 2005, P.L. 109-58, Sec. 1334(a), added Code Sec. 45M, effective for appliances produced after 12/31/2005.

Sec. 45N. Mine rescue team training credit.

(a) Amount of credit.

For purposes of section 38, the mine rescue team training credit determined under this section with respect to each qualified mine rescue team employee of an eligible employer for any taxable year is an amount equal to the lesser of—

(1) 20 percent of the amount paid or incurred by the taxpayer during the taxable year with respect to the training program costs of such qualified mine rescue team employee (including wages of such employee while attending such program), or

(2) $10,000.

(b) Qualified mine rescue team employee.

For purposes of this section, the term "qualified mine rescue team employee" means with respect to any taxable year any full-time employee of the taxpayer who is—

(1) a miner eligible for more than 6 months of such taxable year to serve as a mine rescue team member as a result of completing, at a minimum, an initial 20-hour course of instruction as prescribed by the Mine Safety and Health Administration's Office of Educational Policy and Development, or

(2) a miner eligible for more than 6 months of such taxable year to serve as a mine rescue team member by virtue of receiving at least 40 hours of refresher training in such instruction.

(c) Eligible employer.

For purposes of this section, the term "eligible employer" means any taxpayer which employs individuals as miners in underground mines in the United States.

(d) Wages.

For purposes of this section, the term "wages" has the meaning given to such term by subsection (b) of section 3306 (determined without regard to any dollar limitation contained in such section).

(e) Termination.

This section shall not apply to taxable years beginning after December 31, 2011.

In 2010, P.L. 111-312, Sec. 735(a), substituted "December 31, 2011" for "December 31, 2009" in subsec. (e), effective for tax. yrs. begin. after 12/31/2009.

In 2008, P.L. 110-343, Sec. 310DivC, substituted "December 31, 2009" for "December 31, 2008" in subsec. (e), effective 10/3/2008.

In 2006, P.L. 109-432, Sec. 405(a), added Code Sec. 45N, effective for tax. yrs. begin. after 12/31/2005

Sec. 45O. Agricultural chemicals security credit.

(a) In general.

For purposes of section 38, in the case of an eligible agricultural business, the agricultural chemicals security credit determined under this section for the taxable year is 30 percent of the qualified security expenditures for the taxable year.

(b) Facility limitation.

The amount of the credit determined under subsection (a) with respect to any facility for any taxable year shall not exceed—

(1) $100,000, reduced by

(2) the aggregate amount of credits determined under subsection (a) with respect to such facility for the 5 prior taxable years.

(c) Annual limitation.

The amount of the credit determined under subsection (a) with respect to any taxpayer for any taxable year shall not exceed $2,000,000.

(d) Qualified chemical security expenditure.

For purposes of this section, the term "qualified chemical security expenditure" means, with respect to any eligible agricultural business for any taxable year, any amount paid or incurred by such business during such taxable year for—

(1) employee security training and background checks,

(2) limitation and prevention of access to controls of specified agricultural chemicals stored at the facility,

(3) tagging, locking tank valves, and chemical additives to prevent the theft of specified agricultural chemicals or to render such chemicals unfit for illegal use,

(4) protection of the perimeter of specified agricultural chemicals,

(5) installation of security lighting, cameras, recording equipment, and intrusion detection sensors,

(6) implementation of measures to increase computer or computer network security,

(7) conducting a security vulnerability assessment,

(8) implementing a site security plan, and

(9) such other measures for the protection of specified agricultural chemicals as the Secretary may identify in regulation.

Amounts described in the preceding sentence shall be taken into account only to the extent that such amounts are paid or incurred for the purpose of protecting specified agricultural chemicals.

(e) Eligible agricultural business.

For purposes of this section, the term "eligible agricultural business" means any person in the trade or business of—

(1) selling agricultural products, including specified agricultural chemicals, at retail predominantly to farmers and ranchers, or

(2) manufacturing, formulating, distributing, or aerially applying specified agricultural chemicals.

(f) Specified agricultural chemical.

For purposes of this section, the term "specified agricultural chemical" means—

(1) any fertilizer commonly used in agricultural operations which is listed under—

  (A) section 302(a)(2) of the Emergency Planning and Community Right-to-Know Act of 1986,

  (B) section 101 of part 172 of title 49, Code of Federal Regulations, or

  (C) part 126, 127, or 154 of title 33, Code of Federal Regulations, and

(2) any pesticide (as defined in section 2(u) of the Federal Insecticide, Fungicide, and Rodenticide Act), including all active and inert ingredients thereof, which is customarily used on crops grown for food, feed, or fiber.

(g) Controlled groups.

Rules similar to the rules of paragraphs (1) and (2) of section 41(f) shall apply for purposes of this section.

(h) Regulations.

The Secretary may prescribe such regulations as may be necessary or appropriate to carry out the purposes of this section, including regulations which—

(1) provide for the proper treatment of amounts which are paid or incurred for purpose of protecting any specified agricultural chemical and for other purposes, and

(2) provide for the treatment of related properties as one facility for purposes of subsection (b).

(i) Termination.

This section shall not apply to any amount paid or incurred after December 31, 2012.

In 2008, P.L. 110-246, Sec. 4, Repeals the duplicative enactment and provides effective date provisions of the Act entitled "An Act to provide for the continuation of agricultural programs through fiscal year 2012, and for other purposes" Sec. 4, P.L. 110-246 reads as follows:

"Sec. 4. Repeal of duplicative enactment.

"(a) In General- The Act entitled 'An Act to provide for the continuation of agricultural programs through fiscal year 2012, and for other purposes' (H.R. 2419 of the 110th Congress), and the amendments made by that Act, are repealed, effective on the date of enactment of that Act.

"(b) Effective Date- Except as otherwise provided in this Act, this Act and the amendments made by this Act shall take effect on the earlier of--

"(1) the date of enactment of this Act; or

"(2) the date of the enactment of the Act entitled 'An Act to provide for the continuation of agricultural programs through fiscal year 2012, and for other purposes' (H.R. 2419 of the 110th Congress)."

—P.L. 110-246, Sec. 15343(a), added Code Sec. 45O, effective for amounts paid or incurred after 5/22/2008. [Ed. Note: May 22, 2008 was the date of enactment for H.R. 2419 (PL 110-234), which was repealed by (2008 Farm Act § 4(a)) (PL 110-246, 6/18/2008), in connection with the reenactment of the farm bill to correct a technical deficiency in its original passage.]

Sec. 45P. Employer wage credit for employees who are active duty members of the uniformed services.

(a) General rule.

For purposes of section 38, in the case of an eligible small business employer, the differential wage payment credit for any taxable year is an amount equal to 20 percent of the sum of the eligible differential wage payments for each of the qualified employees of the taxpayer during such taxable year.

(b) Definitions.

For purposes of this section—

(1) Eligible differential wage payments. The term "eligible differential wage payments" means, with respect to each qualified employee, so much of the differential wage payments (as defined in section 3401(h)(2)) paid to such employee for the taxable year as does not exceed $20,000.

(2) Qualified employee. The term "qualified employee" means a person who has been an employee of the taxpayer for the 91-day period immediately preceding the period for which any differential wage payment is made.

(3) Eligible small business employer.

(A) In general. The term "eligible small business employer" means, with respect to any taxable year, any employer which—

  (i) employed an average of less than 50 employees on business days during such taxable year, and

  (ii) under a written plan of the employer, provides eligible differential wage payments to every qualified employee of the employer.

(B) Controlled groups. For purposes of subparagraph (A), all persons treated as a single employer under subsection (b), (c), (m), or (o) of section 414 shall be treated as a single employer.

Tax credits   **Code Sec. 45Q**

(c) Coordination with other credits.

The amount of credit otherwise allowable under this chapter with respect to compensation paid to any employee shall be reduced by the credit determined under this section with respect to such employee.

(d) Disallowance for failure to comply with employment or reemployment rights of members of the reserve components of the Armed Forces of the United States.

No credit shall be allowed under subsection (a) to a taxpayer for—

(1) any taxable year, beginning after the date of the enactment of this section, in which the taxpayer is under a final order, judgment, or other process issued or required by a district court of the United States under section 4323 of title 38 of the United States Code with respect to a violation of chapter 43 of such title, and

(2) the 2 succeeding taxable years.

(e) Certain rules to apply.

For purposes of this section, rules similar to the rules of subsections (c), (d), and (e) of section 52 shall apply.

(f) Termination.

This section shall not apply to any payments made after December 31, 2011.

In 2010, P.L. 111-312, Sec. 736(a), substituted "December 31, 2011" for "December 31, 2009" in subsec. (f), effective for payments made after 12/31/2009.

In 2008, P.L. 110-245, Sec. 111(a), added Code Sec. 45P, effective for amounts paid after 6/17/2008.

Sec. 45Q. Credit for carbon dioxide sequestration.

(a) General rule.

For purposes of section 38, the carbon dioxide sequestration credit for any taxable year is an amount equal to the sum of—

(1) $20 per metric ton of qualified carbon dioxide which is—

(A) captured by the taxpayer at a qualified facility, and

(B) disposed of by the taxpayer in secure geological storage and not used by the taxpayer as described in paragraph (2)(B), and

(2) $10 per metric ton of qualified carbon dioxide which is—

(A) captured by the taxpayer at a qualified facility,

(B) used by the taxpayer as a tertiary injectant in a qualified enhanced oil or natural gas recovery project, and

(C) disposed of by the taxpayer in secure geological storage.

(b) Qualified carbon dioxide.

For purposes of this section—

(1) **In general.** The term "qualified carbon dioxide" means carbon dioxide captured from an industrial source which—

(A) would otherwise be released into the atmosphere as industrial emission of greenhouse gas, and

(B) is measured at the source of capture and verified at the point of disposal or injection.

(2) **Recycled carbon dioxide.** The term "qualified carbon dioxide" includes the initial deposit of captured carbon dioxide used as a tertiary injectant. Such term does not include carbon dioxide that is re-captured, recycled, and re-injected as part of the enhanced oil and natural gas recovery process.

(c) Qualified facility.

For purposes of this section, the term "qualified facility" means any industrial facility—

(1) which is owned by the taxpayer,

(2) at which carbon capture equipment is placed in service, and

(3) which captures not less than 500,000 metric tons of carbon dioxide during the taxable year.

(d) Special rules and other definitions.

For purposes of this section—

(1) **Only carbon dioxide captured and disposed of or used within the United States taken into account.** The credit under this section shall apply only with respect to qualified carbon dioxide the capture and disposal or use of which is within—

(A) the United States (within the meaning of section 638(1)), or

(B) a possession of the United States (within the meaning of section 638(2)).

(2) **Secure geological storage.** The Secretary, in consultation with the Administrator of the Environmental Protection Agency the Secretary of Energy, and the Secretary of the Interior, shall establish regulations for determining adequate security measures for the geological storage of carbon dioxide under paragraph (1)(B) or (2)(C) of subsection (a) such that the carbon dioxide does not escape into the atmosphere. Such term shall include storage at deep saline formations, oil and gas reservoirs, and unminable coal seams under such conditions as the Secretary may determine under such regulations.

(3) **Tertiary injectant.** The term "tertiary injectant" has the same meaning as when used within section 193(b)(1).

(4) **Qualified enhanced oil or natural gas recovery project.** The term "qualified enhanced oil or natural gas recovery project" has the meaning given the term "qualified enhanced oil recovery project" by section 43(c)(2), by substituting "crude oil or natural gas" for "crude oil" in subparagraph (A)(i) thereof.

(5) **Credit attributable to taxpayer.** Any credit under this section shall be attributable to the person that captures and physically or contractually ensures the disposal of or the use as a tertiary injectant of the qualified carbon dioxide, except to the extent provided in regulations prescribed by the Secretary.

(6) **Recapture.** The Secretary shall, by regulations, provide for recapturing the benefit of any credit allowable under subsection (a) with respect to any qualified carbon dioxide which ceases to be captured, disposed of, or used as a tertiary injectant in a manner consistent with the requirements of this section.

(7) **Inflation adjustment.** In the case of any taxable year beginning in a calendar year after 2009, there shall be substituted for each dollar amount contained in subsection (a) an amount equal to the product of—

(A) such dollar amount, multiplied by

(B) the inflation adjustment factor for such calendar year determined under section 43(b)(3)(B) for such calendar year, determined by substituting "2008" for "1990".

(e) Application of section.

The credit under this section shall apply with respect to qualified carbon dioxide before the end of the calendar year in which the Secretary, in consultation with the Administrator of the Environmental Protection Agency, certifies that 75,000,000 metric tons of qualified carbon dioxide have been taken into account in accordance with subsection (a).

In 2009, P.L. 111-5, Sec. 1131(a), deleted "and" at the end of subpara. (a)(2)(A), substituted ", and" for the period in subpara (a)(2)(B), and added subpara. (a)(2)(C).... Sec. 1131(b)(1)(A), substituted "paragraph (1)(B) or (2)(C) of subsection (a)" for "subsection (a)(1)(B)" in para. (d)(2).... Sec. 1131(b)(1)(B), substituted ", oil and gas reservoirs, and unminable coal seams" for "and unminable coal seams" in para. (d)(2).... Sec. 1131(b)(1)(C), added "the Secretary of Energy, and the Secretary of the Interior," after "Environmental Protection Agency" in para. (d)(2).... Sec. 1131(b)(2), added "and not used by the taxpayer as described in paragraph (2)(B)" after "storage" in subpara. (a)(1)(B).... Sec. 1131(b)(3), substituted "taken into account in accordance with subsection (a)" for "captured and disposed of or used as a tertiary injectant" in subsec. (e), effective for carbon dioxide captured after 2/17/2009.

In 2008, P.L. 110-343, Sec. 115(a)DivB, added Code Sec. 45Q, effective for carbon dioxide captured after 10/3/2008.

Sec. 45R. Employee health insurance expenses of small employers.

(a) General rule.

For purposes of section 38, in the case of an eligible small employer, the small employer health insurance credit determined under this section for any taxable year in the credit period is the amount determined under subsection (b).

(b) Health insurance credit amount.

Subject to subsection (c), the amount determined under this subsection with respect to any eligible small employer is equal to 50 percent (35 percent in the case of a tax-exempt eligible small employer) of the lesser of—

(1) the aggregate amount of nonelective contributions the employer made on behalf of its employees during the taxable year under the arrangement described in subsection (d)(4) for premiums for qualified health plans offered by the employer to its employees through an Exchange, or

(2) the aggregate amount of nonelective contributions which the employer would have made during the taxable year under the arrangement if each employee taken into account under paragraph (1) had enrolled in a qualified health plan which had a premium equal to the average premium (as determined by the Secretary of Health and Human Services) for the small group market in the rating area in which the employee enrolls for coverage.

(c) Phaseout of credit amount based on number of employees and average wages.

The amount of the credit determined under subsection (b) without regard to this subsection shall be reduced (but not below zero) by the sum of the following amounts:

(1) Such amount multiplied by a fraction the numerator of which is the total number of full-time equivalent employees of the employer in excess of 10 and the denominator of which is 15.

(2) Such amount multiplied by a fraction the numerator of which is the average annual wages of the employer in excess of the dollar amount in effect under subsection (d)(3)(B) and the denominator of which is such dollar amount.

(d) Eligible small employer.

For purposes of this section—

(1) **In general.** The term "eligible small employer" means, with respect to any taxable year, an employer—

(A) which has no more than 25 full-time equivalent employees for the taxable year,

(B) the average annual wages of which do not exceed an amount equal to twice the dollar amount in effect under paragraph (3)(B) for the taxable year, and

(C) which has in effect an arrangement described in paragraph (4).

(2) **Full-time equivalent employees.**

(A) In general. The term "full-time equivalent employees" means a number of employees equal to the number determined by dividing—

(i) the total number of hours of service for which wages were paid by the employer to employees during the taxable year, by

(ii) 2,080.

Such number shall be rounded to the next lowest whole number if not otherwise a whole number.

(B) Excess hours not counted. If an employee works in excess of 2,080 hours of service during any taxable year, such excess shall not be taken into account under subparagraph (A).

(C) Hours of service. The Secretary, in consultation with the Secretary of Labor, shall prescribe such regulations, rules, and guidance as may be necessary to determine the hours of service of an employee, including rules for the application of this paragraph to employees who are not compensated on an hourly basis.

(3) **Average annual wages.**

(A) In general. The average annual wages of an eligible small employer for any taxable year is the amount determined by dividing—

(i) the aggregate amount of wages which were paid by the employer to employees during the taxable year, by

(ii) the number of full-time equivalent employees of the employee determined under paragraph (2) for the taxable year.

Such amount shall be rounded to the next lowest multiple of $1,000 if not otherwise such a multiple.

(B) Dollar amount. For purposes of paragraph (1)(B) and subsection (c)(2)—

(i) 2010, 2011, 2012, and 2013. The dollar amount in effect under this paragraph for taxable years beginning in 2010, 2011, 2012, or 2013 is $25,000.

(ii) Subsequent years. In the case of a taxable year beginning in a calendar year after 2013, the dollar amount in effect under this paragraph shall be equal to $25,000, multiplied by the cost-of-living adjustment under section 1(f)(3) for the calendar year, determined by substituting "calendar year 2012" for "calendar year 1992" in subparagraph (B) thereof.

(4) **Contribution arrangement.** An arrangement is described in this paragraph if it requires an eligible small employer to make a nonelective contribution on behalf of each employee who enrolls in a qualified health plan offered to employees by the employer through an exchange in an amount equal to a uniform percentage (not less than 50 percent) of the premium cost of the qualified health plan.

(5) **Seasonal worker hours and wages not counted.** For purposes of this subsection—

(A) In general. The number of hours of service worked by, and wages paid to, a seasonal worker of an employer shall not be taken into account in determining the full-time equivalent employees and average annual wages of the employer unless the worker works for the employer on more than 120 days during the taxable year.

(B) Definition of seasonal worker. The term "seasonal worker" means a worker who performs labor or services on a seasonal basis as defined by the Secretary of Labor, including workers covered by section 500.20(s)(1) of title 29, Code of Federal Regulations and retail workers employed exclusively during holiday seasons.

(e) Other rules and definitions.

For purposes of this section—

(1) **Employee.**

(A) Certain employees excluded. The term "employee" shall not include—

(i) an employee within the meaning of section 401(c)(1),

(ii) any 2-percent shareholder (as defined in section 1372(b)) of an eligible small business which is an S corporation,

(iii) any 5-percent owner (as defined in section 416(i)(1)(B)(i)) of an eligible small business, or

(iv) any individual who bears any of the relationships described in subparagraphs (A) through (G) of section 152(d)(2) to, or is a dependent described in section 152(d)(2)(H) of, an individual described in clause (i), (ii), or (iii).

(B) Leased employees. The term "employee" shall include a leased employee within the meaning of section 414(n).

(2) Credit period. The term "credit period" means, with respect to any eligible small employer, the 2-consecutive-taxable year period beginning with the 1st taxable year in which the employer (or any predecessor) offers 1 or more qualified health plans to its employees through an Exchange.

(3) Nonelective contribution. The term "nonelective contribution" means an employer contribution other than an employer contribution pursuant to a salary reduction arrangement.

(4) Wages. The term "wages" has the meaning given such term by section 3121(a) (determined without regard to any dollar limitation contained in such section).

(5) Aggregation and other rules made applicable.

(A) Aggregation rules. All employers treated as a single employer under subsection (b), (c), (m), or (o) of section 414 shall be treated as a single employer for purposes of this section.

(B) Other rules. Rules similar to the rules of subsections (c), (d), and (e) of section 52 shall apply.

(f) Credit made available to tax-exempt eligible small employers.

(1) In general. In the case of a tax-exempt eligible small employer, there shall be treated as a credit allowable under subpart C (and not allowable under this subpart) the lesser of—

(A) the amount of the credit determined under this section with respect to such employer, or

(B) the amount of the payroll taxes of the employer during the calendar year in which the taxable year begins.

(2) Tax-exempt eligible small employer. For purposes of this section, the term "taxexempt eligible small employer" means an eligible small employer which is any organization described in section 501(c) which is exempt from taxation under section 501(a).

(3) Payroll taxes. For purposes of this subsection—

(A) In general. The term "payroll taxes" means—

(i) amounts required to be withheld from the employees of the tax-exempt eligible small employer under section 3401(a),

(ii) amounts required to be withheld from such employees under section 3101(b), and

(iii) amounts of the taxes imposed on the tax-exempt eligible small employer under section 3111(b).

(B) Special rule. A rule similar to the rule of section 24(d)(2)(C) shall apply for purposes of subparagraph (A).

(g) Application of section for calendar years 2010, 2011, 2012, and 2013.

In the case of any taxable year beginning in 2010, 2011, 2012, or 2013, the following modifications to this section shall apply in determining the amount of the credit under subsection (a):

(1) No credit period required. The credit shall be determined without regard to whether the taxable year is in a credit period and for purposes of applying this section to taxable years beginning after 2013, no credit period shall be treated as beginning with a taxable year beginning before 2014.

(2) Amount of credit. The amount of the credit determined under subsection (b) shall be determined—

(A) by substituting "35 percent (25 percent in the case of a tax-exempt eligible small employer)" for "50 percent (35 percent in the case of a tax-exempt eligible small employer)",

(B) by reference to an eligible small employer's nonelective contributions for premiums paid for health insurance coverage (within the meaning of section 9832(b)(1)) of an employee, and

(C) by substituting for the average premium determined under subsection (b)(2) the amount the Secretary of Health and Human Services determines is the average premium for the small group market in the State in which the employer is offering health insurance coverage (or for such area within the State as is specified by the Secretary).

(3) Contribution arrangement. An arrangement shall not fail to meet the requirements of subsection (d)(4) solely because it provides for the offering of insurance outside of an Exchange.

(h) Insurance definitions.

Any term used in this section which is also used in the Public Health Service Act or subtitle A of title I of the Patient Protection and Affordable Care Act shall have the meaning given such term by such Act or subtitle.

(i) Regulations.

The Secretary shall prescribe such regulations as may be necessary to carry out the provisions of this section, including regulations to prevent the avoidance of the 2-year limit on the credit period through the use of successor entities and the avoidance of the limitations under subsection (c) through the use of multiple entities.

In 2010, P.L. 111-148, Sec. 1421(a), added Code Sec. 45R, effective for amounts paid or incurred in tax. yrs. begin. after 12/31/2009 [as amended by Sec. 10105(e)(4) of this Act, see below].

—P.L. 111-148, Sec. 10105(e)(1), amended subpara. (d)(3)(B) [as added by Sec. 1421(a) of this Act, see above].

—P.L. 111-148, Sec. 10105(e)(2), substituted "2010, 2011" for "2011" in subsec. (g) [as added by Sec. 1421(a) of this Act, see above], effective for amounts paid or incurred in tax. yrs. begin. after 12/31/2009, as if included in the provisions of Sec. 1421(f)(1) of this Act [as amended by Sec. 10105(e)(4) of this Act, see below].

Prior to amendment, subpara. (d)(3)(B) read as follows:

"(B) Dollar amount. For purposes of paragraph (1)(B)—

"(i) 2011, 2012, and 2013. The dollar amount in effect under this paragraph for taxable years beginning in 2011, 2012, or 2013 is $20,000.

"(ii) Subsequent years. In the case of a taxable year beginning in a calendar year after 2013, the dollar amount in effect under this paragraph shall be equal to $20,000, multiplied by the cost-of-living adjustment determined under section 1(f)(3) for the calendar year, determined by substituting 'calendar year 2012' for 'calendar year 1992' in subparagraph (B) thereof."

—P.L. 111-148, Sec. 10105(e)(4), substituted "2009" for "2010" both places it appeared in Sec. 1421(f) [the effective date provided for the enactment of Code Sec. 45R, by Sec. 1421(a) of this Act, see above].

SUBPART E.—RULES FOR COMPUTING INVESTMENT CREDIT

Sec. 46. Amount of credit.
Sec. 47. Rehabilitation credit.
Sec. 48. Energy credit.
Sec. 48A. Qualifying advanced coal project credit.
Sec. 48B. Qualifying gasification project credit.
Sec. 48C. Qualifying advanced energy project credit.
Sec. 48D. Qualifying therapeutic discovery project credit.
Sec. 49. At-risk rules.
Sec. 50. Other special rules.
Sec. 50. Repealed. [Restoration of credit.]

In 2010, P.L. 111-148, Sec. 9023(a), added item 48D.
In 2009, P.L. 111-5, Sec. 1302(c)(2), added item 48C.
In 2005, P.L. 109-58, Sec. 1307(c)(2), added items 48A and 48B.
In 2004, P.L. 108-357, Sec. 322(d)(2)(C), amended item 48.
Prior to amendment, item 48 read as follows:
"48. Energy credit; reforestation credit."
In 1990, P.L. 101-508, Sec. 11813(a), amended subpart E, of part IV of subchapter A of chapter 1, effective for property placed in service after 12/31/90, except as provided in Sec. 11813(c) of this Act, reproduced in note following Code Sec 46.
Prior to amendment, subpart E, of part IV of subchapter A of chapter 1, read as follows:
"SUBPART E—RULES FOR COMPUTING CREDIT FOR INVESTMENT IN CERTAIN DEPRECIABLE PROPERTY
"Sec.
"46. Amount of credit.
"47. Certain dispositions, etc., of section 38 property.
"48. Definitions; special rules.
"49. Termination of regular percentage.
"50. Repealed. [Restoration of credit.]"

In 1986, P.L. 99-514, Sec. 211(c), added item 49.
In 1984, P.L. 98-369, Sec. 474(n)(1), redesignated subpart B as E.
In 1978, P.L. 95-600, Sec. 312(c)(5), repealed items 49 and 50.
Prior to repeal, items 49 and 50 read as follows:
"49. Termination for period beginning April 19, 1969, and ending during 1971."
"50. Restoration of credit."
In 1971, P.L. 92-178, Sec. 101(b)(5), amended item 49 and added item 50.
Prior to amendment, item 49 read as follows:
"49. Termination of credit."
In 1969, P.L. 91-172, Sec. 703(d), added item 49.
In 1962, P.L. 87-834, Sec. 2(g)(1), added subpart B.

"SEC. 46. AMOUNT OF CREDIT.
"(a) Amount of investment credit. For purposes of section 38, the amount of the investment credit determined under this section for any taxable year shall be an amount equal to the sum of the following percentages of the qualified investment (as determined under subsections (c) and (d)):
"(1) the regular percentage,
"(2) in the case of energy property, the energy percentage, and
"(3) in the case of that portion of the basis of any property which is attributable to qualified rehabilitation expenditures, the rehabilitation percentage.
"(b) Determination of percentages. For purposes of subsection (a)—
"(1) Regular percentage. The regular percentage is 10 percent.
"(2) Energy percentage.
"(A) In general. The energy percentage shall be determined in accordance with the following table:

"Column A— Description	Column B— Percentage	Column C— Period
In the case of:	The energy percentage is:	For the period: Beginning on: And ending on:
"(i) General Rule.—Property not described in any of the following provisions of this column	10 percent	Oct. 1, 1978 Dec. 31, 1982
"(ii) Solar Wind, or Geothermal Property.— Property described in section 48(l)(2)(A)(ii) or 48(l)(3)(A)(viii)...	A. 10 percent	Oct. 1, 1978 Dec. 31, 1979
	B. 15 percent	Jan. 1, 1980 Dec. 31, 1985
"(iii) Ocean Thermal Property.— Property described in section 48(l)(3)(A)(ix)...	15 percent	Jan. 1, 1980 Dec. 31, 1985
"(iv) Qualified Hydroelectric Generating Property.— Property described in section 48(l)(2)(A)(vii)...	11 percent	Jan. 1, 1980 Dec. 31, 1985
"(v) Qualified Intercity Buses.— Property described in section 48(l)(2)(A)(ix)...	10 percent	Jan. 1, 1980 Dec. 31, 1985
"(vi) Biomass Property.— Property described in section 48(l)(15)...	10 percent	Oct. 1, 1978 Dec. 31, 1985
"(vii) Chlor-Alkali Electrolytic Cells.— Property described in section 48(l)(5)(M)...	10 percent	Jan. 1, 1980 Dec. 31, 1982
"(viii) Solar Energy Property. Property described in section 48(l)(4) (other than wind energy property)...	A. 15 percent	Jan. 1, 1986 Dec. 31, 1986.
	B. 12 percent	Jan. 1, 1987 Dec. 31, 1987.
	C. 10 percent	Jan. 1, 1988 Dec. 31, 1991.
"(ix) Geothermal Property. Property described in section 48(l)(3)(A)(viii)...	A. 15 percent	Jan. 1, 1986 Dec. 31, 1986.
	B. 10 percent	Jan. 1, 1987 Dec. 31, 1991.
"(x) Ocean Thermal Property. Property described in section 48(l)(3)(A)(ix)...	15 percent	Jan. 1, 1986 Sept. 30, 1990.
"(xi) Biomass Property. Property described in section 48(l)(15).	A. 15 percent	Jan. 1, 1986 Dec. 31, 1986.
	B. 10 percent	Jan. 1, 1987 Dec. 31, 1987.

"(B) Periods for which percentage not specified. In the case of any energy property, the energy percentage shall be zero for any period for which an energy percentage is not specified for such property under subparagraph (A) as modified by subparagraphs (C) and (D)).
"(C) Longer period for certain long-term projects. For the purpose of applying the energy percentage contained in clause (i) of subparagraph (A) with respect to property which is part of a project with a normal construction period of 2 years or more (within the meaning of subsection (d)(2)(A)(i)), 'December 31, 1990' shall be substituted for 'December 31, 1982' if—
"(i) before January 1, 1983, all engineering studies in connection with the commencement of the construction of the project have been completed and all environmental and construction permits required under Federal, State, or local law in connection with the commencement of the construction of the project have been applied for, and
"(ii) before January 1, 1986, the taxpayer has entered into binding contracts for the acquisition, construction, reconstruction, or erection of equipment specially designed for the project and the aggregate cost to the taxpayer of that equipment is at least 50 percent of the reasonably estimated cost for all such equipment which is to be placed in service as part of the project upon its completion.
"(D) Longer period for certain hydroelectric generating property. If an application has been docketed with the Federal Energy Regulatory Commission before January 1, 1986, with respect to the installation of any qualified hydroelectric generating property, for purposes of applying the energy percentage contained in clause (iv) of subparagraph (A) with respect to such property, 'December 31, 1988' shall be substituted for 'December 31, 1985.'
"(E) Certain rules made applicable. Rules similar to the rules of subsections (c) and (d) of section 49 shall apply to any credit allowable by reason of subparagraph (C) or (D).
"(3) Special rule for certain energy property. The regular percentage shall not apply to any energy property which, but for section 48(l)(1), would not be section 38 property. In the case of any qualified hydroelectric generating property which is a fish passageway, the preceding sentence shall not apply to any period after 1979 for which the energy percentage for such property is greater than zero.
"(4) Rehabilitation percentage.
"(A) In general. The term 'rehabilitation percentage' means—

"(i) 10 percent in the case of qualified rehabilitation expenditures with respect to a qualified rehabilitated building other than a certified historic structure, and

"(ii) 20 percent in the case of such expenditure with respect to a certified historic structure.

"(B) Regular and energy percentages not to apply. The regular percentage and the energy percentages shall not apply to that portion of the basis of any property which is attributable to qualified rehabilitation expenditures.

"(c) Qualified investment.

"(1) In general. For purposes of this subpart, the term 'qualified investment' means, with respect to any taxable year, the aggregate of—

"(A) the applicable percentage of the basis of each new section 38 property (as defined in section 48(b)) placed in service by the taxpayer during such taxable year, plus

"(B) the applicable percentage of the cost of each used section 38 property (as defined in section 48(c)(1)) placed in service by the taxpayer during such taxable year.

"(2) Applicable percentage in certain cases. Except as provided in paragraphs (3), (6), and (7), the applicable percentage for purposes of paragraph (1) for any property shall be determined under the following table:

If the useful life is—	The applicable percentage is—
"3 years or more but less than 5 years	33⅓
"5 years or more but less than 7 years	66⅔
"7 years or more	100

For purposes of this subpart, the useful life of any property shall be the useful life used in computing the allowance for depreciation under section 167 for the taxable year in which the property is placed in service.

"(3) Public utility property.

"(A) To the extent that the credit allowed by section 38 with respect to any public utility property is determined at the rate of 7 percent, in the case of any property which is public utility property, the amount of the qualified investment shall be 4/7 of the amount determined under paragraph (1). The preceding sentence shall not apply for purposes of applying the energy percentage.

"(B) For purposes of subparagraph (A), the term 'public utility property' means property used predominantly in the trade or business of the furnishing or sale of—

"(i) electrical energy, water, or sewage disposal services,

"(ii) gas through a local distribution system, or

"(iii) telephone service, telegraph service by means of domestic telegraph operations (as defined in section 222(a)(5) of the Communications Act of 1934, as amended; 47 U.S.C. 222(a)(5)), or other communication services (other than international telegraph service),

if the rates for such furnishing or sale, as the case may be, have been established or approved by a State or political subdivision thereof, by an agency or instrumentality of the United States, or by a public service or public utility commission or other similar body of any State or political subdivision thereof. Such term also means communication property of the type used by persons engaged in providing telephone or microwave communication services to which clause (iii) applies, if such property is used predominantly for communication purposes.

"(C) In the case of any interest in a submarine cable circuit used to furnish telegraph service between the United States and a point outside the United States of a taxpayer engaged in furnishing international telegraph service (if the rates for such furnishing have been established or approved by a governmental unit, agency, instrumentality, commission, or similar body described in subparagraph (B)), the qualified investment shall not exceed the qualified investment attributable to so much of the interest of the taxpayer in the circuit as does not exceed 50 percent of all interests in the circuit.

"(4) Coordination with subsection (d). The amount which would (but for this paragraph) be treated as qualified investment under this subsection with respect to any property shall be reduced (but not below zero) by any amount treated by the taxpayer or a predecessor of the taxpayer (or, in the case of a sale and leaseback described in section 47(a)(3)(C), by the lessee) as qualified investment with respect to such property under subsection (d), to the extent the amount so treated has not been required to be recaptured by reason of section 47(a)(3).

"(5) Applicable percentage in the case of certain pollution control facilities.

"(A) In general. Notwithstanding paragraph (2), in the case of property—

"(i) with respect to which an election under section 169 applies, and

"(ii) the useful life of which (determined without regard to section 169) is not less than 5 years.

100 percent shall be the applicable percentage for purposes of applying paragraph (1) with respect to so much of the adjusted basis of the property as (after the application of section 169(f)) constitutes the amortizable basis for purposes of section 169.

"(B) Special rule where property is financed by private activity bonds. To the extent that any property is financed by the proceeds of a private activity bond (within the meaning of section 141) the interest on which is exempt from tax under section 103, subparagraph (A) shall be applied by substituting '50 percent' for '100 percent'. This subparagraph shall not apply for purposes of applying the energy percentage.

"(6) Special rule for commuter highway vehicles.

"(A) In general. Notwithstanding paragraph (2) or (3), in the case of a commuter highway vehicle the useful life of which is 3 years or more, or which is recovery property (within the meaning of section 168), the applicable percentage for purposes of paragraph (1) shall be 100 percent.

"(B) Definition of commuter highway vehicle. For purposes of subparagraph (A), the term 'commuter highway vehicle' means a highway vehicle—

"(i) the seating capacity of which is at least 8 adults (not including the driver),

"(ii) at least 80 percent of the mileage use of which can reasonably be expected to be (I) for purposes of transporting the taxpayer's employees between their residences and their place of employment, and (II) on trips during which the number of employees transported for such purposes is at least one-half of the adult seating capacity of such vehicle (not including the driver),

"(iii) which is acquired by the taxpayer on or after the date of the enactment of the Energy Tax Act of 1978, and placed in service by the taxpayer before January 1, 1986, and

"(iv) with respect to which the taxpayer makes an election under this paragraph on his return for the taxable year in which such vehicle is placed in service.

"(7) Applicable percentage for property to which section 168 applies. Notwithstanding paragraph (2), the applicable percentage for purposes of paragraph (1) shall be—

"(A) in the case of property to which section 168 applies other than 3-year property (within the meaning of section 168(e)), 100 percent, and

"(B) in the case of 3-year property (within the meaning of section 168(e)), 60 percent.

For purposes of subparagraph (A), RRB replacement property (within the meaning of section 168(f)(3)(B) (as in effect on the day before the date of the enactment of the Tax Reform Act of 1986)) shall be treated as property which is not 3-year property.

"(8) Certain nonrecourse financing excluded from credit base.

"(A) Limitation. The credit base of any property to which this paragraph applies shall be reduced by the nonqualified nonrecourse financing with respect to such property (as of the close of the taxable year in which placed in service).

"(B) Property to which paragraph applies. This paragraph applies to any property which—

"(i) is placed in service during the taxable year by a taxpayer described in section 465(a)(1), and

"(ii) is used in connection with an activity with respect to which any loss is subject to limitation under section 465.

"(C) Credit base defined. For purposes of this paragraph, the term 'credit base' means—

"(i) in the case of new section 38 property, the basis of the property, or

"(ii) in the case of used section 38 property, the cost of such property.

"(D) Nonqualified nonrecourse financing.

"(i) In general. For purposes of this paragraph and paragraph (9), the term 'nonqualified nonrecourse financing' means any nonrecourse financing which is not qualified commercial financing.

"(ii) Qualified commercial financing. For purposes of this paragraph, the term 'qualified commercial financing' means any financing with respect to any property if—

"(I) such property is acquired by the taxpayer from a person who is not a related person,

"(II) the amount of the nonrecourse financing with respect to such property does not exceed 80 percent of the credit base of such property, and

"(III) such financing is borrowed from a qualified person or represents a loan from any Federal, State, or local government or instrumentality thereof, or is guaranteed by any Federal, State, or local government.

Such term shall not include any convertible debt.

"(iii) Nonrecourse financing. For purposes of this subparagraph, the term 'nonrecourse financing' includes—

"(I) any amount with respect to which the taxpayer is protected against loss through guarantees, stop-loss agreements, or other similar arrangements, and

"(II) except to the extent provided in regulations, any amount borrowed from a person who has an interest (other than as a creditor) in the activity in which the property is used or from a related person to a person (other than the taxpayer) having such an interest.

In the case of amounts borrowed by a corporation from a shareholder, subclause (II) shall not apply to an interest as a shareholder.

"(iv) Qualified person. For purposes of this paragraph, the term 'qualified person' means any person which is actively and regularly engaged in the business of lending money and which is not—

"(I) a related person with respect to the taxpayer,

"(II) a person from which the taxpayer acquired the property (or a related person to such person), or

"(III) a person who receives a fee with respect to the taxpayer's investment in the property (or a related person to such person).

"(v) Related person. For purposes of this subparagraph, the term 'related person' has the meaning given such term by section 465(b)(3)(C). Except as otherwise provided in regulations prescribed by the Secretary, the determination of whether a person is a related person shall be made as of the close of the taxable year in which the property is placed in service.

"(E) Application to partnerships and S corporations. For purposes of this paragraph and paragraph (9)—

"(i) In general. Except as otherwise provided in this subparagraph, in the case of any partnership or S corporation, the determination of whether a partner's or shareholder's allocable share of any financing is nonqualified nonrecourse financing shall be made at the partner or shareholder level.

"(ii) Special rule for certain recourse financing of S corporation. A shareholder of an S corporation shall be treated as liable for his allocable share of any financing provided by a qualified person to such corporation if—

"(I) such financing is recourse financing (determined at the corporate level), and

"(II) such financing is provided with respect to qualified business property of such corporation.

1,185

"(iii) Qualified business property. For purposes of clause (ii), the term 'qualified business property' means any property if—
"(I) such property is used by the corporation in the active conduct of a trade or business,
"(II) during the entire 12-month period ending on the last day of the taxable year, such corporation had at least 3 full-time employees who were not owner-employees (as defined in section 465(c)(7)(E)(i)) and substantially all the services of whom were services directly related to such trade or business, and
"(III) during the entire 12-month period ending on the last day of such taxable year, such corporation had at least 1 full-time employee substantially all of the services of whom were in the active management of the trade or business.
Such term shall not include any master sound recording or other tangible or intangible asset associated with literary, artistic, or musical properties.
"(iv) Determination of allocable share. The determination of any partner's or shareholder's allocable share of any financing shall be made in the same manner as the credit allowable by section 38 with respect to such property.
"(F) Special rule for certain energy property.
"(i) In general. Subparagraph (A) shall not apply with respect to qualified energy property.
"(ii) Qualified energy property. The term 'qualified energy property' means energy property to which (but for this subparagraph) subparagraph (A) applies and—
"(I) which is described in clause (iii),
"(II) with respect to which the energy percentage determined under subsection (b)(2) at the time such property is placed in service is greater than zero,
"(III) as of the close of the taxable year in which the property is placed in service, not more than 75 percent of the basis of such property is attributable to nonqualified nonrecourse financing, and
"(IV) with respect to which any nonqualified nonrecourse financing in connection with such property consists of a level payment loan.
For purposes of subclause (II), the energy percentage for property described in clause (iii)(V) shall be treated as being greater than zero during any period the energy percentage for property described in section 48(l)(14) is greater than zero.
"(iii) Property to which this subparagraph applies. Energy property is described in this clause if such property is—
"(I) described in clause (ii), (iv), or (vii) or section 48(l)(2),
"(II) described in section 48(l)(15),
"(III) described in section 48(l)(3)(A)(iii) (but only to the extent such property is used for converting an alternate substance into alcohol for fuel purposes),
"(IV) described in clause (i) of section 48(l)(2)(A) (but only to the extent such property is also described in section 48(l)(3)(A)(viii) or (ix)), or
"(V) property comprising a system for using the same energy source for the sequential generation of electrical power, mechanical shaft power, or both, in combination with steam, heat, or other forms of useful energy.
"(iv) Level payment loan defined. The term 'level payment loan' means a loan in which each installment is substantially equal, a portion of each installment is attributable to the repayment of principal, and that portion is increased commensurate with decreases in the portion of the payment attributable to interest.
"(9) Subsequent decreases in nonqualified nonrecourse financing with respect to the property.
"(A) In general. If, at the close of a taxable year following the taxable year in which the property was placed in service, there is a net decrease in the amount of nonqualified nonrecourse financing with respect to such property, such net decrease shall be taken into account as an increase in the credit base for such property in accordance with subparagraph (C).
"(B) Certain transactions not taken into account. For purposes of this paragraph, nonqualified nonrecourse financing shall not be treated as decreased through the surrender or other use of property financed by nonqualified nonrecourse financing.
"(C) Manner in which taken into account.
"(i) Credit determined by reference to taxable year property placed in service. For purposes of determining the amount of credit allowable under section 38 and the amount of credit subject to the early disposition or cessation rules under section 47, any increase in a taxpayer's credit base for any property by reason of this paragraph shall be taken into account as if it were property placed in service by the taxpayer in the taxable year in which the property referred to in subparagraph (A) was first placed in service.
"(ii) Credit allowed for year of decrease in nonqualified nonrecourse financing. Any credit allowable under this subpart for any increase in qualified investment by reason of this paragraph shall be treated as earned during the taxable year of the decrease in the amount of nonqualified nonrecourse financing.
"(d) Qualified progress expenditures.
"(1) Increase in qualified investment.
"(A) In general. In the case of any taxpayer who has made an election under paragraph (6), the amount of the qualified investment of such taxpayer for the taxable year (determined under subsection (c) without regard to this subsection) shall be increased by an amount equal to the aggregate of the applicable percentage of each qualified progress expenditure for the taxable year with respect to progress expenditure property.
"(B) Applicable percentage.
"(i) Recovery property. For purposes of subparagraph (A), the applicable percentage for property to which section 168 applies shall be determined under subsection (c)(7) based on a reasonable expectation of what the character of the property will be when it is placed in service.
"(ii) Nonrecovery property. For purposes of subparagraph (A), the applicable percentage for property to which section 168 does not apply shall be determined under subsection (c)(2) based on a reasonable expectation of what the useful life of the property will be when it is placed in service.

"(iii) Application on basis of facts known. Clauses (i) and (ii) shall be applied on the basis of the facts known at the close of the taxable year of the taxpayer in which the expenditure is made.
"(2) Progress expenditure property defined.
"(A) In general. For purposes of this subsection, the term 'progress expenditure property' means any property which is being constructed by or for the taxpayer and which—
"(i) has a normal construction period of two years or more, and
"(ii) it is reasonable to believe will be new section 38 property in the hands of the taxpayer when it is placed in service.
Clauses (i) and (ii) of the preceding sentence shall be applied on the basis of facts known at the close of the taxable year of the taxpayer in which construction begins (or, if later, at the close of the first taxable year to which an election under this subsection applies).
"(B) Normal construction period. For purposes of subparagraph (A), the term 'normal construction period' means the period reasonably expected to be required for the construction of the property—
"(i) beginning with the date on which physical work on the construction begins (or, if later, the first day of the first taxable year to which an election under this subsection applies), and
"(ii) ending on the date on which it is expected that the property will be available for placing in service.
"(3) Qualified progress expenditures defined. For purposes of this subsection—
"(A) Self-constructed property. In the case of any self-constructed property, the term 'qualified progress expenditures' means the amount which, for purposes of this subpart, is, properly chargeable (during such taxable year) to capital account with respect to such property.
"(B) Non-self-constructed property. In the case of non-self-constructed property, the term 'qualified progress expenditures' means the lesser of—
"(i) the amount paid during the taxable year to another person for the construction of such property, or
"(ii) the amount which represents that proportion of the overall cost to the taxpayer of the construction by such other person which is properly attributable to that portion of such construction which is completed during such taxable year.
"(4) Special rules for applying paragraph (3). For purposes of paragraph (3)—
"(A) Component parts, etc. Property which is to be a component part of, or is otherwise to be included in, any progress expenditure property shall be taken into account—
"(i) at a time not earlier than the time at which it becomes irrevocably devoted to use in the progress expenditure property, and
"(ii) as if (at the time referred to in clause (i)) the taxpayer had expended an amount equal to that portion of the cost to the taxpayer of such component or other property which, for purposes of this subpart, is properly chargeable (during such taxable year) to capital account with respect to such property.
"(B) Certain borrowings disregarded. Any amount borrowed directly or indirectly by the taxpayer from the person constructing the property for him shall not be treated as an amount expended for such construction.
"(C) Certain unused expenditures carried over. In the case of non-self-constructed property, if for the taxable year—
"(i) the amount under clause (i) of paragraph (3)(B) exceeds the amount under clause (ii) of paragraph (3)(B), then the amount of such excess shall be taken into account under such clause (i) for the succeeding taxable year, or
"(ii) the amount under clause (ii) of paragraph (3)(B) exceeds the amount under clause (i) of paragraph (3)(B), then the amount of such excess shall be taken into account under such clause (ii) for the succeeding taxable year.
"(D) Determination of percentage of completion. In the case of non-self-constructed property, the determination under paragraph (3)(B)(ii) of the proportion of the overall cost to the taxpayer of the construction of any property which is properly attributable to construction completed during any taxable year shall be made, under regulations prescribed by the Secretary or his delegate, on the basis of engineering or architectural estimates or on the basis of cost accounting records. Unless the taxpayer establishes otherwise by clear and convincing evidence, the construction shall be deemed to be completed not more rapidly than ratably over the normal construction period.
"(E) No qualified progress expenditures for certain prior periods. In the case of any property, no qualified progress expenditures shall be taken into account under this subsection for any period before January 22, 1975 (or, if later, before the first day of the first taxable year to which an election under this subsection applies).
"(F) No qualified progress expenditures for property for year it is placed in service, etc. In the case of any property, no qualified progress expenditures shall be taken into account under this subsection for the earlier of—
"(i) the taxable year in which the property is placed in service, or
"(ii) the first taxable year for which recapture is required under section 47(a)(3) with respect to such property,
or for any taxable year thereafter.
"(5) Other definitions. For purposes of this subsection—
"(A) Self-constructed property. The term 'self-constructed property' means property more than half of the construction expenditures for which it is reasonable to believe will be made directly by the taxpayer.
"(B) Non-self-constructed property. The term 'non-self-constructed property' means property which is not self-constructed property.
"(C) Construction, etc. The term 'construction' includes reconstruction and erection, and the term 'constructed' includes reconstructed and erected.
"(D) Only construction of section 38 property to be taken into account. Construction shall be taken into account only if, for purposes of this subpart, expenditures therefor are properly chargeable to capital account with respect to the property.

"(6) Election. An election under this subsection may be made at such time and in such manner as the Secretary may by regulations prescribe. Such an election shall apply to the taxable year for which made and to all subsequent taxable years. Such an election, once made, may not be revoked except with the consent of the Secretary.

"(7) Transitional rules. The qualified investment taken into account under this subsection for any taxable year beginning before January 1, 1980, with respect to any property shall be (in lieu of the full amount) an amount equal to the sum of—

"(A) the applicable percentage of the full amount determined under the following table:

For a taxable year beginning in:	The applicable percentage is:
1974 or 1975	20
1976	40
1977	60
1978	80
1979	100;

plus

"(B) in the case of any property to which this subsection applied for one or more preceding taxable years, 20 percent of the full amount for each such preceding taxable year.

For purposes of this paragraph, the term 'full amount', when used with respect to any property for any taxable year, means the amount of the qualified investment for such property for such year determined under this subsection without regard to this paragraph.

"(e) Limitations with respect to certain persons.

"(1) In general. In the case of—

"(A) an organization to which section 593 applies, and

"(B) a regulated investment company or a real estate investment trust subject to taxation under subchapter M (sec. 851 and following),

the qualified investment shall equal such person's ratable share of such qualified investment.

"(2) Ratable share. For purposes of paragraph (1), the ratable share of any person for any taxable year qualified investment shall be—

"(A) in the case of an organization referred to in paragraph (1)(A), 50 percent thereof, and

"(B) in the case of a regulated investment company or a real estate investment trust, the ratio (i) the numerator of which is its taxable income and (ii) the denominator of which is its taxable income computed without regard to the deduction for dividends paid provided by section 852(b)(2)(D) or 857(b)(2)(B), as the case may be.

For purposes of subparagraph (B) of the preceding sentence, the term 'taxable income' means in the case of a regulated investment company its investment company taxable income (within the meaning of section 852(b)(2)), and in the case of a real estate investment trust its real estate investment trust taxable income (within the meaning of section 857(b)(2)) determined without regard to any deduction for capital gains dividends (as defined in section 857(b)(3)(C)) and by excluding any net capital gain.

"(3) Noncorporate lessors. A credit shall be allowed by section 38 to a person which is not a corporation with respect to property of which such person is the lessor only if—

"(A) the property subject to the lease has been manufactured or produced by the lessor, or

"(B) the term of the lease (taking into account options to renew) is less than 50 percent of the useful life of the property, and for the period consisting of the first 12 months after the date on which the property is transferred to the lessee the sum of the deductions with respect to such property which are allowable to the lessor solely by reason of section 162 (other than rents and reimbursed amounts with respect to such property) exceeds 15 percent of the rental income produced by such property.

In the case of property of which a partnership is the lessor, the credit otherwise allowable under section 38 with respect to such property to any partner which is a corporation shall be allowed notwithstanding the first sentence of this paragraph. For purposes of this paragraph, an S corporation shall be treated as a person which is not a corporation. This paragraph shall not apply with respect to any property which is treated as section 38 property by reason of section 48(a)(1)(E). For purposes of subparagraph (B), in the case of any property to which section 168 applies the useful life shall be the class life for such property (as defined in section 168(i)(1)).

"(4) Special rules where section 593 organization is lessee.

"(A) In general. For purposes of paragraph (1)(A), if an organization described in section 593 is the lessee of any section 38 property, the lessor of such property shall be treated as an organization described in section 593 with respect to such property.

"(B) Exception for short-term leases. This paragraph shall not apply to any property by reason of use under a lease with a term of less than 6 months (determined under section 168(i)(3)).

"(C) Election not to have subparagraph (A) apply. Subparagraph (A) shall not apply for any taxable year to an organization described in section 593 if such organization elects to compute for such year and all subsequent taxable years the amount of the deduction for a reasonable addition to a reserve for bad debts on the basis of actual experience. Any such election shall apply to any successor organization engaged in substantially similar activities and, once made, shall be irrevocable. Notwithstanding the preceding provisions of this subparagraph, any such election shall terminate effective with respect to the 1st taxable year of the organization making such election which begins after 1986 and during which such organization (or any successor organization) was not at any time the lessee under any lease of regular investment tax credit property. For purposes of the preceding sentence, the term 'regular investment tax credit property' means any section 38 property if the regular percentage applied to such property and the amount of qualified investment with respect to such property would have been reduced under paragraph (1) but for an election under this subparagraph.

"(D) Special rules for partnerships, etc. For purposes of paragraph (1)(A), rules similar to the rules of paragraphs (5) and (6) of section 168(h) shall apply.

"(E) Exception for qualified rehabilitated buildings leased to section 593 organizations. Subparagraph (A) shall not apply to qualified investment attributable to qualified rehabilitation expenditures for any portion of a building if such portion of the building would not be tax-exempt use property (as defined in section 168(h)) if the section 593 organization were a tax-exempt entity (as defined in section 168(h)(2)).

"(f) Limitation in case of certain regulated companies.

"(1) General rule. Except as otherwise provided in this subsection, no credit determined under subsection (a) shall be allowed by section 38 with respect to any property described in section 50 (as in effect before its repeal by the Revenue Act of 1978) which is public utility property (as defined in paragraph (5)) of the taxpayer—

"(A) Cost of service reduction. If the taxpayer's cost of service for ratemaking purposes is reduced by reason of any portion of the credit determined under subsection (a) and allowable by section 38 (determined without regard to this subsection); or

"(B) Rate base reduction. If the base to which the taxpayer's rate of return for ratemaking purposes is applied is reduced by reason of any portion of the credit determined under subsection (a) and allowable by section 38 (determined without regard to this subsection).

Subparagraph (B) shall not apply if the reduction in the rate base is restored not less rapidly than ratably. If the taxpayer makes an election under this sentence within 90 days after the date of the enactment of this paragraph in the manner prescribed by the Secretary, the immediately preceding sentence shall not apply to property described in paragraph (5)(B) if any agency or instrumentality of the United States having jurisdiction for ratemaking purposes with respect to such taxpayer's trade or business referred to in paragraph (5)(B) determines that the natural domestic supply of the product furnished by the taxpayer in the course of such trade or business is insufficient to meet the present and future requirements of the domestic economy.

"(2) Special rule for ratable flow-through. If the taxpayer makes an election under this paragraph within 90 days after the date of the enactment of this paragraph in the manner prescribed by the Secretary, paragraph (1) shall not apply, but no credit determined under subsection (a) shall be allowed by section 38 with respect to any property described in section 50 (as in effect before its repeal by the Revenue Act of 1978) which is public utility property (as defined in paragraph (5)) of the taxpayer—

"(A) Cost of service reduction. If the taxpayer's cost of service for ratemaking purposes or in its regulated books of account is reduced by more than a ratable portion of the credit determined under subsection (a) and allowable by section 38 (determined without regard to this subsection), or

"(B) Rate base reduction. If the base to which the taxpayer's rate of return for ratemaking purposes is applied is reduced by reason of any portion of the credit determined under subsection (a) and allowable by section 38 (determined without regard to this subsection).

"(3) Special rule for immediate flow-through in certain cases. In the case of property to which section 167(l)(2)(C) applies, if the taxpayer makes an election under this paragraph within 90 days after the date of the enactment of this paragraph in the manner prescribed by the Secretary, paragraphs (1) and (2) shall not apply to such property.

"(4) Limitation.

"(A) In general. The requirements of paragraphs (1), (2), and (9) regarding cost of service and rate base adjustments shall not be applied to public utility property of the taxpayer to disallow the credit with respect to such property before the first final determination which is inconsistent with paragraph (1), (2), or (9) (as the case may be) is put into effect with respect to public utility property (to which this subsection applies) of the taxpayer. Thereupon, paragraph (1), (2), or (9) shall apply to disallow the credit with respect to public utility property (to which this subsection applies) placed in service by the taxpayer—

"(i) before the date that the first final determination, or a subsequent determination, which is inconsistent with paragraph (1), (2), or (9) (as the case may be) is put into effect, and

"(ii) on or after the date that a determination referred to in clause (i) is put into effect and before the date that a subsequent determination thereafter which is consistent with paragraph (1), (2), or (9) (as the case may be) is put into effect.

"(B) Determinations. For purposes of this paragraph a determination is a determination made with respect to public utility property (to which this subsection applies) by a governmental unit, agency, instrumentality, or commission or similar body described in subsection (c)(3)(B) which determines the effect of the credit determined under subsection (a) and allowed by section 38 (determined without regard to this subsection)—

"(i) on the taxpayer's cost of service or rate base for ratemaking purposes, or

"(ii) in the case of a taxpayer which made an election under paragraph (2) or the election described in paragraph (9), on the taxpayer's cost of service for ratemaking purposes or in its regulated books of account or rate base for ratemaking purposes.

"(C) Special rules. For purposes of this paragraph—

"(i) a determination is final if all rights to appeal or to request a review, a rehearing, or a redetermination, have been exhausted or have lapsed, "(ii) the first final determination is the first final determination made after the date of the enactment of this subsection, and

"(iii) a subsequent determination is a determination subsequent to a final determination.

"(5) Public utility property. For purposes of this subsection, the term 'public utility property' means—

"(A) property which is public utility property within the meaning of subsection (c)(3)(B), and

"(B) property used predominantly in the trade or business of the furnishing or sale of (i) steam through a local distribution system or (ii) the transportation of gas or steam by pipeline, if the rates for such furnishings or sale are established or approved by a governmental unit, agency, instrumentality, or commission described in subsection (c)(3)(B).

"(6) Ratable portion. For purposes of determining ratable restoration to base under paragraph (1) and for purposes of determining ratable portions under paragraph (2)(A), the period of time used in computing depreciation expense for purposes of reflecting operating results in the taxpayer's regulated books of account shall be used.

"(7) Reorganizations, assets acquisitions, etc. If by reason of a corporate reorganization, by reason of any other acquisition of the assets of one taxpayer by another taxpayer, by reason of the fact that any trade or business of the taxpayer is subject to ratemaking by more than one body, or by reason of other circumstances, the application of any provisions of this subsection to any public utility property does not carry out the purposes of this subsection, the Secretary shall provide by regulations for the application of such provisions in a manner consistent with the purposes of this subsection.

"(8) Prohibition of immediate flowthrough. An election made under paragraph (3) shall apply only to the amount of the credit determined under subsection (a) and allowable under section 38 with respect to public utility property (within the meaning of the first sentence of subsection (c)(3)(B)) determined as if the Tax Reduction Act of 1975, the Tax Reform Act of 1976 and the Energy Tax Act of 1978 and the Revenue Act of 1978, had not been enacted. Any taxpayer who had timely made an election under paragraph (3) may, at his own option and without regard to any requirement imposed by an agency described in subsection (c)(3)(B), elect within 90 days after the date of the enactment of the Tax Reduction Act of 1975 (in such manner as the Secretary shall prescribe) to have the provisions of paragraph (3) apply with respect to the amount of the credit determined under subsection (a) and allowable under section 38 with respect to such property which is in excess of the amount determined under the preceding sentence. If such taxpayer does not make such an election, paragraph (1) or (2) (whichever paragraph is applicable without regard to this paragraph) shall apply to such excess credit, except that if neither paragraph (1) nor (2) is applicable (without regard to this paragraph), paragraph (1) shall apply unless the taxpayer elects (in such manner as the Secretary shall prescribe) within 90 days after the date of the enactment of the Tax Reduction Act of 1975 to have the provisions of paragraph (2) apply. The provisions of this paragraph shall not be applied to disallow such excess credit before the first final determination which is inconsistent with such requirements is made, determined in the same manner as under paragraph (4).

"(9) Repealed.

"(10) Use of inconsistent estimates and projections, etc., for purposes of paragraphs (1) and (2).

"(A) In general. One way in which the requirements of paragraph (1) or (2) are not met is if the taxpayer, for ratemaking purposes, uses a procedure or adjustment which is inconsistent with the requirements of paragraph (1) or paragraph (2), as the case may be.

"(B) Use of inconsistent estimates and projections. The procedures and adjustments which are to be treated as inconsistent for purposes of subparagraph (A) shall include any procedure or adjustment for ratemaking purposes which uses an estimate or projection of the taxpayer's qualified investment for purposes of the credit allowable by section 38 unless such estimate or projection is consistent with the estimates and projections of property which are used, for ratemaking purposes, with respect to the taxpayer's depreciation expense and rate base.

"(C) Regulatory authority. The Secretary may by regulations prescribe procedures and adjustments (in addition to those specified in subparagraph (B)) which are to be treated as inconsistent for purposes of subparagraph (A).

"(g) 50 percent credit in the case of certain vessels.

"(1) In general. In the case of a qualified withdrawal out of the untaxed portion of a capital gain account or out of an ordinary income account in a capital construction fund established under section 607 of the Merchant Marine Act, 1936 (46 U.S.C. 1177), for—

"(A) the acquisition, construction, or reconstruction of a qualified vessel, or

"(B) the acquisition, construction, or reconstruction of barges or containers which are part of the complement of a qualified vessel and to which subsection (f)(1)(B) of such section 607 applies,

for purposes of section 38 there shall be deemed to have been made (at the time of such withdrawal) a qualified investment (within the meaning of subsection (c)) or qualified progress expenditures (within the meaning of subsection (d)), whichever is appropriate, with respect to property which is section 38 property.

"(2) Amount of credit. For purposes of paragraph (1), the amount of the qualified investment shall be 50 percent of the applicable percentage of the qualified withdrawal referred to in paragraph (1), or the amount of the qualified progress expenditures shall be 50 percent of such withdrawal, as the case may be. For purposes of determining the amount of the credit allowable by reason of this subsection for any taxable year, the limitation of section 38(c) shall be determined without regard to subsection (d)(1)(A) of such section 607.

"(3) Coordination with section 38. The amount of the credit allowable by reason of this subsection with respect to any property shall be the minimum amount allowable under section 38 with respect to such property. If, without regard to this subsection, a greater amount is allowable under section 38 with respect to such property, then such greater amount shall apply and this subsection shall not apply.

"(4) Coordination with section 47. Section 47 shall be applied—

"(A) to any property to which this subsection applies, and

"(B) to the payment (out of the untaxed portion of a capital gain account or out of the ordinary income account of a capital construction fund established under section 607 of the Merchant Marine Act, 1936) of the principal of any indebtedness incurred in connection with property with respect to which a credit was allowed under section 38.

For purposes of section 47, any payment described in subparagraph (B) of the preceding sentence shall be treated as a disposition occurring less than 3 years after the property was placed in service; but, in the case of a credit allowable without regard to this subsection, the aggregate amount which may be recaptured by reason of this sentence shall not exceed 50 percent of such credit.

"(5) Definitions. Any term used in section 607 of the Merchant Marine Act, 1936, shall have the same meaning when used in this subsection.

"(6) No inference. Nothing in this subsection shall be construed to infer that any property described in this subsection is or is not section 38 property, and any determination of such issue shall be made as if this subsection had not been enacted.

"(h) Special rules for cooperatives. In the case of a cooperative organization described in section 1381(a)—

"(1) that portion of the credit determined under subsection (a) and allowable to the organization under section 38 which the organization cannot use for the taxable year to which the qualified investment is attributable because of the limitation contained in section 38(c) shall be allocated to the patrons of the organization,

"(2) section 47 (relating to certain dispositions, etc., of section 38 property) shall be applied as if any allocated portion of the credit had been retained by the organization, and

"(3) the rules necessary to carry out the purposes of this subsection shall be determined under regulations prescribed by the Secretary."

In 1990, P.L. 101-508, Sec. 11406, substituted "Dec. 31, 1991" for "Sept. 30, 1990" in clauses (b)(2)(A)(viii) and (ix), effective 11/5/90.

In 1989, P.L. 101-239, Sec. 7106, substituted "Sept. 30, 1990" for "Dec. 31, 1989" in clauses (b)(2)(A)(viii), (ix), and (x), effective 12/19/89.

—P.L. 101-239, Sec. 7814(d)(1), and (2), corrected Sec. 4006 of P.L. 100-647, see below, by substituting "Dec. 31, 1988" for "December 31, 1988" and by substituting "Dec. 31, 1989" for "December 31, 1989".

In 1988, P.L. 100-647, Sec. 1002(a)(4)(A), substituted "168(i)(3)" for "168(j)(6)" in subpara. (e)(4)(B) . . . Sec. 1002(a)(4)(B), substituted "paragraphs (5) and (6) of section 168(h)" for "paragraphs (8) and (9) of section 168(j)" in subpara. (e)(4)(D) . . . Sec. 1002(a)(4)(C), substituted "168(h)" for "168(j)" in subpara. (e)(4)(E) . . . Sec. 1002(e)(4)(D), substituted "168(h)(2)" for "168(j)(4)" in subpara. (e)(4)(E) . . . Sec. 1002(a)(15), substituted "property to which section 168 applies" for "recovery property (within the meaning of section 168", substituted "class life" for "present class life" and substituted "168(i)(1)" for "168(g)(2)" in the last sentence of para. (e)(3) . . . Sec. 1002(a)(17)(A), substituted "property to which section 168 applies" for "recovery property" in para. (c)(7) . . . Sec. 1002(a)(17)(B), substituted "168(e)" for "168(c)" each place it appeared in para. (c)(7) . . . Sec. 1002(a)(17)(C), substituted "168(f)(3)(B) (as in effect on the day before the date of enactment of the Tax Reform Act of 1986)" for "168(f)(3)(B)" in para. (c)(7) . . . Sec. 1002(a)(17)(D), substituted "property to which section 168 applies" for "recovery property" in the heading of para. (c)(7) . . . Sec. 1002(a)(25)(A), substituted "property to which section 168 applies" for "recovery property (within the meaning of section 168)" in clause (d)(1)(B)(i) . . . Sec. 1002(a)(25)(B), substituted "to which section 168 does not apply" for "which is not recovery property within the meaning of section 168)" in clause (d)(1)(B)(ii), effective for property placed in service after 12/31/86, in tax. yrs. end. after 12/31/86. See Sec. 203(a)(1)(B) and Sec. 203(b)-(e) of P.L. 99-514, reproduced in note following Code Sec. 168.

—P.L. 100-647, Sec. 1002(f)(1), amended Sec. 212(f)(2) of P.L. 99-514, reproduced below, by substituting "(2) Special rule.—In the case of a LTV corporation, in lieu of the requirements of paragraph (1)—" for "(2) General rules. If this section applies to LTV Corporation then in lieu of the requirements of paragraph (1)—" . . . Sec. 1002(f)(2), amended Sec. 212(f)(2)(B)(i)(I) of P.L. 99-514, reproduced below, by substituting "when the corporation receives the refund" for "such involvement begins" . . . Sec. 1002(f)(3), added Sec. 212(g)(3) of P.L. 99-514, reproduced below . . . Sec. 1002(f)(4), added Sec. 212(h) of P.L. 99-514, reproduced below . . . Sec. 1002(f)(5), amended Sec. 212(g)(2)(B) of P.L. 99-514, reproduced below, by substituting "determined for periods before January 1, 1986, under" for "determined under" . . . Sec. 1002(f)(6), added Sec. 212(f)(3) of P.L. 99-514, reproduced below.

—P.L. 100-647, Sec. 1002(g), amended Sec. 213(e)(2)(B) of P.L. 99-514, reproduced below, by substituting "determined for periods before January 1, 1986, under" for "determined under".

—P.L. 100-647, Sec. 1002(k)(1), amended Sec. 251(d)(2)(B) of P.L. 99-514 [reproduced below], special rules for amendments made by Sec. 251(a) of P.L. 99-514, by deleting Sec. 251(d)(2)(B)(i) and redesignating Sec. 251(d)(2)(B)(ii) and (iii) as Sec. 251 (d)(2)(B)(i) and (ii) . . . Sec. 1002(k)(2), amended Sec. 251(d)(3)(P) of P.L. 99-514, reproduced below, by substituting "San Jose, California" for "San Francisco" . . . Sec. 1002(k)(3)(A)-(C), amended Sec. 251(d)(4) of P.L. 99-514, reproduced below, by substituting "Marble Arcade office building" for "Lakeland marbel Arcade" in Sec. 251(d)(4)(K) of P.L. 99-514 by deleting "and" at the end of Sec. 251(d)(4)(Y) of P.L. 99-514 by amending Sec. 251(d)(4)(Z) of P.L. 99-514 and by adding Sec. 251(d)(4)(AA)-(OO) of P.L. 99-514 . . . Sec. 1002(k)(4), amended Sec. 251(d)(6) of P.L. 99-514, reproduced below . . . Sec. 1002(k)(5), amended Sec. 251(d)(3)(B) of P.L. 99-514, reproduced

Tax credits   Subpart E

below, by substituting "Pontalba" for "Pontabla" ... Sec. 1002(k)(6), amended Sec. 251(d)(4)(T) of P.L. 99-514, reproduced below, by substituting "Covington" for "Louisville".

Prior to deletion, Sec. 251(d)(2)(B)(i) of P.L. 99-514 read as follows:

"(i) the rehabilitation was completed pursuant to a written contract that was binding on March 1, 1986,"

Prior to amendment, Sec. 251(d)(4)(Z) of P.L. 99-514 read as follows:

"(Z) the Apollo and Bishop Building Complex on 125th Street, the Bigelow-Hartford Carpet Mill in New York, New York."

Prior to amendment, Sec. 251(d)(6) of P.L. 99-514 read as follows:

"(6) Expensing of rehabilitation expenditures for the Frankford Arsenal. In the case of any expenditures paid or incurred in connection with the rehabilitation of the Frankford Arsenal during the 8-year period beginning on January 1, 1987, such expenditures (including expenditures for repair and maintenance of the building and property) shall be allowable as a deduction in the taxable year in which paid or incurred in an amount not in excess of the submissions made by the taxpayer before September 16, 1986."

—P.L. 100-647, Sec. 1009(a)(1), added the last sentence of subpara. (e)(4)(C), effective for tax. yrs. after 12/31/86.

—P.L. 100-647, Sec. 1013(a)(44)(A), substituted "private activity bonds" for "industrial development bonds" in the heading of subpara. (c)(5)(B) ... Sec. 1013(a)(44)(B), substituted "a private activity bond (within the meaning of section 141)" for "an industrial development bond (within the meaning of section 103(b)(2))" in subpara. (c)(5)(B), effective for bonds issued after 8/15/86.

—P.L. 100-647, Sec. 4006(1)-(3), [as amended by Sec. 7814(d)(1) and (2) of P.L. 101-239, see above] substituted "Dec. 31, 1989" for "Dec. 31, 1988" in clauses (b)(2)(A)(viii), (ix), and (x), effective 11/10/88.

In 1986, P.L. 99-514, Sec. 201(d)(7)(B), substituted "section 465(b)(3)(C)" for "section 168(e)(4)" in clause (c)(8)(D)(v), effective for property placed in service after 12/31/86, in tax. yrs. end. after 12/31/86. For exception for certain aircraft used in Alaska, see Sec. 211(d) of this Act reproduced in note following Code Sec. 49.

—P.L. 99-514, Sec. 212, [as amended by Sec. 1002(f)(1)-(6) of P.L. 100-647, see above.], provides:

"Sec. 212. Effective 15-year carryback of existing carryforwards of steel companies.

"(a) General rule. If a qualified corporation makes an election under this section for its 1st taxable year beginning after December 31, 1986, with respect to any portion of its existing carryforwards, the amount determined under subsection (b) shall be treated as a payment against the tax imposed by chapter 1 of the Internal Revenue Code of 1986 made by such corporation on the last day prescribed by law (without regard to extensions) for filing its return of tax under chapter 1 of such Code for such 1st taxable year.

"(b) Amount. For purposes of subsection (a), the amount determined under this subsection shall be the lesser of—

"(1) 50 percent of the portion of the corporation's existing carryforwards to which the election under subsection (a) applies, or

"(2) the corporation's net tax liability for the carryback period.

"(c) Corporation making election may not use same amounts under section 38. In the case of a qualified corporation which makes an election under subsection (a), the portion of such corporation's existing carryforwards to which such an election applies shall not be taken into account under section 38 of the Internal Revenue Code of 1986 for any taxable year beginning after December 31, 1986.

"(d) Net tax liability for carryback period. For purposes of this section—

"(1) In general. A corporation's net tax liability for the carryback period is the aggregate of such corporation's net tax liability for taxable years in the carryback period.

"(2) Net tax liability. The term 'net tax liability' means, with respect to any taxable year, the amount of the tax imposed by chapter 1 of the Internal Revenue Code of 1954 for such taxable year, reduced by the sum of the credits allowable under part IV of subchapter A of such chapter 1 (other than section 34 thereof). For purposes of the preceding sentence, any tax treated as not imposed by chapter 1 of such Code under section 26(b)(2) of such Code shall not be treated as tax imposed by such chapter 1.

"(3) Carryback period. The term 'carryback period' means the period—

"(A) which begins with the corporation's 15th taxable year preceding the 1st taxable year from which there is an unused credit included in such corporation's existing carryforwards (but in no event shall such period begin before the corporation's 1st taxable year ending after December 31, 1961), and

"(B) which ends with the corporation's last taxable year beginning before January 1, 1986.

"(e) No recomputation of minimum tax, etc. Nothing in this section shall be construed to affect—

"(1) the amount of the tax imposed by section 56 of the Internal Revenue Code of 1986, or

"(2) the amount of any credit allowable under such Code, for any taxable year in the carryback period.

"(f) Reinvestment requirement.

"(1) In general. Any amount determined under this section must be committed to reinvestment in, and modernization of the steel industry through investment in modern plant and equipment, research and development, and other appropriate projects, such as working capital for steel operations and programs for the retraining of steel workers.

"(2) Special rule. In the case of the LTV Corporation, in lieu of the requirements of paragraph (1)—

"(A) such corporation shall place such refund in a separate account; and

"(B) amounts in such separate account—

"(i) shall only be used by the corporation—

"(I) to purchase an insurance policy which provides that, in the event the corporation becomes involved in a title 11 or similar case (as defined in section 368(a)(3)(A) of the Internal Revenue Code of 1954), the insurer will provide life and health insurance coverage during the 1-year period beginning on the date when the corporation receives the refund to any individual with respect to whom the corporation would (but for such involvement) have been obligated to provide such coverage the coverage provided by the insurer will be identical to the coverage which the corporation would (but for such involvement) have been obligated to provide, and provides that the payment of insurance premiums will not be required during such 1-year period to keep such policy in force, or

"(II) directly in connection with the trade or business of the corporation in the manufacturer or production of steel; and

"(ii) shall be used (or obligated) for purposes described in clause (i) not later than 3 months after the corporation receives the refund.

"(3) In the case of a qualified corporation, no offset to any refund under this section may be made by reason of any tax imposed by section 4971 of the Internal Revenue Code of 1986 (or any interest or penalty attributable to any such tax), and the date on which any such refund is to be paid shall be determined without regard to such corporation's status under title 11, United States Code.

"(g) Definitions. For purposes of this section—

"(1) Qualified corporation.

"(A) In general. The term 'qualified corporation' means any corporation which is described in section 806(b) of the Steel Import Stabilization Act and a company which was incorporated on February 11, 1983, in Michigan.

"(B) Certain predecessors included. In the case of any qualified corporation which has carryforward attributable to a predecessor corporation described in such section 806(b), the qualified corporation and the predecessor corporation shall be treated as 1 corporation for purposes of subsections (d) and (e).

"(2) Existing carryforwards. The term 'existing carryforward' means the aggregate of the amounts which—

"(A) are unused business credit carryforwards to the taxpayer's 1st taxable year beginning after December 31, 1986 (determined without regard to the limitations of section 38(c) and any reduction under section 49 of the Internal Revenue Code of 1986), and

"(B) are attributable to the amount of the regular investment credit determined for periods before January 1, 1986, under section 46(a)(1) of such Code (relating to regular percentage), or any corresponding provision of prior law, determined on the basis that the regular investment audit was used first.

"(3) Special rule for restructuring. In the case of any corporation, any restructuring shall not limit, increase, or otherwise affect the benefits which would have been available under this section but for such restructuring.

"(h) Tentative refunds. Rules similar to the rules of section 6425 of the Internal Revenue Code of 1986 shall apply to any overpayment resulting from the application of this section."

—P.L. 99-514, Sec. 213, [as amended by Sec. 1002(g) of P.L. 100-647, see above] provides:

"SEC. 213. EFFECTIVE 15-YEAR CARRYBACK OF EXISTING CARRYFORWARDS OF QUALIFIED FARMERS.

"(a) General rule. If a taxpayer who is a qualified farmer makes an election under this section for its 1st taxable year beginning after December 31, 1986, with respect to any portion of its existing carryforwards, the amount determined under subsection (b) shall be treated as a payment against the tax imposed by chapter 1 of the Internal Revenue Code of 1986 made by such taxpayer on the last day prescribed by law (without regard to extensions) for filing its return of tax under chapter 1 of such Code for such 1st taxable year.

"(b) Amount. For purposes of subsection (a), the amount determined under this subsection shall be equal to the smallest of—

"(1) 50 percent of the portion of the taxpayer's existing carryforwards to which the election under subsection (a) applies,

"(2) the taxpayer's net tax liability for the carryback period (within the meaning of section 212(d) of this Act), or

"(3) $750.

"(c) Taxpayer making election may not use same amounts under section 38. In the case of a qualified farmer who makes an election under subsection (a), the portion of such farmer's existing carryforwards to which such an election applies shall not be taken into account under section 38 of the Internal Revenue Code of 1986 for any taxable year beginning after December 31, 1986.

"(d) No recomputation of minimum tax, etc. Nothing in this section shall be construed to affect—

"(1) the amount of the tax imposed by section 56 of the Internal Revenue Code of 1954, or

"(2) the amount of any credit allowable under such Code, for any taxable year in the carryback period (within the meaning of section 212(d)(3) of this Act).

"(e) Definitions and special rules. For purposes of this section—

"(1) Qualified farmer. The term 'qualified farmer' means any taxpayer who, during the 3-taxable year period preceding the taxable year for which an election is made under subsection (a), derived 50 percent or more of the taxpayer's gross income from the trade or business of farming.

"(2) Existing carryforward. The term 'existing carryforward' means the aggregate of the amounts which—

"(A) are unused business credit carryforwards to the taxpayer's 1st taxable year beginning after December 31, 1986 (determined without regard to the limitations of section 38(c) of the Internal Revenue Code of 1986), and

"(B) are attributable to the amount of the investment credit determined for periods before January 1, 1986, under section 46(a) of such Code (or any corresponding provision of prior law) with respect to section 38 property which was used by the taxpayer in the trade or business of farming, determined on the basis that such credit was used first.

"(3) Farming. The term 'farming' has the meaning given such term by section 2032A(e)(4) and (5) of such Code."

—P.L. 99-514, Sec. 251(a), amended para. (b)(4), effective for property placed in service after 12/31/86, in tax. yrs. end. after 12/31/86, with special rules provided by Sec. 251(d)(2)-(6) [as amended by Sec. 1002(k)(1) of P.L. 100-647-(b), see above] of this Act, which reads as follows:

"(2) General transitional rule. The amendments made by this section and section 201 shall not apply to any property placed in service before January 1, 1994, if such property is placed in service as part of—

"(A) a rehabilitation which was completed pursuant to a written contract which was binding on March 1, 1986, or

"(B) a rehabilitation incurred in connection with property (including any leasehold interest) acquired before March 2, 1986, or acquired on or after such date pursuant to a written contract that was binding on March 1, 1986, if—

"(i) parts 1 and 2 of the Historic Preservation Certification Application were filed with the Department of the Interior (or its designee) before March 2, 1986, or

"(ii) the lesser of $1,000,000 or 5 percent of the cost of the rehabilitation is incurred before March 2, 1986, or is required to be incurred pursuant to a written contract which was binding on March 1, 1986.

"(3) Certain additional rehabilitations. The amendments made by this section and section 201 shall not apply to—

"(A) the rehabilitation of 8 bathhouses within the Hot Springs National Park or of buildings in the Central Avenue Historic District at such Park,

"(B) the rehabilitation of the Upper Pontalba Building in New Orleans, Louisiana,

"(C) the rehabilitation of at least 60 buildings listed on the National Register at the Frankford Arsenal,

"(D) the rehabilitation of De Baliveriere Arcade, St. Louis Centre, and Drake Apartments in Missouri,

"(E) the rehabilitation of The Tides in Bristol, Rhode Island,

"(F) the rehabilitation and renovation of the Outlet Company building and garage in Providence, Rhode Island,

"(G) the rehabilitation of 10 structures in Harrisburg, Pennsylvania, with respect to which the Harristown Development Corporation was designated redeveloper and received an option to acquire title to the entire project site for $1 on June 27, 1984,

"(H) the rehabilitation of a project involving the renovation of 3 historic structures on the Minneapolis riverfront, with respect to which the developer of the project entered into a redevelopment agreement with a municipality dated January 4, 1985, and industrial development bonds were sold in 3 separate issues in May, July, and October 1985,

"(I) the rehabilitation of a bank's main office facilities of approximately 120,000 square feet, in connection with which the bank's board of directors authorized a $3,300,000 expenditure for the renovation and retrofit on March 20, 1984,

"(J) the rehabilitation of 10 warehouse buildings built between 1906 and 1910 and purchased under a contract dated February 17, 1986,

"(K) the rehabilitation of a facility which is customarily used for conventions and sporting events if an analysis of operations and recommendations of utilization of such facility was prepared by a certified public accounting firm pursuant to an engagement authorized on March 6, 1984, and presented on June 11, 1984, to officials of the city in which such facility is located,

"(L) Mount Vernon Mills in Columbia, South Carolina,

"(M) the Barbara Jordan II Apartments,

"(N) the rehabilitation of the Federal Building and Post Office, 120 Hanover Street, Manchester, New Hampshire,

"(O) the rehabilitation of the Charleston Waterfront project in South Carolina,

"(P) the Hayes Mansion in San Jose, California,

"(Q) the renovation of a facility owned by the National Railroad Passenger Corporation ('Amtrak') for which project Amtrak engaged a development team by letter agreement dated August 23, 1985, as modified by letter agreement dated September 9, 1985,

"(R) the rehabilitation of a structure or its components which is listed in the National Register of Historic Places, is located in Allegheny County, Pennsylvania, will be substantially rehabilitated (as defined in section 48(g)(1)(C) prior to amendment by this Act), prior to December 31, 1989; and was previously utilized as a market and an auto dealership,

"(S) The Bellevue Stratford Hotel in Philadelphia, Pennsylvania,

"(T) the Dixon Mill Housing project in Jersey City, New Jersey,

"(U) Motor Square Garden,

"(V) the Blackstone Apartments, and the Shriver-Johnson building, in Sioux Falls, South Dakota,

"(W) the Holy Name Academy in Spokane, Washington,

"(X) the Nike/Clemson Mill in Exeter, New Hampshire,

"(Y) the Central Bank Building in Grand Rapids, Michigan, and

"(Z) the Heritage Hotel, in the City of Marquette, Michigan.

"(4) Additional rehabilitations. The amendments made by this section and section 201 shall not apply to—

"(A) the Fort Worth Town Square Project in Texas,

"(B) the American Youth Hostel in New York, New York,

"(C) The Riverwest Loft Development (including all three phases, two of which do not involve rehabilitations),

"(D) the Gaslamp Quarter Historic District in California,

"(E) the Eberhardt & Ober Brewery, in Pennsylvania,

"(F) the Captain's Walk Limited Partnership-Harris Place Development, in Connecticut,

"(G) the Velvet Mills in Connecticut,

"(H) the Roycroft Inn, in New York,

"(I) Old Main Village, in Mankato, Minnesota,

"(J) the Washburn-Crosby A Mill, in Minneapolis, Minnesota,

"(K) the Marble Arcade office building in Lakeland, Florida,

"(L) the Willard Hotel, in Washington, D.C.,

"(M) the H. P. Lau Building in Lincoln, Nebraska,

"(N) the Starks Building, in Louisville, Kentucky,

"(O) the Bellevue High School, in Bellevue, Kentucky,

"(P) the Major Hampden Smith House, in Owensboro, Kentucky,

"(Q) the Doe Run Inn, in Brandenburg, Kentucky,

"(R) the State National Bank, in Frankfort, Kentucky,

"(S) the Captain Jack House, in Fleming, Kentucky,

"(T) the Elizabeth Arlinghaus House, in Covington, Kentucky,

"(U) Limerick Shamrock, in Louisville, Kentucky,

"(V) the Robert Mills Project, in South Carolina,

"(W) the 620 Project, consisting of 3 buildings, in Kentucky,

"(X) the Warrior Hotel, Ltd., the first two floors of the Martir Hotel, and the 105,000 square foot warehouse constructed in 1910, all in Sioux City, Iowa,

"(Y) the waterpark condominium residential project, to the extent of $2 million of expenditures,

"(Z) the Bigelow-Hartford Carpet Mill in Enfield, Connecticut,

"(AA) properties abutting 125th Street in New York County from 7th Avenue west to Morningside and the pier area on the Hudson River at the end of such 125th Street,

"(BB) the City of Los Angeles Central Library project pursuant to an agreement dated December 28, 1983,

"(CC) the Warehouse Row project in Chattanooga, Tennessee,

"(DD) any project described in section 204(a)(1)(F) of this Act,

"(EE) the Wood Street Commons project in Pittsburgh, Pennsylvania,

"(FF) any project described in section 803(d)(6) of this Act,

"(GG) Union Station, Indianapolis, Indiana,

"(HH) the Mattress Factory project in Pittsburgh, Pennsylvania,

"(II) Union Station in Providence, Rhode Island,

"(JJ) South Pack Plaza, Asheville, North Carolina,

"(KK) Old Louisville Trust Project, Louisville, Kentucky,

"(LL) Stewarts Rehabilitation Project, Louisville, Kentucky,

"(MM) Bernheim Officenter, Louisville, Kentucky,

"(NN) Springville Mill Project, Rockville, Connecticut, and

"(OO) the D.J. Stewart Company building, State and Main Streets, Rockford, Illinois.

"(5) Reduction in credit for property under transitional rules. In the case of property placed in service after December 31, 1986, and to which the amendments made by this section do not apply, subparagraph (A) of section 46(b)(4) of the Internal Revenue Code of 1954 (as in effect before the enactment of this Act) shall be applied—

"(A) by substituting '10 percent' for '15 percent', and

"(B) by substituting '13 percent' for '20 percent'.

"(6) Expensing of rehabilitation expenses for the Frankford Arsenal. In the case of any expenditures paid or incurred in connection with improvements (including repairs and maintenance) of the Frankford Arsenal pursuant to a contract and partnership agreement during the 8-year period specified in the contract or agreement, all such expenditures to be made during the period 1986 through and including 1993 shall—

"(A) be treated as made (and allowable as a deduction) during 1986,

"(B) be treated as qualified rehabilitation expenditures made during 1986, and

"(C) be allocated in accordance with the partnership agreement regardless of when the interest in the partnership was acquired, except that—

"(i) if the taxpayer is not the original holder of such interest, no person (other than the taxpayer) had claimed any benefits by reason of this paragraph,

"(ii) no interest under section 6611 of the 1986 Code on any refund of income taxes which is solely attributable to this paragraph shall be paid for the period—

"(I) beginning on the date which is 45 days after the later of April 15, 1987, or the date on which the return for such taxes was filed, and

"(II) ending on the date the taxpayer acquired the interest in the partnership, and

"(iii) if the expenditures to be made under this provision are not paid or incurred before January 1, 1994, then the tax imposed by chapter 1 of such Code for the taxpayer's last taxable year beginning in 1993 shall be increased by the amount of the tax benefits by reason of this paragraph which are attributable to the expenditures not so paid or incurred.

"(7) Special rule. In the case of the rehabilitation of the Willard Hotel in Washington, D.C., section 205(c)(1)(B)(ii) of the Tax Equity and Fiscal Responsibility Act of 1982 shall be applied by substituting '1987' for '1986'.

Prior to amendment, para. (b)(4) read as follows:

"(4) Rehabilitation percentage.

"(A) In general.

Tax credits   Subpart E

"In the case of qualified rehabilitation expenditures with respect to a:	The rehabilitation percentage is:
30-year building	15
40-year building	20
Certified historic structure	25

"(B) Regular and energy percentages not to apply. The regular percentages and the energy percentages shall not apply to that portion of the basis of any property which is attributable to qualified rehabilitation expenditures.

"(C) Definitions. For purpose of this paragraph

"(i) 30-year building. The term '30-year building' means a qualified rehabilitated building other than a 40-year building and other than a certified historic structure.

"(ii) 40-year building. The term '40-year building' means a qualified rehabilitated building (other than a certified historic structure) which would meet the requirements of section 48(g)(1)(B) if '40' were substituted for '30' each place it appears in subparagraph (B) thereof

"(iii) Certified historic structure. The term 'certified historic structure' means a qualified rehabilitated building which meets the requirements of section 48(g)(3)"
—P.L. 99-514, Sec. 421(a), added items (viii)-(xi) to the table in subpara. (b)(2)(A) ... Sec. 421(b), added subpara. (b)(2)(E), effective for periods beginning after 12/31/85, under rules similar to rules under Code Sec. 48(m) (as amended by this Act).

—P.L. 99-514, Sec. 1802(a)(6), added subpara. (e)(4)(D) ... Sec. 1802(a)(8), added subpara. (e)(4)(E), effective for property placed in service by the taxpayer after 11/5/83, in tax. yrs. end. after 11/5/83, and for property placed in service by the taxpayer on or before 11/5/83, if the lease to the tax-exempt entity is entered into after 11/5/83, and subject to the special provisions in Sec. 31(g) of P.L. 98-369, reproduced in the note following Code Sec. 168

—P.L. 99-514, Sec. 1844(a), substituted "this subparagraph" for "clause (i)" in clause (c)(8)(D)(v) ... Sec. 1844(b)(3), substituted "an increase in the credit base for" for "additional qualified investment in" in subpara. (c)(9)(A) ... Sec. 1844(b)(5), amended clause (c)(9)(C)(i), effective for property placed in service after 7/18/84 in tax. yrs. end. after 7/18/84, except that such amendments shall not apply to any property to which the amendments made by Sec. 211(f) of P.L. 97-34 do not apply.

Prior to amendment, clause (c)(9)(C)(i) read as follows:

"(i) Credit determined by reference to taxable year property placed in service. For purposes of determining the amount of credit allowable under section 38 and the amount of credit subject to the early disposition or cessation rules under section 47, any increase in a taxpayer's qualified investment in property by reason of this paragraph shall be deemed to be additional qualified investment made by the taxpayer in the year in which the property referred to in subparagraph (A) was first placed in service."

—P.L. 99-514, Sec. 1847(b)(11), substituted "48(l)(3)(A)(viii)" for "48(l)(3)(A)(vii)" in subpara. (b)(2)(A), effective for tax yrs. begin. after 12/31/83, and to carrybacks from tax. yrs. begin after 12/31/83.

—P.L. 99-514, Sec. 1848(a), repealed para. (f)(9), effective for obligations issued after 12/31/83.

Prior to repeal, para. (f)(9) read as follows:

"(9) Special rule for additional credit. If the taxpayer makes an election under subsection (E) of subsection (a)(2), for a taxable year beginning after December 31, 1975, then, notwithstanding the prior paragraphs of this subsection, no credit shall be allowed by section 38 in excess of the amount which would be allowed without regard to the provisions of subparagraph (E) of subsection (a)(2) if—

"(A) the taxpayer's cost of service for ratemaking purposes or in its regulated books of account is reduced by reason for any portion of such credit which results from the transfer of employer securities or cash to a tax credit employee stock ownership plan which meets the requirements of section 409A;

"(B) the base to which the taxpayer's rate of return for ratemaking purposes is applied is reduced by reason of any portion of such credit which results from a transfer described in subparagraph (A) to such employee stock ownership plan; or

"(C) any portion of the amount of such credit which results from a transfer described in subparagraph (A) to such employee stock ownership plan is treated for ratemaking purposes in any way other than as though it had been contributed by the taxpayer's common shareholders."

In 1984, P.L. 98-369, Sec. 16(a), repealed as if not enacted Sec. 302(c)(3) of P.L. 97-34 which amended subpara. (c)(8)(D) by substituting "subparagraph (A) or (B) of section 128(c)(1)" for "clause (i), (ii), (iii) of subparagraph (A) or subparagraph (B) of section 128(c)(2)", effective for tax. yrs. begin. after 12/31/84

—P.L. 98-369, Sec. 31(f), added para. (e)(4), effective for amendments made to property placed in service by the taxpayer after 11/5/83, in taxable years ending after such date and to property placed in service by the taxpayer on or before 11/5/83, if the lease to the tax-exempt entity is entered into after 11/5/83, and subject to the special provisions in Sec. 31(g) of this Act reproduced in note following Code Sec. 168.

—P.L. 98-369, Sec. 113(b)(2)(B), added "recovery" before "property" the first place it appears in subpara. (c)(7)(A), effective for property placed in service after 12/31/80.

—P.L. 98-369, Sec. 431(a), amended as much of para. (c)(8) as precedes subpara. (c)(8)(F) ... Sec. 431(b)(1), amended para. (c)(9) ... Sec. 431(d)(1), amended clause (c)(8)(F)(i) ... Sec. 431(d)(2), amended subclause (c)(8)(F)(ii)(III) ... Sec. 431(d)(3), substituted "nonqualified nonrecourse financing" for "nonrecourse financing (other than financing described in section 46(c)(8)(B)(ii))" in subclause (c)(8)(F)(ii)(IV), effective for property placed in service after 7/18/84 in tax. yrs. ending after 7/18/84 except that such amendments shall not apply to any

property to which the amendments made by Sec. 211(f) of P.L. 97-34 do not apply.

Prior to amendment, para. (c)(8) read as follows:

"(8) Limitation to amount at risk.

"(A) In general. In the case of new or used section 38 property which—

"(i) is placed in service during the taxable year by a taxpayer described in section 465(a)(1), and

"(ii) is used in connection with an activity with respect to which any loss is subject to limitation under section 465,

the basis of such property for purposes of paragraph (1) shall not exceed the amount the taxpayer is at risk with respect to such property as of the close of such taxable year.

"(B) Amount at risk.

"(i) In general. Except as provided in clause (ii), the term 'at risk' has the same meaning given such term by section 465(b) (without regard to paragraph (5) thereof).

"(ii) Certain financing. In the case of a taxpayer who at all times is at risk (determined without regard to this clause) in an amount equal to at least 20 percent of the basis (determined under section 168(d)(1)(A)(1)) of property described in subparagraph (A) and who acquired such property from a person who is not a related person, such taxpayer shall for purposes of this paragraph be considered at risk with respect to any amount borrowed in connection with such property (other than convertible debt) to the extent that such amount—

"(I) is borrowed from a qualified person, or

"(II) represents a loan from any Federal, State, or local government or instrumentality thereof, or is guaranteed by, any Federal, State, or local government.

"(C) Special rule for partnerships and Subchapter S corporations. In the case of any partnership or S corporation, any amount treated as at risk under subparagraph (B)(ii) shall be allocated among the partners or shareholders (and treated as an amount at risk with respect to such persons) in the same manner as the credit allowable by section 38.

"(D) Qualified person. For purposes of this paragraph, the term 'qualified person' means any person—

"(i) which—

"(I) is an institution described in clause (i), (ii), or (iii) of subparagraph (A) or subparagraph (B) of section 128(c)(2) or an insurance company to which subchapter L applies, or

"(II) is a pension trust qualified under section 401(a) or a person not described in subclause (I) and which is actively and regularly engaged in the business of lending money,

"(ii) which is not a related person with respect to the taxpayer,

"(iii) which is not a person who receives a fee with respect to the taxpayer's investment in property described in subparagraph (A) or a related person to such person, and

"(iv) which is not a person from which the taxpayer acquired the property described in subparagraph (A) or a related person to such person.

"(E) Related person. For purposes of this paragraph, the term 'related person' has the same meaning as such term is used in section 168(e)(4), except that in applying section 168(e)(4)(D)(i) in the case of a person described in subparagraph (D)(i)(II) of this paragraph, sections 267(b) and 707(b)(1) shall be applied by substituting '0 percent' for '50 percent'.

"(F) Special rule for certain energy property.

"(i) In general. The provisions of subparagraph (A) shall not apply to amounts borrowed with respect to qualified energy property (other than amounts described in subparagraph (B)).

"(ii) Qualified energy property. The term 'qualified energy property' means energy property to which (but for this subparagraph) subparagraph (A) applies and—

"(I) which is described in clause (iii),

"(II) with respect to which the energy percentage determined under section 46(a)(2)(C) at the time such property is placed in service is greater than zero,

"(III) with respect to which the taxpayer, as of the close of the taxable year in which the property is placed in service, is at risk (within the meaning of section 465(b) without regard to paragraph (5) thereof) in an amount equal to at least 25 percent of the basis of the property, and

"(IV) with respect to which any nonrecourse financing (other than financing described in section 46(c)(8)(B)(ii)) in connection with such property consists of a level payment loan.

For purposes of subclause (II), the energy percentage for property described in clause (iii)(V) shall be treated as being greater than zero during any period the energy percentage for property described in section 48(l)(14) is greater than zero.

"(iii) Property to which this subparagraph applies. Energy property is described in this clause if such property is—

"(I) described in clause (ii), (iv), or (vii) or section 48(l)(2),

"(II) described in section 48(l)(15),

"(III) described in section 48(l)(3)(A)(iii) (but only to the extent such property is used for converting an alternate substance into alcohol for fuel purposes),

"(IV) described in clause (i) of section 48(l)(2)(A) (but only to the extent such property is also described in section 48(l)(3)(A)(viii) or (ix)), or

"(V) property comprising a system for using the same energy source for the sequential generation of electrical power, mechanical shaft power, or both, in combination with steam, heat, or other forms of useful energy.

"(iv) Level payment loan defined. The term 'level payment loan' means a loan in which each installment is substantially equal, a portion of each installment is attributable to the repayment of principal, and that portion is increased commensurate with decreases in the portion of the payment attributable to interest."

Prior to amendment, para. (c)(9) read as follows:

"(9) Subsequent increases in the taxpayer's amount at risk with respect to the property.

"(A) In general. If, at the close of a taxable year subsequent to the year in which property was placed in service, the amount which the taxpayer has at risk with respect to such property has increased (as determined under subparagraph (B)), such increase shall be taken into account as additional qualified investment in such property in accordance with subparagraph (C).

"(B) Increases to be taken into account. For purposes of subparagraphs (A) and (C), the amount which a taxpayer has at risk with respect to the property shall be treated as increased by the sum of the cash and the fair market value of property (other than property with respect to which the taxpayer is not at risk) used during the taxable year to reduce the principal sum of any amount with respect to which the taxpayer is not at risk.

"(C) Manner in which taken into account. For purposes of determining the amount of credit allowed under section 38 and the amount of credit subject to the early disposition rules under section 47, an increase in a taxpayer's qualified investment in property (determined under subparagraph (B)) shall be deemed to be additional qualified investment made by the taxpayer in the year in which the property referred to in subparagraph (A) was first placed in service. However, the credit determined by taking into account the increase in qualified investment under this paragraph shall be considered a credit earned in the taxable year of such increase."

—P.L. 98-369, Sec. 474(o)(1), amended subsecs. (a) and (b)... Sec. 474(o)(2), substituted "subsection (b)(2)" for "section 46(a)(2)(C)" in subclause (c)(8)(F)(ii)(II)... Sec. 474(o)(3)(A)(i), and (ii), deleted "and the $25,000 amount specified under subparagraph (A) and (B) of subsection (a)(3)" after "the qualified investment" and substituted "such qualified investment" for "such items" in para. (e)(1)... Sec. 474(o)(3)(B), substituted "qualified investment" for "the items described therein" in para. (e)(2)... Sec. 474(o)(4)(A), substituted "no credit determined under subsection (a) shall be allowed by section 38" for "no credit shall be allowed by section 38" in para. (f)(1) and (2)... Sec. 474(o)(4)(B), substituted "the credit determined under subsection (a) and allowable by section 38" for "the credit allowable by section 38" each place it appears in paras. (f)(1) and (2)... Sec. 474(o)(4)(C), substituted "the credit determined under subsection (a) and allowed by section 38" for "the credit allowed by section 38" in subpara. (f)(4)(B)... Sec. 474(o)(5)(A), substituted "the credit determined under subsection (a) and allowable under section 38" for "the credit allowable under section 38" each place it appears in para. (f)(8)... Sec. 474(o)(5)(B), substituted "(within the meaning of subsection (c)(3)(B)" for "(within the meaning of subsection (a)(7)(C))" in para. (f)(8)... Sec. 474(o)(6), substituted "the limitation of section 38(c)" for "the limitation of subsection (a)(3)" in para. (g)(2)... Sec. 474(o)(7)(A), and (B), substituted "the credit determined under subsection (a) and allowable to the organization under section 38" for "the credit allowable to the organization under section 38" and substituted "the limitation contained in section 38(c)" for "the limitation contained in subsection (a)(3)" in para. (h)(1), effective for tax. yrs. begin. after 12/31/83 and to carrybacks from tax. yrs. begin after 12/31/83. Sec. 475(c) of this Act provides:

"(c) Clarification of effect of amendments on investment tax credit. Nothing in the amendments made by section 474(o) shall be construed as reducing the amount of any credit allowable for qualified investment in taxable years beginning before January 1, 1984."

Prior to amendment, subsecs. (a) and (b) read as follows:

"(a) General rule.

"(1) First-in-first-out rule. The amount of the credit allowed by section 38 for the taxable year shall be an amount equal to the sum of—

"(A) the investment credit carryovers carried to such taxable year,

"(B) the amount of the credit determined under paragraph (2) for such taxable year, plus

"(C) the investment credit carrybacks carried to such taxable year.

"(2) Amount of credit.

"(A) In general. The amount of the credit determined under this paragraph for the taxable year shall be an amount equal to the sum of the following percentages of the qualified investment (as determined under subsections (c) and (d)):

"(i) the regular percentage,

"(ii) in the case of energy property, the energy percentage,

"(iii) the employee plan percentage, and

"(iv) in the case of that portion of the basis of any property which is attributable to qualified rehabilitation expenditures, the rehabilitation percentage.

"(B) Regular percentage. For purposes of this paragraph, the regular percentage is 10 percent.

"(C) Energy percentage. For purposes of this paragraph—

"(i) In general. The energy percentage shall be determined in accordance with the following table:

Column A— Description	Column B— Percentage	Column C— Period
In the case of:	The energy percentage is:	For the period: Beginning on: And ending on:
I. General Rule— Property not described in any of the following provisions of this column	10 percent	Oct. 1, 1978 Dec. 31, 1982.
II. Solar, Wind, or Geothermal Property— Property described in section 48(l)(2)(A)(ii) or 48(l)(3)(A)(viii)	A. 10 percent B. 15 percent	Oct. 1, 1978 Dec. 31, 1979. Jan. 1, 1980 Dec. 31, 1985.
III. Ocean Thermal Property— Property described in section 48(l)(3)(A)(ix)	15 percent	Jan. 1, 1980 Dec. 31, 1985.
IV. Qualified Hydroelectric Generating Property— Property described in section 48(l)(2)(A)(vii)	11 percent	Jan. 1, 1980 Dec. 31, 1985.
V. Qualified Intercity Buses.— Property described in section 48(l)(2)(A)(ix)	10 percent	Jan. 1, 1980 Dec. 31, 1985.
VI. Biomass Property— Property described in section 48(l)(15)	10 percent	Oct. 1, 1978 Dec. 31, 1985.
VII. Chlor-Alkali Electrolytic Cells — Property described in section 48(l)(5)(M)	10 percent	Jan. 1, 1980 Dec. 31, 1982.

"(ii) Periods for which percentage not specified. In the case of any energy property, the energy percentage shall be zero for any period for which an energy percentage is not specified for such property under clause (i) (as modified by clauses (iii) and (iv)).

"(iii) Longer period for certain long-term projects. For the purpose of applying the energy percentage contained in subclause (I) of clause (i) with respect to property which is a part of a project with a normal construction period of 2 years or more (within the meaning of section 46(d)(2)(A)(i)), 'December 31, 1990' shall be substituted for 'December 31, 1982' if—

"(I) before January 1, 1983, the taxpayer has completed all engineering studies in connection with the commencement of the construction of the project, and has applied for all environmental and construction permits required under Federal, State, or local law in connection with the commencement of the construction of the project, and

"(II) before January 1, 1986, the taxpayer has entered into binding contracts for the acquisition, construction, reconstruction, or erection of equipment specially designed for the project and the aggregate cost to the taxpayer of that equipment is at least 50 percent of the reasonably estimated cost for all such equipment which is to be placed in service as part of the project upon its completion.

"(iv) Longer period for certain hydroelectric generating property. If an application has been docketed by the Federal Energy Regulatory Commission before January 1, 1986, with respect to the installation of any qualified hydroelectric generating property, for purposes of applying the energy percentage contained in subclause (IV) of clause (i) with respect to such property, 'December 31, 1988' shall be substituted for 'December 31, 1985'.

"(D) Special rule for certain energy property. For purposes of this paragraph, the regular percentage shall not apply to any energy property which, but for section 48(l)(1), would not be section 38 property. In the case of any qualified hydroelectric generating property which is a fish passageway, the preceding sentence shall not apply to any period after 1979 for which the energy percentage for such property is greater than zero.

"(E) Employee plan percentage. For purposes of this paragraph, the employee plan percentage is—

"(i) with respect to the period beginning on January 21, 1975, and ending on December 31, 1982, 1 percent,

"(ii) with respect to the period beginning on January 1, 1977, and ending on December 31, 1982, an additional percentage (not in excess of ½ of 1 percent) which results in an amount equal to the amount determined under section 48(n)(1)(B), and

"(iii) with respect to any period beginning after December 31, 1982, zero.

This subparagraph shall apply to a corporation only if it meets the requirements of section 409A and only if it elects (at such time, in such form, and in such manner as the Secretary prescribes) to have this subparagraph apply.

"(F) Rehabilitation percentage. for purposes of this paragraph—

"(i) In general.

In the case of qualified rehabilitation expenditures with respect to a:	The rehabilitation percentage is:
30-year building	15
40-year building	20
Certified historic structure	25

"(ii) Regular and energy percentages not to apply. The regular percentage and the energy percentage shall not apply to that portion of the basis of any property which is attributable to qualified rehabilitation expenditures.

"(iii) Definitions.

"(I) 30-year building. The term '30-year building' means a qualified rehabilitated building other than a 40-year building and other than a certified historic structure.

"(II) 40-year building. The term '40-year building' means a qualified rehabilitated building (other than a certified historic structure) which would meet the requirements of section 48(g)(1)(B) if '40' were substituted for '30' each place it appears in subparagraph (B) thereof.

"(III) Certified historic structure. The term 'certified historic structure' means a qualified rehabilitated building which meets the requirements of section 48(g)(3).

"(3) Limitation based on amount of tax. Notwithstanding paragraph (1), the credit allowed by section 38 for the taxable year shall not exceed—

"(A) so much of the liability for tax for the taxable year as does not exceed $25,000, plus

"(B) 85 percent of so much of the liability for tax for the taxable year as exceeds $25,000.

"(4) Liability for tax. For purposes of paragraph (3), the liability for tax for the taxable year shall be the tax imposed by this chapter for such year, reduced by the sum of the credits allowable under—

"(A) section 33 (relating to foreign tax credit), and

"(B) section 37 (relating to credit for the elderly and the permanently and totally disabled).

For purposes of this paragraph, any tax imposed for the taxable year by section 56 (relating to corporate minimum tax), section 72(m)(5)(B) (relating to 10 percent tax on premature distributions to key employees) section 72(q)(1) (relating to 5-percent tax on premature distributions under annuity contracts), section 402(e) (relating to tax on lump sum distributions), section 408(f) (relating to additional tax on income from certain retirement accounts), section 531 (relating to accumulated earnings tax, section 541 (relating to personal holding company tax) or section 1374 (relating to tax on certain capital gains of S corporations), and any additional tax imposed for the taxable year by section 1351(d)(1) (relating to recoveries of foreign expropriation losses), shall not be considered tax imposed by this chapter for such year.

"(5) Married individuals. In the case of a husband or wife who files a separate return, the amount specified under subparagraphs (A) and (B) of paragraph (3) shall be $12,500 in lieu of $25,000. This paragraph shall not apply if the spouse of the taxpayer has no qualified investment for, and no unused credit carryback or carryover to, the taxable year of such spouse which ends within or with the taxpayer's taxable year.

"(6) Controlled groups. In the case of a controlled group, the $25,000 amount specified under paragraph (3) shall be reduced for each component member of such group by apportioning $25,000 among the component members of such group in such manner as the Secretary shall by regulations prescribe. For purposes of the preceding sentence, the term 'controlled group' has the meaning assigned to such term by section 1563(a).

"(7) Special rules in the case of energy property. Under regulations prescribed by the Secretary—

"(A) In general. This subsection and subsection (b) shall be applied separately—

"(i) first with respect to so much of the credit allowed by section 38 as is not attributable to the energy percentage, and

"(ii) second with respect to so much of the credit allowed by section 38 as is attributable to the application of the energy percentage to energy property.

"(B) Rules of application for energy property. In applying this subsection and subsection (b) for taxable years ending after September 30, 1978, with respect to so much of the credit allowed by section 38 as is described in subparagraph (A)(ii)—

"(i) paragraph (3)(B) shall be applied by substituting '100 percent' for '85 percent', and

"(ii) the liability for tax shall be the amount determined under paragraph (4) reduced by so much of the credit allowed by section 38 as is described in subparagraph (A)(i)."

"(b) Carryback and carryover of unused credits.

"(1) In general. If the sum of the amount of the investment credit carryovers to the taxable year under subsection (a)(1)(A) plus the amount determined under subsection (a)(1)(B) for the taxable year exceeds the amount of the limitation imposed by subsection (a)(3) for such taxable year (hereinafter in this subsection referred to as the 'unused credit year'), such excess attributable to the amount determined under subsection (a)(1)(B) shall be—

"(A) an investment credit carryback to each of the 3 taxable years preceding the unused credit year, and

"(B) an investment credit carryover to each of the 7 taxable years following the unused credit year,

and, subject to the limitations imposed by paragraphs (2) and (3), shall be taken into account under the provisions of subsection (a)(1) in the manner provided in such subsection. The entire amount of the unused credit for an unused credit year shall be carried to the earliest of the 10 taxable years to which (by reason of subparagraphs (A) and (B)) such credit may be carried and then to each of the other 9 taxable years to the extent, because of the limitations imposed by paragraphs (2) and (3), such unused credit may not be taken into account under subsection (a)(1) for a prior taxable year to which such unused credit may be carried. In the case of an unused credit for an unused credit year ending before January 1, 1971, which is an investment credit carryover to a taxable year beginning after December 31, 1970 (determined without regard to this sentence), this paragraph shall be applied—

"(C) by substituting '10 taxable years' for '7 taxable years' in subparagraph (B), and by substituting '13 taxable years' for '10 taxable years', and '12 taxable years' for '9 taxable years' in the preceding sentence, and

"(D) by carrying such an investment credit carryover to a later taxable year (than the taxable year to which it would, but for this subparagraph, be carried) to which it may be carried if, because of the amendments made by section 802(b)(2) of the Tax Reform Act of 1976, carrying such carryover to the taxable year to which it would, but for this subparagraph, be carried would cause a portion of an unused credit from an unused credit year ending after December 31, 1970 to expire.

In the case of an unused credit for an unused credit year ending after December 31, 1973, this paragraph shall be applied by substituting '15' for '7' in subparagraph (B), and by substituting '18' for '10', and '17' for '9' in the second sentence.

"(2) Limitation of carrybacks. The amount of the unused credit which may be taken into account under subsection (a)(1) for any preceding taxable year shall not exceed the amount by which the limitation imposed by subsection (a)(3) for such taxable year exceeds the sum of—

"(A) the amounts determined under subparagraphs (A) and (B) of subsection (a)(1) for such taxable year, plus

"(B) the amounts which (by reason of this subsection) are carried back to such taxable year and are attributable to taxable years preceding the unused credit year.

"(3) Limitation on carryovers. The amount of the unused credit which may be taken into account under subsection (a)(1)(A) for any succeeding taxable year shall not exceed the amount by which the limitation imposed by subsection (a)(3) for such taxable year exceeds the sum of the amounts which, by reason of this subsection, are carried to such taxable year and are attributable to taxable years preceding the unused credit year."

—P.L. 98-369, Sec. 713(c)(1)(C) substituted "tax on premature distributions to key employees" for "tax on premature distributions to owner-employees" in para. (a)(4) (before amendment by Sec. 470(o)(1) of this Act), effective for distributions after 12/31/82.

In 1983, P.L. 98-21, Sec. 122(c)(1), substituted "relating to credit for the elderly and the permanently and totally disabled" for "relating to credit for the elderly" in subpara. (a)(4)(B), effective for tax. yrs. begin. after 12/31/83.

—P.L. 97-448, Sec. 102(d)(2), added para. (c)(3) to Sec. 209 of P.L. 97-34, effective date for amendments made by Sec. 207(c)(1) of P.L. 97-34, see below.

—P.L. 97-448, Sec. 102(e)(1)(A), amended subpara. (c)(7)(A) ... Sec. 102(e)(1)(B), substituted "shall be treated as property which is not 3-year property" for "shall be treated as 5-year property", effective for property placed in service after 12/31/80.

Prior to amendment, subpara. (c)(7)(A) read as follows:

"(A) in the case of 15-year public utility, 10-year, or 5-year property (within the meaning of section 168(c)), 100 percent, and"

—P.L. 97-448, Sec. 102(f)(1), amended Sec. 212(e)(2)(B) of P.L. 97-34, part of the effective date for changes made by Sec. 212(a)(1) of P.L. 97-34, see below.

Prior to amendment, Sec. 212(e)(2)(B) of P.L. 97-448 read as follows:

"(B) such building meets the requirements of paragraph (1) of section 48(g) of the Internal Revenue Code of 1954 (as in effect on the day before the date of enactment of this Act) but does not meet the requirements of such paragraph (1) (as amended by this Act)."

—P.L. 97-448, Sec. 102(f)(5)(A), substituted "a qualified rehabilitated building" for "any building" in subclause (a)(2)(F)(iii)(II) ... Sec. 102(f)(5)(B), substituted "means a qualified rehabilitated building which meets the requirements of section 48(g)(3)" for "has the meaning given to such term by section 48(g)(3)" in subclause (a)(2)(F)(iii)(III), effective for expenditures incurred after 12/31/81, in tax. yrs. end. after 12/31/81.

—P.L. 97-448, Sec. 202(f), amended subclause (a)(2)(C)(iii)(I).

Prior to amendment, subclause (a)(2)(C)(iii)(I) read as follows:

"(I) 30-year building. The term '30-year building' means a qualified rehabilitated building other than a 40-year building and other than a certified historic structure."

—P.L. 97-448, Sec. 306(a)(1)(A)(i), redesignated the second Sec. 201(c) of P.L. 97-248 as Sec. 201(d) of P.L. 97-248, see below.

—P.L. 97-424, Sec. 541(b), added para. (f)(10), effective for tax. yrs. begin. after 12/31/79.

—P.L. 97-424, Sec. 541(c)(2)-(5), provided a special rule on tax treatment of public utility property which is reproduced in the note following Code Sec. 167.

—P.L. 97-424, Sec. 546(b), added item VII to the table in clause (a)(2)(C)(i), effective 1/6/83.

In 1982, P.L. 97-354, Sec. 5(a)(4), substituted "section 1374 (relating to tax on certain capital gains of S corporations)," for "section 1378 (relating to tax on certain capital gains of subchapter S corporations)," in the second sentence of para. (a)(4) ... Sec. 5(a)(5), substituted "S corporation" for "electing small business corporation (within the meaning of section 1371(b))" in subpara. (c)(8)(C) ... Sec. 5(a)(6), substituted "an S corporation" for "an electing small business corporation (as defined in section 1371)" in para. (e)(3), effective for tax. yrs. begin. after 12/31/82.

—P.L. 97-248, Sec. 201(d)(8)(A), [as amended by Sec. 306(a)(1)(A)(i) of P.L. 97-448] substituted "(relating to corporate minimum tax)" for "(relating to mini-

mum tax for tax preferences)" in para. (a)(4), effective for distributions after 12/31/82.
— P.L. 97-248, Sec. 205(b)(1), amended subpara. (a)(3)(B) . . . Sec. 205(b)(2)(A), deleted paras. (a)(7) and (a)(8), and redesignated para. (a)(9) as para. (a)(7) . . . Sec. 205(b)(2)(B), amended clause (a)(7)(A)(i) (as redesignated by Sec. 205(b)(2)(A) of this Act) . . . Sec. 205(b)(2)(C), deleted clause (a)(7)(B)(ii) and redesignated clause (a)(7)(B)(iii) as clause (a)(7)(B)(ii) (as redesignated by Sec. 205(b)(2)(A) of this Act), effective for tax. yrs. begin. after 12/31/82.
Prior to amendment, subpara. (a)(3)(B) read as follows:
"(B) the following percentage of so much of the liability for tax for the taxable year as exceeds $25,000:

"If the taxable year ends in:	The percentage is:
"1979	60
"1980	70
"1981	80
"1982 or thereafter	90."

Prior to deletion, paras. (a)(7) and (a)(8) read as follows:
"(7) Alternative limitation in the case of certain utilities.
"(A) In general. If, for the taxable year ending in 1979 —
"(i) the amount of the qualified investment of the taxpayer which is attributable to public utility property is 25 percent or more of his aggregate qualified investment, and
"(ii) the application of this paragraph results in a percentage higher than 60 percent,
then subparagraph (B) of paragraph (3) of this subsection shall be applied by substituting for '60 percent' the taxpayer's applicable percentage for such year.
"(B) Applicable percentage. The applicable percentage for any taxpayer for any taxable year ending in 1979 is —
"(i) 50 percent, plus
"(ii) that portion of 20 percent which the taxpayer's amount of qualified investment which is public utility property bears to his aggregate qualified investment. If the proportion referred to in clause (ii) is 75 percent or more, the applicable percentage of the taxpayer for the year shall be 70 percent.
"(C) Public utility property defined. For purposes of this paragraph, the term 'public utility property' has the meaning given to such term by the first sentence of subsection (c)(3)(B).
"(8) Alternative limitation in the case of certain railroads and airlines.
"(A) In general. If, for a taxable year ending in 1979 or 1980 —
"(i) the amount of the qualified investment of the taxpayer which is attributable to railroad property or to airline property, as the case may be, is 25 percent or more of his aggregate qualified investment, and
"(ii) the application of this paragraph results in a percentage higher than 60 percent (70 percent in the case of a taxable year ending in 1980),
then subparagraph (B) of paragraph (3) of this subsection shall be applied by substituting for '60 percent' ('70 percent' in the case of a taxable year ending in 1980) the taxpayer's applicable percentage for such year.
"(B) Applicable percentage. The applicable percentage of any taxpayer for any taxable year under this paragraph is —
"(i) 50 percent, plus
"(ii) that portion of the tentative percentage for the taxable year which the taxpayer's amount of qualified investment which is railroad property or airline property (as the case may be) bears to his aggregate qualified investment.
If the proportion referred to in clause (ii) is 75 percent or more, the applicable percentage of the taxpayer for the taxable year shall be 90 percent (80 percent in the case of a taxable year ending in 1980).
"(C) Tentative percentage. For purposes of subparagraph (B), the tentative percentage shall be determined under the following table:

If the taxable year ends in:	The tentative percentage is:
1979	40
1980	30

"(D) Railroad property defined. For purposes of this paragraph, the term 'railroad property' means section 38 property used by the taxpayer directly in connection with the trade or business carried on by the taxpayer of operating a railroad (including a railroad switching or terminal company).
"(E) Airline property defined. For purposes of this paragraph, the term 'airline property' means section 38 property used by the taxpayer directly in connection with the trade or business carried on by the taxpayer of the furnishing or sale of transportation as a common carrier by air subject to the jurisdiction of the Civil Aeronautics Board of the Federal Aviation Administration."
Prior to amendment, clause (a)(7)(B)(i) read as follows:
"(i) paragraph (3)(B) shall be applied by substituting '100 percent' for the percentage determined under the table contained in such paragraph,"
Prior to deletion, clause (a)(7)(B)(ii) read as follows:
"(ii) paragraphs (7) and (8) shall not apply, and"
— P.L. 97-248, Sec. 265(b)(2)(A)(i), added "section 72(q)(1) (relating to 5-percent tax on premature distributions under annuity contracts)," after "owner-employees)" in para. (a)(4), effective for distributions after 12/31/82.
In 1981, P.L. 97-34, Sec. 207(c)(1), added the last sentence to para. (b)(1), effective for unused credit years end. after 12/31/73. Sec. 209(c)(3) of this Act provides:
"(3) Carryover must have been alive in 1981. The amendments made by subsections (a), (b), and (c) of section 207 [P.L. 97-34] shall not apply to any amount which, under the law in effect on the day before the date of the enactment of this Act, could not be carried to a taxable year ending in 1981."
Sec. 209(d)(2) of this Act provides:
"(2) Transitional rule for requirements of section 46(f). If, by the terms of the applicable rate order last entered before the date of the enactment of this Act by a regulatory commission having appropriate jurisdiction, a regulated public utility would (but for this provision) fail to meet the requirements of paragraph (1) or (2) of section 46(f) of the Internal Revenue Code of 1954 with respect to property for an accounting period ending after December 31, 1980, such regulated public utility shall not fail to meet such requirements if, by the terms of its first rate order determining cost of service with respect to such property which becomes effective after the date of the enactment of this Act and on or before January 1, 1983, such regulated public utility meets such requirements. This provision shall not apply to any rate order which, under the rules in effect before the date of the enactment of this Act, was inconsistent with the requirements of paragraph (1) or (2) of section 46(f) of such Code (whichever would have been applicable)."
— P.L. 97-34, Sec. 211(a)(1), added para. (c)(7), effective for property placed in service after 12/31/80.
— P.L. 97-34, Sec. 211(b)(1), amended para. (d)(1) . . . Sec. 211(b)(2), deleted "having a useful life of 7 years or more" after "section 38 property" in clause (d)(2)(A)(ii), effective for progress expenditures made after 12/31/80.
Prior to amendment, para. (d)(1) read as follows:
"(1) In general. In the case of any taxpayer who has made an election under paragraph (6), the amount of his qualified investment for the taxable year (determined under subsection (c) without regard to this subsection) shall be increased by an amount equal to his aggregate qualified progress expenditures for the taxable year with respect to progress expenditure property."
— P.L. 97-34, Sec. 211(d), added the last sentence to the end of para. (e)(3), effective for leases entered into after 6/25/81.
— P.L. 97-34, Sec. 211(e)(1), substituted "(2) Applicable percentage in certain cases. Except as provided in paragraphs (3), (6), and (7), the applicable percentage for purposes of paragraph (1) for any property shall be determined under the following table:" for "(2) Applicable percentage. For purposes of paragraph (1), the applicable percentage for any property shall be determined under the following tables:" . . . Sec. 211(e)(2), amended, subpara. (c)(6)(A), effective for property placed in service after 12/31/80.
Prior to amendment, subpara. (c)(6)(A) read as follows:
"(A) In general. Notwithstanding paragraph (2), in the case of a commuter highway vehicle the useful life of which is 3 years or more, the applicable percentage for purposes of paragraph (1) shall be 100 percent."
— P.L. 97-34, Sec. 211(f)(1), added paras. (c)(8) and (c)(9). Sec. 211(i)(5) of this Act provides:
"(5) At risk rules.
"(A) In general. The amendment made by subsection (f) shall not apply to —
"(i) property placed in service by the taxpayer on or before February 18, 1981, and
"(ii) property placed in service by the taxpayer after February 18, 1981, where such property is acquired by the taxpayer pursuant to a binding contract entered into on or before that date.
"(B) Binding contract. For purposes of subparagraph (A)(ii), property acquired pursuant to a binding contract shall, under regulations prescribed by the Secretary, include property acquired in a manner so that it would have qualified as pretermination property under section 49(b) (as in effect before its repeal by the Revenue Act of 1978)."
— P.L. 97-34, Sec. 212(a)(1), amended subpara. (a)(2)(A) by deleting "and" at the end of clause (a)(2)(A)(ii), by substituting ", and" for the period at the end of clause (a)(2)(A)(iii), and by adding clause (a)(2)(A)(iv) . . . Sec. 212(a)(2), added subpara. (a)(2)(F), effective for expenditures incurred after 12/31/81, in tax. yrs. ending after 12/31/81, except as provided in Sec. 212(e)(2) of this Act which reads as follows:
"(2) Transitional rule. The amendments made by this section shall not apply with respect to any rehabilitation of a building if —
"(A) the physical work on such rehabilitation began before January 1, 1982, and
"(B) such building does not meet the requirements of paragraph (1) of section 48(g) of the Internal Revenue Code of 1954 (as amended by this Act)."
— P.L. 97-34, Sec. 302(c)(3), [repealed as if not enacted by Sec. 16(a) of P.L. 98-369, see above] substituted "subparagraph (A) or (B) of section 128(c)(1)" for "clause (i), (ii), (iii) of subparagraph (A) or subparagraph (B) of section 128(c)(1)" in subpara. (c)(8)(D), effective for tax. yrs. begin. after 12/31/84.
— P.L. 97-34, Sec. 332(a)(1), substituted "December 31, 1982" for "December 31, 1983" in clauses (a)(2)(E)(i) and (ii) . . . Sec. 332(a)(3), deleted "and" at the end of clause (a)(2)(E)(i) . . . Sec. 332(a)(3), substituted ", and" for the period at the end of clause (a)(2)(E)(ii) . . . Sec. 332(a)(4), added clause (a)(2)(E)(iii), effective 8/13/81.
In 1980, P.L. 96-223, Sec. 221(a), amended subpara. (a)(2)(C).
Prior to amendment, subpara. (a)(2)(C) read as follows:
"(C) Energy percentage. For purposes of this paragraph, the energy percentage is —
"(i) 10 percent with respect to the period beginning on October 1, 1978, and ending on December 31, 1982, and
"(ii) zero with respect to any other period."
— P.L. 96-223, Sec. 222(e)(2), added "In the case of any qualified hydroelectric generating property which is a fish passageway, the preceding sentence shall not apply to any period after 1979 for which the energy percentage for such property is greater than zero." to the end of subpara. (a)(2)(D), effective for periods after 12/31/79, under rules similar to the rules of Code Sec. 48(m).

—P.L. 96-223, Sec. 223(b)(1)(A)(i), added "and" at the end of clause (a)(10)(A)(i) [redesignated para. (a)(9) by P.L. 96-223, see below] . . . P.L. 223(b)(1)(A)(ii), substituted a period for "(other than solar or wind energy property), and" at the end of clause (a)(10)(A)(ii) [redesignated para. (a)(9) by P.L. 96-223, see below] . . . Sec. 223(b)(1)(A)(iii), deleted clause (a)(10)(A)(iii) [redesignated para. (a)(9) by P.L. 96-223, see below] . . . Sec. 223(b)(1)(B), deleted "other than solar or wind energy property" from the heading of subpara. (a)(10)(B) [redesignated para. (a)(9) by P.L. 96-223, see below] . . . Sec. 223(b)(1)(C), deleted subpara. (a)(10)(C) [redesignated para. (a)(9) by P.L. 96-223, see below], effective for qualified investment for tax. yrs. begin. after 12/31/79.

Prior to amendment, clause (a)(10)(A)(iii) read as follows:

"(iii) then with respect to so much of the credit allowed by section 38 as is attributable to the application of the energy percentage to solar or wind energy property."

Prior to amendment, subpara. (a)(10)(C) read as follows:

"(C) Refundable credit for solar or wind energy property. In the case of so much of the credit allowed by section 38 as is described in subparagraph (A)(iii)—

"(i) paragraph (3) shall not apply, and

"(ii) for purposes of this title (other than section 38, this subpart, and chapter 63), such credit shall be treated as if it were allowed by section 39 and not by section 38."

—P.L. 96-222, Sec. 101(a)(7)(A), substituted "subparagraph (E) of subsection (a)(2)" for "subparagraph (B) of subsection (a)(2)" each place it appeared in para. (f)(9) and substituted "a tax credit employee stock ownership plan which meets the requirements of section 409A" for "an employee stock ownership plan which meets the requirements of section 301(d) of the Tax Reduction Act of 1975" in subpara. (f)(9)(A), presumably intended by Congress to be effective with respect to qualified investment for tax. yrs. begin. after '78 [Sec. 101(b)(2)] although technically effective with respect to estates of decedents dying after 4/1/80 [Sec. 101(b)(1)(D)].

—P.L. 96-222, Sec. 101(a)(7)(B), corrected Sec. 141(g) of P.L. 95-600 [see below].

Prior to corrections, Sec. 141(g) of P.L. 95-600 read as follows:

"(g) Effective dates.

"(1) In general. The amendments made by this section (other than by subsection (f)(3)) shall apply with respect to qualified investment for taxable years beginning after December 31, 1978. The amendment made by subsection (f)(7) shall apply to years beginning after December 31, 1978.

"(2) Retroactive application of amendment made by subsection (d). In determining the regular tax deduction under section 6 of the Internal Revenue Code of 1954 for any taxable year beginning before January 1, 1979, the amount of the credit allowable under section 38 shall be determined without regard to section 46(a)(2)(B) of such Code (as in effect before the enactment of the Energy Tax Act of 1978)."

—P.L. 96-222, Sec. 101(a)(7)(L)(iii)(I), substituted "employee plan" for "ESOP" each place it appeared in para. (a)(2) . . . Sec. 101(a)(7)(L)(v)(I), substituted "Employee plan" for "ESOP" in the heading of subpara. (a)(2)(E), presumably intended by Congress to be effective for qualified investment for tax. yrs. begin. after '78 [Sec. 101(b)(2)] although technically effective with respect to estates of decedents dying after 4/1/80 [Sec. 101(b)(1)(D)].

—P.L. 96-222, Sec. 101(a)(7)(M)(i), added "and ending on" before "before December 31, 1983" each place it appeared in subpara. (a)(2)(e) [unable to make amendment as Code Sec. presently reads, see Sec. 301(a)(1) of P.L. 95-618, below].

—P.L. 96-222, Sec. 103(a)(2)(A), amended Sec. 312(c) of P.L. 95-600 which amended paras. (f)(1) and (2) by substituting "described in section 50 (as in effect before its repeal by the Revenue Act of 1978)" for "described in section 50" [see below].

—P.L. 96-222, Sec. 103(a)(2)(B)(i), redesignated para. (a)(10) as para. (a)(9) . . . Sec. 103(a)(2)(B)(ii), amended redesignated clause (a)(9)(B)(i) . . . Sec. 103(a)(2)(B)(iii), substituted "(7) and (8)" for "(7), (8) and (9)" in redesignated clause (a)(9)(B)(ii), effective 11/9/78.

Prior to amendment, clause (a)(9)(B)(i) read as follows:

"(i) paragraph (3)(C) shall be applied by substituting '100 percent' for '50 percent'."

—P.L. 96-222, Sec. 103(a)(3), added the last sentence to subpara. (c)(5)(B), effective for property acquired by the taxpayer after '78 and for property, the construction, reconstruction or erection of which was completed by taxpayer after '78 (but only to the extent of the basis thereof attributable to construction, reconstruction or erection after '78).

—P.L. 96-222, Sec. 103(a)(4)(A), added the last sentence to para. (e)(3), effective for tax. yrs. end. after 10/31/78.

—P.L. 96-222, Sec. 107(a)(3)(A), substituted "subsection (a)(7)(C)" for "subsection (a)(7)(D)" in the first sentence of para. (f)(8), effective 10/4/76.

In 1978, P.L. 95-618, Sec. 241(a), added para. (c)(6), effective 11/9/78.

—P.L. 95-618, Sec. 301(a)(1), amended para. (a)(2), (which is further amended by Sec. 311(a) of P.L. 95-600, see below) effective 11/9/78.

Prior to amendment, para. (a)(2) read as follows:

"(2) Amount of credit for current taxable year.

"(A) 10 percent credit. Except as otherwise provided in subparagraph (B), in the case of a property described in subparagraph (D), the amount of the credit determined under this paragraph for the taxable year shall be an amount equal to 10 percent of the qualified investment (as determined under subsections (c) and (d)).

"(B) Additional credit. In the case of a corporation which elects (at such time, in such form, and in such manner as the Secretary prescribes) to have the provisions of this subparagraph apply, the amount of the credit determined under this paragraph shall be an amount equal to—

"(i) 11 percent of the qualified investment (as determined under subsections (c) and (d)), plus

"(ii) an additional percent (not in excess of one-half percent) of the qualified investment (as determined under such subsections) equal in amount to the amount determined under section 301(e) of the Tax Reduction Act of 1975.

An election may not be made to have the provisions of this subparagraph apply unless the corporation meets the requirements of section 301(d) of the Tax Reduction Act of 1975.

"(C) 7 percent credit. In the case of property not described in subparagraph (D), the amount of credit determined under this paragraph for the taxable year shall be an amount equal to 7 percent of the qualified investment (as determined under subsections (c) and (d)).

"(D) Transitional rules. The provisions of subparagraphs (A) and (B) shall apply only to—

"(i) property to which subsection (d) does not apply, the construction, reconstruction, or erection of which is completed by the taxpayer after January 21, 1975, but only to the extent of the basis thereof attributable to the construction, reconstruction, or erection after January 21, 1975, and before January 1, 1981,

"(ii) property to which subsection (d) does not apply, acquired by the taxpayer after January 21, 1975, and before January 1, 1981, and placed in service by the taxpayer before January 1, 1981, and

"(iii) property to which subsection (d) applies, but only to the extent of the qualified investment (as determined under subsections (c) and (d)) with respect to qualified progress expenditures made after January 21, 1975, and before January 1, 1981.

For purposes of applying clause (ii) of subparagraph (B), the date 'December 31, 1976,' shall be substituted for the date 'January 21, 1975,' each place it appears in this subparagraph."

—P.L. 95-618, Sec. 301(a)(2)(A), amended subpara. (c)(3)(A), effective 11/9/78.

Prior to amendment, subpara. (c)(3)(A) read as follows:

"(A) to the extent that subsection (a)(2)(C) applies to property which is public utility property, the amount of the qualified investment shall be ½ of the amount determined under paragraph (1)."

—P.L. 95-618, Sec. 301(a)(2)(B), substituted ", the Tax Reform Act of 1976, and the Energy Act of 1978" for "and the Tax Reform Act of 1976" in para. (f)(8), effective 11/9/78.

—P.L. 95-618, Sec. 301(c)(1), added para. (a)(10), effective 11/9/78.

—P.L. 95-600, Sec. 141(e), substituted "December 31, 1983" for "December 31, 1980" each place it appeared in subpara. (a)(2)(E), as added by Sec. 301(a)(1) of P.L. 95-618 . . . Sec. 141(f)(1), deleted Secs. 301(d), (e) and (f), of P.L. 94-12, (which were further amended by Secs. 803(c), (d) and (e) of P.L. 94-455 [This amendment merely deletes historical background, and does not effect actual Internal Revenue Code Secs., see below.] . . . Sec. 141(f)(2), substituted "section 48(n)(1)(B)" for "section 301(e) of the Tax Reduction Act of 1975" and substituted "section 409A" for "section 301(d) of the Tax Reduction Act of 1975" in subpara. (a)(2)(E), as added by Sec. 301(a)(1) of P.L. 95-618, effective with respect to qualified investment for tax. yrs. begin. after '78. Sec. 141(g)(2) of this Act provides as follows:

"(2) Election to have amendments apply during 1978. At the election of the taxpayer, paragraph (1) shall be applied by substituting 'December 31, 1977' for 'December 31, 1978'; except that in the case of a plan in existence before December 31, 1978, any such election shall not affect the required allocation of employer securities attributable to qualified investment for taxable years beginning before January 1, 1979. An election under the preceding sentence shall be made at such time and in such manner as the Secretary of the Treasury or his delegate shall prescribe. Such an election, once made, shall be irrevocable."

—P.L. 95-600, Sec. 311(a), amended subpara. (a)(2)(B), as added by Sec. 301(a)(1) of P.L. 95-615 . . . Sec. 311(c)(1), substituted "To the extent that the credit allowed by section 38 with respect to any public utility property is determined at the rate of 7 percent" for "For the period beginning on January 1, 1981" in subpara. (c)(3)(A) as amended by Sec. 301(a)(2)(A) of P.L. 95-615 . . . Sec. 311(c)(2), substituted "the Energy Tax Act of 1978, and the Revenue Act of 1978" for "and the Energy Tax Act of 1978" in para. (f)(8) (as amended by Sec. 301(a)(2)(B) of P.L. 95-615), effective 11/6/78.

Prior to amendment, subpara. (a)(2)(B), as added by Sec. 301(a)(1) of P.L. 95-615, read as follows:

"(B) Regular percentage. For purposes of this paragraph, the regular percentage is—

"(i) 10 percent with respect to the period beginning on January 21, 1975, and ending on December 31, 1980, or

"(ii) 7 percent with respect to the period beginning on January 1, 1981."

—P.L. 95-600, Sec. 312(a), amended para. (a)(3) . . . Sec. 312(b), amended paras. (a)(7) and (a)(8) . . . deleted para. (a)(9) . . . Sec. 312(c)(2), substituted "described in section 50 (as in effect before its repeal by the Revenue Act of 1978)" for "described in section 50" in paras. (f)(1) and (2), for tax. yrs. end. after '78.

Prior to amendment, para. (a)(3) read as follows:

"(3) Limitation based on amount of tax. Notwithstanding paragraph (1), the credit allowed by section 38 for the taxable year shall not exceed—

"(A) so much of the liability for tax for the taxable year as does not exceed $25,000, plus

"(B) for taxable years ending on or before the last day of the suspension period (as defined in section 48(j)), 25 percent of so much of the liability for tax for the taxable year as exceeds $25,000, or

"(C) for taxable years ending after the last day of such suspension period, 50 percent of so much of the liability for tax for the taxable year as exceeds $25,000.

Subpart E — Tax credits

In applying subparagraph (C) to a taxable year beginning on or before the last day of such suspension period and ending after the last day of such suspension period, the percent referred to in such subparagraph shall be the sum of 25 percent plus the percent which bears the same ratio to 25 percent as the number of days in such year after the last day of the suspension period bears to the total number of days in such year. The amount otherwise determined under this paragraph shall be reduced (but not below zero) by the credit which would have been allowable under paragraph (1) for such taxable year with respect to suspension period property but for the application of section 48(h)(1)."

Prior to amendment, paras. (a)(7)-(9) read as follows:

"(7) Alternative limitation in the case of certain utilities.

"(A) In general. If, for a taxable year ending after calendar year 1974 and before calendar year 1981, the amount of the qualified investment of the taxpayer which is attributable to public utility property is 25 percent or more of his aggregate qualified investment, then subparagraph (C) of paragraph (3) of this subsection shall be applied by substituting for 50 percent his applicable percentage for such year.

"(B) Applicable percentage. The applicable percentage of any taxpayer for any taxable year is—

"(i) 50 percent, plus

"(ii) that portion of the tentative percentage for the taxable year which the taxpayer's amount of qualified investment which is public utility property bears to his aggregate qualified investment.

If the proportion referred to in clause (ii) is 75 percent or more, the applicable percentage of the taxpayer for the year shall be 50 percent plus the tentative percentage for such year.

"(C) Tentative percentage. For purposes of subparagraph (B), the tentative percentage shall be determined under the following table:

"If the taxable year ends in:	The tentative percentage is:
1975 or 1976	50
1977	40
1978	30
1979	20
1980	10

"(D) Public utility property defined. For purposes of this paragraph, the term 'public utility property' has the meaning given to such term by the first sentence of subsection (c)(3)(B).

"(8) Alternative limitation in the case of certain railroads.

"(A) In general. If, for a taxable year ending after calendar year 1976, and before calendar year 1983, the amount of the qualified investment of the taxpayer which is attributable to railroad property is 25 percent or more of his aggregate qualified investment, then subparagraph (C) of paragraph (3) of this subsection shall be applied by substituting for 50 percent his applicable percentage for such year.

"(B) Applicable percentage. The applicable percentage of any taxpayer for any taxable year under this paragraph is—

"(i) 50 percent, plus

"(ii) that portion of the tentative percentage for the taxable year which the taxpayer's amount of qualified investment which is railroad property bears to his aggregate qualified investment.

If the proportion referred to in clause (ii) is 75 percent or more, the applicable percentage of the taxpayer for the year shall be 50 percent plus the tentative percentage for such year.

"(C) Tentative percentage. For purposes of subparagraph (B), the tentative percentage shall be determined under the following table:

"If the taxable year ends in:	The tentative percentage is:
1977 or 1978	50
1979	40
1980	30
1981	20
1982	10

"(D) Railroad property defined. For purposes of this paragraph, the term 'railroad property' means section 38 property used by the taxpayer directly in connection with the trade or business carried on by the taxpayer of operating a railroad (including a railroad switching or terminal company).

"(9) Alternative limitation in the case of certain airlines.

"(A) In general. If, for a taxable year ending after calendar year 1976 and before calendar year 1983, the amount of the qualified investment of the taxpayer which is attributable to airline property is 25 percent or more of his aggregate qualified investment, then subparagraph (C) of paragraph (3) of this subsection shall be applied by substituting for 50 percent his applicable percentage for such year.

"(B) Applicable percentage. The applicable percentage of any taxpayer for any taxable year under this paragraph is—

"(i) 50 percent, plus

"(ii) that portion of the tentative percentage for the taxable year which the taxpayer's amount of qualified investment which is airline property bears to his aggregate qualified investment.

If the proportion referred to in clause (ii) is 75 percent or more, the applicable percentage of the taxpayer for the year shall be 50 percent plus the tentative percentage for such year.

"(C) Tentative percentage. For purposes of subparagraph (B), the tentative percentage shall be determined under the following table:

"If the taxable year ends in:	The tentative percentage is:
1977 or 1978	50
1979	40
1980	30
1981	20
1982	10

"(D) Airline property defined. For purposes of this paragraph, the term 'airline property' means section 38 property used by the taxpayer directly in connection with the trade or business carried on by the taxpayer of the furnishing or sale of transportation as a common carrier by air subject to the jurisdiction of the Civil Aeronautics Board or the Federal Aviation Administration."

—P.L. 95-600, Sec. 313(a), amended para. (c)(5), effective for property acquired by the taxpayer after '78 and for property, the construction, reconstruction or erection of which was completed by taxpayer after '78 (but only to the extent of the basis thereof attributable to construction, reconstruction or erection after '78).

Prior to amendment, para. (c)(5) read as follows:

"(5) Applicable percentage in the case of certain pollution control facilities. Notwithstanding subsection (c)(2), in the case of property—

"(A) with respect to which an election under section 169 applies, and

"(B) the useful life of which (determined without regard to section 169) is not less than 5 years,

50 percent shall be the applicable percentage for purposes of applying paragraph (1) with respect to so much of the adjusted basis of the property as (after the application of section 169(f)) constitutes the amortizable basis for purposes of section 169."

—P.L. 95-600, Sec. 316(a), added subpara. (h)... Sec. 316(b)(1)(A), added "and" at the end of subpara. (e)(1)(A)... Sec. 316(b)(1)(B), deleted "and" at the end of subpara. (e)(1)(B)... Sec. 316(b)(1)(C), deleted subpara. (e)(1)(C)... Sec. 316(b)(2)(A), added "and" at the end of subpara. (e)(2)(A)... Sec. 316(b)(2)(B), substituted a period for ", and" at the end of subpara. (e)(2)(B)... Sec. 316(b)(2)(C), deleted subpara. (e)(2)(C), effective for tax. yrs. end. after 10/31/78.

Prior to amendment, subpara. (e)(1)(C) read as follows:

"(C) a cooperative organization described in section 1381(a),"

Prior to amendment, subpara. (e)(2)(C) read as follows:

"(C) in the case of a cooperative organization, the ratio (i) the numerator of which is its taxable income and (ii) the denominator of which is its taxable income increased by amounts to which section 1382(b) or (c) applies and similar amounts the tax treatment of which is determined without regard to subchapter T (sec. 1381 and following),"

—P.L. 95-600, Sec. 703(a)(1), substituted "subsection (a)(7)(D)" for "subsection (a)(6)(D)" in para. (f)(8)... Sec. 703(a)(2), substituted "Merchant Marine Act, 1936" for "Merchant Marine Act, 1970" in para. (g)(5), effective 10/4/76.

—P.L. 95-600, Sec. 703(j)(9), corrected the instructions in Sec. 1901(b)(1)(C) of P.L. 94-455, to amend para. (a)(4) instead of para. (a)(3).

In 1976, P.L. 94-455, Sec. 503(b)(4), substituted "credit for the elderly" for "retirement income" in subpara. (a)(3)(C), effective for tax. yrs. begin. after '75.

—P.L. 94-455, Sec. 802(a)(1), redesignated paras. (a)(2) through (a)(6) as paras. (a)(3) through (a)(7)... Sec. 802(a)(2), amended para. (a)(1) and added para. (a)(2), effective for tax. yrs. begin. after '75.

Prior to amendment, para. (a)(1) read as follows:

"(1) General rule.

"(A) Ten percent credit. Except as otherwise provided in this paragraph, in the case of a property described in subparagraph (D), the amount of the credit allowed by section 38 for the taxable year shall be an amount equal to 10 percent of the qualified investment (as determined under subsections (c) and (d)).

"(B) Eleven percent credit. Except as otherwise provided in this paragraph, in the case of a corporation which elects to have the provisions of this subparagraph apply, the amount of the credit allowed by section 38 for the taxable year with respect to property described in subparagraph (D) shall be an amount equal to 11 percent of the qualified investment (as determined under subsections (c) and (d)). An election may not be made to have the provisions of this subparagraph apply for the taxable year unless the corporation meets the requirements of section 301(d) of the Tax Reduction Act of 1975. An election by a corporation to have the provisions of this subparagraph apply shall be made at such time, in such form, and in such manner as the Secretary or his delegate may prescribe.

"(C) Seven percent credit. Except as otherwise provided in this paragraph, the amount of credit allowed by section 38 for the taxable year shall be an amount equal to 7 percent of the qualified investment (as determined under subsections (c) and (d)).

"(D) Transitional rules. The provisions of subparagraphs (A) and (B) shall apply only to—

"(i) property to which subsection (d) does not apply, the construction, reconstruction, or erection of which is completed by the taxpayer after January 21, 1975, but only to the extent of the basis thereof attributable to the construction, reconstruction, or erection after January 21, 1975, and before January 1, 1977.

"(ii) property to which subsection (d) does not apply, acquired by the taxpayer after January 21, 1975, and before January 1, 1977, and placed in service by the taxpayer before January 1, 1977, and

"(iii) property to which subsection (d) applies, but only to the extent of the qualified investment (as determined under subsections (c) and (d)) with respect to qualified progress expenditures made after January 21, 1975, and before January 1, 1977."

—P.L. 94-455, Sec. 802(b)(1), substituted "paragraph (3)" for "paragraph (2)" in paras. (a)(4), (a)(5), (a)(6), (a)(7) as redesignated by Sec. 802(a) of this Act... Sec. 802(b)(2), amended subsec. (b)... Sec. 802(b)(3), substituted "subsection

Tax credits — Subpart E

"(a)(2)(C)" for "subsection (a)(1)(C)" in subpara. (c)(3)(A) . . . Sec. 802(b)(4), substituted "subsection (a)(3)" for "subsection (a)(2)" in para. (e)(1) . . . Sec. 802(b)(5), added "and the Tax Reform Act of 1976" after "the Tax Reduction Act of 1975" in the first sentence of para. (f)(8), effective for tax. yrs. begin. after '75.

Prior to amendment, subsec. (b) read as follows:

"(b) Carryback and carryover of unused credits.

"(1) Allowance of credit. If the amount of the credit determined under subsection (a)(1) for any taxable year exceeds the limitation provided by subsection (a)(2) for such taxable year (hereinafter in this subsection referred to as 'unused credit year'), such excess shall be—

"(A) an investment credit carryback to each of the 3 taxable years preceding the unused credit year, and

"(B) an investment credit carryover to each of the 7 taxable years following the unused credit year,

and shall be added to the amount allowable as a credit by section 38 for such years, except that such excess may be a carryback only to a taxable year ending after December 31, 1961. The entire amount of the unused credit for an unused credit year shall be carried to the earliest of the 10 taxable years to which (by reason of subparagraphs (A) and (B)) such credit may be carried, and then to each of the other 9 taxable years to the extent that, because of the limitation contained in paragraph (2), such unused credit may not be added for a prior taxable year to which such unused credit may be carried. In the case of an unused credit for an unused credit year ending before January 1, 1971, which is an investment credit carryover to a taxable year beginning after December 31, 1970 (determined without regard to this sentence), this paragraph shall be applied by substituting '10 taxable years' for '7 taxable years' in subparagraph (B) and by substituting '13 taxable years' for 10 taxable years and '12 taxable years' for '9 taxable years' in the preceding sentence.

"(2) Limitation. The amount of the unused credit which may be added under paragraph (1) for any preceding or succeeding taxable year shall not exceed the amount by which the limitation provided by subsection (a)(2) for such taxable year exceeds the sum of—

"(A) the credit allowable under subsection (a)(1) for such taxable year, and

"(B) the amounts which, by reason of this subsection, are added to the amount allowable for such taxable year and attributable to taxable years preceding the unused credit year.

"(3) Special rules for carryovers from pre-1971 unused credit years. The extent to which an investment credit carryover from an unused credit year ending before January 1, 1971, may be added under paragraph (1) for a taxable year beginning after December 31, 1970, shall be determined without regard to paragraph (2)(A). In determining the excess under paragraph (1) for any taxable year beginning after December 31, 1970, the limitation provided by subsection (a)(2) for such taxable year shall be reduced by the investment credit carryovers from such unused credit years (to the extent such unused credit may not be added for a prior taxable year).

"(4) Taxable year beginning before January 1, 1962. For purposes of determining the amount of an investment credit carryback that may be added under paragraph (1) for a taxable year beginning before January 1, 1962, and ending after December 31, 1961, the amount of the limitation provided by subsection (a)(2) is the amount which bears the same ratio to such limitation as the number of days in such taxable year after December 31, 1961, bears to the total number of days in such year.

"(5) Certain taxable years ending in 1969, 1970, or 1971. The amount which may be added under this subsection for any taxable year beginning after December 31, 1968, and ending after April 18, 1969, and before January 1, 1972, shall not exceed 20 percent of the higher of—

"(A) the aggregate of the investment credit carrybacks and investment credit carryovers to the taxable year, or

"(B) the highest amount computed under subparagraph (A) for any preceding taxable year which began after December 31, 1968, and ended after April 18, 1969,

In the case of a taxable year ending after August 15, 1971, and before January 1, 1972, the percentage contained in the preceding sentence shall be increased by 6 percentage points for each month (or portion thereof) in the taxable year after August 15, 1971.

"(6) Additional 3-year carryover period in certain cases. Any portion of an investment credit carryback or carryover to any taxable year beginning after December 31, 1968, and ending after April 18, 1969, and before January 1, 1971, which—

"(A) may be added under this subsection under the limitation provided by paragraph (2), and

"(B) may not be added under the limitation provided by paragraph (5),

shall be an investment credit carryover to each of the 3 taxable years following the 7th taxable year after the unused credit year, and shall (subject to the provisions of paragraphs (1), (2), and (5)) be added to the amount allowable as a credit by section 38 for such years."

—P.L. 94-455, Sec. 803(a), added para. (f)(9), effective for tax. yrs. begin. after '74.

—P.L. 94-455, Sec. 803(b)(1)(A), substituted "paragraphs (1), (2), and (9)" for "paragraphs (1) and (2)" each place it appeared in subpara. (f)(4)(A) . . . Sec. 803(b)(1)(B), substituted "paragraph (1), (2), or (9)" for "paragraph (1) or (2)" each place it appeared in subpara. (f)(4)(A) . . . Sec. 803(b)(1)(C), substituted "paragraph (2) or the election described in paragraph (9)" for "paragraph (2)" in clause (f)(4)(B)(ii), effective for tax. yrs. begin. after '74.

—P.L. 94-455, Sec. 803(c), and (e), amended Sec. 301(d) of P.L. 94-12, effective for tax. yrs. begin. after '74. Sec. 301(d) of P.L. 94-12, as amended, reads as follows:

"(d) Plan requirements for taxpayers electing additional credit. In order to meet the requirements of this subsection—

"(1) Except as expressly provided in subsections (e) and (f), a corporation (hereinafter in this subsection referred to as the 'employer') must establish an employee stock ownership plan (described in paragraph (2)) which is funded by transfers of employer securities in accordance with the provisions of paragraph (6) and which meets all other requirements of this subsection.

"(2) The plan referred to in paragraph (1) must be a defined contribution plan established in writing which—

"(A) is a stock bonus plan, a stock bonus and a money purchase pension plan, or a profit-sharing plan,

"(B) is designed to invest primarily in employer securities, and

"(C) meets such other requirements (similar to requirements applicable to employee stock ownership plans as defined in section 4975(e)(7) of the Internal Revenue Code of 1954) as the Secretary of the Treasury or his delegate may prescribe.

"(3) The plan must provide for the allocation of all employer securities transferred to it or purchased by it (because of the requirements of section 46(a)(1)(B) of the Internal Revenue Code of 1954) to the account of each participant (who was a participant at any time during the plan year, whether or not he is a participant at the close of the plan year) as of the close of each plan year in an amount which bears substantially the same proportion to the amount of all such securities allocated to all participants in the plan for that plan year as the amount of compensation paid to such participant (disregarding any compensation in excess of the first \$100,000 per year) bears to the compensation paid to all such participants during that year (disregarding any compensation in excess of the first \$100,000 with respect to any participant). Notwithstanding the first sentence of this paragraph, the allocation to participants' accounts may be extended over whatever period may be necessary to comply with the requirements of section 415 of the Internal Revenue Code of 1954. For purposes of this paragraph, the amount of compensation paid to a participant for a year is the amount of such participant's compensation within the meaning of section 415(c)(3) of such Code for such year.

"(4) The plan must provide that each participant has a nonforfeitable right to any stock allocated to his account under paragraph (3), and that no stock allocated to a participant's account may be distributed from that account before the end of the eighty-fourth month beginning after the month in which the stock is allocated to the account except in the case of separation from the service, death, or disability.

"(5) The plan must provide that each participant is entitled to direct the plan as to the manner in which any employer securities allocated to the account of the participant are to be voted.

"(6) On making a claim for credit, adjustment, or refund under section 38 of the Internal Revenue Code of 1954, the employer states in such claim that it agrees, as a condition of receiving any such credit, adjustment, or refund—

"(A) in the case of a taxable year beginning before January 1, 1977, to transfer employer securities forthwith to the plan having an aggregate value at the time of the claim of 1 percent of the amount of the qualified investment (as determined under section 46 (c) and (d) of such Code) of the taxpayer for the taxable year, and

"(B) in the case of a taxable year beginning after December 31, 1976—

"(i) to transfer employer securities to the plan having an aggregate value at the time of the claim of 1 percent of the amount of the qualified investment (as determined under section 46(c) and (d) of such Code) of the employer for the taxable year,

"(ii) except as provided in clause (iii), to effect the transfer not later than 30 days after the time (including extensions) for filing its income tax return for a taxable year, and

"(iii) in the case of an employer whose credit (as determined under section 46(a)(2)(B) of such Code) for a taxable year beginning after December 31, 1976, exceeds the limitations of paragraph (3) of section 46(a) of such Code—

"(I) to effect that portion of the transfer allocable to investment credit carrybacks of such excess credit at the time required under clause (ii) for the unused credit year (within the meaning of section 46(b) of such Code), and

"(II) to effect that portion of the transfer allocable to investment credit carryovers of such excess credit at the time required under clause (ii) for the taxable year to which such portion is carried over.

For purposes of meeting the requirements of this paragraph, a transfer of cash shall be treated as a transfer of employer securities if the cash is, under the plan, used to purchase employer securities.

"(7) Notwithstanding any other provision of law to the contrary, if the plan does not meet the requirements of section 401 of the Internal Revenue Code of 1954—

"(A) stock transferred under paragraph (6) or subsection (e)(3) and allocated to the account of any participant under paragraph (3) and dividends thereon shall not be considered income of the participant or his beneficiary under the Internal Revenue Code of 1954 until actually distributed or made available to the participant or his beneficiary and, at such time, shall be taxable under section 72 of such Code (treating the participant or his beneficiary as having a basis of zero in the contract),

"(B) no amount shall be allocated to any participant in excess of the amount which might be allocated if the plan met the requirements of section 401 of such Code, and

"(C) the plan must meet the requirements of sections 410 and 415 of such Code.

"(8)(A) Except as provided in subparagraph (B)(iii), if the amount of the credit determined under section 46(a)(2)(B) of the Internal Revenue Code of 1954 is recaptured or redetermined in accordance with the provisions of such Code, the amounts transferred to the plan under this subsection and subsection (e) and allocated under the plan shall remain in the plan or in participant accounts, as the case may be, and continue to be allocated in accordance with the plan.

"(B) If the amount of the credit determined under section 46(a)(2)(B) of the Internal Revenue Code of 1954 is recaptured in accordance with the provisions of such Code—

"(i) the employer may reduce the amount required to be transferred to the plan under paragraph (6) of this subsection, or under paragraph (3) of subsection (e), for the current taxable year or any succeeding taxable years by the portion of the amount so recaptured which is attributable to the contribution to such plan,

"(ii) notwithstanding the provisions of paragraph (12), the employer may deduct such portion, subject to the limitations of section 404 of such Code (relating to deductions for contributions to an employees' trust or plan), or

"(iii) if the requirements of subsection (f)(1) are met, the employer may withdraw from the plan an amount not in excess of such portion.

"(C) If the amount of the credit claimed by an employer for a prior taxable year under section 38 of the Internal Revenue Code of 1954 is reduced because of a redetermination which becomes final during the taxable year, and the employer transferred amounts to a plan which were taken into account for purposes of this subsection for that prior taxable year, then—

"(i) the employer may reduce the amount it is required to transfer to the plan under paragraph (6) of this subsection, or under paragraph (3) of subsection (e), for the taxable year or any succeeding taxable year by the portion of the amount of such reduction in the credit or increase in tax which is attributable to the contribution to such plan, or

"(ii) notwithstanding the provisions of paragraph (12), the employer may deduct such portion subject to the limitations of section 404 of such Code.

"(9) For purposes of this subsection, the term—

"(A) 'employer securities' means common stock issued by the employer or a corporation which is a member of a controlled group of corporations which includes the employer (within the meaning of section 1563(a) of the Internal Revenue Code of 1954, determined without regard to section 1563(a)(4) and (e)(3)(C) of such Code) with voting power and dividend rights no less favorable than the voting power and dividend rights of other common stock issued by the employer or such controlling corporation, or securities issued by the employer or such controlling corporation, convertible into such stock, and

"(B) 'value' means the average of closing prices of the employer's securities, as reported by a national exchange on which securities are listed, for the 20 consecutive trading days immediately preceding the date of transfer or allocation of such securities or, in the case of securities not listed on a national exchange, the fair market value as determined in good faith and in accordance with regulations issued by the Secretary of the Treasury or his delegate.

"(10) The Secretary of the Treasury or his delegate shall prescribe such regulations and require such reports as may be necessary to carry out the provisions of this subsection and subsections (e) and (f).

"(11) If the employer fails to meet any requirement imposed under this subsection and subsections (e) and (f) or under any obligation undertaken to comply with the requirement of this subsection and subsections (e) and (f), he is liable to the United States for a civil penalty of an amount equal to the amount involved in such failure. The preceding sentence shall not apply if the taxpayer corrects such failure (as determined by the Secretary of the Treasury or his delegate) within 90 days after notice thereof. For purposes of this paragraph, the term 'amount involved' means an amount determined by the Secretary or his delegate, but not in excess of 1 percent of the qualified investment of the taxpayer for the taxable year under section 46(a)(1)(B) and not less than the product of one-half of one percent of such amount multiplied by the number of months (or parts thereof) during which such failure continues. The amount of such penalty may be collected by the Secretary of the Treasury in the same manner in which a deficiency in the payment of Federal income tax may be collected.

"(12) Notwithstanding any provision of the Internal Revenue Code of 1954 to the contrary, no deductions shall be allowed under section 162, 212, or 404 of such Code for amounts transferred to an employee stock ownership plan and taken into account under this subsection.

"(13)(A) As reimbursement for the expense of establishing the plan, the employer may withhold from amounts due the plan for the taxable year for which the plan is established, or the plan may pay, so much of the amounts paid or incurred in connection with the establishment of the plan as does not exceed the sum of 10 percent of the first $100,000 that the employer is required to transfer to the plan for that taxable year under paragraph (6) (including any amounts transferred under subsection (e) (3)) and 5 percent of any amount in excess of the first $100,000 of such amount.

"(B) As reimbursement for the expense of administering the plan, the employer may withhold from amounts due the plan, or the plan may pay, so much of the amounts paid or incurred during the taxable year as expenses of administering the plan as does not exceed the smaller of—

"(i) the sum of 10 percent of the first $100,000 and 5 percent of any amount in excess of $100,000 of the income from dividends paid to the plan with respect to stock of the employer during the plan year ending with or within the employer's taxable year, or

"(ii) $100,000.

"(14) The return of a contribution made by an employer to an employee stock ownership plan designed to satisfy the requirements of this subsection or subsection (e) (or a provision for such a return) does not fail to satisfy the requirements of this subsection, subsection (e), section 401(a) of the Internal Revenue Code of 1954, or section 403(c)(1) of the Employee Retirement Income Security Act of 1974 if—

"(A) the contribution is conditioned under the plan upon determination by the Secretary of the Treasury that such plan meets the applicable requirements of this subsection, subsection (e), or section 401(a) of such Code,

"(B) the application for such a determination is filed with the Secretary not later than 90 days after the date on which the credit under section 38 is allowed, and

"(C) the contribution is returned within one year after the date on which the Secretary issues notice to the employer that such plan does not satisfy the requirements of this subsection, subsection (e), or section 401(a) of such Code."

—P.L. 94-455, Sec. 803(d), amended Sec. 301 of P.L. 94-12, by adding subsec. (e), effective for tax. yrs. begin. after '76, and by adding subsec. (f), effective for tax. yrs. begin. after '74. Sec. 301(e) of P.L. 94-12 and (f) read as follows:

"(e) Plan requirements for taxpayers electing additional one-half percent credit.

"(1) General rule. For purposes of clause (ii) of section 46(a)(2)(B) of the Internal Revenue Code of 1954, the amount determined under this subsection for a taxable year is an amount equal to the sum of the matching employee contributions for the taxable year which meet the requirements of this subsection.

"(2) Election; basic plan requirements. No amount shall be determined under this subsection for the taxable year unless the corporation elects to have this subsection apply for that year. A corporation may not elect to have the provisions of this subsection apply for a taxable year unless the corporation meets the requirements of subsection (d) and the requirements of this subsection.

"(3) Employer contribution. On making a claim for credit, adjustment, or refund under section 38 of the Internal Revenue Code of 1954, the employer shall state in such claim that the employer agrees, as a condition of receiving any such credit, adjustment, or refund attributable to the provisions of section 46(a)(2)(B)(ii) of such Code, to transfer at the time described in subsection (d)(6)(B) employer securities (as defined in subsection (d)(9)(A)) to the plan having an aggregate value at the time of the transfer of not more than one-half of one percent of the amount of the qualified investment (as determined under subsections (c) and (d) of section 46 of such Code) of the taxpayer for the taxable year. For purposes of meeting the requirements of this paragraph, a transfer of cash shall be treated as a transfer of employer securities if the cash is, under the plan, used to purchase employer securities.

"(4) Requirements relating to matching employee contributions—

"(A) An amount contributed by an employee under a plan described in subsection (d) for the taxable year may not be treated as a matching employee contribution for that taxable year under this subsection unless—

"(i) each employee who participates in the plan described in subsection (d) is entitled to make such a contribution,

"(ii) the contribution is designated by the employee as a contribution intended to be used for matching employer amounts transferred under paragraph (3) to a plan which meets the requirements of this subsection, and

"(iii) the contribution is in the form of an amount paid in cash to the employer or plan administrator not later than 24 months after the close of the taxable year in which the portion of the credit allowed by section 38 of such Code (and determined under clause (ii) of section 46(a)(2)(B) of such Code which the contribution is to match) is allowed, and is invested forthwith in employer securities (as defined in subsection (d)(9)(A)).

"(B) The sum of the amounts of matching employee contributions taken into account for purposes of this subsection for any taxable year may not exceed the value (at the time of transfer) of the employer securities transferred to the plan in accordance with the requirements of paragraph (3) for the year for which the employee contributions are designated as matching contributions.

"(C) The employer may not make participation in the plan a condition of employment and the plan may not require matching employee contributions as a condition of participation in the plan.

"(D) Employee contributions under the plan must meet the requirements of section 401(a)(4) of such Code (relating to contributions).

"(5) A plan must provide for allocation of all employer securities transferred to it or purchased by it under this subsection to the account of each participant (who was a participant at any time during the plan year, whether or not he is a participant at the close of plan year) as of the close of the plan year in an amount equal to his matching employee contributions for the year. Matching employee contributions and amounts so allocated shall be deemed to be allocated under subsection (d)(3).

"(f) Recapture.

"(1) General rule. Amounts transferred to a plan under subsection (d)(6) or (e)(3) may be withdrawn from the plan by the employer if the plan provides that while subject to recapture—

"(A) amounts so transferred with respect to a taxable year are segregated from other plan assets, and

"(B) separate accounts are maintained for participants on whose behalf amounts so transferred have been allocated for a taxable year.

"(2) Coordination with other law. Notwithstanding any other law or rule of law, an amount withdrawn by the employer will neither fail to be considered to be nonforfeitable nor fail to be for the exclusive benefit of participants or their beneficiaries merely because of the withdrawal from the plan of—

"(A) amounts described in paragraph (1), or

"(B) employer amounts transferred under subsection (e)(3) to the plan which are not matched by matching employee contributions or which are in excess of the limitations of section 415 of such Code,

nor will the withdrawal of any such amount be considered to violate the provisions of section 403(c)(1) of the Employee Retirement Income Security Act of 1974."

—P.L. 94-455, Sec. 805(a), added subsec. (g), effective for tax. yrs. begin. after '75 in the case of property placed in service after 12/31/75.

—P.L. 94-455, Sec. 1607(b)(1)(B)(i), substituted "857(b)(2)(B)" for "857(b)(2)(C)" following "section 852(b)(2)(D) or" in subpara. (e)(2)(B) . . . Sec. 1607(b)(1)(B)(ii), added "determined without regard to any deduction for capital gains dividends (as defined in section 857(b)(3)(C)) and by excluding any net

Tax credits   Subpart E

capital gain" immediately before the period at the end of para. (e)(2), effective for tax. yrs. end. after 10/4/76. Sec. 1608(c) of this Act provided the following exceptions to the effective date:

"(c) Alternative tax and net operating loss. The amendments made by sections 1606 and 1607 shall apply to taxable years ending after the date of the enactment of this Act, except that in the case of a taxpayer which has a net operating loss (as defined in section 172(c) of the Internal Revenue Code of 1954) for any taxable year ending after the date of enactment of this Act for which the provisions of part II of subchapter M of chapter 1 of subtitle A of such Code apply to such taxpayer, such loss shall not be a net operating loss carryback under section 172 of such Code to any taxable year ending on or before the date of enactment of this Act."

—P.L. 94-455, Sec. 1701(b), added para. (a)(8), effective for tax. yrs. begin. 10/4/76.

—P.L. 94-455, Sec. 1703, added para. (a)(9), effective for tax. yrs. end. after '76 and before '83.

—P.L. 94-455, Sec. 1901(a)(4)(A), substituted "section 408(f)" for "section 408(e)" following "distributions to owner-employees" in the second sentence of para. (a)(4), as previously redesignated by this Act, effective for tax. yrs. begin. after '76.

—P.L. 94-455, Sec. 1901(a)(4)(B), substituted "47 U.S.C. 222(a)(5)" for "47 U.S.C., sec. 222(a)(5)" in clause (c)(3)(B)(iii), effective for tax. yrs. begin. after '76.

—P.L. 94-455, Sec. 1901(b)(1)(C), deleted subpara. (a)(3)(B), added "and" at the end of subpara. (a)(3)(A), redesignated subpara. (a)(3)(C) as subpara. (a)(3)(B), (all of which were redesignated by Sec. 802(a) of this Act as being in para. (a)(4)), effective for tax. yrs. begin. after '76.

Prior to amendment, subpara. (a)(3)(B) read as follows:

"(B) section 35 (relating to partially tax-exempt interest, and"

—P.L. 94-455, Sec. 1901(b)(13)(A), substituted "Secretary" for "Secretary or his delegate" in paras. (a)(6), (d)(4), (d)(6), (f)(1), (f)(2), (f)(3), (f)(7), and each place it appeared in (f)(8), effective for tax. yrs. begin. after '76.

—P.L. 94-455, Sec. 2112(a)(2), added para. (c)(5), effective for property acquired by taxpayer, and which construction, reconstruction, etc., was completed after '76, in tax. yrs. begin. after '76.

In 1975, P.L. 94-12, Sec. 301(a), amended para. (a)(1), effective date of enactment (3/29/75).

Prior to amendment, para. (a)(1) read as follows:

"(1) General rule. The amount of the credit allowed by section 38 for the taxable year shall be equal to 7 percent of the qualified investment (as defined in subsection (c))."

—P.L. 94-12, Sec. 301(a), "Plan requirements for taxpayers electing additional credit", was retroactively amended by Sec. 803(c) of P.L. 94-455, see above.

—P.L. 94-12, Sec. 301(b)(2), added para. (a)(6), effective for tax. yrs. end. after 12/31/74.

—P.L. 94-12, Sec. 301(b)(1), rewrote subpara. (c)(3)(A), effective with respect to property placed in service after 1/21/75, in tax. yrs. end. after 1/21/75.

Prior to amendment, subpara. (c)(3)(A) read as follows:

"(A) In the case of section 38 property which is public utility property, the amount of the qualified investment shall be 4/7 of the amount determined under paragraph (1)"

—P.L. 94-12, Sec. 302(b)(1), added para. (c)(4), effective for tax. yrs. end. after 12/31/74.

—P.L. 94-12, Sec. 302(a), redesignated subsecs. (d) and (e) as (e) and (f) and added new subsec. (d), effective for tax. yrs. end. after 12/31/74.

—P.L. 94-12, Sec. 301(b)(3), added para. (f)(8), effective for tax. yrs. end. after 12/31/74.

In 1974, P.L. 93-406, Sec. 2001(g)(2)(B), added "section 72(m)(5)(B) (relating to 10 percent tax on premature distributions to owner-employees)," in para. (a)(3), effective for distributions made in taxable years beginning after 12/31/75.

—P.L. 93-406, Sec. 2002(g)(2), added "section 408(e) (relating to additional tax on income from certain retirement accounts)," in para. (a)(3), effective 1/1/75.

—P.L. 93-406, Sec. 2005(c)(4), added "section 402(e) (relating to lump sum distributions)," in para. (a)(3), effective for distributions or payments made after 12/31/73 in taxable years beginning after 12/31/73.

In 1971, P.L. 92-178, Sec. 102(a)(1)(A), substituted "3 years" for "4 years" in subsec. (c)(2) . . . Sec. 102(a)(1)(B), substituted "5 years" for "6 years" each place it appeared in subsec. (c)(2) . . . Sec. 102(a)(1)(C), substituted "7 years" for "8 years" each place it appeared in subsec. (c)(2), effective for property described in Code Sec. 50.

—P.L. 92-178, Sec. 102(b), substituted a new second sentence for "For purposes of this paragraph, the useful life of any property shall be determined as of the time such property is placed in service by the taxpayer." in subsec. (c)(2), effective for property described in Code Sec. 50.

—P.L. 92-178, Sec. 105(a), substituted "4/7" for "3/7" in subpara. (c)(3)(A) . . . Sec. 105(b)(1), inserted "or" to the end of clause (c)(3)(B)(ii), struck out clauses (c)(3)(B)(iii) & (iv) and added new clause (c)(3)(B)(iii) . . . Sec. 105(b)(2), added a new sentence to the end of subpara. (c)(3)(B) . . . Sec. 105(b)(3), and added new subpara. (c)(3)(C), effective for property described in Code Sec. 50.

Prior to amendment, clauses (c)(3)(B)(iii) and (iv) read as follows:

"(iii) telephone service, or

"(iv) telegraph service by means of domestic telegraph operations (as defined in section 222(a)(5) of the Communications Act of 1934, as amended: 47 U.S.C., sec. 222(a)(5))."

—P.L. 92-178, Sec. 105(c), added subsec. (e), effective for property described in Code Sec. 50

—P.L. 92-178, Sec. 105(e), provided as follows:

"(e) Application of Section 203(e) of Revenue Act of 1964. Section 203(e) of the Revenue Act of 1964 shall not apply to public utility property to which section 46(e) of the Internal Revenue Code of 1954 (as added by subsection (c)) applies."

—P.L. 92-178, Sec. 106(a), added para. (b)(3) . . . Sec. 106(b), added a sentence to the end of para. (b)(1), effective for tax. yrs. begin. after 12/31/70

—P.L. 92-178, Sec. 106(c)(1), amended para. (b)(5), effective for tax. yrs. end. after 8/15/71.

Prior to amendment, para. (b)(5) read as follows:

"(5) Taxable years beginning after December 31, 1968, and ending after April 18, 1969. The amount which may be added under this subsection for any taxable year beginning after December 31, 1968, and ending after April 18, 1969, shall not exceed 20 percent of the higher of—

"(A) the aggregate of the investment credit carrybacks and investment credit carryovers to the taxable year, or

"(B) the highest amount computed under subparagraph (A) for any preceding taxable year which began after December 31, 1968, and ended after April 18, 1969."

—P.L. 92-178, Sec. 106(c)(2), inserted "and before January 1, 1971," after "April 18, 1969," and substituted "following the 7th taxable year after the unused credit year" for "following the last taxable year for which such portion may be added under paragraph (1)", effective for tax. yrs. begin. after 12/31/70

—P.L. 92-178, Sec. 107(a), repealed para. (c)(4), effective for casualties and thefts occurring after 8/15/71.

Prior to repeal, para. (c)(4) read as follows:

"(4) Certain replacement property. For purposes of paragraph (1), if section 38 property is placed in service by the taxpayer to replace property which was—

"(A) destroyed or damaged by fire, storm, shipwreck, or other casualty, or

"(B) stolen,

the basis of such section 38 property (in the case of new section 38 property), or the cost of such section 38 property (in the case of used section 38 property), which (but for this paragraph) would be taken into account under paragraph (1) shall be reduced by an amount equal to the amount received by the taxpayer as compensation, by insurance or otherwise, for the property so destroyed, damaged, or stolen, or to the adjusted basis of such property, whichever is the lesser. No reduction in basis or cost shall be made under the preceding sentence in any case in which the reduction in qualified investment attributable to the substitution required by section 47(a)(1) with respect to the property so destroyed, damaged, or stolen (determined without regard to section 47(a)(4)) is greater than the reduction described in the preceding sentence."

—P.L. 92-178, Sec. 108(a), added para. (d)(3), effective for leases entered into after 9/22/71.

In 1969, P.L. 91-172, Sec. 301(b)(4), inserted "section 56 (relating to minimum tax for tax preferences)," before "section 531" in para. (a)(3), effective for tax. yrs. end. after 12/31/69.

—P.L. 91-172, Sec. 401(e)(1), amended para. (a)(5), effective for tax. yrs. end. on or after 12/31/70.

Prior to amendment, para. (a)(5) read as follows:

"(5) Affiliated groups. In the case of an affiliated group, the $25,000 amount specified under subparagraphs (A) and (B) of paragraph (2) shall be reduced for each member of the group by apportioning $25,000 among the members of such group in such manner as the Secretary or his delegate shall by regulations prescribe. For purposes of the preceding sentence, the term 'affiliated group' has the meaning assigned to such term by section 1504(a), except that all corporations shall be treated as includible corporations (without any exclusion under section 1504(b))."

—P.L. 91-172, Sec. 703(b), added paras. (b)(5) and (6), effective 12/30/69.

In 1967, P.L. 90-225, Sec. 2(a), deleted para. (b)(3), effective for investment credit carrybacks from taxable years ending after 7/31/67.

Prior to repeal, para. (b)(3) read as follows:

"(3) Effect of net operating loss carryback. To the extent that the excess described in paragraph (1) arises by reason of a net operating loss carryback, subparagraph (A) of paragraph (1) shall not apply."

In 1966, P.L. 89-800, Sec. 3(a), amended para. (a)(2) read as follows, effective tax. yrs. end. after 10/9/66.

Prior to amendment, para.(a)(2) read as follows:

"(2) Limitation based on amount of tax. Notwithstanding paragraph (1), the credit allowed by section 38 for the taxable year shall not exceed—

"(A) so much of the liability for tax for the taxable year as does not exceed $25,000, plus

"(B) 25 percent of so much of the liability for tax for the taxable year as exceeds $25,000."

—P.L. 89-800, Sec. 3(b)(1), amended subpara. (b)(1)(B) . . . Sec. 3(b)(2), substituted "10 taxable years" for "8 taxable years" and substituted "other 9 taxable years" for "other 7 taxable years" in para. (b)(1), effective as provided in Sec. 4 of this Act, which provides:

"Sec. 4. The amendments made by this Act shall apply to taxable years ending after October 9, 1966, except that the amendments made by section 3(b) shall apply only if the fifth taxable year following the unused credit year ends after December 31, 1966."

Prior to amendment, subpara. (b)(1)(B) read as follows:

"(B) an investment credit carryover to each of the 5 taxable years following the unused credit year,"

—P.L. 89-384, Sec. 1(c)(1), added "and any additional tax imposed for the taxable year by section 1351(d)(1) (relating to recoveries by reason of foreign expropriation losses)," in para. (a)(3), effective for amounts received after 12/31/64 in respect of foreign expropriation losses (as defined in Code Sec. 1351(b)) sustained after 12/31/58.

1,199

—P.L. 89-389, Sec. 2(b)(5), substituted ", section 154 (relating to personal holding company tax, or section 1378 (relating to tax on certain capital gains of subchapter S corporations)," for "or by section 541 (relating to personal holding company tax)" in para. (a)(3), effective for taxable years of electing small business corporations beginning after 4/14/66, but not to sales or exchanges occurring before 2/24/66.

In **1964**, P.L. 88-272, Sec. 201(d)(4), deleted subpara. (a)(3)(B), and redesignated subparas. (a)(3)(C) and (D) as (a)(3)(B) and (C), effective for tax. yrs. in which dividends received credit not allowed.

In **1962**, P.L. 87-834, Sec. 2, added Code Sec. 46, effective for tax. yrs. end. after '61.

"SEC. 47. CERTAIN DISPOSITIONS, ETC., OF SECTION 38 PROPERTY.

"(a) General rule. Under regulations prescribed by the Secretary—

"(1) Early disposition, etc. If during any taxable year any property is disposed of, or otherwise ceases to be section 38 property with respect to the taxpayer, before the close of the useful life which was taken into account in computing the credit under section 38, then the tax under this chapter for such taxable year shall be increased by an amount equal to the aggregate decrease in the credits allowed under section 38 for all prior taxable years which would have resulted solely from substituting, in determining qualified investment, for such useful life the period beginning with the time such property was placed in service by the taxpayer and ending with the time such property ceased to be section 38 property.

"(2) Property becomes public utility property. If during any taxable year any property taken into account in determining qualified investment becomes public utility property (within the meaning of section 46(c)(3)(B)), then the tax under this chapter for such taxable year shall be increased by an amount equal to the aggregate decrease in the credits allowed under section 38 for all prior taxable years which would have resulted solely from treating the property, for purposes of determining qualified investment, as public utility property (after giving due regard to the period before such change in use). If the application of this paragraph to any property is followed by the application of paragraph (1) to such property, proper adjustment shall be made in applying paragraph (1).

"(3) Property ceases to be progress expenditure property.

"(A) In general. If during any taxable year any property taken into account in determining qualified investment under section 46(d) ceases (by reason of sale or other disposition, cancellation or abandonment of contract, or otherwise) to be, with respect to the taxpayer, property which, when placed in service, will be new section 38 property, then the tax under this chapter for such taxable year shall be increased by an amount equal to the aggregate decrease in the credits allowed under section 38 for all prior taxable years which would have resulted solely from reducing to zero the qualified investment taken into account with respect to such property.

"(B) Certain excess credit recaptured. Any amount which would have been applied as a reduction of the qualified investment in property by reason of paragraph (4) of section 46(c) but for the fact that a reduction under such paragraph cannot reduce qualified investment below zero shall be treated as an amount required to be recaptured under subparagraph (A) for the taxable year in which the property is placed in service.

"(C) Certain sales and leasebacks. Under regulations prescribed by the Secretary a sale by, and leaseback to, a taxpayer who, when the property is placed in service, will be a lessee to whom section 48(d) applies shall not be treated as a cessation described in subparagraph (A) to the extent that the qualified investment which will be passed through to the lessee under section 48(d) with respect to such property is not less than the qualified progress expenditures properly taken into account by the lessee with respect to such property.

"(D) Coordination with paragraphs (1) and (5). If, after property is placed in service, there is a disposition or other cessation described in paragraph (1), or a disposition, cessation, or change in expected use described in paragraph (5), then paragraph (1) or (5), as the case may be, shall be applied as if any credit, which was allowable by reason of section 46(d) and which has not been required to be recaptured before such disposition, cessation, or change in use were allowable for the taxable year the property was placed in service.

"(4) Special rules for commuter highway vehicles.

"(A) Useful life. For purposes of this subsection, 3 years shall be treated as the useful life which was taken into account in computing the credit under section 38 with respect to any commuter highway vehicle (as defined in section 46(c)(6)(B)).

"(B) Change in use. If less than 80 percent of the mileage use of any commuter highway vehicle by the taxpayer during that portion of any taxable year which is within the first 36 months of the operation of such vehicle by the taxpayer meets the requirements of section 46(c)(6)(B), then the tax under this chapter for such taxable year shall be increased by an amount equal to the aggregate decrease in the credits allowed under section 38 for all prior taxable years which would have resulted solely from treating such vehicle, for purposes of determining qualified investment, as not being a commuter highway vehicle. If the application of this subparagraph to any property is followed by the application of paragraph (1) to such property, proper adjustment shall be made in applying paragraph (1).

"(5) Special rules for recovery property.

"(A) General rule. If, during any taxable year, section 38 recovery property is disposed of, or otherwise ceases to be section 38 property with respect to the taxpayer before the close of the recapture period, then, except as provided in subparagraph (D), the tax under this chapter for such taxable year shall be increased by the recapture percentage of the aggregate decrease in the credits allowed under section 38 for all prior taxable years which would have resulted solely from reducing to zero the qualified investment taken into account with respect to such property.

"(B) Recapture percentage. For purposes of subparagraph (A), the recapture percentage shall be determined in accordance with the following table:

If the recovery property ceases to be section 38 property within—	The recapture percentage is: For property other than 3-year property	For 3-year property
One full year after placed in service	100	100
One full year after the close of the period described in clause (i)	80	66
One full year after the close of the period described in clause (ii)	60	33
One full year after the close of the period described in clause (iii)	40	0
One full year after the close of the period described in clause (iv)	20	0

"(C) Property ceases to be progress expenditure property. If, during any taxable year, any recovery property taken into account in determining qualified investment under section 46(d)(1) ceases to be progress expenditure property (as determined under paragraph (3)) or becomes, with respect to the taxpayer, recovery property of a character other than that expected in determining the applicable percentage under section 46(d)(1)(B)(i), then the tax under this chapter for such taxable year shall be adjusted in accordance with regulations prescribed by the Secretary.

"(D) Limitation. The tax for the taxable year shall be increased under subparagraph (A) only with respect to the credits allowed under section 38 which were used to reduce tax liability. In the case of credits not so used to reduce tax liability, the carrybacks and carryovers under section 39 shall be appropriately adjusted.

"(E) Definitions and special rules.

"(i) Section 38 recovery property. For purposes of this paragraph, the term 'section 38 recovery property' means any section 38 property which is recovery property (within the meaning of section 168).

"(ii) Recapture period. For purposes of this paragraph, the term 'recapture period' means, with respect to any recovery property, the period consisting of the first full year after the property is placed in service and the 4 succeeding full years (the 2 succeeding full years in the case of 3-year property).

"(iii) Classification of property. For purposes of this paragraph, property shall be classified as provided in section 168(e).

"(iv) Paragraph (1) not to apply. Paragraph (1) shall not apply with respect to any recovery property.

"(v) Treatment as recovery property. Any reference in this paragraph to recovery property shall be treated as including a reference to any property to which section 168 (as amended by the Tax Reform Act of 1986) applies.

"(6) Carrybacks and carryovers adjusted. In the case of any cessation described in paragraph (1), (3), or (5) or any change in use described in paragraph (2) or (4), the carrybacks and carryovers under section 39 shall be adjusted by reason of such cessation (or change in use).

"(7) Aircraft used outside the United States after April 18, 1969.

"(A) General rule. Any aircraft which was new section 38 property for the taxable year in which it was placed in service and which is used outside the United States under a qualifying lease or leases shall be treated as not ceasing to be section 38 property by reason of such use until such aircraft has been so used for a period or periods exceeding 3½ years in total. For purposes of the preceding sentence, the registration of such aircraft under the laws of a foreign country shall be treated as use outside the United States.

"(B) Computation of qualified investment. If an aircraft described in subparagraph (A) is disposed of or otherwise ceases to be section 38 property, the increase under paragraph (1) and the adjustment under paragraph (6) shall not be greater than the increase or adjustment which would result if the qualified investment of such aircraft were based upon a useful life equal to the lesser of (i) the actual useful life of such aircraft with respect to the taxpayer, or, (ii) twice the number of full calendar months during which such aircraft was registered by the Administrator of the Federal Aviation Agency and was used in the United States, operated to and from the United States, or operated under contract with the United States. For purposes of the preceding sentence, an aircraft shall be treated as used in the United States for any calendar month beginning after such aircraft was placed in service, if such month is included in a taxable year ending before January 1, 1971, for which such aircraft was section 38 property (determined without regard to this paragraph).

"(C) Qualifying lease defined. For purposes of subparagraph (A), the term 'qualifying lease' means a lease from an air carrier (as defined in section 101 of the Federal Aviation Act of 1958, as amended (49 U.S.C. 1301)) which complies with the provisions of the Federal Aviation Act of 1958, as amended, and the rules and regulations promulgated by the Secretary of Transportation thereunder, but only if such lease was executed after April 18, 1969.

"(8) Motion picture films and video tapes.

"(A) Disposition where depreciation exceeds 90 percent of basis or cost. A qualified film (within the meaning of section 48(k)(1)(B)) which has an applicable percentage determined under section 48(k)(3) shall cease to be section 38 property with respect to the taxpayer at the close of the first day on which the aggregate amount allowable as a deduction under section 167 equals or exceeds 90 percent of the basis or cost of such film (adjusted for any partial dispositions).

"(B) Other dispositions. In the case of a disposition of the exclusive right to display a qualified film which has an applicable percentage determined under section 48(k)(3) in one or more mediums of publication or exhibition in one or more specifically defined geographical areas over the remaining initial period of commercial exploitation of the film or tape in such geographical areas, the taxpayer shall be considered to have disposed of all or part of such film or tape and shall recompute the credit earned on all of his basis or cost or on that part of the basis or cost properly allocable to that part of the film or tape disposed of. In the case of an affiliated group of corporations, a transfer within the affiliated group shall not be treated as a disposition until there is a transfer outside the group. For purposes of the preceding sentence, the term 'affiliated group' has the meaning given to such term by section 1504 (determined as if section 1504(b) did not include paragraph (3) thereof. For purposes of this paragraph, section 1504(a) shall be applied by substituting '50 percent' for '80 percent' each place it appears.

"(9) Aircraft leased to foreign persons or entities.

"(A) In general. Any aircraft which was new section 38 property for the taxable year in which it was placed in service and which is used by any foreign person or entity (as defined in section 168(h)(2)) under a qualified lease (as defined in paragraph (7)(C)) entered into before January 1, 1990, shall not be treated as ceasing to be section 38 property by reason of such use until such aircraft has been so used for a period or periods exceeding 3 years in total.

"(B) Recapture period extended. For purposes of paragraphs (1) and (5)(B) of this subsection, any period during which there was use described in subparagraph (A) of an aircraft shall be disregarded.

"(b) Section not to apply in certain cases. Subsection (a) shall not apply to—

"(1) a transfer by reason of death, or

"(2) a transaction to which section 381(a) applies.

For purposes of subsection (a), property shall not be treated as ceasing to be section 38 property with respect to the taxpayer by reason of a mere change in the form of conducting the trade or business so long as the property is retained in such trade or business as section 38 property and the taxpayer retains a substantial interest in such trade or business.

"(c) Special rule. Any increase in tax under subsection (a) shall not be treated as tax imposed by this chapter for purposes of determining the amount of any credit allowable under subpart A, B, D, or G.

"(d) Increases in nonqualified nonrecourse financing.

"(1) In general. If, as of the close of the taxable year, there is a net increase with respect to the taxpayer in the amount of nonqualified nonrecourse financing (within the meaning of section 46(c)(8)) with respect to any property to which section 46(c)(8) applied, then the tax under this chapter for such taxable year shall be increased by an amount equal to the aggregate decrease in credits allowed under section 38 for all prior taxable years which would have resulted from reducing the credit base (as defined in section 46(c)(8)(C)) taken into account with respect to such property by the amount of such net increase. For purposes of determining the amount of credit subject to the early disposition or cessation rules of subsection (a), the net increase in the amount of the nonqualified nonrecourse financing with respect to the property shall be treated as reducing the property's credit base (and correspondingly reducing the qualified investment in the property) in the year in which the property was first placed in service.

"(2) Transfers of debt more than 1 year after initial borrowing not treated as increasing nonqualified nonrecourse financing. For purposes of paragraph (1), the amount of nonqualified nonrecourse financing (within the meaning of section 46(c)(8)(D)) with respect to the taxpayer shall not be treated as increased by reason of a transfer of (or agreement to transfer) any evidence of an indebtedness if such transfer occurs (or such agreement is entered into) more than 1 year after the date such indebtedness was incurred.

"(3) Special rules for certain energy property.

"(A) In general. In the case of the second taxable year following the taxable year in which any qualified energy property (within the meaning of section 46(c)(8)(F)) is placed in service by the taxpayer and any succeeding taxable year, the taxpayer, for purposes of paragraph (1), shall be treated as increasing the amount of nonqualified nonrecourse financing (within the meaning of section 46(c)(8)) with respect to such property for such taxable year in an amount equal to the credit recapture amount (if any).

"(B) Credit recapture amount. For purposes of this paragraph, the term 'credit recapture amount' means an amount equal to the excess (if any) of—

"(i) the total amount of principal to be paid as of the close of any taxable year under a nonrecourse level payment loan (as defined in section 46(c)(8)(F)(iv)) with respect to such property, over

"(ii) the sum of —

"(I) the amount of principal actually paid as of the close of such taxable year, plus

"(II) the sum of the credit recapture amounts with respect to such property for all preceding taxable years.

"(C) Special rules for determining principal to be paid. For purposes of subparagraph (B)(i), in determining the amount of the principal to be paid under a level payment loan, such determination shall be made as if such loan was to be fully repaid by the end of a period equal to the earlier of—

"(i) the class life (as defined in section 168(i)(1)) of the property or, if the property has no class life, a similar period determined by the Secretary, or

"(ii) the period at the end of which full repayment is to occur under the terms of the loan.

"(D) Special rule for certain cumulative deficiencies. If the excess of—

"(i) the amount of the total scheduled principal payments under a loan described in subparagraph (B)(i) as of the close of the taxable year, over

"(ii) the total principal actually paid under such loan as of the close of such taxable year,

is equal to or greater than the amount of such total scheduled payments for the 5-taxable year period ending with such taxable year, then, notwithstanding subparagraph (B), the credit recapture amount for such taxable year shall be equal to the principal remaining to be paid as of the close of such taxable year over the sum of the credit recapture amounts with respect to such property for all preceding taxable years.

"(E) Special rule for certain dispositions.

"(i) In general. If any property which is held by the taxpayer and to which this paragraph applies is disposed of by the taxpayer, then for purposes of paragraph (1) and notwithstanding subparagraph (B), the credit recapture amount for the taxpayer shall be an amount equal to the unpaid principal on the loan described in subparagraph (B)(i) as of the date of disposition reduced by the sum of the credit recapture amounts with respect to such property for all preceding taxable years;

"(ii) Assumptions, etc. Any amount of the loan described in subparagraph (B)(i) which is assumed or taken subject to by any person shall be treated for purposes of clause (i) as not reducing unpaid principal with respect to such loan.

"(F) Deleted

"(G) Additional interest. In the case of any increase in tax under paragraph (1) by reason of the application of this paragraph, there shall be added to such tax interest on such tax (determined at the underpayment rate established under section 6621) as if the increase in tax under paragraph (1) was for the taxable year in which the property was placed in service.

"(e) Transfers between spouses or incident to divorce. In the case of any transfer described in subsection (a) of section 1041

"(1) subsection (a) of this section shall not apply, and

"(2) the same tax treatment under this section with respect to the transferred property shall apply to the transferee as would have applied to the transferor."

In 1990, P.L. 101-508, Sec. 11801(c)(8)(A), substituted ", or" for the comma at the end of para. (b)(1), substituted a period for ", or" at the end of para. (b)(2), and deleted para. (b)(3), effective 11/5/90, except as provided in Sec. 11821(b) of this Act, which reads as follows:

"(b) Savings provision. If —

"(1) any provision amended or repealed by this part applied to—

"(A) any provision amended or repealed by this part applied to—

"(A) any transaction occurring before the date of the enactment of this Act [11/5/90],

"(B) any property acquired before such date of enactment [11/5/90], or

"(C) any item of income, loss, deduction, or credit taken into account before such date of enactment [11/5/90], and

"(2) the treatment of such transaction, property, or item under such provision would (without regard to the amendments made by this part) affect liability for tax for periods ending after such date of enactment [11/5/90],

nothing in the amendments made by this part shall be construed to affect the treatment of such transaction, property, or item for purposes of determining liability for tax for periods ending after such date of enactment [11/5/90]."

Prior to amendment, para. (b)(3) read as follows:

"(3) a transfer to which subsection (c) of section 374 (relating to exchanges under the final system plan of ConRail) applies."

In 1988, P.L. 100-647, Sec. 1002(a)(18), substituted "46(c)(8)(C)" for "48(c)(8)(C)" in para. (d)(1) . . . Sec. 1002(a)(26)(A), added clause (a)(5)(E)(v) . . . Sec. 1002(a)(26)(B), deleted the last sentence of subpara. (a)(5)(D) . . . Sec. 1002(a)(26)(C), substituted "168(e)" for "168(c)" in clause (a)(5)(E)(iii) . . . Sec. 1002(a)(27), substituted "section 168(h)(2)" for "section 168(j)(4)(C)" in subpara. (a)(9)(A) . . . Sec. 1002(a)(28), substituted "class life (as defined in section 168(i)(1))" for "present class life (as defined in section 168(g)(2))" and substituted "no class life (as defined in section 168(i)(1))" for "no present class life (as defined in section 168(g)(2))" in clause (d)(3)(C)(i), effective for property placed in service after 12/31/86, in tax. yrs. end. after 12/31/86.

Prior to deletion, the last sentence of subpara. (d)(5)(D) read as follows:

"If, prior to a disposition to which this subsection applies, any portion of any credit is not allowable with respect to any property by reason of section 168(i)(3), such portion shall be treated (for purposes of this subparagraph) as not having been used to reduce tax liability."

—P.L. 100-647, Sec. 1007(g)(3)(A), substituted "D, or G" for "or D" in subsec. (c), effective for tax. yrs. begin. after 12/31/86.

In 1986, P.L. 99-514, Sec. 1511(c)(2), substituted "determined at the underpayment rate established under section 6621" for "determined under section 6621" in subpara. (d)(3)(G), effective for purposes of determining interest for periods after 12/31/86.

—P.L. 99-514, Sec. 1802(a)(5)(A), added para. (a)(9), effective for property placed in service by the taxpayer after 5/23/83, in tax. yrs. end. after 5/23/83, and for property placed in service by the taxpayer on or before 5/23/83, if the lease to the tax-exempt entity is entered into after 5/23/83. Exceptions and special rules are provided by Sec. 31(g)(2)-(20) of P.L. 98-369, reproduced in the notes following Code Sec. 168.

—P.L. 99-514, Sec. 1844(b)(1), substituted "reducing the credit base (as defined in section 48(c)(8)(C))" for "reducing the qualified investment" in, and added the last sentence to, para. (d)(1) . . . Sec. 1844(b)(2), deleted subpara. (d)(3)(F) . . . Sec. 1844(d)(4), added "reduced by the sum of the credit recapture amounts with respect to such property for all preceding taxable years" before the semicolon in clause (d)(3)(E)(i), effective for property placed in service after 7/18/84 in tax. yrs. end. after 7/18/84, except in the case of any property to which the amendments made by Sec. 211(f) of P.L. 97-34 do not apply.

Prior to deletion, subpara. (d)(3)(F) read as follows:

"(F) Application with subsection (a). The amount of any increase in tax under subsection (a) with respect to any property to which this paragraph applies shall be determined by reducing the qualified investment with respect to such property by the aggregate credit recapture amounts for all taxable years under this paragraph."

In 1985, P.L. 99-121, Sec. 103(b)(6), substituted "For property other than 3-year property" for "For 15-year, 10-year, and 5-year property" in the table in subpara. (a)(5)(B), effective for property placed in service by the taxpayer after 3/15/84. For exceptions and special rules, see Sec. 111(g)(2)-(4) of P.L. 98-369, reproduced in note following Code Sec. 168.

In 1984, P.L. 98-443, Sec. 9(p), substituted "Secretary of Transportation" for "Civil Aeronautics Board" in subpara. (a)(7)(C), effective 1/1/85.

—P.L. 98-369, Sec. 421(b)(7), added subsec. (e), effective for transfers after 7/18/84 in tax. yrs. ending after 7/18/84. Sec. 421(d)(2), (3) and (4) of this Act provides:

"(2) Election to have amendments apply to transfers after 1983. If both spouses or former spouses make an election under this paragraph, the amendments made by this section shall apply to all transfers made by such spouses (or former spouses) after December 31, 1983.

"(3) Exception for transfers pursuant to existing decrees. Except in the case of an election under paragraph (2), the amendments made by this section shall not apply to transfers under any instrument in effect on or before the date of the enactment of this Act unless both spouses (or former spouses) elect to have such amendments apply to transfers under such instrument.

"(4) Election. Any election under paragraph (2) or (3) shall be made in such manner, at such time, and subject to such conditions, as the Secretary of the Treasury or his delegate may by regulations prescribe."

—P.L. 98-369, Sec. 431(b)(2), amended the heading of subsec. (d) and paras. (d)(1) and (2) . . . Sec. 431(d)(4), substituted "increasing the amount of nonqualified nonrecourse financing (within the meaning of section 46(c)(8))" for "ceasing to be at risk" in subpara. (d)(3)(A) . . . Sec. 431(d)(5), deleted "other than a loan described in section 46(c)(8)(B)(ii)" in clause (d)(3)(B)(i), effective for property placed in service after 7/18/84 in tax. yrs. ending after 7/18/84, except not effective for any property to which the amendments made by section 211(f) of the Economic Recovery Tax Act of 1981 do not apply. Sec. 431(e) of the Act provides:

"(2) Amendments may be elected retroactively. At the election of the taxpayer, the amendments made by this section shall apply as if included in the amendments made by section 211(f) of the Economic Recovery Tax Act of 1981. Any election made under the preceding sentence shall apply to all property of the taxpayer to which the amendments made by such section 211(f) apply and shall be made at such time and in such manner as the Secretary of the Treasury or his delegate may by regulations prescribe."

Prior to amendment, the heading of subsec. (d) and paras. (d)(1) and (2) read as follows:

"(d) Property ceasing to be at risk.

"(1) In general. If the taxpayer ceases to any extent to be at risk (within the meaning of section 46(c)(8)(B)) with respect to any amount in connection with section 38 property, then the tax under this chapter for such taxable year shall be increased by an amount equal to the aggregate decrease in credits allowed under section 38 for all prior taxable years which would have resulted from substituting, in determining qualified investment, the amount determined under section 46(c)(8) with respect to such property if, on the date the property was placed in service, the taxpayer had not been at risk with respect to the amount he ceased to be at risk to.

"(2) Certain transfers not treated as ceasing to be at risk. If, after the 12-month period after the date on which a taxpayer borrows an amount from a qualified person (within the meaning of section 46(c)(8)(D)) with respect to which such taxpayer is considered at risk under section 46(c)(8)(B), the qualified person transfers or agrees to transfer any evidence of such indebtedness to a person who is not a qualified person, then, for purposes of paragraph (1), the taxpayer shall not be treated as ceasing to be at risk with respect to such amount."

—P.L. 98-369, Sec. 474(o)(8), substituted "under section 39" for "under section 46(b)" in paras. (a)(5) and (6) . . . Sec. 474(o)(9), substituted "subpart A, B, or D" for "subpart A" in subsec. (c), effective for tax. yrs. begin. after 12/31/83 and for carrybacks from tax. yrs. begin. after 12/31/83 except as provided in Sec. 475(c) which reads as follows:

"(c) Clarification of effect of amendments on investment tax credit. Nothing in the amendments made by section 474(o) [P.L. 98-369] shall be construed as reducing the amount of any credit allowable for qualified investment in taxable years beginning before January 1, 1984."

In 1983, P.L. 97-448, Sec. 102(e)(3)(A), substituted "section 46(c)(8)(D)" for "section 48(c)(8)(D)" and substituted "section 46(c)(8)(B)" for "section 48(c)(8)(B)" in para. (d)(2) . . . Sec. 102(c)(3)(B), substituted "section 46(c)(8)(F)" for "section 46(c)(8)(E)" in subpara. (d)(3)(A), effective for property placed in service after 12/31/80 in tax. yrs. end. after 12/31/80.

In 1982, P.L. 97-248, Sec. 208(a)(2)(B), added the last sentence at end of subpara. (a)(5)(D), effective for agreements entered into after 7/1/82, or to property placed in service after 7/1/82. For transitional rules see Sec. 208(d)(2)-(6) of this Act reproduced in note following Code Sec. 168.

In 1981, P.L. 97-34, Sec. 211(f)(2), added subsec. (d), effective as provided in Sec. 211(i)(5) of this Act which reads as follows:

"(5) At risk rules.

"(A) In general. The amendment made by subsection (f) shall not apply to—

"(i) property placed in service by the taxpayer on or before February 18, 1981, and

"(ii) property placed in service by the taxpayer after February 18, 1981, where such property is acquired by the taxpayer pursuant to a binding contract entered into on or before that date.

"(B) Binding contract. For purposes of subparagraph (A)(ii), property acquired pursuant to a binding contract shall, under regulations prescribed by the Secretary, include property acquired in a manner so that it would have qualified as pretermination property under section 49(b) (as in effect before its repeal by the Revenue Act of 1978)."

—P.L. 97-34, Sec. 211(g)(1), redesignated paras. (a)(5), (6) and (7) as paras. (a)(6), (7) and (8) and added new para. (a)(5) . . . Sec. 211(g)(2)(A), amended subpara. (a)(3)(D) . . . Sec. 211(g)(2)(B), substituted "paragraph (1), (3), or (5)" for "paragraph (1) or (3)" in para. (a)(6) as redesignated by Sec. 211(g)(1) of this Act . . . Sec. 211(g)(2)(C), substituted "paragraph (6)" for "paragraph (5)" in subpara. (a)(7)(B) as redesignated by Sec. 211(g)(1) of this Act, effective for property placed in service after 12/31/80.

Prior to amendment, subpara. (a)(3)(D) read as follows:

"(D) Coordination with paragraph (1). If, after property is placed in service, there is a disposition or other cessation described in paragraph (1), paragraph (1) shall be applied as if any credit which was allowable by reason of section 46(d) and which has not been required to be recaptured before such cessation were allowable for the taxable year the property was placed in service."

In 1978, P.L. 95-618, Sec. 241(b)(1), redesignated para. (a)(4) as para. (a)(5) and added new para. (a)(4) . . . Sec. 241(b)(2), substituted "paragraph (2) or (4)" for "paragraph (2)" in para. (a)(5) as redesignated . . . Sec. 241(b)(3), substituted "paragraph (5)" for "paragraph (4)" in subpara. (a)(6)(B), effective 11/9/78.

—P.L. 95-600, Sec. 317(a), deleted "or" at the end of para. (b)(1), substituted ", or" for the period at the end of para. (b)(2), and added para. (b)(3), effective for tax. yrs. end. after 3/31/76.

In 1976, P.L. 94-455, Sec. 804(b), added para. (a)(7), effective for tax. yrs. begin. after '74.

—P.L. 94-455, Sec. 1906(b)(13)(A), substituted "Secretary" for "Secretary or his delegate" each place it appeared in subsec (a), effective for tax. yrs. begin. after '76.

In 1975, P.L. 94-12, Sec. 302(b)(2), redesignated former para. (3) as (4) and added new para. (3), effective for tax. yrs. end. after 12/31/74.

—P.L. 94-12, Sec. 302(c)(1), substituted "paragraph (1) or (3)" for "paragraph (1)" in para. (a)(4), as redesignated by Sec. 302(b)(2) of this Act, effective for tax. yrs. end. after 12/31/74.

—P.L. 94-12, Sec. 302(c)(2), substituted "paragraph (4)" for "paragraph (3)" in para. (a)(5) and subpara. (a)(6)(B), effective for tax. yrs. end. after 12/31/74.

In 1971, P.L. 92-178, Sec. 102(c), substituted "3½ years" for "4 years" in subsec. (a)(6)(A), effective for leases executed after 4/18/69. Sec. 102(d)(2) of this Act provides:

"(2) In redetermining qualified investment for purposes of section 47(a) of the Internal Revenue Code of 1954 in the case of any property which ceases to be section 38 property with respect to the taxpayer after August 15, 1971, or which becomes public utility property after such date, section 46(c)(2) of such Code shall be applied as amended by subsection (a)."

—P.L. 92-178, Sec. 107(a), repealed para. (a)(4), effective for casualties and thefts occurring after 8/15/71.

Prior to repeal, para. (a)(4) read as follows:

"(4) Property destroyed by casualty, etc. No increase shall be made under paragraph (1) and no adjustment shall be made under paragraph (3) in any case in which—

"(A) any property is disposed of, or otherwise ceases to be section 38 property with respect to the taxpayer, on account of its destruction or damage by fire, storm, shipwreck, or other casualty, or by reason of its theft,

"(B) section 38 property is placed in service by the taxpayer to replace the property described in subparagraph (A), and

"(C) the reduction in basis or cost of such section 38 property described in the first sentence of section 46(c)(4) is equal to or; greater than the reduction in qualified investment which (but for this paragraph) would be made by reason of the substitution required by paragraph (1) with respect to the property described in subparagraph (A).

Subparagraphs (B) and (C) shall not apply with respect to any casualty or theft occurring after April 18, 1969."

—P.L. 92-178, Sec. 107(b), repealed para. (a)(5), except if replacement property described in subpara. 47(a)(5)(B) is not property described in Code Sec. 50.

Prior to repeal, para. (a)(5) read as follows:

"(5) Certain property replaced after April 18, 1969. In any case in which—

"(A) section 38 property is disposed of, and

"(B) property which would be section 38 property but for section 49 is placed in service by the taxpayer to replace the property disposed of,

the increase under paragraph (1) and the adjustment under paragraph (4) shall not be greater than the increase or adjustment which would result if the qualified investment of the property described in subparagraph (B) (determined as if such property were section 38 property) were substituted for the qualified investment of the property disposed of (as determined under paragraph (1)). Except in the case of a disposition by reason of a casualty or theft occurring before April 19, 1969, the preceding sentence shall apply only if the section 38 property disposed of is replaced within 6 months after the date of such disposition."

—added para. (a)(6), effective for tax. yrs. end. after 4/18/69.

In 1969, P.L. 91-172, Sec. 703(c), added the last sentence of subsec. (a)(4) and added para. (a)(5).

In 1962, P.L. 87-834, Sec. 2, added Code Sec. 47, effective for tax. yrs. end. after '61.

"SEC. 48. DEFINITIONS; SPECIAL RULES.

"(a) Section 38 property.

"(1) In general. Except as provided in this subsection, the term 'section 38 property means'—

"(A) tangible personal property, (other than an air conditioning or heating unit), or

"(B) other tangible property (not including a building and its structural components) but only if such property—

"(i) is used as an integral part of manufacturing, production, or extraction or of furnishing transportation, communications, electrical energy, gas, water, or sewage disposal services, or

"(ii) constitutes a research facility used in connection with any of the activities referred to in clause (i), or

"(iii) constitutes a facility used in connection with any of the activities referred to in clause (i) for the bulk storage of fungible commodities (including commodities in a liquid or gaseous state), or

"(C) elevators and escalators, but only if—

"(i) the construction, reconstruction, or erection of the elevator or escalator is completed by the taxpayer after June 30, 1963, or

"(ii) the elevator or escalator is acquired after June 30, 1963, and the original use of such elevator or escalator commences with the taxpayer and commences after such date, or

"(D) single purpose agricultural or horticultural structures; or

"(E) in the case of a qualified rehabilitated building, that portion of the basis which is attributable to qualified rehabilitation expenditures (within the meaning of subsection (g)), or

"(F) in the case of qualified timber property (within the meaning of section 194(c)(1)), that portion of the basis of such property constituting the amortizable basis acquired during the taxable year (other than that portion of such amortizable basis attributable to property which otherwise qualifies as section 38 property) and taken into account under section 194 (after the application of section 194(b)(1)), or

"(G) a storage facility (not including a building or its structural components) used in connection with the distribution of petroleum or any primary product of petroleum.

Such term includes only property to which section 168 applies without regard to any useful life) and any other property with respect to which depreciation (or amortization in lieu of depreciation) is allowable and having a useful life (determined as of the time such property is placed in service) of 3 years or more. The preceding sentence shall not apply to property described in subparagraph (F) and, for purposes of this subpart, the useful life of such property shall be treated as its normal growing period.

"(2) Property used outside the United States.

"(A) In general. Except as provided in subparagraph (B), the term 'section 38 property' does not include property which is used predominantly outside the United States.

"(B) Exceptions. Subparagraph (A) shall not apply to—

"(i) any aircraft which is registered by the Administrator of the Federal Aviation Agency and which is operated to and from the United States or is operated under contract with the United States;

"(ii) rolling stock which is used within and without the United States and which is—

"(I) of a domestic railroad corporation providing transportation subject to subchapter I of chapter 105 of title 49, or

"(II) of a United States person (other than a corporation described in subclause (I)) but only if the rolling stock is not leased to one or more foreign persons for periods aggregating more than 12 months in any 24-month period;

"(iii) any vessel documented under the laws of the United States which is operated in the foreign or domestic commerce of the United States;

"(iv) any motor vehicle of a United States person (as defined in section 7701(a)(30)) which is operated to and from the United States;

"(v) any container of a United States person which is used in the transportation of property to and from the United States;

"(vi) any property (other than a vessel or an aircraft) of a United States person which is used for the purpose of exploring for, developing, removing, or transporting resources from the outer Continental Shelf (within the meaning of section 2 of the Outer Continental Shelf Lands Act, as amended and supplemented; 43 U.S.C. 1331);

"(vii) any property which is owned by a domestic corporation (other than a corporation which has an election in effect under section 936) or by a United States citizen (other than a citizen entitled to the benefits of section 931 or 933) and which is used predominantly in a possession of the United States by such a corporation or such a citizen, or by a corporation created or organized in, or under the law of, a possession of the United States;

"(viii) any communications satellite (as defined in section 103(3) of the Communications Satellite Act of 1962, 47 U.S.C. 702(3)), or any interest therein, of a United States person;

"(ix) any cable, or any interest therein, of a domestic corporation engaged in furnishing telephone service to which section 46(c)(3)(B)(iii) applies (or of a wholly owned domestic subsidiary of such a corporation), if such cable is part of a submarine cable system which constitutes part of a communication link exclusively between the United States and one or more foreign countries;

"(x) any property (other than a vessel or an aircraft) of a United States person which is used in international or territorial waters within the northern portion of the Western Hemisphere for the purpose of exploring for, developing, removing, or transporting resources from ocean waters or deposits under such waters, and

"(xi) any property described in subsection (l)(3)(A)(ix) which is owned by a United States person and which is used in international or territorial waters to generate energy for use in the United States.

"For purposes of clause (x), the term 'northern portion of the Western Hemisphere' means the area lying west of the 30th meridian west of Greenwich, east of the international dateline, and north of the Equator, but not including any foreign country which is a country of South America.

"(3) Property used for lodging. Property which is used predominantly to furnish lodging or in connection with the furnishing of lodging shall not be treated as section 38 property. The preceding sentence shall not apply to—

"(A) nonlodging commercial facilities which are available to persons not using the lodging facilities on the same basis as they are available to persons using the lodging facilities,

"(B) property used by a hotel or motel in connection with the trade or business of furnishing lodging where the predominant portion of the accommodations is used by transients,

"(C) coin-operated vending machines and coin-operated washing machines and dryers, and

"(D) a certified historic structure to the extent of that portion of the basis which is attributable to qualified rehabilitation expenditures.

"(4) Property used by certain tax-exempt organizations. Property used by an organization (other than a cooperative described in section 521) which is exempt from the tax imposed by this chapter shall be treated as section 38 property only if such property is used predominantly in an unrelated trade or business the income of which is subject to tax under section 511. If the property is debt-financed property (as defined in section 514(b)), the basis or cost of such property for purposes of computing qualified investment under section 46(c) shall include only that percentage of the basis or cost which is the same percentage as is used under section 514(a), for the year the property is placed in service, in computing the amount of gross income to be taken into account during such taxable year with respect to such property. If any qualified rehabilitated building is used by the tax-exempt organization pursuant to a lease, this paragraph shall not apply to that portion of the basis of such building which is attributable to qualified rehabilitation expenditures.

"(5) Property used by governmental units or foreign persons or entities.

"(A) In general. Property used—

"(i) by the United States, any State or political subdivision thereof, any possession of the United States, or any agency or instrumentality of any of the foregoing, or

"(ii) by any foreign person or entity (as defined in section 168(h)(2)(C)), but only with respect to property to which section 168(h)(2)(A)(iii) applies (determined after the application of section 168(h)(2)(B)),

"shall not be treated as section 38 property.

"(B) Exception for short-term leases.

"(i) In general. This paragraph and paragraph (4) shall not apply to any property by reason of use under a lease with a term of less than 6 months (determined under section 168(i)(3)).

"(ii) Exception for certain oil drilling property and certain containers. For purposes of this paragraph and paragraph (4), clause (i) shall be applied by substituting the lease term limitation in section 168(h)(1)(C)(ii) for the lease term limitation in clause (i) in the case of property which is leased to a foreign person or entity and—

"(I) which is used in offshore drilling for oil and gas (including drilling vessels, barges, platforms, and drilling equipment) and support vessels with respect to such property, or

"(II) which is a container described in section 48(a)(2)(B)(v) (without regard to whether such container is used outside the United States) or container chassis or trailer but only if such container, chassis, or trailer has a present class life of not more than 6 years.

"(C) Exception for qualified rehabilitated buildings leased to governments, etc. If any qualified rehabilitated building is leased to a governmental unit (or a foreign person or entity), this paragraph shall not apply to that portion of the basis of such building which is attributable to qualified rehabilitation expenditures.

"(D) Special rules for partnerships, etc. For purposes of this paragraph and paragraph (4), rules similar to the rules of paragraphs (5) and (6) of section 168(h) shall apply.

"(E) Cross reference. For provision providing special rules for the application of this paragraph and paragraph (4), see section 168(h).

"(6) Livestock. Livestock (other than horses) acquired by the taxpayer shall be treated as section 38 property, except that if substantially identical livestock is sold or otherwise disposed of by the taxpayer during the one-year period beginning 6 months before the date of such acquisition and if section 47(a) (relating to certain dispositions, etc., of section 38 property) does not apply to such sale or other disposition, then, unless such sale or other disposition constitutes an involuntary conversion (within the meaning of section 1033), the cost of the livestock acquired shall, for purposes of this subpart, be reduced by an amount equal to the amount realized on such sale or other disposition. Horses shall not be treated as section 38 property.

"(7) Property completed abroad or predominantly of foreign origin.

"(A) In general. Property shall not be treated as section 38 property if—

"(i) such property was completed outside the United States, or

"(ii) less than 50 percent of the basis of such property is attributable to value added within the United States.

"For purposes of this subparagraph, the term 'United States' includes the Commonwealth of Puerto Rico and the possessions of the United States.

"(B) Period of application of paragraph. Except as provided in subparagraph (D), subparagraph (A) shall apply only with respect to property described in section 50 (as in effect before its repeal by the Revenue Act of 1978)—

"(i) the construction, reconstruction, or erection of which by the taxpayer is begun after August 15, 1971, and on or before the date of termination of Proclamation 4074, or

"(ii) which is acquired pursuant to an order placed on or before the date of termination of Proclamation 4074, unless acquired pursuant to an order which the taxpayer establishes was placed before August 16, 1971.

"(C) President may exempt articles. If the President of the United States shall at any time determine that the application of subparagraph (A) to any article or class of articles is not in the public interest, he may by Executive order specify that subparagraph (A) shall not apply to such article or class of articles. Subparagraph

(A) shall not apply to an article or class of articles for the period specified in such Executive order. Any period specified under the preceding sentence shall not apply to property ordered before (or to property the construction, reconstruction, or erection of which began before) the date of the Executive order specifying such period, except that, if the President determines it to be in the public interest, such period shall apply to property ordered (or property the construction, reconstruction, or erection of which began) after a date (before the date of the Executive order) specified in the Executive order.

"(D) Countries maintaining trade restrictions or engaging in discriminatory acts. If, on or after the date of the termination of Proclamation 4074, the President determines that a foreign country—

"(i) maintains nontariff trade restrictions, including variable import fees, which substantially burden United States commerce in a manner inconsistent with provisions of trade agreements, or

"(ii) engages in discriminatory or other acts (including tolerance of international cartels) or policies unjustifiably restricting United States commerce,

"he may provide by Executive order for the application of subparagraph (A) to any article or class of articles manufactured or produced in such foreign country for such period as may be provided by Executive order.

"(8) Repealed.
"(9) Repealed.
"(10) Boilers fueled by oil or gas.

"(A) In general. The term section 38 property does not include any boiler primarily fueled by petroleum or petroleum products (including natural gas) unless the use of coal is precluded by Federal air pollution regulations (or by State air pollution regulations in effect on October 1, 1978) or unless the use of such boiler will be an exempt use within the meaning of subparagraph (B). For purposes of the preceding sentence, the term 'petroleum or petroleum products' does not include petroleum coke or petroleum pitch.

"(B) Exempt use defined. For purposes of subparagraph (A), the term 'exempt use' means—

"(i) use in an apartment, hotel, motel, or other residential facility,

"(ii) use in a vehicle, aircraft, or vessel, or in transportation by pipeline,

"(iii) use on a farm for farming purposes (within the meaning of section 6420(c)),

"(iv) use in—
"(I) a shopping center,
"(II) an office building,
"(III) a wholesale or retail establishment,
"(IV) any other facility which is not an integral part of manufacturing, processing, or mining, or
"(V) any facility for the production of electric power having a heat rate of less than 9,500 Btu's per kilowatt hour and which is capable of converting to synthetic fuels (as certified by the Secretary),

"(v) use in the exploration for, or the development, extraction, transmission, or storage of, crude oil, natural gas, or natural gas liquids, and

"(vi) use in Hawaii.

"Except as provided in clauses (iv)(V) and (vi) of the preceding sentence, the term 'exempt use' does not include use of a boiler which is public utility property (within the meaning of section 46(f)(5)).

"(b) New section 38 property.

" For purposes of this subpart—

"(1) In general. The term 'new section 38 property' means section 38 property the original use of which commences with the taxpayer. Such term includes any section 38 property the reconstruction of which is completed by the taxpayer, but only with respect to that portion of the basis which is properly attributable to such reconstruction.

"(2) Special rule for sale-leasebacks. For purposes of the first sentence of paragraph (1), in the case of any section 38 property which—

"(A) is originally placed in service by a person, and

"(B) is sold and leased back by such person, or is leased to such person, within 3 months after the date such property was originally placed in service,

such property shall be treated as originally placed in service not earlier than the date on which such property is used under the leaseback (or lease) referred to in subparagraph (B). The preceding sentence shall not apply to any property if the lessee and lessor of such property make an election under this sentence. Such an election, once made, may be revoked only with the consent of the Secretary.

"(3) Special rule for energy property. The principles of paragraph (2) shall be applicable in determining whether the original use of property commences with the taxpayer for purposes of section 48(l)(2)(B)(ii).

"(c) Used section 38 property.

"(1) In general. For purposes of this subpart, the term 'used section 38 property' means section 38 property acquired by purchase after December 31, 1961, which is not new section 38 property. Property shall not be treated as 'used section 38 property' if, after its acquisition by the taxpayer, it is used by a person who used such property before such acquisition (or by a person who bears a relationship described in section 179(d)(2)(A) or (B) to a person who used such property before such acquisition).

"(2) Dollar limitation.

"(A) In general. The cost of used section 38 property taken into account under section 46(c)(1)(B) for any taxable year shall not exceed $125,000 ($150,000 for taxable years beginning after 1987). If such cost exceeds $125,000 (or $150,000 as the case may be), the taxpayer shall select (at such time and in such manner as the Secretary shall by regulations prescribe) the items to be taken into account, but only to the extent of an aggregate cost of $125,000 (or $150,000). Such a selection, once made, may be changed only in the manner, and to the extent, provided by such regulations.

"(B) Married individuals. In the case of a husband or wife who files a separate return, the limitation under subparagraph (A) shall be $62,500 ($75,000 for taxable years beginning after 1987). This subparagraph shall not apply if the spouse of the taxpayer has no used section 38 property which may be taken into account as qualified investment for the taxable year of such spouse which ends within or with the taxpayer's taxable year.

"(C) Controlled groups. In the case of a controlled group, the amount specified under subparagraph (A) shall be reduced for each component member of the group by apportioning such amount among the component members of such group in accordance with their respective amounts of used section 38 property which may be taken into account.

"(D) Partnerships and S corporations. In the case of a partnership, the limitation contained in subparagraph (A) shall apply with respect to the partnership and with respect to each partner. A similar rule shall apply in the case of an S corporation and its shareholders.

"(3) Definitions. For purposes of this subsection—

"(A) Purchase. The term 'purchase' has the meaning assigned to such term by section 179(d)(2).

"(B) Cost. The cost of used section 38 property does not include so much of the basis of such property as is determined by reference to the adjusted basis of other property held at any time by the person acquiring such property. If property is disposed of (other than by reason of its destruction or damage by fire, storm, shipwreck, or other casualty, or its theft) and used section 38 property similar or related in service or use is acquired as a replacement therefor in a transaction to which the preceding sentence does not apply, the cost of the used section 38 property acquired shall be its basis reduced by the adjusted basis of the property replaced. The cost of used section 38 property shall not be reduced with respect to the adjusted basis of any property disposed of if, by reason of section 47, such disposition involved an increase of tax or a reduction of the unused credit carrybacks or carryovers described in section 39.

"(C) Controlled group. The term 'controlled group' has the meaning assigned to such term by section 1563(a), except that the phrase 'more than 50 percent' shall be substituted for the phrase 'at least 80 percent' each place it appears in section 1563(a)(1).

"(d) Certain leased property.

"(1) General rule. A person (other than a person referred to in section 46(e)(1)) who is a lessor of property may (at such time, in such manner, and subject to such conditions as are provided by regulations prescribed by the Secretary) elect with respect to any new section 38 property (other than property described in paragraph (4)) to treat the lessee as having acquired such property for an amount equal to—

"(A) except as provided in subparagraph (B), the fair market value of such property, or

"(B) if the property is leased by a corporation which is a component member of a controlled group (within the meaning of section 38(c)(3)(B)) to another corporation which is a component member of the same controlled group, the basis of such property to the lessor.

"(2) Special rule for certain short term leases.

"(A) In general. A person (other than a person referred to in section 46(e)(1)) who is a lessor of property described in paragraph (4) may (at such time, in such manner, and subject to conditions as are provided by regulations prescribed by the Secretary) elect with respect to such property to treat the lessee as having acquired a portion of such property for the amount determined under subparagraph (B).

"(B) Determination of lessee's investment. The amount for which a lessee of property described in paragraph (4) shall be treated as having acquired a portion of such property is an amount equal to a fraction, the numerator of which is the term of the lease and the denominator of which is the class life of the property leased (determined under section 167(m)), of the amount for which the lessee would be treated as having acquired the property under paragraph (1).

"(C) Determination of lessor's qualified investment. The qualified investment of a lessor of property described in paragraph (4) in any such property with respect to which he has made an election under this paragraph is an amount equal to his qualified investment in such property (as determined under section 46(c)) multiplied by a fraction equal to the excess of one over the fraction used under subparagraph (B) to determine the lessee's investment in such property.

"(3) Limitations. The elections provided by paragraphs (1) and (2) may be made with respect to property which would be new section 38 property if acquired by the lessee. For purposes of the preceding sentence and section 46(c), the useful life of property in the hands of the lessee is the useful life of such property in the hands of the lessor. If a lessor makes the election provided by paragraph (1) with respect to any property, the lessee shall be treated for all purposes of this subpart as having acquired such property. If a lessor makes the election provided by paragraph (2) with respect to any property, the lessee shall be treated for all purposes of this subpart as having acquired a fractional portion of such property, equal to the fraction determined under paragraph (2)(B) with respect to such property.

"(4) Property to which paragraph (2) applies. Paragraph (2) shall apply only to property which—

"(A) is new section 38 property,
"(B) has a class life (determined under section 167(m)) in excess of 14 years,
"(C) is leased for a period which is less than 80 percent of its class life, and
"(D) is not leased subject to a net lease (within the meaning of section 57(c)(1)(B) (as in effect on the day before the date of enactment of the Tax Reform Act of 1986)).

"(5) Coordination with basis adjustment. In the case of any property with respect to which an election is made under this subsection—

"(A) subsection (q) (other than paragraph (4)) shall not apply with respect to such property,

"(B) the lessee of such property shall include ratably in gross income over the shortest recovery period which could be applicable under section 168 with respect to such property an amount equal to 50 percent of the amount of the credit allowable under section 38 to the lessee with respect to such property, and

"(C) in the case of a disposition of such property to which section 47 applies, this paragraph shall be applied in accordance with regulations prescribed by the Secretary.

"(6) Coordination with at-risk rules.

"(A) Extension of at-risk rules to certain lessors.

"(i) In general. If —

"(I) a lessor makes an election under this subsection with respect to any at-risk property leased to an at-risk lessee, and

"(II) but for this clause, section 46(c)(8) would not apply to such property in the hands of the lessor,

"section 46(c)(8) shall apply to the lessor with respect to such property.

"(ii) Exceptions. Clause (i) shall not apply —

"(I) if the lessor manufactured or produced the property,

"(II) if the property has a readily ascertainable fair market value, or

"(III) in circumstances which the Secretary determines by regulations to be circumstances where the application of clause (i) is not necessary to carry out the purposes of section 46(c)(8).

"(B) Requirement that lessor be at risk. In the case of any property which, in the hands of the lessor, is property to which section 46(c)(8) applies, the amount of the credit allowable to the lessee under section 38 with respect to such property by reason of an election under this subsection shall at no time exceed the credit which would have been allowable to the lessor with respect to such property (determined without regard to section 46(e)(3)) if —

"(i) the lessor's basis in such property were equal to the lessee acquisition amount, and

"(ii) no election had been made under this subsection.

"(C) Lessee subject to at-risk limitations.

"(i) In general. In the case of any lease where —

"(I) the lessee is an at-risk lessee,

"(II) the property is at-risk property, and

"(III) the at-risk percentage is less than the required percentage,

"any credit allowable under section 38 to the lessee by reason of an election under this subsection (hereinafter in this paragraph referred to as the 'total credit') shall be allowable only as provided in subparagraph (D).

"(ii) At-risk percentage. For purposes of this paragraph, the term 'at-risk percentage' means the percentage obtained by dividing —

"(I) the present value (as of the time the lease is entered into) of the aggregate lease at-risk payments, by

"(II) the lessee acquisition amount.

"For purposes of subclause (I), the present value shall be determined by using a discount rate equal to the underpayment rate in effect under section 6621 as of the time the lease is entered into.

"(iii) Required percentage. For purposes of clause (i)(III), the term 'required percentage' means the sum of —

"(I) 2 times the sum of the percentages applicable to the property under section 46(a), plus

"(II) 10 percent.

"In the case of 3-year property, such term means 60 percent of the required percentage determined under the preceding sentence.

"(iv) Lessee acquisition amount. For purposes of this paragraph, the term 'lessee acquisition amount' means the amount for which the lessee is treated as having acquired the property by reason of an election under this subsection.

"(v) Lease at-risk payment. For purposes of this paragraph, the term 'lease at-risk payment' means any rental payment —

"(I) which the lessee is required to make under the lease in all events, and

"(II) with respect to which the lessee is not protected against loss through nonrecourse financing, guarantees, stop-loss agreements, or other similar arrangements.

"(D) Year for which credit allowable.

"(i) In general. Except as provided in clause (ii), in any case to which subparagraph (C)(i) applies, the portion of the total credit allowable for any taxable year shall be an amount which bears the same ratio to such total credit as —

"(I) the aggregate rental payments made by the lessee under the lease during such taxable year, bears to

"(II) the lessee acquisition amount.

"(ii) Remaining amount allowable for year in which aggregate rental payments exceed required percentage of acquisition amount. The total credit (to the extent not allowable for a preceding taxable year) shall be allowable for the first taxable year as of the close of which the aggregate rental payments made by the lessee under the lease equal or exceed the required percentage (as defined in subparagraph (C)(iii)) of the lessee acquisition amount.

"(E) Definition of at-risk lessee and at-risk property. For purposes of this paragraph —

"(i) At-risk lessee. The term 'at-risk lessee' means any lessee who is a taxpayer described in section 465(a)(1).

"(ii) At-risk property. The term 'at-risk property' means any property used by an at-risk lessee in connection with an activity with respect to which any loss is subject to limitation under section 465.

"(F) Special rules for subparagraphs (C) and (D).

"(i) Subparagraphs (C) and (D) apply in lieu of other at-risk rules. In the case of any election under this subsection, paragraphs (8) and (9) of section 46(c) and subsection (d) of section 47 shall only apply with respect to the lessor.

"(ii) Application to partnerships and S corporations. For purposes of subparagraphs (C) and (D), rules similar to the rules of subparagraph (E) of section 46(c)(8) shall apply.

"(iii) Subsequent reductions in at-risk amount. Under regulations prescribed by the Secretary, the principles of subsection (d) of section 47 shall apply for purposes of subparagraphs (C) and (D).

"(G) Regulations. The Secretary shall prescribe such regulations as may be necessary to carry out the purposes of this paragraph, including regulations —

"(i) providing for such adjustments as may be appropriate where expenses connected with the lease are borne by the lessor, and

"(ii) providing the extent to which contingencies in the lease will be disregarded.

"(e) [Repealed.]

"(f) Estates and trusts.

"In the case of an estate or trust —

"(1) the qualified investment for any taxable year shall be apportioned between the estate or trust and the beneficiaries on the basis of the income of the estate or trust allocable to each, and

"(2) any beneficiary to whom any investment has been apportioned under paragraph (1) shall be treated (for purposes of this subpart) as the taxpayer with respect to such investment, and such investment shall not (by reason of such apportionment) lose its character as an investment in new section 38 property or used section 38 property, as the case may be.

"(g) Special rules for qualified rehabilitated buildings.

" For purposes of this subpart —

"(1) Qualified rehabilitated building. For purposes of this subsection —

"(A) In general. The term 'qualified rehabilitated building' means any building (and its structural components) if —

"(i) such building has been substantially rehabilitated,

"(ii) such building was placed in service before the beginning of the rehabilitation, and

"(iii) in the case of any building other than a certified historic structure, in the rehabilitation process —

"(I) 50 percent or more of the existing external walls of such building are retained in place as external walls,

"(II) 75 percent or more of the existing external walls of such building are retained in place as internal or external walls, and

"(III) 75 percent or more of the existing internal structural framework of such building is retained in place.

"(B) Building must be first placed in service before 1936. In the case of a building other than a certified historic structure, a building shall not be a qualified rehabilitated building unless the building was first placed in service before 1936.

"(C) Substantially rehabilitated defined.

"(i) In general. For purposes of subparagraph (A)(i), a building shall be treated as having been substantially rehabilitated only if the qualified rehabilitation expenditures during the 24-month period selected by the taxpayer (at the time and in the manner prescribed by regulations) and ending with or within the taxable year exceed the greater of —

"(I) the adjusted basis of such building (and its structural components), or

"(II) $5,000.

"The adjusted basis of the building (and its structural components) shall be determined as of the beginning of the 1st day of such 24-month period, or of the holding period of the building, whichever is later. For purposes of the preceding sentence, the determination of the beginning of the holding period shall be made without regard to any reconstruction by the taxpayer in connection with the rehabilitation.

"(ii) Special rule for phased rehabilitation. In the case of any rehabilitation which may reasonably be expected to be completed in phases set forth in architectural plans and specifications completed before the rehabilitation begins, clause (i) shall be applied by substituting '60-month period' for '24-month period'.

"(iii) Lessees. The Secretary shall prescribe by regulation rules for applying this subparagraph to lessees.

"(D) Reconstruction. Rehabilitation includes reconstruction.

"(2) Qualified rehabilitation expenditure defined. For purposes of this section —

"(A) In general. The term 'qualified rehabilitation expenditure' means any amount properly chargeable to capital account —

"(i) for property for which depreciation is allowable under section 168 and which is —

"(I) nonresidential real property,

"(II) residential rental property,

"(III) real property which has a class life of more than 12.5 years, or

"(IV) an addition or improvement to property or housing described in subclause (I), (II), or (III), and

"(ii) in connection with the rehabilitation of a qualified rehabilitated building.

"(B) Certain expenditures not included. The term 'qualified rehabilitation expenditure' does not include —

"(i) Straight line depreciation must be used. Any expenditure with respect to which the taxpayer does not use the straight line method over a recovery period determined under subsection (c) or (g) of section 168. The preceding sentence shall not apply to any expenditure to the extent the alternative depreciation system of section 168(g) applies to such expenditure by reason of subparagraph (B) or (C) of section 168(g)(1).

"(ii) Cost of acquisition. The cost of acquiring any building or interest therein.

"(iii) Enlargements. Any expenditure attributable to the enlargement of an existing building.

"(iv) Certified historic structure, etc. Any expenditure attributable to the rehabilitation of a certified historic structure or a building in a registered historic district, unless the rehabilitation is a certified rehabilitation (within the meaning of subparagraph (C)). The preceding sentence shall not apply to a building in a registered historic district if—

"(I) such building was not a certified historic structure,

"(II) the Secretary of the Interior certified to the Secretary that such building is not of historic significance to the district, and

"(III) if the certification referred to in subclause (II) occurs after the beginning of the rehabilitation of such building, the taxpayer certifies to the Secretary that, at the beginning of such rehabilitation, he in good faith was not aware of the requirement of subclause (II).

"(v) Tax-exempt use property.

"(I) In general. Any expenditure in connection with the rehabilitation of a building which is allocable to that portion of such building which is (or may reasonably be expected to be) tax-exempt use property (within the meaning of section 168(h)).

"(II) Clause not to apply for purposes of paragraph (1)(C). This clause shall not apply for purposes of determining under paragraph (1)(C) whether a building has been substantially rehabilitated.

"(vi) Expenditures of lessee. Any expenditure of a lessee of a building if, on the date the rehabilitation is completed, the remaining term of the lease (determined without regard to any renewal periods) is less than the recovery period determined under section 168(c).

"(C) Certified rehabilitation. For purposes of subparagraph (B), the term 'certified rehabilitation' means any rehabilitation of a certified historic structure which the Secretary of the Interior has certified to the Secretary as being consistent with the historic character of such property or the district in which such property is located.

"(D) Nonresidential real property; residential rental property; class life. For purposes of subparagraph (A), the terms 'nonresidential real property', 'residential rental property', and 'class life' have the respective meanings given such terms by section 168.

"(3) Certified historic structure defined. For purposes of this subsection—

"(A) In general. The term 'certified historic structure' means any building (and its structural components) which—

"(i) is listed in the National Register, or

"(ii) is located in a registered historic district and is certified by the Secretary of the Interior to the Secretary as being of historic significance to the district.

"(B) Registered historic district. The term 'registered historic district' means—

"(i) any district listed in the National Register, and

"(ii) any district—

"(I) which is designated under a statute of the appropriate State or local government, if such statute is certified by the Secretary of the Interior to the Secretary as containing criteria which will substantially achieve the purpose of preserving and rehabilitating buildings of historic significance to the district, and

"(II) which is certified by the Secretary of the Interior to the Secretary as meeting substantially all of the requirements for the listing of districts in the National Register.

"(4) Property treated as new section 38 property. Property which is treated as section 38 property by reason of subsection (a)(1)(E) shall be treated as new section 38 property,

"(h) Repealed.

"(i) Repealed.

"(j) Repealed.

"(k) Movie and television films.

"(1) Entitlement to credit.

"(A) In general. A credit shall be allowable under section 38 to a taxpayer with respect to any motion picture film or video tape—

"(i) only if such film or tape is new section 38 property (determined without regard to useful life) which is a qualified film, and

"(ii) only to the extent the taxpayer has an ownership interest in such film or tape.

"(B) Qualified film defined. For purposes of this subsection, the term 'qualified film' means any motion picture film or video tape created primarily for use as public entertainment or for educational purposes. Such term does not include any film or tape the market for which is primarily topical or is otherwise essentially transitory in nature.

"(C) Ownership interest. For purposes of this subsection, a person's 'ownership interest' in a qualified film shall be determined on the basis of his proportionate share of any loss which may be incurred with respect to the production costs of such film.

"(2) Applicable percentage to be 66⅔. Except as provided in paragraph (3), the applicable percentage under section 46(c)(2) for any qualified film shall be 66⅔ percent.

"(3) Election of 90-percent rule.

"(A) In general. If the taxpayer makes an election under this paragraph, the applicable percentage under section 46(c)(2) shall be determined as if the useful life of the film would have expired at the close of the first taxable year by the close of which the aggregate amount allowable as a deduction under section 167 would equal or exceed 90 percent of the basis of the film.

"(B) Making of election. An election under this paragraph shall be made at such time and in such manner as the Secretary may by regulations prescribe. Such an election shall apply for the taxable year for which it is made and for all subsequent taxable years and may be revoked only with the consent of the Secretary.

"(C) Who may elect. If for any prior taxable year paragraph (2) of this subsection applied to the taxpayer or any related business entity, or if for the taxable year paragraph (2) applies to any related business entity, an election under this paragraph may be made by the taxpayer only with the consent of the Secretary.

"(D) Related business entity. Two or more corporations, partnerships, trusts, estates, proprietorships, or other entities shall be treated as related business entities if 50 percent or more of the beneficial interest in each of such entities is owned by the same or related persons (taking into account only persons who own at least 10 percent of such beneficial interest). For purposes of this subparagraph, a person is a related person to another person if—

"(i) such persons are component members of a controlled group of corporations (within the meaning of section 1563(a), except that section 1563(b)(2) shall not apply and except that 'more than 50 percent' shall be substituted for 'at least 80 percent' each place it appears in section 1563(a)), or

"(ii) the relationship between such persons would result in a disallowance of losses under section 267 or 707(b), except that for these purposes a family of an individual includes only his spouse and minor children.

"For purposes of this subparagraph, the term 'beneficial interest' means voting stock in the case of a corporation, profits interest or capital interest in the case of a partnership, or beneficial interest in the case of a trust or estate.

"(4) Predominant use test or at-risk rules; qualified investment. In the case of any qualified film—

"(A) section 48(a)(2), section 46(c)(8), or section 46(c)(9) shall not apply, and

"(B) in determining qualified investment under section 46(c)(1), there shall be used (in lieu of the basis of the property) an amount equal to the qualified United States production costs (as defined in paragraph (5)).

"(5) Qualified United States production costs.

"(A) In general. For purposes of this subsection, the term 'qualified United States production costs' means with respect to any film—

"(i) direct production costs allocable to the United States, plus

"(ii) if 80 percent or more of the direct production costs are allocable to the United States, all other production costs other than direct production costs allocable outside the United States.

"(B) Production costs. For purposes of this subsection, the term 'production costs' includes—

"(i) a reasonable allocation of general overhead costs,

"(ii) compensation (other than participations described in clause (vi)) for services performed by actors, production personnel, directors, and producers,

"(iii) costs of 'first' distribution of prints,

"(iv) the cost of the screen rights and other material being filmed,

"(v) 'residuals' payable under contracts with labor organizations, and

"(vi) participations payable as compensation to actors, production personnel, directors, and producers.

"Participations in all qualified films placed in service by a taxpayer during a taxable year shall be taken into account under clause (vi) only to the extent of the lesser of 25 percent of each such participation or 12½ percent of the aggregate qualified United States production costs (other than costs described in clauses (v) and (vi) of this subparagraph) for such films, but taking into account for both the 25 percent limit and 12½ percent limit no more than $1,000,000 in participations for any one individual with respect to any one film. For purposes of this subparagraph (other than clauses (v) and (vi) and the preceding sentence), costs shall be taken into account only if they are capitalized.

"(C) Direct production costs. For purposes of this paragraph, the term 'direct production costs' does not include items referred to in clause (i), (iv), (v), or (vi) of subparagraph (B). The term also does not include advertising and promotional costs and such other costs as may be provided in regulations prescribed by the Secretary.

"(D) Allocation of direct production costs. For purposes of this paragraph—

"(i) Compensation for services performed shall be allocated to the country in which the services are performed, except that payments to United States persons for services performed outside the United States shall be allocated to the United States. For purposes of the preceding sentence, payments to an S corporation or a partnership shall be considered payments to a United States person only to the extent that such payments are included in the gross income of a United States person other than an S corporation or partnership.

"(ii) Amounts for equipment and supplies shall be allocated to the country in which, with respect to the production of the film, the predominant use occurs.

"(iii) All other items shall be allocated under regulations prescribed by the Secretary which are consistent with the allocation principle set forth in clause (ii).

"(6) United States. For purposes of this subsection, the term 'United States' includes the possessions of the United States.

"(l) Energy property.

"For purposes of this subpart—

"(1) Treatment as section 38 property. For any period for which the energy percentage determined under section 46(b)(2) for any energy property is greater than zero—

"(A) such energy property shall be treated as meeting the requirements of paragraph (1) of subsection (a), and

"(B) paragraph (3) of subsection (a) shall not apply to such property.

"(2) Energy property defined. The term 'energy property' means property—

"(A) which is—

"(i) alternative energy property,

"(ii) solar wind energy property,

"(iii) specially defined energy property,

"(iv) recycling equipment,

"(v) shale oil equipment,

"(vi) equipment for producing natural gas from geopressured brine,

"(vii) qualified hydroelectric generating property,
"(viii) cogeneration equipment, or
"(ix) qualified intercity buses,
"(B)(i) the construction, reconstruction, or erection of which is completed by the taxpayer after September 30, 1978, or
"(ii) which is acquired after September 30, 1978, if the original use of such property commences with the taxpayer and commences after such date, and
"(C) with respect to which depreciation (or amortization in lieu of depreciation) is allowable, and which has a useful life (determined as of the time such property is placed in service) of 3 years or more or to which section 168 applies.

"(3) Alternative energy property.
"(A) In general. The term 'alternative energy property' means—
"(i) a boiler the primary fuel for which will be an alternate substance,
"(ii) a burner (including necessary on-site equipment to bring the alternate substance to the burner) for a combustor other than a boiler if the primary fuel for such burner will be an alternate substance,
"(iii) equipment for converting an alternate substance into a synthetic liquid, gaseous, or solid fuel,
"(iv) equipment designed to modify existing equipment which uses oil or natural gas as a fuel or as feedstock so that such equipment will use either a substance other than oil and natural gas, or oil mixed with a substance other than oil and natural gas (where such other substance will provide not less than 25 percent of the fuel or feedstock),
"(v) equipment to convert—
"(I) coal (including lignite), or any nonmarketable substance derived therefrom, into a substitute for a petroleum or natural gas derived feedstock for the manufacture of chemicals or other products, or
"(II) coal (including lignite), or any substance derived therefrom, into methanol, ammonia, or a hydroprocessed coal liquid or solid,
"(vi) pollution control equipment required (by Federal, State, or local regulations) to be installed on or in connection with equipment described in clause (i), (ii), (iii), (iv), or (v),
"(vii) equipment used for the unloading, transfer, storage, reclaiming from storage, and preparation (including, but not limited to, washing, crushing, drying, and weighing) at the point of use of an alternate substance for use in equipment described in clause (i), (ii), (iii), (iv), (v), or (vi),
"(viii) equipment used to produce, distribute, or use energy derived from a geothermal deposit (within the meaning of section 613(e)(3)), but only, in the case of electricity generated by geothermal power, up to (but not including) the electrical transmission stage, and
"(ix) equipment, placed in service at either of 2 locations designated by the Secretary after consultation with the Secretary of Energy, which converts ocean thermal energy to usable energy.
"The equipment described in clause (vii) includes equipment used for the storage of fuel derived from garbage at the site at which such fuel was produced from garbage.

"(B) Alternate substance. The term 'alternate substance' means any substance other than—
"(i) oil and natural gas, and
"(ii) any product of oil and natural gas.
"(C) Special rule for certain pollution control equipment. The term 'pollution control equipment' does not include any equipment which—
"(i) is installed on or in connection with property which, as of October 1, 1978, was using coal (including lignite), and
"(ii) was required to be installed by Federal, State, or local regulations in effect on such date.
"For purposes of the preceding sentence, in the case of property which is alternative energy property solely by reason of the amendments made by section 222(b) of the Crude Oil Windfall Profit Tax Act of 1980, 'January 1, 1980' shall be substituted for 'October 1, 1978'.

"(4) Solar or wind energy property. The term 'solar or wind energy property' means any equipment which uses solar or wind energy—
"(A) to generate electricity,
"(B) to heat or cool (or provide hot water for use in) a structure, or
"(C) to provide solar process heat.

"(5) Specially defined energy property. The term 'specially defined energy property' means—
"(A) a recuperator,
"(B) a heat wheel,
"(C) a regenerator,
"(D) a heat exchanger,
"(E) a waste heat boiler,
"(F) a heat pipe,
"(G) an automatic energy control system,
"(H) a turbulator,
"(I) A preheater,
"(J) a combustible gas recovery system,
"(K) an economizer,
"(L) modifications to alumina electrolytic cells,
"(M) modifications to chlor-alkali electrolytic cells, or
"(N) any other property of a kind specified by the Secretary by regulations, the principal purpose of which is reducing the amount of energy consumed in any existing industrial or commercial process and which is installed in connection with an existing industrial or commercial facility. The Secretary shall not specify any property under subparagraph (N) unless he determines that such specification meets the requirements of paragraph (9) of section 23(c) for specification of items under section 23(c)(4)(A)(viii).

"(6) Recycling equipment.
"(A) In general. The term 'recycling equipment' means any equipment which is used exclusively—
"(i) to sort and prepare solid waste for recycling, or
"(ii) in the recycling of solid waste.
"(B) Certain equipment not included. The term 'recycling equipment' does not include—
"(i) any equipment used in a process after the first marketable product is produced, or
"(ii) in the case of recycling iron or steel, any equipment used to reduce the waste to a molten state and in any process thereafter.
"(C) 10 percent virgin material allowed. Any equipment used in the recycling of material which includes some virgin materials shall not be treated as failing to meet the exclusive use requirements of subparagraph (A) if the amount of such virgin materials is 10 percent or less.
"(D) Certain equipment included. The term 'recycling equipment' includes any equipment which is used in the conversion of solid waste into a fuel or into useful energy such as steam, electricity, or hot water.

"(7) Shale oil equipment. The term 'shale oil equipment' means equipment for producing or extracting oil from oil-bearing shale rock but does not include equipment for hydrogenation, refining, or other process subsequent to retorting.

"(8) Equipment for producing natural gas from geopressured brine. The term 'equipment for producing natural gas from geopressured brine' means equipment which is used exclusively to extract natural gas described in section 613A(b)(3)(C)(i).

"(9) Equipment must meet certain standards to qualify. Equipment qualifies under paragraph (3), (4), (5), (6), (7), or (8) only if it meets the performance and quality standards (if any) which—
"(A) have been prescribed by the Secretary by regulations (after consultation with the Secretary of Energy), and
"(B) are in effect as of the time of the acquisition of the property.

"(10) Existing. For purposes of this subsection, the term 'existing' means—
"(A) when used in connection with a facility, 50 percent or more of the basis of such facility is attributable to construction, reconstruction, or erection before October 1, 1978, or
"(B) when used in connection with an industrial or commercial process, such process was carried on in the facility as of October 1, 1978.

"(11) Special rule for property financed by subsidized energy financing or industrial development bonds.
"(A) Reduction of qualified investment. For purposes of applying the energy percentage to any property, if such property is financed in whole or in part by—
"(i) subsidized energy financing, or
"(ii) the proceeds a private activity bond (within the meaning of section 141) the interest on which is exempt from tax under section 103,
the amount taken into account as qualified investment shall not exceed the amount which (but for this subparagraph) would be the qualified investment multiplied by the fraction determined under subparagraph (B).
"(B) Determination of fraction. For purposes of subparagraph (A), the fraction determined under this subparagraph is 1 reduced by a fraction—
"(i) the numerator of which is that portion of the qualified investment in the property which is allocable to such financing or proceeds, and
"(ii) the denominator of which is the qualified investment in the property.
"(C) Subsidized energy financing. For purposes of subparagraph (A), the term 'subsidized energy financing' means financing provided under a Federal, State, or local program a principal purpose of which is to provide subsidized financing for projects designed to conserve or produce energy.

"(12) Industrial includes agricultural. The term 'industrial' includes agricultural.

"(13) Qualified hydroelectric generating property.
"(A) In general. The term 'qualified hydroelectric generating property' means property installed at a qualified hydroelectric site which is—
"(i) equipment for increased capacity to generate electricity by water (up to, but not including, the electrical transmission stage), and
"(ii) structures for housing such generating equipment, fish passageways, and dam rehabilitation property, required by reason of the installation of equipment described in clause (i).
"(B) Qualified hydroelectric site. The term 'qualified hydroelectric site' means any site—
"(i) at which—
"(I) there is a dam the construction of which was completed before October 18, 1979, and which was not significantly enlarged after such date, or
"(II) electricity is to be generated without any dam or other impoundment of water, and
"(ii) the installed capacity of which is less than 125 megawatts.
"(C) Limitation on credit when installed capacity exceeds 25 megawatts. For purposes of applying the energy percentage to any qualified hydroelectric generating property placed in service in connection with a site the installed capacity of which exceeds 25 megawatts, the amount taken into account as qualified investment shall not exceed the amount which (but for this subparagraph) would be the qualified investment multiplied by a fraction—
"(i) the numerator of which is 25 reduced by 1 for each whole megawatt by which such installed capacity exceeds 100 megawatts, and
"(ii) the denominator of which is the number of megawatts of such installed capacity but not in excess of 100.
"(D) Dam rehabilitation property. For purposes of this paragraph, the term 'dam rehabilitation property' means any amount properly chargeable to capital account for property (or additions or improvements to property) in connection with the rehabilitation of a dam.

"(E) Installed capacity. The term 'installed capacity' means, with respect to any site, the installed capacity of all electrical generating equipment placed in service at such site. Such term includes the capacity of equipment installed during the 3 taxable years following the taxable year in which the equipment is placed in service.

"(14) Cogeneration equipment.

"(A) In general. The term 'cogeneration equipment' means property which is an integral part of a system for using the same fuel to produce both qualified energy and electricity at an industrial or commercial facility at which, as of January 1, 1980, electricity or qualified energy was produced.

"(B) Only cogeneration increases taken into account. The term 'cogeneration equipment' includes property only to the extent that such property increases the capacity of the system to produce qualified energy or electricity, whichever is the secondary energy product of the system.

"(C) Limitation on use of oil or gas. The term 'cogeneration equipment' does not include any property which is part of a system if—

"(i) such system uses oil or natural gas (or a product of oil or natural gas) as a fuel for any purpose other than—

"(I) start-up,
"(II) flame control, or
"(III) back-up, or

"(ii) more than 20 percent (determined on a Btu basis) of the fuel for such system for any taxable year consists of oil or natural gas (or a product of oil or natural gas).

"(D) Qualified energy. The term 'qualified energy' means steam, heat, or other forms of useful energy (other than electric energy) to be used for industrial, commercial, or space-heating purposes (other than in the production of electricity).

"(E) Industrial includes purification and desalinization of water. The term 'industrial' includes the purification of water and the desalinization of water.

"(15) Biomass property.

"(A) In general. The term 'biomass property' means—

"(i) any property described in clause (i), (ii), or (iii) of paragraph (3)(A), as modified by the last sentence of paragraph (3)(A) and by subparagraph (B) of this paragraph, and

"(ii) any equipment described in so much of clause (vi) or (vii) of paragraph (3)(A) as relates to property described in clause (i) of this subparagraph.

"(B) Modifications. For purposes of subparagraph (A)—

"(i) the term 'alternate substance' has the meaning given to such term by paragraph (3)(B), except that such term does not include any inorganic substance and does not include coal (including lignite) or any product of such coal, and

"(ii) clause (iii) of paragraph (3)(A) shall be applied by substituting 'a qualified fuel' for 'a synthetic liquid, gaseous, or solid fuel'.

"(C) Qualified fuel. For purposes of subparagraph (B), the term 'qualified fuel' means—

"(i) any synthetic solid fuel, and

"(ii) alcohol for fuel purposes if the primary source of energy for the facility producing the alcohol is not oil or natural gas or a product of oil or natural gas.

"(16) Qualified intercity buses.

"(A) In general. Paragraph (2)(A)(ix) shall apply only with respect to the qualified investment in qualified intercity buses of a taxpayer—

"(i) which is a common carrier regulated by the Interstate Commerce Commission or an appropriate State agency (as determined by the Secretary), and

"(ii) which is engaged in the trade or business of furnishing intercity passenger transportation or intercity charter service by bus.

"(B) Qualified intercity bus. The term 'qualified intercity bus' means an automobile bus—

"(i) the chassis of which is an automobile bus chassis and the body of which is an automobile bus body,

"(ii) which has—

"(I) a seating capacity of more than 35 passengers (in addition to the driver), and

"(II) 1 or more baggage compartments, separated from the passenger area, with a capacity of at least 200 cubic feet, and

"(iii) which is used predominantly by the taxpayer in the trade or business of furnishing intercity passenger transportation or intercity charter service.

"(C) Operating capacity must increase. Under regulations prescribed by the Secretary—

"(i) In general. The amount of qualified investment taken into account under paragraph (2)(A)(ix) for any taxable year shall not exceed the amount of the qualified investment which is attributable to an increase in the taxpayer's total operating seating capacity for the taxable year over such capacity as of the close of the preceding taxable year.

"(ii) Special rules. The regulations prescribed under this subparagraph—

"(I) shall provide that only buses used predominantly on a full-time basis in the trade or business of furnishing intercity passenger or intercity charter service shall be taken into account in determining the taxpayer's total operating seating capacity, and

"(II) shall provide rules treating related taxpayers as 1 person.

"(17) Exclusion for public utility property. The terms 'alternative energy property', 'biomass property', 'solar or wind energy property', 'recycling equipment', and 'cogeneration property' do not include property which is public utility property (within the meaning of section 46(f)(5)).

"(m) Application of certain transitional rules.

"Where the application of any provision of subsection (l) of this section or subsection (b) or (c)(3) of section 46 is expressed in terms of a period, such provision shall apply only to—

"(1) property to which section 46(d) does not apply, the construction, reconstruction, or erection of which is completed by the taxpayer on or after the first day of such period, but only to the extent of the basis thereof attributable to the construction, reconstruction, or erection during such period,

"(2) property to which section 46(d) does not apply, acquired by the taxpayer during such period and placed in service by the taxpayer during such period, and

"(3) property to which section 46(d) applies, but only to the extent of the qualified investment (as determined under subsections(c) and (d) of section 46) with respect to qualified progress expenditures made during such period.

"(n) Repealed.

"(o) Certain credits defined.

"For purposes of this title—

"(1) Regular investment credit. The term 'regular investment credit' means that portion of the credit allowable by section 38 which is attributable to the regular percentage.

"(2) Energy investment credit. The term 'energy investment credit' means that portion of the credit allowable by section 38 which is attributable to the energy percentage.

"(3) Rehabilitation investment credit. The term 'rehabilitation investment credit' means that portion of the credit allowable by section 38 which is attributable to the rehabilitation percentage.

"(p) Single purpose agricultural or horticultural structure defined.

" For purposes of this section—

"(1) In general. The term 'single purpose agricultural or horticultural structure' means—

"(A) a single purpose livestock structure, and

"(B) a single purpose horticultural structure.

"(2) Single purpose livestock structure. The term 'single purpose livestock structure' means any enclosure or structure specifically designed, constructed, and used—

"(A) for housing, raising, and feeding a particular type of livestock and their produce, and

"(B) for housing the equipment (including any replacements) necessary for the housing, raising, and feeding referred to in subparagraph (A).

"(3) Single purpose horticultural structure. The term 'single purpose horticultural structure' means—

"(A) a greenhouse specifically designed, constructed, and used for the commercial production of plants, and

"(B) a structure specifically designed, constructed and used for the commercial production of mushrooms.

"(4) Structures which include work space. An enclosure or structure which provides work space shall be treated as a single purpose agricultural or horticultural structure only if such work space is solely for—

"(A) the stocking, caring for, or collecting of livestock or plants (as the case may be) or their produce,

"(B) the maintenance of the enclosure or structure, and

"(C) the maintenance or replacement of the equipment or stock enclosed or housed therein.

"(5) Special rule for applying section 47. For purposes of section 47, any single purpose agricultural or horticultural structure shall be treated as meeting the requirements of this subsection for any period during which such structure is held for the use under which it qualified under this subsection.

"(6) Livestock. The term 'livestock' includes poultry.

"(q) Basis adjustment to section 38 property.

"(1) In general. For purposes of this subtitle, if a credit is determined under section 46(a) with respect to section 38 property, the basis of such property shall be reduced by 50 percent of the amount of the credit so determined.

"(2) Certain dispositions. If during any taxable year there is a recapture amount determined with respect to any section 38 property the basis of which was reduced under paragraph (1), the basis of such property (immediately before the event resulting in such recapture) shall be increased by an amount equal to 50 percent of such recapture amount. For purposes of the preceding sentence, the term 'recapture amount' means any increase in tax (or adjustment in carrybacks or carryovers) determined under section 47.

"(3) Special rule for qualified rehabilitated buildings. In the case of any credit determined under section 46(a) for any qualified rehabilitation expenditure in connection with a qualified rehabilitated building, paragraphs (1) and (2) of this subsection and paragraph (5) of subsection (d) shall be applied without regard to the phrase '50 percent of'.

"(4) Election of reduced credit in lieu of basis adjustment for regular percentage.

"(A) In general. If the taxpayer elects to have this paragraph apply with respect to any recovery property—

"(i) paragraphs (1) and (2) shall not apply to so much of the credit determined under section 46(a) with respect to such property as is attributable to the regular percentage set forth in section 46(b)(1); and

"(ii) the amount of the credit allowable under section 38 with respect to such property shall be determined under subparagraph (b).

"(B) Reduction in credit. In the case of any recovery property to which an election under subparagraph (A) applies—

"(i) solely for the purposes of applying the regular percentage, the applicable percentage under subsection (c) or (d) of section 46 shall be deemed to be 100 percent, and

"(ii) notwithstanding section 46(b)(1), the regular percentage shall be—

"(I) 8 percent in the case of recovery property other than 3-year property, or

"(II) 4 percent in the case of recovery property which is 3-year property.

"For purposes of the preceding sentence, RRB replacement property (within the meaning of section 168(f)(3)(B) shall be treated as property which is not 3-year property.

"(C) Time and manner of making election.

"(i) In general. An election under this subsection with respect to any property shall be made on the taxpayer's return of the tax imposed by this chapter for the taxpayer's taxable year in which such property is placed in service (or in the case of property to which an election under section 46(d) applies, for the first taxable year for which qualified progress expenditures were taken into account with respect to such property).

"(ii) Revocable only with consent. An election under this subsection with respect to any property, once made, may be revoked only with the consent of the Secretary.

"(5) Recapture of reductions.

"(A) In general. For purposes of sections 1245 and 1250, any reduction under this subsection shall be treated as a deduction allowed for depreciation.

"(B) Special rule for section 1250. For purposes of section 1250(b), the determination of what would have been the depreciation adjustments under the straight line method shall be made as if there had been no reduction under this section.

"(6) Adjustment in basis of interest in partnership or S corporation. The adjusted basis of—

"(A) a partner's interest in a partnership, and

"(B) stock in an S corporation,

shall be appropriately adjusted to take into account adjustments made under this subsection in the basis of property held by the partnership or S corporation (as the case may be).

"(7) Special rule for qualified films. If a credit is allowed under section 38 with respect to any qualified film (within the meaning of subsection (k)(1)(B)) then, in lieu of any reduction under paragraph (1)—

"(A) to the extent that the credit is determined with respect to any amount described in clause (v) or (vi) of subsection (k)(5)(B), any deduction allowable under this chapter with respect to such amount shall be reduced by 50 percent of the amount of the credit so determined, and

"(B) the basis of the taxpayer's ownership interest (within the meaning of subsection (k)(1)(C)) shall be reduced by the excess of—

"(i) 50 percent of the amount of the credit determined under subsection (k), over

"(ii) the amount of the reduction under subparagraph (A).

"(r) Certain section 501(d) organizations.

"(1) In general. In the case of eligible section 501(d) organizations—

"(A) any business engaged in by such organization for the common benefit of its members and the taxable income from which is included in the gross income of its members shall be treated as an unrelated business for purposes of paragraph (4) of subsection (a),

"(B) the qualified investment for each taxable year with respect to such business shall be apportioned pro rata among such members in the same manner as the taxable income of such organization, and

"(C) any individual to whom any investment has been apportioned under subparagraph (B) shall be treated for purposes of this subpart (other than section 47) as the taxpayer with respect to such investment, and such investment shall not (by reason of such apportionment) lose its character as an investment in new section 38 property or used section 38 property, as the case may be.

"(2) Limitation on used section 38 property applied at organization level. The limitation under subparagraph (A) of subsection (c)(2) shall apply with respect to the section 501(d) organization.

"(3) Recapture. For purposes of applying section 47 to any property for which credit was allowed under section 38 by reason of this subsection—

"(A) the section 501(d) organization shall be treated as the taxpayer to which the credit under section 38 was allowed,

"(B) the amount of such credit allowed with respect to the property shall be treated as the amount which would have been allowed to the section 501(d) organization were such credit allowable to such organizations,

"(C) subparagraph (D) of section 47(a)(5) shall not apply, and

"(D) the amount of the increase in tax under section 47 for any taxable year with respect to property to which this subsection applies shall be allocated pro rata among the members of such organization in the same manner as such organization's taxable income for such year is allocated among such members.

"(4) No investment credit allowed to member if member claims other investment credit. No credit shall be allowed to an individual by reason of this subsection if such individual claims a credit under section 38 without regard to this subsection. The amount of the credit not allowed by reason of the preceding sentence shall not be allowed to any other person.

"(5) Eligible section 501(d) organization. For this subsection, the term 'eligible section 501(d) organization' means any organization—

"(A) which elects to be treated as an organization described in section 501(d) and which is exempt from tax under section 501(a), and

"(B) which does not provide a substantially higher standard of living for any person or persons than it does for the majority of the members of the community.

"(s) Special rules relating to sound recordings.

"(1) In general. For purposes of this title, in the case of any sound recording, the original use of which commences with the taxpayer, the taxpayer may elect to treat such recording as recovery property which is 3-year property to the extent that the taxpayer has an ownership interest in such recording.

"(2) Failure to make election. If a taxpayer does not make an election under paragraph (1) with respect to any sound recording—

"(A) no credit shall be allowed under section 38 with respect to such recording, and

"(B) such recording shall not be treated as recovery property.

"(3) Predominant use test and at risk rules not to apply; qualified investment. In the case of any sound recording—

"(A) sections 46(c)(8), 46(c)(9), and 48(a)(2) shall not apply, and

"(B) in determining the qualified investment under section 46(c)(1), there shall be used (in lieu of the basis of the property) an amount equal to the production costs which are allocable to the United States (as determined under rules similar to the rules of section 48(k)(5)(D)).

"(4) Ownership interest. For purposes of determining the credit allowable under section 38, the ownership interest of any person in a sound recording shall be determined on the basis of his proportionate share of any loss which may be incurred with respect to the production costs of such sound recording.

"(5) Sound recording. For purposes of this subsection, the term 'sound recording' means works which result from the fixation of a series of musical, spoken, or other sounds, regardless of the nature of the material objects (such as discs, tapes, or other phonorecordings) in which such sounds are embodied.

"(6) Production costs.

"(A) In general. For purposes of this subsection, the term 'production costs' includes—

"(i) a reasonable allocation of general overhead costs,

"(ii) compensation for services performed by song writers, artists, production personnel, directors, producers, and similar personnel,

"(iii) costs of 'first' distribution of records or tapes, and

"(iv) the cost of the material being recorded.

"(B) Certain costs not taken into account. Except as provided in subparagraph (C), the term 'production costs' shall not include—

"(i) 'residuals' payable under contracts with labor organizations, or

"(ii) participations or royalties payable as compensation to song writers, artists, production personnel, directors, producers, and similar personnel, or

"(iii) any other contingent amounts.

"(C) Certain contingent amounts taken into account. In the case of any amount which is described in subparagraph (B) and which is incurred in the taxable year in which the sound recording is placed in service or the next taxable year—

"(i) subparagraph (B) shall not apply, and

"(ii) for purposes of sections 38 and 168, the taxpayer shall be treated as having placed in service in each such taxable year 3-year recovery property with a basis equal to the amount so incurred in such taxable year.

"(7) Election made separately. An election under paragraph (1) shall be made separately with respect to each sound recording and must be made by all persons having an ownership interest in such recording.

"(8) United States. For purposes of this subsection, the term 'United States' includes the possessions of the United States.

"(9) Termination. This subsection shall not apply to any property placed in service after December 31, 1985, unless such property is transition property (as defined in section 49(e)(1)).

"(t) Cross reference.

"For application of this subpart to certain acquiring corporations, see section 381(c)(26)."

In 1990, P.L. 101-508, Sec. 11801(c)(6)(A), deleted para. (a)(8), effective 11/5/90 except as provided in Sec. 11821(b) of this Act, reproduced below:

"(b) Savings provision. If—

"(1) any provision amended or repealed by this part applied to—

"(A) any transaction occurring before the date of the enactment of this Act [11/5/90],

"(B) any property acquired before such date of enactment [11/5/90], or

"(C) any item of income, loss, deduction, or credit taken into account before such date of enactment [11/5/90], and

"(2) the treatment of such transaction, property, or item under such provision would (without regard to the amendments made by this part) affect liability for tax for periods ending after such date of enactment [11/5/90],

nothing in the amendments made by this part shall be construed to affect the treatment of such transaction, property, or item for purposes of determining liability for tax for periods ending after such date of enactment [11/5/90]."

Prior to repeal, para. (a)(8) read as follows:

"(8) Amortized property. Any property with respect to which an election under section 167(k), 184, or 188 applies shall not be treated as section 38 property."

In 1988, P.L. 100-647, Sec. 1002(a)(14)(A), substituted "168(h)(2)(C)" for "168(j)(4)(C)"... Sec. 1002(a)(14)(B), substituted "168(h)(2)(A)(iii)" for "168(j)(4)(A)(iii)"... Sec. 1002(a)(14)(C), substituted "168(h)(2)(B)" for "168(j)(4)(B)"... Sec. 1002(a)(14)(D), substituted "168(i)(3)" for "168 (j)(6)"... Sec. 1002(a)(14)(E), substituted "168(h)(1)(C)(ii)" for "168(j)(3)(C)(ii)"... Sec. 1002(a)(14)(F), substituted "paragraph (5) and (6) of section 168(h)" for "paragraph (8) and (9) of section 168(j)"... Sec. 1002(a)(14)(G), amended subpara. (a)(5)(E) in para. (a)(5)... Sec. 1002(a)(16)(A), added para. (s)(9)... Sec. 1002(a)(20), redesignated subsec. (s) relating to cross references as subsec. (t)... Sec. 1002(a)(29), substituted "property to which section 168 applies" for "recovery property (within the meaning of section 168)" in para. (a)(1)... Sec. 1002(a)(30), substituted "to which section 168 applies" for "which is recovery property (within the meaning of section 168)" in subpara. (l)(2)(C), effective for property placed in service after 12/31/86, in tax. yrs. end. after 12/31/86.

Prior to amendment, subpara. (a)(5)(E) read as follows:

"(E) Cross reference.

"For provisions providing special rules for the application of this paragraph and paragraph (4), see section 168(j)."

—P.L. 100-647, Sec. 1013(a)(41), substituted "a private activity bond (within the meaning of section 141)" for "an industrial development bond (within the meaning of section 103(b)(2))" in clause (l)(11)(A)(ii), effective for bonds issued after 8/15/86.

In 1986, P.L. 99-514, Sec. 251(b), amended subsec. (g) . . . Sec. 251(c), deleted "other than a certified historic structure" after "qualified rehabilitated building" in para. (q)(3), effective for property placed in service after 12/31/86, in tax. yrs. end. after 12/31/86, except as provided in Sec. 251(d)(2)-(6) of this Act, reproduced in the note following Code Sec. 46.

Prior to amendment, subsec. (g) [as amended by Sec. 1802(a)(9)(B) of this Act, see below] read as follows:

"(g) Special rules for qualified rehabilitated buildings.

"For purposes of this subpart—

"(1) Qualified rehabilitated building defined.

"(A) In general. The term 'qualified rehabilitated building' means any building (and its structural components)—

"(i) which has been substantially rehabilitated,

"(ii) which was placed in service before the beginning of the rehabilitation, and

"(iii) 75 percent or more of the existing external walls of which are retained in place as external walls in the rehabilitation process.

"(B) 30 years must have elapsed since construction. In the case of a building other than a certified historic structure, a building shall not be a qualified rehabilitated building unless there is a period of at least 30 years between the date the physical work on the rehabilitation began and the date the building was first placed in service.

"(C) Substantially rehabilitated defined.

"(i) In general. For purposes of subparagraph (A)(i), a building shall be treated as having been substantially rehabilitated only if the qualified rehabilitation expenditures during the 24-month period selected by the taxpayer (at the time and in the manner prescribed by regulations) and ending with or within the taxable year exceed the greater of—

"(I) the adjusted basis of such building, (and its structural components) or

"(II) $5,000.

The adjusted basis of the building (and its structural components) shall be determined as of the beginning of the first day of such 24-month period, or of the holding period of the building (within the meaning of section 1250(e)), whichever is later. For purposes of the preceding sentence, the determination of the beginning of the holding period shall be made without regard to any reconstruction by the taxpayer in connection with the rehabilitation.

"(ii) Special rule for phased rehabilitation. In the case of any rehabilitation which may reasonably be expected to be completed in phases set forth in architectural plans and specifications completed before the rehabilitation begins, clause (i) shall be applied by substituting '60-month period' for '24-month period.'.

"(iii) Lessees. The Secretary shall prescribe by regulation rules for applying this provision to lessees.

"(D) Reconstruction. Rehabilitation includes reconstruction.

"(E) Alternative test for definition of qualified rehabilitated building. The requirement in clause (iii) of subparagraph (A) shall be deemed to be satisfied if in the rehabilitation process—

"(i) 50 percent or more of the existing external walls of the building are retained in place as external walls,

"(ii) 75 percent or more of the existing external walls of such building are retained in place as internal or external walls, and

"(iii) 75 percent or more of the existing internal structural framework of such building is retained in place.

"(2) Qualified rehabilitation expenditure defined.

"(A) In general. The term 'qualified rehabilitation expenditure' means any amount properly chargeable to capital account which is incurred after December 31, 1981—

"(i) for real property (or additions or improvements to real property) which have a recovery period (within the meaning of section 168) of 19 (15 years in the case of low-income housing) years, and

"(ii) in connection with the rehabilitation of a qualified rehabilitated building.

"(B) Certain expenditures not included. The term 'qualified rehabilitation expenditure' does not include—

"(i) Accelerated methods of depreciation may not be used. Any expenditures with respect to which an election has not been made under section 168(b)(3) (to use the straight-line method of depreciation). The preceding sentence shall not apply to any expenditure to the extent subsection (f)(12) or (j) of section 168 applies to such expenditure.

"(ii) Cost of acquisition. The cost of acquiring any building or interest therein.

"(iii) Enlargements. Any expenditure attributable to the enlargement of an existing building.

"(iv) Certified historic structure, etc. Any expenditure attributable to the rehabilitation of a certified historic structure or a building in a registered historic district, unless the rehabilitation is a certified rehabilitation (within the meaning of subparagraph (C). The preceding sentence shall not apply to a building in a registered historic district if—

"(I) such building was not a certified historic structure,

"(II) the Secretary of the Interior certified to the Secretary that such building is not of historic significance to the district, and

"(III) if the certification referred to in subclause (II) occurs after the beginning of the rehabilitation of such building, the taxpayer certifies to the Secretary that, at the beginning of such rehabilitation, he in good faith was not aware of the requirements of subclause (II).

"(v) Expenditures of lessee. Any expenditure of a lessee of a building if, on the date the rehabilitation is completed, the remaining term of the lease (determined without regard to any renewal periods) is less than 19 years (15 years in the case of low-income housing).

"(vi) Tax-exempt use property.

"(I) In general. Any expenditure in connection with the rehabilitation of a building which is allocable to that portion of such building which is (or may reasonably be expected to be) tax-exempt use property (within the meaning of section 168(j)).

"(II) Clause not to apply for purposes of paragraph (1)(C). This clause shall not apply for purposes of determining under paragraph (1)(C) whether a building has been substantially rehabilitated.

"(C) Certified rehabilitation. For purposes of subparagraph (B), the term 'certified rehabilitation' means any rehabilitation of a certified historic structure which the Secretary of the Interior has certified to the Secretary as being consistent with the historic character of such property or the district in which such property is located.

"(D) Low-income housing. For purposes of subparagraph (B), the term 'low-income housing' has the meaning given such term by section 168(c)(2)(F).

"(3) Certified historic structure defined.

"(A) In general. The term 'certified historic structure' means any building (and its structural components) which—

"(i) is listed in the National Register, or

"(ii) is located in a registered historic district and is certified by the Secretary of the Interior to the Secretary as being of historic significance to the district.

"(B) Registered historic district. The term 'registered historic district' means—

"(i) any district listed in the National Register, and

"(ii) any district—

"(I) which is designated under a statute of the appropriate State or local government, if such statute is certified by the Secretary of the Interior to the Secretary as containing criteria which will substantially achieve the purpose of preserving and rehabilitating buildings of historic significance to the district, and

"(II) which is certified by the Secretary of the Interior to the Secretary as meeting substantially all of the requirements for the listing of districts in the National Register.

"(4) Property treated as new section 38 property. Property which is treated as section 38 property by reason of subsection (a)(1)(E) shall be treated as new section 38 property."

— P.L. 99-514, Sec. 701(e)(4)(C), added "(as in effect on the day before the date of the enactment of the Tax Reform Act of 1986)" in subpara. (d)(4)(D), effective for tax. yrs. begin. after 12/31/86.

— P.L. 99-514, Sec. 803(b)(2)(B), amended para. (r)(5) [sic (s)(5); see Sec. 1879(j)(1) of this Act, below], effective for costs incurred after 12/31/86, in tax. yrs. end. after 12/31/86.

Prior to amendment, para. (r)(5) [sic (s)(5)] read as follows:

"(5) Sound recording. For purposes of this subsection, the term 'sound recording' means any sound recording described in section 280(c)(2)."

— P.L. 99-514, Sec. 1272(d)(5), deleted "932," after "931," in clause (a)(2)(B)(vii) . . . Sec. 1275(c)(5), substituted "or 933" for ", 933, or 934(c)" in clause (a)(2)(B)(vii), effective for tax. yrs. begin. after 12/31/86.

— P.L. 99-514, Sec. 1511(c)(3), substituted "the underpayment rate" for "the rate" in clause (d)(6)(C)(ii), effective for purposes of determining interest for periods after 12/31/86.

— P.L. 99-514, Sec. 1802(a)(4)(C), redesignated subpara. (a)(5)(D) as (a)(5)(E) and added new subpara. (a)(5)(D) . . . Sec. 1802(a)(5)(B), deleted clause (a)(5)(B)(iii) . . . Sec. 1802(a)(9)(A), substituted "514(b)" for "514(c)" and "514(a)" for "514(b)" in para. (a)(4) . . . Sec. 1802(a)(9)(B), substituted "section 168(j)" for "section 168(j)(3)" in subclause (g)(2)(B)(vi)(I) [before amendment by Sec. 251(b) of this Act, see above], effective for property placed in service by the taxpayer after 5/23/83, in tax. yrs. end. after 5/23/83, and for property placed in service by the taxpayer on or before 5/23/83, if the lease to the tax-exempt entity is entered into after 5/23/83. Special rules are provided by Sec. 31(g) of P.L. 98-369, reproduced in the note following Code Sec. 168.

Prior to deletion, clause (a)(5)(B)(iii) read as follows:

"(iii) Exception for certain aircraft.

"(I) In general. In the case of any aircraft used under a qualifying lease (as defined in section 47(a)(7)(C) and which is leased to a foreign person or entity before January 1, 1990, clause (i) shall be applied by substituting '3 years' for '6 months.'

"(II) Recapture period extended. For purposes of applying subparagraph (B) of section 47(a)(5) and paragraph (1) of section 47(a), there shall not be taken into account any period of a lease to which subclause (I) applies."

— P.L. 99-514, Sec. 1809(d)(2), redesignated para. (q)(6) (concerning special rule for qualified films) as para. (q)(7), effective for periods after 12/31/82.

— P.L. 99-514, Sec. 1809(e)(1), added the last sentence to para. (b)(1) . . . Sec. 1809(e)(2)(A), added "the first sentence of" before "paragraph (1)" in para. (b)(2) . . . Sec. 1809(e)(2)(B), substituted "used under the leaseback (or lease) referred to in subparagraph (B)" for "used under the lease" in para. (b)(2) . . . Sec. 1809(e)(2)(C), added the last two sentences to para. (b)(2) . . . Sec. 1809(e)(2)(D), substituted "3 months after" for "3 months of" in subpara. (b)(2)(B), effective for property originally placed in service after 4/11/84.

— P.L. 99-514, Sec. 1847(b)(6), substituted "section 23(c)" for "section 44C(c)" and "section 23(c)(4)(A)(viii)" for "section 44C(c)(4)(A)(viii)" in para. (1)(5), effective for tax. yrs. begin. after 12/31/83 and for carrybacks from tax. yrs. begin. after 12/31/83.

— P.L. 99-514, Sec. 1879(j)(1), redesignated subsec. (r) as subsec. (s) and added new subsec. (r), effective for periods after 12/31/78 (under rules similar to the rules of Code Sec. 48(m), as amended by this Act), in tax. yrs. end. after 12/31/78. Sec. 1879(j)(3) of this Act provides:

"(3) Special rule. If refund or credit of any overpayment of tax resulting from the application of this subsection is prevented at any time before the close of the date which is 1 year after the date of the enactment of this Act by operation of any law or rule of law (including res judicata), refund or credit of such overpayment (to the extent attributable to the application of the amendments made by this subsection) may, nevertheless, be made or allowed if claim therefor is filed before the close of such 1-year period."

In 1985, P.L. 99-121, Sec. 103(b)(5), substituted "19" for "18" in clauses (g)(2)(A)(i) and (g)(2)(B)(v), effective for property placed in service by the taxpayer after 5/8/85, except as provided in Sec. 105(b)(5) of this Act which reads as follows:

"(5) Special rule for leasing of qualified rehabilitated buildings.—The amendment made by paragraph (5) of section 103(b) [of this Act] to section 48(g)(2)(B)(v) of the Internal Revenue Code of 1954 shall not apply to leases entered into before May 22, 1985, but only if the lessee signed the lease before May 17, 1985."

In 1984, P.L. 98-369, Sec. 11(a)(1), substituted "$125,000 ($150,000 for taxable years beginning after 1987)" for "$150,000 ($125,000 for taxable years beginning in 1981, 1982, 1983, or 1984)" in subpara. (c)(2)(A) . . . Sec. 11(a)(2), substituted "$125,000 (or $150,000" for "$150,000 (or $125,000" in each place it appeared in subpara. (c)(2)(A) . . . Sec. 11(b), substituted "$62,500 ($75,000 for taxable years beginning after 1987)" for "$75,000 ($62,500 for taxable years beginning in 1981, 1982, 1983, or 1984)" in subpara. (c)(2)(B), effective for tax. yrs. end. after 12/31/83.

—P.L. 98-369, Sec. 31(b), amended para. (a)(5) . . . Sec. 31(c)(1), added clause (g)(2)(B)(vi) . . . Sec. 31(c)(2), added a sentence to the end of clause (g)(2)(B)(i), effective for property placed in service by the taxpayer after 5/23/83, in tax. yrs. ending after such date and to property placed in service by the taxpayer on or before 5/23/83, if the lease to the tax-exempt entity is entered into after 5/23/83, except as provided in Sec. 31(g)(18) of this Act (following) and subject to the special provisions in Sec. 31(g) of this Act reproduced in note following Code Sec. 168.

"(18) Special rule for amendment made by subsection (c)(1).—

"(A) In general. The amendment made by subsection (c)(1) shall not apply to property—

"(i) leased by the taxpayer on or before November 1, 1983, or

"(ii) leased by the taxpayer after November 1, 1983, if on or before such date the taxpayer entered into a written binding contract requiring the taxpayer to lease such property.

"(B) Limitation. Subparagraph (A) shall apply to the amendment made by subsection (c)(1) only to the extent such amendment relates to property described in subclause (II), (III), or (IV) of section 168(j)(3)(B)(ii) of the Internal Revenue Code of 1954 (as added by this section)."

Prior to amendment, para. (a)(5) read as follows:

"(5) Property used by governmental units. Property used by the United States, any State or political subdivision thereof, any international organization, or any agency or instrumentality of any of the foregoing shall not be treated as section 38 property. For purposes of the preceding sentence, the International Telecommunications Satellite Consortium, the International Maritime Satellite Organization, and any successor organization of such Consortium or Organization shall not be treated as an international organization. If any qualified rehabilitated building is used by the governmental unit pursuant to a lease, this paragraph shall not apply to that portion of the basis of such building which is attributable to qualified rehabilitation expenditures."

—P.L. 98-369, Sec. 111(e)(8)(A), substituted "real property" for "property" in clause (g)(2)(A)(i) . . . Sec. 111(e)(8)(B), substituted "18 (15 years in the case of low-income housing) ["] for "15" in clause (g)(2)(A)(i) . . . Sec. 111(e)(8)(C), substituted "18 years (15 years in the case of low-income housing)" for "15 years" in clause (g)(2)(B)(v) . . . Sec. 111(e)(8)(D), added subpara. (g)(2)(D), effective for property placed in service by the taxpayer after 3/15/84. For exceptions and special rules see Sec. 111(g)(2)-(4) of this Act reproduced in note following Code Sec. 168.

—P.L. 98-369, Sec. 113(a)(1), redesignated subsec. (r) as subsec. (s) and added new subsec. (r), effective for property placed in service after 3/15/84, in tax. yrs. end. after 3/15/84.

—P.L. 98-369, Sec. 113(b)(3)(A), added ", section 46(c)(8), or section 46(c)(9)" after "section 48(a)(2)" in subpara. (k)(4)(A) . . . Sec. 113(b)(3)(B), added "or at-risk rules" after "test" in the heading of para. (k)(4) . . . Sec. 113(b)(3)(C), substituted "used" for "issued" in subpara. (k)(4)(B), effective as provided in Sec. 211(i)(5) of P.L. 97-34, reproduced in note following Code Sec. 46.

—P.L. 98-369, Sec. 113(b)(4), added para. (q)(6), effective for periods after 12/31/82 except as provided in Sec. 205(c)(1)(B)-(E) of P.L. 97-248, reproduced below.

—P.L. 98-369, Sec. 114(a), amended subsec. (b), effective for property originally placed in service after 4/11/84 (determined without regard to such amendment).

Prior to amendment, subsec. (b) read as follows:

"(b) New section 38 property.

"For purposes of this subpart, the term 'new section 38 property' means section 38 property—

"(1) the construction, reconstruction, or erection of which is completed by the taxpayer after December 31, 1961, or

"(2) acquired after December 31, 1961, if the original use of such property commences with the taxpayer and commences after such date.

In applying section 46(c)(1)(A) in the case of property described in paragraph (1), there shall be taken into account only that portion of the basis which is properly attributable to construction, reconstruction, or erection after December 31, 1961. For purposes of determining whether section 38 property subject to a lease is new section 38 property, such property shall be treated as originally placed in service not earlier than the date such property is used under the lease but only if such property is leased within 3 months after such property is placed in service."

—P.L. 98-369, Sec. 431(c), added para. (d)(6), effective for property placed in service after 7/18/84 in tax. yrs. end. after 7/18/84, except for any property to which the amendments made by Sec. 211(f) of P.L. 97-34 apply. Sec. 431(e)(2) of this Act provides:

"(2) Amendments may be elected retroactively.— At the election of the taxpayer, the amendments made by this section shall apply as if included in the amendments made by section 211(f) of the Economic Recovery Tax Act of 1981 [P.L. 97-34]. Any election made under the preceding sentence shall apply to all property of the taxpayer to which the amendments made by such section 211(f) apply and shall be made at such time and in such manner as the Secretary of the Treasury or his delegate may by regulations prescribe."

—P.L. 98-369, Sec. 474(o)(10), substituted "section 39" for "section 46(b)" in subpara. (c)(3)(B) . . . Sec. 474(o)(11), substituted "section 38(c)(3)(B)" for "section 46(a)(6)" in subpara. (d)(1)(B) . . . Sec. 474(o)(12), added "and" at end of para. (f)(1), substituted a period for ", and" at end of para. (f)(2), and deleted para. (f)(3) . . . Sec. 474(o)(13), substituted "section 46(b)(2)" for "section 46(a)(2)(C)" in para. (l)(1) . . . Sec. 474(o)(14), substituted "subsection (b)" for "subsection (a)(2)" in subsec. (m) . . . Sec. 474(o)(15), repealed subsec. (n) except that para. (n)(4) (as in effect before its repeal by Sec. 474(o)(15) of this Act) shall continue to apply in the case of any recapture under Code Sec. 47(f) of a credit allowable for a tax. yr. begin. before 1/1/84, . . . Sec. 474(o)(16), deleted paras. (o)(3), (4), (5), (6), and (7) and redesignated para. (o)(8) as para. (o)(3) . . . Sec. 474(o)(17), substituted "section 46(a)" for "section 46(a)(2)" and "section 46(b)(1)" for "section 46(a)(2)(B)" each place it appeared in subsec. (q) . . . Sec. 474(o)(18), substituted "section 381(c)(26)" for "section 381(c)(23)" in subsec. (r) (redesignated subsec. (s) by Sec. 113(a)(1) of this Act, see above), effective for tax. yrs. begin. after 12/31/83 and to carrybacks from tax. yrs. begin. after 12/31/83. Sec. 475(c) of this Act provides:

"(c) Clarification of effect of amendments on investment tax credit. Nothing in the amendments made by section 474(o) [P.L. '98-369] shall be construed as reducing the amount of any credit allowable for qualified investment in taxable years beginning before January 1, 1984."

Prior to deletion, para. (f)(3) read as follows:

"(3) the $25,000 amount specified under subparagraphs (A) and (B) of section 46(a)(3) applicable to such estate or trust shall be reduced to an amount which bears the same ratio to $25,000 as the amount of the qualified investment allocated to the estate or trust under paragraph (1) bears to the entire amount of the qualified investment."

Prior to repeal, subsec. (n) read as follows:

"(n) Requirements for allowance or employee plan percentage.

"(1) In general.

"(A) Basic employee plan percentage. The basic employee plan percentage shall not apply to any taxpayer for any taxable year unless the taxpayer on his return for such taxable year agrees, as a condition for the allowance of such percentage—

"(i) to make transfers of employer securities to a tax credit employee stock ownership plan maintained by the taxpayer having an aggregate value which does not exceed 1 percent of the amount of the qualified investment (as determined under subsections (c) and (d) of section 46) for the taxable year, and

"(ii) to make such transfers at the times prescribed in subparagraph (C).

"(B) Matching employee plan percentage. The matching employee plan percentage shall not apply to any taxpayer for any taxable year unless the basic employee plan percentage applies to such taxpayer for such taxable year, and the taxpayer on his return for such taxable year agrees, as a condition for the allowance of the matching employee plan percentage—

"(i) to make transfers of employer securities to a tax credit employee stock ownership plan maintained by the employer having an aggregate value equal to the lesser of—

"(I) the sum of the qualified matching employee contributions made to such plan for the taxable year, or

"(II) one-half of 1 percent of the amount of the qualified investment (as determined under subsections (c) and (d) of section 46) for the taxable year, and

"(ii) to make such transfers at the times prescribed in subparagraph (C).

"(C) Times for making transfers. The aggregate of the transfers required under subparagraphs (A) and (B) shall be made—

"(i) to the extent allocable to that portion of the employee plan credit allowed for the taxable year or allowed as a carryback to a preceding taxable year, not later than 30 days after the due date (including extensions) for filing the return for the taxable year, or

"(ii) to the extent allocable to that portion of the employee plan credit which is allowed as a carryover in a succeeding taxable year, not later than 30 days after the due date (including extensions) for filing the return for such succeeding taxable year.

The Secretary may by regulations provide that transfers may be made later than the times prescribed in the preceding sentence where the amount of any credit or carryover or carryback for any taxable year exceeds the amount shown on the return for the taxable year (including where such excess is attributable to qualified matching employee contributions made after the close of the taxable year).

"(D) Ordering rules. For purposes of subparagraph (C), the portion of the employee plan credit allowed for the current year or as a carryover or carryback shall be determined—

"(i) first by treating the credit or carryover or carryback as attributable to the regular percentage,

"(ii) second by treating the portion (not allocated under clause (i)) of such credit or carryover or carryback as attributable to the basic employee plan percentage, and

"(iii) finally by treating the portion (not allocated under clause (i) or (ii) as attributable to the matching employee plan percentage.

"(2) Qualified matching employee contribution defined.

"(A) In general. For purposes of this subsection, the term 'qualified matching employee contribution' means, with respect to any taxable year, any contribution made by an employee to a tax credit employee stock ownership plan maintained by the taxpayer if—

"(i) each employee who is entitled to an allocation of employer securities transferred to the tax credit employee stock ownership plan under paragraph (1)(A) is entitled to make such a contribution, and

"(ii) the contribution is paid in cash to the employer or plan administrator not later than 24 months after the close of the taxable year, and is invested forthwith in employer securities, and

"(iii) the tax credit employee stock ownership plan meets the requirements of subparagraph (B).

"(B) Plan requirements. For purposes of subparagraph (A), a tax credit employee stock ownership plan meets the requirements of this subparagraph if—

"(i) participation in the tax credit employee stock ownership plan is not required as a condition of employment and the tax credit employee stock ownership plan does not require matching employee contributions as a condition of participation in the tax credit employee stock ownership plan,

"(ii) employee contributions under the tax credit employee stock ownership plan meet the requirements of section 401(a)(4), and

"(iii) the tax credit employee stock ownership plan provides for allocation of all employer securities transferred to it or purchased by it (because of the requirements of paragraph (1)(B)) to the account of each participant in an amount equal to such participant's matching employee contributions for the year.

"(3) Certain contributions of cash treated as contributions of employer securities. For purposes of this subsection, a transfer of cash shall be treated as a transfer of employer securities if the cash is, under the tax credit employee stock ownership plan, used within 30 days to purchase employer securities.

"(4) Adjustments if employee plan credit recaptured. If any portion of the employee plan credit is recaptured under section 47 of the employee plan credit is reduced by a final determination—

"(A) the employer may reduce the amount required to be transferred to the tax credit employee stock ownership plan under paragraph (1) for the current taxable year or any succeeding taxable year by an amount equal to such portion (or reduction), or

"(B) notwithstanding the provisions of paragraph (5) and to the extent not taken into account under subparagraph (A), the employer may deduct an amount equal to such portion (or reduction), subject to the limitations of section 404.

"(5) Disallowance of deduction. No deduction shall be allowed under section 162, 212, or 404 for amounts required to be transferred to a tax credit employee stock ownership plan under this subsection.

"(6) Definitions. For purpose of this subsection—

"(A) Employer securities. The term 'employer securities' has the meaning given to such term by section 409A(l).

"(B) Value. The term 'value' means—

"(i) in the case of securities listed on a national exchange, the average of closing prices of such securities for the 20 consecutive trading days immediately preceding the due date on which the securities are contributed to the plan, or

"(ii) in the case of securities not listed on a national exchange, the fair market value as determined in good faith and in accordance with regulations prescribed by the Secretary."

Prior to deletion, paras. (o)(3), (4), (5), (6) and (7) read as follows:

"(3) Employee plan credit. The term 'employee plan credit' means the sum of—

"(A) the basic employee plan credit, and

"(B) the matching employee plan credit.

"(4) Basic employee plan credit. The term 'basic employee plan credit' means that portion of the credit allowable by section 38 which is attributable to the basic employee plan percentage.

"(5) Matching employee plan credit. The term 'matching employee plan credit' means that portion of the credit allowable by section 38 which is attributable to the matching employee plan percentage.

"(6) Basic employee plan percentage. The term 'basic employee plan percentage' means the 1-percent employee plan percentage set forth in section 46(a)(2)(E)(i).

"(7) Matching employee plan percentage. The term 'matching employee plan percentage' means the additional employee plan percentage (not to exceed ½ of 1 percent) set forth in section 46(a)(2)(E)(ii)."

—P.L. 98-369, Sec. 712(b), added para. (q)(6) [sic (7)], effective for periods after 12/31/82 except as provided in Sec. 205(c)(1)(B)–(E) of P.L. 97-248, reproduced below.

—P.L. 98-369, Sec. 721(x)(1), substituted "S corporation" for "electing small business corporation" in clause (k)(5)(D)(i), effective for tax. yrs. begin. after 12/31/82.

—P.L. 98-369, Sec. 735(c)(1), amended clause (l)(16)(B)(i), effective 1/7/83.

Prior to amendment, clause (l)(16)(B)(i) read as follows:

"(i) the chassis and body of which is exempt under section 4063(a)(6) from the tax imposed by section 4061(a),"

—P.L. 98-369, Sec. 1043(a), added subpara. (g)(1)(E), effective for expenditures incurred after 12/31/83, in tax. yrs. end. after 12/31/83.

In 1983, P.L. 97-448, Sec. 102(e)(2)(A), added "(not including a building or its structural components)" after "storage facility" in subpara. (a)(1)(G), effective for periods after 12/31/80, under rules similar to the rules under Code Sec. 48(m).

—P.L. 97-448, Sec. 102(f)(1), amended Sec. 212(e)(2)(B) of P.L. 97-34, part of the effective date for changes made by Sec. 212(a)(3) of P.L. 97-34, see below.

Prior to amendment, Sec. 212(e)(2)(B) of P.L. 97-34 read as follows:

"(B) such building meets the requirements of paragraph (1) of section 48(g) of the Internal Revenue Code of 1954 (as in effect on the day before the date of enactment of this Act) but does not meet the requirements of such paragraph (1) (as amended by this Act)."

—P.L. 97-448, Sec. 102(f)(2), substituted "the 24-month period selected by the taxpayer (at the time and in the manner prescribed by regulations) and ending with or within the taxable year" for "the 24-month period ending on the last day of the taxable year" in clause (g)(1)(C)(i) . . . Sec. 102(f)(3)(A), substituted "a credit is determined under section 46(a)(2)" for "a credit is allowed under this section" in subpara. (g)(5)(A) . . . Sec. 102(f)(3)(B), substituted "the credit so determined" for "the credit so allowed" in subpara. (g)(5)(A) . . . Sec. 102(f)(6)(A), substituted "building (and its structural components)" for "property" the first two places it appeared in clause (g)(1)(C)(i) . . . Sec. 102(f)(6)(B), substituted "building" for "property" the third place it appeared in clause (g)(1)(C)(i) . . . Sec. 102(f)(6)(C), added the last sentence to clause (g)(1)(C)(i), effective for expenditures incurred after 12/31/81 in tax. yrs. end. after 12/31/81.

—P.L. 97-448, Sec. 102(g), amended Sec. 213(b) of P.L. 97-34, the effective date for changes made by Sec. 213(a) of P.L. 97-34, by substituting "taxable years beginning after December 31, 1980" for "property placed in service after December 31, 1980", see below.

—P.L. 97-448, Sec. 202(c), corrected Sec. 223(a)(1) of P.L. 97-223 to amend subpara. (a)(10)(A) instead of para. (a)(10), see below.

—P.L. 97-448, Sec. 306(a)(3), substituted "paragraphs (1) and (2) of this subsection and paragraph (5) of subsection (d)" for "paragraphs (1) and (2)" in para. (q)(3), effective for periods after 12/31/82.

—P.L. 97-424, Sec. 546(a)(1), deleted "or" from the end of subpara. (l)(5)(L) . . . Sec. 546(a)(2), redesignated subpara. (l)(5)(M) as (l)(5)(N) and added new subpara. (l)(5)(M) . . . Sec. 546(a)(3), substituted "(N)" for "(M)" in the second sentence of para. (l)(5), effective 1/6/83.

In 1982, P.L. 97-362, Sec. 104(a), substituted "; except that such term does not include equipment for hydrogenation, refining, or other process subsequent to retorting other than hydrogenation or other process which is applied in the vicinity of the property from which the shale was extracted and which is applied to bring the shale oil to a grade and quality suitable for transportation to and processing in a refinery." for "but does not include equipment for hydrogenation refining, or other process subsequent to retorting." in para. (l)(7), effective for periods begin. after 12/31/80 and before 1/1/83, under rules similar to the rules of Code Sec. 48(m).

—P.L. 97-354, Sec. 3(d)(1), added the last sentence to subpara. (c)(2)(D) . . . Sec. 3(d)(2), substituted "Partnerships and S corporations" for "Partnerships" in the heading of subpara. (c)(2)(D) . . . Sec. 5(a)(7), repealed subsec. (e) . . . Sec. 5(a)(8), substituted "an S corporation" for "an electing small business corporation (within the meaning of section 1371)" in clause (k)(5)(D)(i), effective for tax. yrs. begin. after 12/31/82.

Prior to repeal, subsec. (e) read as follows:

"(e) Subchapter S corporations.

"In the case of an electing small business corporation (as defined in section 1371)—

"(1) the qualified investment for each taxable year shall be apportioned pro rata among the persons who are shareholders of such corporation on the last day of such taxable year; and

"(2) any person to whom any investment has been apportioned under paragraph (1) shall be treated (for purposes of this subpart) as the taxpayer with respect to such investment, and such investment shall not (by reason of such apportionment) lost its character as an investment in new section 38 property or used section 38 property, as the case may be."

—P.L. 97-248, Sec. 205(a)(1), redesignated subsec. (q) as subsec. (r) and added new subsec. (q) . . . Sec. 205(a)(4), added para. (d)(5) . . . Sec. 205(a)(5)(A), deleted para. (g)(5), effective for periods after 12/31/82. Sec. 205(c)(1)(B)–(E) of this Act also provide:

"(B) Exception.—The amendments made by subsection (a) shall not apply to any property which—

"(i) is constructed, reconstructed, erected, or acquired pursuant to a contract which was entered into after August 13, 1981, and was, on July 1, 1982, and at all times thereafter, binding on the taxpayer,

"(ii) is placed in service after December 31, 1982, and before January 1, 1986,

"(iii) with respect to which an election under section 168(f)(8)(A) of such Code is not in effect at any time, and

"(iv) is not described in section 167(l)(3)(A) of such Code.

"(C) Special rule for integrated manufacturing facilities.—

"(i) in general.—In the case of any integrated manufacturing facility, the requirements of clause (i) of subparagraph (B) shall be treated as met if—

"(I) the on-site construction of the facility began before July 1, 1982, and

"(II) during the period beginning after August 13, 1981, and ending on July 1, 1982, the taxpayer constructed (or entered into binding contracts for the construction of) more than 20 percent of the cost of such facility.

"(ii) Integrated manufacturing facility.—For purposes of clause (i), the term 'integrated manufacturing facility' means 1 or more facilities—

"(I) located on a single site,

"(II) for the manufacture of 1 or more manufactured products from raw materials by the application of 2 or more integrated manufacturing processes.

"(D) Special rule for historic structures.—In the case of any certified historic structure (as defined in section 48(g)(3) of the Internal Revenue Code of 1954), clause (i) of subparagraph (B) shall be applied by substituting 'December 31, 1980' for 'August 13, 1981.'

"(E) Certain projects with respect to historic structures.—In the case of any certified historic structure (as so defined), the requirements of clause (i) of subparagraph (B) shall be treated as met with respect to such property

"(i) if the rehabilitation begins after December 31, 1980, and before July 1, 1982, or

"(ii) if—

"(I) before July 1, 1982, a public offering with respect to interests in such property was registered with the Securities and Exchange Commission,

"(II) before such date an application with respect to such property was filed under section 8 of the United States Housing Act of 1937, and

"(III) such property is placed in service before July 1, 1984."

Prior to deletion, para. (g)(5) read as follows:

"(5) Adjustment to basis.

"(A) In general. For purposes of this subtitle, if a credit is allowed under this section for any qualified rehabilitation expenditure in connection with a qualified rehabilitated building other than a certified historic structure, the increase in basis of such property which would (but for this paragraph) result from such expenditure shall be reduced by the amount of the credit so allowed.

"(B) Certain dispositions. If during any taxable year there is a recapture amount determined with respect to any qualified rehabilitated building the basis of which was reduced under subparagraph (A), the basis of such building (immediately before the event resulting in such recapture) shall be increased by an amount equal to such recapture amount. For purposes of the preceding sentence, the term 'recapture amount' means any increase in tax (or adjustment in carrybacks or carryovers) determined under section 47(a)(5)."

—P.L. 97-248, Sec. 209(c), added the last sentence to subsec. (b), effective for property placed in service after 12/31/83.

In 1981, P.L. 97-34, Sec. 211(a)(2), deleted paragraph (a)(9), effective for property placed in service after 12/31/80.

Prior to deletion, para. (a)(9) read as follows:

"(9) Railroad track. In the case of a railroad (including a railroad switching or terminal company) which uses the retirement-replacement method of accounting for depreciation of its railroad track, the term 'section 38 property' includes replacement track material, if—

"(A) the replacement is made pursuant to a scheduled program for replacement,

"(B) the replacement is made pursuant to observations by maintenance-of-way personnel of specific track material needing replacement,

"(C) the replacement is made pursuant to the detection by a rail-test car of specific track material needing replacement, or

"(D) the replacement is made as a result of a casualty.

Replacements made as a result of a casualty shall be section 38 property only to the extent that, in the case of each casualty, the qualified investment with respect to the replacement track material exceeds $50,000. For purposes of this paragraph, the term 'track material' includes ties, rail, other track material, and ballast."

—P.L. 97-34, Sec. 211(c), substituted ", or" for the period at the end of subpara. (a)(1)(F) and added subpara. (a)(1)(G), effective for periods after 12/31/80, under rules similar to the rules under Code Sec. 48(m).

—P.L. 97-34, Sec. 211(e)(3), added "or which is recovery property (within the meaning of section 168" before the period at the end of subpara. (l)(2)(C) ... Sec. 211(e)(4), substituted "includes only recovery property (within the meaning of section 168 without regard to any useful life) and any other property" for "includes only property" in the second sentence of para. (a)(1), effective for property placed in service after 12/31/80.

—P.L. 97-34, Sec. 211(h), amended clause (a)(2)(B)(ii), effective for tax. yrs. begin. after 12/31/80.

Prior to amendment, clause (a)(2)(B)(ii) read as follows:

"(ii) rolling stock, of a domestic railroad corporation providing transportation subject to subchapter I of chapter 105 of title 49, which is used within and without the United States;".

—P.L. 97-34, Sec. 212(a)(3), added para. (o)(8) ... Sec. 212(b), amended subsec. (g) ... Sec. 212(c), deleted "and" at the end of subpara. (a)(3)(B), substituted ", and" for the period at the end of subpara. (a)(3)(C) and added new subpara. (a)(3)(D) ... Sec. 212(d)(2)(A), substituted "or 188" for "188, or 191" in para. (a)(8), effective for expenditures incurred after 12/31/81, in tax. yrs. end. after 12/31/81. Sec. 212(e)(2) of this Act provides:

"(2) Transitional rule. The amendments made by this section shall not apply with respect to any rehabilitation of a building if—

"(A) the physical work on such rehabilitation began before January 1, 1982, and

"(B) such building does not meet the requirements of paragraph (1) of section 48(g) of the Internal Revenue Code of 1954 (as amended by this Act)."

Prior to amendment, subsec. (g) read as follows:

"(g) Special rules for qualified rehabilitated buildings.

"For purposes of this subpart—

"(1) Qualified rehabilitated building defined.

"(A) In general. The term 'qualified rehabilitated building' means any building (and its structural components)—

"(i) which has been rehabilitated,

"(ii) which was placed in service before the beginning of the rehabilitation,

"(iii) 75 percent or more of the existing external walls of which are retained in place as external walls in the rehabilitation process.

"(B) 20 years must have elapsed since construction or prior rehabilitation. A building shall not be a qualified rehabilitated building unless there is a period of at least 20 years between—

"(i) the date the physical work on this rehabilitation of the building began, and

"(ii) the later of—

"(I) the date such building was first placed in service, or

"(II) the date such building was placed in service in connection with a prior rehabilitation with respect to which a credit was allowed by reason of subsection (a)(1)(E).

"(C) Major portion treated as separate building in certain cases. Where there is a separate rehabilitation of a major portion of a building, such major portion shall be treated as a separate building.

"(D) Rehabilitation includes reconstruction. Rehabilitation includes reconstruction.

"(2) Qualified rehabilitation expenditure defined.

"(A) In general. The term 'qualified rehabilitation expenditure' means any amount properly chargeable to capital account which is incurred after October 31, 1978—

"(i) for property (or additions or improvements to property) with a useful life of 5 years or more, and

"(ii) in connection with the rehabilitation of a qualified rehabilitated building.

"(B) Certain expenditures not included. The term 'qualified rehabilitation expenditure' does not include—

"(i) Property otherwise section 38 property. Any expenditure for property which constitutes section 38 property (determined without regard to subsections (a)(1)(E) and (I)).

"(ii) Cost of acquisition. The cost of acquiring any building or any interest therein.

"(iii) Enlargements. Any expenditure attributable to the enlargement of the existing building.

"(iv) Certified historic structures. Any expenditure attributable to the rehabilitation of a certified historic structure (within the meaning of section 191(d)(1)), unless the rehabilitation is a certified rehabilitation (within the meaning of section 191(d)(4)).

"(3) Property treated as new section 38 property. Property which is treated as section 38 property by reason of subsection (a)(1)(E) shall be treated as new section 38 property."

—P.L. 97-34, Sec. 213(a), amended subparas. (c)(2)(A), (B), and (C), effective for tax. yrs. begin. after 12/31/80.

Prior to amendment, subparas. (c)(2)(A), (B) and (C) read as follows:

"(2) Dollar limitation.

"(A) In general. The cost of used section 38 property taken into account under section 46(c)(1)(B) for any taxable year shall not exceed $100,000. If such cost exceeds $100,000, the taxpayer shall select (at such time and in such manner as the Secretary or his delegate shall by regulations prescribe) the items to be taken into account, but only to the extent of an aggregate cost of $100,000. Such a selection, once made, may be changed only in the manner, and to the extent, provided by such regulations.

"(B) Married individuals. In the case of a husband or wife who files a separate return, the limitation under subparagraph (A) shall be $50,000 in lieu of $100,000. This subparagraph shall not apply if the spouse of the taxpayer has no used section 38 property which may be taken into account as qualified investment for the taxable year of such spouse which ends within or with the taxpayer's taxable year.

"(C) Controlled groups. In the case of a controlled group, the $100,000 amount specified under subparagraph (A) shall be reduced for each component member of the group by apportioning $100,000 among the component members of such group in accordance with their respective amounts of used section 38 property which may be taken into account."

—P.L. 97-34, Sec. 214(a), added the last sentence to para. (a)(4) ... Sec. 214(b), added the last sentence to para. (a)(5), effective for uses after 7/29/80, in tax. yrs. ending after 7/29/80.

—P.L. 97-34, Sec. 332(b), substituted "which does not exceed" for "equal to" in clause (n)(1)(A)(i), effective for qualified investments made after 12/31/81.

In 1980, P.L. 96-605, Sec. 109(a), amended para. (a)(5), effective for tax. yrs. begin. after 12/31/79.

Prior to amendment, para. (a)(5) read as follows:

"(5) Property used by governmental units. Property used by the United States, any State or political subdivision thereof, any international organization (other than the International Telecommunications Satellite Consortium or any successor organization), or any agency or instrumentality of any of the foregoing shall not be treated as section 38 property."

—P.L. 96-605, Sec. 223(a), substituted "the date on which the securities are contributed to the plan" for "the due date for filing the return for the taxable year (determined without regard to extensions)" in clause (n)(6)(B)(i), effective for tax. yrs. begin. after 12/31/80.

—P.L. 96-451, Sec. 302(a)(1), substituted ", or" for the period at the end of subpara. (a)(1)(E) ... Sec. 302(a)(2), added subpara. (a)(1)(F) ... Sec. 302(a)(3), added the last sentence to para. (a)(1), effective for additions to capital account made after 12/31/79.

—P.L. 96-223, Sec. 221(b), amended para. (l)(1) and substituted "one-half of the energy percentage determined under section 46(a)(2)(C)" for "5 percent" in para. (l)(11).

Prior to amendment, para. (l)(1) read as follows:

"(1) Treatment as section 38 property. For the period beginning on October 1, 1978, and ending on December 31, 1982—

"(A) any energy property shall be treated as meeting the requirements of paragraph (1) of subsection (a), and

"(B) paragraph (3) of subsection (a) shall not apply to any energy property."

—P.L. 96-223, Sec. 222(a)(1), deleted "or" at the end of clause (l)(2)(A)(v) ... Sec. 222(a)(2), and added clauses (l)(2)(A)(vii), (viii), and (ix) ... Sec. 222(b)(1), deleted "(other than coke or coke gas)" after "solid fuel" in clause (l)(3)(A)(iii) ... Sec. 222(b)(2), amended clause (l)(3)(A)(v) ... Sec. 222(b)(3), deleted "and" at the end of clause (l)(3)(A)(vii) ... Sec. 222(b)(4), substituted ", and" for the period at the end of clause (l)(3)(A)(viii) ... Sec. 222(b)(5), added new clause (l)(3)(A)(ix) ... Sec. 222(c)(1), deleted "or" at the end of subpara. (l)(4)(A) ... Sec. 222(c)(2), substituted ", or" for the period at the end of subpara. (l)(4)(B)

1,213

... Sec. 222(c)(3), added new subpara. (l)(4)(C), effective for periods after 12/31/79, under rules similar to the rules of Code Sec. 48(m).
Prior to amendment, clause (l)(3)(A)(v) read as follows:
"(v) equipment which uses coal (including lignite) as a feedstock for the manufacture of chemicals or other products (other than coke or coke gas),"
—P.L. 96-223, Sec. 222(d)(1), amended para. (l)(5) by deleting "or" at the end of subpara. (K), by redesignating subpara. (L) as (M), and by adding new subpara. (L), effective for periods after 9/30/78 under rules similar to the rules of Code Sec. 48(m).
—P.L. 96-223, Sec. 222(d)(2), added the last sentence to para. (l)(5) . . . Sec. 222(e)(1), added para. (l)(13) . . . Sec. 222(f), added para. (l)(14) . . . Sec. 222(g), added para. (l)(15) and added the last sentence to para. (l)(3) . . . Sec. 222(h), added para. (l)(16) . . . Sec. 222(i)(1)(A), deleted subpara. (l)(3)(B) and redesignated subparas. (l)(3)(C) and (D) as (B) and (C) . . . Sec. 222(i)(1)(B), added para. (l)(17) . . . Sec. 222(i)(2), amended subpara. (a)(2)(B) by deleting "and" at the end of clause (ix), by substituting ", and" for the period at the end of clause (x) and by adding new clause (xi) . . . Sec. 222(i)(3), added the last sentence to subpara. (l)(3)(C) [as redesignated by Sec. 222(i)(1)], effective for periods after 12/31/79, under rules similar to Code Sec. 48(m).
Prior to amendment, subpara. (l)(3)(B) read as follows:
"(B) Exclusion for public utility property. The terms 'alternative energy property', 'solar or wind energy property', and 'recycling equipment' do not include property which is public utility property (within the meaning of section 46(f)(5))."
Sec. 223(a)(1) of P.L. 96-223, added the last sentence to subpara. (a)(10)(A), effective for periods after 12/31/79 under rules similar to the rules of Code Sec. 48(m).
—P.L. 96-223, Sec. 223(c)(1), amended para. (l)(11), effective for periods after 12/31/82 under rules similar to the rules of Code Sec. 48(m) except as provided by Sec. 223(c)(2)(B), (C) and (D) of this Act which reads as follows:
"(B) Earlier application for certain property. In the case of property which is—
"(i) qualified hydroelectric generating property (described in section 48(l)(2)(A)(viii) of such Code),
"(ii) cogeneration equipment (described in section 48(l)(2)(A)(viii) of such Code),
"(iii) qualified intercity buses (described in section 48(l)(2)(A)(ix) of such Code), or
"(IV) ocean thermal property (described in section 48(l)(3)(A)(ix) of such Code), or
"(v) expanded energy credit property,
the amendment made by paragraph (1) shall apply to periods after December 31, 1979, under rules similar to the rules of section 48(m) of the Internal Revenue Code of 1954.
"(C) Expanded energy credit property. For purposes of subparagraph (B), the term 'expanded energy credit property' means—
"(i) property to which section 48(l)(3)(A) of such Code applies because of the amendments made by paragraphs (1) and (2) of section 222(b),
"(ii) property described in section 48(l)(3)(C) of such Code (relating to solar process heat),
"(iii) property described in section 48(l)(5)(L) of such Code (relating to alumina electrolytic cells), and
"(iv) property described in the last sentence of section 48(l)(3)(A) of such Code (relating to storage equipment for refuse-derived fuel).
"(D) Financing taken into account. For the purpose of applying the provisions of section 48(l)(11) of such Code in the case of property financed in whole or in part by subsidized energy financing (within the meaning of section 48(l)(11)(C) of such Code), no financing made before January 1, 1980, shall be taken into account. The preceding sentence shall not apply to financing provided from the proceeds of any tax-exempt industrial development bond (within the meaning of section 103(b)(2) of such Code)."
—P.L. 96-222, Sec. 101(a)(7)(B), corrected Sec. 141(g) of P.L. 95-600 [see below].
Prior to corrections, Sec. 141(g) of P.L. 95-600 read as follows:
"(g) Effective dates.
"(1) In general. The amendments made by this section (other than by subsection (f)(3)) shall apply with respect to qualified investment for taxable years beginning after December 31, 1978. The amendment made by subsection (f)(7) shall apply to years beginning after December 31, 1978."
—P.L. 96-222, Sec. 101(a)(7)(G), amended clause (n)(1)(B)(i) . . . Sec. 101(a)(7)(H), added "(including where such excess is attributable to qualified matching employee contributions made after the close of the taxable year)" before the period in the last sentence of subpara. (n)(1)(C) . . . Sec. 101(a)(7)(i)(I) thru (IV), substituted "a tax credit employee stock ownership plan" for "an ESOP" each place it appeared in clause (n)(1)(A)(i), para. (n)(2), subpara. (n)(2)(A) and para. (n)(5) . . . Sec. 101(a)(7)(L)(ii)(III), thru (VI), substituted "tax credit employee stock ownership plan" for "ESOP" each place it appeared in clause (n)(1)(B)(i) [inoperative change made by 101(a)(7)(G), see above], paras. (n)(2) and (3) and subpara. (n)(4)(A) . . . Sec. 101(a)(7)(L)(iii)(II), and (III), substituted "employee plan" for "ESOP" each place it appeared in subsecs. (n) and (o) . . . Sec. 101(a)(7)(L)(v)(II), thru (V), substituted "employee plan" for "ESOP" in the headings of para. (n), subparas. (n)(1)(A) and (B), and paras. (n)(4), and (o)(3), (4), (5), (6) and (7) . . . Sec. 101(a)(7)(M)(ii), added "and" to the end of clause (n)(2)(B)(i), deleted clause (n)(2)(B)(ii), redesignated clause (n)(2)(B)(iii) as (ii) and redesignated clause (n)(2)(B)(iv) as (iii) . . . Sec. 101(a)(7)(M)(iii), added "percentage" after "attributable to the matching employee plan" in para. (o)(5) [as amended by 101(a)(7)(L)(iii), see above], presumably intended by Congress to be effective with respect to qualified investment for tax. yrs. begin. after '78 [Sec. 101(b)(2)] although technically effective with respect to the estates of decedents dying after 4/1/80 [Sec. 101(b)(1)(D)].

Prior to amendment, clause (n)(1)(B)(i) read as follows:
"(i) to make transfers of employer securities to an ESOP maintained by the taxpayer having an aggregate value equal to the sum of the qualified matching employee contributions made to such ESOP for the taxable year, and"
Prior to amendment, clause (n)(2)(B)(ii) read as follows:
"(ii) employee contributions under the ESOP meet the requirements of section 401(a)(4), and"
—P.L. 96-222, Sec. 103(a)(2)(A), amended Sec. 312(c) of P.L. 95-600 which amended subpara. (a)(7)(B) by substituting "described in section 50 (as in effect before its repeal by the Revenue Act of 1978)" for "described in section 50" [see below].
—P.L. 96-222, Sec. 103(a)(4)(B), substituted "subsections (a)(1)(E) and (l))" for "subsection (a)(1)(E)" at the end of clause (g)(2)(B)(i), effective for tax. yrs. end. after 10/31/78.
—P.L. 96-222, Sec. 108(c)(6), substituted "5" for "51" in the last sentence of subpara. (a)(10)(B), effective 5/1/80.
In 1978, P.L. 95-618, Sec. 301(b), redesignated subsec. (l) as subsec. (n) . . . added new subsecs. (l) and (m), effective 11/9/78.
—P.L. 95-618, Sec. 301(d)(1), amended subpara. (a)(1)(A) . . . Sec. 301(d)(2), added para. (a)(10), effective for property placed in service after 9/30/78. . . . Sec. 301(d)(4)(B), of this Act provides:
"(B) Binding contracts. The amendments made by this subsection shall not apply to property which is constructed, reconstructed, erected, or acquired pursuant to a contract which, on October 1, 1978, and at all times thereafter, was binding on the taxpayer."
Prior to amendment, subpara. (a)(1)(A) read as follows:
"(A) tangible personal property, or"
—P.L. 95-600, Sec. 141(b), redesignated subsec. (n) [as redesignated by Sec. 301(b) of P.L. 95-618] as subsec. (p) and added new subsecs. (n) and (o), effective for qualified investment for tax. yrs. begin. after '78. Sec. 141(g)(2) of this Act provides:
"(2) Election to have amendments apply during 1978. At the election of the taxpayer, paragraph (1) shall be applied by substituting 'December 31, 1977' for 'December 31, 1978'; except that in the case of a plan in existence before December 31, 1978, any such election shall not affect the required allocation of employer securities attributable to qualified investment for taxable years beginning before January 1, 1979. An election under the preceding sentence shall be made at such time and in such manner as the Secretary of the Treasury or his delegate shall prescribe. Such an election, once made, shall be irrevocable."
—P.L. 95-600, Sec. 311(b), extended the $100,000 limitation on used property indefinitely, by deleting "January 1, 1981" in Sec. 301(c)(2) of P.L. 94-12 [as amended by Sec. 801 of P.L. 94-455].
—P.L. 95-600, Sec. 312(c)(1), deleted subsecs. (h), (i) and (j) . . . Sec. 312(c)(2), substituted "described in section 50 (as in effect before its repeal by the Revenue Act of 1978)" for "described in section 50" in subpara. (a)(7)(B) . . . Sec. 312(c)(3), deleted "(other than pre-termination property)" following "Property" in subpara. (a)(7)(A), effective for tax. yrs. end. after '78.
Prior to deletion, subsecs. (h), (i) and (j) read as follows:
"(h) Suspension of investment credit.
"For purposes of this subpart—
"(1) General rule. Section 38 property which is suspension period property shall not be treated as new or used section 38 property.
"(2) Suspension period property defined. Except as otherwise provided in this subsection and subsection (i), the term 'suspension period property' means section 38 property—
"(A) the physical construction, reconstruction, or erection of which (i) is begun during the suspension period, or (ii) is begun, pursuant to an order placed during such period, before May 24, 1967, or
"(B) which (i) is acquired by the taxpayer during the suspension period, or (ii) is acquired by the taxpayer, pursuant to an order placed during such period, before May 24, 1967.
"In applying subparagraph (A) to any section 38 property, there shall be taken into account only that portion of the basis which is properly attributable to construction, reconstruction, or erection before May 24, 1967.
"(3) Binding contracts. To the extent that any property is constructed, reconstructed, erected, or acquired pursuant to a contract which was, on October 9, 1966, and at all times thereafter, binding on the taxpayer, such property shall not be deemed to be suspension period property.
"(4) Equipped building rule. If—
"(A) pursuant to a plan of the taxpayer in existence on October 9, 1966 (which plan was not substantially modified at any time after such date and before the taxpayer placed the equipped building in service), the taxpayer has constructed, reconstructed, erected, or acquired a building and the machinery and equipment necessary to the planned use of the building by the taxpayer, and
"(B) more than 50 percent of the aggregate adjusted basis of all the property of a character subject to the allowance for depreciation making up such building as so equipped is attributable to either property the construction, reconstruction, or erection of which was begun by the taxpayer before October 10, 1966, or property the acquisition of which by the taxpayer occurred before such date,
then all section 38 property comprising such building as so equipped (and any incidental section 38 property adjacent to such building which is necessary to the planned use of the building) shall be treated as section 38 property which is not suspension period property. For purposes of subparagraph (B) of the preceding sentence, the rules of paragraphs (3) and (6) shall be applied. For purposes of this paragraph, a special purpose structure shall be treated as a building.
"(5) Plant facility rule.
"(A) General rule. If—

"(i) pursuant to a plan of the taxpayer in existence on October 9, 1966 (which plan was not substantially modified at any time after such date and before the taxpayer placed the plant facility in service), the taxpayer has constructed, reconstructed, or erected a plant facility, and either

"(ii) the construction, reconstruction, or erection of such plant facility was commenced by the taxpayer before October 10, 1966, or

"(iii) more than 50 percent of the aggregate adjusted basis of all the property of a character subject to the allowance for depreciation making up such plant facility is attributable to either property the construction, reconstruction, or erection of which was begun by the taxpayer before October 10, 1966, or property the acquisition of which by the taxpayer occurred before such date,

then all section 38 property comprising such plant facility shall be treated as section 38 property which is not suspension period property. For purposes of clause (iii) of the preceding sentence, the rules of paragraphs (3) and (6) shall be applied.

"(B) Plant facility defined. For purposes of this paragraph, the term 'plant facility' means a facility which does not include any building (or of which buildings constitute an insignificant portion) and which is—

"(i) a self-contained, single operating unit or processing operation,

"(ii) located on a single site, and

"(iii) identified, on October 9, 1966, in the purchasing and internal financial plans of the taxpayer as a single unitary project.

"(C) Special rule. For purposes of this subsection, if—

"(i) a certificate of convenience and necessity has been issued before October 10, 1966, by a Federal regulatory agency with respect to two or more plant facilities which are included under a single plan of the taxpayer to construct, reconstruct, or erect such plant facilities, and

"(ii) more than 50 percent of the aggregate adjusted basis of all the property of a character subject to the allowance for depreciation making up such plant facilities is attributable to either property the construction, reconstruction, or erection of which was begun by the taxpayer before October 10, 1966, or property the acquisition of which by the taxpayer occurred before such date,

such plant facilities shall be treated as a single plant facility.

"(D) Commencement of construction. For purposes of subparagraph (A)(ii), the construction, reconstruction, or erection of a plant facility shall not be considered to have commenced until construction, reconstruction, or erection has commenced at the site of such plant facility. The preceding sentence shall not apply if the site of such plant facility is not located on land.

"(6) Machinery or equipment rule. Any piece of machinery or equipment—

"(A) more than 50 percent of the parts and components of which (determined on the basis of cost) were held by the taxpayer on October 9, 1966, or are acquired by the taxpayer pursuant to a binding contract which was in effect on such date, for inclusion or use in such piece of machinery or equipment, and

"(B) the cost of the parts and components of which is not an insignificant portion of the total cost,

shall be treated as property which is not suspension period property.

"(7) Certain lease-back transactions, etc. Where a person who is a party to a binding contract described in paragraph (3)transfers rights in such contract (or in the property to which such contract relates) to another person but a party to such contract retains a right to use the property under a lease with such other person, then to the extent of the transferred rights such other person shall, for purposes of paragraph (3), succeed to the position of the transferor with respect to such binding contract and such property. The preceding sentence shall apply, in any case in which the lessor does not make an election under subsection (d), only if a party to such contract retains a right to use the property under a long-term lease.

"(8) Certain lease and contract obligations. Where, pursuant to a binding lease or contract to lease in effect on October 9, 1966, a lessor or lessee is obligated to construct, reconstruct, erect, or acquire property specified in such lease or contract, any property so constructed, reconstructed, erected, or acquired by the lessor or lessee which is section 38 property shall be treated as property which is not suspension period property. In the case of any project which includes property other than the property to be leased to such lessee, the preceding sentence shall be applied, in the case of the lessor, to such other property only if the binding leases and contracts with all lessees in effect on October 9, 1966, cover real property constituting 25 percent or more of the project (determined on the basis of rental value). For purposes of the preceding sentences of this paragraph, in the case of any project where one or more vendor-vendee relationships exist, such vendors and vendees shall be treated as lessors and lessees. Where, pursuant to a binding contract in effect on October 9, 1966, (i) the taxpayer is required to construct, reconstruct, erect, or acquire property specified in the contract, to be used to produce one or more products, and (ii) the other party is required to take substantially all of the products to be produced over a substantial portion of the expected useful life of the property, then such property shall be treated as property which is not suspension period property. Clause (ii) of the preceding sentence shall not apply if a political subdivision of a State is the other party to the contract and is required by the contract to make substantial expenditures which benefit the taxpayer.

"(9) Certain transfers to be disregarded.

"(A) If property or rights under a contract are transferred in—

"(i) a transfer by reason of death, or

"(ii) a transaction as a result of which the basis of the property in the hands of the transferee is determined by reference to its basis in the hands of the transferor by reason of the application of section 332, 351, 361, 371(a), 374(a), 721, or 731, and such property (or the property acquired under such contract) would not be treated as suspension period property in the hands of the decedent or the transferor, such property shall not be treated as suspension period property in the hands of the transferee.

"(B) If—

"(i) property or rights under a contract are acquired in a transaction to which section 334(b)(2) applies,

"(ii) the stock of the distributing corporation was acquired before October 10, 1966, or pursuant to a binding contract in effect October 9, 1966, and

"(iii) such property (or the property acquired under such contract) would not be treated as suspension period property in the hands of the distributing corporation, such property shall not be treated as suspension period property in the hands of the distributee.

"(10) Property acquired from affiliated corporation. For purposes of this subsection, in the case of property acquired by a corporation which is a member of an affiliated group from another member of the same group—

"(A) such corporation shall be treated as having acquired such property on the date on which it was acquired by such other member,

"(B) such corporation shall be treated as having entered into a binding contract for the construction, reconstruction, erection, or acquisition of such property on the date on which such other member entered into a contract for the construction, reconstruction, erection, or acquisition of such property, and

"(C) such corporation shall be treated as having commenced the construction, reconstruction, or erection of such property on the date on which such other member commenced such construction, reconstruction, or erection.

"For purposes of the preceding sentence, the term 'affiliated group' has the meaning assigned to it by section 1504(a), except that all corporations shall be treated as includible corporations (without any exclusion under section 1504(b).

"(11) Certain tangible property constructed during suspension period and leased new thereafter. Tangible personal property constructed or reconstructed by a person shall not be suspension period property if—

"(A) such person leases such property after the close of the suspension period and the original use of such property commences after the close of such period,

"(B) such construction or reconstruction, and such lease transaction, was not pursuant to an order placed during the suspension period, and

"(C) an election is made under subsection (d) with respect to such property which satisfies the requirements of such subsection.

"(12) Water and air pollution control facilities.

"(A) In general. Any water pollution control facility or air pollution control facility shall be treated as property which is not suspension period property.

"(B) Water pollution control facility. For purposes of subparagraph (A), the term 'water pollution control facility' means any section 38 property which—

"(i) is used primarily to control water pollution by removing, altering, or disposing of wastes, including the necessary intercepting sewers, outfall sewers, pumping, power, and other equipment, and their appurtenances; and

"(ii) is certified by the State water pollution control agency (as defined in section 13(a) of the Federal Water Pollution Control Act) as being in conformity with the State program or requirements for control of water pollution and is certified by the Secretary of Interior as being in compliance with the applicable regulations of Federal agencies and the general policies of the United States for cooperation with the States in the prevention and abatement of water pollution under the Federal Water Pollution Control Act.

"(C) Air pollution control facility. For purposes of subparagraph (A), the term 'air pollution control facility' means any section 38 property which—

"(i) is used primarily to control atmospheric pollution or contamination by removing, altering, or disposing of atmospheric pollutants or contaminants; and

"(ii) is certified by the State air pollution control agency (as defined in section 302(b) of the Clean Air Act) as being in conformity with the State program or requirements for control of air pollution and is certified by the Secretary of Health, Education, and Welfare as being in compliance with the applicable regulations of Federal agencies and the general policies of the United States for cooperation with the States in the prevention and abatement of air pollution under the Clean Air Act.

"(D) Standards for facility. Subparagraph (A) shall apply in the case of any facility only if the taxpayer constructs, reconstructs, erects, or acquires such facility in furtherance of Federal, State, or local standards for the control of water pollution or atmospheric pollution or contaminants.

"(13) Certain replacement property. Section 38 property constructed, reconstructed, erected, or acquired by the taxpayer shall be treated as property which is not suspension period property to the extent such property is placed in service to replace property which was—

"(A) destroyed or damaged by fire, storm, shipwreck, or other casualty, or

"(B) stolen, but only to the extent the basis (in the case of new section 38 property) or cost (in the case of used section 38 property) of such section 38 property does not exceed the adjusted basis of the property destroyed, damaged or stolen.

"(i) Exemption from suspension of $20,000 of investment.

"(1) In general. In the case of property acquired by the taxpayer by purchase for use in his trade or business which would (but for this subsection) be suspension period property, the taxpayer may select items to which this subsection applies, to the extent of an aggregate cost, for the suspension period, of $20,000. Any item so selected shall be treated as property which is not suspension period property for purposes of this subpart (other than for purposes of paragraphs (4), (5), (6), (7), (8), (9), and (10) of subsection (h)).

"(2) Applicable rules. Under regulations prescribed by the Secretary, rules similar to the rules provided by paragraphs (2) and (3) of subsection (c) shall be applied for purposes of this subsection. Subsection (d) shall not apply with respect to any item to which this subsection applies.

"(j) Suspension period.

"For purposes of this subpart, the term 'suspension period' means the period beginning on October 10, 1966, and ending on March 9, 1967."

—P.L. 95-600, Sec. 314(a), substituted ", or" for the period at the end of subpara. (a)(1)(C) and added subpara. (a)(1)(D) . . . Sec. 314(b), redesignated subsec.

(p) [as redesignated by Sec. 141(b) of this Act] as subsec. (q) and added new subsec. (p), effective for tax. yrs. end. after 8/15/71.

—P.L. 95-600, Sec. 315(a), substituted "; or" for the period at the end of subpara. (a)(1)(D) (as added by Sec. 314(a), of this Act) . . . Sec. 315(b), added subsec. (g), effective for tax. yrs. end. after 10/31/78.

—P.L. 95-600, Sec. 315(c), substituted "188, or 191" for "or 188" in para. (a)(8), effective for property placed in service after 10/31/78.

—P.L. 95-600, Sec. 703(a)(3), substituted "section 46(a)(6)" for "section 46(a)(5)" in subpara. (d)(1)(B) . . . Sec. 703(a)(4), substituted "section 57(c)(1)(B)" for "section 57(c)(2)" in subpara. (d)(4)(B), effective 10/4/76.

—P.L. 95-473, Sec. 2(a)(2)(A), substituted "providing transportation subject to subchapter I of chapter 105 of title 49" for "subject to part I of the Interstate Commerce Act" in clause (a)(2)(B)(ii), effective 10/17/78.

In 1976, P.L. 94-455, Sec. 801, extended the $100,000 limitation on used property for 4 years by substituting "January 1, 1981" for "January 1, 1977" in Sec. 301(c)(2) of P.L. 94-12.

—P.L. 94-455, Sec. 802(b)(6), substituted "section 46(a)(3)" for "section 46(a)(2)" following "under subparagraphs (A) and (B) of" in subsec. (f), effective for tax. yrs. begin. after '75.

—P.L. 94-455, Sec. 804(a), redesignated subsec. (k) as subsec. (l) and added a new subsec. (k), effective for tax. yrs. begin. after '74. Sec. 804(d) of this Act provides the following with respect to entitlement to credit:

"(d) Entitlement to credit.

"Paragraph (1) of section 48(k) of the Internal Revenue Code of 1954 (relating to entitlement of credit) shall apply to any motion picture film or video tape placed in service in any taxable year beginning before January 1, 1975."

In 1976, P.L. 94-445, Sec. 804(c), provided the following alternative methods of computing credit for past periods.

"(c) Alternative methods of computing credit for past periods.

"(1) General rule for determining useful life, predominant foreign use, etc.—In the case of a qualified film (within the meaning of section 48(k)(1)(B) of the Internal Revenue Code of 1954) placed in service in a taxable year beginning before January 1, 1975, with respect to which neither an election under paragraph (2) of this subsection nor an election under subsection (e)(2) applies—

"(A) the applicable percentage under section 46(c)(2) of such Code shall be determined as if the useful life of the film would have expired at the close of the first taxable year by the close of which the aggregate amount allowable as a deduction under section 167 of such Code would equal or exceed 90 percent of the basis of such property (adjusted for any partial dispositions),

"(B) for purposes of section 46(c)(1) of such Code, the basis of the property shall be determined by taking into account the total production costs (within the meaning of section 48(k)(5)(B) of such Code),

"(C) for purposes of section 48(a)(2) of such Code, such film shall be considered to be used predominantly outside the United States in the first taxable year for which 50 percent or more of the gross revenues received or accrued during the taxable year from showing the film were received or accrued from showing the film outside the United States, and

"(D) Section 47(a)(7) of such Code shall apply.

"(2) Election of 40-percent method.—

"(A) In general.—A taxpayer may elect to have this paragraph apply to all qualified films placed in service during taxable years beginning before January 1, 1975 (other than films to which an election under subsection (e)(2) of this section applies).

"(B) Effect of election.—If the taxpayer makes an election under this paragraph, then section 48(k) of the Internal Revenue Code of 1954 shall apply to all qualified films described in subparagraph (A) with the following modifications:

"(i) subparagraph (B) of paragraph (4) shall not apply, but in determining qualified investment under section 46(c)(1) of such Code, there shall be used (in lieu of the basis of such property) an amount equal to 40 percent of the aggregate production costs (within the meaning of paragraph (5)(B) of such section 48(k)),

"(ii) paragraph (2) shall be applied by substituting '100 percent' for '66⅔ percent', and

"(iii) paragraph (3) and paragraph (5) (other than subparagraph (B)) shall not apply.

"(C) Rules relating to elections.—An election under this paragraph shall be made not later than the day which is 6 months after the date of the enactment of this Act and shall be made in such manner as the Secretary of the Treasury or his delegate shall by regulations prescribe. Such an election may be revoked only with the consent of the Secretary of the Treasury or his delegate.

"(D) The taxpayer must consent to join in certain proceedings.—No election may be made under this paragraph or subsection (e)(2) by any taxpayer unless he consents, under regulations prescribed by the Secretary of the Treasury or his delegate, to treat the determination of the investment credit allowable on each film subject to an election as a separate cause of action, and to join in any judicial proceeding for determining the person entitled to, and the amount of, the credit allowable under section 38 of the Internal Revenue Code of 1954 with respect to any film covered by such election.

"(3) Election to have credit determined in accordance with previous litigation.—

"(A) In general.—A taxpayer described in subparagraph (B) may elect to have this paragraph apply to all films (whether or not qualified) placed in service in taxable years beginning before January 1, 1975, and with respect to which an election under subsection (e)(2) is not made.

"(B) Who may elect.—A taxpayer may make an election under this paragraph if he has filed an action in any court of competent jurisdiction, before January 1, 1976, for a determination of such taxpayer's rights to the allowance of a credit against tax under section 38 of the Internal Revenue Code of 1954 for any taxable year beginning before January 1, 1975, with respect to any film.

"(C) Effect of election.—If the taxpayer makes an election under this paragraph—

"(i) paragraphs (1) and (2) of this subsection, and subsection (d) shall not apply to any film placed in service by the taxpayer, and

"(ii) subsection 48(k) of the Internal Revenue Code of 1954 shall not apply to any film placed in service by the taxpayer in any taxable year beginning before January 1, 1975, and with respect to which an election under subsection (e)(2) is not made,

and the right of the taxpayer to the allowance of a credit against tax under section 38 of such Code with respect to any film placed in service in any taxable year beginning before January 1, 1975, and as to which an election under subsection (e)(2) is not made, shall be determined as though this section (other than this paragraph) has not been enacted.

"(D) Rules relating to elections.—An election under this paragraph shall be made not later than the day which is 90 days after the date of the enactment of this Act, by filing a notification of such election with the national office of the Internal Revenue Service. Such an election, once made, shall be irrevocable."

—P.L. 94-455, Sec. 1051(h)(1), substituted "(other than a corporation which has an election in effect under section 936 or which is entitled to the benefits of section 934(b))" for "(other than a corporation entitled to the benefits of section 931 or 934(b))" in clause (a)(2)(B)(vii), effective for tax. yrs. begin. after '75, except that "qualified possession source investment income" as defined in section 936(d)(2) of the Internal Revenue Code of 1954 shall include income from any source outside the United States if the taxpayer establishes to the satisfaction of the Secretary of the Treasury or his delegate that the income from such sources was earned before 10/1/76.

—P.L. 94-455, Sec. 1901(a)(5)(A), substituted "43 U.S.C. 1331)" for "43 U.S.C., sec. 1331)" in clause (a)(2)(B)(vi) . . . Sec. 1901(a)(5)(B), substituted "47 U.S.C. 702(3)" for "47 U.S.C., sec. 702(3)" in clause (a)(2)(B)(viii), effective for tax. yrs. begin. after '76.

—P.L. 94-455, Sec. 1901(b)(11)(A), deleted "187," following "184," in para. (a)(8), effective for tax. yrs. begin. after '76.

—P.L. 94-455, Sec. 1906(b)(13)(A), substituted "Secretary" for "Secretary or his delegate" each place it appeared in subsec. (d) and subsec. (i), effective for tax. yrs. begin. after '76.

—P.L. 94-455, Sec. 2112(a)(1), deleted "169," following "167(k)," in para. (a)(8) and deleted the second sentence of para. (a)(8), effective for property acquired by taxpayer, and which construction, reconstruction, etc, was completed after '76, in tax. yrs. begin. after '76.

Prior to amendment, the second sentence of para. (a)(8) read as follows:

"In the case of any property to which section 169 applies, the preceding sentence shall apply only to so much of the adjusted basis of the property as (after the application of section 169(f)) constitutes the amortizable basis for purposes of section 169."

In 1975, P.L. 94-12, Sec. 604(a), substituted "territorial waters within the northern portion of the Western Hemisphere" for "territorial waters" in clause (a)(2)(B)(x) and added the final sentence to subpara. (a)(2)(B), effective as provided in Sec. 604(b), which reads as follows:

"(b) Effective date.

"(1) In general. The amendments made by subsection (a) shall apply to property, the construction, reconstruction, or erection of which was completed after March 18, 1975, or the acquisition of which by the taxpayer occurred after such date.

"(2) Binding contract. The amendments made by subsection (a) shall not apply to property constructed, reconstructed, erected, or acquired pursuant to a contract which was on April 1, 1974, and at all times thereafter, binding on the taxpayer.

"(3) Certain lease-back transactions, etc. Where a person who is a party to a binding contract described in paragraph (2) transfers rights in such contract (or in the property to which such contract relates) to another person but a party to such contract retains a right to use the property under a lease with such other person, then to the extent of the transferred rights such other person shall, for purposes of paragraph (2), succeed to the position of the transferor with respect to such binding contract and such property. The preceding sentence shall apply, in any case in which the lessor does not make an election under section 48(d) of the Internal Revenue Code of 1954, only if a party to such contract retains a right to use the property under a long-term lease."

—P.L. 94-12, Sec. 301(c)(1)(A), and (B), substituted "$100,000" for "$50,000" each place it appeared in para. (c)(2) and substituted "$50,000" for "$25,000" in para. (c)(2), effective for tax. yrs. begin. after 12/31/74 and before 1/1/77.

Prior to amendment, para. (c)(2) read as follows:

"(2) Dollar limitation.

"(A) In general. The cost of used section 38 property taken into account under section 46(c)(1)(B) for any taxable year shall not exceed $50,000. If such cost exceeds $50,000, the taxpayer shall select (at such time and in such manner as the Secretary or his delegate shall by regulations prescribe) the items to be taken into account, but only to the extent of an aggregate cost of $50,000. Such a selection, once made, may be changed only in the manner, and to the extent, provided by such regulations.

"(B) Married individuals. In the case of a husband or wife who files a separate return, the limitation under subparagraph (A) shall be $25,000 in lieu of $50,000. This subparagraph shall not apply if the spouse of the taxpayer has no used section 38 property which may be taken into account as qualified investment for the taxable year of such spouse which ends within or with the taxpayer's taxable year.

"(C) Controlled groups. In the case of a controlled group, the $50,000 amount specified under subparagraph (A) shall be reduced for each component member of the group by apportioning $50,000 among the component members of such group in accordance with their respective amounts of used section 38 property which may be taken into account.

Tax credits   Subpart E

"(D) Partnerships. In the case of a partnership, the limitation contained in subparagraph (A) shall apply with respect to the partnership and with respect to each partner."

—P.L. 94-12, Sec. 302(c)(3), substituted "46(e)(1)" for "46(d)(1)" each place it appeared in paras. (d)(1) and (d)(2), effective for tax. yrs. end. after 12/31/74.

In 1971, P.L. 92-178, Sec. 102(a)(2), substituted "3 years" for "4 years" in the second sentence of subsec. (a)(1), effective for property described in Code Sec. 50.

—P.L. 92-178, Sec. 103, 12/10/71, added subsec. (a)(7), effective 12/10/71.

—P.L. 92-178, Sec. 104(a)(1), deleted clause (ii) and added new clauses (ii) and (iii) in subsec. (a)(1)(B), effective for property described in Code Sec. 50.

Prior to deletion, clause (ii) read as follows:

"(ii) constitutes a research or storage facility used in connection with any of the activities referred to in clause (i), or."

—P.L. 92-178, Sec. 104(b), struck out "and" at the end of subpara. (a)(3)(A), substituted ", and" for the period at the end of subpara. (a)(3)(B) and added new subpara. (a)(3)(C), effective for property described in Code Sec. 50.

—P.L. 92-178, Sec. 104(c)(1), inserted "(other than the International Telecommunications Satellite Consortium or any successor organization)" after "international organization" in para. (a)(5), effective for tax. yrs. end. after 12/31/61.

—P.L. 92-178, Sec. 104(c)(2), deleted "and" at the end of clause (a)(2)(B)(vi), substituted a semicolon for the period at the end of clause (a)(2)(B)(vii) and added new clause (a)(2)(B)(viii), effective for tax. yrs. end. after 12/31/61.

—P.L. 92-178, Sec. 104(c)(3), added new clause (a)(2)(B)(ix), effective for property described in Code Sec. 50.

—P.L. 92-178, Sec. 104(d), added new clause (a)(2)(B)(x), effective for property described in Code Sec. 50.

—P.L. 92-178, Sec. 104(e), amended para. (a)(6), effective for property described in Code Sec. 50.

Prior to amendment, para. (a)(6) read as follows:

"(6) Livestock. Livestock shall not be treated as section 38 property."

—P.L. 92-178, Sec. 104(f)(1), added para. (a)(8), effective for property described in Code Sec. 50.

—P.L. 92-178, Sec. 104(g), added para. (a)(9), effective for tax. yrs. end. after 12/31/61.

—P.L. 92-178, Sec. 108(b), substituted "section 46(d)(1)" for "section 46(d)" in subsec. (d) [prior to amend. by Sec. 108(c) of P.L. 92-178], effective for leases entered into after Sept. 22, 1971

—P.L. 92-178, Sec. 108(c), amended subsec. (d), effective for leases entered into after 11/8/71.

Prior to amendment, subsec. (d) read as follows:

"(d) Certain leased property.

A person (other than a person referred to in section 46(d)) who is a lessor of property may (at such time, in such manner, and subject to such conditions as are provided by regulations prescribed by the Secretary or his delegate) elect with respect to any new section 38 property to treat the lessee as having acquired such property for an amount equal to—

"(1) except as provided in paragraph (2), the fair market value of such property, or

"(2) if such property is leased by a corporation which is a component member of a controlled group (within the meaning of section 46(a)(5)) to another corporation which is a component member of the same controlled group, the basis of such property to the lessor.

"The election provided by the preceding sentence may be made only with respect to property which would be new section 38 property if acquired by the lessee. For purposes of the preceding sentence and section 46(c), the useful life of property in the hands of the lessee is the useful life of such property in the hands of the lessor. If a lessor makes the election provided by this subsection with respect to any property, the lessee shall be treated for all purposes of this subpart as having acquired such property.

"In the case of suspension period property which is leased and is property of a kind which the lessor ordinarily leases to one lessee for a substantial portion of the useful life of the property, the lessor of the property shall be deemed to have elected to treat the first such lessee as having acquired such property for purposes of applying the last sentence of section 46(a)(2). In the case of section 38 property which (i) is leased after October 9, 1966 (other than pursuant to a binding contract to lease entered into before October 10, 1966), (ii) is not suspension period property with respect to the lessor but is suspension period property if acquired by the lessee, and (iii) is property of the same kind which the lessor ordinarily sold to customers before October 10, 1966, or ordinarily leased before such date and made an election under this subsection, the lessor of such property shall be deemed to have made an election under this subsection with respect to such property."

In 1969, P.L. 91-172, Sec. 121(d)(2)(A), added the last sentence of para. (a)(4), effective for tax. yrs. begin. after 12/31/69.

—P.L. 91-172, Sec. 401(e)(2), amended subpara. (c)(2)(C), effective for tax. yrs. end. on or after 12/31/70.

Prior to amendment, subpara. (c)(2)(C) read as follows:

"(C) Affiliated groups. In the case of an affiliated group, the $50,000 amount specified under subparagraph (A) shall be reduced for each member of the group by apportioning $50,000 among the members of such group in accordance with their respective amounts of used section 38 property which may be taken into account."

—P.L. 91-172, Sec. 401(e)(3), amended subpara. (c)(3)(C), effective for tax. yrs. end. on or after 12/31/70.

Prior to amendment, subpara. (c)(3)(C) read as follows:

"(C) Affiliated group. The term 'affiliated group' has the meaning assigned to such term by section 1504(a), except that—

"(i) the phrase 'more than 50 percent' shall be substituted for the phrase 'at least 80 percent' each place it appears in section 1504(a), and

"(ii) all corporations shall be treated as includible corporations (without any exclusion under section 1504(b))."

—P.L. 91-172, Sec. 401(e)(4), amended para. (d)(2), effective for tax. yrs. end. on or after 12/31/70.

Prior to amendment, para. (d)(2) read as follows:

"(2) if such property is leased by a corporation which is a member of an affiliated group (within the meaning of section 46(a)(5)) to another corporation which is a member of the same affiliated group, the basis of such property to the lessor."

In 1967, P.L. 90-26, Sec. [1], substituted March 9, 1967 for December 31, 1967 in subsec. (j)... Sec. 2(a), amended subparas. (h)(2)(A) and (B)... Sec. 3, amended clause. (a)(2)(B)(i) by inserting at the end the phrase "or is operated under contract with the United States", effective for tax. yrs. end. after 3/9/67.

Prior to amendment, subparas. (h)(2)(A) and (B) read as follows:

"(A) the physical construction, reconstruction, or erection of which begins either during the suspension period or pursuant to an order placed during such period, or

"(B) which is acquired by the taxpayer either during the suspension period or pursuant to an order placed during such period."

In 1966, P.L. 89-809, Sec. 201(a), added clause (a)(2)(B)(vii), effective as provided in Sec. 201(b), which provides:

"(b) Effective date. The amendments made by subsection (a) shall apply to taxable years ending after December 31, 1965, but only with respect to property placed in service after such date. In applying section 46(b) of the Internal Revenue Code of 1954 (relating to carryback and carryover of unused credits), the amount of any investment credit carryback to any taxable year ending on or before December 31, 1965, shall be determined without regard to the amendments made by this section."

—P.L. 89-800, Sec. [1](a), redesignated former subsec. (h) as (k) and added subsecs. (h)–(j)... Sec. [1](b), added the last two sentences to subsec. (d), effective for tax. yrs. end. after 10/8/66.

In 1964, P.L. 88-272, Sec. 203(a)(1), repealed subsec. (g) (requiring that the basis of section 38 property be reduced by 7 percent of the qualified investment)... Sec. 203(a)(3)(A), deleted the last sentence of subsec. (d), effective as provided in Sec. 203(a)(4) of this Act, which provides:

"(4) Effective date. Paragraphs (1) and (3) of this subsection shall apply—

"(A) In the case of property placed in service after December 31, 1963, with respect to taxable years ending after such date, and

"(B) In the case of property placed in service before January 1, 1964, with respect to taxable years beginning after December 31, 1963."

Prior to deletion, the last sentence of subsec. (d) read as follows:

"If a lessor made an election under this subsection, subsec. (g) would not apply with respect to such property, and deductions otherwise allowable under section 162 to the lessee for amounts paid the lessor would be adjusted consistent with subsec. (g)."

—P.L. 88-272, Sec. 203(b), amended paras. (d)(1) and (2), effective for property possession of which is transferred to a lessee on or after the date of enactment of this Act. [2/26/64]

Prior to amendment, paras. (d)(1) and (2) read as follows:

"(1) if such property was constructed by the lessor (or by a corporation which controls or is controlled by the lessor within the meaning of section 368(c)), the fair market value of such property, or

"(2) if paragraph (1) does not apply, the basis of such property to the lessor."

—P.L. 88-272, Sec. 203(c)(1), substituted ", or" for the period at the end of subpara. (a)(1)(B)... Sec. 203(c)(2), added subpara. (a)(1)(C), effective for tax. yrs. end. after 6/30/63.

—P.L. 88-272, Sec. 203(a)(2), also provided with respect to property placed in service before '64 that:

"(A) The basis of any section 38 property (as defined in section 48(a) of the Internal Revenue Code of 1954) placed in service before January 1, 1964, shall be increased, under regulations prescribed by the Secretary of the Treasury or his delegate, by an amount equal to 7 percent of the qualified investment with respect to such property under section 46(c) of the Internal Revenue Code of 1954. If there has been any increase with respect to such property under section 48(g)(2) of such Code, the increase under the preceding sentence shall be appropriately reduced therefor.

"(B) If a lessor made the election provided by section 48(d) of the Internal Revenue Code of 1954 with respect to property placed in service before January 1, 1964—

"(i) subparagraph (A) shall not apply with respect to such property, but

"(ii) under regulations prescribed by the Secretary of the Treasury or his delegate, the deductions otherwise allowable under section 162 of such Code to the lessee for amounts paid to the lessor under the lease (or, if such lessee has purchased such property, the basis of such property) shall be adjusted in a manner consistent with subparagraph (A).

"(C) The adjustments under this paragraph shall be made as of the first day of the taxpayer's first taxable year which begins after December 31, 1963."

In 1962, P.L. 87-834, Sec. 2, added Code Sec. 48, effective for tax. yrs. end. after '61.

"SEC. 49. TERMINATION OF REGULAR PERCENTAGE.

"(a) General rule.

1,217

" For purposes of determining the amount of the investment tax credit determined under section 46, the regular percentage shall not apply to any property placed in service after December 31, 1985.

"(b) Exceptions.

" Subject to the provisions of subsections (c) and (d), subsection (a) shall not apply to the following:

"(1) Transition property. Property which is transition property (within the meaning of subsection (e)).

"(2) Qualified progress expenditure for periods before January 1, 1986. In the case of any taxpayer who has made an election under section 46(d)(6), the portion of the adjusted basis of any progress expenditure property attributable to qualified progress expenditures for periods before January 1, 1986.

"(3) Qualified timber property. The portion of the adjusted basis of qualified timber property which is treated as section 38 property under section 48(a)(1)(F).

"(c) 35-percent reduction in credit for taxable years after 1986.

"(1) Reduction in current year investment credit. Any portion of the current year business credit under section 38(b) for any taxable year beginning after June 30, 1987, which is attributable to the regular investment credit shall be reduced by 35 percent.

"(2) Unexpired carryforwards to 1st taxable year beginning after June 30, 1987. Any portion of the business credit carryforward under section 38(a)(1) attributable to the regular investment credit which has not expired as of the close of the taxable year preceding the 1st taxable year of the taxpayer beginning after June 30, 1987, shall be reduced by 35 percent.

"(3) Special rule for taxable years beginning before and ending after July 1, 1987. In the case of any taxable year beginning before and ending after July 1, 1987—

"(A) any portion of the current year business credit under section 38(b) for such taxable year, or

"(B) any portion of the business credit carryforward under section 38(a)(1) for such year,

"which is attributable to the regular investment credit shall be reduced by the applicable percentage.

"(4) Treatment of disallowed credit.

"(A) In general. The amount of the reduction of the regular investment credit under paragraphs (1) and (2) shall not be allowed as a credit for any taxable year.

"(B) No carryback for years straddling July 1, 1987; gross up of carryforwards. In any case to which paragraph (3) applies—

"(i) the amount of the reduction under paragraph (3) may not be carried back to any taxable year, but

"(ii) there shall be added to the carryforwards from the taxable year (before applying paragraph (2)) an amount equal to the amount which bears the same ratio to the carryforwards from such taxable year (determined without regard to this clause) as—

"(I) the applicable percentage, bears to

"(II) 1 minus the applicable percentage.

"(5) Definitions and special rules. For purposes of this subsection—

"(A) Applicable percentage. The term 'applicable percentage' means, with respect to a taxable year beginning before and ending after July 1, 1987, the percentage which bears the same ratio to 35 percent as—

"(i) the number of months in such taxable year after June 30, 1987, bears to

"(ii) the number of months in such taxable year.

"(B) Regular investment credit.

"(i) In general. The term 'regular investment credit' means the credit determined under section 46(a) to the extent attributable to the regular percentage.

"(ii) Exception for timber property. The term 'regular investment credit' shall not include any portion of the regular investment credit which is attributable to section 38 property described in section 48(a)(1)(F).

"(d) Full basis adjustment.

"(1) In general. In the case of periods after December 31, 1985, with respect to so much of the credit determined under section 46(a) with respect to transition property as is attributable to the regular investment credit (as defined in subsection (c)(5)(B))—

"(A) paragraphs (1), (2), and (7) of section 48(q) and section 48(d)(5) shall be applied by substituting '100 percent' for '50 percent' each place it appears, and

"(B) sections 48(q)(4) and 196(d) shall not apply.

"(2) Special rule for qualified progress expenditures. If the taxpayer made an election under section 48(q)(4) with respect to any qualified progress expenditures for periods before January 1, 1986—

"(A) paragraph (1) shall not apply to the portion of the adjusted basis attributable to such expenditures, and

"(B) such election shall not apply to such expenditures for periods after December 31, 1985.

"(e) Transition property.

" For purposes of this section—

"(1) Transition property. The term 'transition property' means any property placed in service after December 31, 1985, and to which the amendments made by section 201 of the Tax Reform Act of 1986 do not apply, except that in making such determination—

"(A) section 203(a)(1)(A) of such Act shall be applied by substituting '1986' for '1986',

"(B) sections 203(b)(1) and 204(a)(3) of such Act shall be applied by substituting 'December 31, 1985' for 'March 1, 1986',

"(C) in the case of transition property with a class life of less than 7 years—

"(i) section 203(b)(2) of such Act shall apply, and

"(ii) in the case of property with a class life—

"(I) of less than 5 years, the applicable date shall be July 1, 1986, and

"(II) at least 5 years, but less than 7 years, the applicable date shall be January 1, 1987, and

"(D) section 203(b)(3) shall be applied by substituting '1986' for '1987'.

"(2) Treatment of progress expenditures. No progress expenditures for periods after December 31, 1985, with respect to any property shall be taken into account for purposes of applying the regular percentage unless it is reasonable to expect that such property will be transition property when placed in service. If any progress expenditures are taken into account by reason of the preceding sentence and subsequently there is not a reasonable expectation that such property would be transition property when placed in service, the credits attributable to progress expenditures with respect to such property shall be recaptured under section 47."

In 1988, P.L. 100-647, Sec. 1002(e)(1), amended para. (d)(1) . . . Sec. 1002(e)(2), amended subpara. (c)(4)(B) . . . Sec. 1002(e)(3), amended clause (c)(5)(B)(i), effective as provided in Secs. 211(e)(1)-(4) of P.L. 99-514, reproduced below.

Prior to amendment, para. (d)(1) read as follows:

"(1) In general. In the case of periods after December 31, 1985, section 48(q) (relating to basis adjustment to section 38) property shall be applied with respect to transaction property—

"(A) by substituting '100 percent' for '50 percent' in paragraph (1), and

"(B) without regard to paragraph (4) thereof (relating to election of reduced credit in lieu of basis adjustment)."

Prior to amendment, subpara. (c)(4)(B) read as follows:

"(B) No carryback for year straddling July 1, 1987; gross up of carryforwards. The amount of the reduction of the regular investment credit under paragraph (3)—

"(i) may not be carried back to any taxable year, but

"(ii) shall be added to the carryforwards from the taxable year before applying paragraph (2)."

Prior to amendment, clause (C)(5)(B)(i) read as follows:

"(i) In general. The term 'regular investment credit' has the meaning given such term by section 48(o)."

— P.L. 100-647, Sec. 1002(e)(4), amended Sec. 211(e)(1) of P.L. 99-514 [reproduced below], part of the effective date for changes made by Sec. 211(a) of P.L. 99-514, by adding the last sentence, see below . . . Sec. 1002(e)(5), amended Sec. 211(e)(4)(A) of P.L. 99-514 [reproduced below], by substituting "Subsections (c) and (d) of section 49 of the Internal Revenue Code of 1986" for "Paragraphs (c) and (d) of section 49 of the Internal Revenue Code of 1954" and substituting "1985" for "1935", see below . . . Sec. 1002(e)(6), amended Sec. 211(e)(4)(B) of P.L. 99-514 [reproduced below], by substituting "shall be treated as transition property and subsections (c) and (d) of section 49 of such Code shall not apply to such property" for "shall be treated as transition property" . . . Sec. 1002(e)(7), added Sec. 211(e)(4)(C), (D) and (E) of P.L. 99-514, reproduced below.

— P.L. 100-647, Sec. 1002(e)(8)(B), repealed subpara. (c)(5)(C), effective for tax. yrs. begin. after 12/31/83, and to carrybacks from tax. yrs. begin. after 12/31/83. Prior to repeal, subpara. (c)(5)(C) read as follows:

"(C) Portion of credits attributable to regular investment credit. The portion of any current year business credit or business credit carryforward which is attributable to the regular investment credit shall be determined on the basis that the regular investment credit is used first."

In 1986, P.L. 99-514, Sec. 211(a), added Code Sec. 49, effective as provided in Sec. 211(e)(1)-(4) of this Act, reproduced below [as amended by Sec. 1002(e)(4) of P.L. 100-647-(7)]. For normalization rules and exceptions, see Secs. 211(b) and (d) of this Act reproduced below. Sec. 211(e)(1)-(4) of this Act provides:

"(e) Effective date.

"(1) In general. Except as provided in this subsection, the amendments made by this section shall apply to property placed in service after December 31, 1985, in taxable years ending after such date. Section 49(c) of the Internal Revenue Code of 1986 (as added by subsection (a)) shall apply to taxable years ending after June 30, 1987, and to amounts carried to such taxable years. Sec. 211(b) of this Act provides:

"(2) Exceptions for certain films. For purposes of determining whether any property is transition property within the meaning of section 49(e) of the Internal Revenue Code of 1986—

"(A) in the case of any motion picture or television film, construction shall be treated as including production for purposes of section 203(b)(1) of this Act, and written contemporary evidence of an agreement (in accordance with industry practice) shall be treated as a written binding contract for such purposes,

"(B) in the case of any television film, a license agreement or agreement for production services between a television network and a producer shall be treated as a binding contract for purposes of section 203(b)(1)(A) of this Act, and

"(C) a motion picture film shall be treated as described in section 203(b)(1)(A) of this Act if—

"(i) funds were raised pursuant to a public offering before September 26, 1985, for the production of such film,

"(ii) 40 percent of the funds raised pursuant to such public offering are being spent on films the production of which commenced before such date, and

"(iii) all of the films funded by such public offering are required to be distributed pursuant to distribution agreements entered into before September 26, 1985.

"(3) Normalization rules. — The provisions of subsection (b) shall apply to any violation of the normalization requirements under paragraph (1) or (2) of section 46(f) of the Internal Revenue Code of 1986 occurring in taxable years ending after December 31, 1985.

"(4) Additional exceptions. —

"(A) Subsections (c) and (d) of section 49 of the Internal Revenue Code of 1986 shall not apply to any continuous caster facility for slabs and blooms which

Tax credits Subpart E

is subject to a lease and which is part of a project the second phase of which is a continuous slab caster which was placed in service before December 31, 1985.

"(B) For purposes of determining whether an automobile manufacturing facility (including equipment and incidental appurtenances) is transition property within the meaning of section 49(e) property with respect to which the Board of Directors of an automobile manufacturer formally approved the plan for the project on January 7, 1985 shall be treated as transition property and subsections (c) and (d) of section 49 of such Code shall not apply to such property, but only with respect to $70,000,000 of regular investment tax credits.

"(C) Any solid waste disposal facility which will process and incinerate solid waste of one or more public or private entities including Dakota County, Minnesota, and with respect to which a bond carryforward from 1985 was elected in an amount equal to $12,500,000 shall be treated as transition property within the meaning of section 49(e) of the Internal Revenue Code of 1986.

"(D) For purposes of section 49 of such Code, the following property shall be treated as transition property:

"(i) 2 catamarans built by a shipbuilder incorporated in the State of Washington in 1964, the contracts for which were signed on April 22, 1986 and November 12, 1985, and 1 barge built by such shipbuilder the contract for which was signed on August 7, 1985.

"(ii) 2 large passenger ocean-going United States flag cruise ships with a passenger rated capacity of up to 250 which are built by the shipbuilder described in clause (i), which are the first such ships built in the United States since 1952, and which were designed at the request of a Pacific Coast cruise line pursuant to a contract entered into in October 1985. This clause shall apply only to that portion of the cost of each ship which does not exceed $40,000,000.

"(iii) Property placed in service during 1986 by Satellite Industries, Inc., with headquarters in Minneapolis, Minnesota, to the extent that the cost of such property does not exceed $1,950,000.

"(E) Subsections (c) and (d) of section 49 of such Code shall not apply to property described in section 204(a)(4) of this Act."

"(b) Normalization rules.

"If, for any taxable year beginning after December 31, 1985, the requirements of paragraph (1) or (2) of section 46(f) of the Internal Revenue Code of 1986 are not met with respect to public utility property to which the regular percentage applied for purposes of determining the amount of the investment tax credit—

"(1) all credits for open taxable years as of the time of the final determination referred to in section 46(f)(4)(A) of such Code shall be recaptured, and

"(2) if the amount of the taxpayer's unamortized credits (or the credits not previously restored to rate base) with respect to such property (whether or not for open years) exceeds the amount referred to in paragraph (1), the taxpayer's tax for the taxable year shall be increased by the amount of such excess.

"If any portion of the excess described in paragraph (2) is attributable to a credit which is allowable as a carryover to a taxable year beginning after December 31, 1985, in lieu of applying paragraph (2) with respect to such portion, the amount of such carryover shall be reduced by the amount of such portion. Rules similar to the rules of this subsection shall apply in the case of any property with respect to which the requirements of section 46(f)(9) of such Code are met."

Sec. 211(d) of this Act provides:

"(d) Exception for certain aircraft used in Alaska.

"(1) The amendments made by subsection (a) shall not apply to property originally placed in service after December 29, 1982, and before August 1, 1985, by a corporation incorporated in Alaska on May 21, 1953, and used by it—

"(A) in part, for the transportation of mail for the United States Postal Service in the State of Alaska, and

"(B) in part, to provide air service in the State of Alaska on routes which had previously been served by an air carrier that received compensation from the Civil Aeronautics Board for providing service.

"(2) In the case of property described in subparagraph (A)—

"(A) such property shall be treated as recovery property described in section 208(d)(5) of the Tax Equity and Fiscal Responsibility Act of 1982 ('TEFRA');

"(B) '48 months' shall be substituted for '3 months' each place it appears in applying—

"(i) section 48(b)(2)(B) of the Code, and

"(ii) section 168(f)(8)(D) of the Code (as in effect after the amendments made by the Technical Corrections Act of 1982 but before the amendments made by TEFRA); and

"(C) the limitation of section 168(f)(8)(D)(ii)(III) (as then in effect) shall be read by substituting 'the lessee's original cost basis.', for 'the adjusted basis of the lessee at the time of the lease.'.

"(3) The aggregate amount of property to which this paragraph shall apply shall not exceed $60,000,000."

"SEC. 49 REPEALED.

In 1978, P.L. 95-600, Sec. 312(c)(1), repealed Code Sec. 49, effective for tax. yrs. end. after '78.

Prior to repeal, Code Sec. 49 read as follows:

"Sec. 49. Termination for period beginning April 19, 1969, and ending during 1971.

"(a) General rule.

"For purposes of this subpart, the term 'section 38 property' does not include property—

"(1) the physical construction, reconstruction, or erection of which is begun after April 18, 1969, or

"(2) which is acquired by the taxpayer after April 18, 1969, other than pre-termination property.

"This subsection shall not apply to property described in section 50.

"(b) Pre-termination property.

"For purposes of this subpart—

"(1) Binding contracts. Any property shall be treated as pre-termination property to the extent that such property is constructed, reconstructed, erected, or acquired pursuant to a contract which was, on April 18, 1969, and at all times thereafter, binding on the taxpayer.

"(2) Equipped building rule. If—

"(A) pursuant to a plan of the taxpayer in existence on April 18, 1969 (which plan was not substantially modified at any time after such date and before the taxpayer placed the equipped building in service), the taxpayer has constructed, reconstructed, erected, or acquired a building and the machinery and equipment necessary to the planned use of the building by the taxpayer, and

"(B) more than 50 percent of the aggregate adjusted basis of all the property of a character subject to the allowance for depreciation making up such building as so equipped is attributable to either property the construction, reconstruction, or erection of which was begun by the taxpayer before April 19, 1969, or property the acquisition of which by the taxpayer occurred before such date,

then all property comprising such building as so equipped (and any incidental property adjacent to such building which is necessary to the planned use of the building) shall be pre-termination property. For purposes of subparagraph (B) of the preceding sentence, the rules of paragraphs (1) and (4) shall be applied. For purposes of this paragraph, a special purpose structure shall be treated as a building.

"(3) Plant facility rule.

"(A) General rule. If—

"(i) pursuant to a plan of the taxpayer in existence on April 18, 1969 (which plan was not substantially modified at any time after such date and before the taxpayer placed the plant facility in service), the taxpayer has constructed, reconstructed, or erected a plant facility, and either

"(ii) the construction, reconstruction, or erection of such plant facility was commenced by the taxpayer before April 19, 1969, or

"(iii) more than 50 percent of the aggregate adjusted basis of all the property of a character subject to the allowance for depreciation making up such plant facility is attributable to either property the construction, reconstruction, or erection of which was begun by the taxpayer before April 19, 1969, or property the acquisition of which by the taxpayer occurred before such date,

then all property comprising such plant facility shall be pre-termination property. For purposes of clause (iii) of the preceding sentence, the rules of paragraphs (1) and (4) shall be applied.

"(B) Plant facility defined. For purposes of this paragraph, the term 'plant facility' means a facility which does not include any building (or of which buildings constitute an insignificant portion) and which is—

"(i) a self-contained, single operating unit or processing operation,

"(ii) located on a single site, and

"(iii) identified, on April 18, 1969, in the purchasing and internal financial plans of the taxpayer as a single unitary project.

"(C) Special rule. For purposes of this subsection, if—

"(i) a certificate of convenience and necessity has been issued before April 19, 1969, by a Federal regulatory agency with respect to two or more plant facilities which are included under a single plan of the taxpayer to construct, reconstruct, or erect such plant facilities, and

"(ii) more than 50 percent of the aggregate adjusted basis of all the property of a character subject to the allowance for depreciation making up such plant facilities is attributable to either property the construction, reconstruction, or erection of which was begun by the taxpayer before April 19, 1969, or property the acquisition of which by the taxpayer occurred before such date,

such plant facilities shall be treated as a single plant facility.

"(D) Commencement of construction. For purposes of subparagraph (A)(ii), the construction, reconstruction, or erection of a plant facility shall not be considered to have commenced until construction, reconstruction, or erection has commenced at the site of such plant facility. The preceding sentence shall not apply if the site of such plant facility is not located on land.

"(4) Machinery or equipment rule. Any piece of machinery or equipment—

"(A) more than 50 percent of the parts and components of which (determined on the basis of cost) were held by the taxpayer on April 18, 1969, or are acquired by the taxpayer pursuant to a binding contract which was in effect on such date, for inclusion or use in such piece of machinery or equipment, and

"(B) the cost of the parts and components of which is not an insignificant portion of the total cost,

shall be treated as property which is pre-termination property.

"(5) Certain lease-back transactions, etc.

"(A) Where a person who is a party to a binding contract described in paragraph (1) transfers rights in such contract (or in the property to which such contract relates) to another person but a party to such contract retains a right to use the property under a lease with such other person, than to the extent of the transferred rights such other person shall, for purposes of paragraph (1), succeed to the position of the transferor with respect to such binding contract and such property.

In any case in which the lessor does not make an election under section 48(d)—

"(i) the preceding sentence shall apply only if a party to the contract retains the right to use the property under a lease for a term of at least 1 year; and

"(ii) if such use is retained (other than under a long-term lease), the lessor shall be deemed for the purposes of section 47 as having made a disposition of the property at such time as the lessee loses the right to use the property.

"For purposes of clause (ii), if the lessee transfers the lease in a transfer described in paragraph (7), the lessee shall be considered as having the right to use of the property so long as the transferee has such use.

"(B) For purposes of subparagraph (A)—

"(i) a person who holds property (or rights in property) which is pre-termination property by reason of the application of paragraph (4) shall, with respect to such property, be treated as a party to a binding contract described in paragraph (1), and

"(ii) a corporation which is a member of the same affiliated group (as defined in paragraph (8)) as the transferor described in subparagraph (A) and which simultaneously with the transfer of property to another person acquires a right to use such property under a lease with such other person shall be treated as the transferor and as a party to the contract.

"(6) Certain lease and contract obligations.

"(A) Where, pursuant to a binding lease or contract to lease in effect on April 18, 1969, a lessor or lessee is obligated to construct, reconstruct, erect, or acquire property specified in such lease or contract or in a related document filed before April 19, 1969, with a Federal regulatory agency, or property, the specifications of which are readily ascertainable from the terms of such lease or contract or from such related document, any property so constructed, reconstructed, erected, or acquired by the lessor or lessee shall be pre-termination property. In the case of any project which includes property other than the property to be leased to such lessee, the preceding sentence shall be applied, in the case of the lessor, to such other property only if the binding leases and contracts with all lessees in effect on April 18, 1969, cover real property constituting 25 percent or more of the project (determined on the basis of rental value). For purposes of the preceding sentences of this paragraph, in the case of any project where one or more vendor-vendee relationships exist, such vendors and vendees shall be treated as lessors and lessees.

"(B) Where, in order to perform a binding contract or contracts in effect on April 18, 1969, (i) the taxpayer is required to construct, reconstruct, erect, or acquire property specified in any order of a Federal regulatory agency for which application was filed before April 19, 1969, (ii) the property is to be used to transport one or more products under such contract or contracts, and (iii) one or more parties to the contract or contracts are required to take or to provide more than 50 percent of the products to be transported over a substantial portion of the expected useful life of the property, then such property shall be pre-termination property.

"(C) Where, in order to perform a binding contract in effect on April 18, 1969, the taxpayer is required to construct, reconstruct, erect, or acquire property specified in the contract to be used to produce one or more products and (unless the other party to the contract is a State or a political subdivision of a State which is required by the contract to make substantial expenditures which benefit the taxpayer) the other party to the contract is required to take substantially all of the products to be produced over a substantial portion of the expected useful life of the property, then such property shall be pre-termination property. For purposes of applying the preceding sentence in the case of a contract for the extraction of minerals, property shall be treated as specified in the contract if (i) the specifications for such property are readily ascertainable from the location and characteristics of the mineral properties specified in such contract from which the minerals are to be extracted; (ii) such property is necessary for and is to be used solely in the extraction of minerals under such contract; (iii) the physical construction, reconstruction, or erection of such property is begun by the taxpayer before April 19, 1970, such property is acquired by the taxpayer before April 19, 1970, or such property is constructed, reconstructed, erected, or acquired pursuant to a contract which was, on April 18, 1970, and at all times thereafter, binding on the taxpayer; (iv) such property is placed in service on or before December 31, 1972; (v) such contract is a fixed price contract (except for provisions for price changes under which the loss of the credit allowed by section 38 would not result in a price change); and (vi) such property is not placed in service to replace other property used in extracting minerals under such contract.

"(7) Certain transfers to be disregarded.

"(A) If property or rights under a contract are transferred in—

"(i) a transfer by reason of death,

"(ii) a transaction as a result of which the basis of the property in the hands of the transferee is determined by reference to its basis in the hands of the transferor by reason of the application of section 332, 351, 361, 371(a), 374(a), 721, or 731, or

"(iii) a sale of substantially all of the assets of the transferor pursuant to the terms of a contract, which was on April 18, 1969, and at all times thereafter, binding on the transferee,

and such property (or the property acquired under such contract) would be treated as pre-termination property in the hands of the decedent or the transferor, such property shall be treated as pre-termination property in the hands of the transferee.

"(B) If—

"(i) property or rights under a contract are acquired in a transaction to which section 334(b)(2) applies,

"(ii) the stock of the distributing corporation was acquired before April 19, 1969, or pursuant to a binding contract in effect April 18, 1969, and

"(iii) such property (or the property acquired under such contract) would be treated as pre-termination property in the hands of the distributing corporation, such property shall be treated as pre-termination property in the hands of the distributee.

"(8) Property acquired from affiliated corporation. In the case of property acquired by a corporation which is a member of an affiliated group from another member of the same group—

"(A) such corporation shall be treated as having acquired such property on the date on which it was acquired by such other member,

"(B) such corporation shall be treated as having entered into a binding contract for the construction, reconstruction, erection, or acquisition of such property on the date on which such other member entered into a contract for the construction, reconstruction, erection, or acquisition of such property, and

"(C) such corporation shall be treated as having commenced the construction, reconstruction, or erection of such property on the date on which such other member commenced such construction, reconstruction, or erection.

For purposes of this subsection and subsection (c), a contract between two corporations which are members of the same affiliated group shall not be treated as a binding contract as between such corporations, unless, at all times after June 30, 1969, and prior to the completion of performance of such contract, such corporations are not members of the same affiliated group. For purposes of the preceding sentences, the term 'affiliated group' has the meaning assigned to it by section 1504(a), except that all corporations shall be treated as includible corporations (without any exclusion under section 1504(b)).

"(9) Barges for ocean-going vessels. Barges specifically designed and constructed, reconstructed, erected, or acquired for use with ocean-going vessels which are designed to carry barges and which are pre-termination property, but not in excess of—

"(A) the number to be used with such vessels specified in applications for mortgage or construction loan insurance filed with the Secretary of Commerce on or before April 18, 1969, under title XI of the Merchant Marine Act, 1936, or

"(B) if subparagraph (A) does not apply and if more than 50 percent of the barges which the taxpayer establishes as necessary to the initial planned use of such vessels are pre-termination property (determined without regard to this paragraph), the number which the taxpayer establishes as so necessary,

together with the machinery and equipment to be installed on such barges and necessary for their planned use, shall be treated as pre-termination property.

"(10) Certain new-design products. Where—

"(A) on April 18, 1969, the taxpayer had undertaken a project to produce a product of a new design pursuant to binding contracts in effect on such date which—

"(i) were fixed-price contracts (except for provisions requiring or permitting price changes resulting from changes in rates of pay or costs of materials), and

"(ii) covered more than 50 percent of the entire production of such design to be delivered by the taxpayer before January 1, 1973, and

"(B) on or before April 18, 1969, more than 50 percent of the aggregate adjusted basis of all property of a character subject to the allowance for depreciation required to carry out such binding contracts was property the construction, reconstruction, or erection of which had begun by the taxpayer, or had been acquired by the taxpayer (or was under a binding contract for such construction, reconstruction, erection, or acquisition),

then all tangible personal property placed in service by the taxpayer before January 1, 1972, which is required to carry out such binding contracts shall be deemed to be pre-termination property. For purposes of subparagraph (B) of the preceding sentence, jigs, dies, templates, and similar items which can be used only for the manufacture or assembly of the production under the project and which were described in written engineering and internal financial plans of the taxpayer in existence on April 18, 1969, shall be treated as property which on such date was under a binding contract for construction.

"(c) Leased property.

"In the case of property which is leased after April 18, 1969 (other than pursuant to a binding contract to lease entered into before April 19, 1969), which is section 38 property with respect to the lessor but is property which would not be section 38 property because of the application of subsection (a) if acquired by the lessee, and which is property of the same kind which the lessor ordinarily sold to customers before April 19, 1969, or ordinarily leased before such date and made an election under section 48(d), such property shall not be section 38 property with respect to either the lessor or the lessee."

In 1971, P.L. 92-178, Sec. 101(b)(1), added the last sentence of subsec. (a), effective 12/10/71.

—P.L. 92-178, Sec. 101(b)(2), substituted "For purposes of this subpart" for "For purposes of this section" in subsec. (b), effective 12/10/71.

—P.L. 92-178, Sec. 101(b)(3), repealed subsec. (d), effective 12/10/71.

Prior to repeal, subsec. (d) read as follows:

"(d) Property placed in service after 1975.

"For purposes of this subpart, the term 'section 38 property' does not include any property placed in service after December 31, 1975."

—P.L. 92-178, Sec. 101(b)(4), amended the title of Code Sec. 49, effective 12/10/71.

Prior to amendment, the title of Code Sec. 49 read as follows:

"Termination of credit."

In 1969, P.L. 91-172, Sec. 703(a), added Code Sec. 49.

"SEC. 50. REPEALED.

In 1978, P.L. 95-600, Sec. 312(c)(1), repealed Code Sec. 50, effective for tax. yrs. end. after '78.

Prior to repeal, Code Sec. 50 read as follows:

"SEC. 50. RESTORATION OF CREDIT.

"(a) General rule.

"Section 49(a) (relating to termination of credit) shall not apply to property—

"(1) the construction, reconstruction, or erection of which—

"(A) is completed by the taxpayer after August 15, 1971, or

"(B) is begun by the taxpayer after March 31, 1971, or

"(2) which is acquired by the taxpayer—

"(A) after August 15, 1971, or

"(B) after March 31, 1971, and before August 16, 1971, pursuant to an order which the taxpayer establishes was placed after March 31, 1971.

"(b) Transitional rule.

Tax credits   Code Sec. 46

"In applying section 46(c)(1)(A) in the case of property described in subsection (a)(1)(A) the construction, reconstruction, or erection of which is begun before April 1, 1971, there shall be taken into account only that portion of the basis which is properly attributable to construction, reconstruction, or erection after August 15, 1971. This subsection shall not apply to pre-termination property (within the meaning of section 49(b))."

In 1976, P.L. 94-455, Sec. 804(e)(2), provided the following with respect to elections described in subsec. (a);

"(2) Election may also apply to property described in section 50(a). — At the election of the taxpayer, made within 1 year after the date of the enactment of this Act in such manner as the Secretary of the Treasury or his delegate may by regulations prescribe, the amendments made by subsections (a) and (b) shall also apply to property which is property described in section 50(a) of the Internal Revenue Code of 1954 and which is placed in service in taxable years beginning before January 1, 1975."

(For amendments made by subsecs. (a) and (b) of this Act, see notes for Code Secs. 48 and 47, respectively.)

In 1971, P.L. 92-178, Sec. 101(a), enacted 12/10/71, added Code Sec. 50.

Sec. 46. Amount of credit.

For purposes of section 38, the amount of the investment credit determined under this section for any taxable year shall be the sum of—

(1) the rehabilitation credit,
(2) the energy credit,
(3) the qualifying advanced coal project credit,
(4) the qualifying gasification project credit
(5) the qualifying advanced energy project credit, and
(6) the qualifying therapeutic discovery project credit.

In 2010, P.L. 111-148, Sec. 9023(b)(1), added a comma at the end of para. (2) . . . Sec. 9023(b)(2), substituted ", and" for the period at the end of para. (5) . . . Sec. 9023(b)(2), added para. (6), effective for amounts paid or incurred after 12/31/2008, in taxable years beginning after such date.

In 2009, P.L. 111-5, Sec. 1302(a), deleted "and" at the end of para. (3), deleted the period at the end of para. (4) and added para. (5), effective for periods after 2/17/2009, under rules similar to the rules of Code Sec. 48(m) (as in effect on the day before the date of the enactment of the Revenue Reconciliation Act of 1990 [enacted 11/5/90]).

In 2005, P.L. 109-58, Sec. 1307(a), deleted "and" at the end of para. (1), deleted the period at the end of para. (2), and added paras. (3) and (4), effective for periods after 8/8/2005, under rules similar to the rules of Code Sec. 48(m) (as in effect on the day before the date of the enactment of the Revenue Reconciliation Act of 1990 [enacted 11/5/90]).

In 2004, P.L. 108-357, Sec. 322(d)(1)(A), added "and" at the end of para. (1) . . . Sec. 322(d)(1)(B), substituted a period for ", and" at the end of para. (2) . . . Sec. 322(d)(1)(C), deleted para. (3), effective for expenditures paid or incurred after 10/22/2004.

Prior to deletion, para. (3) read as follows:

"(3) the reforestation credit."

In 1990, P.L. 101-508, Sec. 11813(a), amended Code Sec. 46 as part of the amendment to subpart E, of part IV of subchapter A of chapter 1, effective for property placed in service after 12/31/90 except as provided in Sec. 11813(c)(2) of this Act, which reads as follows:

"(2) Exceptions. — The amendments made by this section shall not apply to—

"(A) any transition property (as defined in section 49(e) of the Internal Revenue Code of 1986 (as in effect on the day before the date of the enactment of this Act) [11/5/90],

"(B) any property with respect to which qualified progress expenditures were previously taken into account under section 46(d) of such Code (as so in effect), and

"(C) any property described in section 46(b)(2)(C) of such Code (as so in effect)."

In 1990, P.L. 101-508, Sec. 11406, substituted "Dec. 31, 1991" for "Sept. 30, 1990" in clauses (b)(2)(A)(viii) and (ix), effective 11/5/90.

In 1989, P.L. 101-239, Sec. 7106, substituted "Sept. 30, 1990" for "Dec. 31, 1989" in clauses (b)(2)(A)(viii), (ix), and (x), effective 12/19/89.

— P.L. 101-239, Sec. 7814(d)(1), and (2), corrected Sec. 4006 of P.L. 100-647, see below, by substituting "Dec. 31, 1988" for "December 31, 1988" and by substituting "Dec. 31, 1989" for "December 31, 1989"

In 1988, P.L. 100-647, Sec. 1002(a)(4)(A), substituted "168(i)(3)" for "168(j)(6)" in subpara. (e)(4)(B) . . . Sec. 1002(a)(4)(B), substituted "paragraphs (5) and (6) of section 168(h)" for "paragraphs (8) and (9) of section 168(j)" in subpara. (e)(4)(D) . . . Sec. 1002(a)(4)(C), substituted "168(h)" for "168(j)" in subpara. (e)(4)(E) . . . Sec. 1002(a)(4)(D), substituted "168(h)(2)" for "168(j)(4)" in subpara. (e)(4)(E) . . . Sec. 1002(a)(15), substituted "property to which section 168 applies" for "recovery property (within the meaning of section 168", substituted "class life" for "present class life" and substituted "168(i)(1)" for "168(g)(2)" in the last sentence of para. (e)(4) . . . Sec. 1002(a)(17)(A), substituted 'property to which section 168 applies' for 'recovery property' in para. (c)(7) . . . Sec. 1002(a)(17)(B), substituted '168(e)' for '168(c)' each place it appeared in para. (c)(7) . . . Sec. 1002(a)(17)(C), substituted '168(f)(3)(B) (as in effect on the day before the date of enactment of the Tax Reform Act of 1986)' for '168(f)(3)(B)" in para. (c)(7) . . . Sec. 1002(a)(17)(D), substituted 'property to which section 168 applies' for 'recovery property' in the heading of para. (c)(7) . . . Sec. 1002(a)(25)(A), substituted 'property to which section 168 applies' for 'recovery property (within the meaning of section 168)' in clause (d)(1)(B)(i) . . . Sec. 1002(a)(25)(B), substituted 'to which section 168 does not apply' for 'which is not recovery property within the meaning of section 168)' in clause (d)(1)(B)(ii), effective for property placed in service after 12/31/86, in tax. yrs. end. after 12/31/86. See Sec. 203(a)(1)(B) and 203(b)-(e) of P.L. 99-514, reproduced in note following Code Sec. 168.

— P.L. 100-647, Sec. 1002(f)(1), amended Sec. 212(f)(2) of P.L. 99-514, reproduced below, by substituting '(2) Special rule. — In the case of a LTV corporation, in lieu of the requirements of paragraph (1) —' for '(2) General rules. If this section applies to LTV Corporation then in lieu of the requirements of paragraph (1) —' . . . Sec. 1002(f)(2), amended Sec. 212(f)(2)(B)(i)(I) of P.L. 99-514, reproduced below, by substituting 'when the corporation receives the refund' for 'such involvement begins' . . . Sec. 1002(f)(3), added Sec. 212(g)(3) of P.L. 99-514, reproduced below . . . Sec. 1002(f)(4), added Sec. 212(h) of P.L. 99-514, reproduced below . . . Sec. 1002(f)(5), amended Sec. 212(g)(2)(B) of P.L. 99-514, reproduced below, by substituting 'determined for periods before January 1, 1986, under' for 'determined under' . . . Sec. 1002(f)(6), added Sec. 212(f)(3) of P.L. 99-514, reproduced below.

— P.L. 100-647, Sec. 1002(g), amended Sec. 213(e)(2)(B) of P.L. 99-514, reproduced below, by substituting 'determined for periods before January 1, 1986, under' for 'determined under'.

— P.L. 100-647, Sec. 1002(k)(1), amended Sec. 251(d)(2)(B) of P.L. 99-514 [reproduced below], special rules for amendments made by Sec. 251(a) of P.L. 99-514, by deleting Sec. 251(d)(2)(B)(i) and redesignating Sec. 251(d)(2)(B)(ii) and (iii) as Sec. 251 (d)(2)(B)(i) and (ii) . . . Sec. 1002(k)(2), amended Sec. 251(d)(3)(P) of P.L. 99-514, reproduced below, by substituting 'San Jose, California' for 'San Francisco' . . . Sec. 1002(k)(3)(A)-(C), amended Sec. 251(d)(4) of P.L. 99-514, reproduced below, by substituting 'Marble Arcade office building' for 'Lakeland marbel Arcade' in Sec. 251(d)(4)(K) of P.L. 99-514 by deleting 'and' at the end of Sec. 251(d)(4)(Y) of P.L. 99-514 by amending Sec. 251(d)(4)(Z) of P.L. 99-514 and by adding Sec. 251(d)(4)(AA)-(OO) of P.L. 99-514 . . . Sec. 1002(k)(4), amended Sec. 251(d)(6) of P.L. 99-514, reproduced below . . . Sec. 1002(k)(5), amended Sec. 251(d)(3)(B) of P.L. 99-514, reproduced below, by substituting 'Pontalba' for 'Pontabla' . . . Sec. 1002(k)(6), amended Sec. 251(d)(4)(T) of P.L. 99-514, reproduced below, by substituting 'Covington' for 'Louisville.'

Prior to deletion Sec. 251(d)(2)(B)(i) of P.L. 99-514 read as follows:

"(i) the rehabilitation was completed pursuant to a written contract that was binding on March 1, 1986,"

Prior to amendment, Sec. 251(d)(4)(Z) of P.L. 99-514 read as follows:

"(Z) the Apollo and Bishop Building Complex on 125th Street, the Bigelow-Hartford Carpet Mill in New York, New York."

Prior to amendment, Sec. 251(d)(6) of P.L. 99-514 read as follows:

"(6) Expensing of rehabilitation expenditures for the Frankford Arsenal. In the case of any expenditures paid or incurred in connection with the rehabilitation of the Frankford Arsenal during the 8-year period beginning on January 1, 1987, such expenditures (including expenditures for repair and maintenance of the building and property) shall be allowable as a deduction in the taxable year in which paid or incurred in an amount not in excess of the submissions made by the taxpayer before September 16, 1986."

— P.L. 100-647, Sec. 1009(a)(1), added the last sentence of subpara. (e)(4)(C), effective for tax. yrs. after 12/31/86.

— P.L. 100-647, Sec. 1013(a)(44)(A), and (B), substituted "private activity bonds" for "industrial development bonds" in the heading of subpara. (c)(5)(B) and substituted "a private activity bond (within the meaning of section 141)" for "an individual development bond (within the meaning of section 103(b)(2))" in subpara. (c)(5)(B), effective for bonds issued after 8/15/86.

— P.L. 100-647, Sec. 4006(1)-(3), [as amended by Sec. 7814(d)(1) and (2) of P.L. 101-239, see above] substituted "Dec. 31, 1989" for "Dec. 31, 1988" in clauses (b)(2)(A)(viii), (ix), and (x), effective 11/10/88.

In 1986, P.L. 99-514, Sec. 201(d)(7)(B), substituted "section 465(b)(3)(C)" for "section 168(e)(4)" in clause (c)(8)(D)(v), effective for property placed in service after 12/31/86, in tax. yrs. end. after 12/31/86. For exception for certain aircraft used in Alaska, see Sec. 211(d) of this Act reproduced in note following Code Sec. 49.

— P.L. 99-514, Sec. 212, [as amended by Sec. 1002(f)(1)-(6) of P.L. 100-647, see above.], provides:

"Sec. 212. Effective 15-year carryback of existing carryforwards of steel companies.

"(a) General rule. —

"If a qualified corporation makes an election under this section for its 1st taxable year beginning after December 31, 1986, with respect to any portion of its existing carryforwards, the amount determined under subsection (b) shall be treated as a payment against the tax imposed by chapter 1 of the Internal Revenue Code of 1986 made by such corporation on the last day prescribed by law (without regard to extensions) for filing its return of tax under chapter 1 of such Code for such 1st taxable year.

"(b) Amount. —

"For purposes of subsection (a), the amount determined under this subsection shall be the lesser of—

"(1) 50 percent of the portion of the corporation's existing carryforwards to which the election under subsection (a) applies, or

"(2) the corporation's net tax liability for the carryback period.

1,221

"(c) Corporation making election may not use same amounts under section 38. — "In the case of a qualified corporation which makes an election under subsection (a), the portion of such corporation's existing carryforwards to which such an election applies shall not be taken into account under section 38 of the Internal Revenue Code of 1986 for any taxable year beginning after December 31, 1986.

"(d) Net tax liability for carryback period.

"For purposes of this section—

"(1) In general. — A corporation's net tax liability for the carryback period is the aggregate of such corporation's net tax liability for taxable years in the carryback period.

"(2) Net tax liability. — The term 'net tax liability' means, with respect to any taxable year, the amount of the tax imposed by chapter 1 of the Internal Revenue Code of 1954 for such taxable year, reduced by the sum of the credits allowable under part IV of subchapter A of such chapter 1 (other than section 34 thereof). For purposes of the preceding sentence, any tax treated as not imposed by chapter 1 of such Code under section 26(b)(2) of such Code shall not be treated as tax imposed by such chapter 1.

"(3) Carryback period. — The term 'carryback period' means the period—

"(A) which begins with the corporation's 15th taxable year preceding the 1st taxable year from which there is an unused credit included in such corporation's existing carryforwards (but in no event shall such period begin before the corporation's 1st taxable year ending after December 31, 1961), and

"(B) which ends with the corporation's last taxable year beginning before January 1, 1986.

"(e) No recomputation of minimum tax, etc.

"Nothing in this section shall be construed to affect—

"(1) the amount of the tax imposed by section 56 of the Internal Revenue Code of 1986, or

"(2) the amount of any credit allowable under such Code, for any taxable year in the carryback period.

"(f) Reinvestment requirement.

"(1) In general. — Any amount determined under this section must be committed to reinvestment in, and modernization of the steel industry through investment in modern plant and equipment, research and development, and other appropriate projects, such as working capital for steel operations and programs for the retraining of steel workers.

"(2) Special rule. In the case of the LTV Corporation, in lieu of the requirements of paragraph (1)—

"(A) such corporation shall place such refund in a separate account; and

"(B) amounts in such separate account—

"(i) shall only be used by the corporation—

"(I) to purchase an insurance policy which provides that, in the event the corporation becomes involved in a title 11 or similar case (as defined in section 368(a)(3)(A) of the Internal Revenue Code of 1954), the insurer will provide life and health insurance coverage during the 1-year period beginning on the date when the corporation receives the refund to any individual with respect to whom the corporation would (but for such involvement) have been obligated to provide such coverage the coverage provided by the insurer will be identical to the coverage which the corporation would (but for such involvement) have been obligated to provide, and provides that the payment of insurance premiums will not be required during such 1-year period to keep such policy in force, or

"(II) directly in connection with the trade or business of the corporation in the manufacturer or production of steel; and

"(ii) shall be used (or obligated) for purposes described in clause (i) not later than 3 months after the corporation receives the refund.

"(3) In the case of a qualified corporation, no offset to any refund under this section may be made by reason of any tax imposed by section 4971 of the Internal Revenue Code of 1986 (or any interest or penalty attributable to any such tax), and the date on which any such refund is to be paid shall be determined without regard to such corporation's status under title 11, United States Code.

"(g) Definitions.

"For purposes of this section—

"(1) Qualified corporation.—

"(A) In general. — The term 'qualified corporation' means any corporation which is described in section 806(b) of the Steel Import Stabilization Act and a company which was incorporated on February 11, 1983, in Michigan.

"(B) Certain predecessors included. — In the case of any qualified corporation which has carryforward attributable to a predecessor corporation described in such section 806(b), the qualified corporation and the predecessor corporation shall be treated as 1 corporation for purposes of subsections (d) and (e).

"(2) Existing carryforwards. — The term 'existing carryforward' means the aggregate of the amounts which—

"(A) are unused business credit carryforwards to the taxpayer's 1st taxable year beginning after December 31, 1986 (determined without regard to the limitations of section 38(c) and any reduction under section 49 of the Internal Revenue Code of 1986), and

"(B) are attributable to the amount of the regular investment credit determined for periods before January 1, 1986, under section 46(a)(1) of such Code (relating to regular percentage), or any corresponding provision of prior law, determined on the basis that the regular investment audit was used first.

"(3) Special rule for restructuring. In the case of any corporation, any restructuring shall not limit, increase, or otherwise affect the benefits which would have been available under this section but for such restructuring.

"(h) Tentative refunds. Rules similar to the rules of section 6425 of the Internal Revenue Code of 1986 shall apply to any overpayment resulting from the application of this section."

—P.L. 99-514, Sec. 213, [as amended by Sec. 1002(g) of P.L. 100-647, see above] provides:

"SEC. 213. EFFECTIVE 15-YEAR CARRYBACK OF EXISTING CARRYFORWARDS OF QUALIFIED FARMERS.

"(a) General rule.

"If a taxpayer who is a qualified farmer makes an election under this section for its 1st taxable year beginning after December 31, 1986, with respect to any portion of its existing carryforwards, the amount determined under subsection (b) shall be treated as a payment against the tax imposed by chapter 1 of the Internal Revenue Code of 1986 made by such taxpayer on the last day prescribed by law (without regard to extensions) for filing its return of tax under chapter 1 of such Code for such 1st taxable year.

"(b) Amount.

"For purposes of subsection (a), the amount determined under this subsection shall be equal to the smallest of—

"(1) 50 percent of the portion of the taxpayer's existing carryforwards to which the election under subsection (a) applies,

"(2) the taxpayer's net tax liability for the carryback period (within the meaning of section 212(d) of this Act), or

"(3) $750.

"(c) Taxpayer making election may not use same amounts under section 38.

"In the case of a qualified farmer who makes an election under subsection (a), the portion of such farmer's existing carryforwards to which such an election applies shall not be taken into account under section 38 of the Internal Revenue Code of 1986 for any taxable year beginning after December 31, 1986.

"(d) No recomputation of minimum tax, etc.

"Nothing in this section shall be construed to affect—

"(1) the amount of the tax imposed by section 56 of the Internal Revenue Code of 1954, or

"(2) the amount of any credit allowable under such Code, for any taxable year in the carryback period (within the meaning of section 212(d)(3) of this Act).

"(e) Definitions and special rules.

"For purposes of this section—

"(1) Qualified farmer. — The term 'qualified farmer' means any taxpayer who, during the 3-taxable year period preceding the taxable year for which an election is made under subsection (a), derived 50 percent or more of the taxpayer's gross income from the trade or business of farming.

"(2) Existing carryforward. — The term 'existing carryforward' means the aggregate of the amounts which—

"(A) are unused business credit carryforwards to the taxpayer's 1st taxable year beginning after December 31, 1986 (determined without regard to the limitations of section 38(c) of the Internal Revenue Code of 1986), and

"(B) are attributable to the amount of the investment credit determined for periods before January 1, 1986, under section 46(a) of such Code (or any corresponding provision of prior law) with respect to section 38 property which was used by the taxpayer in the trade or business of farming, determined on the basis that such credit was used first.

"(3) Farming. — The term 'farming' has the meaning given such term by section 2032A(e)(4) and (5) of such Code."

—P.L. 99-514, Sec. 251(a), amended para. (b)(4), effective for property placed in service after 12/31/86, in tax. yrs. end. after 12/31/86, with special rules provided by Sec. 251(d)(2)-(6) [as amended by Sec. 1002(k)(1) of P.L. 100-647(b), see above] of this Act, which reads as follows:

"(2) General transitional rule. — The amendments made by this section and section 201 shall not apply to any property placed in service before January 1, 1994, if such property is placed in service as part of—

"(A) a rehabilitation which was completed pursuant to a written contract which was binding on March 1, 1986, or

"(B) a rehabilitation incurred in connection with property (including any leasehold interest) acquired before March 2, 1986, or acquired on or after such date pursuant to a written contract that was binding on March 1, 1986, if—

"(i) parts 1 and 2 of the Historic Preservation Certification Application were filed with the Department of the Interior (or its designee) before March 2, 1986, or

"(ii) the lesser of $1,000,000 or 5 percent of the cost of the rehabilitation is incurred before March 2, 1986, or is required to be incurred pursuant to a written contract which was binding on March 1, 1986.

"(3) Certain additional rehabilitations. — The amendments made by this section and section 201 shall not apply to—

"(A) the rehabilitation of 8 bathhouses within the Hot Springs National Park or of buildings in the Central Avenue Historic District at such Park,

"(B) the rehabilitation of the Upper Pontalba Building in New Orleans, Louisiana,

"(C) the rehabilitation of at least 60 buildings listed on the National Register at the Frankford Arsenal,

"(D) the rehabilitation of De Baliveriere Arcade, St. Louis Centre, and Drake Apartments in Missouri,

"(E) the rehabilitation of The Tides in Bristol, Rhode Island,

"(F) the rehabilitation and renovation of the Outlet Company building and garage in Providence, Rhode Island,

"(G) the rehabilitation of 10 structures in Harrisburg, Pennsylvania, with respect to which the Harristown Development Corporation was designated redeveloper and received an option to acquire title to the entire project site for $1 on June 27, 1984,

"(H) the rehabilitation of a project involving the renovation of 3 historic structures on the Minneapolis riverfront, with respect to which the developer of the project entered into a redevelopment agreement with a municipality dated January

Tax credits — Code Sec. 46

4, 1985, and industrial development bonds were sold in 3 separate issues in May, July, and October 1985,

"(I) the rehabilitation of a bank's main office facilities of approximately 120,000 square feet, in connection with which the bank's board of directors authorized a $3,300,000 expenditure for the renovation and retrofit on March 20, 1984,

"(J) the rehabilitation of 10 warehouse buildings built between 1906 and 1910 and purchased under a contract dated February 17, 1986,

"(K) the rehabilitation of a facility which is customarily used for conventions and sporting events if an analysis of operations and recommendations of utilization of such facility was prepared by a certified public accounting firm pursuant to an engagement authorized on March 6, 1984, and presented on June 11, 1984, to officials of the city in which such facility is located,

"(L) Mount Vernon Mills in Columbia, South Carolina,

"(M) the Barbara Jordan II Apartments,

"(N) the rehabilitation of the Federal Building and Post Office, 120 Hanover Street, Manchester, New Hampshire,

"(O) the rehabilitation of the Charleston Waterfront project in South Carolina,

"(P) the Hayes Mansion in San Jose, California,

"(Q) the renovation of a facility owned by the National Railroad Passenger Corporation ('Amtrak') for which project Amtrak engaged a development team by letter agreement dated August 23, 1985, as modified by letter agreement dated September 9, 1985,

"(R) the rehabilitation of a structure or its components which is listed in the National Register of Historic Places, is located in Allegheny County, Pennsylvania, will be substantially rehabilitated (as defined in section 48(g)(1)(C) prior to amendment by this Act), prior to December 31, 1989; and was previously utilized as a market and an auto dealership,

"(S) The Bellevue Stratford Hotel in Philadelphia, Pennsylvania,

"(T) the Dixon Mill Housing project in Jersey City, New Jersey,

"(U) Motor Square Garden,

"(V) the Blackstone Apartments, and the Shriver-Johnson building, in Sioux Falls, South Dakota,

"(W) the Holy Name Academy in Spokane, Washington,

"(X) the Nike/Clemson Mill in Exeter, New Hampshire,

"(Y) the Central Bank Building in Grand Rapids, Michigan, and

"(Z) the Heritage Hotel, in the City of Marquette, Michigan.

"(4) Additional rehabilitations. — The amendments made by this section and section 201 shall not apply to —

"(A) the Fort Worth Town Square Project in Texas,

"(B) the American Youth Hostel in New York, New York,

"(C) The Riverwest Loft Development (including all three phases, two of which do not involve rehabilitations),

"(D) the Gaslamp Quarter Historic District in California,

"(E) the Eberhardt & Ober Brewery, in Pennsylvania,

"(F) the Captain's Walk Limited Partnership-Harris Place Development, in Connecticut,

"(G) the Velvet Mills in Connecticut,

"(H) the Roycroft Inn, in New York,

"(I) Old Main Village, in Mankato, Minnesota,

"(J) the Washburn-Crosby A Mill, in Minneapolis, Minnesota,

"(K) the Marble Arcade office building in Lakeland, Florida,

"(L) the Willard Hotel, in Washington, D.C.,

"(M) the H. P. Lau Building in Lincoln, Nebraska,

"(N) the Starks Building, in Louisville, Kentucky,

"(O) the Bellevue High School, in Bellevue, Kentucky,

"(P) the Major Hampden Smith House, in Owensboro, Kentucky,

"(Q) the Doe Run Inn, in Brandenburg, Kentucky,

"(R) the State National Bank, in Frankfort, Kentucky,

"(S) the Captain Jack House, in Fleming, Kentucky,

"(T) the Elizabeth Arlinghaus House, in Covington, Kentucky,

"(U) Limerick Shamrock, in Louisville, Kentucky,

"(V) the Robert Mills Project, in South Carolina,

"(W) the 620 Project, consisting of 3 buildings, in Kentucky,

"(X) the Warrior Hotel, Ltd., the first two floors of the Martin Hotel, and the 105,000 square foot warehouse constructed in 1910, all in Sioux City, Iowa,

"(Y) the waterpark condominium residential project, to the extent of $2 million of expenditures,

"(Z) the Bigelow-Hartford Carpet Mill in Enfield, Connecticut,

"(AA) properties abutting 125th Street in New York County from 7th Avenue west to Morningside and the pier area on the Hudson River at the end of such 125th Street,

"(BB) the City of Los Angeles Central Library project pursuant to an agreement dated December 28, 1983,

"(CC) the Warehouse Row project in Chattanooga, Tennessee,

"(DD) any project described in section 204(a)(1)(F) of this Act,

"(EE) the Wood Street Commons project in Pittsburgh, Pennsylvania,

"(FF) any project described in section 803(d)(6) of this Act,

"(GG) Union Station, Indianapolis, Indiana,

"(HH) the Mattress Factory project in Pittsburgh, Pennsylvania,

"(II) Union Station in Providence, Rhode Island,

"(JJ) South Pack Plaza, Asheville, North Carolina,

"(KK) Old Louisville Trust Project, Louisville, Kentucky,

"(LL) Stewarts Rehabilitation Project, Louisville, Kentucky,

"(MM) Bernheim Officenter, Louisville, Kentucky,

"(NN) Springville Mill Project, Rockville, Connecticut, and

"(OO) the D.J. Stewart Company building, State and Main Streets, Rockford, Illinois.

"(5) Reduction in credit for property under transitional rules. — In the case of property placed in service after December 31, 1986, and to which the amendments made by this section do not apply, subparagraph (A) of section 46(b)(4) of the Internal Revenue Code of 1954 (as in effect before the enactment of this Act) shall be applied —

"(A) by substituting '10 percent' for '15 percent', and

"(B) by substituting '13 percent' for '20 percent'.

"(6) Expensing of rehabilitation expenses for the Frankford Arsenal. In the case of any expenditures paid or incurred in connection with improvements (including repairs and maintenance) of the Frankford Arsenal pursuant to a contract and partnership agreement during the 8-year period specified in the contract or agreement, all such expenditures to be made during the period 1986 through and including 1993 shall —

"(A) be treated as made (and allowable as a deduction) during 1986,

"(B) be treated as qualified rehabilitation expenditures made during 1986, and

"(C) be allocated in accordance with the partnership agreement regardless of when the interest in the partnership was acquired, except that —

"(i) if the taxpayer is not the original holder of such interest, no person (other than the taxpayer) had claimed any benefits by reason of this paragraph,

"(ii) no interest under section 6611 of the 1986 Code on any refund of income taxes which is solely attributable to this paragraph shall be paid for the period —

"(I) beginning on the date which is 45 days after the later of April 15, 1987, or the date on which the return for such taxes was filed, and

"(II) ending on the date the taxpayer acquired the interest in the partnership, and

"(iii) if the expenditures to be made under this provision are not paid or incurred before January 1, 1994, then the tax imposed by chapter 1 of such Code for the taxpayer's last taxable year beginning in 1993 shall be increased by the amount of the tax benefits by reason of this paragraph which are attributable to the expenditures not so paid or incurred.

"(7) Special rule. In the case of the rehabilitation of the Willard Hotel in Washington, D.C., section 205(c)(1)(B)(ii) of the Tax Equity and Fiscal Responsibility Act of 1982 shall be applied by substituting '1987' for '1986'.

Prior to amendment, para. (b)(4) read as follows:

"(4) Rehabilitation percentage

"(A) In general

"In the case of qualified rehabilitation expenditures with respect to a:	The rehabilitation percentage is:
30-year building	15
40-year building	20
Certified historic structure	25

"(B) Regular and energy percentages not to apply. The regular percentages and the energy percentages shall not apply to that portion of the basis of any property which is attributable to qualified rehabilitation expenditures.

"(C) Definitions. For purpose of this paragraph

"(i) 30-year building. The term '30-year building' means a qualified rehabilitated building other than a 40-year building and other than a certified historic structure.

"(ii) 40-year building. The term '40-year building' means a qualified rehabilitated building (other than a certified historic structure) which would meet the requirements of section 48(g)(1)(B) if '40' were substituted for '30' each place it appears in subparagraph (B) thereof

"(iii) Certified historic structure. The term 'certified historic structure' means a qualified rehabilitated building which meets the requirements of section 48(g)(3)"

—P.L. 99-514, Sec. 421(a), added items (viii)-(xi) to the table in subpara. (b)(2)(A)... Sec. 421(b), added subpara. (b)(2)(E), effective for periods beginning after 12/31/85, under rules similar to rules under Code Sec. 48(m) (as amended by this Act).

—P.L. 99-514, Sec. 1802(a)(6), added subpara. (e)(4)(D)... Sec. 1802(a)(8), added subpara. (e)(4)(E), effective for property placed in service by the taxpayer after 11/5/83, in tax. yrs. end. after 11/5/83, and for property placed in service by the taxpayer on or before 11/5/83, if the lease to the tax-exempt entity is entered into after 11/5/83, and subject to the special provisions in Sec. 31(g) of P.L. 98-369, reproduced in the note following Code Sec. 168.

—P.L. 99-514, Sec. 1844(a), substituted "this subparagraph" for "clause (i)" in clause (c)(8)(D)(v)... Sec. 1844(b)(3), substituted "an increase in the credit base for" for "additional qualified investment in" in subpara. (c)(9)(A)... Sec. 1844(b)(5), amended clause (c)(9)(C)(i), effective for property placed in service after 7/18/84 in tax. yrs. end. after 7/18/84, except that such amendments shall not apply to any property to which the amendments made by Sec. 211(f) of P.L. 97-34 do not apply.

Prior to amendment, clause (c)(9)(C)(i) read as follows:

"(i) Credit determined by reference to taxable year property placed in service. For purposes of determining the amount of credit allowable under section 38 and the amount of credit subject to the early disposition or cessation rules under section 47, any increase in a taxpayer's qualified investment in property by reason of this paragraph shall be deemed to be additional qualified investment made by the taxpayer in the year in which the property referred to in subparagraph (A) was first placed in service."

—P.L. 99-514, Sec. 1847(b)(11), substituted "48(1)(3)(A)(viii)" for "48(1)(3)(A)(vii)" in subpara. (b)(2)(A), effective for tax. yrs. begin. after 12/31/83, and to carrybacks from tax. yrs. begin after 12/31/83.

—P.L. 99-514, Sec. 1848(a), repealed para. (f)(9), effective for obligations issued after 12/31/83.

Prior to repeal, para. (f)(9) read as follows:

"(9) Special rule for additional credit. If the taxpayer makes an election under subparagraph (E) of subsection (a)(2), effective for a taxable year beginning after December 31, 1975, then, notwithstanding the prior paragraphs of this subsection, no credit shall be allowed by section 38 in excess of the amount which would be allowed without regard to the provisions of subparagraph (E) of subsection (a)(2) if—

"(A) the taxpayer's cost of service for ratemaking purposes or in its regulated books of account is reduced by reason for any portion of such credit which results from the transfer of employer securities or cash to a tax credit employee stock ownership plan which meets the requirements of section 409A;

"(B) the base to which the taxpayer's rate of return for ratemaking purposes is applied is reduced by reason of any portion of such credit which results from a transfer described in subparagraph (A) to such employee stock ownership plan; or

"(C) any portion of the amount of such credit which results from a transfer described in subparagraph (A) to such employee stock ownership plan is treated for ratemaking purposes in any way other than as though it had been contributed by the taxpayer's common shareholders."

In 1984, P.L. 98-369, Sec. 16(a), repealed as if not enacted Sec. 302(c)(3) of P.L. 97-34 which amended subpara. (c)(8)(D) by substituting "subparagraph (A) or (B) of section 128(c)(1)" for "clause (i), (ii), (iii) of subparagraph (A) or subparagraph (B) of section 128(c)(2)", effective for tax. yrs. begin. after 12/31/84

—P.L. 98-369, Sec. 31(f), added para. (e)(4), effective for amendments made to property placed in service by the taxpayer after 11/5/83, in taxable years ending after such date and to property placed in service by the taxpayer on or before 11/5/83, if the lease to the tax-exempt entity is entered into after 11/5/83, and subject to the special provisions in Sec. 31(g) of the Act reproduced in note following Code Sec. 168.

—P.L. 98-369, Sec. 113(b)(2)(B), added "recovery" before "property" the first place it appears in subpara. (c)(7)(A), effective for property placed in service after 12/31/80.

—P.L. 98-369, Sec. 431(a), amended as much of para. (c)(8) as precedes subpara. (c)(8)(F) . . . Sec. 431(b)(1), amended para. (c)(9) . . . Sec. 431(d)(1), amended clause (c)(8)(F)(i) . . . Sec. 431(d)(2), amended subclause (c)(8)(F)(ii)(III) . . . Sec. 431(d)(3), substituted "nonqualified nonrecourse financing" for "nonrecourse financing (other than financing described in section 46(c)(8)(B)(ii))" in subclause (c)(8)(F)(ii)(IV), effective for property placed in service after 7/18/84 in tax. yrs. ending after 7/18/84 except that such amendments shall not apply to any property to which the amendments made by Sec. 211(f) of P.L. 97-34 do not apply.

Prior to amendment, para. (c)(8) read as follows:

"(8) Limitation to amount at risk.

"(A) In general. In the case of new or used section 38 property which—

"(i) is placed in service during the taxable year by a taxpayer described in section 465(a)(1), and

"(ii) is used in connection with an activity with respect to which any loss is subject to limitation under section 465,

the basis of such property for purposes of paragraph (1) shall not exceed the amount the taxpayer is at risk with respect to such property as of the close of such taxable year.

"(B) Amount at risk.

"(i) In general. Except as provided in clause (ii), the term 'at risk' has the same meaning given such term by section 465(b) (without regard to paragraph (5) thereof);

"(ii) Certain financing. In the case of a taxpayer who at all times is at risk (determined without regard to this clause) in an amount equal to at least 20 percent of the basis (determined under section 168(d)(1)(A)(1)) of property described in subparagraph (A) and who acquired such property from a person who is not a related person, such taxpayer shall for purposes of this paragraph be considered at risk with respect to any amount borrowed in connection with such property (other than convertible debt) to the extent that such amount—

"(I) is borrowed from a qualified person, or

"(II) represents a loan from any Federal, State, or local government or instrumentality thereof, or is guaranteed by, any Federal, State, or local government.

"(C) Special rule for partnerships and Subchapter S corporations. In the case of any partnership or S corporation, any amount treated as at risk under subparagraph (B)(ii) shall be allocated among the partners or shareholders (and treated as an amount at risk with respect to such persons) in the same manner as the credit allowable by section 38.

"(D) Qualified person. For purposes of this paragraph, the term 'qualified person' means any person—

"(i) which—

"(I) is an institution described in clause (i), (ii), or (iii) of subparagraph (A) or subparagraph (B) of section 128(c)(2) or an insurance company to which subchapter L applies, or

"(II) is a pension trust qualified under section 401(a) or a person not described in subclause (I) and which is actively and regularly engaged in the business of lending money,

"(ii) which is not a related person with respect to the taxpayer,

"(iii) which is not a person who receives a fee with respect to the taxpayer's investment in property described in subparagraph (A) or a related person to such person, and

"(iv) which is not a person from which the taxpayer acquired the property described in subparagraph (A) or a related person to such person.

"(E) Related person. For purposes of this paragraph, the term 'related person' has the same meaning as such term is used in section 168(e)(4), except that in applying section 168(e)(4)(D)(i) in the case of a person described in subparagraph (D)(i)(II) of this paragraph, sections 267(b) and 707(b)(1) shall be applied by substituting '0 percent' for '50 percent'.

"(F) Special rule for certain energy property.

"(i) In general. The provisions of subparagraph (A) shall not apply to amounts borrowed with respect to qualified energy property (other than amounts described in subparagraph (B)).

"(ii) Qualified energy property. The term 'qualified energy property' means energy property to which (but for this subparagraph) subparagraph (A) applies and—

"(I) which is described in clause (iii),

"(II) with respect to which the energy percentage determined under section 46(a)(2)(C) at the time such property is placed in service is greater than zero,

"(III) with respect to which the taxpayer, as of the close of the taxable year in which the property is placed in service, is at risk (within the meaning of section 465(b)) without regard to paragraph (5) thereof) in an amount equal to at least 25 percent of the basis of the property, and

"(IV) with respect to which any nonrecourse financing (other than financing described in section 46(c)(8)(B)(ii)) in connection with such property consists of a level payment loan.

For purposes of subclause (II), the energy percentage for property described in clause (iii)(V) shall be treated as being greater than zero during any period the energy percentage for property described in section 48(l)(14) is greater than zero.

"(iii) Property to which this subparagraph applies. Energy property is described in this clause if such property is—

"(I) described in clause (ii), (iv), or (vii) or section 48(l)(2),

"(II) described in section 48(l)(15),

"(III) described in section 48(l)(3)(A)(iii) (but only to the extent such property is used for converting an alternate substance into alcohol for fuel purposes),

"(IV) described in clause (i) of section 48(l)(2)(A) (but only to the extent such property is also described in section 48(l)(3)(A)(viii) or (ix)), or

"(V) property comprising a system for using the same energy source for the sequential generation of electrical power, mechanical shaft power, or both, in combination with steam, heat, or other forms of useful energy.

"(iv) Level payment loan defined. The term 'level payment loan' means a loan in which each installment is substantially equal, a portion of each installment is attributable to the repayment of principal, and that portion is increased commensurate with decreases in the portion of the payment attributable to interest."

Prior to amendment, para. (c)(9) read as follows:

"(9) Subsequent increases in the taxpayer's amount at risk with respect to the property.

"(A) In general. If, at the close of a taxable year subsequent to the year in which property was placed in service, the amount which the taxpayer has at risk with respect to such property has increased (as determined under subparagraph (B)), such increase shall be taken into account as additional qualified investment in such property in accordance with subparagraph (C).

"(B) Increases to be taken into account. For purposes of subparagraphs (A) and (C), the amount which a taxpayer has at risk with respect to the property shall be treated as increased by the sum of the cash and the fair market value of property (other than property with respect to which the taxpayer is not at risk) used during the taxable year to reduce the principal sum of any amount with respect to which the taxpayer is not at risk.

"(C) Manner in which taken into account. For purposes of determining the amount of credit allowed under section 38 and the amount of credit subject to the early disposition rules under section 47, an increase in a taxpayer's qualified investment in property (determined under subparagraph (B)) shall be deemed to be additional qualified investment made by the taxpayer in the year in which the property referred to in subparagraph (A) was first placed in service. However, the credit determined by taking into account the increase in qualified investment under this paragraph shall be considered a credit earned in the taxable year of such increase."

—P.L. 98-369, Sec. 474(o)(1), amended subsecs. (a) and (b) . . . Sec. 474(o)(2), substituted "subsection (b)(2)" for "section 46(a)(2)(C)" in subclause (c)(8)(F)(ii)(II) . . . Sec. 474(o)(3)(A)(i), and (ii), deleted "and the $25,000 amount specified under subparagraph (A) and (B) of subsection (a)(3)" after "the qualified investment" and substituted "such qualified investment" for "such items" in para. (e)(1) . . . Sec. 474(o)(3)(B), substituted "qualified investment" for "the items described therein" in para. (e)(2) . . . Sec. 474(o)(4)(A), substituted "no credit determined under subsection (a) shall be allowed by section 38" for "no credit shall be allowed by section 38" in para. (f)(1) and (2) . . . Sec. 474(o)(4)(B), substituted "the credit determined under subsection (a) and allowable by section 38" for "the credit allowable by section 38" each place it appears in paras. (f)(1) and (2) . . . Sec. 474(o)(4)(C), substituted "the credit determined under subsection (a) and allowed by section 38" for "the credit allowed by section 38" in subpara. (f)(4)(B) . . . Sec. 474(o)(5)(A), substituted "the credit determined under subsection (a) and allowable under section 38" for "the credit allowable under section 38" each place it appears in para. (f)(8) . . . Sec. 474(o)(5)(B), substituted "(within the meaning of the first sentence of subsection (c)(3)(B)" for "(within the meaning of subsection (a)(7)(C))" in para. (f)(8) . . . Sec. 474(o)(6), substituted "the limitation of section 38(c)" for "the limitation of subsection (a)(3)" in para. (g)(2) . . . Sec. 474(o)(7)(A), and (B), substituted "the credit determined under subsection (a) and allowable to the organization under section 38" for "the credit allowable to the organization under section 38" and substituted "the limitation contained in section 38(c)" for "the limitation contained in subsection (a)(3)" in para. (h)(1), effective for tax. yrs. begin. after 12/31/83 and to carrybacks from tax. yrs. begin after 12/31/83. Sec. 475(c) of the Act provides:

"(c) Clarification of effect of amendments on investment tax credit.

Tax credits   Code Sec. 46

"Nothing in the amendments made by section 474(o) shall be construed as reducing the amount of any credit allowable for qualified investment in taxable years beginning before January 1, 1984."

Prior to amendment, subsecs. (a) and (b) read as follows:

"(a) General rule

"(1) First-in-first-out rule. The amount of the credit allowed by section 38 for the taxable year shall be an amount equal to the sum of—

"(A) the investment credit carryovers carried to such taxable year,

"(B) the amount of the credit determined under paragraph (2) for such taxable year, plus

"(C) the investment credit carrybacks carried to such taxable year.

"(2) Amount of credit.

"(A) In general. The amount of the credit determined under this paragraph for the taxable year shall be an amount equal to the sum of the following percentages of the qualified investment (as determined under subsections (c) and (d)):

"(i) the regular percentage,

"(ii) in the case of energy property, the energy percentage,

"(iii) the employee plan percentage, and

"(iv) in the case of that portion of the basis of any property which is attributable to qualified rehabilitation expenditures, the rehabilitation percentage.

"(B) Regular percentage. For purposes of this paragraph, the regular percentage is 10 percent.

"(C) Energy percentage. For purposes of this paragraph—

"(i) In general. The energy percentage shall be determined in accordance with the following table:

Column A — Description	Column B — Percentage	Column C — Period	
	The energy percentage is:	For the period:	
In the case of:		Beginning on:	And ending on:
I. General Rule — Property not described in any of the following provisions of this column	10 percent	Oct. 1, 1978	Dec. 31, 1982.
II. Solar, Wind, or Geothermal Property — Property described in section 48(l)(2)(A)(ii) or 48(l)(3)(A)(viii)	A. 10 percent B. 15 percent	Oct. 1, 1978 Jan. 1, 1980	Dec. 31, 1979. Dec. 31, 1985.
III. Ocean Thermal Property — Property described in section 48(l)(3)(A)(ix)	15 percent	Jan. 1, 1980	Dec. 31, 1985.
IV. Qualified Hydroelectric Generating Property — Property described in section 48(l)(2)(A)(vii)	11 percent	Jan. 1, 1980	Dec. 31, 1985.
V. Qualified Intercity Buses. — Property described in section 48(l)(2)(A)(ix)	10 percent	Jan. 1, 1980	Dec. 31, 1985.
VI. Biomass Property — Property described in section 48(l)(15)	10 percent	Oct. 1, 1978	Dec. 31, 1985.
VII. Chlor-Alkali Electrolytic Cells — Property described in section 48(l)(5)(M)	10 percent	Jan. 1, 1980	Dec. 31, 1982.

"(ii) Periods for which percentage not specified. In the case of any energy property, the energy percentage shall be zero for any period for which an energy percentage is not specified for such property under clause (i) (as modified by clauses (iii) and (iv)).

"(iii) Longer period for certain long-term projects. For the purpose of applying the energy percentage contained in subclause (I) of clause (i) with respect to property which is a part of a project with a normal construction period of 2 years or more (within the meaning of section 46(d)(2)(A)(i)), 'December 31, 1990' shall be substituted for 'December 31, 1982' if—

"(I) before January 1, 1983, the taxpayer has completed all engineering studies in connection with the commencement of the construction of the project, and has applied for all environmental and construction permits required under Federal, State, or local law in connection with the commencement of the construction of the project, and

"(II) before January 1, 1986, the taxpayer has entered into binding contracts for the acquisition, construction, reconstruction, or erection of equipment specially designed for the project and the aggregate cost to the taxpayer of that equipment is at least 50 percent of the reasonably estimated cost for all such equipment which is to be placed in service as part of the project upon its completion.

"(iv) Longer period for certain hydroelectric generating property. If an application has been docketed by the Federal Energy Regulatory Commission before January 1, 1986, with respect to the installation of any qualified hydroelectric generating property, for purposes of applying the energy percentage contained in subclause (IV) of clause (i) with respect to such property, 'December 31, 1988' shall be substituted for 'December 31, 1985'.

"(D) Special rule for certain energy property. For purposes of this paragraph, the regular percentage shall not apply to any energy property which, but for section 48(l)(1), would not be section 38 property. In the case of any qualified hydroelectric generating property which is a fish passageway, the preceding sentence shall not apply to any period after 1979 for which the energy percentage for such property is greater than zero.

"(E) Employee plan percentage. For purposes of this paragraph, the employee plan percentage is—

"(i) with respect to the period beginning on January 21, 1975, and ending on December 31, 1982, 1 percent,

"(ii) with respect to the period beginning on January 1, 1977, and ending on December 31, 1982, an additional percentage (not in excess of ½ of 1 percent) which results in an amount equal to the amount determined under section 48(n)(1)(B), and

"(iii) with respect to any period beginning after December 31, 1982, zero.

This subparagraph shall apply to a corporation only if it meets the requirements of section 409A and only if it elects (at such time, in such form, and in such manner as the Secretary prescribes) to have this subparagraph apply.

"(F) Rehabilitation percentage. for purposes of this paragraph—

"(i) In general.

In the case of qualified rehabilitation expenditures with respect to a:	The rehabilitation percentage is:
30-year building	15
40-year building	20
Certified historic structure	25

"(ii) Regular and energy percentages not to apply. The regular percentage and the energy percentage shall not apply to that portion of the basis of any property which is attributable to qualified rehabilitation expenditures.

"(iii) Definitions.

"(I) 30-year building. The term '30-year building' means a qualified rehabilitated building other than a 40-year building and other than a certified historic structure.

"(II) 40-year building. The term '40-year building' means a qualified rehabilitated building (other than a certified historic structure) which would meet the requirements of section 48(g)(1)(B) if '40' were substituted for '30' each place it appears in subparagraph (B) thereof.

"(III) Certified historic structure. The term 'certified historic structure' means a qualified rehabilitated building which meets the requirements of section 48(g)(3).

"(3) Limitation based on amount of tax. Notwithstanding paragraph (I), the credit allowed by section 38 for the taxable year shall not exceed—

"(A) so much of the liability for tax for the taxable year as does not exceed $25,000, plus

"(B) 85 percent of so much of the liability for tax for the taxable year as exceeds $25,000.

"(4) Liability for tax. For purposes of paragraph (3), the liability for tax for the taxable year shall be the tax imposed by this chapter for such year, reduced by the sum of the credits allowable under—

"(A) section 33 (relating to foreign tax credit), and

"(B) section 37 (relating to credit for the elderly and the permanently and totally disabled).

For purposes of this paragraph, any tax imposed for the taxable year by section 56 (relating to corporate minimum tax), section 72(m)(5)(B) (relating to 10 percent tax on premature distributions to key employees) section 72(q)(1) (relating to 5-percent tax on premature distributions under annuity contracts), section 402(e) (relating to tax on lump sum distributions), section 408(f) (relating to additional tax on income from certain retirement accounts), section 531 (relating to accumulated earnings tax, section 541 (relating to personal holding company tax) or section 1374 (relating to tax on certain capital gains of S corporations), and any additional tax imposed for the taxable year by section 1351(d)(1) (relating to recov-

1,225

eries of foreign expropriation losses), shall not be considered tax imposed by this chapter for such year.

"(5) Married individuals. In the case of a husband or wife who files a separate return, the amount specified under subparagraphs (A) and (B) of paragraph (3) shall be $12,500 in lieu of $25,000. This paragraph shall not apply if the spouse of the taxpayer has no qualified investment for, and no unused credit carryback or carryover to, the taxable year of such spouse which ends within or with the taxpayer's taxable year.

"(6) Controlled groups. In the case of a controlled group, the $25,000 amount specified under paragraph (3) shall be reduced for each component member of such group by apportioning $25,000 among the component members of such group in such manner as the Secretary shall by regulations prescribe. For purposes of the preceding sentence, the term 'controlled group' has the meaning assigned to such term by section 1563(a).

"(7) Special rules in the case of energy property. Under regulations prescribed by the Secretary—

"(A) In general. This subsection and subsection (b) shall be applied separately—

"(i) first with respect to so much of the credit allowed by section 38 as is not attributable to the energy percentage, and

"(ii) second with respect to so much of the credit allowed by section 38 as is attributable to the application of the energy percentage to energy property.

"(B) Rules of application for energy property. In applying this subsection and subsection (b) for taxable years ending after September 30, 1978, with respect to so much of the credit allowed by section 38 as is described in subparagraph (A)(ii)—

"(i) paragraph (3)(B) shall be applied by substituting '100 percent' for '85 percent', and

"(ii) the liability for tax shall be the amount determined under paragraph (4) reduced by so much of the credit allowed by section 38 as is described in subparagraph (A)(i)."

"(b) Carryback and carryover of unused credits.

"(1) In general. If the sum of the amount of the investment credit carryovers to the taxable year under subsection (a)(1)(A) plus the amount determined under subsection (a)(1)(B) for the taxable year exceeds the amount of the limitation imposed by subsection (a)(3) for such taxable year (hereinafter in this subsection referred to as the 'unused credit year'), such excess attributable to the amount determined under subsection (a)(1)(B) shall be—

"(A) an investment credit carryback to each of the 3 taxable years preceding the unused credit year, and

"(B) an investment credit carryover to each of the 7 taxable years following the unused credit year,

and, subject to the limitations imposed by paragraphs (2) and (3), shall be taken into account under the provisions of subsection (a)(1) in the manner provided in such subsection. The entire amount of the unused credit for an unused credit year shall be carried to the earliest of the 10 taxable years to which (by reason of subparagraphs (A) and (B)) such credit may be carried and then to each of the other 9 taxable years to the extent, because of the limitations imposed by paragraphs (2) and (3), such unused credit may not be taken into account under subsection (a)(1) for a prior taxable year to which such unused credit may be carried. In the case of an unused credit for an unused credit year ending before January 1, 1971, which is an investment credit carryover to a taxable year beginning after December 31, 1970 (determined without regard to this sentence), this paragraph shall be applied—

"(C) by substituting '10 taxable years' for '7 taxable years' in subparagraph (B), and by substituting '13 taxable years' for '10 taxable years', and '12 taxable years' for '9 taxable years' in the preceding sentence, and

"(D) by carrying such an investment credit carryover to a later taxable year (than the taxable year to which it would, but for this subparagraph, be carried) to which it may be carried if, because of the amendments made by section 802(b)(2) of the Tax Reform Act of 1976, carrying such carryover to the taxable year to which it would, but for this subparagraph, be carried would cause a portion of an unused credit from an unused credit year ending after December 31, 1970 to expire.

In the case of an unused credit for an unused credit year ending after December 31, 1973, this paragraph shall be applied by substituting '15' for '7' in subparagraph (B), and by substituting '18' for '10', and '17' for '9' in the second sentence.

"(2) Limitation of carrybacks. The amount of the unused credit which may be taken into account under subsection (a)(1) for any preceding taxable year shall not exceed the amount by which the limitation imposed by subsection (a)(3) for such taxable year exceeds the sum of—

"(A) the amounts determined under subparagraphs (A) and (B) of subsection (a)(1) for such taxable year, plus

"(B) the amounts which (by reason of this subsection) are carried back to such taxable year and are attributable to taxable years preceding the unused credit year.

"(3) Limitation on carryovers. The amount of the unused credit which may be taken into account under subsection (a)(1)(A) for any succeeding taxable year shall not exceed the amount by which the limitation imposed by subsection (a)(3) for such taxable year exceeds the sum of the amounts which, by reason of this subsection, are carried to such taxable year and are attributable to taxable years preceding the unused credit year."

—P.L. 98-369, Sec. 713(c)(1)(C), substituted "tax on premature distributions to key employees" for "tax on premature distributions to owner-employees" in para. (a)(4) (before amend. by Sec. 470(o)(1) of this Act) effective for distributions after 12/31/82.

In 1983, P.L. 98-21, Sec. 122(c)(1), substituted "relating to credit for the elderly and the permanently and totally disabled" for "relating to credit for the elderly" in subpara. (a)(4)(B), effective for tax. yrs. begin. after 12/31/83.

—P.L. 97-448, Sec. 102(d)(2), added para. (c)(3) to Sec. 209 of P.L. 97-34, the effective date for amendments made by Sec. 207(c)(1) of P.L. 97-34, see below.

—P.L. 97-448, Sec. 102(e)(1)(A), amended subpara. (c)(7)(A)... Sec. 102(e)(1)(B), substituted "shall be treated as property which is not 3-year property" for "shall be treated as 5-year property", effective for property placed in service after 12/31/80.

Prior to amendment, subpara. (c)(7)(A) read as follows:

"(A) in the case of 15-year public utility, 10-year, or 5-year property (within the meaning of section 168(c)), 100 percent, and"

—P.L. 97-448, Sec. 102(f)(1), amended Sec. 212(e)(2)(B) of P.L. 97-34, part of the effective date for changes made by Sec. 212(a)(1) of P.L. 97-34, see below.

Prior to amendment, Sec. 212(e)(2)(B) of P.L. 97-34 read as follows:

"(B) such building meets the requirements of paragraph (1) of section 48(g) of the Internal Revenue Code of 1954 (as in effect on the day before the date of enactment of this Act) but does not meet the requirements of such paragraph (1) (as amended by this Act)."

—P.L. 97-448, Sec. 102(f)(5)(A), substituted "a qualified rehabilitated building" for "any building" in subclause (a)(2)(F)(iii)(II)... Sec. 102(f)(5)(B), substituted "means a qualified rehabilitated building which meets the requirements of section 48(g)(3)" for "has the meaning given to such term by section 48(g)(3)" in subclause (a)(2)(F)(iii)(III), effective for expenditures incurred after 12/31/81, in tax. yrs. end. after 12/31/81.

—P.L. 97-448, Sec. 202(f), amended subclause (a)(2)(C)(iii)(I).

Prior to amendment, subclause (a)(2)(C)(iii)(I) read as follows:

"(I) 30-year building. The term '30-year building' means a qualified rehabilitated building other than a 40-year building and other than a certified historic structure."

—P.L. 97-448, Sec. 306(a)(1)(A)(i), redesignated the second Sec. 201(c) of P.L. 97-248 as Sec. 201(d) of P.L. 97-248, see below.

—P.L. 97-424, Sec. 541(b), added para. (f)(10), effective for tax. yrs. begin. after 12/31/79.

—P.L. 97-424, Sec. 541(c)(2)-(5), provided a special rule on tax treatment of public utility property which is reproduced in the note following Code Sec. 167.

—P.L. 97-424, Sec. 546(b), added item VII to the table in clause (a)(2)(C)(i), effective 1/6/83.

In 1982, P.L. 97-354, Sec. 5(a)(4), substituted "section 1374 (relating to tax on certain capital gains of S corporations)," for "section 1378 (relating to tax on certain capital gains of subchapter S corporations)," in the second sentence of para. (a)(4)... Sec. 5(a)(5), substituted "S corporation" for "electing small business corporation (within the meaning of section 1371(b))" in subpara. (c)(8)(C)... Sec. 5(a)(6), substituted "an S corporation" for "an electing small business corporation (as defined in section 1371)" in para. (e)(3), effective for tax. yrs. begin. after 12/31/82.

—P.L. 97-248, Sec. 201(d)(8)(A), substituted "(relating to corporate minimum tax)" for "(relating to minimum tax for tax preferences)" in para. (a)(4), effective for distributions after 12/31/82.

—P.L. 97-248, Sec. 205(b)(1), amended subpara. (a)(3)(B)... Sec. 205(b)(2)(A), deleted paras. (a)(7) and (a)(8), and redesignated para. (a)(9) as para. (a)(7)... Sec. 205(b)(2)(B), amended clause (a)(7)(A)(i) (as redesignated by Sec. 205(b)(2)(A) of this Act)... Sec. 205(b)(2)(C), deleted clause (a)(7)(B)(ii) and redesignated clause (a)(7)(B)(iii) as clause (a)(7)(B)(ii) (as redesignated by Sec. 205(b)(2)(A) of this Act), effective for tax. yrs. begin. after 12/31/82.

Prior to amendment, subpara. (a)(3)(B) read as follows:

"(B) the following percentage of so much of the liability for tax for the taxable year as exceeds $25,000:

"If the taxable year ends in:	The percentage is:
"1979	60
"1980	70
"1981	80
"1982 or thereafter	90."

Prior to deletion, paras. (a)(7) and (a)(8) read as follows:

"(7) Alternative limitation in the case of certain utilities.

"(A) In general. If, for the taxable year ending in 1979—

"(i) the amount of the qualified investment of the taxpayer which is attributable to public utility property is 25 percent or more of his aggregate qualified investment, and

"(ii) the application of this paragraph results in a percentage higher than 60 percent,

then subparagraph (B) of paragraph (3) of this subsection shall be applied by substituting for '60 percent' the taxpayer's applicable percentage for such year.

"(B) Applicable percentage. The applicable percentage for any taxpayer for any taxable year ending in 1979 is—

"(i) 50 percent, plus

"(ii) that portion of 20 percent which the taxpayer's amount of qualified investment which is public utility property bears to his aggregate qualified investment. If the proportion referred to in clause (ii) is 75 percent or more, the applicable percentage of the taxpayer for the year shall be 70 percent.

"(C) Public utility property defined. For purposes of this paragraph, the term 'public utility property' has the meaning given to such term by the first sentence of subsection (c)(3)(B).

"(8) Alternative limitation in the case of certain railroads and airlines.

"(A) In general. If, for a taxable year ending in 1979 or 1980—

Tax credits Code Sec. 46

"(i) the amount of the qualified investment of the taxpayer which is attributable to railroad property or to airline property, as the case may be, is 25 percent or more of his aggregate qualified investment, and

"(ii) the application of this paragraph results in a percentage higher than 60 percent (70 percent in the case of a taxable year ending in 1980),

then subparagraph (B) of paragraph (3) of this subsection shall be applied by substituting for '60 percent' ('70 percent' in the case of a taxable year ending in 1980) the taxpayer's applicable percentage for such year.

"(B) Applicable percentage. The applicable percentage of any taxpayer for any taxable year under this paragraph is—

"(i) 50 percent, plus

"(ii) that portion of the tentative percentage for the taxable year which the taxpayer's amount of qualified investment which is railroad property or airline property (as the case may be) bears to his aggregate qualified investment.

If the proportion referred to in clause (ii) is 75 percent or more, the applicable percentage of the taxpayer for the taxable year shall be 90 percent (80 percent in the case of a taxable year ending in 1980).

"(C) Tentative percentage. For purposes of subparagraph (B), the tentative percentage shall be determined under the following table:

If the taxable year ends in:	The tentative percentage is:
1979	40
1980	30

"(D) Railroad property defined. For purposes of this paragraph, the term 'railroad property' means section 38 property used by the taxpayer directly in connection with the trade or business carried on by the taxpayer of operating a railroad (including a railroad switching or terminal company).

"(E) Airline property defined. For purposes of this paragraph, the term 'airline property' means section 38 property used by the taxpayer directly in connection with the trade or business carried on by the taxpayer of the furnishing or sale of transportation as a common carrier by air subject to the jurisdiction of the Civil Aeronautics Board of the Federal Aviation Administration."

Prior to amendment, clause (a)(7)(B)(i) read as follows:

"(i) paragraph (3)(B) shall be applied by substituting '100 percent' for the percentage determined under the table contained in such paragraph,"

Prior to deletion, clause (a)(7)(B)(ii) read as follows:

"(ii) paragraphs (7) and (8) shall not apply, and"

—P.L. 97-248, Sec. 265(b)(2)(A)(i), added "section 72(q)(1) (relating to 5-percent tax on premature distributions under annuity contracts)," after "owner-employees)" in para. (a)(4), effective for distributions after 12/31/82.

In 1981, P.L. 97-34, Sec. 207(c)(1), added the last sentence to para. (b)(1), effective for unused credit years end. after 12/31/73. Sec. 209(c)(3) of this Act provides:

"(3) Carryover must have been alive in 1981. The amendments made by subsections (a), (b), and (c) of section 207 [P.L. 97-34] shall not apply to any amount which, under the law in effect on the day before the date of the enactment of this Act, could not be carried to a taxable year ending in 1981."

Sec. 209(d)(2) of this Act provides:

"(2) Transitional rule for requirements of section 46(f).— If, by the terms of the applicable rate order last entered before the date of the enactment of this Act by a regulatory commission having appropriate jurisdiction, a regulated public utility would (but for this provision) fail to meet such requirements of paragraph (1) or (2) of section 46(f) of the Internal Revenue Code of 1954 with respect to property for an accounting period ending after December 31, 1980, such regulated public utility shall not fail to meet such requirements if, by the terms of its first rate order determining cost of service with respect to such property which becomes effective after the date of the enactment of this Act and on or before January 1, 1983, such regulated public utility meets such requirements. This provision shall not apply to any rate order which, under the rules in effect before the date of the enactment of this Act, was inconsistent with the requirements of paragraph (1) or (2) of section 46(f) of such Code (whichever would have been applicable)."

—P.L. 97-34, Sec. 211(a)(1), added para. (c)(7), effective for property placed in service after 12/31/80.

—P.L. 97-34, Sec. 211(b)(1), amended para. (d)(1) ... Sec. 211(b)(2), deleted "having a useful life of 7 years or more" after "section 38 property" in clause (d)(2)(A)(ii), effective for progress expenditures made after 12/31/80.

Prior to amendment, para. (d)(1) read as follows:

"(d) Qualified progress expenditures.—

"(1) In general. In the case of any taxpayer who has made an election under paragraph (6), the amount of his qualified investment for the taxable year (determined under subsection (c) without regard to this subsection) shall be increased by an amount equal to his aggregate qualified progress expenditures for the taxable year with respect to progress expenditure property."

—P.L. 97-34, Sec. 211(d), added the last sentence to the end of para. (e)(3), effective for leases entered into after 6/25/81.

—P.L. 97-34, Sec. 211(e)(1), substituted "(2) Applicable percentage in certain cases. Except as provided in paragraphs (3), (6), and (7), the applicable percentage for purposes of paragraph (1) for any property shall be determined under the following table:" for "(2) Applicable percentage. For purposes of paragraph (1), the applicable percentage for any property shall be determined under the following tables:" ... Sec. 211(e)(2), amended, subpara. (c)(6)(A), effective for property placed in service after 12/31/80.

Prior to amendment, subpara. (c)(6)(A) read as follows:

"(A) In general. Notwithstanding paragraph (2), in the case of a commuter highway vehicle the useful life of which is 3 years or more, the applicable percentage for purposes of paragraph (1) shall be 100 percent."

—P.L. 97-34, Sec. 211(f)(1), added paras. (c)(8) and (c)(9). Sec. 211(i)(5) of this Act provides:

"(5) At risk rules.—

"(A) In general.— The amendment made by subsection (f) shall not apply to—

"(i) property placed in service by the taxpayer on or before February 18, 1981, and

"(ii) property placed in service by the taxpayer after February 18, 1981, where such property is acquired by the taxpayer pursuant to a binding contract entered into on or before that date.

"(B) Binding contract.— For purposes of subparagraph (A)(ii), property acquired pursuant to a binding contract shall, under regulations prescribed by the Secretary, include property acquired in a manner so that it would have qualified as pretermination property under section 49(b) (as in effect before its repeal by the Revenue Act of 1978)."

—P.L. 97-34, Sec. 212(a)(1), amended subpara. (a)(2)(A) by deleting "and" at the end of clause (a)(2)(A)(ii), by substituting ", and" for the period at the end of clause (a)(2)(A)(iii), and by adding clause (a)(2)(A)(iv) ... Sec. 212(a)(2), added subpara. (a)(2)(F), effective for expenditures incurred after 12/31/81, in tax. yrs. ending after 12/31/81, except as provided in Sec. 212(e)(2) of this Act which reads as follows:

"(2) Transitional rule.— The amendments made by this section shall not apply with respect to any rehabilitation of a building if—

"(A) the physical work on such rehabilitation began before January 1, 1982, and

"(B) such building does not meet the requirements of paragraph (1) of section 48(g) of the Internal Revenue Code of 1954 (as amended by this Act)."

—P.L. 97-34, Sec. 332(a), amended subpara. (a)(2)(E) by substituting "December 31, 1982" for "December 31, 1983" in clauses (a)(2)(E)(i) and (ii) ... by deleting "and" at the end of clause (a)(2)(E)(i) ... by substituting ", and" for the period at the end of clause (a)(2)(E)(ii) ... by adding clause (a)(2)(E)(iii), effective 8/13/81.

In 1980, P.L. 96-223, Sec. 221(a), amended subpara. (a)(2)(C).

Prior to amendment, subpara. (a)(2)(C) read as follows:

"(C) Energy percentage. For purposes of this paragraph, the energy percentage is—

"(i) 10 percent with respect to the period beginning on October 1, 1978, and ending on December 31, 1982, or

"(ii) zero with respect to any other period."

—P.L. 96-223, Sec. 222(e)(2), added "In the case of any qualified hydroelectric generating property which is a fish passageway, the preceding sentence shall not apply to any period after 1979 for which the energy percentage for such property is greater than zero." to the end of subpara. (a)(2)(D), effective for periods after 12/31/79, under rules similar to the rules of Code Sec. 48(m).

—P.L. 96-223, Sec. 223(b)(1), amended para. (a)(10) [redesignated para. (a)(9) by P.L. 96-223, see below] by inserting "and" at the end of clause (a)(10)(A)(i) ... substituting a period for "(other than solar or wind energy property), and" at the end of clause (a)(10)(A)(ii) ... deleting clause (a)(10)(A)(iii) ... deleting "other than solar or wind energy property" from the heading of subpara. (a)(10)(B) ... deleting subpara. (a)(10)(C), effective for qualified investment for tax. yrs. begin. after 12/31/79.

Prior to amendment, clause (a)(10)(A)(iii) read as follows:

"(iii) then with respect to so much of the credit allowed by section 38 as is attributable to the application of the energy percentage to solar or wind energy property."

Prior to amendment, subpara. (a)(10)(C) read as follows:

"(C) Refundable credit for solar or wind energy property. In the case of so much of the credit allowed by section 38 as is described in subparagraph (A)(iii)—

"(i) paragraph (3) shall not apply, and

"(ii) for purposes of this title (other than section 38, this subpart, and chapter 63), such credit shall be treated as if it were allowed by section 39 and not by section 38."

—P.L. 96-222, Sec. 101(a)(7)(A), substituted "subparagraph (E) of subsection (a)(2)" for "subparagraph (B) of subsection (a)(2)" each place it appeared in para. (f)(9) and substituted "a tax credit employee stock ownership plan which meets the requirements of section 409A" for "an employee stock ownership plan which meets the requirements of section 301(d) of the Tax Reduction Act of 1975" in subpara. (f)(9)(A), presumably intended by Congress to be effective with respect to qualified investment for tax. yrs. begin. after '78 [Sec. 101(b)(2)] although technically effective with respect to estates of decedents dying after 4/1/80 [Sec. 101(b)(1)(D)].

—P.L. 96-222, Sec. 101(a)(7)(B), corrected Sec. 141(g) of P.L. 95-600 [see below].

Prior to corrections, Sec. 141(g) of P.L. 95-600 read as follows:

"(g) Effective dates.—

"(1) In general. The amendments made by this section (other than by subsection (f)(3)) shall apply with respect to qualified investment for taxable years beginning after December 31, 1978. The amendment made by subsection (f)(7) shall apply to years beginning after December 31, 1978."

—P.L. 96-222, Sec. 101(a)(7)(L)(iii)(I), substituted "employee plan" for "ESOP" each place it appeared in para. (a)(2) ... Sec. 101(a)(7)(L)(v)(I), substituted "Employee plan" for "ESOP" in the heading of subpara. (a)(2)(E), presumably intended by Congress to be effective for qualified investment for tax. yrs. begin. after '78 [Sec. 101(b)(2)] although technically effective with respect to estates of decedents dying after 4/1/80 [Sec. 101(b)(1)(D)].

—P.L. 96-222, Sec. 101(a)(7)(M)(i), added "and ending on" before "before December 31, 1983" each place it appeared in subpara. (a)(2)(e) [inoperative, see Sec. 301(a)(1) of P.L. 95-618, below].

—P.L. 96-222, Sec. 103(a)(2)(A), amended Sec. 312(c) of P.L. 95-600 which amended paras. (f)(1) and (2) by substituting "described in section 50 (as in effect before its repeal by the Revenue Act of 1978)" for "described in section 50" [see below].

—P.L. 96-222, Sec. 103(a)(2)(B)(i), redesignated para. (a)(10) as para. (a)(9) . . . Sec. 103(a)(2)(B)(ii), amended redesignated clause (a)(9)(B)(i) . . . Sec. 103(a)(2)(B)(iii), substituted "(7) and (8)" for "(7), (8) and (9)" in redesignated clause (a)(9)(B)(ii), effective 11/9/78.

Prior to amendment, clause (a)(9)(B)(i) read:

"(i) paragraph (3)(C) shall be applied by substituting '100 percent' for '50 percent'."

—P.L. 96-222, Sec. 103(a)(3), added the last sentence to subpara. (c)(5)(B), effective for property acquired by the taxpayer after '78 and for property, the construction, reconstruction or erection of which was completed by taxpayer after '78 (but only to the extent of the basis thereof attributable to construction, reconstruction or erection after '78).

—P.L. 96-222, Sec. 103(a)(4)(A), added the last sentence to para. (e)(3), effective for tax. yrs. end. after 10/31/78.

—P.L. 96-222, Sec. 107(a)(3)(A), substituted "subsection (a)(7)(C)" for "subsection (a)(7)(D)" in the first sentence of para. (f)(8), effective 10/4/76.

In 1978, P.L. 95-618, Sec. 241(a), added para. (c)(6), effective 11/9/78.

—P.L. 95-618, Sec. 301(a)(1), amended para. (a)(2), (which is further amended by Sec. 311(a) of P.L. 95-600, see below) effective 11/9/78.

Prior to amendment, para. (a)(2) read as follows:

"(2) Amount of credit for current taxable year. —

"(A) 10 percent credit. Except as otherwise provided in subparagraph (B), in the case of a property described in subparagraph (D), the amount of the credit determined under this paragraph for the taxable year shall be an amount equal to 10 percent of the qualified investment (as determined under subsections (c) and (d)).

"(B) Additional credit. In the case of a corporation which elects (at such time, in such form, and in such manner as the Secretary prescribes) to have the provisions of this subparagraph apply, the amount of the credit determined under this paragraph shall be an amount equal to—

"(i) 11 percent of the qualified investment (as determined under subsections (c) and (d)), plus

"(ii) an additional percent (not in excess of one-half percent) of the qualified investment (as determined under such subsections) equal in amount to the amount determined under section 301(e) of the Tax Reduction Act of 1975.

"An election may not be made to have the provisions of this subparagraph apply unless the corporation meets the requirements of section 301(d) of the Tax Reduction Act of 1975.

"(C) 7 percent credit. In the case of property not described in subparagraph (D), the amount of credit determined under this paragraph for the taxable year shall be an amount equal to 7 percent of the qualified investment (as determined under subsections (c) and (d)).

"(D) Transitional rules. The provisions of subparagraphs (A) and (B) shall apply only to—

"(i) property to which subsection (d) does not apply, the construction, reconstruction, or erection of which is completed by the taxpayer after January 21, 1975, but only to the extent of the basis thereof attributable to the construction, reconstruction, or erection after January 21, 1975, and before January 1, 1981,

"(ii) property to which subsection (d) does not apply, acquired by the taxpayer after January 21, 1975, and before January 1, 1981, and placed in service by the taxpayer before January 1, 1981, and

"(iii) property to which subsection (d) applies, but only to the extent of the qualified investment (as determined under subsections (c) and (d)) with respect to qualified progress expenditures made after January 21, 1975, and before January 1, 1981.

"For purposes of applying clause (ii) of subparagraph (B), the date 'December 31, 1976,' shall be substituted for the date 'January 21, 1975,' each place it appears in this subparagraph."

—P.L. 95-618, Sec. 301(a)(2)(A), amended subpara. (c)(3)(A), effective 11/9/78.

Prior to amendment, subpara. (c)(3)(A) read as follows:

"(A) to the extent that subsection (a)(2)(C) applies to property which is public utility property, the amount of the qualified investment shall be ⅘ of the amount determined under paragraph (1)."

—P.L. 95-618, Sec. 301(a)(2)(B), substituted ", the Tax Reform Act of 1976, and the Energy Tax Act of 1978" for "and the Tax Reform Act of 1976" in para. (f)(8), effective 11/9/78.

—P.L. 95-618, Sec. 301(c)(1), added para. (a)(10), effective 11/9/78.

—P.L. 95-600, Sec. 141(e), substituted "December 31, 1983" for "December 31, 1980" each place it appeared in subpara. (a)(2)(E), as added by Sec. 301(a)(1) of P.L. 95-618 . . . Sec. 141(f)(1), deleted Secs. 301(d), (e) and (f), of P.L. 94-12, (which were further amended by Secs. 803(c), (d) and (e) of P.L. 94-455). [This amendment merely deletes historical background, and does not effect actual Internal Revenue Code Secs., see below.] . . . Sec. 141(f)(2), substituted "section 48(n)(1)(B)" for "section 301(e) of the Tax Reduction Act of 1975" and substituted "section 409A" for "section 301(d) of the Tax Reduction Act of 1975" in subpara. (a)(2)(E), as added by Sec. 301(a)(1) of P.L. 95-618, effective with respect to qualified investment for tax. yrs. begin. after '78. Para. (g)(2) of Sec. 141 provides as follows:

"(2) Election to have amendments apply during 1978. At the election of the taxpayer, paragraph (1) shall be applied by substituting 'December 31, 1977' for 'December 31, 1978'; except that in the case of a plan in existence before December 31, 1978, any such election shall not affect the required allocation of employer securities attributable to qualified investment for taxable years beginning before January 1, 1979. An election under the preceding sentence shall be made at such time and in such manner as the Secretary of the Treasury or his delegate shall prescribe. Such an election, once made, shall be irrevocable."

—P.L. 95-600, Sec. 311(a), amended subpara. (a)(2)(B), as added by Sec. 301(a)(1) of P.L. 95-615 . . . Sec. 311(c)(1), substituted "To the extent that the credit allowed by section 38 with respect to any public utility property is determined at the rate of 7 percent" for "For the period beginning on January 1, 1981" in subpara. (c)(3)(A) as amended by Sec. 301(a)(2)(A) of P.L. 95-615 . . . Sec. 311(c)(2), substituted "the Energy Tax Act of 1978, and the Revenue Act of 1978" for "and the Energy Tax Act of 1978" in para. (f)(8) (as amended by Sec. 301(a)(2)(B) of P.L. 95-615), effective 11/6/78.

Prior to amendment, subpara. (a)(2)(B), as added by Sec. 301(a)(1) of P.L. 95-615, read as follows:

"(B) Regular percentage. For purposes of this paragraph, the regular percentage is—

"(i) 10 percent with respect to the period beginning on January 21, 1975, and ending on December 31, 1980, or

"(ii) 7 percent with respect to the period beginning on January 1, 1981."

—P.L. 95-600, Sec. 312(a), amended para. (a)(3) . . . Sec. 312(b), amended paras. (a)(7) and (a)(8) . . . added para. (a)(9) . . . Sec. 312(c)(2) substituted "described in section 50 (as in effect before its repeal by the Revenue Act of 1978)" for "described in section 50" in paras. (f)(1) and (2), effective for tax. yrs. end. after '78.

Prior to amendment, paras. (a)(3) read as follows:

"(3) Limitation based on amount of tax. Notwithstanding paragraph (1), the credit allowed by section 38 for the taxable year shall not exceed—

"(A) so much of the liability for tax for the taxable year as does not exceed $25,000, plus

"(B) for taxable years ending on or before the last day of the suspension period (as defined in section 48(j)), 25 percent of so much of the liability for tax for the taxable year as exceeds $25,000, or

"(C) for taxable years ending after the last day of such suspension period, 50 percent of so much of the liability for tax for the taxable year as exceeds $25,000. "In applying subparagraph (C) to a taxable year beginning on or before the last day of such suspension period and ending after the last day of such suspension period, the percent referred to in such subparagraph shall be the sum of 25 percent plus the percent which bears the same ratio to 25 percent as the number of days in such year after the last day of the suspension period bears to the total number of days in such year. The amount otherwise determined under this paragraph shall be reduced (but not below zero) by the credit which would have been allowable under paragraph (1) for such taxable year with respect to suspension period property but for the application of section 48(h)(1)."

Prior to amendment, paras. (a)(7), (8) and (9) read as follows:

"(7) Alternative limitation in the case of certain utilities. —

"(A) In general. — If, for a taxable year ending after calendar year 1974 and before calendar year 1981, the amount of the qualified investment of the taxpayer which is attributable to public utility property is 25 percent or more of his aggregate qualified investment, then subparagraph (C) of paragraph (3) of this subsection shall be applied by substituting for 50 percent his applicable percentage for such year.

"(B) Applicable percentage. — The applicable percentage of any taxpayer for any taxable year is —

"(i) 50 percent, plus

"(ii) that portion of the tentative percentage for the taxable year which the taxpayer's amount of qualified investment which is public utility property bears to his aggregate qualified investment.

"If the proportion referred to in clause (ii) is 75 percent or more, the applicable percentage of the taxpayer for the year shall be 50 percent plus the tentative percentage for such year.

"(C) Tentative percentage. — For purposes of subparagraph (B), the tentative percentage shall be determined under the following table:

"If the taxable year ends in:	The tentative percentage is:
1975 or 1976	50
1977	40
1978	30
1979	20
1980	10

"(D) Public utility property defined. — For purposes of this paragraph, the term 'public utility property' has the meaning given to such term by the first sentence of subsection (c)(3)(B).

"(8) Alternative limitation in the case of certain railroads.

"(A) In general. If, for a taxable year ending after calendar year 1976, and before calendar year 1983, the amount of the qualified investment of the taxpayer which is attributable to railroad property is 25 percent or more of his aggregate qualified investment, then subparagraph (C) of paragraph (3) of this subsection shall be applied by substituting for 50 percent his applicable percentage for such year.

"(B) Applicable percentage. The applicable percentage of any taxpayer for any taxable year under this paragraph is —

"(i) 50 percent, plus

"(ii) that portion of the tentative percentage for the taxable year which the taxpayer's amount of qualified investment which is railroad property bears to his aggregate qualified investment.

Tax credits   **Code Sec. 46**

"If the proportion referred to in clause (ii) is 75 percent or more, the applicable percentage of the taxpayer for the year shall be 50 percent plus the tentative percentage for such year.

"(C) Tentative percentage. For purposes of subparagraph (B), the tentative percentage shall be determined under the following table:

"If the taxable year ends in:	The tentative percentage is:
1977 or 1978	50
1979	40
1980	30
1981	20
1982	10

"(D) Railroad property defined. For purposes of this paragraph, the term 'railroad property' means section 38 property used by the taxpayer directly in connection with the trade or business carried on by the taxpayer of operating a railroad (including a railroad switching or terminal company).

"(9) Alternative limitation in the case of certain airlines.

"(A) In general. If, for a taxable year ending after calendar year 1976 and before calendar year 1983, the amount of the qualified investment of the taxpayer which is attributable to airline property is 25 percent or more of his aggregate qualified investment, then subparagraph (C) of paragraph (3) of this subsection shall be applied by substituting for 50 percent his applicable percentage for such year.

"(B) Applicable percentage. The applicable percentage of any taxpayer for any taxable year under this paragraph is—

"(i) 50 percent, plus

"(ii) that portion of the tentative percentage for the taxable year which the taxpayer's amount of qualified investment which is airline property bears to his aggregate qualified investment.

If the proportion referred to in clause (ii) is 75 percent or more, the applicable percentage of the taxpayer for the year shall be 50 percent plus the tentative percentage for such year.

"(C) Tentative percentage. For purposes of subparagraph (B), the tentative percentage shall be determined under the following table:

"If the taxable year ends in:	The tentative percentage is:
1977 or 1978	50
1979	40
1980	30
1981	20
1982	10

"(D) Airline property defined. For purposes of this paragraph, the term 'airline property' means section 38 property used by the taxpayer directly in connection with the trade or business carried on by the taxpayer of the furnishing or sale of transportation as a common carrier by air subject to the jurisdiction of the Civil Aeronautics Board or the Federal Aviation Administration."

—P.L. 95-600, Sec. 313(a), amended para. (c)(5), effective for property acquired by the taxpayer after '78 and for property, the construction, reconstruction or erection of which was completed by taxpayer after '78 (but only to the extent of the basis thereof attributable to construction, reconstruction or erection after '78). Prior to amendment, para. (c)(5) read as follows:

"(5) Applicable percentage in the case of certain pollution control facilities. Notwithstanding subsection (c)(2), in the case of property—

"(A) with respect to which an election under section 169 applies, and

"(B) the useful life of which (determined without regard to section 169) is not less than 5 years,

50 percent shall be the applicable percentage for purposes of applying paragraph (1) with respect to so much of the adjusted basis of the property as (after the application of section 169(f)) constitutes the amortizable basis for purposes of section 169."

—P.L. 95-600, Sec. 316(a), added subpara. (h) . . . Sec. 316(b)(1), added "and" at the end of subpara. (e)(1)(A) . . . deleted "and" at the end of subpara. (e)(1)(B) . . . deleted subpara. (e)(1)(C) . . . Sec. 316(b)(2), added "and" at the end of subpara. (e)(2)(A) . . . substituted a period for ", and" at the end of subpara. (e)(2)(B) . . . deleted subpara. (e)(2)(C), effective for tax. yrs. end. after 10/31/78.

Prior to amendment, subpara. (e)(1)(C) read as follows:

"(C) a cooperative organization described in section 1381(a),"

Prior to amendment, subpara. (e)(2)(C) read as follows:

"(C) in the case of a cooperative organization, the ratio (i) the numerator of which is its taxable income and (ii) the denominator of which is its taxable income increased by amounts to which section 1382(b) or (c) applies and similar amounts the tax treatment of which is determined without regard to subchapter T (sec. 1381 and following)."

—P.L. 95-600, Sec. 703(a)(1), substituted "subsection (a)(7)(D)" for "subsection (a)(6)(D)" in para. (f)(8) . . . Sec. 703(a)(2), substituted "Merchant Marine Act, 1936" for "Merchant Marine Act, 1970" in para. (g)(5), effective 10/4/76.

—P.L. 95-600, Sec. 703(j)(9), corrected the instructions in Sec. 1901(b)(1)(C) of P.L. 94-455, to amend para. (a)(4) instead of para. (a)(3).

In 1976, P.L. 94-455, Sec. 503(b)(4), substituted "credit for the elderly" for "retirement income" in subpara. (a)(3)(C), effective for tax. yrs. begin. after '75.

—P.L. 94-455, Sec. 802(a), redesignated paras. (a)(2) through (a)(6) as paras. (a)(3) through (a)(7) . . . amended para. (a)(1) . . . added para. (a)(2), effective for tax. yrs. begin. after '75.

Prior to amendment, para. (a)(1) read as follows:

"(1) General rule.

"(A) Ten percent credit. Except as otherwise provided in this paragraph, in the case of a property described in subparagraph (D), the amount of the credit allowed by section 38 for the taxable year shall be an amount equal to 10 percent of the qualified investment (as determined under subsections (c) and (d)).

"(B) Eleven percent credit. Except as otherwise provided in this paragraph, in the case of a corporation which elects to have the provisions of this subparagraph apply, the amount of the credit allowed by section 38 for the taxable year with respect to property described in subparagraph (D) shall be an amount equal to 11 percent of the qualified investment (as determined under subsections (c) and (d)). An election may not be made to have the provisions of this subparagraph apply for the taxable year unless the corporation meets the requirements of section 301(d) of the Tax Reduction Act of 1975. An election by a corporation to have the provisions of this subparagraph apply shall be made at such time, in such form, and in such manner as the Secretary or his delegate may prescribe.

"(C) Seven percent credit. Except as otherwise provided in this paragraph, the amount of credit allowed by section 38 for the taxable year shall be an amount equal to 7 percent of the qualified investment (as determined under subsections (c) and (d)).

"(D) Transitional rules. The provisions of subparagraphs (A) and (B) shall apply only to—

"(i) property to which subsection (d) does not apply, the construction, reconstruction, or erection of which is completed by the taxpayer after January 21, 1975, but only to the extent of the basis thereof attributable to the construction, reconstruction, or erection after January 21, 1975, and before January 1, 1977.

"(ii) property to which subsection (d) does not apply, acquired by the taxpayer after January 21, 1975, and before January 1, 1977, and placed in service by the taxpayer before January 1, 1977, and

"(iii) property to which subsection (d) applies, but only to the extent of the qualified investment (as determined under subsections (c) and (d)) with respect to qualified progress expenditures made after January 21, 1975, and before January 1, 1977."

—P.L. 94-455, Sec. 802(b)(1), substituted "paragraph (3)" for "paragraph (2)" in paras. (a)(4), (a)(5), (a)(6), (a)(7) as redesignated by Sec. 802(a) of the Act . . . Sec. 802(b)(2), amended subsec. (b) . . . Sec. 802(b)(3), substituted "subsection (a)(2)(C)" for "subsection (a)(1)(C)" in subpara. (c)(3)(A) . . . Sec. 802(b)(4), substituted "subsection (a)(3)" for "subsection (a)(2)" in para. (e)(1) . . . Sec. 802(b)(5), added "and the Tax Reform Act of 1976" after "the Tax Reduction Act of 1975" in the first sentence of para. (f)(8), effective for tax. yrs. begin. after 1975.

Prior to amendment, subsec. (b) read as follows:

"(b) Carryback and carryover of unused credits.

"(1) Allowance of credit. If the amount of the credit determined under subsection (a)(1) for any taxable year exceeds the limitation provided by subsection (a)(2) for such taxable year (hereinafter in this subsection referred to as 'unused credit year'), such excess shall be—

"(A) an investment credit carryback to each of the 3 taxable years preceding the unused credit year, and

"(B) an investment credit carryover to each of the 7 taxable years following the unused credit year,

and shall be added to the amount allowable as a credit by section 38 for such years, except that such excess may be a carryback only to a taxable year ending after December 31, 1961. The entire amount of the unused credit for an unused credit year shall be carried to the earliest of the 10 taxable years to which (by reason of subparagraphs (A) and (B)) such credit may be carried, and then to each of the other 9 taxable years to the extent that, because of the limitation contained in paragraph (2), such unused credit may not be added for a prior taxable year to which such unused credit may be carried. In the case of an unused credit for an unused credit year ending before January 1, 1971, which is an investment credit carryover to a taxable year beginning after December 31, 1970 (determined without regard to this sentence), this paragraph shall be applied by substituting '10 taxable years' for '7 taxable years' in subparagraph (B) and by substituting '13 taxable years' for 10 taxable years' and '12 taxable years' for '9 taxable years' in the preceding sentence.

"(2) Limitation. The amount of the unused credit which may be added under paragraph (1) for any preceding or succeeding taxable year shall not exceed the amount by which the limitation provided by subsection (a)(2) for such taxable year exceeds the sum of—

"(A) the credit allowable under subsection (a)(1) for such taxable year, and

"(B) the amounts which, by reason of this subsection, are added to the amount allowable for such taxable year and attributable to taxable years preceding the unused credit year.

"(3) Special rules for carryovers from pre-1971 unused credit years. The extent to which an investment credit carryover from an unused credit year ending before January 1, 1971, may be added under paragraph (1) for a taxable year beginning after December 31, 1970, shall be determined without regard to paragraph (2)(A). In determining the excess under paragraph (1) for any taxable year beginning after December 31, 1970, the limitation provided by subsection (a)(2) for such taxable year shall be reduced by the investment credit carryovers from such unused credit years (to the extent such unused credit may not be added for a prior taxable year).

"(4) Taxable year beginning before January 1, 1962. For purposes of determining the amount of an investment credit carryback that may be added under paragraph (1) for a taxable year beginning before January 1, 1962, and ending after December 31, 1961, the amount of the limitation provided by subsection (a)(2) is the amount which bears the same ratio to such limitation as the number of days in such taxable year after December 31, 1961, bears to the total number of days in such year.

"(5) Certain taxable years ending in 1969, 1970, or 1971. The amount which may be added under this subsection for any taxable year beginning after December 31, 1968, and ending after April 18, 1969, and before January 1, 1972, shall not exceed 20 percent of the higher of—

"(A) the aggregate of the investment credit carrybacks and investment credit carryovers to the taxable year, or

"(B) the highest amount computed under subparagraph (A) for any preceding taxable year which began after December 31, 1968, and ended after April 18, 1969.

In the case of a taxable year ending after August 15, 1971, and before January 1, 1972, the percentage contained in the preceding sentence shall be increased by 6 percentage points for each month (or portion thereof) in the taxable year after August 15, 1971.

"(6) Additional 3-year carryover period in certain cases. Any portion of an investment credit carryback or carryover to any taxable year beginning after December 31, 1968, and ending after April 18, 1969, and before January 1, 1971, which—

"(A) may be added under this subsection under the limitation provided by paragraph (2), and

"(B) may not be added under the limitation provided by paragraph (5),

shall be an investment credit carryover to each of the 3 taxable years following the 7th taxable year after the unused credit year, and shall (subject to the provisions of paragraphs (1), (2), and (5)) be added to the amount allowable as a credit by section 38 for such years."

—P.L. 94-455, Sec. 803(a), added para. (f)(9), effective for tax. yrs. begin. after '74.

—P.L. 94-455, Sec. 803(b)(1), substituted "paragraphs (1), (2), and (9)" for "paragraphs (1) and (2)" each place it appeared in subpara. (f)(4)(A) ... substituted "paragraph (1), (2), or (9)" for "paragraph (1) or (2)" each place it appeared in subpara. (f)(4)(A) ... substituted "paragraph (2) or the election described in paragraph (9)" for "paragraph (2)" in clause (f)(4)(B)(ii), effective for tax. yrs. begin. after '74.

—P.L. 94-455, Sec. 803(c), and (e), amended Sec. 301(d) of P.L. 94-12, effective for tax. yrs. begin. after '74. Sec. 301(d) of P.L. 94-12, as amended, reads as follows:

"(d) Plan requirements for taxpayers electing additional credit.

"In order to meet the requirements of this subsection—

"(1) Except as expressly provided in subsections (e) and (f), a corporation (hereinafter in this subsection referred to as the 'employer') must establish an employee stock ownership plan (described in paragraph (2)) which is funded by transfers of employer securities in accordance with the provisions of paragraph (6) and which meets all other requirements of this subsection.

"(2) The plan referred to in paragraph (1) must be a defined contribution plan established in writing which—

"(A) is a stock bonus plan, a stock bonus and a money purchase pension plan, or a profit-sharing plan,

"(B) is designed to invest primarily in employer securities, and

"(C) meets such other requirements (similar to requirements applicable to employee stock ownership plans as defined in section 4975(e)(7) of the Internal Revenue Code of 1954) as the Secretary of the Treasury or his delegate may prescribe.

"(3) The plan must provide for the allocation of all employer securities transferred to it or purchased by it (because of the requirements of section 46(a)(1)(B) of the Internal Revenue Code of 1954) to the account of each participant (who was a participant at any time during the plan year, whether or not he is a participant at the close of the plan year) as of the close of each plan year in an amount which bears substantially the same proportion to the amount of all such securities allocated to all participants in the plan for that plan year as the amount of compensation paid to such participant (disregarding any compensation in excess of the first $100,000 per year) bears to the compensation paid to all such participants during that year (disregarding any compensation in excess of the first $100,000 with respect to any participant). Notwithstanding the first sentence of this paragraph, the allocation to participants' accounts may be extended over whatever period may be necessary to comply with the requirements of section 415 of the Internal Revenue Code of 1954. For purposes of this paragraph, the amount of compensation paid to a participant for a year is the amount of such participant's compensation within the meaning of section 415(c)(3) of such Code for such year.

"(4) The plan must provide that each participant has a nonforfeitable right to any stock allocated to his account under paragraph (3), and that no stock allocated to a participant's account may be distributed from that account before the end of the eighty-fourth month beginning after the month in which the stock is allocated to the account except in the case of separation from the service, death, or disability.

"(5) The plan must provide that each participant is entitled to direct the plan as to the manner in which any employer securities allocated to the account of the participant are to be voted.

"(6) On making a claim for credit, adjustment, or refund under section 38 of the Internal Revenue Code of 1954, the employer states in such claim that it agrees, as a condition of receiving any such credit, adjustment, or refund—

"(A) in the case of a taxable year beginning before January 1, 1977, to transfer employer securities forthwith to the plan having an aggregate value at the time of the claim of 1 percent of the amount of the qualified investment (as determined under section 46 (c) and (d) of such Code) of the taxpayer for the taxable year, and

"(B) in the case of a taxable year beginning after December 31, 1976—

"(i) to transfer employer securities to the plan having an aggregate value at the time of the claim of 1 percent of the amount of the qualified investment (as determined under section 46(c) and (d) of such Code) of the employer for the taxable year,

"(ii) except as provided in clause (iii), to effect the transfer not later than 30 days after the time (including extensions) for filing its income tax return for a taxable year, and

"(iii) in the case of an employer whose credit (as determined under section 46(a)(2)(B) of such Code) for a taxable year beginning after December 31, 1976, exceeds the limitations of paragraph (3) of section 46(a) of such Code—

"(I) to effect that portion of the transfer allocable to investment credit carrybacks of such excess credit at the time required under clause (ii) for the unused credit year (within the meaning of section 46(b) of such Code), and

"(II) to effect that portion of the transfer allocable to investment credit carryovers of such excess credit at the time required under clause (ii) for the taxable year to which such portion is carried over.

For purposes of meeting the requirements of this paragraph, a transfer of cash shall be treated as a transfer of employer securities if the cash is, under the plan, used to purchase employer securities.

"(7) Notwithstanding any other provision of law to the contrary, if the plan does not meet the requirements of section 401 of the Internal Revenue Code of 1954—

"(A) stock transferred under paragraph (6) or subsection (e)(3) and allocated to the account of any participant under paragraph (3) and dividends thereon shall not be considered income of the participant or his beneficiary under the Internal Revenue Code of 1954 until actually distributed or made available to the participant or his beneficiary and, at such time, shall be taxable under section 72 of such Code (treating the participant or his beneficiary as having a basis of zero in the contract),

"(B) no amount shall be allocated to any participant in excess of the amount which might be allocated if the plan met the requirements of section 401 of such Code, and

"(C) the plan must meet the requirements of sections 410 and 415 of such Code.

"(8)(A) Except as provided in subparagraph (B)(iii), if the amount of the credit determined under section 46(a)(2)(B) of the Internal Revenue Code of 1954 is recaptured or redetermined in accordance with the provisions of such Code, the amounts transferred to the plan under this subsection and subsection (e) and allocated under the plan shall remain in the plan or in participant accounts, as the case may be, and continue to be allocated in accordance with the plan.

"(B) If the amount of the credit determined under section 46(a)(2)(B) of the Internal Revenue Code of 1954 is recaptured in accordance with the provisions of such Code—

"(i) the employer may reduce the amount required to be transferred to the plan under paragraph (6) of this subsection, or under paragraph (3) of subsection (e), for the current taxable year or any succeeding taxable years by the portion of the amount so recaptured which is attributable to the contribution to such plan,

"(ii) notwithstanding the provisions of paragraph (12), the employer may deduct such portion, subject to the limitations of section 404 of such Code (relating to deductions for contributions to an employees' trust or plan), or

"(iii) if the requirements of subsection (f)(1) are met, the employer may withdraw from the plan an amount not in excess of such portion.

"(C) If the amount of the credit claimed by an employer for a prior taxable year under section 38 of the Internal Revenue Code of 1954 is reduced because of a redetermination which becomes final during the taxable year, and the employer transferred amounts to a plan which were taken into account for purposes of this subsection for that prior taxable year, then—

"(i) the employer may reduce the amount it is required to transfer to the plan under paragraph (6) of this subsection, or under paragraph (3) of subsection (e), for the taxable year or any succeeding taxable year by the portion of the amount of such reduction in the credit or increase in tax which is attributable to the contribution to such plan, or

"(ii) notwithstanding the provisions of paragraph (12), the employer may deduct such portion subject to the limitations of section 404 of such Code.

"(9) For purposes of this subsection, the term—

"(A) 'employer securities' means common stock issued by the employer or a corporation which is a member of a controlled group of corporations which includes the employer (within the meaning of section 1563(a) of the Internal Revenue Code of 1954, determined without regard to section 1563(a)(4) and (e)(3)(C) of such Code) with voting power and dividend rights no less favorable than the voting power and dividend rights of other common stock issued by the employer or such controlling corporation, or securities issued by the employer or such controlling corporation, convertible into such stock, and

"(B) 'value' means the average of closing prices of the employer's securities, as reported by a national exchange on which securities are listed, for the 20 consecutive trading days immediately preceding the date of transfer or allocation of such securities or, in the case of securities not listed on a national exchange, the fair market value as determined in good faith and in accordance with regulations issued by the Secretary of the Treasury or his delegate.

"(10) The Secretary of the Treasury or his delegate shall prescribe such regulations and require such reports as may be necessary to carry out the provisions of this subsection and subsections (e) and (f).

"(11) If the employer fails to meet any requirement imposed under this subsection and subsections (e) and (f) or under any obligation undertaken to comply with the requirement of this subsection and subsections (e) and (f), he is liable to the United States for a civil penalty of an amount equal to the amount involved in such failure. The preceding sentence shall not apply if the taxpayer corrects such failure (as determined by the Secretary of the Treasury or his delegate) within 90 days after notice thereof. For purposes of this paragraph, the term 'amount involved' means an amount determined by the Secretary or his delegate, but not in

Tax credits Code Sec. 46

excess of 1 percent of the qualified investment of the taxpayer for the taxable year under section 46(a)(1)(B) and not less than the product of one-half of one percent of such amount multiplied by the number of months (or parts thereof) during which such failure continues. The amount of such penalty may be collected by the Secretary of the Treasury in the same manner in which a deficiency in the payment of Federal income tax may be collected.

"(12) Notwithstanding any provision of the Internal Revenue Code of 1954 to the contrary, no deductions shall be allowed under section 162, 212, or 404 of such Code for amounts transferred to an employee stock ownership plan and taken into account under this subsection.

"(13)(A) As reimbursement for the expense of establishing the plan, the employer may withhold from amounts due the plan for the taxable year for which the plan is established, or the plan may pay, so much of the amounts paid or incurred in connection with the establishment of the plan as does not exceed the sum of 10 percent of the first $100,000 that the employer is required to transfer to the plan for that taxable year under paragraph (6) (including any amounts transferred under subsection (e) (3)) and 5 percent of any amount in excess of the first $100,000 of such amount.

"(B) As reimbursement for the expense of administering the plan, the employer may withhold from amounts due the plan, or the plan may pay, so much of the amounts paid or incurred during the taxable year as expenses of administering the plan as does not exceed the smaller of—

"(i) the sum of 10 percent of the first $100,000 and 5 percent of any amount in excess of $100,000 of the income from dividends paid to the plan with respect to stock of the employer during the plan year ending with or within the employer's taxable year, or

"(ii) $100,000.

"(14) The return of a contribution made by an employer to an employee stock ownership plan designed to satisfy the requirements of this subsection or subsection (e) (or a provision for such a return) does not fail to satisfy the requirements of this subsection, subsection (e), section 401(a) of the Internal Revenue Code of 1954, or section 403(c)(1) of the Employee Retirement Income Security Act of 1974 if—

"(A) the contribution is conditioned under the plan upon determination by the Secretary of the Treasury that such plan meets the applicable requirements of this subsection, subsection (e), or section 401(a) of such Code,

"(B) the application for such a determination is filed with the Secretary not later than 90 days after the date on which the credit under section 38 is allowed, and

"(C) the contribution is returned within one year after the date on which the Secretary issues notice to the employer that such plan does not satisfy the requirements of this subsection, subsection (e), or section 401(a) of such Code."

—P.L. 94-455, Sec. 803(d), amended Sec. 301 of P.L. 94-12, by adding subsec. (e), effective for tax. yrs. begin. after '76, and by adding subsec. (f), effective for tax. yrs. begin. after '74. Sec. 301(e) of P.L. 94-12 read as follows:

"(e) Plan requirements for taxpayers electing additional one-half percent credit

"(1) General rule. For purposes of clause (ii) of section 46(a)(2)(B) of the Internal Revenue Code of 1954, the amount determined under this subsection for a taxable year is an amount equal to the sum of the matching employee contributions for the taxable year which meet the requirements of this subsection.

"(2) Election; basic plan requirements. No amount shall be determined under this subsection for the taxable year unless the corporation elects to have this subsection apply for that year. A corporation may not elect to have the provisions of this subsection apply for a taxable year unless the corporation meets the requirements of subsection (d) and the requirements of this subsection.

"(3) Employer contribution. On making a claim for credit, adjustment, or refund under section 38 of the Internal Revenue Code of 1954, the employer shall state in such claim that the employer agrees, as a condition of receiving any such credit, adjustment, or refund attributable to the provisions of section 46(a)(2)(B)(ii) of such Code, to transfer at the time described in subsection (d)(6)(B) employer securities (as defined in subsection (d)(9)(A)) to the plan having an aggregate value at the time of the transfer of not more than one-half of one percent of the amount of the qualified investment (as determined under subsections (c) and (d) of section 46 of such Code) of the taxpayer for the taxable year. For purposes of meeting the requirements of this paragraph, a transfer of cash shall be treated as a transfer of employer securities if the cash is, under the plan, used to purchase employer securities.

"(4) Requirements relating to matching employee contributions—

"(A) An amount contributed by an employee under a plan described in subsection (d) for the taxable year may not be treated as a matching employee contribution for that taxable year under this subsection unless—

"(i) each employee who participates in the plan described in subsection (d) is entitled to make such a contribution,

"(ii) the contribution is designated by the employee as a contribution intended to be used for matching employer amounts transferred under paragraph (3) to a plan which meets the requirements of this subsection, and

"(iii) the contribution is in the form of an amount paid in cash to the employer or plan administrator not later than 24 months after the close of the taxable year in which the portion of the credit allowed by section 38 of such Code (and determined under clause (ii) of section 46(a)(2)(B) of such Code which the contribution is to match) is allowed, and is invested forthwith in employer securities (as defined in subsection (d)(9)(A)).

"(B) The sum of the amounts of matching employee contributions taken into account for purposes of this subsection for any taxable year may not exceed the value (at the time of transfer) of the employer securities transferred to the plan in accordance with the requirements of paragraph (3) for the year for which the employee contributions are designated as matching contributions.

"(C) The employer may not make participation in the plan a condition of employment and the plan may not require matching employee contributions as a condition of participation in the plan.

"(D) Employee contributions under the plan must meet the requirements of section 401(a)(4) of such Code (relating to contributions).

"(5) A plan must provide for allocation of all employer securities transferred to it or purchased by it under this subsection to the account of each participant (who was a participant at any time during the plan year, whether or not he is a participant at the close of plan year) as of the close of the plan year in an amount equal to his matching employee contributions for the year. Matching employee contributions and amounts so allocated shall be deemed to be allocated under subsection (d)(3).

"(f) Recapture

"(1) General rule. Amounts transferred to a plan under subsection (d)(6) or (e)(3) may be withdrawn from the plan by the employer if the plan provides that while subject to recapture—

"(A) amounts so transferred with respect to a taxable year are segregated from other plan assets, and

"(B) separate accounts are maintained for participants on whose behalf amounts so transferred have been allocated for a taxable year.

"(2) Coordination with other law. Notwithstanding any other law or rule of law, an amount withdrawn by the employer will neither fail to be considered to be nonforfeitable nor fail to be for the exclusive benefit of participants or their beneficiaries merely because of the withdrawal from the plan of—

"(A) amounts described in paragraph (1), or

"(B) employer amounts transferred under subsection (e)(3) to the plan which are not matched by matching employee contributions or which are in excess of the limitations of section 415 of such Code,

nor will the withdrawal of any such amount be considered to violate the provisions of section 403(c)(1) of the Employee Retirement Income Security Act of 1974."

—P.L. 94-455, Sec. 805(a), added subsec. (g), effective for tax. yrs. begin. after '75 in the case of property placed in service after 12/31/75.

—P.L. 94-455, Sec. 1607(b)(1)(B), substituted "857(b)(2)(B)" for "857(b)(2)(C)" following "section 852(b)(2)(D) or" in subpara. (e)(2)(B) ... added "determined without regard to any deduction for capital gains dividends (as defined in section 857(b)(3)(C)) and by excluding any net capital gain" immediately before the period at the end of para. (e)(2), effective for tax. yrs. end. after 10/4/76. Sec. 1608(c) of the Act provided the following exceptions to the effective date:

"(c) Alternative tax and net operating loss.

"The amendments made by sections 1606 and 1607 shall apply to taxable years ending after the date of the enactment of this Act, except that in the case of a taxpayer which has a net operating loss (as defined in section 172(c) of the Internal Revenue Code of 1954) for any taxable year ending after the date of enactment of this Act for which the provisions of part II of subchapter M of chapter 1 of subtitle A of such Code apply to such taxpayer, such loss shall not be a net operating loss carryback under section 172 of such Code to any taxable year ending on or before the date of enactment of this Act."

—P.L. 94-455, Sec. 1701(b), added para. (a)(8), effective for tax. yrs. begin. 10/4/76.

—P.L. 94-455, Sec. 1703, added para. (a)(9), effective for tax. yrs. end. after 1976 and before 1983.

—P.L. 94-455, Sec. 1901(a)(4)(A), substituted "section 408(f)" for "section 408(e)" following "distributions to owner-employees)" in the second sentence of para. (a)(4), as previously redesignated by the Act, for tax. yrs. begin. after '76.

—P.L. 94-455, Sec. 1901(a)(4)(B), substituted "47 U.S.C. 222(a)(5)" for "47 U.S.C., sec. 222(a)(5)" in clause (c)(3)(B)(iii), for tax. yrs. begin. after '76.

—P.L. 94-455, Sec. 1901(b)(1)(C), deleted subpara. (a)(3)(B) ... added "and" at the end of subpara. (a)(3)(A) ... redesignated subpara. (a)(3)(C) as subpara. (a)(3)(B), (all of which were redesignated by Sec. 802(a) of the Act as being in para. (a)(4)), effective for tax. yrs. begin. after '76.

Prior to amendment, subpara. (a)(3)(B) read as follows:

"(B) section 35 (relating to partially tax-exempt interest, and"

—P.L. 94-455, Sec. 1901(b)(13)(A), substituted "Secretary" for "Secretary or his delegate" in paras. (a)(6), (a)(4), (d)(6), (f)(1), (f)(2), (f)(3), (f)(7), and each place it appeared in (f)(8), effective for tax. yrs. begin. after '76.

—P.L. 94-455, Sec. 2112(a)(2), added para. (c)(5), effective for property acquired by taxpayer, and which construction, reconstruction, etc., was completed after '76, in tax. yrs. begin. after '76.

In 1975, P.L. 94-12, Sec. 301(a), rewrote para. (a)(1), effective date of enactment (3/29/75).

Prior to amendment, para. (a)(1) read as follows:

"(1) General rule. The amount of the credit allowed by section 38 for the taxable year shall be equal to 7 percent of the qualified investment (as defined in subsection (c))."

—P.L. 94-12, Sec. 301(d), "Plan requirements for taxpayers electing additional credit", was retroactively amended by Sec. 803(c) of P.L. 94-455, see above.

—P.L. 94-12, Sec. 301(b)(2), added new para. (a)(6), effective for tax. yrs. end. after 12/31/74.

—P.L. 94-12, Sec. 301(b)(1), rewrote subpara. (c)(3)(A), effective with respect to property placed in service after 1/21/75, in tax. yrs. end. after 1/21/75.

Prior to amendment, subpara. (c)(3)(A) read as follows:

"(A) In the case of section 38 property which is public utility property, the amount of the qualified investment shall be 4/7 of the amount determined under paragraph (1)"

1,231

—P.L. 94-12, Sec. 302(b)(1), added new para. (c)(4), effective for tax. yrs. end. after 12/31/74.
—P.L. 94-12, Sec. 302(a), redesignated former subsecs. (d) and (e) as (e) and (f) and added new subsec. (d), effective for tax. yrs. end. after 12/31/74.
—P.L. 94-12, Sec. 301(b)(3), added new para. (f)(8), effective for tax. yrs. end. after 12/31/74.

In **1974**, P.L. 93-406, Sec. 2001(g)(2)(B), added in subsec. (a)(3) "section 72(m)(5)(B) (relating to 10 percent tax on premature distributions to owner-employees)," for distributions made in taxable years beginning after 12/31/75.
—P.L. 93-406, Sec. 2002(g)(2), added in subsec. (a)(3) "section 408(e) (relating to additional tax on income from certain retirement accounts)," effective 1/1/75.
—P.L. 93-406, Sec. 2005(c)(4), added in subsec. (a)(3) "section 402(e) (relating to lump sum distributions)," for distributions or payments made after 12/31/73 in taxable years beginning after 12/31/73.

In **1971**, P.L. 92-178, Sec. 102(a)(1), substituted "3 years" for "4 years" in para. (c)(2) ... substituted "5 years" for "6 years" each place it appeared in subsec. (c)(2) ... substituted "7 years" for "8 years" each place it appeared in para. (c)(2), effective for property described in Code Sec. 50. ... Sec. 102(b), substituted a new second sentence for "For purposes of this paragraph, the useful life of any property shall be determined as of the time such property is placed in service by the taxpayer." in subsec. (c)(2), effective for property described in Code Sec. 50. ... Sec. 105(a), substituted "4/7" for "3/7" in subpara. (c)(3)(A) ... Sec. 105(b), inserted "or" to the end of clause (c)(3)(ii), struck out clauses (c)(3)(iii) & (iv) and added new clause (c)(3)(iii), added a new sentence to the end of subpara. (c)(3)(B) and added new subpara. (c)(3)(C), effective for property described in Code Sec. 50.

Prior to amendment, clauses (c)(3)(iii) & (iv) read as follows:
"(iii) telephone service, or
"(iv) telegraph service by means of domestic telegraph operations (as defined in section 222(a)(5) of the Communications Act of 1934, as amended: 47 U.S.C., sec. 222(a)(5))." ... Sec. 105(c), added new subsec. (e), effective for property described in Code Sec. 50. ... Sec. 105(e), provided as follows:
"(e) Application of Section 203(e) of Revenue Act of 1964.
"Section 203(e) of the Revenue Act of 1964 shall not apply to public utility property to which section 46(e) of the Internal Revenue Code of 1954 (as added by subsection (c)) applies." ... Sec. 106(a), added new para. (b)(3) ... Sec. 106(b), added a sentence to the end of para. (b)(1), effective for tax. yrs. begin. after 12/31/70 ... Sec. 106(c)(1), substituted new para. (b)(5), effective for tax. yrs. end. after 8/15/71.

Prior to amendment, para. (b)(5) read as follows:
"(5) Taxable years beginning after December 31, 1968, and ending after April 18, 1969. The amount which may be added under this subsection for any taxable year beginning after December 31, 1968, and ending after April 18, 1969, shall not exceed 20 percent of the higher of—
"(A) the aggregate of the investment credit carrybacks and investment credit carryovers to the taxable year, or
"(B) the highest amount computed under subparagraph (A) for any preceding taxable year which began after December 31, 1968, and ended after April 18, 1969." ... Sec. 106(c)(2), inserted "and before January 1, 1971," after "April 18, 1969," and substituted "following the 7th taxable year after the unused credit year" for "following the last taxable year for which such portion may be added under paragraph (1)", for tax. yrs. begin. after 12/31/70. ... Sec. 107(a), repealed para. (c)(4), effective for casualties and thefts occurring after 8/15/71.

Prior to repeal para. (c)(4) read as follows:
"(4) Certain replacement property. For purposes of paragraph (1), if section 38 property is placed in service by the taxpayer to replace property which was—
"(A) destroyed or damaged by fire, storm, shipwreck, or other casualty, or
"(B) stolen,
the basis of such section 38 property (in the case of new section 38 property), or the cost of such section 38 property (in the case of used section 38 property), which (but for this paragraph) would be taken into account under paragraph (1) shall be reduced by an amount equal to the amount received by the taxpayer as compensation, by insurance or otherwise, for the property so destroyed, damaged, or stolen, or to the adjusted basis of such property, whichever is the lesser. No reduction in basis or cost shall be made under the preceding sentence in any case in which the reduction in qualified investment attributable to the substitution required by section 47(a)(1) with respect to the property so destroyed, damaged, or stolen (determined without regard to section 47(a)(4)) is greater than the reduction described in the preceding sentence." ... Sec. 108(a), added new para. (d)(3) for leases entered into after 9/22/71.

In **1969**, P.L. 91-172, Sec. 301(b)(4), inserted "section 56 (relating to minimum tax for tax preferences)," before "section 531" in para. (a)(3), effective for tax. yrs. end. after 12/31/69.
—P.L. 91-172, Sec. 401(e)(1), amended para. (a)(5), effective for tax. yrs. end. on or after 12/31/70.

Prior to amendments subsec. (a)(5) read as follows:
"(5) Affiliated groups. In the case of an affiliated group, the $25,000 amount specified under subparagraphs (A) and (B) of paragraph (2) shall be reduced for each member of the group by apportioning $25,000 among the members of such group in such manner as the Secretary or his delegate shall by regulations prescribe. For purposes of the preceding sentence, the term 'affiliated group' has the meaning assigned to such term by section 1504(a), except that all corporations shall be treated as includible corporations (without any exclusion under section 1504(b))."
—P.L. 91-172, Sec. 703(b), added paras. (b)(5) and (6).

In **1967**, P.L. 90-225, Sec. 2(a), amended Code Sec. 46(b) by deleting subpar. (3), effective for investment credit carrybacks from tax. yrs. end. after 7/31/67.

Prior to repeal, subpar. (3) read as follows:
"(3) Effect of net operating loss carryback.
To the extent that the excess described in paragraph (1) arises by reason of a net operating loss carryback, subparagraph (A) of paragraph (1) shall not apply."

In **1966**, P.L. 89-800, Sec. 3(a), added "for taxable years ending on or before the last day of the suspension period (as defined in section 48 (jj))," at the beginning of subpara. (a)(2)(B), and added subpara. (a)(2)(C) covering the application of subpara. (a)(2)(C) and the reduction of the amount otherwise determined under para. (a)(2) by the credit allowable but for the application of section 48(h)(1). ... Sec. 3(b), substituted "7 taxable years" for "5 taxable years" in subpara. (b)(1)(B) and "10 taxable years" and "other 9 taxable years" for "8 taxable years" and "other 7 taxable years" respectively in text following subpara. (b)(1)(B).
—P.L. 89-389, added reference to tax imposed for the taxable year by section 1378 (relating to tax on certain capital gains of subchapter S corporations) in the list of taxes not to be considered tax imposed by this chapter for purposes of para. (a)(3).
—P.L. 89-384, added any additional tax imposed for the taxable year by section 1351 (relating to recoveries of foreign expropriation losses) to the list of taxes not to be considered a tax imposed by this chapter for purposes of para. (a)(3).

In **1964**, P.L. 88-272, deleted subpara. (a)(3)(B) relating to Code Sec. 34, and redesignated subpars. (a)(3)(C) and (D) as (a)(3)(B) and (C), respectively, effective for tax. yrs. in which dividends received credit not allowed.

In **1962**, P.L. 87-834, Sec. 2, added Code Sec. 46, effective for tax. yrs. end. after 1961.

Sec. 47. Rehabilitation credit.
(a) General rule.
For purposes of section 46, the rehabilitation credit for any taxable year is the sum of—

(1) 10 percent of the qualified rehabilitation expenditures with respect to any qualified rehabilitated building other than a certified historic structure, and

(2) 20 percent of the qualified rehabilitation expenditures with respect to any certified historic structure.

(b) When expenditures taken into account.
(1) **In general.** Qualified rehabilitation expenditures with respect to any qualified rehabilitated building shall be taken into account for the taxable year in which such qualified rehabilitated building is placed in service.

(2) **Coordination with subsection (d).** The amount which would (but for this paragraph) be taken into account under paragraph (1) with respect to any qualified rehabilitated building shall be reduced (but not below zero) by any amount of qualified rehabilitation expenditures taken into account under subsection (d) by the taxpayer or a predecessor of the taxpayer (or, in the case of a sale and leaseback described in section 50(a)(2)(C), by the lessee), to the extent any amount so taken into account has not been required to be recaptured under section 50(a).

(c) Definitions.
For purposes of this section—

(1) **Qualified rehabilitated building.**

(A) In general. The term "qualified rehabilitated building" means any building (and its structural components) if—

(i) such building has been substantially rehabilitated,

(ii) such building was placed in service before the beginning of the rehabilitation,

(iii) in the case of any building other than a certified historic structure, in the rehabilitation process—

(I) 50 percent or more of the existing external walls of such building are retained in place as external walls,

(II) 75 percent or more of the existing external walls of such building are retained in place as internal or external walls, and

(III) 75 percent or more of the existing internal structural framework of such building is retained in place, and

(iv) depreciation (or amortization in lieu of depreciation) is allowable with respect to such building.

(B) Building must be first placed in service before 1936. In the case of a building other than a certified historic structure, a building shall not be a qualified rehabilitated building unless the building was first placed in service before 1936.

(C) Substantially rehabilitated defined.

(i) In general. For purposes of subparagraph (A)(i), a building shall be treated as having been substantially rehabilitated only if the qualified rehabilitation expenditures during the 24-month period selected by the taxpayer (at the time and in the manner prescribed by regulation) and ending with or within the taxable year exceed the greater of—

(I) the adjusted basis of such building (and its structural components), or

(II) $5,000.

The adjusted basis of the building (and its structural components) shall be determined as of the beginning of the 1st day of such 24-month period, or of the holding period of the building, whichever is later. For purposes of the preceding sentence, the determination of the beginning of the holding period shall be made without regard to any reconstruction by the taxpayer in connection with the rehabilitation.

(ii) Special rule for phased rehabilitation. In the case of any rehabilitation which may reasonably be expected to be completed in phases set forth in architectural plans and specifications completed before the rehabilitation begins, clause (i) shall be applied by substituting "60-month period" for "24-month period".

(iii) Lessees. The Secretary shall prescribe by regulation rules for applying this subparagraph to lessees.

(D) Reconstruction. Rehabilitation includes reconstruction.

(2) Qualified rehabilitation expenditure defined.

(A) In general. The term "qualified rehabilitation expenditure" means any amount properly chargeable to capital account—

(i) for property for which depreciation is allowable under section 168 and which is—

(I) nonresidential real property,

(II) residential rental property,

(III) real property which has a class life of more than 12.5 years, or

(IV) an addition or improvement to property described in subclause (I), (II), or (III), and

(ii) in connection with the rehabilitation of a qualified rehabilitated building.

(B) Certain expenditures not included. The term "qualified rehabilitation expenditure" does not include—

(i) Straight line depreciation must be used. Any expenditure with respect to which the taxpayer does not use the straight line method over a recovery period determined under subsection (c) or (g) of section 168. The preceding sentence shall not apply to any expenditure to the extent the alternative depreciation system of section 168(g) applies to such expenditure by reason of subparagraph (B) or (C) of section 168(g)(1).

(ii) Cost of acquisition. The cost of acquiring any building or interest therein.

(iii) Enlargements. Any expenditure attributable to the enlargement of an existing building.

(iv) Certified historic structure, etc. Any expenditure attributable to the rehabilitation of a certified historic structure or a building in a registered historic district, unless the rehabilitation is a certified rehabilitation (within the meaning of subparagraph (C)). The preceding sentence shall not apply to a building in a registered historic district if—

(I) such building was not a certified historic structure,

(II) the Secretary of the Interior certified to the Secretary that such building is not of historic significance to the district, and

(III) if the certification referred to in subclause (II) occurs after the beginning of the rehabilitation of such building, the taxpayer certifies to the Secretary that, at the beginning of such rehabilitation, he in good faith was not aware of the requirements of subclause (II).

(v) Tax-exempt use property.

(I) In general. Any expenditure in connection with the rehabilitation of a building which is allocable to the portion of such property which is (or may reasonably be expected to be) tax-exempt use property (within the meaning of section 168(h), except that "50 percent" shall be substituted for "35 percent" in paragraph (1)(B)(iii) thereof.

(II) Clause not to apply for purposes of paragraph (1)(C). This clause shall not apply for purposes of determining under paragraph (1)(C) whether a building has been substantially rehabilitated.

(vi) Expenditures of lessee. Any expenditure of a lessee of a building if, on the date the rehabilitation is completed, the remaining term of the lease (determined without regard to any renewal periods) is less than the recovery period determined under section 168(c).

(C) Certified rehabilitation. For purposes of subparagraph (B), the term "certified rehabilitation" means any rehabilitation of a certified historic structure which the Secretary of the Interior has certified to the Secretary as being consistent with the historic character of such property or the district in which such property is located.

(D) Nonresidential real property; residential rental property; class life. For purposes of subparagraph (A), the terms "nonresidential real property," "residential rental property," and "class life" have the respective meanings given such terms by section 168.

(3) Certified historic structure defined.

(A) In general. The term "certified historic structure" means any building (and its structural components) which—

(i) is listed in the National Register, or

(ii) is located in a registered historic district and is certified by the Secretary of the Interior to the Secretary as being of historic significance to the district.

(B) Registered historic district. The term "registered historic district" means—

(i) any district listed in the National Register, and

(ii) any district—

(I) which is designated under a statute of the appropriate State or local government, if such statute is certified by the Secretary of the Interior to the Secretary as containing criteria which will substantially achieve the purpose of preserving and rehabilitating buildings of historic significance to the district, and

(II) which is certified by the Secretary of the Interior to the Secretary as meeting substantially all of the requirements for the listing of districts in the National Register.

(d) Progress expenditures.

(1) In general. In the case of any building to which this subsection applies, except as provided in paragraph (3)—

(A) if such building is self-rehabilitated property, any qualified rehabilitation expenditure with respect to such building shall be taken into account for the taxable year for which such expenditure is properly chargeable to capital account with respect to such building, and

(B) if such building is not self-rehabilitated property, any qualified rehabilitation expenditure with respect to such building shall be taken into account for the taxable year in which paid.

(2) Property to which subsection applies.

(A) In general. This subsection shall apply to any building which is being rehabilitated by or for the taxpayer if—

(i) the normal rehabilitation period for such building is 2 years or more, and

(ii) it is reasonable to expect that such building will be a qualified rehabilitated building in the hands of the taxpayer when it is placed in service.

Clauses (i) and (ii) shall be applied on the basis of facts known as of the close of the taxable year of the taxpayer in which the rehabilitation begins (or, if later, at the close of the first taxable year to which an election under this subsection applies).

(B) Normal rehabilitation period. For purposes of subparagraph (A), the term "normal rehabilitation period" means the period reasonably expected to be required for the rehabilitation of the building—

(i) beginning with the date on which physical work on the rehabilitation begins (or, if later, the first day of the first taxable year to which an election under this subsection applies), and

(ii) ending on the date on which it is expected that the property will be available for placing in service.

(3) Special rules for applying paragraph (1). For purposes of paragraph (1)—

(A) Component parts, etc. Property which is to be a component part of, or is otherwise to be included in, any building to which this subsection applies shall be taken into account—

(i) at a time not earlier than the time at which it becomes irrevocably devoted to use in the building, and

(ii) as if (at the time referred to in clause (i)) the taxpayer had expended an amount equal to that portion of the cost to the taxpayer of such component or other property which, for purposes of this subpart, is properly chargeable (during such taxable year) to capital account with respect to such building.

(B) Certain borrowing disregarded. Any amount borrowed directly or indirectly by the taxpayer from the person rehabilitating the property for him shall not be treated as an amount expended for such rehabilitation.

(C) Limitation for buildings which are not self-rehabilitated.

(i) In general. In the case of a building which is not self-rehabilitated, the amount taken into account under paragraph (1)(B) for any taxable year shall not exceed the amount which represents the portion of the overall cost to the taxpayer of the rehabilitation which is properly attributable to the portion of the rehabilitation which is completed during such taxable year.

(ii) Carry-over of certain amounts. In the case of a building which is not a self-rehabilitated building, if for the taxable year—

(I) the amount which (but for clause (i)) would have been taken into account under paragraph (1)(B) exceeds the limitation of clause (i), then the amount of such excess shall be taken into account under paragraph (1)(B) for the succeeding taxable year, or

(II) the limitation of clause (i) exceeds the amount taken into account under paragraph (1)(B), then the amount of such excess shall increase the limitation of clause (i) for the succeeding taxable year.

(D) Determination of percentage of completion. The determination under subparagraph (C)(i) of the portion of the overall cost to the taxpayer of the rehabilitation which is properly attributable to rehabilitation completed during any taxable year shall be made, under regulations prescribed by the Secretary, on the basis of engineering or architectural estimates or on the basis of cost accounting records. Unless the taxpayer establishes otherwise by clear and convincing evidence, the rehabilitation shall be deemed to be completed not more rapidly than ratably over the normal rehabilitation period.

(E) No progress expenditures for certain prior periods. No qualified rehabilitation expenditures shall be taken into account under this subsection for any period before the first day of the first taxable year to which an election under this subsection applies.

(F) No progress expenditures for property for year it is placed in service, etc. In the case of any building, no qualified rehabilitation expenditures shall be taken into account under this subsection for the earlier of—

(i) the taxable year in which the building is placed in service, or

(ii) the first taxable year for which recapture is required under section 50(a)(2) with respect to such property,

or for any taxable year thereafter.

(4) Self-rehabilitated building. For purposes of this subsection, the term "self-rehabilitated building" means any building if it is reasonable to believe that more than half of the qualified rehabilitation expenditures for such building will be made directly by the taxpayer.

(5) Election. This subsection shall apply to any taxpayer only if such taxpayer has made an election under this paragraph. Such an election shall apply to the taxable year for which made and all subsequent taxable years. Such an election, once made, may be revoked only with the consent of the Secretary.

In 2008, P.L. 110-289, Sec. 3025(a), substituted "section 168(h), except that '50 percent' shall be substituted for '35 percent' in paragraph (1)(B)(iii) thereof" for "section 168(h)" in subclause (c)(2)(B)(v)(I), effective for expenditures properly taken into account for periods after 12/31/2007.

In 1990, P.L. 101-508, Sec. 11813(a), amended Code Sec. 47 as part of the amendment to subpart E, of part IV of subchapter A of chapter 1, effective for property placed in service after 12/31/90 except as provided in Sec. 11813(c)(2) of this Act, reproduced in note following Code Sec. 46.

In 1990, P.L. 101-508, Sec. 11801(c)(8)(A), substituted ", or" for the comma at the end of para. (b)(1), substituted a period for ", or" at the end of para. (b)(2), and deleted para. (b)(3), effective 11/5/90, except as provided in Sec. 11821(b) of this Act, reproduced below:

"(b) Savings provision. If

"(1) any provision amended or repealed by this part applied to—

"(A) any provision amended or repealed by this part applied to—

"(A) any transaction occurring before the date of the enactment of this Act [11/5/90],

"(B) any property acquired before such date of enactment [11/5/90], or

"(C) any item of income, loss, deduction, or credit taken into account before such date of enactment [11/5/90], and

"(2) the treatment of such transaction, property, or item under such provision would (without regard to the amendments made by this part) affect liability for tax for periods ending after such date of enactment [11/5/90],

nothing in the amendments made by this part shall be construed to affect the treatment of such transaction, property, or item for purposes of determining liability for tax for periods ending after such date of enactment [11/5/90]."

Prior to amendment, para. (b)(3) read as follows:

"(3) a transfer to which subsection (c) of section 374 (relating to exchanges under the final system plan of ConRail) applies."

In 1988, P.L. 100-647, Sec. 1002(a)(18), substituted "46(c)(8)(C)" for "48(c)(8)(C)" in para. (d)(1) . . . Sec. 1002(a)(26)(A), added clause (a)(5)(E)(v) . . . Sec. 1002(a)(26)(B), deleted the last sentence of subpara. (a)(5)(D) . . . Sec. 1002(a)(26)(C), substituted "168(e)" for "168(c)" in clause (a)(5)(E)(iii) . . . Sec. 1002(a)(27), substituted "section 168(h)(2)" for "section 168(j)(4)(C)" in subpara. (a)(9)(A) . . . Sec. 1002(a)(28), substituted "class life (as defined in section 168(i)(1))" for "present class life (as defined in section 168(g)(2))" and substituted "no class life (as defined in section 168(i)(1))" for "no present class life (as defined in section 168(g)(2))" in clause (d)(3)(C)(i), effective for property placed in service after 12/31/86, in tax. yrs. end. after 12/31/86.

Prior to deletion the last sentence of subpara. (d)(5)(D) read as follows: "If, prior to a disposition to which this subsection applies, any portion of any credit is not allowable with respect to any property by reason of section 168(i)(3), such portion shall be treated (for purposes of this subparagraph) as not having been used to reduce tax liability."

—P.L. 100-647, Sec. 1007(g)(3)(A), substituted "D, or G" for "or D" in subsec. (c), effective for tax. yrs. begin. after 12/31/86.

In 1986, P.L. 99-514, Sec. 1511(c)(2), substituted "determined at the underpayment rate established under section 6621" for "determined under section 6621" in subpara. (d)(3)(G), effective for purposes of determining interest for periods after 12/31/86.

—P.L. 99-514, Sec. 1802(a)(5)(A), added para. (a)(9), effective for property placed in service by the taxpayer after 5/23/83, in tax. yrs. end. after 5/23/83, and for property placed in service by the taxpayer on or before 5/23/83, if the lease to the tax-exempt entity is entered into after 5/23/83. Exceptions and special rules are provided by Sec. 31(g)(2)-(20) of P.L. 98-369, reproduced in the notes following Code Sec. 168.

—P.L. 99-514, Sec. 1844(b)(1), substituted "reducing the credit base (as defined in section 48(c)(8)(C))" for "reducing the qualified investment" in, and added the last sentence to, para. (d)(1) . . . Sec. 1844(b)(2), deleted subpara. (d)(3)(F) . . . Sec. 1844(d)(4), added "reduced by the sum of the credit recapture amounts with respect to such property for all preceding taxable years" before the semicolon in clause (d)(3)(E)(i), effective for property placed in service after 7/18/84 in tax. yrs. end. after 7/18/84, except in the case of any property to which the amendments made by Sec. 211(f) of P.L. 97-34 do not apply.

Prior to deletion, subpara. (d)(3)(F) read as follows:

"(F) Application with subsection (a). The amount of any increase in tax under subsection (a) with respect to any property to which this paragraph applies shall be determined by reducing the qualified investment with respect to such property by the aggregate credit recapture amounts for all taxable years under this paragraph."

In 1985, P.L. 99-121, Sec. 103(b)(6), substituted "For property other than 3-year property" for "For 15-year, 10-year, and 5-year property" in the table in subpara. (a)(5)(B), effective for property placed in service by the taxpayer after 3/15/84. For exceptions and special rules, see Sec. 111(g)(2)-(4) of P.L. 98-369, reproduced in note following Code Sec. 168.

In 1984, P.L. 98-443, Sec. 9(p), substituted "Secretary of Transportation" for "Civil Aeronautics Board" in subpara. (a)(7)(C), effective 1/1/85.

—P.L. 98-369, Sec. 421(b)(7), added subsec. (e), effective for transfers after 7/18/84 in tax. yrs. ending after 7/18/84. Sec. 421(d)(2), (3) and (4) of the Act provides:

"(2) Election to have amendments apply to transfers after 1983.—If both spouses or former spouses make an election under this paragraph, the amendments made by this section shall apply to all transfers made by such spouses (or former spouses) after December 31, 1983.

"(3) Exception for transfers pursuant to existing decrees.—Except in the case of an election under paragraph (2), the amendments made by this section shall not apply to transfers under any instrument in effect on or before the date of the enactment of this Act unless both spouses (or former spouses) elect to have such amendments apply to transfers under such instrument.

"(4) Election.—Any election under paragraph (2) or (3) shall be made in such manner, at such time, and subject to such conditions, as the Secretary of the Treasury or his delegate may by regulations prescribe."

—P.L. 98-369, Sec. 431(b)(2), amended the heading of subsec. (d) and paras. (d)(1) and (2) . . . Sec. 431(d)(4), substituted "increasing the amount of nonqualified nonrecourse financing (within the meaning of section 46(c)(8))" for "ceasing to be at risk" in subpara. (d)(3)(A) . . . Sec. 431(d)(5), deleted "other than a loan described in section 46(c)(8)(B)(ii)" in clause (d)(3)(B)(i), effective for property placed in service after 7/18/84 in tax. yrs. ending after 7/18/84, except not effective for any property to which the amendments made by section 211(f) of the Economic Recovery Tax Act of 1981 do not apply. Sec. 431(e) of the Act provides:

"(2) Amendments may be elected retroactively.— At the election of the taxpayer, the amendments made by this section shall apply as if included in the amendments made by section 211(f) of the Economic Recovery Tax Act of 1981. Any election made under the preceding sentence shall apply to all property of the taxpayer to which the amendments made by such section 211(f) apply and shall be made at such time and in such manner as the Secretary of the Treasury or his delegate may by regulations prescribe."

Prior to amendment, the heading of subsec. (d) and paras. (d)(1) and (2) read as follows:

"(d) Property ceasing to be at risk.

"(1) In general. If the taxpayer ceases to any extent to be at risk (within the meaning of section 46(c)(8)(B)) with respect to any amount in connection with section 38 property, then the tax under this chapter for such taxable year shall be increased by an amount equal to the aggregate decrease in credits allowed under section 38 for all prior taxable years which would have resulted from substituting, in determining qualified investment, the amount determined under section 46(c)(8) with respect to such property if, on the date the property was placed in service, the taxpayer had not been at risk with respect to the amount he ceased to be at risk to.

"(2) Certain transfers not treated as ceasing to be at risk. If, after the 12-month period after the date on which a taxpayer borrows an amount from a qualified person (within the meaning of section 46(c)(8)(D)) with respect to which such taxpayer is considered at risk under section 46(c)(8)(B), the qualified person transfers or agrees to transfer any evidence of such indebtedness to a person who is not a qualified person, then, for purposes of paragraph (1), the taxpayer shall not be treated as ceasing to be at risk with respect to such amount."

—P.L. 98-369, Sec. 474(o)(8), substituted "under section 39" for "under section 46(b)" in paras. (a)(5) and (6) . . . Sec. 474(o)(9), substituted "subpart A, B, or D" for "subpart A" in subsec. (c), effective for tax. yrs. begin. after 12/31/83 and for carrybacks from tax. yrs. begin. after 12/31/83 except as provided in Sec. 475(c) which reads as follows:

"(c) Clarification of effect of amendments on investment tax credit.—Nothing in the amendments made by section 474(o) [P.L. 98-369] shall be construed as reducing the amount of any credit allowable for qualified investment in taxable years beginning before January 1, 1984."

In 1983, P.L. 97-448, Sec. 102(e)(3)(A), substituted "section 46(c)(8)(D)" for "section 48(c)(8)(D)" and substituted "section 46(c)(8)(B)" for "section 48(c)(8)(B)" in para. (d)(2) . . . Sec. 102(c)(3)(B), substituted "section 46(c)(8)(F)" for "section 46(c)(8)(E)" in subpara. (d)(3)(A), effective for property placed in service after 12/31/80 in tax. yrs. end. after 12/31/80.

In 1982, P.L. 97-248, Sec. 208(a)(2)(B), added the last sentence at end of subpara. (a)(5)(D), effective for agreements entered into after 7/1/82, or to property placed in service after 7/1/82. For transitional rules see Sec. 208(d)(2)-(6) of this Act reproduced in note following Code Sec. 168.

In 1981, P.L. 97-34, Sec. 211(f)(2), added subsec. (d). Sec. 211(i)(5) of this Act provides:

"(5) At risk rules.

"(A) In general. The amendment made by subsection (f) shall not apply to—

"(i) property placed in service by the taxpayer on or before February 18, 1981, and

"(ii) property placed in service by the taxpayer after February 18, 1981, where such property is acquired by the taxpayer pursuant to a binding contract entered into on or before that date.

"(B) Binding contract. For purposes of subparagraph (A)(ii), property acquired pursuant to a binding contract shall, under regulations prescribed by the Secretary, include property acquired in a manner so that it would have qualified as pretermination property under section 49(b) (as in effect before its repeal by the Revenue Act of 1978)."

—P.L. 97-34, Sec. 211(g)(1), redesignated paras. (a)(5), (6) and (7) as paras. (a)(6), (7) and (8) and added new para. (a)(5) . . . Sec. 211(g)(2)(A), amended subpara. (a)(3)(D) . . . Sec. 211(g)(2)(B), substituted "paragraph (1), (3), or (5)" for "paragraph (1) or (3)" in para. (a)(6) as redesignated by Sec. 211(g)(1) of this Act . . . Sec. 211(g)(2)(C), substituted "paragraph (6)" for "paragraph (5)" in subpara. (a)(7)(B) as redesignated by Sec. 211(g)(1) of this Act, effective for property placed in service after 12/31/80.

Prior to amendment, subpara. (a)(3)(D) read as follows:

"(D) Coordination with paragraph (1). If, after property is placed in service, there is a disposition or other cessation described in paragraph (1), paragraph (1) shall be applied as if any credit which was allowable by reason of section 46(d) and which has not been required to be recaptured before such cessation were allowable for the taxable year the property was placed in service."

In 1978, P.L. 95-618, Sec. 241(b), redesignated para. (a)(4) as para. (a)(5) . . . added new para. (a)(4) . . . substituted "paragraph (2) or (4)" for "paragraph (2)" in para. (a)(5) as redesignated . . . substituted "paragraph (5)" for "paragraph (4)" in subpara. (a)(6)(B), effective 11/9/78.

—P.L. 95-600, Sec. 317(a), deleted "or" at the end of para. (b)(1) . . . substituted ", or" for the period at the end of para. (b)(2) . . . added para. (b)(3), effective for tax. yrs. end. after 3/31/76.

In 1976, P.L. 94-455, Sec. 804(b), added para. (a)(7), effective for tax. yrs. begin. after '74.

—P.L. 94-455, Sec. 1906(b)(13)(A), substituted "Secretary" for "Secretary or his delegate" each place it appeared in subsec (a), effective for tax. yrs. begin. after '76.

In 1975, P.L. 94-12, Sec. 302(b)(2), redesignated former para. (3) as (4) and added new para. (3), effective for tax. yrs. end. after 12/31/74.

—P.L. 94-12, Sec. 302(c)(1), substituted "paragraph (1) or (3)" for "paragraph (1)" in para. (a)(4), as redesignated by Sec. 302(b)(2) of the Act, effective for tax. yrs. end. after 12/31/74.

—P.L. 94-12, Sec. 302(c)(2), substituted "paragraph (4)" for "paragraph (3)" in para. (a)(5) and subpara. (a)(6)(B), effective for tax. yrs. end. after 12/31/74.

In 1971, P.L. 92-178, Sec. 102(c), substituted "3½ years" for "4 years" in subsec. (a)(6)(A), effective for leases executed after 4/18/69. . . . Sec. 102(d)(2), pro-

vided as follows: "In redetermining qualified investment for purposes of section 47(a) of the Internal Revenue Code of 1954 in the case of any property which ceases to be section 38 property with respect to the taxpayer after August 15, 1971, or which becomes public utility property after such date, section 46(c)(2) of such Code shall be applied as amended by subsection (a)." ... Sec. 107(a), repealed para. (a)(4), effective for casualties and thefts occurring after 8/15/71.
Prior to repeal, para. (a)(4) read as follows:
"(4) Property destroyed by casualty, etc. No increase shall be made under paragraph (1) and no adjustment shall be made under paragraph (3) in any case in which—
"(A) any property is disposed of, or otherwise ceases to be section 38 property with respect to the taxpayer, on account of its destruction or damage by fire, storm, shipwreck, or other casualty, or by reason of its theft,
"(B) section 38 property is placed in service by the taxpayer to replace the property described in subparagraph (A), and
"(C) the reduction in basis or cost of such section 38 property described in the first sentence of section 46(c)(4) is equal to or; greater than the reduction in qualified investment which (but for this paragraph) would be made by reason of the substitution required by paragraph (1) with respect to the property described in subparagraph (A).
Subparagraphs (B) and (C) shall not apply with respect to any casualty or theft occurring after April 18, 1969." ... Sec. 107(b), repealed para. (a)(5), except if replacement property described in subpara. 47(a)(5)(B) is not property described in Code Sec. 50.
Prior to repeal, para. (a)(5) read as follows:
"(5) Certain property replaced after April 18, 1969. In any case in which—
"(A) section 38 property is disposed of, and
"(B) property which would be section 38 property but for section 49 is placed in service by the taxpayer to replace the property disposed of,
the increase under paragraph (1) and the adjustment under paragraph (4) shall not be greater than the increase or adjustment which would result if the qualified investment of the property described in subparagraph (B) (determined as if such property were section 38 property) were substituted for the qualified investment of the property disposed of (as determined under paragraph (1)). Except in the case of a disposition by reason of a casualty or theft occurring before April 19, 1969, the preceding sentence shall apply only if the section 38 property disposed of is replaced within 6 months after the date of such disposition."
—P.L. 91-676, added para. (a)(6), effective for tax. yrs. end. after 4/18/69.
In 1969, P.L. 91-172, Sec. 703(c), added the last sentence of subsec. (a)(4) and added para. (a)(5).
In 1962, P.L. 87-834, Sec. 2, added Code Sec. 47, for tax. yrs. end. after '61.

Sec. 48. Energy credit.
(a) Energy credit.

(1) In general. For purposes of section 46, except as provided in paragraphs (1)(B), and (2)(B), (3)(B), and (4)(B) of subsection (c), the energy credit for any taxable year is the energy percentage of the basis of each energy property placed in service during such taxable year.

(2) Energy percentage.

(A) In general. The energy percentage is—

(i) 30 percent in the case of—

(I) qualified fuel cell property,

(II) energy property described in paragraph (3)(A)(i) but only with respect to periods ending before January 1, 2017,

(III) energy property described in paragraph (3)(A)(ii), and

(IV) qualified small wind energy property, and

(ii) in the case of any energy property to which clause (i) does not apply, 10 percent.

(B) Coordination with rehabilitation credit. The energy percentage shall not apply to that portion of the basis of any property which is attributable to qualified rehabilitation expenditures.

(3) Energy property. For purposes of this subpart, the term "energy property" means any property—

(A) which is—

(i) equipment which uses solar energy to generate electricity, to heat or cool (or provide hot water for use in) a structure, or to provide solar process heat, excepting property used to generate energy for the purposes of heating a swimming pool,

(ii) equipment which uses solar energy to illuminate the inside of a structure using fiber-optic distributed sunlight but only with respect to periods ending before January 1, 2017,

(iii) equipment used to produce, distribute, or use energy derived from a geothermal deposit (within the meaning of section 613(e)(2)), but only, in the case of electricity generated by geothermal power, up to (but not including) the electrical transmission stage,

(iv) qualified fuel cell property or qualified microturbine property,

(v) combined heat and power system property,

(vi) qualified small wind energy property, or

(vii) equipment which uses the ground or ground water as a thermal energy source to heat a structure or as a thermal energy sink to cool a structure, but only with respect to periods ending before January 1, 2017,

(B)(i) the construction, reconstruction, or erection of which is completed by the taxpayer, or

(ii) which is acquired by the taxpayer if the original use of such property commences with the taxpayer,

(C) with respect to which depreciation (or amortization in lieu of depreciation) is allowable, and

(D) which meets the performance and quality standards (if any) which—

(i) have been prescribed by the Secretary by regulations (after consultation with the Secretary of Energy), and

(ii) are in effect at the time of the acquisition of the property.

Such term shall not include any property which is part of a facility the production from which is allowed as a credit under section 45 for the taxable year or any prior taxable year.

(4) Special rule for property financed by subsidized energy financing or industrial development bonds.

(A) Reduction of basis. For purposes of applying the energy percentage to any property, if such property is financed in whole or in part by—

(i) subsidized energy financing, or

(ii) the proceeds of a private activity bond (within the meaning of section 141) the interest on which is exempt from tax under section 103,

the amount taken into account as the basis of such property shall not exceed the amount which (but for this subparagraph) would be so taken into account multiplied by the fraction determined under subparagraph (B).

(B) Determination of fraction. For purposes of subparagraph (A), the fraction determined under this subparagraph is 1 reduced by a fraction—

(i) the numerator of which is that portion of the basis of the property which is allocable to such financing or proceeds, and

(ii) the denominator of which is the basis of the property.

(C) Subsidized energy financing. For purposes of subparagraph (A), the term "subsidized energy financing" means financing provided under a Federal, State, or local program a principal purpose of which is to provide subsidized financing for projects designed to conserve or produce energy.

(D) Termination. This paragraph shall not apply to periods after December 31, 2008, under rules similar to the rules of section 48(m) (as in effect on the day before the date of the enactment of the Revenue Reconciliation Act of 1990).

(5) Election to treat qualified facilities as energy property.

(A) In general. In the case of any qualified property which is part of a qualified investment credit facility—

(i) such property shall be treated as energy property for purposes of this section, and

(ii) the energy percentage with respect to such property shall be 30 percent.

(B) Denial of production credit. No credit shall be allowed under section 45 for any taxable year with respect to any qualified investment credit facility.

(C) Qualified investment credit facility. For purposes of this paragraph, the term "qualified investment credit facility" means any of the following facilities if no credit has been allowed under section 45 with respect to such facility and the taxpayer makes an irrevocable election to have this paragraph apply to such facility:

(i) Wind facilities. Any qualified facility (within the meaning of section 45) described in paragraph (1) of section 45(d) if such facility is placed in service in 2009, 2010, 2011, or 2012.

(ii) Other facilities. Any qualified facility (within the meaning of section 45) described in paragraph (2), (3), (4), (6), (7), (9), or (11) of section 45(d) if such facility is placed in service in 2009, 2010, 2011, 2012, or 2013.

(D) Qualified property. For purposes of this paragraph, the term "qualified property" means property—

(i) which is—

(I) tangible personal property, or

(II) other tangible property (not including a building or its structural components), but only if such property is used as an integral part of the qualified investment credit facility, and

(ii) with respect to which depreciation (or amortization in lieu of depreciation) is allowable.

(b) Certain progress expenditure rules made applicable.

Rules similar to the rules of subsections (c)(4) and (d) of section 46 (as in effect on the day before the date of the enactment of the Revenue Reconciliation Act of 1990) shall apply for purposes of subsection (a).

(c) Definitions.

For purposes of this section—

(1) Qualified fuel cell property.

(A) In general. The term "qualified fuel cell property" means a fuel cell power plant which—

(i) has a nameplate capacity of at least 0.5 kilowatt of electricity using an electrochemical process, and

(ii) has an electricity-only generation efficiency greater than 30 percent.

(B) Limitation. In the case of qualified fuel cell property placed in service during the taxable year, the credit otherwise determined under subsection (a) for such year with respect to such property shall not exceed an amount equal to $1,500 for each 0.5 kilowatt of capacity of such property.

(C) Fuel cell power plant. The term "fuel cell power plant" means an integrated system comprised of a fuel cell stack assembly and associated balance of plant components which converts a fuel into electricity using electrochemical means.

(D) Termination. The term "qualified fuel cell property" shall not include any property for any period after December 31, 2016.

(2) Qualified microturbine property.

(A) In general. The term "qualified microturbine property" means a stationary microturbine power plant which—

(i) has a nameplate capacity of less than 2,000 kilowatts, and

(ii) has an electricity-only generation efficiency of not less than 26 percent at International Standard Organization conditions.

(B) Limitation. In the case of qualified microturbine property placed in service during the taxable year, the credit otherwise determined under subsection (a) for such year with respect to such property shall not exceed an amount equal $200 for each kilowatt of capacity of such property.

(C) Stationary microturbine power plant. The term "stationary microturbine power plant" means an integrated system comprised of a gas turbine engine, a combustor, a recuperator or regenerator, a generator or alternator, and associated balance of plant components which converts a fuel into electricity and thermal energy. Such term also includes all secondary components located between the existing infrastructure for fuel delivery and the existing infrastructure for power distribution, including equipment and controls for meeting relevant power standards, such as voltage, frequency, and power factors.

(D) Termination. The term "qualified microturbine property" shall not include any property for any period after December 31, 2016.

(3) Combined heat and power system property.

(A) Combined heat and power system property. The term "combined heat and power system property" means property comprising a system—

(i) which uses the same energy source for the simultaneous or sequential generation of electrical power, mechanical shaft power, or both, in combination with the generation of steam or other forms of useful thermal energy (including heating and cooling applications),

(ii) which produces—

(I) at least 20 percent of its total useful energy in the form of thermal energy which is not used to produce electrical or mechanical power (or combination thereof), and

(II) at least 20 percent of its total useful energy in the form of electrical or mechanical power (or combination thereof),

(iii) the energy efficiency percentage of which exceeds 60 percent, and

(iv) which is placed in service before January 1, 2017.

(B) Limitation.

(i) In general. In the case of combined heat and power system property with an electrical capacity in excess of the applicable capacity placed in service during the taxable year, the credit under subsection (a)(1) (determined without regard to this paragraph) for such year shall be equal to the amount which bears the same ratio to such credit as the applicable capacity bears to the capacity of such property.

(ii) Applicable capacity. For purposes of clause (i), the term "applicable capacity" means 15 megawatts or a mechanical energy capacity of more than 20,000 horsepower or an equivalent combination of electrical and mechanical energy capacities.

(iii) Maximum capacity. The term "combined heat and power system property" shall not include any property comprising a system if such system has a capacity in excess of 50 megawatts or a mechanical energy capacity in excess of 67,000 horsepower or an equivalent combination of electrical and mechanical energy capacities.
  (C) Special rules.
    (i) Energy efficiency percentage. For purposes of this paragraph, the energy efficiency percentage of a system is the fraction—
      (I) the numerator of which is the total useful electrical, thermal, and mechanical power produced by the system at normal operating rates, and expected to be consumed in its normal application, and
      (II) the denominator of which is the lower heating value of the fuel sources for the system.
    (ii) Determinations made on Btu basis. The energy efficiency percentage and the percentages under subparagraph (A)(ii) shall be determined on a Btu basis.
    (iii) Input and output property not included. The term "combined heat and power system property" does not include property used to transport the energy source to the facility or to distribute energy produced by the facility.
  (D) Systems using biomass. If a system is designed to use biomass (within the meaning of paragraphs (2) and (3) of section 45(c) without regard to the last sentence of paragraph (3)(A)) for at least 90 percent of the energy source—
    (i) subparagraph (A)(iii) shall not apply, but
    (ii) the amount of credit determined under subsection (a) with respect to such system shall not exceed the amount which bears the same ratio to such amount of credit (determined without regard to this subparagraph) as the energy efficiency percentage of such system bears to 60 percent.
 (4) Qualified small wind energy property.
  (A) In general. The term "qualified small wind energy property" means property which uses a qualifying small wind turbine to generate electricity.
  (B) Qualifying small wind turbine. The term "qualifying small wind turbine" means a wind turbine which has a nameplate capacity of not more than 100 kilowatts.
  (C) Termination. The term "qualified small wind energy property" shall not include any property for any period after December 31, 2016.
(d) Coordination with Department of Treasury grants.
  In the case of any property with respect to which the Secretary makes a grant under section 1603 of the American Recovery and Reinvestment Tax Act of 2009—
  (1) Denial of production and investment credits. No credit shall be determined under this section or section 45 with respect to such property for the taxable year in which such grant is made or any subsequent taxable year.
  (2) Recapture of credits for progress expenditures made before grant. If a credit was determined under this section with respect to such property for any taxable year ending before such grant is made—
    (A) the tax imposed under subtitle A on the taxpayer for the taxable year in which such grant is made shall be increased by so much of such credit as was allowed under section 38,
    (B) the general business carryforwards under section 39 shall be adjusted so as to recapture the portion of such credit which was not so allowed, and
    (C) the amount of such grant shall be determined without regard to any reduction in the basis of such property by reason of such credit.
  (3) Treatment of grants. Any such grant shall—
    (A) not be includible in the gross income of the taxpayer, but
    (B) shall be taken into account in determining the basis of the property to which such grant relates, except that the basis of such property shall be reduced under section 50(c) in the same manner as a credit allowed under subsection (a).

In **2010,** P.L. 111-312, Sec. 707(a)(1), substituted "2009, 2010, or 2011" for "2009 or 2010" in Sec. 1603(a)(1), Div. B of P.L. 111-5 [see below] effective 2/17/2009 . . . Sec. 707(a)(2)(A), substituted "after 2011" for "after 2010" in Sec. 1603(a)(2), Div. B of P.L. 111-5 [see below] . . . Sec. 707(a)(2)(B), substituted "2009, 2010, or 2011" for "2009 or 2010" in Sec. 1603(a)(2), Div. B of P.L. 111-5 [see below] . . . Sec. 707(b), substituted "2012" for "2011" in Sec. 1603(j), Div. B of P.L. 111-5 [see below]
In **2009,** P.L. 111-5, Sec. 1102(a), added para. (a)(5), effective for facilities placed in service after 12/31/2008.
  —P.L. 111-5, Sec. 1103(a), deleted subpara. (c)(4)(B), and redesignated subparas. (c)(4)(C) and (c)(4)(D) as subparas. (c)(4)(B) as (c)(4)(C) . . . Sec. 1103(b)(1), added subpara. (a)(4)(D), effective for periods after 12/31/2008, under rules similar to the rules of Code Sec. 48(m) (as in effect on the day before the date of the enactment of the Revenue Reconciliation Act of 1990 [enacted 11/5/90]).
Prior to deletion, subpara. (c)(4)(B) read as follows:
  "(B) Limitation. In the case of qualified small wind energy property placed in service during the taxable year, the credit otherwise determined under subsection (a)(1) for such year with respect to all such property of the taxpayer shall not exceed $4,000."
  —P.L. 111-5, Sec. 1103(b)(1), added subpara. (a)(4)(D), effective for periods after 12/31/2008, under rules similar to the rules of section 48(m) of the Internal Revenue Code of 1986 (as in effect on the day before the date of the enactment of the Revenue Reconciliation Act of 1990 [enacted 11/5/90]).
  —P.L. 111-5, Sec. 1104, added subsec. (d), enacted 2/17/2009.
  —P.L. 111-5, Sec. 1603, of this Act, as amended by Sec. 707(a) and (b), P.L. 111-312, 12/17/2010 (see below) provides:
"Sec. 1603. Grants for specified energy property in lieu of tax credits.
"(a) In general. Upon application, the Secretary of the Treasury shall, subject to the requirements of this section, provide a grant to each person who places in service specified energy property to reimburse such person for a portion of the expense of such property as provided in subsection (b). No grant shall be made under this section with respect to any property unless such property—
"(1) is placed in service during 2009, 2010, or 2011
"(2) is placed in service after 2011 and before the credit termination date with respect to such property, but only if the construction of such property began during 2009, 2010, or 2011
"(b) Grant amount.
"(1) In general. The amount of the grant under subsection (a) with respect to any specified energy property shall be the applicable percentage of the basis of such property.
"(2) Applicable percentage. For purposes of paragraph (1), the term 'applicable percentage' means—
"(A) 30 percent in the case of any property described in paragraphs (1) through (4) of subsection (d), and
"(B) 10 percent in the case of any other property.
"(3) Dollar limitations. In the case of property described in paragraph (2), (6), or (7) of subsection (d), the amount of any grant under this section with respect to such property shall not exceed the limitation described in section 48(c)(1)(B), 48(c)(2)(B), or 48(c)(3)(B) of the Internal Revenue Code of 1986, respectively, with respect to such property.
"(c) Time for payment of grant. The Secretary of the Treasury shall make payment of any grant under subsection (a) during the 60-day period beginning on the later of—
"(1) the date of the application for such grant, or
"(2) the date the specified energy property for which the grant is being made is placed in service.
"(d) Specified energy property. For purposes of this section, the term 'specified energy property' means any of the following:
"(1) Qualified facilities. Any qualified property (as defined in section 48(a)(5)(D)) which is part of a qualified facility (within the meaning of section 45) described in paragraph (1), (2), (3), (4), (6), (7), (9), or (11) of section 45(d) of the Internal Revenue Code of 1986.
"(2) Qualified fuel cell property. Any qualified fuel cell property (as defined in section 48(c)(1) of such Code).
"(3) Solar property. Any property described in clause (i) or (ii) of section 48(a)(3)(A) of such Code.
"(4) Qualified small wind energy property. Any qualified small wind energy property (as defined in section 48(c)(4) of such Code).
"(5) Geothermal property. Any property described in clause (iii) of section 48(a)(3)(A) of such Code.

"(6) Qualified microturbine property. Any qualified microturbine property (as defined in section 48(c)(2) of such Code).

"(7) Combined heat and power system property. Any combined heat and power system property (as defined in section 48(c)(3) of such Code).

"(8) Geothermal heat pump property. Any property described in clause (vii) of section 48(a)(3)(A) of such Code.

"Such term shall not include any property unless depreciation (or amortization in lieu of depreciation) is allowable with respect to such property.

"(e) Credit termination date. For purposes of this section, the term 'credit termination date' means—

"(1) in the case of any specified energy property which is part of a facility described in paragraph (1) of section 45(d) of the Internal Revenue Code of 1986, January 1, 2013,

"(2) in the case of any specified energy property which is part of a facility described in paragraph (2), (3), (4), (6), (7), (9), or (11) of section 45(d) of the Internal Revenue Code of 1986, January 1, 2014, and

"(3) in the case of any specified energy property described in section 48, January 1, 2017.

"In the case of any property which is described in paragraph (3) and also in another paragraph of this subsection, paragraph (3) shall apply with respect to such property.

"(f) Application of certain rules. In making grants under this section, the Secretary of the Treasury shall apply rules similar to the rules of section 50 of the Internal Revenue Code of 1986. In applying such rules, if the property is disposed of, or otherwise ceases to be specified energy property, the Secretary of the Treasury shall provide for the recapture of the appropriate percentage of the grant amount in such manner as the Secretary of the Treasury determines appropriate.

"(g) Exception for certain non-taxpayers. The Secretary of the Treasury shall not make any grant under this section to—

"(1) any Federal, State, or local government (or any political subdivision, agency, or instrumentality thereof),

"(2) any organization described in section 501(c) of the Internal Revenue Code of 1986 and exempt from tax under section 501(a) of such Code,

"(3) any entity referred to in paragraph (4) of section 54(j) of such Code, or

"(4) any partnership or other pass-thru entity any partner (or other holder of an equity or profits interest) of which is described in paragraph (1), (2) or (3).

"(h) Definitions. Terms used in this section which are also used in section 45 or 48 of the Internal Revenue Code of 1986 shall have the same meaning for purposes of this section as when used in such section 45 or 48. Any reference in this section to the Secretary of the Treasury shall be treated as including the Secretary's delegate.

"(i) Appropriations. There is hereby appropriated to the Secretary of the Treasury such sums as may be necessary to carry out this section.

"(j) Termination. The Secretary of the Treasury shall not make any grant to any person under this section unless the application of such person for such grant is received before October 1, 2012."

In 2008, P.L. 110-343, Sec. 103(a)(1)DivB, substituted "January 1, 2017" for "January 1, 2009" in subcl. (a)(2)(A)(i)(II) and clause (a)(3)(A)(ii) . . . Sec. 103(a)(2)DivB, substituted "December 31, 2016" for "December 31, 2008" in subpara. (c)(1)(E) . . . Sec. 103(a)(3)DivB, substituted "December 31, 2016" for "December 31, 2008" in subpara. (c)(2)(E), effective 10/3/2008.

—P.L. 110-343, Sec. 103(c)(1)DivB, deleted "or" at the end of clause (a)(3)(A)(iii), added "or" at the end of clause (a)(3)(A)(iv) and added clause (a)(3)(A)(v) . . . Sec. 103(c)(2)(A)DivB, substituted "Definitions" for "Qualified fuel cell property; qualified microturbine property" in the heading of subsec. (c) . . . Sec. 103(c)(2)(B)DivB, added para. (c)(3) . . . Sec. 103(c)(3)DivB, substituted "paragraphs (1)(B), (2)(B), and (3)(B)" for "paragraphs (1)(B) and (2)(B)" in para. (a)(1) . . . Sec. 103(d)DivB, substituted "$1,500" for "$500" in subpara. (c)(1)(B), effective for periods after 10/3/2008, in tax. yrs. end. after 10/3/2008, under rules similar to the rules of Code Sec. 48(m) (as in effect on the day before the date of the enactment of the Revenue Reconciliation Act of 1990).

—P.L. 110-343, Sec. 103(e)(1)DivB, deleted "The term 'energy property" shall not include any property which is public utility property (as defined in section 46(f)(5) as in effect on the day before the date of the enactment of the Revenue Reconciliation Act of 1990)." before "Such term shall not include any property which is part of a facility the production from which is allowed as a credit under section 45 for the taxable year or any prior taxable year." in para. (a)(3) . . . Sec. 103(e)(2)(A)DivB, deleted subpara. (c)(1)(D) and redesignated subpara. (c)(1)(E) as (D) [as amended by Sec. 103(a)(2) Div B, of this Act, see above] . . . Sec. 103(e)(2)(B)DivB, deleted subpara. (c)(2)(D) and redesignated subpara. (c)(2)(E) as (D) [as amended by Sec. 103(a)(3) Div B, of this Act, see above], effective for periods after 2/13/2008, in tax. yrs. end. after 2/13/2008, under rules similar to the rules of Code Sec. 48(m) (as in effect on the day before the date of the enactment of the Revenue Reconciliation Act of 1990).

Prior to deletion, subpara. (c)(1)(D) read as follows:

"(D) Special rule. The first sentence of the matter in subsection (a)(3) which follows subparagraph (D) thereof shall not apply to qualified fuel cell property which is used predominantly in the trade or business of the furnishing or sale of telephone service, telegraph service by means of domestic telegraph operations, or other telegraph services (other than international telegraph services)."

Prior to deletion, subpara. (c)(2)(D) read as follows:

"(D) Special rule. The first sentence of the matter in subsection (a)(3) which follows subparagraph (D) thereof shall not apply to qualified microturbine property which is used predominantly in the trade or business of the furnishing or sale of telephone service, telegraph service by means of domestic telegraph operations, or other telegraph services (other than international telegraph services)."

—P.L. 110-343, Sec. 104(a)DivB, deleted "or" at the end of clause (a)(3)(A)(iv) [as amended by Sec. 103(c)(1) Div B, of this Act, see above], added "or" at the end of clause (a)(3)(A)(v) [as added by Sec. 103(c)(1) Div B, of this Act, see above], and added clause (a)(3)(A)(vi) . . . Sec. 104(b)DivB, deleted "and" at the end of subcl. (a)(2)(A)(i)(II) and added subcl. (a)(2)(A)(i)(IV) . . . Sec. 104(c)DivB, added para. (c)(4) . . . Sec. 104(d)DivB, substituted "paragraphs (1)(B), (2)(B), (3)(B), and (4)(B)" for "paragraphs (1)(B), (2)(B), and (3)(B)" in para. (a)(1) [as amended by Sec. 103(c)(3) Div B, of this Act, see above], effective for periods after 10/3/2008, in tax. yrs. end. after 10/3/2008, under rules similar to the rules of Code Sec. 48(m) (as in effect on the day before the date of the enactment of the Revenue Reconciliation Act of 1990).

—P.L. 110-343, Sec. 105(a)DivB, deleted "or" at the end of clause (a)(3)(A)(v) [as amended by Sec. 104(a) Div B, of this Act, see above], added "or" at the end of clause (a)(3)(A)(vi) [as added by Sec. 104(a) Div B, of this Act, see above] and added clause (a)(3)(A)(vii), effective for periods after 10/3/2008, in tax. yrs. end. after 10/3/2008, under rules similar to the rules of Code Sec. 48(m) (as in effect on the day before the date of the enactment of the Revenue Reconciliation Act of 1990).

In 2007, P.L. 110-172, Sec. 11(a)(8), substituted "section" for "subsection" in the text preceding para. (c)(1) . . . Sec. 11(a)(9), substituted "subsection (a)" for "paragraph (1)" in subpara. (c)(1)(B) and subpara. (c)(2)(B), enacted 12/29/2007.

In 2006, P.L. 109-432, Sec. 207(1), substituted "January 1, 2009" for "January 1, 2008" in subclause (a)(2)(A)(i)(II) and clause (a)(3)(A)(iii). . . . Sec. 207(2), substituted "December 31, 2008" for "December 31, 2007" in subparas. (c)(1)(E) and (c)(2)(E), enacted 12/20/2006.

In 2005, P.L. 109-135, Sec. 412(m), substituted "paragraphs (1)(B) and (2)(B) of subsection (c)" for "paragraph (1)(B) or (2)(B) of subsection (d)" in para. (a)(1) . . . Sec. 412(n)(1), redesignated clause (a)(3)(A)(iii) [as added by Sec. 1336(a) of P.L. 109-58, see below] as (a)(3)(A)(iv) . . . Sec. 412(n)(2), deleted "or" at the end of clause (a)(3)(A)(ii), effective 12/21/2005.

—P.L. 109-58, Sec. 1336(a), deleted "or" at the end of clause (a)(3)(A)(i), added "or" at the end of clause (a)(3)(A)(ii), and added clause (a)(3)(A)(iii) . . . Sec. 1336(b), added subsec. (c) . . . Sec. 1336(c), amended subpara. (a)(2)(A) . . . Sec. 1336(d), added "except as provided in paragraph (1)(B) or (2)(B) of subsection (d)," before "the energy" in para. (a)(1), effective for periods after 12/31/2005, in tax. yrs. end. after 12/31/2005, under rules similar to the rules of section 48(m) of the Internal Revenue Code of 1986 (as in effect on the day before the date of the enactment of the Revenue Reconciliation Act of 1990 [enacted 11/5/90]).

Prior to amendment, subpara. (a)(2)(A) read as follows:

"(A) In general. The energy percentage is 10 percent."

—P.L. 109-58, Sec. 1337(a), amended subpara. (a)(2)(A) . . . Sec. 1337(b), deleted "or" at the end of clause (a)(3)(A)(i) [Sec. 1336(a) of this Act already deleted "or" at the end of clause (a)(3)(A)(i), see above], redesignated clause (a)(3)(A)(ii) as clause (a)(3)(A)(iii), and added clause (a)(3)(A)(ii) . . . Sec. 1337(c), added "excepting property used to generate energy for the purposes of heating a swimming pool," after "solar process heat," in clause (a)(3)(A)(i), effective for periods after 12/31/2005, in tax. yrs. end. after 12/31/2005, under rules similar to the rules of section 48(m) of the Internal Revenue Code of 1986 (as in effect on the day before the date of the enactment of the Revenue Reconciliation Act of 1990 [enacted 11/5/90]).

Prior to amendment, subpara. (a)(2)(A) read as follows:

"(A) In general. The energy percentage is—

"(i) in the case of qualified fuel cell property, 30 percent, and

"(ii) in the case of any other energy property, 10 percent."

In 2004, P.L. 108-357, Sec. 322(d)(2)(A)(i), deleted subsec. (b) . . . Sec. 322(d)(2)(A)(ii), substituted "subsection (a)" for "this subsection" in para. (a)(5) . . . Sec. 322(d)(2)(A)(iii), redesignated para. (a)(5) [as amended by Sec. 322(d)(2)(A)(ii) of this Act, see above] as subsec. (b) . . . Sec. 322(d)(2)(B), deleted "; reforestation credit" after "Energy credit" in the heading of Code Sec. 48, effective for expenditures paid or incurred after 10/22/2004.

Prior to deletion, subsec. (b) read as follows:

"*(b) Reforestation credit.*

"(1) In general. For purposes of section 46, the reforestation credit for any taxable year is 10 percent of the portion of the amortizable basis of any qualified timber property which was acquired during such taxable year and which is taken into account under section 194 (after the application of section 194(b)(1)).

"(2) Definitions. For purposes of this subpart, the terms 'amortizable basis' and 'qualified timber property' have the respective meanings given to such terms by section 194."

—P.L. 108-357, Sec. 710(e), added "Such term shall not include any property which is part of a facility the production from which is allowed as a credit under section 45 for the taxable year or any prior taxable year." at the end of para. (a)(3), effective for electricity produced and sold after 10/22/2004, in tax. yrs. end. after 10/22/2004. For special provisions, see Sec. 710(g)(2)-(4) of P.L. 108-357, reproduced in the history of Code Sec. 45.

In 1992, P.L. 102-486, Sec. 1916(a)(1), substituted "The" for "Except as provided in subparagraph (B), the" in subpara. (a)(2)(A) . . . Sec. 1916(a)(2), deleted subpara. (a)(2)(B) . . . Sec. 1916(a)(3), redesignated subpara. (a)(2)(C) as subpara. (a)(2)(B), effective 6/30/92.

Prior to deletion, subpara. (a)(2)(B) read as follows:

"(B) Termination. Effective with respect to periods after June 30, 1992, the energy percentage is zero. For purposes of the preceding sentence, rules similar to the rules of section 48(m) (as in effect on the day before the date of the enactment of the Revenue Reconciliation Act of 1990) shall apply."

In 1991, P.L. 102-227, Sec. 106, substituted "June 30, 1992" for "December 31, 1991" in subpara. (a)(2)(B), effective 12/11/91.

In 1990, P.L. 101-508, Sec. 11813(a), amended Code Sec. 48 as part of the amendment to subpart E, of part IV of subchapter A of chapter 1, effective for property placed in service after 12/31/90 except as provided in Sec. 11813(c)(2) of this Act, reproduced in note following Code Sec. 46.

Sec. 48A. Qualifying advanced coal project credit.
(a) In general.
For purposes of section 46, the qualifying advanced coal project credit for any taxable year is an amount equal to—
(1) 20 percent of the qualified investment for such taxable year in the case of projects described in subsection (d)(3)(B)(i),
(2) 15 percent of the qualified investment for such taxable year in the case of projects described in subsection (d)(3)(B)(ii), and
(3) 30 percent of the qualified investment for such taxable year in the case of projects described in clause (iii) of subsection (d)(3)(B).
(b) Qualified investment.
(1) **In general.** For purposes of subsection (a), the qualified investment for any taxable year is the basis of eligible property placed in service by the taxpayer during such taxable year which is part of a qualifying advanced coal project—
(A)(i) the construction, reconstruction, or erection of which is completed by the taxpayer, or
(ii) which is acquired by the taxpayer if the original use of such property commences with the taxpayer, and
(B) with respect to which depreciation (or amortization in lieu of depreciation) is allowable.
(2) **Special rule for certain subsidized property.** Rules similar to section 48(a)(4) (without regard to subparagraph (D) thereof) shall apply for purposes of this section.
(3) **Certain qualified progress expenditures rules made applicable.** Rules similar to the rules of subsections (c)(4) and (d) of section 46 (as in effect on the day before the enactment of the Revenue Reconciliation Act of 1990) shall apply for purposes of this section.
(c) Definitions.
For purposes of this section—
(1) **Qualifying advanced coal project.** The term "qualifying advanced coal project" means a project which meets the requirements of subsection (e).
(2) **Advanced coal-based generation technology.** The term "advanced coal-based generation technology" means a technology which meets the requirements of subsection (f).
(3) **Eligible property.** The term "eligible property" means—
(A) in the case of any qualifying advanced coal project using an integrated gasification combined cycle, any property which is a part of such project and is necessary for the gasification of coal, including any coal handling and gas separation equipment, and
(B) in the case of any other qualifying advanced coal project, any property which is a part of such project.
(4) **Coal.** The term "coal" means anthracite, bituminous coal, subbituminous coal, lignite, and peat.
(5) **Greenhouse gas capture capability.** The term "greenhouse gas capture capability" means an integrated gasification combined cycle technology facility capable of adding components which can capture, separate on a long-term basis, isolate, remove, and sequester greenhouse gases which result from the generation of electricity.
(6) **Electric generation unit.** The term "electric generation unit" means any facility at least 50 percent of the total annual net output of which is electrical power, including an otherwise eligible facility which is used in an industrial application.
(7) **Integrated gasification combined cycle.** The term "integrated gasification combined cycle" means an electric generation unit which produces electricity by converting coal to synthesis gas which is used to fuel a combined-cycle plant which produces electricity from both a combustion turbine (including a combustion turbine/fuel cell hybrid) and a steam turbine.
(d) Qualifying advanced coal project program.
(1) **Establishment.** Not later than 180 days after the date of enactment of this section, the Secretary, in consultation with the Secretary of Energy, shall establish a qualifying advanced coal project program for the deployment of advanced coal-based generation technologies.
(2) **Certification.**
(A) Application period. Each applicant for certification under this paragraph shall submit an application meeting the requirements of subparagraph (B). An applicant may only submit an application—
(i) for an allocation from the dollar amount specified in clause (i) or (ii) of paragraph (3)(B) during the 3-year period beginning on the date the Secretary establishes the program under paragraph (1), and
(ii) for an allocation from the dollar amount specified in paragraph (3)(B)(iii) during the 3-year period beginning at the earlier of the termination of the period described in clause (i) or the date prescribed by the Secretary.
(B) Requirements for applications for certification. An application under subparagraph (A) shall contain such information as the Secretary may require in order to make a determination to accept or reject an application for certification as meeting the requirements under subsection (e)(1). Any information contained in the application shall be protected as provided in section 552(b)(4) of title 5, United States Code.
(C) Time to act upon applications for certification. The Secretary shall issue a determination as to whether an applicant has met the requirements under subsection (e)(1) within 60 days following the date of submittal of the application for certification.
(D) Time to meet criteria for certification. Each applicant for certification shall have 2 years from the date of acceptance by the Secretary of the application during which to provide to the Secretary evidence that the criteria set forth in subsection (e)(2) have been met.
(E) Period of issuance. An applicant which receives a certification shall have 5 years from the date of issuance of the certification in order to place the project in service and if such project is not placed in service by that time period then the certification shall no longer be valid.
(3) **Aggregate credits.**
(A) In general. The aggregate credits allowed under subsection (a) for projects certified by the Secretary under paragraph (2) may not exceed $2,550,000,000.
(B) Particular projects. Of the dollar amount in subparagraph (A), the Secretary is authorized to certify—
(i) $800,000,000 for integrated gasification combined cycle projects the application for which is submitted during the period described in paragraph (2)(A)(i),
(ii) $500,000,000 for projects which use other advanced coal-based generation technologies the application for which is submitted during the period described in paragraph (2)(A)(i), and

Tax credits Code Sec. 48A(f)(1)(B)

(iii) $1,250,000,000 for advanced coal-based generation technology projects the application for which is submitted during the period described in paragraph (2)(A)(ii).

(4) Review and redistribution.

(A) Review. Not later than 6 years after the date of enactment of this section, the Secretary shall review the credits allocated under this section as of the date which is 6 years after the date of enactment of this section.

(B) Redistribution. The Secretary may reallocate credits available under clauses (i) and (ii) of paragraph (3)(B) if the Secretary determines that—

(i) there is an insufficient quantity of qualifying applications for certification pending at the time of the review, or

(ii) any certification made pursuant to paragraph (2) has been revoked pursuant to paragraph (2)(D) because the project subject to the certification has been delayed as a result of third party opposition or litigation to the proposed project.

(C) Reallocation. If the Secretary determines that credits under clause (i) or (ii) of paragraph (3)(B) are available for reallocation pursuant to the requirements set forth in paragraph (2), the Secretary is authorized to conduct an additional program for applications for certification.

(5) Disclosure of allocations. The Secretary shall, upon making a certification under this subsection or section 48B(d), publicly disclose the identity of the applicant and the amount of the credit certified with respect to such applicant.

(e) Qualifying advanced coal projects.

(1) Requirements. For purposes of subsection (c)(1), a project shall be considered a qualifying advanced coal project that the Secretary may certify under subsection (d)(2) if the Secretary determines that, at a minimum—

(A) the project uses an advanced coal-based generation technology—

(i) to power a new electric generation unit; or

(ii) to retrofit or repower an existing electric generation unit (including an existing natural gas-fired combined cycle unit);

(B) the fuel input for the project, when completed, is at least 75 percent coal;

(C) the project, consisting of one or more electric generation units at one site, will have a total nameplate generating capacity of at least 400 megawatts;

(D) the applicant provides evidence that a majority of the output of the project is reasonably expected to be acquired or utilized;

(E) the applicant provides evidence of ownership or control of a site of sufficient size to allow the proposed project to be constructed and to operate on a long-term basis;

(F) the project will be located in the United States; and

(G) in the case of any project the application for which is submitted during the period described in subsection (d)(2)(A)(ii), the project includes equipment which separates and sequesters at least 65 percent (70 percent in the case of an application for reallocated credits under subsection (d)(4)) of such project's total carbon dioxide emissions.

(2) Requirements for certification. For the purpose of subsection (d)(2)(D), a project shall be eligible for certification only if the Secretary determines that—

(A) the applicant for certification has received all Federal and State environmental authorizations or reviews necessary to commence construction of the project; and

(B) the applicant for certification, except in the case of a retrofit or repower of an existing electric generation unit, has purchased or entered into a binding contract for the purchase of the main steam turbine or turbines for the project, except that such contract may be contingent upon receipt of a certification under subsection (d)(2).

(3) Priority for certain projects. In determining which qualifying advanced coal projects to certify under subsection (d)(2), the Secretary shall—

(A) certify capacity, in accordance with the procedures set forth in subsection (d), in relatively equal amounts to—

(i) projects using bituminous coal as a primary feedstock,

(ii) projects using subbituminous coal as a primary feedstock, and

(iii) projects using lignite as a primary feedstock,

(B) give high priority to projects which include, as determined by the Secretary—

(i) greenhouse gas capture capability,

(ii) increased by-product utilization,

(iii) applicant participants who have a research partnership with an eligible educational institution (as defined in section 529(e)(5)), and

(iv) other benefits , and

(C) give highest priority to projects with the greatest separation and sequestration percentage of total carbon dioxide emissions.

(f) Advanced coal-based generation technology.

(1) In general. For the purpose of this section, an electric generation unit uses advanced coal-based generation technology if—

(A) the unit—

(i) uses integrated gasification combined cycle technology, or

(ii) except as provided in paragraph (3), has a design net heat rate of 8530 Btu/kWh (40 percent efficiency), and

(B) the unit is designed to meet the performance requirements in the following table:

1,241

Code Sec. 48A(f)(1)(B) — Tax credits

Performance characteristic:	Design level for project:
SO₂ (percent removal)	99 percent
NOₓ (emissions)	0.07 lbs/MMBTU
PM* (emissions)	0.015 lbs/MMBTU
Hg (percent removal)	90 percent

For purposes of the performance requirement specified for the removal of SO_2 in the table contained in subparagraph (B), the SO_2 removal design level in the case of a unit designed for the use of feedstock substantially all of which is subbituminous coal shall be 99 percent SO_2 removal or the achievement of an emission level of 0.04 pounds or less of SO_2 per million Btu, determined on a 30-day average.

(2) Design net heat rate. For purposes of this subsection, design net heat rate with respect to an electric generation unit shall—

(A) be measured in Btu per kilowatt hour (higher heating value),

(B) be based on the design annual heat input to the unit and the rated net electrical power, fuels, and chemicals output of the unit (determined without regard to the cogeneration of steam by the unit),

(C) be adjusted for the heat content of the design coal to be used by the unit—

(i) if the heat content is less than 13,500 Btu per pound, but greater than 7,000 Btu per pound, according to the following formula: design net heat rate=unit net heat rate x [1−[((13,500−design coal heat content, Btu per pound)/1,000)* 0.013]], and

(ii) if the heat content is less than or equal to 7,000 Btu per pound, according to the following formula: design net heat rate=unit net heat rate x [1−[((13,500−design coal heat content, Btu per pound)/1,000)* 0.018]], and

(D) be corrected for the site reference conditions of—

(i) elevation above sea level of 500 feet,

(ii) air pressure of 14.4 pounds per square inch absolute,

(iii) temperature, dry bulb of 63°F,

(iv) temperature, wet bulb of 54°F, and

(v) relative humidity of 55 percent.

(3) Existing units. In the case of any electric generation unit in existence on the date of the enactment of this section, such unit uses advanced coal-based generation technology if, in lieu of the requirements under paragraph (1)(A)(ii), such unit achieves a minimum efficiency of 35 percent and an overall thermal design efficiency improvement, compared to the efficiency of the unit as operated, of not less than—

(A) 7 percentage points for coal of more than 9,000 Btu,

(B) 6 percentage points for coal of 7,000 to 9,000 Btu, or

(C) 4 percentage points for coal of less than 7,000 Btu.

(g) Applicability.

No use of technology (or level of emission reduction solely by reason of the use of the technology), and no achievement of any emission reduction by the demonstration of any technology or performance level, by or at one or more facilities with respect to which a credit is allowed under this section, shall be considered to indicate that the technology or performance level is—

(1) adequately demonstrated for purposes of section 111 of the Clean Air Act (42 U.S.C. 7411);

(2) achievable for purposes of section 169 of that Act (42 U.S.C. 7479); or

(3) achievable in practice for purposes of section 171 of such Act (42 U.S.C. 7501).

(h) Competitive certification awards modification authority.

In implementing this section or section 48B, the Secretary is directed to modify the terms of any competitive certification award and any associated closing agreement where such modification—

(1) is consistent with the objectives of such section,

(2) is requested by the recipient of the competitive certification award, and

(3) involves moving the project site to improve the potential to capture and sequester carbon dioxide emissions, reduce costs of transporting feedstock, and serve a broader customer base,

unless the Secretary determines that the dollar amount of tax credits available to the taxpayer under such section would increase as a result of the modification or such modification would result in such project not being originally certified. In considering any such modification, the Secretary shall consult with other relevant Federal agencies, including the Department of Energy.

(i) Recapture of credit for failure to sequester.

The Secretary shall provide for recapturing the benefit of any credit allowable under subsection (a) with respect to any project which fails to attain or maintain the separation and sequestration requirements of subsection (e)(1)(G).

In 2009, P.L. 111-5, Sec. 1103(b)(2)(C), added "(without regard to subparagraph (D) thereof)" after "section 48(a)(4)" in para. (b)(2), effective for periods after 12/31/2008, under rules similar to the rules of section 48(m) of the Internal Revenue Code of 1986 (as in effect on the day before the date of the enactment of the Revenue Reconciliation Act of 1990 [enacted 11/5/90]).

In 2008, P.L. 110-343, Sec. 111(a)DivB, deleted "and" at the end of para. (a)(1), substituted ", and" for the period at the end of para. (a)(2), and added para. (a)(3) ... Sec. 111(b)DivB, substituted "$2,550,000,000" for "$1,300,000,000" in subpara. (d)(3)(A) ... Sec. 111(c)(1)DivB, amended subpara. (d)(3)(B) ... Sec. 111(c)(2)DivB, amended subpara. (d)(2)(A) ... Sec. 111(c)(3)(A)DivB, deleted "and" at the end of subpara. (e)(1)(E), substituted "; and" for the period at the end of subpara. (e)(1)(F), and added subpara. (e)(1)(G) ... Sec. 111(c)(3)(B)DivB, deleted "and" at the end of clause (e)(3)(A)(iii), substituted ", and" for the period at the end of clause (e)(3)(B)(iii), and added subpara. (e)(3)(C) ... Sec. 111(c)(3)(C)DivB, added subsec. (i) ... Sec. 111(c)(4)(A)DivB, deleted "and" at the end of clause (e)(3)(B)(ii) ... Sec. 111(c)(4)(B)DivB, redesignated clause (e)(3)(B)(iii) as clause (e)(3)(B)(iv) ... Sec. 111(c)(4)(C)DivB, added new clause (e)(3)(B)(iii), effective for credits the application for which is submitted during the period described in Code Sec. 48A(d)(2)(A)(ii) and which are allocated or reallocated after 10/3/2008.

Prior to amendment, subpara. (d)(3)(B) read as follows:

"(B) Particular projects. Of the dollar amount in subparagraph (A), the Secretary is authorized to certify—

"(i) $800,000,000 for integrated gasification combined cycle projects, and

"(ii) $500,000,000 for projects which use other advanced coal-based generation technologies."

Prior to amendment, subpara. (d)(2)(A) read as follows:

"(A) Application period. Each applicant for certification under this paragraph shall submit an application meeting the requirements of subparagraph (B). An applicant may only submit an application during the 3-year period beginning on the date the Secretary establishes the program under paragraph (1) ."

—P.L. 110-343, Sec. 111(c)(5)DivB, substituted "certain" for "integrated gasification combined cycle" in the heading of para. (e)(5), effective [as if included in the amendment made by P.L. 109-58, Sec. 1307(b)] for periods after 8/8/2005, under rules similar to the rules of Code Sec. 48(m) (as in effect on the day before the date of enactment of the Revenue Reconciliation Act of 1990 [enacted 11/5/90]).

Tax credits   Code Sec. 48B(d)(3)

—P.L. 110-343, Sec. 111(d)DivB, added para. (d)(5), effective for certifications made after 10/3/2008.
—P.L. 110-246, Sec. 4, Repeals the duplicative enactment and provides effective date provisions of the Act entitled "An Act to provide for the continuation of agricultural programs through fiscal year 2012, and for other purposes" Sec. 4, P.L. 110-246 reads as follows:
"Sec. 4. Repeal of duplicative enactment.
"(a) In General- The Act entitled 'An Act to provide for the continuation of agricultural programs through fiscal year 2012, and for other purposes' (H.R. 2419 of the 110th Congress), and the amendments made by that Act, are repealed, effective on the date of enactment of that Act.
"(b) Effective Date- Except as otherwise provided in this Act, this Act and the amendments made by this Act shall take effect on the earlier of—
"(1) the date of enactment of this Act; or
"(2) the date of the enactment of the Act entitled 'An Act to provide for the continuation of agricultural programs through fiscal year 2012, and for other purposes' (H.R. 2419 of the 110th Congress)."
—P.L. 110-246, Sec. 15346(a), added subsec. (h), effective 5/22/2008 and is applicable to all competitive certification awards entered into under section 48A or 48B of the Internal Revenue Code of 1986, whether such awards were issued before, on, or after 5/22/2008. [Ed. Note: May 22, 2008 was the date of enactment for H.R. 2419 (PL 110-234), which was repealed by (2008 Farm Act § 4(a)) (PL 110-246, 6/18/2008), in connection with the reenactment of the farm bill to correct a technical deficiency in its original passage.]
In 2007, P.L. 110-172, Sec. 11(a)(10), deleted "subsection" before "paragraph (2)" and "paragraph (2)(D)" in clause (d)(4)(B)(ii), enacted 12/29/2007.
In 2006, P.L. 109-432, Sec. 203(a), added the flush matter at the end of para. (f)(1), effective for applications for certification under Code Sec. 48A(d)(2) submitted after 10/2/2006.
In 2005, P.L. 109-58, Sec. 1307(b), added Code Sec. 48A, effective for periods after 8/8/2005, under rules similar to the rules of Code Sec. 48(m) (as in effect on the day before the date of enactment of the Revenue Reconciliation Act of 1990 [enacted 11/5/90]).

Sec. 48B. Qualifying gasification project credit.
(a) In general.
For purposes of section 46, the qualifying gasification project credit for any taxable year is an amount equal to 20 percent (30 percent in the case of credits allocated under subsection (d)(1)(B)) of the qualified investment for such taxable year.
(b) Qualified investment.
  (1) In general. For purposes of subsection (a), the qualified investment for any taxable year is the basis of eligible property placed in service by the taxpayer during such taxable year which is part of a qualifying gasification project—
    (A)(i) the construction, reconstruction, or erection of which is completed by the taxpayer, or
    (ii) which is acquired by the taxpayer if the original use of such property commences with the taxpayer, and
    (B) with respect to which depreciation (or amortization in lieu of depreciation) is allowable.
  (2) Special rule for certain subsidized property. Rules similar to section 48(a)(4) (without regard to subparagraph (D) thereof) shall apply for purposes of this section.
  (3) Certain qualified progress expenditures rules made applicable. Rules similar to the rules of subsections (c)(4) and (d) of section 46 (as in effect on the day before the enactment of the Revenue Reconciliation Act of 1990) shall apply for purposes of this section.
(c) Definitions.
For purposes of this section—
  (1) Qualifying gasification project. The term "qualifying gasification project" means any project which—
    (A) employs gasification technology,
    (B) will be carried out by an eligible entity, and
    (C) any portion of the qualified investment of which is certified under the qualifying gasification program as eligible for credit under this section in an amount (not to exceed $650,000,000) determined by the Secretary.
  (2) Gasification technology. The term "gasification technology" means any process which converts a solid or liquid product from coal, petroleum residue, biomass, or other materials which are recovered for their energy or feedstock value into a synthesis gas composed primarily of carbon monoxide and hydrogen for direct use or subsequent chemical or physical conversion.
  (3) Eligible property. The term "eligible property" means any property which is a part of a qualifying gasification project and is necessary for the gasification technology of such project.
  (4) Biomass.
    (A) In general. The term "biomass" means any—
      (i) agricultural or plant waste,
      (ii) byproduct of wood or paper mill operations, including lignin in spent pulping liquors, and
      (iii) other products of forestry maintenance.
    (B) Exclusion. The term "biomass" does not include paper which is commonly recycled.
  (5) Carbon capture capability. The term "carbon capture capability" means a gasification plant design which is determined by the Secretary to reflect reasonable consideration for, and be capable of, accommodating the equipment likely to be necessary to capture carbon dioxide from the gaseous stream, for later use or sequestration, which would otherwise be emitted in the flue gas from a project which uses a nonrenewable fuel.
  (6) Coal. The term "coal" means anthracite, bituminous coal, subbituminous coal, lignite, and peat.
  (7) Eligible entity. The term "eligible entity" means any person whose application for certification is principally intended for use in a domestic project which employs domestic gasification applications related to—
    (A) chemicals,
    (B) fertilizers,
    (C) glass,
    (D) steel,
    (E) petroleum residues,
    (F) forest products,
    (G) agriculture, including feedlots and dairy operations, and
    (H) transportation grade liquid fuels.
  (8) Petroleum residue. The term "petroleum residue" means the carbonized product of highboiling hydrocarbon fractions obtained in petroleum processing.
(d) Qualifying gasification project program.
  (1) In general. Not later than 180 days after the date of the enactment of this section, the Secretary, in consultation with the Secretary of Energy, shall establish a qualifying gasification project program to consider and award certifications for qualified investment eligible for credits under this section to qualifying gasification project sponsors under this section. The total amounts of credit that may be allocated under the program shall not exceed—
    (A) $350,000,000, plus
    (B) $250,000,000 for qualifying gasification projects that include equipment which separates and sequesters at least 75 percent of such project's total carbon dioxide emissions.
  (2) Period of issuance. A certificate of eligibility under paragraph (1) may be issued only during the 10-fiscal year period beginning on October 1, 2005.
  (3) Selection criteria. The Secretary shall not make a competitive certification award for qualified investment for credit eligibility under this section unless the recipient has documented to the satisfaction of the Secretary that—

(A) the award recipient is financially viable without the receipt of additional Federal funding associated with the proposed project,

(B) the recipient will provide sufficient information to the Secretary for the Secretary to ensure that the qualified investment is spent efficiently and effectively,

(C) a market exists for the products of the proposed project as evidenced by contracts or written statements of intent from potential customers,

(D) the fuels identified with respect to the gasification technology for such project will comprise at least 90 percent of the fuels required by the project for the production of chemical feedstocks, liquid transportation fuels, or coproduction of electricity,

(E) the award recipient's project team is competent in the construction and operation of the gasification technology proposed, with preference given to those recipients with experience which demonstrates successful and reliable operations of the technology on domestic fuels so identified, and

(F) the award recipient has met other criteria established and published by the Secretary.

(4) Selection priorities. In determining which qualifying gasification projects to certify under this section, the Secretary shall—

(A) give highest priority to projects with the greatest separation and sequestration percentage of total carbon dioxide emissions, and

(B) give high priority to applicant participants who have a research partnership with an eligible educational institution (as defined in section 529(e)(5)).

(e) Denial of double benefit.

A credit shall not be allowed under this section for any qualified investment for which a credit is allowed under section 48A.

(f) Recapture of credit for failure to sequester.

The Secretary shall provide for recapturing the benefit of any credit allowable under subsection (a) with respect to any project which fails to attain or maintain the separation and sequestration requirements for such project under subsection (d)(1).

In 2009, P.L. 111-5, Sec. 1103(b)(2)(D), added "(without regard to subparagraph (D) thereof)" after "section 48(a)(4)" in para. (b)(2), effective for periods after 12/31/2008, under rules similar to the rules of section 48(m) of the Internal Revenue Code of 1986 (as in effect on the day before the date of the enactment of the Revenue Reconciliation Act of 1990).

In 2008, P.L. 110-343, Sec. 112(a)DivB, added "(30 percent in the case of credits allocated under subsection (d)(1)(B))" after "20 percent"... Sec. 112(b)DivB, substituted "shall not exceed—

"(A) $350,000,000, plus

"(B) $250,000,000 for qualifying gasification projects that include equipment which separates and sequesters at least 75 percent of such project's total carbon dioxide emissions." for "shall not exceed $350,000,000" and all that follows in para. (d)(1)... Sec. 112(c)DivB, added subsec. (f)... Sec. 112(d)DivB, added para. (d)(4)... Sec. 112(e)DivB, deleted "and" at the end of subpara. (c)(7)(F), substituted ", and" for the period at the end of subpara. (c)(7)(G) and added subpara. (c)(7)(H), effective for credits described in section 48B(d)(1)(B) of the Internal Revenue Code of 1986 which are allocated or reallocated after 10/3/2008.

In 2005, P.L. 109-58, Sec. 1307(b), added Code Sec. 48B, effective for periods after 8/8/2005, under rules similar to the rules of Code Sec. 48(m) (as in effect on the day before the date of enactment of the Revenue Reconciliation Act of 1990 [enacted 11/5/90]).

Sec. 48C. Qualifying advanced energy project credit.
(a) In general.

For purposes of section 46, the qualifying advanced energy project credit for any taxable year is an amount equal to 30 percent of the qualified investment for such taxable year with respect to any qualifying advanced energy project of the taxpayer.

(b) Qualified investment.
(1) In general. For purposes of subsection (a), the qualified investment for any taxable year is the basis of eligible property placed in service by the taxpayer during such taxable year which is part of a qualifying advanced energy project.

(2) Certain qualified progress expenditures rules made applicable. Rules similar to the rules of subsections (c)(4) and (d) of section 46 (as in effect on the day before the enactment of the Revenue Reconciliation Act of 1990) shall apply for purposes of this section.

(3) Limitation. The amount which is treated for all taxable years with respect to any qualifying advanced energy project shall not exceed the amount designated by the Secretary as eligible for the credit under this section.

(c) Definitions.
(1) Qualifying advanced energy project.

(A) In general. The term "qualifying advanced energy project" means a project—

(i) which re-equips, expands, or establishes a manufacturing facility for the production of—

(I) property designed to be used to produce energy from the sun, wind, geothermal deposits (within the meaning of section 613(e)(2)), or other renewable resources,

(II) fuel cells, microturbines, or an energy storage system for use with electric or hybrid-electric motor vehicles,

(III) electric grids to support the transmission of intermittent sources of renewable energy, including storage of such energy,

(IV) property designed to capture and sequester carbon dioxide emissions,

(V) property designed to refine or blend renewable fuels or to produce energy conservation technologies (including energy-conserving lighting technologies and smart grid technologies),

(VI) new qualified plug-in electric drive motor vehicles (as defined by section 30D), qualified plug-in electric vehicles (as defined by section 30(d)), or components which are designed specifically for use with such vehicles, including electric motors, generators, and power control units, or

(VII) other advanced energy property designed to reduce greenhouse gas emissions as may be determined by the Secretary, and

(ii) any portion of the qualified investment of which is certified by the Secretary under subsection (d) as eligible for a credit under this section.

(B) Exception. Such term shall not include any portion of a project for the production of any property which is used in the refining or blending of any transportation fuel (other than renewable fuels).

(2) Eligible property. The term "eligible property" means any property—

(A) which is necessary for the production of property described in paragraph (1)(A)(i),

(B) which is—

(i) tangible personal property, or

(ii) other tangible property (not including a building or its structural components), but only if such property is used as an integral part of the qualified investment credit facility, and

(C) with respect to which depreciation (or amortization in lieu of depreciation) is allowable.

Tax credits   Code Sec. 48D(c)(1)(A)

(d) Qualifying advanced energy project program.
(1) Establishment.
(A) In general. Not later than 180 days after the date of enactment of this section, the Secretary, in consultation with the Secretary of Energy, shall establish a qualifying advanced energy project program to consider and award certifications for qualified investments eligible for credits under this section to qualifying advanced energy project sponsors.

(B) Limitation. The total amount of credits that may be allocated under the program shall not exceed $2,300,000,000.

(2) Certification.
(A) Application period. Each applicant for certification under this paragraph shall submit an application containing such information as the Secretary may require during the 2-year period beginning on the date the Secretary establishes the program under paragraph (1).

(B) Time to meet criteria for certification. Each applicant for certification shall have 1 year from the date of acceptance by the Secretary of the application during which to provide to the Secretary evidence that the requirements of the certification have been met.

(C) Period of issuance. An applicant which receives a certification shall have 3 years from the date of issuance of the certification in order to place the project in service and if such project is not placed in service by that time period, then the certification shall no longer be valid.

(3) Selection criteria. In determining which qualifying advanced energy projects to certify under this section, the Secretary—

(A) shall take into consideration only those projects where there is a reasonable expectation of commercial viability, and

(B) shall take into consideration which projects—
(i) will provide the greatest domestic job creation (both direct and indirect) during the credit period,
(ii) will provide the greatest net impact in avoiding or reducing air pollutants or anthropogenic emissions of greenhouse gases,
(iii) have the greatest potential for technological innovation and commercial deployment,
(iv) have the lowest levelized cost of generated or stored energy, or of measured reduction in energy consumption or greenhouse gas emission (based on costs of the full supply chain), and
(v) have the shortest project time from certification to completion.

(4) Review and redistribution.
(A) Review. Not later than 4 years after the date of enactment of this section, the Secretary shall review the credits allocated under this section as of such date.

(B) Redistribution. The Secretary may reallocate credits awarded under this section if the Secretary determines that—
(i) there is an insufficient quantity of qualifying applications for certification pending at the time of the review, or
(ii) any certification made pursuant to paragraph (2) has been revoked pursuant to paragraph (2)(B) because the project subject to the certification has been delayed as a result of third party opposition or litigation to the proposed project.

(C) Reallocation. If the Secretary determines that credits under this section are available for reallocation pursuant to the requirements set forth in paragraph (2), the Secretary is authorized to conduct an additional program for applications for certification.

(5) Disclosure of allocations. The Secretary shall, upon making a certification under this subsection, publicly disclose the identity of the applicant and the amount of the credit with respect to such applicant.

(e) Denial of double benefit.
A credit shall not be allowed under this section for any qualified investment for which a credit is allowed under section 48, 48A, or 48B.

In **2009**, P.L. 111-5, Sec. 1302(b), added Code Sec. 48C, effective for periods after 2/17/2009, under rules similar to the rules of section 48(m) of the Internal Revenue Code of 1986 (as in effect on the day before the date of the enactment of the Revenue Reconciliation Act of 1990 [enacted 11/5/90]).

Sec. 48D. Qualifying therapeutic discovery project credit.
(a) In general.
For purposes of section 46, the qualifying therapeutic discovery project credit for any taxable year is an amount equal to 50 percent of the qualified investment for such taxable year with respect to any qualifying therapeutic discovery project of an eligible taxpayer.

(b) Qualified investment.
(1) In general. For purposes of subsection (a), the qualified investment for any taxable year is the aggregate amount of the costs paid or incurred in such taxable year for expenses necessary for and directly related to the conduct of a qualifying therapeutic discovery project.

(2) Limitation. The amount which is treated as qualified investment for all taxable years with respect to any qualifying therapeutic discovery project shall not exceed the amount certified by the Secretary as eligible for the credit under this section.

(3) Exclusions. The qualified investment for any taxable year with respect to any qualifying therapeutic discovery project shall not take into account any cost—
(A) for remuneration for an employee described in section 162(m)(3),
(B) for interest expenses,
(C) for facility maintenance expenses,
(D) which is identified as a service cost under section 1.263A-1(e)(4) of title 26, Code of Federal Regulations, or
(E) for any other expense as determined by the Secretary as appropriate to carry out the purposes of this section.

(4) Certain progress expenditure rules made applicable. In the case of costs described in paragraph (1) that are paid for property of a character subject to an allowance for depreciation, rules similar to the rules of subsections (c)(4) and (d) of section 46 (as in effect on the day before the date of the enactment of the Revenue Reconciliation Act of 1990) shall apply for purposes of this section.

(5) Application of subsection. An investment shall be considered a qualified investment under this subsection only if such investment is made in a taxable year beginning in 2009 or 2010.

(c) Definitions.
(1) Qualifying therapeutic discovery project. The term "qualifying therapeutic discovery project" means a project which is designed—
(A) to treat or prevent diseases or conditions by conducting pre-clinical activities, clinical trials, and clinical studies, or carrying out research protocols, for the pur-

1,245

pose of securing approval of a product under section 505(b) of the Federal Food, Drug, and Cosmetic Act or section 351(a) of the Public Health Service Act,

(B) to diagnose diseases or conditions or to determine molecular factors related to diseases or conditions by developing molecular diagnostics to guide therapeutic decisions, or

(C) to develop a product, process, or technology to further the delivery or administration of therapeutics.

(2) Eligible taxpayer.

(A) In general. The term "eligible taxpayer" means a taxpayer which employs not more than 250 employees in all businesses of the taxpayer at the time of the submission of the application under subsection (d)(2).

(B) Aggregation rules. All persons treated as a single employer under subsection (a) or (b) of section 52, or subsection (m) or (o) of section 414, shall be so treated for purposes of this paragraph.

(3) Facility maintenance expenses. The term "facility maintenance expenses" means costs paid or incurred to maintain a facility, including—

(A) mortgage or rent payments,

(B) insurance payments,

(C) utility and maintenance costs, and

(D) costs of employment of maintenance personnel.

(d) Qualifying therapeutic discovery project program.

(1) Establishment.

(A) In general. Not later than 60 days after the date of the enactment of this section, the Secretary, in consultation with the Secretary of Health and Human Services, shall establish a qualifying therapeutic discovery project program to consider and award certifications for qualified investments eligible for credits under this section to qualifying therapeutic discovery project sponsors.

(B) Limitation. The total amount of credits that may be allocated under the program shall not exceed $1,000,000,000 for the 2-year period beginning with 2009.

(2) Certification.

(A) Application period. Each applicant for certification under this paragraph shall submit an application containing such information as the Secretary may require during the period beginning on the date the Secretary establishes the program under paragraph (1).

(B) Time for review of applications. The Secretary shall take action to approve or deny any application under subparagraph (A) within 30 days of the submission of such application.

(C) Multi-year applications. An application for certification under subparagraph (A) may include a request for an allocation of credits for more than 1 of the years described in paragraph (1)(B).

(3) Selection criteria. In determining the qualifying therapeutic discovery projects with respect to which qualified investments may be certified under this section, the Secretary—

(A) shall take into consideration only those projects that show reasonable potential—

(i) to result in new therapies—

(I) to treat areas of unmet medical need, or

(II) to prevent, detect, or treat chronic or acute diseases and conditions,

(ii) to reduce long-term health care costs in the United States, or

(iii) to significantly advance the goal of curing cancer within the 30-year period beginning on the date the Secretary establishes the program under paragraph (1), and

(B) shall take into consideration which projects have the greatest potential—

(i) to create and sustain (directly or indirectly) high quality, high-paying jobs in the United States, and

(ii) to advance United States competitiveness in the fields of life, biological, and medical sciences.

(4) Disclosure of allocations. The Secretary shall, upon making a certification under this subsection, publicly disclose the identity of the applicant and the amount of the credit with respect to such applicant.

(e) Special rules.

(1) Basis adjustment. For purposes of this subtitle, if a credit is allowed under this section for an expenditure related to property of a character subject to an allowance for depreciation, the basis of such property shall be reduced by the amount of such credit.

(2) Denial of double benefit.

(A) Bonus depreciation. A credit shall not be allowed under this section for any investment for which bonus depreciation is allowed under section 168(k), 1400L(b)(1), or 1400N(d)(1).

(B) Deductions. No deduction under this subtitle shall be allowed for the portion of the expenses otherwise allowable as a deduction taken into account in determining the credit under this section for the taxable year which is equal to the amount of the credit determined for such taxable year under subsection (a) attributable to such portion. This subparagraph shall not apply to expenses related to property of a character subject to an allowance for depreciation the basis of which is reduced under paragraph (1), or which are described in section 280C(g).

(C) Credit for research activities.

(i) In general. Except as provided in clause (ii), any expenses taken into account under this section for a taxable year shall not be taken into account for purposes of determining the credit allowable under section 41 or 45C for such taxable year.

(ii) Expenses included in determining base period research expenses. Any expenses for any taxable year which are qualified research expenses (within the meaning of section 41(b)) shall be taken into account in determining base period research expenses for purposes of applying section 41 to subsequent taxable years.

(f) Coordination with department of treasury grants.

In the case of any investment with respect to which the Secretary makes a grant under section 9023(e) of the Patient Protection and Affordable Care Act of 2009—

(1) Denial of credit. No credit shall be determined under this section with respect to such investment for the taxable year in which such grant is made or any subsequent taxable year.

(2) Recapture of credits for progress expenditures made before grant. If a credit was determined under this section with respect to such investment for any taxable year ending before such grant is made—

(A) the tax imposed under subtitle A on the taxpayer for the taxable year in which such grant is made shall be increased by so much of such credit as was allowed under section 38,

(B) the general business carryforwards under section 39 shall be adjusted so as to recapture the portion of such credit which was not so allowed, and

Tax credits

(C) the amount of such grant shall be determined without regard to any reduction in the basis of any property of a character subject to an allowance for depreciation by reason of such credit.

(3) Treatment of grants. Any such grant shall not be includible in the gross income of the taxpayer.

In 2010, P.L. 111-148, Sec. 9023(a), added Code Sec. 48D, effective for amounts paid or incurred after 12/31/2008, in taxable years beginning after such date. Sec. 9023(e) of this Act, provides:

"(e) Grants for qualified investments in therapeutic discovery projects in lieu of tax credits.

"(1) In general. Upon application, the Secretary of the Treasury shall, subject to the requirements of this subsection, provide a grant to each person who makes a qualified investment in a qualifying therapeutic discovery project in the amount of 50 percent of such investment. No grant shall be made under this subsection with respect to any investment unless such investment is made during a taxable year beginning in 2009 or 2010.

"(2) Application.

"(A) In general. at the stated election of the applicant, an application for certification under section 48D(d)(2) of the Internal Revenue Code of 1986 for a credit under such section for the taxable year of the applicant which begins in 2009 shall be considered to be an application for a grant under paragraph (1) for such taxable year.

"(B) Taxable years beginning in 2010.—An application for a grant under paragraph (1) for a taxable year beginning in 2010 shall be submitted—

"(i) not earlier than the day after the last day of such taxable year, and "'(ii) not later than the due date (including extensions) for filing the return of tax for such taxable year.

"(C) Information to be submitted. An application for a grant under paragraph (1) shall include such information and be in such form as the Secretary may require to state the amount of the credit allowable (but for the receipt of a grant under this subsection) under section 48D for the taxable year for the qualified investment with respect to which such application is made.

"(3) Time for payment of grant.

"(A) In general. The Secretary of the Treasury shall make payment of the amount of any grant under paragraph (1) during the 30-day period beginning on the later of—

"(i) the date of the application for such grant, or

"(ii) the date the qualified investment for which the grant is being made is made.

"(B) Regulations. In the case of investments of an ongoing nature, the Secretary shall issue regulations to determine the date on which a qualified investment shall be deemed to have been made for purposes of this paragraph.

"(4) Qualified investment. For purposes of this subsection, the term 'qualified investment' means a qualified investment that is certified under section 48D(d) of the Internal Revenue Code of 1986 for purposes of the credit under such section 48D.

"(5) Application of certain rules.

"(A) In general. In making grants under this subsection, the Secretary of the Treasury shall apply rules similar to the rules of section 50 of the Internal Revenue Code of 1986. In applying such rules, any increase in tax under chapter 1 of such Code by reason of an investment ceasing to be a qualified investment shall be imposed on the person to whom the grant was made.

"(B) Special rules.

"(i) Recapture of excessive grant amounts. If the amount of a grant made under this subsection exceeds the amount allowable as a grant under this subsection, such excess shall be recaptured under subparagraph (A) as if the investment to which such excess portion of the grant relates had ceased to be a qualified investment immediately after such grant was made.

"(ii) Grant information not treated as return information. In no event shall the amount of a grant made under paragraph (1), the identity of the person to whom such grant was made, or a description of the investment with respect to which such grant was made be treated as return information for purposes of section 6103 of the Internal Revenue Code of 1986.

"(6) Exception for certain non-taxpayers. The Secretary of the Treasury shall not make any grant under this subsection to—

"(A) any Federal, State, or local government (or any political subdivision, agency, or instrumentality thereof),

"(B) any organization described in section 501(c) of the Internal Revenue Code of 1986 and exempt from tax under section 501(a) of such Code,

"(C) any entity referred to in paragraph (4) of section 54(j) of such Code, or

"(D) any partnership or other pass-thru entity any partner (or other holder of an equity or profits interest) of which is described in subparagraph (A), (B) or (C).

"In the case of a partnership or other pass-thru entity described in subparagraph (D), partners and other holders of any equity or profits interest shall provide to such partnership or entity such information as the Secretary of the Treasury may require to carry out the purposes of this paragraph.

"(7) Secretary. Any reference in this subsection to the Secretary of the Treasury shall be treated as including the Secretary's delegate.

"(8) Other terms. Any term used in this subsection which is also used in section 48D of the Internal Revenue Code of 1986 shall have the same meaning for purposes of this subsection as when used in such section.

"(9) Denial of double benefit. No credit shall be allowed under section 46(6) of the Internal Revenue Code of 1986 by reason of section 48D of such Code for any investment for which a grant is awarded under this subsection.

"(10) Appropriations. There is hereby appropriated to the Secretary of the Treasury such sums as may be necessary to carry out this subsection.

"(11) Termination. The Secretary of the Treasury shall not make any grant to any person under this subsection unless the application of such person for such grant is received before January 1, 2013.

"(12) Protecting middle class families from tax increases. It is the sense of the Senate that the Senate should reject any procedural maneuver that would raise taxes on middle class families, such as a motion to commit the pending legislation to the Committee on Finance, which is designed to kill legislation that provides tax cuts for American workers and families, including the affordability tax credit and the small business tax credit."

Sec. 49. At-risk rules.
(a) General rule.
(1) Certain nonrecourse financing excluded from credit base.

(A) Limitation. The credit base of any property to which this paragraph applies shall be reduced by the nonqualified nonrecourse financing with respect to such credit base (as of the close of the taxable year in which placed in service).

(B) Property to which paragraph applies. This paragraph applies to any property which—

(i) is placed in service during the taxable year by a taxpayer described in section 465(a)(1), and

(ii) is used in connection with an activity with respect to which any loss is subject to limitation under section 465.

(C) Credit base defined. For purposes of this paragraph, the term "credit base" means—

(i) the portion of the basis of any qualified rehabilitated building attributable to qualified rehabilitation expenditures,

(ii) the basis of any energy property,

(iii) the basis of any property which is part of a qualifying advanced coal project under section 48A,

(iv) the basis of any property which is part of a qualifying gasification project under section 48B,

(v) the basis of any property which is part of a qualifying advanced energy project under section 48C, and

(vi) the basis of any property to which paragraph (1) of section 48D(e) applies which is part of a qualifying therapeutic discovery project under such section 48D.

(D) Nonqualified nonrecourse financing.

(i) In general. For purposes of this paragraph and paragraph (2), the term "nonqualified nonrecourse financing" means any nonrecourse financing which is not qualified commercial financing.

(ii) Qualified commercial financing. For purposes of this paragraph, the term "qualified commercial financing" means any financing with respect to any property if—

(I) such property is acquired by the taxpayer from a person who is not a related person,

(II) the amount of the nonrecourse financing with respect to such property does not exceed 80 percent of the credit base of such property, and

(III) such financing is borrowed from a qualified person or represents a loan from any Federal, State, or local government or instrumentality thereof, or is guaranteed by any Federal, State, or local government.

Such term shall not include any convertible debt.

(iii) Nonrecourse financing. For purposes of this subparagraph, the term "nonrecourse financing" includes—

(I) any amount with respect to which the taxpayer is protected against loss through guarantees, stop-loss agreements, or other similar arrangements, and

(II) except to the extent provided in regulations, any amount borrowed from a person who has an interest (other than as a creditor) in the activity in which the property is used or from a related person to a person (other than the taxpayer) having such an interest.

In the case of amounts borrowed by a corporation from a shareholder, subclause (II) shall not apply to an interest as a shareholder.

(iv) Qualified person. For purposes of this paragraph, the term "qualified person" means any person which is actively and regularly engaged in the business of lending money and which is not—

(I) a related person with respect to the taxpayer,

(II) a person from which the taxpayer acquired the property (or a related person to such person), or

(III) a person who receives a fee with respect to the taxpayer's investment in the property (or a related person to such person).

(v) Related person. For purposes of this subparagraph, the term "related person" has the meaning given such term by section 465(b)(3)(C). Except as otherwise provided in regulations prescribed by the Secretary, the determination of whether a person is a related person shall be made as of the close of the taxable year in which the property is placed in service.

(E) Application to partnerships and S corporations. For purposes of this paragraph and paragraph (2)—

(i) In general. Except as otherwise provided in this subparagraph, in the case of any partnership or S corporation, the determination of whether a partner's or shareholder's allocable share of any financing is nonqualified nonrecourse financing shall be made at the partner or shareholder level.

(ii) Special rule for certain recourse financing of S corporation. A shareholder of an S corporation shall be treated as liable for his allocable share of any financing provided by a qualified person to such corporation if—

(I) such financing is recourse financing (determined at the corporate level), and

(II) such financing is provided with respect to qualified business property of such corporation.

(iii) Qualified business property. For purposes of clause (ii), the term "qualified business property" means any property if—

(I) such property is used by the corporation in the active conduct of a trade or business,

(II) during the entire 12-month period ending on the last day of the taxable year, such corporation had at least 3 full-time employees who were not owner-employees (as defined in section 465(c)(7)(E)(i)) and substantially all the services of whom were services directly related to such trade or business, and

(III) during the entire 12-month period ending on the last day of such taxable year, such corporation had at least 1 full-time employee substantially all of the services of whom were in the active management of the trade or business.

(iv) Determination of allocable share. The determination of any partner's or shareholder's allocable share of any financing shall be made in the same manner as the credit allowable by section 38 with respect to such property.

(F) Special rules for energy property. Rules similar to the rules of subparagraph (F) of section 46(c)(8) (as in effect on the day before the date of the enactment [11/5/90] of the Revenue Reconciliation Act of 1990) shall apply for purposes of this paragraph.

(2) Subsequent decreases in nonqualified nonrecourse financing with respect to the property.

(A) In general. If, at the close of a taxable year following the taxable year in which the property was placed in service, there is a net decrease in the amount of nonqualified nonrecourse financing with respect to such property, such net decrease shall be taken into account as an increase in the credit base for such property in accordance with subparagraph (C).

(B) Certain transactions not taken into account. For purposes of this paragraph, nonqualified nonrecourse financing shall not be treated as decreased through the surrender or other use of property financed by nonqualified nonrecourse financing.

(C) Manner in which taken into account.

(i) Credit determined by reference to taxable year property placed in service. For purposes of determining the amount of credit allowable under section 38 and the amount of credit subject to the early disposition or cessation rules under section 50(a), any increase in a taxpayer's credit base for any property by reason of this paragraph shall be taken into account as if it were property placed in service by the taxpayer in the taxable year in which the property referred to in subparagraph (A) was first placed in service.

(ii) Credit allowed for year of decrease in nonqualified nonrecourse financing. Any credit allowable under this subpart for any increase in qualified investment by reason of this paragraph shall be treated as earned during the taxable year of the decrease in the amount of nonqualified nonrecourse financing.

(b) Increases in nonqualified nonrecourse financing.

(1) In general. If, as of the close of the taxable year, there is a net increase with respect to the taxpayer in the amount of nonqualified nonrecourse financing (within the meaning of subsection (a)(1)) with respect to any property to which subsection (a)(1) applied, then the tax under this chapter for such taxable year shall be increased by an amount equal to the aggregate decrease in credits allowed under section 38 for all prior taxable years which would have resulted from reducing the credit base (as defined in subsection (a)(1)(C)) taken into account with respect to such property by the amount of such net increase. For purposes of determining the amount of credit subject to the early disposition or cessation rules of section 50(a), the net increase in the amount of the nonqualified nonrecourse financing with respect to the property shall be treated as reducing the property's credit base in the year in which the property was first placed in service.

(2) Transfers of debt more than 1 year after initial borrowing not treated as increasing nonqualified nonrecourse financing. For purposes of paragraph (1), the amount of nonqualified nonrecourse financing (within the meaning of subsection (a)(1)(D)) with respect to the taxpayer shall not be treated as increased by reason of a transfer of (or agreement to transfer) any evidence of any indebtedness if such transfer occurs (or such agreement is

Tax credits   Code Sec. 49

entered into) more than 1 year after the date such indebtedness was incurred.

(3) Special rules for certain energy property. Rules similar to the rules of section 47(d)(3) (as in effect on the day before the date of the enactment [11/5/90] of the Revenue Reconciliation Act of 1990) shall apply for purposes of this subsection.

(4) Special rule. Any increase in tax under paragraph (1) shall not be treated as tax imposed by this chapter for purposes of determining the amount of any credit allowable under this chapter.

In 2010, P.L. 111-148, Sec. 9023(c)(1)(A), deleted "and" at the end of clause (a)(1)(C)(iv)... Sec. 9023(c)(1)(B), substituted ", and" for the period at the end of clause (a)(1)(C)(v)... Sec. 9023(c)(1)(C), added clause (a)(1)(C)(vi), effective for amounts paid or incurred after 12/31/2008, in taxable years beginning after such date.

In 2009, P.L. 111-5, Sec. 1302(c)(1), deleted "and" at the end of clause (a)(1)(C)(iii), substituted ", and" for the period at the end of clause (a)(1)(C)(iv), and added clause (a)(1)(C)(v), effective for periods after 2/17/2009, under rules similar to the rules of section 48(m) of the Internal Revenue Code of 1986 (as in effect on the day before the date of enactment of the Revenue Reconciliation Act of 1990 [enacted 11/5/90]).

In 2005, P.L. 109-58, Sec. 1307(c)(1), deleted "and" at the end of clause (a)(1)(C)(ii), deleted clause (a)(1)(C)(iii), and added clauses (a)(1)(C)(iii) and (iv), effective for periods after 8/8/2005, under rules similar to the rules of Code Sec. 48(m) (as in effect on the day before the date of enactment of the Revenue Reconciliation Act of 1990 [enacted 11/5/90]).

Prior to deletion, clause (a)(1)(C)(iii) read as follows:
"(iii) the amortizable basis of any qualified timber property."

In 1998, P.L. 105-206, Sec. 6004(g)(6), substituted "this chapter" for "subpart A, B, D, or G" in para. (b)(4), effective for obligations issued after 12/31/97.

In 1990, P.L. 101-508, Sec. 11813(a), amended Code Sec. 49 as part of the amendment to subpart E, of part IV of subchapter A of chapter 1, effective for property placed in service after 12/31/90, except as provided in Sec. 11813(c)(2) of this Act reproduced in note following Code Sec. 46.

In 1978, P.L. 95-600, Sec. 312(c)(1), repealed Code Sec. 49, effective for tax. yrs. end. after 1978.
Prior to repeal, Code Sec. 49 read as follows:
"Sec. 49. Termination for period beginning April 19, 1969, and ending during 1971.
"(a) General rule.
"For purposes of this subpart, the term 'section 38 property' does not include property—
"(1) the physical construction, reconstruction, or erection of which is begun after April 18, 1969, or
"(2) which is acquired by the taxpayer after April 18, 1969, other than pre-termination property.
"This subsection shall not apply to property described in section 50.
"(b) Pre-termination property.
"For purposes of this subpart—
"(1) Binding contracts. Any property shall be treated as pre-termination property to the extent that such property is constructed, reconstructed, erected, or acquired pursuant to a contract which was, on April 18, 1969, and at all times thereafter, binding on the taxpayer.
"(2) Equipped building rule. If—
"(A) pursuant to a plan of the taxpayer in existence on April 18, 1969 (which plan was not substantially modified at any time after such date and before the taxpayer placed the equipped building in service), the taxpayer has constructed, reconstructed, erected, or acquired a building and the machinery and equipment necessary to the planned use of the building by the taxpayer, and
"(B) more than 50 percent of the aggregate adjusted basis of all the property of a character subject to the allowance for depreciation making up such building as so equipped is attributable to either property the construction, reconstruction, or erection of which was begun by the taxpayer before April 19, 1969, or property the acquisition of which by the taxpayer occurred before such date,
then all property comprising such building as so equipped (and any incidental property adjacent to such building which is necessary to the planned use of the building) shall be pre-termination property. For purposes of subparagraph (B) of the preceding sentence, the rules of paragraphs (1) and (4) shall be applied. For purposes of this paragraph, a special purpose structure shall be treated as a building.
"(3) Plant facility rule.
"(A) General rule. If—
"(i) pursuant to a plan of the taxpayer in existence on April 18, 1969 (which plan was not substantially modified at any time after such date and before the taxpayer placed the plant facility in service), the taxpayer has constructed, reconstructed, or erected a plant facility, and either
"(ii) the construction, reconstruction, or erection of such plant facility was commenced by the taxpayer before April 19, 1969, or

"(iii) more than 50 percent of the aggregate adjusted basis of all the property of a character subject to the allowance for depreciation making up such plant facility is attributable to either property the construction, reconstruction, or erection of which was begun by the taxpayer before April 19, 1969, or property the acquisition of which by the taxpayer occurred before such date,
then all property comprising such plant facility shall be pre-termination property. For purposes of clause (iii) of the preceding sentence, the rules of paragraphs (1) and (4) shall be applied.
"(B) Plant facility defined. For purposes of this paragraph, the term 'plant facility' means a facility which does not include any building (or of which buildings constitute an insignificant portion) and which is—
"(i) a self-contained, single operating unit or processing operation,
"(ii) located on a single site, and
"(iii) identified, on April 18, 1969, in the purchasing and internal financial plans of the taxpayer as a single unitary project.
"(C) Special rule. For purposes of this subsection, if—
"(i) a certificate of convenience and necessity has been issued before April 19, 1969, by a Federal regulatory agency with respect to two or more plant facilities which are included under a single plan of the taxpayer to construct, reconstruct, or erect such plant facilities, and
"(ii) more than 50 percent of the aggregate adjusted basis of all the property of a character subject to the allowance for depreciation making up such plant facilities is attributable to either property the construction, reconstruction, or erection of which was begun by the taxpayer before April 19, 1969, or property the acquisition of which by the taxpayer occurred before such date,
such plant facilities shall be treated as a single plant facility.
"(D) Commencement of construction. For purposes of subparagraph (A)(ii), the construction, reconstruction, or erection of a plant facility shall not be considered to have commenced until construction, reconstruction, or erection has commenced at the site of such plant facility. The preceding sentence shall not apply if the site of such plant facility is not located on land.
"(4) Machinery or equipment rule. Any piece of machinery or equipment—
"(A) more than 50 percent of the parts and components of which (determined on the basis of cost) were held by the taxpayer on April 18, 1969, or are acquired by the taxpayer pursuant to a binding contract which was in effect on such date, for inclusion or use in such piece of machinery or equipment, and
"(B) the cost of the parts and components of which is not an insignificant portion of the total cost,
shall be treated as property which is pre-termination property.
"(5) Certain lease-back transactions, etc.
"(A) Where a person who is a party to a binding contract described in paragraph (1) transfers rights in such contract (or in the property to which such contract relates) to another person but a party to such contract retains a right to use the property under a lease with such other person, than to the extent of the transferred rights such other person shall, for purposes of paragraph (1), succeed to the position of the transferor with respect to such binding contract and such property. In any case in which the lessor does not make an election under section 48(d)—
"(i) the preceding sentence shall apply only if a party to the contract retains the right to use the property under a lease for a term of at least 1 year; and
"(ii) if such use is retained (other than under a long-term lease), the lessor shall be deemed for the purposes of section 47 as having made a disposition of the property at such time as the lessee loses the right to use the property.
"For purposes of clause (ii), if the lessee transfers the lease in a transfer described in paragraph (7), the lessee shall be considered as having the right to use of the property so long as the transferee has such use.
"(B) For purposes of subparagraph (A)—
"(i) a person who holds property (or rights in property) which is pre-termination property by reason of the application of paragraph (4) shall, with respect to such property, be treated as a party to a binding contract described in paragraph (1), and
"(ii) a corporation which is a member of the same affiliated group (as defined in paragraph (8)) as the transferor described in subparagraph (A) and which simultaneously with the transfer of property to another person acquires a right to use such property under a lease with such other person shall be treated as the transferor and as a party to the contract.
"(6) Certain lease and contract obligations.
"(A) Where, pursuant to a binding lease or contract to lease in effect on April 18, 1969, a lessor or lessee is obligated to construct, reconstruct, erect, or acquire property specified in such lease or contract or in a related document filed before April 19, 1969, with a Federal regulatory agency, or property, the specifications of which are readily ascertainable from the terms of such lease or contract or from such related document, any property so constructed, reconstructed, erected, or acquired by the lessor or lessee shall be pre-termination property. In the case of any project which includes property other than the property to be leased to such lessee, the preceding sentence shall be applied, in the case of the lessor, to such other property only if the binding leases and contracts with all lessees in effect on April 18, 1969, cover real property constituting 25 percent or more of the project (determined on the basis of rental value). For purposes of the preceding sentences of this paragraph, in the case of any project where one or more vendor-vendee relationships exist, such vendors and vendees shall be treated as lessors and lessees.
"(B) Where, in order to perform a binding contract or contracts in effect on April 18, 1969, (i) the taxpayer is required to construct, reconstruct, erect, or acquire property specified in any order of a Federal regulatory agency for which application was filed before April 19, 1969, (ii) the property is to be used to transport one or more products under such contract or contracts, and (iii) one or more parties to the contract or contracts are required to take or to provide more than 50 percent of the products to be transported over a substantial portion of the expected useful life of the property, then such property shall be pre-termination property.

1,249

"(C) Where, in order to perform a binding contract in effect on April 18, 1969, the taxpayer is required to construct, reconstruct, erect, or acquire property specified in the contract to be used to produce one or more products and (unless the other party to the contract is a State or a political subdivision of a State which is required by the contract to make substantial expenditures which benefit the taxpayer) the other party to the contract is required to take substantially all of the products to be produced over a substantial portion of the expected useful life of the property, then such property shall be pre-termination property. For purposes of applying the preceding sentence in the case of a contract for the extraction of minerals, property shall be treated as specified in the contract if (i) the specifications for such property are readily ascertainable from the location and characteristics of the mineral properties specified in such contract from which the minerals are to be extracted; (ii) such property is necessary for and is to be used solely in the extraction of minerals under such contract; (iii) the physical construction, reconstruction, or erection of such property is begun by the taxpayer before April 19, 1970, such property is acquired by the taxpayer before April 19, 1970, or such property is constructed, reconstructed, erected, or acquired pursuant to a contract which was, on April 18, 1970, and at all times thereafter, binding on the taxpayer; (iv) such property is placed in service on or before December 31, 1972; (v) such contract is a fixed price contract (except for provisions for price changes under which the loss of the credit allowed by section 38 would not result in a price change); and (vi) such property is not placed in service to replace other property used in extracting minerals under such contract.

"(7) Certain transfers to be disregarded.
"(A) If property or rights under a contract are transferred in—
"(i) a transfer by reason of death,
"(ii) a transaction as a result of which the basis of the property in the hands of the transferee is determined by reference to its basis in the hands of the transferor by reason of the application of section 332, 351, 361, 371(a), 374(a), 721, or 731, or
"(iii) a sale of substantially all of the assets of the transferor pursuant to the terms of a contract, which was on April 18, 1969, and at all times thereafter, binding on the transferee,
and such property (or the property acquired under such contract) would be treated as pre-termination property in the hands of the decedent or the transferor, such property shall be treated as pre-termination property in the hands of the transferee.
"(B) If—
"(i) property or rights under a contract are acquired in a transaction to which section 334(b)(2) applies,
"(ii) the stock of the distributing corporation was acquired before April 19, 1969, or pursuant to a binding contract in effect April 18, 1969, and
"(iii) such property (or the property acquired under such contract) would be treated as pre-termination property in the hands of the distributing corporation, such property shall be treated as pre-termination property in the hands of the distributee.

"(8) Property acquired from affiliated corporation. In the case of property acquired by a corporation which is a member of an affiliated group from another member of the same group—
"(A) such corporation shall be treated as having acquired such property on the date on which it was acquired by such other member,
"(B) such corporation shall be treated as having entered into a binding contract for the construction, reconstruction, erection, or acquisition of such property on the date on which such other member entered into a contract for the construction, reconstruction, erection, or acquisition of such property, and
"(C) such corporation shall be treated as having commenced the construction, reconstruction, or erection of such property on the date on which such other member commenced such construction, reconstruction, or erection.
For purposes of this subsection and subsection (c), a contract between two corporations which are members of the same affiliated group shall not be treated as a binding contract as between such corporations, unless, at all times after June 30, 1969, and prior to the completion of performance of such contract, such corporations are not members of the same affiliated group. For purposes of the preceding sentences, the term 'affiliated group' has the meaning assigned to it by section 1504(a), except that all corporations shall be treated as includible corporations (without any exclusion under section 1504(b)).

"(9) Barges for ocean-going vessels. Barges specifically designed and constructed, reconstructed, erected, or acquired for use with ocean-going vessels which are designed to carry barges and which are pre-termination property, but not in excess of—
"(A) the number to be used with such vessels specified in applications for mortgage or construction loan insurance filed with the Secretary of Commerce on or before April 18, 1969, under title XI of the Merchant Marine Act, 1936, or
"(B) if subparagraph (A) does not apply and if more than 50 percent of the barges which the taxpayer establishes as necessary to the initial planned use of such vessels are pre-termination property (determined without regard to this paragraph), the number which the taxpayer establishes as so necessary,
together with the machinery and equipment to be installed on such barges and necessary for their planned use, shall be treated as pre-termination property.

"(10) Certain new-design products. Where—
"(A) on April 18, 1969, the taxpayer had undertaken a project to produce a product of a new design pursuant to binding contracts in effect on such date which—
"(i) were fixed-price contracts (except for provisions requiring or permitting price changes resulting from changes in rates of pay or costs of materials), and
"(ii) covered more than 50 percent of the entire production of such design to be delivered by the taxpayer before January 1, 1973, and
"(B) on or before April 18, 1969, more than 50 percent of the aggregate adjusted basis of all property of a character subject to the allowance for depreciation required to carry out such binding contracts was property the construction, reconstruction, or erection of which had begun by the taxpayer, or had been acquired by the taxpayer (or was under a binding contract for such construction, reconstruction, erection, or acquisition),
then all tangible personal property placed in service by the taxpayer before January 1, 1972, which is required to carry out such binding contracts shall be deemed to be pre-termination property. For purposes of subparagraph (B) of the preceding sentence, jigs, dies, templates, and similar items which can be used only for the manufacture or assembly of the production under the project and which were described in written engineering and internal financial plans of the taxpayer in existence on April 18, 1969, shall be treated as property which on such date was under a binding contract for construction.

"(c) Leased property.
"In the case of property which is leased after April 18, 1969 (other than pursuant to a binding contract to lease entered into before April 19, 1969), which is section 38 property with respect to the lessor but is property which would not be section 38 property because of the application of subsection (a) if acquired by the lessee, and which is property of the same kind which the lessor ordinarily sold to customers before April 19, 1969, or ordinarily leased before such date and made an election under section 48(d), such property shall not be section 38 property with respect to either the lessor or the lessee."

In 1971, P.L. 92-178, Sec. 101(b)(1), added the last sentence of subsec. (a), effective 12/10/71.
—P.L. 92-178, Sec. 101(b)(2), substituted "For purposes of this subpart" for "For purposes of this section" in subsec. (b), effective 12/10/71.
—P.L. 92-178, Sec. 101(b)(3), repealed subsec. (d), effective 12/10/71.
Prior to repeal, subsec. (d) read as follows:
"(d) Property placed in service after 1975.
"For purposes of this subpart, the term 'section 38 property' does not include any property placed in service after December 31, 1975."
—P.L. 92-178, Sec. 101(b)(4), amended the title of Code Sec. 49, effective 12/10/71.
Prior to amendment, the title of Code Sec. 49 read as follows:
"Termination of credit."
In 1969, P.L. 91-172, Sec. 703(a), added Code Sec. 49.

Sec. 50. Other special rules.
(a) Recapture in case of dispositions, etc.
Under regulations prescribed by the Secretary—
(1) Early disposition, etc.
(A) General rule. If, during any taxable year, investment credit property is disposed of, or otherwise ceases to be investment credit property with respect to the taxpayer, before the close of the recapture period, then the tax under this chapter for such taxable year shall be increased by the recapture percentage of the aggregate decrease in the credits allowed under section 38 for all prior taxable years which would have resulted solely from reducing to zero any credit determined under this subpart with respect to such property.
(B) Recapture percentage. For purposes of subparagraph (A), the recapture percentage shall be determined in accordance with the following table:

If the property ceases to be investment credit property within—	The recapture percentage is:
(i) One full year after placed in service	100
(ii) One full year after the close of the period described in clause (i)	80
(iii) One full year after the close of the period described in clause (ii)	60
(iv) One full year after the close of the period described in clause (iii)	40
(v) One full year after the close of the period described in clause (iv)	20

(2) Property ceases to qualify for progress expenditures.
(A) In general. If during any taxable year any building to which section 47(d) applied ceases (by reason of sale or other disposition, cancellation or abandonment of contract, or otherwise) to be, with respect to the taxpayer, property which, when placed in service, will be a qualified rehabilitated building, then the tax under this chapter for such taxable year shall be increased by an

amount equal to the aggregate decrease in the credits allowed under section 38 for all prior taxable years which would have resulted solely from reducing to zero the credit determined under this subpart with respect to such building.

(B) Certain excess credit recaptured. Any amount which would have been applied as a reduction under paragraph (2) of section 47(b) but for the fact that a reduction under such paragraph cannot reduce the amount taken into account under section 47(b)(1) below zero shall be treated as an amount required to be recaptured under subparagraph (A) for the taxable year during which the building is placed in service.

(C) Certain sales and leasebacks. Under regulations prescribed by the Secretary, a sale by, and leaseback to, a taxpayer who, when the property is placed in service, will be a lessee to whom the rules referred to in subsection (d)(5) apply shall not be treated as a cessation described in subparagraph (A) to the extent that the amount which will be passed through to the lessee under such rules with respect to such property is not less than the qualified rehabilitation expenditures properly taken into account by the lessee under section 47(d) with respect to such property.

(D) Coordination with paragraph (1). If, after property is placed in service, there is a disposition or other cessation described in paragraph (1), then paragraph (1) shall be applied as if any credit which was allowable by reason of section 47(d) and which has not been required to be recaptured before such disposition, cessation, or change in use were allowable for the taxable year the property was placed in service.

(E) Special rules. Rules similar to the rules of this paragraph shall apply in cases where qualified progress expenditures were taken into account under the rules referred to in section 48(b).

(3) **Carrybacks and carryovers adjusted.** In the case of any cessation described in paragraph (1) or (2), the carrybacks and carryovers under section 39 shall be adjusted by reason of such cessation.

(4) **Subsection not to apply in certain cases.** Paragraphs (1) and (2) shall not apply to—

(A) a transfer by reason of death, or

(B) a transaction to which section 381(a) applies.

For purposes of this subsection, property shall not be treated as ceasing to be investment credit property with respect to the taxpayer by reason of a mere change in the form of conducting the trade or business so long as the property is retained in such trade or business as investment credit property and the taxpayer retains a substantial interest in such trade or business.

(5) **Definitions and special rules.**

(A) Investment credit property. For purposes of this subsection, the term "investment credit property" means any property eligible for a credit determined under this subpart.

(B) Transfer between spouses or incident to divorce. In the case of any transfer described in subsection (a) of section 1041—

(i) the foregoing provisions of this subsection shall not apply, and

(ii) the same tax treatment under this subsection with respect to the transferred property shall apply to the transferee as would have applied to the transferor.

(C) Special rule. Any increase in tax under paragraph (1) or (2) shall not be treated as tax imposed by this chapter for purposes of determining the amount of any credit allowable under this chapter.

(b) **Certain property not eligible.**

No credit shall be determined under this subpart with respect to—

(1) **Property used outside United States.**

(A) In general. Except as provided in subparagraph (B), no credit shall be determined under this subpart with respect to any property which is used predominantly outside the United States.

(B) Exceptions. Subparagraph (A) shall not apply to any property described in section 168(g)(4).

(2) **Property used for lodging.** No credit shall be determined under this subpart with respect to any property which is used predominantly to furnish lodging or in connection with the furnishing of lodging. The preceding sentence shall not apply to—

(A) nonlodging commercial facilities which are available to persons not using the lodging facilities on the same basis as they are available to persons using the lodging facilities;

(B) property used by a hotel or motel in connection with the trade or business of furnishing lodging where the predominant portion of the accommodations is used by transients;

(C) a certified historic structure to the extent of that portion of the basis which is attributable to qualified rehabilitation expenditures; and

(D) any energy property.

(3) **Property used by certain tax-exempt organization.** No credit shall be determined under this subpart with respect to any property used by an organization (other than a cooperative described in section 521) which is exempt from the tax imposed by this chapter unless such property is used predominantly in an unrelated trade or business the income of which is subject to tax under section 511. If the property is debt-financed property (as defined in section 514(b)), the amount taken into account for purposes of determining the amount of the credit under this subpart with respect to such property shall be that percentage of the amount (which but for this paragraph would be so taken into account) which is the same percentage as is used under section 514(a), for the year the property is placed in service, in computing the amount of gross income to be taken into account during such taxable year with respect to such property. If any qualified rehabilitated building is used by the tax-exempt organization pursuant to a lease, this paragraph shall not apply for purposes of determining the amount of the rehabilitation credit.

(4) **Property used by governmental units or foreign persons or entities.**

(A) In general. No credit shall be determined under this subpart with respect to any property used—

(i) by the United States, any State or political subdivision thereof, any possession of the United States, or any agency or instrumentality of any of the foregoing, or

(ii) by any foreign person or entity (as defined in section 168(h)(2)(C)), but only with respect to property to which section 168(h)(2)(A)(iii) applies (determined after the application of section 168(h)(2)(B)).

(B) Exception for short-term leases. This paragraph and paragraph (3) shall not apply to any property by reason of use under a lease with a term of less than 6 months (determined under section 168(i)(3)).

Code Sec. 50(b)(4)(C)   **Tax credits**

(C) Exception for qualified rehabilitated buildings leased to governments, etc. If any qualified rehabilitated building is leased to a governmental unit (or a foreign person or entity) this paragraph shall not apply for purposes of determining the rehabilitation credit with respect to such building.

(D) Special rules for partnerships, etc. For purposes of this paragraph and paragraph (3), rules similar to the rules of paragraphs (5) and (6) of section 168(h) shall apply.

(E) Cross reference. For special rules for the application of this paragraph and paragraph (3), see section 168(h).

(c) Basis adjustment to investment credit property.

(1) In general. For purposes of this subtitle, if a credit is determined under this subpart with respect to any property, the basis of such property shall be reduced by the amount of the credit so determined.

(2) Certain dispositions. If during any taxable year there is a recapture amount determined with respect to any property the basis of which was reduced under paragraph (1), the basis of such property (immediately before the event resulting in such recapture) shall be increased by an amount equal to such recapture amount. For purposes of the preceding sentence, the term "recapture amount" means any increase in tax (or adjustment in carrybacks or carryovers) determined under subsection (a).

(3) Special rule. In the case of any energy credit—

(A) only 50 percent of such credit shall be taken into account under paragraph (1), and

(B) only 50 percent of any recapture amount attributable to such credit shall be taken into account under paragraph (2).

(4) Recapture of reductions.

(A) In general. For purposes of sections 1245 and 1250, any reduction under this subsection shall be treated as a deduction allowed for depreciation.

(B) Special rule for section 1250. For purposes of section 1250(b), the determination of what would have been the depreciation adjustments under the straight line method shall be made as if there had been no reduction under this section.

(5) Adjustment in basis of interest in partnership or S corporation. The adjusted basis of—

(A) a partner's interest in a partnership, and

(B) stock in an S corporation,

shall be appropriately adjusted to take into account adjustments made under this subsection in the basis of property held by the partnership or S corporation (as the case may be).

(d) Certain rules made applicable.

For purposes of this subpart, rules similar to the rules of the following provisions (as in effect on the day before the date of the enactment [11/5/90] of the Revenue Reconciliation Act of 1990) shall apply:

(1) Section 46(e) (relating to limitations with respect to certain persons).

(2) Section 46(f) (relating to limitation in case of certain regulated companies).

(3) Section 46(h) (relating to special rules for cooperatives).

(4) Paragraphs (2) and (3) of section 48(b) (relating to special rule for sale-leasebacks).

(5) Section 48(d) (relating to certain leased property).

(6) Section 48(f) (relating to estates and trusts).

(7) Section 48(r) (relating to certain 501(d) organizations).

Paragraphs (1)(A), (2)(A), and (4) of section 46(e) referred to in paragraph (1) of this subsection shall not apply to any taxable year beginning after December 31, 1995.

In **2005**, P.L. 109-135, Sec. 412(o), substituted "section 48(b)" for "section 48(a)(5)" in subpara. (a)(2)(E), effective 12/21/2005.

In **2004**, P.L. 108-357, Sec. 322(d)(2)(D), deleted "or reforestation credit" after "energy credit" in para. (c)(3), effective for expenditures paid or incurred after 10/22/2004.

In **1998**, P.L. 105-206, Sec. 6004(g)(7), substituted "this chapter" for "subpart A, B, D, or G" in subpara. (a)(5)(C), effective for obligations issued after 12/31/97.

In **1996**, P.L. 104-188, Sec. 1616(b)(1), added the sentence at the end of subsec. (d), effective for tax. yrs. begin. after 12/31/95.

—P.L. 104-188, Sec. 1702(h)(11), substituted "section 48(a)(5)" for "section 48(a)(5)(A)" in subpara. (a)(2)(E), effective for property placed in service after 12/31/90, except as provided in Sec. 11813(c)(2) of this Act, reproduced in note following Code Sec. 46.

—P.L. 104-188, Sec. 1704(t)(29), substituted "subsection (d)(5)" for "subsection (c)(4)" in subpara. (a)(2)(C), effective 8/20/96.

In **1990**, P.L. 101-508, Sec. 11813(a), added Code Sec. 50 as part of the amendment to subpart E, of part IV of subchapter A of chapter 1, effective for property placed in service after 12/31/90, except as provided in Sec. 11813(c)(2) of this Act, reproduced in note following Code Sec. 46.

Sec. 50. Repealed.

In **1978**, P.L. 95-600, Sec. 312(c)(1), repealed Code Sec. 50, effective for tax. yrs. end. after 12/31/78.

Prior to repeal, Code Sec. 50 read as follows:

"SEC. 50. RESTORATION OF CREDIT.

"(a) General rule.

"Section 49(a) (relating to termination of credit) shall not apply to property—

"(1) the construction, reconstruction, or erection of which—

"(A) is completed by the taxpayer after August 15, 1971, or

"(B) is begun by the taxpayer after March 31, 1971, or

"(2) which is acquired by the taxpayer—

"(A) after August 15, 1971, or

"(B) after March 31, 1971, and before August 16, 1971, pursuant to an order which the taxpayer establishes was placed after March 31, 1971.

"(b) Transitional rule.

"In applying section 46(c)(1)(A) in the case of property described in subsection (a)(1)(A) the construction, reconstruction, or erection of which is begun before April 1, 1971, there shall be taken into account only that portion of the basis which is properly attributable to construction, reconstruction, or erection after August 15, 1971. This subsection shall not apply to pre-termination property (within the meaning of section 49(b))."

In **1976**, P.L. 94-455, Sec. 804(e)(2), provided the following with respect to elections described in subsec. (a);

"(2) Election may also apply to property described in section 50(a).— At the election of the taxpayer, made within 1 year after the date of the enactment of this Act in such manner as the Secretary of the Treasury or his delegate may by regulations prescribe, the amendments made by subsections (a) and (b) shall also apply to property which is property described in section 50(a) of the Internal Revenue Code of 1954 and which is placed in service in taxable years beginning before January 1, 1975."

(For amendments made by subsecs. (a) and (b) of the Act, see notes for Code Secs. 48 and 47, respectively.)

In **1971**, P.L. 92-178, Sec. 101(a), added Code Sec. 50.

SUBPART C. REPEALED

Sec.

50A. [Repealed.]

50B. [Repealed.]

In **1984**, P.L. 98-369, Sec. 474(m)(2), repealed subpart C and items 50A and 50B. Prior to repeal subpart C and items 50A and 50B read as follows:

"SUBPART C — RULES FOR COMPUTING CREDIT FOR EXPENSES OF WORK INCENTIVE PROGRAMS

"Sec.

"50A. Amount of credit.

"50B. Definitions; special rules."

In **1971**, P.L. 92-178, Sec. 601(b), added Subpart C.

Sec. 50A. Repealed.

In **1984**, P.L. 98-369, Sec. 474(m)(2), repealed Code Sec. 50A, effective for tax. yrs. begin. after 12/31/83 and to carrybacks from tax. yrs. begin. after 12/31/83.

Prior to repeal, Code Sec. 50A read as follows.

"SEC. 50A. AMOUNT OF CREDIT.

"(a) Determination of amount.

1,252

"(1) General rule. The amount of the credit allowed by section 40 for the taxable year shall be equal to the sum of—
"(A) 50 percent of the first-year work incentive program expenses, and
"(B) 25 percent of the second-year work incentive program expenses.
"(2) Limitation based on amount of tax. Notwithstanding paragraph (1), the amount of the credit allowed by section 40 for the taxable year shall not exceed the liability for tax for the taxable year.
"(3) Liability for tax. For purposes of paragraph (2), the liability for tax for the taxable year shall be the tax imposed by this chapter for such year, reduced by the sum of the credit allowable under—
"(A) section 33 (relating to foreign tax credit),
"(B) section 37 (relating to credit for the elderly),
"(C) section 38 (relating to investment in certain depreciable property), and
"(D) section 41 (relating to contributions to candidates for public office).
For purposes of this paragraph, any tax imposed for the taxable year by section 56 (relating to minimum tax for tax preferences), section 72(m)(5)(B) (relating to 10 percent tax on premature distributions to owner-employees) section 72(q)(1) (relating to 5-percent tax on premature distributions under annuity contracts), section 402(e) (relating to tax on lump sum distributions), section 408(f) (relating to additional tax on income from certain retirement accounts), section 531 (relating to accumulated earnings tax), section 541 (relating to personal holding company tax), or section 1374 (relating to tax on certain capital gains of S corporations), and any additional tax imposed for the taxable year by section 1351(d)(1) (relating to recoveries of foreign expropriation losses), shall not be considered tax imposed by this chapter for such year.
"(4) Limitation with respect to nonbusiness eligible employees.
"(A) In general. In the case of any work incentive program expenses paid or incurred by the taxpayer during the taxable year to eligible employees whose services are not performed in connection with a trade or business of the taxpayer—
"(i) paragraph (1)(A) shall be applied by substituting '35 percent' for '50 percent',
"(ii) subparagraph (B) of paragraph (1) shall not apply, and
"(iii) the aggregate amount of such work incentive program expenses which may be taken into account under paragraph (1) for such taxable year may not exceed $12,000.
"(B) Dependent care credit may not be claimed. No credit shall be allowed under section 44A with respect to any amounts paid or incurred by the taxpayer with respect to which the taxpayer is allowed a credit under section 40.
"(C) Married individuals. In the case of a husband or wife who files a separate return, subparagraph (A) shall be applied by substituting '$6,000' for '$12,000'. The preceding sentence shall not apply if the spouse of the taxpayer has no work incentive program expenses described in such subparagraph for the taxable year.
"(b) Carryback and carryover of unused credit.
"(1) Allowance of credit. If the amount of the credit determined under subsection (a)(1) for any taxable year exceeds the limitation provided by subsection (a)(2) for such taxable year (hereinafter in this subsection referred to as 'unused credit year'), such excess shall be—
"(A) a work incentive program credit carryback to each of the 3 taxable years preceding the unused credit year, and
"(B) a work incentive program credit carryover to each of the 7 taxable years following the unused credit year,
and shall be added to the amount allowable as a credit by section 40 for such years, except that such excess may be a carryback only to a taxable year beginning after December 31, 1971. The entire amount of the unused credit for an unused credit year shall be carried to the earliest of the 10 taxable years to which (by reason of subparagraphs (A) and (B)) such credit may be carried, and then to each of the other 9 taxable years to the credit that, because of the limitation contained in paragraph (2), such unused credit may not be added for a prior taxable year to which such unused credit may be carried. In the case of an unused credit for an unused credit year ending after December 31, 1973, this paragraph shall be applied by substituting '15' for '7' in subparagraph (B), and by substituting '18' for '10', and '17' for '9' in the second sentence.
"(2) Limitation. The amount of the unused credit which may be added under paragraph (1) for any preceding or succeeding taxable year shall not exceed the amount by which the limitation provided by subsection (a)(2) for such taxable year exceeds the sum of—
"(A) the credit allowable under subsection (a)(1) for such taxable year, and
"(B) the amounts which, by reason of this subsection, are added to the amount allowable for such taxable year and attributable to taxable years preceding the unused credit year."
In **1983**, P.L. 97-448, Sec. 102(d)(2), added para. (c)(3) to Sec. 209 of P.L. 97-34, the effective date for amendments made by Sec. 207(c)(1) of P.L. 97-34, see below.
In **1982**, P.L. 97-354, Sec. 5(a)(9), substituted "section 1374 (relating to tax on certain capital gains of S corporations)," for "section 1378 (relating to tax on certain capital gains of subchapter S corporations)," in the second sentence of para. (a)(3), effective for tax. yrs. begin. after 12/31/82.
—P.L. 97-248, Sec. 265(b)(2)(A)(ii), added "section 72(q)(1) (relating to 5-percent tax on premature distributions under annuity contracts) after 'owner-employees)' in para. (a)(3), effective for distributions after 12/31/82.
In **1981**, P.L. 97-34, Sec. 207(c)(1), added the sentence at the end of para. (b)(1), effective for unused credit years end. after 12/31/73. Sec. 209(c)(3) of the Act provides:
"(3) Carryover must have been alive in 1981. The amendments made by subsections (a), (b), and (c) of section 207 shall not apply to any amount which, under the law in effect on the day before the date of the enactment of this Act, could not be carried to a taxable year ending in 1981."

In **1980**, P.L. 96-222, Sec. 103(a)(7)(D)(i), substituted " '$6,000' for " '$6,000' and" in subpara. (a)(4)(C) [Inoperative, corrected by Sec. 6(c)(1) of P.L. 96-178, see below].
—P.L. 96-178, Sec. 6(c)(1), substituted " '$6,000' for" for " '$6000' and" in subpara. (a)(4)(C).
—P.L. 96-178, Sec. 6(a), added a new last sentence to Sec. 322(e)(1) of P.L. 95-600, reproduced below.
In **1978**, P.L. 95-600, Sec. 322(a), amended paras. (a)(1) and (2) . . . Sec. 322(b), deleted paras. (a)(4), (5) and (6) and added new para. (a)(4) . . . Sec. 322(c), repealed subsecs. (c) and (d). . . . Sec. 322(e)(1), of this Act provides
"(1) In general. Except as otherwise provided in this subsection, the amendments made by this section shall apply to work incentive program expenses paid or incurred after December 31, 1978, in taxable years ending after such date; except that so much of the amendment made by subsection (a) as affects section 50A(a)(2) of the Internal Revenue Code of 1954 shall apply to taxable years beginning after December 31, 1978. For purposes of applying 50A(a)(2) of the Internal Revenue Code of 1954 with respect to a taxable year beginning before January 1, 1979, the rules of sections 50A(a)(4), 50A(a)(5), and 50B(e)(3) of such Code (as in effect on the day before the date of the enactment of this Act shall apply)."
Prior to amendment, paras. (a)(1), and (2) read as follows:
"(1) General rule. The amount of the credit allowed by section 40 for the taxable year shall be equal to 20 percent of the work incentive program expenses (as defined in section 50B(a)).
"(2) Limitation based on amount of tax. Notwithstanding paragraph (1), the credit allowed by section 40 for the taxable year shall not exceed—
"(A) so much of the liability for tax for the taxable year as does not exceed $50,000, plus
"(B) 50 percent of so much of the liability for tax for the taxable year as exceeds $50,000.
The preceding sentence shall not apply to so much of the credit allowed by section 40 as is attributable to Federal welfare recipient employment incentive expenses described in subsection (a)(6)(B)."
Prior to deletion, paras. (a)(4)-(6) read as follows:
"(4) Married individuals. In the case of a husband or wife who files a separate return, the amount specified under subparagraphs (A) and (B) of paragraph (2) shall be $25,000 in lieu of $50,000. This paragraph shall not apply if the spouse of the taxpayer has no work incentive program expenses for, and no unused credit carryback or carryover to, the taxable year of such spouse which ends within or with the taxpayer's taxable year.
"(5) Controlled groups. In the case of a controlled group, the $50,000 amount specified under paragraph (2) shall be reduced for each component member of such group by apportioning $50,000 among the component members of such group in such manner as the Secretary shall by regulations prescribe. For purposes of the preceding sentence, the term 'controlled group' has the meaning assigned to such term by section 1563(a).
"(6) Limitation with respect to certain eligible employees.
"(A) Nonbusiness eligible employees. Notwithstanding paragraph (1), the credit allowed by section 40 with respect to Federal welfare recipient employment incentive expenses paid or incurred by the taxpayer during the taxable year to an eligible employee whose services are not performed in connection with a trade or business of the taxpayer shall not exceed $1,000.
"(B) Child day care services eligible employees. Notwithstanding paragraph (1), the credit allowed by section 40 with respect to Federal welfare recipient employment incentive expenses paid or incurred by the taxpayer during the taxable year to an eligible employee whose services are performed in connection with a child day care services program, conducted by the taxpayer, shall not exceed $1,000."
Prior to repeal, subsecs. (c) and (d) read as follows:
"(c) Early termination of employment by employer, etc.
"(1) General rule. Under regulations prescribed by the Secretary—
"(A) Work incentive program expenses. If the employment of any employee with respect to whom work incentive program expenses are taken into account under subsection (a) is terminated by the taxpayer at any time during the first 90 days of such employment (whether or not consecutive) or before the close of the 90th calendar day after the day in which such employee completes 90 days of employment with the taxpayer, the tax under this chapter for the taxable year in which such employment is terminated shall be increased by an amount (determined under such regulations) equal to the credits allowed under section 40 for such taxable year and all prior taxable years attributable to work incentive program expenses paid or incurred with respect to such employee.
"(B) Carrybacks and carryovers adjusted. In the case of any termination of employment to which subparagraph (A) applies, the carrybacks and carryovers under subsection (b) shall be properly adjusted.
"(2) Subsection not to apply in certain cases.
"(A) In General. Paragraph (1) shall not apply to—
"(i) a termination of employment of an employee who voluntarily leaves the employment of the taxpayer,
"(ii) a termination of employment of an individual who, before the close of the period referred to in paragraph (1)(A), becomes disabled to perform the services of such employment, unless such disability is removed before the close of such period and the taxpayer fails to offer reemployment to such individual,
"(iii) a termination of employment of an individual, if it is determined under the applicable State unemployment compensation law that the termination was due to the misconduct of such individual,
"(iv) a termination of employment of an individual with respect to whom Federal welfare recipient employment incentive expenses (as described in section 50B(a)(2)) are taken into account under subsection (a); or

"(v) a termination of employment of an individual due to a substantial reduction in the trade or business operations of the taxpayer.

"(B) Change in form of business, etc. For purposes of paragraph (1), the employment relationship between the employee and an employer shall not be treated as terminated—

"(i) by a transaction to which section 381(a) applies, if the employee continues to be employed by the acquiring corporation, or

"(ii) by reason of a mere change in the form of conducting the trade or business of the taxpayer, if the employee continues to be employed in such trade or business and the taxpayer retains a substantial interest in such trade or business.

"(3) Special rule. Any increase in tax under paragraph (1) shall not be treated as tax imposed by this chapter for purposes of determining the amount of any credit allowable under subpart A.

"(d) Failure to pay comparable wages.

"(1) General rule. Under regulations prescribed by the Secretary, if during the period described in subsection (c)(1)(A), the taxpayer pays wages (as defined in section 50B(b)) to an employee with respect to whom work incentive program expenses are taken into account under subsection (a) which are less than the wages paid to other employees who perform comparable services, the tax under this chapter for the taxable year in which such wages are so paid shall be increased by an amount (determined under such regulations) equal to the credits allowed under section 40 for such taxable year and all prior taxable years attributable to work incentive program expenses paid or incurred with respect to such employee, and the carrybacks and carryovers under subsection (b) shall be properly adjusted.

"(2) Special rule. Any increase in tax under paragraph (1) shall not be treated as tax imposed by this chapter for purposes of determining the amount of any credit allowable under subpart A."

In 1976, P.L. 94-455, Sec. 503(b)(4), substituted "credit for the elderly" for "retirement income" in subpara. (a)(3)(C), effective for tax. yrs. begin. after 12/31/75.

—P.L. 94-455, Sec. 1901(a)(6), substituted "section 408(f)" for "section 408(e)" in the second sentence of para. (a)(3), effective for tax. yrs. begin. after 12/31/76.

—P.L. 94-455, Sec. 1901(b)(1)(D), deleted subpara. (a)(3)(B) and redesignated subparas. (a)(3)(C), (D) and (E) subparas. (a)(3)(B), (C) and (D), effective for tax. yrs. begin. after 12/31/76.

Prior to amendment, subpara. (a)(3)(B) read as follows:

"(B) section 35 (relating to partially tax exempt interest),"

—P.L. 94-455, Sec. 1906(b)(13)(A), substituted "Secretary" for "Secretary or his delegate" in subsecs. (a), (c), and (d), effective for tax. yrs. begin. after 12/31/76.

—P.L. 94-455, Sec. 2107(a), substituted "$50,000" for "$25,000" each place it appeared in para. (a)(2), substituted "$25,000" for "$12,500", and substituted "$50,000" for "$25,000" in para. (a)(4), substituted "$50,000" for "$25,000" each place it appeared in para. (a)(5), effective 10/4/76.

—P.L. 94-455, Sec. 2107(b), substituted "90 days" for "12 months" each place it appeared in subpara. (c)(1)(A), substituted "90th calendar day" for "12th calendar month" in subpara. (c)(1)(A), substituted "the day" for "the calendar month" in subpara. (c)(1)(A) . . . Sec. 2107(c), deleted "or" at the end of clause (c)(2)(A)(iii), substituted ", or" for the period at the end of clause (c)(2)(A)(iv) and added clause (c)(2)(A)(v), effective 10/4/76.

—P.L. 94-401, Sec. 4(a)(1), added the last sentence in para. (a)(2) . . . Sec. 4(a)(2), amended para. (a)(6), effective for Federal welfare recipient employment incentive expenses paid or incurred by the taxpayer to an eligible employee whose services are performed in connection with a child day care services program of the taxpayer shall apply to such expenses paid or incurred by a taxpayer to an eligible employee whom such taxpayer hires after 9/7/76.

Prior to amendment, para. (a)(6) read as follows:

"(6) Limitation with respect to nonbusiness eligible employees. Notwithstanding paragraph (1), the credit allowed by section 40 with respect to Federal welfare recipient employment incentive expenses paid or incurred by the taxpayer during the taxable year to an eligible employee whose services are not performed in connection with a trade or business of the taxpayer shall not exceed $1,000."

In 1975, P.L. 94-12, Sec. 401(a)(1), added para. (a)(6), effective with respect to welfare recipient employment incentive expenses paid or incurred by a taxpayer to an eligible employee whom such taxpayer hires after 3/29/75.

—P.L. 94-12, Sec. 401(a)(2), struck out the "or" in clause (c)(2)(A)(ii), substituted ", or" for the period at the end of clause (c)(2)(A)(iii), and added clause (c)(2)(A)(iv), effective with respect to welfare recipient employment incentive expenses paid or incurred by a taxpayer to an eligible employee whom such taxpayer hires after 3/29/75.

In 1974, P.L. 93-406, Sec. 2001(g)(2)(B), added "section 72(m)(5)(B) (relating to 10 percent tax on premature distributions to owner-employees)," in the second sentence of para. (a)(3), effective for distributions in tax. yrs. beginning after 12/31/75.

—P.L. 93-406, Sec. 2002(g)(2), added "section 408(e) (relating to additional tax on income from certain retirement accounts)," in the second sentence of para. (a)(3), effective 1/1/75.

—P.L. 93-406, Sec. 2005(c)(4), added "section 402(e) (relating to lump sum distributions)," in the second sentence of para. (a)(3), effective for distributions or payments made after 12/31/73 in tax. yrs. beginning after 12/31/73.

In 1971, P.L. 92-178, Sec. 601(b), added Code Sec. 50A, effective for tax. yrs. begin. after 12/31/71.

Sec. 50B. Repealed.

In 1989, P.L. 101-239, Sec. 7644(a), amended that part of subpara.(h)(1)(A) that preceded clause (h)(1)(A)(i), [prior to repeal by Sec. 474(m)(2) of P.L. 98-369, see below], effective for purposes of credits first claimed after 3/11/87.

Prior to amendment, that part of subpara. (h)(1)(A) that preceded clause (h)(1)(A)(i) read as follows:

"(A) who has been certified by the Secretary of Labor or by the appropriate agency of State or local government as—"

In 1984, P.L. 98-369, Sec. 474(m)(2), repealed Code Sec. 50B, effective for tax. yrs. begin. after 12/31/83 and for carrybacks from tax. yrs. begin. after 12/31/83.

Prior to repeal, Code Sec. 50B read as follows:

"SEC. 50B. DEFINITIONS; SPECIAL RULES.

"(a) Work incentive program expenses. For purposes of this subpart.

"(1) In general. The term 'work incentive program expenses' means the amount of wages paid or incurred by the taxpayer for services rendered by eligible employees.

"(2) First-year work incentive program expenses. The term 'first-year work incentive program expenses' means, with respect to any eligible employee, work incentive program expenses attributable to service rendered during the one-year period which begins on the day the eligible employee begins work for the taxpayer.

"(3) Second-year work incentive program expenses. The term 'second-year work incentive program expenses' means, with respect to any eligible employee, work incentive program expenses attributable to service rendered during the one-year period which begins on the day after the last day of the one-year period described in paragraph (2).

"(4) Limitation on amount of work incentive program expenses. The amount of the work incentive program expenses taken into account with respect to any eligible employee for any one-year period described in paragraph (2) or (3) (as the case may be) shall not exceed $6,000.

"(5) Termination. The term 'work incentive program expenses' shall not include any amount paid or incurred in any taxable year beginning after December 31, 1981.

"(b) Wages.

"For purposes of subsection (a), the term 'wages' means only cash remuneration (including amounts deducted and withheld).

"(c) Limitations.

"(1) Reimbursed expenses. No item shall be taken into account under subsection (a) to the extent that the taxpayer is reimbursed for such item.

"(2) Geographical limitation. No item shall be taken into account under subsection (a) with respect to any expense paid or incurred by the taxpayer with respect to employment outside the United States.

"(3) Ineligible individuals. No item shall be taken into account under subsection (a) with respect to an individual who—

"(A) bears any of the relationships described in paragraphs (1) through (8) of section 152(a) to the taxpayer, or, if the taxpayer is a corporation, to an individual who owns, directly or indirectly, more than 50 percent in value of the outstanding stock of the corporation (determined with the application of section 267(c)),

"(B) if the taxpayer is an estate or trust, is a grantor, beneficiary, or fiduciary of the estate or trust, or is an individual who bears any of the relationships described in paragraphs (1) through (8) of section 152(a) to a grantor, beneficiary, or fiduciary of the estate or trust, or

"(C) is a dependent (described in section 152(a)(9)) of the taxpayer, or, if the taxpayer is a corporation, of an individual described in subparagraph (A), or, if the taxpayer is an estate or trust, of a grantor, beneficiary, or fiduciary of the estate or trust.

"(d) Repealed.

"(e) Estates and trusts.

"In the case of an estate or trust—

"(1) the work incentive program expenses for any taxable year shall be apportioned between the estate or trust and the beneficiaries on the basis of the income of the estate or trust allocable to each, and

"(2) any beneficiary to whom any expenses have been apportioned under paragraph (1) shall be treated (for purposes of this subpart) as the taxpayer with respect to such expenses.

"(f) Limitations with respect to certain persons.

"In the case of—

"(1) an organization to which section 593 applies,

"(2) a regulated investment company or a real estate investment trust subject to taxation under subchapter M (section 851 and following), and

"(3) a cooperative organization described in section 1381(a),

rules similar to the rules provided in subsections (e) and (h) of section 46 shall apply under regulations prescribed by the Secretary.

"(g) Special rules for controlled groups.

"(1) Controlled group of corporations. For purposes of this subpart, all employees of all corporations which are members of the same controlled group of corporations shall be treated as employed by a single employer. In any such case, the credit (if any) allowable by section 40 to each such member shall be its proportionate share of the work incentive program expenses giving rise to such credit. For purposes of this subsection, the term 'controlled group of corporations' has the meaning given to such term by section 1563(a), except that—

"(A) 'more than 50 percent' shall be substituted for 'at least 80 percent' each place it appears in section 1563(a)(1), and

"(B) the determination shall be made without regard to subsections (a)(4) and (e)(3)(C) of section 1563.

Tax credits   Code Sec. 50B

"(2) Employees of partnerships, proprietorships, etc., which are under common control. For purposes of this subpart, under regulations prescribed by the Secretary—

"(A) all employees of trades or business (whether or not incorporated) which are under common control shall be treated as employed by a single employer, and

"(B) the credit (if any) allowable by section 40 with respect to each trade or business shall be its proportionate share of the work incentive program expenses giving rise to such credit.

The regulations prescribed under this paragraph shall be based on principles similar to the principles which apply in the case of paragraph (1).

"(h) Eligible employee.

"(1) Eligible employee. For purposes of this subpart the term 'eligible employee' means an individual—

"(A) who has been certified (or for whom a written request for certification has been made) on or before the day the individual began work for the taxpayer by the Secretary of Labor or by the appropriate agency of State or local government as—

"(i) being eligible for financial assistance under part A of title IV of the Social Security Act and as having continually received such financial assistance during the 90-day period which immediately precedes the date on which such individual is hired by the employer, or

"(ii) having been placed in employment under a work incentive program established under 432(b)(1) of the Social Security Act,

"(B) who has been employed by the taxpayer for a period in excess of 30 consecutive days on a substantially full-time basis (except as provided in subsection (i)),

"(C) who has not displaced any other individual from employment by the taxpayer, and

"(D) who is not a migrant worker.

The term 'eligible employee' includes an employee of the taxpayer whose services are not performed in connection with a trade or business of the taxpayer.

"(2) Migrant worker. For purposes of paragraph (1), the term 'migrant worker' means an individual who is employed for services for which the customary period of employment by one employer is less than 30 days if the nature of such services requires that such individual travel from place to place over a short period of time.

"(i) Special rules with respect to employment of day care workers.

"(1) Eligible employee. An individual who would be an 'eligible employee' (as that term is defined for purposes of this section) except for the fact that such individual's employment is not on a substantially full-time basis, shall be deemed to be an eligible employee as so defined, if such employee's employment is related to the provision of child day care services and is performed on either a full-time or part-time basis.

"(2) Alternative computation with respect to child day care services eligible employees paid from funds made available under title XX of the Social Security Act.

The amount of the credit allowed a taxpayer under section 40, as determined under section 50A and the preceding provisions of this section, with respect to work incentive program expenses paid or incurred by him with respect to an eligible employee whose services are performed in connection with a child day care services program conducted by the taxpayer, and with respect to whom the taxpayer is reimbursed (in whole or in part) from funds made available pursuant to section 2007 of the Social Security Act, at the option of the taxpayer shall be equal to 100 percent of the unreimbursed wages paid or incurred by the taxpayer with respect to such employee, but not more than the amount of the limitation in paragraph (4).

"(3) Unreimbursed wages. For purposes of this subsection, the term 'unreimbursed wages' means work incentive program expenses for which the taxpayer was not reimbursed under section 2007 of the Social Security Act or under any other grant or program.

"(4) Limitation. The amount of the credit, as determined under paragraph (2), with respect to any employee shall not exceed the lesser of—

"(A) an amount equal to $6,000 minus the amount of the funds reimbursed to the taxpayer with respect to such employee from funds made available pursuant to section 2007 of the Social Security Act; or

"(B) with respect to work incentive program expenses attributable to service rendered—

"(i) during the one-year period which begins on the day such employee begins work for the taxpayer, an amount equal to the lesser of—

"(I) $3,000, or

"(II) 50 percent of the sum of the amount of the unreimbursed wages of such employee and the amount reimbursed to the taxpayer with respect to such employee from funds made available pursuant to section 2007 of the Social Security Act; or

"(ii) during the one-year period which begins on the day after the last day of the one-year period described in clause (i), an amount equal to the lesser of—

"(I) $1,500, or

"(II) 25 percent of the sum of the amount of the unreimbursed wages of such employee and the amount reimbursed to the taxpayer with respect to such employee from funds made available pursuant to section 2007 of the Social Security Act.

"(j) Cross reference.

"For application of this subpart to certain acquiring corporations, see section 381(c)(24)."

In **1983**, P.L. 97-448, Sec. 102(1)(2), substituted "subsection (b)(2)" for "subsection (b)(2)(A)" in Sec. 261(g)(1)(B) of P.L. 97-34, the effective date for changes made by Sec. 261(b)(2) of P.L. 97-34, see below.

In **1982**, P.L. 97-354, Sec. 5(a)(10), repealed subsec. (d), effective for tax. yrs. begin. after 12/31/82.

Prior to repeal, subsec. (d) read as follows:

"(d) Subchapter S corporations.

"In case of an electing small business corporation (as defined in section 1371)—

"(1) the work incentive program expenses for each taxable year shall be apportioned pro rata among the persons who are shareholders of such corporation on the last day of such taxable year, and

"(2) any person to whom any expenses have been apportioned under paragraph (1) shall be treated (for purposes of this subpart) as the taxpayer with respect to such expenses."

In **1981**, P.L. 97-34, Sec. 261(b)(2)(B)(i), added para. (a)(5), effective as provided in Sec. 261(g)(1)(B) of this Act which reads as follows:

"(B) Eligible work incentive employees.—The amendments made by subsection (b)(2) [P.L. 97-34] to the extent relating to the designation of eligible work incentive employees (within the meaning of section 51(d)(9) of the Internal Revenue Code of 1954) as members of a targeted group and subsection (b)(2)(B)(ii) [P.L. 97-34] shall apply to taxable years beginning after December 31, 1981. In the case of an eligible work incentive employee, subsections (a) and (b) of section 51 of such Code shall be applied for taxable years beginning after December 31, 1981, as if such employees had been members of a targeted group for taxable years beginning before January 1, 1982."

In **1980**, P.L. 96-272, Sec. 208(b)(1), amended subsec. (i) . . . Sec. 208(b)(2), added "(except as provided in subsection (i)" after "full-time basis" in subpara. (h)(1)(B), effective for tax. yrs. begin. after 12/31/79.

Prior to amendment, subsec. (i) read as follows:

"(i) Special rules with respect to employment of day care workers.

"(1) Eligible employee. An individual who would be an 'eligible employee' (as that term is defined for purposes of this section) except for the fact that such individual's employment is not on a substantially full-time basis, shall be deemed to be an eligible employee as so defined, if such employee's employment consists of services performed in connection with a child day care program of the taxpayer, on either a full-time or part-time basis.

"(2) Alternative limitation with respect to child day care services eligible employees. The amount of the credit allowed a taxpayer under the preceding provisions of this section with respect to work incentive program expenses paid or incurred by him with respect to an eligible employee whose services are performed in connection with a child day care services program conducted by the taxpayer shall, at the election of the taxpayer, be determined by including (in computing the amount of such expenses so paid or incurred by him) any amount with respect to such employee for which he was reimbursed from funds made available pursuant to Sec. 3(c) of P.L. 94-401 or section 2007 of title XX of the Social Security Act, except that, if the total amount of such credit, as so computed, plus such amount reimbursed to him under such sections, exceeds the lesser of $6,000 or 100 percent of the total expenses paid or incurred by him with respect to such employee, the amount of such credit shall be reduced (but not below zero) so as to provide that such total does not exceed the lesser of $6,000 or 100 percent of the total expenses paid or incurred by him with respect to such employee."

—P.L. 96-272, Sec. 208(b)(3)(B), provides that the redesignation of subsec. (i) as (j) by Sec. 3(a)(10 of P.L. 96-178 remains in effect for tax. yrs. begin. after 12/31/79.

—P.L. 96-222, Sec. 103(a)(5), substituted "subsections (e) and (h) of section 46" for "section 46(e)" in para. (f)(3), effective for tax. yrs. end. after 10/31/78.

—P.L. 96-222, Sec. 103(a)(7)(B), made inoperative amendments to Sec. 322(e)(2) of P.L. 95-600 [reproduced below]. The same amendments were made by Sec. 6(b) of P.L. 96-178 [see below] .

—P.L. 96-222, Sec. 103(a)(7)(C) and 103(a)(7)(D)(i), and (ii), made inoperative changes to subpara. (a)(2)(B), subpara. (g)(2)(B) and subpara. (h)(1)(A). The same amendments were made by Secs. 3(a)(3) and 6(c)(2) and (3) of P.L. 97-178 [see below].

—P.L. 96-178, Sec. 3(a)(1), redesignated subsec. (i) as subsec. (j) . . . added new subsec. (i), effective 1/2/80 for tax. yrs. beginning after 12/31/78 and before 1/1/80.

—P.L. 96-178, Sec. 3(a)(3), substituted "January 1, 1979" for "October 1, 1978" in subpara. (a)(2)(B), as in effect prior to amendment by P.L. 95-600, see below.

—P.L. 96-178, Sec. 6(a), added the last sentence to Sec. 322(e)(1) of P.L. 95-600, reproduced below.

—P.L. 96-178, Sec. 6(b), amended Sec. 322(e)(2)(B) (reproduced below) by substituting "September 26, 1978, for purposes of applying the amendments made by this section" for "September 27, 1978" and substituting "January 1, 1979, and any wages paid or incurred after December 31, 1978, with respect to such individual shall be considered to be attributable to services rendered after that date" for "January 1, 1979."

—P.L. 96-178, Sec. 6(c)(2), substituted "giving rise to such credit" for "giving to such credit" in subpara. (g)(2)(B).

—P.L. 96-178, Sec. 6(c)(3), substituted "90-day" for "9-day" in clause (h)(1)(A)(i).

In **1978**, P.L. 95-600, Sec. 322(d)(1), amended subsec. (a) . . . Sec. 322(d)(2), deleted paras. (c)(1) and (4) and redesignated paras. (c)(2), (3) and (5) as (c)(1), (2) and (3), . . . Sec. 322(d)(3), inserted "and" at the end of para. (e)(1), substituted a period for ", and" at the end of para. (e)(2) and deleted para. (e)(3) . . . Sec. 322(d)(4), redesignated subsecs. (g) and (h) as subsecs. (h) and (i) and added new subsec. (g) . . . Sec. 322(d)(5), amended para. (h)(1), as redesignated by Sec. 322(d)(4) of this Act.

Sec. 322(e) of the Act provides:

1,255

"(e) Effective date.
"(1) In general. — Except as otherwise provided in this subsection, the amendments made by this section shall apply to work incentive program expenses paid or incurred after December 31, 1978, in taxable years ending after such date; except that so much of the amendment made by subsection (a) as affects section 50A(a)(2) of the Internal Revenue Code of 1954 shall apply to taxable years beginning after December 31, 1978. For purposes of applying section 50A(a)(2) of the Internal Revenue Code of 1954 with respect to a taxable year beginning before January 1, 1979, the rules of sections 50A(a)(4), 50A(a)(5), and 50B(e)(3) of such Code (as in effect on the day before the date of the enactment of this Act shall apply."

"(2) Special rules for certain eligible employees.—
"(A) Eligible employees hired before September 26, 1978, for purposes of applying the amendments made by this section. In the case of any eligible employee (as defined in section 50B(h)) hired before September 26, 1978, for purposes of applying the amendments made by this section, no credit shall be allowed under section 40 with respect to second-year work incentive program expenses (as defined in section 50B(a)) attributable to service performed by such employee.

"(B) Eligible employees hired after September 26, 1978, for purposes of applying the amendments made by this section. In the case of any eligible employee (as defined in section 50B(h)) hired after September 26, 1978, for purposes of applying the amendments made by this section, such individual shall be treated for purposes of the credit allowed by section 40 as having first begun work for the taxpayer not earlier than January 1, 1979, and any wages paid or incurred after December 31, 1978, with respect to such individual shall be considered to be attributable to service rendered after that date."

Prior to amendment, subsec. (a) read as follows:
"(a) Work incentive program expenses.
"(1) In general. For purposes of this subpart, the term 'work incentive program expenses' means the sum of—
"(A) the amount of wages paid or incurred by the taxpayer for services rendered during the first 12 months of employment (whether or not consecutive) of employees who are certified by the Secretary of Labor as —
"(i) having been placed in employment under a work incentive program established under section 432(b)(1) of the Social Security Act, and
"(ii) not having displaced any individual from employment, plus
"(B) the amount of Federal welfare recipient employment incentive expenses paid or incurred by the taxpayer for services rendered during the first 12 months of employment (whether or not consecutive).
"(2) Definitions. For purposes of this section, the term 'Federal welfare recipient employment incentive expenses' means the amount of wages paid or incurred by the taxpayer for services rendered to the taxpayer by an eligible employee—
"(A) before January 1, 1980 or
"(B) in the case of an eligible employee whose services are performed in connection with a child day care services program of the taxpayer, before January 1, 1979.
"(3) Exclusion. No item taken into account under paragraph (1)(A) shall be taken into account under paragraph (1)(B). No item taken into account under paragraph (1)(B) shall be taken into account under paragraph 1(A)."

Prior to amendment paras. (c)(1) and (4) read as follows:
"(1) Trade or business expenses. No item shall be taken into account under subsection (a)(1)(A) unless such item is incurred in a trade or business of the taxpayer."
* * *
"(4) Maximum period of training or instruction. No item with respect to any employee shall be taken into account under subsection (a)(1)(A) after the end of the 24-month period beginning with the date of initial employment of such employee by the taxpayer."

Prior to deletion, para. (e)(3) read as follows:
"(3) the $50,000 amount specified under subparagraphs (A) and (B) of section 50A(a)(2) applicable to such estate or trust shall be reduced to an amount which bears the same ratio to $50,000 as the amount of the expenses allocated to the trust under paragraph (1) bears to the entire amount of such expenses."

Prior to amendment para. (h)(1) read as follows:
"(1) Eligible employee. For purposes of subsection (a)(1)(B), the term 'eligible employee' means an individual—
"(A) who has been certified by the appropriate agency of State or local government as being eligible for financial assistance under part A of title IV of the Social Security Act and as having continuously received such financial assistance during the 90 day period which immediately precedes the date on which such individual is hired by the taxpayer,
"(B) who has been employed by the taxpayer for a period in excess of 30 consecutive days on a substantially full-time basis,
"(C) who has not displaced any other individual from employment by the taxpayer, and
"(D) who is not a migrant worker.
"The term 'eligible employee' includes an employee of the taxpayer whose services are not performed in connection with a trade or business of the taxpayer.
"(2) Migrant worker. For purposes of paragraph (1), the term 'migrant worker' means an individual who is employed for services for which the customary period of employment by one employer is less than 30 days if the nature of such services requires that such individual travel from place to place over a short period of time."

In **1977**, P.L. 95-171, Sec. 1(e), substituted "October 1, 1978" for "October 1, 1977" in subpara. (a)(2)(B), effective 10/1/77.

In **1976**, P.L. 94-455, Sec. 1906(b)(13)(A), substituted "Secretary" for "Secretary or his delegate" in subsec. (f), effective for tax. yrs. begin. after 12/31/76.

—P.L. 94-455, Sec. 2107(a)(4), substituted "$50,000" for "$25,000" each place it appeared in para. (e)(3), effective 10/4/76.
—P.L. 94-455, Sec. 2107(d), substituted "January 1, 1980," for "July 1, 1976," in para. (a)(2) . . . Sec. 2107(e), amended subpara. (a)(1)(B), effective 10/4/76.

Prior to amendment subpara. (a)(1)(B) read as follows:
"(B) the amount of Federal welfare recipient employment incentive expenses paid or incurred by the taxpayer during the taxable year."
—P.L. 94-455, Sec. 2107(f), added "the Secretary of Labor or by" after "certified by" in subpara. (g)(1)(A), effective 10/4/76.
—P.L. 94-401, Sec. 4(b), amended para. (a)(2), effective for Federal welfare recipient employment incentive expenses paid or incurred by the taxpayer to an eligible employee whose services are performed in connection with a child day care service program of the taxpayer shall apply to such expenses paid or incurred by a taxpayer to an eligible employee whom such taxpayer hires after 10/4/76.

Prior to amendment, para. (a)(2) read as follows:
"(2) Definition. For purposes of this section, the term 'Federal welfare recipient employment incentive expenses' means the amount of wages paid or incurred by the taxpayer for services rendered to the taxpayer before July 1, 1976, by an eligible employee."

In **1975**, P.L. 94-12, Sec. 401(a)(3), amended subsec. (a) . . . Sec. 401(a)(4), substituted 'subsection (a)(1)(A)' for 'subsection (a)' in paras. (c)(1) and (c)(4), effective with respect to welfare recipient employment incentive expenses paid or incurred by a taxpayer to an eligible employee whom such taxpayer hires after 3/29/75.

Prior to amendment, subsec. (a) read as follows:
"(a) Work incentive program expenses.
"For purposes of this subpart, the term 'work incentive program expenses' means the wages paid or incurred by the taxpayer for services rendered during the first 12 months of employment (whether or not consecutive) of employees who are certified by the Secretary of Labor as —
"(1) having been placed in employment under a work incentive program established under section 432(b)(1) of the Social Security Act, and
"(2) not having displaced any individual from employment."
—P.L. 94-12, Sec. 401(a)(5), redesignated subsec. (g) as (h) and added new subsec. (g), effective with respect to federal welfare recipient employment incentive expenses paid or incurred by a taxpayer to an eligible employee whom taxpayer hires after 3/29/75.
—P.L. 94-12, Sec. 302(c)(4), substituted "46(e)" for "46(d)" in subsec. (f), effective for tax. yrs. end. after 12/31/74.

In **1971**, P.L. 92-178, Sec. 601(b), added Code Sec. 50B, effective for tax. yrs. begin. after 12/31/71.

SUBPART F.—RULES FOR COMPUTING WORK OPPORTUNITY CREDIT

Sec.
51. Amount of credit.
51A. Repealed. [Temporary incentives for employing long-term family assistance recipients.]
52. Special rules.

In **1997**, P.L. 105-34, Sec. 801(b), added item 51A.

In **1996**, P.L. 104-188, Sec. 1201(e)(2), substituted "work opportunity credit" for "targeted jobs credit" in the heading of subpart F.

In **1984**, P.L. 98-369, Sec. 474(n)(1), redesignated Subpart D as F . . . Sec. 474(n)(2), amended the heading of Subpart F . . . Sec. 474(p)(9), deleted item 53.
Prior to amendment, the heading of Subpart F read as follows:
"SUBPART F—RULES FOR COMPUTING CREDIT FOR EMPLOYMENT OF CERTAIN NEW EMPLOYEES"
Prior to deletion, item 53 read as follows:
"Sec. 53. Limitation based on amount of tax."

In **1977**, P.L. 95-30, Sec. 202(b), added the table of sections for Subpart D.

Sec. 51. Amount of credit.
(a) Determination of amount.

For purposes of section 38, the amount of the work opportunity credit determined under this section for the taxable year shall be equal to 40 percent of the qualified first-year wages for such year.

(b) Qualified wages defined.

For purposes of this subpart—

(1) In general. The term "qualified wages" means the wages paid or incurred by the employer during the taxable year to individuals who are members of a targeted group.

(2) Qualified first-year wages. The term "qualified first-year wages" means, with respect to any individual, qualified wages attributable to service rendered during the 1-year period beginning with the day the individual begins work for the employer.

(3) Limitation on wages per year taken into account. The amount of the qualified first-year wages which may be taken into account with respect to any individual shall not exceed $6,000 per year ($12,000 per year in the case of any individual who is a qualified veteran by reason of subsection (d)(3)(A)(ii)).

(c) Wages defined.

For purposes of this subpart—

(1) In general. Except as otherwise provided in this subsection and subsection (h)(2), the term "wages" has the meaning given to such term by subsection (b) of section 3306 (determined without regard to any dollar limitation contained in such section).

(2) On-the-job training and work supplementation payments.

(A) Exclusion for employers receiving on-the-job training payments. The term "wages" shall not include any amounts paid or incurred by an employer for any period to any individual for whom the employer receives federally funded payments for on-the-job training of such individual for such period.

(B) Reduction for work supplementation payments to employers. The amount of wages which would (but for this subparagraph) be qualified wages under this section for an employer with respect to an individual for a taxable year shall be reduced by an amount equal to the amount of the payments made to such employer (however utilized by such employer) with respect to such individual for such taxable year under a program established under section 482(e) of the Social Security Act.

(3) Payments for services during labor disputes. If—

(A) the principal place of employment of an individual with the employer is at a plant or facility, and

(B) there is a strike or lockout involving employees at such plant or facility,

the term "wages" shall not include any amount paid or incurred by the employer to such individual for services which are the same as, or substantially similar to, those services performed by employees participating in, or affected by, the strike or lockout during the period of such strike or lockout.

(4) Termination. The term "wages" shall not include any amount paid or incurred to an individual who begins work for the employer—

(A) after December 31, 1994, and before October 1, 1996, or

(B) after December 31, 2011.

(5) Coordination with payroll tax forgiveness. The term "wages" shall not include any amount paid or incurred to a qualified individual (as defined in section 3111(d)(3)) during the 1-year period beginning on the hiring date of such individual by a qualified employer (as defined in section 3111(d)) unless such qualified employer makes an election not to have section 3111(d) apply.

(d) Members of targeted groups.

For purposes of this subpart—

(1) In general. An individual is a member of a targeted group if such individual is—

(A) a qualified IV-A recipient,

(B) a qualified veteran,

(C) a qualified ex-felon,

(D) a designated community resident,

(E) a vocational rehabilitation referral,

(F) a qualified summer youth employee,

(G) a qualified supplemental nutrition assistance program benefits recipient,

(H) a qualified SSI recipient, or

(I) a long-term family assistance recipient.

(2) Qualified IV-A recipient.

(A) In general. The term "qualified IV-A recipient" means any individual who is certified by the designated local agency as being a member of a family receiving assistance under a IV-A program for any 9 months during the 18-month period ending on the hiring date.

(B) IV-A program. For purposes of this paragraph, the term "IV-A program" means any program providing assistance under a State program funded under part A of title IV of the Social Security Act and any successor of such program.

(3) Qualified veteran.

(A) In general. The term "qualified veteran" means any veteran who is certified by the designated local agency as—

(i) being a member of a family receiving assistance under a supplemental nutrition assistance program under the Food and Nutrition Act of 2008 for at least a 3-month period ending during the 12-month period ending on the hiring date, or

(ii) entitled to compensation for a service-connected disability, and—

(I) having a hiring date which is not more that 1 year after having been discharged or released from active duty in the Armed Forces of the United States, or

(II) having aggregate periods of unemployment during the 1-year period ending on the hiring date which equal or exceed 6 months.

(B) Veteran. For purposes of subparagraph (A), the term "veteran" means any individual who is certified by the designated local agency as—

(i)(I) having served on active duty (other than active duty for training) in the Armed Forces of the United States for a period of more than 180 days, or

(II) having been discharged or released from active duty in the Armed Forces of the United States for a service-connected disability, and

(ii) not having any day during the 60-day period ending on the hiring date which was a day of extended active duty in the Armed Forces of the United States. For purposes of clause (ii), the term "extended active duty" means a period of more than 90 days during which the individual was on active duty (other than active duty for training).

(C) Other definitions. For purposes of subparagraph (A), the terms "compensation" and "service-connected" have the meanings given such terms under section 101 of title 38, United States Code.

(4) Qualified ex-felon. The term "qualified ex-felon" means any individual who is certified by the designated local agency—

(A) as having been convicted of a felony under any statute of the United States or any State, and

(B) as having a hiring date which is not more than 1 year after the last date on which such individual was so convicted or was released from prison.

(5) Designated community residents.

(A) In general. The term "designated community resident" means any individual who is certified by the designated local agency—

(i) as having attained age 18 but not age 40 on the hiring date, and

(ii) as having his principal place of abode within an empowerment zone, enterprise community, renewal community, or rural renewal county.

(B) Individual must continue to reside in zone, community, or county. In the case of a designated community resident, the term "qualified wages" shall not include wages paid or incurred for services performed while the individual's principal place of abode is outside an empowerment zone, enterprise community, renewal community, or rural renewal county.

(C) Rural renewal county. For purposes of this paragraph, the term "rural renewal county" means any county which—

(i) is outside a metropolitan statistical area (defined as such by the Office of Management and Budget), and

(ii) during the 5-year periods 1990 through 1994 and 1995 through 1999 had a net population loss.

(6) Vocational rehabilitation referral. The term "vocational rehabilitation referral" means any individual who is certified by the designated local agency as—

(A) having a physical or mental disability which, for such individual, constitutes or results in a substantial handicap to employment, and

(B) having been referred to the employer upon completion of (or while receiving) rehabilitative services pursuant to—

(i) an individualized written plan for employment under a State plan for vocational rehabilitation services approved under the Rehabilitation Act of 1973,

(ii) a program of vocational rehabilitation carried out under chapter 31 of title 38, United States Code, or

(iii) an individual work plan developed and implemented by an employment network pursuant to subsection (g) of section 1148 of the Social Security Act with respect to which the requirements of such subsection are met.

(7) Qualified summer youth employee.

(A) In general. The term "qualified summer youth employee" means any individual—

(i) who performs services for the employer between May 1 and September 15,

(ii) who is certified by the designated local agency as having attained age 16 but not 18 on the hiring date (or if later, on May 1 of the calendar year involved),

(iii) who has not been an employee of the employer during any period prior to the 90-day period described in subparagraph (B)(i), and

(iv) who is certified by the designated local agency as having his principal place of abode within an empowerment zone, enterprise community, or renewal community.

(B) Special rules for determining amount of credit. For purposes of applying this subpart to wages paid or incurred to any qualified summer youth employee—

(i) subsection (b)(2) shall be applied by substituting "any 90-day period between May 1 and September 15" for "the 1-year period beginning with the day the individual begins work for the employer", and

(ii) subsection (b)(3) shall be applied by substituting "$3,000" for "$6,000".

The preceding sentence shall not apply to an individual who, with respect to the same employer, is certified as a member of another targeted group after such individual has been a qualified summer youth employee.

(C) Youth must continue to reside in zone or community. Paragraph (5)(B) shall apply for purposes of subparagraph (A)(iv).

(8) Qualified supplemental nutrition assistance program benefits recipient.

(A) In general. The term "qualified supplemental nutrition assistance program benefits recipient" means any individual who is certified by the designated local agency—

(i) as having attained age 18 but not age 40 on the hiring date, and

(ii) as being a member of a family—

(I) receiving assistance under a supplemental nutrition assistance program under the Food and Nutrition Act of 2008 for the 6-month period ending on the hiring date, or

(II) receiving such assistance for at least 3 months of the 5-month period ending on the hiring date, in the case of a member of a family who ceases to be eligible for such assistance under section 6(o) of the Food and Nutrition Act of 2008.

(B) Participation information. Notwithstanding any other provision of law, the Secretary of the Treasury and the Secretary of Agriculture shall enter into an agreement to provide information to designated local agencies with respect to participation in the supplemental nutrition assistance program.

(9) Qualified SSI recipient. The term "qualified SSI recipient" means any individual who is certified by the designated local agency as receiving supplemental security income benefits under title XVI of the Social Security Act (including supplemental security income benefits of the type described in section 1616 of such Act or section 212 of Public Law 93-66) for any month ending within the 60-day period ending on the hiring date.

(10) Long-term family assistance recipient. The term "long-term family assistance recipient" means any individual who is certified by the designated local agency—

(A) as being a member of a family receiving assistance under a IV-A program (as defined in paragraph (2)(B)) for at least the 18-month period ending on the hiring date,

(B)(i) as being a member of a family receiving such assistance for 18 months beginning after August 5, 1997, and

(ii) as having a hiring date which is not more than 2 years after the end of the earliest such 18-month period, or

(C)(i) as being a member of a family which ceased to be eligible for such assistance by reason of any limitation imposed by Federal or State law on the maximum period such assistance is payable to a family, and

(ii) as having a hiring date which is not more than 2 years after the date of such cessation.

(11) Hiring date. The term "hiring date" means the day the individual is hired by the employer.

(12) Designated local agency. The term "designated local agency" means a State employment security agency established in accordance with the Act of June 6, 1933, as amended (29 U.S.C. 49-49n).

(13) Special rules for certifications.

(A) In general. An individual shall not be treated as a member of a targeted group unless—

(i) on or before the day on which such individual begins work for the employer, the employer has received a certification from a designated local agency that such individual is a member of a targeted group, or

(ii)(I) on or before the day the individual is offered employment with the employer, a pre-screening notice is completed by the employer with respect to such individual, and

(II) not later than the 28th day after the individual begins work for the employer, the employer submits such notice, signed by the employer and the individual under penalties of perjury, to the designated local agency as part of a written request for such a certification from such agency.

For purposes of this paragraph, the term "pre-screening notice" means a document (in such form as the Secretary shall prescribe) which contains information provided by the individual on the basis of which the employer believes that the individual is a member of a targeted group.

(B) Incorrect certifications. If—

(i) an individual has been certified by a designated local agency as a member of a targeted group, and

(ii) such certification is incorrect because it was based on false information provided by such individual,

the certification shall be revoked and wages paid by the employer after the date on which notice of revocation is received by the employer shall not be treated as qualified wages.

(C) Explanation of denial of request. If a designated local agency denies a request for certification of membership in a targeted group, such agency shall provide to the person making such request a written explanation of the reasons for such denial.

(14) Credit allowed for unemployed veterans and disconnected youth hired in 2009 or 2010.

(A) In general. Any unemployed veteran or disconnected youth who begins work for the employer during 2009 or 2010 shall be treated as a member of a targeted group for purposes of this subpart.

(B) Definitions. For purposes of this paragraph—

(i) Unemployed veteran. The term "unemployed veteran" means any veteran (as defined in paragraph (3)(B), determined without regard to clause (ii) thereof) who is certified by the designated local agency as—

(I) having been discharged or released from active duty in the Armed Forces at any time during the 5-year period ending on the hiring date, and

(II) being in receipt of unemployment compensation under State or Federal law for not less than 4 weeks during the 1-year period ending on the hiring date.

(ii) Disconnected youth. The term "disconnected youth" means any individual who is certified by the designated local agency—

(I) as having attained age 16 but not age 25 on the hiring date,

(II) as not regularly attending any secondary, technical, or post-secondary school during the 6-month period preceding the hiring date,

(III) as not regularly employed during such 6-month period, and

(IV) as not readily employable by reason of lacking a sufficient number of basic skills.

(e) Credit for second-year wages for employment of long-term family assistance recipients.

(1) In general. With respect to the employment of a long-term family assistance recipient—

(A) the amount of the work opportunity credit determined under this section for the taxable year shall include 50 percent of the qualified second-year wages for such year, and

(B) in lieu of applying subsection (b)(3), the amount of the qualified first-year wages, and the amount of qualified second-year wages, which may be taken into account with respect to such a recipient shall not exceed $10,000 per year.

(2) Qualified second-year wages. For purposes of this subsection, the term "qualified second-year wages" means qualified wages—

(A) which are paid to a long-term family assistance recipient, and

(B) which are attributable to service rendered during the 1-year period beginning on the day after the last day of the 1-year period with respect to such recipient determined under subsection (b)(2).

(3) Special rules for agricultural and railway labor. If such recipient is an employee to whom subparagraph (A) or (B) of subsection (h)(1) applies, rules similar to the rules of such subparagraphs shall apply except that—

(A) such subparagraph (A) shall be applied by substituting "$10,000" for "$6,000", and

(B) such subparagraph (B) shall be applied by substituting "$833.33" for "$500".

(f) Remuneration must be for trade or business employment.

(1) In general. For purposes of this subpart, remuneration paid by an employer to an employee during any taxable year shall be taken into account only if more than one-half of the remuneration so paid is for services performed in a trade or business of the employer.

(2) Special rule for certain determination. Any determination as to whether paragraph (1), or subparagraph (A) or (B) of subsection (h)(1), applies with respect to any employee for any taxable year shall be made without regard to subsections (a) and (b) of section 52.

(g) United States Employment Service to notify employers of availability of credit.

The United States Employment Service, in consultation with the Internal Revenue Service, shall take such steps as may be necessary or appropriate to keep employers apprised of the availability of the work opportunity credit determined under this subpart.

(h) Special rules for agricultural labor and railway labor. For purposes of this subpart—

(1) Unemployment insurance wages.

(A) Agricultural labor. If the services performed by any employee for an employer during more than one-half of any pay period (within the meaning of section 3306(d)) taken into account with respect to any year constitute agricultural labor (within the meaning of section 3306(k)), the term "unemployment insurance wages" means, with respect to the remuneration paid by the employer to such employee for such year, an amount equal to so much of such remuneration as constitutes "wages" within the meaning of section 3121(a), except that the contribution and benefit base for each calendar year shall be deemed to be $6,000.

(B) Railway labor. If more than one-half of remuneration paid by an employer to an employee during any year is remuneration for service described in section 3306(c)(9), the term "unemployment insurance wages" means, with respect to such employee for such year, an amount equal to so much of the remuneration paid to such employee during such year which would be subject to contributions under section 8(a) of the Railroad Unemployment Insurance Act (45 U.S.C. 358(a)) if the maximum amount subject to such contributions were $500 per month.

(2) Wages. In any case to which subparagraph (A) or (B) of paragraph (1) applies, the term "wages" means unemployment insurance wages (determined without regard to any dollar limitation).

(i) Certain individuals ineligible.

(1) Related individuals. No wages shall be taken into account under subsection (a) with respect to an individual who—

(A) bears any of the relationships described in subparagraphs (A) through (G) of section 152(d)(2) to the taxpayer, or, if the taxpayer is a corporation, to an individual who owns, directly or indirectly, more than 50 percent in value of the outstanding stock of the corporation, or, if the taxpayer is an entity other than a corporation, to any individual who owns, directly or indirectly, more than 50 percent of the capital and profits interests in the entity, (determined with the application of section 267(c)),

(B) if the taxpayer is an estate or trust, is a grantor, beneficiary, or fiduciary of the estate or trust, or is an individual who bears any of the relationships described in subparagraphs (A) through (G) of section 152(d)(2) to a grantor, beneficiary, or fiduciary of the estate or trust, or

(C) is a dependent (described in section 152(d)(2)(H)) of the taxpayer, or, if the taxpayer is a corporation, of an individual described in subparagraph (A), or, if the taxpayer is an estate or trust, of a grantor, beneficiary, or fiduciary of the estate or trust.

(2) Nonqualifying rehires. No wages shall be taken into account under subsection (a) with respect to any individual if, prior to the hiring date of such individual, such individual had been employed by the employer at any time.

(3) Individuals not meeting minimum employment periods.

(A) Reduction of credit for individuals performing fewer than 400 hours of service. In the case of an individual who has performed at least 120 hours, but less than 400 hours, of service for the employer, subsection (a) shall be applied by substituting "25 percent" for "40 percent".

(B) Denial of credit for individuals performing fewer than 120 hours of service. No wages shall be taken into account under subsection (a) with respect to any individual unless such individual has performed at least 120 hours of service for the employer.

(j) Election to have work opportunity credit not apply.

(1) In general. A taxpayer may elect to have this section not apply for any taxable year.

(2) Time for making election. An election under paragraph (1) for any taxable year may be made (or revoked) at any time before the expiration of the 3-year period beginning on the last date prescribed by law for filing the return for such taxable year (determined without regard to extensions).

(3) Manner of making election. An election under paragraph (1) (or revocation thereof) shall be made in such manner as the Secretary may by regulations prescribe.

(k) Treatment of successor employers; treatment of employees performing services for other persons.

(1) Treatment of successor employers. Under regulations prescribed by the Secretary, in the case of a successor employer referred to in section 3306(b)(1), the determination of the amount of the credit under this section with respect to wages paid by such successor employer shall be made in the same manner as if such wages were paid by the predecessor employer referred to in such section.

(2) Treatment of employees performing services for other persons. No credit shall be determined under this section with respect to remuneration paid by an employer to an employee for services performed by such employee for another person unless the amount reasonably expected to be received by the employer for such services from such other person exceeds the remuneration paid by the employer to such employee for such services.

In **2010,** P.L. 111-312, Sec. 757(a), substituted "December 31, 2011" for "August 31, 2011" in subpara. (c)(4)(B), effective for individuals who begin work for the employer after 12/17/2010.
—P.L. 111-147, Sec. 101(b), added para. (c)(5), effective for wages paid after 3/18/2010.

In **2009,** P.L. 111-5, Sec. 1221(a), added para. (d)(14), effective for individuals who begin work for the employer after 12/31/2008.

In **2008,** P.L. 110-343, Sec. 319(a)DivC, substituted "4-year" for "2-year" in Sec. 201(b)(1), P.L. 109-73, reproduced below, effective for individuals hired after 8/27/2007.
—P.L. 110-246, Sec. 4002(b)(1)(A), substituted "supplemental nutrition assistance program" for "food stamp program" in clause (d)(3)(A)(i), subclause (d)(8)(A)(ii)(I), subpara. (d)(8)(B), . . . Sec. 4002(b)(1)(B), substituted "Food and Nutrition Act of 2008" for "Food Stamp Act of 1977" in clause (d)(3)(A)(i), subclause (d)(8)(A)(ii)(I) and (II) . . . Sec. 4002(b)(1)(D), substituted "supplemental nutrition assistance program benefits" for "food stamp" in clause (d)(3)(A)(i), para. (d)(8), subpara. (d)(8)(A), enacted 5/22/2008. [Ed. Note: May 22, 2008 was the date of enactment for H.R. 2419 (PL 110-234), which was repealed by (2008 Farm Act § 4(a)) (PL 110-246, 6/18/2008), in connection with the reenactment of the Farm Bill to correct a technical deficiency in its original passage.]

In **2007,** P.L. 110-28, Sec. 8211(a), substituted "August 31, 2011" for "December 31, 2007" in subpara. (c)(4)(B) . . . Sec. 8211(b)(1), amended para. (d)(5) . . . Sec. 8211(b)(2), amended subpara. (d)(1)(D) . . . Sec. 8211(c), deleted "or" at the end of clause (d)(6)(B)(i), substituted ", or" for the period at the end of clause (d)(6)(B)(ii), and added clause (d)(6)(B)(iii) . . . Sec. 8211(d)(1)(A), amended subpara. (d)(3)(A) . . . Sec. 8211(d)(1)(B), added subpara. (d)(3)(C) . . . Sec. 8211(d)(2)(A), added "($12,000 per year in the case of any individual who is a qualified veteran by reason of subsection (d)(3)(A)(ii))" before the period at the end of para. (b)(3) . . . Sec. 8211(d)(2)(B), substituted "Limitation on" for "Only first $6,000 of" in the heading of para (b)(3), effective for individuals who begin work for the employer after the 5/25/2007.
Prior to amendment, subpara. (d)(1)(D) read as follows:
"(D) a high-risk youth,"
Prior to amendment, subpara. (d)(3)(A) read as follows:
"(A) In general. The term 'qualified veteran' means any veteran who is certified by the designated local agency as being a member of a family receiving assistance under a food stamp program under the Food Stamp Act of 1977 for at least a 3-month period ending during the 12-month period ending on the hiring date."
Prior to amendment, para. (d)(5) read as follows:
"(5) High-risk youth.
"(A) In general. The term "high-risk youth" means any individual who is certified by the designated local agency—
"(i) as having attained age 18 but not age 25 on the hiring date, and
"(ii) as having his principal place of abode within an empowerment zone, enterprise community, or renewal community.
"(B) Youth must continue to reside in zone or community. In the case of a high-risk youth, the term "qualified wages" shall not include wages paid or incurred for services performed while such youth's principal place of abode is outside an empowerment zone, enterprise community, or renewal community."

In **2006,** P.L. 109-432, Sec. 105(a), substituted "2007" for "2005" in subpara. (c)(4)(B), effective for individuals who begin work for the employer after 12/31/2005.
—P.L. 109-432, Sec. 105(b), added "and" at the end of subpara. (d)(4)(A), substituted a period for ', and" at end of subpara. (d)(4)(B), and deleted all following subpara (d)(4)(B), which included subpara. (d)(4)(C) and the flush sentence at the end of para. (d)(4) . . . Sec. 105(c), substituted "40" for "25" in subpara. (d)(8)(A). . . . Sec. 105(d), substituted "28th day" for "21st day" in subclause (d)(12)(A)(ii)(II). . . . Sec. 105(e)(1), deleted "or" at end of subpara. (d)(1)(G), substituted ", or" for the period at end of subpara. (d)(1)(H), and added subpara. (d)(1)(I). . . . Sec. 105(e)(2), redesignated paras. (d)(10), (11) and (12) as paras. (d)(11), (12) and (13), added new para. (d)(10). . . . Sec. 105(e)(3), added new

Tax credits Code Sec. 51

subsec. (e), effective for individuals who begin work for the employer after 12/31/2006.

Prior to amendment, subpara. (d)(4)(C) and the flush sentence at the end of para. (d)(4) read as follows:

"(C) as being a member of a family which had an income during the 6 months immediately preceding the earlier of the month in which such income determination occurs or the month in which the hiring date occurs, which, on an annual basis, would be 70 percent or less of the Bureau of Labor Statistics lower living standard.

"Any determination under subparagraph (C) shall be valid for the 45-day period beginning on the date such determination is made."

In **2005**, P.L. 109-73, Sec. 201, as amended by Sec. 319(a) Div C, P.L. 110-343 [see above] of this Act, reads as follows:

"SEC. 201. WORK OPPORTUNITY TAX CREDIT FOR HURRICANE KATRINA EMPLOYEES.

"(a) In general. For purposes of section 51 of the Internal Revenue Code of 1986, a Hurricane Katrina employee shall be treated as a member of a targeted group.

"(b) Hurricane Katrina employee. For purposes of this section, the term 'Hurricane Katrina employee' means—

"(1) any individual who on August 28, 2005, had a principal place of abode in the core disaster area and who is hired during the 4-year period beginning on such date for a position the principal place of employment of which is located in the core disaster area, and

"(2) any individual who on such date had a principal place of abode in the core disaster area, who is displaced from such abode by reason of Hurricane Katrina, and who is hired during the period beginning on such date and ending on December 31, 2005.

"(c) Reasonable identification acceptable. In lieu of the certification requirement under subparagraph (A) of section 51(d)(12) of such Code, an individual may provide to the employer reasonable evidence that the individual is a Hurricane Katrina employee, and subparagraph (B) of such section shall be applied as if such evidence were a certification described in such subparagraph.

"(d) Special rules for determining credit. For purposes of applying subpart F of part IV of subchapter A of chapter 1 of such Code to wages paid or incurred to any Hurricane Katrina employee—

"(1) section 51(c)(4) of such Code shall not apply, and

"(2) section 51(i)(2) of such Code shall not apply with respect to the first hire of such employee as a Hurricane Katrina employee, unless such employee was an employee of the employer on August 28, 2005."

In **2004**, P.L. 108-311, Sec. 207(5)(A), substituted "subparagraphs (A) through (G) of section 152(d)(2)" for "paragraphs (1) through (8) of section 152(a)" each place it appeared in subparas. (i)(1)(A) and (B)... Sec. 207(5)(B), substituted "152(d)(2)(H)" for "152(a)(9)" in subpara. (i)(1)(C), effective for tax. yrs. begin. after 12/31/2004.

—P.L. 108-311, Sec. 303(a)(1), substituted "December 31, 2005" for "December 31, 2003" in para. (c)(4), effective for individuals who begin work for the employer after 12/31/2003.

In **2002**, P.L. 107-147, Sec. 604(a), substituted "2003" for "2001" in subpara. (c)(4)(B), effective for individuals who begin work for the employer after 12/31/2001.

In **2000**, P.L. 106-554, Sec. 1(a)(7), [which enacted into law Sec. 102(a) of P.L. 106-554] substituted "empowerment zone, enterprise community, or renewal community" for "empowerment zone or enterprise community" in clause (d)(5)(A)(ii) and subpara. (d)(5)(B)... Sec. 1(a)(7), [which enacted into law Sec. 102(b) of P.L. 106-554] substituted "empowerment zone, enterprise community, or renewal community" for "empowerment zone or enterprise community" in clause (d)(7)(A)(iv)... Sec. 1(a)(7), [which enacted into law Sec. 102(c) of P.L. 106-554] added "or community" after "zone" in the heading of subparas. (d)(5)(B) and (d)(7)(C), effective for individuals who begin work for the employer after 12/31/2001.

—P.L. 106-554, Sec. 1(a)(7), [which enacted into law Sec. 316(a)(1) of P.L. 106-554] substituted "program funded" for "plan approved" in subpara. (d)(2)(B)... Sec. 1(a)(7), [which enacted into law Sec. 316(a)(2) of P.L. 106-554] deleted "(relating to assistance for needy families with minor children)" after "Security Act" in subpara. (d)(2)(B), effective for individuals who begin work for the employer after 9/30/96.

In **1999**, P.L. 106-170, Sec. 505(a), substituted "December 31, 2001" for "June 30, 1999" in subpara. (c)(4)(B)... Sec. 505(b), deleted "during which he was not a member of a targeted group" after "at any time" in para. (i)(2), effective for individuals who begin work for the employer after 6/30/99.

In **1998**, P.L. 105-277, Sec. 1002(a), substituted "June 30, 1999" for "June 30, 1998" in subpara. (c)(4)(B), effective for individuals who begin work for the employer after 6/30/98.

—P.L. 105-277, Sec. 4006(c)(1), substituted "plan for employment" for "rehabilitation plan" in clause (d)(6)(B)(i), effective 10/21/98. The reference to "plan for employment" in clause (d)(6)(B)(i) shall be treated as including a reference to the rehabilitation plan referred to in such clause as in effect before the amendment made by Sec. 4006(c)(1) of this Act.

In **1997**, P.L. 105-34, Sec. 603(a), substituted "June 30, 1998" for "September 30, 1997" in subpara. (c)(4)(B)... Sec. 603(b)(1), substituted "for any 9 months during the 18-month period ending on the hiring date." for "for at least a 9-month period ending during the 9-month period ending on the hiring date." in subpara. (d)(2)(A)... Sec. 603(b)(2), amended subpara. (d)(3)(A)... Sec. 603(c)(1), deleted "or" at the end of subpara. (d)(1)(F), substituted ", or" for the period at the end of subpara. (d)(1)(G), and added subpara. (d)(1)(H)... Sec. 603(c)(2), redesignated paras. (d)(9)-(11) as (d)(10)-(12) and added new para. (d)(9)... Sec. 603(d)(1), substituted "40 percent" for "35 percent" in subsec. (a)... Sec.

603(d)(2), amended para. (i)(3), effective for individuals who begin work for the employer after 9/30/97.

Prior to amendment, subpara. (d)(3)(A) read as follows:

"(A) In general. The term 'qualified veteran' means any veteran who is certified by the designated local agency as being—

"(i) a member of a family receiving assistance under a IV-A program (as defined in paragraph (2)(B)) for at least a 9-month period ending during the 12-month period ending on the hiring date, or

"(ii) a member of a family receiving assistance under a food stamp program under the Food Stamp Act of 1977 for at least a 3-month period ending during the 12-month period ending on the hiring date."

Prior to amendment, para. (i)(3) read as follows:

"(3) Individuals not meeting minimum employment period. No wages shall be taken into account under subsection (a) with respect to any individual unless such individual either—

"(A) is employed by the employer at least 180 days (20 days in the case of a qualified summer youth employee), or

"(B) has completed at least 400 hours (120 hours in the case of a qualified summer youth employee) of services performed for the employer."

—P.L. 105-33, Sec. 5514(a)(1), deleted Sec. 110(l)(1) of P.L. 104-193 [see below], effective 7/1/97.

In **1996**, P.L. 104-193, Sec. 110(l)(1), substituted "being eligible for financial assistance under part A of title IV of the Social Security Act and as having continually received such financial assistance during the 90-day period which immediately precedes the date on which such individual is hired by the employer." for

"(A) being eligible for financial assistance under part A of title IV of the Social Security Act and as having continually received such financial assistance during the 90-day period which immediately precedes the date on which such individual is hired by the employer, or

"(B) having been placed in employment under a work incentive program established under section 432(b)(1) or 445 of the Social Security Act." in para. (d)(9) [prior to deletion by Sec. 5514(a)(1) of P.L. 105-33, see above], effective 7/1/97.

—P.L. 104-188, Sec. 1201(a), substituted "35 percent" for "40 percent" in subsec. (a)... Sec. 1201(b), amended subsec. (d)... Sec. 1201(c), amended para. (i)(3)... Sec. 1201(d), amended para. (c)(4)... Sec. 1201(e)(1), substituted "work opportunity credit" for "targeted jobs credit" each place it appeared in subsecs. (a) and (g)... Sec. 1201(e)(5), substituted "work opportunity credit" for "targeted jobs credit" in the heading of subsec. (j)... Sec. 1201(f), deleted ", subsection (d)(8)(D)," after "provided in this subsection" in para. (c)(1), effective for individuals who begin work for the employer after 9/30/96.

Prior to amendment, para. (c)(4) read as follows:

"(4) Termination. The term 'wages' shall not include any amount paid or incurred to an individual who begins work for the employer after December 31, 1994."

Prior to amendment, subsec. (d) read as follows:

"(d) Members of targeted groups. For purposes of this subpart—

"(1) In general.

"An individual is a member of a targeted group if such individual is—

"(A) a vocational rehabilitation referral,

"(B) an economically disadvantaged youth,

"(C) an economically disadvantaged Vietnam-era veteran,

"(D) an SSI recipient,

"(E) a general assistance recipient,

"(F) a youth participating in a cooperative education program,

"(G) an economically disadvantaged ex-convict,

"(H) an eligible work incentive employee,

"(I) an involuntarily terminated CETA employee, or

"(J) a qualified summer youth employee.

"(2) Vocational rehabilitation referral.

"The term 'vocational rehabilitation referral' means any individual who is certified by the designated local agency as—

"(A) having a physical or mental disability which, for such individual, constitutes or results in a substantial handicap to employment, and

"(B) having been referred to the employer upon completion of (or while receiving) rehabilitative services pursuant to—

"(i) an individualized written rehabilitation plan under a State plan for vocational rehabilitation services approved under the Rehabilitation Act of 1973, or

"(ii) a program of vocational rehabilitation carried out under chapter 31 of title 38, United States Code.

"(3) Economically disadvantaged youth.

"(A) In general. The term 'economically disadvantaged youth' means any individual who is certified by the designated local agency as—

"(i) meeting the age requirements of subparagraph (B), and

"(ii) being a member of an economically disadvantaged family (as determined under paragraph (11)).

"(B) Age requirements. An individual meets the age requirements of this subparagraph if such individual has attained age 18 but not age 23 on the hiring date.

"(4) Vietnam veteran who is a member of an economically disadvantaged family. The term 'Vietnam veteran who is a member of an economically disadvantaged family' means any individual who is certified by the designated local agency as—

"(A)(i) having served on active duty (other than active duty for training) in the Armed Forces of the United States for a period of more than 180 days, any part of which occurred after August 4, 1964, and before May 8, 1975, or

"(ii) having been discharged or released from active duty in the Armed Forces of the United States for a service-connected disability if any part of such active duty was performed after August 4, 1964, and before May 8, 1975,

1,261

"(B) not having any day during the preemployment period which was a day of extended active duty in the Armed Forces of the United States, and

"(C) being a member of an economically disadvantaged family (determined under paragraph (11)).

For purposes of subparagraph (B), the term 'extended active duty' means a period of more than 90 days during which the individual was on active duty (other than active duty for training).

"(5) SSI recipients. The term 'SSI recipient' means any individual who is certified by the designated local agency as receiving supplemental security income benefits under title XVI of the Social Security Act (including supplemental security income benefits of the type described in section 1616 of such Act or Sec. 212 of P.L.93-66 for any month ending in the preemployment period.

"(6) General assistance recipients.

"(A) In general. The term 'general assistance recipient' means any individual who is certified by the designated local agency as receiving assistance under a qualified general assistance program for any period of not less than 30 days ending within the preemployment period.

"(B) Qualified general assistance program. The term 'qualified general assistance program' means any program of a State or a political subdivision of a State—

"(i) which provides general assistance or similar assistance which—

"(I) is based on need, and

"(II) consists of money payments or voucher or scrip, and

"(ii) which is designated by the Secretary (after consultation with the Secretary of Health and Human Services) as meeting the requirements of clause (i).

"(7) Economically disadvantaged ex-convict. The term 'economically disadvantaged ex-convict' means any individual who is certified by the designated local agency—

"(A) as having been convicted of a felony under any statute of the United States or any State,

"(B) as being a member of an economically disadvantaged family (as determined under paragraph (11)), and

"(C) as having a hiring date which is not more than 5 years after the last date on which such individual was so convicted or was released from prison.

"(8) Youth participating in a qualified cooperative education program.

"(A) In general. The term 'youth participating in a qualified cooperative education program' means any individual who is certified by the school participating in the program as—

"(i) having attained age 16 and not having attained age 20,

"(ii) not having graduated from a high school or vocational school,

"(iii) being enrolled in and actively pursuing a qualified cooperative education program, and

"(iv) being a member of an economically disadvantaged family (as determined under paragraph (11)).

"(B) Qualified cooperative education program defined. The term 'qualified cooperative education program' means a program of vocational education for individuals who (through written cooperative arrangements between a qualified school and 1 or more employers) receive instruction (including required academic instruction) by alternation of study and school with a job in any occupational field (but only if these 2 experiences are planned by the school and employer so that each contributes to the student's education and employability).

"(C) Qualified school defined. The term 'qualified school' means—

"(i) a specialized high school used exclusively or principally for the provision of vocational education to individuals who are available for study in preparation for entering the labor market,

"(ii) the department of a high school exclusively or principally used for providing vocational education to persons who are available for study in preparation for entering the labor market, or

"(iii) a technical or vocational school used exclusively or principally for the provision of vocational education to persons who have completed or left high school and who are available for study in preparation for entering the labor market.

A school which is not a public school shall be treated as a qualified school only if it is exempt from tax under section 501(a).

"(D) Wages. In the case of remuneration attributable to services performed while the individual meets the requirements of clauses (i), (ii), and (iii) of subparagraph (A), wages, and unemployment insurance wages, shall be determined without regard to section 3306(c)(10)(C).

"(9) Eligible work incentive employees. The term 'eligible work incentive employee' means an individual who has been certified by the designated local agency as—

"(A) being eligible for financial assistance under part A of title IV of the Social Security Act and as having continually received such financial assistance during the 90-day period which immediately precedes the date on which such individual is hired by the employer, or

"(B) having been placed in employment under a work incentive program established under section 432(b)(1) or 445 of the Social Security Act.

"(10) Involuntarily terminated CETA employee. The term 'involuntarily terminated CETA employee' means an individual who is certified by the designated local agency as having been involuntarily terminated after December 31, 1980, from employment financed in whole or in part under a program under part D of title II or title VI of the Comprehensive Employment and Training Act. This paragraph shall not apply to any individual who begins work for the employer after December 31, 1982.

"(11) Members of economically disadvantaged families. An individual is a member of an economically disadvantaged family if the designated local agency determines that such individual was a member of a family which had an income during the 6 months immediately preceding the earlier of the month in which such determination occurs or the month in which the hiring date occurs, which, on an annual basis, would be 70 percent or less of the Bureau of Labor Statistics lower living standard. Any such determination shall be valid for the 45-day period beginning on the date such determination is made. Any such determination with respect to an individual who is a qualified summer youth employee or youth participating in a qualified cooperative education program with respect to any employer shall also apply for purposes of determining whether such individual is a member of another targeted group with respect to such employer.

"(12) Qualified summer youth employee.

"(A) In general. The term 'qualified summer youth employee' means an individual—

"(i) who performs services for the employer between May 1 and September 15,

"(ii) who is certified by the designated local agency as having attained age 16 but not 18 on the hiring date (or if later, on May 1 of the calendar year involved),

"(iii) who has not been an employee of the employer during any period prior to the 90-day period described in subparagraph (B)(ii), and

"(iv) who is certified by the designated local agency as being a member of an economically disadvantaged family (as determined under paragraph (11)).

"(B) Special rules for determining amount of credit. For purposes of applying this subpart to wages paid or incurred to any qualified summer youth employee—

"(i) subsection (b)(2) shall be applied by substituting 'any 90-day period between May 1 and September 15' for 'the 1-year period beginning with the day the individual begins work for the employer', and

"(ii) subsection (b)(3) shall be applied by substituting '$3,000' for '$6,000'.

"(C) Special rule for continued employment for same employer. In the case of an individual who, with respect to the same employer, is certified as a member of another targeted group after such individual has been a qualified summer youth employee, paragraph (14) shall be applied by substituting 'certified' for 'hired by the employer'.

"(13) Preemployment period. The term 'preemployment period' means the 60-day period ending on the hiring date.

"(14) Hiring date. The term 'hiring date' means the day the individual is hired by the employer.

"(15) Designated local agency. The term 'designated local agency' means a State employment security agency established in accordance with the Act of June 6, 1933, as amended (29 U.S.C. 49–49n).

"(16) Special rules for certifications.

"(A) In general. An individual shall not be treated as a member of a targeted group unless, on or before the day on which such individual begins work for the employer, the employer—

"(i) has received a certification from a designated local agency that such individual is a member of a targeted group, or

"(ii) has requested in writing such certification from the designated local agency.

For purposes of the preceding sentence, if on or before the day on which such individual begins work for the employer, such individual has received from a designated local agency (or other agency or organization designated pursuant to a written agreement with such designated local agency) a written preliminary determination that such individual is a member of a targeted group, then 'the fifth day' shall be substituted for 'the day' in such sentence.

"(B) Incorrect certifications. If—

"(i) an individual has been certified as a member of a targeted group, and

"(ii) such certification is incorrect because it was based on false information provided by such individual,

the certification shall be revoked and wages paid by the employer after the date on which notice of revocation is received by the employer shall not be treated as qualified wages.

"(C) Employer request must specify potential basis for eligibility. In any request for a certification of an individual as a member of a targeted group, the employer shall—

"(i) specify each subparagraph (but not more than 2) of paragraph (1) by reason of which the employer believes that such individual is such a member, and

"(ii) certify that a good faith effort was made to determine that such individual is such a member."

Prior to amendment, para. (i)(3) read as follows:

"(3) Individuals not meeting minimum employment period. No wages shall be taken into account under subsection (a) with respect to any individual unless such individual either—

"(A) is employed by the employer at least 90 days (14 days in the case of an individual described in subsection (d)(12)), or

"(B) has completed at least 120 hours (20 hours in the case of an individual described in subsection (d)(12)) of services performed for the employer."

In 1993, P.L. 103-66, Sec. 13102(a), substituted "December 31, 1994" for "June 30, 1992" in para. (c)(4), effective for individuals who begin work for the employer after 6/30/92.

—P.L. 103-66, Sec. 13302(d), added ", or, if the taxpayer is an entity other than a corporation, to any individual who owns, directly or indirectly, more than 50 percent of the capital and profits interests in the entity," after "of the corporation" in subpara. (i)(1)(A), effective 8/10/93.

In 1991, P.L. 102-227, Sec. 105(a), substituted "June 30, 1992" for "December 31, 1991" in para. (c)(4), effective for individuals who begin work for the employer after 12/31/91.

In 1990, P.L. 101-508, Sec. 11405(a), substituted "December 31, 1991" for "September 30, 1990" in para. (c)(4), effective for individuals who begin work for the employer after 9/30/90.

Tax credits
Code Sec. 51

In 1989, P.L. 101-239, Sec. 7103(a), substituted "September 30, 1990" for "December 31, 1989" in para. (c)(4), effective 12/19/89.

—P.L. 101-239, Sec. 7103(c)(1), added subpara. (d)(16)(C), effective for individuals who begin work for the employer after 12/31/89.

In 1988, P.L. 100-647, Sec. 1017(a), substituted "subsection (a)" for "subsection (a)(1)" in clause (d)(12)(B)(i), before deletion by Sec. 4010(d)(1) of this Act, effective with respect to individuals who begin work for the employer after 12/31/85.

—P.L. 100-647, Sec. 4010(a), substituted "December 31, 1989" for "December 31, 1988" in para. (c)(4), effective 11/10/88.

—P.L. 100-647, Sec. 4010(c)(1), substituted "age 23" for "age 25" in subpara. (d)(3)(B) . . . Sec. 4010(d)(1), deleted clause (d)(12)(B)(i), and redesignated clauses (d)(12)(B)(ii) and (iii) as clauses (d)(12)(B)(i) and (ii), effective for individuals who begin work for the employer after 12/31/88.

Prior to deletion, clause (d)(12)(B)(i) read as follows:

"(i) subsection (a) shall be applied by substituting '85 percent' for '40 percent'",

—P.L. 100-485, Sec. 202(c)(6), substituted "section 482(e)" for "section 414" in subpara. (c)(2)(B), effective on 10/1/90.

In 1987, P.L. 100-203, Sec. 10601(a), redesignated para. (c)(3) as (c)(4) and added new para. (c)(3), effective for amounts paid or incurred on or after 1/1/87, for services rendered on or after 1/1/87.

In 1986, P.L. 99-514, Sec. 1701(a), substituted "December 31, 1988" for "December 31, 1985" in para. (c)(3) . . . Sec. 1701(b)(1), amended subsec. (a) . . . Sec. 1701(b)(2)(A)(i), deleted para. (b)(3) and redesignated para. (b)(4) as (b)(3) . . . Sec. 1701(b)(2)(A)(ii), deleted ", and the amount of the qualified second-year wages," after "first-year wages" in para. (b)(3) [as so redesignated] . . . Sec. 1701(b)(2)(B)(i), substituted "40 percent" for "50 percent" in clause (d)(12)(B)(i) . . . Sec. 1701(b)(2)(B)(ii), deleted clause (d)(12)(B)(ii) and redesignated clauses (d)(12)(B)(iii) and (iv) as clauses (d)(12)(B)(ii) and (iii) . . . Sec. 1701(b)(2)(B)(iii), substituted "subsection (b)(3)" for "subsection (b)(4)" in clause (d)(12)(B)(iii) [as so redesignated] . . . Sec. 1701(c), added para. (i)(3), effective with respect to individuals who begin work for the employer after 12/31/85.

Prior to amendment, subsec. (a) read as follows:

"(a) Determination of amount.

"For purposes of section 38, the amount of the targeted jobs credit determined under this section for the taxable year shall be the sum of—

"(1) 50 percent of the qualified first-year wages for such year, and

"(2) 25 percent of the qualified second-year wages for such year."

Prior to deletion, para. (b)(3) read as follows:

"(3) Qualified second-year wages. The term 'qualified second-year wages' means, with respect to any individual, the qualified wages attributable to service rendered during the 1-year period beginning on the day after the last day of the 1-year period with respect to such individual determined under paragraph (2)."

Prior to deletion, clause (d)(12)(B)(ii) read as follows:

"(ii) subsections (a)(2) and (b)(3) shall not apply,"

—P.L. 99-514, Sec. 1878(f)(1), redesignated the subsec. (j) added by Sec. 1041(c)(1) of P.L. 98-369, as subsec. (k), effective for individuals who begin work for the employer after 7/18/84.

—P.L. 99-514, Sec. 1878(f)(2), amended Sec. 1041(c)(5)(B) of P.L.98-369 [reproduced below], exceptions to the effective date for changes made by Sec. 1041(c) of P.L.98-369, by substituting "section 51(k)" for "section 51(j)".

In 1984, P.L. 98-369, Sec. 474(p)(1), amended subsec. (a) . . . Sec. 474(p)(2), substituted "the targeted jobs credit determined under this subpart" for "the credit provided by section 44B" in subsec. (g) . . . Sec. 474(p)(3), added subsec. (j), effective for tax. yrs. begin. after 12/31/83, and for carrybacks from tax. yrs. begin. after 12/31/83.

Prior to amendment, subsec. (a) read as follows:

"(a) Determination of amount. The amount of the credit allowable by section 44B for the taxable year shall be the sum of—

"(1) 50 percent of the qualified first-year wages for such year, and

"(2) 25 percent of the qualified second-year wages for such year."

—P.L. 98-369, Sec. 712(n), added the last sentence of para. (d)(11), effective for amounts paid or incurred after 4/30/83 to individuals beginning work for the employer after 4/30/83.

—P.L. 98-369, Sec. 1041(a), substituted "December 31, 1985" for "December 31, 1984" in para. (c)(3), effective for individuals who begin work for the employer after 7/18/84.

—P.L. 98-369, Sec. 1041(c)(1), added subsec. (j) [sic , (k)] . . . Sec. 1041(c)(2), added the last sentence of subpara. (d)(16)(A) . . . Sec. 1041(c)(3), substituted "(or if later, on May 1 of the calendar year involved)" for "(as defined in paragraph (14))" in clause (d)(12)(A)(ii) . . . Sec. 1041(c)(4), deleted "(or, in the case of a vocational rehabilitation referral, the day the individual begins work for the employer on or after the beginning of such individual's rehabilitation plan)" before the period at the end of para. (b)(2), effective for individuals who begin work for the employer after 7/18/84, except as provided in Sec. 1041(c)(5)(B) [as amended by Sec. 1878(f)(2) of P.L. 99-514, see above] of this Act which reads as follows:

"(B) Special rule for employees performing services for other persons.—Paragraph (2) of section 51(k) of the Internal Revenue Code of 1954 (as added by this subsection [Sec. 1041 of P.L.96-369 and the amendment made by paragraph (3) of this subsection [Sec. 1041of P.L.96-369] shall apply to individuals who begin work for the employer after December 31, 1984."

—P.L. 98-369, Sec. 2638(b), amended para. (c)(2), effective for payments made on or after 7/18/84.

Prior to amendment, para. (c)(2) read as follows:

"(2) Exclusion for employers receiving on-the-job training payments. The term 'wages' shall not include any amounts paid or incurred by an employer for any period to any individual for whom the employer receives federally funded payments for on-the-job training of such individual for such period."

—P.L. 98-369, Sec. 2663(j)(5)(A), substituted "Health and Human Services" for "Health, Education and Welfare" in clause (d)(6)(B)(ii), effective 7/18/84; but such amendment shall not be construed as changing or affecting any right, liability, status, or interpretation which existed (under the provisions of law involved) before 7/18/84.

In 1983, P.L. 97-448, Sec. 102(1)(1), substituted "clauses (i), (ii), and (iii) of subparagraph (A)" for "subparagraph (A)" in subpara. (d)(8)(D), effective for wages paid or incurred after 12/31/81, in tax. yrs. end. after 12/31/81.

—P.L. 97-448, Sec. 102(1)(2), substituted "subsection (b)(2)" for "subsection (b)(2)(A)" in Sec. 261(g)(1)(B) of P.L. 97-34, the effective date for changes made by Sec. 261(b)(2) of P.L.97-34, see below.

—P.L. 97-448, Sec. 102(1)(3), substituted "section 432(b)(1) or 445" for "section 432(b)(1)" in subpara. (d)(9)(B), effective as provided in Sec. 261(g)(1)(B) of P.L. 97-34, reproduced below.

—P.L. 97-448, Sec. 102(1)(4), substituted "the earlier of the month in which such determination occurs or the month in which the hiring date occurs" for "the month in which such determination occurs" in para. (d)(11), effective for certifications made after 1/12/83 for individuals beginning work for an employer after 5/11/82.

In 1982, P.L. 97-248, Sec. 233(a), substituted "1984" for "1982" in para. (c)(3), effective 9/3/82.

—P.L. 97-248, Sec. 233(b)(1), deleted "or" at the end of subpara. (d)(1)(H) . . . Sec. 233(b)(2), substituted ", or" for the period in subpara. (d)(1)(I) . . . Sec. 233(b)(3), added subpara. (d)(1)(J) . . . Sec. 233(b)(4), redesignated paras. (d)(12), (d)(13), (d)(14) and (d)(15) as paras. (d)(13), (d)(14), (d)(15), and (d)(16) . . . Sec. 233(b)(5), added new para. (d)(12), effective for amounts paid or incurred after 4/30/83 to individuals beginning work for the employer after 4/30/83.

—P.L. 97-248, Sec. 233(c), added the last sentence to para. (d)(10), effective 9/3/82.

—P.L. 97-248, Sec. 233(d), added "or voucher or scrip" before ", and" in clause (d)(6)(B)(i)(II), for amounts paid or incurred after 7/1/82 to individuals beginning work for the employer after 7/1/82.

—P.L. 97-248, Sec. 233(f), substituted "on or before the day" for "before the day" in subpara. (d)(15)(A), (before amendment by Sec. 233(b)(4) of this Act, see above), effective for individuals who begin work for the taxpayer after 5/11/82.

In 1981, P.L. 97-34, Sec. 261(a), amended para. (c)(4), effective for wages paid or incurred with respect to individuals first beginning work for an employer after 8/13/81 in tax. yrs. end. after 8/13/81.

Prior to amendment, para. (c)(4) read as follows:

"(4) Termination. The term 'wages' shall not include any amount paid or incurred after December 31, 1981."

—P.L. 97-34, Sec. 261(b)(1), deleted "or" at the end of subpara. (d)(1)(F), substituted a comma for the period at the end of subpara. (d)(1)(G), added subparas. (d)(1)(H) and (d)(1)(I), effective for wages paid or incurred with respect to individuals first beginning work for an employer after 8/13/81 in tax. yrs. ending after 8/13/81.

—P.L. 97-34, Sec. 261(b)(2)(A), redesignated paras. (d)(9), (10), (11) and (12) as paras. (d)(11), (12), (13) and (14), and added new paras. (d)(9) and (10) . . . Sec. 261(b)(2)(B)(ii), deleted para. (c)(3) and redesignated para. (c)(4) (as amended by Sec. 261(a) of this Act) as para. (c)(3) . . . Sec. 261(b)(2)(B)(iii), substituted "paragraph (11)" for "paragraph (9)" in clause (d)(3)(A)(ii), subpara. (d)(4)(C), and subpara. (d)(7)(B), effective for wages paid or incurred with respect to individuals first beginning to work for an employer after 8/13/81 in tax. yrs. end. after 8/13/81, except as provided in Sec. 261(g)(1)(B) of this Act which reads as follows:

"(B) Eligible work incentive employees. The amendments made by subsection (b)(2)(A) [P.L.97-34] to the extent relating to the designation of eligible work incentive employees (within the meaning of section 51(d)(9) of the Internal Revenue Code of 1954) as members of a targeted group and subsection (b)(2)(B)(ii) [P.L.97-34] shall apply to taxable years beginning after December 31, 1981. In the case of an eligible work incentive employee, subsections (a) and (b) of section 51 of such Code shall be applied for taxable years beginning after December 31, 1981, as if such employees had been members of a targeted group for taxable years beginning before January 1, 1982."

Prior to amendment, para. (c)(3) read as follows:

"(3) Individuals for whom WIN credit claimed. The term 'wages' does not include any amount paid or incurred by the employer to an individual with respect to whom the employer claims credit under section 40."

—P.L. 97-34, Sec. 261(b)(3), added "and" at the end of subpara. (d)(4)(B), substituted a period for ", and" at the end of subpara. (d)(4)(C), and deleted subpara. (d)(4)(D), effective for wages paid or incurred with respect to individuals first beginning work for an employer after 8/13/81, in tax. yrs. ending after 8/13/81.

Prior to deletion, subpara. (d)(4)(D) read as follows:

"(D) not having attained the age of 35 on the hiring date."

—P.L. 97-34, Sec. 261(b)(4), deleted "and" at the end of clause (d)(8)(A)(ii), substituted ", and" for the period at the end of clause (d)(8)(A)(iii) and added clause (d)(8)(A)(iv), effective for wages paid or incurred after 12/31/81, in tax. yrs. ending after 12/31/81.

—P.L. 97-34, Sec. 261(c)(1), added para. (d)(15), effective for all individuals whether such individuals began to work for their employer before, on, or after 8/13/81. Sec. 261(g)(2)(B) and (C) of this Act provide:

"(B) Special rule for individuals who began work for the employer before 45th day before date of enactment. In the case of any individual (other than an individual described in section 51(d)(8) of the Internal Revenue Code of 1954) who began work for the employer before the date 45 days before the date of the enactment of this Act, paragraph (15) of section 51(d) of the Internal Revenue Code of 1954 (as added by subsection (c)(1)) shall be applied by substituting 'July 23, 1981,' for the day on which such individual begins work for the employer.

"(C) Individuals who begin work for employer within 45 days before or after date of enactment. In the case of any individual (other than an individual described in section 51(d)(8) of the Internal Revenue Code of 1954) who begins work for the employer during the 90-day period beginning with the date 45 days before the date of the enactment of this Act, and in the case of an individual described in section 51(d)(8) of such Code who begins work before the end of such 90-day period, paragraph (15) of section 51(d) of such Code (as added by subsection (c)(1)) shall be applied by substituting 'the last day of the 90-day period beginning with the date 45 days before the date of the enactment of this Act' for the day on which such individual begins work for the employer."

—P.L. 97-34, Sec. 261(c)(2), amended para. (d)(11) (as redesignated by Sec. 261(b)(2)(A) of this Act, see above) . . . Sec. 261(d), added subsec. (i), effective for wages paid or incurred with respect to individuals first beginning work for an employer after 8/13/81, in tax. yrs. end. after 8/13/81.

Prior to amendment, para. (d)(11) read as follows:

"(11) Members of economically disadvantaged families. An individual is a member of an economically disadvantaged family if the designated local agency determines that such individual was a member of a family which had an income during the 6 months immediately preceding the month in which the hiring date occurs, which, on an annual basis would be less than 70 percent of the bureau of Labor Statistics lower living standard."

—P.L. 97-34, Sec. 261(e)(1), deleted subsec. (e) . . . Sec. 261(e)(2), substituted "any taxable year" for "any year" in paras. (f)(1) and (2) and deleted para. (f)(3), effective for tax. yrs. begin. after 12/31/81.

Prior to deletion, subsec. (e) read as follows:

"(e) Qualified first-year wages cannot exceed 30 percent of FUTA wages for all employees. The amount of the qualified first-year wages which may be taken into account under subsection (a)(1) for any taxable year shall not exceed 30 percent of the aggregate unemployment insurance wages paid by the employer during the calendar year ending in such taxable year. For purposes of the preceding sentence, except as provided in subsection (h)(1) the term 'unemployment insurance wages' has the meaning given to the term 'wages' by section 3306(b)."

Prior to deletion, para. (f)(3) read as follows:

"(3) Year defined. For purposes of this subsection and subsection (h), the term 'year' means the taxable year; except that, for purposes of applying so much of such subsections as relates to subsection (e), such term means the calendar year."

—P.L. 97-34, Sec. 261(f)(1)(A), amended para. (d)(14) (as redesignated by Sec. 261(b)(2)(A) of this Act, see above) . . . Sec. 261(f)(1)(B), substituted "United States Employment Service" for "Secretary of Labor" in both the heading and text of subsec. (g), effective 10/12/81.

Prior to amendment, para. (d)(14) read as follows:

"(14) Designated local agency. The term 'designated local agency' means the agency for any locality designated jointly by the Secretary and the Secretary of Labor to perform certification of employees for employers in that locality."

In 1980, P.L. 96-222, Sec. 103(a)(6)(A), substituted "December 31, 1981" for "December 31, 1980" in para. (c)(4) . . . Sec. 103(a)(6)(E)(i), amended subpara. (d)(8)(D) . . . Sec. 106(a)(6)(E)(ii), substituted ", subsection (d)(8)(D), and subsection (h)(2)," for "and subsection (h)(2)" in para. (c)(1), effective for amounts paid or incurred after '78, in tax. yrs. end. after 12/31/78.

Prior to amendment, subpara. (d)(8)(D) read as follows:

"(D) Individual must be currently pursuing program. Wages shall be taken into account with respect to a qualified cooperative education program only if the wages are attributable to services performed while the individual meets the requirements of subparagraph (A)."

—P.L. 96-222, Sec. 103(a)(6)(F), substituted "age 20" for "age 19" in clause (d)(8)(A)(i), presumably intended by Congress to be effective with respect to wages paid or incurred on or after 11/27/79 in tax. yrs. end. on or after 11/27/79 [Sec. 103(b)(1)], although technically effective for amounts paid or incurred after '78, in tax. yrs. end. after 12/31/78 [Sec. 103(b)(2)].

—P.L. 96-222, Sec. 103(a)(6)(G)(iii), substituted "amounts paid or incurred" for "amounts paid" in para. (c)(2) . . . Sec. 103(a)(6)(G)(iv), deleted "or" at the end of subpara. (d)(1)(E) . . . Sec. 103(a)(6)(G)(v), substituted "active duty" for "active day" in clause (d)(4)(A)(i) . . . Sec. 103(a)(6)(G)(vi), substituted "preemployment" for "preemployment" in subpara. (d)(4)(B) . . . Sec. 103(a)(6)(G)(vii), substituted "preemployment" for "pre-employment" in para. (d)(5) . . . Sec. 103(a)(6)(G)(viii), substituted "employers" for "employer" in para. (d)(12) . . . Sec. 103(a)(6)(G)(ix), added "except as provided in subsection (h)(1)," after "the preceding sentence" in subsec. (e), effective for amounts paid or incurred after 12/31/78, in tax. yrs. end. after 12/31/78.

In 1978, P.L. 95-600, Sec. 321(a), amended Code Sec. 51, for amounts paid or incurred after 12/31/78, in tax. yrs. end. after 12/31/78. See Sec. 321(d)(2) and (3) reproduced in note at Code Sec. 44B.

Prior to amendment, Code Sec. 51 read as follows:

"Sec. 51. Amount of credit.

"(a) Determination of amount.

"The amount of the credit allowable by section 44B shall be—

"(1) for a taxable year beginning in 1977, an amount equal to 50 percent of the excess of the aggregate unemployment insurance wages paid during 1977 over 102 percent of the aggregate unemployment insurance wages paid during 1976, and

"(2) for a taxable year beginning in 1978, an amount equal to 50 percent of the excess of the aggregate unemployment insurance wages paid during 1978 over 102 percent of the aggregate unemployment insurance wages paid during 1977.

"(b) Minimum preceding year wages.

"For purposes of determining the amount of the credit under subsection (a) with respect to 1977 or 1978, 102 percent of the amount of the aggregate unemployment insurance wages paid during the preceding calendar year shall be deemed to be not less than 50 percent of the amount of such wages paid during 1977 or 1978, as the case may be.

"(c) Total wages must increase.

"The amount of the credit allowable by section 44B for any taxable year shall not exceed the amount which would be determined for such year under subsection (a) (without regard to subsection (b)) if—

"(1) the aggregate amounts taken into account as unemployment insurance wages were determined without any dollar limitation, and

"(2) '105 percent' were substituted for '102 percent' in the appropriate paragraph of subsection (a).

"(d) $100,000 per year limitation on credit.

"Except as provided in subsection (e), the amount of the credit determined under this subpart for any employer (and the amount of the credit allowable by section 44B to any taxpayer) with respect to any calendar year shall not exceed $100,000.

"(e) Additional 10 percent credit for vocational rehabilitation referrals.

"(1) In general. The amount of the credit allowable by section 44B for any taxable year beginning in 1977 or 1978 (determined without regard to this subsection) shall be increased by an amount equal to 10 percent of the unemployment insurance wages paid by the employer to vocational rehabilitation referrals during the calendar year in which such taxable year begins.

"(2) Only first year taken into account. For purposes of this subsection, unemployment insurance wages may be taken into account with respect to any individual—

"(A) only to the extent attributable to services rendered during the 1-year period beginning with his first payment of wages by the employer after the beginning of such individual's rehabilitation plan, and

"(B) only if such first payment occurs after December 31, 1976.

"(3) Only first $4,200 of wages taken into account for any individual. For purposes of this subsection, the unemployment insurance wages paid during 1978 which are taken into account with respect to any individual shall not exceed $4,200 reduced by the amount of unemployment insurance wages paid by the employer to such individual during 1977.

"(4) 20-percent limitation. The amount of the credit allowable by reason of this subsection for any taxable year shall not exceed one-fifth of the credit determined for such year under this section without regard to this subsection and subsection (d).

"(f) Definitions.

"For purposes of this subpart—

"(1) Unemployment insurance wages. Except as otherwise provided in this subpart, the term 'unemployment insurance wages' has the meaning given to the term 'wages' by section 3306(b), except that, in the case of amounts paid during 1978, '$4,200' shall be substituted for '$6,000' each place it appears in section 3306(b).

"(2) Agricultural labor. If the services performed by any employee for an employer during more than one-half of any pay period (within the meaning of section 3306(d)) taken into account with respect to any calendar year constitute agricultural labor (within the meaning of section 3306(k)), the term 'unemployment insurance wages' means, with respect to the remuneration paid by the employer to such employee for such year, an amount equal to so much of such remuneration as constitutes 'wages' within the meaning of section 3121(a), except that the contribution and benefit base for each calendar year shall be deemed to be $4,200.

"(3) Railway labor. If more than one-half of the remuneration paid by an employer to an employee during the calendar year is remuneration for service described in section 3306(c)(9), the term 'unemployment insurance wages' means, with respect to such employee for such year, an amount equal to ⅞ of so much of the remuneration paid to such employee during such year as is subject to contributions under section 8(a) of the Railroad Unemployment Insurance Act (45 U.S.C. 358(a)).

"(4) Vocational rehabilitation referral. The term 'vocational rehabilitation referral' means any individual who—

"(A) has a physical or mental disability which, for such individual, constitutes or results in a substantial handicap to employment, and

"(B) has been referred to the employer upon completion of (or while receiving) rehabilitative services pursuant to—

"(i) an individualized rehabilitation plan under a State plan for vocational rehabilitation services approved under the Rehabilitation Act of 1973, or

"(ii) a program of vocational rehabilitation carried out under chapter 31 of title 38, United States Code.

"(g) Rules for application of section.

"For purposes of this subpart—

"(1) Remuneration must be for trade or business employment within United States. Remuneration paid by an employer to an employee during any calendar year shall be taken into account only if more than one-half of the remuneration so paid is for services performed in the United States in a trade or business of the employer.

"(2) Special rule for certain determinations. Any determination as to whether paragraph (1) of this subsection, or paragraph (2) or (3) of subsection (f), applies with respect to any employee for any calendar year shall be made without regard to subsections (a) and (b) of section 52."

Tax credits — Code Sec. 52(c)

In 1977, P.L. 95-30, Sec. 202(b), added Code Sec. 51, effective for tax. yrs. begin. after 12/31/76 and for credit carrybacks from such yrs.

Sec. 51A. Repealed.

In 2010, P.L. 111-312, Sec. 101(a)(1), substituted "December 31, 2012" for "December 31, 2010" both places it appeared in Sec. 901 of P.L. 107-16, [see below] effective as if included in the enactment of P.L. 107-16, EGTRRA, 6/7/2001.

In 2006, P.L. 109-432, Sec. 105(a), substituted "2007" for "2005" in subsec. (f) . . . Sec. 105(e)(4)(A), repealed Code Sec. 51A, effective for individuals who begin work for the employer after 12/31/2005.

Prior to repeal, Code Sec. 51A read as follows:

"SEC. 51A. TEMPORARY INCENTIVES FOR EMPLOYING LONG-TERM FAMILY ASSISTANCE RECIPIENTS.

"(a) Determination of amount.

"For purposes of section 38, the amount of the welfare-to-work credit determined under this section for the taxable year shall be equal to—

"(1) 35 percent of the qualified first-year wages for such year, and

"(2) 50 percent of the qualified second-year wages for such year.

"(b) Qualified wages defined. For purposes of this section—

"(1) In general.

"The term 'qualified wages' means the wages paid or incurred by the employer during the taxable year to individuals who are long-term family assistance recipients.

"(2) Qualified first-year wages.

"The term 'qualified first-year wages' means, with respect to any individual, qualified wages attributable to service rendered during the 1-year period beginning with the day the individual begins work for the employer.

"(3) Qualified second-year wages. The term 'qualified second-year wages' means, with respect to any individual, qualified wages attributable to service rendered during the 1-year period beginning on the day after the last day of the 1-year period with respect to such individual determined under paragraph (2).

"(4) Only the first $10,000 of wages per year taken into account.

"The amount of the qualified first-year wages, and the amount of qualified second-year wages, which may be taken into account with respect to any individual shall not exceed $10,000 per year.

"(5) Wages.

"(A) In general. The term 'wages' has the meaning given such term by section 51(c), without regard to paragraph (4) thereof.

"(B) Certain amounts treated as wages. The term 'wages' includes amounts paid or incurred by the employer which are excludable from such recipient's gross income under—

"(i) section 105 (relating to amounts received under accident and health plans),

"(ii) section 106 (relating to contributions by employer to accident and health plans),

"(iii) section 127 (relating to educational assistance programs), but only to the extent paid or incurred to a person not related to the employer, or

"(iv) section 129 (relating to dependent care assistance programs).

"The amount treated as wages by clause (i) or (ii) for any period shall be based on the reasonable cost of coverage for the period, but shall not exceed the applicable premium for the period under section 4980B(f)(4).

"(C) Special rules for agricultural and railway labor. If such recipient is an employee to whom subparagraph (A) or (B) of section 51(h)(1) applies, rules similar to the rules of such subparagraphs shall apply except that—

"(i) such subparagraph (A) shall be applied by substituting '$10,000' for '$6,000', and

"(ii) such subparagraph (B) shall be applied by substituting '$833.33' for '$500'.

"(c) Long-term family assistance recipients. For purposes of this section—

"(1) In general. The term 'long-term family assistance recipient' means any individual who is certified by the designated local agency (as defined in section 51(d)(11))—

"(A) as being a member of a family receiving assistance under a IV-A program (as defined in section 51(d)(2)(B)) for at least the 18-month period ending on the hiring date,

"(B)(i) as being a member of a family receiving such assistance for 18 months beginning after the date of the enactment of this section, and

"(ii) as having a hiring date which is not more than 2 years after the end of the earliest such 18-month period, or

"(C)(i) as being a member of a family which ceased to be eligible after the date of the enactment of this section for such assistance by reason of any limitation imposed by Federal or State law on the maximum period such assistance is payable to a family, and

"(ii) as having a hiring date which is not more than 2 years after the date of such cessation.

"(2) Hiring date. The term 'hiring date' has the meaning given such term by section 51(d).

"(d) Certain rules to apply.

"(1) In general. Rules similar to the rules of section 52, and subsections (d)(11), (f), (g), (i) (as in effect on the day before the date of the enactment of the Taxpayer Relief Act of 1997), (j), and (k) of section 51, shall apply for purposes of this section.

"(2) Credit to be part of general business credit, etc. References to section 51 in section 38(b), 280C(a), and 1396(c)(3) shall be treated as including references to this section.

"(e) Coordination with work opportunity credit. If a credit is allowed under this section to an employer with respect to an individual for any taxable year, then for purposes of applying section 51 to such employer, such individual shall not be treated as a member of a targeted group for such taxable year.

"(f) Termination. This section shall not apply to individuals who begin work for the employer after December 31, 2007."

In 2004, P.L. 108-311, Sec. 303(a)(2), substituted "December 31, 2005" for "December 31, 2003" in subsec. (f), effective for individuals who begin work for the employer after 12/31/2003.

In 2002, P.L. 107-358, Sec. 2, added subsec. (c) in Sec. 901 of P.L. 107-16 [see below], effective 12/17/2002.

—P.L. 107-147, Sec. 417(4), substituted "51(d)(11)" for "51(d)(10)" in para. (c)(1), effective 3/9/2002.

—P.L. 107-147, Sec. 605(a), substituted "2003" for "2001" in subsec. (f), effective for individuals who begin work for the employer after 12/31/2001.

In 2001, P.L. 107-16, Sec. 411(c), deleted "or would be so excludable but for section 127(d)" after "assistance programs)" in clause (b)(5)(B)(iii), effective for expenses relating to courses begin. after 12/31/2001.

—P.L. 107-16, Sec. 901, of this Act [as amended by Sec. 2 of P.L. 107-358, and Sec. 101(a)(1) of P.L. 111-312, see above], reads as follows:

"SEC. 901. SUNSET OF PROVISIONS OF ACT.

"(a) In general. All provisions of, and amendments made by, this Act shall not apply—

"(1) to taxable, plan, or limitation years beginning after December 31, 2012, or

"(2) in the case of title V, to estates of decedents dying, gifts made, or generation skipping transfers, after December 31, 2012.

"(b) Application of certain laws. The Internal Revenue Code of 1986 and the Employee Retirement Income Security Act of 1974 shall be applied and administered to years, estates, gifts, and transfers described in subsection (a) as if the provisions and amendments described in subsection (a) had never been enacted.

"(c) Exception. Subsection (a) shall not apply to section 803 (relating to no federal income tax on restitution received by victims of the Nazi regime or their heirs or estates)."

In 1999, P.L. 106-170, Sec. 505(a), substituted "December 31, 2001" for "June 30, 1999" in subsec. (f), effective for individuals who begin work for the employer after 6/30/99.

In 1998, P.L. 105-277, Sec. 1003, substituted "June 30, 1999" for "April 30, 1999" in subsec. (f), effective 10/21/98.

In 1997, P.L. 105-34, Sec. 801(a), added Code Sec. 51A, effective for individuals who begin work for the employer after 12/31/97.

Sec. 52. Special rules.
(a) Controlled group of corporations.

For purposes of this subpart, all employees of all corporations which are members of the same controlled group of corporations shall be treated as employed by a single employer. In any such case, the credit (if any) determined under section 51(a) with respect to each such member shall be its proportionate share of the wages giving rise to such credit. For purposes of this subsection, the term "controlled group of corporations" has the meaning given to such term by section 1563(a), except that—

(1) "more than 50 percent" shall be substituted for "at least 80 percent" each place it appears in section 1563(a)(1), and

(2) the determination shall be made without regard to subsections (a)(4) and (e)(3)(C) of section 1563.

(b) Employees of partnerships, proprietorships, etc., which are under common control.

For purposes of this subpart, under regulations prescribed by the Secretary—

(1) all employees of trades or business (whether or not incorporated) which are under common control shall be treated as employed by a single employer, and

(2) the credit (if any) determined under section 51(a) with respect to each trade or business shall be its proportionate share of the wages giving rise to such credit.

The regulations prescribed under this subsection shall be based on principles similar to the principles which apply in the case of subsection (a).

(c) Tax-exempt organizations.

No credit shall be allowed under section 38 for any work opportunity credit determined under this subpart to any organization (other than a cooperative described in section 521) which is exempt from income tax under this chapter.

(d) Estates and trusts.

In the case of an estate or trust—

(1) the amount of the credit determined under this subpart for any taxable year shall be apportioned between the estate or trust and the beneficiaries on the basis of the income of the estate or trust allocable to each, and

(2) any beneficiary to whom any amount has been apportioned under paragraph (1) shall be allowed, subject to section 38(c), a credit under section 38(a) for such amount.

(e) Limitations with respect to certain persons.

Under regulations prescribed by the Secretary, in the case of—

(1) a regulated investment company or a real estate investment trust subject to taxation under subchapter M (section 851 and following), and

(2) a cooperative organization described in section 1381(a),

rules similar to the rules provided in subsections (e) and (h) of section 46 (as in effect on the day before the date of the enactment [11/5/90] of the Revenue Reconciliation Act of 1990) shall apply in determining the amount of the credit under this subpart.

In 1997, P.L. 105-34, Sec. 1601(b), substituted "work opportunity credit" for "targeted jobs credit" in subsec. (c), effective for individuals who begin work for the employer after 9/30/96.

In 1996, P.L. 104-188, Sec. 1616(b)(2), deleted para. (e)(1) and redesignated paras. (e)(2) and (3) as (1) and (2), effective for tax. yrs. begin. after 12/31/95.

Prior to deletion, para. (e)(1) read as follows:

"(1) an organization to which section 593 (relating to reserves for losses on loans) applies,"

In 1990, P.L. 101-508, Sec. 11813(b)(4), substituted "section 46 (as in effect on the day before the date of the enactment of the Revenue Reconciliation Act of 1990)" for "section 46" in subsec. (e), effective for property placed in service after 12/31/90 except as provided in Sec. 11813(c)(2) of this Act, reproduced in note following Code Sec. 46.

In 1984, P.L. 98-369, Sec. 474(p)(4), substituted "the credit (if any) determined under section 51(a) with respect to each such member" for "the credit (if any) allowable by section 44B to each such member" in subsec. (a) . . . Sec. 474(p)(5), substituted "the credit (if any) determined under section 51(a)" for "the credit (if any) allowable by section 44B" in para. (b)(2) . . . Sec. 474(p)(6), substituted "credit shall be allowed under section 38 for any targeted jobs credit determined under this subpart" for "credit shall be allowed under section 44B" in subsec. (c) . . . Sec. 474(p)(7), substituted "subject to section 38(c), a credit under section 38(a)" for "subject to section 53, a credit under section 44B" in para. (d)(2), effective for tax. yrs. begin. after 12/31/83 and to carrybacks from tax. yrs. begin. after 12/31/83.

In 1982, P.L. 97-354, Sec. 5(a)(11), deleted subsec. (d) and redesignated subsecs. (e) and (f) as subsecs. (d) and (e), effective for tax. yrs. begin. after 12/31/82.

Prior to deletion, subsec. (d) read as follows:

"(d) Subchapter S Corporations. In the case of an electing small business corporation (as defined in section 1371)—

"(1) the amount of the credit determined under this subpart for any taxable year shall be apportioned pro rata among the persons who are shareholders of such corporation on the last day of such taxable year, and

"(2) any person to whom an amount is apportioned under paragraph (1) shall be allowed, subject to section 53, a credit under section 44B for such person."

In 1980, P.L. 96-222, Sec. 103(a)(5), substituted "subsections (e) and (h) of section 46" for "section 46(e)", in subsec. (f), effective for amounts paid or incurred after 12/31/78, in tax. yrs. end. after 12/31/78.

In 1978, P.L. 95-600, Sec. 321(c)(1)(A)(i), deleted subsecs. (c),(e), (i) and (j) . . . Sec. 321(c)(1)(A)(ii), redesignated subsecs. (d), (f), (g) and (h) as subsecs. (c), (d), (e) and (f), respectively . . . Sec. 321(c)(1)(B), substituted "proportionate share of the wages" for "proportionate contribution to the increase in unemployment insurance wages" in subsecs. (a) and (b) . . . Sec. 321(c)(1)(C)(i), added "and" at the end of para. (e)(1) . . . Sec. 321(c)(1)(C)(ii), substituted a period for ", and" at the end of para. (e)(2) . . . Sec. 321(c)(1)(C)(iii), deleted para. (e)(3), as redesignated by Sec. 321(c)(1)(A) of this Act, effective for amounts paid or incurred after '78, in tax. yrs. end. after 12/31/78.

Prior to amendment, subsecs. (c), read as follows:

"(c) Adjustments for certain acquisitions, etc.

"Under regulations prescribed by the Secretary—

"(1) Acquisitions. If, after December 31, 1975, an employer acquires the major portion of a trade or business of another person (hereinafter in this paragraph referred to as the 'predecessor') or the major portion of a separate unit of a trade or business of a predecessor, then, for purposes of applying this subpart for any calendar year ending after such acquisition, the amount of unemployment insurance wages deemed paid by the employer during periods before such acquisition shall be increased by so much of such wages paid by the predecessor with respect to the acquired trade or business as is attributable to the portion of such trade or business acquired by the employer.

"(2) Dispositions. If, after December 31, 1975—

"(A) an employer disposes of the major portion of any trade or business of the employer or the major portion of a separate unit of a trade or business of the employer in a transaction to which paragraph (1) applies, and

"(B) the employer furnishes the acquiring person such information as is necessary for the application of paragraph (1),

then, for purposes of applying this subpart for any calendar year ending after such disposition, the amount of unemployment insurance wages deemed paid by the employer during periods before such disposition shall be decreased by so much of such wages as is attributable to such trade or business or separate unit."

Prior to amendment, subsec. (e) read as follows:

"(e) Change in status from self-employed to employee.

"If—

"(1) during 1976 or 1977 an individual has net earnings from self-employment (as defined in section 1402(a)) which are attributable to such trade or business, and

"(2) for any portion of the succeeding calendar year such individual is an employee of such trade or business,

then, for purposes of determining the credit allowable for a taxable year beginning in such succeeding calendar year, the employer's aggregate unemployment insurance wages for 1976 or 1977, as the case may be, shall be increased by an amount equal to so much of the net earnings referred to in paragraph (1) as does not exceed $4,200."

Prior to amendment, subsecs. (i) and (j) read as follows

"(i) $50,000 limitation in the case of married individuals filing separate returns.

"In the case of a husband or wife who files a separate return, the limitation under section 51(d) shall be $50,000 in lieu of $100,000. This subsection shall not apply if the spouse of the taxpayer has no interest in a trade or business for the taxable year of such spouse which ends within or with the taxpayer's taxable year.

"(j) Certain short taxable years.

"If the employer has more than one taxable year beginning in 1977 or 1978, the credit under this subpart shall be determined for the employer's last taxable year beginning in 1977 or 1978, as the case may be."

Prior to amendment para. (e)(3), as redesignated by this Act, read as follows:

"(3) the $100,000 amount specified in section 51(d) applicable to such estate or trust shall be reduced to an amount which bears the same ratio to $100,000 as the portion of the credit allocable to the estate or trust under paragraph (1) bears to the entire amount of such credit."

In 1977, P.L. 95-30, Sec. 202(b), added Code Sec. 52, effective for tax. yrs. begin. after 12/31/76, and for credit carrybacks from such yrs.

SUBPART G.—CREDIT AGAINST REGULAR TAX FOR PRIOR YEAR MINIMUM TAX LIABILITY

Sec.

53. Credit for prior year minimum tax liability.

53. Repealed. [Limitation based on amount of tax.]

In 1986, P.L. 99-514, Sec. 701(b), added subpart G to Part IV of subchapter A of Chapter 1.

Sec. 53. Credit for prior year minimum tax liability.

(a) Allowance of credit.

There shall be allowed as a credit against the tax imposed by this chapter for any taxable year an amount equal to the minimum tax credit for such taxable year.

(b) Minimum tax credit.

For purposes of subsection (a), the minimum tax credit for any taxable year is the excess (if any) of—

(1) the adjusted net minimum tax imposed for all prior taxable years beginning after 1986, over

(2) the amount allowable as a credit under subsection (a) for such prior taxable years.

(c) Limitation.

The credit allowable under subsection (a) for any taxable year shall not exceed the excess (if any) of—

(1) the regular tax liability of the taxpayer for such taxable year reduced by the sum of the credits allowable under subparts A, B, D, E, and F of this part, over

(2) the tentative minimum tax for the taxable year.

(d) Definitions.

For purposes of this section—

(1) Net minimum tax.

(A) In general. The term "net minimum tax" means the tax imposed by section 55.

(B) Credit not allowed for exclusion preferences.
(i) Adjusted net minimum tax. The adjusted net minimum tax for any taxable year is—
(I) the amount of the net minimum tax for such taxable year, reduced by
(II) the amount which would be the net minimum tax for such taxable year if the only adjustments and items of tax preference taken into account were those specified in clause (ii).
(ii) Specified items. The following are specified in this clause—
(I) the adjustments provided for in subsection (b)(1) of section 56, and
(II) the items of tax preference described in paragraphs (1), (5) and (7) of section 57(a).
(iii) Credit allowable for exclusion preferences of corporations. In the case of a corporation—
(I) the preceding provisions of this subparagraph shall not apply, and
(II) the adjusted net minimum tax for any taxable year is the amount of the net minimum tax for such year.
(2) Tentative minimum tax. The term "tentative minimum tax" has the meaning given to such term by section 55(b).
(e) Special rule for individuals with long-term unused credits.
(1) **In general.** If an individual has a long-term unused minimum tax credit for any taxable year beginning before January 1, 2013, the amount determined under subsection (c) for such taxable year shall not be less than the AMT refundable credit amount for such taxable year.
(2) **AMT refundable credit amount.** For purposes of paragraph (1), the term "AMT refundable credit amount" means, with respect to any taxable year, the amount (not in excess of the long term unused minimum tax credit for such taxable year) equal to the greater of—
(A) 50 percent of the long-term unused minimum tax credit for such taxable year, or
(B) the amount (if any) of the AMT refundable credit amount determined under this paragraph for the taxpayer's preceding taxable year (determined without regard to subsection (f)(2)).
(3) **Long-term unused minimum tax credit.**
(A) In general. For purposes of this subsection, the term "long-term" unused minimum tax credit' means, with respect to any taxable year, the portion of the minimum tax credit determined under subsection (b) attributable to the adjusted net minimum tax for taxable years before the 3rd taxable year immediately preceding such taxable year.
(B) First-in, first-out ordering rule. For purposes of subparagraph (A), credits shall be treated as allowed under subsection (a) on a first-in, first-out basis.
(4) **Credit refundable.** For purposes of this title (other than this section), the credit allowed by reason of this subsection shall be treated as if it were allowed under subpart C.
(f) Treatment of certain underpayments, interest, and penalties attributable to the treatment of incentive stock options.
(1) **Abatement.** Any underpayment of tax outstanding on the date of the enactment of this subsection which is attributable to the application of section 56(b)(3) for any taxable year ending before January 1, 2008, and any interest or penalty with respect to such underpayment which is outstanding on such date of enactment, is hereby abated.

The amount determined under subsection (b)(1) shall not include any tax abated under the preceding sentence.
(2) **Increase in credit for certain interest and penalties already paid.** The AMT refundable credit amount, and the minimum tax credit determined under subsection (b), for the taxpayer's first 2 taxable years beginning after December 31, 2007, shall each be increased by 50 percent of the aggregate amount of the interest and penalties which were paid by the taxpayer before the date of the enactment of this subsection and which would (but for such payment) have been abated under paragraph (1).

In 2009, P.L. 111-5, Sec. 1142(b)(4)(A), deleted clause (d)(1)(B)(iii) and redesignated clause (d)(1)(B)(iv) as clause (d)(1)(B)(iii) ... Sec. 1142(b)(4)(B), deleted "increased in the manner provided in clause (iii)" in subclause (d)(1)(B)(iii)(II) [as redesignated], effective for vehicles acquired after 2/17/2009. Prior to deletion, clause (d)(1)(B)(iii) read as follows:
"(iii) Special rule. The adjusted net minimum tax for the taxable year shall be increased by the amount of the credit not allowed under section 30 solely by reason of the application of section 30(b)(3)(B).
In 2008, P.L. 110-343, Sec. 103(a)DivC, amended para. (e)(2), effective for tax. yrs. begin. after 12/31/2007.
Prior to amendment, para. (e)(2) read as follows:
"(2) AMT refundable credit amount. For purposes of paragraph (1)—
"(A) In general. The term 'AMT refundable credit amount' means, with respect to any taxable year, the amount (not in excess of the long-term unused minimum tax credit for such taxable year) equal to the greater of—
"(i) $5,000,
"(ii) 20 percent of the long-term unused minimum tax credit for such taxable year, or
"(iii) the amount (if any) of the AMT refundable credit amount determined under this paragraph for the taxpayer's preceding taxable year (as determined before any reduction under subparagraph (B)).
"(B) Phaseout of AMT refundable credit amount.
"(i) In general. In the case of an individual whose adjusted gross income for any taxable year exceeds the threshold amount (within the meaning of section 151(d)(3)(C)), the AMT refundable credit amount determined under subparagraph (A) for such taxable year shall be reduced by the applicable percentage (within the meaning of section 151(d)(3)(B)).
"(ii) Adjusted gross income. For purposes of clause (i), adjusted gross income shall be determined without regard to sections 911, 931, and 933."
—P.L. 110-343, Sec. 103(b)DivC, added subsec. (f), effective 10/3/2008.
In 2007, P.L. 110-172, Sec. 2(a), amended subpara. (e)(2)(A), effective for tax. yrs. begin. after 12/20/2006.
Prior to amendment, subpara. (e)(2)(A) read as follows:
"(A) In general. The term 'AMT refundable credit amount' means, with respect to any taxable year, the amount equal to the greater of—
"(i) the lesser of—
"(I) $5,000, or
"(II) the amount of long-term unused minimum tax credit for such taxable year, or
"(ii) 20 percent of the amount of such credit."
In 2006, P.L. 109-432, Sec. 402(a), added subsec. (e), effective for tax. yrs. begin. after 12/20/2006.
In 2005, P.L. 109-58, Sec. 1322(a)(3)(G), deleted "under section 29 (relating to credit for producing fuel from a nonconventional source) solely by reason of the application of section 29(b)(6)(B), or not allowed" after "credit not allowed" in clause (d)(1)(B)(iii), effective for credits determined under the Internal Revenue Code of 1986 for tax. yrs. end. after 12/31/2005.
In 2004, P.L. 108-357, Sec. 421(a)(2), deleted "and if section 59(a)(2) did not apply" after "specified in clause (ii)" in subclause (d)(1)(B)(i)(II), effective for tax. yrs. begin. after 12/31/2004.
In 1996, P.L. 104-188, Sec. 1205(d)(5)(A), deleted "[or] not allowed under section 28 solely by reason of the application of section 28(d)(2)(B)," after "section 29(d)(2)(B)," in clause (d)(1)(B)(iii) ... Sec. 1205(d)(5)(B), deleted "or not allowed under section 28 solely by reason of the application of section 28(d)(2)(B)" after "section 29(d)(5)(B)" in subclause (d)(1)(B)(iv)(II), effective for amounts paid or incurred in tax. yrs. end. after 6/30/96. [As directed by Sec. 1701 of this Act, the amendments made by Sec. 1704(j)(1) of this Act should be treated as being made before Sec. 1205(d)(5)(B). However, it is not possible to make the amendments accurately if the Sec. 1704(j)(1) changes are made first. The amendments have been made in the order in which the appear in the Act.]
—P.L. 104-188, Sec. 1702(e)(5), amended the effective date of amendments made by Sec. 1913(b)(2)(C)(i) of P.L. 102-486, from effective for property placed in service after 6/30/93, to effective for tax. yrs. begin. after 12/31/90. [see below].
—P.L. 104-188, Sec. 1704(j)(1), amended subclause (d)(1)(B)(iv)(II), effective for tax. yrs. begin. after 12/31/96.
Prior to amendment, subclause (d)(1)(B)(iv)(II) [as amended by section 1205(d)(5)(B) of this Act, see above] read as follows:
"(II) the adjusted net minimum tax for any taxable year is the amount of the net minimum tax for such year increased by the amount of any credit not allowed under section 29 solely by reason of the application of section 29(b)(5)(B)."

Code Sec. 53 — Tax credits

[As directed by Sec. 1701 of this Act, the amendments made by Sec. 1704(j)(1) of this Act should be treated as being made before Sec. 1205(d)(5)(B). However, it is not possible to make the amendments accurately if the Sec. 1704(j)(1) changes are made first. The amendments have been made in the order in which they appear in the Act.]

In 1993, P.L. 103-66, Sec. 13113(b)(2), substituted "(6), and (8)" for "and (6)" in subclause (d)(1)(B)(ii)(II), effective for stock issued after 8/10/93.

—P.L. 103-66, Sec. 13171(c), substituted "(5), and (7)" for "(5), (6) and (8)" in subclause (d)(1)(B)(ii)(II) [as amended by Sec. 13113(b)(2) of this Act], effective for contributions made after 6/30/92, except in the case of any contribution of capital gain property which is not tangible personal property, such amendments shall apply only if the contribution is made after 12/31/92.

In 1992, P.L. 102-486, Sec. 1913(b)(2)(C)(i), substituted "section 29(b)(6)(B)," for "section 29(b)(5)(B) or" in clause (d)(1)(B)(iii), effective for tax. yrs. begin. after 12/31/90 [as amended by Sec. 1702(e)(5) of P.L. 104-188, see above]

—P.L. 102-486, Sec. 1913(b)(2)(C)(ii), added ", or not allowed under section 30 solely by reason of the application of section 30(b)(3)(B)" before the period at the end of clause (d)(1)(B)(iii), effective for property placed in service after 6/30/93.

In 1989, P.L. 101-239, Sec. 7612(a)(1), added clause (d)(1)(B)(iv) . . . Sec. 7612(a)(2), substituted "subsection (b)(1)" for "subsections (b)(1) and (c)(3)" and deleted the last sentence in clause (d)(1)(B)(ii), effective for purposes of determining the adjusted net minimum tax for tax. yrs. begin. after 12/31/89.

Prior to amendment, the last sentence of clause (d)(1)(B)(ii) read as follows:

"In the case of taxable years beginning after 1989, the adjustments provided in section 56(g) shall be treated as specified in this clause to the extent attributable to items which are excluded from gross income for any taxable year for purposes of the regular tax, or are not deductible for any taxable year under the adjusted current earnings method of section 56(g)."

—P.L. 101-239, Sec. 7612(b)(1), added "or not allowed under section 28 solely by reason of the application of section 28(d)(2)(B)" after "section 29(d)(5)(B)" in clauses (d)(1)(B)(iii) and (d)(1)(B)(iv) [as added by Sec. 7612(a)(1) of this Act], effective for purposes of determining the amount of the minimum tax credit for tax. yrs. begin. after 12/31/89 except that, for such purposes, Code Sec. 53(b)(1) shall be applied as if such amendment had been in effect for all prior yrs.

—P.L. 101-239, Sec. 7811(d)(2), added "and if section 59(a)(2) did not apply" before the period at the end of subclause (d)(1)(B)(i)(II), effective for tax. yrs. begin. after 12/31/86

In 1988, P.L. 100-647, Sec. 1007(g)(4), substituted "current earnings" for "earnings and profits" in the last sentence of clause (d)(1)(B)(ii) . . . Sec. 6304(a), added clause (d)(1)(B)(iii), effective for tax. yrs. begin. after 12/31/86.

In 1986, P.L. 99-514, Sec. 701(b), added Code Sec. 53, as part of subpart G of Part IV of subchapter A of chapter 1, effective for tax. yrs. begin. after 12/31/86.

Sec. 53. Repealed.

In 1984, P.L. 98-369, Sec. 713(c)(1)(C), substituted "tax on premature distributions to key employees" for "tax on premature distributions to owner employees" in subsec. (a) (before repeal by Sec. 474(p)(8) of this Act, see below), effective for tax. yrs. begin. after 12/31/83.

—P.L. 98-369, Sec. 474(p)(8), repealed Code Sec. 53, effective for tax. yrs. begin. after 12/31/83 and to carrybacks from such yrs. begin. after 12/31/83.

Prior to repeal Code Sec. 53 read as follows:

"SEC. 53. LIMITATION BASED ON AMOUNT OF TAX.

"(a) General rule.

"Notwithstanding section 51, the amount of the credit allowed by section 44B for the taxable year shall not exceed 90 percent of the excess of the tax imposed by this chapter for the taxable year over the sum of the credits allowable under—

"(1) section 33 (relating to foreign tax credit),

"(2) section 37 (relating to credit for the elderly and permanently and totally disabled),

"(3) section 38 (relating to investment in certain depreciable property),

"(4) section 40 (relating to expenses of work incentive programs),

"(5) section 41 (relating to contributions to candidates for public office),

"(6) section 42 (relating to general tax credit), and

"(7) section 44A (relating to expenses for household and dependent care services necessary for gainful employment).

For purposes of this subsection, any tax imposed for the taxable year by section 56 (relating to corporate minimum tax), section 72(m)(5)(B) (relating to 10 percent tax on premature distributions to key employees section 72(q)(1) (relating to 5-percent tax on premature distributions under annuity contracts), section 402(e) (relating to tax on lump-sum distributions), section 408(f) (relating to additional tax on income from certain retirement accounts), section 531 (relating to accumulated earnings tax), section 541 (relating to personal holding company tax), or section 1374 (relating to tax on certain capital gains of S corporations), and any additional tax imposed for the taxable year by section 1351(d)(1) (relating to recoveries of foreign expropriation losses), shall not be considered tax imposed by this chapter for such year.

"(b) Carryback and carryover of unused credit.

"(1) Allowance of credit. If the amount of the credit determined under section 51 for any taxable year exceeds the limitation provided by subsection (a) for such taxable year (hereinafter in this subsection referred to as the 'unused credit year'), such excess shall be—

"(A) a new employee credit carryback to each of the 3 taxable years preceding the unused credit year, and

"(B) a new employee credit carryover to each of the 15 taxable years following the unused credit year,

and shall be added to the amount allowable as a credit by section 44B for such years. If any portion of such excess is a carryback to a taxable year beginning before January 1, 1977, section 44B shall be deemed to have been in effect for such taxable year for purposes of allowing such carryback as a credit under such section. The entire amount of the unused credit for an unused credit year shall be carried to the earliest of the 18 taxable years to which (by reason of subparagraphs (A) and (B)) such credit may be carried, and then to each of the other 17 taxable years to the extent that, because of the limitation contained in paragraph (2), such unused credit may not be added for a prior taxable year to which such unused credit may be carried.

"(2) Limitation. The amount of the unused credit which may be added under paragraph (1) for any preceding or succeeding taxable year shall not exceed the amount by which the limitation provided by subsection (a) for such taxable year exceeds the sum of—

"(A) the credit allowable under section 44B for such taxable year, and

"(B) the amounts which, by reason of this subsection, are added to the amount allowable for such taxable year and which are attributable to taxable years preceding the unused credit year."

In 1983, P.L. 98-21, Sec. 122(c)(1), substituted "relating to credit for the elderly and the permanently and totally disabled" for "relating to credit for the elderly" in para. (a)(2), for tax. yrs. begin. after 12/31/83.

—P.L. 97-448, Sec. 102(d)(2), added para. (c)(3) to Sec. 209 of P.L. 97-34, the effective date for amendments made by Sec. 207(c)(2) of P.L. 97-34, see below.

—P.L. 97-448, Sec. 102(d)(3), corrected Sec. 207(c)(2) of P.L. 97-34 to amend para. (b)(1) instead of para. (c)(2), [see below].

—P.L. 97-448, Sec. 306(a)(1)(A)(i), redesignated the second Sec. 201(c) of P.L. 97-248 as Sec. 201(d) of P.L. 97-248, see below.

In 1982, P.L. 97-354, Sec. 5(a)(12), substituted "section 1374 (relating to tax on certain capital gains of S corporations)," for "section 1378 (relating to tax on certain capital gains of Subchapter S corporations),", in the second sentence of subsec. (a), effective for tax. yrs. begin. after 12/31/82.

—P.L. 97-248, Sec. 201(d)(8)(A), substituted "(relating to corporate minimum tax)" for "(relating to minimum tax for tax preferences)" in subsec. (a), effective for tax. yrs. begin. after 12/31/82.

—P.L. 97-248, Sec. 265(b)(2)(A)(iii), added "section 72(q)(1) (relating to 5-percent tax on premature distributions under annuity contracts)" after "owner-employees)" in subsec. (a), effective for distributions after 12/31/82.

In 1981, P.L. 97-34, Sec. 207(c)(2), substituted "15" for "7", "18" for "10" and "17" for "9" in subpara. (b)(1)(B), effective for unused credit years begin. after 12/31/76.

Sec. 209(c)(3) of this Act provides:

"(3) Carryover must have been alive in 1981.—The amendments made by subsections (a), (b), and (c) of section 207 shall not apply to any amount which, under the law in effect on the day before the date of the enactment of this act, could not be carried to a taxable year ending in 1981."

In 1980, P.L. 96-222, Sec. 103(a)(6)(G)(xii), corrected Sec. 321(d)(4) of P.L. 95-600, the effective date for changes made by Sec. 321(c)(2) of P.L. 95-600, by substituting "subsection (c)(2)" for "subsection (u)(2)" [see below].

In 1978, P.L. 95-600, Sec. 321(c)(2)(A), substituted "90 percent of the excess of the tax imposed by this chapter for the taxable year over the sum of" for "the amount of the tax imposed by this chapter for the taxable year, reduced by" in subsec. (a) . . . Sec. 321(c)(2)(B), deleted subsec. (b) and redesignated subsec. (c) as subsec. (b), effective for tax. yrs. begin. after 12/31/78.

Prior to amendment, subsec. (b) read as follows:

"(b) Special rule for pass-thru of credit.

"In the case of a partner in a partnership, a beneficiary of an estate or trust, and a shareholder in a subchapter S corporation, the limitation provided by subsection (a) for the taxable year shall not exceed a limitation separately computed with respect to such person's interest in such entity by taking an amount which bears the same relationship to such limitation as—

"(1) that portion of the person's taxable income which is allocable or apportionable to the person's interest in such entity, bears to

"(2) the person's taxable income for such year reduced by his zero bracket amount (determined under section 63), if any."

In 1977, P.L. 95-30, Sec. 202(b), added Code Sec. 53, effective for tax. yrs. begin. after 12/31/76, and for credit carrybacks from such yrs.

SUBPART H.—NONREFUNDABLE CREDIT TO HOLDERS OF CLEAN RENEWABLE ENERGY BONDS

Sec. 54. Credit to holders of clean renewable energy bonds.

In 2008, P.L. 110-234, Sec. 15316(c)(4), substituted "Clean Renewable Energy Bonds" for "Certain Bonds", effective for obligations issued after 5/22/2008.

In 2005, P.L. 109-58, Sec. 1303(c)(1), added item 54 as part of new subpart H, effective for bonds issued after 12/31/2005.

Sec. 54. Credit to holders of clean renewable energy bonds.

(a) Allowance of credit.

If a taxpayer holds a clean renewable energy bond on 1 or more credit allowance dates of the bond occurring during any taxable year, there shall be allowed as a credit against

1,268

Tax credits
Code Sec. 54(f)(2)

the tax imposed by this chapter for the taxable year an amount equal to the sum of the credits determined under subsection (b) with respect to such dates.

(b) Amount of credit.

(1) In general. The amount of the credit determined under this subsection with respect to any credit allowance date for a clean renewable energy bond is 25 percent of the annual credit determined with respect to such bond.

(2) Annual credit. The annual credit determined with respect to any clean renewable energy bond is the product of—

(A) the credit rate determined by the Secretary under paragraph (3) for the day on which such bond was sold, multiplied by

(B) the outstanding face amount of the bond.

(3) Determination. For purposes of paragraph (2), with respect to any clean renewable energy bond, the Secretary shall determine daily or cause to be determined daily a credit rate which shall apply to the first day on which there is a binding, written contract for the sale or exchange of the bond. The credit rate for any day is the credit rate which the Secretary or the Secretary's designee estimates will permit the issuance of clean renewable energy bonds with a specified maturity or redemption date without discount and without interest cost to the qualified issuer.

(4) Credit allowance date. For purposes of this section, the term "credit allowance date" means—

(A) March 15,

(B) June 15,

(C) September 15, and

(D) December 15.

Such term also includes the last day on which the bond is outstanding.

(5) Special rule for issuance and redemption. In the case of a bond which is issued during the 3-month period ending on a credit allowance date, the amount of the credit determined under this subsection with respect to such credit allowance date shall be a ratable portion of the credit otherwise determined based on the portion of the 3-month period during which the bond is outstanding. A similar rule shall apply when the bond is redeemed or matures.

(c) Limitation based on amount of tax.

The credit allowed under subsection (a) for any taxable year shall not exceed the excess of—

(1) the sum of the regular tax liability (as defined in section 26(b)) plus the tax imposed by section 55, over

(2) the sum of the credits allowable under this part (other than subparts C, I, and J, section 1400N(l), and this section).

(d) Clean renewable energy bond.

For purposes of this section—

(1) In general. The term "clean renewable energy bond" means any bond issued as part of an issue if—

(A) the bond is issued by a qualified issuer pursuant to an allocation by the Secretary to such issuer of a portion of the national clean renewable energy bond limitation under subsection (f)(2),

(B) 95 percent or more of the proceeds of such issue are to be used for capital expenditures incurred by qualified borrowers for 1 or more qualified projects,

(C) the qualified issuer designates such bond for purposes of this section and the bond is in registered form, and

(D) the issue meets the requirements of subsection (h).

(2) Qualified project; special use rules.

(A) In general. The term "qualified project" means any qualified facility (as determined under section 45(d) without regard to paragraph (10) and to any placed in service date) owned by a qualified borrower.

(B) Refinancing rules. For purposes of paragraph (1)(B), a qualified project may be refinanced with proceeds of a clean renewable energy bond only if the indebtedness being refinanced (including any obligation directly or indirectly refinanced by such indebtedness) was originally incurred by a qualified borrower after the date of the enactment of this section.

(C) Reimbursement. For purposes of paragraph (1)(B), a clean renewable energy bond may be issued to reimburse a qualified borrower for amounts paid after the date of the enactment of this section with respect to a qualified project, but only if—

(i) prior to the payment of the original expenditure, the qualified borrower declared its intent to reimburse such expenditure with the proceeds of a clean renewable energy bond,

(ii) not later than 60 days after payment of the original expenditure, the qualified issuer adopts an official intent to reimburse the original expenditure with such proceeds, and

(iii) the reimbursement is made not later than 18 months after the date the original expenditure is paid.

(D) Treatment of changes in use. For purposes of paragraph (1)(B), the proceeds of an issue shall not be treated as used for a qualified project to the extent that a qualified borrower or qualified issuer takes any action within its control which causes such proceeds not to be used for a qualified project. The Secretary shall prescribe regulations specifying remedial actions that may be taken (including conditions to taking such remedial actions) to prevent an action described in the preceding sentence from causing a bond to fail to be a clean renewable energy bond.

(e) Maturity limitations.

(1) Duration of term. A bond shall not be treated as a clean renewable energy bond if the maturity of such bond exceeds the maximum term determined by the Secretary under paragraph (2) with respect to such bond.

(2) Maximum term. During each calendar month, the Secretary shall determine the maximum term permitted under this paragraph for bonds issued during the following calendar month. Such maximum term shall be the term which the Secretary estimates will result in the present value of the obligation to repay the principal on the bond being equal to 50 percent of the face amount of such bond. Such present value shall be determined without regard to the requirements of subsection (l)(6) and using as a discount rate the average annual interest rate of tax-exempt obligations having a term of 10 years or more which are issued during the month. If the term as so determined is not a multiple of a whole year, such term shall be rounded to the next highest whole year.

(f) Limitation on amount of bonds designated.

(1) National limitation. There is a national clean renewable energy bond limitation of $1,200,000,000.

(2) Allocation by Secretary. The Secretary shall allocate the amount described in paragraph (1) among qualified projects in such manner as the Secretary determines appropriate, except that the Secretary may not allocate more than $750,000,000 of the national clean renewable energy bond limitation to finance qualified projects of qualified borrowers which are governmental bodies.

Code Sec. 54(g)

(g) Credit included in gross income.
Gross income includes the amount of the credit allowed to the taxpayer under this section (determined without regard to subsection (c)) and the amount so included shall be treated as interest income. [Sec. 11(g)(2), P.L. 110-172, 12/29/2007, directs Code Sec. 54(g) be amended. It appears as if the amendment should be made to Code Sec. 56(g), see notes following this Code Sec. for details.]

(h) Special rules relating to expenditures.
   (1) In general. An issue shall be treated as meeting the requirements of this subsection if, as of the date of issuance, the qualified issuer reasonably expects—
   (A) at least 95 percent of the proceeds of such issue are to be spent for 1 or more qualified projects within the 5-year period beginning on the date of issuance of the clean energy bond,
   (B) a binding commitment with a third party to spend at least 10 percent of the proceeds of such issue will be incurred within the 6-month period beginning on the date of issuance of the clean energy bond or, in the case of a clean energy bond the proceeds of which are to be loaned to 2 or more qualified borrowers, such binding commitment will be incurred within the 6-month period beginning on the date of the loan of such proceeds to a qualified borrower, and
   (C) such projects will be completed with due diligence and the proceeds of such issue will be spent with due diligence.
   (2) Extension of period. Upon submission of a request prior to the expiration of the period described in paragraph (1)(A), the Secretary may extend such period if the qualified issuer establishes that the failure to satisfy the 5-year requirement is due to reasonable cause and the related projects will continue to proceed with due diligence.
   (3) Failure to spend required amount of bond proceeds within 5 years. To the extent that less than 95 percent of the proceeds of such issue are expended by the close of the 5-year period beginning on the date of issuance (or if an extension has been obtained under paragraph (2), by the close of the extended period), the qualified issuer shall redeem all of the nonqualified bonds within 90 days after the end of such period. For purposes of this paragraph, the amount of the nonqualified bonds required to be redeemed shall be determined in the same manner as under section 142.

(i) Special rules relating to arbitrage.
A bond which is part of an issue shall not be treated as a clean renewable energy bond unless, with respect to the issue of which the bond is a part, the qualified issuer satisfies the arbitrage requirements of section 148 with respect to proceeds of the issue.

(j) Cooperative electric company; qualified energy tax credit bond lender; governmental body; qualified borrower.
For purposes of this section—
   (1) Cooperative electric company. The term "cooperative electric company" means a mutual or cooperative electric company described in section 501(c)(12) or section 1381(a)(2)(C), or a not-for-profit electric utility which has received a loan or loan guarantee under the Rural Electrification Act.
   (2) Clean renewable energy bond lender. The term "clean renewable energy bond lender" means a lender which is a cooperative which is owned by, or has outstanding loans to, 100 or more cooperative electric companies and is in existence on February 1, 2002, and shall include any affiliated entity which is controlled by such lender.
   (3) Governmental body. The term "governmental body" means any State, territory, possession of the United States, the District of Columbia, Indian tribal government, and any political subdivision thereof.
   (4) Qualified issuer. The term "qualified issuer" means—
   (A) a clean renewable energy bond lender,
   (B) a cooperative electric company, or
   (C) a governmental body.
   (5) Qualified borrower. The term "qualified borrower" means—
   (A) a mutual or cooperative electric company described in section 501(c)(12) or 1381(a)(2)(C), or
   (B) a governmental body.

(k) Special rules relating to pool bonds.
No portion of a pooled financing bond may be allocable to any loan unless the borrower has entered into a written loan commitment for such portion prior to the issue date of such issue.

(l) Other definitions and special rules.
For purposes of this section—
   (1) Bond. The term "bond" includes any obligation.
   (2) Pooled financing bond. The term "pooled financing bond" shall have the meaning given such term by section 149(f)(6)(A).
   (3) Partnership; S corporation; and other pass-thru entities.
   (A) In general. Under regulations prescribed by the Secretary, in the case of a partnership, trust, S corporation, or other pass-thru entity, rules similar to the rules of section 41(g) shall apply with respect to the credit allowable under subsection (a).
   (B) No basis adjustment. In the case of a bond held by a partnership or an S corporation, rules similar to the rules under section 1397E(l) shall apply.
   (4) Ratable principal amortization required. A bond shall not be treated as a clean renewable energy bond unless it is part of an issue which provides for an equal amount of principal to be paid by the qualified issuer during each calendar year that the issue is outstanding.
   (5) Reporting. Issuers of clean renewable energy bonds shall submit reports similar to the reports required under section 149(e).

(m) Termination.
This section shall not apply with respect to any bond issued after December 31, 2009.

In 2009, P.L. 111-5, Sec. 1531(c)(3), substituted ", I, and J' for "and I" in para. (c)(2), effective for obligations issued after 2/17/2009.
—P.L. 111-5, Sec. 1541(b)(1), repealed para. (l)(4), redesignated paras. (l)(5) and (6) as paras. (l)(4) and (5), effective for tax. yrs. end. after 2/17/2009.
Prior to repeal, para. (l)(4) read as follows:
"(4) Bonds held by regulated investment companies. If any clean renewable energy bond is held by a regulated investment company, the credit determined under subsection (a) shall be allowed to shareholders of such company under procedures prescribed by the Secretary."
In 2008, P.L. 110-343, Sec. 107(c)DivB, substituted "December 31, 2009" for "December 31, 2008" in subsec. (m), effective for obligations issued after 10/3/2008.
—P.L. 110-246, Sec. 4, Repeals the duplicative enactment and provides effective date provisions of the Act entitled "An Act to provide for the continuation of agricultural programs through fiscal year 2012, and for other purposes". Sec. 4, P.L. 110-246 reads as follows:
"Sec. 4. Repeal of duplicative enactment.
"(a) In General- The Act entitled 'An Act to provide for the continuation of agricultural programs through fiscal year 2012, and for other purposes' (H.R. 2419 of the 110th Congress), and the amendments made by that Act, are repealed, effective on the date of enactment of that Act.

Tax credits   Code Sec. 54A(d)(2)(B)(i)

"(b) Effective Date- Except as otherwise provided in this Act, this Act and the amendments made by this Act shall take effect on the earlier of--
"(1) the date of enactment of this Act; or
"(2) the date of the enactment of the Act entitled 'An Act to provide for the continuation of agricultural programs through fiscal year 2012, and for other purposes' (H.R. 2419 of the 110th Congress)."
— P.L. 110-246, Sec. 15316(c)(1), substituted "subparts C and I" for "subpart C" in para. (c)(2), effective for obligations issued after 5/22/2008. [Ed. Note: May 22, 2008 was the date of enactment for H.R. 2419 (PL 110-234), which was repealed by (2008 Farm Act § 4(a)) (PL 110-246, 6/18/2008), in connection with the reenactment of the farm bill to correct a technical deficiency in its original passage.]
In 2007, P.L. 110-172, Sec. 11(g)(2), directs that "an organization to which part I of subchapter T (relating to tax treatment of cooperatives) applies which is engaged in the marketing of agricultural or horticultural products" is substituted for "a cooperative described in section 927(a)(4)" in clause Code Sec. 54(g)(4)(C)(iv). It appears as if the amendment should be made to Code Sec. 56(g)(4)(C)(iv) and has been incorporated in Code Sec. 56(g)(4)(C)(iv), enacted 12/29/2007.
In 2006, P.L. 109-432, Sec. 107(b)(2), substituted "section 1397E(l)" for "section 1397E(i)" in subpara. (l)(3)(B), effective for obligations issued after 12/20/2006 for allocations of the national zone academy bond limitation for calendar years after 2005.
— P.L. 109-432, Sec. 202(a)(1), substituted "$1,200,000,000" for "$800,000,000" in para. (f)(1), effective for bonds issued after 12/31/2006.
— P.L. 109-432, Sec. 202(a)(2), substituted "$750,000,000" for "$500,000,000" in para. (f)(2), effective for allocations or reallocations after 12/31/2006.
— P.L. 109-432, Sec. 202(a)(3), substituted "December 31, 2008" for "December 31, 2007" in subsec. (m), effective for bonds issues after 12/31/2006.
— P.L. 109-222, Sec. 508(d)(3), substituted "section 149(f)(6)(A)" for "section 149(f)(4)(A)" in para. (l)(2), effective for bonds issued after 5/17/2006.
In 2005, P.L. 109-135, Sec. 101(b)(1), added ", section 1400N(l)," after "subpart C" in para. (c)(2), effective for tax. yrs. end. on or after 8/28/2005.
— P.L. 109-135, Sec. 402(c)(1), deleted para. (l)(5) and redesignated paras. (l)(6) and (7) as paras. (l)(5) and (6), effective for bonds issued after 12/31/2005 as if included in Sec. 1303 of the Energy Tax Incentives Act of 2005, P.L. 109-58. Prior to deletion, para. (l)(5) read as follows:
"(5) Treatment for estimated tax purposes. Solely for purposes of sections 6654 and 6655, the credit allowed by this section (determined without regard to subsection (c)) to a taxpayer by reason of holding a clean renewable energy bond on a credit allowance date shall be treated as if it were a payment of estimated tax made by the taxpayer on such date."
— P.L. 109-58, Sec. 1303(a), added Code Sec. 54, effective for bonds issued after 12/31/2005.

SUBPART I.— QUALIFIED TAX CREDIT BONDS.

Sec. 54A. Credit to holders of qualified tax credit bonds.
Sec. 54B. Qualified forestry conservation bonds.
Sec. 54C. New clean renewable energy bonds.
Sec. 54D. Qualified energy conservation bonds.
Sec. 54E. Qualified zone academy bonds.
Sec. 54F. Qualified school construction bonds.

In 2009, P.L. 111-5, Sec. 1521(b)(3), added item 54F
In 2008, P.L. 110-343, Sec. 107(b)(3) Div B, added item 54C... Sec. 301(b)(3) Div B, added item 54D ... Sec. 313(b)(4) Div C, added item 54E, effective for obligations issued after 10/3/2008.
— P.L. 110-234, Sec. 15316(a), added items 54A and 54B as part of new subpart I, effective for obligations issued after 5/22/2008.

Sec. 54A. Credit to holders of qualified tax credit bonds.

(a) Allowance of credit.
If a taxpayer holds a qualified tax credit bond on one or more credit allowance dates of the bond during any taxable year, there shall be allowed as a credit against the tax imposed by this chapter for the taxable year an amount equal to the sum of the credits determined under subsection (b) with respect to such dates.

(b) Amount of credit.
(1) In general. The amount of the credit determined under this subsection with respect to any credit allowance date for a qualified tax credit bond is 25 percent of the annual credit determined with respect to such bond.
(2) Annual credit. The annual credit determined with respect to any qualified tax credit bond is the product of—
(A) the applicable credit rate, multiplied by
(B) the outstanding face amount of the bond.
(3) Applicable credit rate. For purposes of paragraph (2), the applicable credit rate is the rate which the Secretary estimates will permit the issuance of qualified tax credit bonds with a specified maturity or redemption date without discount and without interest cost to the qualified issuer. The applicable credit rate with respect to any qualified tax credit bond shall be determined as of the first day on which there is a binding, written contract for the sale or exchange of the bond.
(4) Special rule for issuance and redemption. In the case of a bond which is issued during the 3-month period ending on a credit allowance date, the amount of the credit determined under this subsection with respect to such credit allowance date shall be a ratable portion of the credit otherwise determined based on the portion of the 3-month period during which the bond is outstanding. A similar rule shall apply when the bond is redeemed or matures.

(c) Limitation based on amount of tax.
(1) In general. The credit allowed under subsection (a) for any taxable year shall not exceed the excess of—
(A) the sum of the regular tax liability (as defined in section 26(b)) plus the tax imposed by section 55, over
(B) the sum of the credits allowable under this part (other than subparts C and J and this subpart).
(2) Carryover of unused credit. If the credit allowable under subsection (a) exceeds the limitation imposed by paragraph (1) for such taxable year, such excess shall be carried to the succeeding taxable year and added to the credit allowable under subsection (a) for such taxable year (determined before the application of paragraph (1) for such succeeding taxable year).

(d) Qualified tax credit bond.
For purposes of this section—
(1) Qualified tax credit bond. The term "qualified tax credit bond" means—
(A) a qualified forestry conservation bond,
(B) a new clean renewable energy bond,
(C) a qualified energy conservation bond,
(D) a qualified zone academy bond, or
(E) a qualified school construction bond,
which is part of an issue that meets requirements of paragraphs (2), (3), (4), (5), and (6).

(2) Special rules relating to expenditures.
(A) In general. An issue shall be treated as meeting the requirements of this paragraph if, as of the date of issuance, the issuer reasonably expects—
(i) 100 percent or more of the available project proceeds to be spent for 1 or more qualified purposes within the 3-year period beginning on such date of issuance, and
(ii) a binding commitment with a third party to spend at least 10 percent of such available project proceeds will be incurred within the 6-month period beginning on such date of issuance.
(B) Failure to spend required amount of bond proceeds within 3 years.
(i) In general. To the extent that less than 100 percent of the available project proceeds of the issue are expended by the close of the expenditure period for 1 or more qualified purposes, the issuer shall redeem all of the nonqualified bonds within 90 days after the end of such period. For purposes of this paragraph, the amount of the nonqualified bonds required to be

redeemed shall be determined in the same manner as under section 142.

(ii) Expenditure period. For purposes of this subpart, the term "expenditure period" means, with respect to any issue, the 3-year period beginning on the date of issuance. Such term shall include any extension of such period under clause (iii).

(iii) Extension of period. Upon submission of a request prior to the expiration of the expenditure period (determined without regard to any extension under this clause), the Secretary may extend such period if the issuer establishes that the failure to expend the proceeds within the original expenditure period is due to reasonable cause and the expenditures for qualified purposes will continue to proceed with due diligence.

(C) Qualified purpose. For purposes of this paragraph, the term "qualified purpose" means—

(i) in the case of a qualified forestry conservation bond, a purpose specified in section 54B(e),

(ii) in the case of a new clean renewable energy bond, a purpose specified in section 54C(a)(1),

(iii) in the case of a qualified energy conservation bond, a purpose specified in section 54D(a)(1),

(iv) in the case of a qualified zone academy bond, a purpose specified in section 54E(a)(1), and

(v) in the case of a qualified school construction bond, a purpose specified in section 54F(a)(1).

(D) Reimbursement. For purposes of this subtitle, available project proceeds of an issue shall be treated as spent for a qualified purpose if such proceeds are used to reimburse the issuer for amounts paid for a qualified purpose after the date that the Secretary makes an allocation of bond limitation with respect to such issue, but only if—

(i) prior to the payment of the original expenditure, the issuer declared its intent to reimburse such expenditure with the proceeds of a qualified tax credit bond,

(ii) not later than 60 days after payment of the original expenditure, the issuer adopts an official intent to reimburse the original expenditure with such proceeds, and

(iii) the reimbursement is made not later than 18 months after the date the original expenditure is paid.

(3) **Reporting.** An issue shall be treated as meeting the requirements of this paragraph if the issuer of qualified tax credit bonds submits reports similar to the reports required under section 149(e).

(4) **Special rules relating to arbitrage.**

(A) In general. An issue shall be treated as meeting the requirements of this paragraph if the issuer satisfies the requirements of section 148 with respect to the proceeds of the issue.

(B) Special rule for investments during expenditure period. An issue shall not be treated as failing to meet the requirements of subparagraph (A) by reason of any investment of available project proceeds during the expenditure period.

(C) Special rule for reserve funds. An issue shall not be treated as failing to meet the requirements of subparagraph (A) by reason of any fund which is expected to be used to repay such issue if—

(i) such fund is funded at a rate not more rapid than equal annual installments,

(ii) such fund is funded in a manner reasonably expected to result in an amount not greater than an amount necessary to repay the issue, and

(iii) the yield on such fund is not greater than the discount rate determined under paragraph (5)(B) with respect to the issue.

(5) **Maturity limitation.**

(A) In general. An issue shall be treated as meeting the requirements of this paragraph if the maturity of any bond which is part of such issue does not exceed the maximum term determined by the Secretary under subparagraph (B).

(B) Maximum term. During each calendar month, the Secretary shall determine the maximum term permitted under this paragraph for bonds issued during the following calendar month. Such maximum term shall be the term which the Secretary estimates will result in the present value of the obligation to repay the principal on the bond being equal to 50 percent of the face amount of such bond. Such present value shall be determined using as a discount rate the average annual interest rate of tax-exempt obligations having a term of 10 years or more which are issued during the month. If the term as so determined is not a multiple of a whole year, such term shall be rounded to the next highest whole year.

(6) **Prohibition on financial conflicts of interest.** An issue shall be treated as meeting the requirements of this paragraph if the issuer certifies that—

(A) applicable State and local law requirements governing conflicts of interest are satisfied with respect to such issue, and

(B) if the Secretary prescribes additional conflicts of interest rules governing the appropriate Members of Congress, Federal, State, and local officials, and their spouses, such additional rules are satisfied with respect to such issue.

(e) **Other definitions.**

For purposes of this subchapter—

(1) **Credit allowance date.** The term "credit allowance date" means—

(A) March 15,

(B) June 15,

(C) September 15, and

(D) December 15.

Such term includes the last day on which the bond is outstanding.

(2) **Bond.** The term "bond" includes any obligation.

(3) **State.** The term "State" includes the District of Columbia and any possession of the United States.

(4) **Available project proceeds.** The term "available project proceeds" means—

(A) the excess of—

(i) the proceeds from the sale of an issue, over

(ii) the issuance costs financed by the issue (to the extent that such costs do not exceed 2 percent of such proceeds), and

(B) the proceeds from any investment of the excess described in subparagraph (A).

(f) **Credit treated as interest.**

For purposes of this subtitle, the credit determined under subsection (a) shall be treated as interest which is includible in gross income.

(g) **S corporations and partnerships.**

In the case of a tax credit bond held by an S corporation or partnership, the allocation of the credit allowed by this

Tax credits

Code Sec. 54B(e)(4)

section to the shareholders of such corporation or partners of such partnership shall be treated as a distribution.

(h) Bonds held by real estate investment trusts.

If any qualified tax credit bond is held by a real estate investment trust, the credit determined under subsection (a) shall be allowed to beneficiaries of such trust (and any gross income included under subsection (f) with respect to such credit shall be distributed to such beneficiaries) under procedures prescribed by the Secretary.

(i) Credits may be stripped.

Under regulations prescribed by the Secretary—

(1) In general. There may be a separation (including at issuance) of the ownership of a qualified tax credit bond and the entitlement to the credit under this section with respect to such bond. In case of any such separation, the credit under this section shall be allowed to the person who on the credit allowance date holds the instrument evidencing the entitlement to the credit and not to the holder of the bond.

(2) Certain rules to apply. In the case of a separation described in paragraph (1), the rules of section 1286 shall apply to the qualified tax credit bond as if it were a stripped bond and to the credit under this section as if it were a stripped coupon.

In 2009, P.L. 111-5, Sec. 1521(b)(1), deleted "or" at the end of subpara. (d)(1)(C), added "or" at the end of subpara. (d)(1)(D) and added subpara. (d)(1)(E) . . . Sec. 1521(b)(2), deleted "and" at the end of clause (d)(2)(C)(iii), deleted the period at the end of clause (d)(2)(C)(iv) and added clause (d)(2)(C)(v), effective for obligations issued after 2/17/2009.

—P.L. 111-5, Sec. 1531(c)(2), substituted "subparts C and J" for "subpart C", effective for tax. yrs. end. after 2/17/2009.

—P.L. 111-5, Sec. 1541(b)(2), amended subsec. (h)
Prior to amendment, subsec. (h) read as follows:

"(h) Bonds held by regulated investment companies and real estate investment trusts. If any qualified tax credit bond is held by a regulated investment company or a real estate investment trust, the credit determined under subsection (a) shall be allowed to shareholders of such company or beneficiaries of such trust (and any gross income included under subsection (f) with respect to such credit shall be treated as distributed to such shareholders or beneficiaries) under procedures prescribed by the Secretary."

In 2008, P.L. 110-343, Sec. 107(b)(1)DivB, amended para. (d)(1) . . . Sec. 107(b)(2)DivB, amended subpara. (d)(2)(C), effective for obligations issued after 10/3/2008.

Prior to amendment, para. (d)(1) read as follows:

"(1) Qualified tax credit bond. The term 'qualified tax credit bond' means a qualified forestry conservation bond which is part of an issue that meets the requirements of paragraphs (2), (3), (4), (5), and (6)."

Prior to amendment, subpara. (d)(2)(C) read as follows:

"(C) Qualified purpose. For purposes of this paragraph, the term 'qualified purpose' means a purpose specified in section 54B(e)."

—P.L. 110-343, Sec. 301(b)(1)DivB, amended para. (d)(1) [as amended by Sec. 107(b)(1) Div B, of this Act, see above] . . . Sec. 301(b)(2)DivB, amended subpara. (d)(2)(C) [as amended by Sec. 107(b)(2) Div B, of this Act, see above], effective for obligations issued after 10/3/2008.

Prior to amendment, para. (d)(1) [as amended by Sec. 107(b)(1) Div B, of this Act, see above] read as follows:

"(1) Qualified tax credit bond. The term 'qualified tax credit bond' means—
"(A) a qualified forestry conservation bond, or
"(B) a new clean renewable energy bond,
which is part of an issue that meets requirements of paragraphs (2), (3), (4), (5), and (6)."

Prior to amendment, subpara. (d)(2)(C) [as amended by Sec. 107(b)(2) Div B, of this Act, see above] read as follows:

"(C) Qualified purpose. For purposes of this paragraph, the term 'qualified purpose' means—
"(i) in the case of a qualified forestry conservation bond, a purpose specified in section 54B(e), and
"(ii) in the case of a new clean renewable energy bond, a purpose specified in section 54C(a)(1)."

—P.L. 110-343, Sec. 313(b)(1)DivC, deleted "or" at the end of subpara. (d)(1)(B) [as amended by Sec. 301(b)(1) Div B, of this Act, see above], added "or" at the end of subpara. (d)(1)(C) [as amended by Sec. 301(b)(1) Div B, of this Act, see above] and added subpara. (d)(1)(D) . . . Sec. 313(b)(2)DivC, deleted "and" at the end of clause (d)(2)(C)(ii) [as amended by Sec. 301(b)(2) Div B, of this Act, see above], substituted ", and" for the period at the end of clause (d)(2)(C)(iii) [as amended by Sec. 301(b)(2) Div B, of this Act, see above] and added clause (d)(2)(C)(iv), effective for obligations issued after 10/3/2008.

—P.L. 110-246, Sec. 4, Repeals the duplicative enactment and provides effective date provisions of the Act entitled "An Act to provide for the continuation of agricultural programs through fiscal year 2012, and for other purposes" Sec. 4, P.L. 110-246 reads as follows:

"Sec. 4. Repeal of duplicative enactment.

"(a) In General- The Act entitled 'An Act to provide for the continuation of agricultural programs through fiscal year 2012, and for other purposes' (H.R. 2419 of the 110th Congress), and the amendments made by that Act, are repealed, effective on the date of enactment of that Act.

"(b) Effective Date- Except as otherwise provided in this Act, this Act and the amendments made by this Act shall take effect on the earlier of--
"(1) the date of enactment of this Act; or
"(2) the date of the enactment of the Act entitled 'An Act to provide for the continuation of agricultural programs through fiscal year 2012, and for other purposes' (H.R. 2419 of the 110th Congress)."

—P.L. 110-234, Sec. 15316(a), added new Code. Sec. 54A, effective for obligations issued after 5/22/2008. [Ed. Note: May 22, 2008 was the date of enactment for H.R. 2419 (PL 110-234), which was repealed by (2008 Farm Act § 4(a)) (PL 110-246, 6/18/2008), in connection with the reenactment of the farm bill to correct a technical deficiency in its original passage.]

Sec. 54B. Qualified forestry conservation bonds.

(a) Qualified forestry conservation bond.

For purposes of this subchapter, the term "qualified forestry conservation bond" means any bond issued as part of an issue if—

(1) 100 percent of the available project proceeds of such issue are to be used for one or more qualified forestry conservation purposes,

(2) the bond is issued by a qualified issuer, and

(3) the issuer designates such bond for purposes of this section.

(b) Limitation on amount of bonds designated.

The maximum aggregate face amount of bonds which may be designated under subsection (a) by any issuer shall not exceed the limitation amount allocated to such issuer under subsection (d).

(c) National limitation on amount of bonds designated.

There is a national qualified forestry conservation bond limitation of $500,000,000.

(d) Allocations.

(1) In general. The Secretary shall make allocations of the amount of the national qualified forestry conservation bond limitation described in subsection (c) among qualified forestry conservation purposes in such manner as the Secretary determines appropriate so as to ensure that all of such limitation is allocated before the date which is 24 months after the date of the enactment of this section.

(2) Solicitation of applications. The Secretary shall solicit applications for allocations of the national qualified forestry conservation bond limitation described in subsection (c) not later than 90 days after the date of the enactment of this section.

(e) Qualified forestry conservation purpose.

For purposes of this section, the term "qualified forestry conservation purpose" means the acquisition by a State or any political subdivision or instrumentality thereof or a 501(c)(3) organization (as defined in section 150(a)(4)) from an unrelated person of forest and forest land that meets the following qualifications:

(1) Some portion of the land acquired must be adjacent to United States Forest Service Land.

(2) At least half of the land acquired must be transferred to the United States Forest Service at no net cost to the United States and not more than half of the land acquired may either remain with or be conveyed to a State.

(3) All of the land must be subject to a native fish habitat conservation plan approved by the United States Fish and Wildlife Service.

(4) The amount of acreage acquired must be at least 40,000 acres.

1,273

(f) Qualified issuer.
For purposes of this section, the term "qualified issuer" means a State or any political subdivision or instrumentality thereof or a 501(c)(3) organization (as defined in section 150(a)(4)).

(g) Special arbitrage rule.
In the case of any qualified forestry conservation bond issued as part of an issue, section 54A(d)(4)(C) shall be applied to such issue without regard to clause (i).

(h) Election to treat 50 percent of bond allocation as payment of tax.
  (1) In general. If—
    (A) a qualified issuer receives an allocation of any portion of the national qualified forestry conservation bond limitation described in subsection (c), and
    (B) the qualified issuer elects the application of this subsection with respect to such allocation,
  then the qualified issuer (without regard to whether the issuer is subject to tax under this chapter) shall be treated as having made a payment against the tax imposed by this chapter, for the taxable year preceding the taxable year in which the allocation is received, in an amount equal to 50 percent of the amount of such allocation.
  (2) Treatment of deemed payment.
    (A) In general. Notwithstanding any other provision of this title, the Secretary shall not use the payment of tax described in paragraph (1) as an offset or credit against any tax liability of the qualified issuer but shall refund such payment to such issuer.
    (B) No interest. Except as provided in paragraph (3)(A), the payment described in paragraph (1) shall not be taken into account in determining any amount of interest under this title.
  (3) Requirement for, and effect of, election.
    (A) Requirement. No election under this subsection shall take effect unless the qualified issuer certifies to the Secretary that any payment of tax refunded to the issuer under this subsection will be used exclusively for 1 or more qualified forestry conservation purposes. If the qualified issuer fails to use any portion of such payment for such purpose, the issuer shall be liable to the United States in an amount equal to such portion, plus interest at the overpayment rate under section 6621 for the period from the date such portion was refunded to the date such amount is paid. Any such amount shall be assessed and collected in the same manner as tax imposed by this chapter, except that subchapter B of chapter 63 (relating to deficiency procedures) shall not apply in respect of such assessment or collection.
    (B) Effect of election on allocation. If a qualified issuer makes the election under this subsection with respect to any allocation—
      (i) the issuer may issue no bonds pursuant to the allocation, and
      (ii) the Secretary may not reallocate such allocation for any other purpose.

In 2008, P.L. 110-246, Sec. 4, Repeals the duplicative enactment and provides effective date provisions of the Act entitled "An Act to provide for the continuation of agricultural programs through fiscal year 2012, and for other purposes" Sec. 4, P.L. 110-246 reads as follows:

"Sec. 4. Repeal of duplicative enactment.

"(a) In General. The Act entitled 'An Act to provide for the continuation of agricultural programs through fiscal year 2012, and for other purposes' (H.R. 2419 of the 110th Congress), and the amendments made by that Act, are repealed, effective on the date of enactment of that Act.

"(b) Effective Date- Except as otherwise provided in this Act, this Act and the amendments made by this Act shall take effect on the earlier of--

"(1) the date of enactment of this Act; or

"(2) the date of the enactment of the Act entitled 'An Act to provide for the continuation of agricultural programs through fiscal year 2012, and for other purposes' (H.R. 2419 of the 110th Congress)."

—P.L. 110-246, Sec. 15316(a), added new Code. Sec. 54B, effective for obligations issued after 5/22/2008. [Ed. Note: May 22, 2008 was the date of enactment for H.R. 2419 (PL 110-234), which was repealed by (2008 Farm Act § 4(a)) (PL 110-246, 6/18/2008), in connection with the reenactment of the farm bill to correct a technical deficiency in its original passage.]

Sec. 54C. New clean renewable energy bonds.
(a) New clean renewable energy bonds.
For purposes of this subpart, the term "new clean renewable energy bond" means any bond issued as part of an issue if—
  (1) 100 percent of the available project proceeds of such issue are to be used for capital expenditures incurred by governmental bodies, public power providers, or cooperative electric companies for one or more qualified renewable energy facilities,
  (2) the bond is issued by a qualified issuer, and
  (3) the issuer designates such bond for purposes of this section.

(b) Reduced credit amount.
The annual credit determined under section 54A(b) with respect to any new clean renewable energy bond shall be 70 percent of the amount so determined without regard to this subsection.

(c) Limitation on amount of bonds designated.
  (1) In general. The maximum aggregate face amount of bonds which may be designated under subsection (a) by any issuer shall not exceed the limitation amount allocated under this subsection to such issuer.
  (2) National limitation on amount of bonds designated. There is a national new clean renewable energy bond limitation of $800,000,000 which shall be allocated by the Secretary as provided in paragraph (3), except that—
    (A) not more than 33⅓ percent thereof may be allocated to qualified projects of public power providers,
    (B) not more than 33⅓ percent thereof may be allocated to qualified projects of governmental bodies, and
    (C) not more than 33⅓ percent thereof may be allocated to qualified projects of cooperative electric companies.
  (3) Method of allocation.
    (A) Allocation among public power providers. After the Secretary determines the qualified projects of public power providers which are appropriate for receiving an allocation of the national new clean renewable energy bond limitation, the Secretary shall, to the maximum extent practicable, make allocations among such projects in such manner that the amount allocated to each such project bears the same ratio to the cost of such project as the limitation under paragraph (2)(A) bears to the cost of all such projects.
    (B) Allocation among governmental bodies and cooperative electric companies. The Secretary shall make allocations of the amount of the national new clean renewable energy bond limitation described in paragraphs (2)(B) and (2)(C) among qualified projects of governmental bodies and cooperative electric companies, respectively, in such manner as the Secretary determines appropriate.
  (4) Additional limitation. The national new clean renewable energy bond limitation shall be increased by $1,600,000,000. Such increase shall be allocated by the Secretary consistent with the rules of paragraphs (2) and (3).

Tax credits

(d) Definitions.
For purposes of this section—
(1) Qualified renewable energy facility. The term "qualified renewable energy facility" means a qualified facility (as determined under section 45(d) without regard to paragraphs (8) and (10) thereof and to any placed in service date) owned by a public power provider, a governmental body, or a cooperative electric company.
(2) Public power provider. The term "public power provider" means a State utility with a service obligation, as such terms are defined in section 217 of the Federal Power Act (as in effect on the date of the enactment of this paragraph).
(3) Governmental body. The term "governmental body" means any State or Indian tribal government, or any political subdivision thereof.
(4) Cooperative electric company. The term "cooperative electric company" means a mutual or cooperative electric company described in section 501(c)(12) or section 1381(a)(2)(C).
(5) Clean renewable energy bond lender. The term "clean renewable energy bond lender" means a lender which is a cooperative which is owned by, or has outstanding loans to, 100 or more cooperative electric companies and is in existence on February 1, 2002, and shall include any affiliated entity which is controlled by such lender.
(6) Qualified issuer. The term "qualified issuer" means a public power provider, a cooperative electric company, a governmental body, a clean renewable energy bond lender, or a not-for-profit electric utility which has received a loan or loan guarantee under the Rural Electrification Act.

In 2009, P.L. 111-5, Sec. 1111, added para. (c)(4), effective 2/17/2009.
—P.L. 111-5, Sec. 1601, of this Act provide:
"SEC. 1601. APPLICATION OF CERTAIN LABOR STANDARDS TO PROJECTS FINANCED WITH CERTAIN TAX FAVORED BONDS.
"Subchapter IV of chapter 31 of the title 40, United States Code, shall apply to projects financed with the proceeds of—
"(1) any new clean renewable energy bond (as defined in section 54C of the Internal Revenue Code of 1986) issued after the date of the enactment of this Act,
"(2) any qualified energy conservation bond (as defined in section 54D of the Internal Revenue Code of 1986) issued after the date of the enactment of this Act,
"(3) any qualified zone academy bond (as defined in section 54E of the Internal Revenue Code of 1986) issued after the date of the enactment of this Act,
"(4) any qualified school construction bond (as defined in section 54F of the Internal Revenue Code of 1986), and
"(5) any recovery zone economic development bond (as defined in section 1400U-2 of the Internal Revenue Code of 1986)."
In 2008, P.L. 110-343, Sec. 107(a)DivB, added Code Sec. 54C, effective for obligations issued after 10/3/2008.

Sec. 54D. Qualified energy conservation bonds.
(a) Qualified energy conservation bond.
For purposes of this subchapter, the term "qualified energy conservation bond" means any bond issued as part of an issue if—
(1) 100 percent of the available project proceeds of such issue are to be used for one or more qualified conservation purposes,
(2) the bond is issued by a State or local government, and
(3) the issuer designates such bond for purposes of this section.
(b) Reduced credit amount.
The annual credit determined under section 54A(b) with respect to any qualified energy conservation bond shall be 70 percent of the amount so determined without regard to this subsection.

(c) Limitation on amount of bonds designated.
The maximum aggregate face amount of bonds which may be designated under subsection (a) by any issuer shall not exceed the limitation amount allocated to such issuer under subsection (e).
(d) National limitation on amount of bonds designated.
There is a national qualified energy conservation bond limitation of $3,200,000,000.
(e) Allocations.
(1) In general. The limitation applicable under subsection (d) shall be allocated by the Secretary among the States in proportion to the population of the States.
(2) Allocations to largest local governments.
(A) In general. In the case of any State in which there is a large local government, each such local government shall be allocated a portion of such State's allocation which bears the same ratio to the State's allocation (determined without regard to this subparagraph) as the population of such large local government bears to the population of such State.
(B) Allocation of unused limitation to state. The amount allocated under this subsection to a large local government may be reallocated by such local government to the State in which such local government is located.
(C) Large local government. For purposes of this section, the term "large local government" means any municipality or county if such municipality or county has a population of 100,000 or more.
(3) Allocation to issuers; restriction on private activity bonds. Any allocation under this subsection to a State or large local government shall be allocated by such State or large local government to issuers within the State in a manner that results in not less than 70 percent of the allocation to such State or large local government being used to designate bonds which are not private activity bonds.
(4) Special rules for bonds to implement green community programs. In the case of any bond issued for the purpose of providing loans, grants, or other repayment mechanisms for capital expenditures to implement green community programs, such bond shall not be treated as a private activity bond for purposes of paragraph (3).
(f) Qualified conservation purpose.
For purposes of this section—
(1) In general. The term "qualified conservation purpose" means any of the following:
(A) Capital expenditures incurred for purposes of—
(i) reducing energy consumption in publicly-owned buildings by at least 20 percent,
(ii) implementing green community programs (including the use of loans, grants, or other repayment mechanisms to implement such programs),
(iii) rural development involving the production of electricity from renewable energy resources, or
(iv) any qualified facility (as determined under section 45(d) without regard to paragraphs (8) and (10) thereof and without regard to any placed in service date).
(B) Expenditures with respect to research facilities, and research grants, to support research in—
(i) development of cellulosic ethanol or other nonfossil fuels,
(ii) technologies for the capture and sequestration of carbon dioxide produced through the use of fossil fuels,
(iii) increasing the efficiency of existing technologies for producing nonfossil fuels,

(iv) automobile battery technologies and other technologies to reduce fossil fuel consumption in transportation, or

(v) technologies to reduce energy use in buildings.

(C) Mass commuting facilities and related facilities that reduce the consumption of energy, including expenditures to reduce pollution from vehicles used for mass commuting.

(D) Demonstration projects designed to promote the commercialization of—

(i) green building technology,

(ii) conversion of agricultural waste for use in the production of fuel or otherwise,

(iii) advanced battery manufacturing technologies,

(iv) technologies to reduce peak use of electricity, or

(v) technologies for the capture and sequestration of carbon dioxide emitted from combusting fossil fuels in order to produce electricity.

(E) Public education campaigns to promote energy efficiency.

(2) Special rules for private activity bonds. For purposes of this section, in the case of any private activity bond, the term "qualified conservation purposes" shall not include any expenditure which is not a capital expenditure.

(g) Population.

(1) In general. The population of any State or local government shall be determined for purposes of this section as provided in section 146(j) for the calendar year which includes the date of the enactment of this section.

(2) Special rule for counties. In determining the population of any county for purposes of this section, any population of such county which is taken into account in determining the population of any municipality which is a large local government shall not be taken into account in determining the population of such county.

(h) Application to Indian tribal governments.

An Indian tribal government shall be treated for purposes of this section in the same manner as a large local government, except that—

(1) an Indian tribal government shall be treated for purposes of subsection (e) as located within a State to the extent of so much of the population of such government as resides within such State, and

(2) any bond issued by an Indian tribal government shall be treated as a qualified energy conservation bond only if issued as part of an issue the available project proceeds of which are used for purposes for which such Indian tribal government could issue bonds to which section 103(a) applies.

In 2009, P.L. 111-5, Sec. 1112(a), substituted "$3,200,000,000" for "$800,000,000" in subsec. (d) . . . Sec. 1112(b)(1), added "(including the use of loans, grants, or other repayment mechanisms to implement such programs)" after "green community programs" in clause (f)(1)(A)(ii) . . . Sec. 1112(b)(2), added para. (e)(4), effective 2/17/2009.

—P.L. 111-5, Sec. 1601, of this Act provides:

"SEC. 1601. APPLICATION OF CERTAIN LABOR STANDARDS TO PROJECTS FINANCED WITH CERTAIN TAX FAVORED BONDS.

"Subchapter IV of chapter 31 of the title 40, United States Code, shall apply to projects financed with the proceeds of—

"(1) any new clean renewable energy bond (as defined in section 54C of the Internal Revenue Code of 1986) issued after the date of the enactment of this Act,

"(2) any qualified energy conservation bond (as defined in section 54D of the Internal Revenue Code of 1986) issued after the date of the enactment of this Act,

"(3) any qualified zone academy bond (as defined in section 54E of the Internal Revenue Code of 1986) issued after the date of the enactment of this Act,

"(4) any qualified school construction bond (as defined in section 54F of the Internal Revenue Code of 1986), and

"(5) any recovery zone economic development bond (as defined in section 1400U-2 of the Internal Revenue Code of 1986)."

In 2008, P.L. 110-343, Sec. 301(a)DivB, added Code Sec. 54D, effective for obligations issued after 10/3/2008.

Sec. 54E. Qualified zone academy bonds.

(a) Qualified zone academy bonds.

For purposes of this subchapter, the term "qualified zone academy bond" means any bond issued as part of an issue if—

(1) 100 percent of the available project proceeds of such issue are to be used for a qualified purpose with respect to a qualified zone academy established by an eligible local education agency,

(2) the bond is issued by a State or local government within the jurisdiction of which such academy is located, and

(3) the issuer—

(A) designates such bond for purposes of this section,

(B) certifies that it has written assurances that the private business contribution requirement of subsection (b) will be met with respect to such academy, and

(C) certifies that it has the written approval of the eligible local education agency for such bond issuance.

(b) Private business contribution requirement.

For purposes of subsection (a), the private business contribution requirement of this subsection is met with respect to any issue if the eligible local education agency that established the qualified zone academy has written commitments from private entities to make qualified contributions having a present value (as of the date of issuance of the issue) of not less than 10 percent of the proceeds of the issue.

(c) Limitation on amount of bonds designated.

(1) National limitation. There is a national zone academy bond limitation for each calendar year. Such limitation is $400,000,000 for 2008, $1,400,000,000 for 2009 and 2010, and $400,000,000 for 2011 and, except as provided in paragraph (4), zero thereafter.

(2) Allocation of limitation. The national zone academy bond limitation for a calendar year shall be allocated by the Secretary among the States on the basis of their respective populations of individuals below the poverty line (as defined by the Office of Management and Budget). The limitation amount allocated to a State under the preceding sentence shall be allocated by the State education agency to qualified zone academies within such State.

(3) Designation subject to limitation amount. The maximum aggregate face amount of bonds issued during any calendar year which may be designated under subsection (a) with respect to any qualified zone academy shall not exceed the limitation amount allocated to such academy under paragraph (2) for such calendar year.

(4) Carryover of unused limitation.

(A) In general. If for any calendar year—

(i) the limitation amount for any State, exceeds

(ii) the amount of bonds issued during such year which are designated under subsection (a) with respect to qualified zone academies within such State,

the limitation amount for such State for the following calendar year shall be increased by the amount of such excess.

(B) Limitation on carryover. Any carryforward of a limitation amount may be carried only to the first 2 years following the unused limitation year. For purposes of the preceding sentence, a limitation amount shall be treated as used on a first-in first-out basis.

(C) Coordination with section 1397E. Any carryover determined under section 1397E(e)(4) (relating to carryover of unused limitation) with respect to any State to calendar year 2008 or 2009 shall be treated for purposes of this section as a carryover with respect to such State for such calendar year under subparagraph (A), and the limitation of subparagraph (B) shall apply to such carryover taking into account the calendar years to which such carryover relates.

(d) Definitions.

For purposes of this section—

(1) Qualified zone academy. The term "qualified zone academy" means any public school (or academic program within a public school) which is established by and operated under the supervision of an eligible local education agency to provide education or training below the post-secondary level if—

(A) such public school or program (as the case may be) is designed in cooperation with business to enhance the academic curriculum, increase graduation and employment rates, and better prepare students for the rigors of college and the increasingly complex workforce,

(B) students in such public school or program (as the case may be) will be subject to the same academic standards and assessments as other students educated by the eligible local education agency,

(C) the comprehensive education plan of such public school or program is approved by the eligible local education agency, and

(D)(i) such public school is located in an empowerment zone or enterprise community (including any such zone or community designated after the date of the enactment of this section), or

(ii) there is a reasonable expectation (as of the date of issuance of the bonds) that at least 35 percent of the students attending such school or participating in such program (as the case may be) will be eligible for free or reduced-cost lunches under the school lunch program established under the National School Lunch Act.

(2) Eligible local education agency. For purposes of this section, the term "eligible local education agency" means any local educational agency as defined in section 9101 of the Elementary and Secondary Education Act of 1965.

(3) Qualified purpose. The term "qualified purpose" means, with respect to any qualified zone academy—

(A) rehabilitating or repairing the public school facility in which the academy is established,

(B) providing equipment for use at such academy,

(C) developing course materials for education to be provided at such academy, and

(D) training teachers and other school personnel in such academy.

(4) Qualified contributions. The term "qualified contribution" means any contribution (of a type and quality acceptable to the eligible local education agency) of—

(A) equipment for use in the qualified zone academy (including state-of-the-art technology and vocational equipment),

(B) technical assistance in developing curriculum or in training teachers in order to promote appropriate market driven technology in the classroom,

(C) services of employees as volunteer mentors,

(D) internships, field trips, or other educational opportunities outside the academy for students, or

(E) any other property or service specified by the eligible local education agency.

In 2010, P.L. 111-312, Sec. 758(a)(1), substituted "2008," for "2008 and" in para. (c)(1) ... Sec. 758(a)(2), added "and $400,000,000 for 2011" after "2010," in para. (c)(1), effective for obligations issued after 12/31/2010.

In 2009, P.L. 111-5, Sec. 1522(a), substituted "and $1,400,000,000 for 2009 and 2010" for "and 2009" in para. (c)(1), effective for obligations issued after 12/31/2008.

—P.L. 111-5, Sec. 1601, of this Act provides:

"SEC. 1601. APPLICATION OF CERTAIN LABOR STANDARDS TO PROJECTS FINANCED WITH CERTAIN TAX FAVORED BONDS.

"Subchapter IV of chapter 31 of the title 40, United States Code, shall apply to projects financed with the proceeds of—

"(1) any new clean renewable energy bond (as defined in section 54C of the Internal Revenue Code of 1986) issued after the date of the enactment of this Act,

"(2) any qualified energy conservation bond (as defined in section 54D of the Internal Revenue Code of 1986) issued after the date of the enactment of this Act,

"(3) any qualified zone academy bond (as defined in section 54E of the Internal Revenue Code of 1986) issued after the date of the enactment of this Act,

"(4) any qualified school construction bond (as defined in section 54F of the Internal Revenue Code of 1986), and

"(5) any recovery zone economic development bond (as defined in section 1400U-2 of the Internal Revenue Code of 1986)."

In 2008, P.L. 110-343, Sec. 313(a)DivC, added Code Sec. 54E, effective for obligations issued after 10/3/2008.

Sec. 54F. Qualified school construction bonds.

(a) Qualified school construction bond.

For purposes of this subchapter, the term "qualified school construction bond" means any bond issued as part of an issue if—

(1) 100 percent of the available project proceeds of such issue are to be used for the construction, rehabilitation, or repair of a public school facility or for the acquisition of land on which such a facility is to be constructed with part of the proceeds of such issue,

(2) the bond is issued by a State or local government within the jurisdiction of which such school is located, and

(3) the issuer designates such bond for purposes of this section.

(b) Limitation on amount of bonds designated.

The maximum aggregate face amount of bonds issued during any calendar year which may be designated under subsection (a) by any issuer shall not exceed the limitation amount allocated under subsection (d) for such calendar year to such issuer.

(c) National limitation on amount of bonds designated.

There is a national qualified school construction bond limitation for each calendar year. Such limitation is—

(1) $11,000,000,000 for 2009,

(2) $11,000,000,000 for 2010, and

(3) except as provided in subsection (e), zero after 2010.

(d) Allocation of limitation.

(1) Allocation among states. Except as provided in paragraph (2)(C), the limitation applicable under subsection (c) for any calendar year shall be allocated by the Secretary among the States in proportion to the respective amounts each such State is eligible to receive under section 1124 of the Elementary and Secondary Education Act of 1965 (20 U.S.C. 6333) for the most recent fiscal year ending before such calendar year. The limitation amount allocated to a State under the preceding sentence shall be allocated by the State education agency (or such other agency as is authorized under State law to make such allocation) to issuers within such State.

(2) 40 percent of limitation allocated among largest school districts.

(A) In general. 40 percent of the limitation applicable under subsection (c) for any calendar year shall be allocated under subparagraph (B) by the Secretary among local educational agencies which are large local educational agencies for such year.

(B) **Allocation formula.** The amount to be allocated under subparagraph (A) for any calendar year shall be allocated among large local educational agencies in proportion to the respective amounts each such agency received under section 1124 of the Elementary and Secondary Education Act of 1965 (20 U.S.C. 6333) for the most recent fiscal year ending before such calendar year.

(C) **Reduction in state allocation.** The allocation to any State under paragraph (1) shall be reduced by the aggregate amount of the allocations under this paragraph to large local educational agencies within such State.

(D) **Allocation of unused limitation to state.** The amount allocated under this paragraph to a large local educational agency for any calendar year may be reallocated by such agency to the State in which such agency is located for such calendar year. Any amount reallocated to a State under the preceding sentence may be allocated as provided in paragraph (1).

(E) **Large local educational agency.** For purposes of this paragraph, the term "large local educational agency" means, with respect to a calendar year, any local educational agency if such agency is—

　(i) among the 100 local educational agencies with the largest numbers of children aged 5 through 17 from families living below the poverty level, as determined by the Secretary using the most recent data available from the Department of Commerce that are satisfactory to the Secretary, or

　(ii) 1 of not more than 25 local educational agencies (other than those described in clause (i)) that the Secretary of Education determines (based on the most recent data available satisfactory to the Secretary) are in particular need of assistance, based on a low level of resources for school construction, a high level of enrollment growth, or such other factors as the Secretary deems appropriate.

(3) **Allocations to certain possessions.** The amount to be allocated under paragraph (1) to any possession of the United States other than Puerto Rico shall be the amount which would have been allocated if all allocations under paragraph (1) were made on the basis of respective populations of individuals below the poverty line (as defined by the Office of Management and Budget). In making other allocations, the amount to be allocated under paragraph (1) shall be reduced by the aggregate amount allocated under this paragraph to possessions of the United States.

(4) **Allocations for Indian schools.** In addition to the amounts otherwise allocated under this subsection, $200,000,000 for calendar year 2009, and $200,000,000 for calendar year 2010, shall be allocated by the Secretary of the Interior for purposes of the construction, rehabilitation, and repair of schools funded by the Bureau of Indian Affairs. In the case of amounts allocated under the preceding sentence, Indian tribal governments (as defined in section 7701(a)(40)) shall be treated as qualified issuers for purposes of this subchapter.

(e) **Carryover of unused limitation.**

If for any calendar year—

(1) the amount allocated under subsection (d) to any State, exceeds

(2) the amount of bonds issued during such year which are designated under subsection (a) pursuant to such allocation,

the limitation amount under such subsection for such State for the following calendar year shall be increased by the amount of such excess. A similar rule shall apply to the amounts allocated under paragraphs (2) and (4) of subsection (d).

In 2010, P.L. 111-147, Sec. 301(b)(1), substituted "by the State education agency (or such other agency as is authorized under State law to make such allocation)" for "by the State" in para. (d)(1). . . . Sec. 301(b)(2), substituted "paragraphs (2) and (4) of subsection (d)" for "subsection (d)(4)" in the second sentence of para. (e), effective for obligations issued after 2/17/2009, as if included in Sec. 1521 of the American Recovery and Reinvestment Tax Act of 2009 [P.L. 111-5, see below]..

In 2009, P.L. 111-5, Sec. 1521(a), added Code Sec. 54F, effective for obligations issued after 2/17/2009. . . . Sec. 1601, of this Act provides:

"Sec. 1601. Application of certain labor standards to projects financed with certain tax favored bonds.

"Subchapter IV of chapter 31 of the title 40, United States Code, shall apply to projects financed with the proceeds of—

"(1) any new clean renewable energy bond (as defined in section 54C of the Internal Revenue Code of 1986) issued after the date of the enactment of this Act,

"(2) any qualified energy conservation bond (as defined in section 54D of the Internal Revenue Code of 1986) issued after the date of the enactment of this Act,

"(3) any qualified zone academy bond (as defined in section 54E of the Internal Revenue Code of 1986) issued after the date of the enactment of this Act,

"(4) any qualified school construction bond (as defined in section 54F of the Internal Revenue Code of 1986), and

"(5) any recovery zone economic development bond (as defined in section 1400U-2 of the Internal Revenue Code of 1986)."

Subpart J.—Build America Bonds

Sec. 54AA. Build America Bonds.

In 2009, P.L. 111-5, Sec. 1531(a), added subpart J and item 54AA, effective for obligations issued after 2/17/2009.

Sec. 54AA. Build America bonds.

(a) **In general.**

If a taxpayer holds a build America bond on one or more interest payment dates of the bond during any taxable year, there shall be allowed as a credit against the tax imposed by this chapter for the taxable year an amount equal to the sum of the credits determined under subsection (b) with respect to such dates.

(b) **Amount of credit.**

The amount of the credit determined under this subsection with respect to any interest payment date for a build America bond is 35 percent of the amount of interest payable by the issuer with respect to such date.

(c) **Limitation based on amount of tax.**

　(1) **In general.** The credit allowed under subsection (a) for any taxable year shall not exceed the excess of—

　　(A) the sum of the regular tax liability (as defined in section 26(b)) plus the tax imposed by section 55, over

　　(B) the sum of the credits allowable under this part (other than subpart C and this subpart).

　(2) **Carryover of unused credit.** If the credit allowable under subsection (a) exceeds the limitation imposed by paragraph (1) for such taxable year, such excess shall be carried to the succeeding taxable year and added to the credit allowable under subsection (a) for such taxable year (determined before the application of paragraph (1) for such succeeding taxable year).

(d) **Build America bond.**

　(1) **In general.** For purposes of this section, the term "build America bond" means any obligation (other than a private activity bond) if—

　　(A) the interest on such obligation would (but for this section) be excludable from gross income under section 103,

　　(B) such obligation is issued before January 1, 2011, and

　　(C) the issuer makes an irrevocable election to have this section apply.

Tax credits   Part VI

(2) Applicable rules. For purposes of applying paragraph (1)—

(A) for purposes of section 149(b), a build America bond shall not be treated as federally guaranteed by reason of the credit allowed under subsection (a) or section 6431,

(B) for purposes of section 148, the yield on a build America bond shall be determined without regard to the credit allowed under subsection (a), and

(C) a bond shall not be treated as a build America bond if the issue price has more than a de minimis amount (determined under rules similar to the rules of section 1273(a)(3)) of premium over the stated principal amount of the bond.

(e) Interest payment date.

For purposes of this section, the term "interest payment date" means any date on which the holder of record of the build America bond is entitled to a payment of interest under such bond.

(f) Special rules.

(1) Interest on build America bonds includible in gross income for federal income tax purposes. For purposes of this title, interest on any build America bond shall be includible in gross income.

(2) Application of certain rules. Rules similar to the rules of subsections (f), (g), (h), and (i) of section 54A shall apply for purposes of the credit allowed under subsection (a).

(g) Special rule for qualified bonds issued before 2011.

In the case of a qualified bond issued before January 1, 2011—

(1) Issuer allowed refundable credit. In lieu of any credit allowed under this section with respect to such bond, the issuer of such bond shall be allowed a credit as provided in section 6431.

(2) Qualified bond. For purposes of this subsection, the term "qualified bond" means any build America bond issued as part of an issue if—

(A) 100 percent of the excess of—

(i) the available project proceeds (as defined in section 54A) of such issue, over

(ii) the amounts in a reasonably required reserve (within the meaning of section 150(a)(3)) with respect to such issue,

are to be used for capital expenditures, and

(B) the issuer makes an irrevocable election to have this subsection apply.

(h) Regulations.

The Secretary may prescribe such regulations and other guidance as may be necessary or appropriate to carry out this section and section 6431.

In **2009**, P.L. 111-5, Sec. 1531(a), added section 54AA, effective for obligations issued after 2/17/2009.

—P.L. 111-5, Sec. 1531(d), of this Act, provides:

"(d) TRANSITIONAL COORDINATION WITH STATE LAW.

"Except as otherwise provided by a State after the date of the enactment of this Act, the interest on any build America bond (as defined in section 54AA of the Internal Revenue Code of 1986, as added by this section) and the amount of any credit determined under such section with respect to such bond shall be treated for purposes of the income tax laws of such State as being exempt from Federal income tax."

PART VI.— ALTERNATIVE MINIMUM TAX

Sec.

55. Alternative minimum tax imposed.

56. Adjustments in computing alternative minimum taxable income.

57. Items of tax preference.

58. Denial of certain losses.

59. Other definitions and special rules

In **1986**, P.L. 99-514, Sec. 701(a), amended Part VI of subchapter A of chapter 1. Prior to amendment, Part VI of subchapter A of chapter 1 read as follows:

"PART VI.— MINIMUM TAX FOR TAX PREFERENCES

"Sec.

"55. Alternative minimum tax for taxpayers other than corporations.

"56. Corporate minimum tax.

"57. Items of tax preference.

"58. Rules for application of this part."

In **1983**, P.L. 97-448, Sec. 306(a)(1)(A)(i), redesignated the second Sec. 201(c) of P.L. 97-248 as Sec. 201(d) of P.L. 97-248, see below.

In **1982**, P.L. 97-248, Sec. 201(d)(2), [as redesignated by Sec. 306(a)(1)(A)(i) of P.L. 92-448, see above] amended item 56.

Prior to amendment, item 56 read as follows:

"56. Imposition of tax."

In **1978**, P.L. 95-600, Sec. 421(f), added item 55.

In **1969**, P.L. 91-172, Sec. 301(a), added Part VI.

SEC. 55. ALTERNATIVE MINIMUM TAX FOR TAXPAYERS OTHER THAN CORPORATIONS.

"(a) Tax imposed.

"In the case of a taxpayer other than a corporation, there is imposed (in addition to any other tax imposed by this subtitle) a tax equal to the excess (if any) of—

"(1) an amount equal to 20 percent of so much of the alternative minimum taxable income as exceeds the exemption amount, over

"(2) the regular tax for the taxable year.

"(b) Alternative minimum taxable income.

"For purposes of this title, the term 'alternative minimum taxable income' means the adjusted gross income (determined without regard to the deduction allowed by section 172) of the taxpayer for the taxable year—

"(1) reduced by the sum of—

"(A) the alternative tax net operating loss deduction, plus

"(B) the alternative tax itemized deductions, plus

"(C) any amount included in income under section 87 or 667, and

"(2) increased by the amount of items of tax preference.

"(c) Credits.

"(1) In general. For purposes of determining any credit allowable under subpart A, B, or D of part IV of this subchapter (other than the foreign tax credit allowed under section 27(a))—

"(A) the tax imposed by this section shall not be treated as a tax imposed by this chapter, and

"(B) the amount of the foreign tax credit allowed by section 27(a) shall be determined without regard to this section.

"(2) Foreign tax credit allowed against alternative minimum tax.

"(A) Determination of foreign tax credit. The total amount of the foreign tax credit which can be taken against the tax imposed by subsection (a) shall be determined under subpart A of part III of subchapter N (section 901 and following).

"(B) Increase in amount of foreign taxes taken into account. For purposes of the determination provided by subparagraph (A), the amount of the taxes paid or accrued to foreign countries or possessions of the United States during the taxable year shall be increased by an amount equal to the lesser of—

"(i) the foreign tax credit allowable under section 27(a) in computing the regular tax for the taxable year, or

"(ii) the tax imposed by subsection (a).

"(C) Section 904(a) limitation. For purposes of the determination provided by subparagraph (A), the limitation of section 904(a) shall be an amount equal to the same proportion of the sum of the tax imposed by subsection (a) against which such credit is taken and the regular tax as—

"(i) the taxpayer's alternative minimum taxable income from sources without the United States (but not in excess of the taxpayer's entire alternative minimum taxable income), bears to

"(ii) his entire alternative minimum taxable income.

"For such purpose, the amount of the limitation of section 904(a) shall not exceed the tax imposed by subsection (a).

"(D) Definition of alternative minimum taxable income from sources without the United States. For purposes of subparagraph (C), the term 'alternative minimum taxable income from sources without the United States' means adjusted gross income from sources without the United States, adjusted as provided in paragraphs (1) and (2) of subsection (b) (taking into account in such adjustment only items described in such paragraphs which are properly attributable to items of gross income from sources without the United States).

"(E) Special rule for applying section 904(c). In determining the amount of foreign taxes paid or accrued during the taxable year which may be deemed to be paid or accrued in a preceding or succeeding taxable year under section 904(c)—

"(i) the limitation of section 904(a) shall be deemed to be the amount of foreign tax credit allowable under section 27(a) in computing the regular tax for the taxable year increased by the amount of the limitation determined under subparagraph (C), and

"(ii) any increase under subparagraph (B) shall be taken into account.

"(3) Carryover and carryback of certain credits. In the case of any taxable year for which a tax is imposed by this section, for purposes of determining the amount of any carryover or carryback to any other taxable year of any credit allowable under section 23, 25, 30, or 38, the amount of the limitation under section 26, 30(g), or 38(c) (as the case may be) shall be deemed to be—

"(A) the amount of such credit allowable for such taxable year (determined without regard to this paragraph), reduced (but not below zero) by

"(B) the amount of the tax imposed by this section for the taxable year, reduced by—

"(i) the amount of the credit allowable under section 27(a),

"(ii) in the case of the limitation under section 30(g), the amount of such tax taken into account under this subparagraph with respect to the limitation under section 26, and

"(iii) in the case of the limitation under section 38(c), the amount of such tax taken into account under this subparagraph with respect to limitations under sections 26 and 30(g).

"(d) Alternative tax net operating loss deduction defined.

For purposes of this section—

"(1) In general. The term 'alternative tax net operating loss deduction' means the net operating loss deduction allowable for the taxable year under section 172, except that in determining the amount of such deduction—

"(A) in the case of taxable years beginning after December 31, 1982, section 172(b)(2) shall be applied by substituting 'alternative minimum taxable income' for 'taxable income' each place it appears, and

"(B) the net operating loss (within the meaning of section 172(c)) for any loss year shall be adjusted as provided in paragraph (2).

"(2) Adjustments to net operating loss computation.

"(A) Post-1982 loss years. In the case of a loss year beginning after December 31, 1982, the net operating loss for such year under section 172(c) shall—

"(i) be reduced by the amount of the items of tax preference arising in such year which are taken into account in computing the net operating loss, and

"(ii) be computed by taking into account only itemized deductions which are alternative tax itemized deductions for the taxable year and which are otherwise described in section 172(c).

"(B) Pre-1983 years. In the case of loss years beginning before January 1, 1983, the amount of the net operating loss which may be carried over to taxable years beginning after December 31, 1982, for purposes of paragraph (1), shall be equal to the amount which may be carried from the loss year to the first taxable year of the taxpayer beginning after December 31, 1982.

"(e) Alternative tax itemized deductions.

"For purposes of this section—

"(1) In general. The term 'alternative tax itemized deductions' means an amount equal to the sum of any amount allowable as a deduction for the taxable year (other than a deduction allowable in computing adjusted gross income) under—

"(A) section 165(a) for losses described in subsection (c)(3) or (d) of section 165,

"(B) section 170 (relating to charitable deductions),

"(C) section 213 (relating to medical deductions),

"(D) this chapter for qualified interest, or

"(E) section 691(c) (relating to deduction for estate tax).

"(2) Amounts which may be carried over. No amount shall be taken into account under paragraph (1) to the extent such amount may be carried to another taxable year for purposes of the regular tax.

"(3) Qualified interest. The term 'qualified interest' means the sum of—

"(A) any qualified housing interest, and

"(B) any amount allowed as a deduction for interest (other than qualified housing interest) to the extent such amount does not exceed the qualified net investment income of the taxpayer for the taxpayer year.

"(4) Qualified housing interest.

"(A) In general. The term 'qualified housing interest' means interest which is paid or accrued during the taxable year on indebtedness which is incurred in acquiring, constructing, or substantially rehabilitating any property which—

"(i) is the principal residence (within the meaning of section 1034) of the taxpayer at the time such interest accrues or is paid, or

"(ii) is a qualified dwelling used by the taxpayer (or any member of his family within the meaning of section 267(c)(4)) during the taxable year.

"(B) Qualified dwelling. The term 'qualified dwelling' means any—

"(i) house,

"(ii) apartment,

"(iii) condominium, or

"(iv) mobile home not used on a transient basis (within the meaning of section 7701(a)(19)(C)(v)),

including all structures or other property appurtenant thereto.

"(C) Special rule for indebtedness incurred before July 1, 1982. The term 'qualified housing interest' includes interest paid or accrued on indebtedness which—

"(i) was incurred by the taxpayer before July 1, 1982, and

"(ii) is secured by property which, at the time such indebtedness was incurred, was—

"(I) the principal residence (within the meaning of section 1034) of the taxpayer, or

"(II) a qualified dwelling used by the taxpayer (or any member of his family (within the meaning of section 267(c)(4)).

"(5) Qualified net investment income. For purposes of this subsection—

"(A) In general. The term 'qualified net investment income' means the excess of—

"(i) qualified investment income, over

"(ii) qualified investment expenses.

"(B) Qualified investment income. The term 'qualified investment income' means the sum of—

"(i) investment income (within the meaning of section 163(d)(3)(B) other than clause (ii) thereof),

"(ii) any capital gain net income attributable to the disposition of property held for investment, and

"(iii) the amount of items of tax preference described in paragraph (I) of section 57(a).

"(C) Qualified investment expenses. The term 'qualified investment expenses' means the deductions directly connected with the production of qualified investment income to the extent that—

"(i) such deductions are allowable in computing adjusted gross income, and

"(ii) such deductions are not items of tax preference.

"(6) Special rules for estates and trusts.

"(A) In general. In the case of an estate or trust, the alternative tax itemized deductions for any taxable year includes the deductions allowable under sections 642(c), 651(a), and 661(a).

"(B) Determination of adjusted gross income. The adjusted gross income of an estate or trust shall be computed in the same manner as in the case of an individual, except that the deductions for costs paid or incurred in connection with the administration of the estate or trust shall be treated as allowable in arriving at adjusted gross income.

"(7) Limitation on medical deduction. In applying subparagraph (C) of paragraph (1), the amount allowable as a deduction under section 213 shall be determined by substituting '10 percent' for '5 percent' in section 213(a).

"(8) Treatment of interests in limited partnerships and subchapter S corporations.

"(A) Certain interest treated as not allowable in computing adjusted gross income. Any amount allowable as a deduction for interest on indebtedness incurred or continued to purchase or carry a limited business interest shall be treated as not allowable in computing adjusted gross income.

"(B) Income and losses taken into account in computing qualified net investment income. Any income or loss derived from a limited business interest shall be taken into account in computing qualified net investment income.

"(C) Limited business interest. The term 'limited business interest' means an interest—

"(i) as a limited partner in a partnership, or

"(ii) as a shareholder in an S corporation if the taxpayer does not actively participate in the management of such corporation.

"(f) Other definitions.

For purposes of this section—

"(1) Exemption amount. The term 'exemption amount' means—

"(A) $40,000 in the case of—

"(i) a joint return, or

"(ii) a surviving spouse (as defined in section 2(a)),

"(B) $30,000 in the case of an individual who—

"(i) is not a married individual (as defined in section 143), and

"(ii) is not a surviving spouse (as so defined), and

"(C) $20,000 in the case of—

"(i) a married individual (as so defined) who files a separate return, or

"(ii) an estate or trust.

"(2) Regular tax. The term 'regular tax' means the taxes imposed by this chapter for the taxable year (computed without regard to this section and without regard to the taxes imposed by sections 47(a), 72(m)(5)(B), 72(q), 402(e), 408(f), and 667(b)) reduced by the sum of the credits allowable under subparts A, B, and D of part IV of this subchapter. For purposes of this paragraph, the amount of the credits allowable under such subpart shall be determined without regard to this section."

In 1986, P.L. 99-514, Sec. 231(a)(2), amended Sec. 221(d) of P.L. 97-34, the effective date for changes made by Sec. 221(b)(1)(A) of P.L. 97-34, by substituting "amounts paid or incurred after June 30, 1981" for "amounts paid or incurred after June 30, 1981 and before January 1, 1986" [see below].

—P.L. 99-514, Sec. 1847(a)(1), substituted "of such credit allowable" for "of such limitation" in subpara. (c)(3)(A) . . . Sec. 1847(a)(2), amended clause (c)(2)(E)(i), effective for tax. yrs begin. after 12/31/83 and to carrybacks from tax. yrs. begin. after 12/31/83.

Prior to amendment, clause (c)(2)(E)(i) read as follows:

"(i) the limitation of section 904(a) shall be increased by the amount of the limitation determined under subparagraph (C), and"

In 1984, P.L. 98-369, Sec. 474(q)(1)(A), substituted "subpart A, B, or D of part IV" for "subpart A of part IV" in para (c)(1) . . . Sec. 474(q)(1)(B), substituted "section 27(a)" for "section 33(a)" each place it appeared in para. (c)(1) . . . Sec. 474(q)(2), substituted "section 27(a)" for "section 33(a)" in clause (c)(2)(B)(i) . . . Sec. 474(q)(3), amended para. (c)(3) . . . Sec. 474(q)(4), substituted "allowable under subparts A,B, and D of part IV of this subchapter" for "allowable under subpart A of part IV of this subchapter (other than under sections 31, 39, and 43)" in para. (f)(2), effective for tax. yrs. begin. after 12/31/83 and to carrybacks from tax. yrs. begin. after 12/31/83.

Prior to amendment, para. (c)(3) read as follows:

"(3) Carryover and carryback of certain credits.

"(A) In general. In the case of any taxable year in which a tax is imposed by this section, for purposes of determining the amount of any carryback or carryover of any applicable credit to any other taxable year, the amount of the applicable credit limitation for such taxable year shall be deemed to be—

1,280

Tax credits — Part VI

"(i) the amount of the applicable credit allowable for such taxable year (determined without regard to this paragraph), reduced (but not below zero) by—

"(ii) the amount of the tax imposed by this section for the taxable year, reduced by—

"(I) the amount of the credit allowable under section 33(a), and

"(II) the amount of such tax taken into account under this clause with respect to any applicable credit having a lower number or letter designation.

"(B) Applicable credits, etc. For purposes of this paragraph—

"(i) Applicable credit. The term 'applicable credit' means any credit allowable under section 38, 40, 44B, 44C, 44E, or 44F.

"(ii) Applicable credit limitation. The term 'applicable credit limitation' means, with respect to any applicable credit, the limitation under section 46(a)(3), 53(a), 44C(b)(5), 44E(e)(1), 44F(g)(1), or 50A(a)(2), whichever is appropriate."

—P.L. 98-369, Sec. 491(d)(1), deleted "409(c)," after "408(f)," from para. (f)(2), effective for obligations issued after 12/31/83.

—P.L. 98-369, Sec. 612(e)(3)(A), substituted "26" for "25" each place it appeared in para. (c)(3)... Sec. 612(e)(3)(B), substituted "section 23, 25, 30, or 38" for "section 23, 30, or 38" in para. (c)(3), effective for interest paid or accrued after 12/31/84, on indebtedness incurred after 12/31/84.

—P.L. 98-369, Sec. 632, provided various exceptions to the amendments made by Title VI of this Act. See note following Code Sec. 103A.

—P.L. 98-369, Sec. 711(a)(1), substituted "sections 47(a), 72(m)(5)(B)" for "sections 72(m)(5)(B)" in para. (f)(2)... Sec. 711(a)(4), amended subpara. 55(e)(8)(B)... Sec. 711(a)(5), substituted "section 87 or 667" for "section 667" in subpara. (b)(1)(C), effective for tax. yrs. begin. after 12/31/82.

Prior to amendment, subpara. (e)(8)(B) read as follows:

"(B) Income treated as qualified investment income. Any income derived from a limited business interest shall be treated as qualified investment income."

In 1983, P.L. 97-448, Sec. 103(g)(2)(E), deleted "44G(b)(1)" after "44C(b)(1) and (2)" in para. (c)(4), effective for tax. yrs. end. after 9/30/81.

—P.L. 97-448, Sec. 305(c), substituted "subparagraph (A) (and in determining the sum of itemized deductions for purposes of subparagraph (C)(i))" for "subparagraph (A)" in the last sentence of para. (b)(1), for tax. yrs. begin. after 12/31/78.

—P.L. 97-448, Sec. 306(a)(1)(B), substituted "capital gain net income" for "net capital gain" in clause (e)(5)(b)(ii)... Sec. 306(a)(1)(C), substituted "paragraph (1)" for "subparagraph (A)" in subpara. (d)(2)(B), effective for tax. yrs. begin. after 12/31/82.

In 1982, P.L. 97-354, Sec. 5(a)(13), substituted "an S corporation" for "an electing small business corporation (as defined in section 1371(b))" in subpara. (e)(8)(C), effective for tax. yrs. begin. after 12/31/82.

—P.L. 97-248, Sec. 201(a), amended Code Sec. 55, effective for tax. yrs. begin. after 12/31/82.

Prior to amendment, Code Sec. 55 read as follows:

"Sec. 55. Alternative minimum tax for taxpayers other than corporations.
"(a) Alternative minimum tax imposed.

"In the case of a taxpayer other than a corporation, if—

"(1) an amount equal to the sum of—

"(A) 10 percent of so much of the alternative minimum taxable income as exceeds $20,000 but does not exceed $60,000 plus

"(B) 20 percent of so much of the alternative minimum taxable income as exceeds $60,000, exceeds

"(2) the regular tax for the taxable year, then there is imposed (in addition to all other taxes imposed by this title) a tax equal to the amount of such excess.

"(b) Definitions.

"For purposes of this section—

"(1) Alternative minimum taxable income. The term 'alternative minimum taxable income' means gross income—

"(A) reduced by the sum of the deductions allowed for the taxable year,

"(B) reduced by the sum of any amounts included in income under section 86 or 667, and

"(C) increased by an amount equal to the sum of the tax preference items for—

"(i) adjusted itemized deductions (within the meaning of section 57(a)(1)), and

"(ii) capital gains (within the meaning of section 57(a)(9)).

For purposes of subparagraph (A), a deduction shall not be taken into account to the extent such deduction may be carried to another taxable year.

"(2) Regular tax. The term 'regular tax' means the taxes imposed by this chapter for the taxable year (computed without regard to this section and without regard to the taxes imposed by sections 72(m)(5)(B), 402(e), 408(f), 409(c), and 667(b)) reduced by the sum of the credits allowable under subpart A of part IV of this subchapter (other than under sections 31, 39 and 43). For purposes of this paragraph, the amount of the credit allowable under such subpart shall be determined without regard to this section.

"(3) Treatment of zero bracket amount. In the case of an individual who does not itemize his itemized deductions, the zero bracket amount shall be treated as a deduction allowed.

"(c) Credits.

"(1) In general. For purposes of—

"(A) determining the amount of any credit allowable under subpart A of part IV of this subchapter (other than the foreign tax credit allowable under section 33(a)) against the tax imposed by subsection (a), the tax imposed by subsection (a) shall be treated as a tax imposed by this chapter only to the extent of the amount which would be determined under subsection (a)(1) if the alternative minimum taxable income was reduced by the sum of—

"(i) the net capital gain, and

"(ii) the adjusted itemized deductions, and

"(B) determining the amount of any such credit (including the credit allowable under section 33(a)) against the tax imposed by this chapter (other than the tax imposed by this section) for the current taxable year, this section shall be disregarded.

"(2) Rules for determining amount of credit allowable. For purposes of determining the amount of any credit allowable under subpart A of part IV of this subchapter (other than the credits imposed by sections 31, 39, and 43) which can be taken against the tax imposed by subsection (a)—

"(A) the amount of such credit shall be increased by an amount equal to the lesser of—

"(i) the amount of such credit allowable in computing the regular tax for the current taxable year, or

"(ii) the excess of—

"(I) the amount of the tax imposed by subsection (a), over

"(II) the sum of the amounts determined under this subparagraph with respect to credits allowed under a section of such subpart having a higher number designation than such credit (other than the credits allowable by sections 31, 39, and 43), and

"(B) in the case of any credit under section 38, 40, or 44B, such credit shall be reduced, under regulations prescribed by the Secretary, by that portion of such credit which is not attributable to an active trade or business of the taxpayer.

"(3) Foreign tax credit allowed against alternative minimum tax.

"(A) Determination of foreign tax credit. The total amount of the foreign tax credit which can be taken against the tax imposed by subsection (a) shall be determined under subpart A of part III of subchapter N (sec. 901 and following).

"(B) Section 904(a) limitation. For purposes of the determination provided by subparagraph (A), the limitation of section 904(a) shall be an amount equal to the same proportion of the sum of the tax imposed by subsection (a) against which such credit is taken and the regular tax (excluding the tax imposed by section 56) as—

"(i) the taxpayer's alternative minimum taxable income from sources without the United States (but not in excess of the taxpayer's entire alternative minimum taxable income), bears to

"(ii) his entire alternative minimum taxable income. For such purpose, the amount of the limitation of section 904(a) shall not exceed the tax imposed by subsection (a).

"(C) Definition of alternative minimum taxable income from sources without the United States. For purposes of subparagraph (B), the term 'alternative minimum taxable income from sources without the United States' means the items of gross income from sources without the United States adjusted as provided in subparagraph (A), (B), and (C) of section 55(b)(1) (taking into account in such adjustment only items described in such subparagraphs which are properly attributable to items of gross income from sources without the United States).

"(D) Special rule for applying section 904(c). In determining the amount of foreign taxes paid or accrued during the taxable year which may be deemed to be paid or accrued in a preceding or succeeding taxable year under section 904(c)—

"(i) the limitation of section 904(a) shall be increased by the amount of the limitation determined under subparagraph (B), and

"(ii) any increase under paragraph (2)(A) shall be taken into account.

"(4) Carryover and carryback of certain credits.

"(A) In general. For purposes of determining the amount of any carryover or carryback to any other taxable year of any credit allowable under subpart A of part IV of this subchapter (other than section 33), the amount of the limitation under section 44F(g)(1), 44E(e)(1), 44C(b)(1) and (2), 44G(b)(1), 53(b), 50A(a)(2), or 46(a)(3) (to the extent such limitation does not exceed the amount of the credit allowable in computing the regular tax for the current taxable year) shall be increased for the current taxable year by the amount determined under subparagraph (A) of paragraph (1) of this subsection, and decreased by—

"(i) the sum of the credits allowed under a section having a lower number designation than the section allowing such credit (other than the credits allowable by sections 31, 33, 39, and 43) against the tax imposed by subsection (a), and

"(ii) the amount determined with respect to such credit under paragraph (2)(B) for the current taxable year.

"(B) Amount of credit. Any increase under paragraph (2)(A) shall be taken into account in determining the amount of any carryover or carryback from the current taxable year."

In 1981, P.L. 97-34, Sec. 101(d)(1), substituted ", exceeds" for "but does not exceed $100,000, plus" in subpara. (a)(1)(B) and deleted subpara. (a)(1)(C), effective for tax. yrs. begin. after 12/31/81.

Prior to deletion, subpara. (a)(1)(C) read as follows:

"(C) 25 percent of so much of the alternative minimum taxable income as exceeds $100,000, exceeds"

—P.L. 97-34, Sec. 221(b)(1)(A), [as amended by Sec. 231(a) of P.L. 99-514, see above], substituted "section 44F(g)(1), 44E(e)(1)" for "section 44E(e)(1)" in subpara. (c)(4)(A), effective [as amended by Sec. 231(a) of P.L. 99-514, see above] for amounts paid or incurred after 6/30/81. For transitional rule, see Sec. 221(d)(2) of this Act reproduced in note following Code Sec. 44F.

—P.L. 97-34, Sec. 331(d)(1)(A), added "44G(b)(1)," before "53(b)" in subpara. (c)(4)(A), effective for tax. yrs. begin. after 12/31/81.

In 1980, P.L. 96-603, Sec. 4(a)(1), amended para. (c)(1)... Sec. 4(a)(2), redesignated paras. (c)(2) and (c)(3) as paras. (c)(3) and (c)(4), and added new para. (c)(2)... Sec. 4(a)(3), amended para. (c)(4) (as redesignated by Sec. 4(a)(2) of this Act)... Sec. 4(b)(1), substituted "credits allowable under such subpart" for "credit allowable under section 33" in para. (b)(2)... Sec. 4(b)(2)(A), deleted subpara. (c)(3)(B) [as redesignated by Sec. 4(a)(2) of this Act] and redesignated subparas. (c)(3)(C), (D), and (E) as subparas. (c)(3)(B), (C), and (D)... Sec. 4(b)(2)(B), substituted "subparagraph (B)" for "subparagraph (C)" in subparas.

Part VI — Tax credits

(c)(3)(C) and (D) [as redesignated by Sec. 4(a)(2) of this Act] ... Sec. 4(b)(2)(C), amended clause (c)(3)(D)(ii) [as redesignated by Sec. 4(a)(2) of this Act], effective for tax. yrs. begin. after 12/31/79.

Prior to amendment, para. (c)(1) read as follows:

"(1) Credits other than foreign tax credit not allowable, etc. For purposes of determining the amount of any credit allowable under subpart A of part IV of this subchapter (other than the foreign tax credit allowed under section 33(A))

"(A) the tax imposed by this section shall not be treated as a tax imposed by this chapter, and

"(B) the amount of the foreign tax credit allowed under section 33(a) shall be determined without regard to this section."

Prior to amendment, subpara. (c)(3)(B) (as redesignated by Sec. 4(a)(2) of this Act) read as follows:

"(B) Increase in amount of foreign taxes taken into account. For purposes of the determination provided by subparagraph (A), the amount of taxes paid or accrued to foreign countries or possessions of the United States during the taxable year shall be increased by an amount equal to the lesser of—

"(i) the foreign tax credit allowable under section 33(a) in computing the regular tax for the taxable year, or

"(ii) the tax imposed by subsection (a)."

Prior to amendment, clause (c)(3)(D)(ii) read as follows:

"(ii) any increase under subparagraph (B) shall be taken into account."

Prior to amendment, para. (c)(4) (as redesignated by Sec. 4(a)(2) of this Act) read as follows:

"(4) Carryover and carryback of certain credits. In any taxable year in which a tax is imposed by this section (referred to as the current taxable year)—

"(A) Employment credit. For purposes of determining under section 53(b) the amount of any jobs credit carryback or carryover to any other taxable year, the amount of the limitation under section 53(a) for the current taxable year shall be deemed to be—

"(i) the amount of the credit allowable under section 44B for the current taxable year without regard to this subparagraph, reduced by

"(ii) the amount equal to the lesser of (I) the amount of the credit allowable under section 44B for the current taxable year without regard to this subparagraph, or (II) the net tax imposed by this section for the current taxable year.

"(B) Work incentive program credit. For purposes of determining under section 50A(b) the amount of any work incentive program credit carryback or carryover to any other taxable year, the amount of the limitation under section 50A(a)(2) for the current taxable year shall be deemed to be—

"(i) the amount of the credit allowable under section 40 for the current taxable year without regard to this subparagraph, reduced by

"(ii) the amount equal to the lesser of (I) the amount of the credit allowable under section 40 for the current taxable year without regard to this subparagraph, or, (II) the net tax imposed by this section for the current taxable year reduced by the amount of reduction described in clause (ii) of subparagraph (A).

"(C) Investment credit. For purposes of determining under section 46(b) the amount of any investment credit carryback or carryover to any other taxable year, the amount of the limitation under section 46(a)(3) for the current taxable year shall be deemed to be—

"(i) the amount of the credit allowable under section 38 for the current taxable year without regard to this subparagraph, reduced by

"(ii) the amount equal to the lesser of (I) the amount of the credit allowable under section 38 for the current taxable year without regard to this subparagraph, or (II) the net tax imposed by this section for the current taxable year reduced by the sum of the amounts of reduction described in clause (ii) of subparagraphs (A) and (B).

"(D) Net tax imposed by this section. For purposes of this paragraph, the term 'net tax imposed by this section' means the tax imposed by this section reduced by the foreign tax credit allowed under section 33 (a), as modified by paragraph (2).

"In determining any carryover under subsection 44C(b)(6), a rule similar to the rule set forth in subparagraph (A) shall be treated as inserted in this paragraph before subparagraph (A), and the applications of subparagraphs (A), (B), and (C) shall be adjusted accordingly.

"In determining any carryover under subsection 44E(e)(2), a rule similar to the rule set forth in subparagraph (A) shall be treated as inserted in this paragraph before subparagraph (A), and the applications of subparagraphs (A), (B), and (C) shall be adjusted accordingly.

—P.L. 96-223, Sec. 232(b)(2)(A), added the last sentence of para. (c)(3) ... Sec. 232(c)(2), substituted "section 86 or 667" for "section 667" in subpara. (b)(1)(B), effective for sales or uses after 9/30/80, in tax. yrs. end. after 9/30/80.

—P.L. 96-222, Sec. 104(a)(4)(A), added the last sentence of para. (b)(1) ... Sec. 104(a)(4)(B), amended paras. (c)(1) and (2) ... Sec. 104(a)(4)(C), added the last sentence of para. (b)(2) ... Sec. 104(a)(4)(D), added para. (b)(3) ... Sec. 104(a)(4)(G), added "In determining any carryover under subsection 44C(b)(6), a rule similar to the rule set forth in subparagraph (A) shall be treated as inserted in this paragraph before subparagraph (A), and the applications of subparagraphs (A), (B), and (C) shall be adjusted accordingly." to the end of para. (c)(3) ... Sec. 104(a)(4)(H)(i), amended para. (a)(2) ... Sec. 104(a)(4)(H)(ii), substituted "section 53(b)" for "section 53(c)" in subpara. (c)(3)(A) ... Sec. 104(a)(4)(H)(viii), added "409(c)," after "408(f)," in para. (b)(2), effective for tax. yrs. begin. after 12/31/78.

Prior to amendment, para. (a)(2) read as follows:

"(2) the regular tax for the taxable year, then there is imposed (in addition to all other taxes imposed by this title) a tax equal to the amount of such excess."

Prior to amendment, paras. (c)(1) and (2) read as follows:

"(1) Credits other than the foreign tax credit not allowable. For purposes of determining the amount of any credit allowable under subpart A of part IV of this subchapter (other than the foreign tax credit allowed under section 33(a)), the tax imposed by this section shall not be treated as a tax imposed by this chapter.

"(2) Foreign tax credit allowed against alternative minimum tax. The total amount of the foreign tax credit which can be taken against the tax imposed by subsection (a) shall be determined under section 901 and sections 903 through 908. For purposes of this determination—

"(A) the amount of taxes paid or accrued to foreign countries or possessions of the United States in the taxable year shall be deemed to include an amount equal to the lesser of (i) the foreign tax credit allowed under section 33(a) in computing the regular tax for the taxable year, or (ii) the tax imposed under subsection (a);

"(B) the limitation of section 904(a) shall be an amount equal to the same proportion of the sum of the tax imposed by this section against which such credit is taken and the regular tax (excluding the tax imposed by section 56) which the taxpayer's alternative minimum taxable income from sources without the United States (but not in excess of the taxpayer's entire alternative minimum taxable income) bears to his entire alternative minimum taxable income for the same taxable year. For purposes of the preceding sentence, the entire alternative minimum taxable income shall be reduced by an amount equal to the zero bracket amount;

"(C) the term 'alternative minimum taxable income from sources without United States' means the excess of the items of gross income from sources without the United States over that portion of the deductions taken into account in computing alternative minimum taxable income which are deducted from those items of gross income in computing taxable income from sources without the United States; for purposes of this subparagraph. and except as provided in section 904, gross and taxable income from sources without the United States shall be determined under part I of subchapter N of chapter 1; and

"(D) the amount of foreign taxes paid during the taxable year which may be deemed to be paid in a preceding or succeeding year under section 904(c) the limitation of section 904(a) shall be increased by the lesser of (i) the amount described in subparagraph (B) or (ii) the tax imposed under subsection (a)."

In 1978, P.L. 95-600, Sec. 421(a), added Code Sec. 55, effective for tax. yrs. begin. after 12/31/78.

"SEC. 56. CORPORATE MINIMUM TAX.

"(a) General rule.

"In addition to the other taxes imposed by this chapter, there is hereby imposed for each taxable year, with respect to the income of every corporation, a tax equal to 15 percent of the amount by which the sum of the items of tax preference exceeds the greater of—

"(1) $10,000, or

"(2) the regular tax deduction for the taxable year (as determined under subsection (c)).

"(b) Deferral of tax liability in case of certain net operating losses.

"(1) In general. If for any taxable year a corporation—

"(A) has a net operating loss any portion of which (under section 172) remains as a net operating loss carryover to a succeeding taxable year, and

"(B) has items of tax preference in excess of $10,000,

then an amount equal to the lesser of the tax imposed by subsection (a) or 15 percent of the amount of the net operating loss carryover described in subparagraph (A) shall be treated as tax liability not imposed for the taxable year, but as imposed for the succeeding taxable year or years pursuant to paragraph (2).

"(2) Year of liability. In any taxable year in which any portion of the net operating loss carryover attributable to the excess described in paragraph (1)(B) reduces taxable income, the amount of tax liability described in paragraph (1) shall be treated as tax liability imposed in such taxable year in an amount equal to 15 percent of such reduction.

"(3) Priority of application. For purposes of paragraph (2), if any portion of the net operating loss carryover described in paragraph (1)(A) is not attributable to the excess described in paragraph (1)(B), such portion shall be considered as being applied in reducing taxable income before such other portion.

"(c) Regular tax deduction defined.

"For purposes of this section, the term 'regular tax deduction' means an amount equal to the taxes imposed by this chapter for the taxable year (computed without regard to this part and without regard to the taxes imposed by sections 531 and 541), reduced by the sum of the credits allowable under subparts A, B, and D of part IV.

"(d) Regular tax deduction adjustment for timber.

"In the case of a corporation, the regular tax deduction (as determined under subsection (c)) shall be reduced by an amount equal to the lesser of—

"(1) one-third of the amount determined under subsection (c) without regard to this subsection, or

"(2) the preference reduction for timber determined under section 57(a)(9)(C).

"(e) Tax carryover for timber.

"(1) In general. In the case of a corporation, if for any taxable year, including a taxable year beginning before January 1, 1976—

"(A) the taxes imposed by this chapter (computed without regard to this part and without regard to the tax imposed by section 531) which, under regulations prescribed by the Secretary, are attributable to income from timber, reduced by the sum of the credits allowable under—

"(i) section 27 (relating to foreign tax credit), and

"(ii) section 38 (relating to general business credit), exceed

"(B) the items of tax preference (as determined under section 57),

then the excess of the taxes described in subparagraph (A) over the items of tax preference shall be a tax carryover to each of the 7 taxable years following such year. The entire amount of the excess shall be carried to the first of such 7 taxa-

Tax credits — Part VI

ble years, and then to each of the other such taxable years to the extent that such excess is not used to reduce the amount subject to tax under subsection (a) for a prior taxable year to which such excess may be carried.

"(2) Limitation. The amount of any carryover under paragraph (1) which may be deducted in a taxable year shall be limited to—

"(A) the excess of—

"(i) the amount of timber preference income for the taxable year (as defined in section 57(e)), over

"(ii) the amount determined under section 57(a)(9)(C) for the taxable year,

"(B) reduced by the excess of—

"(i) the regular tax deduction for the taxable year (as determined under subsection (c) without regard to this subsection), over

"(ii) the amount determined under subsection (d) for the taxable year."

In 1986, P.L. 99-514, Sec. 1171(b)(3), deleted the last sentence of subsec. (c), effective for compensation paid or accrued after 12/31/86 in tax. yrs. end. after 12/31/86.

—P.L. 99-514, Sec. 1171(a), of this Act provides

"(a) Section 1171.

"The amendments made by section 1171 shall not apply in the case of a tax credit employee stock ownership plan if—

"(1) such plan was favorably approved on September 23, 1983, by employees, and

"(2) not later than January 11, 1984, the employer of such employees was 100 percent owned by such plan."

Prior to amendment, subsec. (c) read as follows:

"(c) Regular tax deduction defined.

"For purposes of this section, the term 'regular tax deduction' means an amount equal to the taxes imposed by this chapter for the taxable year (computed without regard to this part and without regard to the taxes imposed by sections 531 and 541), reduced by the sum of the credits allowable under subparts A, B, and D of part IV. For purposes of the preceding sentence, the amount of the credit determined under section 38 for any taxable year shall be determined without regard to the employee stock ownership credit determined under section 41."

In 1984, P.L. 98-369, Sec. 441(b)(1), amended Sec. 2123 of P.L. 94-455 (reproduced below), effective for information published after 7/18/84 (date of enactment of P.L. 98-369).

Prior to amendment, Sec. 2123 of P.L. 94-455 read as follows:

"Sec. 2123. High income taxpayer report.

"The Secretary of the Treasury shall publish annually information on the amount of tax paid by individual taxpayers with high total incomes. Total income for this purpose is to be calculated and set forth in three ways:

"(1) by adding to adjusted gross income any items of tax preference excluded from, or deducted in arriving at, adjusted gross income,

"(2) by subtracting any investment expenses incurred in the production of such income to the extent of the investment income, and

"(3) by making both of the adjustments referred to in paragraphs (1) and (2).

In any event these data are to include the number of such individuals with total income over $200,000 who owe no Federal income tax after credits] and the deductions, exclusions or credits used by them to avoid tax."

—P.L. 98-369, Sec. 474(r)(1)(A), substituted "subparts A, B, and D of part IV" for "subpart A of part IV other than sections 39 and 44G" in subsec (c) and amended the last sentence in subsec. (c)... Sec. 474(r)(1)(B), amended subpara. (e)(1)(A), effective for tax. yrs. begin. after 12/31/83, and to carrybacks from tax. yrs. begin. after 12/31/83.

Prior to amendment, the last sentence in subsec. (c) read as follows:

"For purposes of the preceding sentence, the amount of the credit allowable under section 38 shall be determined without regard to the employee plan percentage set forth in section 46(a)(2)(E)."

Prior to amendment, subpara. (e)(1)(A) read as follows:

"(A) the taxes imposed by this chapter (computed without regard to this part and without regard to the tax imposed by section 531) which, under regulations prescribed by the Secretary, are attributable to income from timber, reduced by the sum of the credits allowable under—

"(i) section 33 (relating to foreign tax credit),

"(ii) section 38 (relating to investment credit), and

"(iii) section 40 (relating to expenses of work incentive programs), and

"(iv) section 44B (relating to credit for employment of certain new employees), exceed"

In 1983, P.L. 97-448, Sec. 306(a)(1)(A)(i), redesignated the second Sec. 201(c) of P.L. 97-248 as Sec. 201(d) of P.L. 97-248, see below... Sec. 306(a)(1)(A)(ii), substituted "subsection (d)(1)" for "subsection (c)(1)" in Sec. 201(e)(2) of P.L. 97-248, reproduced below.

In 1982, P.L. 97-248, Sec. 201(d)(1)(A), [as redesignated by Sec. 306(a)91)(A)(i) of P.L. 97-448, see above] substituted "corporation" for "person" each place it appeared in Code Sec. 56 . . . Sec. 201(d)(1)(B), [as redesignated by Sec. 306(a)91)(A)(i) of P.L. 97-448, see above] deleted "one-half (or in the case of a corporation, an amount equal to)" in subsec. (c) . . . Sec. 201(d)(1)(C), [as redesignated by Sec. 306(a)91)(A)(i) of P.L. 97-448, see above] substituted "sections 531 and 541" for "sections 72(m)(5)(B), 402(e), 408(f), 531, and 541" after "means an amount equal to" in subsec. (c) . . . Sec. 201(d)(1)(D), [as redesignated by Sec. 306(a)91)(A)(i) of P.L. 97-448, see above] substituted "39 and 44G" for "31, 39, 43, and 44G" in subsec. (c) . . . Sec. 201(d)(1)(E), [as redesignated by Sec. 306(a)91)(A)(i) of P.L. 97-448, see above] substituted "Corporate minimum tax" for "Imposition of tax" in the heading of Code Sec. 56, effective as provided in Sec. 201(e)(2) of this Act [as amended by Sec. 306(a)(1)(A)(ii) of P.L. 97-448, see above] which reads as follows:

"(2) Special rule for pre-1983 section 56(b) tax deferrals. The amendments made by subsection (d)(1) of this section to section 56(b) of the Internal Revenue Code of 1954 shall not apply to any net operating loss carryover from any taxable year beginning before January 1, 1983, which is attributable to any excess described in section 56(b)(1)(B) of such Code for such taxable year."

In 1981, P.L. 97-34, Sec. 331(c)(2), substituted "43, and 44G" for "and 43" in subsec. (c), effective for tax. yrs. ending after 12/31/82.

In 1980, P.L. 96-222, Sec. 101(a)(7)(B), amended Sec. 141(g) of P.L. 95-600 [see below].

Prior to amendment, Sec. 141(g) of P.L. 95-600 read as follows:

"(g) Effective dates.

"(1) In general. The amendments made by this section (other than by subsection (f)(3)) shall apply with respect to qualified investment for taxable years beginning after December 31, 1978. The amendment made by subsection (f)(7) shall apply to years beginning after December 31, 1978.

"(2) Retroactive application of amendment made by subsection (d). In determining the regular tax deduction under section 6 of the Internal Revenue Code of 1954 for any taxable year beginning before January 1, 1979, the amount of the credit allowable under section 38 shall be determined without regard to section 46(a)(2)(B) of such Code (as in effect before the enactment of the Energy Tax Act of 1978)."

—P.L. 96-222, Sec. 101(a)(7)(L)(iii)(iv), substituted "employee plan" for "ESOP" in subsec. (c), presumably intended by Congress to be effective with respect to qualified investment for tax. yrs. begin. after 12/31/78 [Sec. 101(b)(2)] although technically effective with respect to estates of decedents dying after 4/1/80. [Sec. 101(b)(1)(D)].

In 1978, P.L. 95-618, Sec. 101(b)(2), amended subsec. (c), effective for tax. yrs. end. on or after 4/20/77.

Prior to amendment, subsec. (c) read as follows:

"(c) Regular tax deduction defined.

"For purposes of this section, the term regular tax deduction means an amount equal to one-half of (or in the case of a corporation, an amount equal to) the taxes imposed by this chapter for the taxable year (computed without regard to this part and without regard to the taxes imposed by sections 72(m)(5)(B), 402(e), 408(f), 531, and 541), reduced by the sum of the credits allowable under—

"(1) section 33 (relating to foreign tax credit),

"(2) section 37 (relating to credit for the elderly),

"(3) section 38 (relating to investment credit),

"(4) section 40 (relating to expenses of work incentive program),

"(5) section 41 (relating to contributions to candidates for public office),

"(6) section 42 (relating to general tax credit),

"(7) section 44 (relating to purchase of new principal residence),

"(8) section 44A (relating to expenses for household and dependent care services necessary for gainful employment), and

"(9) section 44B (relating to credit for employment of certain new employees)."

—P.L. 95-600, Sec. 141(d), added the last sentence of subsec. (c), effective with respect to qualified investment for tax. yrs. begin. after 12/31/78, except as provided in Sec. 141(g)(2) and (6) [as amended by Sec. 101(a)(7)(B) of P.L. 96-222, see above] of this Act,, which reads as follows:.

"(2) Election to have amendments apply during 1978. At the election of the taxpayer, paragraph (1) shall be applied by substituting 'December 31, 1977' for 'December 31, 1978'; except that in the case of a plan in existence before December 31, 1978, any such election shall not affect the required allocation of employer securities attributable to qualified investment for taxable years beginning before January 1, 1979. An election under the preceding sentence shall be made at such time and in such manner as the Secretary of the Treasury or his delegate shall prescribe. Such an election, once made, shall be irrevocable."

* * *

"(6) Retroactive application of amendment made by subsection (d). In determining the regular tax deduction under section 56(c) of the Internal Revenue Code of 1954 for any taxable year beginning before January 1, 1979, the amount of the credit allowable under section 38 of such Code shall be determined without regard to section 46(a)(2)(B) of such Code (as in effect before the enactment of the Energy Tax Act of 1978)."

In 1977, P.L. 95-30, Sec. 202(d)(2)(A), deleted "and" at the end of para. (c)(7), substituted ", and" for the period at the end of para. (c)(8) and added para. (c)(9) . . . Sec. 202(d)(2)(B)(i), deleted "and" at the end of clause (e)(1)(A)(ii) . . . Sec. 202(d)(2)(B)(ii), substituted "and" for "exceed" at the end of clause (e)(1)(A)(iii) . . . Sec. 202(d)(2)(B)(iii), added clause (e)(1)(A)(iv), effective for tax. yrs. begin. after 12/31/76 and to credit carrybacks from such yrs.

In 1976, P.L. 94-568, Sec. 3(a), amended Sec. 301(g)(2) of P.L. 94-455 [see below], effective 10/4/76.

Prior to amendment, Sec. 301(g)(2) of P.L. 94-455 read as follows:

"(2) Tax carryover. Except as provided in paragraph (4) and in section 56(e) of the Internal Revenue Code of 1954, the amount of any tax carryover under section 56(c) of such Code from a taxable year beginning before January 1, 1976, shall not be allowed as a tax carryover for any taxable year beginning after December 31, 1975."

—P.L. 94-455, Sec. 301(a), amended subsec. (a) . . . Sec. 301(b)(1), substituted "$10,000" for "$30,000" in subpara. (b)(1)(B) and substituted "15 percent" for "10 percent" in paras. (b)(1) and (b)(2) . . . Sec. 301(b)(2), amended subsec. (c) . . . Sec. 301(c)(4)(B), added subsecs. (d) and (e), effective for tax. yrs. end. after '75, except as provided in Sec. 301(g)(2)-(4) [as amended by Sec. 3(a) of P.L. 94-568, see above], which reads as follows:

"(2) Tax carryover.

1,283

"(A) In general. Except as provided in subparagraph (B), the amount of any tax carryover under section 56(c) of the Internal Revenue Code of 1954 from a taxable year beginning before January 1, 1976, shall not be allowed as a tax carryover for any taxable year beginning after December 31, 1975.

"(B) Except as provided by paragraph (4) and in section 56(e) of the Internal Revenue Code of 1954, in the case of a corporation which is not an electing small business corporation (as defined in section 1371(b) of such Code) or a personal holding company (as defined in section 524 of such Code), the amount of any tax carryover under section 56(c) of such Code from a taxable year beginning before July 1, 1976, shall not be allowed as a tax carryover for any taxable year beginning after June 30, 1976.

"(3) Special rule for taxable year 1976 in the case of a corporation. Notwithstanding any provision of the Internal Revenue Code of 1954 to the contrary, in the case of a corporation which is not an electing small business corporation or a personal holding company the tax imposed by section 56 of such Code for taxable years beginning in 1976, is an amount equal to the sum of—

"(A) the amount of the tax which would have been imposed for such taxable year under such section as such section was in effect on the day before the date of the enactment of the Tax Reform Act of 1976, and

"(B) one-half of the amount by which the amount of the tax which would be imposed for such taxable year under such section as amended by the Tax Reform Act of 1976 (but for this paragraph) exceeds the amount determined under subparagraph (A).

"(4) Certain financial institutions. In the case of a taxpayer which is a financial institution to which section 585 or 593 of the Internal Revenue Code of 1954 applies, the amendments made by this section shall apply only to taxable years beginning after December 31, 1977, and paragraph (2) shall be applied by substituting 'January 1, 1978' for 'January 1, 1976' and by substituting 'December 31, 1977' for 'December 31, 1975'."

—P.L. 94-455, Sec. 301(f), of this Act, provides:

"(f) For purposes of section 21 of the Internal Revenue Code of 1954, the amendments made by this section shall not be treated as a change in rate of tax."

Prior to amendment, subsec. (a) read as follows:

"(a) In general.

"In addition to the other taxes imposed by this chapter, there is hereby imposed for each taxable year, with respect to the income of every person, a tax equal to 10 percent of the amount (if any) by which—

"(1) the sum of the items of tax preference in excess of $30,000, is greater than

"(2) the sum of—

"(A) the taxes imposed by this chapter for the taxable year (computed without regard to this part and without regard to the taxes imposed by sections 72(m)(5)(B), 402(e), 408(f), 531, and 541) reduced by the sum of the credits allowable under—

"(i) section 33 (relating to foreign tax credit),
"(ii) section 37 (relating to retirement income),
"(iii) section 38 (relating to investment credit),
"(iv) section 40 (relating to expenses of work incentive program),
"(v) section 41 (relating to contributions to candidates for public office),
"(vi) section 42 (relating to credit for personal exemptions), and
"(vii) section 44 (relating to credit for purchase of new principal residence); and

"(B) the tax carry-overs to the taxable year."

Prior to amendment, subsec. (c) read as follows:

"(c) Tax carry overs.

"If for any taxable year—

"(1) the taxes imposed by this chapter (computed without regard to this part and without regard to the taxes imposed by sections 72(m)(5)(B), 402(e), 408(f), 531, and 541) reduced by the sum of the credits allowable under—

"(A) section 33 (relating to foreign tax credit),
"(B) section 37 (relating to retirement income),
"(C) section 38 (relating to investment credit),
"(D) section 40 (relating to expenses of work incentive program),
"(E) section 41 (relating to contributions to candidates for public office),
"(F) section 42 (relating to credit for personal exemptions), and
"(G) section 44 (relating to credit for purchase of new principal residence), exceed

"(2) the sum of the items of tax preferences in excess of $30,000,

then the excess of the taxes described in paragraph (1) over the sum described in paragraph (2) shall be a tax carry over to each of the 7 taxable years following such year. The entire amount of the excess for a taxable year shall be carried to the first of such 7 taxable years, and then to each of the other such taxable years to the extent that such excess is not used to reduce the amount subject to tax under subsection (a) for a prior taxable year to which excess may be carried."

—P.L. 94-455, Sec. 2123, [as amended by Sec. 441(b)(1) of P.L. 98-369, see above] effective for information published after 7/18/84, provides:

"Sec. 2123. High income taxpayer report.

"The Secretary of the Treasury shall publish annually information on the amount of tax paid by individual taxpayers with high total incomes. Total income for this purpose is to be calculated and set forth by adding to adjusted gross income any items of tax preference excluded from, or deducted in arriving at, adjusted gross income, and by subtracting any investment expenses incurred in the production of such income to the extent of the investment income. These data are to include the number of such individuals with total income over $200,000 who owe no Federal income tax (after credits) and the deductions, exclusions, or credits used by them to avoid tax."

In 1975, P.L. 94-164, Sec. 2(e), extended the effective date for amendments made by Sec. 203 of P.L. 94-12, to include tax. yrs. end. after 12/31/74 and before 1/1/77.

—P.L. 94-12, Sec. 203(b)(2), amended subpara. (a)(2)(A) by striking out "and" at the end of clause (iv), by substituting ", and" for "; and" in clause (v), and by adding new clause (vi), effective for taxable years ending after 12/31/74 and before 1/1/76.

—P.L. 94-12, Sec. 208(d)(2), deleted "and" at the end of clause (a)(2)(A)(v), substituted ", and" for "; and" in clause (a)(2)(A)(vi), and added new clause (a)(2)(A)(vii), effective date of enactment [3/29/75].

—P.L. 94-12, Sec. 203(b)(3), deleted "and" at the end of subpara. (c)(1)(D), substituted "and" for "exceed" in subpara. (c)(1)(E), and added new subpara. (c)(1)(F), effective for taxable years ending after 12/31/74 and before 1/1/76.

—P.L. 94-12, Sec. 208(d)(3), deleted "and" at the end of subpara. (c)(1)(E), substituted "and" for "exceed" in subpara. (c)(1)(F), and added new subpara. (c)(1)(G), effective date of enactment [3/29/75].

In 1974, P.L. 93-406, Sec. 2001(g)(2)(D), substituted "72(m)(5)(B)," for "402(e)" in subpara. (a)(1)(A), effective for tax. yrs. begin. after 12/31/75.

—P.L. 93-406, Sec. 2002(g)(4), substituted "408(f), 531" for "531" in subpara. (a)(1)(A), effective 1/1/75.

—P.L. 93-406, Sec. 2005(c)(7), added "402(e)," before "531" in subpara. (a)(2)(A) and para. (c)(1), effective for distributions or payments made after 12/31/75 in tax. yrs. begin. after 12/31/75.

In 1971, P.L. 92-178, Sec. 601(c)(4)(A), deleted "and" at the end of clause (a)(2)(ii) . . . Sec. 601(c)(4)(B), inserted a comma in place of "; and" at the end of clause (a)(2)(iii) . . . Sec. 601(c)(4)(C), added clauses (iv) and (v) to para. (a)(2) . . . Sec. 601(c)(5)(A), deleted "and" at the end of subpara. (c)(1)(B) . . . Sec. 601(c)(5)(B), deleted "exceed" at the end of subpara. (c)(1)(C) . . . Sec. 601(c)(5)(C), added subpara. (c)(1)(D), and (E), effective for tax. yrs. begin. after 12/31/71.

In 1970, P.L. 91-614, Sec. 501(a)(1), amended para. (a)(2) . . . Sec. 501(a)(2), added subsec. (c), effective as provided in Sec. 501(b) of this Act, which provides:

"(b) Effective date. The amendments made by subsection (a) shall apply to taxable years ending after December 13, 1969. In the case of a taxable year beginning in 1969 and ending in 1970, the excess referred to in section 56(c) of the Internal Revenue Code of 1954 (as added by subsection (a)) shall be an amount equal to the excess determined under such section (without regard to the [sic this] sentence), multiplied by a fraction—

"(1) the numerator of which is the number of days in the taxable year occurring after 12/31/69, and

"(2) the denominator of which is the number of days in the entire taxable year."

Prior to amendment, para. (a)(2) read as follows:

"(2) the taxes imposed by this chapter for the taxable year (computed without regard to this part and without regard to the taxes imposed by sections 531 and 541) reduced by the sum of the credits allowable under—

"(A) section 33 (relating to foreign tax credit),
"(B) section 37 (relating to retirement income), and
"(C) section 38 (relating to investment credit)."

In 1969, P.L. 91-172, Sec. 301(a), added Code Sec. 56, effective as provided in Sec. 301(c), which reads as follows:

"(c) Effective date. The amendments made by this section shall apply to taxable years ending after December 31, 1969. In the case of a taxable year beginning in 1969 and ending in 1970, the tax imposed by section 56 of the Internal Revenue Code of 1954 shall be an amount equal to the tax imposed by such section (determined without regard to this sentence) multiplied by a fraction—

"(1) the numerator of which is the number of days in the taxable year occurring after December 31, 1969, and

"(2) the denominator of which is the number of days in the entire taxable year."

"SEC. 57. ITEMS OF TAX PREFERENCE.

"(a) In general.

"For purposes of this part, the items of tax preference are—

"(1) Exclusion of dividends. Any amount excluded from gross income for the taxable year under section 116.

"(2) Accelerated depreciation on real property. With respect to each section 1250 property (as defined in section 1250(c)), the amount by which the deduction allowable for the taxable year for exhaustion, wear and tear, obsolescence, or amortization exceeds the depreciation deduction which would have been allowable for the taxable year had the taxpayer depreciated the property under the straight line method for each taxable year of its useful life (determined without regard to section 167(k)) for for which the taxpayer has held the property.

"(3) Accelerated depreciation on leased personal property. With respect to each item of section 1245 property (as defined in section 1245(a)(3)) which is subject to a lease, the amount by which—

"(A) the deduction allowable for the taxable year for depreciation or amortization, exceeds

"(B) the deduction which would have been allowable for the taxable year had the taxpayer depreciated the property under the straight-line method for each taxable year of its useful life for which the taxpayer has held the property.

For purposes of subparagraph (B), useful life shall be determined as if section 167(m)(1) (relating to asset depreciation range) did not include the last sentence thereof.

"(4) Amortization of certified pollution control facilities. With respect to each certified pollution control facility for which an election is in effect under section 169, the amount by which the deduction allowable for the taxable year under such

Tax credits — Part VI

section exceeds the depreciation deduction which would otherwise be allowable under section 167.

"(5) Mining exploration and development costs. With respect to each mine or other natural deposit (other than an oil or gas well) of the taxpayer, an amount equal to the excess of—

"(A) the amount allowable as a deduction under section 616(a) or 617, over

"(B) the amount which would have been allowable if the expenditures had been capitalized and amortized ratably over the 10-year period beginning with the taxable year in which such expenditures were made.

"(6) Circulation and research and experimental expenditures. An amount equal to the excess of—

"(A) the amount allowable as a deduction under section 173 or 174(a) for the taxable year, over

"(B) the amount which would have been allowable for the taxable year with respect to expenditures paid or incurred during such taxable year if—

"(i) the circulation expenditures described in section 173 had been capitalized and amortized ratably over the 3-year period beginning with the taxable year in which such expenditures were made, or

"(ii) the research and experimental expenditures described in section 174 had been capitalized and amortized ratably over the 10-year period beginning with the taxable year in which such expenditures were made.

"(7) Reserves for losses on bad debts of financial institutions. In the case of a financial institution to which section 585 or 593 applies, the amount by which the deduction allowable for the taxable year for a reasonable addition to a reserve for bad debts exceeds the amount that would have been allowable had the institution maintained its bad debt reserve for all taxable years on the basis of actual experience.

"(8) Depletion. With respect to each property (as defined in section 614), the excess of the deduction for depletion allowable under section 611 for the taxable year over the adjusted basis of the property at the end of the taxable year (determined without regard to the depletion deduction for the taxable year).

"(9) Capital gains.

"(A) Individuals. In the case of a taxpayer other than a corporation, an amount equal to the net capital gain deduction for the taxable year determined under section 1202.

"(B) Corporations. In the case of a corporation having a net capital gain for the taxable year, an amount equal to the product obtained by multiplying the net capital gain by a fraction the numerator of which is the highest rate of tax specified in section 11(b), minus the alternative tax rate under section 1201(a), for the taxable year, and the denominator of which is the highest rate of tax specified in section 11(b) for the taxable year. In the case of a corporation to which section 1201(a) does not apply, the amount under this subparagraph shall be determined under regulations prescribed by the Secretary in a manner consistent with the preceding sentence.

"(C) Preference reduction for timber. In the case of a corporation, the amount of the tax preference under subparagraph (B) shall be reduced (but not below zero) by the sum of—

"(i) one-third of the corporation's timber preference income (as defined in subsection (e)), plus

"(ii) $20,000,

but in no event shall this reduction exceed the amount of timber preference income.

"(D) Principal residence. For purposes of subparagraph (a), gain from the sale or exchange of a principal residence (within the meaning of section 1034) shall not be taken into account.

"(E) Special rule for certain insolvent taxpayers.

"(i) In general. The amount of the tax preference under subparagraph (A) shall be reduced (but not below zero) by the excess (if any) of—

"(I) the applicable percentage of gain from any farm insolvency transaction, over

"(II) the applicable percentage of any loss from any farm insolvency transaction which offsets such gain.

"(ii) Reduction limited to amount of insolvency. The amount of the reduction determined under clause (i) shall not exceed the amount by which the taxpayer is insolvent immediately before the transaction (reduced by any portion of such amount previously taken into account under this clause).

"(iii) Farm insolvency transaction. For purposes of this subparagraph, the term 'farm insolvency transaction' means—

"(I) the transfer by a farmer of farmland to a creditor in cancellation of indebtedness or

"(II) the sale or exchange by the farmer of property described in subclause (I) under the threat of foreclosure.

but only if the farmer is insolvent immediately before such transaction.

"(iv) Insolvent. For purposes of this subparagraph, the term 'insolvent' means the excess of liabilities over the fair market value of assets.

"(v) Applicable percentage. For purposes of this subparagraph, the term 'applicable percentage' means that percentage of net capital gain with respect to which a deduction is allowed under section 1202(a).

"(vi) Farmland. For purposes of this subparagraph, the term 'farmland' means any land used or held for use in the trade or business of farming (within the meaning of section 2032A(e)(5)).

"(vii) Farmer. For purposes of this subparagraph, the term 'farmer' means any taxpayer if 50 percent or more of the average annual gross income of the taxpayer for the 3 preceding taxable years is attributable to the trade or business of farming (within the meaning of section 2032A(e)(5)).

"(10) Incentive stock options. With respect to the transfer of a share of stock pursuant to the exercise of an incentive stock option (as defined in section 422A),

the amount by which the fair market value of the share at the time of exercise exceeds the option price. For purposes of this paragraph, the fair market value of a share of stock shall be determined without regard to any restriction other than a restriction which, by its terms, will never lapse.

"(11) Intangible drilling costs.

"(A) In general. With respect to all oil, gas and geothermal properties of the taxpayer, the amount (if any) by which the amount of the excess intangible drilling costs arising in the taxable year is greater than the amount of the net income of the taxpayer from oil and gas properties for the taxable year.

"(B) Excess intangible drilling costs. For purposes of subparagraph (A), the amount of the excess intangible drilling costs arising in the taxable year is the excess of—

"(i) the intangible drilling and development costs described in section 263(c) paid or incurred in connection with oil, gas and geothermal wells (other than costs incurred in drilling a nonproductive well) allowable under this chapter for the taxable year, over

"(ii) the amount which would have been allowable for the taxable year if such costs had been capitalized and straight line recovery of intangibles (as defined in subsection (d)) had been used with respect to such costs.

"(C) Net income from oil, gas and geothermal properties. For purposes of subparagraph (A), the amount of the net income of the taxpayer from oil and gas properties for the taxable year is the excess of—

"(i) the aggregate amount of gross income (within the meaning of section 613(a)) from all oil, gas and geothermal properties of the taxpayer received or accrued by the taxpayer during the taxable year, over

"(ii) the amount of any deductions allocable to such properties reduced by the excess described in subparagraph (B) for such taxable year.

"(D) Paragraph applied separately with respect to geothermal properties and oil and gas properties. This paragraph shall be applied separately with respect to—

"(i) all oil and gas properties which are not described in clause (ii), and

"(ii) all properties which are geothermal deposits (as defined in section 613(e)(3)).

"(12) Accelerated cost recovery deduction.

"(A) In general. With respect to each recovery property (other than 19-year real property and low-income housing) which is subject to a lease, the amount (if any) by which the deduction allowed under section 168(a) for the taxable year exceeds the deduction which would have been allowable for the taxable year had the property been depreciated using the straight-line method (with a half-year convention and without regard to salvage value) and a recovery period determined in accordance with the following table:

In the case of:	The recovery period is:
3-year property	5 years.
5-year property	8 years.
10-year property	15 years.
15-year public utility property	22 years.

"(B) 19-year real property and low-income housing. With respect to each recovery property which is 19-year real property or low-income housing, the amount (if any) by which the deduction allowed under section 168(a) (or, in the case of property described in section 167(k), under section 167) for the taxable year exceeds the deduction which would have been allowable for a taxable year had the property been depreciated using a straight-line method (without regard to salvage value) over a recovery period of—.

"(i) 19 years in the case of 19-year real property, and

"(ii) 15 years in the case of low-income housing property.

"(C) Subparagraphs (A) and (B) inapplicable where longer recovery periods apply. If, pursuant to section 168(b)(3) or 168(f)(2), the recovery period for any property is longer than the recovery period for such property set forth in subparagraph (A) or (B), subparagraph (A) or (B) (as the case may be) shall not apply to such property.

"(D) Paragraphs (2) and (3) shall not apply. Paragraphs (2) and (3) shall not apply to recovery property.

"(E) Definitions. For purposes of this paragraph, the terms '3-year property', '5-year property', '10-year property', '15-year public utility property', '19-year real property', 'low-income housing', and 'recovery property', shall have the same meanings given such terms under section 168.

Paragraphs (1), (3), (5), (6), (11), and (12)(A) shall not apply to a corporation other than a personal holding company (as defined in section 542).

"(b) Application with section 291.

"(1) In general.

"(A) Pollution control facilities; bad debt reserves. In the case of any item of tax preference of a corporation described in paragraph (4) or (7) of subsection (a), only 59% percent of the amount of such item of tax preference (determined without regard to this subsection) shall be taken into account as an item of tax preference.

"(B) Iron ore and coal. In the case of any item of tax preference of a corporation described in paragraph (8) of subsection (a) (but only to the extent such item is allocable to a deduction for depletion for iron ore and coal, including lignite), only 71.6 percent of the amount of such item of tax preference (determined without regard to this subsection) shall be taken into account as an item of tax preference.

"(2) Certain capital gains. In determining the net capital gain of any corporation for purposes of paragraph (9)(B) of subsection (a), there shall be taken into account only 59% percent of any gain from the sale or exchange of section 1250 property which is equal to 80 percent of the excess determined under section 291(a)(1) with respect to such property.

1,285

"(c) Net leases.

"(1) In general. For purposes of this section, property shall be considered to be subject to a net lease for a taxable year if—

"(A) for such taxable year the sum of the deductions of the lessor with respect to such property which are allowable solely by reason of section 162 (other than rents and reimbursed amounts with respect to such property) is less than 15 percent of the rental income produced by such property, or

"(B) the lessor is either guaranteed a specified return or is guaranteed in whole or in part against loss of income.

"(2) Multiple leases of single parcel of real property. If a parcel of real property of the taxpayer is leased under two or more leases, paragraph (1)(A) shall, at the election of the taxpayer, be applied by treating all leased portions of such property as subject to a single lease.

"(3) Elimination of 15-percent test after 5 years in case of real property. At the election of the taxpayer, paragraph (1)(A) shall not apply with respect to real property of the taxpayer which has been in use for more than 5 years.

"(4) Elections. An election under paragraph (2) or (3) shall be made at such time and in such manner as the Secretary or his delegate prescribes by regulations.

"(d) Straight line recovery of intangibles defined.

"For purposes of paragraph (11) of subsection (a)—

"(1) In general. The term 'straight line recovery of intangibles', when used with respect to intangible drilling and development costs for any well, means (except in the case of an election under paragraph (2)) ratable amortization of such costs over the 120-month period beginning with the month in which production from such well begins.

"(2) Election. If the taxpayer elects, at such time and in such manner as the Secretary may by regulations prescribe, with respect to the intangible drilling and development costs for any well, the term 'straight line recovery of intangibles' means any method which would be permitted for purposes of determining cost depletion with respect to such well and which is selected by the taxpayer for purposes of subsection (a)(11).

"(e) Timber preference income defined.

"For purposes of this part, the term 'timber preference income' means the sum of—

"(1) the gains referred to in section 631(a) and section 631(b),

"(2) long-term capital gains on timber, and

"(3) gains on the sale of timber included in paragraph 1231(b)(1), multiplied by the fraction determined in paragraph 57(a)(9)(B)."

In **1986,** P.L. 99-514, Sec. 1804(k)(2)(A), and (B), amended Sec. 68(e)(2) and (3) of P.L. 98-369 [reproduced in note following Code Sec. 291], part of the effective date for changes made by Sec. 68(c)(1) and (2) of P.L. 98-369, see below.

—P.L. 99-514, Sec. 1804(k)(3)(C), amended subpara. (b)(1)(B)... Sec. 1804(k)(3)(D), substituted "80 percent" for "85 percent" in para. (b)(2), effective for tax. yrs. begin. after 12/31/84.

Prior to amendment, subpara. (b)(1)(B) read as follows:

"(B) Iron ore and coal. In the case of any item of tax preference of a corporation described in paragraph (8) of subsection (a) (but only to the extent such item is allocable to a deduction for depletion for iron ore and coal (including legnite)),"

—P.L. 99-514, Sec. 1809(a)(3), amended subpara. (a)(12)(B), effective for property placed in service by taxpayer after 3/15/84. For special rules and exceptions, see Secs. 111(g)(2)-(4) of P.L. 98-369 reproduced below.

Prior to amendment, subpara. (a)(12)(B) read as follows:

"(B) 19-year real property and low-income housing. With respect to each recovery property which is 19-year real property or low-income housing, the amount (if any) by which the deduction allowed under section 168(a) (or, in the case of property described in section 167(k), under section 167) for the taxable year exceeds the deduction which would have been allowable for a taxable year had the property been depreciated using the straight-line method (without regard to salvage value) over a recovery period of—"

—P.L. 99-514, Sec. 1855(a), amended Sec. 555(c)(2) of P.L. 98-369 [see below], the effective date for changes made by Sec. 555(a)(2) of P.L. 98-369, by substituting "subsection (a)(2)" for "subsection (b)" and by deleting "after March 20, 1984," for "option issued", see below.

—P.L. 99-272, Sec. 13208(a), added subpara. (a)(9)(E), effective for transfers, sales or exchanges after 12/31/81, in tax. yrs. end. after 12/31/81.

In **1985,** P.L. 99-121, Sec. 103(b)(1)(B), substituted "19-year recovery period" for "18-year recovery period" each place it appeared in the text and headings of para. (a)(12)... Sec. 103(b)(7), substituted "19 years" for "18 years" in clause (a)(12)(B)(i), effective for property placed in service by the taxpayer after 5/8/85, except as provided in Sec. 105(b)(2) and (3) of this Act reproduced in note following Code Sec. 168.

In **1984,** P.L. 98-369, Sec. 16(b), amended para. (a)(1), effective for tax. yrs. end. after 12/31/83.

Prior to amendment, para. (a)(1) read as follows:

"(1) Exclusion of interest and dividends. Any amount excluded from gross income for the taxable year under section 116 or 128."

—P.L. 98-369, Sec. 68(c)(2), amended para. (b)(1), effective for tax. yrs. begin. after 12/31/84, except relating to pollution control facilities effective for property placed in service after 12/31/84, in tax. yrs. end. after 12/31/84.

Prior to amendment, para. (b)(1) read as follows:

"(1) In general. In the case of any item of tax preference of a corporation described in —

"(A) paragraph (4) or (7) of subsection (a), or

"(B) paragraph (8) of subsection (a) (but only to the extent such item is allocable to a deduction for depletion for iron ore and coal (including lignite)), only 71.6 percent of the amount of such item of tax preference (determined without regard to this subsection) shall be taken into account as an item of tax preference."

—P.L. 98-369, Sec. 68(c)(2), substituted "59% percent" for "71.6 percent" in para. (b)(2), effective to sales or other dispositions after 12/31/84 in tax. yrs. end. after 12/31/84.

—P.L. 98-369, Sec. 111(e)(5), substituted "18-year real property, low-income housing" for "15-year real property" in subpara. (a)(12)(A)... Sec. 111(e)(6), amended subpara. (a)(12)(B)... Sec. 111(e)(7), substituted "18-year real property", "low-income housing," for "15-year real property," in subpara. (a)(12)(E), effective for property placed in service by the taxpayer after 3/15/84. For special rules and exceptions, Sec. 111(g)(2)-(4) of the Act, which reads as follows:

"(2) Exception. The amendments made by this section shall not apply to property placed in service by the taxpayer before January 1, 1987, if—

"(A) the taxpayer or a qualified person entered into a binding contract to purchase or construct such property before March 16, 1984, or

"(B) construction of such property was commenced by or for the taxpayer or a qualified person before March 16, 1984.

For purposes of this paragraph the term 'qualified person' means any person who transfers his rights in such a contract or such property to the taxpayer, but only if such property is not placed in service by such person before such rights are transferred to the taxpayer.

"(3) Special rules for application of paragraph (2).—

"(A) Certain inventory. In the case of any property which—

"(i) is held by a person as property described in section 1221(1), and

"(ii) is disposed of by such person before January 1, 1985,

such person shall not, for purposes of paragraph (2), be treated as having placed such property in service before such property is disposed of merely because such person rented such property or held such property for rental. No deduction for depreciation or amortization shall be allowed to such person with respect to such property,

"(B) Certain property financed by bonds. In the case of any property with respect to which—

"(i) bonds were issued to finance such property before 1984, and

"(ii) an architectural contract was entered into before March 16, 1984,

paragraph (2) shall be applied by substituting 'May 2' for 'March 16'.

"(4) Special rule for components. For purposes of applying section 168(f)(1)(B) of the Internal Revenue Code of 1954 (as amended by this section) to components placed in service after December 31, 1986, property to which paragraph (2) applies shall be treated as placed in service by the taxpayer before March 16, 1984."

Prior to amendment, subpara. (a)(12)(B) read as follows:

"(B) 15-year real property. With respect to each recovery property which is 15-year real property, the amount (if any) by which the deduction which would have been allowable for the taxable year had the property been depreciated using a 15-year period and the straight-line method (without regard to salvage value)."

—P.L. 98-369, Sec. 555(a)(2), added the last sentence to para. (a)(10), effective as provided in Sec. 555(c)(2) of this Act [as amended by Sec. 1855(a) of P.L. 99-514, see above]:

"(2) Items of tax preference. The amendment made by subsection (a)(2) shall apply to options exercised after March 20, 1984. In the case of an option issued pursuant to a plan adopted or corporate action taken by the board of directors of the grantor corporation before May 15, 1984, the preceding sentence shall be applied by substituting 'December 31, 1984' for 'March 20, 1984'."

—P.L. 98-369, Sec. 711(a)(3)(A), amended subpara. (a)(6)(B)... Sec. 722(a)(1)(A), deleted "(or, in the case of property described in section 167(k), under section 167)" in subpara. 57(a)(12)(A)... Sec. 722(a)(1)(B), inserted "(or, in the case of property described in section 167(k), under section 167)" after "section 168(a)" in subpara. (a)(12)(B) [as amended by Sec. 111(e)(6) of the Act], effective for tax. yrs. begin. after 12/31/82.

Prior to amendment, subpara. (a)(6)(B) read as follows:

"(B) the amount which would have been allowable for the taxable year if the circulation expenditures described in section 173 or the research and experimental expenditures described in section 174 had been capitalized and amortized ratably over the 10-year period beginning with the taxable year in which such expenditures were made."

In **1983,** P.L. 97-448, Sec. 102(b)(1)(A), substituted "and (12)(A)" for "and (12)" in the next to last sentence of subsec. (a), effective for property placed in service after 12/31/80 in tax. yrs. end. after 12/31/80 and before 1/1/83 [Sec. 102(b)(1)(B) of P.L. 97-448].

—P.L. 97-448, Sec. 102(b)(3), redesignated subparas. (a)(12)(C) and (D) as subparas. (a)(12)(E) and (F) and added new subpara. (a)(12)(C)... Sec. 102(b)(4), substituted "under section 168(a)(or, in the case of property described in section 167(k) under section 167)" for "under section 168(a)" in subpara. (a)(12)(A), effective for property placed in service after 12/31/80 in tax. yrs. end. after 12/31/80.

In **1982,** P.L. 97-354, Sec. 5(a)(14), deleted "an electing small business corporation (as defined in section 1371(b) and" after "shall not apply to a corporation other than" in the last sentence of subsec. (a)... Sec. 5(a)(15)(A), substituted "a corporation" for "an applicable corporation" in para. (b)(1)... Sec. 5(a)(15)(B), substituted "corporation" for "applicable corporation" in para. (b)(2)... Sec. 5(a)(15)(C), deleted para. (b)(3), effective for tax. yrs. begin. after 12/31/82.

Prior to deletion, para. (b)(3) read as follows:

"(3) Applicable corporation defined. For purposes of this subsection, the term 'applicable corporation' has the meaning given such term by section 291(e)(2).".

—P.L. 97-248, Sec. 201(b)(1)(A), amended para. (a)(1)... Sec. 201(b)(1)(B), amended paras. (a)(5) and (a)(6)... Sec. 201(b)(1)(C), amended para. (a)(10)...

Tax credits Part VI

Sec. 201(b)(2)(A), substituted "(1), (3), (5), (6), (11), and (12)(A)" for "(3), (11), and (12)" in the next to last sentence of subsec. (a)... Sec. 201(b)(2)(B), deleted the last sentence in subsec. (a), effective for tax. yrs. begin. after 12/31/82.

Prior to amendment, para. (a)(1) read as follows:

"(1) Adjusted itemized deductions. In the case of an individual, an amount equal to the adjusted itemized deductions for the taxable year (as determined under subsection (b))".

Prior to amendment, paras. (a)(5) and (a)(6) read as follows:

"(5) Amortization of railroad rolling stock. With respect to each unit of railroad rolling stock for which an election is in effect under section 184, the amount by which the deduction allowable for the taxable year under such section exceeds the depreciation deduction which would otherwise be allowable under section 167.

"(6) Stock options. With respect to the transfer of a share of stock pursuant to the exercise of a qualified stock option (as defined in section 422(b)) or a restricted stock option (as defined in section 424(b)), the amount by which the fair market value of the share at the time of exercise exceeds the option price."

Prior to amendment, para. (a)(10) read as follows:

"(10) Amortization of child care facilities. With respect to each item of section 188 property for which an election is in effect under section 188, the amount by which the deduction allowable for the taxable year under such section exceeds the depreciation deduction which would otherwise be allowable under section 167."

Prior to amendment, the last sentence in subsec. (a) read as follows:

"For purposes of section 56, in the case of a taxpayer other than a corporation, the adjusted itemized deductions described in paragraph (1) and capital gains described in paragraph (9) shall not be treated as items of tax preference."

—P.L. 97-248, Sec. 204(b), amended subsec. (b), effective as provided in Sec. 204(d)(6) of this Act which reads as follows:

"(6) Minimum tax.—The amendment made by subsection (b) [Sec. 204(b) of P.L. 97-248] shall apply to taxable years ending after December 31, 1982, with respect to items of tax preference described in section 57(b) of such Code to which section 291 of such Code applies; except that in the case of an item described in section 291(a)(2) of such Code, such amendment shall apply to taxable years beginning after December 31, 1983."

Prior to amendment, subsec. (b) read as follows:

"(b) Adjusted itemized deductions.

"(1) In general. For purposes of paragraph (1) of subsection (a), the amount of the adjusted itemized deductions for any taxable year is the amount by which the sum of the itemized deductions (as defined in section 63(f)) without regard to paragraph (3) thereof other than—

"(A) the deduction for State and local, and foreign, taxes provided by section 164(a),

"(B) the deduction for medical, dental, etc., expenses provided by section 213,

"(C) the deduction for casualty losses described in section 165(c)(3), and

"(D) the deduction allowable under section 691(c),

exceeds 60 percent of the taxpayer's adjusted gross income reduced by the items in subparagraphs (A) through (D) for the taxable year.

"(2) Special rules for estates and trusts—

"(A) In general. In the case of an estate or trust, for purposes of paragraph (1) of subsection (a), the amount of the adjusted itemized deductions for any taxable year is the amount by which the sum of the deductions for the taxable year other than—

"(i) the deductions allowable in arriving at adjusted gross income,

"(ii) the deduction for personal exemption provided by section 642(b),

"(iii) the deduction for casualty losses described in section 165(c)(3),

"(iv) the deductions allowable under section 651(a), 661(a), or 691(c),

"(v) the deduction for State and local, and foreign, taxes provided by section 164(a), and

"(vi) the deductions allowable to a trust under section 642(c) to the extent that a corresponding amount is included in the gross income of the beneficiary under section 622(a)(1) for the taxable year of the beneficiary with which or within which the taxable year of the trust ends,

exceeds 60 percent of the adjusted gross income reduced by the items in clauses (iii) through (vi) for the taxable year.

"(B) Determination of adjusted gross income. For purposes of this paragraph, the adjusted gross income of an estate or trust shall be computed in the same manner as in the case of an individual, except that—

"(i) the deductions for costs paid or incurred in connection with the administration of the estate or trust, and

"(ii) to the extent provided in subparagraph (C), the deductions under section 642(c),

shall be treated as allowable in arriving at adjusted gross income.

"(C) Treatment of certain charitable contributions. For purposes of this paragraph, the following deductions under section 642(c) (relating to deductions for amounts paid or permanently set aside for charitable purposes) shall be treated as deductions allowable in arriving at adjusted gross income:

"(i) deductions allowable to an estate,

"(ii) deductions allowable to a trust all of the unexpired interests in which are devoted to one or more of the purposes described in section 170(c) (determined without regard to section 170(c)(2)(A)),

"(iii) deductions allowable to a trust which is a pooled income fund within the meaning of section 642(c)(5),

"(iv) deductions allowable to a trust—

"(I) all the income interest in which are devoted to one or more of the purposes described in section 170(c) (determined without regard to section 170(c)(2)(A)),

"(II) all of the interests (other than income interests) in which are held by a corporation, and

"(III) the grantor of which is a corporation.

"(v) deductions allowable to a trust which are attributable to transfers to the trust before January 1, 1977, and

"(vi) deductions allowable to a trust, all of the income interest of which is devoted solely to one or more of the purposes described in section 170(c) (determined without regard to section 170(c)(2)(A)), which are attributable to transfers pursuant to a will or pursuant to an inter vivos trust in which the grantor had the power to revoke at the date of his death.")

In 1981, P.L. 97-34, Sec. 121(c)(1), added "without regard to paragraph (3) thereof" after "section 63(f)" in para. (b)(1), effective for contributions made after 12/31/81, in tax. yrs. begin. after 12/31/81.

—P.L. 97-34, Sec. 205(a), added para. (a)(12)... Sec. 205(b), substituted ", (11), and (12)" for "and (11)" in the next to last sentence of subsec. (a), effective for property placed in service after 12/31/80, in tax. yrs. ending after 12/31/80.

—P.L. 97-34, Sec. 212(d)(2)(B), deleted "or 191" which followed "section 167(k)" in para. (a)(2), effective for expenditures incurred after 12/31/81, in tax. yrs. ending after 12/31/81. For transitional rule see Sec. 212(e)(2) reproduced in note following Code Sec. 46.

In 1980, P.L. 96-596, Sec. 3(a), redesignated clauses (b)(2)(C)(iv) and (v) as clauses (b)(2)(C)(v) and (vi), and added new clause (b)(2)(C)(iv), effective for tax. yrs. begin. after 12/31/75.

—P.L. 96-222, Sec. 104(a)(4)(E), added ", and foreign," after "State and local" in subpara. (b)(1)(A) and clause (b)(2)(A)(v)... Sec. 104(a)(4)(F), substituted "clauses (iii) through (vi)" for "clauses (i) through (vi)" in subpara. (b)(2)(A) ... Sec. 107(a)(1)(A), substituted "section 170(c) (determined without regard to section 170(c)(2)(A))" for "section 170(c)(2)(B)" in subpara. (b)(2)(C), effective for tax. yrs. begin. after 12/31/75.

In 1978, P.L. 95-618, Sec. 401, makes the same amendment to the effective date of Sec. 308(a) of P.L. 95-30 as Sec. 422 of P.L. 95-600.

—P.L. 95-618, Sec. 402(b)(1), substituted "oil, gas, and geothermal properties" for "Oil and gas properties" each place it appeared in para. (a)(11)... Sec. 402(b)(2), substituted "oil, gas, and geothermal wells" for "oil and gas wells" in clause (a)(11)(B)(i)... Sec. 402(b)(3), added subpara. (a)(11)(D), effective for wells commenced on or after 10/1/78, in tax. yrs. end. on or after 10/1/78. Sec. 402(e)(2) of this Act provides as follows:

"(2) Election. The taxpayer may elect to capitalize or deduct any costs to which section 263(c) of the Internal Revenue Code of 1954 applies by reason of the amendments made by this section. Any such election shall be made before the expiration of the time for filing claim for credit or refund of any overpayment of tax imposed by chapter 1 of such Code with respect to the taxpayer's first taxable year to which the amendments made by this section apply and for which he pays or incurs costs to which such section 263(c) applies by reason of the amendments made by this section. Any election under this paragraph may be changed or revoked at any time before the expiration of the time referred to in the preceding sentence, but after the expiration of such time such election may not be changed or revoked."

—P.L. 95-600, Sec. 301(b)(2), substituted "the highest rate of tax specified in section 11(b)" for "the sum of the normal tax rate and the surtax rate under section 11" each place it appeared in subpara. (a)(9)(B), effective for tax. yrs. begin. after 12/31/78.

—P.L. 95-600, Sec. 402(b)(1), amended subpara. (a)(9)(A), effective for tax. yrs. end. after 10/31/78.

Prior to amendment, subpara. (a)(9)(A) read as follows:

"(A) Individuals. In the case of a taxpayer other than a corporation, an amount equal to one-half of the net capital gain for the taxable year."

—P.L. 95-600, Sec. 421(b)(1), added subpara. (a)(9)(D), effective for sales and exchanges made after 7/26/78, in tax. yrs. end. after 7/26/78.

—P.L. 95-600, Sec. 421(b)(2), amended the last sentence of subsec. (a)... Sec. 421(b)(3), amended para. (b)(1)... Sec. 421(b)(4), amended subpara. (b)(2)(A) (as amended by Sec. 701(b)(3) of this Act), effective for tax. yrs. begin. after 12/31/78.

Prior to amendment, the last sentence of subsec. (a) read as follows:

"Paragraphs (3), and (11) shall not apply to a corporation."

Prior to amendment, para. (b)(1) read as follows:

"(1) In general. For purposes of paragraph (1) of subsection (a), the amount of the adjusted itemized deductions for any taxable year is the amount by which the sum of the deductions for the taxable year other than—

"(A) deductions allowable in arriving at adjusted gross income,

"(B) the deduction for personal exemptions provided by section 151,

"(C) the deduction for medical, dental, etc., expenses provided by section 213,

"(D) the deduction for casualty losses described in section 165(c)(3), and

"(E) the deduction allowable under section 691(c),

exceeds 60 percent (but does not exceed 100 percent) of the taxpayer's adjusted gross income for the taxable year."

Prior to amendment, subpara. (b)(2)(A) read as follows:

"(A) In general. In the case of an estate or trust, for purposes of paragraph (1) of subsection (a), the amount of the adjusted itemized deductions for any taxable year is the amount by which the sum of the deductions for the taxable year other than—

"(i) the deductions allowable in arriving at adjusted gross income,

"(ii) the deduction for personal exemption provided by section 642(b),

"(iii) the deduction for casualty losses described in section 165(c)(3),

"(iv) the deductions allowable under section 651(a), 661(a), or 691(c), and

"(v) the deductions allowable to a trust under section 642(c) to the extent that a corresponding amount is included in the gross income of the beneficiary under section 662(a)(1) for the taxable year of the beneficiary with which or within which the taxable year of the trusts ends,

exceeds 60 percent (but does not exceed 100 percent) of the adjusted gross income of the estate or trust for the taxable year."
—P.L. 95-600, Sec. 422, amended Sec. 308(b) of P.L. 95-30 [see below], the effective date for changes made by Sec. 308(a) of P.L. 95-30 [see below] by deleting "and before January 1, 1978".
Prior to amendment, Sec. 308(b) of P.L. 95-40 read as follows:
"(b) Effective date. The amendments made by subsection (a) shall apply with respect to taxable years beginning after December 31, 1976, and before January 1, 1978."
—P.L. 95-600, Sec. 701(b)(1)(A), substituted "In the case of an individual, an amount" for "An amount" in para. (a)(1) . . . Sec. 701(b)(1)(B), substituted "Paragraphs (3) and" for "Paragraphs (1), (3), and" in the last sentence of subsec. (a) . . . Sec. 701(b)(3), amended para. (b)(2) . . . Sec. 701(b)(4), amended para. (b)(1) by deleting "and" at the end of subpara. (b)(1)(C), by adding "and" at the end of subpara. (b)(1)(D) and by adding new subpara. (b)(1)(E), effective for tax. yrs. begin. after 12/31/75.

Prior to amendment, para. (b)(2) read as follows:
"(2) Special rule for trusts and estates. In the case of a trust or estate, any deduction allowed or allowable for the taxable year—
"(A) under section 642(c) (but only to the extent that the amount of the deduction allowable under such section is included in the income of the beneficiary under section 662(a)(1) for the taxable year of the beneficiary with which or within which the taxable year of the trust ends);
"(B) under section 642(d), 642(e), 642(f), 651(a), 661(a), or 691; or
"(C) for cost paid or incurred in connection with the administration of the trust or estate;
shall, for purposes of paragraph (1), be treated as a deduction allowable in arriving at an adjusted gross income."
—P.L. 95-600, Sec. 701(f)(3)(D), added "or 191" after "167(k)" in para. (a)(2), for additions to capital account made after 6/14/76 and before 6/15/81.

In 1977, P.L. 95-30, Sec. 101(d)(5)(A), substituted "adjusted" for "excess" in the heading and text of para. (a)(1) . . . Sec. 101(d)(5)(B), substituted "adjusted" for "excess" in the heading and so much of para. (b)(1) as precedes subpara. (b)(1)(A) . . . Sec. 101(d)(5)(C)(i), deleted subpara. (b)(1)(B) . . . Sec. 101(d)(5)(C)(ii), redesignated subparas. (b)(1)(C) through (b)(1)(E) as (b)(1)(B) through (b)(1)(D), effective for tax. yrs. begin. after 12/31/76.
Prior to deletion, subpara. (b)(1)(B) read as follows:
"(B) the standard deduction provided by section 141,"
—P.L. 95-30, Sec. 308(a), amended para. (a)(11), effective [as amended by Sec. 422 of P.L. 95-600, and Sec. 401 of P.L. 95-618, see above] for tax. yrs. begin. after 12/31/76.
Prior to amendment, para. (a)(11) read as follows:
"(11) Intangible drilling costs. The excess of the intangible drilling and development costs described in section 263(c) paid or incurred in connection with oil and gas wells (other than costs incurred in drilling a nonproductive well) allowable under this chapter for the taxable year over the amount which would have been allowable for the taxable year if such costs had been capitalized and straight line recovery of intangibles (as defined in subsection (d)) had been used with respect to such costs."
—P.L. 95-30, Sec. 402(a)(5), deleted "on-the-job training and" following "Amortization of" in the heading of subpara. (a)(10), effective for expenditures made after 12/31/76.

In 1976, P.L. 94-455, Sec. 301(c)(1), amended paras. (a)(1) and (a)(3) and substituted new para. (a)(11) for so much of subsec. (a) that followed para. (a)(10) . . . Sec. 301(c)(2), amended subsec. (b) . . . Sec. 301(c)(3), added subsec. (d) . . . Sec. 301(c)(4)(A), added subpara. (a)(9)(C) . . . Sec. 301(c)(4)(C), added subsec. (e), effective for tax. yrs. end. after '77 except in the case of financial institutions which apply to tax. yrs. begin. after '77. Sec. 301(f) of the Act provides:
"(f) For purposes of Sec. 21 of the Internal Revenue Code of 1954, the amendments made by this section shall not be treated as a change in a rate of tax."
Prior to amendment, para. (a)(1) read as follows:
"(1) Excess investment interest. The amount of the excess investment interest for the taxable year (as determined under subsection (b))."
Prior to amendment, para. (a)(3) read as follows:
"(3) Accelerated depreciation on personal property subject to a net lease. With respect to each item of section 1245 property (as defined in section 1245(a)(3)) which is the subject of a net lease, the amount by which the deduction allowable for the taxable year for exhaustion, wear and tear, obsolescence, or amortization exceeds the depreciation deduction which would have been allowable for the taxable year had the taxpayer depreciated the property under the straight line method for each taxable year of its useful life for which the taxpayer has held the property."
Prior to amendment, the material following para. (a)(10) read as follows:
"Paragraph (1) shall apply only to taxable years beginning before January 1, 1972, Paragraphs (1) and (3) shall not apply to a corporation other than an electing small business corporation (as defined in section 1371(b)) and a personal holding company (as defined in section 542)."
Prior to amendment, subsec. (b) read as follows:
"(b) Excess investment interest.
"(1) In general. For purposes of paragraph (1) of subsection (a), the excess investment interest for any taxable year is the amount by which the investment interest expense for the taxable year exceeds the sum of—
"(A) the net investment income for the taxable year, and
"(B) the amount (if any) by which the deductions allowable under sections 162, 163, 164(a)(1) or (2), and 212 attributable to property of the taxpayer subject to a net lease exceeds the gross rental income produced by such property for the taxable year.

"(2) Definitions. For purposes of this subsection—
"(A) Net investment income. The term 'net investment income' means the excess of investment income over investment expenses.
"(B) Investment income. The term 'investment income' means—
"(i) the gross income from interest, dividends, rents, and royalties,
"(ii) the net short-term capital gain attributable to the disposition of property held for investment, and
"(iii) amounts treated under sections 1245 and 1250 as gain from the sale or exchange of property which is neither a capital asset nor property described in section 1231,
but only to the extent such income, gain, and amounts are not derived from the conduct of a trade or business.
"(C) Investment expenses. The term 'investment expenses' means the deductions allowable under sections 162, 164(a)(1) or (2), 166, 167, 171, 212, 243, 244, 245, or 611 directly connected with the production of investment income. For purposes of this subparagraph, the deduction allowable under section 167 with respect to any property may be treated as the amount which would have been allowable had the taxpayer depreciated the property under the straight line method for each taxable year of its useful life for which the taxpayer has held the property, and the deduction allowable under section 611 with respect to any property may be treated as the amount which would have been allowable had the taxpayer determined the deduction under section 611 without regard to section 613 for each taxable year for which the taxpayer has held the property.
"(D) Investment interest expense. The term 'investment interest expense' means interest paid or accrued on indebtedness incurred or continued to purchase or carry property held for investment. For purposes of the preceding sentence, interest paid or accrued on indebtedness incurred or continued in the construction of property to be used in a trade or business shall not be treated as an investment interest expense.
"(3) Property subject to net lease. For purposes of this subsection, property which is subject to a net lease entered into after October 9, 1969, shall be treated as property held for investment, and not as property used in a trade or business."
—P.L. 94-455, Sec. 1901(b)(33)(A), and (B), substituted "the net capital gain" for "the amount by which the net long-term capital gain exceeds the net short-term capital loss" in subpara. (a)(9)(A) and substituted "In the case of a corporation having a net capital gain for the taxable year, an amount equal to the product obtained by multiplying the net capital gain" for "In the case of a corporation, if the net long-term capital gain exceeds the net short-term capital loss for the taxable year, an amount equal to the product obtained by multiplying such excess" before "by a fraction" in subpara. (a)(9)(B), effective for tax. yrs. begin. after 12/31/76.
—P.L. 94-455, Sec. 1906(b)(13)(A), substituted "Secretary" for "Secretary or his delegate" in subpara. (a)(9)(B), effective for tax. yrs. begin. after 12/31/76.

In 1971, P.L. 92-178, Sec. 303(b), added para. (10) to subsec. (a), effective for tax. yrs. end. after 12/31/71 . . . Sec. 304(a)(1), amended subsec. (c), effective for tax. yrs. begin. after 12/31/69.
Prior to amendment, subsec. (c) read as follows:
"(c) Net leases.
"For purposes of this section, property shall be considered to be subject to a net lease for a taxable year if—
"(1) for such taxable year the sum of the deductions with respect to such property which are allowable solely by reason of section 162 is less than 15 percent of the rental income produced by such property, or
"(2) the lessor is either guaranteed a specified return or is guaranteed in whole or in part against loss of income."
—P.L. 92-178, Sec. 304(a), substituted "exceeds the sum of—" for "exceeds the net investment income for the taxable year," in para. (b)(1) and added new subparas. (b)(1)(A) & (B) . . . Sec. 304(d), inserted "162," before "164(a)(1) or (2)," in subpara. (b)(2)(C), effective for tax. yrs. begin. after 12/31/69.

In 1969, P.L. 91-172, Sec. 301(a), added Code Sec. 57, effective for tax. yrs. end. after 12/31/69.

"Sec. 58. Rules for application of this part.
"(a) Repealed.
"(b) Members of controlled groups.
"In the case of a controlled group of corporations (as defined in section 1563(a)), the $10,000 amount specified in section 56 shall be divided among the component members of such group in proportion to their respective regular tax deductions (within the meaning of section 56(c)) for the taxable year.
"(c) Estates and trusts.
"In the case of an estate or trust, the items of tax preference (and any itemized deductions) for any taxable year shall be apportioned between the estate or trust and the beneficiaries in accordance with regulations prescribed by the Secretary.
"(d) Certain capital gains of S corporations.
"If for a taxable year of an S corporation a tax is imposed on the income of such corporation under section 1374, such corporation shall be subject to the tax imposed by section 56, but computed only with reference to the item of tax preference set forth in section 57(a)(9)(B) to the extent attributable to gains subject to the tax imposed by section 1374.
"(e) Participants in a common trust fund.
"The items of tax preference of a common trust fund (as defined in section 584(a)) for each taxable year of the fund shall be treated as items of tax preference of the participants of such fund and shall be apportioned pro rata among such participants. For purposes of this subsection, this part shall be treated as applying to such fund.
"(f) Regulated investment companies, etc.

"In the case of a regulated investment company to which part I of subchapter M applies or a real estate investment trust to which part II of subchapter M applies—

"(1) the item of tax preference set forth in section 57(a)(9) shall not be treated as an item of tax preference of such company or such trust for each taxable year to the extent that such item is attributable to amounts taken into account as income by the shareholders of such company under section 852(b)(3), or by the shareholders or holders of beneficial interests of such trust under section 857(b)(3), and

"(2) the items of tax preference of such company or such trust for each taxable year (other than the item of tax preference set forth in section 57(a)(9) and, in the case of a real estate investment trust, the items of tax preference set forth in paragraphs (2) and (12)(B) of section 57(a)) shall be treated as items of tax preference of the shareholders of such company, or the shareholders or holders of beneficial interests of such trust (and not as items of tax preference of such company or such trust), in the same proportion that the dividends (other than capital gain dividends) paid to each such shareholder, or holder of beneficial interest, bears to the taxable income of such company or such trust determined without regard to the deduction for dividends paid.

"(g) Tax preferences attributable to foreign sources.

"(1) In general. For purposes of section 56, the items of tax preference set forth in section 57(a) (other than in paragraph (9) of such section) which are attributable to sources within any foreign country or possession of the United States shall be taken into account only to the extent that such items reduce the tax imposed by this chapter (other than the tax imposed by section 56) on income derived from sources within the United States. For purposes of the preceding sentence, items of tax preference shall be treated as reducing the tax imposed by this chapter before items which are not items of tax preference.

"(2) Capital gains. For purposes of section 56, the items of tax preference set forth in section 57(a)(9) which are attributable to sources within any foreign country or possession of the United States shall not be taken into account if preferential treatment is not accorded gain from the sale or exchange of capital assets (or property treated as capital assets).

For purposes of this paragraph, preferential treatment is accorded such items which are attributable to a foreign country or possession of the United States if such country or possession imposes no significant amount of tax with respect to such items; except that, for purposes of subparagraph (B), preferential treatment shall be deemed not to be accorded to capital gain recognized on the receipt of property (other than money) in exchange for stock of a corporation which is engaged in the active conduct of a trade or business within one or more foreign countries or possessions if (i) such exchange is described in section 332, 351, 354, 355, 356, or 361, (ii) such exchange is made in the foreign country or possession in which such corporation's business is primarily carried on, (iii) such exchange is not subject to tax by such foreign country or possession because it is regarded under the laws of such country or possession as a transaction in which gain or loss is either not realized or not recognized, and (iv) such gain, if it had been realized and recognized under the laws of such country or possession, would not have been accorded preferential treatment and would have been subject to tax at a rate of at least 28 percent (30 percent if the exchange occurs before January 1, 1979). For purposes of computing the minimum tax, if any, which may be payable on a subsequent transaction involving any property received upon the exchange of stock described in the preceding sentence, the property received shall be treated as having the same basis in the taxpayer's hands immediately after such exchange as such stock had immediately before such exchange.

"(h) Regulations to include tax benefit rule.

"The Secretary shall prescribe regulations under which items of tax preference shall be properly adjusted where the tax treatment giving rise to such items will not result in the reduction of the taxpayer's tax under this subtitle for any taxable years.

"(i) Optional 10-year writeoff of certain tax preferences.

"(1) In general. For purposes of this title, in the case of an individual, any qualified expenditure to which an election under this paragraph applies shall be allowed as a deduction ratably over the 10-year period (3-year period in the case of circulation expenditures described in section 173) beginning with the taxable year in which such expenditure was made.

"(2) Qualified expenditure. For purposes of this subsection, the term 'qualified expenditure' means any amount which, but for an election under this subsection, would have been allowable as a deduction for the taxable year in which paid or incurred under—

"(A) section 173 (relating to circulation expenditures),

"(B) section 174(a) (relating to research and experimental expenditures),

"(C) section 263(c) (relating to intangible drilling and development expenditures),

"(D) section 616(a) (relating to development expenditures), or

"(E) section 617 (relating to deduction of certain mining exploration expenditures).

"(3) Other sections not applicable. Except as provided in this subsection, no deduction shall be allowed under any other section for any qualified expenditure to which an election under this subsection applies.

"(4) Special election for intangible drilling and development costs not allocable to limited business interest.

"(A) In general. In the case of any nonlimited partnership intangible drilling costs (with respect to wells located in the United States) to which an election under this paragraph applies—

"(i) the applicable percentage of such cost (adjusted as provided in section 48(q)) shall be allowed as a deduction for the taxable year in which paid or incurred and for each of the 4 succeeding taxable years, and

"(ii) such costs shall be treated, for purposes of determining the amount of the credit allowable under section 38 for the taxable year in which paid or incurred, as qualified investment (within the meaning of subsections (c) and (d) of section 46) with respect to property placed in service during such year.

"(B) Applicable percentage. For purposes of subparagraph (A), the term 'applicable percentage' means the percentage determined in accordance with the following table:

"Taxable Year:	Applicable percentage:
1	15
2	22
3	21
4	21
5	21

"(C) Nonlimited intangible drilling costs. For purposes of this paragraph, the term 'nonlimited intangible drilling costs' means any qualified expenditure described in paragraph (2)(C) of an individual which is not allocable to a limited business interest (as defined in section 55(e)(8)(C)) of such individual.

"(5) Election.

"(A) In general. An election may be made under this subsection with respect to any qualified expenditure.

"(B) Revocable only with consent. An election under this subsection with respect to any qualified expenditure may be revoked only with the consent of the Secretary.

"(C) Time and manner. An election under this subsection shall be made at such time and in such manner as the Secretary shall by regulations prescribe.

"(D) Partners and shareholders of S corporations. In the case of a partnership, any election under this subsection shall be made separately by each partner with respect to the partner's allocable share of any qualified expenditure. A similar rule shall apply in the case of an S corporation and its shareholders.

"(6) Dispositions.

"(A) Oil, gas, and geothermal property. In the case of any disposition of any oil, gas, or geothermal property to which section 1254 applies (determined without regard to this section)—

"(i) any deduction under paragraph (1) or (4)(A) with respect to costs which are allocable to such property shall, for purposes of section 1254, be treated as a deduction allowable under section 263(c), and

"(ii) in the case of any credit allowable under section 38 by reason of paragraph (4)(B) which is allocable to such property, such disposition shall, for purposes of section 47, be treated as a disposition of section 38 recovery property which is not 3-year property.

"(B) Application of section 617(d). In the case of any disposition of mining property to which section 617(d) applies (determined without regard to this subsection), any amount allowable as a deduction under paragraph (1) which is allocable to such property shall, for purposes of section 617(d), be treated as a deduction allowable under section 617(a).

"(7) Amounts to which election apply not treated as tax preference. Any qualified expenditure to which an election under paragraph (1) or (4) applies shall not be treated as an item of tax preference under section 57(a)."

In 1989, P.L. 101-239, Sec. 7811(d)(1)(B), of this Act, regarding amendments related to section 1007 of the 1988 act, provides:

"(B) The repeal of section 58(h) of the Internal Revenue Code of 1954 by the Tax Reform Act of 1986 shall be effective only with respect to items of tax preference arising in taxable years beginning after December 31, 1986."

In 1986, P.L. 99-514, Sec. 1875(a), substituted "of tax preference (and any itemized deductions)" for "of tax preference" in subsec. (c), effective for tax. yrs. begin. after 12/31/82.

In 1984, P.L. 98-369, Sec. 711(a)(2), added "(with respect to wells located in the United States)" after "intangible drilling costs" in subpara. (i)(4)(A) . . . Sec. 711(a)(3)(B), substituted "10-year period (3-year period in the case of circulation expenditures described in section 173)" for "10-year period" in para. (i)(1), effective for tax. yrs. begin. after 12/31/82.

In 1983, P.L. 97-448, Sec. 102(b)(2), substituted "the items of tax preference set forth in paragraphs (2) and (12)(B) of section 57(a)" for "the item of tax preference set forth in section 57(a)(2) in para. (f)(2), effective for property placed in service after 12/31/80 in tax. yrs. end. after 12/31/80.

—P.L. 97-448, Sec. 306(a)(1)(A)(i), redesignated the second Sec. 201(c) of P.L. 97-248 as Sec. 201(d) of P.L. 97-248, see below.

In 1982, P.L. 97-354, Sec. 3(c)(1), amended subpara. (i)(4)(C) . . . Sec. 3(c)(2)(A), added the last sentence of subpara. (i)(5)(D) . . . Sec. 3(c)(2)(B), substituted 'Partners and shareholders of S corporations' for 'Partners' in the heading of subpara. (i)(5)(D) . . . Sec. 3(c)(3), substituted 'limited business interest' for 'interest as limited partner' in the heading of para. (i)(4) . . . Sec. 5(a)(16), amended subsec. (d), effective for tax. yrs. begin. after 12/31/82.

Prior to amendment, subpara. (i)(4)(C) read as follows:

"(C) Nonlimited partnership intangible drilling costs. For purposes of this paragraph, the term 'nonlimited partnership intangible drilling costs' means any qualified expenditure described in paragraph (2)(C) of an individual which is not allocable to such individual's interest as a limited partner in a limited partnership."

Prior to amendment, subsec. (d) read as follows:

"(d) Electing small business corporations and their shareholders.

"(1) In general. Except as provided in paragraph (2), the items of tax preference of an electing small business corporation (as defined in section 1371(b)) for each taxable year of the corporation shall be treated as items of tax preference of the shareholders of such corporation, and, except as provided in paragraph (2), shall not be treated as items of tax preference of such corporation. The sum of the

1,289

Part VI **Tax credits**

items so treated shall be apportioned pro rata among such shareholders in a manner consistent with section 1374(c)(1). For purposes of this paragraph, this part shall be treated as applying to such corporation.

"(2) Certain capital gains. If for a taxable year of an electing small business corporation a tax is imposed on the income of such corporation under section 1378, such corporation shall be subject to the tax imposed by section 56, but computed only with reference to the item of tax preference set forth in section 57(a)(9)(B) to the extent attributable to gains subject to the tax imposed by section 1378."

—P.L. 97-248, Sec. 201(c)(1), added subsec. (i) . . . Sec. 201(d)(3)(A), [as redesignated by Sec. 306(a)91](A)(i) of P.L. 97-448, see above] repealed subsec. (a) . . . Sec. 201(d)(3)(B), [as redesignated by Sec. 306(a)91)(A)(i) of P.L. 97-448, see above]amended subsec. (c) . . . Sec. 201(d)(3)(C)(i), [as redesignated by Sec. 306(a)91)(A)(i) of P.L. 97-448, see above] substituted "paragraph" for "paragraphs (6) and" in para. (g)(1) . . . Sec. 201(d)(3)(C)(ii), [as redesignated by Sec. 306(a)91)(A)(i) of P.L. 97-448, see above] amended para. (g)(2), effective for tax. yrs. begin after 12/31/82.

Prior to repeal, subsec. (a) read as follows:

"(a) Married individuals filing separate returns.

"In the case of a married individual who files a separate return for the taxable year, section 56 shall be applied by substituting $5,000 for $10,000 each place it appears. In the case of a married individual who files a separate return for the taxable year, the amount determined under paragraph (1) of section 55(a) shall be an amount equal to one-half of the amount which would be determined under such paragraph if the amount of the individual's alternative minimum taxable income were multiplied by 2."

Prior to amendment, subsec. (c) read as follows:

"(c) Estates and trusts.

"In the case of an estate or trust—

"(1) the sum of the items of tax preference for any taxable year of the estate or trust shall be apportioned between the estate or trust and the beneficiaries in accordance with regulations prescribed by the Secretary

"(2) the $10,000 amount specified in section 56 applicable to such estate or trust shall be reduced to an amount which bears the same ration to $10,000 as the portion of the sum of the items of tax preference allocated to the estate or trust under paragraph (1) bears to such sum, and

"(3) the liability for the tax imposed by section 55(a) shall be determined as in the case of a married individual filing separately."

Prior to amendment, para. (g)(2) read as follows:

"(2) Capital gains and stock options. For purposes of section 56, the items of tax preference set forth in paragraphs (6) and (9) of section 57(a) which are attributable to sources within any foreign country or possession of the United States shall not be taken into account if, under the tax laws of such country or possession—

"(A) in the case of the item set forth in paragraph (6) of section 57(a), preferential treatment is not accorded transfers of shares of stock pursuant to stock options described in such paragraph, and

"(B) in the case of the item set forth in paragraph (9) of section 57(a), preferential treatment is not accorded gain from the sale or exchange of capital assets (or property treated as capital assets).

For purposes of this paragraph, preferential treatment is accorded such items which are attributable to a foreign country or possession of the United States if such country or possession imposes no significant amount of tax with respect to such items; except that, for purposes of subparagraph (B), preferential treatment shall be deemed not to be accorded to capital gain recognized on the receipt of property (other than money) in exchange for stock of a corporation which is engaged in the active conduct of a trade or business within one or more foreign countries or possessions if (i) such exchange is described in section 332, 351, 354, 355, 356, or 361, (ii) such exchange is made in the foreign country or possession in which such corporation's business is primarily carried on, (iii) such exchange is not subject to tax by such foreign country or possession because it is regarded under the laws of such country or possession as a transaction in which gain or loss is either not realized or not recognized, and (iv) such gain, if it had been realized and recognized under the laws of such country or possession, would not have been accorded preferential treatment and would have been subject to tax at a rate of at least 28 percent (30 percent if the exchange occurs before January 1, 1979). For purposes of computing the minimum tax, if any, which may be payable on a subsequent transaction involving any property received upon the exchange of stock described in the preceding sentence, the property received shall be treated as having the same basis in the taxpayer's hands immediately after such exchange as such stock had immediately before such exchange."

In 1980, P.L. 96-222, Sec. 107(a)(1)(C), substituted "in accordance with regulations prescribed by the Secretary" for "on the basis of the income of the estate or trust allocable to each" in para. (c)(1), effective for tax. yrs. begin. after 12/31/78.

In 1978, P.L. 95-600, Sec. 421(c)(1), added a new sentence at the end of subsec. (a) . . . Sec. 421(c)(2), amended subsec. (c) . . . Sec. 421(c)(3), repealed subsec. (i), effective for tax. yrs. begin. after 12/31/78.

Prior to amendment, subsec. (c) read as follows:

"(c) Estates and trusts.

"In the case of an estate or trust—

"(1) the sum of the items of tax preference for any taxable year of the estate or trust shall be apportioned between the estate or trust and the beneficiaries on the basis of the income of the estate or trust allocable to each, and

"(2) the $10,000 amount specified in section 56 applicable to such estate or trust shall be reduced to an amount which bears the same ratio to $10,000 as the portion of the sum of the items of tax preference allocated to the estate or trust under paragraph (1) bears to such sum."

Prior to repeal, subsec. (i) read as follows:

"(i) Corporation defined.

"Except as provided in subsection (d)(2), for purposes of this part, the term 'corporation' does not include an electing small business corporation (as defined in section 1371(b)) or a personal holding company (as defined in section 542)."

—P.L. 95-600, Sec. 423(a), substituted ";" and all the material following for the period in the last sentence of para. (g)(2), effective 11/6/78.

—P.L. 95-600, Sec. 701(b)(2), amended subsec. (b), effective for tax. yrs. begin. after 12/31/75.

Prior to amendment, subsec. (b) read as follows:

"(b) Members of controlled groups.

"In the case of a controlled group of corporations (as defined in section 1563(a)), the $10,000 amount specified in section 56 shall be divided equally among the component members of such group unless all component members consent (at such time and in such manner as the Secretary prescribes by regulations) to an apportionment plan providing for an unequal allocation of such amount."

—P.L. 94-427, Sec. 2, of this Act provides:

"Sec. 2. Commuting expenses.

"With respect to transportation costs paid or incurred after December 31, 1976, and on or before December 31, 1979, the application of sections 62, 162, and 262 and of chapters 21, 23, and 24 of the Internal Revenue Code of 1954 to transportation expenses in traveling between a taxpayer's residence and place of work shall be determined—

"(1) without regard to Revenue Ruling 76-453 (and without regard to any other regulation, ruling, or decision reaching the same result as, or a result similar to, the result set forth in such Revenue Ruling); and

"(2) with full regard to the rules in effect before Revenue Ruling 76-453."

In 1976, P.L. 94-455, Sec. 301(d)(1), amended subsec. (a) . . . Sec. 301(d)(2), substituted "$10,000" for "$30,000" in subsec. (b) and para. (c)(2) . . . Sec. 301(d)(3), added subsecs. (h) and (i), effective for tax. yrs. end. after '75 except in the case of financial institutions which apply to tax. yrs. begin. after '77. Sec. 301(f) of the Act provides:

"(f) For purposes of Sec. 21 of the Internal Revenue Code of 1954, the amendments made by this section shall not be treated as a change in a rate of tax."

Prior to amendment, subsec. (a) read as follows:

"(a) Husband and wife.

"In the case of a husband or wife who files a separate return for the taxable year, the $30,000 amount specified in section 56 shall be $15,000."

—P.L. 94-455, Sec. 1901(b)(40), deleted ", notwithstanding the provisions of section 1371(b)(1)," after "such corporation shall" in para. (d)(2), effective for tax. yrs. begin. after '76.

—P.L. 94-455, Sec. 1906(b)(13)(A), substituted "Secretary" for "Secretary or his delegate" in subsec. (b), effective for tax. yrs. begin. after '76.

In 1971, P.L. 92-178, Sec. 308, added a sentence to the end of para. (g)(2), effective for tax. yrs. begin. after 12/31/69.

In 1969, P.L. 91-172, Sec. 301(a), added Code Sec. 58, effective for tax. yrs. end. after 12/31/69.

Sec. 55. Alternative minimum tax imposed.

> • **Caution:** Code Sec. 55, following, was amended by P.L. 107-16, the Economic Growth and Tax Relief Reconciliation Act of 2001 (EGTRRA), P.L. 108-27 and P.L. 108-311. Sec. 201(c), P.L. 111-312, reproduced in notes to this Code Sec., provides that those amendments are no longer subject to the EGTRRA sunsets.

(a) General rule.

There is hereby imposed (in addition to any other tax imposed by this subtitle) a tax equal to the excess (if any) of—

(1) the tentative minimum tax for the taxable year, over

(2) the regular tax for the taxable year.

(b) Tentative minimum tax.

For purposes of this part—

(1) Amount of tentative tax.

(A) Noncorporate taxpayers.

(i) In general. In the case of a taxpayer other than a corporation, the tentative minimum tax for the taxable year is the sum of—

(I) 26 percent of so much of the taxable excess as does not exceed $175,000, plus

(II) 28 percent of so much of the taxable excess as exceeds $175,000.

The amount determined under the preceding sentence shall be reduced by the alternative minimum tax foreign tax credit for the taxable year.

(ii) **Taxable excess.** For purposes of this subsection, the term "taxable excess" means so much of the alternative minimum taxable income for the taxable year as exceeds the exemption amount.

(iii) **Married individual filing separate return.** In the case of a married individual filing a separate return, clause (i) shall be applied by substituting "$87,500" for "$175,000" each place it appears. For purposes of the preceding sentence, marital status shall be determined under section 7703.

(B) **Corporations.** In the case of a corporation, the tentative minimum tax for the taxable year is—

(i) 20 percent of so much of the alternative minimum taxable income for the taxable year as exceeds the exemption amount, reduced by

(ii) the alternative minimum tax foreign tax credit for the taxable year.

(2) Alternative minimum taxable income. The term "alternative minimum taxable income" means the taxable income of the taxpayer for the taxable year—

(A) determined with the adjustments provided in section 56 and section 58, and

(B) increased by the amount of the items of tax preference described in section 57.

If a taxpayer is subject to the regular tax, such taxpayer shall be subject to the tax imposed by this section (and, if the regular tax is determined by reference to an amount other than taxable income, such amount shall be treated as the taxable income of such taxpayer for purposes of the preceding sentence).

(3) Maximum rate of tax on net capital gain of noncorporate taxpayers. The amount determined under the first sentence of paragraph (1)(A)(i) shall not exceed the sum of—

(A) the amount determined under such first sentence computed at the rates and in the same manner as if this paragraph had not been enacted on the taxable excess reduced by the lesser of—

(i) the net capital gain; or

(ii) the sum of—

(I) the adjusted net capital gain, plus

(II) the unrecaptured section 1250 gain, plus

(B) 5 percent (0 percent in the case of taxable years beginning after 2007) of so much of the adjusted net capital gain (or, if less, taxable excess) as does not exceed an amount equal to the excess described in section 1(h)(1)(B), plus

(C) 15 percent of the adjusted net capital gain (or, if less, taxable excess) in excess of the amount on which tax is determined under subparagraph (B), plus

(D) 25 percent of the amount of taxable excess in excess of the sum of the amounts on which tax is determined under the preceding subparagraphs of this paragraph.

Terms used in this paragraph which are also used in section 1(h) shall have the respective meanings given such terms by section 1(h) but computed with the adjustments under this part.

(4) Maximum rate of tax on qualified timber gain of corporations. In the case of any taxable year to which section 1201(b) applies, the amount determined under clause (i) of subparagraph (B) shall not exceed the sum of—

(A) 20 percent of so much of the taxable excess (if any) as exceeds the qualified timber gain (or, if less, the net capital gain), plus

(B) 15 percent of the taxable excess in excess of the amount on which a tax is determined under subparagraph (A).

Any term used in this paragraph which is also used in section 1201 shall have the meaning given such term by such section, except to the extent such term is subject to adjustment under this part.

(c) Regular tax.

(1) In general. For purposes of this section, the term "regular tax" means the regular tax liability for the taxable year (as defined in section 26(b)) reduced by the foreign tax credit allowable under section 27(a), the section 936 credit allowable under section 27(b), and the Puerto Rico economic activity credit under section 30A. Such term shall not include any increase in tax under section 45(e)(11)(C), 49(b) or 50(a) or subsection (j) or (k) of section 42.

(2) Coordination with income averaging for farmers and fishermen. Solely for purposes of this section, section 1301 (relating to averaging of farm and fishing income) shall not apply in computing the regular tax liability.

(3) Cross references. For provisions providing that certain credits are not allowable against the tax imposed by this section, see sections 26(a), 30C(d)(2), and 38(c).

(d) Exemption amount.

For purposes of this section—

(1) Exemption amount for taxpayers other than corporations. In the case of a taxpayer other than a corporation, the term "exemption amount" means—

(A) $45,000 ($72,450 in the case of taxable years beginning in 2010 and $74,450 in the case of taxable years beginning in 2011) in the case of—

(i) a joint return, or

(ii) a surviving spouse,

(B) $33,750 ($47,450 in the case of taxable years beginning in 2010 and $48,450 in the case of taxable years beginning in 2011) in the case of an individual who—

(i) is not a married individual, and

(ii) is not a surviving spouse,

(C) 50 percent of the dollar amount applicable under paragraph (1)(A) in the case of a married individual who files a separate return, and

(D) $22,500 in the case of an estate or trust.

For purposes of this paragraph, the term "surviving spouse" has the meaning given to such term by section 2(a), and marital status shall be determined under section 7703.

(2) Corporations. In the case of a corporation, the term "exemption amount" means $40,000.

(3) Phase-out of exemption amount. The exemption amount of any taxpayer shall be reduced (but not below zero) by an amount equal to 25 percent of the amount by which the alternative minimum taxable income of the taxpayer exceeds—

(A) $150,000 in the case of a taxpayer described in paragraph (1)(A) or (2),

(B) $112,500 in the case of a taxpayer described in paragraph (1)(B), and

(C) $75,000 in the case of a taxpayer described in subparagraph (C) or (D) of paragraph (1).

In the case of a taxpayer described in paragraph (1)(C), alternative minimum taxable income shall be increased by the lesser of (i) 25 percent of the excess of alternative minimum taxable income (determined without regard to this sentence) over the minimum amount of such income (as so determined) for which the exemption amount under paragraph (1)(C) is zero, or (ii) such exemption amount (determined without regard to this paragraph).

(e) Exemption for small corporations.
(1) In general.
(A) $7,500,000 gross receipts test. The tentative minimum tax of a corporation shall be zero for any taxable year if the corporation's average annual gross receipts for all 3-taxable-year periods ending before such taxable year does not exceed $7,500,000. For purposes of the preceding sentence, only taxable years beginning after December 31, 1993, shall be taken into account.

(B) $5,000,000 gross receipts test for first 3-year period. Subparagraph (A) shall be applied by substituting "$5,000,000" for "$7,500,000" for the first 3-taxable-year period (or portion thereof) of the corporation which is taken into account under subparagraph (A).

(C) First taxable year corporation in existence. If such taxable year is the first taxable year that such corporation is in existence, the tentative minimum tax of such corporation for such year shall be zero.

(D) Special rules. For purposes of this paragraph, the rules of paragraphs (2) and (3) of section 448(c) shall apply.

(2) Prospective application of minimum tax if small corporation ceases to be small. In the case of a corporation whose tentative minimum tax is zero for any prior taxable year by reason of paragraph (1), the application of this part for taxable years beginning with the first taxable year such corporation ceases to be described in paragraph (1) shall be determined with the following modifications:

(A) Section 56(a)(1) (relating to depreciation) and section 56(a)(5) (relating to pollution control facilities) shall apply only to property placed in service on or after the change date.

(B) Section 56(a)(2) (relating to mining exploration and development costs) shall apply only to costs paid or incurred on or after the change date.

(C) Section 56(a)(3) (relating to treatment of long-term contracts) shall apply only to contracts entered into on or after the change date.

(D) Section 56(a)(4) (relating to alternative net operating loss deduction) shall apply in the same manner as if, in section 56(d)(2), the change date were substituted for "January 1, 1987" and the day before the change date were substituted for "December 31, 1986" each place it appears.

(E) Section 56(g)(2)(B) (relating to limitation on allowance of negative adjustments based on adjusted current earnings) shall apply only to prior taxable years beginning on or after the change date.

(F) Section 56(g)(4)(A) (relating to adjustment for depreciation to adjusted current earnings) shall not apply.

(G) Subparagraphs (D) and (F) of section 56(g)(4) (relating to other earnings and profits adjustments and depletion) shall apply in the same manner as if the day before the change date were substituted for "December 31, 1989" each place it appears therein.

(3) Exception. The modifications in paragraph (2) shall not apply to—

(A) any item acquired by the corporation in a transaction to which section 381 applies, and

(B) any property the basis of which in the hands of the corporation is determined by reference to the basis of the property in the hands of the transferor,

if such item or property was subject to any provision referred to in paragraph (2) while held by the transferor.

(4) Change date. For purposes of paragraph (2), the change date is the first day of the first taxable year for which the taxpayer ceases to be described in paragraph (1).

(5) Limitation on use of credit for prior year minimum tax liability. In the case of a taxpayer whose tentative minimum tax for any taxable year is zero by reason of paragraph (1), section 53(c) shall be applied for such year by reducing the amount otherwise taken into account under section 53(c)(1) by 25 percent of so much of such amount as exceeds $25,000. Rules similar to the rules of section 38(c)(6)(B) shall apply for purposes of the preceding sentence.

In 2010, P.L. 111-312, Sec. 101(a)(1), substituted "December 31, 2012" for "December 31, 2010" both places it appeared in Sec. 901, P.L. 107-16 [see below], effective as if included in the enactment of P.L. 107-16, EGTRRA, 6/7/2001.

—P.L. 111-312, Sec. 102(a), substituted "December 31, 2012" for "December 31, 2010" in Sec. 303, P.L. 108-27 [see below], effective as if included in the enactment of the Jobs and Growth Tax Relief Reconciliation Act of 2003, P.L. 108-27, 5/28/2003.

—P.L. 111-312, Sec. 201(a)(1), substituted "$72,450 in the case of taxable years beginning in 2010 and $74,450 in the case of taxable years beginning in 2011" for "$70,950 in the case of taxable years beginning in 2009" in subpara. (d)(1)(A) ... Sec. 201(a)(2), substituted "$47,450 in the case of taxable years beginning in 2010 and $48,450 in the case of taxable years beginning in 2011" for "$46,700 in the case of taxable years beginning in 2009" in subpara. (d)(1)(B), effective for tax. yrs. begin. after 12/31/2009.

—P.L. 111-312, Sec. 201(c), of this Act, provides:
"(c) Repeal of EGTRRA sunset. Title IX of the Economic Growth and Tax Relief Reconciliation Act of 2001 [P.L. 107-16, see below] (relating to sunset of provisions of such Act) shall not apply to title VII of such Act (relating to alternative minimum tax)."

—P.L. 111-240, Sec. 2013(b), substituted "38(c)(6)(B)" for "38(c)(3)(B)" in para. (e)(5), effective for credits determined in tax. yrs. begin. after December 31, 2009, and to carrybacks of such credits.

In 2009, P.L. 111-5, Sec. 1012(a)(1), substituted "($70,950 in the case of taxable years beginning in 2009)" for "($69,950 in the case of taxable years beginning in 2008)" in subpara. (d)(1)(A) ... Sec. 1012(a)(2), substituted "($46,700 in the case of taxable years beginning in 2009)" for "($46,200 in the case of taxable years beginning in 2008)" in subpara. (d)(1)(B), effective for tax. yrs. begin. after 12/31/2008.

—P.L. 111-5, Sec. 1142(b)(5), deleted "30(b)(3)," in para. (c)(3), effective for vehicles acquired after 2/17/2009

—P.L. 111-5, Sec. 1144(b)(3), deleted "30B(g)(2)," in para. (c)(3), effective for tax. yrs. begin. after 12/31/2008.

In 2008, P.L. 110-343, Sec. 102(a)(1)DivC, substituted "($69,950 in the case of taxable years beginning in 2008)" for "($66,250 in the case of taxable years beginning in 2007)" in subpara. (d)(1)(A).

—P.L. 110-343, Sec, 102(a)(2)DivC, substituted "($46,200 in the case of taxable years beginning in 2008)" for "($44,350 in the case of taxable years beginning in 2007)" in subpara. (d)(1)(B), effective for tax. yrs. begin. after 12/31/2007.

—P.L. 110-246, Sec. 4, Repeals the duplicative enactment and provides effective date provisions of the Act entitled "An Act to provide for the continuation of agricultural programs through fiscal year 2012, and for other purposes" Sec. 4, P.L. 110-246 reads as follows:

"Sec. 4. Repeal of duplicative enactment.

"(a) In General- The Act entitled 'An Act to provide for the continuation of agricultural programs through fiscal year 2012, and for other purposes' (H.R. 2419 of the 110th Congress), and the amendments made by that Act, are repealed, effective on the date of enactment of that Act.

"(b) Effective Date- Except as otherwise provided in this Act, this Act and the amendments made by this Act shall take effect on the earlier of--

"(1) the date of enactment of this Act; or

"(2) the date of the enactment of the Act entitled 'An Act to provide for the continuation of agricultural programs through fiscal year 2012, and for other purposes' (H.R. 2419 of the 110th Congress)."

—P.L. 110-246, Sec. 15311(b), added para. (b)(4), effective for tax. yrs. ending after 5/22/2008. [Ed. Note: May 22, 2008 was the date of enactment for H.R. 2419 (PL 110-234), which was repealed by (2008 Farm Act Sec. 4(a)) (PL 110-246, 6/18/2008), in connection with the reenactment of the farm bill to correct a technical deficiency in its original passage.]

In 2007, P.L. 110-166, Sec. 2(a)(1), substituted "($66,250 in the case of taxable years beginning in 2007)" for "($62,550 in the case of taxable years beginning in 2006)" in subpara. (d)(1)(A) ... Sec. 2(a)(2), substituted "($44,350 in the case of taxable years beginning in 2007)" for "($42,500 in the case of taxable years beginning in 2006)" in subpara. (d)(1)(B), effective for tax. yrs. begin. after 12/31/2006.

In 2006, P.L. 109-222, Sec. 102, substituted "December 31, 2010" for "December 31, 2008" in Sec. 303 of P.L. 108-27 [see below], effective 5/17/2006.

Minimum tax — Code Sec. 55

—P.L. 109-222, Sec. 301(a)(1), substituted "$62,550 in the case of taxable years beginning in 2006" for "$58,000 in the case of taxable years beginning in 2003, 2004, and 2005" in subpara. (d)(1)(A)... Sec. 301(a)(2), substituted "$42,500 in the case of taxable years beginning in 2006" for "$40,250 in the case of taxable years beginning in 2003, 2004, and 2005" in subpara. (d)(1)(B), effective for tax. yrs. begin. after 12/31/2005.

In 2005, P.L. 109-135, Sec. 403(h), substituted "regular tax liability" for "regular tax" in para. (c)(2), effective for tax. yrs. begin. after 12/31/2003 as if included in Sec. 314 of the American Jobs Creation Act of 2004, P.L. 108-357.

—P.L. 109-135, Sec. 412(p)(1), added "30B(g)(2), 30C(d)(2)," after "30(b)(3)," in para. (c)(3)... Sec. 412(p)(2), repealed Sec. 1341(b)(3) of P.L. 109-58 [see below]... Sec. 412(p)(3), repealed Sec. 1342(b)(3) of P.L. 109-58 [see below], effective 12/21/2005.

—P.L. 109-58, Sec. 1302(b), added "45(e)(11)(C)," after "section" in the last sentence of para. (c)(1), effective for tax. yrs. of cooperative organizations end. after 8/8/2005.

—P.L. 109-58, Sec. 1322(a)(3)(H), deleted "29(b)(6)," after "sections 26(a)," in para. (c)(3), effective for credits determined under the Internal Revenue Code of 1986 for tax. yrs. end. after 12/31/2005.

—P.L. 109-58, Sec. 1341(b)(3), added "30B(g)(2)," after "30(b)(2)," in para. (c)(2), effective for property placed in service after 12/31/2005, in tax. yrs. end. after 12/31/2005. [Note: This amendment has been repealed by Sec. 412(p)(2) of P.L. 109-135, see above.]

—P.L. 109-58, Sec. 1342(b)(3), added "30C(d)(2)," after "30B(g)(2)," in para. (c)(2) [as amended by Sec. 1341(b)(3) of this Act, see above], effective for property placed in service after 12/31/2005, in tax. yrs. end. after 12/31/2005. [Note: This amendment has been repealed by Sec. 412(p)(3) of P.L. 109-135, see above.]

In 2004, P.L. 108-357, Sec. 314(a), redesignated para. (c)(2) as (c)(3) and added para. (c)(2), effective for tax. yrs. begin. after 12/31/2003.

—P.L. 108-311, Sec. 103(a), substituted "2003, 2004, and 2005" for "2003 and 2004" in subparas. (d)(1)(A) and (B), effective for tax. yrs. begin. after 12/31/2004.

—P.L. 108-311, Sec. 105, of this Act, reads as follows:

"SEC. 105. APPLICATION OF EGTRRA SUNSET TO THIS TITLE. Each amendment made by this title [Secs. 101-104] shall be subject to title IX of the Economic Growth and Tax Relief Reconciliation Act of 2001 [Sec. 901 of P.L. 107-16] to the same extent and in the same manner as the provision of such Act to which such amendment relates."

—P.L. 108-311, Sec. 406(d), substituted "an amount equal to the excess described in" for "the amount on which a tax is determined under" in subpara. (b)(3)(B), effective for tax. yrs. end. after 5/6/97 as if included in Sec. 311 of the Taxpayer Relief Act of 1997, P.L. 105-34.

In 2003, P.L. 108-27, Sec. 106(a)(1), substituted "$58,000 in the case of taxable years beginning in 2003 and 2004" for "$49,000 in the case of taxable years beginning in 2001, 2002, 2003, and 2004" in subpara. (d)(1)(A)... Sec. 106(a)(2), substituted "$40,250 in the case of taxable years beginning in 2003 and 2004" for "$35,750 in the case of taxable years beginning in 2001, 2002, 2003, and 2004" in subpara. (d)(1)(B), effective for tax. yrs. begin. after 12/31/2002.

—P.L. 108-27, Sec. 107, of this Act, reads as follows:

"SEC. 107. APPLICATION OF EGTRRA SUNSET TO THIS TITLE. Each amendment made by this title [Secs. 101-106] shall be subject to title IX of the Economic Growth and Tax Relief Reconciliation Act of 2001 to the same extent and in the same manner as the provision of such Act to which such amendment relates."

—P.L. 108-27, Sec. 301(a)(1), substituted "5 percent (0 percent in the case of taxable years beginning after 2007)" for "10 percent" in subpara. (b)(3)(B)... Sec. 301(a)(2)(B), substituted "15 percent" for "20 percent" in subpara (b)(3)(C) ... Sec. 301(b)(2), deleted "In the case of taxable years beginning after December 31, 2000, rules similar to the rules of section 1(h)(9) shall apply for purposes of subparagraphs (B) and (C)." before "Terms used in this paragraph" in para. (b)(3), effective for tax. yrs. end. on or after 5/6/2003.

—P.L. 108-27, Sec. 301(c), of this Act, reads as follows:

"(c) Transitional rules for taxable years which include May 6, 2003. For purposes of applying section 1(h) of the Internal Revenue Code of 1986 in the case of a taxable year which includes May 6, 2003—

"(1) The amount of tax determined under subparagraph (B) of section 1(h)(1) of such Code shall be the sum of—

"(A) 5 percent of the lesser of—

"(i) the net capital gain determined by taking into account only gain or loss properly taken into account for the portion of the taxable year on or after May 6, 2003 (determined without regard to collectibles gain or loss, gain described in section 1(h)(6)(A)(i) of such Code, and section 1202 gain), or

"(ii) the amount on which a tax is determined under such subparagraph (without regard to this subsection), plus

"(B) 8 percent of the lesser of—

"(i) the qualified 5-year gain (as defined in section 1(h)(9) of the Internal Revenue Code of 1986, as in effect on the day before the date of the enactment of this Act) properly taken into account for the portion of the taxable year before May 6, 2003, or

"(ii) the excess (if any) of—

"(I) the amount on which a tax is determined under such subparagraph (without regard to this subsection), over

"(II) the amount on which a tax is determined under subparagraph (A), plus

"(C) 10 percent of the excess (if any) of—

"(i) the amount on which a tax is determined under such subparagraph (without regard to this subsection), over

"(ii) the sum of the amounts on which a tax is determined under subparagraphs (A) and (B).

"(2) The amount of tax determined under subparagraph (C) of section (1)(h)(1) of such Code shall be the sum of—

"(A) 15 percent of the lesser of—

"(i) the excess (if any) of the amount of net capital gain determined under subparagraph (A)(i) of paragraph (1) of this subsection over the amount on which a tax is determined under subparagraph (A) of paragraph (1) of this subsection, or

"(ii) the amount on which a tax is determined under such subparagraph (C) (without regard to this subsection), plus

"(B) 20 percent of the excess (if any) of—

"(i) the amount on which a tax is determined under such subparagraph (C) (without regard to this subsection), over

"(ii) the amount on which a tax is determined under subparagraph (A) of this paragraph.

"(3) For purposes of applying section 55(b)(3) of such Code, rules similar to the rules of paragraphs (1) and (2) of this subsection shall apply.

"(4) In applying this subsection with respect to any pass-thru entity, the determination of when gains and losses are properly taken into account shall be made at the entity level.

"(5) For purposes of applying section 1(h)(11) of such Code, as added by section 302 of this Act, to this subsection, dividends which are qualified dividend income shall be treated as gain properly taken into account for the portion of the taxable year on or after May 6, 2003.

"(6) Terms used in this subsection which are also used in section 1(h) of such Code shall have the respective meanings that such terms have in such section."

—P.L. 108-27, Sec. 303, of this Act [as amended by Sec. 102 of P.L. 109-222, and Sec. 102(a) of P.L. 111-312, see above], reads as follows:

"SEC. 303. SUNSET OF TITLE. All provisions of, and amendments made by, this title [Secs. 301 and 302] shall not apply to taxable years beginning after December 31, 2012, and the Internal Revenue Code of 1986 shall be applied and administered to such years as if such provisions and amendments had never been enacted."

In 2002, P.L. 107-358, Sec. 2, added subsec. (c) in Sec. 901 of P.L. 107-16 [see below], effective 12/17/2002.

In 2001, P.L. 107-16, Sec. 701(a)(1), substituted "$45,000 ($49,000 in the case of taxable years beginning in 2001, 2002, 2003, and 2004)" for "$45,000" in subpara. (d)(1)(A)... Sec. 701(a)(2), substituted "$33,750 ($35,750 in the case of taxable years beginning in 2001, 2002, 2003, and 2004)" for "$33,750" in subpara. (d)(1)(B)... Sec. 701(b)(1), deleted "and" at the end of subpara. (d)(1)(B), deleted subpara. (d)(1)(C), and added subparas. (d)(1)(C) and (D)... Sec. 701(b)(2), substituted "subparagraph (C) or (D) of paragraph (1)" for "paragraph (1)(C)" in subpara. (d)(3)(C)... Sec. 701(b)(3)(A), substituted "paragraph (1)(C)" for "paragraph (1)(C)(i)" in the last sentence of para. (d)(3)... Sec. 701(b)(3)(B), substituted "the minimum amount of such income (as so determined) for which the exemption amount under paragraph (1)(C) is zero, or (ii) such exemption amount (determined without regard to this paragraph)" for "$165,000 or (ii) $22,500" in the last sentence of para. (d)(3), effective for tax. yrs. begin. after 12/31/2000.

Prior to deletion, subpara. (d)(1)(C) read as follows:

"(C) $22,500 in the case of—

"(i) a married individual who files a separate return, or

"(ii) an estate or trust."

—P.L. 107-16, Sec. 901, of this Act [as amended by Sec. 2 of P.L. 107-358, and Sec. 101(a)(1), P.L. 111-312, see above], reads as follows:

"Sec. 901. Sunset of provisions of Act.

"(a) In general. All provisions of, and amendments made by, this Act shall not apply—

"(1) to taxable, plan, or limitation years beginning after December 31, 2012, or

"(2) in the case of title V, to estates of decedents dying, gifts made, or generation skipping transfers, after December 31, 2012.

"(b) Application of certain laws. The Internal Revenue Code of 1986 and the Employee Retirement Income Security Act of 1974 shall be applied and administered to years, estates, gifts, and transfers described in subsection (a) as if the provisions and amendments described in subsection (a) had never been enacted.

"(c) Exception. Subsection (a) shall not apply to section 803 (relating to no federal income tax on restitution received by victims of the Nazi regime or their heirs or estates)."

In 1998, P.L. 105-206, Sec. 6005(d)(2), amended para. (b)(3), effective for tax. yrs. end. after 5/6/97.

Prior to amendment, para. (b)(3) read as follows:

"(3) Maximum rate of tax on net capital gain of noncorporate taxpayers. The amount determined under the first sentence of paragraph (1)(A)(i) shall not exceed the sum of—

"(A) the amount determined under such first sentence computed at the rates and in the same manner as if this paragraph had not been enacted on the taxable excess reduced by the lesser of—

"(i) the net capital gain, or

"(ii) the sum of—

"(I) the adjusted net capital gain, plus

"(II) the unrecaptured section 1250 gain, plus

"(B) 25 percent of the lesser of—

"(i) the unrecaptured section 1250 gain, or

"(ii) the amount of taxable excess in excess of the sum of—

"(I) the adjusted net capital gain, plus

"(II) the amount on which a tax is determined under subparagraph (A), plus

"(C) 10 percent of so much of the taxpayer's adjusted net capital gain (or, if less, taxable excess) as does not exceed the amount on which a tax is determined under section 1(h)(1)(D), plus

1,293

"(D) 20 percent of the taxpayer's adjusted net capital gain (or, if less, taxable excess) in excess of the amount on which tax is determined under subparagraph (C).
In the case of taxable years beginning after December 31, 2000, rules similar to the rules of section 1(h)(2) shall apply for purposes of subparagraphs (C) and (D). Terms used in this paragraph which are also used in section 1(h) shall have the respective meanings given such terms by section 1(h)."
—P.L. 105-206, Sec. 6006(a), amended para. (e)(1), effective or tax. yrs. begin. after 12/31/97.
Prior to amendment, para. (e)(1) read as follows:
"(1) In general. The tentative minimum tax of a corporation shall be zero for any taxable year if—
"(A) such corporation met the $5,000,000 gross receipts test of section 448(c) for its first taxable year beginning after December 31, 1996, and
"(B) such corporation would meet such test for the taxable year and all prior taxable years beginning before such first taxable year if such test were applied by substituting '$7,500,000' for '$5,000,000'."
In 1997, P.L. 105-34, Sec. 311(b)(1), added para. (b)(3)... Sec. 311(b)(2)(A), substituted "this subsection" for "clause (i)" in clause (b)(1)(A)(ii), effective for tax. yrs. end. after 5/6/97.
—P.L. 105-34, Sec. 401(a), added subsec. (e), effective for tax. yrs. begin. after 12/31/97.
—P.L. 105-34, Sec. 1601(f)(1)(C), substituted "Puerto Rico" for "Puerto Rican" in para. (c)(1), effective for tax. yrs. begin. after 12/31/95. For special rules, see Sec. 1601(c)(2)-(3), of P.L. 104-188, reproduced below.
In 1996, P.L. 104-188, Sec. 1205(d)(6), deleted "28(d)(2)," after "sections 26(a)," in para. (c)(2), effective for amounts paid or incurred in tax. yrs. end. after 6/30/96.
—P.L. 104-188, Sec. 1401(b)(3), deleted "shall not include any tax imposed by section 402(d) and" after "Such term" in para. (c)(1), effective for tax. yrs. begin. after 12/31/99. For transitional rules, see Sec. 1401(c)(2), of this Act, which reads as follows:
"(2) Retention of certain transition rules. The amendments made by this section shall not apply to any distribution for which the taxpayer is eligible to elect the benefits of section 1122(h)(3) or (5) of the Tax Reform Act of 1986. Notwithstanding the preceding sentence, individuals who elect such benefits after December 31, 1999, shall not be eligible for 5-year averaging under section 402(d) of the Internal Revenue Code of 1986 (as in effect immediately before such amendments)."
—P.L. 104-188, Sec. 1601(b)(2)(A), substituted ", the section 936 credit allowable under 27(b), and the Puerto Rican economic activity credit under section 30A" for "and the section 936 credit allowable under section 27(b)" in para. (c)(1), effective for tax. yrs. begin. after 12/31/95. For special rules, see Sec. 1601(c)(2)-(3), of this Act, which reads as follows:
"(2) Special rule for qualified possession source investment income. The amendments made by this section shall not apply to qualified possession source investment income received or accrued before July 1, 1996, without regard to the taxable year in which received or accrued.
"(3) Special transition rule for payment of estimated tax installments. In determining the amount of any installment due under section 6655 of the Internal Revenue Code of 1986 after the date of the enactment of this Act and before October 1, 1996, only ½ of any increase in tax (for the taxable year for which such installment is made) by reason of the amendments made by subsections (a) and (b) shall be taken into account. Any reduction in such installment by reason of the preceding sentence shall be recaptured by increasing the next required installment for such year by the amount of such reduction."
In 1993, P.L. 103-66, Sec. 13203(a), amended para. (b)(1)... Sec. 13203(b)(1), substituted "$45,000" for "$40,000" in subpara. (d)(1)(A)... Sec. 13203(b)(2), substituted "$33,750" for "$30,000" in subpara. (d)(1)(B)... Sec. 13203(b)(3), substituted "$22,500" for "$20,000" in subpara. (d)(1)(C)... Sec. 13203(c)(1), substituted "$165,000 or (ii) $22,500" for "$155,000 or (ii) $20,000" in para. (d)(3), effective for tax. yrs. begin. after 12/31/92.
Prior to amendment, para. (b)(1) read as follows:
"(1) In general. The tentative minimum tax for the taxable year is—
"(A) 20 percent (24 percent in the case of a taxpayer other than a corporation) of so much of the alternative minimum taxable income for the taxable year as exceeds the exemption amount, reduced by
"(B) the alternative minimum tax foreign tax credit for the taxable year."
In 1992, P.L. 102-486, Sec. 1913(b)(2)(D), substituted "29(b)(6), 30(b)(3)," for "29(b)(5)," in para. (c)(2), effective for property placed in service after 6/30/93.
—P.L. 102-318, Sec. 521(b)(1), substituted "section 402(d)" for "section 402(e)" in para. (c)(1), effective for distributions after 12/31/92. For special rule, see Sec. 521(e)(2) of this Act which reads as follows:
"(2) Special rule for partial distributions. For purposes of section 402(a)(5)(D)(i)(II) of the Internal Revenue Code of 1986 (as in effect before the amendments made by this section), a distribution before January 1, 1993, which is made before or at the same time as a series of periodic payments shall not be treated as one of such series if it is not substantially equal in amount to other payments in such series."
In 1990, P.L. 101-508, Sec. 11102(a), substituted "24 percent" for "21 percent" in subpara. (b)(1)(A), effective for tax. yrs. begin. after 12/31/90.
—P.L. 101-508, Sec. 11813(b)(5), substituted "section 49(b) or 50(a)" for "section 47" in para. (c)(1), effective for property placed in service after 12/31/90 except as provided in Sec. 11813(c)(2) of this Act, reproduced in note following Code Sec. 46.

In 1988, P.L. 100-647, Sec. 1002(l)(27), substituted "subsection (j) or (k) of section 42" for "section 42(j)" in para. (c)(1), effective for buildings placed in service after 12/31/86, in tax. yrs. end. after 12/31/86.
—P.L. 100-647, Sec. 1007(a)(1), added "and the section 936 credit allowable under section 27(b)" before the period at the end of the first sentence in para. (c)(1)... Sec. 1007(a)(2), added a sentence to the end of para. (b)(2), effective for tax. yrs. begin. after 12/31/86.
—P.L. 100-647, Sec. 1007(a)(3), added a sentence to the end of para. (d)(3), effective for tax. yrs. end. after 11/10/88. Sec. 1007(f)(1) provides the following transitional rule:
"(1) In the case of the taxable year of an estate or trust which begins before January 1, 1987, and ends on or after such date, the items of tax preference apportioned to any beneficiary of such estate or trust under section 58(c) of the Internal Revenue Code of 1954 (as in effect on 10/21/86 shall be taken into account for purposes of determining the amount of the tax imposed by '86 Code section 55 (as amended by the Tax Reform Act of 1986) on such beneficiary for such beneficiary's taxable year in which such taxable year of the estate or trust ends."
In 1986, P.L. 99-514, Sec. 252(c), added "or section 42(j)" after "section 47", in subsec. (c), effective for buildings placed in service after 12/31/86, in tax. yrs. end. after 12/31/86.
—P.L. 99-514, Sec. 701(a), added Code Sec. 55 as part of the amendments to Part VI of subchapter A of Chapter 1, effective for tax. yrs. begin. after 12/31/86.

Sec. 56. Adjustments in computing alternative minimum taxable income.

(a) Adjustments applicable to all taxpayers.

In determining the amount of the alternative minimum taxable income for any taxable year the following treatment shall apply (in lieu of the treatment applicable for purposes of computing the regular tax):

(1) Depreciation.

(A) In general.

(i) Property other than certain personal property. Except as provided in clause (ii), the depreciation deduction allowable under section 167 with respect to any tangible property placed in service after December 31, 1986, shall be determined under the alternative system of section 168(g). In the case of property placed in service after December 31, 1998, the preceding sentence shall not apply but clause (ii) shall continue to apply.

(ii) 150-percent declining balance method for certain property. The method of depreciation used shall be—

(I) the 150 percent declining balance method,

(II) switching to the straight line method for the 1st taxable year for which using the straight line method with respect to the adjusted basis as of the beginning of the year will yield a higher allowance.

The preceding sentence shall not apply to any section 1250 property (as defined in section 1250(c)) (and the straight line method shall be used for such section 1250 property) or to any other property if the depreciation deduction determined under section 168 with respect to such other property for purposes of the regular tax is determined by using the straight line method.

(B) Exception for certain property. This paragraph shall not apply to property described in paragraph (1), (2), (3), or (4) of section 168(f), or in section 168(e)(3)(C)(iv).

(C) Coordination with transitional rules.

(i) In general. This paragraph shall not apply to property placed in service after December 31, 1986, to which the amendments made by section 201 of the Tax Reform Act of 1986 do not apply by reason of section 203, 204, or 251(d) of such Act.

(ii) Treatment of certain property placed in service before 1987. This paragraph shall apply to any property to which the amendments made by section 201 of the Tax Reform Act of 1986 apply by reason of an election under section 203(a)(1)(B) of such Act with-

Minimum tax Code Sec. 56(b)(1)(E)

out regard to the requirement of subparagraph (A) that the property be placed in service after December 31, 1986.

(D) Normalization rules. With respect to public utility property described in section 168(i)(10), the Secretary shall prescribe the requirements of a normalization method of accounting for this section.

(2) Mining exploration and development costs.

(A) In general. With respect to each mine or other natural deposit (other than an oil, gas, or geothermal well) of the taxpayer, the amount allowable as a deduction under section 616(a) or 617(a) (determined without regard to section 291(b)) in computing the regular tax for costs paid or incurred after December 31, 1986, shall be capitalized and amortized ratably over the 10-year period beginning with the taxable year in which the expenditures were made.

(B) Loss allowed. If a loss is sustained with respect to any property described in subparagraph (A), a deduction shall be allowed for the expenditures described in subparagraph (A) for the taxable year in which such loss is sustained in an amount equal to the lesser of—

(i) the amount allowable under section 165(a) for the expenditures if they had remained capitalized, or

(ii) the amount of such expenditures which have not previously been amortized under subparagraph (A).

(3) Treatment of certain long-term contracts. In the case of any long-term contract entered into by the taxpayer on or after March 1, 1986, the taxable income from such contract shall be determined under the percentage of completion method of accounting (as modified by section 460(b)). For purposes of the preceding sentence, in the case of a contract described in section 460(e)(1), the percentage of the contract completed shall be determined under section 460(b)(1) by using the simplified procedures for allocation of costs prescribed under section 460(b)(3). The first sentence of this paragraph shall not apply to any home construction contract (as defined in section 460(e)(6)).

(4) Alternative tax net operating loss deduction. The alternative tax net operating loss deduction shall be allowed in lieu of the net operating loss deduction allowed under section 172.

(5) Pollution control facilities. In the case of any certified pollution control facility placed in service after December 31, 1986, the deduction allowable under section 169 (without regard to section 291) shall be determined under the alternative system of section 168(g). In the case of such a facility placed in service after December 31, 1998, such deduction shall be determined under section 168 using the straight line method.

(6) Adjusted basis. The adjusted basis of any property to which paragraph (1) or (5) applies (or with respect to which there are any expenditures to which paragraph (2) or subsection (b)(2) applies) shall be determined on the basis of the treatment prescribed in paragraph (1), (2), or (5), or subsection (b)(2), whichever applies.

(7) Section 87 not applicable. Section 87 (relating to alcohol fuel credit) shall not apply.

(b) Adjustments applicable to individuals.

In determining the amount of the alternative minimum taxable income of any taxpayer (other than a corporation), the following treatment shall apply (in lieu of the treatment applicable for purposes of computing the regular tax):

(1) Limitation on deductions.

(A) In general. No deduction shall be allowed—

(i) for any miscellaneous itemized deduction (as defined in section 67(b)), or

(ii) for any taxes described in paragraph (1), (2), or (3) of section 164(a) or clause (ii) of section 164(b)(5)(A).

Clause (ii) shall not apply to any amount allowable in computing adjusted gross income.

> • *Caution:* Code Sec. 56(b)(1)(B), following, is effective for tax. yrs. begin. before 1/1/2013. For Code Sec. 56(b)(1)(B), effective for tax. yrs. begin. after 12/31/2012, see below.

(B) Medical expenses. In determining the amount allowable as a deduction under section 213, subsection (a) of section 213 shall be applied by substituting "10 percent" for "7.5 percent".

> • *Caution:* Code Sec. 56(b)(1)(B), following, is effective for tax. yrs. begin. after 12/31/2012. For Code Sec. 56(b)(1)(B), effective for tax. yrs. begin. before 1/1/2013, see above.

(B) Medical expenses. In determining the amount allowable as a deduction under section 213, subsection (a) of section 213 shall be applied without regard to subsection (f) of such section.

(C) Interest. In determining the amount allowable as a deduction for interest, subsections (d) and (h) of section 163 shall apply, except that—

(i) in lieu of the exception under section 163(h)(2)(D), the term "personal interest" shall not include any qualified housing interest (as defined in subsection (e)),

(ii) sections 163(d)(6) and 163(h)(5) (relating to phase-ins) shall not apply,

(iii) interest on any specified private activity bond (and any amount treated as interest on a specified private activity bond under section 57(a)(5)(B)), and any deduction referred to in section 57(a)(5)(A), shall be treated as includible in gross income (or as deductible) for purposes of applying section 163(d),

(iv) in lieu of the exception under section 163(d)(3)(B)(i), the term "investment interest" shall not include any qualified housing interest (as defined in subsection (e)), and

(v) the adjustments of this section and sections 57 and 58 shall apply in determining net investment income under section 163(d).

(D) Treatment of certain recoveries. No recovery of any tax to which subparagraph (A)(ii) applied shall be included in gross income for purposes of determining alternative minimum taxable income.

(E) Standard deduction and deduction for personal exemptions not allowed. The standard deduction under section 63(c), the deduction for personal exemptions under section 151, and the deduction under section 642(b) shall not be allowed. The preceding sentence shall not apply to so much of the standard deduction as is determined under subparagraphs (D) and (E) of section 63(c)(1).

(F) **Section 68 not applicable.** Section 68 shall not apply.

(2) **Circulation and research and experimental expenditures.**

(A) In general. The amount allowable as a deduction under section 173 or 174(a) in computing the regular tax for amounts paid or incurred after December 31, 1986, shall be capitalized and—

(i) in the case of circulation expenditures described in section 173, shall be amortized ratably over the 3-year period beginning with the taxable year in which the expenditures were made, or

(ii) in the case of research and experimental expenditures described in section 174(a), shall be amortized ratably over the 10-year period beginning with the taxable year in which the expenditures were made.

(B) Loss allowed. If a loss is sustained with respect to any property described in subparagraph (A), a deduction shall be allowed for the expenditures described in subparagraph (A) for the taxable year in which such loss is sustained in an amount equal to the lesser of—

(i) the amount allowable under section 165(a) for the expenditures if they had remained capitalized, or

(ii) the amount of such expenditures which have not previously been amortized under subparagraph (A).

(C) Special rule for personal holding companies. In the case of circulation expenditures described in section 173, the adjustments provided in this paragraph shall apply also to a personal holding company (as defined in section 542).

(D) Exception for certain research and experimental expenditures. If the taxpayer materially participates (within the meaning of section 469(h)) in an activity, this paragraph shall not apply to any amount allowable as a deduction under section 174(a) for expenditures paid or incurred in connection with such activity.

(3) **Treatment of incentive stock options.** Section 421 shall not apply to the transfer of stock acquired pursuant to the exercise of an incentive stock option (as defined in section 422). Section 422(c)(2) shall apply in any case where the disposition and the inclusion for purposes of this part are within the same taxable year and such section shall not apply in any other case. The adjusted basis of any stock so acquired shall be determined on the basis of the treatment prescribed by this paragraph.

(c) **Adjustments applicable to corporations.**

In determining the amount of the alternative minimum taxable income of a corporation, the following treatment shall apply:

(1) **Adjustment for adjusted current earnings.** Alternative minimum taxable income shall be adjusted as provided in subsection (g).

(2) **Merchant marine capital construction funds.** In the case of a capital construction fund established under chapter 535 of title 46, United States Code—

(A) subparagraphs (A), (B), and (C) of section 7518(c)(1) (and the corresponding provisions of such chapter 535) shall not apply to—

(i) any amount deposited in such fund after December 31, 1986, or

(ii) any earnings (including gains and losses) after December 31, 1986, on amounts in such fund, and

(B) no reduction in basis shall be made under section 7518(f) (or the corresponding provisions of such chapter 535) with respect to the withdrawal from the fund of any amount to which subparagraph (A) applies.

For purposes of this paragraph, any withdrawal of deposits or earnings from the fund shall be treated as allocable first to deposits made before (and earnings received or accrued before) January 1, 1987.

(3) **Special deduction for certain organizations not allowed.** The deduction determined under section 833(b) shall not be allowed.

(d) **Alternative tax net operating loss deduction defined.**

(1) **In general.** For purposes of subsection (a)(4), the term "alternative tax net operating loss deduction" means the net operating loss deduction allowable for the taxable year under section 172, except that—

(A) the amount of such deduction shall not exceed the sum of—

(i) the lesser of—

(I) the amount of such deduction attributable to net operating losses (other than the deduction described in clause (ii)(I)), or

(II) 90 percent of alternative minimum taxable income determined without regard to such deduction and the deduction under section 199, plus

(ii) the lesser of—

(I) the amount of such deduction attributable to an applicable net operating loss with respect to which an election is made under section 172(b)(1)(H), or

(II) alternative minimum taxable income determined without regard to such deduction and the deduction under section 199 reduced by the amount determined under clause (i), and

(B) in determining the amount of such deduction—

(i) the net operating loss (within the meaning of section 172(c)) for any loss year shall be adjusted as provided in paragraph (2), and

(ii) appropriate adjustments in the application of section 172(b)(2) shall be made to take into account the limitation of subparagraph (A).

(2) **Adjustments to net operating loss computation.**

(A) Post-1986 loss years. In the case of a loss year beginning after December 31, 1986, the net operating loss for such year under section 172(c) shall—

(i) be determined with the adjustments provided in this section and section 58, and

(ii) be reduced by the items of tax preference determined under section 57 for such year.

An item of tax preference shall be taken into account under clause (ii) only to the extent such item increased the amount of the net operating loss for the taxable year under section 172(c).

(B) Pre-1987 years. In the case of loss years beginning before January 1, 1987, the amount of the net operating loss which may be carried over to taxable years beginning after December 31, 1986, for purposes of paragraph (2), shall be equal to the amount which may be carried from the loss year to the first taxable year of the taxpayer beginning after December 31, 1986.

(3) **Net operating loss attributable to federally declared disasters.** In the case of a taxpayer which has a qualified disaster loss (as defined by section 172(b)(1)(J)) for the taxable year, paragraph (1) shall be applied by increasing the amount determined under subparagraph (A)(ii)(I) thereof by the sum of the carrybacks and carryovers of such loss.

(e) **Qualified housing interest.**

For purposes of this part—

(1) **In general.** The term "qualified housing interest" means interest which is qualified residence interest (as de-

fined in section 163(h)(3)) and is paid or accrued during the taxable year on indebtedness which is incurred in acquiring, constructing, or substantially improving any property which—
  (A) is the principal residence (within the meaning of section 121) of the taxpayer at the time such interest accrues, or
  (B) is a qualified dwelling which is a qualified residence (within the meaning of section 163(h)(4)).
Such term also includes interest on any indebtedness resulting from the refinancing of indebtedness meeting the requirements of the preceding sentence; but only to the extent that the amount of the indebtedness resulting from such refinancing does not exceed the amount of the refinanced indebtedness immediately before the refinancing.

(2) Qualified dwelling. The term "qualified dwelling" means any—
  (A) house,
  (B) apartment,
  (C) condominium, or
  (D) mobile home not used on a transient basis (within the meaning of section 7701(a)(19)(C)(v)),
including all structures or other property appurtenant thereto.

(3) Special rule for indebtedness incurred before July 1, 1982. The term "qualified housing interest" includes interest which is qualified residence interest (as defined in section 163(h)(3)) and is paid or accrued on indebtedness which—
  (A) was incurred by the taxpayer before July 1, 1982, and
  (B) is secured by property which, at the time such indebtedness was incurred, was—
    (i) the principal residence (within the meaning of section 121) of the taxpayer, or
    (ii) a qualified dwelling used by the taxpayer (or any member of his family (within the meaning of section 267(c)(4))).

(f) Repealed.

(g) Adjustments based on adjusted current earnings.
  (1) In general. The alternative minimum taxable income of any corporation for any taxable year shall be increased by 75 percent of the excess (if any) of—
    (A) the adjusted current earnings of the corporation, over
    (B) the alternative minimum taxable income (determined without regard to this subsection and the alternative tax net operating loss deduction).
  (2) Allowance of negative adjustments.
    (A) In general. The alternative minimum taxable income for any corporation of any taxable year, shall be reduced by 75 percent of the excess (if any) of—
      (i) the amount referred to in subparagraph (B) of paragraph (1), over
      (ii) the amount referred to in subparagraph (A) of paragraph (1).
    (B) Limitation. The reduction under subparagraph (A) for any taxable year shall not exceed the excess (if any) of—
      (i) the aggregate increases in alternative minimum taxable income under paragraph (1) for prior taxable years, over
      (ii) the aggregate reductions under subparagraph (A) of this paragraph for prior taxable years.
  (3) Adjusted current earnings. For purposes of this subsection, the term "adjusted current earnings" means the alternative minimum taxable income for the taxable year—
    (A) determined with the adjustments provided in paragraph (4), and
    (B) determined without regard to this subsection and the alternative tax net operating loss deduction.
  (4) Adjustments. In determining adjusted current earnings, the following adjustments shall apply:
    (A) Depreciation.
      (i) Property placed in service after 1989. The depreciation deduction with respect to any property placed in service in a taxable year beginning after 1989 shall be determined under the alternative system of section 168(g). The preceding sentence shall not apply to any property placed in service after December 31, 1993, and the depreciation deduction with respect to such property shall be determined under the rules of subsection (a)(1)(A).
      (ii) Property to which new ACRS system applies. In the case of any property to which the amendments made by section 201 of the Tax Reform Act of 1986 apply and which is placed in service in a taxable year beginning before 1990, the depreciation deduction shall be determined—
        (I) by taking into account the adjusted basis of such property (as determined for purposes of computing alternative minimum taxable income) as of the close of the last taxable year beginning before January 1, 1990, and
        (II) by using the straight-line method over the remainder of the recovery period applicable to such property under the alternative system of section 168(g).
      (iii) Property to which original ACRS system applies. In the case of any property to which section 168 (as in effect on the day before the date of the enactment [10/22/86] of the Tax Reform Act of 1986 and without regard to subsection (d)(1)(A)(ii) thereof) applies and which is placed in service in a taxable year beginning before 1990, the depreciation deduction shall be determined—
        (I) by taking into account the adjusted basis of such property (as determined for purposes of computing the regular tax) as of the close of the last taxable year beginning before January 1, 1990, and
        (II) by using the straight line method over the remainder of the recovery period which would apply to such property under the alternative system of section 168(g).
      (iv) Property placed in service before 1981. In the case of any property not described in clause (i), (ii), or (iii), the amount allowable as depreciation or amortization with respect to such property shall be determined in the same manner as for purposes of computing taxable income.
      (v) Special rule for certain property. In the case of any property described in paragraph (1), (2), (3), or (4) of section 168(f), the amount of depreciation allowable for purposes of the regular tax shall be treated as the amount allowable under the alternative system of section 168(g).
    (B) Inclusion of items included for purposes of computing earnings and profits.
      (i) In general. In the case of any amount which is excluded from gross income for purposes of computing alternative minimum taxable income but is taken into

account in determining the amount of earnings and profits—

(I) such amount shall be included in income in the same manner as if such amount were includible in gross income for purposes of computing alternative minimum taxable income, and

(II) the amount of such income shall be reduced by any deduction which would have been allowable in computing alternative minimum taxable income if such amount were includible in gross income.

The preceding sentence shall not apply in the case of any amount excluded from gross income under section 108 (or the corresponding provisions of prior law) or under section 139A or 1357. In the case of any insurance company taxable under section 831(b), this clause shall not apply to any amount not described in section 834(b).

(ii) Inclusion of buildup in life insurance contracts. In the case of any life insurance contract—

(I) the income on such contract (as determined under section 7702(g)) for any taxable year shall be treated as includible in gross income for such year, and

(II) there shall be allowed as a deduction that portion of any premium which is attributable to insurance coverage.

(iii) Tax exempt interest on certain housing bonds. Clause (i) shall not apply in the case of any interest on a bond to which section 57(a)(5)(C)(iii) applies.

(iv) Tax exempt interest on bonds issued in 2009 and 2010.

(I) In general. Clause (i) shall not apply in the case of any interest on a bond issued after December 31, 2008, and before January 1, 2011.

(II) Treatment of refunding bonds. For purposes of subclause (I), a refunding bond (whether a current or advance refunding) shall be treated as issued on the date of the issuance of the refunded bond (or in the case of a series of refundings, the original bond).

(III) Exception for certain refunding bonds. Subclause (II) shall not apply to any refunding bond which is issued to refund any bond which was issued after December 31, 2003, and before January 1, 2009.

(C) Disallowance of items not deductible in computing earnings and profits.

(i) In general. A deduction shall not be allowed for any item if such item would not be deductible for any taxable year for purposes of computing earnings and profits.

(ii) Special rule for certain dividends.

(I) In general. Clause (i) shall not apply to any deduction allowable under section 243 or 245 for any dividend which is a 100-percent dividend or which is received from a 20-percent owned corporation (as defined in section 243(c)(2)), but only to the extent such dividend is attributable to income of the paying corporation which is subject to tax under this chapter (determined after the application of sections 30A, 936 (including subsections (a)(4), (i), and (j) thereof) and 921 (as in effect before its repeal by the FSC Repeal and Extraterritorial Income Exclusion Act of 2000)).

(II) 100-percent dividend. For purposes of subclause (I), the term "100 percent dividend" means any dividend if the percentage used for purposes of determining the amount allowable as a deduction under section 243 or 245 with respect to such dividend is 100 percent.

(iii) Treatment of taxes on dividends from 936 corporations.

(I) In general. For purposes of determining the alternative minimum foreign tax credit, 75 percent of any withholding or income tax paid to a possession of the United States with respect to dividends received from a corporation eligible for the credit provided by section 936 shall be treated as a tax paid to a foreign country by the corporation receiving the dividend.

(II) Limitation. If the aggregate amount of the dividends referred to in subclause (I) for any taxable year exceeds the excess referred to in paragraph (1), the amount treated as tax paid to a foreign country under subclause (I) shall not exceed the amount which would be so treated without regard to this subclause multiplied by a fraction the numerator of which is the excess referred to in paragraph (1) and the denominator of which is the aggregate amount of such dividends.

(III) Treatment of taxes imposed on 936 corporation. For purposes of this clause, taxes paid by any corporation eligible for the credit provided by section 936 to a possession of the United States shall be treated as a withholding tax paid with respect to any dividend paid by such corporation to the extent such taxes would be treated as paid by the corporation receiving the dividend under rules similar to the rules of section 902 (and the amount of any such dividend shall be increased by the amount so treated).

(IV) Separate application of foreign tax credit limitations. In determining the alternative minimum foreign tax credit, section 904(d) shall be applied as if dividends from a corporation eligible for the credit provided by section 936 were a separate category of income referred to in a subparagraph of section 904(d)(1).

(V) Coordination with limitation on 936 credit. Any reference in this clause to a dividend received from a corporation eligible for the credit provided by section 936 shall be treated as a reference to the portion of any such dividend for which the dividends received deduction is disallowed under clause (i) after the application of clause (ii)(I).

(VI) Application to section 30A corporations. References in this clause to section 936 shall be treated as including references to section 30A.

(iv) Special rule for certain dividends received by certain cooperatives. In the case of an organization to which part I of subchapter T (relating to tax treatment of cooperatives) applies which is engaged in the marketing of agricultural or horticultural products, clause (i) shall not apply to any amount allowable as a deduction under section 245(c). [Sec. 11(g)(2), P.L. 110-172, 12/29/2007, directs that Code Sec. 54(g)(4)(C)(iv) be amended. It appears as if the amendment should be made to Code Sec. 56(g)(4)(C)(iv) and is in place here. See notes following this Code Sec.]

(v) Deduction for domestic production. Clause (i) shall not apply to any amount allowable as a deduction under section 199.

Minimum tax   Code Sec. 56

(vi) Special rule for certain distributions from controlled foreign corporations. Clause (i) shall not apply to any deduction allowable under section 965.

(D) Certain other earnings and profits adjustments.

(i) Intangible drilling costs. The adjustments provided in section 312(n)(2)(A) shall apply in the case of amounts paid or incurred in taxable years beginning after December 31, 1989. In the case of a taxpayer other than an integrated oil company (as defined in section 291(b)(4)), in the case of any oil or gas well, this clause shall not apply in the case of amounts paid or incurred in taxable years beginning after December 31, 1992.

(ii) Certain amortization provisions not to apply. Sections 173 and 248 shall not apply to expenditures paid or incurred in taxable years beginning after December 31, 1989.

(iii) LIFO inventory adjustments. The adjustments provided in section 312(n)(4) shall apply, but only with respect to taxable years beginning after December 31, 1989.

(iv) Installment sales. In the case of any installment sale in a taxable year beginning after December 31, 1989, adjusted current earnings shall be computed as if the corporation did not use the installment method. The preceding sentence shall not apply to the applicable percentage (as determined under section 453A) of the gain from any installment sale with respect to which section 453A(a)(1) applies.

(E) Disallowance of loss on exchange of debt pools. No loss shall be recognized on the exchange of any pool of debt obligations for another pool of debt obligations having substantially the same effective interest rates and maturities.

(F) Depletion.

(i) In general. The allowance for depletion with respect to any property placed in service in a taxable year beginning after December 31, 1989, shall be cost depletion determined under section 611.

(ii) Exception for independent oil and gas producers and royalty owners. In the case of any taxable year beginning after December 31, 1992, clause (i) (and subparagraph (C)(i)) shall not apply to any deduction for depletion computed in accordance with section 613A(c).

(G) Treatment of certain ownership changes. If—

(i) there is an ownership change (within the meaning of section 382) in a taxable year beginning after 1989 with respect to any corporation, and

(ii) there is a net unrealized built-in loss (within the meaning of section 382(h)) with respect to such corporation,

then the adjusted basis of each asset of such corporation (immediately after the ownership change) shall be its proportionate share (determined on the basis of respective fair market values) of the fair market value of the assets of such corporation (determined under section 382(h)) immediately before the ownership change.

(H) Adjusted basis. The adjusted basis of any property with respect to which an adjustment under this paragraph applies shall be determined by applying the treatment prescribed in this paragraph.

(I) Treatment of charitable contributions. Notwithstanding subparagraphs (B) and (C), no adjustment related to the earnings and profits effects of any charitable contribution shall be made in computing adjusted current earnings.

(5) **Other definitions.** For purposes of paragraph (4)—

(A) Earnings and profits. The term "earnings and profits" means earnings and profits computed for purposes of subchapter C.

(B) Treatment of alternative minimum taxable income. The treatment of any item for purposes of computing alternative minimum taxable income shall be determined without regard to this subsection.

(6) **Exception for certain corporations.** This subsection shall not apply to any S corporation, regulated investment company, real estate investment trust, or REMIC.

In 2010, P.L. 111-148, Sec. 9013(c), substituted "without regard to subsection (f) of such section" for "by substituting '10 percent' for '7.5 percent'" in subpara. (b)(1)(B), effective for tax. yrs. begin. after 12/31/2012.

In 2009, P.L. 111-92, Sec. 13(b), amended subclause (d)(1)(A)(ii)(I), effective for tax. yrs. end. after 12/31/2002

Prior to amendment, subclause (d)(1)(A)(ii)(I) read as follows:

"(I) the amount of such deduction attributable to the sum of carrybacks of net operating losses from taxable years ending during 2001 or 2002 and carryovers of net operating losses to taxable years ending during 2001 and 2002, or"

—P.L. 111-92, Sec. 13(d), of this Act, provides:

"(d) Anti-abuse rules. The Secretary of Treasury or the Secretary's designee shall prescribe such rules as are necessary to prevent the abuse of the purposes of the amendments made by this section, including anti-stuffing rules, anti-churning rules (including rules relating to sale-leasebacks), and rules similar to the rules under section 1091 of the Internal Revenue Code of 1986 relating to losses from wash sales."

—P.L. 111-92, Sec. 13(f), of this Act, provides:

"(f) Exception for tarp recipients. The amenfments made by this section shall not apply to—

"(1) any taxpayer if—

"(A) the Federal Government acquired before the date of the enactment of this Act an equity interest in the taxpayer pursuant to the Emergency Economic Stabilization Act of 2008,

"(B) the Federal Government acquired before such date of enactment any warrant (or other right) to acquire any equity interest with respect to the taxpayer pursuant to the Emergency Economic Stabilization Act of 2008, or

"(C) such taxpayer receives after such date of enactment funds from the Federal Government in exchange for an interest described in subparagraph (A) or (B) pursuant to a program established under title I of division A of the Emergency Economic Stabilization Act of 2008 (unless such taxpayer is a financial institution (as defined in section 3 of such Act) and the funds are received pursuant to a program established by the Secretary of the Treasury for the stated purpose of increasing the availability of credit to small businesses using funding made available under such Act), or

"(2) the Federal National Mortgage Association and the Federal Home Loan Mortgage Corporation, and

"(3) any taxpayer which at any time in 2008 or 2009 was or is a member of the same affiliated group (as defined in section 1504 of the Internal Revenue Code of 1986, determined without regard to subsection (b) thereof) as a taxpayer described in paragraph (1) or (2)."

—P.L. 111-5, Sec. 1008(d), substituted "subparagraphs (D) and (E) of section 63(c)(1)" for "section 63(c)(1)(D)" in subpara. (b)(1)(E), effective for purchases on or after 2/17/2009 in tax. yrs. end. after 2/17/2009.

—P.L. 111-5, Sec. 1503(b), added clause (g)(4)(B)(iv), effective for obligations issued after 12/31/2008.

In 2008, P.L. 110-343, Sec. 706(b)(3)DivC, added a sentence at the end of subpara. (b)(1)(E), effective for disasters declared in tax. yrs. begin. after 12/31/2007.

—P.L. 110-343, Sec. 708(c)DivC, added para. (d)(3), effective for losses arising in tax. yrs. begin. after 12/31/2007, in connection with disasters declared after 10/3/2008.

—P.L. 110-343, Sec. 712DivC, of this Act, provides:

"Sec. 712. Coordination with heartland disaster relief.

"The amendments made by this subtitle, other than the amendments made by sections 706(a)(2), 710, and 711, shall not apply to any disaster described in section 702(c)(1)(A), or to any expenditure or loss resulting from such disaster."

—P.L. 110-289, Sec. 3022(a)(2), added clause (g)(4)(B)(iii), effective for bonds issued after 7/30/2008.

In 2007, P.L. 110-172, Sec. 11(g)(1), substituted "921 (as in effect before its repeal by the FSC Repeal and Extraterritorial Income Exclusion Act of 2000)" for "921" in subclause (g)(4)(C)(ii)(I) ... Sec. 11(g)(2), directs that "an organization to which part I of subchapter T (relating to tax treatment of cooperatives) applies which is engaged in the marketing of agricultural or horticultural products" is substituted for "a cooperative described in section 927(a)(4)" in clause Code Sec. 54(g)(4)(C)(iv). It appears as if the amendment should be made to Code Sec. 56(g)(4)(C)(iv) and has been incorporated in Code Sec. 56(g)(4)(C)(iv), enacted 12/29/2007.

In 2006, P.L. 109-304, Sec. 17(e)(1)(A), substituted "chapter 535 of title 46, United States Code" for "section 607 of the Merchant Marine Act, 1936 (46 U.S.C. 1177)" in para. (c)(2) ... Sec. 17(e)(1)(B), substituted "such chapter 535" for "such section 607" in subparas. (c)(2)(A) and (B), enacted 10/6/2006.

1,299

—P.L. 109-222, Sec. 513(a), amended Sec. 5(c)(1) of P.L. 106-519 [see below]... Sec. 513(b), repealed Sec. 101(f) of P.L. 108-357 [see below], effective for tax. yrs. begin. after 5/17/2006.

Prior to amendment, Sec. 5(c)(1) of P.L. 106-519 read as follows:

"(1) In general. In the case of a FSC (as so defined) in existence on September 30, 2000, and at all times thereafter, the amendments made by this Act shall not apply to any transaction in the ordinary course of trade or business involving a FSC which occurs—

"(A) before January 1, 2002; or

"(B) after December 31, 2001, pursuant to a binding contract—

"(i) which is between the FSC (or any related person) and any person which is not a related person; and

"(ii) which is in effect on September 30, 2000, and at all times thereafter.

For purposes of this paragraph, a binding contract shall include a purchase option, renewal option, or replacement option which is included in such contract and which is enforceable against the seller or lessor."

Prior to repeal, Sec. 101(f) of P.L. 108-357 read as follows:

"(f) Binding contracts. The amendments made by this section shall not apply to any transaction in the ordinary course of a trade or business which occurs pursuant to a binding contract—

"(1) which is between the taxpayer and a person who is not a related person (as defined in section 943(b)(3) of such Code, as in effect on the day before the date of the enactment of this Act), and

"(2) which is in effect on September 17, 2003, and at all times thereafter.

"For purposes of this subsection, a binding contract shall include a purchase option, renewal option, or replacement option which is included in such contract and which is enforceable against the seller or lessor."

In 2005, P.L. 109-135, Sec. 403(a)(14), substituted "such deduction and the deduction under section 199" for "such deduction" in subclauses (d)(1)(A)(i)(II) and (d)(1)(A)(ii)(II), effective for tax. yrs. begin. after 12/31/2004 as if included in Sec. 102 of the American Jobs Creation Act of 2004, P.L. 108-357 [as amended by Sec. 403(a)(19) of P.L. 109-135, see below].

—P.L. 109-135, Sec. 403(a)(19), of this Act, provides:

"(19) Subsection (e) of section 102 of the American Jobs Creation Act of 2004 is amended to read as follows:

"(e) Effective date.

"(1) In general. The amendments made by this section shall apply to taxable years beginning after December 31, 2004.

"(2) Application to pass-thru entities, etc. In determining the deduction under section 199 of the Internal Revenue Code of 1986 (as added by this section), items arising from a taxable year of a partnership, S corporation, estate, or trust beginning before January 1, 2005, shall not be taken into account for purposes of subsection (d)(1) of such section."

—P.L. 109-135, Sec. 403(r)(2), added "or clause (ii) of section 164(b)(5)(A)" before the period at the end of clause (b)(1)(A)(ii), effective for tax. yrs. begin. after 12/31/2003 as if included in Sec. 501 of the American Jobs Creation Act of 2004, P.L. 108-357.

—P.L. 109-58, Sec. 1326(d), added ", or in section 168(e)(3)(C)(iv)" after "section 168(f)" in subpara. (a)(1)(B), effective for property placed in service after 4/11/2005, except as provided in Sec. 1326(e)(2) of this Act, which reads as follows:

"(2) Exception. The amendments made by this section shall not apply to any property with respect to which the taxpayer or a related party has entered into a binding contract for the construction thereof on or before April 11, 2005, or, in the case of self-constructed property, has started construction on or before such date."

In 2004, P.L. 108-357, Sec. 101(b)(4), deleted "114 or" after "or under section" in clause (g)(4)(B)(i), effective for transactions after 12/31/2004. Sec. 101(d)-(f) [subsec. (f) was repealed by Sec. 513(b) of P.L. 109-222, see above] of this Act, reads as follows:

"(d) Transitional rule for 2005 and 2006.

"(1) In general. In the case of transactions during 2005 or 2006, the amount includible in gross income by reason of the amendments made by this section shall not exceed the applicable percentage of the amount which would have been so included but for this subsection.

"(2) Applicable percentage. For purposes of paragraph (1), the applicable percentage shall be as follows:

"(A) For 2005, the applicable percentage shall be 20 percent.

"(B) For 2006, the applicable percentage shall be 40 percent.

"(e) Revocation of election to be treated as domestic corporation. If, during the 1-year period beginning on the date of the enactment of this Act, a corporation for which an election is in effect under section 943(e) of the Internal Revenue Code of 1986 revokes such election, no gain or loss shall be recognized with respect to property treated as transferred under clause (ii) of section 943(e)(4)(B) of such Code to the extent such property—

"(1) was treated as transferred under clause (i) thereof, or

"(2) was acquired during a taxable year to which such election applies and before May 1, 2003, in the ordinary course of its trade or business.

The Secretary of the Treasury (or such Secretary's delegate) may prescribe such regulations as may be necessary to prevent the abuse of the purposes of this subsection.

"(f) [Repealed by Sec. 513(b) of P.L. 109-222, see above]

—P.L. 108-357, Sec. 102(b), added clause (g)(4)(C)(v), effective for tax. yrs. begin. after 12/31/2004.

—P.L. 108-357, Sec. 248(b)(1), added 'or 1357' after 'section 139A' in clause (g)(4)(B)(i), effective for tax. yrs. begin. after 10/22/2004.

—P.L. 108-357, Sec. 422(b), added clause (g)(4)(C)(vi), effective for tax. yrs. end. on or after 10/22/2004.

—P.L. 108-357, Sec. 835(b)(1), substituted 'or REMIC' for 'REMIC, or FASIT' in para. (g)(6), effective 1/1/2005, except as provided in Sec. 835(c)(2) of this Act, which reads as follows:

"(2) Exception for existing FASITs. Paragraph (1) shall not apply to any FASIT in existence on the date of the enactment of this Act to the extent that regular interests issued by the FASIT before such date continue to remain outstanding in accordance with the original terms of issuance."

—P.L. 108-311, Sec. 403(b)(3), substituted "after December 31, 1990" for "before January 1, 2003" in Sec. 102(c)(2) of P.L. 107-147, the effective date for amendments made by Sec. 102(c)(1) of P.L. 107-147 [see below].

—P.L. 108-311, Sec. 403(b)(4)(A), deleted "attributable to carryovers" after "other than the deduction" in subclause (d)(1)(A)(i)(I)... Sec. 403(b)(4)(B)(i), substituted "from taxable years" for "for taxable years" in subclause (d)(1)(A)(ii)(I)... Sec. 403(b)(4)(B)(ii), substituted "carryovers" for "carryforwards" in subclause (d)(1)(A)(ii)(I), effective [as amended by Sec. 403(b)(3) of P.L. 108-311, see above] for tax. yrs. end. after 12/13/90 (as provided by Sec. 102(c)(2) of P.L. 107-147).

In 2003, P.L. 108-173, Sec. 1202(b), added "or 139A" after "section 114" in subpara. (g)(4)(B), effective for tax. yrs. end. after 12/8/2003.

In 2002, P.L. 107-147, Sec. 102(c)(1), amended subpara. (d)(1)(A), effective [as amended by Sec. 403(b)(3) of P.L. 108-311, see above] for tax. yrs. end. after 12/13/1990.

Prior to amendment, subpara. (d)(1)(A) read as follows:

"(A) the amount of such deduction shall not exceed 90 percent of alternate minimum taxable income determined without regard to such deduction, and"

—P.L. 107-147, Sec. 417(5), substituted "such section 1250" for "such 1250" in subpara. (a)(1)(A), effective 3/9/2002.

In 2000, P.L. 106-554, Sec. 1(a)(7), [which enacted into law Sec. 314(d) of P.L. 106-554] added "(and the straight line method shall be used for such 1250 property)" after "defined in section 1250(c))" in clause (a)(1)(A)(ii), effective 8/5/97.

—P.L. 106-519, Sec. 4(1), added "or under section 114" after "prior law)" in clause (g)(4)(B)(i), effective for transactions after 9/30/2000. Sec. 5(b)–(d) [para. (c)(1) as amended by Sec. 513(a) of P.L. 109-222, see above] of this Act, provides:

"(b) No new FSCs; termination of inactive FSCs—

"(1) No new FSCs. No corporation may elect after September 30, 2000, to be a FSC (as defined in section 922 of the Internal Revenue Code of 1986, as in effect before the amendments made by this Act).

"(2) Termination of inactive FSCs. If a FSC has no foreign trade income (as defined in section 923(b) of such Code, as so in effect) for any period of 5 consecutive taxable years beginning after December 31, 2001, such FSC shall cease to be treated as a FSC for purposes of such Code for any taxable year beginning after such period.

"(c) Transition period for existing Foreign Sales Corporations.

"(1) In general. In the case of a FSC (as so defined) in existence on September 30, 2000, and at all times thereafter, the amendments made by this Act shall not apply to any transaction in the ordinary course of trade or business involving a FSC which occurs before January 1, 2002.

"(2) Election to have amendments apply earlier. A taxpayer may elect to have the amendments made by this Act apply to any transaction by a FSC or any related person to which such amendments would apply but for the application of paragraph (1). Such election shall be effective for the taxable year for which made and all subsequent taxable years, and, once made, may be revoked only with the consent of the Secretary of the Treasury.

"(3) Exception for old earnings and profits of certain corporations.

"(A) In general. In the case of a foreign corporation to which this paragraph applies—

"(i) earnings and profits of such corporation accumulated in taxable years ending before October 1, 2000, shall not be included in the gross income of the persons holding stock in such corporation by reason of section 943(e)(4)(B)(i), and

"(ii) rules similar to the rules of clauses (ii), (iii), and (iv) of section 953(d)(4)(B) shall apply with respect to such earnings and profits.

The preceding sentence shall not apply to earnings and profits acquired in a transaction after September 30, 2000, to which section 381 applies unless the distributor or transferor corporation was immediately before the transaction a foreign corporation to which this paragraph applies.

"(B) Existing FSCs. This paragraph shall apply to any controlled foreign corporation (as defined in section 957) if—

"(i) such corporation is a FSC (as so defined) in existence on September 30, 2000,

"(ii) such corporation is eligible to make the election under section 943(e) by reason of being described in paragraph (2)(B) of such section, and

"(iii) such corporation makes such election not later than for its first taxable year beginning after December 31, 2001.

"(C) Other corporations. This paragraph shall apply to any controlled foreign corporation (as defined in section 957), and such corporation shall (notwithstanding any provision of section 943(e)) be treated as an applicable foreign corporation for purposes of section 943(e), if—

"(i) such corporation is in existence on September 30, 2000;

"(ii) as of such date, such corporation is wholly owned (directly or indirectly) by a domestic corporation (determined without regard to any election under section 943(e));

"(iii) for each of the 3 taxable years preceding the first taxable year to which the election under section 943(e) by such controlled foreign corporation applies—

# Minimum tax	Code Sec. 56

"(I) all of the gross income of such corporation is subpart F income (as defined in section 952), including by reason of section 954(b)(3)(B); and

"(II) in the ordinary course of such corporation's trade or business, such corporation regularly sold (or paid commissions) to a FSC which on September 30, 2000, was a related person to such corporation;

"(iv) such corporation has never made an election under section 922(a)(2) (as in effect before the date of the enactment of this paragraph) to be treated as a FSC; and

"(v) such corporation makes the election under section 943(e) not later than for its first taxable year beginning after December 31, 2001.

The preceding sentence shall cease to apply as of the date that the domestic corporation referred to in clause (ii) ceases to wholly own (directly or indirectly) such controlled foreign corporation.

"(4) Related person. For purposes of this subsection, the term 'related person' has the meaning given to such term by section 943(b)(3).

"(5) Section references. Except as otherwise expressly provided, any reference in this subsection to a section or other provision shall be considered to be a reference to a section or other provision of the Internal Revenue Code of 1986, as amended by this Act.

"(d) Special rules relating to leasing transactions.

"(1) Sales income. If foreign trade income in connection with the lease or rental of property described in section 927(a)(1)(B) of such Code (as in effect before the amendments made by this Act) is treated as exempt foreign trade income for purposes of section 921(a) of such Code (as so in effect) such property shall be treated as property described in section 941(c)(1)(B) of such Code (as added by this Act) for purposes of applying section 941(c)(2) of such Code (as so added) to any subsequent transaction involving such property to which the amendments made by this Act apply.

"(2) Limitation on use of gross receipts method. If any person computed its foreign trade income from any transaction with respect to any property on the basis of a transfer price determined under the method described in section 925(a)(1) of such Code (as in effect before the amendments made by this Act), then the qualifying foreign trade income (as defined in section 941(a) of such Code, as in effect after such amendment) of such person (or any related person) with respect to any other transaction involving such property (and to which the amendments made by this Act apply) shall be zero."

In 1998, P.L. 105-277, Sec. 4006(c)(2), substituted "section 460(b)(1)" for "section 460(b)(2)" and "section 460(b)(3)" for "section 460(b)(4)" in para. (a)(3), effective 10/21/98.

—P.L. 105-206, Sec. 6005(c)(3), added "on or" before "before" each place it appeared in the heading and text of Sec. 312(d)(2)[sic (e)] of P.L. 105-34, see below.

In 1997, P.L. 105-34, Sec. 312(d)(1), substituted "section 121" for "section 1034" in subpara. (e)(1)(A) and clause (e)(3)(B)(i), effective for sales and exchanges after 5/6/97, except as provided in Secs. 312(d)(2)-(4) [sic (e)(2)-(4)] of this Act [as amended by Sec. 6005(e)(3) of P.L. 105-206, see above], which read as follows:

"(2) Sales on or before date of enactment. At the election of the taxpayer, the amendments made by this section shall not apply to any sale or exchange on or before the date of the enactment of this Act.

"(3) Certain sales within 2 years after date of enactment. Section 121 of the Internal Revenue Code of 1986 (as amended by this section) shall be applied without regard to subsection (c)(2)(B) thereof in the case of any sale or exchange of property during the 2-year period beginning on the date of the enactment of this Act if the taxpayer held such property on the date of the enactment of this Act and fails to meet the ownership and use requirements of subsection (a) thereof with respect to such property.

"(4) Binding contracts. At the election of the taxpayer, the amendments made by this section shall not apply to a sale or exchange after the date of the enactment of this Act, if—

"(A) such sale or exchange is pursuant to a contract which was binding on such date, or

"(B) without regard to such amendments, gain would not be recognized under section 1034 of the Internal Revenue Code of 1986 (as in effect on the day before the date of the enactment of this Act) on such sale or exchange by reason of a new residence acquired on or before such date or with respect to the acquisition of which by the taxpayer a binding contract was in effect on such date.

This paragraph shall not apply to any sale or exchange by an individual if the treatment provided by section 877(a)(1) of the Internal Revenue Code of 1986 applies to such individual."

—P.L. 105-34, Sec. 402(a), added the sentence at the end of clause (g)(1)(A)(i) ... Sec. 402(b), added the sentence at the end of para. (a)(5), effective date of enactment.

—P.L. 105-34, Sec. 403(a), deleted para. (a)(6), and redesignated paras. (a)(7) and (8) as paras. (a)(6) and (7), effective for dispositions in tax. yrs. begin. after 12/31/87, except as provided in Sec. 403(b)(2) of this Act, which reads as follows:

"(2) Special rule for 1987.—In the case of taxable years beginning in 1987, the last sentence of section 56(a)(6) of the Internal Revenue Code of 1986 (as in effect for such taxable years) shall be applied by inserting 'or in the case of a taxpayer using the cash receipts and disbursements method of accounting, any disposition described in section 453C(e)(1)(B)(ii)' after 'section 453C(e)(4).'"

Prior to amendment, para. (a)(6) read as follows:

"(6) Installment sales of certain property.

"In the case of any disposition after March 1, 1986, of any property described in section 1221(1), income from such disposition shall be determined without regard to the installment method under section 453. This paragraph shall not apply to any disposition with respect to which an election is in effect under section 453(1)(2)(B)."

—P.L. 105-34, Sec. 1212(a), added a sentence at the end of clause (g)(4)(B)(i), effective for tax. yrs. begin. after 12/31/97.

In 1996, P.L. 104-188, Sec. 1601(b)(2)(B)(i), added "30A," before "936" in subclause (g)(4)(C)(ii)(I) ... Sec. 1601(b)(2)(B)(ii), substituted ", (i), and (j)" for "and (i)" in subclause (g)(4)(C)(ii)(I) ... Sec. 1601(b)(2)(C), added subclause (g)(4)(C)(iii)(VI), effective for tax. yrs. begin. after 12/31/95.

—P.L. 104-188, Sec. 1601(c)(2)-(3), of this Act provides:

"(2) Special rule for qualified possession source investment income. The amendments made by this section shall not apply to qualified possession source investment income received or accrued before July 1, 1996, without regard to the taxable year in which received or accrued.

"(3) Special transition rule for payment of estimated tax installments. In determining the amount of any installment due under section 6655 of the Internal Revenue Code of 1986 after the date of the enactment of this Act and before October 1, 1996, only ½ of any increase in tax (for the taxable year for which such installment is made) by reason of the amendments made by subsections (a) and (b) shall be taken into account. Any reduction in such installment by reason of the preceding sentence shall be recaptured by increasing the next required installment for such year by the amount of such reduction."

—P.L. 104-188, Sec. 1621(b)(2), substituted "REMIC, or FASIT" for "or REMIC" in para. (g)(6), effective 9/1/97.

—P.L. 104-188, Sec. 1702(c)(1), redesignated subparas. (g)(4)(I) and (J) as subparas. (g)(4)(H) and (I), effective as provided in Sec. 11301(d)(2) of P.L. 101-508, see below.

—P.L. 104-188, Sec. 1702(e)(1)(A), amended clause (d)(1)(B)(ii), effective for tax. yrs. begin. after 12/31/90.

Prior to amendment, clause (d)(1)(B)(ii) read as follows:

"(ii) in the case of taxable years beginning after December 31, 1986, section 172(b)(2) shall be applied by substituting '90 percent of the alternative minimum taxable income determined without regard to the alternative tax net operating loss deduction' for 'taxable income' each place it appears."

—P.L. 104-188, Sec. 1702(e)(1)(B), of this Act provides:

"(B) For purposes of applying sections 56(g)(1) and 56(g)(3) of the Internal Revenue Code of 1986 with respect to taxable years beginning in 1991 and 1992, the reference in such sections to the alternative tax net operating loss deduction shall be treated as including a reference to the deduction under section 56(h) of such Code as in effect before the amendments made by section 1915 of the Energy Policy Act of 1992."

—P.L. 104-188, Sec. 1702(e)(4), added ", but only with respect to taxable years beginning after December 31, 1989" before the period at the end of clause (g)(4)(D)(iii), effective 11/5/90.

—P.L. 104-188, Sec. 1702(h)(12), corrected Sec. 11801(c)(9)(G)(ii) of P.L. 101-508, so that it substituted "Section 422(c)(2)" for "Section 422A(c)(2)" instead of "section 422(c)(2)" for "section 422A(c)(2)", in para. (b)(3), see below, effective as provided in Sec. 11821(b) of P.L. 101-508, see below.

—P.L. 104-188, Sec. 1704(t)(1), substituted "of subclause " for "of the subclause" in subclause (g)(4)(C)(ii)(II) ... Sec. 1704(t)(48), substituted "section 56(g)" for "section 59(g)" in Sec. 11801(c)(2)(B) of P.L. 101-508 [see below], so that the amendments made by Sec. 11801(c)(2)(B) of P.L. 101-508 are made to Code Sec. 56, rather than Code Sec. 59, effective date of enactment.

In 1993, P.L. 103-66, Sec. 13115(a), added a sentence at the end of clause (g)(4)(A)(i), effective for property placed in service after 12/31/93, except as provided in Sec. 13115(b)(2) of this Act, which reads as follows:

"(2) Coordination with transitional rules. The amendments made by this section shall not apply to any property to which paragraph (1) of section 56(a) of the Internal Revenue Code of 1986 does not apply by reason of subparagraph (C)(i) thereof."

—P.L. 103-66, Sec. 13171(b), added subpara. (g)(4)(J), effective for contributions made after 6/30/92, except that in the case of any contribution of capital gain property which is not tangible personal property, such amendments shall apply only if the contribution is made after 12/31/92.

—P.L. 103-66, Sec. 13227(c)(1), substituted "sections 936 (including subsections (a)(4) and (i) thereof) and 921" for "sections 936 and 921" in subclause (g)(4)(C)(ii)(I) ... Sec. 13227(c)(2), added subclauses (g)(4)(C)(iii)(IV) and (V), effective for tax. yrs. begin. after 12/31/93.

In 1992, P.L. 102-486, Sec. 1915(a)(2), amended subpara. (g)(4)(F) ... Sec. 1915(b)(2), added a sentence at the end of clause (g)(4)(D)(i) ... Sec. 1915(c)(1), deleted subsec. (h) ... Sec. 1915(c)(2), amended subpara. (d)(1)(A), effective for tax. yrs. begin. after 12/31/92.

Prior to amendment, subpara. (g)(4)(F) read as follows:

"(F) Depletion. The allowance for depletion with respect to any property placed in service in a taxable year beginning after 1989 shall be cost depletion determined under section 611."

Prior to deletion, subsec. (h) read as follows:

"(h) Adjustment based on energy preferences.

"(1) In general. In computing the alternative minimum taxable income of any taxpayer other than an integrated oil company for any taxable year beginning after 1990, there shall be allowed as a deduction an amount equal to the lesser of—

"(A) the alternative tax energy preference deduction, or

"(B) 40 percent of alternative minimum taxable income.

"(2) Phase-out of deduction as oil prices increase. The amount of the deduction under paragraph (1) (determined without regard to this paragraph) shall be reduced (but not below zero) by the amount which bears the same ratio to such amount as—

1,301

"(A) the excess of the reference price of crude oil for the calendar year preceding the calendar year in which the taxable year begins over $28, bears to
"(B) $6.
For purposes of this paragraph, the reference price for any calendar year shall be determined under section 29(d)(2)(C) and the $28 amount under subparagraph (A) shall be adjusted at the same time and in the same manner as under section 43(b)(3).
"(3) Alternative tax energy preference deduction. For purposes of paragraph (1), the term 'alternative tax energy preference deduction' means an amount equal to the sum of—
"(A) in the case of the intangible drilling cost preference, an amount equal to the sum of—
"(i) 75 percent of the portion of the intangible drilling cost preference attributable to qualified exploratory costs, plus
"(ii) 15 percent of the excess (if any) of—
"(I) the intangible drilling cost preference, over
"(II) the portion of the intangible drilling cost preference attributable to qualified exploratory costs, plus
"(B) 50 percent of the marginal production depletion preference.
"(4) Intangible drilling cost preference. For purposes of this subsection—
"(A) In general. The term 'intangible drilling cost preference' means the amount by which alternative minimum taxable income would be reduced if it were computed without regard to section 57(a)(2) and subsection (g)(4)(D)(i).
"(B) Portion attributable to qualified exploratory costs. For purposes of subparagraph (A), the portion of the intangible drilling cost preference attributable to qualified exploratory costs is an amount which bears the same ratio to the intangible drilling cost preference as—
"(i) the qualified exploratory costs of the taxpayer for the taxable year, bear to
"(ii) the total intangible drilling and development costs with respect to which the taxpayer may make an election under section 263(c) for the taxable year.
"(5) Marginal production depletion preference. For purposes of this subsection, the term 'marginal production depletion preference' means the amount by which alternative minimum taxable income would be reduced if it were computed as if section 57(a)(1) and subsection (g)(4)(G) did not apply to any allowance for depletion determined under section 613A(c)(6).
"(6) Qualified exploratory costs. For purposes of this subsection—
"(A) In general. The term 'qualified exploratory costs' means intangible drilling and development costs of a taxpayer other than an integrated oil company which—
"(i) the taxpayer may elect to deduct as expenses under section 263(c), and
"(ii) are paid or incurred in connection with the drilling of an exploratory well located in the United States (within the meaning of section 638(1)).
"(B) Exploratory well. The term 'exploratory well' means any of the following oil or gas wells:
"(i) An oil or gas well which is completed (or if not completed, with respect to which drilling operations cease) before the completion of any other well which—
"(I) is located within 1.25 miles from the well, and
"(II) is capable of production in commercial quantities.
"(ii) An oil or gas well which is not described in clause (i) but which has a total depth which is at least 800 feet below the deepest completion depth of any well within 1.25 miles which is capable of production in commercial quantities.
"(iii) An oil or gas well capable of production in commercial quantities which is not described in clause (i) or (ii) but which is completed into a new reservoir, except that this clause shall not apply to a gas well if the gas is produced (or to be produced) from Devonian shale, coal seams, or a tight formation (determined in a manner similar to the manner under section 29(c)(2)).
A well shall not be treated as an exploratory well unless the operator submits to the Secretary (at such time and in such manner as the Secretary may provide) a certification from a petroleum engineer that the well is described in one of the preceding clauses.
"(C) Certain costs not included. The term 'qualified exploratory costs' shall not include any cost paid or incurred—
"(i) in constructing, acquiring, transporting, erecting, or installing an offshore platform, or
"(ii) with respect to the drilling of a well from an offshore platform unless it is the first well which penetrates a reservoir.
"(D) Integrated oil company. For purposes of this paragraph, the term 'integrated oil company' means, with respect to any taxable year, any producer of crude oil to whom subsection (c) of section 613A does not apply by reason of paragraph (2) or (4) of section 613A(d).
"(7) Special rules.
"(A) Alternative minimum taxable income. For purposes of paragraphs (1)(B), (4)(A), and (5), alternative minimum taxable income shall be determined without regard to the deduction allowable under this subsection and the alternative tax net operating loss deduction under subsection (a)(4).
"(B) Geothermal deposits. For purposes of this subsection, intangible drilling and development costs shall not include costs with respect to wells drilled for any geothermal deposits (as defined in section 613(e)(3)).
"(8) Regulations. The Secretary may by regulation provide for appropriate adjustments in computing alternative minimum taxable income or adjusted current earnings for any taxable year following a taxable year for which a deduction was allowed under this subsection to ensure that no double benefit is allowed by reason of such deduction.
Prior to amendment, subpara. (d)(1)(A) read as follows:
"(A) the amount of such deduction shall not exceed the excess (if any) of—
"(i) 90 percent of alternative minimum taxable income determined without regard to such deduction and the deduction under subsection (h), over

"(ii) the deduction under subsection (h), and
In 1990, P.L. 101-508, Sec. 11103(b), added subpara. (b)(1)(F), effective for tax. yrs. begin. after 12/31/90.
—P.L. 101-508, Sec. 11301(b), deleted subpara. (g)(4)(F) and redesignated subparas. (g)(4)(G) and (g)(4)(H) as subparas. (g)(4)(F) and (g)(4)(G), effective as provided in Sec. 11301(d)(2) of this Act, which reads as follows:
"(2) Subsection (b).
"(A) In general. The amendment made by subsection (b) shall apply to taxable years beginning on or after September 30, 1990, except that, in the case of a small insurance company, such amendment shall apply to taxable years beginning after December 31, 1989. For purposes of this paragraph, the term 'small insurance company' means any insurance company which meets the requirements of section 806(a)(3) of the Internal Revenue Code of 1986; except that paragraph (2) of section 806(c) of such Code shall not apply.
"(B) Special rules for year which includes September 30, 1990. In the case of any taxable year which includes September 30, 1990, the amount of acquisition expenses which is required to be capitalized under section 56(g)(4)(F) of the Internal Revenue Code of 1986 (as in effect before the amendment made by subsection (b)) by a company which is not a small insurance company shall be the amount which bears the same ratio to the amount which (but for this subparagraph) would be so required to be capitalized as the number of days in such taxable year before September 30, 1990, bears to the total number of days in such taxable year. A similar reduction shall be made in the amount amortized for such taxable year under such section 56(g)(4)(F)."
Prior to deletion, subpara. (g)(4)(F) read as follows:
"(F) Acquisition expenses of life insurance companies. Acquisition expenses of life insurance companies shall be capitalized and amortized in accordance with the treatment generally required under generally accepted accounting principles as if this subparagraph applied to all taxable years."
—P.L. 101-508, Sec. 11531(a), added subsec. (h) . . . Sec. 11531(b)(1), amended subpara. (d)(1)(A), effective for tax. yrs. begin. after 12/31/90.
Prior to amendment, subsec. (d)(1)(A) read as follows:
"(A) the amount of such deduction shall not exceed 90 percent of alternative minimum taxable income determined without regard to such deduction, and"
—P.L. 101-508, Sec. 11704(a)(1), substituted "years" for "year" in clause (g)(4)(D)(ii), effective 11/5/90.
—P.L. 101-508, Sec. 11801(a)(3), deleted subsec. (f) . . . Sec. 11801(c)(2)(A), amended para. (c)(1) . . . Sec. 11801(c)(2)(B), [amended by Sec. 1704(t)(48) of P.L. 104-188, see above] deleted "beginning after 1989" after "taxable year" in (g)(1) and (2) . . . Sec. 11801(c)(2)(C), amended clause (g)(4)(C)(iii) . . . Sec. 11801(c)(9)(G)(i), substituted "section 422" for "section 422A" in para. (b)(3) . . . Sec. 11801(c)(9)(G)(ii), substituted "Section 422(c)(2)" for "Section 422A(c)(2)", in para. (b)(3), [as amended by Sec. 1702(h)(12) of P.L. 104-188, see above] effective 11/5/90 except as provided in Sec. 11821(b) of this Act, which reads as follows:
"(b) Savings provision. If—
"(1) any provision amended or repealed by this part applied to—
"(A) any transaction occurring before the date of the enactment of this Act [11/5/90],
"(B) any property acquired before such date of enactment [11/5/90], or
"(C) any item of income, loss, deduction, or credit taken into account before such date of enactment [11/5/90], and
"(2) the treatment of such transaction, property, or item under such provision would (without regard to the amendments made by this part) affect liability for tax for periods ending after such date of enactment [11/5/90],
nothing in the amendments made by this part shall be construed to affect the treatment of such transaction, property, or item for purposes of determining liability for tax for periods ending after such date of enactment [11/5/90]."
Prior to deletion, subsec. (f) read as follows:
"(f) Adjustments for book income of corporations.
"(1) In general. The alternative minimum taxable income of any corporation for any taxable year beginning in 1987, 1988, or 1989 shall be increased by 50 percent of the amount (if any) by which—
"(A) the adjusted net book income of the corporation, exceeds
"(B) the alternative minimum taxable income for the taxable year (determined without regard to this subsection and the alternative tax net operating loss deduction).
"(2) Adjusted net book income. For purposes of this subsection—
"(A) In general. The term 'adjusted net book income' means the net income or loss of the taxpayer set forth on the taxpayer's applicable financial statement, adjusted as provided in this paragraph.
"(B) Adjustments for certain taxes. The amount determined under subparagraph (A) shall be appropriately adjusted to disregard any Federal income taxes, or income, war profits, or excess profits taxes imposed by any foreign country or possession of the United States, which are directly or indirectly taken into account on the taxpayer's applicable financial statement. The preceding sentence shall not apply to any such taxes (otherwise eligible for the credit provided by section 901 without regard to section 901(j)) imposed by a foreign country or possession of the United States if the taxpayer does not choose to take, to any extent, the benefits of section 901. No adjustment shall be made under this subparagraph for the tax imposed by section 59A.
"(C) Special rules for related corporations.
"(i) Consolidated returns. If the taxpayer files a consolidated return for any taxable year, adjusted net book income for such taxable year shall take into account items on the taxpayer's applicable financial statement which are properly allocable to members of such group included on such return.

Minimum tax Code Sec. 56

"(ii) Treatment of dividends. In the case of any corporation which is not included on a consolidated return with the taxpayer, adjusted net book income shall take into account the earnings of such other corporation only to the extent of the sum of the dividends received from such other corporation and other amounts required to be included in gross income under this chapter in respect of the earnings of such other corporation.

"(D) Statements covering different periods. Appropriate adjustments shall be made in adjusted net book income in any case in which an applicable financial statement covers a period other than the taxable year.

"(E) Special rule for cooperatives. In the case of a cooperative to which section 1381 applies, the amount determined under subparagraph (A) shall be reduced by the amounts referred to in section 1382(b) (relating to patronage dividends and per-unit retain allocations) to the extent such amounts were not otherwise taken into account in determining adjusted net book income.

"(F) Treatment of taxes on dividends from 936 corporations.

"(i) In general. For purposes of determining the alternative minimum tax foreign tax credit, 50 percent of any withholding tax or income tax paid to a possession of the United States with respect to dividends received from a corporation eligible for the credit provided by section 936 shall be treated as a tax paid to a foreign country by the corporation receiving the dividend.

"(ii) Limitation. If the aggregate amount of the dividends referred to in clause (i) for any taxable year exceeds the excess referred to in paragraph (1), the amount treated as a tax paid to a foreign country under clause (i) shall not exceed the amount which would be so treated without regard to this clause multiplied by a fraction—

"(I) the numerator of which is the excess referred to in paragraph (1), and

"(II) the denominator of which is the aggregate amount of such dividends.

"(iii) Treatment of taxes imposed on 936 corporation. For purposes of this subparagraph, taxes paid by any corporation eligible for the credit provided by section 936 to a possession of the United States shall be treated as a withholding tax paid with respect to any dividend paid by such corporation to the extent such taxes would be treated as paid by the corporation receiving the dividend under rules similar to the rules of section 902 (and the amount of any such dividend shall be increased by the amount so treated).

"(G) Rules for Alaska native corporations. The amount determined under subparagraph (A) shall be appropriately adjusted to allow:

"(i) cost recovery and depletion attributable to property the basis of which is determined under section 21(c) of the Alaska Native Claims Settlement Act (43 U.S.C. 1620(c)), and

"(ii) deductions for amounts payable made pursuant to section 7(i) or section 7(j) of such Act (43 U.S.C. 1606(i) and 1606(j)) only at such time as the deductions are allowed for tax purposes.

"(H) Special rules for life insurance companies.

"(i) Policyholder dividends of mutual companies. In determining the adjusted net book income of any mutual life insurance company, a reduction shall be allowed for policyholder dividends with respect to any taxable year only to the extent such dividends exceed the differential earnings amount determined for such taxable year under section 809.

"(ii) Other adjustments. To the extent provided by the Secretary, such additional adjustments shall be made as may be necessary to make the calculation of adjusted net book income in the case of any life insurance company consistent with the calculation of adjusted net book income generally.

"(I) Exclusion of certain income from transfer of stock for debt. In determining adjusted net book income, there shall not be taken into account any income resulting from the transfer of stock by the corporation issuing such stock to a creditor in satisfaction of its indebtedness. The preceding sentence shall apply only in the case of a debtor in a title 11 case (as defined in section 108(d)(2)) or to the extent the debtor is insolvent (as defined in section 108(d)(3)).

"(J) Secretarial authority to adjust items. Under regulations, adjusted net book income shall be properly adjusted to prevent the omission or duplication of any item.

"(3) Applicable financial statement. For purposes of this subsection—

"(A) In general. The term 'applicable financial statement' means, with respect to any taxable year, any statement covering such taxable year—

"(i) which is required to be filed with the Securities and Exchange Commission,

"(ii) which is a certified audited income statement to be used for the purposes of a statement or report—

"(I) for credit purposes,

"(II) to shareholders, or

"(III) for any other substantial nontax purpose,

"(iii) which is an income statement for a substantial nontax purpose required to be provided to—

"(I) the Federal Government or any agency thereof,

"(II) a State government or any agency thereof, or

"(III) a political subdivision of a State or any agency thereof, or

"(iv) which is an income statement to be used for the purposes of a statement or report—

"(I) for credit purposes,

"(II) to shareholders, or

"(III) for any other substantial nontax purpose.

"(B) Earnings and profits used in certain cases. If—

"(i) a taxpayer has no applicable financial statement, or

"(ii) a taxpayer has only a statement described in subparagraph (A)(iv) and the taxpayer elects the application of this subparagraph,

"the net income or loss set forth on the taxpayer's applicable financial statement shall, for purposes of this subsection, be treated as being equal to the taxpayer's earnings and profits for the taxable year (without diminution by reason of distributions during the tax year). Such election, once made, shall remain in effect for any taxable year for which the taxpayer is described in this subparagraph unless revoked with the consent of the Secretary.

"(C) Special rule where more than 1 statement. For purposes of subparagraph (A), if a taxpayer has a statement described in more than 1 clause or subclause, the applicable financial statement shall be the statement described in the clause or subclause with the lowest number designation. If the taxpayer has 2 or more statements described in the clause (or subclause) with the lowest number designation, the applicable financial statement shall be the one of such statements specified in regulations.

"(4) Exception for certain corporations. This subsection shall not apply to any S corporation, regulated investment company, real estate investment trust, or REMIC."

Prior to amendment, para. (c)(1) read as follows:

"(1) Adjustment for book income or adjusted current earnings.

"(A) Book income adjustment. For taxable years beginning in 1987, 1988, and 1989, alternative minimum taxable income shall be adjusted as provided under subsection (f).

"(B) Adjusted current earnings. For taxable years beginning after 1989, alternative minimum taxable income shall be adjusted as provided under subsection (g)."

Prior to amendment, clause (g)(4)(C)(iii) read as follows:

"(iii) Special rule for dividends from section 936 companies. In the case of any dividend received from a corporation eligible for the credit provided by section 936, rules similar to the rules of subparagraph (F) of subsection (f)(1) shall apply, except that '75 percent' shall be substituted for '50 percent' in clause (i) thereof."

—P.L. 101-508, Sec. 11812(b)(4), substituted "section 168(i)(10)" for "section 167(1)(3)(A)" in subpara. (a)(1)(D), effective for property placed in service after 11/5/90 except as provided in Sec. 11812(c)(2) and (c)(3) of this Act, which reads as follows:

"(2) Exception. The amendments made by this section shall not apply to any property to which section 168 of the Internal Revenue Code of 1986 does not apply by reason of subsection (f)(5) thereof.

"(3) Exception for previously grandfather expenditures. The amendments made by this section shall not apply to rehabilitation expenditures described in section 252(f)(5) of the Tax Reform Act of 1986 (as added by section 1002(1)(31) of the Technical and Miscellaneous Revenue Act of 1988)."

In 1989, P.L. 101-239, Sec. 7205(b), amended clause (g)(4)(H)(ii), effective for ownership changes and acquisitions after 10/2/89, in tax. yrs. end. after 10/2/89, except as provided in Sec. 7205(c)(2)-(4) of this Act which reads as follows:

"(2) Binding contract.—The amendments made by this section shall not apply to any ownership change or acquisition pursuant to a written binding contract in effect on October 2, 1989, and at all times thereafter before such change or acquisition.

"(3) Bankruptcy proceedings.—In the case of a reorganization described in section 368(a)(1)(G) of the Internal Revenue Code of 1986, or an exchange of debt for stock in a title 11 or similar case (as defined in section 368(a)(3) of such Code), the amendments made by this section shall not apply to any ownership change resulting from such a reorganization or proceeding if a petition in such case was filed with the court before October 3, 1989.

"(4) Subsidiaries of bankrupt parent.—The amendments made by this section shall not apply to any built-in loss of a corporation which is a member (on October 2, 1989) of an affiliated group the common parent of which (on such date) was subject to title 11 or similar case (as defined in section 368(a)(3) of such Code). The preceding sentence shall apply only if the ownership change or acquisition is pursuant to the plan approved in such proceeding and is before the date 2 years after the date on which the petition which commenced such proceeding was filed."

Prior to amendment, clause (g)(4)(H)(ii) read as follows:

"(ii)(I) the aggregate adjusted bases of the assets of such corporation (immediately after the change), exceed

"(II) the value of the stock of such corporation (as determined for purposes of section 382), properly adjusted for liabilities and other relevant items, then the adjusted basis of each asset of such corporation (as of such time) shall be its proportionate share (determined on the basis of respective fair market values) of the amount referred to in clause (ii)(II)."

—P.L. 101-239, Sec. 7611(a)(1)(A), amended clause (g)(4)(A)(i) ... Sec. 7611(a)(1)(B), deleted clauses (g)(4)(A)(v) and (vi) and redesignated clause (g)(4)(A)(vii) as clause (g)(4)(A)(v) ... Sec. 7611(a)(2), added "and which is placed in service in a taxable year beginning before 1990" after "thereof) applies" in clause (g)(4)(A)(iii) ... Sec. 7611(b), amended subpara. (g)(4)(D) [as amended by Sec. 7815(e)(4) of this Act, see below] ... Sec. 7611(c), amended subpara. (g)(4)(G) ... Sec. 7611(d), amended clause (g)(4)(C)(ii) ... Sec. 7611(e), added clause (g)(4)(C)(iv) ... Sec. 7611(f)(1), substituted "in a taxable year beginning after 1989" for "after the date of the enactment of the Tax Reform Act of 1986" in clause (g)(4)(H)(i) ... Sec. 7611(f)(2), added the last sentence to clause (g)(4)(B)(i) ... Sec. 7611(f)(3), deleted clause (g)(4)(B)(iii) ... Sec. 7611(f)(4), deleted subparas. (g)(5)(A) and (C) and redesignated subparas. (g)(5)(B) and (D) as subparas. (g)(5)(A) and (B), effective for tax. yrs. begin. after 12/31/89.

Prior to amendment, clause (g)(4)(A)(i) read as follows:

"(i) Property placed in service after 1989. The depreciation deduction with respect to any property placed in service in a taxable year beginning after 1989 shall be determined under whichever of the following methods yields deductions with a smaller present value:

"(I) The alternative system of section 168(g), or

"(II) The method used for book purposes."

Prior to deletion, clauses (g)(4)(A)(v) and (vi) read as follows:

"(v) Slower method used if used for book purposes. In the case of any property to which clause (ii), (iii), or (iv) applies, if the depreciation method used for book purposes yields deductions for taxable years beginning after 1989 with a smaller present value than the method which would otherwise be used under such clause, the method used for book purposes shall be used in lieu of the method which would otherwise be used under such clause.

"(vi) Election to have cumulative limitation.

"(I) In general. In the case of any property placed in service during a taxable year to which an election under this clause applies, in lieu of applying clause (i), the depreciation deduction for such property for any taxable year shall be the lesser of the accumulated 168(g) depreciation or the accumulated book depreciation; reduced by the aggregate amount of the depreciation deductions determined under this subclause with respect to such property for prior taxable years.

"(II) Accumulated 168(g) depreciation. For purposes of this clause, the term 'accumulated section 168(g) depreciation' means the aggregate amount of the depreciation deductions determined under the alternative system of section 168(g) with respect to the property for all periods before the close of the taxable year.

"(III) Accumulated book depreciation. For purposes of this clause, the term 'accumulated book depreciation' means the aggregate amount of the depreciation deductions determined under the method used for book purposes with respect to the property for all periods before the close of the taxable year.

"(IV) Election. The taxpayer may make an election under this clause for any taxable year beginning after 1989. Such an election, once made with respect to any such taxable year, shall apply to all property placed in service during such taxable year, and shall be irrevocable.

"(V) Similar rules for property described in clause (i), (iii), or (iv). Rules similar to the rules of the preceding provisions of this clause shall also apply in the case of property to which clause (ii), (iii), or (iv) applies."

Prior to amendment, subpara. (g)(4)(D), as amended by Sec. 7815(e)(4) of this Act, see below, read as follows:

"(D) Certain other earnings and profits adjustments.

"(i) In general. The adjustments provided in section 312(n) shall apply; except that—

"(I) paragraphs (1), (2), and (3) shall apply only to amounts paid or incurred in taxable years beginning after December 31, 1989,

"(II) paragraph (4) shall apply only to taxable years beginning after December 31, 1989,

"(III) paragraph (5) shall apply only to installment sales in taxable years beginning after December 31, 1989, and

"(IV) paragraphs (6), (7), and (8) shall not apply.

"(ii) Special rule for intangible drilling costs and mineral exploration and development costs. If—

"(I) the present value of the deductions provided under subparagraph (A)(ii) or (B)(ii) of section 312(n)(2) with respect to amounts paid or incurred in taxable years beginning after December 31, 1989, exceeds

"(II) the present value of the deductions for such amounts under the method used for book purposes,

such amounts shall be deductible under the method used for book purposes in lieu of that provided in such subparagraph."

Prior to amendment subpara. (g)(4)(G) read as follows:

"(G) Depletion. The allowances for depletion with respect to any property placed in service in a taxable year beginning after 1989, shall be determined under whichever of the following methods yields deductions with a smaller present value:

"(i) cost depletion determined under section 611, or

"(ii) the method used for book purposes."

Prior to amendment, clause (g)(4)(C)(ii) read as follows:

"(ii) Special rule for 100-percent dividends. Clause (i) shall not apply to any deduction allowable under section 243 or 245 for a 100-percent dividend—

"(I) if the corporation receiving such dividend and the corporation paying such dividend could not be members of the same affiliated group under section 1504 by reason of section 1504(b),

"(II) but only to the extent such dividend is attributable to income of the paying corporation which is subject to tax under this chapter (determined after the application of sections 936 and 921).

For purposes of the preceding sentence, the term '100 percent dividend' means any dividend if the percentage used for purposes of determining the amount allowable as a deduction under section 243 or 245 with respect to such dividend is 100 percent."

Prior to deletion, clause (g)(4)(B)(iii) read as follows:

"(iii) Inclusion of income on annuity contract. In the case of any annuity contract, the income on such contract (as determined under section 72(u)(2)) shall be treated as includible in gross income for such year. The preceding sentence shall not apply to any annuity contract which is held under a plan described in section 403(a) or which is described in section 72(u)(3)(C)."

Prior to deletion, subparas. (g)(5)(A) and (C) read as follows:

"(A) Book purposes. The term 'book purposes' means the treatment for purposes of preparing the applicable financial statement referred to in subsection (f).

* * *

"(C) Present value. Present value shall be determined as of the time the property is placed in service (or, if later, as of the beginning of the first taxable year beginning after 1989) and under regulations prescribed by the Secretary."

—P.L. 101-239, Sec. 7611(g)(3), of this Act provides:

"(3) Regulations on earnings and profits rules. Not later than March 15, 1991, the Secretary of the Treasury or his delegate shall prescribe initial regulations providing guidance as to which items of income are included in adjusted current earnings under section 56(g)(4)(B)(i) of the Internal Revenue Code of 1986 and which items of deduction are disallowed under section 56(g)(4)(C) of such Code."

—P.L. 101-239, Sec. 7612(c)(1), deleted "with respect to which the requirements of clauses (i) and (ii) of section 460(e)(1)(B) are met" which followed "(as defined in section 460(e)(6))" in para. (a)(3) [as amended by Sec. 7815(e)(2)(B) of this Act, see below] effective for contracts entered into in tax. yrs. begin. after 9/30/90.

—P.L. 101-239, Sec. 7612(d)(1), added subpara. (b)(2)(D), effective for tax. yrs. begin. after 12/31/90.

—P.L. 101-239, Sec. 7811(d)(3)(A), added the second sentence in para. (b)(3) . . . Sec. 7811(d)(3)(B), substituted "this paragraph" for "the preceding sentence" in para. (b)(3), effective for tax. yrs. begin. after 12/31/86, except as provided in Sec. 701(f)(2), (3) and (5) of P.L. 99-514, reproduced below.

—P.L. 101-239, Sec. 7815(e)(2)(B), substituted "The first sentence of this paragraph shall not" for "The preceding sentence shall not" in para. (a)(3) . . . Sec. 7815(e)(4), added "and" at the end of subclause (g)(4)(D)(i)(III), deleted subclauses (g)(4)(D)(i)(IV) and (V) and added subclause (g)(4)(D)(i)(IV) [amendments made to clause (g)(4)(D)(i) prior to amendments made by Sec. 7611(b) of this Act, see above] effective as provided by Sec. 5041(e)(1) of P.L. 100-647, reproduced below.

Prior to deletion, subclauses (g)(4)(D)(i)(IV) and (V) read as follows:

"(IV) paragraph (6) shall apply only to contracts entered into on or after March 1, 1986, and

"(V) paragraph (7) and (8) shall not apply."

—P.L. 101-239, Sec. 7815(e)(3), amended Sec. 5041(e)(1)(C) of P.L. 100-647 [reproduced below], the effective date for changes made by Sec. 5041(b)(4) of P.L. 100-647, by substituting "subsections (a) and (b)" for "subsections (a), (b), and (c)", see below.

—P.L. 101-239, Sec. 7821(a)(5), provides:

"(5) In the case of taxable years beginning in 1987, the reference to section 453 contained in section 56(a)(6) of the Internal Revenue Code of 1986 shall be treated as including a reference to section 453A."

In 1988, P.L. 100-647, Sec. 1002(a)(12), substituted "do not apply by reason of section 203, 204, or 251(d) of such Act" for "do not apply" in clause (a)(1)(C)(i), effective for property placed in service after 12/31/86, in tax. yrs. end. after 12/31/86, except as provided in Sec. 203(a)(1)(B) through 203(e) of P.L. 99-514 reproduced in note following Code Sec. 168.

—P.L. 100-647, Sec. 1007(b)(1), added "For purposes of the preceding sentence, in the case of a contract described in section 460(e)(1), the percentage of the contract completed shall be determined under section 460(b)(2) by using the simplified procedures for allocation of costs prescribed under section 460(b)(4)" at the end of para. (a)(3) . . . Sec. 1007(b)(2), amended subpara. (b)(1)(E) . . . Sec. 1007(b)(3), deleted "and" at the end of clause (b)(1)(C)(ii), substituted a comma for the period at the end of clause (b)(1)(C)(iii), and added clauses (b)(1)(C)(iv) and (b)(1)(C)(v) . . . Sec. 1007(b)(4)(A), substituted "specified private activity bond" for "specified activity bond" in clause (b)(1)(C)(iii) . . . Sec. 1007(b)(4)(B), substituted "section 57(a)(5)(B)" for "section 56(a)(5)(B)" in clause (b)(1)(C)(iii) . . . Sec. 1007(b)(5)(A), deleted "(other than subsection (a)(6) thereof)" after "for such year" in clause (d)(2)(A)(ii) . . . Sec. 1007(b)(5)(B), added "An item of tax preference shall be taken into account under clause (ii) only to the extent such item increased the amount of the net operating loss for the taxable year under section 172(c)." at the end of subpara. (d)(2)(A) . . . Sec. 1007(b)(6)(A)(i), substituted "interest which is qualified residence interest (as defined in section 163(h)(3))" for "interest which is" in para. (e)(1) . . . Sec. 1007(b)(6)(A)(ii), substituted "section 163(h)(4)" for "section 163(h)(3)" in para. (e)(1) . . . Sec. 1007(b)(6)(B), substituted "interest which is qualified residence interest (as defined in section 163(h)(3)) and is paid or accrued" for "interest paid or accrued" in para. (e)(3) . . . Sec. 1007(b)(7), substituted "any such taxes (otherwise eligible for the credit provided by section 901 without regard to section 901(j))" for "any such taxes" in subpara. (f)(2)(B) . . . Sec. 1007(b)(8), substituted "an income statement for a substantial nontax purpose" for "an income statement" in clause (f)(3)(A)(iii) . . . Sec. 1007(b)(9), substituted "this subsection" for "paragraph (3)(A)" in subpara. (f)(3)(B) . . . Sec. 1007(b)(10), added the last sentence of subpara. (f)(3)(C) . . . Sec. 1007(b)(11)(A), amended subpara. (f)(2)(F) . . . Sec. 1007(b)(11)(B), substituted "clause (i)" for "clause (ii)(I)" in clause (g)(4)(C)(iii) . . . Sec. 1007(b)(12), added the last sentence of clause (g)(4)(B)(iii) (later amended by Sec. 6079(a)(1) of this Act, see below) . . . Sec. 1007(b)(13)(A), substituted "adjusted current earnings" for "adjusted earnings and profits" in the heading of para. (c)(1) . . . Sec. 1007(b)(13)(B), substituted "adjusted current earnings" for "adjusted earnings and profits" in the heading of subpara. (c)(1)(B), effective for tax. yrs. begin. after 12/31/86, except as provided in Sec. 701(f)(2), (3) and (5) of P.L. 99-514, reproduced below.

—P.L. 100-647, Sec. 1007(b)(14)(A), added para. (b)(3), effective for options exercised after 12/31/87.

—P.L. 100-647, Sec. 1007(b)(15), substituted "personal" for "real" in the heading of clause (a)(1)(A)(i) . . . Sec. 1007(b)(16), deleted "itemized" from before "deductions" in the heading of para. (b)(1) . . . Sec. 1007(b)(17), added clauses (g)(4)(A)(vi) and (g)(4)(A)(vii) . . . Sec. 1007(b)(18), added subpara. (g)(4)(I) . . . Sec. 1007(b)(19), added para. (a)(8), effective for tax. yrs. begin. after 12/31/86, except as provided in Sec. 701(e)(2), (3) and (5) of P.L. 99-514, reproduced below.

Prior to amendment, subpara. (b)(1)(E) read as follows:

"(E) Standard deduction not allowed. The standard deduction provided in section 63(c) shall not be allowed."

Prior to amendment, subpara. (f)(2)(F) read as follows:

"(F) Treatment of dividends from 936 corporations.

"(i) In general. In determining the amount of adjusted net book income, any dividend received from a corporation eligible for the credit provided by section 936 shall be increased by the amount of any withholding tax paid to a possession of the United States with respect to such dividend.

"(ii) Treatment as foreign taxes.

"(I) In general. 50 percent of any withholding tax paid to a possession of the United States with respect to dividends referred to in clause (i) (to the extent such dividends do not exceed the excess referred to in paragraph (1), determined without regard to clause (ii)) shall, for purposes of this part, be treated as a tax paid by the corporation receiving the dividend to a foreign country.

"(II) Treatment of taxes imposed on 936 corporation. For purposes of this subparagraph, taxes paid by any corporation eligible for the credit provided by section 936 to a possession of the United States, shall be treated as a withholding tax paid with respect to any dividend paid by such corporation to the extent such taxes would be treated as paid by the corporation receiving the dividend under rules similar to the rules of section 902."

—P.L. 100-647, Sec. 2001(c)(3)(A), added the last sentence of subpara. (f)(2)(B), effective for tax yrs. begin. after 12/31/86.

—P.L. 100-647, Sec. 2004(b)(2), substituted "163(h)(5)" for "163(h)(6)" in clause (b)(1)(C)(ii) . . . Sec. 2004(b)(3)(A), substituted "substantially improving" for "substantially rehabilitating" in para. (e)(1) . . . Sec. 2004(b)(3)(B), deleted "or is paid" after "interest accrues" in subpara. (e)(1)(A), effective for tax yrs. begin. after 12/31/86.

—P.L. 100-647, Sec. 5041(b)(4), added the last sentence to para. (a)(3), effective as provided by Sec. 5041(e)(1) [as amended by Sec. 7815(e)(3) of P.L. 101-239, see above] which reads as follows:

"(1) Subsections (a), (b), and (c).—

"(A) In general.—Except as otherwise provided in this paragraph, the amendments made by subsections (a), (b), and (c) shall apply to contracts entered into on or after June 21, 1988.

"(B) Binding bids.—The amendments made by subsections (a), (b), and (c) shall not apply to any contract resulting from the acceptance of a bid made before June 21, 1988. The preceding sentence shall apply only if the bid could not have been revoked or altered at any time on or after June 21, 1988.

"(C) Special rule for certain ship contracts.—The amendments made by subsections (a) and (b) shall not apply in the case of a qualified ship contract (as defined in section 10203(b)(2)(B) of the Revenue Act of 1987)."

—P.L. 100-647, Sec. 6079(a)(1), amended the last sentence of clause (g)(4)(B)(iii) (as added by Sec. 1007(b)(12) of this Act), effective for tax yrs. begin. after 12/31/86, except as provided in Sec. 701(f)(2), (3) and (5) of P.L. 99-514, reproduced below.

Prior to amendment, the last sentence of clause (g)(4)(B)(iii) read as follows: "The preceding sentence shall not apply to any annuity contract held under a plan described in section 403(a)."

—P.L. 100-647, Sec. 6303(a), redesignated subpara. (f)(2)(I) as subpara. (f)(2)(J) and added new subpara. (f)(2)(I), effective for tax. yrs. begin. after 12/31/86, except as provided in Sec. 701(f)(2), (3) and (5) of P.L. 99-514, reproduced below.

In 1987, P.L. 100-203, Sec. 10202(d), amended para. (a)(6), effective for dispositions in tax. yrs. begin. after 12/31/86.

Prior to amendment, para. (a)(6) read as follows:

"(6) Installment sales of certain property. In the case of any—

"(A) disposition after March 1, 1986, of property described in section 1221(1), or

"(B) other disposition if an obligation arising from such disposition would be an applicable installment obligation (as defined in section 453C(e)) to which section 453C applies,

income from such disposition shall be determined without regard to the installment method under section 453 or 453A and all payments to be received for the disposition shall be deemed received in the taxable year of the disposition. This paragraph shall not apply to any disposition with respect to which an election is in effect under section 453C(e)(4)."

—P.L. 100-203, Sec. 10243(a), redesignated subpara. (f)(2)(H) as (f)(2)(I) and added new subpara. (f)(2)(H), effective for tax. yrs. begin. after 12/31/87.

In 1986, P.L. 99-514, Sec. 701(a), added Code Sec. 56, as part of the amendments to Part VI of subchapter A of chapter 1, effective for tax. yrs. begin. after 12/31/86. Sec. 701(f)(2), (3) and (5) of this Act provides:

"(2) Adjustment of net operating loss.

"(A) Individuals.—In the case of a net operating loss of an individual for a taxable year beginning after December 31, 1982, and before January 1, 1987, for purposes of determining the amount of such loss which may be carried to a taxable year beginning after December 31, 1986, for purposes of the minimum tax, such loss shall be adjusted in the manner provided in section 55(d)(2) of the Internal Revenue Code of 1954 as in effect on the day before the date of the enactment of this Act.

"(B) Corporations.—If the minimum tax of a corporation was deferred under section 56(b) of the Internal Revenue Code of 1954 (as in effect on the day before the date of the enactment of this Act) for any taxable year beginning before January 1, 1987, and the amount of such tax has not been paid for any taxable year beginning before January 1, 1987, the amount of the net operating loss carryovers of such corporation which may be carried to taxable years beginning after December 31, 1986, for purposes of the minimum tax shall be reduced by the amount of tax preferences a tax on which was so deferred.

"(3) Installment sales.—Section 56(a)(6) of the Internal Revenue Code of 1986 (as amended by this section) shall not apply to any disposition to which the amendments made by section 811 of this Act (relating to allocation of dealer's indebtedness to installment obligations) do not apply by reason of section 811(c)(2) of this Act.

* * *

"(5) Book income.

"(A) In general.—In the case of a corporation to which this paragraph applies, the amount of any increase for any taxable year under section 56(c)(1)(A) of the Internal Revenue Code of 1986 (as added by this section) shall be reduced (but not below zero) by the excess (if any) of—

"(i) 50 percent of the excess of taxable income for the 5-taxable year period ending with the taxable year preceding the 1st taxable year to which such section applies over the adjusted net book income for such period, over

"(ii) the aggregate amounts taken into account under this paragraph for preceding taxable years.

"(B) Taxpayer to whom paragraph applies.—This paragraph applies to a taxpayer which was incorporated in Delaware on May 31, 1912.

"(C) Terms.—Any term used in this paragraph which is used in section 56 of such Code (as so added) shall have the same meaning as when used in such section."

Sec. 57. Items of tax preference.

(a) General rule.

For purposes of this part, the items of tax preference determined under this section are—

(1) Depletion. With respect to each property (as defined in section 614), the excess of the deduction for depletion allowable under section 611 for the taxable year over the adjusted basis of the property at the end of the taxable year (determined without regard to the depletion deduction for the taxable year). Effective with respect to taxable years beginning after December 31, 1992, this paragraph shall not apply to any deduction for depletion computed in accordance with section 613A(c).

(2) Intangible drilling costs.

(A) In general. With respect to all oil, gas, and geothermal properties of the taxpayer, the amount (if any) by which the amount of the excess intangible drilling costs arising in the taxable year is greater than 65 percent of the net income of the taxpayer from oil, gas, and geothermal properties for the taxable year.

(B) Excess intangible drilling costs. For purposes of subparagraph (A), the amount of the excess intangible drilling costs arising in the taxable year is the excess of—

(i) the intangible drilling and development costs paid or incurred in connection with oil, gas, and geothermal wells (other than costs incurred in drilling a nonproductive well) allowable under section 263(c) or 291(b) for the taxable year, over

(ii) the amount which would have been allowable for the taxable year if such costs had been capitalized and straight line recovery of intangibles (as defined in subsection (b)) had been used with respect to such costs.

(C) Net income from oil, gas, and geothermal properties. For purposes of subparagraph (A), the amount of the net income of the taxpayer from oil, gas, and geothermal properties for the taxable year is the excess of—

(i) the aggregate amount of gross income (within the meaning of section 613(a)) from all oil, gas, and geothermal properties of the taxpayer received or accrued by the taxpayer during the taxable year, over

(ii) the amount of any deductions allocable to such properties reduced by the excess described in subparagraph (B) for such taxable year.

(D) Paragraph applied separately with respect to geothermal properties and oil and gas properties. This paragraph shall be applied separately with respect to—

(i) all oil and gas properties which are not described in clause (ii), and

(ii) all properties which are geothermal deposits (as defined in section 613(e)(2)).

(E) Exception for independent producers. In the case of any oil or gas well—

(i) In general. In the case of any taxable year beginning after December 31, 1992, this paragraph shall not apply to any taxpayer which is not an integrated oil company (as defined in section 291(b)(4)).

(ii) Limitation on benefit. The reduction in alternative minimum taxable income by reason of clause (i) for any taxable year shall not exceed 40 percent (30 percent in case of taxable years beginning in 1993) of the alternative minimum taxable income for such year determined without regard to clause (i) and the alternative tax net operating loss deduction under section 56(a)(4).

(3) Repealed.
(4) Repealed.
(5) Tax-exempt interest.

(A) In general. Interest on specified private activity bonds reduced by any deduction (not allowable in computing the regular tax) which would have been allowable if such interest were includible in gross income.

(B) Treatment of exempt-interest dividends. Under regulations prescribed by the Secretary, any exempt-interest dividend (as defined in section 852(b)(5)(A)) shall be treated as interest on a specified private activity bond to the extent of its proportionate share of the interest on such bonds received by the company paying such dividend.

(C) Specified private activity bonds.

(i) In general. For purposes of this part, the term "specified private activity bond" means any private activity bond (as defined in section 141) which is issued after August 7, 1986, and the interest on which is not includible in gross income under section 103.

(ii) Exception for qualified 501(c)(3) bonds. For purposes of clause (i), the term "private activity bond" shall not include any qualified 501(c)(3) bond (as defined in section 145).

(iii) Exception for certain housing bonds. For purposes of clause (i), the term "private activity bond" shall not include any bond issued after the date of the enactment of this clause if such bond is—

(I) an exempt facility bond issued as part of an issue 95 percent or more of the net proceeds of which are to be used to provide qualified residential rental projects (as defined in section 142(d)),

(II) a qualified mortgage bond (as defined in section 143(a)), or

(III) a qualified veterans' mortgage bond (as defined in section 143(b)).

The preceding sentence shall not apply to any refunding bond unless such preceding sentence applied to the refunded bond (or in the case of a series of refundings, the original bond).

(iv) Exception for refundings. For purposes of clause (i), the term "private activity bond" shall not include any refunding bond (whether a current or advance refunding) if the refunded bond (or in the case of a series of refundings, the original bond) was issued before August 8, 1986.

(v) Certain bonds issued before September 1, 1986. For purposes of this subparagraph, a bond issued before September 1, 1986, shall be treated as issued before August 8, 1986, unless such bond would be a private activity bond if—

(I) paragraphs (1) and (2) of section 141(b) were applied by substituting "25 percent" for "10 percent" each place it appears,

(II) paragraphs (3), (4), and (5) of section 141(b) did not apply, and

(III) subparagraph (B) of section 141(c)(1) did not apply.

(vi) Exception for bonds issued in 2009 and 2010.

(I) In general. For purposes of clause (i), the term "private activity bond" shall not include any bond issued after December 31, 2008, and before January 1, 2011.

(II) Treatment of refunding bonds. For purposes of subclause (I), a refunding bond (whether a current or advance refunding) shall be treated as issued on the date of the issuance of the refunded bond (or in the case of a series of refundings, the original bond).

(III) Exception for certain refunding bonds. Subclause (II) shall not apply to any refunding bond which is issued to refund any bond which was issued after December 31, 2003, and before January 1, 2009.

(6) Accelerated depreciation or amortization on certain property placed in service before January 1, 1987. The amounts which would be treated as items of tax preference with respect to the taxpayer under paragraphs (2), (3), (4), and (12) of this subsection (as in effect on the day before the date of the enactment [10/22/86] of the Tax Reform Act of 1986). The preceding sentence shall not apply to any property to which section 56(a)(1) or (5) applies.

> • *Caution:* Code Sec. 57(a)(7), following, was amended by Sec. 301(b)(3), P.L. 108-27. These provisions generally sunset for tax years beginning after 12/31/2012. For specific sunset provisions see Sec. 303, P.L. 108-27, as amended by Sec. 102(a), P.L. 111-312, reproduced in history notes for this Code Sec.

(7) Exclusion for gains on sale of certain small business stock. An amount equal to 7 percent of the amount excluded from gross income for the taxable year under section 1202.

(b) Straight line recovery of intangibles defined.

For purposes of paragraph (2) of subsection (a)—

(1) In general. The term "straight line recovery of intangibles", when used with respect to intangible drilling and development costs for any well, means (except in the case of an election under paragraph (2)) ratable amortization of such costs over the 120-month period beginning with the month in which production from such well begins.

(2) Election. If the taxpayer elects with respect to the intangible drilling and development costs for any well, the term "straight line recovery of intangibles" means any method which would be permitted for purposes of determining cost depletion with respect to such well and which is selected by the taxpayer for purposes of subsection (a)(2).

In 2010, P.L. 111-312, Sec. 102(a), substituted "December 31, 2012" for "December 31, 2010" in Sec. 303 of P.L. 108-27 [see below], effective as if included in the enactment of the Jobs and Growth Tax Relief Act of 2003, P.L. 108-27, 5/28/2003.

In 2009, P.L. 111-5, Sec. 1503(a), added clause (a)(5)(C)(vi), effective for obligations issued after 12/31/2008.

In 2008, P.L. 110-289, Sec. 3022(a)(1), redesignated clauses (a)(5)(C)(iii) and (iv) as clauses (a)(5)(C)(iv) and (v) and added new clause (a)(5)(C)(iii), effective for bonds issued after 7/30/2008.

Minimum tax   Code Sec. 58(c)(2)

In 2006, P.L. 109-222, Sec. 102, substituted "December 31, 2010" for "December 31, 2008" in Sec. 303 of P.L. 108-27 [see below], effective 5/17/2006.

In 2003, P.L. 108-27, Sec. 301(b)(3)(A), substituted "7 percent" for "42 percent" the first place it appeared in para. (a)(7) . . . Sec. 301(b)(3)(B), deleted "In the case of stock the holding period of which begins after December 31, 2000 (determined with the application of the last sentence of section 1(h)(2)(B)), the preceding sentence shall be applied by substituting '28 percent' for '42 percent'." at the end of para. (a)(7), effective for dispositions on or after 5/6/2003.

—P.L. 108-27, Sec. 303, of this Act [as amended by Sec. 102, P.L. 109-222 and Sec. 102(a), P.L. 111-312, see above], reads as follows:

"Sec. 303. Sunset of title. All provisions of, and amendments made by, this title [Secs. 301 and 302] shall not apply to taxable years beginning after December 31, 2012, and the Internal Revenue Code of 1986 shall be applied and administered to such years as if such provisions and amendments had never been enacted."

In 1998, P.L. 105-206, Sec. 6005(d)(3), added a sentence at the end of para. (a)(7), effective for tax. yrs end. after 5/6/97.

In 1997, P.L. 105-34, Sec. 311(b)(2)(B), substituted "42 percent" for "one-half" in para. (a)(7), effective for tax. yrs end. after 5/6/97.

In 1996, P.L. 104-188, Sec. 1616(b)(3), deleted para. (a)(4), effective for tax. yrs. begin. after 12/31/95.

Prior to deletion, para. (a)(4) read as follows:

"(4) Reserves for losses on bad debts of financial institutions. In the case of a financial institution to which section 593 applies, the amount by which the deduction allowable for the taxable year for a reasonable addition to a reserve for bad debts exceeds the amount that would have been allowable had the institution maintained its bad debt reserve for all taxable years on the basis of actual experience."

In 1993, P.L. 103-66, Sec. 13113(b)(1), added para. (a)(8), effective for stock issued after date of enactment.

—P.L. 103-66, Sec. 13171(a), deleted para. (a)(6) and redesignated paras. (a)(7) and (8) as paras. (a)(6) and (7), effective for contributions made after 6/30/92, except that in the case of any contribution of capital gain property which is not tangible personal property, such amendments shall apply only if the contribution is made after 12/31/92.

Prior to deletion, para. (a)(6) read as follows:

"(6) Appreciated property charitable deduction.

"(A) In general. The amount by which the deduction allowable under section 170 or 642(c) would be reduced if all capital gain property were taken into account at its adjusted basis.

"(B) Capital gain property. For purposes of subparagraph (A), the term 'capital gain property' has the meaning given to such term by section 170(b)(1)(C)(iv). Such term shall not include any property to which an election under section 170(b)(1)(C)(iii) applies. In the case of any taxable year beginning in 1991, such term shall not include any tangible personal property. In the case of a contribution made before July 1, 1992, in a taxable year beginning in 1992, such term shall not include any tangible personal property."

In 1992, P.L. 102-486, Sec. 1915(a)(1), added a sentence at the end of para. (a)(1) . . . Sec. 1915(b)(1), added subpara. (a)(2)(E), effective for tax. yrs. begin. after 12/31/92.

In 1991, P.L. 102-227, Sec. 112, added the sentence at the end of subpara. (a)(6)(B), effective 12/11/91.

In 1990, P.L. 101-508, Sec. 11344, added the last sentence to subpara. (a)(6)(B), effective 11/5/90.

—P.L. 101-508, Sec. 11801(c)(12)(A), deleted "585 or" before "593 applies," in para. (a)(4) . . . Sec. 11815(b)(3), substituted "section 613(e)(2)" for "section 613(e)(3)" in clause (a)(2)(D)(ii), effective 11/5/90 except as provided in Sec. 11821(b) of this Act, reproduced in note following Code Sec. 585.

In 1988, P.L. 100-647, Sec. 1007(b)(14)(B), deleted para. (a)(3), effective for options exercised after 12/31/87.

Prior to deletion, para. (a)(3) read as follows:

"(3) Incentive stock options.

"(A) In general. With respect to the transfer of a share of stock pursuant to the exercise of an incentive stock option (as defined in section 422A), the amount by which the fair market value of the share at the time of exercise exceeds the option price. For purposes of this paragraph, the fair market value of a share of stock shall be determined without regard to any restriction other than a restriction which, by its terms, will never lapse.

"(B) Basis adjustment. In determining the amount of gain or loss recognized for purposes of this part on any disposition of a share of stock acquired pursuant to an exercise (in a taxable year beginning after December 31, 1986) of an incentive stock option, the basis of such stock shall be increased by the amount of the excess referred to in subparagraph (A)."

—P.L. 100-647, Sec. 1007(c)(1), added "(whether a current or advance refunding)" after "any refunding bond" in clause (a)(5)(C)(iii) . . . Sec. 1007(c)(2), amended clause (a)(5)(C)(i) . . . Sec. 1007(c)(3), added "or 642(c)" after "section 170" in subpara. (a)(6)(A), effective for tax. yrs. begin. after 12/31/86.

Prior to amendment, clause (a)(5)(C)(i) read as follows:

"(i) In general. For purposes of this part, the term 'specified private activity bonds' means any private activity bond (as defined in section 141) issued after August 7, 1986."

—P.L. 100-647, Sec. 1007(f)(4)(A), and (B) provides the following transitional provisions:

"(4)(A) If any property to which this paragraph applies is placed in service in a taxable year which begins before January 1, 1987, and ends on or after August 1, 1986, the item of tax preference determined under section 57(a) of the Internal Revenue Code of 1954 (as in effect on the day before the date of the enactment of the Tax Reform Act of 1986) with respect to such property shall be the excess of—

"(i) the amount allowable as a deduction for depreciation or amortization for such taxable year, over

"(ii) the amount which would be determined for such taxable year under the rules of paragraph (1) or (5) (whichever is appropriate) of section 56(a) of the Internal Revenue Code of 1954 (as amended by the Tax Reform Act of 1986).

"(B) This paragraph shall apply to any property—

"(i) which is described in paragraph (4) or (12) of section 57(a) of the Internal Revenue Code of 1954 (as so in effect), and

"(ii) to which paragraph (1) or (5) of section 56(a) of the Internal Revenue Code of 1986 would apply if the taxable year referred to in subparagraph (A) began after December 31, 1986."

In 1986, P.L. 99-514, Sec. 701(a), added Code Sec. 57, as part of the amendments to Part VI of subchapter A of chapter 1, effective for tax. yrs. begin. after 12/31/86. Sec. 701(f)(4) of this Act provides:

"(4) Exception for charitable contributions before August 16, 1986.—Section 57(a)(6) of the Internal Revenue Code of 1986 (as amended by this section) shall not apply to any deduction attributable to contributions made before August 16, 1986."

Sec. 58. Denial of certain losses.

(a) Denial of farm loss.

(1) In general. For purposes of computing the amount of the alternative minimum taxable income for any taxable year of a taxpayer other than a corporation—

(A) Disallowance of farm loss. No loss of the taxpayer for such taxable year from any tax shelter farm activity shall be allowed.

(B) Deduction in succeeding taxable year. Any loss from a tax shelter farm activity disallowed under subparagraph (A) shall be treated as a deduction allocable to such activity in the 1st succeeding taxable year.

(2) Tax shelter farm activity. For purposes of this subsection, the term "tax shelter farm activity" means—

(A) any farming syndicate as defined in section 464(c), and

(B) any other activity consisting of farming which is a passive activity (within the meaning of section 469(c)).

(3) Application to personal service corporations. For purposes of paragraph (1), a personal service corporation (within the meaning of section 469(j)(2)) shall be treated as a taxpayer other than a corporation.

(4) Determination of loss. In determining the amount of the loss from any tax shelter farm activity, the adjustments of sections 56 and 57 shall apply.

(b) Disallowance of passive activity loss.

In computing the alternative minimum taxable income of the taxpayer for any taxable year, section 469 shall apply, except that in applying section 469—

(1) the adjustments of sections 56 and 57 shall apply,

(2) the provisions of section 469(m) (relating to phase-in of disallowance) shall not apply, and

(3) in lieu of applying section 469(j)(7), the passive activity loss of a taxpayer shall be computed without regard to qualified housing interest (as defined in section 56(e)).

(c) Special rules.

For purposes of this section—

(1) Special rule for insolvent taxpayers.

(A) In general. The amount of losses to which subsection (a) or (b) applies shall be reduced by the amount (if any) by which the taxpayer is insolvent as of the close of the taxable year.

(B) Insolvent. For purposes of this paragraph, the term "insolvent" means the excess of liabilities over the fair market value of assets.

(2) Loss allowed for year of disposition of farm shelter activity. If the taxpayer disposes of his entire interest in any tax shelter farm activity during any taxable year, the amount of the loss attributable to such activity (determined after carryovers under subsection (a)(1)(B)) shall (to the extent otherwise allowable) be allowed for such taxable year in computing alternative minimum taxable income and not treated as a loss from a tax shelter farm activity.

In **1988**, P.L. 100-647, Sec. 1007(d)(1)(A), deleted "(as modified by section 461(i)(4)(A))" after "section 464(c)" in subpara. (a)(2)(A) . . . Sec. 1007(d)(1)(B), substituted "section 469(c)" for "section 469(d), without regard to paragraph (1)(B) thereof" in subpara. (a)(2)(B) . . . Sec. 1007(d)(2), substituted "469(j)(2)" for "469(g)(1)(C)" in para. (a)(3) . . . Sec. 1007(d)(3), added para. (a)(4) . . . Sec. 1007(d)(4), amended paras. (b)(1), (2) and (3), effective for tax. yrs. begin. after 12/31/86.

Prior to amendment, paras. (b)(1), (2) and (3) read as follows:

"(1) the adjustments of section 56 shall apply,

"(2) any deduction to the extent such deduction is an item of tax preference under section 57(a) shall not be taken into account, and

"(3) the provisions of section 469(m) (relating to phase-in of disallowance) shall not apply."

In **1987**, P.L. 100-203, Sec. 10212(b), substituted "469(m)" for "469(l)" in para. (b)(3), effective for tax. yrs. begin. after 12/31/87. Sec. 501(c)(2) of P.L. 99-514 provides:

"(2) Special rule for carryovers.— The amendments made by this section shall not apply to any loss, deduction, or credit carried to a taxable year beginning after December 31, 1986, from a taxable year beginning before January 1, 1987.

"(3) Special rule for low-income housing.—

"(A) In general.— Except as provided in subparagraph (B), section 469(i)(6)(B)(i) of the Internal Revenue Code of 1986 (as added by this section) shall not apply to any property placed in service before December 31, 1989.

"(B) Exception where at least 10 percent of costs incurred.— In the case of property placed in service after December 31, 1989, and before January 1, 1991, section 469(i)(6)(B)(i) of such Code shall apply to such property if at least 10 percent of the costs of such property were incurred before January 1, 1989."

In **1986**, P.L. 99-514, Sec. 701(a), added Code Sec. 58 as part of the amendments to Part VI of subchapter A of chapter 1, effective for tax. yrs. begin. after 12/31/86.

Sec. 59. Other definitions and special rules.
(a) Alternative minimum tax foreign tax credit.

For purposes of this part—

(1) In general. The alternative minimum tax foreign tax credit for any taxable year shall be the credit which would be determined under section 27(a) for such taxable year if—

(A) the pre-credit tentative minimum tax were the tax against which such credit was taken for purposes of section 904 for the taxable year and all prior taxable years beginning after December 31, 1986,

(B) section 904 were applied on the basis of alternative minimum taxable income instead of taxable income, and

(C) the determination of whether any income is high-taxed income for purposes of section 904(d)(2) were made on the basis of the applicable rate specified in subparagraph (A)(i) or (B)(i) of section 55(b)(1) (whichever applies) in lieu of the highest rate of tax specified in section 1 or 11 (whichever applies).

(2) Pre-credit tentative minimum tax. For purposes of this subsection, the term "pre-credit tentative minimum tax" means—

(A) in the case of a taxpayer other than a corporation, the amount determined under the first sentence of section 55(b)(1)(A)(i), or

(B) in the case of a corporation, the amount determined under section 55(b)(1)(B)(i).

(3) Election to use simplified section 904 limitation.

(A) In general. In determining the alternative minimum tax foreign tax credit for any taxable year to which an election under this paragraph applies—

(i) subparagraph (B) of paragraph (1) shall not apply, and

(ii) the limitation of section 904 shall be based on the proportion which—

(I) the taxpayer's taxable income (as determined for purposes of the regular tax) from sources without the United States (but not in excess of the taxpayer's entire alternative minimum taxable income), bears to

(II) the taxpayer's entire alternative minimum taxable income for the taxable year.

(B) Election.

(i) In general. An election under this paragraph may be made only for the taxpayer's first taxable year which begins after December 31, 1997, and for which the taxpayer claims an alternative minimum tax foreign tax credit.

(ii) Election revocable only with consent. An election under this paragraph, once made, shall apply to the taxable year for which made and all subsequent taxable years unless revoked with the consent of the Secretary.

(b) Minimum tax not to apply to income eligible for credits under section 30A or 936.

In the case of any corporation for which a credit is allowable for the taxable year under section 30A or 936, alternative minimum taxable income shall not include any income with respect to which a credit is determined under section 30A or 936.

(c) Treatment of estates and trusts.

In the case of any estate or trust, the alternative minimum taxable income of such estate or trust and any beneficiary thereof shall be determined by applying part I of subchapter J with the adjustments provided in this part.

(d) Apportionment of differently treated items in case of certain entities.

(1) In general. The differently treated items for the taxable year shall be apportioned (in accordance with regulations prescribed by the Secretary)—

(A) Regulated investment companies and real estate investment trusts. In the case of a regulated investment company to which part I of subchapter M applies or a real estate investment company to which part II of subchapter M applies, between such company or trust and shareholders and holders of beneficial interest in such company or trust.

(B) Common trust funds. In the case of a common trust fund (as defined in section 584(a)), pro rata among the participants of such fund.

(2) Differently treated items. For purposes of this section, the term "differently treated item" means any item of tax preference or any other item which is treated differently for purposes of this part than for purposes of computing the regular tax.

(e) Optional 10-year writeoff of certain tax preferences.

(1) In general. For purposes of this title, any qualified expenditure to which an election under this paragraph applies shall be allowed as a deduction ratably over the 10-year period (3-year period in the case of circulation expenditures described in section 173) beginning with the taxable year in which such expenditure was made (or, in the case of a qualified expenditure described in paragraph (2)(C), over the 60-month period beginning with the month in which such expenditure was paid or incurred).

(2) Qualified expenditure. For purposes of this subsection, the term "qualified expenditure" means any amount which, but for an election under this subsection, would have been allowable as a deduction (determined without regard to section 291) for the taxable year in which paid or incurred under—

(A) section 173 (relating to circulation expenditures),

(B) section 174(a) (relating to research and experimental expenditures),

(C) section 263(c) (relating to intangible drilling and development expenditures),

(D) section 616(a) (relating to development expenditures), or

(E) section 617(a) (relating to mining exploration expenditures).

(3) Other sections not applicable. Except as provided in this subsection, no deduction shall be allowed under any other section for any qualified expenditure to which an election under this subsection applies.

(4) Election.

(A) In general. An election may be made under paragraph (1) with respect to any portion of any qualified expenditure.

(B) Revocable only with consent. Any election under this subsection may be revoked only with the consent of the Secretary.

(C) Partners and shareholders of S corporations. In the case of a partnership, any election under paragraph (1) shall be made separately by each partner with respect to the partner's allocable share of any qualified expenditure. A similar rule shall apply in the case of an S corporation and its shareholders.

(5) Dispositions.

(A) Application of section 1254. In the case of any disposition of property to which section 1254 applies (determined without regard to this section), any deduction under paragraph (1) with respect to amounts which are allocable to such property shall, for purposes of section 1254, be treated as a deduction allowable under section 263(c), 616(a), or 617(a), whichever is appropriate.

(B) Application of Section 617(d). In the case of any disposition of mining property to which section 617(d) applies (determined without regard to this subsection), any deduction under paragraph (1) with respect to amounts which are allocable to such property shall, for purposes of section 617(d), be treated as a deduction allowable under section 617(a).

(6) Amounts to which election apply not treated as tax preference. Any portion of any qualified expenditure to which an election under paragraph (1) applies shall not be treated as an item of tax preference under section 57(a) and section 56 shall not apply to such expenditure.

(f) Coordination with section 291.

Except as otherwise provided in this part, section 291 (relating to cutback of corporate preferences) shall apply before the application of this part.

(g) Tax benefit rule.

The Secretary may prescribe regulations under which differently treated items shall be properly adjusted where the tax treatment giving rise to such items will not result in the reduction of the taxpayer's regular tax for the taxable year for which the item is taken into account or for any other taxable year.

(h) Coordination with certain limitations.

The limitations of sections 704(d), 465, and 1366(d) (and such other provisions as may be specified in regulations) shall be applied for purposes of computing the alternative minimum taxable income of the taxpayer for the taxable year with the adjustments of sections 56, 57, and 58.

(i) Special rule for amounts treated as tax preference.

For purposes of this subtitle (other than this part), any amount shall not fail to be treated as wholly exempt from tax imposed by this subtitle solely by reason of being included in alternative minimum taxable income.

(j) Treatment of unearned income of minor children.

(1) In general. In the case of a child to whom section 1(g) applies, the exemption amount for purposes of section 55 shall not exceed the sum of—

(A) such child's earned income (as defined in section 911(d)(2)) for the taxable year, plus

(B) $5,000.

(2) Inflation adjustment. In the case of any taxable year beginning in a calendar year after 1998, the dollar amount in paragraph (1)(B) shall be increased by an amount equal to the product of—

(A) such dollar amount, and

(B) the cost-of-living adjustment determined under section 1(f)(3) for the calendar year in which the taxable year begins, determined by substituting "1997" for "1992" in subparagraph (B) thereof.

If any increase determined under the preceding sentence is not a multiple of $50, such increase shall be rounded to the nearest multiple of $50.

In 2004, P.L. 108-357, Sec. 421(a)(1), deleted para. (a)(2) and redesignated paras. (a)(3) and (4) as paras. (a)(2) and (3), effective for tax. yrs. begin. after 12/31/2004.

Prior to deletion, para. (a)(2) read as follows:

"(2) Limitation to 90 percent of tax.

"(A) In general. The alternative minimum tax foreign tax credit for any taxable year shall not exceed the excess (if any) of—

"(i) the pre-credit tentative minimum tax for the taxable year, over

"(ii) 10 percent of the amount which would be the pre-credit tentative minimum tax without regard to the alternative tax net operating loss deduction and section 57(a)(2)(E).

"(B) Carryback and carryforward. If the alternative minimum tax foreign tax credit exceeds the amount determined under subparagraph (A), such excess shall, for purposes of this part, be treated as an amount to which section 904(c) applies."

In 1998, P.L. 105-206, Sec. 6011(a), redesignated para. (a)(3) [sic (4)] as (a)(4), effective for tax. yrs. begin. after 12/31/97.

—P.L. 105-206, Sec. 6023(2), substituted "credits under section 30A or 936" for "section 936 credit" in the heading of subsec. (b), effective 7/22/98.

In 1997, P.L. 105-34, Sec. 1057(a), deleted subsec. (a)(2)(C), effective for tax. yrs. begin. after 8/5/97.

Prior to deletion, subpara. (a)(2)(C) read as follows:

"(C) Exception. Subparagraph (A) shall not apply to any domestic corporation if—

"(i) more than 50 percent of the stock of such domestic corporation (by vote and value) is owned by United States persons who are not members of an affiliated group (as defined in section 1504 of such Code) which includes such corporation,

"(ii) all of the activities of such corporation are conducted in 1 foreign country with which the United States has an income tax treaty in effect and such treaty provides for the exchange of information between such foreign country and the United States,

"(iii) all of the current earnings and profits of such corporation are distributed at least annually (other than current earnings and profits retained for normal maintenance or capital replacements or improvements of an existing business), and

"(iv) all of such distributions by such corporation to United States persons are used by such persons in a trade or business conducted in the United States."

—P.L. 105-34, Sec. 1103(a), added para. (a)(3) [sic (4)], effective for tax. yrs. begin. after 12/31/97.

—P.L. 105-34, Sec. 1201(b), amended subsec. (j), effective for tax. yrs. begin. after 12/31/97.

Prior to amendment, subsec. (j) read as follows:

"(j) Treatment of unearned income of minor children.

"(1) Limitation on exemption amount. In the case of a child to whom section 1(g) applies, the exemption amount for purposes of section 55 shall not exceed the sum of—

"(A) such child's earned income (as defined in section 911(d)(2)) for the taxable year, plus

"(B) twice the amount in effect for the taxable year under section 63(c)(5)(A) (or, if greater, the child's share of the unused parental minimum tax exemption).

"(2) Limitation based on parental minimum tax.

"(A) In general. In the case of a child to whom section 1(g) applies, the amount of the tax imposed by section 55 shall not exceed such child's share of the allocable parental minimum tax.

"(B) Allocable parental minimum tax. For purposes of this paragraph, the term 'allocable parental minimum tax' means the excess of—

"(i) the tax which would be imposed by section 55 on the parent if—

"(I) the amount of the parent's tentative minimum tax were increased by the aggregate of the tentative minimum taxes of all children of the parent to whom section 1(g) applies, and

"(II) the amount of the parent's regular tax were increased by the aggregate of the regular taxes of all children of the parent to whom section 1(g) applies, over

"(ii) the tax imposed by section 55 on the parent without regard to this subparagraph.

"(C) Child share. A child's share of any allocable parental minimum tax shall be determined under rules similar to the rules of section 1(g)(3)(B).

"(D) Other rules made applicable. For purposes of this paragraph, rules similar to the rules of paragraphs (3)(D), (5), and (6) of section 1(g) shall apply.

"(3) Unused parental minimum tax exemption.

"(A) In general. For purposes of this subsection, the term 'unused parental minimum tax exemption' means the excess (if any) of—

"(i) the exemption amount applicable to the parent under section 55(d), over

"(ii) the parent's alternative minimum taxable income.

"(B) Certain rules made applicable. A child's share of any unused parental minimum tax exemption shall be determined under rules similar to the rules of section 1(g)(3)(B), and rules similar to the rules of paragraphs (3)(D) and (5) of section 1(g) shall apply for purposes of this paragraph."

In 1996, P.L. 104-188, Sec. 1601(b)(2)(D), substituted "section 30A or 936, alternative minimum taxable income shall not include any amount with respect to which a credit is determined under section 30A or 936." for "section 936, alternative minimum taxable income shall not include any amount with respect to which the requirements of subparagraph (A) or (B) of section 936(a)(1) are met." in subsec. (b), effective for tax. yrs. begin. after 12/31/95.

—P.L. 104-188, Sec. 1601(c)(2) and (3), of this Act provides:

"(2) Special rule for qualified possession source investment income. The amendments made by this section shall not apply to qualified possession source investment income received or accrued before July 1, 1996, without regard to the taxable year in which received or accrued.

"(3) Special transition rule for payment of estimated tax installment. In determining the amount of any installment due under section 6655 of the Internal Revenue Code of 1986 after the date of the enactment of this Act and before October 1, 1996, only ½ of any increase in tax (for the taxable year for which such installment is made) by reason of the amendments made by subsections (a) and (b) shall be taken into account. Any reduction in such installment by reason of the preceding sentence shall be recaptured by increasing the next required installment for such year by the amount of such reduction."

—P.L. 104-188, Sec. 1702(a)(1), substituted "section 1(g)(3)(B)" for "section 1(i)(3)(B)" in subpara. (j)(3)(B), effective for tax. yrs. begin. after 12/31/92.

—P.L. 104-188, Sec. 1703(e)(1), substituted "the pre-credit tentative minimum tax" for "the amount determined under section 55(b)(1)(A)" in subpara. (a)(1)(A) and clause (a)(2)(A)(i) ... Sec. 1703(e)(2), substituted "specified in subparagraph (A)(i) or (B)(i) of section 55(b)(1) (whichever applies)" for "specified in section 55(b)(1)(A)" in subpara. (a)(1)(C) ... Sec. 1703(e)(3), substituted "which would be the pre-credit tentative minimum tax" for "which would be determined under section 55(b)(1)(A)" in clause (a)(2)(A)(ii) ... Sec. 1703(e)(4), added para. (a)(3), effective for tax. yrs. begin. after 12/31/92.

—P.L. 104-188, Sec. 1704(m)(3), substituted "twice the amount in effect for the taxable year under section 63(c)(5)(A)" for "$1,000" in subpara. (j)(1)(B), effective for tax. yrs. begin. after 12/31/95.

In 1992, P.L. 102-486, Sec. 1915(c)(3), substituted "and section 57(a)(2)(E)" for "and the alternative tax energy preference deduction under section 56(h)" in clause (a)(2)(A)(ii), effective for tax. yrs. begin. after 12/31/92.

In 1990, P.L. 101-508, Sec. 11101(d)(3)(A), substituted "section 1(g)" for "section 1(i)" each place it appeared in subsec. (j) ... Sec. 11101(d)(3)(B), substituted "section 1(g)(3)(B)" for "section 1(i)(3)(B)" in subpara. (j)(2)(C), effective for tax. yrs. begin. after 12/31/90.

—P.L. 101-508, Sec. 11531(b)(2), added "and the alternative tax energy preference deduction under section 56(h)" before the period in clause (a)(2)(A)(ii), effective for tax. yrs. begin. after 12/31/90.

—P.L. 101-508, Sec. 11702(d)(1), added "(or, if greater, the child's share of the unused parental minimum tax exemption)" before the period at the end of subpara. (j)(1)(B) ... Sec. 11702(d)(2), added para. (j)(3) ... Sec. 11702(d)(2), substituted "paragraphs (3)(D), (5), and (6)" for "paragraphs (5) and (6)" in subpara. (j)(2)(D), effective for tax. yrs. begin. after 12/31/88.

—P.L. 101-508, Sec. 11801(c)(2)(D), added "and" at the end of subpara. (a)(1)(B), deleted subpara. (a)(1)(C), and redesignated subpara. (a)(1)(D) as subpara. (a)(1)(C), effective 11/5/90 except as provided in Sec. 11821(b) of this Act, reproduced in note following Code Sec. 56.

Prior to deletion, subpara. (a)(1)(C) read as follows:

"(C) for purposes of section 904, any increase in alternative minimum taxable income by reason of section 56(c)(1)(A) (relating to adjustment for book income) shall have the same proportionate source (and character) as alternative minimum taxable income determined without regard to such increase, and"

In 1989, P.L. 101-239, Sec. 7611(f)(5)(B), added "(or, in the case of a qualified expenditure described in paragraph (2)(C), over the 60-month period beginning with the month in which such expenditure was paid or incurred)" before the period at the end of para. (e)(1), effective for costs paid or incurred in tax. yrs. begin. after 12/31/89.

—P.L. 101-239, Sec. 7611(f)(6)(A), substituted "any amount shall" for "interest shall" in subsec. (i) ... Sec. 7611(f)(6)(B), substituted "amounts" for "interest" in heading of subsec. (i), effective for tax. yrs. begin. after 12/31/89. Sec. 7611(g)(3) of this Act provides:

"(3) Regulations on earnings and profits rules. Not later than March 15, 1991, the Secretary of the Treasury or his delegate shall prescribe initial regulations providing guidance as to which items of income are included in adjusted current earnings under section 56(g)(4)(B)(i) of the Internal Revenue Code of 1986 and which items of deduction are disallowed under section 56(g)(4)(C) of such Code."

—P.L. 101-239, Sec. 7612(e)(1), added subpara. (a)(2)(C), effective for tax. yrs. begin. after 3/31/90 except as provided in Sec. 7612(e)(2)(B) of this Act which reads as follows:

"(B) Special rule for year which includes March 31, 1990. — In the case of any taxable year (of a corporation described in subparagraph (C) of section 59(a)(2) of the Internal Revenue Code of 1986 (as added by paragraph (1)) [Sec. 7612(e)(1)]) which begins after December 31, 1989, and includes March 31, 1990, the amount determined under clause (ii) of section 59(a)(2)(A) of such Code shall be an amount which bears the same ratio to the amount which would have been determined under such clause without regard to this subparagraph as the number of days in such taxable year on or before March 31, 1990, bears to the total number of days in such taxable year."

—P.L. 101-239, Sec. 7811(d)(1)(A), substituted "for the taxable year for which the item is taken into account or for any other taxable year" for "for any taxable year" in subsec. (g), effective for tax. yrs. begin. after 12/31/86.

—P.L. 101-239, Sec. 7811(j)(7), substituted "Other" for "Others" in the heading of subpara. (j)(2)(D), effective for tax. yrs. begin. after 12/31/88.

In 1988, P.L. 100-647, Sec. 1007(e)(1), substituted "would have been allowable as a deduction (determined without regard to section 291)" for "would have been allowable as a deduction" in para. (e)(2) ... Sec. 1007(e)(2), substituted "taxable year with the adjustments of sections 56, 57, and 58." for "taxable year—

"(1) with the adjustments of section 56, and

"(2) by not taking into account any deduction to the extent such deduction is an item of tax preference under section 57(a)." in subsec (h) ... Sec. 1007(e)(3), deleted "and" at the end of subpara. (a)(1)(B), substituted ", and " for the period at the end of subpara. (a)(1)(C), and added subpara. (a)(1)(D) ... Sec. 1007(e)(4)(A) and (B), substituted "of this subtitle (other than this part)" for "of this subtitle" and substituted "by this subtitle" for "by this title" in subsec. (i), effective for tax. yrs. begin. after 12/31/86.

—P.L. 100-647, Sec. 1007(f)(5), of this Act provides:

"(5) In determining the amount of the alternative minimum tax foreign tax credit under section 59 of the 1986 Code, there shall not be taken into account any taxes paid or accrued in a taxable year beginning after December 31, 1986, which are treated under section 904(c) of the 1986 Code as paid or accrued in a taxable year beginning on or before December 31, 1986."

—P.L. 100-647, Sec. 1014(e)(5)(A), added subsec. (j), effective for tax. yrs. begin. after 12/31/88.

—P.L. 100-647, Sec. 1012(aa)(2)(B) and (4), provides:

"(2) Certain amendments to apply notwithstanding treaties. — The following amendments made by the Reform Act shall apply notwithstanding any treaty obligation of the United States in effect on the date of the enactment of the Reform Act:

* * *

"(B) The amendments made by title VII of the Reform Act to the extent such amendments relate to the alternative minimum tax foreign tax credit."

* * *

"(4) Treatment of technical corrections. — For purposes of paragraphs (2) and (3), any amendment made by this title shall be treated as if it had been included in the provision of the Reform Act to which such amendment relates."

In 1986, P.L. 99-514, Sec. 701(a), added Code Sec. 59, as part of the amendments to Part VI of subchapter A of chapter 1, effective for tax. yrs. begin. after 12/31/86 (see Sec. 1012 of P.L. 100-647(aa)(2)(B) and (4), above).

PART VII. — ENVIRONMENTAL TAX

Sec.

59A. Environmental tax.

In 1986, P.L. 99-499, Sec. 516(b)(5), added Part VII to Subchapter A of Chapter 1.

Sec. 59A. Environmental tax.
(a) Imposition of tax.

In the case of a corporation, there is hereby imposed (in addition to any other tax imposed by this subtitle) a tax equal to 0.12 percent of the excess of—

(1) the modified alternative minimum taxable income of such corporation for the taxable year, over

(2) $2,000,000.

(b) Modified alternative minimum taxable income.

For purposes of this section, the term "modified alternative minimum taxable income" means alternative minimum taxable income (as defined in section 55(b)(2)) but determined without regard to—

(1) the alternative tax net operating loss deduction (as defined in section 56(d)), and

(2) the deduction allowed under section 164(a)(5).

Income Code Sec. 61(b)

(c) Exception for RIC's and REIT's.
The tax imposed by subsection (a) shall not apply to—
(1) a regulated investment company to which part I of subchapter M applies, and
(2) a real estate investment trust to which part II of subchapter M applies.
(d) Special rules.
(1) Short taxable years. The application of this section to taxable years of less than 12 months shall be in accordance with regulations prescribed by the Secretary.
(2) Section 15 not to apply. Section 15 shall not apply to the tax imposed by this section.
(e) Application of tax.
(1) In general. The tax imposed by this section shall apply to taxable years beginning after December 31, 1986, and before January 1, 1996.
(2) Earlier termination. The tax imposed by this section shall not apply to taxable years—
(A) beginning during a calendar year during which no tax is imposed under section 4611(a) by reason of paragraph (2) of section 4611(e), and
(B) beginning after the calendar year which includes the termination date under paragraph (3) of section 4611(e).

In 1992, P.L. 102-486, Sec. 1915(c)(4), deleted "or the alternative tax energy preference deduction under section 56(h)" after "(as defined in section 56(d))" in para. (b)(1), effective for tax. yrs. begin. after 12/31/92.
In 1990, P.L. 101-508, Sec. 11231(a)(1)(A), substituted "January 1, 1996" for "January 1, 1992" in para. (e)(1), effective 11/5/90.
—P.L. 101-508, Sec. 11531(b)(3), added "or the alternative tax energy preference deduction under section 56(h)" before ", and" in para. (b)(1), effective for tax. yrs. begin. after 12/31/90.
—P.L. 101-508, Sec. 11801(c)(2)(E), deleted "(and the last sentence of section 56(f)(2)(B))" after "164(a)(5)" in para. (b)(2), effective 11/5/90 except as provided in Sec. 11821(b) of this Act, reproduced at note following Code Sec. 56.
In 1988, P.L. 100-647, Sec. 2001(c)(1), redesignated subsecs. (c) and (d) as subsecs. (d) and (e) and added new subsec. (c)... Sec. 2001(c)(3)(B), added "(and the last sentence of section 56(f)(2)(B))" before the period at the end of para. (b)(2), effective for tax yrs. begin. after 12/31/86.
In 1986, P.L. 99-499, Sec. 516(a), added Code Sec. 59A, as part of Part VII of subchapter A of chapter 1, effective for tax. yrs. begin. after 12/31/86.

PART VIII.—SUPPLEMENTAL MEDICARE PREMIUM [REPEALED]
Sec.
59B. Repealed [Supplemental medicare premium.]

In 1989, P.L. 101-234, Sec. 102(a), repealed as if not enacted Sec. 111(a) of P.L. 100-360, which added Part VIII to Subchapter A of chapter 1.
Prior to repeal, Part VIII read as follows:
"PART VIII. SUPPLEMENTAL MEDICARE PREMIUM
"Sec.
"59B. Supplemental medicare premium."
In 1988, P.L. 100-360, Sec. 111(a), [repealed as if not enacted by Sec. 102(a) of P.L. 101-234, see above] added Part VIII to Subchapter A of chapter 1.

Sec. 59B. Repealed.

In 1989, P.L. 101-234, Sec. 102(a), repealed as if not enacted Sec. 111(a) of P.L. 100-360, which added Code Sec. 59B, effective tax. yrs. begin. after 12/31/88.
In 1988, P.L. 100-360, Sec. 111(a), [repealed as if not enacted by Sec. 102(a) of P.L. 101-234, see above] added Code Sec. 59B as part of Part VIII of subchapter A of chapter 1, effective for tax. yrs. begin. after 12/31/88. Sec. 111(d) of this Act provides:

Subchapter B.—Computation of Taxable Income
Part
I. Definition of gross income, adjusted gross income, taxable income, etc.
II. Items specifically included in gross income.
III. Items specifically excluded from gross income.
IV. Determination of marital status. [Tax exemption requirements for State and local bonds.]
V. Deductions for personal exemptions.
VI. Itemized deductions for individuals and corporations.
VII. Additional itemized deductions for individuals.
VIII. Special deductions for corporations.
IX. Items not deductible.
X. Terminal railroad corporations and their shareholders.
XI. Special rules relating to corporate preference items.

In 1986, P.L. 99-514, Sec. 1301(b), amended Part IV. This Act did not amend the item for Part IV on the list of Parts for Subchapter B, but Congress presumably intended to do so.
In 1982, P.L. 97-248, Sec. 204(c)(2), added part XI.
In 1977, P.L. 95-30, Sec. 101(e)(3), amended the item for Part IV.
Prior to amendment, the item for Part IV read as follows:
"IV. Standard deduction for individuals."
In 1976, P.L. 94-455, Sec. 1901(b)(4)(C), substituted "taxable income, etc." for "and taxable income" in the item for Part I.
In 1962, P.L. 87-870, Sec. 1, added part X.

PART I.—DEFINITION OF GROSS INCOME, ADJUSTED GROSS INCOME, TAXABLE INCOME, ETC.
Sec.
61. Gross income defined.
62. Adjusted gross income defined.
63. Taxable income defined.
64. Ordinary income defined.
65. Ordinary loss defined.
66. Treatment of community income.
67. 2-percent floor on miscellaneous itemized deductions.
68. Overall limitation on itemized deductions.

In 1990, P.L. 101-508, Sec. 11103(d), added item 68.
In 1986, P.L. 99-514, Sec. 132(d), added item 67.
In 1984, P.L. 98-369, Sec. 424(b)(2)(C), deleted "where spouses live apart" from the end of item 66.
In 1980, P.L. 96-605, Sec. 101(b), added item 66.
In 1976, P.L. 94-455, Sec. 1901(b)(4)(A), added items 64 and 65.... Sec. 1901(b)(4)(B), substituted "taxable income, etc." for "and taxable income" in the heading for Part I.

Sec. 61. Gross income defined.
(a) General definition.
Except as otherwise provided in this subtitle, gross income means all income from whatever source derived, including (but not limited to) the following items:
(1) Compensation for services, including fees, commissions, fringe benefits, and similar items;
(2) Gross income derived from business;
(3) Gains derived from dealings in property;
(4) Interest;
(5) Rents;
(6) Royalties;
(7) Dividends;
(8) Alimony and separate maintenance payments;
(9) Annuities;
(10) Income from life insurance and endowment contracts;
(11) Pensions;
(12) Income from discharge of indebtedness;
(13) Distributive share of partnership gross income;
(14) Income in respect of a decedent; and
(15) Income from an interest in an estate or trust.
(b) Cross references.
For items specifically included in gross income, see part II (sec. 71 and following). For items specifically excluded from gross income, see part III (sec. 101 and following).

In 2009, P.L. 111-32, Sec. 1302, relating to Consumer Assistance to Recycle and Save Program, reads as follows:

"Sec. 1302. Consumer Assistance to Recycle and Save Program.

"(a) Establishment. There is established in the National Highway Traffic Safety Administration a voluntary program to be known as the 'Consumer Assistance to Recycle and Save Program' through which the Secretary, in accordance with this section and the regulations promulgated under subsection (d), shall—

"(1) authorize the issuance of an electronic voucher, subject to the specifications set forth in subsection (c), to offset the purchase price or lease price for a qualifying lease of a new fuel efficient automobile upon the surrender of an eligible tradein vehicle to a dealer participating in the Program;

"(2) register dealers for participation in the Program and require that all registered dealers—

"(A) accept vouchers as provided in this section as partial payment or down payment for the purchase or qualifying lease of any new fuel efficient automobile offered for sale or lease by that dealer; and

"(B) in accordance with subsection (c)(2), to transfer each eligible trade-in vehicle surrendered to the dealer under the Program to an entity for disposal;

"(3) in consultation with the Secretary of the Treasury, make electronic payments to dealers for eligible transactions by such dealers, in accordance with the regulations issued under subsection (d); and

"(4) in consultation with the Secretary of the Treasury and the Inspector General of the Department of Transportation, establish and provide for the enforcement of measures to prevent and penalize fraud under the program.

"(b) Qualifications for and value of vouchers. A voucher issued under the Program shall have a value that may be applied to offset the purchase price or lease price for a qualifying lease of a new fuel efficient automobile as follows:

"(1) $3,500 Value. The voucher may be used to offset the purchase price or lease price of the new fuel efficient automobile by $3,500 if—

"(A) the new fuel efficient automobile is a passenger automobile and the combined fuel economy value of such automobile is at least 4 miles per gallon higher than the combined fuel economy value of the eligible trade-in vehicle;

"(B) the new fuel efficient automobile is a category 1 truck and the combined fuel economy value of such truck is at least 2 miles per gallon higher than the combined fuel economy value of the eligible trade-in vehicle;

"(C) the new fuel efficient automobile is a category 2 truck that has a combined fuel economy value of at least 15 miles per gallon and—

"(i) the eligible trade-in vehicle is a category 2 truck and the combined fuel economy value of the new fuel efficient automobile is at least 1 mile per gallon higher than the combined fuel economy value of the eligible trade-in vehicle; or

"(ii) the eligible trade-in vehicle is a category 3 truck of model year 2001 or earlier; or

"(D) the new fuel efficient automobile is a category 3 truck and the eligible trade-in vehicle is a category 3 truck of model year of 2001 or earlier and is of similar size or larger than the new fuel efficient automobile as determined in a manner prescribed by the Secretary.

"(2) $4,500 Value. The voucher may be used to offset the purchase price or lease price of the new fuel efficient automobile by $4,500 if—

"(A) the new fuel efficient automobile is a passenger automobile and the combined fuel economy value of such automobile is at least 10 miles per gallon higher than the combined fuel economy value of the eligible tradein vehicle;

"(B) the new fuel efficient automobile is a category 1 truck and the combined fuel economy value of such truck is at least 5 miles per gallon higher than the combined fuel economy value of the eligible trade-in vehicle; or

"(C) the new fuel efficient automobile is a category 2 truck that has a combined fuel economy value of at least 15 miles per gallon and the combined fuel economy value of such truck is at least 2 miles per gallon higher than the combined fuel economy value of the eligible tradein vehicle and the eligible trade-in vehicle is a category 2 truck.

"(c) Program specifications.

"(1) Limitations.

"(A) General period of eligibility. A voucher issued under the Program shall be used only in connection with the purchase or qualifying lease of new fuel efficient automobiles that occur between July 1, 2009, and November 1, 2009.

"(B) Number of vouchers per person and per tradein vehicle. Not more than 1 voucher may be issued for a single person and not more than 1 voucher may be issued for the joint registered owners of a single eligible trade-in vehicle.

"(C) No combination of vouchers. Only 1 voucher issued under the Program may be applied toward the purchase or qualifying lease of a single new fuel efficient automobile.

"(D) Cap on funds for category 3 trucks. Not more than 7.5 percent of the total funds made available for the Program shall be used for vouchers for the purchase or qualifying lease of category 3 trucks.

"(E) Combination with other incentives permitted. The availability or use of a Federal, State, or local incentive or a State-issued voucher for the purchase or lease of a new fuel efficient automobile shall not limit the value or issuance of a voucher under the Program to any person otherwise eligible to receive such a voucher.

"(F) No additional fees. A dealer participating in the program may not charge a person purchasing or leasing a new fuel efficient automobile any additional fees associated with the use of a voucher under the Program.

"(G) Number and amount. The total number and value of vouchers issued under the Program may not exceed the amounts appropriated for such purpose.

"(2) Disposition of eligible trade-in vehicles.

"(A) In general. For each eligible trade-in vehicle surrendered to a dealer under the Program, the dealer shall certify to the Secretary, in such manner as the Secretary shall prescribe by rule, that the dealer—

"(i) has not and will not sell, lease, exchange, or otherwise dispose of the vehicle for use as an automobile in the United States or in any other country; and

"(ii) will transfer the vehicle (including the engine block), in such manner as the Secretary prescribes, to an entity that will ensure that the vehicle—

"(I) will be crushed or shredded within such period and in such manner as the Secretary prescribes; and

"(II) has not been, and will not be, sold, leased, exchanged, or otherwise disposed of for use as an automobile in the United States or in any other country.

"(B) Savings provision. Nothing in subparagraph (A) may be construed to preclude a person who is responsible for ensuring that the vehicle is crushed or shredded from—

"(i) selling any parts of the disposed vehicle other than the engine block and drive train (unless with respect to the drive train, the transmission, drive shaft, or rear end are sold as separate parts); or

"(ii) retaining the proceeds from such sale.

"(C) Coordination. The Secretary shall coordinate with the Attorney General to ensure that the National Motor Vehicle Title Information System and other publicly accessible systems are appropriately updated on a timely basis to reflect the crushing or shredding of vehicles under this section and appropriate reclassification of the vehicles' titles. The commercial market shall also have electronic and commercial access to the vehicle identification numbers of vehicles that have been disposed of on a timely basis.

"(d) Regulations. Notwithstanding the requirements of section 553 of title 5, United States Code, the Secretary shall promulgate final regulations to implement the Program not later than 30 days after the date of the enactment of this Act. Such regulations shall—

"(1) provide for a means of registering dealers for participation in the Program;

"(2) establish procedures for the reimbursement of dealers participating in the Program to be made through electronic transfer of funds for the amount of the vouchers as soon as practicable but no longer than 10 days after the submission of information supporting the eligible transaction, as deemed appropriate by the Secretary;

"(3) require the dealer to use the voucher in addition to any other rebate or discount advertised by the dealer or offered by the manufacturer for the new fuel efficient automobile and prohibit the dealer from using the voucher to offset any such other rebate or discount;

"(4) require dealers to disclose to the person trading in an eligible trade-in vehicle the best estimate of the scrappage value of such vehicle and to permit the dealer to retain $50 of any amounts paid to the dealer for scrappage of the automobile as payment for any administrative costs to the dealer associated with participation in the Program;

"(5) consistent with subsection (c)(2), establish requirements and procedures for the disposal of eligible trade-in vehicles and provide such information as may be necessary to entities engaged in such disposal to ensure that such vehicles are disposed of in accordance with such requirements and procedures, including—

"(A) requirements for the removal and appropriate disposition of refrigerants, antifreeze, lead products, mercury switches, and such other toxic or hazardous vehicle components prior to the crushing or shredding of an eligible trade-in vehicle, in accordance with rules established by the Secretary in consultation with the Administrator of the Environmental Protection Agency, and in accordance with other applicable Federal or State requirements;

"(B) a mechanism for dealers to certify to the Secretary that each eligible trade-in vehicle will be transferred to an entity that will ensure that the vehicle is disposed of, in accordance with such requirements and procedures, and to submit the vehicle identification numbers of the vehicles disposed of and the new fuel efficient automobile purchased with each voucher;

"(C) a mechanism for obtaining such other certifications as deemed necessary by the Secretary from entities engaged in vehicle disposal; and

"(D) a list of entities to which dealers may transfer eligible trade-in vehicles for disposal; and

"(6) provide for the enforcement of the penalties described in subsection (e).

"(e) Anti-fraud provisions.

"(1) Violation. It shall be unlawful for any person to violate any provision under this section or any regulations issued pursuant to subsection (d) (other than by making a clerical error).

"(2) Penalties. Any person who commits a violation described in paragraph (1) shall be liable to the United States Government for a civil penalty of not more than $15,000 for each violation. The Secretary shall have the authority to assess and compromise such penalties, and shall have the authority to require from any entity the records and inspections necessary to enforce this program. In determining the amount of the civil penalty, the severity of the violation and the intent and history of the person committing the violation shall be taken into account.

"(f) Information to consumers and dealers. Not later than 30 days after the date of the enactment of this Act, and promptly upon the update of any relevant information, the Secretary, in consultation with the Administrator of the Environmental Protection Agency, shall make available on an Internet website and through other means determined by the Secretary information about the Program, including—

"(1) how to determine if a vehicle is an eligible tradein vehicle;

"(2) how to participate in the Program, including how to determine participating dealers; and

"(3) a comprehensive list, by make and model, of new fuel efficient automobiles meeting the requirements of the Program. Once such information is available, the Secretary shall conduct a public awareness campaign to inform consumers about the Program and where to obtain additional information.

"(g) Record keeping and report.

"(1) Database. The Secretary shall maintain a database of the vehicle identification numbers of all new fuel efficient vehicles purchased or leased and all eligible trade-in vehicles disposed of under the Program.

"(2) Report on efficacy of the program. Not later than 60 days after the termination date described in subsection (c)(1)(A), the Secretary shall submit a report to the Committee on Energy and Commerce of the House of Representatives and the Committee on Commerce, Science, and Transportation of the Senate describing the efficacy of the Program, including—

"(A) a description of Program results, including—

"(i) the total number and amount of vouchers issued for purchase or lease of new fuel efficient automobiles by manufacturer (including aggregate information concerning the make, model, model year) and category of automobile;

"(ii) aggregate information regarding the make, model, model year, and manufacturing location of vehicles traded in under the Program; and

"(iii) the location of sale or lease;

"(B) an estimate of the overall increase in fuel efficiency in terms of miles per gallon, total annual oil savings, and total annual greenhouse gas reductions, as a result of the Program; and

"(C) an estimate of the overall economic and employment effects of the Program.

"(h) Exclusion of vouchers from income.

"(1) For purposes of all federal and state programs. A voucher issued under this program or any payment made for such a voucher pursuant to subsection (a)(3) shall not be regarded as income and shall not be regarded as a resource for the month of receipt of the voucher and the following 12 months, for purposes of determining the eligibility of the recipient of the voucher (or the recipient's spouse or other family or household members) for benefits or assistance, or the amount or extent of benefits or assistance, under any Federal or State program.

"(2) For purposes of taxation. A voucher issued under the program or any payment made for such a voucher pursuant to subsection (a)(3) shall not be considered as gross income of the purchaser of a vehicle for purposes of the Internal Revenue Code of 1986.

"(i) Definitions. As used in this section—

"(1) the term 'passenger automobile' means a passenger automobile, as defined in section 32901(a)(18) of title 49, United States Code, that has a combined fuel economy value of at least 22 miles per gallon;

"(2) the term 'category 1 truck' means a nonpassenger automobile, as defined in section 32901(a)(17) of title 49, United States Code, that has a combined fuel economy value of at least 18 miles per gallon, except that such term does not include a category 2 truck;

"(3) the term 'category 2 truck' means a large van or a large pickup, as categorized by the Secretary using the method used by the Environmental Protection Agency and described in the report entitled 'Light-Duty Automotive Technology and Fuel Economy Trends: 1975 through 2008';

"(4) the term 'category 3 truck' means a work truck, as defined in section 32901(a)(19) of title 49, United States Code;

"(5) the term 'combined fuel economy value' means—

"(A) with respect to a new fuel efficient automobile, the number, expressed in miles per gallon, centered below the words 'Combined Fuel Economy' on the label required to be affixed or caused to be affixed on a new automobile pursuant to subpart D of part 600 of title 40, Code of Federal Regulations;

"(B) with respect to an eligible trade-in vehicle, the equivalent of the number described in subparagraph (A), and posted under the words 'Estimated New EPA MPG' and above the word 'Combined' for vehicles of model year 1984 through 2007, or posted under the words 'New EPA MPG' and above the word 'Combined' for vehicles of model year 2008 or later on the fueleconomy.gov website of the Environmental Protection Agency for the make, model, and year of such vehicle; or

"(C) with respect to an eligible trade-in vehicle manufactured between model years 1978 through 1985, the equivalent of the number described in subparagraph (A) as determined by the Secretary (and posted on the website of the National Highway Traffic Safety Administration) using data maintained by the Environmental Protection Agency for the make, model, and year of such vehicle.

"(6) the term 'dealer' means a person licensed by a State who engages in the sale of new automobiles to ultimate purchasers;

"(7) the term 'eligible trade-in vehicle' means an automobile or a work truck (as such terms are defined in section 32901(a) of title 49, United States Code) that, at the time it is presented for trade-in under this section—

"(A) is in drivable condition;

"(B) has been continuously insured consistent with the applicable State law and registered to the same owner for a period of not less than 1 year immediately prior to such trade-in;

"(C) was manufactured less than 25 years before the date of the trade-in; and

"(D) in the case of an automobile, has a combined fuel economy value of 18 miles per gallon or less;

"(8) the term 'new fuel efficient automobile' means an automobile described in paragraph (1), (2), (3), or (4)—

"(A) the equitable or legal title of which has not been transferred to any person other than the ultimate purchaser;

"(B) that carries a manufacturer's suggested retail price of $45,000 or less;

"(C) that—

"(i) in the case of passenger automobiles, category 1 trucks, or category 2 trucks, is certified to applicable standards under section 86.1811—04 of title 40, Code of Federal Regulations; or

"(ii) in the case of category 3 trucks, is certified to the applicable vehicle or engine standards under section 86.1816—08, 86—007—11 or 86.008—10 of title 40, Code of Federal Regulations; and

"(D) that has the combined fuel economy value of at least—

"(i) 22 miles per gallon for a passenger automobile;

"(ii) 18 miles per gallon for a category 1 truck; or

"(iii) 15 miles per gallon for a category 2 truck;

"(9) the term 'Program' means the Consumer Assistance to Recycle and Save Program established by this section;

"(10) the term 'qualifying lease' means a lease of an automobile for a period of not less than 5 years;

"(11) the term 'scrappage value' means the amount received by the dealer for a vehicle upon transferring title of such vehicle to the person responsible for ensuring the dismantling and destroying of the vehicle;

"(12) the term 'Secretary' means the Secretary of Transportation acting through the National Highway Traffic Safety Administration;

"(13) the term 'ultimate purchaser' means, with respect to any new automobile, the first person who in good faith purchases such automobile for purposes other than resale;

"(14) the term 'vehicle identification number' means the 17 character number used by the automobile industry to identify individual automobiles; and

"(15) the term 'voucher' means an electronic transfer of funds to a dealer based on an eligible transaction under this program.

"(j) Appropriation. There is hereby appropriated to the Secretary of Transportation $1,000,000,000, of which up to $50,000,000 is available for administration, to remain available until expended to carry out this section."

In 2002, P.L. 107-134, Sec. 105, of this Act, reads as follows:

"Sec. 105. Exclusion of certain cancellations of indebtedness.

"(a) In general. For purposes of the Internal Revenue Code of 1986—

"(1) gross income shall not include any amount which (but for this section) would be includible in gross income by reason of the discharge (in whole or in part) of indebtedness of any taxpayer if the discharge is by reason of the death of an individual incurred as the result of the terrorist attacks against the United States on September 11, 2001, or as the result of illness incurred as a result of an attack involving anthrax occurring on or after September 11, 2001, and before January 1, 2002, and

"(2) return requirements under section 6050P of such Code shall not apply to any discharge described in paragraph (1).

"(b) Effective date. This section shall apply to discharges made on or after September 11, 2001, and before January 1, 2002."

In 2001, P.L. 107-16, Sec. 803, of this Act, reads as follows:

"Sec. 803. No federal income tax on restitution received by victims of the Nazi regime or their heirs or estates.

"(a) In general. For purposes of the Internal Revenue Code of 1986, any excludable restitution payments received by an eligible individual (or the individual's heirs or estate) and any excludable interest—

"(1) shall not be included in gross income; and

"(2) shall not be taken into account for purposes of applying any provision of such Code which takes into account excludable income in computing adjusted gross income, including section 86 of such Code (relating to taxation of Social Security benefits).

For purposes of such Code, the basis of any property received by an eligible individual (or the individual's heirs or estate) as part of an excludable restitution payment shall be the fair market value of such property as of the time of the receipt.

"(b) Eligible individual. For purposes of this section, the term 'eligible individual' means a person who was persecuted on the basis of race, religion, physical or mental disability, or sexual orientation by Nazi Germany, any other Axis regime, or any other Nazi-controlled or Nazi-allied country.

"(c) Excludable restitution payment. For purposes of this section, the term 'excludable restitution payment' means any payment or distribution to an individual (or the individual's heirs or estate) which—

"(1) is payable by reason of the individual's status as an eligible individual, including any amount payable by any foreign country, the United States of America, or any other foreign or domestic entity, or a fund established by any such country or entity, any amount payable as a result of a final resolution of a legal action, and any amount payable under a law providing for payments or restitution of property;

"(2) constitutes the direct or indirect return of, or compensation or reparation for, assets stolen or hidden from, or otherwise lost to, the individual before, during, or immediately after World War II by reason of the individual's status as an eligible individual, including any proceeds of insurance under policies issued on eligible individuals by European insurance companies immediately before and during World War II; or

"(3) consists of interest which is payable as part of any payment or distribution described in paragraph (1) or (2).

"(d) Excludable interest. For purposes of this section, the term 'excludable interest' means any interest earned by—

"(1) escrow accounts or settlement funds established pursuant to the settlement of the action entitled 'In re: Holocaust Victim Assets Litigation,' (E.D.N.Y.) C.A. No. 96-4849,

"(2) funds to benefit eligible individuals or their heirs created by the International Commission on Holocaust Insurance Claims as a result of the Agreement between the Government of the United States of America and the Government of the Federal Republic of Germany concerning the Foundation 'Remembrance, Responsibility, and Future,' dated July 17, 2000, or

"(3) similar funds subject to the administration of the United States courts created to provide excludable restitution payments to eligible individuals (or eligible individuals' heirs or estates).

"(e) Effective date.

"(1) In general. This section shall apply to any amount received on or after January 1, 2000.

"(2) No inference. Nothing in this Act shall be construed to create any inference with respect to the proper tax treatment of any amount received before January 1, 2000."

In 1988, P.L. 100-647, Sec. 6252(a)(1), repealed Sec. 6 of P.L. 98-4 [reproduced below].

Prior to repeal, Sec. 6 of P.L. 98-4 read as follows:

"Sec. 6. Study.

"(a) General rule.

"The Secretary of the Treasury or his delegate, after consultation with the Secretary of Agriculture, shall conduct a study of

"(1) the 1983 payment-in-kind program, and

"(2) the tax treatment provided with respect to such program by this Act.

"(b) Report.

"Not later than September 1, 1983, the Secretary of the Treasury shall submit to the Congress a report on the study conducted under subsection (a), together with such recommendations as he may deem advisable."

In 1986, P.L. 99-272, Sec. 13207(d), redesignated Sec. 531(g) of P.L. 98-369 as Sec. 531(h) [reproduced below].

In 1984, P.L. 98-369, Sec. 531(c), substituted "commissions, fringe benefits, and similar items" for "commissions, and similar items" in para. (a)(1), effective on 1/1/85. Sec. 531(h) of this Act [as amended by Sec. 13207(d) of P.L. 99-272, see above] provides:

"(h) Moratorium on issuance of regulations relating to faculty housing.

"(1) In general. Any regulation providing for the inclusion in gross income under section 61 of the Internal Revenue Code of 1954 of the excess (if any) of the fair market value of qualified campus lodging over the greater of—

"(A) the operating costs paid or incurred in furnishing such lodging, or

"(B) the rent received for such lodging,

shall not be issued before January 1, 1986.

"(2) Qualified campus lodging. For purposes of this subsection, the term 'qualified campus lodging' means lodging which is—

"(A) located on (or in close proximity to) a campus of an educational institution (described in section 170(b)(1)(A)(ii) of the Internal Revenue Code of 1954), and

"(B) provided by such institution to an employee of such institution, or to a spouse or dependent (within the meaning of section 152 of such Code) of such employee.

"(3) Application of subsection. This subsection shall apply with respect to lodging furnished after December 31, 1983, and before January 1, 1986."

—P.L. 98-369, Sec. 1026, provides:

"Sec. 1026. No gain recognized from net gifts made before March 4, 1981.

"(a) In general. In the case of any transfer of property subject to gift tax made before March 4, 1981, for purposes of subtitle A of the Internal Revenue Code of 1954, gross income of the donor shall not include any amount attributable to the donee's payment of (or agreement to pay) any gift tax imposed with respect to such gift.

"(b) Gift tax defined. For purposes of subsection (a), the term 'gift tax' means—

"(1) the tax imposed by chapter 12 of such Code, and

"(2) any tax imposed by a State (or the District of Columbia) on transfers by gifts.

"(c) Statute of limitations. If refund or credit of any overpayment of tax resulting from subsection (a) is prevented on the date of the enactment of this Act (or at any time within 1 year after such date) by the operation of any law or rule of law (including res judicata), refund or credit of such overpayment (to the extent attributable to subsection (a)) may nevertheless be made or allowed if claim therefor is filed within 1 year after the date of the enactment of this Act."

—P.L. 98-369, Sec. 1061, amended Sec. 5 of P.L. 98-4 (reproduced below), by redesignating Sec. 5(b) as (c) and adding new Sec. 5(b) and by amending Sec. 5(a)(2), effective for commodities received for the 1984 crop year (as described in Sec. 5(a)(2) of P.L. 98-4].

Prior to amendment, Sec. 5(a)(2) of P.L. 98-4 read as follows:

"(2) 1983 crop year. The term '1983 crop year' means the crop year for any crop the harvesting or planting period for which occurs during 1983."

In 1983, P.L. 98-4, of this Act, [as amended by P.L. 98-369, Sec. 1061(a); P.L. 99-514, Sec. 2; and P.L. 100-647, Sec. 6252(a)(1)] provides:

"SECTION 1. SHORT TITLE.

"This Act may be cited as the 'Payment-in-Kind Tax Treatment Act of 1983'.

"SEC. 2. INCOME TAX TREATMENT OF AGRICULTURAL COMMODITIES RECEIVED UNDER A 1983 PAYMENT-IN-KIND PROGRAM.

"(a) Income Tax Deferral, Etc. Except as otherwise provided in this Act, for purposes of the Internal Revenue Code of 1986—

"(1) a qualified taxpayer shall not be treated as having realized income when he receives a commodity under a 1983 payment-in-kind program,

"(2) such commodity shall be treated as if it were produced by such taxpayer, and

"(3) the unadjusted basis of such commodity in the hands of such taxpayer shall be zero.

"(b) Effective Date. This section shall apply to taxable years ending after December 31, 1982, but only with respect to commodities received for the 1983 crop year.

"SEC. 3. LAND DIVERTED UNDER 1983 PAYMENT-IN-KIND PROGRAM TREATED AS USED IN FARMING BUSINESS, ETC.

"(a) General Rule. For purposes of the provisions specified in subsection (b), in the case of any land diverted from the production of an agricultural commodity under a 1983 payment-in-kind program—

"(1) such land shall be treated as used during the 1983 crop year by the qualified taxpayer in the active conduct of the trade or business of farming, and

"(2) any qualified taxpayer who materially participates in the diversion and devotion to conservation uses required under a 1983 payment-in-kind program shall be treated as materially participating in the operation of such land during such crop year.

"(b) Provisions to Which Subsection (a) Applies. The provisions specified in this subsection are—

"(1) section 2032A of the Internal Revenue Code of 1986 (relating to valuation of certain farm, etc., real property),

"(2) section 6166 of such Code (relating to extension of time for payment of estate tax where estate consists largely of interest in closely held business),

"(3) chapter 2 of such Code (relating to tax on self-employment income), and

"(4) title II of the Social Security Act [42 U.S.C. 401 et seq.] (relating to Federal old-age, survivors, and disability insurance benefits).

"SEC. 4. ANTIABUSE RULES.

"(a) General Rule. In the case of any person, sections 2 and 3 of this Act shall not apply with respect to any land acquired by such person after February 23, 1983, unless such land was acquired in a qualified acquisition.

"(b) Qualified Acquisition. For purposes of this section, the term 'qualified acquisition' means any acquisition—

"(1) by reason of the death of a qualified transferor,

"(2) by reason of a gift from a qualified transferor, or

"(3) from a qualified transferor who is a member of the family of the person acquiring the land.

"(c) Definitions and Special Rules. For purposes of this section—

"(1) Qualified transferor. The term 'qualified transferor' means any person—

"(A) who held the land on February 23, 1983, or

"(B) who acquired the land after February 23, 1983, in a qualified acquisition.

"(2) Member of family. The term 'member of the family' has the meaning given such term by section 2032A(e)(2) of the Internal Revenue Code of 1986.

"(3) Mere change in form of business. Subsection (a) shall not apply to any change in ownership by reason of a mere change in the form of conducting the trade or business so long as the land is retained in such trade or business and the person holding the land before such change retains a direct or indirect 80-percent interest in such land.

"(4) Treatment of certain acquisitions of right to the crop. The acquisition of a direct or indirect interest in 80 percent or more of the crop from any land shall be treated as an acquisition of such land.

"SEC. 5. DEFINITIONS AND SPECIAL RULES.

"(a) General Rule. For purposes of this Act—

"(1) 1983 payment-in-kind program. The term '1983 payment-in-kind program' means any program for the 1983 crop year—

"(A) under which the Secretary of Agriculture (or his delegate) makes payments in kind of any agricultural commodity to any person in return for—

"(i) the diversion of farm acreage from the production of an agricultural commodity, and

"(ii) the devotion of such acreage to conservation uses, and

"(B) which the Secretary of Agriculture certifies to the Secretary of the Treasury as being described in subparagraph (A).

"(2) Crop year. The term '1983 crop year' means the crop year for any crop the planting or harvesting period for which occurs during 1983. The term '1984 crop year' means the crop year for wheat the planting and harvesting period for which occurs during 1984.

"(3) Qualified taxpayer. The term 'qualified taxpayer' means any producer of agricultural commodities (within the meaning of the 1983 payment-in-kind programs) who receives any agricultural commodity in return for meeting the requirements of clauses (i) and (ii) of paragraph (1)(A).

"(4) Receipt includes right to receive, etc. A right to receive (or other constructive receipt of) a commodity shall be treated the same as actual receipt of such commodity.

"(5) Amounts received by the taxpayer as reimbursement for storage. A qualified taxpayer reporting on the cash receipts and disbursements method of accounting shall not be treated as being entitled to receive any amount as reimbursement for storage of commodities received under a 1983 payment-in-kind program until such amount is actually received by the taxpayer.

"(6) Commodity credit loans treated separately. Subsection (a) of section 2 shall apply to the receipt of any commodity under a 1983 payment-in-kind program separately from, and without taking into account, any related transaction or series of transactions involving the satisfaction of loans from the Commodity Credit Corporation.

"(b) Extension to Wheat Planted and Harvested in 1984. In the case of wheat—

"(1) any reference in this Act to the 1983 crop year shall include a reference to the 1984 crop year, and

"(2) any reference to the 1983 payment-in-kind program shall include a reference to any program for the 1984 year for wheat which meets the requirements of subparagraphs (A) and (B) of subsection (a)(1).

"(c) Regulations. The Secretary of the Treasury or his delegate (after consultation with the Secretary of Agriculture) shall prescribe such regulations as may be necessary to carry out the purposes of this Act, including (but not limited to) such regulations as may be necessary to carry out the purposes of this Act where the commodity is received by a cooperative on behalf of the qualified taxpayer."

In 1981, P.L. 97-34, Sec. 801, substituted "December 31, 1983" for "May 31, 1981" each place it appears in Sec. 1 of P.L. 95-427, reproduced below.

In 1979, P.L. 96-167, Sec. 1, substituted "May 31, 1981" for "December 31, 1979" each place it appears in Sec. 1 of P.L. 95-427, reproduced below.

In 1978, P.L. 95-600, Sec. 162, extended the effective date of amendments made by Sec. 2117 of P.L. 94-455 (reproduced below) to discharges of indebtedness made before 1/1/83 with respect to cancellation of certain student loans. Sec. 163(c)(2) of the Act provides as follows:

"(2) Expenses. Amounts received by volunteers serving in any program [tax counseling for elderly] carried out under this section as reimbursement for expenses are exempt from taxation under chapters 1 and 21 of the Internal Revenue Code of 1954."

—P.L. 95-427, Sec. 1, provided as follows:

"Section 1. Fringe Benefit Regulations.

"(a) In General.

No fringe benefit regulation shall be issued—

"(1) in final form on or after May 1, 1978, and on or before December 31, 1983 or

"(2) in proposed or final form on or after May 1, 1978, if such regulation has an effective date on or before December 31, 1983.

"(b) Definition of fringe benefit regulation.

For purposes of subsection (a), the term 'fringe benefit regulation' means a regulation providing for the inclusion of any fringe benefit in gross income by reason of section 61 of the Internal Revenue Code of 1954."

In 1976, P.L. 94-455, Sec. 2117, provided the following with respect to cancellation of certain student loans, effective for discharges of indebtedness made before 1/1/79:

"Sec. 2117. Cancellation of certain student loans.

"(a) In General.

"In the case of an individual, no amount shall be included in gross income for purposes of section 61 of the Internal Revenue Code of 1954 by reason of the discharge of all or part of the indebtedness of the individual under a student loan if such discharge was pursuant to a provision of such loan under which all or part of the indebtedness of the individual would be discharged if the individual worked for a certain period of time in certain geographical areas or for certain classes of employers.

"(b) Student Loan.

"For purposes of this section the term 'student loan' means any loan to an individual to assist the individual in attending an educational organization described in section 170(b)(1)(A)(ii) of such Code—

"(1) by the United States, or an instrumentality or agency thereof, or a State, territory, or possession of the United States, or any political subdivision thereof, or the District of Columbia, or

"(2) by any such educational organization pursuant to an agreement with the United States, or an instrumentality or agency thereof, or a State, territory, or possession of the United States, or any political subdivision thereof, or the District of Columbia under which the funds from which the loan was made were provided to such educational organization."

—P.L. 94-455, Sec. 2119, covers the application of Code Sec. 61 (as it relates to costs of goods sold) to publisher's prepublication expenditures. See note to Code Sec. 174.

In 1960, P.L. 86-780, Sec. 5, provided with respect to employee moving expenses that:

"Any amount received after December 31, 1949, and before October 1, 1955, from a corporation which—

"(1) was formed exclusively for the purpose of, and was engaged exclusively in, operating without profit a scientific laboratory for the Atomic Energy Commission, and

"(2) operated solely on funds appropriated to the Atomic Energy Commission, by an individual as reimbursement for moving himself and his immediate family, household goods, and personal effects to a new place of residence in order to accept employment with such corporation shall, for Federal income tax purposes, be treated as an amount which was not includible in the gross income of the individual, to the extent that such amount did not exceed the actual expenses paid or incurred by the individual for such purposes, if the individual was advised, at the time of his employment, by an authorized officer, employee, or agent of such corporation that the amount of such reimbursement would not be includible in gross income. If refund or credit of any overpayment resulting from the application of this section is prevented on the date of enactment of this Act [9/14/60], or within six months after such date, by the operation of any law or rule of law (other than chapter 74 of the Internal Revenue Code of 1954, relating to closing agreements and compromises, and the corresponding provisions of prior law), refund or credit of such overpayment may, nevertheless, be made or allowed if claim therefore is filed within six months after such date. No interest shall be paid or allowed on any overpayment resulting from the application of the preceding sentence."

Sec. 62. Adjusted gross income defined.
(a) General rule.

For purposes of this subtitle, the term "adjusted gross income" means, in the case of an individual, gross income minus the following deductions:

(1) Trade and business deductions. The deductions allowed by this chapter (other than by part VII of this subchapter) which are attributable to a trade or business carried on by the taxpayer, if such trade or business does not consist of the performance of services by the taxpayer as an employee.

(2) Certain trade and business deductions of employees.

(A) Reimbursed expenses of employees. The deductions allowed by part VI (section 161 and following) which consist of expenses paid or incurred by the taxpayer, in connection with the performance by him of services as an employee, under a reimbursement or other expense allowance arrangement with his employer. The fact that the reimbursement may be provided by a third party shall not be determinative of whether or not the preceding sentence applies.

(B) Certain expenses of performing artists. The deductions allowed by section 162 which consist of expenses paid or incurred by a qualified performing artist in connection with the performances by him of services in the performing arts as an employee.

(C) Certain expenses of officials. The deductions allowed by section 162 which consist of expenses paid or incurred with respect to services performed by an official as an employee of a State or a political subdivision thereof in a position compensated in whole or in part on a fee basis.

(D) Certain expenses of elementary and secondary school teachers. In the case of taxable years beginning during 2002, 2003, 2004, 2005, 2006, 2007, 2008, 2009, 2010, or 2011 the deductions allowed by section 162 which consist of expenses, not in excess of $250, paid or incurred by an eligible educator in connection with books, supplies (other than nonathletic supplies for courses of instruction in health or physical education), computer equipment (including related software and services) and other equipment, and supplementary materials used by the eligible educator in the classroom.

(E) Certain expenses of members of reserve components of the Armed Forces of the United States. The deductions allowed by section 162 which consist of expenses, determined at a rate not in excess of the rates for travel expenses (including per diem in lieu of subsistence) authorized for employees of agencies under subchapter I of chapter 57 of title 5, United States Code, paid or incurred by the taxpayer in connection with the performance of services by such taxpayer as a member of a reserve component of the Armed Forces of the United States for any period during which such individual is more than 100 miles away from home in connection with such services.

(3) Losses from sale or exchange of property. The deductions allowed by part VI (Sec. 161 and following) as losses from the sale or exchange of property.

(4) Deductions attributable to rents and royalties. The deductions allowed by part VI (Sec. 161 and following), by section 212 (relating to expenses for production of income), and by section 611 (relating to depletion) which are attributable to property held for the production of rents or royalties.

(5) Certain deductions of life tenants and income beneficiaries of property. In the case of a life tenant of property, or an income beneficiary of property held in trust, or an heir, legatee, or devisee of an estate, the deduction for depreciation allowed by section 167 and the deduction allowed by section 611.

(6) Pension, profit-sharing, and annuity plans of self-employed individuals. In the case of an individual who is an employee within the meaning of section 401(c)(1), the deduction allowed by section 404.

(7) Retirement savings. The deduction allowed by section 219 (relating to deduction of certain retirement savings).

(8) Repealed.

(9) Penalties forfeited because of premature withdrawal of funds from time savings accounts or deposits. The deductions allowed by section 165 for losses incurred in any transaction entered into for profit, though not connected with a trade or business, to the extent that such losses include amounts forfeited to a bank, mutual savings bank, savings and loan association, building and loan association, cooperative bank or homestead association as a penalty for premature withdrawal of funds from a time savings account, certificate of deposit, or similar class of deposit.

(10) Alimony. The deduction allowed by section 215.

(11) Reforestation expenses. The deduction allowed by section 194.

(12) Certain required repayments of supplemental unemployment compensation benefits. The deduction allowed by section 165 for the repayment to a trust described in paragraph (9) or (17) of section 501(c) of supplemental unemployment compensation benefits received from such trust if such repayment is required because of the receipt of trade readjustment allowances under section 231 or 232 of the Trade Act of 1974 (19 U.S.C. 2291 and 2292).

(13) Jury duty pay remitted to employer. Any deduction allowable under this chapter by reason of an individual remitting any portion of any jury pay to such individual's employer in exchange for payment by the employer of compensation for the period such individual was performing jury duty. For purposes of the preceding sentence, the term "jury pay" means any payment received by the individual for the discharge of jury duty.

(14) Deduction for clean-fuel vehicles and certain refueling property. The deduction allowed by section 179A.

(15) Moving expenses. The deduction allowed by section 217.

(16) Archer MSAs. The deduction allowed by section 220.

(17) Interest on education loans. The deduction allowed by section 221.

• *Caution:* Code Sec. 62(a)(18), following, was amended by Sec. 431(b), P.L. 107-16, the Economic Growth and Tax Relief Reconciliation Act of 2001 (EGTRRA). These provisions generally sunset for tax years beginning after 12/31/2012. For specific sunset provisions, see Sec. 901 of P.L. 107-16 (as amended) reproduced in history notes for this Code Sec.

---

(18) Higher education expenses. The deduction allowed by section 222.

(19) Health savings accounts. The deduction allowed by section 223.

(20) Costs involving discrimination suits, etc. Any deduction allowable under this chapter for attorney fees and court costs paid by, or on behalf of, the taxpayer in connection with any action involving a claim of unlawful discrimination (as defined in subsection (e)) or a claim of a violation of subchapter III of chapter 37 of title 31, United States Code or a claim made under section 1862(b)(3)(A) of the Social Security Act (42 U.S.C. 1395y(b)(3)(A)). The preceding sentence shall not apply to any deduction in excess of the amount includible in the taxpayer's gross income for the taxable year on account of a judgment or settlement (whether by suit or agreement and whether as lump sum or periodic payments) resulting from such claim.

(21) Attorneys fees relating to awards to whistleblowers. Any deduction allowable under this chapter for attorney fees and court costs paid by, or on behalf of, the taxpayer in connection with any award under section 7623(b) (relating to awards to whistleblowers). The preceding sentence shall not apply to any deduction in excess of the amount includible in the taxpayer's gross income for the taxable year on account of such award.

Nothing in this section shall permit the same item to be deducted more than once.

(b) Qualified performing artist.

(1) In general. For purposes of subsection (a)(2)(B), the term "qualified performing artist" means, with respect to any taxable year, any individual if—

(A) such individual performed services in the performing arts as an employee during the taxable year for at least 2 employers,

(B) the aggregate amount allowable as a deduction under section 162 in connection with the performance of such services exceeds 10 percent of such individual's gross income attributable to the performance of such services, and

(C) the adjusted gross income of such individual for the taxable year (determined without regard to subsection (a)(2)(B)) does not exceed $16,000.

(2) Nominal employer not taken into account. An individual shall not be treated as performing services in the performing arts as an employee for any employer during any taxable year unless the amount received by such individual from such employer for the performance of such services during the taxable year equals or exceeds $200.

(3) Special rules for married couples.

(A) In general. Except in the case of a husband and wife who lived apart at all times during the taxable year, if the taxpayer is married at the close of the taxable year, subsection (a)(2)(B) shall apply only if the taxpayer and his spouse file a joint return for the taxable year.

(B) Application of paragraph (1). In the case of a joint return—

(i) paragraph (1) (other than subparagraph (C) thereof) shall be applied separately with respect to each spouse, but

(ii) paragraph (1)(C) shall be applied with respect to their combined adjusted gross income.

(C) Determination of marital status. For purposes of this subsection, marital status shall be determined under section 7703(a).

(D) Joint return. For purposes of this subsection, the term "joint return" means the joint return of a husband and wife made under section 6013.

(c) Certain arrangements not treated as reimbursement arrangements.

For purposes of subsection (a)(2)(A), an arrangement shall in no event be treated as a reimbursement or other expense allowance arrangement if—

(1) such arrangement does not require the employee to substantiate the expenses covered by the arrangement to the person providing the reimbursement, or

(2) such arrangement provides the employee the right to retain any amount in excess of the substantiated expenses covered under the arrangement.

The substantiation requirements of the preceding sentence shall not apply to any expense to the extent that substantiation is not required under section 274(d) for such expense by reason of the regulations prescribed under the 2nd sentence thereof.

(d) Definition; special rules.

(1) Eligible educator.

(A) In general. For purposes of subsection (a)(2)(D), the term "eligible educator" means, with respect to any taxable year, an individual who is a kindergarten through grade 12 teacher, instructor, counselor, principal, or aide in a school for at least 900 hours during a school year.

(B) School. The term "school" means any school which provides elementary education or secondary education (kindergarten through grade 12), as determined under State law.

(2) Coordination with exclusions. A deduction shall be allowed under subsection (a)(2)(D) for expenses only to the extent the amount of such expenses exceeds the amount excludable under section 135, 529(c)(1), or 530(d)(2) for the taxable year.

(e) Unlawful discrimination defined.

For purposes of subsection (a)(20), the term "unlawful discrimination" means an act that is unlawful under any of the following:

(1) Section 302 of the Civil Rights Act of 1991 (2 U.S.C. 1202).

(2) Section 201, 202, 203, 204, 205, 206, or 207 of the Congressional Accountability Act of 1995 (2 U.S.C. 1311, 1312, 1313, 1314, 1315, 1316, or 1317).

(3) The National Labor Relations Act (29 U.S.C. 151 et seq.).

(4) The Fair Labor Standards Act of 1938 (29 U.S.C. 201 et seq.).

(5) Section 4 or 15 of the Age Discrimination in Employment Act of 1967 (29 U.S.C. 623 or 633a).

(6) Section 501 or 504 of the Rehabilitation Act of 1973 (29 U.S.C. 791 or 794).

(7) Section 510 of the Employee Retirement Income Security Act of 1974 (29 U.S.C. 1140).

(8) Title IX of the Education Amendments of 1972 (20 U.S.C. 1681 et seq.).

(9) The Employee Polygraph Protection Act of 1988 (29 U.S.C. 2001 et seq.).

(10) The Worker Adjustment and Retraining Notification Act (29 U.S.C. 2102 et seq.).

(11) Section 105 of the Family and Medical Leave Act of 1993 (29 U.S.C. 2615).

(12) Chapter 43 of title 38, United States Code (relating to employment and reemployment rights of members of the uniformed services).

(13) Section 1977, 1979, or 1980 of the Revised Statutes (42 U.S.C. 1981, 1983, or 1985).

(14) Section 703, 704, or 717 of the Civil Rights Act of 1964 (42 U.S.C. 2000e-2, 2000e-3, or 2000e-16).

(15) Section 804, 805, 806, 808, or 818 of the Fair Housing Act (42 U.S.C. 3604, 3605, 3606, 3608, or 3617).

(16) Section 102, 202, 302, or 503 of the Americans with Disabilities Act of 1990 (42 U.S.C. 12112, 12132, 12182, or 12203).

(17) Any provision of Federal law (popularly known as whistleblower protection provisions) prohibiting the discharge of an employee, the discrimination against an employee, or any other form of retaliation or reprisal against an employee for asserting rights or taking other actions permitted under Federal law.

(18) Any provision of Federal, State, or local law, or common law claims permitted under Federal, State, or local law—

(i) providing for the enforcement of civil rights, or

(ii) regulating any aspect of the employment relationship, including claims for wages, compensation, or benefits, or prohibiting the discharge of an employee, the discrimination against an employee, or any other form of retaliation or reprisal against an employee for asserting rights or taking other actions permitted by law.

In 2010, P.L. 111-312, Sec. 101(a)(1), substituted "December 31, 2012" for "December 31, 2010" both places it appeared in Sec. 901, P.L. 107-16 [see below], effective as if included in the enactment of P.L. 107-16, EGTRRA, 6/7/2001.

—P.L. 111-312, Sec. 721(a), substituted "2009, 2010, or 2011" for "or 2009" in subpara. (a)(2)(D), effective for tax. yrs. begin. after 12/31/2009.

In 2008, P.L. 110-343, Sec. 203(a)DivC, substituted "2007, 2008, or 2009" for "or 2007" in subpara. (a)(2)(D), effective for tax. yrs. begin. after 12/31/2007.

In 2006, P.L. 109-432, Sec. 108(a), substituted "2005, 2006, or 2007" for "or 2005" in subpara. (a)(2)(D), effective for tax. yrs. begin. after 12/31/2005.

—P.L. 109-432, Sec. 406(a)(3), added para. (a)(21), effective for information provided on or after 12/20/2006.

In 2005, P.L. 109-135, Sec. 412(q)(1)(A), redesignated para. (a)(19) [as added by Sec. 703(a) of P.L. 108-357, see below] as para. (a)(20)... Sec. 412(q)(1)(B), redesignated text of para. (a)(19) [as added by Sec. 703(a) of P.L. 108-357, see below] as text of para. (a)(20)... Sec. 412(q)(2), substituted "subsection (a)(20)" for "subsection (a)(19)" in subsec. (e), effective 12/21/2005.

In 2004, P.L. 108-357, Sec. 703(a), added para. (a)(19) [sic (a)(20) as clarified by Sec. 412(q)(1)(A) and (B) of P.L. 109-135, see above]... Sec. 703(b), added subsec. (e), effective for fees and costs paid after 10/22/2004 with respect to any judgment or settlement occurring after 10/22/2004.

—P.L. 108-311, Sec. 307(a), substituted ", 2003, 2004, or 2005" for "or 2003" in subpara. (a)(2)(D), effective for expenses paid or incurred in tax. yrs. begin. after 12/31/2003.

In 2003, P.L. 108-173, Sec. 1201(b), added para. (a)(19), effective for tax. yrs. begin. after 12/31/2003.

—P.L. 108-121, Sec. 109(b), added subpara. (a)(2)(E), effective for amounts paid or incurred in tax. yrs. begin. after 12/31/2002.

In 2002, P.L. 107-358, Sec. 2, added subsec. (c) in Sec. 901 of P.L. 107-16 [see below], effective 12/17/2002.

—P.L. 107-147, Sec. 406(a), added subpara. (a)(2)(D)... Sec. 406(b), added subsec. (d), effective for tax. yrs. begin. after 12/31/2001.

In 2001, P.L. 107-16, Sec. 431(b), added para. (a)(18), effective for payments made in tax. yrs. begin. after 12/31/2001.

—P.L. 107-16, Sec. 901, of this Act [as amended by Sec. 2, P.L. 107-358, and Sec. 101(a)(1), P.L. 111-312, see above], reads as follows:

"Sec. 901. Sunset of provisions of Act.

"(a) In general. All provisions of, and amendments made by, this Act shall not apply—

"(1) to taxable, plan, or limitation years beginning after December 31, 2012, or

"(2) in the case of title V, to estates of decedents dying, gifts made, or generation skipping transfers, after December 31, 2012.

"(b) Application of certain laws. The Internal Revenue Code of 1986 and the Employee Retirement Income Security Act of 1974 shall be applied and administered to years, estates, gifts, and transfers described in subsection (a) as if the provisions and amendments described in subsection (a) had never been enacted.

"(c) Exception. Subsection (a) shall not apply to section 803 (relating to no federal income tax on restitution received by victims of the Nazi regime or their heirs or estates)."

In 2000, P.L. 106-554, Sec. 1(a)(7), [which enacted into law Sec. 202(b)(1) of P.L. 106-554] amended para. (a)(16), effective 12/21/2000.

Prior to amendment, para. (a)(16) read as follows:

"(16) Medical savings accounts. The deduction allowed by section 220."

In 1997, P.L. 105-34, Sec. 202(b), added para. (a)(17), effective as provided in Sec. 202(e) of this Act, which reads as follows:

"(e) Effective date. The amendments made by this section shall apply to any qualified education loan as defined in Code Section 221(e)(1) of the Internal Revenue Code as incurred on, before, or after the date of enactment of this Act [8/5/97], but only with respect to—

"(1) any loan interest payment due and paid after December 31, 1997, and

"(2) the portion of the 60-month period referred to in section 221(d) of the Internal Revenue Code of 1986 (as added by this section) after December 31, 1997."

—P.L. 105-34, Sec. 975(a), added subpara. (a)(2)(C), effective for expenses paid or incurred in tax. yrs. begin. after 12/31/86.

In 1996, P.L. 104-191, Sec. 301(b), added para. (a)(16), effective for tax. yrs. begin. after 12/31/96.

—P.L. 104-188, Sec. 1401(b)(4), deleted para. (a)(8), effective for tax. yrs. begin. after 12/31/99. For transitional rules, see Sec. 1401(c)(2), of this Act, which reads as follows:

"(2) Retention of certain transition rules. The amendments made by this section shall not apply to any distribution for which the taxpayer is eligible to elect the benefits of section 1122(h)(3) or (5) of the Tax Reform Act of 1986. Notwithstanding the preceding sentence, individuals who elect such benefits after December 31, 1999, shall not be eligible for 5-year averaging under section 402(d) of the Internal Revenue Code of 1986 (as in effect immediately before such amendments)."

Prior to deletion, para. (a)(8) read as follows:

"(8) Certain portion of lump-sum distributions from pension plans taxed under section 402(d). The deduction allowed by section 402(d)(3)"

In 1993, P.L. 103-66, Sec. 13213(c)(1), added para. (a)(15), effective for expenses incurred after 12/31/93.

In 1992, P.L. 102-486, Sec. 1913(a)(2), added para. (a)(14), effective for property placed in service after 6/30/93.

—P.L. 102-318, Sec. 521(b)(2), substituted "402(d)" for "402(e)" each place it appeared in para. (a)(8), effective for distributions after 12/31/92. For special rule, see Sec. 521(e)(2) of this Act which reads as follows:

"(2) Special rule for partial distributions. For purposes of section 402(a)(5)(D)(i)(II) of the Internal Revenue Code of 1986 (as in effect before the amendments made by this section), a distribution before January 1, 1993, which is made before or at the same time as a series of periodic payments shall not be treated as one of such series if it is not substantially equal in amount to other payments in such series."

In 1990, P.L. 101-508, Sec. 11802(e)(1), amended para. (a)(13), effective 11/5/90 except as provided in Sec. 11821(b) of this Act, reproduced in note following Code Sec. 220.

Prior to amendment, para. (a)(13) read as follows:

"(13) Jury duty pay remitted to employer. The deduction allowed by section 220."

In 1988, P.L. 100-647, Sec. 1001(b)(3)(A), added the last sentence to subpara. (a)(2)(A) . . . Sec. 6007(b), added para. (a)(13), effective for tax. yrs. begin. after 12/31/86.

—P.L. 100-485, Sec. 702(a), added subsec. (c), effective for tax. yrs. begin. after 12/31/88.

In 1986, P.L. 99-514, Sec. 131(b)(1), deleted para. (16) . . . Sec. 132(b)(1), amended para. (2) . . . Sec. 132(b)(2), substituted "(a) General rule. For purposes of this subtitle" for "For purposes of this subtitle" in matter preceding para. (1), and added subsec. (b) . . . Sec. 132(c), deleted para. (a)(8) [as amended] . . . Sec. 301(b)(1), deleted para. (a)(3) [as amended] and redesignated paras. (a)(4), (a)(5), (a)(6), (a)(7), (a)(10), (a)(11), (a)(12), (a)(13) (a)(14), and (a)(15) [as amended] as paras. (a)(3) through (a)(12), effective for tax. yrs. begin. after 12/31/86.

Prior to deletion, para. (16) read as follows:

"(16) Deduction for two-earner married couples. The deduction allowed by section 221."

Prior to amendment, para. (2) read as follows:

"(2) Trade and business deductions of employees.

"(A) Reimbursed expenses. The deductions allowed by part VI (Sec. 161 and following) which consist of expenses paid or incurred by the taxpayer, in connection with the performance by him of services as an employee, under a reimbursement or other expense allowance arrangement with his employer.

"(B) Expenses for travel away from home. The deductions allowed by part VI (Sec. 161 and following) which consist of expenses of travel, meals, and lodging while away from home, paid or incurred by the taxpayer in connection with the performance by him of services as an employee.

"(C) Transportation expenses. The deductions allowed by part VI (Sec. 161 and following) which consist of expenses of transportation paid or incurred by the taxpayer in connection with the performance by him of services as an employee.

"(D) Outside salesmen. The deductions allowed by part VI (Sec. 161 and following) which are attributable to a trade or business carried on by the taxpayer, if such trade or business consists of the performance of services by the taxpayer as an employee and if such trade or business is to solicit, away from the employer's place of business, business for the employer."

Prior to deletion, para (a)(8) [as amended] read as follows:

"(8) Moving expense deduction. The deduction allowed by section 217."

Prior to deletion, para. (a)(3) [as amended] read as follows:

"(3) Long-term capital gains. The deduction allowed by section 1202."

—P.L. 99-514, Sec. 1875(c)(3), deleted "to the extent attributable to contributions made on behalf of such individual" after "section 404" in para. (7) [redesignated as para. (a)(6) by Sec. 301 of this Act, see above], effective for tax. yrs. begin. after 12/31/83.

In 1984, P.L. 98-369, Sec. 491(d)(2)(A), substituted "the deduction allowed by section 404" for "the deductions allowed by section 404 and section 405(c)" in para. (7) . . . Sec. 491(d)(2)(B), substituted "and annuity" for "annuity, and bond purchase" in the heading of para. (7), effective for obligations issued after 12/31/83.

In 1982, P.L. 97-354, Sec. 5(a)(17), deleted para. (9), effective for yrs. begin. after 12/31/83.

Prior to deletion, para. (9) read as follows:

"(9) Pension, etc., plans of electing small business corporations. The deduction allowed by section 1379(b)(3)."

In 1981, P.L. 97-34, Sec. 103(b), added para. (16) after para. (15) (as redesignated by Sec. 112(b)(2) of this Act, see below), effective for tax. yrs. end. after 12/31/81.

—P.L. 97-34, Sec. 112(b)(2), deleted para. (14) and redesignated paras. (15) and (16) as paras. (14) and (15), effective for tax. yrs. begin. after 12/31/81.

Prior to deletion, para. (14) read as follows:

"(14) Deduction for certain expenses of living abroad. The deduction allowed by section 913."

—P.L. 97-34, Sec. 311(h)(1), deleted "and the deduction allowed by section 220 (relating to retirement savings for certain married individuals)" following "certain retirement savings)" in para. (10), effective for tax. yrs. begin. after 12/31/81. Sec. 311(i)(2) of this Act provides:

"(2) Transitional rule. For purposes of the Internal Revenue Code of 1954, any amount allowed as a deduction under section 220 of such Code (as in effect before its repeal by this Act) shall be treated as if it were allowed by section 219 of such Code."

In 1980, P.L. 96-608, Sec. 3(a), added para. (16), effective for repayments made in tax. yrs. begin. after 12/28/80.

—P.L. 96-451, Sec. 301(b), added para. (15), effective for additions to capital account made after 12/31/79.

In 1979, P.L. 96-167, Sec. 2, substituted "May 31, 1981" for "December 31, 1979" each place it appeared in Sec. 2 of P.L. 95-427, reproduced below.

In 1978, P.L. 95-615, Sec. 203(b), added para. (14), effective for tax. yrs. begin. after 12/31/77. Sec. 209(c) of the Act provides:

"(c) Election of Prior Law.

"(1) A taxpayer may elect not to have the amendments made by this title apply with respect to any taxable year beginning after December 31, 1977, and before January 1, 1979.

"(2) An election under this subsection shall be filed with a taxpayer's timely filed return for the first taxable year beginning after December 31, 1977."

—P.L. 95-427, Sec. 2, provides as follows:

"Sec. 2. Commuting Expenses.

With respect to transportation costs paid or incurred after December 31, 1976, and on or before May 31, 1981, the application of sections 62, 162, and 262 and of chapters 21, 23, and 24 of the Internal Revenue Code of 1954 to transportation expenses in traveling between a taxpayer's residence and place of work shall be determined—

"(1) without regard to Revenue Ruling 76-453 (and without regard to any other regulation, ruling, or decision reaching the same result as, or a result similar to, the result set forth in such Revenue Ruling); and

"(2) with full regard to the rules in effect before Revenue Ruling 76-453."

In 1976, P.L. 94-455, Sec. 502(a), added para. (13), effective for tax. yrs. begin. after 12/31/76.

—P.L. 94-455, Sec. 1501(b)(1), added "and the deduction allowed by section 220 (relating to retirement savings for certain married individuals)" after "(relating to deduction of certain retirement savings)" in para. (10), effective for tax. yrs. begin. after 12/31/76.

—P.L. 94-455, Sec. 1901(a)(8), redesignated para. (11) as added by Sec. 6(a) of P.L. 93-483, as para. (12), effective for tax. yrs. begin. after 12/31/76.

—P.L. 94-455, Sec. 1901(a)(9), substituted "trade or business, to the extent" for "trade or business to the extent" in para. (12), as redesignated by Sec. 1901(a)(8) of this Act, effective for tax. yrs. begin. after 12/31/76.

In 1974, P.L. 93-483, Sec. 6(a), added para. (11), titled "Penalties forfeited because of premature withdrawal of funds from time savings accounts or deposits.", effective for tax. yrs. begin. after 12/31/72.

—P.L. 93-406, Sec. 2002(a)(2), added para. (10), effective for tax. yrs. begin. after 12/31/74.

—P.L. 93-406, Sec. 2005(c)(9), added para. (11), effective for distributions or payments made after '73, in tax. yrs. begin. after '73.

In 1969, P.L. 91-172, Sec. 531(b), added para. (9), effective for tax. yrs. of electing small business corporations begin. after 12/31/70.

In 1964, P.L. 88-272, Sec. 213(b), added para. (8), effective for expenses incurred after 12/31/63, in tax. yrs. end. after 12/31/63.

In 1962, P.L. 87-792, Sec. 7, added para. (7), effective for tax. yrs. begin. after 12/31/62.

⎡ • **Caution:** Code Sec. 63, following, was amended by P.L. 107-16, EGTRRA, P.L. 107-147 and P.L. 108-311. These provisions generally sunset for tax years beginning after 12/31/2012. For specific sunset provisions, see Sec. 901, P.L. 107-16 (as amended) and Sec. 105 of P.L. 108-311, reproduced in history notes for this Code Sec. ⎦

Sec. 63. Taxable income defined.
(a) In general.

Except as provided in subsection (b), for purposes of this subtitle, the term "taxable income" means gross income minus the deductions allowed by this chapter (other than the standard deduction).

(b) Individuals who do not itemize their deductions.

In the case of an individual who does not elect to itemize his deductions for the taxable year, for purposes of this sub-

title, the term "taxable income" means adjusted gross income, minus—
   (1) the standard deduction, and
   (2) the deduction for personal exemptions provided in section 151.
(c) Standard deduction.
For purposes of this subtitle—
   (1) In general. Except as otherwise provided in this subsection, the term "standard deduction" means the sum of—
      (A) the basic standard deduction,
      (B) the additional standard deduction,
      (C) in the case of any taxable year beginning in 2008 or 2009, the real property tax deduction,
      (D) the disaster loss deduction, and
      (E) the motor vehicle sales tax deduction.
   (2) Basic standard deduction. For purposes of paragraph (1), the basic standard deduction is—
      (A) 200 percent of the dollar amount in effect under subparagraph (C) for the taxable year in the case of—
         (i) a joint return, or
         (ii) a surviving spouse (as defined in section 2(a)),
      (B) $4,400 in the case of a head of household (as defined in section 2(b)), or
      (C) $3,000 in any other case.
   (3) Additional standard deduction for aged and blind. For purposes of paragraph (1), the additional standard deduction is the sum of each additional amount to which the taxpayer is entitled under subsection (f).
   (4) Adjustments for inflation. In the case of any taxable year beginning in a calendar year after 1988, each dollar amount contained in paragraph (2)(B), (2)(C), or (5) or subsection (f) shall be increased by an amount equal to—
      (A) such dollar amount, multiplied by
      (B) the cost-of-living adjustment determined under section 1(f)(3) for the calendar year in which the taxable year begins, by substituting for "calendar year 1992" in subparagraph (B) thereof—
         (i) "calendar year 1987" in the case of the dollar amounts contained in paragraph (2)(B), (2)(C), or (5)(A) or subsection (f), and
         (ii) "calendar year 1997" in the case of the dollar amount contained in paragraph (5)(B).
   (5) Limitation on basic standard deduction in the case of certain dependents. In the case of an individual with respect to whom a deduction under section 151 is allowable to another taxpayer for a taxable year beginning in the calendar year in which the individual's taxable year begins, the basic standard deduction applicable to such individual for such individual's taxable year shall not exceed the greater of—
      (A) $500, or
      (B) the sum of $250 and such individual's earned income.
   (6) Certain individuals, etc., not eligible for standard deduction. In the case of—
      (A) a married individual filing a separate return where either spouse itemizes deductions,
      (B) a nonresident alien individual,
      (C) an individual making a return under section 443(a)(1) for a period of less than 12 months on account of a change in his annual accounting period, or
      (D) an estate or trust, common trust fund, or partnership,
the standard deduction shall be zero.

   (7) Real property tax deduction. For purposes of paragraph (1), the real property tax deduction is the lesser of—
      (A) the amount allowable as a deduction under this chapter for State and local taxes described in section 164(a)(1), or
      (B) $500 ($1,000 in the case of a joint return).
Any taxes taken into account under section 62(a) shall not be taken into account under this paragraph.
   (8) Disaster loss deduction. For the purposes of paragraph (1), the term "disaster loss deduction" means the net disaster loss (as defined in section 165(h)(3)(B)).
   (9) Motor vehicle sales tax deduction. For purposes of paragraph (1), the term "motor vehicle sales tax deduction" means the amount allowable as a deduction under section 164(a)(6). Such term shall not include any amount taken into account under section 62(a).
(d) Itemized deductions.
For purposes of this subtitle, the term "itemized deductions" means the deductions allowable under this chapter other than—
   (1) the deductions allowable in arriving at adjusted gross income, and
   (2) the deduction for personal exemptions provided by section 151.
(e) Election to itemize.
   (1) In general. Unless an individual makes an election under this subsection for the taxable year, no itemized deduction shall be allowed for the taxable year. For purposes of this subtitle, the determination of whether a deduction is allowable under this chapter shall be made without regard to the preceding sentence.
   (2) Time and manner of election. Any election under this subsection shall be made on the taxpayer's return, and the Secretary shall prescribe the manner of signifying such election on the return.
   (3) Change of election. Under regulations prescribed by the Secretary, a change of election with respect to itemized deductions for any taxable year may be made after the filing of the return for such year. If the spouse of the taxpayer filed a separate return for any taxable year corresponding to the taxable year of the taxpayer, the change shall not be allowed unless, in accordance with such regulations—
      (A) the spouse makes a change of election with respect to itemized deductions, for the taxable year covered in such separate return, consistent with the change of treatment sought by the taxpayer, and
      (B) the taxpayer and his spouse consent in writing to the assessment (within such period as may be agreed on with the Secretary) of any deficiency, to the extent attributable to such change of election, even though at the time of the filing of such consent the assessment of such deficiency would otherwise be prevented by the operation of any law or rule of law.
This paragraph shall not apply if the tax liability of the taxpayer's spouse for the taxable year corresponding to the taxable year of the taxpayer has been compromised under section 7122.
(f) Aged or blind additional amounts.
   (1) Additional amounts for the aged. The taxpayer shall be entitled to an additional amount of $600—
      (A) for himself if he has attained age 65 before the close of his taxable year, and
      (B) for the spouse of the taxpayer if the spouse has attained age 65 before the close of the taxable year and

an additional exemption is allowable to the taxpayer for such spouse under section 151(b).

(2) Additional amount for blind. The taxpayer shall be entitled to an additional amount of $600—

(A) for himself if he is blind at the close of the taxable year, and

(B) for the spouse of the taxpayer if the spouse is blind as of the close of the taxable year and an additional exemption is allowable to the taxpayer for such spouse under section 151(b).

For purposes of subparagraph (B), if the spouse dies during the taxable year the determination of whether such spouse is blind shall be made as of the time of such death.

(3) Higher amount for certain unmarried individuals. In the case of an individual who is not married and is not a surviving spouse, paragraphs (1) and (2) shall be applied by substituting "$750" for "$600".

(4) Blindness defined. For purposes of this subsection, an individual is blind only if his central visual acuity does not exceed 20/200 in the better eye with correcting lenses, or if his visual acuity is greater than 20/200 but is accompanied by a limitation in the fields of vision such that the widest diameter of the visual field subtends an angle no greater than 20 degrees.

(g) Marital status.

For purposes of this section, marital status shall be determined under section 7703.

In 2010, P.L. 111-312, Sec. 101(a)(1), substituted "December 31, 2012" for "December 31, 2010" both places it appeared in Sec. 901, P.L. 107-16 [see below], effective as if included in the enactment of P.L. 107-16, EGTRRA, 6/7/2001.

In 2009, P.L. 111-5, Sec. 1008(c)(1), deleted "and" at the end of subpara. (c)(1)(C), substituted ", and" for the period at the end of subpara. (c)(1)(D) and added subpara. (c)(1)(E) ... Sec. 1008(c)(2), added para. (c)(9), effective for purchases on or after 2/17/2009 in tax. yrs. end. after 2/17/2009.

In 2008, P.L. 110-343, Sec. 204(a)DivC, added "or 2009" after "2008" in subpara. (c)(1)(C), effective for tax. yrs. begin. after 12/31/2008.

—P.L. 110-343, Sec. 706(b)(1)DivC, deleted "and" at the end of subpara. (c)(1)(B), substituted ", and" for the period at the end of subpara. (c)(1)(C), and added subpara. (c)(1)(D)

—P.L. 110-343, Sec. 706(b)(2)DivC, added para. (c)(8), effective for disasters declared in tax. yrs. begin. after 12/31/2007.

—P.L. 110-343, Sec. 712DivC, of this Act, provides:

"Sec. 712. Coordination with heartland disaster relief.

"The amendments made by this subtitle, other than the amendments made by sections 706(a)(2), 710, and 711, shall not apply to any disaster described in section 702(c)(1)(A), or to any expenditure or loss resulting from such disaster."

—P.L. 110-289, Sec. 3012(a), struck out "and" at the end of subpara. (c)(1)(A), substituted ", and" for the period at the end of subpara. (c)(1)(B) and added subpara. (c)(1)(C). ... Sec. 3012(b), added para. (c)(7), effective for tax. yrs. begin. after 12/31/2007.

In 2004, P.L. 108-311, Sec. 101(b)(1), amended para. (c)(2) ... Sec. 101(b)(2)(A), substituted "(2)(C)" for "(2)(D)" each place it appeared in para. (c)(4) ... Sec. 101(b)(2)(B), deleted para. (c)(7), effective for tax. yrs. begin. after 12/31/2003.

Prior to amendment, para. (c)(2) read as follows:

"(2) Basic standard deduction. For purposes of paragraph (1), the basic standard deduction is—

"(A) the applicable percentage of the dollar amount in effect under subparagraph (D) for the taxable year in the case of—

"(i) a joint return, or

"(ii) a surviving spouse (as defined in section 2(a)),

"(B) $4,400 in the case of a head of household (as defined in section 2(b)),

"(C) one-half of the amount in effect under subparagraph (A) in the case of a married individual filing a separate return, or

"(D) $3,000 in any other case.

"If any amount determined under subparagraph (A) is not a multiple of $50, such amount shall be rounded to the next lowest multiple of $50."

Prior to deletion, para. (c)(7) read as follows:

"(7) Applicable percentage. For purposes of paragraph (2), the applicable percentage shall be determined in accordance with the following table:

For taxable years beginning in calendar year—	The applicable percentage is—
2003 and 2004	200
2005	174
2006	184
2007	187
2008	190
2009 and thereafter	200.

—P.L. 108-311, Sec. 105, of this Act, reads as follows:

"Sec. 105. Application of EGTRRA sunset to this title. Each amendment made by this title [Secs. 101-104] shall be subject to title IX of the Economic Growth and Tax Relief Reconciliation Act of 2001 [P.L. 107-16, see below] to the same extent and in the same manner as the provision of such Act to which such amendment relates."

In 2003, P.L. 108-27, Sec. 103(a), amended the table in para. (c)(7), effective for tax. yrs. begin. after 12/31/2002.

Prior to amendment, the table in para. (c)(7) read as follows:

"For taxable years beginning in calendar year—	The applicable percentage is—
2005	174
2006	184
2007	187
2008	190
2009 and thereafter	200."

... Sec. 103(b), substituted "2002" for "2004" in Sec. 301(d) of P.L. 107-16 [relating to the effective date of amendments by Sec. 301 of P.L. 107-16, see below]

—P.L. 108-27, Sec. 107, of this Act reads as follows:

"Sec. 107. Application of EGTRRA sunset to this title.

"Each amendment made by this title [Secs. 101-106] shall be subject to title IX of the Economic Growth and Tax Relief Reconciliation Act of 2001 to the same extent and in the same manner as the provision of such Act to which such amendment relates."

In 2002, P.L. 107-358, Sec. 2, added subsec. (c) in Sec. 901 of P.L. 107-16 [see below], effective 12/17/2002.

—P.L. 107-147, Sec. 411(e)(1)(A), substituted "subparagraph (D)" for "subparagraph (C)" in subpara. (c)(2)(A) ... Sec. 411(e)(1)(B), deleted "or" at the end of subpara. (c)(2)(B) ... Sec. 411(e)(1)(C), redesignated subpara. (c)(2)(C) as (c)(2)(D) ... Sec. 411(e)(1)(D), added new subpara. (c)(2)(C) ... Sec. 411(e)(1)(E), added a flush sentence at the end of para. (c)(2) ... Sec. 411(e)(2)(A), substituted "paragraph (2)(B), (2)(D), or (5)" for "paragraph (2) or (5)" in para. (c)(4) ... Sec. 411(e)(2)(B), substituted "paragraph (2)(B), (2)(D)," for "paragraph (2)" in clause (c)(4)(B)(i) ... Sec. 411(e)(2)(C), deleted "The preceding sentence shall not apply to the amount referred to in paragraph (2)(A)." at the end of para. (c)(4), effective for tax. yrs. begin. after 12/31/2004.

In 2001, P.L. 107-16, Sec. 301(a)(1), substituted "the applicable percentage of the dollar amount in effect under subparagraph (C) for the taxable year" for "$5,000" in subpara. (c)(2)(A) ... Sec. 301(a)(2), added "or" at the end of subpara. (c)(2)(B) ... Sec. 301(a)(3), substituted "in any other case." for "in the case of an individual who is not married and who is not a surviving spouse or head of household, or" in subpara. (c)(2)(C) ... Sec. 301(a)(4), deleted subpara. (c)(2)(D) ... Sec. 301(b), added para. (c)(7) ... Sec. 301(c)(2), added a flush sentence at the end of para. (c)(4), effective for tax. yrs. begin. after 12/31/2002 [as amended by Sec. 103(b) of P.L. 108-27, see above].

Prior to deletion, subpara. (c)(2)(D) read as follows:

"(D) $2,500 in the case of a married individual filing a separate return."

—P.L. 107-16, Sec. 901, of this Act [as amended by Sec. 2, P.L. 107-358, and Sec. 101(a)(1), P.L. 111-312, see above], reads as follows:

"Sec. 901. Sunset of provisions of Act.

"(a) In general. All provisions of, and amendments made by, this Act shall not apply—

"(1) to taxable, plan, or limitation years beginning after December 31, 2012, or

"(2) in the case of title V, to estates of decedents dying, gifts made, or generation skipping transfers, after December 31, 2012.

"(b) Application of certain laws. The Internal Revenue Code of 1986 and the Employee Retirement Income Security Act of 1974 shall be applied and administered to years, estates, gifts, and transfers described in subsection (a) as if the provisions and amendments described in subsection (a) had never been enacted.

"(c) Exception. Subsection (a) shall not apply to section 803 (relating to no federal income tax on restitution received by victims of the Nazi regime or their heirs or estates)."

In 1997, P.L. 105-34, Sec. 1201(a)(1), amended para. (c)(5) ... Sec. 1201(a)(2)(A), substituted "(5)" for "(5)(A)" in para. (c)(4) ... Sec. 1201(a)(2)(B), amended subpara. (c)(4)(B), effective for tax. yrs. begin. after 12/31/97.

Prior to amendment, subpara. (c)(4)(B) read as follows:

"(B) the cost-of-living adjustment determined under section 1(f)(3) for the calendar year in which the taxable year begins, by substituting 'calendar year 1987' for 'calendar year 1992' in subparagraph (B) thereof."

Prior to amendment, para. (c)(5) read as follows:

"(5) Limitation on basic standard deduction in the case of certain dependents. In the case of an individual with respect to whom a deduction under section 151 is allowable to another taxpayer for a taxable year beginning in the calendar year in which the individual's taxable year begins, the basic standard deduction applicable to such individual for such individual's taxable year shall not exceed the greater of—

"(A) $500, or

"(B) such individual's earned income."

In 1993, P.L. 103-66, Sec. 13201(b)(3)(D), substituted "1992" for "1989" in subpara. (c)(4)(B), effective for tax. yrs. begin. after 12/31/92.

In 1990, P.L. 101-508, Sec. 11101(d)(1)(D), added ", by substituting 'calendar year 1987' for 'calendar year 1989'" in subparagraph (B) thereof" before the period in subpara. (c)(4)(B), effective for tax. yrs. begin. after 12/31/90.

Income   Code Sec. 64

—P.L. 101-508, Sec. 11801(a)(4), deleted subsec. (h), effective 11/5/90 except as provided in Sec. 11821(b) of this Act, which reads as follows:

"(b) Savings provision. If—

"(1) any provision amended or repealed by this part applied to—

"(A) any transaction occurring before the date of the enactment of this Act [11/5/90],

"(B) any property acquired before such date of enactment [11/5/90], or

"(C) any item of income, loss, deduction, or credit taken into account before such date of enactment [11/5/90], and

"(2) the treatment of such transaction, property, or item under such provision would (without regard to the amendments made by this part) affect liability for tax for periods ending after such date of enactment [11/5/90],

nothing in the amendments made by this part shall be construed to affect the treatment of such transaction, property, or item for purposes of determining liability for tax for periods ending after such date of enactment [11/5/90]."

Prior to deletion, subsec. (h) read as follows:

"(h) Transitional rule for taxable years beginning in 1987. In the case of any taxable year beginning in 1987, paragraph (2) of subsection (c) shall be applied—

"(1) by substituting '$3,760' for '$5,000',

"(2) by substituting '$2,540' for '$4,400',

"(3) by substituting '$2,540' for '$3,000', and

"(4) by substituting '$1,880' for '$2,500'.

The preceding sentence shall not apply if the taxpayer is entitled to an additional amount determined under subsection (f) (relating to additional amount for aged and blind) for the taxable year."

In 1988, P.L. 100-647, Sec. 1001(b)(1)(A), substituted "the basic standard deduction applicable" for "the standard deduction applicable" in para. (c)(5)... Sec. 1001(b)(1)(B), substituted "basic standard deduction" for "standard deduction" in the heading of para. (c)(5), effective for tax. yrs. begin. after 12/31/86.

In 1986, P.L. 99-514, Sec. 102(a), amended Code Sec. 63... Sec. 1272(d)(6), deleted subpara. (c)(6)(C) and redesignated subparas. (c)(6)(D) and (E) as (c)(6)(C) and (D), effective for tax. yrs. begin. after 12/31/86. For special rules, see Sec. 1277(b) of this Act, reproduced in note following Code Sec. 931.

Prior to amendment, Code Sec. 63 read as follows:

"SEC. 63. TAXABLE INCOME DEFINED.

"(a) Corporations.

"For purposes of this subtitle, in the case of a corporation, the term 'taxable income' means gross income minus the deductions allowed by this chapter.

"(b) Individuals.

"For purposes of this subtitle, in the case of an individual the term 'taxable income' means adjusted gross income—

"(1) reduced by the sum of—

"(A) the excess itemized deductions,

"(B) the deductions for personal exemptions provided by section 151, and

"(C) the direct charitable deduction, and

"(2) increased (in the case of an individual for whom an unused zero bracket amount computation is provided by subsection (e)) by the unused zero bracket amount (if any).

"(c) Excess itemized deductions.

"For purposes of this subtitle, the term 'excess itemized deductions' means the excess (if any) of—

"(1) the itemized deductions, over

"(2) the zero bracket amount.

"(d) Zero bracket amount.

"For purposes of this subtitle, the term 'zero bracket amount' means—

"(1) in the case of an individual to whom subsection (a), (b), (c), or (d) of section 1 applies, the maximum amount of taxable income on which no tax is imposed by the applicable subsection of section 1, or

"(2) zero in any other case.

"(e) Unused zero bracket amount.

"(1) Individuals for whom computation must be made. A computation for the taxable year shall be made under this subsection for the following individuals:

"(A) a married individual filing a separate return where either spouse itemizes deductions,

"(B) a nonresident alien individual,

"(C) a citizen of the United States entitled to the benefits of section 931 (relating to income from sources within possessions of the United States), and

"(D) an individual with respect to whom a deduction under section 151(e) is allowable to another taxpayer for a taxable year beginning in the calendar year in which the individual's taxable year begins.

"(2) Computation. For purposes of this subtitle, an individual's unused zero bracket amount for the taxable year is an amount equal to the excess (if any) of—

"(A) the zero bracket amount, over

"(B) the itemized deductions.

In the case of an individual referred to in paragraph (1)(D), if such individual's earned income (as defined in section 911(d)(2)) exceeds the itemized deductions, such earned income shall be substituted for the itemized deductions in subparagraph (B).

"(f) Itemized deductions.

"For purposes of this subtitle, the term 'itemized deductions' means the deductions allowable by this chapter other than—

"(1) the deductions allowable in arriving at adjusted gross income,

"(2) the deductions for personal exemptions provided by section 151, and

"(3) the direct charitable deduction.

"(g) Election to itemize.

"(1) In general. Unless an individual makes an election under this subsection for the taxable year, no itemized deduction shall be allowed for the taxable year. For purposes of this subtitle, the determination of whether a deduction is allowable under this chapter shall be made without regard to the preceding sentence.

"(2) Who may elect. Except as provided in paragraph (3), an individual may make an election under this subsection for the taxable year only if such individual's itemized deductions exceed the zero bracket amount.

"(3) Certain individuals treated as electing to itemize. An individual who has an unused zero bracket amount (as determined under subsection (e)(2)) shall be treated as having made an election under this subsection for the taxable year.

"(4) Time and manner of election. Any election under this subsection shall be made on the taxpayer's return, and the Secretary shall prescribe the manner of signifying such election on the return.

"(5) Change of treatment. Under regulations prescribed by the Secretary, a change of treatment with respect to the zero bracket amount and itemized deductions for any taxable year may be made after the filing of the return for such year. If the spouse of the taxpayer filed a separate return for any taxable year corresponding to the taxable year of the taxpayer, the change shall not be allowed unless, in accordance with such regulations—

"(A) the spouse makes a change of treatment with respect to the zero bracket amount and itemized deductions, for the taxable year covered in such separate return, consistent with the change of treatment sought by the taxpayer, and

"(B) the taxpayer and his spouse consent in writing to the assessment, within such period as may be agreed on with the Secretary, of any deficiency, to the extent attributable to such change of treatment, even though at the time of the filing of such consent the assessment of such deficiency would otherwise be prevented by the operation of any law or rule of law.

This paragraph shall not apply if the tax liability of the taxpayer's spouse, for the taxable year corresponding to the taxable year of the taxpayer, has been compromised under section 7122.

"(h) Marital status.

"For purposes of this section, marital status shall be determined under section 143.

"(i) Direct charitable deduction.

"For purposes of this section, the term 'direct charitable deduction' means that portion of the amount allowable under section 170(a) which is taken as a direct charitable deduction for the taxable year under section 170(i)."

Prior to deletion, subpara. (c)(6)(C) read as follows:

"(C) a citizen of the United States entitled to the benefits of section 931 (relating to income from sources within possessions of the United States),"

In 1981, P.L. 97-34, Sec. 104(b), amended subsec. (d), effective for tax. yrs. begin. after 12/31/84.

Prior to amendment, subsec. (d) read as follows:

"(d) Zero bracket amount.

"For purposes of this subtitle, the term 'zero bracket amount' means—

"(1) $3,400 in the case of—

"(A) a joint return under section 6013, or

"(B) a surviving spouse (as defined in section 2(a)),

"(2) $2,300 in the case of an individual who is not married and who is not a surviving spouse (as so defined),

"(3) $1,700 in the case of a married individual filing a separate return, or

"(4) zero in any other case."

—P.L. 97-34, Sec. 111(b)(4), substituted "section 911(d)(2)" for "section 911(b)" in para. (e)(2), effective for tax. yrs. begin. after 12/31/81.

—P.L. 97-34, Sec. 121(b)(1), deleted "and" at the end of subpara. (b)(1)(A), and added subpara. (b)(1)(C)... Sec. 121(b)(2), added subsec. (i)... Sec. 121(c)(2), deleted "and" at the end of para. (f)(1), substituted "; and" for the period at the end of para. (f)(2) and added para. (f)(3), effective for contributions made after 12/31/81, in tax. yrs. begin. after 12/31/81.

In 1978, P.L. 95-600, Sec. 101(b)(1), substituted "$3,400" for "$3,200", in subsec. (d)... Sec. 101(b)(3), substituted "$2,300" for "$2,200" in subsec. (d)... Sec. 101(b)(3), substituted "$1,700" for "$1,600" in subsec. (d), effective for tax. yrs. begin. after 12/31/78.

In 1977, P.L. 95-30, Sec. 102(a), amended Code Sec. 63, effective for tax. yrs. begin. after 12/31/76.

Prior to amendment, Code Sec. 63 read as follows:

"SEC. 63. TAXABLE INCOME DEFINED.

"(a) General rule.

"Except as provided in subsection (b), for purposes of this subtitle the term 'taxable income' means gross income, minus the deductions allowed by this chapter, other than the standard deduction allowed by part IV (sec. 141 and following).

"(b) Individuals electing standard deduction.

"In the case of an individual electing under section 144 to use the standard deduction provided in part IV (sec. 141 and following), for purposes of this subtitle the term 'taxable income' means adjusted gross income, minus—

"(1) such standard deduction, and

"(2) the deductions for personal exemptions provided in section 151."

Sec. 64. Ordinary income defined.

For purposes of this subtitle, the term "ordinary income" includes any gain from the sale or exchange of property which is neither a capital asset nor property described in section 1231(b). Any gain from the sale or exchange of property which is treated or considered, under other provisions of this subtitle, as "ordinary income" shall be treated as gain

1,321

from the sale or exchange of property which is neither a capital asset nor property described in section 1231(b).

In **1976,** P.L. 94-455, Sec. 1901(a)(10), added Code Sec. 64, effective for tax. yrs. begin. after 12/31/76.

Sec. 65. Ordinary loss defined.

For purposes of this subtitle, the term "ordinary loss" includes any loss from the sale or exchange of property which is not a capital asset. Any loss from the sale or exchange of property which is treated or considered, under other provisions of this subtitle, as "ordinary loss" shall be treated as loss from the sale or exchange of property which is not a capital asset.

In **1976,** P.L. 94-455, Sec. 1901(a)(11), added Code Sec. 65, effective for tax. yrs. begin. after 12/31/76.

Sec. 66. Treatment of community income.

(a) Treatment of community income where spouses live apart.

If—

(1) 2 individuals are married to each other at any time during a calendar year;

(2) such individuals—

(A) live apart at all times during the calendar year, and

(B) do not file a joint return under section 6013 with each other for a taxable year beginning or ending in the calendar year;

(3) one or both of such individuals have earned income for the calendar year which is community income; and

(4) no portion of such earned income is transferred (directly or indirectly) between such individuals before the close of the calendar year,

then, for purposes of this title, any community income of such individuals for the calendar year shall be treated in accordance with the rules provided by section 879(a).

(b) Secretary may disregard community property laws where spouse not notified of community income.

The Secretary may disallow the benefits of any community property law to any taxpayer with respect to any income if such taxpayer acted as if solely entitled to such income and failed to notify the taxpayer's spouse before the due date (including extensions) for filing the return for the taxable year in which the income was derived of the nature and amount of such income.

(c) Spouse relieved of liability in certain other cases.

Under regulations prescribed by the Secretary, if—

(1) an individual does not file a joint return for any taxable year,

(2) such individual does not include in gross income for such taxable year an item of community income properly includible therein which, in accordance with the rules contained in section 879(a), would be treated as the income of the other spouse,

(3) the individual establishes that he or she did not know of, and had no reason to know of, such item of community income, and

(4) taking into account all facts and circumstances, it is inequitable to include such item of community income in such individual's gross income,

then, for purposes of this title, such item of community income shall be included in the gross income of the other spouse (and not in the gross income of the individual). Under procedures prescribed by the Secretary, if, taking into account all the facts and circumstances, it is inequitable to hold the individual liable for any unpaid tax or any deficiency (or any portion of either) attributable to any item for which relief is not available under the preceding sentence, the Secretary may relieve such individual of such liability.

(d) Definitions.

For purposes of this section—

(1) Earned income. The term "[foreign] earned income" has the meaning given to such term by section 911(d)(2).

(2) Community income. The term "community income" means income which, under applicable community property laws, is treated as community income.

(3) Community property laws. The term "community property laws" means the community property laws of a State, a foreign country, or a possession of the United States.

In **1998,** P.L. 105-206, Sec. 3201(b), added a sentence at the end of subsec. (c), effective any liability for tax arising after 7/22/98 and any liability for tax arising on or before 7/22/98 but remaining unpaid as of 7/22/98. Sec. 3201(g)(2) of this Act, provides:

"(2) 2-year period. The 2-year period under subsection (b)(1)(E) or (c)(3)(B) of section 6015 of the Internal Revenue Code of 1986 shall not expire before the date which is 2 years after the date of the first collection activity after the date of the enactment of this Act."

In **1989,** P.L. 101-239, Sec. 7841(d)(8), substituted "section 911(d)(2)" for "section 911(b)" in para. (d)(1), effective 12/19/89.

In **1988,** P.L. 100-647, Sec. 6004, added Sec. 424(c)(3) of P.L. 98-369, transitional rules for changes made by Sec. 424(b)(2) of P.L. 98-369, see below.

In **1984,** P.L. 98-369, Sec. 424(b)(1), redesignated subsec. (b) as subsec. (d) and added new subsecs. (b) and (c).... Sec. 424(b)(2)(A), deleted "where spouses live apart" at the end of the heading of Code Sec. 66... Sec. 424(b)(2)(B), substituted "Treatment of community income where spouses live apart" for "General rule" in the heading of subsec. (a), effective as provided in Sec. 424(c) of this Act [as amended by Sec. 6004 of P.L. 100-647, see above] which reads:

"(c) Effective dates.—

"(1) In general.—Except as provided in paragraph (2), the amendments made by subsections (a) and (b) shall apply to all taxable years to which the Internal Revenue Code of 1954 applies. Corresponding provisions shall be deemed to be included in the Internal Revenue Code of 1939 and shall apply to all taxable years to which such Code applies.

"(2) Authority to disregard community property laws.— Subsection (b) of section 66 of the Internal Revenue Code of 1954, as added by subsection (b), shall apply to taxable years beginning after December 31, 1984.

"(3) Transitional rule.— If—

"(A) a joint return under section 6013 of the Internal Revenue Code of 1954 was filed before January 1, 1985,

"(B) on such return there is an understatement (as defined in section 6661(b)(2)(A) of such Code) which is attributable to disallowed deductions attributable to activities of such spouse,

"(C) the amount of such disallowed deductions exceeds the taxable income shown on such return,

"(D) without regard to any determination before October 21, 1988, the other spouse establishes that in signing the return he or she did not know, and had no reason to know, that there was such an understatement, and

"(E) the marriage between such spouses terminated and immediately after such termination the net worth of the other spouse was less than $10,000

notwithstanding any law or rule of law (including res judicata), the other spouse shall be relieved of liability for tax (including interest, penalties, and other amounts) for such taxable year to the extent such liability is attributable to such understatement, and, to the extent the liability so attributable has been collected from such other spouse, it shall be refunded or credited to such other spouse. No credit or refund shall be made under the preceding sentence unless claim therefor has been submitted to the Secretary of the Treasury or his delegate before the date 1 year after the date of the enactment of this paragraph, and no interest on such credit or refund shall be allowed for any period before such date of enactment."

In **1980,** P.L. 96-605, Sec. 101(a), added Code Sec. 66, effective for calendar yrs. begin. after 12/31/80.

Sec. 67. 2-percent floor on miscellaneous itemized deductions.

(a) General rule.

In the case of an individual, the miscellaneous itemized deductions for any taxable year shall be allowed only to the extent that the aggregate of such deductions exceeds 2 percent of adjusted gross income.

(b) Miscellaneous itemized deductions.

For purposes of this section, the term "miscellaneous itemized deductions" means the itemized deductions other than—

(1) the deduction under section 163 (relating to interest),

(2) the deduction under section 164 (relating to taxes),

(3) the deduction under section 165(a) for casualty or theft losses described in paragraph (2) or (3) of section 165(c) or for losses described in section 165(d),

(4) the deductions under section 170 (relating to charitable, etc., contributions and gifts) and section 642(c) (relating to deduction for amounts paid or permanently set aside for a charitable purpose),

(5) the deduction under section 213 (relating to medical, dental, etc., expenses),

(6) any deduction allowable for impairment-related work expenses,

(7) the deduction under section 691(c) (relating to deduction for estate tax in case of income in respect of the decedent),

(8) any deduction allowable in connection with personal property used in a short sale,

(9) the deduction under section 1341 (relating to computation of tax where taxpayer restores substantial amount held under claim of right),

(10) the deduction under section 72(b)(3) (relating to deduction where annuity payments cease before investment recovered),

(11) the deduction under section 171 (relating to deduction for amortizable bond premium), and

(12) the deduction under section 216 (relating to deductions in connection with cooperative housing corporations).

(c) Disallowance of indirect deduction through pass-thru entity.

(1) In general. The Secretary shall prescribe regulations which prohibit the indirect deduction through pass-thru entities of amounts which are not allowable as a deduction if paid or incurred directly by an individual and which contain such reporting requirements as may be necessary to carry out the purposes of this subsection.

(2) Treatment of publicly offered regulated investment companies.

(A) In general. Paragraph (1) shall not apply with respect to any publicly offered regulated investment company.

(B) Publicly offered regulated investment companies. For purposes of this subsection—

(i) In general. The term "publicly offered regulated investment company" means a regulated investment company the shares of which are—

(I) continuously offered pursuant to a public offering (within the meaning of section 4 of the Securities Act of 1933, as amended (15 U.S.C. 77a to 77aa)),

(II) regularly traded on an established securities market, or

(III) held by or for no fewer than 500 persons at all times during the taxable year.

(ii) Secretary may reduce 500 person requirement. The Secretary may by regulation decrease the minimum shareholder requirement of clause (i)(III) in the case of regulated investment companies which experience a loss of shareholders through net redemptions of their shares.

(3) Treatment of certain other entities. Paragraph (1) shall not apply—

(A) with respect to cooperatives and real estate investment trusts, and

(B) except as provided in regulations, with respect to estates and trusts.

(d) Impairment-related work expenses.

For purposes of this section, the term "impairment-related work expenses" means expenses—

(1) of a handicapped individual (as defined in section 190(b)(3)) for attendant care services at the individual's place of employment and other expenses in connection with such place of employment which are necessary for such individual to be able to work, and

(2) with respect to which a deduction is allowable under section 162 (determined without regard to this section).

(e) Determination of adjusted gross income in case of estates and trusts.

For purposes of this section, the adjusted gross income of an estate or trust shall be computed in the same manner as in the case of an individual, except that—

(1) the deductions for costs which are paid or incurred in connection with the administration of the estate or trust and which would not have been incurred if the property were not held in such trust or estate, and

(2) the deductions allowable under sections 642(b), 651, and 661,

shall be treated as allowable in arriving at adjusted gross income. Under regulations, appropriate adjustments shall be made in the application of part I of subchapter J of this chapter to take into account the provisions of this section.

(f) Coordination with other limitation.

This section shall be applied before the application of the dollar limitation of the second sentence of section 162(a) (relating to trade or business expenses).

In 2000, P.L. 106-554, Sec. 1(a)(7) , [which enacted into law Sec. 319(2) of P.L. 106-554] substituted "the second sentence" for "the last sentence" in subsec. (f), effective 12/21/2000.

In 1998, P.L. 105-277, Sec. 4004(b)(1), substituted "for casualty or theft losses described in paragraph (2) or (3) of section 165(c) or for losses described in section 165(d)" for "for losses described in subsection (c)(3) or (d) of section 165" in para. (b)(3), effective for tax. yrs. begin. after 12/31/86.

In 1993, P.L. 103-66, Sec. 13213(c)(2), deleted para. (b)(6) and redesignated paras. (b)(7)-(b)(13) as paras. (b)(6)-(b)(12), effective for expenses incurred after 12/31/93.

Prior to deletion, para. (b)(6) read as follows:

"(6) the deduction under section 217 (relating to moving expenses),"

In 1989, P.L. 101-239, Sec. 7814(f), deleted para. (c)(4), effective for tax. yrs. begin. after 12/31/87.

Prior to deletion, para. (c)(4) read as follows:

"(4) Termination. This subsection shall not apply to any taxable year beginning after December 31, 1989."

In 1988, P.L. 100-647, Sec. 1001(f)(1), added subsec. (f) . . . Sec. 1001(f)(2)(A), and (B), substituted "deductions" for "deduction" and added "and section 642(c) (relating to deduction for amounts paid or permanently set aside for a charitable purpose)" before the comma at the end of para. (b)(4) . . . Sec. 1001(f)(3), amended subsec. (e) . . . Sec. 1001(f)(4), amended the last sentence in subsec. (c), effective for tax. yrs. begin. after 12/31/86, except as provided by Sec. 10104(a) of P.L. 100-203, see below.

Prior to amendment, subsec. (e) read as follows:

"(e) Determination of adjusted gross income in case of estates and trusts.

"For purposes of this section, the adjusted gross income of an estate or trust shall be computed in the same manner as in the case of an individual, except that the deductions for [c]osts which are paid or incurred in connection with the administration of the estate or trust and would not have been incurred if the property were not held in such trust or estate shall be treated as allowable in arriving at adjusted gross income."

Prior to amendment, the last sentence of subsec. (c) read as follows:

"The preceding sentence shall not apply with respect to estates, trusts, cooperatives, and real estate investment trusts."

—P.L. 100-647, Sec. 4011(a), amended subsec. (c), effective for tax. yrs. begin. after 12/31/87.

Prior to amendment, subsec. (c), read as follows:

"(c) Disallowance of indirect deduction through pass-thru entity.

"The Secretary shall prescribe regulations which prohibit the indirect deduction through pass-thru entities of amounts which are not allowable as a deduction if paid or incurred directly by an individual and which contain such reporting requirements as may be necessary to carry out the purposes of this subsection. The preceding sentence shall not apply—

"(1) with respect to cooperatives and real estate investment trusts, and

"(2) except as provided in regulations, with respect to estates and trusts."

In 1987, P.L. 100-203, Sec. 10104(a), provides:

"(a) 1-Year delay in treatment of publicly offered regulated investment companies under 2-percent floor.—

"(1) General rule.— Section 67(c) of the Internal Revenue Code of 1986 to the extent it relates to indirect deductions through a publicly offered regulated investment company shall apply only to taxable years beginning after December 31, 1987.

"(2) Publicly offered regulated investment company defined.— For purposes of this subsection—

"(A) In general.— The term 'publicly offered regulated investment company' means a regulated investment company the shares of which are—

"(i) continuously offered pursuant to a public offering (within the meaning of section 4 of the Securities Act of 1933, as amended (15 U.S.C. 77a to 77aa)),

"(ii) regularly traded on an established securities market, or

"(iii) held by or for no fewer than 500 persons at all times during the taxable year.

"(B) Secretary may reduce 500 person requirement.— The Secretary of the Treasury or his delegate may by regulation decrease the minimum shareholder requirement of subparagraph (A)(iii) in the case of regulated investment companies which experience a loss of shareholders through net redemptions of their shares."

In 1986, P.L. 99-514, Sec. 132(a), added Code Sec. 67, effective for tax. yrs. begin. after 12/31/86, except as provided by Sec. 10104(a) of P.L. 100-203 (see above).

Sec. 68. Overall limitation on itemized deductions.

(a) General rule

In the case of an individual whose adjusted gross income exceeds the applicable amount, the amount of the itemized deductions otherwise allowable for the taxable year shall be reduced by the lesser of—

(1) 3 percent of the excess of adjusted gross income over the applicable amount, or

(2) 80 percent of the amount of the itemized deductions otherwise allowable for such taxable year.

(b) Applicable amount.

(1) **In general.** For purposes of this section, the term "applicable amount" means $100,000 ($50,000 in the case of a separate return by a married individual within the meaning of section 7703).

(2) **Inflation adjustments.** In the case of any taxable year beginning in a calendar year after 1991, each dollar amount contained in paragraph (1) shall be increased by an amount equal to—

(A) such dollar amount, multiplied by

(B) the cost-of-living adjustment determined under section 1(f)(3) for the calendar year in which the taxable year begins, by substituting "calendar year 1990" for "calendar year 1992" in subparagraph (B) thereof.

(c) Exception for certain itemized deductions.

For purposes of this section, the term "itemized deductions" does not include—

(1) the deduction under section 213 (relating to medical, etc. expenses),

(2) any deduction for investment interest (as defined in section 163(d)), and

(3) the deduction under section 165(a) for casualty or theft losses described in paragraph (2) or (3) of section 165(c) or for losses described in section 165(d).

(d) Coordination with other limitations.

This section shall be applied after the application of any other limitation on the allowance of any itemized deduction.

(e) Exception for estates and trusts.

This section shall not apply to any estate or trust.

> • *Caution:* Code Sec. 68(f) and (g), following, were amended by P.L. 107-16, EGTRRA. These provisions generally sunset for tax years beginning after 12/31/2012. For specific sunset provisions, see Sec. 901, P.L. 107-16 (as amended) reproduced in history notes for this Code Sec.

(f) Phaseout of limitation.

(1) **In general.** In the case of taxable years beginning after December 31, 2005, and before January 1, 2010, the reduction under subsection (a) shall be equal to the applicable fraction of the amount which would (but for this subsection) be the amount of such reduction.

(2) **Applicable fraction.** For purposes of paragraph (1), the applicable fraction shall be determined in accordance with the following table:

For taxable years beginning in calendar year—	The applicable fraction is—
2006 and 2007	⅔
2008 and 2009	⅓

(g) Termination.

This section shall not apply to any taxable year beginning after December 31, 2009.

In 2010, P.L. 111-312, Sec. 101(a)(1), substituted "December 31, 2012" for "December 31, 2010" both places it appeared in Sec. 901, P.L. 107-16 [see below], effective as if included in the enactment of P.L. 107-16, EGTRRA, 6/7/2001.

In 2002, P.L. 107-358, Sec. 2, added subsec. (c) in Sec. 901 of P.L. 107-16 [see below], effective 12/17/2002.

In 2001, P.L. 107-16, Sec. 103(a), added subsecs. (f) and (g), effective for tax. yrs. begin. after 12/31/2005.

—P.L. 107-16, Sec. 901, of this Act [as amended by Sec. 2, P.L. 107-358, and Sec. 101(a)(1), P.L. 111-312, see above], reads as follows:

"SEC. 901. SUNSET OF PROVISIONS OF ACT.

"(a) In general. All provisions of, and amendments made by, this Act shall not apply—

"(1) to taxable, plan, or limitation years beginning after December 31, 2012, or

"(2) in the case of title V, to estates of decedents dying, gifts made, or generation skipping transfers, after December 31, 2012.

"(b) Application of certain laws. The Internal Revenue Code of 1986 and the Employee Retirement Income Security Act of 1974 shall be applied and administered to years, estates, gifts, and transfers described in subsection (a) as if the provisions and amendments described in subsection (a) had never been enacted.

"(c) Exception. Subsection (a) shall not apply to section 803 (relating to no federal income tax on restitution received by victims of the Nazi regime or their heirs or estates)."

In 1998, P.L. 105-277, Sec. 4004(b)(2), substituted "for casualty or theft losses described in paragraph (2) or (3) of section 165(c) or for losses described in section 165(d)" for "for losses described in subsection (c)(3) or (d) of section 165" in para. (c)(3), effective for tax. yrs. begin. after 12/31/90.

In 1993, P.L. 103-66, Sec. 13201(b)(3)(E), substituted "1992" for "1989" in subpara. (b)(2)(B), effective for tax. yrs. begin. after 12/31/92.

—P.L. 103-66, Sec. 13204, deleted subsec. (f), effective 8/10/93.

Prior to deletion, subsec. (f) read as follows:

"(f) Termination. This section shall not apply to any taxable year beginning after December 31, 1995."

In 1990, P.L. 101-508, Sec. 11103(a), added Code Sec. 68, effective for tax. yrs. begin. after 12/31/90.

PART II.—ITEMS SPECIFICALLY INCLUDED IN GROSS INCOME

Sec.

71. Alimony and separate maintenance payments.
72. Annuities; certain proceeds of endowment and life insurance contracts.
73. Services of child.
74. Prizes and awards.
75. Dealers in tax-exempt securities.
76. Repealed. [Mortgages made or obligations issued by joint-stock land banks.]
77. Commodity credit loans.
78. Dividends received from certain foreign corporations by domestic corporations choosing foreign tax credit.
79. Group-term life insurance purchased for employees.
80. Restoration of value of certain securities.
81. Repealed. [Increase in vacation pay suspense account.]

82. Reimbursement of moving expenses. [Reimbursement for expenses of moving.]
83. Property transferred in connection with performance of services.
84. Transfer of appreciated property to political organizations.
85. Unemployment compensation.
86. Social security and tier 1 railroad retirement benefits.
87. Alcohol and biodiesel fuels credits.
88. Certain amounts with respect to nuclear decommissioning costs.
89. Repealed. [Benefits provided under certain employee benefit plans.]
90. Illegal federal irrigation subsidies.

In **2004**, P.L. 108-357, Sec. 302(c)(1)(B), amended item 87.
Prior to amendment, item 87 read as follows:
"87. Alcohol fuel credit."
In **1989**, P.L. 101-239, Sec. 7822(c), amended item 90.
Prior to amendment item 90 read as follows:
"90. Federal irrigation subsidies."
—P.L. 101-140, Sec. 202(b), repealed item 89.
Prior to repeal, item 89 read as follows:
"89. Benefits provided under certain employee benefit plans."
In **1987**, P.L. 100-203, Sec. 10201(b)(6), repealed item 81.
Prior to repeal, item 81 read as follows:
"81. Increase in vacation pay suspense account."
—P.L. 100-203, Sec. 10611(b), added item 90.
In **1986**, P.L. 99-514, Sec. 805(c)(1)(B), amended item 81.
Prior to amendment, item 81 read as follows:
"81. Certain increases in suspense accounts."
—P.L. 99-514, Sec. 1151(j)(1), added item 89.
In **1984**, P.L. 98-369, Sec. 91(f)(2), added item 88.
In **1983**, P.L. 98-21, Sec. 121(f)(3), redesignated item 86 as 87 and added new item 86.
In **1980**, P.L. 96-223, Sec. 232(c)(3), added item 86.
In **1978**, P.L. 95-600, Sec. 112(c)(1), added item 85.
In **1976**, P.L. 94-455, Sec. 1901(b)(5), repealed item 76.
Prior to repeal, item 76 read as follows:
"Mortgages made or obligations issued by joint-stock land banks."
In **1975**, P.L. 93-625, Sec. 4(c)(2), amended item 81.
Prior to amendment, item 81 read as follows:
"Increases in suspense account under section 166(g)."
—P.L. 93-625, Sec. 13(a)(2), added item 84.
In **1969**, P.L. 91-172, Sec. 231(c)(1), added item 82.
—P.L. 91-172, Sec. 321(c), added item 83.
In **1966**, P.L. 89-722, Sec. [1](b)(2), added item 81.
—P.L. 89-384, Sec. 1(b)(2), added item 80.
In **1964**, P.L. 88-272, Sec. 204(a)(2), added item 79.
In **1962**, P.L. 87-834, Sec. 9(d)(1), added item 78.

Sec. 71. Alimony and separate maintenance payments.
(a) General rule.
Gross income includes amounts received as alimony or separate maintenance payments.
(b) Alimony or separate maintenance payments defined.
For purposes of this section—
(1) **In general.** The term "alimony or separate maintenance payment" means any payment in cash if—
(A) such payment is received by (or on behalf of) a spouse under a divorce or separation instrument,
(B) the divorce or separation instrument does not designate such payment as a payment which is not includible in gross income under this section and not allowable as a deduction under section 215,
(C) in the case of an individual legally separated from his spouse under a decree of divorce or of separate maintenance, the payee spouse and the payor spouse are not members of the same household at the time such payment is made, and
(D) there is no liability to make any such payment for any period after the death of the payee spouse and there is no liability to make any payment (in cash or property) as a substitute for such payments after the death of the payee spouse.
(2) **Divorce or separation instrument.** The term "divorce or separation instrument" means—
(A) a decree of divorce or separate maintenance or a written instrument incident to such a decree,
(B) a written separation agreement, or
(C) a decree (not described in subparagraph (A)) requiring a spouse to make payments for the support or maintenance of the other spouse.
(c) Payments to support children.
(1) **In general.** Subsection (a) shall not apply to that part of any payment which the terms of the divorce or separation instrument fix (in terms of an amount of money or a part of the payment) as a sum which is payable for the support of children of the payor spouse.
(2) **Treatment of certain reductions related to contingencies involving child.** For purposes of paragraph (1), if any amount specified in the instrument will be reduced—
(A) on the happening of a contingency specified in the instrument relating to a child (such as attaining a specified age, marrying, dying, leaving school, or a similar contingency), or
(B) at a time which can clearly be associated with a contingency of a kind specified in subparagraph (A), an amount equal to the amount of such reduction will be treated as an amount fixed as payable for the support of children of the payor spouse.
(3) **Special rule where payment is less than amount specified in instrument.** For purposes of this subsection, if any payment is less than the amount specified in the instrument, then so much of such payment as does not exceed the sum payable for support shall be considered a payment for such support.
(d) Spouse.
For purposes of this section, the term "spouse" includes a former spouse.
(e) Exception for joint returns.
This section and section 215 shall not apply if the spouses make a joint return with each other.
(f) Recomputation where excess front-loading of alimony payments
(1) **In general.** If there are excess alimony payments—
(A) the payor spouse shall include the amount of such excess payments in gross income for the payor spouse's taxable year beginning in the 3rd post-separation year, and
(B) the payee spouse shall be allowed a deduction in computing adjusted gross income for the amount of such excess payments for the payee's taxable year beginning in the 3rd post-separation year.
(2) **Excess alimony payments.** For purposes of this subsection, the term "excess alimony payments" mean the sum of—
(A) the excess payments for the 1st post-separation year, and
(B) the excess payments for the 2nd post-separation year.
(3) **Excess payments for 1st post-separation year.** For purposes of this subsection, the amount of the excess payments for the 1st post-separation year is the excess (if any) of—
(A) the amount of the alimony or separate maintenance payments paid by the payor spouse during the 1st post-separation year, over

Code Sec. 71(f)(3)(B) — Income

(B) the sum of—
 (i) the average of—
  (I) the alimony or separate maintenance payments paid by the payor spouse during the 2nd post-separation year, reduced by the excess payments for the 2nd post-separation year, and
  (II) the alimony or separate maintenance payments paid by the payor spouse during the 3rd post-separation year, plus
 (ii) $15,000.

(4) Excess payments for 2nd post-separation year. For purposes of this subsection, the amount of the excess payments for the 2nd post-separation year is the excess (if any) of—
 (A) the amount of the alimony or separate maintenance payments paid by the payor spouse during the 2nd post-separation year, over
 (B) the sum of—
  (i) the amount of the alimony or separate maintenance payments paid by the payor spouse during the 3rd post-separation year, plus
  (ii) $15,000.

(5) Exceptions.
 (A) Where payment ceases by reason of death or remarriage. Paragraph (1) shall not apply if—
  (i) either spouse dies before the close of the 3rd post-separation year, or the payee spouse remarries before the close of the 3rd post-separation year, and
  (ii) the alimony or separate maintenance payments cease by reason of such death or remarriage.
 (B) Support payments. For purposes of this subsection, the term "alimony or separate maintenance payment" shall not include any payment received under a decree described in subsection (b)(2)(C).
 (C) Fluctuating payments not within control of payor spouse. For purposes of this subsection, the term "alimony or separate maintenance payment" shall not include any payment to the extent it is made pursuant to a continuing liability (over a period of not less than 3 years) to pay a fixed portion or portions of the income from a business or property or from compensation for employment or self-employment.

(6) Post-separation years. For purposes of this subsection, the term "1st post-separation years" means the 1st calendar year in which the payor spouse paid to the payee spouse alimony or separate maintenance payments to which this section applies. The 2nd and 3rd post-separation years shall be the 1st and 2nd succeeding calendar years, respectively.

(g) Cross References.
 (1) For deduction of alimony or separate maintenance payments, see section 215.
 (2) For taxable status of income of an estate or trust in the case of divorce, etc., see section 682.

In 1986, P.L. 99-514, Sec. 1843(a), added subsec. (g)... Sec. 1843(b), deleted "(and the divorce or separation instrument states that there is no such liability)" after "payee spouse" in subpara. (b)(1)(D)... Sec. 1843(d), substituted "specified in subparagraph (A)" for "specified in paragraph (I)" in subpara. (c)(2)(B), effective for divorce or separation instruments (as defined in Code Sec. 71(b)(2)) executed after 12/31/84, and effective as provided in Sec. 422(e)(2) of P.L. 98-369, reproduced below.

—P.L. 99-514, Sec. 1843(c)(1), amended Subsec. (f), effective for divorce or separation instruments (as defined in Code Sec. 71(b)(2)) executed after 12/31/86. Secs. 1843(c)(2)(B) and 1843(c)(3) of this Act provide:

"(B) Modifications of instruments executed before January 1, 1987. The amendments made by paragraph (1) shall also apply to any divorce or separation instrument (as so defined) executed before January 1, 1987, but modified on or after such date if the modification expressly provides that the amendments made by paragraph (1) shall apply to such modification.

"(3) Transitional rule. In the case of any instrument to which the amendment made by paragraph (1) does not apply, paragraph (2) of section 71(f) of the Internal Revenue Code of 1954 (as in effect on the day before the date of the enactment of this Act) shall apply only with respect to the first 3 post-separation years."

Prior to amendment, subsec. (f) read as follows:
"(f) Special rules to prevent excess front-loading of alimony payments.
"(1) Requirement that payments be for more than 6 years. Alimony or separate maintenance payments (in excess of $10,000 during any calendar year) paid by the payor spouse to the payee spouse shall not be treated as alimony or separate maintenance payments unless such payments are to be made by the payor spouse to the payee spouse in each of the 6 post-separation years (not taking into account any termination contingent on the death of either spouse or the remarriage of the payee spouse).
"(2) Recomputation where payments decrease by more than $10,000. If there is an excess amount determined under paragraph (3) for any computation year—
"(A) the payor spouse shall include such excess amount in gross income for the payor spouse's taxable year beginning in the computation year, and
"(B) the payee spouse shall be allowed a deduction in computing adjusted gross income for such excess amount for the payee spouse's taxable year beginning in the computation year.
"(3) Determination of excess amount. The excess amount determined under this paragraph for any computation year is the sum of—
"(A) the excess (if any) of—
"(i) the amount of alimony or separate maintenance payments paid by the payor spouse during the immediately preceding post-separation year, over
"(ii) the amount of the alimony or separate maintenance payments paid by the payor spouse during the computation year increased by $10,000, plus
"(B) a like excess for each of the other preceding post-separation years.
In determining the amount of the alimony or separate maintenance payments paid by the payor spouse during any preceding post-separation year, the amount paid during such year shall be reduced by any excess previously determined in respect of such year under this paragraph.
"(4) Definitions. For purposes of this subsection—
"(A) Post-separation year. The term 'post-separation year' means any calendar year in the 6 calendar year period beginning with the first calendar year in which the payor spouse paid to the payee spouse alimony or separate maintenance payments to which this section applies.
"(B) Computation year. The term 'computation year' means the post-separation year for which the excess under paragraph (3) is being determined.
"(5) Exceptions.
"(A) Where payments cease by reason of death or remarriage. Paragraph (2) shall not apply to any post-separation year (and subsequent post-separation years) if—
"(i) either spouse dies before the close of such post-separation year or the payee spouse remarries before the close of such post-separation year, and
"(ii) the alimony or separate maintenance payments cease by reason of such death or remarriage.
"(B) Support payments. For purposes of this subsection the term 'alimony or separate maintenance payment' shall not include any payment received under a decree described in subsection (b)(2)(C).
"(C) Fluctuating payments not within control of payor spouse. For purposes of this subsection, the term 'alimony or separate maintenance payment' shall not include any payment to the extent it is made pursuant to a continuing liability (over a period of not less than 6 years) to pay a fixed portion of the income from a business or property or from compensation for employment or self-employment."

In 1984, P.L. 98-369, Sec. 422(a), amended Code Sec. 71, effective for divorce or separation instruments (as defined in Code Sec. 71(b)(2) as amended by this section) executed after 12/31/84. Sec. 422(e)(2) of the Act also provides:

"(2) Modifications of instruments executed before January 1, 1985.— The amendments made by this section shall also apply to any divorce or separation instrument (as so defined) executed before January 1, 1985, but modified on or after such date if the modification expressly provides that the amendments made by this section shall apply to such modification."

Prior to amendment, Code Sec. 71 read as follows:
"SEC. 71. ALIMONY AND SEPARATE MAINTENANCE PAYMENTS.
"(a) General rule.
"(1) Decree of divorce or separate maintenance. If a wife is divorced or legally separated from her husband under a decree of divorce or of separate maintenance, the wife's gross income includes periodic payments (whether or not made at regular intervals) received after such decree in discharge of (or attributable to property transferred, in trust or otherwise, in discharge of) a legal obligation which, because of the marital or family relationship, is imposed on or incurred by the husband under the decree or under a written instrument incident to such divorce or separation.
"(2) Written separation agreement. If a wife is separated from her husband and there is a written separation agreement executed after the date of the enactment of this title, the wife's gross income includes periodic payments (whether or not made at regular intervals) received after such agreement is executed which are made under such agreement and because of the marital or family relationship (or which are attributable to property transferred, in trust or otherwise, under such agreement and because of such relationship). This paragraph shall not apply if the husband and wife make a single return jointly.
"(3) Decree for support. If a wife is separated from her husband, the wife's gross income includes periodic payments (whether or not made at regular intervals) received by her after the date of the enactment of this title from her husband under a decree entered after March 1, 1954, requiring the husband to make the

Income

Code Sec. 72(c)(2)(C)

payments for her support or maintenance. This paragraph shall not apply if the husband and wife make a single return jointly.

"(b) Payments to support minor children.

"Subsection (a) shall not apply to that part of any payment which the terms of the decree, instrument, or agreement fix, in terms of an amount of money or a part of the payment, as a sum which is payable for the support of minor children of the husband. For purposes of the preceding sentence, if any payment is less than the amount specified in the decree, instrument, or agreement, then so much of such payment as does not exceed the sum payable for support shall be considered a payment for such support.

"(c) Principal sum paid in installments.

"(1) General rule. For purposes of subsection (a), installment payments discharging a part of an obligation the principal sum of which is, either in terms of money or property, specified in the decree, instrument, or agreement shall not be treated as periodic payments.

"(2) Where period for payment is more than 10 years. If, by the terms of the decree, instrument, or agreement, the principal sum referred to in paragraph (1) is to be paid or may be paid over a period ending more than 10 years from the date of such decree, instrument, or agreement, then (notwithstanding paragraph (1)) the installment payments shall be treated as periodic payments for purposes of subsection (a), but (in the case of any one taxable year of the wife) only to the extent of 10 percent of the principal sum. For purposes of the preceding sentence, the part of any principal sum which is allocable to a period after the taxable year of the wife in which it is received shall be treated as an installment payment for the taxable year in which it is received.

"(d) Rule for husband in case of transferred property.

"The husband's gross income does not include amounts received which, under subsection (a), are (1) includible in the gross income of the wife, and (2) attributable to transferred property.

"(e) Cross references

"(1) For definitions of 'husband' and 'wife', see section 7701(a)(17).

"(2) For deduction by husband of periodic payments not attributable to transferred property, see section 215.

"(3) For taxable status of income of an estate or trust in case of divorce, etc., see section 682."

Sec. 72. Annuities; certain proceeds of endowment and life insurance contracts.

(a) General rule for annuities.

(1) Income inclusion. Except as otherwise provided in this chapter, gross income includes any amount received as an annuity (whether for a period certain or during one or more lives) under an annuity, endowment, or life insurance contract.

(2) Partial annuitization. If any amount is received as an annuity for a period of 10 years or more or during one or more lives under any portion of an annuity, endowment, or life insurance contract—

(A) such portion shall be treated as a separate contract for purposes of this section,

(B) for purposes of applying subsections (b), (c), and (e), the investment in the contract shall be allocated pro rata between each portion of the contract from which amounts are received as an annuity and the portion of the contract from which amounts are not received as an annuity, and

(C) a separate annuity starting date under subsection (c)(4) shall be determined with respect to each portion of the contract from which amounts are received as an annuity.

(b) Exclusion ratio.

(1) In general. Gross income does not include that part of any amount received as an annuity under an annuity, endowment, or life insurance contract which bears the same ratio to such amount as the investment in the contract (as of the annuity starting date) bears to the expected return under the contract (as of such date).

(2) Exclusion limited to investment. The portion of any amount received as an annuity which is excluded from gross income under paragraph (1) shall not exceed the unrecovered investment in the contract immediately before the receipt of such amount.

(3) Deduction where annuity payments cease before entire investment recovered.

(A) In general. If—

(i) after the annuity starting date, payments as an annuity under the contract cease by reason of the death of an annuitant, and

(ii) as of the date of such cessation, there is unrecovered investment in the contract,

the amount of such unrecovered investment (in excess of any amount specified in subsection (e)(5) which was not included in gross income) shall be allowed as a deduction to the annuitant for his last taxable year.

(B) Payments to other persons. In the case of any contract which provides for payments meeting the requirements of subparagraphs (B) and (C) of subsection (c)(2), the deduction under subparagraph (A) shall be allowed to the person entitled to such payments for the taxable year in which such payments are received.

(C) Net operating loss deductions provided. For purposes of section 172, a deduction allowed under this paragraph shall be treated as if it were attributable to a trade or business of the taxpayer.

(4) Unrecovered investment. For purposes of this subsection, the unrecovered investment in the contract as of any date is—

(A) the investment in the contract (determined without regard to subsection (c)(2)) as of the annuity starting date, reduced by

(B) the aggregate amount received under the contract on or after such annuity starting date and before the date as of which the determination is being made, to the extent such amount was excludable from gross income under this subtitle.

(c) Definitions.

(1) Investment in the contract. For purposes of subsection (b), the investment in the contract as of the annuity starting date is—

(A) the aggregate amount of premiums or other consideration paid for the contract, minus

(B) the aggregate amount received under the contract before such date, to the extent that such amount was excludable from gross income under this subtitle or prior income tax laws.

(2) Adjustment in investment where there is refund feature. If—

(A) the expected return under the contract depends in whole or in part on the life expectancy of one or more individuals;

(B) the contract provides for payments to be made to a beneficiary (or to the estate of an annuitant) on or after the death of the annuitant or annuitants; and

(C) such payments are in the nature of a refund of the consideration paid,

then the value (computed without discount for interest) of such payments on the annuity starting date shall be subtracted from the amount determined under paragraph (1). Such value shall be computed in accordance with actuarial tables prescribed by the Secretary. For purposes of this paragraph and of subsection (e)(2)(A), the term "refund of the consideration paid" includes amounts payable after the death of an annuitant by reason of a provision in the contract for a life annuity with minimum period of payments certain, but (if part of the consideration was contributed by an employer) does not include that part of any payment to a beneficiary (or to the estate of the annuitant) which is not attributable to the consideration paid by the employee for the contract as determined under paragraph (1)(A).

Code Sec. 72(c)(3)

(3) **Expected return.** For purposes of subsection (b), the expected return under the contract shall be determined as follows:

(A) Life expectancy. If the expected return under the contract, for the period on and after the annuity starting date, depends in whole or in part on the life expectancy of one or more individuals, the expected return shall be computed with reference to actuarial tables prescribed by the Secretary.

(B) Installment payments. If subparagraph (A) does not apply, the expected return is the aggregate of the amounts receivable under the contract as an annuity.

(4) **Annuity starting date.** For purposes of this section, the annuity starting date in the case of any contract is the first day of the first period for which an amount is received as an annuity under the contract; except that if such date was before January 1, 1954, then the annuity starting date is January 1, 1954.

(d) **Special rules for qualified employer retirement plans.**
(1) **Simplified method of taxing annuity payments.**

(A) In general. In the case of any amount received as an annuity under a qualified employer retirement plan—

(i) subsection (b) shall not apply, and

(ii) the investment in the contract shall be recovered as provided in this paragraph.

(B) Method of recovering investment in contract.

(i) In general. Gross income shall not include so much of any monthly annuity payment under a qualified employer retirement plan as does not exceed the amount obtained by dividing—

(I) the investment in the contract (as of the annuity starting date), by

(II) the number of anticipated payments determined under the table contained in clause (iii)(or, in the case of a contract to which subsection (c)(3)(B) applies, the number of monthly annuity payments under such contract).

(ii) Certain rules made applicable. Rules similar to the rules of paragraphs (2) and (3) of subsection (b) shall apply for purposes of this paragraph.

(iii) Number of anticipated payments. If the annuity is payable over the life of a single individual, the number of anticipated payments shall be determined as follows:

If the age of the annuitant on the annuity starting date is:	The number of anticipated payments is:
Not more than 55	360
More than 55 but not more than 60	310
More than 60 but not more than 65	260
More than 65 but not more than 70	210
More than 70	160

(iv) Number of anticipated payments where more than one life. If the annuity is payable over the lives of more than 1 individual, the number of anticipated payments shall be determined as follows:

If the combined ages of annuitants are:	The number is:
Not more than 110	410
More than 110 but not more than 120	360
More than 120 but not more than 130	310
More than 130 but not more than 140	260
More than 140	210.

(C) Adjustment for refund feature not applicable. For purposes of this paragraph, investment in the contract shall be determined under subsection (c)(1) without regard to subsection (c)(2).

(D) Special rule where lump sum paid in connection with commencement of annuity payments. If, in connection with the commencement of annuity payments under any qualified employer retirement plan, the taxpayer receives a lump sum payment—

(i) such payment shall be taxable under subsection (e) as if received before the annuity starting date, and

(ii) the investment in the contract for purposes of this paragraph shall be determined as if such payment had been so received.

(E) Exception. This paragraph shall not apply in any case where the primary annuitant has attained age 75 on the annuity starting date unless there are fewer than 5 years of guaranteed payments under the annuity.

(F) Adjustment where annuity payments not on monthly basis. In any case where the annuity payments are not made on a monthly basis, appropriate adjustments in the application of this paragraph shall be made to take into account the period on the basis of which such payments are made.

(G) Qualified employer retirement plan. For purposes of this paragraph, the term "qualified employer retirement plan" means any plan or contract described in paragraph (1), (2), or (3) of section 4974(c).

(2) **Treatment of employee contributions under defined contribution plans.** For purposes of this section, employee contributions (and any income allocable thereto) under a defined contribution plan may be treated as a separate contract.

(e) **Amounts not received as annuities.**
(1) **Application of subsection.**

(A) In general. This subsection shall apply to any amount which—

(i) is received under an annuity, endowment, or life insurance contract, and

(ii) is not received as an annuity,

if no provision of this subtitle (other than this subsection) applies with respect to such amount.

(B) Dividends. For purposes of this section, any amount received which is in the nature of a dividend or similar distribution shall be treated as an amount not received as an annuity.

(2) **General rule.** Any amount to which this subsection applies—

(A) if received on or after the annuity starting date, shall be included in gross income, or

(B) if received before the annuity starting date—

(i) shall be included in gross income to the extent allocable to income on the contract, and

(ii) shall not be included in gross income to the extent allocable to the investment in the contract.

(3) **Allocation of amounts to income and investment.** For purposes of paragraph (2)(B)—

(A) Allocation to income. Any amount to which this subsection applies shall be treated as allocable to income on the contract to the extent that such amount does not exceed the excess (if any) of—

(i) the cash value of the contract (determined without regard to any surrender charge) immediately before the amount is received, over

(ii) the investment in the contract at such time.

(B) Allocation to investment. Any amount to which this subsection applies shall be treated as allocable to investment in the contract to the extent that such amount is not allocated to income under subparagraph (A).

(4) Special rules for application of paragraph (2)(B). For purposes of paragraph (2)(B)—

(A) Loans treated as distributions. If, during any taxable year, an individual—

(i) receives (directly or indirectly) any amount as a loan under any contract to which this subsection applies, or

(ii) assigns or pledges (or agrees to assign or pledge) any portion of the value of any such contract,

such amount or portion shall be treated as received under the contract as an amount not received as an annuity. The preceding sentence shall not apply for purposes of determining investment in the contract, except that the investment in the contract shall be increased by any amount included in gross income by reason of the amount treated as received under the preceding sentence.

(B) Treatment of policyholder dividends. Any amount described in paragraph (1)(B) shall not be included in gross income under paragraph (2)(B)(i) to the extent such amount is retained by the insurer as a premium or other consideration paid for the contract.

(C) Treatment of transfers without adequate consideration.

(i) In general. If an individual who holds an annuity contract transfers it without full and adequate consideration, such individual shall be treated as receiving an amount equal to the excess of—

(I) the cash surrender value of such contract at the time of transfer, over

(II) the investment in such contract at such time,

under the contract as an amount not received as an annuity.

(ii) Exception for certain transfers between spouses or former spouses. Clause (i) shall not apply to any transfer to which section 1041(a) (relating to transfers of property between spouses or incident to divorce) applies.

(iii) Adjustment to investment in contract of transferee. If under clause (i) an amount is included in the gross income of the transferor of an annuity contract, the investment in the contract of the transferee in such contract shall be increased by the amount so included.

(5) Retention of existing rules in certain cases.

(A) In general. In any case to which this paragraph applies—

(i) paragraphs (2)(B) and (4)(A) shall not apply, and

(ii) if paragraph (2)(A) does not apply,

the amount shall be included in gross income, but only to the extent it exceeds the investment in the contract.

(B) Existing contracts. This paragraph shall apply to contracts entered into before August 14, 1982. Any amount allocable to investment in the contract after August 13, 1982, shall be treated as from a contract entered into after such date.

(C) Certain life insurance and endowment contracts. Except as provided in paragraph (10) and except to the extent prescribed by the Secretary by regulations, this paragraph shall apply to any amount not received as an annuity which is received under a life insurance or endowment contract.

(D) Contracts under qualified plans. Except as provided in paragraph (8), this paragraph shall apply to any amount received—

(i) from a trust described in section 401(a) which is exempt from tax under section 501(a),

(ii) from a contract—

(I) purchased by a trust described in clause (i),

(II) purchased as part of a plan described in section 403(a),

(III) described in section 403(b), or

(IV) provided for employees of a life insurance company under a plan described in section 818(a)(3), or

(iii) from an individual retirement account or an individual retirement annuity.

Any dividend described in section 404(k) which is received by a participant or beneficiary shall, for purposes of this subparagraph, be treated as paid under a separate contract to which clause (ii)(I) applies.

(E) Full refunds, surrenders, redemptions, and maturities. This paragraph shall apply to—

(i) any amount received, whether in a single sum or otherwise, under a contract in full discharge of the obligation under the contract which is in the nature of a refund of the consideration paid for the contract, and

(ii) any amount received under a contract on its complete surrender, redemption, or maturity.

In the case of any amount to which the preceding sentence applies, the rule of paragraph (2)(A) shall not apply.

(6) Investment in the contract. For purposes of this subsection, the investment in the contract as of any date is—

(A) the aggregate amount of premiums or other consideration paid for the contract before such date, minus

(B) the aggregate amount received under the contract before such date, to the extent that such amount was excludable from gross income under this subtitle or prior income tax laws.

(7) Repealed.

(8) Extension of paragraph (2)(B) to qualified plans.

(A) In general. Notwithstanding any other provision of this subsection, in the case of any amount received before the annuity starting date from a trust or contract described in paragraph (5)(D), paragraph (2)(B) shall apply to such amounts.

(B) Allocation of amount received. For purposes of paragraph (2)(B), the amount allocated to the investment in the contract shall be the portion of the amount described in subparagraph (A) which bears the same ratio to such amount as the investment in the contract bears to the account balance. The determination under the preceding sentence shall be made as of the time of the distribution or at such other time as the Secretary may prescribe.

(C) Treatment of forfeitable rights. If an employee does not have a nonforfeitable right to any amount under any trust or contract to which subparagraph (A) applies, such amount shall not be treated as part of the account balance.

(D) Investment in the contract before 1987. In the case of a plan which on May 5, 1986, permitted withdrawal of any employee contributions before separation from service, subparagraph (A) shall apply only to the extent that amounts received before the annuity starting date (when increased by amounts previously received under the contract after December 31, 1986) exceed the investment in the contract as of December 31, 1986.

> • *Caution:* Code Sec. 72(e)(9), following, was amended by P.L. 107-16, EGTRRA. These provisions generally sunset for tax years beginning after 12/31/2012. For specific sunset provisions, see Sec. 901, P.L. 107-16 (as amended) reproduced in history notes for this Code Sec.

(9) Extension of paragraph (2)(B) to qualified tuition programs and Coverdell education savings accounts. Notwithstanding any other provision of this subsection, paragraph (2)(B) shall apply to amounts received under a qualified tuition program (as defined in section 529(b)) or under a Coverdell education savings account (as defined in section 530(b)). The rule of paragraph (8)(B) shall apply for purposes of this paragraph.

(10) Treatment of modified endowment contracts.
(A) In general. Notwithstanding paragraph (5)(C), in the case of any modified endowment contract (as defined in section 7702A)—
　(i) paragraphs (2)(B) and (4)(A) shall apply, and
　(ii) in applying paragraph (4)(A), "any person" shall be substituted for "an individual".
(B) Treatment of certain burial contracts. Notwithstanding subparagraph (A), paragraph (4)(A) shall not apply to any assignment (or pledge) of a modified endowment contract if such assignment (or pledge) is solely to cover the payment of expenses referred to in section 7702(e)(2)(C)(iii) and if the maximum death benefit under such contract does not exceed $25,000.

(11) Special rules for certain combination contracts providing long-term care insurance. Notwithstanding paragraphs (2), (5)(C), and (10), in the case of any charge against the cash value of an annuity contract or the cash surrender value of a life insurance contract made as payment for coverage under a qualified long-term care insurance contract which is part of or a rider on such annuity or life insurance contract—
(A) the investment in the contract shall be reduced (but not below zero) by such charge, and
(B) such charge shall not be includible in gross income.

(12) Anti-abuse rules.
(A) In general. For purposes of determining the amount includible in gross income under this subsection—
　(i) all modified endowment contracts issued by the same company to the same policyholder during any calendar year shall be treated as 1 modified endowment contract, and
　(ii) all annuity contracts issued by the same company to the same policyholder during any calendar year shall be treated as 1 annuity contract.
The preceding sentence shall not apply to any contract described in paragraph (5)(D).
(B) Regulatory authority. The Secretary may by regulations prescribe such additional rules as may be necessary or appropriate to prevent avoidance of the purposes of this subsection through serial purchases of contracts or otherwise.

(f) Special rules for computing employees' contributions.
In computing, for purposes of subsection (c)(1)(A), the aggregate amount of premiums or other consideration paid for the contract, and for purposes of subsection (e)(6), the aggregate premiums or other consideration paid, amounts contributed by the employer shall be included, but only to the extent that—
(1) such amounts were includible in the gross income of the employee under this subtitle or prior income tax laws; or
(2) if such amounts had been paid directly to the employee at the time they were contributed, they would not have been includible in the gross income of the employee under the law applicable at the time of such contribution.
Paragraph (2) shall not apply to amounts which were contributed by the employer after December 31, 1962, and which would not have been includible in the gross income of the employee by reason of the application of section 911 if such amounts had been paid directly to the employee at the time of contribution. The preceding sentence shall not apply to amounts which were contributed by the employer, as determined under regulations prescribed by the Secretary, to provide pension or annuity credits, to the extent such credits are attributable to services performed before January 1, 1963, and are provided pursuant to pension or annuity plan provisions in existence on March 12, 1962, and on that date applicable to such services, or to the extent such credits are attributable to services performed as a foreign missionary (within the meaning of section 403(b)(2)(D)(iii), as in effect before the enactment of the Economic Growth and Tax Relief Reconciliation Act of 2001).

(g) Rules for transferee where transfer was for value.
Where any contract (or any interest therein) is transferred (by assignment or otherwise) for a valuable consideration, to the extent that the contract (or interest therein) does not, in the hands of the transferee, have a basis which is determined by reference to the basis in the hands of the transferor, then—
(1) for purposes of this section, only the actual value of such consideration, plus the amount of the premiums and other consideration paid by the transferee after the transfer, shall be taken into account in computing the aggregate amount of the premiums or other consideration paid for the contract;
(2) for purposes of subsection (c)(1)(B), there shall be taken into account only the aggregate amount received under the contract by the transferee before the annuity starting date, to the extent that such amount was excludable from gross income under this subtitle or prior income tax laws; and
(3) the annuity starting date is January 1, 1954, or the first day of the first period for which the transferee received an amount under the contract as an annuity, whichever is the later.
For purposes of this subsection, the term "transferee" includes a beneficiary of, or the estate of, the transferee.

(h) Option to receive annuity in lieu of lump sum.
If—
(1) a contract provides for payment of a lump sum in full discharge of an obligation under the contract, subject to an option to receive an annuity in lieu of such lump sum;
(2) the option is exercised within 60 days after the day on which such lump sum first became payable; and
(3) part or all of such lump sum would (but for this subsection) be includible in gross income by reason of subsection (e)(1),

then, for purposes of this subtitle, no part of such lump sum shall be considered as includible in gross income at the time such lump sum first became payable.

(j) Interest.

Notwithstanding any other provision of this section, if any amount is held under an agreement to pay interest thereon, the interest payments shall be included in gross income.

(k) Repealed.

(l) Face-amount certificates.

For purposes of this section, the term "endowment contract" includes a face-amount certificate, as defined in section 2(a)(15) of the Investment Company Act of 1940 (15 U.S.C., Sec. 80a-2), issued after December 31, 1954.

(m) Special rules applicable to employee annuities and distributions under employee plans.

(1) Repealed.

(2) **Computation of consideration paid by the employee.** In computing—

(A) the aggregate amount of premiums or other consideration paid for the contract for purposes of subsection (c)(1)(A) (relating to the investment in the contract), and

(B) the aggregate premiums or other consideration paid for purposes of subsection (e)(6) (relating to certain amounts not received as an annuity),

any amount allowed as a deduction with respect to the contract under section 404 which was paid while the employee was an employee within the meaning of section 401(c)(1) shall be treated as consideration contributed by the employer, and there shall not be taken into account any portion of the premiums or other consideration for the contract paid while the employee was an owner-employee which is properly allocable (as determined under regulations prescribed by the Secretary) to the cost of life, accident, health, or other insurance.

(3) **Life insurance contracts.**

(A) This paragraph shall apply to any life insurance contract—

(i) purchased as a part of a plan described in section 403(a), or

(ii) purchased by a trust described in section 401(a) which is exempt from tax under section 501(a) if the proceeds of such contract are payable directly or indirectly to a participant in such trust or to a beneficiary of such participant.

(B) Any contribution to a plan described in subparagraph (A)(i) or a trust described in subparagraph (A)(ii) which is allowed as a deduction under section 404, and any income of a trust described in subparagraph (A)(ii), which is determined in accordance with regulations prescribed by the Secretary to have been applied to purchase the life insurance protection under a contract described in subparagraph (A), is includible in the gross income of the participant for the taxable year when so applied.

(C) In the case of the death of an individual insured under a contract described in subparagraph (A), an amount equal to the cash surrender value of the contract immediately before the death of the insured shall be treated as a payment under such plan or a distribution by such trust, and the excess of the amount payable by reason of the death of the insured over such cash surrender value shall not be includible in gross income under this section and shall be treated as provided in section 101.

(4) Repealed.

(5) **Penalties applicable to certain amounts received by 5-percent owners.**

(A) This paragraph applies to amounts which are received from a qualified trust described in section 401(a) or under a plan described in section 403(a) at any time by an individual who is, or has been, a 5-percent owner, or by a successor of such an individual, but only to the extent such amounts are determined, under regulations prescribed by the Secretary, to exceed the benefits provided for such individual under the plan formula.

(B) If a person receives an amount to which this paragraph applies, his tax under this chapter for the taxable year in which such amount is received shall be increased by an amount equal to 10 percent of the portion of the amount so received which is includible in his gross income for such taxable year.

(C) For purposes of this paragraph, the term "5-percent owner" means any individual who, at any time during the 5 plan years preceding the plan year ending in the taxable year in which the amount is received, is a 5-percent owner (as defined in section 416(i)(1)(B)).

(6) **Owner-employee defined.** For purposes of this subsection, the term "owner-employee" has the meaning assigned to it by section 401(c)(3) and includes an individual for whose benefit an individual retirement account or annuity described in section 408(a) or (b) is maintained. For purposes of the preceding sentence, the term "owner-employee" shall include an employee within the meaning of section 401(c)(1).

(7) **Meaning of disabled.** For purposes of this section, an individual shall be considered to be disabled if he is unable to engage in any substantial gainful activity by reason of any medically determinable physical or mental impairment which can be expected to result in death or to be of long-continued and indefinite duration. An individual shall not be considered to be disabled unless he furnishes proof of the existence thereof in such form and manner as the Secretary may require.

(8) Repealed.

(9) Repealed.

(10) **Determination of investment in the contract in the case of qualified domestic relations orders.** Under regulations prescribed by the Secretary, in the case of a distribution or payment made to an alternate payee who is the spouse or former spouse of the participant pursuant to a qualified domestic relations order (as defined in section 414(p)), the investment in the contract as of the date prescribed in such regulations shall be allocated on a pro rata basis between the present value of such distribution or payment and the present value of all other benefits payable with respect to the participant to which such order relates.

(n) Annuities under retired serviceman's family protection plan or survivor benefit plan.

Subsection (b) shall not apply in the case of amounts received after December 31, 1965, as an annuity under chapter 73 of title 10 of the United States Code, but all such amounts shall be excluded from gross income until there has been so excluded (under section 122(b)(1) or this section, including amounts excluded before January 1, 1966) an amount equal to the consideration for the contract (as defined by section 122(b)(2)), plus any amount treated pursuant to section 101(b)(2)(D) (as in effect on the day before the date of the enactment of the Small Business Job Protection Act of 1996) as additional consideration paid by the employee. Thereafter all amounts so received shall be included in gross income.

(o) Special rules for distributions from qualified plans to which employee made deductible contributions.

(1) **Treatment of contributions.** For purposes of this section and sections 402 and 403, notwithstanding section 414(h), any deductible employee contribution made to a qualified employer plan or government plan shall be treated as an amount contributed by the employer which is not includible in the gross income of the employee.

(2) **Repealed.**

(3) **Amounts constructively received.**

(A) In general. For purposes of this subsection, rules similar to the rules provided by subsection (p) (other than the exception contained in paragraph (2) thereof) shall apply.

(B) Purchase of life insurance. To the extent any amount of accumulated deductible employee contributions of an employee are applied to the purchase of life insurance contracts, such amount shall be treated as distributed to the employee in the year so applied.

(4) **Special rule for treatment of rollover amounts.** For purposes of sections 402(c), 403(a)(4), 403(b)(8), 408(d)(3), and 457(e)(16), the Secretary shall prescribe regulations providing for such allocations of amounts attributable to accumulated deductible employee contributions, and for such other rules, as may be necessary to insure that such accumulated deductible employee contributions do not become eligible for additional tax benefits (or freed from limitations) through the use of rollovers.

(5) **Definitions and special rules.** For purposes of this subsection—

(A) Deductible employee contributions. The term "deductible employee contributions" means any qualified voluntary employee contribution (as defined in section 219(e)(2)) made after December 31, 1981, in a taxable year beginning after such date and made for a taxable year beginning before January 1, 1987, and allowable as a deduction under section 219(a) for such taxable year.

(B) Accumulated deductible employee contributions. The term "accumulated deductible employee contributions" means the deductible employee contributions—

(i) increased by the amount of income and gain allocable to such contributions, and

(ii) reduced by the sum of the amount of loss and expense allocable to such contributions and the amounts distributed with respect to the employee which are attributable to such contributions (or income or gain allocable to such contributions).

(C) Qualified employer plan. The term "qualified employer plan" has the meaning given to such term by subsection (p)(3)(A)(i).

(D) Government plan. The term "government plan" has the meaning given such term by subsection (p)(3)(B).

(6) **Ordering rules.** Unless the plan specifies otherwise, any distribution from such plan shall not be treated as being made from the accumulated deductible employee contributions until all other amounts to the credit of the employee have been distributed.

(p) Loans treated as distributions.

For purposes of this section—

(1) **Treatment as distributions.**

(A) Loans. If during any taxable year a participant or beneficiary receives (directly or indirectly) any amount as a loan from a qualified employer plan, such amount shall be treated as having been received by such individual as a distribution under such plan.

(B) Assignments or pledges. If during any taxable year a participant or beneficiary assigns (or agrees to assign) or pledges (or agrees to pledge) any portion of his interest in a qualified employer plan, such portion shall be treated as having been received by such individual as a loan from such plan.

(2) **Exception for certain loans.**

(A) General rule. Paragraph (1) shall not apply to any loan to the extent that such loan (when added to the outstanding balance of all other loans from such plan whether made on, before, or after August 13, 1982), does not exceed the lesser of—

(i) $50,000, reduced by the excess (if any) of—

(I) the highest outstanding balance of loans from the plan during the 1-year period ending on the day before the date on which such loan was made, over

(II) the outstanding balance of loans from the plan on the date on which such loan was made, or

(ii) the greater of (I) one-half of the present value of the nonforfeitable accrued benefit of the employee under the plan, or (II) $10,000.

For purposes of clause (ii), the present value of the nonforfeitable accrued benefit shall be determined without regard to any accumulated deductible employee contributions (as defined in subsection (o)(5)(B)).

(B) Requirement that loan be repayable within 5 years.

(i) In general. Subparagraph (A) shall not apply to any loan unless such loan, by its terms, is required to be repaid within 5 years.

(ii) Exception for home loans. Clause (i) shall not apply to any loan used to acquire any dwelling unit which within a reasonable time is to be used (determined at the time the loan is made) as the principal residence of the participant.

(C) Requirement of level amortization. Except as provided in regulations, this paragraph shall not apply to any loan unless substantially level amortization of such loan (with payments not less frequently than quarterly) is required over the term of the loan.

(D) Related employers and related plans. For purposes of this paragraph—

(i) the rules of subsections (b), (c), and (m) of section 414 shall apply, and

(ii) all plans of an employer (determined after the application of such subsections) shall be treated as 1 plan.

(3) **Denial of interest deductions in certain cases.**

(A) In general. No deduction otherwise allowable under this chapter shall be allowed under this chapter for any interest paid or accrued on any loan to which paragraph (1) does not apply by reason of paragraph (2) during the period described in subparagraph (B).

(B) Period to which subparagraph (A) applies. For purposes of subparagraph (A), the period described in this subparagraph is the period—

(i) on or after the 1st day on which the individual to whom the loan is made is a key employee (as defined in section 416(i)), or

(ii) such loan is secured by amounts attributable to elective deferrals described in subparagraph (A) or (C) of section 402(g)(3).

(4) Qualified employer plan, etc. For purposes of this subsection—
   (A) Qualified employer plan.—
      (i) In general. The term "qualified employer plan" means—
         (I) a plan described in section 401(a) which includes a trust exempt from tax under section 501(a),
         (II) an annuity plan described in section 403(a), and
         (III) a plan under which amounts are contributed by an individual's employer for an annuity contract described in section 403(b).
      (ii) Special rule. The term "qualified employer plan" shall include any plan which was (or was determined to be) a qualified employer plan or a government plan.
   (B) Government plan. The term "government plan" means any plan, whether or not qualified, established and maintained for its employees by the United States, by a State or political subdivision thereof, or by an agency or instrumentality of any of the foregoing.

(5) Special rules for loans, etc., from certain contracts. For purposes of this subsection, any amount received as a loan under a contract purchased under a qualified employer plan (and any assignment or pledge with respect to such a contract) shall be treated as a loan under such employer plan.

(q) 10-percent penalty for premature distributions from annuity contracts

   (1) Imposition of penalty. If any taxpayer receives any amount under an annuity contract, the taxpayer's tax under this chapter for the taxable year in which such amount is received shall be increased by an amount equal to 10 percent of the portion of such amount which is includible in gross income.

   (2) Subsection not to apply to certain distributions. Paragraph (1) shall not apply to any distribution—
      (A) made on or after the date on which the taxpayer attains age 59½,
      (B) made on or after the death of the holder (or, where the holder is not an individual, the death of the primary annuitant (as defined in subsection (s)(6)(B))),
      (C) attributable to the taxpayer's becoming disabled within the meaning of subsection (m)(7),
      (D) which is a part of a series of substantially equal periodic payments (not less frequently than annually) made for the life (or life expectancy) of the taxpayer or the joint lives (or joint life expectancies) of such taxpayer and his designated beneficiary,
      (E) from a plan, contract, account, trust, or annuity described in subsection (e)(5)(D),
      (F) allocable to investment in the contract before August 14, 1982,
      (G) under a qualified funding asset (within the meaning of section 130(d), but without regard to whether there is a qualified assignment),
      (H) to which subsection (t) applies (without regard to paragraph (2) thereof),
      (I) under an immediate annuity contract (within the meaning of section 72(u)(4)), or
      (J) which is purchased by an employer upon the termination of a plan described in section 401(a) or 403(a) and which is held by the employer until such time as the employee separates from service.

   (3) Change in substantially equal payments. If—
      (A) paragraph (1) does not apply to a distribution by reason of paragraph (2)(D), and
      (B) the series of payments under such paragraph are subsequently modified (other than by reason of death or disability)—
         (i) before the close of the 5-year period beginning on the date of the first payment and after the taxpayer attains age 59½, or
         (ii) before the taxpayer attains age 59½,
      the taxpayer's tax for the 1st taxable year in which such modification occurs shall be increased by an amount, determined under regulations, equal to the tax which (but for paragraph (2)(D)) would have been imposed, plus interest for the deferral period (within the meaning of subsection (t)(4)(B)).

(r) Certain railroad retirement benefits treated as received under employer plans.

   (1) In general. Notwithstanding any other provision of law, any benefit provided under the Railroad Retirement Act of 1974 (other than a tier 1 railroad retirement benefit) shall be treated for purposes of this title as a benefit provided under an employer plan which meets the requirements of section 401(a).

   (2) Tier 2 taxes treated as contributions.
      (A) In general. For purposes of paragraph (1)—
         (i) the tier 2 portion of the tax imposed by section 3201 (relating to tax on employees) shall be treated as an employee contribution,
         (ii) the tier 2 portion of the tax imposed by section 3211 (relating to tax on employee representatives) shall be treated as an employee contribution, and
         (iii) the tier 2 portion of the tax imposed by section 3221 (relating to tax on employers) shall be treated as an employer contribution.
      (B) Tier 2 portion. For purposes of subparagraph (A)—
         (i) After 1984. With respect to compensation paid after 1984, the tier 2 portion shall be the taxes imposed by sections 3201(b), 3211(b), and 3221(b).
         (ii) After September 30, 1981, and before 1985. With respect to compensation paid before 1985 for services rendered after September 30, 1981, the tier 2 portion shall be —
            (I) so much of the tax imposed by section 3201 as is determined at the 2 percent rate, and
            (II) so much of the taxes imposed by sections 3211 and 3221 as is determined at the 11.75 percent rate.
         With respect to compensation paid for services rendered after December 31, 1983, and before 1985, subclause (I) shall be applied by substituting "2.75 percent" for "2 percent", and subclause (II) shall be applied by substituting "12.75 percent" for "11.75 percent".
         (iii) Before October 1, 1981. With respect to compensation paid for services rendered during any period before October 1, 1981, the tier 2 portion shall be the excess (if any) of—
            (I) the tax imposed for such period by section 3201, 3211, or 3221, as the case may be (other than any tax imposed with respect to man-hours), over
            (II) the tax which would have been imposed by such section for such period had the rates of the comparable taxes imposed by chapter 21 for such period applied under such section.

(C) Contributions not allocable to supplemental annuity or windfall benefits. For purposes of paragraph (1), no amount treated as an employee contribution under this paragraph shall be allocated to—

(i) any supplemental annuity paid under section 2(b) of the Railroad Retirement Act of 1974, or

(ii) any benefit paid under section 3(h), 4(e), or 4(h) of such Act.

(3) **Tier 1 railroad retirement benefit.** For purposes of paragraph (1), the term "tier 1 railroad retirement benefit" has the meaning given such term by section 86(d)(4).

(s) **Required distributions where holder dies before entire interest is distributed.**

(1) **In general.** A contract shall not be treated as an annuity contract for purposes of this title unless it provides that—

(A) if any holder of such contract dies on or after the annuity starting date and before the entire interest in such contract has been distributed, the remaining portion of such interest will be distributed at least as rapidly as under the method of distributions being used as of the date of his death, and

(B) if any holder of such contract dies before the annuity starting date, the entire interest in such contract will be distributed within 5 years after the death of such holder.

(2) **Exception for certain amounts payable over life of beneficiary.** If—

(A) any portion of the holder's interest is payable to (or for the benefit of) a designated beneficiary,

(B) such portion will be distributed (in accordance with regulations) over the life of such designated beneficiary (or over a period not extending beyond the life expectancy of such beneficiary), and

(C) such distributions begin not later than 1 year after the date of the holder's death or such later date as the Secretary may by regulations prescribe,

then for purposes of paragraph (1), the portion referred to in subparagraph (A) shall be treated as distributed on the day on which such distributions begin.

(3) **Special rule where surviving spouse beneficiary.** If the designated beneficiary referred to in paragraph (2)(A) is the surviving spouse of the holder of the contract, paragraphs (1) and (2) shall be applied by treating such spouse as the holder of such contract.

(4) **Designated beneficiary.** For purposes of this subsection, the term "designated beneficiary" means any individual designated a beneficiary by the holder of the contract.

(5) **Exception for certain annuity contracts.** This subsection shall not apply to any annuity contract—

(A) which is provided—

(i) under a plan described in section 401(a) which includes a trust exempt from tax under section 501, or

(ii) under a plan described in section 403(a),

(B) which is described in section 403(b),

(C) which is an individual retirement annuity or provided under an individual retirement account or annuity, or

(D) which is a qualified funding asset (as defined in section 130(d), but without regard to whether there is a qualified assignment).

(6) **Special rule where holder is corporation or other non-individual.**

(A) In general. For purposes of this subsection, if the holder of the contract is not an individual, the primary annuitant shall be treated as the holder of the contract.

(B) Primary annuitant. For purposes of subparagraph (A), the term "primary annuitant" means the individual, the events in the life of whom are of primary importance in affecting the timing or amount of the payout under the contract.

(7) **Treatment of changes in primary annuitant where holder of contract is not an individual.** For purposes of this subsection, in the case of a holder of an annuity contract which is not an individual, if there is a change in a primary annuitant (as defined in paragraph (6)(B)), such change shall be treated as the death of the holder.

(t) **10-percent additional tax on early distributions from qualified retirement plans.**

(1) **Imposition of additional tax.** If any taxpayer receives any amount from a qualified retirement plan (as defined in section 4974(c)), the taxpayer's tax under this chapter for the taxable year in which such amount is received shall be increased by an amount equal to 10 percent of the portion of such amount which is includible in gross income.

(2) **Subsection not to apply to certain distributions.** Except as provided in paragraphs (3) and (4), paragraph (1) shall not apply to any of the following distributions:

(A) In general. Distributions which are—

(i) made on or after the date on which the employee attains age 59½,

(ii) made to a beneficiary (or to the estate of the employee) on or after the death of the employee,

(iii) attributable to the employee's being disabled within the meaning of subsection (m)(7),

(iv) part of a series of substantially equal periodic payments (not less frequently than annually) made for the life (or life expectancy) of the employee or the joint lives (or joint life expectancies) of such employee and his designated beneficiary,

(v) made to an employee after separation from service after attainment of age 55,

(vi) dividends paid with respect to stock of a corporation which are described in section 404(k), or

(vii) made on account of a levy under section 6331 on the qualified retirement plan.

(B) Medical expenses. Distributions made to the employee (other than distributions described in subparagraph (A), (C), or (D)) to the extent such distributions do not exceed the amount allowable as a deduction under section 213 to the employee for amounts paid during the taxable year for medical care (determined without regard to whether the employee itemizes deductions for such taxable year).

(C) Payments to alternate payees pursuant to qualified domestic relations orders. Any distribution to an alternate payee pursuant to a qualified domestic relations order (within the meaning of section 414(p)(1)).

(D) Distributions to unemployed individuals for health insurance premiums.

(i) In general. Distributions from an individual retirement plan to an individual after separation from employment—

(I) if such individual has received unemployment compensation for 12 consecutive weeks under any Federal or State unemployment compensation law by reason of such separation,

(II) if such distributions are made during any taxable year during which such unemployment compensation is paid or the succeeding taxable year, and

(III) to the extent such distributions do not exceed the amount paid during the taxable year for insurance described in section 213(d)(1)(D) with respect to the individual and the individual's spouse and dependents (as defined in section 152, determined without regard to subsections (b)(1), (b)(2), and (d)(1)(B) thereof).

(ii) Distributions after reemployment. Clause (i) shall not apply to any distribution made after the individual has been employed for at least 60 days after the separation from employment to which clause (i) applies.

(iii) Self-employed individuals. To the extent provided in regulations, a self-employed individual shall be treated as meeting the requirements of clause (i)(I) if, under Federal or State law, the individual would have received unemployment compensation but for the fact the individual was self-employed.

(E) Distributions from individual retirement plans for higher education expenses. Distributions to an individual from an individual retirement plan to the extent such distributions do not exceed the qualified higher education expenses (as defined in paragraph (7)) of the taxpayer for the taxable year. Distributions shall not be taken into account under the preceding sentence if such distributions are described in subparagraph (A), (C), or (D) or to the extent paragraph (1) does not apply to such distributions by reason of subparagraph (B).

(F) Distributions from certain plans for first home purchases. Distributions to an individual from an individual retirement plan which are qualified first-time homebuyer distributions (as defined in paragraph (8)). Distributions shall not be taken into account under the preceding sentence if such distributions are described in subparagraph (A), (C), (D), or (E) or to the extent paragraph (1) does not apply to such distributions by reason of subparagraph (B).

(G) Distributions from retirement plans to individuals called to active duty.

(i) In general. Any qualified reservist distribution.

(ii) Amount distributed may be repaid. Any individual who receives a qualified reservist distribution may, at any time during the 2-year period beginning on the day after the end of the active duty period, make one or more contributions to an individual retirement plan of such individual in an aggregate amount not to exceed the amount of such distribution. The dollar limitations otherwise applicable to contributions to individual retirement plans shall not apply to any contribution made pursuant to the preceding sentence. No deduction shall be allowed for any contribution pursuant to this clause.

(iii) Qualified reservist distribution. For purposes of this subparagraph, the term "qualified reservist distribution" means any distribution to an individual if—

(I) such distribution is from an individual retirement plan, or from amounts attributable to employer contributions made pursuant to elective deferrals described in subparagraph (A) or (C) of section 402(g)(3) or section 501(c)(18)(D)(iii),

(II) such individual was (by reason of being a member of a reserve component (as defined in section 101 of title 37, United States Code)) ordered or called to active duty for a period in excess of 179 days or for an indefinite period, and

(III) such distribution is made during the period beginning on the date of such order or call and ending at the close of the active duty period.

(iv) Application of subparagraph. This subparagraph applies to individuals ordered or called to active duty after September 11, 2001. In no event shall the 2-year period referred to in clause (ii) end on or before the date which is 2 years after the date of the enactment of this subparagraph.

(3) **Limitations.**

(A) Certain exceptions not to apply to individual retirement plans. Subparagraphs (A)(v) and (C) of paragraph (2) shall not apply to distributions from an individual retirement plan.

(B) Periodic payments under qualified plans must begin after separation. Paragraph (2)(A)(iv) shall not apply to any amount paid from a trust described in section 401(a) which is exempt from tax under section 501(a) or from a contract described in section 72(e)(5)(D)(ii) unless the series of payments begins after the employee separates from service.

(4) **Change in substantially equal payments.**

(A) In general. If—

(i) paragraph (1) does not apply to a distribution by reason of paragraph (2)(A)(iv), and

(ii) the series of payments under such paragraph are subsequently modified (other than by reason of death or disability)—

(I) before the close of the 5-year period beginning with the date of the first payment and after the employee attains age 59½, or

(II) before the employee attains age 59½,

the taxpayer's tax for the 1st taxable year in which such modification occurs shall be increased by an amount, determined under regulations, equal to the tax which (but for paragraph (2)(A)(iv)) would have been imposed, plus interest for the deferral period.

(B) Deferral period. For purposes of this paragraph, the term "deferral period" means the period beginning with the taxable year in which (without regard to paragraph (2)(A)(iv)) the distribution would have been includible in gross income and ending with the taxable year in which the modification described in subparagraph (A) occurs.

(5) **Employee.** For purposes of this subsection, the term "employee" includes any participant, and in the case of an individual retirement plan, the individual for whose benefit such plan was established.

(6) **Special rules for simple retirement accounts.** In the case of any amount received from a simple retirement account (within the meaning of section 408(p)) during the 2-year period beginning on the date such individual first participated in any qualified salary reduction arrangement maintained by the individual's employer under section 408(p)(2), paragraph (1) shall be applied by substituting "25 percent" for "10 percent".

(7) **Qualified higher education expenses.** For purposes of paragraph (2)(E)—

(A) In general. The term "qualified higher education expenses" means qualified higher education expenses (as defined in section 529(e)(3)) for education furnished to—

(i) the taxpayer,

(ii) the taxpayer's spouse, or

(iii) any child (as defined in section 152(f)(1)) or grandchild of the taxpayer or the taxpayer's spouse, at an eligible educational institution (as defined in section 529(e)(5)).

(B) Coordination with other benefits. The amount of qualified higher education expenses for any taxable year shall be reduced as provided in section 25A(g)(2).

(8) Qualified first-time homebuyer distributions. For purposes of paragraph (2)(F)—

(A) In general. The term "qualified first-time homebuyer distribution" means any payment or distribution received by an individual to the extent such payment or distribution is used by the individual before the close of the 120th day after the day on which such payment or distribution is received to pay qualified acquisition costs with respect to a principal residence of a first-time homebuyer who is such individual, the spouse of such individual, or any child, grandchild, or ancestor of such individual or the individual's spouse.

(B) Lifetime dollar limitation. The aggregate amount of payments or distributions received by an individual which may be treated as qualified first-time homebuyer distributions for any taxable year shall not exceed the excess (if any) of—

(i) $10,000, over

(ii) the aggregate amounts treated as qualified first-time homebuyer distributions with respect to such individual for all prior taxable years.

(C) Qualified acquisition costs. For purposes of this paragraph, the term "qualified acquisition costs" means the costs of acquiring, constructing, or reconstructing a residence. Such term includes any usual or reasonable settlement, financing, or other closing costs.

(D) First-time homebuyer; other definitions. For purposes of this paragraph—

(i) First-time homebuyer. The term "first-time homebuyer" means any individual if—

(I) such individual (and if married, such individual's spouse) had no present ownership interest in a principal residence during the 2-year period ending on the date of acquisition of the principal residence to which this paragraph applies, and

(II) subsection (h) or (k) of section 1034 (as in effect on the day before the date of the enactment of this paragraph) did not suspend the running of any period of time specified in section 1034 (as so in effect) with respect to such individual on the day before the date the distribution is applied pursuant to subparagraph (A).

(ii) Principal residence. The term "principal residence" has the same meaning as when used in section 121.

(iii) Date of acquisition. The term "date of acquisition" means the date—

(I) on which a binding contract to acquire the principal residence to which subparagraph (A) applies is entered into, or

(II) on which construction or reconstruction of such a principal residence is commenced.

(E) Special rule where delay in acquisition. If any distribution from any individual retirement plan fails to meet the requirements of subparagraph (A) solely by reason of a delay or cancellation of the purchase or construction of the residence, the amount of the distribution may be contributed to an individual retirement plan as provided in section 408(d)(3)(A)(i) (determined by substituting "120th day" for "60th day" in such section), except that—

(i) section 408(d)(3)(B) shall not be applied to such contribution, and

(ii) such amount shall not be taken into account in determining whether section 408(d)(3)(B) applies to any other amount.

(9) Special rule for rollovers to section 457 plans. For purposes of this subsection, a distribution from an eligible deferred compensation plan (as defined in section 457(b)) of an eligible employer described in section 457(e)(1)(A) shall be treated as a distribution from a qualified retirement plan described in 4974(c)(1) to the extent that such distribution is attributable to an amount transferred to an eligible deferred compensation plan from a qualified retirement plan (as defined in section 4974(c)).

(10) Distributions to qualified public safety employees in governmental plans.

(A) In general. In the case of a distribution to a qualified public safety employee from a governmental plan (within the meaning of section 414(d)) which is a defined benefit plan, paragraph (2)(A)(v) shall be applied by substituting "age 50" for "age 55".

(B) Qualified public safety employee. For purposes of this paragraph, the term "qualified public safety employee" means any employee of a State or political subdivision of a State who provides police protection, firefighting services, or emergency medical services for any area within the jurisdiction of such State or political subdivision.

(u) Treatment of annuity contracts not held by natural persons.

(1) In general. If any annuity contract is held by a person who is not a natural person—

(A) such contract shall not be treated as an annuity contract for purposes of this subtitle (other than subchapter L), and

(B) the income on the contract for any taxable year of the policyholder shall be treated as ordinary income received or accrued by the owner during such taxable year.

For purposes of this paragraph, holding by a trust or other entity as an agent for a natural person shall not be taken into account.

(2) Income on the contract.

(A) In general. For purposes of paragraph (1), the term "income on the contract" means, with respect to any taxable year of the policyholder, the excess of—

(i) the sum of the net surrender value of the contract as of the close of the taxable year plus all distributions under the contract received during the taxable year or any prior taxable year, reduced by

(ii) the sum of the amount of net premiums under the contract for the taxable year and prior taxable years and amounts includible in gross income for prior taxable years with respect to such contract under this subsection.

Where necessary to prevent the avoidance of this subsection, the Secretary may substitute "fair market value of the contract" for "net surrender value of the contract" each place it appears in the preceding sentence.

(B) Net premiums. For purposes of this paragraph, the term "net premiums" means the amount of premiums paid under the contract reduced by any policyholder dividends.

Income   Code Sec. 72

(3) **Exceptions.** This subsection shall not apply to any annuity contract which—

  (A) is acquired by the estate of a decedent by reason of the death of the decedent,

  (B) is held under a plan described in section 401(a) or 403(a), under a program described in section 403(b), or under an individual retirement plan,

  (C) is a qualified funding asset (as defined in section 130(d), but without regard to whether there is a qualified assignment),

  (D) is purchased by an employer upon the termination of a plan described in section 401(a) or 403(a) and is held by the employer until all amounts under such contract are distributed to the employee for whom such contract was purchased or the employee's beneficiary, or

  (E) is an immediate annuity.

(4) **Immediate annuity.** For purposes of this subsection, the term "immediate annuity" means an annuity—

  (A) which is purchased with a single premium or annuity consideration,

  (B) the annuity starting date (as defined in subsection (c)(4)) of which commences no later than 1 year from the date of the purchase of the annuity, and

  (C) which provides for a series of substantially equal periodic payments (to be made not less frequently than annually) during the annuity period.

(v) **10-percent additional tax for taxable distributions from modified endowment contracts.**

(1) **Imposition of additional tax.** If any taxpayer receives any amount under a modified endowment contract (as defined in section 7702A), the taxpayer's tax under this chapter for the taxable year in which such amount is received shall be increased by an amount equal to 10 percent of the portion of such amount which is includible in gross income.

(2) **Subsection not to apply to certain distributions.** Paragraph (1) shall not apply to any distribution—

  (A) made on or after the date on which the taxpayer attains age 59½,

  (B) which is attributable to the taxpayer's becoming disabled (within the meaning of subsection (m)(7)), or

  (C) which is part of a series of substantially equal periodic payments (not less frequently than annually) made for the life (or life expectancy) of the taxpayer or the joint lives (or joint life expectancies) of such taxpayer and his beneficiary.

(w) **Application of basis rules to nonresident aliens.**

(1) **In general.** Notwithstanding any other provision of this section, for purposes of determining the portion of any distribution which is includible in gross income of a distributee who is a citizen or resident of the United States, the investment in the contract shall not include any applicable nontaxable contributions or applicable nontaxable earnings.

(2) **Applicable nontaxable contribution.** For purposes of this subsection, the term "applicable nontaxable contribution" means any employer or employee contribution—

  (A) which was made with respect to compensation—

    (i) for labor or personal services performed by an employee who, at the time the labor or services were performed, was a nonresident alien for purposes of the laws of the United States in effect at such time, and

    (ii) which is treated as from sources without the United States, and

  (B) which was not subject to income tax (and would have been subject to income tax if paid as cash compensation when the services were rendered) under the laws of the United States or any foreign country.

(3) **Applicable nontaxable earnings.** For purposes of this subsection, the term "applicable nontaxable earnings" means earnings—

  (A) which are paid or accrued with respect to any employer or employee contribution which was made with respect to compensation for labor or personal services performed by an employee,

  (B) with respect to which the employee was at the time the earnings were paid or accrued a nonresident alien for purposes of the laws of the United States, and

  (C) which were not subject to income tax under the laws of the United States or any foreign country.

(4) **Regulations.** The Secretary shall prescribe such regulations as may be necessary to carry out the provisions of this subsection, including regulations treating contributions and earnings as not subject to tax under the laws of any foreign country where appropriate to carry out the purposes of this subsection.

(x) **Cross reference.**

For limitation on adjustments to basis of annuity contracts sold, see section 1021.

In 2010, P.L. 111-312, Sec. 101(a)(1), substituted "December 31, 2012" for "December 31, 2010" both places it appeared in Sec. 901, P.L. 107-16 [see below], effective as if included in the enactment of P.L. 107-16, EGTRRA, 6/7/2001.

—P.L. 111-240, Sec. 2113(a), amended subsec. (a), effective for tax. yrs. begin. after 12/31/2010.

Prior to amendment, subsec. (a) read as follows:

"(a) General rule for annuities. Except as otherwise provided in this chapter, gross income includes any amount received as an annuity (whether for a period certain or during one or more lives) under an annuity, endowment, or life insurance contract."

In 2008, P.L. 110-458, Sec. 108(a), added "on or" before "before" in clause (t)(2)(G)(iv), effective for distributions after 9/11/2001, as if included in the provisions of Sec. 827 of the Pension Protection Act of 2006, P.L. 109-280.

—P.L. 110-245, Sec. 107(a), deleted ", and before December 31, 2007" after "September 11, 2001" in clause (t)(2)(G)(iv), effective for individuals ordered or called to active duty on or after 12/31/2007.

In 2006, P.L. 109-280, Sec. 811, of this Act [relating to Sec. 901 of P.L. 107-16, see below], provides:

"SEC. 811. PENSIONS AND INDIVIDUAL RETIREMENT ARRANGEMENT PROVISIONS OF ECONOMIC GROWTH AND TAX RELIEF RECONCILIATION ACT OF 2001 MADE PERMANENT.

"Title IX of the Economic Growth and Tax Relief Reconciliation Act of 2001 shall not apply to the provisions of, and amendments made by, subtitles A through F of title VI of such Act (relating to pension and individual retirement arrangement provisions)."

—P.L. 109-280, Sec. 827(a), added subpara. (t)(2)(G), effective for distributions after 9/11/2001, except as provided in Sec. 827(c)(2), of this Act, which reads as follows:

"(2) Waiver of limitations. If refund or credit of any overpayment of tax resulting from the amendments made by this section is prevented at any time before the close of the 1-year period beginning on the date of the enactment of this Act by the operation of any law or rule of law (including res judicata), such refund or credit may nevertheless be made or allowed if claim therefor is filed before the close of such period."

—P.L. 109-280, Sec. 828(a), added para. (t)(10), effective for distributions after 8/17/2006.

—P.L. 109-280, Sec. 844(a), redesignated para. (e)(11) as (e)(12) and added para. (e)(11), effective for contracts issued after 12/31/1996, but only for tax. yrs. begin. after 12/31/2009.

—P.L. 109-280, Sec. 1304(a), of this Act, [relating to Sec. 901 of P.L. 107-16, see below] provides:

"SEC. 1304. QUALIFIED TUITION PROGRAMS.

"(a) Permanent extension of modifications. Section 901 of the Economic Growth and Tax Relief Reconciliation Act of 2001 [P.L. 107-16, see below] (relating to sunset provisions) shall not apply to section 402 of such Act (relating to modifications to qualified tuition programs)."

In 2005, P.L. 109-135, Sec. 201(b)(4)(A), repealed Secs. 101 and 103 of P.L. 109-73, see below.

—P.L. 109-73, Sec. 101, of this Act [repealed by Sec. 201(b)(4)(A) of P.L. 109-135, see above], reads as follows:

"SEC. 101. TAX-FAVORED WITHDRAWALS FROM RETIREMENT PLANS FOR RELIEF RELATING TO HURRICANE KATRINA.

"(a) In general. Section 72(t) of the Internal Revenue Code of 1986 shall not apply to any qualified Hurricane Katrina distribution.

"(b) Aggregate dollar limitation.

"(1) In general. For purposes of this section, the aggregate amount of distributions received by an individual which may be treated as qualified Hurricane Katrina distributions for any taxable year shall not exceed the excess (if any) of—

"(A) $100,000, over

"(B) the aggregate amounts treated as qualified Hurricane Katrina distributions received by such individual for all prior taxable years.

"(2) Treatment of plan distributions. If a distribution to an individual would (without regard to paragraph (1)) be a qualified Hurricane Katrina distribution, a plan shall not be treated as violating any requirement of the Internal Revenue Code of 1986 merely because the plan treats such distribution as a qualified Hurricane Katrina distribution, unless the aggregate amount of such distributions from all plans maintained by the employer (and any member of any controlled group which includes the employer) to such individual exceeds $100,000.

"(3) Controlled group. For purposes of paragraph (2), the term 'controlled group' means any group treated as a single employer under subsection (b), (c), (m), or (o) of section 414 of such Code.

"(c) Amount distributed may be repaid.

"(1) In general. Any individual who receives a qualified Hurricane Katrina distribution may, at any time during the 3-year period beginning on the day after the date on which such distribution was received, make one or more contributions in an aggregate amount not to exceed the amount of such distribution to an eligible retirement plan of which such individual is a beneficiary and to which a rollover contribution of such distribution could be made under section 402(c), 403(a)(4), 403(b)(8), 408(d)(3), or 457(e)(16) of such Code, as the case may be.

"(2) Treatment of repayments of distributions from eligible retirement plans other than IRAs. For purposes of such Code, if a contribution is made pursuant to paragraph (1) with respect to a qualified Hurricane Katrina distribution from an eligible retirement plan other than an individual retirement plan, then the taxpayer shall, to the extent of the amount of the contribution, be treated as having received the qualified Hurricane Katrina distribution in an eligible rollover distribution (as defined in section 402(c)(4) of such Code) and as having transferred the amount to the eligible retirement plan in a direct trustee to trustee transfer within 60 days of the distribution.

"(3) Treatment of repayments for distributions from IRAs. For purposes of such Code, if a contribution is made pursuant to paragraph (1) with respect to a qualified Hurricane Katrina distribution from an individual retirement plan (as defined by section 7701(a)(37) of such Code), then, to the extent of the amount of the contribution, the qualified Hurricane Katrina distribution shall be treated as a distribution described in section 408(d)(3) of such Code and as having been transferred to the eligible retirement plan in a direct trustee to trustee transfer within 60 days of the distribution.

"(d) Definitions. For purposes of this section—

"(1) Qualified Hurricane Katrina distribution. Except as provided in subsection (b), the term 'qualified Hurricane Katrina distribution' means any distribution from an eligible retirement plan made on or after August 25, 2005, and before January 1, 2007, to an individual whose principal place of abode on August 28, 2005, is located in the Hurricane Katrina disaster area and who has sustained an economic loss by reason of Hurricane Katrina.

"(2) Eligible retirement plan. The term 'eligible retirement plan' shall have the meaning given such term by section 402(c)(8)(B) of such Code.

"(e) Income inclusion spread over 3 year period for qualified Hurricane Katrina distributions.

"(1) In general. In the case of any qualified Hurricane Katrina distribution, unless the taxpayer elects not to have this subsection apply for any taxable year, any amount required to be included in gross income for such taxable year shall be so included ratably over the 3-taxable year period beginning with such taxable year.

"(2) Special rule. For purposes of paragraph (1), rules similar to the rules of subparagraph (E) of section 408A(d)(3) of such Code shall apply.

"(f) Special rules.

"(1) Exemption of distributions from trustee to trustee transfer and withholding rules. For purposes of sections 401(a)(31), 402(f), and 3405 of such Code, qualified Hurricane Katrina distributions shall not be treated as eligible rollover distributions.

"(2) Qualified Hurricane Katrina distributions treated as meeting plan distribution requirements. For purposes of such Code, a qualified Hurricane Katrina distribution shall be treated as meeting the requirements of sections 401(k)(2)(B)(i), 403(b)(7)(A)(ii), 403(b)(11), and 457(d)(1)(A) of such Code."

—P.L. 109-73, Sec. 103, of this Act [repealed by Sec. 201(b)(4)(A) of P.L. 109-135, see above], reads as follows:

SEC. 103. LOANS FROM QUALIFIED PLANS FOR RELIEF RELATING TO HURRICANE KATRINA.

"(a) Increase in limit on loans not treated as distributions. In the case of any loan from a qualified employer plan (as defined under section 72(p)(4) of the Internal Revenue Code of 1986) to a qualified individual made after the date of enactment of this Act and before January 1, 2007—

"(1) clause (i) of section 72(p)(2)(A) of such Code shall be applied by substituting '$100,000' for '$50,000', and

"(2) clause (ii) of such section shall be applied by substituting 'the present value of the nonforfeitable accrued benefit of the employee under the plan' for 'one-half of the present value of the nonforfeitable accrued benefit of the employee under the plan'.

"(b) Delay of repayment. In the case of a qualified individual with an outstanding loan on or after August 25, 2005, from a qualified employer plan (as defined in section 72(p)(4) of such Code)—

"(1) if the due date pursuant to subparagraph (B) or (C) of section 72(p)(2) of such Code for any repayment with respect to such loan occurs during the period beginning on August 25, 2005, and ending on December 31, 2006, such due date shall be delayed for 1 year,

"(2) any subsequent repayments with respect to any such loan shall be appropriately adjusted to reflect the delay in the due date under paragraph (1) and any interest accruing during such delay, and

"(3) in determining the 5-year period and the term of a loan under subparagraph (B) or (C) of section 72(p)(2) of such Code, the period described in paragraph (1) shall be disregarded.

"(c) Qualified individual. For purposes of this section, the term 'qualified individual' means an individual whose principal place of abode on August 28, 2005, is located in the Hurricane Katrina disaster area and who has sustained an economic loss by reason of Hurricane Katrina."

In 2004, P.L. 108-357, Sec. 906(a), redesignated subsec. (w) as (x) and added subsec. (w), effective for distributions on or after 10/22/2004.

—P.L. 108-311, Sec. 207(6), added ", determined without regard to subsections (b)(1), (b)(2), and (d)(1)(B) thereof" after "section 152" in subclause (t)(2)(D)(i)(III) . . . Sec. 207(7), substituted "152(f)(1)" for "151(c)(3)" in clause (t)(7)(A)(iii), effective for tax. yrs. begin. after 12/31/2004.

—P.L. 108-311, Sec. 408(a)(4), substituted "Economic Growth and Tax Relief Reconciliation Act of 2001" for "Economic Growth and Tax Relief Reconciliation Act of 2001" in subsec. (f), enacted 10/4/2004.

In 2002, P.L. 107-358, Sec. 2, added subsec. (c) in Sec. 901 of P.L. 107-16 [see below], effective 12/17/2002.

In 2001, P.L. 107-90, Sec. 204(e)(2), substituted "3211(b)" for "3211(a)(2)" in clause (r)(2)(B)(i), effective for calendar yrs. begin. after 12/31/2001.

—P.L. 107-22, Sec. 1(b)(1)(A), substituted "a Coverdell education savings" for "an education individual retirement" in para. (e)(9) . . . Sec. 1(b)(3)(A), substituted "Coverdell education savings" for "education individual retirement" in the heading of para. (e)(9), effective 7/26/2001.

—P.L. 107-16, Sec. 402(a)(4)(A), substituted "qualified tuition" for "qualified State tuition" in para. (e)(9) . . . Sec. 402(a)(4)(B), substituted "qualified tuition" for "qualified State tuition" in the heading of para. (e)(9), effective for tax. yrs. begin. after 12/31/2001.

—P.L. 107-16, Sec. 632(a)(3)(A), substituted "section 403(b)(2)(D)(iii), as in effect before the enactment of the Economic Growth and Tax Relief Reconciliation Act of 2001" for "section 403(b)(2)(D)(iii))" in subsec. (f), effective for yrs. begin. after 12/31/2001.

—P.L. 107-16, Sec. 641(a)(2)(C), added para. (t)(9) . . . Sec. 641(e)(1), substituted "403(b)(8), 408(d)(3), and 457(e)(16)" for "and 408(d)(3)" in para. (o)(4), effective for distributions after 12/31/2001. Sec. 641(f)(2) and (3) of this Act, provides:

"(2) Reasonable notice. No penalty shall be imposed on a plan for the failure to provide the information required by the amendment made by subsection (c) with respect to any distribution made before the date that is 90 days after the date on which the Secretary of the Treasury issues a safe harbor rollover notice after the date of the enactment of this Act, if the administrator of such plan makes a reasonable attempt to comply with such requirement.

"(3) Special rule. Notwithstanding any other provision of law, subsections (h)(3) and (h)(5) of section 1122 of the Tax Reform Act of 1986 shall not apply to any distribution from an eligible retirement plan (as defined in clause (iii) or (iv) of section 402(c)(8)(B) of the Internal Revenue Code of 1986) on behalf of an individual if there was a rollover to such plan on behalf of such individual which is permitted solely by reason of any amendment made by this section."

—P.L. 107-16, Sec. 901, of this Act [as amended by Sec. 2, P.L. 107-358 and Sec. 101(a)(1), P.L. 111-312, and as related to Sec. 811 and 1304(a) of P.L. 109-280, see above], reads as follows:

"Sec. 901. Sunset of provisions of Act.

"(a) In general. All provisions of, and amendments made by, this Act shall not apply—

"(1) to taxable, plan, or limitation years beginning after December 31, 2012, or

"(2) in the case of title V, to estates of decedents dying, gifts made, or generation skipping transfers, after December 31, 2012.

"(b) Application of certain laws. The Internal Revenue Code of 1986 and the Employee Retirement Income Security Act of 1974 shall be applied and administered to years, estates, gifts, and transfers described in subsection (a) as if the provisions and amendments described in subsection (a) had never been enacted.

"(c) Exception. Subsection (a) shall not apply to section 803 (relating to no federal income tax on restitution received by victims of the Nazi regime or their heirs or estates)."

In 1998, P.L. 105-206, Sec. 3436(a), deleted "or" at the end of clauses (t)(2)(A)(iv) [Ed. amendment cannot be made to this clause] and (t)(2)(A)(v), substituted ", or" for the period at the end of clause (t)(2)(A)(vi), and added clause (t)(2)(A)(vii), effective for distributions after 12/31/99.

—P.L. 105-206, Sec. 6004(d)(3)(B), added para. (e)(9), effective for tax. yrs. begin. after 12/31/97.

—P.L. 105-206, Sec. 6005(c)(1)(A), substituted "120th day" for "120 days" in subpara. (t)(8)(E) . . . Sec. 6005(c)(1)(B), substituted "60th day" for "60 days" in subpara. (t)(8)(E), effective for distributions after 12/31/98.

—P.L. 105-206, Sec. 6023(3), added "(as in effect on the day before the date of the enactment of the Small Business Job Protection Act of 1996)" after "section 101(b)(2)(D)" in subsec. (n) . . . Sec. 6023(4), substituted "(A)(v)" for "(A)(v)," in subpara. (t)(3)(A), effective 7/22/98.

In 1997, P.L. 105-34, Sec. 203(a), added subpara. (t)(2)(E) . . . Sec. 203(b), added para. (t)(7), effective for distributions after 12/31/97, for expenses paid after 12/31/97 (in tax. yrs. end. after 12/31/97), for education furnished in academic periods begin. after 12/31/97.

Income   Code Sec. 72

—P.L. 105-34, Sec. 303(a), added subpara. (t)(2)(F) ... Sec. 303(b), added para. (t)(8), effective for payments and distributions in tax. yrs. begin. after 12/31/97.

—P.L. 105-34, Sec. 1075(a), added clause (d)(1)(B)(iv) ... Sec. 1075(b)(1), added "If the annuity is payable over the life of a single individual, the number of anticipated payments shall be determined as follows:" before the table in clause (d)(1)(B)(iii) ... Sec. 1075(b)(2), deleted "primary" before "annuitant" in the table in clause (d)(1)(B)(iii), effective for annuity starting dates begin. after 12/31/97.

In 1996, P.L. 104-191, Sec. 361(a), deleted "(B)," from subpara. (t)(3)(A) ... Sec. 361(b), added subpara. (t)(2)(D) ... Sec. 361(c), substituted ", (C), or (D)" for "or (C)" in subpara. (t)(2)(B), effective for distributions after 12/31/96.

—P.L. 104-188, Sec. 1403(a), amended subsec. (d), effective for cases where the annuity starting date is after the 90th day after 8/20/96.

Prior to amendment, subsec. (d) read as follows:

"(d) Treatment of employee contributions under defined contribution plans as separate contracts. For purposes of this section, employee contributions (and any income allocable thereto) under a defined contribution plan may be treated as a separate contract."

—P.L. 104-188, Sec. 1421(b)(4)(A), added para. (t)(6), effective for tax. yrs. begin. after 12/31/96.

—P.L. 104-188, Sec. 1463(a), added ", or to the extent such credits are attributable to services performed as a foreign missionary (within the meaning of section 403(b)(2)(D)(iii))" before the period at the end of subsec. (f), effective for tax. yrs. begin. after 12/31/96.

—P.L. 104-188, Sec. 1704(l)(1), added "(determined without regard to subsection (c)(2))" after "in the contract" in subpara. (b)(4)(A), effective as provided in Sec. 1122(h)(2)(B) of P.L. 99-514 [as amended by Sec. 1011A(b)(12) of P.L. 100-647, see below], reproduced below.

—P.L. 104-188, Sec. 1704(t)(2), added "and" at the end of subpara. (m)(2)(A), deleted subpara. (d)(2)(B), and redesignated subpara. (m)(2)(C) as subpara. (m)(2)(B) ... Sec. 1704(t)(77), amended clause (p)(4)(A)(ii), effective 8/20/96.

Prior to deletion, subpara. (m)(2)(C) read as follows:

"(B) the consideration for the contract contributed by the employee for purposes of subsection (d)(1) (relating to employee's contributions recoverable in 3 years) and subsection (e)(7) (relating to plans where substantially all contributions are employee contributions) and"

Prior to amendment, clause (p)(4)(A)(ii) read as follows:

"(ii) Special rules. The term 'qualified employer plan' —

"(I) shall include any plan which was (or was determined to be) a qualified employer plan or a government plan, but

"(II) shall not include a plan described in subsection (e)(7)."

In 1993, P.L. 103-66, Sec. 14172, deleted "with respect to benefits received before October 1, 1992 [1990]" in Sec. 224(c)(1)(A) of P.L. 98-76, see below.

—P.L. 103-66, Sec. 14303(d)(2)(A), added subpara. (t)(2)(D) ... Sec. 14303(d)(2)(B), added paras. (t)(6) and (t)(7) ... Sec. 14303(d)(2)(C)(i), substituted ", (C), or (D)" for "or (C)" in subpara. (t)(2)(B), effective 8/10/93.

In 1992, P.L. 102-318, Sec. 521(b)(3), substituted "sections 402(c)" for "sections 402(a)(5), 402(a)(7)" in para. (o)(4), effective for distributions after 12/31/92. For special rule, see Sec. 521(e)(2) of this Act which reads as follows:

"(2) Special rule for partial distributions. For purposes of section 402(a)(5)(D)(i)(II) of the Internal Revenue Code of 1986 (as in effect before the amendments made by this section), a distribution before January 1, 1993, which is made before or at the same time as a series of periodic payments shall not be treated as one of such series if it is not substantially equal in amount to other payments in such series."

In 1990, P.L. 101-508, Sec. 11802(a)(1), deleted subpara. (t)(2)(C) ... Sec. 11802(a)(2), redesignated subpara. (t)(2)(D) as subpara. (t)(2)(C) ... Sec. 11802(a)(3), substituted "and (C)" for "(C), and (D)" in subpara. (t)(3)(A), effective 11/5/90 except as provided in Sec. 11821(b) of this Act, which reads as follows:

"(b) Savings provision. If—

"(1) any provision amended or repealed by this part applied to—

"(A) any transaction occurring before the date of the enactment of this Act [11/5/90],

"(B) any property acquired before such date of enactment [11/5/90], or

"(C) any item of income, loss, deduction, or credit taken into account before such date of enactment [11/5/90], and

"(2) the treatment of such transaction, property, or item under such provision would (without regard to the amendments made by this part) affect liability for tax for periods ending after such date of enactment [11/5/90],

nothing in the amendments made by this part shall be construed to affect the treatment of such transaction, property, or item for purposes of determining liability for tax for periods ending after such date of enactment [11/5/90]."

Prior to deletion, subpara. (t)(2)(C) read as follows:

"(C) Exceptions for distributions from employee stock ownership plans. Any distribution made before January 1, 1990, to an employee from an employee stock ownership plan (as defined in section 4975(e)(7)) or a tax credit employee stock ownership plan (as defined in section 409) if—

"(i) such distribution is attributable to assets which have been invested in employer securities (within the meaning of section 409(l)) at all times during the 5 plan-year period preceding the plan year in which the distribution is made, and

"(ii) at all times during such period the requirements of sections 401(a)(28) and 409 (as in effect at such times) are met with respect to such employer securities."

In 1989, P.L. 101-239, Sec. 7811(m)(4), substituted "subsection (s)(6)(B))" for "subsection (s)(6)(B))" in subpara. (q)(2)(B), effective for distributions made before 4/22/87.

—P.L. 101-239, Sec. 7815(a)(3), added the last sentence to subpara. (e)(11)(A) ... Sec. 7815(a)(5), substituted "calendar year" for "12-month period" [each place it appeared] in subpara. (e)(11)(A), effective for annuity contracts entered into after 10/21/88. For special rules, see Secs. 5012(e)(2)-(4) of P.L. 100-647 reproduced in note following Code Sec. 7702A.

—P.L. 101-239, Sec. 10102, substituted "1990" for "1989" in Sec. 224(c)(1)(A) of P.L. 98-76, reproduced below.

In 1988, P.L. 100-647, Sec. 1011A(b)(1)(A), deleted "for purposes of subsections (d)(1) and (e)(7), the consideration for the contract contributed by the employee" after "consideration paid for the contract" in subpart. (f) ... Sec. 1011A(b)(1)(B), substituted "Subsection (b)" for "Subsections (b) and (d)" in subsec. (n) ... Sec. 1011A(b)(2)(A), added subsec. (d) ... Sec. 1011A(b)(2)(B), deleted para. (e)(9) ... Sec. 1011A(b)(9)(A), deleted para. (e)(7) ... Sec. 1011A(b)(9)(B), substituted "paragraph (8)" for "paragraphs (7) and (8)" in subpara. (e)(5)(D) ... Sec. 1011A(b)(9)(C), deleted "(other than paragraph (7))" after "this subsection" in subpara. (e)(8)(A) ... Sec. 1011A(b)(9)(D), deleted "[,](determined without regard to subsection (e)(7))" after "subsection (e)(5)(D)" in subpara. (q)(2)(E), effective for individuals whose annuities start after 7/1/86.

Prior to deletion, para. (e)(9) read as follows:

"(9) Treatment of employee contribution as separate contract. Any employee contributions (and any income allocable thereto) under a defined contribution plan shall be treated as a separate contract for purposes of this subsection."

Prior to deletion, para. (e)(7) read as follows:

"(7) Special rules for plans where substantially all contributions are employee contributions.

"(A) In general. In the case of any plan or contract to which this paragraph applies, subparagraph (D) of paragraph (5) shall not apply to any amount received from such plan or contract.

"(B) Plans or contracts to which this paragraph applies. This paragraph shall apply to any plan or contract—

"(i) which is described in clause (i) or subclause (I), (II), or (III) of clause (ii) of paragraph (5)(D), and

"(ii) with respect to which 85 percent or more of the total contributions during a representative period are derived from employee contributions.

For purposes of clause (ii), deductible employee contributions (as defined in subsection (o)(5)(A)) shall not be taken into account.

"(C) Special rule for certain federal plans. If the Federal Government or an instrumentality thereof maintains more than 1 plan, subparagraph (B) shall be applied by aggregating all such plans which are actively administered by the Federal Government or such instrumentality."

—P.L. 100-647, Sec. 1011A(b)(11), added Sec. 1122(h)(9) of P.L. 99-514 [reproduced below], special rules for amendments made by Sec. 1122(c)(3)(A) of P.L. 99-514, see below.

—P.L. 100-647, Sec. 1011A(b)(12), amended Sec. 1122(h)(2)(B) of P.L. 99-514, the effective date for changes made by Sec. 1122(c)(2) of P.L. 99-514, see below.

Prior to amendment, Sec. 1122(h)(2)(B) of P.L. 99-514 read as follows:

"(B) Subsection (c)(2). The amendment made by subsection (c)(2) shall apply to individuals whose annuity starting date is after December 31, 1986."

—P.L. 100-647, Sec. 1011A(c)(1), deleted "on account of early retirement under the plan" after "separation from service" in clause (t)(2)(A)(v) ... Sec. 1011A(c)(2), amended subpara. (t)(2)(C) ... Sec. 1011A(c)(3), substituted "(C), and (D)" for "and (C)" in subpara. (t)(3)(A) ... Sec. 1011A(c)(4), substituted a period for the comma at the end of subparas. (q)(2)(D) and (G) ... Sec. 1011A(c)(5), substituted "taxpayer" for "employee" each place it appeared in subpara. (q)(3)(B) ... Sec. 1011A(c)(6), added subpara. (q)(2)(H) ... Sec. 1011A(c)(7), added "designated" before "beneficiary" in clause (t)(2)(A)(iv) and subpara. (q)(2)(D) ... Sec. 1011A(c)(8), deleted para. (o)(2), effective for tax. yrs. begin. after 12/31/86. Sec. 1011A(c)(13) of this Act provides:

"(13) Section 72(t) of the 1986 Code shall apply to any distribution without regard to whether such distribution is made without the consent of the participant pursuant to section 411(a)(11) or section 417(e) of the 1986 Code."

Prior to amendment, subpara. (t)(2)(C) read as follows:

"(C) Certain plans.

"(i) In general. Except as provided in clause (ii), any distribution made before January 1, 1990, to an employee from an employee stock ownership plan defined in section 4975(e)(7) to the extent that, on average, a majority of assets in the plan have been invested in employer securities (as defined in section 409(l)) for the 5-plan-year period preceding the plan year in which the distribution is made.

"(ii) Benefits distributed must be invested in employer securities for 5 years. Clause (i) shall not apply to any distribution which is attributable to assets which have not been invested in employer securities at all times during the period referred to in clause (i)."

Prior to deletion, para. (o)(2) read as follows:

"(2) Additional tax if amount received before age 59½. If—

"(A) any accumulated deductible employee contributions are received from a qualified employer plan or government plan

"(B) such amount is received by the employee before the employee attains the age of 59½, and

"(C) such amount is not attributable to such employee's becoming disabled (within the meaning of subsection (m)(7)),

then the employee's tax under this chapter for the taxable year in which such amount is received shall be increased by an amount equal to 10 percent of the amount so received to the extent that such amount is includible in gross income. For purposes of this title, any tax imposed by this paragraph shall be treated as a tax imposed by subsection (m)(5)(B)."

1,339

Code Sec. 72

—P.L. 100-647, Sec. 1011A(c)(12), added Sec. 1123(e)(5) of P.L. 99-514 [reproduced below], part of the effective date for amendments made by Sec. 1123(b) of P.L. 99-514, see below.

—P.L. 100-647, Sec. 1011A(h)(1), added "to which paragraph (1) does not apply by reason of paragraph (2) during the period" after "loan" in subpara. (p)(3)(A) ... Sec. 1011A(h)(2), amended subpara. (p)(3)(B), effective for loans made, renewed, renegotiated, modified or extended after 12/31/86.

Prior to amendment, subpara. (p)(3)(B) read as follows:

"(B) Loans to which subparagraph (A) applies.

For purposes of subparagraph (A), a loan is described in this subparagraph—

"(i) if paragraph (1) does not apply to such loan by reason of paragraph (2), and

"(ii) if—

"(I) such loan is made to a key employee (as defined in section 416(i)), or

"(II) such loan is secured by amounts attributable to elective 401(k) or 403(b) deferrals (as defined in section 402(g)(3))."

—P.L. 100-647, Sec. 1011A(i)(1), added "(other than subchapter L)" following "subtitle" in subpara. (u)(1)(A) ... Sec. 1011A(i)(2), substituted "until all amounts under such contract are distributed to the employee for whom such contract was purchased or the employee's beneficiary" for "until such time as the employee separates from service" in subpara. (u)(3)(D) ... Sec. 1011A(i)(3), deleted "which" before "is" [each place it appeared in] subpara. (u)(3)(D) and (E) ... Sec. 1011A(i)(4), deleted "and" at the end of subpara. (u)(4)(A), substituted ", and" for the period at the end of subpara (u)(4)(B) and added subpara. (u)(4)(C), effective for contributions to annuity contracts after 2/28/86.

—P.L. 100-647, Sec. 1018(k)(1), deleted "or" at the end of subpara. (s)(5)(B), substituted ", or" for the period at the end of subpara. (s)(5)(C) and added subpara. (s)(5)(D) ... Sec. 1018(k)(2), substituted "certain annuity contracts" for "annuity contracts which are part of qualified plans" in the heading of para. (s)(5), effective for contracts issued after 1/18/85, in tax. yrs. end. after 1/18/85.

—P.L. 100-647, Sec. 1018(t)(1)(A), substituted "primary annuitant" for "primary annuity" in para. (s)(7), effective for contracts issued after 4/22/87, in tax. yrs. end. after 4/22/87.

—P.L. 100-647, Sec. 1018(t)(1)(B), deleted the parenthesis following "(B))" in subpara. (q)(2)(B), effective for distributions made after 4/22/87.

—P.L. 100-647, Sec. 1018(t)(1)(D), changed the effective date for the amendment made by Sec. 1826(c) of P.L. 99-514 so that the amendment is effective for "distributions commencing after the date 6 months after 10/22/86 [date of enactment of P.L. 99-514]" rather than effective for "distributions made after the date 6 months after 10/22/86 [date of enactment of P.L. 99-514]" see below.

—P.L. 100-647, Sec. 1018(u)(8), made the same amendment to subpara. (q)(2)(D) as Sec. 1011A(c)(4) of this Act, see above.

—P.L. 100-647, Sec. 5012(a)(1), added para. (e)(10) ... Sec. 5012(a)(2), substituted "Except as provided in paragraph (10) and except to the extent" for "Except to the extent" in subpara. (e)(5)(C) ... Sec. 5012(b)(1), redesignated subsec. (v) as subsec. (w) and added new subsec. (v), effective for contracts entered into on or after 6/21/88, except as provided in Sec. 5012(e)(2)-(4) of this Act reproduced in note following Code Sec. 7702A.

—P.L. 100-647, Sec. 5012(d)(1), added the last sentence to subpara. (e)(4)(A) ... Sec. 5012(d)(2), added para. (e)(11), effective for contracts entered into on or after 6/21/88, except as provided in Sec. 5012(e)(2)-(4) of this Act reproduced in note following Code Sec. 7702A and Sec. 5012(e)(5) of this Act which reads:

"(5) Special rule for annuity contracts. In the case of annuity contracts, the amendments made by [Sec. 5012(d) of this Act] shall apply to contracts entered into after October 21, 1988."

In 1987, P.L. 100-203, Sec. 9034(1), added "(other than amounts described in subparagraph (B))" after "amounts" in Sec. 224(c)(1)(A) of P.L. 98-76 ... Sec. 9034(2), substituted "1989" for "1988", in Sec. 224(c)(1)(A) of P.L. 98-76 ... Sec. 9034(3), deleted the last sentence of Sec. 224(c)(1)(A) of P.L. 98-76, reproduced below.

Prior to deletion, the last sentence of Sec. 224(c)(1)(A) of P.L. 98-76 read as follows:

"The aggregate amount appropriated under the preceding sentence to the extent attributable to benefits other than windfall benefits shall not exceed $877,000,000."

In 1986, P.L. 99-514, Sec. 1101(b)(2)(B), amended para. (p)(3) ... Sec. 1101(b)(2)(C)(i), added "and made for a taxable year beginning before January 1, 1987" after "date" in subpara. (o)(5)(A) ... Sec. 1101(b)(2)(C)(ii), substituted "subsection (p)(3)(A)(i)" for "section 219(e)(3)" in subpara. (o)(5)(C) ... Sec. 1101(b)(2)(C)(iii), substituted "subsection (p)(3)(B)" for "section 219(e)(4)" in subpara. (o)(5)(D), effective for contributions for tax. yrs. begin. after 12/31/86.

Prior to amendment, para. (p)(3) read as follows:

"(3) Qualified employer plan, etc. For purposes of this subsection, the term 'qualified employer plan' means any plan which was (or was determined to be) a qualified employer plan (as defined in section 219(e)(3) other than a plan described in subsection (e)(7)). For purposes of this subsection, such term includes any government plan (as defined in section 219(e)(4))."

—P.L. 99-514, Sec. 1122(c)(1), deleted subsec. (d), effective for individuals whose annuities start after 7/1/86.

Prior to deletion, subsec. (d) read as follows:

"(d) Employees' annuities.

"(1) Employee's contributions recoverable in 3 years. Where—

"(A) Part of the consideration for an annuity, endowment, or life insurance contract is contributed by the employer, and

"(B) during the 3-year period beginning on the date on which an amount is first received under the contract as an annuity, the aggregate amount receivable by the employee under the terms of the contract is equal to or greater than the consideration for the contract contributed by the employee,

then all amounts received as an annuity under the contract shall be excluded from gross income until there has been so excluded an amount equal to the consideration for the contract contributed by the employee. Thereafter all amounts so received under the contract shall be included in gross income.

"(2) Special rules for application of paragraph (1). For purposes of paragraph (1)—

"(A) if the employee died before any amount was received as an annuity under the contract, the words 'receivable by the employee' shall be read as 'receivable by a beneficiary of the employee'; and

"(B) any contribution made with respect to the contract while the employee is an employee within the meaning of section 401(c)(1) which is not allowed as a deduction under section 404 shall be treated as consideration for the contract contributed by the employee.

"(3) Cross reference. For certain rules for determining whether amounts contributed by employer are includible in the gross income of the employee, see part I of subchapter D (Sec. 401 and following, relating to pension, profit-sharing, and stock bonus plans, etc.)."

—P.L. 99-514, Sec. 1122(c)(2), amended subsec. (b), effective as provided in Sec. 1122(h)(2)(B) [as amended by Sec. 1011A(b)(12) of P.L. 100-647, see above] of this Act, which reads as follows:

"(B) Subsection (c)(2). The amendment made by subsection (c)(2) shall apply to individuals whose annuity starting date is after December 31, 1986, except that section 72(b)(3) of the Internal Revenue Code of 1986 (as added by such subsection) shall apply to individuals whose annuity starting date is after July 1, 1986."

Prior to amendment, subsec. (b) read as follows:

"(b) Exclusion ratio.

"Gross income does not include that part of any amount received as an annuity under an annuity, endowment, or life insurance contract which bears the same ratio to such amount as the investment in the contract (as of the annuity starting date) bears to the expected return under the contract (as of such date). This subsection shall not apply to any amount to which subsection (d)(1) (relating to certain employee annuities) applies."

—P.L. 99-514, Sec. 1122(c)(3)(A), added paras. (e)(8) and (e)(9) ... Sec. 1122(c)(3)(B), substituted "paragraphs (7) and (8)" for "paragraph (7)" in subpara. (e)(5)(D), effective for amounts received after 7/1/86 in the case of any plan not described in section 72(e)(8)(D) of the Internal Revenue Code of 1986 (as added above). Sec. 1122(h)(9) of this Act [as added by Sec. 1011A(b)(11) of P.L. 100-647, see above] provides as follows:

"(9) Special rule for state plans. In the case of a plan maintained by a State which on May 5, 1986, permitted withdrawal by the employee of employee contributions (other than as an annuity), section 72(e) of the Internal Revenue Code of 1986 shall be applied—

"(A) without regard to the phrase 'before separation from service' in paragraph (8)(D), and

"(B) by treating any amount received (other than as an annuity) before or with the 1st annuity payment as having been received before the annuity starting date."

—P.L. 99-514, Sec. 1123(a), redesignated subsec. (t) as subsec. (u) and added new subsec. (t) ... Sec. 1123(b)(1)(A), substituted "10 percent" for "5 percent" in para. (q)(1) ... Sec. 1123(b)(1)(B), substituted "10-percent" for "5-percent" in the heading of subsec. (q) ... Sec. 1123(b)(2), amended subpara. (q)(2)(D) ... Sec. 1123(b)(3), added para. (q)(3) ... Sec. 1123(b)(3), [sic (4)], substituted "Paragraph (1)" for "This subsection" in para. (q)(2) ... Sec. 1123(b)(4), [sic (5)], deleted "or" at the end of subpara. (q)(2)(G) [sic F], deleted the period at the end of subpara. (q)(2)(H) [sic (G)], and added subparas. (q)(2)(I) [sic (H)] and (J) [sic (I)] ... Sec. 1123(d)(1), amended subpara. (m)(5)(A) (as amended by Sec. 1852(a)(2)(A) of this Act), effective for tax. yrs. begin. after 12/31/86. Secs. 1123(e)(3), 1123(e)(4) and (e)(5) [as added by Sec. 1011A(c)(12) of P.L. 100-647, see above] of this Act provide:

"(3) Exception where distribution commences. The amendments made by this section shall not apply to distributions to any employee from a plan maintained by any employer if—

"(A) as of March 1, 1986, the employee separated from service with the employer,

"(B) as of March 1, 1986, the accrued benefit of the employee was in pay status pursuant to a written election providing a specific schedule for the distribution of the entire accrued benefit of the employee, and

"(C) such distribution is made pursuant to such written election.

"(4) Transition rule. The amendments made by this section shall not apply with respect to any benefits with respect to which a designation is in effect under section 242(b)(2) of the Tax Equity and Fiscal Responsibility Act of 1982."

"(5) Special rule for distributions under an annuity contract. The amendments made by paragraphs (1), (2), and (3) of subsection (b) shall not apply to any distribution under an annuity contract if—

"(A) as of March 1, 1986, payments were being made under such contract pursuant to a written election providing a specific schedule for the distribution of the taxpayer's interest in such contract, and

"(B) such distribution is made pursuant to such written election."

Prior to amendment, subpara. (q)(2)(D) read as follows:

"(D) which is one of a series of substantially equal periodic payments made for the life of a taxpayer or over a period extending for at least 60 months after the annuity starting date,"

Prior to amendment, subpara. (m)(5)(A) read as follows:

"(A) This subparagraph shall apply—

"(i) to amounts which—

"(I) are received from a qualified trust described in section 401(a) or under a plan described in section 403(a), and

"(II) are received by a 5-percent owner before such owner attains the age of 59½ years, for any reason other than such owner becoming disabled (within the meaning of paragraph (7) of this section), and

"(ii) to amounts which are received from a qualified trust described in section 401(a) or under a plan described in section 403(a) at any time by a 5-percent owner, or by the successor of such owner, but only to the extent that such amounts are determined (under regulations prescribed by the Secretary) to exceed the benefits provided for such individual under the plan formula.

Clause (i) shall not apply to any amount received by an individual in his capacity as a policyholder of an annuity, endowment, or life insurance contract which is in the nature of a dividend or similar distribution and clause (i) shall not apply to amounts attributable to benefits accrued before January 1, 1985.

—P.L. 99-514, Sec. 1134(a), amended clause (p)(2)(A)(i) redesignated subpara. (p)(2)(C) as (p)(2)(D) and added new subpara. (p)(2)(C) . . . Sec. 1134(c), redesignated paragraphs (p)(3) and (p)(4) as (p)(4) and (p)(5), and added new para. (p)(3) . . . Sec. 1134(d), amended clause (p)(2)(B)(ii), effective for loans made, renewed, renegotiated, modified or extended after 12/31/86.

Prior to amendment, clause (p)(2)(A)(i) read as follows:

"(i) $50,000, or"

Prior to amendment, clause (p)(2)(B)(ii) read as follows:

"(ii) Exception for home loans. Clause (i) shall not apply to any loan used to acquire, construct, reconstruct, or substantially rehabilitate any dwelling unit which within a reasonable time is to be used (determined at the time the loan is made) as a principal residence of the participant or a member of the family (within the meaning of section 267(c)(4)) of the participant."

—P.L. 99-514, Sec. 1135(a), redesignated subsec. (u) as subsec. (v) and added new subsec. (u), effective for contributions to annuity contracts after 2/28/86.

—P.L. 99-514, Sec. 1826(a), added para. (s)(5), effective for contracts issued after 1/18/85 in tax. yrs. end. after 1/18/85. See note to Sec. 222 (c)(2) of P.L. 98-369 below, for transitional rules.

—P.L. 99-514, Sec. 1826(b)(1), added paras. (s)(6) and (s)(7) . . . Sec. 1826(b)(2), substituted "any holder of such contract" for "the holder of such contract" each place it appeared in para. (s)(1) . . . Sec. 1826(b)(3), added subpara. (e)(4)(C), effective for contracts issued after the date which is 6 months after the date of enactment of this Act [10/22/86] in tax. yrs. end. after such date.

—P.L. 99-514, Sec. 1826(c), amended subpara. (q)(2)(B), effective [as amended by Sec. 1018(t)(1)(D) of P.L. 100-647, see above] for distributions commencing after the date 6 months after 10/22/86 [date of enactment].

Prior to amendment, subpara. (q)(2)(B) read as follows:

"(B) made to a beneficiary (or to the estate of an annuitant) on or after the death of an annuitant,"

—P.L. 99-514, Sec. 1826(d), deleted "or" at the end of subpara. (q)(2)(E), substituted ", or" for the period at the end of subpara. (q)(2)(F), and added subpara. (q)(2)(G), effective for contracts issued after 1/18/85 in tax. yrs. end. after 1/18/85. See Sec. 222 of P.L. 98-369, below for transitional rules.

—P.L. 99-514, Sec. 1852(a)(2)(A), amended subpara. (m)(5)(A) . . . Sec. 1852(a)(2)(B), amended subpara. (m)(5)(C), effective for tax. yrs. begin. after 12/31/84.

Prior to amendment, subpara. (m)(5)(A) read as follows:

"(A) This paragraph shall apply—

"(i) to amounts (other than any amount received by an individual in his capacity as a policyholder of an annuity, endowment, or life insurance contract which is in the nature of a dividend or similar distribution) which are received from a qualified trust described in section 401(a) or under a plan described in section 403(a) and which are received by an individual, who is, or has been, a 5-percent owner, before such individual attains the age of 59½ years, for any reason other than the individual's becoming disabled (within the meaning of paragraph (7) of this subsection), but only to the extent that such amounts are attributable to contributions paid on behalf of such individual (other than contributions made by him as a 5-percent owner) while he was a 5-percent owner, and

"(ii) to amounts which are received from a qualified trust described in section 401(a) or under a plan described in section 403(a) at any time by an individual who is, or has been a 5-percent owner, or by the successor of such individual, but only to the extent that such amounts are determined under regulations prescribed by the Secretary, to exceed the benefits provided for such individual under the plan formula."

Prior to amendment, subpara. (m)(5)(C) read as follows:

"(C) For purposes of this paragraph, the term '5-percent owner' have [sic has] the same meanings as when used in section 416."

—P.L. 99-514, Sec. 1852(a)(2)(C), substituted "5-percent owners" for "owner-employees" in the heading of para. (m)(5), effective, generally, for loans, assignments, and pledges made after 8/13/82. For exceptions, see the note following Sec. 236 of P.L. 97-248, below.

—P.L. 99-514, Sec. 1852(c)(1)(A), substituted "any plan or contract" for "any trust or contract" in subpara. (e)(7)(B) . . . Sec. 1852(c)(1)(B), substituted "85 percent or more of" for "85 percent of" in clause (e)(7)(B)(ii) . . . Sec. 1852(c)(1)(C), added the last sentence to subpara. (e)(7)(B) . . . Sec. 1852(c)(2), added "(determined without regard to subsection (e)(7))" after "subsection (e)(5)(D)" in subpara. (q)(2)(E) . . . Sec. 1852(c)(3)(A), substituted "subsections (d)(1) and (e)(7)" for "subsection (d)(1)" in subsec. (f) . . . Sec. 1852(c)(3)(B), substituted "subsection (e)(6)" for "subsection (e)(1)(B)" in subsec. (f) . . . Sec. 1852(c)(4)(A), amended subpara. (m)(2)(B) . . . Sec. 1852(c)(4)(B), substituted "subsection (e)(6)" for "subsection (e)(1)(B)" in subpara. (m)(2)(C), effective for any amount received or loan made after the 90th day after 7/18/84.

Prior to amendment, subpara. (m)(2)(B) read as follows:

"(B) the consideration for the contract contributed by the employee for purposes of subsection (d)(1) (relating to employee's contributions recoverable in 3 years), and"

—P.L. 99-514, Sec. 1854(b)(1), added the flush sentence which follows clause (e)(5)(D)(iii), effective for tax. yrs. begin. after 7/18/84 except as provided in Sec. 1854(b)(6) of this Act, which reads as follows:

"(6) The amendments made by paragraphs (1) and (2) [Sec. 1854 of this Act] shall not apply to dividends paid before January 1, 1986, if the taxpayer treated such dividends in a manner inconsistent with such amendments on a return filed with the Secretary before the date of the enactment [10/22/86] of this Act."

—P.L. 99-514, Sec. 1875(c)(5), corrected the effective date for amendments made by Sec. 713(d)(1) of P.L. 98-369, see below.

—P.L. 99-514, Sec. 1898(c)(1)(B), added "who is the spouse or former spouse of the participant" after "alternate payee" in para. (m)(10), effective for payments made after 10/22/86.

In 1984, P.L. 98-397, Sec. 204(c)(2), added para. (m)(10), effective for plan yrs. begin. after 12/31/84, except as provided in Sec. 302(b) of this Act reproduced in note following Code Sec. 402. For transitional rules see Sec. 303 of this Act, reproduced in note following Code Sec. 401.

—P.L. 98-369, Sec. 211(b)(1), substituted "section 818(a)(3)" for "section 805(d)(3)" in subclause (e)(5)(D)(i)(IV), effective for tax. yrs. begin. after 12/31/83.

—P.L. 98-369, Sec. 222(a), amended para. (q)(1) . . . Sec. 222(b), redesignated subsec. (s) as subsec. (t) and added new subsec. (s), effective for contracts issued after the day which is 6 months after 7/18/84 in tax. yrs. end. after such date. Sec. 222(c)(2) of this Act provides:

"(2) Transitional rules for contracts issued before effective date. In the case of any contract (other than a single premium contract) which is issued on or before the day which is 6 months after the date of the enactment of this Act, for purposes of section 72(q)(1)(A) of the Internal Revenue Code of 1954 (as in effect on the day before the date of the enactment of this Act), any investment in such contract which is made during any calendar year shall be treated as having been made on January 1 of such calendar year."

Prior to amendment, para. (q)(1) read as follows:

"(1) Imposition of penalty.

"(A) In general. If any taxpayer receives any amount under an annuity contract, the taxpayer's tax under this chapter for the taxable year in which such amount is received shall be increased by an amount equal to 5 percent of the portion of such amount includible in gross income which is properly allocable to any investment in the annuity contract made during the 10-year period ending on the date such amount was received by the taxpayer.

"(B) Allocation on first-in, first-out basis. For purposes of subparagraph (A), the amount includible in gross income shall be allocated to the earliest investment in the contract with respect to which amounts have not been previously fully allocated under this paragraph."

—P.L. 98-369, Sec. 421(b)(1), deleted subsec. (k), effective for transfers after 7/18/84 in tax. yrs. ending after 7/18/84. Secs. 421(d)(2)-(4), of this Act provide:

"(2) Election to have amendments apply to transfers after 1983. If both spouses or former spouses make an election under this paragraph, the amendments made by this section shall apply to all transfers made by such spouses (or former spouses) after December 31, 1983.

"(3) Exception for transfers pursuant to existing decrees. Except in the case of an election under paragraph (2), the amendments made by this section shall not apply to transfers under any instrument in effect on or before the date of the enactment of this Act unless both spouses (or former spouses) elect to have such amendments apply to transfers under such instrument.

"(4) Election. Any election under paragraph (2) or (3) shall be made in such manner, at such time, and subject to such conditions, as the Secretary of the Treasury or his delegate may by regulations prescribe."

Prior to deletion, subsec. (k) read as follows:

"(k) Payments in discharge of alimony.

"(1) In general. This section shall not apply to so much of any payment under an annuity, endowment, or life insurance contract (or any interest therein) as is includible in the gross income of the wife under section 71 or section 682 (relating to income of an estate or trust in case of divorce, etc.).

"(2) Cross reference. For definition of 'wife', see section 7701(a)(17)."

—P.L. 98-369, Sec. 491(d)(3), substituted "402 and 403" for "402, 403, and 405" in para. (o)(1) . . . Sec. 491(d)(4), substituted "and 408(d)(3)" for "408(d)(3), and 409(b)(3)(C)" in para. (o)(4), effective for obligations issued after 12/31/83.

—P.L. 98-369, Sec. 521(d)(1)-(3), substituted "5-percent owner" for "key employee" each place it appeared in subpara. (m)(5)(A), deleted "in a top-heavy plan" before ", and" at the end of clause (m)(5)(A)(i), and substituted "the term '5-percent owner'" for "the terms 'key employee' and 'top-heavy plan'" in subpara. (m)(5)(C), effective for yrs. begin. after 12/31/84.

—P.L. 98-369, Sec. 523(a), added para. (e)(7) . . . Sec. 523(b)(1), substituted "Except as provided in paragraph (7), this" for "This" in subpara. (e)(5)(D) . . . Sec. 523(b)(2), added "other than a plan described in subsection (e)(7)" after "section 219(e)(3)" in para. (p)(3), effective for any amount received or loan made after the 90th day after 7/18/84.

—P.L. 98-369, Sec. 554, amended Sec. 236(c) of P.L. 97-248, the effective date for changes made by Sec. 236, by adding subpara. (c)(2)(D), reproduced below.

—P.L. 98-369, Sec. 713(b)(1)(A), substituted "subsection (p) (other than the exception contained in paragraph (2) thereof)" for "subsection (p)" in subpara. (o)(3)(A) . . . Sec. 713(b)(1)(B), added the last sentence of subpara. (p)(2)(A), effective generally, for loans, assignments and pledges made after 8/13/82. For exceptions, see the note following Sec. 236 of P.L. 97-248, below.

—P.L. 98-369, Sec. 713(b)(2), amended Sec. 236(c)(2)(C), part of the effective date for changes made by Sec. 236 of P.L. 97-248 (reproduced below), by adding "or if such loan was payable on demand" before the period.

—P.L. 98-369, Sec. 713(b)(4), amended clause (p)(2)(A)(ii)...Sec. 713(c)(1)(A), substituted "as a key employee" for "as an owner employee" in clause (m)(5)(A)(i)...Sec. 713(c)(1)(B), substituted "key employees" for "owner employees" in the heading of para. (m)(5), effective generally, for loans, assignments and pledges made after 8/13/82. For exceptions, see the note following Sec. 236 of P.L. 97-248, below.

Prior to amendment, clause (p)(2)(A)(ii) read as follows:

"(ii) ½ of the present value of the nonforfeitable accrued benefit of the employee under the plan (but not less than $10,000)."

—P.L. 98-369, Sec. 713(d)(1), [as amended by Sec. 1875(c)(5) of P.L. 99-514, see above], deleted para. (m)(9), effective for contributions made in tax. yrs. begin. after 12/31/83.

Prior to deletion, para. (m)(9) read as follows:

"(9) Return of excess contributions before due date of return.

"(A) In general. If an excess contribution is distributed in a qualified distribution—

"(i) such distribution of such excess contribution shall not be included in gross income, and

"(ii) this section (other than this paragraph) shall be applied as if such excess contribution and such distribution had not been made.

"(B) Excess contribution. For purposes of this paragraph, the term 'excess contribution' means any contribution to a qualified trust described in section 401(a) or under a plan described in section 403(a) or 405(a) made on behalf of an employee (within the meaning of section 401(c)) for any taxable year to the extent such contribution exceeds the amount allowable as a deduction under section 404(a).

"(C) Qualified distribution. The term 'qualified distribution' means any distribution of an excess contribution which meets requirements similar to the requirements of subparagraphs (A), (B), and (C) of section 408(d)(4). In the case of such a distribution, the rules of the last sentence of section 408(d)(4) shall apply."

In 1983, P.L. 98-76, Sec. 224(a), redesignated subsec. (r) as subsec. (s) and added new subsec. (r), effective for benefits received after 12/31/83, in tax. yrs. end. after 12/31/83 except as provided in Sec. 227(b)(2) and (3) of this Act, which reads as follows:

"(2) Treatment of certain lump-sum payments received after December 31, 1983. The amendments made by section 224 shall not apply to any portion of a lump-sum payment received after December 31, 1983, if the generally applicable payment date for such portion was before January 1, 1984.

"(3) No fresh start. For purposes of determining whether any benefit received after December 31, 1983, is includible in gross income by reason of section 72(r) of the Internal Revenue Code of 1954, as added by this Act, the amendments made by section 224 be treated as having been in effect during all periods before 1984."

Sec. 224(c) of P.L. 98-76 [as amended by Sec. 9034 of P.L. 100-203, Sec. 10102 of P.L. 101-239, and Sec. 14172 of P.L. 103-66, see above] provides:

"(c) Section 72(r) revenue increase transferred to certain railroad accounts.

"(1) In general.

"(A) Transfers to railroad retirement account. There are hereby appropriated to the Railroad Retirement Account amounts (other than amounts described in subparagraph (B)) equivalent to the aggregate increase in tax liabilities under chapter 1 of the Internal Revenue Code of 1954 which is attributable to the application of section 72(r) of the Internal Revenue Code of 1954 (as added by this Act).

"(B) Revenue increases attributable to windfall benefits received after September 31, 1988, transferred to dual benefits payments account. There are hereby appropriated to the Dual Benefits Payments Account amounts equivalent to the aggregate increase in tax liabilities under chapter 1 of such Code which is attributable to the application of section 72(r) of such Code (as added by this Act) with respect to windfall benefits received after September 30, 1988.

"(C) Windfall benefits defined. For purposes of this paragraph, the term 'windfall benefits' means any benefit paid under section 3(h), 4(e), or 4(h) of the Railroad Retirement Act of 1974.

"(2) Transfers. The amounts appropriated by paragraph (1) shall be transferred from time to time (but not less frequently than quarterly) from the general fund of the Treasury on the basis of estimates made by the Secretary of the Treasury of the amounts referred to in paragraph (1). Any such quarterly payment shall be made on the first day of such quarter and shall take into account benefits estimated to be received during such quarter. Proper adjustments shall be made in the amounts subsequently transferred to the extent prior estimates were in excess of or less than the amounts required to be transferred.

"(3) Revenue increases from tax on supplemental annuities not included. Paragraph (1) shall not apply to tax liabilities attributable to supplemental annuities paid under section 2(b) of the Railroad Retirement Act of 1974."

—P.L. 97-448, Sec. 103(c)(3)(B)(i), deleted "without regard to subparagraph (D) thereof" in para. (p)(3), effective as provided in Sec. 103(c)(3)(B)(ii) of this Act, which reads as follows:

"(ii) The amendment made by clause (i) [Sec. 103(c)(3)(B)(i) of P.L. 97-448] shall take effect as if the matter struck out had never been included in such paragraph."

—P.L. 97-448, Sec. 103(c)(6), deleted "to which the employee made one or more deductible employee contributions" after "government plan" in subpara. (o)(2)(A), for tax. yrs. begin. after 12/31/81.

—P.L. 97-448, Sec. 103(d)(3), corrected Sec. 312(f)(1) of P.L. 97-34, the effective date for changes made by Sec. 312(d) of P.L. 97-34 to "taxable years beginning after December 31, 1981" from "to plans which include employees within the meaning of section 401(c)(1) with respect to taxable years beginning after 12/31/81" [see below].

—P.L. 97-448, Sec. 306(a)(11), added Sec. 236(c)(3) of P.L. 97-248, the effective date for changes made by Sec. 236 of P.L. 97-248 [reproduced below].

In 1982, P.L. 97-248, Sec. 236(a), redesignated subsec. (p) as subsec. (q) and added new subsec. (p)...Sec. 236(b)(1), deleted paras. (m)(4) and (m)(8)...Sec. 236(b)(2), substituted "subsection (p)" for "subsection (m)(4) and (8)" in subpara. (o)(3)(A), effective as provided in Sec. 236 of this Act [as amended by Sec. 306(a)(11) of P.L. 97-448, Sec. 554 of P.L. 98-369, and Sec. 713(b)(2) of P.L. 98-369, see above] which reads:

"(c) Effective Date.

"(1) In general. The amendments made by this section shall apply to loans, assignments, and pledges made after August 13, 1982. For purposes of the preceding sentence, the outstanding balance of any loan which is renegotiated, extended, renewed, or revised after such date shall be treated as an amount received as a loan on the date of such renegotiation, extension, renewal, or revision.

"(2) Exception for certain loans used to repay outstanding obligations.

"(A) In general. Any qualified refunding loan shall not be treated as a distribution by reason of the amendments made by this section to the extent such loan is repaid before August 14, 1983.

"(B) Qualified refunding loan. For purposes of subparagraph (A), the term 'qualified refunding loan' means any loan made after August 13, 1982, and before August 14, 1983, to the extent such loan is used to make a required principal payment.

"(C) Required principal payment. For purposes of subparagraph (B), the term 'required principal payment' means any principal repayment on a loan under the plan which was outstanding on August 13, 1982, if such repayment is required to be made after August 13, 1982, and before August 14, 1983 or if such loan was payable on demand.

"(D) Special rule for non-key employees. In the case of a non-key employee (within the meaning of section 416(i)(2) of the Internal Revenue Code of 1954), this paragraph shall be applied by substituting 'January 1, 1985' for 'August 14, 1983' each place it appears.

"(3) Treatment of certain renegotiations. If—

"(A) the taxpayer after August 13, 1982, and before September 4, 1982, borrows money from a government plan (as defined in section 219(e)(4) of the Internal Revenue Code of 1954),

"(B) under the applicable State law, such loan requires the renegotiation of all outstanding prior loans made to the taxpayer under such plan, and

"(C) the renegotiation described in subparagraph (B) does not change the interest rate on, or extend the duration of, any such outstanding prior loan,

then the renegotiation described in subparagraph (B) shall not be treated as a renegotiation, extension, renewal, or revision for purposes of paragraph (1). If the renegotiation described in subparagraph (B) does not meet the requirements of subparagraph (C) solely because it extends the duration of any such outstanding prior loan, the requirements of subparagraph (C) shall be treated as met with respect to such renegotiation if, before April 1, 1983, such extension is eliminated."

Prior to deletion, para. (m)(4) read as follows:

"(4) Amounts constructively received.

"(A) Assignments or pledges. If during any taxable year an owner-employee assigns (or agrees to assign) or pledges (or agrees to pledge) any portion of his interest in a trust described in section 401(a) which is exempt from tax under section 501(a), an individual retirement account described in section 408(a), an individual retirement annuity described in section 408(b) or any portion of the value of a contract purchased as part of a plan described in section 403(a), such portion shall be treated as having been received by such owner-employee as a distribution from such trust or as an amount received under the contract.

"(B) Loans on contracts. If during any taxable year, an owner-employee receives, directly or indirectly, any amount from any insurance company as a loan under a contract purchased by a trust described in section 401(a) which is exempt from tax under section 501(a) or purchased as part of a plan described in section 403(a), and issued by such insurance company, such amount shall be treated as an amount received under the contract."

Prior to deletion, para. (m)(8) read as follows:

"(8) Loans to owner-employees. If, during any taxable year, an owner-employee receives, directly or indirectly, any amount as a loan from a trust described in section 401(a) which is exempt from tax under section 501(a), such amount shall be treated as having been received by such owner-employee as a distribution from such trust."

—P.L. 97-248, Sec. 237(d)(1)(A), substituted "a key employee" for "an owner-employee" in clause (m)(5)(A)(i)...Sec. 237(d)(1)(B), substituted "while he was a key employee in a top-heavy plan" for "while he was an owner-employee" in clause (m)(5)(A)(i)...Sec. 237(d)(1)(C), substituted "a key employee" for "an owner-employee" in clause (m)(5)(A)(ii)...Sec. 237(d)(2), added subpara. (m)(5)(C)...Sec. 237(d)(3), deleted "except in applying paragraph (5)" after "owner-employee shall" in para. (m)(6), effective for yrs. begin. after 12/31/83.

—P.L. 97-248, Sec. 265(a), amended subsec. (e), effective 8/13/82.

Prior to amendment, subsec. (e) read as follows:

"(e) Amounts not received as annuities.

"(1) General rule. If any amount is received under an annuity, endowment, or life insurance contract, if such amount is not received as an annuity, and if no other provision of this subtitle applies, then such amount—

"(A) if received on or after the annuity starting date, shall be included in gross income; or

"(B) if subparagraph (A) does not apply, shall be included in gross income, but only to the extent that it (when added to amounts previously received under the contract which were excludable from gross income under this subtitle or prior income tax laws) exceeds the aggregate premiums or other consideration paid.

For purposes of this section, any amount received which is in the nature of a dividend of similar distribution shall be treated as an amount not received as an annuity.

"(2) Special rules for application of paragraph (1). For purposes of paragraph (1), the following shall be treated as amounts not received as an annuity:

"(A) any amount received, whether in a single sum or otherwise, under a contract in full discharge of the obligation under the contract which is in the nature of a refund of the consideration paid for the contract; and

"(B) any amount received under a contract on its surrender, redemption, or maturity.

In the case of any amount to which the preceding sentence applies, the rule of paragraph (1)(B) shall apply (and the rule of paragraph (1)(A) shall not apply)."

—P.L. 97-248, Sec. 265(b)(1), redesignated subsec. (q) [formerly subsec. (p) before redesignation by Sec. 236(a) of this Act, see above] as subsec. (r) and added new subsec. (q), effective for distributions after 12/31/82.

In 1981, P.L. 97-34, Sec. 311(b)(1), redesignated subsec. (o) as subsec. (p) and added new subsec. (o), effective for tax. yrs. begin. after 12/31/81. Sec. 311(i)(2) of this Act provides:

"(2) Transitional Rule. For purposes of the Internal Revenue Code of 1954, any amount allowed as a deduction under section 220 of such Code (as in effect before its repeal by this Act) shall be treated as if it were allowed by section 219 of such Code."

—P.L. 97-34, Sec. 312(d)(1), added the last sentence to para. (m)(6) . . . Sec. 312(d)(2), added para. (m)(8), effective [as amended by Sec. 103(d)(3) of P.L. 97-448, see above] for tax. yrs. begin. after 12/31/81. Sec. 312(f)(2) of this Act provides:

"(2) Transitional Rule. The amendments made by subsection (d) shall not apply to any loan from a plan to a self-employed individual who is an employee within the meaning of section 401(c)(1) which is outstanding on December 31, 1981. For purposes of the preceding sentence, any loan which is renegotiated, extended, renewed, or revised after such date shall be treated as a new loan."

—P.L. 97-34, Sec. 312(e)(1), added para. (m)(9), effective [as amended by Sec. 103(d)(3) of P.L. 97-448, see above] for tax. yrs. begin. after 12/31/81.

In 1977, P.L. 95-30, Sec. 301(b)(3), (4), and (5), amended Sec. 505(d) of P.L. 94-455, to read as follows:

"(d) Special Rule for Coordination With Section 72.

"In the case of an individual who—

"(1) retired on disability before January 1, 1977, and

"(2) on December 31, 1975, or December 31, 1976, was entitled to exclude any amount with respect to such retirement disability from gross income under section 105(d) of the Internal Revenue Code of 1954,

for purposes of section 72 the annuity starting date shall not be deemed to occur before the beginning of the taxable year in which the taxpayer attains age 65, or before the beginning of an earlier taxable year for which the taxpayer makes an irrevocable election not to seek the benefits of such section 105(d) for such year and all subsequent years."

—P.L. 95-30, Sec. 301(c), (d), and (e), provided as follows:

"(c) Revocation of Election.

"Any election made under section 105(d)(7) of the Internal Revenue Code of 1954 or under section 505(d) of the Tax Reform Act of 1976 for a taxable year beginning in 1976 may be revoked (in such manner as may be prescribed by regulations) at any time before the expiration of the period for assessing a deficiency with respect to such taxable year (determined without regard to subsection (d) of this section).

"(d) Period for Assessing Deficiency.

"In the case of any revocation made under subsection (c), the period for assessing a deficiency with respect to any taxable year affected by the revocation shall not expire before the date which is 1 year after the date of the making of the revocation, and, notwithstanding any law or rule of law, such deficiency, to the extent attributable to such revocation, may be assessed at any time during such 1-year period.

"(e) Effective Date.

"The amendments made by this section shall take effect on October 4, 1976, but shall not apply—

"(1) with respect to any taxpayer who makes or has made an election under section 105(d)(7) of the Internal Revenue Code of 1954 or under section 505(d) of the Tax Reform Act of 1976 (as such sections were in effect before the enactment of this Act) for a taxable year beginning in 1976, if such election is not revoked under subsection (c) of this section, and

"(2) with respect to any taxpayer (other than a taxpayer described in paragraph (1)) who has an annuity starting date at the beginning of a taxable year beginning in 1976 by reason of the amendments made by section 505 of the Tax Reform Act of 1976 (as in effect before the enactment of this Act), unless such person elects (in such manner as the Secretary of the Treasury or his delegate may by regulations prescribe) to have such amendments apply."

In 1976, P.L. 94-455, Sec. 505(d), provided a special rule for coordination with Code Sec. 72, see above.

—P.L. 94-455, Sec. 1901(a)(12), deleted "(whether or not before January 1, 1954)" following "during the 3-year period beginning on the date", and deleted "(under this paragraph and prior income tax laws)" following "from gross income until there has been so excluded" in para. (d)(1), effective for tax. yrs. begin. after 12/31/76.

—P.L. 94-455, Sec. 1901(a)(13), substituted "an individual retirement account" for "an individual retirement amount" in subpara. (m)(4)(A), effective for tax. yrs. begin. after '76.

—P.L. 94-455, Sec. 1906(b)(13)(A), substituted "Secretary" for "Secretary or his delegate" each place it appeared in subsecs. (c), (f), and (m), effective for tax. yrs. begin. after 12/31/76.

—P.L. 94-455, Sec. 1951(b)(1)(A), deleted subsec. (i), effective for tax. yrs. begin. after '76, except as provided in Sec. 1951(b)(1)(B) of the Act, which reads as follows:

"(B) Savings provision. Notwithstanding subparagraph (A), if the provisions of section 72(i) applied to amounts received in taxable years beginning before January 1, 1977, under an annuity contract, then amounts received under such contract on or after such date shall be treated as if such provisions were repealed."

Prior to amendment, subsec. (i) read as follows:

"(i) Joint and survivor annuities where first annuitant died in 1951, 1952, or 1953.

"Where an annuitant died after December 31, 1950, and before January 1, 1954, and the basis of a surviving annuitant's interest in the joint and survivor annuity contract was determinable under section 113(a)(5) of the Internal Revenue Code of 1939, then—

"(1) subsection (d) shall not apply with respect to such contract;

"(2) for purposes of this section, the aggregate amount of premiums or other consideration paid for the contract is the basis of the contract determined under such section 113(a)(5);

"(3) for purposes of subsection (c)(1)(B), there shall be taken into account only the aggregate amount received by the surviving annuitant under the contract before the annuity starting date, to the extent that such amount was excludable from gross income under this subtitle or prior income tax laws; and

"(4) the annuity starting date is January 1, 1954, or the first day of the first period for which the surviving annuitant received an amount under the contract as an annuity, whichever is the later."

In 1974, P.L. 93-406, Sec. 2001(h)(2), deleted para. (m)(1), effective for tax. yrs. end. after 9/2/74.

Prior to deletion, para. (m)(1) read as follows:

"(1) Certain amounts received before annuity starting date. Any amounts received under an annuity, endowment, or life insurance contract before the annuity starting date which are not received as an annuity (within the meaning of subsection (e)(2)) shall be included in the recipient's gross income for the taxable year in which received to the extent that—

"(A) such amounts, plus all amounts theretofore received under the contract and includible in gross income under this paragraph, do not exceed

"(B) the aggregate premiums or other consideration paid for the contract while the employee was an owner-employee which were allowed as deductions under section 404 for the taxable year and all prior taxable years.

Any such amounts so received which are not includible in gross income under this paragraph shall be subject to the provisions of subsection (e)."

—P.L. 93-406, Sec. 2002(g)(10)(A), added ", an individual retirement amount described in section 408(a), an individual retirement annuity described in section 408(b)", after "501(a)" in subpara. (m)(4)(A), effective 1/1/75.

—P.L. 93-406, Sec. 2001(h)(3), substituted "(other than contributions made by him as an owner-employee)" for "(whether or not paid by him)" in clause (m)(5)(A)(i), effective for tax. yrs. end. after 9/2/74.

—P.L. 93-406, Sec. 2001(e)(5)(A), added "and" at the end of clause (m)(5)(A)(i) . . . Sec. 2001(e)(5)(B), substituted a period for ", and" at the end of clause (m)(5)(A)(ii) . . . Sec. 2001(e)(5)(C), deleted clause (m)(5)(A)(iii), effective for contributions made in tax. yrs. begin. after 12/31/75.

Prior to deletion, clause (m)(5)(A)(iii) read as follows:

"(iii) to amounts which are received, by an individual who is, or has been, an owner-employee, by reason of the distribution under the provisions of section 401(e)(2)(E) of his entire interest in all qualified trusts described in section 401(a) and in all plans described in section 403(a)."

—P.L. 93-406, Sec. 2001(g)(1), amended subpara. (m)(5)(B), effective for distributions made in tax. yrs. begin. after 12/31/75.

Prior to amendment, subpara. (m)(5)(B) read as follows:

"(B)(i) If the aggregate of the amounts to which this paragraph applies received by any person in his taxable year equals or exceeds $2,500, the increase in his tax for the taxable year in which such amounts are received and attributable to such amounts shall be not less than 110 percent of the aggregate increase in taxes, for the taxable year and the 4 immediately preceding taxable years, which would have resulted if such amounts had been included in such person's gross income ratably over such taxable years.

"(ii) If deductions have been allowed under section 404 for contributions paid on behalf of the individual while he is an owner-employee for a number of prior taxable years less than 4, clause (i) shall be applied by taking into account a number of taxable years immediately preceding the taxable year in which the amount was so received equal to such lesser number."

—P.L. 93-406, Sec. 2001(g)(2)(A), deleted subparas. (m)(5)(C), (D) and (E), effective for distributions made in tax. yrs. begin. after 12/31/75.

Prior to deletion, subparas. (m)(5)(C), (D), and (E) read as follows:

"(C) If subparagraph (B) does not apply to a person for the taxable year, the increase in tax of such person for the taxable year attributable to the amounts to which this paragraph applies shall be 110 percent of such increase (computed without regard to this subparagraph).

"(D) Subparagraph (A)(ii) of this paragraph shall not apply to any amount to which section 402(a)(2) or 403(a)(2) applies.

"(E) For special rules for computation of taxable income for taxable years to which this paragraph applies, see subsection (n)(3)."

—P.L. 93-406, Sec. 2002(g)(10)(B), substituted "401(c)(3) and includes an individual for whose benefit an individual retirement account or annuity described in section 408(a) or (b) is maintained" for "401(c)(3)" in para. (m)(6), effective 1/1/75.

Code Sec. 72   Income

—P.L. 93-406, Sec. 2005(c)(3), deleted subsec. (n) and redesignated subsecs. (o) and (p) as subsecs. (n) and (o), effective for distributions or payments made after 12/31/73, in tax. yrs. begin. after such date.

Prior to deletion, subsec. (n) read as follows:

"(n) Treatment of total distributions.

"(1) Application of subsection.

"(A) General rule. This subsection shall apply to amounts —

"(i) distributed to a distributee, in the case of an employees' trust described in section 401(a) which is exempt from tax under section 501(a), or

"(ii) paid to a payee, in the case of an annuity plan described in section 403(a), "if the total distributions or amounts payable to the distributee or payee with respect to an employee (including an individual who is an employee within the meaning of section 401(c)(1)) are paid to the distributee or payee within one taxable year of the distributee or payee, but only to the extent that section 402(a)(2) or 403(a)(2)(A) does not apply to such amounts.

"(B) Distributions to which applicable. This subsection shall apply only to distributions or amounts paid —

"(i) on account of the employee's death,

"(ii) with respect to an individual who is an employee without regard to section 401(c)(1), on account of his separation from the service,

"(iii) with respect to an employee within the meaning of section 401(c)(1), after he has attained the age of 59½ years, or

"(iv) with respect to an employee within the meaning of section 401(c)(1), after he has become disabled within the meaning of subsection (m)(7)).

"(C) Minimum period of service. This subsection shall apply to amounts distributed or paid to an employee from or under a plan only if he has been a participant in the plan for 5 or more taxable years prior to the taxable year in which such amounts are distributed or paid.

"(D) Amounts subject to penalty. This subsection shall not apply to amounts described in clauses (ii) and (iii) of subparagraph (A) of subsection (m)(5) (but, in the case of amounts described in clause (ii) of such subparagraph, only to the extent that subsection (m)(5) applies to such amounts).

"(2) Limitation of tax. In any case to which this subsection applies, the tax attributable to the amounts to which this subsection applies for the taxable year in which such amounts are received shall not exceed whichever of the following is the greater:

"(A) 5 times the increase in tax would result from the inclusion in gross income of the recipient of 20 percent of so much of the amount so received as is includible in gross income, or

"(B) 5 times the increase in tax which would result if the taxable income of the recipient for such taxable year equaled 20 percent of the amount of the taxable income of the recipient for such taxable year determined under paragraph (3)(A).

"(3) Determination of taxable income. Notwithstanding section 63 (relating to definition of taxable income), for purposes only of computing the tax under this chapter attributable to amounts to which this subsection or subsection (m)(5) applies and which are includible in gross income—

"(A) the taxable income of the recipient for the taxable year of receipt shall be treated as being not less than the amount by which (i) the aggregate of such amounts so includible in gross income exceeds (ii) the amount of the deductions allowed for such taxable year under section 151 (relating to deductions for personal exemptions); and

"(B) in making ratable inclusion computations under paragraph (5)(B) of subsection (m), the taxable income of the recipient for each taxable year involved in such ratable inclusion shall be treated as being not less than the amount required by such paragraph (5)(B) to be treated as includible in gross income for such taxable year.

"In any case in which the preceding sentence results in an increase in taxable income for any taxable year, the resulting increase in the taxes imposed by section 1 or 3 for such taxable year shall not be reduced by any credit under part IV of subchapter A (other than sections 31 and 39 thereof) which, but for this sentence, would be allowable.

"(4) Special rule for employees without regard to section 401(c)(1). In the case of amounts to which this subsection applies which are distributed or paid with respect to an individual who is an employee without regard to section 401(c)(1), paragraph (2) shall be applied with the following modifications:

"(A) '7 times' shall be substituted for '5 times', and '14-2/7 percent' shall be substituted for '20 percent'.

"(B) Any amount which is received during the taxable year by the employee as compensation (other than as deferred compensation within the meaning of section 404) for personal services performed for the employer in respect of whom the amounts distributed or paid are received shall not be taken into account.

"(C) No portion of the total distributions or amounts payable (of which the amounts distributed or paid are a part) to which section 402(a)(2) or 403(a)(2)(A) applies shall be taken into account.

"Subparagraph (B) shall not apply if the employee has not attained the age of 59½ years, unless he has died or become disabled (within the meaning of subsection (m)(7))."

—P.L. 93-406, Sec. 2007(b)(2), added "or survivor benefit plan" after "plan" in the heading of subsec. (n), as redesignated by Sec. 2005(c)(3) of this Act, effective for tax. yrs. end. on or after 9/21/72.

In 1969, P.L. 91-172, Sec. 515(b)(1), amended so much of subsec. (n) as preceded para. (n)(2) . . . Sec. 515(b)(2), added para. (n)(4), effective for tax. yrs. end. after 12/31/69.

Prior to amendment, so much of subsec. (n) as preceded para. (n)(2) read as follows:

"(n) Treatment of certain distributions with respect to contributions by self-employed individuals.

"(1) Application of subsection.

"(A) Distributions by employees' trust. Subject to the provisions of subparagraph (C), this subsection shall apply to amounts distributed to a distributee, in the case of an employees' trust described in section 401(a) which is exempt from tax under section 501(a), if the total distributions payable to the distributee with respect to an employee are paid to the distributee within one taxable year of the distributee —

"(i) on account of the employee's death,

"(ii) after the employee has attained the age of 59½ years, or

"(iii) after the employee has become disabled (within the meaning of subsection (m)(7)).

"(B) Annuity plans. Subject to the provisions of subparagraph (C), this subsection shall apply to amounts paid to a payee, in the case of an annuity plan described in section 403(a), if the total amounts payable to the payee with respect to an employee are paid to the payee within one taxable year of the payee—

"(i) on account of the employee's death,

"(ii) after the employee has attained the age of 59½ years, or

"(iii) after the employee has become disabled (within the meaning of subsection (m)(7)).

"(C) Limitations and exceptions. This subsection shall apply—

"(i) only with respect to so much of any distribution or payment to which (without regard to this subparagraph) subparagraph (A) or (B) applies as is attributable to contributions made on behalf of an employee while he was an employee within the meaning of section 401(c)(1), and

"(ii) if the recipient is the employee on whose behalf such contributions were made, only if contributions which were allowed as a deduction under section 404 have been made on behalf of such employee while he was an employee within the meaning of section 401(c)(1) for 5 or more taxable years prior to the taxable year in which the total distributions payable or total amounts payable, as the case may be, are paid.

"This subsection shall not apply to amounts described in clauses (ii) and (iii) of subparagraph (A) of subsection (m)(5) (but, in the case of amounts described in clause (ii) of each subparagraph, only to the extent that subsection (m)(5) applies to such amounts)."

In 1966, P.L. 89-365, Sec. 1, redesignated subsec. (o) as subsec. (p) and added new subsec. (o), effective for tax. yrs. end. after '65.

In 1965, P.L. 89-97, Sec. 106(d), added para. (m)(7), substituted "paragraph (7) of this subsection" for "section 213(g)(3)" in clause (m)(5)(A)(i), substituted "subsection (m)(7)" for "section 213(g)(3)" in clause (n)(1)(A)(iii) and (B)(iii), effective for tax. yrs. begin. after '66.

—P.L. 89-44, Sec. 809(d)(2), substituted "sections 31 and 39" for "section 31" in subsec. (n)(3), effective for tax. yrs. begin. after June 30, '65.

In 1964, P.L. 88-272, Sec. 232(b), deleted para. (e)(3), effective for tax yrs. begin. after 12/31/63.

Prior to deletion, para. (e)(3) read as follows:

"(3) Limit on tax attributable to receipt of lump sum. If a lump sum is received under an annuity, endowment, or life insurance contract, and the part which is includible in gross income is determined under paragraph (1), then the tax attributable to the inclusion of such part in gross income for the taxable year shall not be greater than the aggregate of the taxes attributable to such part had it been included in the gross income of the taxpayer ratably over the taxable year in which received and the preceding 2 taxable years."

In 1962, P.L. 87-792, Sec. 4, designated existing provisions in para. (d)(2) as subpara. (d)(2)(A) and added subpara. (d)(2)(B) and added subsecs. (m) and (n) and redesignated former (m) as (o), effective for tax. yrs. begin. after 12/31/62.

—P.L. 87-834, Sec. 11(b), added the last two sentences of subsec. (f), effective for tax. yrs. end. after 12/31/62.

Sec. 73. Services of child.
(a) Treatment of amounts received.

Amounts received in respect of the services of a child shall be included in his gross income and not in the gross income of the parent, even though such amounts are not received by the child.

(b) Treatment of expenditures.

All expenditures by the parent or the child attributable to amounts which are includible in the gross income of the child (and not of the parent) solely by reason of subsection (a) shall be treated as paid or incurred by the child.

(c) Parent defined.

For purposes of this section, the term "parent" includes an individual who is entitled to the services of a child by reason of having parental rights and duties in respect of the child.

(d) Cross reference.

For assessment of tax against parent in certain cases, see section 6201(c).

Income Code Sec. 75

Sec. 74. Prizes and awards.
(a) General rule.

Except as otherwise provided in this section or in section 117 (relating to qualified scholarships), gross income includes amounts received as prizes and awards.

(b) Exception for certain prizes and awards transferred to charities.

Gross income does not include amounts received as prizes and awards made primarily in recognition of religious, charitable, scientific, educational, artistic, literary, or civic achievement, but only if—

(1) the recipient was selected without any action on his part to enter the contest or proceeding;

(2) the recipient is not required to render substantial future services as a condition to receiving the prize or award; and

(3) the prize or award is transferred by the payor to a governmental unit or organization described in paragraph (1) or (2) of section 170(c) pursuant to a designation made by the recipient.

(c) Exception for certain employee achievement awards.

(1) **In general.** Gross income shall not include the value of an employee achievement award (as defined in section 274(j)) received by the taxpayer if the cost to the employer of the employee achievement award does not exceed the amount allowable as a deduction to the employer for the cost of the employee achievement award.

(2) **Excess deduction award.** If the cost to the employer of the employee achievement award received by the taxpayer exceeds the amount allowable as a deduction to the employer, then gross income includes the greater of—

(A) an amount equal to the portion of the cost to the employer of the award that is not allowable as a deduction to the employer (but not in excess of the value of the award), or

(B) the amount by which the value of the award exceeds the amount allowable as a deduction to the employer.

The remaining portion of the value of such award shall not be included in the gross income of the recipient.

(3) **Treatment of tax-exempt employers.** In the case of an employer exempt from taxation under this subtitle, any reference in this subsection to the amount allowable as a deduction to the employer shall be treated as a reference to the amount which would be allowable as a deduction to the employer if the employer were not exempt from taxation under this subtitle.

(4) **Cross reference.** For provisions excluding certain de minimis fringes from gross income, see section 132(e).

In 1986, P.L. 99-514, Sec. 122(a)(1)(A), substituted "Except as otherwise provided in this section or" for "Except as provided in subsection (b) and" in subsec. (a) . . . Sec. 122(a)(1)(B), substituted "Exception for certain prizes and awards transferred to charities" for "Exception" in the heading of subsec. (b) . . . Sec. 122(a)(1)(C), deleted "and" at the end of para. (b)(1), substituted "; and" for the period at the end of para. (b)(2), and added para. (b)(3) . . . Sec. 122(a)(1)(D), added subsec. (c), effective for prizes and awards granted after 12/31/86.

—P.L. 99-514, Sec. 123(b)(1), substituted "(relating to qualified scholarships)" for "(relating to scholarship and fellowship grants)" in subsec. (a), effective for tax. yrs. begin. after 12/31/86, but only in the case of scholarships and fellowships granted after 8/16/86.

Sec. 75. Dealers in tax-exempt securities.
(a) Adjustment for bond premium.

In computing the gross income of a taxpayer who holds during the taxable year a municipal bond (as defined in subsection (b)(1)) primarily for sale to customers in the ordinary course of his trade or business—

(1) If the gross income of the taxpayer from such trade or business is computed by the use of inventories and his inventories are valued on any basis other than cost, the cost of securities sold (as defined in subsection (b)(2)) during such year shall be reduced by an amount equal to the amortizable bond premium which would be disallowed as a deduction for such year by section 171(a)(2) (relating to deduction for amortizable bond premium) if the definition in section 171(d) of the term "bond" did not exclude such municipal bond; or

(2) if the gross income of the taxpayer from such trade or business is computed without the use of inventories, or by use of inventories valued at cost, and the municipal bond is sold or otherwise disposed of during such year, the adjusted basis (computed without regard to this paragraph) of the municipal bond shall be reduced by the amount of the adjustment which would be required under section 1016(a)(5) (relating to adjustment to basis for amortizable bond premium) if the definition in section 171(d) of the term "bond" did not exclude such municipal bond.

Notwithstanding the provisions of paragraph (1), no reduction to the cost of securities sold during the taxable year shall be made in respect of any obligation described in subsection (b)(1)(A)(ii) which is held by the taxpayer at the close of the taxable year; but in the taxable year in which any such obligation is sold or otherwise disposed of, if such obligation is a municipal bond (as defined in subsection (b)(1)), the cost of securities sold during such year shall be reduced by an amount equal to the adjustment described in paragraph (2), without regard to the fact that the taxpayer values his inventories on any basis other than cost.

(b) Definitions.

For purposes of subsection (a)—

(1) The term "municipal bond" means any obligation issued by a government or political subdivision thereof if the interest on such obligation is excludable from gross income; but such term does not include such an obligation if—

(A)(i) it is sold or otherwise disposed of by the taxpayer within 30 days after the date of its acquisition by him, or

(ii) its earliest maturity or call date is a date more than 5 years from the date on which it was acquired by the taxpayer; and

(B) when it is sold or otherwise disposed of by the taxpayer—

(i) in the case of a sale, the amount realized, or

(ii) in the case of any other disposition, its fair market value at the time of such disposition,

is higher than its adjusted basis (computed without regard to this section and section 1016(a)(6)).

Determinations under subparagraph (B) shall be exclusive of interest.

(2) The term "cost of securities sold" means the amount ascertained by subtracting the inventory value of the closing inventory of a taxable year from the sum of—

(A) the inventory value of the opening inventory for such year, and

(B) the cost of securities and other property purchased during such year which would properly be included in the inventory of the taxpayer if on hand at the close of the taxable year.

In 1958, P.L. 85-886, Sec. 2(a)(1), substituted "municipal bond" for "short-term municipal bond," redesignated subpara. (b)(1)(A) as clause (b)(1)(A)(i), redesignated subpara. (b)(1)(B), as clause (b)(1)(A)(ii) and added new subpara. (b)(1)(B) . . . Sec. 2(a)(2), deleted "short term" each place it preceded "municipal bond" each place it appeared in subsec. (a) . . . Sec. 2(a)(3), added the sentence at the end of subsec. (a) for tax. yrs. end. after '57, but only with respect to obligations acquired after such date.

Sec. 76. Repealed.

In 1976, P.L. 94-455, Sec. 1901(a)(14), repealed Code Sec. 76, effective for tax. yrs. begin. after 12/31/76.
Prior to amendment, Code Sec. 76 read as follows:
"SEC. 76. MORTGAGES MADE OR OBLIGATIONS ISSUED BY JOINT-STOCK LAND BANKS.
"All income (except interest) derived from mortgages made, or obligations issued, after May 28, 1938, by a joint-stock land bank shall (notwithstanding section 26 of the Federal Farm Loan Act; 12 U.S.C. 931-3) be included in gross income."

Sec. 77. Commodity credit loans.
(a) Election to include loans in income.
Amounts received as loans from the Commodity Credit Corporation shall, at the election of the taxpayer, be considered as income and shall be included in gross income for the taxable year in which received.
(b) Effect of election on adjustments for subsequent years.
If a taxpayer exercises the election provided for in subsection (a) for any taxable year, then the method of computing income so adopted shall be adhered to with respect to all subsequent taxable years unless with the approval of the Secretary a change to a different method is authorized.

In 1976, P.L. 94-455, Sec. 1906(b)(13)(A), substituted "Secretary" for "Secretary or his delegate" in subsec. (b), effective for tax. yrs. begin. after 12/31/76.

Sec. 78. Dividends received from certain foreign corporations by domestic corporations choosing foreign tax credit.
If a domestic corporation chooses to have the benefits of subpart A of part III of subchapter N (relating to foreign tax credit) for any taxable year, an amount equal to the taxes deemed to be paid by such corporation under section 902(a)(relating to credit for corporate stockholder in foreign corporation) or under section 960(a)(1)(relating to taxes paid by foreign corporation) for such taxable year shall be treated for purposes of this title (other than section 245) as a dividend received by such domestic corporation from the foreign corporation.

In 1976, P.L. 94-455, Sec. 1033(b)(1), substituted "section 902(a)" for "section 902(a)(1)," substituted "section 960(a)(1)" for "section 960(a)(1)(C)" in Code Sec. 78. Sec. 1033(c), of the Act provided the following effective dates for amendments made by Sec. 1033 of the Act:
"(c) Effective dates.—The amendments made by this section shall apply—
"(1) in respect of any distribution received by a domestic corporation after December 31, 1977, and
"(2) in respect of any distribution received by a domestic corporation before January 1, 1978, in a taxable year of such corporation beginning after December 31, 1975, but only to the extent that such distribution is made out of the accumulated profits of a foreign corporation for a taxable year (of such foreign corporation) beginning after December 31, 1975.
For purposes of paragraph (2), a distribution made by a foreign corporation out of its profits which are attributable to a distribution received from a foreign corporation to which section 902(b) of the Internal Revenue Code of 1954 applies shall be treated as made out of the accumulated profits of a foreign corporation for a taxable year beginning before January 1, 1976, to the extent that such distribution was paid out of the accumulated profits of such foreign corporation for a taxable year beginning before January 1, 1976."

In 1962, P.L. 87-834, Sec. 9(b), added Code Sec. 78 for any distribution received by a domestic corporation after 12/31/64, and in respect of any distribution received by a domestic corporation before 1/1/65, in a taxable year of such corporation beginning after 12/31/62, but only to the extent that such distribution is made out of the accumulated profits of a foreign corporation for a taxable year (of such foreign corporation) beginning after 12/31/62.

Sec. 79. Group-term life insurance purchased for employees.
(a) General rule.
There shall be included in the gross income of an employee for the taxable year an amount equal to the cost of group-term life insurance on his life provided for part or all of such year under a policy (or policies) carried directly or indirectly by his employer (or employers); but only to the extent that such cost exceeds the sum of—
(1) the cost of $50,000 of such insurance, and
(2) the amount (if any) paid by the employee toward the purchase of such insurance.
(b) Exceptions.
Subsection (a) shall not apply to—
(1) the cost of group-term life insurance on the life of an individual which is provided under a policy carried directly or indirectly by an employer after such individual has terminated his employment with such employer and is disabled (within the meaning of section 72(m)(7)),
(2) the cost of any portion of the group-term life insurance on the life of an employee provided during part or all of the taxable year of the employee under which—
 (A) the employer is directly or indirectly the beneficiary, or
 (B) a person described in section 170(c) is the sole beneficiary,
for the entire period during such taxable year for which the employee receives such insurance, and
(3) the cost of any group-term life insurance which is provided under a contract to which section 72(m)(3) applies.
(c) Determination of cost of insurance.
For purposes of this section and section 6052, the cost of group-term insurance on the life of an employee provided during any period shall be determined on the basis of uniform premiums (computed on the basis of 5-year age brackets) prescribed by regulations by the Secretary.
(d) Nondiscrimination requirements.
(1) In general. In the case of a discriminatory group-term life insurance plan
 (A) subsection (a)(1) shall not apply with respect to any key employee, and
 (B) the cost of group-term life insurance on the life of any key employee shall be the greater of—
  (i) such cost determined without regard to subsection (c), or
  (ii) such cost determined with regard to subsection (c).
(2) Discriminatory group-term life insurance plan. For purposes of this subsection, the term "discriminatory group-term life insurance plan" means any plan of an employer for providing group-term life insurance unless—
 (A) the plan does not discriminate in favor of key employees as to eligibility to participate, and
 (B) the type and amount of benefits available under the plan do not discriminate in favor of participants who are key employees.
(3) Nondiscriminatory eligibility classification.
 (A) In general. A plan does not meet requirements of subparagraph (A) of paragraph (2) unless—
  (i) such plan benefits 70 percent or more of all employees of the employer,
  (ii) at least 85 percent of all employees who are participants under the plan are not key employees,
  (iii) such plan benefits such employees as qualify under a classification set up by the employer and found by the Secretary not to be discriminatory in favor of key employees, or
  (iv) in the case of a plan which is part of a cafeteria plan, the requirements of section 125 are met.

(B) Exclusion of certain employees. For purposes of subparagraph (A), there may be excluded from consideration—

(i) employees who have not completed 3 years of service;

(ii) part-time or seasonal employees;

(iii) employees not included in the plan who are included in a unit of employees covered by an agreement between employee representatives and one or more employers which the Secretary finds to be a collective bargaining agreement, if the benefits provided under the plan were the subject of good faith bargaining between such employee representatives and such employer or employers; and

(iv) employees who are nonresident aliens and who receive no earned income (within the meaning of section 911(d)(2)) from the employer which constitutes income from sources within the United States (within the meaning of section 861(a)(3)).

(4) **Nondiscriminatory benefits.** A plan does not meet the requirements of paragraph (2)(B) unless all benefits available to participants who are key employees are available to all other participants.

(5) **Special rule.** A plan shall not fail to meet the requirements of paragraph (2)(B) merely because the amount of life insurance on behalf of the employees under the plan bears a uniform relationship to the total compensation or the basic or regular rate of compensation of such employees.

(6) **Key employee defined.** For purposes of this subsection, the term "key employee" has the meaning given to such term by paragraph (1) of section 416(i). Such term also includes any former employee if such employee when he retired or separated from service was a key employee.

(7) **Exemption for church plans.**

(A) In general. This subsection shall not apply to a church plan maintained for church employees.

(B) Definitions. For purposes of subparagraph (A), the terms "church plan" and "church employee" have the meaning given such terms by paragraphs (1) and (3)(B) of section 414(e), respectively, except that—

(i) section 414(e) shall be applied by substituting "section 501(c)(3)" for "section 501" each place it appears, and

(ii) the term "church employee" shall not include an employee of—

(I) an organization described in section 170(b)(1)(A)(ii) above the secondary school level (other than a school for religious training),

(II) an organization described in section 170(b)(1)(A)(iii), and

(III) an organization described in section 501(c)(3), the basis of the exemption for which is substantially similar to the basis for exemption of an organization described in subclause (II).

(8) **Treatment of former employees.** To the extent provided in regulations, this subsection shall be applied separately with respect to former employees.

(e) **Employee includes former employee.**

For purposes of this section, the term "employee" includes a former employee.

In 1990, P.L. 101-508, Sec. 11703(e)(1), substituted "any former employee" for "any retired employee" in para. (d)(6), effective for employees separating from service after 11/5/90.

In 1989, P.L. 101-140, Sec. 203(a)(1), repealed as if not enacted Sec. 1151(c) of P.L. 99-514, which amended subsec. (d).

—P.L. 101-140, Sec. 203(b)(1)(A), amended para. (d)(7), effective as provided in Sec. 1151(k)(1) and (4) of P.L. 99-514 reproduced in note following Code Sec. 414.

Prior to amendment, para. (d)(7) read as follows:

"(7) Certain controlled groups, etc. All employees who are treated as employed by a single employer under subsection (b), (c), or (m) of section 414 shall be treated as employed by a single employer for purposes of this section,"

— In '88 Sec. 5013(a) of P.L. 100-647 deleted the last sentence of subsec. (c), effective for tax. yrs. begin. after 12/31/88.

Prior to deletion, the last sentence of subsec. (c) read as follows:

"In the case of an employee who has attained age 64, the cost prescribed shall not exceed the cost with respect to such individual if he were age 63."

In 1986, P.L. 99-514, Sec. 1827(a)(1), amended subpara. (d)(1)(B), effective for tax. yrs. end. after 10/22/86.

Prior to amendment, subpara. (d)(1)(B) read as follows:

"(B) the cost of group-term life insurance on the life of any key employee shall be determined without regard to subsection (c)."

— P.L. 99-514, Sec. 1827(b)(1), amended Sec. 223(d)(2)(A) of P.L. 98-369 [reproduced below], part of the effective date for changes made by Sec. 223 of P.L. 98-369, by substituting "was employed by such employer (or a predecessor employer) at any time during 1983. Such amendments also shall not apply to any employee who retired from employment on or before January 1, 1984, and who, when he retired, was covered by the plan (or a predecessor plan)" in the matter following clause (d)(2)(A)(ii) for "either was employed by such employer at any time during 1983 or retired from employment with such employer on or before January 1, 1984", see below . . . Sec. 1827(b)(2), amended Sec. 223(d)(2)(C) of P.L. 98-369 by deleting "after December 31, 1986," and by substituting "may, at the employer's election, be disregarded" for "shall not be taken into account", see below . . . Sec. 1827(b)(3), added Sec. 223(d)(2)(D) of P.L. 98-369, see below.

— P.L. 99-514, Sec. 1827(c), amended para. (d)(6) . . . Sec. 1827(d), added para. (d)(8), effective for tax. yrs. begin. after 12/31/83. For special rules see Sec. 223(d)(2) of P.L. 98-369, reproduced below.

Prior to amendment, para. (d)(6) read as follows:

"(6) Key employee defined. For purposes of this subsection, the term 'key employee' has the meaning given to such term by paragraph (1) of section 416(i), except that subparagraph (A)(iv) of such paragraph shall be applied by not taking into account employees described in paragraph (3)(B) who are not participants in the plan."

In 1984, P.L. 98-369, Sec. 223(a)(1), added subsec. (e) . . . Sec. 223(a)(2), amended para. (b)(1) . . . Sec. 223(b), amended para. (d)(1), effective for tax. yrs. begin. after 12/31/83. Sec. 223(d)(2) of this Act [as amended by Sec. 1827(b) of P.L. 99-514, see above] also provides:

"(2) Inclusion of former employees in the case of existing group-term life insurance plans.

"(A) In general. The amendments made by subsection (a) shall not apply—

"(i) to any group-term life insurance plan of the employer in existence on January 1, 1984, or

"(ii) to any group-term life insurance plan of the employer (or a successor employer) which is a comparable successor to a plan described in clause (i),

but only with respect to an individual who attained age 55 on or before January 1, 1984, and was employed by such employer (or a predecessor employer) at any time during 1983. Such amendments also shall not apply to any employee who retired from employment on or before January 1, 1984, and who, when he retired, was covered by the plan (or predecessor plan).

"(B) Special rule in the case of discriminatory group-term life insurance plan. In the case of any plan which, after December 31, 1986, is a discriminatory group-term life insurance plan (as defined in section 79(d) of the Internal Revenue Code of 1954), subparagraph (A) shall not apply in the case of any individual retiring under such plan after December 31, 1986.

"(C) Benefits to certain retired individuals not taken into account for purposes of determining whether plan is discriminatory. For purposes of determining whether a plan described in subparagraph (A) meets the requirements of section 79(d) of the Internal Revenue Code of 1954 with respect to group-term life insurance for former employees, coverage provided to employees who retired on or before December 31, 1986, may, at the employer's election, be disregarded.

"(D) Comparable successor plans. For purposes of subparagraph (A), a plan shall not fail to be treated as a comparable successor to a plan described in subparagraph (A)(i) with respect to any employee whose benefits do not increase under the successor plan."

Prior to amendment, para. (b)(1) read as follows:

"(1) The cost of group-term life insurance on the life of an individual which is provided under a policy carried directly or indirectly by an employer after such individual has terminated his employment with such employer and either has reached the retirement age with respect to such employer or is disabled (within the meaning of section 72(m)(7))."

Prior to amendment, para. (d)(1) read as follows:

"(1) In general. In the case of a discriminatory group-term life insurance plan, paragraph (1) of subsection (a) shall not apply with respect to any key employee."

In 1982, P.L. 97-248, Sec. 244(a), added subsec. (d), effective for tax. yrs. begin. after 12/31/83.

In 1976, P.L. 94-455, Sec. 1906(b)(13)(A), substituted "Secretary" for "Secretary or his delegate" in subsec. (c), effective for tax. yrs. begin. after 12/31/76.

In 1965, P.L. 89-97, Sec. 106(d), substituted "section 72(m)(7)" for "paragraph (3) of section 213(g), determined without regard to paragraph (4) thereof" in subsec. (b)(1), effective for tax. yrs. begin. after 12/31/66.

In 1964, P.L. 88-272, Sec. 204, added Code Sec. 79, for group term life insurance provided after 12/31/63 in tax. yrs. end. after 12/31/63. In applying new Code

1,347

Sec. 79(b) to a taxable year beginning before 5/1/64, if paragraph (2)(B) of such section applies with respect to an employee for the period beginning 5/1/64 and ending with the close of his first taxable year ending after 4/30/64, such paragraph (2)(B) shall be treated as applying with respect to such employee for the period beginning 1/1/64, and ending 4/30/64.

Sec. 80. Restoration of value of certain securities.
(a) General rule.

In the case of a domestic corporation subject to the tax imposed by section 11 or 801, if the value of any security (as defined in section 165(g)(2))—

(1) which became worthless by reason of the expropriation, intervention, seizure, or similar taking by the government of any foreign country, any political subdivision thereof, or any agency or instrumentality of the foregoing of property to which such security was related, and

(2) which was taken into account as a loss from the sale or exchange of a capital asset or with respect to which a deduction for a loss was allowed under section 165,

is restored in whole or in part during any taxable year by reason of any recovery of money or other property in respect of the property to which such security was related, the value so restored (to the extent that, when added to the value so restored during prior taxable years, it does not exceed the amount of the loss described in paragraph (2)) shall, except as provided in subsection (b), be included in gross income for the taxable year in which such restoration occurs.

(b) Reduction for failure to receive tax benefit.

The amount otherwise includible in gross income under subsection (a) in respect of any security shall be reduced by an amount equal to the amount (if any) of the loss described in subsection (a)(2) which did not result in a reduction of the taxpayer's tax under this subtitle for any taxable year, determined under regulations prescribed by the Secretary.

(c) Character of income.

For purposes of this subtitle—

(1) Except as provided in paragraph (2), the amount included in gross income under this section shall be treated as ordinary income.

(2) If the loss described in subsection (a)(2) was taken into account as a loss from the sale or exchange of a capital asset, the amount included in gross income under this section shall be treated as long-term capital gain.

(d) Treatment under foreign expropriation loss recovery provision.

This section shall not apply to any recovery of a foreign expropriation loss to which section 1351 applies.

In **1984**, P.L. 98-369, Sec. 211(b)(2), substituted "801" for "802" in subsec. (a), effective for tax. yrs. begin. after 12/31/83.

In **1976**, P.L. 94-455, Sec. 1901(b)(3)(K), substituted "ordinary income" for "gain from the sale or exchange of property which is neither a capital asset nor property described in section 1231" in para. (c)(1), effective for tax. yrs. begin. after 12/31/76.

—P.L. 94-455, Sec. 1906(b)(13)(A), substituted "Secretary" for "Secretary or his delegate" in subsec. (b), effective for tax. yrs. begin. after 12/31/76.

In **1966**, P.L. 89-384, Sec. 1(b), added Code Sec. 80, effective for tax. yrs. begin. after 12/31/65, but only for losses described in Code Sec. 80(a)(2) and sustained after 12/31/58.

Sec. 81. Repealed.

In **1987**, P.L. 100-203, Sec. 10201(b)(1), repealed Code Sec. 81, effective for tax. yrs. begin. after 12/31/87, and as provided in Sec. 10201(c)(2) of the Act, reproduced in the notes following Code Sec. 463.

Prior to repeal, Code Sec. 81 read as follows:

"SEC. 81. INCREASE IN VACATION PAY SUSPENSE ACCOUNT.

"There shall be included in gross income for the taxable year the amount of any increase in any suspense account for such taxable year required by paragraph (2)(B) of section 463(c) (relating to accrual of vacation pay)."

In **1986**, P.L. 99-514, Sec. 805(c)(1)(A), amended Code Sec. 81, effective for tax. yrs. begin. after 12/31/86.

Prior to amendment, Code Sec. 81 read as follows:

"SEC. 81. CERTAIN INCREASES IN SUSPENSE ACCOUNTS.

"There shall be included in gross income for the taxable year for which an increase is required—

"(1) Certain dealers' reserves.—The amount of any increase in the suspense account required by paragraph (4)(B)(ii) of section 166(f) (relating to certain debt obligations guaranteed by dealers).

"(2) Vacation pay.—The amount of any increase in the suspense account required by paragraph (2)(B) of section 463(c) (relating to accrual of vacation pay)."

In **1976**, P.L. 94-455, Sec. 605(b), substituted "section 166(f)" for "section 166(g)" in para. (1) effective, for guarantees made after 12/31/75 in tax. yrs. begin. after 12/31/75.

In **1975**, P.L. 93-625, Sec. 4(c)(1), amended Code Sec. 81, effective for tax. yrs. begin. after 12/31/73, except as provided in Sec. 4(d)(2) of the Act, reproduced below.

Prior to amendment, Code Sec. 81 read as follows:

"Sec. 81. Increases in suspense account under section 166(g).

"The amount of any increase in the suspense account required by paragraph (4)(B)(ii) of section 166(g) (relating to certain debt obligations guaranteed by dealers) shall be included in gross income for the taxable year for which such increase is required."

—P.L. 93-625, Sec. 4(d)(2), reads as follows:

"(2) If the taxpayer maintained an account for vacation pay under section 97 of the Technical Amendments Act of 1958, as amended, for his last taxable year ending before January 1, 1973, the amendments made by this section shall apply to taxable years ending after December 31, 1972."

In **1966**, P.L. 89-722, Sec. 1(b)(1), added Code Sec. 81, effective for tax. yrs. end. after 10/21/65.

Sec. 82. Reimbursement for expenses of moving.

Except as provided in section 132(a)(6), there shall be included in gross income (as compensation for services) any amount received or accrued, directly or indirectly, by an individual as a payment for or reimbursement of expenses of moving from one residence to another residence which is attributable to employment or self-employment.

In **1993**, P.L. 103-66, Sec. 13213(d)(3)(A), substituted "Except as provided in section 132(a)(6), there shall" for "There shall" in Code Sec. 82, effective for reimbursements or other payments in respect of expenses incurred after 12/31/93.

In **1974**, P.L. 93-490, Sec. 2, provides as follows for tax. yrs. end. before 1/1/76 (made permanent, see subsec. 217(g)):

"(a) In General.

"Notwithstanding the provisions of section 82 (relating to reimbursement for expenses of moving) and section 217 (relating to moving expenses), of the Internal Revenue Code of 1954, the Secretary of the Treasury, in the administration of those sections, is authorized—

"(1) to enter into an agreement with the Secretary concerned under which the Secretary concerned will not be required to withhold tax on, or to report, moving expense reimbursements made to members of the armed forces;

"(2) to permit any taxpayer who is a member of the armed forces not to include in adjusted gross income the amount of any reimbursement in kind of moving expenses made by the Secretary concerned; and

"(3) to permit any taxpayer who is a member of the armed forces to deduct any amount paid by him as moving expenses in connection with any move required by the Secretary concerned, in excess of any reimbursement received for such expenses, without regard to the provisions of section 217(c) (relating to conditions), to the extent it is otherwise deductible under section 217.

"(b) Definitions.

"For purposes of this section, the term—

"(1) 'armed forces' has the meaning given it by section 101(4) of title 37, United States Code;

"(2) 'Secretary concerned' means the Secretary of Defense and, with respect to the Coast Guard, the Secretary of Transportation; and

"(3) 'adjusted gross income' and 'moving expenses' have the meanings given them by sections 62 and 217(b), respectively, of the Internal Revenue Code of 1954."

In **1969**, P.L. 91-172, Sec. 231(b), added Code Sec. 82, effective for tax. yrs. begin. after 12/31/69, except that the amendments made by this section shall not apply (at the election of the taxpayer made at such time and manner as the Secretary of the Treasury or his delegate prescribes) with respect to moving expenses paid or incurred before July 1, 1970, in connection with the commencement of work by the taxpayer as an employee at a new principal place of work of which the taxpayer had been notified by his employer on or before December 19, 1969.

Sec. 83. Property transferred in connection with performance of services.
(a) General rule.

If, in connection with the performance of services, property is transferred to any person other than the person for whom such services are performed, the excess of—

Income
Code Sec. 83

(1) the fair market value of such property (determined without regard to any restriction other than a restriction which by its terms will never lapse) at the first time the rights of the person having the beneficial interest in such property are transferable or are not subject to a substantial risk of forfeiture, whichever occurs earlier, over

(2) the amount (if any) paid for such property,

shall be included in the gross income of the person who performed such services in the first taxable year in which the rights of the person having the beneficial interest in such property are transferable or are not subject to a substantial risk of forfeiture, whichever is applicable. The preceding sentence shall not apply if such person sells or otherwise disposes of such property in an arm's length transaction before his rights in such property become transferable or not subject to a substantial risk of forfeiture.

(b) Election to include in gross income in year of transfer.

(1) In general. Any person who performs services in connection with which property is transferred to any person may elect to include in his gross income, for the taxable year in which such property is transferred, the excess of—

(A) the fair market value of such property at the time of transfer (determined without regard to any restriction other than a restriction which by its terms will never lapse), over

(B) the amount (if any) paid for such property.

If such election is made, subsection (a) shall not apply with respect to the transfer of such property, and if such property is subsequently forfeited, no deduction shall be allowed in respect of such forfeiture.

(2) Election. An election under paragraph (1) with respect to any transfer of property shall be made in such manner as the Secretary prescribes and shall be made not later than 30 days after the date of such transfer. Such election may not be revoked except with the consent of the Secretary.

(c) Special rules.

For purposes of this section—

(1) Substantial risk of forfeiture. The rights of a person in property are subject to a substantial risk of forfeiture if such person's rights to full enjoyment of such property are conditioned upon the future performance of substantial services by any individual.

(2) Transferability of property. The rights of a person in property are transferable only if the rights in such property of any transferee are not subject to a substantial risk of forfeiture.

(3) Sales which may give rise to suit under Section 16(b) of the Securities Exchange Act of 1934. So long as the sale of property at a profit could subject a person to suit under section 16(b) of the Securities Exchange Act of 1934, such person's rights in such property are—

(A) subject to a substantial risk of forfeiture, and

(B) not transferable.

(4) For purposes of determining an individual's basis in property transferred in connection with the performance of services, rules similar to the rules of section 72(w) shall apply.

(d) Certain restrictions which will never lapse.

(1) Valuation. In the case of property subject to a restriction which by its terms will never lapse, and which allows the transferee to sell such property only at a price determined under a formula, the price so determined shall be deemed to be the fair market value of the property unless established to the contrary by the Secretary, and the burden of proof shall be on the Secretary with respect to such value.

(2) Cancellation. If, in the case of property subject to a restriction which by its terms will never lapse, the restriction is canceled, then, unless the taxpayer establishes—

(A) that such cancellation was not compensatory, and

(B) that the person, if any, who would be allowed a deduction if the cancellation were treated as compensatory, will treat the transaction as not compensatory, as evidenced in such manner as the Secretary shall prescribe by regulations,

the excess of the fair market value of the property (computed without regard to the restrictions) at the time of cancellation over the sum of—

(C) the fair market value of such property (computed by taking the restriction into account) immediately before the cancellation, and

(D) the amount, if any, paid for the cancellation,

shall be treated as compensation for the taxable year in which such cancellation occurs.

(e) Applicability of section.

This section shall not apply to—

(1) a transaction to which section 421 applies,

(2) a transfer to or from a trust described in section 401(a) or a transfer under an annuity plan which meets the requirements of section 404(a)(2),

(3) the transfer of an option without a readily ascertainable fair market value,

(4) the transfer of property pursuant to the exercise of an option with a readily ascertainable fair market value at the date of grant, or

(5) group-term life insurance to which section 79 applies.

(f) Holding period.

In determining the period for which the taxpayer has held property to which subsection (a) applies, there shall be included only the period beginning at the first time his rights in such property are transferable or are not subject to a substantial risk of forfeiture, whichever occurs earlier.

(g) Certain exchanges.

If property to which subsection (a) applies is exchanged for property subject to restrictions and conditions substantially similar to those to which the property given in such exchange was subject, and if section 354, 355, 356, or 1036 (or so much of section 1031 as relates to section 1036) applied to such exchange, or if such exchange was pursuant to the exercise of a conversion privilege—

(1) such exchange shall be disregarded for purposes of subsection (a), and

(2) the property received shall be treated as property to which subsection (a) applies.

(h) Deduction by employer.

In the case of a transfer of property to which this section applies or a cancellation of a restriction described in subsection (d), there shall be allowed as a deduction under section 162, to the person for whom were performed the services in connection with which such property was transferred, an amount equal to the amount included under subsection (a), (b), or (d)(2) in the gross income of the person who performed such services. Such deduction shall be allowed for the taxable year of such person in which or with which ends the taxable year in which such amount is included in the gross income of the person who performed such services.

In **2004**, P.L. 108-357, Sec. 906(b), added para. (c)(4), effective for distributions on or after 10/22/2004.

In **1990**, P.L. 101-508, Sec. 11801(a)(5), deleted subsec. (i), effective 11/5/90 except as provided in Sec. 11821(b) of this Act, which reads as follows:

"(b) Savings provision. If—
"(1) any provision amended or repealed by this part applied to—
"(A) Any transaction occurring before the date of the enactment of this Act [11/5/90],
"(B) any property acquired before such date of enactment [11/5/90], or
"(C) any item of income, loss, deduction, or credit taken into account before such date of enactment [11/5/90], and
"(2) the treatment of such transaction, property, or item under such provision would (without regard to the amendments made by this part) affect liability for tax for periods ending after such date of enactment,
nothing in the amendments made by this part shall be construed to affect the treatment of such transaction, property, or item for purposes of determining liability for tax for periods ending after such date of enactment [11/5/90]."
Prior to deletion, subsec. (i) read as follows:
"(i) Transition rules. This section shall apply to property transferred after June 30, 1969, except that this section shall not apply to property transferred—
"(1) pursuant to a binding written contract entered into before April 22, 1969,
"(2) upon the exercise of an option granted before April 22, 1969,
"(3) before May 1, 1970, pursuant to a written plan adopted and approved before July 1, 1969,
"(4) before January 1, 1973, upon the exercise of an option granted pursuant to a binding written contract entered into before April 22, 1969, between a corporation and the transferor requiring the transferor to grant options to employees of such corporation (or a subsidiary of such corporation) to purchase a determinable number of shares of stock of such corporation, but only if the transferee was an employee of such corporation (or a subsidiary of such corporation) on or before April 22, 1969, or
"(5) in exchange for (or pursuant to the exercise of a conversion privilege contained in) property transferred before July 1, 1969, or for property to which this section does not apply (by reason of paragraph (1), (2), (3), or (4)), if section 354, 355, 356, or 1036 (or so much of section 1031 as relates to section 1036) applies, or if gain or loss is not otherwise required to be recognized upon the exercise of such conversion privilege, and if the property received in such exchange is subject to restrictions and conditions substantially similar to those to which the property given in such exchange was subject."
In **1988**, P.L. 100-647, Sec. 1018(q)(3), amended Sec. 1879(p) of P.L. 99-514 [reproduced below], by substituting "Paragraph (1)" for "Subsection (a)" and substituted "paragraph (1)" for "Subsection (a)" each place it appeared in paras. (2) and (3), see below.
In **1986**, P.L. 99-514, Sec. 1827(e), deleted "the cost of" before "group-term life insurance" in para. (e)(5), effective for tax. yrs. begin. after 12/31/83. For special rules see Sec. 223(d)(2) of P.L. 98-369, reproduced below.
—P.L. 99-514, Sec. 1855(b), amended the material preceding para. (1) of Sec. 556 of P.L. 98-369 [reproduced below].
Prior to amendment, this material read as follows:
"Sec. 556. Time for making certain section 83(b) elections.
"In the case of any transfer of property in connection with the performance of services after June 30, 1976, and on or before November 18, 1982, the election permitted by section 83(b) of the Internal Revenue Code of 1954 may be made, notwithstanding paragraph (2) of such section 83(b), with the income tax return for the first taxable year ending after the date of the enactment of this Act, if—"
—P.L. 99-514, Sec. 1879(p), [as amended by Sec. 1018(g)(3) of P.L. 100-647, see below] related to Sec. 252 of P.L. 97-34, provides:
"(p) Amendment related to Section 252 of the Economic Recovery Tax Act of 1981.
"(1) Notwithstanding subsection (c) of section 252 of the Economic Recovery Tax Act of 1981, the amendment made by subsection (a) of such section 252 (and the provisions of subsection (b) of such section 252) shall apply to any transfer of stock to any person if—
"(A) such transfer occurred in November or December of 1973 and was pursuant to the exercise of an option granted in November or December of 1971,
"(B) in December 1973 the corporation granting the option was acquired by another corporation in a transaction qualifying as a reorganization under section 368 of the Internal Revenue Code of 1954,
"(C) the fair market value (as of July 1, 1974) of the stock received by such person in the reorganization in exchange for the stock transferred to him pursuant to the exercise of such option was less than 50 percent of the fair market value of the stock so received (as of December 4, 1973),
"(D) in 1975 or 1976 such person sold substantially all of the stock received in such reorganization, and
"(E) such person makes an election under this section at such time and in such manner as the Secretary of the Treasury or his delegate shall prescribe.
"(2) Limitation on amount of benefit.— Paragraph (1) shall not apply to transfers with respect to any employee to the extent that the application of Paragraph (1) with respect to such employee would (but for this paragraph) result in a reduction in liability for income tax with respect to such employee for all taxable years in excess of $100,000 (determined without regard to any interest).
"(3) Statute of limitations.—
"(A) Overpayments.— If refund or credit of any overpayment of tax resulting from the application of Paragraph (1) is prevented on the date of the enactment of this Act (or at any time within 6 months after such date of enactment) by the operation of any law or rule of law, refund or credit of such overpayment (to the extent attributable to the application of Paragraph (1)) may, nevertheless, be made or allowed if claim therefor is filed before the close of such 6-month period.
"(B) Deficiencies.— If the assessment of any deficiency of tax resulting from the application of Paragraph (1) is prevented on the date of the enactment of this Act (or at any time within 6 months after such date of enactment) by the opera-

tion of any law or rule of law, assessment of such deficiency (to the extent attributable to the application of subsection (a)) may, nevertheless, be made within such 6-month period."
In **1984**, P.L. 98-369, Sec. 223(c), deleted "or" at the end of para. (e)(3), substituted ", or" for the period at the end of para. (e)(4), and added para. (e)(5), effective for tax. yrs. begin. after 12/31/83. Sec. 223(d)(2) of this Act provides that:
"(2) Inclusion of former employees in the case of existing group-term insurance plans.
"(A) In general. The amendments made by subsection (a) shall not apply—
"(i) to any group-term life insurance plan of the employer in existence on January 1, 1984, or
"(ii) to any group-term life insurance plan of the employer (or a successor employer) which is a comparable successor to a plan described in clause (i), but only with respect to an individual who attained age 55 on or before January 1, 1984, and either was employed by such employer at any time during 1983 or retired from employment with such employer on or before January 1, 1984.
"(B) Special rule in the case of discriminatory group-term life insurance plan. In the case of any plan which, after December 31, 1986, is a discriminatory group-term life insurance plan (as defined in section 79(d) of the Internal Revenue Code of 1954), subparagraph (A) shall not apply in the case of any individual retiring under such plan after December 31, 1986.
"(C) Benefits to certain retired individuals not taken into account for purposes of determining whether plan is discriminatory. For purposes of determining whether after December 31, 1986, a plan described in subparagraph (A) meets the requirements of section 79(d) of the Internal Revenue Code of 1954 with respect to group-term life insurance for former employees, coverage provided to employees who retired on or before December 31, 1986, shall not be taken into account."
—P.L. 98-369, Sec. 556, [as amended by Sec. 1855(b) of P.L. 99-514 see above] provides as follows:
"Sec. 556. Time for making certain section 83(b) elections.
"In the case of any transfer of property in connection with the performance of services on or before November 18, 1982, the election permitted by section 83(b) of the Internal Revenue Code of 1954 may be made, notwithstanding paragraph (2) of such section 83(b), with the income tax return for any taxable year ending after July 18, 1984, and beginning before the date of the enactment of the Tax Reform Act of 1986 [10/22/86] if—
"(1) the amount paid for such property was not less than its fair market value at the time of transfer (determined without regard to any restriction other than a restriction which by its terms will never lapse), and
"(2) the election is consented to by the person transferring such property.
The election shall contain that information required by the Secretary of the Treasury or his delegate for elections permitted by such section 83(b). The period for assessing any tax attributable to a transfer of property which is the subject of an election made pursuant to this section shall not expire before the date which is 3 years after the date such election was made."
In **1983**, P.L. 97-448, Sec. 102(k)(1), substituted "Securities Exchange Act of 1934" for "Securities and Exchange Act of 1934" each place it appeared in para. (c)(3), effective for transfers after 12/31/81.
—P.L. 97-448, Sec. 102(k)(2), amended Sec. 252(c) of P.L. 97-34 which provides the effective date for amendments made by Sec. 252 of P.L. 97-34, so that the amendments are effective for transfers after 12/31/81 rather than effective tax. yrs. end. after 12/31/81, see below.
In **1981**, P.L. 97-34, Sec. 252(a), added para. (c)(3), effective for transfers after 12/31/81 [see Sec. 1879(p) of P.L. 99-514, above]. Sec. 252(b) of this Act provides:
"(b) Special Rule for Certain Accounting Rules. For purposes of section 83 of the Internal Revenue Code of 1954, property is subject to substantial risk of forfeiture and is not transferable so long as such property is subject to a restriction on transfer to comply with the 'Pooling-of-Interests Accounting' rules set forth in Accounting Series Release Numbered 130 ((10/5/72) 37 FR 20937; 17 CFR 211.130) and Accounting Series Release Numbered 135 ((1/18/73) 38 FR 1734; 17 CFR 211.135)."
In **1976**, P.L. 94-455, Sec. 1901(a)(15), deleted "(or, if later, 30 days after the date of the enactment of the Tax Reform Act of 1969)" after "the date of such transfer" in para. (b)(2), effective for tax. yrs. begin. after 12/31/76.
—P.L. 94-455, Sec. 1906(b)(13)(A), substituted "Secretary" for "Secretary or his delegate" each place it appeared in subsecs. (b) and (d), effective for tax. yrs. begin. after 12/31/76.
In **1969**, P.L. 91-172, Sec. 321(a), added Code Sec. 83, effective for tax. yrs. end. after 6/30/69.

Sec. 84. Transfer of appreciated property to political organization.
(a) General rule.
If—
(1) any person transfers property to a political organization, and
(2) the fair market value of such property exceeds its adjusted basis,
then for purposes of this chapter the transferor shall be treated as having sold such property to the political organization on the date of the transfer, and the transferor shall be

Income

treated as having realized an amount equal to the fair market value of such property on such date.

(b) Basis of property.

In the case of a transfer of property to a political organization to which subsection (a) applies, the basis of such property in the hands of the political organization shall be the same as it would be in the hands of the transferor, increased by the amount of gain recognized to the transferor by reason of such transfer.

(c) Political organization defined.

For purposes of this section, the term "political organization" has the meaning given to such term by section 527(e)(1).

In **1975,** P.L. 93-625, Sec. 13(a)(1), added Code Sec. 84, effective for transfers made after 5/7/74, in tax. yrs. end. after 5/7/74.

Sec. 85. Unemployment compensation.
(a) General rule.

In the case of an individual, gross income includes unemployment compensation.

(b) Unemployment compensation defined.

For purposes of this section, the term "unemployment compensation" means any amount received under a law of the United States or of a State which is in the nature of unemployment compensation.

(c) Special rule for 2009.

In the case of any taxable year beginning in 2009, gross income shall not include so much of the unemployment compensation received by an individual as does not exceed $2,400.

In **2009,** P.L. 111-5, Sec. 1007(a), added subsec. (c), effective for tax. yrs. begin. after 12/31/2008.

In **1986,** P.L. 99-514, Sec. 121, amended Code Sec. 85, effective for amounts received after 12/31/86, in tax. yrs. end. after 12/31/86.

Prior to amendment, Code Sec. 85 read as follows:

"SEC. 85. UNEMPLOYMENT COMPENSATION.

"(a) In general.

"If the sum for the taxable year of the adjusted gross income of the taxpayer (determined without regard to this section, section 86, and section 221) and the unemployment compensation exceeds the base amount, gross income for the taxable year includes unemployment compensation in an amount equal to the lesser of—

"(1) one-half of the amount of the excess of such sum over the base amount, or

"(2) the amount of the unemployment compensation.

"(b) Base amount defined.

"For purposes of this section, the term base amount means—

"(1) except as provided in paragraphs (2) and (3), $12,000,

"(2) $18,000, in the case of a joint return under section 6013, or

"(3) zero, in the case of a taxpayer who—

"(A) is married at the close of the taxable year (within the meaning of section 143) but does not file a joint return for such year, and

"(B) does not live apart from his spouse at all times during the taxable year.

"(c) Unemployment compensation defined.

"For purposes of this section, the term 'unemployment compensation' means any amount received under a law of the United States or of a State which is in the nature of unemployment compensation."

In **1984,** P.L. 98-369, Sec. 1075(a), amended Sec. 112(d) of P.L. 95-600, the effective date for changes made by Sec. 112(a) of P.L. 95-600 . . . Sec. 1075(b), provides:

"*(b) Waiver of statute of limitations.* — If credit or refund of any overpayment of tax resulting from the amendment made by subsection (a) is barred on the date of the enactment of this Act or at any time during the 1-year period beginning on the date of the enactment of this Act by the operation of any law or rule of law (including res judicata), refund or credit of such overpayment (to the extent attributable to the amendment made by subsection (a)) may, nevertheless, be made or allowed if claim therefor is filed before the close of such 1-year period."

Prior to amendment, Sec. 112(d) of P.L. 95-600 read as follows:

"*(d) Effective date.* — the amendments made by this section shall apply to payments of unemployment compensation made after December 31, 1978, in taxable years ending after such date."

In **1983,** P.L. 98-21, Sec. 121(f)(1), substituted "this section, section 86," for "this section," in subsec. (a), effective for benefits received after 12/31/83, in tax. yrs. end. after 12/31/83.

—P.L. 98-21, Sec. 122(c)(2), deleted "section 105(d)(4)" before "and section 221" in subsec. (a), effective for tax. yrs. begin. after 12/31/83.

Code Sec. 86(b)(1)(B)

In **1982,** P.L. 97-248, Sec. 611(a), substituted "$12,000" for "$20,000" in para. (b)(1) and substituted "$18,000" for "$25,000" in para. (b)(2), effective for payments of unemployment compensation made after 12/31/81 in tax. yrs. ending after 12/31/81. Secs. 611(b)(2)-(4) of this Act provide:

"(2) No addition to tax for underpayment of estimated tax attributable to application of amendments to compensation paid in 1982. — No addition to tax shall be made under section 6654 of the Internal Revenue Code of 1954 with respect to any underpayment to the extent such underpayment is attributable to unemployment compensation which is received during 1982 and which (but for the amendments made by subsection (a)) would not be includable in gross income.

"(3) Special rule for fiscal year taxpayers. — In the case of a taxable year (other than a calendar year) which includes January 1, 1982—

"(A) the amendments made by this section shall be applied by taking into account the entire amount of unemployment compensation received during such taxable year, but

"(B) the increase in gross income for such taxable year as a result of such amendments shall not exceed the amount of unemployment compensation paid after December 31, 1981.

"(4) Unemployment compensation defined — For purposes of this subsection, the term 'unemployment compensation' has the meaning given to such term by section 85(c) of the Internal Revenue Code of 1954."

In **1981,** P.L. 97-34, Sec. 103(c)(1), substituted ", section 105(d), and section 221" for "and without regard to section 105(d)" in subsec. (a), effective for tax. yrs. begin. after 12/31/81.

In **1978,** P.L. 95-600, Sec. 112(a), added Code Sec. 85, effective as provided in Sec. 112(d) [amended by Sec. 1075(a) of P.L. 98-369, see above], which reads as follows:

"*(d) Effective date.*—The amendments made by this section shall apply to payments of unemployment compensation made after December 31, 1978, in taxable years ending after such date; except that such amendments shall not apply to payments made for weeks of unemployment ending before December 1, 1978."

Sec. 86. Social security and tier 1 railroad retirement benefits.
(a) In general.

(1) In general. Except as provided in paragraph (2), gross income for the taxable year of any taxpayer described in subsection (b) (notwithstanding section 207 of the Social Security Act) includes social security benefits in an amount equal to the lesser of—

(A) one-half of the social security benefits received during the taxable year, or

(B) one-half of the excess described in subsection (b)(1).

(2) Additional amount. In the case of a taxpayer with respect to whom the amount determined under subsection (b)(1)(A) exceeds the adjusted base amount, the amount included in gross income under this section shall be equal to the lesser of—

(A) the sum of—

(i) 85 percent of such excess, plus

(ii) the lesser of the amount determined under paragraph (1) or an amount equal to one-half of the difference between the adjusted base amount and the base amount of the taxpayer, or

(B) 85 percent of the social security benefits received during the taxable year.

(b) Taxpayers to whom subsection (a) applies.

(1) In general. A taxpayer is described in this subsection if—

(A) the sum of—

(i) the modified adjusted gross income of the taxpayer for the taxable year, plus

(ii) one-half of the social security benefits received during the taxable year, exceeds

(B) the base amount.

• **Caution:** Code Sec. 86(b)(2), following, was amended by P.L. 107-16, EGTRRA. These provisions generally sunset for tax years beginning after 12/31/2012. For specific sunset provisions, see Sec. 901, P.L. 107-16 (as amended) reproduced in history notes for this Code Sec.

(2) Modified adjusted gross income. For purposes of this subsection, the term "modified adjusted gross income" means adjusted gross income—
  (A) determined without regard to this section and sections 135, 137, 199, 221, 222, 911, 931, and 933, and
  (B) increased by the amount of interest received or accrued by the taxpayer during the taxable year which is exempt from tax.

(c) Base amount and adjusted base amount.
For purposes of this section—
  (1) Base amount. The term "base amount" means—
    (A) except as otherwise provided in this paragraph, $25,000,
    (B) $32,000 in the case of a joint return, and
    (C) zero in the case of a taxpayer who—
      (i) is married as of the close of the taxable year (within the meaning of section 7703) but does not file a joint return for such year, and
      (ii) does not live apart from his spouse at all times during the taxable year.
  (2) Adjusted base amount. The term "adjusted base amount" means—
    (A) except as otherwise provided in this paragraph, $34,000,
    (B) $44,000 in the case of a joint return, and
    (C) zero in the case of a taxpayer described in paragraph (1)(C).

(d) Social Security benefit.
  (1) In general. For purposes of this section, the term "social security benefit" means any amount received by the taxpayer by reason of entitlement to—
    (A) a monthly benefit under title II of the Social Security Act, or
    (B) a tier 1 railroad retirement benefit.
  (2) Adjustment for repayments during year.
    (A) In general. For purposes of this section, the amount of social security benefits received during any taxable year shall be reduced by any repayment made by the taxpayer during the taxable year of a social security benefit previously received by the taxpayer (whether or not such benefit was received during the taxable year).
    (B) Denial of deduction. If (but for this subparagraph) any portion of the repayments referred to in subparagraph (A) would have been allowable as a deduction for the taxable year under section 165, such portion shall be allowable as a deduction only to the extent it exceeds the social security benefits received by the taxpayer during the taxable year (and not repaid during such taxable year).
  (3) Workmen's compensation benefits substituted for social security benefits. For purposes of this section, if, by reason of section 224 of the Social Security Act (or by reason of section 3(a)(1) of the Railroad Retirement Act of 1974), any social security benefit is reduced by reason of the receipt of a benefit under a workmen's compensation act, the term "social security benefit" includes that portion of such benefit received under the workmen's compensation act which equals such reduction.
  (4) Tier 1 railroad retirement benefit. For purposes of paragraph (1), the term "tier 1 railroad retirement benefit" means—
    (A) the amount of the annuity under the Railroad Retirement Act of 1974 equal to the amount of the benefit to which the taxpayer would have been entitled under the Social Security Act if all of the service after December 31, 1936, of the employee (on whose employment record the annuity is being paid) had been included in the term "employment" as defined in the Social Security Act, and
    (B) a monthly annuity amount under section 3(f)(3) of the Railroad Retirement Act of 1974.
  (5) Effect of early delivery of benefit checks. For purposes of subsection (a), in any case where section 708 of the Social Security Act causes social security benefit checks to be delivered before the end of the calendar month for which they are issued, the benefits involved shall be deemed to have been received in the succeeding calendar month.

(e) Limitation on amount included where taxpayer receives lump-sum payment.
  (1) Limitation. If—
    (A) any portion of a lump-sum payment of social security benefits received during the taxable year is attributable to prior taxable years, and
    (B) the taxpayer makes an election under this subsection for the taxable year,
  then the amount included in gross income under this section for the taxable year by reason of the receipt of such portion shall not exceed the sum of the increases in gross income under this chapter for prior taxable years which would result solely from taking into account such portion in the taxable years to which it is attributable.
  (2) Special rules.
    (A) Year to which benefit attributable. For purposes of this subsection, a social security benefit is attributable to a taxable year if the generally applicable payment date for such benefit occurred during such taxable year.
    (B) Election. An election under this subsection shall be made at such time and in such manner as the Secretary shall by regulations prescribe. Such election, once made, may be revoked only with the consent of the Secretary.

(f) Treatment as pension or annuity for certain purposes.
For purposes of—
  (1) section 22(c)(3)(A) (relating to reduction for amounts received as pension or annuity),
  (2) section 32(c)(2) (defining earned income),
  (3) section 219(f)(1) (defining compensation), and
  (4) section 911(b)(1) (defining foreign earned income),
any social security benefit shall be treated as an amount received as a pension or annuity.

In **2010**, P.L. 111-312, Sec. 101(a)(1), substituted "December 31, 2012" for "December 31, 2010" both places it appeared in Sec. 901, P.L. 107-16 [see below], effective as if included in the enactment of P.L. 107-16, EGTRRA, 6/7/2001.

In **2005**, P.L. 109-135, Sec. 403(a)(19), amended Sec. 102(e) of P.L. 108-357 [which provides the effective date for the amendment made by Sec. 102(d)(1) of P.L. 108-357, see below] to read as follows:
"(e) Effective date.
  "(1) In general. The amendments made by this section shall apply to taxable years beginning after December 31, 2004.
  "(2) Application to pass-thru entities, etc. In determining the deduction under section 199 of the Internal Revenue Code of 1986 (as added by this section), items arising from a taxable year of a partnership, S corporation, estate, or trust beginning before January 1, 2005, shall not be taken into account for purposes of subsection (d)(1) of such section."

In **2004**, P.L. 108-357, Sec. 102(d)(1), added "199," before "221" in subpara. (b)(2)(A), effective for tax. yrs. begin. after 12/31/2004. For special rule, see Sec. 403(a)(19) of P.L. 109-135, reproduced above.

In **2002**, P.L. 107-358, Sec. 2, added subsec. (c) in Sec. 901 of P.L. 107-16 [see below], effective 12/17/2002.

Income   Code Sec. 89

In 2001, P.L. 107-16, Sec. 431(c)(1), added "222," after "221," in para. (b)(2), effective for payments made in tax. yrs. begin. after 12/31/2001.
— P.L. 107-16, Sec. 901, of this Act [as amended by Sec. 2, P.L. 107-358, and Sec. 101(a)(1), P.L. 111-312, see above], reads as follows:
"SEC. 901. SUNSET OF PROVISIONS OF ACT.
"(a) In general. All provisions of, and amendments made by, this Act shall not apply—
"(1) to taxable, plan, or limitation years beginning after December 31, 2012, or
"(2) in the case of title V, to estates of decedents dying, gifts made, or generation skipping transfers, after December 31, 2012.
"(b) Application of certain laws. The Internal Revenue Code of 1986 and the Employee Retirement Income Security Act of 1974 shall be applied and administered to years, estates, gifts, and transfers described in subsection (a) as if the provisions and amendments described in subsection (a) had never been enacted.
"(c) Exception. Subsection (a) shall not apply to section 803 (relating to no federal income tax on restitution received by victims of the Nazi regime or their heirs or estates)."
In 1998, P.L. 105-277, Sec. 4003(a)(2)(B), added "221," after "137," in subpara. (b)(2)(A), effective as provided in Sec. 202(e) of P.L. 105-34, which reads as follows:
"(e) Effective date. The amendments made by this section shall apply to any qualified education loan (as defined in section 221(e)(1) of the Internal Revenue Code of 1986, as added by this section) incurred on, before, or after the date of the enactment of this Act, but only with respect to—
"(1) any loan interest payment due and paid after December 31, 1997, and
"(2) the portion of the 60-month period referred to in section 221(d) of the Internal Revenue Code of 1986 (as added by this section) after December 31, 1997.
" Effective Date. The amendments made by this section shall take effect as if included in the provisions of the American Jobs Creation Act of 2004 to which they relate."
In 1996, P.L. 104-188, Sec. 1704(t)(3), substituted "adjusted" for "adusted" in para. (b)(2), effective 8/20/96.
— P.L. 104-188, Sec. 1807(c)(2), added "137," before "911" in subpara. (b)(2)(A), effective for tax. yrs. begin. after 12/31/96.
In 1994, P.L. 103-296, Sec. 309(d), deleted the last sentence of para. (d)(1), effective for benefits received after 12/31/95, in tax. yrs. end. after 12/31/95.
Prior to amendment, the last sentence of para. (d)(1) read as follows:
"For purposes of the preceding sentence, the amount received by any taxpayer shall be determined as if the Social Security Act did not contain section 203(i) thereof."
In 1993, P.L. 103-66, Sec. 13215(a)(1), added para. (a)(2) . . . Sec. 13215(a)(2)(A), substituted "(1) In general. Except as provided in paragraph (2), gross" for "Gross" in subsec. (a) . . . Sec. 13215(a)(2)(B), redesignated paras. (a)(1) and (2) as subparas. (a)(1)(A) and (B) . . . Sec. 13215(b), amended subsec. (c), effective for tax. yrs. begin. after 12/31/93.
Prior to amendment, subsec. (c) read as follows:
"(c) Base amount.
For purposes of this section, the term 'base amount' means—
"(1) except as otherwise provided in this subsection, $25,000,
"(2) $32,000, in the case of a joint return, and
"(3) zero, in the case of a taxpayer who—
"(A) is married at the close of the taxable year (within the meaning of section 7703) but does not file a joint return for such year, and
"(B) does not live apart from his spouse at all times during the taxable year."
In 1988, P.L. 100-647, Sec. 1001(e), added "and" at the end of para. (f)(3), deleted para. (f)(4), and redesignated para. (f)(5) as para. (f)(4), effective for tax. yrs. end. after 12/31/86.
Prior to deletion, para. (f)(4) read as follows:
"(4) section 221(b)(2) (defining earned income), and"
— P.L. 100-647, Sec. 6009(c)(1), added "135," before "911" in subpara. (b)(2)(A), effective for tax. yrs. begin. after 12/31/89.
In 1986, P.L. 99-514, Sec. 131(b)(2), substituted "sections" for "sections 221," in subpara. (b)(2)(A), effective for tax. yrs. begin. after 12/31/86.
— P.L. 99-514, Sec. 1301(j)(8), substituted "section 7703" for "section 143" in subpara. (c)(3)(A), effective for bonds issued after 8/15/86.
— P.L. 99-514, Sec. 1847(b)(2), substituted "section 22(c)(3)(A)" for "section 37(c)(3)(A)" in para. (f)(1), effective for benefits received after 12/31/83, in tax. yrs. end. after 12/31/83, except as provided in Sec. 121(g)(2) of P.L. 98-21, reproduced below.
— P.L. 99-272, Sec. 12111(b), added para. (d)(5), effective for benefit checks issued for months end. after 4/7/86.
— P.L. 99-272, Sec. 13204(a), amended para. (d)(4), effective for any monthly benefit for which the generally applicable payment date is after 12/31/85.
Prior to amendment, para. (d)(4) read as follows:
"(4) Tier 1 railroad retirement benefit. For purposes of paragraph (1), the term 'tier 1 railroad retirement benefit' means a monthly benefit under section 3(a), 3(f)(3), 4(a), or 4(f) of the Railroad Retirement Act of 1974."
In 1984, P.L. 98-369, Sec. 474(r)(2), substituted "section 32(c)(2)" for "section 43(c)(2)" in para. (f)(1), (redesignated as para. (f)(2) by Sec. 2661(o)(1) of this Act), for tax. yrs. begin. after 12/31/83, and for carrybacks from such years.
— P.L. 98-369, Sec. 2661(o)(1), redesignated paras. (f)(1), (f)(2), (f)(3) and (f)(4) as paras. (f)(2), (f)(3), (f)(4) and (f)(5), and added a new para. (f)(1) effective as provided in Sec. 121(g) of P.L. 98-21, reproduced below.
In 1983, P.L. 98-76, Sec. 224(d), added "3(f)(3)," after "3(a)," in para. (d)(4), effective for benefits received after 12/31/83, in tax. yrs. end. after 12/31/83, except as provided in Sec. 227(b)(2) and (3) reproduced in note following Code Sec. 72.
— P.L. 98-21, Sec. 121(a), added new Code Sec. 86, effective as provided in Sec. 121(g) which reads as follows:
"(g) Effective dates.
"(1) In general.—Except as provided in paragraph (2), the amendments made by this section shall apply to benefits received after December 31, 1983, in taxable years ending after such date.
"(2) Treatment of certain lump-sum payments received after December 31, 1983.—The amendments made by this section shall not apply to any portion of a lump-sum payment of social security benefits (as defined in section 86(d) of the Internal Revenue Code of 1954) received after December 31, 1983, if the generally applicable payment date for such portion was before January 1, 1984."
— P.L. 98-21, Sec. 335(b)(2)(A), added "(notwithstanding section 207 of the Social Security Act)" before "includes" in subsec. (a).

Sec. 87. Alcohol and biodiesel fuels credits.

Gross income includes—

(1) the amount of the alcohol fuel credit determined with respect to the taxpayer for the taxable year under section 40(a), and

(2) the biodiesel fuels credit determined with respect to the taxpayer for the taxable year under section 40A(a).

In 2004, P.L. 108-357, Sec. 302(c)(1)(A), amended Code Sec. 87, effective for fuel produced, and sold or used, after 12/31/2004, in tax. yrs. end. after 12/31/2004.
Prior to amendment, Code Sec. 87 read as follows:
"SEC. 87. ALCOHOL FUEL CREDIT. Gross income includes the amount of the alcohol fuel credit determined with respect to the taxpayer for the taxable year under section 40(a)."
In 1984, P.L. 98-369, Sec. 474(r)(3), amended Code Sec. 87, effective for tax. yrs. begin. after 12/31/83, and to carrybacks from such years.
Prior to amendment, Code Sec. 87 read as follows:
"SEC. 87. ALCOHOL FUEL CREDIT.
"Gross income includes an amount equal to the amount of the credit allowable to the taxpayer under section 44E for the taxable year (determined without regard to subsection (e) thereof)."
In 1983, P.L. 98-21, Sec. 121(a), redesignated Code Sec. 86 as Code Sec. 87, effective for amounts received after 12/31/83, in tax. yrs. end. after 12/31/83.
In 1980, P.L. 96-223, Sec. 232(c)(1), added Code Sec. 86, effective for sales and uses after 9/30/80, in tax. yrs. end. after 9/30/80.

Sec. 88. Certain amounts with respect to nuclear decommissioning costs.

In the case of any taxpayer who is required to include the amount of any nuclear decommissioning costs in the taxpayer's cost of service for ratemaking purposes, there shall be includible in the gross income of such taxpayer the amount so included for any taxable year.

In 1986, P.L. 99-514, Sec. 1807(a)(4)(E)(vii), substituted "for ratemaking" for "of ratemaking", effective 7/18/84, for tax. yrs. end. after 7/18/84.
In 1984, P.L. 98-369, Sec. 91(f)(1), added Code Sec. 88, effective 7/18/84, for tax. yrs. ending after 7/18/84.

Sec. 89. Repealed.

In 1989, P.L. 101-140, Sec. 202(a), repealed Code Sec. 89 as if the repeal were included in Sec. 1151 of P.L. 99-514 [the law that enacted Code Sec. 89]. The repeal is effective as provided in Sec. 1151(k)(1)-(3) of P.L. 99-514, reproduced below.
— P.L. 101-140, Sec. 203(a)(7), repealed Sec. 3021(c)(1) of P.L. 100-647 (transitional provisions) and repealed Sec. 6070 of P.L. 100-647 (definitions).
Prior to repeal, Sec. 3021(c)(1) of P.L. 100-647 read as follows:
"(c) Transitional provisions for purposes of section 89. —
"(1) Temporary valuation rules.—In the case of testing years beginning before the later of January 1, 1991, or the date 1 year after the Secretary of the Treasury or his delegate first issues such valuation rules as are necessary to apply the provisions of section 89 of the 1986 Code to health plans (or if later the effective date of such rules)—
"(A) Section 89(g)(3)(B) of the 1986 Code shall not apply.
"(B)(i) Except as provided in clause (ii), the value of coverage under a health plan for purposes of section 89 of the 1986 Code shall be determined in substantially the same manner as costs under a health plan are determined under section 4980B(f)(4) of the 1986 Code.
"(ii) For purposes of determining whether an employer meets the requirements of subsections (d), (e), and (f) of section 89 of the 1986 Code, value under clause (i) may be determined under any other reasonable method selected by the employer.

"(2) Former employees.— The amendments made by section 1151 of the Reform Act [P.L. 99-514] shall not apply to former employees who separated from service with the employer before January 1, 1989 (and were not reemployed on or after such date), and such former employees shall not be taken into account in determining whether the requirements of section 89 of the 1986 Code are met with respect to other former employees. The preceding sentence shall not apply to the extent that—

"(A) the value of employer-provided benefits provided to any such former employee exceeds the value of such benefits which were provided under the terms of the plan as in effect on December 31, 1988, or

"(B) the employer-provided benefits provided to such former employees are modified so as to discriminate in favor of such former employees who are highly compensated employees. Any excess value under the preceding sentence shall be determined without regard to any increase required by Federal law, regulation or rule or any increase which is the same for employees separating on or before December 31, 1988, and employees separating after such date and which does not discriminate in favor of highly compensated employees who separated from service after December 31, 1988.

"(3) Written plan requirement.— The requirements of section 89(k)(1)(A) of the 1986 Code shall be treated as met with respect to any testing year beginning in 1989, if—

"(A) the plan is in writing before the close of such year,

"(B) the employees had reasonable notice of the plan's essential features on or before the beginning of such year, and

"(C) the provisions of the written plan apply for the entire year.

"(4) Rules to be prescribed before November 15, 1988.— Not later than November 15, 1988, the Secretary of the Treasury or his delegate shall issue such rules as may be necessary to carry out the provisions of section 89 of the 1986 Code."

Prior to amendment, subpara. (g)(3)(D) read as follows:

"(D) Salary reductions. Except for purposes of subsections (d)(1)(A)(ii) and (j)(5), any salary reduction shall be treated as an employer-provided benefit."

Prior to deletion, the last sentence of para. (j)(5) read as follows:

"The preceding sentence shall apply only where the average work week of employees who are not highly compensated employees is 30 hours or more."

Prior to amendment, clause (j)(8)(A)(ii) read as follows:

"(ii) the coverage under such plan is not significantly changed during the transition period (other than by reason of the change in members of a group)."

Prior to repeal, Sec. 6070 of P.L. 100-647 read as follows:

"SEC. 6070. DEFINITION OF PART-TIME EMPLOYEE FOR PURPOSES OF SECTION 89.

"For purposes of section 89(f) of the 1986 Code, in the case of a plan maintained by an employer which employs fewer than 10 employees on a normal working day during a plan year, section 89(h)(1)(B) of such Code shall be applied—

"(1) by substituting '35 hours' for '17½ hours' in the case of a plan year beginning in 1989, and

"(2) by substituting '25 hours' for '17½ hours' in the case of plan years beginning in 1990. All persons treated as 1 employer for purposes of subsection (b), (c), (m), (n), or (o) section 414 of the 1986 Code shall be treated as 1 employer for purposes of the preceding sentence."

Prior to repeal, Code Sec. 89 read as follows:

"SEC. 89. BENEFITS PROVIDED UNDER CERTAIN EMPLOYEE BENEFIT PLANS.

"(a) Benefits under discriminatory plans.

"(1) In general. Notwithstanding any provision of part III of this subchapter, gross income of a highly compensated employee who is a participant in a discriminatory employee benefit plan during any testing year shall include an amount equal to such employee's excess benefit under such plan for such testing year.

"(2) Year of inclusion.

"(A) In general. Except as provided in subparagraph (B)—

"(i) any amount included in gross income under paragraph (1) shall be taken into account for the taxable year of the employee with or within which the testing year ends, and

"(ii) any deduction of the employer attributable to such amount shall be allowable for the taxable year of the employer with or within which the testing year ends.

"(B) Election to delay inclusion for 1 year. If an employer maintaining a plan with a testing year ending after September 30 and on or before December 31 of a calendar year elects the application of this subparagraph—

"(i) amounts included in gross income under paragraph (1) with respect to employees of such employer shall be taken into account for the taxable year of the employee following the taxable year determined under subparagraph (A), but

"(ii) any deduction of the employer which is attributable to such amounts shall be allowable for the taxable year with or within which the testing year following the testing year in which the excess benefits occurred ends.

"(b) Excess benefit.

"For purposes of this section—

"(1) In general. The excess benefit of any highly compensated employee is the excess of such employee's employer-provided benefit under the plan over the highest permitted benefit.

"(2) Highest permitted benefit. For purposes of paragraph (1), the highest permitted benefit under any plan shall be determined by reducing the nontaxable benefits of highly compensated employees (beginning with the employees with the greatest nontaxable benefits) until such plan would not be treated as a discriminatory employee benefit plan if such reduced benefits were taken into account.

"(3) Plans of same type. In computing the excess benefit with respect to any benefit, there shall be taken into account all plans of the employer of the same type.

"(4) Nontaxable benefits. For purposes of this subsection, the term 'nontaxable benefit' means any benefit provided under a plan to which this section applies which (without regard to subsection (a)(1)) is excludable from gross income under this chapter. Such term includes any group-term life insurance the cost of which is includible in gross income under section 79.

"(c) Discriminatory employee benefit plan.

For purposes of this section, the term 'discriminatory employee benefit plan' means any statutory employee benefit plan unless such plan meets the—

"(1) eligibility requirements of subsection (d), and

"(2) benefit requirements of subsection (e).

"(d) Eligibility requirements.

"(1) In general. A plan meets the eligibility requirements of this subsection for any plan year if—

"(A) at least 90 percent of all employees who are not highly compensated employees—

"(i) are eligible to participate in such plan (or in any other plan of the employer of the same type), and

"(ii) would (if they participated) have available under such plans an employer-provided benefit which is at least 50 percent of the largest employer-provided benefit available under all such plans of the employer to any highly compensated employee,

"(B) at least 50 percent of the employees eligible to participate in such plan are not highly compensated employees, and

"(C) such plan does not contain any provision relating to eligibility to participate which (by its terms or otherwise) discriminates in favor of highly compensated employees.

"(2) Alternative eligibility percentage test. A plan shall be treated as meeting the requirements of paragraph (1)(B) if—

"(A) the percentage determined by dividing the number of highly compensated employees eligible to participate in the plan by the total number of highly compensated employees, does not exceed

"(B) the percentage similarly determined with respect to employees who are not highly compensated employees.

"(e) Benefit requirements.

"(1) In general. A plan meets the benefit requirements of this subsection for any testing year if the average employer-provided benefit received by employees other than highly compensated employees under all plans of the employer of the same type is at least 75 percent of the average employer-provided benefit received by highly compensated employees under all plans of the employer of the same type.

"(2) Average employer-provided benefit. For purposes of this subsection, the term 'average employer-provided benefit' means, with respect to highly compensated employees, an amount equal to—

"(A) the aggregate employer-provided benefits received by highly compensated employees under all plans of the type being tested, divided by

"(B) the number of highly compensated employees (whether or not covered under such plans).

The average employer-provided benefit with respect to employees other than highly compensated employees shall be determined in the same manner as the average employer-provided benefit for highly compensated employees.

"(f) Special rule where health or group-term plan meets 80-percent coverage test.

"If at least 80 percent of the employees who are not highly compensated employees are covered under a health plan or group-term life insurance plan during the testing year, such plan shall be treated as meeting the requirements of subsections (d) and (e) for such year. The preceding sentence shall not apply if the plan does not meet the requirements of subsection (d)(1)(C) (relating to nondiscriminatory provisions).

"(g) Operating rules.

"(1) Aggregation of comparable health plans. In the case of health plans maintained by an employer—

"(A) In general. An employer may treat a group of comparable plans as 1 plan for purposes of applying subsections (d)(1)(B), (d)(2) and (f).

"(B) Comparable plans. For purposes of subparagraph (A), a group of comparable plans is any group (selected by the employer) of plans of the same type if the smallest employer-provided benefit available to any participant in any such plan is at least 95 percent of the largest employer-provided benefit available to any participant in any such plan.

"(C) Employees covered by more than 1 plan. The Secretary may provide that 2 or more plans providing benefits to the same participant shall be treated as 1 plan for purposes of applying subsections (d)(1)(B), (d)(2), and (f).

"(D) Special rules for applying subsection (f).

"(i) In general. For purposes of applying subsection (f)—

"(I) except as provided in clause (ii), subparagraph (B) shall be applied by substituting '90 percent' for '95 percent', and

"(II) a group of plans of the same type shall be treated as comparable plans if the requirements of subparagraph (E) are met.

"(ii) Election to use lower percentage in determining comparability. If an election by the employer under this clause applies for the testing year—

"(I) subclause (I) of clause (i) shall not apply,

"(II) for purposes of applying subsection (f), subparagraph (B) of this paragraph shall be applied by substituting '80 percent' for '95 percent', and

"(III) subsection (f) shall be applied with respect to all health plans maintained by the employer by substituting '90 percent' for '80 percent'.

"(E) Plans treated as comparable if employee cost difference is $100 or less.

"(i) In general. A group of plans of the same type shall be treated as comparable with respect to a group of employees if—

"(I) such plans are available to all employees in the group on the same terms, and

"(II) the difference in annual cost to employees between the plans with the lowest and highest annual employee cost is not greater than $100.

"(ii) Coordination with subparagraph (B). A plan not in the group of plans described in clause (i) shall be treated as part of such group if, under subparagraph (B) (without regard to clause (iii) of this subparagraph), such plan is comparable to the plan in such group with the largest employer-provided benefit.

"(iii) Other plans providing comparable benefits. A plan not in the group of plans described in clause (i) shall be treated as part of such group with respect to an employee if—

"(I) in the case of an employee who is not a highly compensated employee, such employee is eligible to participate in the plan in such group with the largest employer-provided benefit (without regard to clause (ii)),

"(II) in the case of an employee who is not a highly compensated employee, the annual cost to such employee under such plan is not lower than the lowest cost permitted within such group, and

"(III) the employer-provided benefit under such plan is less than the employer-provided benefit under the plan in such group with the largest such benefit (without regard to clause (ii)).

"(iv) Separate application of requirements. If an employer elects the application of paragraph (2)(A)(ii), the amount under clause (i) shall be allocated among plans covering spouses and dependents and plans covering employees in such manner as the employer specifies.

"(v) Cost-of-living adjustment. In the case of testing years beginning after 1989, the $100 amount under clause (i) shall be increased by the percentage (if any) by which—

"(I) the CPI for the calendar year preceding the year in which the testing year begins, exceeds

"(I) the CPI for 1988.

For purposes of this clause, the CPI for any calendar year shall be determined under section 1(f).

"(2) Special rules for applying benefit requirements to health plans.

"(A) Election. For purposes of determining whether the requirements of subsection (e) or (f) are met with respect to health plans, the employer may elect—

"(i) to disregard any employee if such employee and his spouse and dependents (if any) are covered by a health plan providing core benefits maintained by another employer, and

"(ii) to apply subsection (e) or (f) separately with respect to coverage of spouses or dependents by such plans and to take into account with respect to such coverage only employees with a spouse or dependents who are not covered by a health plan providing core benefits maintained by another employer.

The provisions of the preceding sentence shall not apply for purposes of applying subsection (f) unless the requirements of subsection (f) would be met if such subsection were applied without regard to the preceding sentence and on the basis of eligibility to participate rather than coverage.

"(B) Sworn statements. Any employer who elects the application of subparagraph (A) shall obtain and maintain, in such manner as the Secretary may prescribe, adequate sworn statements to demonstrate whether individuals have—

"(i) a spouse or dependents,

"(ii) core health benefits under a plan of another employer, and

"(iii) the health coverage (if any) received by the employee from the employer. The Secretary shall provide a method for meeting the requirements of this subparagraph through the use of valid sampling techniques. No statement shall be required under clause (ii) with respect to any individual eligible for coverage at no cost under a health plan which provides core health benefits and with respect to whom the employee does not elect any core health coverage from the employer.

"(C) Presumption where no statement. In the absence of a statement described in subparagraph (B)—

"(i) an employee who is not a highly compensated employee shall be treated—

"(I) as not covered by another plan of another employer providing core benefits, and

"(II) as having a spouse and dependents not covered by another plan of another employer providing core benefits, and

"(ii) a highly compensated employee shall be treated—

"(I) as covered by another plan of another employer providing core benefits, and

"(II) as not having a spouse or dependents.

"(D) Certain individuals may not be disregarded. In the case of a highly compensated employee who receives employer-provided benefits under all health plans of the employer which are more than 133⅓ percent of the average employer-provided benefit under such plans for employees other than highly compensated employees, the employer may not disregard such employee, or his spouse or dependents for purposes of clause (i) or (ii) of subparagraph (A). The Secretary shall make such adjustments as are necessary in applying the rules of the preceding sentence to subsection (f).

"(E) Special rule. No employee who is not a highly compensated employee may be disregarded under subparagraph (A)(i) with respect to any health plan of the employer unless under such plan such employee is entitled, when the coverage under the other health plan referred to in subparagraph (A)(i) ceases, to elect coverage under the plan of the employer (whether or not an election is otherwise available). Such election is to be on the same terms as if such employee was making such election during a subsequent open season. Rules similar to the rules of the preceding sentences of this subparagraph shall apply in the case of an employee treated as not having a spouse or dependents or having a spouse or dependents covered by a health plan of another employer providing core benefits.

"(3) Employer-provided benefit. For purposes of this section—

"(A) In general. Except as provided in subsection (k), an employee's employer-provided benefit under any statutory employee benefit plan is—

"(i) in the case of any health or group-term life insurance plan, the value of the coverage, or

"(ii) in the case of any other plan, the value of the benefits,

provided during the testing year to or on behalf of such employee to the extent attributable to contributions made by the employer.

"(B) Special rule for health plans. The value of the coverage provided by any health plan shall be determined under procedures prescribed by the Secretary which shall—

"(i) set forth the values of various standard types of coverage involving a representative group, and

"(ii) provide for adjustments to take into account the specific coverage and group involved.

"(C) Special rule for group-term life plans.

"(i) In general. Except as provided in clause (ii), in determining the value of coverage under a group-term life insurance plan, the amount taken into account for any employee shall be based on the cost of the insurance determined under section 79(c) for an employee who is age 40.

"(ii) Excess benefit. For purposes of subsection (b), the excess benefit with respect to coverage under a group-term life insurance plan shall be equal to the greater of—

"(I) the cost of such excess benefit (expressed as dollars of coverage) determined without regard to section 79(c), or

"(II) such cost determined with regard to section 79(c).

"(D) Salary reductions.

"(i) In general. Except for purposes of subsections (d)(1)(A)(ii) and (j)(5), any salary reduction shall be treated as an employer-provided benefit.

"(ii) Special rule for subsection (d)(1)(a)(ii). Notwithstanding clause (i), any salary reduction under a cafeteria plan (within the meaning of section 125) shall be treated as an employer-provided benefit for purposes of subsection (d)(1)(A)(ii) if—

"(I) the percentage of employees who are not highly compensated employees eligible to participate in the plan is not greater than the percentage of highly compensated employees so eligible,

"(II) all employees eligible to participate in the plan are eligible under the same terms and conditions, and

"(III) no highly compensated employee eligible under the plan is eligible to participate in any other plan maintained by the employer for any benefit of the same type unless the benefit is available on the same terms and conditions to every employee who is not a highly compensated employee eligible to participate in the plan.

"(iii) Regulations. Notwithstanding clause (i) or (ii), the Secretary may by regulations provide that any salary reduction shall or shall not be treated as an employer-provided benefit to prevent avoidance of the purposes of this section.

"(E) Special rule for multiemployer plans.

"(i) In general. Except as provided in regulations and clause (ii), an employer may treat the contribution such employer makes to a multiemployer plan on behalf of an employee as the employer-provided benefit of such employee under such plan.

"(ii) Adjustment. If—

"(I) the allocation of plan benefits between highly compensated employees and other employees under a multiemployer plan (or within either of such groups) varies materially from the allocation of employer contributions to such plan, or

"(II) the employer contributions relate to benefits of different types,

the employer-provided benefit determined under clause (i) shall be appropriately adjusted to take into account such material variation or such employer contribution.

"(iii) Exception for professionals. This subparagraph shall not apply to any employer maintaining a multiemployer plan if such employer makes contributions to such plan on behalf of any individual performing services in the field of health, law, engineering, architecture, accounting, actuarial science, financial services, or consulting or in such other field as the Secretary may prescribe.

"(4) Election to test plans of different types together.

"(A) In general. Except as provided in subparagraph (B), the employer may elect to treat all plans of the types specified in such election as plans of the same type for purposes of applying subsection (e).

"(B) Exception for health plans. Subparagraph (A) shall not apply for purposes of determining whether any health plan meets the requirements of subsection (e); except that benefits provided under health plans which meet such requirements may be taken into account in determining whether plans of other types meet the requirements of subsection (e).

"(5) Separate line of business exception. If, under section 414(r), an employer is treated as operating separate lines of business for a year, the employer may apply the preceding provisions of this section separately with respect to employees in each such separate line of business. The preceding sentence shall not apply to any plan unless such plan is available to a group of employees as qualify under a classification set up by the employer and found by the Secretary not to be discriminatory in favor of highly compensated employees. In applying section 414(r)(7) for purposes of this section, an operating unit shall be treated as in a separate geographic area from another unit if such units are at least 35 miles apart.

"(6) Time for testing.

"(A) In general. Except as otherwise provided in this paragraph, the determination of whether any plan is a discriminatory employee benefit plan for any testing year shall be made on the basis of the facts as of the testing day.

"(B) Adjustment where benefit of highly compensated employee changes. If the employer-provided benefit (actually provided or made available) of a highly compensated employee changes during the testing year by reason of any change in the terms of the plan or the making of an election by such employee, the amount taken into account as such employee's employer-provided benefit shall be adjusted to take into account such change and the portion of the testing year during which the changed benefit is provided (or made available).

"(C) Treatment of non-highly compensated employees where change in plan. Rules similar to the rules of subparagraph (B) shall apply in the case of employees who are not highly compensated employees and who are affected by any change in the terms of the plan, except that the determination of such employees' employer-provided benefits (actually provided or made available) shall be determined as of the date after such change selected by the employer and permitted under regulations prescribed by the Secretary.

"(D) Testing day. For purposes of this paragraph, the term 'testing day' means—

"(i) the day designated in the plan as the testing day for purposes of this paragraph, or

"(ii) if there is no day so designated, the last day of the testing year.

"(E) Limitations.

"(i) Designation must be consistent for all plans of same type. No day may be designated under subparagraph (D)(i) with respect to any plan unless the same day is so designated with respect to all other plans of the employer of the same type.

"(ii) Designation binding. Any designation under subparagraph (D)(i) shall apply to the testing year for which made and all subsequent years unless revoked with the consent of the Secretary.

"(F) Special rule for multiple employer plan. In the case of a multiemployer plan or any other plan maintained by more than 1 employer, each employer may, subject to such rules as the Secretary may prescribe, elect its own testing year under paragraph (13) of subsection (j) and its own testing date under this paragraph.

"(7) Sampling. For purposes of determining whether a plan is a discriminatory employee benefit plan (but not for purposes of identifying the highly compensated employees who have a discriminatory excess or the amount of any such excess), determinations under this section may be made on the basis of a statistically valid random sample. The preceding sentence shall apply only if—

"(A) the sampling is conducted by an independent person in a manner not inconsistent with regulations prescribed by the Secretary, and

"(B) the statistical method and sample size result in a 95 percent probability that the results will have a margin of error not greater than 3 percent.

"(h) Excluded employees.

"(1) In general. The following employees shall be excluded from consideration under this section:

"(A) Employees who have not completed 1 year of service (or in the case of core benefits under a health plan, 6 months of service). An employee shall be excluded from consideration until the 1st day of the 1st month (or 1st day of a period of less than 31 days specified by the plan) beginning after completion of the period of service required under the preceding sentence.

"(B) Employees who normally work less than 17½ hours per week.

"(C) Employees who normally work during not more than 6 months during any year.

"(D) Employees who have not attained age 21.

"(E) Employees who are included in a unit of employees covered by an agreement which the Secretary finds to be a collective bargaining agreement between employee representatives and 1 or more employers if there is evidence that the type of benefits provided under the plan was the subject of good faith bargaining between the employee representatives and such employer or employers.

"(F) Employees who are nonresident aliens and who receive no earned income (within the meaning of section 911(d)(2)) from the employer which constitutes income from sources within the United States (within the meaning of section 861(a)(3)).

"(G) Employees who are students if—

"(i) such students are performing services described in section 3121(b)(10), and

"(ii) core health coverage is made available to such students by such employer. Subparagraphs (A), (B), (C), and (D) shall be applied by substituting a shorter period of service, smaller number of hours or months, or lower age specified in the plan for the period of service, number of hours or months, or age (as the case may be) specified in such subparagraph.

"(2) Certain exclusions not to apply if excluded employees covered. Except to the extent provided in regulations, employees shall not be excluded from consideration under any subparagraph of paragraph (1) (other than subparagraph (F)) unless no employee described in such subparagraph (determined with regard to the last sentence of paragraph (1)) is eligible under the plan.

"(3) Exclusion must apply to all plans.

"(A) In general. An exclusion shall apply under any subparagraph of paragraph (1) (other than subparagraph (F) thereof) only if the exclusion applies to all statutory employee benefit plans of the employer of the same type. In the case of a cafeteria plan, all benefits under the cafeteria plan shall be treated as provided under plans of the same type.

"(B) Exception. Subparagraph (A) shall not apply to any difference in waiting periods for core and noncore benefits provided by health plans.

"(4) Exception for separate line of business. If any line of business is treated separately under subsection (g)(5), then paragraphs (2) and (3) shall be applied separately to such line of business.

"(5) Requirements may be met separately with respect to excluded group. Notwithstanding paragraphs (2) and (3), if employees do not meet minimum age or service requirements described in paragraph (1) (without regard to the last sentence thereof) and are covered under a plan of the employer which meets the requirements of this section separately with respect to such employees, such employees may be excluded from consideration in determining whether any plan of the employer meets the requirements of this section.

"(6) Special rule for multiemployer plan. Except as provided in regulations, any multiemployer plan shall not be taken into account in applying subparagraph (A), (B), (C), or (D) of paragraph (1) with respect to other plans of the employer. For purposes of this paragraph, a rule similar to the rule of subsection (g)(3)(E)(iii) shall apply.

"(i) Statutory employee benefit plan.

"For purposes of this section—

"(1) In general. The term 'statutory employee benefit plan' means—

"(A) an accident or health plan (within the meaning of section 105(e)), and

"(B) any plan of an employer for providing group-term life insurance (within the meaning of section 79).

"(2) Employer may elect to treat other plans as statutory employee benefit plan. An employer may elect to treat any of the following plans as statutory employee benefit plans:

"(A) A qualified group legal services plan (within the meaning of section 120(b)).

"(B) An educational assistance program (within the meaning of section 127(b)).

"(C) A dependent care assistance program (within the meaning of section 129(d)).

An election under this paragraph with respect to any plan shall apply with respect to all plans of the same type as such plan.

"(3) Plans of the same type. 2 or more plans shall be treated as of the same type if such plans are described in the same subparagraph of paragraph (1) or (2).

"(4) Church plans. The term 'statutory employee benefit plan' shall not include a plan maintained by a church for church employees. For purposes of this paragraph, the term 'church' has the meaning given such term by section 3121(w)(3)(A), including a qualified church-controlled organization (as defined in section 3121(w)(3)(B)).

"(j) Other definitions and special rules.

"For purposes of this section—

"(1) Highly compensated employee. The term 'highly compensated employee' has the meaning given such term by section 414(q).

"(2) Health plan. The term 'health plan' means any plan described in paragraph (1)(A) of subsection (i).

"(3) Treatment of former employees. Except to the extent provided in regulations, this section shall be applied separately to former employees under requirements similar to the requirements that apply to employees.

"(4) Group-term life insurance plans.

"(A) In general. Any group-term life insurance plan shall not be treated as 2 or more separate plans merely because the amount of life insurance under the plan on behalf of employees bears a uniform relationship to the compensation of such employees.

"(B) Limitation on compensation. For purposes of subparagraph (A), compensation in excess of the amount applicable under section 401(a)(17) shall not be taken into account.

"(C) Limitation. This paragraph shall not apply to any plan if such plan is combined with plans of other types pursuant to an election under subsection (g)(4).

"(D) Compensation. For purposes of applying this paragraph—

"(i) In general. Compensation shall be determined on any basis determined by the employer which does not discriminate in favor of highly compensated employees.

"(ii) Special rules for 1989 and 1990. In the case of testing years beginning in 1989 or 1990, the employer may elect to treat base compensation as compensation.

"(5) Special rule for employees working less than 30 hours per week. Any health plan shall not fail to meet the requirements of this section merely because the employer-provided benefit is proportionately reduced for employees who normally work less than 30 hours per week.

"(6) Treatment of self-employed individuals. In the case of a statutory employee benefit plan—

"(A) Treatment as employee, etc. The term 'employee' includes any self-employed individual (as defined in section 401(c)(1)), and the term 'compensation' includes such individual's earned income (as defined in section 401(c)(2)).

"(B) Employer. An individual who owns the entire interest in an unincorporated trade or business shall be treated as his own employer. A partnership shall be treated as the employer of each partner who is treated as an employee under subparagraph (A).

"(7) Certain plans treated as meeting other nondiscrimination requirements. If an employer makes an election under subsection (i)(2) to have this section apply to any plan and such plan meets the requirements of this section, such plan shall be treated as meeting any other nondiscrimination requirement imposed on such plan (other than any requirement under section 120(c)(3), 127(b)(3), or 129(d)(4)).

"(8) Special rules for certain dispositions or acquisitions.

"(A) In general. If a person becomes, or ceases to be, a member of a group described in subsection (b), (c), (m), or (o) of section 414, then the requirements of this section shall be treated as having been met during the transition period with respect to any plan covering employees of such person or any other member of such group if—

"(i) such requirements were met immediately before each such change, and

"(ii) either—

"(I) the coverage under such plan is not significantly changed during the transition period (other than by reason of the change in members in such group), or

"(II) such plan meets such other requirements as the Secretary may prescribe by regulation.

"(B) Transition period. For purposes of subparagraph (A), the term 'transition period' means the period—

"(i) beginning on the date of the change in members of a group, and

"(ii) ending on the last day of the 1st testing year beginning after the date of such change.

"(9) Coordination with medicare, etc. If a plan may be coordinated with health benefits provided under any Federal, State, or foreign law or under any other health plan covering the employee or family member of the employee, such plan shall not fail to meet the requirements of this section with respect to health benefits merely because the amount of such benefits provided to any employee or family member of any employee are coordinated in a manner which does not discriminate in favor of highly compensated employees.

"(10) Disability benefits.

"(A) In general. If a plan may be coordinated with disability benefits provided under any Federal, State, or foreign law or under any other plan covering the employee, such plan shall not fail to meet the requirements of this section with respect to disability benefits merely because the amount of such benefits provided to an employee are coordinated in a manner which does not discriminate in favor of highly compensated employees.

"(B) Certain disability plans exempt from nondiscrimination rules. Subsection (a) shall not apply to any disability coverage other than disability coverage the benefits of which are excludable from gross income under section 105(b) or (c).

"(11) Separate application in the case of options. Except as provided in subsection (g)(1), each option or different benefit shall be treated as a separate plan.

"(12) Employers with only highly compensated employees. The requirements of subsections (d) and (e) shall not apply to any statutory employee benefit plan for any year for which the only employees of the employer maintaining the plan are highly compensated employees.

"(13) Testing year. The term 'testing year' means—

"(A) any 12-month period beginning with the calendar month designated in the plan for purposes of this section, or

"(B) if there is no such designation, the calendar year.

No period may be designated under subparagraph (A) unless the same period is designated with respect to all other plans of the employer of the same type. Any designation under subparagraph (A) may be changed only with the consent of the Secretary.

"(k) Requirement that plan be in writing, etc.

"(1) In general. Notwithstanding any provision of part III of this subchapter, gross income of an employee shall include an amount equal to such employee's employer-provided benefit for the taxable year under an employee benefit plan to which this subsection applies unless, except to the extent provided in regulations—

"(A) such plan is in writing,

"(B) the employees' rights under such plan are legally enforceable,

"(C) employees are provided reasonable notification of benefits available in the plan,

"(D) such plan is maintained for the exclusive benefit of employees, and

"(E) such plan was established with the intention of being maintained for an indefinite period of time.

Such inclusion shall be coordinated (under regulations prescribed by the Secretary) with any inclusion under subsection (a) with respect to such plan. In the case of a statutory employee benefit plan described in subsection (i)(1)(B), any amount required to be included in gross income under this subsection shall be included in the gross income of the beneficiary.

"(2) Plans to which subsection applies. This subsection shall apply to—

"(A) any statutory employee benefit plan,

"(B) a qualified tuition reduction program (within the meaning of section 117(d)),

"(C) a cafeteria plan (within the meaning of section 125),

"(D) a fringe benefit program providing no-additional-cost services, qualified employee discounts, or employer-operated eating facilities which are excludable from gross income under section 132, and

"(E) a plan to which section 505 applies.

"(3) Special rule for determining inclusion. For purposes of paragraph (1), an employee's employer-provided benefit shall be the value of the benefits provided to the employee.

"(4) Plans to which contributions are made by more than 1 employer. For purposes of paragraph (1)(D), in the case of a plan to which contributions are made by more than 1 employer, each employer shall be treated as employing employees of all other employers.

"(5) Loss of exemption for certain plans. If a plan described in paragraph (2)(E) fails to meet the requirements of paragraph (1), the organization which is part of such plan shall not be exempt from tax under section 501(a).

"(l) Reporting requirements.

"(1) In general. If an employee of an employer maintaining a plan is required to include any amount in gross income under this section for any testing year ending with or within a calendar year, the employer shall separately include such amount on the statement which the employer is required to provide the employee under section 6051(a) (and any statement required to be furnished under section 6051(d)).

"(2) Penalty. For penalty for failing to report, see section 6652(k).

"(m) Regulations.

"The Secretary shall prescribe such regulations as may be necessary or appropriate to carry out the purposes of this section, including regulations providing for appropriate adjustments in case of individuals not employees of the employer throughout the testing year."

—P.L. 101-136, Sec. 528, provides that "no monies appropriated by this Act [for the fiscal year ending September 30, '90] may be used to implement or enforce section 1151 of the Tax Reform Act of '86 [P.L. 99-514] or the amendments made by such section." [See below]

In 1988, P.L. 100-647, Sec. 1011B(a)(1), amended para. (a)(2) ... Sec. 1011B(a)(2), added the last sentence to para. (b)(4) ... Sec. 1011B(a)(3), added subpara. (g)(1)(C) ... Sec. 1011B(a)(4), added the last sentence to subpara. (g)(2)(B) ... Sec. 1011B(a)(5), substituted "under such plans" for "under such plan" in subpara. (g)(2)(D) ... Sec. 1011B(a)(6), deleted para. (g)(6) ... Sec. 1011B(a)(7), added "(or 1st day of a period of less than 31 days specified by the plan)" after "month" in subpara. (h)(1)(A) ... Sec. 1011B(a)(8), added para. (j)(12) ... Sec. 1011B(a)(9), added para. (k)(5) ... Sec. 1011B(a)(21), deleted "described in subparagraph (A), (B), or (C) of subsection (i)(2)" after "employee benefit plan" in para. (j)(6) ... Sec. 1011B(a)(28), substituted "(g)(5)" for "(h)(5)" in para. (h)(4) ... Sec. 1011B(a)(29), deleted the last sentence and inserted two new sentences at the end of para. (k)(1) ... Sec. 1011B(a)(34), substituted "6652(k)" for "6652(l)" in para. (l)(2), effective as provided in Secs. 1151(k)(1)-(3) of P.L. 99-514, reproduced below.

Prior to amendment, para. (a)(2) read as follows:

"(2) Year of inclusion. Any amount included in gross income under paragraph (1) shall be taken into account for the taxable year of the employee with or within which the plan year ends."

Prior to deletion, para. (g)(6) read as follows:

"(6) Special rule for applying eligibility requirements and 80-percent test to health plans. For purposes of determining whether the requirements of subsection (d)(1)(A)(ii) or of subsection (f) are met with respect to health plans, the employer may elect—

"(A) to apply this section separately with respect to coverage of spouses and dependents by such plans, and

"(B) to take into account with respect to such coverage only those employees with a spouse or dependent (determined under rules similar to the rules of paragraphs (2)(B) and (C))."

Prior to deletion, the last sentence of para. (k)(1) read as follows:

"Such inclusion shall be in lieu of any inclusion under subsection (a) with respect to such plan."

—P.L. 100-647, Sec. 1011B(a)(25), added the last sentence to Sec. 1151(k)(1) of P.L. 99-514 [reproduced below], the effective date for amendments made by Sec. 1151(a) of P.L. 99-514, see below.

—P.L. 100-647, Sec. 3021(a)(1)(A), substituted "testing year" for "plan year" each place it appeared in Code Sec. 89 [as amended by Sec. 1011B of this Act] ... Sec. 3021(a)(1)(B), added para. (j)(13) ... Sec. 3021(a)(2)(A), added para. (g)(6) ... Sec. 3021(a)(3), added para. (g)(7) ... Sec. 3021(a)(4), added subpara. (g)(3)(E) ... Sec. 3021(a)(5)(A), added para. (h)(6) ... Sec. 3021(a)(5)(B), added subpara. (h)(1)(G) ... Sec. 3021(a)(6), added subparagraphs (g)(1)(D) and (E) ... Sec. 3021(a)(7)(A)(i), substituted "subsection (e) or (f)" for "subsection (e)" each place it appeared in subpara. (g)(2)(A) ... Sec. 3021(a)(7)(A)(ii), added the last sentence to subpara. (g)(2)(A) ... Sec. 3021(a)(7)(B), added the last sentence to subpara. (g)(2)(D) ... Sec. 3021(a)(9), substituted "Except as provided in subsection (g)(1), each option" for "Each option" in para. (j)(11) ... Sec. 3021(a)(11), amended subpara. (g)(3)(D) ... Sec. 3021(a)(12), deleted the last sentence of subpara. (j)(5) ... Sec. 3021(a)(13)(A), amended clause (j)(8)(A)(ii), effective as provided in Secs. 1151(k)(1)-(3) of P.L. 99-514, [reproduced below] and Secs. 3021(a)(2)(B) of this Act [reproduced below] and Sec. 3021(c) of this Act [repealed by Sec. 203(a)(7) of P.L. 101-140, see above].

—P.L. 100-647, Sec. 3021(a)(2)(B), of this Act provides:

"(B) Designations for 1989 not binding. Any designation of a testing day for a year beginning in 1989 shall be disregarded in determining the day which may be designated as the testing day for years beginning after 1989."

—P.L. 100-647, Sec. 3021(a)(8)(A), added subpara. (g)(2)(E) ... Sec. 3021(a)(8)(B), deleted "and" at the end of clause (g)(2)(B)(i), substituted ", and" for the period at the end of clause (g)(2)(B)(ii), and added clause (g)(2)(B)(iii), effective for testing yrs. begin. after 12/31/89, but see Sec. 3021(a)(2)(B) of this Act, reproduced above. For transitional rules, see Sec. 3021(c) of this Act, reproduced above.

—P.L. 100-647, Sec. 3021(b)(2)(B), added the last sentence to para. (g)(5) ... Sec. 3021(b)(3)(A), added subpara. (j)(4)(D) ... Sec. 3021(b)(3)(B), deleted "(within the meaning of section 414(s))" after "compensation" in subpara. (j)(4)(A), effective for yrs. begin. after 12/31/86, but see Sec. 3021(a)(2)(B) of this Act, reproduced above.

—P.L. 100-647, Sec. 6051(a), added para. (i)(4), effective as provided in Secs. 1151(k)(1)-(3) of P.L. 99-514, reproduced below.

—P.L. 100-647, Sec. 6070, provides definition of part time employee [repealed by Sec. 203(a)(7) of P.L. 101-140, see above].

In 1986, P.L. 99-514, Sec. 1151(a), added Code Sec. 89, effective as provided in Secs. 1151(k)(1)-(3) of this Act [as amended by Sec. 1011(a)(25) of P.L. 100-647] which reads:

"(k) Effective dates.

"(1) In general.—The amendments made by this section shall apply to years beginning after the later of—

"(A) December 31, 1987, or

"(B) the earlier of—

"(i) the date which is 3 months after the date on which the Secretary of the Treasury or his delegate issues such regulations as are necessary to carry out the provisions of section 89 of the Internal Revenue Code of 1986 (as added by this section), or

Code Sec. 89

"(ii) December 31, 1988.
Notwithstanding the preceding sentence, the amendments made by subsections (e)(1) and (i)(3)(C) shall, to the extent they relate to sections 106, 162(i)(2), and 162(k) of the Internal Revenue Code of 1986, apply to years beginning after 1986.

"(2) Special rule for collective bargaining plan.—In the case of a plan maintained pursuant to 1 or more collective bargaining agreements between employee representatives and 1 or more employers ratified before March 1, 1986, the amendments made by this section shall not apply to employees covered by such an agreement in years beginning before the earlier of—

"(A) the date on which the last of such collective bargaining agreements terminates (determined without regard to any extension thereof after February 28, 1986), or

"(B) January 1, 1991.

A plan shall not be required to take into account employees to which the preceding sentence applies for purposes of applying section 89 of the Internal Revenue Code of 1986 (as added by this section) to employees to which the preceding sentence does not apply for any year preceding the year described in the preceding sentence.

"(3) Exception for certain group-term insurance plans.—In the case of a plan described in section 223(d)(2) of the Tax Reform Act of 1984, such plan shall be treated as meeting the requirements of section 89 of the Internal Revenue Code of 1986 (as added by this section) with respect to individuals described in section 223(d)(2) of such Act. An employer may elect to disregard such individuals in applying section 89 of such Code (as so added) to other employees of the employer."

Sec. 90. Illegal Federal irrigation subsidies.
(a) General rule.

Gross income shall include an amount equal to any illegal Federal irrigation subsidy received by the taxpayer during the taxable year.

(b) Illegal Federal irrigation subsidy.

For purposes of this section—

(1) In general. The term "illegal Federal irrigation subsidy" means the excess (if any) of—

(A) the amount required to be paid for any Federal irrigation water delivered to the taxpayer during the taxpayer year, over

(B) the amount paid for such water.

(2) Federal irrigation water. The term "Federal irrigation water" means any water made available for agricultural purposes from the operation of any reclamation or irrigation project referred to in paragraph (8) of section 202 of the Reclamation Reform Act of 1982.

(c) Denial of deduction.

No deduction shall be allowed under this subtitle by reason of any inclusion in gross income under subsection (a).

In **1987**, P.L. 100-203, Sec. 10611(a), added new Code Sec. 90, effective for water delivered to the taxpayer in months beginning after 12/22/87.

PART III.—ITEMS SPECIFICALLY EXCLUDED FROM GROSS INCOME

Sec.
101. Certain death benefits.
102. Gifts and inheritances.
103. Interest on State and local bonds.
103A. Repealed. [Mortgage subsidy bonds.]
104. Compensation for injuries or sickness.
105. Amounts received under accident and health plans.
106. Contributions by employer to accident and health plans.
107. Rental value of parsonages.
108. Income from discharge of indebtedness.
109. Improvements by lessee on lessor's property.
110. Qualified lessee construction allowances for short-term leases.
110. Repealed. [Income taxes paid by lessee corporation.]
111. Recovery of tax benefit items.
112. Certain combat zone compensation of members of the Armed Forces.
113. Repealed. [Mustering-out payments for members of Armed Forces.]
114. Repealed. [Extraterritorial income.]
114. Repealed. [Sports programs conducted for the American National Red Cross.]
115. Income of states, municipalities, etc.
116. Repealed.
117. Qualified scholarships.
118. Contributions to the capital of a corporation.
119. Meals or lodging furnished for the convenience of the employer.
120. Amounts received under qualified group legal services plans.
121. Exclusion of gain from sale of principal residence.
122. Certain reduced uniformed services retirement pay.
123. Amounts received under insurance contracts for certain living expenses.
124. Repealed. [Qualified transportation provided by employer.]
125. Cafeteria plans.
126. Certain cost-sharing payments.
127. Educational assistance programs.
128. Repealed. [Interest on certain savings certificates.]
129. Dependent care assistance programs.
130. Certain personal injury liability assignments.
131. Certain foster care payments.
132. Certain fringe benefits.
133. Repealed. [Interest on certain loans used to acquire employer securities.]
134. Certain military benefits.
135. Income from United States savings bonds used to pay higher education tuition and fees.
136. Energy conservation subsidies provided by public utilities.
137. Adoption assistance programs.
138. Medicare Advantage MSA.
139. Disaster relief payments.
139A. Federal subsidies for prescription drug plans.
139B. Benefits provided to volunteer firefighters and emergency medical responders.
139C. COBRA premium assistance.
139D. Indian Health Care Benefits.
140. Cross references to other Acts.

In **2011**, P.L. HR1473, repealed item 139D[sic E].
Prior to repeal, item 139D[sic E] read as follows:
"139D[sic E] Free choice vouchers."
In **2010**, P.L. 111-148, added items 139D and 139D[sic E].
In **2009**, P.L. 111-5, Sec. 3001(a)(15)(A), added item 139C.
In **2008**, P.L. 110-142, Sec. 5(b), added item 139B.
In **2004**, P.L. 108-357, Sec. 101(b)(3), repealed item 114.
Prior to repeal, item 114 read as follows:
"114. Extraterritorial income."
—P.L. 108-311, Sec. 408(a)(5)(G), amended item 138.
Prior to amendment, item 138 read as follows:
"138. Medicare+Choise MSA."
In **2003**, P.L. 108-173, Sec. 1202(a), added item 139A.
In **2002**, P.L. 107-134, Sec. 111(b), deleted item 139 and added new items 139 and 140.
Prior to deletion, item 139 read as follows:
"Sec. 139. Cross reference to other Acts."
In **2000**, P.L. 106-519, Sec. 4(6), added item 114.
In **1997**, P.L. 105-34, Sec. 1213(d), added item 110 . . . Sec. 312(d)(14), amended item 121.
Prior to amendment, item 121 read as follows:

Exclusions from income — Code Sec. 101(d)(2)(B)(ii)

"121. One-time exclusion of gain from sale of principal residence by individual who has attained age 55."
—P.L. 105-33, Sec. 4006(b)(3), deleted item 138 and added a new item 138 and item 139.
Prior to deletion, item 138 read as follows:
"138. Cross references to other Acts."
In **1996**, P.L. 104-188, Sec. 1602(b)(8), deleted item 133... Sec. 1704(t)(4)(B), substituted "combat zone compensation" for "combat pay" in item 112... Sec. 1807(c)(7), deleted item 137 and added items 137 and 138.
Prior to deletion, item 133 read as follows:
"Sec. 133. Interest on certain loans used to acquire employer securities."
Prior to deletion, item 137 read as follows:
"Sec. 137. Cross reference to other Acts."
In **1992**, P.L. 102-486, Sec. 1912(b), amended item 136, and added item 137.
Prior to amendment, item 136 read as follows:
"136. Cross references to other Acts."
In **1990**, P.L. 101-508, Sec. 11801(b)(2), repealed items 110, 113, 114, 124, 128.
Prior to repeal, item 110 read as follows:
"110. Income taxes paid by lessee corporation."
Prior to repeal, item 113 read as follows:
"113. Mustering-out payments for members of Armed Forces."
Prior to repeal, item 114 read as follows:
"114. Sports programs conducted for the American National Red Cross."
Prior to repeal, item 124 read as follows:
"124. Qualified transportation provided by employer."
Prior to repeal, item 128 read as follows:
"128. Interest on certain savings certificates."
In **1988**, P.L. 100-647, Sec. 1013(a)(37), amended item 103 and repealed item 103A... Sec. 6009(c)(4), repealed item 135 and added new items 135 and 136.
Prior to amendment, item 103 read as follows:
"103. Interest on state and local bonds."
Prior to repeal, item 103A read as follows:
"103A. Mortgage subsidy bonds."
Prior to repeal, item 135 read as follows:
"135. Cross references to other Acts."
In **1986**, P.L. 99-514, Sec. 123(b)(4), amended item 117... Sec. 612(b)(8), repealed item 116... Sec. 1168(b), redesignated item 134 as 135 and added new item 134.
Prior to repeal, item 116 read as follows:
"116. Partial exclusion of dividends and interest received by individuals."
Prior to repeal, item 117 read as follows:
"117. Scholarships and fellowship grants."
In **1984**, P.L. 98-369, Sec. 16(a), repealed as if not enacted Sec. 302(c) of P.L. 97-34, which amended item 128... Sec. 171(b), amended item 111... Sec. 531(a)(2), redesignated item 132 as 133 and added new item 132... Sec. 543(b), redesignated item 133 as 134 and added new item 133.
Prior to amendment, item 111 read as follows:
"111. Recovery of bad debts, prior taxes, and delinquency amounts."
In **1983**, P.L. 97-473, Sec. 101(b)(2), redesignated item 130 as item 131 and added new item 130.
—P.L. 97-473, Sec. 102(b), redesignated item 131 as item 132 and added item 131.
In **1981**, P.L. 97-34, Sec. 124(e)(1), redesignated Code Sec. 129 [as redesignated by Sec. 301(b)(1) of this Act, see below] as Code Sec. 130 and added new Code Sec. 129. This Act did not amend the table of sections for Part III, but Congress presumably intended to do so.... Sec. 301(b)(1), redesignated item 128 as 129 and added new item 128... Sec. 302(c)(1), [repealed as if not enacted by Sec. 16(a) of P.L. 98-369, see above] added new item 128.
In **1980**, P.L. 96-499, Sec. 1102(b), added item 103A.
—P.L. 96-223, Sec. 404(b)(1), amended item 116.
Prior to amendment, item 116 read as follows:
"116. Partial exclusion of dividends received by individuals."
In **1978**, P.L. 95-618, Sec. 242(b), redesignated item 124 as 125 and added new item 124.
—P.L. 95-600, Sec. 134(b), redesignated item 125 [as redesignated by Sec. 242(b) of P.L. 95-618, see above] as 126 and added new item 125.... Sec. 404(c)(3), amended item 121... Sec. 543(b), redesignated item 126 as 127 and added new item 126.
Prior to amendment, item 121 read as follows:
"121. Gain from sale or exchange of residence of individual who has attained age 65."
—P.L. 95-600, Sec. 164(c), redesignated item 124 [sic 127] as item 125 [sic 128] and added new item 124 [sic 127]
In **1976**, P.L. 94-455, Sec. 2134(c), added item 120.
In **1969**, P.L. 91-172, Sec. 901(b), redesignated item 123 as 124 and added new item 123.
In **1966**, P.L. 89-365, Sec. [1](a)(2), redesignated 122 as 123 and added new item 122.
In **1964**, P.L. 88-272, Sec. 206(b)(2), redesignated item 121 as 122, and added new item 121.
In **1958**, P.L. 85-866, Sec. 3(b), repealed item 120.
Prior to repeal, item 120 read as follows:
"Statutory subsistence allowance received by police."

Sec. 101. Certain death benefits.
(a) Proceeds of life insurance contracts payable by reason of death.
(1) General rule. Except as otherwise provided in paragraph (2), subsection (d), subsection (f), and subsection (j), gross income does not include amounts received (whether in a single sum or otherwise) under a life insurance contract, if such amounts are paid by reason of the death of the insured.
(2) Transfer for valuable consideration. In the case of a transfer for a valuable consideration, by assignment or otherwise, of a life insurance contract or any interest therein, the amount excluded from gross income by paragraph (1) shall not exceed an amount equal to the sum of the actual value of such consideration and the premiums and other amounts subsequently paid by the transferee. The preceding sentence shall not apply in the case of such a transfer—
  (A) if such contract or interest therein has a basis for determining gain or loss in the hands of a transferee determined in whole or in part by reference to such basis of such contract or interest therein in the hands of the transferor, or
  (B) if such transfer is to the insured, to a partner of the insured, to a partnership in which the insured is a partner, or to a corporation in which the insured is a shareholder or officer.
The term "other amounts" in the first sentence of this paragraph includes interest paid or accrued by the transferee on indebtedness with respect to such contract or any interest therein if such interest paid or accrued is not allowable as a deduction by reason of section 264(a)(4).
(b) Repealed.
(c) Interest.
If any amount excluded from gross income by subsection (a) is held under an agreement to pay interest thereon, the interest payments shall be included in gross income.
(d) Payment of life insurance proceeds at a date later than death.
(1) General rule. The amounts held by an insurer with respect to any beneficiary shall be prorated (in accordance with such regulations as may be prescribed by the Secretary) over the period or periods with respect to which such payments are to be made. There shall be excluded from the gross income of such beneficiary in the taxable year received any amount determined by such proration. Gross income includes, to the extent not excluded by the preceding sentence, amounts received under agreements to which this subsection applies.
(2) Amount held by an insurer. An amount held by an insurer with respect to any beneficiary shall mean an amount to which subsection (a) applies which is—
  (A) held by any insurer under an agreement provided for in the life insurance contract, whether as an option or otherwise, to pay such amount on a date or dates later than the death of the insured, and
  (B) equal to the value of such agreement to such beneficiary
    (i) as of the date of death of the insured (as if any option exercised under the life insurance contract were exercised at such time), and
    (ii) as discounted on the basis of the interest rate used by the insurer in calculating payments under the agreement and mortality tables prescribed by the Secretary.

(3) **Application of subsection.** This subsection shall not apply to any amount to which subsection (c) is applicable.

(e) **Repealed.**

(f) **Proceeds of flexible premium contracts issued before January 1, 1985 payable by reason of death.**

(1) **In general.** Any amount paid by reason of the death of the insured under a flexible premium life insurance contract issued before January 1, 1985 shall be excluded from gross income only if—

(A) under such contract—

(i) the sum of the premiums paid under such contract does not at any time exceed the guideline premium limitation as of such time, and

(ii) any amount payable by reason of the death of the insured (determined without regard to any qualified additional benefit) is not at any time less than the applicable percentage of the cash value of such contract at such time, or

(B) by the terms of such contract, the cash value of such contract may not at any time exceed the net single premium with respect to the amount payable by reason of the death of the insured (determined without regard to any qualified additional benefit) at such time.

(2) **Guideline premium limitation.** For purposes of this subsection—

(A) Guideline premium limitation. The term "guideline premium limitation" means, as of any date, the greater of—

(i) the guideline single premium, or

(ii) the sum of the guideline level premiums to such date.

(B) Guideline single premium. The term "guideline single premium" means the premium at issue with respect to future benefits under the contract (without regard to any qualified additional benefit), and with respect to any charges for qualified additional benefits, at the time of a determination under subparagraph (A) or (E) and which is based on—

(i) the mortality and other charges guaranteed under the contract, and

(ii) interest at the greater of an annual effective rate of 6 percent or the minimum rate or rates guaranteed upon issue of the contract.

(C) Guideline level premium. The term "guideline level premium" means the level annual amount, payable over the longest period permitted under the contract (but ending not less than 20 years from date of issue or not later than age 95, if earlier), computed on the same basis as the guideline single premium, except that subparagraph (B)(ii) shall be applied by substituting "4 percent" for "6 percent".

(D) Computational rules. In computing the guideline single premium or guideline level premium under subparagraph (B) or (C)—

(i) the excess of the amount payable by reason of the death of the insured (determined without regard to any qualified additional benefit) over the cash value of the contract shall be deemed to be not greater than such excess at the time the contract was issued,

(ii) the maturity date shall be the latest maturity date permitted under the contract, but not less than 20 years after the date of issue or (if earlier) age 95, and

(iii) the amount of any endowment benefit (or sum of endowment benefits) shall be deemed not to exceed the least amount payable by reason of the death of the insured (determined without regard to any qualified additional benefit) at any time under the contract.

(E) Adjustments. The guideline single premium and guideline level premium shall be adjusted in the event of a change in the future benefits or any qualified additional benefit under the contract which was not reflected in any guideline single premiums or guideline level premium previously determined.

(3) **Other definitions and special rules.** For purposes of this subsection—

(A) Flexible premium life insurance contract. The terms "flexible premium life insurance contract" and "contract" mean a life insurance contract (including any qualified additional benefits) which provides for the payment of one or more premiums which are not fixed by the insurer as to both timing and amount. Such terms do not include that portion of any contract which is treated under State law as providing any annuity benefits other than as a settlement option.

(B) Premiums paid. The term "premiums paid" means the premiums paid under the contract less any amounts (other than amounts includible in gross income) to which section 72(e) applies. If, in order to comply with the requirements of paragraph (1)(A), any portion of any premium paid during any contract year is returned by the insurance company (with interest) within 60 days after the end of a contract year—

(i) the amount so returned (excluding interest) shall be deemed to reduce the sum of the premiums paid under the contract during such year, and

(ii) notwithstanding the provisions of section 72(e), the amount of any interest so returned shall be includible in the gross income of the recipient.

(C) Applicable percentage. The term "applicable percentage" means—

(i) 140 percent in the case of an insured with an attained age at the beginning of the contract year of 40 or less, and

(ii) in the case of an insured with an attained age of more than 40 as of the beginning of the contract year, 140 percent reduced (but not below 105 percent) by one percent for each year in excess of 40.

(D) Cash value. The cash value of any contract shall be determined without regard to any deduction for any surrender charge or policy loan.

(E) Qualified additional benefits. The term "qualified additional benefits" means any—

(i) guaranteed insurability,

(ii) accidental death benefit,

(iii) family term coverage, or

(iv) waiver of premium.

(F) Premium payments not disqualifying contract. The payment of a premium which would result in the sum of the premiums paid exceeding the guideline premium limitation shall be disregarded for purposes of paragraph (1)(A)(i) if the amount of such premium does not exceed the amount necessary to prevent the termination of the contract without cash value or on before the end of the contract year.

(G) Net single premium. In computing the net single premium under paragraph (1)(B)—

(i) the mortality basis shall be that guaranteed under the contract (determined by reference to the most recent mortality table allowed under all State laws on the date of issuance),

(ii) interest shall be based on the greater of—

Exclusions from income   Code Sec. 101(g)(4)(D)

(I) an annual effective rate of 4 percent (3 percent for contracts issued before July 1, 1983), or

(II) the minimum rate or rates guaranteed upon issue of the contract, and

(iii) the computational rules of paragraph (2)(D) shall apply, except that the maturity date referred to in clause (ii) thereof shall not be earlier than age 95.

(H) Correction of errors. If the taxpayer establishes to the satisfaction of the Secretary that—

(i) the requirements described in paragraph (1) for any contract year was not satisfied due to reasonable error, and

(ii) reasonable steps are being taken to remedy the error,

the Secretary may waive the failure to satisfy such requirements.

(I) Regulations. The Secretary shall prescribe such regulations as may be necessary or appropriate to carry out the purposes of this subsection.

(g) Treatment of certain accelerated death benefits.

(1) **In general.** For purposes of this section, the following amounts shall be treated as an amount paid by reason of the death of an insured:

(A) Any amount received under a life insurance contract on the life of an insured who is a terminally ill individual.

(B) Any amount received under a life insurance contract on the life of an insured who is a chronically ill individual.

(2) **Treatment of viatical settlements.**

(A) In general. If any portion of the death benefit under a life insurance contract on the life of an insured described in paragraph (1) is sold or assigned to a viatical settlement provider, the amount paid for the sale or assignment of such portion shall be treated as an amount paid under the life insurance contract by reason of the death of such insured.

(B) Viatical settlement provider.

(i) In general. The term "viatical settlement provider" means any person regularly engaged in the trade or business of purchasing, or taking assignments of, life insurance contracts on the lives of insureds described in paragraph (1) if—

(I) such person is licensed for such purposes (with respect to insureds described in the same subparagraph of paragraph (1) as the insured) in the State in which the insured resides, or

(II) in the case of an insured who resides in a State not requiring the licensing of such persons for such purposes with respect to such insured, such person meets the requirements of clause (ii) or (iii), whichever applies to such insured.

(ii) Terminally ill insureds. A person meets the requirements of this clause with respect to an insured who is a terminally ill individual if such person—

(I) meets the requirements of sections 8 and 9 of the Viatical Settlements Model Act of the National Association of Insurance Commissioners, and

(II) meets the requirements of the Model Regulations of the National Association of Insurance Commissioners (relating to standards for evaluation of reasonable payments) in determining amounts paid by such person in connection with such purchases or assignments.

(iii) Chronically ill insureds. A person meets the requirements of this clause with respect to an insured who is a chronically ill individual if such person—

(I) meets requirements similar to the requirements referred to in clause (ii)(I), and

(II) meets the standards (if any) of the National Association of Insurance Commissioners for evaluating the reasonableness of amounts paid by such person in connection with such purchases or assignments with respect to chronically ill individuals.

(3) **Special rules for chronically ill insureds.** In the case of an insured who is a chronically ill individual—

(A) In general. Paragraphs (1) and (2) shall not apply to any payment received for any period unless—

(i) such payment is for costs incurred by the payee (not compensated for by insurance or otherwise) for qualified long-term care services provided for the insured for such period, and

(ii) the terms of the contract giving rise to such payment satisfy—

(I) the requirements of section 7702B(b)(1)(B), and

(II) the requirements (if any) applicable under subparagraph (B).

For purposes of the preceding sentence, the rule of section 7702B(b)(2)(B) shall apply.

(B) Other requirements. The requirements applicable under this subparagraph are—

(i) those requirements of section 7702B(g) and section 4980C which the Secretary specifies as applying to such a purchase, assignment, or other arrangement,

(ii) standards adopted by the National Association of Insurance Commissioners which specifically apply to chronically ill individuals (and, if such standards are adopted, the analogous requirements specified under clause (i) shall cease to apply), and

(iii) standards adopted by the State in which the policyholder resides (and if such standards are adopted, the analogous requirements specified under clause (i) and (subject to section 4980C(f)) standards under clause (ii), shall cease to apply).

(C) Per diem payments. A payment shall not fail to be described in subparagraph (A) by reason of being made on a per diem or other periodic basis without regard to the expenses incurred during the period to which the payment relates.

(D) Limitation on exclusion for periodic payments. For limitation on amount of periodic payments which are treated as described in paragraph (1), see section 7702B(d).

(4) **Definitions.** For purposes of this subsection—

(A) Terminally ill individual. The term "terminally ill individual" means an individual who has been certified by a physician as having an illness or physical condition which can reasonably be expected to result in death in 24 months or less after the date of the certification.

(B) Chronically ill individual. The term "chronically ill individual" has the meaning given such term by section 7702B(c)(2); except that such term shall not include a terminally ill individual.

(C) Qualified long-term care services. The term "qualified long-term care services" has the meaning given such term by section 7702B(c).

(D) Physician. The term "physician" has the meaning given to such term by section 1861(r)(1) of the Social Security Act (42 U.S.C. 1395x(r)(1)).

(5) Exception for business-related policies. This subsection shall not apply in the case of any amount paid to any taxpayer other than the insured if such taxpayer has an insurable interest with respect to the life of the insured by reason of the insured being a director, officer, or employee of the taxpayer or by reason of the insured being financially interested in any trade or business carried on by the taxpayer.

(h) Survivor benefits attributable to service by a public safety officer who is killed in the line of duty.

  (1) In general. Gross income shall not include any amount paid as a survivor annuity on account of the death of a public safety officer (as such term is defined in section 1204 of the Omnibus Crime Control and Safe Streets Act of 1968) killed in the line of duty—

  (A) if such annuity is provided, under a governmental plan which meets the requirements of section 401(a), to the spouse (or a former spouse) of the public safety officer or to a child of such officer; and

  (B) to the extent such annuity is attributable to such officer's service as a public safety officer.

  (2) Exceptions. Paragraph (1) shall not apply with respect to the death of any public safety officer if, as determined in accordance with the provisions of the Omnibus Crime Control and Safe Streets Act of 1968—

  (A) the death was caused by the intentional misconduct of the officer or by such officer's intention to bring about such officer's death;

  (B) the officer was voluntarily intoxicated (as defined in section 1204 of such Act) at the time of death;

  (C) the officer was performing such officer's duties in a grossly negligent manner at the time of death; or

  (D) the payment is to an individual whose actions were a substantial contributing factor to the death of the officer.

(i) Certain employee death benefits payable by reason of death of certain terrorist victims or astronauts.

  (1) In general. Gross income does not include amounts (whether in a single sum or otherwise) paid by an employer by reason of the death of an employee who is a specified terrorist victim (as defined in section 692(d)(4)).

  (2) Limitation.

  (A) In general. Subject to such rules as the Secretary may prescribe, paragraph (1) shall not apply to amounts which would have been payable after death if the individual had died other than as a specified terrorist victim (as so defined).

  (B) Exception. Subparagraph (A) shall not apply to incidental death benefits paid from a plan described in section 401(a) and exempt from tax under section 501(a).

  (3) Treatment of self-employed individuals. For purposes of paragraph (1), the term "employee" includes a self-employed individual (as defined in section 401(c)(1)).

  (4) Relief with respect to astronauts. The provisions of this subsection shall apply to any astronaut whose death occurs in the line of duty.

(j) Treatment of certain employer-owned life insurance contracts.

  (1) General rule. In the case of an employer-owned life insurance contract, the amount excluded from gross income of an applicable policyholder by reason of paragraph (1) of subsection (a) shall not exceed an amount equal to the sum of the premiums and other amounts paid by the policyholder for the contract.

  (2) Exceptions. In the case of an employer-owned life insurance contract with respect to which the notice and consent requirements of paragraph (4) are met, paragraph (1) shall not apply to any of the following:

  (A) Exceptions based on insured's status. Any amount received by reason of the death of an insured who, with respect to an applicable policyholder—

   (i) was an employee at any time during the 12-month period before the insured's death, or

   (ii) is, at the time the contract is issued—

    (I) a director,

    (II) a highly compensated employee within the meaning of section 414(q) (without regard to paragraph (1)(B)(ii) thereof), or

    (III) a highly compensated individual within the meaning of section 105(h)(5), except that "35 percent" shall be substituted for "25 percent" in subparagraph (C) thereof.

  (B) Exception for amounts paid to insured's heirs. Any amount received by reason of the death of an insured to the extent—

   (i) the amount is paid to a member of the family (within the meaning of section 267(c)(4)) of the insured, any individual who is the designated beneficiary of the insured under the contract (other than the applicable policyholder), a trust established for the benefit of any such member of the family or designated beneficiary, or the estate of the insured, or

   (ii) the amount is used to purchase an equity (or capital or profits) interest in the applicable policyholder from any person described in clause (i).

  (3) Employer-owned life insurance contract.

  (A) In general. For purposes of this subsection, the term "employer-owned life insurance contract" means a life insurance contract which—

   (i) is owned by a person engaged in a trade or business and under which such person (or a related person described in subparagraph (B)(ii)) is directly or indirectly a beneficiary under the contract, and

   (ii) covers the life of an insured who is an employee with respect to the trade or business of the applicable policyholder on the date the contract is issued.

For purposes of the preceding sentence, if coverage for each insured under a master contract is treated as a separate contract for purposes of sections 817(h), 7702, and 7702A, coverage for each such insured shall be treated as a separate contract.

  (B) Applicable policyholder. For purposes of this subsection—

   (i) In general. The term "applicable policyholder" means, with respect to any employer-owned life insurance contract, the person described in subparagraph (A)(i) which owns the contract.

   (ii) Related persons. The term "applicable policyholder" includes any person which—

    (I) bears a relationship to the person described in clause (i) which is specified in section 267(b) or 707(b)(1), or

    (II) is engaged in trades or businesses with such person which are under common control (within the meaning of subsection (a) or (b) of section 52).

  (4) Notice and consent requirements. The notice and consent requirements of this paragraph are met if, before the issuance of the contract, the employee—

  (A) is notified in writing that the applicable policyholder intends to insure the employee's life and the maximum face amount for which the employee could be insured at the time the contract was issued,

(B) provides written consent to being insured under the contract and that such coverage may continue after the insured terminates employment, and

(C) is informed in writing that an applicable policyholder will be a beneficiary of any proceeds payable upon the death of the employee.

(5) **Definitions.** For purposes of this subsection—

(A) Employee. The term "employee" includes an officer, director, and highly compensated employee (within the meaning of section 414(q)).

(B) Insured. The term "insured" means, with respect to an employer-owned life insurance contract, an individual covered by the contract who is a United States citizen or resident. In the case of a contract covering the joint lives of 2 individuals, references to an insured include both of the individuals.

In 2006, P.L. 109-280, Sec. 863(a), added subsec. (j) . . . Sec. 863(c)(1), substituted "subsection (f), and subsection (j))" for "and subsection (f)" in para. (a)(1), effective for life insurance contracts issued after 8/17/2006, for a contract issued after 8/17/2006 pursuant to an exchange described in Code Sec. 1035 for a contract issued on or prior 8/17/2006. For purposes of the preceding sentence, any material increase in the death benefit or other material change shall cause the contract to be treated as a new contract except that, in the case of a master contract (within the meaning of Code Sec. 264(f)(4)(E)), the addition of covered lives shall be treated as a new contract only with respect to such additional covered lives.

In 2003, P.L. 108-121, Sec. 110(b)(1), added para. (i)(4) . . . Sec. 110(b)(2), added "or astronauts" after "victims" in the heading of subsec. (i), effective for amounts paid after 12/31/2002, with respect to deaths occurring after 12/31/2002.

In 2002, P.L. 107-134, Sec. 102(a), added subsec. (i), effective for tax. yrs. end. before, on, or after 9/11/2001. Sec. 102(b)(2) of this Act, provides:

"(2) Waiver of limitations. If refund or credit of any overpayment of tax resulting from the amendments made by this section is prevented at any time before the close of the 1-year period beginning on the date of the enactment of this Act by the operation of any law or rule of law (including res judicata), such refund or credit may nevertheless be made or allowed if claim therefor is filed before the close of such period."

In 2001, P.L. 107-15, Sec. 2, substituted ", and to amounts received in taxable years beginning after December 31, 2001, with respect to individuals dying on or before December 31, 1996." for the period in Sec. 1528(b) of P.L. 105-34, see below.

In 1998, P.L. 105-206, Sec. 6010(o)(3)(B), substituted "except that, in the case of a master contract (within the meaning of section 264(f)(4)(E) of the Internal Revenue Code of 1986), the addition of covered lives shall be treated as a new contract only with respect to such additional covered lives." for "but the addition of covered lives shall be treated as a new contract only with respect to such additional covered lives. For purposes of this subsection, an increase in the death benefit under a policy or contract issued in connection with a lapse described in section 501(d)(2) of the Health Insurance Portability and Accountability Act of 1996 shall not be treated as a new contract." in Sec. 1084(d) [sic (f)] of P.L. 105-34 [see below]

In 1997, P.L. 105-34, Sec. 1084(b)(2), added the sentence to the end of para. (a)(2), effective as provided in Sec. 1084(d) [sic (f)] of this Act [as amended by Sec. 6010(o)(3)(B) of 105-206, see above], which reads as follows:

"(d) [sic (f)] Effective date. The amendments made by this section shall apply to contracts issued after June 8, 1997, in taxable years ending after such date. For purposes of the preceding sentence, any material increase in the death benefit or other material change in the contract shall be treated as a new contract except that, in the case of a master contract (within the meaning of section 264(f)(4)(E) of the Internal Revenue Code of 1986), the addition of covered lives shall be treated as a new contract only with respect to such additional covered lives."

—P.L. 105-34, Sec. 1528(a), added subsec. (h), effective for amounts received in tax. yrs. begin. after 12/31/96, with respect to individuals dying after 12/31/96, and to amounts received in tax. yrs. begin. after 12/31/2001, with respect to individuals dying on or before 12/31/96.

In 1996, P.L. 104-188, Sec. 1402(a), deleted subsec. (b) . . . Sec. 1402(b)(1), substituted "subsection (a)" for "subsection (a) or (b)" in subsec. (c), effective for decedents dying after 8/20/96.

Prior to deletion, subsec. (b) read as follows:

"(b) Employees' death benefits.

"(1) General rule. Gross income does not include amounts received (whether in a single sum or otherwise) by the beneficiaries or the estate of an employee, if such amounts are paid by or on behalf of an employer and are paid by reason of the death of the employee.

"(2) Special rules for paragraph (1).

"(A) $5,000 limitation. The aggregate amounts excludable under paragraph (1) with respect to the death of any employee shall not exceed $5,000.

"(B) Nonforfeitable rights. Paragraph (1) shall not apply to amounts with respect to which the employee possessed, immediately before his death, a nonfor-

feitable right to receive the amounts while living. This subparagraph shall not apply to a lump sum distribution (as defined in section 402(e)(4))—

"(i) by a stock bonus, pension, or profit-sharing trust described in section 401(a) which is exempt from tax under section 501(a),

"(ii) under an annuity contract under a plan described in section 403(a), or

"(iii) under an annuity contract purchased by an employer which is an organization referred to in section 170(b)(1)(A)(ii) or (vi) or which is a religious organization (other than a trust) and which is exempt from tax under section 501(a), but only with respect to that portion of such total distributions payable which bears the same ratio to the amount of such total distributions payable which is (without regard to this subsection) includible in gross income, as the amounts contributed by the employer for such annuity contract which are excludable from gross income under section 403(b) bear to the total amounts contributed by the employer for such annuity contract.

"(C) Joint and survivor annuities. Paragraph (1) shall not apply to amounts received by a surviving annuitant under a joint and survivor's annuity contract after the first day of the first period for which an amount was received as an annuity by the employee (or would have been received if the employee had lived).

"(D) Other annuities. In the case of any amount to which section 72 (relating to annuities, etc.) applies, the amount which is excludable under paragraph (1) (as modified by the preceding subparagraphs of this paragraph) shall be determined by reference to the value of such amount as of the day on which the employee died. Any amount so excludable under paragraph (1) shall, for purposes of section 72, be treated as additional consideration paid by the employee. Paragraph (1) shall not apply in the case of an annuity under chapter 73 of title 10 of the United States Code if the member or former member of the uniformed services by reason of whose death such annuity is payable died after attaining retirement age.

"(3) Treatment of self-employed individuals. For purposes of this subsection—

"(A) Self-employed individual not considered employee. Except as provided in subparagraph (B), the term 'employee' does not include a self-employed individual described in section 401(c)(1).

"(B) Special rule for certain distributions. In the case of any amount paid or distributed—

"(i) by a trust described in section 401(a) which is exempt from tax under section 501(a), or

"(ii) under a plan described in section 403(a),

the term 'employee' includes a self-employed individual described in section 401(c)(1)."

—P.L. 104-191, Sec. 331(a), added subsec. (g), effective for amounts received after 12/31/96.

In 1986, P.L. 99-514, Sec. 1001(a), amended the second sentence of para. (d)(1) . . . Sec. 1001(b), amended clause (d)(2)(B)(ii) . . . Sec. 1001(c)(1), deleted para. (d)(3) and redesignated para. (d)(4) as (d)(3) . . . Sec. 1001(c)(2), substituted "equal" for "is equal" in subpara. (d)(2)(B), effective for amounts received for deaths occurring after 10/22/86, in tax. yrs. end. after 10/22/86.

Prior to amendment, the second sentence of para. (d)(1) read as follows:

"There shall be excluded from the gross income of such beneficiary in the taxable year received—

"(A) any amount determined by such proration, and

"(B) in the case of the surviving spouse of the insured, that portion of the excess of the amounts received under one or more agreements specified in paragraph (2)(A) (whether or not payment of any part of such amounts is guaranteed by the insurer) over the amount determined in subparagraph (A) of this paragraph which is not greater than $1,000 with respect to any insured."

Prior to amendment, clause (d)(2)(B)(ii) read as follows:

"(ii) as discounted on the basis of the interest rate and mortality tables used by the insurer in calculating payments under the agreement."

Prior to deletion, para. (d)(3) read as follows:

"(3) Surviving spouse. For purposes of this subsection, the term 'surviving spouse' means the spouse of the insured as of the date of death, including a spouse legally separated but not under a decree of absolute divorce."

—P.L. 99-514, Sec. 1825(d), added Sec. 221(b)(3) to P.L. 98-369 (reproduced below), a transitional rule for changes made by Sec. 221(b) of P.L. 98-369, see below.

In 1984, P.L. 98-369, Sec. 221(b)(1), amended Sec. 266(c)(1) of P.L. 97-248, the effective date for changes made by Sec. 266 of P.L. 97-248, for contracts entered into before 1/1/85 rather than contracts entered into before 1/1/84, see below.

—P.L. 98-369, Sec. 221(b)(2)(A), substituted "flexible premium life insurance contract issued before January 1, 1985" for "flexible premium life insurance contract" in para. (f)(1) . . . Sec. 221(b)(2)(B), substituted "flexible premium contracts issued before January 1, 1985" for "flexible premium contracts" in the heading of subsec. (f), effective 1/1/84. Sec. 221(b)(3) [as added by Sec. 1825(d) of P.L. 99-514, above] of this Act provides:

"(3) Transitional rule.—Any flexible premium contract issued during 1984 which meets the requirements of section 7702 of the Internal Revenue Code of 1954 (as added by this section [Sec. 221]) shall be treated as meeting the requirements of section 101(f) of such Code."

For special rule for certain contracts issued after 6/30/84, see Sec. 421(d)(2) and (3) of this Act reproduced in note following Code Sec. 7702.

—P.L. 98-369, Sec. 421(b)(2), deleted subsec. (e), effective for transfers after 7/18/84 in tax. yrs. ending after 7/18/84, except as provided in Sec. 421(d)(2)-(4) of this Act which reads as follows

"(2) Election to have amendments apply to transfers after 1983.—If both spouses or former spouses make an election under this paragraph, the amendments made by this section shall apply to all transfers made by such spouses (or former spouses) after December 31, 1983.

Code Sec. 101 — Exclusions from income

"(3) **Exception for transfers pursuant to existing decrees.**—Except in the case of an election under paragraph (2), the amendments made by this section shall not apply to transfers under any instrument in effect on or before the date of the enactment of this Act unless both spouses (or former spouses) elect to have such amendments apply to transfers under such instrument.

"(4) **Election.**— Any election under paragraph (2) or (3) shall be made in such manner, at such time, and subject to such conditions, as the Secretary of the Treasury or his delegate may by regulations prescribe."

Prior to deletion, subsec. (e) read as follows:

"(e) **Alimony, etc., payments.**

"(1) **In general.** This section shall not apply to so much of any payment as is includible in the gross income of the wife under section 71 (relating to alimony) or section 682 (relating to income of an estate or trust in case of divorce, etc.).

"(2) **Cross reference.** For definition of 'wife', see section 7701(a)(17)."

—P.L. 98-369, Sec. 713(e), amended subpara. (b)(3)(B), effective for decedents dying after 12/31/83.

Prior to amendment, subpara. (b)(3)(B) read as follows:

"(B) **Special rule for certain lump sum distributions.** In the case of any lump sum distribution described in the second sentence of paragraph (2)(B), the term 'employee' includes a self-employed individual described in section 401(c)(1)."

In 1983, P.L. 97-448, Sec. 306(a)(13), substituted "section 101(f)(2)(C)" for "section 103(f)(2)(C)" in Sec. 266(c)(3) of P.L. 97-248, the effective date for changes made by Sec. 266 of P.L. 97-248, reproduced below.

In 1982, P.L. 97-354, Sec. 6(b)(2), provides:

"(2) **Allowance of exclusion of death benefit.**— Notwithstanding section 241(b) of the Tax Equity and Fiscal Responsibility Act of 1982, in the case of amounts received under a plan of an S corporation, the amendment made by section 239 of such Act shall apply with respect to decedents dying after December 31, 1982."

—P.L. 97-248, Sec. 239, amended para. (b)(3), effective for decedents dying after 12/31/83.

Prior to amendment, para. (b)(3) read as follows:

"(3) **Self-employed individual not considered an employee.** For purposes of this subsection, the term 'employee' does not include an individual who is an employee within the meaning of section 401(c)(1) (relating to self-employed individuals)."

—P.L. 97-248, Sec. 266(a), added subsec. (f) . . . Sec. 266(b), substituted ", subsection (d), and subsection (f)" for "and in subsection (d)", in para. (a)(1), effective for contracts entered into before 1/1/85. Secs. 266 (c)(2) and (3) of this Act provide:

"(2) **Special rule for contracts entered into before January 1, 1983.**— Any contract entered into before January 1, 1983, which meets the requirements of section 101(f) of the Internal Revenue Code of 1954 on the date which is 1 year after the date of the enactment of this Act shall be treated as meeting the requirements of such section for any period before the date on which such contract meets such requirements. Any death benefits paid under a flexible premium life insurance contract (within the meaning of section 101(f)(3)(A) of such Code) before the date which is 1 year after such date of enactment shall be excluded from gross income.

"(3) **Special rule for certain contracts.**— Any contract entered into before January 1, 1983, shall be treated as meeting the requirements of subparagraph (A) of section 101(f)(1) of such Code if such contract would meet such requirements if section 101(f)(2)(C) of such Code were applied by substituting '3 percent' for '4 percent'."

In 1976, P.L. 94-455, Sec. 1901(a)(16), deleted subsec. (f), for tax. yrs. begin. after '76.

Prior to deletion, subsec. (f) read as follows:

"(f) **Effective date of section.**

"This section shall apply only to amounts received by reason of the death of an insured or an employee occurring after the date of enactment of this title. Section 22(b)(1) of the Internal Revenue Code of 1939 shall apply to amounts received by reason of the death of an insured or an employee occurring on or before such date."

—P.L. 94-455, Sec. 1906(b)(13)(A), substituted "Secretary" for "Secretary or his delegate" in para. (d)(1), effective for tax. yrs. begin. after 12/31/76.

In 1974, P.L. 93-406, Sec. 2005(c)(15), substituted "a lump sum distribution (as defined in section 402(e)(4))" for "total distributions payable (as defined in section 402(a)(3)) which are paid to a distributee within one taxable year of the distributee by reason of the employee's death" in subpara. (b)(2)(B), effective with respect to distributions or payments made after 12/31/73, in tax. yrs. begin. after such date.

—P.L. 93-406, Sec. 2007(b)(3), substituted "if the member or former member of the uniformed services by reason of whose death such annuity is payable" for "if the individual who made the election under such chapter" in subpara. (b)(2)(D), effective with respect to individuals dying on or after 9/21/72.

In 1969, P.L. 9-172, Sec. 101(i)(1), substituted "section 170(b)(1)(A)(ii) or (vi) or which is a religious organization (other than a trust)" for "section 503(b)(1), (2), or (3)" in clause (b)(2)(B)(iii), effective 1/1/70.

In 1966, P.L. 89-365, Sec. 1(c), added the last sentence of subpara. (b)(2)(D), effective for individuals making an election under chapter 73 of title 10 of the United States Code who die after 12/31/65.

In 1962, P.L. 87-792, Sec. 7, substituted "described in section 403(a)" for "which meets the requirements of paragraphs (3), (4), (5), and (6) of section 401(a)" in subsec (b)(2)(B)(ii), added subsec. (b)(3), effective for tax. yrs. end. after 12/31/62.

In 1958, P.L. 85-866, Sec. 23(d), substituted in subpara. (b)(2)(B) "This subparagraph shall not apply to total distributions payable (as defined in section 402(a)(3)) which are paid to a distributee within one taxable year of the distributee by reason of the employee's death—" for "(other than total distributions payable, as defined in section 402(a)(3), which are paid to distributee, by a stock bonus, pension, or profit-sharing trust described in section 401(a) which is exempt from tax under section 501(a), or under an annuity contract under a plan which meets the requirements of paragraphs (3), (4), (5), and (6) of section 401(a), within one taxable year of the distributee by reason of the employee's death)", and added clauses (i), (ii), and (iii), effective for tax. yrs. begin. after 12/31/57.

Sec. 102. Gifts and inheritances.

(a) General rule.

Gross income does not include the value of property acquired by gift, bequest, devise, or inheritance.

(b) Income.

Subsection (a) shall not exclude from gross income—

(1) the income from any property referred to in subsection (a); or

(2) where the gift, bequest, devise, or inheritance is of income from property, the amount of such income.

Where, under the terms of the gift, bequest, devise, or inheritance, the payment, crediting, or distribution thereof is to be made at intervals, then, to the extent that it is paid or credited or to be distributed out of income from property, it shall be treated for purposes of paragraph (2) as a gift, bequest, devise, or inheritance of income from property. Any amount included in the gross income of a beneficiary under subchapter J shall be treated for purposes of paragraph (2) as a gift, bequest, devise, or inheritance of income from property.

(c) Employee gifts.

(1) In general. Subsection (a) shall not exclude from gross income any amount transferred by or for an employer to, or for the benefit of, an employee.

(2) Cross references. For provisions excluding certain employee achievement awards from gross income, see section 74(c).

For provisions excluding certain de minimis fringes from gross income, see section 132(e).

In 1986, P.L. 99-514, Sec. 122(b), added subsec. (c), effective for prizes and awards granted after 12/31/86.

Sec. 103. Interest on State and local bonds.

(a) Exclusion.

Except as provided in subsection (b), gross income does not include interest on any State or local bond.

(b) Exceptions.

Subsection (a) shall not apply to—

(1) Private activity bond which is not a qualified bond. Any private activity bond which is not a qualified bond (within the meaning of section 141).

(2) Arbitrage bond. Any arbitrage bond (within the meaning of section 148).

(3) Bond not in registered form, etc. Any bond unless such bond meets the applicable requirements of section 149.

(c) Definitions.

For purposes of this section and part IV—

(1) State or local bond. The term "State or local bond" means an obligation of a State or political subdivision thereof.

(2) State. The term "State" includes the District of Columbia and any possession of the United States.

In 1998, P.L. 105-206, Sec. 3105, of this Act, reads as follows:

"Sec. 3105. Administrative appeal of adverse Internal Revenue Service determination of tax-exempt status of bond issue.

"The Internal Revenue Service shall amend its administrative procedures to provide that if, upon examination, the Internal Revenue Service proposes to an issuer that interest on previously issued obligations of such issuer is not excludable from gross income under section 103(a) of the Internal Revenue Code of 1986, the is-

Exclusions from income Code Sec. 103

suer of such obligations shall have an administrative appeal of right to a senior officer of the Internal Revenue Service Office of Appeals."

In 1989, P.L. 101-239, Sec. 7831(e), added Sec. 1318(8) of P.L. 99-514, part of the special and transitional rules for amendments made by Sec. 1301(a) of P.L. 99-514 reproduced below.

In 1988, P.L. 100-647, Sec. 1013(c)(1), amended Sec. 1313 of P.L. 99-514 [reproduced below], special and transitional rules for amendments made by Sec. 1301(a) of P.L. 99-514, by substituting "the net proceeds" for "the proceeds" in clause (a)(1)(B)(i), see below.

—P.L. 100-647, Sec. 1013(c)(2)(A), amended Sec. 1313 of P.L. 99-514 [reproduced below], special and transitional rules for amendments made by Sec. 1301(a) of P.L. 99-514, by substituting "sections 143(g) and 148" for "section 148" in subpara. (a)(3)(C), see below, effective for bonds issued after 6/30/87.

—P.L. 100-647, Sec. 1013(c)(3), amended Sec. 1313 of P.L. 99-514 [reproduced below], by deleting "of such Code" after "150(b)" in subpara. (a)(3)(E), see below . . . Sec. 1013(c)(4), amended Sec. 1313 of P.L. 99-514 [reproduced below], by adding the last sentence to para. (a)(3), see below . . . Sec. 1013(c)(5), amended Sec. 1313 of P.L. 99-514 [reproduced below], by adding "and by substituting 'September 1, 1986' for 'August 16, 1986' '" at the end of subpara. (a)(4)(A), see below . . . Sec. 1013(c)(6), amended Sec. 1313 of P.L. 99-514 [reproduced below], by adding the last sentence to para. (b)(2), see below . . . Sec. 1013(c)(7), amended Sec. 1313 of P.L. 99-514 [reproduced below], by deleting "of such Code" after "150(b)" in subpara. (b)(3)(F), see below . . . Sec. 1013(c)(8), amended Sec. 1313 of P.L. 99-514 [reproduced below], by adding subpara. (b)(3)(G), see below . . . Sec. 1013(c)(9), amended Sec. 1313 of P.L. 99-514 [reproduced below], by substituting "are or will be" for "are to be" in para. (b)(5), see below . . . Sec. 1013(c)(10)(A), amended Sec. 1313 of P.L. 99-514 [reproduced below], by substituting "certain" for "current" in the heading of subsec. (c), see below . . . Sec. 1013(c)(10)(B), amended Sec. 1313 of P.L. 99-514 [reproduced below], by adding "(or series of bonds)" after "any bond" and substituting "law did not" for "law do not" in para. (c)(1), see below . . . Sec. 1013(c)(11)(A), amended Sec. 1313 of P.L. 99-514 [reproduced below], by amending subpara. (c)(1)(A), see below . . . Sec. 1013(c)(11)(B), amended Sec. 1313 of P.L. 99-514 [reproduced below], by adding the last sentence to para. (c)(1) . . . Sec. 1013(c)(11)(C), amended Sec. 1313 of P.L. 99-514 [reproduced below], by adding "and" at the end of subpara. (c)(1)(B), deleting subpara. (c)(1)(C), and redesignating subpara. (c)(1)(D) as (c)(1)(C), see below . . . Sec. 1013(c)(11)(D), amended Sec. 1313 of P.L. 99-514 [reproduced below], by substituting "and (C)" for "and (D)" in subpara. (c)(2)(B), see below . . . Sec. 1013(c)(13), amended Sec. 1313 of P.L. 99-514 [reproduced below], by adding "(or series of bonds)" after "apply to any bond" in para. (c)(2), substituting "subsection did not" for "subsection does not" in para. (c)(2), and substituting "the net proceeds" for "the proceeds" in clause (c)(1)(A)(i), see below.

Prior to amendment, subpara. (c)(1)(A) read as follows:

"(A) the refunding bond has a maturity date not later than the maturity date of the refunded bond,"

Prior to deletion, subpara. (c)(1)(C) read as follows:

"(C) the interest rate on the refunding bond is lower than the interest rate on the refunded bond, and"

—P.L. 100-647, Sec. 1013(c)(11)(E), provides the following:

"(E) A refunding bond issued before July 1, 1987, shall be treated as meeting the requirement of subparagraph (A) of section 1313(c)(1) of the Reform Act if such bond met the requirement of such subparagraph as in effect before the amendments made by this paragraph."

—P.L. 100-647, Sec. 1013(c)(12)(A), amended 1954 Code Sec. 103(b)(6)(N) [before amended by Sec. 1301(a) of P.L. 99-514, reproduced below], by redesignating clauses (ii) and (iii) as (iii) and (iv), respectively, deleting clause (i), and adding new clauses (i) and (ii), see below.

Sec. 1013(c)(15) provides the following:

"(15) A bond issued to refund an obligation described in section 103(o)(3) of the Internal Revenue Code of 1954 (as in effect on the day before the date of the enactment of the Tax Reform Act of 1986) shall not be treated as described in section 144(b) of the 1986 Code unless it is described in section 144(b)(1)(A) of the 1986 Code."

Prior to amendment, clause (b)(6)(N)(i) of 1954 Code Sec. 103 read as follows:

"(i) In general. This paragraph shall not apply to any obligation issued after December 31, 1986 (including any obligations issued to refund an obligation issued on or before such date)."

—P.L. 100-647, Sec. 1013(c)(14)(A), amended Sec. 1313 of P.L. 99-514 [reproduced below], special and transitional rules for amendments made by Sec. 1301(a) of P.L. 99-514, by adding subsec. (d), see below, effective for refunding bonds issued after 10/16/87.

—P.L. 100-647, Sec. 1013(d)(1), amended Sec. 1314 of P.L. 99-514 [reproduced below], special and transitional rules for amendments made by Sec. 1301(a) of P.L. 99-514, by adding the last sentence to subsec. (a), see below . . . Sec. 1013(d)(2), amended Sec. 1314 of P.L. 99-514 [reproduced below], by substituting "August" for "December" in subsec. (f), see below . . . Sec. 1013(d)(3), amended Sec. 1314 of P.L. 99-514 [reproduced below], by redesignating subsec. (g) as (i) and adding subsecs. (g) and (h), see below.

—P.L. 100-647, Sec. 1013(e)(1), amended Sec. 1315 of P.L. 99-514 [reproduced below], special and transitional rules for amendments made by Sec. 1301(a) of P.L. 99-514, by adding "for calendar year 1986" after "1954 Code" each place it appeared in subsec. (c), substituting "August 15" for "August 16" each place it appeared in subsec. (c), and adding the last sentence to subsec. (c), see below . . . Sec. 1013(e)(2)(A), amended Sec. 1315 of P.L. 99-514 [reproduced below], by adding the last sentence to subsec. (e), see below.

—P.L. 100-647, Sec. 1013(f)(1)(A), amended Sec. 1316 of P.L. 99-514 [reproduced below], special and transitional rules for amendments made by Sec. 1301(a) of P.L. 99-514, by adding "and as having a carryforward purpose described in section 146(f)(5) of such Code" after "the 1986 Code" in paras. (a)(1), (b)(1), (c)(1), and (f)(1), see below, effective only with respect to carryforwards of volume cap for years after 1986.

—P.L. 100-647, Sec. 1013(f)(2), amended Sec. 1316 of P.L. 99-514 [reproduced below], special and transitional rules for amendments made by Sec. 1301(a) of P.L. 99-514, by adding para. (c)(4), see below . . . Sec. 1013(f)(3), amended Sec. 1316 of P.L. 99-514 [reproduced below], by adding "(and section 103(h)(2)(B)(ii) of the 1954 Code)" after "1986 Code" the first place it appears in para. (e)(1) and adding "(and section 103(b)(16) of the 1954 Code)" after "1986 Code" in the last sentence of para. (e)(1), see below . . . Sec. 1013(f)(4)(A), amended Sec. 1316 of P.L. 99-514 [reproduced below], by adding "issued to provide a facility" before "described in paragraph (3)" in para. (g)(2), see below . . . Sec. 1013(f)(4)(B), amended Sec. 1316 of P.L. 99-514 [reproduced below], by adding "such" before "paragraph (3)" in subpara. (g)(2)(C), see below . . . Sec. 1013(f)(5), amended Sec. 1316 of P.L. 99-514 [reproduced below], by adding "(and the provisions of section 1314)" after "section 1301" in para. (g)(6), see below . . . Sec. 1013(f)(6), amended Sec. 1316 of P.L. 99-514 [reproduced below], by amending para. (g)(7), see below . . . Sec. 1013(f)(8), amended Sec. 1316 of P.L. 99-514 [reproduced below], by amending para. (j)(2), see below . . . Sec. 1013(f)(9), amended Sec. 1316 of P.L. 99-514 [reproduced below], by substituting "no more than $55,000,000 shall be outstanding later than November 1, 1987" for "$55,000,000 must be redeemed no later than November 1, 1987" in para. (k)(2), see below . . . Sec. 1013(f)(11), amended Sec. 1316 of P.L. 99-514 [reproduced below], by repealing subsec. (l).

Prior to amendment, para. (g)(7) read as follows:

"(7) In the case of a bond described in section 632(d) of the Tax Reform Act of 1984

"(A) section 141 of the 1986 Code shall be applied without regard to subsection (a)(2) and subsection (b)(5) and paragraphs (1) and (2) of subsection (b) thereof shall be applied by substituting '25 percent' for '10 percent' each place it appears, and

"(B) section 149(b) of the 1986 Code shall not apply."

Prior to amendment, para. (j)(2) read as follows:

"(2) by adding at the end thereof the following new sentence: 'In the case of refunding obligations not to exceed $40,000,000 with respect to the Dade County, Florida, airport, the first sentence of this paragraph shall be applied by substituting 'December 31, 1987' for 'December 31, 1984' and the amendments made by section 1301 of the Tax Reform Act of 1986 shall not apply.' "

Prior to repeal, subsec. (l) read as follows:

"(l) Certain refundings.

"Section 628(g) of the Tax Reform Act of 1984 (and the amendments made by section 1301 of this Act) shall not apply to any refunding obligation if the refunded issue was approved by a city building commission on April 29, 1982, and was issued on May 11, 1982, and the refunding obligations were issued before January 1, 1987."

—P.L. 100-647, Sec. 1013(f)(7), amended Sec. 1316 of P.L. 99-514 [reproduced below], special and transitional rules for amendments made by Sec. 1301(a) of P.L. 99-514, by adding "and as having a carryforward purpose described in section 146(f)(5) of such Code" after "the 1986 Code" in subpara. (g)(8)(A), see below, effective only with respect to carryforwards of volume cap for years after 1986.

—P.L. 100-647, Sec. 1013(g)(1), amended Sec. 1317 of P.L. 99-514 [reproduced below], special and transitional rules for amendments made by Sec. 1301(a) of P.L. 99-514, by substituting ", a subsidiary of Sierra Pacific Resources, began in 1980 work to finance, construct, and operate" for "began construction in 1980" in subpara. (2)(J), see below . . . Sec. 1013(g)(2), amended Sec. 1317 of P.L. 99-514 [reproduced below], by amending subpara. (3)(C), see below . . . Sec. 1013(g)(3)(A), amended Sec. 1317 of P.L. 99-514 [reproduced below], by substituting "authorized" for "approved" and substituting "December 2" for "December 9" in subpara. (3)(P), see below . . . Sec. 1013(g)(3)(B), amended Sec. 1317 of P.L. 99-514 [reproduced below], by deleting "domed" before "stadium" in subpara. (3)(A), see below . . . Sec. 1013(g)(3)(C), amended Sec. 1317 of P.L. 99-514 [reproduced below], by adding ", or is a renovation of an existing stadium located in Oakland, California, and used by an American League baseball team" after "coliseum complex" in subpara. (3)(U), see below . . . Sec. 1013(g)(3)(D), amended Sec. 1317 of P.L. 99-514 [reproduced below], by substituting "$25,000,000" for "225,000,000" in subpara. (2)(W), see below . . . Sec. 1013(g)(4), amended Sec. 1317 of P.L. 99-514 [reproduced below], by adding subpara. (3)(Z), see below . . . Sec. 1013(g)(5), amended Sec. 1317 of P.L. 99-514 [reproduced below], by substituting "1986, and the bonds" for "1986. The bonds" in para. (4), deleting "and" at the end of subpara. (4)(A), and adding "and" at the end of subpara. (4)(B), see below . . . Sec. 1013(g)(6), amended Sec. 1317 of P.L. 99-514 [reproduced below], by amending subpara. (6)(W), see below . . . Sec. 1013(g)(7), amended Sec. 1317 of P.L. 99-514 [reproduced below], by redesignating subpara. (6)(X) as (Z) and adding subparas. (6)(X) and (Y), see below . . . Sec. 1013(g)(8), amended Sec. 1317 of P.L. 99-514 [reproduced below], by adding "and section 149(d)(2) of the 1986 Code shall not apply to bonds so treated" to the end of subpara. (7)(A), see below . . . Sec. 1013(g)(9), amended Sec. 1317 of P.L. 99-514 [reproduced below], by amending subpara. (7)(D), see below . . . Sec. 1013(g)(10), amended Sec. 1317 of P.L. 99-514 [reproduced below], by amending clause (7)(G)(ii), see below . . . Sec. 1013(g)(11), amended Sec. 1317 of P.L. 99-514 [reproduced below], by substituting "aquafestival" for "civic festival" in clause (7)(J)(i), amending clause (7)(J)(ii), and substituting "$10,000,000" for "$5,000,000" in subpara. (7)(J), see below . . . Sec. 1013(g)(12), amended Sec. 1317 of P.L. 99-514 [reproduced below], by substituting "March 6" for "March 5" in subpara. (9)(E), see below . . . Sec. 1013(g)(13), amended Sec. 1317 of P.L. 99-514 [reproduced below], by substituting "in December 1985 by a task force created jointly" for "by a task force created jointly, in December 1985" in clause (9)(J)(iii), see below... Sec. 1013(g)(14), amended Sec. 1317 of P.L. 99-514 [reproduced below], by substituting "in section 142(a)" for "and section 142(a)" in subpara. (11)(A), see below... Sec. 1013(g)(15), amended Sec. 1317 of P.L. 99-514 [reproduced below], by amending subpara. (11)(C), see below... Sec. 1013(g)(16), amended Sec. 1317 of P.L. 99-514 [reproduced below], by deleting the last sentence of subpara. (13)(X)... Sec. 1013(g)(17), amended Sec. 1317 of P.L. 99-514 [reproduced below], by adding subparas. (13)(AA) and (BB), see below... Sec. 1013(g)(18), amended Sec. 1317 of P.L. 99-514 [reproduced below], by substituting "130,000,000" for "90,000,000" and adding "incorporated on February 20, 1985" at the end of para. (14), see below... Sec. 1013(g)(19), amended Sec. 1317 of P.L. 99-514 [reproduced below], by substituting "to provide planning and financial guidance for a possible bond issue, and" for "for possible execution and delivery of tax-exempt certificates of participation by a nonprofit corporation, and" in clause (15)(B)(i) and substituting "bond issue" for "certificates" in clause (15)(B)(ii), see below ... Sec. 1013(g)(20), amended Sec. 1317 of P.L. 99-514 [reproduced below], by deleting the last sentence of para. (16)... Sec. 1013(g)(21), amended Sec. 1317 of P.L. 99-514 [reproduced below], by substituting "fixed guideway" for "light rail transitway" in clause (19)(D)(i), see below... Sec. 1013(g)(22), amended Sec. 1317 of P.L. 99-514 [reproduced below], by substituting "Subsections (c)(2) and (f) of section 148" for "Section 148(f)" in para. (20), see below... Sec. 1013(g)(23), amended Sec. 1317 of P.L. 99-514 [reproduced below], by substituting "Subsections (c)(2)" for "Subsection (c)" and substituting "103A(g)(5)(C)" for "103A(g)(5)(C)1" in subpara. (21)(B), see below... Sec. 1013(g)(24), amended Sec. 1317 of P.L. 99-514 [reproduced below], by amending para. (22), see below... Sec. 1013(g)(25), amended Sec. 1317 of P.L. 99-514 [reproduced below], by adding the last sentence to subpara. (24)(A), see below... Sec. 1013(g)(26)(A), amended Sec. 1317 of P.L. 99-514 [reproduced below], by adding "one or more of" before "3 counties" in clause (25)(A)(i), see below... Sec. 1013(g)(26)(B), amended Sec. 1317 of P.L. 99-514 [reproduced below], by adding the last sentence to clause (25)(B)(i), see below... Sec. 1013(g)(27), amended Sec. 1317 of P.L. 99-514 [reproduced below], by adding the last sentence to subpara. (27)(I), see below... Sec. 1013(g)(28), amended Sec. 1317 of P.L. 99-514 [reproduced below], by substituting "the state of Connecticut, and" for "a State admitted to the Union on June 14, 1776, and" in clause (29)(B)(i), see below... Sec. 1013(g)(29), amended Sec. 1317 of P.L. 99-514 [reproduced below], by deleting "net" before "proceeds" in subpara. (29)(D) see below... Sec. 1013(g)(30), amended Sec. 1317 of P.L. 99-514 [reproduced below], by substituting "dated" for "on" each time it appeared and adding "dated on December 1, 1985" after "(Series 1985 A and 1985 B)" in clause (33)(A)(ii), see below... Sec. 1013(g)(31), amended Sec. 1317 of P.L. 99-514 [reproduced below], by deleting "and before August 7, 1988," before "by the State" and adding the last sentence to subpara. (33)(B), see below... Sec. 1013(g)(32), amended Sec. 1317 of P.L. 99-514 [reproduced below], by substituting "subparagraph (F)" for "subparagraph (G)" in subpara. (33)(G), see below... Sec. 1013(g)(33), amended Sec. 1317 of P.L. 99-514 [reproduced below], by amending clause (33)(H)(ii) and adding the last two sentences to subpara. (33)(H), see below... Sec. 1013(g)(34), amended Sec. 1317 of P.L. 99-514 [reproduced below], by substituting "the issue or issues are" for "the issue is", adding "at least" before "900 units", substituting "245,000 square feet" for "2,000 square feet", and substituting "$112,000,000" for "$150,000,000" in subpara. (33)(K), see below... Sec. 1013(g)(35), amended Sec. 1317 of P.L. 99-514 [reproduced below], by amending subparas. (33)(M), (N) and (O), see below... Sec. 1013(g)(36), amended Sec. 1317 of P.L. 99-514 [reproduced below], by substituting "$400,000,000" for "$80,000,000" in para. (36), see below... Sec. 1013(g)(37), amended Sec. 1317 of P.L. 99-514 [reproduced below], by deleting "and sections 148 and 149" after "section 146" in para. (38)... Sec. 1013(g)(38), amended Sec. 1317 of P.L. 99-514 [reproduced below], by amending paras. (39) and (40), see below... Sec. 1013(g)(39), amended Sec. 1317 of P.L. 99-514 [reproduced below], by amending para. (41), see below... Sec. 1013(g)(40), amended Sec. 1317 of P.L. 99-514 [reproduced below], by adding "and the Internal Revenue Code of 1986 shall be applied without regard to section 149(d)(2)" at the end of para. (43), see below... Sec. 1013(g)(41), amended Sec. 1317 of P.L. 99-514 [reproduced below], by adding "and the temporary period limitation of section 148(c)(2) of the 1986 Code" after "1986 Code", substituting "$200,000,000" for "$100,000,000", and substituting "Hospital Equipment Loan Council" for "Hospitals Bond Pool" in para. (44), see below... Sec. 1013(g)(42), amended Sec. 1317 of P.L. 99-514 [reproduced below], by substituting "any" for "either" after "described in" in para. (48), see below... Sec. 1013(g)(43), amended Sec. 1317 of P.L. 99-514 [reproduced below], by substituting "paragraph (6)(U)" for "subparagraph (O)" in subpara. (48)(B), see below... Sec. 1013(g)(44), amended Sec. 1317 of P.L. 99-514 [reproduced below], by adding subpara. (48)(C), see below... Sec. 1013(g)(45), amended Sec. 1317 of P.L. 99-514 [reproduced below], by substituting "149(d)(2)" for "149(d)" and added "United States" before "Housing Act" in para. (45), see below... Sec. 1013(g)(46), amended Sec. 1317 of P.L. 99-514 [reproduced below], by amending para. (50), see below... Sec. 1013(g)(47), amended Sec. 1317 of P.L. 99-514 [reproduced below], by substituting "Section 141(b)" for "Section 141(a)" and substituting "sections 141(b)(3)" for "sections 141(a)(3)" in para. (51), see below... Sec. 1013(g)(48), amended Sec. 1317 of P.L. 99-514 [reproduced below], by substituting "Except as otherwise provided in this section, this section" for "This section" in para. (52), see below... Sec. 1013(g)(49), amended Sec. 1317 of P.L. 99-514 [reproduced below], by substituting "103(b)(4)(F)" for "103(b)(4)(E)" in para. (2), see below... Sec. 1013(g)(50), amended Sec. 1317 of P.L. 99-514 [reproduced below], by substituting "November 13, 1985" for "November 14, 1985" in clause (27)(H)(ii), see below... Sec. 1013(g)(51), amended Sec. 1317 of P.L. 99-514 [reproduced below], by substituting "November 1, 1985" for "November 11, 1985" in subpara. (33)(I), see below... Sec. 1013(g)(52), amended Sec. 1317 of P.L. 99-514 [repro-

duced below], by substituting "November 5" for "October 29" in subpara. (33)(J), see below.

Prior to amendment, subpara. (3)(C) read as follows:

"(C) A facility is described in this subparagraph if—

"(i) it is a stadium to be used by an American League baseball team currently using a stadium in a city having a population in excess of 2,500,000 and described in section 146(d)(3) of the 1986 Code, or by one or more professional sports teams currently using stadiums in such city (or professional sports teams which locate in such city following the relocation from such city of one or more professional sports teams currently using one or more of such stadiums), and

"(ii) the obligations to be used to provide financing for such stadium are issued pursuant to an inducement resolution adopted by a State agency on November 20, 1985 (whether or not the beneficiary of such issue is the beneficiary (if any) specified in such resolution).

The aggregate face amount of bonds to which this subparagraph applies shall not exceed $250,000,000. In the case of a carryforward of volume cap for a stadium described in the first sentence of this subparagraph, such carryforward shall be permitted whether or not there is a change in the beneficiary of the project."

Prior to amendment, subpara. (6)(W) read as follows:

"(W) A project is described in this paragraph if such project—

"(i) is located on lands submerged under the waters of a Great Lake or on adjacent lands which formerly were submerged under the waters of such lake;

"(ii) project lands were improved with a stadium which was demolished prior to December 31, 1983, and

"(iii) legislation for the project was included in a biennium budget for such the State in which it is to be located prior to December 31, 1983.

The aggregate face amount of bonds to which this subparagraph applies shall not exceed $105,000,000."

Prior to amendment, subpara. (7)(D) read as follows:

"(D) A facility is described in this subparagraph if such facility was initially approved in 1983 and is for San Jose, California. The aggregate face amount of bonds to which this subparagraph applies shall not exceed $100,000,000."

Prior to amendment, clause (7)(G)(ii) read as follows:

"(ii) such facility's location was approved by a task force created jointly, in December 1985, by the Governor or the State within which such facility will be located and the mayor of the capital city of such State, and"

Prior to amendment, clause (7)(J)(ii) read as follows:

"(ii) a referendum was held in the spring of 1985 in which voters permitted the city council to lease 130 acres of dedicated parkland to such festival, and"

Prior to amendment, subpara. (11)(C) read as follows:

"(C) A facility is described in this subparagraph if it is a solid waste disposal facility for Charleston, South Carolina, and a state political subdivision took formal action on April 1, 1980, to commit development funds for such facility."

Prior to deletion, the last sentence of subpara. (13)(X) read as follows:

"In the case of bonds to which this subparagraph applies, the requirements of sections 148 and 149(d) of the 1986 Code shall not be treated as included in section 103 of the 1954 Code and shall apply to such bonds."

Prior to deletion, the last sentence of para. (16) read as follows:

"In the case of bonds to which this paragraph applies, the requirements of sections 148, 149(d), and 149(g) of the 1986 Code shall be treated as included in section 103 of the 1954 Code and shall apply to such bonds."

Prior to amendment, para. (22) read as follows:

"(22) Downtown redevelopment project.

"(A) In the case of a bond described in subparagraph (B), section 141 of the 1986 Code shall be applied without regard to subsection (a)(2), subsection (b)(3), and subsection (b)(5); and paragraphs (1) and (2) of subsection (b) shall be applied by substituting '25 percent' for '10 percent' each place it appears.

"(B) A bond is described in this subparagraph if such bond is issued as part of an issue 95 percent or more of the net proceeds of which are to be used to provide a project to acquire and redevelop a downtown area if

"(i) on August 15, 1985, a downtown redevelopment authority adopted a resolution to issue bonds for such project,

"(ii) before September 26, 1985, the city expended (or entered into binding contracts to expend) more than $10,000,000 in connection with such project, and

"(iii) the state supreme court issued a ruling regarding the proposed finance structure for such project on December 11, 1985.

The aggregate face amount of bonds to which this paragraph applies shall not exceed $85,000,000 and such bonds must be issued before January 1, 1992."

Prior to amendment, clause (33)(H)(ii) read as follows:

"(ii) the request to issue bonds for items to be determined by the issuer was transmitted to Congress on November 7, 1985. The aggregate face amount of bonds to which this subparagraph applies shall not exceed $200,000,000."

Prior to amendment, subparas. (33)(M), (N), and (O) read as follows:

"(M) Proceeds of an issue are described in this subparagraph if—

"(i) such issue would not (if issued before August 16, 1986) be an industrial development bond (as defined in section 103(b)(2) of the 1954 Code), and

"(ii) such bonds were approved by city voters on January 19, 1985, for an art museum and 2 theaters.

The aggregate face amount of obligations to which this subparagraph applies shall not exceed $2,300,000.

"(N) Proceeds of an issue are described in this subparagraph if—

"(i) such issue is issued by a State dormitory authority on behalf of one or more universities described in section 501(c)(3) of the 1986 Code or a foundling hospital, and

"(ii) the application by the university for the issuance of such bond was made before October 27, 1985.

Exclusions from income — Code Sec. 103

The aggregate face amount of bonds to which this paragraph applies shall not exceed $150,000,000. In the case of bonds to which this paragraph applies, the requirements of sections 148 and 149(d) of the 1986 Code shall be treated as included in section 103 of the 1954 Code and shall apply to such bonds.

"(O) Any bond to which section 145(b) of the 1986 Code does not apply by reason of this section shall be taken into account in determining whether such section applies to any later issue.

"(34) Arbitrage rebate. — Section 148(f) of the 1986 Code shall not apply to any period before October 1, 1990, with respect to any bond the proceeds of which are to be used to provide a highspeed rail system for the State of Ohio. The aggregate face amount of bonds to which this paragraph applies shall not exceed $2,000,000,000."

Prior to amendment, paras. (39) and (40) read as follows:

"(39) Certain wastewater treatment facility. — A bond shall not be subject to the provisions of section 146 of the 1986 Code if it is issued to acquire and complete a wastewater treatment facility—

"(A) which was organized by an inter-local agreement dated October 17, 1978,
"(B) for which $78,143,557 has been spent as of July 31, 1986, and
"(C) for which the first construction contract was let on February 27, 1981.

The aggregate face amount of bonds to which this paragraph applies shall not exceed $100,000,000.

"(40) Refunding of certain taxable debt. A bond issued to refinance taxable debt shall not be treated as a qualified 501(c)(3) bond within the meaning of section 141(d)(1)(G) of the 1986 Code if an authorizing resolution as adopted by the issuer on August 14, 1986, for St. Mary's Hospital. The aggregate face amount of bonds to which this paragraph applies shall not exceed $22,314,000."

Prior to amendment, para. (41) read as follows:

"(41) Time to maturity for certain obligations. The requirement of section 147(b) of the 1986 Code shall apply to current refunding bonds issued with respect to two power facilities on which construction has been suspended by measuring the economic life of the facilities from the date of the refunding bonds if the facilities have not been placed in service as of the date of issuance of the refunding bonds. The aggregate face amount of bonds to which this paragraph applies shall not exceed $2,000,000,000."

Prior to amendment, para. (50) read as follows:

"(50) Transition bonds subject to certain rules. In the case of any bond to which any provision of this subsection applies

"(A) Minimum tax treatment. Any bond which, without regard to this section, would be a private activity bond (as defined in section 141(a) of the 1986 Code) shall be so treated for purposes of section 55 of such Code unless such bond would not be described in section 103(b)(2) or (o)(2) of the 1954 Code were such bond issued before August 16, 1986.

"(B) Certain restrictions apply. Except as otherwise expressly provided, sections 103 and 103A of the 1954 Code shall be applied as if the requirements of section 148 and subsections (d) and (g) of section 149 of the 1986 Code were included in each such section."

—P.L. 100-647, Sec. 1013(h)(1), amended Sec. 1318 of P.L. 99-514 [reproduced below], special and transitional rules for amendments made by Sec. 1301(a) of P.L. 99-514, by adding "(a) Definitions.—" before "For purposes of this subtitle" in the heading of subsec. (a), see below... Sec. 1013(h)(2), amended Sec. 1318 of P.L. 99-514 [reproduced below], by adding subsecs. (b)-(d), see below... Sec. 1018(m)(1), amended Sec. 1866 of P.L. 99-514 [reproduced below], transitional rule for amendments made by Sec. 1301(a) of P.L. 99-514, by adding "(or series of obligations)" after "obligation", see below... Sec. 1018(m)(2)(A), amended Sec. 1866 of P.L. 99-514 [reproduced below], by amending para. (1) and adding the last sentence to para. (1), see below... Sec. 1018(m)(3), amended Sec. 1866 of P.L. 99-514 [reproduced below], by substituting "90 days" for "30 days" in para. (4), see below... Sec. 1018(m)(4), amended Sec. 1866 of P.L. 99-514 [reproduced below], by adding "and" at the end of para. (2), deleting para. (3), and redesignating para. (4) as (3), see below... Sec. 1018(m)(5), provides the following:

"(5) A refunding obligation issued before July 1, 1987, shall be treated as meeting the requirement of paragraph (1) of section 1866 of the Reform Act if such obligation met the requirement of such paragraph as enacted by the Reform Act."

Prior to amendment, Sec. 1866(1) of P.L. 99-514 read as follows:

"(2) [sic (1)] the refunding obligation has a maturity date not later than the maturity date of the refunded obligation."

Prior to deletion, Sec. 1866(3) of P.L. 99-514 read as follows:

"(3) the interest rate on the refunding obligation is lower than the interest rate on the refunded issue,"

—P.L. 100-647, Sec. 1018(n)(1), amended Sec. 1869 of P.L. 99-514 [reproduced below], transitional rules for amendments made by 1301(a) of P.L. 99-514, by substituting "(by a governmental unit having the power to exercise eminent domain)" for "pursuant to the exercise of eminent domain" in clause (c)(3)(A)(ii), see below... Sec. 1018(n)(2), amended Sec. 1869 of P.L. 99-514 [reproduced below], by adding "(or similar issues)" after "resulting from the issue" in subpara. (c)(3)(C), see below.

In 1986, P.L. 99-514, Sec. 1301(a), amended Code Sec. 103, effective for bonds issued after 8/15/86. Special and transitional rules are provided by Secs. 1312-1318 of this Act [as amended by Secs. 1013-1018 of P.L. 100-647 and by Sec. 7831(e) of P.L. 101-239] which read as follows:

"Sec. 1312. Transitional rules for construction or binding agreements and certain government bonds issued after August 15, 1986.

"(a) Exception for construction or binding agreements. —

"(1) In general. — The amendments made by section 1301 shall not apply to bonds (other than a refunding bond) with respect to a facility—

"(A)(i) the original use of which commences with the taxpayer, and the construction, reconstruction, or rehabilitation of which began before September 26, 1985, and was completed on or after such date,

"(ii) the original use of which begins with the taxpayer and with respect to which a binding contract to incur significant expenditures for construction, reconstruction, or rehabilitation was entered into before September 26, 1985, and some of such expenditures are incurred on or after such date, or

"(iii) acquired on or after September 26, 1985, pursuant to a binding contract entered into before such date, and

"(B) described in an inducement resolution or other comparable preliminary approval adopted by an issuing authority (or by a voter referendum) before September 26, 1985.

"(2) Significant expenditures. — For purposes of paragraph (1)(A), the term 'significant expenditures' means expenditures greater than 10 percent of the reasonably anticipated cost of the construction, reconstruction, or rehabilitation of the facility involved.

"(b) Certain amendments to apply to bonds under subsection (a) transitional rule.

"(1) In general. — In the case of a bond issued after August 15, 1986, and to which subsection (a) of this section applies, the requirements of the following provisions shall be treated as included in section 103 and section 103A (as appropriate) of the 1954 Code:

"(A) The requirement that 95 percent or more of the net proceeds of an issue are to be used for a purpose described in section 103(b)(4) or (5) of such Code in order for section 103(b)(4) or (5) of such Code to apply, including the application of section 142(b)(2) of the 1986 Code (relating to limitation on office space).

"(B) The requirement that 95 percent or more of the net proceeds of an issue are to be used for a purpose described in section 103(b)(6)(A) of the 1954 Code in order for section 103(b)(6)(A) of such Code to apply.

"(C) The requirements of section 143 of the 1986 Code (relating to qualified mortgage bonds and qualified veterans' mortgage bonds) in order for section 103A(b)(2) of the 1954 Code to apply.

"(D) The requirements of section 144(a)(11) of the 1986 Code (relating to limitation on acquisition of depreciable farm property) in order for section 103(b)(6)(A) of the 1954 Code to apply.

"(E) The requirements of section 147(b) of the 1986 Code (relating to maturity may not exceed 120 percent of economic life).

"(F) The requirements of section 147(f) of the 1986 Code (relating to public approval required for private activity bonds).

"(G) The requirements of section 147(g) of the 1986 Code (relating to restriction on issuance costs financed by issue).

"(H) The requirements of section 148 of the 1986 Code (relating to arbitrage).

"(I) The requirements of section 149(e) of the 1986 Code (relating to information reporting).

"(J) The provisions of section 150(b) of the 1986 Code (relating to changes in use).

"(2) Certain requirements apply only to bonds issued after December 31, 1986. — In the case of subparagraphs (F) and (I) of paragraphs (1), paragraph (1) shall be applied by substituting 'December 31, 1986' for 'August 15, 1986'.

"(3) Application of volume cap. — Except as provided in section 1315, any bond to which this subsection applies shall be treated as a private activity bond for purposes of section 146 of the 1986 Code if such bond would have been taken into account under section 103(n) or 103A(g) of the 1954 Code (determined without regard to any carryforward election) were such bond issued before August 16, 1986.

"(4) Application of provisions. — For purposes of applying the requirements referred to in any subparagraph of paragraph (1) or of subsection (a)(3) or (b)(3) of section 1313 to any bond, such bond shall be treated as described in the subparagraph of section 141(d)(1) of the 1986 Code to which the use of the proceeds of such bond most closely relates.

"(c) Special rules for certain government bonds issued after August 15, 1986. —

"(1) In general. — In the case of any bond described in paragraph (2)—

"(A) section 1311(a) and (c) and subsection (b) of this section shall be applied by substituting 'August 31, 1986' for 'August 15, 1986' each place it appears,

"(B) subsection (b)(1) shall be applied without regard to subparagraphs (F), (G), and (J), and

"(C) such bond shall not be treated as a private activity bond for purposes of applying the requirements referred to in subparagraphs (H) and (I) of subsection (b)(1).

"(2) Bond described. — A bond is described in this paragraph if such bond is not—

"(A) an industrial development bond, as defined in section 103(b)(2) of the 1954 Code but determined—

"(i) by inserting 'directly or indirectly' after 'is' in the material preceding clause (i) of subparagraph (B) thereof, and

"(ii) without regard to subparagraph (B) of section 103(b)(3) of such Code,

"(B) a mortgage subsidy bond (as defined in section 103A(b)(1) of such Code, without regard to any exception from such definition), or

"(C) a private loan bond (as defined in section 103(o)(2)(A) of such Code, without regard to any exception from such definition other than section 103(o)(2)(C) of such Code).

"(d) Election Out. — This section shall not apply to any issue with respect to which the issuer elects not to have this section apply.

"Sec. 1313. Transitional rules relating to refundings.

"(a) Certain current refundings. —

"(1) In general. — Except as provided in paragraph (3), the amendments made by section 1301 shall not apply to any bond the proceeds of which are used exclusively to refund (other than to advance refund) a qualified bond (or a bond which is part of a series of refundings of a qualified bond) if—

"(A) the amount of the refunding bond does not exceed the outstanding amount of the refunded bond, and

"(B)(i) the average maturity of the issue of which the refunding bond is a part does not exceed 120 percent of the average reasonably expected economic life of the facilities being financed with the net proceeds of such issue (determined under section 147(b) of the 1986 Code), or

"(ii) the refunding bond has a maturity date not later than the date which is 17 years after the date on which the qualified bond was issued.

In the case of a qualified bond which was (when issued) a qualified mortgage bond or a qualified veterans' mortgage bond, subparagraph (B)(i) shall not apply and subparagraph (B)(ii) shall be applied by substituting '32 years' for '17 years'.

"(2) Qualified bond. — For purposes of paragraph (1), the term 'qualified bond' means any bond (other than a refunding bond)—

"(A) issued before August 16, 1986, or

"(B) issued after August 15, 1986, if section 1312(a) applies to such bond.

"(3) Certain amendments to apply. — The following provisions of the 1986 Code shall be treated as included in section 103 and section 103A (as appropriate) of the 1954 Code and shall apply to refunding bonds described in paragraph (1):

"(A) The requirements of section 147(f) (relating to public approval required for private activity bonds) but only if the maturity date of the refunding bond is later than the maturity date of the refunded bond.

"(B) The requirements of section 147(g) (relating to restriction on issuance costs financed by issue).

"(C) The requirements of sections 143(g) and 148 (relating to arbitrage).

"(D) The requirements of section 149(e) (relating to information reporting).

"(E) The provisions of section 150(b) (relating to changes in use).

Subparagraphs (A) and (D) shall apply only if the refunding bond is issued after December 31, 1986. In the case of a refunding bond described in paragraph (1) with respect to a qualified bond described in paragraph (2)(B), the requirements of section 1312(b)(1) which applied to such qualified bond shall be treated as specified in this paragraph with respect to such refunding bond.

"(4) Special rules for certain government bonds issued after August 15, 1986. — In the case of any bond described in section 1312(c)(2)—

"(A) paragraph (2) of this subsection shall be applied by substituting 'August 31, 1986' for 'August 15, 1986', and by substituting 'September 1, 1986' for 'August 16, 1986,'

"(B) paragraph (3) shall be applied without regard to subparagraphs (A), (B), and (E), and

"(C) such bond shall not be treated as a private activity bond for purposes of applying the requirements referred to in subparagraphs (C) and (D) of paragraph (3).

"(b) Certain advance refundings. —

"(1) In general. — Except as provided in paragraph (3), the amendments made by section 1301 shall not apply to any bond the proceeds of which are used exclusively to advance refund a bond if—

"(A) the refunded bond is described in paragraph (2), and

"(B) the requirements of subsection (a)(1)(B) are met.

"(2) Non-IDB's, etc. — A bond is described in this paragraph if such bond is not described in subsection (b)(2) or (o)(2)(A) of section 103 of the 1954 Code and was issued (or was issued to refund a bond issued) before August 16, 1986. For purposes of the preceding sentence, the determination of whether a bond is described in such subsection (o)(2)(A) shall be made without regard to any exception other than section 103(o)(2)(C) of such Code.

"(3) Certain amendments to apply. — The following provisions of the 1986 Code shall be treated as included in section 103 and section 103A (as appropriate) of the 1954 Code and shall apply to refunding bonds described in paragraph (1):

"(A) The requirements of section 147(f) (relating to public approval required for private activity bonds).

"(B) The requirements of section 147(g) (relating to restriction on issuance costs financed by issue).

"(C) The requirements of section 148 (relating to arbitrage), except that section 148(d)(3) shall not apply to proceeds of such bonds to be used to discharge the refunded bonds.

"(D) The requirements of paragraphs (3) and (4) of section 149(d) (relating to advance refundings).

"(E) The requirements of section 149(e) (relating to information reporting).

"(F) The provisions of section 150(b) (relating to changes in use).

Subparagraphs (A) and (E) shall apply only if the refunding bond is issued after December 31, 1986.

"(G) Except as provided in the last sentence of subsection (c)(2) of this section, the requirements of section 145(b) (relating to $150,000,000 limitation on bonds other than hospital bonds).

"(4) Special rule for certain government bonds issued after August 15, 1986. — In the case of any bond described in section 1312(c)(2)—

"(A) paragraph (2) of this subsection shall be applied by substituting 'September 1, 1986' for 'August 16, 1986',

"(B) paragraph (3) shall be applied without regard to subparagraphs (A), (B), and (F), and

"(C) such bond shall not be treated as a private activity bond for purposes of applying the requirements referred to in subparagraphs (C) and (E).

"(5) Certain refunding bonds subject to volume cap. — Any refunding bond described in paragraph (1) the proceeds of which are used to refund a bond issued as part of an issue 5 percent or more of the net proceeds of which are or will be used to provide an output facility (within the meaning of section 141(b)(4) of the 1986 Code) shall be treated as a private activity bond for purposes of section 146 of the 1986 Code (to the extent of the nongovernmental use of such issue, under rules similar to the rules of section 146(m)(2) of such Code). For purposes of the preceding sentence, use by a 501(c)(3) organization with respect to its activities which do not constitute unrelated trades or businesses (determined by applying section 513(a) of the 1986 Code) shall not be taken into account.

"(c) Treatment of certain refundings of certain IDB's and 501(c)(3) bonds. —

"(1) $40,000,000 limit for certain small issue bonds. — Paragraph (10) of section 144(a) of the 1986 Code shall not apply to any bond (or series of bonds) the proceeds of which are used exclusively to refund a tax-exempt bond to which such paragraph and the corresponding provision of prior law did not apply if—

"(A) the average maturity date of the issue of which the refunding bond is a part is not later than the average maturity date of the bonds to be refunded by such issue,

"(B) the amount of the refunding bond does not exceed the outstanding amount of the refunded bond, and

"(C) the net proceeds of the refunding bond are used to redeem the refunded bond not later than 90 days after the date of the issuance of the refunding bond. For purposes of subparagraph (A), average maturity shall be determined in accordance with section 147(b)(2)(A) of the 1986 Code.

"(2) $150,000,000 limitation for certain 501(c)(3) bonds. — Subsection (b) of section 145 of the 1986 Code (relating to $150,000,000 limitation for nonhospital bonds) shall not apply to any bond (or series of bonds) the proceeds of which are used exclusively to refund a tax-exempt bond to which such subsection did not apply if—

"(A)(i) the average maturity of the issue of which the refunding bond is a part does not exceed 120 percent of the average reasonably expected economic life of the facilities being financed with the net proceeds of such issue (determined under section 147(b) of the 1986 Code), or

"(ii) the refunding bond has a maturity date not later than the later of the date which is 17 years after the date on which the qualified bond (as defined in subsection (a)(2)) was issued, and

"(B) the requirements of subparagraphs (B) and (C) of paragraph (1) are met with respect to the refunding bond.

Subsection (b) of section 145 of the 1986 Code shall not apply to the 1st advance refunding after March 14, 1986, of a bond issued before January 1, 1986.

"(3) Application to later issues. — Any bond to which section 144(a)(10) or 145(b) of the 1986 Code does not apply by reason of this section shall be taken into account in determining whether such section applies to any later issue.

"(d) Mortgage and student loan targeting rules to apply to loans made more than 3 years after the date of the original issue: Subsections (a)(3) and (b)(3) shall be treated as including the requirements of subsections (e) and (f) of section 143 and paragraphs (3) and (4) of section 144(b) of the 1986 Code with respect to bonds the proceeds of which are used to finance loans made more than 3 years after the date of the issuance of the original bond.

"Sec. 1314. Special rules which override other rules in this subtitle. —

"(a) Arbitrage restriction on investments in annuities. —

"In the case of a bond issued after September 25, 1985, section 103(c) of the 1954 Code shall be applied by treating the reference to securities in paragraph (2) thereof as including a reference to an annuity contract. The preceding sentence shall not apply to the first advance refunding after September 25, 1985, of a bond issued before September 26, 1985.

"(b) Temporary period for advance refundings. —

"In the case of a bond issued after December 31, 1985, to advance refund a bond, the initial temporary period under section 103(c) of the 1954 Code with respect to the proceeds of the refunding bond shall end not later than 30 days after the date of issue of the refunding bond.

"(c) Determination of yield. —

"In the case of a bond issued after December 31, 1985, for purposes of section 103(c) of the 1954 Code, the yield on an issue shall be determined on the basis of the issue price (within the meaning of sections 1273 and 1274 of the 1986 Code).

"(d) Arbitrage rebate requirement. —

"(1) In general. — Except as otherwise provided in this subsection, in the case of a bond issued after December 31, 1985, section 103 of the 1954 Code shall be treated as including the requirements of section 148(f) of the 1986 Code in order for section 103(a) of the 1954 Code to apply.

"(2) Government bonds. — In the case of a bond described in section 1312(c)(2) (and not described in paragraph (3) of this subsection), paragraph (1) shall be applied by substituting 'August 31, 1986' for 'December 31, 1985'.

"(3) Certain pools. —

"(A) In general. — In the case of a bond described in section 1312(c)(2) and issued as part of an issue described in subparagraph (B), (C), (D), or (E), paragraph (1) shall be applied by substituting '3 p.m. E.D.T., July 17, 1986' for 'December 31, 1985'. Such a bond shall not be treated as a private activity bond for purposes of applying section 148(f) of the 1986 Code.

"(B) Loans to unrelated governmental units. — An issue is described in this subparagraph if any portion of the proceeds of the issue is to be used to make or finance loans to any governmental unit other than any governmental unit which is subordinate to the issuer and the jurisdiction of which is within—

"(i) the jurisdiction of the issuer, or

"(ii) the jurisdiction of the governmental unit on behalf of which such issuer issued the issue.

"(C) Less than 75 percent of projects identified. — An issue is described in this subparagraph if less than 75 percent of the proceeds of the issue is to be used to make or finance loans to initial borrowers to finance projects identified (with specificity) by the issuer, on or before the date of issuance of the issue, as projects to be financed with the proceeds of the issue.

"(D) Less than 25 percent of funds committed to be borrowed.—An issue is described in this subparagraph if, on or before the date of issuance of the issue, commitments have not been entered into by initial borrowers to borrow at least 25 percent of the proceeds of the issue.

"(E) Certain long maturity issues.—An issue is described in this subparagraph if—

"(i) the maturity date of any bond issued as part of such issue exceeds 30 years, and

"(ii) any principal payment on any loan made or financed by the proceeds of the issue is to be used to make or finance additional loans.

"(F) Special rules.—

"(i) Exception from subparagraphs (C) and (D) where similar pools issued by issuer.—An issue shall not be treated as described in subparagraph (C) or (D) with respect to any issue to make or finance loans to governmental units if—

"(I) the issuer, before 1986, issued 1 or more similar issues to make or finance loans to governmental units, and

"(II) the aggregate face amount of such issues issued during 1986 does not exceed 250 percent of the average of the annual aggregate face amounts of such similar issues issued during 1983, 1984, or 1985.

"(ii) Determination of issuance.—For purposes of subparagraph (A), an issue shall not be treated as issued until—

"(I) the bonds issued as part of such issue are offered to the public (pursuant to final offering materials), and

"(II) at least 25 percent of such bonds is sold to the public.

For purposes of the preceding sentence, the sale of a bond to a securities firm, broker, or other person acting in the capacity of an underwriter or wholesaler shall not be treated as a sale to the public.

"(e) Information reporting.—

"In the case of a bond issued after December 31, 1986, nothing in section 103(a) of the 1986 Code or any other provision of law shall be construed to provide an exemption from Federal income tax for interest on any bond issued unless such bond satisfies the requirements of section 149(e) of the 1986 Code. A bond described in section 1312(c)(2) shall not be treated as a private activity bond for purposes of applying such requirements.

"(f) Abusive transaction limitation on advance refundings to apply.—

"In the case of a bond issued after August 31, 1986, nothing in section 103(a) of the 1986 Code or any other provision of law shall be construed to provide an exemption from Federal income tax for interest on any bond if the issue of which such bond is a part is described in paragraph (4) of section 149(d) of the 1986 Code (relating to abusive transactions).

"(g) Termination of mortgage bond policy statement requirement.—

"Paragraph (5) of section 103A(j) of the 1954 Code (relating to policy statement) shall not apply to any bond issued after August 15, 1986, and shall not apply to nonissued bond amounts elected under section 25 of the 1986 Code after such date.

"(h) Arbitrage restriction on investments in investment-type property.—

"In the case of a bond issued before August 16, 1986 (September 1, 1986 in the case of a bond described in section 1312(c)(2)), section 103(c) of the 1954 Code shall be applied by treating the reference to securities in paragraph (2) thereof as including a reference to investment-type property but only for purposes of determining whether any bond issued after October 16, 1987, to advance refund such bond (or a bond which is part of a series of refundings of such bond) is an arbitrage bond (within the meaning of section 148(a) of the 1986 Code).

"(i) Section to override other rules.—

"Except as otherwise expressly provided by reference to a provision to which a subsection of this section applies, nothing in any other section of this subtitle shall be construed as exempting any bond from the application of such provision.

"Sec. 1315. Transitional rules relating to volume cap.

"(a) In general.—

"Except as otherwise provided in this section, section 146(f) of the 1986 Code shall not apply with respect to an issuing authority's volume cap under section 103(n) of the 1954 Code, and no carryforward under section 103(n) shall be recognized for bonds issued after August 15, 1986.

"(b) Certain bonds for carryforward projects outside of volume cap.—

"Bonds issued pursuant to an election under section 103(n)(10) of the 1954 Code (relating to elective carryforward of unused limitation for specified project) made before November 1, 1985, shall not be taken into account under section 146 of the 1986 Code if the carryforward project is a facility to which the amendments made by section 1301 do not apply by reason of section 1312(a) of this Act.

"(c) Volume cap not to apply with respect to certain facilities and purposes.—

"Section 146 of the 1986 Code shall not apply to any bond issued with respect to any facility or purpose described in a paragraph of subsection (d) if—

"(1) such bond would not have been taken into account under section 103(n) of the 1954 Code for calendar year 1986 (determined without regard to any carryforward election) were such bond issued before August 15, 1986, or

"(2) such bond would not have been taken into account under section 103(n) of the 1954 Code for calendar year 1986 (determined with regard to any carryforward election made before January 1, 1986) were such bond issued before August 15, 1986.

The preceding sentence shall not apply to the extent section 1313(b)(5) treats any bond as a private activity bond for purposes of section 146 of the 1986 Code.

"(d) Facilities and purposes described.—

"(1) A facility is described in this paragraph if the amendments made by section 201 of this Act (relating to depreciation) do not apply to such facility by reason of section 204(a)(8) of this Act (or, in the case of a facility which is governmentally owned, would not apply to such facility were it owned by a nongovernmental person).

"(2) A facility or purpose is described in this paragraph if the facility or purpose is described in a paragraph of section 1317.

"(3) A facility is described in this paragraph if the facility—

"(A) serves Los Osos, California, and

"(B) would be described in paragraph (1) were it a solid waste disposal facility. The aggregate face amount of bonds to which this paragraph applies shall not exceed $35,000,000.

"(4) A facility is described in this paragraph if it is a sewage disposal facility with respect to which—

"(A) on September 13, 1985, the State public facilities authority took official action authorizing the issuance of bonds for such facility, and

"(B) on December 30, 1985, there was an executive order of the State Governor granting allocation of the State ceiling under section 103(n) of the 1954 Code in the amount of $250,000,000 to the Industrial Development Board of the Parish of East Baton Rouge, Louisiana.

The aggregate face amount of bonds to which this paragraph applies shall not exceed $98,500,000.

"(5) A facility is described in this paragraph if—

"(A) such facility is a solid waste disposal facility in Charleston, South Carolina, and

"(B) a State political subdivision took formal action on April 1, 1980, to commit development funds for such facility.

For purposes of determining whether a bond issued as part of an issue for a facility described in the preceding sentence is an exempt facility bond for purposes of part IV of subchapter B of chapter 1 of the 1986 Code, '90 percent' shall be substituted for '95 percent' in section 142(a) of the 1986 Code.

The aggregate face amount of bonds to which this paragraph applies shall not exceed $75,000,000.

"(6) A facility is described in this paragraph if—

"(A) such facility is a wastewater treatment facility for which site preparation commenced before September 1985, and

"(B) a parish council approved a service agreement with respect to such facility on December 4, 1985.

The aggregate face amount of bonds to which this paragraph applies shall not exceed $120,000,000.

"(e) Treatment of redevelopment bonds.—

"Any bond to which section 1317(6) of this Act applies shall be treated for purposes of this section as described in subsection (c)(1). The preceding sentence shall not apply to any bond which (if issued on August 15, 1986) would have been an industrial development bond (as defined in section 103(b)(2) of the 1954 Code).

"Sec. 1316. Provisions relating to certain established state programs.

"(a) Certain loans to veterans for the purchase of land.—

"(1) In general.—A bond described in paragraph (2) shall be treated as described in section 141(d)(1) of the 1986 Code and as having a carryforward purpose described in section 146(f)(5) of such Code, but subsections (a), (b), (c), and (d) of section 147 of such Code shall not apply to such bond.

"(2) Bond described.—A bond is described in this paragraph if—

"(A) such bond is a private activity bond solely by reason of section 141(c) of such Code, and

"(B) such bond is issued as part of an issue 95 percent or more of the net proceeds of which are to be used to carry out a program established under State law to provide loans to veterans for the purchase of land and which has been in effect in substantially the same form during the 30-year period ending on July 18, 1984, but only if such proceeds are used to make loans or to fund similar obligations—

"(i) in the same manner in which,

"(ii) in the same (or lesser) amount or multiple of acres per participant, and

"(iii) for the same purposes for which, such program was operated on March 15, 1984.

"(b) Renewable energy property.—

"(1) In general.—A bond described in paragraph (2) shall be treated as described in section 141(d)(1) of the 1986 Code and as having a carryforward purpose described in section 146(f)(5) of such Code.

"(2) Bond described.—A bond is described in this paragraph if paragraph (1) of section 103(b) of the 1954 Code would not (without regard to the amendments made by this title) have applied to such bond by reason of section 243 of the Crude Oil Windfall Profit Tax Act of 1980 if—

"(A) such section 243 were applied by substituting '95 percent or more of the net proceeds' for 'substantially all of the proceeds' in subsection (a)(1) thereof, and

"(B) subparagraph (E) of subsection (a)(1) thereof referred to section 149(b) of the 1986 Code.

"(c) Certain state programs.—

"(1) In general.—A bond described in paragraph (2) shall be treated as described in section 141(d)(1) of the 1986 Code and as having a carryforward purpose described in section 146(f)(5) of such Code.

"(2) Bond described.—A bond is described in this paragraph if such bond is issued as part of an issue 95 percent or more of the net proceeds of which are to be used to carry out a program established under sections 280A, 280B, and 280C of the Iowa Code, but only if—

"(A) such program has been in effect in substantially the same form since July 1, 1983, and

"(B) such proceeds are to be used to make loans or fund similar obligations for the same purposes as permitted under such program on July 1, 1986.

"(3) $100,000,000 limitation. — The aggregate face amount of outstanding bonds to which this subsection applies shall not exceed $100,000,000.

"(4) Application of section 147(b). — A bond to which this subsection applies (other than a refunding bond) shall be treated as meeting the requirements of section 147(b) of the 1986 Code if the average maturity (determined in accordance with section 147(b)(2)(A) of such Code) of the issue of which such bond is a part does not exceed 20 years. A bond issued to refund (or which is part of a series of bonds issued to refund) a bond described in the preceding sentence shall be treated as meeting the requirements of such section if the refunding bond has a maturity date not later than the date which is 20 years after the date on which the original bond was issued."

"(d) Use by certain federal instrumentalities treated as use by governmental units.

"Use by an instrumentality of the United States shall be treated as use by a State or local governmental unit for purposes of section 103, and part IV of subchapter B of chapter 1, of the 1986 Code with respect to a program approved by Congress before August 3, 1972, but only if —

"(1) a portion of such program has been financed by bonds issued before such date, to which section 103(a) of the 1954 Code applied pursuant to a ruling issued by the Commissioner of the Internal Revenue Service, and

"(2) construction of 1 or more facilities comprising a part of such program commenced before such date.

"(e) Refunding permitted of certain bonds invested in federally insured deposits.

"(1) In general. — Section 149(b)(2)(B)(ii) of the 1986 Code (and section 103(h)(2)(B)(ii) of the 1954 Code) shall not apply to any bond issued to refund a bond —

"(A) which, when issued, would have been treated as federally guaranteed by reason of being described in clause (ii) of section 103(h)(2)(B) of the 1954 Code if such section had applied to such bond, and

"(B)(i) which was issued before April 15, 1983, or

"(ii) to which such clause did not apply by reason of the except clause in section 631(c)(2) of the Tax Reform Act of 1984.

Section 147(c) of the 1986 Code (and section 103(b)(16) of the 1954 Code) shall not apply to any refunding bond permitted under the preceding sentence if section 103(b)(16) of the 1954 Code did not apply to the refunded bond when issued.

"(2) Requirements. — A refunding bond meets the requirements of this paragraph if —

"(A) the refunding bond has a maturity date not later than the maturity date of the refunded bond,

"(B) the amount of the refunding bond does not exceed the outstanding amount of the refunded bond,

"(C) the weighted average interest rate on the refunding bond is lower than the weighted average interest rate on the refunded bond, and

"(D) the net proceeds of the refunding bond are used to redeem the refunded bond not later than 90 days after the date of the issuance of the refunding bond.

"(f) Certain hydroelectric generating property. —

"(1) In general. — A bond described in paragraph (2) shall be treated as described in section 141(d)(1) of the 1986 Code and as having a carryforward purpose described in section 146(f)(5) of such Code.

"(2) Description. — A bond is described in this paragraph if such bond is issued as part of an issue 95 percent or more of the net proceeds of which are to be used to provide a facility described in section 103(b)(4)(H) of the 1954 Code determined —

"(A) by substituting 'an application for a license' for 'an application' in section 103(b)(8)(E)(ii) of the 1954 Code, and

"(B) by applying the requirements of section 142(b)(2) of the 1986 Code.

"(g) Treatment of bonds subject to transitional rules under tax reform act of 1984.

"(1) Subsections (d)(3) and (f) of section 148 of the 1986 Code shall not apply to any bond described in section 624(c)(2) of the Tax Reform Act of 1984.

"(2)(A) There shall not be taken into account under section 146 of the 1986 Code any bond issued to provide a facility described in the paragraph (3) of section 631(a) of the Tax Reform Act of 1984 relating to exception for certain bonds for a convention center and resource recovery project.

"(B) If a bond issued as part of an issue substantially all of the proceeds of which are used to provide the convention center to which such paragraph (3) applies, such bond shall be treated as an exempt facility bond as defined in section 142(a) of the 1986 Code.

"(C) If a bond which is issued as part of an issue substantially all of the proceeds of which are used to provide the resource recovery project to which such paragraph (3) applies, such bond shall be treated as an exempt facility bond as defined in section 142(a) of the 1986 Code and section 149(b) of such Code shall not apply.

"(3) The amendments made by section 1301 shall not apply to bonds issued to finance any property described in section 631(d)(4) of the Tax Reform Act of 1984.

"(4) The amendments made by section 1301 shall not apply to —

"(A) any bond issued to finance property described in section 631(d)(5) of the Tax Reform Act of 1984,

"(B) any bond described in paragraph (2), (3), (4), (5), (6), or (7) of section 632(a), or section 632(b), of such Act, and

"(C) any bond to which section 632(g)(2) of such Act applies.

In the case of bonds to which this paragraph applies, the requirements of sections 148 and 149(d) shall be treated as included in section 103 of the 1954 Code and shall apply to such bonds.

"(5) The preceding provisions of this subsection shall not apply to any bond issued after December 31, 1988.

"(6) The amendments made by section 1301 (and the provisions of section 1314) shall not apply to any bond issued to finance property described in section 216(b)(3) of the Tax Equity and Fiscal Responsibility Act of 1982.

"(7) In the case of a bond described in section 632(d) of the Tax Reform Act of 1984 —

"(A) section 141 of the 1986 Code shall be applied without regard to subsection (a)(2) and paragraphs (4) and (5) of subsection (b),

"(B) paragraphs (1) and (2) of section 141(b) of the 1986 Code shall be applied by substituting '25 percent' for '10 percent' each place it appears, and

"(C) section 149(b) of the 1986 Code shall not apply.

This paragraph shall not apply to any bond issued after December 31, 1990.

"(8)(A) The amendments made by section 1301 shall not apply to any bond to which section 629(a)(1) of the Tax Reform Act of 1984 applies, but such bond shall be treated as a private activity bond for purposes of section 146 of the 1986 Code and as having a carryforward purpose described in section 146(f)(5) of such Code.

"(B) Section 629 [reproduced below] of the Tax Reform Act of 1984 is amended —

"(i) in subsection (c)(2), by striking out '$625,000,000' and inserting in lieu thereof '$911,000,000',

"(ii) in subsection (c)(3), by adding at the end thereof the following new subparagraphs:

"(D) Improvements to existing generating facilities.

"(E) Transmission lines.

"(F) Electric generating facilities.', and

"(iii) in subsection (a), by adding at the end thereof the following new sentence: 'The preceding sentence shall be applied by inserting 'and a rural electric cooperative utility' after 'regulated public utility' but only if not more than 1 percent of the load of the public power authority is sold to such rural electric cooperative utility.'

"(h) Certain pollution bonds. —

"Any bond which is treated as described in section 103(b)(4)(F) of the 1954 Code by reason of section 13209 of the Consolidated Omnibus Budget Reconciliation Act of 1985 shall be treated as an exempt facility bond for purposes of part IV of subchapter B of chapter 1 of the 1986 Code, and section 147(d) of the 1986 Code shall not apply to such bond.

"(i) Transition rule for aggregate limit per taxpayer. —

"For purposes of section 144(a)(10) of the 1986 Code, tax increment bonds described in section 1869(c)(3) of this Act which are issued before August 16, 1986, shall not be taken into account under subparagraph (B)(ii) thereof.

"(j) Extension of advance refunding exception for qualified public facility. —

"Paragraph (4) of section 631(c) [reproduced below] of the Tax Reform Act of 1984 is amended —

"(1) by striking out 'or the Dade County, Florida, airport' in the last sentence, and

"(2) by adding at the end thereof the following new sentence: 'In the case of refunding obligations not to exceed $100,000,000 issued after October 21, 1986, by Dade County, Florida, for the purpose of advance refunding its Aviation Revenue Bonds (Series J), the first sentence of this paragraph shall be applied by substituting 'the date which is 1 year after the date of the enactment of the Technical and Miscellaneous Revenue Act of 1988' for 'December 31, 1984' and the amendments made by section 1301 of the Tax Reform Act of 1986 shall not apply.'

"(9) Paragraph (2) of section 1316(k) of the Reform Act is amended by striking out '$55,000,000 must be redeemed no later than November 1, 1987' and inserting in lieu thereof 'no more than $55,000,000 shall be outstanding later than November 1, 1987.

"(k) Expansion of exception for river place project. —

"Section 1104 of the Mortgage Subsidy Bond Tax Act of 1980 [reproduced in note following Code Sec. 103A], as added by the Tax Reform Act of 1984, is amended —

"(1) by striking out 'December 31, 1984,' in subsection (p) and inserting in lieu thereof 'December 31, 1984 (other than obligations described in subsection (r)(1)),' and

"(2) by striking out '$55,000,000,' in subsection (r)(1)(B) and inserting in lieu thereof '$110,000,000 of which no more than $55,000,000 shall be outstanding later than November 1, 1987.

"Sec. 1317. Transitional rules for specific facilities.

"(1) Docks and wharves. — A bond issued as part of an issue 95 percent or more of the net proceeds of which are to be used to provide any dock or wharf (within the meaning of section 103(b)(4)(D) of the 1954 Code) shall be treated as an exempt facility bond (for a facility described in section 142(a)(2) of the 1986 Code) for purposes of part IV of subchapter B of chapter 1 of the 1986 Code if such dock or wharf is described in any of the following subparagraphs:

"(A) A dock or wharf is described in this subparagraph if —

"(i) the issue to finance such dock or wharf was approved by official city action on September 3, 1985, and by voters on November 5, 1985, and

"(ii) such dock or wharf is for a slack water harbor with respect to which a Corps of Engineers grant of approximately $2,000,000 has been made under section 107 of the Rivers and Harbors Act.

The aggregate face amount of bonds to which this subparagraph applies shall not exceed $2,500,000.

"(B) A dock or wharf is described in this subparagraph if —

"(i) inducement resolutions were adopted on May 23, 1985, September 18, 1985, and September 24, 1985, for the issuance of the bonds to finance such dock or wharf,

"(ii) a harbor dredging contract with respect thereto was entered into on August 2, 1985, or

"(iii) a construction management and joint venture agreement with respect thereto was entered into on October 1, 1984.

The aggregate face amount of bonds to which this subparagraph applies shall not exceed $625,000,000.

"(C) A facility is described in this subparagraph if—

"(i) the legislature first authorized on June 29, 1981, the State agency issuing the bond to issue at least $30,000,000 of bonds,

"(ii) the developer of the facility was selected on April 26, 1985, and

"(iii) an inducement resolution for the issuance of such issue was adopted on October 9, 1985.

The aggregate face amount of bonds to which this subparagraph applies shall not exceed $200,000,000.

"(D) A facility is described in this subparagraph if—

"(i) an inducement resolution was adopted on October 17, 1985, for such issue, and

"(ii) the city council for the city in which the facility is to be located approved on July 30, 1985, an application for an urban development action grant with respect to such facility.

The aggregate face amount of bonds to which this subparagraph applies shall not exceed $36,500,000. A facility shall be treated as described in this subparagraph if it would be so described if '90 percent' were substituted for '95 percent' in the material preceding subparagraph (A) of this paragraph.

"(2) Pollution control facilities.—A bond issued as part of an issue 95 percent or more of the net proceeds of which are to be used to provide air or water pollution control facilities (within the meaning of section 103(b)(4)(F) of the 1954 Code) shall be treated as an exempt facility bond for purposes of part IV of subchapter B of chapter 1 of the 1986 Code if such facility is described in any of the following subparagraphs:

"(A) A facility is described in this subparagraph if—

"(i) inducement resolutions with respect to such facility were adopted on September 23, 1974, and on April 5, 1985,

"(ii) a bond resolution for such facility was adopted on September 6, 1985, and

"(iii) the issuance of the bonds to finance such facility was delayed by action of the Securities and Exchange Commission (file number 70-7127).

The aggregate face amount of bonds to which this subparagraph applies shall not exceed $120,000,000.

"(B) A facility is described in this subparagraph if—

"(i) there was an inducement resolution for such facility on November 19, 1985, and

"(ii) design and engineering studies for such facility were completed in March of 1985.

The aggregate face amount of bonds to which this subparagraph applies shall not exceed $25,000,000.

"(C) A facility is described in this subparagraph if—

"(i) a resolution was adopted by the county board of supervisors pertaining to an issuance of bonds with respect to such facility on April 10, 1974, and

"(ii) such facility was placed in service on June 12, 1985.

The aggregate face amount of bonds to which this subparagraph applies shall not exceed $90,000,000. For purposes of this subparagraph, a pollution control facility includes a sewage or solid waste disposal facility (within the meaning of section 103(b)(4)(E) of the 1954 Code).

"(D) A facility is described in this subparagraph if—

"(i) the issuance of the bonds for such facility was approved by a State agency on August 22, 1979, and

"(ii) the authority to issue such bonds was scheduled to expire (under terms of the State approval) on August 22, 1989.

The aggregate face amount of bonds to which this subparagraph applies shall not exceed $198,000,000.

"(E) A facility is described in this subparagraph if—

"(i) such facility is 1 of 4 such facilities in 4 States with respect to which the Ball Corporation transmitted a letter of intent to purchase such facilities on February 26, 1986, and

"(ii) inducement resolutions were issued on December 30, 1985, January 15, 1986, January 22, 1986, and March 17, 1986 with respect to bond issuance in the 4 respective States.

The aggregate face amount of bonds to which this subparagraph applies shall not exceed $6,000,000.

"(F) A facility is described in this subparagraph if—

"(i) inducement resolutions for bonds with respect to such facility were adopted on September 27, 1977, May 27, 1980, and October 8, 1981, and

"(ii) such facility is located at a geothermal power complex owned and operated by a single investor-owned utility.

For purposes of this subparagraph and section 103 of the 1986 Code, all hydrogen sulfide air and water pollution control equipment, together with functionally related and subordinate equipment and structures, located or to be located at such power complex shall be treated as a single pollution control facility. The aggregate face amount of bonds to which this subparagraph applies shall not exceed $600,000,000.

"(G) A facility is described in this subparagraph if—

"(i) such facility is an air pollution control facility approved by a State bureau of pollution control on July 10, 1986, and by a State board of economic development on July 17, 1986, and

"(ii) on August 15, 1986, the State bond attorney gave notice to the clerk to initiate validation proceedings with respect to such issue and on August 28, 1986, the validation decree was entered.

The aggregate face amount of bonds to which this subparagraph applies shall not exceed $900,000.

"(I) A facility is described in this subparagraph if—

"(i) a private company met with a State air control board on November 14, 1985, to propose construction of a sulften unit, and

"(ii) the sulften unit is being constructed under a letter of intent to construct which was signed on April 8, 1986.

The aggregate face amount of bonds to which this subparagraph applies shall not exceed $11,000,000.

"(J) A facility is described in this subparagraph if it is part of a 250 megawatt coal-fired electric plant in northeastern Nevada on which the Sierra Pacific Power Company, a subsidiary of Sierra Pacific Resources, began in 1980 work to finance, construct, and operate. The aggregate face amount of bonds to which this subparagraph applies shall not exceed $200,000,000.

"(K) A facility is described in this subparagraph if—

"(i) there was an inducement resolution adopted by a State industrial development authority on January 14, 1976, and

"(ii) such facility is named in a resolution of such authority relating to carryforward of the State's unused 1985 private activity bond limit passed by such industrial development authority on December 18, 1985.

This subparagraph shall apply only to obligations issued at the request of the party pursuant to whose request the January 14, 1976, inducement was given. The aggregate face amount of bonds to which this subparagraph applies shall not exceed $75,000,000.

"(L) A facility is described in this subparagraph if a city council passed an ordinance (ordinance number 4626) agreeing to issue bonds for such project, December 16, 1985. The aggregate face amount of obligations to which this subparagraph applies shall not exceed $45,000,000.

"(3) Sports facilities.—A bond issued as part of an issue 95 percent or more of the net proceeds of which are to be used to provide sports facilities (within the meaning of section 103(b)(4)(B) of the 1954 Code) shall be treated as an exempt facility bond for purposes of part IV of subchapter B of chapter 1 of the 1986 Code if such facilities are described in any of the following subparagraphs:

"(A) A facility is described in this subparagraph if it is a stadium—

"(i) which was the subject of a city ordinance passed on September 23, 1985,

"(ii) for which a loan of approximately $4,000,000 for land acquisition was approved on October 28, 1985, by the State Controlling Board, and

"(iii) a stadium operating corporation with respect to which was incorporated on March 20, 1985.

The aggregate face amount of bonds to which this subparagraph applies shall not exceed $200,000,000.

"(B) A facility is described in this subparagraph if—

"(i) it is a stadium with respect to which a lease agreement for the ground on which the stadium is to be built was entered into between a county and the stadium corporation for such stadium on July 3, 1984,

"(ii) there was a resolution approved on November 14, 1984, by an industrial development authority setting forth the terms under which the bonds to be issued to finance such stadium would be issued, and

"(iii) there was an agreement for consultant and engineering services for such stadium entered into on September 28, 1984.

The aggregate face amount of bonds to which this subparagraph applies shall not exceed $90,000,000.

"(C) A facility is described in this subparagraph if—

"(i) it is one or more stadiums to be used either by an American League baseball team or a National Football League team currently using a stadium in a city having a population in excess of 2,500,000 and described in section 146(d)(3) of the 1986 Code,

"(ii) the bonds to be used to provide financing for one or more such stadiums are issued by a political subdivision or a State agency pursuant to a resolution approving an inducement resolution adopted by a State agency on November 20, 1985, as it may be amended (whether or not the beneficiaries of such issue or issues are the beneficiaries (if any) specified in such inducement resolution and whether or not the number of such stadiums and the locations thereof are as specified in such inducement resolution) or pursuant to P.A. 841470 of the State in which such city is located (and by an agency created thereby), and

"(iii) such stadium or stadiums are located in the city described in (i).

"The aggregate face amount of bonds to which this subparagraph applies shall not exceed $250,000,000. In the case of any carryforward of volume cap for one or more stadiums described in the first sentence of this subparagraph, such carryforward shall be valid with respect to bonds issued for such stadiums notwithstanding any other provision of the 1986 Code or the 1954 Code, and whether or not (i) there is a change in the number of stadiums or the beneficiaries or sites of the stadium or stadiums and (ii) the bonds are issued by either of the state agencies described in the first sentence of this subparagraph.

"(D) A facility is described in this subparagraph if—

"(i) such facility is a stadium or sports arena for Memphis, Tennessee,

"(ii) there was an inducement resolution adopted on November 12, 1985, for the issuance of bonds to expand or renovate an existing stadium and sports arena and/or to construct a new arena, and

"(iii) the city council for such city adopted a resolution on April 19, 1983, to include funds in the capital budget of the city for such facility or facilities.

The aggregate face amount of bonds to which this subparagraph applies shall not exceed $35,000,000.

"(E) A facility is described in this subparagraph if such facility is a baseball stadium located in Bergen, Essex, Union, Middlesex, or Hudson County, New Jersey with respect to which governmental action occurred on November 7, 1985. The aggregate face amount of bonds to which this subparagraph applies shall not exceed $150,000,000.

"(F) A facility is described in this subparagraph if—

"(i) it is a facility with respect to which—

"(I) an inducement resolution dated December 24, 1985, was adopted by the county industrial development authority,

"(II) a public hearing of the county industrial development authority was held on February 6, 1986, regarding such facility, and

"(III) a contract was entered into by the county, dated February 19, 1986, for engineering services for a highway improvement in connection with such project, or

"(ii) it is a domed football stadium adjacent to Cervantes Convention Center in St. Louis, Missouri, with respect to which a proposal to evaluate market demand, financial operations, and economic impact was dated May 9, 1986.

The aggregate face amount of bonds to which this subparagraph applies shall not exceed $175,000,000.

"(G) A project to provide a roof or dome for an existing sports facility is described in this subparagraph if—

"(i) in December 1984 the county sports complex authority filed a carryforward election under section 103(n) of the 1954 Code with respect to such project,

"(ii) in January 1985, the State authorized issuance of $30,000,000 in bonds in the next 3 years for such project, and

"(iii) an 11-member task force was appointed by the county executive in June 1985, to further study the feasibility of the project.

The aggregate face amount of bonds to which this subparagraph applies shall not exceed $30,000,000.

"(H) A sports facility renovation or expansion project is described in this subparagraph if—

"(i) an amendment to the sports team's lease agreement for such facility was entered into on May 23, 1985, and

"(ii) the lease agreement had previously been amended in January 1976, on July 6, 1984, on April 1, 1985, and on May 7, 1985.

The aggregate face amount of bonds to which this subparagraph applies shall not exceed $20,000,000.

"(I) A facility is described in this subparagraph if—

"(i) an appraisal for such facility was completed on March 6, 1985,

"(ii) an inducement resolution was adopted with respect to such facility on June 7, 1985, and

"(iii) a State bond commission granted preliminary approval for such project on September 3, 1985.

The aggregate face amount of bonds to which this subparagraph applies shall not exceed $3,200,000.

"(J) A sports facility renovation or expansion project is described in this subparagraph if—

"(i) such facility is a domed stadium which commenced operations in 1965,

"(ii) such facility has been the subject of an ongoing construction, expansion, or renovation program of planned improvements,

"(iii) part 1 of such improvements began in 1982 with a preliminary renovation program financed by tax-exempt bonds,

"(iv) part 2 of such program was previously scheduled for a bond election on February 25, 1986, pursuant to a Commissioners Court Order of November 5, 1985, and

"(v) the bond election for improvements to such facility was subsequently postponed on December 10, 1985, in order to provide for more comprehensive construction planning.

The aggregate face amount of bonds to which this subparagraph applies shall not exceed $60,000,000.

"(K) A facility is described in this subparagraph if—

"(i) the 1985 State legislature appropriated a maximum sum of $22,500,000 to the State urban development corporation to be made available for such project, and

"(ii) a development and operation agreement was entered into among such corporation, the city, the State budget director, and the county industrial development agency, as of March 1, 1986.

The aggregate face amount of bonds to which this subparagraph applies shall not exceed $28,000,000.

"(L) A facility is described in this subparagraph if—

"(i) it is to consist of 1 or 2 stadiums appropriate for football games and baseball games with related structures and facilities,

"(ii) governmental action was taken on August 7, 1985, by the county commission, and on December 19, 1985, by the city council, concerning such facility, and

"(iii) such facility is located in a city having a National League baseball team.

The aggregate face amount of bonds to which this subparagraph applies shall not exceed $200,000,000.

"(M) A facility is described in this subparagraph if—

"(i) such facility consists of 1 or 2 stadium projects (1 of which may be a stadium renovation or expansion project) with related structures and facilities,

"(ii) a special advisory commission commissioned a study by a national accounting firm with respect to a project for such facility, which study was released in September 1985, and recommended construction of either a new multipurpose or a new baseball-only stadium,

"(iii) a nationally recognized design and architectural firm released a feasibility study with respect to such project in April 1985, and

"(iv) the metropolitan area in which the facility is located is presently the home of an American League baseball team.

The aggregate face amount of bonds to which this subparagraph applies shall not exceed $200,000,000.

"(N) A facility is described in this subparagraph if—

"(i) it is to consist of 1 or 2 stadiums appropriate for football games and baseball games with related structures and facilities,

"(ii) the site for such facility was approved by the council of the city in which such facility is to be located on July 9, 1985, and

"(iii) the request for proposals process was authorized by the council of the city in which such facility is to be located on November 5, 1985, and such requests were distributed to potential developers on November 15, 1985, with responses due by February 14, 1986.

The aggregate face amount of bonds to which this subparagraph applies shall not exceed $200,000,000.

"(O) A facility is described in this subparagraph if—

"(i) such facility is described in a feasibility study dated September 1985, and

"(ii) resolutions were adopted or other actions taken on February 21, 1985, July 18, 1985, August 8, 1985, October 17, 1985, and November 7, 1985, by the Board of Supervisors of the county in which such facility will be located with respect to such feasibility study, appropriations to obtain land for such facility, and approving the location of such facility in the county.

The aggregate face amount of bonds to which this subparagraph applies shall not exceed $20,000,000.

"(P) A facility is described in this subparagraph if such facility constructed on a site acquired with the sale of revenue bonds authorized by a city council on December 2, 1985, (Ordinances No. 669 and 670, series 1985). The aggregate face amount of bonds to which this subparagraph applies shall not exceed $90,000,000.

"(Q) A facility is described in this subparagraph if—

"(i) resolutions were adopted approving a ground lease dated June 27, 1983, by a sports authority (created by a State legislature) with respect to the land on which the facility will be erected,

"(ii) such facility is described in a market study dated June 13, 1983, and

"(iii) such facility was the subject of an Act of the State legislature which was signed on July 1, 1983.

The aggregate face amount of bonds to which this subparagraph applies shall not exceed $81,000,000.

"(R) A facility is described in this subparagraph if such facility is a baseball stadium and adjacent parking facilities with respect to which a city made a carryforward election of $52,514,000 on February 25, 1985. The aggregate face amount of bonds to which this subparagraph applies shall not exceed $50,000,000.

"(S) A facility is described in this subparagraph if—

"(i) such facility is to be used by both a National Hockey League team and a National Basketball Association team,

"(ii) such facility is to be constructed on a platform using air rights over land acquired by a State authority and identified as site B in a report dated May 30, 1984, prepared for a State urban development corporation, and

"(iii) such facility is eligible for real property tax (and power and energy) benefits pursuant to State legislation approved and effective as of July 7, 1982.

The aggregate face amount of bonds to which this subparagraph applies shall not exceed $225,000,000.

"(T) A facility is described in this subparagraph if—

"(i) a resolution authorizing the financing of the facility through an issuance of revenue bonds was adopted by the City Commission on August 5, 1986, and

"(ii) the metropolitan area in which the facility is to be located is currently the spring training home of an American league baseball team located during the regular season in a city described in subparagraph (C).

The aggregate face amount of bonds to which this subparagraph applies shall not exceed $10,000,000.

"(U) A facility is described in this subparagraph if it is a football stadium located in Oakland, California, with respect to which a design was completed by a nationally recognized architectural firm for a stadium seating approximately 72,000, to be located on property adjacent to an existing coliseum complex, or is a renovation of an existing stadium located in Oakland, California, and used by an American League baseball team. The aggregate face amount of bonds to which this subparagraph applies shall not exceed $100,000,000.

"(V) A facility is described in this subparagraph if it is a sports arena (and related parking facility) for Grand Rapids, Michigan. The aggregate face amount of bonds to which this subparagraph applies shall not exceed $80,000,000.

"(W) A facility is described in this subparagraph if such facility is located adjacent to the Anacostia River in the District of Columbia. The aggregate face amount of bonds to which this subparagraph applies shall not exceed $25,000,000.

"(X) A facility is described in this subparagraph if it is a spectator sports facility for the City of San Antonio, Texas. The aggregate face amount of bonds to which this subparagraph applies shall not exceed $125,000,000.

"(Y) A facility is described in this subparagraph if it will be part of, or adjacent to, an existing stadium which has been owned and operated by a State university and if—

"(i) the stadium was the subject of a feasibility report by a certified public accounting firm which is dated December 28, 1984, and

"(ii) a report by an independent research organization was prepared in December 1985 demonstrating support among donors and season ticket holders for the addition of a dome to the stadium.

The aggregate face amount of bonds to which this subparagraph applies shall not exceed $50,000,000.

"(Z) A facility is described in this subparagraph if—

Exclusions from income — Code Sec. 103

"(i) such facility was a redevelopment project that was approved in concept by the city council sitting as the redevelopment agency in October 1984, and

"(ii) $20,000,000 in funds for such facility was identified in a 5-year budget approved by the city redevelopment agency on October 25, 1984.

The aggregate face amount of bonds to which this subparagraph applies shall not exceed $80,000,000.

"(4) Residential rental property.— A bond issued as part of an issue 95 percent or more of the net proceeds of which are to be used to finance a residential rental project within the meaning of section 103(b)(4) of the 1954 Code shall be treated as an exempt facility bond within the meaning of section 142(a)(7) of the 1986 Code if the facility with respect to the bond is issued satisfies all low-income occupancy requirements applicable to such bonds before August 15, 1986, and the bonds are issued pursuant to—

"(A) a contract to purchase such property dated August 12, 1985;

"(B) the county housing authority approved the property and the financing thereof on September 24, 1985, and

"(C) there was an inducement resolution adopted on October 10, 1985, by the county industrial development authority.

The aggregate face amount of bonds to which this paragraph applies shall not exceed $25,400,000.

"(5) Airports.— A bond issued as a part of an issue 95 percent or more of the net proceeds of which are to be used to provide an airport (within the meaning of section 103(b)(4)(D) of the 1954 Code) shall be treated as an exempt facility bond (for facilities described in section 142(a)(1) of the 1986 Code) for purposes of part IV of subchapter B of chapter 1 of the 1986 Code if the facility is described in any of the following subparagraphs:

"(A) A facility is described in this subparagraph if such facility is a hotel at an airport facility serving a city described in section 631(a)(3) of the Tax Reform Act of 1984 (relating to certain bonds for a convention center and resource recovery project). The aggregate face amount of bonds to which this subparagraph applies shall not exceed $40,000,000.

"(B) A facility is described in this subparagraph if such facility is the primary airport for a city described in paragraph (3)(C). The aggregate face amount of bonds to which this subparagraph applies shall not exceed $500,000,000. Section 148(d)(2) of the 1986 Code shall not apply to any issue to which this subparagraph applies. A facility shall be described in this subparagraph if it would be so described if '90 percent' were substituted for '95 percent' in the material preceding subparagraph (A).

"(C) A facility is described in this subparagraph if such facility is a hotel at Logan airport and such hotel is located on land leased from a State authority under a lease contemplating development of such hotel dated May 1, 1983, or under an amendment, renewal, or extension of such a lease. The aggregate face amount of bonds to which this subparagraph applies shall not exceed $40,000,000.

"(D) A facility is described in this subparagraph if such facility is the airport for the County of Sacramento, California. The aggregate face amount of bonds to which this subparagraph applies shall not exceed $150,000,000.

"(6) Redevelopment projects.— A bond issued as part of an issue 95 percent or more of the net proceeds of which are to be used to finance redevelopment activities as part of a project within a specific designated area shall be treated as a qualified redevelopment bond for purposes of part IV of subchapter B of chapter 1 of the 1986 Code if such project is described in any of the following subparagraphs:

"(A) A project is described in this subparagraph if it was the subject of a city ordinance numbered 82-115 and adopted on December 2, 1982, or numbered 9590 and adopted on April 6, 1983. The aggregate face amount of bonds to which this subparagraph applies shall not exceed $9,000,000.

"(B) A project is described in this subparagraph if it is a redevelopment project for an area in a city described in paragraph (3)(C) which was designated as commercially blighted on November 14, 1975, by the city council and the redevelopment plan for which will be approved by the city council before January 31, 1987. The aggregate face amount of bonds to which this subparagraph applies shall not exceed $20,000,000.

"(C) A project is described in this subparagraph if it is a redevelopment project for an area in a city described in paragraph (3)(C) which was designated as commercially blighted on March 28, 1979, by the city council and the redevelopment plan for which was approved by the city council on June 20, 1984. The aggregate face amount of bonds to which this subparagraph applies shall not exceed $100,000,000.

"(D) A project is described in this subparagraph if it is any one of three redevelopment projects in areas in a city described in paragraph (3)(C) designated as blighted by a city council before January 31, 1987 and with respect to which the redevelopment plan is approved by the city council before January 31, 1987. The aggregate face amount of bonds to which this subparagraph applies shall not exceed $20,000,000.

"(E) A project is described in this subparagraph if such project is for public improvements (including street reconstruction and improvement of underground utilities) for Great Falls, Montana, with respect to which engineering estimates are due on October 1, 1986. The aggregate face amount of bonds to which this subparagraph applies shall not exceed $3,000,000.

"(F) A project is described in this subparagraph if—

"(i) such project is located in an area designated as blighted by the governing body of the city on February 15, 1983 (Resolution No. 4573), and

"(ii) such project is developed pursuant to a redevelopment plan adopted by the governing body of the city on March 1, 1983 (Ordinance No. 15073).

The aggregate face amount of bonds to which this subparagraph applies shall not exceed $5,000,000.

"(G) A project is described in this subparagraph if—

"(i) such project is located in an area designated by the governing body of the city in 1983,

"(ii) such project is described in a letter dated August 8, 1985, from the developer's legal counsel to the development agency of the city, and

"(iii) such project consists primarily of retail facilities to be built by the developer named in a resolution of the governing body of the city on August 30, 1985.

The aggregate face amount of bonds to which this subparagraph applies shall not exceed $75,000,000.

"(H) A project is described in this subparagraph if—

"(i) such project is a project for research and development facilities to be used primarily to benefit a State university and related hospital, with respect to which an urban renewal district was created by the city council effective October 11, 1985, and

"(ii) such project was announced by the university and the city in March 1985.

The aggregate face amount of bonds to which this subparagraph applies shall not exceed $40,000,000.

"(I) A project is described in this subparagraph if such project is a downtown redevelopment project with respect to which—

"(i) an urban development action grant was made, but only if such grant was preliminarily approved on November 3, 1983, and received final approval before June 1, 1984, and

"(ii) the issuer of bonds with respect to such facility adopted a resolution indicating the issuer's intent to adopt such redevelopment project on October 6, 1981, and the issuer adopted an ordinance adopting such redevelopment project on December 13, 1983.

The aggregate face amount of bonds to which this subparagraph applies shall not exceed $10,000,000.

"(J) A project is described in this subparagraph if—

"(i) with respect to such project the city council adopted on December 16, 1985, an ordinance directing the urban renewal authority to study blight and produce an urban renewal plan,

"(ii) the blight survey was accepted and approved by the urban renewal authority on March 20, 1986, and

"(iii) the city planning board approved the urban renewal plan on May 7, 1986.

The aggregate face amount of bonds to which this subparagraph applies shall not exceed $60,000,000.

"(K) A project is described in this subparagraph if—

"(i) the city redevelopment agency approved resolutions authorizing issuance of land acquisition and public improvements bonds with respect to such project on August 8, 1978,

"(ii) such resolutions were later amended in June 1979, and

"(iii) the State Supreme Court upheld a lower court decree validating the bonds on December 11, 1980.

The aggregate face amount of bonds to which this subparagraph applies shall not exceed $380,000,000.

"(L) A project is described in this subparagraph if it is a mixed use redevelopment project either—

"(i) in an area (known as the Near South Development Area) with respect to which the planning department of a city described in paragraph 3(C) promulgated a draft development plan dated March 1986, and which was the subject of public hearings held by a subcommittee of the plan commission of such city on May 28, 1986, and June 10, 1986, or

"(ii) in an area located within the boundaries of any 1 or more census tracts which are directly adjacent to a river whose course runs through such city.

The aggregate face amount of bonds to which this subparagraph applies shall not exceed $75,000,000.

"(M) A project is described in this subparagraph if it is a redevelopment project for an area in a city described in paragraph 3(C) and such area—

"(i) was the subject of a report released in May 1986, prepared by the National Park Service, and

"(ii) was the subject of a report released January 1986, prepared by a task force appointed by the Mayor of such city.

The aggregate face amount of bonds to which this subparagraph applies shall not exceed $75,000,000.

"(N) A project is described in this subparagraph if it is a city-university redevelopment project approved by a city ordinance No. 152-0-84 and the development plan for which was adopted on January 28, 1985. The aggregate face amount of bonds to which this subparagraph applies shall not exceed $23,760,000.

"(O) A project is described in this subparagraph if—

"(i) an inducement resolution was passed on March 9, 1984, for issuance of bonds with respect to such project,

"(ii) such resolution was extended by resolutions passed on August 14, 1984, April 2, 1985, August 13, 1985, and July 8, 1986,

"(iii) an urban development action grant was preliminarily approved for part or all of such project on July 3, 1986, and

"(iv) the project is located in a district designated as the Peabody-Gayoso District.

The aggregate face amount of bonds to which this subparagraph applies shall not exceed $140,000,000.

"(P) A project is described in this subparagraph if the project is a 1-block area of a central business district containing a YMCA building with respect to which—

"(i) the city council adopted a resolution expressing an intent to issue bonds for the project on September 27, 1985,

"(ii) the city council approved project guidelines for the project on December 20, 1985, and

1,373

"(iii) the city council by resolution (adopted on July 30, 1986) directed completion of a development agreement.
The aggregate face amount of bonds to which this subparagraph applies shall not exceed $26,000,000.

"(Q) A project is described in this subparagraph if the project is a 2-block area of a central business district designated as blocks E and F with respect to which—
"(i) the city council adopted guidelines and criteria and authorized a request for development proposals on July 22, 1985,
"(ii) the city council adopted a resolution expressing an intent to issue bonds for the project on September 27, 1985, and
"(iii) the city issued requests for development proposals on March 28, 1986.
The aggregate face amount of bonds to which this subparagraph applies shall not exceed $47,000,000.

"(R) A project is described in this subparagraph if the project is an urban renewal project covering approximately 5.9 acres of land in the Shaw area of the northwest section of the District of Columbia and the 1st portion of such project was the subject of a District of Columbia public hearing on June 2, 1986. The aggregate face amount of bonds to which this subparagraph applies shall not exceed $10,000,000.

"(S) A project is described in this subparagraph if such project is a hotel, commercial, and residential project on the east bank of the Grand River in Grand Rapids, Michigan, with respect to which a developer was selected by the city in June 1985 and a planning agreement was executed in August 1985. The aggregate face amount of bonds to which this subparagraph applies shall not exceed $39,000,000.

"(T) A project is described in this subparagraph if such project is the Wurzburg Block Redevelopment Project in Grand Rapids, Michigan. The aggregate face amount of bonds to which this subparagraph applies shall not exceed $60,000,000.

"(U) A project is described in this subparagraph if such project is consistent with an urban renewal plan adopted or ordered prepared before August 28, 1986, by the city council of the most populous city in a state which entered the Union on February 14, 1859. The aggregate face amount of bonds to which this subparagraph applies shall not exceed $83,000,000.

"(V) A project is described in this subparagraph if such project is consistent with an urban renewal plan which was adopted (or ordered prepared) before August 13, 1985, by an appropriate jurisdiction of a state which entered the Union on February 14, 1859. The aggregate face amount of bonds to which this subparagraph applies shall not exceed $135,000,000 and the limitation on the period during which bonds under this section may be issued shall not apply to such bonds.

"(W) A project is described in this subparagraph if such project is—
"(i) a part of the Kenosha Downtown Redevelopment project, and
"(ii) located in an area bounded—
"(I) on the east by the east wall of the Army Corps of Engineers Confined Disposal Facility (extended),
"(II) on the north by 48th Street (extended),
"(III) on the west by the present Chicago & Northwestern Railroad tracks, and
"(IV) on the south by the north line of Eichelman Park (60th Street) (extended).
The aggregate face amount of bonds to which this subparagraph applies shall not exceed $105,000,000.

"(X) A project is described in this subparagraph if a redevelopment plan for such project was approved by the city council of Bell Gardens, California, on June 12, 1979. The aggregate face amount of bonds to which this subparagraph applies shall not exceed $10,000,000.

"(Y) Nothing in this paragraph shall be construed as having the effect of exempting from tax interest on any bond issued after June 10, 1987, if such interest would not have been exempt from tax were such bond issued on August 15, 1986.

"(Z) Any designated area with respect to which a project is described in any subparagraph of this paragraph shall be taken into account in applying section 144(c)(4)(C) of the 1986 Code in determining whether other areas (not so described) may be designated.

"(7) Convention centers.—A bond issued as part of an issue 95 percent or more of the net proceeds of which are to be used to provide any convention or trade show facility (within the meaning of section 103(b)(4)(C) of the 1954 Code) shall be treated as an exempt facility bond for purposes of part IV of subchapter B of chapter 1 of the 1986 Code if such facility is described in any of the following subparagraphs:

"(A) A facility is described in this subparagraph if—
"(i) a feasibility consultant and a design consultant were hired on April 3, 1985, with respect to such facility, and
"(ii) a draft feasibility report with respect to such facility was presented on November 3, 1985, to the Mayor of the city in which such facility is to be located.
The aggregate face amount of bonds to which this subparagraph applies shall not exceed $190,000,000. For purposes of this subparagraph, not more than $20,000,000 of bonds issued to advance refund existing convention facility bonds sold on May 12, 1978, shall be treated as bonds described in this subparagraph and section 149(d)(2) of the 1986 Code shall not apply to bonds so treated.

"(B) A facility is described in this subparagraph if—
"(i) an application for a State loan for such facility was approved by the city council on March 4, 1985, and
"(ii) the city council of the city in which such facility is to be located approved on March 25, 1985, an application for an urban development action grant.
The aggregate face amount of bonds which this subparagraph applies shall not exceed $10,000,000.

"(C) A facility is described in this subparagraph if—
"(i) on November 1, 1983, a convention development tax took effect and was dedicated to financing such facility,

"(ii) the State supreme court of the State in which the facility is to be located validated such tax on February 8, 1985, and
"(iii) an agreement was entered into on November 14, 1985, between the city and county in which such facility is to be located on the terms of the bonds to be issued with respect to such facility.
The aggregate face amount of bonds to which this subparagraph applies shall not exceed $66,000,000.

"(D) A facility is described in this subparagraph if—
"(i) it is a convention, trade, or spectator facility,
"(ii) a regional convention, trade, and spectator facilities study committee was created before March 19, 1985, with respect to such facility, and
"(iii) feasibility and preliminary design consultants were hired on May 1, 1985, and October 31, 1985, with respect to such facility.
The aggregate face amount of bonds to which this subparagraph applies shall not exceed the excess of $175,000,000 over the amount of bonds to which paragraph (48)(B) applies.

"(E) A facility is described in this subparagraph if—
"(i) such facility is meeting rooms for a convention center, and
"(ii) resolutions and ordinances were adopted with respect to such meeting rooms on January 17, 1983, July 11, 1983, December 17, 1984, and September 23, 1985.
The aggregate face amount of bonds to which this subparagraph applies shall not exceed $75,000,000.

"(F) A facility is described in this subparagraph if it is an international trade center which is part of the 125th Street redevelopment project in New York, New York. The aggregate face amount of obligations to which this subparagraph applies shall not exceed $165,000,000.

"(G) A facility is described in this subparagraph if—
"(i) such facility is located in a city which was the subject of a convention center market analysis or study dated March 1983, and prepared by a nationally recognized accounting firm,
"(ii) such facility's location was approved in December 1985 by a task force created jointly by the Governor of the State within which such facility will be located and the mayor of the capital city of such State, and
"(iii) the size of such facility is not more than 200,000 square feet.
The aggregate face amount of bonds to which this subparagraph applies shall not exceed $70,000,000.

"(H) A facility is described in this subparagraph if an analysis of operations and recommendations of utilization of such facility was prepared by a certified public accounting firm pursuant to an engagement authorized on March 6, 1984, and presented on June 11, 1984, to officials of the city in which such facility is located. The aggregate face amount of bonds to which this subparagraph applies shall not exceed $75,000,000.

"(I) A facility is described in this subparagraph if—
"(i) voters approved a bond issue to finance the acquisition of the site for such facility on May 4, 1985,
"(ii) title of the property was transferred from the Illinois Center Gulf Railroad to the city on September 30, 1985, and
"(iii) a United States judge rendered a decision regarding the fair market value of the site of such facility on December 30, 1985.
The aggregate face amount of bonds to which this subparagraph applies shall not exceed $131,000,000.

"(J) A facility is described in this subparagraph if—
"(i) such facility is to be used for an annual aquafestival,
"(ii) a referendum was held on April 6, 1985, in which voters permitted the city council to lease 130 acres of dedicated parkland for the purpose of constructing such facility, and
"(iii) the city council passed an inducement resolution on June 19, 1986.
The aggregate face amount of bonds to which this subparagraph applies shall not exceed $10,000,000.

"(K) A facility is described in this subparagraph if—
"(i) voters approved a bond issued to finance a portion of the cost of such facility on December 1, 1984, and
"(ii) such facility was the subject of a market study and financial projections dated March 21, 1986, prepared by a nationally recognized accounting firm.
The aggregate face amount of bonds to which this subparagraph applies shall not exceed $5,000,000.

"(L) A facility is described in this subparagraph if—
"(i) on July 12, 1984, the city council passed a resolution increasing the local hotel and motel tax to 7 percent to assist in paying for such facility,
"(ii) on October 25, 1984, the city council selected a consulting firm for such facility, and
"(iii) with respect to such facility, the city council appropriated funds for additional work on February 7, 1985, October 3, 1985, and June 26, 1986.
The aggregate face amount of bonds to which this subparagraph applies shall not exceed $120,000,000.

"(M) A facility is described in this subparagraph if—
"(i) a board of county commissioners, in an action dated January 21, 1986, supported an application for official approval of the facility, and
"(ii) the State economic development commission adopted a resolution dated February 25, 1986, determining the facility to be an eligible facility pursuant to State law and the rules adopted by the commission.
The aggregate face amount of bonds to which this subparagraph applies shall not exceed $7,500,000.

"(8) Sports or convention facilities.—A bond issued as a part of an issue 95 percent or more of the net proceeds of which are to be used to provide either a sports facility (within the meaning of section 103(b)(4)(B) of the 1954 Code) or a

Exclusions from income — Code Sec. 103

convention facility (within the meaning of section 103(b)(4)(C) of the 1954 Code) shall be treated as an exempt facility bond for purposes of part IV of subchapter B of chapter 1 of the 1986 Code if such facility is described in any of the following subparagraphs:

"(A) A combined convention and arena facility, or any part thereof (whether on the same or different sites), is described in this subparagraph if—

"(i) bonds for the expansion, acquisition, or construction of such combined facility are payable from a tax and are issued under a plan initially approved by the voters of the taxing authority on April 25, 1978, and

"(ii) such bonds were authorized for expanding a convention center, for acquiring an arena site, and for building an arena or any of the foregoing pursuant to a resolution adopted by the governing body of the bond issuer on March 17, 1986, and superseded by a resolution adopted by such governing body on May 27, 1986.

The aggregate face amount of bonds to which this subparagraph applies shall not exceed $160,000,000.

"(B) A sports or convention facility is described in this subparagraph if—

"(i) on March 4, 1986, county commissioners held public hearings on creation of a county convention facilities authority, and

"(ii) on March 7, 1986, the county commissioners voted to create a county convention facilities authority and to submit to county voters a ½ cent sales and use tax to finance such facility.

The aggregate face amount of bonds to which this subparagraph applies shall not exceed $150,000,000.

"(C) A sports or convention facility is described in this subparagraph if—

"(i) a feasibility consultant and a design consultant were hired prior to October 1980 with respect to such facility,

"(ii) a feasibility report dated October 1980 with respect to such facility was presented to a city or county in which such facility is to be located, and

"(iii) on September 7, 1982, a joint city/county resolution appointed a committee which was charged with the task of independently reviewing the studies and present need for the facility.

The aggregate face amount of bonds to which this subparagraph applies shall not exceed $60,000,000.

"(D) A sports or convention facility is described in this subparagraph if—

"(i) such facility is a multipurpose coliseum facility for which, before January 1, 1985, a city, an auditorium district created by the State legislature within which such facility will be located, and a limited partnership executed an enforceable contract,

"(ii) significant governmental action regarding such facility was taken before May 23, 1983, and

"(iii) inducement resolutions were passed for issuance of bonds with respect to such facility on May 26, 1986.

The aggregate face amount of bonds to which this subparagraph applies shall not exceed $25,000,000.

"(9) Parking facilities.— A bond issued as part of an issue 95 percent or more of the net proceeds of which are to be used to provide a parking facility (within the meaning of section 103(b)(4)(D) of the 1954 Code) shall be treated as an exempt facility bond for purposes of part IV of subchapter B of chapter 1 of the 1986 Code if such facility is described in any of the following subparagraphs:

"(A) A facility is described in this subparagraph if—

"(i) there was an inducement resolution on March 9, 1984, for the issuance of bonds with respect to such facility, and

"(ii) such resolution was extended by resolutions passed on August 14, 1984, April 2, 1985, August 13, 1985, and July 8, 1986.

The aggregate face amount of bonds to which this subparagraph applies shall not exceed $30,000,000.

"(B) A facility is described in this subparagraph if—

"(i) such facility is for a university medical school,

"(ii) the last parcel of land necessary for such facility was purchased on February 4, 1985, and

"(iii) the amount of bonds to be issued with respect to such facility was increased by the State legislature of the State in which the facility is to be located as part of its 1983-1984 general appropriations act.

The aggregate face amount of bonds to which this subparagraph applies shall not exceed $9,000,000.

"(C) A facility is described in this subparagraph if—

"(i) the development agreement with respect to the project of which such facility is a part was entered into during May 1984, and

"(ii) an inducement resolution was passed on October 9, 1985, for the issuance of bonds with respect to the facility.

The aggregate face amount of bonds to which this subparagraph applies shall not exceed $35,000,000.

"(D) A facility is described in this subparagraph if the city council approved a resolution of intent to issue tax-exempt bonds (Resolution 34083) for such facility on April 30, 1986. The aggregate face amount of bonds to which this subparagraph applies shall not exceed $8,000,000. Solely for purposes of this subparagraph, a heliport constructed as part of such facility shall be deemed to be functionally related and subordinate to such facility.

"(E) A facility is described in this subparagraph if—

"(i) resolutions were adopted by a public joint powers authority relating to such facility on March 6, 1985, May 1, 1985, October 2, 1985, December 4, 1985, and February 5, 1986; and

"(ii) such facility is to be located at an exposition park which includes a coliseum and sports arena.

The aggregate face amount of bonds to which this subparagraph applies shall not exceed $150,000,000.

"(F) A facility is described in this subparagraph if—

"(i) it is to be constructed as part of an overall development that is the subject of a development agreement dated October 1, 1983, between a developer and an organization described in section 501(c)(3) of the 1986 Code, and

"(ii) an environmental notification form with respect to the overall development was filed with a State environmental agency on February 28, 1985.

The aggregate face amount of bonds to which this subparagraph applies shall not exceed $60,000,000.

"(G) A facility is described in this subparagraph if—

"(i) an inducement resolution was passed by the city redevelopment agency on December 3, 1984, and a resolution to carryforward the private activity bond limit was passed by such agency on December 21, 1984, with respect to such facility, and

"(ii) the owner participation agreement with respect to such facility was entered into on July 30, 1986.

The aggregate face amount of bonds to which this subparagraph applies shall not exceed $18,000,000.

"(H) A facility is described in this subparagraph if—

"(i) an application (dated August 28, 1986) for financial assistance was submitted to the county industrial development agency with respect to such facility, and

"(ii) the inducement resolution for such facility was passed by the industrial development agency on September 10, 1986.

The aggregate face amount of bonds to which this subparagraph applies shall not exceed $8,000,000.

"(I) A facility is described in this subparagraph if—

"(i) it is located in a city the parking needs of which were comprehensively described in a 'Downtown Parking Plan' dated January 1983, and approved by the city's City Plan Commission on June 1, 1983, and

"(ii) obligations with respect to the construction of which are issued on behalf of a State or local governmental unit by a corporation empowered to issue the same which was created by the legislative body of the State by an Act introduced on May 21, 1985, and thereafter passed, which Act became effective without the governor's signature on June 26, 1985.

The aggregate face amount of bonds to which this subparagraph applies shall not exceed $50,000,000.

"(J) A facility is described in this subparagraph if—

"(i) such facility is located in a city which was the subject of a convention center market analysis or study dated March 1983 and prepared by a nationally recognized accounting firm,

"(ii) such facility is intended for use by, among others, persons attending a convention center located within the same town or city, and

"(iii) such facility's location was approved in December 1985 by a task force created jointly, by the governor of the State within which such facility will be located and the mayor of the capital city of such State.

The aggregate face amount of bonds to which this subparagraph applies shall not exceed $30,000,000.

"(K) A facility is described in this subparagraph if—

"(i) scale and components for the facility were determined by a city downtown plan adopted October 31, 1984 (resolution number 3882), and

"(ii) the site area for the facility is approximately 51,200 square feet.

The aggregate face amount of bonds to which this subparagraph applies shall not exceed $5,000,000.

"(L) A facility is described in this subparagraph if—

"(i) the property for such facility was offered for development by a city renewal agency on March 19, 1986 (resolution number 920), and

"(ii) the site area for the facility is approximately 25,600 square feet.

The aggregate face amount of bonds to which this subparagraph applies shall not exceed $5,000,000.

"(M) A facility is described in this subparagraph if such facility was approved by official action of the city council on July 26, 1984 (resolution number 33718), and is for the Moyer Theatre. The aggregate face amount of bonds to which this subparagraph applies shall not exceed $8,000,000.

"(N) A facility is described in this subparagraph if it is part of a renovation project involving the Outlet Company building in Providence, Rhode Island. The aggregate face amount of obligations to which this subparagraph applies shall not exceed $6,000,000.

"(10) Certain advance refundings.—

"(A) Section 149(d)(3) of the 1986 Code shall not apply to a bond issued by a State admitted to the Union on November 16, 1907, for the advance refunding of not more than $186,000,000 State turnpike obligations.

"(B) A refunding of the Charleston, West Virginia Town Center Garage Bonds shall not be treated for purposes of part IV of subchapter A of chapter 1 of the 1986 Code as an advance refunding if it would not be so treated if '100' were substituted for '90' in section 149(d)(5) of such Code.

"(11) Principal user provisions.—

"(A) In the case of a bond issued as part of an issue the proceeds of which are to be used to provide a facility described in subparagraph (B) or (C), the determination of whether such bond is an exempt facility bond shall be made by substituting '90 percent' for '95 percent' in section 142(a) of the 1986 Code.

"(B) A facility is described in this subparagraph if—

"(i) it is a waste-to-energy project for which a contract for the sale of electricity was executed in September 1984, and

"(ii) the design, construction, and operation contract for such project was signed in March 1985 and the order to begin construction was issued on March 31, 1986.

The aggregate face amount of bonds to which this subparagraph applies shall not exceed $29,100,000.

"(C) A facility is described in this subparagraph if it is described in section 1865(c)(2)(C) of this Act.

"(12) Qualified scholarship funding bonds.— Subsections (d)(3) and (f) of section 148 of the 1986 Code shall not apply to any bond or series of bonds the proceeds of which are used exclusively to refund qualified scholarship funding bonds (as defined in section 150 of the 1986 Code) issued before January 1, 1986, if—

"(A) the amount of the refunding bonds does not exceed the aggregate face amount of the refunded bonds,

"(B) the maturity date of such refunding bond is not later than later of—

"(i) the maturity date of the bond to be refunded, or

"(ii) the date which is 15 years after the date on which the refunded bond was issued (or, in the case of a series of refundings, the date on which the original bond was issued),

"(C) the bonds to be refunded were issued by the California Student Loan Finance Corporation, and

"(D) the face amount of the refunding bonds does not exceed $175,000,000.

"(13) Residential rental property projects.—A bond issued as part of an issue 95 percent or more of the net proceeds of which are to be used to provide a project for residential rental property which satisfies the requirements of section 103(b)(4)(A) of the 1954 Code shall be treated as an exempt facility bond (for projects described in section 142(a)(7) of the 1986 Code) for purposes of part IV of subchapter B of chapter 1 of the 1986 Code if the project is described in any of the following subparagraphs:

"(A) A residential rental property project is described in this subparagraph if—

"(i) a public building development corporation was formed on June 6, 1984, with respect to such project,

"(ii) a partnership of which the corporation is a general partner was formed on June 8, 1984, and

"(iii) the partnership entered into a preliminary agreement with the State public facilities authority effective as of May 4, 1984, with respect to the issuance of the bonds for such project.

The aggregate face amount of bonds to which this subparagraph applies shall not exceed $6,200,000.

"(B) A residential rental property project is described in this subparagraph if—

"(i) the Board of Commissioners of the city housing authority officially selected such project's developer on December 19, 1985,

"(ii) the Board of the City Redevelopment Commission agreed on February 13, 1986, to conduct a public hearing with respect to the project on March 6, 1986,

"(iii) an official action resolution for such project was adopted on March 6, 1986, and

"(iv) an allocation of a portion of the State ceiling was made with respect to such project on July 29, 1986.

The aggregate face amount of bonds to which this subparagraph applies shall not exceed $10,000,000.

"(C) A residential rental property project is described in this subparagraph if—

"(i) the issuance of $1,289,882 of bonds for such project was approved by a State agency on September 11, 1985, and

"(ii) the authority to issue such bonds was scheduled to expire (under the terms of the State approval) on September 9, 1986.

The aggregate face amount of bonds to which this subparagraph applies shall not exceed $1,300,000.

"(D) A residential rental property project is described in this subparagraph if—

"(i) the issuance of $7,020,000 of bonds for such project was approved by a State agency on October 10, 1985, and

"(ii) the authority to issue such bonds was scheduled to expire (under the terms of the State approval) on October 9, 1986.

The aggregate face amount of bonds to which this subparagraph applies shall not exceed $7,020,000.

"(E) A residential rental property project is described in this subparagraph if—

"(i) it is to be located in a city urban renewal project area which was established pursuant to an urban renewal plan adopted by the city council on May 17, 1960,

"(ii) the urban renewal plan was revised in 1972 to permit multifamily dwellings in areas of the urban renewal project designated as a central business district,

"(iii) an inducement resolution was adopted for such project on December 14, 1984, and

"(iv) the city council approved on November 6, 1985, an agreement which provides for conveyance to the city of fee title to such project site.

The aggregate face amount of bonds to which this subparagraph applies shall not exceed $60,000,000.

"(F) A residential rental property project is described in this subparagraph if—

"(i) such project is to be located in a city urban renewal project area which was established pursuant to an urban renewal plan adopted by the city council on May 17, 1960,

"(ii) the urban renewal plan was revised in 1972 to permit multifamily dwellings in areas of the urban renewal project designated as a central business district,

"(iii) the amended urban renewal plan adopted by the city council on May 19, 1972, also provides for the conversion of any public area site in Block J of the urban renewal project area for the development of residential facilities, and

"(iv) acquisition of all of the parcels comprising the Block J project site was completed by the city on December 28, 1984.

The aggregate face amount of bonds to which this subparagraph applies shall not exceed $60,000,000.

"(G) A residential rental property project is described in this subparagraph if—

"(i) such project is to be located on a city-owned site which is to become available for residential development upon the relocation of a bus maintenance facility,

"(ii) preliminary design studies for such project site were completed in December 1985, and

"(iii) such project is located in the same State as the projects described in subparagraphs (E) and (F).

The aggregate face amount of bonds to which this subparagraph applies shall not exceed $100,000,000.

"(H) A residential rental property project is described in this subparagraph if—

"(i) at least 20 percent of the residential units in such project are to be utilized to fulfill the requirements of a unilateral agreement date July 21, 1983, relating to the provision of low- and moderate-income housing,

"(ii) the unilateral agreement was incorporated into ordinance numbers 83-49 and 83-50, adopted by the city council and approved by the mayor on August 24, 1983, and

"(iii) an inducement resolution was adopted for such project on September 25, 1985.

The aggregate face amount of bonds to which this subparagraph applies shall not exceed $8,000,000.

"(I) A residential rental property project is described in this subparagraph if—

"(i) a letter of understanding was entered into on December 11, 1985, between the city and county housing and community development office and the project developer regarding the conveyance of land for such project; and

"(ii) such project is located in the same State as the projects described in subparagraphs (E), (F), (G), and (H).

The aggregate face amount of bonds to which this subparagraph applies shall not exceed an amount which, together with the amounts allowed under subparagraphs (E), (F), (G), and (H), does not exceed $250,000,000.

"(J) A residential rental property project is described in this subparagraph if it is a multifamily residential development located in Arrowhead Springs, within the county of San Bernardino, California, and a portion of the site of which currently is owned by the Campus Crusade for Christ. The aggregate face amount of bonds to which this subparagraph applies shall not exceed $350,000,000.

"(K) A residential rental property project is described in this subparagraph if—

"(i) it is a new residential development with approximately 309 dwelling units located in census tract No. 3202, and

"(ii) there was an inducement ordinance for such project adopted by a city council on November 20, 1985.

The aggregate face amount of bonds to which this subparagraph applies shall not exceed $32,000,000.

"(L) A residential rental property project is described in this subparagraph if—

"(i) it is a new residential development with approximately 70 dwelling units located in census tract No. 3901, and

"(ii) there was an inducement ordinance for such project adopted by a city council on August 14, 1984.

The aggregate face amount of bonds to which this subparagraph applies shall not exceed $4,000,000.

"(M) A residential rental property project is described in this subparagraph if—

"(i) it is a new residential development with approximately 98 dwelling units located in census tract No. 4701, and

"(ii) there was an inducement ordinance for such project adopted by a city council on August 14, 1984.

The aggregate face amount of bonds to which this subparagraph applies shall not exceed $7,000,000.

"(N) A project or projects are described in this subparagraph if they are part of the Willow Road residential improvement plan in Menlo Park, California. The aggregate face amount of obligations to which this subparagraph applies shall not exceed $9,000,000.

"(O) A residential rental property project is described in this subparagraph if—

"(i) an inducement resolution for such project was approved on July 18, 1985, by the city council,

"(ii) such project was approved by such council on August 11, 1986, and

"(iii) such project consists of approximately 22 duplexes to be used for housing qualified low and moderate income tenants.

The aggregate face amount of bonds to which this subparagraph applies shall not exceed $1,500,000.

"(P) A residential rental property project is described in this subparagraph if—

"(i) an inducement resolution for such project was approved on April 22, 1986, by the city council,

"(ii) such project was approved by such council on August 11, 1986, and

"(iii) such project consists of a unit apartment complex (having approximately 60 units) to be used for housing qualified low and moderate income tenants.

The aggregate face amount of bonds to which this subparagraph applies shall not exceed $1,625,000.

"(Q) A residential rental property project is described in this subparagraph if—

"(i) a State housing authority granted a notice of official action for the project on May 24, 1985, and

"(ii) a binding agreement was executed for such project with the State housing finance authority on May 14, 1986, and such agreement was accepted by the State housing authority on June 5, 1986.

The aggregate face amount of bonds to which this subparagraph applies shall not exceed $7,800,000.

"(R) A residential rental property project is described in this subparagraph if such project is either of 2 projects (located in St. Louis, Missouri) which received commitments to provide construction and permanent financing through the issuance of bonds in principal amounts of up to $242,130 and $654,045, on July 16, 1986. The aggregate face amount of bonds to which this subparagraph applies shall not exceed $1,000,000.

"(S) A residential rental property project is described in this subparagraph if—

Exclusions from income　　　　　　　　　　　　　　　　　　　　　　　　　　Code Sec. 103

"(i) a local housing authority approved an inducement resolution for such project on January 28, 1985, and

"(ii) a suit relating to such project was dismissed without right of further appeal on April 4, 1986.

The aggregate face amount of bonds to which this subparagraph applies shall not exceed $13,200,000.

"(T) A residential rental property project is described in this subparagraph if—

"(i) such project is the renovation of a hotel for residents for senior citizens,

"(ii) an inducement resolution for such project was adopted on November 20, 1985, by the State Development Finance Authority, and

"(iii) such project is to be located in the metropolitan area of the city described in paragraph (3)(C).

The aggregate face amount of bonds to which this subparagraph applies shall not exceed $9,500,000.

"(U) A residential rental property project is described in this subparagraph if—

"(i) such project is the renovation of apartment housing,

"(ii) an inducement resolution for such project was adopted on December 20, 1985, by the State Housing Development Authority, and

"(iii) such project is to be located in the metropolitan area of the city described in paragraph (3)(C).

The aggregate face amount of bonds to which this subparagraph applies shall not exceed $12,000,000.

"(V) A residential rental project is described in this subparagraph if it is a renovation and construction project for low-income housing in central Louisville, Kentucky, and local board approval for such project was granted April 22, 1986. The aggregate face amount of bonds to which this subparagraph applies shall not exceed $500,000.

"(W) A residential rental project is described in this subparagraph if—

"(i) such project is 1 of 6 residential rental projects having in the aggregate approximately 1,010 units,

"(ii) inducement resolutions for such projects were adopted by the county residential finance authority on November 21, 1985, and

"(iii) a public hearing of the county residential finance authority was held by such authority on December 19, 1985, regarding such projects to be constructed by an in-commonwealth developer.

The aggregate face amount of bonds to which this subparagraph applies shall not exceed $62,000,000.

"(X) A residential rental project is described in this subparagraph if—

"(i) an inducement resolution with respect to such project was adopted by the State housing development authority on January 25, 1985, and

"(ii) the issuance of bonds for such project was the subject of a law suit filed on October 25, 1985.

"(Y) A project or projects are described in this subparagraph if they are financed with bonds issued by the Tulare, California, County Housing Authority. The aggregate face amount of obligations to which this subparagraph applies shall not exceed $8,000,000.

"(Z) A residential rental project is described in this subparagraph if such project is a multifamily mixed-use housing project located in a city described in paragraph (3)(C), the zoning for which was changed to residential-business planned development on November 26, 1985, and with respect to which both the city on December 4, 1985, and the state housing finance agency on December 20, 1985, adopted inducement resolutions. The aggregate face amount of obligations to which this subparagraph applies shall not exceed $90,000,000.

"(AA) A residential rental property project is described in this subparagraph if it is the Carriage Trace residential rental project in Clinton, Tennessee. The aggregate face amount of bonds to which this subparagraph applies shall not exceed $10,000,000.

"(BB) A residential rental property project is described in this subparagraph if—

"(i) a contract to purchase such property was dated as of August 9, 1985,

"(ii) there was an inducement resolution adopted on September 27, 1985, for the issuance of obligations to finance such property,

"(iii) there was a State court final validation of such financing on November 15, 1985, and

"(iv) the certificate of nonappeal from such validation was available on December 15, 1985.

The aggregate face amount of bonds to which this subparagraph applies shall not exceed $27,750,000.

"(14) Qualified student loans.— The amendments made by section 1301 shall not apply to any qualified student loan bonds (as defined in section 144 of the 1986 Code) issued by the Volunteer State Student Assistance Corporation. The aggregate face amount of bonds to which this paragraph applies shall not exceed $130,000,000. In the case of bonds to which this paragraph applies, the requirements of sections 148 and 149(d) of the 1986 Code shall be treated as included in section 103 of the 1954 Code and shall apply to such bonds incorporated on February 20, 1985.

"(15) Annuity contracts.— The treatment of annuity contracts as investment property under section 148(b)(2) of the 1986 Code shall not apply to any bond described in any of the following subparagraphs:

"(A) A bond is described in this subparagraph if such bond is issued by a city located in a noncontiguous State if—

"(i) the authority to acquire such a contract was approved on September 24, 1985, by city ordinance A085-176, and

"(ii) formal bid requests for such contracts were mailed to insurance companies on September 6, 1985.

The aggregate face amount of bonds to which this subparagraph applies shall not exceed $57,000,000.

"(B) A bond is described in this subparagraph if—

"(i) on or before May 12, 1985, the governing board of the city pension fund authorized an agreement with an underwriter to provide planning and financial guidance for a possible bond issue, and

"(ii) the proceeds of the sale of such bond issue are to be used to purchase an annuity to fund the unfunded liability of the City of Berkeley, California's Safety Members Pension Fund.

The aggregate face amount of bonds to which this subparagraph applies shall not exceed $40,000,000.

"(C) A bond is described in this subparagraph if such bond is issued by the South Dakota Building Authority if on September 18, 1985, representatives of such authority and its underwriters met with bond counsel and approved financing the purchase of an annuity contract through the sale and leaseback of State properties. The aggregate face amount of bonds to which this subparagraph applies shall not exceed $175,000,000.

"(D) A bond is described in this subparagraph if—

"(i) such bond is issued by Los Angeles County, and

"(ii) such county, before September 25, 1985, paid or incurred at least $50,000 of costs related to the issuance of such bonds.

The aggregate face amount of bonds to which this subparagraph applies shall not exceed $500,000,000.

"(16) Solid waste disposal facility.— The amendments made by section 1301 shall not apply to any solid waste disposal facility if—

"(A) construction of such facility was approved by State law I.C. 36-9-31,

"(B) there was an inducement resolution on November 19, 1984, for the bonds with respect to such facility, and

"(C) a carryforward election of unused 1984 volume cap was made for such project on February 25, 1985.

The aggregate face amount of bonds to which this paragraph applies shall not exceed $120,000,000.

"(17) Refunding of bond anticipation notes. — There shall not be taken into account under section 146 of the 1986 Code any refunding of bond anticipation notes—

"(A) issued in December of 1984 by the Rhode Island Housing and Mortgage Finance Corporation,

"(B) which mature in December of 1986,

"(C) which is not an advance refunding within the meaning of section 149(d)(5) of the 1986 Code (determined by substituting '180 days' for '90 days' therein), and

"(D) the aggregate face amount of the refunding bonds does not exceed $25,500,000.

"(18) Certain airports. — The amendments made by section 1301 shall not apply to a bond issued as part of an issue 95 percent or more of the net proceeds of which are to be used to provide any airport (within the meaning of section 103(b)(4)(D) of the 1954 Code) if such airport is a mid-field airport terminal and accompanying facilities at a major air carrier airport which during April 1980 opened a new precision instrument approach runway 10R28L. The aggregate face amount of bonds to which this subparagraph applies shall not exceed $425,000,000.

"(19) Mass commuting facilities. — A bond issued as a part of an issue 95 percent or more of the net proceeds of which are to be used to provide a mass commuting facility (within the meaning of section 103(b)(4)(D) of the 1954 Code) shall be treated as an exempt facility bond (for facilities described in section 142(a)(3) of the 1986 Code) for purposes of part IV of subchapter B of chapter 1 of the 1986 Code if such facility is described in 1 of the following subparagraphs:

"(A) A facility is described in this subparagraph if—

"(i) such facility provides access to an international airport,

"(ii) a corporation was formed in connection with such project in September 1984,

"(iii) the Board of Directors of such corporation authorized the hiring of various firms to conduct a feasibility study with respect to such project in April 1985, and

"(iv) such feasibility study was completed in November 1985.

The aggregate face amount of bonds to which this subparagraph applies shall not exceed $150,000,000.

"(B) A facility is described in this subparagraph if—

"(i) enabling legislation with respect to such project was approved by the State legislature in 1979,

"(ii) a 1-percent local sales tax assessment to be dedicated to the financing of such project was approved by the voters on August 13, 1983, and

"(iii) a capital fund with respect to such project was established upon the issuance of $90,000,000 of notes on October 22, 1985.

The aggregate face amount of bonds to which this subparagraph applies shall not exceed $200,000,000 and such bonds must be issued before January 1, 1996.

"(C) A facility is described in this subparagraph if—

"(i) bonds issued therefor are issued by or on behalf of an authority organized in 1979 pursuant to enabling legislation originally enacted by the State legislature in 1973, and

"(ii) such facility is part of a system connector described in a resolution adopted by the board of directors of the authority on March 27, 1986.

The aggregate face amount of bonds to which this subparagraph applies shall not exceed $400,000,000. Notwithstanding the last paragraph of this subsection, this subparagraph shall apply to bonds issued before January 1, 1996.

"(D) A facility is described in this subparagraph if—

"(i) the facility is a fixed guideway project,

"(ii) enabling legislation with respect to the issuing authority was approved by the State legislature in May 1973,

1,377

"(iii) on October 28, 1985, a board issued a request for consultants to conduct a feasibility study on mass transit corridor analysis in connection with the facility, and

"(iv) on May 12, 1986, a board approved a further binding contract for expenditures of approximately $1,494,963, to be expended on a facility study.

The aggregate face amount of bonds to which this subparagraph applies shall not exceed $250,000,000. Notwithstanding the last paragraph of this subsection, this subparagraph shall apply to bonds issued before January 1, 1996.

"(20) Private colleges.— Subsections (c)(2) and (f) of section 148 of the 1986 Code shall not apply to any bond which is issued as part of an issue if such bond—

"(A) is issued by a political subdivision pursuant to home rule and interlocal cooperation powers conferred by the constitution and laws of a State to provide funds to finance the costs of the purchase and construction of educational facilities for private colleges and universities, and

"(B) was the subject of a resolution of official action by such political subdivision (Resolution No. 86-1039) adopted by the governing body of such political subdivision on March 18, 1986.

The aggregate face amount of bonds to which this paragraph applies shall not exceed $100,000,000.

"(21) Pooled financing programs.—

"(A) Section 147(b) of the 1986 Code shall not apply to any hospital pooled financing program with respect to which—

"(i) a formal presentation was made to a city hospital facilities authority on January 14, 1986, and

"(ii) such authority passed a resolution approving the bond issue in principle on February 5, 1986.

The aggregate face amount of bonds to which this subparagraph applies shall not exceed $95,000,000.

"(B) Subsections (c)(2) and (f) of section 148 of the 1986 Code shall not apply to bonds for which closing occurred on July 16, 1986, and for which a State municipal league served as administrator for use in a State described in section 103A(g)(5)(C) of the Internal Revenue Code of 1954. The aggregate face amount of obligations to which this subparagraph applies shall not exceed $585,000,000.

"(22) Downtown redevelopment project.— Subsection (b) of section 626 of the Tax Reform Act of 1984 is amended by adding at the end thereof the following new paragraph:

"'(7) Exception for certain downtown redevelopment project.— The amendments made by this section shall not apply to any obligation which is issued as part of an issue 95 percent or more of the proceeds of which are to be used to provide a project to acquire and redevelop a downtown area if—

"'(A) on August 15, 1985, a downtown redevelopment authority adopted a resolution to issue obligations for such project, and

"'(B) before September 26, 1985, the city expended, or entered into binding contracts to expend, more than $10,000,000 in connection with such project, and

"'(C) the State supreme court issued a ruling regarding the proposed financing structure for such project on December 11, 1985.

The aggregate face amount of obligations to which this paragraph applies shall not exceed $85,000,000 and such obligations must be issued before January 1, 1992.'

"(23) Mass commuting and parking facilities.— A bond issued as part of an issue 95 percent or more of the net proceeds of which are to be used to provide any mass commuting facility or parking facility (within the meaning of section 103(b)(4)(D) of the 1954 Code) shall be treated as an exempt facility bond for purposes of part IV of subchapter B of chapter 1 of the 1986 Code if such facility is provided in connection with the rehabilitation, renovation, or other improvement to an existing railroad station owned on the date of the enactment of this Act by the National Railroad Passenger Corporation in the Northeast Corridor and which was placed in partial service in 1934 and was placed in the National Register of Historic Places in 1978. The aggregate face amount of bonds to which this paragraph applies shall not exceed $30,000,000.

"(24) Tax-exempt status of bonds of certain educational organizations.—

"(A) In general.— For purposes of section 103 and part IV of subchapter B of chapter 1 of the 1986 Code, a qualified educational organization shall be treated as a governmental unit, but only with respect to a trade or business carried on by such organization which is not an unrelated trade or business (determined by applying section 513(a) of such Code to such organization). The last paragraph of this section shall not apply to the treatment under the preceding sentence.

"(B) Qualified educational organization.— For purposes of subparagraph (A), the term 'qualified educational organization' means a college or university—

"(i) which was reincorporated and renewed with perpetual existence as a corporation by specific act of the legislature of the State within which such college or university is located on March 19, 1913, or

"(ii) which—

"(I) was initially incorporated or created on February 28, 1787, on April 29, 1854, or on May 14, 1888, and

"(II) as an instrumentality of the State, serves as a 'State-related' university by a specific act of the legislature of the State within which such college or university is located.

"(25) Tax-exempt status of bonds of certain public utilities.—

"(A) In general.— Except as provided in subparagraph (B), a bond shall be treated as a qualified bond for purposes of section 103 of the 1986 Code if such bond is issued after the date of the enactment of this Act with respect to a public utility facility if such facility is—

"(i) located at any non-federally owned dam (or on project waters or adjacent lands) located wholly or partially in one or more of 3 counties, 2 of which are contiguous to the third, where the rated capacity of the hydroelectric generating facilities at 5 of such dams on October 18, 1979, was more than 650 megawatts each,

"(ii) located at a dam (or on the project waters or adjacent lands) at which hydroelectric generating facilities were financed with the proceeds of tax-exempt obligations before December 31, 1968,

"(iii) owned and operated by a State, political subdivision of a State, or any agency or instrumentality of any of the foregoing, and

"(iv) located at a dam (or on project waters or adjacent lands) where the general public has access for recreational purposes to such dam or to such project waters or adjacent lands.

"(B) Special rules for subparagraph (A).—

"(i) Bonds subject to cap.— Section 146 of the 1986 Code shall apply to any bond described in subparagraph (A) which (without regard to subparagraph (A)) is a private activity bond. For purposes of applying section 146(k) of the 1986 Code, the public utility facility described in subparagraph (A) shall be treated as described in paragraph (2) of such section and such paragraph shall be applied without regard to the requirement that the issuer establish that a State's share of the use of a facility (or its output) will equal or exceed the State's share of the private activity bonds issued to finance the facility.

"(ii) Limitation on amount of bonds to which subparagraph (A) applies.— The aggregate face amount of bonds to which subparagraph (A) applies shall not exceed $750,000,000, not more than $350,000,000 of which may be issued before January 1, 1992.

"(iii) Limitation on purposes.— Subparagraph (A) shall only apply to bonds issued as part of an issue 95 percent or more of the net proceeds of which are used to provide 1 or more of the following:

"(I) A fish by-pass facility or fisheries enhancement facility.

"(II) A recreational facility or other improvement which is required by Federal licensing terms and conditions or other Federal, State, or local law requirements.

"(III) A project of repair, maintenance, renewal, or replacement, and safety improvement.

"(IV) Any reconstruction, replacement, or improvement, including any safety improvement, which increases, or allows an increase in, the capacity, efficiency, or productivity of the existing generating equipment.

"(26) Convention and parking facilities.— A bond shall not be treated as a private activity bond for purposes of section 103 and part IV of subchapter B of chapter 1 of the 1986 Code if—

"(A) such bond is issued to provide a sports or convention facility described in section 103(b)(4) (B) or (C) of the 1954 Code,

"(B) such bond is not described in section 103 (b)(2) or (o)(2)(A) of such Code,

"(C) legislation by a State legislature in connection with such facility was enacted on July 19, 1985, and was designated Chapter 375 of the Laws of 1985, and

"(D) legislation by a State legislature in connection with the appropriation of funds to a State public benefit corporation for loans in connection with the construction of such facility was enacted on April 17, 1985, and was designated Chapter 41 of the Laws of 1985.

The aggregate face amount of bonds to which this subparagraph applies shall not exceed $35,000,000.

"(27) Small issue termination.— Section 144(a)(12) of the 1986 Code shall not apply to any bond issued as part of an issue 95 percent or more of the net proceeds of which are to be used to provide a facility described in any of the following subparagraphs:

"(A) A facility is described in this subparagraph if—

"(i) the facility is a hotel and office facility located in a State capital,

"(ii) the economic development corporation of the city in which the facility is located adopted an initial inducement resolution on October 30, 1985, and

"(iii) a feasibility consultant was retained on February 21, 1986, with respect to such facility.

The aggregate face amount of bonds to which this subparagraph applies shall not exceed $10,000,000.

"(B) A facility is described in this subparagraph if such facility is financed by bonds issued by a State finance authority which was created in April 1985 by Act 1062 of the State General Assembly, and the Bond Guarantee Act (Act 505 of 1985) allowed such authority to pledge the interest from investment of the State's general fund as a guarantee for bonds issued by such authority. The aggregate face amount of bonds to which this subparagraph applies shall not exceed $75,000,000.

"(C) A facility is described in this subparagraph if such facility is a downtown mall and parking project for Holland, Michigan, with respect to which an initial agreement was formulated with the city in May 1985 and a formal memorandum of understanding was executed on July 2, 1986. The aggregate face amount of bonds to which this subparagraph applies shall not exceed $18,200,000.

"(D) A facility is described in this subparagraph if such facility is a downtown mall and parking ramp project for Traverse City, Michigan, with respect to which a final development agreement was signed in June 1986. The aggregate face amount of bonds to which this subparagraph applies shall not exceed $21,500,000.

"(E) A facility is described in this subparagraph if such facility is the rehabilitation of the Heritage Hotel in Marquette, Michigan. The aggregate face amount of bonds to which this subparagraph applies shall not exceed $5,000,000.

"(F) A facility is described in this subparagraph if it is the Lakeland Center Hotel in Lakeland, Florida. The aggregate face amount of obligations to which this subparagraph applies shall not exceed $10,000,000.

"(G) A facility is described in this subparagraph if it is the Marble Arcade office building renovation project in Lakeland, Florida. The aggregate face amount of obligations to which this subparagraph applies shall not exceed $5,900,000.

Exclusions from income

Code Sec. 103

"(H) A facility is described in this subparagraph if it is a medical office building in Bradenton, Florida, with respect to which—
"(i) a memorandum of agreement was entered into on October 17, 1985, and
"(ii) the city council held a public hearing and approved issuance of the bonds on November 13, 1985.
The aggregate face amount of obligations to which this subparagraph applies shall not exceed $8,500,000.

"(I) A facility is described in this subparagraph if it consists of the rehabilitation of the Andover Town Hall in Andover, Massachusetts. The provisions of section 149(b) of the 1986 Code (relating to federally guaranteed obligations) shall not apply to obligations to finance such project solely as a result of the occupation of a portion of such building by a United States Post Office. For purposes of determining whether any bond to which this subparagraph applies is a qualified small issue bond, there shall not be taken into account under section 144(a) of the 1986 Code capital expenditures with respect to any facility of the United States Government and there shall not be taken into account any bond allocable to the United States Government.

"(J) A facility is described in this subparagraph if it is the Central Bank Building renovation project in Grand Rapids, Michigan. The aggregate face amount of obligations to which this subparagraph applies shall not exceed $1,000,000.

"(28) Certain private loans not taken into account.—For purposes of determining whether any bond is a private activity bond, an amount of loans (but not in excess of $75,000,000) provided from the proceeds of 1 or more issues shall not be taken into account if such loans are provided in furtherance of—

"(A) a city Emergency Conservation Plan as set forth in an ordinance adopted by the city council of such city on February 17, 1983, or

"(B) a resolution adopted by the city council of such city on March 10, 1983, committing such city to a goal of reducing the peak load of such city's electric generation and distribution system by 553 megawatts in 15 years.

"(29) Certain private business use not taken into account.—

"(A) The nonqualified amount of the proceeds of an issue shall not be taken into account under section 141(b)(5) of the 1986 Code or in determining whether a bond described in subparagraph (B) (which is part of such issue) is a private activity bond for purposes of section 103 and part IV of subchapter B of chapter 1 of the 1986 Code.

"(B) A bond is described in this subparagraph if—
"(i) such bond is issued before January 1, 1993, by the state of Connecticut, and
"(ii) such bond is issued pursuant to a resolution of the State Bond Commission adopted before September 26, 1985.

"(C) The nonqualified amount to which this paragraph applies shall not exceed $150,000,000.

"(D) For purposes of this paragraph, the term 'nonqualified amount' has the meaning given such term by section 141(b)(8) of the 1986 Code, except that such term shall include the amount of the proceeds of an issue which is to be used (directly or indirectly) to make or finance loans (other than loans described in section 141(c)(2) of the 1986 Code) to persons other than governmental units.

"(30) Volume cap not to apply to certain facilities.—For purposes of section 146 of the 1986 Code, any exempt facility bond for the following facility shall not be taken into account: The facility is a facility for the furnishing of water which was authorized under P.L. 90-537 of the United States if—

"(A) construction of such facility began on May 6, 1973, and
"(B) forward funding will be provided for the remainder of the project pursuant to a negotiated agreement between State and local water users and the Secretary of the Interior signed April 15, 1986.
"The aggregate face amount of bonds to which this subparagraph applies shall not exceed $391,000,000.

"(31) Certain hydroelectric generating property.—A bond shall be treated as described in paragraph (2) of section 1316(f) of this Act if—
"(A) such bond would be so described but for the substitution specified in such paragraph,
"(B) on January 7, 1983, an application for a preliminary permit was filed for the project for which such bond is issued and received docket no. 6986, and
"(C) on September 20, 1983, the Federal Energy Regulatory Commission issued an order granting the preliminary permit for the project.
The aggregate face amount of bonds to which this paragraph applies shall not exceed $12,000,000.

"(32) Volume cap.—The State ceiling applicable under section 146 of the 1986 Code for calendar year 1987 for the State which ratified the United States Constitution on May 29, 1790, shall be $150,000,000 higher than the State ceiling otherwise applicable under such section for such year.

"(33) Application of $150,000,000 limitation for certain qualified 501(c)(3) bonds.—Proceeds of an issue described in any of the following subparagraphs shall not be taken into account under section 145(b) of the 1986 Code.

"(A) Proceeds of an issue are described in this subparagraph if—
"(i) such proceeds are used to provide medical school facilities or medical research and clinical facilities for a university medical center,
"(ii) such proceeds are of—
"(I) a $21,550,000 issue dated August 1, 1980,
"(II) a $84,400,000 issue dated September 1, 1984, and
"(III) a $48,500,000 issue (Series 1985 A and 1985 B) dated on December 1, 1985, and
"(iii) the issuer of all such issues is the same.

"(B) Proceeds of an issue are described in this subparagraph if such proceeds are for use by Yale University and—
"(i) the bonds are issued after August 8, 1986, by the State of Connecticut Health and Educational Facilities Authority, or

"(ii) the bonds are the 1st or 2nd refundings (including advance refundings) of the bonds described in clause (i), or of original bonds issued before August 7, 1986, by such Authority.
The aggregate face amount of bonds to which this subparagraph applies shall not exceed $90,000,000.

"(C) Proceeds of an issue are described in this subparagraph if—
"(i) such issue is issued on behalf of a university established by Charter granted by King George II of England on October 31, 1754, to accomplish a refunding (including an advance refunding) of bonds issued to finance 1 or more projects, and
"(ii) the application or other request for the issuance of the issue to the appropriate State issuer was made by or on behalf of such university before February 26, 1986.
The aggregate face amount of bonds to which this subparagraph applies shall not exceed $250,000,000.

"(D) Proceeds of an issue are described in this subparagraph if—
"(i) such proceeds are to be used for finance construction of a new student recreation center,
"(ii) a contract for the development phase of the project was signed by the university on May 21, 1986, with a private company for 5 percent of the costs of the project, and
"(iii) a committee of the university board of administrators approved the major program elements for the center on August 11, 1986.
The aggregate face amount of bonds to which this subparagraph applies shall not exceed $25,000,000.

"(E) Proceeds of an issue are described in this subparagraph if—
"(i) such proceeds are to be used in the construction of new life sciences facilities for a university for medical research and education,
"(ii) the president of the university authorized a faculty/administration planning committee for such facilities on September 17, 1982,
"(iii) the trustees of such university authorized site and architect selection on October 30, 1984, and
"(iv) the university negotiated a $2,600,000 contract with the architect on August 9, 1985.
The aggregate face amount of bonds to which this subparagraph applies shall not exceed $47,500,000.

"(F) Proceeds of an issue are described in this subparagraph if such proceeds are to be used to renovate undergraduate chemistry and engineering laboratories, and to rehabilitate other basic science facilities, for an institution of higher education in Philadelphia, Pennsylvania, chartered by legislative Acts of the Commonwealth of Pennsylvania, including an Act dated September 30, 1791. The aggregate face amount of bonds to which this subparagraph applies shall not exceed $6,500,000.

"(G) Proceeds of an issue are described in this subparagraph if such proceeds are of bonds which are the first advance refunding of bonds issued during 1985 for the development of a computer network, and construction and renovation or rehabilitation of other facilities, for an institution of higher education described in subparagraph (F). The aggregate face amount of bonds to which this subparagraph applies shall not exceed $80,000,000.

"(H) Proceeds of an issue are described in this subparagraph if—
"(i) the issue is issued on behalf of a university founded in 1789, and
"(ii) the proceeds of the issue are to be used to finance projects (to be determined by such university and the issuer) which are similar to those projects intended to be financed by bonds that were the subject of a request transmitted to Congress on November 7, 1985.
The aggregate face amount of bonds to which this subparagraph applies shall not exceed $200,000,000. Bonds to which this subparagraph applies shall be treated as qualified 501(c)(3) bonds if such bonds would not (if issued on August 15, 1986) be industrial development bonds (as defined in section 103(b)(2) of the 1954 Code), and section 147(f) of the 1986 Code shall not apply to the issue of which such bonds are a part. Bonds issued to finance facilities described in this subparagraph shall be treated as issued to finance such facilities notwithstanding the fact that a period in excess of 1 year has expired since the facilities were placed in service.

"(I) Proceeds of an issue are described in this subparagraph if the issue is issued on behalf of a university established on August 6, 1872, for a project approved by the trustees thereof on November 1, 1985. The aggregate face amount of bonds to which this subparagraph applies shall not exceed $100,000,000.

"(J) Proceeds of an issue are described in this subparagraph if—
"(i) the issue is issued on behalf of a university for which the founding grant was signed on November 11, 1885, and
"(ii) such bond is issued for the purpose of providing a Near West Campus Redevelopment Project and a Student Housing Project.
The aggregate face amount of bonds to which this subparagraph applies shall not exceed $105,000,000.

"(J) Proceeds of an issue are described in this subparagraph if—
"(i) they are the proceeds of advance refunding obligations issued on behalf of a university established on April 21, 1831, and
"(ii) the application or other request for the issuance of such obligations was made to the appropriate State issuer before July 12, 1986.
The aggregate face amount of obligations to which this subparagraph applies shall not exceed $175,000,000.

"(K) Proceeds of an issue are described in this subparagraph if—
"(i) the issue or issues are for the purpose of financing or refinancing costs associated with university facilities including at least 900 units of housing for students, faculty, and staff in up to two buildings and an office building containing up to 245,000 square feet of space, and

"(ii) a bond act authorizing the issuance of such bonds for such project was adopted on July 8, 1986, and such act under Federal law was required to be transmitted to Congress.

The aggregate face amount of obligations to which this subparagraph applies shall not exceed $112,000,000.

"(L) Proceeds of an issue are described in this subparagraph if such issue is for Cornell University in an aggregate face amount of not more than $150,000,000.

"(M) Proceeds of an issue are described in this subparagraph if such issue is issued on behalf of the Society of the New York Hospital to finance completion of a project commenced by such hospital in 1981 for construction of a diagnostic and treatment center or to refund bonds issued on behalf of such hospital in connection with the construction of such diagnostic and treatment center or to finance construction and renovation projects associated with an inpatient psychiatric care facility. The aggregate face amount of bonds to which this subparagraph applies shall not exceed $150,000,000.

"(N) Any bond to which section 145(b) of the 1986 Code does not apply by reason of this paragraph (other than subparagraph (A) thereof) shall be taken into account in determining whether such section applies to any later issue.

"(O) In the case of any refunding bond—

"(i) to which any subparagraph of this paragraph applies, and

"(ii) to which the last sentence of section 1313(c)(2) applies, such bond shall be treated as having such subparagraph apply (and the refunding bond shall be treated for purposes of such section as issued before January 1, 1986, and as not being an advance refunding) unless the issuer elects the opposite result.

"(34) Arbitrage rebate.—Section 148(f) of the 1986 Code shall not apply to any period before October 1, 1990, with respect to any bond the proceeds of which are to be used to provide a high-speed rail system for the State of Ohio. The aggregate face amount of bonds to which this paragraph applies shall not exceed $2,000,000,000.

"(35) Extension of carryforward period.—

"(A) In the case of a carryforward under section 103(n)(10) of the 1954 Code of $170,000,000 of bond limit for calendar year 1984 for a project described in subparagraph (B), clause (i) of section 103(n)(10)(C) of the 1954 Code shall be applied by substituting '6 calendar years' for '3 calendar years', and such carryforward may be used by any authority designated by the State in which the facility is located.

"(B) A project is described in this subparagraph if—

"(i) such project is a facility for local furnishing of electricity described in section 645 of the Tax Reform Act of 1984, and

"(ii) construction of such facility commenced within the 3-year period following the calendar year in which the carryforward arose.

"(36) Power purchase bonds.—A bond issued to finance purchase of power from a power facility at a dam being renovated pursuant to P.L. 98-381 shall not be treated as a private activity bond if it would not be such under section 141(b)(1) and (2) of the 1986 Code if 25 percent were substituted for 10 percent and the provisions of section 141(b)(3), (4), and (5) of the 1986 Code did not apply. The aggregate face amount of bonds to which this paragraph applies shall not exceed $400,000,000.

"(37) Qualified mortgage bonds.—A bond issued as part of either of 2 issues no later than September 8, 1986, shall be treated as a qualified mortgage bond within the meaning of section 141(d)(1)(B) of the 1986 Code if it satisfies the requirements of section 103A of the 1954 Code and if the issues are issued by the two most populous cities in the Tar Heel State. The aggregate face amount of bonds to which this paragraph applies shall not exceed $4,000,000.

"(38) Exempt facility bonds.—A bond shall be treated as an exempt facility bond within the meaning of section 142(a) of the 1986 Code if it is issued to fund residential, office, retail, light industrial, recreational and parking development known as Tobacco Row. Such bond shall be subject to section 146 of the 1986 Code. The aggregate face amount of bonds to which this paragraph applies shall not exceed $100,000,000.

"(39) Certain bonds treated as qualified 501(c)(3) bonds.—A bond issued as part of an issue shall be treated for purposes of part IV of subchapter B of chapter 1 of the 1986 Code as a qualified 501(c)(3) bond if—

"(A) such bond would not (if issued on August 15, 1986) be an industrial development bond (as defined in section 103(b)(2) of the 1954 Code), and

"(B) such issue was approved by city voters on January 19, 1985, for construction or renovation of facilities for the cultural and performing arts.

The aggregate face amount of bonds to which this paragraph applies shall not exceed $5,000,000.

"(40) Certain library bonds.—In the case of a bond issued before January 1, 1986, by the City of Los Angeles Community Redevelopment Agency to provide the library and related structures associated with the City of Los Angeles Central Library Project, the ownership and use of the land and facilities associated with such project by persons which are not governmental units (or payments from such persons) shall not adversely affect the exclusion from gross income under section 103 of the 1954 Code of interest on such bonds.

"(41) Certain refunding obligations for certain power facilities.—With respect to 2 net billed nuclear power facilities located in the State of Washington on which construction has been suspended, the requirements of section 147(b) of the 1986 Code shall be treated as satisfied with respect to refunding bonds issued before 1992 if—

"(A) each refunding bond has a maturity date not later than the maturity date of the refunded bond, and

"(B) the facilities have not been placed in service as of the date of issuance of the refunding bond. The aggregate face amount of bonds to which this paragraph applies shall not exceed $2,000,000,000. Section 146 of the 1986 Code and the last paragraph of this section shall not apply to bonds to which this paragraph applies.

"(42) Residential rental property.—A bond issued to finance a residential rental project within the meaning of 103(b)(4) of the 1954 Code shall be treated as an exempt facility bond within the meaning of section 142(a)(7) of the 1986 Code if the county housing finance authority adopted an inducement resolution with respect to the project on May 8, 1985, and the project is located in Polk County, Florida. The aggregate face amount of bonds to which this paragraph applies shall not exceed $4,100,000.

"(43) Extension of advance refunding for certain facilities.—Paragraph (4) of section 631(c) of the Tax Reform Act of 1984 is amended—

"(A) by striking out the second sentence thereof,

"(B) by adding at the end thereof the following new sentence: 'In the case of refunding obligations not exceeding $100,000,000 issued by the Alabama State Docks Department, the first sentence of this paragraph shall be applied by substituting 'December 31, 1987' for 'December 31, 1984' and the Internal Revenue Code of 1986 shall be applied without regard to section 149(d)(2),

"(44) Pool bonds.—The following amounts of pool bonds are exempt from the arbitrage rebate requirement of section 148(f) of the 1986 Code and the temporary period limitation of section 148(c)(2) of the 1986 Code:

Pool	Maximum Bond Amount
Tennessee Utility Districts Pool	$ 80,000,000
New Mexico Hospital Equipment Loan Council	$ 35,000,000
Pennsylvania Local Government Investment Trust Pool	$375,000,000
Indiana Bond Bank Pool	$240,000,000
Hernando County, Florida Bond Pool	$300,000,000
Utah Municipal Finance Cooperative Pool	$262,000,000
North Carolina League of Municipalities Pool	$200,000,000
Kentucky Municipal League Bond Pool	$170,000,000
Kentucky Association of Counties Bond Pool	$200,000,000
Homewood Municipal Bond Pool	$ 50,000,000
Colorado Association of School Boards Pool	$300,000,000
Tennessee Municipal League Pooled Bonds	$ 75,000,000
Georgia Municipal Association Pool	$130,000,000

"(45) Certain carryforward elections.—Notwithstanding any other provision of this title—

"(A) In the case of a metropolitan service district created pursuant to State revised statutes, chapter 268, up to $100,000,000 unused 1985 bond authority may be carried forward to any year until 1989 (regardless of the date on which such carryforward election is made).

"(B) If—

"(i) official action was taken by an industrial development board on September 16, 1985, with respect to the issuance of not more than $98,500,000, of waste water treatment revenue bonds, and

"(ii) an executive order of the governor granted a carryforward of State bond authority for such project on December 30, 1985,

such carryforward election shall be valid for any year through 1988. The aggregate face amount of obligations to which this subparagraph applies shall not exceed $98,500,000.

"(46) Treatment of certain obligations to finance hydroelectric generating facility.—If—

"(A) obligations are issued in an amount not exceeding $5,000,000 to finance the construction of a hydroelectric generating facility located on the North Fork of Cache Creek in Lake County, California, which was the subject of a preliminary resolution of the issuer of the obligations on June 29, 1982, or are issued to refund any of such obligations,

"(B) substantially all of the electrical power generated by such facility is to be sold to a nongovernmental person pursuant to a long-term power sales agreement in accordance with the Public Utility Regulatory Policies Act of 1978, and

"(C) the initially issued obligations are issued on or before December 31, 1986, and any of such refunding obligations are issued on or before December 31, 1996, then the person referred to in subparagraph (B) shall not be treated as a principal user of such facilities by reason of such sales for purposes of subparagraphs (D) and (E) of section 103(b)(6) of the 1954 Code.

"(47) Treatment of certain obligations to finance steam and electric cogeneration facility.—If—

"(A) obligations are issued on or before December 31, 1986, in an amount not exceeding $4,400,000 to finance a facility for the generation and transmission of steam and electricity having a maximum electrical capacity of approximately 5.3 megawatts and located within the City of San Jose, California, or are issued to refund any of such obligations,

"(B) substantially all of the electrical power generated by such facility that is not sold to an institution of higher education created by statute of the State of California is to be sold to a nongovernmental person pursuant to a long-term power sales agreement in accordance with the Public Utility Regulatory Policies Act of 1978, and

"(C) the initially issued obligations are issued on or before December 31, 1986, and any of such refunding obligations are issued on or before December 31, 1996, then the nongovernmental person referred to in subparagraph (B) shall not be treated as a principal user of such facilities by reason of such sales for purposes of subparagraphs (D) and (E) of section 103(b)(6) of the Internal Revenue Code of 1954.

"(48) Treatment of certain obligations.—A bond which is not an industrial development bond under section 103(b)(2) of the Internal Revenue Code of 1954 shall not be treated as a private activity bond for purposes of part IV of subchapter B of chapter 1 of the 1986 Code if 95 percent or more of the net proceeds

Exclusions from income Code Sec. 103

of the issue of which such bond is a part are used to provide facilities described in any of the following subparagraphs:

"(A) A facility is described in this subparagraph if it is a governmentally-owned and operated State fair and exposition center with respect to which—

"(i) the 1985 session of the State legislature authorized revenue bonds to be issued in a maximum amount of $10,000,000, and

"(ii) a market feasibility study dated June 30, 1986, relating to a major capital improvement program at the facility was prepared for the advisory board of the State fair and exposition center by a certified public accounting firm.

The aggregate face amount of obligations to which this subparagraph applies shall not exceed $10,000,000.

"(B) A facility is described in this subparagraph if it is a convention, trade, or spectator facility which is to be located in the State with respect to which paragraph (6)(U) applies and with respect to which feasibility and preliminary design consultants were hired on May 1, 1985 and October 31, 1985. The aggregate face amount of obligations to which this subparagraph applies shall not exceed $175,000,000.

"(C) A facility which is part of a project described in paragraph (6)(O). The aggregate face amount of bonds to which this subparagraph applies shall not exceed $20,000,000.

"(49) Transition rule for refunding certain housing bonds. — Sections 146 and 149(d)(2) of the 1986 Code shall not apply to the refunding of any bond issued under section 11(b) of the United States Housing Act of 1937 before December 31, 1983, if —

"(A) the bond has an original term to maturity of at least 40 years,

"(B) the maturity date of the refunding bonds does not exceed the maturity date of the refunded bonds,

"(C) the amount of the refunding bonds does not exceed the outstanding amount of the refunded bonds,

"(D) the interest rate on the refunding bonds is lower than the interest rate of the refunded bonds, and

"(E) the refunded bond is required to be redeemed not later than the earliest date on which such bond could be redeemed at par.

"(50) Transitioned bonds subject to certain rules. — In the case of any bond to which any provision of this section applies, except as otherwise expressly provided, sections 103 and 103A of the 1954 Code shall be applied as if the requirements of sections 147(g), 148, and 149(d) of the 1986 Code were included in each such section.

"(51) Certain additional projects. — Section 141(b) of the 1986 Code shall be applied by substituting '25' for '10' each place it appears and by not applying sections 141(b)(3) and 141(c)(1)(B) to bonds substantially all of the proceeds are used for—

"(A) A project is described in this subparagraph if it consists of a capital improvements program for a metropolitan sewer district, with respect to which a proposition was submitted to voters on August 7, 1984. The aggregate face amount of obligations to which this subparagraph applies shall not exceed $60,000,000.

"(B) Facilities described in this subparagraph if it consists of additions, extensions, and improvements to the wastewater system for Lakeland, Florida. The aggregate face amount of obligations to which this subparagraph applies shall not exceed $20,000,000.

"(C) A project is described in this subparagraph if it is the Central Valley Water Reclamation Project in Utah. The aggregate face amount of obligations to which this subparagraph applies shall not exceed $100,000,000.

"(D) A project is described in this subparagraph if it is a project to construct approximately 26 miles of toll expressways, with respect to which any appeal to validation was filed July 11, 1986. The aggregate face amount of obligations to which this subparagraph applies shall not exceed $450,000,000.

"(52) Termination. Except as otherwise provided in this section, this section shall not apply to any bond issued after December 31, 1990.

"Sec. 1318. Definitions, etc., relating to effective dates and transitional rules.

"(a) Definitions — For purposes of this subtitle —

"(1) 1954 Code. — The term '1954 Code' means the Internal Revenue Code of 1954 as in effect on the day before the date of the enactment of this Act.

"(2) 1986 Code. — The term '1986 Code' means the Internal Revenue Code of 1986 as amended by this Act.

"(3) Bond. — The term 'bond' includes any obligation.

"(4) Advance refund. — A bond shall be treated as issued to advance refund another bond if it is issued more than 90 days before the redemption of the refunded bond.

"(5) Net proceeds. — The term 'net proceeds' has the meaning given such term by section 150(a) of the 1986 Code.

"(6) Continued application of the 1954 code. — Nothing in this subtitle shall be construed to exempt any bond from any provision of the 1954 Code by reason of a delay in (or exemption from) the application of any amendment made by subtitle A.

"(7) Treatment as exempt facility. — Any bond which is treated as an exempt facility bond by section 1316 or 1317 shall not fail to be so treated by reason of subsection (b) of section 142 of the 1986 Code.

"(8) Application of future legislation to transitioned bonds. — In the case of any bond to which the amendments made by section 1301 do not apply by reason of a provision of this Act, any amendment of the 1986 Code (and any other provision applicable to such Code) included in any law enacted after October 22, 1986, shall be treated as included in section 103 and section 103A (as appropriate) of the 1954 Code with respect to such bond unless —

"(A) such law expressly provides that such amendment (or other provision) shall not apply to such bond, or

"(B) such amendment (or other provision) applies to a provision of the 1986 Code —

"(i) for which there is no corresponding provision in section 103 and section 103A (as appropriate) of the 1954 Code, and

"(ii) which is not otherwise treated as included in such sections 103 and 103A with respect to such bond."

"(b) Minimum tax treatment. —

"(1) In general. — Any bond described in paragraph (2) shall not be treated as a private activity bond for purposes of section 57 of the 1986 Code unless such bond would (if issued on August 7, 1986) be —

"(A) an industrial development bond (as defined in section 103(b)(2) of the 1954 Code), or

"(B) a private loan bond (as defined in section 103(o)(2)(A) of the 1954 Code), without regard to any exception from such definition other than section 103(o)(2)(C) of such Code).

"(2) Bonds described. — For purposes of paragraph (1), a bond is described in this paragraph if —

"(A) the amendments made by section 1301 do not apply to such bond by reason of section 1312 or 1316(g),

"(B) any provision of section 1317 applies to such bond, or

"(C) the proceeds of such bond are used to refund any bond referred to in subparagraph (A) or (B) (or any bond which is part of a series of refundings of such a bond) if the requirements of paragraphs (1), (2), and (3) of subsection (c) are met with respect to the refunding bond.

"(c) Current refundings not taken into account in applying aggregate limit on bonds to which transitional rules apply. — The limitation on the aggregate face amount of bonds to which any provision of section 1316(g) or 1317 applies shall not be reduced by the face amount of any bond the proceeds of which are to be used exclusively to refund any bond to which such provision applies (or any bond which is part of a series of refundings of such bond) if —

"(1) the average maturity date of the issue of which the refunding bond is a part is not later than the average maturity date of the bonds to be refunded by such issue,

"(2) the amount of the refunding bond does not exceed the outstanding amount of the refunded bond, and

"(3) the net proceeds of the refunding bond are used to redeem the refunded bond not later than 90 days after the date of the issuance of the refunding bond. For purposes of paragraph (1), average maturity shall be determined in accordance with section 147(b)(2)(A) of the 1986 Code. No limitation in section 1316(g) or 1317 on the period during which bonds may be issued under such section shall apply to any refunding bond which meets the requirements of this subsection.

"(d) Special rule permitting carryforward of volume cap for certain transitioned projects. — A bond to which section 1312 or 1317 applies shall be treated as having a carryforward purpose described in section 146(f)(5) of the 1986 Code, and the requirement of section 146(f)(2)(A) of the 1986 Code shall be treated as met if such project is identified with reasonable specificity. The preceding sentence shall not apply so as to permit a carryforward with respect to any qualified small issue bond.

Prior to amendment by Sec. 1301(a) of P.L. 99-514, Code Sec. 103 [as amended by Sec. 1013(c)(12)(A) of P.L. 100-649 which read as follows.

"Sec. 103. Interest on certain governmental obligations.

"(a) General rule.

"Gross income does not include interest on—

"(1) the obligations of a State, a Territory, or a possession of the United States, or any political subdivision of any of the foregoing, or of the District of Columbia; and

"(2) qualified scholarship funding bonds.

"(b) Industrial development bonds.

"(1) Subsection (a)(1) or (2) not to apply. Except as otherwise provided in this subsection, any industrial development bond shall be treated as an obligation not described in subsection (a)(1) or (2).

"(2) Industrial development bond. For purposes of this section, the term 'industrial development bond' means any obligation —

"(A) which is issued as part of an issue all or a major portion of the proceeds of which are to be used directly or indirectly in any trade or business carried on by any person who is not an exempt person (within the meaning of paragraph (3)), and

"(B) the payment of the principal or interest on which (under the terms of such obligation or any underlying arrangement) is, in whole or in major part —

"(i) secured by any interest in property used or to be used in a trade or business or in payments in respect of such property, or

"(ii) to be derived from payments in respect of property, or borrowed money, used or to be used in a trade or business.

"(3) Exempt person. For purposes of paragraph (2)(A), the term 'exempt person' means —

"(A) a governmental unit, or

"(B) an organization described in section 501(c)(3) and exempt from tax under section 501(a) (but only with respect to a trade or business carried on by such organization which is not an unrelated trade or business, determined by applying section 513(a) to such organization).

"(4) Certain exempt activities. Paragraph (1) shall not apply to any obligation which is issued as part of an issue substantially all of the proceeds of which are to be used to provide —

"(A) projects for residential rental property if at all times during the qualified project period —

"(i) 15 percent or more in the case of targeted area projects, or

"(ii) 20 percent or more in the case of any other project,

1,381

of the units in each project are to be occupied by individuals of low or moderate income,

"(B) sports facilities,

"(C) convention or trade show facilities,

"(D) airports, docks, wharves, mass commuting facilities, parking facilities, or storage or training facilities directly related to any of the foregoing,

"(E) sewage or solid waste disposal facilities or facilities for the local furnishing or electric energy or gas,

"(F) air or water pollution control facilities,

"(G) facilities for the furnishing of water for any purpose if

"(i) the water is or will be made available to members of the general public (including electric utility, industrial, agricultural, or commercial users), and

"(ii) either the facilities are operated by a governmental unit or the rates for the furnishing or sale of the water have been established or approved by a State or political subdivision thereof, by an agency or instrumentality of the United States, or by a public service or public utility commission or other similar body of any State or political subdivision thereof,

"(H) qualified hydroelectric generating facilities,

"(I) qualified mass commuting vehicles, or

"(J) local district heating or cooling facilities.

For purposes of subparagraph (E), the local furnishing of electric energy or gas from a facility shall include furnishing solely within the area consisting of a city and 1 contiguous county.

For purposes of subparagraph (A), any property shall not be treated as failing to be residential rental property merely because part of the building in which such property is located is used for purposes other than residential rental purposes.

"(5) Industrial parks. Paragraph (1) shall not apply to any obligation issued as part of an issue substantially all of the proceeds of which are to be used for the acquisition or development of land as the site for an industrial park. For purposes of the preceding sentence, the term 'development of land' includes the provision of water, sewage, drainage, or similar facilities, or of transportation, power, or communication facilities, which are incidental to use of the site as an industrial park, but, except with respect to such facilities, does not include the provision of structures or buildings.

"(6) Exemption for certain small issues.

"(A) In general. Paragraph (1) shall not apply to any obligation issued as part of an issue the aggregate authorized face amount of which is $1,000,000 or less and substantially all of the proceeds of which are to be used (i) for the acquisition, construction, reconstruction, or improvement of land or property of a character subject to the allowance for depreciation, or (ii) to redeem part or all of a prior issue which was issued for purposes described in clause (i) or this clause.

"(B) Certain prior issues taken into account. If—

"(i) the proceeds of two or more issues of obligations (whether or not the issuer of each such issue is the same) are or will be used primarily with respect to facilities located in the same incorporated municipality or located in the same county (but not in any incorporated municipality),

"(ii) the principal user of such facilities is or will be the same person or two or more related persons, and

"(iii) but for this subparagraph, subparagraph (A) would apply to each such issue,

then, for purposes of subparagraph (A), in determining the aggregate face amount of any later issue there shall be taken into account the face amount of obligations issued under all prior such issues and outstanding at the time of such later issue (not including as outstanding any obligation which is to be redeemed from the proceeds of the later issue).

"(C) Related persons. For purposes of this paragraph and paragraph (13), a person is a related person to another person if—

"(i) the relationship between such persons would result in a disallowance of losses under section 267 or 707(b), or

"(ii) such persons are members of the same controlled group of corporations (as defined in section 1563(a), except that 'more than 50 percent' shall be substituted for 'at least 80 percent' each place it appears therein).

"(D) $10,000,000 limit in certain cases. At the election of the issuer, made at such time and in such manner as the Secretary or his delegate shall by regulations prescribe, with respect to any issue this paragraph shall be applied—

"(i) by substituting '$10,000,000' for '$1,000,000' in subparagraph (A), and

"(ii) in determining the aggregate face amount of such issue, by taking into account not only the amount described in subparagraph (B), but also the aggregate amount of capital expenditures with respect to facilities described in subparagraph (E) paid or incurred during the 6-year period beginning 3 years before the date of such issue and ending 3 years after such date (and financed otherwise than out of the proceeds of outstanding issues to which subparagraph (A) applied), as if the aggregate amount of such capital expenditures constituted the face amount of a prior outstanding issue described in subparagraph (B).

"(E) Facilities taken into account. For purposes of subparagraph (D)(ii), the facilities described in this subparagraph are facilities—

"(i) located in the same incorporated municipality or located in the same county (but not in any incorporated municipality), and

"(ii) the principal user of which is or will be the same person or two or more related persons.

For purposes of clause (i), the determination of whether or not facilities are located in the same governmental unit shall be made as of the date of issue of the issue in question.

"(F) Certain capital expenditures not taken into account. For purposes of subparagraph (D)(ii), any capital expenditure—

"(i) to replace property destroyed or damaged by fire, storm, or other casualty, to the extent of the fair market value of the property replaced,

"(ii) required by a change made after the date of issue of the issue in question in a Federal or State law or local ordinance of general application or required by a change made after such date in rules and regulations of general application issued under such a law or ordinance,

"(iii) required by circumstances which could not be reasonably foreseen on such date of issue or arising out of a mistake of law or fact (but the aggregate amount of expenditures not taken into account under this clause with respect to any issue shall not exceed $1,000,000) or

"(iv) described in clause (i) or (ii) of section 30(b)(2)(A) for which a deduction was allowed under section 174(a),

shall not be taken into account.

"(G) Limitation on loss of tax exemption. In applying subparagraph (D)(ii) with respect to capital expenditures made after the date of any issue, no obligation issued as a part of such issue shall be treated as an obligation not described in subsection (a)(1) by reason of any such expenditure for any period before the date on which such expenditure is paid or incurred.

"(H) Certain refinancing issues. In the case of any issue described in subparagraph (A)(ii), an election may be made under subparagraph (D) only if all of the prior issues being redeemed are issues to which subparagraph (A) applies. In applying subparagraph (D)(ii) with respect to such a refinancing issue, capital expenditures shall be taken into account only for purposes of determining whether the prior issues being redeemed qualified (and would have continued to qualify) under subparagraph (A).

"(I) Aggregate amount of capital expenditures where there is urban development action grant. In the case of any issue substantially all of the proceeds of which are to be used to provide facilities with respect to which an urban development action grant has been made under section 119 of the Housing and Community Development Act of 1974, capital expenditures of not to exceed $10,000,000 shall not be taken into account for purposes of applying subparagraph (D)(ii).

"(J) Issues for residential purposes. This paragraph shall not apply to any obligation which is issued as a part of an issue a significant portion of the proceeds of which are to be used directly or indirectly to provide residential real property for family units.

"(K) Limitations on treatment of obligations as part of the same issue. For purposes of this paragraph, separate lots of obligations which (but for this subparagraph) would be treated as part of the same issue shall be treated as separate issues unless the proceeds of such lots are to be used with respect to 2 or more facilities—

"(i) which are located in more than 1 State, or

"(ii) which have, or will have, as the same principal user the same person or related persons.

"(L) Franchises. For purposes of subparagraph (K), a person (other than a governmental unit) shall be considered a principal user of a facility if such person (or a group of related persons which includes such person)—

"(i) guarantees, arranges, participates in, or assists with the issuance (or pays any portion of the cost of issuance) of any obligation the proceeds of which are to be used to finance or refinance such facility, and

"(ii) provides any property, or any franchise, trademark, or trade name (within the meaning of section 1253), which is to be used in connection with such facility.

"(M) Paragraph not to apply if obligations issued with certain other tax-exempt obligations. This paragraph shall not apply to any obligation which is issued as part of an issue (other than an issue to which subparagraph (D) applies) if the interest on any other obligation which is part of such issue is excluded from gross income under any provision of law other than this paragraph.

"(N) Termination dates.

"(i) In general.—Except as provided in clause (ii), this paragraph shall not apply to any obligation issued after December 31, 1986.

"(ii) Certain refundings.—This paragraph shall apply to any obligation (or series of obligations) issued to refund an obligation issued on or before December 31, 1986, if—

"(I) the average maturity date of the issue of which the refunding obligation is a part is not later than the average maturity date of the obligations to be refunded by such issue,

"(II) the amount of the refunding obligation does not exceed the outstanding amount of the refunded obligation, and

"(III) the proceeds of the refunding obligation are used to redeem the refunded obligation not later than 90 days after the date of the issuance of the refunding obligation.

For purposes of subclause (I), average maturity shall be determined in accordance with subsection (b)(14)(B)(i).

"(iii) Obligations used to finance manufacturing facilities. In the case of any obligation which is part of an issue substantially all of the proceeds of which are to be used to provide a manufacturing facility clause (i) shall be applied by substituting '1988' for '1986'.

"(iv) Manufacturing facility. For purposes of this subparagraph, the term 'manufacturing facility' means any facility which is used in the manufacturing or production of tangible personal property (including the processing resulting in a change in the condition of such property).

"(O) Restrictions on financing certain facilities. This paragraph shall not apply to an issue if—

"(i) more than 25 percent of the proceeds of the issue are used to provide a facility the primary purpose of which is one of the following: retail food and beverage services, automobile sales or service, or the provision of recreation or entertainment; or

"(ii) any portion of the proceeds of the issue is to be used to provide the following: any private or commercial golf course, country club, massage parlor, tennis club, skating facility (including roller skating, skateboard, and ice skating),

Exclusions from income — Code Sec. 103

racquet sports facility (including any handball or racquetball court), hot tub facility, suntan facility, or racetrack.

"(P) Aggregation of issues with respect to single project. For purposes of this paragraph, 2 or more issues part or all of which are to be used with respect to a single building, an enclosed shopping mall, or a strip of offices, stores, or warehouses using substantial common facilities shall be treated as 1 issue (and any person who is a principal user with respect to any of such issues shall be treated as a principal user with respect to the aggregated issue).

"(7) Repealed.

"(8) Qualified hydroelectric generating facilities. For purposes of this section—

"(A) Qualified hydroelectric generating facility. The term 'qualified hydroelectric generating facility' means any qualified hydroelectric generating property which is owned by a State, political subdivision thereof, or agency or instrumentality of any of the foregoing.

"(B) Qualified hydroelectric generating property.

"(i) In general. Except as provided in clause (ii), the term 'qualified hydroelectric generating property' has the meaning given to such term by section 48(l)(13).

"(ii) Dam must be owned by governmental body. The term 'qualified hydroelectric generating property' does not include any property installed at the site of any dam described in section 48(l)(13)(B)(i)(I) unless such dam was owned by one or more governmental bodies described in subparagraph (A) on October 18, 1979, and at all times thereafter until the obligations are no longer outstanding.

"(C) Limitation. Paragraph (4)(II) of this subsection shall not apply to any issue of obligations (otherwise qualifying under paragraph (4)(II)) if the portion of the proceeds of such issue which is used to provide qualified hydroelectric generating facilities exceeds (by more than an insubstantial amount) the product of—

"(i) the eligible cost of the facilities being provided in whole or in part from the proceeds of the issue, and

"(ii) the installed capacity fraction.

"(D) Installed capacity fraction. The term 'installed capacity fraction' means the fraction—

"(i) the numerator of which is 25, reduced by 1 for each megawatt by which the installed capacity exceeds 100 megawatts, and

"(ii) the denominator of which is the number of megawatts of the installed capacity (but not in excess of 100).

For purposes of the preceding sentence, the term 'installed capacity' has the meaning given to such term by section 48(l)(13)(E).

"(E) Eligible cost.

"(i) In general. The eligible cost of any facilities is that portion of the total cost of such facilities which is reasonably expected—

"(I) to be the cost to the governmental body described in subparagraph (A), and

"(II) to be attributable to periods after October 18, 1979, and before 1986 (determined under rules similar to the rules of section 48(m)).

"(ii) Longer period for certain hydroelectric generating property. If an application has been docketed by the Federal Energy Regulatory Commission before January 1, 1986, with respect to the installation of any qualified hydroelectric generating property, clause (i)(II) shall be applied with respect to such property by substituting '1989' for '1986'.

"(F) Certain prior issues taken into account. If the proceeds of 2 or more issues (whether or not the issuer of each issue is the same) are or will be used to finance the same facilities, then, for purposes of subparagraph (C), in determining the amount of the proceeds of any later issue used to finance such facilities, there shall be taken into account the proceeds used to finance such facilities of all prior such issues which are outstanding at the time of such later issue (not including as outstanding any obligation which is to be redeemed from the proceeds of the later issue).

"(9) Qualified mass commuting vehicles.

"(A) In general. For purposes of paragraph (4)(I), the term 'qualified mass commuting vehicle' means any bus, subway car, rail car, ferry, or similar equipment—

"(i) which is leased to a mass transit system wholly owned by 1 or more governmental units (or agencies or instrumentalities thereof), and

"(ii) which is used by such system in providing mass commuting services (or, in the case of a ferry, mass transportation services).

"(B) Termination. Paragraph (4)(I) shall not apply to any obligation issued after December 31, 1984.

"(10) Local district heating or cooling facility. For purposes of this section—

"(A) In general. The term 'local district heating or cooling facility' means property used as an integral part of a local district heating or cooling system.

"(B) Local district heating or cooling system.

"(i) In general. The term 'local district heating or cooling system' means any local system consisting of a pipeline or network (which may be connected to a heating or cooling source) providing hot water, chilled water, or steam to 2 or more users for—

"(I) residential, commercial, or industrial heating or cooling, or

"(II) process steam.

"(ii) Local system. For purposes of this subparagraph, a local system includes facilities furnishing heating and cooling to an area consisting of a city and one contiguous county.

"(11) Repealed

"(12) Projects for residential rental property. For purposes of paragraph (4)(A)—

"(A) Targeted area project. The term 'targeted area project' means—

"(i) a project located in a qualified census tract (within the meaning of section 103A(k)(2)), or

"(ii) an area of chronic economic distress (within the meaning of section 103A(k)(3)).

"(B) Qualified project period. The term 'qualified project period' means the period beginning on the first day on which 10 percent of the units in the project are occupied and ending on the later of—

"(i) the date which is 10 years after the date on which 50 percent of the units in the project are occupied.

"(ii) the date which is a qualified number of days after the date on which any of the units in the project are occupied, or

"(iii) the date on which any assistance provided with respect to the project under section 8 of the United States Housing Act of 1937 terminates.

For purposes of clause (ii), the term 'qualified number' means, with respect to an obligation described in paragraph (4)(A), 50 percent of the number of days which comprise the term of the obligation with the longest maturity.

"(C) Individuals of low and moderate income. Individuals of low and moderate income shall be determined by the Secretary in a manner consistent with determinations of lower income families under section 8 of the United States Housing Act of 1937 (or if such program is terminated, under such program as in effect immediately before such termination), except that the percentage of median gross income which qualifies as low or moderate income shall be 80 percent.

"(13) Exception. Paragraphs (4), (5), and (6) shall not apply with respect to any obligation for any period during which it is held by a person who is a substantial user of the facilities or a related person. For purposes of this paragraph—

"(A) a partnership and each of its partners (and their spouses and minor children) shall be treated as related persons, and

"(B) an S corporation and each of its shareholders (and their spouses and minor children) shall be treated as related persons.

"(14) Maturity may not exceed 120 percent of economic life.

"(A) General rule. Paragraphs (4), (5), and (6) shall not apply to any obligation issued as part of an issue if—

"(i) the average maturity of the obligations which are part of such issue, exceeds

"(ii) 120 percent of the average reasonably expected economic life of the facilities being financed with the proceeds of such issue.

"(B) Determination of averages. For purposes of subparagraph (A)—

"(i) the average maturity of any issue shall be determined by taking into account the respective issue prices of the obligations which are issued as part of such issue, and

"(ii) the average reasonably expected economic life of the facilities being financed with any issue shall be determined by taking into account the respective cost of such facilities.

"(C) Special rules.—

"(i) Determination of economic life. For purposes of this paragraph, the reasonably expected economic life of any facility shall be determined as of the later of—

"(I) the date on which the obligations are issued, or

"(II) the date on which the facility is placed in service (or expected to be placed in service).

"(ii) Treatment of land.

"(I) Land not taken into account. Except as provided in subclause (II), land shall not be taken into account under subparagraph (A)(ii).

"(II) Issues where 25 percent or more of proceeds used to finance land. If 25 percent or more of the proceeds of any issue is used to finance land, such land shall be taken into account under subparagraph (A)(ii) and shall be treated as having an economic life of 50 years.

"(15) Aggregate limit per taxpayer for small issue exception.

"(A) In general. Paragraph (6) of this subsection shall not apply to any issue if the aggregate authorized face amount of such issue allocated to any test-period beneficiary (when increased by the outstanding tax-exempt IDB's of such beneficiary) exceeds $40,000,000.

"(B) Outstanding tax-exempt IDB's of any person. For purposes of applying subparagraph (A) with respect to any issue, the outstanding tax-exempt IDB's of any person who is a test-period beneficiary with respect to such issue is the aggregate face amount of all industrial development bonds the interest on which is exempt from tax under subsection (a)—

"(i) which are allocated to such beneficiary, and

"(ii) which are outstanding at the time of such later issue (not including as outstanding any obligation which is to be redeemed from the proceeds of the later issue).

"(C) Allocation of face amount of an issue.

"(i) In general. Except as otherwise provided in regulations, the portion of the face amount of an issue allocated to any test-period beneficiary of a facility financed by the proceeds of such issue (other than an owner of such facility) is an amount which bears the same relationship to the entire face amount of such issue as the portion of such facility used by such beneficiary bears to the entire facility.

"(ii) Owners. Except as otherwise provided in regulations, the portion of the face amount of an issue allocated to any test-period beneficiary who is an owner of a facility financed by the proceeds of such issue is an amount which bears the same relationship to the entire face amount of such issue as the portion of such facility owned by such beneficiary bears to the entire facility.

"(D) Test-period beneficiary. For purposes of this paragraph, except as provided in regulations, the term 'test-period beneficiary' means any person who was an owner or a principal user of facilities being financed by the issue at any time during the 3-year period beginning on the later of—

"(i) the date such facilities were placed in service, or

"(ii) the date of the issue.

"(E) Treatment of related persons. For purposes of this paragraph, all persons who are related (within the meaning of paragraph (6)(C)) to each other shall be treated as one person.

"(16) Limitation on use for land acquisition.
"(A) In general. Paragraphs (4), (5), and (6) shall not apply with respect to any obligation issued as part of an issue if—
"(i) any portion of the proceeds of such issue are to be used (directly or indirectly) for the acquisition of land (or an interest therein) to be used for farming purposes, or
"(ii) 25 percent or more of the proceeds of such issue are to be used (directly or indirectly) for the acquisition of land not described in clause (i) (or an interest therein).
In the case of an obligation described in paragraph (5) (relating to industrial parks), clause (ii) shall be applied by substituting '50 percent' for '25 percent'.
"(B) Exception for first-time farmers.
"(i) In general. If the requirements of clause (ii) are met with respect to any land, subparagraph (A) shall not apply to such land, and paragraph (17) shall not apply to property located thereon or to property to be acquired within 1 year to be used in farming, but only to the extent of expenditures (financed with the proceeds of the issue) not in excess of $250,000.
"(ii) Acquisition by first-time farmers. The requirements of this clause are met with respect to any land if—
"(I) such land is to be used for farming purposes, and
"(II) such land is to be acquired by an individual who is a first time farmer, who will be the principal user of such land, and who will materially and substantially participate on the farm of which such land is a part in the operation of such farm.
"(iii) First-time farmer. For purposes of this subparagraph, the term 'first-time farmer' means any individual if such individual has not at any time had any direct or indirect ownership interest in substantial farmland in the operation of which such individual materially participated. For purposes of this subparagraph, any ownership or material participation by an individual's spouse or minor child shall be treated as ownership and material participation by the individual.
"(iv) Farm. For purposes of this subparagraph, the term 'farm' has the meaning given such term by section 6420(c)(2).
"(v) Substantial farmland. The term 'substantial farmland' means any parcel of land unless—
"(I) such parcel is smaller than 15 percent of the median size of a farm in the county in which such parcel is located, and
"(II) the fair market value of the land does not at any time while held by the individual exceed $125,000.
"(C) Exception for certain land acquired for environmental purposes. Any land acquired by a public agency in connection with an airport, mass transit, or port development project which consists of facilities described in paragraph (4)(D) shall not be taken into account under subparagraph (A) if—
"(i) such land is acquired for a noise abatement, wetland preservation, future use, or other public purpose, and
"(ii) there is not other significant use of such land.
"(17) Acquisition of existing property not permitted.
"(A) In general. Paragraphs (4), (5), and (6) shall not apply to any obligation issued as part of an issue if any portion of the proceeds of such issue is to be used for the acquisition of any property (or an interest therein) unless the first use of such property is pursuant to such acquisition.
"(B) Exception for certain rehabilitations. Subparagraph (A) shall not apply with respect to any building (and the equipment therefor) if—
"(i) the rehabilitation expenditures with respect to such building equals or exceeds
"(ii) 15 percent of the portion of the cost of acquiring such building (and equipment) financed with the proceeds of the issue.
A rule similar to the rule of the preceding sentence shall apply in the case of facilities other than a building except that clause (ii) shall be applied by substituting '100 percent' for '15 percent'.
"(C) Rehabilitation expenditures. For purposes of this paragraph—
"(i) In general. Except as provided in this subparagraph, the term 'rehabilitation expenditures' means any amount properly chargeable to capital account which is incurred by the person acquiring the building for property (or additions or improvements to property) in connection with the rehabilitation of a building. In the case of an integrated operation contained in a building before its acquisition, such term includes rehabilitating existing equipment in such building or replacing it with equipment having substantially the same function. For purposes of this clause, any amount incurred by a successor to the person acquiring the building or by the seller under a sales contract with such person shall be treated as incurred by such person.
"(ii) Certain expenditures not included. The term 'rehabilitation expenditures' does not include any expenditure described in section 48(g)(2)(B) (other than clause (i) thereof).
"(iii) Period during which expenditures must be incurred. The term 'rehabilitation expenditures' shall not include any amount which is incurred after the date 2 years after the later of—
"(I) the date on which the building was acquired, or
"(II) the date on which the obligation was issued.
"(D) Special rule for certain projects. In the case of a project involving 2 or more buildings, this paragraph shall be applied on a project basis.
"(18) No portion of bonds may be issued for skyboxes, airplanes, gambling establishments, etc. Paragraphs (4), (5), and (6) shall not apply to any obligation issued as part of an issue if any portion of the proceeds of such issue is to be used to provide any airplane, skybox, or other private luxury box, any health club facility, any facility primarily used for gambling, or any store the principal business of which is the sale of alcoholic beverages for consumption off premises.
"(c) Arbitrage.

"(1) Subsection (a)(1) or (2) not to apply to arbitrage bonds. Except as provided in this subsection, any arbitrage bond shall be treated as an obligation not described in subsection (a)(1) or (2).
"(2) Arbitrage bond. For purposes of this subsection, the term 'arbitrage bond' means any obligation which is issued as part of an issue all or a major portion of the proceeds of which are reasonably expected to be used directly or indirectly—
"(A) to acquire securities (within the meaning of section 165(g)(2)(A) or (B)) or obligations (other than obligations described in subsection (a)(1) or (2) which may be reasonably expected at the time of issuance of such issue, to produce a yield over the term of the issue which is materially higher (taking into account any discount or premium) than the yield on obligations of such issue, or
"(B) to replace funds which were used directly or indirectly to acquire securities or obligations described in subparagraph (A).
"(3) Exception. Paragraph (1) shall not apply to any obligation—
"(A) which is issued as part of an issue substantially all of the proceeds of which are reasonably expected to be used to provide permanent financing for real property used or to be used for residential purposes for the personnel of an educational organization described in section 170(b)(1)(A)(ii) which grants baccalaureate or higher degrees, or to replace funds which were so used, and
"(B) the yield on which over the term of the issue is not reasonably expected, at the time of issuance of such issue, to be substantially lower than the yield on obligations acquired or to be acquired in providing such financing.
This paragraph shall not apply with respect to any obligation for any period during which it is held by a person who is a substantial user of property financed by the proceeds of the issue of which such obligation is a part, or by a member of the family (within the meaning of section 318(a)(1)) of any such person.
"(4) Special rules. For purposes of paragraph (1), an obligation shall not be treated as an arbitrage bond solely by reason of the fact that—
"(A) the proceeds of the issue of which such obligation is a part may be invested for a temporary period in securities or other obligations until such proceeds are needed for the purpose for which such issue was issued, or
"(B) an amount of the proceeds of the issue of which such obligation is a part may be invested in securities or other obligations which are part of a reasonably required reserve or replacement fund.
The amount referred to in subparagraph (B) shall not exceed 15 percent of the proceeds of the issue of which such obligation is a part unless the issuer establishes that a higher amount is necessary.
"(5) Student loan incentive payments. Payments made by the Commissioner of Education pursuant to section 438 of the Higher Education Act of 1965 are not to be taken into account, for purposes of paragraph (2)(A), in determining yields on student loan notes.
"(6) Investments in nonpurpose obligations.
"(A) In general. For purposes of this title, any obligation which is part of an issue of industrial development bonds which does not meet the requirements of subparagraphs (C) and (D) shall be treated as an obligation which is not described in subsection (a).
"(B) Exceptions. Subparagraph (A) shall not apply to any obligation described in subsection (b)(4)(A) or to any housing program obligation under section 11(b) of the Housing Act of 1937.
"(C) Limitation on investment in nonpurpose obligations.
"(i) In general. An issue meets the requirements of this subparagraph only if—
"(I) at no time during any bond year, the amount invested in nonpurpose obligations with a yield higher than the yield on the issue exceeds 150 percent of the debt service on the issue for the bond year, and
"(II) the aggregate amount invested as provided in subclause (I) is promptly and appropriately reduced as the amount of outstanding obligations of the issue is reduced.
"(ii) Exception for temporary periods. Clause (i) shall not apply to—
"(I) proceeds of the issue invested for an initial temporary period until such proceeds are needed for the governmental purpose of the issue, and
"(II) temporary investment periods related to debt service.
"(iii) Debt service defined. For purposes of this subparagraph, the debt service on the issue for any bond year is the scheduled amount of interest and amortization of principal payable for such year with respect to such issue. For purposes of the preceding sentence, there shall not be taken into account amounts scheduled with respect to any bond which has been retired before the beginning of the bond year.
"(iv) No disposition in case of loss. This subparagraph shall not require the sale or disposition of any investment if such sale or disposition would result in a loss which exceeds the amount which would be paid to the United States (but for such sale or disposition) at the time of such sale or disposition.
"(D) Rebate to United States. An issue shall be treated as meeting the requirements of this subparagraph only if an amount equal to the sum of—
"(i) the excess of—
"(I) the aggregate amount earned on all nonpurpose obligations (other than investments attributable to an excess described in this clause), over
"(II) the amount which would have been earned if all nonpurpose obligations were invested at a rate equal to the yield on the issue, plus
"(ii) any income attributable to the excess described in clause (i),
is paid to the United States by the issuer in accordance with the requirements of subparagraph (E).
"(E) Due date of payments under subparagraph (D). The amount which is required to be paid to the United States by the issuer shall be paid in installments which are made at least once every 5 years. Each installment shall be in an amount which insures that 90 percent of the amount described in subparagraph (D) with respect to the issue at the time payment of such installment is required will have been paid to the United States. The last installment shall be made no later than 30 days after the day on which the last obligation of the issue is re-

Exclusions from income   Code Sec. 103

deemed and shall be in an amount sufficient to pay the remaining balance of the amount described in subparagraph (D) with respect to such issue.

"(F) Special rules for applying subparagraph (D).

"(i) In general. In determining the aggregate amount earned on nonpurpose obligations for purposes of subparagraph (D)—

"(I) any gain or loss on the disposition of a nonpurpose obligation shall be taken into account, and

"(II) unless the issuer otherwise elects, any amount earned on a bona fide debt service fund shall not be taken into account if the gross earnings on such fund for the bond year is less than $100,000.

"(ii) Temporary investments. Under regulations prescribed by the Secretary, an issue shall, for purposes of this paragraph, be treated as meeting the requirements of subparagraph (D) if the gross proceeds of such issue are expended for the governmental purpose for which the bond was issued by no later than the day which is 6 months after the date of issuance of such issue. Gross proceeds which are held in a bona fide debt service fund shall not be considered gross proceeds for purposes of this clause only.

"(G) Exemption from gross income of sum rebated. Gross income does not include the sum described in subparagraph (D). Notwithstanding any other provision of this title, no deduction shall be allowed for any amount paid to the United States under subparagraph (D).

"(II) Definitions. For purposes of this paragraph—

"(i) Nonpurpose obligations. The term 'nonpurpose obligation' means any security (within the meaning of subparagraph (A) or (B) of section 165(g)(2)) or any obligation not described in subsection (a) which—

"(I) is acquired with the gross proceeds of an issue, and

"(II) is not acquired in order to carry out the governmental purpose of the issue.

"(ii) Gross proceeds. The gross proceeds of an issue include—

"(I) amounts received (including repayments of principal) as a result of investing the original proceeds of the issue, and

"(II) amounts used to pay debt service on the issue.

"(iii) Yield. The yield on the issue shall be determined on the basis of the issue price (within the meaning of section 1273 or 1274).

"(7) Regulations. The Secretary shall prescribe such regulations as may be necessary to carry out the purposes of this subsection.

"(d) Certain irrigation dams.

"A dam for the furnishing of water for irrigation purposes which has a subordinate use in connection with the generation of electric energy by water shall be treated as meeting the requirements of subsection (b)(4)(G) if—

"(1) substantially all of the stored water is contractually available for release from such dam for irrigation purposes, and

"(2) the water so released is available on reasonable demand to members of the general public.

"(e) Qualified scholarship funding bonds.

"For purposes of subsection (a), the term 'qualified scholarship funding bonds' means obligations issued by a corporation which—

"(1) is a corporation not for profit established and operated exclusively for the purpose of acquiring student loan notes incurred under the Higher Education Act of 1965, and

"(2) is organized at the request of a State or one or more political subdivisions thereof or is requested to exercise such power by one or more political subdivisions and required by its corporate charter and bylaws, or required by State law, to devote any income (after payment of expenses, debt service, and the creation of reserves for the same) to the purchase of additional student loan notes or to pay over any income to the State or a political subdivision thereof.

"(f) Certain federally guaranteed obligations.

"Any obligation the payment of interest or principal (or both) of which is guaranteed in whole or in part under title I of the New York City Loan Guarantee Act of 1978 shall, with respect to interest accrued during the period for which such guarantee is in effect, be treated as an obligation not described in subsection (a).

"(g) Qualified steam-generating or alcohol-producing facilities.

"(1) In general. For purposes of subsection (b)(4)(E), the term 'solid waste disposal facility' includes

"(A) a qualified steam-generating facility, and

"(B) a qualified alcohol-producing facility.

"(2) Qualified steam-generating facility defined. For purposes of paragraph (1), the term 'qualified steam-generating facility' means a steam-generating facility for which

"(A) more than half of the fuel (determined on a Btu basis) is solid waste or fuel derived from solid waste, and

"(B) substantially all of the solid waste derived fuel is produced at a facility which is

"(i) located at or adjacent to the site for such steam-generating facility, and

"(ii) owned and operated by the person who owns and operates the steam-generating facility.

"(3) Qualified alcohol-producing facility. For purposes of paragraph (1), the term 'qualified alcohol-producing facility' means a facility

"(A) the primary product of which is alcohol,

"(B) more than half of the feedstock for which is solid waste or a feedstock derived from solid waste, and

"(C) substantially all of the solid waste derived feedstock for which is produced at a facility which is

"(i) located at or adjacent to the site for such alcohol-producing facility, and

"(ii) owned and operated by the person who owns and operates the alcohol-producing facility.

"(4) Special rule in case of steam-generating facility. A facility for producing solid waste derived fuel shall be treated as a facility which meets the requirements of clauses (i) and (ii) of paragraph (2)(B) if

"(A) such facility and the steam-generating facility are owned and operated by or for a State or the same political subdivision or subdivisions of a State, and

"(B) substantially all of the solid waste used in producing the solid waste derived fuel at the facility producing such fuel is collected from the area in which the steam-generating facility is located.

"(h) Obligation must not be guaranteed, etc.

"(1) In general. An obligation shall not be treated as an obligation described in subsection (a) if such obligation is federally guaranteed.

"(2) Federally guaranteed defined. For purposes of paragraph (1), an obligation is federally guaranteed if—

"(A) The payment of principal or interest with respect to such obligation is guaranteed (in whole or in part) by the United States (or any agency or instrumentality thereof),

"(B) such obligation is issued as part of an issue and a significant portion of the proceeds of such issue are to be—

"(i) used in making loans the payment of principal or interest with respect to which are to be guaranteed (in whole or in part) by the United States (or any agency or instrumentality thereof), or

"(ii) invested (directly or indirectly) in federally insured deposits or accounts, or

"(C) the payment of principal or interest on such obligation is otherwise indirectly guaranteed (in whole or in part) by the United States (or any agency or instrumentality thereof).

"(3) Exceptions.

"(A) Certain insurance programs. An obligation shall not be treated as federally guaranteed by reason of—

"(i) any guarantee by the Federal Housing Administration, the Veterans' Administration, the Federal National Mortgage Association, the Federal Home Loan Mortgage Corporation, or the Government National Mortgage Association,

"(ii) any guarantee of student loans and any guarantee by the Student Loan Marketing Association to finance student loans,

"(iii) any guarantee by the Small Business Administration with respect to qualified contracts for pollution control facilities (within the meaning of section 404(a) of the Small Business Investment Act of 1958, as in effect on the date of the enactment of the Tax Reform Act of 1984) if—

"(I) the Administrator of the Small Business Administration charges a fee for making such guarantee, and

"(II) the amount of such fee equals or exceeds 1 percent of the amount guaranteed, or

"(iv) any guarantee by the Bonneville Power Authority pursuant to the Northwest Power Act (16 U.S.C. 839d) as in effect on the date of the enactment of the Tax Reform Act of 1984 with respect to any obligation issued before July 1, 1989.

"(B) Debt service, etc. Paragraph (1) shall not apply to—

"(i) proceeds of the issue invested for an initial temporary period until such proceeds are needed for the purpose for which such issue was issued,

"(ii) investments of a bona fide debt service fund,

"(iii) investments of a reserve which meet the requirements of subsection (c)(4)(B),

"(iv) investments in obligations issued by the United States Treasury, or

"(v) other investments permitted under regulations.

"(C) Exception for housing programs.

"(i) In general. Except as provided in clause (ii), paragraph (1) shall not apply to—

"(I) an obligation described in subsection (b)(4)(A), or a housing program obligation under section 11(b) of the United States Housing Act of 1937,

"(II) a qualified mortgage bond (as defined in section 103A(c)(1)), or

"(III) a qualified veterans' mortgage bond (as defined in section 103A(c)(3)).

"(ii) Exception not to apply where obligation invested in federally insured deposits or accounts. Clause (i) shall not apply to any obligation which is federally guaranteed within the meaning of paragraph (2)(B)(ii),

"(D) Loans to, or guarantees by, financial institutions. Except as provided in paragraph (2)(B)(ii), an obligation which is issued as part of an issue shall not be treated as federally guaranteed merely by reason of the fact that the proceeds of such issue are used in making loans to a financial institution or there is a guarantee by a financial institution.

"(4) Definitions. For purposes of this subsection

"(A) Treatment of certain entities with authority to borrow from United States. To the extent provided in regulations prescribed by the Secretary, any entity with statutory authority to borrow from the United States shall be treated as an instrumentality of the United States. Except in the case of a private activity bond (as defined in subsection (n)(7)), nothing in the preceding sentence shall be construed as treating the District of Columbia or any possession of the United States as an instrumentality of the United States.

"(B) Federally insured deposit or account. The term 'federally insured deposit or account' means any deposit or account in a financial institution to the extent such deposit or account is insured under Federal law by the Federal Deposit Insurance Corporation, the Federal Savings and Loan Insurance Corporation, the National Credit Union Administration, or any similar federally chartered corporation.

"(5) Certain obligations subsidized under energy program.

"(A) In general. An obligation to which this paragraph applies shall be treated as an obligation not described in subsection (a) if the payment of the principal or interest with respect to such obligation is to be made (in whole or in part) under a

1,385

program of a State, or a political subdivision of a State the principal purpose of which is to encourage the production or conservation of energy.

"(B) Obligations to which paragraph applies. This paragraph shall apply to any obligations to which paragraph (1) of subsection (b) does not apply by reason of—

"(i) subsection (b)(4)(II) (relating to qualified hydroelectric generating facilities), or

"(ii) subsection (g) (relating to qualified steam-generating or alcohol-producing facilities).

"(i) Obligations of certain volunteer fire departments.

"(1) In general. An obligation of a volunteer fire department shall be treated as an obligation of a political subdivision of a State if—

"(A) such department is a qualified volunteer fire department with respect to an area within the jurisdiction of such political subdivision, and

"(B) such obligation is issued as part of an issue substantially all of the proceeds of which are to be used for the acquisition, construction, reconstruction, or improvement of a firehouse or firetruck used or to be used by such department.

"(2) Qualified volunteer fire department. For purposes of this subsection, the term 'qualified volunteer fire department' means, with respect to a political subdivision of a State, any organization—

"(A) which is organized and operated to provide firefighting or emergency medical services for persons in an area (within the jurisdiction of such political subdivision) which is not provided with any other firefighting services, and

"(B) which is required (by written agreement) by the political subdivision to furnish firefighting services in such area.

"(j) Obligations must be in registered form to be tax-exempt.

"(1) In general. Nothing in subsection (a) or in any other provision of law shall be construed to provide an exemption from Federal income tax for interest on any registration-required obligation unless the obligation is in registered form.

"(2) Registration-required obligation. The term 'registration-required obligation' means any obligation other than an obligation which—

"(A) is not of a type offered to the public,

"(B) has a maturity (at issue) of not more than 1 year, or

"(C) is described in section 163(1)(2)(B).

"(3) Special rules

"(A) Book entries permitted. For purposes of paragraph (1), a book entry obligation shall be treated as in registered form if the right to the principal of, and stated interest on, such obligation may be transferred only through a book entry consistent with regulations prescribed by the Secretary.

"(B) Nominees. The Secretary shall prescribe such regulations as may be necessary to carry out the purpose of paragraph (1) where there is a nominee or chain of nominees.

"(k) Public approval for industrial development bonds.

"(1) In general. Notwithstanding subsection (b), an industrial development bond shall be treated as an obligation not described in subsection (a) unless the requirements of paragraph (2) of this subsection are satisfied.

"(2) Public approval requirement.

"(A) In general. An obligation shall satisfy the requirements of this paragraph if such obligation is issued as a part of an issue which has been approved by—

"(i) the governmental unit—

"(I) which issued such obligation, or

"(II) on behalf of which such obligation was issued, and

"(ii) each governmental unit having jurisdiction over the area in which any facility, with respect to which financing is to be provided from the proceeds of such issue, is located (except that if more than 1 governmental unit within a State has jurisdiction over the entire area within such State in which such facility is located, only 1 such unit need approve such issue).

"(B) Approval by a governmental unit. For purposes of subparagraph (A), an issue shall be treated as having been approved by any governmental unit if such issue is approved—

"(i) by the applicable elected representative of such governmental unit after a public hearing following reasonable public notice, or

"(ii) by voter referendum of such governmental unit.

"(C) Special rules for approval of facility. If there has been public approval under subparagraph (A) of the plan of financing a facility, such approval shall constitute approval under subparagraph (A) for any issue—

"(i) which is issued pursuant to such plan within 3 years after the date of the first issue pursuant to the approval, and

"(ii) all or substantially all of the proceeds of which are to be used to finance such facility or to refund previous financing under such plan.

"(D) Refunding obligations. No approval under subparagraph (A) shall be necessary with respect to any obligation which is issued to refund an obligation approved under subparagraph (A) (or treated as approved under subparagraph (C)) unless the maturity date of such obligation is later than the maturity date of the obligation to be refunded.

"(E) Applicable elected representative. For purposes of this paragraph—

"(i) In general. The term 'applicable elected representative' means with respect to any governmental unit

"(I) an elected legislative body of such unit, or

"(II) the chief elected executive officer, the chief elected State legal officer of the executive branch, or any other elected official of such unit designated for purposes of this paragraph by such chief elected executive officer or by State law.

"(ii) No applicable elected representative. If (but for this clause) a governmental unit has no applicable elected representative, the applicable elected representative for purposes of clause (i) shall be the applicable elected representative of the governmental unit—

"(I) which is the next higher governmental unit with such a representative, and

"(II) from which the authority of the governmental unit with no such representative is derived.

"(l) Information reporting requirements for certain bonds.

"(1) In general. Notwithstanding subsection (b), any industrial development bond or any other obligation which is issued as part of an issue all or a major portion of the proceeds of which are to be used directly or indirectly—

"(A) to finance loans to individuals for educational expenses, or

"(B) by an organization described in section 501(c)(3) which is exempt from taxation by reason of section 501(a),

shall be treated as an obligation not described in paragraph (1) or (2) of subsection (a) unless such bond satisfies the requirements of paragraph (2).

"(2) Information reporting requirement. An obligation satisfies the requirement of this paragraph if the issuer submits to the Secretary, not later than the 15th day of the 2nd calendar month after the close of the calendar quarter in which the obligation is issued, a statement concerning the issue of which the obligation is a part which contains—

"(A) the name and address of the issuer,

"(B) the date of issue, the amount of lendable proceeds of the issue, and the stated interest rate, term, and face amount of each obligation which is part of the issue,

"(C) where required, the name of the applicable elected representative who approved the issue, or a description of the voter referendum by which the issue was approved,

"(D) the name, address, and employer identification number of—

"(i) each initial principal user of any facilities provided with the proceeds of the issue,

"(ii) the common parent of any affiliated group of corporations (within the meaning of section 1504(a)) of which such initial principal user is a member, and

"(iii) if the issue is treated as a separate issue under subsection (b)(6)(K), any person treated as a principal user under subsection (b)(6)(L),

"(E) a description of any property to be financed from the proceeds of the issue, and

"(F) if such obligation is a private activity bond (as defined in subsection (n)(7)), such information as the Secretary may require for purposes of determining whether the requirements of subsection (n) are met with respect to such obligation.

"(3) Extension of time. The Secretary may grant an extension of time for the filing of any statement required under paragraph (2) if there is reasonable cause for the failure to file such statement in a timely fashion.

"(m) Obligations exempt other than under this title.

"(1) Prior exemptions. For purposes of this title, notwithstanding any provisions of this section or section 103A any obligation the interest on which is exempt from taxation under this title under any provision of law which is in effect on the date of the enactment of this subsection (other than a provision of this title) shall be treated as an obligation described in subsection (a). In the case of an obligation issued after December 31, 1983, such obligation shall not be treated as described in this paragraph unless the appropriate requirements of subsections (b), (c), (h), (j), (k), (l), (n), and (o) of this section and section 103A are met with respect to such obligation. For purposes of applying such requirements, a possession of the United States shall be treated as a State; except that clause (ii) of subsection (n)(4)(A) shall not apply.

"(2) No other interest to be exempt except as provided by this title. Notwithstanding any other provision of law, no interest on any obligation shall be exempt from taxation under this title unless such interest—

"(A) is on an obligation described in paragraph (1), or

"(B) is exempt from tax under this title without regard to any provision of law which is not contained in this title and which is not contained in a revenue Act.

"(3) Exceptions. The following obligations shall be treated as obligations described in paragraph (1) (without regard to the second sentence thereof):

"(A) Any obligation issued pursuant to the Northwest Power Act (16 U.S.C. 839d) as in effect on the date of the enactment of the Tax Reform Act of 1984.

"(B) Any obligation issued pursuant to Sec. 608(a)(6)(A) of P.L. 97-468.

"(C) Any obligation issued before June 19, 1984, under section 11(b) of the United States Housing Act of 1937.

"(n) Limitation on aggregate amount of private activity bonds issued during any calendar year.

"(1) In general. A private activity bond issued as part of an issue shall be treated as an obligation not described in subsection (a) if the aggregate amount of private activity bonds issued pursuant to such issue, when added to the aggregate amount of private activity bonds previously issued by the issuing authority during the calendar year, exceeds such authority's private activity bond limit for such calendar year.

"(2) Private activity bond limit for state agencies. For purposes of this subsection—

"(A) In general. The private activity bond limit for any agency of the State authorized to issue private activity bonds for any calendar year shall be 50 percent of the State ceiling for such calendar year.

"(B) Special rule where state has more than 1 agency. If more than 1 agency of the State is authorized to issue private activity bonds, all such agencies shall be treated as a single agency.

"(3) Private activity bond limit for other issuers. For purposes of this subsection—

"(A) In general. The private activity bond limit for any issuing authority (other than a State agency) for any calendar year shall be an amount which bears the same ratio to 50 percent of the State ceiling for such calendar year as—

"(i) the population of the jurisdiction of such issuing authority, bears to

"(ii) the population for the entire State.

Exclusions from income — Code Sec. 103

"(B) Overlapping jurisdictions. For purposes of subparagraph (A)(i), the rules of section 103A(g)(3)(B) shall apply.

"(4) State ceiling. For purposes of this subsection—

"(A) In general. The State ceiling applicable to any State for any calendar year shall be the greater of—

"(i) an amount equal to $150 multiplied by the State's population, or

"(ii) $200,000,000.

"(B) Phase in of limitation where amount of 1983 private activity bonds exceeds the ceiling.

"(i) In general. In the case of any State which has an excess bond amount for 1983, the State ceiling for calendar year 1984 shall be the sum of the State ceiling determined under subparagraph (A) plus 50 percent of the excess bond amount for 1983.

"(ii) Excess bond amount for 1983. For purposes of clause (i), the excess bond amount for 1983 in any State is the excess (if any) of—

"(I) the aggregate amount of private activity bonds issued by issuing authorities in such State during the first 9 months of calendar year 1983 multiplied by 4/3, over

"(II) the State ceiling determined under subparagraph (A) for calendar year 1984.

"(C) Adjustment of ceiling to reflect partial termination of small issue exemption. In the case of calendar years after 1986, subparagraph (A) shall be applied by substituting '$100' for '$150'.

"(5) Special rule for states with constitutional home rule cities. In the case of any State with 1 or more constitutional home rule cities (as defined in section 103A(g)(5)(C)), the rules of paragraph (5) of section 103A(g) shall apply for purposes of this subsection.

"(6) State may provide for different allocation.

"(A) In general. A State may, by law provide a different formula for allocating the State ceiling among the governmental units or other authorities in such State having authority to issue private activity bonds.

"(B) Interim authority for Governor.

"(i) In general. The Governor of any State may proclaim a different formula for allocating the State ceiling among the governmental units or other authorities in such State having authority to issue private activity bonds.

"(ii) Termination of authority. The authority provided in clause (i) shall not apply after the earlier of—

"(I) the first day of the first calendar year beginning after the legislature has met in regular session for more than 60 days after the date of the enactment of this paragraph, or

"(II) the effective date of any State legislation with respect to the allocation of the State ceiling.

"(C) State may not alter allocation to constitutional home rule cities. The rules of paragraph (6)(C) of section 103A(g) shall apply for purposes of this paragraph.

"(7) Private activity bond. For purposes of this subsection—

"(A) In general. Except as otherwise provided in the paragraph, the term 'private activity bond' means any obligation the interest on which is exempt from tax under subsection (a) and which is—

"(i) an industrial development bond, or

"(ii) a student loan bond.

"(B) Exception for multifamily housing. The term 'private activity bonds' shall not include any obligation described in subsection (b)(4)(A) nor any housing program obligation under section 11(b) of the United States Housing Act of 1937.

"(C) Exception for certain facilities described in section 103(b)(4)(C) or (D).

"(i) In general. The term 'private activity bond' shall not include any obligation described in subparagraph (C) or (D) of subsection (b)(4), but only if all of the property to be financed by the obligation is owned by or on behalf of a governmental unit.

"(ii) Exception not to apply to certain parking facilities. For purposes of clause (i), subparagraph (D) of subsection (b)(4) shall be applied as if it did not contain the phrase 'parking facilities'.

"(iii) Determination of whether property owned by governmental unit. For purposes of clause (i), property shall not be treated as not owned by a governmental unit solely by reason of the length of the lease to which it is subject if the lessee makes an irrevocable election (binding on the lessee and all successors in interest under the lease) not to claim depreciation or an investment credit with respect to such property.

"(iv) Restriction where significant front end loading. Under regulations prescribed by the Secretary, clause (i) shall not apply in any case where the property is leased under a lease which has significant front end loading of rental accruals or payments.

"(D) Refunding issues. The term 'private activity bond' shall not include any obligation which is issued to refund another obligation to the extent that the amount of such obligation does not exceed the amount of the refunded obligation. In the case of any student loan bond, the preceding sentence shall apply only if the maturity date of the refunding obligation is not later than the later of—

"(i) the maturity of the obligation to be refunded, or

"(ii) the date 17 years after the date on which the refunded obligation was issued (or in the case of a series of refundings, the date on which the original obligation was issued).

"(8) Student loan bonds. For purposes of this subsection, the term 'student loan bond' means an obligation which is issued as part of an issue all or a major portion of the proceeds of which are to be used directly or indirectly to finance loans to individuals for educational expenses.

"(9) Population. For purposes of this subsection, determinations of the population of any State (or issuing authority) shall be made with respect to any calendar year on the basis of the most recent census estimate of the resident population of such State (or issuing authority) published by the Bureau of the Census before the beginning of such calendar year.

"(10) Elective carryforward of unused limitation for specified project.

"(A) In general. If—

"(i) an issuing authority's private activity bond limit for any calendar year after 1983, exceeds

"(ii) the aggregate amount of private activity bonds issued during such calendar year by such authority,

such authority may elect to treat all (or any portion) of such excess as a carryforward for 1 or more carryforward projects.

"(B) Election must identify project. In any election under subparagraph (A), the issuing authority shall—

"(i) identify (with reasonable specificity) the project (or projects) for which the carryforward is elected, and

"(ii) specify the portion of the excess described in subparagraph (A) which is to be a carryforward for each such project

"(C) Use of carryforward.

"(i) In general. If any issuing authority elects a carryforward under subparagraph (A) with respect to any carryforward project, any private activity bonds issued by such authority with respect to such project during the 3 calendar years (or, in the case of a project described in subsection (b)(4)(F), 6 calendar years) following the calendar year in which the carryforward arose shall not be taken into account under paragraph (1) to the extent the amount of such bonds do not exceed the amount of the carryforward elected for such project.

"(ii) Order in which carryforward used. Carryforwards elected with respect to any project shall be used in the order of the calendar years in which they arose.

"(D) Election. Any election made under this paragraph shall be made at such time and in such manner as the Secretary shall by regulations prescribe. Any such election (and any identification or specification contained therein), once made, shall be irrevocable.

"(E) Carryforward project. For purposes of this paragraph, the term 'carryforward project' means—

"(i) any project described in paragraph (4) or (5) of subsection (b), and

"(ii) the purpose of issuing student loan bonds.

"(11) Treatment of qualified scholarship funding bonds. In the case of a qualified scholarship funding bond (as defined in subsection (e)), such bond shall be treated for purposes of this subsection as issued by a State or local issuing authority (whichever is appropriate).

"(12) Certification of no consideration for allocation.

"(A) In general. Any private activity bond allocated any portion of the State limit shall not be exempt from tax under subsection (a) unless the public official if any responsible for such allocation certifies under penalty of perjury that the allocation was not made in consideration of any bribe, gift, gratuity, or direct or indirect contribution to any political campaign.

"(B) Any criminal penalty made applicable. Any person willfully making an allocation described in subparagraph (A) in consideration of any bribe, gift, gratuity, or direct or indirect contribution to any political campaign shall be subject to criminal penalty to the same extent as if such allocation were a willful attempt to evade tax imposed by this title.

"(13) Facility must be located within state.

"(A) In general. Except as provided in subparagraph (B), no portion of the State ceiling applicable to any State for any calendar year may be used with respect to financing for a facility located outside such State.

"(B) Exception for certain facilities where state will get proportionate share of benefits. Subparagraph (A) shall not apply to any issue described in subparagraph (E), (G), or (H) of subsection (b)(4) if the issuer establishes that the State's share of the use of the facility (or its output) will equal or exceed the State's share of the private activity bonds issued to finance the facility.

"(o) Private loan bonds.

"(1) Denial of tax exemption. For purposes of this title, any private loan bond shall be treated as an obligation which is not described in subsection (a).

"(2) Private loan bonds. For purposes of this subsection—

"(A) In general. The term 'private loan bond' means any obligation which is issued as part of an issue all or a significant portion of the proceeds of which are reasonably expected to be used directly or indirectly to make or finance loans (other than loans described in subparagraph (C)) to persons who are not exempt persons (within the meaning of subsection (b)(3)).

"(B) Excluded obligations. The term 'private loan bond' shall not include any—

"(i) qualified student loan bond,

"(ii) industrial development bond, or

"(iii) qualified mortgage bond or qualified veterans' mortgage bond.

"(C) Excluded loans. A loan is described in this subparagraph if the loan—

"(i) enables the borrower to finance any governmental tax or assessment of general application for an essential governmental function, or

"(ii) is used to acquire or carry nonpurpose obligations (within the meaning of subsection (c)(6)(H)(i)).

"(3) Qualified student loan bonds. For purposes of this subsection, the term 'qualified student loan bond' means any obligation which is issued as part of an issue all or a major portion of the proceeds of which are reasonably expected to be used directly or indirectly to make or finance student loans under a program of general application to which the Higher Education Act of 1965 applies if—

"(A) limitations are imposed under the program on—

"(i) the maximum amount of loans outstanding to any student, and

"(ii) the maximum rate of interest payable on any loan,

"(B) the loans are directly or indirectly guaranteed by the Federal Government,

Code Sec. 103 — Exclusions from income

"(C) the financing of loans under the program is not limited by Federal law to the proceeds of obligations the interest on which is exempt from taxation under this title, and

"(D) special allowance payments under section 438 of the Higher Education Act of 1965 —

"(i) are authorized to be paid with respect to loans made under the program, or

"(ii) would be authorized to be made with respect to loans under the program if such loans were not financed with the proceeds of obligations the interest on which is exempt from taxation under this title.

Such term shall not include any obligation issued under a State program which discriminates on the basis of the location (in the United States) at which the educational institution is located.

"(p) Cross references.

"For provisions relating to the taxable status of—

"(1) Certain obligations issued by Indian tribal governments (or their subdivisions), see section 7871.

"(2) Exempt interest dividends of regulated investment companies, see section 852(b)(5)(B).

"(3) Puerto Rican bonds, see section 3 of the act of March 2, 1917, as amended (48 U.S.C. 745).

"(4) Virgin Islands insular and municipal bonds, see section 1 of the Act of October 27, 1949 (48 U.S.C. 1403).

"(5) Certain obligations issued under title I of the Housing Act of 1949, see section 102(g) of title I of such Act (42 U.S.C. 1452(g))."

— P.L. 99-514, Sec. 1864(a)(1), added para. (n)(13) (before amendment by Sec. 1301(a) of this Act), effective for obligations issued after 10/22/86 in tax. yrs. end. after 10/22/86 and, at the election of the issuer, for any obligation issued on or before 10/22/86.

— P.L. 99-514, Sec. 1864(b), added "or other authorities" after "governmental units" in subpara. (n)(6)(A) and in clause (n)(6)(B)(i) (before amendment by Sec. 1301(a) of this Act) ... Sec. 1864(c), substituted "all of the property to be financed by the obligation" for "the property described in such subparagraph" in clause (n)(7)(C)(i) (before amendment by Sec. 1301(a)) ... Sec. 1864(d), deleted "and" at the end of subpara. (l)(2)(D), substituted ", and" for the period at the end of subpara. (l)(2)(E), and added subpara. (l)(2)(F) ... Sec. 1864(e), substituted "identify" for "specify" in the heading of subpara. (n)(10)(B) (before amendment by Sec. 1301(a)), substituted "identify (with reasonable specificity)" for "specify" in clause (n)(10)(B)(i) (before amendment by Sec. 1301(a)), and added "identification or" before "specification" in subpara. (n)(10)(D) (before amendment by Sec. 1301(a)), effective for obligations issued after 12/31/83, and as provided in Sec. 631(c)(2)-(3) [sic (4)] of P.L. 98-369, reproduced in the note following Sec. 621 of P.L. 98-369, see below.

— P.L. 99-514, Sec. 1865(a), deleted "the United States," after "program of" in subpara. (h)(5)(A) (before amendment by Sec. 1301(a) of this Act), effective for obligations issued after 12/31/83, and as provided in Sec. 631(c)(2)-(f) of P.L. 98-369, reproduced in the note following Sec. 622 of P.L. 98-369, see below.

— P.L. 99-514, Sec. 1865(c)(1)-(3), provides:

"(c) Treatment of certain obligations used to finance solid waste disposal facility.

"(1) In general. — Any obligation which is part of an issue a substantial portion of the proceeds of which is to be used to finance a solid waste disposal facility described in paragraph (2) shall not, for purposes of section 103(h) of the Internal Revenue Code of 1954, be treated as an obligation which is federally guaranteed by reason of the sale of fuel, steam, electricity, or other forms of usable energy to the Federal Government or any agency or instrumentality thereof.

"(2) Solid waste disposal facility. — A solid waste disposal facility is described in this paragraph if such facility is described in section 103(b)(4)(E) of such Code and—

"(A) if—

"(i) a public State authority created pursuant to State legislation which took effect on July 1, 1980, took formal action before October 19, 1983, to commit development funds for such facility,

"(ii) such authority issues obligations for such facility before January 1, 1988, and

"(iii) expenditures have been made for the development of such facility before October 19, 1983,

"(B) if—

"(i) such facility is operated by the South Eastern Public Service Authority of Virginia, and

"(ii) on December 20, 1984, the Internal Revenue Service issued a ruling concluding that a portion of the obligations with respect to such facility would not be treated as federally guaranteed under section 103(h) of such Code by reason of the transitional rule contained in section 631(c)(3)(A)(i) of the Tax Reform Act of 1984,

"(C) if—

"(i) a political subdivision of a State took formal action on April 1, 1980, to commit development funds for such facility,

"(ii) such facility has a contract to sell steam to a naval base,

"(iii) such political subdivision issues obligations for such facility before January 1, 1988, and

"(iv) expenditures have been made for the development of such facility before October 19, 1983, or

"(D) if—

"(i) such facility is a thermal transfer facility,

"(ii) is to be built and operated by the Elk Regional Resource Authority, and

"(iii) is to be on land leased from the United States Air Force at Arnold Engineering Development Center near Tullahoma, Tennessee.

"(3) Limitations.—

"(A) In the case of a solid waste disposal facility described in paragraph (2)(A), the aggregate face amount of obligations to which paragraph (1) applies shall not exceed $65,000,000.

"(B) In the case of a solid waste disposal facility described in paragraph (2)(B), the aggregate face amount of obligations to which paragraph (1) applies shall not exceed $20,000,000. Such amount shall be in addition to the amount permitted under the Internal Revenue Service ruling referred to in paragraph (2)(B)(ii).

"(C) In the case of a solid waste disposal facility described in paragraph (2)(C), the aggregate face amount of obligations to which paragraph (1) applies shall not exceed $75,000,000.

"(D) In the case of a solid waste disposal facility described in paragraph (2)(D), the aggregate face amount of obligations to which paragraph (1) applies shall not exceed $25,000,000."

— P.L. 99-514, Sec. 1866, [as amended by Sec. 1018(m) of P.L. 100-647], provides:

"Sec. 1866. Transitional rule for limit on small issue exception.

"The amendment made by section 623 of the Tax Reform Act of 1984 [P.L. 98-369, see below] shall not apply to any obligation (or series of obligations) issued to refund another tax-exempt IDB to which the amendment made by such section 623 did not apply if—

"(1) the average maturity of the issue of which the refunding obligation is a part does not exceed the average maturity of the obligations to be refunded by such issue,

For purposes of paragraph (1), average maturity shall be determined in accordance with subsection (b)(14)(B)(i) of such Code.

"(2) the amount of the refunding obligation does not exceed the amount of the refunded obligation, and

"(3) the proceeds of the refunding obligation are used to redeem the refunded obligation not later than 90 days after the date of the issuance of the refunding obligation.

For purposes of the preceding sentence, the term 'tax exempt IDB' means any industrial development bond (as defined in section 103(b) of the Internal Revenue Code of 1954) the interest on which is exempt from tax under section 103(a) of such Code."

— P.L. 99-514, Sec. 1867(a), amended Sec. 624(c)(2) of P.L. 98-369 [reproduced below], exceptions to the effective date for changes made by Sec. 624 of P.L. 98-369, by substituting "for the Essex County New Jersey Resource Recovery Project authorized by the Port Authority of New York and New Jersey on November 10, 1983, as part of an agreement approved" for "by the Essex County Port Authority of New York and New Jersey as part of an issue approved", see below. Sec. 1867(b) of this Act provides:

"(b) The amendment made by section 624 of the Tax Reform Act of 1984 [P.L. 98-369] shall not apply to obligations issued with respect to the Downtown Muskogee Revitalization Project for which a UDAG grant was preliminarily approved on May 5, 1981, if—

"(1) such obligation is issued before January 1, 1986, or

"(2) such obligation is issued after such date to provide additional financing for such project except that the aggregate amount of obligations to which this subsection applies shall not exceed $10,000,000."

— P.L. 99-514, Sec. 1868, amended Sec. 625(a)(3)(C) of P.L. 98-369, reproduced below, by substituting "obligation (or series of refunding obligations) issued exclusively" for "obligation issued exclusively".

— P.L. 99-514, Sec. 1869(a)(1), substituted "private loan bond" for "consumer loan bond" each place it appeared in subsec. (o) (before amendment by Sec. 1301(a) of this Act) ... Sec. 1869(a)(2), and (3), substituted "private loan bonds" for "consumer loan bonds" in the headings of subsec. (o) and para. (o)(2), respectively (before amendment by Sec. 1301(a)) ... Sec. 1869(b)(1), substituted "subsection (c)(6)(H)(i)" for "subsection (c)(6)(G)(i)" in clause (o)(2)(C)(ii) (before amendment by Sec. 1301(a)) ... Sec. 1869(b)(2), redesignated subsec. (o) (relating to cross references) as subsec. (p) (before amendment by Sec. 1301(a)), effective for obligations issued after 7/18/84, except as provided in Sec. 626(b)(2)-(6) of P.L. 98-369, reproduced in the note following Sec. 626(a) of P.L. 98-369, see below.

— P.L. 99-514, Sec. 1869(c)(1), [as amended by Sec. 1018(n) of P.L. 100-647], provides:

"(c) Transitional rules.

"(1) Treatment of certain obligations issued by the city of Baltimore. — Obligations issued by the city of Baltimore, Maryland, after June 30, 1985, shall not be treated as private loan bonds for purposes of section 103(o) of the Internal Revenue Code of 1954 (or as private activity bonds for purposes of section 103 and part IV of subchapter A of chapter 1 of the Internal Revenue Code of 1986, as amended by title XIII of this Act) by reason of the use of a portion of the proceeds of such obligations to finance or refinance temporary advances made by the city of Baltimore in connection with loans to persons who are not exempt persons (within the meaning of section 103(b)(3) of such Code) if—

"(A) such obligations are not industrial development bonds (within the meaning of section 103(b)(2) of the Internal Revenue Code of 1954),

"(B) the portion of the proceeds of such obligations so used is attributable to debt approved by voter referendum on or before November 2, 1982,

"(C) the loans to such nonexempt persons were approved by the Board of Estimates of the city of Baltimore on or before October 19, 1983, and

"(D) the aggregate amount of such temporary advances financed or refinanced by such obligations does not exceed $27,000,000."

— P.L. 99-514, Sec. 1869(c)(2)-(4), added exceptions to the amendments made by Sec. 626(a) of P.L. 98-369, see below. Sec. 1869(c)(2)-(4) of this Act provides:

Exclusions from income
Code Sec. 103

"(2) White Pine Power Project. — The amendment made by section 626(a) of the Tax Reform Act of 1984 shall not apply to any obligation issued during 1984 to provide financing for the White Pine Power Project in Nevada.

"(3) Tax increment bonds. — The amendment made by section 626(a) of the Tax Reform Act of 1984 shall not apply to any tax increment financing obligation issued before August 16, 1986, if —

"(A) substantially all of the proceeds of the issue are to be used to finance —

"(i) sewer, street, lighting, or other governmental improvements to real property,

"(ii) the acquisition of any interest in real property (by a governmental unit having the power to exercise eminent domain), the preparation of such property for new use, or the transfer of such interest to a private developer, or

"(iii) payments of reasonable relocation costs of prior users of such real property,

"(B) all of the activities described in subparagraph (A) are pursuant to a redevelopment plan adopted by the issuing authority before the issuance of such issue,

"(C) repayment of such issue is secured exclusively by pledges of that portion of any increase in real property tax revenues (or their equivalent) attributable to the redevelopment resulting from the issue, (or similar issues) and

"(D) none of the property described in subparagraph (A) is subject to a real property or other tax based on a rate or valuation method which differs from the rate and valuation method applicable to any other similar property located within the jurisdiction of the issuing authority.

"(4) Eastern Maine Electric Cooperative. — The amendment made by section 626(a) of the Tax Reform Act of 1984 shall not apply to obligations issued by Massachusetts Municipal Wholesale Electric Company Project No. 6 if —

"(A) such obligation is issued before January 1, 1986,

"(B) such obligation is issued after such date to refund a prior obligation for such project, except that the aggregate amount of obligations to which this subparagraph applies shall not exceed $100,000,000, or

"(C) such obligation is issued after such date to provide additional financing for such project except that the aggregate amount of obligations to which this subparagraph applies shall not exceed $45,000,000.

Subparagraph (B) shall not apply to any obligation issued for the advance refunding of any obligation."

—P.L. 99-514, Sec. 1869(c)(5), amended Sec. 626(b)(2)(A) of P.L. 98-369 [reproduced below], exceptions to the amendments made by Sec. 626(a) of P.L. 98-369, by substituting "$70 million" for "$11 million" in the table, see below.

—P.L. 99-514, Sec. 1869(c)(6), added exceptions to the amendments made by Sec. 626(a) of P.L. 98-369, see below. Sec. 1869(c)(6) of this Act provides:

"(6) Treatment of obligations to finance St. Johns River Power Park. —

"(A) In general. — The amendment made by section 626(a) of the Tax Reform Act of 1984 shall not apply to any obligation issued to finance the project described in subparagraph (B) if —

"(i) such obligation is issued before September 27, 1985,

"(ii) such obligation is issued after such date to refund a prior tax exemption obligation for such project, the amount of such obligation does not exceed the outstanding amount of the refunded obligation, and such prior tax exempt obligation is retired not later than the date 30 days after the issuance of the refunding obligation, or

"(iii) such obligation is issued after such date to provide additional financing for such project except that the aggregate amount of obligations to which this clause applies shall not exceed $150,000,000.

Clause (ii) shall not apply to any obligation issued for the advance refunding of any obligation.

"(B) Description of project. — The project described in this subparagraph is the St. Johns River Power Park system in Florida which was authorized by legislation enacted by the Florida Legislature in February of 1982."

—P.L. 99-514, Sec. 1870, substituted "clause (ii)" for "clause (i)" in the last sentence of subpara. (b)(16)(A) (before amendment by Sec. 1301(a) of this Act), effective for obligations issued after 12/31/83, and as provided in Sec. 631(c)(2)-(f) of P.L. 98-369, reproduced in the note following Sec. 622 of P.L. 98-369, see below.

—P.L. 99-514, Sec. 1871(a)(1), substituted "(j), (k), (l), (n), and (o)" for "(k), (l) and (n)" in para. (m)(l) (before amendment by Sec. 1301(a) of this Act), effective for obligations issued after 3/28/85 in tax. yrs. end. after 3/28/85.

—P.L. 99-514, Sec. 1871(b), substituted "and (6)" for "(6), and (7)" in para. (b)(13) and in subparas. (b)(14)(A) and (b)(17)(A) (before amendment by Sec. 1301(a) of this Act), effective for obligations issued after 12/31/83, and as provided in Sec. 631(c)(2)-(f) of P.L. 98-369, reproduced below.

—P.L. 99-514, Sec. 1872(a)(2)(A), amended Sec. 631(c)(3)(A) of P.L. 98-369 (reproduced below), part of the effective date for changes made by Secs. 622 and 623 of P.L. 98-369, by substituting "amendments (and provisions) referred to in paragraph (1)" for "amendments made by this subtitle (other than section 621)", see below.

—P.L. 99-514, Sec. 1872(a)(2)(B), amended Secs. 631(c)(3)(A)(i) and (ii), and added Sec. 631(c)(3)(A)(iii), of P.L. 98-369 (reproduced below), part of the effective date for changes made by Secs. 622 and 623 of P.L. 98-369, effective for obligations issued after 3/28/85.

Prior to amendment, Sec. 631(c)(3)(A)(i) and (ii) of P.L. 98-369 read as follows:

"(i) the original use of which commences with the taxpayer and the construction, reconstruction, or rehabilitation of which began before October 19, 1983, or

"(ii) with respect to which a binding contract to incur significant expenditures was entered into before October 19, 1983."

—P.L. 99-514, Sec. 1872(a)(3), added Sec. 631(c)(3)(C) to P.L. 98-369 (reproduced below), part of the effective date for changes made by Secs. 622 and 623 of P.L. 98-369, see below . . . Sec. 1872(a)(4), amended Sec. 631(c)(3)(B) of P.L. 98-369 (reproduced below) by substituting "subsection (b)(2)" for "subsection (b)(2)(A)", see below . . . Sec. 1872(b), added Sec. 631(c)(5) to P.L. 98-369, reproduced below . . . Sec. 1872(c)(1), added Sec. 631(d)(5) to P.L. 98-369, reproduced below.

—P.L. 99-514, Sec. 1899A(2), substituted "guaranteed" for "guaranteed" in subpara. (h)(2)(A) (before amendment by Sec. 1301(a) of this Act) . . . Sec. 1899A(3), substituted "608(a)(6)(A) for '608(6)(A)' in subpara. (m)(3)(B) (before amendment by Sec. 1301(a)) . . . Sec. 1899A(4), substituted 'October 27, 1949' for 'October 27, 1919' in para. (o)[sic (p)](4) (before amendment by Sec. 1301(a)), effective 10/22/86.

—P.L. 99-272, Sec. 13209(a)-(d), provides:

"Sec. 13209. treatment of certain pollution control bonds.

"(a) General rule. — For purposes of subparagraph (F) of section 103(b)(4) of the Internal Revenue Code of 1954 (relating to pollution control facilities), any obligation issued after December 31, 1985, shall be treated as described in such subparagraph if it is part of an issue substantially all of the proceeds of which are used by a qualified regional pollution control authority to acquire existing air or water pollution control facilities which the authority itself will operate in order to maintain or improve control of pollutants. The provisions of section 103(b)(17) of such Code (relating to prohibition on acquisition of existing property not permitted) shall not apply to any obligation described in the preceding sentence.

"(b) $200,000,000 limitation. — The aggregate amount of obligations to which subsection (a) applies shall not exceed $200,000,000, except that the amount of such obligations issued during calendar year 1986 to which subsection (a) applies shall not exceed $100,000,000.

"(c) Restrictions. — Subsection (a) shall apply only if —

"(1) the amount paid (directly or indirectly) for the facilities does not exceed their fair market value,

"(2) the fees or charges imposed (directly or indirectly) on any seller for the use of any facilities after the sale are not less than the amounts charged for the use of such facilities to persons other than the seller,

"(3) the original use of the facilities acquired with the proceeds of such obligations commenced before September 3, 1982, and

"(4) no person other than the qualified regional pollution control authority is considered after the sale as the owner of the facilities for purposes of Federal income taxes.

"(d) Qualified regional pollution control authority defined. — For purposes of this section, the term 'qualified regional pollution control authority' means an authority which —

"(1) is a political subdivision created by State law to control air or water pollution,

"(2) has within its jurisdictional boundaries all or part of at least 2 counties (or equivalent political subdivision),

"(3) operates air or water pollution control facilities, and

"(4) was created on September 1, 1969."

—P.L. 99-272, Sec. 13209(e), deleted para. (b)(11), effective 4/7/86.

Prior to deletion, para. (b)(11) read as follows:

"(11) Pollution control facilities acquired by regional pollution control authorities.

"(A) In general. For purposes of subparagraph (F) of paragraph (4), an obligation shall be treated as described in such subparagraph if it is part of an issue substantially all of the proceeds of which are used by a qualified regional pollution control authority to acquire existing air or water pollution control facilities which the authority itself will operate in order to maintain or improve the control of pollutants.

"(B) Restrictions. Subparagraph (A) shall apply only if —

"(i) the amount paid, directly or indirectly, for the facilities does not exceed their fair market value,

"(ii) the fees or charges imposed, directly or indirectly, on the seller for any use of the facilities after the sale are not less than the amounts that would be charged if the facilities were financed with obligations the interest on which is not exempt from tax, and

"(iii) no person other than the qualified regional pollution control authority is considered after the sale as the owner of the facilities for purposes of Federal income taxes.

"(C) Qualified regional pollution control authority defined. For purposes of this paragraph, the term 'qualified regional pollution control authority' means an authority which —

"(i) is a political subdivision created by State law to control air or water pollution,

"(ii) has within its jurisdictional boundaries all or part of at least 2 counties (or equivalent political subdivisions), and

"(iii) operates air or water pollution control facilities."

In 1984, P.L. 98-369, Sec. 474(r)(4), substituted "section 30(b)(2)(A)" for "section 44F(b)(2)(A)" in clause (b)(6)(F)(iv) effective for tax. yrs. begin. after 12/31/83, and for carrybacks from tax. yrs. begin. after 12/31/83.

—P.L. 98-369, Sec. 621, redesignated subsec. (n) as subsec. (o) [presumably (p)] and added new subsec. (n), for obligations issued after 12/31/83. Sec. 631(a)(2)-(a)(3) [sic (a)(4)] of this Act provides:

"(2) Inducement resolution before June 19, 1984. — The amendment made by section 621 shall not apply to any issue of obligations if —

"(A) there was an inducement resolution (or other comparable preliminary approval) for the issue before June 19, 1984, and

"(B) the issue is issued before January 1, 1985.

"(3) Certain projects preliminarily approved before October 19, 1983, given approval. — If —

"(A) there was an inducement resolution (or other comparable preliminary approval) for a project before October 19, 1983, by any issuing authority,

"(B) a substantial user of such project notifies the issuing authority within 30 days after the date of the enactment of this Act that it intends to claim its rights under this paragraph, and

"(C) construction of such project began before October 19, 1983, or the substantial user was under a binding contract on such date to incur significant expenditures with respect to such project,

such issuing authority shall allocate its share of the limitation under section 103(n) of such Code for the calendar year during which the obligations were to be issued pursuant to such resolution (or other approval) first to such project. If the amount of obligations required by all projects which meet the requirements of the preceding sentence exceeds the issuing authority's share of the limitation under section 103(n) of such Code, priority under the preceding sentence shall be provided first to those projects for which substantial expenditures were incurred before October 19, 1983. If any issuing authority fails to meet the requirements of this paragraph, the limitation under section 103(n) of such Code for the issuing authority for the calendar year following such failure shall be reduced by the amount of obligations with respect to which such failure occurred.

"(3) Exception for certain bonds for a convention center and resource recovery project. — In the case of any city, if —

"(A) the city council of such city authorized a feasibility study for a convention center on June 10, 1982, and

"(B) on November 4, 1983, a municipal authority acting for such city accepted a proposal for the construction of a facility that is capable of generating steam and electricity through the combustion of municipal waste,

the amendment made by section 621 shall not apply to any issue, issued during 1984, 1985, 1986, or 1987 and substantially all of the proceeds of which are to be used to finance the convention center (or access ramps and parking facilities therefor) described in subparagraph (A) or the facility described in subparagraph (B)."

— P.L. 98-369, Sec. 622, amended subsec. (h) . . . Sec. 623, added para. (b)(15), effective for obligations issued after 12/31/83 (see Sec. 1866 of P.L. 99-514, above). Sec. 631(c)(2)-(f) of this Act [as amended by Sec. 1872(a)(2) of P.L. 99-514-(4) and 1872(b), see above] provides:

"(2) Obligations invested in federally insured deposits. — Notwithstanding any other provision of this section, clause (ii) of section 103(h)(2)(B) of the Internal Revenue Code of 1954 (as amended by this subtitle) shall apply to obligations issued after April 14, 1983; except that such clause shall not apply to any obligation issued pursuant to a binding contract in effect on March 4, 1983.

"(3) Exceptions. —

"(A) Construction or binding agreement. — The amendments (and provisions) referred to in paragraph (1) shall not apply to obligations with respect to facilities —

"(i) the original use of which commences with the taxpayer and the construction, reconstruction, or rehabilitation of which began before October 19, 1983, and was completed on or after such date,

"(ii) the original use of which commences with the taxpayer and with respect to which a binding contract to incur significant expenditures for construction, reconstruction, or rehabilitation was entered into before October 19, 1983, and some of such expenditures are incurred on or after such date, or

"(iii) acquired after October 19, 1983, pursuant to a binding contract entered into on or before such date.

"(B) Facilities. — Subparagraph (C) of subsection (b)(2)(A) shall apply for purposes of subparagraph (A) of this paragraph.

"(C) Exception. — Subparagraph (A) shall not apply with respect to the amendment made by section 628(e) and the provisions of sections 628(f) and 629(b).

"(4) Repeal of advance refunding of qualified public facilities. — The amendment made by section 628(g) shall apply to refunding obligations issued after the date of the enactment of this Act; except that if substantially all the proceeds of the refunded issue were used to provide airports or docks, such amendment shall only apply to refunding obligations issued after December 31, 1984. In the case of any refunding obligation with respect to the Alabama State Docks Department or the Dade County Florida Airport, the preceding sentence shall be applied by substituting 'December 31, 1985' for 'December 31, 1984'.

"(5) Special rule for health club facilities. — In the case of any health club facility, with respect to the amendment made by section 627(c) —

"(A) paragraph (1) shall be applied by substituting 'April 12, 1984' for 'December 31, 1983', and

"(B) paragraph (3) shall be applied by substituting 'April 13, 1984' for 'October 19, 1983' each place it appears.

"(d) Provisions of this subtitle not to apply to certain property. —

"The amendments made by this subtitle shall not apply to any property (and shall not apply to obligations issued to finance such property) if such property is described in any of the following paragraphs:

"(1) Any property described in paragraph (5), (6), or (7) of section 31(g) of this Act.

"(2) Any property described in paragraph (4), (8), or (17) of section 31(g) of this Act but only if the obligation is issued before January 1, 1985, and only if before June 19, 1984, the issuer had evidenced an intent to issue obligations exempt from taxation under the Internal Revenue Code of 1954 in connection with such property.

"(3) Any property described in paragraph (3) of section 216(b) of the Tax Equity and Fiscal Responsibility Act of 1982.

"(4) Any solid waste disposal facility described in section 103(b)(4)(E) of the Internal Revenue Code of 1954 if —

"(A) a State public authority created pursuant to State legislation which took effect on June 18, 1973, took formal action before October 19, 1983, to commit development funds for such facility,

"(B) such authority issues obligations for any such facility before January 1, 1987, and

"(C) expenditures have been made for the development of any such facility before October 19, 1983.

"(5) Any solid waste disposal facility described in section 103(b)(4)(E) of the Internal Revenue Code of 1954 if —

"(A) a city government, by resolutions adopted on April 10, 1980, and December 27, 1982, took formal action to authorize the submission of a proposal for a feasibility study for such facility and to authorize the presentation to the Department of the Army (U.S. Army Missile Command) of a proposed agreement to jointly pursue construction and operation of such facility,

"(B) such city government (or a public authority on its behalf) issues obligations for such facility before January 1, 1988, and

"(C) expenditures have been made for the development of such facility before October 19, 1983. Notwithstanding the foregoing provisions of this subsection, the amendments made by section 624 (relating to arbitrage) shall apply to obligations issued to finance property described in paragraph (5).

"(e) Determination of significant expenditure. —

"(1) In general. — For purposes of this section, the term 'significant expenditures' means expenditures which equal or exceed the lesser of —

"(A) $15,000,000, or

"(B) 20 percent of the estimated cost of the facilities.

"(2) Certain grants treated as expenditures. — For purposes of paragraph (1), the amount of any UDAG grant preliminarily approved on May 5, 1981, or April 4, 1983, shall be treated as an expenditure with respect to the facility for which such grant was so approved.

"(f) Exceptions for certain other amendments. —

"If —

"(1) there was an inducement resolution (or other comparable preliminary approval) for an issue before June 19, 1984, by any issuing authority, and

"(2) such issue is issued before January 1, 1985, the following amendments shall not apply:

"(A) the amendments made by section 623,

"(B) the amendments made by subsections (a) and (b) of section 627 (except to the extent such amendments relate to farm land),

"(C) in the case of a race track, the amendment made by section 627(c), and

"(D) the amendments made by section 628(c)."

Prior to amendment, subsec. (h) read as follows:

"(h) Certain obligations must not be guaranteed or subsidized under an energy program.

"(1) In general. An obligation to which this subsection applies shall be treated as an obligation not described in subsection (a) if

"(A) the payment of principal or interest with respect to such obligation is guaranteed (in whole or in part) by the United States under a program a principal purpose of which is to encourage the production or conservation of energy, or

"(B) the payment of the principal or interest with respect to such obligation is to be made (in whole or in part) with funds provided under such a program of the United States, a State, or a political subdivision of a State.

"(2) Obligations to which this subsection applies. This subsection shall apply to any obligations to which paragraph (1) of subsection (b) does not apply by reason of —

"(A) subsection (b)(4)(H) (relating to qualified hydroelectric generating facilities), or

"(B) subsection (g) (relating to qualified steam-generating or alcohol-producing facilities)."

— P.L. 98-369, Sec. 624(a), redesignated para. (c)(6) as para. (c)(7) and added new para. (c)(6) . . . Sec. 624(b)(2), deleted "bonds" from the heading of subsec. (c) . . . Sec. 624(b)(3), added "to arbitrage bonds" in the heading of para. (c)(1), effective for bonds issued after 12/31/84. Sec. 624(c)(2) of this Act [as amended by Sec. 1867(a) of P.L. 99-514 and (b), see above] provides:

"(2) Exception. — The amendments made by this section shall not apply to obligations issued for the Essex County New Jersey Resource Recovery Project authorized by the Port Authority of New York and New Jersey on November 10, 1983, as part of an agreement approved by Essex County, New Jersey, on July 7, 1981, and approved by the State of New Jersey on December 31, 1981. The aggregate face amount of bonds to which this paragraph applies shall not exceed $350,000,000."

— P.L. 98-369, Sec. 625, [as amended by Sec. 1868 of P.L.99-514, see above] provides:

"(a) Arbitrage regulations. —

"(1) In general. — The Secretary shall prescribe regulations which specify the circumstances under which a qualified student loan bond shall be treated as an arbitrage bond for purposes of section 103 of the Internal Revenue Code of 1954. Such regulations may provide that —

"(A) paragraphs (4) and (5) of section 103(c) of such Code shall not apply, and

"(B) rules similar to section 103(c)(6) shall apply,

to qualified student loan bonds.

"(2) Definitions. — For purposes of this subsection —

"(A) Qualified student loan bond. — The term 'qualified student loan bond' has the meaning given to such term by section 103(o)(3) of the Internal Revenue Code of 1954 (as amended by this Act).

"(B) Arbitrage bond. — The term 'arbitrage bond' has the meaning given to such term by section 103(c)(2).

"(3) Effective date. —

"(A) In general. — Except as otherwise provided in this paragraph, any regulations prescribed by the Secretary under paragraph (1) shall apply to obligations issued after the qualified date.

Exclusions from income Code Sec. 103

"(B) Qualified date.—
"(i) In general.— For purposes of this paragraph, the term 'qualified date' means the earlier of—
"(I) the date on which the Higher Education Act of 1965 expires, or
"(II) the date, after the date of enactment of this Act, on which the Higher Education Act of 1965 is reauthorized.
"(ii) Publication of regulations.— Notwithstanding clause (i), the qualified date shall not be a date which is prior to the date that is 6 months after the date on which the regulations prescribed under paragraph (1) are published in the Federal Register.
"(C) Refunding obligations.— Regulations prescribed by the Secretary under paragraph (1) shall not apply to any obligation (or series of refunding obligations) issued exclusively to refund any qualified student loan bond which was issued before the qualified date, except that the requirements of subparagraphs (A) and (B) of section 626(b)(4) of this Act must be met with respect to such refunding.
"(D) Fulfillment of commitments.— Regulations prescribed by the Secretary under paragraph (1) shall not apply to any obligations which are needed to fulfill written commitments to acquire or finance student loans which are originated after June 30, 1984, and before the qualified date, but only if—
"(i) such commitments are binding on the qualified date, and
"(ii) the amount of such commitments is consistent with practices of the issuer which were in effect on March 15, 1984, with respect to establishing secondary markets for student loans.
"(b) Arbitrage limitation on student loan bonds which are not qualified student loan bonds. — Under regulations prescribed by the Secretary of the Treasury or his delegate, any student loan bond (other than a qualified student loan bond) issued after December 31, 1985, shall be treated as an obligation not described in subsection (a)(1) or (2) of section 103 of the Internal Revenue Code of 1954 unless the issue of which such obligation is a part meets requirements similar to those of sections 103(c)(6) and 103A(i) of such Code.
"(c) Issuance of student loan bonds which are not tax-exempt. — Any issuer who may issue obligations described in section 103(a) of the Internal Revenue Code of 1954 may elect to issue student loan bonds which are not described in such section 103(a) of such Code without prejudice to—
"(1) the status of any other obligations issued, or to be issued, by such issuer as obligations described in section 103(a) of such Code, or
"(2) the status of the issuer as an organization exempt from taxation under such Code.
"(d) Federal executive branch jurisdiction over tax-exempt status.— For purposes of Federal law, any determination by the executive branch of the Federal Government of whether interest on any obligation is exempt from taxation under the Internal Revenue Code of 1954 shall be exclusively within the jurisdiction of the Department of the Treasury.
"(e) Study on tax-exempt student loan bonds.—
"(1) In general.— The Comptroller General of the United States and the Director of the Congressional Budget Office, shall conduct studies of—
"(A) the appropriate date of tax-exempt bonds which are issued in connection with the guaranteed student loan program and the PLUS program established under the Higher Education Act of 1965, and
"(B) the appropriate arbitrage rules for such bonds.
"(2) Report. — The Comptroller General of the United States and the Director of the Congressional Budget Office, shall submit to the Committee on Finance and the Committee on Labor and Human Resources of the Senate and the Committee on Ways and Means and the Committee on Education and Labor of the House of Representatives reports on the studies conducted under paragraph (1) by no later than 9 months after the date of enactment of this Act."
—P.L. 98-369, Sec. 626(a), added subsec. (o), for obligations issued after 7/18/84. Sec. 626(b)(2)–(b)(6) of this Act [as amended by Sec. 1869(c)(2) of P.L. 99-514-6), see above] provides:
"(2) Exceptions for certain student loan programs. —
"(A) In general. — The amendments made by this section shall not apply to obligations issued by a program described in the following table to the extent the aggregate face amount of such obligations does not exceed the amount of allowable obligations specified in the following table with respect to such program:

Program	Amount of Allowable Obligations
Colorado Student Obligation Bond Authority	$ 60 million
Connecticut Higher Education Supplementary Loan Authority	$15.5 million
District of Columbia	$ 50 million
Illinois Higher Education Authority	$ 70 million
State of Iowa	$ 16 million
Louisiana Public Facilities Authority	$ 75 million
Maine Health and Higher Education Facilities Authority	$ 5 million
Maryland Higher Education Supplemental Loan Program	$ 24 million
Massachusetts College Student Loan Authority	$ 90 million
Minnesota Higher Education Coordinating Board	$ 60 million
New Hampshire Higher Education and Health Facilities Authority	$ 39 million
New York Dormitory Authority	$ 120 million
Pennsylvania Higher Education Assistance Agency	$ 300 million
Georgia Private Colleges and University Authority	$ 31 million
Wisconsin State Building Commission	$ 60 million
South Dakota Health and Educational Facilities Authority	$ 6 million

"(B) Pennsylvania higher education assistance agency.— Subparagraph (A) shall apply to obligations issued by the Pennsylvania Higher Education Assistance Agency only if such obligations are issued solely for the purpose of refunding student loan bonds outstanding on March 15, 1984.
"(3) Certain tax-exempt mortgage subsidy bonds.— For purposes of applying section 103(o) of the Internal Revenue Code of 1954, the term 'consumer loan bond' shall not include any mortgage subsidy bond (within the meaning of section 103A(b) of such Code) to which the amendments made by section 1102 of the Mortgage Subsidy Bond Tax Act of 1980 do not apply.
"(4) Refunding exception.— The amendments made by this section shall not apply to any obligation or series of obligations the proceeds of which are used exclusively to refund obligations issued before March 15, 1984, except that—
"(A) the amount of the refunding obligations may not exceed 101 percent of the aggregate face amount of the refunded obligations, and
"(B) the maturity date of any refunding obligation may not be later than the date which is 17 years after the date on which the refunded obligation was issued (or, in the case of a series of refundings, the date on which the original obligation was issued).
"(5) Exception for certain established programs.— The amendments made by this section shall not apply to any obligation substantially all of the proceeds of which are used to carry out a program established under State law which has been in effect in substantially the same form during the 30-year period ending on the date of enactment of this Act, but only if such proceeds are used to make loans or to fund similar obligations—
"(A) in the same manner in which,
"(B) in the same (or lesser) amount per participant, and
"(C) for the same purposes for which,
such program was operated on March 15, 1984. This subparagraph shall not apply to obligations issued on or after March 15, 1987.
"(6) Certain bonds for renewable energy property.— The amendments made by this section shall not apply to any obligations described in section 243 of the Crude Oil Windfall Profit Tax Act of 1980."
—P.L. 98-369, Sec. 627(a), added para. (b)(16)... Sec. 627(b), added para. (b)(17)... Sec. 627(c), added para. (b)(18)... Sec. 628(a)(1), added the last sentence to para. (m)(1)... Sec. 628(a)(2), amended subpara. (m)(2)(B)... Sec. 628(a)(3), added para. (m)(3)... Sec. 628(c), added subpara. (b)(6)(P)... Sec. 628(d), added "For purposes of this paragraph—" and subparagraphs (A) and (B) to the end of para. (b)(13)... Sec. 628(e), added the last sentence to para. (b)(4), effective for obligations issued after 12/31/83. For special rules and exceptions, see Sec. 631(c)(2)-(f) of this Act reproduced above following Sec. 622 of P.L. 98-369.
Prior to amendment, subpara. (m)(2)(B) read as follows:
"(B) is exempt from taxation under any provision of this title."
—P.L. 98-369, Sec. 628(f), provides:
"(f) Public approval requirement in the case of public airport.— If —
"(1) the proceeds of any issue are to be used to finance a facility or facilities located on a public airport, and
"(2) the governmental unit issuing such obligations is the owner or operator of such airport,
such governmental unit shall be deemed to be the only governmental unit having jurisdiction over such airport for purposes of subsection (k) of section 103 of the Internal Revenue Code of 1954 (relating to public approval for industrial development bonds)."
—P.L. 98-369, Sec. 628(g), deleted para. (b)(7), as provided in Sec. 631(c)(4) reproduced with the special rules and exceptions provided in Sec. 631(c)(2)-(f) of this Act reproduced above following Sec. 622 of P.L. 98-369.
Prior to deletion para. (b)(7) read as follows:
"(7) Advance refunding of qualified public facilities
"(A) In general. Paragraph (1) shall not apply to a refunding issue if substantially all the proceeds of the refunded issue were used to provide a qualified public facility.
"(B) Qualified public facility defined. For purposes of subparagraph (A), the term 'qualified public facility' means facilities described in subparagraph (C) or (D) of paragraph (4) which are generally available to the general public."
—P.L. 98-369, Sec. 629, provides:
"(a) Certain public utilities. — For purposes of applying section 103(b)(3) of the Internal Revenue Code with respect to—
"(1) any obligations issued after the date of enactment of this Act, and
"(2) any obligations issued after December 31, 1969, which were treated as obligations described in section 103(a) of such Code on the day on which such obligations were issued,
the term 'exempt person' shall include a regulated public utility having any customer service area within a State served by a public power authority which was required as a condition of a Federal Power Commission license specified by an Act of Congress enacted prior to the enactment of section 107 of the Revenue and Expenditure Control Act of 1968 (P.L. 90-364) to contract to sell power to one such utility and which is authorized by State law to sell power to other such utilities, but only with respect to the purchase by any such utility and resale to its customers of any output of any electrical generation facility or any portion thereof or any use of any electrical transmission facility or any portion thereof financed by such power authority and owned by it or by such State, and provided that by agreement between such power authority and any such utility there shall be no markup in the resale price charged by such utility of that component of the resale price which represents the price paid by such utility for such output or use.

1,391

"(b) Certain railroads. — Section 103(b)(1) of the Internal Revenue Code of 1954 shall not apply to any obligation which is described in section 103(b)(6)(A) of such Code if—

"(1) substantially all of the proceeds of such obligation are used to acquire railroad track and right-of-way from a railroad involved in a title 11 or similar proceeding (within the meaning of section 368(a)(3)(A) of such Code), and

"(2) the Federal Railroad Administration provides joint financing for such acquisitions.

"(c) Special rules for subsection (a).—

"(1) Obligations subject to cap. — Any obligation described in subsection (a) shall be treated as a private activity bond for purposes of section 103(n) of the Internal Revenue Code of 1954.

"(2) Limitation on amount of obligations to which subsection (a)(1) applies— The aggregate amount of obligations to which subsection (a)(1) applies shall not exceed $625,000,000.

"(3) Limitation on purposes. — Subsection (a)(1) shall only apply to obligations issued as part of an issue substantially all the proceeds of which are used to provide 1 or more of the following:

"(A) Cable facilities.
"(B) Small hydroelectric facilities.
"(C) The acquisition of an interest in an electrical generating facility."

— P.L. 98-369, Sec. 630, amended subpara. (b)(6)(N), effective for obligations issued after 12/31/83. For special rules and exceptions see Sec. 631(c)(2)-(f) of this Act reproduced above following Sec. 622 of P.L. 98-369.

Prior to amendment, subpara. (b)(6)(N) read as follows:

"(N) Paragraph not to apply to obligations issued after December 31, 1986. This paragraph shall not apply to any obligation issued after December 31, 1986 (including any obligation issued to refund an obligation issued on or before such date)."

— P.L. 98-369, Sec. 632, provided various exceptions to the amendments made by Title VI of this Act. See note following Code Sec. 103A.

— P.L. 98-369, Sec. 644, provides:

"(a) General rule. — For the purposes of section 103(b)(4)(E), facilities for the local furnishing of electric energy also shall include a facility that is part of a system providing service to the general populace (i) if at least 97 percent (measured both by total number of metered customers and by their annual consumption on a kilowatt hour basis) of the retail customers of such system are located in two contiguous counties, and (ii) if the remainder of such customers are located in a portion of a third contiguous county which portion is located on a peninsula not directly connected by land to the rest of the county of which it is a part.

"(b) Election to allocate to 1984 one-half of state limit for 1985, 1986, and 1987. — Solely for purposes of issuing obligations described in subsection (a), the issuing authorities of a State may elect (at such time and in such manner as the Secretary of the Treasury shall by regulations prescribe) to use in 1984 one-half of the amount which would have been the State limit for the calendar years 1985, 1986, and 1987."

— P.L. 98-369, Sec. 645, provides:

"For the purpose of section 103(b)(4)(E), facilities for the local furnishing of electric energy also shall include a facility that is part of a system providing service to the general populace—

"(i) if the facility was initially authorized by the Federal Government in 1962;
"(ii) if the facility receives financing of at least 25 percent by an exempt person;
"(iii) if the electric energy generated by the facility is purchased by an electric cooperative qualified as a rural electric borrower under 7 U.S.C. section 901 et seq. and if;
"(iv) the facility is located in a noncontiguous State."

— P.L. 98-369, Sec. 712(h), amended Sec. 217(e) of P.L. 97-248, the effective date for changes made by Sec. 217, by adding at the end the following: "For purposes of applying section 168(f)(8)(D)(v) of the Internal Revenue Code of 1954, the amendments made by subsection (c) shall apply to agreements entered into after the date of enactment of this Act [9/3/82]", see below.

— P.L. 98-369, Sec. 1065(a)(1), amended Sec. 204 of P.L. 97-473, the effective date for changes made by Sec. 202(b)(2) of P.L. 97-473 (see below), by deleting "and before January 1, 1985" each place it appeared.

In **1984**, P.L. 98-216, Sec. 6(b), repealed Sec. 310(d)(4) of P.L. 97-248, and Sec. 306(b)(2) of P.L. 97-448, the effective date for changes made by Sec. 310 of P.L. 97-248 (reproduced below). Sec. 6 of P.L. 98-216 provides:

"Sec. 6. (a) The repeal of a law enacted by this Act may not be construed as a legislative inference that the provision was or was not in effect before its repeal.
"(b) The laws specified in the following schedule are repealed, except for rights and duties that mature, penalties that were incurred, and proceedings that were begun before the date of enactment of this Act[.]"

Prior to repeal Sec. 310(d)(4) of P.L. 97-248 (as added by Sec. 306(b)(2) of P.L. 97-448) read as follows:

"(4) Effective date for tax-exempt obligations: — In the case of obligations the interest on which is exempt from tax (determined without regard to the amendments made by this section)—

"(A) under section 103 of the Internal Revenue Code of 1954, or
"(B) under other provision of law (without regard to the identity of the holder), the amendments made by this section shall apply only to obligations issued after June 30, 1983. The preceding sentence shall not apply in the case of any obligation which under the Internal Revenue Code of 1954 (as in effect on the day before the date of the enactment of the Tax Equity and Fiscal Responsibility Act of 1982) was required to be in registered form."

In **1983**, P.L. 97-473, Sec. 202(b)(2), amended subsec. (m) [sic , redesignated subsec. (n) by Sec. 547(a) of P.L. 97-424, see below], effective for obligations issued after 12/31/82.

"(n) Cross references.
"For provisions relating to the taxable status of—

"(1) Puerto Rican bonds, see section 3 of the Act of March 2, 1917, as amended (48 U.S.C. 745).
"(2) Virgin Islands insular and municipal bonds, see section 1 of the Act of October 27, 1919 (48 U.S.C. 1403).
"(3) Certain obligations issued under title I of the Housing Act of 1949, see section 102(g) of title I of such Act (42 U.S.C. 1452(g)).
[(24) Exempt-interest dividends. For treatment of exempt-interest dividends, see section 852(b)(5)(B).]"

— P.L. 97-448, Sec. 306(b)(2), added para. (4) to Sec. 310(d) of P.L. 97-248, the effective date for changes made by Sec. 310(b)(1) of P.L. 97-248 [repealed by Sec. 6(b) of P.L. 98-216, see above].

— P.L. 97-424, Sec. 547(a), redesignated subsec. (m) as subsec. (n) and added a new subsec. (m), effective 1/6/83.

In **1982**, P.L. 97-248, Sec. 214(a), added subparas. (b)(6)(K) and (b)(6)(L) . . . Sec. 214(b), added subpara. (b)(6)(M), effective for obligations issued after 9/3/82.

— P.L. 97-248, Sec. 214(c), added subpara. (b)(6)(N), effective 9/3/82.

— P.L. 97-248, Sec. 214(d)(1), deleted "or" at the end of clause (b)(6)(F)(ii) . . . Sec. 214(d)(2), added "or" at the end of clause (b)(6)(F)(iii) . . . Sec. 214(d)(3), added clause (b)(6)(iv), effective for expenditures made after 9/3/82.

— P.L. 97-248, Sec. 214(e), added subpara. (b)(6)(O), effective for obligations issued after 12/31/82.

— P.L. 97-248, Sec. 215(a), redesignated subsec. (k) [formerly subsec. (j) before redesignation by Sec. 310(b)(1) of this Act, see below] as subsec. (l) and added new subsec. (k), effective as provided in Sec. 215(c)(1) of this Act which reads as follows:

"(1) Public approval. — The amendment made by subsection (a) [of this Act] shall apply to obligations issued after December 31, 1982, other than obligations issued solely to refund any obligation which—

"(A) was issued before July 1, 1982, and
"(B) has a maturity which does not exceed 3 years."

— P.L. 97-248, Sec. 215(b)(1), redesignated subsec. (l) [as redesignated by Sec. 215(a) of this Act, see above] as subsec. (m) and added new subsec. (l) . . . Sec. 215(b)(2), substituted "For purposes of this section" for "For purposes of this subsection" in para. (b)(2), effective for obligations issued after 12/31/82, including any obligation issued to refund an obligation issued before 12/31/82.

— P.L. 97-248, Sec. 217(a)(1), deleted "or" at the end of subpara. (b)(4)(H), substituted ",or" for the period at the end of subpara. (b)(4)(I) and added subpara. (b)(4)(J) . . . Sec. 217(a)(2), redesignated para. (b)(10) as para. (b)(13), and added new para. (b)(10) . . . Sec. 217(a)(3), substituted "paragraph (13)" for "paragraph (7)" in subpara. (b)(6)(C) . . . Sec. 217(b), substituted "electric energy or gas from" for "electric energy from"in para. (b)(4) . . . Sec. 217(c)(1), added "ferry," after "rail car" in subpara. (b)(9)(A) . . . Sec. 217(c)(2), added "(or, in the case of a ferry, mass transportation services)" after "mass commuting services" in clause (b)(9)(A)(ii) . . . Sec. 217(d), added para. (b)(11), effective for obligations issued after 9/3/82. For purposes of applying section 168(f)(8)(D)(v) of the Internal Revenue Code of 1954, the amendments made by subsection (c) shall apply to agreements entered into after the date of the enactment of this Act.

— P.L. 97-248, Sec. 218, provides:

"Sec. 218. Treatment of certain refunding obligations.

"(a) General rule. — Paragraph (1) of section 103(b) of the Internal Revenue Code of 1954 shall not apply to any qualified refunding obligation issued by a qualified issuer after the date of the enactment of this Act.

"(b) Qualified refunding obligation. — For purposes of subsection (a), a qualified refunding obligation is any obligation issued as part of an issue if—

"(1) substantially all of the proceeds of such issue are used to defease refunded bonds which were issued under a pooled security arrangement pursuant to a bond resolution which was adopted in 1974 and under which at least 20 facilities have been financed before 1978, and

"(2) each refunded bond is to be retired within 6 months after the first date on which there is no premium for early retirement of such bond.

"(c) Qualified issuer. — For purposes of subsection (a), a qualified issuer is a political subdivision created by a State in 1932 which is engaged primarily in promoting economic development."

— P.L. 97-248, Sec. 219(a), added para. (b)(14), effective for obligations issued after 12/31/82.

— P.L. 97-248, Sec. 221(a), amended subpara. (b)(4)(A) . . . Sec. 221(b), added para. (b)(12) . . . Sec. 221(c)(1), deleted the second sentence of para. (b)(4), effective for obligations issued after 9/3/82 except as provided in Sec. 221(d)(2) of this Act which reads as follows:

"(2) Exception. — The amendments made by this section shall not apply with respect to any obligation to which the amendments made by section 1103 of the Mortgage Subsidy Bond Tax Act of 1980 do not apply by reason of section 1104 [reproduced in note following Code Sec. 103A] of such Act."

Prior to amendment, para. (b)(4)(A) read as follows:

"(A) projects for residential rental property if each obligation issued pursuant to the issue is in registered form and if—

"(i) 15 percent or more in the case of targeted area projects, or
"(ii) 20 percent or more in the case of any other project, of the units in each project are to be occupied by individuals of low or moderate income (within the meaning of section 167(k)(3)(B))."

Prior to amendment, the second sentence of para. (b)(4) read as follows:

Exclusions from income — Code Sec. 103

"For purposes of subparagraph (A), the term 'targeted area project' means a project located in a qualified census tract (within the meaning of section 103A(k)(2)) or an area of chronic economic distress within the meaning of section 103A(k)(3))."

—P.L. 97-248, Sec. 310(b)(1), redesignated subsec. (j) as subsec. (k) and added new subsec. (j), effective for obligations issued after 12/31/82 except as provided in Secs. 310(d)(3) and (4) of this Act which read as follows:

"(3) Exception for certain warrants, etc.—The amendments made by subsection (b) shall not apply to any obligations issued after December 31, 1982, on the exercise of a warrant or the conversion of a convertible obligation if such warrant or obligation was offered or sold outside the United State without registration under the Securities Act of 1933 and was issued before August 10, 1982. A rule similar to the rule of the preceding sentence shall also apply in the case of any regulations issued under section 163(f)(2)(C) of the Internal Revenue Code of 1954 (as added by this section) except that the date on which such regulations take effect shall be substituted for 'August 10, 1982.'

"(4) [repealed by Sec. 6(b) of P.L. 98-216, see above]."

—P.L. 97-248, Sec. 310(c)(1), deleted "if each obligation issued pursuant to the issue is in registered form and" after "rental property" in subpara. (b)(4)(A) . . . Sec. 310(c)(2)(A), deleted subpara. (h)(1)(A) and redesignated subparas. (h)(1)(B) and (h)(1)(C) as subparas. (h)(1)(A) and (h)(1)(B) . . . Sec. 310(c)(2)(B), substituted "must not be" for "must be in registered form and not" in the heading of subsec. (h), effective for obligations issued after 12/31/82.

Prior to deletion subpara. (h)(1)(A) read as follows:
"(A) such obligation is not issued in registered form."

In 1981, P.L. 97-34, Sec. 811(a), amended para. (b)(4) by deleting "or" at the end of subpara. (b)(4)(G) . . . by substituting ", or" for the period at the end of subpara. (b)(4)(H) . . . by adding subpara. (b)(4)(I), effective for obligations issued after 8/13/81.

—P.L. 97-34, Sec. 811(b), redesignated para. (b)(9) as para. (b)(10) and added new para. (b)(9), effective for obligations issued after 8/13/81.

—P.L. 97-34, Sec. 812(a), redesignated subsec. (i) as subsec. (j) and added new subsec. (i), effective for obligations issued after 12/31/80. Sec. 812(b)(2) of this Act provides:

"(2) Special rule for certain obligations issued before effective date.—

"(A) In general. Interest on any obligation described in subparagraph (B) shall be excluded from gross income.

"(B) Obligation to which paragraph applies. For purposes of subparagraph (A), an obligation is described in this subparagraph if the obligation—

"(i) was issued after December 31, 1969, and before January 1, 1981, to the First Bank and Trust Company of Indianapolis, Indiana.

"(ii) was issued by a qualified volunteer fire department (within the meaning of section 103(i)(2) of the Internal Revenue Code of 1954), and

"(iii) was issued for the acquisition, construction, reconstruction, or improvement of firefighting property.

"An obligation shall be treated as described in this subparagraph only for the period which is held by the First Bank and Trust Company of Indianapolis, Indiana.

"(C) Firefighting property. For purposes of subparagraph (B), the term 'firefighting property' means property—

"(i) which is of a character subject to the allowance for depreciation, and

"(ii)(I) which is used in the training for the performance of, or in the performance of, firefighting or ambulance services, or

"(II) which is exclusively used to house the property described in subclause (I)."

In 1980, P.L. 96-499, Sec. 1103(a), amended subpara. (b)(4)(A) . . . Sec. 1103(b), added "For purposes of subparagraph (A), the term 'targeted area project' means a project located in a qualified census tract (within the meaning of section 103A(k)(2)) or an area of chronic economic distress (within the meaning of section 103A(k)(3))." before the last sentence in para. (b)(4) . . . Sec. 1103(c), added subpara. (b)(6)(J), effective for obligations issued after 4/24/79 except as provided in Sec. 1104 of this Act [reproduced in note following Code Sec 103A.]."

Prior to amendment, subpara. (b)(4)(A) read as follows:
"(A) residential real property for family units,"

—P.L. 96-501, Sec. 9(f), provides:

"(f) For purposes of enabling the Administrator to acquire resources necessary to meet the firm load of public bodies, cooperatives, and Federal agencies from a governmental unit at a cost no greater than the cost which would be applicable in the absence of such acquisition, the exemption from gross income of interest on certain governmental obligations provided in section 103(a)(1) of the Internal Revenue Code of 1954 shall not be affected by the Administrator's acquisition of such resources if—

"(1) the Administrator, prior to contracting for such acquisition, certifies to his reasonable belief, that the persons for whom the Administrator is acquiring such resources for sale pursuant to section 5 of this Act are public bodies, cooperatives, and Federal agencies, unless the Administrator also certifies that he is unable to acquire such resources without selling a portion thereof to persons who are not exempt persons (as defined in section 103(b) of such Code), and

"(2) based upon such certification, the Secretary of the Treasury determines in accordance with applicable regulations that less than a major portion of the resource is to be furnished to persons who are not exempt persons (as defined in section 103(b) of such Code).

The certification under paragraph (1) shall be made in accordance with this subsection and a procedure and methodology approved by the Secretary of the Treasury. For purposes of this subsection, the term 'major portion' shall have the meaning provided by regulations issued by the Secretary of the Treasury."

—P.L. 96-223, Sec. 241(a), redesignated subsec. (g) as subsec. (h) and added new subsec. (g), effective with respect to obligations issued after 10/18/79. Sec. 241(b) of the Act provides:

"(b) Certain solid waste and energy-producing facilities.

"(1) General rule. For purposes of section 103 of the Internal Revenue Code of 1954, any obligation issued by an authority for 2 or more political subdivisions of a State which is part of an issue substantially all of the proceeds of which are to be used to provide solid waste-energy producing facilities shall be treated as an obligation of a political subdivision of a State which meets the requirements of section 103(b)(4)(E) of such Code (relating to solid waste disposal, etc., facilities). Nothing in the preceding sentence shall be construed to override the limitations of section 103(c) of such Code (relating to arbitrage bonds).

"(2) Solid waste-energy producing facilities. For purposes of paragraph (1), the term 'solid waste-energy producing facilities' means any solid waste disposal facility and any facility for the production of steam and electrical energy if—

"(A) substantially all of the fuel for the facility producing steam and electrical energy is derived from solid waste from such solid waste disposal facility,

"(B) both such solid waste disposal facility and the facility producing steam and electrical energy are owned and operated by the authority referred to in paragraph (1), and

"(C) all of the electrical energy and steam produced by the facility for producing steam and electricity which is not used by such facility is sold, for purposes other than resale, to an agency or instrumentality of the United States.

"(3) Solid waste disposal facility. For purposes of paragraph (2), the term 'solid waste disposal facility' means any solid waste disposal facility within the meaning of section 103(b)(4)(E) of the Internal Revenue Code of 1954 (determined without regard to section 103(g) of such Code).

"(4) Obligations must be in registered form. This subsection shall not apply to any obligation which is not issued in registered form."

Sec. 241(c) of the Act provides:

"(c) Special rule for certain alcohol-producing facilities.

"(1) In general. Subparagraph (C) of section 103(G)(3) of the Internal Revenue Code of 1954 (as added by subsection a)) shall not apply to any facility for the production of alcohol from solid waste if—

"(A) substantially all of the solid waste derived feedstock for such facility is produced at a facility which—

"(i) went into full production in 1977,

"(ii) is located within the limits of a city, and

"(iii) is located in the same metropolitan area as the alcohol-producing facility, and

"(B) before March 1, 1980, there were negotiations between a governmental body and an organization described in section 501(c)(3) of the Internal Revenue Code of 1954 with respect to the utilization of a special process for the production of alcohol at such alcohol-producing facility.

"(2) Limitation. The aggregate amount of obligations which may be issued by reason of paragraph (1) with respect to any project shall not exceed $30,000,000.

"(3) Termination. This subsection shall not apply to obligations issued after December 31, 1985."

—P.L. 96-223, Sec. 242(a)(1)(A), deleted "or" at the end of subpara. (b)(4)(A) . . . Sec. 242(a)(1)(B), substituted ", or" for the period at the end of subpara. (b)(4)(G) . . . Sec. 242(a)(1)(C), added new subpara. (b)(4)(H) . . . Sec. 242(a)(2), redesignated para. (b)(8) as (b)(9) and added new para. (b)(8), effective with respect to obligations issued after 10/18/79.

Sec. 242(b) of the Act provides:

"(b) Application of Section 103(b)(4)(H) to certain facilities.

"(1) In general. For purposes of section 103(b)(4)(H) of the Internal Revenue Code of 1954 (relating to qualified hydroelectric generating facilities), in the case of a hydroelectric generating facility described in paragraph (2)—

"(A) the facility shall be treated as a qualified hydroelectric generating facility (as defined in section 103(b)(8)(A) of such Code) without regard to clause (ii) of section 48(1)(13)(B) of such Code (relating to maximum generating capacity), and

"(B) the fraction referred to in subparagraph (C) of section 103(b)(8) of such Code shall be deemed to be 1.

"(2) Facilities to which paragraph (1) applies. A facility is described in this paragraph if—

"(A) it would be a qualified hydroelectric generating facility (as defined in section 103(b)(8)(A) of such Code) if clause (ii) of section 48(1)(13)(B) did not apply,

"(B) it constitutes an expansion of generating capacity at an existing hydroelectric generating facility,

"(C) such facility is located at 1 of 2 dams located in the same county where—

"(i) the rated capacity of the hydroelectric generating facilities at each such dam on October 18, 1979, was more than 750 megawatts,

"(ii) the construction of the first such dam began in 1956, power at such first dam was first generated in 1959, and full power production at such first dam began in 1961, and

"(iii) the construction of the second such dam began in 1959, power at such second dam was first generated in 1963, and full power production at such second dam began in 1964,

"(D) acquisition or construction of the existing facility referred to in subparagraph (B) was financed with the proceeds of an obligation described in section 103(a)(1) of such Code,

"(E) the existing facility is owned and operated by a State, political subdivision of a State, or agency or instrumentality of any of the foregoing,

"(F) no more than 60 percent of the electric power and energy produced by such existing facility and of the qualified hydroelectric generating facility is to be sold to anyone other than an exempt person (within the meaning of section 103(b)(3) of such Code), and

"(G) the agency of the State in which the facility is located which has jurisdiction over water rights had granted, before October 18, 1979, a water right under which expanded power and energy generating capacity for the facility was contemplated."

Sec. 243 of the Act provides:

"Sec. 243. Renewable energy property.

"(a) Certain State Obligations for Renewable Energy Property.

"(1) In general. Paragraph (1) of subsection (b) of section 103 of the Internal Revenue Code of 1954 shall not apply to any obligation issued as part of an issue substantially all of the proceeds of which are to be used to provide renewable energy property, if—

"(A) the obligations are general obligations of a State,

"(B) the authority for the issuance of the obligations requires that taxes be levied in sufficient amount to provide for the payment of principal and interest on such obligations,

"(C) the amount of such obligations, when added to the sum of the amounts of all such obligations previously issued by the State which are outstanding, does not exceed the smaller of—

"(i) $500,000,000 or

"(ii) one-half of 1 percent of the value of all property in the State,

"(D) such obligations are issued pursuant to a program to provide financing for small scale energy projects which was established by a State the legislature of which, before October 18, 1979, approved a constitutional amendment to provide for such a program, and

"(E) such obligations meet the requirements of paragraph (1) of section 103(h) of the Internal Revenue Code of 1954.

"(2) Renewable energy property. For purposes of this subsection, the term 'renewable energy property' means property used to produce energy (including heat, electricity, and substitute fuels) from renewable energy sources (including wind, solar, and geothermal energy, waste heat, biomass, and water).

"(b) Effective date.

Subsection (a) shall apply with respect to obligations issued after the date of enactment of this Act."

—P.L. 96-223, Sec. 244(a), redesignated subsec. (h) [as redesignated by Sec. 241(a) of this Act] as subsec. (i) and added new subsec. (h), effective with respect to obligations issued after 10/18/79.

—P.L. 96-222, Sec. 103(a)(3)(C), corrected Sec. 703(q)(1) of P.L. 95-600 to amend para. (c)(5) instead of (d)(5) [see below].

—P.L. 96-222, Sec. 103(a)(8), substituted " of a refund profit" for "or a refund profit" in Sec. 337(a) of P.L. 95-600 [reproduced below].

In 1978, P.L. 95-600, Sec. 331(a), substituted "$10,000,000" for "$5,000,000" in the heading and text of subpara. (b)(6)(D), effective for obligations issued after 1978, in tax. yrs. end. after 12/31/78 and for capital expenditures made after 1978 with respect to obligations issued before 1/1/79.

—P.L. 95-600, Sec. 331(b), added subpara. (b)(6)(I), effective for obligations issued after 9/30/79, in tax. yrs. end. after 9/30/79 and for capital expenditures made after 9/30/79 with respect to obligations issued after 9/30/79.

—P.L. 95-600, Sec. 332(a), added the last sentence in para. (b)(4), for tax. yrs. end. after 4/30/68, but only with respect to obligations issued after 4/30/68.

—P.L. 95-600, Sec. 333(a), amended subpara. (b)(4)(G), for obligations issued after 11/6/78, in tax. yrs. end. after 11/6/78.

Prior to amendment, subpara. (b)(4)(G) read as follows:

"(G) facilities for the furnishing of water, if available on reasonable demand to members of the general public."

—P.L. 95-600, Sec. 334(a), redesignated para. (b)(7) as (b)(8) and added new (b)(7) . . . Sec. 334(b), substituted "(6), and (7)" for "and (6)" in para. (b)(8) as redesignated, for obligations issued after 11/6/78.

—P.L. 95-600, Sec. 337, provides as follows:

"Sec. 337. Disposition of amounts generated by advance refunding of certain governmental obligations.

"(a) General rule.

The payment to a charitable organization of a refund profit held in a trust fund or escrow arrangement, or held by an underwriter or other person under a qualified agreement in accordance with that agreement—

"(1) shall not cause the refunding obligations out of which the refund profit arose to be treated as arbitrage bonds (within the meaning of section 103(c) of the Internal Revenue Code of 1954) and

"(2) may be paid without penalty imposed on the issuer of such obligations.

"(b) Rule for governments which have already paid arbitrage profits to the United States.

In the case of a State or local government which, before January 1, 1977—

"(1) requested in writing a rule by the Internal Revenue Service with respect to the tax consequences of paying refund profit to charitable organizations,

"(2) failed to receive a favorable ruling and did not pay the refund profit to a charitable organization, and

which accounted to the United States for refund profit by direct payment to the United States, or by the purchase of low-interest United States obligations, the Secretary of the Treasury shall pay, out of any amounts in the Treasury not otherwise appropriated, an amount equal to the refund profit for which the State or local government has accounted to the United States. Amounts paid to a State or local government under this subsection shall be distributed to such charitable organizations within 90 days after the date on which the payment is received by the State or local government in the same manner as if the refund profit had not been paid to the United States and met the requirements of subsection (a).

"(c) Definitions.

"For purposes of this section—

"(1) Refund profit. The term 'refund profit' means interest, profit, or other amounts generated by, or arising out of, the advance refunding, before September 24, 1976, of an obligation of a State or local government described in section 103 of such Code.

"(2) Charitable organization. The term 'charitable organization' means an organization described in section 501(c)(3) of such Code and exempt from taxation under section 501(a) of such Code other than an organization described in section 509(a) of such Code.

"(3) Qualified agreement. The term 'qualified agreement' means an agreement (whether or not enforceable) which provides for, or contemplates, the payment of refund profit to one or more charitable organizations.

"(4) Low-interest United States obligations. The term 'low-interest United States obligations' means United States obligations which bear an interest rate lower than the highest rate of interest borne by public debt securities generally available for purchase at the time such obligations were purchased."

—P.L. 95-600, Sec. 703(j)(1)(A), and (B), substituted "(a)(1) or (2)" for "(a)(1) or (4)" in the heading of para. (b)(1) [sic , (c)(1)] and each place it appeared in para. (c)(1) . . . Sec. 703(j)(1)(C), substituted "subsection (a)(1) or (2)" for "subsection (a)(1) or (2) or (4)" in subpara. (c)(2)(A) . . . Sec. 703(j)(1)(D), substituted "paragraph (2)(A)" for "subsection (d)(2)(A)" in para. (c)(5) . . . Sec. 703(j)(1)(E), substituted "subsection (b)(4)(G)" for "subsection (c)(4)(G)" in subsec. (d), effective 10/4/76.

—P.L. 95-600, Sec. 703(q)(1), substituted "section 438 of the Higher Education Act of 1965" for "section 2 of the Emergency Insured Student Loan Act of 1969" in para. (d)(5), effective for payments made by the Commissioner of Education after 1976.

—P.L. 95-339, Sec. 201(a), redesignated subsec. (f) [subsec. (e)[sic]] as subsec. (g) and added new subsec. (f), effective for tax. yrs. end. after 8/8/78.

In 1976, P.L. 94-455, Sec. 2105(a), deleted "or" at the end of para. (a)(2) . . . substituted "; or" for the period at the end of para. (a)(3) . . . added para. (a)(4), for obligations issued on or after 10/4/76.

—P.L. 94-455, Sec. 2105(b), redesignated subsec. (f) as subsec. (g) and added new subsec. (f), for obligations issued on or after 10/4/76.

—P.L. 94-455, Sec. 2105(c), redesignated para. (d)(5) as para. (d)(6) . . . added new para. (d)(5) . . . substituted "(a)(1) or (4)" for "(a)(1)" each place it appeared in paras. (d)(1) and (d)(2), for obligations issued on or after 10/4/76.

—P.L. 94-455, Sec. 2137(d), added para. (g)(24), effective for tax. yrs. begin. after 1975.

—P.L. 94-455, Sec. 1901(a)(17)(A), added "and" at the end of para. (a)(1), deleted paras. (a)(2) and (a)(3) and redesignated para. (a)(4), as added by Sec. 2105(a) of the Act, as para. (a)(2), effective for tax. yrs. begin. after 12/31/76. (But references to para. (a)(4) in para. (c)(1) were not changed from para. (a)(4) to para. (a)(2))

Prior to deletion paras. (a)(2) and (a)(3) read as follows:

"(2) the obligations of the United States;

"(3) the obligations of a corporation organized under Act of Congress, if such corporation is an instrumentality of the United States and if under the respective Act authorizing the issue of the obligations the interest is wholly exempt from the taxes imposed by this subtitle; or"

—P.L. 94-455, Sec. 1901(a)(17)(B), deleted subsec. (b) and redesignated subsecs. (c), (d), (e), (f), and (g), as added by Sec. 2105(b) of the Act, as subsecs. (b), (c), (d), (e) and (f), effective for tax. yrs. begin. after 12/31/76.

Prior to deletion subsec. (b) read as follows:

"(b) Exception.

"Subsection (a)(2) shall not apply to interest on obligations of the United States issued after September 1, 1917 (other than postal savings certificates of deposit, to the extent they represent deposits made before March 1, 1941), unless under the respective Acts authorizing the issuance thereof such interest is wholly exempt from the taxes imposed by this subtitle."

—P.L. 94-455, Sec. 1901(a)(17)(C), added "or (2)" after "(a)(1)" each place it appeared in para. (b)(1), as redesignated by Sec. 1901(a)(17)(B) of the Act, for obligations issued on or after 10/4/76.

—P.L. 94-455, Sec. 1901(a)(17)(D), added "or (2)" after "(a)(1)" in subpara. (c)(2)(A), as redesignated by Sec. 1901(a)(17)(B) of the Act, effective for tax. yrs. begin. after 12/31/76.

—P.L. 94-455, Sec. 1901(a)(17)(E), amended subsec. (e) (relating to certain cross references) [sic], as redesignated by Sec. 1901(a)(17)(B) of the Act, effective for tax. yrs. begin. after 12/31/76.

Prior to amendment, subsec. (e) [sic] read as follows:

"(f) Cross reference.

"For provisions relating to the taxable status of—

"(1) Bonds and certificates of indebtedness authorized by the First Liberty Bond Act, see sections 1 and 6 of that Act (40 Stat. 35, 36; 31 U. S. C. 746, 755);

"(2) Bonds issued to restore or maintain the gold reserve, see section 2 of the Act of March 14, 1900 (31 Stat. 46; 31 U. S. C. 408);

"(3) Bonds, notes, certificates of indebtedness, and Treasury bills authorized by the Second Liberty Bond Act, see sections 4, 5(b) and (d), 7, 18(b), and 22(d) of that Act, as amended (40 Stat. 290; 46 Stat. 20, 775; 40 Stat. 291, 1310; 55 Stat. 8; 31 U. S. C. 752a, 754, 747, 753, 757c);

"(4) Bonds, notes, and certificates of indebtedness of the United States and bonds of the War Finance Corporation owned by certain nonresidents, see section 3 of the Fourth Liberty Bond Act, as amended (40 Stat. 1311, § 4; 31 U. S. C. 750);

"(5) Certificates of indebtedness issued after February 4, 1910, see section 2 of the Act of that date (36 Stat. 192; 31 U. S. C. 769);

Exclusions from income   Code Sec. 103A

"(6) Consols of 1930, see section 11 of the Act of March 14, 1900 (31 Stat. 48; 31 U. S. C. 751;

"(7) Obligations and evidences of ownership issued by the United States or any of its agencies or instrumentalities on or after March 28, 1942, see section 4 of the Public Debt Act of 1941, as amended (c. 147, 61 Stat. 180; 31 U. S. C. 742a);

"(8) Commodity Credit Corporation obligations, see section 5 of the Act of March 8, 1938 (52 Stat. 108; 15 U. S. C. 713a-5);

"(9) Debentures issued by Federal Housing Administrator, see sections 204(d) and 207(i) of the National Housing Act, as amended (52 Stat. 14, 20; 12 U. S. C. 1710, 1713);

"(10) Debentures issued to mortgagees by United States Maritime Commission, see section 1105(c) of the Merchant Marine Act, 1936, as amended (52 Stat. 972; 46 U. S. C. 1275);

"(11) Federal Deposit Insurance Corporation obligations, see section 15 of the Federal Deposit Insurance Act (64 Stat. 890; 12 U. S. C. 1825);

"(12) Federal Home Loan Bank obligations, see section 13 of the Federal Home Loan Bank Act, as amended (49 Stat. 295, § 8; 12 U. S. C. 1433);

"(13) Federal savings and loan association loans, see section 5(h) of the Home Owners' Loan Act of 1933, as amended (48 Stat. 133; 12 U. S. C. 1464);

"(14) Federal Savings and Loan Insurance Corporation obligations, see section 402(e) of the National Housing Act (48 Stat. 1257; 12 U. S. C. 1725);

"(15) Home Owners' Loan Corporation bonds, see section 4(c) of the Home Owners' Loan Act of 1933, as amended (48 Stat. 644, c. 168; 12 U. S. C. 1463);

"(16) Obligations of Central Bank for Cooperatives, production credit corporations, production credit associations, and banks for cooperatives, see section 63 of the Farm Credit Act of 1933 (48 Stat. 267; 12 U. S. C. 1138c);

"(17) Panama Canal bonds, see section 1 of the Act of December 21, 1904 (34 Stat. 5; 31 U. S. C. 743), section 8 of the Act of June 28, 1902 (32 Stat. 484; 31 U. S. C. 744), and section 39 of the Tariff Act of 1909 (36 Stat. 117; 31 U. S. C. 745);

"(18) Philippine bonds, etc., issued before the independence of the Philippines, see section 9 of the Philippine Independence Act (48 Stat. 463; 48 U. S. C. 1239);

"(19) Postal savings bonds, see section 10 of the Act of June 25, 1910 (36 Stat. 817; 39 U. S. C. 760);

"(20) Puerto Rican bonds, see section 3 of the Act of March 2, 1917, as amended (50 Stat. 844; 48 U. S. C. 745);

"(21) Treasury notes issued to retire national bank notes, see section 18 of the Federal Reserve Act (38 Stat. 268; 12 U. S. C. 447;

"(22) United States Housing Authority obligations, see sections 5(e) and 20(b) of the United States Housing Act of 1937 (50 Stat. 890, 898; 42 U. S. C. 1405, 1420);

"(23) Virgin Islands insular and municipal bonds, see section 1 of the Act of October 27, 1949 (63 Stat. 940; 48 U. S. C. 1403)."

—P.L. 94-455, Sec. 1901(b)(8)(B), substituted "educational organization described in section 170(b)(1)(A)(ii)" for "educational institution (within the meaning of section 151(e)(4))" in subpara. (c)(3)(A), as redesignated by Sec. 1901(a)(17)(B) of the Act, effective 2/1/77.

—P.L. 94-455, Sec. 1906(b)(13)(A), substituted "Secretary" for "Secretary or his delegate" in para. (c)(6), as redesignated by Sec. 1901(a)(17)(B) of the Act, effective 2/1/77.

In 1975, P.L. 94-182, Sec. 301(a), made the same change as P.L. 94-164, by redesignating former subsec. (e) [presumably before redesignation by P.L. 94-164] as P.L. 94-164 added, effective with respect to obligation issued after 12/31/75.

—P.L. 94-164, Sec. 7(a), redesignated former subsec. (e) as subsec. (f) and added new subsec. (e), effective with respect to obligations issued after 12/23/75. In P.L. 94-182, Congress also redesignated former subsec. (e) as subsec. (f) and enacted a new subsec. (e), see above.

In 1971, P.L. 92-178, Sec. 315(a), substituted "energy or gas," for "energy, gas, or water, or" in subpara. (c)(4)(E), substituted ", or" for the period at the end of subpara. (c)(4)(G) added subpara. (c)(4)(G), effective for obligations issued after 1/1/69.

—P.L. 92-178, Sec. 315(b), substituted "$1,000,000" for "$250,000" in clause (c)(6)(F)(iii), effective for expenditures incurred after 12/10/71.

In 1969, P.L. 91-172, Sec. 601, redesignated subsec. (d) as (e), and added new subsec. (d), for obligations issued after 10/9/69.

In 1968, P.L. 90-634, Sec. 401(a), amended Sec. 103(c)(6) by adding at the end new subparagraphs (D) through (H), effective with respect to obligations issued after date of enactment (10/24/68).

—P.L. 90-364, Sec. 107(a), redesignated subsec. (c) as subsec. (d) and added new subsec. (d), effective for tax. yrs. end. after 4/30/68, but only with respect to obligations issued after such date except as provided. in Sec. 107(b)(2) of this Act, which reads

"(2) Section 103(c)(1) of the Internal Revenue Code of 1954, as amended by subsection (a), shall not apply with respect to any obligation issued before January 1, 1969, if before May 1, 1968—

"(A) the issuance of the obligation (or the project in connection with which the proceeds of the obligations are to be used) was authorized or approved by the governing body of the governmental unit issuing the obligation or by the voters of such governmental unit;

"(B) in connection with the issuance of such obligation or with the use of the proceeds to be derived from the sale of such obligation or the property to be acquired or improved with such proceeds, a governmental unit has made a significant financial commitment;

"(C) any person (other than a governmental unit) who will use the proceeds to be derived from the sale of such obligation or the property to be acquired or improved with such proceeds has expended (or has entered into a binding contract to expend) for purposes which are related to the use of such proceeds or property, an amount equal to or in excess of 20 percent of such proceeds; or

"(D) in the case of an obligation issued in conjunction with a project where financial assistance will be provided by a governmental agency concerned with economic development, such agency has approved the project or an application for financial assistance is pending."

Sec. 103A. Repealed.

In 1988, P.L. 100-647, Sec. 1013(a)(27), is reproduced in note following Code Sec. 143.

—P.L. 100-647, Sec. 1013(f)(10), added the last sentence to Sec. 1104(r) of P.L. 96-499, see below.

In 1986, P.L. 99-514, Sec. 1301(h), repealed Sec. 611(d)(7) of P.L. 98-369 (reproduced below), part of the special rules and limitations applying to the effective date for changes made by Sec. 611(c) of P.L. 98-369.

Prior to repeal, Sec. 611(d)(7) of P.L. 98-369 read as follows:

"(7) Report to congress.—The Secretary of the Treasury, in consultation with the Secretary of Housing and Urban Development, shall, not later than January 1, 1987, submit a report to the Committee on Finance of the Senate and the Committee on Ways and Means of the House of Representatives regarding the performance of issuers of qualified mortgage bonds and mortgage credit certificates relative to the intent of Congress described in section 103A(j) of the Internal Revenue Code of 1954."

—P.L. 99-514, Sec. 1301(j)(1), repealed Code Sec. 103A, effective for bonds issued after 8/15/86.

Prior to repeal, Code Sec. 103A read as follows:

"SEC. 103A. MORTGAGE SUBSIDY BONDS.

"(a) General rule.

"Except as otherwise provided in this section, any mortgage subsidy bond shall be treated as an obligation not described in subsection (a)(1) or (2) of section 103.

"(b) Mortgage subsidy bond defined.

"(1) In general. For purposes of this title, the term 'mortgage subsidy bond' means any obligation which is issued as part of an issue a significant portion of the proceeds of which are to be used directly or indirectly for mortgages on owner-occupied residences.

"(2) Exceptions. The following shall not be treated as mortgage subsidy bonds:

"(A) any qualified mortgage bond; and

"(B) any qualified veterans' mortgage bond.

"(c) Qualified mortgage bond; qualified mortgage issue; qualified veterans' mortgage bond.

"(1) Qualified mortgage bond defined.

"(A) In general. For purposes of this title, the term 'qualified mortgage bond' means an obligation which is issued as part of a qualified mortgage issue.

"(B) Termination December 31, 1987. No obligation issued after December 31, 1987, may be treated as a qualified mortgage bond.

"(2) Qualified mortgage issue defined.

"(A) Definition. For purposes of this title, the term 'qualified mortgage issue' means an issue by a State or political subdivision thereof of 1 or more obligations, but only if—

"(i) all proceeds of such issue (exclusive of issuance costs and a reasonably required reserve) are to be used to finance owner-occupied residences,

"(ii) such issue meets the requirements of subsections (d), (e), (f), (g), (h), (i), and (j).

"(B) Good faith effort to comply with mortgage eligibility requirements. An issue which fails to meet 1 or more of the requirements of subsections (d), (e), and (f), and (j)(1) and (2) shall be treated as meeting such requirements if—

"(i) the issuer in good faith attempted to meet all such requirements before the mortgages were executed,

"(ii) 95 percent or more of the proceeds devoted to owner-financing was devoted to residences with respect to which (at the time the mortgages were executed) all such requirements were met, and

"(iii) any failure to meet the requirements of such subsections and paragraphs is corrected within a reasonable period after such failure is first discovered.

"(C) Good faith effort to comply with other requirements. An issue which fails to meet 1 or more of the requirements of subsections (g), (h), (i), and (j)(3), (4), and (5) shall be treated as meeting such requirements if—

"(i) the issuer in good faith attempted to meet all such requirements, and

"(ii) any failure to meet such requirements is due to inadvertent error after taking reasonable steps to comply with such requirements.

"(3) Qualified veterans' mortgage bond defined. For purposes of this section, the term 'qualified veterans' mortgage bond' means any obligation—

"(A) which is issued as part of an issue substantially all of the proceeds of which are to be used to provide residences for veterans,

"(B) the payment of the principal and interest on which is secured by the general obligation of a State, and

"(C) which is part of an issue which meets the requirements of subsection (d), paragraphs (1) and (3) of subsection (j), and subsection (o).

"(d) Residence requirements.

"(1) For a residence. A residence meets the requirements of this subsection only if—

"(A) it is a single-family residence which can reasonably be expected to become the principal residence of the mortgagor within a reasonable time after the financing is provided, and

"(B) it is located within the jurisdiction of the authority issuing the obligation.

1,395

"(2) For an issue. An issue meets the requirements of this subsection only if all of the residences for which owner-financing is provided under the issue meet the requirements of paragraph (1).

"(e) 3-Year Requirement.

"(1) In general. An issue meets the requirements of this subsection only if 90 percent or more of the lendable proceeds of such issue are used to finance the residences of mortgagors who had no present ownership interest in their principal residences at any time during the 3-year period ending on the date their mortgage is executed.

"(2) Exceptions. For purposes of paragraph (1), the proceeds of an issue which are used—

"(A) to provide financing with respect to targeted area residences,

"(B) to provide qualified home improvements loans, and

"(C) to provide qualified rehabilitation loans, shall not be taken into account.

"(3) Mortgagor's interest in residence being financed. For purposes of paragraph (1), a mortgagor's interest in the residence with respect to which the financing is being provided shall not be taken into account.

"(f) Purchase price requirement.

"(1) In general. An issue meets the requirements of this subsection only if the acquisition cost of each residence the owner-financing of which is to be provided under the issue does not exceed 110 percent of the average area purchase price applicable to such residence.

"(2) Average area purchase price. For purposes of paragraph (1), the term 'average area purchase price' means, with respect to any residence, the average purchase price of single family residences (in the statistical area in which the residence is located) which were purchased during the most recent 12-month period for which sufficient statistical information is available. The determination under the preceding sentence shall be made as of the date on which the commitment to provide the financing is made (or, if earlier, the date of the purchase of the residence).

"(3) Separate application to new residences and old residences. For purposes of this subsection, the determination of average area purchase price shall be made separately with respect to—

"(A) residences which have not been previously occupied, and

"(B) residences which have been previously occupied.

"(4) Special rule for 2 to 4 family residences. For purposes of this subsection, to the extent provided in regulations, the average area purchase price shall be made separately with respect to 1 family, 2 family, 3 family, and 4 family residences.

"(5) Special rule for targeted area residences. In the case of a targeted area residence, paragraph (1) shall be applied by substituting '120 percent' for '110 percent'.

"(6) Exception for qualified home improvement loans. Paragraph (1) shall not apply with respect to any qualified home improvement loan.

"(g) Limitation on aggregate amount of qualified mortgage bonds issued during any calendar year.

"(1) In general. An issue meets the requirements of this subsection only if the aggregate amount of bonds issued pursuant thereto, when added to the aggregate amount of qualified mortgage bonds previously issued by the issuing authority during the calendar year, does not exceed the applicable limit for such authority for such calendar year.

"(2) Applicable limit for state housing agency. For purposes of this subsection—

"(A) In general. The applicable limit for any State housing finance agency for any calendar year shall be 50 percent of the State ceiling for such year.

"(B) Special rule where more than 1 agency. If any State has more than 1 State housing finance agency, all such agencies shall be treated as a single agency.

"(3) Applicable limit for other issuers. For purposes of this subsection—

"(A) In general. The applicable limit for any issuing authority (other than a State housing finance agency) for any calendar year is an amount which bears the same ratio to 50 percent of the State ceiling for such year as—

"(i) the average annual aggregate principal amount of mortgages executed during the immediately preceding 3 calendar years for single-family owner-occupied residences located within the jurisdiction of such issuing authority, bears to

"(ii) an average determined in the same way for the entire State.

"(B) Overlapping jurisdictions. For purposes of subparagraph (A)(i), if an area is within the jurisdiction of 2 or more governmental units, such area shall be treated as only within the jurisdiction of the unit having jurisdiction over the smallest geographical area unless such unit agrees to surrender all or part of such jurisdiction for such calendar year to the unit with overlapping jurisdiction which has the next smallest geographical area.

"(4) State ceiling. For purposes of this subsection, the State ceiling applicable to any State for any calendar year shall be the greater of—

"(A) 9 percent of the average annual aggregate principal amount of mortgages executed during the immediately preceding 3 calendar years for single-family owner-occupied residences located within the jurisdiction of such State, or

"(B) $200,000,000.

"(5) Special rule for states with constitutional home rule cities. For purposes of this subsection—

"(A) In general.—The applicable limit for any constitutional home rule city for any calendar year shall be determined under subparagraph (A) of paragraph (3) by substituting '100 percent' for '50 percent.'

"(B) Coordination with paragraphs (2) and (3). In the case of any State which contains 1 or more constitutional home rule cities, for purposes of applying paragraphs (2) and (3) with respect to issuing authorities in such State other than constitutional home rule cities, the State ceiling for any calendar year shall be reduced by the aggregate applicable limits determined for such year for all constitutional home rule cities in such State.

"(C) Constitutional home rule city. For purposes of this subsection, the term 'constitutional home rule city' means, with respect to any calendar year, any political subdivision of a State which, under a State constitution which was adopted in 1970 and effective on July 1, 1971, had home rule powers on the first day of the calendar year.

"(6) State may provide for different allocation.

"(A) In general. Except as provided in subparagraph (C), a State may, by law enacted after the date of the enactment of this section, provide a different formula for allocating the State ceiling among the governmental units in such State having authority to issue qualified mortgage bonds.

"(B) Interim authority for governor.

"(i) In general. Except as otherwise provided in subparagraph (C), the Governor of any State may proclaim a different formula for allocating the State ceiling among the governmental units in such State having authority to issue qualified mortgage bonds.

"(ii) Termination of authority. The authority provided in clause (i) shall not apply after the earlier of—

"(I) the first day of the first calendar year beginning after the first calendar year after 1980 during which the legislature of the State met in regular session, or

"(II) the effective date of any State legislation with respect to the allocation of the State ceiling enacted after the date of the enactment of this section.

"(C) State may not alter allocation to constitutional home rule cities. Except as otherwise provided in a State constitutional amendment (or law changing the home rule provision adopted in the manner prescribed by the State constitution), the authority provided in this paragraph shall not apply to that portion of the State ceiling which is allocated to any constitutional home rule city in the State unless such city agrees to such different allocation.

"(7) Transitional rules. In applying this subsection to any calendar year, there shall not be taken into account any bond which, by reason of section 1104 of the Mortgage Subsidy Bond Tax Act of 1980, receives the same tax treatment as bonds issued on or before April 24, 1979.

"(8) Reduction for mortgage credit certificates. The applicable limit of any issuing authority for any calendar year shall be reduced by the sum of—

"(A) the amount of qualified mortgage bonds which such authority elects not to issue under section 25(c)(2)(A)(ii) during such year, plus

"(B) the amount of any reduction in such ceiling under section 25(f) applicable to such authority for such year.

"(h) Portion of loans required to be placed in targeted areas.

"(1) In general. An issue meets the requirements of this subsection only if at least 20 percent of the proceeds of the issue which are devoted to providing owner-financing is made available (with reasonable diligence) for owner-financing of targeted area residences for at least 1 year after the date on which owner-financing is first made available with respect to targeted area residences.

"(2) Limitation. Nothing in paragraph (1) shall be treated as requiring the making available of an amount which exceeds 40 percent of the average annual aggregate principal amount of mortgages executed during the immediately preceding 3 calendar years for single-family owner-occupied residences located in targeted areas within the jurisdiction of the issuing authority.

"(i) Requirements related to arbitrage.

"(1) In general. An issue meets the requirements of this subsection only if such issue meets the requirements of paragraphs (2), (3), and (4) of this subsection. Such requirements shall be in addition to the requirements of section 103(c) (other than section 103(c)(6)).

"(2) Effective rate of mortgage interest cannot exceed bond yield by more than 1.125 percentage points.

"(A) In general. An issue shall be treated as meeting the requirements of this paragraph only if the excess of—

"(i) the effective rate of interest on the mortgages provided under the issue, over

"(ii) the yield on the issue,

is not greater than 1.125 percentage points.

"(B) Effective rate of mortgage interest.

"(i) In general. In determining the effective rate of interest on any mortgage for purposes of this paragraph, there shall be taken into account all fees, charges, and other amounts borne by the mortgagor which are attributable to the mortgage or to the bond issue.

"(ii) Specification of some of the amounts to be treated as borne by the mortgagor. For purposes of clause (i), the following items (among others) shall be treated as borne by the mortgagor:

"(I) all points or similar charges paid by the seller of the property, and

"(II) the excess of the amounts received from any person other than the mortgagor by any person in connection with the acquisition of the mortgagor's interest in the property over the usual and reasonable acquisition costs of a person acquiring like property where owner-financing is not provided through the use of qualified mortgage bonds.

"(iii) Specification of some of the amounts to be treated as not borne by the mortgagor. For purposes of clause (i), the following items shall not be taken into account:

"(I) any expected rebate of arbitrage profits, and

"(II) any application fee, survey fee, credit report fee, insurance charge, or similar amount to the extent such amount does not exceed amounts charged in such area in cases where owner-financing is not provided through the use of qualified mortgage bonds.

Subclause (II) shall not apply to origination fees, points, or similar amounts.

"(iv) Prepayment assumptions. In determining the effective rate of interest—

"(I) it shall be assumed that the mortgage prepayment rate will be the rate set forth in the most recent mortgage maturity experience table published by the Fed-

Exclusions from income — Code Sec. 103A

eral Housing Administration for the State (or, if available, the area within the State) in which the residences are located, and

"(II) prepayments of principal shall be treated as received on the last day of the month in which the issuer reasonably expects to receive such prepayments.

"(C) Yield on the issue. For purposes of this subsection, the yield on the issue shall be determined on the basis of—

"(i) the issue price (within the meaning of sections 1273(b) and 1274), and

"(ii) an expected maturity for the bonds which is consistent with the assumption required under subparagraph (B)(iv).

"(3) Non-mortgage investment requirements.

"(A) In general. An issue meets the requirements of this paragraph only if—

"(i) at no time during any bond year may the amount invested in non-mortgage investments with a yield higher than the yield on the issue exceed 150 percent of the debt service on the issue for the bond year, and

"(ii) the aggregate amount invested as provided in clause (i) is promptly and appropriately reduced as mortgages are repaid.

"(B) Exception for temporary periods. Subparagraph (A) shall not apply to—

"(i) proceeds of the issue invested for an initial temporary period until such proceeds are needed for mortgages, and

"(ii) temporary investment periods related to debt service.

"(C) Debt service defined. For purposes of subparagraph (A), the debt service on the issue for any bond year is the scheduled amount of interest and amortization of principal payable for such year with respect to such issue. For purposes of the preceding sentence, there shall not be taken into account amounts scheduled with respect to any bond which has been retired before the beginning of the bond year.

"(D) No disposition in case of loss. This paragraph shall not require the sale or disposition of any investment if such sale or disposition would result in a loss which exceeds the amount which would be paid or credited to the mortgagors under paragraph (4)(A) (but for such sale or disposition) at the time of such sale or disposition.

"(4) Arbitrage and investment gains to be used to reduce costs of owner-financing.

"(A) In general. An issue shall be treated as meeting the requirements of this paragraph only if an amount equal to the sum of—

"(i) the excess of—

"(I) the amount earned on all non-mortgage investments (other than investments attributable to an excess described in this clause), over

"(II) the amount which would have been earned if the investments were invested at a rate equal to the yield on the issue, plus

"(ii) any income attributable to the excess described in clause (i),

shall be paid or credited to the mortgagors as rapidly as may be practicable.

"(B) Investment gains and losses. For purposes of subparagraph (A), in determining the amount earned on all non-mortgage investments, any gain or loss on the disposition of such investments shall be taken into account.

"(C) Reduction where issuer does not use full 1.125 percentage points under paragraph (2).

"(i) In general. The amount required to be paid or credited to mortgagors under subparagraph (A) (determined under this paragraph without regard to this subparagraph) shall be reduced by the unused paragraph (2) amount.

"(ii) Unused paragraph (2) amount. For purposes of clause (i), the unused paragraph (2) amount is the amount which (if it were treated as an interest payment made by mortgagors) would result in the excess referred to in paragraph (2)(A) being equal to 1.125 percentage points. Such amount shall be fixed and determined as of the yield determination date.

"(D) Election to pay United States. Subparagraph (A) shall be satisfied with respect to any issue if the issuer elects before issuing the obligations to pay over to the United States—

"(i) not less frequently than once each 5 years after the date of issue, an amount equal to 90 percent of the aggregate amount which would be required to be paid or credited to mortgagors under subparagraph (A) (and not theretofore paid to the United States), and

"(ii) not later than 30 days after the redemption of the last obligation, 100 percent of such aggregate amount not theretofore paid to the United States.

"(E) Simplified accounting. The Secretary shall permit any simplified system of accounting for purposes of this paragraph which the issuer establishes to the satisfaction of the Secretary will assure that the purposes of this paragraph are carried out.

"(j) Other requirements.

"(1) Mortgages must be new mortgages.

"(A) In general. An issue meets the requirements of this subsection only if no part of the proceeds of such issue is to be used to acquire or replace existing mortgages.

"(B) Exceptions. Under regulations prescribed by the Secretary, the replacement of—

"(i) construction period loans,

"(ii) bridge loans or similar temporary initial financing, or

"(iii) in the case of a qualified rehabilitation, an existing mortgage,

shall not be treated as the acquisition or replacement of an existing mortgage for purposes of subparagraph (A).

"(2) Certain requirements must be met where mortgage is assumed. An issue meets the requirements of this subsection only if a mortgage with respect to which owner-financing has been provided under such issue may be assumed only if the requirements of subsections (d), (e), and (f), are met with respect to such assumption.

"(3) Information reporting requirement.

"(A) In general. An issue meets the requirements of this subsection only if the issuer submits to the Secretary, not later than the 15th day of the 2nd calendar month after the close of the calendar quarter in which the issue is issued (or such later time as the Secretary may prescribe with respect to any portion of the statement) a statement concerning the issue which contains—

"(i) the name and address of the issuer,

"(ii) the date of the issue, the amount of the lendable proceeds of the issue, and the stated interest rate, term, and face amount of each obligation which is part of the issue,

"(iii) such information as the Secretary may require in order to determine whether such issue meets the requirements of this section and the extent to which proceeds of such issue have been made available to low-income individuals, and

"(iv) such other information as the Secretary may require.

"(B) Extension of time. The Secretary may grant an extension of time for the filing of any statement under subparagraph (A) if there is reasonable cause for the failure to file such statement in a timely fashion.

"(4) State certification requirements.

"(A) In general. An issue meets the requirements of this subsection only if, before the issue is issued, a State official designated by State law (or, where there is no such State official, the Governor) certifies in the manner prescribed by regulations that the issue meets the requirements of subsection (g).

"(B) Certification furnished to secretary. Any certification under subparagraph (A) shall be submitted to the Secretary at the same time as the statement with respect to such issue is submitted under paragraph (3) or such other time as the Secretary may prescribe.

"(C) Special rule for constitutional home rule cities. In the case of any constitutional home rule city (as defined in subsection (g)(5)(C)), the certification under subparagraph (A) shall be made by the chief executive officer of such city.

"(5) Policy statement.

"(A) In general. An issue meets the requirements of this subsection only if the applicable elected representative of the governmental unit—

"(i) which is the issuer, or

"(ii) on whose behalf such issue was issued,

has published (after a public hearing following reasonable public notice) a report described in subparagraph (B) by the last day of the year preceding the year in which such issue is issued and a copy of such report has been submitted to the Secretary on or before such last day.

"(B) Report. The report referred to in subparagraph (A) which is published by the applicable elected representative of the governmental unit shall include—

"(i) a statement of the policies with respect to housing, development, and low-income housing assistance which such governmental unit is to follow in issuing qualified mortgage bonds and mortgage credit certificates, and

"(ii) an assessment of the compliance of such governmental unit during the preceding 1-year period preceding the date of the report with—

"(I) the statement of policy on qualified mortgage bonds and mortgage credit certificates that was set forth in the previous report, if any, of an applicable elected representative of such governmental unit, and

"(II) the intent of Congress that State and local governments are expected to use their authority to issue qualified mortgage bonds and mortgage credit certificates to the greatest extent feasible (taking into account prevailing interest rates and conditions in the housing market) to assist lower income families to afford home ownership before assisting higher income families.

"(C) Extension of time. The Secretary may grant an extension of time for the publishing of a report described in subparagraph (B) or the submittal of such report to the Secretary if there is reasonable cause for the failure to publish or submit such report in a timely fashion.

"(k) Targeted area residences.

"(1) In general. For purposes of this section, the term 'targeted area residence' means a residence in an area which is either—

"(A) a qualified census tract, or

"(B) an area of chronic economic distress.

"(2) Qualified census tract.

"(A) In general. For purposes of paragraph (1), the term 'qualified census tract' means a census tract in which 70 percent or more of the families have income which is 80 percent or less of the statewide median family income.

"(B) Data used. The determination under subparagraph (A) shall be made on the basis of the most recent decennial census for which data are available.

"(3) Area of chronic economic distress.

"(A) In general. For purposes of paragraph (1), the term 'area of chronic economic distress' means an area of chronic economic distress—

"(i) designated by the State as meeting the standards established by the State for purposes of this subsection, and

"(ii) the designation of which has been approved by the Secretary and the Secretary of Housing and Urban Development.

"(B) Criteria to be used in approving state designations. The criteria used by the Secretary and the Secretary of Housing and Urban Development in evaluating any proposed designation of an area for purposes of this subsection shall be—

"(i) the condition of the housing stock, including the age of the housing and the number of abandoned and substandard residential units,

"(ii) the need of area residents for owner-financing under this section, as indicated by low per capita income, a high percentage of families in poverty, a high number of welfare recipients, and high unemployment rates,

"(iii) the potential for use of owner-financing under this section to improve housing conditions in the area, and

"(iv) the existence of a housing assistance plan which provides a displacement program and a public improvements and services program.

"(l) Other definitions and special rules.

"For purposes of this section—
"(1) Mortgage. The term 'mortgage' includes any other owner-financing.
"(2) Bond. The term 'bond' includes any obligation.
"(3) State. The term 'State' includes a possession of the United States and the District of Columbia.
"(4) Statistical area.
"(A) In general. The term 'statistical area' means—
"(i) a standard metropolitan statistical area, and
"(ii) any county (or the portion thereof) which is not within a standard metropolitan statistical area.
"(B) Standard metropolitan statistical area. The term 'standard metropolitan statistical area' means the area in and around a city of 50,000 inhabitants or more (or equivalent area) as defined by the Secretary of Commerce.
"(C) Designation where adequate statistical information not available. For purposes of this paragraph, if there is insufficient recent statistical information with respect to a county (or portion thereof) described in subparagraph (A)(ii), the Secretary may substitute for such county (or portion thereof) another area for which there is sufficient recent statistical information.
"(D) Designation where no county. In the case of any portion of a State which is not within a county, subparagraphs (A)(ii) and (C) shall be applied by substituting for 'county' an area designated by the Secretary which is the equivalent of a county.
"(5) Acquisition cost.
"(A) In general. The term 'acquisition cost' means the cost of acquiring the residence as a completed residential unit.
"(B) Exceptions. The term 'acquisition cost' does not include—
"(i) usual and reasonable settlement or financing costs,
"(ii) the value of services performed by the mortgagor or members of his family in completing the residence, and
"(iii) the cost of land which has been owned by the mortgagor for at least 2 years before the date on which construction of the residence begins.
"(C) Special rule for qualified rehabilitation loans. In the case of a qualified rehabilitation loan, for purposes of subsection (f), the term 'acquisition cost' includes the cost of the rehabilitation.
"(6) Qualified home improvement loan. The term 'qualified home improvement loan' means the financing (in an amount which does not exceed $15,000)—
"(A) of alterations, repairs, and improvements on or in connection with an existing residence by the owner thereof, but
"(B) only of such items as substantially protect or improve the basic livability or energy efficiency of the property.
"(7) Qualified rehabilitation loan.
"(A) In general. The term 'qualified rehabilitation loan' means any owner-financing provided in connection with—
"(i) a qualified rehabilitation, or
"(ii) the acquisition of a residence with respect to which there has been a qualified rehabilitation, but only if the mortgagor to whom such financing is provided is the first resident of the residence after the completion of the rehabilitation.
"(B) Qualified rehabilitation. For purposes of subparagraph (A), the term 'qualified rehabilitation' means any rehabilitation of a building if—
"(i) there is a period of at least 20 years between the date on which the building was first used and the date on which the physical work on such rehabilitation begins,
"(ii) 75 percent or more of the existing external walls of such building are retained in place as external walls in the rehabilitation process, and
"(iii) the expenditures for such rehabilitation are 25 percent or more of the mortgagor's adjusted basis in the residence.
For purposes of clause (iii), the mortgagor's adjusted basis shall be determined as of the completion of the rehabilitation or, if later, the date on which the mortgagor acquires the residence.
"(8) Determinations on actuarial basis. All determinations of yield, effective interest rates, and amounts required to be paid or credited to mortgagors or paid to the United States under subsection (i)(4)(A) shall be made on an actuarial basis taking into account the present value of money.
"(9) Single-family and owner-occupied residences include certain residences with 2 to 4 units. Except for purposes of subsections (g) and (h)(2), the terms 'single-family' and 'owner-occupied', when used with respect to residences, include 2, 3, or 4 family residences—
"(A) one unit of which is occupied by the owner of the units, and
"(B) which were first occupied at least 5 years before the mortgage is executed.
"(10) Cooperative housing corporations
"(A) In general. In the case of any cooperative housing corporation—
"(i) each dwelling unit shall be treated as if it were actually owned by the person entitled to occupy such dwelling unit by reason of his ownership of stock in the corporation, and
"(ii) any indebtedness of the corporation allocable to the dwelling unit shall be treated as if it were indebtedness of the shareholder entitled to occupy the dwelling unit.
"(B) Adjustment to targeted area requirement. In the case of any issue to provide financing to a cooperative housing corporation with respect to cooperative housing not located in a targeted area, to the extent provided in regulations, such issue may be combined with 1 or more other issues for purposes of determining whether the requirements of subsection (h) are met.
"(C) Cooperative housing corporation. The term 'cooperative housing corporation' has the meaning given to such term by section 216(b)(1).
"(m) Special rule for issue used for owner-occupied housing and rental housing.
"In the case of an issue—

"(1) part of the proceeds of which are to be used for mortgages on owner-occupied residences in a manner which meets the requirements of this section, and
"(2) part of the proceeds of which are to be used for rental housing which meets the requirements of section 103(b)(4)(A), under regulations prescribed by the Secretary, each such part shall be treated as a separate issue.
"(n) Advance refunding of mortgage subsidy bonds not permitted.
"On and after the date of the enactment of this section, no obligation may be issued for the advance refunding of a mortgage subsidy bond (determined without regard to subsection (b)(2)).
"(o) Additional Requirements for Qualified Veterans' Mortgage Bonds.
"(1) Veterans to whom financing may be provided. An obligation meets the requirements of this subsection only if each mortgagor to whom financing is provided under the issue is a qualified veteran.
"(2) Requirement that state program be in effect before June 22, 1984. An issue meets the requirements of this subsection only if it is a general obligation of a State which issued qualified veterans' mortgage bonds before June 22, 1984.
"(3) Volume limitation.
"(A) In general. An issue meets the requirements of this subsection only if the aggregate amount of bonds issued pursuant thereto (when added to the aggregate amount of qualified veterans' mortgage bonds previously issued by the State during the calendar year) does not exceed the State veterans limit for such calendar year.
"(B) State veterans limit. A state veterans limit for any calendar year is the amount equal to—
"(i) the aggregate amount of qualified veterans bonds issued by such State during the period beginning on January 1, 1979, and ending on June 22, 1984 (not including the amount of any qualified veterans bond issued by such State during the calendar year (or portion thereof) in such period for which the amount of such bonds so issued was the lowest), divided by
"(ii) the number (not to exceed 5) of calendar years after 1979 and before 1985 during which the State issued qualified veterans bonds (determined by only taking into account bonds issued on or before June 22, 1984).
"(4) Qualified veteran. For purposes of this subsection, the term 'qualified veteran' means any veteran—
"(A) who served on active duty at some time before January 1, 1977, and
"(B) who applied for the financing before the later of—
"(i) the date 30 years after the last date on which such veteran left active service, or
"(ii) January 31, 1985.
"(5) Good faith effort rules made applicable. Rules similar to the rules of subparagraphs (B) and (C) of subsection (c)(2) shall apply to the requirements of this subsection.
"(6) Special rule for certain short-term obligations. In the case of any obligation which has a term of 1 year or less and which was issued to provide financing for property taxes, the amount taken into account under this subsection with respect to such obligation shall be $1/15$ of its principal amount."
—P.L. 99-514, Sec. 1861(a), added subpara. (j)(5)(C), effective for obligations issued after 12/31/84.
—P.L. 99-514, Sec. 1861(b), substituted "January 31, 1985" for "January 1, 1985" in clause (o)(4)(B)(ii), effective for obligations issued after 7/18/84.
—P.L. 99-514, Sec. 1861(c)(1), substituted "and (j)(1) and (2)" for "and (j)" in subpara. (c)(2)(B) . . . Sec. 1861(c)(2), substituted "(i), and (j)(3), (4), and (5)" for "and (i)" in subpara. (c)(2)(C), effective for obligations issued after 12/31/84.
—P.L. 99-514, Sec. 1863(a), amended Sec. 613 of P.L. 98-369 (reproduced below), effective as provided in Sec. 1863(b) of this Act, which reads:
"(b) Effective date. —
"The amendment made by subsection [1863(a), P.L. 99-514] shall take effect on the date of the enactment of this Act [10/22/86], except that such amendment shall not apply with respect to any loan made by the Federal Financing Bank to the State of Oregon pursuant to a credit agreement entered into on April 16, 1985 (as such agreement was in effect on such date). The Secretary of the Treasury shall guarantee any loan made by the Federal Financing Bank to the State of Oregon pursuant to such agreement."
Prior to amendment, Sec. 613 of P.L. 98-369 read as follows:
"SEC. 613. AUTHORITY TO BORROW FROM FEDERAL FINANCING BANK.
"(a) General rule. — Upon application by the appropriate State Housing Agency of Oregon, the Federal Financing Bank shall make qualified cash flow loans to such Agency. Such loans shall bear interest at a rate equal to the average rate on the applicable mortgage bonds with respect to which such loans were made.
"(b) Qualified cash flow loans. — For purposes of this section, the term 'qualified cash flow loan' means any loan with respect to an applicable mortgage bond reasonably necessary to cover any excess determined under subsection (c)(2) on the basis of actual payments. The aggregate amount of such loans which may be outstanding at any 1 time shall not exceed $300,000,000.
"(c) Applicable mortgage bonds. — For purposes of this section, the term 'applicable mortgage bond' means any qualified veterans' mortgage bond issued as part of an issue—
"(1) which was outstanding on December 5, 1980,
"(2) with respect to which the excess of—
"(A) the projected aggregate payments of principal on the applicable mortgage bonds during the 15-fiscal year period beginning with fiscal year 1984, over
"(B) the projected aggregate payments during such period of principal on mortgages financed by the applicable mortgage bonds,
exceeds 12 percent of the aggregate principal amount of such bonds outstanding on July 1, 1983,

Exclusions from income — Code Sec. 103A

"(3) with respect to which the amount of the average annual prepayments during fiscal years 1981, 1982, and 1983 was less than 2 percent of the average of the loan balances as of the beginning of each of such fiscal years, and

"(4) which, for fiscal year 1983, had a prepayment experience rate that did not exceed 20 percent of the prepayment experience rate of the Federal Housing Administration in the State or region in which the issuer is located.

"(d) Definitions. —

"(1) Assumptions used in making projection. — The computation under subsection (c)(2) shall be made by using the following percentage of the prepayment experience of the Federal Housing Administration in the State or region in which the issuer of the applicable mortgage bonds is located:

Fiscal Year:	Percentage:
1984	15
1985	20
1986	25
1987 and thereafter	30

"(2) Qualified veterans' mortgage bonds. — The term 'qualified veterans' mortgage bonds' has the meaning given to such term by section 103A(c)(3) of the Internal Revenue Code of 1954."

—P.L. 99-514, Sec. 1867(a), amended Sec. 624(c)(2) of P.L. 98-369 (reproduced below), exceptions to the effective date for changes made by Sec. 624 of P.L. 98-369, by substituting "for the Essex County New Jersey Resource Recovery Project authorized by the Port Authority of New York and New Jersey on November 10, 1983, as part of an agreement approved" for "by the Essex County Port Authority of New York and New Jersey as part of an issue approved", see below. Sec. 1867(b) of this Act provides:

"(b) The amendment made by section 624 of the Tax Reform Act of 1984 [P.L. 98-369] shall not apply to obligations issued with respect to the Downtown Muskogee Revitalization Project for which a UDAG grant was preliminarily approved on May 5, 1981, if —

"(1) such obligation is issued before January 1, 1986, or

"(2) such obligation is issued after such date to provide additional financing for such project except that the aggregate amount of obligations to which this subsection applies shall not exceed $10,000,000."

—P.L. 99-514, Sec. 1872(c)(2), repealed Sec. 632(a)(1) of P.L. 98-369, (reproduced below), exceptions and special rules for amendments made by Secs. 622-628 of P.L. 98-369, see below . . . Sec. 1873(a), amended Sec. 632(a) of P.L. 98-369 by substituting "section 624" for "section 623" in the matter preceding paragraph (1), see below . . . Sec. 1873(b), added the last sentence to Sec. 632(d) of P.L. 98-369, see below.

Prior to repeal, Sec. 632(a)(1) of P.L. 98-369 read as follows:

"(1) Obligations issued with respect to any waste-to-energy facility authorized by official action on April 10, 1980 and with respect to which a subsequent agreement was signed between a city government and the Department of the Army on December 27, 1982, to jointly pursue construction and operation of such facility."

In 1984, P.L. 98-454, Sec. 204, provides:

"SEC. 204.(a) The Governor of any possession of the United States may for calendar years 1984 and 1985 proclaim a formula (different from that provided by section 103A(g) of the Internal Revenue Code of 1954) for allocating the State ceiling under such section among the governmental units in such possession having authority to issue qualified mortgage bonds (as defined in section 103A(c) of such Code).

"(b) The authority provided by subsection (a) shall not apply after the effective date of any legislation with respect to the allocation of the State ceiling enacted by the legislature of the possession after the date of the enactment of this Act [10/5/84.]"

—P.L. 98-369, Sec. 42(a)(2), substituted "sections 1273(b) and 1274" for "section 1232(b)(2)" in clause (i)(2)(C)(i), effective for tax. yrs. ending after 7/18/84.

—P.L. 98-369, Sec. 611(a), substituted "December 31, 1987" for "December 31, 1983" each place it appeared in subpara. (c)(1)(B), effective for obligations issued after 12/31/84.

—P.L. 98-369, Sec. 611(b)(1), added paras. (j)(3), (j)(4) and (j)(5) for obligations issued after 12/31/84.

—P.L. 98-369, Sec. 611(c)(1), substituted "subsection (d), paragraphs (1) and (3) of subsection (j), and subsection (o)" for "subsection (j)(1)" in subpara. (c)(3)(C) . . . Sec. 611(c)(2), added subsec. (o), effective for obligations issued after 7/18/84. Secs. 611(d)(3)(B)–(d)(6) of the Act [as amended by Sec. 1301(h) of P.L. 99-514, see above] provide:

"(B) Volume limitation. — The requirements of paragraph (3) of section 103A(o) of the Internal Revenue Code of 1954 (as added by this section) shall apply to obligations issued after June 22, 1984. In applying such requirements to obligations issued after such date, obligations issued on or before such date shall not be taken into account under such paragraph (3).

"(C) Qualified veterans' mortgage bonds authorized before October 18, 1983, not taken into account. — The requirements of section 103A(o)(3) of the Internal Revenue Code of 1954 shall not apply to any qualified veterans' mortgage bond if —

"(i) the issuance of such bond was authorized by a State referendum before October 18, 1983, or

"(ii) the issuance of such bond was authorized pursuant to a State referendum before December 1, 1983, where such referendum was authorized by action of the State legislature before October 18, 1983.

"(4) Transitional rule where state formula for allocating state ceiling expires. —

"(A) In general. — If a State law which provided a formula for allocating the State ceiling under section 103A(g) of the Internal Revenue Code of 1954 for calendar year 1983 expires as of the close of calendar year 1983, for purposes of section 103A(g) of such Code, such State law shall be treated as remaining in effect after 1983. In any case to which the preceding sentence applies, where the State's expiring allocation formula requires action by a State official to allocate the State ceiling among issuers, actions of such State official in allocating such ceiling shall be effective.

"(B) Termination. — Subparagraph (A) shall not apply on or after the effective date of any State legislation enacted after the date of the enactment of this Act with respect to the allocation of the State ceiling.

"(C) Special rule for Texas. — In the case of Texas, the Governor of such State may take the actions described in subparagraph (A) pursuant to procedures established by the Governor consistent with the State laws of Texas.

"(5) Special rule for determinations of statistical area. — For purposes of applying section 103A of the Internal Revenue Code of 1954 and any other provision of Federal law —

"(A) Recission. — The Director of the Office of Management and Budget shall rescind the designation of the Kansas City, Missouri primary metropolitan statistical area (KCMO PMSA) and the designation of the Kansas City, Kansas primary metropolitan statistical area (Kansas City, KS PMSA), and shall not take any action to designate such two primary metropolitan statistical areas as a consolidated metropolitan statistical area.

"(B) Designation. — The Director of the Office of Management and Budget shall designate a single metropolitan statistical area which includes the following:

"(i) Kansas City, Kansas.
"(ii) Kansas City, Missouri.
"(iii) The counties of Johnson, Wyandotte, Leavenworth, and Miami in Kansas.
"(iv) The counties of Cass, Clay, Jackson, Platte, Ray, and Lafayette in Missouri.

The metropolitan statistical area designation pursuant to this subsection shall be known as the 'Kansas City Missouri-Kansas Metropolitan Statistical Area'.

"(6) Transitional rule for Kentucky and Nevada. — For purposes of section 103A(g) of the Internal Revenue Code of 1954, in the case of Kentucky and Nevada, subclause (I) of section 103A(g)(6)(B)(ii) of such Code shall be applied as if the first day referred to in such subclause were January 1, 1987."

—P.L. 98-369, Sec. 612(b), added para. (g)(8) for interest paid or accrued after 12/31/84, on indebtedness incurred after 12/31/84. Sec. 612(g)(2) of the Act provides:

"(2) Elections. — The amendments made by this section shall apply to elections under section 25(c)(2)(A)(ii) of the Internal Revenue Code of 1954 (as added by this section) for calendar years after 1983."

—P.L. 98-369, Sec. 613, [as amended by Sec. 1863 of P.L. 99-514, see above] provides:

"SEC. 613. ADVANCE REFUNDING OF CERTAIN VETERANS MORTGAGE BONDS PERMITTED.

"(a) In general. —

"Notwithstanding section 103A(n) of the Internal Revenue Code of 1954, an issuer of applicable mortgage bonds may issue advance refunding bonds with respect to such applicable mortgage bonds.

"(b) Limitation in amount of advanced refunding. —

"(1) In general. — The amount of advanced refunding bonds which may be issued under subsection (a) shall not exceed the lesser of —

"(A) $300,000,000, or

"(B) the excess of —

"(i) the projected aggregate payments of principal on the applicable mortgage bonds during the 15-fiscal year period beginning with fiscal year 1984, over

"(ii) the projected aggregate payments during such period of principal on mortgages financed by the applicable mortgage bonds.

"(2) Assumptions used in making projection. — The computation under paragraph (1)(B) shall be made by using the following percentages of the prepayment experience of the Federal Housing Administration in the State or region in which the issuer of the advance refunding bonds is located:

"Fiscal Year:	Percentage:
1984	15
1985	20
1986	25
1987 and thereafter	30

"(c) Definitions. —

"For purposes of this section. —

"(1) Applicable mortgage bonds. — The term 'applicable mortgage bonds' means any qualified veterans' mortgage bonds issued as part of an issue —

"(A) which was outstanding on December 31, 1981,

"(B) with respect to which the excess determined under subsection (b)(1)(B) exceeds 12 percent of the aggregate principal amount of such bonds outstanding on July 1, 1983,

"(C) with respect to which the amount of the average annual prepayments during fiscal years 1981, 1982, and 1983 was less than 2 percent of the average of the loan balances as of the beginning of each of such fiscal years, and

"(D) which, for fiscal year 1983, had a prepayment experience rate that did not exceed 20 percent of the prepayment experience rate of the Federal Housing Administration in the State or region in which the issuer is located.

"(2) Qualified veterans' mortgage bonds. — The term 'qualified veterans' mortgage bonds' has the meaning given to such term by section 103A(c)(3) of the Internal Revenue Code of 1954.

"(3) Fiscal year — The term 'fiscal year' means the fiscal year of the State."

—P.L. 98-369, Sec. 614, amended Sec. 1104 of P.L. 96-499, the effective date for changes made by Sec. 1102 and 1103 of P.L. 96-499, by adding subsecs. (p), (q) and (r), reproduced below.

—P.L. 98-369, Sec. 624(b)(1), substituted "section 103(c) (other than section 103(c)(6))" for "section 103(c)" in para. (i)(1), for bonds issued after 12/31/84. Sec. 624(c)(2) of the Act [as amended by Sec. 1867(a) of P.L. 99-514 and (b), see above] provides:

"(2) Exception. — The amendments made by this section shall not apply to obligations issued for the Essex County New Jersey Resource Recovery Project authorized by the Port Authority of New York and New Jersey on November 10, 1983, as part of an agreement approved by Essex County, New Jersey, on July 7, 1981, and approved by the State of New Jersey on December 31, 1981. The aggregate face amount of bonds to which this paragraph applies shall not exceed $350,000,000."

—P.L. 98-369, Sec. 632, [as amended by P.L. 99-514, Secs. 1872(c)(2) and 1873(a) and (b), see above] provides:

"Sec. 632. Miscellaneous Exceptions and Special Rules.

"(a) Exception from provisions other than arbitrage and federal guarantees. — Notwithstanding any other provision of this subtitle, the amendments made by this subtitle (other than the amendments made by section 622 (relating to Federal guarantees) and section 624 (relating to arbitrage)) shall not apply to the following obligations:

"(1) [Repealed]

"(2) Obligations issued to finance a redevelopment program on 9 city blocks adjacent to a transit station but only if such program was approved on October 25, 1983.

"(3) Obligations issued pursuant to an inducement resolution adopted on August 8, 1978, for a redevelopment plan for which a redevelopment trust fund was established on September 7, 1977.

"(4) Obligations issued to finance a UDAG project which was preliminarily approved on December 29, 1982, and which received final approval on May 3, 1984.

"(5) Obligations issued to finance a parking garage pursuant to an inducement resolution adopted on March 9, 1984, in connection with a project for which a UDAG grant application was made on January 31, 1984.

"(6) Obligations which—

"(A) are issued to finance a downtown development project with respect to which an urban development action grant is made but only if such grant—

"(i) was preliminarily approved on November 3, 1983, and

"(ii) received final approval before June 1, 1984, and

"(B) are issued in connection with inducement resolutions that were adopted on December 21, 1982, July 5, 1983, and March 1, 1983,

but only to the extent the aggregate face amount of such obligations does not exceed $34,000,000.

"(7) Obligations with respect to which an inducement resolution was adopted on March 5, 1984, for the purpose of acquiring existing airport facilities at more than 12 locations in 1 State but—

"(A) only if the Civil Aeronautics Board certifies that such transaction would reduce the amount of Federal subsidies provided under section 419 of the Airline Deregulation Act of 1978, and

"(B) only to the extent the aggregate face amount of such obligations does not exceed $25,000,000.

"(8) Obligations described in subsection (b).

"(b) Certain parking facility bonds. — For purposes of the Internal Revenue Code of 1954, any obligation issued with respect to a parking facility approved by an agency of a county government on December 1, 1982, as part of an urban revitalization plan shall be treated as an obligation described in section 103(b)(4)(D) of such Code.

"(c) Exception to certain bond limitations. — The amendments made by section 621 (relating to the limitations on amount of private activity bonds) and section 626(a) (relating to the prohibition on acquiring existing facilities) shall not apply to obligations issued before January 1, 1987, in connection with the Claymont, Delaware, regeneration plant of the Delaware Economic Development Authority, but only to the extent the aggregate face amount of such obligation does not exceed $30,000,000.

"(d) Certain obligations treated as not federally guaranteed. — For purposes of section 103(h) of the Internal Revenue Code of 1954, obligations (including refunding obligations) shall not be treated as federally guaranteed if—

"(A) such obligations are issued with respect to any facility, and

"(B) any obligation was issued on June 3, 1982 in the principal amount of $11,312,125 for the purpose of financing the development, study, or related costs incurred with respect to such facility.

The amendment made by section 626 shall not apply to any obligations described in the preceding sentence.

"(e) Certain expenditures treated as significant expenditures. — For purposes of this title, expenditures of $850,000 incurred with respect to any project involving $15,000,000 shall be treated as significant expenditures if such expenditures were incurred pursuant to an agreement entered into on July 13, 1982, relating to the discharge of industrial waste after January 1, 1986.

"(f) Certain ordinances treated as inducement resolutions. — For purposes of this title, any ordinance passed on May 3, 1982, with respect to a planned development district shall be treated as an inducement resolution with respect to obligations issued in 1984 in connection with a mall planned for such district.

"(g) Delayed effective date with respect to certain IDBS. —

"(1) FERC projects. — Notwithstanding any other provision of this title, and amendments made by this title (other than the amendments to section 103(c) of the Internal Revenue Code of 1954) which, but for this paragraph, would apply to industrial development bonds issued after December 31, 1984, shall not apply to any of the following obligations issued before January 1, 1986:

"(A) obligations issued with respect to Federal Energy Regulatory Commission project 4657, but only to the extent the aggregate face amount of such obligations does not exceed $12,900,000;

"(B) obligations issued with respect to Federal Energy Regulatory Commission project 2853, but only to the extent the aggregate face amount of such obligations does not exceed $28,600,000; or

"(C) obligations issued with respect to Federal Energy Regulatory Commission project 4700, but only to the extent the aggregate face amount of such obligations does not exceed $3,850,000.

"(2) Park central new town in town project. — Notwithstanding any other provision of this title, any amendments made by this title (other than the amendments to section 103(c) of the Internal Revenue Code of 1954) which, but for this paragraph, would apply to industrial development bonds issued after December 31, 1984, shall not apply to any obligation issued before January 1, 1988, with respect to Park Central New Town In Town Project located in Port Arthur, Texas, but only to the extent the aggregate face amount of such obligations does not exceed $80,000,000."

In 1982, P.L. 97-248, Sec. 220(a)(1), substituted "1.125 percentage points" for "1 percentage point" in subpara. (i)(2)(A)... Sec. 220(a)(2), amended clause (i)(2)(B)(iv)... Sec. 220(a)(3)(A), substituted "1.125 percentage points" for "1 percentage point" in the heading of para. (i)(2)... Sec. 220(a)(3)(B), substituted "1.125 percentage points" for "1 percentage point" in clause (i)(4)(C)(ii) and in the heading of subpara. (i)(4)(C)... Sec. 220(b), added subpara. (i)(3)(D), effective for obligations issued after 9/3/82.

Prior to amendment, clause (i)(2)(B)(iv) read as follows:

"(iv) Prepayment assumption. In determining the effective rate of interest, it shall be assumed that the mortgage prepayment rate will be the rate set forth in the most recent mortgage maturity experience table published by the Federal Housing Administration for the State (or, if available, the area within the State) in which the residences are located."

—P.L. 97-248, Sec. 220(c), amended subsec. (e), effective for obligations issued after 9/3/82. Sec. 220(f)(2) of this Act provides:

"(2) First time homebuyer requirement. The amendments made by subsection (c) shall also apply to obligations issued after April 24, 1979, and before the date of the enactment of this Act but only to the extent that the proceeds of such obligations are not committed as of the date of the enactment of this Act [9/3/82]."

Prior to amendment, subsec. (e) read as follows:

"(e) 3-Year requirement.

"(1) In general. An issue meets the requirements of this subsection only if each mortgagor to whom financing is provided under the issue had a present ownership interest in a principal residence of such mortgagor at no time during the 3-year period ending on the date the mortgage is executed. For purposes of the preceding sentence, the mortgagor's interest in the residence with respect to which the financing is being provided shall not be taken into account.

"(2) Exceptions. Paragraph (1) shall not apply with respect to—

"(A) any financing provided with respect to a targeted area residence,

"(B) any qualified home improvement loan, and

"(C) any qualified rehabilitation loan."

—P.L. 97-248, Sec. 220(d)(1), substituted "110 percent" for "90 percent" each place it appeared in subsec. (f)... Sec. 220(d)(2), substituted "120 percent" for "110 percent" in para. (f)(5)... Sec. 220(e), added para. (1)(10), effective for obligations issued after 9/3/82.

—P.L. 97-248, Sec. 221(c)(2), repealed Sec. 1104(k) of P.L. 96-499 (see below). Prior to repeal Sec. 1104(k) of P.L. 96-499 read as follows:

"(k) Transitional rule for low- and moderate-income requirement.

"In the case of obligations issued after April 24, 1979, and before January 1, 1984, the period for which the low- and moderate-income requirements of section 103(b)(4)(A) of the Internal Revenue Code of 1954 (as amended by section 1103 of this subtitle) is required to be met shall be 20 years."

—P.L. 97-248, Sec. 310(c)(3)(A), deleted para. (j)(1) and redesignated paras. (j)(2) and (j)(3) as paras. (j)(1) and (j)(2),... Sec. 310(c)(3)(B), substituted "(f), and (j)" for "and (f) and paragraphs (2) and (3) of subsection (j)" in subpara. (c)(2)(B)... Sec. 310(c)(3)(C), deleted ", and paragraph (1) of subsection (j)" in subpara. (c)(2)(C)... Sec. 310(c)(3)(D), substituted "subsection (j)(1)" for "subsection (j)(2)" in para. (c)(3)(C)... Sec. 310(c)(4), deleted "in registered form" after "is issued" in subpara. (c)(3)(A), effective for obligations issued after 12/31/82.

Prior to deletion, para. (j)(1) read as follows:

"(j) Other requirements.

"(1) Obligations must be registered. An issue meets the requirements of this subsection only if each obligation issued pursuant to such issue is in registered form."

In 1980, P.L. 96-595, Sec. 5(a), added subparas. (i)(4)(C), (D) and (E)... Sec. 5(b), added "or paid to the United States" after "credited to mortgagors" in para. (1)(8), effective as if included in the amendments made by P.L. 96-499, see below.

—P.L. 96-499, Sec. 1102(a), added Code Sec. 103A, effective for obligations issued after 4/24/79 except as provided in Sec. 1104 of this Act which reads:

"Sec. 1104. Effective Dates For Bond Provisions.

"(a) General rule.

"(1) In general. Except as otherwise provided in this section, the amendments made by sections 1102 and 1103 shall apply to obligations issued after April 24, 1979.

"(2) Exceptions for certain obligations issued before January 1, 1981. The amendments made by sections 1102 and 1103 shall not apply to obligations issued before January 1, 1981, if such obligations are part of an issue substantially all the proceeds of which (exclusive of issuance costs and a reasonably required reserve) are, before the date which is 1 year after the date of issue of the obligations, committed—

Exclusions from income Code Sec. 103A

"(A) except as provided in subparagraph (B), by firm commitment letters (similar to those used in financing not provided with tax-exempt bonds), and

"(B) in the case of rental housing, by the commencement of construction of the project or by the acquisition of the project.

"(b) Exception for official action taken before April 25, 1979.

"(1) In general. The amendments made by sections 1102 and 1103 shall not apply to obligations if official action before April 25, 1979, of the governing body of the unit having authority to issue such obligations indicated an intent to issue such obligations.

"(2) Action by staff of housing authority treated as action of authority in certain cases. For purposes of paragraph (1), if, before April 25, 1979—

"(A) the permanent professional staff of a State or local housing authority performed substantial work on a bond issue, and

"(B) it was reasonable to expect that the bond issue, as developed by the staff, would be promptly approved by the governing body of the housing authority,

then such action by such staff shall be treated as the official action of such governing body.

"(3) Special rules relating to size of issue.

"(A) In general. Except as provided in subparagraph (B), an issue does not qualify for the exception provided by paragraph (1) if the issue size exceeds the intended issue size.

"(B) Exception. In the case of an issue to provide owner-financing for residences for which as of April 24, 1979, there was no documentation relating to intended issue size, paragraph (1) shall not apply unless—

"(i) substantially all of the proceeds of the issue (exclusive of issuance costs and a reasonably required reserve) are to be used to provide owner-financing for one to four family residences (one unit of which is owner occupied) and not to acquire or replace existing mortgages (within the meaning of section 103A(j)(2) of the Internal Revenue Code of 1954), and

"(ii) substantially all of the proceeds referred to in clause (i) are committed by firm commitment letters (similar to those used in owner-financing not provided with tax-exempt bonds) to such owner-financing before the day which is 9 months after the date of issue of the obligations.

"(C) Issue size defined. For purposes of this paragraph, the term 'issue size' means the aggregate face amount of obligations issued pursuant to the issue.

"(D) Intended issue size. For purposes of this paragraph, the term 'intended issue size' means the aggregate face amount of obligations which a reasonable individual would reasonably conclude from the documentation before April 25, 1979, was the issue size which the governing body of the issuing authority intended to issue.

"(4) Local referendum held before June 13, 1979.

"(A) In general. For purposes of paragraph (1), if—

"(i) on April 25, 1979, legislation was pending in a State legislature,

"(ii) on April 27, 1979, such legislation was amended to authorize local governmental units to issue tax-exempt obligations,

"(iii) before June 13, 1979, such legislation was enacted and a local governmental unit in such State held a referendum with respect to the issuance of obligations to finance owner-occupied residences, and

"(iv) any action with respect to the issuance of such obligations by the governing body of such local governmental unit would have met the requirements of paragraph (1) if such legislation had been in effect, and such referendum had been held, when that action was taken,

then such legislation shall be treated as in effect, and such referendum shall be treated as having been held, at the time when such action was taken.

"(B) Dollar limit for local governmental units. The aggregate amount of obligations which may be issued by local governmental units with respect to the area comprising any local governmental area by reason of subparagraph (A) may not exceed—

"(i) $35,000,000, reduced by

"(ii) the aggregate amount of obligations which are issued (before, on, or after the issue under this paragraph) by local governmental units with respect to such area after April 24, 1979, and to which the amendments made by this subtitle do not apply solely by reason of this subsection (determined without regard to the application of subparagraph (A) of this paragraph).

"(C) Mortgage requirements. Subparagraph (A) shall not apply with respect to any issue unless such issue meets the requirements of paragraph (3)(A) of subsection (c).

"(5) Certain local action pursuant to legislation enacted before September 29, 1979.

"(A) In general. For purposes of paragraph (1), if—

"(i) on April 25, 1979, legislation was pending in a State legislature authorizing a local governmental unit to issue tax-exempt obligations for owner-occupied residences,

"(ii) before September 29, 1979, such legislation was enacted, and

"(iii) any action with respect to the issuance of such obligations by the local governing body would have met the requirements of paragraph (1) if such legislation had been in effect when that action was taken,

then such legislation shall be treated as in effect at the time when such action was taken.

"(B) Dollar limit for local governmental units. The aggregate amount of obligations which may be issued by local governmental units with respect to the area comprising any local governmental area by reason of subparagraph (A) may not exceed the lesser of—

"(i) the aggregate amount authorized by the legislation referred to in subparagraph (A), or

"(ii) $150,000,000.

"(C) Mortgage requirements. Subparagraph (A) shall not apply with respect to any issue unless such issue meets the requirements of paragraph (3)(A) of subsection (c).

"(c) $150,000,000 exception for state housing finance agencies.

"(1) In general. To the extent of the limit set forth in paragraph (2), the amendments made by this subtitle shall not apply to obligations issued by a State housing finance agency.

"(2) Dollar limit for state housing finance agencies. The aggregate amount of obligations which may be issued by State housing finance agencies with respect to any State by reason of paragraph (1) may not exceed—

"(A) $150,000,000, reduced by

"(B) the aggregate amount of obligations which are issued (before, on, or after the issue under this subsection) by the housing finance agencies of such State after April 24, 1979, to finance owner-occupied residences and to which the amendments made by this subtitle do not apply solely by reason of subsection (b).

"(3) Commitments. Paragraph (1) shall not apply with respect to any issue unless substantially all of the proceeds of such issue (exclusive of issuance costs and a reasonably required reserve)—

"(A) are to be used to provide owner-financing for 1 to 4 family residences (1 unit of which is owner-occupied) and not to acquire or replace existing mortgages (within the meaning of section 103A(j)(2) of the Internal Revenue Code of 1954), and

"(B) are committed by firm commitment letters (similar to those used in owner-financing not provided by tax-exempt bonds) to owner-financing before January 1, 1981.

"(4) Special rules for action in 1978 pursuant to mortgage program established in 1970.

"(A) In general. If—

"(i) in 1970 State legislation established a program to issue tax-exempt obligations to finance the purchase of existing mortgages from financial institutions,

"(ii) in August 1978, as a step toward issuing obligations under such program, the governing body of the housing agency administering the program made a finding that there was a shortage of mortgage funds within the State,

"(iii) moneys received by any financial institution on the purchase of mortgages will be reinvested within 90 days in new mortgages, and

"(iv) the issue meets the requirements of subparagraphs (B) and (C),

then paragraph (3) shall not apply with respect to an issue of obligations pursuant to the program referred to in clause (i) and the finding referred to in clause (ii).

"(B) Downpayment requirement. An issue meets the requirements of this subparagraph only if 75 percent or more of the financing provided under the issue is financing for residences where such financing constitutes 95 percent or more of the acquisition cost of the residences.

"(C) Targeted area requirement. An issue meets the requirements of this subparagraph only if at least 20 percent of the financing provided under the issue is owner-financing of targeted area residences. For purposes of the preceding sentence, the term 'targeted area residence' means a residence in an area which is a census tract in which 70 percent or more of the families have income which is 80 percent or less of the statewide median family income (determined on the basis of the most recent decennial census for which data are available).

"(D) Dollar limit. The aggregate amount of obligations which may be issued by a State housing authority by reason of subparagraph (A) may not exceed $125,000,000.

"(d) Special rules.

"(1) Court action was pending to determine scope of authorizing legislation.

"(A) In general. If—

"(i) before April 25, 1979, a State had enacted a law under which counties were authorized to establish public trusts to issue tax-exempt obligations for public purposes,

"(ii) on such date the question of whether or not that law authorized the issuance of obligations to finance certain owner-occupied residences was being litigated in a court of competent jurisdiction,

"(iii) before July 31, 1979, the Supreme Court of such State held that the counties were so authorized, and

"(iv) there is written evidence (which was in existence before April 25, 1979) that before April 25, 1979, the governing body of a county in such State had taken action indicating an intent to issue (or to establish a program for issuing) tax-exempt obligations to finance owner-occupied residences,

then the amendments made by section 1102 shall not apply to obligations issued by the public trust for such county.

"(B) Dollar limit. The aggregate amount of obligations which may be issued with respect to any county by reason of subparagraph (A) may not exceed $50,000,000.

"(2) State legislation enacted before June 8, 1979, where locality had established income limitations before April 25, 1979.

"(A) In general. If—

"(i) on April 25, 1979, legislation was pending in a State legislature authorizing a local governmental unit to issue tax-exempt obligations for owner-occupied residences,

"(ii) there is written evidence (which was in existence before April 25, 1979) that before April 25, 1979, the governing body of the local governmental unit had taken action indicating to its delegation to the State legislature what the income limitation would be for individuals who would be eligible for mortgages under the program, and

"(iii) before June 8, 1979, the legislation referred to in clause (i) was enacted, then the amendments made by section 1102 shall not apply to obligations issued by the local governmental unit.

1,401

"(B) Dollar limit. The aggregate amount of obligations which may be issued with respect to any local governmental area by reason of subparagraph (A) may not exceed $150,000,000.

"(3) Resolutions before city council before enactment of state authorizing legislation.

"(A) In general. If—

"(i) before April 25, 1979, 2 resolutions were submitted to a city council the first of which would create an urban residential finance authority and the second of which would authorize the appointment of the members of such authority,

"(ii) at the time such resolutions were submitted, State authorizing legislation had not been enacted,

"(iii) before April 25, 1979, the State authorizing legislation was enacted, and

"(iv) after April 24, 1979, and before May 17, 1979, a resolution was adopted by the city council which created an urban residential finance authority and which authorized the appointment of members of the authority,

then the amendments made by section 1102 shall not apply with respect to obligations issued on behalf of such city.

"(B) Dollar limit. The aggregate amount of obligations which may be issued with respect to any city by reason of subparagraph (A) may not exceed $50,000,000.

"(4) Special rule where city postponed second half of authorized issue to save interest.

"(A) on March 28, 1979, the council of a city adopted a resolution authorizing the issuance of not to exceed $30,000,000 of mortgage revenue bonds,

"(B) on or about August 1, 1979, approximately one-half of the obligations authorized by such resolution were issued, and

"(C) the reason why the remaining obligations were not issued at that time was to save interest payments until the money was actually needed,

then the amendments made by section 1102 shall not apply with respect to the issuance of the remaining obligations which were authorized by such March 28, 1979, resolution.

"(5) State was in process of permitting localities to establish nonprofit corporations.

"(A) In general. If—

"(i) a State law enacted after April 24, 1979, and before June 16, 1979, provides that local governments may establish nonprofit corporations to issue tax-exempt obligations to finance owner-occupied residences,

"(ii) pursuant to such State law, a local government establishes such a nonprofit corporation and designates it for purposes of this subsection, and

"(iii) on November 7 or 14, 1979, an amount was specified by or for the local government as the maximum amount of obligations which the local government expected the nonprofit corporation to issue with respect to the area under any transitional authority provided by this subtitle,

then the amendments made by section 1102 shall not apply to obligations issued by the nonprofit corporation with respect to the area for which such local government has jurisdiction.

"(B) Dollar limits. The aggregate amount of obligations which may be issued with respect to any area by reason of subparagraph (A) may not exceed the amount referred to in subparagraph (A)(iii) which was specified on November 7 or 14, 1979, by or for the local government.

"(C) Substitution of housing authorities, etc. For purposes of applying so much of paragraph (7) as relates to subparagraph (A)—

"(i) if the local housing authority had the intent referred to in paragraph (7), such local housing authority shall be substituted for the local government, and

"(ii) if the governing body of the local government is a commissioners court, the county judge who was on April 24, 1979, the presiding officer of such court shall be treated as the governing body of such government.

"(6) Obligations issued under this subsection must meet the requirements of subsection (c)(3). No obligations may be issued under this subsection unless the issue meets the requirements of subsection (c)(3).

"(7) Governing body must file affidavits showing intent on April 24, 1979. No obligation may be issued under this subsection with respect to any area unless a majority of the members of the governing body of the local governmental unit having jurisdiction over that area file affidavits with the Secretary of the Treasury (or his delegate) indicating that it was their intent on April 24, 1979, either that tax-exempt obligations be issued to provide financing for owner-occupied residences or that a program be established to issue such obligations.

"(8) Limitations reduced by certain other issues. Any limitation on the amount of obligations which may be issued by any issuer by reason of any paragraph of this subsection shall be reduced by the aggregate amount of obligations which are issued (before, on, or after the issue under this subsection) by local governmental units with respect to the area within the jurisdiction of such issuer after April 24, 1979, and to which the amendments made by this subtitle do not apply solely by reason of subsection (b).

"(e) Ongoing local programs for rehabilitation loans.

"(1) In general. If before April 25, 1979, a local governmental unit had a qualified rehabilitation loan program, then the amendments made by this subtitle shall not apply to obligations issued by such governmental unit for qualified loans if substantially all of the proceeds of such issue (exclusive of issuance costs and a reasonably required reserve) are committed by firm commitment letters (similar to those used in owner financing not provided by tax-exempt bonds) to qualified loans before January 1, 1981.

"(2) Limitation. The aggregate amount of obligations which may be issued by reason of paragraph (1) by local governmental units with respect to the area comprising any local governmental area may not exceed the lesser of—

"(A) $10,000,000, or

"(B) the aggregate amount of loans made with respect to that area under the qualified rehabilitation loan program during the period beginning on January 1, 1977, and ending on April 24, 1979.

The limitation established by the preceding sentence shall be reduced by the aggregate amount of obligations (if any) which are issued (before, on, or after the issue under this subsection) under the qualified rehabilitation loan program after April 24, 1979, with respect to the same local governmental area and to which the amendments made by this subtitle do not apply solely by reason of subsection (b).

"(3) Qualified rehabilitation loan program. For purposes of this subsection, the term 'qualified rehabilitation loan program' means a program for the financing—

"(A) of alterations, repairs, and improvements on or in connection with an existing residence by the owner thereof, but

"(B) only of such items as substantially protect or improve the basic livability of the property.

"(4) Qualified loan. For purposes of this subsection, the term 'qualified loan' means the financing—

"(A) of alterations, repairs, and improvements on or in connection with an existing 1 to 4 family residence (1 unit of which is owner-occupied) by the owner thereof, but

"(B) only of such items as substantially protect or improve the basic livability of the property.

"(5) Dollar limit on qualified loans. For purposes of this subsection, a loan shall not be treated as a qualified loan if the financing is in an amount which exceeds $20,000 plus $2,500 for each unit in excess of 1.

"(f) $50 per capita exception for local governments.

"(1) In general. To the extent of the limit set forth in paragraph (2), the amendments made by section 1102 shall not apply to mortgage subsidy bonds issued by local governmental units after April 24, 1979.

"(2) Limit.

"(A) In general. The aggregate amount of obligations issued with respect to any area by reason of paragraph (1) shall not exceed—

"(i) the amount equal to the product of $50 and the population of that area, reduced by

"(ii) the aggregate amount of obligations which are issued (before, on, or after the issue under this subsection) by local governmental units after April 24, 1979, with respect to that area and to which the amendments made by this subtitle do not apply solely by reason of subsections (b), (d), and (e).

"(B) Determination of population. For purposes of subparagraph (A), the population of any area shall be the population as of July 1, 1976, as determined for purposes of the State and Local Fiscal Assistance Act of 1972.

"(3) Unit must establish that action was taken before April 25, 1979. Paragraph (1) shall not apply with respect to any obligation issued by any local governmental unit unless—

"(A) there is written evidence (which was in existence before April 25, 1979), that before April 25, 1979, the governing body of such local governmental unit had taken action indicating an intent to issue (or to establish a program for issuing) tax-exempt obligations to finance owner-occupied residences,

"(B) on October 30, 1979, such local governmental unit had authority to issue obligations to finance owner-occupied residences, and

"(C) a majority of the members of the governing body of the local governmental unit file with the Secretary of the Treasury (or his delegate) affidavits that the requirement of such subparagraph (A) is met.

For purposes of subparagraph (A), action of the governing body of a second local governmental unit with respect to the same area shall be treated as action of the issuing governmental unit.

"(4) Commitments. Paragraph (1) shall not apply with respect to any issue unless such issue meets the requirements of paragraph (3) of subsection (c).

"(5) Overlapping jurisdictions. For purposes of this subsection, if 2 or more local governmental units meet the requirements of paragraph (3) and have authority to issue mortgage subsidy bonds with respect to residences in the same area, only the unit having jurisdiction over the smallest geographical area shall be treated as having issuing authority with respect to such area unless such unit agrees to surrender part or all of the amount permitted under this subsection to the local governmental unit with overlapping jurisdiction which has the next smallest geographical area.

"(g) Rollover of existing tax-exempt obligations.

"(1) In general. The amendments made by sections 1102 and 1103 shall not apply to the issuance of obligations to refinance for the same purpose tax-exempt indebtedness which was outstanding on April 24, 1979 (or indebtedness which had previously been refinanced pursuant to this subsection), but only if—

"(A) on April 24, 1979, there was an agreed on period for the maturity of the mortgages or other financing, and

"(B) the new obligations have a maturity date which does not exceed by more than 2 years the agreed on period referred to in subparagraph (A).

"(2) Amounts for reserves, issue costs, etc. An issue which otherwise meets the requirements of paragraph (1) shall not be treated as failing to meet such requirements solely because the amount of the new indebtedness exceeds the amount of the old indebtedness by such amount as is reasonably necessary to cover construction period interest, reserves, and the costs of issuing the new indebtedness.

"(h) Special rules for projects under development.

"(1) Rental Housing. The amendment made by section 1103 shall not apply to a project which was in the development stage on April 24, 1979, if—

"(A) a plan specifying the number and location of rental units was approved on or before such date by a governing body of a State or local government or by a state or local housing agency or similar agency, and

"(B) substantial expenditures for site improvement for the project had been incurred on or before such date.

Exclusions from income Code Sec. 103A

"(2) Rental housing projects approved by secretary of HUD. The amendment made by section 1103 shall not apply to a project which was in the development stage on April 24, 1979, if—

"(A) a plan specifying the number and location of rental units was preliminarily approved by the Secretary of Housing and Urban Development pursuant to section 221(d)(4) or section 232 of the National Housing Act on or before such date, and

"(B) fees for processing the project with the Department of Housing and Urban Development and other expenditures for the project had been incurred on or before such date.

"(3) Owner-occupied housing. The amendments made by section 1102 shall not apply to a project which was in the development stage on April 24, 1979, if on or before such date—

"(A) substantial expenditures had been made for detailed plans and specifications, and

"(B) either tax-exempt construction financing had been issued with respect to the project or there is written evidence that a governmental unit intended to issue tax-exempt obligations to finance the acquisition of the units by home buyers. The amendment made by section 1103 shall not apply to construction or other initial temporary financing issued with respect to a project which meets the requirements of the preceding sentence if substantially all of the dwelling units in such project are to be owner-occupied residences.

"(4) Certain redevelopment mortgage bond financing projects. Subparagraph (B) of paragraph (3) shall be treated as satisfied if, before April 25, 1979—

"(A) the developer of a project acquired the land for such project.

"(B) there was approval by the mayor's advisory committee of a city of a comprehensive proposal (under a State law authorizing tax-exempt obligations for use only in redevelopment areas) for such project, subject to revisions to be made, and

"(C) a revised proposal was submitted to the redevelopment agency and city council containing the revisions.

The aggregate amount of obligations which may be issued by local governmental units with respect to the area comprising any local governmental area by reason of this paragraph may not exceed $20,000,000.

"(i) Registration requirements.

"(1) In general. Notwithstanding any other provisions of this section, the amendments made by sections 1102 and 1103, insofar as they require obligations to be in registered form, shall apply to obligations issued after December 31, 1981.

"(2) Bonds under transitional rules. Any obligation issued after December 31, 1981, by reason of this section shall be in registered form.

"(j) Advance refunding. Notwithstanding any other provision of this section —

"(1) subsection (n) of section 103A of the Internal Revenue Code of 1954 (as added by section 1102) shall apply to obligations issued after the date of the enactment of this Act to refund obligations issued before, on, or after such date of enactment, and

"(2) this section shall not apply to obligations issued after such date of enactment for the advance refunding of obligations issued before, on, or after such date of enactment.

"(k) Repealed.

"(l) Substitution of governmental instrumentality for city.

"(1) In general. If—

"(A) a corporation was created on June 17, 1971, pursuant to State law to provide financing for the construction and rehabilitation of low-income housing,

"(B) pursuant to a State law enacted in 1955 a city has made loans to housing developers from the proceeds of short-term bonds and notes issued by the city, and has secured 50-year mortgages from the developers, and

"(C) the corporation agrees to acquire from the city certain of the loans referred to in subparagraph (B) by issuing obligations which will be secured by mortgages referred to in subparagraph (B) on 12 projects (11 of which projects are subsidized with interest-reduction subsidies under section 236 of the National Housing Act),

then the amendments made by this subtitle shall not apply to obligations issued by the corporation to acquire the loans (and mortgages) referred to in subparagraph (C).

"(2) Dollar limit. The aggregate amount of obligations to which paragraph (1) applies shall not exceed $135,000,000.

"(3) Time limit. Paragraph (1) shall not apply to any obligation issued after December 31, 1980.

"(m) State legislation was pending on April 1, 1979, and enacted on April 26, 1979, where locality had taken action to undertake a study of local mortgage market.

"(1) In general. If—

"(A) on April 1, 1979, legislation was pending in a State legislature limiting the authority to local governments within such State to issue tax-exempt obligations for owner-occupied residence under existing home rule authority, and such legislation was enacted on April 26, 1979,

"(B) there is written evidence (which was in existence before April 25, 1979) that not earlier than June 1, 1978, but before April 25, 1979, the governing body of a local government in such State had taken action authorizing the undertaking of a demographic or related study of the local mortgage market, which study was intended to serve as a basis for issuance of tax exempt obligations for owner-occupied residences,

"(C) on December 20, 1979, an amount was specified by or for the local government as the range of obligations which it expected to issue with respect to the area under any transitional authority provided by the Act, and

"(D) a majority of the members of the governing body of the local government certify that the city or county was waiting enactment of the legislation described in subparagraph (A) prior to determining to proceed towards the issuance of tax-exempt obligations for owner-occupied residences.

then the amendments made by section 1102 shall not apply to obligations issued by such city or county.

"(2) Dollar limits. The aggregate amount of obligations which may be issued with respect to any area by reason of paragraph (1) may not exceed the maximum amount referred to in paragraph (1)(C) which was specified on December 20, 1979, by or for such local government.

"(3) Time limits. Paragraph (1) shall not apply with respect to any issue unless substantially all of the proceeds of such issue (exclusive of issuance costs and a reasonably required reserve) are committed by firm commitment letters (similar to those used in owner-financing not provided by tax-exempt bonds) to owner-financing before January 1, 1982.

"(n) Certain additional transitional authority.

"(1) In general. The amendments made by sections 1102 and 1103 shall not apply to issues described in the following table:

City or county	Ceiling amount	Purpose of issue
Baltimore, Maryland	$100,000,000	Financing owner-occupied residences.
Port Arthur, Texas	175,000,000	For financing on New Town In Town project.
Minneapolis, Minnesota	25,000,000	Financing owner-occupied residences.
Minneapolis-St. Paul, Minnesota	235,000,000	Joint program for financing owner-occupied residences involving some UDAG grants and private financing.
Detroit, Michigan	50,000,000	To issue obligations maturing before 1986 for construction on the Riverfront West project.
Brevard County, Florida	150,000,000	Financing owner-occupied residences.
Chicago, Illinois	235,000,000	For financing on the Presidential Towers project.

"(2) Issuing authority. The authority granted by this subsection with respect to any city or county may be used only by the appropriate issuing authority for that city or county.

"(3) Ceiling amount. The ceiling amount specified in paragraph (1) with respect to any item shall be the maximum aggregate amount of obligations which may be issued by the appropriate issuing authority under the authority granted by such item.

"(4) Purpose. The authority under any item may be used to issue obligations only for the purpose set forth in paragraph (1) for such item.

"(o) Special rule for loans to lenders program.

"(1) In general. In the case of any obligations issued during 1981 or 1982 pursuant to a qualified loans to lender program—

"(A) the amendments made by section 1103 shall not apply,

"(B) subsection (i) of section 103A of the Internal Revenue Code of 1954 (other than the last sentence of paragraph (1) of such subsection) shall not apply, and

"(C) the determination of whether the requirements of subsections (d), (e), (f), (h), (j)(2), and (j)(3) of such section 103A are met with respect to such issue shall be made by taking into account the loans made by the financial institutions with the funds provided by the issue (in lieu of the mortgages acquired from the financial institutions with the proceeds of the issue).

"(2) Qualified loans to lender program. For purposes of paragraph (1), the term 'qualified loans to lender program' means any program established pursuant to legislation enacted by New York State in 1970 which finances the purchase of existing mortgages from financial institutions and requires any money received by a financial institution on the purchase of a mortgage to be reinvested within 90 days in new mortgages."

"(p) Most exceptions not to apply to bonds issued after December 31, 1984.

"In addition to any obligations to which the amendments made by section 1102 apply by reason of the provisions of this section, the amendments made by section 1102 shall apply, notwithstanding any other provision of this section (other than subsection (n)), to obligations issued after December 31, 1984, all or a major portion of the proceeds of which are used to finance new mortgages on single-family residences that the owner occupied.

"(q) Reduction of state ceiling by amount of special mortgage bonds issued before 1985.—

"(1) In general. Notwithstanding any other provision of this section (other than subsections (n) and (r)), any obligation—

"(A) which is part of an issue all or a major portion of the proceeds of which are used to finance new mortgages in single-family residences that are owner occupied,

"(B) which were issued by issuing authorities in such State after June 15, 1984, and before January 1, 1985, and

"(C) to which the amendments made by section 1102 do not apply by reason of any provision of this section other than subsection (n),

shall, for purposes of applying the Internal Revenue Code of 1954, be treated as an obligation which is not described in section 103(a) of such Code if the aggregate face amount of such issue exceeds the portion of the State ceiling that is allocated by the State to such issue prior to the date of issuance of such issue.

1,403

Code Sec. 103A — Exclusions from income

"(2) Application of section 103A(g). For purposes of applying section 103A(g) of such Code, the State ceiling for calendar year 1984 shall be reduced by the aggregate amount allocated by the State to any issues described in paragraph (1).

"(3) State ceiling. For purposes of this subsection, the term 'State ceiling' has the meaning given to such term by section 103A(g)(4) of the Internal Revenue Code of 1954.

"(r) Exceptions to subsection (q).

Subsection (q) shall not apply with respect to—

"(1) obligations—

"(A) the proceeds of which are used to finance the River Place Project located in Minneapolis, Minnesota, and

"(B) the aggregate face amount of which does not exceed $55,000,000, or

"(2) obligations—

"(A) the proceeds of which are used to finance the Waseca, Minnesota project, and

"(B) the aggregate face amount of which does not exceed $7,800,000.

Section 148(f) of the Internal Revenue Code of 1986 and the amendments made by section 1301 of the Tax Reform Act of 1986 shall not apply to any bonds described in paragraph (1) which may be issued as a result of the amendments made by the Tax Reform Act of 1986."

Sec. 104. Compensation for injuries or sickness.

(a) In general.

Except in the case of amounts attributable to (and not in excess of) deductions allowed under section 213 (relating to medical, etc., expenses) for any prior taxable year, gross income does not include—

(1) amounts received under workmen's compensation acts as compensation for personal injuries or sickness;

(2) the amount of any damages (other than punitive damages) received (whether by suit or agreement and whether as lump sums or as periodic payments) on account of personal physical injuries or physical sickness;

(3) amounts received through accident or health insurance (or through an arrangement having the effect of accident or health insurance) for personal injuries or sickness (other than amounts received by an employee, to the extent such amounts (A) are attributable to contributions by the employer which were not includible in the gross income of the employee, or (B) are paid by the employer);

(4) amounts received as a pension, annuity, or similar allowance for personal injuries or sickness resulting from active service in the armed forces of any country or in the Coast and Geodetic Survey or the Public Health Service, or as a disability annuity payable under the provisions of section 808 of the Foreign Service Act of 1980; and

(5) amounts received by an individual as disability income attributable to injuries incurred as a direct result of a terroristic or military action (as defined in section 692(c)(2)).

For purposes of paragraph (3), in the case of an individual who is, or has been, an employee within the meaning of section 401(c)(1) (relating to self-employed individuals), contributions made on behalf of such individual while he was such an employee to a trust described in section 401(a) which is exempt from tax under section 501(a), or under a plan described in section 403(a), shall, to the extent allowed as deductions under section 404, be treated as contributions by the employer which were not includible in the gross income of the employee. For purposes of paragraph (2), emotional distress shall not be treated as a physical injury or physical sickness. The preceding sentence shall not apply to an amount of damages not in excess of the amount paid for medical care (described in subparagraph (A) or (B) of section 213(d)(1)) attributable to emotional distress.

(b) Termination of application of subsection (a)(4) in certain cases.

(1) In general. Subsection (a)(4) shall not apply in the case of any individual who is not described in paragraph (2).

(2) Individuals to whom subsection (a)(4) continues to apply. An individual is described in this paragraph if—

(A) on or before September 24, 1975, he was entitled to receive any amount described in subsection (a)(4),

(B) on September 24, 1975, he was a member of any organization (or reserve component thereof) referred to in subsection (a)(4) or under a binding written commitment to become such a member,

(C) he receives an amount described in subsection (a)(4) by reason of a combat-related injury, or

(D) on application therefor, he would be entitled to receive disability compensation from the Veterans' Administration.

(3) Special rules for combat-related injuries. For purposes of this subsection, the term "combat-related injury" means personal injury or sickness—

(A) which is incurred—

(i) as a direct result of armed conflict,

(ii) while engaged in extrahazardous service, or

(iii) under conditions simulating war; or

(B) which is caused by an instrumentality of war.

In the case of an individual who is not described in subparagraph (A) or (B) of paragraph (2), except as provided in paragraph (4), the only amounts taken into account under subsection (a)(4) shall be the amounts which he receives by reason of a combat-related injury.

(4) Amount excluded to be not less than veterans' disability compensation. In the case of any individual described in paragraph (2), the amounts excludable under subsection (a)(4) for any period with respect to any individual shall not be less than the maximum amount which such individual, on application therefor, would be entitled to receive as disability compensation from the Veterans' Administration.

(c) Application of prior law in certain cases.

The phrase "(other than punitive damages)" shall not apply to punitive damages awarded in a civil action—

(1) which is a wrongful death action, and

(2) with respect to which applicable State law (as in effect on September 13, 1995 and without regard to any modification after such date) provides, or has been construed to provide by a court of competent jurisdiction pursuant to a decision issued on or before September 13, 1995, that only punitive damages may be awarded in such an action.

This subsection shall cease to apply to any civil action filed on or after the first date on which the applicable State law ceases to provide (or is no longer construed to provide) the treatment described in paragraph (2).

(d) Cross references.

(1) For exclusion from employee's gross income of employer contributions to accident and health plans, see section 106.

(2) For exclusion of part of disability retirement pay from the application of subsection (a)(4) of this section, see section 1403 of title 10, United States Code (relating to career compensation laws).

In 2002, P.L. 107-134, Sec. 113(a), substituted "a terroristic or military action (as defined in section 692(c)(2))" for "a violent attack which the Secretary of State determines to be a terrorist attack and which occurred while such individual was an employee of the United States engaged in the performance of his official duties outside the United States." in para. (a)(5), effective for tax. yrs. end. on or after 9/11/2001.

In 1998, P.L. 105-206, Sec. 6015(c)(1), amended Sec. 1529(a) of P.L. 105-34 [see below] ... Sec. 6015(c)(2), amended Sec. 1529(b)(1)(B) of P.L. 105-34 [see below]

Prior to amendment, Sec. 1529(a) of P.L. 105-34 read as follows:

"(a) General rule. For purposes of determining whether any amount to which this section applies is excludable from gross income under section 104(a)(1) of the Internal Revenue Code of 1986, the following conditions shall be treated as personal injuries or sickness in the course of employment:

"(1) Heart disease.

Exclusions from income Code Sec. 105(h)(1)

"(2) Hypertension."

Prior to amendment, Sec. 1529(b)(1)(B) of P.L. 105-34 read as follows:

"(B) under a State law (as amended on May 19, 1992) which irrebuttably presumed that heart disease and hypertension are workrelated illnesses but only for employees separating from service before July 1, 1992; or"

In 1997, P.L. 105-34, Sec. 1529, of this Act [as amended by Sec. 6015(c)(1) and (2) of 105-206, see above], provides:

"SEC. 1529. TREATMENT OF CERTAIN DISABILITY BENEFITS RECEIVED BY FORMER POLICE OFFICERS OR FIREFIGHTERS.

"(a) General rule. Amounts to which this section applies which are received by an individual (or the survivors of the individual) as a result of hypertension or heart disease of the individual shall be excludable from gross income under section 104(a)(1) of the Internal Revenue Code of 1986.

"(b) Amounts to which section applies. This section shall apply to any amount—

"(1) which is payable—

"(A) to an individual (or to the survivors of an individual) who was a full-time employee of any police department or fire department which is organized and operated by a State, by any political subdivision thereof, or by any agency or instrumentality of a State or political subdivision thereof, and

"(B) under—

"(i) a State law (as amended on May 19, 1992) which irrebuttably presumed that heart disease and hypertension are work-related illnesses but only for employees hired before July 1, 1992; or

"(ii) any other statute, ordinance, labor agreement, or similar provision as a disability pension payment or in the nature of a disability pension payment attributable to employment as a police officer or fireman, but only if the individual is referred to in the State law described in clause (i); and

"(2) which was received in calendar year 1989, 1990, or 1991.

"(c) Waiver of statute of limitations. If, on the date of the enactment of this Act [8/5/97] (or at any time within the 1-year period beginning on such date of enactment [8/5/97]), credit or refund of any overpayment of tax resulting from the provisions of this section is barred by any law or rule of law (including res judicata), than credit or refund of such overpayment shall, nevertheless, be allowed or made if claim therefore is filed before the date 1 year after such date of enactment [8/5/97]."

In 1996, P.L. 104-188, Sec. 1605(a), amended para. (a)(2)...Sec. 1605(b), substituted "For purposes of paragraph (2), emotional distress shall not be treated as a physical injury or physical sickness. The preceding sentence shall not apply to an amount of damages not in excess of the amount paid for medical care (described in subparagraph (A) or (B) of section 213(d)(1)) attributable to emotional distress." for "Paragraph (2) shall not apply to any punitive damages in connection with a case not involving physical injury or physical sickness." in subsec. (a) ...Sec. 1605(c), redesignated subsec. (c) as subsec. (d) and added a new subsec. (c), effective for amounts received after 8/20/96, in tax. yrs. end. after 8/20/96, except as provided in Sec. 1603(d)(2) of this Act, which reads as follows:

"(2) Exception. The amendments made by this section shall not apply to any amount received under a written binding agreement, court decree, or mediation award in effect on (or issued on or before) September 13, 1995."

Prior to amendment, para. (a)(2) read as follows:

"(2) the amount of any damages received (whether by suit or agreement and whether as lump sums or as periodic payments) on account of personal injuries or sickness;"

—P.L. 104-191, Sec. 311(b), added "(or through an arrangement having the effect of accident or health insurance)" after "health insurance" in para. (a)(3), effective for tax. yrs. begin. after 12/31/96.

In 1989, P.L. 101-239, Sec. 7641(a), added the last sentence to subsec. (a), effective for amounts received after 7/10/89, in tax. yrs. end. after 7/10/89, except as provided in Sec. 7641(b)(2) of this Act which reads:

"(2) Exception.—The amendment made by subsection (a) shall not apply to any amount received—

"(A) under any written binding agreement, court decree, or mediation award in effect on (or issued on or before) July 10, 1989, or

"(B) pursuant to any suit filed on or before July 10, 1989."

In 1983, P.L. 97-473, Sec. 101(a), substituted "whether by suit or agreement and whether as lump sums or as periodic payments" for "whether by suit or agreement" in para. (a)(2), effective for tax. yrs. end. after 12/31/82.

In 1980, P.L. 96-465, Sec. 2206(e)(1), substituted "section 808 of the Foreign Service Act of 1980" for "section 831 of the Foreign Service Act of 1946, as amended (22 U.S.C. 1081)" in para. (a)(4), effective 2/15/81.

In 1976, P.L. 94-455, Sec. 505(b), redesignated subsec. (b) as subsec. (c) and added new subsec. (b), for tax. yrs. begin. after '76.

—P.L. 94-455, Sec. 505(e), deleted "and" at the end of para. (a)(3)...substituted "; and" for the period at the end of para. (a)(4)...added para. (a)(5), for tax. yrs. begin. after '76.

—P.L. 94-455, Sec. 1901(a)(18)(A), deleted "; 60 Stat. 1021" after "(22 U.S.C. 1081" in para. (a)(4)...Sec. 1901(a)(18)(B), amended para. (c)(2) as redesignated by Sec. 505(b) of the Act, effective for tax. yrs. begin. after 12/31/76.

Prior to amendment para. (c)(2) read as follows:

"(2) For exclusion of part of disability retirement pay from the application of subsection (a)(4) of this section, see section 402(h) of the Career Compensation Act of 1949 (37 U.S.C. 272(h))."

In 1962, P.L. 87-792, Sec. 7(d), added the last sentence of subsec. (a), effective for tax. yrs. begin. after 12/31/62.

In 1960, P.L. 86-723, Sec. 51, added "or as a disability annuity ... 60 Stat. 1021)" in subsec. (a)(4), effective for tax. yrs. end. after 9/8/60.

Sec. 105. Amounts received under accident and health plans.

(a) Amounts attributable to employer contributions.

Except as otherwise provided in this section, amounts received by an employee through accident or health insurance for personal injuries or sickness shall be included in gross income to the extent such amounts (1) are attributable to contributions by the employer which were not includible in the gross income of the employee, or (2) are paid by the employer.

(b) Amounts expended for medical care.

Except in the case of amounts attributable to (and not in excess of) deductions allowed under section 213 (relating to medical, etc., expenses) for any prior taxable year, gross income does not include amounts referred to in subsection (a) if such amounts are paid, directly or indirectly, to the taxpayer to reimburse the taxpayer for expenses incurred by him for the medical care (as defined in section 213(d)) of the taxpayer, his spouse, his dependents (as defined in section 152, determined without regard to subsections (b)(1), (b)(2), and (d)(1)(B) thereof), and any child (as defined in section 152(f)(1)) of the taxpayer who as of the end of the taxable year has not attained age 27. Any child to whom section 152(e) applies shall be treated as a dependent of both parents for purposes of this subsection.

(c) Payments unrelated to absence from work.

Gross income does not include amounts referred to in subsection (a) to the extent such amounts—

(1) constitute payment for the permanent loss or loss of use of a member or function of the body, or the permanent disfigurement, of the taxpayer, his spouse, or a dependent (as defined in section 152, determined without regard to subsections (b)(1), (b)(2), and (d)(1)(B) thereof), and

(2) are computed with reference to the nature of the injury without regard to the period the employee is absent from work.

(d) Repealed.

(e) Accident and health plans.

For purposes of this section and section 104—

(1) amounts received under an accident or health plan for employees, and

(2) amounts received from a sickness and disability fund for employees maintained under the law of a State or the District of Columbia,

shall be treated as amounts received through accident or health insurance.

(f) Rules for application of section 213.

For purposes of section 213(a) (relating to medical, dental, etc., expenses) amounts excluded from gross income under subsection (c) or (d) shall not be considered as compensation (by insurance or otherwise) for expenses paid for medical care.

(g) Self-employed individual not considered an employee.

For purposes of this section, the term "employee" does not include an individual who is an employee within the meaning of section 401(c)(1) (relating to self-employed individuals).

(h) Amount paid to highly compensated individuals under a discriminatory self-insured medical expense reimbursement plan.

(1) In general. In the case of amounts paid to a highly compensated individual under a self-insured medical reimbursement plan which does not satisfy the requirements of paragraph (2) for a plan year, subsection (b) shall not ap-

1,405

ply to such amounts to the extent they constitute an excess reimbursement of such highly compensated individual.

(2) Prohibition of discrimination. A self-insured medical reimbursement plan satisfies the requirements of this paragraph only if—

(A) the plan does not discriminate in favor of highly compensated individuals as to eligibility to participate; and

(B) the benefits provided under the plan do not discriminate in favor of participants who are highly compensated individuals.

(3) Nondiscriminatory eligibility classifications.

(A) In general. A self-insured medical reimbursement plan does not satisfy the requirements of subparagraph (A) of paragraph (2) unless such plan benefits—

(i) 70 percent or more of all employees, or 80 percent or more of all the employees who are eligible to benefit under the plan if 70 percent or more of all employees are eligible to benefit under the plan; or

(ii) such employees as qualify under a classification set up by the employer and found by the Secretary not to be discriminatory in favor of highly compensated individuals.

(B) Exclusion of certain employees. For purposes of subparagraph (A), there may be excluded from consideration—

(i) employees who have not completed 3 years of service;

(ii) employees who have not attained age 25;

(iii) part-time or seasonal employees;

(iv) employees not included in the plan who are included in a unit of employees covered by an agreement between employee representatives and one or more employers which the Secretary finds to be a collective bargaining agreement, if accident and health benefits were the subject of good faith bargaining between such employee representatives and such employer or employers; and

(v) employees who are nonresident aliens and who receive no earned income (within the meaning of section 911(d)(2)) from the employer which constitutes income from sources within the United States (within the meaning of section 861(a)(3)).

(4) Nondiscriminatory benefits. A self-insured medical reimbursement plan does not meet the requirements of subparagraph (B) of paragraph (2) unless all benefits provided for participants who are highly compensated individuals are provided for all other participants.

(5) Highly compensated individual defined. For purposes of this subsection, the term "highly compensated individual" means an individual who is—

(A) one of the 5 highest paid officers,

(B) a shareholder who owns (with the application of section 318) more than 10 percent in value of the stock of the employer, or

(C) among the highest paid 25 percent of all employees (other than employees described in paragraph (3)(B) who are not participants).

(6) Self-insured medical reimbursement plan. The term "self-insured medical reimbursement plan" means a plan of an employer to reimburse employees for expenses referred to in subsection (b) for which reimbursement is not provided under a policy of accident and health insurance.

(7) Excess reimbursement of highly compensated individual. For purposes of this section, the excess reimbursement of a highly compensated individual which is attributable to a self-insured medical reimbursement plan is—

(A) in the case of a benefit available to highly compensated individuals but not to all other participants (or which otherwise fails to satisfy the requirements of paragraph (2)(B)), the amount reimbursed under the plan to the employee with respect to such benefit, and

(B) in the case of benefits (other than benefits described in subparagraph (A) paid to a highly compensated individual by a plan which fails to satisfy the requirements of paragraph (2), the total amount reimbursed to the highly compensated individual for the plan year multiplied by a fraction—

(i) the numerator of which is the total amount reimbursed to all participants who are highly compensated individuals under the plan for the plan year, and

(ii) the denominator of which is the total amount reimbursed to all employees under the plan for such plan year.

In determining the fraction under subparagraph (B), there shall not be taken into account any reimbursement which is attributable to a benefit described in subparagraph (A).

(8) Certain controlled groups, etc. All employees who are treated as employed by a single employer under subsection (b), (c), or (m) of section 414 shall be treated as employed by a single employer for purposes of this section.

(9) Regulations. The Secretary shall prescribe such regulations as may be necessary to carry out the provisions of this section.

(10) Time of inclusion. Any amount paid for a plan year that is included in income by reason of this subsection shall be treated as received or accrued in the taxable year of the participant in which the plan year ends.

(i) Sick pay under Railroad Unemployment Insurance Act.

Notwithstanding any other provision of law, gross income includes benefits paid under section 2(a) of the Railroad Unemployment Insurance Act for days of sickness; except to the extent such sickness (as determined in accordance with standards prescribed by the Railroad Retirement Board) is the result of on-the-job injury.

(j) Special rule for certain governmental plans.

(1) In general. For purposes of subsection (b), amounts paid (directly or indirectly) to the taxpayer from an accident or health plan described in paragraph (2) shall not fail to be excluded from gross income solely because such plan, on or before January 1, 2008, provides for reimbursements of health care expenses of a deceased plan participant's beneficiary.

(2) Plan described. An accident or health plan is described in this paragraph if such plan is funded by a medical trust that is established in connection with a public retirement system and that—

(A) has been authorized by a State legislature, or

(B) has received a favorable ruling from the Internal Revenue Service that the trust's income is not includible in gross income under section 115.

In 2010, P.L. 111-152, Sec. 1004(d)(1)(A), substituted "his dependents" for "and his dependents" in the first sentence of subsec. (b)

—P.L. 111-152, Sec. 1004(d)(1)(B), added ", and any child (as defined in section 152(f)(1)) of the taxpayer who as of the end of the taxable year has not attained age 27" before the period in the first sentence of subsec. (b), effective 3/30/2010.

In 2008, P.L. 110-458, Sec. 124(a), added subsec. (j), effective for payments before, on, or after 12/23/2008.

Exclusions from income Code Sec. 105

In 2004, P.L. 108-311, Sec. 207(9), added ", determined without regard to subsections (b)(1), (b)(2), and (d)(1)(B) thereof" after "section 152" in subsec. (b) and para. (c)(1), effective for tax. yrs. begin. after 12/31/2004.

In 1989, P.L. 101-140, Sec. 203(a)(1), repealed as if not enacted Sec. 1151(c)(2) of P.L. 99-514, which deleted subsec. (h) and redesignated subsec. (i) as subsec. (h).

In 1986, P.L. 99-514, Sec. 1301(j)(9), substituted "section 7703(a)" for "section 143(a)" in subpara. (d)(5)(C), effective for bonds issued after 8/15/86.

In 1984, P.L. 98-369, Sec. 423(b)(2), added a new sentence at the end of subsec. (b), effective for tax. yrs. begin. after 12/31/84.

In 1983, P.L. 98-76, Sec. 241(a), added subsec. (i), effective for amounts received after 12/31/83, in tax. yrs. end. after 12/31/83.

—P.L. 98-21, Sec. 122(b), deleted subsec. (d), effective for tax. yrs. begin. after 12/31/83. Sec. 122(d)(2) of the Act provides as follows:

"(2) Transitional rule—If an individual's annuity starting date was deferred under section 105(d)(6) of the Internal Revenue Code of 1954 (as in effect on the day before the date of the enactment of this section), such deferral shall end on the first day of such individual's first taxable year beginning after December 31, 1983."

Prior to deletion, subsec. (d) read as follows:

"(d) Certain disability payments.

"(1) In general. In the case of a taxpayer who—

"(A) has not attained age 65 before the close of the taxable year, and

"(B) retired on disability and, when he retired, was permanently and totally disabled,

gross income does not include amounts referred to in subsection (a) if such amounts constitute wages or payments in lieu of wages for a period during which the employee is absent from work on account of permanent and total disability.

"(2) Limitation. This subsection shall not apply to the extent that the amounts referred to in paragraph (1) exceed a weekly rate of $100.

"(3) Phaseout over $15,000. If the adjusted gross income of the taxpayer for the taxable year (determined without regard to this subsection and section 221) exceeds $15,000, the amount which but for this paragraph would be excluded under this subsection for the taxable year shall be reduced by an amount equal to the excess of the adjusted gross income (as so determined) over $15,000.

"(4) Permanent and total disability defined. For purposes of this subsection, an individual is permanently and totally disabled if he is unable to engage in any substantial gainful activity by reason of any medically determinable physical or mental impairment which can be expected to result in death or which has lasted or can be expected to last for a continuous period of not less than 12 months. An individual shall not be considered to be permanently and totally disabled unless he furnishes proof of the existence thereof in such form and manner, and at such times, as the Secretary may require.

"(5) Special rules for married couples.

"(A) Married couple must file joint return. Except in the case of a husband and wife who live apart at all times during the taxable year, if the taxpayer is married at the close of the taxable year, the exclusion provided by this subsection shall be allowed only if the taxpayer and his spouse file a joint return for the taxable year.

"(B) Application of paragraphs (2) and (3). In the case of a joint return—

"(i) paragraph (2) shall be applied separately with respect to each spouse, but

"(ii) paragraph (3) shall be applied with respect to their combined adjusted gross income.

"(C) Determination of marital status. For purposes of this subsection, marital status shall be determined under section 7703(a).

"(D) Joint return defined. For purposes of this subsection, the term 'joint return' means the joint return of a husband and wife made under section 6013.

"(6) Coordination with section 72. In the case of an individual described in subparagraphs (A) and (B) of paragraph (1), for purposes of section 72 the annuity starting date shall not be deemed to occur before the beginning of the taxable year in which the taxpayer attains age 65, or before the beginning of an earlier taxable year for which the taxpayer makes an irrevocable election not to seek the benefits of this subsection for such year and all subsequent years."

In 1982, P.L. 97-248, Sec. 202(b)(3)(C), substituted "section 213(d)" for "section 213(e)" in subsec. (c), effective for tax. yrs. begin. after 12/31/83.

In 1981, P.L. 97-34, Sec. 103(c)(2), added "and section 221" after "subsection" the first place it appeared in para. (d)(3), effective for tax. yrs. begin. after 12/31/81.

—P.L. 97-34, Sec. 111(b)(4), substituted "section 911(d)(2)" for "911(b)" in clause (h)(3)(B)(v), effective for tax. yrs. begin. after 12/31/81.

In 1980, P.L. 96-613, Sec. 5(b), made the same amendment as Sec. 201(b)(1) of P.L. 96-605, see below.

—P.L. 96-605, Sec. 201(b)(1), substituted "subsection (b), (c), or (m) of section 414" for "subsection (b) or (c) of section 414" in para. (h)(8) and substituted "controlled groups, etc." for "controlled groups" in the heading of para. (h)(8), effective for plan yrs. end. after 11/30/80 except as provided Sec. 201(c)(2) of the Act which read as follows:

"(2) Plans in existence on November 30, 1980. In the case of a plan in existence on November 30, 1980, the amendments made by this section shall apply to plan years beginning after November 30, 1980."

—P.L. 96-222, Sec. 103(a)(13)(B), substituted "highly compensated individuals" for "highly compensated participants" in clause (h)(3)(A)(ii)... Sec. 103(a)(13)(C), amended subpara. (h)(7)(A), effective for amounts reimbursed after 12/31/79. For purposes of applying subsec. (h), there shall not be taken into account any amount reimbursed before 1/1/80.

Prior to amendment, subpara. (h)(7)(A) read as follows:

"(A) in the case of a benefit available to a highly compensated individual but not to a broad cross-section of employees, the amount reimbursed under the plan to the employee with respect to such benefit, and"

—P.L. 96-222, Sec. 103(a)(13)(D), amended Sec. 366(b) of P.L. 95-600 [see below], the effective date for changes made by Sec. 366(a) of P.L. 95-600.

Prior to the amendment of Sec. 366(b) of P.L. 95-600 the amendments made by Sec. 366(a) of P.L. 95-600, were effective for tax. yrs. begin. after. 12/31/79.

In 1978, P.L. 95-600, Sec. 366(a), added subsec. (h), effective [as amended by 103(a)(13)(D) of P.L. 96-222, see above] for amounts reimbursed after 12/31/79. For purposes of applying subsec. (h), there shall not be taken into account any amount reimbursed before 1/1/80.

—P.L. 95-600, Sec. 701(c)(1), deleted paras. (d)(4) and (d)(6), redesignated paras. (d)(5) and (d)(7) as (d)(4) and (d)(6), and added new para. (d)(5), effective as if included in the amendments made by Sec. 505(a) of P.L. 94-455, see below.

Prior to deletion, para. (d)(4) read as follows:

"(4) Married couple must file joint return. Except in the case of a husband and wife who live apart at all times during the taxable year, if the taxpayer is married at the close of the taxable year, the exclusion provided by this subsection shall be allowed only if the taxpayer and his spouse file a joint return for the taxable year. For purposes of this subsection, marital status shall be determined under section 143."

Prior to deletion, para. (d)(6) read as follows:

"(6) Joint return. For purposes of this subsection, the term 'joint return' means the joint return of a husband and wife made under section 6013."

—P.L. 95-600, Sec. 701(c)(2)(A), substituted "section 105(d)(4)" for "section 105(d)(5)" in Sec. 505(c)(3) of P.L. 94-455 (reproduced below).

—P.L. 95-600, Sec. 701(c)(2)(B), substituted "section 105(d)(6)" for "section 105(d)(7)" in Secs. 301(c) and (e)(1) of P.L. 95-30, (reproduced below).

In 1977, P.L. 95-30, Sec. 301(a), changed the effective date for amendments made by Sec. 505(a) of P.L. 94-455, so that the amendments are effective for tax. yrs. begin. after 12/31/76, rather than effective for tax. yrs. begin. after. 12/31/75.

—P.L. 95-30, Sec. 301(b)(1), substituted "1977" for "1976" in Sec. 505(c)(1) of P.L. 94-455... Sec. 301(b)(2), added "or January 1, 1977" after "January 1, 1976" in Sec. 505(c)(3) of P.L. 94-455, see below.

—P.L. 95-30, Sec. 301(c), (d), and (e), provide as follows:

"(c) Revocation of election.

"Any election made under section 105(d)(7) of the Internal Revenue Code of 1954 or under section 505(d) of the Tax Reform Act of 1976 for a taxable year beginning in 1976 may be revoked (in such manner as may be prescribed by regulations) at any time before the expiration of the period for assessing a deficiency with respect to such taxable year (determined without regard to subsection (d) of this section).

"(d) Period for assessing deficiency.

"In the case of any revocation made under subsection (c), the period for assessing a deficiency with respect to any taxable year affected by the revocation shall not expire before the date which is 1 year after the date of the making of the revocation, and, notwithstanding any law or rule of law, such deficiency, to the extent attributable to such revocation, may be assessed at any time during such 1-year period.

"(e) Effective date.

"The amendments made by this section shall take effect on October 4, 1976, but shall not apply—

"(1) with respect to any taxpayer who makes or has made an election under section 105(d)(7) of the Internal Revenue Code of 1954 or under section 505(d) of the Tax Reform Act of 1976 (as such sections were in effect before the enactment of this Act) for a taxable year beginning in 1976, if such election is not revoked under subsection (c) of this section, and

"(2) with respect to any taxpayer (other than a taxpayer described in paragraph (1)) who has an annuity starting date at the beginning of a taxable year beginning in 1976 by reason of the amendments made by section 505 of the tax Reform Act of 1976 (as in effect before the enactment of this Act), unless such person elects (in such manner as the Secretary of the Treasury or his delegate may by regulations prescribe) to have such amendments apply."

In 1976, P.L. 94-455, Sec. 505(a), amended subsec. (d), effective for tax. yrs. begin. after 12/31/76. Sec. 505(c) of this Act [as amended by Sec. 301(b)(1) and (2) of P.L. 95-30 and Sec. 701(c)(2)(A) of P.L. 95-600] provides:

"(c) Special rule for existing permanent and total disability cases.

"In the case of any individual who—

"(1) retired before January 1, 1977,

"(2) either retired on disability or was entitled to retire on disability, and

"(3) on January 1, 1976, or January 1, 1977, was permanently and totally disabled (within the meaning of section 105(d)(4) of the Internal Revenue Code of 1954),

such individual shall be deemed to have met the requirements of section 105(d)(1)(B) of such Code (as amended by subsection (a) of this section)."

Prior to amendment, subsec. (d) read as follows:

"(d) Wage continuation plans.

"Gross income does not include amounts referred to in subsection (a) if such amounts constitute wages or payments in lieu of wages for a period during which the employee is absent from work on account of personal injuries or sickness; but this subsection shall not apply to the extent that such amounts exceed a weekly rate of $100. The preceding sentence shall not apply to amounts attributable to the first 30 calendar days in such period, if such amounts are at a rate which exceeds 75 percent of the regular weekly rate of wages of the employee (as determined under regulations prescribed by the Secretary or his delegate). If amounts attributable to the first 30 calendar days in such period are at a rate which does not exceed 75 percent of the regular weekly rate of wages of the employee, the first sentence of this subsection (1) shall not apply to the extent that such amounts exceed a weekly rate of $75, and (2) shall not apply to amounts attributable to the first 7 calendar days in such period unless the employee is hospitalized on account of personal injuries or sickness for at least one day during such period. If such amounts are not paid on the basis of a weekly pay period, the Secretary or his delegate shall by regulations prescribe the method of determining the weekly rate at which such amounts are paid.''

—P.L. 94-455, Sec. 1901(c)(2), deleted '', a Territory,'' after "law of a State" in para. (e)(2), effective for tax. yrs. begin. after 12/31/76.

In 1964, P.L. 88-272, Sec. 205(a), amended second sentence and added the third sentence of subsec. (d), effective for periods of absence commencing after 12/31/63.

Prior to amendment, the second sentence of subsec. (d) read as follows:
"In the case of period during which the employee is absent from work on account of sickness, the preceding sentence shall not apply to amounts attributable to the first 7 calendar days in such period unless the employee is hospitalized on account of sickness for at least one day during such period."

In 1962, P.L. 87-792, Sec. 7(e), added subsec. (g), effective for tax. yrs. begin. after 12/31/62.

Sec. 106. Contributions by employer to accident and health plans.

(a) General rule.
Except as otherwise provided in this section, gross income of an employee does not include employer-provided coverage under an accident or health plan.

(b) Contributions to Archer MSAs.

(1) **In general.** In the case of an employee who is an eligible individual, amounts contributed by such employee's employer to any Archer MSA of such employee shall be treated as employer-provided coverage for medical expenses under an accident or health plan to the extent such amounts do not exceed the limitation under section 220(b)(1) (determined without regard to this subsection) which is applicable to such employee for such taxable year.

(2) **No constructive receipt.** No amount shall be included in the gross income of any employee solely because the employee may choose between the contributions referred to in paragraph (1) and employer contributions to another health plan of the employer.

(3) **Special rule for deduction of employer contributions.** Any employer contribution to an Archer MSA, if otherwise allowable as a deduction under this chapter, shall be allowed only for the taxable year in which paid.

(4) **Employer MSA contributions required to be shown on return.** Every individual required to file a return under section 6012 for the taxable year shall include on such return the aggregate amount contributed by employers to the Archer MSAs of such individual or such individual's spouse for such taxable year.

(5) **MSA contributions not part of COBRA coverage.** Paragraph (1) shall not apply for purposes of section 4980B.

(6) **Definitions.** For purposes of this subsection, the terms "eligible individual" and "Archer MSA" have the respective meanings given to such terms by section 220.

(7) **Cross reference.** For penalty on failure by employer to make comparable contributions to the Archer MSAs of comparable employees, see section 4980E.

(c) Inclusion of long-term care benefits provided through flexible spending arrangements.

(1) **In general.** Effective on and after January 1, 1997, gross income of an employee shall include employer-provided coverage for qualified long-term care services (as defined in section 7702B(c)) to the extent that such coverage is provided through a flexible spending or similar arrangement.

(2) **Flexible spending arrangement.** For purposes of this subsection, a flexible spending arrangement is a benefit program which provides employees with coverage under which—

(A) specified incurred expenses may be reimbursed (subject to reimbursement maximums and other reasonable conditions), and

(B) the maximum amount of reimbursement which is reasonably available to a participant for such coverage is less than 500 percent of the value of such coverage.

In the case of an insured plan, the maximum amount reasonably available shall be determined on the basis of the underlying coverage.

(d) Contributions to health savings accounts.

(1) **In general.** In the case of an employee who is an eligible individual (as defined in section 223(c)(1)), amounts contributed by such employee's employer to any health savings account (as defined in section 223(d)) of such employee shall be treated as employer-provided coverage for medical expenses under an accident or health plan to the extent such amounts do not exceed the limitation under section 223(b) (determined without regard to this subsection) which is applicable to such employee for such taxable year.

(2) **Special rules.** Rules similar to the rules of paragraphs (2), (3), (4), and (5) of subsection (b) shall apply for purposes of this subsection.

(3) **Cross reference.** For penalty on failure by employer to make comparable contributions to the health savings accounts of comparable employees, see section 4980G.

(e) FSA and HRA terminations to fund HSAs.

(1) **In general.** A plan shall not fail to be treated as a health flexible spending arrangement or health reimbursement arrangement under this section or section 105 merely because such plan provides for a qualified HSA distribution.

(2) **Qualified HSA distribution.** The term "qualified HSA distribution" means a distribution from a health flexible spending arrangement or health reimbursement arrangement to the extent that such distribution—

(A) does not exceed the lesser of the balance in such arrangement on September 21, 2006, or as of the date of such distribution, and

(B) is contributed by the employer directly to the health savings account of the employee before January 1, 2012.

Such term shall not include more than 1 distribution with respect to any arrangement.

(3) **Additional tax for failure to maintain high deductible health plan coverage.**

(A) In general. If, at any time during the testing period, the employee is not an eligible individual, then the amount of the qualified HSA distribution—

(i) shall be includible in the gross in-come of the employee for the taxable year in which occurs the first month in the testing period for which such employee is not an eligible individual, and

(ii) the tax imposed by this chapter for such taxable year on the employee shall be increased by 10 percent of the amount which is so includible.

(B) Exception for disability or death. Clauses (i) and (ii) of subparagraph (A) shall not apply if the employee ceases to be an eligible individual by reason of the death of the employee or the employee becoming disabled (within the meaning of (m)(7)section 72(m)(7)).

(4) **Definition and special rules.** For purposes of this subsection—

(A) Testing period. The term "testing period" means the period beginning with the month in which the quali-

Exclusions from income — Code Sec. 106

fied HSA distribution is contributed to the health savings account and ending on the last day of the 12th month following such month.

(B) Eligible individual. The term "eligible individual" has the meaning given such term by section 223(c)(1).

(C) Treatment as rollover contribution. A qualified HSA distribution shall be treated as a rollover contribution described in section 223(f)(5).

(5) Tax treatment relating to distributions. For purposes of this title—

(A) In general. A qualified HSA distribution shall be treated as a payment described in subsection (d).

(B) Comparability excise tax.

(i) In general. Except as provided in clause (ii), section 4980G shall not apply to qualified HSA distributions.

(ii) Failure to offer to all employees. In the case of a qualified HSA distribution to any employee, the failure to offer such distribution to any eligible individual covered under a high deductible health plan of the employer shall (notwithstanding section 4980G(d)) be treated for purposes of section 4980G as a failure to meet the requirements of section 4980G(b).

(f) Reimbursements for medicine restricted to prescribed drugs and insulin.

For purposes of this section and section 105, reimbursement for expenses incurred for a medicine or a drug shall be treated as a reimbursement for medical expenses only if such medicine or drug is a prescribed drug (determined without regard to whether such drug is available without a prescription) or is insulin.

In 2010, P.L. 111-148, Sec. 9003(c), added subsec. (f), effective for expenses incurred with respect to tax. yrs. begin. after 12/31/2010.

In 2006, P.L. 109-432, Sec. 302(a), added subsec. (e), effective for distributions made on or after 12/20/2006.

In 2003, P.L. 108-173, Sec. 1201(d)(1), added subsec. (d), effective for tax. yrs. begin. after 12/31/2003.

In 2000, P.L. 106-554, Sec. 1(a)(7), [which enacted into law Sec. 202(a)(2) of P.L. 106-554] substituted "Archer MSA" for "medical savings account" each place it appeared in subsec. (b) . . . Sec. 1(a)(7), [which enacted into law Sec. 202(b)(2)(A) of P.L. 106-554] substituted "Archer MSAs" for "medical savings accounts" each place it appeared in paras. (b)(4) and (b)(7) . . . Sec. 1(a)(7), [which enacted into law Sec. 202(b)(6) of P.L. 106-554] substituted "Archer MSAs" for "medical savings accounts" in the heading of subsec. (b) . . . Sec. 1(a)(7), [which enacted into law Sec. 202(b)(10) of P.L. 106-554] substituted "an Archer" for "a Archer" in subsec. (b), effective 12/21/2000.

In 1996, P.L. 104-191, Sec. 301(c)(1), amended the text of Code Sec. 106, effective for tax. yrs. begin. after 12/31/96.

Prior to amendment, the text of Code Sec. 106 read as follows:

"Gross income of an employee does not include employer-provided coverage under an accident or health plan."

—P.L. 104-191, Sec. 321(c)(2), added subsec. (c) [as amended by Sec. 301(c)(1), of this Act, see above] effective for contracts issued after 12/31/96. Sec. 321(f)(2)-(5), of this Act, reads as follows:

"(2) Continuation of existing policies. In the case of any contract issued before January 1, 1997, which met the long-term care insurance requirements of the State in which the contract was situated at the time the contract was issued—

"(A) such contract shall be treated for purposes of the Internal Revenue Code of 1986 as a qualified long-term care insurance contract (as defined in section 7702B(b) of such Code), and

"(B) services provided under, or reimbursed by, such contract shall be treated for such purposes as qualified long-term care services (as defined in section 7702B(c) of such Code).

In the case of an individual who is covered on December 31, 1996, under a State long-term care plan (as defined in section 7702B(f)(2) of such Code), the terms of such plan on such date shall be treated for purposes of the preceding sentence as a contract issued on such date which met the long-term care insurance requirements of such State.

"(3) Exchanges of existing policies. If, after the date of enactment of this Act and before January 1, 1998, a contract providing for long-term care insurance coverage is exchanged solely for a qualified long-term care insurance contract (as defined in section 7702B(b) of such Code), no gain or loss shall be recognized on the exchange. If, in addition to a qualified long-term care insurance contract, money or other property is received in the exchange, then any gain shall be recognized to the extent of the sum of the money and the fair market value of the other property received. For purposes of this paragraph, the cancellation of a contract providing for long-term care insurance coverage and reinvestment of the cancellation proceeds in a qualified long-term care insurance contract within 60 days thereafter shall be treated as an exchange.

"(4) Issuance of certain riders permitted. For purposes of applying sections 101(f), 7702, and 7702A of the Internal Revenue Code of 1986 to any contract—

"(A) the issuance of a rider which is treated as a qualified long-term care insurance contract under section 7702B, and

"(B) the addition of any provision required to conform any other long-term care rider to be so treated,

shall not be treated as a modification or material change of such contract.

"(5) Application of per diem limitation to existing contracts. The amount of per diem payments made under a contract issued on or before July 31, 1996, with respect to an insured which are excludable from gross income by reason of section 7702B of the Internal Revenue Code of 1986 (as added by this section) shall not be reduced under subsection (d)(2)(B) thereof by reason of reimbursements received under a contract issued on or before such date. The preceding sentence shall cease to apply as of the date (after July 31, 1996) such contract is exchanged or there is any contract modification which results in an increase in the amount of such per diem payments or the amount of such reimbursements."

In 1989, P.L. 101-239, Sec. 7862(c)(1)(A), deleted the last sentence of para. (b)(2) [of Code Sec. 106 before amendment by Sec. 3011(b)(1) of P.L. 100-647] effective for yrs. begin. after 12/31/86.

Prior to deletion, the last sentence in subpara. (b)(2) read as follows:

"Under regulations, rules similar to the rules of subsections (a) and (b) of section 52 (relating to employers under common control) shall apply for purposes of subparagraph (A)."

—P.L. 101-136, Sec. 528, provided that "no monies appropriated by this Act [for the fiscal year ending September 30, '90] may be used to implement or enforce section 1151 of the Tax Reform Act of '86 [P.L. 99-514] or the amendments made by such section." [See below]

In 1988, P.L. 100-647, Sec. 1011B(a)(25), amended Sec. 1151(k)(1) of P.L. 99-514 [reproduced below], part of the effective date for changes made by Sec. 1151(j)(2) of P.L. 99-514, by adding the last sentence, see below.

—P.L. 100-647, Sec. 1018(t)(7)(A)(i), substituted "any employer-provided coverage" for "any amount contributed by an employer" in para. (b)(1) . . . Sec. 1018(t)(7)(A)(ii), substituted "under a group" for "to a group" in para. (b)(1), effective for plan yrs. begin. on or after 7/1/86, except as provided in Sec. 1001(e)(2) of P.L. 99-272, reproduced below.

—P.L. 100-647, Sec. 3011(b)(1), amended Code Sec. 106, effective for tax. yrs. begin. after 12/31/88, but not for any plan for any plan year to which Code Sec. 162(k) (as in effect on the day before the date of the enactment of this Act [11/10/88]) did not apply by reason of section 10001(e)(2) of the Consolidated Omnibus Budget Reconciliation Act of 1985 [P.L. 99-272].

Prior to amendment, Code Sec. 106 read as reproduced below.

"SEC. 106. CONTRIBUTIONS BY EMPLOYER TO ACCIDENT AND HEALTH PLANS.

"(a) In general.

"Gross income of an employee does not include employer-provided coverage under an accident or health plan.

"(b) Exception for highly compensated individuals where plan fails to provide certain continuation coverage.

"(1) In general. Subsection (a) shall not apply to any employer-provided coverage on behalf of a highly compensated employee (within the meaning of section 414(q)) under a group health plan maintained by such employer unless all such plans maintained by such employer meet the continuing coverage requirements of section 162(k).

"(2) Exception for certain plans. Paragraph (1) shall not apply to any—

"(A) group health plan for any calendar year if all employers maintaining such plan normally employed fewer than 20 employees on a typical business day during the preceding calendar year,

"(B) governmental plan (within the meaning of section 414(d)), or

"(C) church plan (within the meaning of section 414(e)).

"(3) Group health plan. For purposes of this subsection, the term 'group health plan' has the meaning given such term by section 162(i)(3)."

In 1986, P.L. 99-514, Sec. 1114(b)(1), substituted "highly compensated employee (within the meaning of section 414(q))" for "highly compensated individual (within the meaning of section 105(h)(5))" in para. (b)(1), effective for yrs. begin. after 12/31/86.

—P.L. 99-514, Sec. 1151(j)(2), amended subsec. (a), effective as provided in Sec. 1151(k)(1) [as amended by Sec. 1011B(a)(25) of P.L. 100-647] of this Act, which reads:

"(k) Effective dates.—

"(1) In general.—The amendments made by this section shall apply to years beginning after the later of—

"(A) December 31, 1987, or

"(B) the earlier of—

"(i) the date which is 3 months after the date on which the Secretary of the Treasury or his delegate issues such regulations as are necessary to carry out the provisions of section 89 of the Internal Revenue Code of 1986 (as added by this section), or

"(ii) December 31, 1988.

"Notwithstanding the preceding sentence, the amendments made by subsections (e)(1) and (i)(3)(C) shall, to the extent they relate to sections 106, 162(i)(2), and 162(k) of the Internal Revenue Code of 1986, apply to years beginning after 1986."

Prior to amendment, subsec. (a) read as follows:

"(a) In general.

"Gross income does not include contributions by the employer to accident or health plans for compensation (through insurance or otherwise) to his employees for personal injuries or sickness."

—P.L. 99-272, Sec. 10001(b), added "(a) In general." before "Gross" in Code Sec. 106 and added subsec. (b), for plan years beginning on or after 7/1/86, except as provided in Sec. 10001(e)(2) of this Act, which reads:

"(2) Special rule for collective bargaining agreements.—In the case of a group health plan maintained pursuant to one or more collective bargaining agreements between employee representatives and one or more employers ratified before the date of the enactment of this Act, the amendments made by this section shall not apply to plan years beginning before the later of—

"(A) the date on which the last of the collective bargaining agreements relating to the plan terminates (determined without regard to any extension thereof agreed to after the date of the enactment of this Act), or

"(B) January 1, 1987.

For purposes of subparagraph (A), any plan amendment made pursuant to a collective bargaining agreement relating to the plan which amends the plan solely to conform to any requirement added by this section shall not be treated as a termination of such collective bargaining agreement."

Sec. 107. Rental value of parsonages.

In the case of a minister of the gospel, gross income does not include—

(1) the rental value of a home furnished to him as part of his compensation; or

(2) the rental allowance paid to him as part of his compensation, to the extent used by him to rent or provide a home and to the extent such allowance does not exceed the fair rental value of the home, including furnishings and appurtenances such as a garage, plus the cost of utilities.

In 2002, P.L. 107-181, Sec. 2(a), added "and to the extent such allowance does not exceed the fair rental value of the home, including furnishings and appurtenances such as a garage, plus the cost of utilities" before the period at the end of para. (2), effective for tax. yrs. begin. after 12/31/2001. Sec. 2(b)(2) and (3) of this Act, provides:

(2) Returns positions. The amendment made by this section also shall apply to any taxable year beginning before January 1, 2002, for which the taxpayer—

"(A) on a return filed before April 17, 2002, limited the exclusion under section 107 of the Internal Revenue Code of 1986 as provided in such amendment, or

"(B) filed a return after April 16, 2002.

"(3) Other years before 2002. Except as provided in paragraph (2), notwithstanding any prior regulation, revenue ruling, or other guidance issued by the Internal Revenue Service, no person shall be subject to the limitations added to section 107 of such Code by this Act for any taxable year beginning before January 1, 2002."

Sec. 108. Income from discharge of indebtedness.

(a) Exclusion from gross income.

(1) In general. Gross income does not include any amount which (but for this subsection) would be includible in gross income by reason of the discharge (in whole or in part) of indebtedness of the taxpayer if—

(A) the discharge occurs in a title 11 case,

(B) the discharge occurs when the taxpayer is insolvent,

(C) the indebtedness discharged is qualified farm indebtedness,

(D) in the case of a taxpayer other than a C corporation, the indebtedness discharged is qualified real property business indebtedness, or

(E) the indebtedness discharged is qualified principal residence indebtedness which is discharged before January 1, 2013.

(2) Coordination of exclusions.

(A) Title 11 exclusion takes precedence. Subparagraphs (B), (C) (D), and (E) of paragraph (1) shall not apply to a discharge which occurs in a title 11 case.

(B) Insolvency exclusion takes precedence over qualified farm exclusion and qualified real property business exclusion. Subparagraphs (C) and (D) of paragraph (1) shall not apply to a discharge to the extent the taxpayer is insolvent.

(C) Principal residence exclusion takes precedence over insolvency exclusion unless elected otherwise. Paragraph (1)(B) shall not apply to a discharge to which paragraph (1)(E) applies unless the taxpayer elects to apply paragraph (1)(B) in lieu of paragraph (1)(E).

(3) Insolvency exclusion limited to amount of insolvency. In the case of a discharge to which paragraph (1)(B) applies, the amount excluded under paragraph (1)(B) shall not exceed the amount by which the taxpayer is insolvent.

(b) Reduction of tax attributes.

(1) In general. The amount excluded from gross income under subparagraph (A), (B), or (C) of subsection (a)(1) shall be applied to reduce the tax attributes of the taxpayer as provided in paragraph (2).

(2) Tax attributes affected; order of reduction. Except as provided in paragraph (5), the reduction referred to in paragraph (1) shall be made in the following tax attributes in the following order:

(A) NOL. Any net operating loss for the taxable year of the discharge, and any net operating loss carryover to such taxable year.

(B) General business credit. Any carryover to or from the taxable year of a discharge of an amount for purposes for determining the amount allowable as a credit under section 38 (relating to general business credit).

(C) Minimum tax credit. The amount of the minimum tax credit available under section 53(b) as of the beginning of the taxable year immediately following the taxable year of the discharge.

(D) Capital loss carryovers. Any net capital loss for the taxable year of the discharge, and any capital loss carryover to such taxable year under section 1212.

(E) Basis reduction.

(i) In general. The basis of the property of the taxpayer.

(ii) Cross reference. For provisions for making the reduction described in clause (i), see section 1017.

(F) Passive activity loss and credit carryovers. Any passive activity loss or credit carryover of the taxpayer under section 469(b) from the taxable year of the discharge.

(G) Foreign tax credit carryovers. Any carryover to or from the taxable year of the discharge for purposes of determining the amount of the credit allowable under section 27.

(3) Amount of reduction.

(A) In general. Except as provided in subparagraph (B), the reductions described in paragraph (2) shall be one dollar for each dollar excluded by subsection (a).

(B) Credit carryover reduction. The reductions described in subparagraphs (B), (C), and (G) shall be 33 ⅓ cents for each dollar excluded by subsection (a). The reduction described in subparagraph (F) in any passive activity credit carryover shall be 33 ⅓ cents for each dollar excluded by subsection (a).

(4) Ordering rules.

(A) Reductions made after determination of tax for year. The reductions described in paragraph (2) shall be made after the determination of the tax imposed by this chapter for the taxable year of the discharge.

(B) Reductions under subparagraph (A) or (D) of paragraph (2). The reductions described in subparagraph (A) or (D) of paragraph (2) (as the case may be) shall be made first in the loss for the taxable year of the discharge and then in the carryovers to such taxable year in the order of the taxable years from which each such carryover arose.

Exclusions from income — Code Sec. 108(d)(9)(A)

(C) Reductions under subparagraphs (B) and (G) of paragraph (2). The reductions described in subparagraphs (B) and (G) of paragraph (2) shall be made in the order in which carryovers are taken into account under this chapter for the taxable year of the discharge.

(5) Election to apply reduction first against depreciable property.

(A) In general. The taxpayer may elect to apply any portion of the reduction referred to in paragraph (1) to the reduction under section 1017 of the basis of the depreciable property of the taxpayer.

(B) Limitation. The amount to which an election under subparagraph (A) applies shall not exceed the aggregate adjusted bases of the depreciable property held by the taxpayer as of the beginning of the taxable year following the taxable year in which the discharge occurs.

(C) Other tax attributes not reduced. Paragraph (2) shall not apply to any amount to which an election under this paragraph applies.

(c) Treatment of discharge of qualified real property business indebtedness.

(1) Basis reduction.

(A) In general. The amount excluded from gross income under subparagraph (D) of subsection (a)(1) shall be applied to reduce the basis of the depreciable real property of the taxpayer.

(B) Cross reference. For provisions making the reduction described in subparagraph (A), see section 1017.

(2) Limitations.

(A) Indebtedness in excess of value. The amount excluded under subparagraph (D) of subsection (a)(1) with respect to any qualified real property business indebtedness shall not exceed the excess (if any) of—

(i) the outstanding principal amount of such indebtedness (immediately before the discharge), over

(ii) the fair market value of the real property described in paragraph (3)(A) (as of such time), reduced by the outstanding principal amount of any other qualified real property business indebtedness secured by such property (as of such time).

(B) Overall limitation. The amount excluded under subparagraph (D) of subsection (a)(1) shall not exceed the aggregate adjusted bases of depreciable real property (determined after any reductions under subsections (b) and (g)) held by the taxpayer immediately before the discharge (other than depreciable real property acquired in contemplation of such discharge).

(3) Qualified real property business indebtedness. The term "qualified real property business indebtedness" means indebtedness which—

(A) was incurred or assumed by the taxpayer in connection with real property used in a trade or business and is secured by such real property,

(B) was incurred or assumed before January 1, 1993, or if incurred or assumed on or after such date, is qualified acquisition indebtedness, and

(C) with respect to which such taxpayer makes an election to have this paragraph apply.

Such term shall not include qualified farm indebtedness. Indebtedness under subparagraph (B) shall include indebtedness resulting from the refinancing of indebtedness under subparagraph (B) (or this sentence), but only to the extent it does not exceed the amount of the indebtedness being refinanced.

(4) Qualified acquisition indebtedness. For purposes of paragraph (3)(B), the term "qualified acquisition indebtedness" means, with respect to any real property described in paragraph (3)(A), indebtedness incurred or assumed to acquire, construct, reconstruct, or substantially improve such property.

(5) Regulations. The Secretary shall issue such regulations as are necessary to carry out this subsection, including regulations preventing the abuse of this subsection through cross-collateralization or other means.

(d) Meaning of terms; special rules relating to certain provisions.

(1) Indebtedness of taxpayer. For purposes of this section, the term "indebtedness of the taxpayer" means any indebtedness—

(A) for which the taxpayer is liable, or

(B) subject to which the taxpayer holds property.

(2) Title 11 case. For purposes of this section, the term "title 11 case" means a case under title 11 of the United States Code (relating to bankruptcy), but only if the taxpayer is under the jurisdiction of the court in such case and the discharge of indebtedness is granted by the court or is pursuant to a plan approved by the court.

(3) Insolvent. For purposes of this section, the term "insolvent" means the excess of liabilities over the fair market value of assets. With respect to any discharge, whether or not the taxpayer is insolvent, and the amount by which the taxpayer is insolvent, shall be determined on the basis of the taxpayer's assets and liabilities immediately before the discharge.

(4) Repealed.

(5) Depreciable property. The term "depreciable property" has the same meaning as when used in section 1017.

(6) Certain provisions to be applied at partner level. In the case of a partnership, subsections (a), (b), (c) and (g) shall be applied at the partner level.

(7) Special rules for S corporation.

(A) Certain provisions to be applied at corporate level. In the case of an S corporation, subsections (a), (b), (c), and (g) shall be applied at the corporate level, including by not taking into account under section 1366(a) any amount excluded under subsection (a) of this section.

(B) Reduction in carryover of disallowed losses and deductions. In the case of an S corporation, for purposes of subparagraph (A) of subsection (b)(2), any loss or deduction which is disallowed for the taxable year of the discharge under section 1366(d)(1) shall be treated as a net operating loss for such taxable year. The preceding sentence shall not apply to any discharge to the extent that subsection (a)(1)(D) applies to such discharge.

(C) Coordination with basis adjustments under section 1367(b)(2). For purposes of subsection (e)(6), a shareholder's adjusted basis in indebtedness of an S corporation shall be determined without regard to any adjustments made under section 1367(b)(2).

(8) Reductions of tax attributes in title 11 cases of individuals to be made by estate. In any case under chapter 7 or 11 of title 11 of the United States Code to which section 1398 applies, for purposes of paragraphs (1) and (5) of subsection (b) the estate (and not the individual) shall be treated as the taxpayer. The preceding sentence shall not apply for purposes of applying section 1017 to property transferred by the estate to the individual.

(9) Time for making election, etc.

(A) Time. An election under paragraph (5) of subsection (b) or under paragraph (3)(C) of subsection (c) shall be made on the taxpayer's return for the taxable year in which the discharge occurs or at such other time as may be permitted in regulations prescribed by the Secretary.

(B) Revocation only with consent. An election referred to in subparagraph (A), once made, may be revoked only with the consent of the Secretary.

(C) Manner. An election referred to in subparagraph (A) shall be made in such manner as the Secretary may by regulations prescribe.

(10) Cross reference. For provision that no reduction is to be made in the basis of exempt property of an individual debtor, see section 1017(c)(1).

(e) General rules for discharge of indebtedness (including discharges not in title 11 cases or insolvency).

For purposes of this title—

(1) No other insolvency exception. Except as otherwise provided in this section, there shall be no insolvency exception from the general rule that gross income includes income from the discharge of indebtedness.

(2) Income not realized to extent of lost deductions. No income shall be realized from the discharge of indebtedness to the extent that payment of the liability would have given rise to a deduction.

(3) Adjustments for unamortized premium and discount. The amount taken into account with respect to any discharge shall be properly adjusted for unamortized premium and unamortized discount with respect to the indebtedness discharged.

(4) Acquisition of indebtedness by person related to debtor.

(A) Treated as acquisition by debtor. For purposes of determining income of the debtor from discharge of indebtedness, to the extent provided in regulations prescribed by the Secretary, the acquisition of outstanding indebtedness by a person bearing a relationship to the debtor specified in section 267(b) or 707(b)(1) from a person who does not bear such a relationship to the debtor shall be treated as the acquisition of such indebtedness by the debtor. Such regulations shall provide for such adjustments in the treatment of any subsequent transactions involving the indebtedness as may be appropriate by reason of the application of the preceding sentence.

(B) Members of family. For purposes of this paragraph, sections 267(b) and 707(b)(1) shall be applied as if section 267(c)(4) provided that the family of an individual consists of the individual's spouse, the individual's children, grandchildren, and parents, and any spouse of the individual's children or grandchildren.

(C) Entities under common control treated as related. For purposes of this paragraph, two entities which are treated as a single employer under subsection (b) or (c) of section 414 shall be treated as bearing a relationship to each other which is described in section 267(b).

(5) Purchase-money debt reduction for solvent debtor treated as price reduction. If—

(A) the debt of a purchaser of property to the seller of such property which arose out of the purchase of such property is reduced,

(B) such reduction does not occur—
(i) in a title 11 case, or
(ii) when the purchaser is insolvent, and

(C) but for this paragraph, such reduction would be treated as income to the purchaser from the discharge of indebtedness,

then such reduction shall be treated as a purchase price adjustment.

(6) Indebtedness contributed to capital. Except as provided in regulations, for purposes of determining income of the debtor from discharge of indebtedness, if a debtor corporation acquires its indebtedness from a shareholder as a contribution to capital—

(A) section 118 shall not apply, but

(B) such corporation shall be treated as having satisfied the indebtedness with an amount of money equal to the shareholder's adjusted basis in the indebtedness.

(7) Recapture of gain on subsequent sale of stock.

(A) In general. If a creditor acquires stock of a debtor corporation in satisfaction of such corporation's indebtedness, for purposes of section 1245—

(i) such stock (and any other property the basis of which is determined in whole or in part by reference to the adjusted basis of such stock) shall be treated as section 1245 property,

(ii) the aggregate amount allowed to the creditor—
(I) as deductions under subsection (a) or (b) of section 166 (by reason of the worthlessness or partial worthlessness of the indebtedness), or
(II) as an ordinary loss on the exchange,
shall be treated as an amount allowed as a deduction for depreciation, and

(iii) an exchange of such stock qualifying under section 354(a), 355(a), or 356(a) shall be treated as an exchange to which section 1245(b)(3) applies.

The amount determined under clause (ii) shall be reduced by the amount (if any) included in the creditor's gross income on the exchange.

(B) Special rule for cash basis taxpayers. In the case of any creditor who computes his taxable income under the cash receipts and disbursements method, proper adjustment shall be made in the amount taken into account under clause (ii) of subparagraph (A) for any amount which was not included in the creditor's gross income but which would have been included in such gross income if such indebtedness had been satisfied in full.

(C) Stock of parent corporation. For purposes of this paragraph, stock of a corporation in control (within the meaning of section 368(c)) of the debtor corporation shall be treated as stock of the debtor corporation.

(D) Treatment of successor corporation. For purposes of this paragraph, the term "debtor corporation" includes a successor corporation.

(E) Partnership rule. Under regulations prescribed by the Secretary, rules similar to the rules of the foregoing subparagraphs of this paragraph shall apply with respect to the indebtedness of a partnership.

(8) Indebtedness satisfied by corporate stock or partnership interest. For purposes of determining income of a debtor from discharge of indebtedness, if—

(A) a debtor corporation transfers stock, or

(B) a debtor partnership transfers a capital or profits interest in such partnership,

to a creditor in satisfaction of its recourse or nonrecourse indebtedness, such corporation or partnership shall be treated as having satisfied the indebtedness with an amount of money equal to the fair market value of the stock or interest. In the case of any partnership, any discharge of indebtedness income recognized under this paragraph shall be included in the distributive shares of taxpayers which were the partners in the partnership immediately before such discharge.

Exclusions from income — Code Sec. 108(g)(3)(D)

(9) Discharge of indebtedness income not taken into account in determining whether entity meets REIT qualifications. Any amount included in gross income by reason of the discharge of indebtedness shall not be taken into account for purposes of paragraphs (2) and (3) of section 856(c).

(10) Indebtedness satisfied by issuance of debt instrument.

(A) In general. For purposes of determining income of a debtor from discharge of indebtedness, if a debtor issues a debt instrument in satisfaction of indebtedness, such debtor shall be treated as having satisfied the indebtedness with an amount of money equal to the issue price of such debt instrument.

(B) Issue price. For purposes of subparagraph (A), the issue price of any debt instrument shall be determined under sections 1273 and 1274. For purposes of the preceding sentence, section 1273(b)(4) shall be applied by reducing the stated redemption price of any instrument by the portion of such stated redemption price which is treated as interest for purposes of this chapter.

(f) Student loans.

(1) In general. In the case of an individual, gross income does not include any amount which (but for this subsection) would be includible in gross income by reason of the discharge (in whole or in part) of any student loan if such discharge was pursuant to a provision of such loan under which all or part of the indebtedness of the individual would be discharged if the individual worked for a certain period of time in certain professions for any of a broad class of employers.

(2) Student loan. For purposes of this subsection, the term "student loan" means any loan to an individual to assist the individual in attending an educational organization described in section 170(b)(1)(A)(ii) made by—

(A) the United States, or an instrumentality or agency thereof,

(B) a State, territory, or possession of the United States, or the District of Columbia, or any political subdivision thereof,

(C) a public benefit corporation—

  (i) which is exempt from taxation under section 501(c)(3),

  (ii) which has assumed control over a State, county, or municipal hospital, and

  (iii) whose employees have been deemed to be public employees under State law, or

(D) any educational organization described in section 170(b)(1)(A)(ii) if such loan is made—

  (i) pursuant to an agreement with any entity described in subparagraph (A), (B), or (C) under which the funds from which the loan was made were provided to such educational organization, or

  (ii) pursuant to a program of such educational organization which is designed to encourage its students to serve in occupations with unmet needs or in areas with unmet needs and under which the services provided by the students (or former students) are for or under the direction of a governmental unit or an organization described in section 501(c)(3) and exempt from tax under section 501(a).

The term "student loan" includes any loan made by an educational organization described in section 170(b)(1)(A)(ii) or by an organization exempt from tax under section 501(a) to refinance a loan to an individual to assist the individual in attending any such educational organization but only if the refinancing loan is pursuant to a program of the refinancing organization which is designed as described in subparagraph (D)(ii).

(3) Exception for discharges on account of services performed for certain lenders. Paragraph (1) shall not apply to the discharge of a loan made by an organization described in paragraph (2)(D) if the discharge is on account of services performed for either such organization.

(4) Payments under National Health Service Corps loan repayment program and certain State loan repayment programs. In the case of an individual, gross income shall not include any amount received under section 338B(g) of the Public Health Service Act, under a State program described in section 338I of such Act, or under any other State loan repayment or loan forgiveness program that is intended to provide for the increased availability of health care services in underserved or health professional shortage areas (as determined by such State).

(g) Special rules for discharge of qualified farm indebtedness.

(1) Discharge must be by qualified person.

(A) In general. Subparagraph (C) of subsection (a)(1) shall apply only if the discharge is by a qualified person.

(B) Qualified person. For purposes of subparagraph (A), the term "qualified person" has the meaning given to such term by section 49(a)(1)(D)(iv); except that such term shall include any Federal, State, or local government or agency or instrumentality thereof.

(2) Qualified farm indebtedness. For purposes of this section, indebtedness of a taxpayer shall be treated as qualified farm indebtedness if—

(A) such indebtedness was incurred directly in connection with the operation by the taxpayer of the trade or business of farming, and

(B) 50 percent or more of the aggregate gross receipts of the taxpayer for the 3 taxable years preceding the taxable year in which the discharge of such indebtedness occurs is attributable to the trade or business of farming.

(3) Amount excluded cannot exceed sum of tax attributes and business and investment assets.

(A) In general. The amount excluded under subparagraph (C) of subsection (a)(1) shall not exceed the sum of—

  (i) the adjusted tax attributes of the taxpayer, and

  (ii) the aggregate adjusted bases of qualified property held by the taxpayer as of the beginning of the taxable year following the taxable year in which the discharge occurs.

(B) Adjusted tax attributes. For purposes of subparagraph (A), the term "adjusted tax attributes" means the sum of the tax attributes described in subparagraphs (A), (B), (C), (D), (F), and (G) of subsection (b)(2) determined by taking into account $3 for each $1 of the attributes described in subparagraphs (B), (C), and (G) of subsection (b)(2) and the attribute described in subparagraph (F) of subsection (b)(2) to the extent attributable to any passive activity credit carryover.

(C) Qualified property. For purposes of this paragraph, the term "qualified property" means any property which is used or is held for use in a trade or business or for the production of income.

(D) Coordination with insolvency exclusion. For purposes of this paragraph, the adjusted basis of any qualified property and the amount of the adjusted tax attributes shall be determined after any reduction under

(h) Special rules relating to qualified principal residence indebtedness.

(1) Basis reduction. The amount excluded from gross income by reason of subsection (a)(1)(E) shall be applied to reduce (but not below zero) the basis of the principal residence of the taxpayer.

(2) Qualified principal residence indebtedness. For purposes of this section, the term "qualified principal residence indebtedness" means acquisition indebtedness (within the meaning of section 163(h)(3)(B), applied by substituting "$2,000,000 ($1,000,000" for "$1,000,000 ($500,000" in clause (ii) thereof) with respect to the principal residence of the taxpayer.

(3) Exception for certain discharges not related to taxpayer's financial conditions. Subsection (a)(1)(E) shall not apply to the discharge of a loan if the discharge is on account of services performed for the lender or any other factor not directly related to a decline in the value of the residence or to the financial condition of the taxpayer.

(4) Ordering rules. If any loan is discharged, in whole or in part, and only a portion of such loan is qualified principal residence indebtedness, subsection (a)(1)(E) shall apply only to so much of the amount discharged as exceeds the amount of the loan (as determined immediately before such discharge) which is not qualified principal residence indebtedness.

(5) Principal residences. For purposes of this subsection, the term "principal residence" has the same meaning as when used in section 121.

(i) Deferral and ratable inclusion of income arising from business indebtedness discharged by the reacquisition of a debt instrument.

(1) In general. At the election of the taxpayer, income from the discharge of indebtedness in connection with the reacquisition after December 31, 2008, and before January 1, 2011, of an applicable debt instrument shall be includible in gross income ratably over the 5-taxable-year period beginning with—

(A) in the case of a reacquisition occurring in 2009, the fifth taxable year following the taxable year in which the reacquisition occurs, and

(B) in the case of a reacquisition occurring in 2010, the fourth taxable year following the taxable year in which the reacquisition occurs.

(2) Deferral of deduction for original issue discount in debt for debt exchanges.

(A) In general. If, as part of a reacquisition to which paragraph (1) applies, any debt instrument is issued for the applicable debt instrument being reacquired (or is treated as so issued under subsection (e)(4) and the regulations thereunder) and there is any original issue discount determined under subpart A of part V of subchapter P of this chapter with respect to the debt instrument so issued—

(i) except as provided in clause (ii), no deduction otherwise allowable under this chapter shall be allowed to the issuer of such debt instrument with respect to the portion of such original issue discount which—

(I) accrues before the 1st taxable year in the 5-taxable-year period in which income from the discharge of indebtedness attributable to the reacquisition of the debt instrument is includible under paragraph (1), and

(II) does not exceed the income from the discharge of indebtedness with respect to the debt instrument being reacquired, and

(ii) the aggregate amount of deductions disallowed under clause (i) shall be allowed as a deduction ratably over the 5-taxable-year period described in clause (i)(I).

If the amount of the original issue discount accruing before such 1st taxable year exceeds the income from the discharge of indebtedness with respect to the applicable debt instrument being reacquired, the deductions shall be disallowed in the order in which the original issue discount is accrued.

(B) Deemed debt for debt exchanges. For purposes of subparagraph (A), if any debt instrument is issued by an issuer and the proceeds of such debt instrument are used directly or indirectly by the issuer to reacquire an applicable debt instrument of the issuer, the debt instrument so issued shall be treated as issued for the debt instrument being reacquired. If only a portion of the proceeds from a debt instrument are so used, the rules of subparagraph (A) shall apply to the portion of any original issue discount on the newly issued debt instrument which is equal to the portion of the proceeds from such instrument used to reacquire the outstanding instrument.

(3) Applicable debt instrument. For purposes of this subsection—

(A) Applicable debt instrument. The term "applicable debt instrument" means any debt instrument which was issued by—

(i) a C corporation, or

(ii) any other person in connection with the conduct of a trade or business by such person.

(B) Debt instrument. The term "debt instrument" means a bond, debenture, note, certificate, or any other instrument or contractual arrangement constituting indebtedness (within the meaning of section 1275(a)(1)).

(4) Reacquisition. For purposes of this subsection—

(A) In general. The term "reacquisition" means, with respect to any applicable debt instrument, any acquisition of the debt instrument by—

(i) the debtor which issued (or is otherwise the obligor under) the debt instrument, or

(ii) a related person to such debtor.

(B) Acquisition. The term "acquisition" shall, with respect to any applicable debt instrument, include an acquisition of the debt instrument for cash, the exchange of the debt instrument for another debt instrument (including an exchange resulting from a modification of the debt instrument), the exchange of the debt instrument for corporate stock or a partnership interest, and the contribution of the debt instrument to capital. Such term shall also include the complete forgiveness of the indebtedness by the holder of the debt instrument.

(5) Other definitions and rules. For purposes of this subsection—

(A) Related person. The determination of whether a person is related to another person shall be made in the same manner as under subsection (e)(4).

(B) Election.

(i) In general. An election under this subsection with respect to any applicable debt instrument shall be made by including with the return of tax imposed by chapter 1 for the taxable year in which the reacquisition of the debt instrument occurs a statement which—

(I) clearly identifies such instrument, and

Exclusions from income   Code Sec. 108

(II) includes the amount of income to which paragraph (1) applies and such other information as the Secretary may prescribe.

(ii) *Election irrevocable.* Such election, once made, is irrevocable.

(iii) *Pass through entities.* In the case of a partnership, S corporation, or other pass through entity, the election under this subsection shall be made by the partnership, the S corporation, or other entity involved.

(C) *Coordination with other exclusions.* If a taxpayer elects to have this subsection apply to an applicable debt instrument, subparagraphs (A), (B), (C), and (D) of subsection (a)(1) shall not apply to the income from the discharge of such indebtedness for the taxable year of the election or any subsequent taxable year.

(D) *Acceleration of deferred items.*

(i) *In general.* In the case of the death of the taxpayer, the liquidation or sale of substantially all the assets of the taxpayer (including in a title 11 or similar case), the cessation of business by the taxpayer, or similar circumstances, any item of income or deduction which is deferred under this subsection (and has not previously been taken into account) shall be taken into account in the taxable year in which such event occurs (or in the case of a title 11 case, the day before the petition is filed).

(ii) *Special rule for pass thru entities.* The rule of clause (i) shall also apply in the case of the sale or exchange or redemption of an interest in a partnership, S corporation, or other pass through entity by a partner, shareholder, or other person holding an ownership interest in such entity.

(6) Special rule for partnerships. In the case of a partnership, any income deferred under this subsection shall be allocated to the partners in the partnership immediately before the discharge in the manner such amounts would have been included in the distributive shares of such partners under section 704 if such income were recognized at such time. Any decrease in a partner's share of partnership liabilities as a result of such discharge shall not be taken into account for purposes of section 752 at the time of the discharge to the extent it would cause the partner to recognize gain under section 731. Any decrease in partnership liabilities deferred under the preceding sentence shall be taken into account by such partner at the same time, and to the extent remaining in the same amount, as income deferred under this subsection is recognized.

(7) Secretarial authority. The Secretary may prescribe such regulations, rules, or other guidance as may be necessary or appropriate for purposes of applying this subsection, including—

(A) extending the application of the rules of paragraph (5)(D) to other circumstances where appropriate,

(B) requiring reporting of the election (and such other information as the Secretary may require) on returns of tax for subsequent taxable years, and

(C) rules for the application of this subsection to partnerships, S corporations, and other pass-thru entities, including for the allocation of deferred deductions.

In 2010, P.L. 111-148, Sec. 10908(a), amended para. (f)(4), effective for amounts received by an individual in tax. yrs. begin. after 12/31/2008.
Prior to amendment, para. (f)(4) read as follows:
"(4) Payments under National Health Service Corps loan repayment program and certain State loan repayment programs. In the case of an individual, gross income shall not include any amount received under section 338B(g) of the Public Health Service Act or under a State program described in section 338I of such Act."

In 2009, P.L. 111-5, Sec. 1231(a), added subsec. (i), effective for discharges in tax. yrs. end. after 12/31/2008.

In 2008, P.L. 110-343, Sec. 303(a)DivA, substituted "January 1, 2013" for "January 1, 2010", in subpara. (a)(1)(E), effective for discharges of indebtedness occurring on or after 1/1/2010.

In 2007, P.L. 110-142, Sec. 2(a), deleted "or" at the end of subpara. (a)(1)(C), substituted ", or" for the period at the end of subpara. (a)(1)(D), added new subpara. (a)(1)(E)... Sec. 2(b), added new subsec. (h)... Sec. 2(c)(1), substituted "(D), and (E)" for "and (D)" in subpara. (a)(2)(A)... Sec. 2(c)(2), added new subpara. (a)(2)(C), effective for discharges of indebtedness on or after 1/1/2007.

In 2004, P.L. 108-357, Sec. 320(a), added para. (f)(4), effective for amounts received by an individual in tax. yrs. begin. after 12/31/2003.
—P.L. 108-357, Sec. 896(a), amended para. (e)(8), effective for cancellations of indebtedness occurring on or after 10/22/2004.
Prior to amendment, para. (e)(8) read as follows:
"(8) Indebtedness satisfied by corporation's stock. For purposes of determining income of a debtor from discharge of indebtedness, if a debtor corporation transfers stock to a creditor in satisfaction of its indebtedness, such corporation shall be treated as having satisfied the indebtedness with an amount of money equal to the fair market value of the stock."

In 2002, P.L. 107-147, Sec. 402(a), added ", including by not taking into account under section 1366(a) any amount excluded under subsection (a) of this section" after "corporate level" in subpara. (d)(7)(A), effective for discharges of indebtedness after 10/11/2001, in tax. yrs. end. after 10/11/2001, except as provided in Sec. 402(b)(2) of this Act, which reads as follows:
"(2) Exception. The amendment made by this section shall not apply to any discharge of indebtedness before March 1, 2002, pursuant to a plan of reorganization filed with a bankruptcy court on or before October 11, 2001."

In 1998, P.L. 105-206, Sec. 6004(f)(1), amended the last sentence of para. (f)(2) ... Sec. 6004(f)(2), deleted "(or by an organization described in paragraph (2)(E) from funds provided by an organization described in paragraph (2)(D))" after "described in paragraph (2)(D)" in para. (f)(3), effective for discharges of indebtedness after 8/5/97.
Prior to amendment, the last sentence of para. (f)(2) read as follows:
"The term 'student loan' includes any loan made by an educational organization so described or by an organization exempt from tax under section 501(a) to refinance a loan meeting the requirements of the preceding sentence."

In 1997, P.L. 105-34, Sec. 225(a)(1), deleted "or" at the end of subpara. (f)(2)(B), amended subpara. (f)(2)(D) and added flush language at the end of para. (f)(2) ... Sec. 225(a)(2), added para. (f)(3), effective for discharges of indebtedness after 8/5/97.
Prior to amendment, subpara. (f)(2)(D) read as follows:
"(D) any educational organization so described pursuant to an agreement with any entity described in subparagraph (A), (B), or (C) under which the funds from which the loan was made were provided to such educational organization."

In 1996, P.L. 104-188, Sec. 1703(n)(2), substituted "paragraph (3)(C)" for "paragraph (3)(B)" in subpara. (d)(9)(A), effective for discharges after 12/31/92, in tax. yrs. end. after 12/31/92.

In 1993, P.L. 103-66, Sec. 13150(a), deleted "or" at the end of subpara. (a)(1)(B), substituted ", or" for the period at the end of subpara. (a)(1)(C), and added subpara. (a)(1)(D) ... Sec. 13150(b), added subsec. (c) ... Sec. 13150(c)(1), substituted ", (C), and (D)" for "and (C)" in subpara. (a)(2)(A) ... Sec. 13150(c)(2), amended subpara. (a)(2)(B) ... Sec. 13150(c)(3)(A), substituted "subsections (a), (b), (c), and (g)" for "subsections (a), (b), and (g)" in para. (d)(6) and subpara. (d)(7)(A) ... Sec. 13150(c)(3)(B), substituted "certain provisions" for "subsections (a), (b), and (g)" in the heading of subsec. (d) ... Sec. 13150(c)(3)(C), substituted "Certain provisions" for "Subsections (a), (b), and (g)" in the headings of para. (d)(6) and subpara. (d)(7)(A) ... Sec. 13150(c)(4), added the sentence at the end of subpara. (d)(7)(B) ... Sec. 13150(c)(5), added "or under paragraph (3)(B) of subsection (c)" after "subsection (a)" in subpara. (d)(9)(A), effective for discharges after 12/31/92, in tax. yrs. end. after 12/31/92.
Prior to amendment, subpara. (a)(2)(B) read as follows:
"(B) Insolvency exclusion takes precedence over qualified farm exclusion. Subparagraph (C) of paragraph (1) shall not apply to a discharge to the extent the taxpayer is insolvent."
—P.L. 103-66, Sec. 13226(a)(1)(A), deleted para. (e)(10) and redesignated para. (e)(11) as (e)(10) ... Sec. 13226(a)(1)(B), amended para. (e)(8) ... Sec. 13226(a)(2)(B), substituted "Except as provided in regulations, for" for "For" in para. (e)(6), effective for stock transferred after 12/31/94, in satisfaction of any indebtedness, except as provided in Sec. 13226(a)(3)(B) of this Act, which reads as follows:
"(B) Exception for title 11 cases.—The amendments made by this subsection shall not apply to stock transferred in satisfaction of any indebtedness if such transfer is in a title 11 or similar case (as defined in section 368(a)(3)(A) of the Internal Revenue Code of 1986) which was filed on or before December 31, 1993."
Prior to deletion, para. (e)(10) read as follows:
"(10) Indebtedness satisfied by corporation's stock.
"(A) In general. For purposes of determining income of a debtor from discharge of indebtedness, if a debtor corporation transfers stock to a creditor in satisfaction of its indebtedness, such corporation shall be treated as having satisfied the indebtedness with an amount of money equal to the fair market value of the stock.
"(B) Exception for certain stock in title 11 cases and insolvent debtors.
"(i) In general. Subparagraph (A) shall not apply to any transfer of stock of the debtor (other than disqualified stock)—
"(I) by a debtor in a title 11 case, or
"(II) by any other debtor but only to the extent such debtor is insolvent.

Code Sec. 108 — Exclusions from income

"(ii) Disqualified stock. For purposes of clause (i), the term 'disqualified stock' means any stock with a stated redemption price if—

"(I) such stock has a fixed redemption date,

"(II) the issuer of such stock has the right to redeem such stock at one or more times, or

"(III) the holder of such stock has the right to require its redemption at one or more times."

Prior to amendment, para. (e)(8) read as follows:

"(8) Stock for debt exception not to apply in de minimis cases. For purposes of determining income of the debtor from discharge of indebtedness, the stock for debt exception shall not apply—

"(A) to the issuance of nominal or token shares, or

"(B) with respect to an unsecured creditor, where the ratio of the value of the stock received by such unsecured creditor to the amount of his indebtedness cancelled or exchanged for stock in the workout is less than 50 percent of a similar ratio computed for all unsecured creditors participating in the workout.

Any stock which is disqualified stock (as defined in paragraph (10)(B)(ii)) shall not be treated as stock for purposes of this paragraph."

—P.L. 103-66, Sec. 13226(b)(1), redesignated subparas. (b)(2)(C)-(E) as subparas. (b)(2)(D)-(F) and added new subpara. (b)(2)(C)... Sec. 13226(b)(2), redesignated subpara. (b)(2)(F) [as amended by Sec. 13226(b)(1) of this Act] as subpara. (b)(2)(G) and added new subpara. (b)(2)(F)... Sec. 13226(b)(3)(A), amended subpara. (b)(3)(B)... Sec. 13226(b)(3)(B), substituted "(D)" for "(C)" in the text and heading of subpara. (b)(4)(B)... Sec. 13226(b)(3)(C), substituted "(G)" for "(E)" in the text and heading of subpara. (b)(4)(C)... Sec. 13226(b)(3)(D)(i), substituted "subparagraphs (A), (B), (C), (D), (F), and (G)" for "subparagraphs (A), (B), (C), and (E)" in subpara. (g)(3)(B)... Sec. 13226(b)(3)(D)(ii), substituted "subparagraphs (B), (D), and (G)" for "subparagraphs (B) and (E)" in subpara. (g)(3)(B)... Sec. 13226(b)(3)(D)(iii), added "and the attribute described in subparagraph (F) of subsection (b)(2) to the extent attributable to any passive activity credit carryover" before the period at the end of subpara. (g)(3)(B), effective for discharges of indebtedness in tax. yrs. begin. after 12/31/93.

Prior to amendment, subpara. (b)(3)(B) read as follows:

"(B) Credit carryover reduction. The reductions described in subparagraphs (B) and (E) of paragraph (2) shall be 33⅓ cents for each dollar excluded by subsection (a)."

In 1990, P.L. 101-508, Sec. 11325(b)(1), added para. (e)(11)... Sec. 11325(b)(1), amended subpara. (e)(10)(B)... Sec. 11325(b)(2), added the last sentence to para. (e)(8), effective for debt instruments issued, and stock transferred, after 10/9/90, in satisfaction of any indebtedness, except as provided in Sec. 11325(c)(2) of this Act, which reads as follows:

"(2) Exceptions.—The amendments made by this section shall not apply to any debt instrument issued, or stock transferred, in satisfaction of any indebtedness if such issuance or transfer (as the case may be)—

"(A) is in a title 11 or similar case (as defined in section 368(a)(3)(A) of the Internal Revenue Code of 1986) which was filed on or before October 9, 1990,

"(B) is pursuant to a written binding contract in effect on October 9, 1990, and at all times thereafter before such issuance or transfer,

"(C) is pursuant to a transaction which was described in documents filed with the Securities and Exchange Commission on or before October 9, 1990, or

"(D) is pursuant to a transaction—

"(i) the material terms of which were described in a written public announcement on or before October 9, 1990,

"(ii) which was the subject of a prior filing with the Securities and Exchange Commission, and

"(iii) which is the subject of a subsequent filing with the Securities and Exchange Commission before January 1, 1991."

Prior to amendment, subpara. (e)(10)(B) read as follows:

"(B) Exception for title 11 cases and insolvent debtors. Subparagraph (A) shall not apply in the case of a debtor in a title 11 case or to the extent the debtor is insolvent."

—P.L. 101-508, Sec. 11813(b)(6), substituted "section 49(a)(1)(D)(iv)" for "section 46(c)(8)(D)(iv)" in subpara. (g)(1)(B), effective for property placed in service after 12/31/90, except as provided by Sec. 11813(c)(2) of this Act reproduced in note following Code Sec. 46.

In 1988, P.L. 100-647, Sec. 1004(a)(1), deleted "or" at the end of subpara. (a)(1)(A), substituted ", or" for the period at the end of subpara. (a)(1)(B) and added subpara. (a)(1)(C)... Sec. 1004(a)(2), amended para. (a)(2)... Sec. 1004(a)(3)(A), substituted "subparagraph (A), (B), or (C)" for "subparagraph (A) or (B)" in para. (b)(1)... Sec. 1004(a)(3)(B), deleted "in title 11 case or insolvency" after "attributes" in the heading of subsec. (b)... Sec. 1004(a)(4), amended subsec. (g)... Sec. 1004(a)(6)(A), substituted "subsections (a), (b) and (g)" for "subsections (a) and (b)" in paras. (d)(6) and (7)... Sec. 1004(a)(6)(B), substituted "subsections (a), (b), and (g)" for "subsections (a), (b), and (c)" in the heading of subsec. (d)... Sec. 1004(a)(6)(C), substituted "subsections (a), (b), and (g)" for "subsections (a) and (b)", in the headings of para. (d)(6) and subpara. (d)(7)(A), effective for discharges of indebtedness occurring after 4/9/86, in tax. yrs. end. after 4/9/86.

Prior to amendment, para. (a)(2) read as follows:

"(2) Coordination of exclusions. Subparagraph (B) of paragraph (1) shall not apply to a discharge which occurs in a title 11 case."

Prior to amendment, subsec. (g) read as follows:

"(g) Special rules for discharge of qualified farm indebtedness of solvent farmers.

"(1) In general. For purposes of this section and section 1017, the discharge by a qualified person of qualified farm indebtedness of a taxpayer who is not insolvent at the time of the discharge shall be treated in the same manner as if the discharge had occurred when the taxpayer was insolvent.

"(2) Qualified farm indebtedness. For purposes of this subsection, indebtedness of a taxpayer shall be treated as qualified farm indebtedness if—

"(A) such indebtedness was incurred directly in connection with the operation by the taxpayer of the trade or business of farming, and

"(B) 50 percent or more of the average annual gross receipts of the taxpayer for the 3 taxable years preceding the taxable year in which the discharge of such indebtedness occurs is attributable to the trade or business of farming.

"(3) Qualified person. For purposes of this subsection, the term 'qualified person' means a person described in section 46(c)(8)(D)(iv)."

In 1986, P.L. 99-514, Sec. 104(b)(2), substituted "33⅓ cents" for "50 cents" in subpara. (b)(3)(B), effective for tax. yrs. begin. after 12/31/86.

—P.L. 99-514, Sec. 231(d)(3)(D), amended subpara. (b)(2)(B), effective for tax. yrs. begin. after 12/31/85.

Prior to amendment, subpara. (b)(2)(B) read as follows:

"(B) Research credit and general business credit. Any carryover to or from the taxable year of a discharge of an amount for purposes of determining the amount allowable as a credit under—

"(i) section 30 (relating to credit for increasing research activities), or

"(ii) section 38 (relating to general business credit).

For purposes of this subparagraph, there shall not be taken into account any portion of a carryover which is attributable to the employee stock ownership credit determined under section 41."

—P.L. 99-514, Sec. 405(a), added subsec. (g), effective for discharges of indebtedness occurring after 4/9/86, in tax. yrs. end. after 4/9/86.

—P.L. 99-514, Sec. 621(e)(1), repealed Sec. 59(b) of P.L. 98-369 which added subpara. (e)(10)(C), effective as provided in Sec. 621(f)(2) of this Act reproduced in note following Code Sec. 382.

Prior to repeal, subpara. (e)(10)(C) as added by Sec. 59(b) of P.L. 98-369 read as follows:

"(C) Exception for transfers in certain workouts.

"(i) In general. Subparagraph (A) shall not apply to any transfer of stock in a qualified workout.

"(ii) Qualified workout. For purposes of clause (i), the term 'qualified workout' means any plan under which stock is transferred to creditors in satisfaction of indebtedness if—

"(I) because of cash flow and credit problems, the corporation making such transfer will have trouble in meeting liabilities coming due during the next 12 months to such an extent that there is a substantial threat of involuntary proceedings relating to insolvency or bankruptcy,

"(II) such corporation in any report to its shareholders for the period during which such transfer occurs includes a statement that such corporation believes it meets the requirement of subclause (I) and that it is availing itself of the workout provisions of this subparagraph,

"(III) the holders of more than 50 percent of the total indebtedness of the corporation approve such plan, and

"(IV) at least 25 percent of the total indebtedness of the corporation is extinguished by transfers pursuant to such plan."

—P.L. 99-514, Sec. 805(c)(2), substituted "subsection (a) or (b) of section 166" for "subsection (a), (b) or (c) of section 166" in clause (e)(7)(A)(ii)... Sec. 805(c)(3), deleted subpara. (e)(7)(B) and redesignated subparagraphs (e)(7)(C), (D), (E) and (F) as subparagraphs (e)(7)(B), (C), (D) and (E)... Sec. 805(c)(4), substituted "the foregoing subparagraphs" for "subparagraphs (A), (B), (C), (D) and (E)" in subpara. (e)(7)(E) (as redesignated), effective for tax. yrs. begin. after 12/31/86. See Sec. 805(d)(2) reproduced in note following Code Sec. 166.

Prior to deletion, subpara. (e)(7)(B) read as follows:

"(B) Taxpayers on reserve method. In the case of a taxpayer to whom subsection (c) of section 166 (relating to reserve for bad debts) applies, the amount determined under clause (ii) of subparagraph (A) shall be the aggregate charges to the reserve resulting from the worthlessness or partial worthlessness of the indebtedness."

—P.L. 99-514, Sec. 822(a), deleted para. (a)(1)(C), added "or" at the end of para. (a)(1)(A) and substituted a period for ", or" at the end of para. (a)(1)(B)... Sec. 822(b)(1), amended para. (a)(2)... Sec. 822(b)(2), deleted subsec. (c)... Sec. 822(b)(3)(A), deleted para. (d)(4)... Sec. 822(b)(3)(B), substituted "subsections (a) and (b)" for "subsections (a), (b), and (c)" each place it appeared in the heading and text of paras. (d)(6) and (7)... Sec. 822(b)(3)(C), deleted the last sentence of subpara. (d)(7)(B)... Sec. 822(b)(3)(D), deleted "under paragraph (4) of this subsection or" after "An election" in subpara. (d)(9)(A), effective for discharges after 12/31/86.

Prior to deletion, subpara. (a)(1)(C) read as follows:

"(C) the indebtedness discharged is qualified business indebtedness."

Prior to amendment, para. (a)(2) read as follows:

"(2) Coordination of exclusions.

"(A) Title 11 exclusion takes precedence. Subparagraphs (B) and (C) of paragraph (1) shall not apply to a discharge which occurs in a title 11 case.

"(B) Insolvency exclusion takes precedence over qualified business exclusion. Subparagraph (C) of paragraph (1) shall not apply to a discharge to the extent that the taxpayer is insolvent."

Prior to deletion, subsec. (c) read as follows:

"(c) Tax treatment of discharge of qualified business indebtedness. In the case of a discharge of qualified business indebtedness—

"(1) Basis reduction.

"(A) In general. The amount excluded from gross income under subparagraph (C) of subsection (a)(1) shall be applied to reduce the basis of the depreciable property of the taxpayer.

Exclusions from income   Code Sec. 108

"(B) Cross reference. For provisions for making the reduction described in subparagraph (A), see section 1017.

"(2) Limitation. The amount excluded under subparagraph (C) of subsection (a)(1) shall not exceed the aggregate adjusted bases of the depreciable property held by the taxpayer as of the beginning of the taxable year following the taxable year in which the discharge occurs (determined after any reductions under subsection (b))."

Prior to deletion, para. (d)(4) read as follows:

"(4) Qualified business indebtedness. Indebtedness of the taxpayer shall be treated as qualified business indebtedness if (and only if)—

"(A) the indebtedness was incurred or assumed—

"(i) by a corporation, or

"(ii) by an individual in connection with property used in his trade or business, and

"(B) such taxpayer makes an election under this paragraph with respect to such indebtedness."

Prior to deletion, the last sentence of subpara. (d)(7)(B) read as follows:

"The preceding sentence shall not apply to any discharge to the extent that subsection (a)(1)(C) applies to such discharge."

—P.L. 99-514, Sec. 1171(b)(4), deleted the last sentence of subpara. (b)(2)(B), effective for compensation paid or accrued after 12/31/86, in tax. yrs. end. after 12/31/86. Sec. 1177(a) of this Act provides:

"(a) Section 1171.

"The amendments made by section 1171 [P.L. 99-514] shall not apply in the case of a tax credit employee stock ownership plan if—

"(1) such plan was favorably approved on September 23, 1983, by employees, and

"(2) not later than January 11, 1984, the employer of such employees was 100 percent owned by such plan."

Prior to deletion, the last sentence of (b)(2)(B) read as follows:

"For purposes of this subparagraph, there shall not be taken into account any portion of a carryover which is attributable to the employee stock ownership credit determined under section 41."

—P.L. 99-514, Sec. 1847(b)(7), substituted "section 27" for "section 33" in subpara. (b)(2)(E), effective for tax. yrs. begin. after 12/31/83, and to carrybacks from tax. yrs. begin. after 12/31/83.

—P.L. 99-509, Sec. 8021(b), and (e), reproduced in note following Code Sec. 338, provides tax treatment of Conrail public sale.

In 1984, P.L. 98-369, Sec. 59(a), added para. (e)(10), effective for transfers after 7/18/84 in tax. yrs. ending after 7/18/84. Secs. 59(b)(2)–(b)(4) [sic (c)(2)–(c)(4)] of this Act provide:

"(2) Transitional rule. The amendment made by subsection (a) shall not apply to the transfer by a corporation of its stock in exchange for debt of the corporation after the date of the enactment of this Act if such transfer is—

"(A) pursuant to a written contract requiring such transfer which was binding on the corporation at all times on June 7, 1984, and at all times after such date but only if the transfer takes place before January 1, 1985, and only if the transferee held the debt at all times on June 7, 1984, or

"(B) pursuant to the exercise of an option to exchange debt for stock but only if such option was in effect at all times on June 7, 1984, and at all times after such date and only if at all times on June 7, 1984, the option and the debt were held by the same person.

"(3) Certain transfers to controlling shareholder. The amendment made by subsection (a) shall not apply to any transfer before January 1, 1985, by a corporation of its stock in exchange for debt of the corporation if—

"(A) such transfer is to another corporation which at all times on June 7, 1984, owned 75 percent or more of the total value of the stock of the corporation making such transfer, and

"(B) immediately after such transfer, the transferee corporation owns 80 percent or more of the total value of the stock of the transferor corporation.

"(4) Certain transfers pursuant to debt restructure agreement. The amendment made by subsection (a) shall not apply to the transfer by a corporation of its stock in exchange for debt of the corporation after the date of the enactment of this Act and before January 1, 1985, if—

"(A) such transfer is covered by a debt restructure agreement entered into by the corporation during November 1983, and

"(B) such agreement was specified in a registration statement filed with the Securities and Exchange Commission by the corporation on March 7, 1984."

—P.L. 98-369, Sec. 59(b)(1), [repealed by Sec. 621(e)(1) of P.L. 99-514, see above] added subpara. (e)(10)(C), effective for tax. yrs. begin. after 6/30/78.

—P.L. 98-369, Sec. 474(r)(5), amended subpara. (b)(2)(B) for tax. yrs. begin. after 12/31/83 and to carrybacks from tax. yrs. begin. after 12/31/83.

Prior to amendment, subpara. (b)(2)(B) read as follows:

"(B) Certain credit carryovers. Any carryover to or from the taxable year of the discharge of an amount for purposes of determining the amount of a credit allowable under—

"(i) section 38 (relating to investment in certain depreciable property),

"(ii) section 40 (relating to expenses of work incentive programs),

"(iii) section 44B (relating to credit for employment of certain new employees),

"(iv) section 44E (relating to alcohol used as a fuel), or

"(v) section 44F (relating to credit for increasing research activities).

For purposes of clause (i), there shall not be taken into account any portion of a carryover which is attributable to the employee plan credit (within the meaning of section 48(o)(3))."

—P.L. 98-369, Sec. 721(b)(2), redesignated paras. (d)(7), (d)(8) and (d)(9) as paras. (d)(8), (d)(9), and (d)(10), deleted para. (d)(6), and added new paras. (d)(6) and (d)(7), effective for tax. yrs. begin. after 12/31/82, except that Code Sec.

108(d)(7)(C) applies to contributions to capital after 12/31/80 in tax. yrs. ending after 12/31/80.

Prior to deletion, para. (d)(6) read as follows:

"(6) Subsections (a), (b), and (c) to be applied at partner level or S corporation shareholder level. In the case of a partnership, subsections (a), (b), and (c) shall be applied at the partner level. In the case of an S corporation, subsections (a), (b), and (c) shall be applied at the shareholder level."

—P.L. 98-369, Sec. 1076(a), added subsec. (f) effective for discharges of indebtedness made after 12/31/82.

In 1983, P.L. 97-448, Sec. 102(h)(l), amended subpara. (b)(2)(B) by deleting "or" at the end of clause (iii), by substituting ", or" for the period at the end of clause (iv), and by adding clause (v), effective for amounts paid or incurred after 6/30/81 and before 1/1/86.

—P.L. 97-448, Sec. 304(d)(1)–(3), amended subpara. (e)(7)(A) by deleting "and" from the end of clause (i), by substituting ", and" for the period at the end of clause (ii), and by adding clause (iii), effective 1/12/83.

In 1982, P.L. 97-354, Sec. 3(e), amended para. (d)(6), effective for tax. yrs. begin. after 12/31/82.

Prior to amendment, para. (d)(6) read as follows:

"(6) Subsections (a), (b), and (c) to be applied at partner level. In the case of a partnership, subsections (a), (b), and (c) shall be applied at the partner level."

In 1980, P.L. 96-589, Sec. 2(a), amended Code Sec. 108, effective for any transaction which occurs after 12/31/80, other than a transaction which occurs in a proceeding in a bankruptcy case or similar judicial proceeding (or in a proceeding under the Bankruptcy Act) commencing on or before 12/31/80.

Sec. 7(a)(2) of this Act provides:

"(2) Transitional rule. In the case of any discharge of indebtedness to which subparagraph (A) or (B) of section 108(a)(1) of the Internal Revenue Code of 1954 (relating to exclusion from gross income), as amended by section 2, applies and which occurs before January 1, 1982, or which occurs in a proceeding in a bankruptcy case or similar judicial proceedings commencing before January 1, 1982, then—

"(A) section 108(b)(2) of the such Code (relating to reduction of tax attributes), as so amended, shall be applied without regard to subparagraphs (A), (B), (C), and (E) thereof, and

"(B) the basis of any property shall not be reduced under section 1017 of such Code (relating to reduction in basis in connection with discharges of indebtedness), as so amended, below the fair market value of such property on the date the debt is discharged."

Secs. 7(f) and (g) of this Act provides:

"(f) Election to substitute September 30, 1979, for December 31, 1980.

"(1) In general. The debtor (or debtors) in a bankruptcy case or similar judicial proceeding may (with the approval of the court) elect to apply [subsection 7(a) of this Act] by substituting 'September 30, 1979' for 'December 31, 1980' each place it appears in such subsections.

"(2) Effect of election. Any election made under paragraph (1) with respect to any proceeding shall apply to all parties to the proceeding.

"(3) Revocation only with consent. Any election under this subsection may be revoked only with the consent of the Secretary of the Treasury or his delegate.

"(4) Time and manner of election. Any election under this subsection shall be made at such time, and in such manner, as the Secretary of the Treasury or his delegate may by regulations prescribe.

"(g) Definitions.

"For purposes of this section—

"(1) Bankruptcy case. The term 'bankruptcy case' means any case under title 11 of the United States Code (as recodified by P.L. 95-598).

"(2) Similar judicial proceeding. The term 'similar judicial proceeding' means a receivership, foreclosure, or similar proceeding in a Federal or State court (as modified by section 368(a)(3)(D) of the Internal Revenue Code of 1954)."

Prior to amendment, Code Sec. 108 read as follows:

"SEC. 108. INCOME FROM DISCHARGE OF INDEBTEDNESS.

"No amount shall be included in gross income by reason of the discharge, in whole or in part, within the taxable year, of any indebtedness for which the taxpayer is liable, or subject to which the taxpayer holds property, if—

"(1) the indebtedness was incurred or assumed—

"(A) by a corporation, or

"(B) by an individual in connection with property used in his trade or business, and

"(2) such taxpayer makes and files a consent to the regulations prescribed under section 1017 (relating to adjustment of basis) then in effect at such time and in such manner as the Secretary by regulations prescribes. In such case, the amount of any income of such taxpayer attributable to any unamortized premium (computed as of the first day of the taxable year in which such discharge occurred) with respect to such indebtedness shall not be included in gross income, and the amount of the deduction attributable to any unamortized discount (computed as of the first day of the taxable year in which such discharge occurred) with respect to such indebtedness shall not be allowed as a deduction."

In 1976, P.L. 94-455, Sec. 1906(b)(13)(A), substituted "Secretary" for "Secretary or his delegate" in para. (2), for tax. yrs. begin. after '76.

—P.L. 94-455, Sec. 1951(b)(2)(A), deleted subsec. (b) and deleted the heading, "(a) Special rule of exclusion." from subsec. (a), effective for tax. yrs. begin. after 12/31/76 except as provided by Sec. 1951(b)(2)(B) of the Act:

"(B) Savings provision. If any discharge, cancellation, or modification of indebtedness of a railroad corporation occurs in a taxable year beginning after December 31, 1976, pursuant to an order of a court in a proceeding referred to in section 108(b) (A) or (B) which commenced before January 1, 1960, then, notwithstanding the amendments made by subparagraph (A), the provisions of sub-

1,417

section (b) of section 108 shall be considered as not repealed with respect to such discharge, cancellation, or modification of indebtedness."
Prior to deletion subsec. (b) read as follows:
"(b) Railroad corporations.
"No amount shall be included in gross income by reason of the discharge, cancellation, or modification, in whole or in part, within the taxable year, of any indebtedness of a railroad corporation, as defined in section 77(m) of the Bankruptcy Act (11 U. S. C. 205(m)), if such discharge, cancellation, or modification is effected pursuant to an order of a court—
"(A) in a receivership proceeding, or
"(B) in a proceeding under section 77 of the Bankruptcy Act,
commenced before January 1, 1960. In such cases, the amount of any income of the taxpayer attributable to any unamortized premium (computed as of the first day of the taxable year in which such discharge occurred) with respect to such indebtedness shall not be included in gross income, and the amount of the deduction attributable to any unamortized discount (computed as of the first day of the taxable year in which such discharge occurred) with respect to such indebtedness shall not be allowed as a deduction. Subsection (a) of this section shall not apply with respect to any discharge of indebtedness to which this subsection applies."
In 1960, P.L. 86-496, Sec. 1(a), provided in subsec. (b) that if the discharge, cancellation, or modification of any indebtedness is effected pursuant to a court order in a receivership proceeding or in a proceeding under section 77 of the Bankruptcy Act, commenced before '60, then no amount is to be included in gross income with respect to it, and eliminated provisions which made subsection inapplicable to discharges occurring in a taxable year beginning after '57, for tax. yrs. end. after '59, but only with respect to discharges after '59.
In 1956, Act June 29, 1956, ch. 463, Sec. 5, substituted "December 31, 1957" for "December 31, 1955" in subsec. (b).

Sec. 109. Improvements by lessee on lessor's property.

Gross income does not include income (other than rent) derived by a lessor of real property on the termination of a lease, representing the value of such property attributable to buildings erected or other improvements made by the lessee.

Sec. 110. Qualified lessee construction allowances for short-term leases.

(a) In general.

Gross income of a lessee does not include any amount received in cash (or treated as a rent reduction) by a lessee from a lessor—

(1) under a short-term lease of retail space, and
(2) for the purpose of such lessee's constructing or improving qualified long-term real property for use in such lessee's trade or business at such retail space,

but only to the extent that such amount does not exceed the amount expended by the lessee for such construction or improvement.

(b) Consistent treatment by lessor.

Qualified long-term real property constructed or improved in connection with any amount excluded from a lessee's income by reason of subsection (a) shall be treated as nonresidential real property of the lessor (including for purposes of section 168(i)(8)(B)).

(c) Definitions.

For purposes of this section—

(1) Qualified long-term real property. The term "qualified long-term real property" means nonresidential real property which is part of, or otherwise present at, the retail space referred to in subsection (a) and which reverts to the lessor at the termination of the lease.

(2) Short-term lease. The term "short-term lease" means a lease (or other agreement for occupancy or use) of retail space for 15 years or less (as determined under the rules of section 168(i)(3)).

(3) Retail space. The term "retail space" means real property leased, occupied, or otherwise used by a lessee in its trade or business of selling tangible personal property or services to the general public.

(d) Information required to be furnished to Secretary.

Under regulations, the lessee and lessor described in subsection (a) shall, at such times and in such manner as may be provided in such regulations, furnish to the Secretary—

(1) information concerning the amounts received (or treated as a rent reduction) and expended as described in subsection (a), and
(2) any other information which the Secretary deems necessary to carry out the provisions of this section.

In 1997, P.L. 105-34, Sec. 1213(a), added Code Sec. 110, effective for leases entered into after 8/5/97.

Sec. 110. Repealed.

In 1990, P.L. 101-508, Sec. 11801(a)(6), repealed Code Sec. 110, effective 11/5/90 except as provided in Sec. 11821(b) of this Act, which reads as follows:
"(b) Savings provision. If —
"(1) any provision amended or repealed by this part applied to—
"(A) any transaction occurring before the date of the enactment of this Act [11/5/90],
"(B) any property acquired before such date of enactment [11/5/90], or
"(C) any item of income, loss, deduction, or credit taken into account before such date of enactment [11/5/90], and
"(2) the treatment of such transaction, property, or item under provision would (without regard to the amendments made by this part) affect liability for tax for periods ending after such date of enactment [11/5/90],
nothing in the amendments made by this part shall be construed to affect the treatment of such transaction, property, or item for purposes of determining liability for tax for periods ending after such date of enactment [11/5/90]."
Prior to repeal, Code Sec. 110 read as follows:
"SEC. 110. INCOME TAXES PAID BY LESSEE CORPORATION.
"If—
"(1) a lease was entered into before January 1, 1954,
"(2) both lessee and lessor are corporations, and
"(3) under the lease, the lessee is obligated to pay, or to reimburse the lessor for, any part of the tax imposed by this subtitle on the lessor with respect to the rentals derived by the lessor from the lessee, then gross income of the lessor does not include such payment or reimbursement, and no deduction for such payment or reimbursement shall be allowed to the lessee.
For purposes of the preceding sentence, a lease shall be considered to have been entered into before January 1, 1954, if it is a renewal or continuance of a lease entered into before such date and if such renewal or continuance was made in accordance with an option contained in the lease on December 31, 1953."

Sec. 111. Recovery of tax benefit items.

(a) Deductions.

Gross income does not include income attributable to the recovery during the taxable year of any amount deducted in any prior taxable year to the extent such amount did not reduce the amount of tax imposed by this chapter.

(b) Credits.

(1) In general. If—

(A) a credit was allowable with respect to any amount for any prior taxable year, and
(B) during the taxable year there is a downward price adjustment or similar adjustment,

the tax imposed by this chapter for the taxable year shall be increased by the amount of the credit attributable to the adjustment.

(2) Exception where credit did not reduce tax. Paragraph (1) shall not apply to the extent that the credit allowable for the recovered amount did not reduce the amount of tax imposed by this chapter.

(3) Exception for investment tax credit and foreign tax credit. This subsection shall not apply with respect to the credit determined under section 46 and the foreign tax credit.

(c) Treatment of carryovers.

For purposes of this section, an increase in a carryover which has not expired before the beginning of the taxable year in which the recovery or adjustment takes place shall be treated as reducing tax imposed by this chapter.

(d) Special rules for accumulated earnings tax and for personal holding company tax.

In applying subsection (a) for the purpose of determining the accumulated earnings tax under section 531 or the tax

Exclusions from income — Code Sec. 112(c)(5)

under section 541 (relating to personal holding companies)—

(1) any excluded amount under subsection (a) allowed for the purposes of this subtitle (other than section 531 or section 541) shall be allowed whether or not such amount resulted in a reduction of the tax under section 531 or the tax under section 541 for the prior taxable year; and

(2) where any excluded amount under subsection (a) was not allowable as a deduction for the prior taxable year for purposes of this subtitle other than of section 531 or section 541 but was allowable for the same taxable year under section 531 or section 541, then such excluded amount shall be allowable if it did not result in a reduction of the tax under section 531 or the tax under section 541.

In 1986, P.L. 99-514, Sec. 1812(a)(1), substituted "did not reduce the amount of tax imposed by this chapter" for "did not reduce income subject to tax" in subsec. (a)... Sec. 1812(a)(2), substituted "reducing tax imposed by this chapter" for "reducing income subject to tax or reducing tax imposed by this chapter, as the case may be" in subsec. (c), effective for amounts recovered after 12/31/83, in tax. yrs. end. after 12/31/83.

In 1984, P.L. 98-369, Sec. 171(a), amended Code Sec. 111, effective for amounts recovered after 12/31/83, in tax. yrs. end. after 12/31/83.

Prior to amendment, Code Sec. 111 read as follows:

"Sec. 111. Recovery of bad debts, prior taxes, and delinquency amounts.

"(a) General rule.

"Gross income does not include income attributable to the recovery during the taxable year of a bad debt, prior tax, or delinquency amount, to the extent of the amount of the recovery exclusion with respect to such debt, tax, or amount.

"(b) Definitions.

"For purposes of subsection (a)—

"(1) Bad debt. The term 'bad debt' means a debt on account of the worthlessness or partial worthlessness of which a deduction was allowed for a prior taxable year.

"(2) Prior tax. The term 'prior tax' means a tax on account of which a deduction or credit was allowed for a prior taxable year.

"(3) Delinquency amount. The term 'delinquency amount' means an amount paid or accrued on account of which a deduction or credit was allowed for a prior taxable year and which is attributable to failure to file return with respect to a tax, or pay a tax, within the time required by the law under which the tax is imposed, or to failure to file return with respect to a tax or pay a tax.

"(4) Recovery exclusion. The term 'recovery exclusion', with respect to a bad debt, prior tax, or delinquency amount, means the amount, determined in accordance with regulations prescribed by the Secretary, of the deductions or credits allowed, on account of such bad debt, prior tax, or delinquency amount, which did not result in a reduction of the taxpayer's tax under this subtitle (not including the accumulated earnings tax imposed by section 531 or the tax on personal holding companies imposed by section 541) or corresponding provisions of prior income tax laws (other than subchapter E of chapter 2 of the Internal Revenue Code of 1939, relating to World War II excess profits tax), reduced by the amount excludable in previous taxable years with respect to such debt, tax, or amount under this section.

"(c) Special rules for accumulated earnings tax and for personal holding company tax.

"In applying subsections (a) and (b) for the purpose of determining the accumulated earnings tax under section 531 or the tax under section 541 (relating to personal holding companies)—

"(1) a recovery exclusion allowed for purposes of this subtitle (other than section 531 or section 541) shall be allowed whether or not the bad debt, prior tax, or delinquency amount resulted in a reduction of the tax under section 531 or the tax under section 541 for the prior taxable year; and

"(2) where a bad debt, prior tax, or delinquency amount was not allowable as a deduction or credit for the prior taxable year for purposes of this subtitle other than of section 531 or section 541 but was allowable for the same taxable year under section 531 or section 541, then a recovery exclusion shall be allowable if such bad debt, prior tax, or delinquency amount did not result in a reduction of the tax under section 531 or the tax under section 541.

"(d) Increase in carryover treated as yielding tax benefit.

"For purposes of paragraph (4) of subsection (b), an increase in a carryover which has not expired shall be treated as a reduction in tax."

In 1980, P.L. 96-589, Sec. 2(c), added subsec. (d), effective for any transaction which occurs after 12/31/80, other than a transaction which occurs in a proceeding in a bankruptcy case or similar judicial proceeding (or in a proceeding under the Bankruptcy Act) commencing on or before 12/31/80. Sec. 7(f) and (g) of this Act provides:

"(f) Election to substitute September 30, 1979, for December 31, 1980.

"(1) In general. The debtor (or debtors) in a bankruptcy case or similar judicial proceeding may (with the approval of the court) elect to apply [subsection 7(a) of this Act by substituting 'September 30, 1979' for 'December 31, 1980' each place it appears in such subsections.

"(2) Effect of election. Any election made under paragraph (1) with respect to any proceeding shall apply to all parties to the proceeding.

"(3) Revocation only with consent. Any election under this subsection may be revoked only with the consent of the Secretary of the Treasury or his delegate.

"(4) Time and manner of election. Any election under this subsection shall be made at such time, and in such manner, as the Secretary of the Treasury or his delegate may by regulations prescribe.

"(g) Definitions.

"For purposes of this section—

"(1) Bankruptcy case. The term 'bankruptcy case' means any case under title 11 of the United States Code (as recodified by P.L. 95-598).

"(2) Similar judicial proceeding. The term 'similar judicial proceeding' means a receivership, foreclosure, or similar proceeding in a Federal or State court (as modified by section 368(a)(3)(D) of the Internal Revenue Code of 1954)."

In 1976, P.L. 94-455, Sec. 1906(b)(13)(A), substituted "Secretary" for "Secretary or his delegate" in para. (b)(4), effective for tax. yrs. begin. after 12/31/76.

Sec. 112. Certain combat zone compensation of members of the Armed Forces.

(a) Enlisted personnel.

Gross income does not include compensation received for active service as a member below the grade of commissioned officer in the Armed Forces of the United States for any month during any part of which such member—

(1) served in a combat zone, or

(2) was hospitalized as a result of wounds, disease, or injury incurred while serving in a combat zone; but this paragraph shall not apply for any month beginning more than 2 years after the date of the termination of combatant activities in such zone.

With respect to service in the combat zone designated for purposes of the Vietnam conflict, paragraph (2) shall not apply to any month after January 1978.

(b) Commissioned officers.

Gross income does not include so much of the compensation as does not exceed the maximum enlisted amount received for active service as a commissioned officer in the Armed Forces of the United States for any month during any part of which such officer—

(1) served in a combat zone, or

(2) was hospitalized as a result of wounds, disease, or injury incurred while serving in a combat zone; but this paragraph shall not apply for any month beginning more than 2 years after the date of the termination of combatant activities in such zone.

With respect to service in the combat zone designated for purposes of the Vietnam conflict, paragraph (2) shall not apply to any month after January 1978.

(c) Definitions.

For purposes of this section—

(1) The term "commissioned officer" does not include a commissioned warrant officer.

(2) The term "combat zone" means any area which the President of the United States by Executive Order designates, for purposes of this section or corresponding provisions of prior income tax laws, as an area in which Armed Forces of the United States are or have (after June 24, 1950) engaged in combat.

(3) Service is performed in a combat zone only if performed on or after the date designated by the President by Executive Order as the date of the commencing of combatant activities in such zone, and on or before the date designated by the President by Executive Order as the date of the termination of combatant activities in such zone; except that June 25, 1950, shall be considered the date of the commencing of combatant activities in the combat zone designated in Executive order 10195.

(4) The term "compensation" does not include pensions and retirement pay.

(5) The term "maximum enlisted amount" means, for any month, the sum of—

(A) the highest rate of basic pay payable for such month to any enlisted member of the Armed Forces of the United States at the highest pay grade applicable to enlisted members, and

(B) in the case of an officer entitled to special pay under section 310 of title 37, United States Code, for such month, the amount of such special pay payable to such officer for such month.

(d) Prisoners of war, etc.

(1) Members of the armed forces. Gross income does not include compensation received for active service as a member of the Armed Forces of the United States for any month during any part of which such member is in a missing status (as defined in section 551(2) of title 37, United States Code) during the Vietnam conflict as a result of such conflict, other than a period with respect to which it is officially determined under section 552(c) of such title 37 that he is officially absent from his post of duty without authority.

(2) Civilian employees. Gross income does not include compensation received for active service as an employee for any month during any part of which such employee is in a missing status during the Vietnam conflict as a result of such conflict. For purposes of this paragraph, the terms "active service," "employee," and "missing status" have the respective meanings given to such terms by section 5561 of title 5 of the United States Code.

(3) Period of conflict. For purposes of this subsection, the Vietnam conflict began February 28, 1961, and ends on the date designated by the President by Executive order as the date of the termination of combatant activities in Vietnam. For purposes of this subsection, an individual is in a missing status as a result of the Vietnam conflict if immediately before such status began he was performing service in Vietnam or was performing service in Southeast Asia in direct support of military operations in Vietnam.

In **1996**, P.L. 104-188, Sec. 1704(t)(4)(A), substituted "combat zone compensation" for "combat pay" in the heading of Code Sec. 112, effective 8/20/96.

— P.L. 104-117, Sec. 1(a)(2) and (b), of this Act, regarding treatment of certain individuals performing services in certain hazardous duty areas, effective 11/21/95, provides:

"(a) General rule. For purposes of the following provisions of the Internal Revenue Code of 1986, a qualified hazardous duty area shall be treated in the same manner as if it were a combat zone (as determined under section 112 of such Code):

* * *

"(2) Section 112 (relating to the exclusion of certain combat pay of members of the Armed Forces).

* * *

"(b) Qualified hazardous duty area. For purposes of this section, the term 'qualified hazardous duty area' means Bosnia and Herzegovina, Croatia, or Macedonia, if as of the date of the enactment [3/20/96] of this section any member of the Armed Forces of the United States is entitled to special pay under section 310 of title 37, United States Code (relating to special pay; duty subject to hostile fire or imminent danger) for services performed in such country. Such term includes any such country only during the period such entitlement is in effect. Solely for purposes of applying section 7508 of the Internal Revenue Code of 1986, in the case of an individual who is performing services as part of Operation Joint Endeavor outside the United States while deployed away from such individual's permanent duty station, the term 'qualified hazardous duty area' includes, during the period for which such entitlement is in effect, any area in which such services are performed."

— P.L. 104-117, Sec. 1(d)(1), substituted "the maximum enlisted amount" for "$500" in subsec. (b). . . Sec. 1(d)(2), added para. (c)(5), effective 11/21/95.

In **1976**, P.L. 94-569, Sec. 3(b), substituted "after January 1978" for "beginning more than 2 years after the date of the enactment of this sentence" in the last sentence of subsecs. (a) and (b), effective 10/20/76.

In **1975**, P.L. 93-597, Sec. 2(a), deleted "during an induction period" in paras. (a)(1) and (b)(1); substituted ", but this paragraph shall not apply for any month beginning more than 2 years after the date of the termination of combatant activities in such zone" for "during an induction period; but this paragraph shall not apply for any month during any part of which there are no combatant activities in any combat zone as determined under subsection (c)(3) of this section" in paras. (a)(2) and (b)(2); added the final sentence in subsecs. (a) and (b), effective 7/1/73.

— P.L. 93-597, Sec. 2(b), deleted para. (c)(5), effective 7/1/73.
Prior to deletion, para. (c)(5) read as follows:
"(5) The term 'induction period' means any period during which, under laws heretofore or hereafter enacted relating to the induction of individuals for training and service in the Armed Forces of the United States, individuals (other than individuals liable for induction by reason of a prior deferment) are liable for induction for such training and service."

In **1972**, P.L. 92-279, Sec. 1, added subsec. (d), effective for tax. yrs. end. on or after 2/28/61. Sec. 3(a)(2) and (3), of this Act, provides as follows:

"(2) If refund or credit of any overpayment for any taxable year resulting from the application of the amendment made by the first section of this Act (including interest, additions to the tax, and additional amounts) is prevented at any time before the expiration of the applicable period specified in paragraph (3) by the operation of any law or rule of law, such refund or credit of such overpayment may, nevertheless, be made or allowed if claim therefor is filed before the expiration of such applicable period.

"(3) For purposes of paragraph (2), the applicable period for any individual with respect to any compensation is the period ending on whichever of the following days is the later:

"(A) the day which is one year after the date of the enactment of this Act, or

"(B) the day which is 2 years after the date on which it is determined that the individual's missing status (within the meaning of section 112(d) of the Internal Revenue Code of 1954) has terminated for purposes of such section 112."

In **1966**, P.L. 89-739, Sec. [1](b), substituted "$500" for "$200" in subsec. (b), effective for compensation received in tax. yrs. end. after 12/31/65, for periods of active service after such date.

Sec. 113. Repealed.

In **1990**, P.L. 101-508, Sec. 11801(a)(7), repealed Code Sec. 113, effective 11/5/90 except as provided in Sec. 11821(b) of this Act, reproduced in note following Code Sec. 110.

Prior to repeal, Code Sec. 113 read as follows:

"Sec. 113. Mustering-out payments for members of the Armed Forces.

"Gross income does not include amounts received during the taxable year as mustering-out payments with respect to service in the Armed Forces of the United States."

Sec. 114. Repealed.

In **2006**, P.L. 109-222, Sec. 513(a), amended Sec. 5(c)(1) of P.L. 106-519 [see below] . . . Sec. 513(b), repealed Sec. 101(f) of P.L. 108-357 [see below], effective for tax. yrs. begin. after 5/17/2006.

Prior to amendment, Sec. 5(c)(1) of P.L. 106-519 read as follows:

"(1) In general. In the case of a FSC (as so defined) in existence on September 30, 2000, and at all times thereafter, the amendments made by this Act shall not apply to any transaction in the ordinary course of trade or business involving a FSC which occurs—

"(A) before January 1, 2002; or

"(B) after December 31, 2001, pursuant to a binding contract—

"(i) which is between the FSC (or any related person) and any person which is not a related person; and

"(ii) which is in effect on September 30, 2000, and at all times thereafter.

For purposes of this paragraph, a binding contract shall include a purchase option, renewal option, or replacement option which is included in such contract and which is enforceable against the seller or lessor."

Prior to repeal, Sec. 101(f) of P.L. 108-357 read as follows:

"(f) Binding contracts. The amendments made by this section shall not apply to any transaction in the ordinary course of a trade or business which occurs pursuant to a binding contract—

"(1) which is between the taxpayer and a person who is not a related person (as defined in section 943(b)(3) of such Code, as in effect on the day before the date of the enactment of this Act), and

"(2) which is in effect on September 17, 2003, and at all times thereafter.

"For purposes of this subsection, a binding contract shall include a purchase option, renewal option, or replacement option which is included in such contract and which is enforceable against the seller or lessor."

In **2004**, P.L. 108-357, Sec. 101(a), repealed Code Sec. 114, effective for transactions after 12/31/2004. Sec. 101(d)-(f) [subsec. (f) was repealed by Sec. 513(b) of P.L. 109-222, see above] of this Act, reads as follows:

"(d) Transitional rule for 2005 and 2006.

"(1) In general. In the case of transactions during 2005 or 2006, the amount includible in gross income by reason of the amendments made by this section shall not exceed the applicable percentage of the amount which would have been so included but for this subsection.

"(2) Applicable percentage. For purposes of paragraph (1), the applicable percentage shall be as follows:

"(A) For 2005, the applicable percentage shall be 20 percent.

"(B) For 2006, the applicable percentage shall be 40 percent.

"(e) Revocation of election to be treated as domestic corporation. If, during the 1-year period beginning on the date of the enactment of this Act, a corporation for which an election is in effect under section 943(e) of the Internal Revenue Code of 1986 revokes such election, no gain or loss shall be recognized with respect to property treated as transferred under clause (ii) of section 943(e)(4)(B) of such Code to the extent such property—

"(1) was treated as transferred under clause (i) thereof, or

Exclusions from income   Code Sec. 115

"(2) was acquired during a taxable year to which such election applies and before May 1, 2003, in the ordinary course of its trade or business.

The Secretary of the Treasury (or such Secretary's delegate) may prescribe such regulations as may be necessary to prevent the abuse of the purposes of this subsection.

"(f) [Repealed by Sec. 513(b) of P.L. 109-222, see above]

Prior to repeal, Code Sec. 114 read as follows:

"SEC. 114. EXTRATERRITORIAL INCOME.

"(a) *Exclusion.* Gross income does not include extraterritorial income.

"(b) *Exception.* Subsection (a) shall not apply to extraterritorial income which is not qualifying foreign trade income as determined under subpart E of part III of subchapter N.

"(c) *Disallowance of deductions.*

"(1) In general. Any deduction of a taxpayer allocated under paragraph (2) to extraterritorial income of the taxpayer excluded from gross income under subsection (a) shall not be allowed.

"(2) Allocation. Any deduction of the taxpayer properly apportioned and allocated to the extraterritorial income derived by the taxpayer from any transaction shall be allocated on a proportionate basis between—

"(A) the extraterritorial income derived from such transaction which is excluded from gross income under subsection (a), and

"(B) the extraterritorial income derived from such transaction which is not so excluded.

"(d) *Denial of credits for certain foreign taxes.* Notwithstanding any other provision of this chapter, no credit shall be allowed under this chapter for any income, war profits, and excess profits taxes paid or accrued to any foreign country or possession of the United States with respect to extraterritorial income which is excluded from gross income under subsection (a).

"(e) *Extraterritorial income.* For purposes of this section, the term 'extraterritorial income' means the gross income of the taxpayer attributable to foreign trading gross receipts (as defined in section 942) of the taxpayer."

In 2000, P.L. 106-519, Sec. 3(a), added Code Sec. 114, effective for transactions after 9/30/2000. Sec. 5(b)–(d) [para. (c)(1) as amended by Sec. 513(a) of P.L. 109-222, see above] of this Act, provides:

"(b) No new FSCs; termination of inactive FSCs —

"(1) No new FSCs. No corporation may elect after September 30, 2000, to be a FSC (as defined in section 922 of the Internal Revenue Code of 1986, as in effect before the amendments made by this Act).

"(2) Termination of inactive FSCs. If a FSC has no foreign trade income (as defined in section 923(b) of such Code, as so in effect) for any period of 5 consecutive taxable years beginning after December 31, 2001, such FSC shall cease to be treated as a FSC for purposes of such Code for any taxable year beginning after such period.

"(c) Transition period for existing Foreign Sales Corporations.

"(1) In general. In the case of a FSC (as so defined) in existence on September 30, 2000, and at all times thereafter, the amendments made by this Act shall not apply to any transaction in the ordinary course of trade or business involving a FSC which occurs before January 1, 2002.

"(2) Election to have amendments apply earlier. A taxpayer may elect to have the amendments made by this Act apply to any transaction by a FSC or any related person to which such amendments would apply but for the application of paragraph (1). Such election shall be effective for the taxable year for which made and all subsequent taxable years, and, once made, may be revoked only with the consent of the Secretary of the Treasury.

"(3) Exception for old earnings and profits of certain corporations.

"(A) In general. In the case of a foreign corporation to which this paragraph applies —

"(i) earnings and profits of such corporation accumulated in taxable years ending before October 1, 2000, shall not be included in the gross income of the persons holding stock in such corporation by reason of section 943(e)(4)(B)(i), and

"(ii) rules similar to the rules of clauses (ii), (iii), and (iv) of section 953(d)(4)(B) shall apply with respect to such earnings and profits.

The preceding sentence shall not apply to earnings and profits acquired in a transaction after September 30, 2000, to which section 381 applies unless the distributor or transferor corporation was immediately before the transaction a foreign corporation to which this paragraph applies.

"(B) Existing FSCs. This paragraph shall apply to any controlled foreign corporation (as defined in section 957) if —

"(i) such corporation is a FSC (as so defined) in existence on September 30, 2000,

"(ii) such corporation is eligible to make the election under section 943(e) by reason of being described in paragraph (2)(B) of such section, and

"(iii) such corporation makes such election not later than for its first taxable year beginning after December 31, 2001.

"(C) Other corporations. This paragraph shall apply to any controlled foreign corporation (as defined in section 957), and such corporation shall (notwithstanding any provision of section 943(e)) be treated as an applicable foreign corporation for purposes of section 943(e), if —

"(i) such corporation is in existence on September 30, 2000;

"(ii) as of such date, such corporation is wholly owned (directly or indirectly) by a domestic corporation (determined without regard to any election under section 943(e));

"(iii) for each of the 3 taxable years preceding the first taxable year to which the election under section 943(e) by such controlled foreign corporation applies —

"(I) all of the gross income of such corporation is subpart F income (as defined in section 952), including by reason of section 954(b)(3)(B); and

"(II) in the ordinary course of such corporation's trade or business, such corporation regularly sold (or paid commissions) to a FSC which on September 30, 2000, was a related person to such corporation;

"(iv) such corporation has never made an election under section 922(a)(2) (as in effect before the date of the enactment of this paragraph) to be treated as a FSC; and

"(v) such corporation makes the election under section 943(e) not later than for its first taxable year beginning after December 31, 2001.

The preceding sentence shall cease to apply as of the date that the domestic corporation referred to in clause (ii) ceases to wholly own (directly or indirectly) such controlled foreign corporation.

"(4) Related person. For purposes of this subsection, the term 'related person' has the meaning given to such term by section 943(b)(3).

"(5) Section references. Except as otherwise expressly provided, any reference in this subsection to a section or other provision shall be considered to be a reference to a section or other provision of the Internal Revenue Code of 1986, as amended by this Act.

"(d) Special rules relating to leasing transactions.

"(1) Sales income. If foreign trade income in connection with the lease or rental of property described in section 927(a)(1)(B) of such Code (as in effect before the amendments made by this Act) is treated as exempt foreign trade income for purposes of section 921(a) of such Code (as so in effect), such property shall be treated as property described in section 941(c)(1)(B) of such Code (as added by this Act) for purposes of applying section 941(c)(2) of such Code (as so added) to any subsequent transaction involving such property to which the amendments made by this Act apply.

"(2) Limitation on use of gross receipts method. If any person computed its foreign trade income from any transaction with respect to any property on the basis of a transfer price determined under the method described in section 925(a)(1) of such Code (as in effect before the amendments made by this Act), then the qualifying foreign trade income (as defined in section 941(a) of such Code, as in effect after such amendment) of such person (or any related person) with respect to any other transaction involving such property (and to which the amendments made by this Act apply) shall be zero."

Sec. 114.   Repealed.

In 1990, P.L. 101-508, Sec. 11801(a)(8), repealed Code Sec. 114, effective 11/5/90, except as provided in Sec. 11821(b) of this Act reproduced in note following Code Sec. 110.

Prior to repeal, Code Sec. 114 read as follows:

"SEC. 114. SPORTS PROGRAMS CONDUCTED FOR THE AMERICAN NATIONAL RED CROSS.

"(a) General rule.

"In the case of a taxpayer which is a corporation primarily engaged in the furnishing of sports programs, gross income does not include amounts received as proceeds from a sports program conducted by the taxpayer if —

"(1) the taxpayer agrees in writing with the American National Red Cross to conduct such sports program exclusively for the benefit of the American National Red Cross;

"(2) the taxpayer turns over to the American National Red Cross the proceeds from such sports program, minus the expenses paid or incurred by the taxpayer —

"(A) which would not have been so paid or incurred but for such sports program, and

"(B) which would be allowable as a deduction under section 162 (relating to trade or business expenses) but for subsection (b) of this section; and

"(3) the facilities used for such program are not regularly used during the taxable year for the conduct of sports programs to which this subsection applies.

For purposes of this subsection, the term 'proceeds from such sports program' includes all amounts paid for admission to the sports program, plus all proceeds received by the taxpayer from such program or activities carried on in connection therewith.

"(b) Treatment of expenses.

"Expenses described in subsection (a)(2) shall be allowed as a deduction under section 162 only to the extent that such expenses exceed the amount excluded from gross income by subsection (a) of this section."

Sec. 115.   Income of states, municipalities, etc.

Gross income does not include —

(1) income derived from any public utility or the exercise of any essential governmental function and accruing to a State or any political subdivision thereof, or the District of Columbia; or

(2) income accruing to the government of any possession of the United States, or any political subdivision thereof.

In 1976, P.L. 94-455, Sec. 1901(a)(19), amended Code Sec. 115, effective for tax. yrs. begin. after 12/31/76.

Prior to amendment Code Sec. 115 read as follows:

"SEC. 115. INCOME OF STATES, MUNICIPALITIES, ETC.

"(a) General rule.

"Gross income does not include —

1,421

Code Sec. 115

"(1) income derived from any public utility or the exercise of any essential governmental function and accruing to a State or Territory, or any political subdivision thereof, or the District of Columbia; or

"(2) income accruing to the government of any possession of the United States or any political subdivision thereof.

"(b) *Contracts made before September 8, 1916, relating to public utilities.*

"Where a State or Territory, or any political subdivision thereof, or the District of Columbia, before September 8, 1916, entered in good faith into a contract with any person, the object and purpose of which was to acquire, construct, operate, or maintain a public utility—

"(1) If—

"(A) by the terms of such contract the tax imposed by this subtitle is to be paid out of the proceeds from the operation of such public utility before any division of such proceeds between the person and the State, Territory, political subdivision, or the District of Columbia, and

"(B) a part of such proceeds for the taxable year would (but for the imposition of the tax imposed by this subtitle) accrue directly to or for the use of such State, Territory, political subdivision, or the District of Columbia, then a tax on the taxable income from the operation of such public utility shall be levied, assessed, collected, and paid in the manner and at the rates prescribed in this subtitle, but there shall be refunded to such State, Territory, political subdivision, or the District of Columbia (under regulations prescribed by the Secretary or his delegate) an amount which bears the same relation to the amount of the tax as the amount which (but for the imposition of the tax imposed by this subtitle) would have accrued directly to or for the use of such State, Territory, political subdivision, or the District of Columbia, bears to the amount of the taxable income from the operation of such public utility for such taxable year.

"(2) If by the terms of such contract no part of the proceeds from the operation of the public utility for the taxable year would, irrespective of the tax imposed by this subtitle, accrue directly to or for the use of such State, Territory, political subdivision, or the District of Columbia, then the tax on the taxable income of such person from the operation of such public utility shall be levied, assessed, collected, and paid in the manner and at the rates prescribed in this subtitle.

"(c) *Contracts made before May 29, 1928, relating to bridge acquisitions.*

"Where a State or political subdivision thereof, pursuant to a contract entered into before May 29, 1928, to which it is not a party, is to acquire a bridge—

"(1) If—

"(A) by the terms of such contract the tax imposed by this subtitle is to be paid out of the proceeds from the operation of such bridge before any division of such proceeds, and

"(B) a part of such proceeds for the taxable year would (but for the imposition of the tax imposed by this subtitle) accrue directly to or for the use of or would be applied for the benefit of such State or political subdivision,

then a tax on the taxable income from the operation of such bridge shall be levied, assessed, collected, and paid in the manner and at the rates prescribed in this subtitle, but there shall be refunded to such State or political subdivision (under regulations to be prescribed by the Secretary or his delegate) an amount which bears the same relation to the amount of the tax as the amount which (but for the imposition of the tax imposed by this subtitle) would have accrued directly to or for the use of or would be applied for the benefit of such State or political subdivision bears to the amount of the taxable income from the operation of such bridge for such taxable year. No such refund shall be made unless the entire amount of the refund is to be applied in part payment for the acquisition of such bridge.

"(2) If by the terms of such contract no part of the proceeds from the operation of the bridge for the taxable year would, irrespective of the tax imposed by this subtitle, accrue directly to or for the use of or be applied for the benefit of such State or political subdivision, then the tax on the taxable income from the operation of such bridge shall be levied, assessed, collected, and paid in the manner and at the rates prescribed in this subtitle."

Sec. 116. Repealed.

In 1986, P.L. 99-514, Sec. 612(a), repealed Code Sec. 116, effective for tax. yrs. begin. after 12/31/86.
Prior to repeal, Code Sec. 116 read as follows:
"SEC. 116. PARTIAL EXCLUSION OF DIVIDENDS RECEIVED BY INDIVIDUALS.
"(a) *Exclusion from gross income.*

"(1) In general. Gross income does not include amounts received by an individual as dividends from domestic corporations.

"(2) Maximum dollar amount. The aggregate amount excluded under subsection (a) for any taxable year shall not exceed $100 ($200 in the case of a joint return under section 6013).

"(b) *Certain dividends excluded.*

"Subsection (a) shall not apply to any dividend from—

"(1) a corporation which, for the taxable year of the corporation in which the distribution is made, or for the next preceding taxable year of the corporation, is a corporation exempt from tax under section 501 (relating to certain charitable, etc., organizations) or section 521 (relating to farmers' cooperative associations); or

"(2) a real estate investment trust which, for the taxable year of the trust in which the dividend is paid, qualifies under part II of subchapter M (sec. 856 and following).

"(c) *Special rules for certain distributions.*

"For purposes of subsection (a)—

"(1) Any amount allowed as a deduction under section 591 (relating to deduction for dividends paid by mutual savings banks, etc.) shall not be treated as a dividend.

Exclusions from income

"(2) A dividend received from a regulated investment company shall be subject to the limitations prescribed in section 854.

"(3) The amount of dividends properly allocable to a beneficiary under section 652 or 662 shall be deemed to have been received by the beneficiary ratably on the same date that the dividends were received by the estate or trust.

"(d) *Certain nonresident aliens ineligible for exclusion.*

"In the case of a nonresident alien individual, subsection (a) shall apply only—

"(1) in determining the tax imposed for the taxable year pursuant to section 871(b)(1) and only in respect of dividends which are effectively connected with the conduct of a trade or business within the United States, or

"(2) in determining the tax imposed for the taxable year pursuant to section 877(b).

"(e) *Dividends from employee stock ownership plans.*

"Subsection (a) shall not apply to any dividend described in section 404(k)."

In 1984, P.L. 98-369, Sec. 542(b), added subsec. (e), effective for tax. yrs. begin. after 7/18/84.

In 1981, P.L. 97-34, Sec. 302(b)(1), amended the effective date for changes made by Sec. 404(a) of P.L. 96-223 from tax. yrs. begin. after 12/31/80 and before 1/1/83 to tax. yrs. begin. after 12/31/80 and before 1/1/82 [see below].

—P.L. 97-34, Sec. 302(b)(2), amended subsec. (a), effective for tax. yrs. begin. after 12/31/81.

Prior to amendment, subsec. (a) read as follows:
"(a) *Exclusion from gross income.*

"Gross income does not include amounts received by an individual as dividends from domestic corporations, to the extent that the dividends do not exceed $100. If the dividends received in a taxable year exceed $100, the exclusion provided by the preceding sentence shall apply to the dividends first received in such year."

In 1980, P.L. 96-223, Sec. 404(a), amended Code Sec. 116, effective [as amended by Sec. 302(b)(1) of P.L. 97-34, see above] for tax. yrs. begin. after 12/31/80, and before 1/1/82.

Prior to amendment Code Sec. 116 read as follows:
"SEC. 116. PARTIAL EXCLUSION OF DIVIDENDS AND INTEREST RECEIVED BY INDIVIDUALS.
"(a) *Exclusion from gross income.*

Gross income does not include the sum of the amounts received during the taxable year by an individual as

"(1) a dividend from a domestic corporation, or

"(2) interest.

"(b) *Limitations.*

"(1) Maximum dollar amount. The aggregate amount excluded under subsection (a) for any taxable year shall not exceed $200 ($400 in the case of a joint return under section 6013).

"(2) Certain dividends excluded. Subsection (a)(1) shall not apply to any dividend from a corporation which, for the taxable year of the corporation in which the distribution is made, or for the next preceding taxable year of the corporation, is a corporation exempt from tax under section 501 (relating to certain charitable, etc., organizations) or section 521 (relating to farmers' cooperative associations).

"(c) *Definitions; special rules.*

"For purposes of this section

"(1) Interest defined. The term 'interest' means

"(A) interest on deposits with a bank (as defined in section 581),

"(B) amounts (whether or not designated as interest) paid, in respect of deposits, investment certificates, or withdrawable or repurchasable shares, by

"(i) a mutual savings bank, cooperative bank, domestic building and loan association, industrial loan association or bank, or credit union, or

"(ii) any other savings or thrift institution which is chartered and supervised under Federal or State law,

the deposits or accounts in which are insured under Federal or State law or which are protected and guaranteed under State law,

"(C) interest on

"(i) evidences of indebtedness (including bonds, debentures, notes, and certificates) issued by a domestic corporation in registered form, and

"(ii) to the extent provided in regulations prescribed in by the Secretary, other evidences of indebtedness issued by a domestic corporation of a type offered by corporations to the public,

"(D) interest on obligations of the United States, a State, or a political subdivision of a State (not excluded from gross income of the taxpayer under any other provision of law), and

"(E) interest attributable to participation shares in a trust established and maintained by a corporation established pursuant to Federal law.

"(2) Distributions from regulated investment companies and real estate investment trusts. Subsection (a) shall apply with respect to any dividend from

"(A) a regulated investment company, subject to the limitations provided in section 854(b)(2), or

"(B) real estate investment trust, subject to the limitations provided in section 857(c).

"(3) Certain nonresident aliens ineligible for exclusion. In the case of a nonresident alien individual, subsection (a) shall apply only

"(A) in determining the tax imposed for the taxable year pursuant to section 871(b)(1) and only in respect of dividends and interest which are effectively connected with the conduct of a trade or business within the United States, or

"(B) in determining the tax imposed for the taxable year pursuant to section 877(b)."

In 1976, P.L. 94-455, Sec. 1051(h)(2), amended para. (b)(2), effective for tax. yrs. begin. after 12/31/75, except that "'qualified possession source investment income' as defined in section 936(d)(2) of the Internal Revenue Code of 1954 shall include income from any source outside the United States as the taxpayer estab-

Exclusions from income — Code Sec. 117

lishes to the satisfaction of the Secretary of the Treasury or his delegate that the income from such sources was earned before October 1, 1976."
Prior to amendment para. (b)(2) read as follows:
"(2) a corporation which, for the taxable year of the corporation in which the distribution is made, or for the next preceding taxable year of the corporation, is—
"(A) a corporation exempt from tax under section 501 (relating to certain charitable, etc., organizations) or section 521 (relating to farmers' cooperative associations); or
"(B) a corporation to which section 931 (relating to income from sources within possessions of the United States) applies; or"
—P.L. 94-455, Sec. 1053(d)(1), deleted para. (b)(1) and redesignated paras. (b)(2) and (b)(3) as (b)(1) and (b)(2), effective for tax. yrs. begin. after 12/31/77.
Prior to amendment para. (b)(1) read as follows:
"(1) a corporation organized under the China Trade Act, 1922 (see sec. 941);"
—P.L. 94-455, Sec. 1901(a)(20), substituted "Gross income" for "Effective with respect to any taxable year ending after July 31, 1954, gross income", effective for tax. yrs. begin. after 12/31/76.
In 1966, P.L. 89-809, Sec. 103, amend. subsec. (d), effective for tax. yrs. begin. after 12/31/66.
Prior to amendment, subsec. (d) read as follows:
"(d) Certain nonresident aliens ineligible for exclusion. Subsection (a) does not apply to a nonresident alien individual with respect to whom a tax is imposed for the taxable year under section 871(a)."
In 1964, P.L. 88-272, Sec. 201(c), substituted "$100" for "$50" each place it appeared in subsec. (a), effective for tax. yrs. begin. after 12/31/63.... Sec. 201(d)(6)(C), added subsec. (c)(3), effective for dividends received after 12/31/64 in tax. yrs. end. after 12/31/64.
In 1960, P.L. 86-779, Sec. 10(f), added para. (b)(3), effective for tax. yrs. of real estate invest. trust begin. after 12/31/60.
In 1959, P.L. 86-69, Sec. 3(a)(2), deleted para. (b)(1) and redesignated paras. (b)(2) and (3) as paras. (b)(1) and (2), effective for dividends received after 12/31/58, in tax. yrs. end. after 12/31/58.
Prior to deletion, para. (b)(1) read as follows:
"(1) an insurance company subject to a tax imposed by part I or II of subchapter L (sec. 801 and following);"

Sec. 117. Qualified scholarships.

(a) General rule.
Gross income does not include any amount received as a qualified scholarship by an individual who is a candidate for a degree at an educational organization described in section 170(b)(1)(A)(ii).

(b) Qualified scholarship.
For purposes of this section—
(1) In general. The term "qualified scholarship" means any amount received by an individual as a scholarship or fellowship grant to the extent the individual establishes that, in accordance with the conditions of the grant, such amount was used for qualified tuition and related expenses.
(2) Qualified tuition and related expenses. For purposes of paragraph (1), the term "qualified tuition and related expenses" means—
(A) tuition and fees required for the enrollment or attendance of a student at an educational organization described in section 170(b)(1)(A)(ii), and
(B) fees, books, supplies, and equipment required for courses of instruction at such an educational organization.

> • *Caution:* Code Sec. 117(c), following, was amended by P.L. 107-16, EGTRRA. These provisions generally sunset for tax years beginning after 12/31/2012. For specific sunset provisions, see Sec. 901, P.L. 107-16 (as amended) reproduced in history notes for this Code Sec.

(c) Limitation.
(1) In general. Except as provided in paragraph (2), subsections (a) and (d) shall not apply to that portion of any amount received which represents payment for teaching, research, or other services by the student required as a condition for receiving the qualified scholarship or qualified tuition reduction.

(2) Exceptions. Paragraph (1) shall not apply to any amount received by an individual under—
(A) the National Health Service Corps Scholarship Program under section 338A(g)(1)(A) of the Public Health Service Act, or
(B) the Armed Forces Health Professions Scholarship and Financial Assistance program under subchapter I of chapter 105 of title 10, United States Code.

(d) Qualified tuition reduction.
(1) In general. Gross income shall not include any qualified tuition reduction.
(2) Qualified tuition reduction. For purposes of this subsection, the term "qualified tuition reduction" means the amount of any reduction in tuition provided to an employee of an organization described in section 170(b)(1)(A)(ii) for the education (below the graduate level) at such organization (or another organization described in section 170(b)(1)(A)(ii)) of—
(A) such employee, or
(B) any person treated as an employee (or whose use is treated as an employee use) under the rules of section 132(h).
(3) Reduction must not discriminate in favor of highly compensated, etc. Paragraph (1) shall apply with respect to any qualified tuition reduction provided with respect to any highly compensated employee only if such reduction is available on substantially the same terms to each member of a group of employees which is defined under a reasonable classification set up by the employer which does not discriminate in favor of highly compensated employees (within the meaning of section 414(q)). For purposes of this paragraph, the term "highly compensated employee" has the meaning given such term by section 414(q).
(5) [sic (4)] Special rules for teaching and research assistants. In the case of the education of an individual who is a graduate student at an educational organization described in section 170(b)(1)(A)(ii) and who is engaged in teaching or research activities for such organization, paragraph (2) shall be applied as if it did not contain the phrase "(below the graduate level)".

In 2010, P.L. 111-312, Sec. 101(a)(1), substituted "December 31, 2012" for "December 31, 2010" both places it appeared in Sec. 901, P.L. 107-16 [see below], effective as if included in the enactment of P.L. 107-16, EGTRRA, 6/7/2001.
In 2002, P.L. 107-358, Sec. 2, added subsec. (c) in Sec. 901 of P.L. 107-16 [see below], effective 12/17/2002.
In 2001, P.L. 107-16, Sec. 413(a)(1), substituted "(1) In general. Except as provided in paragraph (2), subsections (a)" for "Subsections (a)" in subsec. (c)... Sec. 413(a)(2), added para. (c)(2), effective for amounts received in tax. yrs. begin. after 12/31/2001.
—P.L. 107-16, Sec. 901, of this Act [as amended by Sec. 2, P.L. 107-358, and Sec. 101(a)(1), P.L. 111-312, see above], reads as follows:
"SEC. 901. SUNSET OF PROVISIONS OF ACT.
"(a) In general. All provisions of, and amendments made by, this Act shall not apply—
"(1) to taxable, plan, or limitation years beginning after December 31, 2012, or
"(2) in the case of title V, to estates of decedents dying, gifts made, or generation skipping transfers, after December 31, 2012.
"(b) Application of certain laws. The Internal Revenue Code of 1986 and the Employee Retirement Income Security Act of 1974 shall be applied and administered to years, estates, gifts, and transfers described in subsection (a) as if the provisions and amendments described in subsection (a) had never been enacted.
"(c) Exception. Subsection (a) shall not apply to section 803 (relating to no federal income tax on restitution received by victims of the Nazi regime or their heirs or estates)."
In 1996, P.L. 104-188, Sec. 1703(n)(14), substituted "section 132(h)" for "section 132(f)" in subpara. (d)(2)(B), effective for reimbursements or other payments in respect of expenses incurred after 12/31/93.
In 1989, P.L. 101-140, Sec. 203(a)(1), repealed as if not enacted Sec. 1151(g)(2) of P.L. 99-514, which added para. (d)(4).
—P.L. 101-140, Sec. 203(a)(2), repealed as if not enacted Sec. 1011B(a)(31)(B), which amended para. (d)(4).
In 1988, P.L. 100-647, Sec. 1012(aa)(3)(J) and (4), provides:

"(3) Certain amendments not to apply to the extent inconsistent with treaties. The following amendments made by the Reform Act shall not apply to the extent the application of such amendments would be contrary to any treaty obligation of the United States in effect on the date of the enactment of the Reform Act:

"(J) The amendments made by section 123 of the Reform Act.

"(4) Treatment of technical corrections. For purposes of paragraphs (2) and (3), any amendment made by this title shall be treated as if it had been included in the provision of the Reform Act to which such amendment relates."

— P.L. 100-647, Sec. 4001(b)(2), added new para. (d)(5), effective for tax. yrs. begin. after 12/31/87.

— P.L. 100-647, Sec. 6005, of this Act provides:

"(a) In general.

"In the case of an individual who is a Christa McAuliffe Fellow (as defined in section 561(b) of the Higher Education Act of 1965) and is awarded a fellowship pursuant to section 561 of such Act, for purposes of the 1986 Code, gross income shall not include any amount of such fellowship award—

"(1) which is expended for a project approved by the Secretary of Education pursuant to section 563(b) of such Act, and

"(2) which is not expended directly or indirectly for the personal use or benefit of such individual, effective for amounts received in tax. yrs. begin. before 7/1/90."

"(b) Effective date. Subsection (a) shall apply to amounts received before July 1, 1990, in taxable years beginning before such date."

In 1986, P.L. 99-514, Sec. 123(a), amended Code Sec. 117, effective for tax. yrs. begin. after 12/31/86, but only in the case of scholarships and fellowships granted after 8/16/86 (see Sec. 1012 of P.L. 100-647(aa)(3)(J) and (4), above).

Prior to amendment, Code Sec. 117 read as follows:

"SEC. 117. SCHOLARSHIPS AND FELLOWSHIP GRANTS.

"(a) General rule.

"In the case of an individual, gross income does not include—

"(1) any amount received—

"(A) as a scholarship at an educational organization described in section 170(b)(1)(A)(ii), or

"(B) as a fellowship grant,

including the value of contributed services and accommodations; and

"(2) any amount received to cover expenses for—

"(A) travel,

"(B) research,

"(C) clerical help, or

"(D) equipment,

which are incident to such a scholarship or to a fellowship grant, but only to the extent that the amount is so expended by the recipient.

"(b) Limitations.

"(1) Individuals who are candidates for degrees. In the case of an individual who is a candidate for a degree at an educational organization described in section 170(b)(1)(A)(ii), subsection (a) shall not apply to that portion of any amount received which represents payment for teaching, research, or other services in the nature of part-time employment required as a condition to receiving the scholarship or the fellowship grant. If teaching, research, or other services are required of all candidates (whether or not recipients of scholarships or fellowship grants) for a particular degree as a condition to receiving such degree, such teaching, research, or other services shall not be regarded as part-time employment within the meaning of this paragraph.

"(2) Individuals who are not candidates for degrees. In the case of an individual who is not a candidate for a degree at an educational organization described in section 170(b)(1)(A)(ii), subsection (a) shall apply only if the condition in subparagraph (A) is satisfied and then only within the limitations provided in subparagraph (B).

"(A) Conditions for exclusion. The grantor of the scholarship or fellowship grant is—

"(i) an organization described in section 501(c)(3) which is exempt from tax under section 501(a),

"(ii) a foreign government,

"(iii) an international organization, or a binational or multinational education and cultural foundation or commission created or continued pursuant to the Mutual Educational and Cultural Exchange Act of 1961, or

"(iv) the United States, or an instrumentality or agency thereof, or a State, or a possession of the United States, or any political subdivision thereof, or the District of Columbia.

"(B) Extent of exclusion. The amount of the scholarship or fellowship grant excluded under subsection (a)(1) in any taxable year shall be limited to an amount equal to $300 times the number of months for which the recipient received amounts under the scholarship or fellowship grant during such taxable year, except that no exclusion shall be allowed under subsection (a) after the recipient has been entitled to exclude under this section for a period of 36 months (whether or not consecutive) amounts received as a scholarship or fellowship grant while not a candidate for a degree at an educational institution (as defined in section 151(e)(4)).

"(c) Federal grants for tuition and related expenses not includable merely because there is requirement of future service as federal employee.

"(1) In general. If—

"(A) an amount received by an individual under a Federal program would be excludable under subsections (a) and (b) as a scholarship or fellowship grant but for the fact that the individual is required to perform future service as a Federal employee, and

"(B) the individual establishes that, in accordance with the terms of the grant, such amount was used for qualified tuition and related expenses, gross income shall not include such amount.

"(2) Qualified tuition and related expenses defined. For purposes of this subsection—

"(A) In general. The term 'qualified tuition and related expenses' means—

"(i) tuition and fees required for the enrollment or attendance of a student at an institution of higher education, and

"(ii) fees, books, supplies, and equipment required for courses of instruction at an institution of higher education.

"(B) Institution of higher education. The term 'institution of higher education' means an educational institution in any State which—

"(i) admits as regular students only individuals having a certificate of graduation from a high school, or the recognized equivalent of such a certificate,

"(ii) is legally authorized within such State to provide a program of education beyond high school,

"(iii) provides an educational program for which it awards a bachelor's or higher degree, provides a program which is acceptable for full credit toward such a degree, or offers a program of training to prepare students for gainful employment in a recognized health profession, and

"(iv) is a public or other nonprofit institution.

"(3) Service as federal employee. For purposes of this subsection, service in a health manpower shortage area shall be treated as service as a Federal employee.

"(d) Qualified tuition reductions.

"(1) In general. Gross income shall not include any qualified tuition reduction.

"(2) Qualified tuition reduction. For purposes of this subsection, the term 'qualified tuition reduction' means the amount of any reduction in tuition provided to an employee of an organization described in section 170(b)(1)(A)(ii) for the education (below the graduate level) at such organization (or another organization described in section 170(b)(1)(A)(ii)) of—

"(A) such employee, or

"(B) any person treated as an employee (or whose use is treated as an employee use) under the rules of section 132(f).

"(3) Reduction must not discriminate in favor of highly compensated, etc. Paragraph (1) shall apply with respect to any qualified tuition reduction provided with respect to any officer, owner, or highly compensated employee only if such reduction is available on substantially the same terms to each member of a group of employees which is defined under a reasonable classification set up by the employer which does not discriminate in favor of officers, owners, or highly compensated employees."

— P.L. 99-514, Sec. 1114(b)(2), deleted "officer, owner, or" after "with respect to any", and deleted in para. (d)(2), and added the sentence at the end of para. (d)(2), "officers, owners, or" after "discriminate in favor of" effective for tax. yrs. begin. after 12/31/87.

— P.L. 99-514, Sec. 1853(f)(1)-(3), provides:

"(f) Transitional rules for treatment of certain reductions in tuition—

"(1) A tuition reduction plan shall be treated as meeting the requirements of section 117(d)(3) of the Internal Revenue Code of 1954 if—

"(A) such plan would have met the requirements of such section (as amended by this section but without regard to the lack of evidence that benefits under such plan were the subject of good faith bargaining) on the day on which eligibility to participate in the plan was closed,

"(B) at all times thereafter, the tuition reductions available under such plan are available on substantially the same terms to all employees eligible to participate in such plan, and

"(C) the eligibility to participate in such plan closed on June 30, 1972, June 30, 1974, or December 31, 1975.

"(2) For purposes of applying section 117(d)(3) of the Internal Revenue Code of 1954 to all tuition reduction plans of an employer with at least 1 such plan described in paragraph (1) of this subsection, there shall be excluded from consideration employees not included in the plan who are included in a unit of employees covered by an agreement that the Secretary of the Treasury or his delegate finds to be a collective bargaining agreement, between employee representatives and 1 or more employers, if, with respect to plans other than plans described in paragraph (1), there is evidence that such benefits were the subject of good faith bargaining.

"(3) Any reduction in tuition provided with respect to a full-time course of education furnished at the graduate level before July 1, 1988, shall not be included in gross income if—

"(A) such reduction would not be included in gross income under the Internal Revenue Service regulations in effect on the date of the enactment of the Tax Reform Act of 1984, and

"(B) such reduction is provided with respect to a student who was accepted for admission to such course of education before July 1, 1984, and began such course of education before June 30, 1985."

In 1984, P.L. 98-369, Sec. 532(a), added subsec. (d), effective for qualified tuition reductions (as defined in Code Sec. 117(d)(2)) for education furnished after 6/30/85, in tax. yrs. end. after 6/30/85. [See Sec. 1853(f)(2) of P.L. 99-514, reproduced above.]

In 1982, P.L. 97-248, Sec. 248, substituted "1983" for "1981" in Sec. 161(b)(2) of P.L. 95-600 (as amended by Sec. 161(b) of P.L. 96-541), reproduced below.

In 1980, P.L. 96-541, Sec. 5(a)(1), added subsec. (c), effective for tax. yrs. begin. after 12/31/80.

— P.L. 96-541, Sec. 161(b), substituted "1981" for "1980" in Sec. 161(b)(2) of P.L. 95-600, reproduced below.

—P.L. 96-330, Sec. 201(a)(1), which added Subchapter IV to Chapter 73 of title 38, USC, [Veterans' Administration Health Professional Scholarship Program] provides as follows:

"4145. Exemption of scholarship payments from taxation

"Notwithstanding any other law, any payment to, or on behalf of, a participant in the Scholarship Program for tuition, education expenses, or a stipend under this subchapter shall be exempt from taxation."

In **1979**, P.L. 96-167, Sec. 9(a), substituted "1981" for "1980" and "1985" for "1984" in Sec. 4(c) of P.L. 93-483, reproduced below.

—P.L. 96-167, Sec. 9(b), substituted "1980" for "1979" in Sec. 161(b)(2) of P.L. 95-600, reproduced below.

In **1978**, Sec. 161(a)(1), substituted "1980" for "1979" in Sec. 4(c) of P.L. 93-483, see below... Sec. 161(a)(2), substituted "1984" for "1983" in Sec. 4(c) of P.L. 93-483, see below.

—P.L. 95-600, Sec. 161(b), provides as follows:

"(b) National research service awards.—

"(1) General rule.— Any amount paid to, or on behalf of, an individual from appropriated funds as a national research service award under section 472 of the Public Health Service Act shall be treated as a scholarship or fellowship grant under section 117 of the Internal Revenue Code of 1954.

"(2) Effective date.— The provisions of subsection (b) shall apply to awards made during calendar years 1974 through 1983."

In **1977**, P.L. 95-171, Sec. 5, substituted "and 1975, and in the case of a member of a uniformed service receiving training after 1975 and before 1979 in programs described in subsection (a), with respect to amounts received after 1975 and before 1983." for "and 1975, and in the case of a member of a uniformed services receiving training in programs described in subsection (a) during calendar year 1976, with respect to amounts received during calendar years 1976, 1977, 1978, and 1979." in Sec. 4(c) of P.L. 93-483, reproduced below.

In **1976**, P.L. 94-455, Sec. 1901(b)(8)(A), substituted "educational organization described in section 170(b)(1)(A)(ii)" for "educational institution (as defined in section 151(e)(4))" in subpara. (a)(1)(A) and paras. (b)(1) and (b)(2), effective for tax. yrs. begin. after 12/31/76.

—P.L. 94-455, Sec. 1901(c)(3), deleted "a territory," after "or a State," in clause (b)(2)(A)(iv), effective for tax. yrs. begin. after '76.

—P.L. 95-455, Sec. 2130, substituted "and 1975, and, in the case of a member of a uniformed service receiving training in programs described in subsection (a) during calendar year 1976, with respect to amounts received during calendar years 1976, 1977, 1978, and 1979." for "and 1975" in Sec. 4(c) of P.L. 93-483, reproduced below.

In **1974**, P.L. 93-483, Sec. 4, [as amended by Sec. 5 of P.L. 95-171 and Sec. 9(a) of P.L. 96-167, see above] provides as follows:

"(a) In general.

"Any amount received from appropriated funds as a scholarship, including the value of contributed services and accommodations, by a member of a uniformed service who is receiving training under the Armed Forces Health Professions Scholarship Program (or any other program determined by the Secretary of the Treasury or his delegate to have substantially similar objectives) from an educational institution (as defined in section 151(e)(4) of the Internal Revenue Code of 1954) shall be treated as a scholarship under section 117 of such Code, whether that member is receiving training while on active duty or in an off-duty or inactive status, and without regard to whether a period of active duty is required of the member as a condition of receiving those payments.

"(b) Definition of uniformed services.

"For purposes of this section, the term 'uniformed service' has the meaning given it by section 101(3) of title 37, United States Code.

"(c) Effective date.

"The provisions of this section shall apply with respect to amounts received during calendar years 1973, 1974, and 1975, and, in the case of a member of a uniformed service receiving training after 1975 and before 1981 in programs described in subsection (a), with respect to amounts received after 1975 and before 1985."

In **1961**, P.L. 87-256, Sec. 110(a), added clauses (b)(2)(A)(ii) and (iii), effective for tax. yrs. begin. after '61.

Sec. 118. Contributions to the capital of a corporation.

(a) General rule.

In the case of a corporation, gross income does not include any contribution to the capital of the taxpayer.

(b) Contributions in aid of construction, etc.

For purposes of subsection (a), except as provided in subsection (c), the term "contribution to the capital of the taxpayer" does not include any contribution in aid of construction or any other contribution as a customer or potential customer.

(c) Special rules for water and sewerage disposal utilities.

(1) General rule. For purposes of this section, the term "contribution to the capital of the taxpayer" includes any amount of money or other property received from any person (whether or not a shareholder) by a regulated public utility which provides water or sewerage disposal services if—

(A) such amount is a contribution in aid of construction,

(B) in the case of contribution of property other than water or sewerage disposal facilities, such amount meets the requirements of the expenditure rule of paragraph (2), and

(C) such amount (or any property acquired or constructed with such amount) is not included in the taxpayer's rate base for rate-making purposes.

(2) Expenditure rule. An amount meets the requirements of this paragraph if—

(A) an amount equal to such amount is expended for the acquisition or construction of tangible property described in section 1231(b)—

(i) which is the property for which the contribution was made or is of the same type as such property, and

(ii) which is used predominantly in the trade or business of furnishing water or sewerage disposal services,

(B) the expenditure referred to in subparagraph (A) occurs before the end of the second taxable year after the year in which such amount was received, and

(C) accurate records are kept of the amounts contributed and expenditures made, the expenditures to which contributions are allocated, and the year in which the contributions and expenditures are received and made.

(3) Definitions. For purposes of this subsection—

(A) Contribution in aid of construction. The term "contribution in aid of construction" shall be defined by regulations prescribed by the Secretary, except that such term shall not include amounts paid as service charges for starting or stopping services.

(B) Predominantly. The term "predominantly" means 80 percent or more.

(C) Regulated public utility. The term "regulated public utility" has the meaning given such term by section 7701(a)(33), except that such term shall not include any utility which is not required to provide water or sewerage disposal services to members of the general public in its service area.

(4) Disallowance of deductions and credits; adjusted basis. Notwithstanding any other provision of this subtitle, no deduction or credit shall be allowed for, or by reason of, any expenditure which constitutes a contribution in aid of construction to which this subsection applies. The adjusted basis of any property acquired with contributions in aid of construction to which this subsection applies shall be zero.

(d) Statute of limitations.

If the taxpayer for any taxable year treats an amount as a contribution to the capital of the taxpayer described in subsection (c), then—

(1) the statutory period for the assessment of any deficiency attributable to any part of such amount shall not expire before the expiration of 3 years from the date the Secretary is notified by the taxpayer (in such manner as the Secretary may prescribe) of—

(A) the amount of the expenditure referred to in subparagraph (A) of subsection (c)(2),

(B) the taxpayer's intention not to make the expenditures referred to in such subparagraph, or

(C) a failure to make such expenditure within the period described in subparagraph (B) of subsection (c)(2), and

(2) such deficiency may be assessed before the expiration of such 3-year period notwithstanding the provisions of any other law or rule of law which would otherwise prevent such assessment.

(e) Cross references.

(1) For basis of property acquired by a corporation through a contribution to its capital, see section 362.

(2) For special rules in the case of contributions of indebtedness, see section 108(e)(6).

In 1996, P.L. 104-188, Sec. 1613(a)(1)(A), redesignated subsec. (c) as subsec. (e) . . . Sec. 1613(a)(1)(B), added subsecs. (c) and (d) . . . Sec. 1613(a)(2), added "except as provided in subsection (c)," before "the term" in subsec. (b), effective for amounts received after 6/12/96.

In 1988, P.L. 100-647, Sec. 1008(j)(a), amended Sec. 824(c)(4) [reproduced below] of P.L. 99-514, part of the effective date for changes made by Sec. 824(a) of P.L. 99-514, by substituting "an underwriting agreement" for "an indemnity agreement," see below.

In 1986, P.L. 99-514, Sec. 824(a), deleted subsecs. (b) and (c), redesignated subsec. (d) as (c), and added new subsec. (b), effective for amounts received after 12/31/86, in tax. yrs. end. after 12/31/86, except as provided in Sec. 824(c)(2)-(4) [as amended by Sec. 1008(j)(2) of P.L. 100-647, see above] of this Act, which provides:

"(2) Treatment of certain water supply projects.— The amendments made by this section shall not apply to amounts which are paid by the New Jersey Department of Environmental Protection for construction of alternative water supply projects in zones of drinking water contamination and which are designated by such department as being taken into account under this paragraph. Not more than $4,631,000 of such amounts may be designated under the preceding sentence.

"(3) Treatment of certain contributions by transportation authority.— The amendments made by this section shall not apply to contributions in aid of construction by a qualified transportation authority which were clearly identified in a master plan in existence on September 13, 1984, and which are designated by such authority as being taken into account under this paragraph. Not more than $68,000,000 of such contributions may be designated under the preceding sentence. For purposes of this paragraph, a qualified transportation authority is an entity which was created on February 20, 1967, and which was established by an interstate compact and consented to by Congress in P.L. 89-774, 80 Stat. 1324 (1966).

"(4) Treatment of certain partnerships.— In the case of a partnership with a taxable year beginning May 1, 1986, if such partnership realized net capital gain during the period beginning on the 1st day of such taxable year and ending on May 29, 1986, pursuant to an underwriting agreement dated May 6, 1986, then such partnership may elect to treat each asset to which such net capital gain relates as having been distributed to the partners of such partnership in proportion to their distributive share of the capital gain or loss realized by the partnership with respect to such asset and to treat each such asset as having been sold by each partner on the date of the sale of the asset by the partnership. If such an election is made, the consideration received by the partnership in connection with the sale of such assets shall be treated as having been received by the partners in connection with the deemed sale of such assets. In the case of a tiered partnership, for purposes of this paragraph each partnership shall be treated as having realized net capital gain equal to its proportionate share of the net capital gain of each partnership in which it is a partner, and the election provided by this paragraph shall apply to each tier."

Prior to deletion, subsec. (b) and (c) read as follows:

"(b) Contributions in aid of construction.

"(1) General rule. For purposes of this section, the term 'contribution to the capital of the taxpayer' includes any amount of money or other property received from any person (whether or not a shareholder) by a regulated public utility which provides electric energy, gas (through a local distribution system or transportation by pipeline), water, or sewerage disposal services if—

"(A) such amount is a contribution in aid of construction,

"(B) where the contribution is in property which is other than electric energy, gas, steam, water, or sewage disposal facilities, such amount meets the requirements of the expenditure rule of paragraph (2), and

"(C) such amounts (or any property acquired or constructed with such amounts) are not included in the taxpayer's rate base for rate-making purposes.

"(2) Expenditure rule. An amount meets the requirements of this paragraph if—

"(A) an amount equal to such amount is expended for the acquisition or construction of tangible property described in section 1231(b)—

"(i) which was the purpose motivating the contribution, and

"(ii) which is used predominantly in the trade or business of furnishing electric energy, gas, steam, water, or sewerage disposal services,

"(B) the expenditure referred to in subparagraph (A) occurs before the end of the second taxable year after the year in which such amount was received, and

"(C) accurate records are kept of the amounts contributed and expenditures made on the basis of the project for which the contribution was made and on the basis of the year of contribution or expenditure.

"(3) Definitions. For purposes of this section—

"(A) Contribution in aid of construction. The term 'contribution in aid of construction' shall be defined by regulations prescribed by the Secretary; except that such term shall not include amounts paid as customer connection fees (including amounts paid to connect the customer's line to an electric line, a gas main, a steam line, or a main water or sewer line and amounts paid as service charges for starting or stopping services).

"(B) Predominantly. The term 'predominantly' means 80 percent or more.

"(C) Regulated public utility. The term 'regulated public utility' has the meaning given such term by section 7701(a)(33); except that such term shall not include any such utility which is not required to provide electric energy, gas, water, or sewerage disposal services to members of the general public (including in the case of a gas transmission utility, the provision of gas services by sale for resale to the general public) in its service area.

"(4) Disallowance of deductions and investment credit; adjusted basis. Notwithstanding any other provision of this subtitle, no deduction or credit shall be allowed for, or by reason of, the expenditure which constitutes a contribution in aid of construction to which this subsection applies. The adjusted basis of any property acquired with contributions in aid of construction to which this subsection applies shall be zero.

"(c) Statute of limitations.

"If the taxpayer for any taxable year treats an amount as a contribution to the capital of the taxpayer described in subsection (b), then—

"(1) the statutory period for the assessment of any deficiency attributable to any part of such amount shall not expire before the expiration of 3 years from the date the Secretary is notified by the taxpayer (in such manner as the Secretary may prescribe) of—

"(A) the amount of the expenditure referred to in subparagraph (A) of subsection (b)(2),

"(B) the taxpayer's intention not to make the expenditures referred to in such subparagraph, or

"(C) a failure to make such expenditure within the period described in subparagraph (B) of subsection (b)(2); and

"(2) such deficiency may be assessed before the expiration of such 3-year period notwithstanding the provisions of any other law or rule of law which would otherwise prevent such assessment."

In 1984, P.L. 98-369, Sec. 163(a), redesignated subsec. (c) as subsec. (d) and added new subsec. (c), effective for expenditures with respect to which the second tax. yr. described in Code Sec. 118(b)(2)(B) ends after 12/31/84.

In 1980, P.L. 96-589, Sec. 2(e)(2), amended subsec. (c), effective for any transaction which occurs after 12/31/80, other than a transaction which occurs in a proceeding in a bankruptcy case or similar judicial proceeding (or in a proceeding under the Bankruptcy Act) commencing on or before 12/31/80. Sec. 7(f) and (g) of this Act provides:

"(f) Election to substitute September 30, 1979, for December 31, 1980.

"(1) In general. The debtor (or debtors) in a bankruptcy case or similar judicial proceeding may (with the approval of the court) elect to apply [subsections 7(a) and (d) of this Act] by substituting 'September 30, 1979' for 'December 31, 1980' each place it appears in such subsections.

"(2) Effect of election. Any election made under paragraph (1) with respect to any proceeding shall apply to all parties to the proceeding.

"(3) Revocation only with consent. Any election under this subsection may be revoked only with the consent of the Secretary of the Treasury or his delegate.

"(4) Time and manner of election. Any election under this subsection shall be made at such time, and in such manner, as the Secretary of the Treasury or his delegate may by regulations prescribe.

"(g) Definitions.

"For purposes of this section—

"(1) Bankruptcy case. The term 'bankruptcy case' means any case under title 11 of the United States Code (as recodified by P.L. 95-598).

"(2) Similar judicial proceeding. The term 'similar judicial proceeding' means a receivership, foreclosure, or similar proceeding in a Federal or State court (as modified by section 368(a)(3)(D) of the Internal Revenue Code of 1954)."

Prior to amendment, subsec. (c) read as follows:

"(c) Cross reference.

"For basis of property acquired by a corporation through a contribution to its capital, see section 362."

In 1978, P.L. 95-600, Sec. 364(a)(1), substituted "electric energy, gas (through a local distribution system or transportation by pipeline), water," for "water" in para. (b)(1) . . . Sec. 364(a)(2), substituted "electric energy, gas, steam, water," for "water" in subpara. (b)(1)(B) . . . Sec. 364(a)(3), substituted "electric energy, gas, steam, water," for "water" in clause (b)(2)(A)(ii) . . . Sec. 364(a)(4), substituted "line" for "property" in subpara. (b)(3)(A), and substituted "an electric line, a gas main, a steam line, or a main water or sewer line" for "a main water or sewer line" in subpara. (b)(3)(A) . . . Sec. 364(a)(5), amended subpara. (b)(3)(C), effective for contributions made after 1/31/76.

Prior to amendment subpara. (b)(3)(C) read as follows:

"(C) Regulated public utility. The term 'regulated public utility' has the meaning given such term by section 7701(a)(33); except that such term shall not include any such utility which is not required to provide water or sewerage disposal services to members of the general public in its service area."

In 1976, P.L. 94-455, Sec. 2120(a), redesignated subsec. (b) as subsec. (c) and added new subsec. (b), effective for contributions made after 1/31/76.

Sec. 119. Meals or lodging furnished for the convenience of the employer.

(a) Meals and lodging furnished to employee, his spouse, and his dependents, pursuant to employment.

There shall be excluded from gross income of an employee the value of any meals or lodging furnished to him, his spouse, or any of his dependents by or on behalf of his employer for the convenience of the employer, but only if—

Exclusions from income   Code Sec. 119

(1) in the case of meals, the meals are furnished on the business premises of the employer, or

(2) in the case of lodging, the employee is required to accept such lodging on the business premises of his employer as a condition of his employment.

(b) Special rules.

For purposes of subsection (a)—

(1) Provisions of employment contract or state statute not to be determinative. In determining whether meals or lodging are furnished for the convenience of the employer, the provisions of an employment contract or of a State statute fixing terms of employment shall not be determinative of whether the meals or lodging are intended as compensation.

(2) Certain factors not taken into account with respect to meals. In determining whether meals are furnished for the convenience of the employer, the fact that a charge is made for such meals, and the fact that the employee may accept or decline such meals, shall not be taken into account.

(3) Certain fixed charges for meals.

(A) In general. If—

(i) an employee is required to pay on a periodic basis a fixed charge for his meals, and

(ii) such meals are furnished by the employer for the convenience of the employer,

there shall be excluded from the employee's gross income an amount equal to such fixed charge.

(B) Application of subparagraph (A). Subparagraph (A) shall apply—

(i) whether the employee pays the fixed charge out of his stated compensation or out of his own funds, and

(ii) only if the employee is required to make the payment whether he accepts or declines the meals.

(4) Meals furnished to employees on business premises where meals of most employees are otherwise excludable. All meals furnished on the business premises of an employer to such employer's employees shall be treated as furnished for the convenience of the employer if, without regard to this paragraph, more than half of the employees to whom such meals are furnished on such premises are furnished such meals for the convenience of the employer.

(c) Employees living in certain camps.

(1) In general. In the case of an individual who is furnished lodging in a camp located in a foreign country by or on behalf of his employer, such camp shall be considered to be part of the business premises of the employer.

(2) Camp. For purposes of this section, a camp constitutes lodging which is—

(A) provided by or on behalf of the employer for the convenience of the employer because the place at which such individual renders services is in a remote area where satisfactory housing is not available on the open market,

(B) located, as near as practicable, in the vicinity of the place at which such individual renders services, and

(C) furnished in a common area (or enclave) which is not available to the public and which normally accommodates 10 or more employees.

(d) Lodging furnished by certain educational institutions to employees.

(1) In general. In the case of an employee of an educational institution, gross income shall not include the value of qualified campus lodging furnished to such employee during the taxable year.

(2) Exception in cases of inadequate rent. Paragraph (1) shall not apply to the extent of the excess of—

(A) the lesser of—

(i) 5 percent of the appraised value of the qualified campus lodging, or

(ii) the average of the rentals paid by individuals (other than employees or students of the educational institution) during such calendar year for lodging provided by the educational institution which is comparable to the qualified campus lodging provided to the employee, over

(B) the rent paid by the employee for the qualified campus lodging during such calendar year.

The appraised value under subparagraph (A)(i) shall be determined as of the close of the calendar year in which the taxable year begins, or, in the case of a rental period not greater than 1 year, at any time during the calendar year in which such period begins.

(3) Qualified campus lodging. For purposes of this subsection, the term "qualified campus lodging" means lodging to which subsection (a) does not apply and which is—

(A) located on, or in the proximity of, a campus of the educational institution, and

(B) furnished to the employee, his spouse, and any of his dependents by or on behalf of such institution for use as a residence.

(4) Educational institution, etc. For purposes of this subsection—

(A) In general. The term "educational institution" means—

(i) an institution described in section 170(b)(1)(A)(ii) (or an entity organized under State law and composed of public institutions so described), or

(ii) an academic health center.

(B) Academic health center. For purposes of subparagraph (A), the term "academic health center" means an entity—

(i) which is described in section 170(b)(1)(A)(iii),

(ii) which receives (during the calendar year in which the taxable year of the taxpayer begins) payments under subsection (d)(5)(B) or (h) of section 1886 of the Social Security Act (relating to graduate medical education), and

(iii) which has as one of its principal purposes or functions the providing and teaching of basic and clinical medical science and research with the entity's own faculty.

In **1998,** P.L. 105-206, Sec. 5002(a), added para. (b)(4), effective for tax. yrs. begin. before, on, or after 7/22/98.

In **1996,** P.L. 104-188, Sec. 1123(a), amended para. (d)(4), effective for tax. yrs. begin. after 12/31/95.

Prior to amendment, para. (d)(4) read as follows:

"(4) Educational institution. For purposes of this paragraph, the term 'educational institution' means an institution described in section 170(b)(1)(A)(ii)."

In **1988,** P.L. 100-647, Sec. 1011B(d)(1), and (2), deleted "(as of the close of the calendar year in which the taxable year begins)" after "of the appraised value" in clause (d)(2)(A)(i) and added a sentence to the end of para. (d)(2), effective for tax. yrs. begin. after 12/31/85.

In **1986,** P.L. 99-514, Sec. 1164(a), added subsec. (d), effective for tax. yrs. begin. after 12/31/85.

In **1981,** P.L. 97-34, Sec. 113, added subsec. (c), effective for tax. yrs. begin. after 12/31/81.

In **1980,** P.L. 96-605, Sec. 107(a), substituted "January 1, 1974" for "January 1, 1977", substituted "calendar year 1974, 1975, 1976 or 1977" for "calendar year 1977", in subsec. (b) of Sec. 3 of P.L. 95-427 [reproduced below] . . . Sec. 107(b), substituted "December 28, 1981" [one yr. after date of enactment of this Act (12/28/80)] for "April 15, 1979" each place it appears in Sec. 3 of P.L. 95-427 [reproduced below].

—P.L. 96-222, Sec. 108(a)(1)(G), corrected Sec. 205 of P.L. 95-615 to amend para. (a) by substituting "(a) General rule. There shall" for "There shall" [see below].

Code Sec. 119 — Exclusions from income

In 1978, P.L. 95-615, Sec. 205(1), substituted "furnished to him, his spouse, or any of his dependents by or on behalf of his employer for the convenience of the employer" for "furnished to him by his employer for the convenience of the employer" in Code Sec. 119 ... Sec. 205(2), substituted "(a) Meals and lodging furnished to employee, his spouse, and his dependents, pursuant to employment.—There shall" for "There shall" in Code Sec. 119, effective for tax. yrs. begin. after 12/31/77.

—P.L. 95-427, Sec. 4(a), amended Code Sec. 119, effective for tax. yrs. begin. after 12/31/53 and end. after 8/16/54. Sec. 3 of this Act provides as follows:

"Sec. 3. Treatment of certain statutory subsistence allowances or subsistence allowances negotiated in accordance with state law received by state police officers before January 1, 1978.

"(a) General rule.

"If—

"(1) an individual who was employed as a State police officer received a statutory subsistence allowance or a subsistence allowance negotiated in accordance with State law while so employed,

"(2) such individual elects, on or before December 28, 1981, and in such manner and form as the Secretary of the Treasury may prescribe, to have this section apply to such allowance, and

"(3) this section applies to such allowance, then, for purposes of the Internal Revenue Code of 1954, such allowance shall not be included in such individual's gross income.

"(b) Allowances to which section applies.

"For purposes of this section, this section applies to any statutory subsistence allowance or subsistence allowance negotiated in accordance with State law which was received—

"(1) after December 31, 1969, and before January 1, 1974, to the extent such individual did not include such allowance in gross income on his income tax return for the taxable year in which such allowance was received, or

"(2) during the calendar year 1974, 1975, 1976, or 1977.

"(c) Other definitions.

"For purposes of this section—

"(1) State police officer. The term 'State police officer' means any police officer (including a highway patrolman) employed by a State (or the District of Columbia) on a full-time basis with the power to arrest.

"(2) Income tax return. The term 'income tax return' means the return of the taxes imposed by subtitle A of the Internal Revenue Code of 1954. If an individual filed before November 29, 1977, an amended return for any taxable year, such amended return shall be treated as the return for such taxable year.

"(d) Limitation on deduction.

"If any individual receives a subsistence allowance which is excluded from gross income under subsection (a), no deduction shall be allowed under any provision of chapter 1 of the Internal Revenue Code of 1954 for expenses in respect of which he has received such allowance, except to the extent that such expenses exceed the amount excludable from gross income under subsection (a) and the excess is otherwise allowed as a deduction under such chapter 1.

"(e) Statute of limitations.

"If refund or credit of any overpayment of tax resulting from the application of this section is prevented at any time on or before December 28, 1981, by the operation of any law or rule of law (including res judicata), refund or credit of such overpayment (to the extent attributable to the application of this section) may, nevertheless, be made or allowed if claim therefor is filed on or before December 28, 1981."

Prior to amendment Code Sec. 119 read as follows:

"SEC. 119. MEALS OR LODGING FURNISHED FOR THE CONVENIENCE OF THE EMPLOYER.

"There shall be excluded from gross income of an employee the value of any meals or lodging furnished to him by his employer for the convenience of the employer, but only if—

"(1) in the case of meals, the meals are furnished on the business premises of the employer, or

"(2) in the case of lodging, the employee is required to accept such lodging on the business premises of his employer as a condition of his employment.

In determining whether meals or lodging are furnished for the convenience of the employer, the provisions of an employment contract or of a State statute fixing terms of employment shall not be determinative of whether the meals or lodging are intended as compensation."

Sec. 120. Amounts received under qualified group legal services plans.

(a) Exclusion by employee for contributions and legal services provided by employer.

Gross income of an employee, his spouse, or his dependents, does not include—

(1) amounts contributed by an employer on behalf of an employee, his spouse, or his dependents under a qualified group legal services plan (as defined in subsection (b)); or

(2) the value of legal services provided, or amounts paid for legal services, under a qualified group legal services plan (as defined in subsection (b)) to, or with respect to, an employee, his spouse, or his dependents.

No exclusion shall be allowed under this section with respect to an individual for any taxable year to the extent that the value of insurance (whether through an insurer or self-insurance) against legal costs incurred by the individual (or his spouse or dependents) provided under a qualified group legal services plan exceeds $70.

(b) Qualified group legal services plan.

For purposes of this section, a qualified group legal services plan is a separate written plan of an employer for the exclusive benefit of his employees or their spouses or dependents to provide such employees, spouses, or dependents with specified benefits consisting of personal legal services through prepayment of, or provision in advance for, legal fees in whole or in part by the employer, if the plan meets the requirements of subsection (c).

(c) Requirements.

(1) Discrimination. The contributions or benefits provided under the plan shall not discriminate in favor of employees who are highly compensated employees (within the meaning of section 414(q)).

(2) Eligibility. The plan shall benefit employees who qualify under a classification set up by the employer and found by the Secretary not to be discriminatory in favor of employees who are described in paragraph (1). For purposes of this paragraph, there shall be excluded from consideration employees not included in the plan who are included in a unit of employees covered by an agreement which the Secretary of Labor finds to be a collective bargaining agreement between employee representatives and one or more employers, if there is evidence that group legal services plan benefits were the subject of good faith bargaining between such employee representatives and such employer or employers.

(3) Contribution limitation. Not more than 25 percent of the amounts contributed under the plan during the year may be provided for the class of individuals who are shareholders or owners (or their spouses or dependents),each of whom (on any day of the year) owns more than 5 percent of the stock or of the capital or profits interest in the employer.

(4) Notification. The plan shall give notice to the Secretary, in such manner as the Secretary may by regulations prescribe, that it is applying for recognition of the status of a qualified group legal services plan.

(5) Contributions. Amounts contributed under the plan shall be paid only (A) to insurance companies, or to organizations or persons that provide personal legal services, or indemnification against the cost of personal legal services, in exchange for a prepayment or payment of a premium, (B) to organizations or trusts described in section 501(c)(20), (C) to organizations described in section 501(c) which are permitted by that section to receive payments from an employer for support of one or more qualified group legal services plan or plans, except that such organizations shall pay or credit the contribution to an organization or trust described in section 501(c)(20), (D) as prepayments to providers of legal services under the plan, or (E) a combination of the above.

(d) Other definitions and special rules.

For purposes of this section—

(1) Employee. The term "employee" includes, for any year, an individual who is an employee within the meaning of section 401(c)(1) (relating to self-employed individuals).

(2) Employer. An individual who owns the entire interest in an unincorporated trade or business shall be treated as his own employer. A partnership shall be treated as the employer of each partner who is an employee within the meaning of paragraph (1).

Exclusions from income Code Sec. 121(a)

(3) **Allocations.** Allocations of amounts contributed under the plan shall be made in accordance with regulations prescribed by the Secretary and shall take into account the expected relative utilization of benefits to be provided from such contributions or plan assets and the manner in which any premium or other charge was developed.

(4) **Dependent.** The term "dependent" has the meaning given to it by section 152 (determined without regard to subsections (b)(1), (b)(2), and (d)(1)(B) thereof).

(5) **Exclusive benefit.** In the case of a plan to which contributions are made by more than one employer, in determining whether the plan is for the exclusive benefit of an employer's employees or their spouses or dependents, the employees of any employer who maintains the plan shall be considered to be the employees of each employer who maintains the plan.

(6) **Attribution rules.** For purposes of this section—

(A) ownership of stock in a corporation shall be determined in accordance with the rules provided under subsections (d) and (e) of section 1563 (without regard to section 1563(e)(3)(C)), and

(B) the interest of an employee in a trade or business which is not incorporated shall be determined in accordance with regulations prescribed by the Secretary, which shall be based on principles similar to the principles which apply in the case of subparagraph (A).

(7) **Time of notice to secretary.** A plan shall not be a qualified group legal services plan for any period prior to the time notification was provided to the Secretary in accordance with subsection (c)(4), if such notice is given after the time prescribed by the Secretary by regulations for giving such notice.

(e) **Termination.**

This section and section 501(c)(20) shall not apply to taxable years beginning after June 30, 1992.

(f) **Cross reference.**

For reporting and recordkeeping requirements, see section 6039D.

In 2004, P.L. 108-311, Sec. 207(10), added "(determined without regard to subsections (b)(1), (b)(2), and (d)(1)(B) thereof)" after "section 152" in para. (d)(4), effective for tax. yrs. begin. after 12/31/2004.

In 1991, P.L. 102-227, Sec. 104(a)(1), substituted "June 30, 1992" for "December 31, 1991" in subsec. (e), effective for tax. yrs. begin. after 12/31/91.

—P.L. 102-227, Sec. 104(a)(2), of this Act provides:

"(2) Special rule.— In the case of any taxable year beginning in 1992, only amounts paid before July 1, 1992, by the employer for coverage for the employee, his spouse, or his dependents, under a qualified group legal services plan for periods before July 1, 1992, shall be taken into account in determining the amount excluded under section 120 of the Internal Revenue Code of 1986 with respect to such employee for such taxable year."

In 1990, P.L. 101-508, Sec. 11404(a), substituted "December 31, 1991" for "September 30, 1990" in subsec. (e), effective for tax. yrs. begin. after 12/31/89.

—P.L. 101-508, Sec. 11404(b), deleted sec. 7102(a)(2) of P.L. 101-239.

Prior to deletion, Sec. 7102(a)(2) of P.L. 101-239 read as follows:

"(2) Special rule.— In the case of any taxable year beginning in 1990, only amounts paid before October 1, 1990, by the employer for coverage for the employee, his spouse, or his dependents under a qualified group legal services plan for periods before October 1, 1990, shall be taken into account in determining the amount excluded under section 120 of the Internal Revenue Code of 1986 with respect to such employee for such taxable year."

In 1989, P.L. 101-239, Sec. 7102(a)(1), substituted "beginning after September 30, 1990" for "ending after December 31, 1988" in subsec. (e), effective for tax. yrs. end. after 12/31/88.

—P.L. 101-239, Sec. 7102(a)(2), [as repealed by Sec. 11404(b) of P.L. 101-508] see above.

—P.L. 101-140, Sec. 203(a)(1), repealed as if not enacted Sec. 1151(c) of P.L. 99-514 which amended subsec. (b) and repealed as if not enacted Sec. 1151(g) of P.L. 99-514 which amended the last sentence of para. (c)(2).

—P.L. 101-140, Sec. 203(a)(2), repealed as if not enacted Sec. 1011B(a)(31) of P.L. 100-647, which amended para. (c)(2).

In 1988, P.L. 100-647, Sec. 4002(a), substituted "1988" for "1987", in subsec. (e)... Sec. 4002(b)(1), added the last sentence to subsec. (a), effective for tax. yrs. end. after 12/31/87

In 1986, P.L. 99-514, Sec. 1114(b)(3)(A), substituted "highly compensated employees (within the meaning of section 414(q))" for "officers, shareholders, self-employed individuals, or highly compensated" in subsec. (b)... Sec. 1114(b)(3)(B), deleted "self-employed individual;" from before "employee." in the heading of para. (d)(1), and substituted "The" for "The term 'self-employed individual' means, and the" in para. (d)(1), effective for years begin. after 12/31/87.

—P.L. 99-514, Sec. 1162(b), substituted "1987" for "1985" in subsec. (e), effective for yrs. ending after 12/31/85. Sec. 1162(c)(3) of this Act provides:

"(3) Cafeteria plan with group legal benefits. If, within 60 days after the date of the enactment of this Act, an employee elects under a cafeteria plan under section 125 of the Internal Revenue Code of 1986 coverage for group legal benefits to which section 120 of such Code applies, such election may, at the election of the taxpayer, apply to all legal services provided during 1986. The preceding sentence shall not apply to any plan which on August 16, 1986, offered such group legal benefits under such plan."

In 1984, P.L. 98-612, Sec. 1(a), substituted "December 31, 1985" for "December 31, 1984" in subsec. (e), effective for tax. yrs. end. after 12/31/84.

—P.L. 98-612, Sec. 1(b)(3)(A), added subsec. (f), effective 1/1/85.

In 1983, P.L. 97-448, Sec. 108(a), substituted "This section and section 501(c)(20)" for "This section" in subsec. (e), effective 8/13/81.

In 1981, P.L. 97-34, Sec. 802(a), added subsec. (e), effective 8/13/81.

—P.L. 97-34, Sec. 802(b), amended Sec. 2134(e)(1) of P.L. 94-455, the effective date for changes made by Sec. 2134(a), from tax. yrs. begin. after 12/31/76 and end. before 1/1/82 to tax. yrs. begin. after 12/31/76 [see below].

In 1978, P.L. 95-600, Sec. 703(b)(1), substituted "section 120(d)(7)" for "section 120(d)(6)" in Sec. 2134(e)(2) of P.L. 94-455, see below.

In 1976, P.L. 94-455, Sec. 2134(a), added new Code Sec. 120, effective [as amended by Sec. 802(b) of P.L. 97-34, see above] for tax. yrs. begin. after 12/31/76.

Sec. 2134(e)(2) and (e)(3) [as amended by Sec. 703(b)(1) of P.L. 95-600, see above] provide:

"(2) Notice requirement.— For purposes of section 120(d)(7) of the Internal Revenue Code of 1954, the time prescribed by the Secretary of the Treasury by regulations for giving the notice required by section 120(c)(4) of such Code shall not expire before the 90th day after the day on which regulations prescribed under such section 120(c)(4) first become final.

"(3) Existing plans.—

"(A) For purposes of section 120 of the Internal Revenue Code of 1954, a written group legal services plan which was in existence on June 4, 1976, shall be considered as satisfying the requirements of subsections (b) and (c) of such section 120 for the period ending with the compliance date (determined under subparagraph (B)).

"(B) Compliance date.— For purposes of this paragraph, the term 'compliance date' means—

"(i) the date occurring 180 days after the date of the enactment of this Act, or

"(ii) if later, in the case of a plan which is maintained pursuant to one or more agreements which the Secretary of Labor finds to be collective bargaining agreements, the earlier of December 31, 1981, or the date on which the last of the collective bargaining agreements relating to the plan terminates (determined without regard to any extension thereof agreed to after the date of the enactment of this Act)."

Sec. 2134(d) provided as follows:

"(d) Study and report by secretaries of treasury and labor.—

"(1) A complete study and investigation with respect to the desirability and feasibility of continuing the exclusion from income of certain prepaid group legal services benefits under section 120 of the Internal Revenue Code of 1954 shall be made by the Secretary of Labor and by the Secretary of the Treasury.

"(2) The Secretary of Labor and the Secretary of the Treasury shall report to the President and the Congress with respect to the study and investigation conducted under paragraph (1) not later than December 31, 1980.

In 1958, P.L. 85-866, Sec. 3(a), (c), repealed Code Sec. 120, for tax. yrs. end. after 9/30/58, but only with respect to amounts received as a statutory subsistence allowance for any day after 9/30/58.

Prior to repeal, Code Sec. 120 read as follows:

"SEC. 120. STATUTORY SUBSISTENCE ALLOWANCE RECEIVED BY POLICE.

"(a) General rule.

"Gross income does not include any amount received as a statutory subsistence allowance by an individual who is employed as a police official by a State, a Territory, or a possession of the United States, by any political subdivision of any of the foregoing, or by the District of Columbia.

"(b) Limitations.—

"(1) Amounts to which subsection (a) applies shall not exceed $5 per day.

"(2) If any individual receives a subsistence allowance to which subsection (a) applies, no deduction shall be allowed under any other provision of this chapter for expenses in respect of which he has received such allowance, except to the extent that such expenses exceed the amount excludable under subsection (a) and the excess is otherwise allowable as a deduction under this chapter."

Sec. 121. Exclusion of gain from sale of principal residence.

(a) **Exclusion.**

Gross income shall not include gain from the sale or exchange of property if, during the 5-year period ending on the date of the sale or exchange, such property has been owned

1,429

and used by the taxpayer as the taxpayer's principal residence for periods aggregating 2 years or more.

(b) Limitations.

(1) In general. The amount of gain excluded from gross income under subsection (a) with respect to any sale or exchange shall not exceed $250,000.

(2) Special rules for joint returns. In the case of a husband and wife who make a joint return for the taxable year of the sale or exchange of the property—

(A) $500,000 limitation for certain joint returns. Paragraph (1) shall be applied by substituting "$500,000" for "$250,000" if—

(i) either spouse meets the ownership requirements of subsection (a) with respect to such property;

(ii) both spouses meet the use requirements of subsection (a) with respect to such property; and

(iii) neither spouse is ineligible for the benefits of subsection (a) with respect to such property by reason of paragraph (3).

(B) Other joint returns. If such spouses do not meet the requirements of subparagraph (A), the limitation under paragraph (1) shall be the sum of the limitations under paragraph (1) to which each spouse would be entitled if such spouses had not been married. For purposes of the preceding sentence, each spouse shall be treated as owning the property during the period that either spouse owned the property.

(3) Application to only 1 sale or exchange every 2 years.

(A) In general. Subsection (a) shall not apply to any sale or exchange by the taxpayer if, during the 2-year period ending on the date of such sale or exchange, there was any other sale or exchange by the taxpayer to which subsection (a) applied.

(B) Pre-May 7, 1997, sales not taken into account. Subparagraph (A) shall be applied without regard to any sale or exchange before May 7, 1997.

(4) Special rule for certain sales by surviving spouses. In the case of a sale or exchange of property by an unmarried individual whose spouse is deceased on the date of such sale, paragraph (1) shall be applied by substituting "$500,000" for "$250,000" if such sale occurs not later than 2 years after the date of death of such spouse and the requirements of paragraph (2)(A) were met immediately before such date of death.

(4 [sic (5)]) Exclusion of gain allocated to nonqualified use.

(A) In general. Subsection (a) shall not apply to so much of the gain from the sale or exchange of property as is allocated to periods of nonqualified use.

(B) Gain allocated to periods of nonqualified use. For purposes of subparagraph (A), gain shall be allocated to periods of nonqualified use based on the ratio which—

(i) the aggregate periods of nonqualified use during the period such property was owned by the taxpayer, bears to

(ii) the period such property was owned by the taxpayer.

(C) Period of nonqualified use. For purposes of this paragraph—

(i) In general. The term "period of nonqualified use" means any period (other than the portion of any period preceding January 1, 2009) during which the property is not used as the principal residence of the taxpayer or the taxpayer's spouse or former spouse.

(ii) Exceptions. The term "period of nonqualified use" does not include—

(I) any portion of the 5-year period described in subsection (a) which is after the last date that such property is used as the principal residence of the taxpayer or the taxpayer's spouse,

(II) any period (not to exceed an aggregate period of 10 years) during which the taxpayer or the taxpayer's spouse is serving on qualified official extended duty (as defined in subsection (d)(9)(C)) described in clause (i), (ii), or (iii) of subsection (d)(9)(A), and

(III) any other period of temporary absence (not to exceed an aggregate period of 2 years) due to change of employment, health conditions, or such other unforeseen circumstances as may be specified by the Secretary.

(D) Coordination with recognition of gain attributable to depreciation. For purposes of this paragraph—

(i) subparagraph (A) shall be applied after the application of subsection (d)(6), and

(ii) subparagraph (B) shall be applied without regard to any gain to which subsection (d)(6) applies.

(c) Exclusion for taxpayers failing to meet certain requirements.

(1) In general. In the case of a sale or exchange to which this subsection applies, the ownership and use requirements of subsection (a), and subsection (b)(3), shall not apply; but the dollar limitation under paragraph (1) or (2) of subsection (b), whichever is applicable, shall be equal to—

(A) the amount which bears the same ratio to such limitation (determined without regard to this paragraph) as

(B)(i) the shorter of—

(I) the aggregate periods, during the 5-year period ending on the date of such sale or exchange, such property has been owned and used by the taxpayer as the taxpayer's principal residence; or

(II) the period after the date of the most recent prior sale or exchange by the taxpayer to which subsection (a) applied and before the date of such sale or exchange, bears to

(ii) 2 years.

(2) Sales and exchanges to which subsection applies. This subsection shall apply to any sale or exchange if—

(A) subsection (a) would not (but for this subsection) apply to such sale or exchange by reason of—

(i) a failure to meet the ownership and use requirements of subsection (a), or

(ii) subsection (b)(3), and

(B) such sale or exchange is by reason of a change in place of employment, health, or, to the extent provided in regulations, unforeseen circumstances.

(d) Special rules.

(1) Joint returns. If a husband and wife make a joint return for the taxable year of the sale or exchange of the property, subsections (a) and (c) shall apply if either spouse meets the ownership and use requirements of subsection (a) with respect to such property.

(2) Property of deceased spouse. For purposes of this section, in the case of an unmarried individual whose spouse is deceased on the date of the sale or exchange of property, the period such unmarried individual owned and used such property shall include the period such deceased spouse owned and used such property before death.

(3) Property owned by spouse or former spouse. For purposes of this section—

(A) Property transferred to individual from spouse or former spouse. In the case of an individual holding property transferred to such individual in a transaction described in section 1041(a), the period such individual owns such property shall include the period the transferor owned the property.

(B) Property used by former spouse pursuant to divorce decree, etc. Solely for purposes of this section, an individual shall be treated as using property as such individual's principal residence during any period of ownership while such individual's spouse or former spouse is granted use of the property under a divorce or separation instrument (as defined in section 71(b)(2)).

(4) Tenant-stockholder in cooperative housing corporation. For purposes of this section, if the taxpayer holds stock as a tenant-stockholder (as defined in section 216) in a cooperative housing corporation (as defined in such section), then—

(A) the holding requirements of subsection (a) shall be applied to the holding of such stock, and

(B) the use requirements of subsection (a) shall be applied to the house or apartment which the taxpayer was entitled to occupy as such stockholder.

(5) Involuntary conversions.

(A) In general. For purposes of this section, the destruction, theft, seizure, requisition, or condemnation of property shall be treated as the sale of such property.

(B) Application of section 1033. In applying section 1033 (relating to involuntary conversions), the amount realized from the sale or exchange of property shall be treated as being the amount determined without regard to this section, reduced by the amount of gain not included in gross income pursuant to this section.

(C) Property acquired after involuntary conversion. If the basis of the property sold or exchanged is determined (in whole or in part) under section 1033(b) (relating to basis of property acquired through involuntary conversion), then the holding and use by the taxpayer of the converted property shall be treated as holding and use by the taxpayer of the property sold or exchanged.

(6) Recognition of gain attributable to depreciation. Subsection (a) shall not apply to so much of the gain from the sale of any property as does not exceed the portion of the depreciation adjustments (as defined in section 1250(b)(3)) attributable to periods after May 6, 1997, in respect of such property.

(7) Determination of use during periods of out-of-residence care. In the case of a taxpayer who—

(A) becomes physically or mentally incapable of self-care, and

(B) owns property and uses such property as the taxpayer's principal residence during the 5-year period described in subsection (a) for periods aggregating at least 1 year,

then the taxpayer shall be treated as using such property as the taxpayer's principal residence during any time during such 5-year period in which the taxpayer owns the property and resides in any facility (including a nursing home) licensed by a State or political subdivision to care for an individual in the taxpayer's condition.

(8) Sales of remainder interests. For purposes of this section—

(A) In general. At the election of the taxpayer, this section shall not fail to apply to the sale or exchange of an interest in a principal residence by reason of such interest being a remainder interest in such residence, but this section shall not apply to any other interest in such residence which is sold or exchanged separately.

(B) Exception for sales to related parties. Subparagraph (A) shall not apply to any sale to, or exchange with, any person who bears a relationship to the taxpayer which is described in section 267(b) or 707(b).

(9) Uniformed services, foreign service, and intelligence community.

(A) In general. At the election of an individual with respect to a property, the running of the 5-year period described in subsections (a) and (c)(1)(B) and paragraph (7) of this subsection with respect to such property shall be suspended during any period that such individual or such individual's spouse is serving on qualified official extended duty—

(i) as a member of the uniformed services,

(ii) as a member of the Foreign Service of the United States, or

(iii) as an employee of the intelligence community.

(B) Maximum period of suspension. The 5-year period described in subsection (a) shall not be extended more than 10 years by reason of subparagraph (A).

(C) Qualified official extended duty. For purposes of this paragraph—

(i) In general. The term "qualified official extended duty" means any extended duty while serving at a duty station which is at least 50 miles from such property or while residing under Government orders in Government quarters.

(ii) Uniformed services. The term "uniformed services" has the meaning given such term by section 101(a)(5) of title 10, United States Code, as in effect on the date of the enactment of this paragraph.

(iii) Foreign Service of the United States. The term "member of the Foreign Service of the United States" has the meaning given the term "member of the Service" by paragraph (1), (2), (3), (4), or (5) of section 103 of the Foreign Service Act of 1980, as in effect on the date of the enactment of this paragraph.

(iv) Employee of intelligence community. The term "employee of the intelligence community" means an employee (as defined by section 2105 of title 5, United States Code) of—

(I) the Office of the Director of National Intelligence,

(II) the Central Intelligence Agency,

(III) the National Security Agency,

(IV) the Defense Intelligence Agency,

(V) the National Geospatial-Intelligence Agency,

(VI) the National Reconnaissance Office,

(VII) any other office within the Department of Defense for the collection of specialized national intelligence through reconnaissance programs,

(VIII) any of the intelligence elements of the Army, the Navy, the Air Force, the Marine Corps, the Federal Bureau of Investigation, the Department of Treasury, the Department of Energy, and the Coast Guard,

(IX) the Bureau of Intelligence and Research of the Department of State, or

(X) any of the elements of the Department of Homeland Security concerned with the analyses of foreign intelligence information.

(v) Extended duty. The term "extended duty" means any period of active duty pursuant to a call or order to such duty for a period in excess of 90 days or for an indefinite period.

(vi) Repealed.

(D) Special rules relating to election.

(i) Election limited to 1 property at a time. An election under subparagraph (A) with respect to any property may not be made if such an election is in effect with respect to any other property.

(ii) Revocation of election. An election under subparagraph (A) may be revoked at any time.

(10) Property acquired in like-kind exchange. If a taxpayer acquires property in an exchange with respect to which gain is not recognized (in whole or in part) to the taxpayer under subsection (a) or (b) of section 1031, subsection (a) shall not apply to the sale or exchange of such property by such taxpayer (or by any person whose basis in such property is determined, in whole or in part, by reference to the basis in the hands of such taxpayer) during the 5-year period beginning with the date of such acquisition.

• *Caution:* Code Sec. 121(d)(11), redesignated as such by Sec. 101(a) of P.L. 108-121, and further redesignated by Sec. 403(ee)(1) of P.L. 109-135, was originally added by Sec. 542(c), P.L. 107-16, EGTRRA. As provided in Sec. 301(a), P.L. 111-312, this amendment will apply as if never enacted, effective for estates of decedents dying, and transfers made, after 12/31/2009.

(11) Property acquired from a decedent. The exclusion under this section shall apply to property sold by—

(A) the estate of a decedent,

(B) any individual who acquired such property from the decedent (within the meaning of section 1022), and

(C) a trust which, immediately before the death of the decedent, was a qualified revocable trust (as defined in section 645(b)(1)) established by the decedent,

determined by taking into account the ownership and use by the decedent.

(12) Peace corps.

(A) In general. At the election of an individual with respect to a property, the running of the 5-year period described in subsections (a) and (c)(1)(B) and paragraph (7) of this subsection with respect to such property shall be suspended during any period that such individual or such individual's spouse is serving outside the United States—

(i) on qualified official extended duty (as defined in paragraph (9)(C)) as an employee of the Peace Corps, or

(ii) as an enrolled volunteer or volunteer leader under section 5 or 6 (as the case may be) of the Peace Corps Act (22 U.S.C. 2504, 2505).

(B) Applicable rules. For purposes of subparagraph (A), rules similar to the rules of subparagraphs (B) and (D) shall apply.

(e) Denial of exclusion for expatriates.

This section shall not apply to any sale or exchange by an individual if the treatment provided by section 877(a)(1) applies to such individual.

(f) Election to have section not apply.

This section shall not apply to any sale or exchange with respect to which the taxpayer elects not to have this section apply.

(g) Residences acquired in rollovers under section 1034.

For purposes of this section, in the case of property the acquisition of which by the taxpayer resulted under section 1034 (as in effect on the day before the date of the enactment of this section) in the nonrecognition of any part of the gain realized on the sale or exchange of another residence, in determining the period for which the taxpayer has owned and used such property as the taxpayer's principal residence, there shall be included the aggregate periods for which such other residence (and each prior residence taken into account under section 1223(6) in determining the holding period of such property) had been so owned and used.

In 2010, P.L. 111-312, Sec. 101(a)(1), substituted "December 31, 2012" for "December 31, 2010" both places it appears in Sec. 901, P.L. 107-16 [see below], effective as if included in the enactment of P.L. 107-16, EGTRRA, 6/7/2001.

—P.L. 111-312, Sec. 301(a), provides that Code Sec. 121, as amended Sec. 542(c), P.L. 107-16, EGTRRA, 6/7/2001 (added para. (d)(11) [originally para. (d)(9), redesignated by Sec. 101(a), P.L. 108-121 and Sec. 403(ee)(1), P.L. 109-135], see below) will read as if such provision had never been enacted, effective for estates of decedents dying, and transfers made, after 12/31/2009.

Sec. 301(a), 111-312, 12/17/2010, provides:

"(a) In general. Each provision of law amended by subtitle A or E of title V of the Economic Growth and Tax Relief Reconciliation Act of 2001 is amended to read as such provision would read if such subtitle had never been enacted."

—P.L. 111-312, Sec. 301(c), of this Act, provides

"(c) Special election with respect to estates of decedents dying in 2010. Notwithstanding subsection (a), in the case of an estate of a decedent dying after December 31, 2009, and before January 1, 2011, the executor (within the meaning of section 2203 of the Internal Revenue Code of 1986) may elect to apply such Code as though the amendments made by subsection (a) do not apply with respect to chapter 11 of such Code and with respect to property acquired or passing from such decedent (within the meaning of section 1014(b) of such Code). Such election shall be made at such time and in such manner as the Secretary of the Treasury or the Secretary's delegate shall provide. Such an election once made shall be revocable only with the consent of the Secretary of the Treasury or the Secretary's delegate. For purposes of section 2652(a)(1) of such Code, the determination of whether any property is subject to the tax imposed by such chapter 11 shall be made without regard to any election made under this subsection."

—P.L. 111-312, Sec. 301(d), of this Act, provides

" (d) Extension of time for performing certain acts.

" (1) Estate tax. In the case of the estate of a decedent dying after December 31, 2009, and before the date of the enactment of this Act, the due date for—

" (A) filing any return under section 6018 of the Internal Revenue Code of 1986 (including any election required to be made on such a return) as such section is in effect after the date of the enactment of this Act without regard to any election under subsection (c),

" (B) making any payment of tax under chapter 11 of such Code, and

" (C) making any disclaimer described in section 2518(b) of such Code of an interest in property passing by reason of the death of such decedent, shall not be earlier than the date which is 9 months after the date of the enactment of this Act.

" (2) Generation-skipping tax. In the case of any generation-skipping transfer made after December 31, 2009, and before the date of the enactment of this Act, the due date for filing any return under section 2662 of the Internal Revenue Code of 1986 (including any election required to be made on such a return) shall not be earlier than the date which is 9 months after the date of the enactment of this Act."

In 2008, P.L. 110-289, Sec. 3092(a), added para. (b)(4) [sic (5)], effective for sales and exchanges after 12/31/2008.

—P.L. 110-245, Sec. 110(a), added para (d)(12), effective for tax. yrs. begin. after 12/31/2007.

—P.L. 110-245, Sec. 113(a), deleted subpara. (d)(9)(E) . . . Sec. 113(b), deleted clause (d)(9)(C)(vi), effective for sales or exchanges after 7/30/2008.

Prior to deletion, subpara. (d)(9)(E) read as follows:

"(E) Termination with respect to employees of intelligence community.

"Clause (iii) of subparagraph (A) shall not apply with respect to any sale or exchange after December 31, 2010.

Prior to deletion, clause (d)(9)(C)(vi) read as follows:

"(vi) Special rule relating to intelligence community. An employee of the intelligence community shall not be treated as serving on qualified extended duty unless such duty is at a duty station located outside the United States."

In 2007, P.L. 110-172, Sec. 11(a)(11)(A), added subpara. (d)(9)(E) . . . Sec. 11(a)(11)(B), deleted "and before January 1, 2011" before the period at the end of the effective date for the amendments made by Sec. 417 of P.L. 109-432 [see below], enacted 12/29/2007.

—P.L. 110-142, Sec. 7(a), added new para. (b)(4), effective for sales or exchanges after 12/31/2007.

Exclusions from income

In 2006, P.L. 109-432, Sec. 417(a), substituted "duty— (i) as a member of the uniformed services, (ii) as a member of the Foreign Service of the United States, or (iii) as an employee of the intelligence community." for "duty as a member of the uniformed services or of the Foreign Service of the United States." in subpara. (d)(9)(A)... Sec. 417(b), redesignated clause (d)(9)(C)(iv) as (d)(9)(C)(v) and added clause (d)(9)(C)(iv)... Sec. 417(c), added clause (d)(9)(C)(vi)... Sec. 417(d), amended the heading of para. (d)(9), effective for sales or exchanges after 12/20/2006 [as amended by Sec. 11(a)(11)(B) of P.L. 110-172, see above].
Prior to amendment, the heading for para. (d)(9) read as follows:
"Members of uniformed services and foreign service."

In 2005, P.L. 109-135, Sec. 402(a)(3), substituted "1223(6)" for "1223(7)" in subsec. (g), effective 8/8/2005 as if included in Sec. 1263 of the Energy Policy Act of 2005, P.L. 109-58. Sec. 402(m)(2) of this Act, reads as follows:

"2: Repeal of Public Utility Holding Company Act of 1935. The amendments made by subsection (a) shall not apply with respect to any transaction ordered in compliance with the Public Utility Holding Company Act of 1935 before its repeal."

—P.L. 109-135, Sec. 403(ee)(1), redesignated para. (d)(10) [as redesignated by Sec. 101(a) of P.L. 108-21, see below] as para. (d)(11)... Sec. 403(ee)(2), amended para. (d)(10) [as added by Sec. 840(a) of P.L. 108-357, see below], effective for sales or exchanges after 10/22/2004 as if included in Sec. 840 of the American Jobs Creation Act of 2004, P.L. 108-357.

Prior to amendment, para. (d)(10) [as added by Sec. 840(a) of P.L. 108-357, see below] read as follows:

"(10) Property acquired in like-kind exchange. If a taxpayer acquired property in an exchange to which section 1031 applied, subsection (a) shall not apply to the sale or exchange of such property if it occurs during the 5-year period beginning with the date of the acquisition of such property."

In 2004, P.L. 108-357, Sec. 840(a), added para. (d)(10), effective for sales or exchanges after 10/22/2004.

In 2003, P.L. 108-121, Sec. 101(a), redesignated para. (d)(9) as (10) and added para. (d)(9), effective for sales and exchanges after 5/6/97. For special rules, see Sec. 312(d)(2)-(4) of P.L. 105-34, reproduced below.

—P.L. 108-121, Sec. 101(b)(2), of this Act, provides:

"(2) Waiver of limitations. If refund or credit of any overpayment of tax resulting from the amendments made by this section is prevented at any time before the close of the 1-year period beginning on the date of the enactment of this Act by the operation of any law or rule of law (including res judicata), such refund or credit may nevertheless be made or allowed if claim therefor is filed before the close of such period."

In 2002, P.L. 107-358, Sec. 2, added subsec. (c) in Sec. 901 of P.L. 107-16 [see below], effective 12/17/2002.

In 2001, P.L. 107-16, Sec. 542(c), added para. (d)(9), effective for estates of decedents dying after 12/31/2009.

—P.L. 107-16, Sec. 901, of this Act [as amended by Sec. 2 of P.L. 107-358, and Sec. 101(a)(1) of P.L. 111-312, see above], reads as follows:

"Sec. 901. Sunset of provisions of Act.

"(a) In general. All provisions of, and amendments made by, this Act shall not apply—

"(1) to taxable, plan, or limitation years beginning after December 31, 2012, or

"(2) in the case of title V, to estates of decedents dying, gifts made, or generation skipping transfers, after December 31, 2012.

"(b) Application of certain laws. The Internal Revenue Code of 1986 and the Employee Retirement Income Security Act of 1974 shall be applied and administered to years, estates, gifts, and transfers described in subsection (a) as if the provisions and amendments described in subsection (a) had never been enacted.

"(c) Exception. Subsection (a) shall not apply to section 803 (relating to no federal income tax on restitution received by victims of the Nazi regime or their heirs or estates)."

In 1998, P.L. 105-206, Sec. 6005(e)(1), amended para. (b)(2)... Sec. 6005(e)(2), amended para. (c)(1), effective for sales or exchanges after 5/6/97, except as provided in Sec. 312(d)(2)-(4) [sic (e)(2)-(4)] of P.L. 105-34 [see below].
Prior to amendment, para. (b)(2) read as follows:

"(2) $500,000 limitation for certain joint returns. Paragraph (1) shall be applied by substituting '$500,000' for '$250,000' if—

"(A) a husband and wife make a joint return for the taxable year of the sale or exchange of the property,

"(B) either spouse meets the ownership requirements of subsection (a) with respect to such property,

"(C) both spouses meet the use requirements of subsection (a) with respect to such property, and

"(D) neither spouse is ineligible for the benefits of subsection (a) with respect to such property by reason of paragraph (3)."
Prior to amendment, para. (c)(1) read as follows:

"(1) In general. In the case of a sale or exchange to which this subsection applies, the ownership and use requirements of subsection (a) shall not apply and subsection (b)(3) shall not apply; but the amount (b) of gain excluded from gross income under subsection (a) with respect to such sale or exchange shall not exceed—

"(A) the amount which bears the same ratio to the amount which would be so excluded under this section if such requirements had been met, as

"(B) the shorter of—

"(i) the aggregate periods, during the 5-year period ending on the date of such sale or exchange, such property has been owned and used by the taxpayer as the taxpayer's principal residence, or

"(ii) the period after the date of the most recent prior sale or exchange by the taxpayer to which subsection (a) applied and before the date of such sale or exchange,

bears to 2 years."

—P.L. 105-206, Sec. 6005(e)(3), added "on or" before "before" each place it appeared in Sec. 312(d)(2) [sic (e)(2)] of P.L. 105-34, see below.

In 1997, P.L. 105-34, Sec. 312(a), amended Code Sec. 121, effective for sales and exchanges after 5/6/97, except as provided in Sec. 312(d)(2)-(4) [sic (e)(2)-(4)] of this Act [as amended by Sec. 6005(e)(3) of 105-206, see above] which reads as follows:

"(2) Sales on or before date of enactment. At the election of the taxpayer, the amendments made by this section shall not apply to any sale or exchange on or before the date of the enactment of this Act. [8/5/97]

"(3) Certain sales within 2 years after date of enactment. Section 121 of the Internal Revenue Code of 1986 (as amended by this section) shall be applied without regard to subsection (c)(2)(B) thereof in the case of any sale or exchange of property during the 2-year period beginning on the date of the enactment of this Act if the taxpayer held such property on the date of the enactment of this Act and fails to meet the ownership and use requirements of subsection (a) thereof with respect to such property.

"(4) Binding contracts. At the election of the taxpayer, the amendments made by this section shall not apply to a sale or exchange after the date of the enactment of this Act, if—

"(A) such sale or exchange is pursuant to a contract which was binding on such date, or

"(B) without regard to such amendments, gain would not be recognized under section 1034 of the Internal Revenue Code of 1986 (as in effect on the day before the date of the enactment of this Act) on such sale or exchange by reason of a new residence acquired on or before such date or with respect to the acquisition of which by the taxpayer a binding contract was in effect on such date.

This paragraph shall not apply to any sale or exchange by an individual if the treatment provided by section 877(a)(1) of the Internal Revenue Code of 1986 applies to such individual."

Prior to amendment, Code Sec. 121 read as follows:

" Sec. 121. One-time exclusion of gain from sale of principal residence by individual who has attained age 55.

"(a) General rule. At the election of the taxpayer, gross income does not include gain from the sale or exchange of property if—

"(1) the taxpayer has attained the age of 55 before the date of such sale or exchange, and

"(2) during the 5-year period ending on the date of the sale or exchange, such property has been owned and used by the taxpayer as his principal residence for periods aggregating 3 years or more.

"(b) Limitations.

"(1) Dollar limitation. The amount of the gain excluded from gross income under subsection (a) shall not exceed $125,000 ($62,500 in the case of a separate return by a married individual).

"(2) Application to only 1 sale or exchange. Subsection (a) shall not apply to any sale or exchange by the taxpayer if an election by the taxpayer or his spouse under subsection (a) with respect to any other sale or exchange is in effect.

"(3) Additional election if prior sale was made on or before July 26, 1978. In the case of any sale or exchange after July 26, 1978, this section shall be applied by not taking into account any election made with respect to a sale or exchange on or before such date.

"(c) Election. An election under subsection (a) may be made or revoked at any time before the expiration of the period for making a claim for credit or refund of the tax imposed by this chapter for the taxable year in which the sale or exchange occurred, and shall be made or revoked in such manner as the Secretary shall by regulations prescribe. In the case of a taxpayer who is married, an election under subsection (a) or a revocation thereof may be made only if his spouse joins in such election or revocation.

"(d) Special rules.

"(1) Property held jointly by husband and wife. For purposes of this section, if—

"(A) property is held by a husband and wife as joint tenants, tenants by the entirety, or community property,

"(B) such husband and wife make a joint return under section 6013 for the taxable year of the sale or exchange, and

"(C) one spouse satisfies the age, holding, and use requirements of subsection (a) with respect to such property,

then both husband and wife shall be treated as satisfying the age, holding, and use requirements of subsection (a) with respect to such property.

"(2) Property of deceased spouse. For purposes of this section, in the case of an unmarried individual whose spouse is deceased on the date of the sale or exchange of property, if—

"(A) the deceased spouse (during the 5-year period ending on the date of the sale or exchange) satisfied the holding and use requirements of subsection (a)(2) with respect to such property, and

"(B) no election by the deceased spouse under subsection (a) is in effect with respect to a prior sale or exchange,

then such individual shall be treated as satisfying the holding and use requirements of subsection (a)(2) with respect to such property.

"(3) Tenant-stockholder in cooperative housing corporation. For purposes of this section, if the taxpayer holds stock as a tenant-stockholder (as defined in section 216) in a cooperative housing corporation (as defined in such section), then—

"(A) the holding requirements of subsection (a)(2) shall be applied to the holding of such stock, and

"(B) the use requirements of subsection (a)(2) shall be applied to the house or apartment which the taxpayer was entitled to occupy as such stockholder.

"(4) Involuntary conversions. For purposes of this section, the destruction, theft, seizure, requisition, or condemnation of property shall be treated as the sale of such property.

"(5) Property used in part as principal residence. In the case of property only a portion of which, during the 5-year period ending on the date of the sale or exchange, has been owned and used by the taxpayer as his principal residence for periods aggregating 3 years or more, this section shall apply with respect to so much of the gain from the sale or exchange of such property as is determined, under regulations prescribed by the Secretary, to be attributable to the portion of the property so owned and used by the taxpayer.

"(6) Determination of marital status. In the case of any sale or exchange, for purposes of this section—

"(A) the determination of whether an individual is married shall be made as of the date of the sale or exchange; and

"(B) an individual legally separated from his spouse under a decree of divorce or of separate maintenance shall not be considered as married.

"(7) Application of sections 1033 and 1034. In applying sections 1033 (relating to involuntary conversions) and 1034 (relating to sale or exchange of residence), the amount realized from the sale or exchange of property shall be treated as being the amount determined without regard to this section, reduced by the amount of gain not included in gross income pursuant to an election under this section.

"(8) Property acquired after involuntary conversion. If the basis of the property sold or exchanged is determined (in whole or in part) under subsection (b) of section 1033 (relating to basis of property acquired through involuntary conversion), then the holding and use by the taxpayer of the converted property shall be treated as holding and use by the taxpayer of the property sold or exchanged.

"(9) Determination of use during periods of out-of-residence care. In the case of a taxpayer who—

"(A) becomes physically or mentally incapable of self-care, and

"(B) owns property and uses such property as the taxpayer's principal residence during the 5-year period described in subsection (a)(2) for periods aggregating at least 1 year,

then the taxpayer shall be treated as using such property as the taxpayer's principal residence during any time during such 5-year period in which the taxpayer owns the property and resides in any facility (including a nursing home) licensed by a State or political subdivision to care for an individual in the taxpayer's condition."

In 1988, P.L. 100-647, Sec. 6011(a), added para. (d)(9), effective for any sale or exchange after 9/30/88 in tax. yrs. end. after 9/30/88.

In 1981, P.L. 97-34, Sec. 123(a), substituted "$125,000 ($62,500)" for "$100,000 ($50,000)" in para. (b)(1), effective for residences sold or exchanged after 7/20/81.

In 1978, P.L. 95-600, Sec. 404(a), amended the heading of Code Sec. 121 and subsecs. (a) and (b) . . . Sec. 404(b), added para (d)(8) . . . Sec. 404(c)(1), substituted "5-year period" for "8-year period" in subpara. (d)(2)(A) . . . Sec. 404(c)(2), substituted "5-year period" for "8-year period" and "3 years" for "5 years" in para. (d)(5), effective for sales or exchanges after 7/26/78, in tax. yrs. end. after 7/26/78 except as provided in Sec. 404(d)(2) of this Act which reads:

"(2) Transitional Rule. In the case of a sale or exchange of a residence before July 26, 1981, a taxpayer who has attained age 65 on the date of such sale or exchange may elect to have section 121 of the Internal Revenue Code of 1954 applied by substituting '8-year period' for '5-year period' and '5 years' for '3 years' in subsections (a), (d)(2), and (d)(5) of such section."

Prior to amendment, the heading of Code Sec. 121 and subsecs. (a) and (b) read as follows:

"SEC. 121. GAIN FROM SALE OR EXCHANGE OF RESIDENCE OF INDIVIDUAL WHO HAS ATTAINED AGE 65.

"(a) General rule.

"At the election of the taxpayer, gross income does not include gain from the sale or exchange of property if—

"(1) the taxpayer has attained the age of 65 before the date of such sale or exchange, and

"(2) during the 8-year period ending on the date of the sale or exchange, such property has been owned and used by the taxpayer as his principal residence for periods aggregating 5 years or more.

"(b) Limitations.

"(1) Where adjusted sales price exceeds $35,000. If the adjusted sales price of the property sold or exchanged exceeds $35,000, subsection (a) shall apply to that portion of the gain which bears the same ratio to the total amount of such gain as $35,000 bears to such adjusted sales price. For purposes of the preceding sentence, the term 'adjusted sales price' has the meaning assigned to such term by section 1034(b)(1) (determined without regard to subsection (d)(7) of this section).

"(2) Application to only one sale or exchange. Subsection (a) shall not apply to any sale or exchange by the taxpayer if an election by the taxpayer or his spouse under subsection (a) with respect to any other sale or exchange is in effect."

In 1976, P.L. 94-455, Sec. 1404, substituted "$35,000" for "$20,000" each place it appeared in para. (b)(1), effective for tax. yrs. begin. after 12/31/76.

—P.L. 94-455, Sec. 1906(b)(13)(A), substituted "Secretary" for "Secretary or his delegate" in subsec. (c) and para. (d)(5), effective for tax. yrs. begin. after 12/31/76.

In 1964, P.L. 88-272, Sec. 206(a), added Code Sec. 121, effective for dispositions after 12/31/63 in tax. yrs. end. after 12/31/63.

Sec. 122. Certain reduced uniformed services retirement pay.

(a) General rule.

In the case of a member or former member of the uniformed services of the United States, gross income does not include the amount of any reduction in his retired or retainer pay pursuant to the provisions of chapter 73 of title 10, United States Code.

(b) Special rule.

(1) Amount excluded from gross income. In the case of any individual referred to in subsection (a), all amounts received after December 31, 1965, as retired or retainer pay shall be excluded from gross income until there has been so excluded an amount equal to the consideration for the contract. The preceding sentence shall apply only to the extent that the amounts received would, but for such sentence, be includible in gross income.

(2) Consideration for the contract. For purposes of paragraph (1) and section 72(n), the term "consideration for the contract" means, in respect of any individual, the sum of—

(A) the total amount of the reductions before January 1, 1966, in his retired or retainer pay by reason of an election under chapter 73 of title 10 of the United States Code, and

(B) any amounts deposited at any time by him pursuant to section 1438 or 1452(d) of such title 10.

In 1974, P.L. 93-406, Sec. 2007(a), amended subsec. (a), effective for tax. yrs. end. on or after 9/21/72.

Prior to amendment, subsec. (a) read as follows:

"(a) General rule.

"In the case of a member or former member of the uniformed services of the United States who has made an election under chapter 73 of title 10 of the United States Code to receive a reduced amount of retired or retainer pay, gross income does not include the amount of any reduction after December 31, 1965, in his retired or retainer pay by reason of such election."

—P.L. 93-406, Sec. 2005(c)(10), substituted "72(n)" for "72(o)" in para. (b)(2), effective for distributions or payments made after 12/31/73, in tax. yrs. begin. after 12/31/73.

—P.L. 93-406, Sec. 2007(b)(1), added "or 1452(d)" after "section 1438" in para. (b)(2), effective for tax. yrs. end. on or after 9/21/72.

In 1966, P.L. 89-365, Sec. 1, redesignated Code Sec. 122 as 123, and added new Code Sec. 122, effective for tax. yrs. end. after 12/31/65.

Sec. 123. Amounts received under insurance contracts for certain living expenses.

(a) General rule.

In the case of an individual whose principal residence is damaged or destroyed by fire, storm, or other casualty, or who is denied access to his principal residence by governmental authorities because of the occurrence or threat of occurrence of such a casualty, gross income does not include amounts received by such individual under an insurance contract which are paid to compensate or reimburse such individual for living expenses incurred for himself and members of his household resulting from the loss of use or occupancy of such residence.

(b) Limitation.

Subsection (a) shall apply to amounts received by the taxpayer for living expenses incurred during any period only to the extent the amounts received do not exceed the amount by which—

(1) the actual living expenses incurred during such period for himself and members of his household resulting from the loss of use or occupancy of their residence, exceed

(2) the normal living expenses which would have been incurred for himself and members of his household during such period.

Exclusions from income   Code Sec. 125(e)(2)

In 1969, P.L. 91-172, Sec. 901(a), added Code Sec. 123, for amounts received on or after 1/1/69.

Sec. 124. Repealed.

In 1990, P.L. 101-508, Sec. 11801(a)(9), repealed Code Sec. 124, effective 11/5/90, except as provided in Sec. 11821(b) of this Act, reproduced in note following Code Sec. 110.
Prior to repeal, Code Sec. 124 read as follows:
"SEC. 124. QUALIFIED TRANSPORTATION PROVIDED BY EMPLOYER.
"(a) General rule.
"Gross income of an employee does not include the value of qualified transportation provided by the employer between the employee's residence and place of employment.
"(b) Qualified transportation.
"For purposes of this section, the term 'qualified transportation' means transportation in a commuter highway vehicle (as defined in section 46(c)(6)(B) but without regard to clause (iii) or (iv) thereof).
"(c) Additional requirements.
"Subsection (a) does not apply to the value of transportation provided by an employer unless —
"(1) such transportation is provided under a separate written plan of the employer which does not discriminate in favor of employees who are officers, shareholders, or highly compensated employees, and
"(2) the plan provides that the value of such transportation is provided in addition to (and not in lieu of) any compensation otherwise payable to the employee.
"(d) Definitions.
"For purposes of this section —
"(1) Provided by the employer. Transportation shall be considered to be provided by an employer if the transportation is furnished in a commuter highway vehicle (described in subsection (b)) operated by or for the employer.
"(2) Employee. The term 'employee' does not include an individual who is an employee (within the meaning of section 401(c)(1)).
"(e) Effective date.
"Subsection (a) applies with respect to qualified transportation provided in taxable years beginning after December 31, 1978, and before January 1, 1986."

In 1978, P.L. 95-618, Sec. 242(a), added Code Sec. 124, effective 11/10/78. Sec. 242(c) of this Act provides:
"(c) Transition rule.
"The plan requirements of section 124(c) of the Internal Revenue Code of 1954 shall be considered to be met with respect to transportation provided before July 1, 1979, if there is a plan meeting such requirements of the employer in effect on that date."

Sec. 125. Cafeteria plans.

(a) In general.
Except as provided in subsection (b), no amount shall be included in the gross income of a participant in a cafeteria plan solely because, under the plan, the participant may choose among the benefits of the plan.

(b) Exception for highly compensated participants and key employees.

    (1) Highly compensated participants. In the case of a highly compensated participant, subsection (a) shall not apply to any benefit attributable to a plan year for which the plan discriminates in favor of—

        (A) highly compensated individuals as to eligibility to participate, or

        (B) highly compensated participants as to contributions and benefits.

    (2) Key employees. In the case of a key employee (within the meaning of section 416(i)(1)), subsection (a) shall not apply to any benefit attributable to a plan for which the statutory nontaxable benefits provided to key employees exceed 25 percent of the aggregate of such benefits provided for all employees under the plan. For purposes of the preceding sentence, statutory nontaxable benefits shall be determined without regard to the second sentence of subsection (f).

    (3) Year of inclusion. For purposes of determining the taxable year of inclusion, any benefit described in paragraph (1) or (2) shall be treated as received or accrued in the taxable year of the participant or key employee in which the plan year ends.

(c) Discrimination as to benefits or contributions.
For purposes of subparagraph (B) of subsection (b)(1), a cafeteria plan does not discriminate where qualified benefits and total benefits (or employer contributions allocable to qualified benefits and employer contributions for total benefits) do not discriminate in favor of highly compensated participants.

(d) Cafeteria plan defined.
For purposes of this section

    (1) In general. The term "cafeteria plan" means a written plan under which—

        (A) all participants are employees, and

        (B) the participants may choose among 2 or more benefits consisting of cash and qualified benefits.

    (2) Deferred compensation plans excluded.

        (A) In general. The term "cafeteria plan" does not include any plan which provides for deferred compensation.

        (B) Exception for cash and deferred arrangements. Subparagraph (A) shall not apply to a profit-sharing or stock bonus plan or rural cooperative plan (within the meaning of section 401(k)(7)) which includes a qualified cash or deferred arrangement (as defined in section 401(k)(2)) to the extent of amounts which a covered employee may elect to have the employer pay as contributions to a trust under such plan on behalf of the employee.

        (C) Exception for certain plans maintained by educational institutions. Subparagraph (A) shall not apply to a plan maintained by an educational organization described in section 170(b)(1)(A)(ii) to the extent of amounts which a covered employee may elect to have the employer pay as contributions for post-retirement group life insurance if—

            (i) all contributions for such insurance must be made before retirement, and

            (ii) such life insurance does not have a cash surrender value at any time.

For purposes of section 79, any life insurance described in the preceding sentence shall be treated as group-term life insurance.

        (D) Exception for health savings accounts. Subparagraph (A) shall not apply to a plan to the extent of amounts which a covered employee may elect to have the employer pay as contributions to a health savings account established on behalf of the employee.

(e) Highly compensated participant and individual defined.
For purposes of this section—

    (1) Highly compensated participant. The term "highly compensated participant" means a participant who is—

        (A) an officer,

        (B) a shareholder owning more than 5 percent of the voting power or value of all classes of stock of the employer,

        (C) highly compensated, or

        (D) a spouse or dependent (within the meaning of section 152, determined without regard to subsections (b)(1), (b)(2), and (d)(1)(B) thereof) of an individual described in subparagraph (A), (B), or (C).

    (2) Highly compensated individual. The term "highly compensated individual" means an individual who is described in subparagraphs (A), (B), (C), or (D) of paragraph (1).

Code Sec. 125(e)(2) — Exclusions from income

> • *Caution:* Code Sec. 125(f), following, is effective for tax. yrs. begin. before 1/1/2014. For Code Sec. 125(f), effective for tax. yrs. begin. after 12/31/2013, see below.

(f) Qualified benefits defined.

For purposes of this section, the term "qualified benefit" means any benefit which, with the application of subsection (a), is not includible in the gross income of the employee by reason of an express provision of this chapter (other than section 106(b), 117, 127, or 132). Such term includes any group term life insurance which is includible in gross income only because it exceeds the dollar limitation of section 79 and such term includes any other benefit permitted under regulations. Such term shall not include any product which is advertised, marketed, or offered as long-term care insurance.

> • *Caution:* Code Sec. 125(f), following, is effective for tax. yrs. begin. after 12/31/2013. For Code Sec. 125(f), effective for tax. yrs. begin. before 1/1/2014, see above.

(f) Qualified benefits defined.

For purposes of this section—

(1) In general. the term "qualified benefit" means any benefit which, with the application of subsection (a), is not includible in the gross income of the employee by reason of an express provision of this chapter (other than section 106(b), 117, 127, or 132). Such term includes any group term life insurance which is includible in gross income only because it exceeds the dollar limitation of section 79 and such term includes any other benefit permitted under regulations.

(2) Long-term care insurance not qualified. The term "qualified benefit" shall not include any product which is advertised, marketed, or offered as long-term care insurance.

(3) Certain exchange-participating qualified health plans not qualified.

(A) In general. The term "qualified benefit" shall not include any qualified health plan (as defined in section 1301(a) of the Patient Protection and Affordable Care Act) offered through an Exchange established under section 1311 of such Act.

(B) Exception for exchange-eligible employers. Subparagraph (A) shall not apply with respect to any employee if such employee's employer is a qualified employer (as defined in section 1312(f)(2) of the Patient Protection and Affordable Care Act) offering the employee the opportunity to enroll through such an Exchange in a qualified health plan in a group market.

(g) Special rules.

(1) Collectively bargained plan not considered discriminatory. For purposes of this section, a plan shall not be treated as discriminatory if the plan is maintained under an agreement which the Secretary finds to be a collective bargaining agreement between employee representatives and one or more employers.

(2) Health benefits. For purposes of subparagraph (B) of subsection (b)(1), a cafeteria plan which provides health benefits shall not be treated as discriminatory if—

(A) contributions under the plan on behalf of each participant include an amount which—

(i) equals 100 percent of the cost of the health benefit coverage under the plan of the majority of the highly compensated participants similarly situated, or

(ii) equals or exceeds 75 percent of the cost of the health benefit coverage of the participant (similarly situated) having the highest cost health benefit coverage under the plan, and

(B) contributions or benefits under the plan in excess of those described in subparagraph (A) bear a uniform relationship to compensation.

(3) Certain participation eligibility rules not treated as discriminatory. For purposes of subparagraph (A) of subsection (b)(1), a classification shall not be treated as discriminatory if the plan—

(A) benefits a group of employees described in section 410(b)(2)(A)(i), and

(B) meets the requirements of clauses (i) and (ii):

(i) No employee is required to complete more than 3 years of employment with the employer or employers maintaining the plan as a condition of participation in the plan, and the employment requirement for each employee is the same.

(ii) Any employee who has satisfied the employment requirement of clause (i) and who is otherwise entitled to participate in the plan commences participation no later than the first day of the first plan year beginning after the date the employment requirement was satisfied unless the employee was separated from service before the first day of that plan year.

(4) Certain controlled groups, etc. All employees who are treated as employed by a single employer under subsection (b), (c), or (m) of section 414 shall be treated as employed by a single employer for purposes of this section.

(h) Special rule for unused benefits in health flexible spending arrangements of individuals called to active duty.

(1) In general. For purposes of this title, a plan or other arrangement shall not fail to be treated as a cafeteria plan or health flexible spending arrangement merely because such arrangement provides for qualified reservist distributions.

(2) Qualified reservist distribution. For purposes of this subsection, the term "qualified reservist distribution" means, any distribution to an individual of all or a portion of the balance in the employee's account under such arrangement if—

(A) such individual was (by reason of being a member of a reserve component (as defined in section 101 of title 37, United States Code)) ordered or called to active duty for a period in excess of 179 days or for an indefinite period, and

(B) such distribution is made during the period beginning on the date of such order or call and ending on the last date that reimbursements could otherwise be made under such arrangement for the plan year which includes the date of such order or call.

> • *Caution:* Code Sec. 125(i), prior to amendment by Sec. 9005(a)(2), P.L. 111-148, and Sec. 10902(a)

(i) Cross reference.

For reporting and recordkeeping requirements, see section 6039D.

Exclusions from income Code Sec. 125(j)(5)(A)

> • **Caution:** Code Sec. 125(i), following, as added by Sec. 9005(a)

(i) Limitation on health flexible spending arrangements. For purposes of this section, if a benefit is provided under a cafeteria plan through employer contributions to a health flexible spending arrangement, such benefit shall not be treated as a qualified benefit unless the cafeteria plan provides that an employee may not elect for any taxable year to have salary reduction contributions in excess of $2,500 made to such arrangement.

> • **Caution:** Code Sec. 125(i), as amended by P.L. 111-148, Sec. 9005(a)(2), Sec. 10902(a) and 111-152, Sec. 1403(a) generally effective for tax yrs. begin. after 12/31/2013.

(i) Limitation on health flexible spending arrangements.
  (1) In general. For purposes of this section, if a benefit is provided under a cafeteria plan through employer contributions to a health flexible spending arrangement, such benefit shall not be treated as a qualified benefit unless the cafeteria plan provides that an employee may not elect for any taxable year to have salary reduction contributions in excess of $2,500 made to such arrangement.
  (2) Adjustment for inflation. In the case of any taxable year beginning after December 31, 2013, the dollar amount in paragraph (1) shall be increased by an amount equal to—
    (A) such amount, multiplied by
    (B) the cost-of-living adjustment determined under section 1(f)(3) for the calendar year in which such taxable year begins by substituting "calendar year 2012" for "calendar year 1992" in subparagraph (B) thereof.
  If any increase determined under this paragraph is not a multiple of $50, such increase shall be rounded to the next lowest multiple of $50.

(j) Simple cafeteria plan for small businesses.
  (1) In general. An eligible employer maintaining a simple cafeteria plan with respect to which the requirements of this subsection are met for any year shall be treated as meeting any applicable nondiscrimination requirement during such year.
  (2) Simple cafeteria plan. For purposes of this subsection, the term "simple cafeteria plan" means a cafeteria plan—
    (A) which is established and maintained by an eligible employer, and
    (B) with respect to which the contribution requirements of paragraph (3), and the eligibility and participation requirements of paragraph (4), are met.
  (3) Contribution requirements.
    (A) In general. The requirements of this paragraph are met if, under the plan the employer is required, without regard to whether a qualified employee makes any salary reduction contribution, to make a contribution to provide qualified benefits under the plan on behalf of each qualified employee in an amount equal to—
      (i) a uniform percentage (not less than 2 percent) of the employee's compensation for the plan year, or
      (ii) an amount which is not less than the lesser of—
        (I) 6 percent of the employee's compensation for the plan year, or
        (II) twice the amount of the salary reduction contributions of each qualified employee.
    (B) Matching contributions on behalf of highly compensated and key employees. The requirements of subparagraph (A)(ii) shall not be treated as met if, under the plan, the rate of contributions with respect to any salary reduction contribution of a highly compensated or key employee at any rate of contribution is greater than that with respect to an employee who is not a highly compensated or key employee.
    (C) Additional contributions. Subject to subparagraph (B), nothing in this paragraph shall be treated as prohibiting an employer from making contributions to provide qualified benefits under the plan in addition to contributions required under subparagraph (A).
    (D) Definitions. For purposes of this paragraph—
      ((i)) Salary reduction contribution. The term "salary reduction contribution" means, with respect to a cafeteria plan, any amount which is contributed to the plan at the election of the employee and which is not includible in gross income by reason of this section.
      ((ii)) Qualified employee. The term "qualified employee" means, with respect to a cafeteria plan, any employee who is not a highly compensated or key employee and who is eligible to participate in the plan.
      ((iii)) Highly compensated. The term "highly compensated employee" has the meaning given such term by section 414(q).
      ((iv)) Key employee. The term "key employee" has the meaning given such term by section 416(i).
  (4) Minimum eligibility and participation requirements.
    (A) In general. The requirements of this paragraph shall be treated as met with respect to any year if, under the plan—
      (i) all employees who had at least 1,000 hours of service for the preceding plan year are eligible to participate, and
      (ii) each employee eligible to participate in the plan may, subject to terms and conditions applicable to all participants, elect any benefit available under the plan.
    (B) Certain employees may be excluded. For purposes of subparagraph (A)(i), an employer may elect to exclude under the plan employees—
      (i) who have not attained the age of 21 before the close of a plan year,
      (ii) who have less than 1 year of service with the employer as of any day during the plan year,
      (iii) who are covered under an agreement which the Secretary of Labor finds to be a collective bargaining agreement if there is evidence that the benefits covered under the cafeteria plan were the subject of good faith bargaining between employee representatives and the employer, or
      (iv) who are described in section 410(b)(3)(C) (relating to nonresident aliens working outside the United States). A plan may provide a shorter period of service or younger age for purposes of clause (i) or (ii).
  (5) Eligible employer. For purposes of this subsection—
    (A) In general. The term "eligible employer" means, with respect to any year, any employer if such employer employed an average of 100 or fewer employees on business days during either of the 2 preceding years. For purposes of this subparagraph, a year may only be taken into account if the employer was in existence throughout the year.

(B) **Employers not in existence during preceding year.** If an employer was not in existence throughout the preceding year, the determination under subparagraph (A) shall be based on the average number of employees that it is reasonably expected such employer will employ on business days in the current year.

(C) **Growing employers retain treatment as small employer.**

(i) **In general.** If—

(I) an employer was an eligible employer for any year (a "qualified year"), and

(II) such employer establishes a simple cafeteria plan for its employees for such year, then, notwithstanding the fact the employer fails to meet the requirements of subparagraph (A) for any subsequent year, such employer shall be treated as an eligible employer for such subsequent year with respect to employees (whether or not employees during a qualified year) of any trade or business which was covered by the plan during any qualified year.

(ii) **Exception.** This subparagraph shall cease to apply if the employer employs an average of 200 or more employees on business days during any year preceding any such subsequent year.

(D) **Special rules.**

(i) **Predecessors.** Any reference in this paragraph to an employer shall include a reference to any predecessor of such employer.

(ii) **Aggregation rules.** All persons treated as a single employer under subsection (a) or (b) of section 52, or subsection (n) or (o) of section 414, shall be treated as one person.

(6) **Applicable nondiscrimination requirement.** For purposes of this subsection, the term "applicable nondiscrimination requirement" means any requirement under subsection (b) of this section, section 79(d), section 105(h), or paragraph (2), (3), (4), or (8) of section 129(d).

(7) **Compensation.** The term "compensation" has the meaning given such term by section 414(s).

(k) Cross reference.

For reporting and recordkeeping requirements, see section 6039D.

(l) Regulations.

The Secretary shall prescribe such regulations as may be necessary to carry out the provisions of this section.

In 2010, P.L. 111-152, Sec. 1403(a), of this Act, reads as follows:

"(a) In general. Section 10902(b) of the Patient Protection and Affordable Care Act [relating to Sec. 10902(a) of such Act, which amended Code Sec. 125(i), see below] is amended by striking 'December 31, 2010' and inserting 'December 31, 2012'." . . . Sec. 1403(b)(1), substituted "December 31, 2013" for "December 31, 2011" in the matter preceding subpara. (i)(2)(A) [as added by Sec. 9005(a)(2) of P.L. 111-148, and amended by Sec. 10902(a) of P.L. 111-148] . . . Sec. 1403(b)(2), substituted "2012" for "2010" in subpara. (i)(2)(B) [as added by Sec. 9005(a)(2) of P.L. 111-148, and amended by Sec. 10902(a) of P.L. 111-148], enacted 3/30/2010.

—P.L. 111-148, Sec. 1515(a), added para. (f)(3) . . . Sec. 1515(b)(1), substituted "For purposes of this section— (1) In general. The term" for "For purposes of this section, the term" in subsec. (f) . . . Sec. 1515(b)(2), substituted "(2) Long-term care insurance not qualified. The term 'qualified benefit' shall not include" for "Such term shall not include" in subsec. (f), effective for tax. yrs. begin. after 12/31/2013.

—P.L. 111-148, Sec. 9005(a)(1), redesignated subsecs. (i)-(j) as subsecs. (j)-(k) . . . Sec. 9005(a)(2), added subsec. (i), effective for tax. yrs. begin. after 12/31/2010. [Ed. Note: We believe the intent of Congress was to change the effective date for subsec. (i) amde by P.L. 111-152, 1403(a) to P.L. 111-148, 10902(b) to 12/31/2012.]

—P.L. 111-148, Sec. 9022(a), redesignated subsecs. (j)-(k), as amended by Sec. 9005(a)(1) of this Act, above, as subsecs. (k)-(l), and added subsec. (j), effective for yrs. begin. after 12/31/2010.

—P.L. 111-148, Sec. 10902(a), amended subsec. (i), as added by Sec. 9005(a)(2) of this Act, [Ed. Note: We believe the intent of Congress was for the amendment made by P.L. 111-148, Sec. 10902 to completely replace the amendment made by P.L. 111-148, Sec. 9005] see above, effective [as amended by P.L. 111-152, Sec. 1403(a), see above] for tax. yrs. begin. after 12/31/2013.

Prior to amendment, subsec. (i) read as follows:

"(i) Limitation on health flexible spending arrangements.

"For purposes of this section, if a benefit is provided under a cafeteria plan through employer contributions to a health flexible spending arrangement, such benefit shall not be treated as a qualified benefit unless the cafeteria plan provides that an employee may not elect for any taxable year to have salary reduction contributions in excess of $2,500 made to such arrangement."

In 2008, P.L. 110-245, Sec. 114(a), redesignated subsecs. (h) and (i) as subsecs. (i) and (j) and added new subsec. (h), effective for distributions made after 6/17/2008.

In 2007, P.L. 110-172, Sec. 11(a)(12), substituted "second sentence" for "last sentence" in para. (b)(2), enacted 12/29/2007.

In 2004, P.L. 108-311, Sec. 207(11), added ", determined without regard to subsections (b)(1), (b)(2), and (d)(1)(B) thereof" after "section 152" in subpara. (e)(1)(D), effective for tax. yrs. begin. after 12/31/2004.

In 2003, P.L. 108-173, Sec. 1201(i), added subpara. (d)(2)(D), effective for tax. yrs. begin. after 12/31/2003.

In 1996, P.L. 104-191, Sec. 301(d), added "106(b)," before "117" in subsec. (f), effective for tax. yrs. begin. after 12/31/96.

—P.L. 104-191, Sec. 321(c)(1), added a sentence at the end of subsec. (f), effective for contracts issued after 12/31/96. Sec. 321(f)(2)-(5), of this Act, reads as follows:

"(2) Continuation of existing policies. In the case of any contract issued before January 1, 1997, which met the long-term care insurance requirements of the State in which the contract was sitused at the time the contract was issued—

"(A) such contract shall be treated for purposes of the Internal Revenue Code of 1986 as a qualified long-term care insurance contract (as defined in section 7702B(b) of such Code), and

"(B) services provided under, or reimbursed by, such contract shall be treated for such purposes as qualified long-term care services (as defined in section 7702B(c) of such Code).

In the case of an individual who is covered on December 31, 1996, under a State long-term care plan (as defined in section 7702B(f)(2) of such Code), the terms of such plan on such date shall be treated for purposes of the preceding sentence as a contract issued on such date which met the long-term care insurance requirements of such State.

"(3) Exchanges of existing policies. If, after the date of enactment of this Act and before January 1, 1998, a contract providing for long-term care insurance coverage is exchanged solely for a qualified long-term care insurance contract (as defined in section 7702B(b) of such Code), no gain or loss shall be recognized on the exchange. If, in addition to a qualified long-term care insurance contract, money or other property is received in the exchange, then any gain shall be recognized to the extent of the sum of the money and the fair market value of the other property received. For purposes of this paragraph, the cancellation of a contract providing for long-term care insurance coverage and reinvestment of the cancellation proceeds in a qualified long-term care insurance contract within 60 days thereafter shall be treated as an exchange.

"(4) Issuance of certain riders permitted. For purposes of applying sections 101(f), 7702, and 7702A of the Internal Revenue Code of 1986 to any contract—

"(A) the issuance of a rider which is treated as a qualified long-term care insurance contract under section 7702B, and

"(B) the addition of any provision required to conform any other long-term care rider to be so treated,

shall not be treated as a modification or material change of such contract.

"(5) Application of per diem limitation to existing contracts. The amount of per diem payments made under a contract issued on or before July 31, 1996, with respect to an insured which are excludable from gross income by reason of section 7702B of the Internal Revenue Code of 1986 (as added by this section) shall not be reduced under subsection (d)(2)(B) thereof by reason of reimbursements received under a contract issued on or before such date. The preceding sentence shall cease to apply as of the date (after July 31, 1996) such contract is exchanged or there is any contract modification which results in an increase in the amount of such per diem payments or the amount of such reimbursements."

In 1990, P.L. 101-508, Sec. 11801(c)(3), substituted "section 117," for "section 117, 124," in subsec. (f), effective 11/5/90 except as provided in Sec. 11821(b) of this Act, reproduced in note following Code Sec. 110.

In 1989, P.L. 101-239, Sec. 7814(b), substituted "includible" for "includable" in subpara. (e)(2)(C) [inoperative, see Sec. 203(a)(1) of P.L. 101-140, below].

—P.L. 101-140, Sec. 203(a)(1), repealed as if not enacted Sec. 1151(d)(1) of P.L. 99-514, which amended Code Sec 125.

—P.L. 101-140, Sec. 203(a)(3), substituted "section 410(b)(2)(A)(i)" for "subparagraph (B) of section 410(b)(1)" in subpara. (g)(3)(A) . . . Sec. 203(b)(2), amended para. (d)(2), effective as provided in Sec. 1151(k)(1) of P.L. 99-514, reproduced in note following Code Sec. 414.

Prior to amendment, para. (d)(2) read as follows:

"(2) Deferred compensation plans excluded. The term 'cafeteria plan' does not include any plan which provides for deferred compensation. The preceding sentence shall not apply in the case of a profit-sharing or stock bonus plan which includes a qualified cash or deferred arrangement (as defined in section 401(k)(2)) to the extent of amounts which a covered employee may elect to have the employer pay as contributions to a trust under such plan on behalf of the employee.

In 1988, P.L. 100-647, Sec. 1011B(a)(11)(A)-(C), Sec. 1011B(a)(12), Sec. 1011B(a)(13)(A)-(B), Sec. 1018(t)(6), Sec. 4002(b)(2), and Sec. 6051(b) amended

Exclusions from income Code Sec. 126(a)(4)

Code Sec. 125 as amended by Sec. 1151(d)(1) of P.L. 99-514 which is repealed as if not enacted by Sec. 203(a)(1) of P.L. 101-140, see above.

—P.L. 100-647, Sec. 6063, provides:

"SEC. 6063. TREATMENT OF PRE-1989 ELECTIONS FOR DEPENDENT CARE ASSISTANCE UNDER CAFETERIA PLANS.

"For purposes of section 125 of the 1986 Code, a plan shall not be treated as failing to be a cafeteria plan solely because under the plan a participant elected before January 1, 1989, to receive reimbursement under the plan for dependant care assistance for periods after December 31, 1988, and such assistance is includible in gross income under the provisions of the Family Support Act of 1988."

In **1986**, P.L. 99-514, Sec. 1853(b)(1)(A), substituted "qualified benefits" for "statutory nontaxable benefits" each place it appears in subsec. (c) and in subpara. (d)(1)(B)... Sec. 1853(b)(1)(B), amended subsec. (f) effective 1/1/85 except as provided by Sec. 531(b)(5) of P.L. 98-369 [see below].

Prior to amendment, subsec. (f) read as follows:

"*(f) Statutory nontaxable benefits defined.*

"For purposes of this section, the term 'statutory nontaxable benefit' means any benefit which, with the application of subsection (a) is not includible in the gross income of the employee by reason of an express provision of this chapter (other than section 117, 124, 127, or 132). Such term includes any group term life insurance which is includible in gross income only because it exceeds the dollar limitation of section 79."

—P.L. 99-514, Sec. 1853(b)(2), and (3), added Sec. 531(b)(5)(D) and (E) to P.L. 98-369 [reproduced below], exceptions to the effective date for changes made by Sec. 531(b) of P.L. 98-369, see below.

In **1984**, P.L. 98-612, Sec. 1(b)(3)(B), amended subsec. (h), effective 1/1/85. [Inoperative, same amendment made by P.L. 98-611, Sec. (d)(3)(A), below.]

—P.L. 98-611, Sec. 1(d)(3)(A), amended subsec. (h), effective 1/1/85.

Prior to amendment, subsec. (h) read as follows:

"*(h) Reporting requirements.*

"(1) In general. Each employer maintaining a cafeteria plan during any year which begins after December 31, 1984, and to which this section applies shall file a return (at such time and in such manner as the Secretary shall by regulations prescribe) with respect to such plan showing for such year—

"(A) the number of employees of the employer,

"(B) the number of employees participating under the plan,

"(C) the total cost of the plan during the year, and

"(D) the name, address, and taxpayer identification number of the employer and the type of business in which the employer is engaged.

"(2) Recordkeeping requirement. Each employer maintaining a cafeteria plan during any year shall keep such records as may be necessary for purposes of determining whether the requirements of this section are met.

"(3) Additional information when required by the Secretary. Any employer—

"(A) who maintains a cafeteria plan during any year for which a return is required under paragraph (1), and

"(B) who is required by the Secretary to file an additional return for such year, shall file such additional return. Such additional return shall be filed at such time and in such manner as the Secretary shall prescribe and shall contain such information as the Secretary shall prescribe."

—P.L. 98-369, Sec. 531(b)(1), amended para. (d)(1)... Sec. 531(b)(2)(A), amended subsec. (f)... Sec. 531(b)(2)(B), substituted "statutory nontaxable benefits" for "nontaxable benefits" each place it appeared in subsec. (c)... Sec. 531(b)(3), amended subsec. (b)... Sec. 531(b)(4)(A), redesignated subsec. (h) as subsec. (i) and added new subsec. (h), effective on 1/1/85 except as provided by Sec. 531(b)(5) [as amended by Sec. 1853(b)(2) and (3) of P.L. 99-514, see above] of this Act which reads as follows:

"(5) Exception for certain cafeteria plans and benefits.—

"(A) General transitional rule.—Any cafeteria plan in existence on February 10, 1984, which failed as of such date and continued to fail thereafter to satisfy the rules relating to section 125 under proposed Treasury regulations, and any benefit offered under such a cafeteria plan which failed as of such date and continued to fail thereafter to satisfy the rules of section 105, 106, 120, or 129 under proposed Treasury regulations, will not fail to be a cafeteria plan under section 125 or a nontaxable benefit under section 105, 106, 120, or 129 solely because of such failures. The preceding sentence shall apply only with respect to cafeteria plans and benefits provided under cafeteria plans before the earlier of—

"(i) January 1, 1985, or

"(ii) the effective date of any modification to provide additional benefits after February 10, 1984.

"(B) Special transition rule for advance election benefit banks.—Any benefit offered under a cafeteria plan in existence on February 10, 1984, which failed as of such date and continued to fail thereafter to satisfy the rules of section 105, 106, 120, or 129 under proposed Treasury regulations because an employee was assured of receiving (in cash or any other benefit) amounts available but unused for covered reimbursement during the year without regard to whether he incurred covered expenses, will not fail to be a nontaxable benefit under such applicable section solely because of such failure. The preceding sentence shall apply only with respect to benefits provided under cafeteria plans before the earlier of—

"(i) July 1, 1985, or

"(ii) the effective date of any modification to provide additional benefits after February 10, 1984.

Except as provided in Treasury regulations, the special transition rule is available only for benefits with respect to which, after December 31, 1984, contributions are fixed before the period of coverage and taxable cash is not available until the end of such period of coverage.

"(C) Plans for which substantial implementation costs were incurred.—For purposes of this paragraph, any plan with respect to which substantial implementation costs had been incurred before February 10, 1984, shall be treated as in existence on February 10, 1984.

"(D) Collective bargaining agreements.—In the case of any cafeteria plan in existence on February 10, 1984, and maintained pursuant to 1 or more collective bargaining agreements between employee representatives and 1 or more employers, the date on which the last of such collective bargaining agreements terminates (determined without regard to any extension thereof agreed to after July 18, 1984) shall be substituted for 'January 1, 1985' in subparagraph (A) and for 'July 1, 1985' in subparagraph (B). For purposes of the preceding sentence, any plan amendment made pursuant to a collective bargaining agreement relating to the plan which amends the plan solely to conform to any requirement added by this section (or any requirement in the regulations under section 125 of the Internal Revenue Code of 1954 proposed on May 6, 1984) shall not be treated as a termination of such collective bargaining agreement.

"(E) Special rule where contributions or reimbursements suspended.—For purposes of subparagraphs (A) and (B), a plan shall not be treated as not continuing to fail to satisfy the rules referred to in such subparagraphs with respect to any benefit provided in the form of a flexible spending arrangement merely because contributions or reimbursements (or both) with respect to such plan were suspended before January 1, 1985."

Sec. 531(b)(6)(A) of this Act provides:

"(6) Study of effects of cafeteria plans on health care costs.—

"(A) Study.—The Secretary of Health and Human Services, in cooperation with the Secretary of the Treasury, shall conduct a study of the effects of cafeteria plans (within the meaning of section 125 of the Internal Revenue Code of 1954) on the containment of health care costs."

Prior to amendment, para. (d)(1) read as follows:

"(1) In general. The term 'cafeteria plan' means a written plan under which—

"(A) all participants are employees, and

"(B) the participants may choose among two or more benefits.

The benefits which may be chosen may be nontaxable benefits, or cash, property, or other taxable benefits."

Prior to amendment, subsec. (f) read as follows:

"*(f) Nontaxable benefit defined.*

"For purposes of this section, the term 'nontaxable benefit' means any benefit which, with the application of subsection (a), is not includible in the gross income of the employee."

Prior to amendment, subsec. (b) read as follows:

"*(b) Exception for highly compensated participants where plan is discriminatory.*

"(1) In general. In the case of a highly compensated participant, subsection (a) shall not apply to any benefit attributable to a plan year for which the plan discriminates in favor of—

"(A) highly compensated individuals as to eligibility to participate, or

"(B) highly compensated participants as to contributions and benefits.

"(2) Year of inclusion. For purposes of determining the taxable year of inclusion, any benefit described in paragraph (1) shall be treated as received or accrued in the participant's taxable year in which the plan year ends."

In **1980**, P.L. 96-613, Sec. 5(b)(2), made the same amendment to para. (g)(4) as Sec. 201(b)(2) of P.L. 96-605, see below.

—P.L. 96-605, Sec. 226(a), added the last sentence to para. (d)(2); effective for tax. yrs. begin. after 12/31/80.

—P.L. 96-605, Sec. 201(b)(2), substituted "subsection (b), (c), or (m) of section 414" for "subsection (b) or (c) or section 414" in para. (g)(4) and substituted "controlled groups, etc." for "controlled groups" in the heading of para. (g)(4), for plan yrs. ending after 11/30/80 except as provided in Sec. 201(c)(2) of this Act, which reads as follows:

"(2) Plans in existence on November 30, 1980. In the case of a plan in existence on November 30, 1980, the amendments made by this section shall apply to plan years beginning after November 30, 1980."

—P.L. 96-222, Sec. 101(a)(6)(A), substituted "employment requirement" for "service requirement" each place it appeared in subpara. (g)(3)(B), for plan yrs. begin. after '78 [see below].

—P.L. 96-222, Sec. 101(a)(6)(B), changed the effective date for changes made by Sec. 134(a) of P.L. 95-600 from tax. yrs. begin. after 12/31/78 to plan yrs. begin. after 12/31/78 [see below].

In **1978**, P.L. 95-600, Sec. 134(a), added Code Sec. 125, effective [as amended by Sec. 101(a)(6)(B) of P.L. 96-222, see above] for plan yrs. begin. after 12/31/78.

Sec. 126. Certain cost-sharing payments.

(a) General rule.

Gross income does not include the excludable portion of payments received under—

(1) The rural clean water program authorized by section 208(j) of the Federal Water Pollution Control Act (33 U.S.C. 1288(j)).

(2) The rural abandoned mine program authorized by section 406 of the Surface Mining Control and Reclamation Act of 1977 (30 U.S.C. 1236).

(3) The water bank program authorized by the Water Bank Act (16 U.S.C. 1301 *et seq.*).

(4) The emergency conservation measures program authorized by title IV of the Agricultural Credit Act of 1978.

Code Sec. 126(a)(5)   **Exclusions from income**

(5) The agricultural conservation program authorized by the Soil Conservation and Domestic Allotment Act (16 U.S.C. 590a).

(6) The great plains conservation program authorized by section 16 of the Soil Conservation and Domestic Policy Act (16 U.S.C. 590p(b)).

(7) The resource conservation and development program authorized by the Bankhead-Jones Farm Tenant Act and by the Soil Conservation and Domestic Allotment Act (7 U.S.C. 1010; 16 U.S.C. 590a *et seq.*).

(8) The forestry incentives program authorized by section 4 of the Cooperative Forestry Assistance Act of 1978 (16 U.S.C. 2103).

(9) Any small watershed program administered by the Secretary of Agriculture which is determined by the Secretary of the Treasury or his delegate to be substantially similar to the type of programs described in paragraphs (1) through (8).

(10) Any program of a State, possession of the United States, a political subdivision of any of the foregoing, or the District of Columbia under which payments are made to individuals primarily for the purpose of conserving soil, protecting or restoring the environment, improving forests, or providing a habitat for wildlife.

(b) Excludable portion.

For purposes of this section—

(1) In general. The term "excludable portion" means that portion (or all) of a payment made to any person under any program described in subsection (a) which—

(A) is determined by the Secretary of Agriculture to be made primarily for the purpose of conserving soil and water resources, protecting or restoring the environment, improving forests, or providing a habitat for wildlife, and

(B) is determined by the Secretary of the Treasury or his delegate as not increasing substantially the annual income derived from the property.

(2) Payments not chargeable to capital account. The term "excludable portion" does not include that portion of any payment which is properly associated with an amount which is allowable as a deduction for the taxable year in which such amount is paid or incurred.

(c) Election for section not to apply.

(1) In general. The taxpayer may elect not to have this section (and section 1255) apply to any excludable portion (or portion thereof).

(2) Manner and time for making election. Any election under paragraph (1) shall be made in the manner prescribed by the Secretary by regulations and shall be made not later than the due date prescribed by law (including extensions) for filing the return of tax under this chapter for the taxable year in which the payment was received or accrued.

(d) Denial of double benefits.

No deduction or credit shall be allowed with respect to any expenditure which is properly associated with any amount excluded from gross income under subsection (a).

(e) Basis of property not increased by reason of excludable payments.

Notwithstanding any provision of section 1016 to the contrary, no adjustment to basis shall be made with respect to property acquired or improved through the use of any payment, to the extent that such adjustment would reflect any amount which is excluded from gross income under subsection (a).

In 1980, P.L. 96-222, Sec. 105(a)(7)(A), amended subsecs. (b) and (c) and added subsecs. (d) and (e)... Sec. 105(a)(7)(C), added "or his delegate" after "Secretary of the Treasury" in para. (a)(9)... Sec. 105(a)(7)(E), substituted "Any program of a State, possession of the United States, a political subdivision of any of the foregoing, or the District of Columbia" for "Any State program" in para. (a)(10), effective for grants made under programs after 9/30/79.

Prior to amendment, subsecs. (b) and (c) read as follows:

"*(b) Excludable portion.*

"For purposes of this section, the term 'excludable portion' means that portion (or all) of a payment made to any person under any program described in subsection (a) which—

"(1) is determined by the Secretary of Agriculture to be made primarily for the purpose of conserving soil and water resources, protecting or restoring the environment, improving forests, or providing a habitat for wildlife, and

"(2) is determined by the Secretary of the Treasury as not increasing substantially the annual income derived from the property.

"*(c) Application with other sections.*

"No deduction or credit allowable under any other provision of this chapter shall be allowed with respect to any expenditure made with the use of payments described in subsection (a) or with respect to any property acquired with any payment described in subsection (a) (to the extent that the basis is allocable to the use of such payments). Notwithstanding any provision of section 1016 to the contrary, no adjustment to basis shall be made with respect to property acquired through the use of such payments, to the extent that such adjustment would reflect the amount of such payment."

In 1978, P.L. 95-600, Sec. 543(a), added Code Sec. 126, effective for grants made under programs after 9/30/79.

Sec. 127. Educational assistance programs.

(a) Exclusion from gross income.

(1) In general. Gross income of an employee does not include amounts paid or expenses incurred by the employer for educational assistance to the employee if the assistance is furnished pursuant to a program which is described in subsection (b).

(2) $5,250 maximum exclusion. If, but for this paragraph, this section would exclude from gross income more than $5,250 of educational assistance furnished to an individual during a calendar year, this section shall apply only to the first $5,250 of such assistance so furnished.

(b) Educational assistance program.

(1) In general. For purposes of this section, an educational assistance program is a separate written plan of an employer for the exclusive benefit of his employees to provide such employees with educational assistance. The program must meet the requirements of paragraphs (2) through (6) of this subsection.

(2) Eligibility. The program shall benefit employees who qualify under a classification set up by the employer and found by the Secretary not to be discriminatory in favor of employees who are highly compensated employees (within the meaning of section 414(q)) or their dependents. For purposes of this paragraph, there shall be excluded from consideration employees not included in the program who are included in a unit of employees covered by an agreement which the Secretary of Labor finds to be a collective bargaining agreement between employee representatives and one or more employers, if there is evidence that educational assistance benefits were the subject of good faith bargaining between such employee representatives and such employer or employers.

(3) Principal shareholders or owners. Not more than 5 percent of the amounts paid or incurred by the employer for educational assistance during the year may be provided for the class of individuals who are shareholders or owners (or their spouses or dependents), each of whom (on any day of the year) owns more than 5 percent of the stock or of the capital or profits interest in the employer.

(4) Other benefits as an alternative. A program must not provide eligible employees with a choice between educational assistance and other remuneration includible in gross income. For purposes of this section, the business

Exclusions from income   Code Sec. 127

practices of the employer (as well as the written program) will be taken into account.

(5) No funding required. A program referred to in paragraph (1) is not required to be funded.

(6) Notification of employees. Reasonable notification of the availability and terms of the program must be provided to eligible employees.

(c) Definitions; special rules.

For purposes of this section—

> • *Caution:* Code Sec. 127(c)(1), following, was amended by P.L. 107-16, EGTRRA. These provisions generally sunset for tax years beginning after 12/31/2012. For specific sunset provisions, see Sec. 901, P.L. 107-16 (as amended) reproduced in history notes for this Code Sec.

(1) Educational assistance. The term "educational assistance" means—

(A) the payment, by an employer, of expenses incurred by or on behalf of an employee for education of the employee (including, but not limited to, tuition, fees, and similar payments, books, supplies, and equipment), and

(B) the provision, by an employer, of courses of instruction for such employee (including books, supplies, and equipment),

but does not include payment for, or the provision of, tools or supplies which may be retained by the employee after completion of a course of instruction, or meals, lodging, or transportation. The term "educational assistance" also does not include any payment for, or the provision of any benefits with respect to, any course or other education involving sports, games, or hobbies.

(2) Employee. The term "employee" includes, for any year, an individual who is an employee within the meaning of section 401(c)(1) (relating to self-employed individuals).

(3) Employer. An individual who owns the entire interest in an unincorporated trade or business shall be treated as his own employer. A partnership shall be treated as the employer of each partner who is an employee within the meaning of paragraph (2).

(4) Attribution rules.

(A) Ownership of stock. Ownership of stock in a corporation shall be determined in accordance with the rules provided under subsections (d) and (e) of section 1563 (without regard to section 1563(e)(3)(C)).

(B) Interest in unincorporated trade or business. The interest of an employee in a trade or business which is not incorporated shall be determined in accordance with regulations prescribed by the Secretary, which shall be based on principles similar to the principles which apply in the case of subparagraph (A).

(5) Certain tests not applicable. An educational assistance program shall not be held or considered to fail to meet any requirements of subsection (b) merely because—

(A) of utilization rates for the different types of educational assistance made available under the program; or

(B) successful completion, or attaining a particular course grade, is required for or considered in determining reimbursement under the program.

(6) Relationship to current law. This section shall not be construed to affect the deduction or inclusion in income of amounts (not within the exclusion under this section) which are paid or incurred, or received as reimbursement, for educational expenses under section 117, 162 or 212.

(7) Disallowance of excluded amounts as credit or deduction. No deduction or credit shall be allowed to the employee under any other section of this chapter for any amount excluded from income by reason of this section.

> • *Caution:* Code Sec. 127(d), following, was amended by P.L. 107-16, EGTRRA. These provisions generally sunset for tax years beginning after 12/31/2012. For specific sunset provisions, see Sec. 901, P.L. 107-16 (as amended) reproduced in history notes for this Code Sec.

(d) Cross reference.

For reporting and recordkeeping requirements, see section 6039D.

In 2010, P.L. 111-312, Sec. 101(a)(1), substituted "December 31, 2012" for "December 31, 2010" both places it appeared in Sec. 901, P.L. 107-16 [see below], effective as if included in the enactment of P.L. 107-16, EGTRRA, 6/7/2001.

In 2002, P.L. 107-358, Sec. 2, added subsec. (c) in Sec. 901 of P.L. 107-16 [see below], effective 12/17/2002.

In 2001, P.L. 107-16, Sec. 411(a), deleted subsec. (d) and redesignated subsec. (e) as (d)... Sec. 411(b), deleted ", and such term also does not include any payment for, or the provision of any benefits with respect to, any graduate level course of a kind normally taken by an individual pursuing a program leading to a law, business, medical, or other advanced academic or professional degree" after "games, or hobbies" in para (c)(1), effective for expenses relating to courses begin. after 12/31/2001.

Prior to deletion subsec. (d) read as follows:

"(d) Termination. This section shall not apply to expenses paid with respect to courses beginning after December 31, 2001."

—P.L. 107-16, Sec. 901, of this Act [as amended by Sec. 2, P.L. 107-358, and Sec. 101(a)(1), P.L. 111-312, see above], reads as follows:

"Sec. 901. Sunset of provisions of Act.

"(a) In general. All provisions of, and amendments made by, this Act shall not apply—

"(1) to taxable, plan, or limitation years beginning after December 31, 2012, or

"(2) in the case of title V, to estates of decedents dying, gifts made, or generation skipping transfers, after December 31, 2012.

"(b) Application of certain laws. The Internal Revenue Code of 1986 and the Employee Retirement Income Security Act of 1974 shall be applied and administered to years, estates, gifts, and transfers described in subsection (a) as if the provisions and amendments described in subsection (a) had never been enacted.

"(c) Exception. Subsection (a) shall not apply to section 803 (relating to no federal income tax on restitution received by victims of the Nazi regime or their heirs or estates)."

In 1999, P.L. 106-170, Sec. 506(a), substituted "December 31, 2001" for "May 31, 2000" in subsec. (d), effective for courses begin. after 5/31/2000.

In 1997, P.L. 105-34, Sec. 221(a), amended subsec. (d), effective for tax. yrs. begin. after 12/31/96.

Prior to amendment, subsec. (d) read as follows:

"(d) Termination. This section shall not apply to taxable years beginning after May 31, 1997. In the case of any taxable year beginning in 1997, only expenses paid with respect to courses beginning before July 1, 1997, shall be taken into account in determining the amount excluded under this section."

In 1996, P.L. 104-188, Sec. 1202(a), substituted "May 31, 1997. In the case of any taxable year beginning in 1997, only expenses paid with respect to courses beginning before July 1, 1997, shall be taken into account in determining the amount excluded under this section." for "December 31, 1994." in subsec. (d), effective for tax. yrs. begin. after 12/31/94.

—P.L. 104-188, Sec. 1202(b), added ", and such term also does not include any payment for, or the provision of any benefits with respect to, any graduate level course of a kind normally taken by an individual pursuing a program leading to a law, business, medical, or other advanced academic or professional degree" before the period in the last sentence of para. (c)(1), effective for expenses relating to courses beginning after 6/30/96.

—P.L. 104-188, Sec. 1202(c)(3), of this Act provides:

"(3) Expedited procedures. The Secretary of the Treasury shall establish expedited procedures for the refund of any overpayment of taxes imposed by the Internal Revenue Code of 1986 which is attributable to amounts excluded from gross income during 1995 or 1996 under section 127 of such Code, including procedures waiving the requirement that an employer obtain an employee's signature where the employer demonstrates to the satisfaction of the Secretary that any refund collected by the employer on behalf of the employer will be paid to the employee."

In 1993, P.L. 103-66, Sec. 13101(a)(1), amended subsec. (d)... Sec. 13101(a)(2), repealed Sec. 103(a)(2) of P.L. 102-227, effective for tax. yrs. end. after 6/30/92.

1,441

Code Sec. 127 — Exclusions from income

Prior to amendment, subsec. (d) read as follows:
"(d) Termination. This section shall not apply to taxable years beginning after June 30, 1992."

Prior to repeal, Sec. 103(a)(2) of P.L. 102-227 read as follows:

"(2) Special rule.— In the case of any taxable year beginning in 1992, only amounts paid before July 1, 1992, by the employer for educational assistance for the employee shall be taken into account in determining the amount excluded under section 127 of the Internal Revenue Code of 1986 with respect to such employee for such taxable year."

In 1991, P.L. 102-227, Sec. 103(a)(1), substituted "June 30, 1992" for "December 31, 1991" in subsec. (d), effective for tax. yrs. begin. after 12/31/91.

—P.L. 102-227, Sec. 103(a)(2), of this Act is repealed by Sec. 13101(a)(2) of P.L. 103-66, see above.

In 1990, P.L. 101-508, Sec. 11403(a), substituted "December 31, 1991" for "September 30, 1990" in subsec. (d), effective for tax. yrs. begin. after 12/31/89.

—P.L. 101-508, Sec. 11403(b), deleted the last sentence of para. (c)(1), effective for tax. yrs. begin. after 12/31/90.

Prior to deletion, the last sentence of para. (c)(1) read as follows:

"The term 'educational assistance' also does not include any payment for, or the provision of any benefits with respect to, any graduate level course of a kind normally taken by an individual pursuing a program leading to a law, business, medical, or other advanced academic or professional degree."

—P.L. 101-508, Sec. 11403(c), deleted Sec. 7101(a)(2) of P.L. 101-239, effective for tax. yrs. begin. after 12/31/89.

Prior to deletion, Sec. 7101(a)(2) of P.L. 101-239 read as follows:

"(2) Special rule.— In the case of any taxable year beginning in 1990, only amounts paid before October 1, 1990, by the employer for coverage for the employee, his spouse, or his dependents under a qualified group legal services plan for periods before October 1, 1990, shall be taken into account in determining the amount excluded under section 120 of the Internal Revenue Code of 1986 with respect to such employee for such taxable year."

In 1989, P.L. 101-239, Sec. 7101(a)(1), substituted "September 30, 1990" for "December 31, 1988" in subsec. (d), effective for tax. yrs. begin. after 12/31/88. Sec. 7101(a)(2), which provided a special rule, was repealed by Sec. 11403(c) of P.L. 101-239, see above.

—P.L. 101-239, Sec. 7814(a), deleted para. (c)(8), effective for tax. yrs. begin. after 12/31/87.

Prior to deletion, para. (c)(8) read as follows:

"(8) Coordination with section 117(d). In the case of the education of an individual who is a graduate student at an educational organization described in section 170(b)(1)(A)(ii) and who is engaged in teaching or research activities for such organization, section 117(d)(2) shall be applied as if it did not contain the phrase '(below the graduate level)'."

—P.L. 101-140, Sec. 203(a)(1), repealed as if not enacted Sec. 1151(c) of P.L. 99-514, which amended para. (b)(1) and deleted para. (b)(6) and repealed as if not enacted Sec. 1151(g) of P.L. 99-514, which amended the last sentence of para. (b)(2) ... Sec. 203(a)(2), repealed as if not enacted Sec. 1011B(a)(31) of P.L. 100-647, which amended para. (b)(2).

In 1988, P.L. 100-647, Sec. 4001(a), substituted "December 31, 1988" for "December 31, 1987", in subsec. (d) ... Sec. 4001(b)(1), added the last sentence to para. (c)(1), effective for tax. yrs. begin. after 12/31/87.

In 1986, P.L. 99-514, Sec. 1114(b)(4), substituted "highly compensated employees (within the meaning of section 414(q))" for "officers, owners, or highly compensated," in para. (b)(2), effective for yrs. begin. after 12/31/87.

—P.L. 99-514, Sec. 1162(a)(1), substituted "1987" for "1985" in subsec. (d) ... Sec. 1162(a)(2), substituted "$5,250" for "$5,000" in the heading and each time it appeared in subpara. (a)(2), effective for tax. yrs. begin. after 12/31/85.

In 1984, P.L. 98-611, Sec. 1(a), substituted "December 31, 1985" for "December 31, 1983" in subsec. (d) ... Sec. 1(b), amended subsec. (a) ... Sec. 1(c), added para. (c)(8) ... Sec. 1(e), added "to the employee" after "allowed" in para. (c)(7), effective for tax. yrs. begin. after 12/31/83. Sec. 1(g)(4) and (5) of this Act provide:

"(4) No penalties or interest on failure to withhold.— No penalty or interest shall be imposed on any failure to withhold under subtitle C of the Internal Revenue Code of 1954 (relating to employment taxes) with respect to amounts excluded from gross income under section 127 of such Code (as amended by this section and determined without regard to subsection (a)(2) thereof) with respect to periods during 1984.

"(5) Coordination with section 117(d).— In the case of education described in section 127(c)(8) of the Internal Revenue Code of 1954, as added by this section, section 117(d) of such Code shall be treated as in effect on and after January 1, 1984."

Prior to amendment, subsec. (a) read as follows:

"(a) General rule.

"Gross income of an employee does not include amounts paid or expenses incurred by the employer for educational assistance to the employee if the assistance is furnished pursuant to a program which is described in subsection (b)."

—P.L. 98-611, Sec. 1(d)(3)(B), added subsec. (e), effective 1/1/85. Secs. 1(h)(1) and (2) of this Act provide:

"(h) Study.

"(1) In general. The Secretary of the Treasury shall conduct a study of the effect of the provisions of section 127 of the Internal Revenue Code of 1954.

"(2) Report. Not later than October 1, 1985, the Secretary of the Treasury shall submit a report to the Committee on Ways and Means of the House of Representatives and the Committee on Finance of the Senate on the study conducted under paragraph (1) (together with such recommendations as he may deem advisable)."

In 1978, P.L. 95-600, Sec. 164(a), added Code Sec. 127, for tax. yrs. begin. after '78.

Sec. 128. Repealed.

In 1990, P.L. 101-508, Sec. 11801(a)(10), repealed Code Sec. 128, effective 11/5/90 except as provided in Sec. 11821(b) of this Act, reproduced in note following Code Sec. 110.

Prior to repeal, Code Sec. 128 read as follows:

"Sec. 128. INTEREST ON CERTAIN SAVINGS CERTIFICATES.

"(a) In general.

"Gross income does not include any amount received by any individual during the taxable year as interest on a depository institution tax-exempt savings certificate.

"(b) Maximum dollar amount.

"(1) In general. The aggregate amount excludable under subsection (a) for any taxable year shall not exceed the excess of—

"(A) $1,000 ($2,000 in the case of a joint return under section 6013), over

"(B) the aggregate amount received by the taxpayer which was excludable under subsection (a) for any prior taxable year.

"(2) Special rule. For purposes of paragraph (1)(B), one-half of the amount excluded under subsection (a) on any joint return shall be treated as received by each spouse.

"(c) Depository institution tax-exempt savings certificate.

"For purposes of this section—

"(1) In general. The term 'depository institution tax-exempt savings certificate' means any certificate—

"(A) which is issued by a qualified savings institution after September 30, 1981, and before January 1, 1983,

"(B) which has a maturity of 1 year,

"(C) which has an investment yield equal to 70 percent of the average investment yield for the most recent auction (before the week in which the certificate is issued) of United States Treasury bills with maturities of 52 weeks, and

"(D) which is made available in denominations of $500.

"(2) Qualified institution. The term 'qualified institution' means—

"(A)(i) a bank (as defined in section 581),

"(ii) a mutual savings bank, cooperative bank, domestic building and loan association, or other savings institution chartered and supervised as a savings and loan or similar institution under Federal or State law,

"(iii) a credit union, the deposits or accounts of which are insured under Federal or State law or are protected or guaranteed under State law, or

"(iv) a banking facility (whether or not insured under Federal or State law) which is operated under a cost plus agreement with the Department of Defense for members of the Armed Forces of the United States serving outside the United States and their dependents, or

"(B) an industrial loan association or bank chartered and supervised under Federal or State law in a manner similar to a savings and loan institution.

"The term 'qualified institution' does not include any foreign branch or international banking facility of an institution described in the preceding sentence and such a branch or facility shall not be taken into account under subsection (d).

"(d) Institutions required to provide residential property financing.

"(1) In general. If a qualified savings institution (other than an institution described in subsection (c)(2)(A)(iii)) issues any depository institution tax-exempt savings certificate during any calendar quarter, the amount of the qualified residential financing provided by such institution shall during the succeeding calendar quarter not be less than the lesser of—

"(A) 75 percent of the face amount of depository institution tax-exempt savings certificates issued during the calendar quarter, or

"(B) 75 percent of the qualified net savings for the calendar quarter.

"The aggregate amount of qualified tax-exempt savings certificates issued by any institution described in subsection (c)(2)(A)(iii) which are outstanding at the close of any calendar quarter may not exceed the limitation determined under paragraph (4) with respect to such institution for such quarter.

"(2) Penalty for failure to meet requirements. If, as of the close of any calendar quarter, a qualified institution has not met the requirements of paragraph (1) with respect to the preceding calendar quarter, such institution may not issue any certificates until it meets such requirements.

"(3) Qualified residential financing. The term 'qualified residential financing' includes, and is limited to—

"(A) any loan secured by a lien on a single-family or multifamily residence,

"(B) any secured or unsecured qualified home improvement loan (within the meaning of section 103A(l)(6) without regard to the $15,000 limit),

"(C) any mortgage (within the meaning of section 103A(l)(1)) on a single-family or multifamily residence which is insured or guaranteed by the Federal, State, or local government or any instrumentality thereof,

"(D) any loan to acquire a mobile home,

"(E) any construction loan for the construction or rehabilitation of a single-family or multifamily residence,

"(F) the purchase of mortgages secured by single-family or multifamily residences on the secondary market but only to the extent the amount of such purchases exceed the amount of sales of such mortgages by an institution,

"(G) the purchase of securities issued or guaranteed by the Federal National Mortgage Association, the Government National Mortgage Association, or the Federal Home Loan Mortgage Corporation, or securities issued by any other person if such securities are secured by mortgages originated by a qualified institution, but only to the extent the amount of such purchases exceed the amount of sales of such securities by an institution, and

"(H) any loan for agricultural purposes.

"For purposes of this paragraph, the term 'single-family residence' includes 2-, 3-, and 4-family residences, and the term 'residence' includes stock in a cooperative housing corporation (as defined in section 216(b)).

"(4) Limitation for credit unions. For purposes of paragraph (1), the limitation determined under this paragraph with respect to any institution described in subsection (c)(2)(A)(iii) for any calendar quarter is the sum of—

"(A) the aggregate of the amounts described in subparagraph (A) of paragraph (5) with respect to such institution as of September 30, 1981, plus

"(B) 10 percent of the excess of—

"(i) the aggregate of such amounts as of the close of such calendar quarter, over

"(ii) the amount referred to in subparagraph (A).

"For purposes of this paragraph, the amounts described in subparagraph (A) of paragraph (5) shall include amounts paid into credit union share accounts.

"(5) Qualified net savings. The term 'qualified net savings' means, with respect to any qualified institution, the excess of—

"(A) the amounts paid into passbook savings account, 6-month money market certificates, 30-month small-saver certificates, time deposits with a face amount of less than $100,000, and depository institution tax-exempt savings certificates issued by such institution, over

"(B) the amounts withdrawn or redeemed in connection with the accounts and certificates described in subparagraph (A).

"(6) Consolidated groups. For purposes of this subsection, all members of the same affiliated group (as defined in section 1504) which file a consolidated return for the taxable year shall be treated as 1 corporation.

"(e) Penalty for early withdrawals.

"(1) In general. If any portion of a depository institution tax-exempt savings certificate is redeemed before the date on which it matures—

"(A) subsection (a) shall not apply to any interest on such certificate for the taxable year of redemption and any subsequent taxable year, and

"(B) there shall be included in gross income for the taxable year of redemption the amount of any interest on such certificate excluded under subsection (a) for any preceding taxable year.

"(2) Certificate pledged as collateral. For purposes of paragraph (1), if the taxpayer uses any depository institution tax-exempt savings certificate (or portion thereof) as collateral or security for a loan, the taxpayer shall be treated as having redeemed such certificate.

"(f) Other special rules.

"(1) Coordination with section 116. Section 116 shall not apply to the interest on any depository institution tax-exempt savings certificate.

"(2) Estates and trusts.

"(A) In general. Except as provided in subparagraph (B), the exclusion provided by this section shall not apply to estates and trusts.

"(B) Certificates acquired by estate from decedent. In the case of a depository institution tax-exempt savings certificate acquired by an estate by reason of the death of the decedent—

"(i) subparagraph (A) shall not apply, and

"(ii) subsection (b) shall be applied as if the estate were the decedent."

In 1984, P.L. 98-369, Sec. 16(a), repealed as if not enacted Sec. 302(a) of P.L. 97-34 which amended Code Sec. 128 for tax. yrs. begin after 12/31/84.

—P.L. 97-448, Sec. 103(a)(1), added a sentence to the end of para. (d)(4) . . . Sec. 103(a)(5)(A), deleted "or" from the end of clause (c)(2)(A)(ii) . . . Sec. 103(a)(5)(B), added clause (c)(2)(A)(iv), effective for tax. yrs. end. after 9/30/81.

In 1981, P.L. 97-34, Sec. 301(a), added Code Sec. 128, effective for tax. yrs. end. after 9/30/81. Sec. 301(c) of this Act provides:

"(c) Study.

"The Secretary of the Treasury or his delegate shall conduct a study of the exemption from income of interest earned on depository institution tax-exempt savings certificates established by this section to determine the exemption's effectiveness in generating additional savings. Such report shall be submitted to the Congress before June 1, 1983."

Sec. 129. Dependent care assistance programs.
(a) Exclusion.

(1) In general. Gross income of an employee does not include amounts paid or incurred by the employer for dependent care assistance provided to such employee if the assistance is furnished pursuant to a program which is described in subsection (d).

(2) Limitation of exclusion.

(A) In general. The amount which may be excluded under paragraph (1) for dependent care assistance with respect to dependent care services provided during a taxable year shall not exceed $5,000 ($2,500 in the case of a separate return by a married individual).

(B) Year of inclusion. The amount of any excess under subparagraph (A) shall be included in gross income in the taxable year in which the dependent care services were provided (even if payment of dependent care assistance for such services occurs in a subsequent taxable year).

(C) Marital status. For purposes of this paragraph, marital status shall be determined under the rules of paragraphs (3) and (4) of section 21(e).

(b) Earned income limitation.

(1) In general. The amount excluded from the income of an employee under subsection (a) for any taxable year shall not exceed—

(A) in the case of an employee who is not married at the close of such taxable year, the earned income of such employee for such taxable year, or

(B) in the case of an employee who is married at the close of such taxable year, the lesser of—

(i) the earned income of such employee for such taxable year, or

(ii) the earned income of the spouse of such employee for such taxable year.

(2) Special rule for certain spouses. For purposes of paragraph (1), the provisions of section 21(d)(2) shall apply in determining the earned income of a spouse who is a student or incapable of caring for himself.

(c) Payments to related individuals.

No amount paid or incurred during the taxable year of an employee by an employer in providing dependent care assistance to such employee shall be excluded under subsection (a) if such amount was paid or incurred to an individual—

(1) with respect to whom, for such taxable year, a deduction is allowable under section 151(c) (relating to personal exemptions for dependents) to such employee or the spouse of such employee, or

(2) who is a child of such employee (within the meaning of section 152(f)(1)) under the age of 19 at the close of such taxable year.

(d) Dependent care assistance program.

(1) In general. For purposes of this section a dependent care assistance program is a separate written plan of an employer for the exclusive benefit of his employees to provide such employees with dependent care assistance which meets the requirements of paragraphs (2) through (8) of this subsection. If any plan would qualify as a dependent care assistance program but for a failure to meet the requirements of this subsection, then, notwithstanding such failure, such plan shall be treated as a dependent care assistance program in the case of employees who are not highly compensated employees.

(2) Discrimination. The contributions or benefits provided under the plan shall not discriminate in favor of employees who are highly compensated employees (within the meaning of section 414(q)) or their dependents.

(3) Eligibility. The program shall benefit employees who qualify under a classification set up by the employer and found by the Secretary not to be discriminatory in favor of employees described in paragraph (2), or their dependents.

(4) Principal shareholders or owners. Not more than 25 percent of the amounts paid or incurred by the employer for dependent care assistance during the year may be provided for the class of individuals who are shareholders or owners (or their spouses or dependents), each of whom (on any day of the year) owns more than 5 percent of the stock or of the capital or profits interest in the employer.

(5) No funding required. A program referred to in paragraph (1) is not required to be funded.

(6) Notification of eligible employees. Reasonable notification of the availability and terms of the program shall be provided to eligible employees.

(7) Statement of expenses. The plan shall furnish to an employee, on or before January 31, a written statement showing the amounts paid or expenses incurred by the employer in providing dependent care assistance to such employee during the previous calendar year.

(8) Benefits.

(A) In general. A plan meets the requirements of this paragraph if the average benefits provided to employees who are not highly compensated employees under all plans of the employer is at least 55 percent of the average benefits provided to highly compensated employees under all plans of the employer.

(B) Salary reduction agreements. For purposes of subparagraph (A), in the case of any benefits provided through a salary reduction agreement, a plan may disregard any employees whose compensation is less than $25,000. For purposes of this subparagraph, the term "compensation" has the meaning given such term by section 414(q)(4), except that, under rules prescribed by the Secretary, an employer may elect to determine compensation on any other basis which does not discriminate in favor of highly compensated employees.

(9) Excluded employees. For purposes of paragraphs (3) and (8), there shall be excluded from consideration—

(A) subject to rules similar to the rules of section 410(b)(4), employees who have not attained the age of 21 and completed 1 year of service (as defined in section 410(a)(3)), and

(B) employees not included in a dependent care assistance program who are included in a unit of employees covered by an agreement which the Secretary finds to be a collective bargaining agreement between employee representatives and 1 or more employees, if there is evidence that dependent care benefits were the subject of good faith bargaining between such employee representatives and such employer or employers.

(e) Definitions and special rules.

For purposes of this section—

(1) Dependent care assistance. The term "dependent care assistance" means the payment of, or provision of, those services which if paid for by the employee would be considered employment-related expenses under section 21(b)(2) (relating to expenses for household and dependent care services necessary for gainful employment).

(2) Earned income. The term "earned income" shall have the meaning given such term in section 32(c)(2), but such term shall not include any amounts paid or incurred by an employer for dependent care assistance to an employee.

(3) Employee. The term "employee" includes, for any year, an individual who is an employee within the meaning of section 401(c)(1) (relating to self-employed individuals).

(4) Employer. An individual who owns the entire interest in an unincorporated trade or business shall be treated as his own employer. A partnership shall be treated as the employer of each partner who is an employee within the meaning of paragraph (3).

(5) Attribution rules.

(A) Ownership of stock. Ownership of stock in a corporation shall be determined in accordance with the rules provided under subsections (d) and (e) of section 1563 (without regard to section 1563(e)(3)(C)).

(B) Interest in unincorporated trade or business. The interest of an employee in a trade or business which is not incorporated shall be determined in accordance with regulations prescribed by the Secretary, which shall be based on principles similar to the principles which apply in the case of subparagraph (A).

(6) Utilization test not applicable. A dependent care assistance program shall not be held or considered to fail to meet any requirements of subsection (d) (other than paragraphs (4) and (8) thereof) merely because of utilization rates for the different types of assistance made available under the program.

(7) Disallowance of excluded amounts as credit or deduction. No deduction or credit shall be allowed to the employee under any other section of this chapter for any amount excluded from the gross income of the employee by reason of this section.

(8) Treatment of onsite facilities. In the case of an onsite facility maintained by an employer, except to the extent provided in regulations, the amount of dependent care assistance provided to an employee excluded with respect to any dependent shall be based on—

(A) utilization of the facility by a dependent of the employee, and

(B) the value of the services provided with respect to such dependent.

(9) Identifying information required with respect to service provider. No amount paid or incurred by an employer for dependent care assistance provided to an employee shall be excluded from the gross income of such employee unless—

(A) the name, address, and taxpayer identification number of the person performing the services are included on the return to which the exclusion relates, or

(B) if such person is an organization described in section 501(c)(3) and exempt from tax under section 501(a), the name and address of such person are included on the return to which the exclusion relates.

In the case of a failure to provide the information required under the preceding sentence, the preceding sentence shall not apply if it is shown that the taxpayer exercised due diligence in attempting to provide the information so required.

In 2004, P.L. 108-311, Sec. 207(12), substituted "152(f)(1)" for "151(c)(3)" in para. (c)(2), effective for tax. yrs. begin. after 12/31/2004.

In 1996, P.L. 104-188, Sec. 1431(c)(1)(B), substituted "section 414(q)(4)" for "section 414(q)(7)" in subpara. (d)(8)(B), effective as provided in Sec. 1431(d)(1), of this Act, which reads as follows:

"(1) In general. The amendments made by this section shall apply to years beginning after December 31, 1996, except that in determining whether an employee is a highly compensated employee for year beginning in 1997, such amendments shall be treated as having been in effect for years beginning in 1996."

In 1989, P.L. 101-239, Sec. 7811(h)(2), deleted the last sentence of subsec. (a), effective for tax yrs. begin. after 12/31/87, except as provided in Sec. 1011B(c)(2)(C)(ii) and (iii) of P.L. 100-647, see below.

Prior to amendment, the last sentence of subsec. (a) read as follows:

"For purposes of the preceding sentence, marital status shall be determined under the rules of paragraphs (3) and (4) of section 21(e)."

—P.L. 101-140, Sec. 203(a)(1), repealed as if not enacted Sec. 1151(c)(5)(A) of P.L. 99-514, which amended para. (d)(1) . . . Sec. 203(a)(1), repealed as if not enacted Sec. 1151(c)(5)(B) of P.L. 99-514, which deleted para. (d)(6) and redesignated para. (d)(7) as para. (d)(6).

—P.L. 101-140, Sec. 203(a)(1), repealed as if not enacted Sec. 1151(g)(4) of P.L. 99-514, which amended para. (d)(3).

—P.L. 101-140, Sec. 203(a)(2), repealed as if not enacted Sec. 1011B(a)(31) of P.L. 100-647, which amended para. (d)(3) and added para. (d)(8).

—P.L. 101-140, Sec. 204(a)(1), added the last sentence of para. (d)(1) . . . Sec. 204(a)(2)(A), added para. (d)(9) . . . Sec. 204(a)(2)(B), deleted the last sentence of para. (d)(3), effective for yrs. begin. after 12/31/88.

Prior to deletion, the last sentence of para. (d)(3) read as follows:

"For purposes of this paragraph, there shall be excluded from consideration employees not included in the program who are included in a unit of employees covered by an agreement which the Secretary of labor finds to be a collective bargaining agreement between employee representatives and one or more employers, if there is evidence that dependent care benefits were the subject of good faith bargaining between such employee representatives and such employer or employers."

Exclusions from income — Code Sec. 130

—P.L. 101-140, Sec. 204(a)(3)(A), redesignated para. (d)(7) as para. (d)(8)... Sec. 204(a)(3)(B), substituted "paragraphs (2) through (8)" for "paragraphs (2) through (7)" in para. (d)(1)... Sec. 204(a)(3)(C), substituted "(8)" for "(7)" in para. (e)(6), effective for plan yrs. begin. after 12/31/89.

—P.L. 101-136, Sec. 528, provided that "no monies appropriated by this Act [for the fiscal year ending September 30, '90] may be used to implement or enforce section 1151 of the Tax Reform Act of '86 [P.L. 99-514] or the amendments made by such section." [See below]

In **1988**, P.L. 100-647, Sec. 1011B(a)(14), redesignated para. (d)(8) as (d)(7)... Sec. 1011B(a)(15)(A), added "under all plans of the employer" after "employees" the 2nd and 3rd time it appeared in subpara. (d)(7)(A)... Sec. 1011B(a)(15)(B), substituted "a plan may disregard" for "there shall be disregarded" in subpara. (d)(7)(B)... Sec. 1011B(a)(15)(C), substituted "414(q)(7)" for "415(q)(7)" in para. (d)(7)... Sec. 1011B(a)(18), added "(other than paragraphs (4) and (7) thereof)" after "subsection (d)" in para. (e)(6), effective as provided in Sec. 1151(k)(1) of P.L. 99-514.

—P.L. 100-647, Sec. 1011B(a)(25), amended Sec. 1151(k)(1) of P.L. 99-514 [reproduced below], part of the effective date for changes made by Sec. 1151(k)(1) of P.L. 99-514.

—P.L. 100-647, Sec. 1011B(a)(30), substituted "(7)" for "(6)" in subpara. (d)(1)(B) effective as provided in Sec. 1151(k)(1) of P.L. 99-514 [as amended by Sec. 1011B(a)(25) of this Act], reproduced in the note following Code Sec. 414.

—P.L. 100-647, Sec. 1011B(c)(1)(A), added "maintained by an employer" after "onsite facility" in para. (e)(8)... Sec. 1011B(c)(1)(B), added "of dependent care assistance provided to an employee" after "the amount" in para. (e)(8)... Sec. 1011B(c)(1)(C), added "of the facility by a dependent of the employee" after "utilization" in subpara. (e)(8)(A)... Sec. 1011B(c)(1)(D), added "with respect to such dependent" after "provided" in subpara. (e)(8)(B), effective for tax. yrs. begin. after 12/31/86.

—P.L. 100-647, Sec. 1011B(c)(2)(A), amended para. (a)(2), effective for tax. yrs. begin. after 12/31/87 except as provided in Sec. 1011B(c)(2)(C)(ii) and (iii) of this Act which read as follows:

"(ii) A taxpayer may elect to have the amendment made by subparagraph (A) apply to taxable years beginning in 1987.

"(iii) In the case of a taxpayer not making an election under clause (ii), any dependent care assistance provided in a taxable year beginning in 1987 with respect to which reimbursement was not received in such taxable year shall be treated as provided in the taxpayer's first taxable year beginning after December 31, 1987."

Prior to amendment, para. (a)(2) read as follows:

"(2) Limitation of exclusion. The aggregate amount excluded from the gross income of the taxpayer under this section for any taxable year shall not exceed $5,000 ($2,500 in the case of a separate return by a married individual)."

—P.L. 100-647, Sec. 3021(a)(14)(A), deleted "(within the meaning of section 414(q)(7))" after "compensation" in subpara. (d)(7)(B) [as redesignated and amended by 1011B of this Act]... Sec. 3021(a)(14)(B), added the last sentence to subpara. (d)(7)(B), effective as provided in Sec. 1151(k)(1) of P.L. 99-514 [reproduced below].

—P.L. 100-485, Sec. 703(c)(2), added para. (e)(9), effective for tax. yrs. begin. after 12/31/88.

In **1986**, P.L. 99-514, Sec. 104(b)(1)(A), substituted "section 151(c)" for "section 151(e)" in para. (c)(1)... Sec. 104(b)(1)(B), substituted "section 151(c)(3)" for "section 151(c)(5)", effective for tax. yrs. begin. after 12/31/86.

—P.L. 99-514, Sec. 1114(b)(4), substituted "highly compensated employees (within the meaning of section 414(q))" for "officers, owners, or highly compensated", in para. (d)(2) effective for tax. yrs. begin. after 12/31/87.

—P.L. 99-514, Sec. 1151(f), added para. (d)(8), effective as provided in Sec. 1151(k)(1) [as amended by Sec. 1011B(a)(25) of P.L. 100-647, see above], reproduced in the note following Code Sec. 414.

—P.L. 99-514, Sec. 1163(a), amended subsec. (a)... Sec. 1163(b), added para. (e)(8), effective for tax. yrs. begin after 12/31/86.

Prior to amendment, subsec. (a) read as follows:

"(a) In general.

"Gross income of an employee does not include amounts paid or incurred by the employer for dependent care assistance provided to such employee if the assistance is furnished pursuant to a program which is described in subsection (d)."

In **1984**, P.L. 98-369, Sec. 474(r)(6)(A), substituted "section 21(d)(2)" for "section 44A(e)(2)" in para. (b)(2)... Sec. 474(r)(6)(B), substituted "section 21(b)(2)" for "section 44A(c)(2)" in para. (e)(1)... Sec. 474(r)(6)(C), substituted "section 32(c)(2)" for "section 43(c)(2)" in para. (e)(2), effective for tax. yrs. begin. after 12/31/83, and to carrybacks from tax. yrs. begin. after 12/31/83.

In **1983**, P.L. 97-448, Sec. 101(e)(1)(A), redesignated paras. (d)(2) through (d)(6) as paras. (d)(3) through (d)(7), and added new para. (d)(2)... Sec. 101(e)(1)(B), substituted "employees described in paragraph (2), or their dependents" for "employees who are officers, owners, or highly compensated, or their dependents" in para. (d)(3) (as redesignated by Sec. 101(e)(1)(A) of this Act)... Sec. 101(e)(1)(C), substituted "paragraphs (2) through (7)" for "paragraphs (2) through (6)" in para. (d)(1)... Sec. 101(e)(1)(A), substituted "shall be allowed to the employee" for "shall be allowed" in para (e)(7)... Sec. 101(e)(2)(B), substituted "excluded from the gross income of the employee" for "excluded from income" in para. (e)(7), effective for tax. yrs. begin. after 12/31/81.

In **1981**, P.L. 97-34, Sec. 124(e)(1), added Code Sec. 129, effective for tax. yrs. begin. after 12/31/81.

Sec. 130. Certain personal injury liability assignments.

(a) In general.

Any amount received for agreeing to a qualified assignment shall not be included in gross income to the extent that such amount does not exceed the aggregate cost of any qualified funding assets.

(b) Treatment of qualified funding asset.

In the case of any qualified funding asset—

(1) the basis of such asset shall be reduced by the amount excluded from gross income under subsection (a) by reason of the purchase of such asset, and

(2) any gain recognized on a disposition of such asset shall be treated as ordinary income.

(c) Qualified assignment.

For purposes of this section, the term "qualified assignment" means any assignment of a liability to make periodic payments as damages (whether by suit or agreement), or as compensation under any workmen's compensation act, on account of personal injury or sickness (in a case involving physical injury or physical sickness)—

(1) if the assignee assumes such liability from a person who is a party to the suit or agreement, or the workmen's compensation claim, and

(2) if—

(A) such periodic payments are fixed and determinable as to amount and time of payment,

(B) such periodic payments cannot be accelerated, deferred, increased, or decreased by the recipient of such payments,

(C) the assignee's obligation on account of the personal injuries or sickness is no greater than the obligation of the person who assigned the liability, and

(D) such periodic payments are excludable from the gross income of the recipient under paragraph (1) or (2) of section 104(a).

The determination for purposes of this chapter of when the recipient is treated as having received any payment with respect to which there has been a qualified assignment shall be made without regard to any provision of such assignment which grants the recipient rights as a creditor greater than those of a general creditor.

(d) Qualified funding asset.

For purposes of this section, the term "qualified funding asset" means any annuity contract issued by a company licensed to do business as an insurance company under the laws of any State, or any obligation of the United States, if—

(1) such annuity contract or obligation is used by the assignee to fund periodic payments under any qualified assignment,

(2) the periods of the payments under the annuity contract or obligation are reasonably related to the periodic payments under the qualified assignment, and the amount of any such payment under the contract or obligation does not exceed the periodic payment to which it relates,

(3) such annuity contract or obligation is designated by the taxpayer (in such manner as the Secretary shall by regulations prescribe) as being taken into account under this section with respect to such qualified assignment, and

(4) such annuity contract or obligation is purchased by the taxpayer not more than 60 days before the date of the qualified assignment and not later than 60 days after the date of such assignment.

In **1997**, P.L. 105-34, Sec. 962(a)(1), added ", or as compensation under any workmen's compensation act," after "(whether by suit or agreement)" in subsec. (c)... Sec. 962(a)(2), added "or the workmen's compensation claim," after "suit

1,445

or agreement," in para. (c)(1)... Sec. 962(a)(3), substituted "paragraph (1) or (2) of section 104(a)" for "section 104(a)(2)" in subpara. (c)(2)(D), effective for claims under workmen's compensation acts filed after 8/5/97.

In 1988, P.L. 100-647, Sec. 6079(b)(1)(A), deleted subpara. (c)(2)(C) and redesignated subpara. (c)(2)(D) and (c)(2)(E) as subparas. (c)(2)(C) and (c)(2)(D) ... Sec. 6079(b)(1)(B), added the last sentence to subsec. (c), effective for assignments made after 11/10/88.

Prior to amendment, subpara. (c)(2)(C) read as follows:

"(C) the assignee does not provide to the recipient of such payments rights against the assignee which are greater than those of a general creditor."

In 1986, P.L. 99-514, Sec. 1002(a), added "(in a case involving physical injury or physical sickness)" after "injury or sickness", in subsec. (c), effective for assignments entered into after 12/31/86, in tax. yrs. end. after 12/31/86.

In 1983, P.L. 97-473, Sec. 101(b)(1), added new Code Sec. 130, effective for tax. yrs. end. after 12/31/82.

Sec. 131. Certain foster care payments.
(a) General rule.

Gross income shall not include amounts received by a foster care provider during the taxable year as qualified foster care payments.

(b) Qualified foster care payment defined.

For purposes of this section

(1) In general. The term "qualified foster care payment" means any payment made pursuant to a foster care program of a State or political subdivision thereof—

(A) which is paid by—

(i) a State or political subdivision thereof, or

(ii) a qualified foster care placement agency, and

(B) which is—

(i) paid to the foster care provider for caring for a qualified foster individual in the foster care provider's home, or

(ii) a difficulty of care payment.

(2) Qualified foster individual. The term "qualified foster individual" means any individual who is living in a foster family home in which such individual was placed by—

(A) an agency of a State or political subdivision thereof, or

(B) a qualified foster care placement agency.

(3) Qualified foster care placement agency. The term "qualified foster care placement agency" means any placement agency which is licensed or certified by—

(A) a State or political subdivision thereof, or

(B) an entity designated by a State or political subdivision thereof,

for the foster care program of such State or political subdivision to make foster care payments to providers of foster care.

(4) Limitation based on number of individuals over the age of 18. In the case of any foster home in which there is a qualified foster care individual who has attained age 19, foster care payments (other than difficulty of care payments) for any period to which such payments relate shall not be excludable from gross income under subsection (a) to the extent such payments are made for more than 5 such qualified foster individuals.

(c) Difficulty of care payments.

For purposes of this section

(1) Difficulty of care payments. The term "difficulty of care payments" means payments to individuals which are not described in subsection (b)(1)(B)(i), and which—

(A) are compensation for providing the additional care of a qualified foster individual which is—

(i) required by reason of a physical, mental, or emotional handicap of such individual with respect to which the State has determined that there is a need for additional compensation, and

(ii) provided in the home of the foster care provider, and

(B) are designated by the payor as compensation described in subparagraph (A).

(2) Limitation based on number of individuals. In the case of any foster home, difficulty of care payments for any period to which such payments relate shall not be excludable from gross income under subsection (a) to the extent such payments are made for more than—

(A) 10 qualified foster individuals who have not attained age 19, and

(B) 5 qualified foster individuals not described in subparagraph (A).

In 2002, P.L. 107-147, Sec. 404(a), amended para. (b)(1)... Sec. 404(b), amended subpara. (b)(2)(B)... Sec. 404(c), redesignated para. (b)(3) as (4) and added para. (b)(3), effective for tax. yrs. begin. after 12/31/2001.

Prior to amendment, para. (b)(1) read as follows:

"(1) In general. The term 'qualified foster care payment' means any amount—

"(A) which is paid by a State or political subdivision thereof or by a placement agency which is described in section 501(c)(3) and exempt from tax under section 501(a), and

"(B) which is—

"(i) paid to the foster care provider for caring for a qualified foster individual in the foster care provider's home, or

"(ii) a difficulty of care payment."

Prior to amendment, subpara. (b)(2)(B) read as follows:

"(B) in the case of an individual who has not attained age 19, an organization which is licensed by a State (or political subdivision thereof) as a placement agency and which is described in section 501(c)(3) and exempt from tax under section 501(a)."

In 1986, P.L. 99-514, Sec. 1707(a), amended Code Sec. 131, effective for tax. yrs. begin. after 12/31/85.

Prior to amendment, Code Sec. 131 read as follows:

"SEC. 131. CERTAIN FOSTER CARE PAYMENTS.

"(a) General rule.

"Gross income shall not include amounts received by a foster parent during the taxable year as qualified foster care payments.

"(b) Qualified foster care payment defined.

"For purposes of this section—

"(1) In general. The term 'qualified foster care payment' means any amount—

"(A) which is paid by a State or political subdivision thereof or by a child-placing agency which is described in section 501(c)(3) and exempt from tax under section 501(a), and

"(B) which is—

"(i) paid to reimburse the foster parent for the expenses of caring for a qualified foster child in the foster parent's home, or

"(ii) a difficulty of care payment.

"(2) Qualified foster child. The term 'qualified foster child' means any individual who—

"(A) has not attained age 19, and

"(B) is living in a foster family home in which such individual was placed by—

"(i) an agency of a State or political subdivision thereof, or

"(ii) an organization which is licensed by a State (or political subdivision thereof) as a child-placing agency and which is described in section 501(c)(3) and exempt from tax under section 501(a).

"(c) Difficulty of care payments.

"For purposes of this section—

"(1) Difficulty of care payments. The term 'difficulty of care payments' means payments to individuals which are not described in subsection (b)(1)(B)(i), and which—

"(A) are compensation for providing the additional care of a qualified foster child which is—

"(i) required by reason of a physical, mental, or emotional handicap of such child with respect to which the State has determined that there is a need for additional compensation, and

"(ii) provided in the home of the foster parent, and

"(B) are designated by the payor as compensation described in subparagraph (A).

"(2) Limitation based on number of children. In the case of any foster home, difficulty of care payments for any period to which such payments relate shall not be excludable from gross income under subsection (a) to the extent such payments are made for more than 10 qualified foster children."

In 1983, P.L. 97-473, Sec. 102(a), added Code Sec. 131, effective for tax. yrs. begin. after 12/31/78.

Sec. 132. Certain fringe benefits.
(a) Exclusion from gross income.

Gross income shall not include any fringe benefit which qualifies as a—

Exclusions from income — Code Sec. 132(f)(2)(C)

(1) no-additional-cost service,
(2) qualified employee discount,
(3) working condition fringe,
(4) de minimis fringe,

> • *Caution:* Code Sec. 132(a)(5)-(7), following, was amended by Sec. 665(a), P.L. 107-16, the Economic Growth and Tax Relief Reconciliation Act of 2001 (EGTRRA), and further amended by Sec. 103(a), P.L. 108-121. These provisions generally sunset for tax years beginning after 12/31/2012. For specific sunset provisions see Sec. 901, P.L. 107-16 (as amended) reproduced in history notes for this Code Sec.

(5) qualified transportation fringe,
(6) qualified moving expense reimbursement,
(7) qualified retirement planning services, or
(8) qualified military base realignment and closure fringe.

(b) No-additional-cost service defined.
For purposes of this section, the term "no-additional-cost service" means any service provided by an employer to an employee for use by such employee if—
(1) such service is offered for sale to customers in the ordinary course of the line of business of the employer in which the employee is performing services, and
(2) the employer incurs no substantial additional cost (including forgone revenue) in providing such service to the employee (determined without regard to any amount paid by the employee for such service).

(c) Qualified employee discount defined.
For purposes of this section—
(1) **Qualified employee discount.** The term "qualified employee discount" means any employee discount with respect to qualified property or services to the extent such discount does not exceed—
(A) in the case of property, the gross profit percentage of the price at which the property is being offered by the employer to customers, or
(B) in the case of services, 20 percent of the price at which the services are being offered by the employer to customers.
(2) **Gross profit percentage.**
(A) In general. The term "gross profit percentage" means the percent which—
(i) the excess of the aggregate sales price of property sold by the employer to customers over the aggregate cost of such property to the employer, is of
(ii) the aggregate sale price of such property.
(B) Determination of gross profit percentage. Gross profit percentage shall be determined on the basis of—
(i) all property offered to customers in the ordinary course of the line of business of the employer in which the employee is performing services (or a reasonable classification of property selected by the employer), and
(ii) the employer's experience during a representative period.
(3) **Employee discount defined.** The term "employee discount" means the amount by which—
(A) the price at which the property or services are provided by the employer to an employee for use by such employee, is less than

(B) the price at which such property or services are being offered by the employer to customers.
(4) **Qualified property or services.** The term "qualified property or services" means any property (other than real property and other than personal property of a kind held for investment) or services which are offered for sale to customers in the ordinary course of the line of business of the employer in which the employee is performing services.

(d) Working condition fringe defined.
For purposes of this section, the term "working condition fringe" means any property or services provided to an employee of the employer to the extent that, if the employee paid for such property or services, such payment would be allowable as a deduction under section 162 or 167.

(e) De minimis fringe defined.
For purposes of this section—
(1) **In general.** The term "de minimis fringe" means any property or service the value of which is (after taking into account the frequency with which similar fringes are provided by the employer to the employer's employees) so small as to make accounting for it unreasonable or administratively impracticable.
(2) **Treatment of certain eating facilities.** The operation by an employer of any eating facility for employees shall be treated as a de minimis fringe if—
(A) such facility is located on or near the business premises of the employer, and
(B) revenue derived from such facility normally equals or exceeds the direct operating costs of such facility.
The preceding sentence shall apply with respect to any highly compensated employee only if access to the facility is available on substantially the same terms to each member of a group of employees which is defined under a reasonable classification set up by the employer which does not discriminate in favor of highly compensated employees. For purposes of subparagraph (B), an employee entitled under section 119 to exclude the value of a meal provided at such facility shall be treated as having paid an amount for such meal equal to the direct operating costs of the facility attributable to such meal.

(f) Qualified transportation fringe.
(1) **In general.** For purposes of this section, the term "qualified transportation fringe" means any of the following provided by an employer to an employee:
(A) Transportation in a commuter highway vehicle if such transportation is in connection with travel between the employee's residence and place of employment.
(B) Any transit pass.
(C) Qualified parking.
(D) Any qualified bicycle commuting reimbursement.
(2) **Limitation on exclusion.** The amount of the fringe benefits which are provided by an employer to any employee and which may be excluded from gross income under subsection (a)(5) shall not exceed—
(A) $100 per month in the case of the aggregate of the benefits described in subparagraphs (A) and (B) of paragraph (1),
(B) $175 per month in the case of qualified parking, and
(C) the applicable annual limitation in the case of any qualified bicycle commuting reimbursement.
In the case of any month beginning on or after the date of the enactment of this sentence and before January 1, 2012, subparagraph (A) shall be applied as if the dollar amount therein were the same as the dollar amount in effect for such month under subparagraph (B).

1,447

(3) Cash reimbursements. For purposes of this subsection, the term "qualified transportation fringe" includes a cash reimbursement by an employer to an employee for a benefit described in paragraph (1). The preceding sentence shall apply to a cash reimbursement for any transit pass only if a voucher or similar item which may be exchanged only for a transit pass is not readily available for direct distribution by the employer to the employee.

(4) No constructive receipt. No amount shall be included in the gross income of an employee solely because the employee may choose between any qualified transportation fringe (other than a qualified bicycle commuting reimbursement) and compensation which would otherwise be includible in gross income of such employee.

(5) Definitions. For purposes of this subsection—

(A) Transit pass. The term "transit pass" means any pass, token, farecard, voucher, or similar item entitling a person to transportation (or transportation at a reduced price) if such transportation is—

(i) on mass transit facilities (whether or not publicly owned), or

(ii) provided by any person in the business of transporting persons for compensation or hire if such transportation is provided in a vehicle meeting the requirements of subparagraph (B)(i).

(B) Commuter highway vehicle. The term "commuter highway vehicle" means any highway vehicle—

(i) the seating capacity of which is at least 6 adults (not including the driver), and

(ii) at least 80 percent of the mileage use of which can reasonably be expected to be—

(I) for purposes of transporting employees in connection with travel between their residences and their place of employment, and

(II) on trips during which the number of employees transported for such purposes is at least ½ of the adult seating capacity of such vehicle (not including the driver).

(C) Qualified parking. The term "qualified parking" means parking provided to an employee on or near the business premises of the employer or on or near a location from which the employee commutes to work by transportation described in subparagraph (A), in a commuter highway vehicle, or by carpool. Such term shall not include any parking on or near property used by the employee for residential purposes.

(D) Transportation provided by employer. Transportation referred to in paragraph (1)(A) shall be considered to be provided by an employer if such transportation is furnished in a commuter highway vehicle operated by or for the employer.

(E) Employee. For purposes of this subsection, the term "employee" does not include an individual who is an employee within the meaning of section 401(c)(1).

(F) Definitions related to bicycle commuting reimbursement.

(i) Qualified bicycle commuting reimbursement. The term "qualified bicycle commuting reimbursement" means, with respect to any calendar year, any employer reimbursement during the 15-month period beginning with the first day of such calendar year for reasonable expenses incurred by the employee during such calendar year for the purchase of a bicycle and bicycle improvements, repair, and storage, if such bicycle is regularly used for travel between the employee's residence and place of employment.

(ii) Applicable annual limitation. The term "applicable annual limitation" means, with respect to any employee for any calendar year, the product of $20 multiplied by the number of qualified bicycle commuting months during such year.

(iii) Qualified bicycle commuting month. The term "qualified bicycle commuting month" means, with respect to any employee, any month during which such employee—

(I) regularly uses the bicycle for a substantial portion of the travel between the employee's residence and place of employment, and

(II) does not receive any benefit described in subparagraph (A), (B), or (C) of paragraph (1).

(6) Inflation adjustment.

(A) In general. In the case of any taxable year beginning in a calendar year after 1999, the dollar amounts contained in subparagraphs (A) and (B) of paragraph (2) shall be increased by an amount equal to—

(i) such dollar amount, multiplied by

(ii) the cost-of-living adjustment determined under section 1(f)(3) for the calendar year in which the taxable year begins, by substituting "calendar year 1998" for "calendar year 1992".

In the case of any taxable year beginning in a calendar year after 2002, clause (ii) shall be applied by substituting "calendar year 2001" for "calendar year 1998" for purposes of adjusting the dollar amount contained in paragraph (2)(A).

(B) Rounding. If any increase determined under subparagraph (A) is not a multiple of $5, such increase shall be rounded to the next lowest multiple of $5.

(7) Coordination with other provisions. For purposes of this section, the terms "working condition fringe" and "de minimis fringe" shall not include any qualified transportation fringe (determined without regard to paragraph (2)).

(g) Qualified moving expense reimbursement.

For purposes of this section, the term "qualified moving expense reimbursement" means any amount received (directly or indirectly) by an individual from an employer as a payment for (or a reimbursement of) expenses which would be deductible as moving expenses under section 217 if directly paid or incurred by the individual. Such term shall not include any payment for (or reimbursement of) an expense actually deducted by the individual in a prior taxable year.

(h) Certain individuals treated as employees for purposes of subsections (a)(1) and (2).

For purposes of paragraphs (1) and (2) of subsection (a)—

(1) Retired and disabled employees and surviving spouse of employee treated as employee. With respect to a line of business of an employer, the term "employee" includes—

(A) any individual who was formerly employed by such employer in such line of business and who separated from service with such employer in such line of business by reason of retirement or disability, and

(B) any widow or widower of any individual who died while employed by such employer in such line of business or while an employee within the meaning of subparagraph (A).

(2) Spouses and dependent children.

(A) In general. Any use by the spouse or a dependent child of the employee shall be treated as use by the employee.

Exclusions from income — Code Sec. 132(l)

(B) **Dependent child.** For purposes of subparagraph (A), the term "dependent child" means any child (as defined in section 152(f)(1)) of the employee—
  (i) who is a dependent of the employee, or
  (ii) both of whose parents are deceased and who has not attained age 25.

For purposes of the preceding sentence, any child to whom section 152(e) applies shall be treated as the dependent of both parents.

(3) Special rule for parents in the case of air transportation. Any use of air transportation by a parent of an employee (determined without regard to paragraph (1)(B)) shall be treated as use by the employee.

(i) Reciprocal agreements.

For purposes of paragraph (1) of subsection (a), any service provided by an employer to an employee of another employer shall be treated as provided by the employer of such employee if—
(1) such service is provided pursuant to a written agreement between such employers, and
(2) neither of such employers incurs any substantial additional costs (including foregone revenue) in providing such service or pursuant to such agreement.

(j) Special rules.

(1) Exclusions under subsection (a)(1) and (2) apply to highly compensated employees only if no discrimination. Paragraphs (1) and (2) of subsection (a) shall apply with respect to any fringe benefit described therein provided with respect to any highly compensated employee only if such fringe benefit is available on substantially the same terms to each member of a group of employees which is defined under a reasonable classification set up by the employer which does not discriminate in favor of highly compensated employees.

(2) Special rule for leased sections of department stores.
  (A) In general. For purposes of paragraph (2) of subsection (a), in the case of a leased section of a department store—
    (i) such section shall be treated as part of the line of business of the person operating the department store, and
    (ii) employees in the leased section shall be treated as employees of the person operating the department store.
  (B) Leased section of department store. For purposes of subparagraph (A), a leased section of a department store is any part of a department store where over-the-counter sales of property are made under a lease or similar arrangement where it appears to the general public that individuals making such sales are employed by the person operating the department store.

(3) Auto salesmen.
  (A) In general. For purposes of subsection (a)(3), qualified automobile demonstration use shall be treated as a working condition fringe.
  (B) Qualified automobile demonstration use. For purposes of subparagraph (A), the term "qualified automobile demonstration use" means any use of an automobile by a full-time automobile salesman in the sales area in which the automobile dealer's sales office is located if—
    (i) such use is provided primarily to facilitate the salesman's performance of services for the employer, and
    (ii) there are substantial restrictions on the personal use of such automobile by such salesman.

(4) On-premises gyms and other athletic facilities.
  (A) In general. Gross income shall not include the value of any on-premises athletic facility provided by an employer to his employees.
  (B) On-premises athletic facility. For purposes of this paragraph, the term "on-premises athletic facility" means any gym or other athletic facility—
    (i) which is located on the premises of the employer,
    (ii) which is operated by the employer, and
    (iii) substantially all the use of which is by employees of the employer, their spouses, and their dependent children (within the meaning of subsection (h)).

(5) Special rule for affiliates of airlines.
  (A) In general. If—
    (i) a qualified affiliate is a member of an affiliated group another member of which operates an airline, and
    (ii) employees of the qualified affiliate who are directly engaged in providing airline-related services are entitled to no-additional-cost service with respect to air transportation provided by such other member,
  then, for purposes of applying paragraph (1) of subsection (a) to such no-additional-cost service provided to such employees, such qualified affiliate shall be treated as engaged in the same line of business as such other member.
  (B) Qualified affiliate. For purposes of this paragraph, the term "qualified affiliate" means any corporation which is predominantly engaged in airline-related services.
  (C) Airline-related services. For purposes of this paragraph, the term "airline-related services" means any of the following services provided in connection with air transportation:
    (i) Catering.
    (ii) Baggage handling.
    (iii) Ticketing and reservations.
    (iv) Flight planning and weather analysis.
    (v) Restaurants and gift shops located at an airport.
    (vi) Such other similar services provided to the airline as the Secretary may prescribe.
  (D) Affiliated group. For purposes of this paragraph, the term "affiliated group" has the meaning given such term by section 1504(a).

(6) Highly compensated employee. For purposes of this section, the term "highly compensated employee" has the meaning given such term by section 414(q).

(7) Air cargo. For purposes of subsection (b), the transportation of cargo by air and the transportation of passengers by air shall be treated as the same service.

(8) Application of section to otherwise taxable educational or training benefits. Amounts paid or expenses incurred by the employer for education or training provided to the employee which are not excludable from gross income under section 127 shall be excluded from gross income under this section if (and only if) such amounts or expenses are a working condition fringe.

(k) Customers not to include employees.

For purposes of this section (other than subsection (c)(2)), the term "customers" shall only include customers who are not employees.

(l) Section not to apply to fringe benefits expressly provided for elsewhere.

This section (other than subsections (e) and (g)) shall not apply to any fringe benefits of a type the tax treatment of

Code Sec. 132(l) — Exclusions from income

which is expressly provided for in any other section of this chapter.

> • **Caution:** Code Sec. 132(m)-(n), following, was amended by Sec. 665(b), P.L. 107-16, the Economic Growth and Tax Relief Reconciliation Act of 2001 (EGTRRA), and further amended by Sec. 103(a), P.L. 108-121. These provisions generally sunset for tax years beginning after 12/31/2012. For specific sunset provisions see Sec. 901, P.L. 107-16 (as amended) reproduced in history notes for this Code Sec.

(m) Qualified retirement planning services.

(1) In general. For purposes of this section, the term "qualified retirement planning services" means any retirement planning advice or information provided to an employee and his spouse by an employer maintaining a qualified employer plan.

(2) Nondiscrimination rule. Subsection (a)(7) shall apply in the case of highly compensated employees only if such services are available on substantially the same terms to each member of the group of employees normally provided education and information regarding the employer's qualified employer plan.

(3) Qualified employer plan. For purposes of this subsection, the term "qualified employer plan" means a plan, contract, pension, or account described in section 219(g)(5).

(n) Qualified military base realignment and closure fringe.

For purposes of this section—

(1) In general. The term "qualified military base realignment and closure fringe" means 1 or more payments under the authority of section 1013 of the Demonstration Cities and Metropolitan Development Act of 1966 (42 U.S.C. 3374) (as in effect on the date of the enactment of the American Recovery and Reinvestment Tax Act of 2009).

(2) Limitation. With respect to any property, such term shall not include any payment referred to in paragraph (1) to the extent that the sum of all of such payments related to such property exceeds the maximum amount described in subsection (c) of such section (as in effect on such date).

(o) Regulations.

The Secretary shall prescribe such regulations as may be necessary or appropriate to carry out the purposes of this section.

In 2010, P.L. 111-312, Sec. 101(a)(1), substituted "December 31, 2012" for "December 31, 2010" both places it appeared in Sec. 901 of P.L. 107-16 [see below], effective as if included in the enactment of P.L. 107-16, EGTRRA, 6/7/2001.

—P.L. 111-312, Sec. 727(a), substituted "January 1, 2012" for "January 1, 2011" in para. (f)(2), effective for months after 12/31/2010.

In 2009, P.L. 111-92, Sec. 14(a)(1), substituted "the American Recovery and Reinvestment Tax Act of 2009)" for "this subsection) to offset the adverse effects on housing values as a result of a military base realignment or closure" in para. (n)(1)

—P.L. 111-92, Sec. 14(a)(2), deleted "clause (1) of" in para. (n)(2), effective for payments made after 2/17/2009.

—P.L. 111-5, Sec. 1151(a), added a flush sentence at the end of para. (f)(2), effective for months begin. on or after 2/17/2009.

In 2008, P.L. 110-343, Sec. 211(a)DivB, added subpara. (f)(1)(D) ... Sec. 211(b)DivB, deleted "and" at the end of subpara. (f)(2)(A), substituted ", and" for the period at the end of subpara. (f)(2)(B), and added subpara. (f)(2)(C) ... Sec. 211(c)DivB, added subpara. (f)(5)(F) ... Sec. 211(d)DivB, added "(other than a qualified bicycle commuting reimbursement)" after "qualified transportation fringe" in para. (f)(4), effective for tax. yrs. begin. after 12/31/2008.

In 2006, P.L. 109-280, Sec. 811, of this Act [relating to Sec. 901 of P.L. 107-16, see below], provides:

"Sec. 811. Pensions and individual retirement arrangement provisions of Economic Growth and Tax Relief Reconciliation Act of 2001 made permanent.

"Title IX of the Economic Growth and Tax Relief Reconciliation Act of 2001 shall not apply to the provisions of, and amendments made by, subtitles A through F of title VI of such Act (relating to pension and individual retirement arrangement provisions)."

In 2004, P.L. 108-311, Sec. 207(13), substituted "152(f)(1)" for "151(c)(3)" in subpara. (h)(2)(B), effective for tax. yrs. begin. after 12/31/2004.

In 2003, P.L. 108-121, Sec. 103(a), deleted "or" at the end of para. (a)(6), substituted ", or" for the period at the end of para. (a)(7), and added para. (a)(8) ... Sec. 103(b), redesignated subsec. (n) as (o) and added subsec. (n), effective for payments made after 11/11/2003.

In 2002, P.L. 107-358, Sec. 2, added subsec. (c) in Sec. 901 of P.L. 107-16 [see below], effective 12/17/2002.

In 2001, P.L. 107-16, Sec. 665(a), deleted "or" at the end of para. (a)(5), substituted ", or" for the period at the end of para. (a)(6), and added para. (a)(7) ... Sec. 665(b), redesignated subsec. (m) as (n) and added subsec. (m), effective for yrs. begin. after 12/31/2001.

—P.L. 107-16, Sec. 901, of this Act [as amended by Sec. 2 of P.L. 107-358 and Sec. 101(a)(1) of P.L. 111-312, and as related to Sec. 811 of P.L. 109-280, see above], reads as follows:

"SEC. 901. SUNSET OF PROVISIONS OF ACT.

"(a) In general. All provisions of, and amendments made by, this Act shall not apply—

"(1) to taxable, plan, or limitation years beginning after December 31, 2012, or

"(2) in the case of title V, to estates of decedents dying, gifts made, or generation skipping transfers, after December 31, 2012.

"(b) Application of certain laws. The Internal Revenue Code of 1986 and the Employee Retirement Income Security Act of 1974 shall be applied and administered to years, estates, gifts, and transfers described in subsection (a) as if the provisions and amendments described in subsection (a) had never been enacted.

"(c) Exception. Subsection (a) shall not apply to section 803 (relating to no federal income tax on restitution received by victims of the Nazi regime or their heirs or estates)."

In 1998, P.L. 105-178, Sec. 9010(a)(1), amended para. (f)(4), effective for tax. yrs. begin. after 12/31/97.

Prior to amendment, para. (f)(4) read as follows:

"(4) Benefit not in lieu of compensation. Subsection (a)(5) shall not apply to any qualified transportation fringe unless such benefit is provided in addition to (and not in lieu of) any compensation otherwise payable to the employee. This paragraph shall not apply to any qualified parking provided in lieu of compensation which otherwise would have been includible in gross income of the employee, and no amount shall be included in the gross income of the employee solely because the employee may choose between the qualified parking and compensation."

—P.L. 105-178, Sec. 9010(b)(1), amended para. (f)(6) ... Sec. 9010(b)(2)(A), substituted "$65" for "$60" in subpara. '(f)(2)(A) ... Sec. 9010(b)(2)(B), substituted "$175" for "$155" in subpara. (f)(2)(B), effective for tax. yrs. begin. after 12/31/98.

Prior to amendment, para. (f)(6) read as follows:

"(6) Inflation adjustment. In the case of any taxable year beginning in a calendar year after 1993, the dollar amounts contained in paragraph (2)(A) and (B) shall be increased by an amount equal to—

"(A) such dollar amount, multiplied by

"(B) the cost-of-living adjustment determined under section 1(f)(3) for the calendar year in which the taxable year begins.

If any increase determined under the preceding sentence is not a multiple of $5, such increase shall be rounded to the next lowest multiple of $5."

—P.L. 105-178, Sec. 9010(c)(1), substituted "$100" for "$65" in subpara. (f)(2)(A) ... Sec. 9010(c)(2), added a flush sentence at the end of subpara. (f)(6)(A), effective for tax. yrs. begin. after 12/31/2001.

In 1997, P.L. 105-34, Sec. 970(a), added a sentence at the end of para. (e)(2), effective for tax. yrs. begin. after 12/31/97.

—P.L. 105-34, Sec. 1072(a), added a sentence at the end of para. (f)(4), effective for tax. yrs. begin. after 12/31/97.

In 1993, P.L. 103-66, Sec. 13101(b), amended para. (i)(8), effective for tax. yrs. begin. after 12/31/88.

Prior to amendment, para. (i)(8) read as follows:

"(8) Application of section to otherwise taxable employer-provided educational assistance. Amounts which would be excludible from gross income under section 127 but for subsection (a)(2) thereof or the last sentence of subsection (c)(1) thereof shall be excluded from gross income under this section if (and only if) such amounts are a working condition fringe."

—P.L. 103-66, Sec. 13201(b)(3)(F), substituted a period for ", determined by substituting 'calendar year 1992' for 'calendar year 1989' in subparagraph (B) thereof." in subpara. (f)(6)(B), effective for tax. yrs. begin. after 12/31/92.

—P.L. 103-66, Sec. 13213(d)(1), deleted "or" at the end of para. (a)(4), substituted ", or" for the period at the end of para. (a)(5), and added para. (a)(6) ... Sec. 13213(d)(2), redesignated subsecs. (g) through (l) as subsecs. (h) through (m) and added subsec. (g) ... Sec. 13213(d)(3)(B), substituted "subsection (h)" for "subsection (f)" in clause (j)(4)(B)(iii) (as redesignated by Sec. 13213(d)(2) of this Act) ... Sec. 13213(d)(3)(C), substituted "subsections (e) and (g)" for "subsection (e)" in subsec. (l) (as redesignated by Sec. 13213(d)(2) of this Act), effective for reimbursements or other payments in respect of expenses incurred after 12/31/93.

In 1992, P.L. 102-486, Sec. 1911(a), deleted "or" at the end of para. (a)(3), substituted ", or" for the period at the end of para. (a)(4) and added para. (a)(5) ...

Exclusions from income

Sec. 1911(b), redesignated subsecs. (f) through (k) as subsecs. (g) through (l) and added new subsec. (f) . . . Sec. 1911(c), deleted para. (i)(4) and redesignated paras. (i)(5) through (9) as (i)(4) through (8), effective for benefits provided after 12/31/92.

Prior to deletion, para. (i)(4) read as follows:

"(4) Parking. The term 'working condition fringe' includes parking provided to an employee on or near the business premises of the employer."

In 1989, P.L. 101-239, Sec. 7101(b), added para. (h)(9), effective for tax. yrs. begin. after 12/31/88.

—P.L. 101-239, Sec. 7841(d)(7), substituted "highly compensated employees" for "officers, etc.," in the heading of para. (h)(1) . . . Sec. 7841(d)(19), substituted "section 151(c)(3)" for "section 151(e)(3)" in subpara. (f)(2)(B), effective 12/19/89.

—P.L. 101-140, Sec. 203(a)(1), repealed as if not enacted Sec. 1151(g)(5) of P.L. 99-514 which amended para. (h)(1) . . . Sec. 203(a)(2), repealed as if not enacted Sec. 1011B(a)(31)(B) of P.L. 100-647, which amended para. (h)(1).

—P.L. 101-136, Sec. 528, provided that "no monies appropriated by this Act [for the fiscal year ending September 30, '90] may be used to implement or enforce section 1151 of the Tax Reform Act of '86 [P.L. 99-514] or the amendments made by such section." [See below]

In 1988, P.L. 100-647, Sec. 1011B(a)(25), amended Sec. 1151(k)(1) of P.L. 99-514 [reproduced below], part of the effective date for changes made by Secs. 1151(e)(2)(A) of P.L. 99-514, by adding the last sentence, see below.

—P.L. 100-647, Sec. 6066(a), added para. (h)(8), effective for transportation furnished after 12/31/87, in tax. yrs. end. after 12/31/87.

In 1986, P.L. 99-514, Sec. 1114(b)(5)(A), deleted "officer, owner, or" after "respect to any" and "officers, owners," after "in favor of" in paras. (e)(2) and (h)(1) . . . Sec. 1114(b)(5)(B), added para. (h)(7), effective for tax. yrs. begin after 12/31/87.

—P.L. 99-514, Sec. 1151(e)(2)(A), amended subsec. (g), effective as provided in Sec. 1151(k)(1) of this Act [as amended by Sec. 1011B(a)(25) of P.L. 100-647, see above]:

"(1) In general.—The amendments made by this section shall apply to years beginning after the later of—

"(A) December 31, 1987, or

"(B) the earlier of—

"(i) the date which is 3 months after the date on which the Secretary of the Treasury or his delegate issues such regulations as are necessary to carry out the provisions of section 89 of the Internal Revenue Code of 1986 (as added by this section), or

"(ii) December 31, 1988.

Not withstanding the preceding sentence, the amendments made by subsections (e)(1) and (i)(3)(C) shall, to the extent they relate to sections 106, 162(i)(2), and 162(k) of the Internal Revenue Code of 1986, apply to years beginning after 1986."

Prior to amendment, subsec. (g) read as follows:

"(g) Special rules relating to employer. For purposes of this section—

"(1) Controlled groups, etc. All employees treated as employed by a single employer under subsection (b), (c), or (m) of section 414 shall be treated as employed by a single employer for purposes of this section.

"(2) Reciprocal agreements. For purposes of paragraph (1) of subsection (a), any service provided by an employer to an employee of another employer shall be treated as provided by the employer of such employee if—

"(A) such service is provided pursuant to a written agreement between such employers, and

"(B) neither of such employers incurs any substantial additional cost (including forgone revenue) in providing such service or pursuant to such agreement."

—P.L. 99-514, Sec. 1567, provides:

"SEC. 1567. CERTAIN RECORDKEEPING REQUIREMENTS.

"(a) In general. For purposes of sections 132 and 274 of the Internal Revenue Code of 1954, use of an automobile by a special agent of the Internal Revenue Service shall be treated in the same manner as use of an automobile by an officer of any other law enforcement agency.

"(b) Effective date. The provisions of this section shall take effect on January 1, 1985."

—P.L. 99-514, Sec. 1853(a)(1), substituted "are deceased and who has not attained age 25" for "are deceased" in clause (f)(2)(B)(ii) . . . Sec. 1853(a)(2), substituted "are provided by the employer to an employee for use by such employee" for "are provided to the employee by the employer" in subpara. (c)(3)(A) . . . Sec. 1853(a)(3), substituted "subsection (c)(2)" for "subsection (c)(2)(B)", effective 1/1/85. Sec. 1853(e), of this Act provides:

"(e) Treatment of certain leased operations of department stores. For purposes of section 132(h)(2)(B) of the Internal Revenue Code of 1954, a leased section of a department store which, in connection with the offering of beautician services, customarily makes sales of beauty aids in the ordinary course of business shall be treated as engaged in over-the-counter sales of property."

For special rules see Secs. 531(f) and (g) of P.L. 98-369 reproduced below.

—P.L. 99-514, Sec. 1899A(5), substituted "such use is" for "such use in" in clause (h)(3)(B)(i), effective 10/22/86.

—P.L. 99-272, Sec. 13207(a)(1), added para. (f)(3), . . . Sec. 13207(b)(1), added para. (h)(6), effective 1/1/85. Sec. 13207(c) of this Act provides:

"(c) Transitional rule for determination of line of business in case of affiliated group operating airline. If, as of September 12, 1984—

"(1) an individual—

"(A) was an employee (within the meaning of section 132 of the Internal Revenue Code of 1954, including subsection (f) thereof) of one member of an affili-

Code Sec. 133

ated group (as defined in section 1504 of such Code), hereinafter referred to as the 'first corporation', and

"(B) was eligible for no-additional-cost service in the form of air transportation provided by another member of such affiliated group, hereinafter referred to as the 'second corporation',

"(2) at least 50 percent of the individuals performing service for the first corporation were or had been employees of, or had previously performed services for, the second corporation, and

"(3) the primary business of the affiliated group was air transportation of passengers,

then, for purposes of applying paragraphs (1) and (2) of section 132(a) of the Internal Revenue Code of 1954, with respect to no-additional-cost services and qualified employee discounts provided after December 31, 1984, for such individual by the second corporation, the first corporation shall be treated as engaged in the same air transportation line of business as the second corporation. For purposes of the preceding sentence, an employee of the second corporation who is performing services for the first corporation shall also be treated as an employee of the first corporation."

—P.L. 99-272, Sec. 13207(d), redesignated Sec. 531(g) and (h) of P.L. 98-369 as Sec. 531(h) and (i) and added new Sec. 531(g) to P.L. 98-369 [reproduced below].

In 1984, P.L. 98-369, Sec. 531(a)(1), added Code Sec. 132, effective 1/1/85. Secs. 531(f) and (g) [as amended by Sec. 13207(d) of P.L. 99-272, above] of this Act provide:

"(f) Determination of line of business in case of affiliated group operating retail department stores. If—

"(1) as of October 5, 1983, the employees of one member of an affiliated group (as defined in section 1504 of the Internal Revenue Code of 1954 without regard to subsections (b)(2) and (b)(4) thereof) were entitled to employee discounts at the retail department stores operated by another member of such affiliated group, and

"(2) the primary business of the affiliated group is the operation of retail department stores,

then, for purposes of applying section 132(a)(2) of the Internal Revenue Code of 1954, with respect to discounts provided for such employees at the retail department stores operated by such other member, the employer shall be treated as engaged in the same line of business as such other member.

"(g) Special rule for certain services related to air transportation.

"(1) In general. If—

"(A) an individual performs services for a qualified air transportation organization, and

"(B) such services are performed primarily for persons engaged in providing air transportation and are of the kind which (if performed on September 12, 1984) would qualify such individual for no-additional-cost services in the form of air transportation,

then, with respect to such individual, such qualified air transportation organization shall be treated as engaged in the line of business of providing air transportation.

"(2) Qualified air transportation organization. For purposes of paragraph (1), the term 'qualified air transportation organization' means any organization—

"(A) if such organization (or a predecessor) was in existence on September 12, 1984,

"(B) if—

"(i) such organization is described in section 501(c)(6) of the Internal Revenue Code of 1954 and the membership of such organization is limited to entities engaged in the transportation by air of individuals or property for compensation or hire, or

"(ii) such organization is a corporation all the stock of which is owned entirely by entities referred to in clause (i), and

"(C) if such organization is operated in furtherance of the activities of its members or owners."

Sec. 133. Repealed.

In 1996, P.L. 104-188, Sec. 1602(a), repealed Code Sec. 133, effective for loans made after 8/20/96. For notes regarding refinancings and exceptions, see Secs. 1602(c)(2) and (3) of this Act, which read as follows:

"(2) Refinancings. The amendments made by this section shall not apply to loans made after the date of the enactment of this Act to refinance securities acquisition loans (determined without regard to section 133(b)(1)(D) of the Internal Revenue Code of 1986, as in effect on the day before the date of the enactment of this Act) made on or before such date or to refinance loans described in this paragraph if—

"(A) the refinancing loans meet the requirements of section 133 of such Code (as so in effect),

"(B) immediately after the refinancing the principal amount of the loan resulting from the refinancing does not exceed the principal amount of the refinanced loan (immediately before the refinancing), and

"(C) the term of such refinancing loan does not extend beyond the last day of the term of the original securities acquisition loan.

For purposes of this paragraph, the term 'securities acquisition loan' includes a loan from a corporation to an employee stock ownership plan described in section 133(b)(3) of such Code (as so in effect).

"(3) Exception. Any loan made pursuant to a binding written contract in effect before June 10, 1996, and at all times thereafter before such loan is made, shall be treated for purposes of paragraphs (1) and (2) as a loan made on or before the date of the enactment of this Act."

Prior to repeal, Code Sec. 133 read as follows:

"CODE SEC. 133. INTEREST ON CERTAIN LOANS USED TO ACQUIRE EMPLOYER SECURITIES.

"(a) In general. Gross income does not include 50 percent of the interest received by—
"(1) a bank (within the meaning of section 581),
"(2) an insurance company to which subchapter L applies,
"(3) a corporation actively engaged in the business of lending money, or
"(4) a regulated investment company (as defined in section 851),
with respect to a securities acquisition loan.

"(b) Securities acquisition loan.
"(1) In general. For purposes of this section, the term 'securities acquisition loan' means—
"(A) any loan to a corporation or to an employee stock ownership plan to the extent that the proceeds are used to acquire employer securities for the plan, or
"(B) any loan to a corporation to the extent that, within 30 days, employer securities are transferred to the plan in an amount equal to the proceeds of such loan and such securities are allocable to accounts of plan participants within 1 year of the date of such loan.

For purposes of this paragraph, the term 'employer securities' has the meaning given such term by section 409(l). The term 'securities acquisition loan' shall not include a loan with a term greater than 15 years.

"(2) Loans between related persons. The term 'securities acquisition loan' shall not include—
"(A) any loan made between corporations which are members of the same controlled group of corporations, or
"(B) any loan made between an employee stock ownership plan and any person that is—
"(i) the employer of any employees who are covered by the plan; or
"(ii) a member of a controlled group of corporations which includes such employer.

For purposes of this paragraph, subparagraphs (A) and (B) shall not apply to any loan which, but for such subparagraphs, would be a securities acquisition loan if such loan was not originated by the employer of any employees who are covered by the plan or by any member of the controlled group of corporations which includes such employer, except that this section shall not apply to any interest received on such loan during such time as such loan is held by such employer (or any member of such controlled group).

"(3) Terms applicable to certain securities acquisition loans. A loan to a corporation shall not fail to be treated as a securities acquisition loan merely because the proceeds of such loan are lent to an employee stock ownership plan sponsored by such corporation (or by any member of the controlled group of corporations which includes such corporation) if such loan includes—
"(A) repayment terms which are substantially similar to the terms of the loan of such corporation from a lender described in subsection (a), or
"(B) repayment terms providing for more rapid repayment of principal or interest on such loan, but only if allocations under the plan attributable to such repayment do not discriminate in favor of highly compensated employees (within the meaning of section 414(q)).

"(4) Controlled group of corporations. For purposes of this paragraph, the term 'controlled group of corporations' has the meaning given such term by section 409(l)(4).

"(5) Treatment of refinancings. The term 'securities acquisition loan' shall include any loan which—
"(A) is (or is part of a series of loans) used to refinance a loan described in subparagraph (A) or (B) of paragraph (1), and
"(B) meets the requirements of paragraphs (2) and (3).

"(6) Plan must hold more than 50 percent of stock after acquisition or transfer.
"(A) In general. A loan shall not be treated as a securities acquisition loan for purposes of this section unless, immediately after the acquisition or transfer referred to in subparagraph (A) or (B) of paragraph (1), respectively, the employee stock ownership plan owns more than 50 percent of—
"(i) each class of outstanding stock of the corporation issuing the employer securities, or
"(ii) the total value of all outstanding stock of the corporation.
"(B) Failure to retain minimum stock interest.
"(i) In general. Subsection (a) shall not apply to any interest received with respect to a securities acquisition loan which is allocable to any period during which the employee stock ownership plan does not own stock meeting the requirements of subparagraph (A).
"(ii) Exception. To the extent provided by the Secretary, clause (i) shall not apply to any period if, within 90 days of the first date on which the failure occurred (or such longer period not in excess of 180 days as the Secretary may prescribe), the plan acquires stock which results in its meeting the requirements of subparagraph (A).
"(C) Stock. For purposes of subparagraph (A)—
"(i) In general. The term 'stock' means stock other than stock described in section 1504(a)(4).
"(ii) Treatment of certain rights. The Secretary may provide that warrants, options, contracts to acquire stock, convertible debt interests and other similar interests be treated as stock for 1 or more purposes under subparagraph (A).
"(D) Aggregation rule. For purposes of determining whether the requirements of subparagraph (A) are met, an employee stock ownership plan shall be treated as owning stock in the corporation issuing the employer securities which is held by any other employee stock ownership plan which is maintained by—
"(i) the employer maintaining the plan, or
"(ii) any member of a controlled group of corporations (within the meaning of section 409(l)(4)) of which the employer described in clause (i) is a member.

"(7) Voting rights of employer securities. A loan shall not be treated as a securities acquisition loan for purposes of this section unless—
"(A) the employee stock ownership plan meets the requirements of section 409(e)(2) with respect to all employer securities acquired by, or transferred to, the plan in connection with such loan (without regard to whether or not the employer has a registration-type class of securities), and
"(B) no stock described in section 409(l)(3) is acquired by, or transferred to, the plan in connection with such loan unless—
"(i) such stock has voting rights equivalent to the stock to which it may be converted, and
"(ii) the requirements of subparagraph (A) are met with respect to such voting rights.

"(c) Employee stock ownership plan. For purposes of this section, the term 'employee stock ownership plan' has the meaning given to such term by section 4975(e)(7).

"(d) Application with section 483 and original issue discount rules. In applying section 483 and subpart A of part V of subchapter P to any obligation to which this section applies, appropriate adjustments shall be made to the applicable Federal rate to take into account the exclusion under subsection (a).

"(e) Period to which interest exclusion applies.
"(1) In general. In the case of —
"(A) an original securities acquisition loan, and
"(B) any securities acquisition loan (or series of such loans) used to refinance the original securities acquisition loan, subsection (a) shall apply only to interest accruing during the excludable period with respect to the original securities acquisition loan.
"(2) Excludable period. For purposes of this subsection, the term 'excludable period' means, with respect to any original securities acquisition loan—
"(A) In general. The 7-year period beginning on the date of such loan.
"(B) Loans described in subsection (b)(1)(A). If the term of an original securities acquisition loan described in subsection (b)(1)(A) is greater than 7 years, the term of such loan. This subparagraph shall not apply to a loan described in subsection (b)(3)(B).
"(3) Original securities acquisition loan. For the purposes of this subsection, the term 'original securities acquisition loan' means a securities acquisition loan described in subparagraph (A) or (B) of subsection (b)(1)."

In 1989, P.L. 101-239, Sec. 7301(a), added para. (b)(6) . . . Sec. 7301(b), added a sentence to the end of para. (b)(1) . . . Sec. 7301(c), added para. (b)(7), effective for loans made after 7/10/89, except as provided in Secs. 7301(f)(2)-(6) of this Act, which read as follows:

"(2) Binding commitment exceptions.—
"(A) The amendments made by this section shall not apply to any loan—
"(i) which is made pursuant to a binding written commitment in effect on June 6, 1989, and at all times thereafter before such loan is made, or
"(ii) to the extent that the proceeds of such loan are used to acquire employer securities pursuant to a written binding contract (or tender offer registered with the Securities and Exchange Commission) in effect on June 6, 1989, and at all times thereafter before such securities are acquired.
"(B) The amendments made by this section shall not apply to any loan to which subparagraph (A) does not apply which is made pursuant to a binding written commitment in effect on July 10, 1989, and at all times thereafter before such loan is made. The preceding sentence shall only apply to the extent that the proceeds of such loan are used to acquire employer securities pursuant to a written binding contract (or tender offer registered with the Securities and Exchange Commission) in effect on July 10, 1989, and at all times thereafter before such securities are acquired.
"(C) The amendments made by this section shall not apply to any loan made on or before July 10, 1992, pursuant to a written agreement entered into on or before July 10, 1989, if such agreement evidences the intent of the borrower on a periodic basis to enter into securities acquisition loans described in section 133(b)(1)(B) of the Internal Revenue Code of 1986 (as in effect on the day before the date of the enactment of this Act). The preceding sentence shall apply only if one or more securities acquisition loans were made to the borrower on or before July 10, 1989.
"(3) Refinancings.— The amendments made by this section shall not apply to loans made after July 10, 1989, to refinance securities acquisition loans (determined without regard to section 133(b)(2) of the Internal Revenue Code of 1986) made on or before such date or to refinance loans described in this paragraph or paragraph (2), (4), or (5) if—
"(A) such refinancing loans meet the requirements of such section 133 of such Code (as in effect before such amendments) applicable to such loans,
"(B) immediately after the refinancing the principal amount of the loan resulting from the refinancing does not exceed the principal amount of the refinanced loan (immediately before the refinancing), and
"(C) the term of such refinancing loan does not extend beyond the later of—
"(i) the last day of the term of the original securities acquisition loan, or
"(ii) the last day of the 7-year period beginning on the date the original securities acquisition loan was made.

"For purposes of this paragraph, the term 'securities acquisition loan' shall include a loan from a corporation to an employee stock ownership plan described in section 133(b)(3) of such Code.
"(4) Collective bargaining agreements.— The amendments made by this section shall not apply to any loan to the extent such loan is used to acquire employer securities for an employee stock ownership plan pursuant to a collective bargaining agreement which sets forth the material terms of such employee stock ownership plan and which was agreed to on or before June 6, 1989, by one or more employers and employee representatives (and ratified on or before such date or within a reasonable period thereafter).

"(5) Filings with United States. — The amendments made by this section shall not apply to any loan the aggregate principal amount of which was specified in a filing with an agency of the United States on or before June 6, 1989, if—

"(A) such filing specifies such loan is to be a securities acquisition loan for purposes of section 133 of the Internal Revenue Code of 1986 and such filing is for the registration required to permit the offering of such loan, or

"(B) such filing is for the approval required in order for the employee stock ownership plan to acquire more than a certain percentage of the stock of the employer.

"(6) 30-percent test substituted for 50-percent test in case of certain loans. — In the case of a loan to which the amendments made by this section apply—

"(A) which is made before November 18, 1989, or

"(B) with respect to which such amendments would not apply if paragraph (2)(A) were applied by substituting 'November 17, 1989' for 'June 6, 1989' each place it appears,

section 133(b)(6)(A) of the Internal Revenue Code of 1986 (as added by subsection (a)) shall be applied by substituting 'at least 30 percent' for 'more than 50 percent' and section 4978B(c)(1)(B) of such Code (as added by subsection (d)) shall be applied by substituting 'less than 30 percent' for '50 percent or less'. The preceding sentence shall apply to any loan which is used to refinance a loan described in such sentence if the requirements of subparagraphs (A), (B), and (C) of paragraph (3) are met with respect to the refinancing loan."

—P.L. 101-239, Sec. 7816(i)(1), and (2), amended Sec. 6061 of P.L. 100-647 [reproduced below] relating to loans to acquire employer securities, by substituting "section 1011B(h)(5)(A)" for "section 111B(h)(5)(A)", and by substituting "section 1011B(h)" for "section 111B(h)".

In 1988, P.L. 100-647, Sec. 1011B(h)(1), added subsec. (e) ... Sec. 1011B(h)(2)(A)(i), deleted "or are used to refinance such a loan," after "for the plan" in subpara. (b)(1)(A) ... Sec. 1011B(h)(2)(A)(ii), deleted ", except that this subparagraph shall not apply to any loan the commitment period of which exceeds 7 years" before the period at the end of subpara. (b)(1)(B) ... Sec. 1011B(h)(2)(A)(iii), added para. (b)(5) ... Sec. 1011B(h)(2)(B), amended subpara. (b)(3)(B), effective as provided in Sec. 1011B(h)(5)(A) of this Act which reads as follows:

"(5)(A) The amendments made by paragraphs (1) and (2) shall apply to—

"(i) any loan used to acquire employer securities after July 18, 1984, and

"(ii) loans made after July 18, 1984, which were used (or were part of a series of loans used) to refinance any loan which—

"(I) was used to acquire employer securities after May 23, 1984 (July 18, 1984, in the case of a loan described in section 133(b)(3)(B) of the Internal Revenue Code of 1986), and

"(II) met the requirements of section 133 (other than subsection (b)(2) thereof) of such Code as in effect as of the later of the date on which the loan was made, or July 19, 1984.

In no event shall such amendments apply to any loan described in section 133(b)(1)(B) of such Code which is made before October 22, 1986 (or loan used, or part of a series of loans used, to refinance such a loan)."

Prior to amendment subpara. (b)(3)(B) read as follows:

"(B) repayment terms providing for more rapid repayment of principal or interest on such loan but only if—

"(i) allocations under the plan attributable to such repayment do not discriminate in favor of highly compensated employees (within the meaning of section 414(q)), and

"(ii) the total commitment period of such loan to the corporation does not exceed 7 years."

—P.L. 100-647, Sec. 1011(h)(5)(B), amended Sec. 1173(c)(2)(B) of P.L. 99-514 [reproduced below], part of the effective date for changes made by Sec. 1173(b)(2) of P.L. 99-514, see below.

Prior to amendment Sec. 1173(c)(2)(B) of P.L. 99-514 read as follows:

"(B)(i) Section 133(b)(1)(A) of the Internal Revenue Code of 1986, as amended by subsection (b)(2), shall apply to any loan used to refinance a loan which

"(I) met the requirements of section 133(b)(1) (as in effect when such loan was entered into), and

"(II) was used to acquire securities after July 18, 1984

"(ii) If a loan described in clause (i) shall apply only to interest accruing on such loan during the first 7 years"

—P.L. 100-647, Sec. 6061, of this Act [as amended by Sec. 7816(b)(1) and (2) of P.L. 101-239, see above] provides:

"Sec. 6061. LOANS TO ACQUIRE EMPLOYER SECURITIES.

"Notwithstanding the last sentence of section 1011B(h)(5)(A) of this Act, the amendments made by paragraphs (1) and (2) of section 1011B(h) of this Act shall not apply to any loan used to refinance a loan described in section 133(b)(1)(A) of the 1986 Code which is made before October 22, 1986, if the terms of the refinanced loan do not extend the total commitment period beyond the later of—

"(1) the term of the original securities acquisition loan, or

"(2) the amortization period used to determine the regular payments (prior to any final or balloon payment) applicable to the original securities acquisition loan."

In 1986, P.L. 99-514, Sec. 1173(b)(1)(A), deleted "or" from the end of para. (a)(2), added "or" to the end of para. (a)(3), and added para. (a)(4), effective as provided in subpara. 1173(c)(2)(A) of this Act, which reads as follows:

"(A) The amendments made by subsection (b)(1) shall apply to loans used to acquire employer securities after the date of the enactment of this Act [10/22/86], including loans used to refinance loans used to acquire employer securities before such date if such loans were used to acquire employer securities after May 28, 1984."

—P.L. 99-514, Sec. 1173(b)(2), amended para. (b)(1), effective as provided in subparas. 1173(c)(2)(B) [as amended by Sec. 1011B(h)(5)(B) of P.L. 100-647, see above] and (C) of this Act, which read as follows:

"(B) Section 133(b)(1)(A) of the Internal Revenue Code of 1986, as amended by subsection (b)(2), shall apply to any loan used (or part of a series of loans used) to refinance a loan which—

"(i) was used to acquire employer securities after May 23, 1984, and

"(ii) met the requirements of section 133 of the Internal Revenue Code of 1986 as in effect as of the later of—

"(I) the date on which the loan was made, or

"(II) July 19, 1984.

"(C) Section 133(b)(1)(B) of the Internal Revenue Code of 1986, as added by subsection (b)(2), shall apply to loans incurred after the date of enactment of this Act [10/22/86]."

Prior to amendment, para. (b)(1) read as follows:

"(1) In general. For purposes of this section, the term 'securities acquisition loan' means any loan to a corporation, or to an employee stock ownership plan, to the extent that the proceeds are used to acquire employer securities (within the meaning of section 409(1)) for the plan."

—P.L. 99-514, Sec. 1854(c)(2)(A), added subsec. (d) ... Sec. 1854(c)(2)(C), added the flush sentence at the end of para. (b)(2) ... Sec. 1854(c)(2)(D), redesignated para. (b)(3) as (b)(4) and added new para. (b)(3), effective for loans used to acquire employer securities after 7/18/84.

In 1984, P.L. 98-369, Sec. 543(a), added Code Sec. 133, effective for loans used to acquire employer securities after 7/18/84.

Sec. 134. Certain military benefits.
(a) General rule.

Gross income shall not include any qualified military benefit.

(b) Qualified military benefit.

For purposes of this section—

(1) In general. The term "qualified military benefit" means any allowance or in-kind benefit *(other than personal use of a vehicle)* which—

(A) is received by any member or former member of the uniformed services of the United States or any dependent of such member by reason of such member's status or service as a member of such uniformed services, and

(B) was excludable from gross income on September 9, 1986, under any provision of law, regulation, or administrative practice which was in effect on such date (other than a provision of this title).

(2) No other benefit to be excludable except as provided by this title. Notwithstanding any other provision of law, no benefit shall be treated as a qualified military benefit unless such benefit—

(A) is a benefit described in paragraph (1), or

(B) is excludable from gross income under this title without regard to any provision of law which is not contained in this title and which is not contained in a revenue Act.

(3) Limitations on modifications.

(A) In general. Except as provided in subparagraphs (B) and (C) and paragraphs (4) and (5), no modification or adjustment of any qualified military benefit after September 9, 1986, shall be taken into account.

(B) Exception for certain adjustments to cash benefits. Subparagraph (A) shall not apply to any adjustment to any qualified military benefit payable in cash which—

(i) is pursuant to a provision of law or regulation (as in effect on September 9, 1986), and

(ii) is determined by reference to any fluctuation in cost, price, currency, or other similar index.

(C) Exception for death gratuity adjustments made by law. Subparagraph (A) shall not apply to any adjustment to the amount of death gratuity payable under chapter 75 of title 10, United States Code, which is pursuant to a provision of law enacted after September 9, 1986.

(4) Clarification of certain benefits. For purposes of paragraph (1), such term includes any dependent care assistance program (as in effect on the date of the enactment of this paragraph) for any individual described in paragraph (1)(A).

(5) Travel benefits under operation hero miles. The term "qualified military benefit" includes a travel benefit provided under section 2613 of title 10, United States Code (as in effect on the date of the enactment of this paragraph).

(6) Certain State payments. The term "qualified military benefit" includes any bonus payment by a State or political subdivision thereof to any member or former member of the uniformed services of the United States or any dependent of such member only by reason of such member's service in an combat zone (as defined in section 112(c)(2), determined without regard to the parenthetical).

In 2008, P.L. 110-245, Sec. 112(a), added para. (b)(6), effective for payments made before, on, or after 6/17/2008.

In 2004, P.L. 108-375, Sec. 585(b)(1), added para. (b)(5) ... Sec. 585(b)(2)(A), substituted "paragraphs (4) and (5)" for "paragraph (4)" in subpara. (b)(3)(A), effective for travel benefits provided after 10/28/2004.

In 2003, P.L. 108-121, Sec. 102(b)(1), added subpara. (b)(3)(C) ... Sec. 102(b)(2), substituted "subparagraphs (B) and (C)" for "subparagraph (B)" in subpara. (b)(3)(A), effective for deaths occurring after 9/10/2001.

—P.L. 108-121, Sec. 106(a), added para. (b)(4) ... Sec. 106(b)(1), added "and paragraph (4)" after "subparagraphs (B) and (C)" in subpara. (b)(3)(A) [as amended by Sec. 102(b)(2) of this Act, see above], effective for tax. yrs. begin. after 12/31/2002. Sec. 106(d) of this Act, provides:

"(d) No inference. No inference may be drawn from the amendments made by this section with respect to the tax treatment of any amounts under the program described in section 134(b)(4) of the Internal Revenue Code of 1986 (as added by this section) for any taxable year beginning before January 1, 2003."

In 1988, P.L. 100-647, Sec. 1011B(f)(1), substituted ", regulation, or administrative practice" for "or regulation thereunder" in subpara. (b)(1)(B) ... Sec. 1011B(f)(3), deleted "under any provision of law or regulation described in paragraph (1)" after "September 9, 1986," in subpara. (b)(3)(A), effective for tax. yrs. begin. after 12/31/84.

—P.L. 100-647, Sec. 1011B(f)(2)(A), added "(other than personal use of a vehicle)" after "in-kind benefit" in para. (b)(1), effective for tax. yrs. begin. after 12/31/86.

—P.L. 100-647, Sec. 1011B(f)(4), amended Sec. 1168(c) of P.L. 99-514, the effective date for changes made by Sec. 1168(a) of P.L. 99-514, by substituting "1984" for "1986", see below.

In 1986, P.L. 99-514, Sec. 1168(a), added new Code Sec. 134, effective [as amended by Sec. 1011B(f)(4) of P.L. 100-647, see above] for tax. yrs. begin. after 12/31/84.

Sec. 135. Income from United States savings bonds used to pay higher education tuition and fees.

(a) General rule.
In the case of an individual who pays qualified higher education expenses during the taxable year, no amount shall be includible in gross income by reason of the redemption during such year of any qualified United States savings bond.

(b) Limitations.

(1) Limitation where redemption proceeds exceed higher education expenses.

(A) In general. If—

(i) the aggregate proceeds of qualified United States savings bonds redeemed by the taxpayer during the taxable year exceed

(ii) the qualified higher education expenses paid by the taxpayer during such taxable year,

the amount excludable from gross income under subsection (a) shall not exceed the applicable fraction of the amount excludable from gross income under subsection (a) without regard to this subsection.

(B) Applicable fraction. For purposes of subparagraph (A), the term "applicable fraction" means the fraction the numerator of which is the amount described in subparagraph (A)(ii) and the denominator of which is the amount described in subparagraph (A)(i).

(2) Limitation based on modified adjusted gross income.

(A) In general. If the modified adjusted gross income of the taxpayer for the taxable year exceeds $40,000 ($60,000 in the case of a joint return), the amount which would (but for this paragraph) be excludable from gross income under subsection (a) shall be reduced (but not below zero) by the amount which bears the same ratio to the amount which would be so excludable as such excess bears to $15,000 ($30,000 in the case of a joint return).

(B) Inflation adjustment. In the case of any taxable year beginning in a calendar year after 1990, the $40,000 and $60,000 amounts contained in subparagraph (A) shall be increased by an amount equal to—

(i) such dollar amount, multiplied by

(ii) the cost-of-living adjustment under section 1(f)(3) for the calendar year in which the taxable year begins, determined by substituting "calendar year 1989" for "calendar year 1992" in subparagraph (B) thereof.

(C) Rounding. If any amount as adjusted under subparagraph (B) is not a multiple of $50, such amount shall be rounded to the nearest multiple of $50 (or if such amount is a multiple of $25, such amount shall be rounded to the next highest multiple of $50).

(c) Definitions.
For purposes of this section—

(1) Qualified United States Savings bond. The term "qualified United States savings bond" means any United States savings bond issued—

(A) after December 31, 1989,

(B) to an individual who has attained age 24 before the date of issuance, and

(C) at discount under section 3105 of title 31, United States Code.

(2) Qualified higher education expenses.

(A) In general. The term "qualified higher education expenses" means tuition and fees required for the enrollment or attendance of—

(i) the taxpayer,

(ii) the taxpayer's spouse, or

(iii) any dependent of the taxpayer with respect to whom the taxpayer is allowed a deduction under section 151,

at an eligible educational institution.

(B) Exception for education involving sports, etc. Such term shall not include expenses with respect to any course or other education involving sports, games, or hobbies other than as part of a degree program.

• *Caution:* Code Sec. 135(c)(2)(C), following, was amended by P.L. 107-16, EGTRRA. These provisions generally sunset for tax years beginning after 12/31/2012. For specific sunset provisions, see Sec. 901, P.L. 107-16 (as amended) reproduced in history notes for this Code Sec.

(C) Contributions to qualified tuition program and Coverdell education savings accounts. Such term shall include any contribution to a qualified tuition program (as defined in section 529) on behalf of a designated beneficiary (as defined in such section), or to a Coverdell education savings account (as defined in section 530) on behalf of an account beneficiary, who is an individ-

Exclusions from income   Code Sec. 135

ual described in subparagraph (A); but there shall be no increase in the investment in the contract for purposes of applying section 72 by reason of any portion of such contribution which is not includible in gross income by reason of this subparagraph.

(3) Eligible educational institution. The term "eligible educational institution" has the meaning given such term by section 529(e)(5).

> • **Caution:** Code Sec. 135(c)(4), following, was amended by P.L. 107-16, EGTRRA. These provisions generally sunset for tax years beginning after 12/31/2012. For specific sunset provisions, see Sec. 901, P.L. 107-16 (as amended) reproduced in history notes for this Code Sec.

(4) Modified adjusted gross income. The term "modified adjusted gross income" means the adjusted gross income of the taxpayer for the taxable year determined—
  (A) without regard to this section and sections 137, 199, 221, 222, 911, 931, and 933, and
  (B) after the application of sections 86, 469, and 219.

(d) Special rules.
(1) Adjustment for certain scholarships and veterans benefits. The amount of qualified higher education expenses otherwise taken into account under subsection (a) with respect to the education of an individual shall be reduced (before the application of subsection (b)) by the sum of the amounts received with respect to such individual for the taxable year as—
  (A) a qualified scholarship which under section 117 is not includable in gross income,
  (B) an educational assistance allowance under chapter 30, 31, 32, 34, or 35 of title 38, United States Code,
  (C) a payment (other than a gift, bequest, devise, or inheritance within the meaning of section 102(a)) for educational expenses, or attributable to attendance at an eligible educational institution, which is exempt from income taxation by any law of the United States, or

> • **Caution:** Code Sec. 135(d)(1)(D), following, was amended by P.L. 107-16, EGTRRA. These provisions generally sunset for tax years beginning after 12/31/2012. For specific sunset provisions, see Sec. 901, P.L. 107-16 (as amended) reproduced in history notes for this Code Sec.

  (D) a payment, waiver, or reimbursement of qualified higher education expenses under a qualified tuition program (within the meaning of section 529(b)).

(2) Coordination with other higher education benefits. The amount of the qualified higher education expenses otherwise taken into account under subsection (a) with respect to the education of an individual shall be reduced (before the application of subsection (b)) by—

> • **Caution:** Code Sec. 135(d)(2)(A)-(B), following, were amended by P.L. 107-16, EGTRRA. These provisions generally sunset for tax years beginning after 12/31/2012. For specific sunset provisions, see Sec. 901,

P.L. 107-16 (as amended) reproduced in history notes for this Code Sec.

  (A) the amount of such expenses which are taken into account in determining the credit allowed to the taxpayer or any other person under section 25A with respect to such expenses; and
  (B) the amount of such expenses which are taken into account in determining the exclusions under sections 529(c)(3)(B) and 530(d)(2).

(3) No exclusion for married individuals filing separate returns. If the taxpayer is a married individual (within the meaning of section 7703), this section shall apply only if the taxpayer and his spouse file a joint return for the taxable year.

(4) Regulations. The Secretary may prescribe such regulations as may be necessary or appropriate to carry out this section, including regulations requiring record keeping and information reporting.

In 2010, P.L. 111-312, Sec. 101(a)(1), substituted "December 31, 2012" for "December 31, 2010" both places it appeared in Sec. 901, P.L. 107-16 [see below], effective as if included in the enactment of P.L. 107-16, EGTRRA, 6/7/2001.

In 2006, P.L. 109-280, Sec. 1304(a), of this Act [relating to Sec. 901 of P.L. 107-16], provides:
"(a) Permanent extension of modifications. Section 901 of the Economic Growth and Tax Relief Reconciliation Act of 2001 [P.L. 107-16] (relating to sunset provisions) shall not apply to section 402 of such Act (relating to modifications to qualified tuition programs)."

In 2005, P.L. 109-135, Sec. 403(a)(19), of this Act [which amended Sec. 102(e) of P.L. 108-357], provides:
"(e) Effective date.
"(1) In general. The amendments made by this section shall apply to taxable years beginning after December 31, 2004.
"(2) Application to pass-thru entities, etc. In determining the deduction under section 199 of the Internal Revenue Code of 1986 (as added by this section [Sec. 102(a) of P.L. 108-357]), items arising from a taxable year of a partnership, S corporation, estate, or trust beginning before January 1, 2005, shall not be taken into account for purposes of subsection (d)(1) of such section."

In 2004, P.L. 108-357, Sec. 102(e)(1), added "199," before "221" in subpara. (c)(4)(A), effective for tax. yrs. begin. after 12/31/2004. Sec. 102(e)(2) of this Act [as added by Sec. 403(a)(19) of P.L. 109-135, see above] reads as follows:
"(2) Application to pass-thru entities, etc. In determining the deduction under section 199 of the Internal Revenue Code of 1986 (as added by this section [Sec. 102(a) of P.L. 108-357]), items arising from a taxable year of a partnership, S corporation, estate, or trust beginning before January 1, 2005, shall not be taken into account for purposes of subsection (d)(1) of such section."

In 2002, P.L. 107-358, Sec. 2, added subsec. (c) in Sec. 901 of P.L. 107-16 [see below], effective 12/17/2002.

In 2001, P.L. 107-22, Sec. 1(b)(1)(B), substituted "a Coverdell education savings" for "an education individual retirement" in subpara. (c)(2)(C) . . . Sec. 1(b)(3)(B), substituted "Coverdell education savings" for "education individual retirement" in the heading of subpara. (c)(2)(C), effective 7/26/2001.
—P.L. 107-16, Sec. 401(g)(2)(B), substituted "allowed" for "allowable" in subpara. (d)(2)(A), effective for tax. yrs. begin. after 12/31/2001.
—P.L. 107-16, Sec. 402(a)(4)(A), substituted "qualified tuition" for "qualified State tuition" in subparas. (c)(2)(C) and (d)(1)(D) . . . Sec. 402(a)(4)(B), substituted "qualified tuition" for "qualified State tuition" in the heading of subpara. (c)(2)(C) . . . Sec. 402(b)(2)(A), substituted "the exclusions under sections 529(c)(3)(B) and 530(d)(2)" for "the exclusion under section 530(d)(2)" in subpara. (d)(2)(B), effective for tax. yrs. begin. after 12/31/2001.
—P.L. 107-16, Sec. 431(c)(1), added "222," after "221," in para. (c)(4), effective for payments made in tax. yrs. begin. after 12/31/2001.
—P.L. 107-16, Sec. 901, of this Act [as amended by Sec. 2, P.L. 107-358 and Sec. 101(a)(1), P.L. 111-312, and as related to Sec. 1304(a) of P.L. 109-280, see above], reads as follows:
"SEC. 901. SUNSET OF PROVISIONS OF ACT.
"(a) In general. All provisions of, and amendments made by, this Act shall not apply—
"(1) to taxable, plan, or limitation years beginning after December 31, 2012, or
"(2) in the case of title V, to estates of decedents dying, gifts made, or generation skipping transfers, after December 31, 2012.
"(b) Application of certain laws. The Internal Revenue Code of 1986 and the Employee Retirement Income Security Act of 1974 shall be applied and administered to years, estates, gifts, and transfers described in subsection (a) as if the provisions and amendments described in subsection (a) had never been enacted.
"(c) Exception. Subsection (a) shall not apply to section 803 (relating to no federal income tax on restitution received by victims of the Nazi regime or their heirs or estates)."

1,455

In 1998, P.L. 105-277, Sec. 4003(a)(2)(B), added "221," after "137," in subpara. (c)(4)(A), effective as provided in Sec. 202(e) of P.L. 105-34, which reads as follows:

"(e) Effective date. The amendments made by this section shall apply to any qualified education loan (as defined in section 221(e)(1) of the Internal Revenue Code of 1986, as added by this section) incurred on, before, or after the date of the enactment of this Act, but only with respect to—

"(1) any loan interest payment due and paid after December 31, 1997, and

"(2) the portion of the 60-month period referred to in section 221(d) of the Internal Revenue Code of 1986 (as added by this section) after December 31, 1997."

—P.L. 105-206, Sec. 6004(c)(1), amended para. (c)(3), effective for tax. yrs. begin. after 12/31/97, except as provided in Sec. 211(f)(6) of P.L. 105-34, [see below].

Prior to amendment, para. (c)(3) read as follows:

"(3) Eligible educational institution. The term 'eligible educational institution' means—

"(A) an institution described in section 1201(a) or subparagraph (C) or (D) of section 481(a)(1) of the Higher Education Act of 1965 (as in effect on October 21, 1988), and

"(B) an area vocational education school (as defined in subparagraph (C) or (D) of section 521(3) of the Carl D. Perkins Vocational Education Act) which is in any State (as defined in section 521(27) of such Act), as such sections are in effect on October 21, 1988."

—P.L. 105-206, Sec. 6004(d)(4), amended para. (d)(2) . . . Sec. 6004(d)(9)(A), added "and education individual retirement accounts" after "program" in the heading of subpara. (c)(2)(C) . . . Sec. 6004(d)(9)(B), substituted "section 72" for "section 529(c)(3)(A)" in subpara. (c)(2)(C), effective for tax. yrs. begin. after 12/31/97.

Prior to amendment, para. (d)(2) read as follows:

"(2) Coordination with higher education credit. The amount of the qualified higher education expenses otherwise taken into account under subsection (a) with respect to the education of an individual shall be reduced (before the application of subsection (b)) by the amount of such expenses which are taken into account in determining the credit allowable to the taxpayer or any other person under section 25A with respect to such expenses."

In 1997, P.L. 105-34, Sec. 201(d), redesignated paras. (d)(2) and (3) as paras. (d)(3) and (4) and added a new para. (d)(2), effective for expenses paid after 12/31/97 (in tax. yrs. end. after 12/31/97), for education furnished in academic periods begin. after 12/31/97.

—P.L. 105-34, Sec. 211(c), added subpara. (c)(2)(C), effective for tax. yrs. begin. after 12/31/97, except as provided in Sec. 211(f)(6), which reads as follows:

"(6) Transition rule for pre-August 20, 1996 contracts. In the case of any contract issued prior to August 20, 1996, section 529(c)(3)(C) of the Internal Revenue Code of 1986 shall be applied for taxable years ending after August 20, 1996, without regard to the requirement that a distribution be transferred to a member of the family or the requirement that a change in beneficiaries may be made only to a member of the family."

—P.L. 105-34, Sec. 213(e)(2), added ", or to an education individual retirement account (as defined in section 530) on behalf of an account beneficiary" after "(as defined in such section)" in subpara. (c)(2)(C) [as added by Sec. 211(c), see above], effective for tax. yrs. begin. after 12/31/97.

—P.L. 105-34, Sec. 1601(h)(1)(C), substituted "then such program (as in effect on August 20, 1996), shall be treated as a qualified State tuition program with respect to contributions (and earnings allocable thereto) pursuant to contracts entered into under such program before the first date on which such program meets such requirements (determined without regard to this paragraph) and the provisions of such program (as so in effect) shall apply in lieu of section 529(b) of the Internal Revenue Code of 1986, with respect to such contributions and earnings." for "the amendments made by this section shall apply to contributions (and earnings allocable thereto) made before the date such program meets the requirements of such amendments without regard to whether any requirements of such amendments are met with respect to such contributions and earnings." in Sec. 1806(c)(2) of P.L. 104-188, reproduced below.

In 1996, P.L. 104-188, Sec. 1703(d), added ", determined by substituting 'calendar year 1989' for 'calendar year 1992' in subparagraph (B) thereof", before the period in clause (b)(2)(B)(ii), effective for tax. yrs. begin. after 12/31/92.

—P.L. 104-188, Sec. 1806(b)(1), deleted "or" at the end of subpara. (d)(1)(B), substituted ", or" for the period at the end of subpara. (d)(1)(C), and added subpara. (d)(1)(D), effective for tax. yrs. end. after 8/20/96. Sec. 1806(c)(2) [as amended by Sec. 1501(h)(1)(C) of P.L. 105-34, see above] of this Act provides:

"(2) Transition rule. If —

"(A) a State or agency or instrumentality thereof maintains, on the date of the enactment of this Act, a program under which persons may purchase tuition credits or certificates on behalf of, or make contributions for education expenses of, a designated beneficiary, and

"(B) such program meets the requirements of a qualified State tuition program before the later of—

"(i) the date which is 1 year after such date of enactment, or

"(ii) the first day of the first calendar quarter after the close of the first regular session of the State legislature that begins after such date of enactment, then such program (as in effect on August 20, 1996), shall be treated as a qualified State tuition program with respect to contributions (and earnings allocable thereto) pursuant to contracts entered into under such program before the first date on which such program meets such requirements (determined without regard to this paragraph) and the provisions of such program (as so in effect) shall apply in lieu of section 529(b) of the Internal Revenue Code of 1986, with respect to such contributions and earnings.

For purposes of subparagraph (B)(ii), if a State has a 2-year legislative session, each year of such session shall be deemed to be a separate regular session of the State legislature."

—P.L. 104-188, Sec. 1807(c)(2), added "137" before "911" in subpara. (c)(4)(A), effective for tax. yrs. begin. after 12/31/96.

In 1990, P.L. 101-508, Sec. 11101(d)(1)(E), deleted ", determined by substituting 'calendar year 1989' for 'calendar year 1987' in subparagraph (B) thereof" after "the taxable year begins" in clause (b)(2)(B)(ii), effective for tax. yrs. begin. after 12/31/90.

—P.L. 101-508, Sec. 11702(h)(1), substituted "the $40,000 and $60,000 amounts" for "each dollar amount" in subpara. (b)(2)(B) . . . Sec. 11702(h)(2), deleted "(A) or" after "subparagraph" in subpara. (b)(2)(C), effective for tax. yrs. begin. after 12/31/89.

In 1989, P.L. 101-239, Sec. 7816(c)(2), substituted "subsection (a) with respect to" for "subsection (a) respect to" in para. (d)(1), effective for tax. yrs. begin. after 12/31/89.

In 1988, P.L. 100-647, Sec. 6009(a), added Code Sec. 135, effective for tax. yrs. begin. after 12/31/89. Secs. 6009(b) and (e) of this Act provide:

"(b) Promotion of public awareness of program. The Secretary of the Treasury or his delegate shall take such actions as may be necessary to make the general public aware of the program established by this section."

Sec. 6009(e) of this Act provides:

"(e) Parental assistance with tuition stamp study. The Secretary of the Treasury or his delegate, after consultation with the Secretary of Education or his delegate, shall conduct a study of the feasibility of using stamps or similar programs to encourage and facilitate savings by parents towards the purchase of Series EE bonds eligible for the exclusion provided under the amendments made by this section. Not later than December 31, 1989, the Secretary of the Treasury or his delegate shall submit the results of such study, together with any recommendations deemed appropriate, to the Committee on Ways and Means of the House of Representatives and the Committee on Finance of the Senate."

Sec. 136. Energy conservation subsidies provided by public utilities.

(a) Exclusion.

Gross income shall not include the value of any subsidy provided (directly or indirectly) by a public utility to a customer for the purchase or installation of any energy conservation measure.

(b) Denial of double benefit. Notwithstanding any other provision of this subtitle, no deduction or credit shall be allowed for, or by reason of, any expenditure to the extent of the amount excluded under subsection (a) for any subsidy which was provided with respect to such expenditure. The adjusted basis of any property shall be reduced by the amount excluded under subsection (a) which was provided with respect to such property.

(c) Energy conservation measure.

(1) In general. For purposes of this section, the term "energy conservation measure" means any installation or modification primarily designed to reduce consumption of electricity or natural gas or to improve the management of energy demand with respect to a dwelling unit.

(2) Other definitions. For purposes of this subsection—

(A) Dwelling unit. The term "dwelling unit" has the meaning given such term by section 280A(f)(1).

(B) Public utility. The term "public utility" means a person engaged in the sale of electricity or natural gas to residential, commercial, or industrial customers for use by such customers. For purposes of the preceding sentence, the term "person" includes the Federal Government, a State or local government or any political subdivision thereof, or any instrumentality of any of the foregoing.

(d) Exception.

This section shall not apply to any payment to or from a qualified cogeneration facility or qualifying small power production facility pursuant to section 210 of the Public Utility Regulatory Policy Act of 1978.

In 1996, P.L. 104-188, Sec. 1617(a), substituted "energy demand with respect to a dwelling unit" for "energy demand—

"(A) with respect to a dwelling unit, and

"(B) on or after January 1, 1995, with respect to property other than dwelling units."

Exclusions from income Code Sec. 137(b)(1)

The purchase and installation of specially defined energy property shall be treated as an energy conservation measure described in subparagraph (B)." in para. (c)(1) ... Sec. 1617(b)(1), amended subsec. (a) ... Sec. 1617(b)(2)(A), deleted subpara. (c)(2)(A), redesignated subparas. (c)(2)(B) and (C) as subparas. (c)(2)(A) and (B) ... Sec. 1617(b)(2)(B), deleted 'and special rules" after "definitions" in the heading of para. (c)(2), effective as provided in Sec. 1617(c) of this Act, which reads as follows:

"(c) Effective date. The amendments made by this section shall apply to amounts received after December 31, 1996, unless received pursuant to a written binding contract in effect on September 13, 1995, and at all times thereafter."
Prior to amendment, subsec. (a) read as follows:
"(a) Exclusion.
"(1) In general. Gross income shall not include the value of any subsidy provided (directly or indirectly) by a public utility to a customer for the purchase or installation of any energy conservation measure.
"(2) Limitation on exclusion for nonresidential property.
"(A) In general. In the case of any subsidy provided with respect to any energy conservation measure referred to in subsection (c)(1)(B), only the applicable percentage of such subsidy shall be excluded from gross income under paragraph (1).
"(B) Applicable percentage. For purposes of subparagraph (A), the term 'applicable percentage' means —
"(i) 40 percent in the case of subsidies provided during 1995,
"(ii) 50 percent in the case of subsidies provided during 1996, and
"(iii) 65 percent in the case of subsidies provided after 1996."
Prior to deletion, subpara. (c)(2)(A) read as follows:
"(A) Specially defined energy property. The term 'specially defined energy property' means —
"(i) a recuperator,
"(ii) a heat wheel,
"(iii) a regenerator,
"(iv) a heat exchanger,
"(v) a waste heat boiler,
"(vi) a heat pipe,
"(vii) an automatic energy control system,
"(viii) a turbulator,
"(ix) a preheater,
"(x) a combustible gas recovery system,
"(xi) an economizer,
"(xii) modifications to alumina electrolytic cells,
"(xiii) modifications to chlor-alkali electrolytic cells, or
"(xiv) any other property of a kind specified by the Secretary by regulations, the principal purpose of which is reducing the amount of energy consumed in any existing industrial or commercial process and which is installed in connection with an existing industrial or commercial facility."
In 1992, P.L. 102-486, Sec. 1912(a), added new Code Sec. 136, effective for amounts received after 12/31/92.

> • *Caution:* Code Sec. 137, following, was amended by P.L. 107-16, the Economic Growth and Tax Relief Reconciliation Act of 2001 (EGTRRA), and further amended by P.L. 107-147 and P.L. 108-311. These provisions will sunset as provided in Sec. 901 of P.L. 107-16 (as amended). For specific sunset provisions, see Sec. 901, P.L. 107-16 (as amended) reproduced in notes following this Code Sec.

Sec. 137. Adoption assistance programs.
(a) Exclusion.
(1) In general. Gross income of an employee does not include amounts paid or expenses incurred by the employer for qualified adoption expenses in connection with the adoption of a child by an employee if such amounts are furnished pursuant to an adoption assistance program.

> • *Caution:* Code Sec. 137(a)(2), following, reflects amendments made by Sec. 10909(a)(2)(B)(i). As provided in Sec. 10909(c), P.L. 111-148 as amended by Sec. 101(b)(1) of P.L. 111-312, Code Sec. 137(a)(2) will read as if those amendments had never been enacted, effective for tax. yrs. begin. after 12/31/2011. For Code Sec. 137(a)(2), as it will read for tax. yrs. begin. after 12/31/2011, see below.

(2) $13,170 exclusion for adoption of child with special needs regardless of expenses. In the case of an adoption of a child with special needs which becomes final during a taxable year, the qualified adoption expenses with respect to such adoption for such year shall be increased by an amount equal to the excess (if any) of $13,170 over the actual aggregate qualified adoption expenses with respect to such adoption during such taxable year and all prior taxable years.

> • *Caution:* Code Sec. 137(a)(2), following, is effective for tax. yrs. begin. after 12/31/2011, and reflects the sunset of the amendments made by Sec. 10909(a)(2)(B)(i), P.L. 111-148. For details of those amendments, effective date and sunset provisions see the history for this Code Sec. For Code Sec. 137(a)(2), effective for tax. yrs. begin. before 1/1/2012, see above.

(2) $10,000 exclusion for adoption of child with special needs regardless of expenses. In the case of an adoption of a child with special needs which becomes final during a taxable year, the qualified adoption expenses with respect to such adoption for such year shall be increased by an amount equal to the excess (if any) of $10,000 over the actual aggregate qualified adoption expenses with respect to such adoption during such taxable year and all prior taxable years.

(b) Limitations.

> • *Caution:* Code Sec. 137(b)(1), following, reflects amendments made by Sec. 10909(a)(2)(A), P.L. 111-148. As provided in Sec. 10909(c), P.L. 111-148, as amended by Sec. 101(b)(1), P.L. 111-312, Code Sec. 137(b)(1) will read as if those amendments had never been enacted, effective for tax. yrs. begin. after 12/31/2011. For Code Sec. 137(b)(1), as it will read for tax. yrs. begin. after 12/31/2011, see below.

(1) Dollar limitation. The aggregate of the amounts paid or expenses incurred which may be taken into account under subsection (a) for all taxable years with respect to the adoption of a child by the taxpayer shall not exceed $13,170.

> • *Caution:* Code Sec. 137(b)(1), following, is effective for tax. yrs. begin. after 12/31/2011, and reflects the sunset of the amendments made by Sec. 10909(a)(2)(A), P.L. 111-148. For details of those amendments, effective date and sunset provisions see the history for this Code Sec. For Code Sec. 137(b)(1), effective for tax. yrs. begin. before 1/1/2012, see above.

(1) Dollar limitation. The aggregate of the amounts paid or expenses incurred which may be taken into account under subsection (a) for all taxable years with respect to the adoption of a child by the taxpayer shall not exceed $10,000.

Code Sec. 137(b)(2) — Exclusions from income

(2) **Income limitation.** The amount excludable from gross income under subsection (a) for any taxable year shall be reduced (but not below zero) by an amount which bears the same ratio to the amount so excludable (determined without regard to this paragraph but with regard to paragraph (1)) as—
  (A) the amount (if any) by which the taxpayer's adjusted gross income exceeds $150,000, bears to
  (B) $40,000.

(3) **Determination of adjusted gross income.** For purposes of paragraph (2), adjusted gross income shall be determined—
  (A) without regard to this section and sections 199, 221, 222, 911, 931, and 933, and
  (B) after the application of sections 86, 135, 219, and 469.

(c) **Adoption assistance program.**
For purposes of this section, an adoption assistance program is a separate written plan of an employer for the exclusive benefit of such employer's employees—
  (1) under which the employer provides such employees with adoption assistance, and
  (2) which meets requirements similar to the requirements of paragraphs (2), (3), (5), and (6) of section 127(b).
An adoption reimbursement program operated under section 1052 of title 10, United States Code (relating to armed forces) or section 514 of title 14, United States Code (relating to members of the Coast Guard) shall be treated as an adoption assistance program for purposes of this section.

> • *Caution:* Code Sec. 137(d), following, reflects amendments made by Sec. 10909(a)(2)(J)(i) of P.L. 111-148. As provided in Sec. 10909(c), P.L. 111-148, as amended by Sec. 101(b)(1) of P.L. 111-312, Code Sec. 137(d) will read as if those amendments had never been enacted, effective for tax. yrs. begin. after 12/31/2011. For Code Sec. 137(d), as it will read for tax. yrs. begin. after 12/31/2011, see below.

(d) **Qualified adoption expenses.**
For purposes of this section, the term "qualified adoption expenses" has the meaning given such term by section 36C(d) (determined without regard to reimbursements under this section).

> • *Caution:* Code Sec. 137(d), following, is effective for tax. yrs. begin. after 12/31/2011, and reflects the sunset of the amendments made by Sec. 10909(a)(2)(J)(i), P.L. 111-148. For details of those amendments, effective date and sunset provisions, see the history for this Code Sec. For Code Sec. 137(d), effective for tax. yrs. begin. before 1/1/2012, see above.

(d) **Qualified adoption expenses.**
For purposes of this section, the term "qualified adoption expenses" has the meaning given such term by section 23(d) (determined without regard to reimbursements under this section).

> • *Caution:* Code Sec. 137(e), following, reflects amendments made by Sec. 10909(a)(2)(J)(ii) of P.L. 111-148. As provided in Sec. 10909(c), P.L. 111-148, as amended by Sec. 101(b)(1), P.L. 111-312, Code Sec. 137(e) will read as if those amendments had never been enacted, effective for tax. yrs. begin. after 12/31/2011. For Code Sec. 137(e), as it will read for tax. yrs. begin. after 12/31/2011, see below.

(e) **Certain rules to apply.**
Rules similar to the rules of subsections (e), (f), and (g) of section 36C shall apply for purposes of this section.

> • *Caution:* Code Sec. 137(e), following, is effective for tax. yrs. begin. after 12/31/2011, and reflects the sunset of the amendments made by Sec. 10909(a)(2)(J)(ii), P.L. 111-148. For details of those amendments, effective date and sunset provisions, see the history for this Code Sec. For Code Sec. 137(e), effective for tax. yrs. begin. before 1/1/2012, see above.

(e) **Certain rules to apply.**
Rules similar to the rules of subsections (e), (f), and (g) of section 23 shall apply for purposes of this section.

> • *Caution:* Code Sec. 137(f), following, reflects amendments made by Sec. 10909(a)(2)(C), P.L. 111-148. As provided in Sec. 10909(c), P.L. 111-148, as amended by Sec. 101(b)(1) of P.L. 111-312, Code Sec. 137(f) will read as if those amendments had never been enacted, effective for tax. yrs. begin. after 12/31/2011. For Code Sec. 137(f), as it will read for tax. yrs. begin. after 12/31/2011, see below.

(f) **Adjustments for inflation.**
(1) **Dollar limitations.** In the case of a taxable year beginning after December 31, 2010, each of the dollar amounts in subsections (a)(2) and (b)(1) shall be increased by an amount equal to—
  (A) such dollar amount, multiplied by
  (B) the cost-of-living adjustment determined under section 1(f)(3) for the calendar year in which the taxable year begins, determined by substituting "calendar year 2009" for "calendar year 1992" in subparagraph (B) thereof.
If any amount as increased under the preceding sentence is not a multiple of $10, such amount shall be rounded to the nearest multiple of $10.

(2) **Income limitation.** In the case of a taxable year beginning after December 31, 2002, the dollar amount in subsection (b)(2)(A) shall be increased by an amount equal to—
  (A) such dollar amount, multiplied by
  (B) the cost-of-living adjustment determined under section 1(f)(3) for the calendar year in which the taxable year begins, determined by substituting "calendar year 2001" for "calendar year 1992" in subparagraph (B) thereof.
If any amount as increased under the preceding sentence is not a multiple of $10, such amount shall be rounded to the nearest multiple of $10.

> • *Caution:* Code Sec. 137(f), following, is effective for tax. yrs. begin. after 12/31/2011, and reflects the sunset of the amendments made by Sec. 10909(a)(2)(C), P.L. 111-148. For details of those amendments, effective date and sunset provisions, see the history for this Code Sec. For

Exclusions from income — Code Sec. 138(b)

Code Sec. 137(f), effective for tax. yrs. begin. before 1/1/2012, see above.

(f) Adjustments for inflation.

(In the case of a taxable year beginning after December 31, 2002, each of the dollar amounts in subsection (a)(2) and paragraphs (1) and (2)(A) of subsection (b) shall be increased by an amount equal to—

(1) such dollar amount, multiplied by

(2) the cost-of-living adjustment determined under section 1(f)(3) for the calendar year in which the taxable year begins, determined by substituting 'calendar year 2001' for 'calendar year 1992' in subparagraph (B) thereof.

If any amount as increased under the preceding sentence is not a multiple of $10, such amount shall be rounded to the nearest multiple of $10.

In **2010,** P.L. 111-312, Sec. 101(a)(1), substituted "December 31, 2012" for "December 31, 2010" both places it appeared in Sec. 901, P.L. 107-16, effective as if included in the enactment of P.L. 107-16, EGTRRA, 6/7/2001 [see below].

—P.L. 111-312, Sec. 101(b)(1), amended Sec. 10909(c), P.L. 111-148 [see below].

Prior to amendment, Sec. 10909(c), P.L. 111-148, read as follows:

"(c) Application and Extension of EGTRRA Sunset. Notwithstanding section 901 of the Economic Growth and Tax Relief Reconciliation Act of 2001, such section shall apply to the amendments made by this section and the amendments mad by section 202 of such Act by substituting 'December 31, 2011' for 'December 31, 2010' in subsection (a)(1) thereof."

—P.L. 111-312, Sec. 10909(c)(2), substituted "Except as provided in subsection (c), the amendments" for "The amendments" in Sec. 10909(d), P.L. 111-148 (the effective date section for amendments made by Sec. 10909, P.L. 111-148, see below).

Prior to amendment, Sec. 10909(d) of P.L. 111-148, read as follows:

"(d) Effective date. The amendments made by this section shall apply to taxable years beginning after December 31, 2009."

—P.L. 111-148, Sec. 10909(a)(2)(A), substituted "$13,170" for "$10,000" in para. (b)(1)... Sec. 10909(a)(2)(B)(i), substituted "$13,170" for "$10,000" in para. (a)(2)... Sec. 10909(a)(2)(B)(ii), substituted "$13,170" for "$10,000" in the heading of para. (a)(2)... Sec. 10909(a)(2)(C), amended subsec. (f)... Sec. 10909(a)(2)(J)(i), substituted "section 36C(d)" for "section 23(d)" in subsec. (d) ... Sec. 10909(a)(2)(J)(ii), substituted "section 36C" for "section 23" in subsec. (e), effective for tax. yrs. begin. after 12/31/2009, except as provided in Sec. 10909(c) of this Act, [see below].

Prior to amendment, subsec. (f) read as follows:

"(f) Adjustments for inflation.

"(In the case of a taxable year beginning after December 31, 2002, each of the dollar amounts in subsection (a)(2) and paragraphs (1) and (2)(A) of subsection (b) shall be increased by an amount equal to—

"(1) such dollar amount, multiplied by

"(2) the cost-of-living adjustment determined under section 1(f)(3) for the calendar year in which the taxable year begins, determined by substituting 'calendar year 2001' for 'calendar year 1992' in subparagraph (B) thereof.

"If any amount as increased under the preceding sentence is not a multiple of $10, such amount shall be rounded to the nearest multiple of $10."

—P.L. 111-148, Sec. 10909(c), of this Act, relating to the application and extension of EGTRRA sunset provisions [as amended by Sec. 101(b)(1), P.L. 111-312, see above], provides:

"(c) Sunset provision. Each provision of law amended by this section [Sec. 10909] is amended to read as such provision would read if this section had never been enacted. The amendments made by the preceding sentence shall apply to taxable years beginning after 12/31/2011."

—P.L. 111-148, Sec. 10909(d), of this Act, [as amended by Sec. 101(b)(2), P.L. 111-312, see above] reads as follows:

"(d) Effective date. Except as provided in subsection (c) [Sec. 10909(c) of this Act], the amendments made by this section shall apply to taxable years beginning after December 31, 2009."

In **2005,** P.L. 109-135, Sec. 403(a)(19), of this Act [which amended Sec. 102(e) of P.L. 108-357], provides:

"(e) Effective date.

"(1) In general. The amendments made by this section shall apply to taxable years beginning after December 31, 2004.

"(2) Application to pass-thru entities, etc. In determining the deduction under section 199 of the Internal Revenue Code of 1986 (as added by this section [Sec. 102(a) of P.L. 108-357]), items arising from a taxable year of a partnership, S corporation, estate, or trust beginning before January 1, 2005, shall not be taken into account for purposes of subsection (d)(1) of such section."

In **2004,** P.L. 108-357, Sec. 102(d)(1), added "199," before "221" in subpara. (b)(3)(A), effective for tax. yrs. begin. after 12/31/2004. Sec. 102(e)(2) of this Act [as added by Sec. 403(a)(19) of P.L. 109-135, see above], reads as follows:

"(2) Application to pass-thru entities, etc. In determining the deduction under section 199 of the Internal Revenue Code of 1986 (as added by this section [Sec. 102(a) of P.L. 108-357]), items arising from a taxable year of a partnership, S corporation, estate, or trust beginning before January 1, 2005, shall not be taken into account for purposes of subsection (d)(1) of such section."

—P.L. 108-311, Sec. 403(e), substituted "paragraph (1)" for "paragraph (2)" in Sec. 411(c)(2)(B) of P.L. 107-147 [see below], effective for tax. yrs. begin. after 12/31/2001 as if included in Sec. 411 of the Job Creation and Worker Assistance Act of 2002, P.L. 107-147.

In **2002,** P.L. 107-358, Sec. 2, added subsec. (c) in Sec. 901 of P.L. 107-16 [see below], effective 12/17/2002.

—P.L. 107-147, Sec. 411(c)(2)(A), amended subsec. (a), effective for tax. yrs. begin. after 12/31/2002.... Sec. 411(c)(2)(B), substituted "subsection (a)" for "subsection (a)(1)" in para. (b)(2) [sic (b)(1)], effective for tax. yrs. begin. after 12/31/2001.

Prior to amendment, subsec. (a) read as follows:

"(a) In general. Gross income of an employee does not include amounts paid or expenses incurred by the employer for adoption expenses in connection with the adoption of a child by an employee if such amounts are furnished pursuant to an adoption assistance program. The amount of the exclusion shall be—

"(1) in the case of an adoption of a child other than a child with special needs, the amount of the qualified adoption expenses paid or incurred by the taxpayer, and

"(2) in the case of an adoption of a child with special needs, $10,000."

—P.L. 107-147, Sec. 418(a)(2), added a flush sentence at the end of subsec. (f), effective for tax. yrs. begin. after 12/31/2001.

In **2001,** P.L. 107-16, Sec. 202(a)(2), amended subsec. (a), effective for tax. yrs. begin. after 12/31/2002.

Prior to amendment, subsec. (a) read as follows:

"(a) In general. Gross income of an employee does not include amounts paid or expenses incurred by the employer for qualified adoption expenses in connection with the adoption of a child by an employee if such amounts are furnished pursuant to an adoption assistance program."

—P.L. 107-16, Sec. 202(b)(1)(B)(i), substituted "$10,000" for "$5,000" in para. (b)(1)... Sec. 202(b)(1)(B)(ii), deleted "($6,000, in the case of a child with special needs)" at the end of para. (b)(1)... Sec. 202(b)(1)(B)(iii), substituted "subsection (a)(1)" for "subsection (a)" in para. (b)(1)... Sec. 202(b)(2)(B), substituted "$150,000" for "$75,000" in subpara. (b)(2)(A)... Sec. 202(d)(2), deleted subsec, (f)... Sec. 202(e)(2), added subsec. (f), effective for tax. yrs. begin. after 12/31/2001.

Prior to deletion, subsec. (f) read as follows:

"(f) Termination. This section shall not apply to amounts paid or expenses incurred after December 31, 2001."

—P.L. 107-16, Sec. 431(c)(1), added "222," after "221," in para. (b)(3), effective for payments made in tax. yrs. begin. after 12/31/2001.

—P.L. 107-16, Sec. 901, of this Act [as amended by Sec. 2, P.L. 107-358, and Sec. 101(a)(1), P.L. 111-312, see above], reads as follows:

"Sec. 901. Sunset of provisions of Act.

"(a) In general. All provisions of, and amendments made by, this Act shall not apply—

"(1) to taxable, plan, or limitation years beginning after December 31, 2012, or

"(2) in the case of title V, to estates of decedents dying, gifts made, or generation skipping transfers, after December 31, 2012.

"(b) Application of certain laws. The Internal Revenue Code of 1986 and the Employee Retirement Income Security Act of 1974 shall be applied and administered to years, estates, gifts, and transfers described in subsection (a) as if the provisions and amendments described in subsection (a) had never been enacted.

"(c) Exception. Subsection (a) shall not apply to section 803 (relating to no federal income tax on restitution received by victims of the Nazi regime or their heirs or estates)."

In **1998,** P.L. 105-277, Sec. 4003(a)(2)(C), added "221," before "911," in subpara. (b)(3)(A), effective as provided in Sec. 202(e) of P.L. 105-34, which reads as follows:

"(e) Effective date. The amendments made by this section shall apply to any qualified education loan (as defined in section 221(e)(1) of the Internal Revenue Code of 1986, as added by this section) incurred on, before, or after the date of the enactment of this Act, but only with respect to—

"(1) any loan interest payment due and paid after December 31, 1997, and

"(2) the portion of the 60-month period referred to in section 221(d) of the Internal Revenue Code of 1986 (as added by this section) after December 31, 1997."

In **1997,** P.L. 105-34, Sec. 1601(h)(2)(C), substituted "of the amounts paid or expenses incurred which may be taken into account" for "amount excludable from gross income" in para. (b)(1), effective for tax. yrs. begin. after 12/31/96.

In **1996,** P.L. 104-188, Sec. 1807(b), added new Code Sec. 137, effective for tax. yrs. begin. after 12/31/96.

Sec. 138. Medicare Advantage MSA.

(a) Exclusion.

Gross income shall not include any payment to the Medicare Advantage MSA of an individual by the Secretary of Health and Human Services under part C of title XVIII of the Social Security Act.

(b) Medicare Advantage MSA.

For purposes of this section, the term "Medicare Advantage MSA" means an Archer MSA (as defined in section 220(d))—

1,459

(1) which is designated as a Medicare Advantage MSA,
(2) with respect to which no contribution may be made other than—
   (A) a contribution made by the Secretary of Health and Human Services pursuant to part C of title XVIII of the Social Security Act, or
   (B) a trustee-to-trustee transfer described in subsection (c)(4),
(3) the governing instrument of which provides that trustee-to-trustee transfers described in subsection (c)(4) may be made to and from such account, and
(4) which is established in connection with an MSA plan described in section 1859(b)(3) of the Social Security Act.

(c) Special rules for distributions.
(1) Distributions for qualified medical expenses. In applying section 220 to a Medicare Advantage MSA—
   (A) qualified medical expenses shall not include amounts paid for medical care for any individual other than the account holder, and
   (B) section 220(d)(2)(C) shall not apply.
(2) Penalty for distributions from Medicare Advantage MSA not used for qualified medical expenses if minimum balance not maintained.
   (A) In general. The tax imposed by this chapter for any taxable year in which there is a payment or distribution from a Medicare Advantage MSA which is not used exclusively to pay the qualified medical expenses of the account holder shall be increased by 50 percent of the excess (if any) of—
      (i) the amount of such payment or distribution, over
      (ii) the excess (if any) of—
         (I) the fair market value of the assets in such MSA as of the close of the calendar year preceding the calendar year in which the taxable year begins, over
         (II) an amount equal to 60 percent of the deductible under the Medicare Advantage MSA plan covering the account holder as of January 1 of the calendar year in which the taxable year begins.
   Section 220(f)(4) shall not apply to any payment or distribution from a Medicare Advantage MSA.
   (B) Exceptions. Subparagraph (A) shall not apply if the payment or distribution is made on or after the date the account holder—
      (i) becomes disabled within the meaning of section 72(m)(7), or
      (ii) dies.
   (C) Special rules. For purposes of subparagraph (A)—
      (i) all Medicare Advantage MSAs of the account holder shall be treated as 1 account,
      (ii) all payments and distributions not used exclusively to pay the qualified medical expenses of the account holder during any taxable year shall be treated as 1 distribution, and
      (iii) any distribution of property shall be taken into account at its fair market value on the date of the distribution.
(3) Withdrawal of erroneous contributions. Section 220(f)(2) and paragraph (2) of this subsection shall not apply to any payment or distribution from a Medicare Advantage MSA to the Secretary of Health and Human Services of an erroneous contribution to such MSA and of the net income attributable to such contribution.
(4) Trustee-to-trustee transfers. Section 220(f)(2) and paragraph (2) of this subsection shall not apply to any trustee-to-trustee transfer from a Medicare Advantage MSA of an account holder to another Medicare Advantage MSA of such account holder.

(d) Special rules for treatment of account after death of account holder.
In applying section 220(f)(8)(A) to an account which was a Medicare Advantage MSA of a decedent, the rules of section 220(f) shall apply in lieu of the rules of subsection (c) of this section with respect to the spouse as the account holder of such Medicare Advantage MSA.

(e) Reports.
In the case of a Medicare Advantage MSA, the report under section 220(h)—
(1) shall include the fair market value of the assets in such Medicare Advantage MSA as of the close of each calendar year, and
(2) shall be furnished to the account holder—
   (A) not later than January 31 of the calendar year following the calendar year to which such reports relate, and
   (B) in such manner as the Secretary prescribes in such regulations.

(f) Coordination with limitation on number of taxpayers having Archer MSAs.
Subsection (i) of section 220 shall not apply to an individual with respect to a Medicare Advantage MSA, and Medicare Advantage MSAs shall not be taken into account in determining whether the numerical limitations under section 220(j) are exceeded.

In **2004,** P.L. 108-311, Sec. 408(a)(5)(A), substituted "Medicare Advantage MSA" for "Medicare+Choice MSA" each place it appeared in Code Sec. 138 ... Sec. 408(a)(5)(B), substituted "Medicare Advantage MSA" for "Medicare+Choice MSA" in the heading of Code Sec. 138 ... Sec. 408(a)(5)(C), substituted "Medicare Advantage MSA" for "Medicare+Choice MSA" in the heading of subsec. (b) ... Sec. 408(a)(5)(D), substituted "Medicare Advantage MSA" for "Medicare+Choice MSA" in the heading of para. (c)(2) ... Sec. 408(a)(5)(E), substituted "Medicare Advantage MSAs" for "Medicare+Choice MSAs" in clause (c)(2)(C)(i) ... Sec. 408(a)(5)(F), substituted "Medicare Advantage MSAs" for "Medicare+Choice MSAs" in subsec. (f), enacted 10/4/2004.
In **2000,** P.L. 106-554, Sec. 1(a)(7), [which enacted into law Sec. 202(a)(3) of P.L. 106-554] substituted "Archer MSA" for "medical savings account" in subsec. (b) ... Sec. 1(a)(7), [which enacted into law Sec. 202(b)(6) of P.L. 106-554] substituted "Archer MSAs" for "medical savings accounts" in the heading of subsec. (f) ... Sec. 1(a)(7), [which enacted into law Sec. 202(b)(10) of P.L. 106-554] substituted "an Archer" for "a Archer" in subsec. (b), effective 12/21/2000.
In **1997,** P.L. 105-33, Sec. 4006(a), added new Code Sec. 138, effective for tax. yrs. begin. after 12/31/98.

Sec. 139. Disaster relief payments.
(a) General rule.
Gross income shall not include any amount received by an individual as a qualified disaster relief payment.
(b) Qualified disaster relief payment defined.
For purposes of this section, the term "qualified disaster relief payment" means any amount paid to or for the benefit of an individual—
(1) to reimburse or pay reasonable and necessary personal, family, living, or funeral expenses incurred as a result of a qualified disaster,
(2) to reimburse or pay reasonable and necessary expenses incurred for the repair or rehabilitation of a personal residence or repair or replacement of its contents to the extent that the need for such repair, rehabilitation, or replacement is attributable to a qualified disaster,
(3) by a person engaged in the furnishing or sale of transportation as a common carrier by reason of the death or personal physical injuries incurred as a result of a qualified disaster, or
(4) if such amount is paid by a Federal, State, or local government, or agency or instrumentality thereof, in con-

Exclusions from income Code Sec. 139B(c)(1)

nection with a qualified disaster in order to promote the general welfare,
but only to the extent any expense compensated by such payment is not otherwise compensated for by insurance or otherwise.

(c) Qualified disaster defined.
For purposes of this section, the term "qualified disaster" means—
(1) a disaster which results from a terroristic or military action (as defined in section 692(c)(2)),
(2) federally declared disaster (as defined by section 165(h)(3)(C)(i)),
(3) a disaster which results from an accident involving a common carrier, or from any other event, which is determined by the Secretary to be of a catastrophic nature, or
(4) with respect to amounts described in subsection (b)(4), a disaster which is determined by an applicable Federal, State, or local authority (as determined by the Secretary) to warrant assistance from the Federal, State, or local government or agency or instrumentality thereof.

(d) Coordination with employment taxes.
For purposes of chapter 2 and subtitle C, qualified disaster relief payments and qualified disaster mitigation payments shall not be treated as net earnings from self-employment, wages, or compensation subject to tax.

(e) No relief for certain individuals.
Subsections (a), (f), and (g) shall not apply with respect to any individual identified by the Attorney General to have been a participant or conspirator in a terroristic action (as so defined), or a representative of such individual.

(f) Exclusion of certain additional payments.
Gross income shall not include any amount received as payment under section 406 of the Air Transportation Safety and System Stabilization Act.

(g) Qualified disaster mitigation payments.
(1) In general. Gross income shall not include any amount received as a qualified disaster mitigation payment.
(2) Qualified disaster mitigation payment defined. For purposes of this section, the term "qualified disaster mitigation payment" means any amount which is paid pursuant to the Robert T. Stafford Disaster Relief and Emergency Assistance Act (as in effect on the date of the enactment of this subsection) or the National Flood Insurance Act (as in effect on such date) to or for the benefit of the owner of any property for hazard mitigation with respect to such property. Such term shall not include any amount received for the sale or disposition of any property.
(3) No increase in basis. Notwithstanding any other provision of this subtitle, no increase in the basis or adjusted basis of any property shall result from any amount excluded under this subsection with respect to such property.

(h) Denial of double benefit.
Notwithstanding any other provision of this subtitle, no deduction or credit shall be allowed (to the person for whose benefit a qualified disaster relief payment or qualified disaster mitigation payment is made) for, or by reason of, any expenditure to the extent of the amount excluded under this section with respect to such expenditure.

In 2008, P.L. 110-343, Sec. 706(a)(2)(D)(iv)DivC, amended para. (c)(2), effective for disasters declared in tax. yrs. begin. after 12/31/2007.
Prior to amendment, para. (c)(2) read as follows:
"(2) a Presidentially declared disaster (as defined in section 1033(h)(3))."
In 2005, P.L. 109-7, Sec. 1(a)(1), added subsecs. (g) and (h) . . . Sec. 1(a)(2)(A), substituted "qualified disaster relief payments and qualified disaster mitigation payments" for "a qualified disaster relief payment" in subsec. (d) . . . Sec. 1(a)(2)(B), substituted ", (f), and (g)" for "and (f)" in subsec. (e), effective for amounts received before, on, or after 4/15/2005.
In 2002, P.L. 107-134, Sec. 111(a), redesignated Code Sec. 139 as Code Sec. 140 and added new Code Sec. 139, effective for tax. yrs. end. on or after 9/11/2001.

Sec. 139A. Federal subsidies for prescription drug plans.

> • **Caution:** The text of Code Sec. 139A, following, is effective for tax. yrs. begin. before 1/1/2013. For the text of Code Sec. 139A, effective for tax. yrs. begin. after 12/31/2012, see below.

Gross income shall not include any special subsidy payment received under section 1860D-22 of the Social Security Act. This section shall not be taken into account for purposes of determining whether any deduction is allowable with respect to any cost taken into account in determining such payment.

> • **Caution:** The text of Code Sec. 139A, following, is effective for tax. yrs. begin. after 12/31/2012. For the text of Code Sec. 139A, effective for tax. yrs. begin. before 1/1/2013, see above.

Gross income shall not include any special subsidy payment received under section 1860D-22 of the Social Security Act.

In 2010, P.L. 111-152, Sec. 1407, of this Act, reads as follows:
"Sec. 1407. Delay of elimination of deduction for expenses allocable to Medicare Part D subsidy.
"Section 9012(b) of the Patient Protection and Affordable Care Act is amended by striking "2010" and inserting "2012"."
—P.L. 111-148, Sec. 9012(a), amended Code Sec. 139A, effective for tax. yrs. begin. after 12/31/2012.
Prior to amendment, Code Sec. 139A read as follows:
"Gross income shall not include any special subsidy payment received under section 1860D-22 of the Social Security Act. This section shall not be taken into account for purposes of determining whether any deduction is allowable with respect to any cost taken into account in determining such payment."
In 2003, P.L. 108-173, Sec. 1202(a), added Code Sec. 139A, effective for tax. yrs. end. after 12/8/2003.

Sec. 139B. Benefits provided to volunteer firefighters and emergency medical responders.

(a) In general.
In the case of any member of a qualified volunteer emergency response organization, gross income shall not include—
(1) any qualified State and local tax benefit, and
(2) any qualified payment.

(b) Denial of double benefits.
In the case of any member of a qualified volunteer emergency response organization—
(1) the deduction under 164 shall be determined with regard to any qualified State and local tax benefit, and
(2) expenses paid or incurred by the taxpayer in connection with the performance of services as such a member shall be taken into account under section 170 only to the extent such expenses exceed the amount of any qualified payment excluded from gross income under subsection (a).

(c) Definitions.
For purposes of this section—
(1) **Qualified State and local tax benefit.** The term "qualified state and local tax benefit" means any reduc-

1,461

tion or rebate of a tax described in paragraph (1), (2), or (3) of section 164(a) provided by a State or political division thereof on account of services performed as a member of a qualified volunteer emergency response organization.

(2) Qualified payment.

(A) In general. The term "qualified payment" means any payment (whether reimbursement or otherwise) provided by a State or political division thereof on account of the performance of services as a member of a qualified volunteer emergency response organization.

(B) Applicable dollar limitation. The amount determined under subparagraph (A) for any taxable year shall not exceed $30 multiplied by the number of months during such year that the taxpayer performs such services.

(3) Qualified volunteer emergency response organization. The term "qualified volunteer emergency response organization" means any volunteer organization—

(A) which is organized and operated to provide firefighting or emergency medical services for persons in the State or political subdivision, as the case may be, and

(B) which is required (by written agreement) by the State or political subdivision to furnish firefighting or emergency medical services in such State or political subdivision.

(d) Termination.

This section shall not apply with respect to taxable years beginning after December 31, 2010.

In 2007, P.L. 110-142, Sec. 5(a), added new Code Sec. 139B, effective for tax. yrs. begin. after 12/31/2007.

Sec. 139C. COBRA premium assistance.

In the case of an assistance eligible individual (as defined in section 3001 of title III of division B of the American Recovery and Reinvestment Act of 2009), gross income does not include any premium reduction provided under subsection (a) of such section.

In 2010, P.L. 111-144, Sec. 3(b)(5)(B), substituted "3001 of title III of division B of the American Recovery and Reinvestment Act of 2009" for "section 3002 of the Health Insurance Assistance for the Unemployed Act of 2009" in Code Sec. 139C, effective for tax. yrs. end. after 2/17/2009.

In 2009, P.L. 111-5, Sec. 3001(a)(15)(A), added Code Sec. 139C, effective for tax. yrs. end. after 2/17/2009.

Sec. 139D.   Indian Health Care Benefits.

(a) General rule.

Except as otherwise provided in this section, gross income does not include the value of any qualified Indian health care benefit.

(b) Qualified Indian Health Care Benefit.

For purposes of this section, the term "qualified Indian health care benefit" means—

(1) any health service or benefit provided or purchased, directly or indirectly, by the Indian Health Service through a grant to or a contract or compact with an Indian tribe or tribal organization, or through a third-party program funded by the Indian Health Service,

(2) medical care provided or purchased by, or amounts to reimburse for such medical care provided by, an Indian tribe or tribal organization for, or to, a member of an Indian tribe, including a spouse or dependent of such a member,

(3) coverage under accident or health insurance (or an arrangement having the effect of accident or health insurance), or an accident or health plan, provided by an Indian tribe or tribal organization for medical care to a member of an Indian tribe, include a spouse or dependent of such a member, and

(4) any other medical care provided by an Indian tribe or tribal organization that supplements, replaces, or substitutes for a program or service relating to medical care provided by the Federal government to Indian tribes or members of such a tribe.

(c) Definitions.

For purposes of this section—

(1) Indian tribe. The term "Indian tribe" has the meaning given such term by section 45A(c)(6).

(2) Tribal organization. The term "tribal organization" has the meaning given such term by section 4(l) of the Indian Self-Determination and Education Assistance Act.

(3) Medical care. The term "medical care" has the same meaning as when used in section 213.

(4) Accident or health insurance; accident or health plan. The terms "accident or health insurance" and "accident or health plan" have the same meaning as when used in section 105.

(5) Dependent. The term "dependent" has the meaning given such term by section 152, determined without regard to subsections (b)(1), (b)(2), and (d)(1)(B) thereof.

(d) Denial of double benefit.

Subsection (a) shall not apply to the amount of any qualified Indian health care benefit which is not includible in gross income of the beneficiary of such benefit under any other provision of this chapter, or to the amount of any such benefit for which a deduction is allowed to such beneficiary under any other provision of this chapter.

In 2010, P.L. 111-148, Sec. 9021(a), added Code Sec. 139D, effective for benefits and coverage provided after 3/23/2010. . . . Sec. 9021(c), provides:

"(d) No inference. Nothing in the amendments made by this section shall be construed to create an inference with respect to the exclusion from gross income of—

"(1) benefits provided by an Indian tribe or tribal organization that are not within the scope of this section, and

"(2) benefits provided prior to the date of the enactment of this Act."

Sec. 139D[sic 139E].   Repealed.

In 2011, P.L. 112-10, Sec. 1858(b)(2)(A), repealed Code Sec. 139D [sic 139E], effective for vouchers provided after 12/31/2013, as provided in Sec. 10108(f) of P.L. 111-148 [see below].

Prior to repeal, Code Sec. 139D read as follows:

"Sec. 139D. Free choice vouchers.

"Gross income shall not include the amount of any free choice voucher provided by an employer under section 10108 of the Patient Protection and Affordable Care Act to the extent that the amount of such voucher does not exceed the amount paid for a qualified health plan (as defined in section 1301 of such Act) by the taxpayer."

In 2010, P.L. 111-148, Sec. 10108(f)(1), added Code Sec. 139D [sic 139E] effective for vouchers provided after 12/31/2013.

Sec. 140.   Cross references to other acts.

(a) For exemption of—

(1) Allowances and expenditures to meet losses sustained by persons serving the United States abroad, due to appreciation of foreign currencies, see section 5943 of title 5, United States Code.

(2) Amounts credited to the Maritime Administration under section 9(b)(6) of the Merchant Ship Sales Act of 1946, see section 9(c)(1) of that Act (50 U.S.C. App. 1742).

(3) Benefits under laws administered by the Veterans' Administration, see section 5301 of title 38, United States Code.

(4) Earnings of ship contractors deposited in special reserve funds, see section 53507 of title 46, United States Code.

Exclusions from income Code Sec. 140

(5) Income derived from Federal Reserve banks, including capital stock and surplus, see section 7 of the Federal Reserve Act (12 U.S.C. 531).

(6) Special pensions of persons on Army and Navy medal of honor roll, see 38 U.S.C. 1562(a)–(c).

(b) For extension of military income-tax-exemption benefits to commissioned officers of Public Health Service in certain circumstances, see section 212 of the Public Health Service Act (42 U.S.C. 213).

In 2006, P.L. 109-304, Sec. 17(e)(2), substituted "section 53507 of title 46, United States Code" for "section 607(d) of the Merchant Marine Act, 1936 (46 U.S.C. 1177)" in para. (a)(4), enacted 10/6/2006.

In 2002, P.L. 107-134, Sec. 111(a), redesignated Code Sec. 139 as Code Sec. 140, effective for tax. yrs. end. on or after 9/11/2001.

In 1997, P.L. 105-33, Sec. 4006(a), redesignated Code Sec. 138 as Code Sec. 139, effective for tax. yrs. begin. after 12/31/98.

In 1996, P.L. 104-188, Sec. 1807(b), redesignated Code Sec. 137 as Code Sec. 138, effective for tax. yrs. begin. after 12/31/96.

In 1992, P.L. 102-486, Sec. 1912(a), redesignated Code Sec. 136 as Code Sec. 137, effective for amounts received after 12/31/92.

In 1991, P.L. 102-40, Sec. 402(d)(2), substituted "section 5301 of title 38," for "section 3101 of title 38," effective 5/7/91.

In 1988, P.L. 100-647, Sec. 1011B(f)(4), amended Sec. 1168(c) of P.L. 99-514, the effective date for changes made by Sec. 1168(a), by substituting "1984" for "1986", see below.

—P.L. 100-647, Sec. 6009(a), redesignated Code Sec. 135 as Code Sec. 136, effective for tax. yrs. begin. after 12/31/89.

In 1986, P.L. 99-514, Sec. 1168(a), redesignated Code Sec. 134 as Code Sec. 135, effective for tax. yrs. begin. after 12/31/86 [as amended by Sec. 1011B(f)(4) of P.L. 100-647, see above].

In 1984, P.L. 98-369, Sec. 531(a)(1), redesignated Code Sec. 132 as Code Sec. 133 and added new Code Sec. 132, effective after 12/31/84.

—P.L. 98-369, Sec. 543(a), redesignated Code Sec. 133 (as redesignated by Sec. 531(a), see above) as Code Sec. 134 and added new Code Sec. 133, effective for loans used to acquire employer securities after 7/18/84.

—P.L. 98-369, Sec. 2661(o)(2), deleted paras. (a)(6) and (a)(7) and redesignated para. (a)(8) as (a)(6), effective for benefits received after 12/31/83, in tax. yrs. end. after 12/31/83. Sec. 121(g)(2) of P.L. 98-21, provides:

"(2) Treatment of certain lump-sum payments received after December 31, 1983. The amendments made by this section shall not apply to any portion of a lump-sum payment of social security benefits (as defined in section 86(d) of the Internal Revenue Code of 1954) received after December 31, 1983, if the generally applicable payment date for such portion was before January 1, 1984."

Prior to deletion, paras. (a)(6) and (a)(7) read as follows:

"(6) Railroad retirement annuities and pensions, see section 12 of the Railroad Retirement Act of 1935 (45 U.S.C. 2281).

"(7) Railroad unemployment benefits which are not includible in gross income under section 85, section 2(e) of the Railroad Unemployment Insurance Act (45 U.S.C. 352)."

In 1983, P.L. 97-473, Sec. 102(a), redesignated Code Sec. 131 [as redesignated by Sec. 101(b) of P.L. 97-473, see below] as Code Sec. 132, for tax. yrs. begin. after 12/31/78.

—P.L. 97-473, Sec. 101(b), redesignated Code Sec. 130 as Code Sec. 131, for tax yrs. end. after 12/31/82.

In 1981, P.L. 97-34, Sec. 301(a), redesignated Code Sec. 128 as Code Sec. 129, for tax. yrs. end. after 9/30/81.

—P.L. 97-34, Sec. 124(e)(1), redesignated Code Sec. 129 [Code Sec. 128 as redesignated by Sec. 301(a) of this Act, see above] as Code Sec. 130, for tax. yrs. begin. after 12/31/81.

In 1980, P.L. 96-589, Sec. 6(i)(1), deleted para. (a)(1) and redesignated paras. (a)(2) through (a)(9) as paras. (a)(1) through (a)(8), effective 10/1/79, except for any proceeding under the Bankruptcy Act commenced before 10/1/79. Sec. 7(g) of this Act provides:

"(g) Definitions.

"For purposes of this section—

"(1) Bankruptcy case. The term 'bankruptcy case' means any case under title 11 of the United States Code (as recodified by P.L. 95-598).

"(2) Similar judicial proceeding. The term 'similar judicial proceeding' means a receivership, foreclosure, or similar proceeding in a Federal or State court (as modified by section 368(a)(3)(D) of the Internal Revenue Code of 1954)."

Prior to deletion, para. (a)(1) read as follows:

"(1) Adjustments of indebtedness under wage earners' plans, see section 679 of the Bankruptcy Act (11 U.S.C. 1079)."

—P.L. 96-222, Sec. 101(a)(3), substituted "benefits which are not includible in gross income under section 85," for "benefits, see" in para. (a)(8), effective for plan yrs. begin. after 12/31/78.

—P.L. 96-222, Sec. 101(a)(6)(B), corrected the effective date for changes made by Sec. 134(a) of P.L. 95-600 from tax. yrs. begin. after '78 to plan yrs. begin. after '78 [see below].

In 1978, P.L. 95-618, Sec. 242(a), redesignated Code Sec. 124 as Code Sec. 125, effective 11/9/78.

—P.L. 95-600, Sec. 134(a), redesignated Code Sec. 125 (as redesignated by P.L. 95-618, see above) as Code Sec. 126, effective for plan yrs. begin. after 12/31/78.

—P.L. 95-600, Sec. 543(a), redesignated Code Sec. 126 (as redesignated by Sec. 134(a) of this Act) as Code Sec. 127, effective for grants made under programs after 9/30/79.

—P.L. 95-600, Sec. 164(a), redesignated Code Sec. 127 (as redesignated by Sec. 543(a) of this Act) as Code Sec. 128, effective for tax. yrs. begin. after 12/31/78.

In 1976, P.L. 94-455, Sec. 1901(a)(21), amended Code Sec. 124, effective for tax. yrs. begin. after 12/31/76.

Prior to amendment Code Sec. 124 read as follows:

"SEC. 124. CROSS REFERENCES TO OTHER ACTS.

"(a) For exemption of—

"(1) Adjustments of indebtedness under wage earners' plans, see section 679 of the Bankruptcy Act (52 Stat. 938; 11 U. S. C. 1079);

"(2) Allowances and expenditures to meet losses sustained by persons serving the United States abroad, due to appreciation of foreign currencies, see the Acts of March 6, 1934 (48 Stat. 466; 5 U. S. C. 118c) and April 25, 1938 (52 Stat. 221; 5 U. S. C. 118c-1);

"(3) Amounts credited to the Maritime Administration under section 9(b)(6) of the Merchant Ship Sales Act of 1946, see section 9(c)(1) of that Act (60 Stat. 48; 50 U. S. C. App. 1742);

"(4) Benefits under World War Adjusted Compensation Act, see section 308 of that Act, as amended (43 Stat. 125; 44 Stat. 827, § 3; (58 U.S. C. 618);

"(5) Benefits under World War Veterans' Act, 1924, see section 3 of the Act of August 12, 1935 (49 Stat. 609; 38 U. S. C. 454a);

"(6) Dividends and interest derived from certain preferred stock by Reconstruction Finance Corporation, see section 304 of the Act of March 9, 1933, as amended (49 Stat. 1185; 12 U. S. C. 51d);

"(7) Earnings of ship contractors deposited in special reserve funds, see section 607(h) of the Merchant Marine Act, 1936, as amended (52 Stat. 961, § 28; (46 U. S. C. 1177);

"(8) Income derived from Federal Reserve banks, including capital stock and surplus, see section 7 of the Federal Reserve Act (38 Stat. 258; (12 U. S. C. 531).

"(9) Income derived from Ogdensburg bridge across Saint Lawrence River, see section 4 of the Act of June 14, 1933, as amended (54 Stat. 259, § 2);

"(10) Income derived from Owensboro bridge across Ohio River and nearby ferries, see section 4 of the Act of August 14, 1937 (50 Stat. 643);

"(11) Income derived from Saint Clair River bridge and ferries, see section 4 of the Act of June 25, 1930, as amended (48 Stat. 140, § 1);

"(12) Leave compensation payments under section 6 of Armed Forces Leave Act of 1946, see section 7 of that Act (60 Stat. 967; 37 U. S. C. 36);

"(13) Mustering-out payments made to or on account of veterans under the Mustering-Out Payment Act of 1944, see section 5(a) of that Act (58 Stat. 10; 38 U. S. C. 691e);

"(14) Railroad retirement annuities and pensions, see section 12 of the Railroad Retirement Act of 1935, as amended (50 Stat. 316; 45 U. S. C. 2281);

"(15) Railroad unemployment benefits, see section 2(e) of the Railroad Unemployment Insurance Act, as amended (52 Stat. 1097; 53 Stat. 845, § 9; 45 U. S. C. 352);

"(16) Special pensions of persons on Army and Navy medal of honor roll, see section 3 of the Act of April 27, 1916 (39 Stat. 54; (38 U. S. C. 393);

"(17) Gain derived from the sale or other disposition of Treasury Bills, issued after June 17, 1930, under the Second Liberty Bond Act, as amended, see Act of June 17, 1930 (C. 512, 46 Stat. 775; 31 U. S. C. 754);

"(18) Benefits under laws administered by the Veterans' Administration, see section 3101 of title 38, United States Code.

"(b) For extension of military income tax-exemption benefits to commissioned officers of Public Health Service in certain circumstances, see section 212 of the Public Health Service Act (58 Stat. 689; 42 U. S. C. 213)."

In 1971, provided in 42 USC § 4636 that payments made under the Uniform Relocation Assistance provisions of the Relocation Assistance and Real Property Acquisition Policies Act of 1970 are not considered to be income for federal tax purposes.

In 1969, P.L. 91-172, Sec. 901(a), redesignated former Code Sec. 123 as 124.

In 1966, P.L. 89-365, Sec. 1(a)(1), redesignated former Code Sec. 122 as 123.

In 1962, P.L. 87-834, Sec. 27, provided

"SEC. 27. EXCLUSION FROM GROSS INCOME OF CERTAIN AWARDS MADE PURSUANT TO EVACUATION CLAIMS OF JAPANESE-AMERICAN PERSONS.

"(a) In general.

"No amount received as an award under the Act entitled 'An Act to authorize the Attorney General to adjudicate certain claims resulting from evacuation of certain persons of Japanese ancestry under military orders', approved July 2, 1948, as amended by Public Law 116, Eighty-second Congress, and Public Law 673, Eighty-fourth Congress (50 U.S.C. App., Secs. 1981–1987), shall be included in gross income for purposes of chapter 1 of the internal revenue code of 1939 or chapter 1 of the Internal Revenue Code of 1954.

"(b) Effective date, etc.

"Subsection (a) shall apply with respect to taxable years ending after July 2, 1948. If refund or credit of any overpayment of Federal income tax resulting from the application of subsection (a) (including interest, additions to the tax, additional amounts, and penalties) is prevented on the date of the enactment of this Act, or within one year from such date, by the operation of any law or rule of law, the refund or credit of such overpayment may nevertheless be made or allowed if claim therefor is filed within one year after the date of enactment of this Act. In the case of a claim to which the preceding sentence applies, the amount to be refunded or credited as an overpayment shall not be diminished by any credit or set-off based upon any item other than the amount of the award referred to in subsec-

Code Sec. 140 — Exclusions from income

tion (a). No interest shall be allowed or paid on any overpayment resulting from the application of this section."
In 1958, P.L. 85-857, Sec. 13(t), substituted "section 3101 of Title 38, United States Code" for "section 1001 of the Veterans' Benefits Act of 1957" in subsec. (a)(18).
In 1957, P.L. 85-56, Sec. 2201, amended para. (a)(18).
Prior to amendment, para. (a)(18) read as follows:
"(18) Dependency and indemnity compensation paid to survivors of members of a uniformed service and certain other persons, see section 210 of the Servicemen's and Veteran's Survivor Benefits Act."
In 1956, P.L. 881, Sec. 501(t), added para. (a)(18).

PART IV.— TAX EXEMPTION REQUIREMENTS FOR STATE AND LOCAL BONDS
Subpart
A. Private activity bonds.
B. Requirements applicable to all State and local bonds.
C. Definitions and special rules.

In 1986, P.L. 99-514, Sec. 1301(b), amended Part IV of subchapter B of chapter 1.
Prior to amendment, Part IV of subchapter B of chapter 1 read as follows:
"PART IV— DETERMINATION OF MARITAL STATUS
"Sec.
"143. Determination of marital status.
In 1977, P.L. 95-30, Sec. 101(e)(2), amended the table of Code Secs. for Part IV.
Prior to amendment, that table read as follows:
"PART IV.— STANDARD DEDUCTION FOR INDIVIDUALS
"Sec.
"141. Standard deduction.
"142. Individuals not eligible for standard deduction.
"143. Determination of marital status.
"144. Election of standard deduction.
"145. Cross reference."

"SEC. 141. REPEALED.
In 1977, P.L. 95-30, Sec. 101(d)(1), repealed Code Sec. 141, effective for tax. yrs. begin. after '76.
Prior to amendment, Code Sec. 141 read as follows:
"SEC. 141. STANDARD DEDUCTION.
"(a) Standard deduction.
"Except as otherwise provided in this section, the standard deduction referred to in this title is the larger of the percentage standard deduction or the low income allowance.
"(b) Percentage standard deduction.
"The percentage standard deduction is an amount equal to 16 percent of adjusted gross income, but not more than—
"(1) $2,800 in the case of—
"(A) a joint return under section 6013, or
"(B) a surviving spouse (as defined in section 2(a)),
"(2) $2,400 in the case of an individual who is not married and who is not a surviving spouse (as so defined), or
"(3) $1,400 in the case of a married individual filing a separate return.
"(c) Low income allowance.
"The low income allowance is—
"(1) $2,100 in the case of—
"(A) a joint return under section 6013, or
"(B) a surviving spouse (as defined in section 2(a)),
"(2) $1,700 in the case of an individual who is not married and who is not a surviving spouse (as so defined), or
"(3) $1,050 in the case of a married individual filing a separate return.
"(d) Married individuals filing separate returns.
"Notwithstanding subsection (a)—
"(1) The low income allowance shall not apply in the case of a separate return by a married individual if the tax of the other spouse is determined with regard to the percentage standard deduction.
"(2) A married individual filing a separate return may, if the low income allowance is less than the percentage standard deduction, and if the low income allowance of his spouse is greater than the percentage standard deduction of such spouse, elect (under regulations prescribed by the Secretary) to have his tax determined with regard to the low income allowance in lieu of being determined with regard to the percentage standard deduction.
"(e) Limitations in case of certain dependent taxpayers.
"In the case of a taxpayer with respect to whom a deduction under section 151(e) is allowable to another taxpayer for the taxable year—
"(1) the percentage standard deduction shall be computed only with reference to so much of his adjusted gross income as is attributable to his earned income (as defined in section 911(b)), and
"(2) the low income allowance shall not exceed his earned income for the taxable year."
In 1976, P.L. 94-455, Sec. 401(b)(1), and (2), amended subsecs. (c) and (b), effective for tax. yrs. end. after '75.

Prior to amendment, subsecs. (b) and (c) read as follows:
"(b) Percentage Standard Deduction.
"(1) General rule. The percentage standard deduction is an amount equal to 16 percent of adjusted gross income but not to exceed—
"(A) $2,800 in the case of—
"(i) a joint return under section 6013, or
"(ii) a surviving spouse (as defined in section 2(a)),
"(B) $2,400 in the case of an individual who is not married and who is not a surviving spouse (as so defined), or
"(C) $1,400 in the case of a married individual filing a separate return.
"(2) Application of 6-month rule. Notwithstanding the provisions of paragraph (1) of this subsection, the following amounts shall be substituted for the amounts set forth in paragraph (1)—
"(A) '$2,400' for '$2,800' in subparagraph (A),
"(B) '$2,200' for '$2,400' in subparagraph (B), and
"(C) '$1,200' for '$1,400' in subparagraph (C).
"(c) Low income allowance.
"(1) In general. The low income allowance is—
"(A) $2,100 in the case of—
"(i) a joint return under section 6013, or
"(ii) a surviving spouse (as defined in section 2(a)),
"(B) $1,700 in the case of an individual who is not married and who is not a surviving spouse (as so defined), or
"(C) $1,050 in the case of a married individual filing a separate return.
"(2) Application of 6-month rule. Notwithstanding the provisions of paragraph (1), the following amounts shall be substituted for the amount set forth in paragraph (1)—
"(A) '$1,700' for '$2,100' in subparagraph (A),
"(B) '$1,500' for '$1,700' in subparagraph (B), and
"(C) '$850' for '$1,050' in subparagraph (C)."
— P.L. 94-455, Sec. 1906(b)(13)(A), substituted "Secretary" for "Secretary or his delegate" in para. (d)(2), effective for tax. yrs. begin. after '76.
In 1975, P.L. 94-164, Sec. 2(a)(1), amended subsec. (c) . . . Sec. 2(b)(1), amended subsec. (b), effective for tax. yrs. end. after 12/31/75 and before 1/1/77.
Prior to amendment, subsecs. (b) and (c) read as follows:
"(b) Percentage standard deduction.
"The percentage standard deduction is an amount equal to 16 percent of adjusted gross income but not to exceed—
"(1) $2,600 in the case of—
"(A) a joint return under section 6013, or
"(B) a surviving spouse (as defined in section 2(a)),
"(2) $2,300 in the case of an individual who is not married and who is not a surviving spouse (as so defined), or
"(3) $1,300 in the case of a married individual filing a separate return.
"(c) Low income allowance.
"The low income allowance is—
"(1) $1,900 in the case of—
"(A) a joint return under section 6013, or
"(B) a surviving spouse (as defined in section 2(a)),
"(2) $1,600 in the case of an individual who is not married and who is not a surviving spouse (as so defined), or
"(3) $950 in the case of a married individual filing a separate return."
— P.L. 94-12, Sec. 202(a), amended subsec. (b), effective for tax. yrs. end. after 12/31/74 and before 1/1/76.
Prior to amendment, subsec. (b) read as follows:
"(b) Percentage standard deduction.
"The percentage standard deduction is an amount equal to the applicable percentage of adjusted gross income shown in the following table, but not to exceed the maximum amount shown in such table (or one-half of such maximum amount in the case of a separate return by a married individual):

"Taxable years beginning in—	Applicable percentage	Maximum amount
1970	10	$1,000
1971	13	1,500
1972 and thereafter	15	2,000

— P.L. 94-12, Sec. 201(a), amended subsec. (c), effective for tax. yrs. after 12/31/74 and before 1/1/76.
Prior to amendment, subsec. (c) read as follows:
"(c) Low income allowance.
"The low income allowance is $1,300 ($650 in the case of a married individual filing a separate return)."
In 1971, P.L. 92-178, Sec. 202, substituted the last line in the table in subsec. (b) for the last two lines which read as follows:

| "1972 | 14 | $2,000 |
| "1973 and thereafter | 15 | 2,000", |

for tax. yrs. begin. after 12/31/71.
— P.L. 92-178, Sec. 203(b), amended subsec. (c), effective for tax. yrs. begin. after '71
— P.L. 92-178, Sec. 203(a), amended subsec. (c), effective for tax. yrs. begin. during '71.
Prior to amendment, subsec. (c) read as follows for tax yrs. begin. after '71:
"(c) Low income allowance.
"The low income allowance is $1,000 ($500, in the case of a married individual filing a separate return)."

Exclusions from income — Part IV

Prior to amendment, subsec. (c) reads as follows for tax yrs. begin. before '72.
"(c) Low income allowance.
"(1) In general. The low income allowance is an amount equal to the sum of—
"(A) the basic allowance, and
"(B) the additional allowance.
"(2) Basic allowance. For purposes of this subsection, the basic allowance is an amount equal to the sum of—
"(A) $200, plus
"(B) $100, multiplied by the number of exemptions.
"The basic allowance shall not exceed $1,000.
"(3) Additional allowance.
"(A) In general. For purposes of this subsection, the additional allowance is an amount equal to the excess (if any) of $900 over the sum of—
"(i) $100, multiplied by the number of exemptions, plus
"(ii) the income phase-out.
"(B) Income phase-out. For purposes of subparagraph (A)(ii), the income phase-out is an amount equal to one-half of the amount by which the adjusted gross income for the taxable year exceeds the sum of—
"(i) $1,100, plus
"(ii) $625, multiplied by the number of exemptions.
"(4) Married individuals filing separate returns. In the case of a married taxpayer filing a separate return—
"(A) the low income allowance is an amount equal to the basic allowance, and
"(B) the basic allowance is an amount (not in excess of $500) equal to the sum of—
"(i) $100, plus
"(ii) $100, multiplied by the number of exemptions.
"(5) Number of exemptions. For purposes of this subsection, the number of exemptions is the number of exemptions allowed as a deduction for the taxable year under section 151.
"(6) Special rule for 1971. For a taxable year beginning after December 31, 1970, and before January 1, 1972,—
"(A) paragraph (3)(A) shall be applied by substituting '$850' for '$900',
"(B) paragraph (3)(B) shall be applied by substituting 'one-fifteenth' for 'one-half',
"(C) paragraph (3)(B)(i) shall be applied by substituting '$1050' for '$1100', and
"(D) paragraph (3)(B)(ii) shall be applied by substituting '$650' for '$625'."
—P.L. 92-178, Sec. 301(a), added subsec. (e), effective for tax. yrs. begin. after 12/31/71.
In 1969, P.L. 91-172, Sec. 802(a), amended subsecs. (a), (b), and (c), effective for tax. yrs. begin. after 12/31/69.
Prior to amendment, subsecs. (a), (b), and (c) read as follows:
"(a) Standard deduction.
"Except as otherwise provided in this section, the standard deduction referred to in this title is the larger of the 10-percent standard deduction or the minimum standard deduction. The standard deduction shall not exceed $1,000, except that in the case of a separate return by a married individual the standard deduction shall not exceed $500.
"(b) Ten-percent standard deduction.
"The 10-percent standard deduction is an amount equal to 10 percent of the adjusted gross income.
"(c) Minimum standard deduction.
"The minimum standard deduction is an amount equal to the sum of—
"(1) $100, multiplied by the number of exemptions allowed for the taxable year as a deduction under section 151, plus
"(2)(A) $200, in the case of a joint return of a husband and wife under section 6013,
"(B) $200, in the case of a return of an individual who is not married, or
"(C) $100, in the case of a separate return by a married individual."
—P.L. 91-172, Sec. 802(c)(4), substituted "low income allowance" for "minimum standard deduction" and substituted "percentage" for "10-percent" each time they appeared in subsec. (d), effective for tax. yrs. begin. after 12/31/69.
—P.L. 91-172, Sec. 802(e), substituted new subsec. (c) as shown above, effective for tax. yrs. begin. after 12/31/71.
In 1964, designated existing provisions as subsec. (a), substituted "Except as otherwise provided in this section, the standard deduction referred to in this title is the larger of the 10-percent standard deduction or the minimum standard deduction. The standard deduction shall not exceed $1,000" for "The standard deduction referred to in section 63(b) (defining taxable income in case of individual electing standard deduction) shall be an amount equal to 10 percent of the adjusted gross income or $1,000, whichever is the lesser" therein, and added subsecs. (b)–(d), effective for tax. yrs. begin. after '63, except for purposes of Code Sec. 21.

"Sec. 142. Repealed.
In 1977, P.L. 95-30, Sec. 101(d)(1), repealed Code Sec. 142, effective for tax. yrs. begin. after '76.
Prior to amendment, Code Sec. 142 read as follows:
"Sec. 142. Individuals not eligible for standard deduction.
"(a) Husband and wife.
"The standard deduction shall not be allowed to a husband or wife if the tax of the other spouse is determined under section 1 on the basis of the taxable income computed without regard to the standard deduction.
"(b) Certain other taxpayers ineligible.

"The standard deduction shall not be allowed in computing the taxable income of—
"(1) a nonresident alien individual;
"(2) a citizen of the United States entitled to the benefits of section 931 (relating to income from sources within possessions of the United States);
"(3) an individual making a return under section 443(a)(1) for a period of less than 12 months on account of change in his annual accounting period; or
"(4) an estate or trust, common trust fund, or partnership."
Prior to the amendment of Part IV of Subchapter B of Chapter 1 by Sec. 1301(b) of P.L. 99-514, Code Sec. 143 read as follows:
"Sec. 143. Determination of marital status.
"(a) General rule.
"For purposes of part V—
"(1) The determination of whether an individual is married shall be made as of the close of his taxable year; except that if his spouse dies during his taxable year such determination shall be made as of the time of such death; and
"(2) An individual legally separated from his spouse under a decree of divorce or of separate maintenance shall not be considered as married.
"(b) Certain married individuals living apart.
"For purposes of those provisions of this title which refer to this subsection, if—
"(1) an individual who is married (within the meaning of subsection (a)) and who files a separate return maintains as his home a household which constitutes for more than one-half of the taxable year the principal place of abode of a child (within the meaning of section 151(e)(3)) with respect to whom such individual is entitled to a deduction for the taxable year under section 151 (or would be so entitled but for paragraph (2) or (4) of section 152(e)),
"(2) such individual furnishes over one-half of the cost of maintaining such household during the taxable year, and
"(3) during the last 6 months of the taxable year, such individual's spouse is not a member of such household, such individual shall not be considered as married."
In 1984, P.L. 98-369, Sec. 423(c)(1), amended subsec. (b), effective for x yrs. begin. after 12/31/84.
Prior to amendment, subsec. (b) read as follows:
"(b) Certain married individuals living apart.
"For purposes of part V, if—
"(1) an individual who is married (within the meaning of subsection (a)) and who files a separate return maintains as his home a household which constitutes for more than one-half of the taxable year the principal place of abode of a dependent (A) who (within the meaning of section 152) is a son, stepson, daughter, or stepdaughter of the individual, and (B) with respect to whom such individual is entitled to a deduction for the taxable year under section 151,
"(2) such individual furnishes over half of the cost of maintaining such household during the taxable year, and
"(3) during the entire taxable year such individual's spouse is not a member of such household,
such individual shall not be considered as married."
In 1977, P.L. 95-30, Sec. 101(d)(4), deleted "this part and" each place it appeared in Code Sec. 143, effective for tax. yrs. begin. after '76.
In 1976, P.L. 94-455, Sec. 1901(a)(22), substituted "this part and part V" for "this part" each place it appeared in Code Sec. 143, effective for tax. yrs. begin. after '76.
In 1969, P.L. 91-172, Sec. 802(b), substituted "(a) General rule. For purposes of this part—" for "For purposes of this part—" and added subsec. (b), effective for tax. yrs. begin. after 12/31/69.

"Sec. 144. Repealed.
In 1977, P.L. 95-30, Sec. 101(d)(1), repealed Code Sec. 144, effective for tax. yrs. begin. after '76.
Prior to amendment, Code Sec. 144 read as follows:
"144. Election of standard deduction.
"(a) Method of election.
"The standard deduction shall be allowed if the taxpayer so elects in his return, and the Secretary shall prescribe the manner of signifying such election in the return.
"(b) Change of election.
"Under regulations prescribed by the Secretary, a change of election with respect to the standard deduction for any taxable year may be made after the filing of the return for such year. If the spouse of the taxpayer filed a separate return for any taxable year corresponding, for purposes of section 142(a), to the taxable year of the taxpayer, the change shall not be allowed unless, in accordance with such regulations—
"(1) the spouse makes a change of election with respect to the standard deduction for the taxable year covered in such separate return, consistent with the change of election sought by the taxpayer, and
"(2) the taxpayer and his spouse consent in writing to the assessment, within such period as may be agreed on with the Secretary, of any deficiency, to the extent attributable to such change of election, even though at the time of the filing of such consent the assessment of such deficiency would otherwise be prevented by the operation of any law or rule of law.
"This subsection shall not apply if the tax liability of the taxpayer's spouse, for the taxable year corresponding (for purposes of section 142(a)) to the taxable year of the taxpayer, has been compromised under section 7122.
"(c) Change of election defined.

"For purposes of this title, the term 'change of election with respect to the standard deduction' means—
 "(1) a change of an election to take (or not to take) the standard deduction or;
 "(2) a change of an election under section 141(d)(2)."

In **1976**, P.L. 94-455, Sec. 501(b)(3), amended subsec. (a), effective for tax. yrs. begin. after '75.
Prior to amendment, subsec. (a) read as follows:
"(a) Method and effect of election.
 "(1) If the adjusted gross income shown on the return is $10,000 or more, the standard deduction shall be allowed if the taxpayer so elects in his return, and the Secretary or his delegate shall by regulations prescribe the manner of signifying such election in the return. If the adjusted gross income shown on the return is $10,000 or more, but the correct adjusted gross income is less than $10,000, then an election by the taxpayer under the preceding sentence to take the standard deduction shall be considered as his election to pay the tax imposed by section 3 (relating to tax based on tax table); and his failure to make under the preceding sentence an election to take the standard deduction shall be considered his election not to pay the tax imposed by section 3.
 "(2) If the adjusted gross income shown on the return is less than $10,000, the standard deduction shall be allowed only if the taxpayer elects, in the manner provided in section 4, to pay the tax imposed by section 3. If the adjusted gross income shown on the return is less than $10,000, but the correct adjusted gross income is $10,000 or more, then an election by the taxpayer to pay the tax imposed by section 3 shall be considered as his election to take the standard deduction; and his failure to elect to pay the tax imposed by section 3 shall be considered his election not to take the standard deduction.
 "(3) If the taxpayer on making his return fails to signify, in the manner provided by paragraph (1) or (2), his election to take the standard deduction or to pay the tax imposed by section 3, as the case may be, such failure shall be considered his election not to take the standard deduction.
 "(4) If the adjusted gross income shown on the return is less than $10,000, and if the taxpayer cannot elect to pay the tax imposed by section 3 by reason of section 4(d)(5), the standard deduction (after the application of section 141(e)) shall be allowed, notwithstanding paragraph (2), if the taxpayer so elects in his return."
—P.L. 94-455, Sec. 501(b)(4), deleted para. (c)(2), inserted "or" at the end of para. (c)(1), and redesignated para. (c)(3) as para. (c)(2), effective for tax. yrs. begin. after '75.
Prior to deletion, para. (c)(2) read as follows:
 "(2) a change of an election to pay (or not to pay) the tax under section 3; or"
—P.L. 94-455, Sec. 501(b)(5), deleted subsec. (d), effective for tax. yrs. begin. after '75.
Prior to amendment, subsec. (d) read as follows:
"(d) Individuals electing income averaging.
 "In the case of a taxpayer who chooses to have the benefits of part I of subchapter Q (relating to income averaging) for the taxable year—
 "(1) subsection (a) shall not apply for such taxable year, and
 "(2) the standard deduction shall be allowed if the taxpayer so elects in his return for such taxable year.
The Secretary or his delegate shall by regulations prescribe the manner of signifying such election in the return. If the taxpayer on making his return fails to signify, in the manner so prescribed, his election to take the standard deduction, such failure shall be considered his election not to take the standard deduction."
—P.L. 94-455, Sec. 1906(b)(13)(A), substituted "Secretary" for "Secretary or his delegate" in each place it appeared in subsec. (b), effective for tax. yrs. begin. after '76.
In **1971**, P.L. 92-178, Sec. 206, substituted "$10,000" for "$5,000" each place it appeared in Code Sec. 144, effective for tax. yrs. begin. after 12/31/70.
—P.L. 92-178, Sec. 301(c), added para. (4) to subsec. (a), effective for tax. yrs. begin. after 12/31/71.
In **1964**, P.L. 88-272, Sec. 112, substituted "with respect to the standard deduction for any taxable year" for "for any taxable year to take, or not to take, the standard deduction, or to pay, or not to pay, the tax under section 3" in subsec. (b) and added subsecs. (c) and (d), effective for tax. yrs. begin. after '63, except for purposes of Code Sec. 21.

"SEC. 145. REPEALED.
In **1977**, P.L. 95-30, Sec. 101(d)(1), repealed Code Sec. 145, effective for tax. yrs. begin. after '76.
Prior to amendment, Code Sec. 145 read as follows:
"SEC. 145. CROSS REFERENCE.
 "For disallowance of certain credits against the tax in the case of individuals electing the standard deduction, see section 36."

SUBPART A.—PRIVATE ACTIVITY BONDS

Sec.
141. Private activity bond; qualified bond.
142. Exempt facility bond.
143. Mortgage revenue bonds: qualified mortgage and qualified veterans' mortgage bond.
144. Qualified small issue bond; qualified student loan bond; qualified redevelopment bond.
145. Qualified 501(c)(3) bond.
146. Volume cap.
147. Other requirements applicable to certain private activity bonds.

In **1986**, P.L. 99-514, Sec. 1301(b), added Subpart A as part of the changes made to Part IV.

Sec. 141. Private activity bond; qualified bond.
(a) Private activity bond.
 For purposes of this title, the term "private activity bond" means any bond issued as part of an issue—
 (1) which meets—
  (A) the private business use test of paragraph (1) of subsection (b), and
  (B) the private security or payment test of paragraph (2) of subsection (b), or
 (2) which meets the private loan financing test of subsection (c).
(b) Private business tests.
 (1) Private business use test. Except as otherwise provided in this subsection, an issue meets the test of this paragraph if more than 10 percent of the proceeds of the issue are to be used for any private business use.
 (2) Private security or payment test. Except as otherwise provided in this subsection, an issue meets the test of this paragraph if the payment of the principal of, or the interest on, more than 10 percent of the proceeds of such issue is (under the terms of such issue or any underlying arrangement) directly or indirectly—
  (A) secured by any interest in—
   (i) property used or to be used for a private business use, or
   (ii) payments in respect of such property, or
  (B) to be derived from payments (whether or not to the issuer) in respect of property, or borrowed money, used or to be used for a private business use.
 (3) 5 percent test for private business use not related or disproportionate to government use financed by the issue.
  (A) In general. An issue shall be treated as meeting the tests of paragraphs (1) and (2) if such tests would be met if such paragraphs were applied—
   (i) by substituting "5 percent" for "10 percent" each place it appears, and
   (ii) by taking into account only—
    (I) the proceeds of the issue which are to be used for any private business use which is not related to any government use of such proceeds,
    (II) the disproportionate related business use proceeds of the issue, and
    (III) payments, property, and borrowed money with respect to any use of proceeds described in subclause (I) or (II).
  (B) Disproportionate related business use proceeds. For purposes of subparagraph (A), the disproportionate related business use proceeds of an issue is an amount equal to the aggregate of the excesses (determined under the following sentence) for each private business use of the proceeds of an issue which is related to a government use of such proceeds. The excess determined under this sentence is the excess of—
   (i) the proceeds of the issue which are to be used for the private business use, over
   (ii) the proceeds of the issue which are to be used for the government use to which such private business use relates.

Private activity bonds — Code Sec. 141(d)(3)(C)

(4) **Lower limitation for certain output facilities.** An issue 5 percent or more of the proceeds of which are to be used with respect to any output facility (other than a facility for the furnishing of water) shall be treated as meeting the tests of paragraphs (1) and (2) if the nonqualified amount with respect to such issue exceeds the excess of—
  (A) $15,000,000, over
  (B) the aggregate nonqualified amounts with respect to all prior tax-exempt issues 5 percent or more of the proceeds of which are or will be used with respect to such facility (or any other facility which is part of the same project).
There shall not be taken into account under subparagraph (B) any bond which is not outstanding at the time of the later issue or which is to be redeemed (other than in an advance refunding) from the net proceeds of the later issue.

(5) **Coordination with volume cap where nonqualified amount exceeds $15,000,000.** If the nonqualified amount with respect to an issue—
  (A) exceeds $15,000,000, but
  (B) does not exceed the amount which would cause a bond which is part of such issue to be treated as a private activity bond without regard to this paragraph,
such bond shall nonetheless be treated as a private activity bond unless the issuer allocates a portion of its volume cap under section 146 to such issue in an amount equal to the excess of such nonqualified amount over $15,000,000.

(6) **Private business use defined.**
  (A) In general. For purposes of this subsection, the term "private business use" means use (directly or indirectly) in a trade or business carried on by any person other than a governmental unit. For purposes of the preceding sentence, use as a member of the general public shall not be taken into account.
  (B) Clarification of trade or business. For purposes of the 1st sentence of subparagraph (A), any activity carried on by a person other than a natural person shall be treated as a trade or business.

(7) **Government use.** The term "government use" means any use other than a private business use.

(8) **Nonqualified amount.** For purposes of this subsection, the term "nonqualified amount" means, with respect to an issue, the lesser of—
  (A) the proceeds of such issue which are to be used for any private business use, or
  (B) the proceeds of such issue with respect to which there are payments (or property or borrowed money) described in paragraph (2).

(9) **Exception for qualified 501(c)(3) bonds.** There shall not be taken into account under this subsection or subsection (c) the portion of the proceeds of an issue which (if issued as a separate issue) would be treated as a qualified 501(c)(3) bond if the issuer elects to treat such portion as a qualified 501(c)(3) bond.

(c) **Private loan financing test.**
(1) **In general.** An issue meets the test of this subsection if the amount of the proceeds of the issue which is to be used (directly or indirectly) to make or finance loans (other than loans described in paragraph (2)) to persons other than governmental units exceeds the lesser of—
  (A) 5 percent of such proceeds, or
  (B) $5,000,000.

(2) **Exception for tax assessment, etc., loans.** For purposes of paragraph (1), a loan is described in this paragraph if such loan—
  (A) enables the borrower to finance any governmental tax or assessment of general application for a specific essential governmental function,
  (B) is a nonpurpose investment (within the meaning of section 148(f)(6)(A)), or
  (C) is a qualified natural gas supply contract (as defined in section 148(b)(4)).

(d) **Certain issues used to acquire nongovernmental output property treated as private activity bonds.**
(1) **In general.** For purposes of this title, the term "private activity bond" includes any bond issued as part of an issue if the amount of the proceeds of the issue which are to be used (directly or indirectly) for the acquisition by a governmental unit of nongovernmental output property exceeds the lesser of—
  (A) 5 percent of such proceeds, or
  (B) $5,000,000.

(2) **Nongovernmental output property.** Except as otherwise provided in this subsection, for purposes of paragraph (1), the term "nongovernmental output property" means any property (or interest therein) which before such acquisition was used (or held for use) by a person other than a governmental unit in connection with an output facility (within the meaning of subsection (b)(4)) (other than a facility for the furnishing of water). For purposes of the preceding sentence, use (or the holding for use) before October 14, 1987, shall not be taken into account.

(3) **Exception for property acquired to provide output to certain areas.** For purposes of paragraph (1)—
  (A) In general. The term "nongovernmental output property" shall not include any property which is to be used in connection with an output facility 95 percent or more of the output of which will be consumed in—
    (i) a qualified service area of the governmental unit acquiring the property, or
    (ii) a qualified annexed area of such unit.
  (B) Definitions. For purposes of subparagraph (A)—
    (i) Qualified service area. The term "qualified service area" means, with respect to the governmental unit acquiring the property, any area throughout which such unit provided (at all times during the 10-year period ending on the date such property is acquired by such unit) output of the same type as the output to be provided by such property. For purposes of the preceding sentence, the period before October 14, 1987, shall not be taken into account.
    (ii) Qualified annexed area. The term "qualified annexed area" means, with respect to the governmental unit acquiring the property, any area if—
      (I) such area is contiguous to, and annexed for general governmental purposes into, a qualified service area of such unit,
      (II) output from such property is made available to all members of the general public in the annexed area, and
      (III) the annexed area is not greater than 10 percent of such qualified service area.
  (C) Limitation on size of annexed area not to apply where output capacity does not increase by more than 10 percent. Subclause (III) of subparagraph (B)(ii) shall not apply to an annexation of an area by a governmental unit if the output capacity of the property acquired in connection with the annexation, when added to the output capacity of all other property which is not treated as nongovernmental output property by reason of subparagraph (A)(ii) with respect to such annexed area, does not exceed 10 percent of the output capacity

of the property providing output of the same type to the qualified service area into which it is annexed.

(D) Rules for determining relative size, etc. For purposes of subparagraphs (B)(ii) and (C)—

(i) The size of any qualified service area and the output capacity of property serving such area shall be determined as the close of the calendar year preceding the calendar year in which the acquisition of nongovernmental output property or the annexation occurs.

(ii) A qualified annexed area shall be treated as part of the qualified service area into which it is annexed for purposes of determining whether any other area annexed in a later year is a qualified annexed area.

(4) Exception for property converted to nonoutput use. For purposes of paragraph (1)—

(A) In general. The term "nongovernmental output property" shall not include any property which is to be converted to a use not in connection with an output facility.

(B) Exception. Subparagraph (A) shall not apply to any property which is part of the output function of a nuclear power facility.

(5) Special rules. In the case of a bond which is a private activity bond solely by reason of this subsection—

(A) subsections (c) and (d) of section 147 (relating to limitations on acquisition of land and existing property) shall not apply, and

(B) paragraph (8) of section 142(a) shall be applied as if it did not contain "local".

(6) Treatment of joint action agencies. With respect to nongovernmental output property acquired by a joint action agency the members of which are governmental units, this subsection shall be applied at the member level by treating each member as acquiring its proportionate share of such property.

(7) Exception for qualified electric and natural gas supply contracts. The term "nongovernmental output property" shall not include any contract for the prepayment of electricity or natural gas which is not investment property under section 148(b)(2).

(e) Qualified bond.

For purposes of this part, the term "qualified bond" means any private activity bond if—

(1) **In general.** Such bond is—

(A) an exempt facility bond,

(B) a qualified mortgage bond,

(C) a qualified veterans' mortgage bond,

(D) a qualified small issue bond,

(E) a qualified student loan bond,

(F) a qualified redevelopment bond, or

(G) a qualified 501(c)(3) bond.

(2) **Volume cap.** Such bond is issued as part of an issue which meets the applicable requirements of section 146, and

(3) **Other requirements.** Such bond meets the applicable requirements of each subsection of section 147.

In **2005**, P.L. 109-58, Sec. 1327(a), deleted "or" at the end of subpara. (c)(2)(A), substituted ", or " for the period at the end of subpara. (c)(2)(B), and added subpara. (c)(2)(C) ... Sec. 1327(c), added para. (d)(7), effective for obligations issued after 8/8/2005.

In **1988**, P.L. 100-647, Sec. 1013(a)(38), substituted "which would cause a bond" for "which would cause bond" in subpara. (b)(5)(B), effective for bonds issued after 8/15/86.

—P.L. 100-647, Sec. 6179, provides:

"Before January 1, 1989, the Secretary of the Treasury or his delegate shall issue guidance concerning the application of the private security or payment test under section 141(b)(2) of the Internal Revenue Code of 1986 to tax-exempt bond financing by State and local governments of hazardous waste clean-up activities conducted by such governments where some of the activities occur on privately owned land."

In **1987**, P.L. 100-203, Sec. 10631(a), redesignated subsec. (d) as subsec. (e) and added new subsec. (d), effective for bonds issued after 10/31/87 (other than bonds issued to refund bonds issued on or before 10/13/87) Sec. 10631(c)(2) and (c)(3) of the Act also provides:

"(2) Binding agreements. The amendments made by this section shall not apply to bonds (other than advance refunding bonds) with respect to a facility acquired after October 13, 1987, pursuant to a binding contract entered into on or before such date.

"(3) Transitional rule. The amendments made by this section shall not apply to bonds issued—

"(A) after October 13, 1987, by an authority created by a statute—

"(i) approved by the State Governor on July 24, 1986, and

"(ii) sections 1 through 10 of which became effective on January 15, 1987, and

"(B) to provide facilities serving the area specified in such statute on the date of its enactment."

In **1986**, P.L. 99-514, Sec. 1301(b), added Code Sec. 141 as part of the amendments to Part IV of subchapter B of chapter 1, effective for bonds issued after 8/15/86. Secs. 1301(d), 1301(e) and 1301(i) of this Act provide:

"(d) State and local government series modifications.—

"Notwithstanding any other provision of law or any regulations promulgated thereunder (including the provisions of 31 CFR part 344) the Secretary of the Treasury shall extend by January 1, 1987, the State and Local Government Series program to provide—

"(1) instruments allowing flexible investment of bond proceeds in a manner eliminating the earning of rebatable arbitrage,

"(2) demand deposits under such program by eliminating advance notice and minimum maturity requirements related to the purchase of bonds,

"(3) operation of such program at no net cost to the Federal Government, and

"(4) deposits for a stated maturity under reasonable advance notice requirements.

"(e) Management contracts.—

"The Secretary of the Treasury or his delegate shall modify the Secretary's advance ruling guidelines relating to when use of property pursuant to a management contract is not considered a trade or business use by a private person for purposes of section 141(c) of the Internal Revenue Code of 1986 to provide that use pursuant to a management contract generally shall not be treated as trade or business use as long as—

"(1) the term of such contract (including renewal options) does not exceed 5 years,

"(2) the exempt owner has the option to cancel such contract at the end of any 3-year period,

"(3) the manager under the contract is not compensated (in whole or in part) on the basis of a share of net profits, and

"(4) at least 50 percent of the annual compensation of the manager under such contract is based on a periodic fixed fee."

"(i) Amendment to output regulations.—

"The Secretary of the Treasury or his delegate shall amend the provision in the Federal income tax regulations relating to when use pursuant to certain output contracts is considered to satisfy the private business tests of paragraphs (1) and (2) of section 141(b) of the Internal Revenue Code of 1986 to eliminate the requirement of a 3 percent guaranteed minimum payment."

For transitional rules, see Secs. 1312—1318 of this Act reproduced in the note following Code Sec. 103.

Sec. 142. Exempt facility bond.

(a) General rule.

For purposes of this part, the term "exempt facility bond" means any bond issued as part of an issue 95 percent or more of the net proceeds of which are to be used to provide—

(1) airports,

(2) docks and wharves,

(3) mass commuting facilities,

(4) facilities for the furnishing of water,

(5) sewage facilities,

(6) solid waste disposal facilities,

(7) qualified residential rental projects,

(8) facilities for the local furnishing of electric energy or gas,

(9) local district heating or cooling facilities,

(10) qualified hazardous waste facilities,

• **Caution:** Code Sec. 142(a)(11)-(13), following, were amended by P.L. 107-16, EGTRRA. These provisions generally sunset for tax years beginning after 12/31/2012. For specific sunset provisions, see Sec. 901, P.L. 107-16 (as amended) reproduced in history notes for this Code Sec.

(11) high-speed intercity rail facilities,
(12) environmental enhancements of hydro-electric generating facilities,
(13) qualified public educational facilities,
(14) qualified green building and sustainable design projects, or
(15) qualified highway or surface freight transfer facilities.

(b) Special exempt facility bond rules.
For purposes of subsection (a)—
(1) Certain facilities must be governmentally owned.
(A) In general. A facility shall be treated as described in paragraph (1), (2), (3), or (12) of subsection (a) only if all of the property to be financed by the net proceeds of the issue is to be owned by a governmental unit.
(B) Safe harbor for leases and management contracts. For purposes of subparagraph (A), property leased by a governmental unit shall be treated as owned by such governmental unit if—
(i) the lessee makes an irrevocable election (binding on the lessee and all successors in interest under the lease) not to claim depreciation or an investment credit with respect to such property,
(ii) the lease term (as defined in section 168(i)(3)) is not more than 80 percent of the reasonably expected economic life of the property (as determined under section 147(b)), and
(iii) the lessee has no option to purchase the property other than at fair market value (as of the time such option is exercised).
Rules similar to the rules of the preceding sentence shall apply to management contracts and similar types of operating agreements.
(2) Limitation on office space. An office shall not be treated as described in a paragraph of subsection (a) unless—
(A) the office is located on the premises of a facility described in such a paragraph, and
(B) not more than a de minimis amount of the functions to be performed at such office is not directly related to the day-to-day operations at such facility.

(c) Airports, docks and wharves, mass commuting facilities and high-speed intercity rail facilities.
For purposes of subsection (a)—
(1) Storage and training facilities. Storage or training facilities directly related to a facility described in paragraph (1), (2), (3), or (11) of subsection (a) shall be treated as described in the paragraph in which such facility is described.
(2) Exception for certain private facilities. Property shall not be treated as described in paragraph (1), (2), (3), or (11) of subsection (a) if such property is described in any of the following subparagraphs and is to be used for any private business use (as defined in section 141(b)(6)).
(A) Any lodging facility.
(B) Any retail facility (including food and beverage facilities) in excess of a size necessary to serve passengers and employees at the exempt facility.
(C) Any retail facility (other than parking) for passengers or the general public located outside the exempt facility terminal.

(D) Any office building for individuals who are not employees of a governmental unit or of the operating authority for the exempt facility.
(E) Any industrial park or manufacturing facility.

(d) Qualified residential rental project.
For purposes of this section—
(1) In general. The term "qualified residential rental project" means any project for residential rental property if, at all times during the qualified project period, such project meets the requirements of subparagraph (A) or (B), whichever is elected by the issuer at the time of the issuance of the issue with respect to such project:
(A) 20-50 test. The project meets the requirements of this subparagraph if 20 percent or more of the residential units in such project are occupied by individuals whose income is 50 percent or less of area median gross income.
(B) 40-60 test. The project meets the requirements of this subparagraph if 40 percent or more of the residential units in such project are occupied by individuals whose income is 60 percent or less of area median gross income.
For purposes of this paragraph, any property shall not be treated as failing to be residential rental property merely because part of the building in which such property is located is used for purposes other than residential rental purposes.
(2) Definitions and special rules. For purposes of this subsection—
(A) Qualified project period. The term "qualified project period" means the period beginning on the 1st day on which 10 percent of the residential units in the project are occupied and ending on the latest of—
(i) the date which is 15 years after the date on which 50 percent of the residential units in the project are occupied,
(ii) the 1st day on which no tax-exempt private activity bond issued with respect to the project is outstanding, or
(iii) the date on which any assistance provided with respect to the project under section 8 of the United States Housing Act of 1937 terminates.
(B) Income of individuals; area median gross income.
(i) In general. The income of individuals and area median gross income shall be determined by the Secretary in a manner consistent with determinations of lower income families and area median gross income under section 8 of the United States Housing Act of 1937 (or, if such program is terminated, under such program as in effect immediately before such termination). Determinations under the preceding sentence shall include adjustments for family size. Subsections (g) and (h) of section 7872 shall not apply in determining the income of individuals under this subparagraph.
(ii) Special rule relating to basic housing allowances. For purposes of determining income under this subparagraph, payments under section 403 of title 37, United States Code, as a basic pay allowance for housing shall be disregarded with respect to any qualified building.
(iii) Qualified building. For purposes of clause (ii), the term "qualified building" means any building located—
(I) in any county in which is located a qualified military installation to which the number of members of the Armed Forces of the United States as-

signed to units based out of such qualified military installation, as of June 1, 2008, has increased by not less than 20 percent, as compared to such number on December 31, 2005, or

(II) in any county adjacent to a county described in subclause (I).

(iv) Qualified military installation. For purposes of clause (iii), the term "qualified military installation" means any military installation or facility the number of members of the Armed Forces of the United States assigned to which, as of June 1, 2008, is not less than 1,000.

(C) Students. Rules similar to the rules of 42(i)(3)(D) shall apply for purposes of this subsection.

(D) Single-room occupancy units. A unit shall not fail to be treated as a residential unit merely because such unit is a single-room occupancy unit (within the meaning of section 42).

(E) Hold harmless for reductions in area median gross income.

(i) In general. Any determination of area median gross income under subparagraph (B) with respect to any project for any calendar year after 2008 shall not be less than the area median gross income determined under such subparagraph with respect to such project for the calendar year preceding the calendar year for which such determination is made.

(ii) Special rule for certain census changes. In the case of a HUD hold harmless impacted project, the area median gross income with respect to such project for any calendar year after 2008 (hereafter in this clause referred to as the current calendar year) shall be the greater of the amount determined without regard to this clause or the sum of—

(I) the area median gross income determined under the HUD hold harmless policy with respect to such project for calendar year 2008, plus

(II) any increase in the area median gross income determined under subparagraph (B) (determined without regard to the HUD hold harmless policy and this subparagraph) with respect to such project for the current calendar year over the area median gross income (as so determined) with respect to such project for calendar year 2008.

(iii) HUD hold harmless policy. The term "HUD hold harmless policy" means the regulations under which a policy similar to the rules of clause (i) applied to prevent a change in the method of determining area median gross income from resulting in a reduction in the area median gross income determined with respect to certain projects in calendar years 2007 and 2008.

(iv) HUD hold harmless impacted project. The term "HUD hold harmless impacted project" means any project with respect to which area median gross income was determined under subparagraph (B) for calendar year 2007 or 2008 if such determination would have been less but for the HUD hold harmless policy.

(3) **Current income determinations.** For purposes of this subsection—

(A) In general. The determination of whether the income of a resident of a unit in a project exceeds the applicable income limit shall be made at least annually on the basis of the current income of the resident. The preceding sentence shall not apply with respect to any project for any year if during such year no residential unit in the project is occupied by a new resident whose income exceeds the applicable income limit.

(B) Continuing resident's income may increase above the applicable limit. If the income of a resident of a unit in a project did not exceed the applicable income limit upon commencement of such resident's occupancy of such unit (or as of any prior determination under subparagraph (A)), the income of such resident shall be treated as continuing to not exceed the applicable income limit. The preceding sentence shall cease to apply to any resident whose income as of the most recent determination under subparagraph (A) exceeds 140 percent of the applicable income limit if after such determination, but before the next determination, any residential unit of comparable or smaller size in the same project is occupied by a new resident whose income exceeds the applicable income limit.

(C) Exception for projects with respect to which affordable housing credit is allowed. In the case of a project with respect to which credit is allowed under section 42, the second sentence of subparagraph (B) shall be applied by substituting "building (within the meaning of section 42)" for "project".

(4) **Special rule in case of deep rent skewing.**

(A) In general. In the case of any project described in subparagraph (B), the 2d sentence of subparagraph (B) of paragraph (3) shall be applied by substituting—

(i) "170 percent" for "140 percent", and

(ii) "any low-income unit in the same project is occupied by a new resident whose income exceeds 40 percent of area median gross income" for "any residential unit of comparable or smaller size in the same project is occupied by a new resident whose income exceeds the applicable income limit".

(B) Deep rent skewed project. A project is described in this subparagraph if the owner of the project elects to have this paragraph apply and, at all times during the qualified project period, such project meets the requirements of clauses (i), (ii), and (iii):

(i) The project meets the requirements of this clause if 15 percent or more of the low-income units in the project are occupied by individuals whose income is 40 percent or less of area median gross income.

(ii) The project meets the requirements of this clause if the gross rent with respect to each low-income unit in the project does not exceed 30 percent of the applicable income limit which applies to individuals occupying the unit.

(iii) The project meets the requirements of this clause if the gross rent with respect to each low-income unit in the project does not exceed ½ of the average gross rent with respect to units of comparable size which are not occupied by individuals who meet the applicable income limit.

(C) Definitions applicable to subparagraph (B). For purposes of subparagraph (B)—

(i) Low-income unit. The term "low-income unit" means any unit which is required to be occupied by individuals who meet the applicable income limit.

(ii) Gross rent. The term "gross rent" includes—

(I) any payment under section 8 of the United States Housing Act of 1937, and

(II) any utility allowance determined by the Secretary after taking into account such determinations under such section 8.

(5) **Applicable income limit.** For purposes of paragraphs (3) and (4), the term "applicable income limit" means—

(A) the limitation under subparagraph (A) or (B) of paragraph (1) which applies to the project, or

(B) in the case of a unit to which paragraph (4)(B)(i) applies, the limitation which applies to such unit.

(6) Special rule for certain high cost housing area. In the case of a project located in a city having 5 boroughs and a population in excess of 5,000,000, subparagraph (B) of paragraph (1) shall be applied by substituting "25 percent" for "40 percent".

(7) Certification to secretary. The operator of any project with respect to which an election was made under this subsection shall submit to the Secretary (at such time and in such manner as the Secretary shall prescribe) an annual certification as to whether such project continues to meet the requirements of this subsection. Any failure to comply with the provisions of the preceding sentence shall not affect the tax-exempt status of any bond but shall subject the operator to penalty, as provided in section 6652(j).

(e) Facilities for the furnishing of water.

For purposes of subsection (a)(4), the term "facilities for the furnishing of water" means any facility for the furnishing of water if—

(1) the water is or will be made available to members of the general public (including electric utility, industrial, agricultural, or commercial users), and

(2) either the facility is operated by a governmental unit or the rates for the furnishing or sale of the water have been established or approved by a State or political subdivision thereof, by an agency or instrumentality of the United States, or by a public service or public utility commission or other similar body of any State or political subdivision thereof.

(f) Local furnishing of electric energy or gas.

For purposes of subsection (a)(8)—

(1) In general. The local furnishing of electric energy or gas from a facility shall only include furnishing solely within the area consisting of—

(A) a city and 1 contiguous county, or

(B) 2 contiguous counties.

(2) Treatment of certain electric energy transmitted outside local area.

(A) In general. A facility shall not be treated as failing to meet the local furnishing requirement of subsection (a)(8) by reason of electricity transmitted pursuant to an order of the Federal Energy Regulatory Commission under section 211 or 213 of the Federal Power Act (as in effect on the date of the enactment of this paragraph) if the portion of the cost of the facility financed with tax-exempt bonds is not greater than the portion of the cost of the facility which is allocable to the local furnishing of electric energy (determined without regard to this paragraph).

(B) Special rule for existing facilities. In the case of a facility financed with bonds issued before the date of an order referred to in subparagraph (A) which would (but for this subparagraph) cease to be tax-exempt by reason of subparagraph (A), such bonds shall not cease to be tax-exempt bonds (and section 150(b)(4) shall not apply) if, to the extent necessary to comply with subparagraph (A)—

(i) an escrow to pay principal of, premium (if any), and interest on the bonds is established within a reasonable period after the date such order becomes final, and

(ii) bonds are redeemed not later than the earliest date on which such bonds may be redeemed.

(3) Termination of future financing. For purposes of this section, no bond may be issued as part of an issue described in subsection (a)(8) with respect to a facility for the local furnishing of electric energy or gas on or after the date of the enactment of this paragraph unless—

(A) the facility will—

(i) be used by a person who is engaged in the local furnishing of that energy source on January 1, 1997, and

(ii) be used to provide service within the area served by such person on January 1, 1997 (or within a county or city any portion of which is within such area), or

(B) the facility will be used by a successor in interest to such person for the same use and within the same service area as described in subparagraph (A).

(4) Election to terminate tax-exempt bond financing by certain furnishers.

(A) In general. In the case of a facility financed with bonds issued before the date of the enactment of this paragraph which would cease to be tax-exempt by reason of the failure to meet the local furnishing requirement of subsection (a)(8) as a result of a service area expansion, such bonds shall not cease to be tax-exempt bonds (and section 150(b)(4) shall not apply) if the person engaged in such local furnishing by such facility makes an election described in subparagraph (B).

(B) Election. An election is described in this subparagraph if it is an election made in such manner as the Secretary prescribes, and such person (or its predecessor in interest) agrees that—

(i) such election is made with respect to all facilities for the local furnishing of electric energy or gas, or both, by such person.

(ii) no bond exempt from tax under section 103 and described in subsection (a)(8) may be issued on or after the date of the enactment of this paragraph with respect to all such facilities of such person,

(iii) any expansion of the service area—

(I) is not financed with the proceeds of any exempt facility bond described in subsection (a)(8) and

(II) is not treated as a nonqualifying use under the rules of paragraph (2), and

(iv) all outstanding bonds used to finance the facilities for such person are redeemed not later than 6 months after the later of—

(I) the earliest date on which such bonds may be redeemed, or

(II) the date of the election.

(C) Related persons. For purposes of this paragraph, the term "person" includes a group of related persons (within the meaning of section 144(a)(3)) which includes such person.

(g) Local district heating or cooling facility.

(1) In general. For purposes of subsection (a)(9), the term "local district heating or cooling facility" means property used as an integral part of a local district heating or cooling system.

(2) Local district heating or cooling system.

(A) In general. For purposes of paragraph (1), the term "local district heating or cooling system" means any local system consisting of a pipeline or network (which may be connected to a heating or cooling source) providing hot water, chilled water, or steam to 2 or more users for—

(i) residential, commercial, or industrial heating or cooling, or

(ii) process steam.

(B) **Local system.** For purposes of this paragraph, a local system includes facilities furnishing heating and cooling to an area consisting of a city and 1 contiguous county.

(h) Qualified hazardous waste facilities.

For purposes of subsection (a)(10), the term "qualified hazardous waste facility" means any facility for the disposal of hazardous waste by incineration or entombment but only if—

(1) the facility is subject to final permit requirements under subtitle C of title II of the Solid Waste Disposal Act (as in effect on the date of the enactment of the Tax Reform Act of 1986), and

(2) the portion of such facility which is to be provided by the issue does not exceed the portion of the facility which is to be used by persons other than—

(A) the owner or operator of such facility, and

(B) any related person (within the meaning of section 144(a)(3)) to such owner or operator.

(i) High-speed intercity rail facilities.

(1) In general. For purposes of subsection (a)(11), the term "high-speed intercity rail facilities" means any facility (not including rolling stock) for the fixed guideway rail transportation of passengers and their baggage between metropolitan statistical areas (within the meaning of section 143(k)(2)(B)) using vehicles that are reasonably expected to be capable of attaining a maximum speed in excess of 150 miles per hour between scheduled stops, but only if such facility will be made available to members of the general public as passengers.

(2) Election by nongovernmental owners. A facility shall be treated as described in subsection (a)(11) only if any owner of such facility which is not a governmental unit irrevocably elects not to claim—

(A) any deduction under section 167 or 168, and

(B) any credit under this subtitle,

with respect to the property to be financed by the net proceeds of the issue.

(3) Use of proceeds. A bond issued as part of an issue described in subsection (a)(11) shall not be considered an exempt facility bond unless any proceeds not used within a 3-year period of the date of the issuance of such bond are used (not later than 6 months after the close of such period) to redeem bonds which are part of such issue.

(j) Environmental enhancements of hydro-electric generating facilities.

(1) In general. For purposes of subsection (a)(12), the term "environmental enhancements of hydroelectric generating facilities" means property—

(A) the use of which is related to a federally licensed hydroelectric generating facility owned and operated by a governmental unit, and

(B) which—

(i) protects or promotes fisheries or other wildlife resources, including any fish by-pass facility, fish hatchery, or fisheries enhancement facility, or

(ii) is a recreational facility or other improvement required by the terms and conditions of any Federal licensing permit for the operation of such generating facility.

(2) Use of proceeds. A bond issued as part of an issue described in subsection (a)(12) shall not be considered an exempt facility bond unless at least 80 percent of the net proceeds of the issue of which it is a part are used to finance property described in paragraph (1)(B)(i).

> • **Caution:** Code Sec. 142(k), following, was added by P.L. 107-16, EGTRRA. These provisions generally sunset for tax years beginning after 12/31/2012. For specific sunset provisions, see Sec. 901, P.L. 107-16 (as amended) reproduced in history notes for this Code Sec.

(k) Qualified public educational facilities.

(1) In general. For purposes of subsection (a)(13), the term "qualified public educational facility" means any school facility which is—

(A) part of a public elementary school or a public secondary school, and

(B) owned by a private, for-profit corporation pursuant to a public-private partnership agreement with a State or local educational agency described in paragraph (2).

(2) Public-private partnership agreement described. A public-private partnership agreement is described in this paragraph if it is an agreement—

(A) under which the corporation agrees—

(i) to do 1 or more of the following: construct, rehabilitate, refurbish, or equip a school facility, and

(ii) at the end of the term of the agreement, to transfer the school facility to such agency for no additional consideration, and

(B) the term of which does not exceed the term of the issue to be used to provide the school facility.

(3) School facility. For purposes of this subsection, the term "school facility" means—

(A) any school building,

(B) any functionally related and subordinate facility and land with respect to such building, including any stadium or other facility primarily used for school events, and

(C) any property, to which section 168 applies (or would apply but for section 179), for use in a facility described in subparagraph (A) or (B).

(4) Public schools. For purposes of this subsection, the terms "elementary school" and "secondary school" have the meanings given such terms by section 14101 of the Elementary and Secondary Education Act of 1965 (20 U.S.C. 8801), as in effect on the date of the enactment of this subsection.

(5) Annual aggregate face amount of tax-exempt financing.

(A) In general. An issue shall not be treated as an issue described in subsection (a)(13) if the aggregate face amount of bonds issued by the State pursuant thereto (when added to the aggregate face amount of bonds previously so issued during the calendar year) exceeds an amount equal to the greater of—

(i) $10 multiplied by the State population, or

(ii) $5,000,000.

(B) Allocation rules.

(i) In general. Except as otherwise provided in this subparagraph, the State may allocate the amount described in subparagraph (A) for any calendar year in such manner as the State determines appropriate.

(ii) Rules for carryforward of unused limitation. A State may elect to carry forward an unused limitation for any calendar year for 3 calendar years following the calendar year in which the unused limitation arose under rules similar to the rules of section

146(f), except that the only purpose for which the carryforward may be elected is the issuance of exempt facility bonds described in subsection (a)(13).

(l) Qualified green building and sustainable design projects.

(1) In general. For purposes of subsection (a)(14), the term "qualified green building and sustainable design project" means any project which is designated by the Secretary, after consultation with the Administrator of the Environmental Protection Agency, as a qualified green building and sustainable design project and which meets the requirements of clauses (i), (ii), (iii), and (iv) of paragraph (4)(A).

(2) Designations.

(A) In general. Within 60 days after the end of the application period described in paragraph (3)(A), the Secretary, after consultation with the Administrator of the Environmental Protection Agency, shall designate qualified green building and sustainable design projects. At least one of the projects designated shall be located in, or within a 10-mile radius of, an empowerment zone as designated pursuant to section 1391, and at least one of the projects designated shall be located in a rural State. No more than one project shall be designated in a State. A project shall not be designated if such project includes a stadium or arena for professional sports exhibitions or games.

(B) Minimum conservation and technology innovation objectives. The Secretary, after consultation with the Administrator of the Environmental Protection Agency, shall ensure that, in the aggregate, the projects designated shall—

(i) reduce electric consumption by more than 150 megawatts annually as compared to conventional generation,

(ii) reduce daily sulfur dioxide emissions by at least 10 tons compared to coal generation power,

(iii) expand by 75 percent the domestic solar photovoltaic market in the United States (measured in megawatts) as compared to the expansion of that market from 2001 to 2002, and

(iv) use at least 25 megawatts of fuel cell energy generation.

(3) Limited designations. A project may not be designated under this subsection unless—

(A) the project is nominated by a State or local government within 180 days of the enactment of this subsection, and

(B) such State or local government provides written assurances that the project will satisfy the eligibility criteria described in paragraph (4).

(4) Application.

(A) In general. A project may not be designated under this subsection unless the application for such designation includes a project proposal which describes the energy efficiency, renewable energy, and sustainable design features of the project and demonstrates that the project satisfies the following eligibility criteria:

(i) Green building and sustainable design. At least 75 percent of the square footage of commercial buildings which are part of the project is registered for United States Green Building Council's LEED certification and is reasonably expected (at the time of the designation) to receive such certification. For purposes of determining LEED certification as required under this clause, points shall be credited by using the following:

(I) For wood products, certification under the Sustainable Forestry Initiative Program and the American Tree Farm System.

(II) For renewable wood products, as credited for recycled content otherwise provided under LEED certification.

(III) For composite wood products, certification under standards established by the American National Standards Institute, or such other voluntary standards as published in the Federal Register by the Administrator of the Environmental Protection Agency.

(ii) Brownfield redevelopment. The project includes a brownfield site as defined by section 101(39) of the Comprehensive Environmental Response, Compensation, and Liability Act of 1980 (42 U.S.C. 9601), including a site described in subparagraph (D)(ii)(II)(aa) thereof.

(iii) State and local support. The project receives specific State or local government resources which will support the project in an amount equal to at least $5,000,000. For purposes of the preceding sentence, the term "resources" includes tax abatement benefits and contributions in kind.

(iv) Size. The project includes at least one of the following:

(I) At least 1,000,000 square feet of building.

(II) At least 20 acres.

(v) Use of tax benefit. The project proposal includes a description of the net benefit of the tax-exempt financing provided under this subsection which will be allocated for financing of one or more of the following:

(I) The purchase, construction, integration, or other use of energy efficiency, renewable energy, and sustainable design features of the project.

(II) Compliance with certification standards cited under clause (i).

(III) The purchase, remediation, and foundation construction and preparation of the brownfields site.

(vi) Prohibited facilities. An issue shall not be treated as an issue described in subsection (a)(14) if any proceeds of such issue are used to provide any facility the principal business of which is the sale of food or alcoholic beverages for consumption on the premises.

(vii) Employment. The project is projected to provide permanent employment of at least 1,500 full time equivalents (150 full time equivalents in rural States) when completed and construction employment of at least 1,000 full time equivalents (100 full time equivalents in rural States).

The application shall include an independent analysis which describes the project's economic impact, including the amount of projected employment.

(B) Project description. Each application described in subparagraph (A) shall contain for each project a description of—

(i) the amount of electric consumption reduced as compared to conventional construction,

(ii) the amount of sulfur dioxide daily emissions reduced compared to coal generation,

(iii) the amount of the gross installed capacity of the project's solar photovoltaic capacity measured in megawatts, and

(iv) the amount, in megawatts, of the project's fuel cell energy generation.

(5) Certification of use of tax benefit. No later than 30 days after the completion of the project, each project must certify to the Secretary that the net benefit of the tax-exempt financing was used for the purposes described in paragraph (4).

(6) Definitions. For purposes of this subsection—

(A) Rural State. The term "rural State" means any State which has—

(i) a population of less than 4,500,000 according to the 2000 census,

(ii) a population density of less than 150 people per square mile according to the 2000 census, and

(iii) increased in population by less than half the rate of the national increase between the 1990 and 2000 censuses.

(B) Local government. The term "local government" has the meaning given such term by section 1393(a)(5).

(C) Net benefit of tax-exempt financing. The term "net benefit of tax-exempt financing" means the present value of the interest savings (determined by a calculation established by the Secretary) which result from the tax-exempt status of the bonds.

(7) Aggregate face amount of tax-exempt financing.

(A) In general. An issue shall not be treated as an issue described in subsection (a)(14) if the aggregate face amount of bonds issued by the State or local government pursuant thereto for a project (when added to the aggregate face amount of bonds previously so issued for such project) exceeds an amount designated by the Secretary as part of the designation.

(B) Limitation on amount of bonds. The Secretary may not allocate authority to issue qualified green building and sustainable design project bonds in an aggregate face amount exceeding $2,000,000,000.

(8) Termination. Subsection (a)(14) shall not apply with respect to any bond issued after September 30, 2012.

(9) Treatment of current refunding bonds. Paragraphs (7)(B) and (8) shall not apply to any bond (or series of bonds) issued to refund a bond issued under subsection (a)(14) before October 1, 2012, if—

(A) the average maturity date of the issue of which the refunding bond is a part is not later than the average maturity date of the bonds to be refunded by such issue,

(B) the amount of the refunding bond does not exceed the outstanding amount of the refunded bond, and

(C) the net proceeds of the refunding bond are used to redeem the refunded bond not later than 90 days after the date of the issuance of the refunding bond.

For purposes of subparagraph (A), average maturity shall be determined in accordance with section 147(b)(2)(A).

(m) Qualified highway or surface freight transfer facilities.

(1) In general. For purposes of subsection (a)(15), the term "qualified highway or surface freight transfer facilities" means—

(A) any surface transportation project which receives Federal assistance under title 23, United States Code (as in effect on the date of the enactment of this subsection),

(B) any project for an international bridge or tunnel for which an international entity authorized under Federal or State law is responsible and which receives Federal assistance under title 23, United States Code (as so in effect), or

(C) any facility for the transfer of freight from truck to rail or rail to truck (including any temporary storage facilities directly related to such transfers) which receives Federal assistance under either title 23 or title 49, United States Code (as so in effect).

(2) National limitation on amount of tax-exempt financing for facilities.

(A) National limitation. The aggregate amount allocated by the Secretary of Transportation under subparagraph (C) shall not exceed $15,000,000,000.

(B) Enforcement of national limitation. An issue shall not be treated as an issue described in subsection (a)(15) if the aggregate face amount of bonds issued pursuant to such issue for any qualified highway or surface freight transfer facility (when added to the aggregate face amount of bonds previously so issued for such facility) exceeds the amount allocated to such facility under subparagraph (C).

(C) Allocation by Secretary of Transportation. The Secretary of Transportation shall allocate the amount described in subparagraph (A) among qualified highway or surface freight transfer facilities in such manner as the Secretary determines appropriate.

(3) Expenditure of proceeds. An issue shall not be treated as an issue described in subsection (a)(15) unless at least 95 percent of the net proceeds of the issue is expended for qualified highway or surface freight transfer facilities within the 5-year period beginning on the date of issuance. If at least 95 percent of such net proceeds is not expended within such 5-year period, an issue shall be treated as continuing to meet the requirements of this paragraph if the issuer uses all unspent proceeds of the issue to redeem bonds of the issue within 90 days after the end of such 5-year period. The Secretary, at the request of the issuer, may extend such 5-year period if the issuer establishes that any failure to meet such period is due to circumstances beyond the control of the issuer.

(4) Exception for current refunding bonds. Paragraph (2) shall not apply to any bond (or series of bonds) issued to refund a bond issued under subsection (a)(15) if—

(A) the average maturity date of the issue of which the refunding bond is a part is not later than the average maturity date of the bonds to be refunded by such issue,

(B) the amount of the refunding bond does not exceed the outstanding amount of the refunded bond, and

(C) the refunded bond is redeemed not later than 90 days after the date of the issuance of the refunding bond.

For purposes of subparagraph (A), average maturity shall be determined in accordance with section 147(b)(2)(A).

In 2010, P.L. 111-312, Sec. 101(a)(1), substituted "December 31, 2012" for "December 31, 2010" both places it appeared in Sec. 901, P.L. 107-16 [see below], effective as if included in the enactment of P.L. 107-16, EGTRRA, 6/7/2001.

In 2009, P.L. 111-5, Sec. 1504(a), substituted "be capable of attaining a maximum speed in excess of" for "operate at speeds in excess of" in para (i)(1), effective for obligations issued after 2/17/2009.

In 2008, P.L. 110-343, Sec. 307(a)DivB, substituted "September 30, 2012" for "September 30, 2009" in para. (l)(8) . . . Sec. 307(b)DivB, substituted "October 1, 2012" for "October 1, 2009" in para. (l)(9) . . . Sec. 307(c)DivA, substituted "issuance of the last issue with respect to such project," for "issuance" in Sec. 701(d), P.L. 108-357, reproduced below, effective 10/3/2008.

—P.L. 110-289, Sec. 3005(a)(1), substituted "(i) In general. The income" for "The income" in subpara. (d)(2)(B) . . . Sec. 3005(a)(2), added subparas. (d)(2)(B)(ii)-(iv), effective as provided in Sec. 3005(b) of this Act, which reads as follows:

"(b) The amendments made by this section shall apply to—

"(1) determinations made after the date of the enactment of this Act and before January 1, 2012, in the case of any qualified building (as defined in section 142(d)(2)(B)(iii) of the Internal Revenue Code of 1986)—

"(A) with respect to which housing credit dollar amounts have been allocated on or before the date of the enactment of this Act, or

"(B) with respect to buildings placed in service before such date of enactment, to the extent paragraph (1) of section 42(h) of such Code does not apply to such building by reason of paragraph (4) thereof, but only with respect to bonds issued before such date of enactment, and

"(2) determinations made after the date of enactment of this Act, in the case of qualified buildings (as so defined)—

"(A) with respect to which housing credit dollar amounts are allocated after the date of the enactment of this Act and before January 1, 2012, or

"(B) with respect to which buildings placed in service after the date of enactment of this Act and before January 1, 2012, to the extent paragraph (1) of section 42(h) of such Code does not apply to such building by reason of paragraph (4) thereof, but only with respect to bonds issued after such date of enactment and before January 1, 2012."

—P.L. 110-289, Sec. 3008(a), added subpara. (d)(3)(C) . . . Sec. 3008(b), added subpara. (d)(2)(C) . . . Sec. 3008(c), added subpara. (d)(2)(D), effective for determinations of the status of qualified residential rental projects for periods begin. after 7/30/2008, for bonds issued before, on, or after 7/30/2008.

—P.L. 110-289, Sec. 3009(a), added subpara. (d)(2)(E), effective for determinations of area median gross income for calendar years after 2008.

—P.L. 110-289, Sec. 3010(a), added a sentence to the end of subpara. (d)(3)(A), effective for yrs. end. after the 7/30/2008.

In 2006, P.L. 109-280, Sec. 1303, of this Act, provides:

"SEC. 1303. EXCEPTION TO THE LOCAL FURNISHING REQUIREMENT OF THE TAX-EXEMPT BOND RULES.

"(a) Snettisham hydroelectric facility. For purposes of determining whether any private activity bond issued before May 31, 2006, and used to finance the acquisition of the Snettisham hydroelectric facility is a qualified bond for purposes of section 142(a)(8) of the Internal Revenue Code of 1986, the electricity furnished by such facility to the City of Hoonah, Alaska, shall not be taken into account for purposes of section 142(f)(1) of such Code.

"(b) Lake Dorothy hydroelectric facility. For purposes of determining whether any private activity bond issued before May 31, 2006, and used to finance the Lake Dorothy hydroelectric facility is a qualified bond for purposes of section 142(a)(8) of the Internal Revenue Code of 1986, the electricity furnished by such facility to the City of Hoonah, Alaska, shall not be taken into account for purposes of paragraphs (1) and (3) of section 142(f) of such Code.

"(c) Definitions. For purposes of this section—

"(1) Lake Dorothy hydroelectric facility. The term 'Lake Dorothy hydroelectric facility' means the hydroelectric facility located approximately 10 miles south of Juneau, Alaska, and commonly referred to as the 'Lake Dorothy project'.

"(2) Snettisham hydroelectric facility. The term 'Snettisham hydroelectric facility' means the hydroelectric project described in section 1804 of the Small Business Job Protection Act of 1996."

In 2006, P.L. 109-222, Sec. 209(b)(2), substituted "Subsections (g) and (h) of section 7872" for "Section 7872(g)" in subpara. (d)(2)(B), effective for calendar yrs. begin. after 12/31/2005, with respect to loans made before, on, or after 12/31/2005.

In 2005, P.L. 109-59, Sec. 11143(a), deleted "or" at the end of para. (a)(13), substituted ", or" for the period at the end of para. (a)(14), and added para. (a)(15) . . . Sec. 11143(b), added subsec. (m), effective for bonds issued after 8/10/2005.

In 2004, P.L. 108-357, Sec. 701(a), deleted "or" at the end of para. (a)(12), substituted ", or" for the period at the end of para. (a)(13), and added para. (a)(14) . . . Sec. 701(b), added subsec. (l), effective for bonds issued after 12/31/2004.

—P.L. 108-357, Sec. 701(d), of this Act, reads as follows:

"*(d) Accountability.* Each issuer shall maintain, on behalf of each project, an interest bearing reserve account equal to 1 percent of the net proceeds of any bond issued under this section for such project. Not later than 5 years after the date of issuance of the last issue with respect to such project, the Secretary of the Treasury, after consultation with the Administrator of the Environmental Protection Agency, shall determine whether the project financed with such bonds has substantially complied with the terms and conditions described in section 142(l)(4) of the Internal Revenue Code of 1986 (as added by this section). If the Secretary, after such consultation, certifies that the project has substantially complied with such terms and conditions and meets the commitments set forth in the application for such project described in section 142(l)(4) of such Code, amounts in the reserve account, including all interest, shall be released to the project. If the Secretary determines that the project has not substantially complied with such terms and conditions, amounts in the reserve account, including all interest, shall be paid to the United States Treasury."

In 2002, P.L. 107-358, Sec. 2, added subsec. (c) in Sec. 901 of P.L. 107-16 [see below], effective 12/17/2002.

In 2001, P.L. 107-16, Sec. 422(a), deleted "or" at the end of para. (a)(11), substituted ", or" for the period at the end of para. (a)(12), and added para. (a)(13) . . . Sec. 422(b), added subsec. (k), effective for bonds issued after 12/31/2001.

—P.L. 107-16, Sec. 901, of this Act [as amended by Sec. 2, P.L. 107-358, and Sec. 101(a)(1), P.L. 111-312, see above], reads as follows:

"SEC. 901. SUNSET OF PROVISIONS OF ACT.

"(a) In general. All provisions of, and amendments made by, this Act shall not apply—

"(1) to taxable, plan, or limitation years beginning after December 31, 2012, or

"(2) in the case of title V, to estates of decedents dying, gifts made, or generation skipping transfers, after December 31, 2012.

"(b) Application of certain laws. The Internal Revenue Code of 1986 and the Employee Retirement Income Security Act of 1974 shall be applied and administered to years, estates, gifts, and transfers described in subsection (a) as if the provisions and amendments described in subsection (a) had never been enacted.

"(c) Exception. Subsection (a) shall not apply to section 803 (relating to no federal income tax on restitution received by victims of the Nazi regime or their heirs or estates)."

In 1998, P.L. 105-206, Sec. 6023(5), substituted "1997 (" for "1997, (" in clause (f)(3)(A)(ii), effective 7/22/98.

In 1996, P.L. 104-188, Sec. 1608(a), added paras. (f)(3) and (4), effective 8/20/96.

—P.L. 104-188, Sec. 1608(b), of this Act, provides:

"(b) No interference with respect to outstanding bonds. The use of the term 'person' in section 142(f)(3) of the Internal Revenue Code of 1986, as added by subsection (a), shall not be construed to affect the tax-exempt status of interest on any bonds issued before the date of the enactment of this Act."

—P.L. 104-188, Sec. 1704(j)(4), amended Sec. 1921(b)(2) of P.L. 102-486 by adding a comma after "(2)" in the material proposed to be stricken, see below.

—P.L. 104-188, Sec. 1804, of this Act, provides:

"Sec. 1804. Tax-exempt bonds for sale of Alaska Power Administration facility.

"Sections 142(f)(3) (as added by section 1608) and 147(d) of the Internal Revenue Code of 1986 shall not apply in determining whether any private activity bond issued after the date of the enactment of this Act and used to finance the acquisition of the Snettisham hydroelectric project from the Alaska Power Administration is a qualified bond for purposes of such Code."

In 1992, P.L. 102-486, Sec. 1919(a), amended subsec. (f), effective for obligations issued before, on, or after 10/24/92.

Prior to amendment, subsec. (f) read as follows:

"(f) Local furnishing of electric energy or gas.

For purposes of subsection (a)(8), the local furnishing of electric energy or gas from a facility shall only include furnishing solely within the area consisting of—

"(1) a city and 1 contiguous county, or

"(2) 2 contiguous counties."

—P.L. 102-486, Sec. 1921(a)(1), deleted "or" at the end of para. (a)(10) . . . Sec. 1921(a)(2), substituted ", or" for the period at the end of para. (a)(11) . . . Sec. 1921(a)(3), added para. (a)(12) . . . Sec. 1921(b)(1), added subsec. (j) . . . Sec. 1921(b)(2), [as amended by Sec. 1704(j)(7) of P.L. 104-188, see above] substituted "(2), (3), or (12)" for "(2), or (3)" in subpara. (b)(1)(A), effective for bonds issued after 10/24/92.

In 1989, P.L. 101-239, Sec. 7108(e)(3), added the last sentence to subpara. (d)(2)(B) . . . Sec. 7108(n)(1), substituted "½" for "⅓" in clause (d)(4)(B)(iii), effective for determinations under Code Sec. 42 for housing credit dollar amounts allocated from State housing credit ceilings for calendar yrs. after '89, except as provided in Sec. 7108(r)(2) through (r)(8) of this Act which reads:

"(2) Buildings not subject to allocation limits.—Except as otherwise provided in this subsection, to the extent paragraph (1) of section 42(h) of such Code does not apply to any building by reason of paragraph (4) thereof, the amendments made by this section shall apply to buildings placed in service after December 31, 1989.

"(3) 1-year carryover of unused credit authority, etc.—The amendments made by subsection (b) shall apply to calendar years after 1989, but clauses (ii), (iii), and (iv) of section 42(h)(3)(C) of such Code (as added by this section) shall be applied without regard to allocations for 1989 or any preceding year.

"(4) Additional buildings eligible for waiver of 10-year rule.—The amendments made by subsection (f) shall take effect on the date of the enactment of this Act.

"(5) Certifications with respect to 1st year of credit period.—The amendment made by subsection (p) shall apply to taxable years ending on or after December 31, 1989.

"(6) Certain rules which apply to bonds.— Paragraphs (1)(D) and (2)(D) of section 42(m) of such Code, as added by this section, shall apply to obligations issued December 31, 1989.

"(7) Clarifications.—The amendments made by the following provisions of this section shall apply as if included in the amendments made by section 252 of the Tax Reform Act of 1986:

"(A) Paragraph (1) of subsection (h) (relating to units rented on a monthly basis).

"(B) Subsection (1) (relating to eligible basis for new buildings to include expenditures before close of 1st year of credit period).

"(8) Guidance on difficult development areas and posting of bond to avoid recapture.—Not later than 180 days after the date of the enactment of this Act—

"(A) the Secretary of Housing and Urban Development shall publish initial guidance on the designation of difficult development areas under section 42(d)(5)(C) of such Code, as added by this section, and

"(B) the Secretary of the Treasury shall publish initial guidance under section 42(j)(6) of such Code (relating to no recapture on disposition of building (or interest therein) where bond posted)."

—P.L. 101-239, Sec. 7816(s)(1), added "In general.—" after "(1)" in para. (i)(1), effective for bonds issued after 11/10/88.

In 1988, P.L. 100-647, Sec. 1013(a)(1), substituted "average gross rent" for "average rent" in clause (d)(4)(B)(iii) . . . Sec. 1013(a)(39), substituted "(as defined in section 168(i)(3))" for "(as defined in 168(i)(3))" in clause (b)(1)(B)(ii), effective for bonds issued after 8/15/86. For transitional rules, see Secs. 1312-1318 of P.L. 99-514 reproduced in the note following Code Sec. 103.

—P.L. 100-647, Sec. 6180(a)(1), deleted "or" at the end of para. (a)(9) . . . Sec. 6180(a)(2), substituted "or" for the period at the end of para. (a)(10) . . . Sec. 6180(a)(3), added para. (a)(11) . . . Sec. 6180(b)(1), added subsec. (i) . . . Sec. 6180(b)(2)(A), substituted "paragraph (1), (2), (3), or (11) of subsection (a)" for "paragraph (1), (2), or (3) of subsection (a)" each place it appeared in paras. (c)(1) and (2) . . . Sec. 6180(b)(2)(B), substituted "mass commuting facilities and high-speed intercity rail facilities" for "and mass commuting facilities" in the heading of subsec. (c), effective for bonds issued after 11/10/88 [date of enactment].

In 1986, P.L. 99-514, Sec. 1301(b), added Code Sec. 142 as part of the amendments to Part IV of subchapter B of chapter 1, effective for bonds issued after 8/15/86. For transitional rules, see Secs. 1312–1318 of this Act reproduced in the note following Code Sec. 103.

Sec. 143. Mortgage revenue bonds: qualified mortgage bond and qualified veterans' mortgage bond.

(a) Qualified mortgage bond.

(1) Qualified mortgage bond defined. For purposes of this title, the term "qualified mortgage bond" means a bond which is issued as part of a qualified mortgage issue.

(2) Qualified mortgage issue defined.

(A) Definition. For purposes of this title, the term "qualified mortgage issue" means an issue by a State or political subdivision thereof of 1 or more bonds, but only if—

(i) all proceeds of such issue (exclusive of issuance costs and a reasonably required reserve) are to be used to finance owner-occupied residences,

(ii) such issue meets the requirements of subsections (c), (d), (e), (f), (g), (h), (i), and (m)(7)

(iii) such issue does not meet the private business tests of paragraphs (1) and (2) of section 141(b), and

(iv) except as provided in subparagraph (D)(ii), repayments of principal on financing provided by the issue are used not later than the close of the 1st semiannual period beginning after the date the prepayment (or complete repayment) is received to redeem bonds which are part of such issue.

Clause (iv) shall not apply to amounts received within 10 years after the date of issuance of the issue (or, in the case of refunding bond, the date of issuance of the original bond).

(B) Good faith effort to comply with mortgage eligibility requirements. An issue which fails to meet 1 or more of the requirements of subsections (c), (d), (e), (f), and (i) shall be treated as meeting such requirements if—

(i) the issuer in good faith attempted to meet all such requirements before the mortgages were executed,

(ii) 95 percent or more of the proceeds devoted to owner-financing was devoted to residences with respect to which (at the time the mortgages were executed) all such requirements were met, and

(iii) any failure to meet the requirements of such subsections is corrected within a reasonable period after such failure is first discovered.

(C) Good faith effort to comply with other requirements. An issue which fails to meet 1 or more of the requirements of subsections (g), (h), and (m)(7) shall be treated as meeting such requirements if—

(i) the issuer in good faith attempted to meet all such requirements, and

(ii) any failure to meet such requirements is due to inadvertent error after taking reasonable steps to comply with such requirements.

(D) Proceeds must be used within 42 months of date of issuance.

(i) In general. Except as otherwise provided in this subparagraph, an issue shall not meet the requirement of subparagraph (A)(i) unless—

(I) all proceeds of the issue required to be used to finance owner-occupied residences are so used within the 42-month period beginning on the date of issuance of the issue (or, in the case of a refunding bond, within the 42-month period beginning on the date of issuance of the original bond) or, to the extent not so used within such period, are used within such period to redeem bonds which are part of such issue, and

(II) no portion of the proceeds of the issue are used to make or finance any loan (other than a loan which is a nonpurpose investment within the meaning of section 148(f)(6)(A)) after the close of such period.

(ii) Exception. Clause (i) (and clause (iv) of subparagraph (A)) shall not be construed to require amounts of less than $250,000 to be used to redeem bonds. The Secretary may by regulation treat related issues as 1 issue for purposes of the preceding sentence.

(b) Qualified veterans' mortgage bond defined.

For purposes of this part, the term "qualified veterans' mortgage bond" means any bond—

(1) which is issued as part of an issue 95 percent or more of the net proceeds of which are to be used to provide residences for veterans,

(2) the payment of the principal and interest on which is secured by the general obligation of a State,

(3) which is part of an issue which meets the requirements of subsections (c), (g), (i)(1), and (l), and

(4) which is part of an issue which does not meet the private business tests of paragraphs (1) and (2) of section 141(b).

Rules similar to the rules of subparagraphs (B) and (C) of subsection (a)(2) shall apply to the requirements specified in paragraph (3) of this subsection.

(c) Residence requirements.

(1) For a residence. A residence meets the requirements of this subsection only if—

(A) it is a single-family residence which can reasonably be expected to become the principal residence of the mortgagor within a reasonable time after the financing is provided, and

(B) it is located within the jurisdiction of the authority issuing the bond.

(2) For an issue. An issue meets the requirements of this subsection only if all of the residences for which owner-financing is provided under the issue meet the requirements of paragraph (1).

(d) 3-year requirement.

(1) In general. An issue meets the requirements of this subsection only if 95 percent or more of the net proceeds of such issue are used to finance the residences of mortgagors who had no present ownership interest in their principal residences at any time during the 3-year period ending on the date their mortgage is executed.

(2) Exceptions. For purposes of paragraph (1), the proceeds of an issue which are used to provide—

(A) financing with respect to targeted area residences,

(B) qualified home improvement loans and qualified rehabilitation loans,

(C) financing with respect to land described in subsection (i)(1)(C) and the construction of any residence thereon, and

(D) in the case of bonds issued after the date of the enactment of this subparagraph, financing of any residence for a veteran (as defined in section 101 of title 38, United States Code), if such veteran has not previously qualified for and received such financing by reason of this subparagraph,

shall be treated as used as described in paragraph (1).

(3) Mortgagor's interest in residence being financed. For purposes of paragraph (1), a mortgagor's interest in the residence with respect to which the financing is being provided shall not be taken into account.

(e) Purchase price requirement.

(1) **In general.** An issue meets the requirements of this subsection only if the acquisition cost of each residence the owner-financing of which is provided under the issue does not exceed 90 percent of the average area purchase price applicable to such residence.

(2) **Average area purchase price.** For purposes of paragraph (1), the term "average area purchase price" means, with respect to any residence, the average purchase price of single family residences (in the statistical area in which the residence is located) which were purchased during the most recent 12-month period for which sufficient statistical information is available. The determination under the preceding sentence shall be made as of the date on which the commitment to provide the financing is made (or, if earlier, the date of the purchase of the residence).

(3) **Separate application to new residences and old residences.** For purposes of this subsection, the determination of average area purchase price shall be made separately with respect to—
  (A) residences which have not been previously occupied, and
  (B) residences which have been previously occupied.

(4) **Special rule for 2 to 4 family residences.** For purposes of this subsection, to the extent provided in regulations, the determination of average area purchase price shall be made separately with respect to 1 family, 2 family, 3 family, and 4 family residences.

(5) **Special rule for targeted area residences.** In the case of a targeted area residence, paragraph (1) shall be applied by substituting "110 percent" for "90 percent".

(6) **Exception for qualified home improvement loans.** Paragraph (1) shall not apply with respect to any qualified home improvement loan.

(f) Income requirements.

(1) **In general.** An issue meets the requirements of this subsection only if all owner-financing provided under the issue is provided for mortgagors whose family income is 115 percent or less of the applicable median family income.

(2) **Determination of family income.** For purposes of this subsection, the family income of mortgagors, and area median gross income, shall be determined by the Secretary after taking into account the regulations prescribed under section 8 of the United States Housing Act of 1937 (or, if such program is terminated, under such program as in effect immediately before such termination).

(3) **Special rule for applying paragraph (1) in the case of targeted area residences.** In the case of any financing provided under any issue for targeted area residences—
  (A) ⅓ of the amount of such financing may be provided without regard to paragraph (1), and
  (B) paragraph (1) shall be treated as satisfied with respect to the remainder of the owner financing if the family income of the mortgagor is 140 percent or less of the applicable median family income.

(4) **Applicable median family income.** For purposes of this subsection, the term "applicable median family income" means, with respect to a residence, whichever of the following is the greater:
  (A) the area median gross income for the area in which such residence is located, or
  (B) the statewide median gross income for the State in which such residence is located.

(5) **Adjustment of income requirement based on relation of high housing costs to income.**
  (A) In general. If the residence (for which financing is provided under the issue) is located in a high housing cost area and the limitation determined under this paragraph is greater than the limitation otherwise applicable under paragraph (1), there shall be substituted for the income limitation in paragraph (1), a limitation equal to the percentage determined under subparagraph (B) of the area median gross income for such area.
  (B) Income requirements for residences in high housing cost area. The percentage determined under this subparagraph for a residence located in a high housing cost area is the percentage (not greater than 140 percent) equal to the product of—
    (I) 115 percent, and
    (II) the amount by which the housing cost/income ratio for such area exceeds 0.2.
  (C) High housing cost areas. For purposes of this paragraph, the term "high housing cost area" means any statistical area for which the housing cost/income ratio is greater than 1.2.
  (D) Housing cost/income ratio. For purposes of this paragraph—
    (i) In general. The term "housing cost/income ratio" means, with respect to any statistical area, the number determined by dividing—
      (I) the applicable housing price ratio for such area, by
      (II) the ratio which the area median gross income for such area bears to the median gross income for the United States.
    (ii) Applicable housing price ratio. For purposes of clause (i), the applicable housing price ratio for any area is the new housing price ratio or the existing housing price ratio, whichever results in the housing cost/income ratio being closer to 1.
    (iii) New housing price ratio. The new housing price ratio for any area is the ratio which—
      (I) the average area purchase price (as defined in subsection (e)(2)) for residences described in subsection (e)(3)(A) which are located in such area bears to
      (II) the average purchase price (determined in accordance with the principles of subsection (e)(2)) for residences so described which are located in the United States.
    (iv) Existing housing price ratio. The existing housing price ratio for any area is the ratio determined in accordance with clause (iii) but with respect to residences described in subsection (e)(3)(B).

(6) **Adjustment to income requirements based on family size.** In the case of a mortgagor having a family of fewer than 3 individuals, the preceding provisions of this subsection shall be applied by substituting—
  (A) "100 percent" for "115 percent" each place it appears, and
  (B) "120 percent" for "140 percent" each place it appears.

(g) Requirements related to arbitrage.

(1) **In general.** An issue meets the requirements of this subsection only if such issue meets the requirements of paragraph (2) of this subsection and, in the case of an issue described in subsection (b)(1), such issue also meets the requirements of paragraph (3) of this subsection. Such requirements shall be in addition to the requirements of section 148.

(2) Effective rate of mortgage interest cannot exceed bond yield by more than 1.125 percentage points.

(A) In general. An issue shall be treated as meeting the requirements of this paragraph only if the excess of—

(i) the effective rate of interest on the mortgages provided under the issue, over

(ii) the yield on the issue, is not greater than 1.125 percentage points.

(B) Effective rate of mortgage interest.

(i) In general. In determining the effective rate of interest on any mortgage for purposes of this paragraph, there shall be taken into account all fees, charges, and other amounts borne by the mortgagor which are attributable to the mortgage or to the bond issue.

(ii) Specification of some of the amounts to be treated as borne by the mortgagor. For purposes of clause (i), the following items (among others) shall be treated as borne by the mortgagor:

(I) all points or similar charges paid by the seller of the property, and

(II) the excess of the amounts received from any person other than the mortgagor by any person in connection with the acquisition of the mortgagor's interest in the property over the usual and reasonable acquisition costs of a person acquiring like property where owner-financing is not provided through the use of qualified mortgage bonds or qualified veterans' mortgage bonds.

(iii) Specification of some of the amounts to be treated as not borne by the mortgagor. For purposes of clause (i), the following items shall not be taken into account:

(I) any expected rebate of arbitrage profits, and

(II) any application fee, survey fee, credit report fee, insurance charge, or similar amount to the extent such amount does not exceed amounts charged in such area in cases where owner-financing is not provided through the use of qualified mortgage bonds or qualified veterans' mortgage bonds.

Subclause (II) shall not apply to origination fees, points, or similar amounts.

(iv) Prepayment assumptions. In determining the effective rate of interest—

(I) it shall be assumed that the mortgage prepayment rate will be the rate set forth in the most recent applicable mortgage maturity experience table published by the Federal Housing Administration, and

(II) prepayments of principal shall be treated as received on the last day of the month in which the issuer reasonably expects to receive such prepayments.

The Secretary may by regulation adjust the mortgage prepayment rate otherwise used in determining the effective rate of interest to the extent the Secretary determines that such an adjustment is appropriate by reason of the impact of subsection (m).

(C) Yield on the issue. For purposes of this subsection, the yield on an issue shall be determined on the basis of—

(i) the issue price (within the meaning of sections 1273 and 1274), and

(ii) an expected maturity for the bonds which is consistent with the assumptions required under subparagraph (B)(iv).

(3) Arbitrage and investment gains to be used to reduce costs of owner-financing.

(A) In general. An issue shall be treated as meeting the requirements of this paragraph only if an amount equal to the sum of—

(i) the excess of—

(I) the amount earned on all nonpurpose investments (other than investments attributable to an excess described in this clause), over

(II) the amount which would have been earned if such investments were invested at a rate equal to the yield on the issue, plus

(ii) any income attributable to the excess described in clause (i),

is paid or credited to the mortgagors as rapidly as may be practicable.

(B) Investment gains and losses. For purposes of subparagraph (A), in determining the amount earned on all nonpurpose investments, any gain or loss on the disposition of such investments shall be taken into account.

(C) Reduction where issuer does not use full 1.125 percentage points under paragraph (2).

(i) In general. The amount required to be paid or credited to mortgagors under subparagraph (A) (determined under this paragraph without regard to this subparagraph) shall be reduced by the unused paragraph (2) amount.

(ii) Unused paragraph (2) amount. For purposes of clause (i), the unused paragraph (2) amount is the amount which (if it were treated as an interest payment made by mortgagors) would result in the excess referred to in paragraph (2)(A) being equal to 1.125 percentage points. Such amount shall be fixed and determined as of the yield determination date.

(D) Election to pay United States. Subparagraph (A) shall be satisfied with respect to any issue if the issuer elects before issuing the bonds to pay over to the United States—

(i) not less frequently than once each 5 years after the date of issue, an amount equal to 90 percent of the aggregate amount which would be required to be paid or credited to mortgagors under subparagraph (A) (and not theretofore paid to the United States), and

(ii) not later than 60 days after the redemption of the last bond, 100 percent of such aggregate amount not theretofore paid to the United States.

(E) Simplified accounting. The Secretary shall permit any simplified system of accounting for purposes of this paragraph which the issuer establishes to the satisfaction of the Secretary will assure that the purposes of this paragraph are carried out.

(F) Nonpurpose investment. For purposes of this paragraph, the term "nonpurpose investment" has the meaning given such term by section 148(f)(6)(A).

(h) Portion of loans required to be placed in targeted areas.

(1) In general. An issue meets the requirements of this subsection only if at least 20 percent of the proceeds of the issue which are devoted to providing owner-financing is made available (with reasonable diligence) for owner-financing of targeted area residences for at least 1 year after the date on which owner-financing is first made available with respect to targeted area residences.

(2) Limitation. Nothing in paragraph (1) shall be treated as requiring the making available of an amount which exceeds 40 percent of the average annual aggregate principal amount of mortgages executed during the immediately preceding 3 calendar years for single-family, owner-occupied residences located in targeted areas within the jurisdiction of the issuing authority.

(i) Other requirements.

(1) Mortgages must be new mortgages.

(A) In general. An issue meets the requirements of this subsection only if no part of the proceeds of such issue is used to acquire or replace existing mortgages.

(B) Exceptions. Under regulations prescribed by the Secretary, the replacement of—

(i) construction period loans,

(ii) bridge loans or similar temporary initial financing, and

(iii) in the case of a qualified rehabilitation, an existing mortgage,

shall not be treated as the acquisition or replacement of an existing mortgage for purposes of subparagraph (A).

(C) Exception for certain contract for deed agreements.

(i) In general. In the case of land possessed under a contract for deed by a mortgagor—

(I) whose principal residence (within the meaning of section 121) is located on such land, and

(II) whose family income (as defined in subsection (f)(2)) is not more than 50 percent of applicable median family income (as defined in subsection (f)(4)),

the contract for deed shall not be treated as an existing mortgage for purposes of subparagraph (A).

(ii) Contract for deed defined. For purposes of this subparagraph, the term "contract for deed" means a seller-financed contract for the conveyance of land under which—

(I) legal title does not pass to the purchaser until the consideration under the contract is fully paid to the seller, and

(II) the seller's remedy for nonpayment is forfeiture rather than judicial or nonjudicial foreclosure.

(2) Certain requirements must be met where mortgage is assumed. An issue meets the requirements of this subsection only if each mortgage with respect to which owner-financing has been provided under such issue may be assumed only if the requirements of subsections (c), (d), and (e), and the requirements of paragraph (1) or (3)(B) of subsection (f) (whichever applies), are met with respect to such assumption.

(j) Targeted area residences.

(1) In general. For purposes of this section, the term "targeted area residence" means a residence in an area which is either—

(A) a qualified census tract, or

(B) an area of chronic economic distress.

(2) Qualified census tract.

(A) In general. For purposes of paragraph (1), the term "qualified census tract" means a census tract in which 70 percent or more of the families have income which is 80 percent or less of the statewide median family income.

(B) Data used. The determination under subparagraph (A) shall be made on the basis of the most recent decennial census for which data are available.

(3) Area of chronic economic distress.

(A) In general. For purposes of paragraph (1), the term "area of chronic economic distress" means an area of chronic economic distress—

(i) designated by the State as meeting the standards established by the State for purposes of this subsection, and

(ii) the designation of which has been approved by the Secretary and the Secretary of Housing and Urban Development.

(B) Criteria to be used in approving state designations. The criteria used by the Secretary and the Secretary of Housing and Urban Development in evaluating any proposed designation of an area for purposes of this subsection shall be—

(i) the condition of the housing stock, including the age of the housing and the number of abandoned and substandard residential units,

(ii) the need of area residents for owner-financing under this section, as indicated by low per capita income, a high percentage of families in poverty, a high number of welfare recipients, and high unemployment rates,

(iii) the potential for use of owner-financing under this section to improve housing conditions in the area, and

(iv) the existence of a housing assistance plan which provides a displacement program and a public improvements and services program.

(k) Other definitions and special rules.

For purposes of this section—

(1) Mortgage. The term "mortgage" means any owner-financing.

(2) Statistical area.

(A) In general. The term "statistical area" means—

(i) a metropolitan statistical area, and

(ii) any county (or the portion thereof) which is not within a metropolitan statistical area.

(B) Metropolitan statistical area. The term "metropolitan statistical area" includes the area defined as such by the Secretary of Commerce.

(C) Designation where adequate statistical information not available. For purposes of this paragraph, if there is insufficient recent statistical information with respect to a county (or portion thereof) described in subparagraph (A)(ii), the Secretary may substitute for such county (or portion thereof) another area for which there is sufficient recent statistical information.

(D) Designation where no county. In the case of any portion of a State which is not within a county, subparagraphs (A)(ii) and (C) shall be applied by substituting for "county" an area designated by the Secretary which is the equivalent of a county.

(3) Acquisition cost.

(A) In general. The term "acquisition cost" means the cost of acquiring the residence as a completed residential unit.

(B) Exceptions. The term "acquisition cost" does not include—

(i) usual and reasonable settlement or financing costs,

(ii) the value of services performed by the mortgagor or members of his family in completing the residence, and

(iii) the cost of land (other than land described in subsection (i)(1)(C)(i)) which has been owned by the mortgagor for at least 2 years before the date on which construction of the residence begins.

(C) Special rule for qualified rehabilitation loans. In the case of a qualified rehabilitation loan, for purposes of subsection (e), the term "acquisition cost" includes the cost of the rehabilitation.

(4) Qualified home improvement loan. The term "qualified home improvement loan" means the financing (in an amount which does not exceed $15,000)—

(A) of alterations, repairs, and improvements on or in connection with an existing residence by the owner thereof, but

(B) only of such items as substantially protect or improve the basic livability or energy efficiency of the property.

(5) Qualified rehabilitation loan.

(A) In general. The term "qualified rehabilitation loan" means any owner-financing provided in connection with—

(i) a qualified rehabilitation, or

(ii) the acquisition of a residence with respect to which there has been a qualified rehabilitation,

but only if the mortgagor to whom such financing is provided is the first resident of the residence after the completion of the rehabilitation.

(B) Qualified rehabilitation. For purposes of subparagraph (A), the term "qualified rehabilitation" means any rehabilitation of a building if—

(i) there is a period of at least 20 years between the date on which the building was first used and the date on which the physical work on such rehabilitation begins,

(ii) in the rehabilitation process—

(I) 50 percent or more of the existing external walls of such building are retained in place as external walls,

(II) 75 percent or more of the existing external walls of such building are retained in place as internal or external walls, and

(III) 75 percent or more of the existing internal structural framework of such building is retained in place, and

(iii) the expenditures for such rehabilitation are 25 percent or more of the mortgagor's adjusted basis in the residence.

For purposes of clause (iii), the mortgagor's adjusted basis shall be determined as of the completion of the rehabilitation or, if later, the date on which the mortgagor acquires the residence.

(6) Determinations on actuarial basis. All determinations of yield, effective interest rates, and amounts required to be paid or credited to mortgagors or paid to the United States under subsection (g) shall be made on an actuarial basis taking into account the present value of money.

(7) Single-family and owner-occupied residences include certain residences with 2 to 4 units. Except for purposes of subsection (h)(2), the terms "single-family" and "owner-occupied", when used with respect to residences, include 2, 3, or 4 family residences—

(A) one unit of which is occupied by the owner of the units, and

(B) which were first occupied at least 5 years before the mortgage is executed.

Subparagraph (B) shall not apply to any 2-family residence if the residence is a targeted area residence and the family income of the mortgagor meets the requirement of subsection (f)(3)(B).

(8) Cooperative housing corporations.

(A) In general. In the case of any cooperative housing corporation—

(i) each dwelling unit shall be treated as if it were actually owned by the person entitled to occupy such dwelling unit by reason of his ownership of stock in the corporation, and

(ii) any indebtedness of the corporation allocable to the dwelling unit shall be treated as if it were indebtedness of the shareholder entitled to occupy the dwelling unit.

(B) Adjustment to targeted area requirement. In the case of any issue to provide financing to a cooperative housing corporation with respect to cooperative housing not located in a targeted area, to the extent provided in regulations, such issue may be combined with 1 or more other issues for purposes of determining whether the requirements of subsection (h) are met.

(C) Cooperative housing corporation. The term "cooperative housing corporation" has the meaning given to such term by section 216(b)(1).

(9) Treatment of limited equity cooperative housing.

(A) Treatment as residential rental property. Except as provided in subparagraph (B), for purposes of this part—

(i) any limited equity cooperative housing shall be treated as residential rental property and not as owner-occupied housing, and

(ii) bonds issued to provide such housing shall be subject to the same requirements and limitations as bonds the proceeds of which are to be used to provide qualified residential rental projects (as defined in section 142(d)).

(B) Bonds subject to qualified mortgage bond termination date. Subparagraph (A) shall not apply to any bond issued after the date specified in subsection (a)(1)(B).

(C) Limited equity cooperative housing. For purposes of this paragraph, the term "limited equity cooperative housing" means any dwelling unit which a person is entitled to occupy by reason of his ownership of stock in a qualified cooperative housing corporation.

(D) Qualified cooperative housing corporation. For purposes of this paragraph, the term "qualified cooperative housing corporation" means any cooperative housing corporation (as defined in section 216(b)(1)) if—

(i) the consideration paid for stock held by any stockholder entitled to occupy any house or apartment in a building owned or leased by the corporation may not exceed the sum of—

(I) the consideration paid for such stock by the first such stockholder, as adjusted by a cost-of-living adjustment determined by the Secretary,

(II) payments made by any stockholder for improvements to such house or apartment, and

(III) payments (other than amounts taken into account under subclause (I) or (II)) attributable to any stockholder to amortize the principal of the corporation's indebtedness arising from the acquisition or development of real property, including improvements thereof,

(ii) the value of the corporation's assets (reduced by any corporate liabilities), to the extent such value exceeds the combined transfer values of the outstanding corporate stock, shall be used only for public benefit or charitable purposes, or directly to benefit the corporation itself, and shall not be used directly to benefit any stockholder, and

Private activity bonds   Code Sec. 143(l)(1)

(iii) at the time of issuance of the issue, such corporation makes an election under this paragraph.

(E) Effect of election. If a cooperative housing corporation makes an election under this paragraph, section 216 shall not apply with respect to such corporation (or any successor thereof) during the qualified project period (as defined in section 142(d)(2)).

(F) Corporation must continue to be qualified cooperative. Subparagraph (A)(i) shall not apply to limited equity cooperative housing unless the cooperative housing corporation continues to be a qualified cooperative housing corporation at all times during the qualified project period (as defined in section 142(d)(2)).

(G) Election irrevocable. Any election under this paragraph, once made, shall be irrevocable.

(10) Treatment of resale price control and subsidy lien programs.

(A) In general. In the case of a residence which is located in a high housing cost area (as defined in section 143(f)(5)), the interest of a governmental unit in such residence by reason of financing provided under any qualified program shall not be taken into account under this section (other than subsection (m)), and the acquisition cost of the residence which is taken into account under subsection (e) shall be such cost reduced by the amount of such financing.

(B) Qualified program. For purposes of subparagraph (A), the term "qualified program" means any governmental program providing mortgage loans (other than 1st mortgage loans) or grants—

(i) which restricts (throughout the 9-year period beginning on the date the financing is provided) the resale of the residence to a purchaser qualifying under this section and to a price determined by an index that reflects less than the full amount of any appreciation in the residence's value, or

(ii) which provides for deferred or reduced interest payments on such financing and grants the governmental unit a share in the appreciation of the residence,

but only if such financing is not provided directly or indirectly through the use of any tax-exempt private activity bond.

(11) Special rules for residences located in disaster areas. In the case of a residence located in an area determined by the President to warrant assistance from the Federal Government under the Robert T. Stafford Disaster Relief and Emergency Assistance Act (as in effect on the date of the enactment [8/5/97] of the Taxpayer Relief Act of 1997), this section shall be applied with the following modifications to financing provided with respect to such residence within 2 years after the date of the disaster declaration:

(A) Subsection (d) (relating to 3-year requirement) shall not apply.

(B) Subsections (e) and (f) (relating to purchase price requirement and income requirement) shall be applied as if such residence were a targeted area residence.

The preceding sentence shall apply only with respect to bonds issued after May 1, 2008, and before January 1, 2010.

(12) Special rules for subprime refinancings.

(A) In general. Notwithstanding the requirements of subsection (i)(1), the proceeds of a qualified mortgage issue may be used to refinance a mortgage on a residence which was originally financed by the mortgagor through a qualified subprime loan.

(B) Special rules. In applying subparagraph (A) to any refinancing—

(i) subsection (a)(2)(D)(i) shall be applied by substituting "12-month period" for "42-month period" each place it appears,

(ii) subsection (d) (relating to 3-year requirement) shall not apply, and

(iii) subsection (e) (relating to purchase price requirement) shall be applied by using the market value of the residence at the time of refinancing in lieu of the acquisition cost.

(C) Qualified subprime loan. The term "qualified subprime loan" means an adjustable rate single-family residential mortgage loan made after December 31, 2001, and before January 1, 2008, that the bond issuer determines would be reasonably likely to cause financial hardship to the borrower if not refinanced.

(D) Termination. This paragraph shall not apply to any bonds issued after December 31, 2010.

(12 [sic (13)]) Special rules for residences destroyed in federally declared disasters.

(A) Principal residence destroyed. At the election of the taxpayer, if the principal residence (within the meaning of section 121) of such taxpayer is—

(i) rendered unsafe for use as a residence by reason of a federally declared disaster occurring before January 1, 2010, or

(ii) demolished or relocated by reason of an order of the government of a State or political subdivision thereof on account of a federally declared disaster occurring before such date,

then, for the 2-year period beginning on the date of the disaster declaration, subsection (d)(1) shall not apply with respect to such tax payer and subsection (e) shall be applied by substituting "110" for "90" in paragraph (1) thereof.

(B) Principal residence damaged.

(i) In general. At the election of the taxpayer, if the principal residence (within the meaning of section 121) of such taxpayer was damaged as the result of a federally declared disaster occurring before January 1, 2010, any owner-financing provided in connection with the repair or reconstruction of such residence shall be treated as a qualified rehabilitation loan.

(ii) Limitation. The aggregate owner-financing to which clause (i) applies shall not exceed the lesser of—

(I) the cost of such repair or reconstruction, or

(II) $150,000.

(C) Federally declared disaster. For purposes of this paragraph, the term "federally declared disaster" has the meaning given such term by section 165(h)(3)(C)(i).

(D) Election; denial of double benefit.

(i) Election. An election under this paragraph may not be revoked except with the consent of the Secretary.

(ii) Denial of double benefit. If a taxpayer elects the application of this paragraph, paragraph (11) shall not apply with respect to the purchase or financing of any residence by such taxpayer.

(l) Additional requirements for qualified veterans' mortgage bonds.

An issue meets the requirements of this subsection only if it meets the requirements of paragraphs (1), (2), and (3).

(1) Veterans to whom financing may be provided. An issue meets the requirements of this paragraph only if

1,481

each mortgagor to whom financing is provided under the issue is a qualified veteran.

(2) Requirement that state program be in effect before June 22, 1984. An issue meets the requirements of this paragraph only if it is a general obligation of a State which issued qualified veterans' mortgage bonds before June 22, 1984.

(3) Volume limitation.

(A) In general. An issue meets the requirements of this paragraph only if the aggregate amount of bonds issued pursuant thereto (when added to the aggregate amount of qualified veterans' mortgage bonds previously issued by the State during the calendar year) does not exceed the State veterans limit for such calendar year.

(B) State veterans limit.

(i) In general. In the case of any State to which clause (ii) does not apply, the State veterans limit for any calendar year is the amount equal to—

(I) the aggregate amount of qualified veterans bonds issued by such State during the period beginning on January 1, 1979, and ending on June 22, 1984 (not including the amount of any qualified veterans bond issued by such State during the calendar year (or portion thereof) in such period for which the amount of such bonds so issued was the lowest), divided by

(II) the number (not to exceed 5) of calendar years after 1979 and before 1985 during which the State issued qualified veterans bonds (determined by only taking into account bonds issued on or before June 22, 1984).

(ii) Alaska, Oregon, and Wisconsin. In the case of the following States, the State veterans limit for any calendar year is the amount equal to—

(I) $100,000,000 for the State of Alaska,
(II) $100,000,000 for the State of Oregon, and
(III) $100,000,000 for the State of Wisconsin.

(iii) Phasein. In the case of calendar years beginning before 2010, clause (ii) shall be applied by substituting for each of the dollar amounts therein an amount equal to the applicable percentage of such dollar amount. For purposes of the preceding sentence, the applicable percentage shall be determined in accordance with the following table:

For Calendar Year:	Applicable percentage is:
2006	20 percent
2007	40 percent
2008	60 percent
2009	80 percent.

(C) Treatment of refunding issues.

(i) In general. For purposes of subparagraph (A), the term "qualified veterans' mortgage bond" shall not include any bond issued to refund another bond but only if the maturity date of the refunding bond is not later than the later of—

(I) the maturity date of the bond to be refunded, or
(II) the date 32 years after the date on which the refunded bond was issued (or in the case of a series of refundings, the date on which the original bond was issued).

The preceding sentence shall apply only to the extent that the amount of the refunding bond does not exceed the outstanding amount of the refunded bond.

(ii) Exception for advance refunding. Clause (i) shall not apply to any bond issued to advance refund another bond.

(4) Qualified veteran. For purposes of this subsection, the term "qualified veteran" means any veteran who—

(A) served on active duty, and
(B) applied for the financing before the date 25 years after the last date on which such veteran left active service.

(5) Special rule for certain short-term bonds. In the case of any bond—

(A) which has a term of 1 year or less,
(B) which is authorized to be issued under O.R.S. 407.435 (as in effect on the date of the enactment of this subsection), to provide financing for property taxes, and
(C) which is redeemed at the end of such term,

the amount taken into account under this subsection with respect to such bond shall be $1/15$ of its principal amount.

(m) Recapture of portion of federal subsidy from use of qualified mortgage bonds and mortgage credit certificates.

(1) In general. If, during the taxable year, any taxpayer disposes of an interest in a residence with respect to which there is or was any federally-subsidized indebtedness for the payment of which the taxpayer was liable in whole or part, then the taxpayer's tax imposed by this chapter for such taxable year shall be increased by the lesser of—

(A) the recapture amount with respect to such indebtedness, or
(B) 50 percent of the gain (if any) on the disposition of such interest.

(2) Exceptions. Paragraph (1) shall not apply to—

(A) any disposition by reason of death, and
(B) any disposition which is more than 9 years after the testing date.

(3) Federally-subsidized indebtedness. For purposes of this subsection—

(A) In general. The term "federally-subsidized indebtedness" means any indebtedness if—

(i) financing for the indebtedness was provided in whole or part from the proceeds of any tax-exempt qualified mortgage bond, or
(ii) any credit was allowed under section 25 (relating to interest on certain home mortgages) to the taxpayer for interest paid or incurred on such indebtedness.

(B) Exception for home improvement loans. Such term shall not include any indebtedness to the extent such indebtedness is federally-subsidized indebtedness solely by reason of being a qualified home improvement loan (as defined in subsection (k)(4)).

(4) Recapture amount. For purposes of this subsection—

(A) In general. The recapture amount with respect to any indebtedness is the amount equal to the product of—

(i) the federally-subsidized amount with respect to the indebtedness,
(ii) the holding period percentage, and
(iii) the income percentage.

(B) Federally-subsidized amount. The federally-subsidized amount with respect to any indebtedness is the amount equal to 6.25 percent of the highest principal amount of the indebtedness for which the taxpayer was liable.

Private activity bonds — Code Sec. 143(m)(8)(C)

(C) Holding period percentage.
(i) In general. The term "holding period percentage" means the percentage determined in accordance with the following table:

If the disposition occurs during a year after the testing date which is:	The holding period percentage is:
The 1st such year	20
The 2d such year	40
The 3d such year	60
The 4th such year	80
The 5th such year	100
The 6th such year	80
The 7th such year	60
The 8th such year	40
The 9th such year	20

(ii) Retirements of indebtedness. If the federally-subsidized indebtedness is completely repaid during any year of the 4-year period beginning on the testing date the holding period percentage for succeeding years shall be determined by reducing ratably to zero over the succeeding 5 years the holding period percentage which would have been determined under this subparagraph had the taxpayer disposed of his interest in the residence on the date of the repayment.

(D) Testing date. The term "testing date" means the earliest date on which all of the following requirements are met:
(i) The indebtedness is federally-subsidized indebtedness.
(ii) The taxpayer is liable in whole or part for payment of the indebtedness.

(E) Income percentage. The term "income percentage" means the percentage (but not greater than 100 percent) which—
(i) the excess of—
(I) the modified adjusted gross income of the taxpayer for the taxable year in which the disposition occurs, over
(II) the adjusted qualifying income for such taxable year, bears to
(ii) $5,000.
The percentage determined under the preceding sentence shall be rounded to the nearest whole percentage point (or, if it includes a half of a percentage point, shall be increased to the nearest whole percentage point).

(5) Adjusted qualifying income; modified adjusted gross income.
(A) Adjusted qualifying income. For purposes of paragraph (4), the term "adjusted qualifying income" means the product of—
(i) the highest family income which (as of the date the financing was provided) would have met the requirements of subsection (f) with respect to the residents, and
(ii) 1.05 to the nth power where "n" equals the number of full years during the period beginning on the date the financing was provided and ending on the date of the disposition.
For purposes of clause (i), highest family income shall be determined without regard to subsection (f)(3)(A) and on the basis of the number of members of the taxpayer's family as of the date of the disposition.

(B) Modified adjusted gross income. For purposes of paragraph (4), the term "modified adjusted gross income" means adjusted gross income—
(i) increased by the amount of interest received or accrued by the taxpayer during the taxable year which is excluded from gross income under section 103, and
(ii) decreased by the amount of gain (if any) included in gross income of the taxpayer by reason of the disposition to which this subsection applies.

(6) Special rules relating to limitation on recapture amount based on gain realized.
(A) In general. For purposes of paragraph (1), gain shall be taken into account whether or not recognized, and the adjusted basis of the taxpayer's interest in the residence shall be determined without regard to sections 1033(b) and 1034(e) (as in effect on the day before the date of the enactment of the Taxpayer Relief Act of 1997) for purposes of determining gain.
(B) Dispositions other than sales, exchanges, and involuntary conversions. In the case of a disposition other than a sale, exchange, or involuntary conversion, gain shall be determined as if the interest had been sold for its fair market value.
(C) Involuntary conversions resulting from casualties. In the case of property which (as a result of its destruction in whole or in part by fire, storm, or other casualty) is compulsorily or involuntarily converted, paragraph (1) shall not apply to such conversion if the taxpayer purchases (during the period specified in section 1033(a)(2)(B)) property for use as his principal residence on the site of the converted property. For purposes of subparagraph (A), the adjusted basis of the taxpayer in the residence shall not be adjusted for any gain or loss on a conversion to which this subparagraph applies.

(7) Issuer to inform mortgagor of federally-subsidized amount and family income limits. The issuer of the issue which provided the federally-subsidized indebtedness to the mortgagor shall—
(A) at the time of settlement, provide a written statement informing the mortgagor of the potential recapture under this subsection, and
(B) not later than 90 days after the date such indebtedness is provided, provide a written statement to the mortgagor specifying—
(i) the federally-subsidized amount with respect to such indebtedness, and
(ii) the adjusted qualifying income (as defined in paragraph (5)) for each category of family size for each year of the 9-year period beginning on the date the financing was provided.

(8) Special rules.
(A) No basis adjustment. No adjustment shall be made to the basis of any property for the increase in tax under this subsection.
(B) Special rule where 2 or more persons hold interests in residence. Except as provided in subparagraph (C) and in regulations prescribed by the Secretary, if 2 or more persons hold interests in any residence and are jointly liable for the federally-subsidized indebtedness, the recapture amount shall be determined separately with respect to their respective interests in the residence.
(C) Transfers to spouses and former spouses. Paragraph (1) shall not apply to any transfer on which no gain or

loss is recognized under section 1041. In any such case, the transferee shall be treated under this subsection in the same manner as the transferor would have been treated had such transfer not occurred.

(D) Regulations. The Secretary shall prescribe such regulations as may be necessary or appropriate to carry out this subsection, including regulations dealing with dispositions of partial interests in a residence.

In 2008, P.L. 110-343, Sec. 709DivC, added para. (k)(12) [sic (13)], effective for disasters occurring after 12/31/2007.
— P.L. 110-343, Sec. 712DivC, of this Act, provides:
"SEC. 712. Coordination with heartland disaster relief.
"The amendments made by this subtitle, other than the amendments made by sections 706(a)(2), 710, and 711, shall not apply to any disaster described in section 702(c)(1)(A), or to any expenditure or loss resulting from such disaster."
— P.L. 110-289, Sec. 3021(b)(1), added para. (k)(12), effective for bonds issued after 7/30/2008.
— P.L. 110-289, Sec. 3026(a)(1), substituted "May 1, 2008" for "December 31, 1996" in para. (k)(11) ... Sec. 3026(a)(2), substituted "January 1, 2010" for "January 1, 1999" in para. (k)(11), effective for bonds issued after 5/1/2008.
— P.L. 110-245, Sec. 103(a), struck out "and before January 1, 2008", in subpara. (d)(2)(D) ... Sec. 103(b), substituted "$100,000,000" for "$25,000,000" each place it appears in clause (l)(3)(B)(ii), ... Sec. 103(c), amended para. (l)(4), effective for bonds issued after 12/31/2007. Sec. 103(e) of this Act, provides:
"(e) Transition rule. In the case of any bond issued after December 31, 2007, and before the date of the enactment of this Act, subparagraph (B) of section 143(l)(4) of the Internal Revenue Code of 1986, as amended by this section, shall be applied by substituting '30 years' for '25 years'."
Prior to amendment, para. (l)(4) read as follows:
"(4) Qualified veteran. For purposes of this subsection, the term 'qualified veteran' means —
"(A) in the case of the States of Alaska, Oregon, and Wisconsin, any veteran —
"(i) who served on active duty, and
"(ii) who applied for the financing before the date 25 years after the last date on which such veteran left active service, and
"(B) in the case of any other State, any veteran —
"(i) who served on active duty at some time before January 1, 1977, and
"(ii) who applied for the financing before the later of —
"(I) the date 30 years after the last date on which such veteran left active service, or
"(II) January 31, 1985."
In 2006, P.L. 109-432, Sec. 411(a), deleted clause (l)(3)(B)(iv), effective for allocations of State volume limit after 4/5/2006.
Prior to deletion, clause (l)(3)(B)(iv) reads as follows:
"(iv) Termination. The State veterans limit for the States specified in clause (ii) for any calendar year after 2010 is zero."
— P.L. 109-432, Sec. 416(a), deleted "and" at the end of subpara. (d)(2)(B), added "and" at the end of subpara. (d)(2)(C), and added subpara. (d)(2)(D), effective for bonds issued after 12/20/2006.
— P.L. 109-222, Sec. 203(a)(1), amended para. (l)(4), effective for bonds issued on or after 5/17/2006.
Prior to amendment, para. (l)(4) read as follows:
"(4) Qualified veteran. For purposes of this subsection, the term 'qualified veteran' means any veteran—
"(A) who served on active duty at some time before January 1, 1977, and
"(B) who applied for the financing before the later of —
"(i) the date 30 years after the last date on which such veteran left active service, or
"(ii) January 31, 1985."
— P.L. 109-222, Sec. 203(b)(1)(A), redesignated clauses (l)(3)(B)(i) and (ii) as subclauses (l)(3)(B)(i)(I) and (II) ... Sec. 203(b)(1)(B), substituted "(B) State veterans limit. (i) In general. In the case of any State to which clause (ii) does not apply, the State veterans limit for any calendar year is the amount equal to —" for "(B) State veterans limit. A State veterans limit for any calendar year is the amount equal to —" in the matter preceding subclause (l)(3)(B)(i)(I) [as redes. by Sec. 203(b)(1)(A) of this Act, see above] ... Sec. 203(b)(1)(C), added clauses (l)(3)(B)(ii)-(iv), effective for allocations of State volume limit after 4/5/2006.
In 2005, P.L. 109-135, Sec. 104, of this Act [which amends Sec. 404(d) of P.L. 109-73, see below] reads as follows:
"SEC. 104. EXTENSION OF SPECIAL RULES FOR MORTGAGE REVENUE BONDS.
"Section 404(d) of the Katrina Emergency Tax Relief Act of 2005 is amended by striking "December 31, 2007" and inserting "December 31, 2010"."
— P.L. 109-73, Sec. 404, of this Act [prior to amendment by Sec. 104 of P.L. 109-135, see above], reads as follows:
"SEC. 404. SPECIAL RULES FOR MORTGAGE REVENUE BONDS.
"(a) In General. In the case of financing provided with respect to a qualified Hurricane Katrina recovery residence, subsection (d) of section 143 of the Internal Revenue Code of 1986 shall be applied as if such residence were a targeted area residence.
"(b) Qualified Hurricane Katrina Recovery Residence. For purposes of this section, the term 'qualified Hurricane Katrina recovery residence' means—
"(1) any residence in the core disaster area, and
"(2) any other residence if—

"(A) such other residence is located in the same State as the principal residence referred to in subparagraph (B), and
"(B) the mortgagor with respect to such other residence owned a principal residence on August 28, 2005, which—
"(i) was located in the Hurricane Katrina disaster area, and
"(ii) was rendered uninhabitable by reason of Hurricane Katrina.
"(c) Special Rule for Home Improvement Loans. In the case of any loan with respect to a residence in the Hurricane Katrina disaster area, section 143(k)(4) of such Code shall be applied by substituting $150,000 for the dollar amount contained therein to the extent such loan is for the repair of damage by reason of Hurricane Katrina.
"(d) Application. Subsection (a) shall not apply to financing provided after December 31, 2007."
In 1998, P.L. 105-206, Sec. 6005(e)(3), added "on or" before "before" each place it appeared in the heading and text of Sec. 312(d)(2)[sic (e)] of P.L. 105-34, see below.
In 1997, P.L. 105-34, Sec. 312(d)(1), substituted "section 121" for "section 1034" in subclause (i)(1)(C)(i)(I) ... Sec. 312(d)(3), added "(as in effect on the day before the date of the enactment of the Taxpayer Relief Act of 1997)" after "1034(e)" in subpara. (m)(6)(A), effective for sales and exchanges after 5/6/97, except as provided in Secs. 312(d)(2)-(4) [sic (e)-(4)] of this Act [as amended by Sec. 6005(e)(3), 105-206, see above], which read as follows:
"(2) Sales on or before date of enactment [8/5/97]. — At the election of the taxpayer, the amendments made by this section shall not apply to any sale or exchange on or before the date of the enactment of this Act.
"(3) Certain sales within 2 years after date of enactment [8/5/97]. Section 121 of the Internal Revenue Code of 1986 (as amended by this section) shall be applied without regard to subsection (c)(2)(B) thereof in the case of any sale or exchange of property during the 2-year period beginning on the date of the enactment [8/5/97] of this Act if the taxpayer held such property on the date of the enactment [8/5/97] of this Act and fails to meet the ownership and use requirements of subsection (a) thereof with respect to such property.
"(4) Binding contracts. — At the election of the taxpayer, the amendments made by this section shall not apply to a sale or exchange after the date of the enactment [8/5/97] of this Act, if—
"(A) such sale or exchange is pursuant to a contract which was binding on such date, or
"(B) without regard to such amendments, gain would not be recognized under section 1034 of the Internal Revenue Code of 1986 (as in effect on the day before the date of the enactment [8/5/97] of this Act) on such sale or exchange by reason of a new residence acquired on or before such date or with respect to the acquisition of which by the taxpayer a binding contract was in effect on such date.
This paragraph shall not apply to any sale or exchange by an individual if the treatment provided by section 877(a)(1) of the Internal Revenue Code of 1986 applies to such individual."
— P.L. 105-34, Sec. 914, added para. (k)(11), effective 8/5/97.
In 1996, P.L. 104-188, Sec. 1702(d)(2)(A), substituted "any year of the 4-year period" for "any month of the 10-year period" in clause (m)(4)(C)(ii) ... Sec. 1702(d)(2)(B), substituted "succeeding years" for "succeeding months" in clause (m)(4)(C)(ii) ... Sec. 1702(d)(2)(C), substituted "to zero over the succeeding 5 years" for "over the remainder of such period (or, if lesser, 5 years)" in clause (m)(4)(C)(ii), effective as provided in Sec. 4005(h)(3) of P.L. 100-647, reproduced below.
— P.L. 104-188, Sec. 1703(n)(3), substituted a comma for the period at the end of subpara. (d)(2)(C), effective for loans originated and credit certificates provided after 8/10/93.
In 1993, P.L. 103-66, Sec. 13141(a), amended para. (a)(1), effective for bonds issued after 6/30/92.
Prior to amendment, para. (a)(1) read as follows:
"(1) Qualified mortgage bond defined.
"(A) In general. For purposes of this title, the term 'qualified mortgage bond' means a bond which is issued as part of a qualified mortgage issue.
"(B) Termination on June 30, 1992. No bond issued after June 30, 1992, may be treated as a qualified mortgage bond."
— P.L. 103-66, Sec. 13141(c), added para. (k)(10) ... Sec. 13141(e), added the flush sentence at the end of para., (k)(7), effective for qualified mortgage bonds issued and mortgage credit certificates provided on or after 8/10/93.
— P.L. 103-66, Sec. 13141(d)(1)(A), deleted "and" at the end of subpara. (d)(2)(A) ... Sec. 13141(d)(1)(B), added "and" at the end of subpara. (d)(2)(B) ... Sec. 13141(d)(1)(C), added subpara. (d)(2)(C) ... Sec. 13141(d)(2), added subpara. (i)(1)(C) ... Sec. 13141(d)(3), added "(other than land described in subsection (i)(1)(C)(i))" after "cost of land" in clause (k)(3)(B)(iii), effective for loans originated and credit certificates provided after 8/10/93.
In 1991, P.L. 102-227, Sec. 108(a), substituted "June 30, 1992" for "December 31, 1991" each place it appeared in subpara. (a)(1)(B), effective for bonds issued after 12/31/91.
In 1990, P.L. 101-508, Sec. 11408(a), substituted "December 31, 1991" for "September 30, 1990" each place it appeared in subpara. (a)(1)(B), effective for bonds issued after 9/30/90.
— P.L. 101-508, Sec. 11408(c)(1)(A), amended clause (m)(4)(C)(i) ... Sec. 11408(c)(1)(B), deleted clause (m)(4)(C)(ii) and redesignated clause (m)(4)(C)(iii) as clause (m)(4)(C)(ii) ... Sec. 11408(c)(1)(C), substituted "9 years" for "10 years" in subpara. (m)(2)(B) ... Sec. 11408(c)(2)(A), deleted "and" at the end of clause (m)(4)(A)(i), substituted ", and" for the period at the end of clause (m)(4)(A)(ii) and added clause (m)(4)(A)(iii) ... Sec. 11408(c)(2)(B), added subpara. (m)(4)(E) ... Sec. 11408(c)(2)(C)(i), amended the heading of para. (m)(5), amended subpara. (m)(5)(A) and deleted subpara. (m)(5)(B) ... Sec.

Private activity bonds　　　　　　　　　　　　　　　　　　　　　　　Code Sec. 144(a)(2)(C)

11408(c)(2)(C)(ii), redesignated subpara. (m)(5)(C) as subpara. (m)(5)(B) and substituted "paragraph (4)" for "this paragraph" in subpara. (m)(5)(B) [as redesignated] . . . Sec. 11408(c)(3)(A), amended para. (m)(1) . . . Sec. 11408(c)(3)(B)(i), substituted "Special rules relating to limitation" for "Limitation" in heading of para. (m)(6) . . . Sec. 11408(c)(3)(B)(ii), deleted first sentence of subpara. (m)(6)(A) . . . Sec. 11408(c)(3)(B)(iii), substituted "paragraph (1)" for "the preceding sentence" in subpara. (m)(6)(A) . . . Sec. 11408(c)(3)(C), amended clause (m)(7)(B)(ii), effective as provided in Sec. 4005(h)(3) of P.L. 100-647, reproduced below.

Prior to amendment, clause (m)(4)(C)(i) read as follows:

"(i) Dispositions during 1st 5 years. If the disposition of the taxpayer's interest in the residence occurs during the 5-year period beginning on the testing date, the holding period percentage is the percentage determined by dividing the number of full months during which the requirements of subparagraph (D) were met by 60."

Prior to deletion, clause (m)(4)(C)(ii) read as follows:

"(ii) Dispositions during 2d 5 years. If the disposition of the taxpayer's interest in the residence occurs during the 5-year period following the 5-year period described in clause (i), the holding period percentage is the percentage determined by dividing—

"(I) the excess of 120 over the number of full months during which such requirements were met by

"(II) 60."

Prior to amendment, para. (m)(5) heading and subparas. (m)(5)(A) and (m)(5)(B) read as follows:

"(5) Reduction of recapture amount if taxpayer meets certain income limitations.

"(A) In general. The recapture amount which would (but for this paragraph) apply with respect to any disposition during a taxable year shall be reduced (but not below zero) by 2 percent of such amount for each $100 by which adjusted qualifying income exceeds the modified adjusted gross income of the taxpayer for such year.

"(B) Adjusted qualifying income. For purposes of this paragraph, the term 'adjusted qualifying income' means the amount equal to the sum of—

"(i) $5,000, plus

"(ii) the product of—

"(I) the highest family income which (as of the date the financing was provided) would have met the requirement of subsection (f) with respect to the residence, and

"(II) the percentage equal to the sum of 100 percent plus 5 percent for each full year during the period beginning on such date and ending on the date of the disposition.

"For purposes of clause (ii)(I), highest family income shall be determined without regard to subsection (f)(3)(A) and on the basis of the number of members of the taxpayer's family as of the date of the disposition."

Prior to amendment, para. (m)(1) read as follows:

"(1) In general. If, during the taxable year, any taxpayer disposes of an interest in a residence with respect to which there is or was any federally-subsidized indebtedness for the payment of which the taxpayer was liable in whole or in part, then the taxpayer's tax imposed by this chapter for such taxable year shall be increased by the recapture amount with respect to such indebtedness."

Prior to deletion, the first sentence of subpara. (m)(6)(A) read as follows:

"In no event shall the recapture amount of the taxpayer with respect to any indebtedness exceed 50 percent of the gain (if any) on the disposition of the taxpayer's interest in the residence."

Prior to amendment, clause (m)(7)(B)(ii) read as follows:

"(ii) the amounts described in paragraph (5)(B)(ii) for each category of family size for each year of the 10-year period beginning on the date the financing was provided."

In 1989, P.L. 101-239, Sec. 7104(a), substituted "September 30, 1990" for "December 31, 1989" each place it appeared in subpara. (a)(1)(B), effective 12/19/89.

In 1988, P.L. 100-647, Sec. 1013(a)(2), substituted "such issue does not meet" for "no bond which is part of such issue meets" in clause (a)(2)(A)(iii) . . . Sec. 1013(a)(3), added "is part of an issue which" after "which" in para. (b)(4), effective for bonds issued after 8/15/86. For transitional rules, see Secs. 1312 and 1318 of P.L. 99-514 reproduced in the note following Code Sec. 103.

—P.L. 100-647, Sec. 1013(a)(27), provides:

"(27) The date contained in section 143(a)(1)(B) of the 1986 Code shall be treated as contained in section 103A(c)(1)(B) of the Internal Revenue Code of 1954, as in effect on the day before the date of the enactment of the Reform Act, for purposes of any bond issued to refund a bond to which such 103A(c)(1) applies."

—P.L. 100-647, Sec. 4005(a)(1), substituted "December 31, 1989" for "December 31, 1988" each place it appeared in subpara. (a)(1)(B), effective for bonds issued, and nonissued bond amounts elected, after 12/31/88.

—P.L. 100-647, Sec. 4005(b), added para. (f)(5) . . . Sec. 4005(c), added para. (f)(6), effective for bonds issued, and nonissued bond amounts elected, after 12/31/88, except as provided in Sec. 4005(h)(2)(A) of this Act, which reads as follows:

"(2) Special rules relating to certain requirements and refunding bonds.—In the case of a bond issued to refund (or which is part of a series of bonds issued to refund) a bond issued before January 1, 1989—

"(A) the amendments made by subsections (b) and (c) shall apply to financing provided after the date of issuance of the refunding issue, and"

—P.L. 100-647, Sec. 4005(d)(1)(A), substituted "paragraph (2) of this subsection and, in the case of an issue described in subsection (b)(1), such issue also meets the requirements of paragraph (3) of this subsection" for "paragraphs (2) and (3) of this subsection" in para. (g)(1) . . . Sec. 4005(d)(1)(B), deleted "(other than subsection (f) thereof)" after "section 148" in para. (g)(1) . . . Sec. 4005(e), added subpara. (a)(2)(D), effective for bonds issued, and nonissued bond amounts elected, after 12/31/88.

—P.L. 100-647, Sec. 4005(f), deleted "and" at the end of clause (a)(2)(A)(ii) and substituted ", and" for the period at the end of clause (a)(2)(A)(iii) and added clause (a)(2)(A)(iv), effective for bonds issued, and nonissued bond amounts elected, after 12/31/88, except as provided by Sec. 4005(h)(2)(B) of this Act, which reads as follows:

"(2) Special rules relating to certain requirements and refunding bonds.—In the case of a bond issued to refund (or which is part of a series of bonds issued to refund) a bond issued before January 1, 1989—

* * *

"(B) the amendment made by subsection (f) shall apply to payments (including on loans made before such date of issuance) received on or after such date of issuance."

—P.L. 100-647, Sec. 4005(g)(1), added subsec. (m) . . . Sec. 4005(g)(2)(A), substituted "(i), and (m)(7)" for "and (i)" in clause (a)(2)(A)(ii) . . . Sec. 4005(g)(2)(B), substituted ", (h), and (m)(7)" for "and (h)" in subpara. (a)(2)(C) . . . Sec. 4005(g)(6), added a new sentence to the end of clause (g)(2)(B)(iv), effective as provided by Sec. 4005(h)(3) of this Act, which reads as follows:

"(3) Subsection (g).—

"(A) In general.—Except as provided in subparagraph (B), the amendments made by subsection (g) shall apply to financing provided, and mortgage credit certificates issued, after December 31, 1990.

"(B) Exception.—The amendments made by subsection (g) shall not apply to financing provided pursuant to a binding contract (entered into before June 23, 1988) with a homebuilder, lender, or mortgagor if the bonds (the proceeds of which are used to provide such financing) are issued—

"(i) before June 23, 1988, or

"(ii) before August 1, 1988, pursuant to a written application (made before July 1, 1988) for State bond volume authority."

—P.L. 100-647, Sec. 4005(i), of this Act provides:

"(i) Study of recapture provisions.—The Comptroller General of the United States shall conduct a study of section 143(m) of the 1986 Code (as added by this section) and of alternatives to accomplish the purposes of such section. A report of such study shall be submitted not later than July 1, 1990, to the Committee on Ways and Means of the House of Representatives and the Committee on Finance of the Senate."

In 1986, P.L. 99-514, Sec. 1301(b), added Code Sec. 143 as part of the amendments to Part IV of subchapter B of chapter 1, effective for bonds issued after 8/15/86. For transitional rules, see Secs. 1312—1318 of this Act reproduced in the note following Code Sec. 103.

Sec. 144. Qualified small issue bond; qualified student loan bond; qualified redevelopment bond.

(a) Qualified small issue bond.

(1) In general. For purposes of this part, the term "qualified small issue bond" means any bond issued as part of an issue the aggregate authorized face amount of which is $1,000,000 or less and 95 percent or more of the net proceeds of which are to be used—

(A) for the acquisition, construction, reconstruction, or improvement of land or property of a character subject to the allowance for depreciation, or

(B) to redeem part or all of a prior issue which was issued for purposes described in subparagraph (A) or this subparagraph.

(2) Certain prior issues taken into account. If—

(A) the proceeds of 2 or more issues of bonds (whether or not the issuer of each such issue is the same) are or will be used primarily with respect to facilities located in the same incorporated municipality or located in the same county (but not in any incorporated municipality),

(B) the principal user of such facilities is or will be the same person or 2 or more related persons, and

(C) but for this paragraph, paragraph (1) (or the corresponding provision of prior law) would apply to each such issue,

then, for purposes of paragraph (1), in determining the aggregate face amount of any later issue there shall be taken into account the aggregate face amount of tax-exempt bonds issued under all prior such issues and outstanding at the time of such later issue (not including as outstanding any bond which is to be redeemed (other than in an advance refunding) from the net proceeds of the later issue).

1,485

(3) **Related persons.** For purposes of this subsection, a person is a related person to another person if—
(A) the relationship between such persons would result in a disallowance of losses under section 267 or 707(b), or
(B) such persons are members of the same controlled group of corporations (as defined in section 1563(a), except that "more than 50 percent" shall be substituted for "at least 80 percent" each place it appears therein).

(4) **$10,000,000 limit in certain cases.**
(A) In general. At the election of the issuer with respect to any issue, this subsection shall be applied—
(i) by substituting "$10,000,000" for "$1,000,000" in paragraph (1), and
(ii) in determining the aggregate face amount of such issue, by taking into account not only the amount described in paragraph (2), but also the aggregate amount of capital expenditures with respect to facilities described in subparagraph (B) paid or incurred during the 6-year period beginning 3 years before the date of such issue and ending 3 years after such date (and financed otherwise than out of the proceeds of outstanding tax-exempt issues to which paragraph (1) (or the corresponding provision of prior law) applied), as if the aggregate amount of such capital expenditures constituted the face amount of a prior outstanding issue described in paragraph (2).
(B) Facilities taken into account. For purposes of subparagraph (A)(ii), the facilities described in this subparagraph are facilities—
(i) located in the same incorporated municipality or located in the same county (but not in any incorporated municipality), and
(ii) the principal user of which is or will be the same person or 2 or more related persons.
For purposes of clause (i), the determination of whether or not facilities are located in the same governmental unit shall be made as of the date of issue of the issue in question.
(C) Certain capital expenditures not taken into account. For purposes of subparagraph (A)(ii), any capital expenditure—
(i) to replace property destroyed or damaged by fire, storm, or other casualty, to the extent of the fair market value of the property replaced,
(ii) required by a change made after the date of issue of the issue in question in a Federal or State law or local ordinance of general application or required by a change made after such date in rules and regulations of general application issued under such a law or ordinance,
(iii) required by circumstances which could not be reasonably foreseen on such date of issue or arising out of a mistake of law or fact (but the aggregate amount of expenditures not taken into account under this clause with respect to any issue shall not exceed $1,000,000), or
(iv) described in clause (i) or (ii) of section 41(b)(2)(A) for which a deduction was allowed under section 174(a),
shall not be taken into account.
(D) Limitation on loss of tax exemption. In applying subparagraph (A)(ii) with respect to capital expenditures made after the date of any issue, no bond issued as a part of such issue shall cease to be treated as a qualified small issue bond by reason of any such expenditure for any period before the date on which such expenditure is paid or incurred.
(E) Certain refinancing issues. In the case of any issue described in paragraph (1)(B), an election may be made under subparagraph (A) of this paragraph only if all of the prior issues being redeemed are issues to which paragraph (1) (or the corresponding provision of prior law) applied. In applying subparagraph (A)(ii) with respect to such a refinancing issue, capital expenditures shall be taken into account only for purposes of determining whether the prior issues being redeemed qualified (and would have continued to qualify) under paragraph (1) (or the corresponding provision of prior law).
(F) Aggregate amount of capital expenditures where there is urban development action grant. In the case of any issue 95 percent or more of the net proceeds of which are to be used to provide facilities with respect to which an urban development action grant has been made under section 119 of the Housing and Community Development Act of 1974, capital expenditures of not to exceed $10,000,000 shall not be taken into account for purposes of applying subparagraph (A)(ii). This subparagraph shall not apply to bonds issued after December 31, 2006.
(G) Additional capital expenditures not taken into account. With respect to bonds issued after December 31, 2006, in addition to any capital expenditure described in subparagraph (C), capital expenditures of not to exceed $10,000,000 shall not be taken into account for purposes of applying subparagraph (A)(ii).

(5) **Issues for residential purposes.** This subsection shall not apply to any bond issued as part of an issue 5 percent or more of the net proceeds of which are to be used directly or indirectly to provide residential real property for family units.

(6) **Limitations on treatment of bonds as part of the same issue.**
(A) In general. For purposes of this subsection, separate lots of bonds which (but for this subparagraph) would be treated as part of the same issue shall be treated as separate issues unless the proceeds of such lots are to be used with respect to 2 or more facilities—
(i) which are located in more than 1 State, or
(ii) which have, or will have, as the same principal user the same person or related persons.
(B) Franchises. For purposes of subparagraph (A), a person (other than a governmental unit) shall be considered a principal user of a facility if such person (or a group of related persons which includes such person)—
(i) guarantees, arranges, participates in, or assists with the issuance (or pays any portion of the cost of issuance) of any bond the proceeds of which are to be used to finance or refinance such facility, and
(ii) provides any property, or any franchise, trademark, or trade name (within the meaning of section 1253), which is to be used in connection with such facility.

(7) **Subsection not to apply if bonds issued with certain other tax-exempt bonds.** This subsection shall not apply to any bond issued as part of an issue (other than an issue to which paragraph (4) applies) if the interest on any other bond which is part of such issue is excluded from gross income under any provision of law other than this subsection.

(8) **Restrictions on financing certain facilities.** This subsection shall not apply to an issue if—

(A) more than 25 percent of the net proceeds of the issue are to be used to provide a facility the primary purpose of which is one of the following: retail food and beverage services, automobile sales or service, or the provision of recreation or entertainment; or

(B) any portion of the proceeds of the issue is to be used to provide the following: any private or commercial golf course, country club, massage parlor, tennis club, skating facility (including roller skating, skateboard, and ice skating), racquet sports facility (including any handball or racquetball court), hot tub facility, suntan facility, or racetrack.

(9) Aggregation of issues with respect to single project. For purposes of this subsection, 2 or more issues part or all of the net proceeds of which are to be used with respect to a single building, an enclosed shopping mall, or a strip of offices, stores, or warehouses using substantial common facilities shall be treated as 1 issue (and any person who is a principal user with respect to any of such issues shall be treated as a principal user with respect to the aggregated issue).

(10) Aggregate limit per taxpayer.
(A) In general. This subsection shall not apply to any issue if the aggregate authorized face amount of such issue allocated to any test-period beneficiary (when increased by the outstanding tax-exempt facility-related bonds of such beneficiary) exceeds $40,000,000.

(B) Outstanding tax-exempt facility-related bonds.
(i) In general. For purposes of applying subparagraph (A) with respect to any issue, the outstanding tax-exempt facility-related bonds of any person who is a test-period beneficiary with respect to such issue is the aggregate amount of tax-exempt bonds referred to in clause (ii)—
(I) which are allocated to such beneficiary, and
(II) which are outstanding at the time of such later issue (not including as outstanding any bond which is to be redeemed (other than in an advance refunding) from the net proceeds of the later issue).
(ii) Bonds taken into account. For purposes of clause (i), the bonds referred to in this clause are—
(I) exempt facility bonds, qualified small issue bonds, and qualified redevelopment bonds, and
(II) industrial development bonds (as defined in section 103(b)(2), as in effect on the day before the date of the enactment [10/22/86] of the Tax Reform Act of 1986) to which section 141(a) does not apply.

(C) Allocation of face amount of issue.
(i) In general. Except as otherwise provided in regulations, the portion of the face amount of an issue allocated to any test-period beneficiary of a facility financed by the proceeds of such issue (other than an owner of such facility) is an amount which bears the same relationship to the entire face amount of such issue as the portion of such facility used by such beneficiary bears to the entire facility.
(ii) Owners. Except as otherwise provided in regulations, the portion of the face amount of an issue allocated to any test-period beneficiary who is an owner of a facility financed by the proceeds of such issue is an amount which bears the same relationship to the entire face amount of such issue as the portion of such facility owned by such beneficiary bears to the entire facility.

(D) Test-period beneficiary. For purposes of this paragraph, except as provided in regulations, the term "test-period beneficiary" means any person who is an owner or a principal user of facilities being financed by the issue at any time during the 3-year period beginning on the later of—
(i) the date such facilities were placed in service, or
(ii) the date of issue.
(E) Treatment of related persons. For purposes of this paragraph, all persons who are related (within the meaning of paragraph (3)) to each other shall be treated as 1 person.

(11) Limitation on acquisition of depreciable farm property.
(A) In general. This subsection shall not apply to any issue if more than $250,000 of the net proceeds of such issue are to be used to provide depreciable farm property with respect to which the principal user is or will be the same person or 2 or more related persons.
(B) Depreciable farm property. For purposes of this paragraph, the term "depreciable farm property" means property of a character subject to the allowance for depreciation which is to be used in a trade or business of farming.
(C) Prior issues taken into account. In determining the amount of proceeds of an issue to be used as described in subparagraph (A), there shall be taken into account the aggregate amount of each prior issue to which paragraph (1) (or the corresponding provisions of prior law) applied which were or will be so used.

(12) Termination dates.
(A) In general. This subsection shall not apply to—
(i) any bond (other than a bond described in clause (ii)) issued after December 31, 1986, or
(ii) any bond (or series of bonds) issued to refund a bond issued on or before such date unless—
(I) the average maturity date of the issue of which the refunding bond is a part is not later than the average maturity date of the bonds to be refunded by such issue,
(II) the amount of the refunding bond does not exceed the outstanding amount of the refunded bond, and
(III) the net proceeds of the refunding bond are used to redeem the refunded bond not later than 90 days after the date of the issuance of the refunding bond.
For purposes of clause (ii)(I), average maturity shall be determined in accordance with section 147(b)(2)(A).
(B) Bonds issued to finance manufacturing facilities and farm property. Subparagraph (A) shall not apply to any bond issued as part of an issue 95 percent or more of the net proceeds of which are to be used to provide—
(i) any manufacturing facility, or
(ii) any land or property in accordance with section 147(c)(2).
(C) Manufacturing facility.
For purposes of this paragraph—
(i) In general. The term "manufacturing facility" means any facility which is used in the manufacturing or production of tangible personal property (including the processing resulting in a change in the condition of such property). A rule similar to the rule of section 142(b)(2) shall apply for purposes of the preceding sentence. For purposes of the 1st sentence of this subparagraph, the term "manufacturing facil-

ity" includes facilities which are directly related and ancillary to a manufacturing facility (determined without regard to this sentence) if—

(ii) *Certain facilities included.* Such term includes facilities which are directly related and ancillary to a manufacturing facility (determined without regard to this clause) if—

(I) such facilities are located on the same site as the manufacturing facility, and

(II) not more than 25 percent of the net proceeds of the issue are used to provide such facilities.

(iii) *Special rules for bonds issued in 2009 and 2010.* In the case of any issue made after the date of enactment of this clause and before January 1, 2011, clause (ii) shall not apply and the net proceeds from a bond shall be considered to be used to provide a manufacturing facility if such proceeds are used to provide—

(I) a facility which is used in the creation or production of intangible property which is described in section 197(d)(1)(C)(iii), or

(II) a facility which is functionally related and subordinate to a manufacturing facility (determined without regard to this subclause) if such facility is located on the same site as the manufacturing facility.

(b) Qualified student loan bond.

For purposes of this part—

(1) In general. The term "qualified student loan bond" means any bond issued as part of an issue the applicable percentage or more of the net proceeds of which are to be used directly or indirectly to make or finance student loans under—

(A) a program of general application to which the Higher Education Act of 1965 applies if—

(i) limitations are imposed under the program on—

(I) the maximum amount of loans outstanding to any student, and

(II) the maximum rate of interest payable on any loan,

(ii) the loans are directly or indirectly guaranteed by the Federal Government,

(iii) the financing of loans under the program is not limited by Federal law to the proceeds of tax-exempt bonds, and

(iv) special allowance payments under section 438 of the Higher Education Act of 1965—

(I) are authorized to be paid with respect to loans made under the program, or

(II) would be authorized to be made with respect to loans under the program if such loans were not financed with the proceeds of tax-exempt bonds, or

(B) a program of general application approved by the State if no loan under such program exceeds the difference between the total cost of attendance and other forms of student assistance (not including loans pursuant to section 428B(a)(1) of the Higher Education Act of 1965 (relating to parent loans) or subpart I of part C of title VII of the Public Health Service Act (relating to student assistance)) for which the student borrower may be eligible. A program shall not be treated as described in this subparagraph if such program is described in subparagraph (A).

A bond shall not be treated as a qualified student loan bond if the issue of which such bond is a part meets the private business tests of paragraphs (1) and (2) of section 141(b) (determined by treating 501(c)(3) organizations as governmental units with respect to their activities which do not constitute unrelated trades or businesses, determined by applying section 513(a)).

(2) Applicable percentage. For purposes of paragraph (1), the term "applicable percentage" means—

(A) 90 percent in the case of the program described in paragraph (1)(A), and

(B) 95 percent in the case of the program described in paragraph (1)(B).

(3) Student borrowers must be residents of issuing state, etc. A student loan shall be treated as being made or financed under a program described in paragraph (1) with respect to an issue only if the student is—

(A) a resident of the State from which the volume cap under section 146 for such loan was derived, or

(B) enrolled at an educational institution located in such State.

(4) Discrimination on basis of school location not permitted. A program shall not be treated as described in paragraph (1)(A) if such program discriminates on the basis of the location (in the United States) of the educational institution in which the student is enrolled.

(c) Qualified redevelopment bond.

For purposes of this part—

(1) In general. The term "qualified redevelopment bond" means any bond issued as part of an issue 95 percent or more of the net proceeds of which are to be used for 1 or more redevelopment purposes in any designated blighted area.

(2) Additional requirements. A bond shall not be treated as a qualified redevelopment bond unless—

(A) the issue described in paragraph (1) is issued pursuant to—

(i) a State law which authorizes the issuance of such bonds for redevelopment purposes in blighted areas, and

(ii) a redevelopment plan which is adopted before such issuance by the governing body described in paragraph (4)(A) with respect to the designated blighted area,

(B)(i) the payment of the principal and interest on such issue is primarily secured by taxes of general applicability imposed by a general purpose governmental unit, or

(ii) any increase in real property tax revenues (attributable to increases in assessed value) by reason of the carrying out of such purposes in such area is reserved exclusively for debt service on such issue (and similar issues) to the extent such increase does not exceed such debt service,

(C) each interest in real property located in such area—

(i) which is acquired by a governmental unit with the proceeds of the issue, and

(ii) which is transferred to a person other than a governmental unit,

is transferred for fair market value,

(D) the financed area with respect to such issue meets the no additional charge requirements of paragraph (5), and

(E) the use of the proceeds of the issue meets the requirements of paragraph (6).

(3) Redevelopment purposes. For purposes of paragraph (1)—

(A) *In general.* The term "redevelopment purposes" means, with respect to any designated blighted area—

(i) the acquisition (by a governmental unit having the power to exercise eminent domain) of real property located in such area,

(ii) the clearing and preparation for redevelopment of land in such area which was acquired by such governmental unit,

(iii) the rehabilitation of real property located in such area which was acquired by such governmental unit, and

(iv) the relocation of occupants of such real property.

(B) New construction not permitted. The term "redevelopment purposes" does not include the construction (other than the rehabilitation) of any property or the enlargement of an existing building.

(4) Designated blighted area. For purposes of this subsection—

(A) In general. The term "designated blighted area" means any blighted area designated by the governing body of a local general purpose governmental unit in the jurisdiction of which such area is located.

(B) Blighted area. The term "blighted area" means any area which the governing body described in subparagraph (A) determines to be a blighted area on the basis of the substantial presence of factors such as excessive vacant land on which structures were previously located, abandoned or vacant buildings, substandard structures, vacancies, and delinquencies in payment of real property taxes.

(C) Designated areas may not exceed 20 percent of total assessed value of real property in government's jurisdiction.

(i) In general. An area may be designated by a governmental unit as a blighted area only if the designation percentage with respect to such area, when added to the designation percentages of all other designated blighted areas within the jurisdiction of such governmental unit, does not exceed 20 percent.

(ii) Designation percentage. For purposes of this subparagraph, the term "designation percentage" means, with respect to any area, the percentage (determined at the time such area is designated) which the assessed value of real property located in such area is of the total assessed value of all real property located within the jurisdiction of the governmental unit which designated such area.

(iii) Exception where bonds not outstanding. The designation percentage of a previously designated blighted area shall not be taken into account under clause (i) if no qualified redevelopment bond (or similar bond) is or will be outstanding with respect to such area.

(D) Minimum designated area.

(i) In general. Except as provided in clause (ii), an area shall not be treated as a designated blighted area for purposes of this subsection unless such area is contiguous and compact and its area equals or exceeds 100 acres.

(ii) 10-acre minimum in certain cases. Clause (i) shall be applied by substituting "10 acres" for "100 acres" if not more than 25 percent of the financed area is to be provided (pursuant to the issue and all other such issues) to 1 person. For purposes of the preceding sentence, all related persons (as defined in subsection (a)(3)) shall be treated as 1 person. For purposes of this clause, an area provided to a developer on a short-term interim basis shall not be treated as provided to such developer.

(5) No additional charge requirements. The financed area with respect to any issue meets the requirements of this paragraph if, while any bond which is part of such issue is outstanding—

(A) no owner or user of property located in the financed area is subject to a charge or fee which similarly situated owners or users of comparable property located outside such area are not subject, and

(B) the assessment method or rate of real property taxes with respect to property located in the financed area does not differ from the assessment method or rate of real property taxes with respect to comparable property located outside such area.

For purposes of the preceding sentence, the term "comparable property" means property which is of the same type as the property to which it is being compared and which is located within the jurisdiction of the designating governmental unit.

(6) Use of proceeds requirements. The use of the proceeds of an issue meets the requirements of this paragraph if—

(A) not more than 25 percent of the net proceeds of such issue are to be used to provide (including the provision of land for) facilities described in subsection (a)(8) or section 147(e), and

(B) no portion of the proceeds of such issue is to be used to provide (including the provision of land for) any private or commercial golf course, country club, massage parlor, hot tub facility, suntan facility, racetrack or other facility used for gambling, or any store the principal business of which is the sale of alcoholic beverages for consumption off premises.

(7) Financed area. For purposes of this subsection, the term "financed area" means, with respect to any issue, the portion of the designated blighted area with respect to which the proceeds of such issue are to be used.

(8) Restriction on acquisition of land not to apply. Section 147(c) (other than paragraphs (1)(B) and (2) thereof) shall not apply to any qualified redevelopment bond.

In **2009**, P.L. 111-5, Sec. 1301(a)(1), substituted "For purposes of this paragraph— (i) In general. The term" for "For purposes of this paragraph, the term" in subpara. (a)(12)(C)

—P.L. 111-5, Sec. 1301(a)(2), deleted the last sentence in subpara. (a)(12)(C) and added clauses (ii) and (iii), effective for obligations issued after 2/17/2009. Prior to amendment, clause (a)(12)(C)(i) and (ii) read as follows:

"(i) such facilities are located on the same site as the manufacturing facility, and

"(ii) not more than 25 percent of the net proceeds of the issue are used to provide such facilities."

In **2006**, P.L. 109-222, Sec. 208(a), substituted 'December 31, 2006' for 'September 30, 2009' in subpara. (a)(4)(G) . . . Sec. 208(b), substituted 'December 31, 2006' for 'September 30, 2009' in subpara. (a)(4)(F), enacted 5/17/2006.

In **2004**, P.L. 108-357, Sec. 340(a), added subpara. (a)(4)(G) . . . Sec. 340(b), added 'This subparagraph shall not apply to bonds issued after September 30, 2009.' at the end of subpara. (a)(4)(F), effective 10/22/2004.

In **1993**, P.L. 103-66, Sec. 13122(a), amended subpara. (a)(12)(B), effective for bonds issued after 6/30/92.

Prior to amendment, subpara. (a)(12)(B) read as follows:

"(B) Bonds issued to finance manufacturing facilities and farm property. In the case of any bond issued as part of an issue 95 percent or more of the net proceeds of which are to be used to provide—

"(i) any manufacturing facility, or

"(ii) any land or property in accordance with section 147(c)(2),

subparagraph (A) shall be applied by substituting 'June 30, 1992' for 'December 31, 1986'."

In **1991**, P.L. 102-227, Sec. 109(a), substituted "June 30, 1992" for "December 31, 1991" in subpara. (a)(12)(B), effective for bonds issued after 12/31/91.

In **1990**, P.L. 101-508, Sec. 11409(a), substituted "December 31, 1991" for "September 30, 1990" in subpara. (a)(12)(B), effective for bonds issued after 9/30/90.

Code Sec. 144   Private activity bonds

In **1989**, P.L. 101-239, Sec. 7105, substituted "substituting 'September 30, 1990' for 'December 31, 1986'" for "substituting '1989' for '1986'" in subpara. (a)(12)(B), effective 12/19/89.

In **1988**, P.L. 100-647, Sec. 1013(a)(4)(A), added "(or series of bonds)" before "issued to refund" in clause (a)(12)(A)(ii)... Sec. 1013(a)(4)(B)(i), amended subclause (a)(12)(A)(ii)(I)... Sec. 1013(a)(4)(B)(ii), added the last sentence of subpara. (a)(12)(A), effective for bonds issued after 8/15/86. For transitional rules see Sec. 1312-1318 of P.L. 99-514 reproduced in note following Code Sec. 103. Sec. 1013(a)(4)(B)(iii) of this Act provides:

"(iii) A refunding bond issued before July 1, 1987, shall be treated as meeting the requirement of subclause (I) of section 144(a)(12)(A)(ii) of the 1986 Code if such bond met the requirement of such subclause as in effect before the amendments made by this subparagraph."

Prior to amendment, subclause (a)(12)(A)(ii)(I) read as follows:

"(I) the refunding bond has a maturity date not later than the maturity date of the refunded bond,"

—P.L. 100-647, Sec. 1013(a)(4)(C), added "and" at the end of subclause (a)(12)(A)(ii)(II), deleted subclause (a)(12)(A)(ii)(III), and redesignated subclause (a)(12)(A)(ii)(IV) as subclause (a)(12)(A)(ii)(III)... Sec. 1013(a)(5)(A)-(C), amended subpara. (b)(1)(B) by deleting "to which part B of title IV of the Higher Education Act of 1965 (relating to guaranteed student loans) does not apply" before "if no loan", by substituting "of the Higher Education Act of 1965" for "of such Act" and substituted "A program shall not be treated as described in this subparagraph if such program is described in subparagraph (A)." for "A bond issued as part of an issue shall be treated as a qualified student loan bond only if no bond which is part of such issue meets the private business tests of paragraphs (1) and (2) of section 141(b)." at the end of subpara. (b)(1)(B), and added the last sentence of para. (b)(1), effective for bonds issued after 8/15/86. For transitional rules see Sec. 1312-1318 of P.L. 99-514 reproduced in note following Code Sec. 103.

Prior to deletion, subclause (a)(12)(A)(ii)(III) read as follows:

"(III) the interest rate on the refunding bond is lower than the interest rate on the refunded bond, and".

—P.L. 100-647, Sec. 1013(c)(12)(B), of this Act provides:

"(B) The date applicable under section 144(a)(12)(B) of the 1986 Code shall be treated as contained in section 103(b)(6)(N)(iii) of the Internal Revenue Code of 1954, as in effect on the day before the date of the enactment of the Reform Act, for purposes of any bond issued to refund a bond in which such section 103(b)(6)(N)(iii) applies."

—P.L. 100-647, Sec. 6176(a), added the sentence at the end of subpara. (a)(12)(C), effective as provided in Sec. 6176(b) of this Act:

"(b) Effective date.—

"(1) In general.—The amendment made by subsection (a) [6176(a)] shall apply to bonds issued after the date of the enactment of this Act [11/10/88].

"(2) Refundings.—The amendment made by subsection (a) shall not apply to any bond issued to refund (or which is part of a series of bonds issued to refund) a bond issued on or before the date of the enactment of this Act if—

"(A) the average maturity date of the issue of which the refunding bond is a part is not later than the average maturity date of the bonds to be refunded by such issue, and

"(B) the amount of the refunding bond does not exceed the outstanding amount of the refunded bond.

For purposes of subparagraph (A), average maturity shall be determined in accordance with section 147(b) of the 1986 Code."

In **1986**, P.L. 99-514, Sec. 1301(b), added Code Sec. 144 as part of the amendments to Part IV of subchapter B of chapter 1, effective for bonds issued after 8/15/86. For transitional rules, see Secs. 1312— 1318 of this Act reproduced in the note following Code Sec. 103.

Sec. 145. Qualified 501(c)(3) bond.

(a) In general.

For purposes of this part, except as otherwise provided in this section, the term "qualified 501(c)(3) bond" means any private activity bond issued as part of an issue if—

(1) all property which is to be provided by the net proceeds of the issue is to be owned by a 501(c)(3) organization or a governmental unit, and

(2) such bond would not be a private activity bond if—

(A) 501(c)(3) organizations were treated as governmental units with respect to their activities which do not constitute unrelated trades or businesses, determined by applying section 513(a), and

(B) paragraphs (1) and (2) of section 141(b) were applied by substituting "5 percent" for "10 percent" each place it appears and by substituting "net proceeds" for "proceeds" each place it appears.

(b) $150,000,000 limitation on bonds other than hospital bonds.

(1) In general. A bond (other than a qualified hospital bond) shall not be treated as a qualified 501(c)(3) bond if the aggregate authorized face amount of the issue (of which such bond is a part) allocated to any 501(c)(3) organization which is a test-period beneficiary (when increased by the outstanding tax-exempt nonhospital bonds of such organization) exceeds $150,000,000.

(2) Outstanding tax-exempt nonhospital bonds.

(A) In general. For purposes of applying paragraph (1) with respect to any issue, the outstanding tax-exempt nonhospital bonds of any organization which is a test-period beneficiary with respect to such issue is the aggregate amount of tax-exempt bonds referred to in subparagraph (B)—

(i) which are allocated to such organization, and

(ii) which are outstanding at the time of such later issue (not including as outstanding any bond which is to be redeemed (other than in an advance refunding) from the net proceeds of the later issue).

(B) Bonds taken into account. For purposes of subparagraph (A), the bonds referred to in this subparagraph are—

(i) any qualified 501(c)(3) bond other than a qualified hospital bond, and

(ii) any bond to which section 141(a) does not apply if—

(I) such bond would have been an industrial development bond (as defined in section 103(b)(2), as in effect on the day before the date of the enactment [10/22/86] of the Tax Reform Act of 1986) if 501(c)(3) organizations were not exempt persons, and

(II) such bond was not described in paragraph (4), (5), or (6) of such section 103(b) (as in effect on the date such bond was issued).

(C) Only nonhospital portion of bonds taken into account.

(i) In general. A bond shall be taken into account under subparagraph (B) only to the extent that the proceeds of the issue of which such bond is a part are not used with respect to a hospital.

(ii) Special rule. If 90 percent or more of the net proceeds of an issue are used with respect to a hospital, no bond which is part of such issue shall be taken into account under subparagraph (B)(ii).

(3) Aggregation rule. For purposes of this subsection, 2 or more organizations under common management or control shall be treated as 1 organization.

(4) Allocation of face amount of issue; test-period beneficiary. Rules similar to the rules of subparagraphs (C), (D), and (E) of section 144(a)(10) shall apply for purposes of this subsection.

(5) Termination of limitation. This subsection shall not apply with respect to bonds issued after the date of the enactment of this paragraph as part of an issue 95 percent or more of the net proceeds of which are to be used to finance capital expenditures incurred after such date.

(c) Qualified hospital bond.

For purposes of this section, the term "qualified hospital bond" means any bond issued as part of an issue 95 percent or more of the net proceeds of which are to be used with respect to a hospital.

(d) Restrictions on bonds used to provide residential rental housing for family units.

(1) In general. Except as otherwise provided in this subsection, a bond which is part of an issue shall not be a qualified 501(c)(3) bond if any portion of the net proceeds of the issue are to be used directly or indirectly to provide residential rental property for family units.

(2) Exception for bonds used to provide qualified residential rental projects. Paragraph (1) shall not apply to any bond issued as part of an issue if the portion of such issue which is to be used as described in paragraph (1) is to be used to provide—

(A) a residential rental property for family units if the first use of such property is pursuant to such issue,

(B) qualified residential rental projects (as defined in section 142(d)), or

(C) property which is to be substantially rehabilitated in a rehabilitation beginning within the 2-year period ending 1 year after the date of the acquisition of such property.

(3) Certain property treated as new property. Solely for purposes of determining under paragraph (2)(A) whether the 1st use of property is pursuant to tax-exempt financing—

(A) In general. If—

(i) the 1st use of property is pursuant to taxable financing,

(ii) there was a reasonable expectation (at the time such taxable financing was provided) that such financing would be replaced by tax-exempt financing, and

(iii) the taxable financing is in fact so replaced within a reasonable period after the taxable financing was provided,

then the 1st use of such property shall be treated as being pursuant to the tax-exempt financing.

(B) Special rule where no operating state or local program for tax-exempt financing. If, at the time of the 1st use of property, there was no operating State or local program for tax-exempt financing of the property, the 1st use of the property shall be treated as pursuant to the 1st tax-exempt financing of the property.

(C) Definitions. For purposes of this paragraph—

(i) Tax-exempt financing. The term "tax-exempt financing" means financing provided by tax-exempt bonds.

(ii) Taxable financing. The term "taxable financing" means financing which is not tax-exempt financing.

(4) Substantial rehabilitation.

(A) In general. Except as provided in subparagraph (B), rules similar to the rules of section 47(c)(1)(C) shall apply in determining for purposes of paragraph (2)(C) whether property is substantially rehabilitated.

(B) Exception. For purposes of subparagraph (A), clause (ii) of section 47(c)(1)(C) shall not apply, but the Secretary may extend the 24-month period in section 47(c)(1)(C)(i) where appropriate due to circumstances not within the control of the owner.

(e) Election out.

This section shall not apply to an issue if—

(1) the issuer elects not to have this section apply to such issue, and

(2) such issue is an issue of exempt facility bonds, or qualified redevelopment bonds, to which section 146 applies.

In 1997, P.L. 105-34, Sec. 222, added para. (b)(5), effective 8/5/97.

In 1990, P.L. 101-508, Sec. 11813(b)(7)(A), substituted "section 47(c)(1)(C)" for "section 48(g)(1)(C)" each place it appeared in para. (d)(4) . . . Sec. 11813(b)(7)(B), substituted "section 47(c)(1)(C)(i)" for "section 48(g)(1)(C)(i)" in subpara. (d)(4)(B), effective for property placed in service after 12/31/90 except as provided in Sec. 11813(c)(2) of this Act, reproduced in note following Code Sec. 46.

In 1989, P.L. 101-239, Sec. 7815(f), redesignated para. (d)(3) as (d)(4) and added new para. (d)(3), effective for obligations issued after 10/21/88.

In 1988, P.L. 100-647, Sec. 1013(a)(6), substituted "103(b)(2)" for "103(b)" in subclause (b)(2)(B)(ii)(I) . . . Sec. 1013(a)(7), substituted "subparagraph (B)" for "subparagraph (B)(ii)" in clause (b)(2)(C)(i) . . . Sec. 1013(a)(8), substituted "subparagraphs (C), (D), and (E)" for "subparagraphs (C) and (D)" in para. (b)(4), effective for bonds issued after 8/15/86.

—P.L. 100-647, Sec. 5053(a), redesignated subsec. (d) as subsec. (e), and added new subsec. (d), effective for obligations issued after 10/21/88, except as provided in Sec. 5053(c)(2) and (3), which reads:

"(2) Exception for construction or binding agreement.—

"(A) The amendments made by this section shall not apply to bonds (other than refunding bonds) with respect to a facility—

"(i)(I) the original use of which begins with the taxpayer, and the construction, reconstruction, or rehabilitation of which began before July 14, 1988, and was completed on or after such date, or

"(II) the original use of which begins with the taxpayer and with respect to which a binding contract to incur significant expenditures for construction, reconstruction, or rehabilitation was entered into before July 14, 1988, and some of such expenditures are incurred on or after such date, and

"(ii) described in an inducement resolution or other comparable preliminary approval adopted by an issuing authority (or by a voter referendum) before July 14, 1988.

For purposes of the preceding sentence, the term 'significant expenditures' means expenditures greater than 10 percent of the reasonably anticipated cost of the construction, reconstruction, or rehabilitation of the facility involved.

"(B) Subparagraph (A) shall not apply to any bond issued after December 31, 1989, and shall not apply unless it is reasonably expected (at the time of issuance of the bond) that the facility will be placed in service before January 1, 1990.

"(3) Refundings.—The amendments made by this section shall not apply to any bond issued to refund (or which is part of a series of bonds issued to refund) a bond issued before July 15, 1988, if—

"(A) the average maturity date of the issue of which the refunding bond is a part is not later than the average maturity date of the bonds to be refunded by such issue,

"(B) the amount of the refunding bond does not exceed the outstanding amount of the refunded bond, and

"(C) the proceeds of the refunding bond are used to redeem the refunded bond not later than 90 days after the date of the issuance of the refunding bond.

For purposes of subparagraph (A), average maturity shall be determined in accordance with section 147(b) of the 1986 Code."

In 1986, P.L. 99-514, Sec. 1301(b), added Code Sec. 145 as part of the amendments to Part IV of subchapter B of chapter 1, effective for bonds issued after 8/15/86. For transitional rules, see Secs. 1312–1318 of this Act reproduced in the note following Code Sec. 103.

Sec. 146. Volume cap.

(a) General rule.

A private activity bond issued as part of an issue meets the requirements of this section if the aggregate face amount of the private activity bonds issued pursuant to such issue, when added to the aggregate face amount of tax-exempt private activity bonds previously issued by the issuing authority during the calendar year, does not exceed such authority's volume cap for such calendar year.

(b) Volume cap for state agencies.

For purposes of this section—

(1) In general. The volume cap for any agency of the State authorized to issue tax-exempt private activity bonds for any calendar year shall be 50 percent of the State ceiling for such calendar year.

(2) Special rule where state has more than 1 agency. If more than 1 agency of the State is authorized to issue tax-exempt private activity bonds, all such agencies shall be treated as a single agency.

(c) Volume cap for other issuers.

For purposes of this section—

(1) In general. The volume cap for any issuing authority (other than a State agency) for any calendar year shall be an amount which bears the same ratio to 50 percent of the State ceiling for such calendar year as—

(A) the population of the jurisdiction of such issuing authority, bears to

(B) the population of the entire State.

(2) Overlapping jurisdictions. For purposes of paragraph (1)(A), if an area is within the jurisdiction of 2 or more governmental units, such area shall be treated as only within the jurisdiction of the unit having jurisdiction over the smallest geographical area unless such unit agrees to surrender all or part of such jurisdiction for such calendar year to the unit with overlapping jurisdiction which has the next smallest geographical area.

(d) State ceiling.

For purposes of this section—

(1) In general. The State ceiling applicable to any State for any calendar year shall be the greater of—

(A) an amount equal to $75 ($62.50 in the case of calendar year 2001) multiplied by the State population, or

(B) $225,000,000 ($187,500,000 in the case of calendar year 2001).

(2) Cost-of-living adjustment. In the case of a calendar year after 2002, each of the dollar amounts contained in paragraph (1) shall be increased by an amount equal to—

(A) such dollar amount, multiplied by

(B) the cost-of-living adjustment determined under section 1(f)(3) for such calendar year by substituting "calendar year 2001" for "calendar year 1992" in subparagraph (B) thereof.

If any increase determined under the preceding sentence is not a multiple of $5 ($5,000 in the case of the dollar amount in paragraph (1)(B)), such increase shall be rounded to the nearest multiple thereof.

(3) Special rule for states with constitutional home rule cities. For purposes of this section—

(A) In general. The volume cap for any constitutional home rule city for any calendar year shall be determined under paragraph (1) of subsection (c) by substituting "100 percent" for "50 percent".

(B) Coordination with other allocations. In the case of any State which contains 1 or more constitutional home rule cities, for purposes of applying subsections (b) and (c) with respect to issuing authorities in such State other than constitutional home rule cities, the State ceiling for any calendar year shall be reduced by the aggregate volume caps determined for such year for all constitutional home rule cities in such State.

(C) Constitutional home rule city. For purposes of this section, the term "constitutional home rule city" means, with respect to any calendar year, any political subdivision of a State which, under a State constitution which was adopted in 1970 and effective on July 1, 1971, had home rule powers on the 1st day of the calendar year.

(4) Special rule for possessions with populations of less than the population of the least populous state.

(A) In general. If the population of any possession of the United States for any calendar year is less than the population of the least populous State (other than a possession) for such calendar year, the limitation under paragraph (1)(A) shall not be less than the amount determined under subparagraph (B) for such calendar year.

(B) Limitation. The limitation determined under this subparagraph, with respect to a possession, for any calendar year is an amount equal to the product of—

(i) the fraction—

(I) the numerator of which is the amount applicable under paragraph (1)(B) for such calendar year, and

(II) the denominator of which is the State population of the least populous State (other than a possession) for such calendar year, and

(ii) the population of such possession for such calendar year.

(5) Increase and set aside for housing bonds for 2008.

(A) Increase for 2008. In the case of calendar year 2008, the State ceiling for each State shall be increased by an amount equal to $11,000,000,000 multiplied by a fraction—

(i) the numerator of which is the State ceiling applicable to the State for calendar year 2008, determined without regard to this paragraph, and

(ii) the denominator of which is the sum of the State ceilings determined under clause (i) for all States.

(B) Set aside.

(i) In general. Any amount of the State ceiling for any State which is attributable to an increase under this paragraph shall be allocated solely for one or more qualified housing issues.

(ii) Qualified housing issue. For purposes of this paragraph, the term "qualified housing issue" means—

(I) an issue described in section 142(a)(7) (relating to qualified residential rental projects), or

(II) a qualified mortgage issue (determined by substituting "12-month period" for "42-month period" each place it appears in section 143(a)(2)(D)(i)).

(e) State may provide for different allocation.

For purposes of this section—

(1) In general. Except as provided in paragraph (3), a State may, by law provide a different formula for allocating the State ceiling among the governmental units (or other authorities) in such State having authority to issue tax-exempt private activity bonds.

(2) Interim authority for governor.

(A) In general. Except as otherwise provided in paragraph (3), the Governor of any State may proclaim a different formula for allocating the State ceiling among the governmental units (or other authorities) in such State having authority to issue private activity bonds.

(B) Termination of authority. The authority provided in subparagraph (A) shall not apply to bonds issued after the earlier of—

(i) the last day of the 1st calendar year after 1986 during which the legislature of the State met in regular session, or

(ii) the effective date of any State legislation with respect to the allocation of the State ceiling.

(3) State may not alter allocation to constitutional home rule cities. Except as otherwise provided in a State constitutional amendment (or law changing the home rule provision adopted in the manner provided by the State constitution), the authority provided in this subsection shall not apply to that portion of the State ceiling which is allocated to any constitutional home rule city in the State unless such city agrees to such different allocation.

(f) Elective carryforward of unused limitation for specified purpose.

(1) In general. If—

(A) an issuing authority's volume cap for any calendar year after 1985, exceeds

(B) the aggregate amount of tax-exempt private activity bonds issued during such calendar year by such authority,

such authority may elect to treat all (or any portion) of such excess as a carryforward for 1 or more carryforward purposes.

(2) Election must identify purpose. In any election under paragraph (1), the issuing authority shall—

(A) identify the purpose for which the carryforward is elected, and
(B) specify the portion of the excess described in paragraph (1) which is to be a carryforward for each such purpose.

(3) Use of carryforward.
(A) In general. If any issuing authority elects a carryforward under paragraph (1) with respect to any carryforward purpose, any private activity bonds issued by such authority with respect to such purpose during the 3 calendar years following the calendar year in which the carryforward arose shall not be taken into account under subsection (a) to the extent the amount of such bonds does not exceed the amount of the carryforward elected for such purpose.
(B) Order in which carryforward used. Carryforwards elected with respect to any purpose shall be used in the order of the calendar years in which they arose.

(4) Election. Any election under this paragraph (and any identification or specification contained therein), once made, shall be irrevocable.

(5) Carryforward purpose. The term "carryforward purpose" means—
(A) the purpose of issuing exempt facility bonds described in 1 of the paragraphs of section 142(a),
(B) the purpose of issuing qualified mortgage bonds or mortgage credit certificates,
(C) the purpose of issuing qualified student loan bonds, and
(D) the purpose of issuing qualified redevelopment bonds.

(6) Special rules for increased volume cap under subsection (d)(5). No amount which is attributable to the increase under subsection (d)(5) may be used—
(A) for any issue other than a qualified housing issue (as defined in subsection (d)(5)), or
(B) to issue any bond after calendar year 2010.

(g) Exception for certain bonds.
Only for purposes of this section, the term "private activity bond" shall not include—
(1) any qualified veterans' mortgage bond,
(2) any qualified 501(c)(3) bond,

> • *Caution:* Code Sec. 146(g)(3), following, was amended by P.L. 107-16, EGTRRA. These provisions generally sunset for tax years beginning after 12/31/2012. For specific sunset provisions, see Sec. 901, P.L. 107-16 (as amended) reproduced in history notes for this Code Sec.

(3) any exempt facility bond issued as part of an issue described in paragraph (1), (2), (12), (13), (14), or (15) of section 142(a), and
(4) 75 percent of any exempt facility bond issued as part of an issue described in paragraph (11) of section 142(a) (relating to high-speed intercity rail facilities).

Paragraph (4) shall be applied without regard to "75 percent of" if all of the property to be financed by the net proceeds of the issue is to be owned by a governmental unit (within the meaning of section 142(b)(1)).

(h) Exception for government-owned solid waste disposal facilities.
(1) In general. Only for purposes of this section, the term "private activity bond" shall not include any exempt facility bond described in section 142(a)(6) which is issued as part of an issue if all of the property to be financed by the net proceeds of such issue is to be owned by a governmental unit.

(2) Safe harbor for determination of government ownership. In determining ownership for purposes of paragraph (1), section 142(b)(1)(B) shall apply, except that a lease term shall be treated as satisfying clause (ii) thereof if it is not more than 20 years.

(i) Treatment of refunding issues.
For purposes of the volume cap imposed by this section—
(1) In general. The term "private activity bond" shall not include any bond which is issued to refund another bond to the extent that the amount of such bond does not exceed the outstanding amount of the refunded bond.

(2) Special rules for student loan bonds. In the case of any qualified student loan bond, paragraph (1) shall apply only if the maturity date of the refunding bond is not later than the later of—
(A) the average maturity date of the qualified student loan bonds to be refunded by the issue of which the refunding bond is a part, or
(B) the date 17 years after the date on which the refunded bond was issued (or in the case of a series of refundings, the date on which the original bond was issued).

(3) Special rules for qualified mortgage bonds. In the case of any qualified mortgage bond, paragraph (1) shall apply only if the maturity date of the refunding bond is not later than the later of—
(A) the average maturity date of the qualified mortgage bonds to be refunded by the issue of which the refunding bond is a part, or
(B) the date 32 years after the date on which the refunded bond was issued (or in the case of a series of refundings, the date on which the original bond was issued).

(4) Average maturity. For purposes of paragraphs (2) and (3), average maturity shall be determined in accordance with section 147(b)(2)(A).

(5) Exception for advance refunding. This subsection shall not apply to any bond issued to advance refund another bond.

(6) Treatment of certain residential rental project bonds as refunding bonds irrespective of obligor.
(A) In general. If, during the 6-month period beginning on the date of a repayment of a loan financed by an issue 95 percent or more of the net proceeds of which are used to provide projects described in section 142(d), such repayment is used to provide a new loan for any project so described, any bond which is issued to refinance such issue shall be treated as a refunding issue to the extent the principal amount of such refunding issue does not exceed the principal amount of the bonds refunded.
(B) Limitations. Subparagraph (A) shall apply to only one refunding of the original issue and only if—
(i) the refunding issue is issued not later than 4 years after the date on which the original issue was issued,
(ii) the latest maturity date of any bond of the refunding issue is not later than 34 years after the date on which the refunded bond was issued, and
(iii) the refunding issue is approved in accordance with section 147(f) before the issuance of the refunding issue.

(j) Population.

For purposes of this section, determinations of the population of any State (or issuing authority) shall be made with respect to any calendar year on the basis of the most recent census estimate of the resident population of such State (or issuing authority) released by the Bureau of Census before the beginning of such calendar year.

(k) Facility must be located within state.

(1) In general. Except as provided in paragraphs (2) and (3) no portion of the State ceiling applicable to any State for any calendar year may be used with respect to financing for a facility located outside such State.

(2) Exception for certain facilities where state will get proportionate share of benefits. Paragraph (1) shall not apply to any exempt facility bond described in paragraph (4), (5), (6), or (10) of section 142(a) if the issuer establishes that the State's share of the use of the facility (or its output) will equal or exceed the State's share of the private activity bonds issued to finance the facility.

(3) Treatment of governmental bonds to which volume cap allocated. Paragraph (1) shall not apply to any bond to which volume cap is allocated under section 141(b)(5)—

(A) for an output facility, or

(B) for a facility of a type described in paragraph (4), (5), (6), or (10) of section 142(a),

if the issuer establishes that the State's share of the private business use (as defined by section 141(b)(6)) of the facility will equal or exceed the State's share of the volume cap allocated with respect to bonds issued to finance the facility.

(l) Issuer of qualified scholarship funding bonds.

In the case of a qualified scholarship funding bond, such bond shall be treated for purposes of this section as issued by a State or local issuing authority (whichever is appropriate).

(m) Treatment of amounts allocated to private activity portion of government use bonds.

(1) In general. The volume cap of an issuer shall be reduced by the amount allocated by the issuer to an issue under section 141(b)(5).

(2) Advance refundings. Except as otherwise provided by the Secretary, any advance refunding of any part of an issue to which an amount was allocated under section 141(b)(5) (or would have been allocated if such section applied to such issue) shall be taken into account under this section to the extent of the amount of the volume cap which was (or would have been) so allocated.

(n) Reduction for mortgage credit certificates, etc.

The volume cap of any issuing authority for any calendar year shall be reduced by the sum of—

(1) the amount of qualified mortgage bonds which such authority elects not to issue under section 25(c)(2)(A)(ii) during such year, plus

(2) the amount of any reduction in such ceiling under section 25(f) applicable to such authority for such year.

In 2010, P.L. 111-312, Sec. 101(a)(1), substituted "December 31, 2012" for "December 31, 2010" both places it appeared in Sec. 901, P.L. 107-16 [see below], effective as if included in the enactment of P.L. 107-16, EGTRRA, 6/7/2001.

In 2008, P.L. 110-289, Sec. 3007(a), added para. (i)(6), effective for repayments of loans received after 7/30/2008.

—P.L. 110-289, Sec. 3021(a)(1), added para. (d)(5) ... Sec. 3021(a)(2), added para. (f)(6), effective for bonds issued after 7/30/2008.

In 2005, P.L. 109-59, Sec. 11143(c), substituted "(14), or (15) of section 142(a), and" for "or (14) of section 142(a) (relating to airports, docks and wharves, environmental enhancements of hydroelectric generating facilities, qualified public educational facilities, and qualified green building and sustainable design projects), and" in para. (g)(3), effective for bonds issued after 8/10/2005.

In 2004, P.L. 108-357, Sec. 701(c)(1), substituted "(13), or (14)" for "or (13)" in para. (g)(3) ... Sec. 701(c)(2), substituted "qualified public educational facilities, and qualified green building and sustainable design projects" for "and qualified public educational facilities" in para. (g)(3), effective for bonds issued after 12/31/2004.

In 2002, P.L. 107-358, Sec. 2, added subsec. (c) in Sec. 901 of P.L. 107-16 [see below], effective 12/17/2002.

In 2001, P.L. 107-16, Sec. 422(c)(1), substituted "(12), or (13)" for "or (12)" in para. (g)(3) ... Sec. 422(c)(2), substituted "environmental enhancements of hydroelectric generating facilities, and qualified public educational facilities" for "and environmental enhancements of hydroelectric generating facilities" in para. (g)(3), effective for bonds issued after 12/31/2001.

—P.L. 107-16, Sec. 901, of this Act [as amended by Sec. 2, P.L. 107-358, and Sec. 101(a)(1), P.L. 111-312, see above], reads as follows:

"SEC. 901. SUNSET OF PROVISIONS OF ACT.

"(a) In general. All provisions of, and amendments made by, this Act shall not apply—

"(1) to taxable, plan, or limitation years beginning after December 31, 2012, or

"(2) in the case of title V, to estates of decedents dying, gifts made, or generation skipping transfers, after December 31, 2012.

"(b) Application of certain laws. The Internal Revenue Code of 1986 and the Employee Retirement Income Security Act of 1974 shall be applied and administered to years, estates, gifts, and transfers described in subsection (a) as if the provisions and amendments described in subsection (a) had never been enacted.

"(c) Exception. Subsection (a) shall not apply to section 803 (relating to no federal income tax on restitution received by victims of the Nazi regime or their heirs or estates)."

In 2000, P.L. 106-554, Sec. 1(a)(7), [which enacted into law Sec. 161(a) of P.L. 106-554] amended paras. (d)(1) and (2), effective for calendar yrs. after 2000.

Prior to amendment, paras. (d)(1) and (2) read as follows:

"(1) In general. The State ceiling applicable to any State for any calendar year shall be the greater of—

"(A) an amount equal to the per capita limit for such year multiplied by the State population, or

"(B) the aggregate limit for such year.

Subparagraph (B) shall not apply to any possession of the United States.

"(2) Per capita limit; aggregate limit. For purposes of paragraph (1), the per capita limit, and the aggregate limit, for any calendar year shall be determined in accordance with the following table:

Calendar Year	Per Capita Limit	Aggregate Limit
1999 through 2002	$50	$150,000,000
2003	55	165,000,000
2004	60	180,000,000
2005	65	195,000,000
2006	70	210,000,000
2007 and thereafter	75	225,000,000.

In 1998, P.L. 105-277, Sec. 2021(a), amended paras. (d)(1) and (2), effective for calendar yrs. after 1998.

Prior to amendment, paras. (d)(1) and (2) read as follows:

"(1) In general. The State ceiling applicable to any State for any calendar year shall be the greater of—

"(A) an amount equal to $75 multiplied by the State population, or

"(B) $250,000,000.

Subparagraph (B) shall not apply to any possession of the United States.

"(2) Adjustment after 1987. In the case of calendar years after 1987, paragraph (1) shall be applied by substituting—

"(A) '$50' for '$75', and

"(B) '$150,000,000' for '$250,000,000'."

In 1993, P.L. 103-66, Sec. 13121(a), added the flush sentence at the end of para. (g)(4), effective for bonds issued after 12/31/93.

In 1992, P.L. 102-486, Sec. 1921(b)(3)(A), substituted ", (2), or (12)" for "or (2)" in para. (g)(3) ... Sec. 1921(b)(3)(B), substituted ", docks and wharves, and environmental enhancements of hydroelectric generating facilities" for "and docks and wharves" in para. (g)(3), effective for bonds issued after 10/24/92.

In 1989, P.L. 101-239, Sec. 7816(s)(2), redesignated para. (g)(3) added by Sec. 6180(b)(3)(C) of P.L. 100-647 [see below] as (g)(4), effective for bonds issued after 11/10/88.

In 1988, P.L. 100-647, Sec. 1013(a)(9), amended subpara. (f)(5)(A) [as in effect before amendment by Sec. 10631(b) of P.L. 100-203] ... Sec. 1013(a)(10)(A), substituted "paragraphs (2) and (3)" for "paragraph (2)" in para. (k)(1) ... Sec. 1013(a)(10)(B), added para. (k)(3) ... Sec. 1013(a)(28)(A), amended subpara. (i)(2)(A) ... Sec. 1013(a)(28)(B), amended subpara. (i)(3)(A) ... Sec. 1013(a)(28)(C), redesignated para. (i)(4) as (i)(5) and added new para. (i)(4) ... Sec. 1013(a)(40), substituted "with respect to a possession" for "with respect to a possession" in subpara. (d)(4)(B), effective for bonds issued after 8/15/86. For transitional rules, see Secs. 1312-1318 of P.L. 99-514, reproduced in note following Code Sec. 103.

Prior to amendment subpara. (f)(5)(A) [as added by Sec. 1301(b) of P.L. 99-514] read as follows:

"(A) the purpose of issuing bonds referred to in one of the clauses of section 141(d)(1)(A),".

Prior to amendment subpara. (i)(2)(A) read as follows:

"(A) the maturity date of the bond to be refunded, or".

Prior to amendment subpara. (i)(3)(A) read as follows:

Private activity bonds   Code Sec. 147(c)(1)(B)

"(A) the maturity date of the bond to be refunded, or".
— P.L. 100-647, Sec. 6180(b)(3)(A), deleted "and" at the end of para. (g)(2) . . . Sec. 6180(b)(3)(B), substituted ", and" for the period at the end of para. (g)(3) . . . Sec. 6180(b)(3)(C), added new para. (g)(3) [sic (4)], effective for bonds issued after 11/10/88.

In 1987, P.L. 100-203, Sec. 10631(b), amended subpara. (f)(5)(A), effective for bonds issued after 10/13/87 (other than bonds issued to refund bonds issued on or before 10/13/87), except as provided in Sec. 10631(c)(2) and (c)(3), which reads:

"(2) Binding agreements. The amendments made by this section shall not apply to bonds (other than advance refunding bonds) with respect to a facility acquired after October 13, 1987, pursuant to a binding contract entered into on or before such date.

"(3) Transitional rule. The amendments made by this section shall not apply to bonds issued —

"(A) after October 13, 1987, by an authority created by a statute —

"(i) approved by the State Governor on July 24, 1986, and

"(ii) sections 1 through 10 of which became effective on January 15, 1987, and

"(B) to provide facilities serving the area specified in such statute on the date of its enactment."

Prior to amendment, subpara. (f)(5)(A) [as amended by Sec. 1013(a)(9) of P.L. 100-647, see above] read as follows:

"(A) the purpose of issuing bonds referred to in one of the clauses of section 141(d)(1)(A),".

In 1986, P.L. 99-514, Sec. 1301(b), added Code Sec. 146 as part of the amendments to Part IV of subchapter B of chapter 1, effective for bonds issued after 8/15/86. For transitional rules, see Secs. 1312– 1318 of this Act reproduced in the note following Code Sec. 103.

Sec. 147. Other requirements applicable to certain private activity bonds.

(a) Substantial user requirement.

(1) In general. Except as provided in subsection (h), a private activity bond shall not be a qualified bond for any period during which it is held by a person who is a substantial user of the facilities or by a related person of such a substantial user.

(2) Related person. For purposes of paragraph (1), the following shall be treated as related persons —

(A) 2 or more persons if the relationship between such persons would result in a disallowance of losses under section 267 or 707(b),

(B) 2 or more persons which are members of the same controlled group of corporations (as defined in section 1563(a), except that "more than 50 percent" shall be substituted for "at least 80 percent" each place it appears therein),

(C) a partnership and each of its partners (and their spouses and minor children), and

(D) an S corporation and each of its shareholders (and their spouses and minor children).

(b) Maturity may not exceed 120 percent of economic life.

(1) General rule. Except as provided in subsection (h), a private activity bond shall not be a qualified bond if it is issued as part of an issue and—

(A) the average maturity of the bonds issued as part of such issue, exceeds

(B) 120 percent of the average reasonably expected economic life of the facilities being financed with the net proceeds of such issue.

(2) Determination of averages. For purposes of paragraph (1)—

(A) the average maturity of any issue shall be determined by taking into account the respective issue prices of the bonds issued as part of such issue, and

(B) the average reasonably expected economic life of the facilities being financed with any issue shall be determined by taking into account the respective cost of such facilities.

(3) Special rules.

(A) Determination of economic life. For purposes of this subsection, the reasonably expected economic life of any facility shall be determined as of the later of—

(i) the date on which the bonds are issued, or

(ii) the date on which the facility is placed in service (or expected to be placed in service).

(B) Treatment of land.

(i) Land not taken into account. Except as provided in clause (ii), land shall not be taken into account under paragraph (1)(B).

(ii) Issues where 25 percent or more of proceeds used to finance land. If 25 percent or more of the net proceeds of any issue is to be used to finance land, such land shall be taken into account under paragraph (1)(B) and shall be treated as having an economic life of 30 years.

(4) Special rule for pooled financing of 501(c)(3) organization.

(A) In general. At the election of the issuer, a qualified 501(c)(3) bond shall be treated as meeting the requirements of paragraph (1) if such bond meets the requirements of subparagraph (B).

(B) Requirements. A qualified 501(c)(3) bond meets the requirements of this subparagraph if—

(i) 95 percent or more of the net proceeds of the issue of which such bond is a part are to be used to make or finance loans to 2 or more 501(c)(3) organizations or governmental units for acquisition of property to be used by such organizations,

(ii) each loan described in clause (i) satisfies the requirements of paragraph (1) (determined by treating each loan as a separate issue),

(iii) before such bond is issued, a demand survey was conducted which shows a demand for financing greater than an amount equal to 120 percent of the lendable proceeds of such issue, and

(iv) 95 percent or more of the net proceeds of such issue are to be loaned to 501(c)(3) organizations or governmental units within 1 year of issuance and, to the extent there are any unspent proceeds after such 1-year period, bonds issued as part of such issue are to be redeemed as soon as possible thereafter (and in no event later than 18 months after issuance).

A bond shall not meet the requirements of this subparagraph if the maturity date of any bond issued as part of such issue is more than 30 years after the date on which the bond was issued (or, in the case of a refunding or series of refundings, the date on which the original bond was issued).

(5) Special rule for certain FHA insured loans. Paragraph (1) shall not apply to any bond issued as part of an issue 95 percent or more of the net proceeds of which are to be used to finance mortgage loans insured under FHA 242 or under a similar Federal Housing Administration program (as in effect on the date of the enactment [10/22/86] of the Tax Reform Act of 1986) where the loan term approved by such Administration plus the maximum maturity of debentures which could be issued by such Administration in satisfaction of its obligations exceeds the term permitted under paragraph (1).

(c) Limitation on use for land acquisition.

(1) In general. Except as provided in subsection (h), a private activity bond shall not be a qualified bond if—

(A) it is issued as part of an issue and 25 percent or more of the net proceeds of such issue are to be used (directly or indirectly) for the acquisition of land (or an interest therein), or

(B) any portion of the proceeds of such issue is to be used (directly or indirectly) for the acquisition of land (or an interest therein) to be used for farming purposes.

(2) Exception for first-time farmers.
(A) In general. If the requirements of subparagraph (B) are met with respect to any land, paragraph (1) shall not apply to such land, and subsection (d) shall not apply to property to be used thereon for farming purposes, but only to the extent of expenditures (financed with the proceeds of the issue) not in excess of $450,000.
(B) Acquisition by first-time farmers. The requirements of this subparagraph are met with respect to any land if—
  (i) such land is to be used for farming purposes, and
  (ii) such land is to be acquired by an individual who is a first-time farmer, who will be the principal user of such land, and who will materially and substantially participate on the farm of which such land is a part in the operation of such farm.
(C) First-time farmer. For purposes of this paragraph—
  (i) In general. The term "first-time farmer" means any individual if such individual—
    (I) has not at any time had any direct or indirect ownership interest in substantial farmland in the operation of which such individual materially participated, and
    (II) has not received financing under this paragraph in an amount which, when added to the financing to be provided under this paragraph, exceeds the amount in effect under subparagraph (A).
  (ii) Aggregation rules. Any ownership or material participation, or financing received, by an individual's spouse or minor child shall be treated as ownership and material participation, or financing received, by the individual.
  (iii) Insolvent farmer. For purposes of clause (i), farmland which was previously owned by the individual and was disposed of while such individual was insolvent shall be disregarded if section 108 applied to indebtedness with respect to such farmland.
(D) Farm. For purposes of this paragraph, the term "farm" has the meaning given such term by section 6420(c)(2).
(E) Substantial farmland. For purposes of this paragraph, the term "substantial farmland" means any parcel of land unless such parcel is smaller than 30 percent of the median size of a farm in the county in which such parcel is located.
(F) Used equipment limitation. For purposes of this paragraph, in no event may the amount of financing provided by reason of this paragraph to a first-time farmer for personal property—
  (i) of a character subject to the allowance for depreciation,
  (ii) the original use of which does not begin with such farmer, and
  (iii) which is to be used for farming purposes, exceed $62,500. A rule similar to the rule of subparagraph (C)(ii) shall apply for purposes of the preceding sentence.
(G) Acquisition from related person. For purposes of this paragraph and section 144(a), the acquisition by a first-time farmer of land or personal property from a related person (within the meaning of section 144(a)(3)) shall not be treated as an acquisition from a related person, if—
  (i) the acquisition price is for the fair market value of such land or property, and
  (ii) subsequent to such acquisition, the related person does not have a financial interest in the farming operation with respect to which the bond proceeds are to be used.
(H) Adjustments for inflation. In the case of any calendar year after 2008, the dollar amount in subparagraph (A) shall be increased by an amount equal to—
  (i) such dollar amount, multiplied by
  (ii) the cost-of-living adjustment determined under section 1(f)(3) for the calendar year, determined by substituting "calendar year 2007" for "calendar year 1992" in subparagraph (B) thereof.
If any amount as increased under the preceding sentence is not a multiple of $100, such amount shall be rounded to the nearest multiple of $100.
(3) Exception for certain land acquired for environmental purposes, etc. Any land acquired by a governmental unit (or issuing authority) in connection with an airport, mass commuting facility, high-speed intercity rail facility, dock, or wharf shall not be taken into account under paragraph (1) if—
(A) such land is acquired for noise abatement or wetland preservation, or for future use as an airport, mass commuting facility, high-speed intercity rail facility, dock, or wharf, and
(B) there is not other significant use of such land.
(d) Acquisition of existing property not permitted.
(1) In general. Except as provided in subsection (h), a private activity bond shall not be a qualified bond if issued as part of an issue and any portion of the net proceeds of such issue is to be used for the acquisition of any property (or an interest therein) unless the 1st use of such property is pursuant to such acquisition.
(2) Exception for certain rehabilitations. Paragraph (1) shall not apply with respect to any building (and the equipment therefor) if—
(A) the rehabilitation expenditures with respect to such building, equal or exceed
(B) 15 percent of the portion of the cost of acquiring such building (and equipment) financed with the net proceeds of the issue.
A rule similar to the rule of the preceding sentence shall apply in the case of structures other than a building except that subparagraph (B) shall be applied by substituting "100 percent" for "15 percent".
(3) Rehabilitation expenditures. For purposes of this subsection—
(A) In general. Except as provided in this paragraph, the term "rehabilitation expenditures" means any amount properly chargeable to capital account which is incurred by the person acquiring the building for property (or additions or improvements to property) in connection with the rehabilitation of a building. In the case of an integrated operation contained in a building before its acquisition, such term includes rehabilitating existing equipment in such building or replacing it with equipment having substantially the same function. For purposes of this subparagraph, any amount incurred by a successor to the person acquiring the building or by the seller under a sales contract with such person shall be treated as incurred by such person.
(B) Certain expenditures not included. The term "rehabilitation expenditures" does not include any expenditure described in section 47(c)(2)(B).
(C) Period during which expenditures must be incurred. The term "rehabilitation expenditures" shall not include

any amount which is incurred after the date 2 years after the later of—
(i) the date on which the building was acquired, or
(ii) the date on which the bond was issued.

(4) Special rule for certain projects. In the case of a project involving 2 or more buildings, this subsection shall be applied on a project basis.

(e) No portion of bonds may be issued for skyboxes, airplanes, gambling establishments, etc.

A private activity bond shall not be a qualified bond if issued as part of an issue and any portion of the proceeds of such issue is to be used to provide any airplane, skybox or other private luxury box, health club facility, facility primarily used for gambling, or store the principal business of which is the sale of alcoholic beverages for consumption off premises.

(f) Public approval required for private activity bonds.

(1) In general. A private activity bond shall not be a qualified bond unless such bond satisfies the requirements of paragraph (2).

(2) Public approval requirement.

(A) In general. A bond shall satisfy the requirements of this paragraph if such bond is issued as a part of an issue which has been approved by—
 (i) the governmental unit—
  (I) which issued such bond, or
  (II) on behalf of which such bond was issued, and
 (ii) each governmental unit having jurisdiction over the area in which any facility, with respect to which financing is to be provided from the net proceeds of such issue, is located (except that if more than 1 governmental unit within a State has jurisdiction over the entire area within such State in which such facility is located, only 1 such unit need approve such issue).

(B) Approval by a governmental unit. For purposes of subparagraph (A), an issue shall be treated as having been approved by any governmental unit if such issue is approved—
 (i) by the applicable elected representative of such governmental unit after a public hearing following reasonable public notice, or
 (ii) by voter referendum of such governmental unit.

(C) Special rules for approval of facility. If there has been public approval under subparagraph (A) of the plan for financing a facility, such approval shall constitute approval under subparagraph (A) for any issue—
 (i) which is issued pursuant to such plan within 3 years after the date of the 1st issue pursuant to the approval, and
 (ii) all or substantially all of the proceeds of which are to be used to finance such facility or to refund previous financing under such plan.

(D) Refunding bonds. No approval under subparagraph (A) shall be necessary with respect to any bond which is issued to refund (other than to advance refund) a bond approved under subparagraph (A) (or treated as approved under subparagraph (C)) unless the average maturity date of the issue of which the refunding bond is a part is later than the average maturity date of the bonds to be refunded by such issue. For purposes of the preceding sentence, average maturity shall be determined in accordance with subsection (b)(2)(A).

(E) Applicable elected representative. For purposes of this paragraph—

 (i) In general. The term "applicable elected representative" means with respect to any governmental unit—
  (I) an elected legislative body of such unit, or
  (II) the chief elected executive officer, the chief elected State legal officer of the executive branch, or any other elected official of such unit designated for purposes of this paragraph by such chief elected executive officer or by State law.

If the office of any elected official described in subclause (II) is vacated and an individual is appointed by the chief elected executive officer of the governmental unit and confirmed by the elected legislative body of such unit (if any) to serve the remaining term of the elected official, the individual so appointed shall be treated as the elected official for such remaining term.

 (ii) No applicable elected representative. If (but for this clause) a governmental unit has no applicable elected representative, the applicable elected representative for purposes of clause (i) shall be the applicable elected representative of the governmental unit-
  (I) which is the next higher governmental unit with such a representative, and
  (II) from which the authority of the governmental unit with no such representative is derived.

(3) Special rule for approval of airports or high-speed intercity rail facilities. If—
(A) the proceeds of an issue are to be used to finance a facility or facilities located at an airport or high-speed intercity rail facilities, and
(B) the governmental unit issuing such bonds is the owner or operator of such airport or high-speed intercity rail facilities,

such governmental unit shall be deemed to be the only governmental unit having jurisdiction over such airport or high-speed intercity rail facilities for purposes of this subsection.

(4) Special rules for scholarship funding bond issues and volunteer fire department bond issues.

(A) Scholarship funding bonds. In the case of a qualified scholarship funding bond, any governmental unit which made a request described in section 150(d)(2)(B) with respect to the issuer of such bond shall be treated for purposes of paragraph (2) of this subsection as the governmental unit on behalf of which such bond was issued. Where more than one governmental unit within a State has made a request described in section 150(d)(2)(B), the State may also be treated for purposes of paragraph (2) of this subsection as the governmental unit on behalf of which such bond was issued.

(B) Volunteer fire department bonds. In the case of a bond of a volunteer fire department which meets the requirements of section 150(e), the political subdivision described in section 150(e)(2)(B) with respect to such department shall be treated for purposes of paragraph (2) of this subsection as the governmental unit on behalf of which such bond was issued.

(g) Restriction on issuance costs financed by issue.

(1) In general. A private activity bond shall not be a qualified bond if the issuance costs financed by the issue (of which such bond is a part) exceed 2 percent of the proceeds of the issue.

(2) Special rule for small mortgage revenue bond issues. In the case of an issue of qualified mortgage bonds or qualified veterans' mortgage bonds, paragraph (1) shall

Code Sec. 147(g)(2)   **Private activity bonds**

be applied by substituting "3.5 percent" for "2 percent" if the proceeds of the issue do not exceed $20,000,000.

> • *Caution:* The heading of Code Sec. 147(h), following, was amended by P.L. 107-16 EGTRRA. These provisions generally sunset for tax years beginning after 12/31/2012. For specific sunset provisions, see Sec. 901, P.L. 107-16 (as amended) reproduced in history notes for this Code Sec.

(h) Certain rules not to apply to certain bonds.
(1) Mortgage revenue bonds and qualified student loan bonds. Subsections (a), (b), (c), and (d) shall not apply to any qualified mortgage bond, qualified veterans' mortgage bond, or qualified student loan bond.
(2) Qualified 501(c)(3) bonds. Subsections (a), (c), and (d) shall not apply to any qualified 501(c)(3) bond and subsection (e) shall be applied as if it did not contain "health club facility" with respect to such a bond.

> • *Caution:* Code Sec. 147(h)(3), following, was amended by P.L. 107-16 EGTRRA. These provisions generally sunset for tax years beginning after 12/31/2012. For specific sunset provisions, see Sec. 901, P.L. 107-16 (as amended) reproduced in history notes for this Code Sec.

(3) Exempt facility bonds for qualified public-private schools. Subsection (c) shall not apply to any exempt facility bond issued as part of an issue described in section 142(a)(13) (relating to qualified public educational facilities).

In 2010, P.L. 111-312, Sec. 101(a)(1), substituted "December 31, 2012" for "December 31, 2010" both places it appeared in Sec. 901, P.L. 107-16 [see below], effective as if included in the enactment of P.L. 107-16, EGTRRA, 6/7/2001.

In 2008, P.L. 110-246, Sec. 4, Repeals the duplicative enactment and provides effective date provisions of the Act entitled "An Act to provide for the continuation of agricultural programs through fiscal year 2012, and for other purposes" Sec. 4, P.L. 110-246 reads as follows:

"Sec. 4. Repeal of duplicative enactment.

"(a) In General- The Act entitled 'An Act to provide for the continuation of agricultural programs through fiscal year 2012, and for other purposes' (H.R. 2419 of the 110th Congress), and the amendments made by that Act, are repealed, effective on the date of enactment of that Act.

"(b) Effective Date- Except as otherwise provided in this Act, this Act and the amendments made by this Act shall take effect on the earlier of--

"(1) the date of enactment of this Act; or

"(2) the date of the enactment of the Act entitled 'An Act to provide for the continuation of agricultural programs through fiscal year 2012, and for other purposes' (H.R. 2419 of the 110th Congress)."

—P.L. 110-246, Sec. 15341(a), substituted "$450,000" for "$250,000" in subpara. (c)(2)(A) . . . Sec. 15341(b), added subpara. (c)(2)(H) . . . Sec. 15341(c), substituted "unless such parcel is smaller than 30 percent of the median size of a farm in the county in which such parcel is located." for "unless— (i) such parcel is smaller than 30 percent of the median size of a farm in the county in which such parcel is located, and (ii) the fair market value of the land does not at any time while held by the individual exceed $125,000." in subpara. (c)(2)(E) . . . Sec. 15341(d), substituted "the amount in effect under subparagraph (A)" for "$250,000" in subcl. (c)(2)(C)(i)(II), effective for bonds issued after 5/22/08. [Ed. Note: May 22, 2008 was the date of enactment for H.R. 2419 (PL 110-234), which was repealed by (2008 Farm Act sect;4(a)) (PL 110-246, 6/18/2008), in connection with the reenactment of the farm bill to correct a technical deficiency in its original passage.]

In 2002, P.L. 107-358, Sec. 2, added subsec. (c) in Sec. 901 of P.L. 107-16 [see below], effective 12/17/2002.

In 2001, P.L. 107-16, Sec. 422(d), added para. (h)(3) . . . Sec. 422(e), substituted "certain bonds" for "mortgage revenue bonds, qualified student loan bonds, and qualified 501(c)(3) bonds" in the heading of subsec. (h), effective for bonds issued after 12/31/2001.

—P.L. 107-16, Sec. 901, of this Act [as amended by Sec. 2, P.L. 107-358, and Sec. 101(a)(1), P.L. 111-312 see above], reads as follows:

"SEC. 901. SUNSET OF PROVISIONS OF ACT.

"(a) In general. All provisions of, and amendments made by, this Act shall not apply—

"(1) to taxable, plan, or limitation years beginning after December 31, 2012, or

"(2) in the case of title V, to estates of decedents dying, gifts made, or generation skipping transfers, after December 31, 2012.

"(b) Application of certain laws. The Internal Revenue Code of 1986 and the Employee Retirement Income Security Act of 1974 shall be applied and administered to years, estates, gifts, and transfers described in subsection (a) as if the provisions and amendments described in subsection (a) had never been enacted.

"(c) Exception. Subsection (a) shall not apply to section 803 (relating to no federal income tax on restitution received by victims of the Nazi regime or their heirs or estates)."

In 1996, P.L. 104-188, Sec. 1117(a), added subpara. (c)(2)(G) . . . Sec. 1117(b), substituted "30 percent" for "15 percent" in clause (c)(2)(E)(i), effective for bonds issued after 8/20/96.

—P.L. 104-188, Sec. 1804, of this Act provides:

"Sec. 1804. Tax-exempt bonds for sale of Alaska Power Administration facility. Sections 142(f)(3) (as added by section 1608) and 147(d) of the Internal Revenue Code of 1986 shall not apply in determining whether any private activity bond issued after the date of the enactment of this Act and used to finance the acquisition of the Snettisham hydroelectric project from the Alaska Power Administration is a qualified bond for purposes of such Code."

In 1990, P.L. 101-508, Sec. 11813(b)(8), substituted "section 47(c)(2)(B)" for "section 48(g)(2)(B)" in subpara. (d)(3)(B), effective for property placed in service after 12/31/90, except as provided in Sec. 11813(c)(2) of this Act, reproduced in note following Code Sec. 46.

In 1989, P.L. 101-239, Sec. 7816(s)(3), added a comma after "mass commuting facility" each place it appeared in para. (c)(3), effective for bonds issued after 11/10/88.

In 1988, P.L. 100-647, Sec. 1013(a)(11), deleted "treated as" after "shall not be" in subsec. (e), effective for bonds issued after 8/15/86.

—P.L. 100-647, Sec. 1013(a)(12), added para. (f)(4), effective for bonds issued after 12/31/86. For transitional rules, see Secs. 1312-1318 of P.L. 99-514 [reproduced in the note following Code Sec. 103].

—P.L. 100-647, Sec. 1013(a)(13)(A), substituted "proceeds of the issue" for "aggregate face amount of the issue" in para. (g)(1) . . . Sec. 1013(a)(13)(B), substituted "proceeds of the issue do not" for "aggregate authorized face amount of the issue does not" in para. (g)(2), effective for bonds issued after 6/30/87.

—P.L. 100-647, Sec. 1013(a)(29), substituted "the average maturity date of the issue of which the refunded bond is a part is later than the average maturity date of the bonds to be refunded by such issue. For purposes of the preceding sentence, average maturity shall be determined in accordance with subsection (b)(2)(A)" for "the maturity date of such bond is later than the maturity date of the bond to be refunded" in para. (f)(2)(D) . . . Sec. 1013(a)(36), added a sentence to the end of clause (f)(2)(E)(i), effective for bonds issued after 12/31/86. For transitional rules, see Secs. 1312-1318 of P.L. 99-514 [reproduced in the note following Code Sec. 103].

—P.L. 100-647, Sec. 1013(b)(1), added Sec. 1311(d) of P.L. 99-514 [reproduced below], part of the effective date for changes made by Sec. 1301(b) of P.L. 99-514, see below.

—P.L. 100-647, Sec. 6180(b)(4), added "high-speed intercity rail facility" after "mass commuting facility" each place it appeared in para. (c)(3) . . . Sec. 6180(b)(5)(A), added "or high-speed intercity rail facilities" after "airport" each place it appeared in para. (f)(3) . . . Sec. 6180(b)(5)(B), added "or high-speed intercity rail facilities" after "airports" in the heading of para. (f)(3), effective for bonds issued after 11/10/88.

In 1986, P.L. 99-514, Sec. 1301(b), added Code Sec. 147, as part of the amendments to Part IV of subchapter B of chapter 1, effective for bonds issued after 8/15/86. Sec. 1311(d) of this Act. [added by Sec. 1013(b)(1) of P.L. 100-647, see above] provides:

"(d) Public approval and information reporting. Sections 147(f) and 149(e) of the 1986 Code shall apply to bonds issued after December 31, 1986." For transitional rules, see Secs. 1312–1318 of this Act reproduced in the note following Code Sec. 103.

SUBPART B.—REQUIREMENTS APPLICABLE TO ALL STATE AND LOCAL BONDS

Sec.
148. Arbitrage.
149. Bonds must be registered to be tax exempt; other requirements.

In 1986, P.L. 99-514, Sec. 1301(b), added Subpart B as part of the changes made to Part IV.

Sec. 148.   Arbitrage.
(a) Arbitrage bond defined.

For purposes of section 103, the term "arbitrage bond" means any bond issued as part of an issue any portion of the proceeds of which are reasonably expected (at the time of issuance of the bond) to be used directly or indirectly—

(1) to acquire higher yielding investments, or
(2) to replace funds which were used directly or indirectly to acquire higher yielding investments.

For purposes of this subsection, a bond shall be treated as an arbitrage bond if the issuer intentionally uses any portion of the proceeds of the issue of which such bond is a part in a manner described in paragraph (1) or (2).

(b) Higher yielding investments.

For purposes of this section—

(1) In general. The term "higher yielding investments" means any investment property which produces a yield over the term of the issue which is materially higher than the yield on the issue.

(2) Investment property. The term "investment property" means—

(A) any security (within the meaning of section 165(g)(2)(A) or (B)),

(B) any obligation,

(C) any annuity contract,

(D) any investment-type property, or

(E) in the case of a bond other than a private activity bond, any residential rental property for family units which is not located within the jurisdiction of the issuer and which is not acquired to implement a court ordered or approved housing desegregation plan.

(3) Alternative minimum tax bonds treated as investment property in certain cases.

(A) In general. Except as provided in subparagraph (B), the term "investment property" does not include any tax-exempt bond.

(B) Exception. With respect to an issue other than an issue a part of which is a specified private activity bond (as defined in section 57(a)(5)(C)), the term "investment property" includes a specified private activity bond (as so defined).

(4) Safe harbor for prepaid natural gas.

(A) In general. The term "investment-type property" does not include a prepayment under a qualified natural gas supply contract.

(B) Qualified natural gas supply contract. For purposes of this paragraph, the term "qualified natural gas supply contract" means any contract to acquire natural gas for resale by a utility owned by a governmental unit if the amount of gas permitted to be acquired under the contract by the utility during any year does not exceed the sum of—

(i) the annual average amount during the testing period of natural gas purchased (other than for resale) by customers of such utility who are located within the service area of such utility, and

(ii) the amount of natural gas to be used to transport the prepaid natural gas to the utility during such year.

(C) Natural gas used to generate electricity. Natural gas used to generate electricity shall be taken into account in determining the average under subparagraph (B)(i)—

(i) only if the electricity is generated by a utility owned by a governmental unit, and

(ii) only to the extent that the electricity is sold (other than for resale) to customers of such utility who are located within the service area of such utility.

(D) Adjustments for changes in customer base.

(i) New business customers. If—

(I) after the close of the testing period and before the date of issuance of the issue, the utility owned by a governmental unit enters into a contract to supply natural gas (other than for resale) for a business use at a property within the service area of such utility, and

(II) the utility did not supply natural gas to such property during the testing period or the ratable amount of natural gas to be supplied under the contract is significantly greater than the ratable amount of gas supplied to such property during the testing period,

then a contract shall not fail to be treated as a qualified natural gas supply contract by reason of supplying the additional natural gas under the contract referred to in subclause (I).

(ii) Lost customers. The average under subparagraph (B)(i) shall not exceed the annual amount of natural gas reasonably expected to be purchased (other than for resale) by persons who are located within the service area of such utility and who, as of the date of issuance of the issue, are customers of such utility.

(E) Ruling requests. The Secretary may increase the average under subparagraph (B)(i) for any period if the utility owned by the governmental unit establishes to the satisfaction of the Secretary that, based on objective evidence of growth in natural gas consumption or population, such average would otherwise be insufficient for such period.

(F) Adjustment for natural gas otherwise on hand.

(i) In general. The amount otherwise permitted to be acquired under the contract for any period shall be reduced by—

(I) the applicable share of natural gas held by the utility on the date of issuance of the issue, and

(II) the natural gas (not taken into account under subclause (I)) which the utility has a right to acquire during such period (determined as of the date of issuance of the issue).

(ii) Applicable share. For purposes of the clause (i), the term "applicable share" means, with respect to any period, the natural gas allocable to such period if the gas were allocated ratably over the period to which the prepayment relates.

(G) Intentional acts. Subparagraph (A) shall cease to apply to any issue if the utility owned by the governmental unit engages in any intentional act to render the volume of natural gas acquired by such prepayment to be in excess of the sum of—

(i) the amount of natural gas needed (other than for resale) by customers of such utility who are located within the service area of such utility, and

(ii) the amount of natural gas used to transport such natural gas to the utility.

(H) Testing period. For purposes of this paragraph, the term "testing period" means, with respect to an issue, the most recent 5 calendar years ending before the date of issuance of the issue.

(I) Service area. For purposes of this paragraph, the service area of a utility owned by a governmental unit shall be comprised of—

(i) any area throughout which such utility provided at all times during the testing period—

(I) in the case of a natural gas utility, natural gas transmission or distribution services, and

(II) in the case of an electric utility, electricity distribution services,

(ii) any area within a county contiguous to the area described in clause (i) in which retail customers of such utility are located if such area is not also served by another utility providing natural gas or electricity services, as the case may be, and

(iii) any area recognized as the service area of such utility under State or Federal law.

(c) Temporary period exception.

(1) **In general.** For purposes of subsection (a), a bond shall not be treated as an arbitrage bond solely by reason of the fact that the proceeds of the issue of which such bond is a part may be invested in higher yielding investments for a reasonable temporary period until such proceeds are needed for the purpose for which such issue was issued.

(2) **Limitation on temporary period for pooled financings.**

(A) In general. The temporary period referred to in paragraph (1) shall not exceed 6 months with respect to the proceeds of an issue which are to be used to make or finance loans (other than nonpurpose investments) to 2 or more persons.

(B) Shorter temporary period for loan repayments, etc. Subparagraph (A) shall be applied by substituting "3 months" for "6 months" with respect to the proceeds from the sale or repayment of any loan which are to be used to make or finance any loan. For purposes of the preceding sentence, a nonpurpose investment shall not be treated as a loan.

(C) Bonds used to provide construction financing. In the case of an issue described in subparagraph (A) any portion of which is used to make or finance loans for construction expenditures (within the meaning of subsection (f)(4)(C)(iv))—

(i) rules similar to the rules of subsection (f)(4)(C)(v) shall apply, and

(ii) subparagraph (A) shall be applied with respect to such portion by substituting "2 years" for "6 months".

(D) Exception for mortgage revenue bonds. This paragraph shall not apply to any qualified mortgage bond or qualified veterans' mortgage bond.

(d) Special rules for reasonably required reserve or replacement fund.

(1) **In general.** For purposes of subsection (a), a bond shall not be treated as an arbitrage bond solely by reason of the fact that an amount of the proceeds of the issue of which such bond is a part may be invested in higher yielding investments which are part of a reasonably required reserve or replacement fund. The amount referred to in the preceding sentence shall not exceed 10 percent of the proceeds of such issue unless the issuer establishes to the satisfaction of the Secretary that a higher amount is necessary.

(2) **Limitation on amount in reserve or replacement fund which may be financed by issue.** A bond issued as part of an issue shall be treated as an arbitrage bond if the amount of the proceeds from the sale of such issue which is part of any reserve or replacement fund exceeds 10 percent of the proceeds of the issue (or such higher amount which the issuer establishes is necessary to the satisfaction of the Secretary).

(e) Minor portion may be invested in higher yielding investments.

Notwithstanding subsections (a), (c), and (d), a bond issued as part of an issue shall not be treated as an arbitrage bond solely by reason of the fact that an amount of the proceeds of such issue (in addition to the amounts under subsections (c) and (d)) is invested in higher yielding investments if such amount does not exceed the lesser of—

(1) 5 percent of the proceeds of the issue, or

(2) $100,000.

(f) Required rebate to the United States.

(1) **In general.** A bond which is part of an issue shall be treated as an arbitrage bond if the requirements of paragraphs (2) and (3) are not met with respect to such issue. The preceding sentence shall not apply to any qualified veterans' mortgage bond.

(2) **Rebate to United States.** An issue shall be treated as meeting the requirements of this paragraph only if an amount equal to the sum of—

(A) the excess of—

(i) the amount earned on all nonpurpose investments (other than investments attributable to an excess described in this subparagraph), over

(ii) the amount which would have been earned if such nonpurpose investments were invested at a rate equal to the yield on the issue, plus

(B) any income attributable to the excess described in subparagraph (A),

is paid to the United States by the issuer in accordance with the requirements of paragraph (3).

(3) **Due date of payments under paragraph (2).** Except to the extent provided by the Secretary, the amount which is required to be paid to the United States by the issuer shall be paid in installments which are made at least once every 5 years. Each installment shall be in an amount which ensures that 90 percent of the amount described in paragraph (2) with respect to the issue at the time payment of such installment is required will have been paid to the United States. The last installment shall be made no later than 60 days after the day on which the last bond of the issue is redeemed and shall be in an amount sufficient to pay the remaining balance of the amount described in paragraph (2) with respect to such issue. A series of issues which are redeemed during a 6-month period (or such longer period as the Secretary may prescribe) shall be treated (at the election of the issuer) as 1 issue for purposes of the preceding sentence if no bond which is part of any issue in such series has a maturity of more than 270 days or is a private activity bond. In the case of a tax and revenue anticipation bond, the last installment shall not be required to be made before the date 8 months after the date of issuance of the issue of which the bond is a part.

(4) **Special rules for applying paragraph (2).**

(A) In general. In determining the aggregate amount earned on nonpurpose investments for purposes of paragraph (2)—

(i) any gain or loss on the disposition of a nonpurpose investment shall be taken into account, and

(ii) any amount earned on a bona fide debt service fund shall not be taken into account if the gross earnings on such fund for the bond year is less than $100,000.

In the case of an issue no bond of which is a private activity bond, clause (ii) shall be applied without regard to the dollar limitation therein if the average maturity of the issue (determined in accordance with section 147(b)(2)(A)) is at least 5 years and the rates of interest on bonds which are part of the issue do not vary during the term of the issue.

(B) Temporary investments. Under regulations prescribed by the Secretary—

(i) In general. An issue shall, for purposes of this subsection, be treated as meeting the requirements of paragraph (2) if—

(I) the gross proceeds of such issue are expended for the governmental purposes for which the issue was issued no later than the day which is 6 months after the date of issuance of the issue, and

(II) the requirements of paragraph (2) are met with respect to amounts not required to be spent as provided in subclause (I) (other than earnings on amounts in any bona fide debt service fund).

Gross proceeds which are held in a bona fide debt service fund or a reasonably required reserve or replacement fund, and gross proceeds which arise after such 6 months and which were not reasonably anticipated as of the date of issuance, shall not be considered gross proceeds for purposes of subclause (I) only.

(ii) Additional period for certain bonds.

(I) In general. In the case of an issue described in subclause (II), clause (i) shall be applied by substituting "1 year" for "6 months" each place it appears with respect to the portion of the proceeds of the issue which are not expended in accordance with clause (i) if such portion does not exceed 5 percent of the proceeds of the issue.

(II) Issues to which subclause (I) applies. An issue is described in this subclause if no bond which is part of such issue is a private activity bond (other than a qualified 501(c)(3) bond) or a tax or revenue anticipation bond.

(iii) Safe harbor for determining when proceeds of tax and revenue anticipation bonds are expended.

(I) In general. For purposes of clause (i), in the case of an issue of tax or revenue anticipation bonds, the net proceeds of such issue (including earnings thereon) shall be treated as expended for the governmental purpose of the issue on the 1st day after the date of issuance that the cumulative cash flow deficit to be financed by such issue exceeds 90 percent of the proceeds of such issue.

(II) Cumulative cash flow deficit. For purposes of subclause (I), the term "cumulative cash flow deficit" means, as of the date of computation, the excess of the expenses paid during the period described in subclause (III) which would ordinarily be paid out of or financed by anticipated tax or other revenues over the aggregate amount available (other than from the proceeds of the issue) during such period for the payment of such expenses.

(III) Period involved. For purposes of subclause (II), the period described in this subclause is the period beginning on the date of issuance of the issue and ending on the earlier of the date 6 months after such date of issuance or the date of the computation of cumulative cash flow deficit.

(iv) Payments of principal not to affect requirements. For purposes of this subparagraph, payments of principal on the bonds which are part of an issue shall not be treated as expended for the governmental purposes of the issue.

(C) Exception from rebate for certain proceeds to be used to finance construction expenditures.—

(i) In general. In the case of a construction issue, paragraph (2) shall not apply to the available construction proceeds of such issue if the spending requirements of clause (ii) are met.

(ii) Spending requirements. The spending requirements of this clause are met if at least—

(I) 10 percent of the available construction proceeds of the construction issue are spent for the governmental purposes of the issue within the 6-month period beginning on the date the bonds are issued,

(II) 45 percent of such proceeds are spent for such purposes within the 1-year period beginning on such date,

(III) 75 percent of such proceeds are spent for such purposes within the 18-month period beginning on such date, and

(IV) 100 percent of such proceeds are spent for such purposes within the 2-year period beginning on such date.

(iii) Exception for reasonable retainage. The spending requirement of clause (ii)(IV) shall be treated as met if—

(I) such requirement would be met at the close of such 2-year period but for a reasonable retainage (not exceeding 5 percent of the available construction proceeds of the construction issue), and

(II) 100 percent of the available construction proceeds of the construction issue are spent for the governmental purposes of the issue within the 3-year period beginning on the date the bonds are issued.

(iv) Construction issue. For purposes of this subparagraph, the term "construction issue" means any issue if—

(I) at least 75 percent of the available construction proceeds of such issue are to be used for construction expenditures with respect to property which is to be owned by a governmental unit or a 501(c)(3) organization, and

(II) all of the bonds which are part of such issue are qualified 501(c)(3) bonds, bonds which are not private activity bonds, or private activity bonds issued to finance property to be owned by a governmental unit or a 501(c)(3) organization.

For purposes of this subparagraph, the term "construction" includes reconstruction and rehabilitation, and rules similar to the rules of section 142(b)(1)(B) shall apply.

(v) Portions of issues used for construction. If—

(I) all of the construction expenditures to be financed by an issue are to be financed from a portion thereof, and

(II) the issuer elects to treat such portion as a construction issue for purposes of this subparagraph,

then, for purposes of this subparagraph and subparagraph (B), such portion shall be treated as a separate issue.

(vi) Available construction proceeds. For purposes of this subparagraph—

(I) In general. The term "available construction proceeds" means the amount equal to the issue price (within the meaning of sections 1273 and 1274) of the construction issue, increased by earnings on the issue price, earnings on amounts in any reasonably required reserve or replacement fund not funded from the issue, and earnings on all of the foregoing earnings, and reduced by the amount of the issue price in any reasonably required reserve or replacement fund and the issuance costs financed by the issue.

(II) Earnings on reserve included only for certain periods. The term "available construction proceeds" shall not include amounts earned on any reasonably required reserve or replacement fund after the earlier of the close of the 2-year period described in clause (ii) or the date the construction is substantially completed.

(III) Payments on acquired purpose obligations excluded. The term "available construction proceeds" shall not include payments on any obligation acquired to carry out the governmental purposes of the issue and shall not include earnings on such payments.

(IV) Election to rebate on earnings on reserve. At the election of the issuer, the term "available construction proceeds" shall not include earnings on any reasonably required reserve or replacement fund.

(vii) Election to pay penalty in lieu of rebate.

(I) In general. At the election of the issuer, paragraph (2) shall not apply to available construction proceeds which do not meet the spending requirements of clause (ii) if the issuer pays a penalty, with respect to each 6-month period after the date the bonds were issued, equal to 1 ½ percent of the amount of the available construction proceeds of the issue which, as of the close of such 6-month period, is not spent as required by clause (ii).

(II) Termination. The penalty imposed by this clause shall cease to apply only as provided in clause (viii) or after the latest maturity date of any bond in the issue (including any refunding bond with respect thereto).

(viii) Election to terminate 1 ½ percent penalty. At the election of the issuer (made not later than 90 days after the earlier of the end of the initial temporary period or the date the construction is substantially completed), the penalty under clause (vii) shall not apply to any 6-month period after the initial temporary period under subsection (c) if the requirements of subclauses (I), (II), and (III) are met.

(I) 3 Percent Penalty. The requirement of this subclause is met if the issuer pays a penalty equal to 3 percent of the amount of available construction proceeds of the issue which is not spent for the governmental purposes of the issue as of the close of such initial temporary period multiplied by the number of years (including fractions thereof) in the initial temporary period.

(II) Yield restriction at close of temporary period. The requirement of this subclause is met if the amount of the available construction proceeds of the issue which is not spent for the governmental purposes of the issue as of the close of such initial temporary period is invested at a yield not exceeding the yield on the issue or which is invested in any tax-exempt bond which is not investment property.

(III) Redemption of bonds at earliest call date. The requirement of this subclause is met if the amount of the available construction proceeds of the issue which is not spent for the governmental purposes of the issue as of the earliest date on which bonds may be redeemed is used to redeem bonds on such date.

(ix) Election to terminate 1 ½ percent penalty before end of temporary period. If—

(I) the construction to be financed by a construction issue is substantially completed before the end of the initial temporary period,

(II) the issuer identifies an amount of available construction proceeds which will not be spent for the governmental purposes of the issue,

(III) the issuer has made the election under clause (viii), and

(IV) the issuer makes an election under this clause before the close of the initial temporary period and not later than 90 days after the date the construction is substantially completed,

then clauses (vii) and (viii) shall be applied to the available construction proceeds so identified as if the initial temporary period ended as of the date the election is made.

(x) Failure to pay penalties. In the case of a failure (which is not due to willful neglect) to pay any penalty required to be paid under clause (vii) or (viii) in the amount or at the time prescribed therefor, the Secretary may treat such failure as not occurring if, in addition to paying such penalty, the issuer pays a penalty equal to the sum of—

(I) 50 percent of the amount which was not paid in accordance with clauses (vii) and (viii), plus

(II) interest (at the underpayment rate established under section 6621) on the portion of the amount which was not paid on the date required for the period beginning on such date.

The Secretary may waive all or any portion of the penalty under this clause. Bonds which are part of an issue with respect to which there is a failure to pay the amount required under this clause (and any refunding bond with respect thereto) shall be treated as not being, and as never having been, tax-exempt bonds.

(xi) Election for pooled financing bonds. At the election of the issuer of an issue the proceeds of which are to be used to make or finance loans (other than nonpurpose investments) to 2 or more persons, the periods described in clauses (ii) and (iii) shall begin on—

(I) the date the loan is made, in the case of loans made within the 1-year period after the date the bonds are issued, and

(II) the date following such 1-year period, in the case of loans made after such 1-year period.

If such an election applies to an issue, the requirements of paragraph (2) shall apply to amounts earned before the beginning of the periods determined under the preceding sentence.

(xii) Payments of principal not to affect requirements. For purposes of this subparagraph, payments of principal on the bonds which are part of the construction issue shall not be treated as an expenditure of the available construction proceeds of the issue.

(xiii) Refunding bonds.

(I) In general. Except as provided in this clause, clause (vii)(II), and the last sentence of clause (x), this subparagraph shall not apply to any refunding bond and no proceeds of a refunded bond shall be treated for purposes of this subparagraph as proceeds of a refunding bond.

(II) Determination of construction portion of issue. For purposes of clause (v), any portion of an issue which is used to refund any issue (or portion thereof) shall be treated as a separate issue.

(III) Coordination with rebate requirement on refunding bonds. The requirements of paragraph (2) shall be treated as met with respect to earnings for any period if a penalty is paid under clause (vii) or (viii) with respect to such earnings for such period.

(xiv) Determination of initial temporary period. For purposes of this subpargraph[sic], the end of the initial temporary period shall be determined without regard to section 149(d)(3)(A)(iv).

(xv) Elections. Any election under this subparagraph (other than clauses (viii) and (ix)) shall be made on or before the date the bonds are issued; and, once made, shall be irrevocable.

(xvi) Time for payment of penalties. Any penalty under this subparagraph shall be paid to the United States not later than 90 days after the period to which the penalty relates.

(xvii) Treatment of bona fide debt service funds. If the spending requirements of clause (ii) are met with respect to the available construction proceeds of a construction issue, then paragraph (2) shall not apply to earnings on a bona fide debt service fund for such issue.

(D) Exception for governmental units issuing $5,000,000 or less of bonds.—

(i) In general. An issue shall, for purposes of this subsection, be treated as meeting the requirements of paragraphs (2) and (3) if—

(I) the issue is issued by a governmental unit with general taxing powers,

(II) no bond which is part of such issue is a private activity bond,

(III) 95 percent or more of the net proceeds of such issue are to be used for local governmental activities of the issuer (or of a governmental unit the jurisdiction of which is entirely within the jurisdiction of the issuer), and

(IV) the aggregate face amount of all tax-exempt bonds (other than private activity bonds) issued by such unit during the calendar year in which such issue is issued is not reasonably expected to exceed $5,000,000.

(ii) Aggregation of issuers. For purpose of subclause (IV) of clause (i)—

(I) an issuer and all entities which issue bonds on behalf of such issuer shall be treated as 1 issuer,

(II) all bonds issued by a subordinate entity shall, for purposes of applying such subclause to each other entity to which such entity is subordinate, be treated as issued by such other entity, and

(III) an entity formed (or, to the extent provided by the Secretary, availed of) to avoid the purposes of such subclause (IV) and all other entities benefiting thereby shall be treated as 1 issuer.

(iii) Certain refunding bonds not taken into account in determining small issuer status. There shall not be taken into account under subclause (IV) of clause (i) any bond issued to refund (other than to advance refund) any bond to the extent the amount of the refunding bond does not exceed the outstanding amount of the refunded bond.

(iv) Certain issues issued by subordinate governmental units, etc., exempt from rebate requirement. An issue issued by a subordinate entity of a governmental unit with general taxing powers shall be treated as described in clause (i)(I) if the aggregate face amount of such issue does not exceed the lesser of—

(I) $5,000,000, or

(II) the amount which, when added to the aggregate face amount of other issues issued by such entity, does not exceed the portion of the $5,000,000 limitation under clause (i)(IV) which such governmental unit allocates to such entity.

For purposes of the preceding sentence, an entity which issues bonds on behalf of a governmental unit with general taxing powers shall be treated as a subordinate entity of such unit. An allocation shall be taken into account under subclause (II) only if it is irrevocable and made before the issuance date of such issue and only to the extent that the limitation so allocated bears a reasonable relationship to the benefits received by such governmental unit from issues issued by such entity.

(v) Determination of whether refunding bonds eligible for exception from rebate requirement. If any portion of an issue is issued to refund other bonds, such portion shall be treated as a separate issue which does not meet the requirements of paragraphs (2) and (3) by reason of this subparagraph unless—

(I) the aggregate face amount of such issue does not exceed $5,000,000,

(II) each refunded bond was issued as part of an issue which was treated as meeting the requirements of paragraphs (2) and (3) by reason of this subparagraph,

(III) the average maturity date of the refunding bonds issued as part of such issue is not later than the average maturity date of the bonds to be refunded by such issue, and

(IV) no refunding bond has a maturity date which is later than the date which is 30 years after the date the original bond was issued.

Subclause (III) shall not apply if the average maturity of the issue of which the original bond was a part (and of the issue of which the bonds to be refunded are a part) is 3 years or less. For purposes of this clause, average maturity shall be determined in accordance with section 147(b)(2)(A).

(vi) Refundings of bonds issued under law prior to Tax Reform Act of 1986. If section 141(a) did not apply to any refunded bond, the issue of which such refunded bond was a part shall be treated as meeting the requirements of subclause (II) of clause (v) if—

(I) such issue was issued by a governmental unit with general taxing powers,

(II) no bond issued as part of such issue was an industrial development bond (as defined in section 103(b)(2), but without regard to subparagraph (B) of section 103(b)(3)) or a private loan bond (as defined in section 103(o)(2)(A), but without regard to any exception from such definition other than section 103(o)(2)(C)), and

(III) the aggregate face amount of all tax-exempt bonds (other than bonds described in subclause (II)) issued by such unit during the calendar year in which such issue was issued did not exceed $5,000,000.

References in subclause (II) to section 103 shall be to such section as in effect on the day before the date of the enactment [10/22/86] of the Tax Reform Act of 1986. Rules similar to the rules of clauses (ii) and (iii) shall apply for purposes of subclause (III). For purposes of subclause (II) of clause (i), bonds described in subclause (II) of this clause to which section 141(a) does not apply shall not be treated as private activity bonds.

> • **Caution:** Code Sec. 148(f)(4)(D)(vii), following, was amended by P.L. 107-16 EGTRRA. These provisions generally sunset for tax years beginning after 12/31/2012. For specific sunset provisions, see Sec. 901, P.L. 107-16 (as amended) reproduced in history notes for this Code Sec.

(vii) Increase in exception for bonds financing public school capital expenditures. Each of the $5,000,000 amounts in the preceding provisions of this subparagraph shall be increased by the lesser of $10,000,000 or so much of the aggregate face amount of the bonds as are attributable to financing the construction (within the meaning of subparagraph (C)(iv)) of public school facilities.

(5) Exemption from gross income of sum rebated. Gross income shall not include the sum described in paragraph (2). Notwithstanding any other provision of this title, no deduction shall be allowed for any amount paid to the United States under paragraph (2).

(6) Definitions. For purposes of this subsection and subsections (c) and (d)—

(A) Nonpurpose investment. The term "nonpurpose investment" means any investment property which—

(i) is acquired with the gross proceeds of an issue, and

(ii) is not acquired in order to carry out the governmental purpose of the issue.

(B) Gross proceeds. Except as otherwise provided by the Secretary, the gross proceeds of an issue include—

(i) amounts received (including repayments of principal) as a result of investing the original proceeds of the issue, and

(ii) amounts to be used to pay debt service on the issue.

(7) Penalty in lieu of loss of tax exemption. In the case of an issue which would (but for this paragraph) fail to meet the requirements of paragraph (2) or (3), the Secretary may treat such issue as not failing to meet such requirements if—

(A) no bond which is part of such issue is a private activity bond (other than a qualified 501(c)(3) bond),

(B) the failure to meet such requirements is not due to willful neglect, and

(C) the issuer pays to the United States a penalty in an amount equal to the sum of—

(i) 50 percent of the amount which was not paid in accordance with paragraphs (2) and (3), plus

(ii) interest (at the underpayment rate established under section 6621) on the portion of the amount which was not paid on the date required under paragraph (3) for the period beginning on such date.

The Secretary may waive all or any portion of the penalty under this paragraph.

(g) Student loan incentive payments.

Except to the extent otherwise provided in regulations, payments made by the Secretary of Education pursuant to section 438 of the Higher Education Act of 1965 are not to be taken into account, for purposes of subsection (a)(1), in determining yields on student loan notes.

(h) Determinations of yield.

For purposes of this section, the yield on an issue shall be determined on the basis of the issue price (within the meaning of sections 1273 and 1274).

(i) Regulations.

The Secretary shall prescribe such regulations as may be necessary or appropriate to carry out the purposes of this section.

In 2010, P.L. 111-312, Sec. 101(a)(1), substituted "December 31, 2012" for "December 31, 2010" both places it appeared in Sec. 901, P.L. 107-16 [see below], effective as if included in the enactment of P.L. 107-16, EGTRRA, 6/7/2001.

In 2006, P.L. 109-432, Sec. 414(a), deleted "and before August 31, 2009" after "the date of enactment" in Sec. 206 of P.L. 109-222 [see below]. Sec. 414(b) of P.L. 109-432 provides the effective date for the amendment made by Sec. 414(a) of such Act.

—P.L. 109-222, Sec. 206, of this Act [as amended by Sec. 414(a) of P.L. 109-432, see above], provides:

"SEC. 206. MODIFICATION OF SPECIAL ARBITRAGE RULE FOR CERTAIN FUNDS. In the case of bonds issued after the date of the enactment of this Act—

"(1) the requirement of paragraph (1) of section 648 of the Deficit Reduction Act of 1984 (98 Stat. 941) shall be treated as met with respect to the securities or obligations referred to in such section if such securities or obligations are held in a fund the annual distributions from which cannot exceed 7 percent of the average fair market value of the assets held in such fund except to the extent distributions are necessary to pay debt service on the bond issue, and

"(2) paragraph (3) of such section shall be applied by substituting 'distributions from' for 'the investment earnings of' both places it appears."

—P.L. 109-222, Sec. 508(c), deleted subclause (f)(4)(D)(ii)(II) and redesignated subclauses (f)(4)(D)(ii)(III) and (IV) as subclauses (f)(4)(D)(ii)(II) and (III), effective for bonds issued after 5/17/2006.

Prior to deletion, subclause (f)(4)(D)(ii)(II) read as follows:

"(II) all bonds issued by a governmental unit to make loans to other governmental units with general taxing powers not subordinate to such unit shall, for purposes of applying such subclause to such unit, be treated as not issued by such unit,"

In 2005, P.L. 109-58, Sec. 1327(a), added para. (b)(4), effective for obligations issued after 8/8/2005.

In 2002, P.L. 107-358, Sec. 2, added subsec. (c) in Sec. 901 of P.L. 107-16 [see below], effective 12/17/2002.

In 2001, P.L. 107-16, Sec. 421(a), substituted "$10,000,000" for "$5,000,000" the second place it appeared in clause (f)(4)(D)(vii), effective for obligations issued in calendar yrs. begin. after 12/31/2001.

—P.L. 107-16, Sec. 901, of this Act [as amended by Sec. 2, P.L. 107-358, and Sec. 101(a)(1), P.L. 111-312, see above], reads as follows:

"SEC. 901. SUNSET OF PROVISIONS OF ACT.

"(a) In general. All provisions of, and amendments made by, this Act shall not apply—

"(1) to taxable, plan, or limitation years beginning after December 31, 2012, or

"(2) in the case of title V, to estates of decedents dying, gifts made, or generation skipping transfers, after December 31, 2012.

"(b) Application of certain laws. The Internal Revenue Code of 1986 and the Employee Retirement Income Security Act of 1974 shall be applied and administered to years, estates, gifts, and transfers described in subsection (a) as if the provisions and amendments described in subsection (a) had never been enacted.

"(c) Exception. Subsection (a) shall not apply to section 803 (relating to no federal income tax on restitution received by victims of the Nazi regime or their heirs or estates)."

In 1997, P.L. 105-34, Sec. 223(a), added clause (f)(4)(D)(vii), effective for bonds issued after 12/31/97.

—P.L. 105-34, Sec. 1441, substituted "5 percent of the proceeds of the issue" for "the lesser of 5 percent of the proceeds of the issue or $100,000" in subclause (f)(4)(B)(ii)(I) . . . Sec. 1442, added clause (f)(4)(C)(xvii) . . . Sec. 1443, deleted para. (d)(3) . . . Sec. 1444(a), deleted subpara. (c)(2)(B) and redesignated subparas. (c)(2)(C)-(E) as subparas. (c)(2)(B)-(D) . . . Sec. 1444(b), deleted subpara. (f)(4)(E), effective for bonds issued after 8/5/97.

Prior to deletion, subpara. (c)(2)(B) read as follows:

"(B) Special rule for certain student loan pools. In the case of the proceeds of an issue to be used to make or finance loans under a program described in section 144(b)(1)(A), subparagraph (A) shall be applied by substituting '18 months' for '6 months'. The preceding sentence shall not apply to any bond issued after December 31, 1988."

Prior to deletion, para. (d)(3) read as follows:

"(3) Limitation on investment in nonpurpose investments.

"(A) In general. A bond which is part of an issue which does not meet the requirements of subparagraph (B) shall be treated as an arbitrage bond.

"(B) Requirements. An issue meets the requirements of this subparagraph only if—

"(i) at no time during any bond year may the amount invested in nonpurpose investments with a yield materially higher than the yield on the issue exceed 150 percent of the debt service on the issue for the bond year, and

"(ii) the aggregate amount invested as provided in clause (i) is promptly and appropriately reduced as the amount of outstanding bonds of the issue is reduced (or, in the case of a qualified mortgage bond or a qualified veterans' mortgage bond, as the mortgages are repaid).

"(C) Exceptions for temporary period. Subparagraph (B) shall not apply to—

"(i) proceeds of the issue invested for an initial temporary period until such proceeds are needed for the governmental purpose of the issue, and

"(ii) temporary investment periods related to debt service.

"(D) Debt service defined. For purposes of this paragraph, the debt service on the issue for any bond year is the scheduled amount of interest and amortization of principal payable for such year with respect to such issue. For purposes of the preceding sentence, there shall not be taken into account amounts scheduled with respect to any bond which has been redeemed before the beginning of the bond year.

"(E) No disposition in case of loss. This paragraph shall not require the sale or disposition of any investment if such sale or disposition would result in a loss which exceeds the amount which, but for such sale or disposition, would at the time of such sale or disposition—

"(i) be paid to the United States, or,

"(ii) in the case of a qualified veterans' mortgage bond, be paid or credited mortgagors under section 143(g)(3)(A).

"(F) Exception for governmental use bonds and qualified 501(c)(3) bonds. This paragraph shall not apply to any bond which is not a private activity bond or which is a qualified 501(c)(3) bond."

Prior to deletion, subpara. (f)(4)(E) read as follows:

"(E) Exception for certain qualified student loan bonds.

"(i) In general. In determining the aggregate amount earned on nonpurpose investments acquired with gross proceeds of an issue of bonds for a program described in section 144(b)(1)(A), the amount earned from investment of net proceeds of such issue during the initial temporary period under subsection (c) shall not be taken into account to the extent that the amount so earned is used to pay the reasonable—

"(I) administrative costs of such program attributable to such issue and the costs of carrying such issue, and

"(II) costs of issuing such issue,

but only to the extent such costs were financed with proceeds of such issue and for which the issuer was not reimbursed. Amounts designated as interest on student loans shall not be taken into account in determining whether the issuer is reimbursed for such costs. Except as otherwise hereafter provided in regulations prescribed by the Secretary, costs described in subclause (I) paid from amounts earned as described in the first sentence of this clause may also be taken into account in determining the yield on the student loans under a program described in section 144(b)(1)(A).

"(ii) Only arbitrage on amounts loaned during temporary period taken into account for administrative costs, etc. The amount earned from investment of net proceeds of an issue during the initial temporary period under subsection (c) shall be taken into account under clause (i)(I) only to the extent attributable to proceeds which were used to make or finance (not later than the close of such period) student loans under a program described in section 144(b)(1)(A).

"(iii) Election. This subparagraph shall not apply to any issue if the issuer elects not to have this subparagraph apply to such issue.

"(iv) Termination. This subparagraph shall not apply to any bond issued after December 31, 1988."

In 1990, P.L. 101-508, Sec. 11701(j)(1), amended subclause (f)(4)(B)(i)(II) . . . Sec. 11701(j)(2), amended the last sentence of clause (f)(4)(B)(i) . . . Sec. 11701(j)(3)(A), redesignated subparas. (f)(4)(C) and (D) as subparas. (f)(4)(D) and (E) . . . Sec. 11701(j)(3)(B), added new subpara. (f)(4)(C) . . . Sec. 11701(j)(4), amended clause (f)(4)(B)(iv) . . . Sec. 11701(j)(5)(A), substituted "subsection (f)(4)(C)(iv)" for "subsection (f)(4)(B)(iv)(IV)" in subpara. (c)(2)(D) . . . Sec. 11701(j)(5)(B), substituted "subsection (f)(4)(C)(v)" for "subsection (f)(4)(B)(iv)(VIII)" in subpara. (c)(2)(D)(i), effective for bonds issued after 12/19/89.

Prior to amendment, subclause (f)(4)(B)(i)(II) read as follows:

"(II) the requirements of paragraph (2) are met after such 6 months with respect to earnings on amounts in any reasonably required reserve or replacement fund."

Prior to amendment, the last sentence of clause (f)(4)(B)(i) read as follows:

"Gross proceeds which are held in a bona fide debt service fund or a reasonably required reserve or replacement fund shall not be considered gross proceeds for purposes of this subparagraph only."

Prior to amendment, clause (f)(4)(B)(iv) read as follows:

"(iv) 2-year period for certain construction bonds.

"(I) In general. In the case of an issue described in subclause (IV), clause (i) shall be applied by substituting '2 years' for '6 months' each place it appears.

"(II) Proceeds must be spent within certain periods. Subclause (I) shall not apply to any issue if less than 10 percent of the net proceeds of the issue are spent for the governmental purposes of the issue within the 6-month period beginning on the date the bonds are issued, less than 45 percent of such proceeds are spent for such purposes within the 1-year period beginning on such date, less than 75 percent of such proceeds are spent for such purposes within the 18-month period beginning on such date, or less than 100 percent of such proceeds are spent for such purposes within the 2-year period beginning on such date. For purposes of the preceding sentence, the term 'net proceeds' includes investment proceeds earned before the close of the period involved on the investment of the sale proceeds of the issue.

"(III) Exception for reasonable retainage. For purposes of subclause (II), 100 percent of the net proceeds of an issue shall be treated as spent for the governmental purposes of the issue within the 2-year period beginning on the date the bonds are issued if such requirement is met within the 3-year period beginning on such date and such requirement would have been met within such 2-year period but for a reasonable retainage (not exceeding 5 percent of the net proceeds of the issue).

"(IV) Issues to which subclause (I) applies. An issue is described in this subclause if at least 75 percent of the net proceeds of the issue are to be used for construction expenditures with respect to property which is owned by a governmental unit or a 501(c)(3) organization. For purposes of the preceding sentence, the term 'construction' includes reconstruction and rehabilitation, and section 142(b)(1) shall apply. An issue is not described in this subclause if any bond which is part of such issue is a bond other than a qualified 501(c)(3) bond, a bond which is not a private activity bond, or a private activity bond to finance property to be owned by a governmental unit or a 501(c)(3) organization.

"(V) Election to pay penalty in lieu of rebate. In the case of an issue described in subclause (IV) which fails to meet the requirements of subclause (II), if the issuer elected the application of this subclause, the requirements of paragraph (2) shall be treated as met if the issuer pays the penalty under paragraph (7) or pays a penalty with respect to the close of each 6 month period after the date the bonds are issued equal to 1½ percent of the amount of the net proceeds of the issue which, as of the close of such period, are not spent as required by subclause (II). The penalty under this subclause shall cease to apply only after the bonds (including any refunding bonds with respect thereto) are no longer outstanding.

"(VI) Election to rebate on earnings on reserve. If the issuer so elects, the term 'net proceeds' for purposes of subclause (II) shall not include earnings on any reasonably required reserve or replacement fund and the requirements of paragraph (2) shall apply to such earnings.

"(VII) Pooled financing bonds. At the election of the issuer of an issue the proceeds of which are to be used to make or finance loans (other than nonpurpose investments) to 2 or more persons, the periods described in clause (i) and this clause shall begin on the date the loan is made in the case of loans made within the 1-year period after the date the bonds were issued. In the case of loans made after such 1-year period, the periods described in clause (i) and this clause shall begin at the close of such 1-year period.

"(VIII) Portions of issue may be treated separately. If only a portion of an issue is to be used for construction expenditures referred to in subclause (IV), such portion and the other portion of such issue may, at the election of the issuer, be treated as separate issues for purposes of this clause and clause (i).

"(IX) Elections. Any election under this clause shall be made on or before the date the bonds are issued; and, once made, shall be irrevocable."

—P.L. 101-508, Sec. 11701(j)(7), provides:

"(7) In the case of a bond issued before the date of the enactment of this Act, the period for making the election under section 148(f)(4)(C)(viii) of the Internal Revenue Code of 1986 (as added by this subsection) shall not expire before the date which is 180 days after such date of enactment."

—P.L. 101-508, Sec. 11701(j)(8), provides:

"(8) Section 148(f)(4)(D)(xiii)(II) of such Code (as added by this subsection) shall apply only to refunding bonds issued after August 3, 1990."

In 1989, P.L. 101-239, Sec. 7652(a), amended clause (f)(4)(B)(i) . . . Sec. 7652(b), added clause (f)(4)(B)(iv) . . . Sec. 7652(c), redesignated subpara. (c)(2)(D) as (c)(2)(E) and added new subpara. (c)(2)(D) . . . Sec. 7652(d), added "each place it appears" after "6 months"' in subclause (f)(4)(B)(ii)(I), effective for bonds issued after 12/19/89.

Prior to amendment, clause (f)(4)(B)(i) read as follows:

"(1) In general. An issue shall, for purposes of this subsection, be treated as meeting the requirements of paragraph (2) if the gross proceeds of such issue are expended for the governmental purpose for which the issue was issued by no later than the day which is 6 months after the date of issuance of such issue. Gross proceeds which are held in a bona fide debt service fund shall not be considered gross proceeds for purposes of this subparagraph only."

—P.L. 101-239, Sec. 7814(c)(2), deleted "a qualified mortgage bond or" after "of" in clause (d)(3)(E)(ii), effective for bonds issued, and nonissued bond amounts elected after 12/31/88. For special rules, see Sec. 4005(h)(2)(B) of P.L. 100-647 reproduced in notes at Code Sec. 143.

—P.L. 101-239, Sec. 7816(r), substituted "such date of issuance or the date" for "such date of issuance, or the date", effective for bonds issued after 11/10/88.

—P.L. 101-239, Sec. 7816(t), substituted "to make loans to" for "on behalf of", in subclause (f)(4)(C)(ii)(II), effective for bonds issued after 12/31/88.

In 1988, P.L. 100-647, Sec. 1013(a)(14), substituted "any reserve or replacement fund" for "any fund described in paragraph (1)" in para. (d)(2) . . . Sec. 1013(a)(15), added the last sentence to para. (f)(3), effective for bonds issued after 8/15/86, except as provided in Sec. 1301(c) of P.L. 99-514, reproduced below.

—P.L. 100-647, Sec. 1013(a)(16)(A), substituted "proceeds of such issue" for "aggregate face amount of such issue" in subclause (f)(4)(B)(iii)(I), effective for bonds issued after 6/30/87.

—P.L. 100-647, Sec. 1013(a)(17)(A)(i), amended the name of subpara. (f)(4)(C) and added clause (f)(4)(C)(i) . . . Sec. 1013(a)(17)(A)(ii), redesignated clauses (f)(4)(C)(i) through (iv) as subclauses (f)(4)(C)(i)(I) through (IV) . . . Sec. 1013(a)(17)(A)(iii), substituted new clauses (f)(4)(C)(ii) through (vi) for "Clause (iv) shall not take into account any bond which is not outstanding at the time of a later issue or which is redeemed (other than in an advance refunding) from the net proceeds of the later issue." in subpara. (f)(4)(C) . . . Sec. 1013(a)(17)(B), deleted "(and all subordinate entities thereof)" which followed "such unit" in subclause (f)(4)(C)(i)(IV), effective for bonds issued after 6/30/87 except as provided in Sec. 1013(a)(17)(C)(ii) of this Act, which reads:

"At the election of an issuer (made at such time and in such manner as the Secretary of the Treasury or his delegate may prescribe), the amendments made by this paragraph shall apply to such issuer as if included in the amendments made by section 1301(a) of the Tax Reform Act of 1986."

Prior to amendment, the name of subpara. (f)(4)(C) read as follows:

for "(C) Exception for small governmental units."

Code Sec. 148 — Private activity bonds

—P.L. 100-647, Sec. 1013(a)(18)(A)-(C), added "for a program" before "described in section 144(b)(1)(A)" in clause (f)(4)(D)(i), substituted "such program" for "such a program" in subclause (f)(4)(D)(i)(I) and added two sentences to the end of clause (f)(4)(D)(i) ... Sec. 1013(a)(19), substituted "not due" for "due to reasonable cause and not" in subpara. (f)(7)(B), effective for bonds issued after 8/15/86, except as provided in Sec. 1301(c) of P.L. 99-514, reproduced below.

—P.L. 100-647, Sec. 1013(a)(43)(A), added para. (b)(3) ... Sec. 1013(a)(43)(B), deleted the last sentence in para. (b)(2), effective for obligations issued after 3/31/88.
Prior to deletion, the last sentence in para. (b)(2) read as follows:
"Such term shall not include any tax-exempt bond."

—P.L. 100-647, Sec. 4005(d)(2), deleted "qualified mortgage bond or" following "to any" in para. (f)(1), effective for bonds issued, and nonissued bond amounts elected after 12/31/88. For special rules see Sec. 4005(h)(2)(B), reproduced in note reproduced at Code Sec. 143.

—P.L. 100-647, Sec. 5053(b), deleted "or" at the end of subpara. (b)(2)(C), substituted ", or" for the period at the end of subpara. (b)(2)(D), and added subpara. (b)(2)(E), effective for obligations issued after 10/21/88, except as provided in Sec. 5053(c)(2) and (3) of this Act, which reads:
"(2) Exception for construction or binding agreement.—
"(A) The amendments made by this section shall not apply to bonds (other than refunding bonds) with respect to a facility—
"(i)(I) the original use of which begins with the taxpayer, and the construction, reconstruction, or rehabilitation of which began before July 14, 1988, and was completed on or after such date, or
"(II) the original use of which begins with the taxpayer and with respect to which a binding contract to incur significant expenditures for construction, reconstruction, or rehabilitation was entered into before July 14, 1988, and some of such expenditures are incurred on or after such date, and
"(ii) described in an inducement resolution or other comparable preliminary approval adopted by an issuing authority (or by a voter referendum) before July 14, 1988.
For purposes of the preceding sentence, the term 'significant expenditures' means expenditures greater than 10 percent of the reasonably anticipated cost of the construction, reconstruction, or rehabilitation of the facility involved.
"(B) Subparagraph (A) shall not apply to any bond issued after December 31, 1989, and shall not apply unless it is reasonably expected (at the time of issuance of the bond) that the facility will be placed in service before January 1, 1990.
"(3) Refundings.— The amendments made by this section shall not apply to any bond issued to refund (or which is part of a series of bonds issued to refund) a bond issued before July 15, 1988, if—
"(A) the average maturity date of the issue of which the refunding bond is a part is not later than the average maturity date of the bonds to be refunded by such issue,
"(B) the amount of the refunding bond does not exceed the outstanding amount of the refunded bond, and
"(C) the proceeds of the refunding bond are used to redeem the refunded bond not later than 90 days after the date of the issuance of the refunding bond.
For purposes of subparagraph (C), average maturity shall be determined in accordance with section 147(b) of the 1986 Code."

—P.L. 100-647, Sec. 6177(a), substituted "the earlier of the date 6 months after such date of issuance," for "the earliest of the maturity date of the issue, the date 6 months after such date of issuance," in subclause (f)(4)(B)(iii)(III) ... Sec. 6177(b), added the last sentence to the end of para. (f)(3), [as amended by Sec. 1013(a)(15) of this Act, see above] effective for bonds issued after 11/10/88.

—P.L. 100-647, Sec. 6181(a), deleted "unless the issuer otherwise elects" before "any amount" from clause (f)(4)(A)(ii) ... Sec. 6181(b), added the last sentence at the end of subpara. (f)(4)(A), effective for bonds issued after 11/10/88. Sec. 6181(c)(2) and (3) of this Act provide:
"(2) Election for outstanding bonds.— Any issue of bonds other than private activity bonds outstanding as of the date of the enactment of this Act shall be allowed a 1-time election to apply the amendments made by subsection (b) to amounts deposited after such date in bona fide debt service funds of such bonds.
"(3) Definition of private activity bond.— For purposes of this section and the last sentence of section 148(f)(4)(A) of the 1986 Code (as added by subsection (b)), the term 'private activity bond' shall include any qualified 501(c)(3) bond (as defined under section 145 of the 1986 Code)."

—P.L. 100-647, Sec. 6183(a), redesignated subclauses (f)(4)(C)(ii)(II) and (III) as (f)(4)(C)(ii)(III) and (IV) and added new subclause (f)(4)(C)(ii)(II), effective for bonds issued after 12/31/88.

In 1986, P.L. 99-514, Sec. 1301(b), added Code Sec. 148 as part of the amendments to Part IV of subchapter B of chapter 1, effective for bonds issued after 8/15/86. Sec. 1301(c) of this Act provides:
"(c) Amendment to arbitrage regulations.
"The provision in the Federal income tax regulations relating to the arbitrage requirements which permits a higher yield on acquired obligations if the issuer elects to waive the benefits of the temporary period provisions shall not apply to bonds issued after August 31, 1986."
For transitional rules, see Secs. 1312—1318 of this Act reproduced in the note following Code Sec. 103.

Sec. 149. Bonds must be registered to be tax exempt; other requirements.

(a) Bonds must be registered to be tax exempt.
(1) General rule. Nothing in section 103(a) or in any other provision of law shall be construed to provide an exemption from Federal income tax for interest on any registration-required bond unless such bond is in registered form.

> • *Caution:* Code Sec. 149(a)(2), following, is effective for obligations issued before 3/18/2012. For Code Sec. 149(a)(2), effective for obligations issued after 3/18/2012, see below.

(2) Registration-required bond. For purposes of paragraph (1), the term "registration-required bond" means any bond other than a bond which—
(A) is not of a type offered to the public,
(B) has a maturity (at issue) of not more than 1 year, or
(C) is described in section 163(f)(2)(B).

> • *Caution:* Code Sec. 149(a)(2), following, is effective for obligations issued after 3/18/2012. For Code Sec. 149(a)(2), effective for obligations issued before 3/18/2012, see above.

(2) Registration-required bond. For purposes of paragraph (1), the term "registration-required bond" means any bond other than a bond which—
(A) is not of a type offered to the public, or
(B) has a maturity (at issue) of not more than 1 year.
(C) Repealed.

(3) Special rules.
(A) Book entries permitted. For purposes of paragraph (1), a book entry bond shall be treated as in registered form if the right to the principal of, and stated interest on, such bond may be transferred only through a book entry consistent with regulations prescribed by the Secretary.
(B) Nominees. The Secretary shall prescribe such regulations as may be necessary to carry out the purpose of paragraph (1) where there is a nominee or chain of nominees.

(b) Federally guaranteed bond is not tax exempt.
(1) In general. Section 103(a) shall not apply to any State or local bond if such bond is federally guaranteed.
(2) Federally guaranteed defined. For purposes of paragraph (1), a bond is federally guaranteed if—
(A) the payment of principal or interest with respect to such bond is guaranteed (in whole or in part) by the United States (or any agency or instrumentality thereof),
(B) such bond is issued as part of an issue and 5 percent or more of the proceeds of such issue is to be—
(i) used in making loans the payment of principal or interest with respect to which are to be guaranteed (in whole or in part) by the United States (or any agency or instrumentality thereof), or
(ii) invested (directly or indirectly) in federally insured deposits or accounts, or
(C) the payment of principal or interest on such bond is otherwise indirectly guaranteed (in whole or in part) by the United States (or an agency or instrumentality thereof).

(3) Exceptions.
(A) Certain insurance programs. A bond shall not be treated as federally guaranteed by reason of—

(i) any guarantee by the Federal Housing Administration, the Veterans' Administration [Department of Veterans Affairs], the Federal National Mortgage Association, the Federal Home Loan Mortgage Corporation, or the Government National Mortgage Association,

(ii) any guarantee of student loans and any guarantee by the Student Loan Marketing Association to finance student loans,

(iii) any guarantee by the Bonneville Power Authority pursuant to the Northwest Power Act (16 U.S.C. 839d) as in effect on the date of the enactment [7/18/84] of the Tax Reform Act of 1984, or

(iv) subject to subparagraph (E), any guarantee by a Federal home loan bank made in connection with the original issuance of a bond during the period beginning on the date of the enactment of this clause and ending on December 31, 2010 (or a renewal or extension of a guarantee so made).

(B) Debt service, etc. Paragraph (1) shall not apply to—

(i) proceeds of the issue invested for an initial temporary period until such proceeds are needed for the purpose for which such issue was issued,

(ii) investments of a bona fide debt service fund,

(iii) investments of a reserve which meet the requirements of section 148(d),

(iv) investments in bonds issued by the United States Treasury, or

(v) other investments permitted under regulations.

(C) Exception for housing programs.

(i) In general. Except as provided in clause (ii), paragraph (1) shall not apply to—

(I) a private activity bond for a qualified residential rental project or a housing program obligation under section 11(b) of the United States Housing Act of 1937,

(II) a qualified mortgage bond, or

(III) a qualified veterans' mortgage bond.

(ii) Exception not to apply where bond invested in federally insured deposits or accounts. Clause (i) shall not apply to any bond which is federally guaranteed within the meaning of paragraph (2)(B)(ii).

(D) Loans to, or guarantees by, financial institutions. Except as provided in paragraph (2)(B)(ii), a bond which is issued as part of an issue shall not be treated as federally guaranteed merely by reason of the fact that the proceeds of such issue are used in making loans to a financial institution or there is a guarantee by a financial institution unless such guarantee constitutes a federally insured deposit or account.

(E) Safety and soundness requirements for federal home loan banks. Clause (iv) of subparagraph (A) shall not apply to any guarantee by a Federal home loan bank unless such bank meets safety and soundness collateral requirements for such guarantees which are at least as stringent as such requirements which apply under regulations applicable to such guarantees by Federal home loan banks as in effect on April 9, 2008.

(4) Definitions. For purposes of this subsection—

(A) Treatment of certain entities with authority to borrow from United States. To the extent provided in regulations prescribed by the Secretary, any entity with statutory authority to borrow from the United States shall be treated as an instrumentality of the United States. Except in the case of an exempt facility bond, a qualified small issue bond, and a qualified student loan bond, nothing in the preceding sentence shall be construed as treating the District of Columbia or any possession of the United States as an instrumentality of the United States.

(B) Federally insured deposit or account. The term "federally insured deposit or account" means any deposit or account in a financial institution to the extent such deposit or account is insured under Federal law by the Federal Deposit Insurance Corporation, the Federal Savings and Loan Insurance Corporation, the National Credit Union Administration, or any similar federally chartered corporation.

(c) Tax exemption must be derived from this title.

(1) General rule. Except as provided in paragraph (2), no interest on any bond shall be exempt from taxation under this title unless such interest is exempt from tax under this title without regard to any provision of law which is not contained in this title and which is not contained in a revenue Act.

(2) Certain prior exemptions.

(A) Prior exemptions continued. For purposes of this title, notwithstanding any provision of this part, any bond the interest on which is exempt from taxation under this title by reason of any provision of law (other than a provision of this title) which is in effect on January 6, 1983, shall be treated as a bond described in section 103(a).

(B) Additional requirements for bonds issued after 1983. Subparagraph (A) shall not apply to a bond (not described in subparagraph (C)) issued after 1983 if the appropriate requirements of this part (or the corresponding provisions of prior law) are not met with respect to such bond.

(C) Description of bond. A bond is described in this subparagraph (and treated as described in subparagraph (A)) if—

(i) such bond is issued pursuant to the Northwest Power Act (16 U.S.C. 839d), as in effect on July 18, 1984;

(ii) such bond is issued pursuant to section 608(a)(6)(A) of Public Law 97-468, as in effect on the date of the enactment [10/22/86] of the Tax Reform Act of 1986; or

(iii) such bond is issued before June 19, 1984 under section 11(b) of the United States Housing Act of 1937.

(d) Advance refundings.

(1) In general. Nothing in section 103(a) or in any other provision of law shall be construed to provide an exemption from Federal income tax for interest on any bond issued as part of an issue described in paragraph (2), (3), or (4).

(2) Certain private activity bonds. An issue is described in this paragraph if any bond (issued as part of such issue) is issued to advance refund a private activity bond (other than a qualified 501(c)(3) bond).

(3) Other bonds.

(A) In general. An issue is described in this paragraph if any bond (issued as part of such issue), hereinafter in this paragraph referred to as the "refunding bond", is issued to advance refund a bond unless—

(i) the refunding bond is only—

(I) the 1st advance refunding of the original bond if the original bond is issued after 1985, or

(II) the 1st or 2nd advance refunding of the original bond if the original bond was issued before 1986,

(ii) in the case of refunded bonds issued before 1986, the refunded bond is redeemed not later than the earliest date on which such bond may be redeemed at par or at a premium of 3 percent or less,

(iii) in the case of refunded bonds issued after 1985, the refunded bond is redeemed not later than the earliest date on which such bond may be redeemed,

(iv) the initial temporary period under section 148(c) ends—

(I) with respect to the proceeds of the refunding bond not later than 30 days after the date of issue of such bond, and

(II) with respect to the proceeds of the refunded bond on the date of issue of the refunding bond, and

(v) in the case of refunded bonds to which section 148(e) did not apply, on and after the date of issue of the refunding bond, the amount of proceeds of the refunded bond invested in higher yielding investments (as defined in section 148(b)) which are nonpurpose investments (as defined in section 148(f)(6)(A)) does not exceed—

(I) the amount so invested as part of a reasonably required reserve or replacement fund or during an allowable temporary period, and

(II) the amount which is equal to the lesser of 5 percent of the proceeds of the issue of which the refunded bond is a part or $100,000 (to the extent such amount is allocable to the refunded bond).

(B) Special rules for redemptions.

(i) Issuer must redeem only if debt service savings. Clause (ii) and (iii) of subparagraph (A) shall apply only if the issuer may realize present value debt service savings (determined without regard to administrative expenses) in connection with the issue of which the refunding bond is a part.

(ii) Redemptions not required before 90th day. For purposes of clauses (ii) and (iii) of subparagraph (A), the earliest date referred to in such clauses shall not be earlier than the 90th day after the date of issuance of the refunding bond.

(4) Abusive transactions prohibited. An issue is described in this paragraph if any bond (issued as part of such issue) is issued to advance refund another bond and a device is employed in connection with the issuance of such issue to obtain a material financial advantage (based on arbitrage) apart from savings attributable to lower interest rates.

(5) Advance refunding. For purposes of this part, a bond shall be treated as issued to advance refund another bond if it is issued more than 90 days before the redemption of the refunded bond.

(6) Special rules for purposes of paragraph (3). For purposes of paragraph (3), bonds issued before the date of the enactment of this subsection shall be taken into account under subparagraph (A)(i) thereof except—

(A) a refunding which occurred before 1986 shall be treated as an advance refunding only if the refunding bond was issued more than 180 days before the redemption of the refunded bond, and

(B) a bond issued before 1986, shall be treated as advance refunded no more than once before March 15, 1986.

(7) Regulations. The Secretary shall prescribe such regulations as may be necessary or appropriate to carry out the purposes of this subsection.

(e) Information reporting.

(1) In general. Nothing in section 103(a) or any other provision of law shall be construed to provide an exemption from Federal income tax for interest on any bond unless such bond satisfies the requirements of paragraph (2).

(2) Information reporting requirements. A bond satisfies the requirements of this paragraph if the issuer submits to the Secretary, not later than the 15th day of the 2d calendar month after the close of the calendar quarter in which the bond is issued (or such later time as the Secretary may prescribe with respect to any portion of the statement), a statement concerning the issue of which the bond is a part which contains—

(A) the name and address of the issuer,

(B) the date of issue, the amount of net proceeds of the issue, the stated interest rate, term, and face amount of each bond which is part of the issue, the amount of issuance costs of the issue, and the amount of reserves of the issue,

(C) where required, the name of the applicable elected representative who approved the issue, or a description of the voter referendum by which the issue was approved,

(D) the name, address, and employer identification number of—

(i) each initial principal user of any facility provided with the proceeds of the issue,

(ii) the common parent of any affiliated group of corporations (within the meaning of section 1504(a)) of which such initial principal user is a member, and

(iii) if the issue is treated as a separate issue under section 144(a)(6)(A), any person treated as a principal user under section 144(a)(6)(B),

(E) a description of any property to be financed from the proceeds of the issue,

(F) a certification by a State official designated by State law (or, where there is no such official, the Governor) that the bond meets the requirements of section 146 (relating to cap on private activity bonds), if applicable, and

(G) such other information as the Secretary may require.

Subparagraphs (C) and (D) shall not apply to any bond which is not a private activity bond. The Secretary may provide that certain information specified in the 1st sentence need not be included in the statement with respect to an issue where the inclusion of such information is not necessary to carry out the purposes of this subsection.

(3) Extension of time. The Secretary may grant an extension of time for the filing of any statement required under paragraph (2) if the failure to file in a timely fashion is not due to willful neglect.

(f) Treatment of certain pooled financing bonds.

(1) In general. Section 103(a) shall not apply to any pooled financing bond unless, with respect to the issue of which such bond is a part, the requirements of paragraphs (2), (3), (4), and (5) are met.

(2) Reasonable expectation requirement.

(A) In general. The requirements of this paragraph are met with respect to an issue if the issuer reasonably expects that—

(i) as of the close of the 1-year period beginning on the date of issuance of the issue, at least 30 percent of the net proceeds of the issue (as of the close of such period) will have been used directly or indirectly to make or finance loans to ultimate borrowers, and

(ii) as of the close of the 3-year period beginning on such date of issuance, at least 95 percent of the net proceeds of the issue (as of the close of such period) will have been so used.

(B) Certain factors may not be taken into account in determining expectations. Expectations as to changes in interest rates or in the provisions of this title (or in the regulations or rulings thereunder) may not be taken into account in determining whether expectations are reasonable for purposes of this paragraph.

(C) Net proceeds. For purposes of subparagraph (A), the term "net proceeds" has the meaning given such term by section 150 but shall not include proceeds used to finance issuance costs and shall not include proceeds necessary to pay interest (during such period) on the bonds which are part of the issue.

(D) Refunding bonds. For purposes of subparagraph (A), in the case of a refunding bond, the date of issuance taken into account is the date of issuance of the original bond.

(3) Cost of issuance payment requirements. The requirements of this paragraph are met with respect to an issue if—

(A) the payment of legal and underwriting costs associated with the issuance of the issue is not contingent, and

(B) at least 95 percent of the reasonably expected legal and underwriting costs associated with the issuance of the issue are paid not later than the 180th day after the date of the issuance of the issue.

(4) Written loan commitment requirement.

(A) In general. The requirement of this paragraph is met with respect to an issue if the issuer receives prior to issuance written loan commitments identifying the ultimate potential borrowers of at least 30 percent of the net proceeds of such issue.

(B) Exception. Subparagraph (A) shall not apply with respect to any issuer which—

(i) is a State (or an integral part of a State) issuing pooled financing bonds to make or finance loans to subordinate governmental units of such State, or

(ii) is a State-created entity providing financing for water-infrastructure projects through the federally-sponsored State revolving fund program.

(5) Redemption requirement. The requirement of this paragraph is met if to the extent that less than the percentage of the proceeds of an issue required to be used under clause (i) or (ii) of paragraph (2)(A) is used by the close of the period identified in such clause, the issuer uses an amount of proceeds equal to the excess of—

(A) the amount required to be used under such clause, over

(B) the amount actually used by the close of such period,

to redeem outstanding bonds within 90 days after the end of such period.

(6) Pooled financing bond. For purposes of this subsection—

(A) In general. The term "pooled financing bond" means any bond issued as part of an issue more than $5,000,000 of the proceeds of which are reasonably expected (at the time of the issuance of the bonds) to be used (or are intentionally used) directly or indirectly to make or finance loans to 2 or more ultimate borrowers.

(B) Exceptions. Such term shall not include any bond if—

(i) section 146 applies to the issue of which such bond is a part (other than by reason of section 141(b)(5)) or would apply but for section 146(i), or

(ii) section 143(1)(3) applies to such issue.

(7) Definition of loan; treatment of mixed use issues.

(A) Loan. For purposes of this subsection, the term "loan" does not include—

(i) any loan which is a nonpurpose investment (within the meaning of section 148(f)(6)(A), determined without regard to section 148(b)(3)), and

(ii) any use of proceeds by an agency of the issuer unless such agency is a political subdivision or instrumentality of the issuer.

(B) Portion of issue to be used for loans treated as separate issue. If only a portion of the proceeds of an issue is reasonably expected (at the time of issuance of the bond) to be used (or is intentionally used) as described in paragraph (6)(A), such portion and the other portion of such issue shall be treated as separate issues for purposes of determining whether such portion meets the requirements of this subsection.

(g) Treatment of hedge bonds.

(1) In general. Section 103(a) shall not apply to any hedge bond unless, with respect to the issue of which such bond is a part—

(A) the requirement of paragraph (2) is met, and

(B) the requirement of subsection (f)(3) is met.

(2) Reasonable expectations as to when proceeds will be spent. An issue meets the requirement of this paragraph if the issuer reasonably expects that—

(A) 10 percent of the spendable proceeds of the issue will be spent for the governmental purposes of the issue within the 1-year period beginning on the date the bonds are issued,

(B) 30 percent of the spendable proceeds of the issue will be spent for such purposes within the 2-year period beginning on such date,

(C) 60 percent of the spendable proceeds of the issue will be spent for such purposes within the 3-year period beginning on such date, and

(D) 85 percent of the spendable proceeds of the issue will be spent for such purposes within the 5-year period beginning on such date.

(3) Hedge bond.

(A) In general. For purposes of this subsection, the term "hedge bond" means any bond issued as part of an issue unless—

(i) the issuer reasonably expects that 85 percent of the spendable proceeds of the issue will be used to carry out the governmental purposes of the issue within the 3-year period beginning on the date the bonds are issued, and

(ii) not more than 50 percent of the proceeds of the issue are invested in nonpurpose investments (as defined in section 148(f)(6)(A)) having a substantially guaranteed yield for 4 years or more.

(B) Exception for investment in tax-exempt bonds not subject to minimum tax.

(i) In general. Such term shall not include any bond issued as part of an issue 95 percent of the net proceeds of which are invested in bonds—

(I) the interest on which is not includible in gross income under section 103, and

(II) which are not specified private activity bonds (as defined in section 57(a)(5)(C)).

(ii) Amounts in bona fide debt service fund. Amounts in a bona fide debt service fund shall be treated as invested in bonds described in clause (i).

(iii) Amounts held pending reinvestment or redemption. Amounts held for not more than 30 days pending reinvestment or bond redemption shall be treated as invested in bonds described in clause (i).

(C) Exception for refunding bonds.

(i) In general. A refunding bond shall be treated as meeting the requirements of this subsection only if the original bond met such requirements.

(ii) General rule for refunding of pre-effective date bonds. A refunding bond shall be treated as meeting the requirements of this subsection if—

(I) this subsection does not apply to the original bond,

(II) the average maturity date of the issue of which the refunding bond is a part is not later than the average maturity date of the bonds to be refunded by such issue, and

(III) the amount of the refunding bond does not exceed the outstanding amount of the refunded bond.

(iii) Refunding of pre-effective date bonds entitled to 5-year temporary period. A refunding bond shall be treated as meeting the requirements of this subsection if—

(I) this subsection does not apply to the original bond,

(II) the issuer reasonably expected that 85 percent of the spendable proceeds of the issue of which the original bond is a part would be used to carry out the governmental purposes of the issue within the 5-year period beginning on the date the original bonds were issued but did not reasonably expect that 85 percent of such proceeds would be so spent within the 3-year period beginning on such date, and

(III) at least 85 percent of the spendable proceeds of the original issue (and all other prior original issues issued to finance the governmental purposes of such issue) were spent before the date the refunding bonds are issued.

(4) Special rules. For purposes of this subsection—

(A) Construction period in excess of 5 years. The Secretary may, at the request of any issuer, provide that the requirement of paragraph (2) shall be treated as met with respect to the portion of the spendable proceeds of an issue which is to be used for any construction project having a construction period in excess of 5 years if it is reasonably expected that such proceeds will be spent over a reasonable construction schedule specified in such request.

(B) Rules for determining expectations. The rules of subsection (f)(2)(B) shall apply.

(5) Regulations. The Secretary may prescribe regulations to prevent the avoidance of the rules of this subsection, including through the aggregation of projects within a single issue.

In 2010, P.L. 111-147, Sec. 502(a)(2)(A), added "or" at the end of subpara. (a)(2)(A), substituted a period for ", or" at the end of subpara. (a)(2)(B) and deleted subpara. (a)(2)(C), effective for obligations issued after 3/18/2012.
Prior to deletion, subpara. (a)(2)(C) read as follows:
"(C) is described in section 163(f)(2)(B)."

In 2008, P.L. 110-289, Sec. 3023(a), deleted "or" at the end of clause (b)(3)(A)(ii), substituted ", or" for the period at the end of clause (b)(3)(A)(iii) and added clause (b)(3)(A)(iv)... Sec. 3023(b), added subpara (b)(3)(E), effective for guarantees made after 7/30/2008.

In 2006, P.L. 109-222, Sec. 508(a), amended subpara. (f)(2)(A)... Sec. 508(b), redesignated paras. (f)(4) and (5) as paras. (f)(6) and (7), and added paras. (f)(4) and (5)... Sec. 508(d)(1), substituted "paragraphs (2), (3), (4), and (5)" for "paragraphs (2) and (3)" in para. (f)(1)... Sec. 508(d)(2), substituted "paragraph (6)(A)" for "paragraph (4)(A)" in subpara. (f)(7)(B) [as redesignated by Sec. 508(b), see above], effective for bonds issued after 5/17/2006.
Prior to amendment, subpara. (f)(2)(A) read as follows:
"(A) In general. The requirements of this paragraph are met with respect to an issue if the issuer reasonably expects that as of the close of the 3-year period beginning on the date of issuance of the issue, at least 95 percent of the net proceeds of the issue (as of the close of such period) will have been used directly or indirectly to make or finance loans to ultimate borrowers."

In 1997, P.L. 105-34, Sec. 967, of this Act provides:
"Sec. 967. Additional advance refunding of certain Virgin Island bonds.
"Subclause (I) of section 149(d)(3)(A)(i) of the Internal Revenue Code of 1986 shall not apply to the second advance refunding of any issue of the Virgin Islands which was first advance refunded before June 9, 1997, if the debt provision of the refunding bonds are changed to repeal the priority first lien requirement of the refunded bonds."

In 1996, P.L. 104-188, Sec. 1704(b)(1), amended clause (g)(3)(B)(iii), effective for bonds issued after 9/14/89, except as provided in Sec. 7651(b)(2)-(5) of P.L. 101-239, reproduced below.
Prior to amendment, clause (g)(3)(B)(iii) read as follows:
"(iii) Investment earnings held pending reinvestment. Investment earnings held for not more than 30 days pending reinvestment shall be treated as invested in bonds described in clause (i)."

In 1989, P.L. 101-239, Sec. 7651(a), added subsec. (g), effective for bonds issued after 9/14/89, except as provided in Secs. 7651(b)(2)-(5) of this Act, which read as follows:
"(2) Bonds sold before September 15, 1989.—The amendment made by subsection (a) shall not apply to any bond sold before September 15, 1989, and issued before October 15, 1989.
"(3) Bonds with respect to which preliminary offering materials mailed.—The amendment made by subsection (a) shall not apply to any issue issued after the date of the enactment of this Act if the preliminary offering materials with respect to such issue were mailed (or otherwise delivered) to members of the underwriting syndicate before September 15, 1989.
"(4) Certain other bonds.—In the case of a bond issued before January 1, 1991, with respect to which official action was taken (or a series of official actions were taken), or other comparable preliminary approval was given, before November 18, 1989, demonstrating an intent to issue such bonds in a maximum specified amount for such issue or with a maximum specified amount of net proceeds of such issue, the issuer may elect to apply section 149(g)(2) of the Internal Revenue Code of 1986 (as added by this section) by substituting '15 percent' for '10 percent' in subparagraph (A) and '50 percent' for '60 percent' in subparagraph (C).
"(5) Bonds issued to finance self-insurance funds.—The amendment made by subsection (a) shall not apply to any bonds issued before July 1, 1990, to finance a self-insurance fund if official action was taken (or a series of official actions were taken), or other comparable preliminary approval was given, before September 15, 1989, demonstrating an intent to issue such bonds in a maximum specified amount for such issue or with a maximum specified amount of net proceeds of such issue."

In 1988, P.L. 100-647, Sec. 1013(a)(20), deleted "with respect to any bond issued before July, 1989" at the end of clause (b)(3)(A)(iii)... Sec. 1013(a)(21), substituted "and a qualified student loan bond" for "a qualified student loan bond, and a qualified redevelopment bond" in subpara. (b)(4)(A), effective for bonds issued after 8/15/86. For transitional rules, see Secs. 1312-1318 of P.L. 99-514 [reproduced in the note following Code Sec. 103].
—P.L. 100-647, Sec. 1013(a)(22), substituted "the failure to file in a timely fashion is not due to willful neglect" for "there is reasonable cause for the failure to file such a statement in a timely fashion" in para. (e)(3), effective for bonds issued after 12/31/86. For transitional rules, see Secs. 1312-1318 of P.L. 99-514 [reproduced in the note following Code Sec. 103].
—P.L. 100-647, Sec. 1013(b)(1), added Sec. 1311(d) of P.L. 99-514 [reproduced below], part of the effective date for changes made by Sec. 1301(b) of P.L. 99-514, see below.
—P.L. 100-647, Sec. 5051(a), added subsec. (f), generally effective for bonds issued after 10/21/88, except as provided in Sec. 5051(b)(2) of this Act which reads as follows:
"(2) Special rule for refunding bonds.—In the case of a bond issued to refund a bond issued before October 22, 1988—
"(A) if the 3-year period described in section 149(f)(2)(A) of the 1986 Code would (but for this paragraph) expire on or before October 22, 1989, such period shall expire on October 21, 1990, and
"(B) if such period expires after October 22, 1989, the portion of the proceeds of the issue of which the refunded bond is a part which is available (on the date of issuance of the refunding issue) to provide loans shall be treated as proceeds of a separate issue (issued after October 21, 1988) for purposes of applying section 149(f) of the 1986 Code."

In 1986, P.L. 99-514, Sec. 1301(b), added Code Sec. 149 as part of the amendments to Part IV of subchapter B of chapter 1, effective for bonds issued after 8/15/86. Sec. 1311(d) of this Act. [added by Sec. 1013(b)(1) of P.L. 100-647, see above] provides:
"(d) Public approval and information reporting.—Sections 147(f) and 149(e) of the 1986 Code shall apply to bonds issued after December 31, 1986."

Private activity bonds Code Sec. 150(c)(1)

For transitional rules, see Secs. 1312—1318 of this Act reproduced in the note following Code Sec. 103.

SUBPART C.—DEFINITIONS AND SPECIAL RULES

Sec.
150. Definitions and special rules.

In 1986, P.L. 99-514, Sec. 1301(b), added Subpart C as part of the changes made to Part IV.

Sec. 150. Definitions and special rules.
(a) General rule.
For purposes of this part—

(1) Bond. The term "bond" includes any obligation.

(2) Governmental unit not to include federal government. The term "governmental unit" does not include the United States or any agency or instrumentality thereof.

(3) Net proceeds. The term "net proceeds" means, with respect to any issue, the proceeds of such issue reduced by amounts in a reasonably required reserve or replacement fund.

(4) 501(c)(3) organization. The term "501(c)(3) organization" means any organization described in section 501(c)(3) and exempt from tax under section 501(a).

(5) Ownership of property. Property shall be treated as owned by a governmental unit if it is owned on behalf of such unit.

(6) Tax-exempt bond. The term "tax-exempt" means, with respect to any bond (or issue), that the interest on such bond (or on the bonds issued as part of such issue) is excluded from gross income.

(b) Change in use of facilities financed with tax-exempt private activity bonds.

(1) Mortgage revenue bonds.

(A) In general. In the case of any residence with respect to which financing is provided from the proceeds of a tax-exempt qualified mortgage bond or qualified veterans' mortgage bond, if there is a continuous period of at least 1 year during which such residence is not the principal residence of at least 1 of the mortgagors who received such financing, then no deduction shall be allowed under this chapter for interest on such financing which accrues on or after the date such period began and before the date such residence is again the principal residence of at least 1 of the mortgagors who received such financing.

(B) Exception. Subparagraph (A) shall not apply to the extent the Secretary determines that its application would result in undue hardship and that the failure to meet the requirements of subparagraph (A) resulted from circumstances beyond the mortgagor's control.

(2) Qualified residential rental projects. In the case of any project for residential rental property—

(A) with respect to which financing is provided from the proceeds of any private activity bond which, when issued, purported to be a tax-exempt bond described in paragraph (7) of section 142(a), and

(B) which does not meet the requirements of section 142(d),

no deduction shall be allowed under this chapter for interest on such financing which accrues during the period beginning on the 1st day of the taxable year in which such project fails to meet such requirements and ending on the date such project meets such requirements. If the provisions of prior law corresponding to section 142(d) apply to a refunded bond, such provisions shall apply (in lieu of section 142(d)) to the refunding bond.

(3) Qualified 501(c)(3) bonds.

(A) In general. In the case of any facility with respect to which financing is provided from the proceeds of any private activity bond which, when issued, purported to be a tax-exempt qualified 501(c)(3) bond, if any portion of such facility—

(i) is used in a trade or business of any person other than a 501(c)(3) organization or a governmental unit, but

(ii) continues to be owned by a 501(c)(3) organization,

then the owner of such portion shall be treated for purposes of this title as engaged in an unrelated trade or business (as defined in section 513) with respect to such portion. The amount of gross income attributable to such portion for any period shall not be less than the fair rental value of such portion for such period.

(B) Denial of deduction for interest. No deduction shall be allowed under this chapter for interest on financing described in subparagraph (A) which accrues during the period beginning on the date such facility is used as described in subparagraph (A)(i) and ending on the date such facility is not so used.

(4) Certain exempt facility bonds and small issue bonds.

(A) In general. In the case of any facility with respect to which financing is provided from the proceeds of any private activity bond to which this paragraph applies, if such facility is not used for a purpose for which a tax-exempt bond could be issued on the date of such issue, no deduction shall be allowed under this chapter for interest on such financing which accrues during the period beginning on the date such facility is not so used and ending on the date such facility is so used.

(B) Bonds to which paragraph applies. This paragraph applies to any private activity bond which, when issued, purported to be a tax-exempt facility bond described in a paragraph (other than paragraph (7)) of section 142(a) or a qualified small issue bond.

(5) Facilities required to be owned by governmental units or 501(c)(3) organizations. If—

(A) financing is provided with respect to any facility from the proceeds of any private activity bond which, when issued, purported to be a tax-exempt bond,

(B) such facility is required to be owned by a governmental unit or a 501(c)(3) organization as a condition of such tax exemption, and

(C) such facility is not so owned,

then no deduction shall be allowed under this chapter for interest on such financing which accrues during the period beginning on the date such facility is not so owned and ending on the date such facility is so owned.

(6) Small issue bonds which exceed capital expenditure limitation. In the case of any financing provided from the proceeds of any bond which, when issued, purported to be a qualified small issue bond, no deduction shall be allowed under this chapter for interest on such financing which accrues during the period such bond is not a qualified small issue bond.

(c) Exception and special rules for purposes of subsection (b).

For purposes of subsection (b)—

(1) Exception. Any use with respect to facilities financed with proceeds of an issue which are not required to be used for the exempt purpose of such issue shall not be taken into account.

(2) Treatment of amounts other than interest. If the amounts payable for the use of a facility are not interest, subsection (b) shall apply to such amounts as if they were interest but only to the extent such amounts for any period do not exceed the amount of interest accrued on the bond financing for such period.

(3) Use of portion of facility. In the case of any person which uses only a portion of the facility, only the interest accruing on the financing allocable to such portion shall be taken into account by such person.

(4) Cessation with respect to portion of facility. In the case of any facility where part but not all of the facility is not used for an exempt purpose, only the interest accruing on the financing allocable to such part shall be taken into account.

(5) Regulations. The Secretary shall prescribe such regulations as may be necessary or appropriate to carry out the purposes of this subsection and subsection (b).

(d) Qualified scholarship funding bond.

For purposes of this part and section 103—

(1) Treatment as state or local bond. A qualified scholarship funding bond shall be treated as a State or local bond.

(2) Qualified scholarship funding bond defined. The term "qualified scholarship funding bond" means a bond issued by a corporation which—

(A) is a corporation not for profit established and operated exclusively for the purpose of acquiring student loan notes incurred under the Higher Education Act of 1965, and

(B) is organized at the request of the State or 1 or more political subdivisions thereof or is requested to exercise such power by 1 or more political subdivisions and required by its corporate charter and bylaws, or required by State law, to devote any income (after payment of expenses, debt service, and the creation of reserves for the same) to the purchase of additional student loan notes or to pay over any income to the United States.

(3) Election to cease status as qualified scholarship funding corporation.

(A) In general. Any qualified scholarship funding bond, and qualified student loan bond, outstanding on the date of the issuer's election under this paragraph (and any bond (or series of bonds) issued to refund such a bond) shall not fail to be a tax-exempt bond solely because the issuer ceases to be described in subparagraphs (A) and (B) of paragraph (2) if the issuer meets the requirements of subparagraphs (B) and (C) of this paragraph.

(B) Assets and liabilities of issuer transferred to taxable subsidiary. The requirements of this subparagraph are met by an issuer if—

(i) all of the student loan notes of the issuer and other assets pledged to secure the repayment of qualified scholarship funding bond indebtedness of the issuer are transferred to another corporation within a reasonable period after the election is made under this paragraph;

(ii) such transferee corporation assumes or otherwise provides for the payment of all of the qualified scholarship funding bond indebtedness of the issuer within a reasonable period after the election is made under this paragraph;

(iii) to the extent permitted by law, such transferee corporation assumes all of the responsibilities of, and succeeds to all of the rights, of the issuer under the issuer's agreements with the Secretary of Education in respect of student loans;

(iv) immediately after such transfer, the issuer, together with any other issuer which has made an election under this paragraph in respect of such transferee, hold all of the senior stock in such transferee corporation; and

(v) such transferee corporation is not exempt from tax under this chapter.

(C) Issuer to operate as independent organization described in section 501(c)(3). The requirements of this subparagraph are met by an issuer if, within a reasonable period after the transfer referred to in subparagraph (B)—

(i) the issuer is described in section 501(c)(3) and exempt from tax under section 501(a);

(ii) the issuer no longer is described in subparagraphs (A) and (B) of paragraph (2); and

(iii) at least 80 percent of the members of the board of directors of the issuer are independent members.

(D) Senior stock. For purposes of this paragraph, the term "senior stock" means stock—

(i) which participates pro rata and fully in the equity value of the corporation with all other common stock of the corporation but which has the right to payment of liquidation proceeds prior to payment of liquidation proceeds in respect of other common stock of the corporation;

(ii) which has a fixed right upon liquidation and upon redemption to an amount equal to the greater of—

(I) the fair market value of such stock on the date of liquidation or redemption (whichever is applicable); or

(II) the fair market value of all assets transferred in exchange for such stock and reduced by the amount of all liabilities of the corporation which has made an election under this paragraph assumed by the transferee corporation in such transfer;

(iii) the holder of which has the right to require the transferee corporation to redeem on a date that is not later than 10 years after the date on which an election under this paragraph was made and pursuant to such election such stock was issued; and

(iv) in respect of which, during the time such stock is outstanding, there is not outstanding any equity interest in the corporation having any liquidation, redemption or dividend rights in the corporation which are superior to those of such stock.

(E) Independent member. The term "independent member" means a member of the board of directors of the issuer who (except for services as a member of such board) receives no compensation directly or indirectly—

(i) for services performed in connection with such transferee corporation, or

(ii) for services as a member of the board of directors or as an officer of such transferee corporation.

For purposes of clause (ii), the term "officer" includes any individual having powers or responsibilities similar to those of officers.

(F) Coordination with certain private foundation taxes. For purposes of sections 4942 (relating to the excise tax on a failure to distribute income) and 4943 (relating to the excise tax on excess business holdings), the transferee corporation referred to in subparagraph (B) shall be treated as a functionally related business (within the meaning of section 4942(j)(4)) with respect to the issuer during the period commencing with the date on which

Deductions   Code Sec. 151(d)(3)(B)

an election is made under this paragraph and ending on the date that is the earlier of—

(i) the last day of the last taxable year for which more than 50 percent of the gross income of such transferee corporation is derived from, or more than 50 percent of the assets (by value) of such transferee corporation consists of, student loan notes incurred under the Higher Education Act of 1965; or

(ii) the last day of the taxable year of the issuer during which occurs the date which is 10 years after the date on which the election under this paragraph is made.

(G) **Election.** An election under this paragraph may be revoked only with the consent of the Secretary.

(e) **Bonds of certain volunteer fire departments.**

For purposes of this part and section 103—

(1) **In general.** A bond of a volunteer fire department shall be treated as a bond of a political subdivision of a State if—

(A) such department is a qualified volunteer fire department with respect to an area within the jurisdiction of such political subdivision, and

(B) such bond is issued as part of an issue 95 percent or more of the net proceeds of which are to be used for the acquisition, construction, reconstruction, or improvement of a firehouse (including land which is functionally related and subordinate thereto) or firetruck used or to be used by such department.

(2) **Qualified volunteer fire department.** For purposes of this subsection, the term "qualified volunteer fire department" means, with respect to a political subdivision of a State, any organization—

(A) which is organized and operated to provide firefighting or emergency medical services for persons in an area (within the jurisdiction of such political subdivision) which is not provided with any other firefighting services, and

(B) which is required (by written agreement) by the political subdivision to furnish firefighting services in such area.

For purposes of subparagraph (A), other firefighting services provided in an area shall be disregarded in determining whether an organization is a qualified volunteer fire department if such other firefighting services are provided by a qualified volunteer fire department (determined with the application of this sentence) and such organization and the provider of such other services have been continuously providing firefighting services to such area since January 1, 1981.

(3) **Treatment as private activity bonds only for certain purposes.** Bonds which are part of an issue which meets the requirements of paragraph (1) shall not be treated as private activity bonds except for purposes of sections 147(f) and 149(d).

In **1996**, P.L. 104-188, Sec. 1614(a), added para. (d)(3), effective 8/20/96.

In **1988**, P.L. 100-647, Sec. 1013(a)(23)(A), added "or a qualified small issue bond" before the period at the end of subpara. (b)(4)(B) . . . Sec. 1013(a)(23)(B), added "and small issue bonds" after "facility bonds" in the heading of para. (b)(4) . . . Sec. 1013(a)(23)(C), added "tax-exempt" before "qualified mortgage bond" in subpara. (b)(1)(A) . . . Sec. 1013(a)(30), added "and before the date such residence is again the principal residence of at least 1 of the mortgagors who received such financing" after "date such period began" in subpara. (b)(1)(A) . . . Sec. 1013(a)(31), substituted "described in paragraph" for "described paragraph" in subpara. (b)(2)(A) . . . Sec. 1013(a)(32), added a sentence to the end of para. (b)(2) . . . Sec. 1013(a)(33), added para. (b)(6), effective for bonds issued after 8/15/86, except as provided in Secs. 1311(d) and (e) of P.L. 99-514, reproduced below. For transitional rules, see Secs. 1312-1318 of P.L. 99-514, reproduced in the note following Code Sec. 103.

—P.L. 100-647, Sec. 1013(a)(24)(A), added para. (e)(3), effective for bonds issued after 10/21/88.

—P.L. 100-647, Sec. 1013(b)(1), added Secs. 1311(d) and (e) of P.L. 99-514 [reproduced below], part of the effective date for changes made by Sec. 1301(b) of P.L. 99-514, see below.

—P.L. 100-647, Sec. 6182(a), added a sentence to the end of para. (e)(2) . . . Sec. 6182(b), added "(including land which is functionally related and subordinate thereto)" after "a firehouse" in subpara. (e)(1)(B), effective for bonds issued after 11/10/88.

In **1986**, P.L. 99-514, Sec. 1301(b), added Code Sec. 150 as part of the amendments to Part IV of subchapter B of chapter 1, effective for bonds issued after 8/15/86. Secs. 1311(c)-(e) of this Act [as amended by Sec. 1013(b)(1) of P.L. 100-647, see above] provide the following:

"(c) Changes in use, etc., of facilities financed with private activity bonds.—Subsection (b) of section 150 of the 1986 Code shall apply to changes in use (and ownership) after August 15, 1986, but only with respect to financing (including refinancings) provided after such date."

"(d) Public approval and information reporting.

"Sections 147(f) and 149(e) of the 1986 Code shall apply to bonds issued after December 31, 1986.

"(e) Rebate requirement for qualified scholarship funding bonds.

"Section 150(d) of the 1986 Code shall apply to payments made after August 15, 1986."

For transitional rules, see Secs. 1312–1318 of this Act reproduced in the note following Code Sec. 103.

PART V.—DEDUCTIONS FOR PERSONAL EXEMPTIONS

Sec.
151. Allowance of deductions for personal exemptions.
152. Dependent defined.
153. Cross references.

In **1976**, P.L. 94-455, Sec. 1901(b)(7)(A)(ii), repealed item 153 and redesignated item 154 as 153.
Prior to repeal, item 153 read as follows:
"153. Determination of marital status."

Sec. 151. Allowance of deductions for personal exemptions.

(a) **Allowance of deductions.**

In the case of an individual, the exemptions provided by this section shall be allowed as deductions in computing taxable income.

(b) **Taxpayer and spouse.**

An exemption of the exemption amount for the taxpayer; and an additional exemption of the exemption amount for the spouse of the taxpayer if a joint return is not made by the taxpayer and his spouse, and if the spouse, for the calendar year in which the taxable year of the taxpayer begins, has no gross income and is not the dependent of another taxpayer.

(c) **Additional exemption for dependents.**

An exemption of the exemption amount for each individual who is a dependent (as defined in section 152) of the taxpayer for the taxable year.

(d) **Exemption amount.**

For purposes of this section—

(1) **In general.** Except as otherwise provided in this subsection, the term "exemption amount" means $2,000.

(2) **Exemption amount disallowed in case of certain dependents.** In the case of an individual with respect to whom a deduction under this section is allowable to another taxpayer for a taxable year beginning in the calendar year in which the individual's taxable year begins, the exemption amount applicable to such individual for such individual's taxable year shall be zero.

(3) **Phaseout.**

(A) **In general.** In the case of any taxpayer whose adjusted gross income for the taxable year exceeds the threshold amount, the exemption amount shall be reduced by the applicable percentage.

(B) **Applicable percentage.** For purposes of subparagraph (A), the term "applicable percentage" means 2

1,513

percentage points for each $2,500 (or fraction thereof) by which the taxpayer's adjusted gross income for the taxable year exceeds the threshold amount. In the case of a married individual filing a separate return, the preceding sentence shall be applied by substituting "$1,250" for "$2,500". In no event shall the applicable percentage exceed 100 percent.

(C) Threshold amount. For purposes of this paragraph, the term "threshold amount" means—

(i) $150,000 in the case of a joint return or a surviving spouse (as defined in section 2(a)),

(ii) $125,000 in the case of a head of a household (as defined in section 2(b)),

(iii) $100,000 in the case of an individual who is not married and who is not a surviving spouse or head of a household, and

(iv) $75,000 in the case of a married individual filing a separate return.

For purposes of this paragraph, marital status shall be determined under section 7703.

(D) Coordination with other provisions. The provisions of this paragraph shall not apply for purposes of determining whether a deduction under this section with respect to any individual is allowable to another taxpayer for any taxable year.

• **Caution:** Code Sec. 151(d)(3)(E)-(F), following, were added by P.L. 107-16 EGTRRA. These provisions generally sunset for tax years beginning after 12/31/2012. For specific sunset provisions, see Sec. 901, P.L. 107-16 (as amended) reproduced in history notes for this Code Sec.

(E) Reduction of phaseout.

(i) In general. In the case of taxable years beginning after December 31, 2005, and before January 1, 2010, the reduction under subparagraph (A) shall be equal to the applicable fraction of the amount which would (but for this subparagraph) be the amount of such reduction.

(ii) Applicable fraction. For purposes of clause (i), the applicable fraction shall be determined in accordance with the following table:

For taxable years beginning in calendar year—	The applicable fraction is—
2006 and 2007	⅔
2008 and 2009	⅓

(F) Termination. This paragraph shall not apply to any taxable year beginning after December 31, 2009.

(4) Inflation adjustments.

(A) Adjustment to basic amount of exemption. In the case of any taxable year beginning in a calendar year after 1989, the dollar amount contained in paragraph (1) shall be increased by an amount equal to—

(i) such dollar amount, multiplied by

(ii) the cost-of-living adjustment determined under section 1(f)(3) for the calendar year in which the taxable year begins, by substituting "calendar year 1988" for "calendar year 1992" in subparagraph (B) thereof.

(B) Adjustment to threshold amounts for years after 1991. In the case of any taxable year beginning in a calendar year after 1991, each dollar amount contained in paragraph (3)(C) shall be increased by an amount equal to—

(i) such dollar amount, multiplied by

(ii) the cost-of-living adjustment determined under section 1(f)(3) for the calendar year in which the taxable year begins, by substituting "calendar year 1990" for "calendar year 1992" in subparagraph (B) thereof.

(e) Identifying information required.

No exemption shall be allowed under this section with respect to any individual unless the TIN of such individual is included on the return claiming the exemption.

In 2010, P.L. 111-312, Sec. 101(a)(1), substituted "December 31, 2012" for "December 31, 2010" both places it appeared in Sec. 901, P.L. 107-16 [see below], effective as if included in the enactment of P.L. 107-16, EGTRRA, 6/7/2001.

In 2004, P.L. 108-311, Sec. 206, amended subsec. (c), effective for tax. yrs. begin. after 12/31/2004.

Prior to amendment, subsec. (c) read as follows:

"(c) Additional exemption for dependents.

"(1) In general. An exemption of the exemption amount for each dependent (as defined in section 152)—

"(A) whose gross income for the calendar year in which the taxable year of the taxpayer begins is less than the exemption amount, or

"(B) who is a child of the taxpayer and who (i) has not attained the age of 19 at the close of the calendar year in which the taxable year of the taxpayer begins, or (ii) is a student who has not attained the age of 24 at the close of such calendar year.

"(2) Exemption denied in case of certain married dependents. No exemption shall be allowed under this subsection for any dependent who has made a joint return with his spouse under section 6013 for the taxable year beginning in the calendar year in which the taxable year of the taxpayer begins.

"(3) Child defined. For purposes of paragraph (1)(B), the term 'child' means an individual who (within the meaning of section 152) is a son, stepson, daughter, or stepdaughter of the taxpayer.

"(4) Student defined. For purposes of paragraph (1)(B)(ii), the term 'student' means an individual who during each of 5 calendar months during the calendar year in which the taxable year of the taxpayer begins—

"(A) is a full-time student at an educational organization described in section 170(b)(1)(A)(ii); or

"(B) is pursuing a full-time course of institutional on-farm training under the supervision of an accredited agent of an educational organization described in section 170(b)(1)(A)(ii) or of a State or political subdivision of a State.

"(5) Certain income of handicapped dependents not taken into account.

"(A) In general. For purposes of paragraph (1)(A), the gross income of an individual who is permanently and totally disabled shall not include income attributable to services performed by the individual at a sheltered workshop if—

"(i) the availability of medical care at such workshop is the principal reason for his presence there, and

"(ii) the income arises solely from activities at such workshop which are incident to such medical care.

"(B) Sheltered workshop defined. For purposes of subparagraph (A), the term 'sheltered workshop' means a school—

"(i) which provides special instruction or training designed to alleviate the disability of the individual, and

"(ii) which is operated by—

"(I) an organization described in section 501(c)(3) and exempt from tax under section 501(a), or

"(II) a State, a possession of the United States, any political subdivision of any of the foregoing, the United States, or the District of Columbia.

"(C) Permanent and total disability defined. An individual shall be treated as permanently and totally disabled for purposes of this paragraph if such individual would be so treated under paragraph (3) of section 22(e).

"(6) Treatment of missing children.

"(A) In general. Solely for the purposes referred to in subparagraph (B), a child of the taxpayer—

"(i) who is presumed by law enforcement authorities to have been kidnapped by someone who is not a member of the family of such child or the taxpayer, and

"(ii) who was (without regard to this paragraph) the dependent of the taxpayer for the portion of the taxable year before the date of the kidnapping,

shall be treated as a dependent of the taxpayer for all taxable years ending during the period that the child is kidnapped.

"(B) Purposes. Subparagraph (A) shall apply solely for purposes of determining—

"(i) the deduction under this section,

"(ii) the credit under section 24 (relating to child tax credit), and

"(iii) whether an individual is a surviving spouse or a head of a household (as such terms are defined in section 2).

"(C) Comparable treatment for principal place of abode requirements. An individual—
"(i) who is presumed by law enforcement authorities to have been kidnapped by someone who is not a member of the family of such individual or the taxpayer, and
"(ii) who had, for the taxable year in which the kidnapping occurred, the same principal place of abode as the taxpayer for more than one-half of the portion of such year before the date of the kidnapping,
shall be treated as meeting the principal place of abode requirements of section 2(a)(1)(B), section 2(b)(1)(A), and section 32(c)(3)(A)(ii) with respect to a taxpayer for all taxable years ending during the period that the individual is kidnapped.
"(D) Termination of treatment. Subparagraphs (A) and (C) shall cease to apply as of the first taxable year of the taxpayer beginning after the calendar year in which there is a determination that the child is dead (or, if earlier, in which the child would have attained age 18)."
In 2002, P.L. 107-358, Sec. 2, added subsec. (c) in Sec. 901 of P.L. 107-16 [see below], effective 12/17/2002.
—P.L. 107-147, Sec. 412(b)(1), substituted "for principal place of abode requirements. An" for "for earned income credit. For purposes of section 32, an" in subpara. (c)(6)(C)... Sec. 412(b)(2), substituted "principal place of abode requirements of section 2(a)(1)(B), section 2(b)(1)(A), and section 32(c)(3)(A)(ii)" for "requirement of section 32(c)(3)(A)(ii)" in subpara. (c)(6)(C), effective for tax. yrs. end. after 12/21/2000.
—P.L. 107-147, Sec. 417(6), added "as" before "such terms" in clause (c)(6)(B)(iii), effective 3/9/2002.
In 2001, P.L. 107-16, Sec. 102(a), added subparas. (d)(3)(E) and (F), effective for tax. yrs. begin. after 12/31/2005.
—P.L. 107-16, Sec. 901, of this Act [as amended by Sec. 2, P.L. 107-358, and Sec. 101(a)(1), P.L. 111-312, see above], reads as follows:
"Sec. 901. Sunset of provisions of Act.
"(a) In general. All provisions of, and amendments made by, this Act shall not apply—
"(1) to taxable, plan, or limitation years beginning after December 31, 2012, or
"(2) in the case of title V, to estates of decedents dying, gifts made, or generation skipping transfers, after December 31, 2012.
"(b) Application of certain laws. The Internal Revenue Code of 1986 and the Employee Retirement Income Security Act of 1974 shall be applied and administered to years, estates, gifts, and transfers described in subsection (a) as if the provisions and amendments described in subsection (a) had never been enacted.
"(c) Exception. Subsection (a) shall not apply to section 803 (relating to no federal income tax on restitution received by victims of the Nazi regime or their heirs or estates)."
In 2000, P.L. 106-554, Sec. 1(a)(7), [which enacted into law Sec. 306(a) of P.L. 106-554] added para. (c)(6), effective for tax. yrs. ending after 12/21/2000.
In 1996, P.L. 104-188, Sec. 1615(a)(1), added subsec. (e), effective for returns the due date for which (without regard to extensions) is on or after the 30th day after 8/20/96, except as provided in Sec. 1615(d)(2) of this Act, which reads as follows:
"(2) Special rule for 1995 and 1996. In the case of returns for taxable years beginning in 1995 or 1996, a taxpayer shall not be required by the amendments made by this section to provide a taxpayer identification number for a child who is born after October 31, 1995, in the case of a taxable year beginning in 1995 or November 30, 1996, in the case of a taxable year beginning in 1996."
—P.L. 104-188, Sec. 1702(a)(2), substituted "joint return" for "joint of a return" in clause (d)(3)(C)(i), effective for tax. yrs. begin. after 12/30/90.
In 1993, P.L. 103-66, Sec. 13201(b)(3)(G), substituted "1992" for "1989" in subclauses (d)(4)(A)(ii) and (d)(4)(B)(ii), effective for tax. yrs. begin. after 12/31/92.
—P.L. 103-66, Sec. 13205, deleted subpara. (d)(3)(E), effective 8/10/93.
Prior to deletion, subpara. (d)(3)(E) read as follows:
"(E) Termination. This paragraph shall not apply to any taxable year beginning after December 31, 1996."
In 1992, P.L. 102-318, Sec. 511, substituted "December 31, 1996" for "December 31, 1995" in subpara. (d)(3)(E), effective 7/3/92.
In 1990, P.L. 101-508, Sec. 11101(d)(1)(F), substituted "1989" for "1987" in subpara. (d)(3)(B)... Sec. 11104(a), amended subsec. (d), effective for tax. yrs. begin. after 12/31/90.
Prior to amendment, subsec. (d) read as follows:
"(d) Exemption amount.
"For purposes of this section—
"(1) In general. Except as provided in paragraph (2), the term 'exemption amount' means—
"(A) $1,900 for taxable years beginning during 1987,
"(B) $1,950 for taxable years beginning during 1988,
"(C) $2,000 for taxable years beginning after December 31, 1988.
"(2) Exemption amount disallowed in the case of certain dependents. In the case of an individual with respect to whom a deduction under this section is allowable to another taxpayer for a taxable year beginning in the calendar year in which the individual's taxable year begins, the exemption amount applicable to such individual for such individual's taxable year shall be zero.
"(3) Inflation adjustment for years after 1989. In the case of any taxable year beginning in a calendar year after 1989, the dollar amount contained in paragraph (1)(C) shall be increased by an amount equal to—
"(A) such dollar amount, multiplied by

"(B) the cost-of-living adjustment determined under section 1(f)(3), for the calendar year in which the taxable year begins, by substituting 'calendar year 1988' for 'calendar year 1989' in subparagraph (B) thereof."
In 1988, P.L. 100-647, Sec. 6010(a), added "who has not attained the age of 24 at the close of such calendar year" after "is a student" in clause (c)(1)(B)(ii), effective for tax. yrs. begin. after 12/31/88.
In 1986, P.L. 99-514, Sec. 103(a), amended subsec. (f)... Sec. 103(b), deleted subsecs. (c) and (d) and redesignated subsecs. (e) and (f) as subsecs. (c) and (d), effective for tax. yrs. begin. after 12/31/86.
Prior to amendment, subsec (f) read as follows:
"(f) Exemption amount.
"For purposes of this section, the term 'exemption amount' means, with respect to any taxable year, $1,000 increased by an amount equal to $1,000 multiplied by the cost-of-living adjustment (as defined in section 1(f)(3)) for the calendar year in which the taxable year begins. If the amount determined under the preceding sentence is not a multiple of $10, such amount shall be rounded to the nearest multiple of $10 (or if such amount is a multiple of $5, such amount shall be increased to the next highest multiple of $10)."
Prior to deletion, subsecs. (c) and (d) read as follows:
"(c) Additional exemption for taxpayer or spouse aged 65 or more.
"(1) For taxpayer. An additional exemption of the exemption amount for the taxpayer if he has attained the age of 65 before the close of his taxable year.
"(2) For spouse. An additional exemption of the exemption amount for the spouse of the taxpayer if a joint return is not made by the taxpayer and his spouse, and if the spouse has attained the age of 65 before the close of such taxable year, and, for the calendar year in which the taxable year of the taxpayer begins, has no gross income and is not the dependent of another taxpayer.
"(d) Additional exemption for blindness of taxpayer or spouse.
"(1) For taxpayer. An additional exemption of the exemption amount for the taxpayer if he is blind at the close of his taxable year.
"(2) For spouse. An additional exemption of the exemption amount for the spouse of the taxpayer if a separate return is made by the taxpayer, and if the spouse is blind and, for the calendar year in which the taxable year of the taxpayer begins, has no gross income and is not the dependent of another taxpayer. For purposes of this paragraph, the determination of whether the spouse is blind shall be made as of the close of the taxable year of the taxpayer; except that if the spouse dies during such taxable year such determination shall be made as of the time of such death.
"(3) Blindness defined. For purposes of this subsection, an individual is blind only if his central visual acuity does not exceed 20/200 in the better eye with correcting lenses, or if his visual acuity is greater than 20/200 but is accompanied by a limitation in the fields of vision such that the widest diameter of the visual field subtends an angle no greater than 20 degrees."
—P.L. 99-514, Sec. 1847(b)(3), substituted "section 22(e)" for "section 37(e)" in subpara. (e)(5)(C), [redesignated subsec. (e) by Sec. 103(b) of this Act, see above] effective for tax. yrs. begin. after 12/31/84.
In 1984, P.L. 98-369, Sec. 426(a), added para. (e)(5), effective for tax. yrs. begin. after 12/31/84.
In 1981, P.L. 97-34, Sec. 104(c)(1), substituted "the exemption amount" for "$1,000" each place it appeared in Code Sec. 151... Sec. 104(c)(2), added subsec. (f), effective for tax. yrs. begin. after 12/31/84.
In 1978, P.L. 95-600, Sec. 102(a), substituted "$1,000" for "$750" each place it appeared in Code Sec. 151, effective for tax. yrs. begin. after 12/31/78.
In 1976, P.L. 94-455, Sec. 1901(a)(23), amended para. (e)(4), effective for tax. yrs. begin. after 12/31/76.
Prior to amendment, para. (e)(4) read as follows:
"(4) Student and educational institution defined. For purposes of paragraph (1)(B)(ii), the term 'student' means an individual who during each of 5 calendar months during the calendar year in which the taxable year of the taxpayer begins—
"(A) is a full-time student at an educational institution; or
"(B) is pursuing a full-time course of institutional on-farm training under the supervision of an accredited agent of an educational institution or of a State or political subdivision of a State.
For purposes of this paragraph, the term 'educational institution' means only an educational institution which normally maintains a regular faculty and curriculum and normally has a regularly organized body of students in attendance at the place where its educational activities are carried on."
In 1971, P.L. 92-178, Sec. 201(a)(1), substituted "$675" for "650" each place it appeared in Code Sec. 151, effective for tax. yrs. begin. after 12/31/70 and before 1/1/72.
—P.L. 92-178, Sec. 201(b)(1), substituted "$750" for "$675" each place it appeared in Code Sec. 151, effective for tax. yrs. begin. after 12/31/71.
In 1969, P.L. 91-172, Sec. 801(a)(1), substituted "$625" for "$600" each place it appeared in Code Sec. 151, effective for tax. yrs. begin. after 12/31/69 and before 1/1/71.
—P.L. 91-172, Sec. 801(b)(1), substituted "$650" for "$625" each place it appeared in Code Sec. 151, effective for tax. yrs. begin. after 12/31/70 and before 1/1/72.
Sec. 801(c)(1) of P.L. 91-172, substituted "$700" for "$650" each place it appeared in Code Sec. 151, effective for tax. yrs. begin. after 12/31/71 and before 1/1/73.
—P.L. 91-172, Sec. 801(d)(1), substituted "$750" for "$700" each place it appeared in Code Sec. 151, effective for tax. yrs. begin. after 12/31/72.

—P.L. 91-172, Sec. 941(b), substituted "if a joint return is made by the taxpayer and his spouse" for "if a separate return is made by the taxpayer" in subsec. (b) and para. (c)(2), effective for tax. yrs. begin. after 12/31/69.

Sec. 152. Dependent defined.
(a) In general.
For purposes of this subtitle, the term "dependent" means—
(1) a qualifying child, or
(2) a qualifying relative.

(b) Exceptions.
For purposes of this section—
(1) **Dependents ineligible.** If an individual is a dependent of a taxpayer for any taxable year of such taxpayer beginning in a calendar year, such individual shall be treated as having no dependents for any taxable year of such individual beginning in such calendar year.
(2) **Married dependents.** An individual shall not be treated as a dependent of a taxpayer under subsection (a) if such individual has made a joint return with the individual's spouse under section 6013 for the taxable year beginning in the calendar year in which the taxable year of the taxpayer begins.
(3) **Citizens or nationals of other countries.**
(A) In general. The term "dependent" does not include an individual who is not a citizen or national of the United States unless such individual is a resident of the United States or a country contiguous to the United States.
(B) Exception for adopted child. Subparagraph (A) shall not exclude any child of a taxpayer (within the meaning of subsection (f)(1)(B)) from the definition of "dependent" if—
(i) for the taxable year of the taxpayer, the child has the same principal place of abode as the taxpayer and is a member of the taxpayer's household, and
(ii) the taxpayer is a citizen or national of the United States.

(c) Qualifying child.
For purposes of this section—
(1) **In general.** The term "qualifying child" means, with respect to any taxpayer for any taxable year, an individual—
(A) who bears a relationship to the taxpayer described in paragraph (2),
(B) who has the same principal place of abode as the taxpayer for more than one-half of such taxable year,
(C) who meets the age requirements of paragraph (3),
(D) who has not provided over one-half of such individual's own support for the calendar year in which the taxable year of the taxpayer begins, and
(E) who has not filed a joint return (other than only for a claim of refund) with the individual's spouse under section 6013 for the taxable year beginning in the calendar year in which the taxable year of the taxpayer begins.
(2) **Relationship.** For purposes of paragraph (1)(A), an individual bears a relationship to the taxpayer described in this paragraph if such individual is—
(A) a child of the taxpayer or a descendant of such a child, or
(B) a brother, sister, stepbrother, or stepsister of the taxpayer or a descendant of any such relative.
(3) **Age requirements.**
(A) In general. For purposes of paragraph (1)(C), an individual meets the requirements of this paragraph if such individual is younger than the taxpayer claiming such individual as a qualifying child and—
(i) has not attained the age of 19 as of the close of the calendar year in which the taxable year of the taxpayer begins, or
(ii) is a student who has not attained the age of 24 as of the close of such calendar year.
(B) Special rule for disabled. In the case of an individual who is permanently and totally disabled (as defined in section 22(e)(3)) at any time during such calendar year, the requirements of subparagraph (A) shall be treated as met with respect to such individual.
(4) **Special rule relating to 2 or more who can claim the same qualifying child.**
(A) In general. Except as provided in subparagraphs (B) and (C), if (but for this paragraph) an individual may be claimed as a qualifying child by 2 or more taxpayers for a taxable year beginning in the same calendar year, such individual shall be treated as the qualifying child of the taxpayer who is—
(i) a parent of the individual, or
(ii) if clause (i) does not apply, the taxpayer with the highest adjusted gross income for such taxable year.
(B) More than 1 parent claiming qualifying child. If the parents claiming any qualifying child do not file a joint return together, such child shall be treated as the qualifying child of—
(i) the parent with whom the child resided for the longest period of time during the taxable year, or
(ii) if the child resides with both parents for the same amount of time during such taxable year, the parent with the highest adjusted gross income.
(C) No parent claiming qualifying child. If the parents of an individual may claim such individual as a qualifying child but no parent so claims the individual, such individual may be claimed as the qualifying child of another taxpayer but only if the adjusted gross income of such taxpayer is higher than the highest adjusted gross income of any parent of the individual.

(d) Qualifying relative.
For purposes of this section—
(1) **In general.** The term "qualifying relative" means, with respect to any taxpayer for any taxable year, an individual—
(A) who bears a relationship to the taxpayer described in paragraph (2),
(B) whose gross income for the calendar year in which such taxable year begins is less than the exemption amount (as defined in section 151(d)),
(C) with respect to whom the taxpayer provides over one-half of the individual's support for the calendar year in which such taxable year begins, and
(D) who is not a qualifying child of such taxpayer or of any other taxpayer for any taxable year beginning in the calendar year in which such taxable year begins.
(2) **Relationship.** For purposes of paragraph (1)(A), an individual bears a relationship to the taxpayer described in this paragraph if the individual is any of the following with respect to the taxpayer:
(A) A child or a descendant of a child.
(B) A brother, sister, stepbrother, or stepsister.
(C) The father or mother, or an ancestor of either.
(D) A stepfather or stepmother.
(E) A son or daughter of a brother or sister of the taxpayer.

Deductions Code Sec. 152(e)(6)

(F) A brother or sister of the father or mother of the taxpayer.

(G) A son-in-law, daughter-in-law, father-in-law, mother-in-law, brother-in-law, or sister-in-law.

(H) An individual (other than an individual who at any time during the taxable year was the spouse, determined without regard to section 7703, of the taxpayer) who, for the taxable year of the taxpayer, has the same principal place of abode as the taxpayer and is a member of the taxpayer's household.

(3) Special rule relating to multiple support agreements. For purposes of paragraph (1)(C), over one-half of the support of an individual for a calendar year shall be treated as received from the taxpayer if—

(A) no one person contributed over one-half of such support,

(B) over one-half of such support was received from 2 or more persons each of whom, but for the fact that any such person alone did not contribute over one-half of such support, would have been entitled to claim such individual as a dependent for a taxable year beginning in such calendar year,

(C) the taxpayer contributed over 10 percent of such support, and

(D) each person described in subparagraph (B) (other than the taxpayer) who contributed over 10 percent of such support files a written declaration (in such manner and form as the Secretary may by regulations prescribe) that such person will not claim such individual as a dependent for any taxable year beginning in such calendar year.

(4) Special rule relating to income of handicapped dependents.

(A) In general. For purposes of paragraph (1)(B), the gross income of an individual who is permanently and totally disabled (as defined in section 22(e)(3)) at any time during the taxable year shall not include income attributable to services performed by the individual at a sheltered workshop if—

(i) the availability of medical care at such workshop is the principal reason for the individual's presence there, and

(ii) the income arises solely from activities at such workshop which are incident to such medical care.

(B) Sheltered workshop defined. For purposes of subparagraph (A), the term "sheltered workshop" means a school—

(i) which provides special instruction or training designed to alleviate the disability of the individual, and

(ii) which is operated by an organization described in section 501(c)(3) and exempt from tax under section 501(a), or by a State, a possession of the United States, any political subdivision of any of the foregoing, the United States, or the District of Columbia.

(5) Special rules for support. For purposes of this subsection—

(A) payments to a spouse which are includible in the gross income of such spouse under section 71 or 682 shall not be treated as a payment by the payor spouse for the support of any dependent, and

(B) in the case of the remarriage of a parent, support of a child received from the parent's spouse shall be treated as received from the parent.

(e) Special rule for divorced parents, etc.

(1) In general. Notwithstanding subsection (c)(1)(B), (c)(4), or (d)(1)(C), if—

(A) a child receives over one-half of the child's support during the calendar year from the child's parents—

(i) who are divorced or legally separated under a decree of divorce or separate maintenance,

(ii) who are separated under a written separation agreement, or

(iii) who live apart at all times during the last 6 months of the calendar year, and—

(B) such child is in the custody of 1 or both of the child's parents for more than one-half of the calendar year, such child shall be treated as being the qualifying child or qualifying relative of the noncustodial parent for a calendar year if the requirements described in paragraph (2) or (3) are met.

(2) Exception where custodial parent releases claim to exemption for the year. For purposes of paragraph (1), the requirements described in this paragraph are met with respect to any calendar year if—

(A) the custodial parent signs a written declaration (in such manner and form as the Secretary may by regulations prescribe) that such custodial parent will not claim such child as a dependent for any taxable year beginning in such calendar year, and

(B) the noncustodial parent attaches such written declaration to the noncustodial parent's return for the taxable year beginning during such calendar year.

(3) Exception for certain pre-1985 instruments.

(A) In general. For purposes of paragraph (1), the requirements described in this paragraph are met with respect to any calendar year if—

(i) a qualified pre-1985 instrument between the parents applicable to the taxable year beginning in such calendar year provides that the noncustodial parent shall be entitled to any deduction allowable under section 151 for such child, and

(ii) the noncustodial parent provides at least $600 for the support of such child during such calendar year.

For purposes of this subparagraph, amounts expended for the support of a child or children shall be treated as received from the noncustodial parent to the extent that such parent provided amounts for such support.

(B) Qualified pre-1985 instrument. For purposes of this paragraph, the term "qualified pre-1985 instrument" means any decree of divorce or separate maintenance or written agreement—

(i) which is executed before January 1, 1985,

(ii) which on such date contains the provision described in subparagraph (A)(i), and

(iii) which is not modified on or after such date in a modification which expressly provides that this paragraph shall not apply to such decree or agreement.

(4) Custodial parent and noncustodial parent. For purposes of this subsection—

(A) Custodial parent. The term "custodial parent" means the parent having custody for the greater portion of the calendar year.

(B) Noncustodial parent. The term "noncustodial parent" means the parent who is not the custodial parent.

(5) Exception for multiple-support agreement. This subsection shall not apply in any case where over one-half of the support of the child is treated as having been received from a taxpayer under the provision of subsection (d)(3).

(6) Special rule for support received from new spouse of parent. For purposes of this subsection, in the case of the remarriage of a parent, support of a child received from the parent's spouse shall be treated as received from the parent.

(f) Other definitions and rules.
For purposes of this section—

(1) Child defined.

(A) In general. The term "child" means an individual who is—

(i) a son, daughter, stepson, or stepdaughter of the taxpayer, or

(ii) an eligible foster child of the taxpayer.

(B) Adopted child. In determining whether any of the relationships specified in subparagraph (A)(i) or paragraph (4) exists, a legally adopted individual of the taxpayer, or an individual who is lawfully placed with the taxpayer for legal adoption by the taxpayer, shall be treated as a child of such individual by blood.

(C) Eligible foster child. For purposes of subparagraph (A)(ii), the term "eligible foster child" means an individual who is placed with the taxpayer by an authorized placement agency or by judgment, decree, or other order of any court of competent jurisdiction.

(2) Student defined. The term "student" means an individual who during each of 5 calendar months during the calendar year in which the taxable year of the taxpayer begins—

(A) is a full-time student at an educational organization described in section 170(b)(1)(A)(ii), or

(B) is pursuing a full-time course of institutional on-farm training under the supervision of an accredited agent of an educational organization described in section 170(b)(1)(A)(ii) or of a State or political subdivision of a State.

(3) Determination of household status. An individual shall not be treated as a member of the taxpayer's household if at any time during the taxable year of the taxpayer the relationship between such individual and the taxpayer is in violation of local law.

(4) Brother and sister. The terms "brother" and "sister" include a brother or sister by the half blood.

(5) Special support test in case of students. For purposes of subsections (c)(1)(D) and (d)(1)(C), in the case of an individual who is—

(A) a child of the taxpayer, and

(B) a student,

amounts received as scholarships for study at an educational organization described in section 170(b)(1)(A)(ii) shall not be taken into account.

(6) Treatment of missing children.

(A) In general. Solely for the purposes referred to in subparagraph (B), a child of the taxpayer—

(i) who is presumed by law enforcement authorities to have been kidnapped by someone who is not a member of the family of such child or the taxpayer, and

(ii) who had, for the taxable year in which the kidnapping occurred, the same principal place of abode as the taxpayer for more than one-half of the portion of such year before the date of the kidnapping,

shall be treated as meeting the requirement of subsection (c)(1)(B) with respect to a taxpayer for all taxable years ending during the period that the child is kidnapped.

(B) Purposes. Subparagraph (A) shall apply solely for purposes of determining—

(i) the deduction under section 151(c),

(ii) the credit under section 24 (relating to child tax credit),

(iii) whether an individual is a surviving spouse or a head of a household (as such terms are defined in section 2), and

(iv) the earned income credit under section 32.

(C) Comparable treatment of certain qualifying relatives. For purposes of this section, a child of the taxpayer—

(i) who is presumed by law enforcement authorities to have been kidnapped by someone who is not a member of the family of such child or the taxpayer, and

(ii) who was (without regard to this paragraph) a qualifying relative of the taxpayer for the portion of the taxable year before the date of the kidnapping,

shall be treated as a qualifying relative of the taxpayer for all taxable years ending during the period that the child is kidnapped.

(D) Termination of treatment. Subparagraphs (A) and (C) shall cease to apply as of the first taxable year of the taxpayer beginning after the calendar year in which there is a determination that the child is dead (or, if earlier, in which the child would have attained age 18).

(7) Cross references. For provision treating child as dependent of both parents for purposes of certain provisions, see sections 105(b), 132(h)(2)(B), and 213(d)(5).

In 2008, P.L. 110-351, Sec. 501(a), added "is younger than the taxpayer claiming such individual as a qualifying child and" after "such individual" in subpara. (c)(3)(A) ... Sec. 501(b), deleted "and" at the end of subpara. (c)(1)(C), substituted ", and" for the period at the end of subpara. (c)(1)(D), and added subpara. (c)(1)(E) ... Sec. 501(c)(2)(A), added subpara. (c)(4)(C) ... Sec. 501(c)(2)(B)(i), substituted "Except as provided in subparagraphs (B) and (C), if (but for this paragraph) an individual may be claimed as a qualifying child by 2 or more taxpayers" for "Except as provided in subparagraph (B), if (but for this paragraph) an individual may be and is claimed as a qualifying child by 2 or more taxpayers" in subpara. (c)(4)(A) ... Sec. 501(c)(2)(B)(ii), substituted "who can claim the same" for "claiming" in the heading of para. (c)(4), effective for tax. yrs. begin. after 12/31/2008.

In 2005, P.L. 109-135, Sec. 404(a), amended subsec. (e), effective for tax. yrs. begin. after 12/31/2004 as if included in Sec. 201 of the Working Families Tax Relief Act of 2004, P.L. 108-311.

Prior to amendment, subsec. (e) read as follows:

"(e) Special rule for divorced parents.

"(1) In general. Notwithstanding subsection (c)(1)(B), (c)(4), or (d)(1)(C), if—

"(A) a child receives over one-half of the child's support during the calendar year from the child's parents—

"(i) who are divorced or legally separated under a decree of divorce or separate maintenance,

"(ii) who are separated under a written separation agreement, or

"(iii) who live apart at all times during the last 6 months of the calendar year, and

"(B) such child is in the custody of 1 or both of the child's parents for more than one-half of the calendar year;

such child shall be treated as being the qualifying child or qualifying relative of the noncustodial parent for a calendar year if the requirements described in paragraph (2) are met.

"(2) Requirements. For purposes of paragraph (1), the requirements described in this paragraph are met if—

"(A) a decree of divorce or separate maintenance or written separation agreement between the parents applicable to the taxable year beginning in such calendar year provides that—

"(i) the noncustodial parent shall be entitled to any deduction allowable under section 151 for such child, or

"(ii) the custodial parent will sign a written declaration (in such manner and form as the Secretary may prescribe) that such parent will not claim such child as a dependent for such taxable year, or

"(B) in the case of such an agreement executed before January 1, 1985, the noncustodial parent provides at least $600 for the support of such child during such calendar year.

For purposes of subparagraph (A), amounts expended for the support of a child or children shall be treated as received from the noncustodial parent to the extent that such parent provided amounts for such support.

"(3) Custodial parent and noncustodial parent. For purposes of this subsection—

"(A) Custodial parent. The term "custodial parent" means the parent with whom a child shared the same principal place of abode for the greater portion of the calendar year.

"(B) Noncustodial parent. The term "noncustodial parent" means the parent who is not the custodial parent.

"(4) Exception for multiple-support agreements. This subsection shall not apply in any case where over one-half of the support of the child is treated as having been received from a taxpayer under the provision of subsection (d)(3)."

In 2004, P.L. 108-311, Sec. 201, amended Code Sec. 152, effective for tax. yrs. begin. after 12/31/2004.

Prior to amendment, Code Sec. 152 read as follows:

"SEC. 152 DEPENDENT DEFINED.

"(a) General definition. For purposes of this subtitle, the term 'dependent' means any of the following individuals over half of whose support, for the calendar year in which the taxable year of the taxpayer begins, was received from the taxpayer (or is treated under subsection (c) or (e) as received from the taxpayer):

"(1) A son or daughter of the taxpayer, or a descendant of either,
"(2) A stepson or stepdaughter of the taxpayer,
"(3) A brother, sister, stepbrother, or stepsister of the taxpayer,
"(4) The father or mother of the taxpayer, or an ancestor of either,
"(5) A stepfather or stepmother of the taxpayer,
"(6) A son or daughter of a brother or sister of the taxpayer,
"(7) A brother or sister of the father or mother of the taxpayer,
"(8) A son-in-law, daughter-in-law, father-in-law, mother-in-law, brother-in-law, or sister-in-law of the taxpayer, or
"(9) An individual (other than an individual who at any time during the taxable year was the spouse, determined without regard to section 7703, of the taxpayer) who, for the taxable year of the taxpayer, has as his principal place of abode the home of the taxpayer and is a member of the taxpayer's household.

"(b) Rules relating to general definition. For purposes of this section—

"(1) The terms 'brother' and 'sister' include a brother or sister by the halfblood.
"(2) In determining whether any of the relationships specified in subsection (a) or paragraph (1) of this subsection exists, a legally adopted child of an individual (and a child who is a member of an individual's household, if placed with such individual by an authorized placement agency for legal adoption by such individual), or a foster child of an individual (if such child satisfies the requirements of subsection (a)(9) with respect to such individual), shall be treated as a child of such individual by blood.
"(3) The term 'dependent' does not include any individual who is not a citizen or national of the United States unless such individual is a resident of the United States or of a country contiguous to the United States. The preceding sentence shall not exclude from the definition of 'dependent' any child of the taxpayer legally adopted by him, if, for the taxable year of the taxpayer, the child has as his principal place of abode the home of the taxpayer and is a member of the taxpayer's household, and if the taxpayer is a citizen or national of the United States.
"(4) A payment to a wife which is includible in the gross income of the wife under section 71 or 682 shall not be treated as a payment by her husband for the support of any dependent.
"(5) An individual is not a member of the taxpayer's household if at any time during the taxable year of the taxpayer the relationship between such individual and the taxpayer is in violation of local law.

"(c) Multiple support agreements. For purposes of subsection (a), over half of the support of an individual for a calendar year shall be treated as received from the taxpayer if—

"(1) no one person contributed over half of such support;
"(2) over half of such support was received from persons each of whom, but for the fact that he did not contribute over half of such support, would have been entitled to claim such individual as a dependent for a taxable year beginning in such calendar year;
"(3) the taxpayer contributed over 10 percent of such support; and
"(4) each person described in paragraph (2) (other than the taxpayer) who contributed over 10 percent of such support files a written declaration (in such manner and form as the Secretary may by regulations prescribe) that he will not claim such individual as a dependent for any taxable year beginning in such calendar year.

"(d) Special support test in case of students. For purposes of subsection (a), in the case of any individual who is—

"(1) a son, stepson, daughter, or stepdaughter of the taxpayer (within the meaning of this section), and
"(2) a student (within the meaning of section 151(c)(4)),

amounts received as scholarships for study at an educational organization described in section 170(b)(1)(A)(ii) shall not be taken into account in determining whether such individual received more than half of his support from the taxpayer.

"(e) Support test in case of children of divorced parents, etc.

"(1) Custodial parent gets exemption. Except as otherwise provided in this subsection, if—

"(A) a child (as defined in section 151(c)(3)) receives over half of his support during the calendar year from his parents—
"(i) who are divorced or legally separated under a decree of divorce or separate maintenance,
"(ii) who are separated under a written separation agreement, or
"(iii) who live apart at all times during the last 6 months of the calendar year, and
"(B) such child is in the custody of one or both of his parents for more than one-half of the calendar year,

such child shall be treated, for purposes of subsection (a), as receiving over half of his support during the calendar year from the parent having custody for a greater portion of the calendar year (hereinafter in this subsection referred to as the 'custodial parent').

"(2) Exception where custodial parent releases claim to exemption for the year. A child of parents described in paragraph (1) shall be treated as having received over half of his support during a calendar year from the noncustodial parent if—

"(A) the custodial parent signs a written declaration (in such manner and form as the Secretary may by regulations prescribe) that such custodial parent will not claim such child as a dependent for any taxable year beginning in such calendar year, and
"(B) the noncustodial parent attaches such written declaration to the noncustodial parent's return for the taxable year beginning during such calendar year.

For purposes of this subsection, the term 'noncustodial parent' means the parent who is not the custodial parent.

"(3) Exception for multiple-support agreement. This subsection shall not apply in any case where over half of the support of the child is treated as having been received from a taxpayer under the provisions of subsection (c).

"(4) Exception for certain pre-1985 instruments.

"(A) In general. A child of parents described in paragraph (1) shall be treated as having received over half his support during a calendar year from the noncustodial parent if—

"(i) a qualified pre-1985 instrument between the parents applicable to the taxable year beginning in such calendar year provides that the noncustodial parent shall be entitled to any deduction allowable under section 151 for such child, and
"(ii) the noncustodial parent provides at least $600 for the support of such child during such calendar year.

For purposes of this subparagraph, amounts expended for the support of a child or children shall be treated as received from the noncustodial parent to the extent that such parent provided amounts for such support.

"(B) Qualified pre-1985 instrument. For purposes of this paragraph, the term 'qualified pre-1985 instrument' means any decree of divorce or separate maintenance or written agreement—

"(i) which is executed before January 1, 1985,
"(ii) which on such date contains the provision described in subparagraph (A)(i), and
"(iii) which is not modified on or after such date in a modification which expressly provides that this paragraph shall not apply to such decree or agreement.

"(5) Special rule for support received from new spouse of parent. For purposes of this subsection, in the case of the remarriage of a parent, support of a child received from the parent's spouse shall be treated as received from the parent.

"(6) Cross reference. For provision treating child as dependent of both parents for purposes of medical expense deduction, see section 213(d)(5)."

In 1986, P.L. 99-514, Sec. 104(b)(1)(B), substituted "section 151(c)(3)" for "section 151(e)(3)" in subpara. (e)(1)(A) . . . Sec. 104(b)(3), substituted "section 151(c)(4)" for "section 151(e)(4)" in para. (d)(2), effective for tax. yrs. begin. after 12/31/86.

—P.L. 99-514, Sec. 1301(j)(8), substituted "section 7703" for "section 143" in para. (a)(9), effective for bonds issued after 8/15/86.

In 1984, P.L. 98-369, Sec. 423(a), amended subsec. (e), effective for tax. yrs. begin. after 12/31/84.

Prior to amendment, subsec. (e) read as follows:

"(e) Support test in case of child of divorced parents, etc.

"(1) General Rule. If—

"(A) a child (as defined in section 151(e)(3)) receives over half of his support during the calendar year from his parents who are divorced or legally separated under a decree of divorce or separate maintenance, or who are separated under a written separation agreement, and
"(B) such child is in the custody of one or both of his parents for more than one-half of the calendar year,

such child shall be treated, for purposes of subsection (a), as receiving over half of his support during the calendar year from the parent having custody for a greater portion of the calendar year unless he is treated, under the provisions of paragraph (2), as having received over half of his support for such year from the other parent (referred to in this subsection as the parent not having custody).

"(2) Special rule. The child of parents described in paragraph (1) shall be treated as having received over half of his support during the calendar year from the parent not having custody if—

"(A)(i) the decree of divorce or of separate maintenance, or a written agreement between the parents applicable to the taxable year beginning in such calendar year, provides that the parent not having custody shall be entitled to any deduction allowable under section 151 for such child, and
"(ii) such parent not having custody provides at least $600 for the support of such child during the calendar year, or
"(B)(i) the parent not having custody provides $1,200 or more for the support of such child (or if there is more than one such child, $1,200 or more for each of such children) for the calendar year, and
"(ii) the parent having custody of such child does not clearly establish that he provided more for the support of such child during the calendar year than the parent not having custody. For the purposes of this paragraph, amounts expended for the support of a child or children shall be treated as received from the parent not having custody to the extent that such parent provided amounts for such support.

"(3) Itemized statement required. If a taxpayer claims that paragraph (2)(B) applies with respect to a child for a calendar year and the other parent claims that paragraph (2)(B)(i) is not satisfied or claims to have provided more for the support of such child during such calendar year than the taxpayer, each parent shall be entitled to receive, under regulations to be prescribed by the Secretary, an itemized statement of the expenditures upon which the other parent's claim of support is based.

1,519

"(4) Exception for multiple-support agreement. The provisions of this subsection shall not apply in any case where over half of the support of the child is treated as having been received from a taxpayer under the provisions of subsection (c).

"(5) Regulations. The Secretary shall prescribe such regulations as may be necessary to carry out the purpose of this subsection."
—Sec. 482(b)(2) of P.L. 98-369, substituted "section 213(d)(5)" for "section 213(d)(4)" in para. (e)(6), as added by Sec. 423(a), effective for tax. yrs. beginning after 12/31/83.

In 1976, P.L. 94-455, Sec. 1901(a)(24), added "or" at the end of para. (a)(8), substituted a period for ", or" at the end para. (a)(9), deleted para. (a)(10), amended para. (b)(3), effective for tax. yrs. begin. after 12/31/76.
Prior to amendment para. (a)(10) read as follows:

"(10) An individual who—
"(A) is a descendant of a brother or sister of the father or mother of the taxpayer,
"(B) for the taxable year of the taxpayer receives institutional care required by reason of a physical or mental disability, and
"(C) before receiving such institutional care, was a member of the same household as the taxpayer."
Prior to amendment para. (b)(3) read as follows:

"(3) The term 'dependent' does not include any individual who is not a citizen or national of the United States unless such individual is a resident of the United States, of a country contiguous to the United States, of the Canal Zone, or of the Republic of Panama. The preceding sentence shall not exclude from the definition of 'dependent' and child of the taxpayer—

"(A) born to him, or legally adopted by him, in the Philippine Islands before January 1, 1956, if the child is a resident of the Republic of the Philippines, and if the taxpayer was a member of the Armed Forces of the United States at the time the child was born to him or legally adopted by him, or
"(B) legally adopted by him, if, for the taxable year of the taxpayer, the child has as his principal place of abode the home of the taxpayer and is a member of the taxpayer's household, and if the taxpayer is a citizen or national of the United States."
—P.L. 94-455, Sec. 1901(b)(7)(B), substituted "section 143" for "section 153" in para. (a)(9), effective for tax. yrs. begin. after 12/31/76.
—P.L. 94-455, Sec. 1901(b)(8)(A), substituted "educational organization described in section 170(b)(1)(A)(ii)" for "educational institution (as defined in section 151(e)(4))" in subsec. (d), effective for tax. yrs. begin. after 12/31/76.
—P.L. 94-455, Sec. 1906(b)(13)(A), substituted "Secretary" for "Secretary or his delegate" in paras. (c)(4), (e)(3) and (e)(5), effective for tax. yrs. begin. after '76.
—P.L. 94-455, Sec. 2139, substituted "each" for "all" in clause (e)(2)(B)(i), effective for tax. yrs. begin. after 10/4/76.

In 1972, P.L. 92-580, Sec. 1(a), substituted "citizen or national of the United States" for "citizen of the United States" each place it appeared in subsec. (b)(3), effective for tax. yrs. begin. after 12/31/71.

In 1969, P.L. 91-172, Sec. 912, added, "or a foster child of an individual (if such child satisfies the requirements of subsection (a)(9) with respect to such individual)," immediately before "shall be treated" in para. (b)(2), effective for tax. yrs. begin. after 12/31/69.

In 1967, P.L. 90-78, Sec. 1(a), added subsec. (e) . . . Sec. 1(b), substituted "subsection (c) or (e)" for "subsection (c)" in subsec. (a), effective for tax. yrs. begin. after 12/31/66.

In 1959, P.L. 86-376, Sec. 1(a), substituted "a legally adopted child of an individual (and a child who is a member of an individual's household, if placed with such individual by an authorized placement agency for legal adoption by such individual" for "a legally adopted child of an individual" in para. (b)(2), effective for tax. yrs. begin. after 12/31/59.

In 1958, P.L. 85-866, Sec. 4(a), added "(other than an individual who at any time during the taxable year was the spouse, determined without regard to section 153, of the taxpayer)" after "individual" in para. (a)(9), effective for tax. yrs. begin. after 12/31/53 and end. after 8/16/54.
—P.L. 85-866, Sec. 4(b), amended the last sentence of para. (b)(3), effective for tax. yrs. begin. after 12/31/57.
Prior to amendment, the last sentence of para. (b)(3) read as follows:
"The preceding sentence shall not exclude from the definition of 'dependent' any child of the taxpayer born to him, or legally adopted by him, in the Philippine Islands before January 1, 1956, if the child is a resident of the Republic of the Philippines, and if the taxpayer was a member of the Armed Forces of the United States at the time the child was born to him or legally adopted by him."
—P.L. 85-866, Sec. 4(c), added para. (b)(5), effective for tax. yrs. begin. after 12/31/53 and end. after 8/16/54.

In 1955, P.L. 333, Sec. 2, substituted "January 1, 1956" for "July 5, 1946" in subsec. (b)(3).

Sec. 153. Cross references.

(1) For deductions of estates and trusts, in lieu of the exemptions under section 151, see section 642(b).

(2) For exemptions of nonresident aliens, see section 873(b)(3).

(3) For determination of marital status, see section 7703.

In 2004, P.L. 108-311, Sec. 207(14), deleted para. (1) and redesignated paras. (2), (3), and (4) as paras. (1), (2), and (3), respectively, effective for tax. yrs. begin. after 12/31/2004.
Prior to deletion, para. (1) read as follows:
"(1) For definitions of 'husband' and 'wife', as used in section 152(b)(4), see section 7701(a)(17)."

In 1986, P.L. 99-514, Sec. 1272(d)(7), deleted para. (4) and redesignated paras. (5) as (4), effective for tax. yrs. begin. after 12/31/86.
Prior to deletion, para. (4) read as follows:
"(4) For exemptions of citizens deriving income mainly from sources within possessions of the United States, see section 931(e)."
—P.L. 99-514, Sec. 1301(j)(8), substituted "section 7703" for "section 143" each place it appeared in para. (5) [redesignated as para. (4) by Sec. 1272(d)(7) of this Act], effective for bonds issued after 8/15/86.

In 1976, P.L. 94-455, Sec. 1901(b)(7)(A), redesignated Code Sec. 154 as Code Sec. 153, effective for tax. yrs. begin. after 12/31/76.
—P.L. 94-455, Sec. 1901(b)(7)(C), added para. (5) to Code Sec. 153 as redesignated by Sec. 1901(b)(7)(A) of this Act, effective for tax. yrs. begin. after 12/31/76.

In 1966, P.L. 89-809, Sec. 103, substituted "section 873(b)(3)" for "section 873(d)" in para. (3), effective for tax. yrs. begin. after 12/31/66.

Sec. 153. Repealed.

In 1976, P.L. 94-455, Sec. 1901(b)(7)(A), repealed Code Sec. 153, effective for tax. yrs. begin. after 12/31/76.
Prior to repeal, Code Sec. 153 read as follows:
"SEC. 153. DETERMINATION OF MARITAL STATUS.
"For purposes of this part—
"(1) The determination of whether an individual is married shall be made as of the close of his taxable year; except that if his spouse dies during his taxable year such determination shall be made as of the time of such death; and
"(2) An individual legally separated from his spouse under a decree of divorce or of separate maintenance shall not be considered as married."

PART VI.—ITEMIZED DEDUCTIONS FOR INDIVIDUALS AND CORPORATIONS

Sec.
161. Allowance of deductions.
162. Trade or business expenses.
163. Interest.
164. Taxes.
165. Losses.
166. Bad debts.
167. Depreciation.
168. Accelerated cost recovery system.
169. Amortization of pollution control facilities.
170. Charitable, etc., contributions and gifts.
171. Amortizable bond premium.
172. Net operating loss deduction.
173. Circulation expenditures.
174. Research and experimental expenditures.
175. Soil and water conservation expenditures; endangered species recovery expenditures.
176. Payments with respect to employees of certain foreign corporations.
177. Repealed. [Trademark and trade name expenditures.]
178. Amortization of cost of acquiring a lease.
179. Election to expense certain depreciable business assets.
179A. Deduction for clean-fuel vehicles and certain refueling property.
179B. Deduction for capital costs incurred in complying with Environmental Protection Agency sulfur regulations.
179C. Election to expense certain refineries.
179D. Energy efficient commercial buildings deduction.
179E. Election to expense advanced mine safety equipment.
180. Expenditures by farmers for fertilizer, etc.

Deductions   Code Sec. 162(a)(3)

181. Treatment of certain qualified film and television productions.
181. Repealed. [Deductions for certain unused investment credit.]
182. Repealed. [Expenditures by farmers for clearing land.]
183. Activities not engaged in for profit.
184. Repealed. [Amortization of certain railroad rolling stock.]
185. Repealed. [Amortization of railroad grading and tunnel bores.]
186. Recoveries of damages for antitrust violations, etc.
187. Repealed. [Amortization of certain coal mine safety equipment.]
188. Repealed. [Amortization of certain expenditures for child care facilities.]
189. Repealed. [Amortization of real property construction period interest and taxes.]
190. Expenditures to remove architectural and transportation barriers to the handicapped and elderly.
191. Repealed. [Amortization of certain rehabilitation expenditures for certified historic structures.]
192. Contributions to black lung benefit trust.
193. Tertiary injectants.
194. Treatment of reforestation expenditures.
194A. Contributions to employer liability trusts.
195. Start-up expenditures.
196. Deduction for certain unused business credits.
197. Amortization of goodwill and certain other intangibles.
198. Expensing of environmental remediation costs.
198A. Expensing of qualified disaster expenses.
199. Income attributable to domestic production activities.

In **2008**, P.L. 110-343, Sec. 707(b)DivC, added item 198A.
—P.L. 110-234, Sec. 15303(a)(2)(C), added "; endangered species recovery expenditures" before the period in item 175.
In **2005**, P.L. 109-58, Sec. 1323(b)(4), added item 179C.
—P.L. 109-58, Sec. 1331(c), added item 179D.
In **2004**, P.L. 108-357, Sec. 102(d)(8), added item 199. . . . Sec. 244(b), added item 181. . . . Sec. 322(c)(5), amended item 194. . . . Sec. 338(b)(6), added item 179B.
Prior to amendment, item 194 read as follows:
"194. Amortization of reforestation expenditures."
In **1997**, P.L. 105-34, Sec. 941(b), added item 198.
In **1993**, P.L. 103-66, Sec. 13261(f)(6), added item 196.
In **1992**, P.L. 102-486, Sec. 1913(a)(3)(B), added item 179A.
In **1990**, P.L. 101-508, Sec. 11801(b)(3), repealed items 184 and 188.
Prior to repeal, item 184 read as follows:
"184. Amortization of certain railroad rolling stock."
Prior to repeal, item 188 read as follows:
"188. Amortization of certain expenditures for child care facilities."
In **1986**, P.L. 99-514, Sec. 201(d)(2)(B), amended item 178 . . . Sec. 241, repealed item 177 . . . Sec. 242(b)(3), repealed item 185 . . . Sec. 402(b)(3), repealed item 182 . . . Sec. 803(c)(2), repealed item 189.
Prior to repeal, item 177 read as follows:
"177. Trademark and trade name expenditures."
Prior to amendment, item 178 read as follows:
"178. Depreciation or amortization of improvements made by lessee on lessor's property."
Prior to repeal, item 182 read as follows:
"182. Expenditures by farmers for clearing land."
Prior to repeal, item 185 read as follows:
"185. Amortization of railroad grading and tunnel bores."
Prior to repeal, item 189 read as follows:
"189. Amortization of real property construction period interest and taxes."
In **1984**, P.L. 98-369, Sec. 94(b), substituted "expenditures" for "expenses" in item 195 . . . Sec. 474(r)(8)(B), substituted "business" for "investment" in item 196.
In **1983**, P.L. 97-448, Sec. 305(b)(2), redesignated item 194 relating to contributions to employer liability trusts as item 194A.
In **1982**, P.L. 97-248, Sec. 205(a)(5)(C), added item 196.
In **1981**, P.L. 97-34, Sec. 201(d), added item 168 . . . Sec. 202(d)(3), amended item 179.

Prior to amendment, item 179 read as follows:
"179. Additional first-year depreciation allowance for small business."
In **1980**, P.L. 96-605, Sec. 102(b), added item 195.
—P.L. 96-451, Sec. 301(c)(2), added item 194[sic 194A].
—P.L. 96-364, Sec. 209(c)(2), added item 194.
—P.L. 96-223, Sec. 251(a)(2)(A), added item 193.
In **1978**, P.L. 95-22, Sec. 4(b)(2), added item 192.
In **1977**, P.L. 95-30, Sec. 402(a)(4), amended item 188.
Prior to amendment, item 188 read as follows:
"188. Amortization of certain expenditures for on-the-job training and child care facilities."
In **1976**, P.L. 94-455, Sec. 201(b), added item 189. . . . Sec. 1901(b)(11)(B), repealed item 187. . . . Sec. 1951(c)(2)(D), repealed item 168. . . . Sec. 2122(b)(1), added item 190. . . . Sec. 2124(a)(3)(A), added item 191.
Prior to repeal, item 187 read as follows:
"187. Amortization of certain coal mine safety equipment."
Prior to repeal, item 168 read as follows:
"168. Amortization of emergency facilities."
In **1971**, P.L. 92-178, Sec. 303(c)(6), added item 188.
In **1969**, P.L. 91-172, Sec. 213(c)(1), added item 183. . . . Sec. 704(b)(1), substituted "pollution control" for "grain storage" in item 169. . . . Sec. 705(b), added items 184 and 185. . . . Sec. 707(b), added item 187. . . . Sec. 904(b), added item 186.
In **1964**, P.L. 88-272, Sec. 203(a)(3)(d), repealed item 181.
Prior to repeal, item 181 read as follows:
"Deductions for certain unused investment credit."
In **1962**, P.L. 87-834, Sec. 2(g)(3), added item 181 . . . Sec. 21(c), added item 182.
In **1960**, P.L. 86-779, Sec. 6(b), added item 180.
In **1958**, P.L. 85-866, Sec. 15(b), added item 178 . . . Sec. 204(b), added item 179.
In **1956**, P.L. 629, Sec. 4(a), added item 177.
In **1954**, P.L. 761, Sec. 210(b), added item 176.

Sec. 161. Allowance of deductions.

In computing taxable income under section 63, there shall be allowed as deductions the items specified in this part, subject to the exceptions provided in part IX (sec. 261 and following, relating to items not deductible).

In **1977**, P.L. 95-30, Sec. 102(b)(1), substituted "section 63" for "section 63(a)" in Code Sec. 161, effective for tax. yrs. begin. after 12/31/76.

Sec. 162. Trade or business expenses.
(a) In general.

There shall be allowed as a deduction all the ordinary and necessary expenses paid or incurred during the taxable year in carrying on any trade or business, including—

(1) a reasonable allowance for salaries or other compensation for personal services actually rendered;

(2) traveling expenses (including amounts expended for meals and lodging other than amounts which are lavish or extravagant under the circumstances) while away from home in the pursuit of a trade or business; and

(3) rentals or other payments required to be made as a condition to the continued use or possession, for purposes of the trade or business, of property to which the taxpayer has not taken or is not taking title or in which he has no equity.

For purposes of the preceding sentence, the place of residence of a Member of Congress (including any Delegate and Resident Commissioner) within the State, congressional district, or possession which he represents in Congress shall be considered his home, but amounts expended by such Members within each taxable year for living expenses shall not be deductible for income tax purposes in excess of $3,000. For purposes of paragraph (2), the taxpayer shall not be treated as being temporarily away from home during any period of employment if such period exceeds 1 year. The preceding sentence shall not apply to any Federal employee during any period for which such employee is certified by the Attorney General (or the designee thereof) as traveling on behalf of the United States in temporary duty status to investigate or prosecute, or provide support services for the investigation or prosecution of, a Federal crime.

(b) Charitable contributions and gifts excepted.
No deduction shall be allowed under subsection (a) for any contribution or gift which would be allowable as a deduction under section 170 were it not for the percentage limitations, the dollar limitations, or the requirements as to the time of payment, set forth in such section.

(c) Illegal bribes, kickbacks, and other payments.

(1) Illegal payments to government officials or employees. No deduction shall be allowed under subsection (a) for any payment made, directly or indirectly, to an official or employee of any government, or of any agency or instrumentality of any government, if the payment constitutes an illegal bribe or kickback or, if the payment is to an official or employee of a foreign government, the payment is unlawful under the Foreign Corrupt Practices Act of 1977. The burden of proof in respect of the issue, for the purposes of this paragraph, as to whether a payment constitutes an illegal bribe or kickback (or is unlawful under the Foreign Corrupt Practices Act of 1977) shall be upon the Secretary to the same extent as he bears the burden of proof under section 7454 (concerning the burden of proof when the issue relates to fraud).

(2) Other illegal payments. No deduction shall be allowed under subsection (a) for any payment (other than a payment described in paragraph (1)) made, directly or indirectly, to any person, if the payment constitutes an illegal bribe, illegal kickback, or other illegal payment under any law of the United States, or under any law of a State (but only if such State law is generally enforced), which subjects the payor to a criminal penalty or the loss of license or privilege to engage in a trade or business. For purposes of this paragraph, a kickback includes a payment in consideration of the referral of a client, patient, or customer. The burden of proof in respect of the issue, for purposes of this paragraph, as to whether a payment constitutes an illegal bribe, illegal kickback, or other illegal payment shall be upon the Secretary to the same extent as he bears the burden of proof under section 7454 (concerning the burden of proof when the issue relates to fraud).

(3) Kickbacks, rebates, and bribes under medicare and medicaid. No deduction shall be allowed under subsection (a) for any kickback, rebate, or bribe made by any provider of services, supplier, physician, or other person who furnishes items or services for which payment is or may be made under the Social Security Act, or in whole or in part out of Federal funds under a State plan approved under such Act, if such kickback, rebate, or bribe is made in connection with the furnishing of such items or services or the making or receipt of such payments. For purposes of this paragraph, a kickback includes a payment in consideration of the referral of a client, patient, or customer.

(d) Capital contributions to Federal National Mortgage Association.
For purposes of this subtitle, whenever the amount of capital contributions evidenced by a share of stock issued pursuant to section 303(c) of the Federal National Mortgage Association Charter Act (12 U.S.C., Sec. 1718) exceeds the fair market value of the stock as of the issue date of such stock, the initial holder of the stock shall treat the excess as ordinary and necessary expenses paid or incurred during the taxable year in carrying on a trade or business.

(e) Denial of deduction for certain lobbying and political expenditures.

(1) In general. No deduction shall be allowed under subsection (a) for any amount paid or incurred in connection with—

(A) influencing legislation,

(B) participation in, or intervention in, any political campaign on behalf of (or in opposition to) any candidate for public office,

(C) any attempt to influence the general public, or segments thereof, with respect to elections, legislative matters, or referendums, or

(D) any direct communication with a covered executive branch official in an attempt to influence the official actions or positions of such official.

(2) Exception for local legislation. In the case of any legislation of any local council or similar governing body—

(A) paragraph (1)(A) shall not apply, and

(B) the deduction allowed by subsection (a) shall include all ordinary and necessary expenses (including, but not limited to, traveling expenses described in subsection (a)(2) and the cost of preparing testimony) paid or incurred during the taxable year in carrying on any trade or business—

(i) in direct connection with appearances before, submission of statements to, or sending communications to the committees, or individual members, of such council or body with respect to legislation or proposed legislation of direct interest to the taxpayer, or

(ii) in direct connection with communication of information between the taxpayer and an organization of which the taxpayer is a member with respect to any such legislation or proposed legislation which is of direct interest to the taxpayer and to such organization,

and that portion of the dues so paid or incurred with respect to any organization of which the taxpayer is a member which is attributable to the expenses of the activities described in clauses (i) and (ii) carried on by such organization.

(3) Application to dues of tax-exempt organizations. No deduction shall be allowed under subsection (a) for the portion of dues or other similar amounts paid by the taxpayer to an organization which is exempt from tax under this subtitle which the organization notifies the taxpayer under section 6033(e)(1)(A)(ii) is allocable to expenditures to which paragraph (1) applies.

(4) Influencing legislation. For purposes of this subsection—

(A) In general. The term "influencing legislation" means any attempt to influence any legislation through communication with any member or employee of a legislative body, or with any government official or employee who may participate in the formulation of legislation.

(B) Legislation. The term "legislation" has the meaning given such term by section 4911(e)(2).

(5) Other special rules.

(A) Exception for certain taxpayers. In the case of any taxpayer engaged in the trade or business of conducting activities described in paragraph (1), paragraph (1) shall not apply to expenditures of the taxpayer in conducting such activities directly on behalf of another person (but shall apply to payments by such other person to the taxpayer for conducting such activities).

(B) De minimis exception.

(i) In general. Paragraph (1) shall not apply to any in-house expenditures for any taxable year if such expenditures do not exceed $2,000. In determining whether a taxpayer exceeds the $2,000 limit under this clause, there shall not be taken into account

Deductions   Code Sec. 162(k)(2)(A)(i)

overhead costs otherwise allocable to activities described in paragraphs (1)(A) and (D).

(ii) In-house expenditures. For purposes of clause (i), the term "in-house expenditures" means expenditures described in paragraphs (1)(A) and (D) other than—

(I) payments by the taxpayer to a person engaged in the trade or business of conducting activities described in paragraph (1) for the conduct of such activities on behalf of the taxpayer, or

(II) dues or other similar amounts paid or incurred by the taxpayer which are allocable to activities described in paragraph (1).

(C) Expenses incurred in connection with lobbying and political activities. Any amount paid or incurred for research for, or preparation, planning, or coordination of, any activity described in paragraph (1) shall be treated as paid or incurred in connection with such activity.

(6) Covered executive branch official. For purposes of this subsection, the term "covered executive branch official" means—

(A) the President,

(B) the Vice President,

(C) any officer or employee of the White House Office of the Executive Office of the President, and the 2 most senior level officers of each of the other agencies in such Executive Office, and

(D) (i) any individual serving in a position in level I of the Executive Schedule under section 5312 of title 5, United States Code, (ii) any other individual designated by the President as having Cabinet level status, and (iii) any immediate deputy of an individual described in clause (i) or (ii).

(7) Special rule for Indian tribal governments. For purposes of this subsection, an Indian tribal government shall be treated in the same manner as a local council or similar governing body.

(8) Cross reference. For reporting requirements and alternative taxes related to this subsection, see section 6033(e).

(f) Fines and penalties.

No deduction shall be allowed under subsection (a) for any fine or similar penalty paid to a government for the violation of any law.

(g) Treble damage payments under the antitrust laws.

If in a criminal proceeding a taxpayer is convicted of a violation of the antitrust laws, or his plea of guilty or nolo contendere to an indictment or information charging such a violation is entered or accepted in such a proceeding, no deduction shall be allowed under subsection (a) for two-thirds of any amount paid or incurred—

(1) on any judgment for damages entered against the taxpayer under section 4 of the Act entitled "An Act to supplement existing laws against unlawful restraints and monopolies, and for other purposes", approved October 15, 1914 (commonly known as the Clayton Act), on account of such violation or any related violation of the antitrust laws which occurred prior to the date of the final judgment of such conviction, or

(2) in settlement of any action brought under such section 4 on account of such violation or related violation.

The preceding sentence shall not apply with respect to any conviction or plea before January 1, 1970, or to any conviction or plea on or after such date in a new trial following an appeal of a conviction before such date.

(h) State legislators' travel expenses away from home.

(1) In general. For purposes of subsection (a), in the case of any individual who is a State legislator at any time during the taxable year and who makes an election under this subsection for the taxable year—

(A) the place of residence of such individual within the legislative district which he represented shall be considered his home,

(B) he shall be deemed to have expended for living expenses (in connection with his trade or business as a legislator) an amount equal to the sum of the amounts determined by multiplying each legislative day of such individual during the taxable year by the greater of—

(i) the amount generally allowable with respect to such day to employees of the State of which he is a legislator for per diem while away from home, to the extent such amount does not exceed 110 percent of the amount described in clause (ii) with respect to such day, or

(ii) the amount generally allowable with respect to such day to employees of the executive branch of the Federal Government for per diem while away from home but serving in the United States, and

(C) he shall be deemed to be away from home in the pursuit of a trade or business on each legislative day.

(2) Legislative days. For purposes of paragraph (1), a legislative day during any taxable year for any individual shall be any day during such year on which—

(A) The legislature was in session (including any day in which the legislature was not in session for a period of 4 consecutive days or less), or

(B) The legislature was not in session but the physical presence of the individual was formally recorded at a meeting of a committee of such legislature.

(3) Election. An election under this subsection for any taxable year shall be made at such time and in such manner as the Secretary shall by regulations prescribe.

(4) Section not to apply to legislators who reside near capitol. For taxable years beginning after December 31, 1980, this subsection shall not apply to any legislator whose place of residence within the legislative district which he represents is 50 or fewer miles from the capitol building of the State.

(i) Repealed.

(j) Certain foreign advertising expenses.

(1) In general. No deduction shall be allowed under subsection (a) for any expenses of an advertisement carried by a foreign broadcast undertaking and directed primarily to a market in the United States. This paragraph shall apply only to foreign broadcast undertakings located in a country which denies a similar deduction for the cost of advertising directed primarily to a market in the foreign country when placed with a United States broadcast undertaking.

(2) Broadcast undertaking. For purposes of paragraph (1), the term "broadcast undertaking" includes (but is not limited to) radio and television stations.

(k) Stock reacquisition expenses.

(1) In general. Except as provided in paragraph (2), no deduction otherwise allowable shall be allowed under this chapter for any amount paid or incurred by a corporation in connection with the reacquisition of its stock or of the stock of any related person (as defined in section 465(b)(3)(C)).

(2) Exceptions. Paragraph (1) shall not apply to—

(A) Certain specific deductions. Any—

(i) deduction allowable under section 163 (relating to interest),

(ii) deduction for amounts which are properly allocable to indebtedness and amortized over the term of such indebtedness, or

(iii) deduction for dividends paid (within the meaning of section 561).

(B) Stock of certain regulated investment companies. Any amount paid or incurred in connection with the redemption of any stock in a regulated investment company which issues only stock which is redeemable upon the demand of the shareholder.

(l) Special rules for health insurance costs of self-employed individuals.

(1) Allowance of deduction. In the case of a taxpayer who is an employee within the meaning of section 401(c)(1), there shall be allowed as a deduction under this section an amount equal to the amount paid during the taxable year for insurance which constitutes medical care for—

(A) the taxpayer,

(B) the taxpayer's spouse,

(C) the taxpayer's dependents, and

(D) any child (as defined in section 152(f)(1)) of the taxpayer who as of the end of the taxable year has not attained age 27.

(2) Limitations.

(A) Dollar amount. No deduction shall be allowed under paragraph (1) to the extent that the amount of such deduction exceeds the taxpayer's earned income (within the meaning of section 401(c)) derived by the taxpayer from the trade or business with respect to which the plan providing the medical care coverage is established.

(B) Other coverage. Paragraph (1) shall not apply to any taxpayer for any calendar month for which the taxpayer is eligible to participate in any subsidized health plan maintained by any employer of the taxpayer or of the spouse of, or any dependent, or individual described in subparagraph (D) of paragraph (1) with respect to, the taxpayer. The preceding sentence shall be applied separately with respect to—

(i) plans which include coverage for qualified long-term care services (as defined in section 7702B(c)) or are qualified long-term care insurance contracts (as defined in section 7702B(b)), and

(ii) plans which do not include such coverage and are not such contracts.

(C) Long-term care premiums. In the case of a qualified long-term care insurance contract (as defined in section 7702B(b)), only eligible long-term care premiums (as defined in section 213(d)(10)) shall be taken into account under paragraph (1).

(3) Coordination with medical deduction. Any amount paid by a taxpayer for insurance to which paragraph (1) applies shall not be taken into account in computing the amount allowable to the taxpayer as a deduction under section 213(a).

(4) Deduction not allowed for self-employment tax purposes. The deduction allowable by reason of this subsection shall not be taken into account in determining an individual's net earnings from self-employment (within the meaning of section 1402(a)) for purposes of chapter 2 for taxable years beginning before January 1, 2010, or after December 31, 2010.

(5) Treatment of certain S corporation shareholders. This subsection shall apply in the case of any individual treated as a partner under section 1372(a), except that—

(A) for purposes of this subsection, such individual's wages (as defined in section 3121) from the S corporation shall be treated as such individual's earned income (within the meaning of section 401(c)(1)), and

(B) there shall be such adjustments in the application of this subsection as the Secretary may by regulations prescribe.

(m) Certain excessive employee remuneration.

(1) In general. In the case of any publicly held corporation, no deduction shall be allowed under this chapter for applicable employee remuneration with respect to any covered employee to the extent that the amount of such remuneration for the taxable year with respect to such employee exceeds $1,000,000.

(2) Publicly held corporation. For purposes of this subsection, the term "publicly held corporation" means any corporation issuing any class of common equity securities required to be registered under section 12 of the Securities Exchange Act of 1934.

(3) Covered employee. For purposes of this subsection, the term "covered employee" means any employee of the taxpayer if—

(A) as of the close of the taxable year, such employee is the chief executive officer of the taxpayer or is an individual acting in such a capacity, or

(B) the total compensation of such employee for the taxable year is required to be reported to shareholders under the Securities Exchange Act of 1934 by reason of such employee being among the 4 highest compensated officers for the taxable year (other than the chief executive officer).

(4) Applicable employee remuneration. For purposes of this subsection—

(A) In general. Except as otherwise provided in this paragraph, the term "applicable employee remuneration" means, with respect to any covered employee for any taxable year, the aggregate amount allowable as a deduction under this chapter for such taxable year (determined without regard to this subsection) for remuneration for services performed by such employee (whether or not during the taxable year).

(B) Exception for remuneration payable on commission basis. The term "applicable employee remuneration" shall not include any remuneration payable on a commission basis solely on account of income generated directly by the individual performance of the individual to whom such remuneration is payable.

(C) Other performance-based compensation. The term "applicable employee remuneration" shall not include any remuneration payable solely on account of the attainment of one or more performance goals, but only if—

(i) the performance goals are determined by a compensation committee of the board of directors of the taxpayer which is comprised solely of 2 or more outside directors,

(ii) the material terms under which the remuneration is to be paid, including the performance goals, are disclosed to shareholders and approved by a majority of the vote in a separate shareholder vote before the payment of such remuneration, and

(iii) before any payment of such remuneration, the compensation committee referred to in clause (i) certifies that the performance goals and any other material terms were in fact satisfied.

(D) **Exception for existing binding contracts.** The term "applicable employee remuneration" shall not include any remuneration payable under a written binding contract which was in effect on February 17, 1993, and which was not modified thereafter in any material respect before such remuneration is paid.

(E) **Remuneration.** For purposes of this paragraph, the term "remuneration" includes any remuneration (including benefits) in any medium other than cash, but shall not include—

(i) any payment referred to in so much of section 3121(a)(5) as precedes subparagraph (E) thereof, and

(ii) any benefit provided to or on behalf of an employee if at the time such benefit is provided it is reasonable to believe that the employee will be able to exclude such benefit from gross income under this chapter.

For purposes of clause (i), section 3121(a)(5) shall be applied without regard to section 3121(v)(1).

(F) **Coordination with disallowed golden parachute payments.** The dollar limitation contained in paragraph (1) shall be reduced (but not below zero) by the amount (if any) which would have been included in the applicable employee remuneration of the covered employee for the taxable year but for being disallowed under section 280G.

(G) **Coordination with excise tax on specified stock compensation.** The dollar limitation contained in paragraph (1) with respect to any covered employee shall be reduced (but not below zero) by the amount of any payment (with respect to such employee) of the tax imposed by section 4985 directly or indirectly by the expatriated corporation (as defined in such section) or by any member of the expanded affiliated group (as defined in such section) which includes such corporation.

(5) Special rule for application to employers participating in the troubled assets relief program.

(A) **In general.** In the case of an applicable employer, no deduction shall be allowed under this chapter—

(i) in the case of executive remuneration for any applicable taxable year which is attributable to services performed by a covered executive during such applicable taxable year, to the extent that the amount of such remuneration exceeds $500,000, or

(ii) in the case of deferred deduction executive remuneration for any taxable year for services performed during any applicable taxable year by a covered executive, to the extent that the amount of such remuneration exceeds $500,000 reduced (but not below zero) by the sum of—

(I) the executive remuneration for such applicable taxable year, plus

(II) the portion of the deferred deduction executive remuneration for such services which was taken into account under this clause in a preceding taxable year.

(B) **Applicable employer.** For purposes of this paragraph—

(i) **In general.** Except as provided in clause (ii), the term "applicable employer" means any employer from whom 1 or more troubled assets are acquired under a program established by the Secretary under section 101(a) of the Emergency Economic Stabilization Act of 2008 if the aggregate amount of the assets so acquired for all taxable years exceeds $300,000,000.

(ii) **Disregard of certain assets sold through direct purchase.** If the only sales of troubled assets by an employer under the program described in clause (i) are through 1 or more direct purchases (within the meaning of section 113(c) of the Emergency Economic Stabilization Act of 2008), such assets shall not be taken into account under clause (i) in determining whether the employer is an applicable employer for purposes of this paragraph.

(iii) **Aggregation rules.** Two or more persons who are treated as a single employer under subsection (b) or (c) of section 414 shall be treated as a single employer, except that in applying section 1563(a) for purposes of either such subsection, paragraphs (2) and (3) thereof shall be disregarded.

(C) **Applicable taxable year.** For purposes of this paragraph, the term "applicable taxable year" means, with respect to any employer—

(i) the first taxable year of the employer—

(I) which includes any portion of the period during which the authorities under section 101(a) of the Emergency Economic Stabilization Act of 2008 are in effect (determined under section 120 thereof), and

(II) in which the aggregate amount of troubled assets acquired from the employer during the taxable Year pursuant to such authorities (other than assets to which subparagraph (B)(ii) applies), when added to the aggregate amount so acquired for all preceding taxable years, exceeds $300,000,000, and

(ii) any subsequent taxable year which includes any portion of such period.

(D) **Covered executive.** For purposes of this paragraph—

(i) **In general.** The term "covered executive" means, with respect to any applicable taxable year, any employee—

(I) who, at any time during the portion of the taxable year during which the authorities under section 101(a) of the Emergency Economic Stabilization Act of 2008 are in effect (determined under section 120 thereof), is the chief executive officer of the applicable employer or the chief financial officer of the applicable employer, or an individual acting in either such capacity, or

(II) who is described in clause (ii).

(ii) **Highest compensated employees.** An employee is described in this clause if the employee is 1 of the 3 highest compensated officers of the applicable employer for the taxable year (other than an individual described in clause (i)(I)), determined—

(I) on the basis of the shareholder disclosure rules for compensation under the Securities Exchange Act of 1934 (without regard to whether those rules apply to the employer), and

(II) by only taking into account employees employed during the portion of the taxable year described in clause (i)(I).

(iii) **Employee remains covered executive.** If an employee is a covered executive with respect to an applicable employer for any applicable taxable year, such employee shall be treated as a covered executive with respect to such employer for all subsequent applicable taxable years and for all subsequent taxable years in which deferred deduction executive remuneration with respect to services performed in all such applicable taxable years would (but for this paragraph) be deductible.

(E) Executive remuneration. For purposes of this paragraph, the term "executive remuneration" means the applicable employee remuneration of the covered executive, as determined under paragraph (4) without regard to subparagraphs (B), (C), and (D) thereof. Such term shall not include any deferred deduction executive remuneration with respect to services performed in a prior applicable taxable year.

(F) Deferred deduction executive remuneration. For purposes of this paragraph, the term "deferred deduction executive remuneration" means remuneration which would be executive remuneration for services performed in an applicable taxable year but for the fact that the deduction under this chapter (determined without regard to this paragraph) for such remuneration is allowable in a subsequent taxable year.

(G) Coordination. Rules similar to the rules of subparagraphs (F) and (G) of paragraph (4) shall apply for purposes of this paragraph.

(H) Regulatory authority. The Secretary may prescribe such guidance, rules, or regulations as are necessary to carry out the purposes of this paragraph and the Emergency Economic Stabilization Act of 2008, including the extent to which this paragraph applies in the case of any acquisition, merger, or reorganization of an applicable employer.

(6) Special rule for application to certain health insurance providers.

(A) In general. No deduction shall be allowed under this chapter—

(i) in the case of applicable individual remuneration which is for any disqualified taxable year beginning after December 31, 2012, and which is attributable to services performed by an applicable individual during such taxable year, to the extent that the amount of such remuneration exceeds $500,000, or

(ii) in the case of deferred deduction remuneration for any taxable year beginning after December 31, 2012, which is attributable to services performed by an applicable individual during any disqualified taxable year beginning after December 31, 2009, to the extent that the amount of such remuneration exceeds $500,000 reduced (but not below zero) by the sum of—

(I) the applicable individual remuneration for such disqualified taxable year, plus

(II) the portion of the deferred deduction remuneration for such services which was taken into account under this clause in a preceding taxable year (or which would have been taken into account under this clause in a preceding taxable year if this clause were applied by substituting "December 31, 2009" for "December 31, 2012" in the matter preceding subclause (I)).

(B) Disqualified taxable year. For purposes of this paragraph, the term "disqualified taxable year" means, with respect to any employer, any taxable year for which such employer is a covered health insurance provider.

(C) Covered health insurance provider. For purposes of this paragraph—

(i) In general. The term "covered health insurance provider" means—

(I) with respect to taxable years beginning after December 31, 2009, and before January 1, 2013, any employer which is a health insurance issuer (as defined in section 9832(b)(2)) and which receives premiums from providing health insurance coverage (as defined in section 9832(b)(1)), and

(II) with respect to taxable years beginning after December 31, 2012, any employer which is a health insurance issuer (as defined in section 9832(b)(2)) and with respect to which not less than 25 percent of the gross premiums received from providing health insurance coverage (as defined in section 9832(b)(1)) is from minimum essential coverage (as defined in section 5000A(f)).

(ii) Aggregation rules. Two or more persons who are treated as a single employer under subsection (b), (c), (m), or (o) of section 414 shall be treated as a single employer, except that in applying section 1563(a) for purposes of any such subsection, paragraphs (2) and (3) thereof shall be disregarded.

(D) Applicable individual remuneration. For purposes of this paragraph, the term "applicable individual remuneration" means, with respect to any applicable individual for any disqualified taxable year, the aggregate amount allowable as a deduction under this chapter for such taxable year (determined without regard to this subsection) for remuneration (as defined in paragraph (4) without regard to subparagraphs (B), (C), and (D) thereof) for services performed by such individual (whether or not during the taxable year). Such term shall not include any deferred deduction remuneration with respect to services performed during the disqualified taxable year.

(E) Deferred deduction remuneration. For purposes of this paragraph, the term "deferred deduction remuneration" means remuneration which would be applicable individual remuneration for services performed in a disqualified taxable year but for the fact that the deduction under this chapter (determined without regard to this paragraph) for such remuneration is allowable in a subsequent taxable year.

(F) Applicable individual. For purposes of this paragraph, the term "applicable individual" means, with respect to any covered health insurance provider for any disqualified taxable year, any individual—

(i) who is an officer, director, or employee in such taxable year, or

(ii) who provides services for or on behalf of such covered health insurance provider during such taxable year.

(G) Coordination. Rules similar to the rules of subparagraphs (F) and (G) of paragraph (4) shall apply for purposes of this paragraph.

(H) Regulatory authority. The Secretary may prescribe such guidance, rules, or regulations as are necessary to carry out the purposes of this paragraph.

• *Caution:* Code Sec. 162(n)-(o), following, are effective for services provided after 2/2/93, and on or before 12/31/95. Code Sec. 162(o) has been redesignated as Code Sec. 162(p) by Sec. 1204(a) of P.L. 105-34. For Code Sec. 162(p) see below. For effective date of the provisions of Sec. 1204(a) of P.L. 105-34, see notes following this Code Sec.

Deductions — Code Sec. 162

(n) Special rule for certain group health plans.
  (1) In general. No deduction shall be allowed under this chapter to an employer for any amount paid or incurred in connection with a group health plan if the plan does not reimburse for inpatient hospital care services provided in the State of New York—
   (A) except as provided in subparagraphs (B) and (C), at the same rate as licensed commercial insurers are required to reimburse hospitals for such services when such reimbursement is not through such a plan,
   (B) in the case of any reimbursement through a health maintenance organization, at the same rate as health maintenance organizations are required to reimburse hospitals for such services for individuals not covered by such a plan (determined without regard to any government-supported individuals exempt from such rate), or
   (C) in the case of any reimbursement through any corporation organized under Article 43 of the New York State Insurance Law, at the same rate as any such corporation is required to reimburse hospitals for such services for individuals not covered by such a plan.
  (2) State law exception. Paragraph (1) shall not apply to any group health plan which is not required under the laws of the State of New York (determined without regard to this subsection or other provisions of Federal law) to reimburse at the rates provided in paragraph (1).
  (3) Group health plan. For purposes of this subsection, the term "group health plan" means a plan of, or contributed to by, an employer or employee organization (including a self-insured plan) to provide health care (directly or otherwise) to any employee, any former employee, the employer, or any other individual associated or formerly associated with the employer in a business relationship, or any member of their family.

(o) Treatment of certain expenses of rural mail carriers.
  (1) General rule. In the case of any employee of the United States Postal Service who performs services involving the collection and delivery of mail on a rural route and who receives qualified reimbursements for the expenses incurred by such employee for the use of a vehicle in performing such services—
   (A) the amount allowable as a deduction under this chapter for the use of a vehicle in performing such services shall be equal to the amount of such qualified reimbursements; and
   (B) such qualified reimbursements shall be treated as paid under a reimbursement or other expense allowance arrangement for purposes of section 62(a)(2)(A) (and section 62(c) shall not apply to such qualified reimbursements).
  (2) Special rule where expenses exceed reimbursements. Notwithstanding paragraph (1)(A), if the expenses incurred by an employee for the use of a vehicle in performing services described in paragraph (1) exceed the qualified reimbursements for such expenses, such excess shall be taken into account in computing the miscellaneous itemized deductions of the employee under section 67.
  (3) Definition of qualified reimbursements. For purposes of this subsection, the term "qualified reimbursements" means the amounts paid by the United States Postal Service to employees as an equipment maintenance allowance under the 1991 collective bargaining agreement between the United States Postal Service and the National Rural Letter Carriers' Association. Amounts paid as an equipment maintenance allowance by such Postal Service under later collective bargaining agreements that supersede the 1991 agreement shall be considered qualified reimbursements if such amounts do not exceed the amounts that would have been paid under the 1991 agreement, adjusted for changes in the Consumer Price Index (as defined in section 1(f)(5)) since 1991.

(p) Treatment of expenses of members of reserve component of Armed Forces of the United States.
For purposes of subsection (a)(2), in the case of an individual who performs services as a member of a reserve component of the Armed Forces of the United States at any time during the taxable year, such individual shall be deemed to be away from home in the pursuit of a trade or business for any period during which such individual is away from home in connection with such service.

(q) Cross reference.
  (1) For special rule relating to expenses in connection with subdividing real property for sale, see section 1237.
  (2) For special rule relating to the treatment of payments by a transferee of a franchise, trademark, or trade name, see section 1253.
  (3) For special rules relating to—
   (A) funded welfare benefit plans, see section 419, and
   (B) deferred compensation and other deferred benefits, see section 404.

In 2011, P.L. 112-10, Sec. 1858(b)(3), deleted "For purposes of paragraph (1), the amount of a free choice voucher provided under section 10108 of the Patient Protection and Affordable Care Act shall be treated as an amount for compensation for personal services actually rendered." at the end of subpara. (a), effective for vouchers provided after 12/31/2013, as if included in the provisions of Sec. 10108(g)(1) of P.L. 111-148 [see below].
In 2010, P.L. 111-240, Sec. 2042(a), added "for taxable years beginning before January 1, 2010, or after December 31, 2010" before the period in para. (l)(4), effective for tax. yrs. begin. after 12/31/2009.
— P.L. 111-152, Sec. 1004(d)(2), amended para. (l)(1)
— P.L. 111-152, Sec. 1004(d)(3), added added ", or any dependent, or individual described in subparagraph (D) of paragraph (1) with respect to," after "spouse of" in subpara. (l)(2)(B), effective 3/30/2010.
Prior to amendment, para. (l)(1) read as follows:
 "(1) Allowance of deduction.
 "(A) In general. In the case of an individual who is an employee within the meaning of section 401(c)(1), there shall be allowed as a deduction under this section an amount equal to the applicable percentage of the amount paid during the taxable year for insurance which constitutes medical care for the taxpayer, his spouse, and dependents.
 "(B) Applicable percentage. For purposes of subparagraph (A), the applicable percentage shall be determined under the following table:

For taxable years beginning in calendar year—	The applicable percentage is—
1999 through 2001	60
2002	70
2003 and thereafter	100.

— P.L. 111-148, Sec. 9014(a), added para. (m)(6), effective for tax. yrs. begin. after 12/31/2009, with respect to services performed after such date.... Sec. 10108(g)(1), added matter at the end of subsec. (a), effective for vouchers provided after 12/31/2013.
In 2008, P.L. 110-343, Sec. 111DivA, of this Act, reads as follows:
 "SEC. 111. EXECUTIVE COMPENSATION AND CORPORATE GOVERNANCE.
 "(a) Applicability. Any financial institution that sells troubled assets to the Secretary under this Act shall be subject to the executive compensation requirements of subsections (b) and (c) and the provisions under the Internal Revenue Code of 1986, as provided under the amendment by section 302, as applicable.
 "(b) Direct purchases.
 "(1) In general. Where the Secretary determines that the purposes of this Act are best met through direct purchases of troubled assets from an individual financial institution where no bidding process or market prices are available, and the Secretary receives a meaningful equity or debt position in the financial institution as a result of the transaction, the Secretary shall require that the financial institution meet appropriate standards for executive compensation and corporate governance. The standards required under this subsection shall be effective for the duration of the period that the Secretary holds an equity or debt position in the financial institution.
 "(2) Criteria. The standards required under this subsection shall include—
 "(A) limits on compensation that exclude incentives for senior executive officers of a financial institution to take unnecessary and excessive risks that threaten the value of the financial institution during the period that the Secretary holds an equity or debt position in the financial institution;

"(B) a provision for the recovery by the financial institution of any bonus or incentive compensation paid to a senior executive officer based on statements of earnings, gains, or other criteria that are later proven to be materially inaccurate; and

"(C) a prohibition on the financial institution making any golden parachute payment to its senior executive officer during the period that the Secretary holds an equity or debt position in the financial institution.

"(3) Definition. For purposes of this section, the term 'senior executive officer' means an individual who is one of the top 5 highly paid executives of a public company, whose compensation is required to be disclosed pursuant to the Securities Exchange Act of 1934, and any regulations issued thereunder, and non-public company counterparts.

"(c) Auction purchases. Where the Secretary determines that the purposes of this Act are best met through auction purchases of troubled assets, and only where such purchases per financial institution in the aggregate exceed $300,000,000 (including direct purchases), the Secretary shall prohibit, for such financial institution, any new employment contract with a senior executive officer that provides a golden parachute in the event of an involuntary termination, bankruptcy filing, insolvency, or receivership. The Secretary shall issue guidance to carry out this paragraph not later than 2 months after the date of enactment of this Act, and such guidance shall be effective upon issuance.

"(d) Sunset. The provisions of subsection (c) shall apply only to arrangements entered into during the period during which the authorities under section 101(a) are in effect, as determined under section 120."

—P.L. 110-343, Sec. 302(a)DivA, added para. (m)(5), effective for tax. yrs. end. on or after 10/3/2008.

—P.L. 110-343, Sec. 702DivC, Sec. 702, P.L. 110-343, relating to tax relief for areas damaged by 2008 Midwestern storms, reads as follows:

"SEC. 702. TEMPORARY TAX RELIEF FOR AREAS DAMAGED BY 2008 MIDWESTERN SEVERE STORMS, TORNADOS, AND FLOODING.

"(a) In general. Subject to the modifications described in this section, the following provisions of or relating to the Internal Revenue Code of 1986 shall apply to any Midwestern disaster area in addition to the areas to which such provisions otherwise apply:

"(1) GO Zone benefits.

"(A) Section 1400N (relating to tax benefits) other than subsections (b), (d), (e), (i), (j), (m), and (o) thereof.

"(B) Section 1400O (relating to education tax benefits).

"(C) Section 1400P (relating to housing tax benefits).

"(D) Section 1400Q (relating to special rules for use of retirement funds).

"(E) Section 1400R(a) (relating to employee retention credit for employers).

"(F) Section 1400S (relating to additional tax relief) other than subsection (d) thereof.

"(G) Section 1400T (relating to special rules for mortgage revenue bonds).

"(2) Other benefits included in Katrina Emergency Tax Relief Act of 2005. Sections 302, 303, 304, 401, and 405 of the Katrina Emergency Tax Relief Act of 2005.

"(b) Midwestern disaster area.

"(1) In general. For purposes of this section and for applying the substitutions described in subsections (d) and (e), the term 'Midwestern disaster area' means an area—

"(A) with respect to which a major disaster has been declared by the President on or after May 20, 2008, and before August 1, 2008, under section 401 of the Robert T. Stafford Disaster Relief and Emergency Assistance Act by reason of severe storms, tornados, or flooding occurring in any of the States of Arkansas, Illinois, Indiana, Iowa, Kansas, Michigan, Minnesota, Missouri, Nebraska, or Wisconsin, and

"(B) determined by the President to warrant individual or individual and public assistance from the Federal Government under such Act with respect to damages attributable to such severe storms, tornados, or flooding.

"(2) Certain benefits available to areas eligible only for public assistance. For purposes of applying this section to benefits under the following provisions, paragraph (1) shall be applied without regard to subparagraph (B):

"(A) Sections 1400Q, 1400S(b), and 1400S(d) of the Internal Revenue Code of 1986.

"(B) Sections 302, 401, and 405 of the Katrina Emergency Tax Relief Act of 2005.

"(c) References.

"(1) Area. Any reference in such provisions to the Hurricane Katrina disaster area or the Gulf Opportunity Zone shall be treated as a reference to any Midwestern disaster area and any reference to the Hurricane Katrina disaster area or the Gulf Opportunity Zone within a State shall be treated as a reference to all Midwestern disaster areas within the State.

"(2) Items attributable to disaster. Any reference in such provisions to any loss, damage, or other item attributable to Hurricane Katrina shall be treated as a reference to any loss, damage, or other item attributable to the severe storms, tornados, or flooding giving rise to any Presidential declaration described in subsection (b)(1)(A).

"(3) Applicable disaster date. For purposes of applying the substitutions described in subsections (d) and (e), the term 'applicable disaster date' means, with respect to any Midwestern disaster area, the date on which the severe storms, tornados, or flooding giving rise to the Presidential declaration described in subsection (b)(1)(A) occurred.

* * * * * * * * * *

"(e) Modifications to Katrina Emergency Tax Relief Act of 2005. The following provisions of the Katrina Emergency Tax Relief Act of 2005 shall be applied with the following modifications:

* * * * * * * * * *

"(3) Mileage reimbursement for charitable volunteers. Section 304—

"(A) by substituting 'beginning on the applicable disaster date and ending on December 31, 2008' for 'beginning on August 25, 2005, and ending on December 31, 2006' in subsection (a), and

"(B) by substituting 'the applicable disaster date' for 'August 25, 2005' in subsection (a).

* * * * * * * * * *

In 2005, P.L. 109-73, Sec. 303, of this Act, reads as follows:
"SEC. 303. INCREASE IN STANDARD MILEAGE RATE FOR CHARITABLE USE OF VEHICLES.
"Notwithstanding section 170(i) of the Internal Revenue Code of 1986, for purposes of computing the deduction under section 170 of such Code for use of a vehicle described in subsection (f)(12)(E)(i) of such section for provision of relief related to Hurricane Katrina during the period beginning on August 25, 2005, and ending on December 31, 2006, the standard mileage rate shall be 70 percent of the standard mileage rate in effect under section 162(a) of such Code at the time of such use. Any increase under this section shall be rounded to the next highest cent."

—P.L. 109-73, Sec. 304, of this Act, reads as follows:
"SEC. 304. MILEAGE REIMBURSEMENTS TO CHARITABLE VOLUNTEERS EXCLUDED FROM GROSS INCOME.

"(a) In general. For purposes of the Internal Revenue Code of 1986, gross income of an individual for taxable years ending on or after August 25, 2005, does not include amounts received, from an organization described in section 170(c) of such Code, as reimbursement of operating expenses with respect to use of a passenger automobile for the benefit of such organization in connection with providing relief relating to Hurricane Katrina during the period beginning on August 25, 2005, and ending on December 31, 2006. The preceding sentence shall apply only to the extent that the expenses which are reimbursed would be deductible under chapter 1 of such Code if section 274(d) of such Code were applied—

"(1) by using the standard business mileage rate in effect under section 162(a) at the time of such use, and

"(2) as if the individual were an employee of an organization not described in section 170(c) of such Code.

"(b) Application to volunteer services only. Subsection (a) shall not apply with respect to any expenses relating to the performance of services for compensation.

"(c) No double benefit. No deduction or credit shall be allowed under any other provision of such Code with respect to the expenses excludable from gross income under subsection (a)."

In 2004, P.L. 108-357, Sec. 318(a), redesignated para. (o)(2) as (o)(3) and added para. (o)(2) . . . Sec. 318(b), deleted "reimbursed" before "expenses" in the heading of subsec. (o), effective for tax. yrs. begin. after 12/31/2003.

—P.L. 108-357, Sec. 802(b)(2), added subpara. (m)(4)(G), effective 3/4/2003; except that periods before 3/4/2003 shall not be taken into account in applying the periods in subsections (a) and (e)(1) of Code Sec. 4985, as added by Sec. 802(a) of this Act.

In 2003, P.L. 108-121, Sec. 109(a), redesignated subsec. (p) as (q) and added subsec. (p), effective for amounts paid or incurred in tax. yrs. begin. after 12/31/2002.

In 1998, P.L. 105-277, Sec. 2002(a), amended the table in subpara. (l)(1)(B), effective for tax. yrs. begin. after 12/31/98.

Prior to amendment, the table in subpara. (l)(1)(B) read as follows:

"For taxable years beginning in calendar year—	The applicable percentage is—
1997	40
1998 and 1999	45
2000 and 2001	50
2002	60
2003 through 2005	80
2006	90
2007 and thereafter	100"

—P.L. 105-206, Sec. 6012(a), substituted "investigate or prosecute, or provide support services for the investigation or prosecution of, a Federal crime." for "investigate, or provide support services for the investigation of, a Federal crime." at the end of subsec. (a), effective for amounts paid or incurred for tax. yrs. end. after 8/5/97.

In 1997, P.L. 105-34, Sec. 934(a), amended the table in subpara. (l)(1)(B), effective for tax. yrs. begin. after 12/31/96.

Prior to amendment, the table in subpara. (l)(1)(B) read as follows:

"For taxable years beginning in calendar year—	The applicable percentage is—
1997	40 percent
1998 through 2002	45 percent
2003	50 percent
2004	60 percent
2005	70 percent
2006 and thereafter	80 percent"

—P.L. 105-34, Sec. 1203(a), redesignated subsec. (o) as subsec. (p) and added new subsec. (o), effective for tax. yrs. begin. after 12/31/97.

—P.L. 105-34, Sec. 1204(a), added the sentence at the end of subsec. (a), effective for amounts paid or incurred for tax. yrs. end. after 8/5/97.

—P.L. 105-34, Sec. 1602(c), added a sentence at the end of subpara. (l)(2)(B) which included clauses (l)(2)(B)(i) and (ii), effective for tax. yrs. begin. after 12/31/96.

Deductions   Code Sec. 162

In 1996, P.L. 104-191, Sec. 311(a), amended para. (l)(1), effective for tax. yrs. begin. after 12/31/96.
Prior to amendment, para. (l)(1) read as follows:
"(1) In general. In the case of an individual who is an employee within the meaning of section 401(c)(1), there shall be allowed as a deduction under this section an amount equal to 30 percent of the amount paid during the taxable year for insurance which constitutes medical care for the taxpayer, his spouse, and dependents."
— P.L. 104-191, Sec. 322(b)(2)(B), added subpara. (l)(2)(C), effective for tax. yrs. begin. after 12/31/96.
— P.L. 104-188, Sec. 1704(p)(1), substituted "the reacquisition of its stock or of the stock of any related person (as defined in section 465(b)(3)(C))" for "the redemption of its stock" in para. (k)(1), effective for amounts paid or incurred after 9/13/95, in tax. yrs. end. after 9/13/95.
— P.L. 104-188, Sec. 1704(p)(2), deleted "or" at the end of clause (k)(2)(A)(i), redesignated clause (k)(2)(A)(ii) as clause (k)(2)(A)(iii), and added a new clause (k)(2)(A)(ii), effective for any amount paid or incurred after 2/28/86, in tax. yrs. end. after 2/28/86.
— P.L. 104-188, Sec. 1704(p)(3), substituted "reacquisition" for "redemption" in the heading of subsec. (k), effective for amounts paid or incurred after 9/13/95, in tax. yrs. end. after 9/13/95.
In 1995, P.L. 104-7, Sec. 1(a), deleted para. (l)(6), effective for tax. yrs. begin. after 12/31/93.
Prior to deletion, para. (l)(6) read as follows:
"(6) Termination. This subsection shall not apply to any taxable year beginning after December 31, 1993."
— P.L. 104-7, Sec. 1(b), substituted "30 percent" for "25 percent" in para. (l)(1), effective for tax. yrs. begin. after 12/31/94.
— P.L. 104-7, Sec. 5, substituted "December 31, 1995" for "May 12, 1995" in Sec. 13442(b) of P.L. 103-66, the effective date for amendments made by Sec. 13442(a) of P.L. 103-66, see below.
In 1993, P.L. 103-66, Sec. 13131(d)(2), amended para. (l)(3), effective for tax. yrs. begin. after 12/31/93.
Prior to amendment, para. (l)(3) read as follows:
"(3) Coordination with medical deduction, etc.
"(A) Medical deduction. Any amount paid by a taxpayer for insurance to which paragraph (1) applies shall not be taken into account in computing the amount allowable to the taxpayer as a deduction under section 213(a).
"(B) Health insurance credit. The amount otherwise taken into account under paragraph (1) as paid for insurance which constitutes medical care shall be reduced by the amount (if any) of the health insurance credit allowable to the taxpayer for the taxable year under section 32."
— P.L. 103-66, Sec. 13174(a)(1), substituted "December 31, 1993" for "June 30, 1992" in para. (l)(6)... Sec. 13174(a)(2), repealed Sec. 110(a)(2) of P.L. 102-227, effective for tax. yrs. end. after 6/30/92.
Prior to repeal, Sec. 110(a)(2) of P.L. 102-227, read as follows:
"(2) Special rule. In the case of any taxable year beginning in 1992—
"(A) only amounts paid before July 1, 1992, by the individual for insurance coverage for periods before July 1, 1992, shall be taken into account in determining the amount deductible under section 162(l) of the Internal Revenue Code of 1986 with respect to such individual for such taxable year, and
"(B) for purposes of subparagraph (A) of section 162(l)(2) of such Code, the amount of the earned income described in such subparagraph taken into account for such taxable year shall be the amount which bears the same ratio to the total amount of such earned income as the number of months in such taxable year ending before July 1, 1992, bears to the number of months in such taxable year."
— P.L. 103-66, Sec. 13174(b)(1), amended subpara. (l)(2)(B), effective for tax. yrs. begin. after 12/31/92.
Prior to amendment, subpara. (l)(2)(B) read as follows:
"(B) Other coverage. Paragraph (1) shall not apply to any taxpayer who is eligible to participate in any subsidized health plan maintained by any employer of the taxpayer or of the spouse of the taxpayer."
— P.L. 103-66, Sec. 13211(a), redesignated subsec. (m) as subsec. (n) and added new subsec. (m), effective for amounts which would otherwise be deductible for tax. yrs. begin. after 1/1/94.
— P.L. 103-66, Sec. 13222(a), amended subsec. (e), effective for amounts paid or incurred after 12/31/93.
Prior to amendment, subsec. (e) read as follows:
"(e) Appearances, etc., with respect to legislation.
"(1) In general. The deduction allowed by subsection (a) shall include all the ordinary and necessary expenses (including, but not limited to, traveling expenses described in subsection (a)(2) and the cost of preparing testimony) paid or incurred during the taxable year in carrying on any trade or business—
"(A) in direct connection with appearances before, submission of statements to, or sending communications to, the committees, or individual members, of Congress or of any legislative body of a State, a possession of the United States, or a political subdivision of any of the foregoing with respect to legislation or proposed legislation of direct interest to the taxpayer, or
"(B) in direct connection with communication of information between the taxpayer and an organization of which he is a member with respect to legislation or proposed legislation of direct interest to the taxpayer and to such organization, and that portion of the dues so paid or incurred with respect to any organization of which the taxpayer is a member which is attributable to the expenses of the activities described in subparagraphs (A) and (B) carried on by such organization.
"(2) Limitation. The provisions of paragraph (1) shall not be construed as allowing the deduction of any amount paid or incurred (whether by way of contribution, gift, or otherwise)—

"(A) for participation in, or intervention in, any political campaign on behalf of any candidate for public office, or
"(B) in connection with any attempt to influence the general public, or segments, thereof, with respect to legislative matters, elections, or referendums."
— P.L. 103-66, Sec. 13442(a), redesignated subsec. (n) [as amended by Sec. 13211(a) of this Act, above] as subsec. (o) and added new subsec. (n), effective for services provided after 2/2/93, and on or before 12/31/95 [as amended by Sec. 5 of P.L. 104-7, see above].
In 1992, P.L. 102-486, Sec. 1938(a), added a new sentence at the end of subsec. (a), effective for costs paid or incurred after 12/31/92.
In 1991, P.L. 102-227, Sec. 110(a)(1), substituted "June 30, 1992" for "December 31, 1991" in para. (l)(6), effective for tax. yrs. begin. after 12/31/91.
— P.L. 102-227, Sec. 110(a)(2), relating to special rules, is repealed by Sec. 13174(a)(2) of P.L. 103-66, see above.
In 1990, P.L. 101-508, Sec. 11111(d)(2), amended para. (l)(3), effective for tax. yrs. begin. after 12/31/90.
Prior to amendment, para. (l)(3) read as follows:
"(3) Coordination with medical deduction. Any amount paid by a taxpayer for insurance to which paragraph (1) applies shall not be taken into account in computing the amount allowable to the taxpayer as a deduction under section 213(a)."
— P.L. 101-508, Sec. 11410(a), substituted "December 31, 1991" for "September 30, 1990" in para. (l)(6)... Sec. 11410(b), deleted Sec. 7107(a)(2) of P.L. 101-239, effective for tax. yrs. begin. after 12/31/89.
Prior to deletion, Sec. 7107(a)(2) of P.L. 101-239, read as follows:
"(2) Special rule. In the case of any taxable year beginning in 1990—
"(A) only amounts paid before October 1, 1990, by the individual for insurance coverage for periods before October 1, 1990, shall be taken into account in determining the amount deductible under section 162(l) of the Internal Revenue Code of 1986 with respect to such individual for such taxable year, and
"(B) for purposes of section 162(l)(2)(A) of such Code, the amount of the earned income described in such paragraph taken into account for such taxable year shall be the amount which bears the same ratio to the total amount of such earned income as the number of months in such taxable year ending before October 1, 1990, bears to the number of months in such taxable year."
In 1989, P.L. 101-239, Sec. 6202(b)(3)(A), deleted subsec. (i), effective for items and services furnished after 12/19/89.
Prior to deletion, subsec. (i) read as follows:
"(i) Group health plans.
"(1) Coverage relating to end stage renal disease. The expenses paid or incurred by an employer for a group health plan shall not be allowed as a deduction under this section if the plan differentiates in the benefits it provides between individuals having end stage renal disease and other individuals covered by such plan on the basis of the existence of end stage renal disease, the need for renal dialysis, or in any other manner.
"(2) Group health plan. For purposes of this subsection the term 'group health plan' means any plan of, or contributed to by, an employer to provide medical care (as defined in section 213(d)) to his employees, former employees, or the families of such employees or former employees, directly or through insurance, reimbursement or otherwise."
— P.L. 101-239, Sec. 7107(a)(1), substituted "September 30, 1990" for "December 31, 1989" in para. (l)(5), [before redesignation as (l)(6) by Sec. 7107(b) of this Act]... Sec. 7107(b), redesignated para. (l)(5) as (l)(6) and added new para. (l)(5), effective for tax. yrs. begin. after 12/31/89.
— P.L. 101-239, Sec. 7107(a)(2), [as repealed in Sec. 11410(b) of P.L. 101-508, see above].
— P.L. 101-239, Sec. 7862(c)(3)(A)(i), substituted "entitlement" for "eligibility" in the heading of clause (k)(2)(B)(iv) [as clause (k)(2)(B)(iv) read before amended by Sec. 3011(b)(3)(A)-(C) of P.L. 100-647, see below]... Sec. 7862(c)(3)(A)(ii), added "which does not contain any exclusion or limitation with respect to any preexisting condition of such beneficiary" after "or otherwise)" in subclause (k)(2)(B)(iv)(II) [as clause (k)(2)(B)(iv) read before amended by Sec. 3011(b)(3)(A)-(C) of P.L. 100-647 see below], effective as provided in Sec 7862(c)(3)(D) which reads:
"(D) the amendments made by this paragraph [Sec. 7862(c)(3)] shall apply to:
"(i) qualifying events occurring after December 31, 1989, and
"(ii) in the case of qualified beneficiaries who elected continuation coverage after December 31, 1988, the period for which the required premium was paid (or was attempted to be paid but was rejected as such)."
— P.L. 101-140, Sec. 203(a)(4), deleted subpara. (1)(2)(B) and redesignated subpara. (1)(2)(C) as subpara. (1)(2)(B), effective as provided in Sec. 1151(k)(1) of P.L. 99-514 reproduced in note following Code Sec. 414.
Prior to deletion, subpara. (1)(2)(B) read as follows:
"(B) Required coverage. Paragraph (1) shall not apply to any taxpayer for any taxable year unless coverage is provided under 1 or more plans meeting the requirements of section 89, treating such coverage as an employer-provided benefit."
In 1988, P.L. 100-647, Sec. 1011B(b)(1), redesignated para. (m)(4) as para. (m)(5) and added new para. (m)(4)... Sec. 1011B(b)(2), redesignated subsec. (m) of the 1986 Code (relating to cross reference) as redesignated by section 1161(a) of the Reform Act, as subsec. (n)... Sec. 1011B(b)(3), added "derived by the taxpayer from the trade or business with respect to which the plan providing the medical care coverage is established" after "401(c))" subpara. (m)(2)(A), effective for tax. yrs. begin. after 12/31/86, except as provided in Secs. 1161(b)(2) and (3) of P.L. 99-514, reproduced below.
— P.L. 100-647, Sec. 1018(t)(7)(B), amended Sec. 1895(d)(5)(A) of P.L. 99-514, by substituting "section 162(k)(5)" for "section 162(k)(2)", see below.

1,529

— P.L. 100-647, Sec. 3011(b)(2), deleted para. (i)(2) and redesignated para. (i)(3) as para. (i)(2) . . . Sec. 3011(b)(3)(A)-(C), deleted subsec. (k), redesignated the subsection relating to stock redemption expenses [subsec. (l)] as subsec. (k), redesignated the subsection relating to special rules for health insurance costs of self-employed individuals [subsec. m] as subsec. (l), and redesignated the subsection relating to cross references [subsec. (n)] as subsec. (m) effective as provided in Sec. 3011(d) of this Act which reads as follows:

"(d) Effective date.

"The amendments made by this section shall apply to taxable years beginning after December 31, 1988, but shall not apply to any plan for any plan year to which section 162(k) of the Internal Revenue Code of 1986 (as in effect on the day before the date of the enactment of this Act) did not apply by reason of section 10001(e)(2) of the Consolidated Omnibus Budget Reconciliation Act of 1985. Prior to amendment, para. (i)(2) read as follows:

"(2) Plans must provide continuation coverage to certain individuals.

"(A) In general. No deduction shall be allowed under this section for expenses paid or incurred by an employer for any group health plan maintained by such employer unless all such plans maintained by such employer meet the continuing coverage requirements of subsection (k).

"(B) Exception for certain small employers, etc. Subparagraph (A) shall not apply to any plan described in section 106(b)(2)."

Prior to amendment, subsec. (k) read as follows:

"(k) Continuation coverage requirements of group health plans.

"(1) In general. For purposes of subsection (i)(2) and section 106(b)(1), a group health plan meets the requirements of this subsection only if each qualified beneficiary who would lose coverage under the plan as a result of a qualifying event is entitled to elect, within the election period, continuation coverage under the plan.

"(2) Continuation coverage. For purposes of paragraph (1), the term 'continuation coverage' means coverage under the plan which meets the following requirements:

"(A) Type of benefit coverage. The coverage must consist of coverage which, as of the time the coverage is being provided, is identical to the coverage provided under the plan to similarly situated beneficiaries under the plan with respect to whom a qualifying event has not occurred. If coverage under the plan is modified for any group of similarly situated beneficiaries, the coverage shall also be modified in the same manner for all individuals who are qualified beneficiaries under the plan pursuant to this subsection in connection with such group.

"(B) Period of coverage. The coverage must extend for at least the period beginning on the date of the qualifying event and ending not earlier than the earliest of the following:

"(i) Maximum required period

"(I) General rule for terminations and reduced hours. In the case of a qualifying event described in paragraph (3)(B), except as provided in subclause (II), the date which is 18 months after the date of the qualifying event.

"(II) Special rule for multiple qualifying events. If a qualifying event (other than a qualifying event described in paragraph (3)(F)) occurs during the 18 months after the date of the qualifying event described in paragraph (3)(B), the date which is 36 months after the date of the qualifying event described in paragraph (3)(B).

"(III) Special rule for certain bankruptcy proceedings. In the case of a qualifying event described in paragraph (3)(F) (relating to bankruptcy proceedings), the date of the death of the covered employee or qualified beneficiary (described in paragraph (7)(B)(iv)(III)), or in the case of the surviving spouse or dependent children of the covered employee, 36 months after the date of the death of the covered employee.

"(IV) General rule for other qualifying events. In the case of a qualifying event not described in paragraph (3)(B) or (3)(F), the date which is 36 months after the date of the qualifying event.

"(ii) End of plan. The date on which the employer ceases to provide any group health plan to any employee.

"(iii) Failure to pay premium. The date on which coverage ceases under the plan by reason of a failure to make timely payment of any premium required under the plan with respect to the qualified beneficiary. The payment of any premium (other than any payment referred to in the last sentence of subparagraph (C)) shall be considered to be timely if made within 30 days after the date due or within such longer period as applies to or under the plan.

"(iv) Group health plan coverage or medicare entitlement. The date on which the qualified beneficiary first becomes, after the date of the election—

"(I) covered under any other group health plan (as an employee or otherwise), which does not contain any exclusion or limitation with respect to any preexisting condition of such beneficiary, or

"(II) in the case of a qualified beneficiary other than a qualified beneficiary described in paragraph (7)(B)(iv), entitled to benefits under the title XVIII of the Social Security Act.

"(C) Premium requirements. The plan may require payment of a premium for any period of continuation coverage, except that such premium—

"(i) shall not exceed 102 percent of the applicable premium for such period, and

"(ii) may, at the election of the payor, be made in monthly installments.

If an election is made after the qualifying event, the plan shall permit payment for continuation coverage during the period preceding the election to be made within 45 days of the date of the election.

"(D) No requirement of insurability. The coverage may not be conditioned upon, or discriminate on the basis of lack of, evidence of insurability.

"(E) Conversion option. In the case of a qualified beneficiary whose period of continuation coverage expires under subparagraph (B)(i), the plan must, during the 180-day period ending on such expiration date, provide to the qualified beneficiary the option of enrollment under a conversion health plan otherwise generally available under the plan.

"(3) Qualifying event. For purposes of this subsection, the term 'qualifying event' means, with respect to any covered employee, any of the following events which, but for the continuation coverage required under this subsection, would result in the loss of coverage of a qualified beneficiary:

"(A) The death of the covered employee.

"(B) The termination (other than by reason of such employee's gross misconduct), or reduction of hours, of the covered employee's employment.

"(C) The divorce or legal separation of the covered employee from the employee's spouse.

"(D) The covered employee becoming entitled to benefits under title XVIII of the Social Security Act.

"(E) A dependent child ceasing to be a dependent child under the generally applicable requirements of the plan.

"(F) A proceeding in a case under title 11, United States Code, commencing on or after July 1, 1986, with respect to the employer from whose employment the covered employee retired at any time.

In the case of an event described in subparagraph (F), a loss of coverage includes a substantial elimination of coverage with respect to a qualified beneficiary described in paragraph (7)(B)(iv) within one year before or after the date of commencement of the proceeding.

"(4) Applicable premium. For purposes of this subsection—

"(A) In general. The term 'applicable premium' means, with respect to any period of continuation coverage of qualified beneficiaries, the cost to the plan for such period of the coverage for similarly situated beneficiaries with respect to whom a qualifying event has not occurred (without regard to whether such cost is paid by the employer or employee).

"(B) Special rule for self-insured plans. To the extent that a plan is a self-insured plan—

"(i) In general. Except as provided in clause (ii), the applicable premium for any period of continuation coverage of qualified beneficiaries shall be equal to a reasonable estimate of the cost of providing coverage for such period for similarly situated beneficiaries which—

"(I) is determined on an actuarial basis, and

"(II) takes into account such factors as the Secretary may prescribe in regulations.

"(ii) Determination on basis of past cost. If a plan administrator elects to have this clause apply, the applicable premium for any period of continuation coverage of qualified beneficiaries shall be equal to—

"(I) the cost to the plan for similarly situated beneficiaries for the same period occurring during the preceding determination period under subparagraph (C), adjusted by

"(II) the percentage increase or decrease in the implicit price deflator of the gross national product (calculated by the Department of Commerce and published in the Survey of Current Business) for the 12-month period ending on the last day of the sixth month of such preceding determination period.

"(iii) Clause (ii) not to apply where significant change. A plan administrator may not elect to have clause (ii) apply in any case in which there is any significant difference, between the determination period and the preceding determination period, in coverage under, or in employees covered by, the plan. The determination under the preceding sentence for any determination period shall be made at the same time as the determination under subparagraph (C).

"(C) Determination period. The determination of any applicable premium shall be made for a period of 12 months and shall be made before the beginning of such period.

"(5) Election. For purposes of this subsection—

"(A) Election period. The term 'election period' means the period which—

"(i) begins not later than the date on which coverage terminates under the plan by reason of a qualifying event,

"(ii) is of at least 60 days' duration, and

"(iii) ends not earlier than 60 days after the later of—

"(I) the date described in clause (i), or

"(II) in the case of any qualified beneficiary who receives notice under paragraph (6)(D), the date of such notice.

"(B) Effect of election on other beneficiaries. Except as otherwise specified in an election, any election of continuation coverage by a qualified beneficiary described in clause (i)(I) or of paragraph (7)(B) shall be deemed to include an election of continuation coverage on behalf of any other qualified beneficiary who would lose coverage under the plan by reason of the qualifying event. If there is a choice among types of coverage under the plan, each qualified beneficiary is entitled to make a separate selection among such type of coverage.

"(6) Notice requirements. In accordance with regulations prescribed by the Secretary—

"(A) the group health plan shall provide, at the time of commencement of coverage under the plan, written notice to each covered employee and spouse of the employee (if any) of the rights provided under this subsection,

"(B) the employer of an employee under a plan must notify the plan administrator of a qualifying event described in subparagraph (A), (B), (D), or (F) of paragraph (3) with respect to such employee within 30 days of the date of the qualifying event,

"(C) each covered employee or qualified beneficiary is responsible for notifying the plan administrator of the occurrence of any qualifying event described in subparagraph (C) or (E) of paragraph (3) within 60 days after the date of the qualifying event, and

"(D) the plan administrator shall notify—

"(i) in the case of a qualifying event described in subparagraph (A), (B), (D), or (F) of paragraph (3), any qualified beneficiary with respect to such event, and

"(ii) in the case of a qualifying event described in subparagraph (C) or (E) of paragraph (3) where the covered employee notifies the plan administrator under subparagraph (C), any qualified beneficiary with respect to such event,

"of such beneficiary's rights under this subsection.

For purposes of subparagraph (D), any notification shall be made within 14 days of the date on which the plan administrator is notified under subparagraph (B) or (C), whichever is applicable, and any such notification to an individual who is a qualified beneficiary as the spouse of the covered employee shall be treated as notification to all other qualified beneficiaries residing with such spouse at the time such notification is made.

"(7) Definitions. For purposes of this subsection—

"(A) Covered employee. The term 'covered employee' means an individual who is (or was) provided coverage under a group health plan by virtue of the individual's employment or previous employment with an employer

"(B) Qualified beneficiary.

"(i) In general. The term 'qualified beneficiary' means, with respect to a covered employee under a group health plan, any other individual who, on the day before the qualifying event for that employee, is a beneficiary under the plan—

"(I) as the spouse of the covered employee, or

"(II) as the dependent child of the employee.

"(ii) Special rule for terminations and reduced employment. In the case of a qualifying event described in paragraph (3)(B), the term 'qualified beneficiary' includes the covered employee.

"(iii) Exception for nonresident aliens. Notwithstanding clauses (i) and (ii), the term 'qualified beneficiary' does not include an individual whose status as a covered employee is attributable to a period in which such individual was a nonresident alien who received no earned income (within the meaning of section 911(d)(2)) from the employer which constituted income from sources within the United States (within the meaning of section 861(a)(3)). If an individual is not a qualified beneficiary pursuant to the previous sentence, a spouse or dependent child of such individual shall not be considered a qualified beneficiary by virtue of the relationship to the individual.

"(iv) Special rule for retirees and widows. In the case of a qualifying event described in paragraph (3)(F), the term 'qualified beneficiary' includes a covered employee who had retired on or before the date of substantial elimination of coverage and any other individual who, on the day before such qualifying event, is a beneficiary under the plan—

"(I) as the spouse of the covered employee,

"(II) as the dependent child of the employee, or

"(III) as the surviving spouse of the covered employee.

"(C) Plan administrator. The term 'plan administrator' has the meaning given the term 'administrator' by section 3(16)(A) of the Employee Retirement Income Security Act of 1974."

In 1986, P.L. 99-514, Sec. 613(a), redesignated subsec. (1) as subsec. (m) and added new subsec. (1), effective for any amount paid or incurred after 2/28/86, in tax. yrs. end. after 2/28/86.

—P.L. 99-514, Sec. 1031(a), provides rules for physicians and surgeons mutual protection and interindemnity arrangements or associations reproduced in note following Code Sec. 831.

—P.L. 99-514, Sec. 1161(a), redesignated subsec. (n) as subsec. (m) [sic , redesignated subsec. (m) as (n)] and added new subsec. (m), effective for tax. yrs. begin. after 12/31/86, except as provided in Sec. 1161(b)(2) and (3) which reads as follows:

"(2) Transitional rule.—In the case of any year to which section 89 of the Internal Revenue Code of 1986 does not apply, section 162(m)(2)(B) of such Code shall be applied by substituting any nondiscrimination requirements otherwise applicable for the requirements of section 89 of such Code.

"(3) Assistance.—The Secretary of the Treasury or his delegate shall provide guidance to self-employed individuals to assist them in meeting the requirements of section 89 of the Internal Revenue Code of 1986 with respect to coverage required by the amendments made by this section."

—P.L. 99-514, Sec. 1895(d)(1)(A), added the sentence at the end of subpara. (k)(2)(A) . . . Sec. 1895(d)(2)(A), amended clause (k)(2)(B)(i) . . . Sec. 1895(d)(3)(A), added the sentence at the end of clause (k)(2)(B)(iii) . . . Sec. 1895(d)(4)(A)(i), deleted clause (k)(2)(B)(v) . . . Sec. 1895(d)(4)(A)(ii), amended subclause (k)(2)(B)(iv)(I) . . . Sec. 1895(d)(4)(A)(iii), substituted "Group health plan coverage" for "Reemployment" in the heading of clause (k)(2)(B)(iv) . . . Sec. 1895(d)(5)(A)(i), [as amended by Sec. 1018(t)(7)(B) of P.L. 100-647, see above] added "of continuation coverage" after "any election" in subpara. (k)(5)(B) . . . Sec. 1895(d)(5)(A)(ii), [as amended by Sec. 1018(t)(7)(B) of P.L. 100-647, see above] added the last sentence to subpara. (k)(5)(B) . . . Sec. 1895(d)(7), added clause (k)(7)(B)(iii), effective for plan yrs. begin. on or after 7/1/86, except as provided in Sec. 10001(d)(2) of P.L. 99-272, reproduced below. Prior to amendment, clause (k)(2)(B)(i) read as follows:

"(i) Maximum period. In the case of—

"(I) a qualifying event described in paragraph (3)(B) (relating to terminations and reduced hours), the date which is 18 months after the date of the qualifying event, and

"(II) any qualifying event not described in subclause (I), the date which is 36 months after the date of the qualifying event."

Prior to deletion, clause (k)(2)(B)(v) read as follows:

"(v) Remarriage of spouse. In the case of an individual who is a qualified beneficiary by reason of being the spouse of a covered employer, the date on which the beneficiary remarries and becomes covered under a group health plan."

Prior to amendment, subclause (k)(2)(B)(iv)(I) read as follows:

"(I) a covered employee under any other group health plan, or"

—P.L. 99-514, Sec. 1895(d)(6)(A), added "within 60 days after the qualifying event" after "paragraph (3)" in subpara. (k)(6)(C), effective for qualifying events occurring after 10/22/86.

—P.L. 99-509, Sec. 8021(c), and (e), reproduced in note following Code Sec. 338, provides tax treatment of Conrail public sale.

—P.L. 99-509, Sec. 9501(a)(1), added subpara. (k)(3)(F) . . . Sec. 9501(b)(1)(A), added "(other than a qualifying event described in paragraph (3)(F)" after "qualifying event" the first time it appeared in subclause (k)(2)(B)(i)(II), added "or (3)(F)" after "(3)(B)" in subclause (k)(2)(B)(i)(III), redesignated subclause (k)(2)(B)(i)(III) as (IV) and added new subclause (k)(2)(B)(i)(III) . . . Sec. 9501(b)(2)(A), added "in the case of a qualified beneficiary other than a qualified beneficiary described in paragraph (7)(B)(iv)," before "entitled" in subclause (k)(2)(B)(iv)(II) . . . Sec. 9501(c)(1), added clause (k)(7)(B)(iv) . . . Sec. 9501(d)(1), substituted "(D), or (F)" for "or (D)" each place it appeared in subpara. (k)(6)(B) and clause (k)(6)(D)(i), effective for plan yrs. begin. on or after 7/1/86, except as provided in Sec. 10001(e)(2) of P.L. 99-272 (reproduced below) and Sec. 9501(e)(2)-(4) of this Act which reads as follows:

"(2) Treatment of certain bankruptcy proceedings.—Notwithstanding paragraph (1), section 10001(e) of the Consolidated Omnibus Budget Reconciliation Act of 1985, and section 10002(d) of such Act, the amendments made by this section and by sections 10001 and 10002 of such Act shall apply in the case of plan years ending during the 12-month period beginning July 1, 1986, but only with respect to—

"(A) a qualifying event described in section 162(k)(3)(F) of the Internal Revenue Code of 1986 or section 603(6) of the Employee Retirement Income Security Act of 1974, and

"(B) a qualifying event described in section 162(k)(3)(A) of the Internal Revenue Code of 1986 or section 603(1) of the Employee Retirement Income Security Act of 1974 relating to the death of a retired employee occurring after the date of the qualifying event described in subparagraph (A).

"(3) Treatment of current retirees.—Section 162(k)(3)(F) of the Internal Revenue Code of 1986 and section 603(6) of the Employee Retirement Income Security Act of 1974 apply to covered employees who retired before, on, or after the date of the enactment of this Act.

"(4) Notice.—In the case of a qualifying event described in section 603(6) of the Employee Retirement Income Security Act of 1974 that occurred before the date of the enactment of this Act, the notice required under section 606(2) of such Act (and under section 162(k)(6)(B) of the Internal Revenue Code of 1986) with respect to such event shall be provided no later than 30 days after the date of the enactment of this Act."

—P.L. 99-272, Sec. 10001(a), redesignated para. (i)(2) as para. (i)(3) and added new para. (i)(2) . . . Sec. 10001(c), redesignated subsec. (k) as subsec. (1) and added new subsec. (k) . . . Sec. 10001(d), substituted "Coverage relating to end stage renal disease" for "General rule" in the heading of para. (i)(1), effective for plan years beginning on or after 7/1/86, except as provided in Sec. 10001 (e)(2) of this Act:

"(2) Special rule for collective bargaining agreements.—In the case of a group health plan maintained pursuant to one or more collective bargaining agreements between employee representatives and one or more employers ratified before the date of the enactment of this Act, the amendments made by this section shall not apply to plan years beginning before the later of—

"(A) the date on which the last of the collective bargaining agreements relating to the plan terminates (determined without regard to any extension thereof agreed to after the date of the enactment of this Act), or

"(B) January 1, 1987.

For purposes of subparagraph (A), any plan amendment made pursuant to a collective bargaining agreement relating to the plan which amends the plan solely to conform to any requirement added by this section shall not be treated as a termination of such collective bargaining agreement."

In 1984, P.L. 98-573, Sec. 232(a), redesignated subsec. (j) as subsec. (k) and added new subsec. (j), effective for tax. yrs. begin. after 10/30/84.

—P.L. 98-369, Sec. 512(b), added para. (j)(3), as redesignated by P.L. 97-248, effective for amounts paid or incurred after 7/18/84, in tax. yrs. end. after 7/18/84. Sec. 512(c)(2) provides:

"(2) Exception for certain extended vacation pay plans. In the case of any extended vacation pay plan maintained pursuant to a collective bargaining agreement—

"(A) between employee representatives and 1 or more employers, and

"(B) in effect on June 22, 1984,

the amendments made by this section shall not apply before the date on which such collective bargaining agreement terminates (determined without regard to any extension thereof agreed to after June 22, 1984). For purposes of the preceding sentence, any plan amendment made pursuant to a collective bargaining agreement relating to the plan which amends the plan solely to conform to any requirement added by this section shall not be treated as a termination of such collective bargaining agreement."

—P.L. 98-369, Sec. 2354(d), substituted "213(d)" for "213(e)" in para. (i)(2), as redesignated by P.L. 97-248, effective 7/18/84. Sec. 2354(e)(1) provides that "none of [the amendments made by Sec. 2354] shall be construed as changing or affecting any right, liability, status, or interpretation which existed (under the provisions of law involved) before that date [7/18/84]."

In 1982, P.L. 97-248, Sec. 128(b)(1), redesignated subsec. (i) [relating to cross references] (as redesignated by P.L. 97-34) as subsec. (j) . . . Sec. 128(b)(2), redesignated subsec. (h) [relating to group health plans] (as added by Sec. 2146(b) of P.L. 97-35) as subsec. (i), effective for tax. yrs. begin. on or after 1/1/82.

—P.L. 97-248, Sec. 288(a)(1), substituted "is unlawful under the Foreign Corrupt Practices Act of 1977" for "would be unlawful under the laws of the United

States if such laws were applicable to such payment and to such official or employee" in para. (c)(1)... Sec. 288(a)(2), substituted "(or is unlawful under the Foreign Corrupt Practices Act of 1977)" for "(or would be unlawful under the laws of the United States)" in para. (c)(2), effective for payments made after 9/3/82.

—P.L. 97-216, Sec. 215(a), added ", but amounts expended by such Members within each taxable year for living expenses shall not be deductible for income tax purposes in excess of $3,000" after "home" in the last sentence of subsec. (a), effective for tax. yrs. begin. after 12/31/81.

—P.L. 97-216, Sec. 215(c), repealed Sec. 139(a) of P.L. 97-51 [see below], effective for tax. yrs. begin. after 12/31/81.

In 1981, P.L. 97-92, Sec. 133(a), amended Sec. 139(b)(3)of P.L. 97-51, the effective date for changes made by Sec. 139(b)(1) of P.L. 97-51, by substituting "1980" for "1981", see below.

—P.L. 97-51, Sec. 139(a), provides:

"Sec. 139. (a) It is the sense of the Congress that the dollar limits on tax deductions for living expenses of Members of Congress while away from home shall be the same as such limits for businessmen and other private citizens."

[repealed by Sec. 215(c) of P.L. 97-216, see above]

—P.L. 97-51, Sec. 139(b)(1), substituted a period for ", but amounts expended by such Members within each taxable year for living expenses shall not be deductible for income tax purposes in excess of $3,000." in the last sentence of subsec. (a), effective for tax. yrs. begin after 12/31/80 [as amended by Sec. 133(a) of P.L. 97-92, see above].

—P.L. 97-35, Sec. 2146(b), redesignated subsec. (h) as subsec. (i) and added new subsec. (h), effective for tax. yrs. begin. on or after 1/1/82.

—P.L. 97-34, Sec. 127(a), redesignated subsec. (h) as subsec. (i) and added new subsec. (h), effective for tax. yrs. begin. on or after 1/1/76.

In 1980, P.L. 96-178, Sec. 1, provided that subsecs. (a) and (d) of Sec. 604 of P.L. 94-455, (reproduced below) were each amended by substituting "January 1, 1979" for "January 1, 1978." These changes are inoperative because of previous amendments made to subsecs. (a) and (d) of Sec. 604 of P.L. 94-455 by Sec. 3 of P.L. 96-167, see below.

In 1979, P.L. 96-167, Sec. 3(a), amended Sec. 604(a) of P.L. 94-455 (reproduced below) by substituting "who, for the taxable year, elects the application" for "who elects the application" and substituting "January 1, 1981" for "January 1, 1978"

—P.L. 96-167, Sec. 3(b), amended Sec. 604(d) of P.L. 94-455 (reproduced below) by eliminating the last sentence.

In 1978, P.L. 95-258, Sec. 2, amended subsecs. (a) and (d) of Sec. 604 of P.L. 94-455, (see below) by substituting "January 1, 1978," for "January 1, 1977," effective 4/7/78.

In 1977, P.L. 95-30, Sec. 307, amended subsecs. (a) and (d) of Sec. 604 of P.L. 94-455(see below), by substituting "January 1, 1977," for "January 1, 1976," and by adding "beginning before January 1, 1976," following "any taxable year" in subsec. (c).

In 1976, P.L. 94-455, Sec. 604, of this Act [as amended by Sec. 307 of P.L. 95-30; Sec. 2 of P.L. 95-258, and Sec. 3(a) of P.L. 96-167, see above], provides:

"Sec. 604. State legislators' travel expenses away from home.

"(a) In general.

For purposes of section 162(a) of the Internal Revenue Code of 1954, in the case of any individual who was a State legislator at any time during any taxable year beginning before January 1, 1981, and who, for the taxable year, elects the application of this section, for any period during such a taxable year in which he was a State legislator—

"(1) the place of residence of such individual within the legislative district which he represented shall be considered his home, and

"(2) he shall be deemed to have expended for living expenses (in connection with his trade or business as a legislator) an amount equal to the sum of the amounts determined by multiplying each legislative day of such individual during the taxable year by the amount generally allowable with respect to such day to employees of the executive branch of the Federal Government for per diem while away from home but serving in the United States.

"(b) Legislative days.

For purposes of subsection (a), a legislative day during any taxable year for any individual shall be any day during such year on which (1) the legislature was in session (including any day in which the legislature was not in session for a period of 4 consecutive days or less), or (2) the legislature was not in session but the physical presence of the individual was formally recorded at a meeting of a committee of such legislature.

"(c) Limitation.

The amount taken into account as living expenses attributable to a trade or business as a State legislator for any taxable year beginning before January 1, 1976 under an election made under this section shall not exceed the amount claimed for such purpose under a return (or amended return) filed before May 21, 1976.

"(d) Making and effect of election.

An election under this section shall be made at such time and in such manner as the Secretary of the Treasury or his delegate shall by regulations prescribe.

—P.L. 94-455, Sec. 1901(c)(4), deleted 'territory' [sic] after 'congressional district,' in subsec. (a), effective for tax. yrs. begin. after 12/31/76.

—P.L. 94-455, Sec. 1906(b)(13)(A), substituted 'Secretary' for 'Secretary or his delegate' in paras. (c)(1) and (c)(2), effective for tax. yrs. begin. after 12/31/76. Sec. 2119 of the Act covers the application of Code Sec. 162 to publishers' prepublication expenditures. See note to Code Sec. 174.

In 1972, P.L. 92-580, Sec. 3, amended Sec. 97 of P.L. 85-866 (see '58) by changing the previously amended cut-off date from January 1, 1971 to January 1, 1973.

In 1971, P.L. 92-178, Sec. 310, amended paras. (c)(2) and (3) and substituted 'Illegal bribes, kickbacks, and other payments' for 'Bribes and illegal kickbacks' in the heading of subsec. (c), effective for payments after 12/30/69, except that para. (c)(3) shall apply only for kickbacks, rebates, and bribes payment of which is made on or after 12/10/71.

Prior to amendment paras. (c)(2) and (c)(3) read as follows:

"(2) Other bribes or kickbacks. If in a criminal proceeding a taxpayer is convicted of making a payment (other than a payment described in paragraph (1)) which is an illegal bribe or kickback, or his plea of guilty or nolo contendere to an indictment or information charging the making of such a payment is entered or accepted in such a proceeding, no deduction shall be allowed under subsection (a) on account of such payment or any related payment made prior to the date of the final judgment in such proceeding.

"(3) Statute of limitations. If a taxpayer claimed a deduction for a payment described in paragraph (2) which is disallowed because of a final judgment entered after the close of the taxable year for which the deduction was claimed, and if the proceeding was based on an indictment returned or an information filed prior to the expiration of the period for the assessment of any deficiency for such taxable year, the period for the assessment of any deficiency attributable to the deduction of such payment shall not expire prior to the expiration of one year from the date of such final judgment, and such deficiency may be assessed prior to the expiration of such one-year period notwithstanding the provision of any other law or rule of law which would otherwise prevent such assessment."

In 1969, P.L. 91-172, Sec. 516(c)(2)(A), added "(1)" at the beginning of subsec. (h), and added para. (2), effective for transfers after 12/31/69.

—P.L. 91-172, Sec. 902(a), redesignated subsec. (f) as subsec. (h) and added new subsecs. (f) and (g)... Sec. 902(b), amended subsec. (c). Subsecs. (c)(1) and (f) shall apply for all tax. yrs. to which such Code applies; subsec. (g) shall apply with respect to amounts paid or incurred after 12/31/69; Paras. (c)(2) and (c)(3) shall apply with respect to payments made after 12/30/69.

Prior to amendment subsec. (c) read as follows:

"(c) Improper payments to officials or employees of foreign countries.

No deduction shall be allowed under subsection (a) for any expenses paid or incurred if the payment thereof is made, directly or indirectly, to an official or employee of a foreign country, and if the making of the payment would be unlawful under the laws of the United States if such laws were applicable to such payment and to such official or employee."... Sec. 903, amended Sec. 97 of P.L. 85-866 (see '58) by changing the previously amended cut-off date from January 1, 1969 to January 1, 1971.

In 1966, P.L. 89-692, amended Sec. 97 of P.L. 85-866 (see '58) by changing the previously amended cut-off date from January 1, 1967 to January 1, 1969.

In 1964, P.L. 88-554, Sec. 1, amended Sec. 97 of P.L. 85-866 (see '58) by changing the previously amended cut-off date from January 1, 1965 to January 1, 1967.

In 1963, P.L. 88-153, amended Sec. 97 of P.L. 85-866 (see '58) by changing the previously amended cut-off date from January 1, 1963 to January 1, 1965.

In 1962, P.L. 87-834, Sec. 3(a), added subsec. (e), and redesignated former subsec. (e) as (f), for tax. yrs. beg. after '62.

—P.L. 87-834, Sec. 4(b), substituted "(including amounts expended for meals and lodging other than amounts which are lavish or extravagant under the circumstances)" for "(including the entire amount expended for meals and lodging)" in para. (a)(2), effective for tax. yrs. end. after 12/31/62, but only in respect of periods after such date.

In 1960, P.L. 86-779, Sec. 7(b), added "the dollar limitations," after "the percentage limitations," in subsec. (b)... Sec. 8(a), added subsec. (d) and redesignated former subsec. (d) as (e), effective for tax. yrs. beg. after 12/31/59.

—P.L. 86-564, Sec. 301, provided that:

"(a) Investigation and report by Joint Committee on Internal Revenue Taxation.

The Joint Committee on Internal Revenue Taxation is hereby authorized and directed to make a full and complete investigation and study of the operation and effects of present law, regulations, and practices relating to the deduction, as ordinary and necessary business expenses, of expenses for entertainment, gifts, dues or initiation fees in social, athletic, or sporting clubs or organizations, and similar or related items. The Joint Committee shall report to the House of Representatives and to the Senate the results of its investigation and study as soon as practicable during the 87th Congress, together with its recommendations for any changes in the law and administrative practices which in its judgment are necessary or appropriate.

"(b) Report by Secretary of the Treasury.

"The Secretary of the Treasury is hereby authorized and directed to report as soon as practicable during the 87th Congress to the House of Representatives and to the Senate the results of the enforcement program of the Internal Revenue Service (announced in Technical Information Release 221, dated April 4, 1960) relating to the deductions, as ordinary and necessary business expenses, of expenses for entertainment, travel, yachts, hunting lodges, club dues, and similar or related items, together with such recommendations with respect thereto as he considers necessary or appropriate to avoid misuse of the business expense deduction.

"(c) Consultation of staffs.

"The staff of the Joint Committee on Internal Revenue Taxation, and the staff of the Secretary of the Treasury, shall consult and cooperate with each other in performing any duties assigned to carry out the purposes of this section."

—P.L. 86-496, Sec. 2, amended Sec. 97 of P.L. 85-866 (see '58) by changing the cut-off date from January 1, 1961 to January 1, 1963.

In 1958, P.L. 85-866, Sec. 5, added subsec. (c) and redesignated former subsec. (c) as (d) applicable "only with respect to expenses paid or incurred after the date of the enactment of this Act [9/2/58]. The determination as to whether any expense paid or incurred on or before the date of the enactment of this Act shall be allowed as a deduction shall be made as if this section had not been enacted and

Deductions　　　　　　　　　　　　　　　　　　　　　　　　　　　　　Code Sec. 163(d)(5)

without inference drawn from the fact that this section is not made applicable with respect to expenses paid or incurred on or before the date of the enactment of this Act."... Sec. 97, [as amended by P.L. 86-496, Sec. 2; P.L. 88-153; P.L. 88-554, Sec. 1; P.L. 89-692; P.L. 91-172, Sec. 903; P.L. 92-580, Sec. 3] provides: "Deduction under section 162 of the Internal Revenue Code of 1954 for accrued vacation pay, computed in accordance with the method of accounting consistently followed by the taxpayer in arriving at such deduction shall not be denied for any taxable year ending before January 1, 1961, solely by reason of the fact that (1) the liability for the vacation pay to a specific person has not been clearly established, or (2) the amount of liability to each individual is not capable of computation with reasonable accuracy if at the time of the accrual the employer in respect of whom the vacation pay is accrued has performed the qualifying service necessary under a plan or policy (communicated to the employee before the beginning of the vacation year) which provides for vacations with pay to qualified employees."

Sec. 163. Interest.
(a) General rule.
There shall be allowed as a deduction all interest paid or accrued within the taxable year on indebtedness.

(b) Installment purchases where interest charge is not separately stated.
(1) General rule. If personal property or educational services are purchased under a contract—
(A) which provides that payment of part or all of the purchase price is to be made in installments, and
(B) in which carrying charges are separately stated but the interest charge cannot be ascertained,
then the payments made during the taxable year under the contract shall be treated for purposes of this section as if they included interest equal to 6 percent of the average unpaid balance under the contract during the taxable year. For purposes of the preceding sentence, the average unpaid balance is the sum of the unpaid balance outstanding on the first day of each month beginning during the taxable year, divided by 12. For purposes of this paragraph, the term "educational services" means any service (including lodging) which is purchased from an educational organization described in section 170(b)(1)(A)(ii) and which is provided for a student of such organization.
(2) Limitation. In the case of any contract to which paragraph (1) applies, the amount treated as interest for any taxable year shall not exceed the aggregate carrying charges which are properly attributable to such taxable year.

(c) Redeemable ground rents.
For purposes of this subtitle, any annual or periodic rental under a redeemable ground rent (excluding amounts in redemption thereof) shall be treated as interest on an indebtedness secured by a mortgage.

(d) Limitation on investment interest.
(1) In general. In the case of a taxpayer other than a corporation, the amount allowed as a deduction under this chapter for investment interest for any taxable year shall not exceed the net investment income of the taxpayer for the taxable year.
(2) Carryforward of disallowed interest. The amount not allowed as a deduction for any taxable year by reason of paragraph (1) shall be treated as investment interest paid or accrued by the taxpayer in the succeeding taxable year.
(3) Investment interest. For purposes of this subsection—
(A) In general. The term "investment interest" means any interest allowable as a deduction under this chapter (determined without regard to paragraph (1)) which is paid or accrued on indebtedness properly allocable to property held for investment.
(B) Exceptions. The term "investment interest" shall not include—

(i) any qualified residence interest (as defined in subsection (h)(3)), or
(ii) any interest which is taken into account under section 469 in computing income or loss from a passive activity of the taxpayer.
(C) Personal property used in short sale. For purposes of this paragraph, the term "interest" includes any amount allowable as a deduction in connection with personal property used in a short sale.
(4) Net investment income. For purposes of this subsection—
(A) In general. The term "net investment income" means the excess of—
(i) investment income, over
(ii) investment expenses.

> • *Caution:* Code Sec. 163(d)(4)(B), following, was amended by Sec. 302(b), P.L. 108-27. These provisions generally sunset for tax years beginning after 12/31/2012. For specific sunset provisions see Sec. 303, P.L. 108-27 reproduced in history notes for this Code Sec.

(B) Investment income. The term "investment income" means the sum of—
(i) gross income from property held for investment (other than any gain taken into account under clause (ii)(I)),
(ii) the excess (if any) of—
(I) the net gain attributable to the disposition of property held for investment, over
(II) the net capital gain determined by only taking into account gains and losses from dispositions of property held for investment, plus
(iii) so much of the net capital gain referred to in clause (ii)(II) (or, if lesser, the net gain referred to in clause (ii)(I)) as the taxpayer elects to take into account under this clause.
Such term shall include qualified dividend income (as defined in section 1(h)(11)(B)) only to the extent the taxpayer elects to treat such income as investment income for purposes of this subsection.
(C) Investment expenses. The term "investment expenses" means the deductions allowed under this chapter (other than for interest) which are directly connected with the production of investment income.
(D) Income and expenses from passive activities. Investment income and investment expenses shall not include any income or expenses taken into account under section 469 in computing income or loss from a passive activity.
(E) Reduction in investment income during phase-in of passive loss rules. Investment income of the taxpayer for any taxable year shall be reduced by the amount of the passive activity loss to which section 469(a) does not apply for such taxable year by reason of section 469(m). The preceding sentence shall not apply to any portion of such passive activity loss which is attributable to a rental real estate activity with respect to which the taxpayer actively participates (within the meaning of section 469(i)(6)) during such taxable year.
(5) Property held for investment. For purposes of this subsection—

1,533

(A) In general. The term "property held for investment" shall include—
  (i) any property which produces income of a type described in section 469(e)(1), and
  (ii) any interest held by a taxpayer in an activity involving the conduct of a trade or business—
    (I) which is not a passive activity, and
    (II) with respect to which the taxpayer does not materially participate.
(B) Investment expenses. In the case of property described in subparagraph (A)(i), expenses shall be allocated to such property in the same manner as under section 469.
(C) Terms. For purposes of this paragraph, the terms "activity", "passive activity", and "materially participate" have the meanings given such terms by section 469.

(6) **Phase-in of disallowance.** In the case of any taxable year beginning in calendar years 1987 through 1990—
(A) In general. The amount of interest paid or accrued during any such taxable year which is disallowed under this subsection shall not exceed the sum of—
  (i) the amount which would be disallowed under this subsection if—
    (I) paragraph (1) were applied by substituting "the sum of the ceiling amount and the net investment income" for "the net investment income", and
    (II) paragraphs (4)(E) and (5)(A)(ii) did not apply, and
  (ii) the applicable percentage of the excess of—
    (I) the amount which (without regard to this paragraph) is not allowable as a deduction under this subsection for the taxable year, over
    (II) the amount described in clause (i).
The preceding sentence shall not apply to any interest treated as paid or accrued during the taxable year under paragraph (2).
(B) Applicable percentage. For purposes of this paragraph, the applicable percentage shall be determined in accordance with the following table:

In the case of taxable years beginning in:	The applicable percentage is:
1987	35
1988	60
1989	80
1990	90

(C) Ceiling amount. For purposes of this paragraph, the term "ceiling amount" means—
  (i) $10,000 in the case of a taxpayer not described in clause (ii) or (iii),
  (ii) $5,000 in the case of a married individual filing a separate return, and
  (iii) zero in the case of a trust.

(e) **Original issue discount.**
(1) **In general.** In the case of any debt instrument issued after July 1, 1982, the portion of the original issue discount with respect to such debt instrument which is allowable as a deduction to the issuer for any taxable year shall be equal to the aggregate daily portions of the original issue discount for days during such taxable year.
(2) **Definitions and special rules.** For purposes of this subsection—
(A) Debt instrument. The term "debt instrument" has the meaning given such term by section 1275(a)(1).

(B) Daily portions. The daily portion of the original issue discount for any day shall be determined under section 1272(a) (without regard to paragraph (7) thereof and without regard to section 1273(a)(3)).
(C) Short-term obligations. In the case of an obligor of a short-term obligation (as defined in section 1283(a)(l)(A)) who uses the cash receipts and disbursements method of accounting, the original issue discount (and any other interest payable) on such obligation shall be deductible only when paid.
(3) **Special rule for original issue discount on obligation held by related foreign person.**
(A) In general. If any debt instrument having original issue discount is held by a related foreign person, any portion of such original issue discount shall not be allowable as a deduction to the issuer until paid. The preceding sentence shall not apply to the extent that the original issue discount is effectively connected with the conduct by such foreign related person of a trade or business within the United States unless such original issue discount is exempt from taxation (or is subject to a reduced rate of tax) pursuant to a treaty obligation of the United States.
(B) Special rule for certain foreign entities.
  (i) In general. In the case of any debt instrument having original issue discount which is held by a related foreign person which is a controlled foreign corporation (as defined in section 957) or a passive foreign investment company (as defined in section 1297), a deduction shall be allowable to the issuer with respect to such original issue discount for any taxable year before the taxable year in which paid only to the extent such original issue discount is includible (determined without regard to properly allocable deductions and qualified deficits under section 952(c)(1)(B)) during such prior taxable year in the gross income of a United States person who owns (within the meaning of section 958(a)) stock in such corporation.
  (ii) Secretarial authority. The Secretary may by regulation exempt transactions from the application of clause (i), including any transaction which is entered into by a payor in the ordinary course of a trade or business in which the payor is predominantly engaged.
(C) Related foreign person. For purposes of subparagraph (A), the term "related foreign person" means any person—
  (i) who is not a United States person, and
  (ii) who is related (within the meaning of section 267(b)) to the issuer.
(4) **Exceptions.** This subsection shall not apply to any debt instrument described in—
(A) subparagraph (D) of section 1272(a)(2) (relating to obligations issued by natural persons before March 2, 1984), and
(B) subparagraph (E) of section 1272(a)(2) (relating to loans between natural persons).
(5) **Special rules for original issue discount on certain high yield obligations.**
(A) In general. In the case of an applicable high yield discount obligation issued by a corporation—
  (i) no deduction shall be allowed under this chapter for the disqualified portion of the original issue discount on such obligation, and

Deductions   Code Sec. 163(f)(2)(B)(ii)(II)

(ii) the remainder of such original issue discount shall not be allowable as a deduction until paid.

For purposes of this paragraph, rules similar to the rules of subsection (i)(3)(B) shall apply in determining the amount of the original issue discount and when the original issue discount is paid.

(B) Disqualified portion treated as stock distribution for purposes of dividend received deduction.

(i) In general. Solely for purposes of sections 243, 245, 246, and 246A, the dividend equivalent portion of any amount includible in gross income of a corporation under section 1272(a) in respect of an applicable high yield discount obligation shall be treated as a dividend received by such corporation from the corporation issuing such obligation.

(ii) Dividend equivalent portion. For purposes of clause (i), the dividend equivalent portion of any amount includible in gross income under section 1272(a) in respect of an applicable high yield discount obligation is the portion of the amount so includible—

(I) which is attributable to the disqualified portion of the original issue discount on such obligation, and

(II) which would have been treated as a dividend if it had been a distribution made by the issuing corporation with respect to stock in such corporation.

(C) Disqualified portion.

(i) In general. For purposes of this paragraph, the disqualified portion of the original issue discount on any applicable high yield discount obligation is the lesser of—

(I) the amount of such original issue discount, or

(II) the portion of the total return on such obligation which bears the same ratio to such total return as the disqualified yield on such obligation bears to the yield to maturity on such obligation.

(ii) Definitions. For purposes of clause (i), the term "disqualified yield" means the excess of the yield to maturity on the obligation over the sum referred to subsection (i)(1)(B) plus 1 percentage point, and the term "total return" is the amount which would have been the original issue discount on the obligation if interest described in the parenthetical in section 1273(a)(2) were included in the stated redemption price at maturity.

(D) Exception for S corporations. This paragraph shall not apply to any obligation issued by any corporation for any period for which such corporation is an S corporation.

(E) Effect on earnings and profits. This paragraph shall not apply for purposes of determining earnings and profits; except that, for purposes of determining the dividend equivalent portion of any amount includible in gross income under section 1272(a) in respect of an applicable high yield discount obligation, no reduction shall be made for any amount attributable to the disqualified portion of any original issue discount on such obligation.

(F) Suspension of application of paragraph.

(i) Temporary suspension. This paragraph shall not apply to any applicable high yield discount obligation issued during the period beginning on September 1, 2008, and ending on December 31, 2009, in exchange (including an exchange resulting from a modification of the debt instrument) for an obligation which is not an applicable high yield discount obligation and the issuer (or obligor) of which is the same as the issuer (or obligor) of such applicable high yield discount obligation. The preceding sentence shall not apply to any obligation the interest on which is interest described in section 871(h)(4) (without regard to subparagraph (D) thereof) or to any obligation issued to a related person (within the meaning of section 108(e)(4)).

(ii) Successive application. Any obligation to which clause (i) applies shall not be treated as an applicable high yield discount obligation for purposes of applying this subparagraph to any other obligation issued in exchange for such obligation.

(iii) Secretarial authority to suspend application. The Secretary may apply this paragraph with respect to debt instruments issued in periods folowing the period described in clause (i) if the Secretary determines that such application is appropriate in light of distressed conditions in the debt capital markets.

(G) Cross reference. For definition of applicable high yield discount obligation, see subsection (i).

(6) Cross references. For provision relating to deduction of original issue discount on tax-exempt obligation, see section 1288.

For special rules in the case of the borrower under certain loans for personal use, see section 1275(b).

(f) Denial of deduction for interest on certain obligations not in registered form.

(1) In general. Nothing in subsection (a) or in any other provision of law shall be construed to provide a deduction for interest on any registration-required obligation unless such obligation is in registered form.

> • *Caution:* Code Sec. 163(f)(2)-(3), following, is effective to obligations issued before 3/19/2012. For Code Sec. 163(f)(2), effective to obligations issued after 3/18/2012, see below.

(2) Registration-required obligation. For purposes of this section—

(A) In general. The term "registration-required obligation" means any obligation (including any obligation issued by a governmental entity) other than an obligation which—

(i) is issued by a natural person,

(ii) is not of a type offered to the public,

(iii) has a maturity (at issue) of not more than 1 year, or

(iv) is described in subparagraph (B).

(B) Certain obligations not included. An obligation is described in this subparagraph if—

(i) there are arrangements reasonably designed to ensure that such obligation will be sold (or resold in connection with the original issue) only to a person who is not a United States person, and

(ii) in the case of an obligation not in registered form—

(I) interest on such obligation is payable only outside the United States and its possessions, and

(II) on the face of such obligation there is a statement that any United States person who holds such

obligation will be subject to limitations under the United States income tax laws.
(C) Authority to include other obligations. Clauses (ii) and (iii) of subparagraph (A), and subparagraph (B), shall not apply to any obligation if—
(i) in the case of—
(I) subparagraph (A), such obligation is of a type which the Secretary has determined by regulations to be used frequently in avoiding Federal taxes, or
(II) subparagraph (B), such obligation is of a type specified by the Secretary in regulations, and
(ii) such obligation is issued after the date on which the regulations referred to in clause (i) take effect.
(3) **Book entries permitted, etc.** For purposes of this subsection, rules similar to the rules of section 149(a)(3) shall apply.

• *Caution:* Code Sec. 163(f)(2)-(3), following, is effective to obligations issued after 3/18/2012. For Code Sec. 163(f)(2), effective to obligations issued before 3/19/2012, see above.

(2) **Registration-required obligation.** For purposes of this section—
(A) In general. The term "registration-required obligation" means any obligation (including any obligation issued by a governmental entity) other than an obligation which—
(i) is issued by a natural person,
(ii) is not of a type offered to the public, or
(iii) has a maturity (at issue) of not more than 1 year.
(B) Authority to include other obligations. Clauses (ii) and (iii) of subparagraph (A) shall not apply to any obligation if—
(i) such obligation is of a type which the Secretary has determined by regulations to be used frequently in avoiding Federal taxes, and
(ii) such obligation is issued after the date on which the regulations referred to in clause (i) take effect.
(3) **Book entries permitted, etc.** For purposes of this subsection, rules similar to the rules of section 149(a)(3) shall apply, except that a dematerialized book entry system or other book entry system specified by the Secretary shall be treated as a book entry system described in such section.
(g) **Reduction of deduction where section 25 credit taken.**
The amount of the deduction under this section for interest paid or accrued during any taxable year on indebtedness with respect to which a mortgage credit certificate has been issued under section 25 shall be reduced by the amount of the credit allowable with respect to such interest under section 25 (determined without regard to section 26).
(h) **Disallowance of deduction for personal interest.**
(1) **In general.** In the case of a taxpayer other than a corporation, no deduction shall be allowed under this chapter for personal interest paid or accrued during the taxable year.
(2) **Personal interest.** For purposes of this subsection, the term "personal interest" means any interest allowable as a deduction under this chapter other than—
(A) interest paid or accrued on indebtedness properly allocable to a trade or business (other than the trade or business of performing services as an employee),

(B) any investment interest (within the meaning of subsection (d)),
(C) any interest which is taken into account under section 469 in computing income or loss from a passive activity of the taxpayer,
(D) any qualified residence interest (within the meaning of paragraph (3)),
(E) any interest payable under section 6601 on any unpaid portion of the tax imposed by section 2001 for the period during which an extension of time for payment of such tax is in effect under section 6163, and
(F) any interest allowable as a deduction under section 221 (relating to interest on educational loans).
(3) **Qualified residence interest.** For purposes of this subsection—
(A) In general. The term "qualified residence interest" means any interest which is paid or accrued during the taxable year on—
(i) acquisition indebtedness with respect to any qualified residence of the taxpayer, or
(ii) home equity indebtedness with respect to any qualified residence of the taxpayer.
For purposes of the preceding sentence, the determination of whether any property is a qualified residence of the taxpayer shall be made as of the time the interest is accrued.
(B) Acquisition indebtedness.
(i) In general. The term "acquisition indebtedness" means any indebtedness which—
(I) is incurred in acquiring, constructing, or substantially improving any qualified residence of the taxpayer, and
(II) is secured by such residence.
Such term also includes any indebtedness secured by such residence resulting from the refinancing of indebtedness meeting the requirements of the preceding sentence (or this sentence); but only to the extent the amount of the indebtedness resulting from such refinancing does not exceed the amount of the refinanced indebtedness.
(ii) $1,000,000 Limitation. The aggregate amount treated as acquisition indebtedness for any period shall not exceed $1,000,000 ($500,000 in the case of a married individual filing a separate return).
(C) Home equity indebtedness.
(i) In general. The term "home equity indebtedness" means any indebtedness (other than acquisition indebtedness) secured by a qualified residence to the extent the aggregate amount of such indebtedness does not exceed—
(I) the fair market value of such qualified residence, reduced by
(II) the amount of acquisition indebtedness with respect to such residence.
(ii) Limitation. The aggregate amount treated as home equity indebtedness for any period shall not exceed $100,000 ($50,000 in the case of a separate return by a married individual).
(D) Treatment of indebtedness incurred on or before October 13, 1987.
(i) In general. In the case of any pre-October 13, 1987, indebtedness—
(I) such indebtedness shall be treated as acquisition indebtedness, and
(II) the limitation of subparagraph (B)(ii) shall not apply.

(ii) Reduction in $1,000,000 limitation. The limitation of subparagraph (B)(ii) shall be reduced (but not below zero) by the aggregate amount of outstanding pre-October 13, 1987, indebtedness.

(iii) Pre-October 13, 1987, indebtedness. The term "pre-October 13, 1987, indebtedness" means—

(I) any indebtedness which was incurred on or before October 13, 1987, and which was secured by a qualified residence on October 13, 1987, and at all times thereafter before the interest is paid or accrued, or

(II) any indebtedness which is secured by the qualified residence and was incurred after October 13, 1987, to refinance indebtedness described in subclause (I) (or refinanced indebtedness meeting the requirements of this subclause) to the extent (immediately after the refinancing) the principal amount of the indebtedness resulting from the refinancing does not exceed the principal amount of the refinanced indebtedness (immediately before the refinancing).

(iv) Limitation on period of refinancing. Subclause (II) of clause (iii) shall not apply to any indebtedness after—

(I) the expiration of the term of the indebtedness described in clause (iii)(I), or

(II) if the principal of the indebtedness described in clause (iii)(I) is not amortized over its term, the expiration of the term of the 1st refinancing of such indebtedness (or if earlier, the date which is 30 years after the date of such 1st refinancing).

(E) Mortgage insurance premiums treated as interest.

(i) In general. Premiums paid or accrued for qualified mortgage insurance by a taxpayer during the taxable year in connection with acquisition indebtedness with respect to a qualified residence of the taxpayer shall be treated for purposes of this section as interest which is qualified residence interest.

(ii) Phaseout. The amount otherwise treated as interest under clause (i) shall be reduced (but not below zero) by 10 percent of such amount for each $1,000 ($500 in the case of a married individual filing a separate return) (or fraction thereof) that the taxpayer's adjusted gross income for the taxable year exceeds $100,000 ($50,000 in the case of a married individual filing a separate return).

(iii) Limitation. Clause (i) shall not apply with respect to any mortgage insurance contracts issued before January 1, 2007.

(iv) Termination. Clause (i) shall not apply to amounts—

(I) paid or accrued after December 31, 2011, or

(II) properly allocable to any period after such date.

(4) Other definitions and special rules. For purposes of this subsection—

(A) Qualified residence.

(i) In general. The term "qualified residence" means—

(I) the principal residence (within the meaning of section 121) of the taxpayer, and

(II) 1 other residence of the taxpayer which is selected by the taxpayer for purposes of this subsection for the taxable year and which is used by the taxpayer as a residence (within the meaning of section 280A(d)(1)).

(ii) Married individuals filing separate returns. If a married couple does not file a joint return for the taxable year—

(I) such couple shall be treated as 1 taxpayer for purposes of clause (i), and

(II) each individual shall be entitled to take into account 1 residence unless both individuals consent in writing to 1 individual taking into account the principal residence and 1 other residence.

(iii) Residence not rented. For purposes of clause (i)(II), notwithstanding section 280A(d)(1), if the taxpayer does not rent a dwelling unit at any time during a taxable year, such unit may be treated as a residence for such taxable year.

(B) Special rule for cooperative housing corporations. Any indebtedness secured by stock held by the taxpayer as a tenant-stockholder (as defined in section 216) in a cooperative housing corporation (as so defined) shall be treated as secured by the house or apartment which the taxpayer is entitled to occupy as such a tenant-stockholder. If stock described in the preceding sentence may not be used to secure indebtedness, indebtedness shall be treated as so secured if the taxpayer establishes to the satisfaction of the Secretary that such indebtedness was incurred to acquire such stock.

(C) Unenforceable security interests. Indebtedness shall not fail to be treated as secured by any property solely because, under any applicable State or local homestead or other debtor protection law in effect on August 16, 1986, the security interest is ineffective or the enforceability of the security interest is restricted.

(D) Special rules for estates and trusts. For purposes of determining whether any interest paid or accrued by an estate or trust is qualified residence interest, any residence held by such estate or trust shall be treated as a qualified residence of such estate or trust if such estate or trust establishes that such residence is a qualified residence of a beneficiary who has a present interest in such estate or trust or an interest in the residuary of such estate or trust.

(E) Qualified mortgage insurance. The term "qualified mortgage insurance" means—

(i) mortgage insurance provided by the Veterans Administration, the Federal Housing Administration, or the Rural Housing Administration, and

(ii) private mortgage insurance (as defined by section 2 of the Homeowners Protection Act of 1998 (12 U.S.C. 4901), as in effect on the date of the enactment of this subparagraph).

(F) Special rules for prepaid qualified mortgage insurance. Any amount paid by the taxpayer for qualified mortgage insurance that is properly allocable to any mortgage the payment of which extends to periods that are after the close of the taxable year in which such amount is paid shall be chargeable to capital account and shall be treated as paid in such periods to which so allocated. No deduction shall be allowed for the unamortized balance of such account if such mortgage is satisfied before the end of its term. The preceding sentences shall not apply to amounts paid for qualified mortgage insurance provided by the Veterans Administration or the Rural Housing Administration.

(5) Phase-in of limitation. In the case of any taxable year beginning in calendar years 1987 through 1990, the amount of interest with respect to which a deduction is disallowed under this subsection shall be equal to the applicable percentage (within the meaning of subsection

Code Sec. 163(h)(5) — Deductions

(d)(6)(B)) of the amount which (but for this paragraph) would have been so disallowed.

(i) Applicable high yield discount obligation.

(1) In general. For purposes of this section, the term "applicable high yield discount obligation" means any debt instrument if—

(A) the maturity date of such instrument is more than 5 years from the date of issue,

(B) the yield to maturity on such instrument equals or exceeds the sum of—

(i) the applicable Federal rate in effect under section 1274(d) for the calendar month in which the obligation is issued, plus

(ii) 5 percentage points, and

(C) such instrument has significant original issue discount.

For purposes of subparagraph (B)(i), the Secretary may by regulation (i) permit a rate to be used with respect to any debt instrument which is higher than the applicable Federal rate if the taxpayer establishes to the satisfaction of the Secretary that such higher rate is based on the same principles as the applicable Federal rate and is appropriate for the term of the instrument , or (ii) permit, on a temporary basis, a rate to be used with respect to any debt instrument which is higher than the applicable Federal rate if the Secretary determines that such rate is appropriate in light of distressed conditions in the debt capital markets.

(2) Significant original issue discount. For purposes of paragraph (1)(C), a debt instrument shall be treated as having significant original issue discount if—

(A) the aggregate amount which would be includible in gross income with respect to such instrument for periods before the close of any accrual period (as defined in section 1272(a)(5)) ending after the date 5 years after the date of issue, exceeds

(B) the sum of—

(i) the aggregate amount of interest to be paid under the instrument before the close of such accrual period, and

(ii) the product of the issue price of such instrument (as defined in sections 1273(b) and 1274(a)) and its yield to maturity.

(3) Special rules. For purposes of determining whether a debt instrument is an applicable high yield discount obligation—

(A) any payment under the instrument shall be assumed to be made on the last day permitted under the instrument, and

(B) any payment to be made in the form of another obligation of the issuer (or a related person within the meaning of section 453(f)(1)) shall be assumed to be made when such obligation is required to be paid in cash or in property other than such obligation.

Except for purposes of paragraph (1)(B), any reference to an obligation in subparagraph (B) of this paragraph shall be treated as including a reference to stock.

(4) Debt instrument. For purposes of this subsection, the term "debt instrument" means any instrument which is a debt instrument as defined in section 1275(a).

(5) Regulations. The Secretary shall prescribe such regulations as may be appropriate to carry out the purposes of this subsection and subsection (e)(5), including—

(A) regulations providing for modifications to the provisions of this subsection and subsection (e)(5) in the case of varying rates of interest, put or call options, indefinite maturities, contingent payments, assumptions of debt instruments, conversion rights, or other circumstances where such modifications are appropriate to carry out the purposes of this subsection and subsection (e)(5), and

(B) regulations to prevent avoidance of the purposes of this subsection and subsection (e)(5) through the use of issuers other than C corporations, agreements to borrow amounts due under the debt instrument, or other arrangements.

(j) Limitation of deduction for interest on certain indebtedness.

(1) Limitation.

(A) In general. If this subsection applies to any corporation for any taxable year, no deduction shall be allowed under this chapter for disqualified interest paid or accrued by such corporation during such taxable year. The amount disallowed under the preceding sentence shall not exceed the corporation's excess interest expense for the taxable year.

(B) Disallowed amount carried to succeeding taxable year. Any amount disallowed under subparagraph (A) for any taxable year shall be treated as disqualified interest paid or accrued in the succeeding taxable year (and clause (ii) of paragraph (2)(A) shall not apply for purposes of applying this subsection to the amount so treated).

(2) Corporations to which subsection applies.

(A) In general. This subsection shall apply to any corporation for any taxable year if—

(i) such corporation has excess interest expense for such taxable year, and

(ii) the ratio of debt to equity of such corporation as of the close of such taxable year (or on any other day during the taxable year as the Secretary may by regulations prescribe) exceeds 1.5 to 1.

(B) Excess interest expense.

(i) In general. For purposes of this subsection, the term "excess interest expense" means the excess (if any) of—

(I) the corporation's net interest expense, over

(II) the sum of 50 percent of the adjusted taxable income of the corporation plus any excess limitation carryforward under clause (ii).

(ii) Excess limitation carryforward. If a corporation has an excess limitation for any taxable year, the amount of such excess limitation shall be an excess limitation carryforward to the 1st succeeding taxable year and to the 2nd and 3rd succeeding taxable years to the extent not previously taken into account under this clause. The amount of such a carryforward taken into account for any such succeeding taxable year shall not exceed the excess interest expense for such succeeding taxable year (determined without regard to the carryforward from the taxable year of such excess limitation).

(iii) Excess limitation. For purposes of clause (ii), the term "excess limitation" means the excess (if any) of—

(I) 50 percent of the adjusted taxable income of the corporation, over

(II) the corporation's net interest expense.

(C) Ratio of debt to equity. For purposes of this paragraph, the term "ratio of debt to equity" means the ratio which the total indebtedness of the corporation bears to the sum of its money and all other assets reduced (but not below zero) by such total indebtedness. For purposes of the preceding sentence—

(i) the amount taken into account with respect to any asset shall be the adjusted basis thereof for purposes of determining gain,

(ii) the amount taken into account with respect to any indebtedness with original issue discount shall be its issue price plus the portion of the original issue discount previously accrued as determined under the rules of section 1272 (determined without regard to subsection (a)(7) or (b)(4) thereof), and

(iii) there shall be such other adjustments as the Secretary may by regulations prescribe.

(3) Disqualified interest. For purposes of this subsection, the term "disqualified interest" means—

(A) any interest paid or accrued by the taxpayer (directly or indirectly) to a related person if no tax is imposed by this subtitle with respect to such interest,

(B) any interest paid or accrued by the taxpayer with respect to any indebtedness to a person who is not a related person if—

(i) there is a disqualified guarantee of such indebtedness, and

(ii) no gross basis tax is imposed by this subtitle with respect to such interest, and

(C) any interest paid or accrued (directly or indirectly) by a taxable REIT subsidiary (as defined in section 856(l)) of a real estate investment trust to such trust.

(4) Related person. For purposes of this subsection—

(A) In general. Except as provided in subparagraph (B), the term "related person" means any person who is related (within the meaning of section 267(b) or 707(b)(1)) to the taxpayer.

(B) Special rule for certain partnerships.

(i) In general. Any interest paid or accrued to a partnership which (without regard to this subparagraph) is a related person shall not be treated as paid or accrued to a related person if less than 10 percent of the profits and capital interests in such partnership are held by persons with respect to whom no tax is imposed by this subtitle on such interest. The preceding sentence shall not apply to any interest allocable to any partner in such partnership who is a related person to the taxpayer.

(ii) Special rule where treaty reduction. If any treaty between the United States and any foreign country reduces the rate of tax imposed by this subtitle on a partner's share of any interest paid or accrued to a partnership, such partner's interests in such partnership shall, for purposes of clause (i), be treated as held in part by a tax-exempt person and in part by a taxable person under rules similar to the rules of paragraph (5)(B).

(5) Special rules for determining whether interest is subject to tax.

(A) Treatment of pass-thru entities. In the case of any interest paid or accrued to a partnership, the determination of whether any tax is imposed by this subtitle on such interest shall be made at the partner level. Rules similar to the rules of the preceding sentence shall apply in the case of any pass-thru entity other than a partnership and in the case of tiered partnerships and other entities.

(B) Interest treated as tax-exempt to extent of treaty reduction. If any treaty between the United States and any foreign country reduces the rate of tax imposed by this subtitle on any interest paid or accrued by the taxpayer, such interest shall be treated as interest on which no tax is imposed by this subtitle to the extent of the same proportion of such interest as—

(i) the rate of tax imposed without regard to such treaty, reduced by the rate of tax imposed under the treaty, bears to

(ii) the rate of tax imposed without regard to the treaty.

(6) Other definitions and special rules. For purposes of this subsection—

(A) Adjusted taxable income. The term "adjusted taxable income" means the taxable income of the taxpayer—

(i) computed without regard to—

(I) any deduction allowable under this chapter for the net interest expense,

(II) the amount of any net operating loss deduction under section 172,

(III) any deduction allowable under section 199, and

(IV) any deduction allowable for depreciation, amortization, or depletion, and

(ii) computed with such other adjustments as the Secretary may by regulations prescribe.

(B) Net interest expense. The term "net interest expense" means the excess (if any) of—

(i) the interest paid or accrued by the taxpayer during the taxable year, over

(ii) the amount of interest includible in the gross income of such taxpayer for such taxable year.

The Secretary may by regulations provide for adjustments in determining the amount of net interest expense.

(C) Treatment of affiliated group. All members of the same affiliated group (within the meaning of section 1504(a)) shall be treated as 1 taxpayer.

(D) Disqualified guarantee.

(i) In general. Except as provided in clause (ii), the term "disqualified guarantee" means any guarantee by a related person which is—

(I) an organization exempt from taxation under this subtitle, or

(II) a foreign person.

(ii) Exceptions. The term "disqualified guarantee" shall not include a guarantee—

(I) in any circumstances identified by the Secretary by regulation, where the interest on the indebtedness would have been subject to a net basis tax if the interest had been paid to the guarantor, or

(II) if the taxpayer owns a controlling interest in the guarantor.

For purposes of subclause (II), except as provided in regulations, the term "a controlling interest" means direct or indirect ownership of at least 80 percent of the total voting power and value of all classes of stock of a corporation, or 80 percent of the profit and capital interests in any other entity. For purposes of the preceding sentence, the rules of paragraphs (1) and (5) of section 267(c) shall apply; except that such rules shall also apply to interest in entities other than corporations.

(iii) Guarantee. Except as provided in regulations, the term "guarantee" includes any arrangement under which a person (directly or indirectly through an entity or otherwise) assures, on a conditional or unconditional basis, the payment of another person's obligation under any indebtedness.

(E) Gross basis and net basis taxation.

(i) Gross basis tax. The term "gross basis tax" means any tax imposed by this subtitle which is determined by reference to the gross amount of any item of income without any reduction for any deduction allowed by this subtitle.

(ii) Net basis tax. The term "net basis tax" means any tax imposed by this subtitle which is not a gross basis tax.

(7) Coordination with passive loss rules, etc. This subsection shall be applied before sections 465 and 469.

(8) Treatment of corporate partners. Except to the extent provided by regulations, in applying this subsection to a corporation which owns (directly or indirectly) an interest in a partnership—

(A) such corporation's distributive share of interest income paid or accrued to such partnership shall be treated as interest income paid or accrued to such corporation,

(B) such corporation's distributive share of interest paid or accrued by such partnership shall be treated as interest paid or accrued by such corporation, and

(C) such corporation's share of the liabilities of such partnership shall be treated as liabilities of such corporation.

(9) Regulations. The Secretary shall prescribe such regulations as may be appropriate to carry out the purposes of this subsection, including—

(A) such regulations as may be appropriate to prevent the avoidance of the purposes of this subsection,

(B) regulations providing such adjustments in the case of corporations which are members of an affiliated group as may be appropriate to carry out the purposes of this subsection,

(C) regulations for the coordination of this subsection with section 884, and

(D) regulations providing for the reallocation of shares of partnership indebtedness, or distributive shares of the partnership's interest income or interest expense.

(k) Section 6166 interest.

No deduction shall be allowed under this section for any interest payable under section 6601 on any unpaid portion of the tax imposed by section 2001 for the period during which an extension of time for payment of such tax is in effect under section 6166.

(l) Disallowance of deduction on certain debt instruments of corporations.

(1) In general. No deduction shall be allowed under this chapter for any interest paid or accrued on a disqualified debt instrument.

(2) Disqualified debt instrument. For purposes of this subsection, the term "disqualified debt instrument" means any indebtedness of a corporation which is payable in equity of the issuer or a related party or equity held by the issuer (or any related party) in any other person.

(3) Special rules for amounts payable in equity. For purposes of paragraph (2), indebtedness shall be treated as payable in equity of the issuer or any other person only if—

(A) a substantial amount of the principal or interest is required to be paid or converted, or at the option of the issuer or a related party is payable in, or convertible into, such equity,

(B) a substantial amount of the principal or interest is required to be determined, or at the option of the issuer or a related party is determined, by reference to the value of such equity, or

(C) the indebtedness is part of an arrangement which is reasonably expected to result in a transaction described in subparagraph (A) or (B).

For purposes of this paragraph, principal or interest shall be treated as required to be so paid, converted, or determined if it may be required at the option of the holder or a related party and there is a substantial certainty the option will be exercised.

(4) Capitalization allowed with respect to equity of persons other than issuer and related parties. If the disqualified debt instrument of a corporation is payable in equity held by the issuer (or any related party) in any other person (other than a related party), the basis of such equity shall be increased by the amount not allowed as a deduction by reason of paragraph (1) with respect to the instrument.

(5) Exception for certain instruments issued by dealers in securities. For purposes of this subsection, the term "disqualified debt instrument" does not include indebtedness issued by a dealer in securities (or a related party) which is payable in, or by reference to, equity (other than equity of the issuer or a related party) held by such dealer in its capacity as a dealer in securities. For purposes of this paragraph, the term "dealer in securities" has the meaning given such term by section 475.

(6) Related party. For purposes of this subsection, a person is a related party with respect to another person if such person bears a relationship to such other person described in section 267(b) or 707(b).

(7) Regulations. The Secretary shall prescribe such regulations as may be necessary or appropriate to carry out the purposes of this subsection, including regulations preventing avoidance of this subsection through the use of an issuer other than a corporation.

(m) Interest on unpaid taxes attributable to nondisclosed reportable transactions.

No deduction shall be allowed under this chapter for any interest paid or accrued under section 6601 on any underpayment of tax which is attributable to the portion of any reportable transaction understatement (as defined in section 6662A(b)) with respect to which the requirement of section 6664(d)(2)(A) is not met.

(n) Cross references.

(1) For disallowance of certain amounts paid in connection with insurance, endowment, or annuity contracts, see section 264.

(2) For disallowance of deduction for interest relating to tax-exempt income, see section 265(a)(2).

(3) For disallowance of deduction for carrying charges chargeable to capital account, see section 266.

(4) For disallowance of interest with respect to transactions between related taxpayers, see section 267.

(5) For treatment of redeemable ground rents and real property held subject to liabilities under redeemable ground rents, see section 1055.

In 2010, P.L. 111-312, Sec. 102(a), substituted "December 31, 2012" for "December 31, 2010" in Sec. 303 of P.L. 108-27 [see below] effective as if included in the enactment of P.L. 108-27.
—P.L. 111-312, Sec. 759(a), substituted "December 31, 2011" for "December 31, 2010" in clause (h)(3)(E)(iv), effective for amounts paid or accrued after 12/31/2010.
—P.L. 111-147, Sec. 502(a)(1), deleted subpara. (f)(2)(B), and redesignated subpara. (f)(2)(C) as subpara. (f)(2)(B)
Prior to deletion, subpara. (f)(2)(B) read as follows:

Deductions   Code Sec. 163

"(B) Certain obligations not included. An obligation is described in this subparagraph if—

"(i) there are arrangements reasonably designed to ensure that such obligation will be sold (or resold in connection with the original issue) only to a person who is not a United States person, and

"(ii) in the case of an obligation not in registered form—

"(I) interest on such obligation is payable only outside the United States and its possessions, and

"(II) on the face of such obligation there is a statement that any United States person who holds such obligation will be subject to limitations under the United States income tax laws." ... Sec. 502(a)(2)(B), added "or" at the end of clause (f)(2)(A)(ii), substituted a period for ", or" at the end of clause (f)(2)(A)(iii), and deleted clause (f)(2)(A)(iv)

Prior to deletion, clause (f)(2)(A)(iv) read as follows:

"(iv) is described in subparagraph (B)." ... Sec. 502(a)(2)(C)(i), deleted ", and subparagraph (B)," in the matter preceding clause (f)(2)(B)(i) ... Sec. 502(a)(2)(C)(ii), amended clause (f)(2)(B)(i)

Prior to amendment, clause (f)(2)(B)(i) read as follows:

"(i) there are arrangements reasonably designed to ensure that such obligation will be sold (or resold in connection with the original issue) only to a person who is not a United States person, and" ... Sec. 502(c), added matter before the period at the end of para. (f)(3), effective for obligations issued after the date which is 2 years after 3/18/2010.

In **2009**, P.L. 111-5, Sec. 1232(a), redesignated subpara. (e)(5)(F) as subpara. (e)(5)(G), and added subpara. (e)(5)(F), effective for obligations issued after 8/31/2008, in tax. yrs. end. after such date.

—P.L. 111-5, Sec. 1232(b)(1), added "(i)" after "regulation" in para. (i)(1) ... Sec. 1232(b)(2), added "or (ii) permit, on a temporary basis, a rate to be used with respect to any debt instrument which is higher than the applicable Federal rate if the Secretary determines that such rate is appropriate in light of distressed conditions in the debt capital markets" before the period in para. (i)(1), effective for obligations issued after 12/31/2009, in tax. yrs. end. after such date.

In **2007**, P.L. 110-142, Sec. 3(a), substituted "December 31, 2010" for "December 31, 2007" in subclause (h)(3)(E)(iv)(I), effective for amounts paid or accrued after 12/31/2007.

In **2006**, P.L. 109-432, Sec. 419(a), added subpara. (h)(3)(E) ... Sec. 419(b), added subpara. (h)(4)(E) and subpara. (h)(4)(F), effective for amounts paid or accrued after 12/31/2006.

—P.L. 109-222, Sec. 102, substituted "December 31, 2010" for "December 31, 2008" in Sec. 303 of P.L. 108-27 [see below], effective 5/17/2006.

—P.L. 109-222, Sec. 501(a), redesignated para. (j)(8) as para. (j)(9), and added para. (j)(8) ... Sec. 501(b), deleted "and" at the end of subpara. (j)(9)(B) [as redesignated by Sec. 501(a) of this Act, see above], substituted ", and" for the period at the end of subpara. (j)(9)(C) [as redesignated by Sec. 501(a) of this Act, see above], and added subpara. (j)(9)(D), effective for tax. yrs. begin. on or after 5/17/2006.

In **2005**, P.L. 109-135, Sec. 403(a)(15), deleted "and" at the end of subclause (j)(6)(A)(i)(II), redesignated subclause (j)(6)(A)(i)(III) as (IV), and added subclause (j)(6)(A)(i)(III), effective for tax. yrs. begin. after 12/31/2004 as if included in Sec. 102 of the American Jobs Creation Act of 2004, P.L. 108-357.

In **2004**, P.L. 108-357, Sec. 424, of this Act, reads as follows:

"SEC. 424. STUDY OF EARNINGS STRIPPING PROVISIONS.

"*(a) In general.* The Secretary of the Treasury or the Secretary's delegate shall conduct a study of the effectiveness of the provisions of the Internal Revenue Code of 1986 applicable to earnings stripping, including a study of—

"(1) the effectiveness of section 163(j) of such Code in preventing the shifting of income outside the United States,

"(2) whether any deficiencies of such provisions place United States-based businesses at a competitive disadvantage relative to foreign-based businesses,

"(3) the impact of earnings stripping activities on the United States tax base,

"(4) whether laws of foreign countries facilitate stripping of earnings out of the United States, and

"(5) whether changes to the earning stripping rules would affect jobs in the United States.

"*(b) Report.* Not later than June 30, 2005, the Secretary shall submit to the Congress a report of the study conducted under this section, including specific recommendations as to how to improve the provisions of such Code applicable to earnings stripping."

—P.L. 108-357, Sec. 838(a), redesignated subsec. (m) as (n), and added subsec. (m), effective for transactions in tax. yrs. begin. after 10/22/2004.

—P.L. 108-357, Sec. 841(a), redesignated subpara. (e)(3)(B) as (e)(3)(C) and added subpara. (e)(3)(B), effective for payments accrued on or after 10/22/2004.

—P.L. 108-357, Sec. 845(a), added "or equity held by the issuer (or any related party) in any other person" after "or a related party" in para. (l)(2) ... Sec. 845(b), redesignated paras. (l)(4)-(5) as (l)(5)-(6) and added para. (l)(4) ... Sec. 845(c), redesignated paras. (l)(5)-(6) as (l)(6)-(7) [as redesignated by Sec. 845(b) of this Act, see above] and added para. (l)(5) ... Sec. 845(d), substituted "or any other person" for "or a related party" in para. (l)(3), effective for debt instruments issued after 10/3/2004.

In **2003**, P.L. 108-27, Sec. 302(b), added a flush sentence at the end of subpara. (d)(4)(B), effective for tax. yrs. begin. after 12/31/2002. Sec. 302(f)(2) of this Act, provides:

"(2) Regulated investment companies and real estate investment trusts. In the case of a regulated investment company or a real estate investment trust, the amendments made by this section shall apply to taxable years ending after December 31, 2002; except that dividends received by such a company or trust on or before such date shall not be treated as qualified dividend income (as defined in section 1(h)(11)(B) of the Internal Revenue Code of 1986, as added by this Act)."

—P.L. 108-27, Sec. 303, of this Act [as amended by Sec. 102 of P.L. 109-222, and Sec. 102(a), P.L. 111-312, see above], reads as follows:

"SEC. 303. SUNSET OF TITLE. All provisions of, and amendments made by, this title [Secs. 301 and 302] shall not apply to taxable years beginning after December 31, 2012, and the Internal Revenue Code of 1986 shall be applied and administered to such years as if such provisions and amendments had never been enacted."

In **1999**, P.L. 106-170, Sec. 544, deleted "and" at the end of subpara. (j)(3)(A), substituted ", and" for the period at the end of subpara. (j)(3)(B) and added subpara. (j)(3)(C), effective for tax. yrs. begin. after 12/31/2000.

In **1998**, P.L. 105-277, Sec. 4003(a)(1), deleted "and" at the end of subpara. (h)(2)(D), substituted ", and" for the period at the end of subpara. (h)(2)(E), and added subpara. (h)(2)(F), effective as provided in Sec. 202(e) of P.L. 105-34, which reads as follows:

"(e) Effective date. The amendments made by this section shall apply to any qualified education loan (as defined in section 221(e)(1) of the Internal Revenue Code of 1986, as added by this section) incurred on, before, or after the date of the enactment of this Act, but only with respect to—

"(1) any loan interest payment due and paid after December 31, 1997, and

"(2) the portion of the 60-month period referred to in section 221(d) of the Internal Revenue Code of 1986 (as added by this section) after December 31, 1997."

—P.L. 105-206, Sec. 6005(e)(3), added "on or" before "before" each place it appeared in the heading and text of Sec. 312(d)(2)[sic (e)] of P.L. 105-34, see below.

In **1997**, P.L. 105-34, Sec. 312(d)(1), substituted "section 121" for "section 1034" in subclause (h)(4)(A)(i)(I), effective for sales and exchanges after 5/6/97, except as provided by Secs. 312(d)(2)-(4) [sic (e)(2)-(4)] of this Act [as amended by Sec. 6005(e)(3), 105-206, see above], which read as follows:

"(2) Sales on or before date of enactment. At the election of the taxpayer, the amendments made by this section shall not apply to any sale or exchange on or before the date of the enactment of this Act.

"(3) Certain sales within 2 years after date of enactment. Section 121 of the Internal Revenue Code of 1986 (as amended by this section) shall be applied without regard to subsection (c)(2)(B) thereof in the case of any sale or exchange of property during the 2-year period beginning on the date of the enactment of this Act if the taxpayer held such property on the date of the enactment of this Act and fails to meet the ownership and use requirements of subsection (a) thereof with respect to such property.

"(4) Binding contracts. At the election of the taxpayer, the amendments made by this section shall not apply to a sale or exchange after the date of the enactment of this Act, if—

"(A) such sale or exchange is pursuant to a contract which was binding on such date, or

"(B) without regard to such amendments, gain would not be recognized under section 1034 of the Internal Revenue Code of 1986 (as in effect on the day before the date of the enactment of this Act) on such sale or exchange by reason of a new residence acquired on or before such date or with respect to the acquisition of which by the taxpayer a binding contract was in effect on such date.

This paragraph shall not apply to any sale or exchange by an individual if the treatment provided by section 877(a)(1) of the Internal Revenue Code of 1986 applies to such individual."

—P.L. 105-34, Sec. 503(b)(2)(A), redesignated subsec. (k) as subsec. (l) and added new subsec. (k) ... Sec. 503(b)(2)(B), deleted "or 6166 or under section 6166A (as in effect before its repeal by the Economic Recovery Tax Act of 1981)" after "section 6163" in subpara. (h)(2)(E), effective for estates of decedents dying after 12/31/97, except as provided in Sec. 503(d)(2) of this Act, which reads as follows:

"(2) Election.—In the case of the estate of any decedent dying before January 1, 1998, with respect to which there is an election under section 6166 of the Internal Revenue Code of 1986, the executor of the estate may elect to have the amendments made by this section apply with respect to installments due after the effective date of the election; except that the 2-percent portion of such installments shall be equal to the amount which would be the 4-percent portion of such installments without regard to such election. Such an election shall be made before January 1, 1999 in the manner prescribed by the Secretary of the Treasury and, once made, is irrevocable."

—P.L. 105-34, Sec. 1005(a), redesignated subsec. (l) [as redesignated] as subsec. (m) and added new subsec. (l), effective for disqualified debt instruments issued after 6/8/97, except as provided in Sec. 1005(b)(2) of this Act, which reads as follows:

"(2) Transition rule.—The amendment made by this section shall not apply to any instrument issued after June 8, 1997, if such instrument is—

"(A) issued pursuant to a written agreement which was binding on such date and at all times thereafter,

"(B) described in a ruling request submitted to the Internal Revenue Service on or before such date, or

"(C) described on or before such date in a public announcement or in a filing with the Securities and Exchange Commission required solely by reason of the issuance."

—P.L. 105-34, Sec. 1604(g)(1), substituted "clause (ii)" for "clause (i)" in clause (j)(2)(B)(iii), effective date of enactment.

In **1996**, P.L. 104-188, Sec. 1703(n)(4), substituted "which is" for "which is a" in clause (j)(6)(E)(ii), effective for interest accrued in tax. yrs. begin. after 12/31/93.

1,541

—P.L. 104-188, Sec. 1704(f)(2)(A), added "(and clause (ii) of paragraph (2)(A) shall not apply for purposes of applying this subsection to the amount so treated)" before the period at the end of subpara. (j)(1)(B).... Sec. 1704(f)(2)(B), redesignated para. (j)(7) as (j)(8) and added new para. (j)(7), effective for interest paid or accrued in tax. yrs. begin. after 7/10/89, except as provided in Sec. 7210(b)(2) of P.L. 101-239, reproduced below.

In 1993, P.L. 103-66, Sec. 13206(d)(1), amended subpara. (d)(4)(B), effective for tax. yrs. begin. after 12/31/92.

Prior to amendment, subpara. (d)(4)(B) read as follows:

"(B) Investment income. The term 'investment income' means the sum of—
"(i) gross income (other than gain taken into account under clause (ii)) from property held for investment, and
"(ii) any net gain attributable to the disposition of property held for investment."

—P.L. 103-66, Sec. 13228(a), amended para. (j)(3)... Sec. 13228(b), added subparas. (j)(6)(D) and (E)... Sec. 13228(c)(1), deleted "to a related person" after "any interest paid or accrued by the taxpayer" in subpara. (j)(5)(B)... Sec. 13228(c)(2), amended the heading of subsec. (j), effective for interest paid or accrued in tax. yrs. begin. after 12/31/93.

Prior to amendment, para. (j)(3) read as follows:

"(3) Disqualified interest. For purposes of this subsection—
"(A) In general. Except as provided in subparagraph (B), the term 'disqualified interest' means any interest paid or accrued by the taxpayer (directly or indirectly) to a related person if no tax is imposed by this subtitle with respect to such interest.
"(B) Exception for certain existing indebtedness. The term 'disqualified interest' does not include any interest paid or accrued under indebtedness with a fixed term—
"(i) which was issued on or before July 10, 1989, or
"(ii) which was issued after such date pursuant to a written binding contract in effect on such date and all times thereafter before such indebtedness was issued."

Prior to amendment, the heading of subsec. (j) read as follows:

"(j) Limitation on deduction for certain interest paid by corporation to related person."

In 1990, P.L. 101-508, Sec. 11701(b)(1), amended the last sentence of subpara. (e)(5)(A)... Sec. 11701(b)(2)(A), deleted "(or stock)" after "obligation" each place it appeared in subpara. (i)(3)(B)... Sec. 11701(b)(2)(B), added the last sentence to para. (i)(3), effective for instruments issued after 7/10/89 except as provided in Sec. 7302(c)(2) of P.L. 101-239, reproduced below.

Prior to amendment, the last sentence of subpara. (e)(5)(A) read as follows:

"For purposes of clause (ii), rules similar to the rules of subsection (i)(3)(B) shall apply in determining the time when the original issue discount is paid."

—P.L. 101-508, Sec. 11701(c)(1), substituted "reduced (but not below zero) by such" for "less such" in subpara. (j)(2)(C)... Sec. 11701(c)(2), substituted "or on any other day" for "and on such other days" in clause (j)(2)(A)(ii), effective for interest paid or accrued in tax. yrs. begin. after 7/10/89 except as provided in Sec 7210(b)(2) of P.L. 101-239, reproduced below.

In 1989, P.L. 101-239, Sec. 7202(a), redesignated para. (e)(5) as (e)(6) and added new para. (e)(5)... Sec. 7202(b), redesignated subsec. (i) as (j) and added new subsec. (i), effective for instruments issued after 7/10/89 except as provided in Sec. 7202(c)(2) of this Act which reads as follows:

"(2) Exceptions.—
"(A) The amendments made by this section shall not apply to any instrument if—
"(i) such instrument is issued in connection with an acquisition—
"(I) which is made on or before July 10, 1989,
"(II) for which there was a written binding contract in effect on July 10, 1989, and at all times thereafter before such acquisition, or
"(III) for which a tender offer was filed with the Securities and Exchange Commission on or before July 10, 1989,
"(ii) the term of such instrument is not greater than—
"(I) the term specified in the written documents described in clause (iii), or
"(II) if no term is determined under subclause (I), 10 years, and
"(iii) the use of such instrument in connection with such acquisition (and the maximum amount of proceeds from such instrument) was determined on or before July 10, 1989, and such determination is evidenced by written documents—
"(I) which were transmitted on or before July 10, 1989, between the issuer and any governmental regulatory bodies or prospective parties to the issuance or acquisition, and
"(II) which are customarily used for the type of acquisition or financing involved.
"(B) The amendments made by this section shall not apply to any instrument issued pursuant to the terms of a debt instrument issued on or before July 10, 1989, or described in subparagraph (A) or (D).
"(C) The amendments made by this section shall not apply to any instrument issued to refinance an original issue discount debt instrument to which the amendments made by this section do not apply if—
"(i) the maturity date of the refinancing instrument is not later than the maturity date of the refinanced instrument,
"(ii) the issue price of the refinancing instrument does not exceed the adjusted issue price of the refinanced instrument,
"(iii) the stated redemption price at maturity of the refinancing instrument is not greater than the stated redemption price at maturity of the refinanced instrument, and

"(iv) the interest payments required under the refinancing instrument before maturity are not less than (and are paid not later than) the interest payments required under the refinanced instrument.
"(D) The amendments made by this section shall not apply to instruments issued after July 10, 1989, pursuant to a reorganization plan in a title 11 or similar case (as defined in section 368(a)(3) of the Internal Revenue Code of 1986) if the amount of proceeds of such instruments, and the maturities of such instruments, do not exceed the amount or maturities specified in the last reorganization plan filed in such case on or before July 10, 1989."

—P.L. 101-239, Sec. 7210(a), redesignated subsec. (j) [as redesignated by Sec. 7202(b) of this Act, see above] as subsec. (k) and added new subsec. (j), effective for interest paid or accrued in tax. yrs. begin. after 7/10/89 except as provided in Sec. 7210(b)(2) of this Act, which reads as follows:

"(2) Special rule for demand loans, etc.—In the case of any demand loan (or other loan without a fixed term) which was outstanding on July 10, 1989, interest on such loan to the extent attributable to periods before September 1, 1989, shall not be treated as disqualified interest for purposes of section 163(j) of the Internal Revenue Code of 1986 (as added by subsection (a))."

In 1988, P.L. 100-647, Sec. 1005(c)(1), substituted "properly allocable to" for "incurred or continued to purchase or carry" in subpara. (d)(3)(A)... Sec. 1005(c)(2), amended subpara. (d)(4)(B)... Sec. 1005(c)(3), amended subpara. (d)(6)(A)... Sec. 1005(c)(4), substituted "properly allocable to" for "incurred or continued in connection with the conduct of" in subpara. (h)(2)(A)... Sec. 1005(c)(5), amended subpara. (h)(3)(C) [as in effect before amended by Sec. 10102 of P.L. 100-203, see below]... Sec. 1005(c)(6)(A), amended the heading of para. (h)(5) [as in effect before amended by Sec. 10102 of P.L. 100-203, see below]... Sec. 1005(c)(6)(B)(i), deleted "For purposes of this section—" after "Qualified residence." in subpara. (h)(5)(A) [as in effect before amended by Sec. 10102 of P.L.100-203, see below]... Sec. 1005(c)(6)(B)(ii), substituted "Any" for "For purposes of this paragraph, any" in subpara. (h)(5)(B) [as in effect before amended by Sec. 10102 of P.L. 100-203, see below]... Sec. 1005(c)(7), deleted "used or" before "rented" in the heading of clause (h)(5)(A)(iii), and deleted "or use" before "a dwelling" in clause (h)(5)(A)(iii) [as in effect before amended by Sec. 10102 of P.L. 100-203, see below]... Sec. 1005(c)(8), added subparas. (C) and (D) to para. (h)(5) [as in effect before amended by Sec. 10102 of 100-203,, see below]... Sec. 1005(c)(9), substituted "(but for this paragraph)" for "(but for this subsection)" in para. (h)(6) [before redesignated as para. (h)(5) by Sec. 2004(b)(1) of this Act]... Sec. 1005(c)(12), added "or under section 6166A (as in effect before its repeal by the Economic Recovery Tax Act of 1981)" before the period in subpara. (h)(2)(E), effective for tax. yrs. begin. after 12/31/86. Sec. 1005(c)(11)(A)-(C) of this Act provides:

"(11) For—
"(A) any amount was disallowed as a deduction under section 163(d) of the Internal Revenue Code of 1954 (as in effect on the day before the date of the enactment of the Reform Act),
"(B) such amount would (but for this paragraph) be treated as investment interest paid or accrued by the taxpayer in the taxpayer's first taxable year beginning after December 31, 1986, and
"(C) the taxpayer makes an election under this paragraph at such time and in such manner as the Secretary of the Treasury or his delegate shall prescribe,
to the extent such amount is attributable to an activity subject to the limitations of section 469 of the 1986 Code, such amount shall not be treated as investment interest but shall be treated as a deduction allocable to such activity for such first taxable year. Subsection (m) of section 469 of the 1986 Code and section 501(c)(2) of the Reform Act shall not apply to any amount so treated."

Sec. 1005(c)(13) of this Act provides:

"(13) For purposes of applying the amendments made by this subsection [Sec. 1005(c)] and the amendments made by section 10102 of the Revenue Act of 1987, the provisions of this subsection shall be treated as having been enacted immediately before the enactment of the Revenue Act of 1987."

Sec. 1005(c)(14) of this Act provides:

"(14)(A) For purposes of applying section 163(h) of the 1986 Code to any taxable year beginning during 1987, if, incident to a divorce or legal separation—
"(i) an individual acquires the interest of a spouse or former spouse in a qualified residence in a transfer to which section 1041 of the 1986 Code applies, and
"(ii) such individual incurs indebtedness which is secured by such qualified residence,
the amount determined under paragraph (3)(B)(ii)(I) of section 163(h) of the 1986 Code (as in effect before the amendments made by the Revenue Act of 1987) with respect to such qualified residence shall be increased by the amount determined under subparagraph (B).
"(B) The amount determined under this subparagraph shall be equal to the excess (if any) of—
"(i) the lesser of the amount of the indebtedness described in subparagraph (A)(ii), or the fair market value of the spouse's or former spouse's interest in the qualified residence as of the time of the transfer, over
"(ii) the basis of the spouse or former spouse in such interest in such residence (adjusted only by the cost of any improvements to such residence)."

Prior to amendment, subpara. (d)(4)(B) read as follows:

"(B) Investment income. The term 'investment income' means the sum of—
"(i) gross income (other than gain described in clause (ii)) from property held for investment, and
"(ii) any net gain attributable to the disposition of property held for investment, but only to the extent such amounts are not derived from the conduct of a trade or business."

Prior to amendment, subpara. (d)(6)(A) read as follows:

"(A) In general. The amount of interest disallowed under this subsection for any such taxable year shall be equal to the sum of—

"(i) the applicable percentage of the amount which (without regard to this paragraph) is not allowed as a deduction under this subsection for the taxable year to the extent such amount does not exceed the ceiling amount,

"(ii) the amount which (without regard to this paragraph) is not allowed as a deduction under this subsection in excess of the ceiling amount, plus

"(iii) the amount of any carryforward to such taxable year under paragraph (2) with respect to which a deduction was disallowed under this subsection for a preceding taxable year.

For purposes of this subparagraph, the amount under clause (i) or (ii) shall be computed without regard to the amount described in clause (iii)."

Prior to amendment, subpara. (h)(3)(C) [added by Sec. 511(b) of P.L. 99-514] read as follows:

"(C) Cost not less than balance of indebtedness incurred on or before August 16, 1986. The amount under subparagraph (B)(ii)(I) at any time after August 16, 1986, shall not be less than the outstanding aggregate principal amount (as of such time) of indebtedness which was incurred on or before August 16, 1986, and which was secured by the qualified residence on August 16, 1986."

Prior to amendment, the heading of para. (h)(5) read as follows:

"(5) Other definitions and special rules."

—P.L. 100-647, Sec. 1006(u)(1), substituted "paragraph (7)" for "paragraph (6)" in subpara. (e)(2)(B), effective for debt instruments issued after 12/31/86, in tax. yrs. end. after 12/31/86.

—P.L. 100-647, Sec. 1009(b)(6), corrected Sec. 902(e)(1) of P.L. 99-514 to amend para. (i)(2) (as redesignated by Sec. 511(b)' of P.L. 99-514) instead of para. (h)(12), see below.

—P.L. 100-647, Sec. 2004(b)(1), redesignated para. (h)(6) as para. (h)(5), effective for tax. yrs. begin. after 12/31/87.

—P.L. 100-647, Sec. 6128(a), amended Sec. 127(g)(3)(B) of P.L. 98-369 [special rules for changes made by Sec. 127(f) of P.L. 98-369] by adding the material following "73-110", effective 11/10/88, see below.

In 1987, P.L. 100-203, Sec. 10102(a), amended para. (h)(3) . . . Sec. 10102(b), deleted para. (h)(4) and redesignated para. (h)(5) as para. (h)(4), effective for tax. yrs. begin. after 12/31/87.

Prior to deletion, para. (h)(3) [as amended by Sec. 1005(c)(5) of P.L.100-647, above] read as follows:

"(3) Qualified residence interest. For purposes of this subsection—

"(A) In general. The term 'qualified residence interest' means interest which is paid or accrued during the taxable year on indebtedness which is secured by any property which (at the time such interest is paid or accrued) is a qualified residence of the taxpayer.

"(B) Limitation on amount of interest. The term 'qualified residence interest' shall not include any interest paid or accrued on indebtedness secured by any qualified residence which is allocable to that portion of the principal amount of such indebtedness which, when added to the outstanding aggregate principal amount of all other indebtedness previously incurred and secured by such qualified residence, exceeds the lesser of—

"(i) the fair market value of such qualified residence, or

"(ii) the sum of—

"(I) the taxpayer's basis in such qualified residence (adjusted only by the cost of any improvements to such residence), plus

"(II) the aggregate amount of qualified indebtedness of the taxpayer with respect to such qualified residence.

"(C) Cost not less than balance of indebtedness incurred on or before August 16, 1986.

"(i) In general. The amount under subparagraph (B)(ii)(I) at any time after August 16, 1986, shall not be less than the outstanding principal amount (as of such time) of indebtedness

"(I) which was incurred on or before August 16, 1986, and which was secured by the qualified residence on August 16, 1986, or

"(II) which is secured by the qualified residence and was incurred after August 16, 1986, to refinance indebtedness described in subclause (I) (or refinanced indebtedness meeting the requirements of this subclause) to the extent (immediately after the refinancing) the principal amount of the indebtedness resulting from the refinancing does not exceed the principal amount of the refinanced indebtedness (immediately before the refinancing).

"(ii) Limitation on period of refinancing. Subclause (II) of clause (i) shall not apply to any indebtedness after—

"(I) the expiration of the term of the indebtedness described in clause (i)(I), or

"(II) if the principal of the indebtedness described in clause (i)(I) is not amortized over its term, the expiration of the term of the 1st refinancing of such indebtedness (or if earlier, the date which is 30 years after the date of such refinancing).

"(D) Time for determination. Except as provided in regulations, any determination under subparagraph (B) shall be made as of the time the indebtedness is incurred."

Prior to amendment, para. (h)(4) read as follows:

"(4) Qualified indebtedness. For purposes of this subsection—

"(A) In general. The term 'qualified indebtedness' means indebtedness secured by a qualified residence of the taxpayer which is incurred after August 16, 1986, to pay for—

"(i) qualified medical expenses, or

"(ii) qualified educational expenses,

which are paid or incurred within a reasonable period of time before or after such indebtedness is incurred.

"(B) Qualified medical expenses. For purposes of this paragraph, the term 'qualified medical expenses' means amounts, not compensated for by insurance or otherwise, incurred for medical care (within the meaning of subparagraphs (A) and (B) of section 213(d)(1)) for the taxpayer, his spouse, or a dependent.

"(C) Qualified educational expenses. For purposes of this paragraph—

"(i) In general. The term 'qualified educational expenses' means qualified tuition and related expenses of the taxpayer, his spouse, or a dependent for attendance at an educational institution described in section 170(b)(1)(A)(ii).

"(ii) Qualified tuition and related expenses. The term 'qualified tuition and related expenses' has the meaning given such term by section 117(b), except that such term shall include any reasonable living expenses while away from home.

"(D) Dependent. For purposes of this paragraph, the term 'dependent' has the meaning given such term by section 152."

—P.L. 100-203, Sec. 10212(b), substituted "469(m)" for "469(l)" in subpara. (d)(4)(E), effective for tax. yrs. begin. after 12/31/86.

In 1986, P.L. 99-514, Sec. 511(a), amended subsec. (d) . . . Sec. 511(b), redesignated subsec. (h) as subsec. (i), and added new subsec. (h), effective for tax. yrs. begin. after 12/31/86.

Prior to amendment, subsec. (d) read as follows:

"(d) Limitation on interest on investment indebtedness.

"(1) In general. In the case of a taxpayer other than a corporation, the amount of investment interest (as defined in paragraph (3)(D)) otherwise allowable as a deduction under this chapter shall be limited, in the following order, to—

"(A) $10,000 ($5,000, in the case of a separate return by a married individual), plus

"(B) the amount of the net investment income (as defined in paragraph (3)(A)), plus the amount (if any) by which the deductions allowable under this section (determined without regard to this subsection) and sections 162, 164(a)(1) or (2), or 212 attributable to property of the taxpayer subject to a net lease exceeds the rental income produced by such property for the taxable year.

In the case of a trust, the $10,000 amount specified in subparagraph (A) shall be zero.

"(2) Carryover of disallowed investment interest. The amount of disallowed investment interest for any taxable year shall be treated as investment interest paid or accrued in the succeeding taxable year.

"(3) Definitions. For purposes of this subsection—

"(A) Net investment income. The term 'net investment income' means the excess of investment income over investment expenses. If the taxpayer has investment interest for the taxable year to which this subsection (as in effect before the Tax Reform Act of 1976) applies, the amount of the net investment income taken into account under this subsection shall be the amount of such income (determined without regard to this sentence) multiplied by a fraction the numerator of which is the excess of the investment interest for the taxable year over the investment interest to which such prior provision applies, and the denominator of which is the investment interest for the taxable year.

"(B) Investment income. The term 'investment income' means—

"(i) the gross income from interest, dividends, rents, and royalties,

"(ii) the net short-term capital gain attributable to the disposition of property held for investment, and

"(iii) any amount treated under sections 1245[,] 1250, and 1254 as ordinary income,

but only to the extent such income, gain, and amounts are not derived from the conduct of a trade or business.

"(C) Investment expenses. The term 'investment expenses' means the deductions allowable under sections 162, 164(a)(1) or (2), 166, 167, 171, 212, or 611 directly connected with the production of investment income. For purposes of this subparagraph, the deduction allowable under section 167 with respect to any property may be treated as the amount which would have been allowable had the taxpayer depreciated the property under the straight line method for each taxable year of its useful life for which the taxpayer has held the property, and the deduction allowable under section 611 with respect to any property may be treated as the amount which would have been allowable had the taxpayer determined the deduction under section 611 without regard to section 613 for each taxable year for which the taxpayer has held the property.

"(D) Investment interest.

"(i) In general. The term 'investment interest' means interest paid or accrued on indebtedness incurred or continued to purchase or carry property held for investment.

"(ii) Certain expenses incurred in connection with short sales. For purposes of clause (i), the term 'interest' includes any amount allowable as a deduction in connection with personal property used in a short sale.

"(E) Disallowed investment interest. The term 'disallowed investment interest' means with respect to any taxable year, the amount not allowable as a deduction solely by reason of the limitation in paragraph (1).

"(4) Special rules.

"(A) Property subject to net lease. For purposes of this subsection, property subject to a lease shall be treated as property held for investment, and not as property used in a trade or business, for a taxable year, if—

"(i) for such taxable year the sum of the deductions of the lessor with respect to such property which are allowable solely by reason of section 162 (other than rents and reimbursed amounts with respect to such property) is less than 15 percent of the rental income produced by such property, or

"(ii) the lessor is either guaranteed a specified return or is guaranteed in whole or in part against loss of income.

"(B) Construction interest. For purposes of this subsection, interest paid or accrued on indebtedness incurred or continued in the construction of property to be used in a trade or business shall not be treated as investment interest.

1,543

"(5) Exceptions. This subsection shall not apply with respect to investment interest, investment income, and investment expenses attributable to a specific item of property, if the indebtedness with respect to such property—

"(A) is for a specified term, and

"(B) was incurred before December 17, 1969, or is incurred after December 16, 1969, pursuant to a written contract or commitment which, on such date and at all times thereafter prior to the incurring of such indebtedness, is binding on the taxpayer.

For taxable years beginning after December 31, 1975, this paragraph shall be applied on an allocation basis rather than a specific item basis.

"(6) Real property leases. For purposes of paragraph (4)(A)—

"(A) if a parcel of real property of the taxpayer is leased under two or more leases, paragraph (4)(A)(i) shall, at the election of the taxpayer, be applied to treating all leased portions of such property as subject to a single lease; and

"(B) at the election of the taxpayer, paragraph (4)(A)(i) shall not apply with respect to real property of the taxpayer which has been in use for more than 5 years.

An election under subparagraph (A) or (B) shall be made at such time and in such manner as the Secretary prescribes by regulations.

"(7) Special rule where taxpayer owns 50 percent or more of enterprise.

"(A) General rule. In the case of any 50 percent owned corporation or partnership, the $10,000 figure specified in paragraph (1) shall be increased by the lesser of—

"(i) $15,000, or

"(ii) the interest paid or accrued during the taxable year on investment indebtedness incurred or continued in connection with the acquisition of the interest in such corporation or partnership.

In the case of a separate return by a married individual, $7,500 shall be substituted for the $15,000 figure in clause (1).

"(B) Ownership requirements. This paragraph shall apply with respect to indebtedness only if the taxpayer, his spouse, and his children own 50 percent or more of the total value of all classes of stock of the corporation or 50 percent or more of all capital interests in the partnership, as the case may be."

—P.L. 99-514, Sec. 902(e)(1), [as amended by Sec. 1009(b)(6) of P.L.100-647, see above] substituted "265(a)(2)" for "265(2)" in para. (4) as redesignated by section 511(b) of this Act, effective for tax. yrs. ending after 12/31/86.

—P.L. 99-514, Sec. 1301(j)(3), substituted "149(a)(3)" for "103(j)(3)" in para. (f)(3), effective for bonds issued after 8/15/86.

—P.L. 99-514, Sec. 1803(a)(4), added subpara. (e)(2)(C), effective for tax. yrs. ending after 7/18/84.

—P.L. 99-514, Sec. 1810(e)(1)(A), added the last sentence to subpara. (e)(3)(A) ... Sec. 1810(e)(1)(B), redesignated para. (e)(4) as para. (e)(5), effective for obligations issued after 6/9/84.

In 1984, P.L. 98-369, Sec. 42(a)(3), amended subsec. (e), effective for tax. yrs. end. after 7/18/84.

Prior to amendment, subsec. (e) read as follows:

"(e) Original issue discount.

"(1) In general. In the case of any bond issued after July 1, 1982, by an issuer (other than a natural person), the portion of the original issue discount with respect to such bond which is allowable as a deduction to the issuer for any taxable year shall be equal to the aggregate daily portions of the original issue discount for days during such taxable year.

"(2) Definitions and special rules. For purposes of this section—

"(A) Bond. The term 'bond' has the meaning given to such term by section 1232A(c)(1).

"(B) Daily portions. The daily portion of the original issue discount for any day shall be determined under section 1232A(a) (without regard to paragraphs (2)(B) and (6) thereof and without regard to the second sentence of section 1232(b)(1))."

—P.L. 98-369, Sec. 56(b), amended subpara. (d)(3)(D), effective for short sales after 7/18/84 in tax. yrs. end. after 7/1/84.

Prior to amendment, subpara. (d)(3)(D) read as follows:

"(D) Investment interest. The term 'investment interest' means interest paid or accrued on indebtedness incurred or continued to purchase or carry property held for investment."

—P.L. 98-369, Sec. 127(f), amended clause (f)(2)(C)(i), effective for interest received after 7/18/84 for obligations issued after 7/18/84, in tax. yrs. end. after 7/18/84. Sec. 127(g)(3) [as amended by Sec. 6128(a) of P.L. 100-647, see above] provides as follows:

"(3) Special rule for certain United States affiliate obligations.

"(A) In general. For purposes of the Internal Revenue Code of 1954, payments of interest on a United States affiliate obligation to an applicable CFC in existence on or before June 22, 1984, shall be treated as payments to a resident of the country in which the applicable CFC is incorporated.

"(B) Exception. Subparagraph (A) shall not apply to any applicable CFC which did not meet requirements which are based on the principles set forth in Revenue Rulings 69-501, 69-377, 70-645, and 73-110 as such principles are applied in Revenue Ruling 86-6, except that the maximum debt-to-equity ratio described in such Revenue Rulings shall be increased from 5-to-1 to 25-to-1.

"(C) Definitions.

"(i) The term 'applicable CFC' has the meaning given such term by section 121(b)(2)(D) of this Act, except that such section shall be applied by substituting 'the date of interest payment' for 'March 31, 1984,' in clause (i) thereof.

"(ii) The term 'United States affiliate obligation' means an obligation described in section 121(b)(2)(F) of this Act which was issued before June 22, 1984."

Prior to amendment, clause (f)(2)(C)(i) read as follows:

"(i) such obligation is of a type which the Secretary has determined by regulations to be used frequently in avoiding Federal taxes, and"

—P.L. 98-369, Sec. 128(c), redesignated para. (e)(3) (as added by Sec. 42(a)(7) of this Act) as para. (e)(4), and added new para. (e)(3), effective for obligations issued after 6/9/84.

—P.L. 98-369, Sec. 612(c), redesignated subsec. (g) as subsec. (h) and added new subsec. (g), effective for interest paid or accrued after 12/31/84, on indebtedness incurred after 12/31/84.

—P.L. 98-369, Sec. 632, provided various exceptions to the amendments made by Title VI of this Act. See note following Code Sec. 103A.

—P.L. 98-369, Sec. 1066, of this Act, provides:

"Sec. 1066. Transitional rule for treatment of certain income from S corporations.

"(a) In general. If—

"(1) a corporation had an election in effect under subchapter S of the Internal Revenue Code of 1954 for the taxable years of such corporation beginning in 1982, 1983, and 1984, and

"(2) a shareholder of such corporation makes an election to have this section apply,

then any qualified income which such shareholder takes into account by reason of holding stock in such corporation for any taxable year of such corporation beginning in 1983 or 1984 shall be treated for purposes of section 163(d) of the Internal Revenue Code of 1954 as such income would have been treated but for the enactment of the Subchapter S Revision Act of 1982.

"(b) Qualified income. For purposes of subsection (a), the term 'qualified income' means any income other than income which is attributable to personal services performed by the shareholder for the corporation.

"(c) Election. The election under subsection (a)(2) shall be made at such time and in such manner as the Secretary of the Treasury or his delegate may by regulations prescribe."

In 1982, P.L. 97-354, Sec. 5(a)(18), deleted subparas. (d)(4)(B) and (C) and redesignated subpara. (d)(4)(D) as subpara. (d)(4)(B), effective for tax. yrs. begin. after 12/31/82.

Prior to deletion, subparas. (d)(4)(B) and (C) read as follows:

"(B) Partnerships. In the case of a partnership, each partner shall, under regulations prescribed by the Secretary, take into account separately his distributive share of the partnership's investment interest and the other items of income and expense taken into account under this subsection.

"(C) Shareholders of electing small business corporations. In the case of an electing small business corporation (as defined in section 1371(b)), the investment interest paid or accrued by such corporation and the other items of income and expense which would be taken into account if this subsection applied to such corporation shall, under regulations prescribed by the Secretary, be treated as investment interest paid or accrued by the shareholders of such corporation and as items of such shareholders, and shall be apportioned pro rata among such shareholders in a manner consistent with section 1374(c)(1)."

—P.L. 97-248, Sec. 231(b), redesignated subsec. (e) as subsec. (f) and added new subsec. (e), effective 9/3/82. Sec. 231(e) of this Act provides:

"(e) Transitional rule.

"For purposes of the amendments made by this section, any evidence of indebtedness issued pursuant to a written commitment which was binding on July 1, 1982, and at all times thereafter shall be treated as issued on July 1, 1982."

—P.L. 97-248, Sec. 310(b)(2), redesignated subsec. (f) as subsec. (g) and added new subsec. (f), effective for obligations issued after 12/31/82. Sec. 310(d)(3) of this Act provides:

"(3) Exception for certain warrants, etc.— The amendments made by subsection (b) shall not apply to any obligations issued after December 31, 1982, on the exercise of a warrant or the conversion of a convertible obligation if such warrant or obligation was offered or sold outside the United States without registration under the Securities Act of 1933 and was issued before August 10, 1982. A rule similar to the rule of the preceding sentence shall also apply in the case of any regulations issued under section 163(f)(2)(C) of the Internal Revenue Code of 1954 (as added by this section) except that the date on which such regulations take effect shall be substituted for 'August 10, 1982'."

In 1976, P.L. 94-455, Sec. 205(c)(3), substituted "1250, and 1254" for "and 1250" in clause (d)(3)(B)(iii) [sic (d)(3)(A)(iii)], effective for tax. yrs. end. after 12/31/75.

—P.L. 94-455, Sec. 209(a)(1), amended paras. (d)(1) and (d)(2) ... Sec. 209(a)(2), added the last sentence in subpara. (d)(3)(A) ... Sec. 209(a)(3), substituted "limitation in paragraph (1)" for "limitations in paragraphs (1) and (2)(A)" in subpara. (d)(3)(E) ... Sec. 209(a)(4), deleted para. (d)(5) and redesignated paras. (d)(6) and (d)(7) as paras. (d)(5) and (d)(6) ... Sec. 209(a)(5), added, the last sentence in redesignated para. (d)(5) ... Sec. 209(a)(7), added new para. (d)(7), effective for tax. yrs. begin. after 12/31/75. Sec. 209(b)(2) of this Act provides as follows:

"(2) Indebtedness incurred before September 11, 1975 — In the case of indebtedness attributable to a specific item of property which—

"(A) is for a specified term, and

"(B) was incurred before September 11, 1975, or is incurred after September 10, 1975, pursuant to a written contract or commitment which on September 11, 1975, and at all times thereafter before the incurring of such indebtedness, is binding on the taxpayer,

the amendments made by this section shall not apply, but section 163(d) of the Internal Revenue Code of 1954 (as in effect before the enactment of this Act) shall apply. For purposes of the preceding sentence, so much of the net investment income (as defined in section 163(d)(3)(A) of such Code) for any taxable year as is not taken into account under section 163(d) of such Code, as amended by this Act, by reason of the last sentence of section 163(d)(3)(A) of such Code, shall be taken into account for purposes of applying such section as in effect before the

Deductions

date of enactment of this Act with respect to interest on indebtedness referred to in the preceding sentence."

Prior to amendment, paras. (d)(1) and (d)(2) read as follows:

"(d) Limitation on interest on investment indebtedness.

"(1) In general. In the case of a taxpayer other than a corporation, the amount of investment interest (as defined in paragraph (3)(D)) otherwise allowable as a deduction under this chapter shall be limited, in the following order, to—

"(A) $25,000 ($12,500, in the case of a separate return by a married individual), plus

"(B) the amount of the net investment income (as defined in paragraph (3)(A)), plus the amount (if any) by which the deductions allowable under this section (determined without regard to this subsection) and sections 162, 164(a)(1) or (2), or 212 attributable to property of the taxpayer subject to a net lease exceeds the rental income produced by such property for the taxable year, plus

"(C) an amount equal to the amount by which the net long-term capital gain exceeds the net short-term capital loss for the taxable year, plus

"(D) one-half of the amount by which investment interest exceeds the sum of the amounts described in subparagraphs (A), (B), and (C).

In the case of a trust, the $25,000 amount specified in subparagraph (A) and in paragraph (2)(A) shall be zero. In determining the amount described in subparagraph (C), only gains and losses attributable to the disposition of property held for investment shall be taken into account.

"(2) Carryover of disallowed investment interest.

"(A) In general. The amount of disallowed investment interest for any taxable year shall be treated as investment interest paid or accrued in the succeeding taxable year. The amount of the interest so treated which is allowable as a deduction by reason of the first sentence of this paragraph for any taxable year shall not exceed one-half of the amount by which—

"(i) the net investment income for such taxable year plus $25,000, exceeds

"(ii) the investment interest paid or accrued during such taxable year (determined without regard to this paragraph) or $25,000, whichever is greater.

"(B) Reduction for capital gain deduction. If—

"(i) an amount of disallowed investment interest treated under subparagraph (A) as investment interest paid or accrued in the taxable year is not allowable as a deduction for such taxable year by reason of the second sentence of subparagraph (A), and

"(ii) the taxpayer is entitled to a deduction under section 1202 for such taxable year (whether or not the taxpayer claims such deduction), the amount of such disallowed investment interest shall be reduced by an amount equal to the amount of the deduction allowable under section 1202."

Prior to amendment, para. (d)(5) read as follows:

"(5) Capital gains. For purposes of sections 1201(b) (relating to alternative capital gains tax), 1202 (relating to deduction for capital gains), and 57(a)(9) (relating to treatment of capital gains as a tax preference), an amount equal to the amount of investment interest which is allowable as a deduction under this chapter by reason of subparagraph (C) of paragraph (1) shall be treated as ordinary income."

—P.L. 94-455, Sec. 1901(b)(3)(K), substituted "ordinary income" for "gain from the sale or exchange of property which is neither a capital asset nor property described in section 1231" in paras. (d)(3) and (5), effective for tax. yrs. begin. after 12/31/76.

—P.L. 94-455, Sec. 1901(b)(8)(C), substituted "educational organization described in section 170(b)(1)(A)(ii) and which is provided for a student of such organization" for "educational institution (as defined in section 151(e)(4)) and which is provided for a student of such institution" in para. (b)(1), effective for tax. yrs. begin. after 12/31/76.

—P.L. 94-455, Sec. 1906(b)(13)(A), substituted "Secretary" for "Secretary or his delegate" each place it appeared in Code Sec. 163, effective for tax. yrs. begin. after 12/31/76.

In 1971, P.L. 92-178, Sec. 304(a)(2)(A), amended clause (d)(4)(A)(i), . . . Sec. 304(a)(2)(B), added para. (d)(7) . . . Sec. 304(b)(2), amended subpara. (d)(1)(B) . . . Sec. 304(d), added "162" before "164(a)(1) or (2)" in subpara. (d)(3)(C), effective for tax. yrs. begin. after 12/31/71.

Prior to amendment, clause (d)(4)(A)(i) read as follows:

"(i) for such taxable year the sum of the deductions with respect to such property which are allowable solely by reason of section 162 is less than 15 percent of the rental income produced by such property, or"

Prior to amendment, subpara. (d)(1)(B) read as follows:

"(B) the amount of the net investment income (as defined in paragraph (3)(A)), plus"

In 1969, P.L. 91-172, Sec. 221(a), redesignated subsec. (d) as (e) and added new subsec. (d), effective for tax. yrs. begin. after 12/31/71.

In 1964, P.L. 88-272, Sec. 224(c), substituted "personal property or educational services are purchased" for "personal property is purchased" and added the last sentence in para. (b)(1), effective for payments made during tax. yrs. begin. after 12/31/63.

In 1963, P.L. 88-9, Sec. 1, added new subsec. (c), redesignated former subsec. (c) as (d) and added para. (d)(5), effective for tax. yrs. end. on or after 1/1/62.

Sec. 164. Taxes.
(a) General rule.

Except as otherwise provided in this section, the following taxes shall be allowed as a deduction for the taxable year within which paid or accrued:

(1) State and local, and foreign, real property taxes.

(2) State and local personal property taxes.

(3) State and local, and foreign, income, war profits, and excess profits taxes.

(4) The GST tax imposed on income distributions.

(5) The environmental tax imposed by section 59A.

(6) Qualified motor vehicle taxes.

In addition, there shall be allowed as a deduction State and local, and foreign, taxes not described in the preceding sentence which are paid or accrued within the taxable year in carrying on a trade or business or an activity described in section 212 (relating to expenses for production of income). Notwithstanding the preceding sentence, any tax (not described in the first sentence of this subsection) which is paid or accrued by the taxpayer in connection with an acquisition or disposition of property shall be treated as part of the cost of the acquired property or, in the case of a disposition, as a reduction in the amount realized on the disposition.

(b) Definitions and special rules.

For purposes of this section—

(1) Personal property taxes. The term "personal property tax" means an ad valorem tax which is imposed on an annual basis in respect of personal property.

(2) State or local taxes. A State or local tax includes only a tax imposed by a State, a possession of the United States, or a political subdivision of any of the foregoing, or by the District of Columbia.

(3) Foreign taxes. A foreign tax includes only a tax imposed by the authority of a foreign country.

(4) Special rules for GST tax.

(A) In general. The GST tax imposed on income distributions is—

(i) the tax imposed by section 2601, and

(ii) any State tax described in section 2604,

but only to the extent such tax is imposed on a transfer which is included in the gross income of the distributee and to which section 666 does not apply.

(B) Special rule for tax paid before due date. Any tax referred to in subparagraph (A) imposed with respect to a transfer occurring during the taxable year of the distributee (or, in the case of a taxable termination, the trust) which is paid not later than the time prescribed by law (including extensions) for filing the return with respect to such transfer shall be treated as having been paid on the last day of the taxable year in which the transfer was made.

(5) General sales taxes. For purposes of subsection (a)—

(A) Election to deduct State and local sales taxes in lieu of State and local income taxes. At the election of the taxpayer for the taxable year, subsection (a) shall be applied—

(i) without regard to the reference to State and local income taxes, and

(ii) as if State and local general sales taxes were referred to in a paragraph thereof.

(B) Definition of general sales tax. The term "general sales tax" means a tax imposed at one rate with respect to the sale at retail of a broad range of classes of items.

(C) Special rules for food, etc. In the case of items of food, clothing, medical supplies, and motor vehicles—

(i) the fact that the tax does not apply with respect to some or all of such items shall not be taken into account in determining whether the tax applies with respect to a broad range of classes of items, and

(ii) the fact that the rate of tax applicable with respect to some or all of such items is lower than the general rate of tax shall not be taken into account in determining whether the tax is imposed at one rate.

(D) Items taxed at different rates. Except in the case of a lower rate of tax applicable with respect to an item described in subparagraph (C), no deduction shall be allowed under this paragraph for any general sales tax imposed with respect to an item at a rate other than the general rate of tax.

(E) Compensating use taxes. A compensating use tax with respect to an item shall be treated as a general sales tax. For purposes of the preceding sentence, the term "compensating use tax" means, with respect to any item, a tax which—

(i) is imposed on the use, storage, or consumption of such item, and

(ii) is complementary to a general sales tax, but only if a deduction is allowable under this paragraph with respect to items sold at retail in the taxing jurisdiction which are similar to such item.

(F) Special rule for motor vehicles. In the case of motor vehicles, if the rate of tax exceeds the general rate, such excess shall be disregarded and the general rate shall be treated as the rate of tax.

(G) Separately stated general sales taxes. If the amount of any general sales tax is separately stated, then, to the extent that the amount so stated is paid by the consumer (other than in connection with the consumer's trade or business) to the seller, such amount shall be treated as a tax imposed on, and paid by, such consumer.

(H) Amount of deduction may be determined under tables.

(i) In general. At the election of the taxpayer for the taxable year, the amount of the deduction allowed under this paragraph for such year shall be—

(I) the amount determined under this paragraph (without regard to this subparagraph) with respect to motor vehicles, boats, and other items specified by the Secretary, and

(II) the amount determined under tables prescribed by the Secretary with respect to items to which subclause (I) does not apply.

(ii) Requirements for tables. The tables prescribed under clause (i)—

(I) shall reflect the provisions of this paragraph,

(II) shall be based on the average consumption by taxpayers on a State-by-State basis (as determined by the Secretary) of items to which clause (i)(I) does not apply, taking into account filing status, number of dependents, adjusted gross income, and rates of State and local general sales taxation, and

(III) need only be determined with respect to adjusted gross incomes up to the applicable amount (as determined under section 68(b)).

(I) Application of paragraph. This paragraph shall apply to taxable years beginning after December 31, 2003, and before January 1, 2012.

(6) Qualified motor vehicle taxes.

(A) In general. For purposes of this section, the term "qualified motor vehicle taxes" means any State or local sales or excise tax imposed on the purchase of a qualified motor vehicle.

(B) Limitation based on vehicle price. The amount of any State or local sales or excise tax imposed on the purchase of a qualified motor vehicle taken into account under subparagraph (A) shall not exceed the portion of such tax attributable to so much of the purchase price as does not exceed $49,500.

(C) Income limitation. The amount otherwise taken into account under subparagraph (A) (after the application of subparagraph (B)) for any taxable year shall be reduced (but not below zero) by the amount which bears the same ratio to the amount which is so treated as—

(i) the excess (if any) of—

(I) the taxpayer's modified adjusted gross income for such taxable year, over

(II) $125,000 ($250,000 in the case of a joint return), bears to

(ii) $10,000.

For purposes of the preceding sentence, the term "modified adjusted gross income" means the adjusted gross income of the taxpayer for the taxable year (determined without regard to sections 911, 931, and 933).

(D) Qualified motor vehicle. For purposes of this paragraph—

(i) In general. The term "qualified motor vehicle" means—

(I) a passenger automobile or light truck which is treated as a motor vehicle for purposes of title II of the Clean Air Act, the gross vehicle weight rating of which is not more than 8,500 pounds, and the original use of which commences with the taxpayer,

(II) a motorcycle the gross vehicle weight rating of which is not more than 8,500 pounds and the original use of which commences with the taxpayer, and

(III) a motor home the original use of which commences with the taxpayer.

(ii) Other terms. The terms "motorcycle" and "motor home" have the meanings given such terms under section 571.3 of title 49, Code of Federal Regulations (as in effect on the date of the enactment of this paragraph).

(E) Qualified motor vehicle taxes not included in cost of acquired property. The last sentence of subsection (a) shall not apply to any qualified motor vehicle taxes.

(F) Coordination with general sales tax. This paragraph shall not apply in the case of a taxpayer who makes an election under paragraph (5) for the taxable year.

(G) Termination. This paragraph shall not apply to purchases after December 31, 2009.

(c) Deduction denied in case of certain taxes.

No deduction shall be allowed for the following taxes:

(1) Taxes assessed against local benefits of a kind tending to increase the value of the property assessed; but this paragraph shall not prevent the deduction of so much of such taxes as is properly allocable to maintenance or interest charges.

(2) Taxes on real property, to the extent that subsection (d) requires such taxes to be treated as imposed on another taxpayer.

(d) Apportionment of taxes on real property between seller and purchaser.

(1) General rule. For purposes of subsection (a), if real property is sold during any real property tax year, then—

(A) so much of the real property tax as is properly allocable to that part of such year which ends on the day before the date of the sale shall be treated as a tax imposed on the seller, and

(B) so much of such tax as is properly allocable to that part of such year which begins on the date of the sale shall be treated as a tax imposed on the purchaser.

Deductions — Code Sec. 164

(2) Special rules.
(A) in the case of any sale of real property, if—
(i) a taxpayer may not, by reason of his method of accounting, deduct any amount for taxes unless paid, and
(ii) the other party to the sale is (under the law imposing the real property tax) liable for the real property tax for the real property tax year,
then for purposes of subsection (a) the taxpayer shall be treated as having paid, on the date of the sale, so much of such tax as, under paragraph (1) of this subsection, is treated as imposed on the taxpayer. For purposes of the preceding sentence, if neither party is liable for the tax, then the party holding the property at the time the tax becomes a lien on the property shall be considered liable for the real property tax for the real property tax year.
(B) In the case of any sale of real property, if the taxpayer's taxable income for the taxable year during which the sale occurs is computed under an accrual method of accounting, and if no election under section 461(c) (relating to the accrual of real property taxes) applies, then, for purposes of subsection (a), that portion of such tax which—
(i) is treated, under paragraph (1) of this subsection, as imposed on the taxpayer, and
(ii) may not, by reason of the taxpayer's method of accounting, be deducted by the taxpayer for any taxable year,
shall be treated as having accrued on the date of the sale.

(e) Taxes of shareholder paid by corporation.
Where a corporation pays a tax imposed on a shareholder on his interest as a shareholder, and where the shareholder does not reimburse the corporation, then—
(1) the deduction allowed by subsection (a) shall be allowed to the corporation; and
(2) no deduction shall be allowed the shareholder for such tax.

(f) Deduction for one-half of self-employment taxes.

> • *Caution:* Code Sec. 164(f)(1), following, is effective with respect to remuneration received, and tax. yrs. beginning, before 1/1/2013. For Code Sec. 164(f)(1), effective with respect to remuneration received, and tax. yrs. beginning, after 12/31/2012, see below.

(1) In general. In the case of an individual, in addition to the taxes described in subsection (a), there shall be allowed as a deduction for the taxable year an amount equal to one-half of the taxes imposed by section 1401 for such taxable year.

> • *Caution:* Code Sec. 164(f)(1), following, is effective with respect to remuneration received, and tax. yrs. beginning, after 12/31/2012. For Code Sec. 164(f)(1), effective with respect to remuneration received, and tax. yrs. beginning, before 1/1/2013, see above.

(1) In general. In the case of an individual, in addition to the taxes described in subsection (a), there shall be allowed as a deduction for the taxable year an amount equal to one-half of the taxes imposed by section 1401 (other than the taxes imposed by section 1401(b)(2)) for such taxable year.

(2) Deduction treated as attributable to trade or business. For purposes of this chapter, the deduction allowed by paragraph (1) shall be treated as attributable to a trade or business carried on by the taxpayer which does not consist of the performance of services by the taxpayer as an employee.

(g) Cross references.
(1) For provisions disallowing any deduction for certain taxes, see section 275.
(2) For treatment of taxes imposed by Indian tribal governments (or their subdivisions), see section 7871.

In **2010**, P.L. 111-312, Sec. 164(b)(5)(I), substituted "January 1, 2012" for "January 1, 2010" in subpara. (b)(5)(I), effective for tax. yrs. begin. after 12/31/2009.
— P.L. 111-148, Sec. 9015(b)(2)(A), inserted "(other than the taxes imposed by section 1401(b)(2))" after "section 1401" in subsec. (f), effective with respect to remuneration received, and tax. yrs. beginning, after 12/31/2012.
In **2009**, P.L. 111-5, Sec. 1008(a), added para. (a)(6)
— P.L. 111-5, Sec. 1008(b), added para. (b)(6), effective for purchases on or after 2/17/2009 in tax. yrs. end. after 2/17/2009.
In **2008**, P.L. 110-343, Sec. 201(a)DivC, substituted "January 1, 2010" for "January 1, 2008" in subpara. (b)(5)(I), effective for tax. yrs. begin. after 12/31/2007.
In **2006**, P.L. 109-432, Sec. 103(a), substituted "2008" for "2006" in subpara. (b)(5)(I), effective for tax. yrs. begin. after 12/31/2005.
In **2005**, P.L. 109-135, Sec. 403(r)(1), amended subpara. (b)(5)(A), effective for tax. yrs. begin. after 12/31/2003 as if included in Sec. 501 of the American Jobs Creation Act of 2004, P.L. 108-357.
Prior to amendment, subpara. (b)(5)(A) read as follows:
"(A) Election to deduct State and local sales taxes in lieu of State and local income taxes.
"(i) In general. At the election of the taxpayer for the taxable year, subsection (a) shall be applied—
"(I) without regard to the reference to State and local income taxes, and
"(II) as if State and local general sales taxes were referred to in a paragraph thereof."
In **2004**, P.L. 108-357, Sec. 501(a), added para. (b)(5), effective for tax. yrs. begin. after 12/31/2003.
In **1996**, P.L. 104-188, Sec. 1704(t)(79), deleted paras. (a)(4) and (5), and added new paras. (a)(4) and (5), effective 8/20/96.
Prior to deletion, paras. (a)(4) and (5) read as follows:
"(4) The environmental tax imposed by section 59A."
"(5) The GST tax imposed on income distributions."
In **1988**, P.L. 100-647, Sec. 1018(u)(11), substituted "The GST tax" for "the GST tax", in para. (a)(5), effective for tax. yrs. begin. after 12/31/86.
— P.L. 100-418, Sec. 1941(b)(2)(A), deleted para. (a)(4), and redesignated paras. (a)(5), and (a)(5)[sic 6] as paras. (a)(4) and (a)(5) effective for crude oil removed from the premises on or after 8/23/88.
Prior to deletion para. (a)(4) read as follows:
"(4) The windfall profit tax imposed by section 4986."
In **1986**, P.L. 99-514, Sec. 134(a)(1), deleted para. (a)(4), and redesignated para. (a)(5) as para. (a)(4) . . . Sec. 134(a)(2), added a sentence to the end of subsec. (a) . . . Sec. 134(b)(1), deleted paras. (b)(2) and (b)(5) . . . Sec. 134(b)(2), redesignated paras. (b)(3) and (4) as paras. (b)(2) and (3), effective for tax. yrs. begin. after 12/31/86.
Prior to deletion, para. (a)(4) read as follows:
"(4) State and legal general sales taxes."
Prior to deletion, para. (b)(2) read as follows:
"(2) General sales taxes.
"(A) In general. The term 'general sales tax' means a tax imposed at one rate in respect of the sale at retail of a broad range of classes of items.
"(B) Special rules for food, etc. In the case of items of food, clothing, medical supplies, and motor vehicles—
"(i) the fact that the tax does not apply in respect of some or all of such items shall not be taken into account in determining whether the tax applies in respect of a broad range of classes of items, and
"(ii) the fact that the rate of tax applicable in respect of some or all of such items is lower than the general rate of tax shall not be taken into account in determining whether the tax is imposed at one rate.
"(C) Items taxed at different rates. Except in the case of a lower rate of tax applicable in respect of an item described in subparagraph (B), no deduction shall be allowed under this section for any general sales tax imposed in respect of an item at a rate other than the general rate of tax.

"(D) Compensating use taxes. A compensating use tax in respect of an item shall be treated as a general sales tax. For purposes of the preceding sentence, the term 'compensating use tax' means, in respect of any item, a tax which—
"(i) is imposed on the use, storage, or consumption of such item, and
"(ii) is complementary to a general sales tax, but only if a deduction is allowable under subsection (a)(4) in respect of items sold at retail in the taxing jurisdiction which are similar to such item.
"(E) Special rule for motor vehicles. In the case of motor vehicles, if the rate of tax exceeds the general rate, such excess shall be disregarded and the general rate shall be treated as the rate of tax."

Prior to deletion, para. (b)(5) read as follows:
"(5) Separately stated general sales taxes. If the amount of any general sales tax or of any tax on the sale of gasoline, diesel fuel, or other motor fuel is separately stated, then, to the extent that the amount so stated is paid by the consumer (otherwise than in connection with the consumer's trade or business) to his seller, such amount shall be treated as a tax imposed on, and paid by such consumer."

—P.L. 99-514, Sec. 1432(a)(1), added para. (a)(5) [sic (a)(6)] . . . Sec. 1432(a)(2), added para. (b)(4), effective for any generation-skipping transfer (within the meaning of Code Sec. 2611) made after 10/22/86.

—P.L. 99-499, Sec. 516(b)(2)(A), added para. (a)(5), effective for tax. yrs. begin. after 12/31/86.

In **1984**, P.L. 98-369, Sec. 474(r)(29)(F), deleted para. (f)(1) (as in effect before its redesignation as para. (g)(1) by Sec. 124(c)(1) of P.L. 98-21) and redesignated paras. (f)(2) and (3) as paras. (f)(1) and (2), respectively, effective as provided in Sec. 475(b) of this Act which reads as follows:

"(b) Tax-Free Covenant Bonds. — The amendments made by subsections (j) and (r)(29) of section 474 shall not apply with respect to obligations issued before January 1, 1984."

Prior to amendment, para. (f)(1) read as follows:
"(1) For provisions disallowing any deduction for the payment of the tax imposed by subchapter B of chapter 3 (relating to tax-free covenant bonds), see section 1451."

—P.L. 98-369, Sec. 1065(a)(1), amended Sec. 204 of P.L. 97-473, the effective date for changes made by Sec. 202(b)(3) of P.L. 97-473' (see below), by deleting "and before January 1, 1985" each place it appeared.

In **1983**, P.L. 98-21, Sec. 124(c)(1), redesignated subsec. (f) as subsec. (g) and added new subsec. (f), effective for tax. yrs. begin. after 12/31/89.

—P.L. 97-473, Sec. 202(b)(3), added para. (f)(3), effective for tax. yrs. begin. after 12/31/82.

In **1980**, P.L. 96-223, Sec. 101(b), added para. (a)(5), effective for periods after 2/29/80.

In **1978**, P.L. 95-600, Sec. 111(a), deleted para. (a)(5) . . . Sec. 111(b), deleted "and gasoline taxes" following "sales tax" in the heading of para. (b)(5) and deleted "or of any tax on the sale of gasoline, diesel fuel, or other motor fuel" after "any general sales tax" in para. (b)(5), effective for tax. yrs. begin. after 12/31/78.

Prior to amendment, para. (a)(5) read as follows:
"(5) State and local taxes on the sale of gasoline, diesel fuel, and other motor fuels."

In **1976**, P.L. 94-455, Sec. 1901(a)(25), deleted subparas. (d)(2)(B) and (d)(2)(C), and redesignated subpara. (d)(2)(D) as (d)(2)(B) effective for tax. yrs. begin. after 12/31/76.

Prior to amendment, subparas. (d)(2)(B) and (d)(2)(C) read as follows:
"(B) Paragraph (1) shall apply to taxable years ending after December 31, 1953, but only in the case of sales after December 31, 1953.
"(C) Paragraph (1) shall not apply to any real property tax, to the extent that such tax was allowable as a deduction under the Internal Revenue Code of 1939 to the seller for a taxable year which ended before January 1, 1954."

—P.L. 94-455, Sec. 1951(b)(3)(A), deleted subsec. (f) and redesignated subsec. (g) as subsec. (f), effective for tax. yrs. begin. after 12/31/76, except as provided in Sec. 1951(b)(3)(B) of the Act, which reads as follows:
"(B) Savings provision. — Notwithstanding subparagraph (A), any amount paid or accrued in a taxable year beginning after December 31, 1976, to the Atomic Energy Commission or its successors for municipal-type services shall be allowed as a deduction under section 164 if such amount would have been deductible by reason of section 164(f) (as in effect for a taxable year ending on December 31, 1976) and if the amount is paid or accrued with respect to real property in a community (within the meaning of section 21 b. of the Atomic Energy Community Act of 1955 (42 U.S.C. 2304(b))) in which the Commission on December 31, 1976, was rendering municipal-type services for which it received compensation from the owners of property within such community."

Prior to deletion, subsec. (f) read as follows:
"(f) Payments for municipal services in atomic energy communities. For purposes of this section, amounts paid or accrued, to compensate the Atomic Energy Commission for municipal-type services, by any owner of real property within any community (within the meaning of section 21b of the Atomic Energy Community Act of 1955) shall be treated as State real property taxes paid or accrued. For purposes of this subsection, the term 'owner' includes a person who holds the real property under a leasehold of 40 or more years and a person who has entered into a contract to purchase under section 61 of the Atomic Energy Community Act of 1955. Subsection (d) of this section shall not apply to a sale by the United States of property with respect to which this subsection applies."

In **1972**, P.L. 92-580, Sec. 4(a), added subpara. (b)(2)(E), effective for tax. yrs. end. on or after 1/1/71.

In **1964**, P.L. 88-272, Sec. 207, amended subsecs. (a)-(c), effective for tax. yrs. begin. after 12/31/63, except as provided in Sec. 207(c)(2) of this Act which reads as follows:

"(2) Special taxing districts. — Section 164(c)(1) of the Internal Revenue Code of 1954 (as amended by subsection (a)) shall not prevent the deduction under section 164 of such Code (as so amended) of taxes levied by a special taxing district which is described in section 164(b)(5) of such Code (as in effect for a taxable year ending on December 31, 1963) and which was in existence on December 31, 1963, for the purpose of retiring indebtedness existing on such date."

Prior to amendment, subsecs. (a)-(c) read as follows:
"(a) General rule.
"Except as otherwise provided in this section, there shall be allowed as a deduction taxes paid or accrued within the taxable year.
"(b) Deduction denied in case of certain taxes.
"No deduction shall be allowed for the following taxes:
"(1) Federal income taxes, including — "(A) the tax imposed by section 3101 (relating to the tax on employees under the Federal Insurance Contributions Act); (B) the taxes imposed by sections 3201 and 3211 (relating to the taxes on railroad employees and railroad employee representatives); and (C) the tax withheld at source on wages under section 3402, and corresponding provisions of prior revenue laws.
"(2) Federal war profits and excess profits taxes.
"(3) Federal import duties, and Federal excise and stamp taxes (not described in paragraph (1), (2), (4), or (5); but this paragraph shall not prevent such duties and taxes from being deducted under section 162 (relating to trade or business expenses); or section 212 (relating to expenses for the production of income).
"(4) Estate, inheritance, legacy, succession, and gift taxes.
"(5) Taxes assessed against local benefits of a kind tending to increase the value of the property assessed; but this paragraph shall not prevent — (A) the deduction of so much of such taxes as is properly allocable to maintenance or interest charges; or (B) the deduction of taxes levied by a special taxing district if — (i) the district covers the whole of at least one county; (ii) at least 1,000 persons are subject to the taxes levied by the district; and (iii) the district levies its assessments annually at a uniform rate on the same assessed value of real property, including improvements, as is used for purposes of the real property tax generally.
"(6) Income, war profits, and excess profits taxes imposed by the authority of any foreign country or possession of the United States, if the taxpayer chooses to take to any extent the benefits of section 901 (relating to the foreign tax credit).
"(7) Taxes on real property, to the extent that subsection (d) requires such taxes to be treated as imposed on another taxpayer.
"(c) Certain retail sales taxes and gasoline taxes.
"(1) General rule. In the case of any State or local sales tax, if the amount of the tax is separately stated, then, to the extent that the amount so stated is paid by the consumer (otherwise than in connection with the consumer's trade or business) to his seller, such amount shall be allowed as a deduction to the consumer as if it constituted a tax imposed on, and paid by, such consumer.
"(2) Definition. For purposes of paragraph (1), the term 'State or local sales tax' means a tax imposed by a State, a Territory, a possession of the United States, or a political subdivision of any of the foregoing, or by the District of Columbia, which tax — (A) is imposed on persons engaged in selling tangible personal property at retail (or on persons selling gasoline or other motor vehicle fuels at wholesale or retail) and is a stated sum per unit of property sold or is measured either by the gross sales price or by the gross receipts from the sale; or (B) is imposed on persons engaged in furnishing services at retail and is measured by the gross receipts for furnishing such services."

—P.L. 88-272, Sec. 207(b)(1), added "State" before "real property taxes" in subsec. (f) . . . Sec. 207(b)(2), amended subsec. (g), effective for tax. yrs. begin. after 12/31/63.

In **1958**, P.L. 85-866, Sec. 6(a), added subsec. (f) and redesignated subsec. (f) as subsec. (g), effective for tax. yrs. begin. after 12/31/57.

Sec. 165. Losses.
(a) General rule.
There shall be allowed as a deduction any loss sustained during the taxable year and not compensated for by insurance or otherwise.

(b) Amount of deduction.
For purposes of subsection (a), the basis for determining the amount of the deduction for any loss shall be the adjusted basis provided in section 1011 for determining the loss from the sale or other disposition of property.

(c) Limitation on losses of individuals.
In the case of an individual, the deduction under subsection (a) shall be limited to
(1) losses incurred in a trade or business;
(2) losses incurred in any transaction entered into for profit, though not connected with a trade or business; and
(3) except as provided in subsection (h), losses of property not connected with a trade or business or a transaction entered into for profit, if such losses arise from fire, storm, shipwreck, or other casualty, or from theft.

Deductions Code Sec. 165(h)(5)(C)

(d) **Wagering losses.**
Losses from wagering transactions shall be allowed only to the extent of the gains from such transactions.

(e) **Theft losses.**
For purposes of subsection (a), any loss arising from theft shall be treated as sustained during the taxable year in which the taxpayer discovers such loss.

(f) **Capital losses.**
Losses from sales or exchanges of capital assets shall be allowed only to the extent allowed in sections 1211 and 1212.

(g) **Worthless securities.**
(1) **General rule.** If any security which is a capital asset becomes worthless during the taxable year, the loss resulting therefrom shall, for purposes of this subtitle, be treated as a loss from the sale or exchange, on the last day of the taxable year, of a capital asset.
(2) **Security defined.** For purposes of this subsection, the term "security" means—
 (A) a share of stock in a corporation;
 (B) a right to subscribe for, or to receive, a share of stock in a corporation; or
 (C) a bond, debenture, note, or certificate, or other evidence of indebtedness, issued by a corporation or by a government or political subdivision thereof, with interest coupons or in registered form.
(3) **Securities in affiliated corporation.** For purposes of paragraph (1), any security in a corporation affiliated with a taxpayer which is a domestic corporation shall not be treated as a capital asset. For purposes of the preceding sentence, a corporation shall be treated as affiliated with the taxpayer only if—
 (A) the taxpayer owns directly stock in such corporation meeting the requirements of section 1504(a)(2); and
 (B) more than 90 percent of the aggregate of its gross receipts for all taxable years has been from sources other than royalties, rents (except rents derived from rental of properties to employees of the corporation in the ordinary course of its operating business), dividends, interest (except interest received on deferred purchase price of operating assets sold), annuities, and gains from sales or exchanges of stocks and securities.
In computing gross receipts for purposes of the preceding sentence, gross receipts from sales or exchanges of stocks and securities shall be taken into account only to the extent of gains therefrom.

(h) **Treatment of casualty gains and losses.**
(1) **$100 limitation per casualty.** Any loss of an individual described in subsection (c)(3) shall be allowed only to the extent that the amount of the loss to such individual arising from each casualty, or from each theft, exceeds $500 ($100 for taxable years beginning after December 31, 2009).
(2) **Net casualty loss allowed only to the extent it exceeds 10 percent of adjusted gross income.**
 (A) In general. If the personal casualty losses for any taxable year exceed the personal casualty gains for such taxable year, such losses shall be allowed for the taxable year only to the extent of the sum of—
  (i) the amount of the personal casualty gains for the taxable year, plus
  (ii) so much of such excess as exceeds 10 percent of the adjusted gross income of the individual.
 (B) Special rule where personal casualty gains exceed personal casualty losses. If the personal casualty gains for any taxable year exceed the personal casualty losses for such taxable year—
  (i) all such gains shall be treated as gains from sales or exchanges of capital assets, and
  (ii) all such losses shall be treated as losses from sales or exchanges of capital assets.
(3) **Special rule for losses in federally declared disasters.**
 (A) In general. If an individual has a net disaster loss for any taxable year, the amount determined under paragraph (2)(A)(ii) shall be the sum of—
  (i) such net disaster loss, and
  (ii) so much of the excess referred to in the matter preceding clause (i) of paragraph (2)(A) (reduced by the amount in clause (i) of this subparagraph) as exceeds 10 percent of the adjusted gross income of the individual.
 (B) Net disaster loss. For purposes of subparagraph (A), the term "net disaster loss" means the excess of—
  (i) the personal casualty losses—
   (I) attributable to a federally declared disaster occurring before January 1, 2010, and
   (II) occurring in a disaster area, over
  (ii) personal casualty gains.
 (C) Federally declared disaster. For purposes of this paragraph—
  (i) Federally declared disaster. The term "federally declared disaster" means any disaster subsequently determined by the President of the United States to warrant assistance by the Federal Government under the Robert T. Stafford Disaster Relief and Emergency Assistance Act.
  (ii) Disaster area. The term "disaster area" means the area so determined to warrant such assistance.
(4) **Definitions of personal casualty gain and personal casualty loss.** For purposes of this subsection—
 (A) Personal casualty gain. The term "personal casualty gain" means the recognized gain from any involuntary conversion of property which is described in subsection (c)(3) arising from fire, storm, shipwreck, or other casualty, or from theft.
 (B) Personal casualty loss. The term "personal casualty loss" means any loss described in subsection (c)(3). For purposes of paragraphs (2) and (3), the amount of any personal casualty loss shall be determined after the application of paragraph (1).
(5) **Special rules.**
 (A) Personal casualty losses allowable in computing adjusted gross income to the extent of personal casualty gains. In any case to which paragraph (2)(A) applies, the deduction for personal casualty losses for any taxable year shall be treated as a deduction allowable in computing adjusted gross income to the extent such losses do not exceed the personal casualty gains for the taxable year.
 (B) Joint returns. For purposes of this subsection, a husband and wife making a joint return for the taxable year shall be treated as 1 individual.
 (C) Determination of adjusted gross income in case of estates and trusts. For purposes of paragraph (2), the adjusted gross income of an estate or trust shall be computed in the same manner as in the case of an individual, except that the deductions for costs paid or incurred in connection with the administration of the estate or trust shall be treated as allowable in arriving at adjusted gross income.

(D) **Coordination with estate tax.** No loss described in subsection (c)(3) shall be allowed if, at the time of filing the return, such loss has been claimed for estate tax purposes in the estate tax return.

(E) **Claim required to be filed in certain cases.** Any loss of an individual described in subsection (c)(3) to the extent covered by insurance shall be taken into account under this section only if the individual files a timely insurance claim with respect to such loss.

(i) **Disaster losses.**

(1) **Election to take deduction for preceding year.** Notwithstanding the provisions of subsection (a), any loss occurring in a disaster area (as defined by clause (ii) of subsection (h)(3)(C)) and attributable to a federally declared disaster (as defined by clause (i) of such subsection) may, at the election of the taxpayer, be taken into account for the taxable year immediately preceding the taxable year in which the disaster occurred.

(2) **Year of loss.** If an election is made under this subsection, the casualty resulting in the loss shall be treated for purposes of this title as having occurred in the taxable year for which the deduction is claimed.

(3) **Amount of loss.** The amount of the loss taken into account in the preceding taxable year by reason of paragraph (1) shall not exceed the uncompensated amount determined on the basis of the facts existing at the date the taxpayer claims the loss.

(4) **Use of disaster loan appraisals to establish amount of loss.** Nothing in this title shall be construed to prohibit the Secretary from prescribing regulations or other guidance under which an appraisal for the purpose of obtaining a loan of Federal funds or a loan guarantee from the Federal Government as a result of a federally declared disaster (as defined by subsection (h)(3)(C)(i)) may be used to establish the amount of any loss described in paragraph (1) or (2).

(j) **Denial of deduction for losses on certain obligations not in registered form.**

(1) **In general.** Nothing in subsection (a) or in any other provision of law shall be construed to provide a deduction for any loss sustained on any registration-required obligation unless such obligation is in registered form (or the issuance of such obligation was subject to tax under section 4701).

(2) **Definitions.** For purposes of this subsection—

> • *Caution:* Code Sec. 165(j)(2)(A), following, is effective for obligations issued before 3/19/2012. For Code Sec. 165(j)(2)(A), effective for obligations issued after 3/18/2012, see below.

(A) **Registration-required obligation.** The term "registration-required obligation" has the meaning given to such term by section 163(f)(2) except that clause (iv) of subparagraph (A), and subparagraph (B), of such section shall not apply.

> • *Caution:* Code Sec. 165(j)(2)(A), following, is effective for obligations issued after 3/18/2012. For Code Sec. 165(j)(2)(A), effective for obligations issued before 3/19/2012, see above.

(A) **Registration-required obligation.** The term "registration-required obligation" has the meaning given to such term by section 163(f)(2).

(B) **Registered form.** The term "registered form" has the same meaning as when used in section 163(f).

(3) **Exceptions.** The Secretary may, by regulations, provide that this subsection and section 1287 shall not apply with respect to obligations held by any person if—

(A) such person holds such obligations in connection with a trade or business outside the United States,

(B) such person holds such obligations as a broker dealer (registered under Federal or State law) for sale to customers in the ordinary course of his trade or business,

(C) such person complies with reporting requirements with respect to ownership, transfers, and payments as the Secretary may require, or

(D) such person promptly surrenders the obligation to the issuer for the issuance of a new obligation in registered form,

but only if such obligations are held under arrangements provided in regulations or otherwise which are designed to assure that such obligations are not delivered to any United States person other than a person described in subparagraph (A), (B), or (C).

(k) **Treatment as disaster loss where taxpayer ordered to demolish or relocate residence in disaster area because of disaster.**

In the case of a taxpayer whose residence is located in an area which has been determined by the President of the United States to warrant assistance by the Federal Government under the Robert T. Stafford Disaster Relief and Emergency Assistance Act, if—

(1) not later than the 120th day after the date of such determination, the taxpayer is ordered, by the government of the State or any political subdivision thereof in which such residence is located, to demolish or relocate such residence, and

(2) the residence has been rendered unsafe for use as a residence by reason of the disaster,

any loss attributable to such disaster shall be treated as a loss which arises from a casualty and which is described in subsection (i).

(l) **Treatment of certain losses in insolvent financial institutions.**

(1) **In general.** If—

(A) as of the close of the taxable year, it can reasonably be estimated that there is a loss on a qualified individual's deposit in a qualified financial institution, and

(B) such loss is on account of the bankruptcy or insolvency of such institution,

then the taxpayer may elect to treat the amount so estimated as a loss described in subsection (c)(3) incurred during the taxable year.

(2) **Qualified individual defined.** For purposes of this subsection, the term "qualified individual" means any individual, except an individual—

(A) who owns at least 1 percent in value of the outstanding stock of the qualified financial institution,

(B) who is an officer of the qualified financial institution,

(C) who is a sibling (whether by the whole or half blood), spouse, aunt, uncle, nephew, niece, ancestor, or lineal descendant of an individual described in subparagraph (A) or (B), or

(D) who otherwise is a related person (as defined in section 267(b)) with respect to an individual described in subparagraph (A) or (B).

(3) Qualified financial institution. For purposes of this subsection, the term "qualified financial institution" means—

(A) any bank (as defined in section 581),

(B) any institution described in section 591,

(C) any credit union the deposits or accounts in which are insured under Federal or State law or are protected or guaranteed under State law, or

(D) any similar institution chartered and supervised under Federal or State law.

(4) Deposit. For purposes of this subsection, the term "deposit" means any deposit, withdrawable account, or withdrawable or repurchasable share.

(5) Election to treat as ordinary loss.

(A) In general. In lieu of any election under paragraph (1), the taxpayer may elect to treat the amount referred to in paragraph (1) for the taxable year as an ordinary loss described in subsection (c)(2) incurred during the taxable year.

(B) Limitations.

(i) Deposit may not be federally insured. No election may be made under subparagraph (A) with respect to any loss on a deposit in a qualified financial institution if part or all of such deposit is insured under Federal law.

(ii) Dollar limitation. With respect to each financial institution, the aggregate amount of losses attributable to deposits in such financial institution to which an election under subparagraph (A) may be made by the taxpayer for any taxable year shall not exceed $20,000 ($10,000 in the case of a separate return by a married individual). The limitation of the preceding sentence shall be reduced by the amount of any insurance proceeds under any State law which can reasonably be expected to be received with respect to losses on deposits in such institution.

(6) Election. Any election by the taxpayer under this subsection for any taxable year—

(A) shall apply to all losses for such taxable year of the taxpayer on deposits in the institution with respect to which such election was made, and

(B) may be revoked only with the consent of the Secretary.

(7) Coordination with section 166. Section 166 shall not apply to any loss to which an election under this subsection applies.

(m) Cross references.

(1) For special rule for banks with respect to worthless securities, see section 582.

(2) For disallowance of deduction for worthlessness of securities to which subsection (g)(2)(C) applies, if issued by a political party or similar organization, see section 271.

(3) For special rule for losses on stock in a small business investment company, see section 1242.

(4) For special rule for losses of a small business investment company, see section 1243.

(5) For special rule for losses on small business stock, see section 1244.

In **2010**, P.L. 111-147, Sec. 502(a)(2)(D), deleted "except that clause (iv) of subparagraph (A), and subparagraph (B), of such section shall not apply" in subpara. (j)(2)(A), effective for obligations issued after 3/18/2012.

In **2008**, P.L. 110-343, Sec. 706(a)(1)DivC, redesignated paras. (h)(3)-(4) as (4)-(5) and added para. (h)(3) . . . Sec. 706(a)(2)(A)DivC, substituted "paragraphs (2) and (3)" for "paragraph (2)" in subpara. (h)(4)(B) . . . Sec. 706(a)(2)(B)DivC, substituted "loss occurring in a disaster area (as defined by clause (ii) of subsection (h)(3)(C)) and attributable to a federally declared disaster (as defined by clause (i) of such subsection" for "loss attributable to a disaster occurring in an area subsequently determined by the President of the United States to warrant assistance by the Federal Government under the Robert T. Stafford Disaster Relief and Emergency Assistance Act" in para. (i)(1) . . . Sec. 706(a)(2)(C)DivC, substituted "federally declared disaster (as defined by subsection (h)(3)(C)(i)" for "Presidentially declared disaster (as defined by section 1033(h)(3))" in para. (i)(4), effective for disasters declared in tax. yrs. begin. after 12/31/2007.

—P.L. 110-343, Sec. 706(c)DivC, substituted "$500 ($100 for taxable years beginning after December 31, 2009)" for "$100" in para. (h)(1), effective for tax. yrs. begin. after 12/31/2008.

—P.L. 110-343, Sec. 712DivC, of this Act, reads as follows:

"Sec. 712. Coordination with Heartland Disaster Relief.

"The amendments made by this subtitle, other than the amendments made by sections 706(a)(2), 710, and 711, shall not apply to any disaster described in section 702(c)(1)(A), or to any expenditure or loss resulting from such disaster."

In **2005**, P.L. 109-135, Sec. 201(b)(4)(B), repealed Sec. 402 of P.L. 109-73, see below.

—P.L. 109-73, Sec. 402, of this Act [prior to repeal by Sec. 201(b)(4)(B) of P.L. 109-135, see above], read as follows:

"Sec. 402. Suspension of Certain Limitations on Personal Casualty Losses.

"Paragraphs (1) and (2)(A) of section 165(h) of the Internal Revenue Code of 1986 shall not apply to losses described in section 165(c)(3) of such Code which arise in the Hurricane Katrina disaster area on or after August 25, 2005, and which are attributable to Hurricane Katrina. In the case of any other losses, section 165(h)(2)(A) of such Code shall be applied without regard to the losses referred to in the preceding sentence."

In **2004**, P.L. 108-311, Sec. 408(a)(7)(A), added "Robert T. Stafford" before "Disaster Relief and Emergency Assistance Act" in para. (i)(1) . . . Sec. 408(a)(7)(B), added "Robert T. Stafford" before "Disaster Relief and Emergency Assistance Act" in subsec. (k), enacted 10/4/2004.

In **2000**, P.L. 106-554, Sec. 1(a)(7), [which enacted into law Sec. 318(b)(1) of P.L. 106-554] amended subpara. (g)(3)(A) . . . Sec. 1(a)(7), [which enacted into law Sec. 318(b)(2) of P.L. 106-554] deleted "As used in subparagraph (A), the term 'stock' does not include nonvoting stock which is limited and preferred as to dividends." after "gains therefrom." in para. (g)(3), effective for tax. yrs. begin. after 12/31/84.

Prior to amendment, subpara. (g)(3)(A) read as follows:

"(A) stock possessing at least 80 percent of the voting power of all classes of its stock and at least 80 percent of each class of its nonvoting stock is owned directly by the taxpayer, and"

In **1997**, P.L. 105-34, Sec. 912(a), added para. (i)(4), effective 8/5/97.

In **1993**, P.L. 103-66, Sec. 13224, of this Act, relating to clarification of treatment of certain FSLIC financial assistance, provides:

"Sec. 13224. Clarification of treatment of certain FSLIC financial assistance.

"(a) General rule.—For purposes of chapter 1 of the Internal Revenue Code of 1986—

"(1) any FSLIC assistance with respect to any loss of principal, capital, or similar amount upon the disposition of any asset shall be taken into account as compensation for such loss for purposes of section 165 of such Code, and

"(2) any FSLIC assistance with respect to any debt shall be taken into account for purposes of section 166, 585, or 593 of such Code in determining whether such debt is worthless (or the extent to which such debt is worthless) and in determining the amount of any addition to a reserve for bad debts arising from the worthlessness or partial worthlessness of such debts.

"(b) FSLIC assistance.—For purposes of this section, the term 'FSLIC assistance' means any assistance (or right to assistance) with respect to a domestic building and loan association (as defined in section 7701(a)(19) of such Code without regard to subparagraph (C) thereof) under section 406(f) of the National Housing Act or section 21A of the Federal Home Loan Bank Act (or under any similar provision of law).

"(c) Effective date.—

"(1) In general.—Except as otherwise provided in this subsection—

"(A) The provisions of this section shall apply to taxable years ending on or after March 4, 1991, but only with respect to FSLIC assistance not credited before March 4, 1991.

"(B) If any FSLIC assistance not credited before March 4, 1991, is with respect to a loss sustained or charge-off in a taxable year ending before March 4, 1991, for purposes of determining the amount of any net operating loss carryover to a taxable year ending on or after March 4, 1991, the provisions of this section shall apply to such assistance for purposes of determining the amount of the net operating loss for the taxable year in which such loss was sustained or debt written off. Except as provided in the preceding sentence, this section shall not apply to any FSLIC assistance with respect to a loss sustained or charge-off in a taxable year ending before March 4, 1991.

"(2) Exceptions.—The provisions of this section shall not apply to any assistance to which the amendments made by section 1401(a)(3) of the Financial Institutions Reform, Recovery, and Enforcement Act of 1989 apply."

In **1988**, P.L. 100-707, Sec. 109(l), substituted "and Emergency Assistance Act" for "Act of 1974" in para. (i)(1) and subsec. (k), effective 11/23/88.

—P.L. 100-647, Sec. 1002(j)(1), redesignated Sec. 243(d) of P.L. 99-514 [reproduced below] as Sec. 243(e) of P.L. 99-514 and added new Sec. 243(d) of P.L. 99-514 [reproduced below] . . . Sec. 1002(j)(2), deleted "to begin in 1987" which followed "period" from heading of Sec. 243(b)(2)(A) of P.L. 99-514 [reproduced below] see below.

Code Sec. 165 — Deductions

—P.L. 100-647, Sec. 1009(d)(1), redesignated para. (l)(6) as (l)(7), deleted para. (l)(5), and added new paras. (l)(5) and (6), effective for tax. yrs. begin. after 12/31/81.

Prior to amendment, para. (l)(5) read as follows:

"(5) Election. Any election by the taxpayer under this subsection may be revoked only with the consent of the Secretary and shall apply to all losses of the taxpayer on deposits in the institution with respect to which such election was made."

—P.L. 100-647, Sec. 1009(d)(2), changed the effective date for changes made by Sec. 905(a) of P.L. 99-514, from effective for tax. yrs. begin. after 12/31/82 to, effective for tax. yrs. begin. after 12/31/81, see below.

—P.L. 100-647, Sec. 1009(d)(4), of this Act provides:

"(4) on the date of the enactment of this Act (or at any time before the date 1 year after such date of enactment) credit or refund of any overpayment of tax attributable to amendments made by section 905 of the Reform Act or by this subsection (or the assessment of any underpayment of tax so attributable) is barred by any law or rule of law—

"(A) credit or refund of any such overpayment may nevertheless be made if claim therefore is filed before the date 1 year after such date of enactment, and

"(B) assessment of any such underpayment may nevertheless be made if made before the date 1 year after such date of enactment."

In 1986, P.L. 99-514, Sec. 243, [as amended by Sec. 1002(j)(1) & (2) of P.L.100-647, see above.] provides:

"Sec. 243. Deduction for bus and freight forwarder operating authority.

"(a) Bus operating authority. —

"(1) In general. — Subject to the modifications contained in paragraph [(c)] (2), section 266 of the Economic Recovery Tax Act of 1981 [P.L. 97-34] shall be applied as if the term 'motor carrier operating authority' included a bus operating authority.

"(2) Modifications. — For purposes of paragraph (1), section 266 of such Act shall be applied—

"(A) by substituting 'November 19, 1982' for 'July 1, 1980' each place it appears, and

"(B) by substituting 'November 1982' for 'July 1980' in subsection (a) thereof.

"(3) Bus operating authority defined. — For purposes of this subsection and section 266 of such Act, the term 'bus operating authority' means —

"(A) a certificate or permit held by a motor common or contract carrier of passengers which was issued pursuant to subchapter II of chapter 109 of title 49, United States Code, and

(B) a certificate or permit held by a motor carrier authorizing the transportation of passengers, as a common carrier, over regular routes in intrastate commerce which was issued by the appropriate State agency.

"(b) Freight forwarder operating authority. —

"(1) In general. — Subject to the modifications contained in paragraph (2), section 266 of the Economic Recovery Tax Act of 1981 shall be applied as if subsection (b) thereof contained 'or a freight forwarder' after 'contract carrier of property'.

"(2) Modifications. — The modifications referred to in this paragraph are:

"(A) 60-month period. — The 60-month period referred to in section 266(a) of such Act shall begin with the later of—

"(i) the deregulation month, or

"(ii) at the election of the taxpayer, the 1st month of the taxpayer's 1st taxable year beginning after the deregulation month.

"(B) Authority must be held as of beginning of 60-month period. — A motor carrier operating authority shall not be taken into account unless such authority is held by the taxpayer at the beginning of the 60-month period applicable to the taxpayer under subparagraph (A).

"(C) Adjusted basis not to exceed adjusted basis at beginning of 60-month period. — The adjusted basis taken into account with respect to any motor carrier operating authority shall not exceed the adjusted basis of such authority as of the beginning of the 60-month period applicable to the taxpayer under subparagraph (A).

"(3) Deregulation month. — For purposes of this section, the term 'deregulation month' means the month in which the Secretary of the Treasury or his delegate determines that a Federal law has been enacted which deregulates the freight forwarding industry.

"(c) Special rule for motor carrier operating authority.

In the case of a corporation which was incorporated on December 29, 1969, in the State of Delaware, notwithstanding any other provision of law, there shall be allowed as a deduction for the taxable year of the taxpayer beginning in 1980 an amount equal to $2,705,188 for its entire loss due to a decline in value of its motor carrier operating authority by reason of deregulation.

"(d) Application of section 334(b)(2). For purposes of subsections (a) and (b), the reference to section 334(b)(2) in section 266(c)(2)(A)(ii) of the Economic Recovery Tax Act of 1981 shall be a reference to such section as in effect before its repeal.

"(e) Effective dates.

"(1) Bus operating authority.

"(A) In general. — Subsection (a) shall apply to taxable years ending after November 18, 1982.

"(B) Statute of limitations. If refund or credit of any overpayment of tax resulting from subsection (a) is prevented at any time on or before the date which is 1 year after the date of the enactment of this Act by the operation of any law or rule of law (including res judicata), refund or credit of such overpayment (to the extent attributable to the application of such subsection) may, notwithstanding such law or rule of law, be made or allowed if claim therefore is filed on or before the date which is 18 months after such date of enactment.

"(2) Freight forwarder operating authority. Subsection (b) shall apply to taxable years ending after the month preceding the deregulation month."

—P.L. 99-514, Sec. 905(a), redesignated subsec. (l) as subsec. (m), and added new subsec. (l), effective [as amended by Sec. 1009(d)(2) of P.L. 100-647, see Sec. 1009(d)(4) of 100-647, see above] for tax. yrs. begin. after 12/31/81.

—P.L. 99-514, Sec. 1004(a), added subpara. (h)(4)(E), effective for losses sustained in tax. yrs. begin. after 12/31/86.

In 1984, P.L. 98-369, Sec. 42(a)(4), substituted "section 1287" for "subsection (d) of section 1232" in para. (j)(3), effective for tax. yrs. end. after 7/18/84.

—P.L. 98-369, Sec. 711(c)(1), redesignated subpara. (h)(2)(B) as subpara. (h)(2)(C) and added new subpara. (h)(2)(B), effective for tax. yrs. begin. after 12/31/82. For exception, see effective date of Sec. 203(b) of P.L. 97-248, below.

—P.L. 98-369, Sec. 711(c)(2)(A)(i), added "or a transaction entered into for profit" after "trade or business" in para. (j)(3)... Sec. 711(c)(2)(A)(ii), amended subsec. (h), effective for tax. yrs. begin. after 12/31/83. Sec. 711(c)(2)(B) of this Act provides:

"(B) Transitional rule. — In the case of taxable years beginning before January 1, 1984 —

"(i) For purposes of paragraph (1)(B) of section 165(h) of the Internal Revenue Code of 1954, adjusted gross income shall be determined without regard to the application of section 1231 of such Code to any gain or loss from an involuntary conversion of property described in subsection (c)(3) of section 165 of such Code arising from fire, storm, shipwreck, or other casualty or from theft.

"(ii) Section 1231 of such Code shall be applied after the application of paragraph (1) of section 165(h) of such Code."

Prior to amendment, subsec. (h) read as follows:

"(h) Casualty and theft losses.

"(1) General rule. Any loss of an individual described in subsection (c)(3) shall be allowed for any taxable year only to the extent that —

"(A) the amount of loss to such individual arising from each casualty, or from each theft, exceeds $100, and

"(B) the aggregate amount of all such losses sustained by such individual during the taxable year (determined after application of subparagraph (A)) exceeds 10 percent of the adjusted gross income of the individual.

"(2) Special rules.

"(A) Joint returns. For purposes of the $100 and 10 percent limitations described in paragraph (1), a husband and wife making a joint return for the taxable year shall be treated as one individual.

"(B) Determination of adjusted gross income in case of estates and trusts. For purposes of paragraph (1), the adjusted gross income of an estate or trust shall be computed in the same manner as in the case of an individual, except that the deductions for costs paid or incurred in connection with the administration of the estate or trust shall be treated as allowable in arriving at adjusted gross income.

"(C) Coordination with estate tax. No loss described in subsection (c)(3) shall be allowed if, at the time of filing the return, such loss has been claimed for estate tax purposes in the estate tax return."

—P.L. 98-369, Sec. 1051(a), redesignated subsec. (k) as subsec. (l) and added new subsec. (k), effective for tax. yrs. end. after 12/31/81, for residences in areas determined by the President of the United States, after 12/31/81, to warrant assistance by the Federal Government under the Disaster Relief Act of 1974.

In 1983, P.L. 97-448, Sec. 102(n), added para. (c)(3) to Sec. 266 of P.L. 97-34, reproduced below.

—P.L. 97-424, Sec. 517(a), amended Sec. 266(c)(2) of P.L. 97-34 by redesignating subpara. (c)(2)(B) as subpara. (c)(2)(C) and adding new subpara. (c)(2)(B), effective for tax. yrs. end. after 7/30/80, see below.

In 1982, P.L. 97-248, Sec. 203(a), deleted subsec. (h), redesignated subsec. (i) as subsec. (j) and added new subsecs. (h) and (i)... Sec. 203(b), amended para. (c)(3), effective for tax. yrs. begin. after 12/31/82, except that "[s]uch amendments shall also apply to the taxpayer's last taxable year beginning before January 1, 1983, solely for purposes of determining the amount allowable as a deduction with respect to any loss taken into account for such year by reason of an election under section 165(i) of the Internal Revenue Code of 1954 (as amended by this section).".

Prior to amendment, para. (c)(3) read as follows:

"(3) losses of property not connected with a trade or business, if such losses arise from fire, storm, shipwreck, or other casualty, or from theft. A loss described in this paragraph shall be allowed only to the extent that the amount of loss to such individual arising from each casualty, or from each theft, exceeds $100. For purposes of the $100 limitation of the preceding sentence, a husband and wife making a joint return under section 6013 for the taxable year in which the loss is allowed as a deduction shall be treated as one individual. No loss described in this paragraph shall be allowed if, at the time of filing the return, such loss has been claimed for estate tax purposes in the estate tax return."

Prior to amendment, subsec. (h) read as follows:

"(h) Disaster losses.

"Notwithstanding the provisions of subsection (a), any loss attributable to a disaster occurring in an area subsequently determined by the President of the United States to warrant assistance by the Federal Government under the Disaster Relief Act of 1974 may, at the election of the taxpayer, be deducted for the taxable year immediately preceding the taxable year in which the disaster occurred. Such deduction shall not be in excess of so much of the loss as would have been deductible in the taxable year in which the casualty occurred, based on facts existing at the date the taxpayer claims the loss. If an election is made under this subsection, the casualty resulting in the loss will be deemed to have occurred in the taxable year for which the deduction is claimed."

—P.L. 97-248, Sec. 310(b)(5), redesignated subsec. (j) (as amended by Sec. 203(a) of this Act) as subsec. (k) and added a new subsec. (j), effective for obli-

Deductions   Code Sec. 165

gations issued after 12/31/82, except as provided in Sec. 310(d)(3) of this Act which reads as follows:

"(3) Exception for certain warrants, etc.—The amendments made by subsection (b) shall not apply to any obligations issued after December 31, 1982, on the exercise of a warrant or the conversion of a convertible obligation if such warrant or obligation was offered or sold outside the United States without registration under the Securities Act of 1933 and was issued before August 10, 1982. A rule similar to the rule of the preceding sentence shall also apply in the case of any regulations issued under section 163(f)(2)(C) of the Internal Revenue Code of 1954 (as added by this section) except that the date on which such regulations take effect shall be substituted for 'August 10, 1982'."

In 1981, P.L. 97-34, Sec. 266, provides:
"SEC. 266. DEDUCTION FOR MOTOR CARRIER OPERATING AUTHORITY.
"(a) General rule.

"For purposes of chapter 1 of the Internal Revenue Code of 1954, in computing the taxable income of a taxpayer who, on July 1, 1980, held one or more motor carrier operating authorities, an amount equal to the aggregate adjusted basis of all motor carrier operating authorities held by the taxpayer on July 1, 1980, or acquired subsequent thereto pursuant to a binding contract in effect on July 1, 1980, shall be allowed as a deduction ratably over a period of 60 months. Such 60-month period shall begin with the month of July 1980 (or if later, the month in which acquired), or at the election of the taxpayer, the first month of the taxpayer's first taxable year beginning after July 1, 1980.

"(b) Definition of motor carrier operating authority.

"For purposes of this section, the term 'motor carrier operating authority' means a certificate or permit held by a motor common or contract carrier of property and issued pursuant to subchapter II of chapter 109 of title 49 of the United States Code.

"(c) Special rules. —

"(1) Adjusted basis. For purposes of the Internal Revenue Code of 1954, proper adjustments shall be made in the adjusted basis of any motor carrier operating authority held by the taxpayer on July 1, 1980, for the amounts allowable as a deduction under this section.

"(2) Certain stock acquisitions. —

"(A) In General. Under regulations prescribed by the Secretary of the Treasury or his delegate, and at the election of the holder of the authority, in any case in which a corporation—

"(i) on or before July 1, 1980 (or after such date pursuant to a binding contract in effect on such date), acquired stock in a corporation which held, directly or indirectly, any motor carrier operating authority at the time of such acquisition, and

"(ii) would have been able to allocate to the basis of such authority that portion of the acquiring corporation's cost basis in such stock attributable to such authority if the acquiring corporation had received such authority in the liquidation of the acquired corporation immediately following such acquisition and such allocation would have been proper under section 334(b)(2) of such Code,

the holder of the authority may, for purposes of this section, allocate a portion of the basis of the acquiring corporation in the stock of the acquired corporation to the basis of such authority in such manner as the Secretary may prescribe in such regulations.

"(B) Treatment of certain noncorporate taxpayers.—Under regulations prescribed by the Secretary of the Treasury or his delegate, and at the election of the holder of the authority, in any case in which—

"(i) a noncorporate taxpayer or group of noncorporate taxpayers on or before July 1, 1980, acquired in one purchase stock in a corporation which held, directly or indirectly, any motor carrier operating authority at the time of such acquisition, and

"(ii) the acquisition referred to in clause (i) would have satisfied the requirements of subparagraph (A) if the stock had been acquired by a corporation,

then, for purposes of subparagraphs (A) and (C), the noncorporate taxpayer or group of noncorporate taxpayers referred to in clause (i) shall be treated as a corporation. The preceding sentence shall apply only if such noncorporate taxpayer (or group of noncorporate taxpayers) on July 1, 1980, held stock constituting control (within the meaning of section 368(c) of the Internal Revenue Code of 1954) of the corporation holding (directly or indirectly) the motor carrier operating authority.

"(C) Adjustment to basis. Under regulations prescribed by the Secretary of the Treasury or his delegate, proper adjustment shall be made to the basis of the stock or other assets in the manner provided by such regulations to take into account any allocation under subparagraph (A).

"(3) Section 381 of the Internal Revenue Code of 1954 to apply. For purposes of section 381 of the Internal Revenue Code of 1954, any item described in this section shall be treated as an item described in subsection (c) of such section 381.
"(d) Effective date.

"The provisions of this section shall apply to taxable years ending after June 30, 1980." [Subpara. (c)(2)(B), above, is effective for tax. yrs. end. after 7/30/80; see Sec. 517(a) of P.L. 97-424, above.]

In 1976, P.L. 94-455, Sec. 1901(a)(26), deleted subsec. (i) and redesignated subsec. (j) as subsec. (i), for tax. yrs. begin. after '76.
Prior to deletion subsec. (i) read as follows:
"(i) Certain property confiscated by the Government of Cuba.

"(1) Treatment as subsection (c)(3) loss. For purposes of this chapter, in the case of an individual who was a citizen of the United States, or a resident alien, on December 31, 1958, any loss of property which—

"(A) was sustained by reason of the expropriation, intervention, seizure, or similar taking of the property, before January 1, 1964, by the government of Cuba, any political subdivision thereof or any agency or instrumentality of the foregoing, and

"(B) was not a loss described in paragraph (1) of subsection (c),

shall be treated as a loss to which paragraph (3) of subsection (c) applies. In the case of tangible property, the preceding sentence shall not apply unless the property was held by the taxpayer, and was located in Cuba, on one or more days in the period beginning on December 31, 1958 and ending on May 16, 1959.

"(2) Special rules.

"(A) For purposes of subsection (a), any loss described in paragraph (1) shall be treated as having been sustained on October 14, 1960, unless it is established that the loss was sustained on some other day.

"(B) For purposes of subsection (a), the fair market value of property held by the taxpayer on one or more days during the period beginning on December 31, 1958, and ending on May 16, 1959, to which paragraph (1) applies, on the day on which the loss of such property was sustained, shall be its fair market value on the first day in such period on which the property was held by the taxpayer.

"(C) For purposes of section 172, a loss described in paragraph (1) shall not be treated as an expropriation loss within the meaning of section 172(k).

"(D) For purposes of section 6601, the amount of any tax imposed by this title shall not be reduced by virtue of this subsection for any period prior to February 26, 1964."

Sec. 2103 of the Act provides as follows:
"SEC. 2103. TAX TREATMENT OF CERTAIN 1972 DISASTER LOSSES.
"(a) Application of section.

This section shall apply to any individual—

"(1) who was allowed a deduction under section 165 of the Internal Revenue Code of 1954 (relating to losses) for a loss attributable to a disaster occurring during calendar year 1972 which was determined by the President, under section 102 of the Disaster Relief Act of 1970, to warrant disaster assistance by the Federal Government,

"(2) who in connection with such disaster—

"(A) received income in the form of cancellation of a disaster loan under section 7 of the Small Business Act or an emergency loan under subtitle C of the Consolidated Farm and Rural Development Act, or

"(B) received income in the form of compensation (not taken into account in computing the amount of the deduction) for such loss in settlement of any claim of the taxpayer against a person for that person's liability in tort for the damage or destruction of that taxpayer's property in connection with the disaster, and

"(3) who elects (at such time and in such manner as the Secretary of the Treasury or his delegate may by regulations prescribe) to take the benefits of this section.

"(b) Effect of election.

In the case of any individual to whom this section applies—

"(1) the tax imposed by chapter 1 of the Internal Revenue Code of 1954 for the taxable year in which the income taken into account is received or accrued which is attributable to such income shall not exceed the additional tax under such chapter which would have been payable for the year in which the deduction for the loss was taken if such deduction had not been taken for such year,

"(2) any amount of tax imposed by chapter 1 attributable to the income taken into account which, on October 1, 1975, was unpaid may be paid in 3 equal annual installments (with the first such installment due and payable on April 15, 1977), and

"(3) no interest on any deficiency shall be payable for any period before April 16, 1977, to the extent such deficiency is attributable to the receipt of such compensation, and no interest on any installment referred to in paragraph (2) shall be payable for any period before the due date of such installment.
"(c) Income taken into account.

For purposes of this section, the income taken into account is—

"(1) in the case of an individual described in subsection (a)(2)(A), the amount of income (not in excess of $5,000) attributable to the cancellation of a disaster loan under section 7 of the Small Business Act or an emergency loan under subtitle C of the Consolidated Farm and Rural Development Act received by reason of the disaster described in subsection (a)(1), or

"(2) in the case of an individual described in subsection (a)(2)(B), the amount of compensation (not in excess of $5,000) for the loss in settlement of any claim of the taxpayer against a person for that person's liability in tort for the damage or destruction of that taxpayer's property in connection with the disaster described in subsection (a)(1).

"(d) Phaseout where adjusted gross income exceeds $15,000.

If for the taxable year for which the deduction for the loss was taken the individual's adjusted gross income exceeded $15,000, the $5,000 limit set forth in paragraph (1) or (2) of subsection (c) (whichever applies) shall be reduced by one dollar for each full dollar that such adjusted gross income exceeds $15,000. In the case of a married individual filing a separate return, the preceding sentence shall be applied by substituting '$7,500' for '$15,000'.
"(e) Statute of limitations.

If refund or credit of any overpayment of income tax resulting from an election made under this section is prevented on the date of the enactment of this Act, or at any time within one year after such date, by the operation of any law, or rule of law, refund or credit of such overpayment (to the extent attributable to such election) may, nevertheless, be made or allowed if claim therefor is filed within one year after such date. If the taxpayer makes an election under this section and if assessment of any deficiency for any taxable year resulting from such election is prevented on the date of the enactment of this Act, or at any time within one year after such date, by the operation of any law or rule of law, such assessment (to the extent attributable to such election) may, nevertheless, be made if made within one year after such date."

In 1974, P.L. 93-288, Sec. 602(h), amended subsec. (h) by striking out "1970" and inserting in lieu thereof "1974", effective 4/1/74.

1,553

Code Sec. 165 — Deductions

In **1972,** P.L. 92-418, Sec. 2(a), amended subsec. (h), effective for disasters occurring after 12/31/71, in tax. yrs. end. after such date.
Prior to amendment subsec. (h) read as follows:
"(h) Disaster losses.
"Notwithstanding the provisions of subsection (a), any loss
"(1) attributable to a disaster which occurs during the period after the close of the taxable year and on or before the last day of the 6th calendar month beginning after the close of the taxable year, and
"(2) occurring in an area subsequently determined by the President of the United States to warrant assistance by the Federal Government under the Disaster Relief Act of 1970, at the election of the taxpayer, may be deducted for the taxable year immediately preceding the taxable year in which the disaster occurred. Such deduction shall not be in excess of so much of the loss as would have been deductible in the taxable year in which the casualty occurred. If an election is made under this subsection, the casualty resulting in the loss will be deemed to have occurred in the taxable year for which the deduction is claimed."
—P.L. 92-336, Sec. 2, amended para. (h)(1), effective for disasters occurring after 12/31/71, in tax. yrs. end. after 12/31/71.
Prior to amendment, para. (h)(1) read as follows:
"(1) attributable to a disaster which occurs during the period following the close of the taxable year and on or before the time prescribed by law for filing the income tax return for the taxable year (determined without regard to any extension of time), and"
In **1971,** P.L. 91-687, Sec. 1, amended subpara. (g)(3)(A)
Prior to amendment, subpara. (g)(3)(A) read as follows: "(A) at least 95 percent of each class of its stock is owned directly by the taxpayer, and" and added a new sentence at the end of para. (g)(3), effective for tax. yrs. begin. or on after 1/1/70.
—P.L. 91-677, Sec. 1(a), substituted "paragraph (1) of subsection (c)" for "paragraph (1) or (2) of subsection (c)," in subpara. (i)(1)(B) substituted "on one or more days in the period beginning on December 31, 1958, and ending on May 16, 1959" for "on December 31, 1958" in the last sentence of para. (i)(1), substituted new subpara. (i)(2)(B), struck out para. (i)(3), effective for losses sustained in tax. yrs. end. after 12/31/58. Notwithstanding any law or rule of law, refund or credit of any overpayment attributable to the amendments made by subsection (a) may be made or allowed if claim therefor is filed after 1/12/71 and before 7/1/71. No interest shall be allowed with respect to any such refund or credit for any period before 1/1/72.
Prior to amendment, subpara. (i)(2)(B) read as follows:
"(B) For purposes of subsection (a), the fair market value of property held by the taxpayer on December 31, 1958, to which paragraph (1) applies, on the day on which the loss of such property was sustained, shall be its fair market value on December 31, 1958."
Prior to amendment, para. (i)(3) read as follows:
"(3) Refunds or credits. Notwithstanding any law or rule of law, refund or credit of any overpayment attributable to the application of paragraph (1) may be made or allowed if claim therefor is filed before January 1, 1965. No interest shall be allowed with respect to any such refund or credit for any period prior to February 26, 1964."
In **1970,** P.L. 91-606, Sec. 301(h), substituted "the Disaster Relief Act of 1970," for "sections 1855 – 1855g of title 42," in para. (h)(2), effective 12/31/70.
In **1964,** P.L. 88-348, Sec. 3(a), amended subsec. (i), effective for losses sustained in tax. yrs. end. after 12/31/58.
Prior to amendment, subsec. (i) read as follows:
"(i) Certain property confiscated by Cuba. For purposes of this chapter, any loss of tangible property, if such loss arises from expropriation, intervention, seizure, or similar taking by the government of Cuba, any political subdivision thereof, or any agency or instrumentality of the foregoing, shall be treated as a loss from a casualty within the meaning of subsection (c)(3).
—P.L. 88-272, Sec. 208(a), amended para. (c)(3), effective for losses sustained after 12/31/63, in tax. yrs. end. after 12/31/63.
Prior to amendment, para. (c)(3) read as follows:
"(3) losses of property not connected with a trade or business, if such losses arise from fire, storm, shipwreck, or other casualty, or from theft. No loss described in this paragraph shall be allowed if, at the time of the filing of the return, such loss has been claimed for estate tax purposes in the estate tax return."
—P.L. 88-272, Sec. 238, added subsec. (i) and redesignated former subsec. (i) as (j).
In **1962,** P.L. 87-426, Sec. 2(a)(2), added subsec. (h), and redesignated former subsec. (h) as (i), effective for any disaster occurring after 12/31/61.
In **1958,** P.L. 85-866, Sec. 7, substituted "rental of" for "rental from" in subpara. (g)(3)(B), as of original date of '54 Code ... Sec. 57(c)(1), added paras. (h)(3) and (4), effective for tax. yrs. begin. after 9/2/58 ... Sec. 202(a), added para. (h)(5), effective 9/2/58.

Sec. 166. Bad debts.
(a) General rule.
  (1) Wholly worthless debts. There shall be allowed as a deduction any debt which becomes worthless within the taxable year.
  (2) Partially worthless debts. When satisfied that a debt is recoverable only in part, the Secretary may allow such debt, in an amount not in excess of the part charged off within the taxable year, as a deduction.

(b) Amount of deduction.
For purposes of subsection (a), the basis for determining the amount of the deduction for any bad debt shall be the adjusted basis provided in section 1011 for determining the loss from the sale or other disposition of property.
(c) Repealed.
(d) Nonbusiness debts.
  (1) General rule. In the case of a taxpayer other than a corporation—
    (A) subsection (a) shall not apply to any nonbusiness debt; and
    (B) where any nonbusiness debt becomes worthless within the taxable year, the loss resulting therefrom shall be considered a loss from the sale or exchange, during the taxable year, of a capital asset held for not more than 1 year.
  (2) Nonbusiness debt defined. For purposes of paragraph (1), the term "nonbusiness debt" means a debt other than—
    (A) a debt created or acquired (as the case may be) in connection with a trade or business of the taxpayer; or
    (B) a debt the loss from the worthlessness of which is incurred in the taxpayer's trade or business.
(e) Worthless securities.
This section shall not apply to a debt which is evidenced by a security as defined in section 165(g)(2)(C).
(f) Cross references.
  (1) For disallowance of deduction for worthlessness of debts owed by political parties and similar organizations, see section 271.
  (2) For special rule for banks with respect to worthless securities, see section 582.

In **1993,** P.L. 103-66, Sec. 13224, of this Act, relating to clarification of treatment of certain FSLIC financial assistance is reproduced in the notes following Code Sec. 165.
In **1988,** P.L. 100-647, Sec. 1008(d)(1), substituted "subsection (a)" for "subsections (a) and (c)" in subpara. (d)(1)(A), effective for tax. yrs. begin. after 12/31/86. For special rules see Sec. 805(d)(2) of P.L. 99-514, reproduced below.
—P.L. 100-647, Sec. 1008(d)(2), amended Sec. 805(b) of P.L. 99-514, part of the changes made to Code Sec. 166 by P.L. 99-514, by adding "as amended by Sec. 901(d)(4)" after "section 166", see below.
In **1986,** P.L. 99-514, Sec. 805(a), deleted subsec. (c) ... Sec. 805(b), [as amended by Sec. 901(d)(4)] deleted subsec. (f), and redesignated subsec. (g) as subsec. (f), effective for tax. yrs. begin. after 12/31/86. Sec. 805(d)(2) of this Act provides:
"(2) Change in method of accounting. In the case of any taxpayer who maintained a reserve for bad debts for such taxpayer's last taxable year beginning before January 1, 1987, and who is required by the amendments made by this section to change its method of accounting for any taxable year—
"(A) such change shall be treated as initiated by the taxpayer,
"(B) such change shall be treated as made with the consent of the Secretary, and
"(C) the net amount of adjustments required by section 481 of the Internal Revenue Code of 1986 to be taken into account by the taxpayer shall—
"(i) in the case of a taxpayer maintaining a reserve under section 166(f), be reduced by the balance in the suspense account under section 166(f)(4) of such Code as of the close of such last taxable year, and
"(ii) be taken into account ratably in each of the first 4 taxable years beginning after December 31, 1986."
Prior to deletion, subsec. (c) read as follows:
"(c) Reserve for bad debts. In lieu of any deduction under subsection (a), there shall be allowed (in the discretion of the Secretary) a deduction for a reasonable addition to a reserve for bad debts."
Prior to deletion, subsec. (f) read as follows:
"(f) Reserve for certain guaranteed debt obligations.
"(1) Allowance of deduction. In the case of a taxpayer who is a dealer in property, in lieu of any deduction under subsection (a), there shall be allowed (in the discretion of the Secretary) for any taxable year ending after October 21, 1965, a deduction—
"(A) for a reasonable addition to a reserve for bad debts which may arise out of his liability as a guarantor, endorser, or indemnitor of debt obligations arising out of the sale by him of real property or tangible personal property (including related services) in the ordinary course of his trade or business; and
"(B) for the amount of any reduction in the suspense account required by paragraph (4)(B)(i).

"(2) Deduction disallowed in other cases. Except as provided in paragraph (1), no deduction shall be allowed to a taxpayer for any addition to a reserve for bad debts which may arise out of his liability as guarantor, endorser, or indemnitor of debt obligations.

"(3) Opening balance. The opening balance of a reserve described in paragraph (1)(A) for the first taxable year ending after October 21, 1965, for which a taxpayer maintains such reserve shall, under regulations prescribed by the Secretary, be determined as if the taxpayer had maintained such reserve for the preceding taxable years.

"(4) Suspense account.

"(A) Requirement. Except as provided by subparagraph (C), each taxpayer who maintains a reserve described in paragraph (1)(A) shall, for purposes of this subsection and section 81, establish and maintain a suspense account. The initial balance of such account shall be equal to the opening balance described in paragraph (3).

"(B) Adjustments. At the close of each taxable year the suspense account shall be—

"(i) reduced by the excess of the suspense account at the beginning of the year over the reserve described in paragraph (1)(A) (after making the addition for such year provided in such paragraph), or

"(ii) increased (but not to an amount greater than the initial balance of the suspense account) by the excess of the reserve described in paragraph (1)(A) (after making the addition for such year provided in such paragraph) over the suspense account at the beginning of such year.

"(C) Limitations. Subparagraphs (A) and (B) shall not apply in the case of the taxpayer who maintained for his last taxable year ending before October 22, 1965, a reserve for bad debts under subsection (c) which included debt obligations described in paragraph (1)(A).

"(D) Section 381 Acquisitions. The application of this paragraph in any acquisition to which section 381(a) applies shall be determined under regulations prescribed by the Secretary."

—P.L. 99-514, Sec. 901(d)(4)(A), deleted paras. (g)(3) and (g)(4) [before redesignation by Sec. 805(b) of this Act], effective for tax. yrs. begin. after 12/31/86. Prior to deletion, paras. (g)(3) and (g)(4), read as follows:

"(3) For special rule for bad debt reserves of certain mutual savings banks, domestic building and loan associations, and cooperative banks, see section 593.

"(4) For special rule for bad debt reserves of banks, small business investment companies, etc., see sections 585 and 586."

In 1984, P.L. 98-369, Sec. 1001(b)(1), substituted "6 months" for "1 year" in subpara. (d)(1)(B), effective for property acquired after 6/22/84 and before 1/1/88.

In 1976, P.L. 94-455, Sec. 605(a), deleted subsec. (f) and redesignated subsecs. (g) and (h) as subsecs. (f) and (g), effective for guarantees made after 12/31/75, in tax. yrs. begin. after 12/31/75.

Prior to deletion, subsec. (f) read as follows:

"(f) Guarantor of certain noncorporate obligations.

"A payment by the taxpayer (other than a corporation) in discharge of part or all of his obligation as a guarantor, endorser, or indemnitor of a noncorporate obligation the proceeds or which were used in the trade or business of the borrower shall be treated as a debt becoming worthless within such taxable year for purposes of this section (except that subsection (d) shall not apply), but only if the obligation of the borrower to the person to whom such payment was made was worthless (without regard to such guaranty, endorsement, or indemnity) at the time of such payment."

—P.L. 94-455, Sec. 1402(b)(1)(A), substituted "9 months" for "6 months" in subpara. (d)(1)(B), effective for tax. yrs. begin. in '77.

—P.L. 94-455, Sec. 1402(b)(2), substituted "1 year" for "9 months" in subpara. (d)(1)(B), effective for tax. yrs. begin. after '77.

—P.L. 94-455, Sec. 1906(b)(13)(A), substituted "Secretary" for "Secretary or his delegate" in subsecs. (a), (c), and (f), effective for tax. yrs. begin. after 12/31/76.

In 1969, P.L. 91-172, Sec. 431(c)(1), added para. (h)(4), effective for tax. yrs. begin. after 7/11/69.

In 1966, P.L. 89-722, Sec. 1(a), redesignated subsec. (g) as (h) and added subsec. (g), effective for tax. yrs. end. after 10/21/65 except that

"(b) If—

"(1) the taxpayer before October 22, 1965, claimed a deduction, for a taxable year ending before such date, under section 166(c) of the Internal Revenue Code of 1954 for an addition to a reserve for bad debts on account of debt obligations described in section 166(g)(1)(A) of such Code (as amended by the first section of this Act), and

"(2) the assessment of a deficiency of the tax imposed by chapter 1 of such Code for such taxable year and each subsequent taxable year ending before October 22, 1965, is not prevented on December 31, 1966, by the operation of any law or rule of law,

then such deduction on account of such debt obligations shall be allowed for each such taxable year under such section 166(c) to the extent that the deduction would have been allowable under the provisions of such section 166(g)(1)(A) if such provisions applied to such taxable years.

"(c) Section 166(g)(2) of the Internal Revenue Code of 1954 (as amended by the first section of this Act) shall apply to taxable years beginning after December 31, 1953, and ending after August 16, 1954."

also provided that

"(c) If the taxpayer establishes a reserve described in section 166(g)(1) of the Internal Revenue Code of 1954 (as amended by subsection (a) of this section) for a taxable year ending after October 21, 1965, and beginning before August 2, 1966, the establishment of such reserve shall not be considered as a change in method of accounting for purposes of section 446(e) of such Code."

In 1958, P.L. 85-866, Sec. 8, substituted "a trade or business of the taxpayer" for "a taxpayer's trade or business" in subpara. (d)(2)(A), effective for tax. yrs. begin. after 12/31/53 and end. after 8/16/54.

Sec. 167. Depreciation.

(a) General rule.

There shall be allowed as a depreciation deduction a reasonable allowance for the exhaustion, wear and tear (including a reasonable allowance for obsolescence)—

(1) of property used in the trade or business, or

(2) of property held for the production of income.

(b) Cross reference.

For determination of depreciation deduction in case of property to which section 168 applies, see section 168.

(c) Basis for depreciation.

(1) In general. The basis on which exhaustion, wear and tear, and obsolescence are to be allowed in respect of any property shall be the adjusted basis provided in section 1011, for the purpose of determining the gain on the sale or other disposition of such property.

(2) Special rule for property subject to lease. If any property is acquired subject to a lease—

(A) no portion of the adjusted basis shall be allocated to the leasehold interest, and

(B) the entire adjusted basis shall be taken into account in determining the depreciation deduction (if any) with respect to the property subject to the lease.

(d) Life tenants and beneficiaries of trusts and estates.

In the case of property held by one person for life with remainder to another person, the deduction shall be computed as if the life tenant were the absolute owner of the property and shall be allowed to the life tenant. In the case of property held in trust, the allowable deduction shall be apportioned between the income beneficiaries and the trustee in accordance with the pertinent provisions of the instrument creating the trust, or, in the absence of such provisions, on the basis of the trust income allocable to each. In the case of an estate, the allowable deduction shall be apportioned between the estate and the heirs, legatees, and devisees on the basis of the income of the estate allocable to each.

(e) Certain term interests not depreciable.

(1) In general. No depreciation deduction shall be allowed under this section (and no depreciation or amortization deduction shall be allowed under any other provision of this subtitle) to the taxpayer for any term interest in property for any period during which the remainder interest in such property is held (directly or indirectly) by a related person.

(2) Coordination with other provisions.

(A) Section 273. This subsection shall not apply to any term interest to which section 273 applies.

(B) Section 305(e). This subsection shall not apply to the holder of the dividend rights which were separated from any stripped preferred stock to which section 305(e)(1) applies.

(3) Basis adjustments. If, but for this subsection, a depreciation or amortization deduction would be allowable to the taxpayer with respect to any term interest in property—

(A) the taxpayer's basis in such property shall be reduced by any depreciation or amortization deductions disallowed under this subsection, and

(B) the basis of the remainder interest in such property shall be increased by the amount of such disallowed deductions (properly adjusted for any depreciation deductions allowable under subsection (d) to the taxpayer).

(4) Special rules.
  (A) Denial of increase in basis of remainderman. No increase in the basis of the remainder interest shall be made under paragraph (3)(B) for any disallowed deductions attributable to periods during which the term interest was held—
    (i) by an organization exempt from tax under this subtitle, or
    (ii) by a nonresident alien individual or foreign corporation but only if income from the term interest is not effectively connected with the conduct of a trade or business in the United States.
  (B) Coordination with subsection (d). If, but for this subsection, a depreciation or amortization deduction would be allowable to any person with respect to any term interest in property, the principles of subsection (d) shall apply to such person with respect to such term interest.
(5) Definitions. For purposes of this subsection—
  (A) Term interest in property. The term "term interest in property" has the meaning given such term by section 1001(e)(2).
  (B) Related person. The term "related person" means any person bearing a relationship to the taxpayer described in subsection (b) or (e) of section 267.
(6) Regulations. The Secretary shall prescribe such regulations as may be necessary to carry out the purposes of this subsection, including regulations preventing avoidance of this subsection through cross-ownership arrangements or otherwise.

(f) Treatment of certain property excluded from section 197.
(1) Computer software.
  (A) In general. If a depreciation deduction is allowable under subsection (a) with respect to any computer software, such deduction shall be computed by using the straight line method and a useful life of 36 months.
  (B) Computer software. For purposes of this section, the term "computer software" has the meaning given to such term by section 197(e)(3)(B); except that such term shall not include any such software which is an amortizable section 197 intangible.
  (C) Tax-exempt use property subject to lease. In the case of computer software which would be tax-exempt use property as defined in subsection (h) of section 168 if such section applied to computer software, the useful life under subparagraph (A) shall not be less than 125 percent of the lease term (within the meaning of section 168(i)(3)).
(2) Certain interests or rights acquired separately. If a depreciation deduction is allowable under subsection (a) with respect to any property described in subparagraph (B), (C), or (D) of section 197(e)(4), such deduction shall be computed in accordance with regulations prescribed by the Secretary. If such property would be tax-exempt use property as defined in subsection (h) of section 168 if such section applied to such property, the useful life under such regulations shall not be less than 125 percent of the lease term (within the meaning of section 168(i)(3)).
(3) Mortgage servicing rights. If a depreciation deduction is allowable under subsection (a) with respect to any right described in section 197(e)(6), such deduction shall be computed by using the straight line method and a useful life of 108 months.

(g) Depreciation under income forecast method.
(1) In general. If the depreciation deduction allowable under this section to any taxpayer with respect to any property is determined under the income forecast method or any similar method—
  (A) the income from the property to be taken into account in determining the depreciation deduction under such method shall be equal to the amount of income earned in connection with the property before the close of the 10th taxable year following the taxable year in which the property was placed in service,
  (B) the adjusted basis of the property shall only include amounts with respect to which the requirements of section 461(h) are satisfied,
  (C) the depreciation deduction under such method for the 10th taxable year beginning after the taxable year in which the property was placed in service shall be equal to the adjusted basis of such property as of the beginning of such 10th taxable year, and
  (D) such taxpayer shall pay (or be entitled to receive) interest computed under the look-back method of paragraph (2) for any recomputation year.
(2) Look-back method. The interest computed under the look-back method of this paragraph for any recomputation year shall be determined by—
  (A) first determining the depreciation deductions under this section with respect to such property which would have been allowable for prior taxable years if the determination of the amounts so allowable had been made on the basis of the sum of the following (instead of the estimated income from such property)—
    (i) the actual income earned in connection with such property for periods before the close of the recomputation year, and
    (ii) an estimate of the future income to be earned in connection with such property for periods after the recomputation year and before the close of the 10th taxable year following the taxable year in which the property was placed in service,
  (B) second, determining (solely for purposes of computing such interest) the overpayment or underpayment of tax for each such prior taxable year which would result solely from the application of subparagraph (A), and
  (C) then using the adjusted overpayment rate (as defined in section 460(b)(7)), compounded daily, on the overpayment or underpayment determined under subparagraph (B).
For purposes of the preceding sentence, any cost incurred after the property is placed in service (which is not treated as a separate property under paragraph (5)) shall be taken into account by discounting (using the Federal mid-term rate determined under section 1274(d) as of the time such cost is incurred) such cost to its value as of the date the property is placed in service. The taxpayer may elect with respect to any property to have the preceding sentence not apply to such property.
(3) Exception from look-back method. Paragraph (1)(D) shall not apply with respect to any property which had a cost basis of $100,000 or less.
(4) Recomputation year. For purposes of this subsection, except as provided in regulations, the term "recomputation year" means, with respect to any property, the 3d and the 10th taxable years beginning after the taxable year in which the property was placed in service, unless the actual income earned in connection with the property for the period before the close of such 3d or 10th taxable year is

Deductions   Code Sec. 167(g)(8)(C)(i)

within 10 percent of the income earned in connection with the property for such period which was taken into account under paragraph (1)(A).

(5) Special rules.

(A) Certain costs treated as separate property. For purposes of this subsection, the following costs shall be treated as separate properties:

(i) Any costs incurred with respect to any property after the 10th taxable year beginning after the taxable year in which the property was placed in service.

(ii) Any costs incurred after the property is placed in service and before the close of such 10th taxable year if such costs are significant and give rise to a significant increase in the income from the property which was not included in the estimated income from the property.

(B) Syndication income from television series. In the case of property which is 1 or more episodes in a television series, income from syndicating such series shall not be required to be taken into account under this subsection before the earlier of—

(i) the 4th taxable year beginning after the date the first episode in such series is placed in service, or

(ii) the earliest taxable year in which the taxpayer has an arrangement relating to the future syndication of such series.

(C) Special rules for financial exploitation of characters, etc. For purposes of this subsection, in the case of television and motion picture films, the income from the property shall include income from the exploitation of characters, designs, scripts, scores, and other incidental income associated with such films, but only to the extent that such income is earned in connection with the ultimate use of such items by, or the ultimate sale of merchandise to, persons who are not related persons (within the meaning of section 267(b)) to the taxpayer.

(D) Collection of interest. For purposes of subtitle F (other than sections 6654 and 6655), any interest required to be paid by the taxpayer under paragraph (1) for any recomputation year shall be treated as an increase in the tax imposed by this chapter for such year.

(E) Treatment of distribution costs. For purposes of this subsection, the income with respect to any property shall be the taxpayer's gross income from such property.

(F) Determinations. For purposes of paragraph (2), determinations of the amount of income earned in connection with any property shall be made in the same manner as for purposes of applying the income forecast method; except that any income from the disposition of such property shall be taken into account.

(G) Treatment of pass-thru entities. Rules similar to the rules of section 460(b)(4) shall apply for purposes of this subsection.

(6) Limitation on property for which income forecast method may be used. The depreciation deduction allowable under this section may be determined under the income forecast method or any similar method only with respect to—

(A) property described in paragraph (3) or (4) of section 168(f),

(B) copyrights,

(C) books,

(D) patents, and

(E) other property specified in regulations.

Such methods may not be used with respect to any amortizable section 197 intangible (as defined in section 197(c)).

(7) Treatment of participations and residuals.

(A) In general. For purposes of determining the depreciation deduction allowable with respect to a property under this subsection, the taxpayer may include participations and residuals with respect to such property in the adjusted basis of such property for the taxable year in which the property is placed in service, but only to the extent that such participations and residuals relate to income estimated (for purposes of this subsection) to be earned in connection with the property before the close of the 10th taxable year referred to in paragraph (1)(A).

(B) Participations and residuals. For purposes of this paragraph, the term "participations and residuals" means, with respect to any property, costs the amount of which by contract varies with the amount of income earned in connection with such property.

(C) Special rules relating to recomputation years. If the adjusted basis of any property is determined under this paragraph, paragraph (4) shall be applied by substituting "for each taxable year in such period" for "for such period".

(D) Other special rules.

(i) Participations and residuals. Notwithstanding subparagraph (A), the taxpayer may exclude participations and residuals from the adjusted basis of such property and deduct such participations and residuals in the taxable year that such participations and residuals are paid.

(ii) Coordination with other rules. Deductions computed in accordance with this paragraph shall be allowable notwithstanding paragraph (1)(B), section 263, 263A, 404, 419, or 461(h).

(E) Authority to make adjustments. The Secretary shall prescribe appropriate adjustments to the basis of property and to the look-back method for the additional amounts allowable as a deduction solely by reason of this paragraph.

(8) Special rules for certain musical works and copyrights.

(A) In general. If an election is in effect under this paragraph for any taxable year, then, notwithstanding paragraph (1), any expense which—

(i) is paid or incurred by the taxpayer in creating or acquiring any applicable musical property placed in service during the taxable year, and

(ii) is otherwise properly chargeable to capital account,

shall be amortized ratably over the 5-year period beginning with the month in which the property was placed in service. The preceding sentence shall not apply to any expense which, without regard to this paragraph, would not be allowable as a deduction.

(B) Exclusive method. Except as provided in this paragraph, no depreciation or amortization deduction shall be allowed with respect to any expense to which subparagraph (A) applies.

(C) Applicable musical property. For purposes of this paragraph—

(i) In general. The term "applicable musical property" means any musical composition (including any accompanying words), or any copyright with respect to a musical composition, which is property to which this subsection applies without regard to this paragraph.

(ii) **Exceptions.** Such term shall not include any property—

(I) with respect to which expenses are treated as qualified creative expenses to which section 263A(h) applies,

(II) to which a simplified procedure established under section 263A(i)(2) applies, or

(III) which is an amortizable section 197 intangible (as defined in section 197(c)).

(D) **Election.** An election under this paragraph shall be made at such time and in such form as the Secretary may prescribe and shall apply to all applicable musical property placed in service during the taxable year for which the election applies.

(E) **Termination.** An election may not be made under this paragraph for any taxable year beginning after December 31, 2010.

(h) **Amortization of geological and geophysical expenditures.**

(1) **In general.** Any geological and geophysical expenses paid or incurred in connection with the exploration for, or development of, oil or gas within the United States (as defined in section 638) shall be allowed as a deduction ratably over the 24-month period beginning on the date that such expense was paid or incurred.

(2) **Half-year convention.** For purposes of paragraph (1), any payment paid or incurred during the taxable year shall be treated as paid or incurred on the mid-point of such taxable year.

(3) **Exclusive method.** Except as provided in this subsection, no depreciation or amortization deduction shall be allowed with respect to such payments.

(4) **Treatment upon abandonment.** If any property with respect to which geological and geophysical expenses are paid or incurred is retired or abandoned during the 24-month period described in paragraph (1), no deduction shall be allowed on account of such retirement or abandonment and the amortization deduction under this subsection shall continue with respect to such payment.

(5) **Special rule for major integrated oil companies.**

(A) **In general.** In the case of a major integrated oil company, paragraphs (1) and (4) shall be applied by substituting "7-year" for "24 month".

(B) **Major integrated oil company.** For purposes of this paragraph, the term "major integrated oil company" means, with respect to any taxable year, a producer of crude oil—

(i) which has an average daily worldwide production of crude oil of at least 500,000 barrels for the taxable year,

(ii) which had gross receipts in excess of $1,000,000,000 for its last taxable year ending during calendar year 2005, and

(iii) to which subsection (c) of section 613A does not apply by reason of paragraph (4) of section 613A(d), determined—

(I) by substituting "15 percent" for "5 percent" each place it occurs in paragraph (3) of section 613A(d), and

(II) without regard to whether subsection (c) of section 613A does not apply by reason of paragraph (2) of section 613A(d).

For purposes of clauses (i) and (ii), all persons treated as a single employer under subsections (a) and (b) of section 52 shall be treated as 1 person and, in case of a short taxable year, the rule under section 448(c)(3)(B) shall apply.

(i) **Cross references.**

(1) For additional rule applicable to depreciation of improvements in the case of mines, oil and gas wells, other natural deposits, and timber, see section 611.

(2) For amortization of goodwill and certain other intangibles, see section 197.

In 2007, P.L. 110-172, Sec. 11(a)(13), substituted "section 263A(i)(2)" for "section 263A(j)(2)" in subclause (g)(8)(C)(ii)(II), enacted 12/29/2007.

—P.L. 110-140, Sec. 1502(a), substituted "7-year" for "5-year", effective for amounts paid or incurred after 12/19/2007.

In 2006, P.L. 109-222, Sec. 207(a), added para. (g)(8), effective for expenses paid or incurred with respect to property placed in service in tax. yrs. begin. after 12/31/2005.

—P.L. 109-222, Sec. 503(a), added para. (h)(5), effective for amounts paid or incurred after 5/17/2006.

In 2005, P.L. 109-135, Sec. 403(ff), of this Act [which amends Sec. 849(a) of P.L. 108-357, see below], reads as follows:

"(ff) Amendment Related to Section 849 of the Act. Subsection (a) of section 849 of the American Jobs Creation Act of 2004 is amended by inserting ', and in the case of property treated as tax-exempt use property other than by reason of a lease, to property acquired after March 12, 2004' before the period at the end."

Sec. 849 provides the effective date for the amendment made by Sec. 847(b)(1) and (2) of P.L. 108-357, see below.

—P.L. 109-135, Sec. 412(r), substituted "section 197(e)(6)" for "section 197(e)(7)" in para. (f)(3), effective 12/21/2005.

—P.L. 109-58, Sec. 1329(a), redesignated subsec. (h) as subsec. (i) and added subsec. (h), effective for amounts paid or incurred in tax. yrs. begin. after 8/8/2005.

In 2004, P.L. 108-357, Sec. 242(a), added para. (g)(7)... Sec. 242(b), redesignated subparas. (g)(5)(E)-(F) as (g)(5)(F)-(G) and added subpara. (g)(5)(E), effective for property placed in service after 10/22/2004.

—P.L. 108-357, Sec. 847(b)(1), added subpara. (f)(1)(C)... Sec. 847(b)(2), added "If such property would be tax-exempt use property as defined in subsection (h) of section 168 if such section applied to such property, the useful life under such regulations shall not be less than 125 percent of the lease term (within the meaning of section 168(i)(3))." at the end of para. (f)(2), effective for leases entered into after 3/12/2004[, and in the case of property treated as tax-exempt use property other than by reason of a lease, to property acquired after March 12, 2004.] [as added by Sec. 403(ff), P.L. 109-135, see above]

—P.L. 108-357, Sec. 849(b), of this Act, reads as follows:

"(b) Exception.

"(1) In general. The amendments made by this part shall not apply to qualified transportation property.

"(2) Qualified transportation property. For purposes of paragraph (1), the term 'qualified transportation property' means domestic property subject to a lease with respect to which a formal application—

"(A) was submitted for approval to the Federal Transit Administration (an agency of the Department of Transportation) after June 30, 2003, and before March 13, 2004,

"(B) is approved by the Federal Transit Administration before January 1, 2006, and

"(C) includes a description of such property and the value of such property.

"(3) Exchanges and conversion of tax-exempt use property. Section 470(c)(4) of the Internal Revenue Code of 1986, as added by section 848, shall apply to property exchanged or converted after the date of the enactment of this Act.

"(4) Intangibles and Indian tribal governments. The amendments made subsections (b)(2), (b)(3), and (e) of section 847, and the treatment of property described in clauses (ii) and (iii) of section 470(c)(2)(B) of the Internal Revenue Code of 1986 (as added by section 848) as tangible property, shall apply to leases entered into after October 3, 2004."

In 1998, P.L. 105-206, Sec. 6018(d)(1), substituted "the Internal Revenue Code of 1986" for "such Code" in Sec. 1604(b)(3) of P.L. 104-188 [see below]... Sec. 6018(d)(2), substituted "the date of the enactment of this Act" for "such date of enactment" in Sec. 1604(b)(3) of P.L. 104-188 [see below].

In 1997, P.L. 105-34, Sec. 1086(a), added para. (g)(6), effective for property placed in service after 8/5/97.

In 1996, P.L. 104-188, Sec. 1604(a), redesignated subsec. (g) as subsec. (h) and added new subsec. (g), effective for property placed in service after 9/13/95, except as provided in Sec. 1604(b)(2) and (3) of this Act [as amended by Sec. 6017(d)(1) and (2) of 105-206, see above], which reads as follows:

"(2) Binding contracts. The amendment made by subsection (a) shall not apply to any property produced or acquired by the taxpayer pursuant to a written contract which was binding on September 13, 1995, and at all times thereafter before such production or acquisition.

"(3) Underpayments of income tax. No addition to tax shall be made under section 6662 of the Internal Revenue Code of 1986 as a result of the application of subsection (d) of that section (relating to substantial understatements of income tax) with respect to any underpayment of income tax for any taxable year ending

Deductions Code Sec. 167

before the date of the enactment of this Act, to the extent such underpayment was created or increased by the amendments made by subsection (a)."

—P.L. 104-188, Sec. 1703(l), amended Sec. 13261(g)(2)(A)(iii) of P.L. 103-66 by substituting "by the taxpayer or a related person" for "by the taxpayer", see below.

In 1993, P.L. 103-66, Sec. 13206(c)(2), amended para. (e)(2), effective 4/30/93. Prior to amendment, para. (e)(2) read as follows:

"(2) Coordination with section 273. This subsection shall not apply to any term interest to which section 273 applies."

—P.L. 103-66, Sec. 13261(b)(1), redesignated subsec. (f) as subsec. (g) and added new subsec. (f)... Sec. 13261(b)(2), amended subsec. (c)... Sec. 13261(f)(1), amended subsec. (g) [as redesignated by Sec. 13261(b)(1) of this Act, see above], effective for property acquired after 8/10/93, except as provided in Sec. 13261(g)(2) [as amended by Sec. 1703(l) of P.L. 104-188, see above] and (3) of this Act, which read as follows:

"(2) Election to have amendments apply to property acquired after July 25, 1991.—

"(A) In general.— If an election under this paragraph applies to the taxpayer—

"(i) the amendments made by this section shall apply to property acquired by the taxpayer after July 25, 1991,

"(ii) subsection (c)(1)(A) of section 197 of the Internal Revenue Code of 1986 (as added by this section) (and so much of subsection (f)(9)(A) of such section 197 as precedes clause (i) thereof) shall be applied with respect to the taxpayer by treating July 25, 1991, as the date of the enactment of such section, and

"(iii) in applying subsection (f)(9) of such section, with respect to any property acquired by the taxpayer or a related person on or before the date of the enactment of this Act, only holding or use on July 25, 1991, shall be taken into account.

"(B) Election.— An election under this paragraph shall be made at such time and in such manner as the Secretary of the Treasury or his delegate may prescribe. Such an election by any taxpayer, once made—

"(i) may be revoked only with the consent of the Secretary, and

"(ii) shall apply to the taxpayer making such election and any other taxpayer under common control with the taxpayer (within the meaning of subparagraphs (A) and (B) of section 41(f)(1) of such Code) at any time after August 2, 1993, and on or before the date on which such election is made.

"(3) Elective binding contract exception.—

"(A) In general.— The amendments made by this section shall not apply to any acquisition of property by the taxpayer if—

"(i) such acquisition is pursuant to a written binding contract in effect on the date of the enactment of this Act and at all times thereafter before such acquisition,

"(ii) an election under paragraph (2) does not apply to the taxpayer, and

"(iii) the taxpayer makes an election under this paragraph with respect to such contract.

"(B) Election.— An election under this paragraph shall be made at such time and in such manner as the Secretary of the Treasury or his delegate shall prescribe. Such an election, once made—

"(i) may be revoked only with the consent of the Secretary, and

"(ii) shall apply to all property acquired pursuant to the contract with respect to which such election was made."

Prior to amendment, subsec. (c) read as follows:

"(c) Basis for depreciation.

"The basis on which exhaustion, wear and tear, and obsolescence are to be allowed in respect of any property shall be the adjusted basis provided in section 1011 for the purpose of determining the gain on the sale or other disposition of such property."

Prior to amendment, subsec. (g) read as follows:

"(g) Depreciation of improvements in the case of mines, etc.

"For additional rule applicable to depreciation of improvements in the case of mines, oil and gas wells, other natural deposits, and timber, see section 611."

In 1990, P.L. 101-508, Sec. 11812(a)(1), deleted subsecs. (b)-(f), (j)-(m), (p), and (q) and redesignated subsecs. (g), (h), (r), and (s) as subsecs. (c), (d), (e), and (f) ... Sec. 11812(a)(2), added new subsec. (b). .. Sec. 11812(b)(1), substituted "(d)" for "(h)" in subparas. (e)(3)(B) and (e)(4)(B), as redesignated, effective for property placed in service after 11/5/90 except as provided in Sec. 11812(c)(2) and (c)(3) of this Act, which read as follows:

"(2) Exception. The amendments made by this section shall not apply to any property to which section 168 of the Internal Revenue Code of 1986 does not apply by reason of subsection (f)(5) thereof.

"(3) Exception for previously grandfather expenditures. The amendments made by this section shall not apply to rehabilitation expenditures described in section 252(f)(5) of the Tax Reform Act of 1986 (as added by section 1002(l)(31) of the Technical and Miscellaneous Revenue Act of 1988)."

Prior to deletion, subsecs. (b)-(f) read as follows:

"(b) Use of certain methods and rates.

"For taxable years ending after December 31, 1953, the term 'reasonable allowance' as used in subsection (a) shall include (but shall not be limited to) an allowance computed in accordance with regulations prescribed by the Secretary, under any of the following methods:

"(1) the straight line method,

"(2) the declining balance method, using a rate not exceeding twice the rate which would have been used had the annual allowance been computed under the method described in paragraph (1),

"(3) the sum of the years-digits method, and

"(4) any other consistent method productive of an annual allowance which, when added to all allowances for the period commencing with the taxpayer's use of the property and including the taxable year, does not, during the first two-thirds of the useful life of the property, exceed the total of such allowances which would have been used had such allowances been computed under the method described in paragraph (2).

Nothing in this subsection shall be construed to limit or reduce an allowance otherwise allowable under subsection (a).

"(c) Limitations on use of certain methods and rates.

Paragraphs (2), (3), and (4) of subsection (b) shall apply only in the case of property (other than intangible property) described in subsection (a) with a useful life of 3 years or more —

"(1) the construction, reconstruction, or erection of which is completed after December 31, 1953, and then only to that portion of the basis which is properly attributable to such construction, reconstruction, or erection after December 31, 1953, or

"(2) acquired after December 31, 1953, if the original use of such property commences with the taxpayer and commences after such date.

Paragraphs (2), (3), and (4) of subsection (b) shall not apply to any motion picture film, video tape, or sound recording.

"(d) Agreement as to useful life on which depreciation rate is based.

"Where, under regulations prescribed by the Secretary, the taxpayer and the Secretary have after August 16, 1954, entered into an agreement in writing specifically dealing with the useful life and rate of depreciation of any property, the rate so agreed upon shall be binding on both the taxpayer and the Secretary in the absence of facts or circumstances not taken into consideration in the adoption of such agreement. The responsibility of establishing the existence of such facts and circumstances shall rest with the party initiating the modification. Any change in the agreed rate and useful life specified in the agreement shall not be effective for taxable years before the taxable year in which notice in writing by certified mail or registered mail is served by the party to the agreement initiating such change. This subsection shall not apply with respect to property to which section 168 applies.

"(e) Change in method.

"(1) Change from declining balance method. In the absence of an agreement under subsection (d) containing a provision to the contrary, a taxpayer may at any time elect in accordance with regulations prescribed by the Secretary to change from the method of depreciation described in subsection (b)(2) to the method described in subsection (b)(1).

"(2) Change with respect to section 1245 property. A taxpayer may, on or before the last day prescribed by law (including extensions thereof) for filing his return for his first taxable year beginning after December 31, 1962, and in such manner as the Secretary shall by regulations prescribe, elect to change his method of depreciation in respect of section 1245 property (as defined in section 1245(a)(3)) from any declining balance or sum of the years-digits method to the straight line method. An election may be made under this paragraph notwithstanding any provision to the contrary in an agreement under subsection (d).

"(3) Change with respect to section 1250 property. A taxpayer may, on or before the last day prescribed by law (including extensions thereof) for filing his return for his first taxable year beginning after December 31, 1975, and in such manner as the Secretary shall by regulation prescribe, elect to change his method of depreciation in respect of section 1250 property (as defined in section 1250(c)) from any declining balance or sum of the years-digits method to the straight line method. An election may be made under this paragraph notwithstanding any provision to the contrary in an agreement under subsection (d).

"(f) Salvage value.

"(1) General rule. Under regulations prescribed by the Secretary, a taxpayer may, for purposes of computing the allowance under subsection (a) with respect to personal property, reduce the amount taken into account as salvage value by an amount which does not exceed 10 percent of the basis of such property (as determined under subsection (g)) as of the time as of which salvage value is required to be determined.

"(2) Personal property defined. For purposes of this subsection, the term 'personal property' means depreciable personal property (other than livestock) with a useful life of 3 years or more acquired after October 16, 1962."

Prior to amendment, subsecs. (j)-(m) read as follows:

"(j) Special rules for section 1250 property.

"(1) General rule. Except as provided in paragraphs (2) and (3), in the case of section 1250 property, subsection (b) shall not apply and the term 'reasonable allowance' as used in subsection (a) shall include an allowance computed in accordance with regulations prescribed by the Secretary, under any of the following methods:

"(A) the straight line method.

"(B) the declining balance method, using a rate not exceeding 150 percent of the rate which would have been used had the annual allowance been computed under the method described in subparagraph (A), or

"(C) any other consistent method productive of an annual allowance which, when added to all allowances for the period commencing with the taxpayer's use of the property and including the taxable year, does not, during the first two-thirds of the useful life of the property, exceed the total of such allowances which would have been used had such allowances been computed under the method described in subparagraph (B).

Nothing in this paragraph shall be construed to limit or reduce an allowance otherwise allowable under subsection (a) except where allowable solely by reason of paragraph (2), (3), or (4) of subsection (b).

"(2) Residential rental property.

"(A) In general. Paragraph (1) of this subsection shall not apply, and subsection (b) shall apply in any taxable year, to a building or structure—

"(i) which is residential rental property located within the United States or any of its possessions, or located within a foreign country if a method of depreciation for such property comparable to the method provided in subsection (b)(2) or (3) is provided by the laws of such country, and

"(ii) the original use of which commences with the taxpayer.

In the case of residential rental property located within a foreign country, the original use of which commences with the taxpayer, if the allowance for depreciation provided under the laws of such country for such property is greater than that provided under paragraph (1) of this subsection, but less than that provided under subsection (b), the allowance for depreciation under subsection (b) shall be limited to the amount provided under the laws of such country.

"(B) Definition. For purposes of subparagraph (A), a building or structure shall be considered to be residential rental property for any taxable year only if 80 percent or more of the gross rental income from such building or structure for such year is rental income from dwelling units (within the meaning of subsection (k)(3)(C)). For purposes of the preceding sentence, if any portion of such building or structure is occupied by the taxpayer, the gross rental income from such building or structure shall include the rental value of the portion so occupied.

"(C) Change in method of depreciation. Any change in the computation of the allowance for depreciation for any taxable year, permitted or required by reason of the application of subparagraph (A), shall not be considered a change in a method of accounting.

"(3) Property constructed, etc., before July 25, 1969. Paragraph (1) of this subsection shall not apply, and subsection (b) shall apply, in the case of property—

"(A) the construction, reconstruction, or erection of which was begun before July 25, 1969, or

"(B) for which a written contract entered into before July 25, 1969, with respect to any part of the construction, reconstruction, or erection or for the permanent financing thereof, was on July 25, 1969, and at all times thereafter, binding on the taxpayer.

"(4) Used section 1250 property. Except as provided in paragraph (5), in the case of section 1250 property acquired after July 24, 1969, the original use of which does not commence with the taxpayer, the allowance for depreciation under this section shall be limited to an amount computed under—

"(A) the straight line method, or

"(B) any other method determined by the Secretary to result in a reasonable allowance under subsection (a), not including—

"(i) any declining balance method,

"(ii) the sum of the years-digits method, or

"(iii) any other method allowable solely by reason of the application of subsection (b)(4) or paragraph (1)(C) of this subsection.

"(5) Used residential rental property. In the case of section 1250 property which is residential rental property (as defined in paragraph (2)(B)) acquired after July 24, 1969, having a useful life of 20 years or more, the original use of which does not commence with the taxpayer, the allowance for depreciation under this section shall be limited to an amount computed under—

"(A) the straight line method,

"(B) the declining balance method, using a rate not exceeding 125 percent of the rate which would have been used had the annual allowance been computed under the method described in subparagraph (A), or

"(C) any other method determined by the Secretary to result in a reasonable allowance under subsection (a), not including—

"(i) the sum of the years-digits method,

"(ii) any declining balance method using a rate in excess of the rate permitted under subparagraph (B), or

"(iii) any other method allowable solely by reason of the application of subsection (b)(4) or paragraph (1)(C) of this subsection.

"(6) Special rules.

"(A) Under regulations prescribed by the Secretary, rules similar to the rules provided in paragraphs (5), (9), (10), and (13) of section 48(h) shall be applied for purposes of paragraphs (3), (4), and (5) of this subsection.

"(B) For purposes of paragraphs (2), (4), and (5), if section 1250 property which is not property described in subsection (a) when its original use commences, becomes property described in subsection (a) after July 24, 1969, such property shall not be treated as property the original use of which commences with the taxpayer.

"(C) Paragraphs (4) and (5) shall not apply in the case of section 1250 property acquired after July 24, 1969, pursuant to a written contract for the acquisition of such property or for the permanent financing thereof, which was, on July 24, 1969, and at all times thereafter, binding on the taxpayer.

"(k) Depreciation of expenditures to rehabilitate low-income rental housing.

"(1) 60-month rule. The taxpayer may elect, in accordance with regulations prescribed by the Secretary, to compute the depreciation deduction provided by subsection (a) attributable to rehabilitation expenditures incurred with respect to low-income rental housing after July 24, 1969, and before January 1, 1987, under the straight line method using a useful life of 60 months and no salvage value. Such method shall be in lieu of any other method of computing the depreciation deduction under subsection (a), and in lieu of any deduction for amortization, for such expenditures.

"(2) Limitations.

"(A) Except as provided in subparagraph (B), the aggregate amount of rehabilitation expenditures paid or incurred by the taxpayer with respect to any dwelling unit in any low-income rental housing which may be taken into account under paragraph (1) shall not exceed $20,000.

"(B) The aggregate amount of rehabilitation expenditures paid or incurred by the taxpayer with respect to any dwelling unit in any low-income rental housing which may be taken into account under paragraph (1) may exceed $20,000, but shall not exceed $40,000, if the rehabilitation is conducted pursuant to a program certified by the Secretary of Housing and Urban Development, or his delegate, or by the government of a State or political subdivision of the United States and if:

"(i) the certification of development costs is required;

"(ii) the tenants occupy units in the property as their principal residence and the program provides for sale of the units to tenants demonstrating home ownership responsibility; and

"(iii) the leasing and sale of such units are pursuant to a program in which the sum of the taxable income, if any, from leasing of each such unit, for the entire period of such leasing, and the amount realized from sale or other disposition of a unit, if sold, normally does not exceed the excess of the taxpayer's cost basis for such unit of property, before adjustment under section 1016 for deductions under section 167, over the net tax benefits realized by the taxpayer, consisting of the tax benefits from such deductions under section 167 minus the tax incurred on such taxable income from leasing, if any.

"(C) Rehabilitation expenditures paid or incurred by the taxpayer in any taxable year with respect to any dwelling unit in any low-income rental housing shall be taken into account under paragraph (1) only if over a period of two consecutive years, including the taxable year, the aggregate amount of such expenditures exceeds $3,000.

"(3) Definitions. For purposes of this subsection—

"(A) Rehabilitation expenditures. The term 'rehabilitation expenditures' means amounts chargeable to capital account and incurred for property or additions or improvements to property (or related facilities) with a useful life of 5 years or more, in connection with the rehabilitation of an existing building for low-income rental housing; but such term does not include the cost of acquisition of such building or any interest therein.

"(B) Low-income rental housing. The term 'low-income rental housing' means any building the dwelling units in which are held for occupancy on a rental basis by families and individuals of low or moderate income, as determined by the Secretary in a manner consistent with the Leased Housing Program under section 8 of the United State Housing Act of 1937 pursuant to regulations prescribed under this subsection.

"(C) Dwelling unit. The term 'dwelling unit' means a house or an apartment used to provide living accommodations in a building or structure, but does not include a unit in a hotel, motel, inn, or other establishment more than one-half of the units in which are used on a transient basis.

"(D) Rehabilitation expenditures incurred. Rehabilitation expenditures incurred pursuant to a binding contract entered into before January 1, 1987, and rehabilitation expenditures incurred with respect to low-income rental housing the rehabilitation of which has begun before January 1, 1987, shall be deemed incurred before January 1, 1987.

"(l) Reasonable allowance in case of property of certain utilities.

"(1) Pre-1970 public utility property.

"(A) In general. In the case of any pre-1970 public utility property, the term 'reasonable allowance' as used in subsection (a) means an allowance computed under—

"(i) a subsection (1) method, or

"(ii) the applicable 1968 method for such property.

Except as provided in subparagraph (B), clause (ii) shall apply only if the taxpayer uses a normalization method of accounting.

"(B) Flow-through method of accounting in certain cases. In the case of any pre-1970 public utility property, the taxpayer may use the applicable 1968 method for such property if—

"(i) the taxpayer used a flow-through method of accounting for such property for its July 1969 accounting period, or

"(ii) the first accounting period with respect to such property is after the July 1969 accounting period, and the taxpayer used a flow-through method of accounting for its July 1969 accounting period for the property on the basis of which the applicable 1968 method for the property in question is established.

"(2) Post-1969 public utility property. In the case of any post-1969 public utility property, the term 'reasonable allowance' as used in subsection (a) means an allowance computed under—

"(A) a subsection (1) method,

"(B) a method otherwise allowable under this section if the taxpayer uses a normalization method of accounting, or

"(C) the applicable 1968 method, if, with respect to its pre-1970 public utility property of the same (or similar) kind most recently placed in service, the taxpayer used a flow-through method of accounting for its July 1969 accounting period.

"(3) Definitions. For purposes of this subsection—

"(A) Public utility property. The term 'public utility property' means property used predominantly in the trade or business of the furnishing or sale of—

"(i) electrical energy, water, or sewage disposal services,

"(ii) gas or steam through a local distribution system,

"(iii) telephone services, or other communication services if furnished or sold by the Communications Satellite Corporation for purposes authorized by the Communications Satellite Act of 1962 (47 U.S.C. 701), or

"(iv) transportation of gas or steam by pipeline,

if the rates for such furnishing or sale, as the case may be, have been established or approved by a State or political subdivision thereof, by any agency or instrumentality of the United States, or by a public service or public utility commission or other similar body of any State or political subdivision thereof.

"(B) Pre-1970 public utility property. The term 'pre-1970 public utility property' means property which was public utility property in the hands of any person at any time before January 1, 1970.

"(C) Post-1969 public utility property. The term 'post-1969 public utility property' means any public utility property which is not pre-1970 public utility property and which is placed in service before January 1, 1981.

"(D) Applicable 1968 method. The term 'applicable 1968 method' means, with respect to any public utility property—

"(i) the method of depreciation used on a return with respect to such property for the latest taxable year for which a return was filed before Aug. 1, 1969,

"(ii) if clause (i) does not apply, the method used by the taxpayer on a return for the latest taxable year for which a return was filed before August 1, 1969, with respect to its public utility property of the same kind (or if there is no property of the same kind, property of the most similar kind) most recently placed in service, or

"(iii) if neither clause (i) nor (ii) applies, a subsection (l) method.

In the case of any section 1250 property to which subsection (j) applies, the term 'applicable 1968 method' means the method permitted under subsection (j) which is most nearly comparable to the applicable 1968 method determined under the preceding sentence.

"(E) Applicable 1968 method in certain cases. If the taxpayer evidenced the intent to use a method of depreciation (other than its applicable 1968 method or a subsection (l) method) with respect to any public utility property in a timely application for change of accounting method filed before August 1, 1969, or in the computation of its tax expense for purposes of reflecting operating results in its regulated books of account for its July 1969 accounting period, such other method shall be deemed to be its applicable 1968 method with respect to such property and public utility property of the same (or similar) kind subsequently placed in service.

"(F) Subsection (l) method. The term 'subsection (l) method' means any method determined by the Secretary to result in a reasonable allowance under subsection (a), other than (i) a declining balance method, (ii) the sum of the years-digits method, or (iii) any other method allowable solely by reason of the application of subsection (b)(4) or (j)(1)(C).

"(G) Normalization method of accounting. In order to use a normalization method of accounting with respect to any public utility property—

"(i) the taxpayer must use the same method of depreciation to compute both its tax expense and its depreciation expense for purposes of establishing its cost of service for ratemaking purposes and for reflecting operating results in its regulated books of account, and

"(ii) if, to compute its allowance for depreciation under this section, it uses a method of depreciation other than the method it used for the purposes described in clause (i), the taxpayer must make adjustments to a reserve to reflect the deferral of taxes resulting from the use of such different methods of depreciation.

For purposes of this subparagraph, rules similar to the rules of section 168(i)(9)(B) shall apply.

"(H) Flow-through method of accounting. The taxpayer used a 'flow-through method of accounting' with respect to any public utility property if it used the same method of depreciation (other than a subsection (l) method) to compute its allowance for depreciation under this section and to compute its tax expense for purposes of reflecting operating results in its regulated books of account.

"(I) July 1969 accounting period. The term 'July 1969 accounting period' means the taxpayer's latest accounting period ending before August 1, 1969, for which it computed its tax expense for purposes of reflecting operating results in its regulated books of account.

For purposes of this paragraph, different declining balance rates shall be treated as different methods of depreciation.

"(4) Special rules as to flow-through method.

"(A) Election as to new property representing growth in capacity. If the taxpayer makes an election under this subparagraph before June 29, 1970, in the manner prescribed by the Secretary, in the case of taxable years beginning after December 31, 1970, paragraph (2)(C) shall not apply with respect to any post-1969 public utility property, to the extent that such property constitutes property which increases the productive or operational capacity of the taxpayer with respect to the goods or services described in paragraph (3)(A) and does not represent the replacement of existing capacity.

"(B) Certain pending applications for changes in method. In applying paragraph (1)(B), the taxpayer shall be deemed to have used a flow-through method of accounting for its July 1969 accounting period with respect to any pre-1970 public utility property for which it filed a timely application for change of accounting method before August 1, 1969, if with respect to public utility property of the same (or similar) kind most recently placed in service, it used a flow-through method of accounting for its July 1969 accounting period.

"(5) Reorganizations, assets acquisitions, etc. If by reason of a corporate reorganization, by reason of any other acquisition of the assets of one taxpayer by another taxpayer, by reason of the fact that any trade or business of the taxpayer is subject to ratemaking by more than one body, or by reason of other circumstances, the application of any provisions of this subsection to any public utility property does not carry out the purposes of this subsection, the Secretary shall provide by regulations for the application of such provisions in a manner consistent with the purposes of this subsection.

"(m) Class Lives.

"(1) In general. In the case of a taxpayer who has made an election under this subsection for the taxable year, the term 'reasonable allowance' as used in subsection (a) means (with respect to property which is placed in service during the taxable year and which is included in any class for which a class life has been prescribed) only an allowance based on the class life prescribed by the Secretary which reasonably reflects the anticipated useful life of that class of property to the industry or other group. The allowance so prescribed may (under regulations prescribed by the Secretary) permit a variance from any class life by not more than 20 percent (rounded to the nearest half year) of such life.

"(2) Certain first-year conventions not permitted. No convention with respect to the time at which assets are deemed placed in service shall be permitted under this section which generally would provide greater depreciation allowances during the taxable year in which the assets are placed in service than would be permitted if all assets were placed in service ratably throughout the year and if depreciation allowances were computed without regard to any convention.

"(3) Making of election. An election under this subsection for any taxable year shall be made at such time, in such manner, and subject to such conditions as may be prescribed by the Secretary by regulations.

"(4) Termination. This subsection shall not apply with respect to any property to which section 168 applies."

Prior to deletion, subsecs. (p) and (q) read as follows:

"(p) Straight line method for boilers fueled by oil or gas.

"In the case of any boiler which, by reason of section 48(a)(10), is not section 38 property—

"(1) subsections (b), (j), and (l) shall not apply, and

"(2) the term 'reasonable allowance' as used in subsection (a) shall mean only an allowance computed under the straight line method using a useful life equal to the class life prescribed by the Secretary under subsection (m) which is applicable to such property (determined without regard to the last sentence of subsection (m)(1)).

"(q) Retirement or replacement of certain boilers, etc., fueled by oil or gas.

"(1) In general. If—

"(A) a boiler or other combustor was in use on October 1, 1978, and as of such date the principal fuel for such combustor was petroleum or petroleum products (including natural gas), and

"(B) the taxpayer establishes to the satisfaction of the Secretary that such combustor will be retired or replaced on or before the date specified by the taxpayer, then for the period beginning with the taxable year in which subparagraph (B) is satisfied, the term 'reasonable allowance' as used in subsection (a) includes an allowance under the straight line method using a useful life equal to the period ending with the date established under subparagraph (B).

"(2) Interest. If the retirement or replacement of any combustor does not occur on or before the date referred to in paragraph (1)(B)—

"(A) this subsection shall cease to apply with respect to such combustor as of such date, and

"(B) interest at the underpayment rate established under section 6621 on the amount of the tax benefit arising from the application of this subsection with respect to such combustor shall be due and payable for the period during which such tax benefit was available to the taxpayer and ending on the date referred to in paragraph (1)(B)."

In 1989, P.L. 101-239, Sec. 7622(b)(1), [sic (d)(1)], repealed subsec. (r), effective for transfers after 10/2/89, except as provided in Sec. 7622(c)(2) [sic Sec. 7622(e)(2)] of this Act which reads as follows:

"(2) Binding contract.—The amendments made by this section [Sec. 7622] shall not apply to any transfer pursuant to a written binding contract in effect on October 2, 1989, and at all times thereafter before the transfer."

Prior to repeal, subsec. (r) read as follows:

"(r) Trademark or trade name expenditures not depreciable.

"(1) In general. No depreciation deduction shall be allowable under this section (and no depreciation or amortization deduction shall be allowable under any other provision of this subtitle) with respect to any trademark or trade name expenditure.

"(2) Trademark or trade name expenditure. For purposes of this subsection, the term 'trademark or trade name expenditure' means any expenditure which is directly connected with the acquisition, protection, expansion, registration (Federal, State, or foreign), or defense of a trademark or trade name."

—P.L. 101-239, Sec. 7645(a), added new subsec. (r), effective for interests created or acquired after 7/27/89, in tax. yrs. end. after 7/27/89.

In 1988, P.L. 100-647, Sec. 1002(a)(22), substituted "section 168(i)(9)(B)" for "section 168(e)(3)(C)" in subpara. (e)(3)(6) . . . Sec. 1002(a)(24), deleted the last sentence of subsec. (a) . . . Sec. 1002(a)(31), substituted "property to which section 168 applies" for "recovery property defined in section 168" in subsec. (d) effective for property placed in service after 12/31/86, in tax. yrs. end. after 12/31/86.

—P.L. 100-647, Sec. 1002(c)(3), of this Act, provides:

"(3) Notwithstanding section 203 of the Reform Act, the amendments made by section 201 of the Reform Act shall apply to any real property which was acquired before January 1, 1987, and was converted on or after such date from personal use to a use for which depreciation is allowable."

Prior to amendment, the last sentence of subsec. (a) read as follows:

"In the case of recovery property (within the meaning of section 168), the deduction allowable under section 168 shall be deemed to constitute the reasonable allowance provided by this section, except with respect to that portion of the basis of such property to which subsection (k) applies."

—P.L. 100-647, Sec. 1002(i)(1), redesignated subsec. (r) as subsec. (s) and added a new subsec. (r), effective for expenditures paid or incurred after 12/31/86. For transitional rules see Sec. 241(c)(2) of P.L. 99-514, reproduced in note following Code Sec. 177.

In 1986, P.L. 99-514, Sec. 201(d)(1), amended para. (m)(4), effective for property placed in service after 12/31/86, in tax. yrs. end. after 12/31/86 [see Sec. 1002(c)(3) of P.L. 100-647, above].

Prior to amendment, para. (m)(4) read as follows:

"(4) Termination. This subsection shall not apply with respect to recovery property (within the meaning of section 168) placed in service after December 31, 1980."

—P.L. 99-514, Sec. 1511(c)(4), substituted "the underpayment rate established under section 6621" for "the rate established under section 6621" in subpara. (q)(2)(B), effective for purposes of determining interest for periods after 12/31/86.
—P.L. 99-514, Sec. 1809(d)(1), added the last (flush) sentence to subsec. (c), effective with respect to property placed in service by the taxpayer after 3/28/85.
In 1984, P.L. 98-369, Sec. 1064, substituted "January 1, 1987" for "January 1, 1984" each place it appeared in subsec. (k).
In 1983, P.L. 97-448, Sec. 102(f)(1), amended Sec. 212(e)(2)(B) of P.L. 97-34, part of the effective date for changes made by Sec. 212((d)(1) of P.L. 97-34 [see below].
Prior to amendment Sec. 212(e)(2)(B) of P.L. 97-34 read as follows:
"(B) such building meets the requirements of paragraph (1) of section 48(g) of the Internal Revenue Code of 1954 (as in effect on the day before the date of enactment of this Act) but does not meet the requirements of such paragraph (1) (as amended by this Act)."
—P.L. 97-424, Sec. 541(a)(2), added the last sentence to subpara. (1)(3)(G), effective for tax. yrs. begin. after 12/31/79. Sec. 541(c)(2) through (c)(5) of this Act provides as follows:
"(2) Special rule for periods beginning before March 1, 1980.—
"(A) In general.—Subject to the provisions of paragraphs (3) and (4), notwithstanding the provisions of sections 167(l) and 46(f) of the Internal Revenue Code of 1954 and of any regulations prescribed by the Secretary of the Treasury (or his delegate) under such sections, the use of ratemaking purposes or for reflecting operating results in the taxpayer's regulated books of account, for any period before March 1, 1980, of—
"(i) any estimates or projections relating to the amounts of the taxpayer's tax expense, depreciation expense, deferred tax reserve, credit allowable under section 38 of such code, or rate base, or
"(ii) any adjustments to the taxpayer's rate of return,
shall not be treated as inconsistent with the requirements of subparagraph (G) of such section 167(l)(3) nor inconsistent with the requirements of paragraph (1) or (2) of such section 46(f), where such estimates or projections, or such rate of return adjustments, were included in a qualified order.
"(B) Qualified order defined.—For purposes of this subsection, the term 'qualified order' means an order—
"(i) by a public utility commission which was entered before March 13, 1980,
"(ii) which used the estimates, projections, or rate of return adjustments referred to in subparagraph (A) to determine the amount of the rates to be collected by the taxpayer or the amount of a refund with respect to rates previously collected, and
"(iii) which ordered such rates to be collected or refunds to be made (whether or not such order actually was implemented or enforced).
"(3) Limitations on application of paragraph (2).—
"(A) Paragraph (2) not to apply to amounts actually flowed through.—Paragraph (2) shall not apply to the amount of any—
"(i) rate reduction, or
"(ii) refund,
which was actually made pursuant to a qualified order.
"(B) Taxpayer must enter into closing agreement before paragraph (2) applies.—Paragraph (2) shall not apply to any taxpayer unless, before the later of—
"(i) July 1, 1983, or
"(ii) 6 months after the refunds or rate reductions are actually made pursuant to a qualified order,
the taxpayer enters into a closing agreement (within the meaning of section 7121 of the Internal Revenue Code of 1954) which provides for the payment by the taxpayer of the amount of which paragraph (2) does not apply by reason of subparagraph (A).
"(4) Special rules relating to payment of refunds or interest by the United States or the taxpayer.—
"(A) Refund defined.—For purposes of this subsection, the term 'refund' shall include any credit allowed by the taxpayer under a qualified order but shall not include interest payable with respect to any refund (or credit) under such order.
"(B) No interest payable by United States.—No interest shall be payable under section 6611 of the Internal Revenue Code of 1954 on any overpayment of tax which is attributable to the application of paragraph (2).
"(C) Payments may be made in two equal installments.—
"(i) In general.—The taxpayer may make any payment required by reason of paragraph (3) in 2 equal installments, the first installment being due on the last date on which a taxpayer may enter into a closing agreement under paragraph (3)(B), and the second payment being due 1 year after the last date for the first payment.
"(ii) Interest payments.—For purposes of section 6601 of such Code, the last date prescribed for payment with respect to any payment required by reason of paragraph (3) shall be the last date on which such payment is due under clause (i).
"(5) No inference.—The application of subparagraph (G) of section 167(l)(3) of the Internal Revenue Code of 1954, and the application of paragraphs (1) and (2) of section 46(f) of such Code, to taxable years beginning before January 1, 1980, shall be determined without any inference drawn from the amendments made by subsections (a) and (b) of this section or from the rules contained in paragraphs (2), (3), and (4). Nothing in the preceding sentence shall be construed to limit the relief provided by paragraphs (2), (3), and (4).
In 1981, P.L. 97-34, Sec. 203(a), added the last sentence to the end of subsec. (a) ... Sec. 203(b), added para. (m)(4), effective for property placed in service after 12/31/80 in tax. yrs. end. after 12/31/80.
—P.L. 97-34, Sec. 203(c)(1), deleted subsec. (r) and redesignated subsec. (s) as subsec. (r), effective 1/1/81 for tax. yrs. end. after 1/1/81.

Prior to deletion, subsec. (r) read as follows:
"(r) Retirement-replacement-betterment method.
"In the case of railroad track used by a common carrier by railroad (including a railroad switching company or a terminal company), the term 'reasonable allowance' as used in subsection (a) includes an allowance for such track computed under the retirement-replacement-betterment method."
—P.L. 97-34, Sec. 203(c)(2), and (3), provides:
"(2) Change in method of accounting. Sections 446 and 481 of the Internal Revenue Code of 1954 shall not apply to the change in the method of depreciation to comply with the provisions of this subsection [i.e., Sec. 203(c)(1)]."
"(3) Transitional rule. The adjusted basis of RRB property (as defined in section 168(g)(6) of such Code) as of December 31, 1980, shall be depreciated using a useful life of no less than 5 years and no more than 50 years and a method described in section 167(b) of such Code, including the method described in section 167(b)(2) of such Code, switching to the method described in section 167(b)(3) of such Code at a time to maximize the deduction."
—P.L. 97-34, Sec. 203(d), added the last sentence to subsec. (d), for property placed in service after 12/31/80 for tax yrs. end. after 12/31/80.
—P.L. 97-34, Sec. 203(e), provides:
"(e) Conforming amendment.
"The Secretary of Health and Human Services is not required to apply any provision of the Internal Revenue Code of 1954, as amended, in calculating depreciation (for the purpose of determining any cost under a program administered by the Secretary), unless a provision of law requires so expressly."
—P.L. 97-34, Sec. 209(d)(3), added "and which is placed in service before January 1, 1981" before the period at the end of subpara. (1)(3)(C).
—P.L. 97-34, Sec. 212(d)(1), deleted subsecs. (n) and (o), for expenditures incurred after 12/31/81, in tax. yrs. end. after 12/3/181. Sec. 212(e)(2) of this Act provides:
"(2) Transitional rule. The amendments made by this section shall not apply with respect to any rehabilitation of a building if—
"(A) the physical work on such rehabilitation began before January 1, 1982, and
"(B) such building does not meet the requirements of paragraph (1) of section 48(g) of the Internal Revenue Code of 1954 (as amended by this Act)."
Prior to amendment, subsecs. (n) and (o) read as follows:
"(n) Straight line method in certain cases.
"(1) In general. In the case of any property in whole or in part constructed, reconstructed, erected, or used on a site which was, on or after June 30, 1976, occupied by a certified historic structure (or by any structure in a registered historic district) which is demolished or substantially altered after such date—
"(A) subsections (b), (j), (k), and (l) shall not apply, and
"(B) the term 'reasonable allowance' as used in subsection (a) means only an allowance computed under the straight line method.
The preceding sentence shall not apply if the last substantial alteration of the structure is a certified rehabilitation.
"(2) Exceptions. The limitations imposed by this subsection shall not apply—
"(A) to personal property, and
"(B) in the case of demolition or substantial alteration of a structure located in a registered historic district, if—
"(i) such structure was not a certified historic structure,
"(ii) the Secretary of the Interior certified to the Secretary that such structure is not of historic significance to the district, and
"(iii) if the certification referred to in clause (ii) occurs after the beginning of the demolition or substantial alteration of such structure, the taxpayer certifies to the Secretary that, at the beginning of such demolition or substantial alteration, he in good faith was not aware of the requirements of clause (ii).
"(3) Definitions. For purposes of this subsection, the terms 'certified historic structure', 'registered historic district', and 'certified rehabilitation' have the respective meanings given such terms by section 191(d).
"(4) Application of subsection. This subsection shall apply to that portion of the basis which is attributable to construction, reconstruction, or erection after December 31, 1975, and before January 1, 1984.
"(o) Substantially rehabilitated historic property.
"(1) General rule. Pursuant to regulations prescribed by the Secretary, the taxpayer may elect to compute the depreciation deduction attributable to substantially rehabilitated historic property (other than property with respect to which an amortization deduction has been allowed to the taxpayer under section 191) as though the original use of such property commenced with him. The election shall be effective with respect to the taxable year referred to in paragraph (2) and all succeeding taxable years.
"(2) Substantially rehabilitated property. For purposes of paragraph (1), the term 'substantially rehabilitated historic property' means any certified historic structure (as defined in section 191(d)(1)) with respect to which the additions to capital account for any certified rehabilitation (as defined in section 191(d)(4)) during the 24-month period ending on the last day of any taxable year, reduced by any amounts allowed or allowable as depreciation or amortization with respect thereto, exceeds the greater of—
"(A) the adjusted basis of such property, or
"(B) $5,000.
The adjusted basis of the property shall be determined as of the beginning of the first day of such 24-month period, or of the holding period of the property (within the meaning of section 1250(e)), whichever is later.
"(3) Application of subsection. This subsection shall apply with respect to additions to capital account occurring after June 30, 1976, and before January 1, 1984."

Deductions Code Sec. 167

—P.L. 97-34, Sec. 264(a), substituted "Except as provided in subparagraph (B), the" for "The" in subsec. (k)(2)(A), redesignated subpara. (k)(2)(B) as subpara. (k)(2)(C) and added new subpara. (k)(2)(B), for rehabilitation expenditures incurred after 12/31/80.

In 1980, P.L. 96-613, Sec. 2(a), redesignated subsec. (r) as subsec. (s) and added new subsec. (r), effective for tax. yrs. end. after 12/31/53.

—P.L. 96-541, Sec. 2(c), added para. (n)(4) . . . Sec. 2(d), added para. (o)(3) . . . Sec. 3, substituted "January 1, 1984" for "January 1, 1982" each place it appeared in subsec. (k), effective 12/17/80.

—P.L. 96-541, Sec. 2(e)(3), and (4), deleted Secs. 2124(c)(2) and (d)(2) of P.L. 94-455, the effective date for changes made by Secs. 2124(c)(1) and (d)(1) of P.L. 94-455, see below.

Prior to deletion Sec. 2124(c)(2) of P.L. 94-455 read as follows:

"(2) Effective date. The amendment made by this subsection shall apply to that portion of the basis which is attributable to construction, reconstruction, or erection after December 31, 1975, and before January 1, 1981."

Prior to deletion Sec. 2124(d)(2) of P.L. 94-455 read as follows:

"(2) Effective date. The amendment made by this subsection shall apply with respect to additions to capital account occurring after June 30, 1976, and before July 1, 1981."

In 1978, P.L. 95-618, Sec. 301(d)(3), redesignated subpara. (p) as subpara. (r) . . . added new subpara. (p), effective for property placed in service after 9/30/78. Sec. 301(d)(4)(B) of the Act provides:

"(B) Binding contracts.

"The amendments made by this subsection shall not apply to property which is constructed, reconstructed, erected, or acquired pursuant to a contract which, on October 1, 1978, and at all times thereafter, was binding on the taxpayer."

—P.L. 95-618, Sec. 301(e)(1), added subsec. (q), effective for tax. yrs. end. after 11/9/78.

—P.L. 95-600, Sec. 312(c)(4), repealed subsec. (i), for tax. yrs. end. after '78.

Prior to repeal, subsec. (i) read as follows:

"(i) Limitation in case of property constructed or acquired during the suspension period.

"(1) In general. Under regulations prescribed by the Secretary, paragraphs (2), (3), and (4) of subsection (b) shall not apply in the case of real property which is not section 38 property (as defined in section 48(a)) if the physical construction, reconstruction, or erection of such property by any person begins during the suspension period, or begins, pursuant to an order placed during such period, before May 24, 1967. Under regulations prescribed by the Secretary, rules similar to the rules provided by paragraphs (3), (4), (7), (8), (9), and (10) of section 48(h) shall be applied for purposes of the preceding sentence. In applying this paragraph to any property, there shall be taken into account only that portion of the basis which is properly attributable to construction, reconstruction, or erection before May 24, 1967.

"(2) Exception. Paragraph (1) shall not apply to any item of real property selected by the taxpayer if the cost of such property (when added to the cost of all other items of real property selected by the taxpayer under this paragraph) does not exceed $50,000. Under regulations prescribed by the Secretary, rules similar to the rules provided by paragraph (2) of section 48(c) shall be applied for purposes of this paragraph.

"(3) Suspension period. For purposes of this subsection, the term 'suspension period' means the period beginning on October 10, 1966, and ending on March 9, 1967.)"

—P.L. 95-600, Sec. 367, substituted "January 1, 1982" for "January 1, 1979" each place it appeared in subsec. (k).

—P.L. 95-600, Sec. 701(f)(4), amended subsec. (n), effective for that portion of the basis which is attributable to construction, reconstruction, or erection after 12/31/75 and before 1/1/81.

Prior to amendment, subsec. (n) read as follows:

"(n) Straight line method in certain cases.

"(1) In general. In the case of any property in whole or in part constructed, reconstructed, erected, or used on a site which was, on or after June 30, 1976, occupied by a certified historic structure (as defined in section 191(d)(1)) which is demolished or substantially altered (other than by virtue of a certified rehabilitation as defined in section 191(d)(3)) after such date—

"(A) subsections (b), (j), (k), and (l) shall not apply,

"(B) the term reasonable allowance as used in subsection (a) shall mean only an allowance computed under the straight line method.

"(2) Exception. The limitations imposed by this subsection shall not apply to personal property."

—P.L. 95-600, Sec. 701(f)(6)(A), added "(other than property with respect to which an amortization deduction has been allowed to the taxpayer under section 191)" following "substantially rehabilitated historic property" in para. (o)(1) . . . substituted "section 191(d)(4)" for "section 191(d)(3)" in para. (o)(2), for additions to capital occurring after 6/30/76 and before 7/1/81.

In 1977, P.L. 95-171, Sec. 4(a), substituted "January 1, 1979" for "January 1, 1978" each place it appeared in subsec. (k) . . . Sec. 4(b), amended Sec. 203(b) of P.L. 94-455 by deleting ", and before January 1, 1978, and expenditures made pursuant to a binding contract entered into before January 1, 1978".

In 1976, P.L. 94-455, Sec. 202(c)(3), substituted "beginning after December 31, 1975," for "beginning after July 24, 1969," in para. (e)(3), for tax. yrs. end. after 1975.

—P.L. 94-455, Sec. 203(a)(1), substituted "January 1, 1978" for "January 1, 1976" in para. (k)(1) . . . Sec. 203(a)(3), substituted "the Leased Housing Program under section 8 of the United States Housing Act of 1937" for "the policies of the Housing and Urban Development Act of 1968" in subpara. (k)(3)(B) . . . Sec. 203(a)(4), added subpara. (k)(3)(D), for expenditures paid or incurred after 12/31/75, and before 1/1/78, and expenditures made pursuant to a binding contract entered into before 1/1/78. [See Sec. 4(b) of P.L. 95-171, above.]

—P.L. 94-455, Sec. 203(a)(2), substituted "$20,000" for "$15,000" in subpara. (k)(2)(A), for expenditures incurred after 1975.

—P.L. 94-455, Sec. 1901(a)(27), substituted "after August 16, 1954" for "after the date of enactment of this title" in subsec. (d) . . . substituted "October 16, 1962" for "the date of the enactment of the Revenue Act of 1962" in para. (f)(2) . . . substituted "before June 29, 1970," for "within 180 days after the date of enactment of this subparagraph" in subpara. (1)(4)(A), effective for tax. yrs. begin. after 12/31/76.

—P.L. 94-455, Sec. 1906(b)(13)(A), substituted "Secretary" for "Secretary or his delegate" in subsecs. (b), (d), (e), (i), (j), (l) and (m) effective for tax. yrs. begin. after 12/31/76.

—P.L. 94-455, Sec. 2124(c), redesignated subsec. (n) as subsec. (p) and added new subsec. (n).

—P.L. 94-455, Sec. 2124(d), added subsec. (o).

In 1975, P.L. 93-625, Sec. 3(c), substituted "January 1, 1976" for "January 1, 1975" in para. (k)(1), effective 1/3/75.

—P.L. 93-625, Sec. 5(a), and (b), effective for property placed in service after 12/31/73, provided as follows:

"(a) General rule.

"In the case of buildings and other items of section 1250 property (within the meaning of section 1250(c) of the Internal Revenue Code of 1954) placed in service before the effective date of the class lives first prescribed by the Secretary of the Treasury or his delegate under section 167(m) of such Code for the class in which such property falls, if an election under such section 167(m) applies to the taxpayer for the taxable year in which such property is placed in service, the taxpayer may, in accordance with regulations prescribed by the Secretary of the Treasury or his delegate, elect to determine the useful life of such property—

"(1) under Revenue Procedure 62-21 (as amended and supplemented) as in effect on December 31, 1970, or

"(2) on the facts and circumstances.

"(b) Repeal of prior transitional rule.

"Paragraph (1) of section 109(e) of the Revenue Act of 1971 (P.L.92-178) is hereby repealed."

In 1974, P.L. 93-482, Sec. 4, specified that, notwithstanding the provisions of section 167(k)(1), subsec. (k) is applicable with respect to rehabilitation expenditures incurred with respect to low income rental housing after 12/31/74, and before 1/1/78, if such expenditures are incurred pursuant to a binding contract entered into before 12/31/74.

In 1971, P.L. 92-178, Sec. 109(a), redesignated subsec. (m) as subsec. (n) and added new subsec. (m), for property placed in service after 12/31/70.

—P.L. 92-178, Sec. 109(e), provided as follows:

"(e) Transitional rules.

"(1) Real property. In the case of buildings and other items of section 1250 property for which a separate guideline life is prescribed in Revenue Procedure 62-21 (as amended and supplemented), the class lives first prescribed by the Secretary of the Treasury or his delegate under section 167(m) of the Internal Revenue Code of 1954 shall be the same as the guideline lives for such property in effect on December 31, 1970. Any such property which is placed in service by the taxpayer during the period beginning on January 1, 1971, and ending on December 31, 1973 (or such earlier date on which a class life subsequently prescribed by the Secretary of the Treasury or his delegate under such section becomes effective for such property) may, in accordance with regulations prescribed by the Secretary of the Treasury or his delegate, be excluded by the taxpayer from an election under such section if a life for such property shorter than the class life prescribed in accordance with the preceding sentence is justified under Revenue Procedure 62-21 (as amended and supplemented).

"(2) Subsidiary assets. If a significant portion of a class of property first prescribed by the Secretary of the Treasury or his delegate under section 167(m) of the Internal Revenue Code of 1954 consists of subsidiary assets, all such subsidiary assets in such class placed in service by the taxpayer during the period beginning on January 1, 1971, and ending on December 31, 1973 (or such earlier date on which a class which includes such subsidiary assets subsequently prescribed by the Secretary of the Treasury or his delegate under such section becomes effective), may, in accordance with regulations prescribed by the Secretary of the Treasury or his delegate, be excluded by the taxpayer from an election under such section."

In 1969, P.L. 91-172, Sec. 441, added subsec. (l), effective for tax. yrs. for which a return has not been filed before 8/1/69.

—P.L. 91-172, Sec. 521(a), redesignated subsec. (j) as subsec. (m) and added new subsecs. (j) and (k) . . . Sec. 521(d), added para. (e)(3), effective for tax. yrs. end. after 7/24/69.

In 1967, P.L. 90-26, Sec. 2(a), amended para. (i)(1) and substituted "March 9, 1967" for "December 31, 1967" in subsec. (i)(3); effective for tax. yrs. end. after 3/9/67.

Prior to amendment, para. (i)(1) read as follows:

"(1) In general. Under regulations prescribed by the Secretary or his delegate, paragraphs (2), (3), and (4) of subsection (b) shall not apply in the case of real property which is not section 38 property (as defined in section 48(a)) if—

"(A) the physical construction, reconstruction, or erection of such property by any person begins during the suspension period, or

"(B) an order for such construction, reconstruction, or erection is placed by any person during the suspension period.

Under regulations prescribed by the Secretary or his delegate, rules similar to the rules provided by paragraphs (3), (4), (7), (8), (9), and (10) of section 48(h) shall be applied for purposes of the preceding sentence."

Code Sec. 167   **Deductions**

In 1966, P.L. 89-800, Sec. 2, redesignated subsec. (i) as (j) and added new subsec. (i), effective for tax. yrs. end. after 10/8/66.

In 1962, P.L. 87-834, Sec. 13(b), designated existing provisions in subsec. (e) as para. (1) and added para. (2), effective for tax. yrs. begin. after 1962 . . . Sec. 13(c), redesignated subsecs. (f), (g) and (h) as subsecs. (g), (h) and (i), respectively, and added new subsec. (f), effective for tax. yrs. begin. after 1961 and end. after 10/16/62.

In 1958, P.L. 85-866, Sec. 89(b), inserted "certified mail or" before "registered mail" in subsec. (d), effective only if mailing occurred after 9/2/58.

Sec. 168. Accelerated cost recovery system.

(a) General rule.

Except as otherwise provided in this section, the depreciation deduction provided by section 167(a) for any tangible property shall be determined by using—

(1) the applicable depreciation method,

(2) the applicable recovery period, and

(3) the applicable convention.

(b) Applicable depreciation method.

For purposes of this section—

(1) In general. Except as provided in paragraphs (2) and (3), the applicable depreciation method is—

(A) the 200 percent declining balance method,

(B) switching to the straight line method for the 1st taxable year for which using the straight line method with respect to the adjusted basis as of the beginning of such year will yield a larger allowance.

(2) 150 percent declining balance method in certain cases. Paragraph (1) shall be applied by substituting "150 percent" for "200 percent" in the case of—

(A) any 15-year or 20-year property not referred to in paragraph (3),

(B) any property used in a farming business (within the meaning of section 263A(e)(4)),

(C) any property (other than property described in paragraph (3)) which is a qualified smart electric meter or qualified smart electric grid system, or

(D) any property (other than property described in paragraph (3)) with respect to which the taxpayer elects under paragraph (5) to have the provisions of this paragraph apply.

(3) Property to which straight line method applies. The applicable depreciation method shall be the straight line method in the case of the following property:

(A) Nonresidential real property.

(B) Residential rental property.

(C) Any railroad grading or tunnel bore.

(D) Property with respect to which the taxpayer elects under paragraph (5) to have the provisions of this paragraph apply.

(E) Property described in subsection (e)(3)(D)(ii).

(F) Water utility property described in subsection (e)(5).

(G) Qualified leasehold improvement property described in subsection (e)(6).

(H) Qualified restaurant property described in subsection (e)(7).

(I) Qualified retail improvement property described in subsection (e)(8).

(4) Salvage value treated as zero. Salvage value shall be treated as zero.

(5) Election. An election under paragraph (2)(C) or (3)(D) may be made with respect to 1 or more classes of property for any taxable year and once made with respect to any class shall apply to all property in such class placed in service during such taxable year. Such an election, once made, shall be irrevocable.

(c) Applicable recovery period.

For purposes of this section, the applicable recovery period shall be determined in accordance with the following table:

In the case of:	The applicable recovery period is:
3-year property	3 years
5-year property	5 years
7-year property	7 years
10-year property	10 years
15-year property	15 years
20-year property	20 years
Water utility property	25 years
Residential rental property	27.5 years
Nonresidential real property	39 years
Any railroad grading or tunnel bore	50 years

(d) Applicable convention.

For purposes of this section—

(1) In general. Except as otherwise provided in this subsection, the applicable convention is the half-year convention.

(2) Real property. In the case of—

(A) nonresidential real property,

(B) residential rental property, and

(C) any railroad grading or tunnel bore,

the applicable convention is the mid-month convention.

(3) Special rule where substantial property placed in service during last 3 months of taxable year.

(A) In general. Except as provided in regulations, if during any taxable year—

(i) the aggregate bases of property to which this section applies placed in service during the last 3 months of the taxable year, exceed

(ii) 40 percent of the aggregate bases of property to which this section applies placed in service during such taxable year,

the applicable convention for all property to which this section applies placed in service during such taxable year shall be the mid-quarter convention.

(B) Certain property not taken into account. For purposes of subparagraph (A), there shall not be taken into account—

(i) any nonresidential real property, residential rental property, and railroad grading or tunnel bore, and

(ii) any other property placed in service and disposed of during the same taxable year.

(4) Definitions.

(A) Half-year convention. The half-year convention is a convention which treats all property placed in service during any taxable year (or disposed of during any taxable year) as placed in service (or disposed of) on the mid-point of such taxable year.

(B) Mid-month convention. The mid-month convention is a convention which treats all property placed in service during any month (or disposed of during any month) as placed in service (or disposed of) on the mid-point of such month.

(C) Mid-quarter convention. The mid-quarter convention is a convention which treats all property placed in service during any quarter of a taxable year (or disposed of during any quarter of a taxable year) as placed in service (or disposed of) on the mid-point of such quarter.

Deductions

(e) Classification of property.

For purposes of this section—

(1) In general. Except as otherwise provided in this subsection, property shall be classified under the following table:

Property shall be treated as:	If such property has a class life (in years) of:
3-year property	4 or less
5-year property	More than 4 but less than 10
7-year property	10 or more but less than 16
10-year property	16 or more but less than 20
15-year property	20 or more but less than 25
20-year property	25 or more.

(2) Residential rental or nonresidential real property.

(A) Residential rental property.

(i) Residential rental property. The term "residential rental property" means any building or structure if 80 percent or more of the gross rental income from such building or structure for the taxable year is rental income from dwelling units.

(ii) Definitions. For purposes of clause (i)—

(I) the term "dwelling unit" means a house or apartment used to provide living accommodations in a building or structure, but does not include a unit in a hotel, motel, or other establishment more than one-half of the units in which are used on a transient basis, and

(II) if any portion of the building or structure is occupied by the taxpayer, the gross rental income from such building or structure shall include the rental value of the portion so occupied.

(B) Nonresidential real property. The term "nonresidential real property" means section 1250 property which is not—

(i) residential rental property, or

(ii) property with a class life of less than 27.5 years.

(3) Classification of certain property.

(A) 3-year property. The term "3-year property" includes—

(i) any race horse—

(I) which is placed in service before January 1, 2014, and

(II) which is placed in service after December 31, 2013, and which is more than 2 years old at the time such horse is placed in service by such purchaser,

(ii) any horse other than a race horse which is more than 12 years old at the time it is placed in service, and

(iii) any qualified rent-to-own property.

(B) 5-year property. The term "5-year property" includes—

(i) any automobile or light general purpose truck,

(ii) any semi-conductor manufacturing equipment,

(iii) any computer-based telephone central office switching equipment,

(iv) any qualified technological equipment,

(v) any section 1245 property used in connection with research and experimentation,

(vi) any property which—

(I) is described in subparagraph (A) of section 48(a)(3) (or would be so described if "solar or wind energy" were substituted for "solar energy" in clause (i) thereof and the last sentence of such section did not apply to such subparagraph),

(II) is described in paragraph (15) of section 48(l) (as in effect on the day before the date of the enactment [11/5/90] of the Revenue Reconciliation Act of 1990) and is a qualifying small power production facility within the meaning of section 3(17)(C) of the Federal Power Act (16 U.S.C. 796(17)(C)), as in effect on September 1, 1986, or

(III) is described in section 48(l)(3)(A)(ix) (as in effect on the date before the date of the enactment of the Revenue Reconciliation Act of 1990), and

(vii) any machinery or equipment (other than any grain bin, cotton ginning asset, fence, or other land improvement) which is used in a farming business (as defined in section 263A(e)(4)), the original use of which commences with the taxpayer after December 31, 2008, and which is placed in service before January 1, 2010.

Nothing in any provision of law shall be construed to treat property as not being described in clause (vi)(I)(or the corresponding provisions of prior law) by reason of being public utility property (within the meaning of section 48(a)(3)).

(C) 7-year property. The term "7-year property" includes—

(i) any railroad track and

(ii) any motorsports entertainment complex,

(iii) any Alaska natural gas pipeline,

(iv) any natural gas gathering line the original use of which commences with the taxpayer after April 11, 2005, and

(v) any property which—

(I) does not have a class life, and

(II) is not otherwise classified under paragraph (2) or this paragraph.

(D) 10-year property. The term "10-year property" includes—

(i) any single purpose agricultural or horticultural structure (within the meaning of subsection (i)(13)),

(ii) any tree or vine bearing fruit or nuts,

(iii) any qualified smart electric meter, and

(iv) any qualified smart electric grid system.

(E) 15-year property. The term "15-year property" includes—

(i) any municipal wastewater treatment plant,

(ii) any telephone distribution plant and comparable equipment used for 2-way exchange of voice and data communications,

(iii) any section 1250 property which is a retail motor fuels outlet (whether or not food or other convenience items are sold at the outlet),

(iv) any qualified leasehold improvement property placed in service before January 1, 2012,

(v) any qualified restaurant property placed in service before January 1, 2012,

(vi) initial clearing and grading land improvements with respect to gas utility property,

(vii) any section 1245 property (as defined in section 1245(a)(3)) used in the transmission at 69 or more kilovolts of electricity for sale and the original use of which commences with the taxpayer after April 11, 2005,

(viii) any natural gas distribution line the original use of which commences with the taxpayer after April 11, 2005, and which is placed in service before January 1, 2011, and

(ix) any qualified retail improvement property placed in service after December 31, 2008, and before January 1, 2012.

(F) 20-year property. The term "20-year property" means initial clearing and grading land improvements with respect to any electric utility transmission and distribution plant.

(4) Railroad grading or tunnel bore. The term "railroad grading or tunnel bore" means all improvements resulting from excavations (including tunneling), construction of embankments, clearings, diversions of roads and streams, sodding of slopes, and from similar work necessary to provide, construct, reconstruct, alter, protect, improve, replace, or restore a roadbed or right-of-way for railroad track.

(5) Water utility property. The term "water utility property" means property—

(A) which is an integral part of the gathering, treatment, or commercial distribution of water, and which, without regard to this paragraph, would be 20-year property, and

(B) any municipal sewer.

(6) Qualified leasehold improvement property. The term "qualified leasehold improvement property" has the meaning given such term in section 168(k)(3) except that the following special rules shall apply:

(A) Improvements made by lessor. In the case of an improvement made by the person who was the lessor of such improvement when such improvement was placed in service, such improvement shall be qualified leasehold improvement property (if at all) only so long as such improvement is held by such person.

(B) Exception for changes in form of business. Property shall not cease to be qualified leasehold improvement property under subparagraph (A) by reason of—

(i) death,

(ii) a transaction to which section 381(a) applies,

(iii) a mere change in the form of conducting the trade or business so long as the property is retained in such trade or business as qualified leasehold improvement property and the taxpayer retains a substantial interest in such trade or business,

(iv) the acquisition of such property in an exchange described in section 1031, 1033, or 1038 to the extent that the basis of such property includes an amount representing the adjusted basis of other property owned by the taxpayer or a related person, or

(v) the acquisition of such property by the taxpayer in a transaction described in section 332, 351, 361, 721, or 731 (or the acquisition of such property by the taxpayer from the transferee or acquiring corporation in a transaction described in such section), to the extent that the basis of the property in the hands of the taxpayer is determined by reference to its basis in the hands of the transferor or distributor.

(7) Qualified restaurant property.

(A) In general. The term "qualified restaurant property" means any section 1250 property which is—

(i) a building, or

(ii) an improvement to a building,

if more than 50 percent of the building's square footage is devoted to preparation of, and seating for on-premises consumption of, prepared meals.

(B) Exclusion from bonus depreciation. Property described in this paragraphshall not be considered qualified property for purposes of subsection (k).

(8) Qualified retail improvement property.

(A) In general. The term "qualified retail improvement property" means any improvement to an interior portion of a building which is nonresidential real property if—

(i) such portion is open to the general public and is used in the retail trade or business of selling tangible personal property to the general public, and

(ii) such improvement is placed in service more than 3 years after the date the building was first placed in service.

(B) Improvements made by owner. In the case of an improvement made by the owner of such improvement, such improvement shall be qualified retail improvement property (if at all) only so long as such improvement is held by such owner. Rules similar to the rules under paragraph (6)(B) shall apply for purposes of the preceding sentence.

(C) Certain improvements not included. Such term shall not include any improvement for which the expenditure is attributable to—

(i) the enlargement of the building,

(ii) any elevator or escalator,

(iii) any structural component benefitting a common area, or

(iv) the internal structural framework of the building.

(D) Exclusion from bonus depreciation. Property described in this paragraph shall not be considered qualified property for purposes of subsection (k).

(E) Repealed.

(f) Property to which section does not apply. This section shall not apply to—

(1) Certain methods of depreciation. Any property if—

(A) the taxpayer elects to exclude such property from the application of this section, and

(B) for the 1st taxable year for which a depreciation deduction would be allowable with respect to such property in the hands of the taxpayer, the property is properly depreciated under the unit-of-production method or any method of depreciation not expressed in a term of years (other than the retirement-replacement-betterment method or similar method).

(2) Certain public utility property. Any public utility property (within the meaning of subsection (i)(10)) if the taxpayer does not use a normalization method of accounting.

(3) Films and video tape. Any motion picture film or video tape.

(4) Sound recordings. Any works which result from the fixation of a series of musical, spoken, or other sounds, regardless of the nature of the material (such as discs, tapes, or other phonorecordings) in which such sounds are embodied.

(5) Certain property placed in service in churning transactions.

(A) In general. Property—

(i) described in paragraph (4) of section 168(e) (as in effect before the amendments made by the Tax Reform Act of 1986), or

(ii) which would be described in such paragraph if such paragraph were applied by substituting "1987"

Deductions Code Sec. 168(g)(4)(F)

for "1981" and "1986" for "1980" each place such terms appear.

(B) Subparagraph (A)(ii) not to apply. Clause (ii) of subparagraph (A) shall not apply to—

(i) any residential rental property or nonresidential real property,

(ii) any property if, for the 1st taxable year in which such property is placed in service—

(I) the amount allowable as a deduction under this section (as in effect before the date of the enactment of this paragraph) with respect to such property is greater than,

(II) the amount allowable as a deduction under this section (as in effect on or after such date and using the half-year convention) for such taxable year, or

(iii) any property to which this section (as amended by the Tax Reform Act of 1986) applied in the hands of the transferor.

(C) Special rule. In the case of any property to which this section would apply but for this paragraph, the depreciation deduction under section 167 shall be determined under the provisions of this section as in effect before the amendments made by section 201 of the Tax Reform Act of 1986.

(g) Alternative depreciation system for certain property.

(1) **In general.** In the case of—

(A) any tangible property which during the taxable year is used predominantly outside the United States,

(B) any tax-exempt use property,

(C) any tax-exempt bond financed property,

(D) any imported property covered by an Executive order under paragraph (6), and

(E) any property to which an election under paragraph (7) applies,

the depreciation deduction provided by section 167(a) shall be determined under the alternative depreciation system.

(2) **Alternative depreciation system.** For purposes of paragraph (1), the alternative depreciation system is depreciation determined by using—

(A) the straight line method (without regard to salvage value),

(B) the applicable convention determined under subsection (d), and

(C) a recovery period determined under the following table:

In the case of:	The recovery period shall be:
(i) Property not described in clause (ii) or (iii)	The class life.
(ii) Personal property with no class life	12 years.
(iii) Nonresidential real and residential rental property	40 years.
(iv) Any railroad grading or tunnel bore or water utility property	50 years.

(3) **Special rules for determining class life.**

(A) Tax-exempt use property subject to lease. In the case of any tax-exempt use property subject to a lease, the recovery period used for purposes of paragraph (2) shall (notwithstanding any other subparagraph of this paragraph) in no event be less than 125 percent of the lease term.

(B) Special rule for certain property assigned to classes. For purposes of paragraph (2), in the case of property described in any of the following subparagraphs of subsection (e)(3), the class life shall be determined as follows:

If property is described in subparagraph:	The class life is:
(A)(iii)	4
(B)(ii)	5
(B)(iii)	9.5
(B)(vii)	10
(C)(i)	10
(C)(iii)	22
(C)(iv)	14
(D)(i)	15
(D)(ii)	20
(E)(i)	24
(E)(ii)	24
(E)(iii)	20
(E)(iv)	39
(E)(v)	39
(E)(vi)	20
(E)(vii)	30
(E)(viii)	35
(E)(ix)	39
(F)	25

(C) Qualified technological equipment. In the case of any qualified technological equipment, the recovery period used for purposes of paragraph (2) shall be 5 years.

(D) Automobiles, etc. In the case of any automobile or light general purpose truck, the recovery period used for purposes of paragraph (2) shall be 5 years.

(E) Certain real property. In the case of any section 1245 property which is real property with no class life, the recovery period used for purposes of paragraph (2) shall be 40 years.

(4) Exception for certain property used outside United States. Subparagraph (A) of paragraph (1) shall not apply to—

(A) any aircraft which is registered by the Administrator of the Federal Aviation Agency and which is operated to and from the United States or is operated under contract with the United States;

(B) rolling stock which is used within and without the United States and which is—

(i) of a rail carrier subject to part A of subtitle IV of title 49, or

(ii) of a United States person (other than a corporation described in clause (i)) but only if the rolling stock is not leased to one or more foreign persons for periods aggregating more than 12 months in any 24-month period;

(C) any vessel documented under the laws of the United States which is operated in the foreign or domestic commerce of the United States;

(D) any motor vehicle of a United States person (as defined in section 7701(a)(30)) which is operated to and from the United States;

(E) any container of a United States person which is used in the transportation of property to and from the United States;

(F) any property (other than a vessel or an aircraft) of a United States person which is used for the purpose of exploring for, developing, removing, or transporting resources from the outer Continental Shelf (within the meaning of section 2 of the Outer Continental Shelf Lands Act, as amended and supplemented; (43 U.S.C. 1331));

(G) any property which is owned by a domestic corporation (other than a corporation which has an election in effect under section 936) or by a United States citizen (other than a citizen entitled to the benefits of section 931 or 933) and which is used predominantly in a possession of the United States by such a corporation or such a citizen, or by a corporation created or organized in, or under the law of, a possession of the United States;

(H) any communications satellite (as defined in section 103(3) of the Communications Satellite Act of 1962, 47 U.S.C. 702(3)), or any interest therein, of a United States person;

(I) any cable, or any interest therein, of a domestic corporation engaged in furnishing telephone service to which section 168(i)(10)(C) applies (or of a wholly owned domestic subsidiary of such a corporation), if such cable is part of a submarine cable system which constitutes part of a communication link exclusively between the United States and one or more foreign countries;

(J) any property (other than a vessel or an aircraft) of a United States person which is used in international or territorial waters within the northern portion of the Western Hemisphere for the purpose of exploring for, developing, removing, or transporting resources from ocean waters or deposits under such waters;

(K) any property described in section 48(l)(3)(A)(ix) (as in effect on the day before the date of the enactment of the Revenue Reconciliation Act of 1990) which is owned by a United States person and which is used in international or territorial waters to generate energy for use in the United States; and

(L) any satellite (not described in subparagraph (H)) or other spacecraft (or any interest therein) held by a United States person if such satellite or other spacecraft was launched from within the United States.

For purposes of subparagraph (J), the term "northern portion of the Western Hemisphere" means the area lying west of the 30th meridian west of Greenwich, east of the international dateline, and north of the Equator, but not including any foreign country which is a country of South America.

(5) Tax-exempt bond financed property. For purposes of this subsection—

(A) In general. Except as otherwise provided in this paragraph, the term "tax-exempt bond financed property" means any property to the extent such property is financed (directly or indirectly) by an obligation the interest on which is exempt from tax under section 103(a).

(B) Allocation of bond proceeds. For purposes of subparagraph (A), the proceeds of any obligation shall be treated as used to finance property acquired in connection with the issuance of such obligation in the order in which such property is placed in service.

(C) Qualified residential rental projects. The term "tax-exempt bond financed property" shall not include any qualified residential rental project (within the meaning of section 142(a)(7)).

(6) Imported property.

(A) Countries maintaining trade restrictions or engaging in discriminatory acts. If the President determines that a foreign country—

(i) maintains nontariff trade restrictions, including variable import fees, which substantially burden United States commerce in a manner inconsistent with provisions of trade agreements, or

(ii) engages in discriminatory or other acts (including tolerance of international cartels) or policies unjustifiably restricting United States commerce,

the President may by Executive order provide for the application of paragraph (1)(D) to any article or class of articles manufactured or produced in such foreign country for such period as may be provided by such Executive order. Any period specified in the preceding sentence shall not apply to any property ordered before (or the construction, reconstruction, or erection of which began before) the date of the Executive order unless the President determines an earlier date to be in the public interest and specifies such date in the Executive order.

(B) Imported property. For purposes of this subsection, the term "imported property" means any property if—

(i) such property was completed outside the United States, or

(ii) less than 50 percent of the basis of such property is attributable to value added within the United States.

For purposes of this subparagraph, the term "United States" includes the Commonwealth of Puerto Rico and the possessions of the United States.

(7) Election to use alternative depreciation system.

(A) In general. If the taxpayer makes an election under this paragraph with respect to any class of property for any taxable year, the alternative depreciation system under this subsection shall apply to all property in such class placed in service during such taxable year. Notwithstanding the preceding sentence, in the case of nonresidential real property or residential rental property, such election may be made separately with respect to each property.

(B) Election irrevocable. An election under subparagraph (A), once made, shall be irrevocable.

(h) Tax-exempt use property.

(1) In general. For purposes of this section—

(A) Property other than nonresidential real property. Except as otherwise provided in this subsection, the term "tax-exempt use property" means that portion of any tangible property (other than nonresidential real property) leased to a tax-exempt entity.

(B) Nonresidential real property.

(i) In general. In the case of nonresidential real property, the term "tax-exempt use property" means that portion of the property leased to a tax-exempt entity in a disqualified lease.

(ii) Disqualified lease. For purposes of this subparagraph, the term "disqualified lease" means any lease of the property to a tax-exempt entity, but only if—

(I) part or all of the property was financed (directly or indirectly) by an obligation the interest on which is exempt from tax under section 103(a) and such entity (or a related entity) participated in such financing,

(II) under such lease there is a fixed or determinable price purchase or sale option which involves such entity (or a related entity) or there is the equivalent of such an option,

(III) such lease has a lease term in excess of 20 years, or

(IV) such lease occurs after a sale (or other transfer) of the property by, or lease of the property from, such entity (or a related entity) and such property has been used by such entity (or a related entity) before such sale (or other transfer) or lease.

(iii) 35-percent threshold test. Clause (i) shall apply to any property only if the portion of such property leased to tax-exempt entities in disqualified leases is more than 35 percent of the property.

(iv) Treatment of improvements. For purposes of this subparagraph, improvements to a property (other than land) shall not be treated as a separate property.

(v) Leasebacks during 1st 3 months of use not taken into account. Subclause (IV) of clause (ii) shall not apply to any property which is leased within 3 months after the date such property is first used by the tax-exempt entity (or a related entity).

(C) Exception for short-term leases.

(i) In general. Property shall not be treated as tax-exempt use property merely by reason of a short-term lease.

(ii) Short-term lease. For purposes of clause (i), the term "short-term lease" means any lease the term of which is—

(I) less than 3 years, and

(II) less than the greater of 1 year or 30 percent of the property's present class life.

In the case of nonresidential real property and property with no present class life, subclause (II) shall not apply.

(D) Exception where property used in unrelated trade or business. The term "tax-exempt use property" shall not include any portion of a property if such portion is predominantly used by the tax-exempt entity (directly or through a partnership of which such entity is a partner) in an unrelated trade or business the income of which is subject to tax under section 511. For purposes of subparagraph (B)(iii), any portion of a property so used shall not be treated as leased to a tax-exempt entity in a disqualified lease.

(E) Nonresidential real property defined. For purposes of this paragraph, the term "nonresidential real property" includes residential rental property.

(2) Tax-exempt entity.

(A) In general. For purposes of this subsection, the term "tax-exempt entity" means—

(i) the United States, any State or political subdivision thereof, any possession of the United States, or any agency or instrumentality of any of the foregoing,

(ii) an organization (other than a cooperative described in section 521) which is exempt from tax imposed by this chapter,

(iii) any foreign person or entity, and

(iv) any Indian tribal government described in section 7701(a)(40).

For purposes of applying this subsection, any Indian tribal government referred to in clause (iv) shall be treated in the same manner as a State.

(B) Exception for certain property subject to United States tax and used by foreign person or entity. Clause (iii) of subparagraph (A) shall not apply with respect to any property if more than 50 percent of the gross income for the taxable year derived by the foreign person or entity from the use of such property is—

(i) subject to tax under this chapter, or

(ii) included under section 951 in the gross income of a United States shareholder for the taxable year with or within which ends the taxable year of the controlled foreign corporation in which such income was derived.

For purposes of the preceding sentence, any exclusion or exemption shall not apply for purposes of determining the amount of the gross income so derived, but shall apply for purposes of determining the portion of such gross income subject to tax under this chapter.

(C) Foreign person or entity. For purposes of this paragraph, the term "foreign person or entity" means—

(i) any foreign government, any international organization, or any agency or instrumentality of any of the foregoing, and

(ii) any person who is not a United States person.

Such term does not include any foreign partnership or other foreign pass-thru entity.

(D) Treatment of certain taxable instrumentalities. For purposes of this subsection, a corporation shall not be treated as an instrumentality of the United States or of any State or political subdivision thereof if—

(i) all of the activities of such corporation are subject to tax under this chapter, and

(ii) a majority of the board of directors of such corporation is not selected by the United States or any State or political subdivision thereof.

(E) Certain previously tax-exempt organizations.

(i) In general. For purposes of this subsection, an organization shall be treated as an organization described in subparagraph (A)(ii) with respect to any property (other than property held by such organization) if such organization was an organization (other than a cooperative described in section 521) exempt from tax imposed by this chapter at any time during the 5-year period ending on the date such property was first used by such organization. The preceding sentence and subparagraph (D)(ii) shall not apply to the Federal Home Loan Mortgage Corporation.

(ii) Election not to have clause (I) apply.

(I) In general. In the case of an organization formerly exempt from tax under section 501(a) as an organization described in section 501(c)(12), clause (i) shall not apply to such organization with respect to any property if such organization elects not to be exempt from tax under section 501(a) during the tax-exempt use period with respect to such property.

(II) Tax-exempt use period. For purposes of subclause (I), the term "tax-exempt use period" means the period beginning with the taxable year in which the property described in subclause (I) is first used by the organization and ending with the close of the 15th taxable year following the last taxable year of the applicable recovery period of such property.

(III) Election. Any election under subclause (I), once made, shall be irrevocable.

(iii) Treatment of successor organizations. Any organization which is engaged in activities substantially similar to those engaged in by a predecessor organization shall succeed to the treatment under this subparagraph of such predecessor organization.

(iv) First used. For purposes of this subparagraph, property shall be treated as first used by the organization—

(I) when the property is first placed in service under a lease to such organization, or

(II) in the case of property leased to (or held by) a partnership (or other pass-thru entity) in which the organization is a member, the later of when such property is first used by such partnership or pass-thru entity or when such organization is first a member of such partnership or pass-thru entity.

(3) Special rules for certain high technology equipment.

(A) Exemption where lease term is 5 years or less. For purposes of this section, the term "tax-exempt use property" shall not include any qualified technological equipment if the lease to the tax-exempt entity has a lease term of 5 years or less. Notwithstanding subsection (i)(3)(A)(i), in determining a lease term for purposes of the preceding sentence, there shall not be taken into account any option of the lessee to renew at the fair market value rent determined at the time of renewal; except that the aggregate period not taken into account by reason of this sentence shall not exceed 24 months.

(B) Exception for certain property.

(i) In general. For purposes of subparagraph (A), the term "qualified technological equipment" shall not include any property leased to a tax-exempt entity if—

(I) part or all of the property was financed (directly or indirectly) by an obligation the interest on which is exempt from tax under section 103(a),

(II) such lease occurs after a sale (or other transfer) of the property by, or lease of such property from, such entity (or related entity) and such property has been used by such entity (or a related entity) before such sale (or other transfer) or lease, or

(III) such tax-exempt entity is the United States or any agency or instrumentality of the United States.

(ii) Leasebacks during 1st 3 months of use not taken into account. Subclause (II) of clause (i) shall not apply to any property which is leased within 3 months after the date such property is first used by the tax-exempt entity (or a related entity).

(4) Related entities. For purposes of this subsection—

(A)(i) Each governmental unit and each agency or instrumentality of a governmental unit is related to each other such unit, agency, or instrumentality which directly or indirectly derives its powers, rights, and duties in whole or in part from the same sovereign authority.

(ii) For purposes of clause (i), the United States, each State, and each possession of the United States shall be treated as a separate sovereign authority.

(B) Any entity not described in subparagraph (A)(i) is related to any other entity if the 2 entities have—

(i) significant common purposes and substantial common membership, or

(ii) directly or indirectly substantial common direction or control.

(C)(i) An entity is related to another entity if either entity owns (directly or through 1 or more entities) a 50 percent or greater interest in the capital or profits of the other entity.

(ii) For purposes of clause (i), entities treated as related under subparagraph (A) or (B) shall be treated as 1 entity.

(D) An entity is related to another entity with respect to a transaction if such transaction is part of an attempt by such entities to avoid the application of this subsection.

(5) Tax-exempt use of property leased to partnerships, etc., determined at partner level. For purposes of this subsection—

(A) In general. In the case of any property which is leased to a partnership, the determination of whether any portion of such property is tax-exempt use property shall be made by treating each tax-exempt entity partner's proportionate share (determined under paragraph (6)(C)) of such property as being leased to such partner.

(B) Other pass-thru entities; tiered entities. Rules similar to the rules of subparagraph (A) shall also apply in the case of any pass-thru entity other than a partnership and in the case of tiered partnerships and other entities.

(C) Presumption with respect to foreign entities. Unless it is otherwise established to the satisfaction of the Secretary, it shall be presumed that the partners of a foreign partnership (and the beneficiaries of any other foreign pass-thru entity) are persons who are not United States persons.

(6) Treatment of property owned by partnerships, etc.

(A) In general. For purposes of this subsection, if—

(i) any property which (but for this subparagraph) is not tax-exempt use property is owned by a partnership which has both a tax-exempt entity and a person who is not a tax-exempt entity as partners, and

(ii) any allocation to the tax-exempt entity of partnership items is not a qualified allocation,

an amount equal to such tax-exempt entity's proportionate share of such property shall (except as provided in paragraph (1)(D)) be treated as tax-exempt use property.

(B) Qualified allocation. For purposes of subparagraph (A), the term "qualified allocation" means any allocation to a tax-exempt entity which—

(i) is consistent with such entity's being allocated the same distributive share of each item of income, gain, loss, deduction, credit, and basis and such share remains the same during the entire period the entity is a partner in the partnership, and

(ii) has substantial economic effect within the meaning of section 704(b)(2).

For purposes of this subparagraph, items allocated under section 704(c) shall not be taken into account.

(C) Determination of proportionate share.

(i) In general. For purposes of subparagraph (A), a tax-exempt entity's proportionate share of any property owned by a partnership shall be determined on the basis of such entity's share of partnership items of income or gain (excluding gain allocated under section 704(c)), whichever results in the largest proportionate share.

(ii) Determination where allocations vary. For purposes of clause (i), if a tax-exempt entity's share of partnership items of income or gain (excluding gain allocated under section 704(c)) may vary during the period such entity is a partner in the partnership, such share shall be the highest share such entity may receive.

Deductions Code Sec. 168(i)(2)(C)

(D) Determination of whether property used in unrelated trade or business. For purposes of this subsection, in the case of any property which is owned by a partnership which has both a tax-exempt entity and a person who is not a tax-exempt entity as partners, the determination of whether such property is used in an unrelated trade or business of such an entity shall be made without regard to section 514.

(E) Other pass-thru entities; tiered entities. Rules similar to the rules of subparagraphs (A), (B), (C), and (D) shall also apply in the case of any pass-thru entity other than a partnership and in the case of tiered partnerships and other entities.

(F) Treatment of certain taxable entities.

(i) In general. For purposes of this paragraph and paragraph (5), except as otherwise provided in this subparagraph, any tax-exempt controlled entity shall be treated as a tax-exempt entity.

(ii) Election. If a tax-exempt controlled entity makes an election under this clause—

(I) such entity shall not be treated as a tax-exempt entity for purposes of this paragraph and paragraph (5), and

(II) any gain recognized by a tax-exempt entity on any disposition of an interest in such entity (and any dividend or interest received or accrued by a tax-exempt entity from such tax-exempt controlled entity) shall be treated as unrelated business taxable income for purposes of section 511.

Any such election shall be irrevocable and shall bind all tax-exempt entities holding interests in such tax-exempt controlled entity. For purposes of subclause (II), there shall only be taken into account dividends which are properly allocable to income of the tax-exempt controlled entity which was not subject to tax under this chapter.

(iii) Tax-exempt controlled entity.

(I) In general. The term "tax-exempt controlled entity" means any corporation (which is not a tax-exempt entity determined without regard to this subparagraph and paragraph (2)(E)) if 50 percent or more (in value) of the stock in such corporation is held by 1 or more tax-exempt entities (other than a foreign person or entity).

(II) Only 5-percent shareholders taken into account in case of publicly traded stock. For purposes of subclause (I), in the case of a corporation the stock of which is publicly traded on an established securities market, stock held by a tax-exempt entity shall not be taken into account unless such entity holds at least 5 percent (in value) of the stock in such corporation. For purposes of this subclause, related entities (within the meaning of paragraph (4)) shall be treated as 1 entity.

(III) Section 318 to apply. For purposes of this clause, a tax-exempt entity shall be treated as holding stock which it holds through application of section 318 (determined without regard to the 50-percent limitation contained in subsection (a)(2)(C) thereof).

(G) Regulations. For purposes of determining whether there is a qualified allocation under subparagraph (B), the regulations prescribed under paragraph (8) for purposes of this paragraph—

(i) shall set forth the proper treatment for partnership guaranteed payments, and

(ii) may provide for the exclusion or segregation of items.

(7) Lease. For purposes of this subsection, the term "lease" includes any grant of a right to use property.

(8) Regulations. The Secretary shall prescribe such regulations as may be necessary or appropriate to carry out the purposes of this subsection.

(i) Definitions and special rules.

For purposes of this section—

(1) Class life. Except as provided in this section, the term "class life" means the class life (if any) which would be applicable with respect to any property as of January 1, 1986, under subsection (m) of section 167 (determined without regard to paragraph (4) and as if the taxpayer had made an election under such subsection). The Secretary, through an office established in the Treasury, shall monitor and analyze actual experience with respect to all depreciable assets. The reference in this paragraph to subsection (m) of section 167 shall be treated as a reference to such subsection as in effect on the day before the date of the enactment of the Revenue Reconciliation Act of 1990 [11/5/90].

(2) Qualified technological equipment.

(A) In general. The term "qualified technological equipment" means—

(i) any computer or peripheral equipment,

(ii) any high technology telephone station equipment installed on the customer's premises, and

(iii) any high technology medical equipment.

(B) Computer or peripheral equipment defined. For purposes of this paragraph—

(i) In general. The term "computer or peripheral equipment" means—

(I) any computer, and

(II) any related peripheral equipment.

(ii) Computer. The term "computer" means a programmable electronically activated device which—

(I) is capable of accepting information, applying prescribed processes to the information, and supplying the results of these processes with or without human intervention, and

(II) consists of a central processing unit containing extensive storage, logic, arithmetic, and control capabilities.

(iii) Related peripheral equipment. The term "related peripheral equipment" means any auxiliary machine (whether on-line or off-line) which is designed to be placed under the control of the central processing unit of a computer.

(iv) Exceptions. The term "computer or peripheral equipment" shall not include—

(I) any equipment which is an integral part of other property which is not a computer,

(II) typewriters, calculators, adding and accounting machines, copiers, duplicating equipment, and similar equipment, and

(III) equipment of a kind used primarily for amusement or entertainment of the user.

(C) High technology medical equipment. For purposes of this paragraph, the term "high technology medical equipment" means any electronic, electromechanical, or computer-based high technology equipment used in the screening, monitoring, observation, diagnosis, or treatment of patients in a laboratory, medical, or hospital environment.

(3) Lease term.
(A) In general. In determining a lease term—
  (i) there shall be taken into account options to renew,
  (ii) the term of a lease shall include the term of any service contract or similar arrangement (whether or not treated as a lease under section 7701(e))—
    (I) which is part of the same transaction (or series of related transactions) which includes the lease, and
    (II) which is with respect to the property subject to the lease or substantially similar property, and
  (iii) 2 or more successive leases which are part of the same transaction (or a series of related transactions) with respect to the same or substantially similar property shall be treated as 1 lease.
(B) Special rule for fair rental options on nonresidential real property or residential rental property. For purposes of clause (i) of subparagraph (A), in the case of nonresidential real property or residential rental property, there shall not be taken into account any option to renew at fair market value determined at the time of renewal.

(4) General asset accounts. Under regulations, a taxpayer may maintain 1 or more general asset accounts for any property to which this section applies. Except as provided in regulations, all proceeds realized on any disposition of property in a general asset account shall be included in income as ordinary income.

(5) Changes in use. The Secretary shall, by regulations, provide for the method of determining the deduction allowable under section 167(a) with respect to any tangible property for any taxable year (and the succeeding taxable years) during which such property changes status under this section but continues to be held by the same person.

(6) Treatments of additions or improvements to property. In the case of any addition to (or improvement of) any property—
(A) any deduction under subsection (a) for such addition or improvement shall be computed in the same manner as the deduction for such property would be computed if such property had been placed in service at the same time as such addition or improvement, and
(B) the applicable recovery period for such addition or improvement shall begin on the later of—
  (i) the date on which such addition (or improvement) is placed in service, or
  (ii) the date on which the property with respect to which such addition (or improvement) was made is placed in service.

(7) Treatment of certain transferees.
(A) In general. In the case of any property transferred in a transaction described in subparagraph (B), the transferee shall be treated as the transferor for purposes of computing the depreciation deduction determined under this section with respect to so much of the basis in the hands of the transferee as does not exceed the adjusted basis in the hands of the transferor. In any case where this section as in effect before the amendments made by section 201 of the Tax Reform Act of 1986 applied to the property in the hands of the transferor, the reference in the preceding sentence to this section shall be treated as a reference to this section as so in effect.
(B) Transactions covered. The transactions described in this subparagraph are—
  (i) any transaction described in section 332, 351, 361, 721, or 731, and
  (ii) any transaction between members of the same affiliated group during any taxable year for which a consolidated return is made by such group.
Subparagraph (A) shall not apply in the case of a termination of a partnership under section 708(b)(1)(B).
(C) Property reacquired by the taxpayer. Under regulations, property which is disposed of and then reacquired by the taxpayer shall be treated for purposes of computing the deduction allowable under subsection (a) as if such property had not been disposed of.

(8) Treatment of leasehold improvements.
(A) In general. In the case of any building erected (or improvements made) on leased property, if such building or improvement is property to which this section applies, the depreciation deduction shall be determined under the provisions of this section.
(B) Treatment of lessor improvements which are abandoned at termination of lease. An improvement—
  (i) which is made by the lessor of leased property for the lessee of such property, and
  (ii) which is irrevocably disposed of or abandoned by the lessor at the termination of the lease by such lessee,
shall be treated for purposes of determining gain or loss under this title as disposed of by the lessor when so disposed of or abandoned.
(C) Cross reference. For treatment of qualified long-term real property constructed or improved in connection with cash or rent reduction from lessor to lessee, see section 110(b).

(9) Normalization rules.
(A) In general. In order to use a normalization method of accounting with respect to any public utility property for purposes of subsection (f)(2)—
  (i) the taxpayer must, in computing its tax expense for purposes of establishing its cost of service for ratemaking purposes and reflecting operating results in its regulated books of account, use a method of depreciation with respect to such property that is the same as, and a depreciation period for such property that is no shorter than, the method and period used to compute its depreciation expense for such purposes; and
  (ii) if the amount allowable as a deduction under this section with respect to such property differs from the amount that would be allowable as a deduction under section 167 using the method (including the period, first and last year convention, and salvage value) used to compute regulated tax expense under clause (i), the taxpayer must make adjustments to a reserve to reflect the deferral of taxes resulting from such difference.
(B) Use of inconsistent estimates and projections, etc.
  (i) In general. One way in which the requirements of subparagraph (A) are not met is if the taxpayer, for ratemaking purposes, uses a procedure or adjustment which is inconsistent with the requirements of subparagraph (A).
  (ii) Use of inconsistent estimates and projections. The procedures and adjustments which are to be treated as inconsistent for purposes of clause (i) shall include any procedure or adjustment for ratemaking purposes which uses an estimate or projection of the taxpayer's tax expense, depreciation expense, or reserve

for deferred taxes under subparagraph (A)(ii) unless such estimate or projection is also used, for ratemaking purposes, with respect to the other 2 such items and with respect to the rate base.

(iii) Regulatory authority. The Secretary may by regulations prescribe procedures and adjustments (in addition to those specified in clause (ii)) which are to be treated as inconsistent for purposes of clause (i).

(C) Public utility property which does not meet normalization rules. In the case of any public utility property to which this section does not apply by reason of subsection (f)(2), the allowance for depreciation under section 167(a) shall be an amount computed using the method and period referred to in subparagraph (A)(i).

(10) Public utility property. The term "public utility property" means property used predominantly in the trade or business of the furnishing or sale of—

(A) electrical energy, water, or sewage disposal services,

(B) gas or steam through a local distribution system,

(C) telephone services, or other communication services if furnished or sold by the Communications Satellite Corporation for purposes authorized by the Communications Satellite Act of 1962 (47 U.S.C. 701), or

(D) transportation of gas or steam by pipeline,

if the rates for such furnishing or sale, as the case may be, have been established or approved by a State or political subdivision thereof, by any agency or instrumentality of the United States, or by a public service or public utility commission or other similar body of any State or political subdivision thereof.

(11) Research and experimentation. The term "research and experimentation" has the same meaning as the term research and experimental has under section 174.

(12) Section 1245 and 1250 property. The terms "section 1245 property" and "section 1250 property" have the meanings given such terms by sections 1245(a)(3) and 1250(c), respectively.

(13) Single purpose agricultural or horticultural structure.

(A) In general. The term "single purpose agricultural or horticultural structure" means—

(i) a single purpose livestock structure, and

(ii) a single purpose horticultural structure.

(B) Definitions. For purposes of this paragraph—

(i) Single purpose livestock structure. The term "single purpose livestock structure" means any enclosure or structure specifically designed, constructed, and used—

(I) for housing, raising, and feeding a particular type of livestock and their produce, and

(II) for housing the equipment (including any replacements) necessary for the housing, raising, and feeding referred to in subclause (I).

(ii) Single purpose horticultural structure. The term "single purpose horticultural structure" means—

(I) a greenhouse specifically designed, constructed, and used for the commercial production of plants, and

(II) a structure specifically designed, constructed, and used for the commercial production of mushrooms.

(iii) Structures which include work space. An enclosure or structure which provides work space shall be treated as a single purpose agricultural or horticultural structure only if such work space is solely for—

(I) the stocking, caring for, or collecting of livestock or plants (as the case may be) or their produce,

(II) the maintenance of the enclosure or structure, and

(III) the maintenance or replacement of the equipment or stock enclosed or housed therein.

(iv) Livestock. The term "livestock" includes poultry.

(14) Qualified rent-to-own property.

(A) In general. The term "qualified rent-to-own property" means property held by a rent-to-own dealer for purposes of being subject to a rent-to-own contract.

(B) Rent-to-own dealer. The term "rent-to-own dealer" means a person that, in the ordinary course of business, regularly enters into rent-to-own contracts with customers for the use of consumer property, if a substantial portion of those contracts terminate and the property is returned to such person before the receipt of all payments required to transfer ownership of the property from such person to the customer.

(C) Consumer property. The term "consumer property" means tangible personal property of a type generally used within the home for personal use.

(D) Rent-to-own contract. The term "rent-to-own contract" means any lease for the use of consumer property between a rent-to-own dealer and a customer who is an individual which—

(i) is titled "Rent-to-Own Agreement" or "Lease Agreement with Ownership Option," or uses other similar language,

(ii) provides for level (or decreasing where no payment is less than 40 percent of the largest payment), regular periodic payments (for a payment period which is a week or month),

(iii) provides that legal title to such property remains with the rent-to-own dealer until the customer makes all the payments described in clause (ii) or early purchase payments required under the contract to acquire legal title to the item of property,

(iv) provides a beginning date and a maximum period of time for which the contract may be in effect that does not exceed 156 weeks or 36 months from such beginning date (including renewals or options to extend),

(v) provides for payments within the 156-week or 36-month period that, in the aggregate, generally exceed the normal retail price of the consumer property plus interest,

(vi) provides for payments under the contract that, in the aggregate, do not exceed $10,000 per item of consumer property,

(vii) provides that the customer does not have any legal obligation to make all the payments referred to in clause (ii) set forth under the contract, and that at the end of each payment period the customer may either continue to use the consumer property by making the payment for the next payment period or return such property to the rent-to-own dealer in good working order, in which case the customer does not incur any further obligations under the contract and is not entitled to a return of any payments previously made under the contract, and

(viii) provides that the customer has no right to sell, sublease, mortgage, pawn, pledge, encumber, or otherwise dispose of the consumer property until all the payments stated in the contract have been made.

(15) Motorsports entertainment complex.
(A) In general. The term "motorsports entertainment complex" means a racing track facility which—
(i) is permanently situated on land, and
(ii) during the 36-month period following the first day of the month in which the asset is placed in service, hosts 1 or more racing events for automobiles (of any type), trucks, or motorcycles which are open to the public for the price of admission.
(B) Ancillary and support facilities. Such term shall include, if owned by the taxpayer who owns the complex and provided for the benefit of patrons of the complex—
(i) ancillary facilities and land improvements in support of the complex's activities (including parking lots, sidewalks, waterways, bridges, fences, and landscaping),
(ii) support facilities (including food and beverage retailing, souvenir vending, and other nonlodging accommodations), and
(iii) appurtenances associated with such facilities and related attractions and amusements (including ticket booths, race track surfaces, suites and hospitality facilities, grandstands and viewing structures, props, walls, facilities that support the delivery of entertainment services, other special purpose structures, facades, shop interiors, and buildings).
(C) Exception. Such term shall not include any transportation equipment, administrative services assets, warehouses, administrative buildings, hotels, or motels.
(D) Termination. Such term shall not include any property placed in service after December 31, 2011.

(16) Alaska natural gas pipeline. The term "Alaska natural gas pipeline" means the natural gas pipeline system located in the State of Alaska which—
(A) has a capacity of more than 500,000,000,000 Btu of natural gas per day, and
(B) is—
(i) placed in service after December 31, 2013, or
(ii) treated as placed in service on January 1, 2014, if the taxpayer who places such system in service before January 1, 2014, elects such treatment.

Such term includes the pipe, trunk lines, related equipment, and appurtenances used to carry natural gas, but does not include any gas processing plant.

(17) Natural gas gathering line. The term "natural gas gathering line" means—
(A) the pipe, equipment, and appurtenances determined to be a gathering line by the Federal Energy Regulatory Commission, and
(B) the pipe, equipment, and appurtenances used to deliver natural gas from the wellhead or a commonpoint to the point at which such gas first reaches—
(i) a gas processing plant,
(ii) an interconnection with a transmission pipeline for which a certificate as an interstate transmission pipeline has been issued by the Federal Energy Regulatory Commission,
(iii) an interconnection with an intrastate transmission pipeline, or
(iv) a direct interconnection with a local distribution company, a gas storage facility, or an industrial consumer.

(18) Qualified smart electric meters.
(A) In general. The term "qualified smart electric meter" means any smart electric meter which—
(i) is placed in service by a taxpayer who is a supplier of electric energy or a provider of electric energy services, and
(ii) does not have a class life (determined without regard to subsection (e)) of less than 10 years.
(B) Smart electric meter. For purposes of subparagraph (A), the term "smart electric meter" means any time-based meter and related communication equipment which is capable of being used by the taxpayer as part of a system that—
(i) measures and records electricity usage data on a time-differentiated basis in at least 24 separate time segments per day,
(ii) provides for the exchange of information between supplier or provider and the customer's electric meter in support of time-based rates or other forms of demand response,
(iii) provides data to such supplier or provider so that the supplier or provider can provide energy usage information to customers electronically, and
(iv) provides net metering.

(19) Qualified smart electric grid systems.
(A) In general. The term "qualified smart electric grid system" means any smart grid property which—
(i) is used as part of a system for electric distribution grid communications, monitoring, and management placed in service by a taxpayer who is a supplier of electric energy or a provider of electric energy services, and
(ii) does not have a class life (determined without regard to subsection (e)) of less than 10 years.
(B) Smart grid property. For the purposes of subparagraph (A), the term "smart grid property" means electronics and related equipment that is capable of—
(i) sensing, collecting, and monitoring data of or from all portions of a utility's electric distribution grid,
(ii) providing real-time, two-way communications to monitor or manage such grid, and
(iii) providing real time analysis of and event prediction based upon collected data that can be used to improve electric distribution system reliability, quality, and performance.

(j) Property on Indian reservations.
(1) In general. For purposes of subsection (a), the applicable recovery period for qualified Indian reservation property shall be determined in accordance with the table contained in paragraph (2) in lieu of the table contained in subsection (c).
(2) Applicable recovery period for Indian reservation property. For purposes of paragraph (1)—

In the case of:	The applicable recovery period is:
3-year property	2 years
5-year property	3 years
7-year property	4 years
10-year property	6 years
15-year property	9 years
20-year property	12 years
Nonresidential real property	22 years

Deductions   Code Sec. 168(k)(2)(B)(ii)

(3) Deduction allowed in computing minimum tax. For purposes of determining alternative minimum taxable income under section 55, the deduction under subsection (a) for property to which paragraph (1) applies shall be determined under this section without regard to any adjustment under section 56.

(4) Qualified Indian reservation property defined. For purposes of this subsection—

(A) In general. The term "qualified Indian reservation property" means property which is property described in the table in paragraph (2) and which is—

(i) used by the taxpayer predominantly in the active conduct of a trade or business within an Indian reservation,

(ii) not used or located outside the Indian reservation on a regular basis,

(iii) not acquired (directly or indirectly) by the taxpayer from a person who is related to the taxpayer (within the meaning of section 465(b)(3)(C)), and

(iv) not property (or any portion thereof) placed in service for purposes of conducting or housing class I, II, or III gaming (as defined in section 4 of the Indian Regulatory Act (25 U.S.C. 2703)).

(B) Exception for alternative depreciation property. The term "qualified Indian reservation property" does not include any property to which the alternative depreciation system under subsection (g) applies, determined—

(i) without regard to subsection (g)(7) (relating to election to use alternative depreciation system), and

(ii) after the application of section 280F(b) (relating to listed property with limited business use).

(C) Special rule for reservation infrastructure investment.

(i) In general. Subparagraph (A)(ii) shall not apply to qualified infrastructure property located outside of the Indian reservation if the purpose of such property is to connect with qualified infrastructure property located within the Indian reservation.

(ii) Qualified infrastructure property. For purposes of this subparagraph, the term "qualified infrastructure property" means qualified Indian reservation property (determined without regard to subparagraph (A)(ii)) which—

(I) benefits the tribal infrastructure,

(II) is available to the general public, and

(III) is placed in service in connection with the taxpayer's active conduct of a trade or business within an Indian reservation.

Such term includes, but is not limited to, roads, power lines, water systems, railroad spurs, and communications facilities.

(5) Real estate rentals. For purposes of this subsection, the rental to others of real property located within an Indian reservation shall be treated as the active conduct of a trade or business within an Indian reservation.

(6) Indian reservation defined. For purposes of this subsection, the term "Indian reservation" means a reservation, as defined in—

(A) section 3(d) of the Indian Financing Act of 1974 (25 U.S.C. 1452(d)), or

(B) section 4(10) of the Indian Child Welfare Act of 1978 (25 U.S.C. 1903(10)).

For purposes of the preceding sentence, such section 3(d) shall be applied by treating the term "former Indian reservations in Oklahoma" as including only lands which are within the jurisdictional area of an Oklahoma Indian tribe (as determined by the Secretary of the Interior) and are recognized by such Secretary as eligible for trust land status under 25 CFR Part 151 (as in effect on the date of the enactment of this sentence).

(7) Coordination with nonrevenue laws. Any reference in this subsection to a provision not contained in this title shall be treated for purposes of this subsection as a reference to such provision as in effect on the date of the enactment of this paragraph.

(8) Termination. This subsection shall not apply to property placed in service after December 31, 2011.

(k) Special allowance for certain property acquired after December 31, 2007, and before January 1, 2013.

(1) Additional allowance. In the case of any qualified property—

(A) the depreciation deduction provided by section 167(a) for the taxable year in which such property is placed in service shall include an allowance equal to 50 percent of the adjusted basis of the qualified property, and

(B) the adjusted basis of the qualified property shall be reduced by the amount of such deduction before computing the amount otherwise allowable as a depreciation deduction under this chapter for such taxable year and any subsequent taxable year.

(2) Qualified property. For purposes of this subsection—

(A) In general. The term "qualified property" means property—

(i)(I) to which this section applies which has a recovery period of 20 years or less,

(II) which is computer software (as defined in section 167(f)(1)(B)) for which a deduction is allowable under section 167(a) without regard to this subsection,

(III) which is water utility property, or

(IV) which is qualified leasehold improvement property,

(ii) the original use of which commences with the taxpayer after December 31, 2007,

(iii) which is—

(I) acquired by the taxpayer after December 31, 2007, and before January 1, 2013, but only if no written binding contract for the acquisition was in effect before January 1, 2008, or

(II) acquired by the taxpayer pursuant to a written binding contract which was entered into after December 31, 2007, and before January 1, 2013, and

(iv) which is placed in service by the taxpayer before January 1, 2013, or, in the case of property described in subparagraph (B) or (C), before January 1, 2014.

(B) Certain property having longer production periods treated as qualified property.

(i) In general. The term "qualified property" includes any property if such property—

(I) meets the requirements of clauses (i), (ii), (iii), and (iv) of subparagraph (A),

(II) has a recovery period of at least 10 years or is transportation property,

(III) is subject to section 263A, and

(IV) meets the requirements of clause (iii) of section 263A(f)(1)(B) (determined as if such clauses also apply to property which has a long useful life (within the meaning of section 263A(f))).

(ii) Only pre-January 1, 2013 basis eligible for additional allowance. In the case of property which is qualified property solely by reason of clause (i), para-

1,575

graph (1) shall apply only to the extent of the adjusted basis thereof attributable to manufacture, construction, or production before January 1, 2013.

(iii) Transportation property. For purposes of this subparagraph, the term "transportation property" means tangible personal property used in the trade or business of transporting persons or property.

(iv) Application of subparagraph. This subparagraph shall not apply to any property which is described in subparagraph (C).

(C) Certain aircraft. The term "qualified property" includes property—

(i) which meets the requirements of clauses (ii), (iii), and (iv) of subparagraph (A),

(ii) which is an aircraft which is not a transportation property (as defined in subparagraph (B)(iii)) other than for agricultural or firefighting purposes,

(iii) which is purchased and on which such purchaser, at the time of the contract for purchase, has made a nonrefundable deposit of the lesser of—

(I) 10 percent of the cost, or
(II) $100,000, and

(iv) which has—

(I) an estimated production period exceeding 4 months, and
(II) a cost exceeding $200,000.

(D) Exceptions.

(i) Alternative depreciation property. The term "qualified property" shall not include any property to which the alternative depreciation system under subsection (g) applies, determined—

(I) without regard to paragraph (7) of subsection (g) (relating to election to have system apply), and
(II) after application of section 280F(b) (relating to listed property with limited business use).

(ii) Qualified New York Liberty Zone leasehold improvement property. The term "qualified property" shall not include any qualified New York Liberty Zone leasehold improvement property (as defined in section 1400L(c)(2)).

(iii) Election out. If a taxpayer makes an election under this clause with respect to any class of property for any taxable year, this subsection shall not apply to all property in such class placed in service during such taxable year.

(E) Special rules.

(i) Self-constructed property. In the case of a taxpayer manufacturing, constructing, or producing property for the taxpayer's own use, the requirements of clause (iii) of subparagraph (A) shall be treated as met if the taxpayer begins manufacturing, constructing, or producing the property after December 31, 2007, and before January 1, 2013.

(ii) Sale-leasebacks. For purposes of clause (iii) and subparagraph (A)(ii), if property is—

(I) originally placed in service after December 31, 2007, by a person, and
(II) sold and leased back by such person within 3 months after the date such property was originally placed in service,

such property shall be treated as originally placed in service not earlier than the date on which such property is used under the leaseback referred to in subclause (II).

(iii) Syndication. For purposes of subparagraph (A)(ii), if—

(I) property is originally placed in service after December 31, 2007, by the lessor of such property,
(II) such property is sold by such lessor or any subsequent purchaser within 3 months after the date such property was originally placed in service (or, in the case of multiple units of property subject to the same lease, within 3 months after the date the final unit is placed in service, so long as the period between the time the first unit is placed in service and the time the last unit is placed in service does not exceed 12 months), and
(III) the user of such property after the last sale during such 3-month period remains the same as when such property was originally placed in service,

such property shall be treated as originally placed in service not earlier than the date of such last sale.

(iv) Limitations related to users and related parties. The term "qualified property" shall not include any property if—

(I) the user of such property (as of the date on which such property is originally placed in service) or a person which is related (within the meaning of section 267(b) or 707(b)) to such user or to the taxpayer had a written binding contract in effect for the acquisition of such property at any time on or before December 31, 2007, or
(II) in the case of property manufactured, constructed, or produced for such user's or person's own use, the manufacture, construction, or production of such property began at any time on or before December 31, 2007.

(F) Coordination with section 280F. For purposes of section 280F—

(i) Automobiles. In the case of a passenger automobile (as defined in section 280F(d)(5)) which is qualified property, the Secretary shall increase the limitation under section 280F(a)(1)(A)(i) by $8,000.

(ii) Listed property. The deduction allowable under paragraph (1) shall be taken into account in computing any recapture amount under section 280F(b)(2).

(G) Deduction allowed in computing minimum tax. For purposes of determining alternative minimum taxable income under section 55, the deduction under subsection (a) for qualified property shall be determined under this section without regard to any adjustment under section 56.

(3) Qualified leasehold improvement property. For purposes of this subsection—

(A) In general. The term "qualified leasehold improvement property" means any improvement to an interior portion of a building which is nonresidential real property if—

(i) such improvement is made under or pursuant to a lease (as defined in subsection (h)(7))—

(I) by the lessee (or any sublessee) of such portion, or
(II) by the lessor of such portion,

(ii) such portion is to be occupied exclusively by the lessee (or any sublessee) of such portion, and

(iii) such improvement is placed in service more than 3 years after the date the building was first placed in service.

(B) Certain improvements not included. Such term shall not include any improvement for which the expenditure is attributable to—

(i) the enlargement of the building,
(ii) any elevator or escalator,
(iii) any structural component benefiting a common area, and
(iv) the internal structural framework of the building.
(C) Definitions and special rules. For purposes of this paragraph—
  (i) Commitment to lease treated as lease. A commitment to enter into a lease shall be treated as a lease, and the parties to such commitment shall be treated as lessor and lessee, respectively.
  (ii) Related persons. A lease between related persons shall not be considered a lease. For purposes of the preceding sentence, the term "related persons" means—
    (I) members of an affiliated group (as defined in section 1504), and
    (II) persons having a relationship described in subsection (b) of section 267; except that, for purposes of this clause, the phrase "80 percent or more" shall be substituted for the phrase "more than 50 percent" each place it appears in such subsection.

(4) Election to accelerate the AMT and research credits in lieu of bonus depreciation.
(A) In general. If a corporation elects to have this paragraph apply for the first taxable year of the taxpayer ending after March 31, 2008, in the case of such taxable year and each subsequent taxable year—
  (i) paragraph (1) shall not apply to any eligible qualified property placed in service by the taxpayer,
  (ii) the applicable depreciation method used under this section with respect to such property shall be the straight line method, and
  (iii) each of the limitations described in subparagraph (B) for any such taxable year shall be increased by the bonus depreciation amount which is—
    (I) determined for such taxable year under subparagraph (C), and
    (II) allocated to such limitation under subparagraph (E).
(B) Limitations to be increased. The limitations described in this subparagraph are—
  (i) the limitation imposed by section 38(c), and
  (ii) the limitation imposed by section 53(c).
(C) Bonus depreciation amount. For purposes of this paragraph—
  (i) In general. The bonus depreciation amount for any taxable year is an amount equal to 20 percent of the excess (if any) of—
    (I) the aggregate amount of depreciation which would be allowed under this section for eligible qualified property placed in service by the taxpayer during such taxable year if paragraph (1) applied to all such property, over
    (II) the aggregate amount of depreciation which would be allowed under this section for eligible qualified property placed in service by the taxpayer during such taxable year if paragraph (1) did not apply to any such property.
  The aggregate amounts determined under subclauses (I) and (II) shall be determined without regard to any election made under subsection (b)(2)(C), (b)(3)(D), or (g)(7) and without regard to subparagraph (A)(ii).
  (ii) Maximum amount. The bonus depreciation amount for any taxable year shall not exceed the maximum increase amount under clause (iii), reduced (but not below zero) by the sum of the bonus depreciation amounts for all preceding taxable years.
  (iii) Maximum increase amount. For purposes of clause (ii), the term "maximum increase amount" means, with respect to any corporation, the lesser of—
    (I) $30,000,000, or
    (II) 6 percent of the sum of the business credit increase amount, and the AMT credit increase amount, determined with respect to such corporation under subparagraph (E).
  (iv) Aggregation rule. All corporations which are treated as a single employer under section 52(a) shall be treated—
    (I) as 1 taxpayer for purposes of this paragraph, and
    (II) as having elected the application of this paragraph if any such corporation so elects.
(D) Eligible qualified property. For purposes of this paragraph, the term "eligible qualified property" means qualified property under paragraph (2), except that in applying paragraph (2) for purposes of this paragraph—
  (i) "March 31, 2008" shall be substituted for "December 31, 2007" each place it appears in subparagraph (A) and clauses (i) and (ii) of subparagraph (E) thereof,
  (ii) "April 1, 2008" shall be substituted for "January 1, 2008" in subparagraph (A)(iii)(I) thereof, and
  (iii) only adjusted basis attributable to manufacture, construction, or production—
    (I) after March 31, 2008, and before January 1, 2010, and
    (II) after December 31, 2010, and before January 1, 2013, shall be taken into account under subparagraph (B)(ii) thereof .
  (iv) Repealed.
  (v) Repealed.
(E) Allocation of bonus depreciation amounts.
  (i) In general. Subject to clauses (ii) and (iii), the taxpayer shall, at such time and in such manner as the Secretary may prescribe, specify the portion (if any) of the bonus depreciation amount for the taxable year which is to be allocated to each of the limitations described in subparagraph (B) for such taxable year.
  (ii) Limitation on allocations. The portion of the bonus depreciation amount which may be allocated under clause (i) to the limitations described in subparagraph (B) for any taxable year shall not exceed—
    (I) in the case of the limitation described in subparagraph (B)(i), the excess of the business credit increase amount over the bonus depreciation amount allocated to such limitation for all preceding taxable years, and
    (II) in the case of the limitation described in subparagraph (B)(ii), the excess of the AMT credit increase amount over the bonus depreciation amount allocated to such limitation for all preceding taxable years.
  (iii) Business credit increase amount. For purposes of this paragraph, the term "business credit increase amount" means the amount equal to the portion of the credit allowable under section 38 (determined without regard to subsection (c) thereof) for the first taxable year ending after March 31, 2008, which is

allocable to business credit carryforwards to such taxable year which are—

(I) from taxable years beginning before January 1, 2006, and

(II) properly allocable (determined under the rules of section 38(d)) to the research credit determined under section 41(a).

(iv) AMT credit increase amount. For purposes of this paragraph, the term "AMT credit increase amount" means the amount equal to the portion of the minimum tax credit under section 53(b) for the first taxable year ending after March 31, 2008, determined by taking into account only the adjusted minimum tax for taxable years beginning before January 1, 2006. For purposes of the preceding sentence, credits shall be treated as allowed on a first-in, first-out basis.

(F) Credit refundable. For purposes of section 6401(b), the aggregate increase in the credits allowable under part IV of subchapter A for any taxable year resulting from the application of this paragraph shall be treated as allowed under subpart C of such part (and not any other subpart).

(G) Other rules.

(i) Election. Any election under this paragraph (including any allocation under subparagraph (E)) may be revoked only with the consent of the Secretary.

(ii) Partnerships with electing partners. In the case of a corporation making an election under subparagraph (A) and which is a partner in a partnership, for purposes of determining such corporation's distributive share of partnership items under section 702—

(I) paragraph (1) shall not apply to any eligible qualified property, and

(II) the applicable depreciation method used under this section with respect to such property shall be the straight line method.

(iii) Special rule for passenger aircraft. In the case of any passenger aircraft, the written binding contract limitation under paragraph (2)(A)(iii)(I) shall not apply for purposes of subparagraphs (C)(i)(I) and (D).

(H) Special rules for extension property.

(i) Taxpayers previously electing acceleration. In the case of a taxpayer who made the election under subparagraph (A) for its first taxable year ending after March 31, 2008—

(I) the taxpayer may elect not to have this paragraph apply to extension property, but

(II) if the taxpayer does not make the election under subclause (I), in applying this paragraph to the taxpayer a separate bonus depreciation amount, maximum amount, and maximum increase amount shall be computed and applied to eligible qualified property which is extension property and to eligible qualified property which is not extension property.

(ii) Taxpayers not previously electing acceleration. In the case of a taxpayer who did not make the election under subparagraph (A) for its first taxable year ending after March 31, 2008—

(I) the taxpayer may elect to have this paragraph apply to its first taxable year ending after December 31, 2008, and each subsequent taxable year, and

(II) if the taxpayer makes the election under subclause (I), this paragraph shall only apply to eligible qualified property which is extension property.

(iii) Extension property. For purposes of this subparagraph, the term "extension property" means property which is eligible qualified property solely by reason of the extension of the application of the special allowance under paragraph (1) pursuant to the amendments made by section 1201(a) of the American Recovery and Reinvestment Tax Act of 2009 (and the application of such extension to this paragraph pursuant to the amendment made by section 1201(b)(1) of such Act).

(I) Special rules for round 2 extension property.

(i) In general. In the case of round 2 extension property, this paragraphshall be applied without regard to—

(I) the limitation described in subparagraph (B)(i) thereof, and

(II) the business credit increase amount under subparagraph (E)(iii)thereof.

(ii) Taxpayers previously electing acceleration. In the case of a tax payer who made the election under subparagraph (A) for its first taxable year ending after March 31, 2008, or a taxpayer who made the election under subparagraph (H)(ii) for its first taxable year ending after December 31, 2008—

(I) the taxpayer may elect not to have this paragraph apply to round 2 extension property, but

(II) if the taxpayer does not make the election under subclause (I), in applying this paragraph to the taxpayer the bonus depreciation amount, maximum amount, and maximum increase amount shall be computed and applied to eligible qualified property which is round 2 extension property.

The amounts described in subclause (II)shall be computed separately from any amounts computed with respect to eligible qualified property which is not round 2 extension property.

(iii) Taxpayers not previously electing acceleration. In the case of a taxpayer who neither made the election under subparagraph (A) for its first taxable year ending after March 31, 2008, nor made the election under subparagraph (H)(ii) for its first taxable year ending after December 31, 2008—

(I) the taxpayer may elect to have this paragraph apply to its first taxable year ending after December 31, 2010, and each subsequent taxable year, and

(II) if the taxpayer makes the election under subclause (I), this paragraph shall only apply to eligible qualified property which is round 2 extension property.

(iv) Round 2 extension property. For purposes of this subparagraph, the term "round 2 extension property" means property which is eligible qualified property solely by reason of the extension of the application of the special allowance under paragraph (1) pursuant to the amendments made by section 401(a) of the Tax Relief, Unemployment Insurance Reauthorization, and Job Creation Act of 2010 (and the application of such extension to this paragraph pursuant to the amendment made by section 401(c)(1) of such Act).

(5) Special rule for property acquired during certain pre-2012 periods. In the case of qualified property acquired by the taxpayer (under rules similar to the rules of clauses (ii) and (iii) of paragraph (2)(A)) after September 8, 2010, and before January 1, 2012, and which is placed in service by the taxpayer before January 1, 2012 (January 1, 2013, in the case of property described in subparagraph (2)(B) or (2)(C)), paragraph (1)(A) shall be applied by substituting "100 percent" for "50 percent".

(l) Special allowance for cellulosic biofuel plant property.
  (1) Additional allowance. In the case of any qualified cellulosic biofuel plant property—
    (A) the depreciation deduction provided by section 167(a) for the taxable year in which such property is placed in service shall include an allowance equal to 50 percent of the adjusted basis of such property, and
    (B) the adjusted basis of such property shall be reduced by the amount of such deduction before computing the amount otherwise allowable as a depreciation deduction under this chapter for such taxable year and any subsequent taxable year.
  (2) Qualified cellulosic biofuel plant property. The term "qualified cellulosic biofuel plant property" means property of a character subject to the allowance for depreciation—
    (A) which is used in the United States solely to produce cellulosic biofuel,
    (B) the original use of which commences with the taxpayer after the date of the enactment of this subsection,
    (C) which is acquired by the taxpayer by purchase (as defined in section 179(d)) after the date of the enactment of this subsection, but only if no written binding contract for the acquisition was in effect on or before the date of the enactment of this subsection, and
    (D) which is placed in service by the taxpayer before January 1, 2013.
  (3) Cellulosic biofuel. The term "cellulosic biofuel" means any liquid fuel which is produced from any lignocellulosic or hemicellulosic matter that is available on a renewable or recurring basis.
  (4) Exceptions.
    (A) Bonus depreciation property under subsection (k). Such term shall not include any property to which section 168(k) applies.
    (B) Alternative depreciation property. Such term shall not include any property described in section 168(k)(2)(D)(i).
    (C) Tax-exempt bond-financed property. Such term shall not include any property any portion of which is financed with the proceeds of any obligation the interest on which is exempt from tax under section 103.
    (D) Election out. If a taxpayer makes an election under this subparagraph with respect to any class of property for any taxable year, this subsection shall not apply to all property in such class placed in service during such taxable year.
  (5) Special rules. For purposes of this subsection, rules similar to the rules of subparagraph (E) of section 168(k)(2) shall apply, except that such subparagraph shall be applied—
    (A) by substituting "the date of the enactment of subsection (l)" for "December 31, 2007" each place it appears therein, and
    (B) by substituting "qualified cellulosic biofuel plant property" for "qualified property" in clause (iv) thereof.
  (6) Allowance against alternative minimum tax. For purposes of this subsection, rules similar to the rules of section 168(k)(2)(G) shall apply.
  (7) Recapture. For purposes of this subsection, rules similar to the rules under section 179(d)(10) shall apply with respect to any qualified cellulosic biofuel plant property which ceases to be qualified cellulosic biofuel plant property.
  (8) Denial of double benefit. Paragraph (1) shall not apply to any qualified cellulosic biofuel plant property with respect to which an election has been made under section 179C (relating to election to expense certain refineries).

(m) Special allowance for certain reuse and recycling property.
  (1) In general. In the case of any qualified reuse and recycling property—
    (A) the depreciation deduction provided by section 167(a) for the taxable year in which such property is placed in service shall include an allowance equal to 50 percent of the adjusted basis of the qualified reuse and recycling property, and
    (B) the adjusted basis of the qualified reuse and recycling property shall be reduced by the amount of such deduction before computing the amount otherwise allowable as a depreciation deduction under this chapter for such taxable year and any subsequent taxable year.
  (2) Qualified reuse and recycling property. For purposes of this subsection—
    (A) In general. The term "qualified reuse and recycling property" means any reuse and recycling property—
      (i) to which this section applies,
      (ii) which has a useful life of at least 5 years,
      (iii) the original use of which commences with the taxpayer after August 31, 2008, and
      (iv) which is—
        (I) acquired by purchase (as defined in section 179(d)(2)) by the taxpayer after August 31, 2008, but only if no written binding contract for the acquisition was in effect before September 1, 2008, or
        (II) acquired by the taxpayer pursuant to a written binding contract which was entered into after August 31, 2008.
    (B) Exceptions.
      (i) Bonus depreciation property under subsection (k). The term "qualified reuse and recycling property" shall not include any property to which section 168(k) applies.
      (ii) Alternative depreciation property. The term "qualified reuse and recycling property" shall not include any property to which the alternative depreciation system under subsection (g) applies, determined without regard to paragraph (7) of subsection (g) (relating to election to have system apply).
      (iii) Election out. If a taxpayer makes an election under this clause with respect to any class of property for any taxable year, this subsection shall not apply to all property in such class placed in service during such taxable year.
    (C) Special rule for self-constructed property. In the case of a taxpayer manufacturing, constructing, or producing property for the taxpayer's own use, the requirements of clause (iv) of subparagraph (A) shall be treated as met if the taxpayer begins manufacturing, constructing, or producing the property after August 31, 2008.
    (D) Deduction allowed in computing minimum tax. For purposes of determining alternative minimum taxable income under section 55, the deduction under subsec-

tion (a) for qualified reuse and recycling property shall be determined under this section without regard to any adjustment under section 56.

(3) **Definitions.** For purposes of this subsection—

(A) Reuse and recycling property.

(i) In general. The term "reuse and recycling property" means any machinery and equipment (not including buildings or real estate), along with all appurtenances thereto, including software necessary to operate such equipment, which is used exclusively to collect, distribute, or recycle qualified reuse and recyclable materials.

(ii) Exclusion. Such term does not include rolling stock or other equipment used to transport reuse and recyclable materials.

(B) Qualified reuse and recyclable materials.

(i) In general. The term "qualified reuse and recyclable materials" means scrap plastic, scrap glass, scrap textiles, scrap rubber, scrap packaging, recovered fiber, scrap ferrous and nonferrous metals, or electronic scrap generated by an individual or business.

(ii) Electronic scrap. For purposes of clause (i), the term "electronic scrap" means—

(I) any cathode ray tube, flat panel screen, or similar video display device with a screen size greater than 4 inches measured diagonally, or

(II) any central processing unit.

(C) Recycling or recycle. The term "recycling" or "recycle" means that process (including sorting) by which worn or superfluous materials are manufactured or processed into specification grade commodities that are suitable for use as a replacement or substitute for virgin materials in manufacturing tangible consumer and commercial products, including packaging.

(n) **Special allowance for qualified disaster assistance property.**

(1) **In general.** In the case of any qualified disaster assistance property—

(A) the depreciation deduction provided by section 167(a) for the taxable year in which such property is placed in service shall include an allowance equal to 50 percent of the adjusted basis of the qualified disaster assistance property, and

(B) the adjusted basis of the qualified disaster assistance property shall be reduced by the amount of such deduction before computing the amount otherwise allowable as a depreciation deduction under this chapter for such taxable year and any subsequent taxable year.

(2) **Qualified disaster assistance property.** For purposes of this subsection—

(A) In general. The term "qualified disaster assistance property" means any property—

(i)(I) which is described in subsection (k)(2)(A)(i), or

(II) which is nonresidential real property or residential rental property,

(ii) substantially all of the use of which is—

(I) in a disaster area with respect to a federally declared disaster occurring before January 1, 2010, and

(II) in the active conduct of a trade or business by the taxpayer in such disaster area,

(iii) which—

(I) rehabilitates property damaged, or replaces property destroyed or condemned, as a result of such federally declared disaster, except that, for purposes of this clause, property shall be treated as replacing property destroyed or condemned if, as part of an integrated plan, such property replaces property which is included in a continuous area which includes real property destroyed or condemned, and

(II) is similar in nature to, and located in the same county as, the property being rehabilitated or replaced,

(iv) the original use of which in such disaster area commences with an eligible taxpayer on or after the applicable disaster date,

(v) which is acquired by such eligible taxpayer by purchase (as defined in section 179(d)) on or after the applicable disaster date, but only if no written binding contract for the acquisition was in effect before such date, and

(vi) which is placed in service by such eligible taxpayer on or before the date which is the last day of the third calendar year following the applicable disaster date (the fourth calendar year in the case of nonresidential real property and residential rental property).

(B) Exceptions.

(i) Other bonus depreciation property. The term "qualified disaster assistance property" shall not include—

(I) any property to which subsection (k) (determined without regard to paragraph (4)), (l), or (m) applies,

(II) any property to which section 1400N(d) applies, and

(III) any property described in section 1400N(p)(3).

(ii) Alternative depreciation property. The term "qualified disaster assistance property" shall not include any property to which the alternative depreciation system under subsection (g) applies, determined without regard to paragraph (7) of subsection (g) (relating to election to have system apply).

(iii) Tax-exempt bond financed property. Such term shall not include any property any portion of which is financed with the proceeds of any obligation the interest on which is exempt from tax under section 103.

(iv) Qualified revitalization buildings. Such term shall not include any qualified revitalization building with respect to which the taxpayer has elected the application of paragraph (1) or (2) of section 1400I(a).

(v) Election out. If a taxpayer makes an election under this clause with respect to any class of property for any taxable year, this subsection shall not apply to all property in such class placed in service during such taxable year.

(C) Special rules. For purposes of this subsection, rules similar to the rules of subparagraph (E) of subsection (k)(2) shall apply, except that such subparagraph shall be applied—

(i) by substituting "the applicable disaster date" for "December 31, 2007" each place it appears therein,

(ii) without regard to "and before January 1, 2013" in clause (i) thereof, and

(iii) by substituting "qualified disaster assistance property" for "qualified property" in clause (iv) thereof.

Deductions — Code Sec. 168

(D) Allowance against alternative minimum tax. For purposes of this subsection, rules similar to the rules of subsection (k)(2)(G) shall apply.

(3) Other definitions. For purposes of this subsection—

(A) Applicable disaster date. The term "applicable disaster date" means, with respect to any federally declared disaster, the date on which such federally declared disaster occurs.

(B) Federally declared disaster. The term "federally declared disaster" has the meaning given such term under section 165(h)(3)(C)(i).

(C) Disaster area. The term "disaster area" has the meaning given such term under section 165(h)(3)(C)(ii).

(D) Eligible taxpayer. The term "eligible taxpayer" means a taxpayer who has suffered an economic loss attributable to a federally declared disaster.

(4) Recapture. For purposes of this subsection, rules similar to the rules under section 179(d)(10) shall apply with respect to any qualified disaster assistance property which ceases to be qualified disaster assistance property.

In 2010, P.L. 111-312, Sec. 401(a)(1), substituted "January 1, 2014" for "January 1, 2012" in clause (k)(2)(A)(iv)... Sec. 401(a)(2), substituted "January 1, 2013" for "January 1, 2011" in subclauses (k)(2)(A)(iii)(I), (k)(2)(A)(iii)(II), clauses (k)(2)(A)(iv), (k)(2)(B)(ii) and the heading of clause (k)(2)(B)(ii), effective for property placed in service after 12/31/2010, in tax yrs. ending after such date. ... Sec. 401(b), added para. (k)(5), effective for property placed in service after 9/8/2010, in tax. yrs. ending after such date. ... Sec. 401(c)(1), substituted "or production (I) after March 31, 2008, and before January 1, 2010, and (II) after December 31, 2010, and before January 1, 2013, shall be taken into account under subparagraph (B)(ii) thereof," for "or production after March 31, 2008, and before January 1, 2010, shall be taken into account under subparagraph (B)(ii) thereof," in clause (k)(4)(D)(iii)... Sec. 401(c)(2), added subpara. (k)(4)(I)... Sec. 401(d)(1), substituted "January 1, 2013" for "January 1, 2011" in the heading of subsec. (k)... Sec. 401(d)(2), substituted "pre-January 1, 2013" for "pre-January 1, 2011" in the heading of clause (k)(2)(B)(ii)... Sec. 401(d)(3)(A), deleted clauses (k)(4)(D)(iv) and (k)(4)(D)(v)... Sec. 401(d)(3)(B), added "and" at the end of clause (k)(4)(D)(ii)... Sec. 401(d)(3)(C), substituted a period for a comma at the end of clause (k)(4)(D)(iii)... Sec. 401(d)(4)(A), added "and" at the end of subpara. (l)(5)(A)... Sec. 401(d)(4)(B), deleted subpara. (d)(4)(B)... Sec. 401(d)(4)(C), redesignated subpara. (d)(4)(C) as (d)(4)(B)... Sec. 401(d)(5), substituted "January 1, 2013" for "January 1, 2011" in clause (n)(2)(C)(ii), effective for property placed in service after 12/31/2010, in tax yrs. ending after such date.

Prior to amendments clauses (k)(4)(D)(iv)-(v) and subpara. (l)(5)(B) read as follows

"(iv) 'January 1, 2011' shall be substituted for 'January 1, 2012' in subparagraph (A)(iv) thereof, and

"(v) 'January 1, 2010' shall be substituted for 'January 1, 2011' each place it appears in subparagraph (A) thereof."

"(B) by substituting 'January 1, 2013' for 'January 1, 2011' in clause (i) thereof, and"

—P.L. 111-312, Sec. 737(a), substituted "January 1, 2012" for "January 1, 2010" in clauses (e)(3)(E)(iv)-(v) and (e)(3)(E)(ix)... Sec. 737(b)(1), deleted "if such building is placed in service after December 31, 2008, and before January 1, 2010" after "a building," in clause (e)(7)(A)(i)... Sec. 737(b)(2), deleted subpara. (e)(8)(E), effective for property placed in service after 12/31/2009.

Prior to amendment, subpara. (e)(8)(E) read as follows:

"(E) Such term shall not include any improvement placed in service after December 31, 2009."

—P.L. 111-312, Sec. 738(a), substituted "December 31, 2011" for "December 31, 2009" in subpara. (i)(15)(D), effective for property placed in service after 12/31/2009. ... Sec. 739(a), substituted "December 31, 2011" for "December 31, 2009" in para. (j)(8), effective for property placed in service after 12/31/2009.

—P.L. 111-240, Sec. 2022(a)(1), substituted "January 1, 2012" for "January 1, 2011" in clause (k)(2)(A)(iv); ... Sec. 2022(a)(2), substituted "January 1, 2011" for "January 1, 2010" each place it appeared in para. (k)(2); ... Sec. 2022(b)(1), substituted "January 1, 2011" for "January 1, 2010" in the heading of subsec. (k); ... Sec. 2022(b)(2), substituted "pre-January 1, 2011" for "pre-January 1, 2010" in the heading of clause (k)(2)(B)(ii); ... Sec. 2022(b)(3), deleted "and" at the end of clause (k)(4)(D)(ii), substituted a comma for the period at the end of clause (k)(4)(D)(iii), and added clauses (k)(4)(D)(iv)-(v); ... Sec. 2022(b)(4), substituted "January 1, 2011" for "January 1, 2010" in subpara. (l)(5)(B); ... Sec. 2022(b)(5), substituted "January 1, 2011" for "January 1, 2010" in subpara. (n)(2)(C), effective for property placed in service after 12/31/2009, in tax. yrs. end. after such date.

In 2009, P.L. 111-5, Sec. 1201(a)(1)(A), substituted "January 1, 2011" for "January 1, 2010" in para. (k)(2)

—P.L. 111-5, Sec. 1201(a)(1)(B), substituted "January 1, 2010" for "January 1, 2009" each place it appears in para. (k)(2)

—P.L. 111-5, Sec. 1201(a)(2)(A), substituted "January 1, 2010" for "January 1, 2009" in the heading of subsec. (k)

—P.L. 111-5, Sec. 1201(a)(2)(B), substituted "pre-January 1, 2010" for "pre-January 1, 2009" in the heading of subsec. (k)(2)(B)(ii)

—P.L. 111-5, Sec. 1201(a)(2)(C), substituted "January 1, 2010" for "January 1, 2009" in subpara. (l)(5)(B)

—P.L. 111-5, Sec. 1201(a)(2)(D), substituted "January 1, 2010" for "January 1, 2009" in subpara. (n)(2)(C), effective for property placed in service after 12/31/2008, in tax. yrs. end. after such date.

—P.L. 111-5, Sec. 1201(a)(3)(A)(i), deleted "and" at the end of clause (k)(4)(D)(i)

—P.L. 111-5, Sec. 1201(a)(3)(A)(ii), redesignated clause (k)(4)(D)(ii) as (k)(4)(D)(iii)

—P.L. 111-5, Sec. 1201(a)(3)(A)(iii), added clause (k)(4)(D)(ii), effective for tax. yrs. end. after 3/31/2008.

—P.L. 111-5, Sec. 1201(b)(1)(A), substituted "2010" for "2009" in subpara. (k)(4)(D)(iii) as redesignated by Law Sec. 1201(a)(3)(A)(ii)

—P.L. 111-5, Sec. 1201(b)(1)(B), added subpara. (k)(4)(H), effective for property placed in service after 12/31/2008, in tax. yrs. end. after such date.

In 2008, P.L. 110-343, Sec. 201(a)DivB, amended para. (l)(3) ... Sec. 201(b)(1)DivB, substituted "cellulosic biofuel" for "cellulosic biomass ethanol" each place it appears in subsec. (l) ... Sec. 201(b)(2)DivB, substituted "cellulosic biofuel" for "cellulosic biomass ethanol" in the heading of subsec. (l) ... Sec. 201(b)(3)DivB, substituted "cellulosic biofuel" for "cellulosic biomass ethanol" in the heading of para. (l)(2), effective for property placed in service after 10/3/2008, in tax. yrs. end. after 10/3/2008.

—P.L. 110-343, Sec. 305(a)(1)DivC, substituted "January 1, 2010" for "January 1, 2008" in clause (e)(3)(E)(iv) and (v), effective for property placed in service after 12/31/2007.

—P.L. 110-343, Sec. 305(b)(1)DivC, amended para. (e)(7), effective for property placed in service after 12/31/2008.

Prior to amendment, para. (e)(7) read as follows:

"(7) Qualified restaurant property. The term 'qualified restaurant property' means any section 1250 property which is an improvement to a building if—

"(A) such improvement is placed in service more than 3 years after the date such building was first placed in service, and

"(B) more than 50 percent of the building's square footage is devoted to preparation of, and seating for on-premises consumption of, prepared meals."

—P.L. 110-343, Sec. 305(c)(1)DivC, deleted "and" at the end of clause (e)(3)(E)(vii), substituted ", and" for the period in clause (e)(3)(E)(viii), added clause (e)(3)(E)(xi), effective for property placed in service after 12/31/2008.

—P.L. 110-343, Sec. 305(c)(2)DivC, added para. (e)(8)

—P.L. 110-343, Sec. 305(c)(3)DivC, added subpara. (b)(3)(I), effective for property placed in service after 12/31/2008.

—P.L. 110-343, Sec. 305(c)(4)DivC, added matter in the table in subpara. (g)(3)(B), effective for property placed in service after 12/31/2008.

—P.L. 110-343, Sec. 306(a)DivB, deleted "and" at the end of clause (e)(3)(D)(i), substituted "," for the period at the end of clause (e)(3)(D)(ii), added clause (e)(3)(D)(iii) and clause (e)(3)(D)(iv), effective for property placed in service after 10/3/2008.

—P.L. 110-343, Sec. 306(b)DivB, added para. (i)(18) and (19), effective for property placed in service after 10/3/2008.

—P.L. 110-343, Sec. 306(c)DivB, deleted "or" at the end of subpara. (b)(2)(B), redesignated subpara. (b)(2)(C) as subpara. (b)(2)(D), added new subpara. (b)(2)(C), effective for property placed in service after 10/3/2008.

—P.L. 110-343, Sec. 308(a)DivB, added subsec. (m), effective for tax. yrs. begin. after 12/31/2008.

—P.L. 110-343, Sec. 315(a)DivC, substituted "December 31, 2009" for "December 31, 2007" in subpara. (j)(8), effective for property placed in service after 12/31/2007.

—P.L. 110-343, Sec. 317(a)DivC, substituted "December 31, 2009" for "December 31, 2007" in subpara. (i)(15)(D), effective for property placed in service after 12/31/2007.

—P.L. 110-343, Sec. 505(a)DivC, deleted "and" at the end of clause. (e)(3)(B)(v), substituted ", and" for the period at the end of clause (e)(3)(B)((vi)(III), added clause (e)(3)(B)(vii), effective for property placed in service after 12/31/2008.

—P.L. 110-343, Sec. 505(b)DivC, added matter in the table in subpara. (g)(3)(B), effective for property placed in service after 12/31/2008.

—P.L. 110-343, Sec. 710(a)DivC, added subsec. (n), effective for property placed in service after 12/31/2007, with respect disasters declared after 12/31/2007.

—P.L. 110-289, Sec. 3081(a), added para. (k)(4), effective for tax. yrs. end. after 3/31/2008.

—P.L. 110-289, Sec. 3081(b), of this Act, reads as follows:

"(b) Application to certain automotive partnerships.

"(1) In general. If an applicable partnership elects the application of this subsection—

"(A) the partnership shall be treated as having made a payment against the tax imposed by chapter 1 of the Internal Revenue Code of 1986 for any applicable taxable year of the partnership in the amount determined under paragraph (3),

"(B) in the case of any eligible qualified property placed in service by the partnership during any applicable taxable year—

"(i) section 168(k) of such Code shall not apply in determining the amount of the deduction allowable with respect to such property under section 168 of such Code,

"(ii) the applicable depreciation method used with respect to such property shall be the straight line method, and

"(C) the amount of the credit determined under section 41 of such Code for any applicable taxable year with respect to the partnership shall be reduced by the amount of the deemed payment under subparagraph (A) for the taxable year.

"(2) Treatment of deemed payment.

"(A) In general. Notwithstanding any other provision of the Internal Revenue Code of 1986, the Secretary of the Treasury or his delegate shall not use the payment of tax described in paragraph (1) as an offset or credit against any tax liability of the applicable partnership or any partner but shall refund such payment to the applicable partnership.

"(B) No interest. The payment described in paragraph (1) shall not be taken into account in determining any amount of interest under such Code.

"(3) Amount of deemed payment. The amount determined under this paragraph for any applicable taxable year shall be the least of the following:

"(A) The amount which would be determined for the taxable year under section 168(k)(4)(C)(i) of the Internal Revenue Code of 1986 (as added by the amendments made by this section) if an election under section 168(k)(4) of such Code were in effect with respect to the partnership.

"(B) The amount of the credit determined under section 41 of such Code for the taxable year with respect to the partnership.

"(C) $30,000,000, reduced by the amount of any payment under this subsection for any preceding taxable year.

"(4) Definitions. For purposes of this subsection—

"(A) Applicable partnership. The term 'applicable partnership' means a domestic partnership that—

"(i) was formed effective on August 3, 2007, and

"(ii) will produce in excess of 675,000 automobiles during the period beginning on January 1, 2008, and ending on June 30, 2008.

"(B) Applicable taxable year. The term 'applicable taxable year' means any taxable year during which eligible qualified property is placed in service.

"(C) Eligible qualified property. The term 'eligible qualified property' has the meaning given such term by section 168(k)(4)(D) of the Internal Revenue Code of 1986 (as added by the amendments made by this section)."

— P.L. 110-246, Sec. 4, Repeals the duplicative enactment and provides effective date provisions of the Act entitled "An Act to provide for the continuation of agricultural programs through fiscal year 2012, and for other purposes" Sec. 4, P.L. 110-246 reads as follows:

"Sec. 4. Repeal of duplicative enactment.

"(a) In General- The Act entitled 'An Act to provide for the continuation of agricultural programs through fiscal year 2012, and for other purposes' (H.R. 2419 of the 110th Congress), and the amendments made by that Act, are repealed, effective on the date of enactment of that Act.

"(b) Effective Date- Except as otherwise provided in this Act, this Act and the amendments made by this Act shall take effect on the earlier of--

"(1) the date of enactment of this Act; or

"(2) the date of the enactment of the Act entitled 'An Act to provide for the continuation of agricultural programs through fiscal year 2012, and for other purposes' (H.R. 2419 of the 110th Congress)."

— P.L. 110-246, Sec. 15344(a), amended clause (e)(3)(A)(i), effective for property placed in service after 12/31/2008.

Prior to amendment, clause (e)(3)(A)(i) read as follows:

"(i) any race horse which is more than 2 years old at the time it is placed in service," [Ed. Note: May 22, 2008 was the date of enactment for H.R. 2419 (PL 110-234), which was repealed by (2008 Farm Act § 4(a)) (PL 110-246, 6/18/2008), in connection with the reenactment of the farm bill to correct a technical deficiency in its original passage.]

— P.L. 110-185, Sec. 103(a)(1), substituted "December 31, 2007" for "September 10, 2001" each place it appears in subsec. (k)... Sec. 103(a)(2), substituted "January 1, 2008" for "September 11, 2001" each place it appears in subsec. (k) ... Sec. 103(a)(3), substituted "January 1, 2009" for "January 1, 2005" each place it appears in subsec. (k)... Sec. 103(a)(4), substituted "January 1, 2010" for "January 1, 2006" each place it appears in subsec. (k)... Sec. 103(b), substituted "50 percent" for "30 percent" in subpara. (k)(1)(A)... Sec. 103(c)(1), substituted "(iii), and (iv)" for "and (iii)" in subclause (k)(2)(B)(i)(I)... Sec. 103(c)(2), substituted "clause (iii)" for "clause (ii) and [sic or] (iii)" in subclause (k)(2)(B)(i)(IV)... Sec. 103(c)(3), substituted ", (iii), and (iv)" for "and (iii)" in clause (k)(2)(C)(i)... Sec. 103(c)(4), substituted "$8,000" for "$4,600" in clause (k)(2)(F)(i)... Sec. 103(c)(5)(A), struck out para. (k)(4)... Sec. 103(c)(5)(B), struck out the last sentence in clause (k)(2)(D)(iii)... Sec. 103(c)(6), redesignated subparas. (l)(4)(A)-(C) as clause (l)(4)(B)-(D) and added a new subpara. (l)(4)(A) ... Sec. 103(c)(7)(A), substituted "December 31, 2007" for "September 10, 2001" in subpara. (l)(5)(A) ... Sec. 103(c)(7)(B), substituted "January 1, 2009" for "January 1, 2005" in subpara. (l)(5)(B)... Sec. 103(c)(11)(A), substituted "DECEMBER 31, 2007" for "SEPTEMBER 10, 2001"... Sec. 103(c)(11)(B), substituted "JANUARY 1, 2009" for "JANUARY 1, 2005" in the heading of subsec. (k)... Sec. 103(c)(12), substituted "PRE-JANUARY 1, 2009" for "PRE-JANUARY 1, 2005" in the heading of subpara. (k)(2)(B)(ii), effective for property placed in service after 12/31/2007, in tax. yrs. end. after such date.

Prior to deletion, the last sentence of clause (k)(2)(D)(iii) read as follows:

"The preceding sentence shall be applied separately with respect to property treated as qualified property by paragraph (4) and other qualified property."

Prior to repeal, para (k)(4) read as follows:

"(4) 50-percent bonus depreciation for certain property.

"(A) In general. In the case of 50-percent bonus depreciation property—

"(i) paragraph (1)(A) shall be applied by substituting '50 percent' for '30 percent', and

"(ii) except as provided in paragraph (2)(D), such property shall be treated as qualified property for purposes of this subsection.

"(B) 50-percent bonus depreciation property. For purposes of this subsection, the term '50-percent bonus depreciation property' means property described in paragraph (2)(A)(i)—

"(i) the original use of which commences with the taxpayer after May 5, 2003,

"(ii) which is—

"(I) acquired by the taxpayer after May 5, 2003, and before January 1, 2005, but only if no written binding contract for the acquisition was in effect before May 6, 2003, or

"(II) acquired by the taxpayer pursuant to a written binding contract which was entered into after May 5, 2003, and before January 1, 2005, and

"(iii) which is placed in service by the taxpayer before January 1, 2005, or, in the case of property described in paragraph (2)(B) (as modified by subparagraph (C) of this paragraph) or paragraph (2)(C) (as so modified), before January 1, 2006.

"(C) Special rules. Rules similar to the rules of subparagraphs (B), (C), and (E) of paragraph (2) shall apply for purposes of this paragraph; except that references to September 10, 2001, shall be treated as references to May 5, 2003.

"(D) Automobiles. Paragraph (2)(F) shall be applied by substituting '$7,650' for '$4,600' in the case of 50-percent bonus depreciation property.

"(E) Election of 30-percent bonus. If a taxpayer makes an election under this subparagraph with respect to any class of property for any taxable year, subparagraph (A)(i) shall not apply to all property in such class placed in service during such taxable year."

In 2007, P.L. 110-172, Sec. 11(b)(1), deleted "enzymatic" after "ethanol produced by" in para. (l)(3), effective for property placed in service after 12/20/2006 in tax. yrs. end. after 12/20/2006.

In 2006, P.L. 109-432, Sec. 112(a), substituted "2007" for "2005" in para. (j)(8), effective for property placed in service after 12/31/2005.

— P.L. 109-432, Sec. 113(a), substituted "2008" for "2006" in clause (e)(3)(E)(iv) and clause (e)(3)(E)(v), effective for property placed in service after 12/31/2005.

— P.L. 109-432, Sec. 209(a), added subsec. (l), effective for property placed in service after 12/20/2006 in tax. yrs. end. after 12/20/2006.

In 2005, P.L. 109-135, Sec. 105, of this Act, reads as follows:

"SEC. 105. SPECIAL EXTENSION OF BONUS DEPRECIATION PLACED IN SERVICE DATE FOR TAXPAYERS AFFECTED BY HURRICANES KATRINA, RITA, AND WILMA.

"In applying the rule under section 168(k)(2)(A)(iv) of the Internal Revenue Code of 1986 to any property described in subparagraph (B) or (C) of section 168(k)(2) of such Code—

"(1) the placement in service of which—

"(A) is to be located in the GO Zone (as defined in section 1400M(1) of such Code), the Rita GO Zone (as defined in section 1400M(3) of such Code), or the Wilma GO Zone (as defined in section 1400M(5) of such Code), and

"(B) is to be made by any taxpayer affected by Hurricane Katrina, Rita, or Wilma, or

"(2) which is manufactured in such Zone by any person affected by Hurricane Katrina, Rita, or Wilma,

the Secretary of the Treasury may, on a taxpayer by taxpayer basis, extend the required date of the placement in service of such property under such section by such period of time as is determined necessary by the Secretary but not to exceed 1 year. For purposes of the preceding sentence, the determination shall be made by only taking into account the effect of one or more hurricanes on the date of such placement by the taxpayer."

— P.L. 109-135, Sec. 403(j)(1), substituted "subparagraph (B) or (C)" for "subparagraphs (B) and (C)" in clause (k)(2)(A)(iv)... Sec. 403(j)(2), substituted "or paragraph (2)(C) (as so modified)" for "and paragraph (2)(C)" in clause (k)(4)(B)(iii), effective for property placed in service after 9/10/2001, in tax. yrs. end. after 9/10/2001 as if included in Sec. 336 of the American Jobs Creation Act of 2004, P.L.108-357.

— P.L. 109-135, Sec. 405(a)(1), amended clause (k)(4)(B)(ii), effective for tax. yrs. end. after 5/5/2003 as if included in Sec. 201 of the Jobs and Growth Tax Relief and Reconciliation Act of 2003, P.L.108-27.

Prior to amendment, clause (k)(4)(B)(ii) read as follows:

"(ii) which is acquired by the taxpayer after May 5, 2003, and before January 1, 2005, but only if no written binding contract for the acquisition was in effect before May 6, 2003, and"

— P.L. 109-135, Sec. 410(a), substituted "if 'solar or wind energy' were substituted for 'solar energy' in clause (i) thereof" for "if 'solar and wind' were substituted for 'solar' in clause (i) thereof" in subclause (e)(3)(B)(vi)(I), effective for property placed in service after 12/31/90, except as provided in Sec. 11813(c)(2) of P.L. 101-508, reproduced in note following Code Sec. 46.

— P.L. 109-135, Sec. 412(s), substituted "Such term shall not include" for "This paragraph shall not apply to" in subpara. (i)(15)(D), effective 12/21/2005.

— P.L. 109-58, Sec. 1301(f)(5), amended subclause (e)(3)(B)(vi)(I), effective for electricity produced and sold after 10/22/2004, in tax. yrs. end. after 10/22/2004 as if included in the amendments made by section 710 of the American Jobs Creation Act of 2004, P.L. 108-357.

Prior to amendment, subclause (e)(3)(B)(vi)(I) read as follows:

"(I) is described in subparagraph (A) of section 48(a)(3) (or would be so described if 'solar and wind' were substituted for 'solar' in clause (i) thereof),"

— P.L. 109-58, Sec. 1308(a), deleted "and" at the end of clause (e)(3)(E)(v), substituted ", and" for the period at the end of clause (e)(3)(E)(vi), and added clause (e)(3)(E)(vii)... Sec. 1308(b), added "(E)(vii)....... 30" after "(E)(vi)...... 20" in the table in subpara. (g)(3)(B), effective for property placed in service after 4/11/2005, except as provided in Sec. 1308(c)(2) of this Act, which reads as follows:

"(2) Exception. The amendments made by this section shall not apply to any property with respect to which the taxpayer or a related party has entered into a binding contract for the construction thereof on or before April 11, 2005, or, in the case of self-constructed property, has started construction on or before such date."

—P.L. 109-58, Sec. 1325(a), deleted "and" at the end of clause (e)(3)(E)(vi) [as amended by Sec. 1308(a) of this Act, see above], substituted ", and" for the period at the end of clause (e)(3)(E)(vii) [as added by Sec. 1308(a) of this Act, see above], and added clause (e)(3)(E)(viii) . . . Sec. 1325(b), added "(E)(viii)...... 35" after "(E)(vii).....30" in the table in subpara. (g)(3)(B) [as amended by Sec. 1308(b) of this Act, see above], effective for property placed in service after 4/11/2005, except as provided in Sec. 1325(c)(2) of this Act, which reads as follows:

"(2) Exception. The amendments made by this section shall not apply to any property with respect to which the taxpayer or a related party has entered into a binding contract for the construction thereof on or before April 11, 2005, or, in the case of self-constructed property, has started construction on or before such date."

—P.L. 109-58, Sec. 1326(a), deleted "and" at the end of clause (e)(3)(C)(iii), redesignated clause (e)(3)(C)(iv) as clause (e)(3)(C)(v), and added clause (e)(3)(C)(iv) . . . Sec. 1326(b), added para. (i)(17) . . . Sec. 1326(c), added "(C)(iv)...... 14" after "(C)(iii)...... 22" in the table in subpara. (g)(3)(B) [as amended by Secs. 1308(b) and 1325(b) of this Act, see above], effective for property placed in service after 4/11/2005, except as provided in Sec. 1326(e)(2) of this Act, which reads as follows:

"(2) Exception. The amendments made by this section shall not apply to any property with respect to which the taxpayer or a related party has entered into a binding contract for the construction thereof on or before April 11, 2005, or, in the case of self-constructed property, has started construction on or before such date."

In 2004, P.L. 108-357, Sec. 211(a), deleted "and" at the end of clause (e)(3)(E)(ii), substituted a comma for the period at the end of clause (e)(3)(E)(iii), and added clauses (e)(3)(E)(iv)-(v) . . . Sec. 211(b), added para. (e)(6) . . . Sec. 211(c), added para. (e)(7) . . . Sec. 211(d)(1), added subparas. (b)(3)(G)-(H) . . . Sec. 211(d)(2), added "not referred to in paragraph (3)" before the comma at the end of subpara. (b)(2)(A) . . . Sec. 211(e), added "(E)(iv) . . . 39" and "(E)(v) . . . 39" in the table in subpara. (g)(3)(B), effective for property placed in service after 10/22/2004.

—P.L. 108-357, Sec. 336(a)(1), redesignated subparas. (k)(2)(C)-(F) as (k)(2)(D)-(G) and added subpara. (k)(2)(C) . . . Sec. 336(a)(2), substituted "subparagraphs (B) and (C)" for "subparagraph (B)" in clause (k)(2)(A)(iv) . . . Sec. 336(b)(1), added clause (k)(2)(B)(iv) . . . Sec. 336(b)(2), substituted "paragraph (2)(D)" for "paragraph (2)(C)" in clause (k)(4)(A)(ii) . . . Sec. 336(b)(3), added "and paragraph (2)(C)" after "of this paragraph)" in clause (k)(4)(B)(iii) . . . Sec. 336(b)(4), substituted "subparagraphs (B), (C), and (E)" for "subparagraphs (B) and (D)" in subpara. (k)(4)(C) . . . Sec. 336(b)(5), substituted "Paragraph (2)(F)" for "Paragraph (2)(E)" in subpara. (k)(4)(D), effective [as if included in Sec. 101 of P.L. 107-147] for property placed in service after 9/10/2001, in tax. yrs. end. after 9/10/2001.

—P.L. 108-357, Sec. 337(a), added "(or, in the case of multiple units of property subject to the same lease, within 3 months after the date the final unit is placed in service, so long as the period between the time the first unit is placed in service and the time the last unit is placed in service does not exceed 12 months)" before the comma at the end of subclause (k)(2)(E)(iii)(II) [as redesignated by Sec. 336(a)(1) of this Act, see above], effective for property sold after 6/4/2004.

—P.L. 108-357, Sec. 704(a), redesignated clause (e)(3)(C)(ii) as (e)(3)(C)(iii) and added clause (e)(3)(C)(ii) . . . Sec. 704(b), added para. (i)(15), effective for property placed in service after 10/22/2004. Sec. 704(c)(2)-(3) of this Act reads as follows:

"(2) Special rule for asset class 80.0. In the case of race track facilities placed in service after the date of the enactment of this Act, such facilities shall not be treated as theme and amusement facilities classified under asset class 80.0.

"(3) No inference. Nothing in this section or the amendments made by this section shall be construed to affect the treatment of property placed in service on or before the date of the enactment of this Act."

—P.L. 108-357, Sec. 706(a), deleted "and" at the end of clause (e)(3)(C)(ii) [as added by Sec. 704(a) of this Act, see above], redesignated clause (e)(3)(C)(iii) as (iv) [as redesignated by Sec. 704(a) of this Act, see above] and added clause (e)(3)(C)(iii) . . . Sec. 706(b), added para. (i)(16) . . . Sec. 706(c), added "(C)(iii) . . . 22" in the table in subpara. (g)(3)(B), effective for property placed in service after 12/31/2004.

—P.L. 108-357, Sec. 847(a), added "(notwithstanding any other subparagraph of this paragraph)" after "paragraph (2) shall" in subpara. (g)(3)(A) . . . Sec. 847(c), deleted "and" at the end of clause (i)(3)(A)(i), redesignated clause (i)(3)(A)(ii) as (iii) and added clause (i)(3)(A)(ii) . . . Sec. 847(d), added a sentence at the end of subpara. (h)(3)(A) . . . Sec. 847(e), deleted "and" at the end of clause (h)(2)(A)(ii), substituted ", and" for the period at the end of clause (h)(2)(A)(iii) and added clause (h)(2)(A)(iv) and a flush sentence at the end of subpara. (h)(2)(A), effective for leases entered into after 3/12/2004.

—P.L. 108-357, Sec. 849(b), of this Act, reads as follows:

"(b) Exception.

"(1) In general. The amendments made by this part shall not apply to qualified transportation property.

"(2) Qualified transportation property. For purposes of paragraph (1), the term 'qualified transportation property' means domestic property subject to a lease with respect to which a formal application—

"(A) was submitted for approval to the Federal Transit Administration (an agency of the Department of Transportation) after June 30, 2003, and before March 13, 2004,

"(B) is approved by the Federal Transit Administration before January 1, 2006, and

"(C) includes a description of such property and the value of such property.

"(3) Exchanges and conversion of tax-exempt use property. Section 470(e)(4) of the Internal Revenue Code of 1986, as added by section 848, shall apply to property exchanged or converted after the date of the enactment of this Act.

"(4) Intangibles and Indian tribal governments. The amendments made subsections (b)(2), (b)(3), and (e) of section 847, and the treatment of property described in clauses (ii) and (iii) of section 470(c)(2)(B) of the Internal Revenue Code of 1986 (as added by section 848) as tangible property, shall apply to leases entered into after October 3, 2004."

—P.L. 108-357, Sec. 901(a), deleted "and" at the end of clause (e)(3)(E)(iv) [as added by Sec. 211(a) of this Act, see above], substituted ", and" for the period at the end of clause (e)(3)(E)(v) [as added by Sec. 211(a) of this Act, see above] and added clause (e)(3)(E)(vi) . . . Sec. 901(b), added subpara. (e)(3)(F) . . . Sec. 901(c), added "(E)(vi) . . . 20" and "(F) . . . 25" in the table in subpara. (g)(3)(B), effective for property placed in service after 10/22/2004.

—P.L. 108-311, Sec. 316, substituted "December 31, 2005" for "December 31, 2004" in para. (j)(8), effective 10/4/2004.

—P.L. 108-311, Sec. 403(a)(1), amended clause (k)(2)(B)(i) . . . Sec. 403(a)(2)(A), added clauses (k)(2)(D)(iii) and (iv) . . . Sec. 403(a)(2)(B), added "clause (iii) and" before "subparagraph (A)(ii)" in clause (k)(2)(D)(ii), effective for property placed in service after 9/10/2001, in tax. yrs. end. after 9/10/2001 as if included in Sec. 101 of the Job Creation and Worker Assistance Act of 2002, P.L.107-147.

Prior to amendment, clause (k)(2)(B)(i) read as follows:

"(i) In general. The term 'qualified property' includes property—

"(I) which meets the requirements of clauses (i), (ii), and (iii) of subparagraph (A),

"(II) which has a recovery period of at least 10 years or is transportation property, and

"(III) which is subject to section 263A by reason of clause (ii) or (iii) of subsection (f)(1)(B) thereof."

—P.L. 108-311, Sec. 408(a)(6)(A), added "is" after "if property" in clause (k)(2)(D)(ii) . . . Sec. 408(a)(6)(B), deleted "is" before "originally placed" in subclause (k)(2)(D)(ii)(I) . . . Sec. 408(a)(8), substituted "minimum" for "miniumum" in the heading of subpara. (k)(2)(F), enacted 10/4/2004.

In 2003, P.L. 108-27, Sec. 201(a), added para. (k)(4) . . . Sec. 201(b)(1)(A), substituted "January 1, 2005" for "September 11, 2004" in clauses (k)(2)(B)(ii) and (k)(2)(D)(i) . . . Sec. 201(b)(1)(B), substituted "pre-January 1, 2005" for "pre-September 11, 2004" in the heading of clause (k)(2)(B)(ii) . . . Sec. 201(b)(2), substituted "January 1, 2005" for "September 11, 2004" each place it appeared in clause (k)(2)(A)(iii) . . . Sec. 201(b)(3), added a sentence at the end of clause (k)(2)(C)(iii) . . . Sec. 201(c)(1), substituted "January 1, 2005" for "September 11, 2004" in the heading of subsec. (k), effective for tax. yrs. end. after 5/5/2003.

In 2002, P.L. 107-147, Sec. 101(a), added subsec. (k), effective for property placed in service after 9/10/2001, in tax. yrs. end. after 9/10/2001.

—P.L. 107-147, Sec. 613(b), substituted "December 31, 2004" for "December 31, 2003" in para. (j)(8), effective 3/9/2002.

In 1998, P.L. 105-277, Sec. 2022, of this Act, reads as follows:

"Sec. 2022. Depreciation study.

"The Secretary of the Treasury (or the Secretary's delegate)—

"(1) shall conduct a comprehensive study of the recovery periods and depreciation methods under section 168 of the Internal Revenue Code of 1986, and

"(2) not later than March 31, 2000, shall submit the results of such study, together with recommendations for determining such periods and methods in a more rational manner, to the Committee on Ways and Means of the House of Representatives and the Committee on Finance of the Senate."

—P.L. 105-206, Sec. 6006(b)(1), deleted para. (c)(2) . . . Sec. 6006(b)(2), amended subsec. (c) and para. (c)(1) preceding the table in (c)(1), effective 8/5/97.

Prior to deletion, para. (c)(2) read as follows:

"(2) Property for which 150 percent method elected. In the case of property to which an election under subsection (b)(2)(C) applies, the applicable recovery period shall be determined under the table contained in subsection (g)(2)(C)."

Prior to amendment, subsec. (c) and para. (c)(1) preceding the table in (c)(1) read as follows:

"(c) Applicable recovery period. For purposes of this section—

"(1) In general. Except as provided in paragraph (2), the applicable recovery period shall be determined in accordance with the following table:"

In 1997, P.L. 105-34, Sec. 1086(b)(1), deleted "and" at the end of clause (e)(3)(A)(i), substituted ", and" for the period at the end of clause (e)(3)(A)(ii), and added clause (e)(3)(A)(iii) . . . Sec. 1086(b)(2), added "(A)(iii) . . . 4" in the table in subpara. (g)(3)(B) . . . Sec. 1086(b)(3), added para. (i)(14), effective for property placed in service after 8/5/97.

—P.L. 105-34, Sec. 1213(c), added subpara. (i)(8)(C), effective for leases entered into after 8/5/97.

—P.L. 105-34, Sec. 1604(c)(1), added the sentence at the end of para. (j)(6), effective for property placed in service after 12/31/93, except as provided in Sec. 1604(c)(2)(A) and (B) of this Act, which reads as follows:

"(A) with respect to property (with an applicable recovery period under section 168(j) of the Internal Revenue Code of 1986 of 6 years or less) held by the taxpayer if the taxpayer claimed the benefits of section 168(j) of such Code with respect to such property on a return filed before March 18, 1997, but only if such

Code Sec. 168 — Deductions

return is the first return of tax filed for the taxable year in which such property was placed in service, or

"(B) with respect to wages for which the taxpayer claimed the benefits of section 45A of such Code for a taxable year on a return filed before March 18, 1997, but only if such return was the first return of tax filed for such taxable year."

In 1996, P.L. 104-188, Sec. 1120(a), deleted "and" at the end of clause (e)(3)(E)(i), substituted ", and" for the period at the end of clause (e)(3)(E)(ii), and added clause (e)(3)(E)(iii) . . . Sec. 1120(b), added "(E)(iii) . . . 20" to the table in subpara. (g)(3)(B), effective as provided in Sec. 1120(c) of this Act, which reads as follows:

"(c) Effective date. The amendments made by this section shall apply to property which is placed in service on or after the date of the enactment of this Act and to which section 168 of the Internal Revenue Code of 1986 applies after the amendment made by section 201 of the Tax Reform Act of 1986. A taxpayer may elect (in such form and manner as the Secretary of the Treasury may prescribe) to have such amendments apply with respect to any property placed in service before such date and to which such section applies."

—P.L. 104-188, Sec. 1121(a), amended para. (i)(8), effective as provided in Sec. 1121(b) of this Act, which reads as follows:

"(b) Effective date. Subparagraph (B) of section 168(i)(8) of the Internal Revenue Code of 1986, as added by the amendment made by subsection (a), shall apply to improvements disposed of or abandoned after June 12, 1996."

Prior to amendment, para. (i)(8) read as follows:

"(8) Treatment of leasehold improvements. In the case of any building erected (or improvements made) on leased property, if such building or improvement is property to which this section applies, the depreciation deduction shall be determined under the provisions of this section."

—P.L. 104-188, Sec. 1613(b)(1), added subpara. (b)(3)(F) . . . Sec. 1613(b)(2), added "Water utility property . . . . 25 years" to the table in para. (c)(1) . . . Sec. 1613(b)(3)(A), added para. (e)(5) . . . Sec. 1613(b)(3)(B)(i), deleted subpara. (e)(3)(F) . . . Sec. 1613(b)(3)(B)(ii), deleted "(F) . . . . 50" from the table in para. (g)(3) . . . Sec. 1613(b)(4), added "or water utility property" after "tunnel bore" in clause (g)(2)(C)(iv), effective for property placed in service after 6/12/96, other than property placed in service pursuant to a binding contract in effect before 6/10/96, and at all times thereafter before the property is placed in service.

Prior to deletion, subpara. (e)(3)(F) read as follows:

"(F) 20-year property. The term '20-year property' includes any municipal sewers."

—P.L. 104-188, Sec. 1702(h)(1)(A), deleted "or" at the end of subclause (e)(3)(B)(vi)(I), substituted ", or" for the period at the end of subclause (e)(3)(B)(vi)(II), and added subclause (e)(3)(B)(vi)(III) . . . Sec. 1702(h)(1)(B), added the sentence at the end of subpara. (e)(3)(B) . . . Sec. 1702(h)(1)(C), substituted "section 48(l)(3)(A)(ix) (as in effect on the day before the date of the enactment of the Revenue Reconciliation Act of 1990)" for "section 48(a)(3)(A)(iii)" in subpara. (g)(4)(K), effective for property placed in service after 12/31/90, except as provided in Sec. 11813(c)(2) of P.L. 101-508, reproduced in note following Code Sec. 46.

—P.L. 104-188, Sec. 1704(t)(54), amended Sec. 11813(b)(9)(A)(i) of P.L. 101-508 by adding a comma after "(3)(A)(ix)" in the material proposed to be stricken, see below.

In 1995, P.L. 104-88, Sec. 304(a), substituted "rail carrier subject to part A of subtitle IV" for "domestic railroad corporation providing transportation subject to subchapter I of chapter 105" in clause (g)(4)(B)(i), effective 12/29/95.

In 1993, P.L. 103-66, Sec. 13151(a), substituted

| "Nonresidential real property . . . . | 39 years" |

for

| "Nonresidential real property . . . . | 31.5 years" |

in para. (c)(1), effective for property placed in service by the taxpayer on or after May 13, 1993, except as provided in Sec. 13151(b)(2) of this Act, which reads as follows:

"(2) Exception.—The amendments made by this section shall not apply to property placed in service by the taxpayer before January 1, 1994, if—

"(A) the taxpayer or a qualified person entered into a binding written contract to purchase or construct such property before May 13, 1993, or

"(B) the construction of such property was commenced by or for the taxpayer or a qualified person before May 13, 1993.

For purposes of this paragraph, the term 'qualified person' means any person who transfers his rights in such a contract or such property to the taxpayer but only if the property is not placed in service by such person before such rights are transferred to the taxpayer."

—P.L. 103-66, Sec. 13321(a), added subsec. (j), effective for property placed in service after 12/31/93.

In 1990, P.L. 101-508, Sec. 11801(c)(8)(B), deleted "371(a), 374(a)," after "361," in clause (i)(7)(B)(i), effective 11/5/90, except as provided in Sec. 11821(b) of this Act, reproduced in note following Code Sec. 370.

—P.L. 101-508, Sec. 11812(b)(2)(A), amended subpara. (i)(2)(A) . . . Sec. 11812(b)(2)(B), amended para. (i)(10) . . . Sec. 11812(b)(2)(C), substituted "subsection (i)(10)" for "section 167(1)(3)(A)" in para. (f)(2) . . . Sec. 11812(b)(2)(D), added the last sentence to para. (i)(1) . . . Sec. 11812(b)(2)(E), deleted "(determined without regard to section 167(l))" after "section 167" in clause (i)(9)(A)(i), effective for property placed in service after 11/5/90, except as provided in Sec. 11812(c)(2)(B) of this Act, reproduced in note following Code Sec. 42.

Prior to amendment, subpara. (e)(2)(A) read as follows:

"(A) Residential rental property. The term 'residential rental property' has the meaning given such term by section 167(j)(2)(B)."

Prior to amendment, para. (i)(10) read as follows:

"(10) Public utility property. The term 'public utility property' has the meaning given such term by section 167(l)(3)(A)."

—P.L. 101-508, Sec. 11813(b)(9)(A)(i), [as amended by Sec. 1704(t)(54) of P.L. 104-188, see above] substituted "subparagraph (A) of section 48(a)(3) (or would be so described if 'solar and wind' were substituted for 'solar' in clause (i) thereof)" for "paragraph (3)(A)(viii), (3)(A)(ix), or (4) of section 48(l)" in subclause (e)(3)(B)(vi)(I) . . . Sec. 11813(b)(9)(A)(ii), added "(as in effect on the day before the date of the enactment of the Revenue Reconciliation Act of 1990)" after "section 48(l)" in subclause (e)(3)(B)(vi)(II) . . . Sec. 11813(b)(9)(B)(i), substituted "subsection (i)(13)" for "section 48(p)" in clause (e)(3)(D)(i) . . . Sec. 11813(b)(9)(B)(ii), added para. (i)(13) . . . Sec. 11813(b)(9)(C), amended para. (g)(4), effective for property placed in service after 12/31/90, except as provided in Sec. 11813(c)(2) of this Act, reproduced in note following Code Sec. 46.

Prior to amendment, para. (g)(4) read as follows:

"(4) Property used predominantly outside the United States. For purposes of this subsection, rules similar to the rules under section 48(a)(2) (including the exceptions contained in subparagraph (B) thereof) shall apply in determining whether property is used predominantly outside the United States. In addition to the exceptions contained in such subparagraph (B), there shall be excepted any satellite or other spacecraft (or any interest therein) held by a United States person if such satellite or spacecraft was launched from within the United States."

In 1989, P.L. 101-239, Sec. 7816(e)(1), substituted "paragraph (2)(C)" for "paragraph (2)(B)" in para. (b)(5) . . . Sec. 7816(e)(2), substituted "subsection (b)(2)(C)" for "subsection (b)(2)(B)" in para. (c)(2), effective for property placed in service after 12/31/88, except as provided in Sec. 6028(b)(2) of P.L. 100-647 reproduced below.

—P.L. 101-239, Sec. 7816(f), redesignated subpara. (b)(3)(D), as added by Sec. 6029(b) of P.L. 100-647 as subpara. (b)(3)(E), effective for property placed in service after 12/31/88.

In 1988, P.L. 100-647, Sec. 1002(a)(5), deleted "and which are" after "section applies" in clause (d)(3)(A)(i) . . . Sec. 1002(a)(6)(A)(i), substituted "1st taxable year" for "1st full taxable year" in clause (f)(5)(B)(ii) . . . Sec. 1002(a)(6)(A)(ii), deleted "or" at the end of clause (f)(5)(B)(i), added ", or" at the end of clause (f)(5)(B)(ii), and added clause (f)(5)(B)(iii) . . . Sec. 1002(a)(6)(B), added subpara. (f)(5)(C) . . . Sec. 1002(a)(7)(A), added the last sentence of subpara. (i)(7)(A) . . . Sec. 1002(a)(7)(B), amended subpara. (i)(7)(B) . . . Sec. 1002(a)(7)(C), deleted subpara. (i)(7)(D) . . . Sec. 1002(a)(8), amended subpara. (h)(2)(B) . . . Sec. 1002(a)(11)(A), amended para. (b)(2) . . . Sec. 1002(a)(11)(B), substituted "under paragraph (2)(B) or (3)(C)" for "under paragraph (3)(C)", in para. (b)(5) . . . Sec. 1002(a)(11)(C), amended subsec. (c) . . . Sec. 1002(a)(16)(B), amended para. (f)(4) . . . Sec. 1002(a)(21), substituted "any section 1245 property" for "any property", in clause (e)(3)(B)(v) . . . Sec. 1002(a)(23)(A), amended subpara (d)(3)(B), effective for property placed in service after 12/31/86, except as provided in Secs. 203(a)(1)(B), (b)-(e) of P.L. 99-514, reproduced below. Sec. 1002(a)(23)(B) of this Act provides:

"(B) Clause (ii) of section 168(d)(3)(B) of the 1986 Code (as added by subparagraph (A)) shall apply to taxable years beginning after March 31, 1988, unless the taxpayer elects, at such time and in such manner as the Secretary of the Treasury or his delegate may prescribe, to have such clause apply to taxable years beginning on or before such date."

Prior to amendment, subpara. (i)(7)(B) read as follows:

"(B) Transactions covered. The transactions described in this subparagraph are any transaction described in section 332, 351, 361, 371(a), 374(a), 721, or 731. Subparagraph (A) shall not apply in the case of a termination of a partnership under section 708(b)(1)(B)."

Prior to deletion, subpara. (i)(7)(D) read as follows:

"(D) Exception. This paragraph shall not apply to any transaction to which subsection (f)(5) applies (relating to churning transactions)."

Prior to amendment, subpara. (h)(2)(B) read as follows:

"(B) Exceptions for certain property subject to United States tax and used by foreign person or entity.

"(i) Income from property subject to United States tax. Clause (iii) of subparagraph (A) shall not apply with respect to any property if more than 50 percent of the gross income for the taxable year derived by the foreign person or entity from the use of such property is—

"(I) subject to tax under this chapter, or

"(II) included under section 951 in the gross income of a United States shareholder for the taxable year with or within which ends the taxable year of the controlled foreign corporation in which such income was derived.

For purposes of the preceding sentence, any exclusion or exemption shall not apply for purposes of determining the amount of the gross income so derived, but shall apply for purposes of determining the portion of such gross income subject to tax under this chapter.

"(ii) Movies and sound recordings. Clause (iii) of subparagraph (A) shall not apply with respect to any qualified film (as defined in section 48(k)(1)(B) or any sound recording as defined in section 48(r)(5))."

Prior to amendment, para. (b)(2) read as follows:

"(2) 15-year and 20-year property. In the case of 15-year and 20-year property, paragraph (1) shall be applied by substituting '150 percent' for '200 percent'."

Prior to amendment, subsec. (c) read as follows:

"(c) Applicable recovery period.

"For purposes of this section, the applicable recovery period shall be determined in accordance with the following table:

Deductions Code Sec. 168

"In the case of:	The applicable recovery period is:
"3-year property	3 years
"5-year property	5 years
"7-year property	7 years
"10-year property	10 years
"15-year property	15 years
"20-year property	20 years
"Residential rental property	27.5 years
"Nonresidential real property	31.5 years."

Prior to amendment, para. (f)(4) read as follows:

"(4) Sound recordings. Any sound recording described in section 48(r)(5)."

Prior to amendment, subpara. (d)(3)(B) read as follows:

"(B) Certain real property not taken into account. For purposes of subparagraph (A), nonresidential real property and residential rental property shall not be taken into account."

—P.L. 100-647, Sec. 1002(c)(1), amended Sec. 203(a)(1)(B) of P.L. 99-514 [reproduced below] part of the effective date for changes made by Sec. 201(a) of P.L. 99-514, by adding the last sentence, see below.

—P.L. 100-647, Sec. 1002(c)(2)(A), and (B), amended Sec. 203(d) of P.L. 99-514 [reproduced below], part of the effective date for changes made by Sec. 201(a) of P.L. 99-514, by substituting "the case of any taxable year beginning before October 1, 1987" for "the case of any taxable year" and by adding the last sentence [see below] in Sec. 203(d) of P.L. 99-514, [reproduced below] . . . Sec. 1002(c)(3), of this Act provides:

"(3) Notwithstanding section 203 of the Reform Act, the amendments made by section 201 of the Reform Act shall apply to any real property which was acquired before January 1, 1987, and was converted on or after such date from personal use to a use for which depreciation is allowable."

—P.L. 100-647, Sec. 1002(c)(4), added the last sentence to Sec. 203(b) of P.L. 99-514, [reproduced below], see below . . . Sec. 1002(c)(5), substituted "Except as otherwise provided in this subsection or section 204, subparagraph" for "Subparagraph" in Sec. 203(c)(1) of P.L. 99-514 [reproduced below], see below . . . Sec. 1002(c)(6), substituted "applies shall be the class life" for "shall be the class life" in Sec. 203(b)(2)(C)(i) of P.L. 99-514, [reproduced below], see below . . . Sec. 1002(c)(7)(A), added "(or would have met such requirements if placed in service by such person" before the comma in Sec. 203(b)(3)(A) of P.L. 99-514 [reproduced below] . . . Sec. 1002(c)(7)(B), added ", or is leased to such person," before "not later than", in Sec. 203(b)(3) of P.L. 99-514 [reproduced below].

—P.L. 100-647, Sec. 1002(d)(1), amended Sec. 204(a)(1)(B) of P.L. 99-514, [reproduced below] transitional rule for amendments made by Sec. 201(a) of P.L. 99-514, by deleting "and" at the end of Sec. 204(a)(1)(B)(ii) of P.L. 99-514, by substituting ", and" for the period at the end of Sec. 204(a)(1)(B)(iii) of P.L. 99-514, and added Sec. 204(a)(1)(B)(iv) of P.L. 99-514 [see below] . . . Sec. 1002(d)(2), substituted "For purposes of this subparagraph, section 203(b)(2) shall be applied by substituting 'January 1, 1994' for 'January 1, 1991' each place it appears" for "For purposes of this subparagraph, subsection (b)(2) shall be applied by substituting 'January 1, 1994' for 'January 1, 1991'", in Sec. 204(a)(1)(C) of P.L. 99-514 [reproduced below] . . . Sec. 1002(d)(3), substituted "For purposes of this subparagraph, section 203(b)(2) shall be applied by substituting 'January 1, 1998' for 'January 1, 1991' each place it appears" for "For purposes of this subparagraph, subsection (b)(2) shall be applied by substituting 'January 1, 1998' for 'January 1, 1991'." in Sec. 204(a)(1)(E) of P.L. 99-514 [reproduced below] . . . Sec. 1002(d)(4)(A)-(C), amended Sec. 204(a)(1)(F) of P.L. 99-514 [reproduced below] by substituting "subparagraph" for "paragraph", substituting a period for ", or" at the end of Sec. 204(a)(1)(F)(iii) of P.L. 99-514, and by substituting "A project is also described in this subparagraph if it is a mixed-use development which is—" for "the mixed use development is", see below . . . Sec. 1002(d)(5), substituted "section 203(b)(2)" for "subsection (b)(2)" and substituted "1998" for "1993" in the last sentence of Sec. 204(a)(1)(F) of P.L. 99-514, [reproduced below], see below . . . Sec. 1002(d)(6), substituted "June 30, 1986" for "July 1, 1986" in Sec. 204(a)(1)(H) of P.L. 99-514 [reproduced below] see below . . . Sec. 1002(d)(7)(A), amended Sec. 204(a)(4) of P.L. 99-514 [reproduced below], see below . . . Sec. 1002(d)(8)(A), deleted "either" which followed "subparagraph if" in Sec. 204(a)(5)(K) of P.L. 99-514 [reproduced below] . . . Sec. 1002(d)(8)(B), substituted "supercalendared" for "super calendar" in Sec. 204(a)(5)(K)(i) of P.L. 99-514 [reproduced below] . . . Sec. 1002(d)(8)(C), substituted "was incurred" for "were incurred" in Sec. 204(a)(5)(K)(i) of P.L. 99-514 [reproduced below] . . . Sec. 1002(d)(8)(D), added "the project" before "involves" in Sec. 204(a)(5)(K)(v) of P.L. 99-514 [reproduced below] . . . Sec. 1002(d)(9), added Sec. 204(a)(5)(Z) of P.L. 99-514 [reproduced below] . . . Sec. 1002(d)(10)(A), substituted a comma for the period at the end of Sec. 204(a)(8)(C) of P.L. 99-514 and added Secs. 204(a)(8)(D) and (E) of P.L. 99-514 [reproduced below], see below . . . Sec. 1002(d)(10)(B), deleted ", and section 203(c)" which followed "section 201" in Sec. 204(a)(8) of P.L. 99-514 [reproduced below] . . . Sec. 1002(d)(11)(A), deleted "either" which followed "facility if" in Sec. 204(a)(10) of P.L. 99-514 [reproduced below] . . . Sec. 1002(d)(11)(B), substituted "wastewater treatment facility serving Greenville, South Carolina" for "wastewater treatment facility" in Sec. 204(a)(10)(C) of P.L. 99-514 [reproduced below] . . . Sec. 1002(d)(11)(C), substituted "such letter of intent and service agreement" for "the letter of intent and service agreement described in subparagraph (A)(2) of this paragraph" in Sec. 204(a)(10)(D) of P.L. 99-514 [reproduced below] . . . Sec. 1002(d)(12)(A), substituted "the United States" for "Kansas, Florida, Georgia, or Texas" in Sec. 204(a)(11)(A) of P.L. 99-514 [reproduced below] . . . Sec. 1002(d)(12)(B), and (C), substituted "the purchaser" for "the purchase" and deleted "Section 211(d)(2)(B) shall not apply to aircraft which meet the requirements of this subparagraph" after "July 1, 1987" in Sec. 204(a)(11)(C) of P.L. 99-514 [reproduced below] . . . Sec. 1002(d)(13), substituted a period for the comma at the end of Sec. 204(a)(14)(E) of P.L. 99-514 and added Secs. 204(a)(14)(F) and (G) of P.L. 99-514 [reproduced below] . . . Sec. 1002(d)(14)(A)-(C), amended Sec. 204(a)(15) of P.L. 99-514 [reproduced below] by adding "located in New Mexico" after "to a project", substituted "$72,000,000" for "72,000", and by substituting "For purposes of this paragraph, section 203(b)(2) shall be applied by substituting 'January 1, 1996' for 'January 1, 1991' each place it appears" for "For purposes of this subparagraph, subsection (b)(2) shall be applied by substituting 'January 1, 1986' for 'January 1, 1991'" . . . Sec. 1002(d)(15), added Secs. 204(a)(24)(E) and (F) of P.L. 99-514 [reproduced below] . . . Sec. 1002(d)(16), substituted "wood energy projects" for "wood energy products" in Sec. 204(a)(25) of P.L. 99-514 [reproduced below] . . . Sec. 1002(d)(17)(A), substituted "540,000" for "525,000" in Sec. 204(a)(27)(B) of P.L. 99-514 [reproduced below] . . . Sec. 1002(d)(17)(B), substituted "$22,000,000" for "$32,000,000" and substituted "before" for "on" in Sec. 204(a)(27)(C) of P.L. 99-514 [reproduced below] . . . Sec. 1002(d)(17)(C), deleted "and 7th Avenue" which followed "57th Street" in Sec. 204(a)(27)(D) of P.L. 99-514 [reproduced below] . . . Sec. 1002(d)(17)(D), substituted "$62,600,000" for "$62,000" in Sec. 204(a)(27)(H) of P.L. 99-514 [reproduced below] . . . Sec. 1002(d)(18), added Sec. 204(a)(27)(I) of P.L. 99-514 [reproduced below] . . . Sec. 1002(d)(19), substituted "$10,500,000" for "$10,200,000" in Sec. 204(a)(31) of P.L. 99-514 [reproduced below] . . . Sec. 1002(d)(20)(A), substituted "December 26, 1985" for "July 30, 1984", substituted "July 2, 1986" for "February 28, 1985", and substituted "in May 1985" for "on June 17, 1985" in Sec. 204(a)(32)(A) of P.L. 99-514 [reproduced below] . . . Sec. 1002(d)(20)(B), substituted "December 26, 1985" for "August 30, 1984", substituted "July 2, 1986" for "May 4, 1985" and substituted "in July 1985" for "on July 3, 1985" in Sec. 204(a)(32)(B) of P.L. 99-514 [reproduced below] . . . Sec. 1002(d)(20)(C), substituted "$5,000,000" for "$2,200,000", substituted "in 1986" for "on January 27, 1986", and added "in Masontown, Pennsylvania," after "plant" in Sec. 204(a)(32)(E) of P.L. 99-514 [reproduced below] . . . Sec. 1002(d)(20)(D), amended Sec. 204(a)(32)(K) of P.L. 99-514 [reproduced below] . . . Sec. 1002(d)(20)(E), added "in connection with" after "housing" in Sec. 204(a)(32)(L) of P.L. 99-514 [reproduced below] . . . Sec. 1002(d)(20)(F), amended Sec. 204(a)(32)(M) of P.L. 99-514 [reproduced below] . . . Sec. 1002(d)(20)(G), substituted "Pensacola, Florida" for "New Orleans, Louisiana" in Sec. 204(a)(32)(O) of P.L. 99-514 [reproduced below] . . . Sec. 1002(d)(20)(H), added "placed" before "to be", added "Coal" before "Company", added "(or any subsidiary thereof)" after "Company" and substituted "by December 31, 1985" for "on December 31, 1985" in Sec. 204(a)(32)(S) of P.L. 99-514 [reproduced below] . . . Sec. 1002(d)(21), amended Sec. 204(a)(32)(T) of P.L. 99-514 [reproduced below] . . . Sec. 1002(d)(22), substituted "constructed" for "placed in service" in Sec. 204(a)(32)(U) of P.L. 99-514 [reproduced below] . . . Sec. 1002(d)(23), substituted "the home rule city on December 4, 1985, and the State housing finance agency on December 20, 1985, adopted inducement resolutions" for "the home rule city and the State housing finance agency adopted inducement resolutions on December 20, 1985" in Sec. 204(a)(32)(X) of P.L. 99-514 [reproduced below] . . . Sec. 1002(d)(24), amended Sec. 204(a)(33)(C) of P.L. 99-514 [reproduced below] . . . Sec. 1002(d)(25), deleted "and" at the end of Sec. 204(a)(33)(J) of P.L. 99-514, substituted ", and" for the period at the end of Sec. 204(a)(33)(K) of P.L. 99-514, and added Sec. 204(a)(33)(L) of P.L. 99-514 [reproduced below] . . . Sec. 1002(d)(26), added Secs. 204(a)(34)-(39) of P.L. 99-514 [reproduced below] . . . Sec. 1002(d)(27), added "(as amended by the Tax Reform Act of 1984)" after the period at the end of Sec. 204(b) of P.L. 99-514 [reproduced below] . . . Sec. 1002(d)(28), added "located in Pennsylvania and" before "constructed pursuant" in Sec. 204(c)(1)(A) of P.L. 99-514 [reproduced below] . . . Sec. 1002(d)(29)(A)-(C), substituted "or, in the case of a project described in subparagraph (b), by substituting 'April 1, 1992') for the applicable date" for "for the applicable date", substituted "on or before April 1, 1986" for "before April 1, 1986" and added the last sentence to Sec. 204(c)(3) of P.L. 99-514 [reproduced below] . . . Sec. 1002(d)(30)(A), amended Secs. 204(c)(4)-(c)(4)(K) of P.L. 99-514 [reproduced below] . . . Sec. 1002(d)(30)(B), amended Secs. 204(c)(4)(M)-(P) and added Sec. 204(c)(4)(Q) of P.L. 99-514 [reproduced below] Sec. 1002(d)(31)(A), substituted "January 25" for "January 18" in Sec. 204(a)(29)(A) of P.L. 99-514 [reproduced below] . . . Sec. 1002(a)(31)(B), substituted "a law suite filed on October 25, 1985" for "law suits filed on June 22, 1984, and November 21, 1985" in Sec. 204(A)(29)(B) of P.L. 99-514 [reproduced below] . . . Sec. 1002(d)(32), amended Sec. 204(a)(33)(J) of P.L. 99-514 (as amended by Sec. 1002(d)(25) of this Act) [reproduced below] . . . Sec. 1002(d)(33), added "and" at the end of Sec. 204(c)(3)(B) [reproduced below] of P.L. 99-514, deleted 204(c)(3)(C) of P.L.99-514, and redesignated Sec. 204(c)(3)(D) of P.L. 99-514 as Sec. 204(c)(3)(C) of P.L. 99-514 [reproduced below] . . . Sec. 1002(d)(34), amended Sec. 204(a)(5)(J)(ii)(II) of P.L. 99-514 [reproduced below] . . . Sec. 1002(d)(35), amended Sec. 204(a)(5)(T) of P.L. 99-514 [reproduced below].

Prior to amendment, Sec.204(c)(3) of P.L. 99-514, read as follows:

"(3) Section 203(b)(2) shall be applied by substituting 'January 1, 1990,' for the applicable date that would otherwise apply in the case of—

"(A) new commercial passenger aircraft used by a domestic airline, if a binding contract with respect to such aircraft was entered into before April 1, 1986, and such aircraft has a present class life of 12 years,

"(B) a pumped storage hydroelectric project with respect to which an application was made to the Federal Energy Regulatory Commission for a license on February 4, 1974, and license was issued August 1, 1977, the project number of which is 2740.

"(C) a facility for the manufacture of an improved particleboard, if— a binding contract to purchase equipment was executed March 3, 1986, such equipment will be placed in service by January 1, 1988, and such facility is located in or near Moncure, North Carolina, and

"(D) a newsprint mill in Pend Oreille county, Washington, costing about $290,000,000."
Prior to amendment, Sec. 204(a)(4) of P.L. 99-514 read as follows:
"(4) Property treated under prior tax acts. The amendments made by section 201 shall not apply to property described in section 12(c)(2) or 31(g)(5) and 31(g)(17)(j) of the Tax Reform Act of 1984, to property described in section 209(d)(1)(B) of the Tax Equity and Fiscal Responsibility Act of 1982, as amended by the Tax Reform Act of 1984 and to property described in section 216(b)(3) of the Tax Equity and Fiscal Responsibility Act of 1982.
Prior to amendment, Sec. 204(a)(32)(K) of P.L. 99-514, read as follows:
"(K) A $600,000,000, 250 megawatt plant placed in service by the Sierra Pacific Power Company,
Prior to amendment Sec. 204(a)(32)(M) of P.L.99-514, read as follows:
"(M) Kenosha Harbor, in Kenosha Wisconsin"
Prior to amendment, Sec. 204(a)(32)(T) of P.L. 99-514, read as follows:
"(T) a fiber optics network placed in service by Kansas City Southern Industries, the total estimated cost of which is $25,000,000,
Prior to amendment, Sec. 204(a)(33)(C) of P.L. 99-514 read as follows:
"(C) a waste-to-energy project in Derry, New Hampshire, costing approximately $60,000,000,
Prior to amendment, Sec. 204(a)(33)(J) of P.L. 99-514 read as follows:
"(J) a 24 megawatt alternative energy facility placed in service by Peat Products, with respect to which certification by the Federal Energy Regulatory Commission on April 3, 1986, and
Prior to amendment, Sec. 204(c)(3)(C) of P.L. 99-514, read as follows:
"(C) a facility for the manufacture of an improved particleboard, if—a binding contract to purchase such equipment was executed March 3, 1986, such equipment will be placed in service by January 1, 1988, and such facility is located in or near Moncure, North Carolina, and
Prior to amendment, Secs. 204(c)(4)(A)-(L) of P.L. 99-514 read as follows:
"(4) The amendments made by section 201 shall not apply to a limited amount of the following property or a limited amount of property set forth in submission before September 16, 1986, by the following taxpayers—
"(A) Arena project, Michigan,
"(B) Campbell Soup Company, Pennsylvania and California,
"(C) Overton, Florida,
"(D) Legett and Platt,
"(E) East Bank Housing Project,
"(F) Standard Telephone Company,
"(G) Presidential Air,
"(H) Ann Arbor Railroad,
"(I) Ada, Michigan Cogeneration,
"(J) Anchor Store Project, Michigan,
"(K) Biogen Power,
"(M) Hardage Company,
"(N) Mesa Airlines,
"(O) Yarn-spinning equipment used at Spring Cotton Mills, and
"(P) 328 units of low-income housing at Angelus Plaza."
Prior to amendment, Sec. 204(a)(5)(J)(ii)(II) of P.L. 99-514 read as follows:
"(II) the Board of Directors of an automobile manufacturer approved a written plan for the conversion of an existing facility to produce a new model of a vehicle currently not produced in the United States, such facility will be placed in service by July 1, 1987, and such Board action recurred in July 1985, with respect to a $523,000,000 expenditure, in June 1983 with respect to a $475,000,000 expenditure, or in July 1984, with respect to a $312,000,000 expenditure."
Prior to amendment, Sec. 205(a)(5)(T) of P.L. 99-514 read as follows:
"(T) A project is described in this subparagraph if it is a plant facility on Alaska's North Slope and
"(i) the approximate cost is $575,000,000 of which approximately $100,000,000 was spent on off-site construction or
"(ii) the approximate cost of which is $450,000,000, of which approximately $100,000,000 was spent on off-site construction, more than 50 percent of the project cost was spent prior to December 31, 1985, and which will be placed in service in 1987."
—P.L. 100-647, Sec. 1002(d)(7)(B), amended Sec. 12(c)(2) of P.L. 98-369 [reproduced below], part of the transitional rules for changes made by Sec. 12(a) of 98-369, by deleting "which is placed in service before January 1, 1988" after "property", see below.
—P.L. 100-647, Sec. 1002(i)(2)(A), added the last item to the table in para. (c)(1) as amended by Sec. 1002(a) of this Act ... Sec. 1002(i)(2)(B)(i), redesignated subpara. (b)(3)(C) as subpara. (b)(3)(D) and added subpara. (b)(3)(C) ... Sec. 1002(i)(2)(B)(ii), substituted "(3)(D)" for "(3)(C)" in para. (b)(5) ... Sec. 1002(i)(2)(C), added para. (e)(4) ... Sec. 1002(i)(2)(D), deleted "and" at the end of subpara. (d)(2)(A), added "and" at the end of subpara. (d)(2)(B) and added subpara. (d)(2)(C) ... Sec. 1002(i)(2)(E), substituted "residential rental property, and railroad grading or tunnel bore" for "and residential rental property" in clause (d)(3)(B)(i), as amended by Sec. 1002(a) of this Act ... Sec. 1002(i)(2)(F), added the last item to the table in subpara. (g)(2)(C) ... Sec. 1002(i)(2)(G), added clause (i)(1)(E)(iii), effective for that portion of the basis of any property which is attributable to expenditures paid or incurred after 12/31/86, except as provided in Sec. 242(c)(2) of P.L. 99-514, reproduced in note following Code Sec. 185.
—P.L. 100-647, Sec. 1018(b)(1), amended Sec. 31(g)(17)(J) of P.L. 98-369 [reproduced below] part of the special rules for amendments made by Sec. 31(a) of P.L. 98-369, by substituting "Register of Deed" for "Registery of Deeds" each place it appears in the last sentence and by substituting "May 7, 1984" for "May 7, 1985" in the last sentence, see below.

—P.L. 100-647, Sec. 1018(b)(2)(A), substituted "this paragraph and paragraph (8)" for "this paragraph" in clauses (j)(9)(E)(i) and (ii)(I) ... Sec. 1018(b)(2)(B), amended clause (j)(9)(E)(iii) as in effect before amendment by Sec. 1802(a)(2) and Sec. 201 of P.L. 99-514, effective for property placed in service by the taxpayer after 5/23/83, in tax. yrs. end. after 5/23/83, and for property placed in service by the taxpayer on or before 5/23/83, if the lease to the tax-exempt entity is entered into after 5/23/83.
Prior to amendment, Sec. 203(j)(9)(E)(iii) [before amendment by Sec. 1802(a)(2) and Sec. 201 of P.L. 99-514], read as follows:
"(iii) Tax-exempt controlled entity. The term 'tax-exempt controlled entity' means any corporation (which is not a tax-exempt entity determined without regard to this subparagraph and paragraph (4)(E)) if 50 percent or more (by value) of the stock in such corporation is held (directly or through the application of section 318 determined without regard to the 50-percent limitation contained in subsection (a)(2)(C) thereof) by 1 or more tax-exempt entities.
—P.L. 100-647, Sec. 6027(a), redesignated subparas. (e)(3)(D) and (E) as subparas. (e)(3)(E) and (F) and added subpara. (e)(3)(D) ... Sec. 6027(b)(1), deleted clause (e)(3)(C)(ii), added 'and' at the end of clause (e)(3)(C)(i) and redesignated clause (e)(3)(C)(iii) as clause (e)(3)(C)(ii) ... Sec. 6027(b)(2), amended the table in subpara. (g)(3)(B), effective for property placed in service after 12/31/88, except as provided in Sec. 6027(c)(2) of this Act which read as follows:
"(2) Exception. The amendments made by this section shall not apply to any property if such property is placed in service before January 1, 1990, and if such property—
"(A) is constructed, reconstructed, or acquired by the taxpayer pursuant to a written contract which was binding on July 14, 1988, or
"(B) is constructed or reconstructed by the taxpayer and such construction or reconstruction began by July 14, 1988."
Prior to deletion, clause (e)(3)(C)(ii) read as follows:
"(ii) any single-purpose agricultural or horticultural structure (within the meaning of section 48(p)), and"
Prior to amendment, the table in subpara. (g)(3)(B) read as follows:

"If property is described in subparagraph:	The class life is:
(B)(ii)	5
(B)(iii)	9.5
(C)(i)	10
(C)(ii)	15
(D)(i)	24
(D)(ii)	24
(E)	50."

—P.L. 100-647, Sec. 6028(a), deleted "or" at the end of subpara. (b)(2)(A) [as amended by Sec. 1002(a)(11)(A) of this Act], redesignated subpara. (b)(2)(B) [as amended by Sec. 1002(a)(11)(A) of this Act], as subpara. (b)(2)(C) and added subpara. (b)(2)(B), effective for property placed in service after 12/31/88, except as provided in Sec. 6028(b)(2) of this Act which reads:
"(2) Exception. The amendments made by this section shall not apply to any property if such property is placed in service before July 1, 1989, and if such property—
"(A) is constructed, reconstructed, or acquired by the taxpayer pursuant to a written contract which was binding on July 14, 1988, or
"(B) is constructed or reconstructed by the taxpayer and such construction or reconstruction began by July 14, 1988."
—P.L. 100-647, Sec. 6029(a), amended subpara. (e)(3)(D) [as added by Sec. 6027 of this Act] ... Sec. 6029(b), added subpara. (b)(3)(D) [sic (E)], ... Sec. 6029(c), amended the item relating to subparagraph (D) in the table in subpara. (g)(3)(B), effective for property placed in service after 12/31/88.
Prior to amendment, subpara. (e)(3)(D) [as amended by Sec. 6027 of this Act] read as follows:
"(D) 10-year property. The term '10-year property' includes any single purpose agricultural or horticultural structure (within the meaning of section 48(p))."
Prior to amendment, the item relating to subparagraph (D) in the table in subpara. (g)(3)(B) read as follows:
"(D) ... 15' with the items for '(D)(i) and (D)(ii)"
—P.L. 100-647, Sec. 6253, amended para. (i)(1), effective, 11/10/88.
Prior to amendment, para. (i)(1) read as follows:
"(1) Class life.
"(A) In general. Except as provided in this section, the term 'class life' means the class life (if any) which would be applicable with respect to any property as of January 1, 1986, under subsection (m) of section 167 (determined without regard to paragraph (4) thereof and as if the taxpayer had made an election under such subsection).
"(B) Secretarial authority. The Secretary, through an office established in the Treasury—
"(i) shall monitor and analyze actual experience with respect to all depreciable assets, and
"(ii) except in the case of residential rental property or nonresidential real property—
"(I) may prescribe a new class life for any property,
"(II) in the case of assigned property, may modify any assigned item, or
"(III) may prescribe a class life for any property which does not have a class life within the meaning of subparagraph (A).
Any class life or assigned item prescribed or modified under the preceding sentence shall reasonably reflect the anticipated useful life, and the anticipated decline in value over time, of the property to the industry or other group.

"(C) Effect of modification. Any class life or assigned item with respect to any property prescribed or modified under subparagraph (B) shall be used in classifying such property under subsection (e) and in applying subsection (g).

"(D) No modification of assigned property before January 1, 1992.

"(i) In general. Except as otherwise provided in this subparagraph, the Secretary may not modify an assigned item under subparagraph (B)(ii)(II) for any assigned property which is placed in service before January 1, 1992.

"(ii) Exception for shorter class life. In the case of assigned property which is placed in service before January 1, 1992, and for which the assigned item reflects a class life which is shorter than the class life under subparagraph (A), the Secretary may modify such assigned item under subparagraph (B)(ii)(II) if such modification results in an item which reflects a shorter class life than such assigned item.

"(E) Assigned property and item. For purposes of this paragraph—

"(i) Assigned property. The term 'assigned property' means property for which a class life, classification, or recovery period is assigned under subsection (e)(3) or subparagraph (B), (C), or (D) of subsection (g)(3).

"(ii) Assigned item. The term 'assigned item' means the class life, classification, or recovery period assigned under section (e)(3) or subparagraph (B), (C), or (D) of subsection (g)(3)."

"(iii) Special rule for railroad grading or tunnel bores. In the case of any property which is a railroad grading or tunnel bore—

"(I) such property shall be treated as an assigned property,

"(II) the recovery period applicable to such property shall be treated as an assigned item, and

"(III) clause (ii) of subparagraph (D) shall not apply."

In 1986, P.L. 99-514, Sec. 201(a), amended Code Sec. 168, effective for property placed in service after 12/31/86, in tax. yrs. end. after 12/31/86. See Secs. 203(b)-(e) and Sec. 204 of this Act [reproduced below] for transitional rules and other provisions Sec. 203(a)(1)(B) [as amended by Sec. 1002(c)(1) of P.L. 100-647, see above] of this Act provides:

"(B) Election to have amendments made by section 201 apply.—A taxpayer may elect (at such time and in such manner as the Secretary of the Treasury or his delegate may prescribe) to have the amendments made by section 201 apply to any property placed in service after July 31, 1986, and before January 1, 1987. No election may be made under this subparagraph with respect to property to which section 168 of the Internal Revenue Code of 1986 would not apply by reason of section 168(f)(5) of such Code if such property were placed in service after December 31, 1986."

Sec. 203(b)–(e) [as amended by P.L. 100-647, Secs. 1002(c)(2)-(7), see above] of this Act provides:

"(b) General transitional rule.

"(1) In general.—The amendments made by section 201 shall not apply to—

"(A) any property which is constructed, reconstructed, or acquired by the taxpayer pursuant to a written contract which was binding on March 1, 1986,

"(B) property which is constructed or reconstructed by the taxpayer if—

"(i) the lesser of (I) $1,000,000 or (II) 5 percent of the cost of such property has been incurred or committed by March 1, 1986, and

"(ii) the construction or reconstruction of such property began by such date, or

"(C) an equipped building or plant facility if construction has commenced as of March 1, 1986, pursuant to a written specific plan and more than one-half of the cost of such equipped building or facility has been incurred or committed by such date.

For purposes of this paragraph, all members of the same affiliated group of corporations (within the meaning of section 1504 of the Internal Revenue Code of 1986) filing a consolidated return shall be treated as one taxpayer.

"(2) Requirement that certain property be placed in service before certain date.—

"(A) In general.—Paragraph (1) and section 204(a) (other than paragraph (8) or (12) thereof) shall not apply to any property unless such property has a class life of at least 7 years and is placed in service before the applicable date determined under the following table:

"In the case of property with a class life of:	The applicable date is
At least 7 but less than 20 years	January 1, 1989
20 years or more	January 1, 1991.

"(B) Residential rental and nonresidential real property.—In the case of residential rental property and nonresidential real property, the applicable date is January 1, 1991.

"(C) Class lives.—For purposes of subparagraph (A)—

"(i) the class life of property to which section 168(g)(3)(B) of the Internal Revenue Code of 1986 (as added by section 201) applies shall be the class life in effect on January 1, 1986, except that computer-based telephone central office switching equipment described in section 168(e)(3)(B)(iii) of such Code shall be treated as having a class life of 6 years,

"(ii) property described in section 204(a) shall be treated as having a class life of 20 years, and

"(iii) property with no class life shall be treated as having a class life of 12 years.

"(D) Substitution of applicable dates.—If any provision of this Act substitutes a date for an applicable date, this paragraph shall be applied by using such date.

"(3) Property qualifies if sold and leased back in 3 months.—Property shall be treated as meeting the requirements of paragraphs (1) and (2) or section 204(a) with respect to any taxpayer if such property is acquired by the taxpayer from a person—

"(A) in whose hands such property met the requirements of paragraphs (1) and (2) or section 204(a), (or would have met such requirements if placed in service by such person) or

"(B) who placed the property in service before January 1, 1987,

and such property is leased back by the taxpayer to such person or is leased to such person not later than the earlier of the applicable date under paragraph (2) or the day which is 3 months after such property was placed in service.

"(4) Plant facility.—For purposes of paragraph (1), the term 'plant facility' means a facility which does not include any building (or with respect to which buildings constitute an insignificant portion) and which is—

"(A) a self-contained single operating unit or processing operation,

"(B) located on a single site, and

"(C) identified as a single unitary project as of March 1, 1986.

"(c) Property financed with tax-exempt bonds.

"(1) In general. Except as otherwise provided in this subsection or section 204, subparagraph (C) of section 168(g)(1) of the Internal Revenue Code of 1986 (as added by this Act) shall apply to property placed in service after December 31, 1986, in taxable years ending after such date, to the extent such property is financed by the proceeds of an obligation (including a refunding obligation) issued after March 1, 1986.

"(2) Exceptions.—

"(A) Construction or binding agreements.— Subparagraph (C) of section 168(g)(1) of such Code (as so added) shall not apply to obligations with respect to a facility—

"(i)(I) the original use of which commences with the taxpayer, and the construction, reconstruction, or rehabilitation of which began before March 2, 1986, and was completed on or after such date,

"(II) with respect to which a binding contract to incur significant expenditures for construction, reconstruction, or rehabilitation was entered into before March 2, 1986, and some of such expenditures are incurred on or after such date, or

"(III) acquired on or after March 2, 1986, pursuant to a binding contract entered into before such date, and

"(ii) described in an inducement resolution or other comparable preliminary approval adopted by the issuing authority (or by a voter referendum) before March 2, 1986.

"(B) Refunding.—

"(i) In general.—Except as provided in clause (ii), in the case of property placed in service after December 31, 1986, which is financed by the proceeds of an obligation which is issued solely to refund another obligation which was issued before March 2, 1986, subparagraph (C) of section 168(g)(1) of such Code (as so added) shall apply only with respect to an amount equal to the basis in such property which has not been recovered before the date such refunded obligation is issued.

"(ii) Significant expenditures.—In the case of facilities the original use of which commences with the taxpayer and with respect to which significant expenditures are made before January 1, 1987, subparagraph (C) of section 168(g)(1) of such Code (as so added) shall not apply with respect to such facilities to the extent such facilities are financed by the proceeds of an obligation issued solely to refund another obligation which was issued before March 2, 1986.

"(C) Facilities.—In the case of an inducement resolution or other comparable preliminary approval adopted by an issuing authority before March 2, 1986, for purposes of subparagraphs (A) and (B)(ii) with respect to obligations described in such resolution, the term 'facilities' means the facilities described in such resolution.

"(D) Significant expenditures.—For purposes of this paragraph, the term 'significant expenditures' means expenditures greater than 10 percent of the reasonably anticipated cost of the construction, reconstruction, or rehabilitation of the facility involved.

"(d) Mid-quarter convention.

"In the case of any taxable year beginning before October 1, 1982 in which property to which the amendments made by section 201 do not apply is placed in service, such property shall be taken into account in determining whether section 168(d)(3) of the Internal Revenue Code of 1986 (as added by section 201) applies for such taxable year to property to which such amendments apply. The preceding sentence shall not apply to property which would be taken into account if such amendments did apply.

"(e) Normalization requirements.

"(1) In general.—A normalization method of accounting shall not be treated as being used with respect to any public utility property for purposes of section 167 or 168 of the Internal Revenue Code of 1986 if the taxpayer, in computing its cost of service for ratemaking purposes and reflecting operating results in its regulated books of account, reduces the excess tax reserve more rapidly or to a greater extent than such reserve would be reduced under the average rate assumption method.

"(2) Definitions.—For purposes of this subsection—

"(A) Excess tax reserve.—The term 'excess tax reserve' means the excess of—

"(i) the reserve for deferred taxes (as described in section 167(l)(3)(G)(ii) or 168(e)(3)(B)(ii) of the Internal Revenue Code of 1954 as in effect on the day before the date of the enactment of this Act), over

"(ii) the amount which would be the balance in such reserve if the amount of such reserve were determined by assuming that the corporate rate reductions provided in this Act were in effect for all prior periods.

"(B) Average rate assumption method.—The average rate assumption method is the method under which the excess in the reserve for deferred taxes is reduced over the remaining lives of the property as used in its regulated books of account which gave rise to the reserve for deferred taxes. Under such method, if timing differences for the property reverse, the amount of the adjustment to the reserve for the deferred taxes is calculated by multiplying—

"(i) the ratio of the aggregate deferred taxes for the property to the aggregate timing differences for the property as of the beginning of the period in question, by

"(ii) the amount of the timing differences which reverse during such period."

Sec. 204 [as amended by P.L. 100-647, Secs. 1002(d)(1)-(35), see above and Sec. 8071 of P.L. 99-509, see below] of this Act provides:

"SEC. 204. ADDITIONAL TRANSITIONAL RULES.

"(a) Other transitional rules.

"(1) Urban renovation projects.—

"(A) In general.—The amendments made by section 201 shall not apply to any property which is an integral part of any qualified urban renovation project.

"(B) Qualified urban renovation project.—For purposes of subparagraph (A), the term 'qualified urban renovation project' means any project—

"(i) described in subparagraph (C), (D), (E), or (G) which before March 1, 1986, was publicly announced by a political subdivision of a State for a renovation of an urban area within its jurisdiction.

"(ii) described in subparagraph (C), (D) or (G) which before March 1, 1986, was identified as a single unitary project in the internal financing plans of the primary developer of the project,

"(iii) described in subparagraph (C) or (D), which is not substantially modified on or after March 1, 1986, and (iv) described in subparagraph (F) or (H).

"(C) Project where agreement on December 19, 1984.—A project is described in this subparagraph if—

"(i) a political subdivision granted on July 11, 1985, development rights to the primary developer-purchaser of such project, and

"(ii) such project was the subject of a development agreement between a political subdivision and a bridge authority on December 19, 1984.

"For purposes of this subparagraph, section 203(b)(2) shall be applied by substituting 'January 1, 1994' for 'January 1, 1991' each place it appears."

"(D) Certain additional projects.—A project is described in this subparagraph if it is described in any of the following clauses of this subparagraph and the primary developer of all such projects is the same person:

"(i) A project is described in this clause if the development agreement with respect thereto was entered into during April 1984 and the estimated cost of the project is approximately $194,000,000.

"(ii) A project is described in this clause if the development agreement with respect thereto was entered into during May 1984 and the estimated cost of the project is approximately $190,000,000.

"(iii) A project is described in this clause if the project has an estimated cost of approximately $92,000,000 and at least $7,000,000 was spent before September 26, 1985, with respect to such project.

"(iv) A project is described in this clause if the estimated project cost is approximately $39,000,000 and at least $2,000,000 of construction cost for such project were incurred before September 26, 1985.

"(v) A project is described in this clause if the development agreement with respect thereto was entered into before September 26, 1985, and the estimated cost of the project is approximately $150,000,000.

"(vi) A project is described in this clause if the board of directors of the primary developer approved such project in December 1982, and the estimated cost of such project is approximately $107,000,000.

"(vii) A project is described in this clause if the board of directors of the primary developer approved such project in December 1982, and the estimated cost of such project is approximately $59,000,000.

"(viii) A project is described in this clause if the Board of Directors of the primary developer approved such project in December 1983, following selection of the developer by a city council on September 26, 1983, and the estimated cost of such project is approximately $107,000,000.

"(E) Project where plan confirmed on October 4, 1984.—A project is described in this subparagraph if—

"(i) a State or an agency, instrumentality, or political subdivision thereof approved the filing of a general project plan on June 18, 1981, and on October 4, 1984, a State or an agency, instrumentality, or political subdivision thereof confirmed such plan,

"(ii) the project plan as confirmed on October 4, 1984, included construction or renovation of office buildings, a hotel, a trade mart, theaters, and a subway complex, and

"(iii) significant segments of such project were the subject of one or more conditional designations granted by a State or an agency, instrumentality, or political subdivision thereof to one or more developers before January 1, 1985.

The preceding sentence shall apply with respect to a property only to the extent that a building on such property site was identified as part of the project plan before September 26, 1985, and only to the extent that the size of the building on such property site was not substantially increased by reason of a modification to the project plan with respect to such property on or after such date. For purposes of this subparagraph, section 203(b)(2) shall be applied by substituting 'January 1, 1998' for 'January 1, 1991' each place it appears."

"(F) A project is described in this subparagraph if it is a sports and entertainment facility which—

"(i) is to be used by both a National Hockey League team and a National Basketball Association team;

"(ii) is to be constructed on a platform utilizing air rights over land acquired by a State authority and identified as site B in a report dated May 30, 1984, prepared for a State urban development corporation; and

"(iii) is eligible for real property tax, and power and energy benefits pursuant to the provisions of State legislation approved and effective July 7, 1982. A project is also described in this subparagraph if it is a mixed-use development which is—

"(I) to be constructed above a public railroad station utilized by the national railroad passenger corporation and commuter railroads serving two States; and

"(II) will include the reconstruction of such station so as to make it a more efficient transportation center and to better integrate the station with the development above, such reconstruction plans to be prepared in cooperation with a State transportation authority.

For purposes of this subparagraph, Section 203 (b)(2) shall be applied by substituting 'January 1, 1998' for the applicable date that would otherwise apply.

"(G) A project is described in this subparagraph if—

"(i) an inducement resolution was passed on March 9, 1984, for the issuance of obligations with respect to such project,

"(ii) such resolution was extended by resolutions passed on August 14, 1984, April 2, 1985, August 13, 1985, and July 8, 1986,

"(iii) an application was submitted on January 31, 1984, for an Urban Development Action Grant with respect to such project, and

"(iv) an Urban Development Action Grant was preliminarily approved for all or part of such project on July 3, 1986.

"(H) A project is described in this subparagraph if it is a redevelopment project, with respect to which $10,000,000 in industrial revenue bonds were approved by a State Development Finance Authority on January 15, 1986, a village transferred approximately $4,000,000 of bond volume authority to the State in June 1986, and a binding Redevelopment Agreement was executed between a city and the development team on June 30, 1986.

"(2) Certain projects granted FERC licenses, etc.—The amendments made by section 201 shall not apply to any property which is part of a project—

"(A) which is certified by the Federal Energy Regulatory Commission before March 2, 1986, as a qualifying facility for purposes of the Public Utility Regulatory Policies Act of 1978,

"(B) which was granted before March 2, 1986, a hydroelectric license for such project by the Federal Energy Regulatory Commission, or

"(C) which is a hydroelectric project of less than 80 megawatts that filed an application for a permit, exemption, or license with the Federal Energy Regulatory Commission before March 2, 1986.

"(3) Supply or service contracts.—The amendments made by section 201 shall not apply to any property which is readily identifiable with and necessary to carry out a written supply or service contract, or agreement to lease, which was binding on March 1, 1986.

"(4) Property treated under prior tax acts. The amendments made by section 201 shall not apply—

"(A) to property described in section 12(c)(2) (as amended by the Technical and Miscellaneous Revenue Act of 1988), 31(g)(5), or 31(g)(17)(J) of the Tax Reform Act of 1984,

"(B) to property described in section 209(d)(1)(B) of the Tax Equity and Fiscal Responsibility Act of 1982, as amended by the Tax Reform Act of 1984, and

"(C) to property described in section 216(b)(3) of the Tax Equity and Fiscal Responsibility Act of 1982."

"(5) Special rules for property included in master plans of integrated projects.—The amendments made by section 201 shall not apply to any property placed in service pursuant to a master plan which is clearly identifiable as of March 1, 1986, for any project described in any of the following subparagraphs of this paragraph:

"(A) A project is described in this subparagraph if—

"(i) the project involves production platforms for offshore drilling, oil and gas pipeline to shore, process and storage facilities, and a marine terminal, and

"(ii) at least $900,000,000 of the costs of such project were incurred before September 26, 1985.

"(B) A project is described in this subparagraph if—

"(i) such project involves a fiber optic network of at least 20,000 miles, and

"(ii) before September 26, 1985, construction commenced pursuant to the master plan and at least $85,000,000 was spent on construction.

"(C) A project is described in this subparagraph if—

"(i) such project passes through at least 10 States and involves intercity communication links (including one or more repeater sites, terminals and junction stations for microwave transmissions, regenerators or fiber optics and other related equipment),

"(ii) the lesser of $150,000,000 or 5 percent of the total project cost has been expended, incurred, or committed before March 2, 1986, by one or more taxpayers each of which is a member of the same affiliated group (as defined in section 1504(a)), and

"(iii) such project consists of a comprehensive plan for meeting network capacity requirements as encompassed within either:

"(I) a November 5, 1985, presentation made to and accepted by the Chairman of the Board and the president of the taxpayer, or

"(II) the approvals by the Board of Directors of the parent company of the taxpayer on May 3, 1985, and September 22, 1985, and of the executive committee of said board on December 23, 1985.

"(D) A project is described in this subparagraph if—

"(i) such project is part of a flat rolled product modernization plan which was initially presented to the Board of Directors of the taxpayer on July 8, 1983,

"(ii) such program will be carried out at 3 locations, and

"(iii) such project will involve a total estimated minimum capital cost of at least $250,000,000.

"(E) A project is described in this subparagraph if the project is being carried out by a corporation engaged in the production of a paint, chemicals, fiberglass, and glass, and if—

Deductions   Code Sec. 168

"(i) the project includes a production line which applies a thin coating to glass in the manufacture of energy efficient residential products, if approved by the management committee of the corporation on January 29, 1986,

"(ii) the project is a turbogenerator which was approved by the president of such corporation and at least $1,000,000 of the cost of which was incurred or committed before such date,

"(iii) the project is a waste-to-energy disposal system which was initially approved by the management committee of the corporation on March 29, 1982, and at least $5,000,000 of the cost of which was incurred before September 26, 1985,

"(iv) the project, which involves the expansion of an existing service facility and the addition of new lab facilities needed to accommodate topcoat and undercoat production needs of a nearby automotive assembly plant, was approved by the corporation's management committee on March 5, 1986, or

"(v) the project is part of a facility to consolidate and modernize the silica production of such corporation and the project was approved by the president of such corporation on August 19, 1985.

"(F) A project is described in this subparagraph if—

"(i) such project involves a port terminal and oil pipeline extending generally from the area of Los Angeles, California, to the area of Midland, Texas, and

"(ii) before September 26, 1985, there is a binding contract for dredging and channeling with respect thereto and a management contract with a construction manager for such project.

"(G) A project is described in this subparagraph if—

"(i) the project is a newspaper printing and distribution plant project with respect to which a contract for the purchase of 8 printing press units and related equipment to be installed in a single press line was entered into on January 8, 1985, and

"(ii) the contract price for such units and equipment represents at least 50 percent of the total cost of such project.

"(H) A project is described in this subparagraph if it is the second phase of a project involving direct current transmission lines spanning approximately 190 miles from the United States-Canadian border to Ayer, Massachusetts, alternating current transmission lines in Massachusetts from Ayers to Millbury to West Medway, DC-AC converted terminals to Monroe, New Hampshire, and Ayer, Massachusetts, and other related equipment and facilities.

"(I) A project is described in this subparagraph if it involves not more than two natural gas-fired combined cycle electric generating units each having a net electrical capability of approximately 233 megawatts, and a sales contract for approximately one-half of the output of the 1st unit was entered into in December 1985.

"(J) A project is described in this subparagraph if—

"(i) the project involves an automobile manufacturing facility (including equipment and incidental appurtenances) to be located in the United States, and

"(ii) either—

"(I) the project was the subject of a memorandum of understanding between 2 automobile manufacturers that was signed before September 25, 1985, the automobile manufacturing facility (including equipment and incidental appurtenances) will involve a total estimated cost of approximately $750,000,000, and will have an annual production capacity of approximately 240,000 vehicles or

"(II) for the Board of Directors of an automobile manufacturer approved a written plan for the conversion of existing facilities to produce new models of a vehicle not currently produced in the United States, such facilities will be placed in service by July 1, 1987, and such Board action occurred in July 1985 with respect to a $602,000,000 expenditure, a $438,000,000 expenditure, and a $321,000,000 expenditure.

"(K) A project is described in this subparagraph if—

"(i) the project involves a joint venture between a utility company and a paper company for a super calendared paper mill, and at least $50,000,000 was incurred or committed with respect to such project before March 1, 1986, or

"(ii) the project involves a paper mill for the manufacture of newsprint (including a cogeneration facility) is generally based on a written design and feasibility study that was completed on December 15, 1981, and will be placed in service before January 1, 1991, or

"(iii) the project is undertaken by a Maine corporation and involves the modernization of pulp and paper mills in Millinocket and/or East Millinocket, Maine, or

"(iv) the project involves the installation of a paper machine for production of coated publication papers, the modernization of a pulp mill, and the installation of machinery and equipment with respect to related processes, as of December 31, 1985, in excess of $50,000,000 was incurred for the project, as of July 1986, in excess of $150,000,000 was incurred for the project, and the project is located in Pine Bluff, Arkansas, or

"(v) the project involves property of a type described in ADR classes 26.1, 26.2, 25, 00.3 and 00.4 included in a paper plant which will manufacture and distribute tissue, towel or napkin products; is located in Effingham County, Georgia; and is generally based upon a written General Description which was submitted to the Georgia Department of Revenue on or about June 13, 1985.

"(L) A project is described in this subparagraph if—

"(i) a letter of intent with respect to such project was executed on June 4, 1985, and

"(ii) a 5-percent downpayment was made in connection with such project for 2 10-unit press lines and related equipment.

"(M) A project is described in this subparagraph if—

"(i) the project involves the retrofit of ammonia plants,

"(ii) as of March 1, 1986, more than $390,000 had been expended for engineering and equipment, and

"(iii) more than $170,000 was expensed in 1985 as a portion of preliminary engineering expense.

"(N) A project is described in this subparagraph if the project involves bulkhead intermodal flat cars which are placed in service before January 1, 1987, and either—

"(i) more than $2,290,000 of expenditures were made before March 1, 1986, with respect to a project involving up to 300 platforms, or

"(ii) more than $95,000 of expenditures were made before March 1, 1986, with respect to a project involving up to 850 platforms.

"(O) A project is described in this subparagraph if—

"(i) the project involves the production and transportation of oil and gas from a well located north of the Arctic Circle, and

"(ii) more than $200,000,000 of cost had been incurred or committed before September 26, 1985.

"(P) A project is described in this subparagraph if—

"(i) a commitment letter was entered into with a financial institution on January 23, 1986, for the financing of the project,

"(ii) the project involves intercity communication links (including microwave and fiber optics communications systems and related property),

"(iii) the project consists of communications links between—

"(I) Omaha, Nebraska, and Council Bluffs, Iowa,

"(II) Waterloo, Iowa and Sioux City, Iowa,

"(III) Davenport, Iowa and Springfield, Illinois, and

"(iv) the estimated cost of such project is approximately $13,000,000.

"(Q) A project is described in this subparagraph if—

"(i) such project is a mining modernization project involving mining, transport, and milling operations,

"(ii) before September 26, 1985, at least $20,000,000 was expended for engineering studies which were approved by the Board of Directors of the taxpayer on January 27, 1983, and

"(iii) such project will involve a total estimated minimum cost of $350,000,000.

"(R) A project is described in this subparagraph if—

"(i) such project is a dragline acquired in connection with a 3-stage program which began in 1980 to increase production from a coal mine,

"(ii) at least $35,000,000 was spent before September 26, 1985, on the 1st 2 stages of the program, and

"(iii) at least $4,000,000 was spent to prepare the mine site for the dragline.

"(S) A project is described in this subparagraph if—it is a project consisting of a mineral processing facility using a heap leaching system (including waste dumps, low-grade dumps, a leaching area, and mine roads) and if—

"(i) convertible subordinated debentures were issued in August 1985, to finance the project,

"(ii) construction of the project was authorized by the Board of Directors of the taxpayer on or before December 31, 1985,

"(iii) at least $750,000 was paid or incurred with respect to the project on or before December 31, 1985, and

"(iv) the project is placed in service on or before December 31, 1986.

"(T) A project is described in this subparagraph if it is a plant facility on Alaska's North Slope which is placed in service before January 1, 1988, and—

"(i) the approximate cost of which is $675,000,000, of which approximately $400,000,000 was spent on off-site construction,

"(ii) the approximate cost of which is $445,000,000, of which approximately $400,000,000 was spent on off-site construction and more than 50 percent of the project cost was spent prior to December 31, 1985, or

"(iii) the approximate cost of which is $375,000,000, of which approximately $260,000,000 was spent on off-site construction.

"(U) A project is described in this subparagraph if it involves the connecting of existing retail stores in the downtown area of a city to a new covered area, the total project will be 250,000 square feet, a formal Memorandum of Understanding relating to development of the project was executed with the city on July 2, 1986, and the estimated cost of the project is $18,186,424.

"(V) A project is described in this subparagraph if it includes a 200,000 square foot office tower, a 200-room hotel, a 300,000 square foot retail center, an 800-space parking facility, the total cost is projected to be $60,000,000, and $1,250,000 was expended with respect to the site before August 25, 1986.

"(W) A project is described in this subparagraph if it is a joint use and development project including an integrated hotel, convention center, office, related retail facilities and public mass transportation terminal, and vehicle parking facilities which satisfies the following conditions:

"(i) is developed within certain air space rights and upon real property exchanged for such joint use and development project which is owned or acquired by a state department of transportation, a regional mass transit district in a county with a population of at least 5,000,000 and a community redevelopment agency;

"(ii) such project affects an existing, approximately 40 acre public mass transportation bus-way terminal facility located adjacent to an interstate highway;

"(iii) a memorandum of understanding with respect to such joint use and development project is executed by a state department of transportation, such a county regional mass transit district and a community redevelopment agency on or before December 31, 1986, and

"(iv) a major portion of such joint use and development project is placed in service by December 31, 1990.

"(X) A project is described in this subparagraph if—

"(i) it is an $8,000,000 project to provide advanced control technology for adipic acid at a plant, which was authorized by the company's Board of Directors in October 1985, at December 31, 1985, $1,400,000 was committed and $400,000 expended with respect to such project, or

"(ii) it is an $8,300,000 project to achieve compliance with State and Federal regulations for particulates emissions, which was authorized by the company's

Board of Directors in December 1985, by March 31, 1986, $250,000 was committed and $250,000 was expended with respect to such project, or

"(iii) it is a $22,000,000 project for the retrofit of a plant that makes a raw material for aspartame, which was approved in the company's December 1985 capital budget, if approximately $3,000,000 of the $22,000,000 was spent before August 1, 1986.

"(Y) A project is described in this subparagraph if such project passes through at least 9 States and involves an intercity communication link (including multiple repeater sites and junction stations for microwave transmissions and amplifiers for fiber optics); the link from Buffalo to New York/Elizabeth was completed in 1984; the link from Buffalo to Chicago was completed in 1985; and the link from New York to Washington is completed in 1986.

"(Z) A project is described in this subparagraph if—

"(i) such project involves a fiber optic network of at least 475 miles, passing through Minnesota and Wisconsin; and

"(ii) before January 1, 1986, at least $15,000,000 was expended or committed for electronic equipment or fiber optic cable to be used in constructing the network."

"(6) Natural gas pipeline. — The amendments made by section 201 shall not apply to any interstate natural gas pipeline (and related equipment) if —

"(A) 3 applications for the construction of such pipeline were filed with the Federal Energy Regulatory Commission before November 22, 1985 (and 2 of which were filed before September 26, 1985), and

"(B) such pipeline has 1 of its terminal points near Bakersfield, California.

"(7) Certain leasehold improvements. — The amendments made by section 201 shall not apply to any reasonable leasehold improvements, equipment and furnishings placed in service by a lessee or its affiliates if—

"(A) the lessee or an affiliate is the original lessee of each building in which such property is to be used,

"(B) such lessee is obligated to lease the building under an agreement to lease entered into before September 26, 1985, and such property is provided for such building, and

"(C) such buildings are to serve as world headquarters of the lessee and its affiliates.

For purposes of this paragraph, a corporation is an affiliate of another corporation if both corporations are members of a controlled group of corporations within the meaning of section 1563(a) of the Internal Revenue Code of 1954 without regard to section 1563(b)(2) of such Code. Such lessee shall include a securities firm that meets the requirements of subparagraph (A), except the lessee is obligated to lease the building under a lease entered into on June 18, 1986.

"(8) Solid waste disposal facilities. — The amendments made by section 201, shall not apply to the taxpayer who originally places in service any qualified solid waste disposal facility (as defined in section 7701(e)(3)(B) of the Internal Revenue Code of 1986) if before March 2, 1986 —

"(A) there is a binding written contract between a service recipient and a service provider with respect to the operation of such facility to pay for the services to be provided by such facility,

"(B) a service recipient and governmental unit (or any entity related to such recipient or unit) made a financial commitment of at least $200,000 for the financing or construction of such facility,

"(C) such facility is the Tri-Cities Solid Waste Recovery Project involving Fremont, Newark, and Union City, California, and has received an authority to construct from the Environmental Protection Agency or from a State or local agency authorized by the Environmental Protection Agency to issue air quality permits under the Clean Air Act,

"(D) a bond volume carryforward election was made for the facility and the facility is for Chattanooga, Knoxville, or Kingsport, Tennessee, or

"(E) such facility is to serve Haverhill, Massachusetts."

"(9) Certain submersible drilling units. — In the case of a binding contract entered into on October 30, 1984, for the purchase of 6 semi-submersible drilling units at a cost of $425,000,000, such units shall be treated as having an applicable date under subsection 203(b)(2) of January 1, 1991.

"(10) Wastewater or sewage treatment facility. — The amendments made by section 201 shall not apply to any property which is part of a wastewater or sewage treatment facility if—

"(A) site preparation for such facility commenced before September 1985, and a parish council approved a service agreement with respect to such facility on December 4, 1985;

"(B) a city-parish advertised in September 1985, for bids for construction of secondary treatment improvements for such facility, in May 1985, the city-parish received statements from 16 firms interested in privatizing the wastewater treatment facilities, and the metropolitan council selected a privatizer at its meeting on November 20, 1985, and adopted a resolution authorizing the Mayor to enter into contractual negotiation with the selected privatizer;

"(C) the property is part of a wastewater treatment facility serving Greenville South Carolina with respect to which a binding service agreement between a privatizer and the Western Carolina Regional Sewer Authority with respect to such facility was signed before January 1, 1986; or

"(D) such property is part of a wastewater treatment facility (located in Cameron County, Texas, within one mile of the City of Harlingen), an application for a wastewater discharge permit was filed with respect to such facility on December 4, 1985, and a City Commission approved a letter of intent relating to a service agreement with respect to such facility on August 7, 1986; or such facility (located in Harlingen, Texas) which is the subject of such letter of intent and service agreement and the design of which was contracted for in a letter of intent dated January 23, 1986.

"(11) Certain aircraft. — The amendments made by section 201 shall not apply to any new aircraft with 19 or fewer passenger seats if—

"(A) the aircraft is manufactured in the United States. For purposes of this subparagraph, an aircraft is 'manufactured' at the point of its final assembly,

"(B) the aircraft was in inventory or in the planned production schedule of the final assembly manufacturer, with orders placed for the engine(s) on or before August 16, 1986, and

"(C) the aircraft is purchased or subject to a binding contract on or before December 31, 1986, and is delivered and placed in service by the purchaser before July 1, 1987.

"(12) Certain satellites. — The amendments made by section 201 shall not apply to any satellite with respect to which—

"(A) on or before January 28, 1986, there was a binding contract to construct or acquire a satellite, and

"(i) an agreement to launch was in existence on that date, or

"(ii) on or before August 5, 1983, the Federal Communications Commission had authorized the construction and for which the authorized party had a specific although undesignated agreement to launch in existence on January 28, 1986;

"(B) by order adopted on July 25, 1985, the Federal Communications Commission granted the taxpayer an orbital slot and authorized the taxpayer to launch and operate 2 satellites with a cost of approximately $300,000,000; or

"(C) the International Telecommunications Satellite Organization or the International Maritime Satellite Organization entered into written binding contracts before May 1, 1985.

"(13) Certain nonwire line cellular telephone systems. — The amendments made by section 201 shall not apply to property that is part of a nonwire line system in the Domestic Public Cellular Radio Telecommunications Service for which the Federal Communications Commission has issued a construction permit before September 26, 1985, but only if such property is placed in service before January 1, 1987.

"(14) Certain cogeneration facilities. — The amendments made by section 201 shall not apply to projects consisting of 1 or more facilities for the cogeneration and distribution of electricity and steam or other forms of thermal energy if—

"(A) at least $100,000 was paid or incurred with respect to the project before March 1, 1986, a memorandum of understanding was executed on September 13, 1985, and the project is placed in service before January 1, 1989,

"(B) at least $500,000 was paid or incurred with respect to the projects before May 6, 1986, the projects involve a 22-megawatt combined cycle gas turbine plant and a 45-megawatt coal waste plant, and applications for qualifying facility status were filed with the Federal Energy Regulatory Commission on March 5, 1986,

"(C) the project cost approximates $125,000,000 to $140,000,000 and an application was made to the Federal Energy Regulatory Commission in July 1985,

"(D) an inducement resolution for such facility was adopted on September 10, 1985, a development authority was given an inducement date of September 10, 1985, for a loan not to exceed $80,000,000 with respect to such facility, and such facility is expected to have a capacity of approximately 30 megawatts of electric power and 70,000 pounds of steam per hour,

"(E) at least $1,000,000 was incurred with respect to the project before May 6, 1986, the project involves a 52-megawatt combined cycle gas turbine plant and a petition was filed with the Connecticut Department of Public Utility Control to approve a power sales agreement with respect to the project on March 27, 1986.

"(F) the project has a planned scheduled capacity of approximately 38,000 kilowatts, the project property is placed in service before January 1, 1991, and the project is operated, established, or constructed pursuant to certain agreements, the negotiation of which began before 1986, with public or municipal utilities conducting business in Massachusetts, or

"(G) the Board of Regents of Oklahoma State University took official action on July 25, 1986, with respect to the project. In the case of the project described in subparagraph (F), section 203(b)(2)(A) shall be applied by substituting 'January 1, 1991' for 'January 1, 1989'."

"(15) Certain electric generating stations. — The amendments made by section 201 shall not apply to a project located in New Mexico consisting of a coal-fired electric generating station (including multiple generating units, coal mine equipment, and transmission facilities) if—

"(A) a tax-exempt entity will own an equity interest in all property included in the project (except the coal mine equipment), and

"(B) at least $72,000,000 was expended in the acquisition of coal leases, land and water rights, engineering studies, and other development costs before May 6, 1986.

For purposes of this paragraph, section 203(b)(2) shall be applied by substituting 'January 1, 1996' for 'January 1, 1991' each place it appears.

"(16) Sports arenas.—

"(A) Indoor sports facility. — The amendments made by section 201 shall not apply to up to $20,000,000 of improvements made by a lessee of any indoor sports facility pursuant to a lease from a State commission granting the right to make limited and specified improvements (including planned seat explanations), if architectural renderings of the project were commissioned and received before December 22, 1985.

"(B) Metropolitan sports arena. — The amendments made by section 201 shall not apply to any property which is part of an arena constructed for professional sports activities in a metropolitan area, provided that such arena is capable of seating no less than 18,000 spectators and a binding contract to incur significant expenditures for its construction was entered into before June 1, 1986.

"(17) Certain waste-to-energy facilities. — The amendments made by section 201 shall not apply to 2 agricultural waste-to-energy powerplants (and required transmission facilities), in connection with which a contract to sell 100 megawatts of electricity to a city was executed in October 1984.

Deductions   Code Sec. 168

"(18) Certain coal-fire plants.— The amendments made by section 201 shall not apply to one of three 540 megawatt coal-fired plants that are placed in service after a sale leaseback occurring after January 1, 1986, if—

"(A) the Board of Directors of an electric power cooperation authorized the investigation of a sale leaseback of a nuclear generation facility by resolution dated January 22, 1985, and

"(B) a loan was extended by the Rural Electrification Administration on February 20, 1986, which contained a covenant with respect to used property leasing from unit II.

"(19) Certain rail systems.—

"(A) The amendments made by section 201 shall not apply to a light rail transit system, the approximate cost of which is $235,000,000, if, with respect to which, the board of directors of a corporation (formed in September 1984 for the purpose of developing, financing, and operating the system) authorized a $300,000 expenditure for a feasibility study in April 1985.

"(B) The amendments made by section 201 shall not apply to any project for rehabilitation of regional railroad rights of way and properties including grade crossings which was authorized by the Board of Directors of such company prior to October 1985; and/or was modified, altered or enlarged as a result of termination of company contracts, but approved by said Board of Directors no later than January 30, 1986, and which is in the public interest, and which is subject to binding contracts or substantive commitments by December 31, 1987.

"(20) Certain detergent manufacturing facility.— The amendments made by section 201 shall not apply to a laundry detergent manufacturing facility, the approximate cost of which is $13,200,000, with respect to which a project agreement was fully executed on March 17, 1986.

"(21) Certain resource recovery facility.— The amendments made by section 201 shall not apply to any of 3 resource recovery plants, the aggregate cost of which approximates $300,000,000, if an industrial development authority adopted a bond resolution with respect to such facilities on December 17, 1984, and the projects were approved by the department of commerce of a Commonwealth on December 27, 1984.

"(22) The amendments made by section 201 shall not apply to a computer and office support center building in Minneapolis, with respect to which the first contract, with an architecture firm, was signed on April 30, 1985, and a construction contract was signed on March 12, 1986.

"(23) Certain district heating and cooling facilities.— The amendments made by section 201 shall not apply to pipes, mains, and related equipment included in district heating and cooling facilities, with respect to which the development authority of a State approved the project through an inducement resolution adopted on October 8, 1985, and in connection with which approximately $11,000,000 of tax-exempt bonds are to be issued.

"(24) Certain vessels.—

"(A) Certain offshore vessels.— The amendments made by section 201 shall not apply to any offshore vessel the construction contract for which was signed on February 28, 1986, and the approximate cost of which is $9,000,000.

"(B) Certain inland river vessel.— The amendments made by section 201 shall not apply to a project involving the reconstruction of an inland river vessel docked on the Mississippi River at St. Louis, Missouri, on July 14, 1986, and with respect to which:

"(i) the estimated cost of reconstruction is approximately $39,000,000;

"(ii) reconstruction was commenced prior to December 1, 1985;

"(iii) at least $17,000,000 was expended before December 31, 1985; and

"(C) Special automobile carrier vessels.— The amendments made by section 201 shall not apply to two new automobile carrier vessels which will cost approximately $47,000,000 and will be constructed by a United States-flag carrier to operate, under the United States-flag and with an American crew, to transport foreign automobiles to the United States, in a case where negotiations for such transportation arrangements commenced in April 1985, formal contract bids were submitted prior to the end of 1985, and definitive transportation contracts were awarded in May 1986.

"(D) The amendments made by section 201 shall not apply to a 562-foot passenger cruise ship, which was purchased in 1980 for the purpose of returning the vessel to United States service, the approximately cost of refurbishment of which is approximately $47,000,000.

"(E) The amendments made by section 201 shall not apply to the Muskegon, Michigan, Cross-Lake Ferry project having a projected cost of approximately $7,200,000.

"(F) The amendments made by section 201 shall not apply to a new automobile carrier vessel, the contract price for which is no greater than $28,000,000, and which will be constructed for and placed in service by OSG Car Carriers, Inc., to transport, under the United States flag and with an American crew, foreign automobiles to North America in a case where negotiations for such transportation arrangements commenced in 1985, and definitive transportation contracts were awarded before June 1986."

"(25) Certain wood energy projects.— The amendments made by section 201 shall not apply to two wood energy projects for which applications with the Federal Energy Regulatory Commission were filed before January 1, 1986, which are described as follows:

"(A) a 26.5 megawatt plant in Fresno, California, and

"(B) a 26.5 megawatt plant in Rocklin, California.

"(26) The amendments made by section 201 shall not apply to property which is a geothermal project of less than 20 megawatts that was certified by the Federal Energy Regulatory Commission on July 14, 1986, as a qualifying small power production facility for purposes of the Public Utility Regulatory Policies Act of 1978 pursuant to an application filed with the Federal Energy Regulatory Commission on April 17, 1986.

"(27) Certain economic development projects.— The amendments made by section 201 shall not apply to any of the following projects:

"(A) A mixed use development on the East River the total cost of which is approximately $400,000,000, with respect to which a letter of intent was executed on January 24, 1984, and with respect to which approximately $2.5 million had been spent by March 1, 1986.

"(B) A 356-room hotel, banquet, and conference facility (including 540,000 square feet of office space) the approximate cost of which is $158,000,000, with respect to which a letter of intent was executed on June 1, 1984, and with respect to which an inducement resolution and bond resolution was adopted on August 20, 1985.

"(C) Phase 1 of a 4-phase project involving the construction of laboratory space and ground-floor retail space the estimated cost of which is $22,000,000 and with respect to which a memorandum of understanding was made before August 29, 1983.

"(D) A project involving the development of a 490,000 square foot mixed-use building at 152 W. 57th Street, New York, New York, the estimated cost of which is $100,000,000, and with respect to which a building permit application was filed in May 1986.

"(E) A mixed-use project containing a 300 unit, 12-story hotel, garage, two multi-rise office buildings, and also included a park, renovated riverboat, and barge with festival marketplace, the capital outlays for which approximate $68,000,000.

"(F) The construction of a three-story office building that will serve as the home office for an insurance group and its affiliated companies, with respect to which a city agreed to transfer its ownership of the land for the project in a Redevelopment Agreement executed on September 18, 1985, once certain conditions are met.

"(G) A commercial bank formed under the laws of the State of New York which entered into an agreement on September 5, 1985, to construct its headquarters at 60 Wall Street, New York, New York, with respect to such headquarters.

"(H) Any property which is part of a commercial and residential project, the first phase of which is currently under construction, to be developed on land which is the subject to an ordinance passed on July 20, 1981, by the city council of the city in which such land is located, designating such land and the improvements to be placed thereon as a residential-business planned development, which development is being financed in part by the proceeds of industrial development bonds in the amount of $62,600,000 issued on December 4, 1985.

"(I) A 600,000 square foot mixed use building known as Flushing Center with respect to which a letter of intent was executed on March 26, 1986.

In the case of the building described in subparagraph (I), section 203(b)(2)(A) shall be applied by substituting 'January 1, 1993' for the applicable date which would otherwise apply."

"(28) The amendments made by section 201 shall not apply to an $80,000,000 capital project steel seamless tubular casings minimill and melting facility located in Youngstown, Ohio, which was purchased by the taxpayer in April 1985, and—

"(A) the purchase and renovation of which was approved, by a committee of the Board of Directors on February 22, 1985, and

"(B) as of December 31, 1985, more than $20,000,000 was incurred or committed with respect to the renovation.

"(29) The amendments made by section 201 shall not apply to any project for residential rental property if—

"(A) an inducement resolution with respect to such project was adopted by the State housing development authority on January 25, 1985, and

"(B) such project was the subject of a lawsuit filed on October 25, 1985 and November 21, 1985.

"(30) The amendments made by section 201 shall not apply to a 30 megawatt electric generating facility fueled by geothermal and wood waste, the approximate cost of which is $55,000,000, and with respect to which a 30-year power sales contract was executed on March 22, 1985.

"(31) The amendments made by section 201 shall not apply to railroad maintenance-of-way equipment, with respect to which a Boston bank entered into a firm binding contract with a major northeastern railroad before March 2, 1986, to finance $10,500,000 of such equipment, if all of the equipment was placed in service before August 1, 1986.

"(32) The amendment made by section 201 shall not apply to—

"(A) a facility constructed on approximately seven acres of land located on Ogle's Poso Creek Oil field, the primary fuel of which will be bituminous coal from Utah or Wyoming, with respect to which an application for an authority to construct was filed on December 26, 1985, an authority to construct was issued on July 2, 1986, and a prevention of significant deterioration permit application was submitted in May 1985,

"(B) a facility constructed on approximately seven acres of land located on Teorco's Jasmin oil field, the primary fuel of which will be bituminous coal from Utah or Wyoming, with respect to which an authority to construct was filed on August 30, 1984, an authority to construct was issued on May 4, 1985, and a prevention of significant deterioration permit application was submitted on July 3, 1985,

"(C) the Mountain View Apartments, in Hadley, Massachusetts,

"(D) a facility expected to have a capacity of not less than 65 megawatts of electricity, the steam from which is to be sold to a pulp and paper mill, with respect to which application was made to the Federal Regulatory Commission for certification as a qualified facility on November 1, 1985, and received such certification on January 24, 1986,

"(E) $5,000,000 of equipment ordered in 1986, in connection with a 60,000 square foot plant in Masontown Pennsylvania, that was completed in 1983,

"(F) a magnetic resonance imaging machine, with respect to which a binding contract to purchase was entered into in April 1986, in connection with the con-

Code Sec. 168 ・ **Deductions**

struction of a magnetic resonance imaging clinic with respect to which a Determination of Need certification was obtained from a State Department of Public Health on October 22, 1985, if such property is placed in service before December 31, 1986,

"(G) a company located in Salina, Kansas, which has been engaged in the construction of highways and city streets since 1946, but only to the extent of $1,410,000 of investment in new section 38 property,

"(H) a $300,000 project undertaken by a small metal finishing company located in Minneapolis, Minnesota, the first parts of which were received and paid for in January 1986, with respect to which the company received Board approval to purchase the largest piece of machinery it has ever ordered in 1985,

"(I) a $1,200,000 finishing machine that was purchased on April 2, 1986 and placed into service in September 1986 by a company located in Davenport, Iowa,

"(J) A 25 megawatt small power production facility, with respect to which Qualifying Facility status numbered QF86-593-000 was granted on March 5, 1986,

"(K) A 250 megawatt coal-fired electric plant in northeastern Nevada estimated to cost $600,000,000 and known as the Thousand Springs project, on which the Sierra Pacific Power Company, a subsidiary of Sierra Pacific Resources, began in 1980 work to design, finance, construct, and operate (and section 203(b)(2) shall be applied with respect to such plant by substituting 'January 1, 1995' for 'January 1, 1991'),"

"(L) 128 units of rental housing in connection with the Point Gloria Limited Partnership,

"(M) property which is part of the Kenosha Downtown Redevelopment Project and which is financed with the proceeds of bonds issued pursuant to section 1317(6)(W),"

"(N) Lakeland Park Phase II, in Baton Rouge, Louisiana,

"(O) the Santa Rosa Hotel, in Pensacola, Florida,

"(P) the Sheraton Baton Rouge, in Baton Rouge, Louisiana,

"(Q) $300,000 of equipment placed in service in 1986, in connection with the renovation of the Best Western Townhouse Convention Center in Cedar Rapids, Iowa,

"(R) the segment of a nationwide fiber optics telecommunications network placed in service by SouthernNet, the total estimated cost of which is $37,000,000,

"(S) two cogeneration facilities to be placed in service by the Reading Anthracite Coal Company (or any subsidiary thereof) costing approximately $110,000,000 each, with respect to which filings were made with the Federal Energy Regulatory Commission by December 31, 1985, and which are located in Pennsylvania,

"(T) a portion of a fiber optics network placed in service by LDX NET after December 31, 1988, but only to the extent the cost of such portion does not exceed $25,000,000.

"(U) 3 newly constructed fishing vessels, and one vessel that is overhauled, constructed by Mid Coast Marine, but only to the extent of $6,700,000 of investment,

"(V) $350,000 of equipment acquired in connection with the reopening of a plant in Bristol, Rhode Island, which plant was purchased by Buttonwoods, Ltd., Associates on February 7, 1986,

"(W) $4,046,000 of equipment placed in service by Brendle's Incorporated, acquired in connection with a Distribution Center,

"(X) a multi-family mixed-use housing project located in a home rule city, the zoning for which was changed to residential business planned development on November 26, 1985, and with respect to which both the home rule city on December 4, 1985, and the State housing finance agency on December 20, 1985 adopted inducement resolutions,

"(Y) the Myrtle Beach Convention Center, in South Carolina, to the extent of $25,000,000 of investment, and

"(Z) railroad cars placed in service by the Pullman Leasing Company, pursuant to an April 3, 1986 purchase order, costing approximately $10,000,000.

"(33) The amendments made by section 201 shall not apply to—

"(A) $400,000 of equipment placed in service by Super Key Market, if such equipment is placed in service before January 1, 1987,

"(B) the Trolley Square project, the total project cost of which is $24,500,000, and the amount of depreciable real property of which is $14,700,000.

"(C)(i) a waste-to-energy project in Derry, New Hampshire, costing approximately $60,000,000, and

"(ii) a waste-to-energy project in Manchester, New Hampshire, costing approximately $60,000,000.

"(D) the City of Los Angeles Co-composting project, the estimated cost of which is $62,000,000, with respect to which, on July 17, 1985, the California Pollution Control Financing Authority issued an initial resolution in the maximum amount of $75,000,000 to finance this project,

"(E) the St. Charles, Missouri Mixed-Use Center,

"(F) Oxford Place in Tulsa, Oklahoma,

"(G) an amount of investment generating $20,000,000 of investment tax credits attributable to property used on the Illinois Diversatech Campus,

"(H) $25,000,000 of equipment used in the Melrose Park Engine Plant that is sold and leased back by Navistar,

"(I) 80,000 vending machines, for a cost approximating $3,400,000 placed into service by Folz Vending Co.,

"(J) A 25.85 megawatt alternative energy facility located in Deblois, Maine, with respect to which certification by the Federal Energy Regulatory Commission was made on April 3, 1986,

"(K) Burbank Manors, in Illinois, and

"(L) a cogeneration facility to be built at a paper company in Turners Falls, Massachusetts, with respect to which a letter of intent was executed on behalf of the paper company on September 26, 1985.

"(34) The amendments made by section 201 shall not apply to an approximately 240,000 square foot beverage container manufacturing plant located in Batesville, Mississippi, or plant equipment used exclusively on the plant premises if—

"(A) a 2-year supply contract was signed by the taxpayer and a customer on November 1, 1985,

"(B) such contract further obligated the customer to purchase beverage containers for an additional 5-year period if physical signs of construction of the plant are present before September 1986,

"(C) ground clearing for such plant began before August 1986, and

"(D) construction is completed, the equipment is installed, and operations are commenced before July 1, 1987.

"(35) The amendments made by section 201 shall not apply to any property which is part of the multifamily housing at the Columbia Point Project in Boston, Massachusetts. A project shall be treated as not described in the preceding sentence and as not described in section 252(f)(1)(D) unless such project includes, at substantially all times throughout the compliance period (within the meaning of section 42(i)(1) of the Internal Revenue Code of 1986), a facility which provides health services to the residents of such project for fees commensurate with the ability of such individuals to pay for such services.

"(36) The amendments made by section 201 shall not apply to any ethanol facility located in Blair, Nebraska, if—

"(A) in July of 1984 an initial binding construction contract was entered into for such facility,

"(B) in June 1986, certain Department of Energy recommended contract changes required a change of contractor, and

"(C) In September of 1986, a new contract to construct such facility, consistent with such recommended changes, was entered into.

"(37) The amendments made by section 201 shall not apply to any property which is part of a sewage treatment facility if, prior to January 1, 1986, the City of Conyers, Georgia, selected a privatizer to construct such facility, received a guaranteed maximum price bid for the construction of such facility, signed a letter of intent and began substantial negotiations of a service agreement with respect to such facility.

"(38) The amendments made by section 201 shall not apply to—

"(A) a $28,000,000 wood resource complex for which construction was authorized by the Board of Directors on August 9, 1985,

"(B) an electrical cogeneration plant in Bethel, Maine which is to generate 2 megawatts of electricity from the burning of wood residues, with respect to which a contract was entered into on July 10, 1984, and with respect to which $200,000 of the expected $2,000,000 cost had been committed before June 15, 1986,

"(C) a mixed income housing project in Portland, Maine which is known as the Back Bay Tower and which is expected to cost $17,300,000,

"(D) the Eastman Place project and office building in Rochester, New York, which is projected to cost $20,000,000, with respect to which an inducement resolution was adopted in December 1986, and for which a binding contract for $500,000 was entered into on April 30, 1986,

"(E) the Marquis Two project in Atlanta, Georgia which has a total budget of $72,000,000 and the construction phase of which began under a contract entered into on March 26, 1986,

"(F) a 166-unit continuing care retirement center in New Orleans, Louisiana, the construction contract for which was signed on February 12, 1986, and is for a maximum amount not to exceed $8,500,000,

"(G) the expansion of the capacity of an oil refining facility in Rosemont, Minnesota from 137,000 to 207,000 barrels per day which is expected to be completed by December 31, 1990, and

"(H) a project in Ransom, Pennsylvania which will burn coal waste (known as 'culm') with an approximate cost of $64,000,000 and for which a certification from the Federal Energy Regulatory Commission was received on March 11, 1986.

"(39) The amendments made by section 201 shall not apply to any facility for the manufacture of an improved particle board if a binding contract to purchase such equipment was executed March 3, 1986, such equipment will be placed in service by January 1, 1988, and such facility is located in or near Moncure, North Carolina.

"(40) Certain trucks, etc.—The amendments made by section 201 shall not apply to trucks, tractor units, and trailers which a privately held truck leasing company headquartered in Des Moines, Iowa, contracted to purchase in September 1985 but only to the extent the aggregate reduction in Federal tax liability by reason of the application of this paragraph does not exceed $8,500,000.

"(b) Special rule for certain property.

"The provisions of section 168(f)(8) of the Internal Revenue Code of 1954 (as amended by section 209 of the Tax Equity and Fiscal Responsibility Act of 1982) shall continue to apply to any transaction permitted by reason of section 12(c)(2) of the Tax Reform Act of 1984 or section 209(d)(1)(B) of the Tax Equity and Fiscal Responsibility Act of 1982 (as amended by the Tax Reform Act of 1984)

"(c) Applicable date in certain cases.

"(1) Section 203(b)(2) shall be applied in substituting 'January 1, 1992' for 'January 1, 1991' in the following cases.

"(A) in the case of a 2-unit nuclear powered electric generating plant (and equipment and incidental appurtenances), constructed pursuant to contracts entered into by the owner operator of the facility before December 31, 1975, including contracts with the engineer/constructor and the nuclear steam system supplier, such contracts shall be treated as contracts described in section 203(b)(1)(A),

"(B) a cogeneration facility with respect to which an application with the Federal Energy Regulatory Commission was filed on August 2, 1985, and approved October 15, 1985.

"(C) in the case of a 1,300 megawatt coal-fired steam powered electric generating plant (and related equipment and incidental appurtenances), which the three owners determined in 1984 to convert from nuclear power to coal power and for which more than $600,000,000 had been incurred or committed for construction before September 25, 1985, except that no investment tax credit will be allowable under section 49(d)(3) added by section 211(a) of this Act for any qualified progress expenditures made after December 31, 1990.

"(2) Section 203(b)(2) shall be applied by substituting 'April 1, 1992' for the applicable date that would otherwise apply, in the case of the second unit of a twin steam electric generating facility and related equipment which was granted a certificate of public convenience and necessity by a public service commission prior to January 1, 1982, if the first unit of the facility was placed in service prior to January 1, 1982, if the first unit of the facility was placed in service prior to January 1, 1985, and before September 26, 1985, more than $100,000,000 had been expended toward the construction of the second unit.

"(3) Section 203(b)(2) shall be applied by substituting 'January 1, 1990,' '(or, in the case of a project described in subparagraph (B), by substituting 'April 1, 1992') for the applicable date, that would otherwise apply in the case of—

"(A) new commercial passenger aircraft used by a domestic airline, if a binding contract with respect to such aircraft was entered into on or before April 1, 1986, and such aircraft has a present class life of 12 years,

"(B) A pumped storage hydroelectric project with respect to which an application was made to the Federal Energy Regulatory Commission for a license on February 4, 1974, and license was issued August 1, 1977, the project number of which is 2740, and

"(C) a newsprint mill in Pend Oreille county, Washington, costing about $290,000,000.

"(4) The amendments made by section 201 shall not apply to a limited amount of the following property or a limited amount of property set forth in a submission before September 16, 1986, by the following taxpayers:

"(A) Arena project, Michigan, but only with respect to $78,000,000 of investments.

"(B) Campbell Soup Company, Pennsylvania, California, North Carolina, Ohio, Maryland, Florida, Nebraska, Michigan, South Carolina, Texas, New Jersey, and Delaware, but only with respect to $9,329,000 of regular investment tax credits.

"(C) The Southeast Overtown/Park West Development, Florida, but only with respect to $200,000,000 of investments.

"(D) Equipment placed in service and operated by Leggett and Platt before July 1, 1987, but only with respect to $2,000,000 of regular investment tax credits, and subsections (c) and (d) of section 49 of the Internal Revenue Code of 1986 shall not apply to such equipment.

"(E) East Bank Housing Project.

"(F) $1,561,215 of investments by Standard Telephone Company.

"(G) Five aircraft placed in service before January 1, 1987, by Presidential Air.

"(H) A rehabilitation project by Ann Arbor Railroad, but only with respect to $2,900,000 of investments.

"(I) Property that is part of a cogeneration project located in Ada, Michigan, but only with respect to $30,000,000 of investments.

"(J) Anchor Store Project, Michigan, but only with respect to $21,000,000 of investments.

"(K) A waste-fired electrical generating facility of Biogen Power, but only with respect to $34,000,000 of investments.

"(L) $14,000,000 of television transmitting towers placed in service by Media General, Inc., which were subject to binding contracts as of January 21, 1986, and will be placed in service before January 1, 1988,

"(M) Interests of Samuel A. Hardage (whether owned individually or in partnership form).

"(N) Two aircraft of Mesa Airlines with an aggregate cost of $5,723,484.

"(O) Yarn-spinning equipment used at Spray Cotton Mills, but only with respect to $3,000,000 of investments.

"(P) 328 units of low-income housing at Angelus Plaza, but only with respect to $20,500,000 of investments.

"(Q) One aircraft of Continental Aviation Services with a cost of approximately $15,000,000 that was purchased pursuant to a contract entered into during March of 1983 and that is placed in service by December 31, 1988.

"(d) Railroad grading and tunnel bores.

"(1) In general.—In the case of expenditures for railroad grading and tunnel bores which were incurred by a common carrier by railroad to replace property destroyed in a disaster occurring on or about April 17, 1983, near Thistel, Utah, such expenditures, to the extent not in excess of $15,000,000 shall be treated as recovery property which is 5-year property under section 168 of the Internal Revenue Code of 1954 (as in effect before the amendments made by this Act) and which is placed in service at the time such expenditures were incurred.

"(2) Business interruption proceeds.—Business interruption proceeds received for loss of use, revenues, or profits in connection with the disaster described in paragraph (1) and devoted by the taxpayer described in paragraph (1) to the construction of replacement track and related grading and tunnel bore expenditures shall be treated as constituting an amount received from the involuntary conversion of property under section 1033(a)(2) of such Code.

"(3) Effective date.—This subsection shall apply to taxable years ending after April 17, 1983.

"(e) Treatment of certain disaster losses.

"(1) In general.—In the case of a disaster described in paragraph (2), at the election of the taxpayer, the amendments made by section 201 of this Act—

"(A) shall not apply to any property placed in service during 1987 or 1988, or

"(B) shall apply to any property placed in service during 1985 or 1986, which is property to replace property lost, damaged, or destroyed in such disaster.

"(2) Disaster to which section applies.—This section shall apply to a flood which occurred on November 3 through 7, 1985, and which was declared a natural disaster area by the President of the United States."

Sec. 251(d)(2)–(4) of this Act [reproduced in the notes following Code Sec. 46] provides further exceptions to the amendments made by Sec. 201 of this Act. Prior to amendment, Code Sec. 168 read as follows:

"SEC. 168. ACCELERATED COST RECOVERY SYSTEM.

"(a) Allowance of deduction.

"There shall be allowed as a deduction for any taxable year the amount determined under this section with respect to recovery property.

"(b) Amount of deduction.

"(1) In general. Except as otherwise provided in this section, the amount of the deduction allowable by subsection (a) for any taxable year shall be the aggregate amount determined by applying to the unadjusted basis of recovery property the applicable percentage determined in accordance with the following table:

If the recovery year is:	3-year	5-year	10-year	15-year public
1	25	15	8	5
2	38	22	14	10
3	37	21	12	9
4		21	10	8
5		21	10	7
6			10	7
7			9	6
8			9	6
9			9	6
10			9	6
11				6
12				6
13				6
14				6
15				6

"(2) 19-year real property.

"(A) In general. In the case of 19-year real property, the applicable percentage shall be determined in accordance with a table prescribed by the Secretary. In prescribing such table, the Secretary shall

"(i) assign to the property a 19-year recovery period, and

"(ii) assign percentages generally determined in accordance with use of the 175 percent declining balance method, switching to the method described in section 167(b)(1) at a time to maximize the deduction allowable under subsection (a).

"(B) Mid-month convention for 19-year real property. In the case of a 19-year real property, the amount of the deduction determined under any provision of this section (or for purposes of section 57(a)(12)(B) or 312(k)) for any taxable year shall be determined on the basis of the number of months (using a mid-month convention) in which the property is in service.

"(3) Election of different recovery percentage.

"(A) In general. Except as provided in subsection (f)(2), in lieu of any applicable percentage under paragraph (1), (2), or (4), the taxpayer may elect, with respect to one or more classes of recovery property placed in service during the taxable year, the applicable percentage determined by use of the straight line method over the recovery period elected by the taxpayer in accordance with the following table:

"In the case of:	The taxpayer may elect a recovery period of:
3-year property	3, 5, or 12 years.
5-year property	5, 12, or 25 years.
10-year property	10, 25, or 35 years.
19-year real property	19, 35, or 45 years.
15-year public utility property	15, 35, or 45 years.
Low-income housing	15, 35, or 45 years.

"(B) Operating rules.

"(i) In general. Except as provided in clause (ii), the taxpayer may elect under subparagraph (A) only a single percentage for property in any class of recovery property placed in service during the taxable year. The percentage so elected shall apply to all property in such class placed in service during such taxable year and shall apply throughout the recovery period elected for such property.

"(ii) Real property. In the case of 19-year real property or low-income housing, the taxpayer shall make the election under subparagraph (A) on a property-by-property basis.

"(iii) Convention. Under regulations prescribed by the Secretary, the half-year convention shall apply to any election with respect to any recovery property (other than 19-year real property or low-income housing) with respect to which an election is made under this paragraph.

"(4) Low-income housing.

"(A) In general. In the case of low-income housing, the applicable percentage shall be determined in accordance with the table prescribed in paragraph (2) (without regard to the mid-month convention), except that in prescribing such table, the Secretary shall—

"(i) assign to the property a 15-year recovery period, and

"(ii) assign percentages generally determined in accordance with use of the 200 percent declining balance method, switching to the method described in section 167(b)(1) at a time to maximize the deduction allowable under subsection (a).

"(B) Monthly convention. In the case of low-income housing, the amount of the deduction determined under any provision of this section (or for purposes of section 57(a)(12)(B) or 312(k)) for any taxable year shall be determined on the basis of the number of months (treating all property placed in service or disposed of during any month as placed in service or disposed of on the first day of such month) in which the property is in service.

"(c) Recovery property.

"For purposes of this title—

"(1) Recovery property defined. Except as provided in subsection (e), the term 'recovery property' means tangible property of a character subject to the allowance for depreciation—

"(A) used in a trade or business, or

"(B) held for the production of income.

"(2) Classes of recovery property. Each item of recovery property shall be assigned to one of the following classes of property:

"(A) 3-year property. The term '3-year property' means section 1245 class property—

"(i) with a present class life of 4 years or less; or

"(ii) used in connection with research and experimentation.

"(B) 5-year property. The term '5-year property' means recovery property which is section 1245 class property and which is not 3-year property, 10-year property, or 15-year public utility property.

"(C) 10-year property. The term '10-year property' means—

"(i) public utility property (other than section 1250 class property or 3-year property) with a present class life of more than 18 years but not more than 25 years; and

"(ii) section 1250 class property with a present class life of 12.5 years or less.

"(D) 19-year real property. The term '19-year real property' means section 1250 class property which—

"(i) does not have a present class life of 12.5 years or less, and

"(ii) is not low-income housing.

"(E) 15-year public utility property. The term '15-year public utility property' means public utility property (other than section 1250 class property or 3-year property) with a present class life of more than 25 years.

"(F) Low-income housing. The term 'low-income housing' means property described in clause (i), (ii), (iii), or (iv) of section 1250(a)(1)(B).

"(G) Special rule for theme parks, etc. For purposes of subparagraphs (C) and (D), a building (and its structural components) shall not be treated as having a present class life of 12.5 years or less by reason of any use other than the use for which such building was originally placed in service.

"(d) Unadjusted basis; adjustments.

"(1) Unadjusted basis defined.

"(A) In general. For purposes of this section, the term 'unadjusted basis' means the excess of—

"(i) the basis of the property determined under part II of subchapter O of chapter 1 for purposes of determining gain (determined without regard to the adjustments described in paragraph (2) or (3) of section 1016(a)), over

"(ii) the sum of—

"(I) that portion of the basis for which the taxpayer property elects amortization (including the deduction allowed under section 167(k)) in lieu of depreciation, and

"(II) that portion of the basis which the taxpayer property elects to treat as an expense under section 179.

"(B) Time for taking basis into account.

"(i) In general. The unadjusted basis of property shall be first taken into account under subsection (b) for the taxable year in which the property is placed in service.

"(ii) Redeterminations. The Secretary shall by regulation provide for the method of determining the deduction allowable under subsection (a) for any taxable year (and succeeding taxable years) in which the basis is redetermined (including any reduction under section 1017).

"(2) Dispositions.

"(A) Mass asset accounts. In lieu of recognizing gain or loss under this chapter, a taxpayer who maintains one or more mass asset accounts of recovery property may, under regulations prescribed by the Secretary, elect to include in income all proceeds realized on the disposition of such property.

"(B) Adjustment to basis. Except as provided under regulations prescribed by the Secretary under paragraph (7) or (10) of subsection (f), if any recovery property (other than 19-year real property or low-income housing or property with respect to which an election under subparagraph (A) is made) is disposed of, the unadjusted basis of such property shall cease to be taken into account in determine any recovery deduction allowable under subsection (a) as of the beginning of the taxable year in which such disposition occurs.

"(C) Disposition includes retirement. For purposes of this subparagraph, the term 'disposition' includes retirement.

"(e) Property excluded from application of section.

"For purposes of this title

"(1) Property placed in service before January 1, 1981. The term 'recovery property' does not include property placed in service by the taxpayer before January 1, 1981.

"(2) Certain methods of depreciation. The term 'recovery property' does not include property if

"(A) the taxpayer elects to exclude such property from the application of this section, and

"(B) for the first taxable year for which a deduction would (but for this election) be allowable under this section with respect to such property in the hands of the taxpayer, the property is properly depreciated under the unit-of-production method or any method of depreciation not expressed in a term of years (other than the retirement-replacement-betterment method).

"(3) Special rule for certain public utility property.

"(A) In general. The term 'recovery property' does not include public utility property (within the meaning of section 167(l)(3)(A)) if the taxpayer does not use a normalization method of accounting.

"(B) Use of normalization method defined. For purposes of subparagraph (A), in order to use a normalization method of accounting with respect to any public utility property

"(i) the taxpayer must, in computing its tax expense for purposes of establishing its cost of service for rate-making purposes and reflecting operating results in its regulated books of account, use a method of depreciation with respect to such property that is the same as, and a depreciation period for such property that is no shorter than, the method and period used to compute its depreciation expense for such purposes; and

"(ii) if the amount allowable as a deduction under this section with respect to such property differs from the amount that would be allowable as a deduction under section 167 (determined without regard to section 167(l)) using the method (including the period, first and last year convention, and salvage value) used to compute regulated tax expense under subparagraph (B)(ii), the taxpayer must make adjustments to a reserve to reflect the deferral of taxes resulting from such difference.

"(C) Use of inconsistent estimates and projections, etc.

"(i) In general. One way in which the requirements of subparagraph (B) are not met is if the taxpayer, for ratemaking purposes, uses a procedure or adjustment which is inconsistent with the requirements of subparagraph (B).

"(ii) Use of inconsistent estimates and projections. The procedures and adjustments which are to be treated as inconsistent for purposes of clause (i) shall include any procedure or adjustment for ratemaking purposes which uses an estimate or projection of the taxpayer's tax expense, depreciation expense, or reserve for deferred taxes under subparagraph (B)(ii) unless such estimate or projection is also used, for ratemaking purposes, with respect to the other 2 such items and with respect to the rate base.

"(iii) Regulatory authority. The Secretary may by regulations prescribe procedures and adjustments (in addition to those specified in clause (ii)) which are to be treated as inconsistent for purposes of clause (i).

"(D) Public utility property which is not recovery property. In the case of public utility property which, by reason of this paragraph, is not treated as recovery property, the allowance for depreciation under section 167(a) shall be an amount computed using the method and period referred to in subparagraph (B)(i).

"(4) Certain transactions in property placed in service before 1981.

"(A) Section 1245 class property. The term 'recovery property' does not include section 1245 class property acquired by the taxpayer after December 31, 1980, if—

"(i) the property was owned or used at any time during 1980 by the taxpayer or a related person,

"(ii) the property is acquired from a person who owned such property at any time during 1980, and, as part of the transaction, the user of such property does not change,

"(iii) the taxpayer leases such property to a person (or a person related to such person) who owned or used such property at any time during 1980, or

"(iv) the property is acquired in a transaction as part of which the user of such property does not change and the property is not recovery property in the hands of the person from which the property is so acquired by reason of clause (ii) or (iii). "For purposes of this subparagraph and subparagraph (B), property shall not be treated as owned before it is placed in service. For purposes of this subparagraph, whether the user of property changes as part of a transaction shall be determined in accordance with regulations prescribed by the Secretary.

"(B) Section 1250 class property. The term 'recovery property' does not include section 1250 class property acquired by the taxpayer after December 31, 1980, if

"(i) such property was owned by the taxpayer or by a related person at any time during 1980;

"(ii) the taxpayer leases such property to a person (or a person related to such person) who owned such property at any time during 1980; or

"(iii) such property is acquired in an exchange described in section 1031, 1033, 1038, or 1039 to the extent that the basis of such property includes an amount representing the adjusted basis of other property owned by the taxpayer or a related person during 1980.

"(C) Certain nonrecognition transactions. The term 'recovery property' does not include property placed in service by the transferor or distributor before January 1, 1981, which is acquired by the taxpayer after December 31, 1980, in a transaction described in section 332, 351, 361, 371(a), 374(a), 721, or 731 (or such property acquired from the transferee or acquiring corporation in a transaction described in such section), to the extent that the basis of the property is determined by reference to the basis of the property in the hands of the transferor or distributor. In the case of property to which this subparagraph applies, rules similar to the rules described in section 381(c)(6) shall apply.

"(D) Related person defined. Except as provided in subparagraph (E), for purposes of this paragraph a person (hereinafter referred to as the related person) is related to any person if

"(i) the related person bears a relationship to such person specified in section 267(b) or section 707(b)(1), or

"(ii) the related person and such person are engaged in trades or businesses under common control (within the meaning of subsections (a) and (b) of section 52).

Deductions   Code Sec. 168

"For purposes of clause (i), in applying section 267(b) and section 707(b)(1) '10 percent' shall be substituted for '50 percent'. The determination of whether a person is related to another person shall be made as of the time the taxpayer acquires the property involved. In the case of the acquisition of property by any partnership which results from the termination of another partnership under section 708(b)(1)(B), the determination of whether the acquiring partnership is related to the other partnership shall be made immediately before the event resulting in such termination occurs.

"(E) Liquidation of subsidiary, etc. For purposes of this paragraph, a corporation is not a related person to the taxpayer

"(i) if such corporation is a distributing corporation in a transaction to which section 334(b)(2)(B) applies and the stock of such corporation referred to in such subparagraph (B) was acquired by the taxpayer by purchase after December 31, 1980, or

"(ii) if such corporation is liquidated in a liquidation to which section 331(a) applies and the taxpayer (or a related person) by himself or together with 1 or more other persons acquires the stock of the liquidated corporation by purchase (meeting the requirements of section 334(b)(2)(B)) after December 31, 1980.

"A similar rule shall apply in the case of a deemed liquidation under section 338.

"(F) Antiavoidance rule. The term 'recovery property' does not include property acquired by the taxpayer after December 31, 1980, which, under regulations prescribed by the Secretary, is acquired in a transaction one of the principal purposes of which is to avoid the principles of paragraph (1) and this paragraph.

"(G) Reduction in unadjusted basis. In the case of an acquisition of property described in subparagraph (B) or (C), the unadjusted basis of the property under subsection (d) shall be reduced to the extent that such property acquired is not recovery property.

"(H) Acquisitions by reason of death. Subparagraphs (A) and (B) shall not apply to the acquisition of any property by the taxpayer if the basis of the property in the hands of the taxpayer is determined under section 1014(a).

"(I) Section 1245 class property acquired incidental to acquisition of section 1250 class property. Under regulations prescribed by the Secretary, subparagraph (B) shall apply (and subparagraph (A) shall not apply) to section 1245 class property which is acquired incidental to the acquisition of section 1250 class property.

"(5) Films and video tapes not recovery property. The term 'recovery property' shall not include any motion picture film or video tape.

"(f) Special rules for application of this section

"For purposes of this section

"(1) Components of section 1250 class property.

"(A) In general. Except as otherwise provided in this paragraph

"(i) the deduction allowable under subsection (a) with respect to any component (which is section 1250 class property) of a building shall be computed in the same manner as the deduction allowable with respect to such building, and

"(ii) the recovery period for such component shall begin on the later of

"(I) the date such component is placed in service, or

"(II) the date on which the building is placed in service.

"(B) Transitional rules.

"(i) Buildings placed in service before 1981. In the case of any building placed in service by the taxpayer before January 1, 1981, for purposes of applying subparagraph (A) to components of such buildings placed in service after December 31, 1980, and before March 16, 1984, the deduction allowable under subsection (a) with respect to such components shall be computed in the same manner as the deduction allowable with respect to the first such component placed in service after December 31, 1980.

"(ii) Buildings placed in service before March 16, 1984. In the case of any building placed in service by the taxpayer before March 16, 1984, for purposes of applying subparagraph (A) to components of such buildings placed in service after March 15, 1984, and before May 9, 1985, the deduction allowable under subsection (a) with respect to such components shall be computed in the same manner as the deduction allowable with respect to the first such component placed in service after March 15, 1984.

"(iii) Buildings placed in service before May 9, 1985. In the case of any building placed in service by the taxpayer before May 9, 1985, for purposes of applying subparagraph (A) to components of such buildings placed in service after May 8, 1985, the deduction allowable under subsection (a) with respect to such components shall be computed in the same manner as the deduction allowable with respect to the first such component placed in service after May 8, 1985.

"(iv) First component treated as separate building. For purposes of clause (i), (ii) or (iii), the method of computing the deduction allowable with respect to the first component described in such clause shall be determined as if it were a separate building.

"(C) Exception for substantial improvements.

"(i) In general. For purposes of this paragraph, a substantial improvement shall be treated as a separate building.

"(ii) Substantial improvement. For purposes of clause (i), the term 'substantial improvement' means the improvements added to capital account with respect to any building during any 24-month period, but only if the sum of the amounts added to such account during such period equals or exceeds 25 percent of the adjusted basis of the building (determined without regard to the adjustments provided in paragraphs (2) and (3) of section 1016(a)) as of the first day of such period.

"(iii) Improvements must be made after building in service for 3 years. For purposes of this paragraph, the term 'substantial improvement' shall not include any improvement made before the date 3 years after the building was placed in service.

"(2) Recovery property used predominantly outside the United States.

"(A) In general. Except as provided in subparagraphs (B) and (C), in the case of recovery property which, during the taxable year, is used predominantly outside the United States, the recovery deduction for the taxable year shall be, in lieu of the amount determined under subsection (b), the amount determined by applying to the unadjusted basis of such property the applicable percentage determined under tables prescribed by the Secretary. For purposes of the preceding sentence, in prescribing such tables, the Secretary shall

"(i) assign the property described in this subparagraph to classes in accordance with the present class life (or 12 years in the case of personal property with no present class life) of such property; and

"(ii) assign percentages (taking into account the half-year convention) determined in accordance with use of the method of depreciation described in section 167(b)(2), switching to the method described in section 167(b)(1) at a time to maximize the deduction allowable under subsection (a).

"(B) Real property. Except as provided in subparagraph (C), in the case of 19-year real property or low-income housing which, during the taxable year, is predominantly used outside the United States, the recovery deduction for the taxable year shall be, in lieu of the amount determined under subsection (b), the amount determined by applying to the unadjusted basis of such property the applicable percentage determined under tables prescribed by the Secretary. For purposes of the preceding sentence, in prescribing such tables, the Secretary shall

"(i) assign to the property described in this subparagraph a 35-year recovery period, and

"(ii) assign percentages determined in accordance with the use of the method of depreciation described n section 167(j)(1)(B), switching to the method described in section 167(b)(1) at a time to maximize the deduction allowable under subsection (a).

"(C) Election of different recovery percentage.

"(i) General rule. The taxpayer may elect, with respect to one or more classes of recovery property described in this paragraph, to determine the applicable percentage under this paragraph by use of the straightline method over the recovery period determined in accordance with the following table:

"In the case of:	The taxpayer may elect a recovery period of:
3-year property	The present class life, 5 or 12 years.
5-year property	The present class life, 12 or 25 years.
10-year property	The present class life, 25 or 35 years.
19-year real property or low-income housing	35 or 45 years.
15-year public utility property	The present class life, 35 or 45 years.

"(ii) Operating rules.

"(I) Period elected by taxpayer. Except as provided in subclause (II), the taxpayer may elect under clause (i) for any taxable year only a single recovery period for recovery property described in this paragraph which is placed in service during such taxable year, which has the same present class life, and which is in the same class under subsection (c)(2). The period so elected shall not be shorter than such present class life.

"(II) Real property. In the case of 19-year real property or low-income housing, the election under clause (i) shall be made on a property-by-property basis.

"(D) Determination of property used predominantly outside the United States. For purposes of this paragraph, under regulations prescribed by the Secretary, rules similar to the rules under section 48(a)(2) (including the exceptions under subparagraph (B)) shall be applied in determining whether property is used predominantly outside the United States.

"(E) Convention. Under regulations prescribed by the Secretary, the half year convention shall apply for purposes of any determination under subparagraph (C) (other than any determination with respect to 19-year real property or low-income housing).

"(3) RRB replacement property.

"(A) In general. In the case of RRB replacement property placed in service before January 1, 1985, the recovery deduction for the taxable year shall be, in lieu of the amount determined under subsection (b), the amount determined by applying to the unadjusted basis of such property the applicable percentage determined under tables prescribed by the Secretary. For purposes of the preceding sentence, in prescribing such tables, the Secretary shall—

"(i) use the recovery period determined in accordance with the following table:

"If the year property is placed in service is:	The recovery period is:
1981	1
1982	2
1983	3
1984	4

"and

"(ii) assign percentages determined in accordance with use of the method of depreciation described in section 167(b)(2), switching to the method described in section 167(b)(3) at a time to maximize the deduction allowable under subsection (a) (taking into account the half-year convention).

"(B) RRB replacement property defined. For purposes of this section, the term 'RRB replacement property' means replacement track material (including rail, ties, other track material, and ballast) installed by a railroad (including a railroad switching or terminal company) if

"(i) the replacement is made pursuant to a scheduled program for replacement,

"(ii) the replacement is made pursuant to observations by maintenance-of-way personnel of specific track material needing replacement, "(iii) the replacement is made pursuant to the detection by a rail-test car of specific track material needing replacement, or

"(iv) the replacement is made as a result of a casualty.

"Replacements made as a result of a casualty shall be RRB replacement property only to the extent that, in the case of each casualty, the replacement cost with respect to the replacement track material exceeds $50,000.

"(4) Manner and time for making elections.

"(A) In general. Any election under this section shall be made for the taxable year in which the property is placed in service.

"(B) Election made on return.

"(i) In general. Except as provided in clause (ii), any election under this section shall be made on the taxpayer's return of the tax imposed by this chapter for the taxable year concerned.

"(ii) Special rule for qualified rehabilitated buildings. In the case of any qualified rehabilitated building (as defined in section 48(g)(1)), an election under subsection (b)(3) may be made at any time before the date 3 years after the building was placed in service.

"(C) Revocation only with consent. Any election under this section, once made, may be revoked only with the consent of the Secretary.

"(5) Short taxable years. In the case of a taxable year that is less than 12 months, the amount of the deduction under this section shall be an amount which bears the same relationship to the amount of the deduction, determined without regard to this paragraph, as the number of months in the short taxable year bears to 12. In such case, the amount of the deduction for subsequent taxable years shall be appropriately adjusted in accordance with regulations prescribed by the Secretary. The determination of when a taxable year begins shall be made in accordance with regulations prescribed by the Secretary. This paragraph shall not apply to any deduction with respect to any property for the first taxable year of the lessor for which an election under paragraph (8) is in effect with respect to such property. In the case of 19-year real property or low-income housing, the first sentence of this paragraph shall not apply to the taxable year in which the property is placed in service or disposed of.

"(6) Leasehold improvements. For purposes of determining whether a leasehold improvement which is recovery property shall be amortized over the term of the lease, the recovery period (taking into account any election under paragraph (2)(C) of this subsection or under subsection (b)(3) with respect to such property) of such property shall be taken into account in lieu of its useful life.

"(7) Special rule for acquisitions and dispositions in nonrecognition transactions. Notwithstanding any other provision of this section, the deduction allowed under this section in the taxable year in which recovery property is acquired or is disposed of in a transaction in which gain or loss is not recognized in whole or in part shall be determined in accordance with regulations prescribed by the Secretary.

"(8) Special rules for finance leases.

"(A) In general. For purposes of this title, except as provided in subsection (i), in the case of any agreement with respect to any finance lease property, the fact that—

"(i) a lessee has the right to purchase the property at a fixed price which is not less than 10 percent of the original cost of the property to the lessor, or

"(ii) the property is of a type not readily usable by any person other than the lessee,

shall not be taken into account in determining whether such agreement is a lease.

"(B) Finance lease property defined. For purposes of this section—

"(i) In general. The term 'finance lease property' means recovery property which is subject to an agreement which meets the requirements of subparagraph (C) and—

"(I) which is new section 38 property of the lessor, which is leased within 3 months after such property was placed in service, and which, if acquired by the lessee, would have been new section 38 property of the lessee, or

"(II) which was new section 38 property of the lessee, which is leased within 3 months after such property is placed in service by the lessee, and with respect to which the adjusted basis of the lessor does not exceed the adjusted basis of the lessee at the time of the lease.

"(ii) Only 40 percent of the lessee's property may be treated as qualified. The cost basis of all finance lease property (determined without regard to this clause)—

"(I) which is placed in service during any calendar year beginning before January 1, 1990, and

"(II) with respect to which the taxpayer is a lessee,

"shall not exceed an amount equal to 40 percent of the cost basis of the taxpayer's qualified base property placed in service during such calendar year.

"(iii) Allocation of disqualified basis. The cost basis not treated as finance lease property under clause (ii) shall be allocated to finance lease property for such calendar year (determined without regard to clause (ii)) in reverse order to when the agreement described in subparagraph (A) with respect to such property was entered into.

"(iv) Certain property may not be treated as finance lease property. The term 'finance lease property' shall not include recovery property—

"(I) which is a qualified rehabilitated building (within the meaning of section 48(g)(1)),

"(II) which is public utility property (within the meaning of section 167(l)(3)(A)),

"(III) which is property with respect to which a deduction is allowable by reason of section 291(e),

"(IV) with respect to which the lessee of the property under the agreement described in subparagraph (A) is a nonqualified tax-exempt organization, or

"(V) property with respect to which the user of such property is a person (other than a United States person) not subject to United States tax on income derived from the use of such property.

"(v) Qualified base property. For purposes of this subparagraph, the term 'qualified base property' means property placed in service during any calendar year which—

"(I) is new section 38 property of the taxpayer,

"(II) is finance lease property (not described in subclause (I)) with respect to which the taxpayer is the lessee, or

"(III) is designated leased property (other than property described in subclause (I) or (II)) with respect to which the taxpayer is the lessee.

"Any designated leased property taken into account by any lessee under the preceding sentence shall not be taken into account by the lessor in determining the lessor's qualified base property. The lessor shall provide the lessee with such information with respect to the cost basis of such property as is necessary to carry out the purposes of this clause.

"(vi) Definition of designated leased property. For purposes of this subparagraph, the term 'designated leased property' means property—

"(I) which is new section 38 property,

"(II) which is subject to a lease with respect to which the lessor of the property is treated (without regard to this paragraph) as the owner of the property for Federal tax purposes,

"(III) with respect to which the term of the lease to which such property is subject is more than 50 percent of the present class life (or, if no present class life, the recovery period under subsection (a)) of such property, and

"(IV) which the lessee designates on his return as designated leased property.

"(vii) Definition; special rules. For purposes of this subparagraph—

"(I) New section 38 property defined. The term 'new section 38 property' has the meaning given such term by section 48(b).

"(II) Lessee limitation not to apply to certain farm property. Clause (ii) shall not apply to any property which is used for farming purposes (within the meaning of section 2032A(e)(5)) and which is placed in service during the calendar year but only if the cost basis of such property, when added to the cost basis of other finance lease property used for such purpose does not exceed $150,000 (determined under rules similar to the rules of section 209(d)(1)(B) of the Tax Equity and Fiscal Responsibility Act of 1982).

"(III) Property placed in service. For purposes of this title (other than clause (i), any finance lease property shall be deemed originally placed in service not earlier than the date such property is used under the lease.

"(C) Agreements must meet certain requirements. The requirements of this subparagraph are met with respect to any agreement if—

"(i) Lessor requirement. Any lessor under the agreement must be—

"(I) a corporation (other than an S corporation or a personal holding company within the meaning of section 542(a)),

"(II) a partnership all of the partners of which are corporations described in subclause (I), or

"(III) a grantor trust with respect to which the grantor and all the beneficiaries of the trust are described in subclause (I) or (II).

"(ii) Characterization of agreement. The parties to the agreement characterize such agreement as a lease.

"(iii) Agreement contains certain provisions. The agreement contains the provision described in clause (i) or (ii) of subparagraph (A), or both.

"(iv) Agreement otherwise lease, etc. For purposes of this title (determined without regard to the provisions described in clause (iii)), the agreement would be treated as a lease and the lessor under the agreement would be treated as the owner of the property.

"(D) Paragraph not to apply to agreements between related persons. This paragraph shall not apply to any agreement if the lessor and lessee are both persons who are members of the same affiliated group (within the meaning of subsection (a) of section 1504 and determined without regard to subsection (b) of section 1504).

"(E) Nonqualified tax-exempt organization.

"(i) In general. The term 'nonqualified tax-exempt organization' means, with respect to any agreement to which subparagraph (A) applies, any organization (or predecessor organization which was engaged in substantially similar activities) which was exempt from taxation under this title at any time during the 5-year period ending on the date such agreement was entered into.

"(ii) Special rule for farmers' cooperatives. The term 'nonqualified tax-exempt organization' shall not include any farmers' cooperative organization which is described in section 521 whether or not exempt from taxation under section 521.

"(iii) Special rule for property used in unrelated trade or business. An organization shall not be treated as a nonqualified tax-exempt organization with respect to any property if such property is used in an unrelated trade or business (within the meaning of section 513) of such organization which is subject to taxation under section 511.

"(F) Cross reference. For special recapture in case where lessee acquires financed recovery property, see section 1245.

"(9) Salvage value. No salvage value shall be taken into account in determining the deduction allowable under subsection (a).

"(10) Transferee bound by transferor's period and method in certain cases.

"(A) In general. In the case of recovery property transferred in a transaction described in subparagraph (B), for purposes of computing the deduction allowable under subsection (a) with respect to so much of the basis in the hands of the transferee as does not exceed the adjusted basis in the hands of the transferor—

"(i) if the transaction is described in subparagraph (B)(i), the transferee shall be treated in the same manner as the transferor, or "(ii) if the transaction is described in clause (ii) or (iii) of subparagraph (B) and the transferor made an election with respect to such property under subsection (b)(3) or (f)(2)(C), the transferee shall be treated as having made the same election (or its equivalent).

"(B) Transfers covered. The transactions described in this subparagraph are

"(i) a transaction described in section 332, 351, 361, 371(a), 374(a), 721, or 731;

"(ii) an acquisition (other than described in clause (i)) from a related person (as defined in subparagraph (D) of subsection (e)(4)); and

"(iii) an acquisition followed by a leaseback to the person from whom the property is acquired.

Clause (i) shall not apply in the case of the termination of a partnership under section 708(b)(1)(B).

"(C) Property reacquired by the taxpayer. Under regulations prescribed by the Secretary, recovery property which is disposed of and then reacquired by the taxpayer shall be treated for purposes of computing the deduction allowable under subsection (a) as if such property had not been disposed of.

"(D) Exception. This paragraph shall not apply to any transaction to which subsection (e)(4) applies.

"(11) Special rules for cooperatives. In the case of a cooperative organization described in section 1381(a), the Secretary may by regulations provide

"(A) for allowing allocation units to make separate elections under this section with respect to recovery property, and

"(B) for the allocation of the deduction allowable under subsection (a) among allocation units.

"(12) Limitations on property financed with tax-exempt bonds.

"(A) In general. Notwithstanding any other provision of this section, to the extent that any property is financed by the proceeds of an industrial development bond (within the meaning of section 103(b)(2)) the interest of which is exempt from taxation under section 103(a), the deduction allowed under subsection (a) (and any deduction allowable in lieu of the deduction allowable under subsection (a)) for any taxable year with respect to such property shall be determined under subparagraph (B).

"(B) Recovery method.

"(i) In general. Except as provided in clause (ii), the amount of the deduction allowed with respect to property described in subparagraph (A) shall be determined by using the straight-line method (with a half-year convention and without regard to salvage value) and a recovery period determined in accordance with the following table:

"In the case of:	The recovery period is:
3-year property	3 years.
5-year property	5 years.
10-year property	10 years.
15-year public utility property	15 years.

"(ii) 19-year real property. In the case of a 19-year real property, the amount of the deduction allowed shall be determined by using the straight-line method (without regard to salvage value) and a recovery period of 19 years.

"(C) Exception for low- and moderate-income housing. Subparagraph (A) shall not apply to—

"(i) any low-income housing, and

"(ii) any other recovery property which is placed in service in connection with projects for residential rental property financed by the proceeds of obligations described in section 103(b)(4)(A).

"(D) Exception where longer recovery period applicable. Subparagraph (A) shall not apply to any recovery property if the recovery period which would be applicable to such property by reason of an election under subsection (b)(3) exceeds the recovery period for such property determined under subparagraph (B).

"(13) Changes in use. The Secretary shall, by regulation, provide for the method of determining the deduction allowable under subsection (a) with respect to any property for any taxable year (and for succeeding taxable years) during which such property changes status under this section but continues to be held by the same person.

"(14) Motor vehicle operating leases.

"(A) In general. For purposes of this title, in the case of a qualified motor vehicle operating agreement which contains a terminal rental adjustment clause—

"(i) such agreement shall be treated as a lease if (but for such terminal rental adjustment clause) such agreement would be treated as a lease under this title, and

"(ii) the lessee shall not be treated as the owner of the property subject to an agreement during any period such agreement is in effect.

"(B) Qualified motor vehicle operating agreement defined. For purposes of this paragraph—

"(i) In general. The term 'qualified motor vehicle operating agreement' means any agreement with respect to a motor vehicle (including a trailer) which meets the requirements of clauses (ii), (iii), and (iv) of this subparagraph.

"(ii) Minimum liability of lessor. An agreement meets the requirements of this clause if under such agreement the sum of—

"(I) the amount the lessor is personally liable to repay, and

"(II) the net fair market value of the lessor's interest in any property pledged as security for property subject to the agreement,

"equals or exceeds all amounts borrowed to finance the acquisition of property subject to the agreement. There shall not be taken into account under subclause (II) any property pledged which is property subject to the agreement or property directly or indirectly financed by indebtedness secured by property subject to the agreement.

"(iii) Certification by lessee; notice of tax ownership. An agreement meets the requirements of this clause if such agreement contains a separate written statement separately signed by the lessee—

"(I) under which the lessee certifies, under penalty of perjury, that it intends that more than 50 percent of the use of the property subject to such agreement is to be in a trade or business of the lessee, and

"(II) which clearly and legibly states that the lessee has been advised that it will not be treated as the owner of the property subject to the agreement for Federal income tax purposes.

"(iv) Lessor must have no knowledge that certification is false. An agreement meets the requirements of this clause if the lessor does not know that the certification described in clause (iii)(I) is false.

"(C) Terminal rental adjustment clause defined.

"(i) In general. For purposes of this paragraph, the term 'terminal rental adjustment clause' means a provision of an agreement which permits or requires the rental price to be adjusted upward or downward by reference to the amount realized by the lessor under the agreement upon sale or other disposition of such property.

"(ii) Special rule for lessee dealers. The term 'terminal rental adjustment clause' also includes a provision of an agreement which requires a lessee who is a dealer in motor vehicles to purchase the motor vehicle for a predetermined price and then resell such vehicle where such provision achieves substantially the same results as a provision described in clause (i).

"(15) Special rules for sound recordings. In the case of a sound recording (within the meaning of section 48(r)), the unadjusted basis of such property shall be equal to the production costs (within the meaning of section 48(r)(6)).

"(g) Definitions.

"For purposes of this section

"(1) Public utility property. The term 'public utility property' means property described in section 167(l)(3)(A).

"(2) Present class life. The term 'present class life' means the class life (if any) which would be applicable with respect to any property as of January 1, 1981, under subsection (m) of section 167 (determined without regard to paragraph (4) thereof and as if the taxpayer had made an election under such subsection). If any property (other than section 1250 class property) does not have a present class life within the meaning of the preceding sentence, the Secretary may prescribe a present class life for such property which reasonably reflects the anticipated useful life of such property to the industry or other group.

"(3) Section 1245 class property. The term 'section 1245 class property' means tangible property described in section 1245(a)(3) other than subparagraphs (C) and (D).

"(4) Section 1250 class property. The term 'section 1250 class property' means property described in section 1250(c) and property described in section 1245(a)(3)(C).

"(5) Research and experimentation. The term 'research and experimentation' has the same meaning as the term research or experimental has under section 174.

"(6) RRB property defined. For purposes of this section, the term 'RRB property' means property which under the taxpayer's method of depreciation before January 1, 1981, would have been depreciated using the retirement-replacement-betterment method.

"(7) Manufactured homes. The term 'manufactured home' has the same meaning as in section 603(6) of the Housing and Community Development Act of 1974, which is 1250 class property used as a dwelling unit.

"(8) Qualified coal utilization property.

"(A) Qualified coal utilization property. The term 'qualified coal utilization property' means that portion of the unadjusted basis of coal utilization property which bears the same ration (but not greater than 1) to such unadjusted basis as

"(i) the Btu's of energy produced by the powerplant or major fuel-burning installation before the conversion or replacement involving coal utilization property, bears to

"(ii) the Btu's of energy produced by such powerplant or installation after such conversion or replacement.

"(B) Coal utilization property. The term 'coal utilization property' means—

"(i) a boiler or burner

"(I) the primary fuel for which is coal (including lignite), and

"(II) which replaces an existing boiler or burner which is part of a powerplant or major fuel-burning installation and the primary fuel for which is oil or natural gas or any product thereof, and

"(ii) equipment for converting an existing boiler or burner described in clause (i)(II) to a boiler or burner the primary fuel for which will be coal.

"(C) Powerplant and major fuel-burning installation. The terms 'powerplant' and 'major fuel-burning installation' have the meanings given such terms by paragraphs (7) and (10) of section 103(a) of the Powerplant and Industrial Fuel Use Act of 1978, respectively.

"(D) Existing boiler or burner. The term 'existing boiler or burner' means a boiler or burner which was placed in service before January 1, 1981.

"(E) Replacement of existing boiler or burner. A boiler or burner shall be treated as replacing a boiler or burner if the taxpayer certifies that the boiler or burner which is to be replaced

"(i) was used during calendar year 1980 for more than 2,000 hours of full load peak use (or equivalent thereof), and

"(ii) will not be used for more than 2,000 hours of such use during any 12-month period after the boiler or burner which is to replace such boiler or burner is placed in service.

"(h) Special rules for recovery property classes.

"For purposes of this section

"(1) Certain horses. The term '3-year property' includes

Code Sec. 168 — Deductions

"(A) any race horse which is more than 2 years old at the time such horse is placed in service; or

"(B) any other horse which is more than 12 years old at such time.

"(2) Railroad tank cars. The term '10-year property' includes railroad tank cars.

"(3) Manufactured homes. The term '10-year property' includes manufactured homes.

"(4) Qualified coal utilization property. The term '10-year property' includes qualified coal utilization property which would otherwise be 15-year public utility property.

"(5) Application with other classes. Any property which is treated as included in a class or property by reason of this subsection shall not be treated as property included in any other class.

"(i) Limitations relating to leases of finance lease property.

"For purposes of this subtitle, in the case of finance lease property, the following limitations shall apply:

"(1) Lessor may not reduce tax liability by more than 50 percent.

"(A) In general. The aggregate amount allowable as deductions or credits for any taxable year which are allocable to all finance lease property with respect to which the taxpayer is the lessor may not reduce the liability for tax of the taxpayer for such taxable year (determined without regard to finance lease items) by more than 50 percent of such liability.

"(B) Carryover of amounts not allowable as deductions or credits. Any amount not allowable as a deduction or credit under subparagraph (A)—

"(i) may be carried over to any subsequent taxable year, and

"(ii) shall be treated as a deduction or credit allocable to finance lease property in such subsequent taxable year.

"(C) Allocation among deductions and credits. The Secretary shall prescribe regulations for determining the amount—

"(i) of any deduction or credit allocable to finance lease property for any taxable year to which subparagraph (A) applies, and

"(ii) of any carryover of any such deduction or credit under subparagraph (B) to any subsequent taxable year.

"(D) Liability for tax and finance lease items defined. For purposes of this paragraph—

"(i) Liability for tax defined. Except as provided in this subparagraph, the term 'liability for tax' means the tax imposed by this chapter, reduced by the sum of the credits allowable under subparts A, B, and D of part IV of subchapter A of this chapter.

"(ii) Finance lease items defined. The term 'finance lease items' means any of the following items which are properly allocable to finance lease property with respect to which the taxpayer is the lessor:

"(I) Any deduction or credit allowable under this chapter.

"(II) Any rental income received by the taxpayer from any lessee of such property.

"(iii) Certain taxes not included. The term 'tax imposed by this chapter' shall not include any tax treated as not imposed by this chapter under section 26(b)(2) (other than the tax imposed by section 56).

"(E) Certain safe harbor lease property taken into account. Under regulations prescribed by the Secretary, deductions and credits and safe harbor lease items which are allocable to safe harbor lease property to which this paragraph (as in effect for taxable years beginning in 1983) applies shall be taken into account for purposes of applying this paragraph.

"(2) Investment credit allowed only over 5-year period. In the case of any credit which would otherwise be allowable under section 38 with respect to any finance lease property for any taxable year (determined without regard to this paragraph), only 20 percent of the amount of such credit shall be allowable in such taxable year and 20 percent of such amount shall be allowable in each of the succeeding 4 taxable years.

"(3) Computation of taxable income of lessee for purposes of percentage depletion.

"(A) In general. For purposes of section 613 or 613A, the taxable income of any taxpayer who is a lessee of any financed recovery property shall be computed as if the taxpayer was the owner of such property, except that the amount of the deduction under subsection (a) of this section shall be determined after application of paragraph (2) of this subsection.

"(B) Coordination with crude oil windfall profit tax. Section 4988(b)(3)(A) shall be applied without regard to subparagraph (A).

"(4) Limitations.

"(A) Termination of certain provisions.

"(i) Paragraph (1). Paragraph (1) shall not apply to property placed in service after September 30, 1989, in taxable years beginning after such date.

"(ii) Paragraph (2). Paragraph (2) shall not apply to property placed in service after September 30, 1989.

"(B) Certain Farm Property. This subsection shall not apply to property which is used for farming purposes (within the meaning of section 2032A(e)(5)) and which is placed in service during the taxable year but only if the cost basis of such property, when added to the cost basis of other finance lease property used for such purpose, does not exceed $150,000 (determined under rules similar to the rules of section 209(d)(1)(B) of the Tax Equity and Fiscal Responsibility Act of 1982).

"(j) Property leased to governments and other tax-exempt entities.

"(1) In general. Notwithstanding any other provision of this section, the deduction allowed under subsection (a) (and any other deduction allowable for depreciation or amortization) for any taxable year with respect to tax-exempt use property shall be determined—

"(A) by using the straight-line method (without regard to salvage value), and

"(B) by using a recovery period determined under the following table:

"In the case of:	The recovery period shall be:
(I) Property not described in subclause (II) or subclause (III)	The present class life.
(II) Personal property with no present class life	12 years.
(III) 19-year real property	40 years.

"(2) Operating rules.

"(A) Recovery period must at least equal 125 percent of lease term. In the case of any tax-exempt use property, the recovery period used for purposes of paragraph (1) shall not be less than 125 percent of the lease term.

"(B) Conventions.

"(i) Property other than 19-year real property. In the case of property other than 19-year real property, the half-year convention shall apply for purposes of paragraph (1).

"(ii) Cross reference.

For other applicable conventions, see paragraphs (2)(B) and (4)(B) of subsection (b).

"(C) Exception where longer recovery period applies. Paragraph (1) shall not apply to any recovery property if the recovery period which applies to such property (without regard to this subsection) exceeds the recovery period for such property determined under this subsection.

"(D) Determination of class for real property which is not recovery property. In the case of any real property which is not recovery property, for purposes of this subsection, the determination of whether such property is 19-year real property shall be made as if such property were recovery property.

"(E) Coordination with subsection (f)(12). Paragraph (12) of subsection (f) shall not apply to any tax-exempt use property to which this subsection applies.

"(F) 19-year real property. For purposes of this subsection, the term '19-year real property' includes—

"(i) low-income housing, and

"(ii) any property which was treated as 15-year real property under this section (as in effect before the amendments made by the Tax Reform Act of 1984).

"(3) Tax-exempt use property. For purposes of this subsection—

"(A) Property other than 19-year real property. Except as otherwise provided in this subsection, the term 'tax-exempt use property' means that portion of any tangible property (other than 19-year real property) leased to a tax-exempt entity.

"(B) 19-year real property.

"(i) In general. In the case of 19-year real property, the term 'tax-exempt use property' means that portion of the property leased to a tax-exempt entity in a disqualified lease.

"(ii) Disqualified lease. For purposes of this subparagraph, the term 'disqualified lease' means any lease of the property to a tax-exempt entity, but only if—

"(I) part or all of the property was financed (directly or indirectly) by an obligation the interest on which is exempt from tax under section 103 and such entity (or a related entity) participated in such financing,

"(II) under such lease there is a fixed or determinable price purchase or sale option which involves such entity (or a related entity) or there is the equivalent of such an option,

"(III) such lease has a lease term in excess of 20 years, or

"(IV) such lease occurs after a sale (or other transfer) of the property by, or lease of the property from, such entity (or a related entity) and such property has been used by such entity (or a related entity) before such sale (or other transfer) or lease.

"(iii) 35-percent threshold test. Clause (i) shall apply to any property only if the portion of such property leased to tax-exempt entities in disqualified leases is more than 35 percent of the property.

"(iv) Treatment of improvements. For purposes of this subparagraph, improvements to a property (other than land) shall not be treated as a separate property.

"(v) Leasebacks during 1st 3 months of use not taken into account. Subclause (IV) of clause (ii) shall not apply to any property which is leased within 3 months after the date such property is first used by the tax-exempt entity (or a related entity).

"(C) Exception for short-term leases.

"(i) In general. Property shall not be treated as tax-exempt use property merely by reason of a short-term lease.

"(ii) Short-term lease. For purposes of clause (i), the term 'short-term lease' means any lease the term of which is—

"(I) less than 3 years, and

"(II) less than the greater of 1 year or 30 percent of the property's present class life.

"In the case of 19-year real property and property with no present class life, subclause (II) shall not apply.

"(D) Exception where property used in unrelated trade or business. The term 'tax-exempt use property' shall not include any portion of a property if such portion is predominantly used by the tax-exempt entity (directly or through a partnership of which such entity is a partner) in an unrelated trade or business the income of which is subject to tax under section 511. For purposes of subparagraph (B)(iii), any portion of a property so used shall not be treated as leased to a tax-exempt entity in a disqualified lease.

"(4) Tax-exempt entity.

"(A) In general. For purposes of this subsection, the term 'tax-exempt entity' means—

"(i) the United States, any State or political subdivision thereof, any possession of the United States, or any agency or instrumentality of any of the foregoing,

"(ii) an organization (other than a cooperative described in section 521) which is exempt from tax imposed by this chapter, and

1,598

Deductions Code Sec. 168

"(iii) any foreign person or entity.

"(B) Exceptions for certain property used by foreign person or entity.

"(i) Income from property subject to United States tax. Clause (iii) of subparagraph (A) shall not apply with respect to any property if more than 50 percent of the gross income for the taxable year derived by the foreign person or entity from the use of such property is—

"(I) subject to tax under this chapter, or

"(II) included under section 951 in the gross income of a United States shareholder for the taxable year with or within which ends the taxable year of the controlled foreign corporation in which such income was derived.

"For purposes of the preceding sentence, any exclusion or exemption shall not apply for purposes of determining the amount of the gross income so derived, but shall apply for purposes of determining the portion of such gross income subject to tax under this chapter.

"(ii) Movies and sound recordings. Clause (iii) of subparagraph (A) shall not apply with respect to any qualified film (as defined in section 48(k)(1)(B)) or any sound recording (as defined in section 48(r)).

"(C) Foreign person or entity. For purposes of this paragraph, the term 'foreign person or entity' means—

"(i) any foreign government, any international organization, or any agency or instrumentality of any of the foregoing, and

"(ii) any person who is not a United States person.

"Such term does not include any foreign partnership or other foreign pass-thru entity.

"(D) Treatment of certain taxable instrumentalities. For purposes of this subsection and paragraph (5) of section 48(a), a corporation shall not be treated as an instrumentality of the United States or of any State or political subdivision thereof if—

"(i) all of the activities of such corporation are subject to tax under this chapter, and

"(ii) a majority of the board of directors of such corporation is not selected by the United States or any State or political subdivision thereof.

"(E) Certain previously tax-exempt organizations.

"(i) In general. For purposes of this subsection and paragraph (4) of section 48(a), an organization shall be treated as an organization described in subparagraph (A)(ii) with respect to any property (other than property held by such organization) if such organization was an organization (other than a cooperative described in section 521) exempt from tax imposed by this chapter at any time during the 5-year period ending on the date such property was first used by such organization. The preceding sentence and subparagraph (D)(ii) shall not apply to the Federal Home Loan Mortgage Corporation.

"(ii) Election not to have clause (i) apply.

"(I) In general. In the case of an organization formerly exempt from tax under section 501(a) as an organization described in section 501(c)(12), clause (i) shall not apply to such organization with respect to any property if such organization elects not to be exempt from tax under section 501(a) during the tax-exempt use period with respect to such property.

"(II) Tax-exempt use period. For purposes of subclause (I), the term 'tax-exempt use period' means the period beginning with the taxable year in which the property described in subclause (I) is first used by the organization and ending with the close of the 15th taxable year following the last taxable year of the recovery period of such property.

"(III) Election. Any election under subclause (I), once made, shall be irrevocable.

"(iii) Treatment of successor organizations. Any organization which is engaged in activities substantially similar to those engaged in by a predecessor organization shall succeed to the treatment under this subparagraph of such predecessor organization.

"(iv) First used. For purposes of this subparagraph, property shall be treated as first used by the organization—

"(I) when the property is first placed in service under a lease to such organization, or

"(II) in the case of property leased to (or held by) a partnership (or other pass-thru entity) in which the organization is a member, the later of when such property is first used by such organization is first a member of such partnership or pass-thru entity.

"(5) Special rules for certain high technology equipment.

"(A) Exemption where lease term is 5 years or less. For purposes of this subsection, the term 'tax-exempt use property' shall not include any qualified technological equipment if the lease to the tax-exempt entity has a lease term of 5 years or less.

"(B) Recovery period where lease term is greater than 5 years. In the case of any qualified technological equipment not described in subparagraph (A) and which is not property to which subsection (f)(2) applies, the recovery period used for purposes of paragraph (1) shall be 5 years.

"(C) Qualified technological equipment. For purposes of this paragraph—

"(i) In general. Except as otherwise provided in this paragraph, the term 'qualified technological equipment' means—

"(I) any computer or peripheral equipment,

"(II) any high technology telephone station equipment installed on the customer's premises, and

"(III) any high technology medical equipment,

"(ii) Exception for certain property. The term 'qualified technological equipment' shall not include any property leased to a tax-exempt entity if—

"(I) part or all of the property was financed (directly or indirectly) by an obligation the interest on which is exempt from tax under section 103,

"(II) such lease occurs after a sale (or other transfer) of the property by, or lease of such property from, such entity (or related entity) and such property has been used by such entity (or a related entity) before such sale (or other transfer) or lease, or

"(III) such tax-exempt entity is the United States or any agency or instrumentality of the United States.

"(iii) Leasebacks during 1st 3 months of use not taken into account. Subclause (II) of clause (ii) shall not apply to any property which is leased within 3 months after the date such property is first used by the tax-exempt entity (or a related entity).

"(D) Computer or peripheral equipment defined. For purposes of this paragraph—

"(i) In general. The term 'computer or peripheral equipment' means

"(I) any computer, and

"(II) any related peripheral equipment.

"(ii) Computer. The term 'computer' means a programmable electronically activated device which

"(I) is capable of accepting information, applying prescribed processes to the information, and supplying the results of these processes with or without human intervention, and

"(II) consists of a central processing unit containing extensive storage, logic, arithmetic, and control capabilities.

"(iii) Related peripheral equipment. The term 'related peripheral equipment' means any auxiliary machine (whether on-line or off-line) which is designed to be placed under the control of the central processing unit of a computer.

"(iv) Exceptions. The term 'computer or peripheral equipment' shall not include—

"(I) any equipment which is an integral part of other property which is not a computer,

"(II) typewriters, calculators, adding and accounting machines, copiers, duplicating equipment, and similar equipment, and

"(III) equipment of a kind used primarily for amusement or entertainment of the user.

"(E) High technology medical equipment. For purposes of this paragraph, the term 'high technology medical equipment' means any electronic, electromechanical, or computer-based high technology equipment used in the screening, monitoring, observation, diagnosis, or treatment of patients in a laboratory, medical, or hospital environment.

"(6) Other special rules. For purposes of this subsection

"(A) Lease. The term 'lease' includes any grant of a right to use property.

"(B) Lease term. In determining a lease term—

"(i) there shall be taken into account options to renew, and

"(ii) 2 or more successive leases which are part of the same transaction (or a series of related transactions) with respect to the same or substantially similar property shall be treated as 1 lease.

"(C) Special rule for fair rental options on 19-year real property. For purposes of clause (i) of subparagraph (B), in the case of 19-year real property, there shall not be taken into account any option to renew at fair market value, determined at the time of renewal.

"(7) Related entities. For purposes of this subsection—

"(A)(i) Each governmental unit and each agency or instrumentality of a governmental unit is related to each other such unit, agency, or instrumentality which directly or indirectly derives its powers, rights, and duties in whole or in part from the same sovereign authority.

"(ii) For purposes of clause (i), the United States, each State, and each possession of the United States shall be treated as a separate sovereign authority.

"(B) Any entity not described in subparagraph (A)(i) is related to any other entity if the 2 entities have—

"(i) significant common purposes and substantial common membership, or

"(ii) directly or indirectly substantial common direction or control.

"(C)(i) An entity is related to another entity if either entity owns (directly or through 1 or more entities) a 50 percent or greater interest in the capital or profits of the other entity.

"(ii) For purposes of clause (i), entities treated as related under subparagraph (A) or (B) shall be treated as 1 entity.

"(D) An entity is related to another entity with respect to a transaction if such transaction is part of an attempt by such entities to avoid the application of this subsection, section 46(e), paragraph (4) or (5) of section 48(a), or clause (vi) of section 48(g)(2)(B).

"(8) Tax-exempt use of property leased to partnerships, etc., determined at partner level. For purposes of this subsection—

"(A) In general. In the case of any property which is leased to a partnership, the determination of whether any portion of such property is tax-exempt use property shall be made by treating each tax-exempt entity partner's proportionate share (determined under paragraph (9)(C)) of such property as being leased to such partner.

"(B) Other pass-thru entities; tiered entities. Rules similar to the rules of subparagraph (A) shall also apply in the case of any pass-thru entity other than a partnership and in the case of tiered partnerships and other entities.

"(C) Presumption with respect to foreign entities. Unless it is otherwise established to the satisfaction of the Secretary, it shall be presumed that the partners of a foreign partnership (and the beneficiaries of any other foreign pass-thru entity) are persons who are not United States persons.

"(9) Treatment of property owned by partnerships, etc.

"(A) In general. For purposes of this subsection, if—

"(i) any property which (but for this subparagraph) is not tax-exempt use property is owned by a partnership which has both a tax-exempt entity and a person who is not a tax-exempt entity as partners, and

"(ii) any allocation to the tax-exempt entity of partnership items is not a qualified allocation,

"an amount equal to such tax-exempt entity's proportionate share of such property shall (except as provided in paragraph (3)(D)) be treated as tax-exempt use property.

"(B) Qualified allocation. For purposes of subparagraph (A), the term 'qualified allocation' means any allocation to a tax-exempt entity which—

"(i) is consistent with such entity's being allocated the same distributive share of each item of income, gain, loss, deduction, credit, and basis and such share remains the same during the entire period the entity is a partner in the partnership, and

"(ii) has substantial economic effect within the meaning of section 704(b)(2).

"For purposes of this subparagraph, items allocated under section 704(c) shall not be taken into account.

"(C) Determination of proportionate share.

"(i) In general. For purposes of subparagraph (A), a tax-exempt entity's proportionate share of any property owned by a partnership shall be determined on the basis of such entity's share of partnership items of income or gain (excluding gain allocated under section 704(c)), whichever results in the largest proportionate share.

"(ii) Determination where allocations vary. For purposes of clause (i), if a tax-exempt entity's share of partnership items of income or gain (excluding gain allocated under section 704(c)) may vary during the period such entity is a partner in the partnership, such share shall be the highest share such entity may receive.

"(D) Determination of whether property used in unrelated trade or business. For purposes of this subsection, in the case of any property which is owned by a partnership which has both a tax-exempt entity and a person who is not a tax-exempt entity as partners, the determination of whether such property is used in an unrelated trade or business of such an entity shall be made without regard to section 514.

"(E) Other pass-thru entities; tiered entities. Rules similar to the rules of subparagraphs (A), (B), (C), and (D) shall also apply in the case of any pass-thru entity other than a partnership and in the case of tiered partnerships and other entities.

"(F) Treatment of certain taxable entities.

"(i) In general. For purposes of this paragraph and paragraph (8) except as otherwise provided in this subparagraph, any tax-exempt controlled entity shall be treated as a tax-exempt entity.

"(ii) Election. If a tax-exempt controlled entity makes an election under this clause—

"(I) such entity shall not be treated as a tax-exempt entity for purposes of this paragraph and paragraph (8) and

"(II) any gain recognized by a tax-exempt entity on any disposition of an interest in such entity (and any dividend or interest received or accrued by a tax-exempt entity from such tax-exempt controlled entity) shall be treated as unrelated business taxable income for purposes of section 511.

Any such election shall be irrevocable and shall bind all tax exempt entities holding interests in such tax-exempt controlled entity. For purposes of subclause (II), there shall only be taken into account dividends which are properly allocable to income of the tax-exempt controlled entity which was not subject to tax under this chapter.

"(iii) Tax-exempt controlled entity.

"(I) In general. The term 'tax-exempt controlled entity' means any corporation (which is not a tax-exempt entity determined without regard to this subparagraph and paragraph (4)(E)) if 50 percent or more (in value) of the stock in such corporation is held by 1 or more tax-exempt entities (other than a foreign person or entity).

"(II) Only 5-Percent shareholders taken into account in case of publicly traded stock. For purposes of subclause (I), in the case of a corporation the stock of which is publicly traded on an established securities market, stock held by a tax-exempt entity shall not be taken into account unless such entity holds at least 5 percent (in value) of the stock in such corporation. For purposes of this subclause, related entities (within the meaning of paragraph (7)) shall be treated as 1 entity.

"(III) Section 318 to apply. For purposes of this clause, a tax-exempt entity shall be treated as holding stock which it holds through application of section 318 (determined without regard to the 50-percent limitation contained in subsection (a)(2)(C) thereof)."

"(G) Regulations. For purposes of determining whether there is a qualified allocation under subparagraph (B), the regulations prescribed under paragraph (10) for purposes of this paragraph—

"(i) shall set forth the proper treatment for partnership guaranteed payments, and

"(ii) may provide for the exclusion or segregation of items.

"(10) Regulations. The Secretary shall prescribe such regulations as may be necessary or appropriate to carry out the purposes of this subsection.

"(k) Cross reference.

"For special rules with respect to certain gain derived from disposition of recovery property, see sections 1245 and 1250."

—P.L. 99-514, Sec. 1801(a)(1), amended Sec. 12(c)(1) of P.L. 98-369 [reproduced below], part of the transitional rules for changes made by Sec. 12 of P.L. 98-369, by adding rules for changes made by Sec. 12 of P.L. 98-369, by adding the last (flush) sentence.

—P.L. 99-514, Sec. 1802(a)(1), added the last sentence to subpara. (j)(3)(D) [before amendment by Sec. 201(a) of this Act, see above]... Sec. 1802(a)(2)(A)(i), and (ii), substituted "any property (other than property held by such organization)" for "any property of which such organization is the lessee" and "first used by" for "first leased to", respectively, in clause (j)(4)(E)(i) [before amendment by Sec. 201(a) of this Act]... Sec. 1802(a)(2)(B), deleted "of which such organization is the lessee" after "with respect to any property" in subclause (j)(4)(E)(ii)(I) [before amendment by Sec. 201(a) of this Act]... Sec. 1802(a)(2)(C), substituted "is first used by the organization" for "is placed in service under the lease" in subclause (j)(4)(E)(ii)(II) [before amendment by Sec. 201(a) of this Act]... Sec. 1802(a)(2)(D), added clause (j)(4)(E)(iv) [before amendment by Sec. 201(a) of this Act], effective for property placed in service by the taxpayer after 5/23/83, in tax. yrs. end. after 5/23/83, and for property placed in service by the taxpayer on or before 5/23/83, if the lease to the tax-exempt entity is entered into after 5/23/83. Exceptions and special rules are provided by Sec. 31(g)(2)–(20) of P.L. 98-369, reproduced below.

—P.L. 99-514, Sec. 1802(a)(2)(E)(i), redesignated subpara. (j)(9)(E) as (j)(9)(F) and added new subpara. (j)(9)(E) [before redesignation by Sec. 1802(a)(7)(A) of this Act, see below; and before amendment by Sec. 201(a) of this Act, see above], effective for property placed in service after 9/27/85; except in the case of any property acquired pursuant to a binding written contract in effect on 9/27/85 (and at all times thereafter). Sec. 1802(a)(2)(E)(ii)(II) of this Act provides:

"(II) If an election under this subclause is made with respect to any property, the amendment made by [Sec. 1802(a)(2)(E)(i)] shall apply to such property whether or not placed in service on or before September 27, 1985."

—P.L. 99-514, Sec. 1802(a)(2)(F), amended Sec. 31(g)(16)(C)(i)(I) of P.L. 98-369 [reproduced below], as part of the special rules relating to changes made by Sec. 31 of P.L. 98-369, by substituting "section 168(j)(4)(E)(i)" for "section 168(j)(4)(E)(i)(I)".

—P.L. 99-514, Sec. 1802(a)(2)(G), substituted "preceding sentence and subparagraph (D)(ii)" for "preceding sentence" in clause (j)(4)(E)(i) [before amendment by Sec. 201(a) of this Act, see above]... Sec. 1802(a)(3), deleted clause (j)(5)(C)(iv) [before amendment by Sec. 201(a) of this Act]... Sec. 1802(a)(4)(A), deleted "and paragraphs (4) and (5) of section 48(a)" after "For purposes of this subsection" in the first sentence of para. (j)(8) [before amendment by Sec. 201(a) of this Act]... Sec. 1802(a)(4)(B)(i), deleted "and paragraphs (4) and (5) of section 48(a)" after "For purposes of this subsection" in subpara. (j)(9)(A) [before amendment by Sec. 201(a) of this Act]... Sec. 1802(a)(4)(B)(ii), substituted "loss, deduction" for "loss deduction" in clause (j)(9)(B)(i) [before amendment by Sec. 201(a) of this Act]... Sec. 1802(a)(7)(A), redesignated subparas. (j)(9)(D)–(F) (as so designated after the amendment made by Sec. 1802(a)(2)(E)(i) of this Act, above) as (j)(9)(E)–(G), and added new subpara. (j)(9)(D) [before amendment by Sec. 201(a) of this Act, see above]... Sec. 1802(a)(7)(B), substituted "(C), and (D)" for "and (C)" in subpara. (j)(9)(E) [as redesignated above; before amendment by Sec. 201(a) of this Act], effective for property placed in service by the taxpayer after 5/23/83, in tax. yrs. end. after 5/23/83, and for property placed in service by the taxpayer on or before 5/23/83, if the lease to the tax-exempt entity is entered into after 5/23/83. Exceptions and special rules are provided by Sec. 31(g)(2)–(20) of P.L. 98-369, reproduced below.

Prior to deletion, clause (j)(5)(c)(iv) read as follows:

"(iv) Property not subject to rapid obsolescence may be excluded. The term 'qualified technological equipment' shall not include any equipment described in subclause (II) or (III) of clause (i)—

"(I) which the Secretary determines by regulations is not subject to rapid obsolescence, and

"(II) which is placed in service after the date on which final regulations implementing such determination are published in the Federal Register."

—P.L. 99-514, Sec. 1802(a)(10)(A), amended Sec. 31(g)(3)(B) of P.L. 98-369 [reproduced below], effective date provisions for the changes made by Sec. 31 of P.L. 98-369, by substituting "Paragraph (9) of section 168(j) of the Internal Revenue Code of 1954 (as added by this section)" for "The amendments made by this section".

—P.L. 99-514, Sec. 1802(a)(10)(B), amended Sec. 31(g)(15)(D)(ii) of P.L. 98-369 [reproduced below], effective date provisions for the changes made by Sec. 31 of P.L. 98-369, with respect to property placed in service by the taxpayer after 7/18/84.

Prior to amendment, Sec. 31(g)(15)(D)(ii) read as follows:

"(ii) such aircraft is placed in service before January 1, 1986."

—P.L. 99-514, Sec. 1802(a)(10)(C), amended Sec. 31(g)(4) of P.L. 98-369 [reproduced below], effective date provisions for the changes made by Sec. 31 of P.L. 98-369, by adding subpara. (C)... Sec. 1802(a)(10)(D)(i), amended Sec. 31(g)(20)(B)(ii) of P.L. 98-369 [reproduced below] by deleting subclauses (I) and (II) and adding new subclauses (I)–(III). Sec. 1802(a)(10)(D)(ii) of P.L. 99-514 provides:

"(ii) The amendment made by [Sec. 1802(a)(10)(D)(i)] shall not apply to any property if—

"(I) on or before March 28, 1985, the taxpayer (or a predecessor in interest under the contract) or the tax-exempt entity entered into a written binding contract to acquire, construct, or rehabilitate the property, or

"(II) the taxpayer or the tax-exempt entity began the construction, reconstruction, or rehabilitation of the property on or before March 28, 1985."

Prior to amendment, clauses (I) and (II) of Sec. 31(g)(20)(B)(ii) of P.L. 98-369 read as follows:

"(I) by substituting '20 percent' for '25 percent' in clause (ii) thereof, and

"(II) without regard to clause (iii) thereof."

—P.L. 99-514, Sec. 1802(a)(10)(E), amended Sec. 31(g)(4) of P.L. 98-369 [reproduced below], effective date provisions for the changes made by Sec. 31 of P.L. 98-369, by adding subparas. (D) and (E)... Sec. 1802(a)(10)(F), amended Sec. 31(g)(17)(H) of P.L. 98-369 [reproduced below] by adding the last (flush)

Deductions
Code Sec. 168

sentence... Sec. 1802(a)(10)(G), amended Sec. 31(g)(17)(L) of P.L. 98-369 [reproduced below] by adding the last (flush) sentence.

—P.L. 99-514, Sec. 1802(b)(1), redesignated paras. (f)(13) and (f)(14) [concerning motor vehicle operating leases and special rules for sound recordings, respectively] as paras. (f)(14) and (f)(15), effective for agreements described in para. (f)(14) (as so redesignated) entered into more than 90 days after 7/18/84.

—P.L. 99-514, Sec. 1809(a)(1), deleted "and low-income housing" after "19-year real property" and added the item relating to low-income housing in the table contained in subpara. (b)(3)(A) [before amendment by Sec. 201(a) of this Act, see above]... Sec. 1809(a)(2)(A)(i)(I), deleted the last sentence of subpara. (b)(2)(A) [before amendment by Sec. 201(a) of this Act]... Sec. 1809(a)(2)(A)(i)(II), amended subpara. (b)(2)(B) [before amendment by Sec. 201(a) of this Act]... Sec. 1809(a)(2)(A)(ii), amended subpara. (f)(2)(B) [before amendment by Sec. 201(a) of this Act]... Sec. 1809(a)(2)(A)(ii), amended subpara. (f)(2)(B) [before amendment by Sec. 201(a) of this Act]... Sec. 1809(a)(2)(B), amended subpara. (b)(4)(B) [before amendment by Sec. 201(a) of this Act], effective for property placed in service by the taxpayer after 3/15/84, with exceptions and special rules provided by Sec. 111(g)(2)–(4) of P.L. 98-369, reproduced below.

Prior to deletion, the last sentence of subpara. (b)(2)(A) read as follows:

"In the case of the 19-year real property, the applicable percentage in the taxable year in which the property is placed in service shall be determined on the basis of the number of months (using a mid-month convention) in such year during which the property was in service."

Prior to amendment, subpara. (b)(2)(B) read as follows:

"(B) Special rule for year of disposition. In the case of a disposition of 19-year real property, the deduction allowable under subsection (a) for the taxable year in which the disposition occurs shall reflect only the months (using a mid-month convention) during such year the property was in service."

Prior to amendment, subpara. (f)(2)(B) read as follows:

"(B) Real property.

"(i) In general. Except as provided in subparagraph (C), in the case of 19-year real property or low-income housing which, during the taxable year, is predominantly used outside the United States, the recovery deduction for the taxable year shall be, in lieu of the amount determined under subsection (b), the amount determined by applying to the unadjusted basis of such property the applicable percentage determined under tables prescribed by the Secretary. For purposes of the preceding sentence in prescribing such tables, the Secretary shall

"(I) assign to the property described in this subparagraph a 35-year recovery period; and

"(II) assign percentages (taking into account the next to the last sentence of subsection (b)(2)(A)) determined in accordance with use of the method of depreciation described in section 167(j)(1)(B), switching to the method described in section 167(b)(1) at a time to maximize the deduction allowable under subsection (a).

"(ii) Special rule for disposition. In the case of a disposition of a 19-year real property or low-income housing described in clause (i) subsection (b)(2)(B) shall apply."

Prior to amendment, subpara. (b)(4)(B) read as follows:

"(B) Special rule for year of disposition. In the case of a disposition of low-income housing, the deduction allowable under subsection (a) for the taxable year in which the disposition occurs shall reflect only the months during such year the property was placed in service."

—P.L. 99-514, Sec. 1809(a)(2)(C)(i), amended clause (j)(2)(B)(ii) [before amendment by Sec. 201(a) of this Act, see above], effective on and after 10/22/86.

Prior to amendment, clause (j)(2)(B)(ii) read as follows:

"(ii) 19-year real property. In the case of 19-year real property, the amount determined under paragraph (1) shall be determined on the basis of the number of months (using a mid-month, convention) in the year in which the property is in service."

—P.L. 99-514, Sec. 1809(a)(4)(A), amended clause (f)(12)(B)(ii) [before amendment by Sec. 201(a) of this Act, see above]... Sec. 1809(a)(4)(B), amended subpara. (f)(12)(C) [before amendment by Sec. 201(a) of this Act], effective for property placed in service by the taxpayer after 3/15/84, with exceptions and special rules provided by Sec. 111(g)(2)–(4) of P.L. 98-369, reproduced below.

Prior to amendment, clause (f)(12)(B)(ii) read as follows:

"(ii) 19-year real property. In the case of a 19-year real property, the amount of the deduction allowed shall be determined by using the straight-line method (determined on the basis of the number of months in the year in which such property was in service and without regard to salvage value) and a recovery period of 19 years."

Prior to amendment, para. (f)(12)(C) read as follows:

"(C) Exception for projects for residential rental property. Subparagraph (A) shall not apply to any recovery property which is placed in service in connection with projects for residential rental property financed by the proceeds of obligations described in section 103(b)(4)(A)."

—P.L. 99-514, Sec. 1809(a)(4)(C), provides:

"(C) Any property described in paragraph (3) of section 631(d) of the Tax Reform Act of 1984 shall be treated as property described in clause (ii) of section 168(f)(12)(C) of the Internal Revenue Code of 1954 as amended by subparagraph (B)."

—P.L. 99-514, Sec. 1809(a)(5), provides:

"(5) Coordination with imputed interest changes. — In the case of any property placed in service before May 9, 1985 (or treated as placed in service before such date by Sec. 105(b)(3) of P.L. 99-121)—

"(A) any reference in any amendment made by this subsection to 19-year real property shall be treated as a reference to 18-year real property, and

"(B) section 168(f)(12)(B)(ii) of the Internal Revenue Code of 1954 (as amended by paragraph (4)(A)) shall be applied by substituting '18 years' for '19 years'."

—P.L. 99-514, Sec. 1809(b)(1), amended subpara. (f)(10)(A) before amendment by Sec. 201(a) of this Act, see above... Sec. 1809(b)(2), added the last (flush) sentence to para. (f)(10)(B) [before amendment by Sec. 201(a) of this Act], effective for property placed in service by the transferee after 12/31/85, in tax. yrs. end. after 12/31/85.

Prior to amendment, subpara. (f)(10)(A) read as follows:

"(A) In general. In the case of recovery property transferred in a transaction described in subpara (B), the transferee shall be treated as the transferor for purposes of computing the deduction allowable under subsection (a) with respect to so much of the basis in the hands of the transferee as does not exceed the adjusted basis in the hands of the transferor."

—P.L. 99-509, Sec. 8071, amended Sec. 204(a) of P.L. 99-514 [reproduced above], transitional rules relating to the changes made by Sec. 201(a) of P.L. 99-514, by adding para. (40) [sic (34)].

In 1985, P.L. 99-121, Sec. 103(a), substituted "19-year recovery period" for "18-year recovery period" in clause (b)(2)(A)(i)... Sec. 103(b)(1)(A), substituted "19-year real property" for "18-year real property" each place it appeared in the text and headings of Code Sec. 168... Sec. 103(b)(2), substituted "19, 35, or 45 years" for "18, 35, or 45 years" in the table in subpara. (b)(3)(A)... Sec. 103(b)(3)(A), redesignated clause (f)(1)(B)(iii) as clause (f)(1)(B)(iv) and added new clause (f)(1)(B)(iii)... Sec. 103(b)(3)(B), substituted "March 15, 1984, and before May, 9, 1985, the" for "March 15, 1984, the" in clause (f)(1)(B)(ii)... Sec. 103(b)(3)(C), substituted ", (ii), or (iii)" for "or (ii)" in clause (f)(1)(B)(iv) (as redesignated)... Sec. 103(b)(4), substituted "19-year real property" for "15-year real property" and substituted "19 years" for "15 years" in the text and heading of clause (f)(12)(B)(ii), effective for property placed in service by the taxpayer after 5/8/85, except as provided in Sec. 105(b)(2) and (3) of this Act which reads as follows:

"(2) Exception.—The amendments made by section 103 shall not apply to property placed in service by the taxpayer before January 1, 1987, if—

"(A) the taxpayer or a qualified person entered into a binding contract to purchase or construct such property before May 9, 1985, or

"(B) construction of such property was commenced by or for the taxpayer or a qualified person before May 9, 1985.

For purposes of this paragraph, the term 'qualified person' means any person whose rights in such a contract or such property are transferred to the taxpayer, but only if such property is not placed in service before such rights are transferred to the taxpayer.

"(3) Special rule for components.—For purposes of applying section 168(f)(1)(B) of the Internal Revenue Code of 1954 (as amended by section 103 [of this Act]) to components placed in service after December 31, 1986, property to which paragraph (2) of this subsection applies shall be treated as placed in service by the taxpayer before May 9, 1985."

In 1984, P.L. 98-369, Sec. 12(a)(1), amended Sec. 209(d)(1)(A) of P.L. 97-248, the effective date for changes made by Sec. 209(a) of P.L. 97-248, by substituting "December 31, 1987" for "December 31, 1983", see below.

—P.L. 98-369, Sec. 12(a)(2), amended Sec. 209(d)(1)(B)(i) of P.L. 97-248 by substituting "January 1, 1988" for "January 1, 1984", reproduced below.

—P.L. 98-369, Sec. 12(a)(3)(A), substituted "1990" for "1986" in subclause (f)(8)(B)(ii)(I), as amended by Sec. 209 of P.L. 97-248.... Sec. 12(a)(3)(B), substituted "1989" for "1985" each place it appeared in para. (i)(4), as amended by Sec. 209 of P.L. 97-248, effective for tax. yrs. end. after 12/31/83. Sec. 12(c) of the Act [as amended by Sec. 1002(d)(7)(B) of P.L. 100-647 and Sec. 1801(a)(1) of P.L. 99-514, see above] provides:

"(c) Transitional rules.

"(1) In general.—The amendments made by subsection (a) shall not apply with respect to any property if—

"(A) a binding contract to acquire or to construct such property was entered into by or for the lessee before March 7, 1984, or

"(B) such property was acquired by the lessee, or the construction of such property was begun, by or for the lessee, before March 7, 1984.

"The preceding sentence shall not apply to any property with respect to which an election is made under this sentence at such time after the date of the enactment of the Tax Reform Act of 1986 as the Secretary of the Treasury or his delegate may prescribe.

"(2) Special rule for certain automotive property.—

"(A) In general. — The amendments made by subsection (a) shall not apply to property.—

"(i) which is automotive manufacturing property, and

"(ii) with respect to which the lessee is a qualified lessee (within the meaning of section 208(d)(6) of the Tax Equity and Fiscal Responsibility Act of 1982).

"(B) $150,000,000 limitation. — The provisions of subparagraph (A) shall not apply to any agreement if the sum of—

"(i) the cost basis of the property subject to the agreement, plus

"(ii) the cost basis of any property subject to an agreement to which subparagraph (A) previously applied and with respect to which the lessee was the lessee under the agreement described in clause (i) (or any related person within the meaning of section 168(e)(4)(D) of the Internal Revenue Code of 1954), exceeds $150,000,000.

"(C) Automotive manufacturing property. — For purposes of this paragraph, the term 'automotive manufacturing property' means—

"(i) property used principally by the taxpayer directly in connection with the trade or business of the taxpayer of the manufacturing of automobiles or trucks (other than truck tractors) with a gross vehicle weight of 13,000 pounds or less, "(ii) machinery, equipment, and special tools of the type included in former depreciation range guideline classes 37.11 and 37.12, and

"(iii) any special tools owned by the taxpayer which are used by a vendor solely for the production of component parts for sale to the taxpayer.

"(3) Special rule for certain cogeneration facilities.—The amendments made by subsection (a) shall not apply with respect to any property which is part of a coal-fired cogeneration facility—

"(A) for which an application for certification was filed with the Federal Energy Regulatory Commission on December 30, 1983,

"(B) for which an application for a construction permit was filed with a State environmental protection agency on February 20, 1984, and

"(C) which is placed in service before January 1, 1988."

—P.L. 98-369, Sec. 12(b), provides:

"(b) Termination of safe harbor leasing rules. Paragraph (8) of section 168(f) of the Internal Revenue Code of 1954 (relating to special rules for leasing), as in effect after the amendments made by section 208 of the Tax Equity and Fiscal Responsibility Act of 1982 but before the amendments made by section 209 of this Act, shall not apply to agreements entered into after December 31, 1983. The preceding sentence shall not apply to property described in paragraph (3)(G) or (5) of section 208(d) of such Act."

—P.L. 98-369, Sec. 31(a), redesignated subsec. (j) as (k) and added new subsec. (j)... Sec. 31(d), added the last sentence to para. (g)(2), effective for property placed in service by the taxpayer after 5/23/83, in tax. yrs. end. after 5/23/83, and for property placed in service by the taxpayer on or before 5/23/83, if the lease to the tax-exempt entity is entered into after 5/23/83. Sec. 31(g)(2)-(20) of this Act [as amended by Sec. 1018(b)(1) of P.L. 100-647, Sec. 1802(a)(2)(F) of P.L. 99-514 and Sec. 1802(a)(10)(A)-(G), see above] provides:

"(2) Leases entered into on or before May 23, 1983.—The amendments made by this section shall not apply with respect to any property leased to a tax-exempt entity if the property is leased pursuant to—

"(A) a lease entered into on or before May 23, 1983 (or a sublease under such a lease), or

"(B) any renewal or extension of a lease entered into on or before May 23, 1983, if such renewal or extension is pursuant to an option exercisable by the tax-exempt entity which was held by the tax-exempt entity on May 23, 1983.

"(3) Binding contracts, etc.—

"(A) The amendments made by this section shall not apply with respect to any property leased to a tax-exempt entity if such lease is pursuant to 1 or more written binding contracts which, on May 23, 1983, and at all times thereafter, required—

"(i) the taxpayer (or his predecessor in interest under the contract) to acquire, construct, reconstruct, or rehabilitate such property, and

"(ii) the tax-exempt entity (or a tax-exempt predecessor thereof) to be the lessee of such property.

"(B) Paragraph (9) of section 168(j) of the Internal Revenue Code of 1954 (as added by this section) shall not apply with respect to any property owned by a partnership if—

"(i) such property was acquired by such partnership on or before October 21, 1983, or

"(ii) such partnership entered into a written binding contract which, on October 21, 1983, and at all times thereafter, required the partnership to acquire or construct such property.

"(C) The amendments made by this section shall not apply with respect to any property leased to a tax-exempt entity (other than any foreign person or entity)—

"(i) if—

"(I) on or before May 23, 1983, the taxpayer (or his predecessor in interest under the contract) or the tax-exempt entity entered into a written binding contract to acquire, construct, reconstruct, or rehabilitate such property and such property had not previously been used by the tax-exempt entity, or

"(II) the taxpayer or the tax-exempt entity acquired the property after June 30, 1982, and on or before May 23, 1983, or completed the construction, reconstruction, or rehabilitation of the property after December 31, 1982, and on or before May 23, 1983, and

"(ii) if such lease is pursuant to a written binding contract entered into before January 1, 1985, which requires the tax-exempt entity to be the lessee of such property.

"(4) Official governmental action on or before November 1, 1983.—

"(A) In general.—The amendments made by this section shall not apply with respect to any property leased to a tax-exempt entity (other than the United States, any agency or instrumentality thereof, or any foreign person or entity) if—

"(i) on or before November 1, 1983, there was significant official governmental action with respect to the project or its design, and

"(ii) the lease to the tax-exempt entity is pursuant to a written binding contract entered into before January 1, 1985, which requires the tax-exempt entity to be the lessee of the property.

"(B) Significant official governmental action.—For purposes of subparagraph (A), the term 'significant official governmental action' does not include granting of permits, zoning changes, environmental impact statements, or similar governmental actions.

"(C) Special rule for credit unions.—In the case of any property leased to a credit union pursuant to a written binding contract with an expiration date of December 31, 1984, which was entered into by such organization on August 23, 1984—

"(i) such credit union shall not be treated as an agency or instrumentality of the United States, and

"(ii) clause (ii) of subparagraph (A) shall be applied by substituting 'January 1, 1987' for 'January 1, 1985'.

"(D) Special rule for Greenville Auditorium Board.—For purposes of this paragraph, significant official governmental action taken by the Greenville County Auditorium Board of Greenville, South Carolina, before May 23, 1983, shall be treated as significant official governmental action with respect to the coliseum facility subject to a binding contract to lease which was in effect on January 1, 1985.

"(E) Treatment of certain historic structures.—If—

"(i) on June 16, 1982, the legislative body of the local governmental unit adopted a bond ordinance to provide funds to renovate elevators in a deteriorating building owned by the local governmental unit and listed in the National Register, and

"(ii) the chief executive officer of the local governmental unit, in connection with the renovation of such building, made an application on June 1, 1983, to a State agency for a Federal historic preservation grant and made an application on June 17, 1983, to the Economic Development Administration of the United States Department of Commerce for a grant,

the requirements of clauses (i) and (ii) of subparagraph (A) shall be treated as met.

"(5) Mass commuting vehicles.—The amendments made by this section shall not apply to any qualified mass commuting vehicle (as defined in section 103(b)(9) of the Internal Revenue Code of 1954) which is financed in whole or in part by obligations the interest on which is excludable from gross income under section 103(a) of such Code if—

"(A) such vehicle is placed in service before January 1, 1988, or

"(B) such vehicle is placed in service on or after such date—

"(i) pursuant to a binding contract or commitment entered into before April 1, 1983, and

"(ii) solely because of conditions which, as determined by the Secretary of the Treasury or his delegate, are not within the control of the lessor or lessee.

"(6) Certain turbines and boilers.—The amendments made by this section shall not apply to any property described in section 208(d)(3)(E) of the Tax Equity and Fiscal Responsibility Act of 1982.

"(7) Certain facilities for which ruling requests filed on or before May 23, 1983.—The amendments made by this section shall not apply with respect to any facilities described in clause (ii) of section 168(f)(12)(C) of the Internal Revenue Code of 1954 (relating to certain sewage or solid waste disposal facilities), as in effect on the day before the date of the enactment of this Act, if a ruling request with respect to the lease of such facility to the tax-exempt entity was filed with the Internal Revenue Service on or before May 23, 1983.

"(8) Recovery period for certain qualified sewage facilities.—

"(A) In general.—In the case of any property (other than 15-year real property) which is part of a qualified sewage facility, the recovery period used for purposes of paragraph (1) of section 168(j) of the Internal Revenue Code of 1954 (as added by this section) shall be 12 years. For purposes of the preceding sentence, the term '15-year real property' includes 18-year real property.

"(B) Qualified sewage facility.—For purposes of subparagraph (A), the term 'qualified sewage facility' means any facility which is part of the sewer system of a city, if

"(i) on June 15, 1983, the City Council approved a resolution under which the city authorized the procurement of equity investments for such facility, and

"(ii) on July 12, 1983, the Industrial Development Board of the city approved a resolution to issue a $100,000,000 industrial development bond issue to provide funds to purchase such facility.

"(9) Property used by the postal service.—In the case of property used by the United States Postal Service, paragraphs (1) and (2) shall be applied by substituting 'October 31' for 'May 23'.

"(10) Existing appropriations.—The amendments made by this section shall not apply to personal property leased to or used by the United States if—

"(A) an express appropriation has been made for rentals under such lease for the fiscal year 1983 before May 23, 1983, and

"(B) the United States or an agency or instrumentality thereof has not provided an indemnification against the loss of all or a portion of the tax benefits claimed under the lease or service contract.

"(11) Special rule for certain partnerships.—

"(A) Partnerships for which qualifying action existed before October 21, 1983.—Paragraph (9) of section 168(j) of the Internal Revenue Code of 1954 (as added by this section) shall not apply to any property acquired, directly or indirectly, before January 1, 1985, by any partnership described in subparagraph (B).

"(B) Application filed before October 21, 1983.—A partnership is described in this subparagraph if—

"(i) before October 21, 1983, the partnership was organized, a request for exemption with respect to such partnership was filed with the Department of Labor, and a private placement memorandum stating the maximum number of units in the partnership that would be offered had been circulated,

"(ii) the interest in the property to be acquired, directly or indirectly (including through acquiring an interest in another partnership) by such partnership was described in such private placement memorandum, and

"(iii) the marketing of partnership units in such partnership is completed not later than two years after the later of the date of the enactment of this Act or the date of publication in the Federal Register of such exemption by the Department of Labor and the aggregate number of units in such partnership sold does not exceed the amount described in clause (i).

"(C) Partnerships for which qualifying action existed before March 6, 1984.—Paragraph (9) of section 168(j) of the Internal Revenue Code of 1954 (as added by this section) shall not apply to any property acquired directly or indirectly, before January 1, 1986, by any partnership described in subparagraph (D). For purposes of this subparagraph, property shall be deemed to have been acquired prior to January 1, 1986, if the partnership had entered into a written binding contract to acquire such property prior to January 1, 1986 and the closing of such contract takes place within 6 months of the date of such contract (24 months in the case of new construction).

"(D) Partnership organized before March 6, 1984. — A partnership is described in this subparagraph if —

"(i) before March 6, 1984, the partnership was organized and publicly announced the maximum amount (as shown in the registration statement, prospectus or partnership agreement, whichever is greater) of interests which would be sold in the partnership, and

"(ii) the marketing or partnership interests in such partnership was completed not later than the 90th day after the date of the enactment of this Act and the aggregate amount of interest in such partnership sold does not exceed the maximum amount described in clause (i).

"(12) Special rule for amendment made by subsection (c)(2). — The amendment made by subsection (c)(2) to the extent it relates to subsection (f)(12) of section 168 of the Internal Revenue Code of 1954 shall take effect as if it had been included in the amendments made by section 216(a) of the Tax Equity and Fiscal Responsibility Act of 1982.

"(13) Special rule for service contracts not involving tax-exempt entities. — In the case of a service contract or other arrangement described in section 7701(e) of the Internal Revenue Code of 1954 (as added by this section) with respect to which no party is a tax-exempt entity, such section 7701(e) shall not apply to—

"(A) such contract or other arrangement if such contract or other arrangement was entered into before November 5, 1983, or

"(B) any renewal or other extension of such contract or other arrangement pursuant to an option contained in such contract or other arrangement on November 5, 1983.

"(14) Property leased to section 593 organizations. — For purposes of the amendment made by subsection (f), paragraphs (1), (2), and (4) shall be applied by substituting —

"(A) 'November 5, 1983' for 'May 23, 1983' and 'November 1, 1983', as the case may be, and

"(B) 'organization described in section 593 of the Internal Revenue Code of 1954' for 'tax-exempt entity'.

"(15) Special rules relating to foreign persons or entities —

"(A) In general. — In the case of tax-exempt use property which is used by a foreign person or entity, the amendments made by this section shall not apply to any property which —

"(i) is placed in service by the taxpayer before January 1, 1984, and

"(ii) is used by such foreign person or entity pursuant to a lease entered into before January 1, 1984.

"(B) Special rule for subleases. — If tax-exempt use property is being used by a foreign person or entity pursuant to a sublease under a lease described in subparagraph (A)(ii), subparagraph (A) shall apply to such property only if such property was used before January 1, 1984, by any foreign person or entity pursuant to such lease.

"(C) Binding contracts, etc. — The amendments made by this section shall not apply with respect to any property (other than aircraft described in subparagraph (D)) leased to a foreign person or entity —

"(i) if —

"(I) on or before May 23, 1983, the taxpayer (or a predecessor in interest under the contract) or the foreign person or entity entered into a written binding contract to acquire, construct, or rehabilitate such property and such property had not previously been used by the foreign person or entity, or

"(II) the taxpayer or the foreign person or entity acquired the property or completed the construction, reconstruction, or rehabilitation of the property after December 31, 1982 and on or before May 23, 1983, and

"(ii) if such lease is pursuant to a written binding contract entered into before January 1, 1984, which requires the foreign person or entity to be the lessee of such property.

"(D) Certain aircraft. — The amendments made by this section shall not apply with respect to any wide-body, four-engine, commercial aircraft used by a foreign person or entity if —

"(i) on or before November 1, 1983, the foreign person or entity entered into a written binding contract to acquire such aircraft, and

"(ii) such aircraft is originally placed in service by such foreign person or entity (or its successor in interest under the contract) after May 23, 1983, and before January 1, 1986.

"(E) Use after 1983. — Qualified container equipment placed in service before January 1, 1984, which is used before such date by a foreign person shall not, for purposes of section 47 of the Internal Revenue Code of 1954, be treated as ceasing to be section 38 property by reason of the use of such equipment before January 1, 1985, by a foreign person or entity. For purposes of this subparagraph, the term 'qualified container equipment' means any container, container chassis, or container trailer of a United States person with a present class life of not more than 6 years.

"(16) Organizations electing exemption from rules relating to previously tax-exempt organizations must elect taxation of exempt arbitrage profits. —

"(A) In general. — An organization may make the election under section 168(j)(4)(E)(ii) of the Internal Revenue Code of 1954 (relating to election not to have rules relating to previously tax-exempt organizations apply) only if such organization elects the tax treatment of exempt arbitrage profits described in subparagraph (B).

"(B) Taxation of exempt arbitrage profits. —

"(i) In general. — In the case of an organization which elects the application of this subparagraph, there is hereby imposed a tax on the exempt arbitrage profits of such organization.

"(ii) Rate of tax, etc. — The tax imposed by clause (i) —

"(I) shall be the amount of tax which would be imposed by section 11 of such Code if the exempt arbitrage profits were taxable income (and there were no other taxable income), and

"(II) shall be imposed for the first taxable year of the tax-exempt use period (as defined in section 168(j)(4)(E)(ii) of such Code).

"(C) Exempt arbitrage profits. —

"(i) In general. — For purposes of this paragraph, the term exempt arbitrage profits means the aggregate amount described in clauses (i) and (ii) of subparagraph (D) of section 103(c)(6) of such Code for all taxable years for which the organization was exempt from tax under section 501(a) of such Code with respect to obligations —

"(I) associated with property described in section 168(j)(4)(E)(i), and

"(II) issued before January 1, 1985.

"(ii) Application of section 103(b)(6). — For purposes of this paragraph, section 103(b)(6) of such Code shall apply to obligations issued before January 1, 1985, but the amount described in clauses (i) and (ii) of subparagraph (D) thereof shall be determined without regard to clauses (i)(II) and (ii) of subparagraph (F) thereof.

"(D) Other laws applicable. —

"(i) In general. — Except as provided in clause (ii), all provisions of law, including penalties, applicable with respect to the tax imposed by section 11 of such Code shall apply with respect to the tax imposed by this paragraph.

"(ii) No credits against tax, etc. — The tax imposed by this paragraph shall not be treated as imposed by section 11 of such Code for purposes of —

"(I) part VI of subchapter A of chapter 1 of such Code (relating to minimum tax for tax preferences), and

"(II) determining the amount of any credit allowable under subpart A of part IV of such subchapter.

"(E) Election. — Any election under subparagraph (A) —

"(i) shall be made at such time and in such manner as the Secretary may prescribe,

"(ii) shall apply to any successor organization which is engaged in substantially similar activities, and

"(iii) once made, shall be irrevocable.

"(17) Certain transitional leased property. — The amendments made by this section shall not apply to property described in section 168(c)(2)(D) of the Internal Revenue Code of 1954, as in effect on the day before the date of the enactment of this Act, and which is described in any of the following subparagraphs:

"(A) Property is described in this subparagraph if such property is leased to a university, and —

"(i) on June 16, 1983, the Board of Administrators of the university adopted a resolution approving the rehabilitation of the property in connection with an overall campus development program; and

"(ii) the property houses a basketball arena and university offices.

"(B) Property is described in this subparagraph if such property is leased to a charitable organization, and —

"(i) on August 21, 1981, the charitable organization acquired the property, with a view towards rehabilitating the property; and

"(ii) on June 12, 1982, an arson fire caused substantial damage to the property, delaying the planned rehabilitation.

"(C) Property is described in this subparagraph if such property is leased to a corporation that is described in section 501(c)(3) of the Internal Revenue Code of 1954 (relating to organizations exempt from tax) pursuant to a contract —

"(i) which was entered into on August 3, 1983; and

"(ii) under which the corporation first occupied the property on December 22, 1983.

"(D) Property is described in this subparagraph if such property is leased to an educational institution for use as an Arts and Humanities Center and with respect to which —

"(i) in November 1982, an architect was engaged to design a planned renovation;

"(ii) in January 1983, the architectural plans were completed;

"(iii) in December 1983, a demolition contract was entered into; and

"(iv) in March 1984, a renovation contract was entered into.

"(E) Property is described in this subparagraph if such property is used by a college as a dormitory, and —

"(i) in October 1981, the college purchased the property with a view towards renovating the property;

"(ii) renovation plans were delayed because of a zoning dispute; and

"(iii) in May 1983, the court of highest jurisdiction in the State in which the college is located resolved the zoning dispute in favor of the college.

"(F) Property is described in this subparagraph if such property is a fraternity house related to a university with respect to which —

"(i) in August 1982, the university retained attorneys to advise the university regarding the rehabilitation of the property;

"(ii) on January 21, 1983, the governing body of the university established a committee to develop rehabilitation plans;

"(iii) on January 10, 1984, the governor of the state in which the university is located approved historic district designation for an area that includes the property; and

"(iv) on February 2, 1984, historic preservation certification applications for the property were filed with a historic landmarks commission.

"(G) Property is described in this subparagraph if such property is leased to a retirement community with respect to which —

"(i) on January 5, 1977, a certificate of incorporation was filed with the appropriate authority of the state in which the retirement community is located; and "(ii) on November 22, 1983, the Board of Trustees adopted a resolution evidencing the intention to begin immediate construction of the property.

"(H) Property is described in this subparagraph if such property is used by a university, and—

"(i) in July 1982, the Board of Trustees of the university adopted a master plan for the financing of the property; and

"(ii) as of August 1, 1983, at least $60,000 in private expenditures had been expended in connection with the property.

"In the case of Clemson University, the preceding sentence applies only to the Continuing Education Center and the component housing project.

"(I) Property is described in this subparagraph if such property is used by a university as a fine arts center and the Board of Trustees of such university authorized the sale-leaseback agreement with respect to such property on March 7, 1984.

"(J) Property is described in this subparagraph if such property is used by a tax-exempt entity as an international trade center, and

"(i) prior to 1982, an environmental impact study for such property was completed;

"(ii) on June 24, 1981, a developer made a written commitment to provide one-third of the financing for the development of such property; and

"(iii) on October 20, 1983, such developer was approved by the Board of Directors of the tax-exempt entity.

"(K) Property is described in this subparagraph if such property is used by university of osteopathic medicine and health sciences, and on or before December 31, 1983, the Board of Trustees of such university approved the construction of such property.

"(L) Property is described in this subparagraph if such property is used by a tax-exempt entity, and—

"(i) such use is pursuant to a lease with a taxpayer which placed substantial improvements in service;

"(ii) on May 23, 1983, there existed architectural plans and specifications (within the meaning of sec. 48(g)(1)(C)(ii) of the Internal Revenue Code of 1954); and

"(iii) prior to May 23, 1983, at least 10 percent of the total cost of such improvements was actually paid or incurred.

Property is described in this subparagraph if such property was leased to a tax-exempt entity pursuant to a lease recorded in the Register of Deed of Essex County, New Jersey, on May 7, 1984, and a deed of such property was recorded in the Register of Deed of Essex County, New Jersey, on May 7, 1984.

"(M) Property is described in this subparagraph if such property is used as a convention center and on June 2, 1983, the City Council of the city in which the center is located provided for over $6 million for the project.

"(18) Special rule for amendment made by subsection (c)(1).—

"(A) In general.— The amendment made by subsection (c)(1) shall not apply to property—

"(i) leased by the taxpayer on or before November 1, 1983, or

"(ii) leased by the taxpayer after November 1, 1983, if on or before such date the taxpayer entered into a written binding contract requiring the taxpayer to lease such property.

"(B) Limitation.— Subparagraph (A) shall apply to the amendment made by subsection (c)(1) only to the extent such amendment relates to property described in subclause (II), (III), or (IV) of section 168(j)(3)(B)(ii) of the Internal Revenue Code of 1954 (as added by this section).

"(19) Special rule for certain energy management contracts.—

"(A) In general.— The amendments made by subsection (e) shall not apply to property used pursuant to an energy management contract that was entered into prior to May 1, 1984.

"(B) Definition of energy management contract.— For purposes of subparagraph (A), the term 'energy management contract' means a contract for the providing of energy conservation or energy management services.

"(20) Definitions.— For purposes of this subsection—

"(A) Tax-exempt entity.— The term 'tax-exempt entity' has the same meaning as when used in section 168(j) of the Internal Revenue Code of 1954 (as added by this section), except that such term shall include any related entity (within the meaning of such section).

"(B) Treatment of improvements.—

"(i) In general.— For purposes of this subsection, an improvement to property shall not be treated as a separate property unless such improvement is a substantial improvement with respect to such property.

"(ii) Substantial improvement.— For purposes of clause (i), the term 'substantial improvement' has the meaning given such term by section 168(f)(1)(C) of such Code determined—

"(I) by substituting 'property' for 'building' each place it appears therein,

"(II) by substituting '20 percent' for '25 percent' in clause (ii) thereof, and

"(III) without regard to clause (iii) thereof.

"(C) Foreign person or entity.— The term 'foreign person or entity' has the meaning given to such term by subparagraph (C) of section 168(j)(4) of such Code (as added by this section). For purposes of this subparagraph and subparagraph (A), such subparagraph (C) shall be applied without regard to the last sentence thereof.

"(D) Leases and subleases.— The determination of whether there is a lease or sublease to a tax-exempt entity shall take into account sections 168(j)(6)(A), 168(j)(8)(A), and 7701(e) of the Internal Revenue Code of 1954 (as added by this section)."

—P.L. 98-369, Sec. 32(a), added para. (f)(13) [sic (14)], effective for agreements described therein entered into more than 90 days after the date of the enactment of the Act (7/18/84).

—P.L. 98-369, Sec. 32(b), amended Sec. 210(a) of P.L. 97-248 by adding "entered into on or before the 90th day after the date of enactment of the Tax Reform Act of 1984 [7/18/84] " after "agreement" the first place it appeared.

—P.L. 98-369, Sec. 111(a)(1), substituted "18-year real property" for "15-year real property" each place it appeared in the text and heading of para. (b)(2) . . . Sec. 111(a)(2), substituted "18-year recovery period" for "15-year recovery period" in clause (b)(2)(A)(i) . . . Sec. 111(a)(3), deleted "(200 percent declining balance method in the case of low-income housing)" after "175 percent declining balance method" in clause (b)(2)(A)(ii) . . . Sec. 111(b)(1), added para. (b)(4) . . . Sec. 111(b)(2), redesignated subpara. (c)(2)(F) as subpara. (c)(2)(G) and added new subpara. (c)(2)(F) . . . Sec. 111(b)(3)(A), deleted the last sentence of subpara. (b)(2)(A) . . . Sec. 111(b)(3)(B), amended subpara. (c)(2)(D) . . . Sec. 111(c), amended subpara. (f)(1)(B), effective for property placed in service by the taxpayer after 3/15/84. Sec. 111(g)(2)-(4) of the Act provides:

"(2) Exception.— The amendments made by this section shall not apply to property placed in service by the taxpayer before January 1, 1987, if—

"(A) the taxpayer or a qualified person entered into a binding contract to purchase or construct such property before March 16, 1984, or

"(B) construction of such property was commenced by or for the taxpayer or a qualified person before March 16, 1984.

For purposes of this paragraph the term 'qualified person' means any person who transfers his rights in such a contract or such property to the taxpayer, but only if such property is not placed in service by such person before such rights are transferred to the taxpayer.

"(3) Special rules for application of paragraph (2).—

"(A) Certain inventory.— In the case of any property which—

"(i) is held by a person as property described in section 1221(1), and

"(ii) is disposed of by such person before January 1, 1985,

such person shall not, for purposes of paragraph (2), be treated as having placed such property in service before such property is disposed of merely because such person rented such property or held such property for rental. No deduction for depreciation or amortization shall be allowed to such person with respect to such property.

"(B) Certain property financed by bonds.— In the case of any property with respect to which—

"(i) bonds were issued to finance such property before 1984, and

"(ii) an architectural contract was entered into before March 16, 1984,

paragraph (2) shall be applied by substituting 'May 2' for 'March 16'.

"(4) Special rule for components.— For purposes of applying section 168(f)(1)(B) of the Internal Revenue Code of 1954 (as amended by this section) to components placed in service after December 31, 1986, property to which paragraph (2) applies shall be treated as placed in service by the taxpayer before March 16, 1984."

Prior to deletion, the last sentence of subpara. (b)(2)(A) read as follows:

"For purposes of this subparagraph, the term 'low-income housing' means property described in clause (i), (ii), (iii), or (iv) of section 1250(a)(1)(B)."

Prior to amendment, subpara. (c)(2)(D) read as follows:

"(D) 15-year real property. The term '15-year real property' means section 1250 class property which does not have a present class life of 12.5 years or less."

Prior to amendment, subpara. (f)(1)(B) read as follows:

"(B) Transitional rule. In the case of any building placed in service by the taxpayer before January 1, 1981, for purposes of applying subparagraph (A) to components of such buildings placed in service after December 31, 1980, the deduction allowable under subsection (a) with respect to such components shall be computed in the same manner as the deduction allowable with respect to the first such component placed in service after December 31, 1980. For purposes of the preceding sentence, the method of computing the deduction allowable with respect to such first component shall be determined as if it were a separate building."

—P.L. 98-369, Sec. 111(d), added "(using a mid-month convention)" after "months" in subparas. (b)(2)(A) and (b)(2)(B), for property placed in service by the taxpayer after 6/22/84. The exceptions and special rules provided by Sec. 111(g)(2)-(4), above, apply to Sec. 111(d), with the substitution (provided by Sec. 111(g)(5)(B)) of "June 23, 1984" for "March 16, 1984" each place it appears in para. (g)(2).

—P.L. 98-369, Sec. 111(e)(1), substituted "18-year real property or low-income housing" for "15-year real property" each place it appeared in clause (b)(3)(B)(iii), subpara. (f)(2)(B), subclause (f)(2)(C)(ii)(II), (f)(2)(E), and para. (f)(5) . . . Sec. 111(e)(2), substituted "18-year real property or low income housing," for "15-year real property" in clause (b)(3)(B)(ii) . . . Sec. 111(e)(3), substituted "18-year real property or low-income housing" for "15-year real property" in subpara. (d)(2)(B), . . . Sec. 111(e)(4), substituted "18-year real property or low-income housing" for "15-year real property" in the table in clause (f)(2)(C)(i), . . . Sec. 111(e)(9)(A), substituted "under paragraph (1), (2), or (4)" for "under paragraphs (1) and (2)" in subpara. (b)(3)(A) . . . Sec. 111(e)(9)(B), substituted

"18-year real property and low-income housing	18, 35, or 45."
for "15-year real property	15, 35, or 45 years"

in subpara. (b)(3)(A), effective for property placed in service by the taxpayer after 3/15/84, with exceptions and special rules provided by Sec. 111(g)(2)-(4), above.

—P.L. 98-369, Sec. 113(a)(2), added para. (f)(14) [sic (15)], effective for property placed in service after 3/15/84, in tax. yrs. end. after 3/15/84.

—P.L. 98-369, Sec. 113(b)(1), added para. (e)(5), effective for any motion picture film or video tape placed in service before, on, or after 7/18/84. Sec. 113(c)(2)(A)(1) & (D) provides the following exceptions:

Deductions   Code Sec. 168

"(i) any qualified film placed in service by the taxpayer before March 15, 1984, if the taxpayer treated such film as recovery property for purposes of section 168 of the Internal Revenue Code of 1954 on a return of tax under chapter 1 of such Code filed before March 16, 1984, or

"(ii) any qualified film placed in service by the taxpayer before January 1, 1985, if—

"(I) 20 percent or more of the production costs of such film were incurred before March 16, 1984, and

"(II) the taxpayer treats such film as recovery property for purposes of section 168 of such Code.

No credit shall be allowable under section 38 of such Code with respect to any qualified film described in clause (ii), except to the extent provided in section 48(k) of such Code."

* * *

"(D) For purposes of this paragraph, the terms 'qualified film' and 'production costs' have the same respective meanings as when used in section 48(k) in the Internal Revenue Code of 1954."

—P.L. 98-369, Sec. 113(b)(2)(A), substituted "title" for "section" in the matter preceding para. (e)(1), effective for property placed in service after 12/31/80, in tax. yrs. end. after 12/31/80.

—P.L. 98-369, Sec. 474(r)(7)(A), substituted "subparts A, B, and D of part IV" for "subpart A of part IV" in clause (i)(1)(D)(i), as added by Sec. 208(a) of P.L. 97-248 . . . Sec. 474(r)(7)(B), substituted "under section 25(b)(2)" for "under the last sentence of section 53(a)" in clause (i)(1)(D)(iii), as added by Sec. 208(a) of P.L. 97-248 . . . Sec. 474(r)(7)(C), substituted "section 38" for "subpart A of part IV of subchapter A of this chapter" in subpara. (i)(4)(A), as added by Sec. 208(a) of P.L. 97-248 . . . Sec. 474(r)(7)(D), substituted "subparts A, B, and D of part IV" for "subpart A of part IV" in clause (i)(1)(D)(i), as added by Sec. 209(b) of P.L. 97-248", Sec. 474(r)(7)(E), substituted "under section 25(b)(2)" for "under the last sentence of section 53(a)" in clause (i)(1)(D)(iii), as added by Sec. 209(b) of P.L. 97-248, effective for tax. yrs. begin. after 12/31/83, and for carrybacks from tax. yrs. begin. after 12/31/83.

—P.L. 98-369, Sec. 612(e)(4), substituted "section 26(b)(2)" for "section 25(b)(2)" in clause (i)(1)(D)(iii), as added by Sec. 208(a) of P.L. 97-248 and amended by Sec. 474(r)(4)(B) of this Act . . . Sec. 612(e)(5), substituted "section 26(b)(2)" for "section 25(b)(2)" in clause (i)(1)(D)(iii), as added by Sec. 209(b) of P.L. 97-248 and amended by Sec. 474(r)(7)(E) of this Act, effective for interest paid or accrued after 12/31/84, on indebtedness incurred after 12/31/84.

—P.L. 98-369, Sec. 628(b)(1), amended subpara. (f)(12)(C) . . . Sec. 628(b)(2), deleted subpara. (f)(12)(D) and redesignated subpara. (f)(12)(E) as subpara. (f)(12)(D), effective for property placed in service after 12/31/83, to the extent such property is financed by the proceeds of an obligation (including a refunding obligation) issued after 10/18/83, except as provided by Sec. 631(b)(2) of this Act:

"(2) Exceptions.—

"(A) Construction or binding agreement.—The amendments made by section 628(b) shall not apply with respect to facilities—

"(i) the original use of which commences with the taxpayer and the construction, reconstruction, or rehabilitation of which began before October 19, 1983, or

"(ii) with respect to which a binding contract to incur significant expenditures was entered into before October 19, 1983.

"(B) Refunding.—

"(i) In general.—Except as provided in clause (ii), in the case of property placed in service after December 31, 1983, which is financed by the proceeds of an obligation which is issued solely to refund another obligation which was issued before October 19, 1983, the amendments made by section 628(b) shall apply only with respect to an amount equal to the basis in such property which has not been recovered before the date such refunded obligation is issued.

"(ii) Significant expenditures.—In the case of facilities the original use of which commences with the taxpayer and with respect to which significant expenditures are made before January 1, 1984, the amendments made by section 628(b) shall not apply with respect to such facilities to the extent such facilities are financed by the proceeds of an obligation issued solely to refund another obligation which was issued before October 19, 1983.

"(C) Facilities.—In the case of an inducement resolution or other comparable preliminary approval adopted by an issuing authority before October 19, 1983, for purposes of applying subparagraphs (A)(i) and (B)(ii) with respect to obligations described in such resolution, the term 'facilities' means the facilities described in such resolution."

Prior to amendment, subpara. (f)(12)(C) read as follows:

"(C) Exceptions. Subparagraph (A) shall not apply to any recovery property which is placed in service—

"(i) in connection with projects for residential rental property financed by the proceeds of obligations described in section 103(b)(4)(A),

"(ii) in connection with a sewage or solid waste disposal facility—

"(I) which provides sewage or solid waste disposal services for the residents of part or all of 1 or more governmental units, and

"(II) with respect to which substantially all of the sewage or solid waste processed is collected from the general public,

"(iii) as an air or water pollution control facility which is—

"(I) installed in connection with an existing facility, or

"(II) installed in connection with the conversion of an existing facility which uses oil or natural gas (or any product of oil or natural gas) as a primary fuel to a facility which uses coal as a primary fuel, or

"(iv) in connection with a facility with respect to which an urban development action grant has been made under section 119 of the Housing and Community Development Act of 1974." Prior to deletion, subpara. (f)(12)(D) read as follows:

"(D) Existing facility. For purposes of this paragraph, the term 'existing facility' means a plant or property in operation before July 1, 1982."

—P.L. 98-369, Sec. 632, provided various exceptions to the amendments made by Title VI of this Act. See note following Code Sec. 103A.

—P.L. 98-369, Sec. 712(d)(1), added the last sentence to Sec. 210(b)(2) of P.L. 97-248, reproduced below.

—P.L. 98-369, Sec. 712(d)(2), added subsec. (c) to Sec. 210 of P.L. 97-248, reproduced below.

—P.L. 98-369, Sec. 1067(a), amended Sec. 208(d)(3) of P.L. 97-248, part of the exception to the effective date for changes made by Sec. 208 of P.L. 97-248 (reproduced below), by adding subpara. (d)(3)(G), effective "as if included in the provision of section 208(d)(3) of [P.L. 97-248]" . . . Sec. 1067(b), provides:

"(b) Special rule for subsection (a) [of Sec. 1067 of P.L. 98-369] The amount of any recapture under section 47 of the Internal Revenue Code of 1954 with respect to the credit allowed under section 38 of such Code with respect to progress expenditures (within the meaning of section 46(d) of such Code) shall apply only to the percentage of the cost basis of the coal gasification facility to which the amendment made by subsection (a) applies."

In 1983, P.L. 97-448, Sec. 102(a)(1), added the last sentence to para. (f)(5) . . . Sec. 102(a)(2), substituted "paragraph (7) or (10) of subsection (f)" for "subsection (f)(7)" in subpara. (d)(2)(B) . . . Sec. 102(a)(3), added para. (f)(13) . . . Sec. 102(a)(4)(A), amended para. (h)(4) . . . Sec. 102(a)(4)(B), amended the heading of subpara. (g)(8)(A) . . . Sec. 102(a)(4)(C), amended the heading of subpara. (g)(8)(B) . . . Sec. 102(a)(5), substituted "In the case of 15-year real property" for "For purposes of this subparagraph" in the third sentence of subpara. (b)(2)(A) . . . Sec. 102(a)(8), added subpara. (c)(2)(F) . . . Sec. 102(a)(9)(A), added the last sentence to subpara. (e)(4)(D) . . . Sec. 102(a)(9)(B), added subparas. (e)(4)(H) and (I), effective for property placed in service after 12/31/80 in tax. yrs. end. after 12/31/80.

Prior to amendment, para. (h)(4) read as follows:

"(4) Qualified coal utilization property. The term '10-year property' includes qualified coal utilization property which is not 3-year property, 5-year property, or 10-year property (determined without regard to this paragraph)."

Prior to amendment the heading of subpara. (g)(8)(A) read as follows:

"(A) In general."

Prior to amendment, the heading of subpara. (g)(8)(B) read as follows:

"(B) In general."

—P.L. 97-448, Sec. 102(a)(10)(A), added the last sentence to subpara. (f)(8)(D) [as in effect before amendments made by Sec. 208(b) of P.L. 97-248, effective as provided in Sec. 102(a)(10)(B), which reads:

"(B) The amendment made by subparagraph (A) shall apply with respect to property to which the provisions of section 168(f)(8) of the Internal Revenue Code of 1954 (as in effect before the amendments made by the Tax Equity and Fiscal Responsibility Act of 1982 [P.L. 97-248] apply."

—P.L. 97-448, Sec. 102(f)(2), amended subpara. (f)(4)(B), for expenditures incurred after 12/31/81 in tax. yrs. end. after 12/31/81.

Prior to amendment, subpara. (f)(4)(B) read as follows:

"(B) Made on return. Any election under this section shall be made on the taxpayer's return of the tax imposed by this chapter for the taxable year concerned."

—P.L. 97-448, Sec. 306(a)(4)(A)(i), substituted "engaged in the furnishing of electric energy to persons in rural areas" for "described in section 1381(a)" in Sec. 208(d)(3)(E)(i) of P.L. 248, reproduced below . . . Sec. 306(a)(4)(A)(ii), added "or section 168(f)(8)(J) of such Code, as added by subsection (b)(4)" after "as added by subsection (a)(1)" in Sec. 208(d)(5) of P.L. 97-248, reproduced below . . . Sec. 306(a)(4)(B), added para. (d)(7) to Sec. 208 of P.L. 97-248, reproduced below . . . Sec. 306(a)(4)(C), amended Sec. 208(d)(3)(C) of P.L. 97-248, reproduced below.

Prior to amendment, Sec. 208(d)(3)(C) of P.L. 97-248 read as follows:

"(C) Manufacturers of certain products.— Property is described in this subparagraph if such property—

"(i) is used to produce a class of products (within the meaning of paragraph (6)(B)) in an industry described in paragraph (6)(A)(ii)(II) (determined without regard to the phrase 'other than the taxpayer'), and

"(ii) would be described in subparagraph (A) if 'October 1' were substituted for 'January 1'."

—P.L. 97-424, Sec. 541(a)(1), redesignated subpara. (e)(3)(C) as (e)(3)(D) and added new subpara. (e)(3)(C), effective for tax. yrs. begin. after 12/31/79.

In 1982, P.L. 97-354, Sec. 5(a)(19), substituted "an S corporation" for "an electing small business corporation (within the meaning of section 1371(b))" in clause (f)(8)(B)(i) as in effect before the enactment of P.L. 97-248 . . . Sec. 5(a)(20), substituted "an S corporation" for "an electing small business corporation (within the meaning of section 1371(b)" in subclause (f)(8)(C)(i)(I) as added by Sec. 209(a) of P.L. 97-248, effective for tax. yrs. begin. after 12/31/82.

—P.L. 97-248, Sec. 206(a), amended para. (b)(1) . . . Sec. 206(b)(1), deleted subpara. (e)(4)(H) . . . Sec. 206(b)(2), substituted "1981" for "1986" in the heading of para. (e)(4), effective 9/3/82.

Prior to amendment, para. (b)(1) read as follows:

"(1) In general. Except as otherwise provided in this section, the amount of the deduction allowable by subsection (a) for any taxable year shall be the aggregate amount determined by applying to the unadjusted basis of recovery property the applicable percentage determined in accordance with the following tables:

"(A) For property placed in service after December 31, 1980, and before January 1, 1985.

1,605

Code Sec. 168 — Deductions

If the recovery year is:	The applicable percentage for the class of property is:			
	3-year	5-year	10-year	15-year public utility
1	25	15	8	5
2	38	22	14	10
3	37	21	12	9
4		21	10	8
5		21	10	7
6			10	7
7			9	6
8			9	6
9			9	6
10			9	6
11				6
12				6
13				6
14				6
15				6

"(B) For property placed in service in 1985.

If the recovery year is:	The applicable percentage for the class of property is:			
	3-year	5-year	10-year	15-year public utility
1	29	18	9	6
2	47	33	19	12
3	24	25	16	12
4		16	14	11
5		8	12	10
6			10	9
7			8	8
8			6	7
9			4	6
10			2	5
11				4
12				4
13				3
14				2
15				1

"(C) For property placed in service after December 31, 1985.

If the recovery year is:	The applicable percentage for the class of property is:			
	3-year	5-year	10-year	15-year public utility
1	33	20	10	7
2	45	32	18	12
3	22	24	16	12
4		16	14	11
5		8	12	10
6			10	9
7			8	8
8			6	7
9			4	6
10			2	5
11				4
12				3
13				3
14				2
15				1"

Prior to deletion, subpara. (e)(4)(H) read as follows:

"(H) Special rules for property placed in service before certain percentages take effect. Under regulations prescribed by the Secretary —

"(i) rules similar to the rules of this paragraph shall be applied in determining whether the tables contained in subparagraph (B) or (C) of subsection (b)(1) apply with respect to recovery property, and

"(ii) if the tables contained in subparagraph (B) or (C) of subsection (b)(1) do not apply to such property by reason of clause (i), the deduction allowable under subsection (a) shall be computed

"(I) In the case of a transaction described in subparagraph (C), under rules similar to the rules described in section 381(c)(6); and

"(II) in the case of a transaction otherwise described in this paragraph, under the recovery period and method (including rates prescribed under subsection (b)(1)) used by the person from whom the taxpayer acquired such property (or, where such person had no recovery method and period for such property, under the recovery period and method (including rates prescribed under subsection (b)(1)) used by the person which transferred such property to such person)."

—P.L. 97-248, Sec. 208(a)(1), redesignated subsec. (i) as subsec. (j) and added a new subsec. (i)... Sec. 208(a)(2)(A), added "except as provided in subsection (i)," before "for purposes of this subtitle" in subpara. (f)(8)(A)... Sec. 208(b)(1),

added "which is not a related person with respect to the lessee" before the comma at the end of subclause (f)(8)(B)(i)(I)... Sec. 208(b)(2), amended clause (f)(8)(B)(iii)... Sec. 208(b)(3), amended subpara. (f)(8)(D)... Sec. 208(b)(4), redesignated subpara. (f)(8)(H) as subpara. (f)(8)(K) and added new subparas. (f)(8)(H), (I) and (J), effective for agreements entered into after 7/1/82 or to property placed in service after 7/1/82, except as provided in Sec. 208(d)(2)–(7) [as amended by Sec. 304(a)(4) of P.L. 97-248 and Sec. 1067(a) of P.L. 98-369, see above] of this Act, which read as follows:

"(2) Transitional rule for certain safe harbor lease property—

"(A) In general.— The amendments made by subsections (a) and (b) shall not apply to transitional safe harbor lease property.

"(B) Special rule for certain provisions.— Subparagraph (A) shall not apply with respect to the provisions of paragraph (6) of section 168(i) of the Internal Revenue Code of 1954 (as added by subsection (a)(1)), to the provisions of section 168(f)(8)(J) of such Code (as added by subsection (b)(4)), or to the amendment made by subsection (b)(1).

"(3) Transitional safe harbor lease property.— For purposes of this subsection, the term 'transitional safe harbor lease property' means property described in any of the following subparagraphs:

"(A) In general.— Property is described in this subparagraph if such property is placed in service before January 1, 1983, if—

"(i) with respect to such property a binding contract to acquire or to construct such property was entered into by the lessee after December 31, 1980, and before July 2, 1982, or

"(ii) such property was acquired by the lessee, or construction of such property was commenced by or for the lessee, after December 31, 1980, and before July 2, 1982.

"(B) Certain qualified lessees.— Property is described in this subparagraph if such property is placed in service before July 1, 1982, and with respect to which—

"(i) an agreement to which section 168(f)(8)(A) of the Internal Revenue Code of 1954 applies was entered into before August 15, 1982, and

"(ii) the lessee under such agreement is a qualified lessee (within the meaning of paragraph (6)).

"(C) Automotive manufacturing property.

"(i) In general. Property is described in this subparagraph if—

"(I) such property is used principally by the taxpayer directly in connection with the trade or business of the taxpayer of the manufacture of automobiles or light-duty trucks.

"(II) such property is automotive manufacturing property, and

"(III) such property would be described in subparagraph (A) if 'October 1' were substituted for 'January 1'.

"(ii) Light-duty truck. For purposes of this subparagraph, the term 'light-duty truck' means any truck with a gross vehicle weight of 13,000 pounds or less. Such term shall not include any truck tractor.

"(iii) Automotive manufacturing property. For purposes of this subparagraph, the term 'automotive manufacturing property' means machinery, equipment, and special tools of the type included in the former asset depreciation range guideline classes 37.11 and 37.12.

"(iv) Special tools used by certain vendors. For purposes of this subparagraph, any special tools owned by a taxpayer described in subclause (I) of clause (i) which are used by a vendor solely for the production of component parts for sale to the taxpayer shall be treated as automotive manufacturing property used directly by such taxpayer.

"(D) Certain aircraft.— Property is described in this subparagraph if such property—

"(i) is a commercial passenger aircraft (other than a helicopter), and

"(ii) would be described in subparagraph (A) if 'January 1, 1984' were substituted for 'January 1, 1983'.

For purposes of determining whether property described in this subparagraph is described in subparagraph (A), subparagraph (A)(ii) shall be applied by substituting 'June 25, 1981' for 'December 31, 1980' and by substituting 'February 20, 1982' for 'July 2, 1982' and construction of the aircraft shall be treated as having been begun during the period referred to in subparagraph (A)(ii) if during such period construction or reconstruction of a subassembly was commenced, or the stub wing join occurred.

"(E) Turbines and boilers.— Property is described in this subparagraph if such property—

"(i) is a turbine or boiler of a cooperative organization engaged in the furnishing of electric energy to persons in rural areas and

"(ii) would be property described in subparagraph (A) if 'July 1' were substituted for 'January 1'.

For purposes of determining whether property described in this subparagraph is described in subparagraph (A), such property shall be treated as having been acquired during the period referred to in subparagraph (A)(ii) if at least 20 percent of the cost of such property is paid during such period.

"(F) Property used in the production of steel.— Property is described in this subparagraph if such property—

"(i) is used by the taxpayer directly in connection with the trade or business of the taxpayer of the manufacture or production of steel, and

"(ii) would be described in subparagraph (A) if 'January 1, 1984' were substituted for 'January 1, 1983'.

"(G) Coal gasification facilities.—

"(i) In general.— Property is described in this subparagraph if such property—

"(I) is used directly in connection with the manufacture or production of low sulfur gaseous fuel from coal, and

Deductions   Code Sec. 168

"(II) would be described in subparagraph (A) if 'July 1, 1984' were substituted for 'January 1, 1983'.

"(ii) Special rule. — For purposes of determining whether property described in this subparagraph is described in subparagraph (A), such property shall be treated as having been acquired during the period referred to in subparagraph (A)(ii) if at least 20 percent of the cost of such property is paid during such period.

"(iii) Limitation on amount. — Clause (i) shall only apply to the lease of an undivided interest in the property in an amount which does not exceed the lesser of—

"(I) 50 percent of the cost basis of such property, or

"(II) $67,500,000.

"(iv) Placed in service. — In the case of property to which this subparagraph applies—

"(I) such property shall be treated as placed in service when the taxpayer receives an operating permit with respect to such property from a State environmental protection agency, and

"(II) the term of the lease with respect to such property shall be treated as being 5 years.

"(4) Special rule for antiavoidance provisions. — The provisions of paragraph (6) of section 168(i) of such Code (as added by subsection (a)(1)), and the amendment made by subsection (b)(1), shall apply to leases entered into after February 19, 1982, in taxable years ending after such date.

"(5) Special rule for mass commuting vehicles. — The amendments made by this section (other than section 168(i)(1) and (7) of such Code, as added by subsection (a)(1)), or section 168(f)(8)(J) of such Code, as added by subsection (b)(4) and section 209 shall not apply to qualified leased property described in section 168(f)(8)(D)(V) of such Code (as in effect after the amendments made by this section) which—

"(A) is placed in service before January 1, 1988, or

"(B) is placed in service after such date—

"(i) pursuant to a binding contract or commitment entered into before April 1, 1983, and

"(ii) solely because of conditions which, as determined by the Secretary of the Treasury or his delegate, are not within the control of the lessor or lessee.

"(6) Qualified lessee defined. —

"(A) In general. — The term 'qualified lessee' means a taxpayer which is a lessee of an agreement to which section 168(f)(8)(A) of such Code applies and which—

"(i) had net operating losses in each of the three most recent taxable years ending before July 1, 1982, and had an aggregate net operating loss for the five most recent taxable years ending before July 1, 1982, and

"(ii) which uses the property subject to the agreement to manufacture and produce within the United States a class of products in an industry with respect to which—

"(I) the taxpayer produced less than 5 percent of the total number of units (or value) of such products during the period covering the three most recent taxable years of the taxpayer ending before July 1, 1982, and

"(II) four or fewer United States persons (including as one person an affiliated group as defined in section 1504(a)) other than the taxpayer manufactured 85 percent or more of the total number of all units (or value) within such class of products manufactured and produced in the United States during such period."

"(B) Class of products. — For purposes of subparagraph (A)—

"(i) the term 'class of products' means any of the categories designated and numbered as a 'class of products' in the 1977 Census of Manufacturers compiled and published by the Secretary of Commerce under title 13 of the United States Code, and

"(ii) information—

"(I) compiled or published by the Secretary of Commerce, as part of or in connection with the Statistical Abstract of the United States or the Census of Manufacturers, regarding the number of units (or value) of a class of products manufactured and produced in the United States during any period, or

"(II) if information under subclause (I) is not available, so compiled or published with respect to the number of such units shipped or sold by such manufacturers during any period,

shall constitute prima facie evidence of the total number of all units of such class of products manufactured and produced in the United States in such period.

"(7) Coordination with at risk rules. — Subparagraph (J) of section 168(f)(8) of the Internal Revenue Code of 1954 (as added by subsection (b)(4)) shall take effect as provided in such subparagraph (J)."

Sec. 208(c) provides:

"(c) Certain leases before October 20, 1981, treated as qualified leases.

"Nothing in paragraph (8) of section 168(f) of the Internal Revenue Code of 1954, or in any regulations prescribed thereunder, shall be treated as making such paragraph inapplicable to any agreement entered into before October 20, 1981, solely because under such agreement 1 party to such agreement is entitled to the credit allowable under section 38 of such Code with respect to property and another party to such agreement is entitled to the deduction allowable under section 168 of such Code with respect to such property. Section 168(f)(8)(B)(ii) of such Code shall not apply to the party entitled to such credit."

Prior to amendment, clause (f)(8)(B)(iii) read as follows:

"(iii) the term of the lease (including any extensions) does not exceed the greater of—

"(I) 90 percent of the useful life of such property for purposes of section 167, or

"(II) 150 percent of the present class life of such property."

Prior to amendment, subpara. (f)(8)(D) read as follows:

"(D) Qualified leased property defined. For purposes, of subparagraph (A), the term 'qualified leased property' means recovery property (other than a qualified rehabilitated building within the meaning of section 48(g)(1)) which is

"(i) new section 38 property (as defined in section 48(b)) of the lessor which is leased within 3 months after such property was placed in service and which, if acquired by the lessee, would have been new section 38 property of the lessee,

"(ii) property

"(I) which was new section 38 property of the lessee,

"(II) which was leased within 3 months after such property was placed in service by the lessee, and

"(III) with respect to which the adjusted basis of the lessor does not exceed the adjusted basis of the lessee at the time of the lease, or

"(iii) property which is a qualified mass commuting vehicle (as defined in section 103(b)(9)) and which is financed in whole or in part by obligations the interest on which is excludable from income under section 103(a).

For purposes of this title (other than this subparagraph), any property described in clause (i) or (ii) to which subparagraph (A) applies shall be deemed originally placed in service not earlier than the date such property is used under the lease. In the case of property placed in service after December 31, 1980, and before the date of the enactment of this subparagraph, this subparagraph shall be applied by submitting 'the date of the enactment of this subparagraph' for 'such property was placed in service'."

—P.L. 97-248, Sec. 209(a), amended para. (f)(8) . . . Sec. 209(b), amended subsec. (i), effective [as amended by Sec. 12(a)(2) of P.L. 98-369, see above] for agreements entered into after 12/31/87, except as provided in Sec. 209(d)(1)(B) [as amended by Sec. 12(a)(2) of P.L. 98-369, see above] of this Act, which reads as follows:

"(B) Special rule for farm property aggregating $150,000 or less. —

"(i) In general. — The amendments made by subsection (a) shall also apply to any agreement entered into after July 1, 1982, and before January 1, 1988, if the property subject to such agreement is section 38 property which is used for farming purposes (within the meaning of section 2032A(e)(5)).

"(ii) $150,000 limitation. — The provisions of clause (i) shall not apply to any agreement if the sum of—

"(I) the cost basis of the property subject to the agreement, plus

"(II) the cost basis of any property subject to an agreement to which this subparagraph previously applied, which was entered into during the same calendar year, and with respect to which the lessee was the lessee of the agreement described in subclause (I) (or any related person within the meaning of section 168(e)(4)(D)),

exceeds $150,000. For purposes of subclause (II), in the case of an individual, there shall not be taken into account any agreement of any individual who is a related person involving property which is used in a trade or business of farming of such related person which is separate from the trade or business of farming of the lessee described in subclause (II)."

Prior to amendment, para. (f)(8) read as follows:

"(8) Special rule for leases.

"(A) In general. In the case of an agreement with respect to qualified leased property, if all of the parties to the agreement characterize such agreement as a lease and elect to have the provisions of this paragraph apply with respect to such agreement, and if the requirements of subparagraph (B) are met, then, except as provided in subsection (i), for purposes of this subtitle

"(i) such agreement shall be treated as a lease entered into by the parties (and any party which is a corporation described in subparagraph (B)(i)(I) shall be deemed to have entered into the lease in the course of carrying on a trade or business), and

"(ii) the lessor shall be treated as the owner of the property and the lessee shall be treated as the lessee of the property.

"(B) Certain requirements must be met. The requirements of this subparagraph are met if

"(i) the lessor is

"(I) a corporation (other than an electing small business corporation (within the meaning of section 1371(b)) or a personal holding company (within the meaning of section 542(a)) which is not a related person with respect to the lessee,

"(II) a partnership all of the partners of which are corporations described in subclause (I), or

"(III) a grantor trust with respect to which the grantor and all beneficiaries of the trust are described in subclause (I) or (II),

"(ii) the minimum investment of the lessor

"(I) at the time the property is first placed in service under the lease, and

"(II) at all times during the term of the lease,

is not less than 10 percent of the adjusted basis of such property, and

"(iii) the term of the lease (including any extensions) does not exceed the greater of—

"(I) 120 percent of the present class life of the property, or

"(II) the period equal to the recovery period determined with respect to such property under subsection (i)(2).

"(C) No other factors taken into account. If the requirements of subparagraphs (A) and (B) are met with respect to any transaction described in subparagraph (A), no other factors shall be taken into account in making a determination as to whether subparagraph (A)(i) or (ii) applies with respect to such transaction.

"(D) Qualified leased property defined. For purposes of this section—

"(i) In general. The term 'qualified leased property' means recovery property—

"(I) which is new section 38 property of the lessor, which is leased within 3 months after such property was placed in service, and which, if acquired by the lessee, would have been new section 38 property of the lessee, or

1,607

"(II) which was new section 38 property of the lessee, which is leased within 3 months after such property is placed in service by the lessee, and with respect to which the adjusted basis of the lessor does not exceed the adjusted basis of the lessee at the time of the lease.

"(ii) Only 45 percent of the lessee's property may be treated as qualified. The cost basis of all safe harbor lease property (determined without regard to this clause)—
"(I) which is placed in service during any calendar year, and
"(II) with respect to which the taxpayer is a lessee,
shall not exceed an amount equal to the 45 percent of the cost basis of the taxpayer's qualified base property placed in service during such calendar year.

"(iii) Allocation of disqualified basis. The cost basis not treated as qualified leased property under clause (ii) shall be allocated to safe harbor lease property for such calendar year (determined without regard to clause (ii)) in reverse order to when the agreement described in subparagraph (A) with respect to such property was entered into.

"(iv) Certain property may not be treated as qualified leased property. The term 'qualified leased property' shall not include recovery property—
"(I) which is a qualified rehabilitated building (within the meaning of section 48(g)(1)),
"(II) which is public utility property (within the meaning of section 167(l)(3)(A)),
"(III) which is property with respect to which a deduction is allowable by reason of section 291(b),
"(IV) with respect to which the lessee of the property (other than property described in clause (v)) under the agreement described in subparagraph (A) is a nonqualified tax-exempt organization, or
"(V) property with respect to which the user of such property is a person (other than a United States person) not subject to United States tax on income derived from the use of such property.

"(v) Qualified mass commuting vehicles included. The term 'qualified leased property' includes recovery property which is a qualified mass commuting vehicle (as defined in section 103(b)(9)) which is financed in whole or in part by obligations the interest on which is excludable under section 103(a).

"(vi) Qualified base property. For purposes of this subparagraph, the term 'qualified base property' means property placed in service during any calendar year which—
"(I) is new section 38 property of the taxpayer,
"(II) is safe harbor lease property (not described in subclause (I)) with respect to which the taxpayer is the lessee, or
"(III) is designated leased property (other than property described in subclause (I) or (II)) with respect which the taxpayer is the lessee.
Any designated leased property taken into account by any lessee under the preceding sentence shall not be taken into account by the lessor in determining the lessor's qualified base property. The lessor shall provide the lessee with such information with respect to the cost basis of such property as is necessary to carry out the purposes of this clause.

"(vii) Definition of designated leased property. For purposes of this subparagraph, the term 'designated leased property' means property—
"(I) which is new section 38 property,
"(II) which is subject to a lease with respect to which the lessor of the property is treated (without regard to this paragraph) as the owner of the property for Federal tax purposes,
"(III) with respect to which the term of the lease to which such property is subject is more than 50 percent of the present class life (or, if no present class life, the recovery period used in subsection (i)(2)) of such property, and
"(IV) which the lessee designates on his return as designated leased property.

"(viii) Definition: special rule. For purposes of this subparagraph—
"(I) New section 38 property. The term 'new section 38 property' has the meaning given such term by section 48(b).
"(II) Property placed in service. For purposes of this title (other than clause (i)), any property described in clause (i) to which subparagraph (A) applies shall be deemed originally placed in service not earlier than the date such property is used under the lease."

"(E) Minimum investment.
"(i) In general. For purposes of subparagraph (A), the term 'minimum investment' means the amount the lessor has at risk with respect to the property (other than financing from the lessee or a related party of the lessee).
"(ii) Special rule for purchase requirement. For purposes of clause (i), an agreement between the lessor and lessee requiring either or both parties to purchase or sell the qualified leased property at some price (whether or not fixed in the agreement) at the end of the lease term shall not affect the amount the lessor is treated as having at risk with respect to the property.

"(F) Characterization by parties. For purposes of this paragraph, any determination as to whether a person is a lessor or lessee or property is leased shall be made on the basis of the characterization of such person or property under the agreement described in subparagraph (A).

"(G) Regulations. The Secretary shall prescribe such regulations as may be necessary to carry out the purposes of this paragraph, including (but not limited to) regulations consistent with such purposes which limit the aggregate amount of (and timing of) deductions and credits in respect of qualified leased property to the aggregate amount (and the timing) allowable without regard to this paragraph.

"(H) Definitions. For purposes of this paragraph—
"(i) Related person. A person is related to another person if both persons are members of the same affiliated group (within the meaning of subsection (a) of section 1504 and determined without regard to subsection (b) of section 1504).
"(ii) Nonqualified tax-exempt organization.

"(I) In general. The term 'nonqualified tax-exempt organization' means, with respect to any agreement to which subparagraph (A) applies, any organization (or predecessor organization) which was engaged in substantially similar activities) which was exempt from taxation under this title at any time during the 5-year period ending on the date such agreement was entered into.
"(II) Special rule for farmers' cooperatives. The term 'nonqualified tax-exempt organization' shall not include any farmers' cooperative organization described in section 521 whether or not exempt from taxation under section 521.
"(III) Special rule for property used in unrelated trade or business. An organization shall not be treated as a nonqualified tax-exempt organization with respect to any property if such property is used in an unrelated trade or business (within the meaning of section 513) of such organization which is subject to tax under section 511.

"(I) Transitional rules for certain transactions.
"(i) In general. Except as provided in clause (ii), clause (ii) of subparagraph (D) shall not apply to any transitional safe harbor lease property (within the meaning of section 208(d)(3) of the Tax Equity and Fiscal Responsibility Act of 1982).
"(ii) Special rules. For purposes of subparagraph (D)(ii)—
"(I) Determination of qualified base property. The cost basis of property described in clause (i) (and other property placed in service during 1982 to which subparagraph (D)(ii) does not apply) shall be taken into account in determining the qualified base property of the taxpayer for the taxable year in which such property was placed in service.
"(II) Reduction in qualified leased property. The cost basis of property which may be treated as qualified leased property under subparagraph (D)(ii) for the taxable year in which such property was placed in service (determined without regard to this subparagraph) shall be reduced by the cost basis of the property taken into account under subclause (I).

"(J) Coordination with at risk rules.
"(i) In general. For purposes of section 465, in the case of property placed in service after the date of the enactment of this subparagraph, if—
"(I) an activity involves the leasing of section 1245 property which is safe harbor lease property, and
"(II) the lessee of such property (as determined under this paragraph) would, but for this paragraph, be treated as the owner of such property for purposes of this title,
then the lessor (as so determined) shall be considered to be at risk with respect to such property in an amount equal to the amount the lessee is considered at risk with respect to such property (determined under section 465 without regard to this paragraph).
"(ii) Subparagraph not to apply to certain service corporations. Clause (i) shall not apply to any lessor which is a corporation the principal function of which is the performance of services in the field of health, law, engineering, architecture, accounting, actuarial science, performing arts, athletics, or consulting.
"(iii) Special rule for property placed in service before date of enactment of this subparagraph. This subparagraph shall apply to property placed in service before the date of enactment of this subparagraph if the provisions of section 465 did not apply to the lessor before such date but become applicable to such lessor after such date.

"(K) Cross reference. For special recapture in cases where lessee acquires qualified leased property, see section 1245."
Prior to amendment, subsec. (i) read as follows:
"(i) Limitations relating to leases of qualified leased property.
"For purposes of this subtitle, in the case of safe harbor lease property, the following limitations shall apply:
"(1) Lessor may not reduce tax liability by more than 50 percent.
"(A) In general. The aggregate amount allowable as deductions or credits for any taxable year which are allocable to all safe harbor lease property with respect to which the taxpayer is the lessor may not reduce the liability for tax of the taxpayer for such taxable year (determined without regard to safe harbor lease items) by more than 50 percent of such liability.
"(B) Carryover of amounts not allowable as deductions or credits. Any amount not allowable as a deduction or credit under subparagraph (A)—
"(i) may be carried over to any subsequent taxable year, and
"(ii) shall be treated as a deduction or credit allocable to safe harbor lease property in such subsequent taxable year.
"(C) Allocation among deductions and credits. The Secretary shall prescribe regulations for determining the amount—
"(i) of any deduction or credit allocable to safe harbor lease property for any taxable year to which subparagraph (A) applies, and
"(ii) of any carryover of any such deduction or credit under subparagraph (B) to any subsequent taxable year.
"(D) Liability for tax and safe harbor lease items defined. For purposes of this paragraph—
"(i) Liability for tax defined. Except as provided in this subparagraph, the term 'liability for tax' means the tax imposed by this chapter, reduced by the sum of the credits allowable under subpart A of part IV of subchapter A of this chapter.
"(ii) Safe harbor lease items defined. The term 'safe harbor lease items' means any of the following items which are properly allocable to safe harbor lease property with respect to which the taxpayer is the lessor:
"(I) Any deduction or credit allowable under this chapter (other than any deduction for interest).
"(II) Any rental income received by the taxpayer from any lessee of such property.
"(III) Any interest allowable as a deduction under this chapter on indebtedness of the taxpayer (or any related person within the meaning of subsection (e)(4)(D)) which is paid or incurred to the lessee of such property (or any person so related to the lessee).

"(iii) Certain taxes not included. The term 'tax imposed by this chapter' shall not include any tax treated as not imposed by this chapter under the last sentence of section 53(a) (other than the tax imposed by section 56).

"(2) Method of cost recovery. The deduction allowable under subsection (a) with respect to any safe harbor lease property shall be determined by using the 150 percent declining balance method, switching to the straight-line method at a time to maximize the deduction (with a half-year convention in the first recovery year and without regard to salvage value) and a recovery period determined in accordance with the following table:

In the case of:	The recovery period is:
3-year property	5 years
5-year property	8 years
10-year property	15 years.

"(3) Investment credit allowed only over 5-year period. In the case of any credit which would otherwise be allowable under section 38 with respect to any safe harbor lease property for any taxable year (determined without regard to this paragraph), only 20 percent of the amount of such credit shall be allowable in such taxable year and 20 percent of such amount shall be allowable in each of the succeeding 4 taxable years.

"(4) No carrybacks of credit or net operating loss allocable to elected qualified leased property.

"(A) Credit carrybacks. In determining the amount of any credit allowable under subpart A of part IV of subchapter A of this chapter which may be carried back to any preceding taxable year—

"(i) the liability for tax for the taxable year from which any such credit is to be carried shall be reduced first by any credit not properly allocable to safe harbor lease property, and

"(ii) no credit which is properly allocable to safe harbor lease property shall be taken into account in determining the amount of any credit which may be carried back.

"(B) Net operating loss carrybacks. The net operating loss carryback provided in section 172(b) for any taxable year shall be reduced by that portion of the amount of such carryback which is properly allocable to the items described in paragraph (1)(D)(ii) with respect to all safe harbor lease property with respect to which the taxpayer is the lessor.

"(5) Limitation on deduction for interest paid by the lessor to the lessee. In the case of interest described in paragraph (1)(D)(ii)(III), the amount allowable as a deduction for any taxable year with respect to such interest shall not exceed the amount which would have been computed if the rate of interest under the agreement were equal to the rate of interest in effect under section 6621 at the time the agreement was entered into.

"(6) Computation of taxable income of lessee for purposes of percentage depletion.

"(A) In general. For purposes of section 613 or 613A, the taxable income of any taxpayer who is a lessee of any safe harbor lease property shall be computed as if the taxpayer was the owner of such property, except that the amount of the deduction under subsection (a) of this section shall be determined after application of paragraph (2) of this subsection.

"(B) Coordination with crude oil windfall profit tax. Section 4988(b)(3)(A) shall be applied without regard to subparagraph (A).

"(7) Transitional rule for application of paragraph (1) to certain transactions. In the case of any deduction or credit with respect to—

"(A) any transitional safe harbor lease property (within the meaning of section 208(d)(3) of the Tax Equity and Fiscal Responsibility Act of 1982), or

"(B) any other safe harbor lease property placed in service during 1982 and to which paragraph (1) does not apply,

paragraph (1) shall not operate to disallow any such deduction or credit for the taxable year for which such deduction or credit would otherwise be allowable but deductions and credits with respect to such property shall be taken into account first in determining whether any deduction or credit is allowable under paragraph (1) with respect to any other safe harbor lease property.

"(8) Safe harbor lease property. For purposes of this section, the term 'safe harbor lease property' means qualified leased property with respect to which an election under section 168(f)(8) is in effect."

—P.L. 97-248, Sec. 210, [as amended by Secs. 32(b), 712(d)(1) and 712(d)(2) of P.L. 98-369, see above] provides:

"SEC. 210. MOTOR VEHICLE OPERATING LEASES.

"(a) In general.

"In the case of any qualified motor vehicle agreement entered into on or before the 90th day after the date of the enactment of the Tax Reform Act of 1984 [7/18/84], the fact that such agreement contains a terminal rental adjustment clause shall not be taken into account in determining whether such agreement is a lease.

"(b) Definitions.

"For purposes of this section—

"(1) Qualified motor vehicle agreement.—The term 'qualified motor vehicle agreement' means any agreement with respect to a motor vehicle (including a trailer)—

"(A) which was entered into before—

"(i) the enactment of any law, or

"(ii) the publication by the Secretary of the Treasury or his delegate of any regulation,

which provides that any agreement with a terminal rental adjustment clause is not a lease,

"(B) with respect to which the lessor under the agreement—

"(i) is personally liable for the repayment of, or

"(ii) has pledged property (but only to the extent of the net fair market value of the lessor's interest in such property), other than property subject to the agreement or property directly or indirectly financed by indebtedness secured by property subject to the agreement, as security for,

all amounts borrowed to finance the acquisition of property subject to the agreement, and

"(C) with respect to which the lessee under the agreement uses the property subject to the agreement in a trade or business or for the production of income.

"(2) Terminal rental adjustment clause.—The term 'terminal rental adjustment clause' means a provision of an agreement which permits or requires the rental price to be adjusted upward or downward by reference to the amount realized by the lessor under the agreement upon sale or other disposition of such property. Such term also includes a provision of an agreement which requires a lessee who is a dealer in motor vehicles to purchase the motor vehicle for a predetermined price and then resell such vehicle where such provision achieves substantially the same results as a provision described in the preceding sentence.

"(c) Exception where lessee took position on return. Subsection (a) shall not apply to deny a deduction for interest paid or accrued claimed by a lessee with respect to a qualified motor vehicle agreement on a return of tax imposed by chapter 1 of the Internal Revenue Code of 1954 which was filed before the date of the enactment of this Act or to deny a credit for investment in depreciable property claimed by the lessee on such a return pursuant to an agreement with the lessor that the lessor would not claim the credit."

—P.L. 97-248, Sec. 216(a), added para. (f)(12), effective as provided in Sec. 216(b) of this Act which reads as follows:

"(b) Effective dates.

"(1) In general.—Except as otherwise provided in this subsection, the amendments made by this section shall apply with respect to property placed in service after December 31, 1982, to the extent such property is financed by the proceeds of an obligation (including a refunding obligation) issued after June 30, 1982.

"(2) Exceptions.—

"(A) Construction or binding agreement.—The amendments made by this section shall not apply with respect to facilities the original use of which commences with the taxpayer and—

"(i) the construction, reconstruction, or rehabilitation of which began before July 1, 1982, or

"(ii) with respect to which a binding agreement to incur significant expenditures was entered into before July 1, 1982.

"(B) Refunding.—

"(i) In general.—Except as provided in clause (ii), in the case of property placed in service after December 31, 1982 which is financed by the proceeds of an obligation which is issued solely to refund another obligation which was issued before July 1, 1982, the amendments made by this section shall apply only with respect to the basis in such property which has not been recovered before the date such refunding obligation is issued.

"(ii) Significant expenditures.—In the case of facilities the original use of which commences with the taxpayer and with respect to which significant expenditures are made before January 1, 1983, the amendments made by this section shall not apply with respect to such facilities to the extent such facilities are financed by the proceeds of an obligation issued solely to refund another obligation which was issued before July 1, 1982.

In the case of an inducement resolution adopted by an issuing authority before July 1, 1982, for purposes of applying subparagraphs (A)(i) and (B)(ii) with respect to obligations described in such resolution, the term 'facilities' means the facilities described in such resolution.

"(3) Certain projects for residential real property.—For purposes of clause (i) of section 168(f)(12)(C) of the Internal Revenue Code of 1954 (as added by this section), any obligation issued to finance a project described in the table contained in paragraph (1) of section 1104(n) of the Mortgage Subsidy Bond Tax Act of 1980 shall be treated as an obligation described in section 103(b)(4)(A) of the Internal Revenue Code of 1954."

—P.L. 97-248, Sec. 224(c)(1), added the last sentence to subpara. (e)(4)(E) ... Sec. 224(c)(2), deleted "(other than a transaction with respect to which the basis is determined under section 334(b)(2))" after "section 332" in clause (f)(10)(B)(i). For effective date see Sec. 224(d) of this Act reproduced in note following Code Sec. 338.

In 1981, P.L. 97-119, Sec. 112, provides:

"SEC. 112. INFORMATION RETURNS WITH RESPECT TO SAFE HARBOR LEASES.

"(a) Requirement of return.

"(1) In general. Except as provided in paragraph (2), paragraph (8) of section 168(f) of the Internal Revenue Code of 1954 (relating to special rule for leases) shall not apply with respect to an agreement unless a return, signed by the lessor and lessee and containing the information required to be included in the return pursuant to subsection (b), has been filed with the Internal Revenue Service not later than the 30th day after the date on which the agreement is executed.

"(2) Special rules for agreements executed before January 1, 1982.—

"(A) In general.—In the case of an agreement executed before January 1, 1982, such agreement shall cease on February 1, 1982, to be treated as a lease under section 168(f)(8) unless a return, signed by the lessor and containing the information required to be included in subsection (b), has been filed with the Internal Revenue Service not later than January 31, 1982.

"(B) Filing by lessee.—If the lessor does not file a return under subparagraph (A), the return requirement under subparagraph(A) shall be satisfied if such return is filed by the lessee before January 31, 1982.

"(3) Certain failure to file.—If—

"(A) a lessor or lessee fails to file any return within the time prescribed by this subsection, and

"(B) such failure is shown to be due to reasonable cause and not due to willful neglect,
the lessor or lessee shall be treated as having filed a timely return if a return is filed within a reasonable time after the failure is ascertained.
"(b) Information required.
The information required to be included in the return pursuant to this subsection is as follows:
"(1) The name, address, and taxpayer identifying number of the lessor and the lessee (and parent company if a consolidated return is filed);
"(2) The district director's office with which the income tax returns of the lessor and lessee are filed;
"(3) A description of each individual property with respect to which the election is made;
"(4) The date on which the lessee places the property in service, the date on which the lease begins and the term of the lease;
"(5) The recovery property class and the ADR midpoint life of the leased property;
"(6) The payment terms between the parties to the lease transaction;
"(7) Whether the ACRS deductions and the investment tax credit are allowable to the same taxpayer;
"(8) The aggregate amount paid to outside parties to arrange or carry out the transaction;
"(9) For the lessor only: the unadjusted basis of the property as defined in section 168(d)(1);
"(10) For the lessor only: if the lessor is a partnership or a grantor trust, the name, address, and taxpayer identifying number of the partners or the beneficiaries, and the district director's office with which the income tax return of each partner or beneficiary is filed; and
"(11) Such other information as may be required by the return or its instructions.
Paragraph (8) shall not apply with respect to any person for any calendar year if it is reasonable to estimate that the aggregate adjusted basis of the property of such person which will be subject to subsection (a) for such year is $1,000,000 or less.
"(c) Coordination with other information requirements.
In the case of agreements executed after December 31, 1982, to the extent provided in regulations prescribed by the Secretary of the Treasury or his delegate, the provisions of this section shall be modified to coordinate such provisions with the other information requirements of the Internal Revenue Code of 1954."
—P.L. 97-34, Sec. 201(a), added new Code Sec. 168, for property placed in service after 12/31/80 in tax. yrs. end. after 12/31/80. For transitional rule see Sec. 203(c)(3) of this Act reproduced in note following Code Sec. 167.
—P.L. 97-34, Sec. 203(e), provides:
"(e) Conforming amendment.
"The Secretary of Health and Human Services is not required to apply any provision of the Internal Revenue Code of 1954, as amended, in calculating depreciation (for the purpose of determining any cost under a program administered by the Secretary), unless a provision of law requires so expressly."
—P.L. 97-34, Sec. 209(d)(1), and (4) provides.
"(d) Special rule for public utilities.
"(1) Transitional rule for normalization requirements. If, by the terms of the applicable rate order last entered before the date of the enactment of this Act by a regulatory commission having appropriate jurisdiction, a regulated public utility would (but for this provision) fail to meet the requirements of section 168(e)(3) of the Internal Revenue Code of 1954 with respect to property because, for an accounting period ending after December 31, 1980, such public utility used a method of accounting other than a normalization method of accounting, such regulated public utility shall not fail to meet such requirements if, by the terms of its first rate order determining cost of service with respect to such property which becomes effective after the date of the enactment of this Act and on or before January 1, 1983, such regulated public utility uses a normalization method of accounting. This provision shall not apply to any rate order which, under the rules in effect before the date of the enactment of this Act, required a regulated public utility to use a method of accounting with respect to the deduction allowable by section 167 which, under section 167(l), it was not permitted to use.
* * *

"(4) Authority to prescribe interim regulations with respect to normalization. Until Congress acts further, the Secretary of the Treasury or his delegate may prescribe such interim regulations as may be necessary or appropriate to determine whether the requirements of section 168(e)(3)(B) of the Internal Revenue Code of 1954 have been met with respect to property placed in service after December 31, 1980."

In 1976, P.L. 94-455, Sec. 1951(b)(4)(A), repealed Code Sec. 168, for tax. yrs. begin. after '76, except as provided in Sec. 1951(b)(4)(B) of the Act:
"(B) Savings provision.—Notwithstanding the repeal made by subparagraph (A), if a certificate was issued before January 1, 1960, with respect to an emergency facility which is or has been placed in service before the date of the enactment of this Act, the provisions of section 168 shall not, with respect to such facility, be considered repealed. The benefit of deductions by reason of the preceding sentence shall be allowed to estates and trusts in the same manner as in the case of an individual. The allowable deduction shall be apportioned between the income beneficiaries and the fiduciary in accordance with regulations prescribed under section 642(f)."
Prior to repeal, Code Sec. 168 read as follows:
"SEC. 168. AMORTIZATION OF EMERGENCY FACILITIES.
"(a) General rule.
"Every person, at his election, shall be entitled to a deduction with respect to the amortization of the adjusted basis (for determining gain) of any emergency facility (as defined in subsection (d)), based on a period of 60 months. Such amortization deduction shall be an amount, with respect to each month of such period within the taxable year, equal to the adjusted basis of the facility at the end of such month divided by the number of months (including the month for which the deduction is computed) remaining in the period. Such adjusted basis at the end of the month shall be computed without regard to the amortization deduction for such month. The amortization deduction above provided with respect to any month shall, except to the extent provided in subsection (f), be in lieu of the depreciation deduction with respect to such facility for such month provided by section 167. The 60-month period shall begin as to any emergency facility, at the election of the taxpayer, with the month following the month in which the facility was completed or acquired, or with the succeeding taxable year.
"(b) Election of amortization.
"The election of the taxpayer to take the amortization deduction and to begin the 60-month period with the month following the month in which the facility was completed or acquired, or with the taxable year succeeding the taxable year in which such facility was completed or acquired, shall be made by filing with the Secretary or his delegate, in such manner, in such form, and within such time, as the Secretary or his delegate may by regulations prescribe, a statement of such election.
"(c) Termination of amortization deduction.
"A taxpayer which has elected under subsection (b) to take the amortization deduction provided in subsection (a) may, at any time after making such election, discontinue the amortization deduction with respect to the remainder of the amortization period, such discontinue to begin as of the beginning of any month specified by the taxpayer in a notice in writing filed with the Secretary or his delegate before the beginning of such month. The depreciation deduction provided under section 167 shall be allowed, beginning with the first month as to which the amortization deduction does not apply and the taxpayer shall not be entitled to any further amortization deduction with respect to such emergency facility.
"(d) Definitions.
"(1) Emergency facility. For purposes of this section, the term 'emergency facility' means any facility, land, building, machinery, or equipment, or any part thereof, the construction, reconstruction, erection, installation, or acquisition of which was completed after December 31, 1949, and with respect to which a certificate under subsection (e) has been made. In no event shall an amortization deduction be allowed in respect of any emergency facility for any taxable year unless a certificate in respect thereof under this paragraph shall have been made before the filing of the taxpayer's return for such taxable year.
"(2) Emergency period. For purposes of this section, the term 'emergency period' means the period beginning January 1, 1950, and ending on the date on which the President proclaims that the utilization of a substantial portion of the emergency facilities with respect to which certifications under subsection (e) have been made is no longer required in the interest of national defense.
"(e) Determination of adjusted basis of emergency facility.
"In determining, for purposes of subsection (a) or (g), the adjusted basis of an emergency facility—
"(1) Certification on or before August 22, 1957. In the case of a certificate made on or before August 22, 1957, there shall be included only so much of the amount of the adjusted basis of such facility (computed without regard to this section) as is properly attributable to such construction, reconstruction, erection, installation, or acquisition after December 31, 1949, as the certifying authority, designated by the President by Executive Order, has certified as necessary in the interest of national defense during the emergency period, and only such portion of such amount as such authority has certified as attributable to defense purposes. Such certification shall be under such regulations as may be prescribed from time to time by such certifying authority with the approval of the President. An application for a certificate must be filed at such time and in such manner as may be prescribed by such certifying authority under such regulations, but in no event shall such certificate have any effect unless an application therefor is filed before March 24, 1951, or before the expiration of 6 months after the beginning of such construction, reconstruction, erection, or installation or the date of such acquisition, whichever is later.
"(2) Certifications after August 22, 1957. In the case of a certificate made after August 22, 1957, there shall be included only so much of the amount of the adjusted basis of such facility (computed without regard to this section) as is properly attributable to such construction, reconstruction, erection, installation, or acquisition after December 31, 1949, as the certifying authority designated by the President by Executive Order, has certified is to be used—
"(A) to produce new or specialized defense items or components of new or specialized defense items (as defined in paragraph (4)) during the emergency period),
"(B) to provide research, developmental, or experimental services during the emergency period for the Department of Defense (or one of the component departments of such Department), or for the Atomic Energy Commission, as a part of the national defense program, or
"(C) to provide primary processing for uranium ore or uranium concentrate under a program of the Atomic Energy Commission for the development of new sources of uranium ore or uranium concentrate,
and only such portion of such amount as such authority has certified is attributable to the national defense program. Such certification shall be under such regulations as may be prescribed from time to time by such certifying authority with the approval of the President. An application for a certificate must be filed at such time and in such manner as may be prescribed by such certifying authority under such regulations but in no event shall such certificate have any effect unless an application therefor is filed before the expiration of 6 months after the beginning of such construction, reconstruction, erection, or installation or the date of such acquisition. For purposes of the preceding sentence, an application which was timely filed under this subsection on or before August 22, 1957, and which was

Deductions Code Sec. 169(d)(1)(B)

pending on such date, shall be considered to be an application timely filed under this paragraph.

"(3) Separate facilities; special rule. After the completion or acquisition of any emergency facility with respect to which a certificate under paragraph (1) or (2) has been made, any expenditure (attributable to such facility and to the period after such completion or acquisition) which does not represent construction, reconstruction, erection, installation, or acquisition included in such certificate, but with respect to which a separate certificate is made under paragraph (1) or (2), shall not be applied in adjustment of the basis of such facility, but a separate basis shall be computed therefor pursuant to paragraph (1) or (2), as the case may be, as if it were a new and separate emergency facility.

"(4) Definitions. For purposes of paragraph (2)—

"(A) New or specialized defense item. The term 'new or specialized defense item' means only an item (excluding services)—

"(i) which is produced, or will be produced, for sale to the Department of Defense (or one of the component departments of such Department), or to the Atomic Energy Commission, for use in the national defense program, and

"(ii) for the production of which existing productive facilities are unsuitable because of its newness or of its specialized defense features.

"(B) Component of new or specialized defense item. The term component of a new or specialized defense item means only an item—

"(i) which is, or will become, a physical part of a new or specialized defense item, and

"(ii) for the production of which existing productive facilities are unsuitable because of its newness or of its specialized defense features.

"(5) Limitation with respect to uranium ore or uranium concentrate processing facilities. No certificate shall be made under paragraph (2)(C) with respect to any facility unless existing facilities for processing the uranium ore or uranium concentrate which will be processed by such facility are unsuitable because of their location.

"(f) Depreciation deduction.

"If the adjusted basis of the emergency facility (computed without regard to this section) is in excess of the adjusted basis computed under subsection (e), the depreciation deduction provided by section 167 shall, despite the provisions of subsection (a) of this section, be allowed with respect to such emergency facility as if its adjusted basis for the purpose of such deduction were an amount equal to the amount of such excess.

"(g) Payment by United States of unamortized cost of facility.

"If an amount is properly includible in the gross income of the taxpayer on account of a payment with respect to an emergency facility and such payment is certified as provided in paragraph (1), then, at the election of the taxpayer in its return for the taxable year in which such amount is so includible—

"(1) The amortization deduction for the month in which such amount is so includible shall (in lieu of the amount of the deduction for such month computed under subsection (a)) be equal to the amount so includible but not in excess of the adjusted basis of the emergency facility as of the end of such month (computed without regard to any amortization deduction for such month). Payments referred to in this subsection shall be payments the amounts of which are certified, under such regulations as the President may prescribe, by the certifying authority designated by the President as compensation to the taxpayer for the unamortized cost of the emergency facility made because—

"(A) a contract with the United States involving the use of the facility has been terminated by its terms or by cancellation, or

"(B) the taxpayer had reasonable ground (either from provisions of a contract with the United States involving the use of the facility, or from written or oral representations made under authority of the United States) for anticipating future contracts involving the use of the facility, which future contracts have not been made.

"(2) In case the taxpayer is not entitled to any amortization deduction with respect to the emergency facility, the depreciation deduction allowable under section 167 on account of the month in which such amount is so includible shall be increased by such amount, but such deduction on account of such month shall not be in excess of the adjusted basis of the emergency facility as of the end of such month (computed without regard to any amount allowable, on account of such month, under section 167 or this paragraph).

"(h) Life tenant and remainderman.

"In the case of property held by one person for life with remainder to another person, the deduction shall be computed as if the life tenant were the absolute owner of the property and shall be allowable to the life tenant.

"(i) Termination.

"No certificate under subsection (e) shall be made with respect to any emergency facility after December 31, 1959.

"(j) Cross reference.

"For special rule with respect to gain derived from the sale or exchange of property the adjusted basis of which is determined with regard to this section, see section 1238."

In 1958, P.L. 85-866, Sec. 9, added subsec. (e)(2)(C) and (e)(5), as of original date of '54 Code.

In 1957, P.L. 85-165, Sec. 4, limited authorization to certifications made on or before Aug. 22, '57, added subsec. (e)(2), redesignated former subsec. (e)(2) as (e)(3), added "or (2)" after "paragraph (i)" wherever appearing and "as the case may be", added subsec. (e)(4), added subsec. (i) and redesignated former subsec. (i) as (j).

Sec. 169. Amortization of pollution control facilities.
(a) Allowance of deduction.

Every person, at his election, shall be entitled to a deduction with respect to the amortization of the amortizable basis of any certified pollution control facility (as defined in subsection (d)), based on a period of 60 months. Such amortization deduction shall be an amount, with respect to each month of such period within the taxable year, equal to the amortizable basis of the pollution control facility at the end of such month divided by the number of months (including the month for which the deduction is computed) remaining in the period. Such amortizable basis at the end of the month shall be computed without regard to the amortization deduction for such month. The amortization deduction provided by this section with respect to any month shall be in lieu of the depreciation deduction with respect to such pollution control facility for such month provided by section 167. The 60-month period shall begin, as to any pollution control facility, at the election of the taxpayer, with the month following the month in which such facility was completed or acquired, or with the succeeding taxable year.

(b) Election of amortization.

The election of the taxpayer to take the amortization deduction and to begin the 60-month period with the month following the month in which the facility is completed or acquired, or with the taxable year succeeding the taxable year in which such facility is completed or acquired, shall be made by filing with the Secretary, in such manner, in such form, and within such time, as the Secretary may by regulations prescribe, a statement of such election.

(c) Termination of amortization deduction.

A taxpayer which has elected under subsection (b) to take the amortization deduction provided in subsection (a) may, at any time after making such election, discontinue the amortization deduction with respect to the remainder of the amortization period, such discontinuance to begin as of the beginning of any month specified by the taxpayer in a notice in writing filed with the Secretary before the beginning of such month. The depreciation deduction provided under section 167 shall be allowed, beginning with the first month as to which the amortization deduction does not apply, and the taxpayer shall not be entitled to any further amortization deduction under this section with respect to such pollution control facility.

(d) Definitions and special rules.

For purposes of this section—

(1) Certified pollution control facility. The term "certified pollution control facility" means a new identifiable treatment facility which is used, in connection with a plant or other property in operation before January 1, 1976, to abate or control water or atmospheric pollution or contamination by removing, altering, disposing, storing, or preventing the creation or emission of pollutants, contaminants, wastes, or heat and which—

(A) the State certifying authority having jurisdiction with respect to such facility has certified to the Federal certifying authority as having been constructed, reconstructed, erected, or acquired in conformity with the State program or requirements for abatement or control of water or atmospheric pollution or contamination;

(B) the Federal certifying authority has certified to the Secretary (i) as being in compliance with the applicable regulations of Federal agencies and (ii) as being in furtherance of the general policy of the United States for cooperation with the States in the prevention and abatement of water pollution under the Federal Water Pollution Control Act, as amended (33 U.S.C. 466 *et seq.*),

1,611

or in the prevention and abatement of atmospheric pollution and contamination under the Clean Air Act, as amended (42 U.S.C. 1857 *et seq.*); and

(C) does not significantly—

(i) increase the output or capacity, extend the useful life, or reduce the total operating costs of such plant or other property (or any unit thereof), or

(ii) alter the nature of the manufacturing or production process or facility.

(2) State certifying authority. The term "State certifying authority" means, in the case of water pollution, the State water pollution control agency as defined in section 13(a) of the Federal Water Pollution Control Act and, in the case of air pollution, the air pollution control agency as defined in section 302(b) of the Clean Air Act. The term "State certifying authority" includes any interstate agency authorized to act in place of a certifying authority of the State.

(3) Federal certifying authority. The term "Federal certifying authority" means, in the case of water pollution, the Secretary of the Interior and, in the case of air pollution, the Secretary of Health and Human Services.

(4) New identifiable treatment facility.

(A) In general. For purposes of paragraph (1), the term "new identifiable treatment facility" includes only tangible property (not including a building and its structural components, other than a building which is exclusively a treatment facility) which is of a character subject to the allowance for depreciation provided in section 167, which is identifiable as a treatment facility, and which is property—

(i) the construction, reconstruction, or erection of which is completed by the taxpayer after December 31, 1968, or

(ii) acquired after December 31, 1968, if the original use of the property commences with the taxpayer and commences after such date.

In applying this section in the case of property described in clause (i)there shall be taken into account only that portion of the basis which is properly attributable to construction, reconstruction, or erection after December 31, 1968.

(B) Certain facilities placed in operation after April 11, 2005. In the case of any facility described in paragraph (1) solely by reason of paragraph (5), subparagraph (A) shall be applied by substituting "April 11, 2005" for "December 31, 1968" each place it appears therein.

(5) Special rule relating to certain atmospheric pollution control facilities. In the case of any atmospheric pollution control facility which is placed in service after April 11, 2005, and used in connection with an electric generation plant or other property which is primarily coal fired—

(A) paragraph (1) shall be applied without regard to the phrase "in operation before January 1, 1976", and

(B) in the case of facility placed in service in connection with a plant or other property placed in operation after December 31, 1975, this section shall be applied by substituting "84" for "60" each place it appears in subsections (a) and (b).

(e) Profitmaking abatement works, etc.

The Federal certifying authority shall not certify any property under subsection (d)(1)(B) to the extent it appears that by reason of profits derived through the recovery of wastes or otherwise in the operation of such property, its costs will be recovered over its actual useful life.

(f) Amortizable basis.

(1) Defined. For purposes of this section, the term "amortizable basis" means that portion of the adjusted basis (for determining gain) of a certified pollution control facility which may be amortized under this section.

(2) Special rules.

(A) If a certified pollution control facility has a useful life (determined as of the first day of the first month for which a deduction is allowable under this section) in excess of 15 years, the amortizable basis of such facility shall be equal to an amount which bears the same ratio to the portion of the adjusted basis of such facility, which would be eligible for amortization but for the application of this subparagraph, as 15 bears to the number of years of useful life of such facility.

(B) The amortizable basis of a certified pollution control facility with respect to which an election under this section is in effect shall not be increased, for purposes of this section, for additions or improvements after the amortization period has begun.

(g) Depreciation deduction.

The depreciation deduction provided by section 167 shall, despite the provisions of subsection (a), be allowed with respect to the portion of the adjusted basis which is not the amortizable basis.

(h) Repealed.

(i) Life tenant and remainderman.

In the case of property held by one person for life with remainder to another person, the deduction under this section shall be computed as if the life tenant were the absolute owner of the property and shall be allowable to the life tenant.

(j) Cross reference.

For special rule with respect to certain gain derived from the disposition of property the adjusted basis of which is determined with regard to this section, see section 1245.

In 2005, P.L. 109-135, Sec. 402(e), added "in the case of facility placed in service in connection with a plant or other property placed in operation after December 31, 1975," at the beginning of subpara. (d)(5)(B), effective for facilities placed in service after 4/11/2005 as if included in Sec. 1309 of the Energy Policy Act of 2005, P.L. 109-58.

—P.L. 109-58, Sec. 1309(a), added para. (d)(5) . . . Sec. 1309(b), amended subpara. (d)(4)(B) . . . Sec. 1309(c), added "and special rules" after "Definitions" in the heading of subsec. (d) . . . Sec. 1309(d), substituted "Health and Human Services" for "Health, Education, and Welfare" in para. (d)(3), effective for facilities placed in service after 4/11/2005.

Prior to amendment, subpara. (d)(4)(B) read as follows:

"(B) Certain plants, etc., placed in operation after 1968. In the case of any treatment facility used in connection with any plant or other property not in operation before January 1, 1969, the preceding sentence shall be applied by substituting December 31, 1975, for December 31, 1968."

In 1976, P.L. 94-455, Sec. 1906(b)(13)(A), substituted "Secretary" for "Secretary or his delegate" in subsecs. (b), (c) and (d), for tax. yrs. begin. after '76.

—P.L. 94-455, Sec. 2112(b), substituted "January 1, 1976" for "January 1, 1969" in para. (d)(1), substituted "storing, or preventing the creation or emission of" for "or storing" in para. (d)(1), deleted "and" at the end of subpara. (d)(1)(A), substituted "and" for the period at the end of subpara. (d)(1)(B), added subpara. (d)(1)(C), effective for tax. yrs. begin. after 12/31/75 except in the case of any property for which the amortization period under Code Sec. 169 has begun before 1/1/76.

—P.L. 94-455, Sec. 2112(c), amended para. (d)(4), effective 10/4/76.

Prior to amendment, para. (d)(4) read as follows:

"(4) New identifiable treatment facility. For purposes of paragraph (1), the term 'new identifiable treatment facility' includes only tangible property (not including a building and its structural components, other than a building which is exclusively a treatment facility) which is of a character subject to the allowance for depreciation provided in section 167, which is identifiable as a treatment facility, and which—

"(A) is property—

"(i) the construction, reconstruction, or erection of which is completed by the taxpayer after December 31, 1968, or

"(ii) acquired after December 31, 1968, if the original use of the property commences with the taxpayer and commences after such date, and

"(B) is placed in service by the taxpayer before January 1, 1976.

Deductions   Code Sec. 170(a)(3)

In applying this section in the case of property described in clause (i) of subparagraph (A), there shall be taken into account only that portion of the basis which is properly attributable to construction, reconstruction, or erection after December 31, 1968."

In 1975, P.L. 93-625, Sec. 3(a), substituted "January 1, 1976" for "January 1, 1975" in subpara. (d)(4)(B), effective 1/3/75.

In 1971, P.L. 92-178, Sec. 104(f)(2), deleted subsec. (h), effective for property described in Code Sec. 50.

Prior to deletion, subsec. (h) read as follows:

"(h) Investment credit not to be allowed. In the case of any property with respect to which an election has been made under subsection (a), so much of the adjusted basis of the property as (after the application of subsection (f)) constitutes the amortizable basis for purposes of this section shall not be treated as section 38 property within the meaning of section 48(a)."

In 1969, P.L. 91-172, Sec. 704(a), amended Code Sec. 169, effective for tax. yrs. end. after 12/31/68.

Prior to amendment, Code Sec. 169 read as follows:

"SEC. 169. AMORTIZATION OF GRAIN-STORAGE FACILITIES.

"(a) Allowance of deduction.

"(1) Original owner. Any person who constructs, reconstructs, or erects a grain-storage facility (as defined in subsection (d)) shall, at his election, be entitled to a deduction with respect to the amortization of the adjusted basis (for determining gain) of such facility based on a period of 60 months. The 60-month period shall begin as to any such facility, at the election of the taxpayer, with the month following the month in which the facility was completed, or with the succeeding taxable year.

"(2) Subsequent owners. Any person who acquires a grain-storage facility from a taxpayer who—

"(A) elected under subsection (b) to take the amortization deduction provided by this subsection with respect to such facility, and

"(B) did not discontinue the amortization deduction pursuant to subsection (c), shall at his election, be entitled to a deduction with respect to the adjusted basis (determined under subsection (a)(2)) of such facility based on the period, if any, remaining (at the time of acquisition) in the 60-month period elected under subsection (b) by the person who constructed, reconstructed, or erected such facility.

"(3) Amount of deduction. The amortization deduction provided in paragraphs (1) and (2) shall be an amount, with respect to each month of the amortization period within the taxable year, equal to the adjusted basis of the facility at the end of such month, divided by the number of months (including the month for which the deduction is computed) remaining in the period. Such adjusted basis at the end of the month shall be computed without regard to the amortization deduction for such month. The amortization deduction above provided with respect to any month shall be in lieu of the depreciation with respect to such facility for such month provided by section 167.

"(b) Election of amortization.

"The election of the taxpayer under subsection (a)(1) to take the amortization deduction and to begin the 60-month period with the month following the month in which the facility was completed shall be made only by a statement to that effect in the return for the taxable year in which the facility was completed. The election of the taxpayer under subsection (a)(1) to take the amortization deduction and to begin such period with the taxable year succeeding such year shall be made only by a statement to that effect in the return for such succeeding taxable year. The election of the taxpayer under subsection (a)(2) to take the amortization deduction shall be made only by a statement to that effect in the return for the taxable year in which the facility was acquired. Notwithstanding the preceding three sentences, the election of the taxpayer under subsection (a)(1) or (2) may be made, under such regulations as the Secretary or his delegate may prescribe, before the time prescribed in the applicable sentence.

"(c) Termination of amortization deduction.

"A taxpayer which has elected under subsection (b) to take the amortization deduction provided in subsection (a) may, at any time after making such election, discontinue the amortization deduction with respect to the remainder of the amortization period, such discontinuance to begin as of the beginning of any month specified by the taxpayer in a notice in writing filed with the Secretary or his delegate before the beginning of such month. The depreciation deduction provided under section 167 shall be allowed, beginning with the first month as to which the amortization deduction does not apply, and the taxpayer shall not be entitled to any further amortization deduction with respect to such facility.

"(d) Definition of grain-storage facility.

"For purposes of this section, the term 'grain-storage facility' means—

"(1) any corn crib, grain bin, or grain elevator, or any similar structure suitable primarily for the storage of grain, which crib, bin, elevator, or structure is intended by the taxpayer at the time of his election to be used for storage of grain produced by him (or, if the election is made by a partnership, produced by the members thereof);

"(2) any public grain warehouse permanently equipped for receiving, elevating, conditioning, and loading out grain.

the construction, reconstruction, or erection of which was completed after December 31, 1952, and on or before December 31, 1956. If any structure described in clause (1) or (2) of the preceding sentence is altered or remodeled so as to increase its capacity for the storage of grain, or if any structure is converted, through alteration or remodeling, into a structure so described, and if such alteration or remodeling was completed after December 31, 1952, and on or before December 31, 1956, such alteration or remodeling shall be treated as the construction of a grain-storage facility. The term 'grain-storage facility' shall include only property of a character which is subject to the allowance for depreciation provided in section 167. The term 'grain-storage facility' shall not include any facility any part of which is an emergency facility within the meaning of section 168 of this title.

"(e) Determination of adjusted basis.

"(1) Original owners. For purposes of subsection (a)(1)—

"(A) in determining the adjusted basis of any grain-storage facility, the construction, reconstruction, or erection of which was begun before January 1, 1953, there shall be included only so much of the amount of the adjusted basis (computed without regard to this subsection) as is properly attributable to such construction, or erection after December 31, 1952; and

"(B) in determining the adjusted basis of any facility which is a grain-storage facility within the meaning of the second sentence of subsection (d), there shall be included only so much of the amount otherwise included in such basis as is properly attributable to the alteration or remodeling.

If any existing grain-storage facility as defined in the first sentence of subsection (d) is altered or remodeled as provided in the second sentence of subsection (d), the expenditures for such remodeling or alteration shall not be applied in adjustment of the basis of such existing facility but a separate basis shall be computed in respect of such facility as if the part altered or remodeled were a new and separate grain-storage facility.

"(2) Subsequent owners. For purposes of subsection (a)(2), the adjusted basis of any grain-storage facility shall be whichever of the following amounts is the smaller:

"(A) The basis (unadjusted) of such facility for purposes of this section in the hands of the transferor, donor, or grantor, adjusted as if such facility in the hands of the taxpayer had a substituted basis within the meaning of section 1016(b), or

"(B) so much of the adjusted basis (for determining gain) of the facility in the hands of the taxpayer (as computed without regard to this subsection) as is properly attributable to construction, reconstruction, or erection after December 31, 1952.

"(f) Depreciation deduction.

"If the adjusted basis of the grain-storage facility (computed without regard to subsection (e)) exceeds the adjusted basis computed under subsection (e), the depreciation deduction provided by section 167 shall, despite the provisions of subsection (a)(3) of this section, be allowed with respect to such grain-storage facility as if the adjusted basis for the purpose of such deduction were an amount equal to the amount of such excess.

"(g) Life tenant and remainderman.

"In the case of property held by one person for life with remainder to another person, the amortization deduction provided in subsection (a) shall be computed as if the life tenant were the absolute owner of the property and shall be allowed to the life tenant."

Sec. 170. Charitable, etc., contributions and gifts.

(a) Allowance of deduction.

(1) General rule. There shall be allowed as a deduction any charitable contribution (as defined in subsection (c)) payment of which is made within the taxable year. A charitable contribution shall be allowable as a deduction only if verified under regulations prescribed by the Secretary.

(2) Corporations on accrual basis. In the case of a corporation reporting its taxable income on the accrual basis, if—

(A) the board of directors authorizes a charitable contribution during any taxable year, and

(B) payment of such contribution is made after the close of such taxable year and on or before the 15th day of the third month following the close of such taxable year,

then the taxpayer may elect to treat such contribution as paid during such taxable year. The election may be made only at the time of the filing of the return for such taxable year, and shall be signified in such manner as the Secretary shall by regulations prescribe.

(3) Future interests in tangible personal property. For purposes of this section, payment of a charitable contribution which consists of a future interest in tangible personal property shall be treated as made only when all intervening interests in, and rights to the actual possession or enjoyment of, the property have expired or are held by persons other than the taxpayer or those standing in a relationship to the taxpayer described in section 267(b) or 707(b). For purposes of the preceding sentence, a fixture which is intended to be severed from the real property shall be treated as tangible personal property.

1,613

(b) Percentage limitations.
(1) Individuals. In the case of an individual, the deduction provided in subsection (a) shall be limited as provided in the succeeding subparagraphs.

(A) General rule. Any charitable contribution to—

(i) a church or a convention or association of churches,

(ii) an educational organization which normally maintains a regular faculty and curriculum and normally has a regularly enrolled body of pupils or students in attendance at the place where its educational activities are regularly carried on,

(iii) an organization the principal purpose or functions of which are the providing of medical or hospital care or medical education or medical research, if the organization is a hospital, or if the organization is a medical research organization directly engaged in the continuous active conduct of medical research in conjunction with a hospital, and during the calendar year in which the contribution is made such organization is committed to spend such contributions for such research before January 1 of the fifth calendar year which begins after the date such contribution is made,

(iv) an organization which normally receives a substantial part of its support (exclusive of income received in the exercise or performance by such organization of its charitable, educational, or other purpose or function constituting the basis for its exemption under section 501(a)) from the United States or any State or political subdivision thereof or from direct or indirect contributions from the general public, and which is organized and operated exclusively to receive, hold, invest, and administer property and to make expenditures to or for the benefit of a college or university which is an organization referred to in clause (ii) of this subparagraph and which is an agency or instrumentality of a State or political subdivision thereof, or which is owned or operated by a State or political subdivision thereof or by an agency or instrumentality of one or more States or political subdivisions,

(v) a governmental unit referred to in subsection (c)(1),

(vi) an organization referred to in subsection (c)(2) which normally receives a substantial part of its support (exclusive of income received in the exercise or performance by such organization of its charitable, educational, or other purpose or function constituting the basis for its exemption under section 501(a)) from a governmental unit referred to in subsection (c)(1) or from direct or indirect contributions from the general public,

(vii) a private foundation described in subparagraph (F), or

(viii) an organization described in section 509(a)(2) or (3),

shall be allowed to the extent that the aggregate of such contributions does not exceed 50 percent of the taxpayer's contribution base for the taxable year.

(B) Other contributions. Any charitable contribution other than a charitable contribution to which subparagraph (A) applies shall be allowed to the extent that the aggregate of such contributions does not exceed the lesser of—

(i) 30 percent of the taxpayer's contribution base for the taxable year, or

(ii) the excess of 50 percent of the taxpayer's contribution base for the taxable year over the amount of charitable contributions allowable under subparagraph (A) (determined without regard to subparagraph (C)).

If the aggregate of such contributions exceeds the limitation of the preceding sentence, such excess shall be treated (in a manner consistent with the rules of subsection (d)(1)) as a charitable contribution (to which subparagraph (A) does not apply) in each of the 5 succeeding taxable years in order of time.

(C) Special limitation with respect to contributions described in subparagraph (A) of certain capital gain property.

(i) In the case of charitable contributions described in subparagraph (A) of capital gain property to which subsection (e)(1)(B) does not apply, the total amount of contributions of such property which may be taken into account under subsection (a) for any taxable year shall not exceed 30 percent of the taxpayer's contribution base for such year. For purposes of this subsection, contributions of capital gain property to which this subparagraph applies shall be taken into account after all other charitable contributions (other than charitable contributions to which subparagraph (D) applies).

(ii) If charitable contributions described in subparagraph (A) of capital gain property to which clause (i) applies exceeds 30 percent of the taxpayer's contribution base for any taxable year, such excess shall be treated, in a manner consistent with the rules of subsection (d)(1), as a charitable contribution of capital gain property to which clause (i) applies in each of the 5 succeeding taxable years in order of time.

(iii) At the election of the taxpayer (made at such time and in such manner as the Secretary prescribes by regulations), subsection (e)(1) shall apply to all contributions of capital gain property (to which subsection (e)(1)(B) does not otherwise apply) made by the taxpayer during the taxable year. If such an election is made, clauses (i) and (ii) shall not apply to contributions of capital gain property made during the taxable year, and, in applying subsection (d)(1) for such taxable year with respect to contributions of capital gain property made in any prior contribution year for which an election was not made under this clause, such contributions shall be reduced as if subsection (e)(1) had applied to such contributions in the year in which made.

(iv) For purposes of this paragraph, the term "capital gain property" means, with respect to any contribution, any capital asset the sale of which at its fair market value at the time of the contribution would have resulted in gain which would have been long-term capital gain. For purposes of the preceding sentence, any property which is property used in the trade or business (as defined in section 1231(b)) shall be treated as a capital asset.

(D) Special limitation with respect to contributions of capital gain property to organizations not described in subparagraph (A).

(i) In general. In the case of charitable contributions (other than charitable contributions to which subparagraph (A) applies) of capital gain property, the total amount of such contributions of such property taken into account under subsection (a) for any taxable year shall not exceed the lesser of—

(I) 20 percent of the taxpayer's contribution base for the taxable year, or
(II) the excess of 30 percent of the taxpayer's contribution base for the taxable year over the amount of the contributions of capital gain property to which subparagraph (C) applies.

For purposes of this subsection, contributions of capital gain property to which this subparagraph applies shall be taken into account after all other charitable contributions.

(ii) Carryover. If the aggregate amount of contributions described in clause (i) exceeds the limitation of clause (i), such excess shall be treated (in a manner consistent with the rules of subsection (d)(1)) as a charitable contribution of capital gain property to which clause (i) applies in each of the 5 succeeding taxable years in order of time.

(E) Contributions of qualified conservation contributions.

(i) In general. Any qualified conservation contribution (as defined in subsection (h)(1)) shall be allowed to the extent the aggregate of such contributions does not exceed the excess of 50 percent of the taxpayer's contribution base over the amount of all other charitable contributions allowable under this paragraph.

(ii) Carryover. If the aggregate amount of contributions described in clause (i) exceeds the limitation of clause (i), such excess shall be treated (in a manner consistent with the rules of subsection (d)(1)) as a charitable contribution to which clause (i) applies in each of the 15 succeeding years in order of time.

(iii) Coordination with other subparagraphs. For purposes of applying this subsection and subsection (d)(1), contributions described in clause (i) shall not be treated as described in subparagraph (A), (B), (C), or (D) and such subparagraphs shall apply without regard to such contributions.

(iv) Special rule for contribution of property used in agriculture or livestock production.

(I) In general. If the individual is a qualified farmer or rancher for the taxable year for which the contribution is made, clause (i) shall be applied by substituting "100 percent" for "50 percent".

(II) Exception. Subclause (I) shall not apply to any contribution of property made after the date of the enactment of this subparagraph which is used in agriculture or livestock production (or available for such production) unless such contribution is subject to a restriction that such property remain available for such production. This subparagraph shall be applied separately with respect to property to which subclause (I) does not apply by reason of the preceding sentence prior to its application to property to which subclause (I) does apply.

(v) Definition. For purposes of clause (iv), the term "qualified farmer or rancher" means a taxpayer whose gross income from the trade or business of farming (within the meaning of section 2032A(e)(5)) is greater than 50 percent of the taxpayer's gross income for the taxable year.

(vi) Termination. This subparagraph shall not apply to any contribution made in taxable years beginning after December 31, 2011.

(F) Certain private foundations. The private foundations referred to in subparagraph (A)(vii) and subsection (e)(1)(B) are—

(i) a private operating foundation (as defined in section 4942(j)(3)),

(ii) any other private foundation (as defined in section 509(a)) which, not later than the 15th day of the third month after the close of the foundation's taxable year in which contributions are received, makes qualifying distributions (as defined in section 4942(g), without regard to paragraph (3) thereof), which are treated, after the application of section 4942(g)(3), as distributions out of corpus (in accordance with section 4942(h)) in an amount equal to 100 percent of such contributions, and with respect to which the taxpayer obtains adequate records or other sufficient evidence from the foundation showing that the foundation made such qualifying distributions, and

(iii) a private foundation all of the contributions to which are pooled in a common fund and which would be described in section 509(a)(3) but for the right of any substantial contributor (hereafter in this clause called "donor") or his spouse to designate annually the recipients, from among organizations described in paragraph (1) of section 509(a), of the income attributable to the donor's contribution to the fund and to direct (by deed or by will) the payment, to an organization described in such paragraph (1), of the corpus in the common fund attributable to the donor's contribution; but this clause shall apply only if all of the income of the common fund is required to be (and is) distributed to one or more organizations described in such paragraph (1) not later than the 15th day of the third month after the close of the taxable year in which the income is realized by the fund and only if all of the corpus attributable to any donor's contribution to the fund is required to be (and is) distributed to one or more of such organizations not later than one year after his death or after the death of his surviving spouse if she has the right to designate the recipients of such corpus.

(G) Contribution base defined. For purposes of this section, the term "contribution base" means adjusted gross income (computed without regard to any net operating loss carryback to the taxable year under section 172).

(2) Corporations. In the case of a corporation—

(A) In general. The total deductions under subsection (a) for any taxable year (other than for contributions to which subparagraph (B) applies) shall not exceed 10 percent of the taxpayer's taxable income.

(B) Qualified conservation contributions by certain corporate farmers and ranchers.

(i) In general. Any qualified conservation contribution (as defined in subsection (h)(1))—

(I) which is made by a corporation which, for the taxable year during which the contribution is made, is a qualified farmer or rancher (as defined in paragraph (1)(E)(v)) and the stock of which is not readily tradable on an established securities market at any time during such year, and

(II) which, in the case of contributions made after the date of the enactment of this subparagraph, is a contribution of property which is used in agriculture or livestock production (or available for such production) and which is subject to a restriction that such property remain available for such production,

shall be allowed to the extent the aggregate of such contributions does not exceed the excess of the tax-

1,615

payer's taxable income over the amount of charitable contributions allowable under subparagraph (A).

(ii) Carryover. If the aggregate amount of contributions described in clause (i) exceeds the limitation of clause (i), such excess shall be treated (in a manner consistent with the rules of subsection (d)(2)) as a charitable contribution to which clause (i) applies in each of the 15 succeeding years in order of time.

(iii) Termination. This subparagraph shall not apply to any contribution made in taxable years beginning after December 31, 2011.

(C) Taxable income. For purposes of this paragraph, taxable income shall be computed without regard to—
(i) this section,
(ii) part VIII (except section 248),
(iii) any net operating loss carryback to the taxable year under section 172,
(iv) section 199, and
(v) any capital loss carryback to the taxable year under section 1212(a)(1).

(3) Temporary suspension of limitations on charitable contributions. In the case of a qualified farmer or rancher (as defined in paragraph (1)(E)(v)), any charitable contribution of food—
(A) to which subsection (e)(3)(C) applies (without regard to clause (ii) thereof), and
(B) which is made during the period beginning on the date of the enactment of this paragraph and before January 1, 2009,
shall be treated for purposes of paragraph (1)(E) or (2)(B), whichever is applicable, as if it were a qualified conservation contribution which is made by a qualified farmer or rancher and which otherwise meets the requirements of such paragraph.

(c) Charitable contribution defined.
For purposes of this section, the term "charitable contribution" means a contribution or gift to or for the use of—
(1) A State, a possession of the United States, or any political subdivision of any of the foregoing, or the United States or the District of Columbia, but only if the contribution or gift is made for exclusively public purposes.
(2) A corporation, trust, or community chest, fund, or foundation—
(A) created or organized in the United States or in any possession thereof, or under the law of the United States, any State, the District of Columbia, or any possession of the United States;
(B) organized and operated exclusively for religious, charitable, scientific, literary, or educational purposes, or to foster national or international amateur sports competition (but only if no part of its activities involve the provision of athletic facilities or equipment), or for the prevention of cruelty to children or animals;
(C) no part of the net earnings of which inures to the benefit of any private shareholder or individual; and
(D) which is not disqualified for tax exemption under section 501(c)(3) by reason of attempting to influence legislation, and which does not participate in, or intervene in (including the publishing or distributing of statements), any political campaign on behalf of (or in opposition to) any candidate for public office.

A contribution or gift by a corporation to a trust, chest, fund, or foundation shall be deductible by reason of this paragraph only if it is to be used within the United States or any of its possessions exclusively for purposes specified in subparagraph (B). Rules similar to the rules of section 501(j) shall apply for purposes of this paragraph.

(3) A post or organization of war veterans, or an auxiliary unit or society of, or trust or foundation for, any such post or organization—
(A) organized in the United States or any of its possessions, and
(B) no part of the net earnings of which inures to the benefit of any private shareholder or individual.

(4) In the case of a contribution or gift by an individual, a domestic fraternal society, order, or association, operating under the lodge system, but only if such contribution or gift is to be used exclusively for religious, charitable, scientific, literary, or educational purposes, or for the prevention of cruelty to children or animals.

(5) A cemetery company owned and operated exclusively for the benefit of its members, or any corporation chartered solely for burial purposes as a cemetery corporation and not permitted by its charter to engage in any business not necessarily incident to that purpose, if such company or corporation is not operated for profit and no part of the net earnings of such company or corporation inures to the benefit of any private shareholder or individual.

For purposes of this section, the term "charitable contribution" also means an amount treated under subsection (g) as paid for the use of an organization described in paragraph (2), (3), or (4).

(d) Carryovers of excess contributions.
(1) Individuals.
(A) In general. In the case of an individual, if the amount of charitable contributions described in subsection (b)(1)(A) payment of which is made within a taxable year (hereinafter in this paragraph referred to as the "contribution year") exceeds 50 percent of the taxpayer's contribution base for such year, such excess shall be treated as a charitable contribution described in subsection (b)(1)(A) paid in each of the 5 succeeding taxable years in order of time, but, with respect to any such succeeding taxable year, only to the extent of the lesser of the two following amounts:
(i) the amount by which 50 percent of the taxpayer's contribution base for such succeeding taxable year exceeds the sum of the charitable contributions described in subsection (b)(1)(A) payment of which is made by the taxpayer within such succeeding taxable year (determined without regard to this subparagraph) and the charitable contributions described in subsection (b)(1)(A) payment of which was made in taxable years before the contribution year which are treated under this subparagraph as having been paid in such succeeding taxable year; or
(ii) in the case of the first succeeding taxable year, the amount of such excess, and in the case of the second, third, fourth, or fifth succeeding taxable year, the portion of such excess not treated under this subparagraph as a charitable contribution described in subsection (b)(1)(A) paid in any taxable year intervening between the contribution year and such succeeding taxable year.
(B) Special rule for net operating loss carryovers. In applying subparagraph (A), the excess determined under subparagraph (A) for the contribution year shall be reduced to the extent that such excess reduces taxable income (as computed for purposes of the second sentence of section 172(b)(2)) and increases the net operating loss deduction for a taxable year succeeding the contribution year.

Deductions   **Code Sec. 170(e)(3)(A)**

(2) **Corporations.**

(A) In general. Any contribution made by a corporation in a taxable year (hereinafter in this paragraph referred to as the "contribution year") in excess of the amount deductible for such year under subsection (b)(2)(A) shall be deductible for each of the 5 succeeding taxable years in order of time, but only to the extent of the lesser of the two following amounts: (i) the excess of the maximum amount deductible for such succeeding taxable year under subsection (b)(2)(A) over the sum of the contributions made in such year plus the aggregate of the excess contributions which were made in taxable years before the contribution year and which are deductible under this subparagraph for such succeeding taxable year; or (ii) in the case of the first succeeding taxable year, the amount of such excess contribution, and in the case of the second, third, fourth, or fifth succeeding taxable year, the portion of such excess contribution not deductible under this subparagraph for any taxable year intervening between the contribution year and such succeeding taxable year.

(B) Special rule for net operating loss carryovers. For purposes of subparagraph (A), the excess of—

(i) the contributions made by a corporation in a taxable year to which this section applies, over

(ii) the amount deductible in such year under the limitation in subsection (b)(2)(A),

shall be reduced to the extent that such excess reduces taxable income (as computed for purposes of the second sentence of section 172(b)(2)) and increases a net operating loss carryover under section 172 to a succeeding taxable year.

(e) **Certain contributions of ordinary income and capital gain property.**

(1) **General rule.** The amount of any charitable contribution of property otherwise taken into account under this section shall be reduced by the sum of—

(A) the amount of gain which would not have been long-term capital gain (determined without regard to section 1221(b)(3)) if the property contributed had been sold by the taxpayer at its fair market value (determined at the time of such contribution), and

(B) in the case of a charitable contribution—

(i) of tangible personal property—

(I) if the use by the donee is unrelated to the purpose or function constituting the basis for its exemption under section 501 (or, in the case of a governmental unit, to any purpose or function described in subsection (c)), or

(II) which is applicable property (as defined in paragraph (7)(C), but without regard to clause (ii) thereof) which is sold, exchanged, or otherwise disposed of by the donee before the last day of the taxable year in which the contribution was made and with respect to which the donee has not made a certification in accordance with paragraph (7)(D),

(ii) to or for the use of a private foundation (as defined in section 509(a)), other than a private foundation described in subsection (b)(1)(F),

(iii) of any patent, copyright (other than a copyright described in section 1221(a)(3) or 1231(b)(1)(C)), trademark, trade name, trade secret, know-how, software (other than software described in section 197(e)(3)(A)(i)), or similar property, or applications or registrations of such property, or

(iv) of any taxidermy property which is contributed by the person who prepared, stuffed, or mounted the property or by any person who paid or incurred the cost of such preparation, stuffing, or mounting,

the amount of gain which would have been long-term capital gain if the property contributed had been sold by the taxpayer at its fair market value (determined at the time of such contribution).

> • **Caution:** Sec. 301(a), P.L. 111-312, (reproduced in the history notes following this Code Sec.) provides that the amendments made by Sec. 542(e)(2)(B), P.L. 107-16, EGTRRA, will apply as if never enacted. Matter at the end of Code Sec. 170(e)(1), following, reflects the removal of these amendments, effective for estates of decedents dying, and transfers made, after 12/31/2009.

For purposes of applying this paragraph (other than in the case of gain to which section 617(d)(1), 1245(a), 1250(a), 1252(a), or 1254(a) applies), property which is property used in the trade or business (as defined in section 1231(b)) shall be treated as a capital asset. For purposes of applying this paragraph in the case of a charitable contribution of stock in an S corporation, rules similar to the rules of section 751 shall apply in determining whether gain on such stock would have been long-term capital gain if such stock were sold by the taxpayer.

> • **Caution:** Matter at the end of Code Sec. 170(e)(1), following, was amended by Sec. 542(e)(2)(B), P.L. 107-16, EGTRRA. As provided in Sec. 301(a), P.L. 111-312, this amendment will apply as if never enacted, effective for estates of decedents dying, and transfers made, after 12/31/2009.

For purposes of applying this paragraph (other than in the case of gain to which section 617(d)(1), 1245(a), 1250(a), 1252(a), or 1254(a) applies), property which is property used in the trade or business (as defined in section 1231(b)) shall be treated as a capital asset. For purposes of applying this paragraph in the case of a charitable contribution of stock in an S corporation, rules similar to the rules of section 751 shall apply in determining whether gain on such stock would have been long-term capital gain if such stock were sold by the taxpayer. For purposes of this paragraph, the determination of whether property is a capital asset shall be made without regard to the exception contained in section 1221(a)(3)(C) for basis determined under section 1022.

(2) **Allocation of basis.** For purposes of paragraph (1), in the case of a charitable contribution of less than the taxpayer's entire interest in the property contributed, the taxpayer's adjusted basis in such property shall be allocated between the interest contributed and any interest not contributed in accordance with regulations prescribed by the Secretary.

(3) **Special rule for certain contributions of inventory and other property.**

(A) Qualified contributions. For purposes of this paragraph, a qualified contribution shall mean a charitable contribution of property described in paragraph (1) or (2) of section 1221(a), by a corporation (other than a corporation which is an S corporation) to an organiza-

1,617

tion which is described in section 501(c)(3) and is exempt under section 501(a) (other than a private foundation, as defined in section 509(a), which is not an operating foundation, as defined in section 4942(j)(3)), but only if—

(i) the use of the property by the donee is related to the purpose or function constituting the basis for its exemption under section 501 and the property is to be used by the donee solely for the care of the ill, the needy, or infants;

(ii) the property is not transferred by the donee in exchange for money, other property, or services;

(iii) the taxpayer receives from the donee a written statement representing that its use and disposition of the property will be in accordance with the provisions of clauses (i) and (ii); and

(iv) in the case where the property is subject to regulation under the Federal Food, Drug, and Cosmetic Act, as amended, such property must fully satisfy the applicable requirements of such Act and regulations promulgated thereunder on the date of transfer and for one hundred and eighty days prior thereto.

(B) Amount of reduction. The reduction under paragraph (1)(A) for any qualified contribution (as defined in subparagraph (A)) shall be no greater than the sum of—

(i) one-half of the amount computed under paragraph (1)(A) (computed without regard to this paragraph), and

(ii) the amount (if any) by which the charitable contribution deduction under this section for any qualified contribution (computed by taking into account the amount determined in clause (i), but without regard to this clause) exceeds twice the basis of such property.

(C) Special rule for contributions of food inventory.

(i) General rule. In the case of a charitable contribution of food from any trade or business of the taxpayer, this paragraph shall be applied—

(I) without regard to whether the contribution is made by a C corporation, and

(II) only to food that is apparently wholesome food.

(ii) Limitation. In the case of a taxpayer other than a C corporation, the aggregate amount of such contributions for any taxable year which may be taken into account under this section shall not exceed 10 percent of the taxpayer's aggregate net income for such taxable year from all trades or businesses from which such contributions were made for such year, computed without regard to this section.

(iii) Apparently wholesome food. For purposes of this subparagraph, the term "apparently wholesome food" has the meaning given to such term by section 22(b)(2) of the Bill Emerson Good Samaritan Food Donation Act (42 U.S.C. 1791(b)(2)), as in effect on the date of the enactment of this subparagraph.

(iv) Termination. This subparagraph shall not apply to contributions made after December 31, 2011.

(D) Special rule for contributions of book inventory to public schools.

(i) Contributions of book inventory. In determining whether a qualified book contribution is a qualified contribution, subparagraph (A) shall be applied without regard to whether the donee is an organization described in the matter preceding clause (i) of subparagraph (A).

(ii) Qualified book contribution. For purposes of this paragraph, the term "qualified book contribution" means a charitable contribution of books to a public school which is an educational organization described in subsection (b)(1)(A)(ii) and which provides elementary education or secondary education (kindergarten through grade 12).

(iii) Certification by donee. Subparagraph (A) shall not apply to any contribution of books unless (in addition to the certifications required by subparagraph (A) (as modified by this subparagraph)), the donee certifies in writing that—

(I) the books are suitable, in terms of currency, content, and quantity, for use in the donee's educational programs, and

(II) the donee will use the books in its educational programs.

(iv) Termination. This subparagraph shall not apply to contributions made after December 31, 2011.

(E) This paragraph shall not apply to so much of the amount of the gain described in paragraph (1)(A) which would be long-term capital gain but for the application of sections 617, 1245, 1250, or 1252.

(4) Special rule for contributions of scientific property used for research.

(A) Limit on reduction. In the case of a qualified research contribution, the reduction under paragraph (1)(A) shall be no greater than the amount determined under paragraph (3)(B).

(B) Qualified research contributions. For purposes of this paragraph, the term "qualified research contribution" means a charitable contribution by a corporation of tangible personal property described in paragraph (1) of section 1221(a), but only if—

(i) the contribution is to an organization described in subparagraph (A) or subparagraph (B) of section 41(e)(6),

(ii) the property is constructed or assembled by the taxpayer,

(iii) the contribution is made not later than 2 years after the date the construction or assembly of the property is substantially completed,

(iv) the original use of the property is by the donee,

(v) the property is scientific equipment or apparatus substantially all of the use of which by the donee is for research or experimentation (within the meaning of section 174), or for research training, in the United States in physical or biological sciences,

(vi) the property is not transferred by the donee in exchange for money, other property, or services, and

(vii) the taxpayer receives from the donee a written statement representing that its use and disposition of the property will be in accordance with the provisions of clauses (v) and (vi).

(C) Construction of property by taxpayer. For purposes of this paragraph, property shall be treated as constructed by the taxpayer only if the cost of the parts used in the construction of such property (other than parts manufactured by the taxpayer or a related person) do not exceed 50 percent of the taxpayer's basis in such property.

(D) Corporation. For purposes of this paragraph, the term "corporation" shall not include—

(i) an S corporation,

(ii) a personal holding company (as defined in section 542), and

(iii) a service organization (as defined in section 414(m)(3)).

(5) Special rule for contributions of stock for which market quotations are readily available.

(A) In general. Subparagraph (B)(ii) of paragraph (1) shall not apply to any contribution of qualified appreciated stock.

(B) Qualified appreciated stock. Except as provided in subparagraph (C), for purposes of this paragraph, the term "qualified appreciated stock" means any stock of a corporation—

(i) for which (as of the date of the contribution) market quotations are readily available on an established securities market, and

(ii) which is capital gain property (as defined in subsection (b)(1)(C)(iv)).

(C) Donor may not contribute more than 10 percent of stock of corporation.

(i) In general. In the case of any donor, the term "qualified appreciated stock" shall not include any stock of a corporation contributed by the donor in a contribution to which paragraph (1)(B)(ii) applies (determined without regard to this paragraph) to the extent that the amount of the stock so contributed (when increased by the aggregate amount of all prior such contributions by the donor of stock in such corporation) exceeds 10 percent (in value) of all of the outstanding stock of such corporation.

(ii) Special rule. For purposes of clause (i), an individual shall be treated as making all contributions made by any member of his family (as defined in section 267(c)(4)).

(6) Special rule for contributions of computer technology and equipment for educational purposes.

(A) Limit on reduction. In the case of a qualified computer contribution, the reduction under paragraph (1)(A) shall be no greater than the amount determined under paragraph (3)(B).

(B) Qualified computer contribution. For purposes of this paragraph, the term "qualified computer contribution" means a charitable contribution by a corporation of any computer technology or equipment, but only if—

(i) the contribution is to—

(I) an educational organization described in subsection (b)(1)(A)(ii),

(II) an entity described in section 501(c)(3) and exempt from tax under section 501(a) other than an entity described in subclause (I)) that is organized primarily for purposes of supporting elementary and secondary education, or

(III) a public library (within the meaning of section 213(1)(A) of the Library Services and Technology Act (20 U.S.C. 9122(1)(A)), as in effect on the date of the enactment [12/21/2000] of the Community Renewal Tax Relief Act of 2000), established and maintained by an entity described in subsection (c)(1),

(ii) the contribution is made not later than 3 years after the date the taxpayer acquired the property (or in the case of property constructed or assembled by the taxpayer, the date the construction or assembling of the property is substantially completed),

(iii) the original use of the property is by the donor or the donee,

(iv) substantially all of the use of the property by the donee is for use within the United States for educational purposes that are related to the purpose or function of the donee,

(v) the property is not transferred by the donee in exchange for money, other property, or services, except for shipping, installation and transfer costs,

(vi) the property will fit productively into the donee's education plan,

(vii) the donee's use and disposition of the property will be in accordance with the provisions of clauses (iv) and (v), and

(viii) the property meets such standards, if any, as the Secretary may prescribe by regulation to assure that the property meets minimum functionality and suitability standards for educational purposes.

(C) Contribution to private foundation. A contribution by a corporation of any computer technology or equipment to a private foundation (as defined in section 509) shall be treated as a qualified computer contribution for purposes of this paragraph if—

(i) the contribution to the private foundation satisfies the requirements of clauses (ii) and (v) of subparagraph (B), and

(ii) within 30 days after such contribution, the private foundation—

(I) contributes the property to a donee described in clause (i) of subparagraph (B) that satisfies the requirements of clauses (iv) through (vii) of subparagraph (B), and

(II) notifies the donor of such contribution.

(D) Donations of property reacquired by manufacturer. In the case of property which is reacquired by the person who constructed or assembled the property—

(i) subparagraph (B)(ii) shall be applied to a contribution of such property by such person by taking into account the date that the original construction or assembly of the property was substantially completed, and

(ii) subparagraph (B)(iii) shall not apply to such contribution.

(E) Special rule relating to construction of property. For the purposes of this paragraph, the rules of paragraph (4)(C) shall apply.

(F) Definitions. For the purposes of this paragraph—

(i) Computer technology or equipment. The term "computer technology or equipment" means computer software (as defined by section 197(e)(3)(B)), computer or peripheral equipment (as defined by section 168(i)(2)(B)), and fiber optic cable related to computer use.

(ii) Corporation. The term "corporation" has the meaning given to such term by paragraph (4)(D).

(G) Termination. This paragraph shall not apply to any contribution made during any taxable year beginning after December 31, 2011.

(7) Recapture of deduction on certain dispositions of exempt use property.

(A) In general. In the case of an applicable disposition of applicable property, there shall be included in the income of the donor of such property for the taxable year of such donor in which the applicable disposition occurs an amount equal to the excess (if any) of—

(i) the amount of the deduction allowed to the donor under this section with respect to such property, over

(ii) the donor's basis in such property at the time such property was contributed.

(B) Applicable disposition. For purposes of this paragraph, the term "applicable disposition" means any sale, exchange, or other disposition by the donee of applicable property—

(i) after the last day of the taxable year of the donor in which such property was contributed, and

(ii) before the last day of the 3-year period beginning on the date of the contribution of such property,

unless the donee makes a certification in accordance with subparagraph (D).

(C) Applicable property. For purposes of this paragraph, the term "applicable property" means charitable deduction property (as defined in section 6050L(a)(2)(A))—

(i) which is tangible personal property the use of which is identified by the donee as related to the purpose or function constituting the basis of the donee's exemption under section 501, and

(ii) for which a deduction in excess of the donor's basis is allowed.

(D) Certification. A certification meets the requirements of this subparagraph if it is a written statement which is signed under penalty of perjury by an officer of the donee organization and—

(i) which—

(I) certifies that the use of the property by the donee was substantial and related to the purpose or function constituting the basis for the donee's exemption under section 501, and

(II) describes how the property was used and how such use furthered such purpose or function, or

(ii) which—

(I) states the intended use of the property by the donee at the time of the contribution, and

(II) certifies that such intended use has become impossible or infeasible to implement.

(f) Disallowance of deduction in certain cases and special rules.

(1) In general. No deduction shall be allowed under this section for a contribution to or for the use of an organization or trust described in section 508(d) or 4948(c)(4) subject to the conditions specified in such sections.

(2) Contributions of property placed in trust.

(A) Remainder interest. In the case of property transferred in trust, no deduction shall be allowed under this section for the value of a contribution of a remainder interest unless the trust is a charitable remainder annuity trust or a charitable remainder unitrust (described in section 664), or a pooled income fund (described in section 642(c)(5)).

(B) Income interests, etc. No deduction shall be allowed under this section for the value of any interest in property (other than a remainder interest) transferred in trust unless the interest is in the form of a guaranteed annuity or the trust instrument specifies that the interest is a fixed percentage distributed yearly of the fair market value of the trust property (to be determined yearly) and the grantor is treated as the owner of such interest for purposes of applying section 671. If the donor ceases to be treated as the owner of such an interest for purposes of applying section 671, at the time the donor ceases to be so treated, the donor shall for purposes of this chapter be considered as having received an amount of income equal to the amount of any deduction he received under this section for the contribution reduced by the discounted value of all amounts of income earned by the trust and taxable to him before the time at which he ceases to be treated as the owner of the interest. Such amounts of income shall be discounted to the date of the contribution. The Secretary shall prescribe such regulations as may be necessary to carry out the purposes of this subparagraph.

(C) Denial of deduction in case of payments by certain trusts. In any case in which a deduction is allowed under this section for the value of an interest in property described in subparagraph (B), transferred in trust, no deduction shall be allowed under this section to the grantor or any other person for the amount of any contribution made by the trust with respect to such interest.

(D) Exception. This paragraph shall not apply in a case in which the value of all interests in property transferred in trust are deductible under subsection (a).

(3) Denial of deduction in case of certain contributions of partial interests in property.

(A) In general. In the case of a contribution (not made by a transfer in trust) of an interest in property which consists of less than the taxpayer's entire interest in such property, a deduction shall be allowed under this section only to the extent that the value of the interest contributed would be allowable as a deduction under this section if such interest had been transferred in trust. For purposes of this subparagraph, a contribution by a taxpayer of the right to use property shall be treated as a contribution of less than the taxpayer's entire interest in such property.

(B) Exceptions. Subparagraph (A) shall not apply to—

(i) a contribution of a remainder interest in a personal residence or farm,

(ii) a contribution of an undivided portion of the taxpayer's entire interest in property, and

(iii) a qualified conservation contribution.

(4) Valuation of remainder interest in real property. For purposes of this section, in determining the value of a remainder interest in real property, depreciation (computed on the straight line method) and depletion of such property shall be taken into account, and such value shall be discounted at a rate of 6 percent per annum, except that the Secretary may prescribe a different rate.

(5) Reduction for certain interest. If, in connection with any charitable contribution, a liability is assumed by the recipient or by any other person, or if a charitable contribution is of property which is subject to a liability, then, to the extent necessary to avoid the duplication of amounts, the amount taken into account for purposes of this section as the amount of the charitable contribution—

(A) shall be reduced for interest (i) which has been paid (or is to be paid) by the taxpayer, (ii) which is attributable to the liability, and (iii) which is attributable to any period after the making of the contribution, and

(B) in the case of a bond, shall be further reduced for interest (i) which has been paid (or is to be paid) by the taxpayer on indebtedness incurred or continued to purchase or carry such bond, and (ii) which is attributable to any period before the making of the contribution.

The reduction pursuant to subparagraph (B) shall not exceed the interest (including interest equivalent) on the bond which is attributable to any period before the making of the contribution and which is not (under the taxpayer's method of accounting) includible in the gross income of the taxpayer for any taxable year. For purposes of this paragraph, the term "bond" means any bond, debenture, note, or certificate or other evidence of indebtedness.

(6) Deductions for out-of-pocket expenditures. No deduction shall be allowed under this section for an out-of-pocket expenditure made by any person on behalf of an

Deductions
Code Sec. 170(f)(10)(F)(i)

organization described in subsection (c) (other than an organization described in section 501(h)(5) (relating to churches, etc.)) if the expenditure is made for the purpose of influencing legislation (within the meaning of section 501(c)(3)).

(7) Reformations to comply with paragraph (2).

(A) In general. A deduction shall be allowed under subsection (a) in respect of any qualified reformation (within the meaning of section 2055(e)(3)(B)).

(B) Rules similar to section 2055(e)(3) to apply. For purposes of this paragraph, rules similar to the rules of section 2055(e)(3) shall apply.

(8) Substantiation requirement for certain contributions.

(A) General rule. No deduction shall be allowed under subsection (a) for any contribution of $250 or more unless the taxpayer substantiates the contribution by a contemporaneous written acknowledgment of the contribution by the donee organization that meets the requirements of subparagraph (B).

(B) Content of acknowledgment. An acknowledgment meets the requirements of this subparagraph if it includes the following information:

(i) The amount of cash and a description (but not value) of any property other than cash contributed.

(ii) Whether the donee organization provided any goods or services in consideration, in whole or in part, for any property described in clause (i).

(iii) A description and good faith estimate of the value of any goods or services referred to in clause (ii) or, if such goods or services consist solely of intangible religious benefits, a statement to that effect.

For purposes of this subparagraph, the term "intangible religious benefit" means any intangible religious benefit which is provided by an organization organized exclusively for religious purposes and which generally is not sold in a commercial transaction outside the donative context.

(C) Contemporaneous. For purposes of subparagraph (A), an acknowledgment shall be considered to be contemporaneous if the taxpayer obtains the acknowledgment on or before the earlier of—

(i) the date on which the taxpayer files a return for the taxable year in which the contribution was made, or

(ii) the due date (including extensions) for filing such return.

(D) Substantiation not required for contributions reported by the donee organization. Subparagraph (A) shall not apply to a contribution if the donee organization files a return, on such form and in accordance with such regulations as the Secretary may prescribe, which includes the information described in subparagraph (B) with respect to the contribution.

(E) Regulations. The Secretary shall prescribe such regulations as may be necessary or appropriate to carry out the purposes of this paragraph, including regulations that may provide that some or all of the requirements of this paragraph do not apply in appropriate cases.

(9) Denial of deduction where contribution for lobbying activities. No deduction shall be allowed under this section for a contribution to an organization which conducts activities to which section 162(e)(1) applies on matters of direct financial interest to the donor's trade or business, if a principal purpose of the contribution was to avoid Federal income tax by securing a deduction for such activities under this section which would be disallowed by reason of section 162(e) if the donor had conducted such activities directly. No deduction shall be allowed under section 162(a) for any amount for which a deduction is disallowed under the preceding sentence.

(10) Split-dollar life insurance, annuity, and endowment contracts.

(A) In general. Nothing in this section or in section 545(b)(2), 642(c), 2055, 2106(a)(2), or 2522 shall be construed to allow a deduction, and no deduction shall be allowed, for any transfer to or for the use of an organization described in subsection (c) if in connection with such transfer—

(i) the organization directly or indirectly pays, or has previously paid, any premium on any personal benefit contract with respect to the transferor, or

(ii) there is an understanding or expectation that any person will directly or indirectly pay any premium on any personal benefit contract with respect to the transferor.

(B) Personal benefit contract. For purposes of subparagraph (A), the term "personal benefit contract" means, with respect to the transferor, any life insurance, annuity, or endowment contract if any direct or indirect beneficiary under such contract is the transferor, any member of the transferor's family, or any other person (other than an organization described in subsection (c)) designated by the transferor.

(C) Application to charitable remainder trusts. In the case of a transfer to a trust referred to in subparagraph (E), references in subparagraphs (A) and (F) to an organization described in subsection (c) shall be treated as a reference to such trust.

(D) Exception for certain annuity contracts. If, in connection with a transfer to or for the use of an organization described in subsection (c), such organization incurs an obligation to pay a charitable gift annuity (as defined in section 501(m)) and such organization purchases any annuity contract to fund such obligation, persons receiving payments under the charitable gift annuity shall not be treated for purposes of subparagraph (B) as indirect beneficiaries under such contract if—

(i) such organization possesses all of the incidents of ownership under such contract,

(ii) such organization is entitled to all the payments under such contract, and

(iii) the timing and amount of payments under such contract are substantially the same as the timing and amount of payments to each such person under such obligation (as such obligation is in effect at the time of such transfer).

(E) Exception for certain contracts held by charitable remainder trusts. A person shall not be treated for purposes of subparagraph (B) as an indirect beneficiary under any life insurance, annuity, or endowment contract held by a charitable remainder annuity trust or a charitable remainder unitrust (as defined in section 664(d)) solely by reason of being entitled to any payment referred to in paragraph (1)(A) or (2)(A) of section 664(d) if—

(i) such trust possesses all of the incidents of ownership under such contract, and

(ii) such trust is entitled to all the payments under such contract.

(F) Excise tax on premiums paid.

(i) In general. There is hereby imposed on any organization described in subsection (c) an excise tax equal to the premiums paid by such organization on any life insurance, annuity, or endowment contract if the payment of premiums on such contract is in connection with a transfer for which a deduction is not allowable under subparagraph (A), determined without regard to when such transfer is made.

(ii) Payments by other persons. For purposes of clause (i), payments made by any other person pursuant to an understanding or expectation referred to in subparagraph (A) shall be treated as made by the organization.

(iii) Reporting. Any organization on which tax is imposed by clause (i) with respect to any premium shall file an annual return which includes—

(I) the amount of such premiums paid during the year and the name and TIN of each beneficiary under the contract to which the premium relates, and

(II) such other information as the Secretary may require.

The penalties applicable to returns required under section 6033 shall apply to returns required under this clause. Returns required under this clause shall be furnished at such time and in such manner as the Secretary shall by forms or regulations require.

(iv) Certain rules to apply. The tax imposed by this subparagraph shall be treated as imposed by chapter 42 for purposes of this title other than subchapter B of chapter 42.

(G) Special rule where state requires specification of charitable gift annuitant in contract. In the case of an obligation to pay a charitable gift annuity referred to in subparagraph (D) which is entered into under the laws of a State which requires, in order for the charitable gift annuity to be exempt from insurance regulation by such State, that each beneficiary under the charitable gift annuity be named as a beneficiary under an annuity contract issued by an insurance company authorized to transact business in such State, the requirements of clauses (i) and (ii) of subparagraph (D) shall be treated as met if—

(i) such State law requirement was in effect on February 8, 1999,

(ii) each such beneficiary under the charitable gift annuity is a bona fide resident of such State at the time the obligation to pay a charitable gift annuity is entered into, and

(iii) the only persons entitled to payments under such contract are persons entitled to payments as beneficiaries under such obligation on the date such obligation is entered into.

(H) Member of family. For purposes of this paragraph, an individual's family consists of the individual's grandparents, the grandparents of such individual's spouse, the lineal descendants of such grandparents, and any spouse of such a lineal descendant.

(I) Regulations. The Secretary shall prescribe such regulations as may be necessary or appropriate to carry out the purposes of this paragraph, including regulations to prevent the avoidance of such purposes.

(11) Qualified appraisal and other documentation for certain contributions.

(A) In general.

(i) Denial of deduction. In the case of an individual, partnership, or corporation, no deduction shall be allowed under subsection (a) for any contribution of property for which a deduction of more than $500 is claimed unless such person meets the requirements of subparagraphs (B), (C), and (D), as the case may be, with respect to such contribution.

(ii) Exceptions.

(I) Readily valued property. Subparagraphs (C) and (D) shall not apply to cash, property described in subsection (e)(1)(B)(iii) or section 1221(a)(1), publicly traded securities (as defined in section 6050L(a)(2)(B)), and any qualified vehicle described in paragraph (12)(A)(ii) for which an acknowledgement under paragraph (12)(B)(iii) is provided.

(II) Reasonable cause. Clause (i) shall not apply if it is shown that the failure to meet such requirements is due to reasonable cause and not to willful neglect.

(B) Property description for contributions of more than $500. In the case of contributions of property for which a deduction of more than $500 is claimed, the requirements of this subparagraph are met if the individual, partnership or corporation includes with the return for the taxable year in which the contribution is made a description of such property and such other information as the Secretary may require. The requirements of this subparagraph shall not apply to a C corporation which is not a personal service corporation or a closely held C corporation.

(C) Qualified appraisal for contributions of more than $5,000. In the case of contributions of property for which a deduction of more than $5,000 is claimed, the requirements of this subparagraph are met if the individual, partnership, or corporation obtains a qualified appraisal of such property and attaches to the return for the taxable year in which such contribution is made such information regarding such property and such appraisal as the Secretary may require.

(D) Substantiation for contributions of more than $500,000. In the case of contributions of property for which a deduction of more than $500,000 is claimed, the requirements of this subparagraph are met if the individual, partnership, or corporation attaches to the return for the taxable year a qualified appraisal of such property.

(E) Qualified appraisal and appraiser. For purposes of this paragraph—

(i) Qualified appraisal. The term "qualified appraisal" means, with respect to any property, an appraisal of such property which—

(I) is treated for purposes of this paragraph as a qualified appraisal under regulations or other guidance prescribed by the Secretary, and

(II) is conducted by a qualified appraiser in accordance with generally accepted appraisal standards and any regulations or other guidance prescribed under subclause (I).

(ii) Qualified appraiser. Except as provided in clause (iii), the term "qualified appraiser" means an individual who—

(I) has earned an appraisal designation from a recognized professional appraiser organization or has otherwise met minimum education and experience requirements set forth in regulations prescribed by the Secretary,

(II) regularly performs appraisals for which the individual receives compensation, and

(III) meets such other requirements as may be prescribed by the Secretary in regulations or other guidance.

(iii) Specific appraisals. An individual shall not be treated as a qualified appraiser with respect to any specific appraisal unless—

(I) the individual demonstrates verifiable education and experience in valuing the type of property subject to the appraisal, and

(II) the individual has not been prohibited from practicing before the Internal Revenue Service by the Secretary under section 330(c) of title 31, United States Code, at any time during the 3-year period ending on the date of the appraisal.

(F) Aggregation of similar items of property. For purposes of determining thresholds under this paragraph, property and all similar items of property donated to 1 or more donees shall be treated as 1 property.

(G) Special rule for pass-thru entities. In the case of a partnership or S corporation, this paragraph shall be applied at the entity level, except that the deduction shall be denied at the partner or shareholder level.

(H) Regulations. The Secretary may prescribe such regulations as may be necessary or appropriate to carry out the purposes of this paragraph, including regulations that may provide that some or all of the requirements of this paragraph do not apply in appropriate cases.

(12) Contributions of used motor vehicles, boats, and airplanes.

(A) In general. In the case of a contribution of a qualified vehicle the claimed value of which exceeds $500—

(i) paragraph (8) shall not apply and no deduction shall be allowed under subsection (a) for such contribution unless the taxpayer substantiates the contribution by a contemporaneous written acknowledgement of the contribution by the donee organization that meets the requirements of subparagraph (B) and includes the acknowledgement with the taxpayer's return of tax which includes the deduction, and

(ii) if the organization sells the vehicle without any significant intervening use or material improvement of such vehicle by the organization, the amount of the deduction allowed under subsection (a) shall not exceed the gross proceeds received from such sale.

(B) Content of acknowledgement. An acknowledgement meets the requirements of this subparagraph if it includes the following information:

(i) The name and taxpayer identification number of the donor.

(ii) The vehicle identification number or similar number.

(iii) In the case of a qualified vehicle to which subparagraph (A)(ii) applies—

(I) a certification that the vehicle was sold in an arm's length transaction between unrelated parties,

(II) the gross proceeds from the sale, and

(III) a statement that the deductible amount may not exceed the amount of such gross proceeds.

(iv) In the case of a qualified vehicle to which subparagraph (A)(ii) does not apply—

(I) a certification of the intended use or material improvement of the vehicle and the intended duration of such use, and

(II) a certification that the vehicle would not be transferred in exchange for money, other property, or services before completion of such use or improvement.

(v) Whether the donee organization provided any goods or services in consideration, in whole or in part, for the qualified vehicle.

(vi) A description and good faith estimate of the value of any goods or services referred to in clause (v) or, if such goods or services consist solely of intangible religious benefits (as defined in paragraph (8)(B)), a statement to that effect.

(C) Contemporaneous. For purposes of subparagraph (A), an acknowledgement shall be considered to be contemporaneous if the donee organization provides it within 30 days of—

(i) the sale of the qualified vehicle, or

(ii) in the case of an acknowledgement including a certification described in subparagraph (B)(iv), the contribution of the qualified vehicle.

(D) Information to Secretary. A donee organization required to provide an acknowledgement under this paragraph shall provide to the Secretary the information contained in the acknowledgement. Such information shall be provided at such time and in such manner as the Secretary may prescribe.

(E) Qualified vehicle. For purposes of this paragraph, the term "qualified vehicle" means any—

(i) motor vehicle manufactured primarily for use on public streets, roads, and highways,

(ii) boat, or

(iii) airplane.

Such term shall not include any property which is described in section 1221(a)(1).

(F) Regulations or other guidance. The Secretary shall prescribe such regulations or other guidance as may be necessary to carry out the purposes of this paragraph. The Secretary may prescribe regulations or other guidance which exempts sales by the donee organization which are in direct furtherance of such organization's charitable purpose from the requirements of subparagraphs (A)(ii) and (B)(iv)(II).

(13) Contributions of certain interests in buildings located in registered historic districts.

(A) In general. No deduction shall be allowed with respect to any contribution described in subparagraph (B) unless the taxpayer includes with the return for the taxable year of the contribution a $500 filing fee.

(B) Contribution described. A contribution is described in this subparagraph if such contribution is a qualified conservation contribution (as defined in subsection (h)) which is a restriction with respect to the exterior of a building described in subsection (h)(4)(C)(ii) and for which a deduction is claimed in excess of $10,000.

(C) Dedication of fee. Any fee collected under this paragraph shall be used for the enforcement of the provisions of subsection (h).

(14) Reduction for amounts attributable to rehabilitation credit. In the case of any qualified conservation contribution (as defined in subsection (h)), the amount of the deduction allowed under this section shall be reduced by an amount which bears the same ratio to the fair market value of the contribution as—

(A) the sum of the credits allowed to the taxpayer under section 47 for the 5 preceding taxable years with respect to any building which is a part of such contribution, bears to

(B) the fair market value of the building on the date of the contribution.

(15) Special rule for taxidermy property.
 (A) Basis. For purposes of this section and notwithstanding section 1012, in the case of a charitable contribution of taxidermy property which is made by the person who prepared, stuffed, or mounted the property or by any person who paid or incurred the cost of such preparation, stuffing, or mounting, only the cost of the preparing, stuffing, or mounting shall be included in the basis of such property.
 (B) Taxidermy property. For purposes of this section, the term "taxidermy property" means any work of art which—
  (i) is the reproduction or preservation of an animal, in whole or in part,
  (ii) is prepared, stuffed, or mounted for purposes of recreating one or more characteristics of such animal, and
  (iii) contains a part of the body of the dead animal.
(16) Contributions of clothing and household items.
 (A) In general. In the case of an individual, partnership, or corporation, no deduction shall be allowed under subsection (a) for any contribution of clothing or a household item unless such clothing or household item is in good used condition or better.
 (B) Items of minimal value. Notwithstanding subparagraph (A), the Secretary may by regulation deny a deduction under subsection (a) for any contribution of clothing or a household item which has minimal monetary value.
 (C) Exception for certain property. Subparagraphs (A) and (B) shall not apply to any contribution of a single item of clothing or a household item for which a deduction of more than $500 is claimed if the taxpayer includes with the taxpayer's return a qualified appraisal with respect to the property.
 (D) Household items. For purposes of this paragraph—
  (i) In general. The term "household items" includes furniture, furnishings, electronics, appliances, linens, and other similar items.
  (ii) Excluded items. Such term does not include—
   (I) food,
   (II) paintings, antiques, and other objects of art,
   (III) jewelry and gems, and
   (IV) collections.
 (E) Special rule for pass-thru entities. In the case of a partnership or S corporation, this paragraph shall be applied at the entity level, except that the deduction shall be denied at the partner or shareholder level.
(17) Recordkeeping. No deduction shall be allowed under subsection (a) for any contribution of a cash, check, or other monetary gift unless the donor maintains as a record of such contribution a bank record or a written communication from the donee showing the name of the donee organization, the date of the contribution, and the amount of the contribution.
(18) Contributions to donor advised funds. A deduction otherwise allowed under subsection (a) for any contribution to a donor advised fund (as defined in section 4966(d)(2)) shall only be allowed if—
 (A) the sponsoring organization (as defined in section 4966(d)(1)) with respect to such donor advised fund is not—
  (i) described in paragraph (3), (4), or (5) of subsection (c), or
  (ii) a type III supporting organization (as defined in section 4943(f)(5)(A)) which is not a functionally integrated type III supporting organization (as defined in section 4943(f)(5)(B)), and
 (B) the taxpayer obtains a contemporaneous written acknowledgment (determined under rules similar to the rules of paragraph (8)(C)) from the sponsoring organization (as so defined) of such donor advised fund that such organization has exclusive legal control over the assets contributed.
(g) Amounts paid to maintain certain students as members of taxpayer's household.
 (1) In general. Subject to the limitations provided by paragraph (2), amounts paid by the taxpayer to maintain an individual (other than a dependent, as defined in section 152 (determined without regard to subsections (b)(1), (b)(2), and (d)(1)(B) thereof), or a relative of the taxpayer) as a member of his household during the period that such individual is—
  (A) a member of the taxpayer's household under a written agreement between the taxpayer and an organization described in paragraph (2), (3), or (4) of subsection (c) to implement a program of the organization to provide educational opportunities for pupils or students in private homes, and
  (B) a full-time pupil or student in the twelfth or any lower grade at an educational organization described in section 170(b)(1)(A)(ii) located in the United States,
 shall be treated as amounts paid for the use of the organization.
 (2) Limitations.
  (A) Amount. Paragraph (1) shall apply to amounts paid within the taxable year only to the extent that such amounts do not exceed $50 multiplied by the number of full calendar months during the taxable year which fall within the period described in paragraph (1). For purposes of the preceding sentence, if 15 or more days of a calendar month fall within such period such month shall be considered as a full calendar month.
  (B) Compensation or reimbursement. Paragraph (1) shall not apply to any amount paid by the taxpayer within the taxable year if the taxpayer receives any money or other property as compensation or reimbursement for maintaining the individual in his household during the period described in paragraph (1).
 (3) Relative defined. For purposes of paragraph (1), the term "relative of the taxpayer" means an individual who, with respect to the taxpayer, bears any of the relationships described in subparagraphs (A) through (G) of section 152(d)(2).
 (4) No other amount allowed as deduction. No deduction shall be allowed under subsection (a) for any amount paid by a taxpayer to maintain an individual as a member of his household under a program described in paragraph (1)(A) except as provided in this subsection.
(h) Qualified conservation contribution.
 (1) In general. For purposes of subsection (f)(3)(B)(iii), the term "qualified conservation contribution" means a contribution—
  (A) of a qualified real property interest,
  (B) to a qualified organization,
  (C) exclusively for conservation purposes.
 (2) Qualified real property interest. For purposes of this subsection, the term "qualified real property interest" means any of the following interests in real property:
  (A) the entire interest of the donor other than a qualified mineral interest,
  (B) a remainder interest, and

(C) a restriction (granted in perpetuity) on the use which may be made of the real property.

(3) Qualified organization. For purposes of paragraph (1), the term "qualified organization" means an organization which—

(A) is described in clause (v) or (vi) of subsection (b)(1)(A), or

(B) is described in section 501(c)(3) and—

(i) meets the requirements of section 509(a)(2), or

(ii) meets the requirements of section 509(a)(3) and is controlled by an organization described in subparagraph (A) or in clause (i) of this subparagraph.

(4) Conservation purpose defined.

(A) In general. For purposes of this subsection, the term "conservation purpose" means—

(i) the preservation of land areas for outdoor recreation by, or the education of, the general public,

(ii) the protection of a relatively natural habitat of fish, wildlife, or plants, or similar ecosystem,

(iii) the preservation of open space (including farmland and forest land) where such preservation is—

(I) for the scenic enjoyment of the general public, or

(II) pursuant to a clearly delineated Federal, State, or local governmental conservation policy,

and will yield a significant public benefit, or

(iv) the preservation of an historically important land area or a certified historic structure.

(B) Special rules with respect to buildings in registered historic districts. In the case of any contribution of a qualified real property interest which is a restriction with respect to the exterior of a building described in subparagraph (C)(ii), such contribution shall not be considered to be exclusively for conservation purposes unless—

(i) such interest—

(I) includes a restriction which preserves the entire exterior of the building (including the front, sides, rear, and height of the building), and

(II) prohibits any change in the exterior of the building which is inconsistent with the historical character of such exterior,

(ii) the donor and donee enter into a written agreement certifying, under penalty of perjury, that the donee—

(I) is a qualified organization (as defined in paragraph (3)) with a purpose of environmental protection, land conservation, open space preservation, or historic preservation, and

(II) has the resources to manage and enforce the restriction and a commitment to do so, and

(iii) in the case of any contribution made in a taxable year beginning after the date of the enactment of this subparagraph, the taxpayer includes with the taxpayer's return for the taxable year of the contribution—

(I) a qualified appraisal (within the meaning of subsection (f)(11)(E)) of the qualified property interest,

(II) photographs of the entire exterior of the building, and

(III) a description of all restrictions on the development of the building.

(C) Certified historic structure. For purposes of subparagraph (A)(iv), the term "certified historic structure" means—

(i) any building, structure, or land area which is listed in the National Register, or

(ii) any building which is located in a registered historic district (as defined in section 47(c)(3)(B)) and is certified by the Secretary of the Interior to the Secretary as being of historic significance to the district.

A building, structure, or land area satisfies the preceding sentence if it satisfies such sentence either at the time of the transfer or on the due date (including extensions) for filing the transferor's return under this chapter for the taxable year in which the transfer is made.

(5) Exclusively for conservation purposes. For purposes of this subsection—

(A) Conservation purpose must be protected. A contribution shall not be treated as exclusively for conservation purposes unless the conservation purpose is protected in perpetuity.

(B) No surface mining permitted.

(i) In general. Except as provided in clause (ii), in the case of a contribution of any interest where there is a retention of a qualified mineral interest, subparagraph (A) shall not be treated as met if at any time there may be extraction or removal of minerals by any surface mining method.

(ii) Special rule. With respect to any contribution of property in which the ownership of the surface estate and mineral interests has been and remains separated, subparagraph (A) shall be treated as met if the probability of surface mining occurring on such property is so remote as to be negligible.

(6) Qualified mineral interest. For purposes of this subsection, the term "qualified mineral interest" means—

(A) subsurface oil, gas, or other minerals, and

(B) the right to access to such minerals.

(i) Standard mileage rate for use of passenger automobile.

For purposes of computing the deduction under this section for use of a passenger automobile, the standard mileage rate shall be 14 cents per mile.

(j) Denial of deduction for certain travel expenses.

No deduction shall be allowed under this section for traveling expenses (including amounts expended for meals and lodging) while away from home, whether paid directly or by reimbursement, unless there is no significant element of personal pleasure, recreation, or vacation in such travel.

(k) Disallowance of deductions in certain cases.

For disallowance of deductions for contributions to or for the use of communist controlled organizations, see section 11(a) of the Internal Security Act of 1950 (50 U.S.C. 790).

(l) Treatment of certain amounts paid to or for the benefit of institutions of higher education.

(1) In general. For purposes of this section, 80 percent of any amount described in paragraph (2) shall be treated as a charitable contribution.

(2) Amount described. For purposes of paragraph (1), an amount is described in this paragraph if—

(A) the amount is paid by the taxpayer to or for the benefit of an educational organization—

(i) which is described in subsection (b)(1)(A)(ii), and

(ii) which is an institution of higher education (as defined in section 3304(f)), and

(B) such amount would be allowable as a deduction under this section but for the fact that the taxpayer receives (directly or indirectly) as a result of paying such amount the right to purchase tickets for seating at an athletic event in an athletic stadium of such institution.

If any portion of a payment is for the purchase of such tickets, such portion and the remaining portion (if any) of such payment shall be treated as separate amounts for purposes of this subsection.

(m) **Certain donee income from intellectual property treated as an additional charitable contribution.**

(1) **Treatment as additional contribution.** In the case of a taxpayer who makes a qualified intellectual property contribution, the deduction allowed under subsection (a) for each taxable year of the taxpayer ending on or after the date of such contribution shall be increased (subject to the limitations under subsection (b)) by the applicable percentage of qualified donee income with respect to such contribution which is properly allocable to such year under this subsection.

(2) **Reduction in additional deductions to extent of initial deduction.** With respect to any qualified intellectual property contribution, the deduction allowed under subsection (a) shall be increased under paragraph (1) only to the extent that the aggregate amount of such increases with respect to such contribution exceed the amount allowed as a deduction under subsection (a) with respect to such contribution determined without regard to this subsection.

(3) **Qualified donee income.** For purposes of this subsection, the term "qualified donee income" means any net income received by or accrued to the donee which is properly allocable to the qualified intellectual property.

(4) **Allocation of qualified donee income to taxable years of donor.** For purposes of this subsection, qualified donee income shall be treated as properly allocable to a taxable year of the donor if such income is received by or accrued to the donee for the taxable year of the donee which ends within or with such taxable year of the donor.

(5) **10-year limitation.** Income shall not be treated as properly allocable to qualified intellectual property for purposes of this subsection if such income is received by or accrued to the donee after the 10-year period beginning on the date of the contribution of such property.

(6) **Benefit limited to life of intellectual property.** Income shall not be treated as properly allocable to qualified intellectual property for purposes of this subsection if such income is received by or accrued to the donee after the expiration of the legal life of such property.

(7) **Applicable percentage.** For purposes of this subsection, the term "applicable percentage" means the percentage determined under the following table which corresponds to a taxable year of the donor ending on or after the date of the qualified intellectual property contribution:

Taxable Year of Donor Ending on or After Date of Contribution:	Applicable Percentage
1st	100
2nd	100
3rd	90
4th	80
5th	70
6th	60
7th	50
8th	40
9th	30
10th	20
11th	10
12th	10

(8) **Qualified intellectual property contribution.** For purposes of this subsection, the term "qualified intellectual property contribution" means any charitable contribution of qualified intellectual property—

(A) the amount of which taken into account under this section is reduced by reason of subsection (e)(1), and

(B) with respect to which the donor informs the donee at the time of such contribution that the donor intends to treat such contribution as a qualified intellectual property contribution for purposes of this subsection and section 6050L.

(9) **Qualified intellectual property.** For purposes of this subsection, the term "qualified intellectual property" means property described in subsection (e)(1)(B)(iii) (other than property contributed to or for the use of an organization described in subsection (e)(1)(B)(ii)).

(10) **Other special rules.**

(A) Application of limitations on charitable contributions. Any increase under this subsection of the deduction provided under subsection (a) shall be treated for purposes of subsection (b) as a deduction which is attributable to a charitable contribution to the donee to which such increase relates.

(B) Net income determined by donee. The net income taken into account under paragraph (3) shall not exceed the amount of such income reported under section 6050L(b)(1).

(C) Deduction limited to 12 taxable years. Except as may be provided under subparagraph (D)(i), this subsection shall not apply with respect to any qualified intellectual property contribution for any taxable year of the donor after the 12th taxable year of the donor which ends on or after the date of such contribution.

(D) Regulations. The Secretary may issue regulations or other guidance to carry out the purposes of this subsection, including regulations or guidance—

(i) modifying the application of this subsection in the case of a donor or donee with a short taxable year, and

(ii) providing for the determination of an amount to be treated as net income of the donee which is properly allocable to qualified intellectual property in the case of a donee who uses such property to further a purpose or function constituting the basis of the donee's exemption under section 501 (or, in the case of a governmental unit, any purpose described in section 170(c)) and does not possess a right to receive any payment from a third party with respect to such property.

(n) **Expenses paid by certain whaling captains in support of native Alaskan subsistence whaling.**

(1) **In general.** In the case of an individual who is recognized by the Alaska Eskimo Whaling Commission as a whaling captain charged with the responsibility of maintaining and carrying out sanctioned whaling activities and who engages in such activities during the taxable year, the amount described in paragraph (2) (to the extent such amount does not exceed $10,000 for the taxable year) shall be treated for purposes of this section as a charitable contribution.

(2) **Amount described.**

(A) In general. The amount described in this paragraph is the aggregate of the reasonable and necessary whaling expenses paid by the taxpayer during the taxable year in carrying out sanctioned whaling activities.

(B) Whaling expenses. For purposes of subparagraph (A), the term "whaling expenses" includes expenses for—

(i) the acquisition and maintenance of whaling boats, weapons, and gear used in sanctioned whaling activities,

(ii) the supplying of food for the crew and other provisions for carrying out such activities, and

(iii) storage and distribution of the catch from such activities.

(3) **Sanctioned whaling activities.** For purposes of this subsection, the term "sanctioned whaling activities" means subsistence bowhead whale hunting activities conducted pursuant to the management plan of the Alaska Eskimo Whaling Commission.

(4) **Substantiation of expenses.** The Secretary shall issue guidance requiring that the taxpayer substantiate the whaling expenses for which a deduction is claimed under this subsection, including by maintaining appropriate written records with respect to the time, place, date, amount, and nature of the expense, as well as the taxpayer's eligibility for such deduction, and that (to the extent provided by the Secretary) such substantiation be provided as part of the taxpayer's return of tax.

(o) **Special rules for fractional gifts.**

(1) **Denial of deduction in certain cases.**

(A) In general. No deduction shall be allowed for a contribution of an undivided portion of a taxpayer's entire interest in tangible personal property unless all interests in the property are held immediately before such contribution by—

(i) the taxpayer, or

(ii) the taxpayer and the donee.

(B) Exceptions. The Secretary may, by regulation, provide for exceptions to subparagraph (A) in cases where all persons who hold an interest in the property make proportional contributions of an undivided portion of the entire interest held by such persons.

(2) **Valuation of subsequent gifts.** In the case of any additional contribution, the fair market value of such contribution shall be determined by using the lesser of—

(A) the fair market value of the property at the time of the initial fractional contribution, or

(B) the fair market value of the property at the time of the additional contribution.

(3) **Recapture of deduction in certain cases; addition to tax.**

(A) Recapture. The Secretary shall provide for the recapture of the amount of any deduction allowed under this section (plus interest) with respect to any contribution of an undivided portion of a taxpayer's entire interest in tangible personal property—

(i) in any case in which the donor does not contribute all of the remaining interests in such property to the donee (or, if such donee is no longer in existence, to any person described in section 170(c)) on or before the earlier of—

(I) the date that is 10 years after the date of the initial fractional contribution, or

(II) the date of the death of the donor, and

(ii) in any case in which the donee has not, during the period beginning on the date of the initial fractional contribution and ending on the date described in clause (i)—

(I) had substantial physical possession of the property, and

(II) used the property in a use which is related to a purpose or function constituting the basis for the organizations' exemption under section 501.

(B) Addition to tax. The tax imposed under this chapter for any taxable year for which there is a recapture under subparagraph (A) shall be increased by 10 percent of the amount so recaptured.

(4) **Definitions.** For purposes of this subsection—

(A) Additional contribution. The term "additional contribution" means any charitable contribution by the taxpayer of any interest in property with respect to which the taxpayer has previously made an initial fractional contribution.

(B) Initial fractional contribution. The term "initial fractional contribution" means, with respect to any taxpayer, the first charitable contribution of an undivided portion of the taxpayer's entire interest in any tangible personal property.

(p) **Other cross references.**

(1) For treatment of certain organizations providing child care, see section 501(k).

(2) For charitable contributions of estates and trusts, see section 642(c).

(3) For nondeductibility of contributions by common trust funds, see section 584.

(4) For charitable contributions of partners, see section 702.

(5) For charitable contributions of nonresident aliens, see section 873.

(6) For treatment of gifts for benefit of or use in connection with the Naval Academy as gifts to or for the use of the United States, see section 6973 of title 10, United States Code.

(7) For treatment of gifts accepted by the Secretary of State, the Director of the International Communication Agency, or the Director of the United States International Development Cooperation Agency, as gifts to or for the use of the United States, see section 25 of the State Department Basic Authorities Act of 1956.

(8) For treatment of gifts of money accepted by the Attorney General for credit to the "Commissary Funds, Federal Prisons" as gifts to or for the use of the United States, see section 4043 of title 18, United States Code.

(9) For charitable contributions to or for the use of Indian Tribal governments (or their subdivisions), see section 7871.

In **2010,** P.L. 111-312, Sec. 101(a)(1), substituted "December 31, 2012" for "December 31, 2010" both places it appears in Sec. 901, P.L. 107-16 [see below], effective as if included in the enactment of P.L. 107-16, EGTRRA, 6/7/2001.

—P.L. 111-312, Sec. 301(a), provides that Code Sec. 170, as amended by Sec. 542(e)(2)(B), P.L. 107-16, EGTRRA, 6/7/2001 (amended para. (e)(1), see below) will read as if such provision had never been enacted, effective for estates of decedents dying, and transfers made, after 12/31/2009.

Sec. 301(a), P.L. 111-312, 12/17/2010, provides:

"(a) In general. Each provision of law amended by subtitle A or E of title V of the Economic Growth and Tax Relief Reconciliation Act of 2001 is amended to read as such provision would read if such subtitle had never been enacted."

—P.L. 111-312, Sec. 301(c), of this Act, provides:

"(c) Special election with respect to estates of decedents dying in 2010. Notwithstanding subsection (a), in the case of an estate of a decedent dying after December 31, 2009, and before January 1, 2011, the executor (within the meaning of section 2203 of the Internal Revenue Code of 1986) may elect to apply such Code as though the amendments made by subsection (a) do not apply with respect to chapter 11 of such Code and with respect to property acquired or passing from such decedent (within the meaning of section 1014(b) of such Code). Such election shall be made at such time and in such manner as the Secretary of the Treasury or the Secretary's delegate shall provide. Such an election once made shall be revocable only with the consent of the Secretary of the Treasury or the Secretary's delegate. For purposes of section 2652(a)(1) of such Code, the determination of whether any property is subject to the tax imposed by such chapter 11 shall be made without regard to any election made under this subsection."

—P.L. 111-312, Sec. 301(d), of this Act, provides:

"(d) Extension of time for performing certain acts.

"(1) Estate tax. In the case of the estate of a decedent dying after December 31, 2009, and before the date of the enactment of this Act, the due date for—

"(A) filing any return under section 6018 of the Internal Revenue Code of 1986 (including any election required to be made on such a return) as such section is in effect after the date of the enactment of this Act without regard to any election under subsection (c),

"(B) making any payment of tax under chapter 11 of such Code, and

"(C) making any disclaimer described in section 2518(b) of such Code of an interest in property passing by reason of the death of such decedent, shall not be earlier than the date which is 9 months after the date of the enactment of this Act.

"(2) Generation-skipping tax. In the case of any generation-skipping transfer made after December 31, 2009, and before the date of the enactment of this Act, the due date for filing any return under section 2662 of the Internal Revenue Code of 1986 (including any election required to be made on such a return) shall not be earlier than the date which is 9 months after the date of the enactment of this Act."

—P.L. 111-312, Sec. 723(a), substituted "December 31, 2011" for "December 31, 2009" in clause. (b)(1)(E)(vi)... Sec. 723(b), substituted "December 31, 2011" for "December 31, 2009" in clause. (b)(2)(B)(iii), effective for contributions made in tax. yrs. begin. after 12/31/2009.

—P.L. 111-312, Sec. 740(a), substituted "December 31, 2011" for "December 31, 2009" in clause. (e)(3)(C)(iv), effective for contributions made after 12/31/2009.

—P.L. 111-312, Sec. 741(a), substituted "December 31, 2011" for "December 31, 2009" in clause. (e)(3)(D)(iv), effective for contributions made after 12/31/2009.

—P.L. 111-312, Sec. 742(a), substituted "December 31, 2011" for "December 31, 2009" in clause. (e)(6)(G), effective for contributions made in tax. yrs. begin. after 12/31/2009.

—P.L. 111-126, Sec. 1, reads as follows:

"Sec 1. Acceleration of income tax benefits for charitable cash contributions for relief of victims of earthquake in Haiti.

"(a) In General. For purposes of section 170 of the Internal Revenue Code of 1986, a taxpayer may treat any contribution described in subsection (b) made after January 11, 2010, and before March 1, 2010, as if such contribution was made on December 31, 2009, and not in 2010.

"(b) Contribution Described. A contribution is described in this subsection if such contribution is a cash contribution made for the relief of victims in areas affected by the earthquake in Haiti on January 12, 2010, for which a charitable contribution deduction is allowable under section 170 of the Internal Revenue Code of 1986.

"(c) Recordkeeping. In the case of a contribution described in subsection (b), a telephone bill showing the name of the donee organization, the date of the contribution, and the amount of the contribution shall be treated as meeting the recordkeeping requirements of section 170(f)(17) of the Internal Revenue Code of 1986.

"(d) Paygo. All applicable provisions in this section are designated as an emergency for purposes of pay-as-you-go principles."

In 2008, P.L. 110-343, Sec. 321(a)DivC, substituted "December 31, 2009" for "December 31, 2007" in subpara. (e)(6)(G), effective for contributions made during tax. yrs. begin. after 12/31/2007.

—P.L. 110-343, Sec. 323(a)(1)DivC, substituted "December 31, 2009" for "December 31, 2007" in clause (e)(3)(C)(iv), effective for contributions made after 12/31/2007.

—P.L. 110-343, Sec. 323(b)(1)DivC, added para. (b)(3), effective for tax. yrs. ending after 10/3/2008.

—P.L. 110-343, Sec. 324(a)DivC, substituted "December 31, 2009" for "December 31, 2007" in clause (e)(3)(D)(iv)... Sec. 324(b)DivC, added "of books" after "to any contribution" in clause (e)(3)(D)(iii), effective for contributions made after 12/31/2007.

—P.L. 110-343, Sec. 702DivC, Sec. 702 Div C, P.L. 110-343, relating to tax relief for areas damaged by 2008 Midwestern storms, reads as follows:

"Sec. 702. Temporary tax relief for areas damaged by 2008 Midwestern severe storms, tornados, and flooding.

"(a) In general. Subject to the modifications described in this section, the following provisions of or relating to the Internal Revenue Code of 1986 shall apply to any Midwestern disaster area in addition to the areas to which such provisions otherwise apply:

"(1) GO Zone benefits.

"(A) Section 1400N (relating to tax benefits) other than subsections (b), (d), (e), (i), (j), (m), and (o) thereof.

"(B) Section 1400O (relating to education tax benefits).

"(C) Section 1400P (relating to housing tax benefits).

"(D) Section 1400Q (relating to special rules for use of retirement funds).

"(E) Section 1400R(a) (relating to employee retention credit for employers).

"(F) Section 1400S (relating to additional tax relief) other than subsection (d) thereof.

"(G) Section 1400T (relating to special rules for mortgage revenue bonds).

"(2) Other benefits included in Katrina Emergency Tax Relief Act of 2005. Sections 302, 303, 304, 401, and 405 of the Katrina Emergency Tax Relief Act of 2005.

"(b) Midwestern disaster area.

"(1) In general. For purposes of this section and for applying the substitutions described in subsections (d) and (e), the term 'Midwestern disaster area' means an area—

"(A) with respect to which a major disaster has been declared by the President on or after May 20, 2008, and before August 1, 2008, under section 401 of the Robert T. Stafford Disaster Relief and Emergency Assistance Act by reason of severe storms, tornados, or flooding occurring in any of the States of Arkansas, Illinois, Indiana, Iowa, Kansas, Michigan, Minnesota, Missouri, Nebraska, and Wisconsin, and

"(B) determined by the President to warrant individual or individual and public assistance from the Federal Government under such Act with respect to damages attributable to such severe storms, tornados, or flooding.

"(2) Certain benefits available to areas eligible only for public assistance. For purposes of applying this section to benefits under the following provisions, paragraph (1) shall be applied without regard to subparagraph (B):

"(A) Sections 1400Q, 1400S(b), and 1400S(d) of the Internal Revenue Code of 1986.

"(B) Sections 302, 401, and 405 of the Katrina Emergency Tax Relief Act of 2005.

"(c) References.

"(1) Area. Any reference in such provisions to the Hurricane Katrina disaster area or the Gulf Opportunity Zone shall be treated as a reference to any Midwestern disaster area and any reference to the Hurricane Katrina disaster area or the Gulf Opportunity Zone within a State shall be treated as a reference to all Midwestern disaster areas within the State.

"(2) Items attributable to disaster. Any reference in such provisions to any loss, damage, or other item attributable to Hurricane Katrina shall be treated as a reference to any loss, damage, or other item attributable to the severe storms, tornados, or flooding giving rise to any Presidential declaration described in subsection (b)(1)(A).

"(3) Applicable disaster date. For purposes of applying the substitutions described in subsections (d) and (e), the term 'applicable disaster date' means, with respect to any Midwestern disaster area, the date on which the severe storms, tornados, or flooding giving rise to the Presidential declaration described in subsection (b)(1)(A) occurred.

* * * * * * * * * *

"(e) Modifications to Katrina Emergency Tax Relief Act of 2005. The following provisions of the Katrina Emergency Tax Relief Act of 2005 shall be applied with the following modifications:

* * * * * * * * * *

"(2) Increase in standard mileage rate. Section 303, by substituting 'beginning on the applicable disaster date and ending on December 31, 2008' for 'beginning on August 25, 2005, and ending on December 31, 2006'.

"(3) Mileage reimbursement for charitable volunteers. Section 304—

"(A) by substituting 'beginning on the applicable disaster date and ending on December 31, 2008' for 'beginning on August 25, 2005, and ending on December 31, 2006' in subsection (a), and

"(B) by substituting 'the applicable disaster date' for 'August 25, 2005' in subsection (a).

* * * * * * * * * *

—P.L. 110-246, Sec. 4, Repeals the duplicative enactment and provides effective date provisions of the Act entitled 'An Act to provide for the continuation of agricultural programs through fiscal year 2012, and for other purposes' Sec. 4, P.L. 110-246 reads as follows:

"Sec. 4. Repeal of duplicative enactment.

"(a) In General- The Act entitled 'An Act to provide for the continuation of agricultural programs through fiscal year 2012, and for other purposes' (H.R. 2419 of the 110th Congress), and the amendments made by that Act, are repealed, effective on the date of enactment of that Act.

"(b) Effective Date- Except as otherwise provided in this Act, this Act and the amendments made by this Act shall take effect on the earlier of--

"(1) the date of enactment of this Act; or

"(2) the date of the enactment of the Act entitled 'An Act to provide for the continuation of agricultural programs through fiscal year 2012, and for other purposes' (H.R. 2419 of the 110th Congress)."

—P.L. 110-246, Sec. 15302(a)(1), substituted "December 31, 2009" for "December 31, 2007" in clause (b)(1)(E)(vi)... Sec. 15302(a)(2), substituted "December 31, 2009" for "December 31, 2007" in clause (b)(2)(B)(iii), effective for contributions made in tax. yrs. begin. after 12/31/2007. [Ed. Note: May 22, 2008 was the date of enactment for H.R. 2419 (PL 110-234), which was repealed by (2008 Farm Act § 4(a)) (PL 110-246, 6/18/2008), in connection with the reenactment of the farm bill to correct a technical deficiency in its original passage.]

In 2007, P.L. 110-172, Sec. 11(a)(14)(a), substituted "subparagraph (F)" for "subparagraph (E)" in clause (b)(1)(A)(vii)... Sec. 11(a)(15), added ", but without regard to clause (ii) thereof" after "paragraph (7)(C)" in subclause (e)(1)(B)(i)(II)... Sec. 11(a)(14)(B), substituted "subsection (b)(1)(F)" for "subsection (b)(1)(E)" in clause (e)(1)(B)(ii), enacted 12/29/2007.

—P.L. 110-172, Sec. 3(c), substituted "substantial and related" for "related" in subclause (e)(7)(D)(i)(I), effective for contributions after 9/1/2006

—P.L. 110-172, Sec. 11(a)(16)(A), substituted "all interests in the property are" for "all interest in the property is" in subpara. (o)(1)(A)... Sec. 11(a)(16)(B)(i), substituted "interests" for "interest" in clause (o)(3)(A)(i)... Sec. 11(a)(16)(B)(ii), substituted "on or before" for "before" in clause (o)(3)(A)(i), enacted 12/29/2007.

In 2006, P.L. 109-432, Sec. 116(a)(1), substituted "2007" for "2005" in subpara. (e)(6)(G), effective for contributions made in tax. yrs. begin. after 12/31/2005.

—P.L. 109-432, Sec. 116(b)(1)(A), added "or assembled" after "constructed" in clause (e)(4)(B)(ii)... Sec. 116(b)(1)(B), added "or assembly" after "construction" in clause (e)(4)(B)(iii)... Sec. 116(b)(2)(A), added "or assembled" after "constructed" and "or assembling" after "construction" in clause (e)(6)(B)(ii)... Sec. 116(b)(2)(B), added "or assembled" after "constructed" and "or assembly" after "construction" in subpara. (e)(6)(D), effective for tax. yrs. begin. after 12/31/2005.

Deductions   Code Sec. 170

—P.L. 109-280, Sec. 1202(a), substituted "2007" for "2005" in clause (e)(3)(C)(iv), effective for contributions made after 12/31/2005.

—P.L. 109-280, Sec. 1204(a), substituted "2007" for "2005" in clause (e)(3)(D)(iv), effective for contributions made after 12/31/2005.

—P.L. 109-280, Sec. 1206(a)(1), redesignated subparas. (b)(1)(E)-(F) as (b)(1)(F)-(G) and added subpara. (b)(1)(E)... Sec. 1206(a)(2), amended para. (b)(2)... Sec. 1206(b)(1), substituted "subsection (b)(2)(A)" for "subsection (b)(2)" each place it appeared in para. (d)(2), effective for contributions made in tax. yrs. begin. after 12/31/2005.

Prior to amendment, para. (b)(2) read as follows:

"(2) Corporations. In the case of a corporation, the total deductions under subsection (a) for any taxable year shall not exceed 10 percent of the taxpayer's taxable income computed without regard to—

"(A) this section,

"(B) part VIII (except section 248),

"(C) section 199,

"(D) any net operating loss carryback to the taxable year under section 172, and

"(E) any capital loss carryback to the taxable year under section 1212(a)(1)."

—P.L. 109-280, Sec. 1213(a)(1) [sic (a)], redesignated subpara. (h)(4)(B) as (C) and added subpara. (h)(4)(B), effective for contributions made after 7/25/2006.

—P.L. 109-280, Sec. 1213(b)(1), deleted "any building, structure, or land area which" after "means" in subpara. (h)(4)(C) [as redesignated by Sec. 1213(a)(1) [sic (a)] of the Act, see above]... Sec. 1213(b)(2), added "any building, structure, or land area which" before "is listed" in clause (h)(4)(C)(i) [as redesignated by Sec. 1213(a)(1) [sic (a)] of the Act, see above]... Sec. 1213(b)(3), added "any building which" before "is located" in clause (h)(4)(C)(ii) [as redesignated by Sec. 1213(a)(1) [sic (a)] of the Act, see above], effective for contributions made after 8/17/2006.

—P.L. 109-280, Sec. 1213(c), added para. (f)(13), effective for contributions made 180 days after 8/17/2006.

—P.L. 109-280, Sec. 1213(d), added para. (f)(14), effective for contributions made after 8/17/2006.

—P.L. 109-280, Sec. 1214(a), deleted "or" at the end of clause (e)(1)(B)(ii), inserted "or" at the end of clause (e)(1)(B)(iii), and added clause (e)(1)(B)(iv)... Sec. 1214(b), added para. (f)(15), effective for contributions made after 7/25/2006.

—P.L. 109-280, Sec. 1215(a)(1), amended clause (e)(1)(B)(i)... Sec. 1215(a)(2), added para. (e)(7), effective for contributions after 9/1/2006.

Prior to amendment, clause (e)(1)(B)(i) read as follows:

"(i) of tangible personal property, if the use by the donee is unrelated to the purpose or function constituting the basis for its exemption under section 501 (or, in the case of a governmental unit, to any purpose or function described in subsection (c))."

—P.L. 109-280, Sec. 1216(a), added para. (f)(16), effective for contributions made after 8/17/2006.

—P.L. 109-280, Sec. 1217(a), added para. (f)(17), effective for contributions made in tax. yrs. begin. after 8/17/2006.

—P.L. 109-280, Sec. 1218(a), redesignated subsec. (o) as (p) and added subsec. (o), effective for contributions, bequests, and gifts made after 8/17/2006.

—P.L. 109-280, Sec. 1219(c)(1), amended subpara. (f)(11)(E), effective for appraisals prepared for returns or submissions filed after the 8/17/2006. Sec. 1219(e)(3) of this Act, provides:

"(3) Special rule for certain easements. In the case of a contribution of a qualified real property interest which is a restriction with respect to the exterior of a building described in section 170(h)(4)(C)(ii) of the Internal Revenue Code of 1986, and an appraisal with respect to the contribution, the amendments made by subsections (a) and (b) shall apply to returns filed after July 25, 2006."

Prior to amendment, subpara. (f)(11)(E) read as follows:

"(E) Qualified appraisal. For purposes of this paragraph, the term 'qualified appraisal' means, with respect to any property, an appraisal of such property which is treated for purposes of this paragraph as a qualified appraisal under regulations or other guidance prescribed by the Secretary."

—P.L. 109-280, Sec. 1234(a), added para. (f)(18), effective for contributions made after the date which is 180 days after 8/17/2006.

—P.L. 109-222, Sec. 204(b), added "(determined without regard to section 1221(b)(3))" after "long-term capital gain" in subpara. (e)(1)(A), effective for sales and exchanges in tax. yrs. begin. after 5/17/2006.

In 2005, P.L. 109-135, Sec. 201(b)(4)(B), repealed Sec. 301 of P.L. 109-73, effective 12/21/2005.

Prior to repeal, Sec. 301 of P.L. 109-73 read as follows:

"SEC. 301. TEMPORARY SUSPENSION OF LIMITATIONS ON CHARITABLE CONTRIBUTIONS.

"(a) In general. Except as otherwise provided in subsection (b), section 170(b) of the Internal Revenue Code of 1986 shall not apply to qualified contributions and such contributions shall not be taken into account for purposes of applying subsections (b) and (d) of section 170 of such Code to other contributions.

"(b) Treatment of excess contributions. For purposes of section 170 of such Code—

"(1) Individuals. In the case of an individual—

"(A) Limitation. Any qualified contribution shall be allowed only to the extent that the aggregate of such contributions does not exceed the excess of the taxpayer's contribution base (as defined in subparagraph (F) of section 170(b)(1) of such Code) over the amount of all other charitable contributions allowed under such section 170(b)(1).

"(B) Carryover. If the aggregate amount of qualified contributions made in the contribution year (within the meaning of section 170(d)(1) of such Code) exceeds the limitation of subparagraph (A), such excess shall be added to the excess described in the portion of subparagraph (A) of such section which precedes clause (i) thereof for purposes of applying such section.

"(2) Corporations. In the case of a corporation—

"(A) Limitation. Any qualified contribution shall be allowed only to the extent that the aggregate of such contributions does not exceed the excess of the taxpayer's taxable income (as determined under paragraph (2) of section 170(b) of such Code) over the amount of all other charitable contributions allowed under such paragraph.

"(B) Carryover. Rules similar to the rules of paragraph (1)(B) shall apply for purposes of this paragraph.

"(c) Exception to overall limitation on itemized deductions. So much of any deduction allowed under section 170 of such Code as does not exceed the qualified contributions paid during the taxable year shall not be treated as an itemized deduction for purposes of section 68 of such Code.

"(d) Qualified contributions.

"(1) In general. For purposes of this section, the term 'qualified contribution' means any charitable contribution (as defined in section 170(c) of such Code)—

"(A) paid during the period beginning on August 28, 2005, and ending on December 31, 2005, in cash to an organization described in section 170(b)(1)(A) of such Code (other than an organization described in section 509(a)(3) of such Code),

"(B) in the case of a contribution paid by a corporation, such contribution is for relief efforts related to Hurricane Katrina, and

"(C) with respect to which the taxpayer has elected the application of this section.

"(2) Exception. Such term shall not include a contribution if the contribution is for establishment of a new, or maintenance in an existing, segregated fund or account with respect to which the donor (or any person appointed or designated by such donor) has, or reasonably expects to have, advisory privileges with respect to distributions or investments by reason of the donor's status as a donor.

"(3) Application of election to partnerships and S corporations. In the case of a partnership or S corporation, the election under paragraph (1)(C) shall be made separately by each partner or shareholder."

—P.L. 109-135, Sec. 403(a)(16), redesignated subparas. (b)(2)(C) and (D) as subparas. (b)(2)(D) and (E) and added subpara. (b)(2)(C), effective for tax. yrs. begin. after 12/31/2004 as if included in Sec. 102 of the American Jobs Creation Act of 2004, P.L. 108-357.

—P.L. 109-135, Sec. 403(gg), added clauses (f)(12)(B)(v) and (vi), effective for contributions made after 12/31/2004 as if included in Sec. 884 of the American Jobs Creation Act of 2004, P.L. 108-357.

—P.L. 109-73, Sec. 303, of this Act, reads as follows:

"SEC. 303. INCREASE IN STANDARD MILEAGE RATE FOR CHARITABLE USE OF VEHICLES.

"Notwithstanding section 170(i) of the Internal Revenue Code of 1986, for purposes of computing the deduction under section 170 of such Code for use of a vehicle described in subsection (f)(12)(E)(i) of such section for provision of relief related to Hurricane Katrina during the period beginning on August 25, 2005, and ending on December 31, 2006, the standard mileage rate shall be 70 percent of the standard mileage rate in effect under section 162(a) of such Code at the time of such use. Any increase under this section shall be rounded to the next highest cent."

—P.L. 109-73, Sec. 304, of this Act, reads as follows:

"SEC. 304. MILEAGE REIMBURSEMENTS TO CHARITABLE VOLUNTEERS EXCLUDED FROM GROSS INCOME.

"(a) In general. For purposes of the Internal Revenue Code of 1986, gross income of an individual for taxable years ending on or after August 25, 2005, does not include amounts received, from an organization described in section 170(c) of such Code, as reimbursement of operating expenses with respect to use of a passenger automobile for the benefit of such organization in connection with providing relief relating to Hurricane Katrina during the period beginning on August 25, 2005, and ending on December 31, 2006. The preceding sentence shall apply only to the extent that the expenses which are reimbursed would be deductible under chapter 1 of such Code if section 274(d) of such Code were applied—

"(1) by using the standard business mileage rate in effect under section 162(a) at the time of such use, and

"(2) as if the individual were an employee of an organization not described in section 170(c) of such Code.

"(b) Application to volunteer services only. Subsection (a) shall not apply with respect to any expenses relating to the performance of services for compensation.

"(c) No double benefit. No deduction or credit shall be allowed under any other provision of such Code with respect to the expenses excludable from gross income under subsection (a)."

—P.L. 109-73, Sec. 305(a), redesignated subpara. (e)(3)(C) as (D) and added subpara. (e)(3)(C), effective for contributions made on or after 8/28/2005, in tax. yrs. end. after 8/28/2005.

—P.L. 109-73, Sec. 306(a), redesignated subpara. (e)(3)(D) as (E) [as redesignated by Sec. 305(a) of this Act, see above] and added subpara. (e)(3)(D), effective for contributions made on or after 8/28/2005, in tax. yrs. end. after 8/28/2005.

—P.L. 109-1, Sec. 1, of this Act, reads as follows:

"SECTION 1. ACCELERATION OF INCOME TAX BENEFITS FOR CHARITABLE CASH CONTRIBUTIONS FOR RELIEF OF INDIAN OCEAN TSUNAMI VICTIMS.

"(a) In general. For purposes of section 170 of the Internal Revenue Code of 1986, a taxpayer may treat any contribution described in subsection (b) made in January 2005 as if such contribution was made on December 31, 2004, and not in January 2005.

"(b) Contribution described. A contribution is described in this subsection if such contribution is a cash contribution made for the relief of victims in areas affected by the December 26, 2004, Indian Ocean tsunami for which a charitable contribution deduction is allowable under section 170 of the Internal Revenue Code of 1986."

In 2004, P.L. 108-357, Sec. 335(a), redesignated subsec. (n) as (o) and added subsec. (n), effective for contributions made after 12/31/2004.

—P.L. 108-357, Sec. 413(c)(30), deleted "556(b)(2)," after "section 545(b)(2)," in subpara. (f)(10)(A), effective for tax. yrs. of foreign corporations begin. after 12/31/2004, and for tax. yrs. of United States shareholders with or within which such tax. yrs. of foreign corporations end.

—P.L. 108-357, Sec. 882(a), deleted "or" at the end of clause (e)(1)(B)(i), added "or" at the end of clause (e)(1)(B)(ii), and added clause (e)(1)(B)(iii)...Sec. 882(b), redesignated subsec. (m) as (n) and added subsec. (m)...Sec. 882(d), added "subsection (e)(1)(B)(iii) or" after "described in" in subclause (f)(11)(A)(ii)(I) [as added by Sec. 883(a) of this Act, see below], effective for contributions made after 6/3/2004.

—P.L. 108-357, Sec. 882(e), of this Act, reads as follows:

"(e) Anti-abuse rules. The Secretary of the Treasury may prescribe such regulations or other guidance as may be necessary or appropriate to prevent the avoidance of the purposes of section 170(e)(1)(B)(iii) of the Internal Revenue Code of 1986 (as added by subsection (a)), including preventing—

"(1) the circumvention of the reduction of the charitable deduction by embedding or bundling the patent or similar property as part of a charitable contribution of property that includes the patent or similar property,

"(2) the manipulation of the basis of the property to increase the amount of the charitable deduction through the use of related persons, pass-thru entities, or other intermediaries, or through the use of any provision of law or regulation (including the consolidated return regulations), and

"(3) a donor from changing the form of the patent or similar property to property of a form for which different deduction rules would apply."

—P.L. 108-357, Sec. 883(a), added para. (f)(11), effective for contributions made after 6/3/2004.

—P.L. 108-357, Sec. 884(a), added para. (f)(12), effective for contributions made after 12/31/2004.

—P.L. 108-311, Sec. 207(15), added "(determined without regard to subsections (b)(1), (b)(2), and (d)(1)(B) thereof)" after "section 152" in para. (g)(1)...Sec. 207(16), substituted "subparagraphs (A) through (G) of section 152(d)(2)" for "paragraphs (1) through (8) of section 152(a)" in para. (g)(3), effective for tax. yrs. begin. after 12/31/2004.

—P.L. 108-311, Sec. 306(a), substituted "2005" for "2003" in subpara. (e)(6)(G), effective for contributions made in tax. yrs. begin. after 12/31/2003.

In 2003, P.L. 108-81, Sec. 503, substituted "section 213(1)(A) of the Library Services and Technology Act (20 U.S.C. 9122(1)(A))" for "section 213(2)(A) of the Library Services and Technology Act (20 U.S.C. 9122(2)(A)" in subclause (e)(6)(B)(i)(III), effective 9/25/2003.

In 2002, P.L. 107-358, Sec. 2, added subsec. (c) in Sec. 901 of P.L.107-16 [see below], effective 12/17/2002.

—P.L. 107-147, Sec. 417(7), substituted "2000)," for "2000," in subclause (e)(6)(B)(i)(III), effective 3/9/2002.

—P.L. 107-147, Sec. 417(22), instructs that Sec. 165(b)(1) of P.L. 106-554 [as enacted into law by P.L. 106-554] shall be applied as if it deleted "in any of the grades K-12" in clause (e)(6)(B)(iv). Sec. 165(b)(1) as originally enacted amended clause (e)(6)(B)(iv) by deleting "in any grades of the K-12", see below.

In 2001, P.L. 107-16, Sec. 542(e)(2)(B), added "For purposes of this paragraph, the determination of whether property is a capital asset shall be made without regard to the exception contained in section 1221(a)(3)(C) for basis determined under section 1022." at the end of para. (e)(1), effective for estates of decedents dying after 12/31/2009.

—P.L. 107-16, Sec. 901, of this Act [as amended by Sec. 2 of P.L. 107-358, and Sec. 101(a)(1), P.L. 111-312, see above], reads as follows:

"SEC. 901. SUNSET OF PROVISIONS OF ACT.

"(a) In general. All provisions of, and amendments made by, this Act shall not apply—

"(1) to taxable, plan, or limitation years beginning after December 31, 2012, or

"(2) in the case of title V, to estates of decedents dying, gifts made, or generation skipping transfers, after December 31, 2012.

"(b) Application of certain laws. The Internal Revenue Code of 1986 and the Employee Retirement Income Security Act of 1974 shall be applied and administered to years, estates, gifts, and transfers described in subsection (a) as if the provisions and amendments described in subsection (a) had never been enacted.

"(c) Exception. Subsection (a) shall not apply to section 803 (relating to no federal income tax on restitution received by victims of the Nazi regime or their heirs or estates)."

In 2000, P.L. 106-554, Sec. 1(a)(7), [which enacted into law Sec. 165(a)(1) of P.L. 106-554] substituted "qualified computer contribution" for "qualified elementary or secondary educational contribution" each place it appeared in para. (e)(6)...Sec. 1(a)(7), [which enacted into law Sec. 165(a)(2) of P.L. 106-554] deleted "or" at the end of subclause (e)(6)(B)(i)(I), added "or" at the end of subclause (e)(6)(B)(i)(II), and added subclause (e)(6)(B)(i)(III)...Sec. 1(a)(7), [which enacted into law Sec. 165(a)(3) of P.L. 106-554] substituted "3 years" for "2 years" in clause (e)(6)(B)(ii)...Sec. 1(a)(7), [which enacted into law Sec. 165(b)(1) of P.L. 106-554] deleted "in any grades of the K-12" after "educational purposes" in clause (e)(6)(B)(iv). Sec. 417(22) of P.L. 107-147, applies the amendment made by Sec. 165(b)(1) as if it deleted "in any of the grades K-12" see above....Sec. 1(a)(7), [which enacted into law Sec. 165(b)(2) of P.L. 106-554] substituted "educational purposes" for "elementary or secondary school purposes" in the heading of para. (e)(6)...Sec. 1(a)(7), [which enacted into law Sec. 165(c) of P.L. 106-554] substituted "December 31, 2003" for "December 31, 2000" in subpara. (e)(6)(F)...Sec. 1(a)(7), [which enacted into law Sec. 165(d)

of P.L. 106-554] deleted "and" at the end of clause (e)(6)(B)(vi), substituted ", and" for the period at the end of clause (e)(6)(B)(vii), and added clause (e)(6)(B)(viii)...Sec. 1(a)(7), [which enacted into law Sec. 165(e) of P.L. 106-554] redesignated subparas. (e)(6)(D)–(F) as (e)(6)(E)–(G) and added subpara. (e)(6)(D), effective for contributions made after 12/31/2000.

In 1999, P.L. 106-170, Sec. 532(c)(1)(A), substituted "section 1221(a)" for "section 1221" in subpara. (e)(3)(A)...Sec. 532(c)(1)(B), substituted "section 1221(a)" for "section 1221" in subpara. (e)(4)(B), effective for any instrument held, acquired, or entered into, any transaction entered into, and supplies held or acquired on or after 12/17/99.

—P.L. 106-170, Sec. 537(a), added para. (f)(10), effective as provided in Sec. 537(b) of this Act, which reads as follows:

"(b) Effective dates.

"(1) In general. Except as otherwise provided in this section, the amendment made by this section shall apply to transfers made after February 8, 1999.

"(2) Excise tax. Except as provided in paragraph (3) of this subsection, section 170(f)(10)(F) of the Internal Revenue Code of 1986 (as added by this section) shall apply to premiums paid after the date of the enactment of this Act.

"(3) Reporting. Clause (iii) of such section 170(f)(10)(F) shall apply to premiums paid after February 8, 1999 (determined as if the tax imposed by such section applies to premiums paid after such date)."

In 1998, P.L. 105-277, Sec. 1004(a)(1), deleted subpara. (e)(5)(D), effective for contributions made after 6/30/98.

Prior to deletion, subpara. (e)(5)(D) read as follows:

"(D) Termination. This paragraph shall not apply to contributions made—

"(i) after December 31, 1994, and before July 1, 1996, or

"(ii) after June 30, 1998."

—P.L. 105-206, Sec. 6004(e)(1), substituted "donee's" for "entity's" in clauses (e)(6)(B)(vi) and (vii)...Sec. 6004(e)(2), substituted "donee" for "organization or entity" in clause (e)(6)(B)(iv)...Sec. 6004(e)(3), substituted "a donee" for "an entity" in subclause (e)(6)(C)(ii)(I)...Sec. 6004(e)(4), substituted "2000" for "1999" in subpara. (e)(6)(F), effective for tax. yrs. begin. after 12/31/97.

In 1997, P.L. 105-34, Sec. 224(a), added para. (e)(6), effective for tax. yrs. begin. after 12/31/97.

—P.L. 105-34, Sec. 508(d), amended clause (h)(5)(B)(ii), effective for easements granted after 12/31/97.

Prior to amendment, clause (h)(5)(B)(ii) read as follows:

"(ii) Special rule. With respect to any contribution of property in which the ownership of the surface estate and mineral interests were separated before June 13, 1976, and remain so separated, subparagraph (A) shall be treated as met if the probability of surface mining occurring on such property is so remote as to be negligible."

—P.L. 105-34, Sec. 602(a), substituted "June 30, 1998" for "May 31, 1997" in clause (e)(5)(D)(ii), effective for contributions made after 5/31/97.

—P.L. 105-34, Sec. 973(a), amended subsec. (i), effective for tax. yrs. begin. after 12/31/97.

Prior to amendment, subsec. (i) read as follows:

"(i) Standard mileage rate for use of passenger automobile. For purposes of computing the deduction under this section for use of a passenger automobile the standard mileage rate shall be 12 cents per mile."

In 1996, P.L. 104-188, Sec. 1206(a), amended subpara. (e)(5)(D), effective for contributions made after 6/30/96.

Prior to amendment, subpara. (e)(5)(D) read as follows:

"(D) Termination. This paragraph shall not apply to contributions made after December 31, 1994."

—P.L. 104-188, Sec. 1316(b), added the sentence at the end of para. (e)(1), effective for tax. yrs. begin. after 12/31/97.

In 1993, P.L. 103-66, Sec. 13172(a), added para. (f)(8), effective for contributions made on or after 1/1/94.

—P.L. 103-66, Sec. 13222(b), added para. (f)(9), effective for amounts paid or incurred after 12/31/93.

In 1990, P.L. 101-508, Sec. 11801(a)(11), deleted subsec. (i)...Sec. 11801(c)(5), redesignated subsecs. (j), (k), (l), (m), and (n) as (i), (j), (k), (l), and (m), effective 11/5/90, except as provided in Sec. 11821(b) of this Act, reproduced in note following Code Sec. 184.

Prior to deletion, subsec. (i) read as follows:

"(i) Rule for nonitemization of deductions.

"(1) In general. In the case of an individual who does not itemize his deductions for the taxable year, the applicable percentage of the amount allowable under subsection (a) for the taxable year shall be taken into account as a direct charitable deduction under section 63.

"(2) Applicable percentage. For purposes of paragraph (1), the applicable percentage shall be determined under the following table:

"For taxable years beginning in—	The applicable percentage is—
1982, 1983 or 1984	25
1985	50
1986 or thereafter	100.

"(3) Limitation for taxable years beginning before 1985. In the case of a taxable year beginning before 1985, the portion of the amount allowable under subsection (a) to which the applicable percentage shall be applied

"(A) shall not exceed $100 for taxable years beginning in 1982 or 1983, and

"(B) shall not exceed $300 for taxable years beginning in 1984.

In the case of a married individual filing a separate return, the limit under subparagraph (A) shall be $50, and the limit under subparagraph (B) shall be $150.

Deductions Code Sec. 170

"(4) Termination. The provisions of this subsection shall not apply to contributions made after December 31, 1986."

—P.L. 101-508, Sec. 11812(b)(10), substituted "section 47(c)(3)(B)" for section 48(g)(3)(B)' in clause (h)(4)(B)(ii), effective for property placed in service after 12/31/90, except as provided in Sec. 11813(c)(2) of this Act, reproduced in note following Code Sec. 46.

In 1988, P.L. 100-647, Sec. 1016(b), repealed Sec. 1608 of P.L. 99-514.

Prior to repeal, Sec. 1608 of P.L. 99-514 read as follows:

"Sec. 1608. Treatment of certain amounts paid to or for the benefit of certain institutions of higher education.

"(a) In general.

"Amounts paid by a taxpayer to or for the benefit of an institution of higher education described in paragraph (1) or (2) of subsection (b) (other than amounts separately paid for tickets) which would otherwise qualify as a charitable contribution within the meaning of section 170 of the Internal Revenue Code of 1986 shall not be disqualified because such taxpayer receives the right to seating or the right to purchase seating in an athletic stadium of such institution.

"(b) Described institutions.

"(1) An institution is described in this paragraph, if—

"(A) such institution was mandated by a State constitution in 1876,

"(B) such institution was established by a State legislature in March 1881, and is located in a State capital pursuant to a statewide election in September 1981,

"(C) the campus of such institution formally opened on September 15, 1883, and

"(D) such institution is operated under the authority of a 9-member board of regents appointed by the governor.

"(2) An institution is described in this paragraph if such institution has an athletic stadium—

"(A) the plans for renovation of which were approved by a board of supervisors in December 1984, and reaffirmed by such board in December 1985 and January 1986, and

"(B) the plans for renovation of which were approved by a State board of ethics for public employees in February 1986."

—P.L. 100-647, Sec. 6001(a), redesignated subsec. (m) as subsec. (n) and added a new subsec. (m), effective for tax. yrs. begin. after 12/31/83. Sec. 6001(b)(2) of this Act, reads as follows:

"(2) Waiver of statute of limitations. If on the date of the enactment of this Act (or at any time within 1 year after such date of enactment) refund or credit of any overpayment of tax resulting from the application of section 170(m) of the 1986 Code (as added by subsection (a)) is barred by any law or rule of law, refund or credit of such overpayment may, nevertheless, be made or allowed if claim therefore is filed before the date 1 year after the date of the enactment [11/10/88] of this Act."

—P.L. 100-647, Sec. 6281, provides:

"Sec. 6281. Authority to waive appraisal requirement for certain charitable contributions of property.

"Notwithstanding paragraph (2) of section 155(a) of the Tax Reform Act of 1984 [P.L. 98-369, reproduced below], the Secretary of the Treasury or his delegate may in the regulations prescribed pursuant to such section waive the requirement of a qualified appraisal in the case of a qualified contribution (within the meaning of section 170(e)(3)(A) of the 1986 Code) of property described in section 1221(1) with a claimed value in excess of $5,000."

In 1987, P.L. 100-203, Sec. 10711(a)(1), substituted "on behalf of (or in opposition to) any candidate" for "on behalf of any candidate" in subpara. (c)(2)(D), effective with respect to activities after 12/22/87.

In 1986, P.L. 99-514, Sec. 142(d), redesignated subsecs. (k) and (l) as subsecs. (l) and (m), and added new subsec. (k), effective for tax. yrs. begin. after 12/31/86.

—P.L. 99-514, Sec. 231(f), amended clause (e)(4)(B)(i), effective for tax. yrs. begin. after 12/31/85.

Prior to amendment, clause (e)(4)(B)(i) read as follows:

"(i) the contribution is to an educational organization which is described in subsection (b)(1)(A)(ii) of this section and which is an institution of higher education (as defined in section 3304(f)),"

—P.L. 99-514, Sec. 301(b)(2), deleted "40 percent (28/46 in the case of a corporation) of" from before "the amount of gain" immediately following subpara. (e)(1)(B), effective for tax. yrs. begin. after 12/31/86.

—P.L. 99-514, Sec. 1608(a), and (b), regarding treatment of amounts paid to or for the benefit of certain institutions of higher education, [repealed by Sec. 1016(b) of P.L. 100-647, see above]

—P.L. 99-514, Sec. 1831, substituted "this paragraph" for "this subparagraph" in clause (b)(1)(C)(iv), effective for contributions made in tax. yrs. ending after 7/18/84.

In 1984, P.L. 98-369, Sec. 155(a)(1), through (6) [see Sec. 6281 of P.L. 100-647, above], provides:

"(a) Substantiation of contributions of property.

"(1) In general.—Not later than December 31, 1984, the Secretary shall prescribe regulations under section 170(a)(1) of the Internal Revenue Code of 1954, which require any individual, closely held corporation, or personal service corporation claiming a deduction under section 170 of such Code for a contribution described in paragraph (2)—

"(A) to obtain a qualified appraisal for the property contributed,

"(B) to attach an appraisal summary to the return on which such deduction is first claimed for such contribution, and

"(C) to include on such return such additional information (including the cost basis and acquisition date of the contributed property) as the Secretary may prescribe in such regulations.

Such regulations shall require the taxpayer to retain any qualified appraisal.

"(2) Contributions to which paragraph (1) applies. For purposes of paragraph (1), a contribution is described in this paragraph—

"(A) if such contribution is of property (other than publicly traded securities), and

"(B) if the claimed value of such property (plus the claimed value of all similar items of property donated to 1 or more donees) exceeds $5,000.

In the case of any property which is nonpublicly traded stock, subparagraph (B) shall be applied by substituting '$10,000' for '$5,000'.

"(3) Appraisal summary. For purposes of this subsection, the appraisal summary shall be in such form and include such information as the Secretary prescribes by regulations. Such summary shall be signed by the qualified appraiser preparing the qualified appraisal and shall contain the TIN of such appraiser. Such summary shall be acknowledged by the donee of the property appraised in such manner as the Secretary prescribes in such regulations.

"(4) Qualified appraisal. The term 'qualified appraisal' means an appraisal prepared by a qualified appraiser which includes—

"(A) a description of the property appraised,

"(B) the fair market value of such property on the date of contribution and the specific basis for the valuation,

"(C) a statement that such appraisal was prepared for income tax purposes,

"(D) the qualifications of the qualified appraiser,

"(E) the signature and TIN of such appraiser, and

"(F) such additional information as the Secretary prescribes in such regulations.

"(5) Qualified appraiser.

"(A) In general. For purposes of this subsection, the term 'qualified appraiser' means an appraiser qualified to make appraisals of the type of property donated, who is not—

"(i) the taxpayer,

"(ii) a party to the transaction in which the taxpayer acquired the property,

"(iii) the donee,

"(iv) any person employed by any of the foregoing persons or related to any of the foregoing persons under section 267(b) of the Internal Revenue Code of 1954, or

"(v) to the extent provided in such regulations, any person whose relationship to the taxpayer would cause a reasonable person to question the independence of such appraiser.

"(B) Appraisal fees. For purposes of this subsection, an appraisal shall not be treated as a qualified appraisal if all or part of the fee paid for such appraisal is based on a percentage of the appraised value of the property. The preceding sentence shall not apply to fees based on a sliding scale that are paid to a generally recognized association regulating appraisers.

"(6) Other definitions. For purposes of this subsection—

"(A) Closely held corporation. The term 'closely held corporation' means any corporation (other than an S corporation) with respect to which the stock ownership requirement of paragraph (2) of section 542(a) of such Code is met.

"(B) Personal service corporation. The term 'personal service corporation' means any corporation (other than an S corporation) which is a service organization (within the meaning of section 414(m)(3) of such Code).

"(C) Publicly traded securities. The term 'publicly traded securities' means securities for which (as of the date of the contribution) market quotations are readily available on an established securities market.

"(D) Nonpublicly traded stock. The term 'nonpublicly traded stock' means any stock of a corporation which is not a publicly traded security.

"(E) The secretary. The term 'Secretary' means the Secretary of the Treasury or his delegate."

—P.L. 98-369, Sec. 174(b)(5)(A), substituted "section 267(b) or 707(b)" for "section 267(b)" in para. (a)(3), effective for transactions after 12/31/83, in tax. yrs. end. after 12/31/83.

—P.L. 98-369, Sec. 301(a)(1), substituted "30 percent" for "20 percent" in clause (b)(1)(B)(i) . . . Sec. 301(a)(2), added the last sentence to subpara. (b)(1)(B), effective for contributions made in tax. yrs. end. after 7/18/84.

—P.L. 98-369, Sec. 301(b), added para. (e)(5), effective for contributions made after 7/18/84, in tax. yrs. end. after 7/18/84.

—P.L. 98-369, Sec. 301(c)(1), redesignated subparas. (b)(1)(D) and (E) as (b)(1)(E) and (F) and added new subpara. (b)(1)(D) . . . Sec. 301(c)(2)(A), substituted "subparagraph (E)" for "subparagraph (D)" in clause (b)(1)(A)(vii) . . . Sec. 301(c)(2)(B), amended the heading of subpara. (b)(1)(C) and amended clause (b)(1)(C)(i) . . . Sec. 301(c)(2)(C), substituted "subsection (b)(1)(E)" for "subsection (b)(1)(D)" in subpara. (e)(1)(B), effective for contributions made in tax. yrs. end. after 7/18/84.

Prior to amendment, the heading of subpara. (b)(1)(C) and clause (b)(1)(C)(i) read as follows:

"(C) Special limitation with respect to contributions of certain capital gain property.

"(i) In the case of charitable contributions of capital gain property to which subsection (e)(1)(B) does not apply, the total amount of contributions of such property which may be taken into account under subsection (a) for any taxable year shall not exceed 30 percent of the taxpayer's contribution base for such year. For purposes of this subsection, contributions of capital gain property to which this paragraph applies shall be taken into account after all other charitable contributions."

—P.L. 98-369, Sec. 492(b)(1)(A), deleted "1251(c)" after "1250(a)" in para. (e)(1) . . . Sec. 492(b)(1)(B), deleted "1251" after "1250" in subpara. (e)(3)(C), effective for tax. yrs. begin. after 12/31/83.

—P.L. 98-369, Sec. 1022(b), added para. (f)(7), effective for reformations after 12/31/78; except that such amendments shall not apply to any reformation to which section 2055(e)(3) of the Internal Revenue Code of 1954 (as in effect on the day before the date of the enactment of this Act [7/18/84]) applies. For purposes of applying clause (iii) of section 2055(e)(3)(C) of such Code [as amended by this section (Sec. 1022 of P.L. 98-369)], the 90th day described in such clause shall be treated as not occurring before 90th day after the date of the enactment of this Act [7/18/84]. Sec. 1022(e)(3) of the Act provides:

"(3) Statutes of limitations.

"(A) In general. If on the date of the enactment of this Act (or at any time before the date 1 year after such date of enactment), credit or refund of any overpayment of tax attributable to the amendments made by this section is barred by any law or rule of law, such credit or refund of such overpayment may nevertheless be made if claim therefor is filed before the date 1 year after the date of the enactment of this Act.

"(B) No interest where statute closed on date of enactment. In any case where the making of the credit or refund of the overpayment described in subparagraph (A) is barred on the date of the enactment of this Act, no interest shall be allowed with respect to such overpayment (or any related adjustment) for the period before the date 180 days after the date on which the Secretary of the Treasury (or his delegate) is notified that the reformation has occurred."

—P.L. 98-369, Sec. 1031(a), redesignated subsecs. (j) and (k) as subsecs. (k) and (l) and added new subsec. (j), effective for tax. yrs. begin. after 12/31/84.

—P.L. 98-369, Sec. 1032(b)(1), redesignated paras. (k)(1) through (8) as paras. (k)(2) through (9) and added new para. (k)(1), effective for tax. yrs. begin. after 7/18/84.

—P.L. 98-369, Sec. 1035(a), amended subpara. (h)(5)(B), effective for contributions made after 7/18/84.

Prior to amendment, subpara. (h)(5)(B) read as follows:

"(B) No surface mining permitted. In the case of a contribution of any interest where there is a retention of a qualified mineral interest, subparagraph (A) shall not be treated as met if at any time there may be extraction or removal of minerals by any surface mining method."

—P.L. 98-369, Sec. 1065(a)(1), amended Sec. 204 of P.L. 97-473, the effective date for changes made by Sec. 202(b)(4) to P.L. 97-473 (see below), by deleting "and before January 1, 1985" each place it appeared.

In 1983, P.L. 98-11, Sec. 207(i), added subsec. (k) to Sec. 7 of the National Trails System Act which reads as follows:

"(k) For the conservation purpose of preserving or enhancing the recreational, scenic, natural, or historical values of components of the national trails system, and environs thereof as determined by the appropriate Secretary, landowners are authorized to donate or otherwise convey qualified real property interests to qualified organizations consistent with section 170(h)(3) of the Internal Revenue Code of 1954, including, but not limited to, right-of-way, open space, scenic, or conservation easements, without regard to any limitation on the nature of the estate or interest otherwise transferable within the jurisdiction where the land is located. The conveyance of any such interest in land in accordance with this subsection shall be deemed to further a Federal conservation policy and yield a significant public benefit for purposes of Sec. 6 of P.L. 96-541."

—P.L. 97-473, Sec. 202(b)(4), added para. (k)(8), effective for tax. yrs. begin. after 12/31/82.

—P.L. 97-448, Sec. 102(f)(7), substituted "section 48(g)(3)(B)" for "section 191(d)(2)" in clause (h)(4)(B)(ii), effective for expenditures incurred after 12/31/81 in tax. yrs. end. after 12/31/81.

In 1982, P.L. 97-354, Sec. 5(a)(21)(A), substituted "an S corporation)" for "an electing small business corporation within the meaning of section 1371(b))" in subpara. (e)(3)(A) ... Sec. 5(a)(21)(B), amended clause (e)(4)(D)(i), effective for tax. yrs. begin. after 12/31/82.

Prior to amendment, clause (e)(4)(D)(i) read as follows:

"(i) an electing small business corporation (as defined in section 1371(b))."

—P.L. 97-258, Sec. 3(f)(1), substituted "section 4043 of title 18, United States Code" for "section 2 of the Act of May 15, 1952, as amended by the Act of July 9, 1952 (31 U.S.C. 725s-4)" in para. (k)(7), effective 9/13/82.

—P.L. 97-248, Sec. 286(b)(1), added the last sentence to the end of para. (c)(2), effective 10/5/76.

In 1981, P.L. 97-34, Sec. 121(a), redesignated subsecs. (i) and (j) as subsecs. (j) and (k) and added new subsec. (i), effective for contributions made after 12/31/81 in tax. yrs. end. after 12/31/81.

—P.L. 97-34, Sec. 222(a), added para. (e)(4), effective for charitable contributions made after 8/13/81 in tax. yrs. end. after 8/13/81.

—P.L. 97-34, Sec. 263(a), substituted "10 percent" for "5 percent" in para. (b)(2), effective for tax. yrs. begin. after 12/31/81.

In 1980, P.L. 96-541, Sec. 6(a), deleted subparas. (f)(3)(B) and (C) and added new subpara. (f)(3)(B) ... Sec. 6(b), redesignated subsecs. (h) and (i) as subsecs. (i) and (j) and added new subsec. (h), effective for transfers made after 12/17/80 in tax. yrs. end. after 12/17/80.

Prior to deletion, subparas. (f)(3)(B) and (C) read as follows:

"(B) Exceptions. Subparagraph (A) shall not apply to a contribution of—

"(i) a remainder interest in a personal residence or farm,

"(ii) an undivided portion of the taxpayer's entire interest in property,

"(iii) a lease on, option to purchase, or easement with respect to real property granted in perpetuity to an organization described in subsection (b)(1)(A) exclusively for conservation purposes, or

"(iv) a remainder interest in real property which is granted to an organization described in subsection (b)(1)(A) exclusively for conservation purposes.

"(C) conservation purposes defined. For purposes of subparagraph (B), the term 'conservation purposes' means—

"(i) the preservation of land areas for public outdoor recreation or education of scenic enjoyment;

"(ii) the preservation of historically important land areas or structures; or

"(iii) the protection of natural environmental systems."

—P.L. 96-541, Sec. 6(c), amended Sec. 309(b)(1) of P.L. 95-30 and Sec. 2124(e)(4) of P.L. 94-455, the effective date for changes made by Sec. 309(a) of P.L. 95-30 and 2124(e)(1) of P.L. 94-455, by deleting ", and before June 14, 1981". See below.

—P.L. 95-465, Sec. 2206(e)(2), amended para. (i)(6), effective 10/17/80.

Prior to amendment, para. (i)(6) read as follows:

"(6) For treatment of gifts accepted by the Secretary of State under the Foreign Service Act of 1946 as gifts to or for the use of the United States, see section 1021(e) of that Act (22 U.S.C. 809(e))."

—P.L. 96-222, Sec. 105(a)(4)(B), amended Sec. 514 of P.L. 95-600 by adding Sec. 514(c)(2) [reproduced below].

In 1979, P.L. 96-74, Sec. 614, provides the following:

"Sec. 614. None of the funds available under this Act [Treasury, Postal Service and General Government Appropriations Act, 1980] may be used to carry out any revenue ruling of the Internal Revenue Service which rules that a taxpayer is not entitled to a charitable deduction for general purpose contributions which are used for educational purposes by a religious organization which is an exempt organization as described in section 170(c)(2) of the Internal Revenue Code of 1954."

In 1978, P.L. 95-600, Sec. 402(b)(2), substituted "40 percent" for "50 percent" in subpara. (e)(1)(B), effective for contributions made after 10/31/78.

—P.L. 95-600, Sec. 403(c)(1), substituted "2⅜₀" for "62½ percent" in subpara. (e)(1)(B), effective for gifts made after 12/31/78. Sec. 514(b) of this Act provides:

"(b) Charitable lead trusts and charitable remainder trusts in the case of income and gift taxes.

"Under regulations prescribed by the Secretary of the Treasury or his delegate, in the case of trusts created before December 31, 1977, provisions comparable to section 2055(e)(3) of the Internal Revenue Code of 1954 (as amended by subsection (a)) shall be deemed to be included in sections 170 and 2522 of the Internal Revenue Code of 1954."

Sec. 514(c)(2) of this Act provides:

"(2) For subsection (b). Subsection (b)—

"(A) insofar as it relates to section 170 of the Internal Revenue Code of 1954 shall apply to transfers in trust and contributions made after July 31, 1969, and

"(B) insofar as it relates to section 2522 of the Internal Revenue Code of 1954 shall apply to transfers made after December 31, 1969."

In 1977, P.L. 95-30, Sec. 309(a), amended clause (f)(3)(B)(iii), effective [as amended by Sec. 6(c) of P.L. 96-541, see above] for contributions or transfers made after 6/13/77.

Prior to amendment, clause (f)(3)(B)(iii) read as follows:

"(iii) a lease on, option to purchase, or easement with respect to real property of not less than 30 years' duration granted to an organization described in subsection (b)(1)(A) exclusively for conservation purposes, or"

—P.L. 95-30, Sec. 309(b)(2), amended Sec. 2124(e) of P.L. 94-455, the effective date of changes made by Sec. 2124(e)(1) of P.L. 94-455, by substituting "June 14, 1981" for "June 14, 1977", see below.

In 1976, P.L. 94-455, Sec. 205(c)(1)(A), substituted "1252(a), or 1254(a)" for "or 1252(a)" in para. (e)(1), effective for tax. yrs. end. after '75.

—P.L. 94-455, Sec. 1052(c)(2), added "and" at the end of subpara. (b)(2)(C), deleted subpara. (b)(2)(D), and redesignated subpara. (b)(2)(E) as subpara. (b)(2)(D), effective for tax. yrs. begin. after 12/31/79.

Prior to amendment, subpara. (b)(2)(D) read as follows:

"(D) section 922 (special deduction for Western Hemisphere trade corporations), and"

—P.L. 94-455, Sec. 1307(c), amended subsec. (f) "by striking out paragraph (6) [sic]" (previously deleted by Sec. 1901(a)(28) of the Act) and substituted new para. (f)(6), effective for tax. yrs. begin. after 12/31/76.

—P.L. 94-455, Sec. 1307(d)(1)(B)(i), substituted "which is not disqualified for tax exemption under section 501(c)(3) by reason of attempting to influence legislation," for "no substantial part of the activities of which is carrying on propaganda, or otherwise attempting, to influence legislation," in subpara. (c)(2)(D), effective for tax. yrs. begin. after 12/31/76.

—P.L. 94-455, Sec. 1313(b)(1), added ", or to foster national or international amateur sports competition (but only if no part of its activities involve the provision of athletic facilities or equipment)," after "or educational purposes" in subpara. (c)(2)(B), effective 10/5/76.

Sec. 1313(c) of this Act provides as follows:

"(c) An organization which (without regard to the amendments made by this section) is an organization described in section 170(c)(2)(B) ... of the Internal Revenue Code of 1954 shall not be treated as an organization not so described as a result of the amendments made by this section."

—P.L. 94-455, Sec. 1901(a)(28)(A)(i), deleted para. (f)(6) and subsec. (g), and redesignated subsecs. (h), (i) and (j) as subsecs. (g), (h) and (i) ... Sec. 1901(a)(28)(A)(ii), deleted subpara. (b)(1)(C) and redesignated subparas. (b)(1)(D), (E) and (F) as subparas. (b)(1)(C), (D) and (E) ... Sec. 1901(a)(28)(A)(iii), substituted "subparagraph (D)" for "subparagraph (E)" in clause (b)(1)(A)(vii) ... Sec. 1901(a)(28)(A)(iv), substituted "subparagraph (C)" for "subparagraph (D)" in clause (b)(1)(B)(ii) ... Sec. 1901(a)(28)(A)(v), substituted "subsection (g)" for "subsection (h)" in the last sentence of subsec. (c) ... Sec. 1901(a)(28)(A)(vi), substituted "subsection (b)(1)(D)" for "subsection (b)(1)(E)" in clause (e)(1)(B)(ii) ... Sec. 1901(a)(2)(B), deleted "(30 percent, in the case of a contribution year beginning before January 1, 1970)" after "exceeds 50 percent" in subpara. (d)(1)(A) ... Sec. 1901(a)(28)(C), deleted "64 Stat. 996;" before "50 U.S.C. 790" in subsec. (h) (as redesignated) ... Sec. 1901(a)(28)(D), amended subsec. (i), effective for tax. yrs. begin. after 12/31/76.

Prior to deletion, para. (f)(6) read as follows:

"(6) Partial reduction of unlimited deduction."

"(A) In general. If the limitations in subsections (b)(1)(A) and (B) do not apply because of the application of subsection (b)(1)(C), the amount otherwise allowable as a deduction under subsection (a) shall be reduced by the amount by which the taxpayer's taxable income computed without regard to this subparagraph is less than the transitional income percentage (determined under subparagraph (C)) of the taxpayer's adjusted gross income. However, in no case shall a taxpayer's deduction under this section be reduced below the amount allowable as a deduction under this section without the applicability of subsection (b)(1)(C).

"(B) Transitional deduction percentage. For purposes of applying subsection (b)(1)(C), the term 'transitional deduction percentage' means—
(i) in the case of a taxable year beginning before 1970, 90 percent, and
(ii) in the case of a taxable year beginning in—

1970	80 percent
1971	74 percent
1972	68 percent
1973	62 percent
1974	56 percent

"(C) Transitional income percentage. For purposes of applying subparagraph (A), the term 'transitional income percentage' means, in the case of a taxable year beginning in—

1970	20 percent
1971	26 percent
1972	32 percent
1973	38 percent
1974	44 percent"

Prior to deletion, subsec. (g) read as follows:
"(g) Application of unlimited charitable contribution deduction.
"(1) Allowance of deduction for taxable years beginning after December 31, 1963. If the taxable year begins after December 31, 1963—
"(A) subsection (b)(1)(C) shall apply only if the taxpayer so elects (at such time and in such manner as the Secretary or his delegate by regulations prescribes); and
"(B) for purposes of subsection (b)(1)(C), the amount of the charitable contributions for the taxable year (and for all prior taxable years beginning after December 31, 1963) shall be determined without the application of subsection (d)(1) and solely by reference to charitable contributions described in paragraph (2).

If the taxpayer elects to have subsection (b)(1)(C) apply for the taxable year, then for such taxable year subsection (a) shall apply only with respect to charitable contributions described in paragraph (2), and no amount of charitable contributions made in the taxable year or any prior taxable year may be treated under subsection (d)(1) as having been made in the taxable year or in any succeeding taxable year.

"(2) Qualified contributions. The charitable contributions referred to in paragraph (1) are—
"(A) any charitable contribution described in subsection (b)(1)(A);
"(B) any charitable contribution, not described in subsection (b)(1)(A), to an organization described in subsection (c)(2) which meets the requirements of paragraph (3) with respect to such charitable contribution; and
"(D) any charitable contribution payment of which is made on or before the date of the enactment of the Revenue Act of 1964.

"(3) Organizations expending at least 50 percent of donor's contributions. An organization shall be an organization referred to in paragraph (2)(C), with respect to any charitable contribution, only if—
"(A) not later than the close of the third year after the organization's taxable year in which the contribution is received (or before such later time as the Secretary or his delegate may allow upon good cause shown by such organization), such organization expends an amount equal to at least 50 percent of such contribution for—
"(i) the active conduct of the activities constituting the purpose or function for which it is organized and operated,
"(ii) assets which are directly devoted to such active conduct,
"(iii) contributions to organizations which are described in subsection (b)(1)(A) or in paragraph (2)(B) of this subsection, or
"(iv) any combination of the foregoing; and
"(B) for the period beginning with the taxable year in which such contribution is received and ending with the taxable year in which subparagraph (A) is satisfied with respect to such contribution, such organization expends all of its net income (determined without regard to capital gains and losses) for the purposes described in clauses (i), (ii), (iii), and (iv) of subparagraph (A).

If the taxpayer so elects (at such time and in such manner as the Secretary or his delegate by regulations prescribes) with respect to contributions made by him to any organization, then, in applying subparagraph (B) with respect to contributions made by him to such organization during his taxable year for which such election is made and during all his subsequent taxable years, amounts expended by the organization after the close of any of its taxable years and on or before the 15th day of the third month following the close of such taxable year shall be treated as expended during such taxable year.

"(4) Disqualifying transactions. An organization shall be an organization referred to in subparagraph (B) or (C) of paragraph (2) only if at no time during the period consisting of the organization's taxable year in which the contribution is received, its 3 preceding taxable years, and its 3 succeeding taxable years, such organization—
"(A) lends any part of its income or corpus to,
"(B) pays compensation (other than reasonable compensation for personal services actually rendered) to,
"(C) makes any of its services available on a preferential basis to,

"(D) purchases more than a minimal amount of securities or other property from, or
"(E) sells more than a minimal amount of securities or other property to, the donor of such contribution, any member of his family (as defined in section 267(c)(4)), any employee of the donor, any officer or employee of a corporation in which he owns (directly or indirectly) 50 percent or more in value of the outstanding stock, or any partner or employee of a partnership in which he owns (directly or indirectly) 50 percent or more of the capital interest or profits interest. This paragraph shall not apply to transactions occurring on or before the date of the enactment of the Revenue Act of 1964 [2/26/64]."

Prior to deletion, subpara. (b)(1)(C) read as follows:
"(C) Unlimited deduction for certain individuals. Subject to the provisions of subsections (f)(6) and (g), the limitations in subparagraphs (A), (B), and (D), and the provisions of subsection (e)(1)(B), shall not apply, in the case of an individual for a taxable year beginning before January 1, 1975, if in such taxable year and in 8 of the 10 preceding taxable years, the amount of the charitable contributions, plus the amount of income tax (determined without regard to chapter 2, relating to tax on self-employment income) paid during such years in respect of such year or preceding taxable years, exceeds the transitional deduction percentage (determined under subsection (f)(6)) of the taxpayer's taxable income for such year, computed without regard to—
"(i) this section,
"(ii) section 151 (allowance of deductions for personal exemption), and
"(iii) any net operating loss carryback to the taxable year under section 172.

In lieu of the amount of income tax paid during any such year, there may be substituted for that year the amount of income tax paid in respect of such year, provided that any amount so included in the year in respect of which payment was made shall not be included in any other year. In the case of a separate return for the taxable year by a married individual who previously filed a joint return with a former deceased spouse for any of the 10 preceding taxable years, the amount of charitable contributions and taxes paid for any such preceding taxable year, for which a joint return was filed with the former deceased spouse, shall be determined in the same manner as if the taxpayer had not remarried after the death of such former spouse."

Prior to amendment, subsec. (i) read as follows:
"(i) Other cross references.
"(1) For charitable contributions of estates and trusts, see section 642(c).
"(2) For nondeductibility of contributions by common trust funds, see section 584.
"(3) For charitable contributions of partners, see section 702.
"(4) For charitable contributions of nonresident aliens, see section 873.
"(5) For treatment of gifts for benefit of or use in connection with the Naval Academy as gifts to or for the use of the United States, see section 3 of the Act of March 31, 1944 (58 Stat. 135; 34 U.S.C. 1115b).
"(6) For treatment of gifts for benefit of the library of the Post Office Department as gifts to or for the use of the United States, see section 2 of the Act of August 8, 1946 (60 Stat. 924; 5 U.S.C. 393).
"(7) For treatment of gifts accepted by the Secretary of State under the Foreign Service Act of 1946 as gifts to or for the use of the United States, see section 1021(e) of that Act (60 Stat. 1032; 22 U.S.C. 809(e)).
"(8) For treatment of gifts of money accepted by the Attorney General for credit to the 'Commissary Funds Federal Prisons' as gifts to or for the use of the United States, see section 2 of the Act of May 15, 1952 (66 Stat. 73, as amended by the Act of July 9, 1952, 66 Stat. 479, 31 U.S.C. 725s-4)."

—P.L. 94-455, Sec. 1901(b)(8)(A), substituted "educational organization described in section 170(b)(1)(A)(ii)" for "educational institution (as defined in section 151(e)(4))" in subpara. (g)(1)(B), as redesignated by this Act, effective for tax. yrs. begin. after '76.

—P.L. 94-455, Sec. 1906(b)(13)(A), substituted "Secretary" for "Secretary or his delegate" each place it appeared in Code Sec. 170, effective for tax. yrs. begin. after 12/31/76.

—P.L. 94-455, Sec. 2124(e)(1), deleted "or" at the end of clause (f)(3)(B)(i) ... substituted "property," for "property." at the end of clause (f)(3)(B)(ii) ... added clauses (f)(3)(B)(iii) and (iv) ... added subpara. (f)(3)(C), effective [as amended by Sec. 6(c) of P.L 96-541 and Sec. 301(b)(2) of P.L. 95-30, see above] for contributions or transfers made after 6/13/76.

—P.L. 94-455, Sec. 2135(a), added para. (e)(3), effective for charitable contributions made after 10/4/76, in tax. yrs. end. after 10/4/76.

In 1972, P.L. 92-603, Sec. 132(c), added subsec. (i) to Sec. 201 of the Social Security Act.

"(i)(1) The Managing Trustee of the Federal Old-Age and Survivors Insurance Trust Fund, The Federal Disability Insurance Trust Fund, The Federal Hospital Insurance Trust Fund, and the Federal Supplementary Medical Insurance Trust Fund is authorized to accept on behalf of the United States money gifts and bequests made unconditionally to any one or more of such Trust Funds or to the Department of Health, Education, and Welfare, or any part or officer thereof, for the benefit of any of such Funds or any activity financed through such Funds.

"(2) Any such gift accepted pursuant to the authority granted in paragraph (1) of this subsection shall be deposited in—
"(A) the specific trust fund designated by the donor or
"(B) if the donor has not so designated, the Federal Old-Age and Survivors Insurance Trust Fund."

Sec. 132(f) and (g) of this Act read as follows:
"(f) The amendments made by this section shall apply with respect to gifts and bequests received after the date of enactment of this Act. [10/31/72]
"(g) For the purpose of Federal income, estate, and gift taxes, any gift or bequest to the Federal Old-Age and Survivors Insurance Trust Fund, the Federal

Disability Insurance Trust Fund, the Federal Hospital Insurance Trust Fund, or the Federal Supplementary Medical Insurance Trust Fund, or to the Department of Health, Education, and Welfare, or any part or officer thereof, for the benefit of any of such Funds or any activity financed through any of such Funds, which is accepted by the Managing Trustee of such Trust Funds under the authority of section 201(i) of the Social Security Act, shall be considered as a gift or bequest to or for the use of the United States and as made for exclusively public purposes."

In 1969, P.L. 91-172, Sec. 101(j)(2), deleted para. (i)(1) and deleted "(2)" preceding "For disallowance" in subsec. (i), effective 1/1/70.

Prior to deletion, para. (i)(1) read as follows:

"(1) For disallowance of deductions in case of contributions or gifts to charitable organizations engaging in prohibited transactions, see section 503(e)."

—P.L. 91-172, Sec. 201(a)(1), redesignated former subsecs. (d), (h) and (i) as subsecs. (h), (i) and (j), added new subsec. (d) and amended subsecs. (a), (b), (c), (e) and (f). Sec. 201(g)(1) provides as follows:

"(1)(A) Except as provided in subparagraphs (B) and (C), the amendments made by subsection (a) shall apply to taxable years beginning after December 31, 1969.

"(B) Subsections (e) and (f)(1) of section 170 of the Internal Revenue Code of 1954 (as amended by subsection (a)) shall apply to contributions paid after December 31, 1969, except that, with respect to a letter or memorandum or similar property described in section 1221(3) of such Code (as amended by section 514 of this Act), such subsection (e) shall apply to contributions paid after July 25, 1969.

"(C) Paragraphs (2), (3), and (4) of section 170(f) of such Code (as amended by subsection (a)) shall apply to transfers in trust and contributions made after July 31, 1969.

"(D) For purposes of applying section 170(d) of such Code (as amended by subsection (a)) with respect to contributions paid in a taxable year beginning before January 1, 1970, subsection (b)(1)(D), subsection (e), and paragraphs (1), (2), (3), and (4) of subsection (f) of section 170 of such Code shall not apply.

Prior to amendment, subsecs. (a), (b) and (c) read as follows:

"(a) Allowance of deduction.

"(1) General rule. There shall be allowed as a deduction any charitable contribution (as defined in subsection (c)) payment of which is made within the taxable year. A charitable contribution shall be allowable as a deduction only if verified under regulations prescribed by the Secretary or his delegate.

"(2) Corporations on accrual basis. In the case of a corporation reporting its taxable income on the accrual basis, if—

"(A) the board of directors authorizes a charitable contribution during any taxable year, and

"(B) payment of such contribution is made after the close of such taxable year and on or before the 15th day of the third month following the close of such taxable year,

then the taxpayer may elect to treat such contribution as paid during such taxable year. The election may be made only at the time of the filing of the return for such taxable year, and shall be signified in such manner as the Secretary or his delegate shall by regulations prescribe.

"(b) Limitations.

"(1) Individuals. In the case of an individual the deduction provided in subsection (a) shall be limited as provided in subparagraphs (A), (B), (C), and (D).

"(A) Special rule. Any charitable contribution to—

"(i) a church or a convention or association of churches,

"(ii) an educational organization referred to in section 503(b)(2),

"(iii) a hospital referred to in section 503(b)(5), or to a medical research organization (referred to in section 503(b)(5)) directly engaged in the continuous active conduct of medical research in conjunction with a hospital, if during the calendar year in which the contribution is made such organization is committed to spend such contributions for such research before January 1 of the fifth calendar year which begins after the date such contribution is made,

"(iv) an organization referred to in section 503(b)(3) organized and operated exclusively to receive, hold, invest, and administer property and to make expenditures to or for the benefit of a college or university which is an organization referred to in clause (ii) of this subparagraph and which is an agency or instrumentality of a State or political subdivision thereof, or which is owned or operated by a State or political subdivision thereof or by an agency or instrumentality of one or more States or political subdivisions,

"(v) a governmental unit referred to in subsection (c)(1), or

"(vi) an organization referred to in subsection (c)(2) which normally receives a substantial part of its support (exclusive of income received in the exercise or performance by such organization of its charitable, educational, or other purpose or function constituting the basis for its exemption under section 501(a)) from a governmental unit referred to in subsection (c)(1) or from direct or indirect contributions from the general public,

shall be allowed to the extent that the aggregate of such contributions does not exceed 10 percent of the taxpayer's adjusted gross income computed without regard to any net operating loss carryback to the taxable year under section 172.

"(B) General limitation. The total deductions under subsection (a) for any taxable year shall not exceed 20 percent of the taxpayer's adjusted gross income computed without regard to any net operating loss carryback to the taxable year under section 172. For purposes of this subparagraph, the deduction under subsection (a) shall be computed without regard to any deduction allowed under subparagraph (A) but shall take into account any charitable contributions described in subparagraph (A) which are in excess of the amount allowable as a deduction under subparagraph (A).

"(C) Unlimited deduction for certain individuals. The limitation in subparagraph (B) shall not apply in the case of an individual if, in the taxable year and in 8 of the 10 preceding taxable years, the amount of the charitable contributions, plus the amount of income tax (determined without regard to chapter 2, relating to tax on self-employment income) paid during such year in respect of such year or preceding taxable years, exceeds 90 percent of the taxpayer's taxable income for such year, computed without regard to—

"(i) this section,

"(ii) section 151 (allowance of deductions for personal exemptions), and

"(iii) any net operating loss carryback to the taxable year under section 172.

In lieu of the amount of income tax paid during any such year, there may be substituted for that year the amount of income tax paid in respect of such year, provided that any amount so included in the year in respect of which payment was made shall not be included in any other year.

"(D) Denial of deduction in case of certain transfers in trust. No deduction shall be allowed under this section for the value of any interest in property transferred after March 9, 1954, to a trust if—

"(i) the grantor has a reversionary interest in the corpus or income of that portion of the trust with respect to which a deduction would (but for this subparagraph) be allowable under this section; and

"(ii) at the time of the transfer the value of such reversionary interest exceeds 5 percent of the value of the property constituting such portion of the trust.

For purposes of this subparagraph, a power exercisable by the grantor or a nonadverse party (within the meaning of section 672(b)), or both, to revest in the grantor property or income therefrom shall be treated as a reversionary interest.

"(2) Corporations. In the case of a corporation the total deductions under subsection (a) for any taxable year shall not exceed 5 percent of the taxpayer's taxable income computed without regard to—

"(A) this section,

"(B) part VIII (except section 248),

"(C) any net operating loss carryback to the taxable year under section 172, and

"(D) section 922 (special deduction for Western Hemisphere trade corporations).

Any contribution made by a corporation in a taxable year (hereinafter in this sentence referred to as the 'contribution year') in excess of the amount deductible for such year under the preceding sentence shall be deductible for each of the 5 succeeding taxable years in order of time, but only to the extent of the lesser of the two following amounts: (i) the excess of the maximum amount deductible for such succeeding taxable year under the preceding sentence over the sum of the contributions made in such year plus the aggregate of the excess contributions which were made in taxable years before the contribution year and which are deductible under this sentence for such succeeding taxable year; or (ii) in the case of the first succeeding taxable year, the amount of such excess contribution, and in the case of the second, third, fourth, or fifth succeeding taxable year, the portion of such excess contribution not deductible under this sentence for any taxable year intervening between the contribution year and such succeeding taxable year.

"(3) Special rule for corporations having net operating loss carryovers. In applying the second sentence of paragraph (2) of this subsection, the excess of—

"(A) the contributions made by a corporation in a taxable year to which this section applies, over

"(B) the amount deductible in such year under the limitation in the first sentence of such paragraph (2).

shall be reduced to the extent that such excess reduces taxable income (as computed for purposes of the second sentence of section 172(b)(2)) and increases a net operating loss carryover under section 172 to a succeeding taxable year.

"(4) Reduction for certain interest. If, in connection with any charitable contribution, a liability is assumed by the recipient or by any other person, or if a charitable contribution is of property which is subject to a liability, then, to the extent necessary to avoid the duplication of amounts, the amount taken into account for purposes of this section as the amount of the charitable contribution—

"(A) shall be reduced for interest (i) which has been paid (or is to be paid) by the taxpayer, (ii) which is attributable to the liability, and (iii) which is attributable to any period after the making of the contribution, and

"(B) in the case of a bond, shall be further reduced for interest (i) which has been paid (or is to be paid) by the taxpayer on indebtedness incurred or continued to purchase or carry such bond, and (ii) which is attributable to any period before the making of the contribution.

The reduction pursuant to subparagraph (B) shall not exceed the interest (including interest equivalent) on the bond which is attributable to any period before the making of the contribution and which is not (under the taxpayer's method of accounting) includible in the gross income of the taxpayer for any taxable year. For purposes of this paragraph, the term 'bond' means any bond, debenture, note, or certificate or other evidence of indebtedness.

"(5) Carryover of certain excess contributions by individuals.

"(A) In the case of an individual, if the amount of charitable contributions described in paragraph (1)(A) payment of which is made within a taxable year (hereinafter in this paragraph referred to as the 'contribution year') beginning after December 31, 1963, exceeds 30 percent of the taxpayer's adjusted gross income for such year (computed without regard to any net operating loss carryback to such year under section 172), such excess shall be treated as a charitable contribution described in paragraph (1)(A) paid in each of the 5 succeeding taxable years in order of time, but, with respect to any such succeeding taxable year, only to the extent of the lesser of the two following amounts:

"(i) the amount by which 30 percent of the taxpayer's adjusted gross income for such succeeding taxable year (computed without regard to any net operating loss carryback to such succeeding taxable year under section 172) exceeds the sum of the charitable contributions described in paragraph (1)(A) payment of which is made by the taxpayer within such succeeding taxable year (determined without regard to this subparagraph) and the charitable contributions described in paragraph (1)(A) payment of which was made in taxable years (beginning after

Deductions

Code Sec. 171(a)(2)

December 31, 1963) before the contribution year which are treated under this subparagraph as having been paid in such succeeding taxable year; or

"(ii) in the case of the first succeeding taxable year, the amount of such excess, and in the case of the second, third, fourth, or fifth succeeding taxable year, the portion of such excess not treated under this subparagraph as a charitable contribution described in paragraph (1)(A) paid in any taxable year intervening between the contribution year and such succeeding taxable year.

"(B) In supplying subparagraph (A), the excess determined under subparagraph (A) for the contribution year shall be reduced to the extent that such excess reduces taxable income (as computed for purposes of the second sentence of section 172(b)(2) and increases the net operating loss deduction for a taxable year succeeding the contribution year.

"(c) Charitable contribution defined.

For purposes of this section, the term 'charitable contribution' means a contribution or gift to or for the use of—

"(1) A State, a Territory, a possession of the United States, or any political subdivision of any of the foregoing, or the United States or the District of Columbia, but only if the contribution or gift is made for exclusively public purposes.

"(2) A corporation, trust, or community chest, fund, or foundation—

"(A) created or organized in the United States or in any possession thereof, or under the law of the United States, any State or Territory, the District of Columbia, or any possession of the United States;

"(B) organized and operated exclusively for religious, charitable, scientific, literary, or educational purposes or for the prevention of cruelty to children or animals;

"(C) no part of the net earnings of which inures to the benefit of any private shareholder or individual; and

"(D) no substantial part of the activities of which is carrying on propaganda, or otherwise attempting, to influence legislation.

A contribution or gift by a corporation to a trust, chest, fund, or foundation shall be deductible by reason of this paragraph only if it is to be used within the United States or any of its possessions exclusively for purposes specified in subparagraph (B).

"(3) A post or organization of war veterans, or an auxiliary unit or society of, or trust or foundation for, any such post or organization—

"(A) organized in the United States or any of its possessions, and

"(B) no part of the net earnings of which inures to the benefit of any private shareholder or individual.

"(4) In the case of a contribution or gift by an individual, a domestic fraternal society, order, or association, operating under the lodge system, but only if such contribution or gift is to be used exclusively for religious, charitable, scientific, literary, or educational purposes, or for the prevention of cruelty to children or animals.

"(5) A cemetery company owned and operated exclusively for the benefit of its members, or any corporation chartered solely for burial purposes as a cemetery corporation and not permitted by its charter to engage in any business not necessarily incident to that purpose, if such company or corporation is not operated for profit and no part of the net earnings of such company or corporation inures to the benefit of any private shareholder or individual.

For purposes of this section, the term 'charitable contribution' also means an amount treated under subsection (d) as paid for the use of an organization described in paragraph (2), (3), or (4)."

Prior to amendment, subsecs. (e) and (f) read as follows:

"(e) Special rule for charitable contributions of certain property.

"The amount of any charitable contribution taken into account under this section shall be reduced by the amount which would have been treated as gain to which section 617(d)(1), 1245(a) or 1250(a) applies if the property contributed has been sold at its fair market value (determined at the time of such contribution).

"(f) Future interests in tangible personal property.

"For purposes of this section, payment of a charitable contribution which consists of a future interest in tangible personal property shall be treated as made only when all intervening interests in, and rights to the actual possession or enjoyment of, the property have expired or are held by persons other than the taxpayer or those standing in a relationship to the taxpayer described in section 267(b). For purposes of the preceding sentence, a fixture which is intended to be severed from the real property shall be treated as tangible personal property."

—P.L. 91-172, Sec. 201(a)(2)(A), substituted "subsection (d)(1)" for "subsection (b)(5)" each place it appeared in subsec. (g) and deleted subpara. (g)(2)(B), effective for tax. yrs. begin. after 12/31/69.

Prior to deletion, subpara. (g)(2)(B) read as follows:

"(B) any charitable contribution, not described in subsection (b)(1)(A), to an organization described in subsection (c)(2) substantially more than half of the assets of which is devoted directly to, and substantially all of the income of which is expended directly for, the active conduct of the activities, constituting the purpose or function for which it is organized and operated."

—P.L. 91-172, Sec. 201(h)(1), added the last sentence to subpara. (b)(1)(C), effective for tax. yrs. begin. after 12/31/68.

In 1966, P.L. 89-570, Sec. [1](b)(1), substituted "section 617(d)(1), 1245(a)" for "section 1245(a)" in subsec. (e), effective for tax. yrs. end. after 9/12/66, but only for expenditures paid or incurred after 9/12/66.

In 1964, P.L. 88-272, Sec. 209(a), deleted "or" at the end of clause (b)(1)(A)(iii), and added clauses (b)(1)(A)(v) and (vi) . . . Sec. 209(b), added subsec. (g) . . . Sec. 209(c)(1), added para. (b)(5), effective for contributions which are paid in tax. yrs. begin. after 12/31/63.

—P.L. 88-272, Sec. 209(d)(1), amended the sentence that followed subpara. (b)(2)(D), effective for tax. yrs. begin. after 12/31/63, for contributions which are paid (or treated as paid under Code Sec. 170(a)(2)) in tax. yrs. begin. after 12/31/61.

Prior to amendment, the sentence that followed subpara. (b)(2)(D) read as follows: "Any contribution by a corporation in a taxable year to which this section applies in excess of the amount deductible in such year under the foregoing limitation shall be deductible in each of the two succeeding taxable years in order of time, but only to the extent of the lesser of the two following amounts: (i) the excess of the maximum amount deductible for such succeeding taxable year under the foregoing limitation over the contributions made in such year; and (ii) in the case of the first succeeding taxable year the amount of such excess contribution, and in the case of the second succeeding taxable year the portion of such excess contribution not deductible in the first succeeding taxable year."

—P.L. 88-272, Sec. 209(e), redesignated subsecs. (f) and (g) as subsecs. (h) and (i) and added new subsec. (f), effective as provided in Sec. 209(f)(3) of this Act, which reads as follows:

"(3) The amendments made by subsection (e) shall apply to transfers of future interests made after December 31, 1963, in taxable years ending after such date, except that such amendments shall not apply to any transfer of a future interest made before July 1, 1964, where—

"(A) the sole intervening interest or right is a nontransferable life interest reserved by the donor, or

"(B) in the case of a joint gift by husband and wife, the sole intervening interest or right is a nontransferable life interest reserved by the donors which expires not later than the death of whichever of such donor dies later.

For purposes of the exception contained in the preceding sentence, a right to make a transfer of the reserved life interest to the donee of the future interest shall not be treated as making a life interest transferable."

—P.L. 88-272, Sec. 231, substituted "certain property" for "section 1245 property" in the subsection heading, and substituted "section 1245(a) or 1250(a)" for "section 1245(a)" in subsec. (e), effective for dispositions after 12/31/63 in tax. yrs. end. after 12/31/63.

In 1962, P.L. 87-858, Sec. 2(a), and (b) added clause (b)(1)(A)(iv), and substituted "any charitable contributions described in subparagraph (A)" for "any charitable contributions to the organizations described in clauses (i), (ii), and (iii)" in subpara. (b)(1)(B), effective for tax. yrs. begin. after 12/31/60.

—P.L. 87-834, Sec. 13(d), redesignated subsecs. (e) and (f) as subsecs. (f) and (g) and added subsec. new (e), effective for tax. yrs. begin. after 12/31/62.

—P.L. 87-834, Sec. 29, provided that:

"For purposes of section 170 of the Internal Revenue Code of 1954 (relating to deduction for charitable, etc., contributions and gifts), a contribution or gift made after December 31, 1961, with respect to a referendum occurring during the calendar year 1962 to or for the use of any nonprofit organization created and operated exclusively—

"(1) to consider proposals for the reorganization of the judicial branch of the government of any State of the United States or political subdivision of such State, and

"(2) to provide information, make recommendations, and seek public support or opposition as to such proposals,

shall be treated as a charitable contribution if no part of the net earnings of such organization inures to the benefit of any private shareholder or individual. The provisions of the preceding sentence shall not apply to any organization which participates in, or intervenes in, any political campaign on behalf of any candidate for public office."

In 1960, P.L. 86-779, Sec. 7(a)(1), added the sentence additionally defining the term "charitable contribution" for the purposes of the section at the end of subsec. (c) . . . Sec. 7(a)(2), redesignated subsecs. (d) and (e) as subsecs. (e) and (f), and added subsec. (d), effective for tax. yrs. begin. after 12/31/59.

In 1958, P.L. 85-866, Sec. 10, added the last sentence to subpara. (b)(1)(C), effective for tax. yrs. begin. after 12/31/57.

—P.L. 85-866, Sec. 11, added para. (b)(3), as of original date of '54 Code.

—P.L. 85-866, Sec. 12, added para. (b)(4), effective for tax. yrs. end. after 12/31/57, but only for charitable contributions made after 12/31/57.

In 1956, P.L. 1022, Sec. [1], added "or to a medical research organization (referred to in section 503(b)(5)) directly engaged in continuous active conduct of medical research in conjunction with a hospital, if during the calendar year in which the contribution is made such organization is committed to spend such contributions for such research before January 1 of the fifth calendar year which begins after the date such contribution is made" after "section 503(b)(5)", effective for tax. yrs. begin. after 12/31/55.

Sec. 171. Amortizable bond premium.
(a) General rule.

In the case of any bond, as defined in subsection (d), the following rules shall apply to the amortizable bond premium (determined under subsection (b)) on the bond:

(1) Taxable bonds. In the case of a bond (other than a bond the interest on which is excludable from gross income), the amount of the amortizable bond premium for the taxable year shall be allowed as a deduction.

(2) Tax-exempt bonds. In the case of any bond the interest on which is excludable from gross income, no deduction shall be allowed for the amortizable bond premium for the taxable year.

1,635

(3) Cross reference. For adjustment to basis on account of amortizable bond premium, see section 1016(a)(5).

(b) Amortizable bond premium.

(1) Amount of bond premium. For purposes of paragraph (2), the amount of bond premium, in the case of the holder of any bond, shall be determined—

(A) with reference to the amount of the basis (for determining loss on sale or exchange) of such bond,

(B)(i) with reference to the amount payable on maturity or on earlier call date, in the case of any bond other than a bond to which clause (ii) applies, or and [sic]

(ii) with reference to the amount payable on maturity (or if it results in a smaller amortizable bond premium attributable to the period to earlier call date, with reference to the amount payable on earlier call date), in the case of any bond described in subsection (a)(1) which is acquired after December 31, 1957, and

(C) with adjustments proper to reflect unamortized bond premium, with respect to the bond, for the period before the date as of which subsection (a) becomes applicable with respect to the taxpayer with respect to such bond.

In no case shall the amount of bond premium on a convertible bond include any amount attributable to the conversion features of the bond.

(2) Amount amortizable. The amortizable bond premium of the taxable year shall be the amount of the bond premium attributable to such year. In the case of a bond to which paragraph (1)(B)(ii) applies and which has a call date, the amount of bond premium attributable to the taxable year in which the bond is called shall include an amount equal to the excess of the amount of the adjusted basis (for determining loss on sale or exchange) of such bond as of the beginning of the taxable year over the amount received on redemption of the bond or (if greater) the amount payable on maturity.

(3) Method of determination.

(A) In general. Except as provided in regulations prescribed by the Secretary, the determinations required under paragraphs (1) and (2) shall be made on the basis of the taxpayer's yield to maturity determined by—

(i) using the taxpayer's basis (for purposes of determining loss on sale or exchange) of the obligation, and

(ii) compounding at the close of each accrual period (as defined in section 1272(a)(5)).

(B) Special rule where earlier call date is used. For purposes of subparagraph (A), if the amount payable on an earlier call date is used under paragraph (1)(B)(ii) in determining the amortizable bond premium attributable to the period before the earlier call date, such bond shall be treated as maturing on such date for the amount so payable and then reissued on such date for the amount so payable.

(4) Treatment of certain bonds acquired in exchange for other property.

(A) In general. If—

(i) a bond is acquired by any person in exchange for other property, and

(ii) the basis of such bond is determined (in whole or in part) by reference to the basis of such other property,

for purposes of applying this subsection to such bond while held by such person, the basis of such bond shall not exceed its fair market value immediately after the exchange. A similar rule shall apply in the case of such bond while held by any other person whose basis is determined (in whole or in part) by reference to the basis in the hands of the person referred to in clause (i).

(B) Special rule where bond exchanged in reorganization. Subparagraph (A) shall not apply to an exchange by the taxpayer of a bond for another bond if such exchange is a part of a reorganization (as defined in section 368). If any portion of the basis of the taxpayer in a bond transferred in such an exchange is not taken into account in determining bond premium by reason of this paragraph, such portion shall not be taken into account in determining the amount of bond premium on any bond received in the exchange.

(c) Election as to taxable bonds.

(1) Eligibility to elect; bonds with respect to which election permitted. In the case of bonds the interest on which is not excludible from gross income, this section shall apply only if the taxpayer has so elected.

(2) Manner and effect of election. The election authorized under this subsection shall be made in accordance with such regulations as the Secretary shall prescribe. If such election is made with respect to any bond (described in paragraph (1)) of the taxpayer, it shall also apply to all such bonds held by the taxpayer at the beginning of the first taxable year to which the election applies and to all such bonds thereafter acquired by him and shall be binding for all subsequent taxable years with respect to all such bonds of the taxpayer, unless, on application by the taxpayer, the Secretary permits him, subject to such conditions as the Secretary deems necessary, to revoke such election. In the case of bonds held by a common trust fund, as defined in section 584(a), the election authorized under this subsection shall be exercisable with respect to such bonds only by the common trust fund. In case of bonds held by an estate or trust, the election authorized under this subsection shall be exercisable with respect to such bonds only by the fiduciary.

(d) Bond defined.

For purposes of this section, the term "bond" means any bond, debenture, note, or certificate or other evidence of indebtedness, but does not include any such obligation which constitutes stock in trade of the taxpayer or any such obligation of a kind which would properly be included in the inventory of the taxpayer if on hand at the close of the taxable year, or any such obligation held by the taxpayer primarily for sale to customers in the ordinary course of his trade or business.

(e) Treatment as offset to interest payments.

Except as provided in regulations, in the case of any taxable bond—

(1) the amount of any bond premium shall be allocated among the interest payments on the bond under rules similar to the rules of subsection (b)(3), and

(2) in lieu of any deduction under subsection (a), the amount of any premium so allocated to any interest payment shall be applied against (and operate to reduce) the amount of such interest payment.

For purposes of the preceding sentence, the term "taxable bond" means any bond the interest of which is not excludable from gross income.

(f) Dealers in tax-exempt securities.

For special rules applicable, in the case of dealers in securities, with respect to premium attributable to certain wholly tax-exempt securities, see section 75.

In 2004, P.L. 108-357, Sec. 413(c)(2)(A), deleted ", or by a foreign personal holding company, as defined in section 552" after "as defined in section 584(a)" in para. (c)(2)... Sec. 413(c)(2)(B), deleted ", or foreign personal holding company" after "only by the common trust fund" in para. (c)(2), effective for tax.

yrs. of foreign corporations begin. after 12/31/2004, and for tax. yrs. of United States shareholders with or within which such tax. yrs. of foreign corporations end.

In 1988, P.L. 100-647, Sec. 1006(j)(1)(A), amended subsec. (e), effective in the case of obligations acquired after 12/31/87; except that the taxpayer may elect to have such amendment apply to obligations acquired after 10/22/86.

Prior to amendment, subsec. (e) read as follows:

"(e) Treatment as interest.

"Except as provided in regulations, the amount of any amortizable bond premium with respect to which a deduction is allowed under subsection (a)(1) for any taxable year shall be treated as interest for purposes of this title."

—P.L. 100-647, Sec. 1006(j)(2), amended Sec. 643(b)(2) of P.L. 99-514, [reproduced below] part of the effective date for amendments made by Sec. 643(a) of P.L. 99-514 by substituting "acquired after" for "issued after", see below.

In 1986, P.L. 99-514, Sec. 643(a), redesignated subsec. (e) as subsec. (f), and added new subsec. (e), effective for obligations acquired after 10/22/86, in tax. yrs. begin. after 10/22/86. Sec. 643(b)(2) [as amended by Sec. 1006(j)(2) of P.L. 100-647, see above] of this Act provides:

"(2) Revocation of election. In the case of a taxpayer with respect to whom an election is in effect on the date of enactment of this Act under section 171(c) of the Internal Revenue Code of 1986, such election shall apply to obligations acquired after the date of the enactment of this Act only if the taxpayer chooses (at such time and in such manner as may be prescribed by the Secretary of the Treasury or his delegate) to have such election apply with respect to such obligations."

—P.L. 99-514, Sec. 1803(a)(11)(A), amended para. (b)(3) . . . Sec. 1803(a)(11)(B), deleted "issued by any corporation and bearing interest (including any like obligation issued by a government or political subdivision thereof)," after "evidence of indebtedness" in subsec. (d), effective for obligations issued after 9/27/85. Sec. 1803(a)(11)(C)(ii) of this Act provides:

"(ii) In the case of a taxpayer with respect to whom an election is in effect on the date of the enactment of this Act under section 171(c) of the Internal Revenue Code of 1954, such election shall apply to obligations issued after September 27, 1985, only if the taxpayer chooses (at such time and in such manner as may be prescribed by the Secretary of the Treasury or his delegate) to have such election apply with respect to such obligations."

Prior to amendment, para. (b)(3) read as follows:

"(3) Method of determination. The determinations required under paragraphs (1) and (2) shall be made—

"(A) in accordance with the method of amortizing bond premium regularly employed by the holder of the bond, if such method is reasonable;

"(B) in all other cases, in accordance with regulations prescribing reasonable methods of amortizing bond premium prescribed by the Secretary."

—P.L. 99-514, Sec. 1803(a)(12)(A), added para. (b)(4), effective for exchanges after 5/6/86.

In 1976, P.L. 94-455, Sec. 1901(b)(1)(E)(i), substituted "(1) Taxable bonds." for "(1) Interest wholly or partially taxable." as the heading for para. (a)(1) . . . Sec. 1901(b)(1)(E)(ii), substituted "(2) Tax-exempt bonds." for "(2) Interest wholly tax-exempt." as the heading for para. (a)(2) . . . Sec. 1901(b)(1)(E)(iii), deleted para. (a)(3) and redesignated para. (a)(4) as (a)(3) . . . Sec. 1901(b)(1)(E)(iv), substituted "subsection (a)(1)" for "subsection (c)(1)(B)" in clause (b)(1)(B)(ii) . . . Sec. 1901(b)(1)(E)(v), amended so much of subsec. (c) as preceded para. (c)(2), effective for tax. yrs. begin. after 12/31/76.

Prior to amendment, para. (a)(3) read as follows:

"(3) Adjustment of credit or deduction for interest partially tax-exempt.

"(A) Individuals. In the case of any bond the interest on which is allowable as a credit under section 35, the amount which would otherwise be taken into account in computing such credit shall be reduced by the amount of the amortizable bond premium for the taxable year.

"(B) Corporations. In the case of any bond the interest on which is allowable as a deduction under section 242, such deduction shall be reduced by the amount of the amortizable bond premium for the taxable year."

Prior to amendment, so much of subsec. (c) as precedes para. (c)(2) read as follows:

"(c) Election as to taxable and partially taxable bonds.

"(1) Eligibility to elect; bonds with respect to which election permitted. This section shall apply with respect to the following classes of taxpayers with respect to the following classes of bonds only if the taxpayer has elected to have this section apply:

"(A) Partially tax-exempt. In the case of a taxpayer other than a corporation, bonds with respect to the interest on which the credit provided in section 35 is allowable; and

"(B) Wholly taxable. In the case of any taxpayer, bonds the interest on which is not excludable from gross income but with respect to which the credit provided in section 35, or the deduction provided in section 242, is not allowable."

—P.L. 94-455, Sec. 1906(b)(13)(A), substituted "Secretary" for "Secretary or his delegate" each place it appeared in paras. (b)(2) and (c)(2), effective for tax. yrs. begin. after 12/31/76.

—P.L. 94-455, Sec. 1951(b)(5)(A)(i), deleted clause (b)(1)(B)(iii) . . . Sec. 1951(b)(5)(a)(ii), substituted "clause (ii) applies, or" for "clause (ii) or (iii) applies," and "by inserting 'and' at the end thereof" in clause (b)(1)(B)(i) . . . Sec. 1951(b)(5)(A)(iii), substituted ", and" for ", or" in clause (b)(1)(B)(ii) . . . Sec. 1951(b)(5)(A)(iv), deleted "or (iii)", which followed "paragraph (1)(B)(ii)", in para. (b)(2), effective for tax. yrs. begin. after 12/31/76. except as provided in Sec. 1(f)(5)(B) of the Act, which reads as follows:

"(B) Savings provision.—Notwithstanding the amendments made by subparagraph (A), in the case of a bond the interest on which is not excludable from gross income—

"(i) which was issued after January 22, 1951, with a call date not more than 3 years after the date of such issue, and

"(ii) which was acquired by the taxpayer after January 22, 1954, and before January 1, 1958,

the bond premium for a taxable year beginning after December 31, 1975, shall not be determined under section 171(b)(1)(B)(i) but shall be determined with reference to the amount payable on maturity, and if the bond is called before its maturity, the bond premium for the year in which the bond is called shall be determined in accordance with the provisions of section 171(b)(2)."

Prior to amendment clause (b)(1)(B)(iii) read as follows:

"(iii) with reference to the amount payable on maturity, in the case of any bond described in subsection (c)(1)(B) which was acquired after January 22, 1954, and before January 1, 1958, but only if such bond was issued after January 22, 1951, and has a call date not more than 3 years after the date of such issue, and"

In 1958, P.L. 85-866, Sec. 13(a)(1), amended subpara. (b)(1)(B) . . . Sec. 13(a)(2), substituted "In the case of a bond to which paragraph (1)(B)(ii) or (iii) applies and which has a call date," for "In the case of a bond described in subsection (c)(1)(B) issued after January 22, 1951, and acquired after January 22, 1954, which has a call date not more than 3 years after the date of such issue," in the second sentence, of para. (b)(2), effective for tax yrs. end. after 12/31/57.

Sec. 172. Net operating loss deduction.
(a) Deduction allowed.

There shall be allowed as a deduction for the taxable year an amount equal to the aggregate of (1) the net operating loss carryovers to such year, plus (2) the net operating loss carrybacks to such year. For purposes of this subtitle, the term "net operating loss deduction" means the deduction allowed by this subsection.

(b) Net operating loss carrybacks and carryovers.
(1) Years to which loss may be carried.

(A) General rule. Except as otherwise provided in this paragraph, a net operating loss for any taxable year—

(i) shall be a net operating loss carryback to each of the 2 taxable years preceding the taxable year of such loss, and

(ii) shall be a net operating loss carryover to each of the 20 taxable years following the taxable year of the loss.

(B) Special rules for REIT's.

(i) In general. A net operating loss for a REIT year shall not be a net operating loss carryback to any taxable year preceding the taxable year of such loss.

(ii) Special rule. In the case of any net operating loss for a taxable year which is not a REIT year, such loss shall not be carried back to any taxable year which is a REIT year.

(iii) REIT year. For purposes of this subparagraph, the term "REIT year" means any taxable year for which the provisions of part II of subchapter M (relating to real estate investment trusts) apply to the taxpayer.

(C) Specified liability losses. In the case of a taxpayer which has a specified liability loss (as defined in subsection (f)) for a taxable year, such specified liability loss shall be a net operating loss carryback to each of the 10 taxable years preceding the taxable year of such loss.

(D) Bad debt losses of commercial banks. In the case of any bank (as defined in section 585(a)(2)), the portion of the net operating loss for any taxable year beginning after December 31, 1986, and before January 1, 1994, which is attributable to the deduction allowed under section 166(a) shall be a net operating loss carryback to each of the 10 taxable years preceding the taxable year of the loss and a net operating loss carryover to each of the 5 taxable years following the taxable year of such loss.

(E) Excess interest loss.

(i) In general. If—

(I) there is a corporate equity reduction transaction, and

(II) an applicable corporation has a corporate equity reduction interest loss for any loss limitation year ending after August 2, 1989,

then the corporate equity reduction interest loss shall be a net operating loss carryback and carryover to the taxable years described in subparagraph (A), except that such loss shall not be carried back to a taxable year preceding the taxable year in which the corporate equity reduction transaction occurs.

(ii) Loss limitation year. For purposes of clause (i) and subsection (h), the term "loss limitation year" means, with respect to any corporate equity reduction transaction, the taxable year in which such transaction occurs and each of the 2 succeeding taxable years.

(iii) Applicable corporation. For purposes of clause (i), the term "applicable corporation" means—

(I) a C corporation which acquires stock, or the stock of which is acquired in a major stock acquisition,

(II) a C corporation making distributions with respect to, or redeeming, its stock in connection with an excess distribution, or

(III) a C corporation which is a successor of a corporation described in subclause (I) or (II).

(iv) Other definitions.

For definitions of terms used in this subparagraph, see subsection (h).

(F) Retention of 3-year carryback in certain cases.

(i) In general. Subparagraph (A)(i) shall be applied by substituting "3 taxable years" for "2 taxable years" with respect to the portion of the net operating loss for the taxable year which is an eligible loss with respect to the taxpayer.

(ii) Eligible loss. For purposes of clause (i), the term "eligible loss" means—

(I) in the case of an individual, losses of property arising from fire, storm, shipwreck, or other casualty, or from theft,

(II) in the case of a taxpayer which is a small business, net operating losses attributable to federally declared disasters (as defined by subsection (h)(3)(C)(i)), and

(III) in the case of a taxpayer engaged in the trade or business of farming (as defined in section 263A(e)(4)), net operating losses attributable to such federally declared disasters.

Such term shall not include any farming loss (as defined in subsection (i)) or or qualified disaster loss (as defined in subsection (j)).

(iii) Small business. For purposes of this subparagraph, the term "small business" means a corporation or partnership which meets the gross receipts test of section 448(c) for the taxable year in which the loss arose (or, in the case of a sole proprietorship, which would meet such test if such proprietorship were a corporation).

(iv) Coordination with paragraph (2). For purposes of applying paragraph (2), an eligible loss for any taxable year shall be treated in a manner similar to the manner in which a specified liability loss is treated.

(G) Farming losses. In the case of a taxpayer which has a farming loss (as defined in subsection (i)) for a taxable year, such farming loss shall be a net operating loss carryback to each of the 5 taxable years preceding the taxable year of such loss.

(H) Carryback for 2008 or 2009 net operating losses.

(i) In general. In the case of an applicable net operating loss with respect to which the taxpayer has elected the application of this subparagraph—

(I) subparagraph (A)(i) shall be applied by substituting any whole number elected by the taxpayer which is more than 2 and less than 6 for "2",

(II) subparagraph (E)(ii) shall be applied by substituting the whole number which is one less than the whole number substituted under subclause (I) for "2", and

(III) subparagraph (F) shall not apply.

(ii) Applicable net operating loss. For purposes of this subparagraph, the term "applicable net operating loss" means the taxpayer's net operating loss for a taxable year ending after December 31, 2007, and beginning before January 1, 2010.

(iii) Election.

(I) In general. Any election under this subparagraph may be made only with respect to 1 taxable year.

(II) Procedure. Any election under this subparagraph shall be made in such manner as may be prescribed by the Secretary, and shall be made by the due date (including extension of time) for filing the return for the taxpayer's last taxable year beginning in 2009. Any such election, once made, shall be irrevocable.

(iv) Limitation on amount of loss carryback to 5th preceding taxable year.

(I) In general. The amount of any net operating loss which may be carried back to the 5th taxable year preceding the taxable year of such loss under clause (i) shall not exceed 50 percent of the taxpayer's taxable income (computed without regard to the net operating loss for the loss year or any taxable year thereafter) for such preceding taxable year.

(II) Carrybacks and carryovers to other taxable years. Appropriate adjustments in the application of the second sentence of paragraph (2) shall be made to take into account the limitation of subclause (I).

(III) Exception for 2008 elections by small businesses. Subclause (I) shall not apply to any loss of an eligible small business with respect to any election made under this subparagraph as in effect on the day before the date of the enactment of the Worker, Homeownership, and Business Assistance Act of 2009.

(v) Special rules for small business.

(I) In general. In the case of an eligible small business which made or makes an election under this subparagraph as in effect on the day before the date of the enactment of the Worker, Homeownership, and Business Assistance Act of 2009, clause (iii)(I) shall be applied by substituting "2 taxable years" for "1 taxable year".

(II) Eligible small business. For purposes of this subparagraph, the term "eligible small business" has the meaning given such term by subparagraph (F)(iii), except that in applying such subparagraph, section 448(c) shall be applied by substituting "$15,000,000" for "$5,000,000" each place it appears.

(I) Transmission property and pollution control investment.

Deductions Code Sec. 172(d)(4)(A)

(i) In general. At the election of the taxpayer for any taxable year ending after December 31, 2005, and before January 1, 2009, in the case of a net operating loss for a taxable year ending after December 31, 2002, and before January 1, 2006, there shall be a net operating loss carryback to each of the 5 taxable years preceding the taxable year of such loss to the extent that such loss does not exceed 20 percent of the sum of the electric transmission property capital expenditures and the pollution control facility capital expenditures of the taxpayer for the taxable year preceding the taxable year for which such election is made.

(ii) Limitations. For purposes of this subsection—

(I) not more than one election may be made under clause (i) with respect to any net operating loss for a taxable year, and

(II) an election may not be made under clause (i) for more than 1 taxable year beginning in any calendar year.

(iii) Coordination with ordering rule. For purposes of applying subsection (b)(2), the portion of any loss which is carried back 5 years by reason of clause (i) shall be treated in a manner similar to the manner in which a specified liability loss is treated.

(iv) Special rules relating to credit or refund. In the case of the portion of the loss which is carried back 5 years by reason of clause (i)—

(I) an application under section 6411(a) with respect to such portion shall not fail to be treated as timely filed if filed within 24 months after the due date specified under such section, and

(II) references in sections 6501(h), 6511(d)(2)(A), and 6611(f)(1) to the taxable year in which such net operating loss arises or results in a net operating loss carryback shall be treated as references to the taxable year for which such election is made.

(v) Definitions. For purposes of this subparagraph—

(I) Electric transmission property capital expenditures. The term "electric transmission property capital expenditures" means any expenditure, chargeable to capital account, made by the taxpayer which is attributable to electric transmission property used by the taxpayer in the transmission at 69 or more kilovolts of electricity for sale. Such term shall not include any expenditure which may be refunded or the purpose of which may be modified at the option of the taxpayer so as to cease to be treated as an expenditure within the meaning of such term.

(II) Pollution control facility capital expenditures. The term "pollution control facility capital expenditures" means any expenditure, chargeable to capital account, made by an electric utility company (as defined in section 2(3) of the Public Utility Holding Company Act (15 U.S.C. 79b(3)), as in effect on the day before the date of the enactment of the Energy Tax Incentives Act of 2005) which is attributable to a facility which will qualify as a certified pollution control facility as determined under section 169(d)(1) by striking "before January 1, 1976," and by substituting "an identifiable" for "a new identifiable". Such term shall not include any expenditure which may be refunded or the purpose of which may be modified at the option of the taxpayer so as to cease to be treated as an expenditure within the meaning of such term.

(J) Certain losses attributable federally declared disasters. In the case of a taxpayer who has a qualified disaster loss (as defined in subsection (j)), such loss shall be a net operating loss carryback to each of the 5 taxable years preceding the taxable year of such loss.

(2) **Amount of carrybacks and carryovers.** The entire amount of the net operating loss for any taxable year (hereinafter in this section referred to as the "loss year") shall be carried to the earliest of the taxable years to which (by reason of paragraph (1)) such loss may be carried. The portion of such loss which shall be carried to each of the other taxable years shall be the excess, if any, of the amount of such loss over the sum of the taxable income for each of the prior taxable years to which such loss may be carried. For purposes of the preceding sentence, the taxable income for any such prior taxable year shall be computed—

(A) with the modifications specified in subsection (d) other than paragraphs (1), (4), and (5) thereof, and

(B) by determining the amount of the net operating loss deduction without regard to the net operating loss for the loss year or for any taxable year thereafter,

and the taxable income so computed shall not be considered to be less than zero.

(3) **Election to waive carryback.** Any taxpayer entitled to a carryback period under paragraph (1) may elect to relinquish the entire carryback period with respect to a net operating loss for any taxable year. Such election shall be made in such manner as may be prescribed by the Secretary, and shall be made by the due date (including extensions of time) for filing the taxpayer's return for the taxable year of the net operating loss for which the election is to be in effect. Such election, once made for any taxable year, shall be irrevocable for such taxable year.

(c) **Net operating loss defined.**

For purposes of this section, the term "net operating loss" means the excess of the deductions allowed by this chapter over the gross income. Such excess shall be computed with the modifications specified in subsection (d).

(d) **Modifications.**

The modifications referred to in this section are as follows:

(1) **Net operating loss deduction.** No net operating loss deduction shall be allowed.

(2) **Capital gains and losses of taxpayers other than corporations.** In the case of a taxpayer other than a corporation—

(A) the amount deductible on account of losses from sales or exchanges of capital assets shall not exceed the amount includable on account of gains from sales or exchanges of capital assets; and

(B) the exclusion provided by section 1202 shall not be allowed.

(3) **Deduction for personal exemptions.** No deduction shall be allowed under section 151 (relating to personal exemptions). No deduction in lieu of any such deduction shall be allowed.

(4) **Nonbusiness deductions of taxpayers other than corporations.** In the case of a taxpayer other than a corporation, the deductions allowable by this chapter which are not attributable to a taxpayer's trade or business shall be allowed only to the extent of the amount of the gross income not derived from such trade or business. For purposes of the preceding sentence—

(A) any gain or loss from the sale or other disposition of—

(i) property, used in the trade or business, of a character which is subject to the allowance for depreciation provided in section 167, or

(ii) real property used in the trade or business,

shall be treated as attributable to the trade or business;

(B) the modifications specified in paragraphs (1), (2)(B), and (3) shall be taken into account;

(C) any deduction for casualty or theft losses allowable under paragraph (2) or (3) of section 165(c) shall be treated as attributable to the trade or business; and

(D) any deduction allowed under section 404 to the extent attributable to contributions which are made on behalf of an individual who is an employee within the meaning of section 401(c)(1) shall not be treated as attributable to the trade or business of such individual.

(5) Computation of deduction for dividends received, etc. The deductions allowed by sections 243 (relating to dividends received by corporations), 244 (relating to dividends received on certain preferred stock of public utilities), and 245 (relating to dividends received from certain foreign corporations) shall be computed without regard to section 246(b) (relating to limitation on aggregate amount of deductions); and the deduction allowed by section 247 (relating to dividends paid on certain preferred stock of public utilities) shall be computed without regard to subsection (a)(1)(B) of such section.

(6) Modifications related to real estate investment trusts. In the case of any taxable year for which part II of subchapter M (relating to real estate investment trusts) applies to the taxpayer—

(A) the net operating loss for such taxable year shall be computed by taking into account the adjustments described in section 857(b)(2) (other than the deduction for dividends paid described in section 857(b)(2)(B)); and

(B) where such taxable year is a "prior taxable year" referred to in paragraph (2) of subsection (b), the term "taxable income" in such paragraph shall mean "real estate investment trust taxable income" (as defined in section 857(b)(2)).

(7) Manufacturing deduction. The deduction under section 199 shall not be allowed.

(e) Law applicable to computations.

In determining the amount of any net operating loss carryback or carryover to any taxable year, the necessary computations involving any other taxable year shall be made under the law applicable to such other taxable year.

(f) Rules relating to specified liability loss.

For purposes of this section—

(1) In general. The term "specified liability loss" means the sum of the following amounts to the extent taken into account in computing the net operating loss for the taxable year:

(A) Any amount allowable as a deduction under section 162 or 165 which is attributable to—

(i) product liability, or

(ii) expenses incurred in the investigation or settlement of, or opposition to, claims against the taxpayer on account of product liability.

(B)(i) Any amount allowable as a deduction under this chapter (other than section 468(a)(1) or 468A(a)) which is in satisfaction of a liability under a Federal or State law requiring—

(I) the reclamation of land,

(II) the decommissioning of a nuclear power plant (or any unit thereof),

(III) the dismantlement of a drilling platform,

(IV) the remediation of environmental contamination, or

(V) a payment under any workers compensation act (within the meaning of section 461(h)(2)(C)(i)).

(ii) A liability shall be taken into account under this subparagraph only if—

(I) the act (or failure to act) giving rise to such liability occurs at least 3 years before the beginning of the taxable year, and

(II) the taxpayer used an accrual method of accounting throughout the period or periods during which such act (or failure to act) occurred.

(2) Limitation. The amount of the specified liability loss for any taxable year shall not exceed the amount of the net operating loss for such taxable year.

(3) Special rule for nuclear powerplants. Except as provided in regulations prescribed by the Secretary, that portion of a specified liability loss which is attributable to amounts incurred in the decommissioning of a nuclear powerplant (or any unit thereof) may, for purposes of subsection (b)(1)(C), be carried back to each of the taxable years during the period—

(A) beginning with the taxable year in which such plant (or unit thereof) was placed in service, and

(B) ending with the taxable year preceding the loss year.

(4) Product liability. The term "product liability" means—

(A) liability of the taxpayer for damages on account of physical injury or emotional harm to individuals, or damage to or loss of the use of property, on account of any defect in any product which is manufactured, leased, or sold by the taxpayer, but only if

(B) such injury, harm, or damage arises after the taxpayer has completed or terminated operations with respect to, and has relinquished possession of, such product.

(5) Coordination with subsection (b)(2). For purposes of applying subsection (b)(2), a specified liability loss for any taxable year shall be treated as a separate net operating loss for such taxable year to be taken into account after the remaining portion of the net operating loss for such taxable year.

(6) Election. Any taxpayer entitled to a 10-year carryback under subsection (b)(1)(C) from any loss year may elect to have the carryback period with respect to such loss year determined without regard to subsection (b)(1)(C). Such election shall be made in such manner as may be prescribed by the Secretary and shall be made by the due date (including extensions of time) for filing the taxpayer's return for the taxable year of the net operating loss. Such election, once made for any taxable year, shall be irrevocable for that taxable year.

(g) Rules relating to bad debt losses of commercial banks.

For purposes of this section—

(1) Portion attributable to deduction for bad debts. The portion of the net operating loss for any taxable year which is attributable to the deduction allowed under section 166(a) shall be the excess of—

(i) the net operating loss for such taxable year, over

(ii) the net operating loss for such taxable year determined without regard to the amount allowed as a deduction under section 166(a) for such taxable year.

(2) Coordination with subsection (b)(2). For purposes of subsection (b)(2), the portion of a net operating loss for any taxable year which is attributable to the deduction allowed under section 166(a) shall be treated in a manner similar to the manner in which a specified liability loss is treated.

(h) Corporate equity reduction interest losses.
For purposes of this section—

(1) In general. The term "corporate equity reduction interest loss" means, with respect to any loss limitation year, the excess (if any) of—

(A) the net operating loss for such taxable year, over

(B) the net operating loss for such taxable year determined without regard to any allocable interest deductions otherwise taken into account in computing such loss.

(2) Allocable interest deductions.

(A) In general. The term "allocable interest deductions" means deductions allowed under this chapter for interest on the portion of any indebtedness allocable to a corporate equity reduction transaction.

(B) Method of allocation. Except as provided in regulations and subparagraph (E), indebtedness shall be allocated to a corporate equity reduction transaction in the manner prescribed under clause (ii) of section 263A(f)(2)(A) (without regard to clause (i) thereof).

(C) Allocable deductions not to exceed interest increases. Allocable interest deductions for any loss limitation year shall not exceed the excess (if any) of—

(i) the amount allowable as a deduction for interest paid or accrued by the taxpayer during the loss limitation year, over

(ii) the average of such amounts for the 3 taxable years preceding the taxable year in which the corporate equity reduction transaction occurred.

(D) De minimis rule. A taxpayer shall be treated as having no allocable interest deductions for any taxable year if the amount of such deductions (without regard to this subparagraph) is less than $1,000,000.

(E) Special rule for certain unforeseeable events. If an unforeseeable extraordinary adverse event occurs during a loss limitation year but after the corporate equity reduction transaction—

(i) indebtedness shall be allocated in the manner described in subparagraph (B) to unreimbursed costs paid or incurred in connection with such event before being allocated to the corporate equity reduction transaction, and

(ii) the amount determined under subparagraph (C)(i) shall be reduced by the amount of interest on indebtedness described in clause (i).

(F) Transition rule. If any of the 3 taxable years described in subparagraph (C)(ii) end on or before August 2, 1989, the taxpayer may substitute for the amount determined under such subparagraph an amount equal to the interest paid or accrued (determined on an annualized basis) during the taxpayer's taxable year which includes August 3, 1989, on indebtedness of the taxpayer outstanding on August 2, 1989.

(3) Corporate equity reduction transaction.

(A) In general. The term "corporate equity reduction transaction" means—

(i) a major stock acquisition, or

(ii) an excess distribution.

(B) Major stock acquisition.

(i) In general. The term "major stock acquisition" means the acquisition by a corporation pursuant to a plan of such corporation (or any group of persons acting in concert with such corporation) of stock in another corporation representing 50 percent or more (by vote or value) of the stock in such other corporation.

(ii) Exception. The term "major stock acquisition" does not include a qualified stock purchase (within the meaning of section 338) to which an election under section 338 applies.

(C) Excess distribution. The term "excess distribution" means the excess (if any) of—

(i) the aggregate distributions (including redemptions) made during a taxable year by a corporation with respect to its stock, over

(ii) the greater of—

(I) 150 percent of the average of such distributions during the 3 taxable years immediately preceding such taxable year, or

(II) 10 percent of the fair market value of the stock of such corporation as of the beginning of such taxable year.

(D) Rules for applying subparagraph (B). For purposes of subparagraph (B)—

(i) Plans to acquire stock. All plans referred to in subparagraph (B) by any corporation (or group of persons acting in concert with such corporation) with respect to another corporation shall be treated as 1 plan.

(ii) Acquisitions during 24-month period. All acquisitions during any 24-month period shall be treated as pursuant to 1 plan.

(E) Rules for applying subparagraph (C). For purposes of subparagraph (C)—

(i) Certain preferred stock disregarded. Stock described in section 1504(a)(4), and distributions (including redemptions) with respect to such stock, shall be disregarded.

(ii) Issuance of stock. The amounts determined under clauses (i) and (ii)(I) of subparagraph (C) shall be reduced by the aggregate amount of stock issued by the corporation during the applicable period in exchange for money or property other than stock in the corporation.

(4) Other rules.

(A) Ordering rule. For purposes of paragraph (1), in determining the allocable interest deductions taken into account in computing the net operating loss for any taxable year, taxable income for such taxable year shall be treated as having been computed by taking allocable interest deductions into account after all other deductions.

(B) Coordination with subsection (b)(2). For purposes of subsection (b)(2)—

(i) a corporate equity reduction interest loss shall be treated in a manner similar to the manner in which a specified liability loss is treated, and

(ii) in determining the net operating loss deduction for any prior taxable year referred to in the 3rd sentence of subsection (b)(2), the portion of any net operating loss which may not be carried to such taxable year under subsection (b)(1)(E) shall not be taken into account.

(C) Members of affiliated groups. Except as provided by regulations, all members of an affiliated group filing a consolidated return under section 1501 shall be treated as 1 taxpayer for purposes of this subsection and subsection (b)(1)(E).

(5) Regulations. The Secretary shall prescribe such regulations as may be necessary to carry out the purposes of this subsection, including regulations—

(A) for applying this subsection to successor corporations and in cases where a taxpayer becomes, or ceases to be, a member of an affiliated group filing a consolidated return under section 1501,

(B) to prevent the avoidance of this subsection through related parties, pass-through entities, and intermediaries, and

(C) for applying this subsection where more than 1 corporation is involved in a corporate equity reduction transaction.

(i) Rules relating to farming losses.

For purposes of this section—

(1) In general. The term "farming loss" means the lesser of—

(A) the amount which would be the net operating loss for the taxable year if only income and deductions attributable to farming businesses (as defined in section 263A(e)(4)) are taken into account, or

(B) the amount of the net operating loss for such taxable year.

Such term shall not include any qualified disaster loss (as defined in subsection (j)).

(2) Coordination with subsection (b)(2). For purposes of applying subsection (b)(2), a farming loss for any taxable year shall be treated in a manner similar to the manner in which a specified liability loss is treated.

(3) Election. Any taxpayer entitled to a 5-year carryback under subsection (b)(1)(G) from any loss year may elect to have the carryback period with respect to such loss year determined without regard to subsection (b)(1)(G). Such election shall be made in such manner as may be prescribed by the Secretary and shall be made by the due date (including extensions of time) for filing the taxpayer's return for the taxable year of the net operating loss. Such election, once made for any taxable year, shall be irrevocable for such taxable year.

(j) Rules relating to qualified disaster losses.

For purposes of this section—

(1) In general. The term "qualified disaster loss" means the lesser of—

(A) the sum of—

(i) the losses allowable under section 165 for the taxable year—

(I) attributable to a federally declared disaster (as defined in section 165(h)(3)(C)(i)) occurring before January 1, 2010, and

(II) occurring in a disaster area (as defined in section 165(h)(3)(C)(ii)), and

(ii) the deduction for the taxable year for qualified disaster expenses which is allowable under section 198A(a) or which would be so allowable if not otherwise treated as an expense, or

(B) the net operating loss for such taxable year.

(2) Coordination with subsection (b)(2). For purposes of applying subsection (b)(2), a qualified disaster loss for any taxable year shall be treated in a manner similar to the manner in which a specified liability loss is treated.

(3) Election. Any taxpayer entitled to a 5-year carryback under subsection (b)(1)(J) from any loss year may elect to have the carryback period with respect to such loss year determined without regard to subsection (b)(1)(J). Such election shall be made in such manner as may be prescribed by the Secretary and shall be made by the due date (including extensions of time) for filing the taxpayer's return for the taxable year of the net operating loss. Such election, once made for any taxable year, shall be irrevocable for such taxable year.

(4) Exclusion. The term "qualified disaster loss" shall not include any loss with respect to any property described in section 1400N(p)(3).

(k) Cross references.

(1) For treatment of net operating loss carryovers in certain corporate acquisitions, see section 381.

(2) For special limitation on net operating loss carryovers in case of a corporate change of ownership, see section 382.

In 2009, P.L. 111-92, Sec. 13(a), amended subpara. (b)(1)(H), effective for net operating losses arising in tax. yrs. end. after 12/31/2007.
Prior to amendment, subpara. (b)(1)(H) read as follows:

"(H) Carryback for 2008 net operating losses of small businesses.

"(i) In general. If an eligible small business elects the application of this subparagraph with respect to an applicable 2008 net operating loss—

"(I) subparagraph (A)(i) shall be applied by substituting any whole number elected by the taxpayer which is more than 2 and less than 6 for '2',

"(II) subparagraph (E)(ii) shall be applied by substituting the whole number which is one less than the whole number substituted under subclause (I) for '2', and

"(III) subparagraph (F) shall not apply.

"(ii) Applicable 2008 net operating loss. For purposes of this subparagraph, the term 'applicable 2008 net operating loss' means—

"(I) the taxpayer's net operating loss for any taxable year ending in 2008, or

"(II) if the taxpayer elects to have this subclause apply in lieu of subclause (I), the taxpayer's net operating loss for any taxable year beginning in 2008.

"(iii) Election. Any election under this subparagraph shall be made in such manner as may be prescribed by the Secretary, and shall be made by the due date (including extension of time) for filing the taxpayer's return for the taxable year of the net operating loss. Any such election, once made, shall be irrevocable. Any election under this subparagraph may be made only with respect to 1 taxable year.

"(iv) Eligible small business. For purposes of this subparagraph, the term 'eligible small business' has the meaning given such term by subparagraph (F)(iii), except that in applying such subparagraph, section 448(c) shall be applied by substituting '$15,000,000' for '$5,000,000' each place it appears."

—P.L. 111-92, Sec. 13(d), of this Act, provides:

"(d) Anti-abuse rules. The Secretary of Treasury or the Secretary's designee shall prescribe such rules as are necessary to prevent the abuse of the purposes of the amendments made by this section, including anti-stuffing rules, anti-churning rules (including rules relating to sale-leasebacks), and rules similar to the rules under section 1091 of the Internal Revenue Code of 1986 relating to losses from wash sales."

—P.L. 111-92, Sec. 13(f), of this Act, provides:

"(f) Exception for tarp recipients. The amenfments made by this section shall not apply to—

"(1) any taxpayer if—

"(A) the Federal Government acquired before the date of the enactment of this Act an equity interest in the taxpayer pursuant to the Emergency Economic Stabilization Act of 2008,

"(B) the Federal Government acquired before such date of enactment any warrant (or other right) to acquire any equity interest with respect to the taxpayer pursuant to the Emergency Economic Stabilization Act of 2008, or

"(C) such taxpayer receives after such date of enactment funds from the Federal Government in exchange for an interest described in subparagraph (A) or (B) pursuant to a program established under title I of division A of the Emergency Economic Stabilization Act of 2008 (unless such taxpayer is a financial institution (as defined in section 3 of such Act) and the funds are received pursuant to a program established by the Secretary of the Treasury for the stated purpose of increasing the availability of credit to small businesses using funding made available under such Act), or

"(2) the Federal National Mortgage Association and the Federal Home Loan Mortgage Corporation, and

"(3) any taxpayer which at any time in 2008 or 2009 was or is a member of the same affiliated group (as defined in section 1504 of the Internal Revenue Code of 1986, determined without regard to subsection (b) thereof) as a taxpayer described in paragraph (1) or (2)."

—P.L. 111-5, Sec. 1211(a), amended subpara. (b)(1)(H)

—P.L. 111-5, Sec. 1211(b), deleted (k) and redesignated subsec. (l) as (k), effective for net operating losses arising in tax. yrs. end. after 12/31/2007.
Prior to amendment, subpara. (b)(1)(H), read as follows:

"(H) In the case of a net operating loss for any taxable year ending during 2001 or 2002, subparagraph (A)(i) shall be applied by substituting '5' for '2' and subparagraph (F) shall not apply."

Prior to deletion, subsec. (k), read as follows:

"(k) Election to disregard 5-year carryback for certain net operating losses

"Any taxpayer entitled to a 5-year carryback under subsection (b)(1)(H) from any loss year may elect to have the carryback period with respect to such loss year determined without regard to subsection (b)(1)(H). Such election shall be made in such manner as may be prescribed by the Secretary and shall be made by the due date (including extensions of time) for filing the taxpayer's return for the taxable year of the net operating loss. Such election, once made for any taxable year, shall be irrevocable for such taxable year."

In 2008, P.L. 110-343, Sec. 706(a)(2)(D)(v) Div C, substituted "federally declared disasters (as defined by subsection (h)(3)(C)(i))" for "Presidentially declared disasters (as defined in section 1033(h)(3))" in subclause (b)(1)(F)(ii)(II) . . . Sec. 706(a)(2)(D)(vi) Div C, substituted "federally declared disasters" for "Presidentially declared disasters" in subclause (b)(1)(F)(ii)(III), effective for disasters declared in tax. yrs. begin. after 12/31/2007.

—P.L. 110-343, Sec. 708(a) Div C, added subpara. (b)(1)(J) . . . Sec. 708(b) Div C, redesignated subsec (j)-(k) as (k)-(l) and added subsec. (j) . . . Sec. 708(d)(1) Div C, added "or qualified disaster loss (as defined in subsection (j))" before the period at the end of the last sentence in clause (b)(1)(F)(ii) . . . Sec. 708(d)(2) Div C, added "Such term shall not include any qualified disaster loss (as defined in subsection (j))." at the the end of para. (i)(1), effective for losses arising in tax. yrs. begin. after 12/31/2007, in connection with disasters declared after such date.

—P.L. 110-343, Sec. 712 Div C, of this Act, reads as follows:

"Sec. 712. Coordination with heartland disaster relief.

"The amendments made by this subtitle, other than the amendments made by sections 706(a)(2), 710, and 711, shall not apply to any disaster described in section 702(c)(1)(A), or to any expenditure or loss resulting from such disaster."

In 2005, P.L. 109-135, Sec. 402(f)(1), amended clause (b)(1)(I)(i) . . . Sec. 402(f)(2), substituted "for a taxable year" for "in a taxable year" in clause (b)(1)(I)(ii) . . . Sec. 402(f)(3), deleted clauses (b)(1)(I)(iv) and (v), added clause (b)(1)(I)(iv), and redesignated clause (b)(1)(I)(vi) as (b)(1)(I)(v), effective 8/8/2005 as if included in Sec. 1311 of the Energy Policy Act of 2005, P.L. 109-58.

Prior to amendment, clause (b)(1)(I)(i) read as follows:

"(i) In general. At the election of the taxpayer in any taxable year ending after December 31, 2005, and before January 1, 2009, in the case of a net operating loss in a taxable year ending after December 31, 2002, and before January 1, 2006, there shall be a net operating loss carryback to each of the 5 years preceding the taxable year of such loss to the extent that such loss does not exceed 20 percent of the sum of electric transmission property capital expenditures and pollution control facility capital expenditures of the taxpayer for the taxable year preceding the taxable year in which such election is made."

Prior to deletion, clauses (b)(1)(I)(iv) and (v) read as follows:

"(iv) Application for adjustment. In the case of any portion of a net operating loss to which an election under clause (i) applies, an application under section 6411(a) with respect to such loss shall not fail to be treated as timely filed if filed within 24 months after the due date specified under such section.

"(v) Special rules relating to refund. For purposes of a net operating loss to which an election under clause (i) applies, references in sections 6501(h), 6511(d)(2)(A), and 6611(f)(1) to the taxable year in which such net operating loss arises or result in a net loss carryback shall be treated as references to the taxable year in which such election occurs."

—P.L. 109-135, Sec. 403(a)(17), added para. (d)(7), effective for tax. yrs. begin. after 12/31/2004 as if included in Sec. 102 of the American Jobs Creation Act of 2004, P.L. 108-357.

—P.L. 109-58, Sec. 1311, added subpara. (b)(1)(I), effective 8/8/2005.

In 2004, P.L. 108-311, Sec. 403(b)(1), deleted "a taxpayer which has" after "In the case of" in subpara. (b)(1)(H), effective for net operating losses for tax. yrs. end. after 12/31/2000 as if included in Sec. 102 of the Job Creation and Worker Assistance Act of 2002, P.L. 107-147. Sec. 403(b)(2) of this Act, reads as follows:

"(2) In the case of a net operating loss for a taxable year ending during 2001 or 2002—

"(A) an application under section 6411(a) of the Internal Revenue Code of 1986 with respect to such loss shall not fail to be treated as timely filed if filed before November 1, 2002,

"(B) any election made under section 172(b)(3) of such Code may (notwithstanding such section) be revoked before November 1, 2002, and

"(C) any election made under section 172(j) of such Code shall (notwithstanding such section) be treated as timely made if made before November 1, 2002."

In 2002, P.L. 107-147, Sec. 102(a), added subpara. (b)(1)(H) . . . Sec. 102(b), redesignated subsec. (j) as (k) and added subsec. (j), effective for net operating losses for tax. yrs. end. after 12/31/2000.

—P.L. 107-147, Sec. 417(8)(A), substituted "3 taxable years" for "3 years" in clause (b)(1)(F)(i) . . . Sec. 417(8)(B), substituted "2 taxable years" for "2 years" in clause (b)(1)(F)(i), effective 3/9/2002.

In 1998, P.L. 105-277, Sec. 2013(a), added subpara. (b)(1)(G) . . . Sec. 2013(b), redesignated subsec. (i) as (j) and added subsec. (i) . . . Sec. 2013(c), added a flush sentence at the end of clause (b)(1)(F)(ii), effective for operating losses for tax. yrs. begin. after 12/31/97.

—P.L. 105-277, Sec. 3004(a), amended subpara. (f)(1)(B), effective for net operating losses arising in tax. yrs. end. after 10/21/98.

Prior to amendment, subpara. (f)(1)(B) read as follows:

"(B) Any amount (not described in subparagraph (A)) allowable as a deduction under this chapter with respect to a liability which arises under a Federal or State law or out of any tort of the taxpayer if—

"(i) in the case of a liability arising out of a Federal or State law, the act (or failure to act) giving rise to such liability occurs at least 3 years before the beginning of the taxable year, or

"(ii) in the case of a liability arising out of a tort, such liability arises out of a series of actions (or failures to act) over an extended period of time a substantial portion of which occurs at least 3 years before the beginning of the taxable year.

A liability shall not be taken into account under subparagraph (B) unless the taxpayer used an accrual method of accounting throughout the period or periods during which the acts or failures to act giving rise to such liability occurred."

—P.L. 105-277, Sec. 4003(h), added clause (b)(1)(F)(iv), effective for net operating losses for tax. yrs. begin. after 8/5/97.

—P.L. 105-277, Sec. 4004(a), amended subpara. (d)(4)(C), effective for tax. yrs. begin. after 12/31/83.

Prior to amendment, subpara. (d)(4)(C) read as follows:

"(C) any deduction allowable under section 165(c)(3) (relating to casualty losses) shall not be taken into account; and"

In 1997, P.L. 105-34, Sec. 1082(a)(1), substituted "2" for "3" in clause (b)(1)(A)(i) . . . Sec. 1082(a)(2), substituted "20" for "15" in clause (b)(1)(A)(ii) . . . Sec. 1082(b), added subpara. (b)(1)(F), effective for net operating losses for tax. yrs. begin. after 8/5/97.

In 1996, P.L. 104-188, Sec. 1702(h)(2), substituted "subsection (h)" for "subsection (m)" in clause (b)(1)(E)(ii) . . . Sec. 1702(h)(16), substituted "subsection (b)(1)(E)" for "subsection (b)(1)(M)" in subpara. (h)(4)(C), effective for acquisitions after 10/9/90, except as provided in Sec. 11324(b)(2) of P.L. 101-508, see below.

—P.L. 104-188, Sec. 1704(t)(5), substituted a period for the comma at the end of clause (h)(3)(B)(i) . . . Sec. 1704(t)(30), substituted "For purposes of subsection (b)(2)—" for "For purposes of subsection (b)(2)" in subpara. (h)(4)(B), effective 8/20/96.

In 1993, P.L. 103-66, Sec. 13113(d)(1)(A), amended para. (d)(2). . . . Sec. 13113(d)(1)(B), added ", (2)(B)" after "paragraphs (1)" in subpara. (d)(4)(B), effective for stock issued after 8/10/93.

Prior to amendment, para. (d)(2) read as follows:

"(2) Capital gains and losses of taxpayers other than corporations.In the case of a taxpayer other than a corporation, the amount deductible on account of losses from sales or exchanges of capital assets shall not exceed the amount includible on account of gains from sales or exchanges of capital assets."

In 1990, P.L. 101-508, Sec. 11324(a), amended clause (m)(3)(B)(ii), effective for acquisitions after 10/9/90, except as provided in Sec. 11324(b)(2) of this Act which reads as follows:

"(2) Binding contract exception.—The amendment made by subsection (a) shall not apply to any acquisition pursuant to a written binding contract in effect on October 9, 1990, and at all times thereafter before such acquisition."

Prior to amendment, clause (m)(3)(B)(ii) read as follows:

"(ii) Exceptions. The term 'major stock acquisition' shall not include—

"(I) a qualified stock purchase (within the meaning of section 338) to which an election under section 338 applies, or

"(II) except as provided in regulations, an acquisition in which a corporation acquires stock of another corporation which, immediately before the acquisition, was a member of an affiliated group (within the meaning of section 1504(a)) other than the common parent of such group."

—P.L. 101-508, Sec. 11701(d)(1), deleted "a C corporation" in the material preceding subclause (b)(1)(M)(iii)(I) . . . Sec. 11701(d)(2), substituted "a C corporation which acquires" for "which acquires" in subclause (b)(1)(M)(iii)(I) . . . Sec. 11701(d)(3), substituted "a C corporation" for "a corporation" in subclause (b)(1)(M)(iii)(II) . . . Sec. 11701(d)(4), substituted "any C corporation which is a successor" for "any successor corporation" in subclause (b)(1)(M)(iii)(III), effective for corporate equity reduction transactions occurring after 8/2/89, in tax. yrs. end. after 8/2/89, except as provided in Sec. 7211(c)(2) of P.L. 101-239, reproduced below.

—P.L. 101-508, Sec. 11704(a)(2), substituted "subsection (b)(2)" for "subsection (B)(2)" in the heading of subpara. (m)(4)(B), effective 11/5/90 [inoperable].

—P.L. 101-508, Sec. 11811(a), amended subsec. (b) . . . Sec. 11811(b)(1), deleted subsecs. (g), (h), (i) and (k), and redesignated subsecs. (j), (l), (m) and (n) as subsecs. (f), (g), (h) and (i) . . . Sec. 11811(b)(2)(A), amended subsec. (f) (as redesignated by Sec. 11811(a) above), effective for net operating losses for tax. yrs. begin. after 12/31/90. Sec. 11811(b)(2)(B) of this Act provides the following:

"(B) The portion of any loss which is attributable to a deferred statutory or tort liability loss (as defined in section 172(k) of the Internal Revenue Code of 1986 as in effect on the day before the date of the enactment of this Act [11/5/90]) may not be carried back to any taxable year beginning before January 1, 1984, by reason of the amendment made by subparagraph (A) [Sec. 11811(b)(2)(A)].

Prior to amendment, subsec. (b) read as follows:

"(b) Net operating loss carrybacks and carryovers.

"(1) Years to which loss may be carried.

"(A) Except as otherwise provided in this paragraph, a net operating loss for any taxable year shall be a net operating loss carryback to each of the 3 taxable years preceding the taxable year of such loss.

"(B) Except as otherwise provided in this paragraph, a net operating loss for any taxable year ending after December 31, 1975, shall be a net operating loss carryover to each of the 15 taxable years following the taxable year of the loss.

"(C) In the case of a taxpayer which is a regulated transportation corporation (as defined in subsection (g)(1)), a net operating loss for any taxable year ending after December 31, 1955, and before January 1, 1976, shall (except as provided in subsection (g)) be a net operating loss carryover to each of the 7 taxable years following the taxable year of such loss.

"(D) In the case of a taxpayer which has a foreign expropriation loss (as defined in subsection (h)) for any taxable year ending after December 31, 1958, the portion of the net operating loss for such year attributable to such foreign expropriation loss shall not be a net operating loss carryback to any taxable year preceding the taxable year of such loss and shall be a net operating loss carryover to each of the 10 taxable years following the taxable year of such loss (or, with respect to that portion of the net operating loss for such year attributable to a Cuban expropriation loss, to each of the 20 taxable years following the taxable year of such loss).

"(E)(i) A net operating loss for a REIT year—

"(I) shall not be a net operating loss carryback to any taxable year preceding the taxable year of such loss, and

"(II) shall be a net operating loss carryover to each of the 15 taxable years following the taxable year of such loss.

"(ii) In the case of any net operating loss for a taxable year which is not a REIT year, such loss shall not be carried back to any taxable year which is a REIT year.

"(iii) For purposes of this subparagraph, the term 'REIT year' means any taxable year for which the provisions of part II of subchapter M (relating to real estate investment trusts) apply to the taxpayer.

"(F) In the case of a financial institution referred to in section 582(c)(5) a net operating loss for any taxable year beginning after December 31, 1975, and before January 1, 1987, shall be a net operating loss carryback to each of the 10 taxable years preceding the taxable year of such loss and shall be a net operating loss carryover to each of the 5 taxable years following the taxable year of such loss.

"(G) In the case of a Bank for Cooperatives (organized and chartered pursuant to section 2 of the Farm Credit Act of 1933 (12 U.S.C. 1134)), a net operating loss for any taxable year beginning after December 31, 1969, and before January 1, 1987, shall be a net operating loss carryback to each of the 10 taxable years preceding the taxable year of such loss and shall be a net operating loss carryover to each of the 5 taxable years following the taxable year of such loss.

"(H) In the case of a net operating loss of the Federal National Mortgage Association for any taxable year beginning after December 31, 1981, and before January 1, 1987, or a net operating loss of the Federal Home Loan Mortgage Corporation for any taxable year beginning after December 31, 1984 and before January 1, 1987—

"(i) such loss, to the extent it exceeds the mortgage disposition loss (within the meaning of subsection (j)), shall be—

"(I) a net operating loss carryback to each of the 10 taxable years preceding the taxable year of the loss, and

"(II) a net operating loss carryover to each of the 5 taxable years following the taxable year of the loss, and

"(ii) the mortgage disposition loss shall be—

"(I) a net operating loss carryback to each of the 3 taxable years preceding the taxable year of the loss, and

"(II) a net operating loss carryover to each of the 15 taxable years following the taxable year of the loss.

"(I) Product liability losses. In the case of a taxpayer which has a product liability loss (as defined in subsection (j)) for a taxable year beginning after September 30, 1979 (referred to in this subparagraph as the 'loss year'), the product liability loss shall be a net operating loss carryback to each of the 10 taxable years preceding the loss year.

"(J) Special rule for deferred statutory or tort liability losses. In the case of a taxpayer which has a deferred statutory or tort liability loss (as defined in subsection (k)) for any taxable year beginning after December 31, 1983, the deferred statutory or tort liability loss shall be a net operating loss carryback to each of the 10 taxable years preceding the taxable year of such loss.

"(K) Bad debt losses of commercial banks. In the case of any bank (as defined in section 585(a)(2)), the portion of the net operating loss for any taxable year beginning after December 31, 1986, and before January 1, 1994, which is attributable to the deduction allowed under section 166(a) shall be a net operating loss carryback to each of the 10 taxable years preceding the taxable year of the loss and a net operating loss carryover to each of the 5 taxable years following the taxable year of such loss.

"(L) Losses of thrift institutions. In the case of an organization to which section 593 applies, in lieu of applying subparagraph (F), a net operating loss for any taxable year beginning after December 31, 1981, and before January 1, 1986, shall be a net operating loss carryback to each of the 10 taxable years preceding the taxable year of such loss and shall be a net operating loss carryover to each of the 8 taxable years following the taxable year of such loss.

"(M) Excess interest loss.

"(i) In general. If—

"(I) there is a corporate equity reduction transaction, and

"(II) an applicable corporation has a corporate equity reduction interest loss for any loss limitation year ending after August 2, 1989,

then the corporate equity reduction interest loss shall be a net operating loss carryback and carryover to the taxable years described in subparagraphs (A) and (B), except that such loss shall not be carried back to a taxable year preceding the taxable year in which the corporate equity reduction transaction occurs.

"(ii) Loss limitation year. For purposes of clause (i) and subsection (m), the term 'loss limitation year' means, with respect to any corporate equity reduction transaction, the taxable year in which such transaction occurs and each of the 2 succeeding taxable years.

"(iii) Applicable corporation. For purposes of clause (i), the term 'applicable corporation' means—

"(I) a C corporation which acquires stock, or the stock of which is acquired, in a major stock acquisition,

"(II) a C corporation making distributions with respect to, or redeeming, its stock in connection with an excess distribution, or

"(III) any C corporation which is a successor of a corporation described in subclause (I) or (II).

"(iv) Other definitions. For definitions of terms used in this subparagraph, see subsection (m).

"(2) Amount of carrybacks and carryovers. Except as provided in subsection (g), the entire amount of the net operating loss for any taxable year (hereinafter in this section referred to as the 'loss year') shall be carried to the earliest of the taxable years to which (by reason of paragraph (1)) such loss may be carried. The portion of such loss which shall be carried to each of the other taxable years shall be the excess, if any, of the amount of such loss over the sum of the taxable income for each of the prior taxable years to which such loss may be carried. For purposes of the preceding sentence, the taxable income for any such prior taxable year shall be computed—

"(A) with the modifications specified in subsection (d) other than paragraphs (1), (4), and (5) thereof; and

"(B) by determining the amount of the net operating loss deduction—

"(i) without regard to the net operating loss for the loss year or for any taxable year thereafter, and

"(ii) without regard to that portion, if any, of a net operating loss for a taxable year attributable to a foreign expropriation loss, if such portion may not, under paragraph (1)(D), be carried back to such prior taxable year,

and the taxable income so computed shall not be considered to be less than zero. For purposes of this paragraph, if a portion of the net operating loss for the loss year is attributable to a foreign expropriation loss to which paragraph (1)(D) applies, such portion shall be considered to be a separate net operating loss for such year to be applied after the other portion of such net operating loss, and, if a portion of a foreign expropriation loss for the loss year is attributable to a Cuban expropriation loss, such portion shall be considered to be a separate foreign expropriation loss for such year to be applied after the portion of such foreign expropriation loss.

"(3) Special rules.

"(A) Paragraph (1)(D) shall apply only if—

"(i) the foreign expropriation loss (as defined in subsection (h) for the taxable year equals or exceeds 50 percent of the net operating loss for the taxable year,

"(ii) in the case of a foreign expropriation loss for a taxable year ending after December 31, 1963, the taxpayer elects (at such time and in such manner as the Secretary by regulations prescribes) to have paragraph (1)(D) apply, and

"(iii) in the case of a foreign expropriation loss for a taxable year ending after December 31, 1958, and before January 1, 1964, the taxpayer elects (in such manner as the Secretary by regulations prescribes) on or before December 31, 1965, to have paragraph (1)(D) apply.

"(B) If a taxpayer makes an election under subparagraph (A)(iii), then (notwithstanding any law or rule of law), with respect to any taxable year ending before January 1, 1964, affected by the election—

"(i) the time for making or changing any choice or election under subpart A of part III of subchapter N (relating to foreign tax credit) shall not expire before January 1, 1966,

"(ii) any deficiency attributable to the election under subparagraph (A)(iii) or to the application of clause (i) of this subparagraph may be assessed at any time before January 1, 1969, and

"(iii) refund or credit of any overpayment attributable to the election under subparagraph (A)(iii) or to the application of clause (i) of this subparagraph may be made or allowed if claim therefor is filed before January 1, 1969.

"(C) Any taxpayer entitled to a carryback period under paragraph (1) may elect to relinquish the entire carryback period with respect to a net operating loss for any taxable year ending after December 31, 1975. Such election shall be made in such manner as may be prescribed by the Secretary, and shall be made by the due date (including extensions of time) for filing the taxpayer's return for the taxable year of the net operating loss for which the election is to be in effect. Such election, once made for any taxable year, shall be irrevocable for that taxable year."

Prior to deletion, subsec. (g) read as follows:

"(g) Carryover of net operating loss for certain regulated transportation corporations.

"(1) Definition. For purposes of subsection (b)(1)(C), the term 'regulated transportation corporation' means a corporation—

"(A)80 percent or more of the gross income of which (computed without regard to dividends and capital gains and losses) for the taxable year is derived from the furnishing or sale of transportation described in subparagraph (A), (C)(i), (E), or (F) of section 7701(a)(33) and taken into account for purposes of the limitation contained in the last two sentences of section 7701(a)(33),

"(B) which is described in subparagraph (G) or (H) of section 7701(a)(33), or

"(C) which is a member of a regulated transportation system.

"(2) Regulated transportation system. For purposes of this subsection, a corporation shall be treated as a member of regulated transportation system for a taxable year if—

"(A) it is a member of an affiliated group of corporations making a consolidated return for such taxable year, and

"(B)80 percent or more of the aggregate gross income of the members of such affiliated group (computed without regard to dividends and capital gains and losses) for such taxable year is derived from sources described in paragraph (1)(A).

For purposes of subparagraph (B), income derived by a corporation described in subparagraph (G) or (H) of section 7701(a)(33) from leases described in subparagraph (G) thereof shall be considered as derived from sources described in paragraph (1)(A).

"(3) Limitation. For purposes of subsection (b)(1)(C)—

"(A) a net operating loss may not be a net operating loss carryover to the 6th taxable year following the loss year unless the taxpayer is a regulated transportation corporation for such 6th taxable year; and

"(B) a net operating loss may not be a net operating loss carryover to the 7th taxable year following the loss year unless the taxpayer is a regulated transporta-

tion corporation for the 6th taxable year following the loss year and for such 7th taxable year."
Prior to deletion, subsec. (h) read as follows:
"(h) Foreign expropriation loss defined.
"For purposes of this section—
"(1) The term 'foreign expropriation loss' means, for any taxable year, the sum of the losses sustained by reason of the expropriation, intervention, seizure, or similar taking of property by the government of any foreign country, any political subdivision thereof, or any agency or instrumentality of the foregoing. For purposes of the preceding sentence, a debt which becomes worthless shall, to the extent of any deduction allowed under section 166(a), be treated as a loss.
"(2) The portion of the net operating loss for any taxable year attributable to a foreign expropriation loss is the amount of the foreign expropriation loss for such year (but not in excess of the net operating loss for such year).
"(3) The term 'Cuban expropriation loss' means, for any taxable year, a foreign expropriation loss sustained by reason of the expropriation, intervention, seizure, or similar taking of property, before January 1, 1964, by the government of Cuba, any political subdivision thereof, or any agency or instrumentality of the foregoing. The portion of a foreign expropriation loss for any taxable year attributable to a Cuban expropriation loss is the amount of the Cuban expropriation loss."
Prior to deletion, subsec. (i) read as follows:
"(i) Rules relating to mortgage disposition loss of the Federal National Mortgage Association or the Federal Home Loan Mortgage Corporation.
"(1) Mortgage disposition loss defined.
"(A) In general. For purposes of subsection (b)(1)(H) and this subsection, the term 'mortgage disposition loss' means for any taxable year the excess (if any) of—
"(i) the losses for such year from the sale or exchange of mortgages, securities, and other evidences of indebtedness, over
"(ii) the gains for such year from the sale or exchange of such assets.
"(B) Mortgage disposition loss cannot exceed the net operating loss for the year. The amount of the mortgage disposition loss for any taxable year shall not be greater than the net operating loss for such year.
"(C) Foreclosure transactions not included. In applying subparagraph (A), any gain or loss which is attributable to a mortgage foreclosure shall not be taken into account.
"(2) Coordination with subsection (b)(2). In applying paragraph (2) of subsection (b), a mortgage disposition loss shall be treated in a manner similar to the manner in which a foreign expropriation loss is treated."
Prior to deletion, subsec. (k) read as follows:
"(k) Definitions and special rules relating to deferred statutory or tort liability losses.
"For purposes of this section—
"(1) Deferred statutory or tort liability loss. The term 'deferred statutory or tort liability loss' means, for any taxable year, the lesser of—
"(A) the net operating loss for such taxable year, reduced by any portion thereof attributable to—
"(i) a foreign expropriation loss, or
"(ii) a product liability loss, or
"(B) the sum of the amounts allowable as a deduction under this chapter (other than any deduction described in subsection (j)(1)(B)) which—
"(i) is taken into account in computing the net operating loss for such taxable year, and
"(ii) is for an amount incurred with respect to a liability which arises under a Federal or State law or out of any tort of the taxpayer and—
"(I) in the case of a liability arising out of a Federal or State law, the act (or failure to act) giving rise to such liability occurs at least 3 years before the beginning of such taxable year, or
"(II) in the case of a liability arising out of a tort, such liability arises out of a series of actions (or failures to act) over an extended period of time a substantial portion of which occurs at least 3 years before the beginning of such taxable year. A liability shall not be taken into account under the preceding sentence unless the taxpayer used an accrual method of accounting throughout the period or periods during which the acts or failures to act giving rise to such liability occurred.
"(2) Special rule for nuclear powerplants. Except as provided in regulations prescribed by the Secretary, that portion of a deferred statutory or tort liability loss which is attributable to amounts incurred in the decommissioning of a nuclear powerplant (or any unit thereof) may, for purposes of subsection (b)(1)(J), be carried back to each of the taxable years during the period—
"(A) beginning with the taxable year in which such plant (or unit thereof) was placed in service, and
"(B) ending with the taxable year preceding the loss year.
"(3) Coordination with subsection (b)(2). In applying paragraph (2) of subsection (b), a deferred statutory or tort liability loss shall be treated in a manner similar to the manner in which a foreign expropriation loss is treated.
"(4) No carryback to taxable years beginning before January 1, 1984. No deferred statutory or tort liability loss may be carried back to a taxable year beginning before January 1, 1984, unless such loss may be carried back to such year without regard to subsection (b)(1)(J)."
Prior to amendment, subsec. (f) (as redesignated by Sec. 11811(b)(2)(A)) read as follows:
"(f) Rules relating to product liability losses.
"For purposes of this section—
"(1) Product liability loss. The term 'product liability loss' means, for any taxable year, the lesser of—
"(A) the net operating loss for such year reduced by any portion thereof which is attributable to a foreign expropriation loss, or

"(B) the sum of the amounts allowable as deductions under sections 162 and 165 which are attributable to—
"(i) product liability, or
"(ii) expenses incurred in the investigation or settlement of, or opposition to, claims against the taxpayer on account of product liability.
"(2) Product liability. The term 'product liability' means—
"(A) liability of the taxpayer for damages on account of physical injury or emotional harm to individuals, or damage to or loss of the use of property, on account of any defect in any product which is manufactured, leased, or sold by the taxpayer, but only if
"(B) such injury, harm, or damage arises after the taxpayer has completed or terminated operations with respect to, and has relinquished possession of, such product.
"(3) Election. Any taxpayer entitled to a 10-year carryback under subsection (b)(1)(I) from any loss year may elect to have the carryback period with respect to such loss year determined without regard to subsection (b)(1)(I). Such election shall be made in such manner as may be prescribed by the Secretary and shall be made by the due date (including extensions of time) for filing the taxpayer's return for the taxable year of the net operating loss. Such election, once made for any taxable year, shall be irrevocable for that taxable year."
— P.L. 101-508, Sec. 11811(b)(3), amended para. (g)(2) (as redesignated by Sec. 11811(a), above)... Sec. 11811(b)(4), amended subpara. (h)(4)(B) (as redesignated by Sec. 11811(a), above), effective for net operating losses for tax. yrs. begin. after 12/31/90.
Prior to amendment, para. (g)(2) (as redesignated) read as follows:
"(2) Coordination with subsection (b)(2). In applying paragraph (2) of subsection (b), the portion of the net operating loss for any taxable year which is attributable to the deduction allowed under section 166(a) shall be treated in a manner similar to the manner in which a foreign expropriation loss is treated."
Prior to amendment, subpara. (h)(4)(B) (as redesignated) read as follows:
"(B) Coordination with subsection (b)(2). In applying paragraph (2) of subsection (b), the corporate equity reduction interest loss shall be treated in a manner similar to the manner in which a foreign expropriation loss is treated."
In 1989, P.L. 101-239, Sec. 7211(a), added subpara. (b)(1)(M)... Sec. 7211(b), redesignated subsec. (m) as subsec. (n) and added new subsec. (m), effective for corporate equity reduction transactions occurring after 8/2/89, in tax. yrs. end. after 8/2/89, except as provided in Sec. 7211(c)(2) which reads as follows:
"(2) Exceptions.—In determining whether a corporate equity reduction transaction has occurred after August 2, 1989, there shall not be taken into account—
"(A) acquisitions or redemptions of stock, or distributions with respect to stock, occurring on or before August 2, 1989,
"(B) acquisitions or redemptions of stock after August 2, 1989, pursuant to a binding written contract (or tender offer filed with the Securities and Exchange Commission) in effect on August 2, 1989, and at all times thereafter before such acquisition or redemption, or
"(C) any distribution with respect to stock after August 2, 1989, which was declared on or before August 2, 1989.
Any distribution to which the preceding sentence applies shall be taken into account under section 172(m)(3)(C)(ii)(I) of the Internal Revenue Code of 1986 (relating to base period for distributions)."
In 1988, P.L. 100-647, Sec. 1003(a)(1), deleted ", (2)(B)," after "paragraphs (1)" in subpara. (d)(4)(B), effective for tax. yrs. begin. after 12/31/86.
— P.L. 100-647, Sec. 1009(c)(1), redesignated subparas. (b)(1)(L) and (M) as subparas. (b)(1)(K) and (L)... Sec. 1009(c)(2), substituted "Except as otherwise provided in this paragraph, a net operating loss" for "Except as provided in subparagraphs (D), (E), (F), (G), (H), (I), (J), (K), (L), and (M), a net operating loss" in subpara. (b)(1)(A)... Sec. 1009(c)(3), amended subpara. (b)(1)(B), effective for losses incurred in tax. yrs. begin. after 12/31/86.
Prior to amendment, subpara. (b)(1)(B) read as follows:
"(B) Except as provided in subparagraphs (C), (D) and (E) a net operating loss for any taxable year ending after December 31, 1955, shall be a net operating loss carryover to each of the 5 taxable years following the taxable year of such loss. Except as provided in subparagraphs (C), (D), (E), (F), (G), (H), (J), (L), and (M) a net operating loss for any taxable year ending after December 31, 1975, shall be a net operating loss carryover to each of the 15 taxable years following the taxable year of such loss."
In 1986, P.L. 99-514, Sec. 104(b)(4), deleted para. (d)(7), effective for tax. yrs. begin. after 12/31/86.
Prior to deletion, para. (d)(7) read as follows:
"(7) Zero bracket amount. In the case of a taxpayer other than a corporation, the zero bracket amount shall be treated as a deduction allowed by this chapter. For purposes of subsection (c)—
"(A) the deduction provided by the preceding sentence shall be in lieu of any itemized deductions of the taxpayer, and
"(B) such sentence shall not apply to an individual who elects to itemize deductions."
— P.L. 99-514, Sec. 301(b)(3), amended para. (d)(2), effective for tax. yrs. begin. after 12/31/86.
Prior to amendment, para. (d)(2) read as follows:
"(2) Capital gains and losses of taxpayers other than corporations. In the case of a taxpayer other than a corporation—
"(A) the amount deductible on account of losses from sales or exchanges of capital assets shall not exceed the amount includible on account of gains from sales or exchanges of capital assets; and
"(B) the deduction for long-term capital gains provided by section 1202 shall not be allowed."

1,645

—P.L. 99-514, Sec. 901(d)(4)(B), substituted "referred to in section 582(c)(5)" for "to which section 585, 586, or 593 applies" in subpara. (b)(1)(F), effective for tax. yrs. begin. after 12/31/86.

—P.L. 99-514, Sec. 903(a)(1), substituted "after December 31, 1975, and before January 1, 1987," for "after December 31, 1975," in subpara. (b)(1)(F) . . . Sec. 903(a)(2), substituted "after December 31, 1969, and before January 1, 1987," for "after December 31, 1969," in subpara. (b)(1)(G) . . . Sec. 903(a)(3)(A), substituted "after December 31, 1981, and before January 1, 1987," for "after December 31, 1981," in subpara. (b)(1)(H) . . . Sec. 903(a)(3)(B), substituted "after December 31, 1984, and before January 1, 1987," for "after December 31, 1984," in subpara. (b)(1)(H) . . . Sec. 903(b)(1), added new subparas. (b)(1)(L), and (b)(1)(M), effective for losses incurred in tax. yrs. begin. after 12/31/86. Sec. 903(c)(2) of this Act provides:

"(2) Additional carryforward period for losses of thrift institutions. Subparagraph (M) of section 172(b)(1) of the Internal Revenue Code of 1986 (as added by this section) shall apply to losses incurred in taxable years beginning after December 31, 1981."

—P.L. 99-514, Sec. 903(b)(2)(A), substituted "(K), (L), and (M)" for "and (K)" in subpara. (b)(1)(A) . . . Sec. 903(b)(2)(B), substituted "(J), (L), and (M)" for "and (J)" in subpara. (b)(1)(B) . . . Sec. 903(b)(2)(C), redesignated subsec. (l) as subsec. (m), and added new subsec. (l), effective for losses incurred in tax. yrs. begin. after 12/31/86.

—P.L. 99-514, Sec. 1303(b)(1), deleted subpara. (b)(1)(J), and redesignated subpara. (b)(1)(K) as (J) . . . Sec. 1303(b)(2), substituted "subsection (b)(1)(J)" for "subsection (b)(1)(K)" in paras. (k)(2) and (k)(4), effective 10/22/86.

Prior to deletion, subpara. (b)(1)(J) read as follows:

"(J) In the case of an electing GSOC which has a net operating loss for any taxable year such loss shall not be a net operating loss carryback to any taxable year preceding the year of such loss, but shall be a net operating loss carryover to each of the 10 taxable years following the year of such loss."

—P.L. 99-514, Sec. 1807(a)(5), added Sec. 91(g)(6) to P.L. 98-369, the effective date for changes made by Sec. 91(d) of P.L. 98-369, see below.

—P.L. 99-514, Sec. 1812(d)(2), amended Sec. 177(d)(4) of P.L. 98-369 [reproduced below], part of the effective date for the amendments made by Sec. 177(b) of P.L. 98-369, see below.

Prior to amendment, Sec. 177(d)(4) of P.L. 98-369 read as follows:

"(4) No accumulated earnings and profits on January 1, 1985,—For purposes of the Internal Revenue Code of 1954, the accumulated profits of the Federal Home Loan Mortgage Corporation as of January 1, 1985, shall be treated as zero."

—P.L. 99-514, Sec. 1899A(6), added "Modifications related to real estate investment trusts." after "(6)" in para. (d)(6), effective 10/22/86.

In 1984, P.L. 98-369, Sec. 91(d)(1), added new subpara. (b)(1)(K) . . . Sec. 91(d)(2), redesignated subsec. (k) as subsec. (l) and added new subsec. (k) . . . Sec. 91(d)(3)(A), substituted "(J), and (K)" for "and (J)" in clause (b)(1)(A)(i) [sic subpara. (b)(1)(A)] . . . Sec. 91(d)(3)(B), substituted "this section" for "subsection (b)" in the matter preceding para. (h)(1) and in the matter preceding para. (j)(1), effective for losses for taxable years begin. after 12/31/83 [as amended by Sec. 1807(a)(5) of P.L. 99-514, see above.].

—P.L. 98-369, Sec. 177(c)(1)(A), added ", or a net operating loss of the Federal Home Loan Mortgage Corporation for any taxable year beginning after December 31, 1984" after "1981" in subpara. (b)(1)(H) . . . Sec. 177(c)(1)(B), and (C), deleted "FNMA" before "mortgage disposition loss" in clause (b)(1)(H)(i) and clause (b)(1)(H)(ii) . . . Sec. 177(c)(2)(A), deleted "FNMA" before "mortgage disposition loss" each place it appeared in subsec. (i) . . . Sec. 177(c)(2)(B), amended the heading for subsec. (i), effective on 1/1/85. Secs. 177(d)(2)–(7) [as amended by Sec. 1812(d)(2) of P.L. 99-514, above] of the Act provide:

"(2) Adjusted basis of assets.—

"(A) In general.—Except as otherwise provided in subparagraph (B), the adjusted basis of any asset of the Federal Home Loan Mortgage Corporation held on January 1, 1985, shall—

"(i) for purposes of determining any loss, be equal to the lesser of the adjusted basis of such asset or the fair market value of such asset as of such date, and

"(ii) for purposes of determining any gain, be equal to the higher of the adjusted basis of such asset or the fair market value of such asset as of such date.

"(B) Special rule for tangible depreciable property.—In the case of any tangible property which—

"(i) is of a character subject to the allowance for depreciation provided by section 167 of the Internal Revenue Code of 1954, and

"(ii) is held by the Federal Home Loan Mortgage Corporation on January 1, 1985,

the adjusted basis of such property shall be equal to the lesser of the basis of such property or the fair market value of such property as of such date.

"(3) Treatment of participation certificates.—

"(A) In general.—Paragraph (2) shall not apply to any right to receive income with respect to any mortgage pool participation certificate or other similar interest in any mortgage (not including any mortgage).

"(B) Treatment of certain sales after March 15, 1984, and before January 1, 1985.—If any gain is realized on the sale or exchange of any right described in subparagraph (A) after March 15, 1984, and before January 1, 1985, the gain shall not be recognized when realized but shall be recognized on January 1, 1985.

"(4) Clarification of earnings and profits of federal home loan mortgage corporation.—

"(A) Treatment of distribution of preferred stock, etc.—For purposes of the Internal Revenue Code of 1954, the distribution of preferred stock by the Federal Home Loan Mortgage Corporation during December of 1984, and the other distributions of such stock by Federal Home Loan Banks during January of 1985, shall be treated as if they were distributions of money equal to the fair market value of the stock on the date of the distribution by the Federal Home Loan Banks (and such stock shall be treated as if it were purchased with the money treated as so distributed). No deduction shall be allowed under section 243 of the Internal Revenue Code of 1954 with respect to any dividend paid by the Federal Home Loan Mortgage Corporation out of earnings and profits accumulated before January 1, 1985.

"(B) Section 246(a) not to apply to distributions out of earnings and profits accumulated during 1985.— Subsection (a) of section 246 of the Internal Revenue Code of 1954 shall not apply to any dividend paid by the Federal Home Loan Mortgage Corporation during 1985 out of earnings and profits accumulated after December 31, 1984.

"(5) Adjusted basis.—For purposes of this subsection, the adjusted basis of any asset shall be determined under part II of subchapter O of the Internal Revenue Code of 1954.

"(6) No carrybacks for years before 1985.—No net operating loss, capital loss, or excess credit of the Federal Home Loan Mortgage Corporation for any taxable year beginning after December 31, 1984, shall be allowed as a carryback to any taxable year beginning before January 1, 1985.

"(7) No deduction allowed for interest on replacement obligations.—

"(A) In general.—The Federal Home Loan Mortgage Corporation shall not be allowed any deduction for interest accruing after December 31, 1984, on any replacement obligation.

"(B) Replacement obligation defined.—For purposes of subparagraph (A), the term 'replacement obligation' means any obligation to any person created after March 15, 1984, which the Secretary of the Treasury or his delegate determines replaces any equity or debt interest of a Federal Home Loan Bank or any other person in the Federal Home Loan Mortgage Corporation existing on such date. The preceding sentence shall not apply to any obligation with respect to which the Federal Home Loan Mortgage Corporation establishes that there is no tax avoidance effect."

Prior to amendment, the heading for subsec. (i) read as follows:

"(i) Rules relating to FNMA mortgage disposition loss."

—P.L. 98-369, Sec. 491(f)(1), deleted "or section 405(c)" after "section 404" in subpara. (d)(4)(D), effective for obligations issued after 12/31/83.

—P.L. 98-369, Sec. 722(a)(4)(A), substituted "and (5)" for "and (6)" in subpara. (b)(2)(A) . . . Sec. 722(a)(4)(B), redesignated paras. (d)(7) and (8) as paras. (d)(6) and (7), respectively, effective for net operating losses in tax. yrs. end. after 12/31/75.

In 1983, P.L. 97-448, Sec. 102(d)(1), added subpara. (c)(1)(C) to Sec. 209 of P.L. 97-34, the effective date for changes made by Sec. 207(a) and(b) of P.L. 97-34, see below.

—P.L. 97-448, Sec. 102(d)(2), added para. (c)(3) to Sec. 209 of P.L. 97-34, the effective date for amendments made by Sec. 207(a) of P.L. 97-34, see below.

In 1982, P.L. 97-354, Sec. 5(a)(22), deleted subsec. (f), effective for tax. yrs. begin. after 12/31/82.

Prior to deletion, subsec. (f) read as follows:

"(f) Disallowance of net operating loss of electing small business corporations. In determining the amount of the net operating loss deduction under subsection (a) of any corporation, there shall be disregarded the net operating loss of such corporation for any taxable year for which such corporation is an electing small business corporation under subchapter S."

—P.L. 97-362, Sec. 102(a), redesignated subparas. (b)(1)(H) and (I) as (b)(1)(I) and (J), and added new subpara. (b)(1)(H) . . . Sec. 102(b), redesignated subsecs. (i) and (j) as subsecs. (j) and (k), and added new subsec. (i) . . . Sec. 102(c)(1), substituted "(H), (I), and (J)" for "(H), and (I)" in subpara. (b)(1)(A) . . . Sec. 102(c)(2), substituted "(H), and (J)" for "and (I)" in subpara. (b)(1)(B) . . . Sec. 102(c)(3), substituted "subsection (j)" for "subsection (i)" in subpara. (b)(1)(I) [as redesignated by Sec. 102(a) of this Act] . . . Sec. 102(c)(4), substituted "subsection (b)(1)(I)" for "subsection (b)(1)(H)" each time it appeared in para. (j)(3) [as redesignated by Sec. 102(b) of this Act], effective for net operating losses for tax. yrs. begin. after 12/31/81.

In 1981, P.L. 97-34, Sec. 207(a)(1), substituted "15" for "7" in subpara. (b)(1)(B) . . . Sec. 207(a)(2)(A), added "and before January 1, 1976," after "1955," in subpara. (b)(1)(C) and deleted the last sentence of subpara. (b)(1)(C), effective for net operating losses in tax. yrs. end. after 12/31/75. Sec. 209(c)(3) of this Act provides:

"(3) Carryover must have been alive in 1981.— The amendments made by subsections (a), (b), and (c) of section 207 shall not apply to any amount which, under the law in effect on the day before the date of the enactment of this Act, could not be carried to a taxable year ending in 1981."

Prior to amendment, the last sentence of subpara. (b)(2)(C) read as follows:

"For any taxable year ending after December 31, 1975, the preceding sentence shall be applied by substituting '9 taxable years' for '7 taxable years'."

—P.L. 97-34, Sec. 207(a)(2)(B)(i), substituted "15" for "8" in subclause (b)(1)(E)(i)(II), effective as if included in the amendments made by Sec. 1(a) of P.L. 96-595 [See Sec. 1(b) of P.L. 96-595, reproduced below], except that the amendments made by Sec. 207(a)(2)(B)(i) shall apply only to net operating losses in tax. yrs. end. after 12/31/72. Sec. 209(c)(1)(C) of this Act provides:

"(C) If any net operating loss for any taxable year ending on or before December 31, 1975, could be a net operating loss carryover to a taxable year ending in 1981 by reason of subclause (II) of section 172(b)(1)(E)(ii) of the Internal Revenue Code of 1954 (as in effect on the day before the date of the enactment of this Act and as modified by Sec. 1(b) of P.L. 96-595'), such net operating loss shall be a net operating loss carryover under section 172 of such Code to each of the 15 taxable years following the taxable year of such loss." See Sec. 209(c)(3) of this Act, reproduced above.

—P.L. 97-34, Sec. 207(a)(2)(B)(ii), amended clause (b)(1)(E)(ii), effective for net operating losses in tax. yrs. end. after 12/31/75. See Sec. 209(c)(3) of this Act, reproduced above.

Prior to amendment, clause (b)(1)(E)(ii) read as follows:

"(ii) In the case of any net operating loss for a taxable year which is not a REIT year—

"(I) such loss shall not be carried back to any taxable year which is a REIT year, and

"(II) the number of taxable years to which such loss may be a net operating loss carryover under subparagraph (B) shall be increased (to a number not greater than 8) by the number of taxable years to which such loss may not be a net operating loss carryback by reason of subclause (I)."

—P.L. 97-34, Sec. 207(a)(2)(C), amended para. (g)(3) by adding "and" at the end of subpara. (g)(3)(A) ... by substituting a period for "; and" at the end of subpara. (g)(3)(B) ... by deleting subpara. (g)(3)(C), effective for net operating losses in tax. yrs. end. after 12/31/75. See Sec. 209(c)(3) of this Act, reproduced above.

Prior to deletion, subpara. (g)(3)(C) read as follows:

"(C) in the case of a net operating loss carryover from a loss year ending after December 31, 1975, subparagraphs (A) and (B) shall be applied by substituting '8th taxable year' for the '6th taxable year' and '9th taxable year' for '7th taxable year.' "

In 1980, P.L. 96-595, Sec. 1(a), amended subpara. (b)(1)(E). Sec. 1(b) of this Act provides as follows:

"(b) Effective date.

"The amendment made by subsection (a) shall apply to the determination of the net operating loss deduction for taxable years ending after October 4, 1976. For purposes of applying the preceding sentence to any net operating loss for a taxable year which is not a REIT year and which ends on or before October 4, 1976, subclause (II) of section 172(b)(1)(E)(ii) of the Internal Revenue Code of 1954 shall be applied by substituting 'the number of REIT years to which such loss was a net operating loss carryback' for 'the number of taxable years to which such loss may not be a net operating loss carryback by reason of subclause (I)'. In the case of a net operating loss for a taxable year described in the preceding sentence, subclause (II) of section 172(b)(1)(E)(ii) of such Code shall not apply to any taxpayer which acted so as to cause it to cease to qualify as a 'real estate investment trust' within the meaning of section 856 of such Code if the principal purpose for such action was to secure the benefit of the allowance of a net operating loss carryover under section 172(b)(1)(B) of such Code."

Prior to amendment, subpara. (b)(1)(E) read as follows:

"(E) In the case of a taxpayer which has a net operating loss for any taxable year for which the provisions of part II of subchapter M (relating to real estate investment trusts) apply to such taxpayer, such loss shall not be a net operating loss carryback to any taxable year preceding the taxable year of such loss and shall be a net operating loss carryover to each of the 8 taxable years following the taxable year of such loss, except, in the case of a net operating loss for a taxable year ending before January 1, 1976, such loss shall not be carried to the 6th, 7th, or 8th taxable year following the taxable year of such loss unless part II of subchapter M applied to the taxpayer for the taxable year to which the loss is carried and for all intervening taxable years following the year of loss. A net operating loss shall not be carried back to a taxable year for which part II of subchapter M applied to the taxpayer."

—P.L. 96-222, Sec. 103(a)(15), corrected Sec. 371(a)(2) of P.L. 95-600 to amend subpara. (b)(1)(A) instead of clause (b)(1)(A)(i) [see below].

—P.L. 96-222, Sec. 106(a)(1), redesignated subpara. (b)(1)(H) (as added by Sec. 601(b) of P.L. 95-600) as subpara. (b)(1)(I) ... Sec. 106(a)(6), substituted ", (H), and (I)" for "and (H)" in subpara. (b)(1)(A) ... Sec. 106(a)(7), substituted "(G), and (I)" for "and (G)" in subpara. (b)(1)(B), effective for corporations chartered after 12/31/78 and before 1/1/84.

In 1978, P.L. 95-600, Sec. 371(a)(1), added subpara. (b)(1)(H) ... Sec. 371(a)(2), substituted "(G), and (H)" for "and (G)" in subpara. (b)(1)(A) [subpara. (b)(1)(A) as amended by Sec. 703(p)(1)(A) of this Act], effective for tax. yrs. begin. after 9/30/79.

—P.L. 95-600, Sec. 371(b), redesignated subsec. (i) as subsec. (j) and added new subsec. (i), effective for tax. yrs. begin. after 9/30/79.

—P.L. 95-600, Sec. 601(b)(1), added subpara. (b)(1)(H), effective for corporations chartered after 12/31/78 and before 1/1/84.

—P.L. 95-600, Sec. 701(d)(1), substituted "(F), and (G)" for "and (F)" in the second sentence of subpara. (b)(1)(B), for losses incurred in tax yrs. after 12/31/75.

—P.L. 95-600, Sec. 703(p)(1)(A), amended subpara. (b)(1)(A), effective for losses sustained in tax. yrs. end. after 11/6/78.

Prior to amendment subpara. (a)(1)(A), read as follows:

"(A)(i) Except as provided in clause (ii) and in subparagraphs (D), (E), (F), and (G), a net operating loss for any taxable year ending after December 31, 1957, shall be a net operating loss carryback to each of the 3 taxable years preceding the taxable year of such loss.

"(ii) In the case of a taxpayer with respect to a taxable year ending on or after December 31, 1962, for which a certification has been issued under section 317 of the Trade Expansion Act of 1962, a net operating loss for such taxable year shall be a net operating loss carryback to each of the 5 taxable years preceding the taxable year of such loss."

—P.L. 95-600, Sec. 703(p)(1)(B), deleted subparas. (b)(3)(A) and (B), and redesignated subparas. (b)(3)(C), (D) and (E) as (b)(3)(A), (B), and (C), effective for losses sustained in tax. yrs. end. after 11/6/78.

Prior to amendment, subparas. (b)(3)(A) and (B) read as follows:

"(A) Paragraph (1)(A)(ii) shall apply only if—

"(i) there has been filed, at such time and in such manner as may be prescribed by the Secretary, a notice of filing of the application under section 317 of the Trade Expansion Act of 1962 for tax assistance, and, after its issuance, a copy of the certification under such section, and

"(ii) the taxpayer consents in writing to the assessment, within such period as may be agreed upon with the Secretary, of any deficiency for any year to the extent attributable to the disallowance of a deduction previously allowed with respect to such net operating loss, even though at the time of filing such consent the assessment of such deficiency would otherwise be prevented by the operation of any law or rule of law.

"(B) In the case of —

"(i) a partnership and its partners, or

"(ii) an electing small business corporation under subchapter S and its shareholders,

paragraph (1)(A)(ii) shall apply as determined under regulations prescribed by the Secretary. Such paragraph shall apply to a net operating loss of a partner or such a shareholder only if it arose predominantly from losses in respect of which certifications under section 317 of the Trade Expansion Act of 1962 were filed under this section."

—P.L. 95-600, Sec. 703(p)(1)(C), substituted "subparagraph (A)(iii)" for "subparagraph (C)(iii)" each place it appeared in subpara. (b)(3)(B), as redesignated by Sec. 703(p)(1)(B) of this Act, effective for losses sustained in tax. yrs. end. after 11/6/78.

In 1977, P.L. 95-30, Sec. 102(b)(2), added para. (d)(8), for tax. yrs. begin. after '76.

In 1976, P.L. 94-455, Sec. 806(a), added the last sentence in subpara. (b)(1)(B), for losses incurred in tax. yrs. end. after 12/31/75.

—P.L. 94-455, Sec. 806(b)(1), added the last sentence in subpara. (b)(1)(C), effective for losses incurred in tax. yrs. end. after 12/31/75.

—P.L. 94-455, Sec. 806(b)(2), deleted "and" at the end of subpara. (g)(3)(A) ... substituted "; and" for the period at the end of subpara. (g)(3)(B) ... added subpara. (g)(3)(C), as previously redesignated by this Act, effective for losses incurred in tax. yrs. end. after 12/31/75.

—P.L. 94-455, Sec. 806(c), added new subpara. (b)(3)(E), as amended by this Act, effective for losses incurred in tax. yrs. end. after 12/31/75.

—P.L. 94-455, Sec. 1052(c)(3), deleted para. (d)(5) and redesignated para. (d)(6) as (d)(5), for tax. yrs. begin. after '79.

Prior to amendment, para. (d)(5) read as follows:

"(5) Special deductions for corporations. No deduction shall be allowed under section 242 (relating to partially tax-exempt interest) or under section 922 (relating to Western Hemisphere trade corporations)."

—P.L. 94-455, Sec. 1606(b), added subpara. (b)(1)(E), effective for tax. yrs. end. after 10/4/76, except for a taxpayer who has a net operating loss as defined in Code Sec. 172(c) for any tax. yr. end. after 10/4/76 for which the provisions of part II of subchapter M of chapter 1 of subtitle A apply to such taxpayer, such loss will not be a net operating loss carryback under Code Sec. 172 to any tax. yr. end. on or before 10/4/76.

—P.L. 94-455, Sec. 1606(c), added para. (d)(7), for tax. yrs. end. after 10/4/76, except for a taxpayer who has a net operating loss as defined in Code Sec. 172(c) for any tax. yr. end. after 10/4/76 for which the provisions of part II of subchapter M of chapter 1 of subtitle A apply to such taxpayer, such loss will not be a net operating loss carryback under Code Sec. 172 to any tax. yr. end. on or before 10/4/76.

—P.L. 94-455, Sec. 1901(a)(29), deleted subpara. (b)(1)(E) ... deleted subparas. (b)(3)(E) and (F) ... deleted "(for any taxable year ending after December 31, 1953)", which followed " 'net operating loss' means", in subsec. (c) ... deleted subsecs. (f), (g) and (i), and redesignated subsecs. (h), (j), (k) and (l) as subsecs. (f), (g), (h) and (i), respectively ... substituted "subsection (g)(1)" and "subsection (g)" for "subsection (j)(1)" and "subsection (j)", respectively, in subpara. (b)(1)(C) ... substituted "subsection (h)" for "subsection (k)" in subpara. (b)(1)(D) and clause (b)(3)(C)(i) ... substituted "subsection (g)" for "subsections (i) and (j)" in para. (b)(2) ... deleted the last sentence in subsec. (e) ... deleted para. (4) in redesignated subsec. (g), effective for tax. yrs. end. after 10/4/76.

Prior to amendment, subpara. (b)(1)(E) read as follows:

"(E) In the case of a taxpayer which is a domestic corporation qualifying under paragraph (3)(E), a net operating loss for any taxable year ending after December 31, 1966, and prior to January 1, 1969, shall be a net operating loss carryback to each of the 5 taxable years preceding the taxable year of such loss and shall be a net operating loss carryover to each of the 3 taxable years following the taxable year of such loss."

Prior to amendment, subparas. (b)(3)(E) and (F) read as follows:

"(E) Paragraph (1)(E) shall apply only if—

"(i) The amount of the taxpayer's net operating loss for the taxable year exceeds the sum of the taxable income (computed as provided in paragraph (2)) for each of the 3 preceding taxable years of the taxpayer,

"(ii) the amount of the taxpayer's net operating loss for the taxable year, increased by the amount of the taxpayer's net operating loss for the preceding taxable year or decreased by the amount of the taxpayer's taxable income for such preceding year, exceeds 15 percent of the sum of the money and other property (in an amount equal to its adjusted basis for determining gain) of the taxpayer, determined as of the close of the taxable year of such loss without regard to any refund or credit of any overpayment of tax to which the taxpayer may be entitled under paragraph (1)(E),

"(iii) the aggregate unadjusted basis of property described in section 1231(b)(1) (without regard to any holding period therein provided), the basis for which was determined under section 1012, which was acquired by the taxpayer during the period beginning with the first day of its fifth taxable year preceding the taxable year of such loss and ending with the last day of the taxable year of such loss, equals or exceeds the aggregate adjusted basis of property of such description of the taxpayer on, and determined as of, the first day of the fifth preceding taxable year, and

"(iv) the taxpayer derived 50 percent or more of its gross receipts (other than gross receipts derived from the conduct of a lending or finance business), for the taxable year of such loss and for each of its 5 preceding taxable years, from the manufacture and production of units within the same single class of products, and 3 or fewer United States persons (including as one person an affiliated group as defined in section 1504(a)) other than the taxpayer manufactured and produced in the United States, in the calendar year ending in or with the taxable year of such loss, 85 percent or more of the total number of all units within such class of products manufactured and produced in the United States in such calendar year.

"(F) For purposes of subparagraph (E)(iv)—

"(i) the term 'class of products' means any of the categories designated and numbered as a 'class of products' in the 1963 Census of Manufacturers compiled and published by the Secretary of Commerce under title 13 of the United States Code, and

"(ii) information compiled or published by the Secretary of Commerce, as part of or in connection with the Statistical Abstract of the United States or the census of manufacturers, regarding the number of units of a class of products manufactured and produced in the United States during a calendar year, or, if such information should not be available, information so compiled or published regarding the number of such units shipped or sold by such manufacturers during a calendar year, shall constitute prima facie evidence of the total number of all units of such class of products manufactured and produced in the United States in such calendar year."

Prior to amendment, subsecs. (f), (g) and (i) read as follows:

"(f) Taxable years beginning in 1953 and ending in 1954.

"In the case of a taxable year beginning in 1953 and ending in 1954—

"(1) In lieu of the amount specified in subsection (c), the net operating loss for such year shall be the sum of—

"(A) that portion of the net operating loss for such year computed without regard to this subsection which the number of days in the loss year after December 31, 1953, bears to the total number of days in such year, and

"(B) that portion of the net operating loss for such year computed under section 122 of the Internal Revenue Code of 1939 as if this section had not been enacted which the number of days in the loss year before January 1, 1954, bears to the total number of days in such year.

"(2) The amount of any net operating loss for such year which shall be carried to the second preceding taxable year is the amount which bears the same ratio to such net operating loss as the number of days in the loss year after December 31, 1953, bears to the total number of days in such year. In determining the amount carried to any other taxable year, the reduction for the second taxable year preceding the loss year shall not exceed the portion of the net operating loss which is carried to the second preceding taxable year.

"(3) The net operating loss deduction for such year shall be, in lieu of the amount specified in section 122(c) of the Internal Revenue Code of 1939, the sum of—

"(A) that portion of the net operating loss deduction for such year, computed as if subsection (a) of this section were applicable to the taxable year, which the number of days in such year after December 31, 1953, bears to the total number of days in such year, and

"(B) that portion of the net operating loss deduction for such year, computed under section 122(c) of the Internal Revenue Code of 1939 as if this paragraph had not been enacted, which the number of days in such year before January 1, 1954, bears to the total number of days in such year.

"(4) For purposes of the second sentence of subsection (b)(2), the taxable income for such year shall be the sum of—

"(A) that portion of the net income for such year, computed without regard to this paragraph, which the number of days in such year before January 1, 1954, bears to the total number of days in such year, and

"(B) that portion of the net income for such year, computed—

"(i) without regard to paragraphs (1) and (2) of section 122(d) of the Internal Revenue Code of 1939, and

"(ii) by allowing as a deduction an amount equal to the sum of the credits provided in subsections (b) and (h) of section 26 of such Code,

which the number of days in such year after December 31, 1953, bears to the total number of days in such year.

"(g) Special transitional rules.

"(1) Losses for taxable years ending before January 1, 1954. For purposes of this section, the determination of the taxable years ending after December 31, 1953, to which a net operating loss for any taxable year ending before January 1, 1954, may be carried shall be made under the Internal Revenue Code of 1939.

"(2) Losses for taxable years ending after December 31, 1953. For purposes of section 122 of the Internal Revenue Code of 1939—

"(A) the determination of the taxable years ending before January 1, 1954, to which a net operating loss for any taxable year ending after December 31, 1953, may be carried shall be made under subsection (b)(1)(A) of this section; and

"(B) in determining the amount of the carryback to the first taxable year preceding the first taxable year ending after December 31, 1953, the portion of the net operating loss carried to such year shall be such net operating loss reduced by—

"(i) the net income for the second preceding taxable year computed as if the second sentence of section 122(b)(2)(B) of the Internal Revenue Code of 1939 applied, or

"(ii) if smaller, the portion of the net operating loss which by reason of subsection (f) of this section is carried to the second preceding taxable year.

"(3) Taxable years beginning after December 31, 1953, and ending before August 17, 1954. In the case of a taxable year which begins after December 31, 1953, and ends before August 17, 1954—

"(A) the net operating loss deduction for such year shall be computed as if subsection (a) of this section applied to such taxable year, and

"(B) for purposes of the second sentence of subsection (b)(2), the taxable income for such taxable year shall be the net income for such taxable year, computed—

"(i) without regard to paragraphs (1) and (2) of section 122(d) of the Internal Revenue Code of 1939, and

"(ii) by allowing as a deduction an amount equal to the sum of the credits provided in subsections (b) and (h) of section 26 of such Code.

"(4) Excess profits tax not affected. For purposes of subchapter D of chapter 1 of the Internal Revenue Code of 1939, excess profits net income shall be computed as if this section had not been enacted and as if section 122 of such Code continued to apply to taxable years to which this subtitle applies.

"(i) Carryback of net operating loss for taxable years beginning in 1957 and ending in 1958.

"In the case of a taxable year beginning in 1957 and ending in 1958, the amount of any net operating loss for such year which shall be carried to the third preceding taxable year is the amount which bears the same ratio to such net operating loss as the number of days in the loss year after December 31, 1957, bears to the total number of days in such year. In determining the amount carried to any other taxable year, the reduction for the third taxable year preceding the loss year shall not exceed the portion of the net operating loss which is carried to the third preceding taxable year."

Prior to amendment, the last sentence in subsec. (e) read as follows:

"The preceding sentence shall apply with respect to all taxable years, whether they begin before, on, or after January 1, 1954."

Prior to amendment, para. (g)(4) read as follows:

"(4) Taxable years beginning in 1955 and ending in 1956. In the case of a net operating loss for a taxable year beginning in 1955 and ending in 1956, the amount of such loss which may be carried—

"(A) to the 6th taxable year following the loss year shall be the amount which bears the same ratio to the amount which (but for this paragraph) would be carried to such 6th taxable year as the number of days in the loss year after December 31, 1955, bears to the total number of days in the loss year, and

"(B) to the 7th taxable year following the loss year shall be the amount (if any) by which (i) the amount carried to the 6th taxable year determined under subparagraph (A), exceeds (ii) the taxable income (computed as provided in subsection (b)(2)) for such 6th taxable year."

—P.L. 94-455, Sec. 1906(b)(13)(A), substituted "Secretary" for "Secretary or his delegate" each place it appeared in para. (b)(3), for tax. yrs. begin. after '76.

—P.L. 94-455, Sec. 2126, substituted "20" for "15" in subpara. (b)(1)(D), effective 10/4/76.

In **1971**, P.L. 91-677, Sec. 2, added the parenthetical phrase at the end of subpara. (b)(1)(D) ... added ", and, if a portion of a foreign expropriation loss for the loss year is attributable to a Cuban expropriation loss, such portion shall be considered to be a separate foreign expropriation loss for such year to be applied after the other portion of such foreign expropriation loss" ... added new para. (k)(3), effective for foreign expropriation losses sustained in tax. yrs. end. after 12/31/58.

In **1969**, P.L. 91-172, Sec. 431(b), (relating to net operating loss deduction), substituted "(E), (F), and (G)" for "and (E)" in clause (b)(1)(A)(i) and added new subparas. (b)(1)(F) and (G) at the end thereof.

In **1967**, P.L. 90-225, Sec. 3(a), substituted "subparagraphs (D) and (E)" for "subparagraph (D)" in clause (b)(1)(A)(i), substituted "subparagraphs (C), (D), and (E)" for "subparagraphs (C) and (D)" in subpara. (b)(1)(B), added subparas. (b)(1)(E), (b)(3)(E), and (b)(3)(F), effective for net operating losses sustained in tax. yrs. end. after 12/31/66.

—P.L. 90-225, Sec. 3(b), provides

"(b) No interest shall be paid or allowed with respect to any overpayment of tax resulting from the application of the amendments made by subsection (a) for any period prior to the date of the enactment of this Act."

In **1964**, P.L. 88-272, Sec. 210, added subpara. (D) in para. (b)(1), references to such subpar. (D) in par. (1)(A)(i) and (1)(B), subparas. (C) and (D) in par. (3), provided that the net operating loss deduction in par. (2)(B) be determined without regard to that portion of a net operating loss due to a foreign expropriation loss, if such portion may not, under par. (1)(D), be carried back to such prior taxable year, and that if a portion of the net operating loss is attributable to foreign expropriation to which par. (1)(D) applied, such portion shall be considered a separate loss for such year to be applied after the other portion of such net operating loss ... added subsec. (k) and redesignated former subsec. (k) as (l), for foreign expropriation losses in tax. yrs. end. after '58.

—P.L. 88-272, Sec. 234, substituted in paras. (j)(1) and (2) references to Code Sec. 7701(a)(33) for references to Code Sec. 1503(c)(1) or (2), wherever appearing, for tax. yrs. begin. after '63.

In **1962**, P.L. 87-710, Sec. 1(a), authorized a carryover of a net operating loss in subsec. (b) for any taxable year ending after '55, to each of the 5 taxable years following the taxable year of loss, or when such loss occurs in the case of regulated transportation corporation, except as provided in subsec. (j), then to each of the 7 taxable years following the taxable year of loss, and eliminated provisions authorizing a net operating loss for any taxable years ending after '57, to be carried over to each of the 5 taxable years following the taxable year of such loss, in par. (1), and added the reference to subsec. (j) in par. (2); ... Sec. 1(b), added subsec. (j) and redesignated former subsec. (j) as (k), with respect to net operating losses for tax. yrs. end. after '55.

—P.L. 87-792, Sec. 7(f), added subpara. (d)(4)(D), effective for tax. yrs. begin. after '62.

—P.L. 87-794, Sec. 317(b), designated existing provisions of subsec. (b)(1) as clause (A)(i) and eliminated provisions which authorized a net operating loss for any taxable year ending after '57, to be a net operating loss carryover to each of the 5 taxable years following the taxable year of such loss, and added clauses (A)(ii), (B), and (C) . . . Sec. 317(b), added the reference to subsection (j) in subsec. (b)(2) and substituted "shall be carried to the earliest of the taxable years to which (by reason of paragraph (1))" for "shall be carried to the earliest of the 8 taxable years to which (by reason of subparagraphs (A) and (B) of paragraph (1))", and "each of the other taxable years" for "each of the other 7 taxable years" . . . Sec. 317(b), added para. (b)(3), with respect to net operating losses for tax. yrs. end. after '55.

In **1958**, P.L. 85-866, Sec. 203, substituted "1957" for "1953", and "3" for "2" in para. (b)(1), substituted "subsection (i)" for "subsection (f)", "8" for "7", and "7" for "6" in para. (b)(2), added redesignated subsec. (i) as (j), effective for net operating losses for tax. yrs. end. after '57.

—P.L. 85-866, Sec. 14, added paras. (f)(3), (f)(4) and (g)(3) and redesignated para. (g)(3) as (g)(4) for all '54 Code yrs.

—P.L. 85-866, Sec. 64, added subsec. (h) and (i) and redesignated former subsec. (h) as (j), effective for tax. yrs. begin. after '67.

—P.L. 85-866, Sec. 14, provided that: "If refund or credit of any overpayment resulting from the application of the amendment made by subsection (a) [to subsecs. (f)(3) and (f)(4) of this section] or (b) [to subsecs. (g)(3) and (g)(4) of this section] is prevented on the date of the enactment of this Act [Sept. 2, 1958], or within 6 months after such date, by the operation of any law or rule of law (other than section 3760 of the Internal Revenue Code of 1939 or section 7121 of the Internal Revenue Code of 1954, relating to closing agreements, and other than section 3761 of the Internal Revenue Code of 1939 or section 7122 of the Internal Revenue Code of 1954, relating to compromises), refund or credit of such overpayment may, nevertheless, be made or allowed if claim therefor is filed within 6 months after such date. No interest shall be paid or allowed on any overpayment resulting from the application of the amendment made by subsection (a) or (b)."

Sec. 173. Circulation expenditures.
(a) General rule.

Notwithstanding section 263, all expenditures (other than expenditures for the purchase of land or depreciable property or for the acquisition of circulation through the purchase of any part of the business of another publisher of a newspaper, magazine, or other periodical) to establish, maintain, or increase the circulation of a newspaper, magazine, or other periodical shall be allowed as a deduction; except that the deduction shall not be allowed with respect to the portion of such expenditures as, under regulations prescribed by the Secretary, is chargeable to capital account if the taxpayer elects, in accordance with such regulations, to treat such portion as so chargeable. Such election, if made, must be for the total amount of such portion of the expenditures which is so chargeable to capital account, and shall be binding for all subsequent taxable years unless, upon application by the taxpayer, the Secretary permits a revocation of such election subject to such conditions as he deems necessary.

(b) Cross reference.

For election of 3-year amortization of expenditures allowable as a deduction under subsection (a), see section 59(e).

In **1988**, P.L. 100-647, Sec. 1007(g)(5), substituted "section 59(e)" for "section 59(d)" in subsec. (b), effective for tax. yrs. begin. after 12/31/86.

In **1986**, P.L. 99-514, Sec. 701(e)(4)(D), substituted "59(d)" for "58(i)" in subsec. (b), effective for tax. yrs. begin. after 12/31/86.

In **1984**, P.L. 98-369, Sec. 711(a)(3)(C), substituted "3-year" for "10-year" in subsec. (b), effective for tax. yrs. begin. after 12/31/82.

In **1983**, P.L. 97-448, Sec. 306(a)(1)(A)(i), redesignated the second Sec. 201(c) of P.L. 97-248 as Sec. 201(d) of P.L. 97-248, see below.

In **1982**, P.L. 97-248, Sec. 201(d)(9)(A), amended Code Sec. 173, effective for tax. yrs. begin. after 12/31/82.

Prior to amendment, Code Sec. 173 read as follows:

"SEC. 173. CIRCULATION EXPENDITURES.

"Notwithstanding section 263, all expenditures (other than expenditures for the purchase of land or depreciable property or for the acquisition of circulation through the purchase of any part of the business of another publisher of a newspaper, magazine, or other periodical) to establish, maintain, or increase the circulation of a newspaper, magazine, or other periodical shall be allowed as a deduction; except that the deduction shall not be allowed with respect to the portion of such expenditures as, under regulations prescribed by the Secretary, is chargeable to capital account if the taxpayer elects, in accordance with such regulations, to treat such portion as so chargeable. Such election, if made, must be for the total amount of such portion of the expenditures which is so chargeable to capital account, and shall be binding for all subsequent taxable years unless, upon application by the taxpayer, the Secretary permits a revocation of such election subject to such conditions as he deems necessary."

In **1976**, P.L. 94-455, Sec. 1906(b)(13)(A), substituted "Secretary" for "Secretary or his delegate" each place it appeared in Code Sec. 173, effective for tax. yrs. begin. after 12/31/76.

Sec. 174. Research and experimental expenditures.
(a) Treatment as expenses.

(1) In general. A taxpayer may treat research or experimental expenditures which are paid or incurred by him during the taxable year in connection with his trade or business as expenses which are not chargeable to capital account. The expenditures so treated shall be allowed as a deduction.

(2) When method may be adopted.

(A) Without consent. A taxpayer may, without the consent of the Secretary, adopt the method provided in this subsection for his first taxable year—

(i) which begins after December 31, 1953, and ends after August 16, 1954, and

(ii) for which expenditures described in paragraph (1) are paid or incurred.

(B) With consent. A taxpayer may, with the consent of the Secretary, adopt at any time the method provided in this subsection.

(3) Scope. The method adopted under this subsection shall apply to all expenditures described in paragraph (1). The method adopted shall be adhered to in computing taxable income for the taxable year and for all subsequent taxable years unless, with the approval of the Secretary, a change to a different method is authorized with respect to part or all of such expenditures.

(b) Amortization of certain research and experimental expenditures.

(1) In general. At the election of the taxpayer, made in accordance with regulations prescribed by the Secretary, research or experimental expenditures which are—

(A) paid or incurred by the taxpayer in connection with his trade or business,

(B) not treated as expenses under subsection (a), and

(C) chargeable to capital account but not chargeable to property of a character which is subject to the allowance under section 167 (relating to allowance for depreciation, etc.) or section 611 (relating to allowance for depletion),

may be treated as deferred expenses. In computing taxable income, such deferred expenses shall be allowed as a deduction ratably over such period of not less than 60 months as may be selected by the taxpayer (beginning with the month in which the taxpayer first realizes benefits from such expenditures). Such deferred expenses are expenditures properly chargeable to capital account for purposes of section 1016(a)(1) (relating to adjustments to basis of property).

(2) Time for and scope of election. The election provided by paragraph (1) may be made for any taxable year beginning after December 31, 1953, but only if made not later than the time prescribed by law for filing the return for such taxable year (including extensions thereof). The method so elected, and the period selected by the taxpayer, shall be adhered to in computing taxable income for the taxable year for which the election is made and for all subsequent taxable years unless, with the approval of the Secretary, a change to a different method (or to a different period) is authorized with respect to part or all of such expenditures. The election shall not apply to any expenditure paid or incurred during any taxable year before the taxable year for which the taxpayer makes the election.

(c) Land and other property.

This section shall not apply to any expenditure for the acquisition or improvement of land, or for the acquisition or improvement of property to be used in connection with the research or experimentation and of a character which is subject to the allowance under section 167 (relating to allowance for depreciation, etc.) or section 611 (relating to allowance for depletion); but for purposes of this section allowances under section 167, and allowances under section 611, shall be considered as expenditures.

(d) Exploration expenditures.

This section shall not apply to any expenditure paid or incurred for the purpose of ascertaining the existence, location, extent, or quality of any deposit of ore or other mineral (including oil and gas).

(e) Only reasonable research expenditures eligible.

This section shall apply to a research or experimental expenditure only to the extent that the amount thereof is reasonable under the circumstances.

(f) Cross references.

(1) For adjustments to basis of property for amounts allowed as deductions as deferred expenses under subsection (b), see section 1016(a)(14).

(2) For election of 10-year amortization of expenditures allowable as a deduction under subsection (a), see section 59(e).

In 1989, P.L. 101-239, Sec. 7110(d), redesignated subsec. (e) as subsec. (f) and added new subsec. (e), effective for tax yrs. begin. after 12/31/89.

In 1988, P.L. 100-647, Sec. 1007(g)(5), substituted "59(e)" for "59(d)" in para. (e)(2), effective for tax. yrs. begin. after 12/31/86.

In 1986, P.L. 99-514, Sec. 701(e)(4)(D), substituted "59(d)" for "58(i)" in para. (e)(2), effective for tax. yrs. begin. after 12/31/86.

In 1983, P.L. 97-448, Sec. 306(a)(1)(A)(i), redesignated the second Sec. 201(c) of P.L. 97-248 as Sec. 201(d) of P.L. 97-248, see below.

In 1982, P.L. 97-248, Sec. 201(d)(9)(B), amended subsec. (e), effective for tax. yrs. begin. after 12/31/82.

Prior to amendment, subsec. (e) read as follows:

"(e) Cross reference.

"For adjustments to basis of property for amounts allowed as deductions as deferred expenses under subsection (b), see section 1016(a)(14)."

In 1981, P.L. 97-34, Sec. 223, provides:

"SEC. 223. SUSPENSION OF REGULATIONS RELATING TO ALLOCATION UNDER SECTION 861 OF RESEARCH AND EXPERIMENTAL EXPENDITURES.

"(a) 2-Year suspension.

"In the case of the taxpayer's first 2 taxable years beginning within 2 years after the date of the enactment of this Act, all research and experimental expenditures (within the meaning of section 174 of the Internal Revenue Code of 1954) which are paid or incurred in such year for research activities conducted in the United States shall be allocated or apportioned to sources within the United States.

"(b) Study.—

"(1) In general. The Secretary of the Treasury shall conduct a study with respect to the impact which section 1.861-8 of the Internal Revenue Service Regulations would have (A) on research and experimental activities conducted in the United States and (B) on the availability of the foreign tax credit.

"(2) Report. Not later than the date 6 months after the date of enactment of this Act, the Secretary of the Treasury shall submit to the Committee on Ways and Means of the House of Representatives and the Committee on Finance of the Senate a report on the study conducted under paragraph (1) (together with such recommendations as he may deem advisable)."

In 1976, P.L. 94-455, Sec. 1901(a)(30), substituted "August 16, 1954," for "the date on which this title is enacted," in clause (a)(2)(A)(i), . . . Sec. 1906(b)(13)(A), substituted "Secretary" for "Secretary or his delegate" each place it appeared in subsecs. (a) and (b), effective for tax. yrs. begin. after 12/31/76.

—P.L. 94-455, Sec. 2119, provided as follows:

"SEC. 2119. REGULATIONS RELATING TO TAX TREATMENT OF CERTAIN PREPUBLICATION EXPENDITURES OF PUBLISHERS.

"(a) General rule.

"With respect to taxable years beginning on or before the date on which regulations dealing with prepublication expenditures are issued after the date of the enactment of this Act, the application of sections 61 (as it relates to cost of goods sold), 162, 174, 263, and 471 of the Internal Revenue Code of 1954 to any prepublication expenditure shall be administered—

"(1) without regard to Revenue Ruling 73-395, and

"(2) in the manner in which such sections were applied consistently by the taxpayer to such expenditures before the date of the issuance of such revenue ruling.

"(b) Regulations to be prospective only.

"Any regulations issued after the date of the enactment of this Act which deal with the application of sections 61 (as it relates to cost of goods sold), 162, 174, 263, and 471 of the Internal Revenue Code of 1954 to prepublication expenditures shall apply only with respect to taxable years beginning after the date on which such regulations are issued.

"(c) Prepublication expenditures defined.

"For purposes of this section, the term 'prepublication expenditures' means expenditures paid or incurred by the taxpayer (in connection with his trade or business of publishing) for the writing, editing, compiling, illustrating, designing, or other development or improvement of a book, teaching aid, or similar product."

Sec. 175. Soil and water conservation expenditures; endangered species recovery expenditures.

(a) In general.

A taxpayer engaged in the business of farming may treat expenditures which are paid or incurred by him during the taxable year for the purpose of soil or water conservation in respect of land used in farming, or for the prevention of erosion of land used in farming, or for endangered species recovery, as expenses which are not chargeable to capital account. The expenditures so treated shall be allowed as a deduction.

(b) Limitation.

The amount deductible under subsection (a) for any taxable year shall not exceed 25 percent of the gross income derived from farming during the taxable year. If for any taxable year the total of the expenditures treated as expenses which are not chargeable to capital account exceeds 25 percent of the gross income derived from farming during the taxable year, such excess shall be deductible for succeeding taxable years in order of time; but the amount deductible under this section for any one such succeeding taxable year (including the expenditures actually paid or incurred during the taxable year) shall not exceed 25 percent of the gross income derived from farming during the taxable year.

(c) Definitions.

For purposes of subsection (a)—

(1) The term "expenditures which are paid or incurred by him during the taxable year for the purpose of soil or water conservation in respect of land used in farming, or for the prevention of erosion of land used in farming, or for endangered species recovery" means expenditures paid or incurred for the treatment or moving of earth, including (but not limited to) leveling, grading and terracing, contour furrowing, the construction, control, and protection of diversion channels, drainage ditches, earthen dams, watercourses, outlets, and ponds, the eradication of brush, and the planting of windbreaks. Such term shall include expenditures paid or incurred for the purpose of achieving site-specific management actions recommended in recovery plans approved pursuant to the Endangered Species Act of 1973. Such term does not include—

(A) the purchase, construction, installation, or improvement of structures, appliances, or facilities which are of a character which is subject to the allowance for depreciation provided in section 167, or

(B) any amount paid or incurred which is allowable as a deduction without regard to this section.

Notwithstanding the preceding sentences, such term also includes any amount, not otherwise allowable as a deduction, paid or incurred to satisfy any part of an assessment levied by a soil or water conservation or drainage district to defray expenditures made by such district (i) which, if paid or incurred by the taxpayer, would without regard to this sentence constitute expenditures deductible under this section, or (ii) for property of a character subject to the allowance for depreciation provided in section 167 and used in the soil or water conservation or drainage district's business as such (to the extent that the taxpayer's share of the assessment levied on the members of the district for such property does not exceed 10 percent of such assessment).

(2) The term "land used in farming" means land used (before or simultaneously with the expenditures described in paragraph (1)) by the taxpayer or his tenant for the production of crops, fruits, or other agricultural products or for the sustenance of livestock.

(3) **Additional limitations.**

(A) Expenditures must be consistent with soil conservation plan or endangered species recovery plan. Notwithstanding any other provision of this section, subsection (a) shall not apply to any expenditures unless such expenditures are consistent with—

(i) the plan (if any) approved by the Soil Conservation Service of the Department of Agriculture or the recovery plan approved pursuant to the Endangered Species Act of 1973 for the area in which the land is located, or

(ii) if there is no plan described in clause (i), any soil conservation plan of a comparable State agency.

(B) Certain wetland, etc., activities not qualified. Subsection (a) shall not apply to any expenditures in connection with the draining or filling of wetlands or land preparation for center pivot irrigation systems.

(d) **When method may be adopted.**

(1) **Without consent.** A taxpayer may, without the consent of the Secretary, adopt the method provided in this section for his first taxable year—

(A) which begins after December 31, 1953, and ends after August 16, 1954, and

(B) for which expenditures described in subsection (a) are paid or incurred.

(2) **With consent.** A taxpayer may, with the consent of the Secretary, adopt at any time the method provided in this section.

(e) **Scope.**

The method adopted under this section shall apply to all expenditures described in subsection (a). The method adopted shall be adhered to in computing taxable income for the taxable year and for all subsequent taxable years unless, with the approval of the Secretary, a change to a different method is authorized with respect to part or all of such expenditures.

(f) **Rules applicable to assessments for depreciable property.**

(1) **Amounts treated as paid or incurred over 9-year period.** In the case of an assessment levied to defray expenditures for property described in clause (ii) of the last sentence of subsection (c)(1), if the amount of such assessment paid or incurred by the taxpayer during the taxable year (determined without the application of this paragraph) is in excess of an amount equal to 10 percent of the aggregate amounts which have been and will be assessed as the taxpayer's share of the expenditures by the district for such property, and if such excess is more than $500, the entire excess shall be treated as paid or incurred ratably over each of the 9 succeeding taxable years.

(2) **Disposition of land during 9-year period.** If paragraph (1) applies to an assessment and the land with respect to which such assessment was made is sold or otherwise disposed of by the taxpayer (other than by the reason of his death) during the 9 succeeding taxable years, any amount of the excess described in paragraph (1) which has not been treated as paid or incurred for a taxable year ending on or before the sale or other disposition shall be added to the adjusted basis of such land immediately prior to its sale or other disposition and shall not thereafter be treated as paid or incurred ratably under paragraph (1).

(3) **Disposition by reason of death.** If paragraph (1) applies to an assessment and the taxpayer dies during the 9 succeeding taxable years, any amount of the excess described in paragraph (1) which has not been treated as paid or incurred for a taxable year ending before his death shall be treated as paid or incurred in the taxable year in which he dies.

In 2008, P.L. 110-246, Sec. 4, Repeals the duplicative enactment and provides effective date provisions of the Act entitled "An Act to provide for the continuation of agricultural programs through fiscal year 2012, and for other purposes" Sec. 4, P.L. 110-246 reads as follows:

"Sec. 4. Repeal of duplicative enactment.

"(a) In General- The Act entitled 'An Act to provide for the continuation of agricultural programs through fiscal year 2012, and for other purposes' (H.R. 2419 of the 110th Congress), and the amendments made by that Act, are repealed, effective on the date of enactment of that Act.

"(b) Effective Date- Except as otherwise provided in this Act, this Act and the amendments made by this Act shall take effect on the earlier of--

"(1) the date of enactment of this Act; or

"(2) the date of the enactment of the Act entitled 'An Act to provide for the continuation of agricultural programs through fiscal year 2012, and for other purposes' (H.R. 2419 of the 110th Congress)."

—P.L. 110-246, Sec. 15303(a)(1), added the second sentence in para. (c)(1) . . . Sec. 15303(a)(2)(A), added ", or for endangered species recovery" after "prevention of erosion of land used in farming" each place it appeared in subsecs. (a) and (c) . . . Sec. 15303(a)(2)(B), added "; endangered species recovery expenditures" before the period in the heading of Code Sec. 175 . . . Sec. 15303(b)(1), added "or endangered species recovery plan" after "conservation plan" in the heading of subpara. (c)(3)(A) . . . Sec. 15303(b)(2), added "or the recovery plan approved pursuant to the Endangered Species Act of 1973" after "Department of Agriculture" in clause (c)(3)(A)(i), effective for expenditures paid or incurred after 12/31/2008. [Ed. Note: May 22, 2008 was the date of enactment for H.R. 2419 (PL 110-234), which was repealed by (2008 Farm Act § 4(a)) (PL 110-246, 6/18/2008), in connection with the reenactment of the farm bill to correct a technical deficiency in its original passage.]

In 1986, P.L. 99-514, Sec. 401(a), added para. (c)(3), effective for amounts paid or incurred after 12/31/86, in tax. yrs. end. after 12/31/86.

In 1976, P.L. 94-455, Sec. 1901(a)(30), substituted "August 16, 1954," for "the date on which this title was enacted," in subpara. (d)(1)(A) . . . Sec. 1906(b)(13)(A), substituted "Secretary" for "Secretary or his delegate" each place it appeared in subsec. (d) and (e), effective for tax. yrs. begin. after 12/31/76.

In 1968, P.L. 90-630, Sec. 5(a), amended the last sentence of subsec. (c)(1) . . . Sec. 5(b), added subsec. (f), effective for assessments levied after the date of enactment (10/22/68) in tax. yrs. end. after such date.

Prior to amendment, the last sentence of (c)(1) read as follows:

"Notwithstanding the preceding sentences, such term also includes any amount, not otherwise allowable as a deduction, paid or incurred to satisfy any part of an assessment levied by a soil or water conservation or drainage district to defray expenditures made by such district which, if paid or incurred by the taxpayer, would without regard to this sentence constitute expenditures deductible under this section."

Sec. 176. Payments with respect to employees of certain foreign corporations.

In the case of a domestic corporation, there shall be allowed as a deduction amounts (to the extent not compensated for) paid or incurred pursuant to an agreement entered into under section 3121(l) with respect to services performed by United States citizens employed by foreign subsidiary corporations. Any reimbursement of any amount previously allowed as a deduction under this section shall be included in gross income for the taxable year in which received.

In 1954, ch. 1206, title II, Sec. 210(a), added Code Sec. 176.

Sec. 177. Repealed.

In 1986, P.L. 99-514, Sec. 241(a), repealed Code Sec. 177, effective for expenditures paid or incurred after 12/31/86, except as provided in Sec. 241(c)(2) of this Act;

"(2) Transitional rule. — The amendments made by this section [Sec. 241] shall not apply to any expenditure incurred—

"(A) pursuant to a binding contract entered into before March 2, 1986, or

"(B) with respect to the development, protection, expansion, registration, or defense of a trademark or trade name commenced before March 2, 1986, but only if not less than the lesser of $1,000,000 or 5 percent of the aggregate cost of such development protection, expansion, registration, or defense has been incurred or committed before such date.

The preceding sentence shall not apply to any expenditure with respect to a trademark or trade name placed in service after December 31, 1987."

Prior to repeal, Code Sec. 177 read as follows:

"SEC. 177. TRADEMARK AND TRADE NAME EXPENDITURES.

"(a) Election to amortize.

"Any trademark or trade name expenditure paid or incurred during a taxable year beginning after December 31, 1955, may, at the election of the taxpayer (made in accordance with regulations prescribed by the Secretary), be treated as a deferred expense. In computing taxable income, all expenditures paid or incurred during the taxable year which are so treated shall be allowed as a deduction ratably over such period of not less than 60 months (beginning with the first month in such taxable year) as may be selected by the taxpayer in making such election. The expenditures so treated are expenditures properly chargeable to capital account for purposes of section 1016(a)(1) (relating to adjustments to basis of property).

"(b) Trademark and trade name expenditures defined.

"For purposes of subsection (a), the term 'trademark or trade name expenditure' means any expenditure which—

"(1) is directly connected with the acquisition, protection, expansion, registration (Federal, State, or foreign), or defense of a trademark or trade name;

"(2) is chargeable to capital account; and

"(3) is not part of the consideration paid for a trademark, trade name, or business.

"(c) Time for and scope of election.

"The election provided by subsection (a) shall be made within the time prescribed by law (including extensions thereof) for filing the return for the taxable year during which the expenditure is paid or incurred. The period selected by the taxpayer under subsection (a) with respect to the expenditures paid or incurred during the taxable year which are treated as deferred expenses shall be adhered to in computing his taxable income for the taxable year for which the election is made and all subsequent years.

"(d) Cross reference.

"For adjustments to basis of property for amounts allowed as deductions for expenditures treated as deferred expenses under this section, see section 1016(a)(16)."

In 1976, P.L. 94-455, Sec. 1906(b)(13)(A), substituted "Secretary" for "Secretary or his delegate" in subsec. (a), effective for tax. yrs. begin. after 12/31/76.

In 1956, ch. 464, Sec. 4(a), added Code Sec. 177.

Sec. 178. Amortization of cost of acquiring a lease.
(a) General rule.

In determining the amount of the deduction allowable to a lessee for exhaustion, wear and tear, obsolescence, or amortization in respect of any cost of acquiring the lease, the term of the lease shall be treated as including all renewal options (and any other period for which the parties reasonably expect the lease to be renewed) if less than 75 percent of such cost is attributable to the period of the term of the lease remaining on the date of its acquisition.

(b) Certain periods excluded.

For purposes of subsection (a), in determining the period of the term of the lease remaining on the date of acquisition, there shall not be taken into account any period for which the lease may subsequently be renewed, extended, or continued pursuant to an option exercisable by the lessee.

In 1988, P.L. 100-647, Sec. 1002(a)(9), substituted "the deduction allowable to a lessee for exhaustion, wear and tear, obsolescence, or amortization" for "the deduction allowable to a lessee of a lease for any taxable year for amortization under section 167, 169, 179, 185, 190, 193, or 194", effective for property placed in service after 12/31/86, in tax. yrs. end. after 12/31/86. Sec. 1002(c)(3) of this Act provides:

"(3) Notwithstanding section 203 of the Reform Act, the amendments made by section 201 of the Reform Act shall apply to any real property which was acquired before January 1, 1987, and was converted on or after such date from personal use to a use for which depreciation is allowable."

In 1986, P.L. 99-514, Sec. 201(d)(2)(A), amended Code Sec. 178 [as amended by Sec. 1812(c)(4)(B), of this Act, see below], effective for property placed in service after 12/31/86, in tax. yrs. ending after 12/31/86. [see Sec. 1002(c)(3) of P.L. 100-647, reproduced above.] Sec. 203(a)(1)(B) of this Act provides:

"(B) Election to have amendments made by section 201 apply.—A taxpayer may elect (at such time and in such manner as the Secretary of the Treasury or his delegate may prescribe) to have the amendments made by section 201 apply to any property placed in service after July 31, 1986, and before January 1, 1987." For transitional and special rules, see Sec. 203(b)-(e) of this Act reproduced in note following Code Sec. 168.

Prior to amendment, Code Sec. 178 [as amended by Sec. 1812(c)(4)(B) of this Act] read as follows:

"SEC. 178. DEPRECIATION OR AMORTIZATION OF IMPROVEMENTS MADE BY LESSEE ON LESSOR'S PROPERTY.

"(a) General rule.

"Except as provided in subsection (b), in determining the amount allowable to a lessee as a deduction for any taxable year for exhaustion, wear and tear, obsolescence, or amortization—

"(1) in respect of any building erected (or other improvement made) on the leased property, if the portion of the term of the lease (excluding any period for which the lease may subsequently be renewed, extended, or continued pursuant to an option exercisable by the lessee) remaining upon the completion of such building or other improvement is less than 60 percent of the useful life of such building or other improvement, or

"(2) in respect of any cost of acquiring the lease, if less than 75 percent of such cost is attributable to the portion of the term of the lease (excluding any period for which the lease may subsequently be renewed, extended, or continued pursuant to an option exercisable by the lessee) remaining on the date of its acquisition, the term of the lease shall be treated as including any period for which the lease may be renewed, extended, or continued pursuant to an option exercisable by the lessee, unless the lessee establishes that (as of the close of the taxable year) it is more probable that the lease will not be renewed, extended, or continued for such period than that the lease will be so renewed, extended, or continued.

"(b) Related lessee and lessor.

"(1) General rule. If a lessee and lessor are related persons (as determined under paragraph (2)) at any time during the taxable year then, in determining the amount allowable to the lessee as a deduction for such taxable year for exhaustion, wear and tear, obsolescence, or amortization in respect of any building erected (or other improvement made) on the leased property, the lease shall be treated as including a period of not less duration than the remaining useful life of such improvement.

"(2) Related persons defined. For purposes of paragraph (1), a lessor and lessee shall be considered to be related persons if—

"(A) the lessor and the lessee are members of an affiliated group (as defined in section 1504), or

"(B) the relationship between the lessor and lessee is one described in subsection (b) of section 267, except that, for purposes of this subparagraph, the phrase '80 percent or more' shall be substituted for the phrase 'more than 50 percent' each place it appears in such subsection and subsec. (f)(1)(A) of such section shall not apply.

For purposes of determining the ownership of stock in applying subparagraph (B), the rules of subsection (c) of section 267 shall apply, except that the family of an individual shall include only his spouse, ancestors, and lineal descendants.

"(c) Reasonable certainty test.

"In any case in which neither subsection (a) nor subsection (b) applies, the determination as to the amount allowable to a lessee as a deduction for any taxable year for exhaustion, wear and tear, obsolescence, or amortization—

"(1) in respect of any building erected (or other improvement made) on the leased property, or

"(2) in respect of any cost of acquiring the lease, shall be made with reference to the term of the lease (excluding any period for which the lease may subsequently be renewed, extended, or continued pursuant to an option exercisable by the lessee), unless the lease has been renewed, extended, or continued or the facts show with reasonable certainty that the lease will be renewed, extended, or continued."

— P.L. 99-514, Sec. 1812(c)(4)(B), added "and subsec. (f)(1)(A) of such section shall not apply" before the period at end of subpara. (b)(2)(B), effective for transactions after 12/31/83, in tax. yrs. end. after 12/31/83.

In 1958, P.L. 85-866, Sec. 15, added Code Sec. 178, effective for costs of acquiring a lease incurred, and improvements begun, after 7/28/58 (other than improvements which, on 7/28/58, and at all times thereafter, the lessee was under a binding legal obligation to make).

Sec. 179. Election to expense certain depreciable business assets.
(a) Treatment as expenses.

A taxpayer may elect to treat the cost of any section 179 property as an expense which is not chargeable to capital account. Any cost so treated shall be allowed as a deduction for the taxable year in which the section 179 property is placed in service.

(b) Limitations.

• *Caution:* Code Sec. 179(b)(1)-(2), following, are effective for tax. yrs. begin. before 1/1/2012. For Code Sec. 179(b)(1)-(2), effective for tax. yrs. begin. after 12/31/2011, see below.

Deductions

(1) Dollar limitation. The aggregate cost which may be taken into account under subsection (a) for any taxable year shall not exceed—
  (A) $250,000 in the case of taxable years beginning after 2007 and before 2010,
  (B) $500,000 in the case of taxable years beginning in 2010 or 2011, and
  (C) $25,000 in the case of taxable years beginning after 2011.

(2) Reduction in limitation. The limitation under paragraph (1) for any taxable year shall be reduced (but not below zero) by the amount by which the cost of section 179 property placed in service during such taxable year exceeds—
  (A) $800,000 in the case of taxable years beginning after 2007 and before 2010,
  (B) $2,000,000 in the case of taxable years beginning in 2010 or 2011, and
  (C) $200,000 in the case of taxable years beginning after 2011.

> • *Caution:* Code Sec. 179(b)(1)-(2), following, are effective for tax. yrs. begin. after 12/31/2011. For Code Sec. 179(b)(1)-(2), effective for tax. yrs. begin. after 1/1/2012, see below.

(1) Dollar limitation. The aggregate cost which may be taken into account under subsection (a) for any taxable year shall not exceed—
  (A) $250,000 in the case of taxable years beginning after 2007 and before 2010,
  (B) $500,000 in the case of taxable years beginning in 2010 or 2011,
  (C) $125,000 in the case of taxable years beginning in 2012, and
  (D) $25,000 in the case of taxable years beginning after 2012.

(2) Reduction in limitation. The limitation under paragraph (1) for any taxable year shall be reduced (but not below zero) by the amount by which the cost of section 179 property placed in service during such taxable year exceeds—
  (A) $800,000 in the case of taxable years beginning after 2007 and before 2010,
  (B) $2,000,000 in the case of taxable years beginning in 2010 or 2011,
  (C) $500,000 in the case of taxable years beginning in 2012, and
  (D) $200,000 in the case of taxable years beginning after 2012.

(3) Limitation based on income from trade or business.
  (A) In general. The amount allowed as a deduction under subsection (a) for any taxable year (determined after the application of paragraphs (1) and (2)) shall not exceed the aggregate amount of taxable income of the taxpayer for such taxable year which is derived from the active conduct by the taxpayer of any trade or business during such taxable year.
  (B) Carryover of disallowed deduction. The amount allowable as a deduction under subsection (a) for any taxable year shall be increased by the lesser of—
    (i) the aggregate amount disallowed under subparagraph (A) for all prior taxable years (to the extent not previously allowed as a deduction by reason of this subparagraph), or
    (ii) the excess (if any) of—
      (I) the limitation of paragraphs (1) and (2) (or if lesser, the aggregate amount of taxable income referred to in subparagraph (A)), over
      (II) the amount allowable as a deduction under subsection (a) for such taxable year without regard to this subparagraph.
  (C) Computation of taxable income. For purposes of this paragraph, taxable income derived from the conduct of a trade or business shall be computed without regard to the deduction allowable under this section.

(4) Married individuals filing separately. In the case of a husband and wife filing separate returns for the taxable year—
  (A) such individuals shall be treated as 1 taxpayer for purposes of paragraphs (1) and (2), and
  (B) unless such individuals elect otherwise, 50 percent of the cost which may be taken into account under subsection (a) for such taxable year (before application of paragraph (3)) shall be allocated to each such individual.

(5) Limitation on cost taken into account for certain passenger vehicles.
  (A) In general. The cost of any sport utility vehicle for any taxable year which may be taken into account under this section shall not exceed $25,000.
  (B) Sport utility vehicle. For purposes of subparagraph (A)—
    (i) In general. The term "sport utility vehicle" means any 4-wheeled vehicle—
      (I) which is primarily designed or which can be used to carry passengers over public streets, roads, or highways (except any vehicle operated exclusively on a rail or rails),
      (II) which is not subject to section 280F, and
      (III) which is rated at not more than 14,000 pounds gross vehicle weight.
    (ii) Certain vehicles excluded. Such term does not include any vehicle which—
      (I) is designed to have a seating capacity of more than 9 persons behind the driver's seat,
      (II) is equipped with a cargo area of at least 6 feet in interior length which is an open area or is designed for use as an open area but is enclosed by a cap and is not readily accessible directly from the passenger compartment, or
      (III) has an integral enclosure, fully enclosing the driver compartment and load carrying device, does not have seating rearward of the driver's seat, and has no body section protruding more than 30 inches ahead of the leading edge of the windshield.

> • *Caution:* Code Sec. 179(b)(6) following, is effective for tax. yrs. begin. after 12/31/2011.

(6) Inflation adjustment.
  (A) In general. In the case of any taxable year beginning in calendar year 2012, the $125,000 and $500,000 amounts in paragraphs (1)(C) and (2)(C) shall each be increased by an amount equal to—
    (i) such dollar amount, multiplied by

Code Sec. 179(b)(6)(A)(ii) — Deductions

(ii) the cost-of-living adjustment determined under section 1(f)(3) for the calendar year in which the taxable year begins, by substituting "calendar year 2006" for "calendar year 1992" in subparagraph (B) thereof.

(B) Rounding.

(i) Dollar limitation. If the amount in paragraph (1) as increased under subparagraph (A) is not a multiple of $1,000, such amount shall be rounded to the nearest multiple of $1,000.

(ii) Phaseout amount. If the amount in paragraph (2) as increased under subparagraph (A) is not a multiple of $10,000, such amount shall be rounded to the nearest multiple of $10,000.

(7) Repealed.

(c) Election.

(1) In general. An election under this section for any taxable year shall—

(A) specify the items of section 179 property to which the election applies and the portion of the cost of each of such items which is to be taken into account under subsection (a), and

(B) be made on the taxpayer's return of the tax imposed by this chapter for the taxable year.

Such election shall be made in such manner as the Secretary may by regulations prescribe.

> • **Caution:** Code Sec. 179(c)(2), following, is effective for tax. yrs. begin. before 1/1/2011. For Code Sec. 179(c)(2), effective for tax. yrs. begin. after 12/31/2010, and Code Sec. 179(c)(2), effective for tax. yrs. begin. after 12/31/2011, see below.

(2) Election irrevocable. Any election made under this section, and any specification contained in any such election, may not be revoked except with the consent of the Secretary. Any such election or specification with respect to any taxable year beginning after 2002 and before 2011 may be revoked by the taxpayer with respect to any property, and such revocation, once made, shall be irrevocable.

> • **Caution:** Code Sec. 179(c)(2), following, is effective for tax. yrs. begin. after 12/31/2010, and before 1/1/2012. For Code Sec. 179(c)(2), effective for tax. yrs. begin. before 1/1/2011, see above. For Code Sec. 179(c)(2), effective for tax. yrs. begin. after 12/31/2011, see below.

(2) Election irrevocable. Any election made under this section, and any specification contained in any such election, may not be revoked except with the consent of the Secretary. Any such election or specification with respect to any taxable year beginning after 2002 and before 2012 may be revoked by the taxpayer with respect to any property, and such revocation, once made, shall be irrevocable.

> • **Caution:** Code Sec. 179(c)(2), following, is effective for tax. yrs. begin. after 12/31/2011. For Code Sec. 179(c)(2), effective for tax. yrs. begin. before 1/1/2012, see above.

(2) Election irrevocable. Any election made under this section, and any specification contained in any such election, may not be revoked except with the consent of the Secretary. Any such election or specification with respect to any taxable year beginning after 2002 and before 2013 may be revoked by the taxpayer with respect to any property, and such revocation, once made, shall be irrevocable.

(d) Definitions and special rules.

(1) Section 179 property. For purposes of this section, the term "section 179 property" means property—

(A) which is—

(i) tangible property (to which section 168 applies), or

> • **Caution:** Code Sec. 179(d)(1)(A)(ii), following, is effective for tax. yrs. begin. before 1/1/2011. For Code Sec. 179(d)(1)(A)(ii) effective for tax. yrs. begin. after 12/31/2010, and Code Sec. 179(d)(1)(A)(ii), effective for tax. yrs. begin. after 12/31/2011, see below.

(ii) computer software (as defined in section 197(e)(3)(B)) which is described in section 197(e)(3)(A)(i), to which section 167 applies, and which is placed in service in a taxable year beginning after 2002 and before 2011,

> • **Caution:** Code Sec. 179(d)(1)(A)(ii), following, is effective for tax. yrs. begin. after 12/31/2010, and before 1/1/2012. For Code Sec. 179(d)(1)(A)(ii) effective for tax. yrs. begin. before 1/1/2011, see above. For Code Sec. 179(d)(1)(A)(ii), effective for tax. yrs. begin. after 12/31/2011, see below.

(ii) computer software (as defined in section 197(e)(3)(B)) which is described in section 197(e)(3)(A)(i), to which section 167 applies, and which is placed in service in a taxable year beginning after 2002 and before 2012,

> • **Caution:** Code Sec. 179(d)(1)(A)(ii), following, is effective for tax. yrs. begin. after 12/31/2011. For Code Sec. 179(d)(1)(A)(ii), effective for tax. yrs. begin. before 1/1/2012, see above.

(ii) computer software (as defined in section 197(e)(3)(B)) which is described in section 197(e)(3)(A)(i), to which section 167 applies, and which is placed in service in a taxable year beginning after 2002 and before 2013,

(B) which is section 1245 property (as defined in section 1245(a)(3)), and

(C) which is acquired by purchase for use in the active conduct of a trade or business.

Such term shall not include any property described in section 50(b) and shall not include air conditioning or heating units.

Deductions

(2) Purchase defined. For purposes of paragraph (1), the term "purchase" means any acquisition of property, but only if—

(A) the property is not acquired from a person whose relationship to the person acquiring it would result in the disallowance of losses under section 267 or 707(b) (but, in applying section 267(b) and (c) for purposes of this section, paragraph (4) of section 267(c) shall be treated as providing that the family of an individual shall include only his spouse, ancestors, and lineal descendants),

(B) the property is not acquired by one component member of a controlled group from another component member of the same controlled group, and

(C) the basis of the property in the hands of the person acquiring it is not determined—

(i) in whole or in part by reference to the adjusted basis of such property in the hands of the person from whom acquired, or

(ii) under section 1014(a) (relating to property acquired from a decedent).

(3) Cost. For purposes of this section, the cost of property does not include so much of the basis of such property as is determined by reference to the basis of other property held at any time by the person acquiring such property.

(4) Section not to apply to estates and trusts. This section shall not apply to estates and trusts.

(5) Section not to apply to certain non-corporate lessors. This section shall not apply to any section 179 property which is purchased by a person who is not a corporation and with respect to which such person is the lessor unless—

(A) the property subject to the lease has been manufactured or produced by the lessor, or

(B) the term of the lease (taking into account options to renew) is less than 50 percent of the class life of the property (as defined in section 168(i)(1)), and for the period consisting of the first 12 months after the date on which the property is transferred to the lessee the sum of the deductions with respect to such property which are allowable to the lessor solely by reason of section 162 (other than rents and reimbursed amounts with respect to such property) exceeds 15 percent of the rental income produced by such property.

(6) Dollar limitation of controlled group. For purposes of subsection (b) of this section—

(A) all component members of a controlled group shall be treated as one taxpayer, and

(B) the Secretary shall apportion the dollar limitation contained in subsection (b)(1) among the component members of such controlled group in such manner as he shall by regulations prescribe.

(7) Controlled group defined. For purposes of paragraphs (2) and (6), the term "controlled group" has the meaning assigned to it by section 1563(a), except that, for such purposes, the phrase "more than 50 percent" shall be substituted for the phrase "at least 80 percent" each place it appears in section 1563(a)(1).

(8) Treatment of partnerships and S corporations. In the case of a partnership, the limitations of subsection (b) shall apply with respect to the partnership and with respect to each partner. A similar rule shall apply in the case of an S corporation and its shareholders.

(9) Coordination with section 38. No credit shall be allowed under section 38 with respect to any amount for which a deduction is allowed under subsection (a).

(10) Recapture in certain cases. The Secretary shall, by regulations, provide for recapturing the benefit under any deduction allowable under subsection (a) with respect to any property which is not used predominantly in a trade or business at any time.

(e) Special rules for qualified disaster assistance property.

(1) In general. For purposes of this section—

(A) the dollar amount in effect under subsection (b)(1) for the taxable year shall be increased by the lesser of—

(i) $100,000, or

(ii) the cost of qualified section 179 disaster assistance property placed in service during the taxable year, and

(B) the dollar amount in effect under subsection (b)(2) for the taxable year shall be increased by the lesser of—

(i) $600,000, or

(ii) the cost of qualified section 179 disaster assistance property placed in service during the taxable year.

(2) Qualified section 179 disaster assistance property. For purposes of this subsection, the term "qualified section 179 disaster assistance property" means section 179 property (as defined in subsection (d)) which is qualified disaster assistance property (as defined in section 168(n)(2)).

(3) Coordination with empowerment zones and renewal communities. For purposes of sections 1397A and 1400J, qualified section 179 disaster assistance property shall not be treated as qualified zone property or qualified renewal property, unless the taxpayer elects not to take such qualified section 179 disaster assistance property into account for purposes of this subsection.

(4) Recapture. For purposes of this subsection, rules similar to the rules under subsection (d)(10) shall apply with respect to any qualified section 179 disaster assistance property which ceases to be qualified section 179 disaster assistance property.

(f) Special rules for qualified real property.

(1) In general. If a taxpayer elects the application of this subsection for any taxable year beginning in 2010 or 2011, the term "section 179 property" shall include any qualified real property which is—

(A) of a character subject to an allowance for depreciation,

(B) acquired by purchase for use in the active conduct of a trade or business, and

(C) not described in the last sentence of subsection (d)(1).

(2) Qualified real property. For purposes of this subsection, the term "qualified real property" means—

(A) qualified leasehold improvement property described in section 168(e)(6),

(B) qualified restaurant property described in section 168(e)(7), and

(C) qualified retail improvement property described in section 168(e)(8).

(3) Limitation. For purposes of applying the limitation under subsection (b)(1)(B), not more than $250,000 of the aggregate cost which is taken into account under subsection (a) for any taxable year may be attributable to qualified real property.

(4) Carryover limitation.

(A) In general. Notwithstanding subsection (b)(3)(B), no amount attributable to qualified real property may be carried over to a taxable year beginning after 2011.

(B) Treatment of disallowed amounts. Except as provided in subparagraph (C), to the extent that any amount is not allowed to be carried over to a taxable year beginning after 2011 by reason of subparagraph (A), this title shall be applied as if no election under this section had been made with respect to such amount.

(C) Amounts carried over from 2010. If subparagraph (B) applies to any amount (or portion of an amount) which is carried over from a taxable year other than the taxpayer's last taxable year beginning in 2011, such amount (or portion of an amount) shall be treated for purposes of this title as attributable to property placed in service on the first day of the taxpayer's last taxable year beginning in 2011.

(D) Allocation of amounts. For purposes of applying this paragraph and subsection (b)(3)(B) to any taxable year, the amount which is disallowed under subsection (b)(3)(A) for such taxable year which is attributed to qualified real property shall be the amount which bears the same ratio to the total amount so disallowed as—

(i) the aggregate amount attributable to qualified real property placed in service during such taxable year, increased by the portion of any amount carried over to such taxable year from a prior taxable year which is attributable to such property, bears to

(ii) the total amount of section 179 property placed in service during such taxable year, increased by the aggregate amount carried over to such taxable year from any prior taxable year.

For purposes of the preceding sentence, only section 179 property with respect to which an election was made under subsection (c)(1) (determined without regard to subparagraph (B) of this paragraph) shall be taken into account.

In 2010, P.L. 111-312, Sec. 402(a), deleted "and" at the end of subpara. (b)(1)(B), deleted subpara. (b)(1)(C), and added new subparas. (b)(1)(C)-(D)
Prior to deletion, subpara. (b)(1)(C) read as follows:
"(C) $25,000 in the case of taxable years beginning after 2011."
—P.L. 111-312, Sec. 402(b), deleted "and" at the end of subpara. (b)(2)(B), deleted subpara. (b)(2)(C), and added new subparas. (b)(2)(C)-(D)
Prior to deletion, subpara. (b)(2)(C) read as follows:
"(C) $200,000 in the case of taxable years beginning after 2011."
—P.L. 111-312, Sec. 402(c), added para. (b)(6) . . . Sec. 402(d), substituted "2013" for "2012" in clause (d)(1)(A)(ii) . . . Sec. 402(e), substituted "2013" for "2012" in para. (c)(2), effective for taxable years beginning after 12/31/2011.
—P.L. 111-312, Sec. 737(b)(3)(A), deleted "(without regard to the dates specified in subparagraph (A)(i) thereof)" after "section 168(e)(7)" in subpara. (f)(2)(B) . . . Sec. 737(b)(3)(B), deleted "without regard to subparagraph (E) thereof" after "section 168(e)(8)" in subpara. (f)(2)(C), effective for property placed in service after 12/31/2009.
—P.L. 111-240, Sec. 2021(a)(1), amended para. (b)(1) . . . Sec. 2021(a)(2), amended para. (b)(2) . . . Sec. 2021(b), added subsec. (f), effective for property placed in service after 12/31/2009, in tax. yrs. begin. after such date.
Prior to amendment paras. (b)(1) and (b)(2) read as follows:
"(1) Dollar limitation.
"The aggregate cost which may be taken into account under subsection (a) for any taxable year shall not exceed $25,000 ($250,000 in the case of taxable years beginning after 2007 and before 2011)."
"(2) Reduction in limitation.
"The limitation under paragraph (1) for any taxable year shall be reduced (but not below zero) by the amount by which the cost of section 179 property placed in service during such taxable year exceeds $200,000 ($800,000 in the case of taxable years beginning after 2007 and before 2011)."
—P.L. 111-240, Sec. 2021(c), substituted "2012" for "2011" in para. (c)(2) . . . Sec. 2021(d), substituted "2012" for "2011" in clause (d)(1)(A)(ii), effective for tax. yrs. begin. after 12/31/2010.
—P.L. 111-147, Sec. 201(a)(1), substituted "($250,000 in the case of taxable years beginning after 2007 and before 2011)" for "($125,000 in the case of taxable years beginning after 2006 and before 2011)" in para. (b)(1) . . . Sec.

201(a)(2), substituted "($800,000 in the case of taxable years beginning after 2007 and before 2011)" for "($500,000 in the case of taxable years beginning after 2006 and before 2011)" in para. (b)(2) . . . Sec. 201(a)(3), deleted paras. (b)(5) and (b)(7) . . . Sec. 201(a)(4), redesignated para. (b)(6) as para. (b)(5), effective for shall apply to tax. yrs. begin. after 12/31/2009.
Prior to deletion paras. (b)(5) and (b)(7) read as follows:
"(5) Inflation adjustments.
"(A) In general. In the case of any taxable year beginning in a calendar year after 2007 and before 2011, the $125,000 and $500,000 amounts in paragraphs (1) and (2) shall each be increased by an amount equal to—
"(i) such dollar amount, multiplied by
"(ii) the cost-of-living adjustment determined under section 1(f)(3) for the calendar year in which the taxable year begins, by substituting 'calendar year 2006' for 'calendar year 1992' in subparagraph (B) thereof.
"(B) Rounding.
"(i) Dollar limitation. If the amount in paragraph (1) as increased under subparagraph (A) is not a multiple of $1,000, such amount shall be rounded to the nearest multiple of $1,000.
"(ii) Phaseout amount. If the amount in paragraph (2) as increased under subparagraph (A) is not a multiple of $10,000, such amount shall be rounded to the nearest multiple of $10,000."
"(7) Increase in limitations for 2008, and 2009.
"In the case of any taxable year beginning in 2008, or 2009—
"(A) the dollar limitation under paragraph (1) shall be $250,000,
"(B) the dollar limitation under paragraph (2) shall be $800,000, and
"(C) the amounts described in subparagraphs (A) and (B) shall not be adjusted under paragraph (5)."
In 2009, P.L. 111-5, Sec. 1202(a)(1), substituted "2008, or 2009" for "2008" in para. (b)(7)
—P.L. 111-5, Sec. 1202(a)(2), substituted "2008, and 2009" for "2008" in the heading of para. (b)(7), effective for tax. yrs. begin. after 12/31/2008.
In 2008, P.L. 110-343, Sec. 711(a)DivC, added subsec. (e), effective for property placed in service after 12/31/2007, for disasters declared after 12/31/2007.
—P.L. 110-185, Sec. 102(a), added para. (b)(7), effective for tax. yrs. begin. after 12/31/2007.
In 2007, P.L. 110-28, Sec. 8212(a), substituted "2011" for "2010" in paras. (b)(1), (b)(2), (b)(5), (c)(2), and clause (d)(1)(A)(ii) . . . Sec. 8212(b)(1), substituted "$125,000 in the case of taxable years beginning after 2006" for "$100,000 in the case of taxable years beginning after 2002" in para. (b)(1) . . . Sec. 8212(b)(2), substituted "$500,000 in the case of taxable years beginning after 2006" for "$400,000 in the case of taxable years beginning after 2002" in para. (b)(2) . . . Sec. 8212(c)(1), substituted "2007" for "2003" in subpara. (b)(5)(A) . . . Sec. 8212(c)(2), substituted "$125,000 and $500,000" for "$100,000 and $400,000" in subpara. (b)(5)(A) . . . Sec. 8212(c)(3), substituted "2006" for "2002" in clause (b)(5)(A)(ii), effective for tax. yrs. begin. after 12/31/2006.
In 2006, P.L. 109-222, Sec. 101, substituted "2010" for "2008" in paras. (b)(1), (b)(2), (b)(5), (c)(2), and clause (d)(1)(A)(ii), enacted 5/17/2006.
In 2004, P.L. 108-357, Sec. 201, substituted "2008" for "2006" each place it appeared in subsecs. (b), (c), and (d), effective 10/22/2004.
—P.L. 108-357, Sec. 910(a), added para. (b)(6), effective for property placed in service after 10/22/2004.
In 2003, P.L. 108-27, Sec. 202(a), amended para. (b)(1) . . . Sec. 202(b), added "($400,000 in the case of taxable years beginning after 2002 and before 2006)" after "$200,000" in para. (b)(2) . . . Sec. 202(c), amended para. (d)(1) . . . Sec. 202(d), added para. (b)(5) . . . Sec. 202(e), added a sentence at the end of para. (c)(2), effective for tax. yrs. begin. after 12/31/2002.
Prior to amendment, para. (d)(1) read as follows:
"(1) Dollar limitation. The aggregate cost which may be taken into account under subsection (a) for any taxable year shall not exceed the following applicable amount:

If the taxable year begins in:	The applicable amount is:
1997	18,000
1998	18,500
1999	19,000
2000	20,000
2001 or 2002	24,000
2003 or thereafter	25,000."

Prior to amendment, para. (d)(1) read as follows:
"(1) Section 179 property. For purposes of this section, the term 'section 179 property' means any tangible property (to which section 168 applies) which is section 1245 property (as defined in section 1245(a)(3)) and which is acquired by purchase for use in the active conduct of a trade or business. Such term shall not include any property described in section 50(b) and shall not include air conditioning or heating units."
In 1996, P.L. 104-188, Sec. 1111(a), amended para. (b)(1), effective for tax. yrs. begin. after 12/31/96.
Prior to amendment, para. (b)(1) read as follows:
"(1) Dollar limitation. The aggregate cost which may be taken into account under subsection (a) for any taxable year shall not exceed $17,500."
—P.L. 104-188, Sec. 1702(h)(10), substituted "a trade or business" for "in a trade or business" in para. (d)(1) . . . Sec. 1702(h)(19), added the sentence at the end of para. (d)(1), effective for property placed in service after 12/30/90, except as provided in Sec. 11813(c)(2) of P.L. 101-508, reproduced in note following Code Sec. 46.

Deductions   Code Sec. 179

In 1993, P.L. 103-66, Sec. 13116(a), substituted "$17,500" for "$10,000" in para. (b)(1), effective for tax. yrs. begin. after 12/31/92.

In 1990, P.L. 101-508, Sec. 11813(b)(11)(A), substituted "section 1245 property (as defined in section 1245(a)(3))" for "section 38 property" in para. (d)(1) . . . Sec. 11813(b)(11)(B), amended para. (d)(5), effective for property placed in service after 12/31/90, except as provided in Sec. 11813(c)(2) reproduced in note following Code Sec. 46.
Prior to amendment, para. (d)(5) read as follows:

"(5) Section not to apply to certain noncorporate lessors. This section shall not apply to any section 179 property purchased by any person described in section 46(e)(3) unless the credit under section 38 is allowable with respect to such person for such property (determined without regard to this section)."

In 1988, P.L. 100-647, Sec. 1002(a)(19), substituted "tangible property (to which section 168 applies)" for "recovery property" in para. (d)(1) . . . Sec. 1002(b)(1), amended para. (b)(3), effective for property placed in service after 12/31/86, in tax. yrs. ending after 12/31/86. Sec. 1002(c)(3) of this Act provides:

"(3) Notwithstanding section 203 of the Reform Act, the amendments made by section 201 of the Reform Act shall apply to any real property which was acquired before January 1, 1987, and was converted on or after such date from personal use to a use for which depreciation is allowable."
Prior to amendment, para. (b)(3) read as follows:

"(3) Limitation based on income from trade or business.

"(A) In general. The aggregate cost of section 179 property taken into account under subsection (a) for any taxable year shall not exceed the aggregate amount of taxable income of the taxpayer for such taxable year which is derived from the active conduct by the taxpayer of any trade or business during such taxable year.

"(B) Carryover of unused cost. The amount of any cost which (but for subparagraph (A)) would have been allowed as a deduction under subsection (a) for any taxable year shall be carried to the succeeding taxable year and added to the amount allowable as a deduction under subsection (a) for such succeeding taxable year.

"(C) Computation of taxable income. For purposes of this paragraph, taxable income derived from the conduct of a trade or business shall be computed without regard to the cost of any section 179 property."

—P.L. 100-647, Sec. 1002(c)(8), amended Sec. 203(a)(2) of P.L. 99-514, the effective date for changes made by Sec. 202 of P.L. 99-514, by adding Sec. 203(a)(2)(B) of P.L. 99-514, reproduced below.

In 1986, P.L. 99-514, Sec. 201(d)(3), amended para. (d)(8), effective for property placed in service after 12/31/86, in tax. yrs. ending after 12/31/86. "[see Sec. 1002(c)(3) of P.L. 100-647, above]." For transitional rules, see Sec. 203(b)-(e) of this Act reproduced in note following Code Sec. 168. Sec. 203(a)(1)(B) of this Act provides:

"(B) Election to have amendments made by section 201 apply.—A taxpayer may elect (at such time and in such manner as the Secretary of the Treasury or his delegate may prescribe) to have the amendments made by section 201 apply to any property placed in service after July 31, 1986, and before January 1, 1987."
Prior to amendment, para. (d)(8) read as follows:

"(8) Dollar limitation in case of partnerships and S corporations. In the case of a partnership, the dollar limitation contained in subsection (b)(1) shall apply with respect to the partnership and with respect to each partner. A similar rule shall apply in the case of an S corporation and its shareholders."

—P.L. 99-514, Sec. 202(a), amended subsec. (b) . . . Sec. 202(b), added "in the active conduct of" after "purchase for use" in para. (d)(1) . . . Sec. 202(c), deleted "before the close of the second taxable year following the taxable year in which it is placed in service by the taxpayer" before the period at the end of the para. (d)(10), effective for property placed in service after 12/31/86, in tax. yrs. end. after 12/31/86. Sec. 203(a)(2)(B) of this Act [as added by Sec. 1002(c)(8) of P.L. 100-647, see above] provides:

"(B) Special rule for fiscal years including January 1, 1987.— In the case of any taxable year (other than a calendar year) which includes January 1, 1987, for purposes of applying the amendments made by section 202 to property placed in service during such taxable year and after December 31, 1986—

"(i) the limitation of section 179(b)(1) of the Internal Revenue Code of 1986 (as amended by section 202) shall be reduced by the aggregate deduction under section 179 (as in effect on the day before the date of the enactment of the Tax Reform Act of 1986) for section 179 property placed in service during such taxable year and before January 1, 1987,

"(ii) the limitation of section 179(b)(2) of such Code (as so amended) shall be applied by taking into account the cost of all section 179 property placed in service during such taxable year, and

"(iii) the limitation of section 179(b)(3) of such Code shall be applied by taking into account the taxable income for the entire taxable year reduced by the amount of any deduction under section 179 of such Code for property placed in service during such taxable year and before January 1, 1987."
Prior to amendment, subsec. (b) read as follows:

"(b) Dollar limitation

"(1) In general. The aggregate cost which may be taken into account under subsection (a) for any taxable year shall not exceed the following applicable amount.

"If the taxable year begins in:	The applicable amount is:
1983, 1984, 1985, 1986, or 1987	$5,000
1988 or 1989	7,500
1990 or thereafter	10,000.

"(2) Married individuals filing separately. In the case of a husband and wife filing separate returns for a taxable year, the applicable amount under paragraph (1) shall be equal to 50 percent of the amount otherwise determined under paragraph (1)."

In 1984, P.L. 98-369, Sec. 13, amended the table in para. (b)(1), effective for tax. yrs. end. after 12/31/83.
Prior to amendment, this table read as follows:

"If the taxable year begins in:	The applicable amount is:
1981	$0
1982	5,000
1983	5,000
1984	7,500
1985	7,500
1986 or thereafter	10,000"

In 1983, P.L. 97-448, Sec. 102(aa), added para. (d)(10), effective for property placed in service after 12/31/80, in tax. yrs. end. after 12/31/80.

In 1982, P.L. 97-354, Sec. 3(f)(1), added the last sentence to para. (d)(8) . . . Sec. 3(f)(2), substituted "partnerships and S corporations" for "partnerships" in the heading of para. (d)(8), effective for tax. yrs. begin. after 12/31/82.

In 1981, P.L. 97-34, Sec. 202(a), added Code Sec. 179, effective for property placed in service after 12/31/80 in tax. yrs. end. after 12/31/80.
Prior to amendment, Code Sec. 179 read as follows:

"SEC. 179. ADDITIONAL FIRST-YEAR DEPRECIATION ALLOWANCE FOR SMALL BUSINESS.
"(a) General rule.

"In the case of section 179 property, the term 'reasonable allowance' as used in section 167(a) may, at the election of the taxpayer, include an allowance, for the first taxable year for which a deduction is allowable under section 167 to the taxpayer with respect to such property, of 20 percent of the cost of such property.
"(b) Dollar limitation.

"If in any one taxable year the cost of section 179 property with respect to which the taxpayer may elect an allowance under subsection (a) for such taxable year exceeds $10,000, then subsection (a) shall apply with respect to those items selected by the taxpayer, but only to the extent of an aggregate cost of $10,000. In the case of a husband and wife who file a joint return under section 6013 for the taxable year, the limitation under the preceding sentence shall be $20,000 in lieu of $10,000.
"(c) Election.

"(1) In general. The election under this section for any taxable year shall be made within the time prescribed by law (including extensions thereof) for filing the return for such taxable year. The election shall be made in such manner as the Secretary may by regulations prescribe.

"(2) Election irrevocable. Any election made under this section may not be revoked except with the consent of the Secretary.
"(d) Definitions and special rules.

"(1) Section 179 property. For purposes of this section, the term 'section 179 property' means tangible personal property—

"(A) of a character subject to the allowance for depreciation under section 167,

"(B) acquired by purchase after December 31, 1957, for use in a trade or business or for holding for production of income, and

"(C) with a useful life (determined at the time of such acquisition) of 6 years or more.

"(2) Purchase defined. For purposes of paragraph (1), the term 'purchase' means any acquisition of property, but only if—

"(A) the property is not acquired from a person whose relationship to the person acquiring it would result in the disallowance of losses under section 267 or 707(b) (but, in applying section 267(b) and (c) for purposes of this section, paragraph (4) of section 267(c) shall be treated as providing that the family of an individual shall include only his spouse, ancestors, and lineal descendants),

"(B) the property is not acquired by one component member of a controlled group from another component member of the same controlled group, and

"(C) the basis of the property in the hands of the person acquiring it is not determined—

"(i) in whole or in part by reference to the adjusted basis of such property in the hands of the person from whom acquired, or

"(ii) under section 1014(a) (relating to property acquired from a decedent).

"(3) Cost. For purposes of this section, the cost of property does not include so much of the basis of such property as is determined by reference to the basis of other property held at any time by the person acquiring such property.

"(4) Section not to apply to trusts. This section shall not apply to trusts.

"(5) Estates. In the case of an estate, any amount apportioned to an heir, legatee, or devisee under section 167(h) shall not be taken into account in applying subsection (b) of this section to section 179 property of such heir, legatee, or devisee not held by such estate.

"(6) Dollar limitation of controlled group. For purposes of subsection (b) of this section—

"(A) all component members of a controlled group shall be treated as one taxpayer, and

"(B) the Secretary shall apportion the dollar limitation contained in such subsection (b) among the component members of such controlled group in such manner as he shall by regulations prescribe.

"(7) Controlled group defined. For purposes of paragraphs (2) and (6), the term 'controlled group' has the meaning assigned to it by section 1563(a); except that, for such purposes, the phrase 'more than 50 percent' shall be substituted for the phrase 'at least 80 percent' each place it appears in section 1563(a)(1).

"(8) Dollar limitation in case of partnerships. In the case of a partnership, the dollar limitation contained in the first sentence of subsection (b) shall apply with respect to the partnership and with respect to each partner.

"(9) Adjustment to basis; when made. In applying section 167(g), the adjustment under section 1016(a)(2) resulting by reason of an election made under this section with respect to any section 179 property shall be made before any other deduction allowed by section 167(a) is computed.

"(e) Regulations.

"The Secretary shall prescribe such regulations as may be necessary to carry out the purposes of this section."

In 1976, P.L. 94-455, Sec. 213(a), redesignated para. (d)(8) as (d)(9) and added new para. (d)(8), effective for partnership tax. yrs. begin. after 12/31/75.

—P.L. 94-455, Sec. 1906(b)(13)(A), substituted "Secretary" for "Secretary or his delegate" each place it appeared in Code Sec. 179, effective for tax. yrs. begin. after 12/31/76.

In 1969, P.L. 91-172, Sec. 401(f)(1), amended subpara. (d)(2)(B), effective for tax. yrs. end. on or after 12/31/70.

Prior to amendment, subpara. (d)(2)(B) read as follows:

"(B) the property is not acquired by one member of an affiliated group from another member of the same affiliated group, and"

—P.L. 91-172, Sec. 401(f)(2), amended paras. (d)(6) and (d)(7), effective for tax. yrs. end. on or after 12/31/70.

Prior to amendment, paras. (d)(6) and (d)(7) read as follows:

"(6) Dollar limitation of affiliated group. For purposes of subsection (b) of this section—

"(A) all members of an affiliated group shall be treated as one taxpayer, and

"(B) the Secretary or his delegate shall apportion the dollar limitation contained in such subsection (b) among the members of such affiliated group in such manner as he shall by regulations prescribe.

"(7) Affiliated group defined. For purposes of paragraphs (2) and (6), the term 'affiliated group' has the meaning assigned to it by section 1504, except that, for such purposes, the phrase 'more than 50 percent' shall be substituted for the phrase 'at least 80 percent' each place it appears in section 1504(a)."

In 1962, P.L. 87-834, Sec. 13(c)(2), substituted "section 167(h)" for "section 167(g)" in para. (d)(5) and "section 167(g)" for "section 167(f)" in para. (d)(8), effective for tax. yrs. begin. after 12/31/61 and end. after 10/16/62.

In 1958, P.L. 85-866, Sec. 204(a), added Code Sec. 179, effective for tax. yrs. end. after 6/30/58.

Sec. 179A. Deduction for clean-fuel vehicles and certain refueling property.

(a) Allowance of deduction.

(1) In general. There shall be allowed as a deduction an amount equal to the cost of—

(A) any qualified clean-fuel vehicle property, and

(B) any qualified clean-fuel vehicle refueling property.

The deduction under the preceding sentence with respect to any property shall be allowed for the taxable year in which such property is placed in service.

(2) Incremental cost for certain vehicles. If a vehicle may be propelled by both a clean-burning fuel and any other fuel, only the incremental cost of permitting the use of the clean-burning fuel shall be taken into account.

(b) Limitations.

(1) Qualified clean-fuel vehicle property.

(A) In general. The cost which may be taken into account under subsection (a)(1)(A) with respect to any motor vehicle shall not exceed—

(i) in the case of a motor vehicle not described in clause (ii) or (iii), $2,000,

(ii) in the case of any truck or van with a gross vehicle weight rating greater than 10,000 pounds but not greater than 26,000 pounds, $5,000, or

(iii) $50,000 in the case of—

(I) a truck or van with a gross vehicle weight rating greater than 26,000 pounds, or

(II) any bus which has a seating capacity of at least 20 adults (not including the driver).

(B) Phaseout. In the case of any qualified clean-fuel vehicle property placed in service after December 31, 2005, the limit otherwise allowable under subparagraph (A) shall be reduced by 75 percent.

(2) Qualified clean-fuel vehicle refueling property.

(A) In general. The aggregate cost which may be taken into account under subsection (a)(1)(B) with respect to qualified clean-fuel vehicle refueling property placed in service during the taxable year at a location shall not exceed the excess (if any) of—

(i) $100,000, over

(ii) the aggregate amount taken into account under subsection (a)(1)(B) by the taxpayer (or any related person or predecessor) with respect to property placed in service at such location for all preceding taxable years.

(B) Related person. For purposes of this paragraph, a person shall be treated as related to another person if such person bears a relationship to such other person described in section 267(b) or 707(b)(1).

(C) Election. If the limitation under subparagraph (A) applies for any taxable year, the taxpayer shall, on the return of tax for such taxable year, specify the items of property (and the portion of costs of such property) which are to be taken into account under subsection (a)(1)(B).

(c) Qualified clean-fuel vehicle property defined.

For purposes of this section—

(1) In general. The term "qualified clean-fuel vehicle property" means property which is acquired for use by the taxpayer and not for resale, the original use of which commences with the taxpayer, with respect to which the environmental standards of paragraph (2) are met, and which is described in either of the following subparagraphs:

(A) Retrofit parts and components. Any property installed on a motor vehicle which is propelled by a fuel which is not a clean-burning fuel for purposes of permitting such vehicle to be propelled by a clean-burning fuel—

(i) if the property is an engine (or modification thereof) which may use a clean-burning fuel, or

(ii) to the extent the property is used in the storage or delivery to the engine of such fuel, or the exhaust of gases from combustion of such fuel.

(B) Original equipment manufacturer's vehicles. A motor vehicle produced by an original equipment manufacturer and designed so that the vehicle may be propelled by a clean-burning fuel, but only to the extent of the portion of the basis of such vehicle which is attributable to an engine which may use such fuel, to the storage or delivery to the engine of such fuel, or to the exhaust of gases from combustion of such fuel.

(2) Environmental standards. Property shall not be treated as qualified clean-fuel vehicle property unless—

(A) the motor vehicle of which it is a part meets any applicable Federal or State emissions standards with respect to each fuel by which such vehicle is designed to be propelled, or

(B) in the case of property described in paragraph (1)(A), such property meets applicable Federal and State emissions-related certification, testing, and warranty requirements.

(3) Exception for qualified electric vehicles. The term "qualified clean-fuel vehicle property" does not include any qualified electric vehicle (as defined in section 30(c)).

(d) Qualified clean-fuel vehicle refueling property defined.

For purposes of this section, the term "qualified clean-fuel vehicle refueling property" means any property (not including a building and its structural components) if—

(1) such property is of a character subject to the allowance for depreciation,

(2) the original use of such property begins with the taxpayer, and
(3) such property is—
  (A) for the storage or dispensing of a clean-burning fuel into the fuel tank of a motor vehicle propelled by such fuel, but only if the storage or dispensing of the fuel is at the point where such fuel is delivered into the fuel tank of the motor vehicle, or
  (B) for the recharging of motor vehicles propelled by electricity, but only if the property is located at the point where the motor vehicles are recharged.
(e) Other definitions and special rules.
  For purposes of this section—
  (1) Clean-burning fuel. The term "clean-burning fuel" means—
    (A) natural gas,
    (B) liquefied natural gas,
    (C) liquefied petroleum gas,
    (D) hydrogen,
    (E) electricity, and
    (F) any other fuel at least 85 percent of which is 1 or more of the following: methanol, ethanol, any other alcohol, or ether.
  (2) Motor vehicle. The term "motor vehicle" means any vehicle which is manufactured primarily for use on public streets, roads, and highways (not including a vehicle operated exclusively on a rail or rails) and which has at least 4 wheels.
  (3) Cost of retrofit parts includes cost of installation. The cost of any qualified clean-fuel vehicle property referred to in subsection (c)(1)(A) shall include the cost of the original installation of such property.
  (4) Recapture. The Secretary shall, by regulations, provide for recapturing the benefit of any deduction allowable under subsection (a) with respect to any property which ceases to be property eligible for such deduction.
  (5) Property used outside United States, etc., not qualified. No deduction shall be allowed under subsection (a) with respect to any property referred to in section 50(b) or with respect to the portion of the cost of any property taken into account under section 179.
  (6) Basis reduction.
    (A) In general. For purposes of this title, the basis of any property shall be reduced by the portion of the cost of such property taken into account under subsection (a).
    (B) Ordinary income recapture. For purposes of section 1245, the amount of the deduction allowable under subsection (a) with respect to any property which is of a character subject to the allowance for depreciation shall be treated as a deduction allowed for depreciation under section 167.
(f) Termination.
  This section shall not apply to any property placed in service after December 31, 2005.

In 2005, P.L. 109-58, Sec. 1348, substituted "December 31, 2005" for "December 31, 2006" in subsec. (f), effective 8/8/2005.
In 2004, P.L. 108-311, Sec. 319(a), amended subpara. (b)(1)(B), effective for property placed in service after 12/31/2003.
Prior to amendment, subpara. (b)(1)(B) read as follows:
  "(B) Phaseout. In the case of any qualified clean-fuel vehicle property placed in service after December 31, 2003, the limit otherwise applicable under subparagraph (A) shall be reduced by—
    "(i) 25 percent in the case of property placed in service in calendar year 2004,
    "(ii) 50 percent in the case of property placed in service in calendar year 2005, and
    "(iii) 75 percent in the case of property placed in service in calendar year 2006."

In 2002, P.L. 107-147, Sec. 606(a)(1)(A), substituted "December 31, 2003," for "December 31, 2001," in subpara. (b)(1)(B)... Sec. 606(a)(1)(B), substituted "2004" for "2002" in clause (b)(1)(B)(i), "2005" for "2003" in clause (b)(1)(B)(ii), and "2006" for "2004" in clause (b)(1)(B)(iii)... Sec. 606(a)(2), substituted "December 31, 2006" for "December 31, 2004" in subsec. (f), effective for property placed in service after 12/31/2001.
In 1996, P.L. 104-188, Sec. 1704(j)(2), redesignated subsec. (g) as subsec. (f), effective 8/20/96.
In 1992, P.L. 102-486, Sec. 1913(a)(1), added Code Sec. 179A, effective for property placed in service after 6/30/93.

Sec. 179B. Deduction for capital costs incurred in complying with Environmental Protection Agency sulfur regulations.
(a) Allowance of deduction.
  In the case of a small business refiner (as defined in section 45H(c)(1)) which elects the application of this section, there shall be allowed as a deduction an amount equal to 75 percent of qualified costs (as defined in section 45H(c)(2)) which are paid or incurred by the taxpayer during the taxable year and which are properly chargeable to capital account.
(b) Reduced percentage.
  In the case of a small business refiner with average daily domestic refinery runs for the 1-year period ending on December 31, 2002, in excess of 155,000 barrels, the number of percentage points described in subsection (a) shall be reduced (not below zero) by the product of such number (before the application of this subsection) and the ratio of such excess to 50,000 barrels.
(c) Basis reduction.
  (1) In general. For purposes of this title, the basis of any property shall be reduced by the portion of the cost of such property taken into account under subsection (a).
  (2) Ordinary income recapture. For purposes of section 1245, the amount of the deduction allowable under subsection (a) with respect to any property which is of a character subject to the allowance for depreciation shall be treated as a deduction allowed for depreciation under section 167.
(d) Coordination with other provisions.
  Section 280B shall not apply to amounts which are treated as expenses under this section.
(e) Election to allocate deduction to cooperative owner.
  (1) In general. If—
    (A) a small business refiner to which subsection (a) applies is an organization to which part I of subchapter T applies, and
    (B) one or more persons directly holding an ownership interest in the refiner are organizations to which part I of subchapter T apply,
  the refiner may elect to allocate all or a portion of the deduction allowable under subsection (a) to such persons. Such allocation shall be equal to the person's ratable share of the total amount allocated, determined on the basis of the person's ownership interest in the taxpayer. The taxable income of the refiner shall not be reduced under section 1382 by reason of any amount to which the preceding sentence applies.
  (2) Form and effect of election. An election under paragraph (1) for any taxable year shall be made on a timely filed return for such year. Such election, once made, shall be irrevocable for such taxable year.
  (3) Written notice to owners. If any portion of the deduction available under subsection (a) is allocated to owners under paragraph (1), the cooperative shall provide any owner receiving an allocation written notice of the amount of the allocation. Such notice shall be provided before the date on which the return described in paragraph (2) is due.

In 2007, P.L. 110-172, Sec. 7(a)(3)(A), substituted "qualified costs" for "qualified capital costs" in subsec. (a) ... Sec. 7(a)(3)(C), added "and which are properly chargeable to capital account" before period at end of subsec. (a), effective for expenses paid or incurred after 12/31/2002, in tax. yrs. end. after such date.

In 2005, P.L. 109-58, Sec. 1324(a), added subsec. (e), effective for expenses paid or incurred after 12/31/2002, in tax. yrs. end. after 12/31/2002 as if included in Sec. 338(a) of P.L. 108-357, the American Jobs Creation Act of 2004.

In 2004, P.L. 108-357, Sec. 338(a), added Code Sec. 179B, effective for expenses paid or incurred after 12/31/2002, in tax. yrs. end. after 12/31/2002.

Sec. 179C. Election to expense certain refineries.

(a) Treatment as expenses.

A taxpayer may elect to treat 50 percent of the cost of any qualified refinery property as an expense which is not chargeable to capital account. Any cost so treated shall be allowed as a deduction for the taxable year in which the qualified refinery property is placed in service.

(b) Election.

(1) **In general.** An election under this section for any taxable year shall be made on the taxpayer's return of the tax imposed by this chapter for the taxable year. Such election shall be made in such manner as the Secretary may by regulations prescribe.

(2) **Election irrevocable.** Any election made under this section may not be revoked except with the consent of the Secretary.

(c) Qualified refinery property.

(1) **In general.** The term "qualified refinery property" means any portion of a qualified refinery—

(A) the original use of which commences with the taxpayer,

(B) which is placed in service by the taxpayer after the date of the enactment of this section and before January 1, 2014,

(C) in the case any portion of a qualified refinery (other than a qualified refinery which is separate from any existing refinery), which meets the requirements of subsection (e),

(D) which meets all applicable environmental laws in effect on the date such portion was placed in service,

(E) no written binding contract for the construction of which was in effect on or before June 14, 2005, and

(F)(i) the construction of which is subject to a written binding construction contract entered into before January 1, 2010,

(ii) which is placed in service before January 1, 2010, or

(iii) in the case of self-constructed property, the construction of which began after June 14, 2005, and before January 1, 2010.

(2) **Special rule for sale-leasebacks.** For purposes of paragraph (1)(A), if property is—

(A) originally placed in service after the date of the enactment of this section by a person, and

(B) sold and leased back by such person within 3 months after the date such property was originally placed in service,

such property shall be treated as originally placed in service not earlier than the date on which such property is used under the leaseback referred to in subparagraph (B).

(3) **Effect of waiver under Clean Air Act.** A waiver under the Clean Air Act shall not be taken into account in determining whether the requirements of paragraph (1)(D) are met.

(d) Qualified refinery.

For purposes of this section, the term "qualified refinery" means any refinery located in the United States which is designed to serve the primary purpose of processing liquid fuel from crude oil or qualified fuels (as defined in section 45K(c)), or directly from shale or tar sands.

(e) Production capacity.

The requirements of this subsection are met if the portion of the qualified refinery—

(1) enables the existing qualified refinery to increase total volume output (determined without regard to asphalt or lube oil) by 5 percent or more on an average daily basis, or

(2) enables the existing qualified refinery to process shale, tar sands, or qualified fuels (as defined in section 45K(c)) at a rate which is equal to or greater than 25 percent of the total throughput of such qualified refinery on an average daily basis.

(f) Ineligible refinery property.

No deduction shall be allowed under subsection (a) for any qualified refinery property—

(1) the primary purpose of which is for use as a topping plant, asphalt plant, lube oil facility, crude or product terminal, or blending facility, or

(2) which is built solely to comply with consent decrees or projects mandated by Federal, State, or local governments.

(g) Election to allocate deduction to cooperative owner.

(1) **In general.** If—

(A) a taxpayer to which subsection (a) applies is an organization to which part I of subchapter T applies, and

(B) one or more persons directly holding an ownership interest in the taxpayer are organizations to which part I of subchapter T apply,

the taxpayer may elect to allocate all or a portion of the deduction allowable under subsection (a) to such persons. Such allocation shall be equal to the person's ratable share of the total amount allocated, determined on the basis of the person's ownership interest in the taxpayer. The taxable income of the taxpayer shall not be reduced under section 1382 by reason of any amount to which the preceding sentence applies.

(2) **Form and effect of election.** An election under paragraph (1) for any taxable year shall be made on a timely filed return for such year. Such election, once made, shall be irrevocable for such taxable year.

(3) **Written notice to owners.** If any portion of the deduction available under subsection (a) is allocated to owners under paragraph (1), the cooperative shall provide any owner receiving an allocation written notice of the amount of the allocation. Such notice shall be provided before the date on which the return described in paragraph (2) is due.

(h) Reporting.

No deduction shall be allowed under subsection (a) to any taxpayer for any taxable year unless such taxpayer files with the Secretary a report containing such information with respect to the operation of the refineries of the taxpayer as the Secretary shall require.

In 2008, P.L. 110-343, Sec. 209(a)(1)DivB, substituted "January 1, 2014" for "January 1, 2012" in subpara. (c)(1)(B) ... Sec. 209(a)(2)DivB, substituted "January 1, 2010" for "January 1, 2008" each place it appeared in subpara. (c)(1)(F) ... Sec. 209(b)(1)DivB, added ", or directly from shale or tar sands" after "(as defined in section 45K(c))" in subsec. (d) ... Sec. 209(b)(2)DivB, added "shale, tar sands, or" before "qualified fuels" in para. (e)(2), effective for property placed in service after 10/3/2008.

In 2005, P.L. 109-58, Sec. 1323(a), added Code Sec. 179C, effective for properties placed in service after 8/8/2005.

Deductions   Code Sec. 179D(f)

Sec. 179D. Energy efficient commercial buildings deduction.

(a) In general.

There shall be allowed as a deduction an amount equal to the cost of energy efficient commercial building property placed in service during the taxable year.

(b) Maximum amount of deduction.

The deduction under subsection (a) with respect to any building for any taxable year shall not exceed the excess (if any) of—

  (1) the product of—

    (A) $1.80, and

    (B) the square footage of the building, over

  (2) the aggregate amount of the deductions under subsection (a) with respect to the building for all prior taxable years.

(c) Definitions.

For purposes of this section—

  (1) Energy efficient commercial building property. The term "energy efficient commercial building property" means property—

    (A) with respect to which depreciation (or amortization in lieu of depreciation) is allowable,

    (B) which is installed on or in any building which is—

      (i) located in the United States, and

      (ii) within the scope of Standard 90.1–2001,

    (C) which is installed as part of—

      (i) the interior lighting systems,

      (ii) the heating, cooling, ventilation, and hot water systems, or

      (iii) the building envelope, and

    (D) which is certified in accordance with subsection (d)(6) as being installed as part of a plan designed to reduce the total annual energy and power costs with respect to the interior lighting systems, heating, cooling, ventilation, and hot water systems of the building by 50 percent or more in comparison to a reference building which meets the minimum requirements of Standard 90.1–2001 using methods of calculation under subsection (d)(2).

  (2) Standard 90.1–2001. The term "Standard 90.1–2001" means Standard 90.1–2001 of the American Society of Heating, Refrigerating, and Air Conditioning Engineers and the Illuminating Engineering Society of North America (as in effect on April 2, 2003).

(d) Special rules.

  (1) Partial allowance.

    (A) In general. Except as provided in subsection (f), if—

      (i) the requirement of subsection (c)(1)(D) is not met, but

      (ii) there is a certification in accordance with paragraph (6) that any system referred to in subsection (c)(1)(C) satisfies the energy-savings targets established by the Secretary under subparagraph (B) with respect to such system,

then the requirement of subsection (c)(1)(D) shall be treated as met with respect to such system, and the deduction under subsection (a) shall be allowed with respect to energy efficient commercial building property installed as part of such system and as part of a plan to meet such targets, except that subsection (b) shall be applied to such property by substituting "$.60" for "$1.80".

    (B) Regulations. The Secretary, after consultation with the Secretary of Energy, shall establish a target for each system described in subsection (c)(1)(C) which, if such targets were met for all such systems, the building would meet the requirements of subsection (c)(1)(D).

  (2) Methods of calculation. The Secretary, after consultation with the Secretary of Energy, shall promulgate regulations which describe in detail methods for calculating and verifying energy and power consumption and cost, based on the provisions of the 2005 California Nonresidential Alternative Calculation Method Approval Manual.

  (3) Computer software.

    (A) In general. Any calculation under paragraph (2) shall be prepared by qualified computer software.

    (B) Qualified computer software. For purposes of this paragraph, the term "qualified computer software" means software—

      (i) for which the software designer has certified that the software meets all procedures and detailed methods for calculating energy and power consumption and costs as required by the Secretary,

      (ii) which provides such forms as required to be filed by the Secretary in connection with energy efficiency of property and the deduction allowed under this section, and

      (iii) which provides a notice form which documents the energy efficiency features of the building and its projected annual energy costs.

  (4) Allocation of deduction for public property. In the case of energy efficient commercial building property installed on or in property owned by a Federal, State, or local government or a political subdivision thereof, the Secretary shall promulgate a regulation to allow the allocation of the deduction to the person primarily responsible for designing the property in lieu of the owner of such property. Such person shall be treated as the taxpayer for purposes of this section.

  (5) Notice to owner. Each certification required under this section shall include an explanation to the building owner regarding the energy efficiency features of the building and its projected annual energy costs as provided in the notice under paragraph (3)(B)(iii).

  (6) Certification.

    (A) In general. The Secretary shall prescribe the manner and method for the making of certifications under this section.

    (B) Procedures. The Secretary shall include as part of the certification process procedures for inspection and testing by qualified individuals described in subparagraph (C) to ensure compliance of buildings with energy-savings plans and targets. Such procedures shall be comparable, given the difference between commercial and residential buildings, to the requirements in the Mortgage Industry National Accreditation Procedures for Home Energy Rating Systems.

    (C) Qualified individuals. Individuals qualified to determine compliance shall be only those individuals who are recognized by an organization certified by the Secretary for such purposes.

(e) Basis reduction.

For purposes of this subtitle, if a deduction is allowed under this section with respect to any energy efficient commercial building property, the basis of such property shall be reduced by the amount of the deduction so allowed.

(f) Interim rules for lighting systems.

Until such time as the Secretary issues final regulations under subsection (d)(1)(B) with respect to property which is part of a lighting system—

(1) **In general.** The lighting system target under subsection (d)(1)(A)(ii) shall be a reduction in lighting power density of 25 percent (50 percent in the case of a warehouse) of the minimum requirements in Table 9.3.1.1 or Table 9.3.1.2 (not including additional interior lighting power allowances) of Standard 90.1–2001.

(2) **Reduction in deduction if reduction less than 40 percent.**

(A) In general. If, with respect to the lighting system of any building other than a warehouse, the reduction in lighting power density of the lighting system is not at least 40 percent, only the applicable percentage of the amount of deduction otherwise allowable under this section with respect to such property shall be allowed.

(B) Applicable percentage. For purposes of subparagraph (A), the applicable percentage is the number of percentage points (not greater than 100) equal to the sum of—

(i) 50, and

(ii) the amount which bears the same ratio to 50 as the excess of the reduction of lighting power density of the lighting system over 25 percentage points bears to 15.

(C) Exceptions. This subsection shall not apply to any system—

(i) the controls and circuiting of which do not comply fully with the mandatory and prescriptive requirements of Standard 90.1–2001 and which do not include provision for bilevel switching in all occupancies except hotel and motel guest rooms, store rooms, restrooms, and public lobbies, or

(ii) which does not meet the minimum requirements for calculated lighting levels as set forth in the Illuminating Engineering Society of North America Lighting Handbook, Performance and Application, Ninth Edition, 2000.

(g) **Regulations.**

The Secretary shall promulgate such regulations as necessary—

(1) to take into account new technologies regarding energy efficiency and renewable energy for purposes of determining energy efficiency and savings under this section, and

(2) to provide for a recapture of the deduction allowed under this section if the plan described in subsection (c)(1)(D) or (d)(1)(A) is not fully implemented.

(h) **Termination.**

This section shall not apply with respect to property placed in service after December 31, 2013.

In **2008,** P.L. 110-343, Sec. 303DivB, substituted "December 31, 2013" for "December 31, 2008" in subsec. (h), effective 10/3/2008.

In **2006,** P.L. 109-432, Sec. 204, substituted "December 31, 2008" for "December 31, 2007" in subsec. (h), enacted 12/20/2006.

In **2005,** P.L. 109-58, Sec. 1331(a), added Code Sec. 179D, effective for property placed in service after 12/31/2005.

Sec. 179E. Election to expense advanced mine safety equipment.

(a) **Treatment as expenses.**

A taxpayer may elect to treat 50 percent of the cost of any qualified advanced mine safety equipment property as an expense which is not chargeable to capital account. Any cost so treated shall be allowed as a deduction for the taxable year in which the qualified advanced mine safety equipment property is placed in service.

(b) **Election.**

(1) **In general.** An election under this section for any taxable year shall be made on the taxpayer's return of the tax imposed by this chapter for the taxable year. Such election shall specify the advanced mine safety equipment property to which the election applies and shall be made in such manner as the Secretary may by regulations prescribe.

(2) **Election irrevocable.** Any election made under this section may not be revoked except with the consent of the Secretary.

(c) **Qualified advanced mine safety equipment property.**

For purposes of this section, the term "qualified advanced mine safety equipment property" means any advanced mine safety equipment property for use in any underground mine located in the United States—

(1) the original use of which commences with the taxpayer, and

(2) which is placed in service by the taxpayer after the date of the enactment of this section.

(d) **Advanced mine safety equipment property.**

For purposes of this section, the term "advanced mine safety equipment property" means any of the following:

(1) Emergency communication technology or device which is used to allow a miner to maintain constant communication with an individual who is not in the mine.

(2) Electronic identification and location device which allows an individual who is not in the mine to track at all times the movements and location of miners working in or at the mine.

(3) Emergency oxygen-generating, self-rescue device which provides oxygen for at least 90 minutes.

(4) Pre-positioned supplies of oxygen which (in combination with self-rescue devices) can be used to provide each miner on a shift, in the event of an accident or other event which traps the miner in the mine or otherwise necessitates the use of such a self rescue device, the ability to survive for at least 48 hours.

(5) Comprehensive atmospheric monitoring system which monitors the levels of carbon monoxide, methane, and oxygen that are present in all areas of the mine and which can detect smoke in the case of a fire in a mine.

(e) **Coordination with section 179.**

No expenditures shall be taken into account under subsection (a) with respect to the portion of the cost of any property specified in an election under section 179.

(f) **Reporting.**

No deduction shall be allowed under subsection (a) to any taxpayer for any taxable year unless such taxpayer files with the Secretary a report containing such information with respect to the operation of the mines of the taxpayer as the Secretary shall require.

(g) **Termination.**

This section shall not apply to property placed in service after December 31, 2011.

In **2010,** P.L. 111-312, Sec. 743(a), substituted "December 31, 2011" for "December 31, 2009" in subsec. (g), effective for property placed in service after 12/31/2009.

In **2008,** P.L. 110-343, Sec. 311DivC, substituted "December 31, 2009" for "December 31, 2008" in subsec. (g), effective 10/3/2008.

In **2006,** P.L. 109-432, Sec. 404(a), added Code Sec. 179E, effective for costs paid or incurred after 12/20/2006.

Sec. 180. Expenditures by farmers for fertilizer, etc.

(a) **In general.**

A taxpayer engaged in the business of farming may elect to treat as expenses which are not chargeable to capital account expenditures (otherwise chargeable to capital account)

Deductions Code Sec. 181

which are paid or incurred by him during the taxable year for the purchase or acquisition of fertilizer, lime, ground limestone, marl, or other materials to enrich, neutralize, or condition land used in farming, or for the application of such materials to such land. The expenditures so treated shall be allowed as a deduction.

(b) Land used in farming.

For purposes of subsection (a), the term "land used in farming" means land used (before or simultaneously with the expenditures described in subsection (a)) by the taxpayer or his tenant for the production of crops, fruits, or other agricultural products or for the sustenance of livestock.

(c) Election.

The election under subsection (a) for any taxable year shall be made within the time prescribed by law (including extensions thereof) for filing the return for such taxable year. Such election shall be made in such manner as the Secretary may by regulations prescribe. Such election may not be revoked except with the consent of the Secretary.

In **1976**, P.L. 94-455, Sec. 1906(b)(13)(A), substituted "Secretary" for "Secretary or his delegate" in subsec. (c), effective for tax. yrs. begin. after 12/31/76.

In **1960**, P.L. 86-779, Sec. 6(a), added Code Sec. 180, effective for tax. yrs. begin. after '59.

Sec. 181. Treatment of certain qualified film and television productions.

(a) Election to treat costs as expenses.

(1) **In general.** A taxpayer may elect to treat the cost of any qualified film or television production as an expense which is not chargeable to capital account. Any cost so treated shall be allowed as a deduction.

(2) **Dollar limitation.**

(A) **In general.** Paragraph (1) shall not apply to so much of the aggregate cost of any qualified film or television production as exceeds $15,000,000.

(B) **Higher dollar limitation for productions in certain areas.** In the case of any qualified film or television production the aggregate cost of which is significantly incurred in an area eligible for designation as—

(i) a low-income community under section 45D, or

(ii) a distressed county or isolated area of distress by the Delta Regional Authority established under section 2009aa-1 of title 7, United States Code,

subparagraph (A) shall be applied by substituting "$20,000,000" for "$15,000,000".

(b) No other deduction or amortization deduction allowable.

With respect to the basis of any qualified film or television production to which an election is made under subsection (a), no other depreciation or amortization deduction shall be allowable.

(c) Election.

(1) **In general.** An election under this section with respect to any qualified film or television production shall be made in such manner as prescribed by the Secretary and by the due date (including extensions) for filing the taxpayer's return of tax under this chapter for the taxable year in which costs of the production are first incurred.

(2) **Revocation of election.** Any election made under this section may not be revoked without the consent of the Secretary.

(d) Qualified film or television production.

For purposes of this section—

(1) **In general.** The term "qualified film or television production" means any production described in paragraph (2) if 75 percent of the total compensation of the production is qualified compensation.

(2) **Production.**

(A) **In general.** A production is described in this paragraph if such production is property described in section 168(f)(3).

(B) **Special rules for television series.** In the case of a television series—

(i) each episode of such series shall be treated as a separate production, and

(ii) only the first 44 episodes of such series shall be taken into account.

(C) **Exception.** A production is not described in this paragraph if records are required under section 2257 of title 18, United States Code, to be maintained with respect to any performer in such production.

(3) **Qualified compensation.** For purposes of paragraph (1)—

(A) **In general.** The term "qualified compensation" means compensation for services performed in the United States by actors, production personnel, directors, and producers.

(B) **Participations and residuals excluded.** The term "compensation" does not include participations and residuals (as defined in section 167(g)(7)(B)).

(e) Application of certain other rules.

For purposes of this section, rules similar to the rules of subsections (b)(2) and (c)(4) of section 194 shall apply.

(f) Termination.

This section shall not apply to qualified film and television productions commencing after December 31, 2011.

In **2010**, P.L. 111-312, Sec. 744(a), substituted "December 31, 2011" for "December 31, 2009" in subsec. (f), effective for productions commencing after 12/31/2009.

In **2008**, P.L. 110-343, Sec. 502(a)DivC, substituted "December 31, 2009" for "December 31, 2008" in subsec. (f)... Sec. 502(b)DivC, amended subpara. (a)(2)(A)... Sec. 502(d)DivC, substituted "actors, production personnel, directors, and producers." for "actors, directors, producers, and other relevant production personnel." in subpara. (d)(3)(A), effective for qualified film and television productions commencing after 12/31/2007.

Prior to amendment subpara. (a)(2)(A) read as follows:

"(A) **In general.** Paragraph (1) shall not apply to any qualified film or television production the aggregate cost of which exceeds $15,000,000."

In **2005**, P.L. 109-135, Sec. 403(e)(1), deleted "For purposes of a television series, only the first 44 episodes of such series may be taken into account." at the end of subpara. (d)(2)(A), redesignated subpara. (d)(2)(B) as (C), and added subpara. (d)(2)(B), effective for qualified film and television productions (as defined in Code Sec. 181(d)(1), as added by Sec. 244(a) of P.L. 108-357) commencing after 10/22/2004.

In **2004**, P.L. 108-357, Sec. 244(a), added Code Sec. 181, effective for qualified film and television productions (as defined in Code Sec. 181(d)(1), as added by Sec. 244(a) of this Act) commencing after 10/22/2004.

Sec. 181. Repealed.

In **1964**, P.L. 88-272, repealed Code Sec. 181 effective for property placed in service after '63, with respect to tax. yrs. end. after '63, and in case of property placed in service before '64, with respect to tax. yrs. begin. after '63. Code Sec. 181 had been added by P.L. 87-834 for tax. yrs. end. after '61 and provided:

"SEC. 181. DEDUCTION FOR CERTAIN UNUSED INVESTMENT CREDIT.

"If the amount of the credit determined under section 46(a)(1) for any taxable year exceeds the limitation provided by section 46(a)(2) for such taxable year and if the amount of such excess has not, after the application of section 46(b), been allowed to the taxpayer as a credit under section 38 for any taxable year, then an amount equal to the amount of such excess not so allowed as a credit shall be allowed to the taxpayer as a deduction for the first taxable year following the last taxable year in which such excess could under section 46(b) have been allowed as a credit. If a taxpayer dies or ceases to exist prior to the first taxable year following the last taxable year in which the excess described in the preceding sentence could under section 46(b) have been allowed as a credit, the amount described in the preceding sentence, or the proper portion thereof, shall, under regulations prescribed by the Secretary or his delegate, be allowed to the taxpayer as a deduction for the taxable year in which such death or cessation occurs."

Sec. 182. Repealed.

In **1986**, P.L. 99-514, Sec. 402(a), repealed Code Sec. 182, effective for amounts paid or incurred after 12/31/85, in tax. yrs. end. after 12/31/85.
Prior to repeal Code Sec. 182 read as follows:

"SEC. 182. EXPENDITURES BY FARMERS FOR CLEARING LAND.

"(a) In general.

"A taxpayer engaged in the business of farming may elect to treat expenditures which are paid or incurred by him during the taxable year in the clearing of land for the purpose of making such land suitable for use in farming as expenses which are not chargeable to capital account. The expenditures so treated shall be allowed as a deduction.

"(b) Limitation.

"The amount deductible under subsection (a) for any taxable year shall not exceed whichever of the following amounts is the lesser:

"(1) $5,000, or

"(2) 25 percent of the taxable income derived from farming during the taxable year.

For purposes of paragraph (2), the term 'taxable income derived from farming' means the gross income derived from farming reduced by the deductions allowed by this chapter (other than by this section) which are attributable to the business of farming.

"(c) Definitions.

"For purposes of subsection (a)—

"(1) The term 'clearing of land' includes (but is not limited to) the eradication of trees, stumps, and brush, the treatment or moving of earth, and the diversion of streams and watercourses.

"(2) The term 'land suitable for use in farming' means land which as a result of the activities described in paragraph (1) is suitable for use by the taxpayer or his tenant for the production of crops, fruits, or other agricultural products or for the sustenance of livestock.

"(d) Exceptions, etc.

"(1) Exceptions. The expenditures to which subsection (a) applies shall not include—

"(A) the purchase, construction, installation, or improvement of structures, appliances, or facilities which are of a character which is subject to the allowance for depreciation provided in section 167, or

"(B) any amount paid or incurred which is allowable as a deduction without regard to this section.

"(2) Certain property used in the clearing of land.

"(A) Allowance for depreciation. The expenditures to which subsection (a) applies shall include a reasonable allowance for depreciation with respect to property of the taxpayer which is used in the clearing of land for the purpose of making such land suitable for use in farming and which, if used in a trade or business, would be property subject to the allowance for depreciation provided by section 167.

"(B) Treatment as depreciation deduction. For purposes of this chapter, any expenditure described in subparagraph (A) shall, to the extent allowed as a deduction under subsection (a), be treated as an amount allowed under section 167 for exhaustion, wear and tear, or obsolescence of the property which is used in the clearing of land.

"(e) Election.

"The election under subsection (a) for any taxable year shall be made within the time prescribed by law (including extensions thereof) for filing the return for such taxable year. Such election shall be made in such manner as the Secretary may by regulations prescribe. Such election may not be revoked except with the consent of the Secretary."

In **1976**, P.L. 94-455, Sec. 1906(b)(13)(A), substituted "Secretary" for "Secretary or his delegate" each place it appeared in subsec. (e), effective for tax. yrs. begin. after 12/31/76.

In **1962**, P.L. 87-834, Sec. 21, added Code Sec. 182, effective for tax. yrs. begin. after 12/31/62.

Sec. 183. Activities not engaged in for profit.

(a) General rule.

In the case of an activity engaged in by an individual or an S corporation, if such activity is not engaged in for profit, no deduction attributable to such activity shall be allowed under this chapter except as provided in this section.

(b) Deductions allowable.

In the case of an activity not engaged in for profit to which subsection (a) applies, there shall be allowed—

(1) the deductions which would be allowable under this chapter for the taxable year without regard to whether or not such activity is engaged in for profit, and

(2) a deduction equal to the amount of the deductions which would be allowable under this chapter for the taxable year only if such activity were engaged in for profit, but only to the extent that the gross income derived from such activity for the taxable year exceeds the deductions allowable by reason of paragraph (1).

(c) Activity not engaged in for profit defined.

For purposes of this section, the term "activity not engaged in for profit" means any activity other than one with respect to which deductions are allowable for the taxable year under section 162 or under paragraph (1) or (2) of section 212.

(d) Presumption.

If the gross income derived from an activity for 3 or more of the taxable years in the period of 5 consecutive taxable years which ends with the taxable year exceeds the deductions attributable to such activity (determined without regard to whether or not such activity is engaged in for profit), then, unless the Secretary establishes to the contrary, such activity shall be presumed for purposes of this chapter for such taxable year to be an activity engaged in for profit. In the case of an activity which consists in major part of the breeding, training, showing, or racing of horses, the preceding sentence shall be applied by substituting "2" for "3" and "7" for "5".

(e) Special rule.

(1) In general. A determination as to whether the presumption provided by subsection (d) applies with respect to any activity shall, if the taxpayer so elects, not be made before the close of the fourth taxable year (sixth taxable year, in the case of an activity described in the last sentence of such subsection) following the taxable year in which the taxpayer first engages in the activity. For purposes of the preceding sentence, a taxpayer shall be treated as not having engaged in an activity during any taxable year beginning before January 1, 1970.

(2) Initial period. If the taxpayer makes an election under paragraph (1), the presumption provided by subsection (d) shall apply to each taxable year in the 5-taxable year (or 7-taxable year) period beginning with the taxable year in which the taxpayer first engages in the activity, if the gross income derived from the activity for 3 (or 2 if applicable) or more of the taxable years in such period exceeds the deductions attributable to the activity (determined without regard to whether or not the activity is engaged in for profit).

(3) Election. An election under paragraph (1) shall be made at such time and manner, and subject to such terms and conditions, as the Secretary may prescribe.

(4) Time for assessing deficiency attributable to activity. If a taxpayer makes an election under paragraph (1) with respect to an activity, the statutory period for the assessment of any deficiency attributable to such activity shall not expire before the expiration of 2 years after the date prescribed by law (determined without extensions) for filing the return of tax under chapter 1 for the last taxable year in the period of 5 taxable years (or 7 taxable years) to which the election relates. Such deficiency may be assessed notwithstanding the provisions of any law or rule of law which would otherwise prevent such an assessment.

In **1988**, P.L. 100-647, Sec. 1001(h)(3), substituted "3 (or 2 if applicable)" for "2", in para. (e)(2), effective for tax. yrs. begin. after 12/31/86.

In **1986**, P.L. 99-514, Sec. 143(a)(1), substituted "3 or more of the taxable years" for "2 or more of the taxable years" in subsec. (d) . . . Sec. 143(a)(2), amended the last sentence of subsec. (d), effective for tax. yrs. begin. after 12/31/86.
Prior to amendment, the last sentence of subsec. (d) read as follows:

"In the case of an activity which consists in major part of the breeding, training, showing, or racing of horses, the preceding sentence shall be applied by substituting the period of 7 consecutive taxable years for the period of 5 consecutive taxable years."

In **1982**, P.L. 97-354, Sec. 5(a)(23), substituted "an S corporation" for "an electing small business corporation (as defined in section 1371(b))" in subsec. (a), effective for tax. yrs. begin. after 12/31/82.

In 1976, P.L. 94-455, Sec. 214(a), added para. (e)(4), effective for tax. yrs. begin. after 12/31/69 but not for any tax. yr. end. before 10/4/76 for which the period for assessing a deficiency expired before 10/4/76.

—P.L. 94-455, Sec. 1906(b)(13)(A), substituted "Secretary" for "Secretary or his delegate" in subsec. (d) and para. (e)(3), effective for tax. yrs. begin. after 12/31/76.

In 1971, P.L. 92-178, Sec. 311, added subsec. (e), effective for tax. yrs. begin. after 12/31/69.

In 1969, P.L. 91-172, Sec. 213(a), added Code Sec. 183, effective for tax. yrs. begin. after 12/31/69.

Sec. 184. Repealed.

In 1990, P.L. 101-508, Sec. 11801(a)(12), repealed Code Sec. 184, effective 11/5/90 except as provided in Sec. 11821(b) of this Act, which reads as follows:
"(b) *Savings provision.*
"If—
"(1) any provision amended or repealed by this part applied to—
"(A) any transaction occurring before the date of the enactment of this Act [11/5/90],
"(B) any property acquired before such date of enactment [11/5/90], or
"(C) any item of income, loss, deduction, or credit taken into account before such date of enactment [11/5/90], and
"(2) the treatment of such transaction, property, or item under such provision would (without regard to the amendments made by this part) affect liability for tax for periods ending after such date of enactment [11/5/90],
nothing in the amendments made by this part shall be construed to affect the treatment of such transaction, property, or item for purposes of determining liability for tax for periods ending after such date of enactment [11/5/90]."
Prior to repeal, Code Sec. 184 reads as follows:
"SEC. 184. AMORTIZATION OF CERTAIN RAILROAD ROLLING STOCK.
"(a) *Allowance of deduction.*
"Every person, at his election, shall be entitled to a deduction with respect to the amortization of the adjusted basis (for determining gain) of any qualified railroad rolling stock (as defined in subsection (d)), based on a period of 60 months. Such amortization deduction shall be an amount, with respect to each month of such period within the taxable year, equal to the adjusted basis of the qualified railroad rolling stock at the end of such month divided by the number of months (including the month for which the deduction is computed) remaining in the period. Such adjusted basis at the end of the month shall be computed without regard to the amortization deduction for such month. The amortization deduction provided by this section with respect to any qualified railroad rolling stock for any month shall be in lieu of the depreciation deduction with respect to such rolling stock for such month provided by section 167. The 60-month period shall begin, as to any qualified railroad rolling stock, at the election of the taxpayer, with the month following the month in which such rolling stock was placed in service or with the succeeding taxable year.
"(b) *Election of amortization.*
"The election of the taxpayer to take the amortization deduction and to begin the 60-month period with the month following the month in which the qualified railroad rolling stock was placed in service, or with the taxable year succeeding the taxable year in which such rolling stock is placed in service, shall be made by filing with the Secretary, in such manner, in such form, and within such time, as the Secretary may by regulations prescribe, a statement of such election.
"(c) *Termination of amortization deduction.*
"A taxpayer which has elected under subsection (b) to take the amortization deduction provided by subsection (a) may, at any time after making such election, discontinue the amortization deduction with respect to the remainder of the amortization period, such discontinuance to begin as of the beginning of any month specified by the taxpayer in a notice in writing filed with the Secretary before the beginning of such month. The depreciation deduction provided under section 167 shall be allowed, beginning with the first month as to which the amortization deduction does not apply, and the taxpayer shall not be entitled to any further amortization deduction under this section with respect to such rolling stock.
"(d) *Qualified railroad rolling stock.*
"Except as provided in subsection (e)(4), the term 'qualified railroad rolling stock' means, for purposes of this section, rolling stock of the type used by a common carrier engaged in the furnishing or sale of transportation by railroad and subject to the jurisdiction of the Interstate Commerce Commission if—
"(1) such rolling stock is—
"(A) used by a domestic common carrier by railroad on a full-time basis, or on a part-time basis if its only additional use is an incidental use by a Canadian or Mexican common carrier by railroad on a per diem basis, or
"(B) owned and used by a switching or terminal company all of whose stock is owned by one or more domestic common carriers by railroad, and
"(2) the original use of such rolling stock commences with the taxpayer after December 31, 1968.
"(e) *Special rules.*
"(1) In general. Except as otherwise provided in this subsection, this section shall apply to qualified railroad rolling stock placed in service after 1968 and before 1976.
"(2) Placed in service in 1969. If any qualified railroad rolling stock is placed in service in 1969—
"(A) the month as to which the amortization period shall begin with respect to such rolling stock shall be determined as if such rolling stock were placed in service on December 31, 1969, and

"(B) subsections (a) and (b) shall be applied by substituting '48' for '60' each place that it appears in such subsections.
This section shall not apply to any qualified railroad rolling stock placed in service in 1969 and owned by any person who is not a domestic common carrier by railroad, or a corporation at least 95 percent of the stock of which is owned by one or more such common carriers.
"(3) Placed in service in 1970. If any qualified railroad rolling stock is placed in service in 1970 by a domestic common carrier by railroad or by a corporation at least 95 percent of the stock of which is owned by one or more such common carriers, then subsection (a) shall be applied, without regard to paragraph (2), as if such rolling stock were placed in service on December 31, 1969.
"(4) Railroad rolling stock not in short supply. The Secretary shall determine (with the assistance of the Secretary of Transportation) which types of railroad rolling stock are not in short supply and shall prescribe regulations designating such types. The term 'qualified railroad rolling stock' shall not include any rolling stock which—
"(A) is of the type of rolling stock designated by such regulations as not in short supply, and
"(B) is placed in service after (i) 1972, or (ii) 30 days after the date on which such regulations are promulgated, whichever is later.
"(5) Adjusted basis.
"(A) The adjusted basis of any qualified railroad rolling stock, with respect to which an election has been made under this section, shall not be increased, for purposes of this section, for amounts chargeable to capital account for additions or improvements after the amortization period has begun.
"(B) Costs incurred in connection with a used unit of railroad rolling stock which are properly chargeable to capital account shall be treated as a separate unit of railroad rolling stock for purposes of this section.
"(C) The depreciation deduction provided by section 167 shall, despite the provisions of subsection (a), be allowed with respect to the portion of the adjusted basis which is not taken into account in applying this section.
"(6) Constructive termination. If at any time during the amortization period any qualified railroad rolling stock ceases to meet the requirements of subsection (d)(1), the taxpayer shall be deemed to have terminated under subsection (c) his election under this section. Such termination shall be effective beginning with the month following the month in which such cessation occurs.
"(7) Method of accounting for date placed in service. For purposes of subsections (a) and (b), in the case of qualified railroad rolling stock placed in service after December 31, 1969, and before January 1, 1976, the taxpayer may elect (unless paragraph (3) is applicable) to begin the 60-month period with the date when such rolling stock is treated as having been placed in service under a method of accounting for acquisitions and retirements of property which—
"(A) prescribes a date when property is placed in service, and
"(B) is consistently followed by the taxpayer.
"(f) *Life tenant and remainderman.*
"In the case of qualified railroad rolling stock leased to a domestic common carrier, and held by one person for life with remainder to another person, the deduction under this section shall be computed as if the life tenant were the absolute owner of the property and shall be allowable to the life tenant.
"(g) *Cross reference.*
"For treatment of certain gain derived from the disposition of property the adjusted basis of which is determined with regard to this section, see section 1245."
In 1976, P.L. 94-455, Sec. 1906(b)(13)(A), substituted "Secretary" for "Secretary or his delegate" each place it appeared in Code Sec. 184, effective for tax. yrs. begin. after 12/31/76.

In 1975, P.L. 93-625, Sec. 3(b), substituted "1976" for "1975" in paras. (e)(1) and (e)(7), effective 1/3/75.

In 1969, P.L. 91-172, Sec. 705(a), added Code Sec. 184, effective for tax. yrs. begin. after 12/31/69.

Sec. 185. Repealed.

In 1986, P.L. 99-514, Sec. 242(a), repealed Code Sec. 185, effective for that portion of the basis of any property which is attributable to expenditures paid or incurred after 12/31/86, except as provided in Sec. 242(c)(2) of this Act:
"(2) Transitional rule.—The amendments made by this section shall not apply to any expenditure incurred—
"(A) pursuant to a binding contract entered into before March 2, 1986, or
"(B) with respect to any improvement commenced before March 2, 1986, but only if not less than the lesser of $1,000,000 or 5 percent of the aggregate cost of such improvement has been incurred or committed before such date.
The preceding sentence shall not apply to any expenditure with respect to an improvement placed in service after December 31, 1987."
Prior to repeal, Code Sec. 185 read as follows:
"SEC. 185. AMORTIZATION OF RAILROAD GRADING AND TUNNEL BORES.
"(a) *General rule.*
"In the case of a domestic common carrier by railroad, the taxpayer shall, at his election, be entitled to a deduction with respect to the amortization of the adjusted basis (for determining gain) of his qualified railroad grading and tunnel bores. The amortization deduction provided by this section with respect to such property shall be in lieu of any depreciation deduction, or other amortization deduction, with respect to such property for any taxable year to which the election applies.
"(b) *Amount of deduction.*
"(1) In general. The deduction allowable under subsection (a) for any taxable year shall be an amount determined by amortizing ratably over a period of 50 years the adjusted basis (for determining gain) of the qualified railroad grading

and tunnel bores of the taxpayer. Such 50-year period shall commence with the first taxable year for which an election under this section is effective.

"(2) Special rule. In the case of qualified railroad grading and tunnel bores placed in service after the beginning of the first taxable year for which an election under this section is effective, the 50-year period with respect to such property shall begin with the year following the year the property is placed in service.

"(c) Election of amortization.

"The election of the taxpayer to take the amortization deduction provided in subsection (a) may be made for any taxable year beginning after December 31, 1969. Such election shall be made by filing with the Secretary, in such manner, in such form, and within such time, as the Secretary may by regulations prescribe, a statement of such election. The election shall remain in effect for all taxable years subsequent to the first year for which it is effective and shall apply to all qualified railroad grading and tunnel bores of the taxpayer, unless, on application by the taxpayer, the Secretary permits him, subject to such conditions as the Secretary deems necessary, to revoke such election.

"(d) Election with respect to pre-1969 property.

"A taxpayer may, for any taxable year beginning after December 31, 1974, elect for purposes of this section to treat the term 'qualified railroad grading and tunnel bores' as including pre-1969 railroad grading and tunnel bores. An election under this subsection shall be made by filing with the Secretary, in such manner, in such form, and within such time, as the Secretary may by regulations prescribe, a statement of such election. The election under this subsection shall remain in effect for all taxable years, after the first year for which it is effective, for which an election under subsection (c) is effective. The election under this subsection shall apply to all pre-1969 railroad grading and tunnel bores of the taxpayer, unless, on application by the taxpayer, the Secretary permits him, subject to such conditions as the Secretary deems necessary, to revoke such election.

"(e) Adjusted basis for pre-1969 railroad grading and tunnel bores.

"(1) In general. The adjusted basis of any pre-1969 railroad grading and tunnel bore shall be determined under this subsection.

"(2) Property acquired or constructed after February 28, 1913.

"(A) In the case of pre-1969 railroad grading and tunnel bores—

"(i) acquired by the taxpayer after February 28, 1913, or

"(ii) the construction of which was completed by the taxpayer after February 28, 1913,

the adjusted basis of such property shall be equal to the adjusted basis (for determining gain) of such property in the hands of the taxpayer.

"(B) In the case of property described in subparagraph (A)(i)—

"(i) which was in existence on February 28, 1913,

"(ii) for which the taxpayer has a substituted basis, and

"(iii) such substituted basis for which would, but for the provisions of this section, be determined under section 1053,

then the adjusted basis of such property shall be determined as if such property were property described in paragraph (3)(A).

"(3) Property acquired or constructed before March 1, 1913.

"(A) In the case of pre-1969 railroad grading and tunnel bores—

"(i) acquired by the taxpayer before March 1, 1913, or

"(ii) the construction of which was completed by the taxpayer before March 1, 1913,

the adjusted basis of such property shall be determined under the provisions of subparagraph (B), (C), or (D) of this paragraph.

"(B) In the case of any property valued under an original valuation made by the Interstate Commerce Commission pursuant to subchapter V of chapter 107 of title 49, the adjusted basis of such property shall be equal to the amount ascertained by the Interstate Commerce Commission as of the date of such valuation to be such property's cost of reproduction new (as the term 'cost of reproduction new' is used in such subchapter V).

"(C) In the case of property which was not valued by the Interstate Commerce Commission in the manner described in subparagraph (B), but which was valued under an original valuation made by a comparable State regulatory body, the adjusted basis of such property shall be equal to the amount ascertained by such State regulatory body as of the date of its original valuation to be such property's value.

"(D) If, in the case of any property to which this paragraph applies—

"(i) neither subparagraph (B) nor (C) applies, or

"(ii) notwithstanding subparagraphs (B) and (C), either the taxpayer or the Secretary can establish the adjusted basis (for purposes of determining gain) of such property in the hands of the taxpayer,

then the adjusted basis of such property shall be equal to its adjusted basis (for purposes of determining gain) in the hands of the taxpayer.

"(f) Definitions.

"For purposes of this section—

"(1) Railroad grading and tunnel bores. The term 'railroad grading and tunnel bores' means all improvements resulting from excavations (including tunneling), construction of embankments, clearings, diversions of roads and streams, sodding of slopes, and from similar work necessary to provide, construct, reconstruct, alter, protect, improve, replace, or restore a roadbed or right-of-way for railroad track. If expenditures for improvements described in the preceding sentence are incurred with respect to an existing roadbed or right-of-way for railroad track, such expenditures shall be considered, in applying this section, as costs for railroad grading or tunnel bores placed in service in the year in which such costs are incurred.

"(2) Qualified railroad grading and tunnel bores. The term 'qualified railroad grading and tunnel bores' means railroad grading and tunnel bores the original use of which commences after December 31, 1968.

"(3) Pre-1969 railroad grading and tunnel bores. The term 'pre-1969 railroad grading and tunnel bores' means railroad grading and tunnel bores the original use of which commences before January 1, 1969.

"(g) Treatment upon retirement.

"If any qualified railroad grading or tunnel bore is retired or abandoned during a taxable year for which an election under this section is in effect, no deduction shall be allowed on account of such retirement or abandonment and the amortization deduction under this section shall continue with respect to such property. This subsection shall not apply if the retirement or abandonment is attributable primarily to fire, storm, or other casualty.

"(h) Investment credit not to be allowed.

"Property eligible to be amortized under this section shall not be treated as section 38 property within the meaning of section 48(a).

"(i) Regulations.

"The Secretary shall prescribe such regulations as may be necessary to carry out the purposes of this section.

"(j) Cross reference.

"For special rule with respect to certain gain derived from the disposition of property the adjusted basis of which is determined with regard to this section, see section 1245."

In 1978, P.L. 95-473, Sec. 2(a)(2)(B), substituted "subchapter V of chapter 107 of title 49" for "section 19a of part I of the Interstate Commerce Act (49 U.S.C. 19a)" and substituted "such subchapter V" for "such section 19a" in subpara. (e)(3)(B), effective 10/17/78.

In 1976, P.L. 94-455, Sec. 1702(a), redesignated subsecs. (d), (e), (f), (g) and (h) as subsecs. (f), (g), (h), (i) and (j), and added new subsecs. (d) and (e), effective 10/4/76.

— P.L. 94-455, Sec. 1702(b), added para. (f)(3), effective 10/4/76.

— P.L. 94-455, Sec. 1906(b)(13)(A), substituted "Secretary" for "Secretary or his delegate" each place it appeared in subsecs, (c) and (i), effective for tax. yrs. begin. after 12/31/76.

In 1969, P.L. 91-172, Sec. 705(a), added Code Sec. 185, for tax. yrs. begin. after 12/31/69.

Sec. 186. Recoveries of damages for antitrust violations, etc.

(a) Allowance of deduction.

If a compensatory amount which is included in gross income is received or accrued during the taxable year for a compensable injury, there shall be allowed as a deduction for the taxable year an amount equal to the lesser of—

(1) the amount of such compensatory amount, or

(2) the amount of the unrecovered losses sustained as a result of such compensable injury.

(b) Compensable injury.

For purposes of this section, the term "compensable injury" means—

(1) injuries sustained as a result of an infringement of a patent issued by the United States,

(2) injuries sustained as a result of a breach of contract or a breach of fiduciary duty or relationship, or

(3) injuries sustained in business, or to property, by reason of any conduct forbidden in the antitrust laws for which a civil action may be brought under section 4 of the Act entitled "An Act to supplement existing laws against unlawful restraints and monopolies, and for other purposes", approved October 15, 1914 (commonly known as the Clayton Act).

(c) Compensatory amount.

For purposes of this section, the term "compensatory amount" means the amount received or accrued during the taxable year as damages as a result of an award in, or in settlement of, a civil action for recovery for a compensable injury, reduced by any amounts paid or incurred in the taxable year in securing such award or settlement.

(d) Unrecovered losses.

(1) In general. For purposes of this section, the amount of any unrecovered loss sustained as a result of any compensable injury is—

(A) the sum of the amount of the net operating losses (as determined under section 172) for each taxable year in whole or in part within the injury period, to the extent that such net operating losses are attributable to such compensable injury, reduced by

Deductions Code Sec. 188

(B) the sum of—

(i) the amount of the net operating losses described in subparagraph (A) which were allowed for any prior taxable year as a deduction under section 172 as a net operating loss carryback or carryover to such taxable year, and

(ii) the amounts allowed as a deduction under subsection (a) for any prior taxable year for prior recoveries of compensatory amounts for such compensable injury.

(2) **Injury period.** For purposes of paragraph (1), the injury period is—

(A) with respect to any infringement of a patent, the period in which such infringement occurred,

(B) with respect to a breach of contract or breach of fiduciary duty or relationship, the period during which amounts would have been received or accrued but for the breach of contract or breach of fiduciary duty or relationship, and

(C) with respect to injuries sustained by reason of any conduct forbidden in the antitrust laws, the period in which such injuries were sustained.

(3) **Net operating losses attributable to compensable injuries.** For purposes of paragraph (1)—

(A) a net operating loss for any taxable year shall be treated as attributable to a compensable injury to the extent of the compensable injury sustained during such taxable year, and

(B) if only a portion of a net operating loss for any taxable year is attributable to a compensable injury, such portion shall (in applying section 172 for purposes of this section) be considered to be a separate net operating loss for such year to be applied after the other portion of such net operating loss.

(e) **Effect on net operating loss carryovers.**

If for the taxable year in which a compensatory amount is received or accrued any portion of a net operating loss carryover to such year is attributable to the compensable injury for which such amount is received or accrued, such portion of such net operating loss carryover shall be reduced by an amount equal to—

(1) the deduction allowed under subsection (a) with respect to such compensatory amount, reduced by

(2) any portion of the unrecovered losses sustained as a result of the compensable injury with respect to which the period for carryover under section 172 has expired.

In **1969**, P.L. 91-172, Sec. 904, added Code Sec. 186, effective for tax. yrs. begin. after 12/31/68.

Sec. 187. Repealed.

In **1976**, P.L. 94-455, Sec. 1901(a)(31), repealed Code Sec. 187, effective for tax. yrs. begin. after '76.
Prior to repeal, Code Sec. 187 read as follows:
"SEC. 187. AMORTIZATION OF CERTAIN COAL MINE SAFETY EQUIPMENT.
"(a) *Allowance of deduction.*
"Every person, at his election, shall be entitled to a deduction with respect to the amortization of the adjusted basis (for determining gain) of any certified coal mine safety equipment (as defined in subsection (d)), based on a period of 60 months. Such amortization deduction shall be an amount, with respect to each month of such period within the taxable year, equal to the adjusted basis of the certified coal mine safety equipment at the end of such month divided by the number of months (including the month for which the deduction is computed) remaining in the period. Such adjusted basis at the end of the month shall be computed without regard to the amortization deduction for such month. The amortization deduction provided by this section with respect to any certified coal mine safety equipment for any month shall be in lieu of the depreciation deduction with respect to such equipment for such month provided by section 167. The 60-month period shall begin, as to any certified coal mine safety equipment, at the election of the taxpayer, with the month following the month in which such equipment was placed in service or with the succeeding taxable year.

"(b) *Election of amortization.*
"The election of the taxpayer to take the amortization deduction and to begin the 60-month period with the month following the month in which the certified coal mine safety equipment was placed in service, or with the taxable year succeeding the taxable year in which such equipment is placed in service, shall be made by filing with the Secretary or his delegate, in such manner, in such form, and within such time, as the Secretary or his delegate may by regulations prescribe, a statement of such election.
"(c) *Termination of amortization deduction.*
"A taxpayer which has elected under subsection (b) to take the amortization deduction provided by subsection (a) may, at any time after making such election, discontinue the amortization deduction with respect to the remainder of the amortization period, such discontinuance to begin as of the beginning of any month specified by the taxpayer in a notice in writing filed with the Secretary or his delegate before the beginning of such month. The depreciation deduction provided under section 167 shall be allowed, beginning with the first month as to which the amortization deduction does not apply, and the taxpayer shall not be entitled to any further amortization deduction under this section with respect to such equipment.
"(d) *Certified coal mine safety equipment.*
"For purposes of this section, the term 'certified coal mine safety equipment' means property which—
"(1) is electric face equipment (within the meaning of section 305 of the Federal Coal Mine Health and Safety Act of 1969) required in order to meet the requirements of section 305(a)(2) of such Act,
"(2) the Secretary of the Interior certifies is permissible within the meaning of such section 305(a)(2), and
"(3) is placed in service before January 1, 1976.
"For purposes of this section, any property placed in service in connection with any used electric face equipment which the Secretary of the Interior certifies makes such electric face equipment permissible shall be treated as a separate item of certified coal mine safety equipment.
"(e) *Special rules.*
"(1) The adjusted basis of any certified coal mine safety equipment, with respect to which an election is made under this section, shall not be increased for purposes of this section, for amounts chargeable to capital account for additions or improvements after the amortization period has begun.
"(2) The depreciation deduction provided by section 167 shall, despite the provisions of subsection (a), be allowed with respect to the portion of the adjusted basis which is not taken into account in applying this section."
In **1975**, P.L. 93-625, Sec. 3(d), substituted "1976" for "1975" in para. (d)(3), effective 1/3/75.
In **1969**, P.L. 91-172, Sec. 707(a), added Code Sec. 187, effective for tax. yrs. end. after 12/31/69.

Sec. 188. Repealed.

In **1990**, P.L. 101-508, Sec. 11801(a)(13), repealed Code Sec. 188, effective 11/5/90 except as provided in Sec. 11821(b) of this Act reproduced in note following Code Sec. 184.
Prior to repeal, Code Sec. 188 read as follows:
"SEC. 188. AMORTIZATION OF CERTAIN EXPENDITURES FOR CHILD CARE FACILITIES.
"(a) *Allowance of deduction.*
"At the election of the taxpayer, made in accordance with regulations prescribed by the Secretary, any expenditure chargeable to capital account made by an employer to acquire, construct, reconstruct, or rehabilitate section 188 property (as defined in subsection (b)) shall be allowable as a deduction ratably over a period of 60 months, beginning with the month in which the property is placed in service. The deduction provided by this section with respect to such expenditure shall be in lieu of any depreciation deduction otherwise allowable on account of such expenditure.
"(b) *Section 188 property.*
"For the purposes of this section, the term 'section 188 property' means tangible property which qualifies under regulations prescribed by the Secretary as a child care center facility primarily for the children of employees of the taxpayer; except that such term shall not include—
"(1) any property which is not of a character subject to depreciation; or
"(2) property located outside the United States.
"(c) *Application of section.*
"This section shall apply only with respect to expenditures made after December 31, 1971, and before January 1, 1982."
In **1977**, P.L. 95-30, Sec. 402(a)(1), substituted "January 1, 1982" for "January 1, 1977" in subsec. (c) . . . Sec. 402(a)(2), deleted "as a facility for on-the-job training of employees (or prospective employees) of the taxpayer, or" after "regulations prescribed by the Secretary" in subsec. (b) . . . Sec. 402(a)(3), deleted "on-the-job training and" from the heading of Code Sec. 188, effective for expenditures made after 12/31/76.
In **1976**, P.L. 94-455, Sec. 1906(b)(13)(A), substituted "Secretary" for "Secretary or his delegate" in subsecs. (a) and (b), effective for tax. yrs. begin. after 12/31/76.
In **1971**, P.L. 92-178, Sec. 303(a), added Code Sec. 188, effective for tax. yrs. end. after 12/31/71.

Sec. 189. Repealed.

In 1986, P.L. 99-514, Sec. 803(b)(1), repealed Code Sec. 189, effective for costs incurred after 12/31/86, in tax. yrs. ending after 12/31/86. Sec. 803(d)(3) of this Act provides:

"(3) Special rule for self-constructed property.—The amendments made by this section shall not apply to any property which is produced by the taxpayer for use by the taxpayer if substantial construction had occurred before March 1, 1986."

For transitional and special rules, see Sec. 803(d)(2)-(7) of this Act, reproduced in note following Code Sec. 263A.

Prior to repeal, Code Sec. 189 read as follows:

"SEC. 189. AMORTIZATION OF REAL PROPERTY CONSTRUCTION PERIOD INTEREST AND TAXES.

"(a) Capitalization of construction period interest and taxes.

"Except as otherwise provided in this section or in section 266 (relating to carrying charges), no deduction shall be allowed for real property construction period interest and taxes.

"(b) Amortization of amounts charged to capital account.

"Any amount paid or accrued which would (but for subsection (a)) be allowable as a deduction for the taxable year shall be allowable for such taxable year and each subsequent amortization year in accordance with the following table:

"If the amount is paid or accrued in a taxable year beginning in—		The percentage of such amount allowable for each amortization year shall be the following percentage of such amount
"Nonresidential real property	Residential real property (other than low-income housing)	
1976		see subsection (f)
	1978	25
1977	1979	20
1978	1980	16⅔
1979	1981	14 2/7
1980	1982	12½
1981	1983	11 1/9
after 1981	after 1983	10

"(c) Amortization year.

"(1) In general. For purposes of this section, the term 'amortization year' means the taxable year in which the amount is paid or accrued, and each taxable year thereafter (beginning with the taxable year after the taxable year in which paid or accrued or, if later, the taxable year in which the real property is ready to be placed in service or is ready to be held for sale) until the full amount has been allowable as a deduction (or until the property is sold or exchanged).

"(2) Rules for sales and exchanges. For purposes of paragraph (1)—

"(A) Proportion of percentage allowed. For the amortization year in which the property is sold or exchanged, a proportionate part of the percentage allowable for such year (determined without regard to the sale or exchange) shall be allowable. If the real property is subject to an allowance for depreciation, the proportion shall be determined in accordance with the convention used for depreciation purposes with respect to such property. In the case of all other real property, under regulations prescribed by the Secretary, the proportion shall be based on that proportion of the amortization year which elapsed before the sale or exchange.

"(B) Unamortized balance. In the case of a sale or exchange of the property, the portion of the amount not allowable shall be treated as an adjustment to basis under section 1016 for purposes of determining gain or loss.

"(C) Certain exchanges. An exchange or transfer after which the property received has a basis determined in whole or in part by reference to the basis of the property to which the amortizable construction period interest and taxes relate, shall not be treated as an exchange.

"(d) Certain property excluded.

"This section shall not apply to any—

"(1) low-income housing,

"(2) real property acquired, constructed, or carried if such property is not, and cannot reasonably expected to be, held in a trade or business, or in an activity conducted for profit.

"(e) Definitions.

"For purposes of this section—

"(1) Real property construction period interest and taxes. The term real property construction period interest and taxes means all—

"(A) interest paid or accrued on indebtedness incurred or continued to acquire, construct, or carry real property, and

"(B) real property taxes,

to the extent such interest and taxes are attributable to the construction period for such property and would be allowable as a deduction under this chapter for the taxable year in which paid or accrued (determined without regard to this section). The Secretary shall prescribe regulations which provide for the allocation of interest to real property under construction.

"(2) Construction period. The term 'construction period', when used with respect to any real property, means the period—

"(A) beginning on the date on which construction of the building or other improvement begins, and

"(B) ending on the date on which the item of property is ready to be placed in service or is ready to be held for sale.

"(3) Nonresidential real property. The term 'nonresidential real property' means real property which is neither residential real property nor low-income housing.

"(4) Residential real property. The term 'residential real property' means property which is or can reasonably be expected to be—

"(A) residential rental property as defined in section 167(j)(2)(B),

"(B) real property described in section 1221(1) held for sale as dwelling units (within the meaning of section 167(k)(3)(C)), or

"(C) real property held by a cooperative housing corporation (as defined in section 216(b)) and used for dwelling purposes.

"(5) Low-income housing. The term 'low-income housing' means property described in clause (i), (ii), (iii), or (iv) of section 1250(a)(1)(B).

"(f) Transitional rule for 1976.

"In the case of amounts paid or accrued by the taxpayer in a taxable year beginning in 1976, the percentage of such amount allowable under this section for—

"(1) the taxable year beginning in 1976 shall be 50 percent, and

"(2) each amortization year thereafter shall be 16⅔ percent.

In 1984, P.L. 98-369, Sec. 93(a)(1), and (2), deleted para. (d)(2) and redesignated para. (d)(3) as (d)(2), effective for tax. yrs. begin. after 12/31/84, for construction begin. after 3/15/84.

Prior to deletion, para. (d)(2) read as follows:

"(2) residential real property (other than low income housing) acquired, constructed, or carried by a corporation other than an S corporation, a personal holding company (within the meaning of section 542), or a foreign personal holding company (within the meaning of section 552), or"

—P.L. 98-369, Sec. 712(c), deleted "or" at the end of subpara. (e)(4)(A), substituted ", or" for the period at the end of subpara. (e)(4)(B) and added subpara. (e)(4)(C), effective for tax. yrs. begin. after 12/31/82, for construction begin. after 12/31/82.

In 1982, P.L. 97-354, Sec. 5(a)(24), substituted "an S corporation" for "an electing small business corporation (within the meaning of section 1371(b))" in para. (d)(2), effective for tax. yrs. begin. after 12/31/82.

—P.L. 97-248, Sec. 207(a), amended subsec. (a) . . . Sec. 207(b)(1), deleted "or" at end of para. (d)(1) . . . Sec. 207(b)(2), redesignated para. (d)(2) as para. (d)(3) . . . Sec. 207(b)(3), added new para. (d)(2) . . . Sec. 207(c), added "The Secretary shall prescribe regulations which provide for the allocation of interest to real property under construction." at the end of para. (e)(1) . . . Sec. 207(d)(1), substituted "real property construction period interest and taxes" for "construction period interest and taxes" in para. (e)(1) . . . Sec. 207(d)(2), substituted "(1) Real property construction period interest and taxes" for "(1) Construction period interest and taxes" in the heading of para. (e)(1), effective for tax. yrs. begin. after 12/31/82, for construction which commences after 12/31/82.

Prior to amendment, subsec. (a) read as follows:

"(a) Capitalization of construction period interest and taxes.

"Except as otherwise provided in this section or in section 266 (relating to carrying charges), in the case of an individual, no deduction shall be allowed for real property construction period interest and taxes. For purposes of this section, an electing small business corporation (as defined in section 1371(b)), a personal holding company (as defined in section 542), and a foreign personal holding company (as defined in section 552) shall be treated as an individual."

In 1981, P.L. 97-34, Sec. 262(a), amended the table in subsec. (b) . . . Sec. 262(b), amended subsec. (d), effective for tax. yrs. begin. after 12/31/81.

Prior to amendment, the table in subsec. (b) read as follows:

Deductions — Code Sec. 191

Nonresidential real property	Residential real property (other than low income housing)	Low-income housing	The percentage of such amount allowable for each amortization year shall be the following percentage of such amount
"1976			see subsection (f)
	1978	1982	25
"1977	1979	1983	20
"1978	1980	1984	16⅔
"1979	1981	1985	14²⁄₇
"1980	1982	1986	12½
"1981	1983	1987	11⅛
after 1981	after 1983	after 1987	10"

Prior to amendment, subsec. (d) read as follows:

"(d) Certain residential property excluded.

"This section shall not apply to any real property acquired, constructed, or carried if such property is not, and cannot reasonably be expected to be, held in a trade or business or in an activity conducted for profit."

In 1978, P.L. 95-600, Sec. 701(e), amended Sec. 201(c)(1) of P.L. 94-455, reproduced below, to read as follows:

"(1) in the case of nonresidential real property, if the construction period begins on or after the first day of the first taxable year beginning after December 31, 1975,"

—P.L. 95-600, Sec. 701(m)(1), deleted "an electing small business corporation (within the meaning of section 1371(b)), or a personal holding company (within the meaning of section 542)," following "in the case of an individual," in subsec. (a) and added the last sentence in subsec. (a), effective as if included in the amendment made by Sec. 201(a) of P.L. 94-455, see below.

In 1976, P.L. 94-455, Sec. 201(a), added Code Sec. 189. Sec. 201(c) of the Act provided as follows:

"(c) Effective date.

"The amendments made by this section shall apply—

"(1) in the case of nonresidential real property, if the construction period begins after December 31, 1975,

"(2) in the case of residential real property (other than low-income housing), to taxable years beginning after December 31, 1977, and

"(3) in the case of low-income housing, to taxable years beginning after December 31, 1981.

"For purposes of this subsection, the terms 'nonresidential real property', 'residential real property (other than low-income housing)', 'low-income housing', and 'construction period' have the same meaning as when used in section 189 of the Internal Revenue Code of 1954 (as added by subsection (a) of this section)."

Sec. 190. Expenditures to remove architectural and transportation barriers to the handicapped and elderly.

(a) Treatment as expenses.

(1) In general. A taxpayer may elect to treat qualified architectural and transportation barrier removal expenses which are paid or incurred by him during the taxable year as expenses which are not chargeable to capital account. The expenditures so treated shall be allowed as a deduction.

(2) Election. An election under paragraph (1) shall be made at such time and in such manner as the Secretary prescribes by regulations.

(b) Definitions.

For purposes of this section—

(1) Architectural and transportation barrier removal expenses. The term "architectural and transportation barrier removal expenses" means an expenditure for the purpose of making any facility or public transportation vehicle owned or leased by the taxpayer for use in connection with his trade or business more accessible to, and usable by, handicapped and elderly individuals.

(2) Qualified architectural and transportation barrier removal expense. The term "qualified architectural and transportation barrier removal expense" means, with respect to any such facility or public transportation vehicle, an architectural or transportation barrier removal expense with respect to which the taxpayer establishes, to the satisfaction of the Secretary, that the resulting removal of any such barrier meets the standards promulgated by the Secretary with the concurrence of the Architectural and Transportation Barriers Compliance Board and set forth in regulations prescribed by the Secretary.

(3) Handicapped individual. The term "handicapped individual" means any individual who has a physical or mental disability (including, but not limited to, blindness or deafness) which for such individual constitutes or results in a functional limitation to employment, or who has any physical or mental impairment (including, but not limited to, a sight or hearing impairment) which substantially limits one or more major life activities of such individual.

(c) Limitation.

The deduction allowed by subsection (a) for any taxable year shall not exceed $15,000.

In 1990, P.L. 101-508, Sec. 11611(c), substituted "$15,000" for "$35,000" in subsec. (c), effective for tax. yrs. end. after 11/5/90.

—P.L. 101-508, Sec. 11801(a)(14), deleted subsec. (d), effective 11/5/90 except as provided in Sec. 11821(b) of this Act, reproduced in note following Code Sec. 184.

Prior to deletion, subsec. (d) read as follows:

"(d) Application of section. This section shall apply to—

"(1) taxable years beginning after December 31, 1976, and before January 1, 1983, and

"(2) taxable years beginning after December 31, 1983."

In 1986, P.L. 99-514, Sec. 244, substituted "1983" for "1983, and before January 1, 1986", in para. d)(2), effective 10/22/86.

In 1984, P.L. 98-369, Sec. 1062(a)(1), amended subsec. (d), effective 7/18/84. Prior to amendment, subsec. (d) read as follows:

"(d) Regulations.

"The Secretary shall prescribe such regulations as may be necessary to carry out the provisions of this section within 180 days after the date of the enactment of the Tax Reform Act of 1976."

—P.L. 98-369, Sec. 1062(a)(2), amended Sec. 2122(c) of P.L. 94-455, the effective date for changes made by Sec. 2122(a) of P.L. 94-455 (as amended by Sec. 9(d) of P.L. 96-167), from tax. yrs. begin. after '76 and before '83 to tax. yrs. begin. after '76, see below.

—P.L. 98-369, Sec. 1062(b), substituted "$35,000" for "$25,000" in subsec. (c), effective for tax. yrs. begin. after 12/31/83.

In 1979, P.L. 96-167, Sec. 9(d), amended Sec. 2122(c) of P.L. 94-455, the effective date for changes made by Sec. 2122(a) of P.L. 94-455, from tax. yrs. begin. after '76 and before '80 to tax. yrs. begin. after '76 and before '83, see below.

In 1976, P.L. 94-455, Sec. 2122(a), added Code Sec. 190, effective [as amended by Sec. 9(d) of P.L. 96-167, and Sec. 1062(a)(2) of P.L. 98-369, see above] for tax. yrs. begin. after 12/31/76.

Sec. 191. Repealed.

In 1981, P.L. 97-34, Sec. 212(d)(1), repealed Code Sec. 191, effective for expenditures incurred after 12/31/81 in tax. yrs. end. after 12/31/81. For transitional rule see Sec. 212(e)(2) of this Act reproduced in note following Code Sec. 46.

Prior to repeal, Code Sec. 191 read as follows:

"SEC. 191. AMORTIZATION OF CERTAIN REHABILITATION EXPENDITURES FOR CERTIFIED HISTORIC STRUCTURES.

"(a) Allowance of deduction.

"Every person, at his election, shall be entitled to a deduction with respect to the amortization of the amortizable basis of any certified historic structure (as defined in subsection (d)) based on a period of 60 months. Such amortization deduction shall be an amount, with respect to each month of such period within the taxable year, equal to the amortizable basis at the end of such month divided by the number of months (including the month for which the deduction is computed) remaining in the period. Such amortizable basis at the end of such month shall be computed without regard to the amortization deduction for such month. The amortization deduction provided by this section with respect to any month shall be in lieu of the depreciation deduction with respect to such basis for such month provided by section 167. The 60-month period shall begin, as to any historic structure, at the election of the taxpayer, with the month following the month in which the basis is acquired, or with the succeeding taxable year.

"(b) Election of amortization.

"The election of the taxpayer to take the amortization deduction and to begin the 60-month period with the month following the month in which the basis is acquired, or with the taxable year succeeding the taxable year in which such basis is acquired, shall be made by filing with the Secretary, in such manner, in such form, and within such time as the Secretary may by regulations prescribe, a statement of such election.

"(c) Termination of amortization deduction.

"A taxpayer who has elected under subsection (b) to take the amortization deduction provided in subsection (a) may, at any time after making such election, discontinue the amortization deduction with respect to the remainder of the amortization period, such discontinuance to begin as of the beginning of any month specified by the taxpayer in a notice in writing filed with the Secretary before the beginning of such month. The depreciation deduction provided under section 167 shall be allowed, beginning with the first month as to which the amortization deduction does not apply, and the taxpayer shall not be entitled to any further amortization deduction under this section with respect to such certified historic structure.

"(d) Definitions.

"For purposes of this section —

"(1) Certified historic structure. The term 'certified historic structure' means a building or structure which is of a character subject to the allowance for depreciation provided in section 167 and which —

"(A) is listed in the National Register, or

"(B) is located in a registered historic district and is certified by the Secretary of the Interior to the Secretary as being of historic significance to the district.

"(2) Registered historic district. The term 'registered historic district' means —

"(A) any district listed in the National Register, and

"(B) any district —

"(i) which is designated under a statute of the appropriate State or local government, if such statute is certified by the Secretary of the Interior to the Secretary as containing criteria which will substantially achieve the purpose of preserving and rehabilitating buildings of historic significance to the district, and

"(ii) which is certified by the Secretary of the Interior to the Secretary as meeting substantially all of the requirements for the listing of districts in the National Register.

"(3) Amortizable basis. The term 'amortizable basis' means the portion of the basis attributable to amounts expended in connection with certified rehabilitation.

"(4) Certified rehabilitation. The term 'certified rehabilitation' means any rehabilitation of a certified historic structure which the Secretary of the Interior has certified to the Secretary as being consistent with the historic character of such property or the district in which such property is located.

"(e) Depreciation deduction.

"The depreciation deduction provided by section 167 shall, despite the provisions of subsection (a), be allowed with respect to the portion of the adjusted basis which is not the amortizable basis.

"(f) Special rules for certain interests.

"(1) Life tenant and remainderman. In the case of property held by one person for life with remainder to another person, the deduction under this section shall be computed as if the life tenant was the absolute owner of the property and shall be allowable to the life tenant.

"(2) Certain lessees

"(A) In general. In the case of a lessee of a certified historic structure who has expended amounts in connection with the certified rehabilitation of such structure which are properly chargeable to capital account, the deduction under this section shall be allowable to such lessee with respect to such amounts.

"(B) Amortizable basis. For purposes of subsection (a), the amortizable basis of such lessee shall not exceed the sum of the amounts described in subparagraph (A).

"(C) Limitation. Subparagraph (A) shall apply only if on the date the certified rehabilitation is completed, the remaining term of the lease (determined without regard to any renewal periods) extends —

"(i) beyond the last day of the useful life (determined without regard to this section) of the improvements for which the amounts described in subparagraph (A) were expended, and

"(ii) for not less than 30 years.

"(g) Application of section.

"This section shall apply with respect to additions to capital account made before June 14, 1976, and before January 1, 1984.

"(h) Cross references.

"(1) For rules relating to the listing of buildings, structures, and historic districts in the National Register, see the Act entitled 'An Act to establish a program for the preservation of additional historic properties throughout the Nation, and for other purposes', approved October 15, 1966 (16 U.S.C. 470 *et seq.*).

"(2) For special rules with respect to certain gain derived from the disposition of property the adjusted basis of which is determined with regard to this section, see sections 1245 and 1250."

In 1980, P.L. 96-541, Sec. 2(a), redesignated subsec. (g) as subsec. (h) and added new subsec. (g).

— P.L. 96-541, Sec. 2(e)(1), deleted Sec. 2124(a)(4) of P.L. 94-455, the effective date for changes made by Sec. 2124(a)(1) of P.L. 94-455, [addition of Code Sec. 191] see below. Sec. 2(a) of P.L. 96-451 added subsec. (g), the effective date for Code Sec. 191, see above.

Prior to deletion Sec. 2124(a)(4) of P.L. 94-455 read as follows:

"(4) Effective date. The amendments made by this subsection shall apply with respect to additions to capital account made after June 14, 1976 and before June 15, 1981."

— P.L. 96-222, Sec. 107(a)(1)(E)(ii), substituted "the date" for "the date of" in subpara. (f)(2)(C).

In 1978, P.L. 95-600, Sec. 701(f)(1), redesignated paras. (d)(2) and (3) as paras. (d)(3) and (4) . . . amended para. (d)(1) and added new para. (d)(2) . . . Sec. 701(f)(2), amended subsec. (g), . . . Sec. 701(f)(7), amended subsec. (f).

Prior to amendment, para. (d)(1) read as follows:

"(1) Certified historic structure. The term 'certified historic structure' means a building or structure which is of a character subject to the allowance for depreciation provided in section 167 which —

"(A) is listed in the National Register,

"(B) is located in a Registered Historic District and is certified by the Secretary of the Interior as being of historic significance to the district, or

"(C) is located in an historic district designated under a statute of the appropriate State or local government if such statute is certified by the Secretary of the Interior to the Secretary as containing criteria which will substantially achieve the purpose of preserving and rehabilitating buildings of historic significance to the district."

Prior to amendment, subsecs. (f) and (g) read as follows:

"(f) Life tenant and remainderman.

"In the case of property held by one person for life with remainder to another person, the deduction under this section shall be computed as if the life tenant were the absolute owner of the property and shall be allowable to the life tenant."

"(g) Cross references.

"(1) For rules relating to the listing of buildings and structures in the National Register and for definitions of 'National Register' and 'Registered Historic District', see section 470 *et seq.* of title 16 of the United States Code.

"(2) For special rule with respect to certain gain derived from the disposition of property the adjusted basis of which is determined with regard to this section, see section 1245."

In 1976, P.L. 94-455, Sec. 2124(a)(1), added Code Sec. 191.

Sec. 192. Contributions to black lung benefit trust.

(a) Allowance of deduction.

There is allowed as a deduction for the taxable year an amount equal to the sum of the amounts contributed by the taxpayer during the taxable year to or under a trust or trusts described in section 501(c)(21).

(b) Limitation.

The maximum amount of the deduction allowed by subsection (a) for any taxpayer for any taxable year shall not exceed the greater of —

(1) the amount necessary to fund (with level funding) the remaining unfunded liability of the taxpayer for black lung claims filed (or expected to be filed) by (or with respect to) past or present employees of the taxpayer, or

(2) the aggregate amount necessary to increase each trust described in section 501(c)(21) to the amount required to pay all amounts payable out of such trust for the taxable year.

(c) Special rules.

(1) Method of determining amounts referred to in subsection (b).

(A) In general. The amounts described in subsection (b) shall be determined by using reasonable actuarial methods and assumptions which are not inconsistent with regulations prescribed by the Secretary.

(B) Funding period. Except as provided in subparagraph (C), the funding period for purposes of subsection (b)(1) shall be the greater of —

(i) the average remaining working life of miners who are present employees of the taxpayer, or

(ii) 10 taxable years.

For purposes of the preceding sentence, the term "miner" has the same meaning as such term has when used in section 402(d) of the Black Lung Benefits Act (30 U.S.C. 902(d)).

(C) Different funding periods. To the extent that —

(i) regulations prescribed by the Secretary provide for a different period, or

(ii) the Secretary consents to a different period proposed by the taxpayer, such different period shall be substituted for the funding period provided in subparagraph (B).

(2) Benefit payments taken into account. In determining the amounts described in subsection (b), only those black lung benefit claims the payment of which is expected to be made from the trust shall be taken into account.

(3) Time when contributions deemed made. For purposes of this section, a taxpayer shall be deemed to have made a payment of a contribution on the last day of a taxable year if the payment is on account of that taxable year and is made not later than the time prescribed by law for filing the return for that taxable year (including extensions thereof).

(4) Contributions to be in cash or certain other items. No deduction shall be allowed under subsection (a) with respect to any contribution to a trust described in section 501(c)(21) other than a contribution in cash or in items in which such trust may invest under subclause (II) of section 501(c)(21)(A)(ii).

(5) Denial of section 162 deduction with respect to liability. No deduction shall be allowed under section 162(a) with respect to any liability taken into account in determining the deduction under subsection (a) of this section of the taxpayer (or a predecessor).

(d) Carryover of excess contributions.

If the amount of the deduction determined under subsection (a) for the taxable year (without regard to the limitation imposed by subsection (b)) with respect to a trust exceeds the limitation imposed by subsection (b) for the taxable year, the excess shall be carried over to the succeeding taxable year and treated as contributed to the trust during that year.

(e) Definition of black lung benefit claim.

For purposes of this section, the term "black lung benefit claim" means a claim for compensation for disability or death due to pneumoconiosis under part C of title IV of the Federal Mine Safety and Health Act of 1977 or under any State law providing for such compensation.

In 1992, P.L. 102-486, Sec. 1940(c), substituted "subclause (II) of section 501(c)(21)(A)(ii)" for "clause (ii) of section 501(c)(21)(B)" in para. (c)(4), effective for tax. yrs. begin. after 12/31/91.

In 1980, P.L. 96-222, Sec. 108(b)(2)(B), substituted "Federal Mine Safety and Health Act of 1977" for "Federal Coal Mine Health and Safety Act of 1969", in subsec. (e), effective for contributions, acts, and expenditures made after 1977, in and for tax yrs. begin. after 1977.

In 1978, P.L. 95-488, Sec. 1(a), amended subsec. (b) . . . Sec. 1(b), amended para. (c)(1) . . . Sec. 1(c), added new para. (c)(5), effective for tax. yrs. begin. after 12/31/77.

Prior to amendment subsec. (b) read as follows:

"*(b) Limitation.*

"(1) In general. The amount of the deduction allowed by subsection (a) for any taxable year with respect to any such trust shall not exceed the amount determined under paragraph (2) or (3), whichever is greater.

"(2) Current year obligations. The amount determined under this paragraph for the taxable year is the amount which, when added to the fair market value of the assets of the trust as of the beginning of the taxable year, is necessary to carry out the purposes of the trust described in subparagraph (A) of section 501(c)(21) for the taxable year.

"(3) Certain future obligations. The amount determined under this paragraph for the taxable year is the sum of—

"(A) the amount which is necessary to meet the expenses of the trust described in clause (iii) of section 501(c)(21)(A) for the taxable year, and

"(B) the lesser of—

"(i) the amount which, when added to the fair market value of the assets of the trust as of the beginning of the taxable year, is necessary to provide all expected future payments with respect to black lung benefit claims which are approved, including any such claims which have been filed and which have not been disapproved, as of the end of the taxable year, or

"(ii) twice the amount which is necessary to provide all expected future payments with respect to the greater of—

"(I) black lung benefit claims filed during the taxable year or any one of the 3 immediately preceding taxable years, or

"(II) such claims approved during any one of those 4 taxable years."

Prior to amendment, para. (c)(1) read as follows:
"*(c) Special rules.*
"(1) Determination of expected future payments. The amounts described in subsection (b) shall be determined by using reasonable actuarial assumptions which are not inconsistent with regulations prescribed by the Secretary."

—P.L. 95-239, Sec. 20(c), provides:

"(c) In accordance with the requirements of section 5 of the Black Lung Benefits Revenue Act of 1977, [P.L. 95-227] it is hereby provided that such Act shall take effect in accordance with the provisions of such Act. The provisions of this subsection are hereby deemed to be in explicit satisfaction of the requirements of section 5 of such Act."

—P.L. 95-227, Sec. 4(b)(1), added Code Sec. 192, effective for contributions, acts, and expenditures made after 1977, in and for tax. yrs. begin. after 1977. Sec. 5 of this Act provides:

"SEC. 5. GENERAL EFFECTIVE DATE RESERVATION.

Notwithstanding any other provision of this Act to the contrary, no provision of this Act (including any amendment made by any such provision) shall take effect or apply unless an Act, enacted after the date of enactment of this Act, contains a provision, explicitly in satisfaction of the requirements of this section, which states that it is the intent of the Congress that the provisions of this Act shall take effect."

Sec. 193. Tertiary injectants.

(a) Allowance of deduction.

There shall be allowed as a deduction for the taxable year an amount equal to the qualified tertiary injectant expenses of the taxpayer for tertiary injectants injected during such taxable year.

(b) Qualified tertiary injectant expenses.

For purposes of this section—

(1) In general. The term "qualified tertiary injectant expenses" means any cost paid or incurred (whether or not chargeable to capital account) for any tertiary injectant (other than a hydrocarbon injectant which is recoverable) which is used as a part of a tertiary recovery method.

(2) Hydrocarbon injectant. The term "hydrocarbon injectant" includes natural gas, crude oil, and any other injectant which is comprised of more than an insignificant amount of natural gas or crude oil. The term does not include any tertiary injectant which is hydrocarbon-based, or a hydrocarbon-derivative, and which is comprised of no more than an insignificant amount of natural gas or crude oil. For purposes of this paragraph, that portion of a hydrocarbon injectant which is not a hydrocarbon shall not be treated as a hydrocarbon injectant.

(3) Tertiary recovery method. The term "tertiary recovery method" means—

(A) any method which is described in subparagraphs (1) through (9) of section 212.78(c) of the June 1979 energy regulations (as defined by section 4996(b)(8)(C) as in effect before its repeal), or

(B) any other method to provide tertiary enhanced recovery which is approved by the Secretary for purposes of this section.

(c) Application with other deductions.

No deduction shall be allowed under subsection (a) with respect to any expenditure—

(1) with respect to which the taxpayer has made an election under section 263(c), or

(2) with respect to which a deduction is allowed or allowable to the taxpayer under any other provision of this chapter.

In 1988, P.L. 100-418, Sec. 1941(b)(7), substituted "section 4996(b)(8)(C) as in effect before its repeal" for "section 4996(b)(8)(C)" in subpara. (b)(3)(A), effective for crude oil removed from the premises on or after 8/23/88.

In 1983, P.L. 97-448, Sec. 202(b), deleted "during the taxable year" after "means any cost paid or incurred" in para. (b)(1), effective for tax. yrs. begin. after 12/31/79.

In 1980, P.L. 96-223, Sec. 251(a)(1), added Code Sec. 193, effective for tax. yrs. begin. after 12/31/79.

Sec. 194. Treatment of reforestation expenditures.
(a) Allowance of deduction.

In the case of any qualified timber property with respect to which the taxpayer has made (in accordance with regulations prescribed by the Secretary) an election under this subsection, the taxpayer shall be entitled to a deduction with respect to the amortization of the amortizable basis of qualified timber property based on a period of 84 months. Such amortization deduction shall be an amount, with respect to each month of such period within the taxable year, equal to the amortizable basis at the end of such month divided by the number of months (including the month for which the deduction is computed) remaining in the period. Such amortizable basis at the end of the month shall be computed without regard to the amortization deduction for such month. The 84-month period shall begin on the first day of the first month of the second half of the taxable year in which the amortizable basis is acquired.

(b) Treatment as expenses.
(1) Election to treat certain reforestation expenditures as expenses.

(A) In general. In the case of any qualified timber property with respect to which the taxpayer has made (in accordance with regulations prescribed by the Secretary) an election under this subsection, the taxpayer shall treat reforestation expenditures which are paid or incurred during the taxable year with respect to such property as an expense which is not chargeable to capital account. The reforestation expenditures so treated shall be allowed as a deduction.

(B) Dollar limitation. The aggregate amount of reforestation expenditures which may be taken into account under subparagraph (A) with respect to each qualified timber property for any taxable year shall not exceed—
  (i) except as provided in clause (ii) or (iii), $10,000,
  (ii) in the case of a separate return by a married individual (as defined in section 7703), $5,000, and
  (iii) in the case of a trust, zero.

(2) Allocation of dollar limit.

(A) Controlled group. For purposes of applying the dollar limitation under paragraph (1)(B)—
  (i) all component members of a controlled group shall be treated as one taxpayer, and
  (ii) the Secretary shall, under regulations prescribed by him, apportion such dollar limitation among the component members of such controlled group.

For purposes of the preceding sentence, the term "controlled group" has the meaning assigned to it by section 1563(a), except that the phrase "more than 50 percent" shall be substituted for the phrase "at least 80 percent" each place it appears in section 1563(a)(1).

(B) Partnerships and S corporations. In the case of a partnership, the dollar limitation contained in paragraph (1)(B) shall apply with respect to the partnership and with respect to each partner. A similar rule shall apply in the case of an S corporation and its shareholders.

(3) Repealed.
(4) Repealed.

(c) Definitions and special rule.
For purposes of this section—

(1) Qualified timber property. The term "qualified timber property" means a woodlot or other site located in the United States which will contain trees in significant commercial quantities and which is held by the taxpayer for the planting, cultivating, caring for, and cutting of trees for sale or use in the commercial production of timber products.

(2) Amortizable basis. The term "amortizable basis" means that portion of the basis of the qualified timber property attributable to reforestation expenditures which have not been taken into account under subsection (b).

(3) Reforestation expenditures.

(A) In general. The term "reforestation expenditures" means direct costs incurred in connection with forestation or reforestation by planting or artificial or natural seeding, including costs—
  (i) for the preparation of the site;
  (ii) of seeds or seedlings; and
  (iii) for labor and tools, including depreciation of equipment such as tractors, trucks, tree planters, and similar machines used in planting or seeding.

(B) Cost-sharing programs. Reforestation expenditures shall not include any expenditures for which the taxpayer has been reimbursed under any governmental reforestation cost-sharing program unless the amounts reimbursed have been included in the gross income of the taxpayer.

(4) Treatment of trusts and estates. The aggregate amount of reforestation expenditures incurred by any trust or estate shall be apportioned between the income beneficiaries and the fiduciary under regulations prescribed by the Secretary. Any amount so apportioned to a beneficiary shall be taken into account as expenditures incurred by such beneficiary in applying this section to such beneficiary.

(5) Application with other deductions. No deduction shall be allowed under any other provision of this chapter with respect to any expenditure with respect to which a deduction is allowed or allowable under this section to the taxpayer.

(d) Life tenant and remainderman.

In the case of property held by one person for life with remainder to another person, the deduction under this section shall be computed as if the life tenant were the absolute owner of the property and shall be allowed to the life tenant.

In **2005**, P.L. 109-135, Sec. 403(i)(1)(A), amended subpara. (b)(1)(B) . . . Sec. 403(i)(1)(B), amended para. (c)(4), effective for expenditures paid or incurred after 10/22/2004 as if included in Sec. 322 of the American Jobs Creation Act of 2004, P.L. 108-357.

Prior to amendment, subpara. (b)(1)(B) read as follows:

"(B) Dollar limitation. The aggregate amount of reforestation expenditures which may be taken into account under subparagraph (A) with respect to each qualified timber property for any taxable year shall not exceed $10,000 ($5,000 in the case of a separate return by a married individual (as defined in section 7703))."

Prior to amendment, para. (c)(4) read as follows:

"(4) Treatment of trusts and estates.

"(A) In general. Except as provided in subparagraph (B), this section shall not apply to trusts and estates.

"(B) Amortization deduction allowed to estates. The benefit of the deduction for amortization provided by subsection (a) shall be allowed to estates in the same manner as in the case of an individual. The allowable deduction shall be apportioned between the income beneficiary and the fiduciary under regulations prescribed by the Secretary. Any amount so apportioned to a beneficiary shall be taken into account for purposes of determining the amount allowable as a deduction under subsection (a) to such beneficiary."

In **2004**, P.L. 108-357, Sec. 322(a), amended the heading of subsec. (b) and para. (b)(1) . . . Sec. 322(b), added "which have not been taken into account under subsection (b)" after "expenditures" in para. (c)(2) . . . Sec. 322(c)(1), deleted paras. (b)(3) and (4) . . . Sec. 322(c)(2), substituted "paragraph (1)(B)" for "paragraph (1)" each place it appeared in para. (b)(2) . . . Sec. 322(c)(3), deleted para. (c)(4) and added paras. (c)(4) and (5) . . . Sec. 322(c)(4), substituted "Treatment" for "Amortization" in the heading of Code Sec. 194, effective for expenditures paid or incurred after 10/22/2004.

Prior to amendment, the heading of subsec. (b) read as follows:
"(b) Limitations."

Prior to amendment, para. (b)(1) read as follows:

"(1) Maximum dollar amount. The aggregate amount of amortizable basis acquired during the taxable year which may be taken into account under subsection (a) for such taxable year shall not exceed $10,000 ($5,000 in the case of a separate return by a married individual (as defined in section 7703))."

Prior to deletion, paras. (b)(3) and (4) read as follows:
"(3) Section not to apply to trusts. This section shall not apply to trusts.
"(4) Estates. The benefit of the deduction for amortization provided by this section shall be allowed to estates in the same manner as in the case of an individual. The allowable deduction shall be apportioned between the income beneficiary and the fiduciary under regulations prescribed by the Secretary. Any amount so apportioned to a beneficiary shall be taken into account for purposes of determining the amount allowable as a deduction under this section to such beneficiary."

Prior to deletion, para. (c)(4) read as follows:
"(4) Basis allocation. If the amount of the amortizable basis acquired during the taxable year of all qualified timber property with respect to which the taxpayer has made an election under subsection (a) exceeds the amount of the limitation under subsection (b)(1), the taxpayer shall allocate that portion of such amortizable basis with respect to which a deduction is allowable under subsection (a) to each such qualified timber property in such manner as the Secretary may by regulations prescribe."

In **1986**, P.L. 99-514, Sec. 1301(j)(8), substituted "section 7703" for "section 143" in para. (b)(1), effective for bonds issued after 8/15/86.

In **1982**, P.L. 97-354, Sec. 3(g)(1), the sentence at the end of subpara. (b)(2)(B) . . . Sec. 3(g)(2), substituted "Partnerships and S corporations" for "Partnerships" in the heading of subpara. (b)(2)(B), effective for tax. yrs. begin. after 12/31/82.

In **1980**, P.L. 96-451, Sec. 301(a), added Code Sec. 194, effective for additions to capital account made after 12/31/79.

Sec. 194A. Contributions to employer liability trusts.
(a) Allowance of deduction.
There shall be allowed as a deduction for the taxable year an amount equal to the amount—
(1) which is contributed by an employer to a trust described in section 501(c)(22) (relating to withdrawal liability payment fund) which meets the requirements of section 4223(h) of the Employee Retirement Income Security Act of 1974, and
(2) which is properly allocable to such taxable year.
(b) Allocation to taxable year.
In the case of a contribution described in subsection (a) which relates to any specified period of time which includes more than one taxable year, the amount properly allocable to any taxable year in such period shall be determined by prorating such amounts to such taxable years under regulations prescribed by the Secretary.
(c) Disallowance of deduction.
No deduction shall be allowed under subsection (a) with respect to any contribution described in subsection (a) which does not relate to any specified period of time.

In **1983**, P.L. 97-448, Sec. 305(b)(1), redesignated Code Sec. 194 as 194A, effective 10/14/82.

In **1980**, P.L. 96-364, Sec. 209(c)(1), added Code Sec. 194, effective for tax. yrs. end. after 9/26/80.

Sec. 195. Start-up expenditures.
(a) Capitalization of expenditures.
Except as otherwise provided in this section, no deduction shall be allowed for start-up expenditures.
(b) Election to deduct.
(1) Allowance of deduction. If a taxpayer elects the application of this subsection with respect to any start-up expenditures—
(A) the taxpayer shall be allowed a deduction for the taxable year in which the active trade or business begins in an amount equal to the lesser of—
(i) the amount of start-up expenditures with respect to the active trade or business, or
(ii) $5,000, reduced (but not below zero) by the amount by which such start-up expenditures exceed $50,000, and
(B) the remainder of such start-up expenditures shall be allowed as a deduction ratably over the 180-month period beginning with the month in which the active trade or business begins.
(2) Dispositions before close of amortization period. In any case in which a trade or business is completely disposed of by the taxpayer before the end of the period to which paragraph (1) applies, any deferred expenses attributable to such trade or business which were not allowed as a deduction by reason of this section may be deducted to the extent allowable under section 165.
(3) Special rule for taxable years beginning in 2010. In the case of a taxable year beginning in 2010, paragraph (1)(A)(ii) shall be applied—
(A) by substituting "$10,000" for "$5,000", and
(B) by substituting "$60,000" for "$50,000".
(c) Definitions.
For purposes of this section—
(1) Start-up expenditures. The term "start-up expenditure" means any amount—
(A) paid or incurred in connection with—
(i) investigating the creation or acquisition of an active trade or business, or
(ii) creating an active trade or business, or
(iii) any activity engaged in for profit and for the production of income before the day on which the active trade or business begins, in anticipation of such activity becoming an active trade or business, and
(B) which, if paid or incurred in connection with the operation of an existing active trade or business (in the same field as the trade or business referred to in subparagraph (A)), would be allowable as a deduction for the taxable year in which paid or incurred.
The term "start-up expenditure" does not include any amount with respect to which a deduction is allowable under section 163(a), 164, or 174.
(2) Beginning of trade or business.
(A) In general. Except as provided in subparagraph (B), the determination of when an active trade or business begins shall be made in accordance with such regulations as the Secretary may prescribe.
(B) Acquired trade or business. An acquired active trade or business shall be treated as beginning when the taxpayer acquires it.
(d) Election.
(1) Time for making election. An election under subsection (b) shall be made not later than the time prescribed by law for filing the return for the taxable year in which the trade or business begins (including extensions thereof).
(2) Scope of election. The period selected under subsection (b) shall be adhered to in computing taxable income for the taxable year for which the election is made and all subsequent taxable years.

In **2010**, P.L. 111-240, Sec. 2031(a), added para. (b)(3), effective for amounts paid or incurred in tax. yrs. begin. after 12/31/2009.

In **2004**, P.L. 108-357, Sec. 902(a)(1), amended para. (b)(1) . . . Sec. 902(a)(2), substituted "deduct" for "amortize" in the heading of subsec. (b), effective for amounts paid or incurred after 10/22/2004.

Prior to amendment, para. (b)(1) read as follows:
"(1) In general. Start-up expenditures may, at the election of the taxpayer, be treated as deferred expenses. Such deferred expenses shall be allowed as a deduction prorated equally over such period of not less than 60 months as may be selected by the taxpayer (beginning with the month in which the active trade or business begins)."

In **1984**, P.L. 98-369, Sec. 94(a), amended Code Sec. 195, effective for tax. yrs. begin. after 6/30/84.

Prior to amendment, Code Sec. 195 read as follows:
"SEC. 195. START-UP EXPENDITURES
"(a) Election to amortize.
"Start-up expenditures may, at the election of the taxpayer, be treated as deferred expenses. Such deferred expenses shall be allowed as a deduction ratably over such period of not less than 60 months as may be selected by the taxpayer (beginning with the month in which the business begins).
"(b) Start-up expenditures.
"For purposes of this section, the term 'start-up expenditure' means any amount—
"(1) paid or incurred in connection with—

(A) investigating the creation or acquisition of an active trade or business, or
(B) creating an active trade or business, and
"(2) which, if paid or incurred in connection with the expansion of an existing trade or business (in the same field as the trade or business referred to in paragraph (1)), would be allowable as a deduction for the taxable year in which paid or incurred.
"(c) Election.
"(1) Time for making election. An election under subsection (a) shall be made not later than the time prescribed by law for filing the return for the taxable year in which the business begins (including extensions thereof).
"(2) Scope of election. The period selected under subsection (a) shall be adhered to in computing taxable income for the taxable year for which the election is made and all subsequent taxable years.
"(3) Manner of making election. An election under subsection (a) shall be made in such manner as the Secretary shall by regulations prescribe.
"(d) Business beginning.
"For purposes of this section, an acquired trade or business shall be treated as beginning when the taxpayer acquires it."
In 1980, P.L. 96-605, Sec. 102(a), added Code Sec. 195, effective for amounts paid or incurred after 7/29/80, in tax. yrs. ending after 7/29/80.

Sec. 196. Deduction for certain unused business credits.

(a) Allowance of deduction.

If any portion of the qualified business credits determined for any taxable year has not, after the application of section 38(c), been allowed to the taxpayer as a credit under section 38 for any taxable year, an amount equal to the credit not so allowed shall be allowed to the taxpayer as a deduction for the first taxable year following the last taxable year for which such credit could, under section 39, have been allowed as a credit.

(b) Taxpayer's dying or ceasing to exist.

If a taxpayer dies or ceases to exist before the first taxable year following the last taxable year for which the qualified business credits could, under section 39, have been allowed as a credit, the amount described in subsection (a) (or the proper portion thereof) shall, under regulations prescribed by the Secretary, be allowed to the taxpayer as a deduction for the taxable year in which such death or cessation occurs.

(c) Qualified business credits.

For purposes of this section, the term "qualified business credits" means—

(1) the investment credit determined under section 46 (but only to the extent attributable to property the basis of which is reduced by section 50(c)),

(2) the work opportunity credit determined under section 51(a),

(3) the alcohol fuels credit determined under section 40(a),

(4) the research credit determined under section 41(a) (other than such credit determined under section 280C(c)(3)) for taxable years beginning after December 31, 1988,

(5) the enhanced oil recovery credit determined under section 43(a),

(6) the empowerment zone employment credit determined under section 1396(a),

(7) the Indian employment credit determined under section 45A(a),

> • *Caution:* Code Sec. 196(c)(8)-(10), following, was amended by Sec. 619(c)(2), P.L. 107-16, the Economic Growth and Tax Relief Reconciliation Act of 2001 (EGTRRA). These provisions generally sunset for tax years beginning after 12/31/2012. For specific sunset provisions see Sec. 901, P.L. 107-16 (as amended) reproduced in history notes for this Code Sec.

(8) the employer Social Security credit determined under section 45B(a),

(9) the new markets tax credit determined under section 45D(a),

(10) the small employer pension plan startup cost credit determined under section 45E(a),

(11) the biodiesel fuels credit determined under section 40A(a),

(12) the low sulfur diesel fuel production credit determined under section 45H(a),

(13) the new energy efficient home credit determined under section 45L(a), and

(14) the small employer health insurance credit determined under section 45R(a).

(d) Special rule for investment tax credit and research credit.

Subsection (a) shall be applied by substituting "an amount equal to 50 percent of" for "an amount equal to" in the case of—

(1) the investment credit determined under section 46 (other than the rehabilitation credit), and

(2) the research credit determined under section 41(a) for a taxable year beginning before January 1, 1990.

In 2010, P.L. 111-312, Sec. 101(a)(1), substituted "December 31, 2012" for "December 31, 2010" both places it appeared in Sec. 901 of P.L. 107-16 [see below], effective as if included in the enactment of P.L. 107-16, EGTRRA, 6/7/2001.
—P.L. 111-148, Sec. 1421(d)(2), deleted "and" at the end of para. (c)(12), substituted ", and" for the period at the end of para. (c)(13), and added para. (c)(14), effective for amounts paid or incurred in tax. yrs. begin. after 12/31/2010.
In 2006, P.L. 109-280, Sec. 811, of this Act [relating to Sec. 901 of P.L. 107-16, see below], provides:
"SEC. 811. PENSIONS AND INDIVIDUAL RETIREMENT ARRANGEMENT PROVISIONS OF ECONOMIC GROWTH AND TAX RELIEF RECONCILIATION ACT OF 2001 MADE PERMANENT.
"Title IX of the Economic Growth and Tax Relief Reconciliation Act of 2001 [P.L. 107-16, see below] shall not apply to the provisions of, and amendments made by, subtitles A through F of title VI of such Act (relating to pension and individual retirement arrangement provisions)."
In 2005, P.L. 109-58, Sec. 1332(d), deleted "and" at the end of para. (c)(11), substituted ", and" for the period at the end of para. (c)(12), and added para. (c)(13), effective for qualified new energy efficient homes acquired after 12/31/2005, in tax. yrs. end. after 12/31/2005.
In 2004, P.L. 108-357, Sec. 302(c)(2), deleted "and" at the end of para. (c)(9), substituted ", and" for the period at the end of para. (c)(10), and added para. (c)(11), effective for fuel produced, and sold or used, after 12/31/2004, in tax. yrs. end. after 12/31/2004.
—P.L. 108-357, Sec. 339(e), deleted "and" at the end of para. (c)(10) [as amended by Sec. 302(c)(2) of this Act, see above], substituted ", and" for the period at the end of para. (c)(11) [as added by Sec. 302(c)(2) of this Act, see above], and added para. (c)(12), effective for expenses paid or incurred after 12/31/2002, in tax. yrs. end. after 12/31/2002.
In 2002, P.L. 107-358, Sec. 2, added subsec. (c) in Sec. 901 of P.L. 107-16 [see below], effective 12/17/2002.
—P.L. 107-147, Sec. 411(n)(2), substituted "first effective" for "established" in Sec. 619(d) of P.L. 107-16, which provides the effective date for amendments made by Sec. 619 of P.L. 107-16, see below.
In 2001, P.L. 107-16, Sec. 619(c)(2), deleted "and" at the end of para. (c)(8), substituted ", and" for the period at the end of para. (c)(9), and added para. (c)(10), effective for costs paid or incurred in tax. yrs. begin. after 12/31/2001, with respect to qualified employer plans first effective after 12/31/2001 [effective date as amended by Sec. 411(n)(2) of P.L. 107-147, see above.].
—P.L. 107-16, Sec. 901, of this Act [as amended by Sec. 2 of P.L. 107-358, and Sec. 101(a)(1) of P.L. 111-312, and as related to Sec. 811 of P.L. 109-280, see above], reads as follows:
"SEC. 901. SUNSET OF PROVISIONS OF ACT.
"(a) In general. All provisions of, and amendments made by, this Act shall not apply—
"(1) to taxable, plan, or limitation years beginning after December 31, 2012, or
"(2) in the case of title V, to estates of decedents dying, gifts made, or generation skipping transfers, after December 31, 2012.
"(b) Application of certain laws. The Internal Revenue Code of 1986 and the Employee Retirement Income Security Act of 1974 shall be applied and administered to years, estates, gifts, and transfers described in subsection (a) as if the provisions and amendments described in subsection (a) had never been enacted.
"(c) Exception. Subsection (a) shall not apply to section 803 (relating to no federal income tax on restitution received by victims of the Nazi regime or their heirs or estates)."

Deductions

In 2000, P.L. 106-554, Sec. 1(a)(7), [which enacted into law Sec. 121(c) of P.L. 106-554 deleted "and" at the end of para. (c)(7), substituted ", and" for the period at the end of para. (c)(8), and added para. (c)(9), effective for investments made after 12/31/2000.

In 1998, P.L. 105-206, Sec. 6020(a), deleted "and" at the end of para. (c)(6), substituted ", and" for the period at the end of para. (c)(7) and added para. (c)(8), effective for taxes paid after 12/31/93, with respect to services performed before, on, or after such date.

In 1996, P.L. 104-188, Sec. 1201(e)(1), substituted "work opportunity credit" for "targeted jobs credit" in para. (c)(2), effective for individuals who begin work for the employer after 9/30/96.

In 1993, P.L. 103-66, Sec. 13302(b)(2), deleted "and" at the end of para. (c)(4), substituted ", and " for the period at the end of para. (c)(5) and added para. (c)(6), effective 8/10/93.

—P.L. 103-66, Sec. 13322(c)(2), deleted "and" from the end of para. (c)(5) [as amended by Sec. 13302(b)(2) of this Act] substituted ", and" for the period at the end of para. (c)(6) [as amended by Sec. 13302(b)(2) of this Act] and added para. (c)(7), effective for wages paid or incurred after 12/31/93.

In 1990, P.L. 101-508, Sec. 11511(b)(3), deleted "and" at the end of para. (c)(3), substituted ", and" for the period at the end of para. (c)(4) and added para. (c)(5), effective for costs paid or incurred in tax. yrs. after 12/31/90 except as provided in Sec. 11511(d)(2) of this Act, which read as follows:

"(2) Special rule for significant expansion of projects. For purposes of section 43(c)(2)(A)(iii) of the Internal Revenue Code of 1986 (as added by subsection (a) [of Sec. 11511 of P.L. 101-508]), any significant expansion after December 31, 1990, of a project begun before January 1, 1991, shall be treated as a project with respect to which the first injection commences after December 31, 1990."

—P.L. 101-508, Sec. 11813(b)(12)(A)(i), substituted "section 46" for "section 46(a)" in para. (c)(1) . . . Sec. 11813(b)(12)(A)(ii), substituted "section 50(c)" for "section 48(q)" in para. (c)(1) . . . Sec. 11813(b)(12)(B)(i), substituted "section 46" for "section 46(a)" in para. (d)(1) . . . Sec. 11813(b)(12)(B)(ii), substituted "other than the rehabilitation credit" for "other than a credit to which section 48(q)(3) applies" in para. (d)(1), effective for property placed in service after 12/31/90 except as provided in Sec. 11813(c)(2) of this Act, reproduced in note following Code Sec. 46.

In 1989, P.L. 101-239, Sec. 7110(c)(2), added "for a taxable year beginning before January 1, 1990" before the period in para. (d)(2), effective for tax. yrs. begin. after 12/31/89.

—P.L. 101-239, Sec. 7814(e)(1), substituted "substituting, 'an amount equal to 50 percent of' for 'an amount equal to' in the case of—" for "substituting an amount equal to 50 percent of for an amount equal to in the case of—" in subsec. (d) . . . Sec. 7814(e)(2)(D), added "(other than such credit determined under section 280C(c)(3))" after "section 41(a)" in para. (c)(4), effective for tax. yrs. begin. after 12/31/88.

In 1988, P.L. 100-647, Sec. 4008(b)(2)(A), deleted "and" at the end of para. (c)(2), substituted ", and" for the period at the end of para. (c)(3), and added para. (c)(4) . . . Sec. 4008(b)(2)(B), amended subsec. (d), effective for tax. yrs. begin. after 12/31/88.

Prior to amendment, subsec. (d) read as follows:
"(d) Special rule for investment tax credit.
"In the case of the investment credit determined under section 46(a) (other than a credit to which section 48(q)(3) applies), subsection (a) shall be applied by substituting 'an amount equal to 50 percent of' for 'an amount equal to'."

In 1984, P.L. 98-369, Sec. 474(r)(8)(A), amended Code Sec. 196, effective for tax. yrs. begin. after 12/31/83, and for carrybacks from tax. yrs. begin. before 12/31/83.

Prior to amendment, Code Sec. 196 read as follows:
"SEC. 196. DEDUCTION FOR CERTAIN UNUSED INVESTMENT CREDITS.
"(a) Allowance of deductions.
"If—
"(1) the amount of the credit determined under section 46(a)(2) for any taxable year exceeds the limitation provided by section 46(a)(3) for such taxable year, and
"(2) the amount of such excess has not, after the application of section 46(b), been allowed to the taxpayer as a credit under section 38 for any taxable year, then an amount equal to 50 percent of the amount of such excess (to the extent attributable to property the basis of which is reduced under section 48(q)) not so allowed as a credit shall be allowed to the taxpayer as a deduction for the first taxable year following the last taxable year in which such excess could under section 46(b) have been allowed as a credit.
"(b) Taxpayers dying or ceasing to exist.
"If a taxpayer dies or ceases to exist prior to the first taxable year following the last taxable year in which the excess described in subsection (a) could under section 46(b) have been allowed as a credit, the amount described in subsection (a), or the proper portion thereof, shall, under regulations prescribed by the Secretary, be allowed to the taxpayer as a deduction for the taxable year in which such death or cessation occurs.
"(c) Special rule for qualified rehabilitated buildings.
"In the case of any credit to which section 48(q)(3) applies, subsection (a) shall be applied without regard to the phrase '50 percent of'."

In 1982, P.L. 97-248, Sec. 205(a)(2), added Code Sec. 196, effective for periods after 12/31/82, under rules similar to the rules of Code Sec. 48(m). Sec. 205(c)(1)(B)-(E) of this Act also provide:

"(B) Exception.— The amendments made by subsection (a) shall not apply to any property which—
"(i) is constructed, reconstructed, erected, or acquired pursuant to a contract which was entered into after August 13, 1981, and was, on July 1, 1982, and at all times thereafter, binding on the taxpayer,

Code Sec. 197(d)(1)(C)

"(ii) is placed in service after December 31, 1982, and before January 1, 1986,
"(iii) with respect to which an election under section 168(f)(8)(A) of such Code is not in effect at any time, and
"(iv) is not described in section 167(1)(3)(A) of such Code.
"(C) Special rule for integrated manufacturing facilities.—
"(i) In general.— In the case of any integrated manufacturing facility, the requirements of clause (i) of subparagraph (B) shall be treated as met if—
"(I) the on-site construction of the facility began before July 1, 1982, and
"(II) during the period beginning after August 13, 1981, and ending on July 1, 1982, the taxpayer constructed (or entered into binding contracts for the construction of) more than 20 percent of the cost of such facility.
"(ii) Integrated manufacturing facility.— For purposes of clause (i), the term 'integrated manufacturing facility' means 1 or more facilities—
"(I) located on a single site,
"(II) for the manufacture of 1 or more manufactured products from raw materials by the application of 2 or more integrated manufacturing processes.
"(D) Special rule for historic structures.— In the case of any certified historic structure (as defined in section 48(g)(3) of the Internal Revenue Code of 1954), clause (i) of subparagraph (B) shall be applied by substituting 'December 31, 1980' for 'August 13, 1981.'
"(E) Certain projects with respect to historic structures.— In the case of any certified historic structure (as so defined), the requirements of clause (i) of subparagraph (B) shall be treated as met with respect to such property—
"(i) if the rehabilitation begins after December 31, 1980, and before July 1, 1982, or
"(ii) if—
"(I) before July 1, 1982, a public offering with respect to interests in such property was registered with the Securities and Exchange Commission,
"(II) before such date an application with respect to such property was filed under section 8 of the United States Housing Act of 1937, and
"(III) such property is placed in service before July 1, 1984."

Sec. 197. Amortization of goodwill and certain other intangibles.

(a) General rule.

A taxpayer shall be entitled to an amortization deduction with respect to any amortizable section 197 intangible. The amount of such deduction shall be determined by amortizing the adjusted basis (for purposes of determining gain) of such intangible ratably over the 15-year period beginning with the month in which such intangible was acquired.

(b) No other depreciation or amortization deduction allowable.

Except as provided in subsection (a), no depreciation or amortization deduction shall be allowable with respect to any amortizable section 197 intangible.

(c) Amortizable section 197 intangible.

For purposes of this section—

(1) In general. Except as otherwise provided in this section, the term "amortizable section 197 intangible" means any section 197 intangible—

(A) which is acquired by the taxpayer after the date of the enactment of this section, and

(B) which is held in connection with the conduct of a trade or business or an activity described in section 212.

(2) Exclusion of self-created intangibles, etc. The term "amortizable section 197 intangible" shall not include any section 197 intangible—

(A) which is not described in subparagraph (D), (E), or (F) of subsection (d)(1), and

(B) which is created by the taxpayer.

This paragraph shall not apply if the intangible is created in connection with a transaction (or series of related transactions) involving the acquisition of assets constituting a trade or business or substantial portion thereof.

(3) Anti-churning rules. For exclusion of intangibles acquired in certain transactions, see subsection (f)(9).

(d) Section 197 intangible.

For purposes of this section—

(1) In general. Except as otherwise provided in this section, the term "section 197 intangible" means—

(A) goodwill,

(B) going concern value,

(C) any of the following intangible items:

1,675

(i) workforce in place including its composition and terms and conditions (contractual or otherwise) of its employment,

(ii) business books and records, operating systems, or any other information base (including lists or other information with respect to current or prospective customers),

(iii) any patent, copyright, formula, process, design, pattern, knowhow, format, or other similar item,

(iv) any customer-based intangible,

(v) any supplier-based intangible, and

(vi) any other similar item,

(D) any license, permit, or other right granted by a governmental unit or an agency or instrumentality thereof,

(E) any covenant not to compete (or other arrangement to the extent such arrangement has substantially the same effect as a covenant not to compete) entered into in connection with an acquisition (directly or indirectly) of an interest in a trade or business or substantial portion thereof, and

(F) any franchise, trademark, or trade name.

(2) Customer-based intangible.

(A) In general. The term "customer-based intangible" means—

(i) composition of market,

(ii) market share, and

(iii) any other value resulting from future provision of goods or services pursuant to relationships (contractual or otherwise) in the ordinary course of business with customers.

(B) Special rule for financial institutions. In the case of a financial institution, the term "customer-based intangible" includes deposit base and similar items.

(3) Supplier-based intangible. The term "supplier-based intangible" means any value resulting from future acquisitions of goods or services pursuant to relationships (contractual or otherwise) in the ordinary course of business with suppliers of goods or services to be used or sold by the taxpayer.

(e) Exceptions.

For purposes of this section, the term "section 197 intangible" shall not include any of the following:

(1) Financial interests. Any interest—

(A) in a corporation, partnership, trust, or estate, or

(B) under an existing futures contract, foreign currency contract, notional principal contract, or other similar financial contract.

(2) Land. Any interest in land.

(3) Computer software.

(A) In general. Any—

(i) computer software which is readily available for purchase by the general public, is subject to a nonexclusive license, and has not been substantially modified, and

(ii) other computer software which is not acquired in a transaction (or series of related transactions) involving the acquisition of assets constituting a trade or business or substantial portion thereof.

(B) Computer software defined. For purposes of subparagraph (A), the term "computer software" means any program designed to cause a computer to perform a desired function. Such term shall not include any data base or similar item unless the data base or item is in the public domain and is incidental to the operation of otherwise qualifying computer software.

(4) Certain interests or rights acquired separately. Any of the following not acquired in a transaction (or series of related transactions) involving the acquisition of assets constituting a trade business or substantial portion thereof:

(A) Any interest in a film, sound recording, video tape, book, or similar property.

(B) Any right to receive tangible property or services under a contract or granted by a governmental unit or agency or instrumentality thereof.

(C) Any interest in a patent or copyright.

(D) To the extent provided in regulations, any right under a contract (or granted by a governmental unit or an agency or instrumentality thereof) if such right—

(i) has a fixed duration of less than 15 years, or

(ii) is fixed as to amount and, without regard to this section, would be recoverable under a method similar to the unit-of-production method.

(5) Interests under leases and debt instruments. Any interest under—

(A) an existing lease of tangible property, or

(B) except as provided in subsection (d)(2)(B), any existing indebtedness.

(6) Mortgage servicing. Any right to service indebtedness which is secured by residential real property unless such right is acquired in a transaction (or series of related transactions) involving the acquisition of assets (other than rights described in this paragraph) constituting a trade or business or substantial portion thereof.

(7) Certain transaction costs. Any fees for professional services, and any transaction costs, incurred by parties to a transaction with respect to which any portion of the gain or loss is not recognized under part III of subchapter C.

(f) Special rules.

(1) Treatment of certain dispositions, etc.

(A) In general. If there is a disposition of any amortizable section 197 intangible acquired in a transaction or series of related transactions (or any such intangible becomes worthless) and one or more other amortizable section 197 intangibles acquired in such transaction or series of related transactions are retained—

(i) no loss shall be recognized by reason of such disposition (or such worthlessness), and

(ii) appropriate adjustments to the adjusted bases of such retained intangibles shall be made for any loss not recognized under clause (i).

(B) Special rule for covenants not to compete. In the case of any section 197 intangible which is a covenant not to compete (or other arrangement) described in subsection (d)(1)(E), in no event shall such covenant or other arrangement be treated as disposed of (or becoming worthless) before the disposition of the entire interest described in such subsection in connection with which such covenant (or other arrangement) was entered into.

(C) Special rule. All persons treated as a single taxpayer under section 41(f)(1) shall be so treated for purposes of this paragraph.

(2) Treatment of certain transfers.

(A) In general. In the case of any section 197 intangible transferred in a transaction described in subparagraph (B), the transferee shall be treated as the transferor for purposes of applying this section with respect to so much of the adjusted basis in the hands of the transferee as does not exceed the adjusted basis in the hands of the transferor.

(B) Transactions covered. The transactions described in this subparagraph are—

(i) any transaction described in section 332, 351, 361, 721, 731, 1031, or 1033, and

(ii) any transaction between members of the same affiliated group during any taxable year for which a consolidated return is made by such group.

(3) Treatment of amounts paid pursuant to covenants not to compete, etc. Any amount paid or incurred pursuant to a covenant or arrangement referred to in subsection (d)(1)(E) shall be treated as an amount chargeable to capital account.

(4) Treatment of franchises, etc.

(A) Franchise. The term "franchise" has the meaning given to such term by section 1253(b)(1).

(B) Treatment of renewals. Any renewal of a franchise, trademark, or trade name (or of a license, a permit, or other right referred to in subsection (d)(1)(D)) shall be treated as an acquisition. The preceding sentence shall only apply with respect to costs incurred in connection with such renewal.

(C) Certain amounts not taken into account. Any amount to which section 1253(d)(1) applies shall not be taken into account under this section.

(5) Treatment of certain reinsurance transactions. In the case of any amortizable section 197 intangible resulting from an assumption reinsurance transaction, the amount taken into account as the adjusted basis of such intangible under this section shall be the excess of—

(A) the amount paid or incurred by the acquirer under the assumption reinsurance transaction, over

(B) the amount required to be capitalized under section 848 in connection with such transaction.

Subsection (b) shall not apply to any amount required to be capitalized under section 848.

(6) Treatment of certain subleases. For purposes of this section, a sublease shall be treated in the same manner as a lease of the underlying property involved.

(7) Treatment as depreciable. For purposes of this chapter, any amortizable section 197 intangible shall be treated as property which is of a character subject to the allowance for depreciation provided in section 167.

(8) Treatment of certain increments in value. This section shall not apply to any increment in value if, without regard to this section, such increment is properly taken into account in determining the cost of property which is not a section 197 intangible.

(9) Anti-churning rules. For purposes of this section—

(A) In general. The term "amortizable section 197 intangible" shall not include any section 197 intangible which is described in subparagraph (A) or (B) of subsection (d)(1) (or for which depreciation or amortization would not have been allowable but for this section) and which is acquired by the taxpayer after the date of the enactment of this section, if—

(i) the intangible was held or used at any time on or after July 25, 1991, and on or before such date of enactment by the taxpayer or a related person,

(ii) the intangible was acquired from a person who held such intangible at any time on or after July 25, 1991, and on or before such date of enactment, and, as part of the transaction, the user of such intangible does not change, or

(iii) the taxpayer grants the right to use such intangible to a person (or a person related to such person) who held or used such intangible at any time on or after July 25, 1991, and on or before such date of enactment.

For purposes of this subparagraph, the determination of whether the user of property changes as part of a transaction shall be determined in accordance with regulations prescribed by the Secretary. For purposes of this subparagraph, deductions allowable under section 1253(d) shall be treated as deductions allowable for amortization.

(B) Exception where gain recognized. If—

(i) subparagraph (A) would not apply to an intangible acquired by the taxpayer but for the last sentence of subparagraph (C)(i), and

(ii) the person from whom the taxpayer acquired the intangible elects, notwithstanding any other provision of this title—

(I) to recognize gain on the disposition of the intangible, and

(II) to pay a tax on such gain which, when added to any other income tax on such gain under this title, equals such gain multiplied by the highest rate of income tax applicable to such person under this title,

then subparagraph (A) shall apply to the intangible only to the extent that the taxpayer's adjusted basis in the intangible exceeds the gain recognized under clause (ii)(I).

(C) Related person defined. For purposes of this paragraph—

(i) Related person. A person (hereinafter in this paragraph referred to as the "related person") is related to any person if—

(I) the related person bears a relationship to such person specified in section 267(b) or section 707(b)(1), or

(II) the related person and such person are engaged in trades or businesses under common control (within the meaning of subparagraphs (A) and (B) of section 41(f)(1)).

For purposes of subclause (I), in applying section 267(b) or 707(b)(1), "20 percent" shall be substituted for "50 percent".

(ii) Time for making determination. A person shall be treated as related to another person if such relationship exists immediately before or immediately after the acquisition of the intangible involved.

(D) Acquisitions by reason of death. Subparagraph (A) shall not apply to the acquisition of any property by the taxpayer if the basis of the property in the hands of the taxpayer is determined under section 1014(a).

(E) Special rule for partnerships. With respect to any increase in the basis of partnership property under section 732, 734, or 743, determinations under this paragraph shall be made at the partner level and each partner shall be treated as having owned and used such partner's proportionate share of the partnership assets.

(F) Anti-abuse rules. The term "amortizable section 197 intangible" does not include any section 197 intangible acquired in a transaction, one of the principal purposes of which is to avoid the requirement of subsection (c)(1) that the intangible be acquired after the date of the enactment of this section or to avoid the provisions of subparagraph (A).

(10) Tax-exempt use property subject to lease. In the case of any section 197 intangible which would be tax-exempt use property as defined in subsection (h) of section 168 if such section applied to such intangible, the amortization period under this section shall not be less than 125 percent of the lease term (within the meaning of section 168(i)(3)).

(g) Regulations.

The Secretary shall prescribe such regulations as may be appropriate to carry out the purposes of this section, including such regulations as may be appropriate to prevent avoidance of the purposes of this section through related persons or otherwise.

In 2005, P.L. 109-135, Sec. 403(ff), added ", and in the case of property treated as tax-exempt use property other than by reason of a lease, to property acquired after March 12, 2004" before the period at the end of Sec. 849(a) of P.L. 108-357. Sec. 849(a) provides the effective date for the amendment made by Sec. 847(b)(3) of P.L. 108-357, see below.

In 2004, P.L. 108-357, Sec. 847(b)(3), added para. (f)(10), effective for leases entered into after 3/12/2004[, and in the case of property treated as tax-exempt use property other than by reason of a lease, to property acquired after March 12, 2004.] [as added by Sec. 403(ff), P.L. 109-135, see above].

—P.L. 108-357, Sec. 849(b), of this Act, reads as follows:

"(b) Exception.

"(1) In general. The amendments made by this part shall not apply to qualified transportation property.

"(2) Qualified transportation property. For purposes of paragraph (1), the term 'qualified transportation property' means domestic property subject to a lease with respect to which a formal application—

"(A) was submitted for approval to the Federal Transit Administration (an agency of the Department of Transportation) after June 30, 2003, and before March 13, 2004,

"(B) is approved by the Federal Transit Administration before January 1, 2006, and

"(C) includes a description of such property and the value of such property.

"(3) Exchanges and conversion of tax-exempt use property. Section 470(e)(4) of the Internal Revenue Code of 1986, as added by section 848, shall apply to property exchanged or converted after the date of the enactment of this Act.

"(4) Intangibles and Indian tribal governments. The amendments made subsections (b)(2), (b)(3), and (e) of section 847, and the treatment of property described in clauses (ii) and (iii) of section 470(c)(2)(B) of the Internal Revenue Code of 1986 (as added by section 848) as tangible property, shall apply to leases entered into after October 3, 2004."

—P.L. 108-357, Sec. 886(a), deleted para. (e)(6) and redesignated paras. (e)(7) and (8) as paras. (e)(6) and (7), effective for property acquired after 10/22/2004. Prior to deletion, para. (e)(6) read as follows:

"(6) Treatment of sports franchises. A franchise to engage in professional football, basketball, baseball, or other professional sport, and any item acquired in connection with such a franchise."

In 1996, P.L. 104-188, Sec. 1703(l), amended Sec. 13261(g)(2)(A)(iii) of P.L. 103-66, relating to elections, by substituting "by the taxpayer or a related person" for "by the taxpayer", see below.

In 1993, P.L. 103-66, Sec. 13261(a), added Code Sec. 197, effective for property acquired after 8/10/93, except as provided in Sec. 13261(g)(2) [as amended by Sec. 1703(l) of P.L. 104-188, see above] and (3) of this Act, which reads as follows:

"(2) Election to have amendments apply to property acquired after July 25, 1991.

"(A) In general. If an election under this paragraph applies to the taxpayer—

"(i) the amendments made by this section shall apply to property acquired by the taxpayer after July 25, 1991,

"(ii) subsection (c)(1)(A) of section 197 of the Internal Revenue Code of 1986 (as added by this section) (and so much of subsection (f)(9)(A) of such section 197 as precedes clause (i) thereof) shall be applied with respect to the taxpayer by treating July 25, 1991, as the date of the enactment of such section, and

"(iii) in applying subsection (f)(9) of such section, with respect to any property acquired by the taxpayer or a related person on or before the date of the enactment of this Act, only holding or use on July 25, 1991, shall be taken into account.

"(B) Election. An election under this paragraph shall be made at such time and in such manner as the Secretary of the Treasury or his delegate may prescribe. Such an election by any taxpayer, once made—

"(i) may be revoked only with the consent of the Secretary, and

"(ii) shall apply to the taxpayer making such election and any other taxpayer under common control with the taxpayer (within the meaning of subparagraphs (A) and (B) of section 41(f)(1) of such Code) at any time after August 2, 1993, and on or before the date on which such election is made.

"(3) Elective binding contract exception.

"(A) In general. The amendments made by this section shall not apply to any acquisition of property by the taxpayer if—

"(i) such acquisition is pursuant to a written binding contract in effect on the date of the enactment of this Act and at all times thereafter before such acquisition,

"(ii) an election under paragraph (2) does not apply to the taxpayer, and

"(iii) the taxpayer makes an election under this paragraph with respect to such contract.

"(B) Election. An election under this paragraph shall be made at such time and in such manner as the Secretary of the Treasury or his delegate shall prescribe. Such an election, once made—

"(i) may be revoked only with the consent of the Secretary, and

"(ii) shall apply to all property acquired pursuant to the contract with respect to which such election was made."

Sec. 198. Expensing of environmental remediation costs.

(a) In general.

A taxpayer may elect to treat any qualified environmental remediation expenditure which is paid or incurred by the taxpayer as an expense which is not chargeable to capital account. Any expenditure which is so treated shall be allowed as a deduction for the taxable year in which it is paid or incurred.

(b) Qualified environmental remediation expenditure.

For purposes of this section—

(1) In general. The term "qualified environmental remediation expenditure" means any expenditure—

(A) which is otherwise chargeable to capital account, and

(B) which is paid or incurred in connection with the abatement or control of hazardous substances at a qualified contaminated site.

(2) Special rule for expenditures for depreciable property. Such term shall not include any expenditure for the acquisition of property of a character subject to the allowance for depreciation which is used in connection with the abatement or control of hazardous substances at a qualified contaminated site; except that the portion of the allowance under section 167 for such property which is otherwise allocated to such site shall be treated as a qualified environmental remediation expenditure.

(c) Qualified contaminated site.

For purposes of this section—

(1) In general. The term "qualified contaminated site" means any area—

(A) which is held by the taxpayer for use in a trade or business or for the production of income, or which is property described in section 1221(a)(1) in the hands of the taxpayer, and

(B) at or on which there has been a release (or threat of release) or disposal of any hazardous substance.

(2) National priorities listed sites not included. Such term shall not include any site which is on, or proposed for, the national priorities list under section 105(a)(8)(B) of the Comprehensive Environmental Response, Compensation, and Liability Act of 1980 (as in effect on the date of the enactment of this section).

(3) Taxpayer must receive statement from State environmental agency. An area shall be treated as a qualified contaminated site with respect to expenditures paid or incurred during any taxable year only if the taxpayer receives a statement from the appropriate agency of the State in which such area is located that such area meets the requirement of paragraph (1)(B).

(4) Appropriate State agency. For purposes of paragraph (3), the chief executive officer of each State may, in consultation with the Administrator of the Environmental Protection Agency, designate the appropriate State environmental agency within 60 days of the date of the enactment of this section. If the chief executive officer of a State has not designated an appropriate environmental agency within such 60-day period, the appropriate environmental agency for such State shall be designated by the Administrator of the Environmental Protection Agency.

(d) Hazardous substance.

For purposes of this section—

(1) In general. The term "hazardous substance" means—

(A) any substance which is a hazardous substance as defined in section 101(14) of the Comprehensive Environmental Response, Compensation, and Liability Act of 1980,

(B) any substance which is designated as a hazardous substance under section 102 of such Act, and

(C) any petroleum product (as defined in section 4612(a)(3)).

(2) Exception. Such term shall not include any substance with respect to which a removal or remedial action is not permitted under section 104 of such Act by reason of subsection (a)(3) thereof.

(e) Deduction recaptured as ordinary income on sale, etc.

Solely for purposes of section 1245, in the case of property to which a qualified environmental remediation expenditure would have been capitalized but for this section—

(1) the deduction allowed by this section for such expenditure shall be treated as a deduction for depreciation, and

(2) such property (if not otherwise section 1245 property) shall be treated as section 1245 property solely for purposes of applying section 1245 to such deduction.

(f) Coordination with other provisions.

Sections 280B and 468 shall not apply to amounts which are treated as expenses under this section.

(g) Regulations.

The Secretary shall prescribe such regulations as may be necessary or appropriate to carry out the purposes of this section.

(h) Termination.

This section shall not apply to expenditures paid or incurred after December 31, 2011.

In 2010, P.L. 111-312, Sec. 745(a), substituted "December 31, 2011" for "December 31, 2009" in subsec. (h), effective for expenditures paid or incurred after 12/31/2009.

In 2008, P.L. 110-343, Sec. 318(a) Div C, substituted "December 31, 2009" for "December 31, 2007" in subsec. (h), effective for expenditures paid or incurred after 12/31/2007.

In 2006, P.L. 109-432, Sec. 109(a), substituted "2007" for "2005" in subsec. (h) ... Sec. 109(b), deleted "and" at the end of subpara. (d)(1)(A), substituted ", and" for the period at the end of subpara. (d)(1)(B), and added subpara. (d)(1)(C), effective for expenditures paid or incurred after 12/31/2005.

In 2004, P.L. 108-311, Sec. 308(a), substituted "December 31, 2005" for "December 31, 2003" in subsec. (h), effective for expenditures paid or incurred after 12/31/2003.

In 2000, P.L. 106-554, Sec. 1(a)(7), [which enacted into law Sec. 162(a) of P.L. 106-554] amended subsec. (c) ... Sec. 1(a)(7) [which enacted into law Sec. 162(b) of P.L. 106-554], substituted "2003" for "2001" in subsec. (h), effective for expenditures paid or incurred after 12/21/2000.

Prior to amendment, subsec. (c) read as follows:

"(c) *Qualified contaminated site.* For purposes of this section—

"(1) Qualified contaminated site.

"(A) In general. The term 'qualified contaminated site' means any area—

"(i) which is held by the taxpayer for use in a trade or business or for the production of income, or which is property described in section 1221(a)(1) in the hands of the taxpayer,

"(ii) which is within a targeted area, and

"(iii) at or on which there has been a release (or threat of release) or disposal of any hazardous substance.

"(B) Taxpayer must receive statement from state environmental agency. An area shall be treated as a qualified contaminated site with respect to expenditures paid or incurred during any taxable year only if the taxpayer receives a statement from the appropriate agency of the State in which such area is located that such area meets the requirements of clauses (ii) and (iii) of subparagraph (A).

"(C) Appropriate State agency. For purposes of subparagraph (B), the chief executive officer of each State may, in consultation with the Administrator of the Environmental Protection Agency, designate the appropriate State environmental agency within 60 days of the date of enactment of this section. If the chief executive officer of a State has not designated an appropriate State environmental agency within such 60-day period, the appropriate environmental agency for such State shall be designated by the Administrator of the Environmental Protection Agency.

"(2) Targeted area.

"(A) In general. The term 'targeted area' means—

"(i) any population census tract with a poverty rate of not less than 20 percent,

"(ii) a population census tract with a population of less than 2,000 if—

"(I) more than 75 percent of such tract is zoned for commercial or industrial use, and

"(II) such tract is contiguous to 1 or more other population census tracts which meet the requirement of clause (i) without regard to this clause,

"(iii) any empowerment zone or enterprise community (and any supplemental zone designated on December 21, 1994), and

"(iv) any site announced before February 1, 1997, as being included as a brownfields pilot project of the Environmental Protection Agency.

"(B) National priorities listed sites not included. Such term shall not include any site which is on, or proposed for, the national priorities list under section 105(a)(8)(B) of the Comprehensive Environmental Response, Compensation, and Liability Act of 1980 (as in effect on the date of the enactment of this section).

"(C) Certain rules to apply. For purposes of this paragraph the rules of sections 1392(b)(4) and 1393(a)(9) shall apply."

In 1999, P.L. 106-170, Sec. 511, substituted "2001" for "2000" in subsec. (h), effective 12/17/99.

— P.L. 106-170, Sec. 532(c)(2)(A), substituted "section 1221(a)(1)" for "section 1221(1)" in clause (c)(1)(A)(i), effective for any instrument held, acquired, or entered into, any transaction entered into, and supplies held or acquired on or after 12/17/99.

In 1997, P.L. 105-34, Sec. 941(a), added Code. Sec. 198, effective for expenditures paid or incurred after 8/5/97, in tax. yrs. end. after 8/5/97.

Sec. 198A. Expensing of qualified disaster expenses.

(a) In general.

A taxpayer may elect to treat any qualified disaster expenses which are paid or incurred by the taxpayer as an expense which is not chargeable to capital account. Any expense which is so treated shall be allowed as a deduction for the taxable year in which it is paid or incurred.

(b) Qualified disaster expense.

For purposes of this section, the term "qualified disaster expense" means any expenditure—

(1) which is paid or incurred in connection with a trade or business or with business-related property,

(2) which is—

(A) for the abatement or control of hazardous substances that were released on account of a federally declared disaster occurring before January 1, 2010,

(B) for the removal of debris from, or the demolition of structures on, real property which is business-related property damaged or destroyed as a result of a federally declared disaster occurring before such date, or

(C) for the repair of business-related property damaged as a result of a federally declared disaster occurring before such date, and

(3) which is otherwise chargeable to capital account.

(c) Other definitions.

For purposes of this section—

(1) Business-related property. The term "business-related property" means property—

(A) held by the taxpayer for use in a trade or business or for the production of income, or

(B) described in section 1221(a)(1) in the hands of the taxpayer.

(2) Federally declared disaster. The term "federally declared disaster" has the meaning given such term by section 165(h)(3)(C)(i).

(d) Deduction recaptured as ordinary income on sale, etc.

Solely for purposes of section 1245, in the case of property to which a qualified disaster expense would have been capitalized but for this section—

(1) the deduction allowed by this section for such expense shall be treated as a deduction for depreciation, and

(2) such property (if not otherwise section 1245 property) shall be treated as section 1245 property solely for purposes of applying section 1245 to such deduction.

(e) Coordination with other provisions.
Sections 198, 280B, and 468 shall not apply to amounts which are treated as expenses under this section.

(f) Regulations.
The Secretary shall prescribe such regulations as may be necessary or appropriate to carry out the purposes of this section.

In 2008, P.L. 110-343, Sec. 707(a)DivC, added Code Sec. 198A, effective for amounts paid or incurred after 12/31/2007 in connection with disaster declared after such date.
—P.L. 110-343, Sec. 712DivC, of this Act, provides:
Sec. 712. Coordination with heartland disaster relief. The amendments made by this subtitle, other than the amendments made by sections 706(a)(2), 710, and 711, shall not apply to any disaster described in section 702(c)(1)(A), or to any expenditure or loss resulting from such disaster."

Sec. 199. Income attributable to domestic production activities.

(a) Allowance of deduction.
(1) In general. There shall be allowed as a deduction an amount equal to 9 percent of the lesser of—
(A) the qualified production activities income of the taxpayer for the taxable year, or
(B) taxable income (determined without regard to this section) for the taxable year.

(2) Phasein. In the case of any taxable year beginning after 2004 and before 2010, paragraph (1) shall be applied by substituting for the percentage contained therein the transition percentage determined under the following table:

For taxable years beginning in:	The transition percentage is:
2005 or 2006	3
2007, 2008, or 2009	6

(b) Deduction limited to wages paid.
(1) In general. The amount of the deduction allowable under subsection (a) for any taxable year shall not exceed 50 percent of the W-2 wages of the taxpayer for the taxable year.

(2) W-2 wages. For purposes of this section—
(A) In general. The term "W-2 wages" means, with respect to any person for any taxable year of such person, the sum of the amounts described in paragraphs (3) and (8) of section 6051(a) paid by such person with respect to employment of employees by such person during the calendar year ending during such taxable year.
(B) Limitation to wages attributable to domestic production. Such term shall not include any amount which is not properly allocable to domestic production gross receipts for purposes of subsection (c)(1).
(C) Return requirement. Such term shall not include any amount which is not properly included in a return filed with the Social Security Administration on or before the 60th day after the due date (including extensions) for such return.
(D) Special rule for qualified film. In the case of a qualified film, such term shall include compensation for services performed in the United States by actors, production personnel, directors, and producers.

(3) Acquisitions and dispositions. The Secretary shall provide for the application of this subsection in cases where the taxpayer acquires, or disposes of, the major portion of a trade or business or the major portion of a separate unit of a trade or business during the taxable year.

(c) Qualified production activities income.
For purposes of this section—
(1) In general. The term "qualified production activities income" for any taxable year means an amount equal to the excess (if any) of—
(A) the taxpayer's domestic production gross receipts for such taxable year, over
(B) the sum of—
(i) the cost of goods sold that are allocable to such receipts, and
(ii) other expenses, losses, or deductions (other than the deduction allowed under this section), which are properly allocable to such receipts.

(2) Allocation method. The Secretary shall prescribe rules for the proper allocation of items described in paragraph (1) for purposes of determining qualified production activities income. Such rules shall provide for the proper allocation of items whether or not such items are directly allocable to domestic production gross receipts.

(3) Special rules for determining costs.
(A) In general. For purposes of determining costs under clause (i) of paragraph (1)(B), any item or service brought into the United States shall be treated as acquired by purchase, and its cost shall be treated as not less than its value immediately after it entered the United States. A similar rule shall apply in determining the adjusted basis of leased or rented property where the lease or rental gives rise to domestic production gross receipts.
(B) Exports for further manufacture. In the case of any property described in subparagraph (A) that had been exported by the taxpayer for further manufacture, the increase in cost or adjusted basis under subparagraph (A) shall not exceed the difference between the value of the property when exported and the value of the property when brought back into the United States after the further manufacture.

(4) Domestic production gross receipts.
(A) In general. The term "domestic production gross receipts" means the gross receipts of the taxpayer which are derived from—
(i) any lease, rental, license, sale, exchange, or other disposition of—
(I) qualifying production property which was manufactured, produced, grown, or extracted by the taxpayer in whole or in significant part within the United States,
(II) any qualified film produced by the taxpayer, or
(III) electricity, natural gas, or potable water produced by the taxpayer in the United States,
(ii) in the case of a taxpayer engaged in the active conduct of a construction trade or business, construction of real property performed in the United States by the taxpayer in the ordinary course of such trade or business, or
(iii) in the case of a taxpayer engaged in the active conduct of an engineering or architectural services trade or business, engineering or architectural services performed in the United States by the taxpayer in the ordinary course of such trade or business with respect to the construction of real property in the United States.
(B) Exceptions. Such term shall not include gross receipts of the taxpayer which are derived from—
(i) the sale of food and beverages prepared by the taxpayer at a retail establishment,

(ii) the transmission or distribution of electricity, natural gas, or potable water, or

(iii) the lease, rental, license, sale, exchange, or other disposition of land.

(C) Special rule for certain government contracts. Gross receipts derived from the manufacture or production of any property described in subparagraph (A)(i)(I) shall be treated as meeting the requirements of subparagraph (A)(i) if—

(i) such property is manufactured or produced by the taxpayer pursuant to a contract with the Federal Government, and

(ii) the Federal Acquisition Regulation requires that title or risk of loss with respect to such property be transferred to the Federal Government before the manufacture or production of such property is complete.

(D) Partnerships owned by expanded affiliated groups. For purposes of this paragraph, if all of the interests in the capital and profits of a partnership are owned by members of a single expanded affiliated group at all times during the taxable year of such partnership, the partnership and all members of such group shall be treated as a single taxpayer during such period.

(5) Qualifying production property. The term "qualifying production property" means—

(A) tangible personal property,

(B) any computer software, and

(C) any property described in section 168(f)(4).

(6) Qualified film. The term "qualified film" means any property described in section 168(f)(3) if not less than 50 percent of the total compensation relating to the production of such property is compensation for services performed in the United States by actors, production personnel, directors, and producers. Such term does not include property with respect to which records are required to be maintained under section 2257 of title 18, United States Code. A qualified film shall include any copyrights, trademarks, or other intangibles with respect to such film. The methods and means of distributing a qualified film shall not affect the availability of the deduction under this section.

(7) Related persons.

(A) In general. The term "domestic production gross receipts" shall not include any gross receipts of the taxpayer derived from property leased, licensed, or rented by the taxpayer for use by any related person.

(B) Related person. For purposes of subparagraph (A), a person shall be treated as related to another person if such persons are treated as a single employer under subsection (a) or (b) of section 52 or subsection (m) or (o) of section 414, except that determinations under subsections (a) and (b) of section 52 shall be made without regard to section 1563(b).

(d) Definitions and special rules.

(1) Application of section to pass-thru entities.

(A) Partnerships and S corporations. In the case of a partnership or S corporation—

(i) this section shall be applied at the partner or shareholder level,

(ii) each partner or shareholder shall take into account such person's allocable share of each item described in subparagraph (A) or (B) of subsection (c)(1) (determined without regard to whether the items described in such subparagraph (A) exceed the items described in such subparagraph (B)),

(iii) each partner or shareholder shall be treated for purposes of subsection (b) as having W-2 wages for the taxable year in an amount equal to such person's allocable share of the W-2 wages of the partnership or S corporation for the taxable year (as determined under regulations prescribed by the Secretary), and

(iv) in the case of each partner of a partnership, or shareholder of an S corporation, who owns (directly or indirectly) at least 20 percent of the capital interests in such partnership or of the stock of such S corporation—

(I) such partner or shareholder shall be treated as having engaged directly in any film produced by such partnership or S corporation, and

(II) such partnership or S corporation shall be treated as having engaged directly in any film produced by such partner or shareholder.

(B) Trusts and estates. In the case of a trust or estate—

(i) the items referred to in subparagraph (A)(ii) (as determined therein) and the W-2 wages of the trust or estate for the taxable year, shall be apportioned between the beneficiaries and the fiduciary (and among the beneficiaries) under regulations prescribed by the Secretary, and

(ii) for purposes of paragraph (2), adjusted gross income of the trust or estate shall be determined as provided in section 67(e) with the adjustments described in such paragraph.

(C) Regulations. The Secretary may prescribe rules requiring or restricting the allocation of items and wages under this paragraph and may prescribe such reporting requirements as the Secretary determines appropriate.

(2) Application to individuals. In the case of an individual, subsections (a)(1)(B) and (d)(9)(A)(iii) shall be applied by substituting "adjusted gross income" for "taxable income". For purposes of the preceding sentence, adjusted gross income shall be determined—

(A) after application of sections 86, 135, 137, 219, 221, 222, and 469, and

(B) without regard to this section.

(3) Agricultural and horticultural cooperatives.

(A) Deduction allowed to patrons. Any person who receives a qualified payment from a specified agricultural or horticultural cooperative shall be allowed for the taxable year in which such payment is received a deduction under subsection (a) equal to the portion of the deduction allowed under subsection (a) to such cooperative which is—

(i) allowed with respect to the portion of the qualified production activities income to which such payment is attributable, and

(ii) identified by such cooperative in a written notice mailed to such person during the payment period described in section 1382(d).

(B) Cooperative denied deduction for portion of qualified payments. The taxable income of a specified agricultural or horticultural cooperative shall not be reduced under section 1382 by reason of that portion of any qualified payment as does not exceed the deduction allowable under subparagraph (A) with respect to such payment.

(C) Taxable income of cooperatives determined without regard to certain deductions. For purposes of this section, the taxable income of a specified agricultural or horticultural cooperative shall be computed without regard to any deduction allowable under subsection (b) or

(c) of section 1382 (relating to patronage dividends, per-unit retain allocations, and nonpatronage distributions).

(D) Special rule for marketing cooperatives. For purposes of this section, a specified agricultural or horticultural cooperative described in subparagraph (F)(ii) shall be treated as having manufactured, produced, grown, or extracted in whole or significant part any qualifying production property marketed by the organization which its patrons have so manufactured, produced, grown, or extracted.

(E) Qualified payment. For purposes of this paragraph, the term "qualified payment" means, with respect to any person, any amount which—

  (i) is described in paragraph (1) or (3) of section 1385(a),
  (ii) is received by such person from a specified agricultural or horticultural cooperative, and
  (iii) is attributable to qualified production activities income with respect to which a deduction is allowed to such cooperative under subsection (a).

(F) Specified agricultural or horticultural cooperative. For purposes of this paragraph, the term "specified agricultural or horticultural cooperative" means an organization to which part I of subchapter T applies which is engaged—

  (i) in the manufacturing, production, growth, or extraction in whole or significant part of any agricultural or horticultural product, or
  (ii) in the marketing of agricultural or horticultural products.

(4) Special rule for affiliated groups.

(A) In general. All members of an expanded affiliated group shall be treated as a single corporation for purposes of this section.

(B) Expanded affiliated group. For purposes of this section, the term "expanded affiliated group" means an affiliated group as defined in section 1504(a), determined—

  (i) by substituting "more than 50 percent" for "at least 80 percent" each place it appears, and
  (ii) without regard to paragraphs (2) and (4) of section 1504(b).

(C) Allocation of deduction. Except as provided in regulations, the deduction under subsection (a) shall be allocated among the members of the expanded affiliated group in proportion to each member's respective amount (if any) of qualified production activities income.

(5) Trade or business requirement. This section shall be applied by only taking into account items which are attributable to the actual conduct of a trade or business.

(6) Coordination with minimum tax. For purposes of determining alternative minimum taxable income under section 55—

(A) qualified production activities income shall be determined without regard to any adjustments under sections 56 through 59, and

(B) in the case of a corporation, subsection (a)(1)(B) shall be applied by substituting "alternative minimum taxable income" for "taxable income".

(7) Unrelated business taxable income. For purposes of determining the tax imposed by section 511, subsection (a)(1)(B) shall be applied by substituting "unrelated business taxable income" for "taxable income".

(8) Treatment of activities in Puerto Rico.

(A) In general. In the case of any taxpayer with gross receipts for any taxable year from sources within the Commonwealth of Puerto Rico, if all of such receipts are taxable under section 1 or 11 for such taxable year, then for purposes of determining the domestic production gross receipts of such taxpayer for such taxable year under subsection (c)(4), the term "United States" shall include the Common-wealth of Puerto Rico.

(B) Special rule for applying wage limitation. In the case of any taxpayer described in subparagraph (A), for purposes of applying the limitation under subsection (b) for any taxable year, the determination of W-60 wages of such taxpayer shall be made without regard to any exclusion under section 3401(a)(8) for remuneration paid for services performed in Puerto Rico.

(C) Termination. This paragraph shall apply only with respect to the first 6 taxable years of the taxpayer beginning after December 31, 2005, and before January 1, 2012.

(9) Special rule for taxpayers with oil related qualified production activities income.

(A) In general. If a taxpayer has oil related qualified production activities income for any taxable year beginning after 2009, the amount otherwise allowable as a deduction under subsection (a) shall be reduced by 3 percent of the least of—

  (i) the oil related qualified production activities income of the taxpayer for the taxable year,
  (ii) the qualified production activities income of the taxpayer for the taxable year, or
  (iii) taxable income (determined without regard to this section).

(B) Oil related qualified production activities income. For purposes of this paragraph, the term "oil related qualified production activities income" means for any taxable year the qualified production activities income which is attributable to the production, refining, processing, transportation, or distribution of oil, gas, or any primary product thereof during such taxable year.

(C) Primary product. For purposes of this paragraph, the term "primary product" has the same meaning as when used in section 927(a)(2)(C), as in effect before its repeal.

(10) Regulations. The Secretary shall prescribe such regulations as are necessary to carry out the purposes of this section, including regulations which prevent more than 1 taxpayer from being allowed a deduction under this section with respect to any activity described in subsection (c)(4)(A)(i).

In 2010, P.L. 111-312, Sec. 746(a)(1), substituted "first 6 taxable years" for "first 4 taxable years" in subpara. (d)(8)(C)
—P.L. 111-312, Sec. 746(a)(2), substituted "January 1, 2012" for "January 1, 2010" in subpara. (d)(8)(C), effective for tax. yrs. begin. after 12/31/2009.
In 2008, P.L. 110-343, Sec. 312(a)(1)DivC, substituted "first 4 taxable years" for "first 2 taxable years" in subpara. (d)(8)(C) . . . Sec. 312(a)(2)DivC, substituted "January 1, 2010" for "January 1, 2008" in subpara. (d)(8)(C), effective for tax. yrs. begin. after 12/31/2007.
—P.L. 110-343, Sec. 401(a)DivB, redesignated para. (d)(9) as (d)(10), and added para. (d)(9) . . . Sec. 401(b)DivB, substituted "subsections (a)(1)(B) and (d)(9)(A)(iii)" for "subsection (a)(1)(B)" in para. (d)(2), effective for tax. yrs. begin. after 12/31/2008.
—P.L. 110-343, Sec. 502(c)(1)DivC, added subpara. (b)(2)(D) . . . Sec. 502(c)(2)DivC, added the last sentence at the end of para. (c)(6) . . . Sec. 502(c)(3)DivC, deleted "and" at the end of clause (d)(1)(A)(ii), substituted ", and" for the period at the end of clause (d)(1)(A)(iii), and added clause (d)(1)(A)(iv), effective for tax. yrs. begin. after 12/31/2007.
In 2006, P.L. 109-432, Sec. 401(a), redesignated para. (d)(8) as para. (d)(9) and added para. (d)(8), effective for tax. yrs. begin. after 12/31/2005.

Deductions — Part VII

—P.L. 109-222, Sec. 514(a), amended para. (b)(2)... Sec. 514(b)(1), amended clause (d)(1)(A)(iii)... Sec. 514(b)(2), deleted "and subsection (d)(1)" after "paragraph (1)" in para. (a)(2), effective for tax. yrs. begin. after 5/17/2006.

Prior to amendment, para. (b)(2) read as follows:

"(2) W-2 wages.

"For purposes of this section, the term 'W-2 wages' means, with respect to any person for any taxable year of such person, the sum of the amounts described in paragraphs (3) and (8) of section 6051(a) paid by such person with respect to employment of employees by such person during the calendar year ending during such taxable year. Such term shall not include any amount which is not properly included in a return filed with the Social Security Administration on or before the 60th day after the due date (including extensions) for such return."

Prior to amendment, clause (d)(1)(a)(iii) read as follows:

"(iii) each partner or shareholder shall be treated for purposes of subsection (b) as having W-2 wages for the taxable year in an amount equal to the lesser of—

"(I) such person's allocable share of the W-2 wages of the partnership or S corporation for the taxable year (as determined under regulations prescribed by the Secretary), or

"(II) 2 times 9 percent of so much of such person's qualified production activities income as is attributable to items allocated under clause (ii) for the taxable year."

In 2005, P.L. 109-135, Sec. 403(a)(1), substituted "the taxpayer" for "the employer" in para. (b)(1)... Sec. 403(a)(2), amended para. (b)(2)... Sec. 403(a)(3), added "and" at the end of clause (c)(1)(B)(i), deleted clauses (c)(1)(B)(ii) and (iii), and added clause (c)(1)(B)(ii)... Sec. 403(a)(4), amended para. (c)(2)... Sec. 403(a)(5), deleted clauses (c)(4)(A)(ii) and (iii) and added clauses (c)(4)(A)(ii) and (iii)... Sec. 403(a)(6), deleted "and" at the end of clause (c)(4)(B)(i), substituted ", or" for the period at the end of clause (c)(4)(B)(ii), and added clause (c)(4)(B)(iii)... Sec. 403(a)(7), added subparas. (c)(4)(C) and (D)... Sec. 403(a)(8), amended para. (d)(1)... Sec. 403(a)(9), amended para. (d)(3)... Sec. 403(a)(10)(A), substituted "more than 50 percent" for "50 percent" in clause (d)(4)(B)(i)... Sec. 403(a)(10)(B), substituted "at least 80 percent" for "80 percent" in para. (d)(4)(B)(i)... Sec. 403(a)(11)(A), amended para. (d)(6)... Sec. 403(a)(11)(B), substituted "subsection (d)(1)" for "subsections (d)(1) and (d)(6)" in para. (a)(2)... Sec. 403(a)(12), redesignated para. (d)(7) as (d)(8) and added para. (d)(7)... Sec. 403(a)(13), added ", including regulations which prevent more than 1 taxpayer from being allowed a deduction under this section with respect to any activity described in subsection (c)(4)(A)(i)" before the period at the end of para. (d)(8) [as redesignated by Sec. 403(a)(12) of this Act, see above], effective for tax. yrs. begin. after 12/31/2004, except as provided in Sec. 102(e)(2) of the American Jobs Creation Act of 2004, P.L. 108-357[as amended by Sec. 403(a)(19) of P.L. 109-135, see below], which reads as follows:

"(2) Application to pass-thru entities, etc. In determining the deduction under section 199 of the Internal Revenue Code of 1986 (as added by this section [Sec. 102(a) of P.L. 108-357]), items arising from a taxable year of a partnership, S corporation, estate, or trust beginning before January 1, 2005, shall not be taken into account for purposes of subsection (d)(1) of such section."

Prior to amendment, para. (b)(2) read as follows:

"(2) W-2 wages. For purposes of paragraph (1), the term 'W-2 wages' means the sum of the aggregate amounts the taxpayer is required to include on statements under paragraphs (3) and (8) of section 6051(a) with respect to employment of employees of the taxpayer during the calendar year ending during the taxpayer's taxable year."

Prior to deletion, clauses (c)(1)(B)(ii) and (iii) read as follows:

"(ii) other deductions, expenses, or losses directly allocable to such receipts, and

"(iii) a ratable portion of other deductions, expenses, and losses that are not directly allocable to such receipts or another class of income."

Prior to amendment, para. (c)(2) read as follows:

"(2) Allocation method. The Secretary shall prescribe rules for the proper allocation of items of income, deduction, expense, and loss for purposes of determining income attributable to domestic production activities."

Prior to deletion, clauses (c)(4)(A)(ii) and (iii) read as follows:

"(ii) construction performed in the United States, or

"(iii) engineering or architectural services performed in the United States for construction projects in the United States."

Prior to amendment, para. (d)(1) read as follows:

"(1) Application of section to pass-thru entities.

"(A) In general. In the case of an S corporation, partnership, estate or trust, or other pass-thru entity—

"(i) subject to the provisions of paragraphs (2) and (3), this section shall be applied at the shareholder, partner, or similar level, and

"(ii) the Secretary shall prescribe rules for the application of this section , including rules relating to—

"(I) restrictions on the allocation of the deduction to taxpayers at the partner or similar level, and

"(II) additional reporting requirements.

"(B) Application of wage limitation. Notwithstanding subparagraph (A)(i), for purposes of applying subsection (b), a shareholder, partner, or similar person which is allocated qualified production activities income from an S corporation, partnership, estate, trust, or other pass-thru entity shall also be treated as having been allocated W-2 wages from such entity in an amount equal to the lesser of—

"(i) such person's allocable share of such wages (without regard to this subparagraph), as determined under regulations prescribed by the Secretary, or

"(ii) 2 times 9 percent of the qualified production activities income allocated to such person for the taxable year."

Prior to amendment, para. (d)(3) read as follows:

"(3) Patrons of agricultural and horticultural cooperatives.

"(A) In general. If any amount described in paragraph (1) or (3) of section 1385(a)—

"(i) is received by a person from an organization to which part I of subchapter T applies which is engaged—

"(I) in the manufacturing, production, growth, or extraction in whole or significant part of any agricultural or horticultural product, or

"(II) in the marketing of agricultural or horticultural products, and

"(ii) is allocable to the portion of the qualified production activities income of the organization which, but for this paragraph, would be deductible under subsection (a) by the organization and is designated as such by the organization in a written notice mailed to its patrons during the payment period described in section 1382(d),

"then such person shall be allowed a deduction under subsection (a) with respect to such amount. The taxable income of the organization shall not be reduced under section 1382 by reason of any amount to which the preceding sentence applies.

"(B) Special rules. For purposes of applying subparagraph (A), in determining the qualified production activities income which would be deductible by the organization under subsection (a)—

"(i) there shall not be taken into account in computing the organization's taxable income any deduction allowable under subsection (b) or (c) of section 1382 (relating to patronage dividends, per-unit retain allocations, and nonpatronage distributions), and

"(ii) in the case of an organization described in subparagraph (A)(i)(II), the organization shall be treated as having manufactured, produced, grown, or extracted in whole or significant part any qualifying production property marketed by the organization which its patrons have so manufactured, produced, grown, or extracted."

Prior to amendment, para. (d)(6) read as follows:

"(6) Coordination with minimum tax. The deduction under this section shall be allowed for purposes of the tax imposed by section 55; except that for purposes of section 55, the deduction under subsection (a) shall be 9 percent of the lesser of—

"(A) qualified production activities income (determined without regard to part IV of subchapter A), or

"(B) alternative minimum taxable income (determined without regard to this section) for the taxable year.

"In the case of an individual, subparagraph (B) shall be applied by substituting 'adjusted gross income' for 'alternative minimum taxable income'. For purposes of the preceding sentence, adjusted gross income shall be determined in the same manner as provided in paragraph (2)."

—P.L. 109-135, Sec. 403(a)(19), amended Sec. 102(e) of P.L. 108-357, see below.

Prior to amendment, Sec. 102(e) of P.L. 108-357 read as follows:

"(e) Effective date. The amendments made by this section shall apply to taxable years beginning after December 31, 2004."

In 2004, P.L. 108-357, Sec. 102(a), added Code Sec. 199, effective for tax. yrs. begin. after 12/31/2004, except as provided in Sec. 102(e)(2) of this Act [as amended by Sec. 403(a)(19) of P.L. 109-135, see above], reads as follows:

"(2) Application to pass-thru entities, etc. In determining the deduction under section 199 of the Internal Revenue Code of 1986 (as added by this section), items arising from a taxable year of a partnership, S corporation, estate, or trust beginning before January 1, 2005, shall not be taken into account for purposes of subsection (d)(1) of such section."

PART VII.—ADDITIONAL ITEMIZED DEDUCTIONS FOR INDIVIDUALS

Sec.
211. Allowance of deductions.
212. Expenses for production of income.
213. Medical, dental, etc., expenses.
214. Repealed. [Expenses for household and dependent care services necessary for gainful employment.]
215. Alimony, etc., payments.
216. Deduction of taxes, interest, and business depreciation by cooperative housing corporation tenant-stockholder.
217. Moving expenses.
218. Contributions to candidates for public office. [Repealed.]
219. Retirement savings.
220. Archer MSAs.
221. Interest on education loans.
222. Qualified tuition and related expenses.
223. Health savings accounts.
224. Cross reference.

Part VII   **Deductions**

In **2003**, P.L. 108-173, Sec. 1201(a), redesignated item 223 as 224, and added new item 223

In **2001**, P.L. 107-16, Sec. 431(c)(4), deleted item 222 and added items 222 and 223.

Prior to deletion, item 222 read as follows:
"222. Cross reference."

In **2000**, P.L. 106-554, Sec. 1(a)(7) [which enacted into law Sec. 202(b)(9) of H.R. 5662], amended item 220.

Prior to amendment, item 220 read as follows:
1. "220. Medical savings accounts."

In **1997**, P.L. 105-34, Sec. 202(d), deleted item 221 and added new 221 and 222.

Prior to deletion, item 221 read as follows:
"221. Cross reference."

In **1996**, P.L. 104-191, Sec. 301(i), deleted item 220 and added new items 220 and 221.

Prior to deletion, item 220 read as follows:
"220. Cross reference."

In **1990**, P.L. 101-508, Sec. 11802(e)(3), repealed items 220 and 221 and added new item 220.

Prior to repeal, items 220 and 221 read as follows:
"220. Jury duty pay remitted to employer.
"221. Cross References."

In **1988**, P.L. 100-647, Sec. 6007(c), repealed item 220 and added items 220 and 221.

Prior to repeal, item 220 read as follows:
"220. Cross references."

In **1986**, P.L. 99-514, Sec. 131(b)(3), repealed item 221.... Sec. 135(b)(2), repealed items 222 and 223 and added item 220.... Sec. 301(b)(5)(B), substituted "reference" for "references" in item 223 [before redesignation by Sec. 135(b)(1) of this Act.]

Prior to repeal, item 221 read as follows:
"221. Deduction for two-earner married couples."

Prior to repeal, items 222 and 223 [as amended by Sec. 301(b)(5) of P.L. 99-514, above] read as follows:
"Sec. 222. Adoption expenses."
"Sec. 223. Cross references."

In **1981**, P.L. 97-34, Sec. 103(c)(3), redesignated item 221 as 222 and added new item 221 ... Sec. 125(b), redesignated item 222 [as redesignated by Sec. 103(c)(3) of this Act] as 223 and added new item 222 ... Sec. 311(h)(11), repealed item 220.

Prior to repeal, item 220 read as follows:
"220. Retirement savings for certain married individuals."

In **1978**, P.L. 95-600, Sec. 113(a)(1), repealed Code Sec. 218. This Act did not amend the list of Code Secs. for Part VII, but presumably Congress intended to.

Prior to repeal, the heading for Code Sec. 218 read as follows:
"Sec. 218. Contributions to candidates for public office."

In **1976**, P.L. 94-455, Sec. 504(b)(2), repealed item 214.

Prior to repeal, item 214 read as follows:
"214. Expenses for household and dependent care services necessary for gainful employment."

—P.L. 94-455, Sec. 1501(c), amended item 220 and added item 221.

Prior to amendment, item 220 read as follows:
"220. Cross references."

In **1974**, P.L. 93-406, Sec. 2002(h)(1), redesignated item 219 as 220 and added new item 219.

In **1971**, P.L. 92-178, Sec. 702(c), redesignated item 218 as 219, and added new item 218 ... Sec. 210(b), amended item 214.

Prior to amendment, item 214 read as follows:
"Expenses for care of certain dependents."

In **1964**, P.L. 82-272, Sec. 213(a)(2), redesignated item 217 as 218, and added new item 217.

In **1962**, P.L. 87-834, Sec. 28(b), amended item 216.

Prior to amendment, item 216 read as follows:
"Amounts representing taxes and interest paid to cooperative housing corporation."

Sec. 211. Allowance of deductions.

In computing taxable income under section 63, there shall be allowed as deductions the items specified in this part, subject to the exceptions provided in part IX (section 261 and following, relating to items not deductible).

In **1977**, P.L. 95-30, Sec. 102(b)(3), substituted "section 63" for "section 63(a)", effective for tax. yrs. begin. after 12/31/76.

Sec. 212. Expenses for production of income.

In the case of an individual, there shall be allowed as a deduction all the ordinary and necessary expenses paid or incurred during the taxable year—

(1) for the production or collection of income;

(2) for the management, conservation, or maintenance of property held for the production of income; or

(3) in connection with the determination, collection, or refund of any tax.

Sec. 213. Medical, dental, etc., expenses.

> • **Caution:** Code Sec. 213(a), following, is effective for tax. yrs. begin. before 1/1/2013. For Code Sec. 213(a), effective for tax. yrs. begin. after 12/31/2012, see below.

(a) Allowance of deduction.

There shall be allowed as a deduction the expenses paid during the taxable year, not compensated for by insurance or otherwise, for medical care of the taxpayer, his spouse, or a dependent (as defined in section 152, determined without regard to subsections (b)(1), (b)(2), and (d)(1)(B) thereof), to the extent that such expenses exceed 7.5 percent of adjusted gross income.

> • **Caution:** Code Sec. 213(a), following, is effective for tax. yrs. begin. after 12/31/2012. For Code Sec. 213(a), effective for tax. yrs. begin. before 1/1/2013, see above.

(a) Allowance of deduction.

There shall be allowed as a deduction the expenses paid during the taxable year, not compensated for by insurance or otherwise, for medical care of the taxpayer, his spouse, or a dependent (as defined in section 152, determined without regard to subsections (b)(1), (b)(2), and (d)(1)(B) thereof), to the extent that such expenses exceed 10 percent of adjusted gross income.

(b) Limitation with respect to medicine and drugs.

An amount paid during the taxable year for medicine or a drug shall be taken into account under subsection (a) only if such medicine or drug is a prescribed drug or is insulin.

(c) Special rule for decedents.

(1) Treatment of expenses paid after death. For purposes of subsection (a), expenses for the medical care of the taxpayer which are paid out of his estate during the 1-year period beginning with the day after the date of his death shall be treated as paid by the taxpayer at the time incurred.

(2) Limitation. Paragraph (1) shall not apply if the amount paid is allowable under section 2053 as a deduction in computing the taxable estate of the decedent, but this paragraph shall not apply if (within the time and in the manner and form prescribed by the Secretary) there is filed—

(A) a statement that such amount has not been allowed as a deduction under section 2053, and

(B) a waiver of the right to have such amount allowed at any time as a deduction under section 2053.

(d) Definitions.

For purposes of this section—

(1) The term "medical care" means amounts paid—

(A) for the diagnosis, cure, mitigation, treatment, or prevention of disease, or for the purpose of affecting any structure or function of the body,

(B) for transportation primarily for and essential to medical care referred to in subparagraph (A),

(C) for qualified long-term care services (as defined in section 7702B(c)), or

(D) for insurance (including amounts paid as premiums under part B of title XVIII of the Social Security Act,

Deductions Code Sec. 213(d)(11)(B)

relating to supplementary medical insurance for the aged) covering medical care referred to in subparagraphs (A) and (B) or for any qualified long-term care insurance contract (as defined in section 7702B(b)).

In the case of a qualified long-term care insurance contract (as defined in section 7702B(b)), only eligible long-term care premiums (as defined in paragraph (10)) shall be taken into account under subparagraph (D).

(2) Amounts paid for certain lodging away from home treated as paid for medical care. Amounts paid for lodging (not lavish or extravagant under the circumstances) while away from home primarily for and essential to medical care referred to in paragraph (1)(A) shall be treated as amounts paid for medical care if—

(A) the medical care referred to in paragraph (1)(A) is provided by a physician in a licensed hospital (or in a medical care facility which is related to, or the equivalent of, a licensed hospital), and

(B) there is no significant element of personal pleasure, recreation, or vacation in the travel away from home.

The amount taken into account under the preceding sentence shall not exceed $50 for each night for each individual.

(3) Prescribed drug. The term "prescribed drug" means a drug or biological which requires a prescription of a physician for its use by an individual.

(4) Physician. The term "physician" has the meaning given to such term by section 1861(r) of the Social Security Act (42 U.S.C. 1395x(r)).

(5) Special rule in the case of child of divorced parents, etc. Any child to whom section 152(e) applies shall be treated as a dependent of both parents for purposes of this section.

(6) In the case of an insurance contract under which amounts are payable for other than medical care referred to in subparagraphs (A), (B), and (C) of paragraph (1)—

(A) no amount shall be treated as paid for insurance to which paragraph (1)(D) applies unless the charge for such insurance is either separately stated in the contract, or furnished to the policyholder by the insurance company in a separate statement,

(B) the amount taken into account as the amount paid for such insurance shall not exceed such charge, and

(C) no amount shall be treated as paid for such insurance if the amount specified in the contract (or furnished to the policyholder by the insurance company in a separate statement) as the charge for such insurance is unreasonably large in relation to the total charges under the contract.

(7) Subject to the limitations of paragraph (6), premiums paid during the taxable year by a taxpayer before he attains the age of 65 for insurance covering medical care (within the meaning of subparagraphs (A), (B), and (C) of paragraph (1)) for the taxpayer, his spouse, or a dependent after the taxpayer attains the age of 65 shall be treated as expenses paid during the taxable year for insurance which constitutes medical care if premiums for such insurance are payable (on a level payment basis) under the contract for a period of 10 years or more or until the year in which the taxpayer attains the age of 65 (but in no case for a period of less than 5 years).

(8) The determination of whether an individual is married at any time during the taxable year shall be made in accordance with the provisions of section 6013(d) (relating to determination of status as husband and wife).

(9) Cosmetic surgery.

(A) In general. The term "medical care" does not include cosmetic surgery or other similar procedures, unless the surgery or procedure is necessary to ameliorate a deformity arising from, or directly related to, a congenital abnormality, a personal injury resulting from an accident or trauma, or disfiguring disease.

(B) Cosmetic surgery defined. For purposes of this paragraph, the term "cosmetic surgery" means any procedure which is directed at improving the patient's appearance and does not meaningfully promote the proper function of the body or prevent or treat illness or disease.

(10) Eligible long-term care premiums.

(A) In general. For purposes of this section, the term "eligible long-term care premiums" means the amount paid during a taxable year for any qualified long-term care insurance contract (as defined in section 7702B(b)) covering an individual, to the extent such amount does not exceed the limitation determined under the following table:

In the case of an individual with an attained age before the close of the taxable year of:	The limitation is:
40 or less	$ 200
More than 40 but not more than 50	375
More than 50 but not more than 60	750
More than 60 but not more than 70	2,000
More than 70	2,500.

(B) Indexing.

(i) In general. In the case of any taxable year beginning in a calendar year after 1997, each dollar amount contained in subparagraph (A) shall be increased by the medical care cost adjustment of such amount for such calendar year. If any increase determined under the preceding sentence is not a multiple of $10, such increase shall be rounded to the nearest multiple of $10.

(ii) Medical care cost adjustment. For purposes of clause (i), the medical care cost adjustment for any calendar year is the percentage (if any) by which—

(I) the medical care component of the Consumer Price Index (as defined in section 1(f)(5)) for August of the preceding calendar year, exceeds

(II) such component for August of 1996.

The Secretary shall, in consultation with the Secretary of Health and Human Services, prescribe an adjustment which the Secretary determines is more appropriate for purposes of this paragraph than the adjustment described in the preceding sentence, and the adjustment so prescribed shall apply in lieu of the adjustment described in the preceding sentence.

(11) Certain payments to relatives treated as not paid for medical care. An amount paid for a qualified long-term care service (as defined in section 7702B(c)) provided to an individual shall be treated as not paid for medical care if such service is provided—

(A) by the spouse of the individual or by a relative (directly or through a partnership, corporation, or other entity) unless the service is provided by a licensed professional with respect to such service, or

(B) by a corporation or partnership which is related (within the meaning of section 267(b) or 707(b)) to the individual.

For purposes of this paragraph, the term "relative" means an individual bearing a relationship to the individual which is described in any of subparagraphs (A) through (G) of section 152(d)(2). This paragraph shall not apply for purposes of section 105(b) with respect to reimbursements through insurance.

(e) Exclusion of amounts allowed for care of certain dependents.

Any expense allowed as a credit under section 21 shall not be treated as an expense paid for medical care.

> • *Caution:* Code Sec. 213(f), following, is effective for tax. yrs. begin. after 12/31/2012.

(f) Special rule for 2013, 2014, 2015, and 2016.

In the case of any taxable year beginning after December 31, 2012, and ending before January 1, 2017, subsection (a) shall be applied with respect to a taxpayer by substituting "7.5 percent" for "10 percent" if such taxpayer or such taxpayer's spouse has attained age 65 before the close of such taxable year.

In 2010, P.L. 111-148, Sec. 9013(a), substituted "10 percent" for "7.5 percent" in subsec. (a)...Sec. 9013(b), added subsec. (f), effective for tax. yrs. begin. after 12/31/2012.

In 2004, P.L. 108-311, Sec. 207(17), added ", determined without regard to subsections (b)(1), (b)(2), and (d)(1)(B) thereof" after "section 152" in subsec. (a)...Sec. 207(18), substituted "subparagraphs (A) through (G) of section 152(d)(2)" for "paragraphs (1) through (8) of section 152(a)" in para. (d)(11), effective for tax. yrs. begin. after 12/31/2004.

In 1996, P.L. 104-191, Sec. 322(a), deleted "or" at the end of subpara. (d)(1)(B), redesignated subpara. (d)(1)(C) as subpara. (d)(1)(D) and added new subpara. (d)(1)(C)...Sec. 322(b)(1), added "or for any qualified long-term care insurance contract (as defined in section 7702B(b))" before the period at the end of subpara. (d)(1)(D) [as redesignated by Sec. 322(a), of this Act, see above]...Sec. 322(b)(2)(A), added a flush sentence at the end of para. (d)(1)...Sec. 322(b)(2)(C), added paras. (d)(10) and (d)(11)...Sec. 322(b)(3)(A), substituted "subparagraphs (A), (B), and (C)" for "subparagraphs (A) and (B)" in para. (d)(6)...Sec. 322(b)(3)(B), substituted "paragraph (1)(D)" for "paragraph (1)(C)" in subpara. (d)(6)(A)...Sec. 322(b)(4), substituted "subparagraphs (A), (B), and (C)" for "subparagraphs (A) and (B)" in para. (d)(7), effective for tax. yrs. begin. after 12/31/96.

In 1993, P.L. 103-66, Sec. 13131(d)(3), deleted subsec. (f), effective for tax. yrs. begin. after 12/31/93.

Prior to deletion, subsec. (f) read as follows:

"(f) Coordination with health insurance credit under section 32. The amount otherwise taken into account under subsection (a) as expenses paid for medical care shall be reduced by the amount (if any) of the health insurance credit allowable to the taxpayer for the taxable year under section 32."

In 1990, P.L. 101-508, Sec. 11111(d)(1), added subsec. (f), effective for tax. yrs. begin. after 12/31/90.

—P.L. 101-508, Sec. 11342(a), added para. (d)(9), effective for tax. yrs. begin. after 12/31/90.

In 1986, P.L. 99-514, Sec. 133, substituted "7.5 percent" for "5 percent" in subsec. (a), effective for tax. yrs. begin. after 12/31/86.

In 1984, P.L. 98-369, Sec. 423(b)(1), redesignated paras. (d)(4), (d)(5), and (d)(6) as paras. (d)(5), (d)(6), and (d)(7), and added new para. (d)(4)...Sec. 423(b)(3), substituted "the limitations of paragraph (5)" for "the limitations of paragraph (4)" in para. (d)(6) [sic (d)(7)], [as redesignated by Secs. 423(b)(1) and 482(a) of the Act and amended by Sec. 711(b) of the Act], effective for tax. yrs. begin. after 12/31/84.

—P.L. 98-369, Sec. 474(r)(9), substituted "section 21" for "section 44A" in subsec. (e), effective for tax. yrs. begin. after 12/31/83, and for carrybacks from tax. yrs. begin. after 12/31/83.

—P.L. 98-369, Sec. 482(a), redesignated paras. (d)(2)-(d)(7) as paras. (d)(3)-(d)(8), and added new para. (d)(2)...Sec. 482(b)(1), substituted "paragraph (6)" for "paragraph (5)" in para. (d)(7), as redesignated by Sec. 482(a) of the Act, effective for tax. yrs. begin. after 12/31/83.

—P.L. 98-369, Sec. 711(b), substituted "paragraph (4)" for "paragraph (2)" in para. (d)(5), effective for tax. yrs. begin. after 12/31/82.

In 1982, P.L. 97-248, Sec. 202(a), amended subsec. (a), effective for tax. yrs. begin. after 12/31/82.

Prior to amendment, subsec. (a) read as follows:

"(a) Allowance of deduction.

"There shall be allowed as a deduction the following amounts, not compensated for by insurance or otherwise—

"(1) the amount by which the amount of the expenses paid during the taxable year (reduced by any amount deductible under paragraph (2)) for medical care of the taxpayer, his spouse, and dependents (as defined in section 152) exceeds 3 percent of the adjusted gross income, and

"(2) an amount (not in excess of $150) equal to one-half of the expenses paid during the taxable year for insurance which constitutes medical care for the taxpayer, his spouse, and dependents."

—P.L. 97-248, Sec. 202(b)(1), amended subsec. (b)...Sec. 202(b)(2), added new paras. (e)(2) and (3)...Sec. 202(b)(3)(A), redesignated paras. (e)(2), (3) and (4) as paras. (e)(4), (5) and (6)...Sec. 202(b)(3)(B), redesignated subsecs. (d), (e) and (f) as subsecs. (c), (d) and (e), effective for tax. yrs. begin. after 12/31/83.

Prior to amendment, subsec. (b) read as follows:

"(b) Limitation with respect to medicine and drugs.

"Amounts paid during the taxable year for medicine and drugs which (but for this subsection) would be taken into account in computing the deduction under subsection (a) shall be taken into account only to the extent that the aggregate of such amounts exceeds 1 percent of the adjusted gross income."

In 1976, P.L. 94-455, Sec. 504(c)(1), substituted "a credit under section 44A" for "a deduction under section 2414" in subsec. (f), effective for tax. yrs. begin. after 12/31/75.

—P.L. 94-455, Sec. 1906(b)(13)(A), substituted "Secretary" for "Secretary or his delegate" in para. (d)(2), effective for tax. yrs. begin. after 12/31/76.

In 1965, P.L. 89-97, Sec. 106(a), amended subsec. (a)...Sec. 106(b), amended subsec. (b)...Sec. 106(c), amended subsec. (e)...Sec. 106(d), deleted subsecs. (c) and (g), effective for tax. yrs. begin. after '66.

Prior to amendment, the subsecs. (a) and (b) read as follows:

"(a) Allowance of deduction.

"There shall be allowed as a deduction the following amounts of the expenses paid during the taxable year, not compensated for by insurance or otherwise, for medical care of the taxpayer, his spouse, or a dependent (as defined in section 152):

"(1) If neither the taxpayer nor his spouse has attained the age of 65 before the close of the taxable year—

"(A) the amount of such expenses for the care of any dependent who—

"(i) is the mother or father of the taxpayer or of his spouse, and

"(ii) has attained the age of 65 before the close of the taxable year, and

"(B) the amount by which such expenses for the care of the taxpayer, his spouse, and such dependents (other than any dependent described in subparagraph (A)) exceed 3 percent of the adjusted gross income.

"(2) If either the taxpayer or his spouse has attained the age of 65 before the close of the taxable year—

"(A) the amount of such expenses for the care of the taxpayer and his spouse,

"(B) the amount of such expenses for the care of any dependent described in paragraph (1)(A), and

"(C) the amount by which such expenses for the care of such dependents (other than any dependent described in paragraph (1)(A)) exceed 3 percent of the adjusted gross income.

"(b) Limitation with respect to medicine and drugs.

"Amounts paid during the taxable year for medicine and drugs which (but for this subsection) would be taken into account in computing the deduction under subsection (a) shall be taken into account only to the extent that the aggregate of such amounts exceeds 1 percent of the adjusted gross income. The preceding sentence shall not apply to amounts paid for the care of—

"(1) the taxpayer and his spouse, if either of them has attained the age of 65 before the close of the taxable year, or

"(2) any dependent described in subsection (a)(1)(A)."

Prior to deletion, subsec. (c) read as follows:

"(c) Maximum limitations. Except as provided in subsection (g), the deduction under this section shall not exceed $5,000, multiplied by the number of exemptions allowed for the taxable year as a deduction under section 151 (other than exemptions allowed by reason of subsection (c) or (d), relating to additional exemptions for age or blindness); except that the maximum deduction under this section shall be—

"(1) $10,000, if the taxpayer is single and not the head of a household (as defined in section 1(b)(2)) and not a surviving spouse (as defined in section 2(b)) or is married but files a separate return; or

"(2) $20,000, if the taxpayer files a joint return with his spouse under section 6013, or is the head of a household (as defined in section 1(b)(2)) or a surviving spouse (as defined in section 2(b))"

Prior to amendment, subsec. (e) read as follows:

"(e) Definitions.

"For purposes of this section—

"(1) The term 'medical care' means amounts paid—

"(A) for the diagnosis, cure, mitigation, treatment, or prevention of disease, or for the purpose of affecting any structure or function of the body (including amounts paid for accident or health insurance), or

"(B) for transportation primarily for and essential to medical care referred to in subparagraph (A).

"(2) The determination of whether an individual is married at any time during the taxable year shall be made in accordance with the provisions of section 6013(d) (relating to determination of status as husband and wife)."

Prior to deletion, subsec. (g) read as follows:

"(g) Maximum limitation if taxpayer or spouse has attained age 65 and is disabled.

"(1) Special rule. Subject to the provisions of paragraph (2), the deduction under this section shall not exceed—

"(A) $20,000, if the taxpayer has attained the age of 65 before the close of the taxable year and is disabled, or if his spouse has attained the age of 65 before the close of the taxable year and is disabled and if his spouse does not make a separate return for the taxable year, or

"(B) $40,000, if both the taxpayer and his spouse have attained the age of 65 before the close of the taxable year and are disabled and if the taxpayer files a joint return with his spouse under section 6013.

"(2) Amounts taken into account. For purposes of paragraph (1)—

"(A) amounts paid by the taxpayer during the taxable year for medical care, other than amounts paid for—

"(i) his medical care, if he has attained the age of 65 before the close of the taxable year and is disabled, or

"(ii) the medical care of his spouse, if his spouse has attained the age of 65 before the close of the taxable year and is disabled, shall be taken into account only to the extent that such amounts do not exceed the maximum limitation provided in subsection (c) which would (but for the provisions of this subsection) apply to the taxpayer for the taxable year;

"(B) if the taxpayer has attained the age of 65 before the close of the taxable year and is disabled, amounts paid by him during the taxable year for his medical care shall be taken into account only to the extent that such amounts do not exceed $20,000; and

"(C) if the spouse of the taxpayer has attained the age of 65 before the close of the taxable year and is disabled, amounts paid by the taxpayer during the taxable year for the medical care of his spouse shall be taken into account only to the extent that such amounts do not exceed $20,000.

"(3) Meaning of disabled. For purposes of paragraph (1), an individual shall be considered to be disabled if he is unable to engage in any substantial gainful activity by reason of any medically determinable physical or mental impairment which can be expected to result in death or to be of long-continued and indefinite duration. An individual shall not be considered to be disabled unless he furnishes proof of the existence thereof in such form and manner as the Secretary or his delegate may require.

"(4) Determination of status. For purposes of paragraph (1), the determination as to whether the taxpayer or his spouse is disabled shall be made as of the close of the taxable year of the taxpayer, except that if his spouse dies during such taxable year such determination shall be made with respect to his spouse as of the time of such death."

In 1964, P.L. 88-272, Sec. 211(a), added a sentence to the end of subsec. (b), effective for tax. yrs. begin. after 12/31/63.

In 1962, P.L. 87-863, Sec. 1, substituted "$5,000" for "$2,500", "$10,000" for "$5,000", and "$20,000" for "$10,000" in subsec. (c), and substituted "$20,000" for "$15,000" in three instances, and "$40,000" for "$30,000" in subsec. (g), effective for tax. yrs. begin. after 12/31/61.

In 1960, P.L. 86-470, Sec. 3, amended subsec. (a), effective for tax. yrs. begin. after 12/31/59.

Prior to amendment, subsec. (a) read as follows:

"(a) Allowance of deduction.

"There shall be allowed as a deduction the expenses paid during the taxable year, not compensated for by insurance or otherwise, for medical care of the taxpayer, his spouse, or a dependent as defined in section 152)—

"(1) if neither the taxpayer nor his spouse has attained the age of 65 before the close of the taxable year, to the extent that such expenses exceed 3 percent of the adjusted gross income; or

"(2) if either the taxpayer or his spouse has attained the age of 65 before the close of the taxable year—

"(A) the amount of such expenses for the care of the taxpayer and his spouse, and

"(B) the amount by which such expenses for the care of such dependents exceed 3 percent of the adjusted gross income.".

In 1958, P.L. 85-866, Sec. 16, deleted, "claimed or" before "allowed" in subpara. (d)(2)(A), effective for tax. yrs. begin. after 12/31/53, and end. after 8/16/54.
—P.L. 85-866, Sec. 17(a), added subsec. (g) . . . Sec. 17(b), substituted "Except as provided in subsection (g), the" for "The" in subsec. (c), effective for tax. yrs. begin. after 12/31/57.

Sec. 214. Repealed.

In 1976, P.L. 94-455, Sec. 504(b)(1), repealed Code Sec. 214, effective for tax. yrs. begin. after 1975.

Prior to repeal, Code Sec. 214 read as follows:

"Sec. 214. Expenses for Household and Dependent Care Services Necessary for Gainful Employment.

"(a) Allowance of deduction.

"In the case of an individual who maintains a household which includes as a member one or more qualifying individuals (as defined in subsection (b)(1)), there shall be allowed as a deduction the employment-related expenses (as defined in subsection (b)(2)) paid by him during the taxable year.

"(b) Definitions, etc.

"(1) Qualifying individual. The term 'qualifying individuals' means—

"(A) a dependent of the taxpayer who is under the age of 15 and with respect to whom the taxpayer is entitled to a deduction under section 151(e).

"(B) a dependent of the taxpayer who is physically or mentally incapable of caring for himself, or

"(C) the spouse of the taxpayer, if he is physically or mentally incapable of caring for himself.

"(2) Employment-related expenses. The term 'employment-related expenses' means amounts paid for the following expenses, but only if such expenses are incurred to enable the taxpayer to be gainfully employed:

"(A) expenses for household services, and

"(B) expenses for the care of a qualifying individual.

"(3) Maintaining a household. An individual shall be treated as maintaining a household for any period only if over half of the cost of maintaining the household during such period is furnished by such individual (or if such individual is married during such period, is furnished by such individual and his spouse).

"(c) Limitations on amounts deductible.

"(1) In general. A deduction shall be allowed under subsection (a) for employment-related expenses incurred during any month only to the extent such expenses do not exceed $400.

"(2) Expenses must be for services in the household.

"(A) In general. Except as provided in subparagraph (B), a deduction shall be allowed under subsection (a) for employment-related expenses only if they are incurred for services in the taxpayer's household.

"(B) Exception. Employment-related expenses described in subsection (b)(2)(B) which are incurred for services outside the taxpayer's household shall be taken into account only if incurred for the care of a qualifying individual described in subsection (b)(1)(A) and only to the extent such expenses incurred during any month do not exceed—

"(i) $200, in the case of one such individual,

"(ii) $300, in the case of two such individuals, and

"(iii) $400, in the case of three or more such individuals.

"(d) Income limitation.

"If the adjusted gross income of the taxpayer exceeds $35,000 for the taxable year during which the expenses are incurred, the amount of the employment-related expenses incurred during any month of such year which may be taken into account under this section shall (after the application of subsections (e)(5) and (c)) be further reduced by that portion of one-half of the excess of the adjusted gross income over $35,000 which is properly allocable to such month. For purposes of the preceding sentence, if the taxpayer is married during any period of the taxable year, there shall be taken into account the combined adjusted gross income of the taxpayer and his spouse for such period.

"(e) Special rules.

"For purposes of this section—

"(1) Married couples must file joint return. If the taxpayer is married at the close of the taxable year, the deduction provided by subsection (a) shall be allowed only if the taxpayer and his spouse file a single return jointly for the taxable year.

"(2) Gainful employment requirement. If the taxpayer is married for any period during the taxable year, there shall be taken into account employment-related expenses incurred during any month of such period only if—

"(A) both spouses are gainfully employed on a substantially full-time basis, or

"(B) the spouse is a qualifying individual described subsection (b)(1)(C).

"(3) Certain married individuals living apart. An individual who for the taxable year would be treated as not married under section 143(b) if paragraph (1) of such section referred to any dependent, shall be treated as not married for such taxable year.

"(4) Payments to related individuals. No deduction shall be allowed under subsection (a) for any amount paid by the taxpayer to an individual bearing a relationship to the taxpayer described in paragraphs (1) through (8) of section 152(a) (relating to definition of dependent) or to a dependent described in paragraph (9) of such section.

"(5) Reduction for certain payments. In the case of employment-related expenses incurred during any taxable year solely with respect to a qualifying individual (other than an individual who is also described in subsection (b)(1)(A)), the amount of such expenses which may be taken into account for purposes of this section shall (before the application of subsection (c)) be reduced—

"(A) if such individual is described in subsection (b)(1)(B), by the amount by which the sum of—

"(i) such individual's adjusted gross income for such taxable year, and

"(ii) the disability payments received by such individual during such year, exceeds $750, or

"(B) in the case of a qualifying individual described in subsection (b)(1)(C), by the amount of disability payments received by such individual during the taxable year.

For purposes of this paragraph, the term 'disability payment' means a payment (other than a gift) which is made on account of the physical or mental condition of an individual and which is not included in gross income.

"(f) Regulations.

"The Secretary or his delegate shall prescribe such regulations as may be necessary to carry out the purposes of this section."

In 1975, P.L. 94-12, Sec. 206, substituted "$35,000" for "$18,000" each place it appeared in subsec. (d), effective for tax. yrs. begin. after 3/29/75.

In 1971, P.L. 92-178, Sec. 210(a), amended Code Sec. 214, effective for tax. yrs. begin. after 12/31/71.

Prior to amendment, Code Sec. 214 read as follows:

"Sec. 214. Expenses for Care of Certain Dependents.

"(a) General rule.

"There shall be allowed as a deduction expenses paid during the taxable year by a taxpayer who is a woman or widower, or is a husband whose wife is incapacitated or is institutionalized, for the care of one or more dependents (as defined in subsection (d)(1)), but only if such care is for the purpose of enabling the taxpayer to be gainfully employed.

"(b) Limitations.

"(1) Dollars limit.

"(A) Except as provided in subparagraph (B), the deduction under subsection (a) shall not exceed $600 for any taxable year.

Code Sec. 214 — Deductions

"(B) The $600 limit of subparagraph (A) shall be increased (to an amount not above $900) by the amount of expenses incurred by the taxpayer for any period during which the taxpayer had 2 or more dependents.

"(2) Working wives and husbands with incapacitated wives.

"In the case of a woman who is married and in the case of a husband whose wife is incapacitated, the deduction under subsection (a)—

"(A) shall not be allowed unless the taxpayer and his spouse file a joint return for the taxable year, and

"(B) shall be reduced by the amount (if any) by which the adjusted gross income of the taxpayer and his spouse exceeds $6,000.

This paragraph shall not apply, in the case of a woman who is married, to expenses incurred while her husband is incapable of self-support because mentally or physically defective, or, in the case of a husband whose wife is incapacitated, to expenses incurred while his wife is institutionalized if such institutionalization is for a period of at least 90 consecutive days (whether or not within one taxable year) or a shorter period if terminated by her death.

"(3) Certain payments not taken into account.

"Subsection (a) shall not apply to any amount paid to an individual with respect to whom the taxpayer is allowed for his taxable year a deduction under section 151 (relating to deductions for personal exemptions).

"(c) Special rule where wife is incapacitated or institutionalized.

"In the case of a husband whose wife is incapacitated or is institutionalized, the deduction under subsection (a) shall be allowed only for expenses incurred while the wife was incapacitated or institutionalized (as the case may be) for a period of at least 90 consecutive days (whether or not within one taxable year) or a shorter period if terminated by her death.

"(d) Definitions.

"For purposes of this section—

"(1) Dependent.

"The term 'dependent' means a person with respect to whom the taxpayer is entitled to an exemption under section 151(e)(1)—

"(A) who has not attained the age of 13 years and who (within the meaning of section 152) is a son, stepson, daughter, or stepdaughter of the taxpayer; or

"(B) who is physically or mentally incapable of caring for himself.

"(2) Widower.

"The term 'widower' includes an unmarried individual who is legally separated from his spouse under a decree of divorce or of separate maintenance.

"(3) Incapacitated wife.

"A wife shall be considered incapacitated only (A) while she is incapable of caring for herself because mentally or physically defective, or (B) while she is institutionalized.

"(4) Institutionalized wife.

"A wife shall be considered institutionalized only while she is, for the purpose of receiving medical care or treatment, an inpatient, resident, or inmate of a public or private hospital, sanitarium, or other similar institution.

"(5) Determination of status.

"A woman shall not be considered as married if—

"(A) she is legally separated from her spouse under a decree of divorce or of separate maintenance at the close of the taxable year, or

"(B) she has been deserted by her spouse, does not know his whereabouts (and has not known his whereabouts at any time during the taxable year), and has applied to a court of competent jurisdiction for appropriate process to compel him to pay support or otherwise to comply with the law or a judicial order, as determined under regulations prescribed by the Secretary or his delegate."

In 1964, P.L. 88-272, Sec. 212(a), amended Code Sec. 214, effective for tax. yrs. begin. after 12/31/63.

Prior to amendment, Code Sec. 214 read as follows:

"SEC. 214. EXPENSES FOR CARE OF CERTAIN DEPENDENTS.

"(a) General rule.

"There shall be allowed as a deduction expenses paid during the taxable year by a taxpayer who is a woman or a widower for the care of one or more dependents (as defined in subsection (c)(1)), but only if such care is for the purpose of enabling the taxpayer to be gainfully employed.

"(b) Limitations.

"(1) In general. The deduction under subsection (a)—

"(A) shall not exceed $600 for any taxable year; and

"(B) shall not apply to any amount paid to an individual with respect to whom the taxpayer is allowed for his taxable year a deduction under section 151 (relating to deductions for personal exemptions).

"(c) Definitions. For purposes of this section—

"(1) Dependent. The term 'dependent' means a person with respect to whom the taxpayer is entitled to an exemption under section 151(e)(1)—

"(A) who has not attained the age of 12 years and who (within the meaning of section 152) is a son, stepson, daughter, or stepdaughter of the taxpayer; or

"(B) who is physically or mentally incapable of caring for himself.

"(2) Widower. The term 'widower' includes an unmarried individual who is legally separated from his spouse under a decree of divorce or of separate maintenance.

"(3) Determination of status. A woman shall not be considered as married if—

"(A) she is legally separated from her spouse under a decree of divorce or of separate maintenance oat the close of the taxable year, or

"(B) she has been deserted by her spouse, does not know his whereabouts (and has not known his whereabouts at any time during the taxable year), and has applied to a court of competent jurisdiction for appropriate process to compel him to pay support or otherwise to comply with the law or a judicial order, as determined under regulations prescribed by the Secretary or his delegate."

In 1963, P.L. 88-4, Sec. [1], designated existing provisions following "as married if" as "(A)", and added clause "(B)" in para. (c)(3), effective for tax. yrs. end. after 4/2/63.

Sec. 215. Alimony, etc., payments.

(a) General rule.

In the case of an individual, there shall be allowed as a deduction an amount equal to the alimony or separate maintenance payments paid during such individual's taxable year.

(b) Alimony or separate maintenance payments defined.

For purposes of this section, the term "alimony or separate maintenance payment" means any alimony or separate maintenance payment (as defined in section 71(b)) which is includible in the gross income of the recipient under section 71.

(c) Requirement of identification number.

The Secretary may prescribe regulations under which—

(1) any individual receiving alimony or separate maintenance payments is required to furnish such individual's taxpayer identification number to the individual making such payments, and

(2) the individual making such payments is required to include such taxpayer identification number on such individual's return for the taxable year in which such payments are made.

(d) Coordination with section 682.

No deduction shall be allowed under this section with respect to any payment if, by reason of section 682 (relating to income of alimony trusts), the amount thereof is not includible in such individual's gross income.

In 1984, P.L. 98-369, Sec. 422(b), amended Code Sec. 215, effective for divorce or separation instruments executed after 12/31/84. Sec. 422(e)(2) and (3) of this Act provides:

"(2) Modifications of instruments executed before January 1, 1985. The amendments made by this section shall also apply to any divorce or separation instrument (as so defined) executed before January 1, 1985, but modified on or after such date if the modification expressly provides that the amendments made by this section shall apply to such modification.

"(3) Requirement of identification number. Section 215(c) of the Internal Revenue Code of 1954 (as amended by subsection 422 (b) of the Act) and the amendments made by subsection (c) shall apply to payments made after December 31, 1984."

Prior to amendment, Code Sec. 215 read as follows:

"SEC. 215. ALIMONY, ETC., PAYMENTS.

"(a) General rule.

"In the case of a husband described in section 71, there shall be allowed as a deduction amounts includible under section 71 in the gross income of his wife, payment of which is made within the husband's taxable year. No deduction shall be allowed under the preceding sentence with respect to any payment if, by reason of section 71(d) or 682, the amount thereof is not includible in the husband's gross income.

"(b) Cross reference.

"For definition of 'husband' and 'wife,' see section 7701(a)(17)."

Sec. 216. Deduction of taxes, interest, and business depreciation by cooperative housing corporation tenant-stockholder.

(a) Allowance of deduction.

In the case of a tenant-stockholder (as defined in subsection (b)(2)), there shall be allowed as a deduction amounts (not otherwise deductible) paid or accrued to a cooperative housing corporation within the taxable year, but only to the extent that such amounts represent the tenant-stockholder's proportionate share of—

(1) the real estate taxes allowable as a deduction to the corporation under section 164 which are paid or incurred by the corporation on the houses or apartment building and on the land on which such houses (or building) are situated, or

(2) the interest allowable as a deduction to the corporation under section 163 which is paid or incurred by the corporation on its indebtedness contracted—

Deductions   Code Sec. 216(c)(2)(B)

(A) in the acquisition, construction, alteration, rehabilitation, or maintenance of the houses or apartment building, or

(B) in the acquisition of the land on which the houses (or apartment building) are situated.

(b) Definitions.

For purposes of this section—

(1) Cooperative housing corporation. The term "cooperative housing corporation" means a corporation—

(A) having one and only one class of stock outstanding,

(B) each of the stockholders of which is entitled, solely by reason of his ownership of stock in the corporation, to occupy for dwelling purposes a house, or an apartment in a building, owned or leased by such corporation,

(C) no stockholder of which is entitled (either conditionally or unconditionally) to receive any distribution not out of earnings and profits of the corporation except on a complete or partial liquidation of the corporation, and

(D) meeting 1 or more of the following requirements for the taxable year in which the taxes and interest described in subsection (a) are paid or incurred:

(i) 80 percent or more of the corporation's gross income for such taxable year is derived from tenant-stockholders.

(ii) At all times during such taxable year, 80 percent or more of the total square footage of the corporation's property is used or available for use by the tenant-stockholders for residential purposes or purposes ancillary to such residential use.

(iii) 90 percent or more of the expenditures of the corporation paid or incurred during such taxable year are paid or incurred for the acquisition, construction, management, maintenance, or care of the corporation's property for the benefit of the tenant-stockholders.

(2) Tenant-stockholder. The term "tenant-stockholder" means a person who is a stockholder in a cooperative housing corporation, and whose stock is fully paid-up in an amount not less than an amount shown to the satisfaction of the Secretary as bearing a reasonable relationship to the portion of the value of the corporation's equity in the houses or apartment building and the land on which situated which is attributable to the house or apartment which such person is entitled to occupy.

(3) Tenant-stockholder's proportionate share.

(A) In general. Except as provided in subparagraph (B), the term "tenant-stockholder's proportionate share" means that proportion which the stock of the cooperative housing corporation owned by the tenant-stockholder is of the total outstanding stock of the corporation (including any stock held by the corporation).

(B) Special rule where allocation of taxes or interest reflect cost to corporation of stockholder's unit.

(i) In general. If, for any taxable year—

(I) each dwelling unit owned or leased by a cooperative housing corporation is separately allocated a share of such corporation's real estate taxes described in subsection (a)(1) or a share of such corporation's interest described in subsection (a)(2), and

(II) such allocations reasonably reflect the cost to such corporation of such taxes, or of such interest, attributable to the tenant-stockholder's dwelling unit (and such unit's share of the common areas),

then the term "tenant-stockholder's proportionate share" means the shares determined in accordance with the allocations described in subclause (II).

(ii) Election by corporation required. Clause (i) shall apply with respect to any cooperative housing corporation only if such corporation elects its application. Such an election, once made, may be revoked only with the consent of the Secretary.

(4) Stock owned by governmental units. For purposes of this subsection, in determining whether a corporation is a cooperative housing corporation, stock owned and apartments leased by the United States or any of its possessions, a State or any political subdivision thereof, or any agency or instrumentality of the foregoing empowered to acquire shares in a cooperative housing corporation for the purpose of providing housing facilities, shall not be taken into account.

(5) Prior approval of occupancy. For purposes of this section, in the following cases there shall not be taken into account the fact that (by agreement with the cooperative housing corporation) the person or his nominee may not occupy the house or apartment without the prior approval of such corporation:

(A) In any case where a person acquires stock of a cooperative housing corporation by operation of law.

(B) In any case where a person other than an individual acquires stock of a cooperative housing corporation.

(C) In any case where the original seller acquires any stock of the cooperative housing corporation from the corporation not later than 1 year after the date on which the apartments or houses (or leaseholds therein) are transferred by the original seller to the corporation.

(6) Original seller defined. For purposes of paragraph (5), the term "original seller" means the person from whom the corporation has acquired the apartments or houses (or leaseholds therein).

(c) Treatment as property subject to depreciation.

(1) In general. So much of the stock of a tenant-stockholder in a cooperative housing corporation as is allocable, under regulations prescribed by the Secretary, to a proprietary lease or right of tenancy in property subject to the allowance for depreciation under section 167(a) shall, to the extent such proprietary lease or right of tenancy is used by such tenant-stockholder in a trade or business or for the production of income, be treated as property subject to the allowance for depreciation under section 167(a). The preceding sentence shall not be construed to limit or deny a deduction for depreciation under section 167(a) by a cooperative housing corporation with respect to property owned by such a corporation and leased to tenant-stockholders.

(2) Deduction limited to adjusted basis in stock.

(A) In general. The amount of any deduction for depreciation allowable under section 167(a) to a tenant-stockholder with respect to any stock for any taxable year by reason of paragraph (1) shall not exceed the adjusted basis of such stock as of the close of the taxable year of the tenant-stockholder in which such deduction was incurred.

(B) Carryforward of disallowed amount. The amount of any deduction which is not allowed by reason of subparagraph (A) shall, subject to the provisions of subparagraph (A), be treated as a deduction allowable under section 167(a) in the succeeding taxable year.

(d) Disallowance of deduction for certain payments to the corporation.

No deduction shall be allowed to a stockholder in a cooperative housing corporation for any amount paid or accrued to such corporation during any taxable year (in excess of the stockholder's proportionate share of the items described in subsections (a)(1) and (a)(2)) to the extent that, under regulations prescribed by the Secretary, such amount is properly allocable to amounts paid or incurred at any time by the corporation which are chargeable to the corporation's capital account. The stockholder's adjusted basis in the stock in the corporation shall be increased by the amount of such disallowance.

(e) Distributions by cooperative housing corporations.

Except as provided in regulations, no gain or loss shall be recognized on the distribution by a cooperative housing corporation of a dwelling unit to a stockholder in such corporation if such distribution is in exchange for the stockholder's stock in such corporation and such dwelling unit is used as his principal residence (within the meaning of section 121).

In 2007, P.L. 110-142, Sec. 4(a), amended subpara. (b)(1)(D), effective for tax. yrs. end. after 12/20/2007.

Prior to amendment, subpara. (b)(1)(D) read as follows:

"(D) 80 percent or more of the gross income of which for the taxable year in which the taxes and interest described in subsection (a) are paid or incurred is derived from tenant-stockholders."

In 1998, P.L. 105-206, Sec. 6005(e)(3), added "on or" before "before" each place it appeared in the heading and text of Sec. 312(d)(2)[sic (e)] of P.L. 105-34, see below.

In 1997, P.L. 105-34, Sec. 312(d)(4), substituted "such dwelling unit is used as his principal residence (within the meaning of section 121)" for "such exchange qualifies for nonrecognition of gain under section 1034(f)" in subsec. (e), effective for sales and exchanges after 5/6/97, except as provided in Sec. 312(d)(2)-(4) [sic (e)(2)-(4)] of this Act [as amended by Sec. 6005(e)(3), 105-206, see above], which reads as follows:

"(2) Sales on or before date of enactment [8/5/97]. At the election of the taxpayer, the amendments made by this section shall not apply to any sale or exchange on or before the date of the enactment [8/5/97] of this Act.

"(3) Certain sales within 2 years after date of enactment [8/5/97]. Section 121 of the Internal Revenue Code of 1986 (as amended by this section) shall be applied without regard to subsection (c)(2)(B) thereof in the case of any sale or exchange of property during the 2-year period beginning on the date of the enactment [8/5/97] of this Act if the taxpayer held such property on the date of the enactment [8/5/97] of this Act and fails to meet the ownership and use requirements of subsection (a) thereof with respect to such property.

"(4) Binding contracts. At the election of the taxpayer, the amendments made by this section shall not apply to a sale or exchange after the date of the enactment [8/5/97] of this Act, if—

"(A) such sale or exchange is pursuant to a contract which was binding on such date, or

"(B) without regard to such amendments, gain would not be recognized under section 1034 of the Internal Revenue Code of 1986 (as in effect on the day before the date of the enactment of this Act) on such sale or exchange by reason of a new residence acquired on or before such date or with respect to the acquisition of which by the taxpayer a binding contract was in effect on such date.

This paragraph shall not apply to any sale or exchange by an individual if the treatment provided by section 877(a)(1) of the Internal Revenue Code of 1986 applies to such individual."

In 1990, P.L. 101-508, Sec. 11702(i)(1), substituted "corporations" for "associations" in heading of subsec. (e) . . . Sec. 11702(i)(2), substituted "corporation" for "association" in subsec. (e), effective for liquidating distributions as provided in Sec. 633(a)(1) of P.L. 99-514, reproduced in note following Code Sec. 336, and effective for nonliquidating distributions as provided in Sec. 633(a)(3) of P.L. 99-514, reproduced in note following Code Sec. 311.

In 1988, P.L. 100-647, Sec. 6282(a), added subsec (e), effective for liquidating distributions as provided in Sec. 633(a)(1) of P.L. 99-514, reproduced in note following Code Sec. 336, and effective for nonliquidating distributions as provided in Sec. 633(a)(3) of P.L. 99-514, reproduced in note following Code Sec. 311.

In 1986, P.L. 99-514, Sec. 644(a)(1)(A), substituted "a person" for "an individual" in para. (b)(2) . . . Sec. 644(a)(1)(B), substituted "such person" for "such individual" in para. (b)(2) . . . Sec. 644(a)(2), amended paras. (b)(5) and (6) . . . Sec. 644(b), amended subsec. (c) . . . Sec. 644(c), added subsec. (d) . . . Sec. 644(d), amended para. (b)(3), effective for tax. yrs. begin. after 12/31/86. Secs. 644(e)(1)-(7) of the Act provide:

"(e) Treatment of amounts received in connection with the refinancing of indebtedness of certain cooperative housing corporations; treatment of amounts paid from qualified refinancing-related reserve.

"(1) Payment of closing costs and creation of reserve excluded from gross income. For purposes of the Internal Revenue Code of 1954, no amount shall be included in the gross income of a qualified cooperative housing corporation by reason of the payment or reimbursement by a city housing development agency or corporation of amounts for—

"(A) closing costs, or

"(B) the creation of reserves for the qualified cooperative housing corporation, in connection with a qualified refinancing.

"(2) Income from reserve fund treated as member income.

"(A) In general. Income from a qualified refinancing-related reserve shall be treated as derived from its members for purposes of—

"(i) section 216 of the Internal Revenue Code of 1954 (relating to deduction of taxes, interest, and business depreciation by cooperative housing corporation tenant-stockholder), and

"(ii) section 277 of such Code (relating to deductions incurred by certain membership organizations in transactions with members).

"(B) No inference. Nothing in the provisions of this paragraph shall be construed to infer that a change in law is intended with respect to the treatment of deductions under section 277 of the Internal Revenue Code of 1954 with respect to cooperative housing corporations, and any determination of such issue shall be made as if such provisions had not been enacted.

"(3) Treatment of certain interest claimed as deduction. Any amount—

"(A) claimed (on a return of tax imposed by chapter 1 of the Internal Revenue Code of 1954) as a deduction by a qualified cooperative housing corporation for interest for any taxable year beginning before January 1, 1986, on a second mortgage loan made by a city housing development agency or corporation in connection with a qualified refinancing, and

"(B) reported (before April 16, 1986) by the qualified cooperative housing corporation to its tenant-stockholders as interest described in section 216(a)(2) of such Code,

shall be treated for purposes of such Code as if such amount were paid by such qualified cooperative housing corporation during such taxable year.

"(4) Qualified cooperative housing corporation.

"(A) In general. For purposes of this subsection, the term 'qualified cooperative housing corporation' means any corporation if—

"(i) such corporation is, after the application of paragraphs (1) and (2), a cooperative housing corporation (as defined in section 216(b) of the Internal Revenue Code of 1954),

"(ii) such corporation is subject to a qualified limited-profit housing companies law, and

"(iii) such corporation either—

"(I) filed for incorporation on July 22, 1965, or

"(II) filed for incorporation on March 5, 1964.

"(B) Qualified limited-profit housing companies law.— For purposes of subparagraph (A), the term 'qualified limited-profit housing companies law' means any limited-profit housing companies law which limits the resale price for a tenant-stockholder's stock in a cooperative housing corporation to the sum of his basis for such stock plus his proportionate share of part or all of the amortization of any mortgage on the building owned by such corporation.

"(5) Qualified refinancing. For purposes of this subsection, the term 'qualified refinancing' means any refinancing—

"(A) which occurred—

"(i) with respect to a qualified cooperative housing corporation described in paragraph (4)(A)(iii)(I) on September 20, 1978, or

"(ii) with respect to a qualified cooperative housing corporation described in paragraph (4)(A)(iii)(II) on November 21, 1978, and

"(B) in which a qualified cooperative housing corporation refinanced a first mortgage loan made to such corporation by a city housing development agency with a first mortgage loan made by a city housing development corporation and insured by an agency of the Federal Government and a second mortgage loan made by such city housing development agency, in the process of which a reserve was created (as required by such Federal agency) and closing costs were paid or reimbursed by such city housing development agency or corporation.

"(6) Qualified refinancing-related reserve. For purposes of this subsection, the term 'qualified refinancing-related reserve' means any reserve of a qualified cooperative housing corporation with respect to the creation of which no amount was included in the gross income of such corporation by reason of paragraph (a).

"(7) Treatment of amounts paid from qualified refinancing-related reserve.

"(A) In general. With respect to any payment from a qualified refinancing-related reserve out of amounts excluded from gross income by reason of paragraph (1)—

"(i) no deduction shall be allowed under chapter 1 of such Code, and

"(ii) the basis of any property acquired with such payment (determined without regard to this subparagraph) shall be reduced by the amount of such payment.

"(B) Ordering rules. For purposes of subparagraph (A), payments from a reserve shall be treated as being made

"(i) first from amounts excluded from gross income by reason of paragraph (1) to the extent thereof, and

"(ii) then from other amounts in the reserve."

Secs. 644(e)(1)-(6) are effective for tax. yrs. begin. after 12/31/86, Sec. 644(e)(7) is effective for amounts paid or incurred, and property acquired, in tax. yrs. begin. after 12/31/85.

Prior to amendment, paras. (b)(5) and (6) read as follows:

"(5) Stock acquired through foreclosure by lending institution. If a bank or other lending institution acquires by foreclosure (or by instrument in lieu of foreclosure) the stock of a tenant-stockholder, and a lease or the right to occupy an apartment or house to which such stock is appurtenant, such bank or other lending institution shall be treated as a tenant-stockholder for a period not to exceed three years from the date of acquisition. The preceding sentence shall apply even though, by agreement with the cooperative housing corporation, the bank (or other lending institution) or its nominee may not occupy the house or apartment without the prior approval of such corporation.

"(6) Stock owned by person from whom the corporation acquired its property.

"(A) In general. If the original seller acquires any stock of the corporation from the corporation or by foreclosure, the original seller shall be treated as a tenant-stockholder for a period not to exceed 3 years from the date of the acquisition of such stock.

"(B) Stock acquisition must take place not later than 1 year after transfer of dwelling units. Except in the case of an acquisition of stock of a corporation by foreclosure, subparagraph (A) shall apply only if the acquisition of stock occurs not later than 1 year after the date on which the apartments or houses (or leaseholds therein) are transferred by the original seller to the corporation. For purposes of this subparagraph and subparagraph (A), the term 'by foreclosure' means by foreclosure (or by instrument in lieu of foreclosure) of any purchase-money security interest in the stock held by the original seller.

"(C) Original seller must have right to occupy apartment or house. Subparagraph (a) shall apply with respect to any acquisition of stock only if, together with such acquisition, the original seller acquires the right to occupy an apartment or house to which such stock is appurtenant.

For purposes of the preceding sentence, there shall not be taken into account the fact that, by agreement with the corporation, the original seller or its nominee may not occupy the house or apartment without the prior approval of the corporation.

"(D) Original seller defined. For purposes of this paragraph, the term 'original seller' means the person from whom the corporation has acquired the apartments or houses (or leaseholds therein). The estate of an original seller shall succeed to, and take into account, the tax treatment of the original seller under this paragraph."

Prior to amendment, subsec. (c) read as follows:

"(c) Treatment as property subject to depreciation.

"So much of the stock of a tenant-stockholder in a cooperative housing corporation as is allocable, under regulations prescribed by the Secretary, to a proprietary lease or right of tenancy in property subject to the allowance for depreciation under section 167(a) shall, to the extent such proprietary lease or right of tenancy is used by such tenant-stockholder in a trade or business or for the production of income, be treated as property subject to the allowance for depreciation under section 167(a). The preceding sentence shall not be construed to limit or deny a deduction for depreciation under 167(a) by a cooperative housing corporation with respect to property owned by such a corporation and leased to tenant-stockholders."

Prior to amendment, para. (b)(3) read as follows:

"(3) The term 'tenant-stockholder's proportionate share' means that proportion which the stock of the cooperative housing corporation owned by the tenant-stockholder is of the total outstanding stock of the corporation (including any stock held by the corporation)."

In 1980, P.L. 96-222, Sec. 105(a)(6)(A), redesignated subparas. (b)(6)(B) and (C) as (b)(6)(C) and (D), deleted subpara. (A), and added new subparas. (b)(6)(A) and (B) . . . Sec. 105(a)(6)(B), added the last sentence to the end of subpara. (b)(6)(D) [as redesignated] effective for stocks acquired after 11/6/78.

Prior to amendment, subpara. (b)(6)(A) read as follows:

"(A) In general. If the original seller acquires any stock of the corporation—

"(i) from the corporation by purchase, or

"(ii) by foreclosure (or by instrument in lieu of foreclosure) of any purchase-money security interest in such stock held by the original seller,

the original seller shall be treated as a tenant-stockholder for a period not to exceed 3 years from the date of acquisition."

In 1978, P.L. 95-600, Sec. 531(a), added para. (b)(6), effective for stocks acquired after 11/6/78.

In 1976, P.L. 94-455, Sec. 1906(b)(13)(A), substituted "Secretary" for "Secretary or his delegate" in para. (b)(2) and subsec. (c), effective for tax. yrs. begin. after 12/31/76.

—P.L. 94-455, Sec. 2101(b), added the last sentence in subsec. (c), effective for tax. yrs. begin. after 12/31/73.

—P.L. 94-455, Sec. 2101(f)(1), added para. (b)(5), effective for stock acquired by banks or other lending institutions after 10/4/76.

In 1969, P.L. 91-172, Sec. 913, added para. (b)(4), effective for tax. yrs. begin. after 12/31/69.

In 1962, P.L. 87-834, changed title from "Amounts representing taxes and interest paid to cooperative housing corporation", and added subsec. (c), for tax. yrs. begin. after '61.

Sec. 217. Moving expenses.
(a) Deduction allowed.

There shall be allowed as a deduction moving expenses paid or incurred during the taxable year in connection with the commencement of work by the taxpayer as an employee or as a self-employed individual at a new principal place of work.

(b) Definition of moving expenses.

(1) In general. For purposes of this section, the term "moving expenses" means only the reasonable expenses—

(A) of moving household goods and personal effects from the former residence to the new residence, and

(B) of traveling (including lodging) from the former residence to the new place of residence.

Such term shall not include any expenses for meals.

(2) Individuals other than taxpayer. In the case of any individual other than the taxpayer, expenses referred to in paragraph (1) shall be taken into account only if such individual has both the former residence and the new residence as his principal place of abode and is a member of the taxpayer's household.

(c) Conditions for allowance.

No deduction shall be allowed under this section unless—

(1) the taxpayer's new principal place of work—

(A) is at least 50 milesfarther from his former residence than was his former principal place of work, or

(B) if he had no former principal place of work, is at least 50 milesfrom his former residence, and

(2) either—

(A) during the 12-month period immediately following his arrival in the general location of his new principal place of work, the taxpayer is a full-time employee, in such general location, during at least 39 weeks, or

(B) during the 24-month period immediately following his arrival in the general location of his new principal place of work, the taxpayer is a full-time employee or performs services as a self-employed individual on a full-time basis, in such general location, during at least 78 weeks, of which not less than 39 weeks are during the 12-month period referred to in subparagraph (A).

For purposes of paragraph (1), the distance between two points shall be the shortest of the more commonly traveled routes between such two points.

(d) Rules for application of subsection (c)(2).

(1) The condition of subsection (c)(2) shall not apply if the taxpayer is unable to satisfy such condition by reason of—

(A) death or disability, or

(B) involuntary separation (other than for willful misconduct) from the service of, or transfer for the benefit of, an employer after obtaining full-time employment in which the taxpayer could reasonably have been expected to satisfy such condition.

(2) If a taxpayer has not satisfied the condition of subsection (c)(2) before the time prescribed by law (including extensions thereof) for filing the return for the taxable year during which he paid or incurred moving expenses which would otherwise be deductible under this section, but may still satisfy such condition, then such expenses may (at the election of the taxpayer) be deducted for such taxable year notwithstanding subsection (c)(2).

(3) If—

(A) for any taxable year moving expenses have been deducted in accordance with the rule provided in paragraph (2), and

(B) the condition of subsection (c)(2) cannot be satisfied at the close of a subsequent taxable year,

then an amount equal to the expenses which were so deducted shall be included in gross income for the first such subsequent taxable year.

(e) Repealed.

(f) Self-employed individual.

For purposes of this section, the term "self-employed individual" means an individual who performs personal services—

(1) as the owner of the entire interest in an unincorporated trade or business, or
(2) as a partner in a partnership carrying on a trade or business.

(g) **Rules for members of the Armed Forces of the United States.**
In the case of a member of the Armed Forces of the United States on active duty who moves pursuant to a military order and incident to a permanent change of station—
  (1) the limitations under subsection (c) shall not apply;
  (2) any moving and storage expenses which are furnished in kind (or for which reimbursement or an allowance is provided, but only to the extent of the expenses paid or incurred) to such member, his spouse, or his dependents, shall not be includible in gross income, and no reporting with respect to such expenses shall be required by the Secretary of Defense or the Secretary of Transportation, as the case may be; and
  (3) if moving and storage expenses are furnished in kind (or if reimbursement or an allowance for such expenses is provided) to such member's spouse and his dependents with regard to moving to a location other than the one to which such member moves (or from a location other than the one from which such member moves), this section shall apply with respect to the moving expenses of his spouse and dependents—
    (A) as if his spouse commenced work as an employee at a new principal place of work at such location; and
    (B) without regard to the limitations under subsection (c).

(h) **Special rules for foreign moves.**
  (1) **Allowance of certain storage fees.** In the case of a foreign move, for purposes of this section, the moving expenses described in subsection (b)(1)(A) include the reasonable expenses—
    (A) of moving household goods and personal effects to and from storage, and
    (B) of storing such goods and effects for part or all of the period during which the new place of work continues to be the taxpayer's principal place of work.
  (2) **Foreign move.** For purposes of this subsection, the term "foreign move" means the commencement of work by the taxpayer at a new principal place of work located outside the United States.
  (3) **United States defined.** For purposes of this subsection and subsection (i), the term "United States" includes the possessions of the United States.

(i) **Allowance of deductions in case of retirees or decedents who were working abroad.**
  (1) **In general.** In the case of any qualified retiree moving expenses or qualified survivor moving expenses—
    (A) this section (other than subsection (h)) shall be applied with respect to such expenses as if they were incurred in connection with the commencement of work by the taxpayer as an employee at a new principal place of work located within the United States, and
    (B) the limitations of subsection (c)(2) shall not apply.
  (2) **Qualified retiree moving expenses.** For purposes of paragraph (1), the term "qualified retiree moving expenses" means any moving expenses—
    (A) which are incurred by an individual whose former principal place of work and former residence were outside the United States, and
    (B) which are incurred for a move to a new residence in the United States in connection with the bona fide retirement of the individual.

  (3) **Qualified survivor moving expenses.** For purposes of paragraph (1), the term "qualified survivor moving expenses" means moving expenses—
    (A) which are paid or incurred by the spouse or any dependent of any decedent who (as of the time of his death) had a principal place of work outside the United States, and
    (B) which are incurred for a move which begins within 6 months after the death of such decedent and which is to a residence in the United States from a former residence outside the United States which (as of the time of the decedent's death) was the residence of such decedent and the individual paying or incurring the expense.

(j) **Regulations.**
The Secretary shall prescribe such regulations as may be necessary to carry out the purposes of this section.

In 1993, P.L. 103-66, Sec. 13213(a)(1), amended subsec. (b)...Sec. 13213(a)(2)(A), repealed subsec. (e)...Sec. 13213(a)(2)(B), amended subsec. (f)...Sec. 13213(a)(2)(C), added "and" at the end of subpara. (g)(3)(A), deleted subpara. (g)(3)(B) and redesignated subpara. (g)(3)(C) as subpara. (g)(3)(B)...Sec. 13213(a)(2)(D), deleted para. (h)(1) and redesignated paras. (h)(2)–(4) as paras. (h)(1)–(3)...Sec. 13213(b), substituted "50 miles" for "35 miles" each place it appeared in para. (c)(1), effective for expenses incurred after 12/31/93. Prior to amendment, subsec. (b) read as follows:
"(b) Definition of moving expenses.
"(1) In general. For purposes of this section, the term 'moving expenses' means only the reasonable expenses—
"(A) of moving household goods and personal effects from the former residence to the new residence,
"(B) of traveling (including meals and lodging) from the former residence to the new place of residence,
"(C) of traveling (including meals and lodging), after obtaining employment, from the former residence to the general location of the new principal place of work and return, for the principal purpose of searching for a new residence,
"(D) of meals and lodging while occupying temporary quarters in the general location of the new principal place of work during any period of 30 consecutive days after obtaining employment, or
"(E) constituting qualified residence sale, purchase, or lease expenses.
"(2) Qualified residence sale, etc., expenses. For purposes of paragraph (1)(E), the term 'qualified residence sale, purchase, or lease expenses' means only reasonable expenses incident to—
"(A) the sale or exchange by the taxpayer or his spouse of the taxpayer's former residence (not including expenses for work performed on such residence in order to assist in its sale) which (but for this subsection and subsection (e)) would be taken into account in determining the amount realized on the sale or exchange,
"(B) the purchase by the taxpayer or his spouse of a new residence in the general location of the new principal place of work which (but for this subsection and subsection (e)) would be taken into account in determining—
"(i) the adjusted basis of the new residence, or
"(ii) the cost of a loan (but not including any amounts which represent payments or prepayments of interest),
"(C) the settlement of an unexpired lease held by the taxpayer or his spouse on property used by the taxpayer as his former residence, or
"(D) the acquisition of a lease by the taxpayer or his spouse on property used by the taxpayer as his new residence in the general location of the new principal place of work (not including amounts which are payments or prepayments of rent).
"(3) Limitations.
"(A) Dollar limits. The aggregate amount allowable as a deduction under subsection (a) in connection with a commencement of work which is attributable to expenses described in subparagraph (C) or (D) of paragraph (1) shall not exceed $1,500. The aggregate amount allowable as a deduction under subsection (a) which is attributable to qualified residence sale, purchase, or lease expenses shall not exceed $3,000, reduced by the aggregate amount so allowable which is attributable to expenses described in subparagraph (C) or (D) of paragraph (1).
"(B) Husband and wife. If a husband and wife both commence work at a new principal place of work within the same general location, subparagraph (A) shall be applied as if there was only one commencement of work. In the case of a husband and wife filing separate returns, subparagraph (A) shall be applied by substituting '$750' for '$1,500', and by substituting '$1,500' for '$3,000'.
"(C) Individuals other than taxpayer. In the case of any individual other than the taxpayer, expenses referred to in subparagraphs (A) through (D) of paragraph (1) shall be taken into account only if such individual has both the former residence and the new residence as his principal place of abode and is a member of the taxpayer's household."
Prior to repeal, subsec. (e) read as follows:
"(e) Denial of double benefit.
The amount realized on the sale of the residence described in subparagraph (A) of subsection (b)(2) shall not be decreased by the amount of any expenses de-

Deductions Code Sec. 218

scribed in such subparagraph which are allowed as a deduction under subsection (a), and the basis of a residence described in subparagraph (B) of subsection (b)(2) shall not be increased by the amount of any expenses described in such subparagraph which are allowed as a deduction under subsection (a). This subsection shall not apply to any expenses with respect to which an amount is included in gross income under subsection (d)(3)."

Prior to amendment, subsec. (f) read as follows:

"(f) Rules for self-employed individuals.

"(1) Definition.For purposes of this section, the term 'self-employed individual' means an individual who performs personal services—

"(A) as the owner of the entire interest in an unincorporated trade or business, or

"(B) as a partner in a partnership carrying on a trade or business.

"(2) Rule for application of subsections (b)(1)(C) and (D).For purposes of subparagraphs (C) and (D) of subsection (b)(1), an individual who commences work at a new principal place of work as a self-employed individual shall be treated as having obtained employment when he has made substantial arrangements to commence such work."

Prior to deletion, subpara. (g)(3)(B) read as follows:

"(B) for purposes of subsection (b)(3), as if such place of work was within the same general location as the member's new principal place of work, and"

Prior to deletion, para. (h)(1) read as follows:

"(1) Increase in limitations.In the case of a foreign move—

"(A) subsection (b)(1)(D) shall be applied by substituting '90 consecutive days' for '30 consecutive days',

"(B) subsection (b)(3)(A) shall be applied by substituting '$4,500' for '$1,500' and by substituting '$6,000' for '$3,000', and

"(C) subsection (b)(3)(B) shall be applied as if the last sentence of such subsection read as follows: 'In the case of a husband and wife filing separate returns, subparagraph (A) shall be applied by substituting '$2,250' for '$4,500', and by substituting '$3,000' for '$6,000.'"

In 1978, P.L. 95-615, Sec. 204, redesignated subsec. (h) as (j) and added new subsecs. (h) and (i), effective for tax. yrs. begin. after 12/31/77. Sec. 209(c) of the Act provides:

"(c) Election of prior law.—

"(1) A taxpayer may elect not to have the amendments made by this title apply with respect to any taxable year beginning after December 31, 1977, and before January 1, 1979.

"(2) An election under this subsection shall be filed with a taxpayer's timely filed return for the first taxable year beginning after December 31, 1977."

In 1976, P.L. 94-455, Sec. 506(a), substituted "35 miles" for "50 miles" each place it appeared in para. (c)(1), effective for tax. yrs. begin. after 12/31/76.

—P.L. 94-455, Sec. 506(b), substituted "$1,500" for "$1,000", and "$3,000" for "$2,500" in subpara. (b)(3)(A) and amended the second sentence in subpara. (b)(3)(B), effective for tax. yrs. begin. after 12/31/76.

Prior to amendment, the second sentence in subpara. (b)(3)(B) read as follows: "In the case of a husband and wife filing separate returns, subparagraph (A) shall be applied by substituting '$500' for '$1,000', and by substituting '$1,250' for '$2,500'."

—P.L. 94-455, Sec. 506(c), redesignated subsec. (g) as (h) and added new subsec. (g), effective for tax. yrs. begin. after 12/31/75.

—P.L. 94-455, Sec. 1906(b)(13)(A), substituted "secretary" for "secretary or his delegate" each place it appeared in Code Sec. 217, effective for tax yrs. begin. after 12/31/76.

In 1974, P.L. 93-490, Sec. 2, provides as follows for tax. yrs. ending before Jan. 1, '76:

"(a) In general.

"Notwithstanding the provisions of section 82 (relating to reimbursement for expenses of moving) and section 217 (relating to moving expenses), of the Internal Revenue Code of 1954, the Secretary of the Treasury, in the administration of those sections, is authorized—

"(1) to enter into an agreement with the Secretary concerned under which the Secretary concerned will not be required to withhold tax on, or to report, moving expense reimbursements made to members of the armed forces;

"(2) to permit any taxpayer who is a member of the armed forces not to include in adjusted gross income the amount of any reimbursement in kind of moving expenses made by the Secretary concerned; and

"(3) to permit any taxpayer who is a member of the armed forces to deduct any amount paid by him as moving expenses in connection with any move required by the Secretary concerned, in excess of any reimbursement received for such expenses, without regard to the provisions of section 217(c) (relating to conditions), to the extent it is otherwise deductible under section 217.

"(b) Definitions.

"For purposes of this section, the term—

"(1) 'armed forces' has the meaning given it by section 101(4) of title 37, United States Code;

"(2) 'Secretary concerned' means the Secretary of Defense and, with respect to the Coast Guard, the Secretary of Transportation; and

"(3) 'adjusted gross income' and 'moving expenses' have the meanings given them by sections 62 and 217(b), respectively, of the Internal Revenue Code of 1954."

In 1971, P.L. 91-642, Sec. 2, amended Sec. 231(d)(1) of the Tax Reform Act of 1969 [below] by striking out "July 1, 1970" and inserting in lieu thereof "January 1, 1971."

In 1969, P.L. 91-172, Sec. 231(a), amended Code Sec. 217, effective for tax. yrs. begin. after 12/31/69, except that Sec. 231(d) [as amended by Sec. 2 of P.L. 642, see above] provides that:

"(1) section 217 of the Internal Revenue Code of 1954 (as amended by subsection (a)) shall not apply to any item to the extent that the taxpayer received or accrued reimbursement or other expense allowance for such item in a taxable year beginning on or before December 31, 1969, which was not included in his gross income; and

"(2) the amendments made by this section shall not apply (at the election of the taxpayer made at such time and manner as the Secretary of the Treasury or his delegate prescribes) with respect to moving expenses paid or incurred before January 1, 1971, in connection with the commencement of work by the taxpayer as an employee at a new principal place of work of which the taxpayer had been notified by his employer on or before December 19, 1969.

Prior to amendment Code Sec. 217 read as follows:

"SEC. 217. MOVING EXPENSES.

"(a) Deduction allowed.

"There shall be allowed as a deduction moving expenses paid or incurred during the taxable year in connection with the commencement of work by the taxpayer as an employee at a new principal place of work.

"(b) Definition of moving expenses.

"(1) In general. For purposes of this section, the term 'moving expenses' means only the reasonable expenses—

"(A) of moving household goods and personal effects from the former residence to the new residence, and

"(B) of traveling (including meals and lodging) from the former residence to the new place of residence.

"(2) Individuals other than taxpayer. In the case of any individual other than the taxpayer, expenses referred to in paragraph (1) shall be taken into account only if such individual has both the former residence and the new residence as his principal place of abode and is a member of the taxpayer's household.

"(c) Conditions for allowance.

"No deduction shall be allowed under this section unless—

"(1) the taxpayer's new principal place of work—

"(A) is at least 20 miles farther from his former residence than was his former principal place of work, or

"(B) if he had no former principal place of work, is at least 20 miles from his former residence, and

"(2) during the 12-month period immediately following his arrival in the general location of his new principal place of work, the taxpayer is a full-time employee, in such general location, during at least 39 weeks.

"(d) Rules for application of subsection (c)(2).

"(1) Subsection (c)(2) shall not apply to any item to the extent that the taxpayer receives reimbursement or other expense allowance from his employer for such item.

"(2) If a taxpayer has not satisfied the condition of subsection (c)(2) before the time prescribed by law (including extensions thereof for filing the return for the taxable year during which he paid or incurred moving expenses which would otherwise be deductible under this section, but may still satisfy such condition, then such expenses may (at the election of the taxpayer) be deducted for such taxable year notwithstanding subsection (c)(2).

"(3) If—

"(A) for any taxable year moving expenses have been deducted in accordance with the rule provided in paragraph (2), and

"(B) the condition of subsection (c)(2) is not satisfied by the close of the subsequent taxable year,

then an amount equal to the expenses which were so deducted shall be included in gross income for such subsequent taxable year.

"(e) Disallowance of deduction with respect to reimbursements not included in gross income.

"No deduction shall be allowed under this section for any item to the extent that the taxpayer receives reimbursement or other expense allowance for such item which is not included in his gross income.

"(f) Regulations.

"The Secretary or his delegate shall prescribe such regulations as may be necessary to carry out the purposes of this section."

In 1964, P.L. 88-272, Sec. 213(a)(1), added Code Sec. 217, effective for expenses incurred after 12/31/63 in tax. yrs. end. after December 31, 1963.

Sec. 218. Repealed.

In 1978, P.L. 95-600, Sec. 113(a)(1), repealed Code Sec. 218, effective for contributions the payment of which is made after 12/31/78, in tax. yrs. begin. after 12/31/78.

Prior to repeal Code Sec. 218 read as follows:

"SEC. 218. CONTRIBUTIONS TO CANDIDATES FOR PUBLIC OFFICE.

"(a) Allowance of deduction.

"In the case of an individual, there shall be allowed as a deduction any political contribution (as defined in section 41(c)(1) or newsletter fund contribution (as defined in section 41(c)(5))) [sic] payment of which is made by such individual within the taxable year.

"(b) Limitations.

1,693

"(1) **Amount.** The deduction under subsection (a) shall not exceed $100 ($200 in the case of a joint return under section 6013).

"(2) **Verification.** The deduction under subsection (a) shall be allowed, with respect to any political contribution or newsletter fund contribution, only if such contribution is verified in such manner as the Secretary shall prescribe by regulations.

"(c) *Election to take credit in lieu of deduction.*

"This section shall not apply in the case of any taxpayer who, for the taxable year, elects to take the credit against tax provided by section 41 (relating to credit against tax for contributions to candidates for public office). Such election shall be made in such manner and at such time as the Secretary shall prescribe by regulations.

"(d) *Cross reference.*

"For disallowance of deduction to estates and trusts, see section 642(i)."

In 1976, P.L. 94-455, Sec. 1906(b)(13)(A), substituted "Secretary" for "Secretary or his delegate" in subsecs. (b) and (c), effective for tax. yrs. begin. after 12/31/76.

In 1975, P.L. 93-625, Sec. 11(d), added "or newsletter fund contributions (as defined in section 41(c)(5))" after "section 41(c)(1)" in subsec. (a), substituted "political contribution or newsletter fund contribution" for "political contribution" the first place it appeared in para. (b)(2), and substituted "contribution" for "political contribution" the second place it appeared in para. (b)(2), effective with respect to any contribution the payment of which is made after 12/31/74, in tax. yrs. begin. after 12/31/74.

—P.L. 93-625, Sec. 12(b), amended para. (b)(1), effective with respect to any contribution the payment of which is made after 12/31/74, in tax. yrs. begin. after 12/31/74.

Prior to amendment, para. (b)(1) read as follows:

"(1) Amount. The deduction under subsection (a) shall not exceed $50 ($100 in the case of a joint return under section 6013)."

In 1971, P.L. 92-178, Sec. 702(a), added Code Sec. 218, effective for tax. yrs. end. after 12/31/71, but only for political contributions, payment of which is made after 12/31/71.

Sec. 219. Retirement savings.
(a) Allowance of deduction.

In the case of an individual, there shall be allowed as a deduction an amount equal to the qualified retirement contributions of the individual for the taxable year.

(b) Maximum amount of deduction.

(1) In general. The amount allowable as a deduction under subsection (a) to any individual for any taxable year shall not exceed the lesser of—

> • *Caution:* Code Sec. 219(b)(1)(A), following, was amended by Sec. 601(a)(1), P.L. 107-16, the Economic Growth and Tax Relief Reconciliation Act of 2001 (EGTRRA). These provisions generally sunset for tax years beginning after 12/31/2012. For specific sunset provisions see Sec. 901, P.L. 107-16 (as amended) reproduced in history notes for this Code Sec.

(A) the deductible amount, or

(B) an amount equal to the compensation includible in the individual's gross income for such taxable year.

(2) Special rule for employer contributions under simplified employee pensions. This section shall not apply with respect to an employer contribution to a simplified employee pension.

(3) Plans under section 501(c)(18). Notwithstanding paragraph (1), the amount allowable as a deduction under subsection (a) with respect to any contributions on behalf of an employee to a plan described in section 501(c)(18) shall not exceed the lesser of—

(A) $7,000, or

(B) an amount equal to 25 percent of the compensation (as defined in section 415(c)(3)) includible in the individual's gross income for such taxable year.

(4) Special rule for simple retirement accounts. This section shall not apply with respect to any amount contributed to a simple retirement account established under section 408(p).

> • *Caution:* Code Sec. 219(b)(5), following, was amended by Sec. 601(a)(2), P.L. 107-16, the Economic Growth and Tax Relief Reconciliation Act of 2001 (EGTRRA). These provisions generally sunset for tax years beginning after 12/31/2012. For specific sunset provisions see Sec. 901, P.L. 107-16 (as amended) reproduced in history notes for this Code Sec.

(5) Deductible amount. For purposes of paragraph (1)(A)—

(A) In general. The deductible amount shall be determined in accordance with the following table:

For taxable years beginning in:	The deductible amount is:
2002 through 2004	$3,000
2005 through 2007	$4,000
2008 and thereafter	$5,000

(B) Catch-up contributions for individuals 50 or older.

(i) In general. In the case of an individual who has attained the age of 50 before the close of the taxable year, the deductible amount for such taxable year shall be increased by the applicable amount.

(ii) Applicable amount. For purposes of clause (i), the applicable amount shall be the amount determined in accordance with the following table:

For taxable years beginning in:	The applicable amount is:
2002 through 2005	$500
2006 and thereafter	$1,000

(C) Catchup contributions for certain individuals.

(i) In general. In the case of an applicable individual who elects to make a qualified retirement contribution in addition to the deductible amount determined under subparagraph (A)—

(I) the deductible amount for any taxable year shall be increased by an amount equal to 3 times the applicable amount determined under subparagraph (B) for such taxable year, and

(II) subparagraph (B) shall not apply.

(ii) Applicable individual. For purposes of this subparagraph, the term "applicable individual" means, with respect to any taxable year, any individual who was a qualified participant in a qualified cash or deferred arrangement (as defined in section 401(k)) of an employer described in clause (iii) under which the employer matched at least 50 percent of the employee's contributions to such arrangement with stock of such employer.

(iii) Employer described. An employer is described in this clause if, in any taxable year preceding the taxable year described in clause (ii)—

(I) such employer (or any controlling corporation of such employer) was a debtor in a case under title 11 of the United States Code, or similar Federal or State law, and

Deductions   Code Sec. 219(f)(5)

(II) such employer (or any other person) was subject to an indictment or conviction resulting from business transactions related to such case.

(iv) Qualified participant. For purposes of clause (ii), the term "qualified participant" means any applicable individual who was a participant in the cash or deferred arrangement described in such clause on the date that is 6 months before the filing of the case described in clause (iii).

(v) Termination. This subparagraph shall not apply to taxable years beginning after December 31, 2009.

(D) Cost-of-living adjustment.

(i) In general. In the case of any taxable year beginning in a calendar year after 2008, the $5,000 amount under subparagraph (A) shall be increased by an amount equal to—

(I) such dollar amount, multiplied by

(II) the cost-of-living adjustment determined under section 1(f)(3) for the calendar year in which the taxable year begins, determined by substituting "calendar year 2007" for "calendar year 1992" in subparagraph (B) thereof.

(ii) Rounding rules. If any amount after adjustment under clause (i) is not a multiple of $500, such amount shall be rounded to the next lower multiple of $500.

(c) Special rules for certain married individuals.

(1) In general. In the case of an individual to whom this paragraph applies for the taxable year, the limitation of paragraph (1) of subsection (b) shall be equal to the lesser of—

(A) the dollar amount in effect under subsection (b)(1)(A) for the taxable year, or

(B) the sum of—

(i) the compensation includible in such individual's gross income for the taxable year, plus

(ii) the compensation includible in the gross income of such individual's spouse for the taxable year reduced by—

(I) the amount allowed as a deduction under subsection (a) to such spouse for such taxable year,

(II) the amount of any designated nondeductible contribution (as defined in section 408(o)) on behalf of such spouse for such taxable year, and

(III) the amount of any contribution on behalf of such spouse to a Roth IRA under section 408A for such taxable year.

(2) Individuals to whom paragraph (1) applies. Paragraph (1) shall apply to any individual if—

(A) such individual files a joint return for the taxable year, and

(B) the amount of compensation (if any) includible in such individual's gross income for the taxable year is less than the compensation includible in the gross income of such individual's spouse for the taxable year.

(d) Other limitations and restrictions.

(1) Beneficiary must be under age 70½. No deduction shall be allowed under this section with respect to any qualified retirement contribution for the benefit of an individual if such individual has attained age 70½ before the close of such individual's taxable year for which the contribution was made.

• *Caution:* Code Sec. 219(d)(2), following, was amended by Sec. 641(e)(2), P.L. 107-16, the Economic Growth and Tax Relief Reconciliation Act of 2001 (EGTRRA). These provisions generally sunset for tax years beginning after 12/31/2012. For specific sunset provisions see Sec. 901, P.L. 107-16 (as amended) reproduced in history notes for this Code Sec.

(2) Recontributed amounts. No deduction shall be allowed under this section with respect to a rollover contribution described in section 402(c), 403(a)(4), 403(b)(8), 408(d)(3), or 457(e)(16).

(3) Amounts contributed under endowment contract. In the case of an endowment contract described in section 408(b), no deduction shall be allowed under this section for that portion of the amounts paid under the contract for the taxable year which is properly allocable, under regulations prescribed by the Secretary, to the cost of life insurance.

(4) Denial of deduction for amount contributed to inherited annuities or accounts. No deduction shall be allowed under this section with respect to any amount paid to an inherited individual retirement account or individual retirement annuity (within the meaning of section 408(d)(3)(C)(ii)).

(e) Qualified retirement contribution.

For purposes of this section, the term "qualified retirement contribution" means—

(1) any amount paid in cash for the taxable year by or on behalf of an individual to an individual retirement plan for such individual's benefit, and

(2) any amount contributed on behalf of any individual to a plan described in section 501(c)(18).

(f) Other definitions and special rules.

(1) Compensation. For purposes of this section, the term "compensation" includes earned income (as defined in section 401(c)(2)). The term "compensation" does not include any amount received as a pension or annuity and does not include any amount received as deferred compensation. The term "compensation" shall include any amount includible in the individual's gross income under section 71 with respect to a divorce or separation instrument described in subparagraph (A) of section 71(b)(2). For purposes of this paragraph, section 401(c)(2) shall be applied as if the term trade or business for purposes of section 1402 included service described in subsection (c)(6). The term compensation includes any differential wage payment (as defined in section 3401(h)(2)).

(2) Married individuals. The maximum deduction under subsection (b) shall be computed separately for each individual, and this section shall be applied without regard to any community property laws.

(3) Time when contributions deemed made. For purposes of this section, a taxpayer shall be deemed to have made a contribution to an individual retirement plan on the last day of the preceding taxable year if the contribution is made on account of such taxable year and is made not later than the time prescribed by law for filing the return for such taxable year (not including extensions thereof).

(4) Reports. The Secretary shall prescribe regulations which prescribe the time and the manner in which reports to the Secretary and plan participants shall be made by the plan administrator of a qualified employer or government plan receiving qualified voluntary employee contributions.

(5) Employer payments. For purposes of this title, any amount paid by an employer to an individual retirement

1,695

Code Sec. 219(f)(5) — Deductions

plan shall be treated as payment of compensation to the employee (other than a self-employed individual who is an employee within the meaning of section 401(c)(1)) includible in his gross income in the taxable year for which the amount was contributed, whether or not a deduction for such payment is allowable under this section to the employee.

(6) Excess contributions treated as contribution made during subsequent year for which there is an unused limitation.

(A) In general. If for the taxable year the maximum amount allowable as a deduction under this section for contributions to an individual retirement plan exceeds the amount contributed, then the taxpayer shall be treated as having made an additional contribution for the taxable year in an amount equal to the lesser of—

(i) the amount of such excess, or

(ii) the amount of the excess contributions for such taxable year (determined under section 4973(b)(2) without regard to subparagraph (C) thereof).

(B) Amount contributed. For purposes of this paragraph, the amount contributed—

(i) shall be determined without regard to this paragraph, and

(ii) shall not include any rollover contribution.

(C) Special rule where excess deduction was allowed for closed year. Proper reduction shall be made in the amount allowable as a deduction by reason of this paragraph for any amount allowed as a deduction under this section for a prior taxable year for which the period for assessing deficiency has expired if the amount so allowed exceeds the amount which should have been allowed for such prior taxable year.

(7) Special rule for compensation earned by members of the armed forces for service in a combat zone. For purposes of subsections (b)(1)(B) and (c), the amount of compensation includible in an individual's gross income shall be determined without regard to section 112.

(8) Election not to deduct contributions. For election not to deduct contributions to individual retirement plans, see section 408(o)(2)(B)(ii).

(g) Limitation on deduction for active participants in certain pension plans.

(1) In general. If (for any part of any plan year ending with or within a taxable year) an individual or the individual's spouse is an active participant, each of the dollar limitations contained in subsections (b)(1)(A) and (c)(1)(A) for such taxable year shall be reduced (but not below zero) by the amount determined under paragraph (2).

(2) Amount of reduction.

(A) In general. The amount determined under this paragraph with respect to any dollar limitation shall be the amount which bears the same ratio to such limitation as—

(i) the excess of —

(I) the taxpayer's adjusted gross income for such taxable year, over

(II) the applicable dollar amount, bears to

(ii) $10,000 ($20,000 in the case of a joint return for a taxable year beginning after December 31, 2006).

(B) No reduction below $200 until complete phaseout. No dollar limitation shall be reduced below $200 under paragraph (1) unless (without regard to this subparagraph) such limitation is reduced to zero.

(C) Rounding. Any amount determined under this paragraph which is not a multiple of $10 shall be rounded to the next lowest $10.

(3) Adjusted gross income; applicable dollar amount. For purposes of this subsection—

(A) Adjusted gross income. Adjusted gross income of any taxpayer shall be determined—

(i) after application of sections 86 and 469, and

> • *Caution:* Code Sec. 219(g)(3)(A)(ii), following, was amended by Sec. 431(c)(1), P.L. 107-16, the Economic Growth and Tax Relief Reconciliation Act of 2001 (EGTRRA). These provisions generally sunset for tax years beginning after 12/31/2012. For specific sunset provisions see Sec. 901, P.L. 107-16 (as amended) reproduced in history notes for this Code Sec.

(ii) without regard to sections 135 [sic], 137, 199, 221, 222, and 911 or the deduction allowable under this section.

(B) Applicable dollar amount. The term "applicable dollar amount" means the following:

(i) In the case of a taxpayer filing a joint return:

For taxable years beginning in:	The applicable dollar amount is:
1998	$ 50,000
1999	$ 51,000
2000	$ 52,000
2001	$ 53,000
2002	$ 54,000
2003	$ 60,000
2004	$ 65,000
2005	$ 70,000
2006	$ 75,000
2007 and thereafter	$ 80,000

(ii) In the case of any other taxpayer (other than a married individual filing a separate return):

For taxable years beginning in:	The applicable dollar amount is:
1998	$ 30,000
1999	$ 31,000
2000	$ 32,000
2001	$ 33,000
2002	$ 34,000
2003	$ 40,000
2004	$ 45,000
2005 and thereafter	$ 50,000

(iii) In the case of a married individual filing a separate return, zero.

(4) Special rule for married individuals filing separately and living apart. A husband and wife who—

(A) file separate returns for any taxable year, and

(B) live apart at all times during such taxable year, shall not be treated as married individuals for purposes of this subsection.

Deductions   Code Sec. 219

(5) **Active participant.** For purposes of this subsection, the term "active participant" means, with respect to any plan year, an individual—
  (A) who is an active participant in—
    (i) a plan described in section 401(a) which includes a trust exempt from tax under section 501(a),
    (ii) an annuity plan described in section 403(a),
    (iii) a plan established for its employees by the United States, by a State or political subdivision thereof, or by an agency or instrumentality of any of the foregoing,
    (iv) an annuity contract described in section 403(b),
    (v) a simplified employee pension (within the meaning of section 408(k)), or
    (vi) any simple retirement account (within the meaning of section 408(p)), or
  (B) who makes deductible contributions to a trust described in section 501(c)(18).

The determination of whether an individual is an active participant shall be made without regard to whether or not such individual's rights under a plan, trust, or contract are nonforfeitable. An eligible deferred compensation plan (within the meaning of section 457(b)) shall not be treated as a plan described in subparagraph (A)(iii).

(6) **Certain individuals not treated as active participants.** For purposes of this subsection, any individual described in any of the following subparagraphs shall not be treated as an active participant for any taxable year solely because of any participation so described:
  (A) Members of reserve components. Participation in a plan described in subparagraph (A)(iii) of paragraph (5) by reason of service as a member of a reserve component of the Armed Forces (as defined in section 10101 of title 10), unless such individual has served in excess of 90 days on active duty (other than active duty for training) during the year.
  (B) Volunteer firefighters. A volunteer firefighter—
    (i) who is a participant in a plan described in subparagraph (A)(iii) of paragraph (5) based on his activity as a volunteer firefighter, and
    (ii) whose accrued benefit as of the beginning of the taxable year is not more than an annual benefit of $1,800 (when expressed as a single life annuity commencing at age 65).

(7) **Special rule for spouses who are not active participants.** If this subsection applies to an individual for any taxable year solely because their spouse is an active participant, then, in applying this subsection to the individual (but not their spouse)—
  (A) the applicable dollar amount under paragraph (3)(B)(i) shall be $150,000; and
  (B) the amount applicable under paragraph (2)(A)(ii) shall be $10,000.

(8) **Inflation adjustment.** In the case of any taxable year beginning in a calendar year after 2006, the dollar amount in the last row of the table contained in paragraph (3)(B)(i), the dollar amount in the last row of the table contained in paragraph (3)(B)(ii), and the dollar amount contained in paragraph (7)(A), shall each be increased by an amount equal to—
  (A) such dollar amount, multiplied by
  (B) the cost-of-living adjustment determined under section 1(f)(3) for the calendar year in which the taxable year begins, determined by substituting "calendar year 2005" for "calendar year 1992" in subparagraph (B) thereof.

Any increase determined under the preceding sentence shall be rounded to the nearest multiple of $1,000.

(h) **Cross reference.**

For failure to provide required reports, see section 6652(g).

In 2010, P.L. 111-312, Sec. 101(a)(1), substituted "December 31, 2012" for "December 31, 2010" both places it appeared in Sec. 901 of P.L. 107-16 [see below], effective as if included in the enactment of P.L. 107-16, EGTRRA, 6/7/2001.

In 2008, P.L. 110-245, Sec. 105(b)(2), added the sentence at the end of para. (f)(1), effective for yrs. begin. after 12/31/2008.

In 2006, P.L. 109-280, Sec. 811, of this Act [relating to Sec. 901 of P.L. 107-16, see below], provides:

"SEC. 811. PENSIONS AND INDIVIDUAL RETIREMENT ARRANGEMENT PROVISIONS OF ECONOMIC GROWTH AND TAX RELIEF RECONCILIATION ACT OF 2001 MADE PERMANENT.

"Title IX of the Economic Growth and Tax Relief Reconciliation Act of 2001 [P.L. 107-16, see below] shall not apply to the provisions of, and amendments made by, subtitles A through F of title VI of such Act (relating to pension and individual retirement arrangement provisions)."

—P.L. 109-280, Sec. 831(a), redesignated subpara. (b)(5)(C) as (D) and added subpara. (b)(5)(C), effective for tax. yrs. begin. after 12/31/2006.

—P.L. 109-280, Sec. 833(b), added para. (g)(8), effective for tax. yrs. begin. after 12/31/2006.

—P.L. 109-227, Sec. 2(a), redesignated para. (f)(7) as (8) and added para. (f)(7), effective for tax. yrs. begin. after 12/31/2003.

—P.L. 109-227, Sec. 2(c), of this Act, provides:

"(c) Contributions for taxable years ending before enactment.

"(1) In general. In the case of any taxpayer with respect to whom compensation was excluded from gross income under section 112 of the Internal Revenue Code of 1986 for any taxable year beginning after December 31, 2003, and ending before the date of the enactment of this Act, any contribution to an individual retirement plan made on account of such taxable year and not later than the last day of the 3-year period beginning on the date of the enactment of this Act shall be treated, for purposes of such Code, as having been made on the last day of such taxable year.

"(2) Waiver of limitations.

"(A) Credit or refund. If the credit or refund of any overpayment of tax resulting from a contribution to which paragraph (1) applies is prevented at any time by the operation of any law or rule of law (including res judicata), such credit or refund may nevertheless be allowed or made if the claim therefor is filed before the close of the 1-year period beginning on the date that such contribution is made (determined without regard to paragraph (1)).

"(B) Assessment of deficiency. The period for assessing a deficiency attributable to a contribution to which paragraph (1) applies shall not expire before the close of the 3-year period beginning on the date that such contribution is made. Such deficiency may be assessed before the expiration of such 3-year period notwithstanding the provisions of any other law or rule of law which would otherwise prevent such assessment.

"(3) Individual retirement plan defined. For purposes of this subsection, the term 'individual retirement plan' has the meaning given such term by section 7701(a)(37) of such Code."

In 2005, P.L. 109-135, Sec. 403(a)(19), of this Act [which amended Sec. 102(e) of P.L. 108-357], provides:

"(e) Effective date.

"(1) In general. The amendments made by this section shall apply to taxable years beginning after December 31, 2004.

"(2) Application to pass-thru entities, etc. In determining the deduction under section 199 of the Internal Revenue Code of 1986 (as added by this section [Sec. 102(a) of P.L. 108-357]), items arising from a taxable year of a partnership, S corporation, estate, or trust beginning before January 1, 2005, shall not be taken into account for purposes of subsection (d)(1) of such section."

In 2004, P.L. 108-357, Sec. 102(d)(1), added "199," before "221" in clause (g)(3)(A)(ii), effective for tax. yrs. begin. after 12/31/2004. For special rule, see Sec. 403(a)(19) of P.L. 109-135, reproduced above.

In 2002, P.L. 107-358, Sec. 2, added subsec. (c) in Sec. 901 of P.L. 107-16 [see below], effective 12/17/2002.

In 2001, P.L. 107-16, Sec. 431(c)(1), added "222," after "221," in clause (g)(3)(A)(ii), effective for payments made in tax. yrs. begin. after 12/31/2001.

—P.L. 107-16, Sec. 601(a)(1), substituted "the deductible amount" for '$2,000' in subpara. (b)(1)(A) . . . Sec. 601(a)(2), added para. (b)(5), effective for tax. yrs. begin. after 12/31/2001.

—P.L. 107-16, Sec. 641(e)(2), substituted "408(d)(3), or 457(e)(16)" for "or 408(d)(3)" in para. (d)(2), effective for distributions after 12/31/2001. Sec. 641(f)(2) and (3) of this Act, provides:

"(2) Reasonable notice. No penalty shall be imposed on a plan for the failure to provide the information required by the amendment made by subsection (c) with respect to any distribution made before the date that is 90 days after the date on which the Secretary of the Treasury issues a safe harbor rollover notice after the date of enactment of this Act, if the administrator of such plan makes a reasonable attempt to comply with such requirement.

"(3) Special rule. Notwithstanding any other provision of law, subsections (h)(3) and (h)(5) of section 1122 of the Tax Reform Act of 1986 shall not apply to any distribution from an eligible retirement plan (as defined in clause (iii) or (iv) of section 402(c)(8)(B) of the Internal Revenue Code of 1986) on behalf of

1,697

Code Sec. 219 — Deductions

an individual if there was a rollover to such plan on behalf of such individual which is permitted solely by reason of any amendment made by this section."
—P.L. 107-16, Sec. 901, of this Act [as amended by Sec. 2 of P.L. 107-358, and Sec. 101(a)(1) of P.L. 111-312, and as related to Sec. 811 of P.L. 109-280, see above], reads as follows:
"Sec. 901. Sunset of provisions of Act.
"(a) In general. All provisions of, and amendments made by, this Act shall not apply—
"(1) to taxable, plan, or limitation years beginning after December 31, 2012, or
"(2) in the case of title V, to estates of decedents dying, gifts made, or generation skipping transfers, after December 31, 2012.
"(b) Application of certain laws. The Internal Revenue Code of 1986 and the Employee Retirement Income Security Act of 1974 shall be applied and administered to years, estates, gifts, and transfers described in subsection (a) as if the provisions and amendments described in subsection (a) had never been enacted.
"(c) Exception. Subsection (a) shall not apply to section 803 (relating to no federal income tax on restitution received by victims of the Nazi regime or their heirs or estates)."
In 2000, P.L. 106-554, Sec. 1(a)(7), [which enacted into law Sec. 316(d) of P.L. 106-554] deleted "and" at the end of subclause (c)(1)(B)(ii)(I), redesignated subclause (c)(1)(B)(ii)(II) as (III), and added subclause (c)(1)(B)(ii)(II), effective for tax. yrs. begin. after 12/31/96.
In 1998, P.L. 105-277, Sec. 4003(a)(2)(B), added "221," after "137," in clause (g)(3)(A)(ii), effective as provided in Sec. 202(e) of P.L. 105-34, which reads as follows:
"(e) Effective date. The amendments made by this section shall apply to any qualified education loan (as defined in section 221(e)(1) of the Internal Revenue Code of 1986, as added by this section) incurred on, before, or after the date of the enactment of this Act, but only with respect to—
"(1) any loan interest payment due and paid after December 31, 1997, and
"(2) the portion of the 60-month period referred to in section 221(d) of the Internal Revenue Code of 1986 (as added by this section) after December 31, 1997."
—P.L. 105-206, Sec. 6005(a)(1)(A), added "or the individual's spouse" after "individual" in para. (g)(1) . . . Sec. 6005(a)(1)(B), amended para. (g)(7) . . . Sec. 6005(a)(2), added "after $10,000" at the end of Sec. 301(a)(2) of P.L. 105-34 [see below], effective for tax. yrs. begin. after 12/31/97.
Prior to amendment, para. (g)(7) read as follows:
"(7) Special rule for certain spouses. In the case of an individual who is an active participant at no time during any plan year ending with or within the taxable year but whose spouse is an active participant for any part of any such plan year—
"(A) the applicable dollar amount under paragraph (3)(B)(i) with respect to the taxpayer shall be $150,000, and
"(B) the amount applicable under paragraph (2)(A)(ii) shall be $10,000."
—P.L. 105-206, Sec. 6018(f)(2), substituted "Clause (ii)" for "Clause (i)" in Sec. 1807(c)(3) of P.L. 104-188 [see below].
In 1997, P.L. 105-34, Sec. 301(a)(1), amended subpara. (g)(3)(B) . . . Sec. 301(a)(2), added "($20,000 in the case of a joint return for a taxable year beginning after December 31, 2006)" at the end of clause (g)(2)(A)(ii) . . . Sec. 301(b)(1), deleted "or the individual's spouse" after "an individual" in para. (g)(1) . . . Sec. 301(b)(2), added para. (g)(7), effective for tax. yrs. begin. after 12/31/97.
Prior to amendment, subpara. (g)(3)(B) read as follows:
"(B) Applicable dollar amount. The term 'applicable dollar amount' means—
"(i) in the case of a taxpayer filing a joint return, $40,000,
"(ii) in the case of any other taxpayer (other than a married individual filing a separate return), $25,000, and
"(iii) in the case of a married individual filing a separate return, zero."
—P.L. 105-34, Sec. 302(c), amended clause (c)(1)(B)(ii), effective for tax. yrs. begin. after 12/31/97.
Prior to amendment, clause (c)(1)(B)(ii) read as follows:
"(ii) the compensation includible in the gross income of such individual's spouse for the taxable year reduced by the amount allowed as a deduction under subsection (a) to such spouse for such taxable year."
In 1996, P.L. 104-188, Sec. 1421(b)(1)(A), amended para. (b)(4) . . . Sec. 1421(b)(1)(B), deleted "or" at the end of clause (g)(5)(A)(iv) and added clause (g)(5)(A)(vi), effective for tax. yrs. begin. after 12/31/96.
—P.L. 104-188, Sec. 1427(a), amended subsec. (c) . . . Sec. 1427(b)(1), substituted "subsection (b)" for "subsections (b) and (c)" in para. (f)(2) . . . Sec. 1427(b)(2), substituted "(c)(1)(A)" for "(c)(2)" in para. (g)(1), effective for tax. yrs. begin. after 12/31/96.
Prior to amendment, subsec. (c) read as follows:
"(c) Special rules for certain married individuals.
"(1) In general. In the case of any individual with respect to whom a deduction is otherwise allowable under subsection (a)—
"(A) who files a joint return under section 6013 for a taxable year, and
"(B) whose spouse—
"(i) has no compensation (determined without regard to section 911) for the taxable year, or
"(ii) elects to be treated for purposes of subsection (b)(1)(B) as having no compensation for the taxable year,
there shall be allowed as a deduction any amount paid in cash for the taxable year by or on behalf of the individual to an individual retirement plan established for the benefit of his spouse.

"(2) Limitation. The amount allowable as a deduction under paragraph (1) shall not exceed the excess of—
"(A) the lesser of—
"(i) $2,250, or
"(ii) an amount equal to the compensation includible in the individual's gross income for the taxable year, over
"(B) the amount allowable as a deduction under subsection (a) for the taxable year.
In no event shall the amount allowable as a deduction under paragraph (1) exceed $2,000."
—P.L. 104-188, Sec. 1807(c)(3), added ", 137," before "and 911" in clause (g)(3)(A)(ii) [amended by Sec. 6018(f)(2), 105-206, see above], effective for tax. yrs. begin. after 12/31/96.
In 1994, P.L. 103-337, Sec. 1677(c), substituted "section 10101 of title 10" for "section 261(a) of title 10" in subpara. (g)(6)(A), effective 10/5/94.
In 1992, P.L. 102-318, Sec. 521(b)(4), substituted "section 402(c)" for "section 402(a)(5), 402(a)(7)" in para. (d)(2), effective for distributions after 12/31/92. For special rule, see Sec. 521(e)(2) of this Act which reads as follows:
"(2) Special rule for partial distributions. For purposes of section 402(a)(5)(D)(i)(II) of the Internal Revenue Code of 1986 (as in effect before the amendments made by this section), a distribution before January 1, 1993, which is made before or at the same time as a series of periodic payments shall not be treated as one of such series if it is not substantially equal in amount to other payments in such series."
In 1989, P.L. 101-239, Sec. 7816(c)(1), corrected Sec. 6009(c)(2) of P.L. 100-647 to amend clause (g)(3)(A)(ii) instead of clause (g)(3)(A)(i), see below.
—P.L. 101-239, Sec. 7841(c)(1), added the sentence to the end of para. (f)(1), effective for contributions after 12/19/89 in tax. yrs. end. after 12/19/89.
In 1988, P.L. 100-647, Sec. 1011(a)(1), amended para. (g)(4), effective for tax. yrs. begin. after 12/31/87, except as provided in Sec. 1011(a)(2)(B) of this Act which reads as follows:
"(B) A taxpayer may elect to have the amendment made by paragraph (1) [Sec. 1011(a)(1)] apply to any taxable year beginning in 1987."
Prior to amendment, para. (g)(4) read as follows:
"(4) Special rule for married individuals filing separately. In the case of a married individual filing a separate return for any taxable year, paragraph (1) shall be applied without regard to whether such individual's spouse is an active participant for any plan year ending with or within such taxable year."
—P.L. 100-647, Sec. 2004(c), amended Sec. 10103(a) P.L. 100-203 [reproduced below] by adding "in a plan established for its employees by the United States" after "participant", see below.
—P.L. 100-647, Sec. 6009(c)(2), [as amended by Sec. 7816(c)(1) of P.L. 101-239, see above] substituted "sections 135 and 911" for "section 911" in clause (g)(3)(A)(ii), effective for tax. yrs. begin. after 12/31/89.
In 1987, P.L. 100-203, Sec. 10103, [as amended by Sec. 2004(c) of P.L. 100-647, see above] provides:
"Sec. 10103. Clarification of treatment of federal judges.
"(a) General Rule — A Federal judge —
"(1) shall be treated as an active participant in a plan established for its employees by the United States for purposes of section 219(g) of the Internal Revenue Code of 1986, and
"(2) shall be treated as an employee for purposes of chapter 1 of such Code.
"(b) Effective Date. — The provisions of subsection (a) shall apply to taxable years beginning after December 31, 1987."
In 1986, P.L. 99-514, Sec. 301(b)(4), substituted "paragraph (6)" for "paragraph (7)", effective for tax. yrs. begin. after 12/31/86.
—P.L. 99-514, Sec. 1101(a)(1), redesignated subsec. (g) as subsec. (h) and added new subsec. (g) . . . Sec. 1101(a)(2), amended para. (f)(3) . . . Sec. 1101(b)(1), amended subsec. (e) . . . Sec. 1101(b)(2)(A), deleted para. (b)(3), effective for contributions for tax. yrs. begin. after 12/31/86.
Prior to amendment, para. (f)(3) read as follows:
"(3) Time when contributions deemed made.
"(A) Individual retirement plans. For purposes of this section, a taxpayer shall be deemed to have made a contribution to an individual retirement plan on the last day of the preceding taxable year if the contribution is made on account of such taxable year and is made not later than the time prescribed by law for filing the return for such taxable year (not including extensions thereof).
"(B) Qualified employer or government plans. For purposes of this section, if a qualified employer or government plan elects to have the provisions of this subparagraph apply, a taxpayer shall be deemed to have made a voluntary contribution to such plan on the last day of the preceding calendar year (if, without regard to this paragraph, such contribution may be made on such date) if the contribution is made on account of the taxable year which includes such last day and by April 15 of the calendar year or such earlier time as is provided by the plan administrator."
Prior to amendment, subsec. (e) read as follows:
"(e) Definition of retirement savings contributions, etc.
For purposes of this section
"(1) Qualified retirement contribution. The term 'qualified retirement contribution' means
"(A) any qualified voluntary employee contribution paid in cash by the individual for the taxable year, and
"(B) any amount paid in cash for the taxable year by or on behalf of such individual for his benefit to an individual retirement plan.
"(2) Qualified voluntary employee contributions

Deductions
Code Sec. 219

"(A) In general. The term 'qualified voluntary employee contribution' means any voluntary contribution

"(i) which is made by an individual as an employee under a qualified employer plan or government plan, which plan allows an employee to make contributions which may be treated as qualified voluntary employee contributions under this section, and

"(ii) with respect to which the individual has not designated such contribution as a contribution which should not be taken into account under this section.

"(B) Voluntary contribution. For purposes of subparagraph (A), the term 'voluntary contribution' means any contribution which is not a mandatory contribution (within the meaning of section 411(c)(2)(C)).

"(C) Designation. For purposes of determining whether or not an individual has made a designation described in subparagraph (A)(ii) with respect to any contribution during any calendar year under a qualified employer plan or government plan, such individual shall be treated as having made such designation if he notifies the plan administrator of such plan, not later than the earlier of

"(i) April 15 of the succeeding calendar year, or

"(ii) the time prescribed by the plan administrator, that the individual does not want such contribution taken into account under this section. Any designation or notification referred to in the preceding sentence shall be made in such manner as the Secretary shall by regulations prescribe and, after the last date on which such designation or notification may be made, shall be irrevocable for such taxable year.

"(3) Qualified employer plan. The term 'qualified employer plan' means—

"(A) a plan described in section 401(a) which includes a trust exempt from tax under section 501(a),

"(B) an annuity plan described in section 403(a), and

"(C) a plan under which amounts are contributed by an individual's employer for an annuity contract described in section 403(b).

"(4) Government plan. The term 'government plan' means any plan, whether or not qualified, established and maintained for its employees by the United States, by a State or political subdivision thereof, or by an agency or instrumentality of any of the foregoing.

"(5) Payments for certain plans. The term 'amounts paid to an individual retirement plan' includes amounts paid for an individual retirement annuity or a retirement bond."

Prior to deletion, para. (b)(3) read as follows:

"(3) Special rule for individual retirement plans. If the individual has paid any qualified voluntary employee contributions for the taxable year, the amount of the qualified retirement contributions (other than employer contributions to a simplified employee pension) which are paid for the taxable year to an individual retirement plan and which are allowable as a deduction under subsection (a) for such taxable year shall not exceed—

"(A) the amount determined under paragraph (1) for such taxable year, reduced by

"(B) the amount of the qualified voluntary employee contributions for the taxable year."

—P.L. 99-514, Sec. 1102(f), added para. (f)(7), effective for contributions and distributions for tax. yrs. begin. after 12/31/86.

—P.L. 99-514, Sec. 1103(a), amended subpara. (c)(1)(B), effective for tax. yrs. begin. before, on, or after 12/31/85.

Prior to amendment, subpara. (c)(1)(B) read as follows:

"(B) whose spouse has no compensation (determined without regard to section 911) for such taxable year,"

—P.L. 99-514, Sec. 1108(g)(2), amended para. (b)(2) . . . Sec. 1108(g)(3), deleted "(determined without regard to so much of the employer contributions to a simplified employee pension as is allowable by reason of paragraph (2) of subsection (b))" in subpara. (c)(2)(B) . . . Sec. 1109(b), added para. (b)(3) [as amended by Sec. 1101(b)(2)(A) of this Act, see above], effective for tax. yrs. begin. after 12/31/86.

Prior to amendment, para. (b)(2) read as follows:

"(2) Special rules for employer contributions under simplified employee pensions.

"(A) Limitation. If there is an employer contribution on behalf of the employee to a simplified employee pension, an employee shall be allowed as a deduction under subsection (a) (in addition to the amount allowable under paragraph (1)) an amount equal to the lesser of

"(i) 15 percent of the compensation from such employer includible in the employee's gross income for the taxable year (determined without regard to the employer contribution to the simplified employee pension), or

"(ii) the amount contributed by such employer to the simplified employee pension and included in gross income (but not in excess of the limitation in effect under Section 415(c)(1)(A)).

"(B) Certain limitations do not apply to employer contribution. Paragraph (1) of this subsection and paragraph (1) of subsection (d) shall not apply with respect to the employer contribution to a simplified employee pension.

"(C) Special rule for applying subparagraph (A)(ii). In the case of an employee who is an officer, shareholder, or owner-employee described in section 408(k)(3), the dollar limitation in effect under section 415(c)(1)(A) shall be reduced by the amount of tax taken into account with respect to such individual under subparagraph (D) of section 408(k)(3)."

—P.L. 99-514, Sec. 1501(d)(1)(B), substituted "6652(g)" for "6652(h)" in subsec. (g) [before redesignation as subsec. (h) by Sec. 1101(a)(1) of this Act, see above], effective for returns due (determined without regard to extensions) after 12/31/86.

—P.L. 99-514, Sec. 1875(c)(4), deleted "reduced by any amount allowable as a deduction to the individual in computing adjusted gross income under paragraph (7) of section 62" in para. (f)(1) . . . Sec. 1875(c)(6)(B), substituted "the dollar limitation in effect under section 415(c)(1)(A)" for "the $15,000 amount specified in subparagraph (A)(ii)" in subpara. (b)(2)(C), effective for yrs. begin. after 12/31/83.

In 1984, P.L. 98-369, Sec. 147(c), substituted "not including" for "including" in subpara. (f)(3)(A), effective for contributions made after 12/31/84.

—P.L. 98-369, Sec. 422(d)(1), substituted "under section 71 (relating to alimony and separate maintenance payments) by reason of a payment under a decree of divorce or separate maintenance or a written instrument incident to such a decree." for "under paragraph (1) of section 71(a) (relating to decree of divorce or separate maintenance)." in subpara. (b)(4)(B), effective for divorce or separation instruments (as defined in Code Sec. 71(b)(2) as amended by this Act) executed after 12/31/84, Secs. 422(e)(2) and (3) of this Act read as follows:

"(2) Modifications of instruments executed before January 1, 1985. The amendments made by this section shall also apply to any divorce or separation instrument (as so defined) executed before January 1, 1985, but modified on or after such date if the modification expressly provides that the amendments made by this section shall apply to such modification.

"(3) Requirement of identification number. Section 215(c) of the Internal Revenue Code of 1954 (as amended by subsection (b)) and the amendments made by subsection (c) shall apply to payments made after December 31, 1984."

—P.L. 98-369, Sec. 491(d)(6), substituted "or 408(d)(3)" for "405(d)(3), 408(d)(3), or 409(b)(3)(C)" in para. (d)(2) . . . Sec. 491(d)(7), deleted the sentence at the end of para. (e)(1) . . . Sec. 491(d)(8), deleted subpara. (e)(3)(C), added "and" at the end of subpara. (e)(3)(B), and redesignated subpara. (e)(3)(D) as (e)(3)(C), effective for obligations issued after 12/31/83.

Prior to deletion, the sentence at the end of para. (e)(1) read as follows:

"For purposes of the preceding sentence, the term 'individual retirement plan' includes a retirement bond described in section 409 only if the bond is not redeemed within 12 months of its issuance."

Prior to deletion, subpara. (e)(3)(C) read as follows:

"(C) a qualified bond purchase plan described in section 405(a), and"

—P.L. 98-369, Sec. 529(a), added the sentence at the end to para. (f)(1) . . . Sec. 529(b), deleted para. (b)(4) [as amended by Sec. 422(d)(1) of this Act, see above], effective for tax. yrs. begin. after 12/31/84.

Prior to deletion, para. (b)(4) read as follows:

"(4) Certain divorced individuals.

"(A) In general. In the case of an individual to whom this paragraph applies, the limitation of paragraph (1) shall not be less than the lesser of

"(i) $1,125, or

"(ii) the sum of the amount referred to in paragraph (1)(B) and any qualifying alimony received by the individual during the taxable year.

"(B) Qualifying alimony. For purposes of this paragraph, the term 'qualifying alimony' means amounts includible in the individual's gross income under section 71 (relating to alimony and separate maintenance payments) by reason of a payment under a decree of divorce or separate maintenance or a written instrument incident to such a decree.

"(C) Individuals to whom paragraph applies. This paragraph shall apply to an individual if

"(i) an individual retirement plan was established for the benefit of the individual at least 5 years before the beginning of the calendar year in which the decree of divorce or separate maintenance was issued, and

"(ii) for at least 3 of the former spouse's most recent 5 taxable years ending before the taxable year in which the decree was issued, such former spouse was allowed a deduction under subsection (c) (or the corresponding provisions of prior law) for contributions to such individual retirement plan."

—P.L. 98-369, Sec. 713(d)(2), substituted "but not in excess of the limitation in effect under section 415(c)(1)(A)" for "but not in excess of $15,000" in clause (b)(2)(A)(ii), effective for tax. yrs. begin. after 12/31/81.

—P.L. 98-369, Sec. 713(g)(1), amended Sec. 243(c) of P.L. 97-248 [the effective date for amendments made by Sec. 243(b)(2) of P.L. 97-248, see below] to apply to individuals dying after 12/31/83.

Prior to amendment, Sec. 243(c) of P.L. 97-248 read as follows:

"(c) Effective dates.

"(1) Subsection (a). The amendments made by subsection (a) shall apply in the case of individuals dying after December 31, 1983.

"(2) Subsection (b). The amendments made by subsection (b) shall apply to taxable years beginning after December 31, 1983."

In 1983, P.L. 97-448, Sec. 103(c)(1), amended subpara. (c)(2)(B) . . . Sec. 103(c)(2), amended para. (d)(1) . . . Sec. 103(c)(3)(A), added "and" at the end of subpara. (e)(3)(C), deleted subpara. (e)(3)(D), and redesignated subpara. (e)(3)(E) as subpara. (e)(3)(D) . . . Sec. 103(c)(4), amended para. (f)(1) . . . Sec. 103(c)(5), substituted "the contribution is made on account of the taxable year which includes such last day and" for "the contribution is made" in subpara. (f)(3)(B) . . . Sec. 103(c)(12)(A), substituted "paragraph (1))" for "paragraph (1)" in subpara. (b)(2)(A), effective for tax. yrs. begin. after 12/31/81.

Prior to amendment, subpara. (c)(2)(B) read as follows:

"(B) the amount allowed as a deduction under subsection (a) for the taxable year."

Prior to amendment, para. (d)(1) read as follows:

"(1) Individuals who have attained age 70½. No deduction shall be allowed under this section with respect to any qualified retirement contribution which is made for a taxable year of an individual if such individual has attained age 70½ before the close of such taxable year."

Prior to deletion, subpara. (e)(3)(D) read as follows:

"(D) a simplified employee pension (within the meaning of section 408(k)), and"

1,699

Code Sec. 219 — Deductions

Prior to amendment, para. (f)(1) read as follows:

"(1) Compensation. For purposes of this section, the term 'compensation' includes earned income as defined in section 401(c)(2)."

—P.L. 97-448, Sec. 103(d)(3), deleted "plans which include employees within the meaning of section 401(c)(1) with respect to" in Sec. 312(f)(1) of P.L. 97-34 [the effective date for amendments made by Sec. 312(c)(1) of P.L. 97-34, see below].

In 1982, P.L. 97-248, Sec. 243(b)(2), added para. (d)(4), effective [as amended by Sec. 713(s)(1) of P.L. 98-369, see above] for individuals dying after 12/31/83.

In 1981, P.L. 97-34, Sec. 311(a), amended Code Sec. 219, effective for tax. yrs. begin. after 12/31/81. Sec. 311(i)(2) of this Act provides transitional rule as follows:

"(2) Transitional rule.— For purposes of the Internal Revenue Code of 1954, any amount allowed as a deduction under section 220 of such Code (as in effect before its repeal by this Act) shall be treated as if it were allowed by section 219 of such Code."

Prior to amendment, Code Sec. 219 read as follows:

"SEC. 219. RETIREMENT SAVINGS.

"(a) Deduction allowed.

"In the case of an individual, there is allowed as a deduction amounts paid in cash for the taxable year by or on behalf of such individual for his benefit—

"(1) to an individual retirement account described in section 408(a),

"(2) for an individual retirement annuity described in section 408(b), or

"(3) for a retirement bond described in section 409 (but only if the bond is not redeemed within 12 months of the date of its issuance);

For purposes of this title, any amount paid by an employer to such a retirement account or for such a retirement annuity or retirement bond constitutes payment of compensation to the employee (other than a self-employed individual who is an employee within the meaning of section 401(c)(1)) includible in his gross income, whether or not a deduction for such payment is allowable under this section to the employee after the application of subsection (b).

"(b) Limitations and restrictions.

"(1) Maximum deduction. The amount allowable as a deduction under subsection (a) to an individual for any taxable year may not exceed an amount equal to 15 percent of the compensation includible in his gross income for such taxable year, or $1,500, whichever is less.

"(2) Covered by certain other plans. No deduction is allowed under subsection (a) for an individual for the taxable year if for any part of such year—

"(A) he was an active participant in—

"(i) a plan described in section 401(a) which includes a trust exempt from tax under section 501(a),

"(ii) an annuity plan described in section 403(a),

"(iii) a qualified bond purchase plan described in section 405(a), or

"(iv) a plan established for its employees by the United States, by a State or political subdivision thereof, or by an agency or instrumentality of any of the foregoing, or

"(B) amounts were contributed by his employer for an annuity contract described in section 403(b) (whether or not his rights in such contract are nonforfeitable).

"(3) Contributions after age 70½ No deduction is allowed under subsection (a) with respect to any payment described in subsection (a) which is made during the taxable year of an individual who has attained age 70½ before the close of such taxable year.

"(4) Recontributed amounts. No deduction is allowed under this section with respect to a rollover contribution described in section 402(a)(5), 402(a)(7), 403(a)(4), 408(b)(3), 408(d)(3), 409(b)(3)(C).

"(5) Amounts contributed under endowment contract. In the case of an endowment contract described in section 408(b), no deduction is allowed under subsection (a) for that portion of the amounts paid under the contract for the taxable year properly allocable, under regulations prescribed by the Secretary, to the cost of life insurance.

"(6) Alternative deduction. No deduction is allowed under subsection (a) for the taxable year if the individual claims the deduction allowed by section 220 for the taxable year.

"(7) Special rules in case of simplified employee pensions.

"(A) Limitation. If there is an employer contribution on behalf of the employee to a simplified employee pension, the limitation under paragraph (1) shall be the lesser of—

"(i) 15 percent of the compensation includible in the employee's gross income for the taxable year (determined without regard to the employer contribution to the simplified employee pension), or

"(ii) the sum of —

"(I) the amount contributed by the employer to the simplified employee pension and included in gross income (but not in excess of $7,500), and

"(II) $1,500, reduced (but not below zero) by the amount described in subclause (I).

"(B) Certain limitations do not apply to employer contribution. Paragraphs (2) and (3) shall not apply with respect to the employer contribution to a simplified employee pension.

"(C) Special rule for applying subparagraph (a)(ii). In the case of an employee who is an officer, shareholder, or owner-employee described in section 408(k)(3), the $7,500 amount specified in subparagraph(A)(ii)(I) shall be reduced by the amount of tax taken into account with respect to such individual under subparagraph (D) of section 408(k)(3).

"(c) Definitions and special rules.

"(1) Compensation. For purposes of this section, the term 'compensation' includes earned income as defined in section 401(c)(2).

"(2) Married individuals. The maximum deduction under subsection (b)(1) shall be computed separately for each individual, and this section shall be applied without regard to any community property laws. For purposes of this section, the determination of whether an individual is married shall be made in accordance with the provisions of section 143(a).

"(3) Time when contributions deemed made. For purposes of this section, a taxpayer shall be deemed to have made a contribution on the last day of the preceding taxable year if the contribution is made on account of such taxable year and is made not later than the time prescribed by law for filing the return for such taxable year (including extensions thereof).

"(4) Participation in governmental plans by certain individuals.

"(A) Members of reserve components. A member of a reserve component of the armed forces (as defined in section 261(a) of title 10) is not considered to be an active participant in a plan described in subsection (b)(2)(A)(iv) for a taxable year solely because he is a member of a reserve component unless he has served in excess of 90 days on active duty (other than active duty for training) during the year.

"(B) Volunteer firefighters. An individual whose participation in a plan described in subsection (b)(2)(A)(iv) is based solely upon his activity as a volunteer firefighter and whose accrued benefit as of the beginning of the taxable year is not more than an annual benefit of $1,800 (when expressed as a single life annuity commencing at age 65) is not considered to be an active participant in such a plan for the taxable year.

"(5) Excess contributions treated as contribution made during subsequent year for which there is an unused limitation.

"(A) In general. If for the taxable year the maximum amount allowable as a deduction under this section exceeds the amount contributed, then the taxpayer shall be treated as having made an additional contribution for the taxable year in an amount equal to the lesser of—

"(i) the amount of such excess, or

"(ii) the amount of the excess contributions for such taxable year (determined under section 4973(b)(2) without regard to subparagraph (C) thereof).

"(B) Amount contributed. For purposes of this paragraph, the amount contributed—

"(i) shall be determined without regard to this paragraph, and

"(ii) shall not include any rollover contribution.

"(C) Special rule where excess deduction was allowed for closed year. Proper reduction shall be made in the amount allowable as a deduction by reason of this paragraph for any amount allowed as a deduction under this section or section 220 for a prior taxable year for which the period for assessing deficiency has expired if the amount so allowed exceeds the amount which should have been allowed for such prior taxable year."

—P.L. 97-34, Sec. 312(c)(1), substituted "$15,000" for "$7,500" in subparas. (b)(2)(A) and (b)(2)(C) [as amended by Sec. 311(a) of this Act, see above], effective [as amended by Sec. 103(d)(3) of P.L. 97-448, see above] for tax. yrs. begin. after 12/31/81.

—P.L. 97-34, Sec. 313(b)(2), added "405(d)(3)," after "403(b)(8)," in para. (d)(2) [as amended by Sec. 311(a) of this Act, see above], effective for redemptions after 8/13/81 in tax. yrs. end. after 8/13/81.

In 1980, P.L. 96-222, Sec. 101(a)(10)(D), amended para. (b)(7), effective for tax. yrs. begin. after 12/31/78.

Prior to amendment, para. (b)(7) read as follows:

"(7) Simplified employee pensions. In the case of an employer contribution on behalf of the employee to a simplified employee pension, paragraph (2) shall not apply with respect to the employer contribution and the limitation under paragraph (1) shall be the lesser of—

"(A) 15 percent of compensation includible in the employee's gross income for the taxable year (determined without regard to the employer contribution to the simplified employee pension), or

"(B) the sum of—

"(i) the amount contributed by the employer to the simplified employee pension and included in gross income (but not in excess of $7,500), and

"(ii) $1,500 reduced (but not below zero) by the amount described in clause (i). In the case of an employee who is an officer, shareholder, or owner-employee described in section 408(k)(3), the amount referred to in subparagraph (b) shall be reduced by the amount of tax taken into account with respect to such individual under subparagraph (D) of section 408(k)(3)."

—P.L. 96-222, Sec. 101(a)(13)(A), substituted "December 31, 1977" for "December 31, 1978" in Sec. 156(d) of P.L. 95-600 [the effective date for amendments made by Sec. 156(c) of P.L. 95-600, see below].

—P.L. 96-222, Sec. 101(a)(14)(B), added "402(a)(7)," after "section 402(a)(5)" in para. (b)(4), effective for distributions or transfers made after 12/31/77, in tax. yrs. begin. after 12/31/77.

In 1978, P.L. 95-600, Sec. 152(c), added para. (b)(7), effective for tax. yrs. begin. after 12/31/78.

—P.L. 95-600, Sec. 156(c)(3), added "403(b)(8)," after "403(a)(4)," in para. (b)(4), effective [as amended by Sec. 101(a)(13)(A) of P.L. 96-222, see above] for distributions or transfers made after 12/31/77, in tax. yrs. begin. after 12/31/77.

—P.L. 95-600, Sec. 157(a)(1), substituted "not later than the time prescribed by law for filing the return for such taxable year (including extensions thereof)" for "not later than 45 days after the end of such taxable year" in para. (c)(3), effective for tax. yrs. begin. after 12/31/77.

—P.L. 95-600, Sec. 157(b)(1), added para. (c)(5), effective for determination of deductions for tax. yrs. begin. after 12/31/75. Sec. 157(b)(4)(B) of this Act provides transitional rule as follows:

"(B) Transitional rule. If, but for this subparagraph, an amount would be allowable as a deduction by reason of section 219(c)(5) or 220(c)(6) of the Internal

Revenue Code of 1954 for a taxable year beginning before January 1, 1978, such amount shall be allowable only for the taxpayer's first taxable year beginning in 1978."

—P.L. 95-600, Sec. 703(c)(1), substituted "subsection (b)(2)(A)(iv)" for "subsection (b)(3)(A)(iv)" each place it appeared in para. (c)(4), effective for tax. yrs. begin. after 12/31/76.

In 1976, P.L. 94-455, Sec. 1501(b)(4)(A), substituted "for" for "during" in subsec. (a) . . . Sec. 1501(b)(4)(B), added para. (b)(6) . . . Sec. 1501(b)(4)(C), added a sentence to the end of para. (c)(2) . . . Sec. 1501(b)(4)(D), added para. (c)(3), effective for tax. yrs. begin. after 12/31/75.

—P.L. 94-455, Sec. 1503(a), added para. (c)(4), effective for tax. yrs. begin. after 12/31/75.

—P.L. 94-455, Sec. 1901(a)(32), substituted "subdivision" for "division" in clause (b)(2)(A)(iv), effective for tax. yrs. begin. after 12/31/76.

—P.L. 94-455, Sec. 1906(b)(13)(A), substituted "Secretary" for "Secretary or his delegate" in Code Sec. 219, effective for tax. yrs. begin. after 12/31/76.

In 1974, P.L. 93-406, Sec. 2002(a), added Code Sec. 219, effective for tax. yrs. begin. after 1974.

Sec. 220. Archer MSAs.

(a) Deduction allowed.

In the case of an individual who is an eligible individual for any month during the taxable year, there shall be allowed as a deduction for the taxable year an amount equal to the aggregate amount paid in cash during such taxable year by such individual to an Archer MSA of such individual.

(b) Limitations.

(1) **In general.** The amount allowable as a deduction under subsection (a) to an individual for the taxable year shall not exceed the sum of the monthly limitations for months during such taxable year that the individual is an eligible individual.

(2) **Monthly limitation.** The monthly limitation for any month is the amount equal to $1/12$ of—

(A) in the case of an individual who has self-only coverage under the high deductible health plan as of the first day of such month, 65 percent of the annual deductible under such coverage, and

(B) in the case of an individual who has family coverage under the high deductible health plan as of the first day of such month, 75 percent of the annual deductible under such coverage.

(3) **Special rule for married individuals.** In the case of individuals who are married to each other, if either spouse has family coverage—

(A) both spouses shall be treated as having only such family coverage (and if such spouses each have family coverage under different plans, as having the family coverage with the lowest annual deductible), and

(B) the limitation under paragraph (1) (after the application of subparagraph (A) of this paragraph) shall be divided equally between them unless they agree on a different division.

(4) **Deduction not to exceed compensation.**

(A) Employees. The deduction allowed under subsection (a) for contributions as an eligible individual described in subclause (I) of subsection (c)(1)(A)(iii) shall not exceed such individual's wages, salaries, tips, and other employee compensation which are attributable to such individual's employment by the employer referred to in such subclause.

(B) Self-employed individuals. The deduction allowed under subsection (a) for contributions as an eligible individual described in subclause (II) of subsection (c)(1)(A)(iii) shall not exceed such individual's earned income (as defined in section 401(c)(1)) derived by the taxpayer from the trade or business with respect to which the high deductible health plan is established.

(C) Community property laws not to apply. The limitations under this paragraph shall be determined without regard to community property laws.

(5) **Coordination with exclusion for employer contributions.** No deduction shall be allowed under this section for any amount paid for any taxable year to an Archer MSA of an individual if—

(A) any amount is contributed to any Archer MSA of such individual for such year which is excludable from gross income under section 106(b), or

(B) if such individual's spouse is covered under the high deductible health plan covering such individual, any amount is contributed for such year to any Archer MSA of such spouse which is so excludable.

(6) **Denial of deduction to dependents.** No deduction shall be allowed under this section to any individual with respect to whom a deduction under section 151 is allowable to another taxpayer for a taxable year beginning in the calendar year in which such individual's taxable year begins.

(7) **Medicare eligible individuals.** The limitation under this subsection for any month with respect to an individual shall be zero for the first month such individual is entitled to benefits under title XVIII of the Social Security Act and for each month thereafter.

(c) Definitions.

For purposes of this section—

(1) **Eligible individual.**

(A) In general. The term "eligible individual" means, with respect to any month, any individual if—

(i) such individual is covered under a high deductible health plan as of the 1st day of such month,

(ii) such individual is not, while covered under a high deductible health plan, covered under any health plan—

(I) which is not a high deductible health plan, and

(II) which provides coverage for any benefit which is covered under the high deductible health plan, and

(iii)(I) the high deductible health plan covering such individual is established and maintained by the employer of such individual or of the spouse of such individual and such employer is a small employer, or

(II) such individual is an employee (within the meaning of section 401(c)(1)) or the spouse of such an employee and the high deductible health plan covering such individual is not established or maintained by any employer of such individual or spouse.

(B) Certain coverage disregarded. Subparagraph (A)(ii) shall be applied without regard to—

(i) coverage for any benefit provided by permitted insurance, and

(ii) coverage (whether through insurance or otherwise) for accidents, disability, dental care, vision care, or long-term care.

(C) Continued eligibility of employee and spouse establishing Archer MSAs. If, while an employer is a small employer—

(i) any amount is contributed to an Archer MSA of an individual who is an employee of such employer or the spouse of such an employee, and

(ii) such amount is excludable from gross income under section 106(b) or allowable as a deduction under this section,

such individual shall not cease to meet the requirement of subparagraph (A)(iii)(I) by reason of such employer ceasing to be a small employer so long as such employee continues to be an employee of such employer.

(D) Limitations on eligibility. for limitations on number of taxpayers who are eligible to have Archer MSAs, see subsection (i).

(2) High deductible health plan.

(A) In general. The term "high deductible health plan" means a health plan—

(i) in the case of self-only coverage, which has an annual deductible which is not less than $1,500 and not more than $2,250,

(ii) in the case of family coverage, which has an annual deductible which is not less than $3,000 and not more than $4,500, and

(iii) the annual out-of-pocket expenses required to be paid under the plan (other than for premiums) for covered benefits does not exceed—

(I) $3,000 for self-only coverage, and

(II) $5,500 for family coverage.

(B) Special rules.

(i) Exclusion of certain plans. Such term does not include a health plan if substantially all of its coverage is coverage described in paragraph (1)(B).

(ii) Safe harbor for absence of preventive care deductible. A plan shall not fail to be treated as a high deductible health plan by reason of failing to have a deductible for preventive care if the absence of a deductible for such care is required by State law.

(3) Permitted insurance. The term "permitted insurance" means—

(A) insurance if substantially all of the coverage provided under such insurance relates to—

(i) liabilities incurred under workers' compensation laws,

(ii) tort liabilities,

(iii) liabilities relating to ownership or use of property, or

(iv) such other similar liabilities as the Secretary may specify by regulations,

(B) insurance for a specified disease or illness, and

(C) insurance paying a fixed amount per day (or other period) of hospitalization.

(4) Small employer.

(A) In general. The term "small employer" means, with respect to any calendar year, any employer if such employer employed an average of 50 or fewer employees on business days during either of the 2 preceding calendar years. For purposes of the preceding sentence, a preceding calendar year may be taken into account only if the employer was in existence throughout such year.

(B) Employers not in existence in preceding year. In the case of an employer which was not in existence throughout the 1st preceding calendar year, the determination under subparagraph (A) shall be based on the average number of employees that it is reasonably expected such employer will employ on business days in the current calendar year.

(C) Certain growing employers retain treatment as small employer. The term "small employer" includes, with respect to any calendar year, any employer if—

(i) such employer met the requirement of subparagraph (A) (determined without regard to subparagraph (B)) for any preceding calendar year after 1996,

(ii) any amount was contributed to the Archer MSA of any employee of such employer with respect to coverage of such employee under a high deductible health plan of such employer during such preceding calendar year and such amount was excludable from gross income under section 106(b) or allowable as a deduction under this section, and

(iii) such employer employed an average of 200 or fewer employees on business days during each preceding calendar year after 1996.

(D) Special rules.

(i) Controlled groups. For purposes of this paragraph, all persons treated as a single employer under subsection (b), (c), (m), or (o) of section 414shall be treated as 1 employer.

(ii) Predecessors. Any reference in this paragraph to an employer shall include a reference to any predecessor of such employer.

(5) Family coverage. The term "family coverage" means any coverage other than self-only coverage.

(d) Archer MSA.

For purposes of this section—

(1) Archer MSA. The term "Archer MSA" means a trust created or organized in the United States as a medical savings account exclusively for the purpose of paying the qualified medical expenses of the account holder, but only if the written governing instrument creating the trust meets the following requirements:

(A) Except in the case of a rollover contribution described in subsection (f)(5), no contribution will be accepted—

(i) unless it is in cash, or

(ii) to the extent such contribution, when added to previous contributions to the trust for the calendar year, exceeds 75 percent of the highest annual limit deductible permitted under subsection (c)(2)(A)(ii) for such calendar year.

(B) The trustee is a bank (as defined in section 408(n)), an insurance company (as defined in section 816), or another person who demonstrates to the satisfaction of the Secretary that the manner in which such person will administer the trust will be consistent with the requirements of this section.

(C) No part of the trust assets will be invested in life insurance contracts.

(D) The assets of the trust will not be commingled with other property except in a common trust fund or common investment fund.

(E) The interest of an individual in the balance in his account is nonforfeitable.

(2) Qualified medical expenses.

(A) In general. The term "qualified medical expenses" means, with respect to an account holder, amounts paid by such holder for medical care (as defined in section 213(d)) for such individual, the spouse of such individual, and any dependent (as defined in section 152, determined without regard to subsections (b)(1), (b)(2), and (d)(1)(B) thereof) of such individual, but only to the extent such amounts are not compensated for by insurance or otherwise. Such term shall include an amount paid for medicine or a drug only if such medicine or drug is a prescribed drug (determined without regard to whether such drug is available without a prescription) or is insulin.

(B) Health insurance may not be purchased from account.

(i) In general. Subparagraph (A) shall not apply to any payment for insurance.

(ii) Exceptions. Clause (i) shall not apply to any expense for coverage under—
(I) a health plan during any period of continuation coverage required under any Federal law,
(II) a qualified long-term care insurance contract (as defined in section 7702B(b)), or
(III) a health plan during a period in which the individual is receiving unemployment compensation under any Federal or State law.
(C) Medical expenses of individuals who are not eligible individuals. Subparagraph (A) shall apply to an amount paid by an account holder for medical care of an individual who is not described in clauses (i) and (ii) of subsection (c)(1)(A) for the month in which the expense for such care is incurred only if no amount is contributed (other than a rollover contribution) to any Archer MSA of such account holder for the taxable year which includes such month. This subparagraph shall not apply to any expense for coverage described in subclause (I) or (III) of subparagraph (B)(ii).

(3) Account holder. The term "account holder" means the individual on whose behalf the Archer MSA was established.

(4) Certain rules to apply. Rules similar to the following rules shall apply for purposes of this section:
(A) Section 219(d)(2) (relating to no deduction for rollovers).
(B) Section 219(f)(3) (relating to time when contributions deemed made).
(C) Except as provided in section 106(b), section 219(f)(5) (relating to employer payments).
(D) Section 408(g) (relating to community property laws).
(E) Section 408(h) (relating to custodial accounts).

(e) Tax treatment of accounts.
(1) In general. An Archer MSA is exempt from taxation under this subtitle unless such account has ceased to be an Archer MSA. Notwithstanding the preceding sentence, any such account is subject to the taxes imposed by section 511 (relating to imposition of tax on unrelated business income of charitable, etc. organizations).
(2) Account terminations. Rules similar to the rules of paragraphs (2) and (4) of section 408(e) shall apply to Archer MSAs, and any amount treated as distributed under such rules shall be treated as not used to pay qualified medical expenses.

(f) Tax treatment of distributions.
(1) Amounts used for qualified medical expenses. Any amount paid or distributed out of an Archer MSA which is used exclusively to pay qualified medical expenses of any account holder shall not be includible in gross income.
(2) Inclusion of amounts not used for qualified medical expenses. Any amount paid or distributed out of an Archer MSA which is not used exclusively to pay the qualified medical expenses of the account holder shall be included in the gross income of such holder.
(3) Excess contributions returned before due date of return.
(A) In general. If any excess contribution is contributed for a taxable year to any Archer MSA of an individual, paragraph (2) shall not apply to distributions from the Archer MSAs of such individual (to the extent such distributions do not exceed the aggregate excess contributions to all such accounts of such individual for such year) if—
(i) such distribution is received by the individual on or before the last day prescribed by law (including extensions of time) for filing such individual's return for such taxable year, and
(ii) such distribution is accompanied by the amount of net income attributable to such excess contribution.
Any net income described in clause (ii) shall be included in the gross income of the individual for the taxable year in which it is received.
(B) Excess contribution. For purposes of subparagraph (A), the term "excess contribution" means any contribution (other than a rollover contribution) which is neither excludable from gross income under section 106(b) nor deductible under this section.

(4) Additional tax on distributions not used for qualified medical expenses.
(A) In general. The tax imposed by this chapter on the account holder for any taxable year in which there is a payment or distribution from an Archer MSA of such holder which is includible in gross income under paragraph (2) shall be increased by 20 percent of the amount which is so includible.
(B) Exception for disability or death. Subparagraph (A) shall not apply if the payment or distribution is made after the account holder becomes disabled within the meaning of section 72(m)(7) or dies.
(C) Exception for distributions after medicare eligibility. Subparagraph (A) shall not apply to any payment or distribution after the date on which the account holder attains the age specified in section 1811 of the Social Security Act.

(5) Rollover contribution. An amount is described in this paragraph as a rollover contribution if it meets the requirements of subparagraphs (A) and (B).
(A) In general. Paragraph (2) shall not apply to any amount paid or distributed from an Archer MSA to the account holder to the extent the amount received is paid into an Archer MSA or a health savings account (as defined in section 223(d)) for the benefit of such holder not later than the 60th day after the day on which the holder receives the payment or distribution.
(B) Limitation. This paragraph shall not apply to any amount described in subparagraph (A) received by an individual from an Archer MSA if, at any time during the 1-year period ending on the day of such receipt, such individual received any other amount described in subparagraph (A) from an Archer MSA which was not includible in the individual's gross income because of the application of this paragraph.

(6) Coordination with medical expense deduction. For purposes of determining the amount of the deduction under section 213, any payment or distribution out of an Archer MSA for qualified medical expenses shall not be treated as an expense paid for medical care.

(7) Transfer of account incident to divorce. The transfer of an individual's interest in an Archer MSA to an individual's spouse or former spouse under a divorce or separation instrument described in subparagraph (A) of section 71(b)(2) shall not be considered a taxable transfer made by such individual notwithstanding any other provision of this subtitle, and such interest shall, after such transfer, be treated as an Archer MSA with respect to which such spouse is the account holder.

(8) Treatment after death of account holder.
(A) Treatment if designated beneficiary is spouse. If the account holder's surviving spouse acquires such holder's interest in an Archer MSA by reason of being the designated beneficiary of such account at the death of the account holder, such Archer MSA shall be treated as if the spouse were the account holder.
(B) Other cases.
(i) In general. If, by reason of the death of the account holder, any person acquires the account holder's interest in an Archer MSA in a case to which subparagraph (A) does not apply—
(I) such account shall cease to be an Archer MSA as of the date of death, and
(II) an amount equal to the fair market value of the assets in such account on such date shall be includible if such person is not the estate of such holder, in such person's gross income for the taxable year which includes such date, or if such person is the estate of such holder, in such holder's gross income for the last taxable year of such holder.
(ii) Special rules.
(I) Reduction of inclusion for predeath expenses. The amount includible in gross income under clause (i) by any person (other than the estate) shall be reduced by the amount of qualified medical expenses which were incurred by the decedent before the date of the decedent's death and paid by such person within 1 year after such date.
(II) Deduction for estate taxes. An appropriate deduction shall be allowed under section 691(c) to any person (other than the decedent or the decedent's spouse) with respect to amounts included in gross income under clause (i) by such person.

(g) Cost-of-living adjustment.
In the case of any taxable year beginning in a calendar year after 1998, each dollar amount in subsection (c)(2) shall be increased by an amount equal to—
(1) such dollar amount, multiplied by
(2) the cost-of-living adjustment determined under section 1(f)(3) for the calendar year in which such taxable year begins by substituting "calendar year 1997" for "calendar year 1992" in subparagraph (B) thereof.
If any increase under the preceding sentence is not a multiple of $50, such increase shall be rounded to the nearest multiple of $50.

(h) Reports.
The Secretary may require the trustee of an Archer MSA to make such reports regarding such account to the Secretary and to the account holder with respect to contributions, distributions, and such other matters as the Secretary determines appropriate. The reports required by this subsection shall be filed at such time and in such manner and furnished to such individuals at such time and in such manner as may be required by the Secretary.

(i) Limitation on number of taxpayers having Archer MSAs.
(1) In general. Except as provided in paragraph (5), no individual shall be treated as an eligible individual for any taxable year beginning after the cut-off year unless—
(A) such individual was an active MSA participant for any taxable year ending on or before the close of the cut-off year, or
(B) such individual first became an active MSA participant for a taxable year ending after the cut-off year by reason of coverage under a high deductible health plan of an MSA-participating employer.
(2) Cut-off year. For purposes of paragraph (1), the term "cut-off year" means the earlier of—
(A) calendar year 2007, or
(B) the first calendar year before 2007 for which the Secretary determines under subsection (j) that the numerical limitation for such year has been exceeded.
(3) Active MSA participant. For purposes of this subsection—
(A) In general. The term "active MSA participant" means, with respect to any taxable year, any individual who is the account holder of any Archer MSA into which any contribution was made which was excludable from gross income under section 106(b), or allowable as a deduction under this section, for such taxable year.
(B) Special rule for cut-off years before 2007. In the case of a cut-off year before 2007—
(i) an individual shall not be treated as an eligible individual for any month of such year or an active MSA participant under paragraph (1)(A) unless such individual is, on or before the cut-off date, covered under a high deductible health plan, and
(ii) an employer shall not be treated as an MSA-participating employer unless the employer, on or before the cut-off date, offered coverage under a high deductible health plan to any employee.
(C) Cut-off date. For purposes of subparagraph (B)—
(i) In general. Except as otherwise provided in this subparagraph, the cut-off date is October 1 of the cut-off year.
(ii) Employees with enrollment periods after October 1. In the case of an individual described in subclause (I) of subsection (c)(1)(A)(iii), if the regularly scheduled enrollment period for health plans of the individual's employer occurs during the last 3 months of the cut-off year, the cut-off date is December 31 of the cut-off year.
(iii) Self-employed individuals. In the case of an individual described in subclause (II) of subsection (c)(1)(A)(iii), the cut-off date is November 1 of the cut-off year.
(iv) Special rules for 1997. If 1997 is a cut-off year by reason of subsection (j)(1)(A)—
(I) each of the cut-off dates under clauses (i) and (iii) shall be 1 month earlier than the date determined without regard to this clause, and
(II) clause (ii) shall be applied by substituting "4 months" for "3 months".
(4) MSA-participating employer. For purposes of this subsection, the term "MSA-participating employer" means any small employer if—
(A) such employer made any contribution to the Archer MSA of any employee during the cut-off year or any preceding calendar year which was excludable from gross income under section 106(b), or
(B) at least 20 percent of the employees of such employer who are eligible individuals for any month of the cut-off year by reason of coverage under a high deductible health plan of such employer each made a contribution of at least $100 to their Archer MSAs for any taxable year ending with or within the cut-off year which was allowable as a deduction under this section.
(5) Additional eligibility after cut-off year. If the Secretary determines under subsection (j)(2)(A) that the numeri-

cal limit for the calendar year following a cut-off year described in paragraph (2)(B) has not been exceeded—
(A) this subsection shall not apply to any otherwise eligible individual who is covered under a high deductible health plan during the first 6 months of the second calendar year following the cut-off year (and such individual shall be treated as an active MSA participant for purposes of this subsection if a contribution is made to any Archer MSA with respect to such coverage), and
(B) any employer who offers coverage under a high deductible health plan to any employee during such 6-month period shall be treated as an MSA-participating employer for purposes of this subsection if the requirements of paragraph (4) are met with respect to such coverage.

For purposes of this paragraph, subsection (j)(2)(A) shall be applied for 1998 by substituting "750,000" for "600,000".

(j) Determination of whether numerical limits are exceeded.

(1) Determination of whether limit exceeded for 1997. The numerical limitation for 1997 is exceeded if, based on the reports required under paragraph (4), the number of Archer MSAs established as of—
(A) April 30, 1997, exceeds 375,000, or
(B) June 30, 1997, exceeds 525,000.

(2) Determination of whether limit exceeded for 1998, 1999, 2001, 2002, 2004, 2005, or 2006.
(A) In general. The numerical limitation for 1998, 1999, 2001, 2002, 2004, 2005, or 2006 is exceeded if the sum of—
(i) the number of MSA returns filed on or before April 15 of such calendar year for taxable years ending with or within the preceding calendar year, plus
(ii) the Secretary's estimate (determined on the basis of the returns described in clause (i)) of the number of MSA returns for such taxable years which will be filed after such date,
exceeds 750,000 (600,000 in the case of 1998). For purposes of the preceding sentence, the term "MSA return" means any return on which any exclusion is claimed under section 106(b) or any deduction is claimed under this section.
(B) Alternative computation of limitation. The numerical limitation for 1998, 1999, 2001, 2002, 2004, 2005, or 2006 is also exceeded if the sum of—
(i) 90 percent of the sum determined under subparagraph (A) for such calendar year, plus
(ii) the product of 2.5 and the number of Archer MSAs established during the portion of such year preceding July 1 (based on the reports required under paragraph (4)) for taxable years beginning in such year,
exceeds 750,000.
(C) No limitation for 2000 or 2003. The numerical limitation shall not apply for 2000 or 2003.

(3) Previously uninsured individuals not included in determination.
(A) In general. The determination of whether any calendar year is a cut-off year shall be made by not counting the Archer MSA of any previously uninsured individual.
(B) Previously uninsured individual. For purposes of this subsection, the term "previously uninsured individual" means, with respect to any Archer MSA, any individual who had no health plan coverage (other than coverage referred to in subsection (c)(1)(B)) at any time during the 6-month period before the date such individual's coverage under the high deductible health plan commences.

(4) Reporting by MSA trustees.
(A) In general. Not later than August 1 of 1997, 1998, 1999, 2001, 2002, 2004, 2005, and 2006 each person who is the trustee of an Archer MSA established before July 1 of such calendar year shall make a report to the Secretary (in such form and manner as the Secretary shall specify) which specifies—
(i) the number of Archer MSAs established before such July 1 (for taxable years beginning in such calendar year) of which such person is the trustee,
(ii) the name and TIN of the account holder of each such account, and
(iii) the number of such accounts which are accounts of previously uninsured individuals.
(B) Additional report for 1997. Not later than June 1, 1997, each person who is the trustee of an Archer MSA established before May 1, 1997, shall make an additional report described in subparagraph (A) but only with respect to accounts established before May 1, 1997.
(C) Penalty for failure to file report. The penalty provided in section 6693(a) shall apply to any report required by this paragraph, except that—
(i) such section shall be applied by substituting "$25" for "$50", and
(ii) the maximum penalty imposed on any trustee shall not exceed $5,000.
(D) Aggregation of accounts. To the extent practical, in determining the number of Archer MSAs on the basis of the reports under this paragraph, all Archer MSAs of an individual shall be treated as 1 account and all accounts of individuals who are married to each other shall be treated as 1 account.

(5) Date of making determinations. Any determination under this subsection that a calendar year is a cut-off year shall be made by the Secretary and shall be published not later than October 1 of such year.

In 2010, P.L. 111-148, Sec. 9003(b), added "Such term shall include an amount paid for medicine or a drug only if such medicine or drug is a prescribed drug (determined without regard to whether such drug is available without a prescription) or is insulin." at the of subpara. (d)(2)(A), effective for amounts paid with respect to tax. yrs. begin. after 12/31/2010. . . . Sec. 9004(b), substituted "20 percent" for "15 percent" in subpara. (f)(4)(A), effective for distributions made after 12/31/2010.

In 2006, P.L. 109-432, Sec. 117(a), substituted "2007" for "2005" each place it appeared in para. (i)(2) and subpara. (i)(3)(B) . . . Sec. 117(b)(1)(A), substituted "2004, 2005, or 2006" for "or 2004" each place it appeared in para. (j)(2) . . . Sec. 117(b)(1)(B), substituted "2004, 2005, or 2006" for "or 2004" in the heading of para. (j)(2) . . . Sec. 117(b)(2), substituted "2004, 2005, and 2006" for "and 2004" in subpara. (j)(4)(A), enacted 12/20/2006. Sec. 117(c) of this Act provides: "(c) Time for filing reports, etc.

"(1) The report required by section 220(j)(4) of the Internal Revenue Code of 1986 to be made on August 1, 2005, or August 1, 2006, as the case may be, shall be treated as timely if made before the close of the 90-day period beginning on the date of the enactment of this Act.

"(2) The determination and publication required by section 220(j)(5) of such Code with respect to calendar year 2005 or calendar year 2006, as the case may be, shall be treated as timely if made before the close of the 120-day period beginning on the date of the enactment of this Act. If the determination under the preceding sentence is that 2005 or 2006 is a cut-off year under section 220(i) of such Code, the cut-off date under such section 220(i) shall be the last day of such 120-day period."

In 2004, P.L. 108-311, Sec. 207(19), added ", determined without regard to subsections (b)(1), (b)(2), and (d)(1)(B) thereof" after "section 152" in subpara. (d)(2)(A), effective for tax. yrs. begin. after 12/31/2004.
—P.L. 108-311, Sec. 322(a), substituted "2005" for "2003" each place it appeared in the text and headings of para. (i)(2) and subpara. (i)(3)(B) . . . Sec. 322(b)(1)(A), substituted "2002, or 2004" for "or 2002" each place it appeared in para. (j)(2) . . . Sec. 322(b)(1)(B), substituted "2002, or 2004" for "or 2002" in

Code Sec. 220 — Deductions

the heading of para. (j)(2)... Sec. 322(b)(2), substituted "2002, and 2004" for "and 2002" in subpara. (j)(4)(A)... Sec. 322(b)(3), amended subpara. (j)(2)(C), effective 1/1/2004.

Prior to amendment, subpara. (j)(2)(C) read as follows:

"(C) No limitation for 2000. The numerical limitation shall not apply for 2000."

—P.L. 108-311, Sec. 322(d), of this Act, provides:

"(d) Time for filing reports, etc.

"(1) The report required by section 220(j)(4) of the Internal Revenue Code of 1986 to be made on August 1, 2004, shall be treated as timely if made before the close of the 90-day period beginning on the date of the enactment of this Act.

"(2) The determination and publication required by section 220(j)(5) of such Code with respect to calendar year 2004 shall be treated as timely if made before the close of the 120-day period beginning on the date of the enactment of this Act. If the determination under the preceding sentence is that 2004 is a cut-off year under section 220(i) of such Code, the cut-off date under such section 220(i) shall be the last day of such 120-day period."

In 2003, P.L. 108-173, Sec. 1201(c), added "or a health savings account (as defined in section 223(d))" after "paid into an Archer MSA" in subpara. (f)(5)(A), effective for tax. yrs. begin. after 12/31/2003.

In 2002, P.L. 107-147, Sec. 612(a), substituted "2003" for "2002" each place it appeared in para. (i)(2) and subpara. (i)(3)(B)... Sec. 612(b)(1), substituted "1998, 1999, 2001, or 2002" for "1998, 1999, or 2001" each place it appeared in para. (j)(2)... Sec. 612(b)(2), substituted "2001, and 2002" for "and 2001" in subpara. (j)(4)(A), effective 1/1/2002.

In 2000, P.L. 106-554, Sec. 1(a)(7), [which enacted into law Sec. 201(a) of P.L. 106-554] substituted "2002" for "2000" each place it appeared in para. (i)(2) and subpara. (i)(3)(B)... Sec. 1(a)(7), [which enacted into law Sec. 201(b)(1)(A) of P.L. 106-554] substituted "1998, 1999, or 2001" for "1998 or 1999" each place it appeared in para. (j)(2)... Sec. 1(a)(7), [which enacted into law Sec. 201(b)(1)(B) of P.L. 106-554] substituted "750,000 (600,000 in the case of 1998)" for "600,000 (750,000 in the case of 1999)" in para. (j)(2)... Sec. 1(a)(7), [which enacted into law Sec. 201(b)(1)(C) of P.L. 106-554]added subpara. (j)(2)(C)... Sec. 1(a)(7), [which enacted into law Sec. 201(b)(2) of P.L. 106-554] substituted "1999, and 2001" for "and 1999" in subpara. (j)(4)(A), effective 12/21/2000.

—P.L. 106-554, Sec. 1(a)(7), [which enacted into law Sec. 202(a)(4) of P.L. 106-554] substituted "Archer MSA" for "medical savings account" each place it appeared... Sec. 1(a)(7), [which enacted into law Sec. 202(b)(2)(B) of P.L. 106-554] substituted "Archer MSAs" for "medical savings accounts" each place it appeared in subsec. (j), para. (e)(2) and subparas. (c)(1)(D), (f)(3)(A) and (i)(4)(B)... Sec. 1(a)(7), [which enacted into law Sec. 202(b)(3) of P.L. 106-554] added "as a medical savings account" after "United States" in para. (d)(1)... Sec. 1(a)(7), [which enacted into law Sec. 202(b)(4) of P.L. 106-554] substituted "Archer MSA" for "Medical savings account" in the heading of subsec. (d)... Sec. 1(a)(7), [which enacted into law Sec. 202(b)(5) of P.L. 106-554] substituted "Archer MSA" for "Medical savings account" in the heading of para. (d)(1)... Sec. 1(a)(7), [which enacted into law Sec. 202(b)(6) of P.L. 106-554] substituted "Archer MSAs" for "medical savings accounts" in the heading of subsec. (i)... Sec. 1(a)(7), [which enacted into law Sec. 202(b)(7) of P.L. 106-554] substituted "Archer MSAs" for "medical savings accounts" in subpara. (c)(1)(C)... Sec. 1(a)(7), [which enacted into law Sec. 202(b)(8) of P.L. 106-554] substituted "Sec. 220. Archer MSAs." for "Sec. 220. Medical savings accounts" in the section heading... Sec. 1(a)(7), [which enacted into law Sec. 202(b)(10) of P.L. 106-554] substituted "an Archer" for "a Archer" each place it appeared in Code Sec. 220... Sec. 1(a)(7), [which enacted into law Sec. 202(b)(11) of P.L. 106-554] substituted "An Archer" for "A Archer" in para. (e)(1), effective 12/21/2000.

In 1997, P.L. 105-34, Sec. 1602(a)(2), deleted subpara. (c)(3)(A) and redesignated subparas. (c)(3)(B)-(D) as subparas. (c)(3)(A)-(C)... Sec. 1602(a)(3), substituted "described in clauses (i) and (ii) of subsection (c)(1)(A)" for "an eligible individual" in subpara. (c)(2)(C), effective for tax. yrs. begin. after 12/31/96.

Prior to deletion, subpara. (c)(3)(A) read as follows:

"(A) Medicare supplemental insurance,"

—P.L. 105-35, Sec. 4006(b)(2), added para. (b)(7), effective for tax. yrs. begin. after 12/31/98.

In 1996, P.L. 104-191, Sec. 301(a), added Code Sec. 220, effective for tax. yrs. begin. after 12/31/96.

Sec. 220. Repealed.

In 1990, P.L. 101-508, Sec. 11802(e)(2), deleted Code Sec. 220, effective 11/5/90, except as provided in Sec. 11821(b) of this Act, reproduced in note following Code Sec. 220 as redesignated from Code Sec. 221.

Prior to repeal, Code Sec. 220 read as follows:

"SEC. 220. JURY DUTY PAY REMITTED TO EMPLOYER.

"If—

"(1) an individual receives payment for the discharge of jury duty, and

"(2) the employer of such individual requires the individual to remit any portion of such payment to the employer in exchange for payment by the employer of compensation for the period the individual was performing jury duty, then there shall be allowed as a deduction the amount so remitted."

In 1988, P.L. 100-647, Sec. 6007(a), added Code Sec. 220, effective for tax. yrs. begin. after 12/31/86.

Sec. 220. Repealed

In 1981, P.L. 97-34, Sec. 311(e), repealed Code Sec. 220, effective for tax. yrs. begin. after 12/31/81. Sec. 311(i)(2) of this Act provides:

"(2) Transitional rule. For purposes of the Internal Revenue Code of 1954, any amount allowed as a deduction under section 220 of such Code (as in effect before its repeal by this Act) shall be treated as if it were allowed by section 219 of such Code."

Prior to repeal, Code Sec. 220 read as follows:

Sec. 220. Retirement savings for certain married individuals.

"(a) Deduction allowed.

"In the case of an individual, there is allowed as a deduction amounts paid in cash for a taxable year by or on behalf of such individual for the benefit of himself and his spouse—

"(1) to an individual retirement account described in section 408(a).

"(2) for an individual retirement annuity described in section 408(b), or

"(3) for a retirement bond described in section 409 (but only if the bond is not redeemed within 12 months of the date of its issuance.

For purposes of this title, any amount paid by an employer to such a retirement account or for such a retirement annuity or retirement bond constitutes payment of compensation to the employee (other than a self-employed individual who is an employee within the meaning of section 401(c)(1)) includible in his gross income, whether or not a deduction for such payment is allowable under this section to the employee after the application of subsection (b).

"Limitations and restrictions.

"(1) Maximum deduction. The amount allowable as a deduction under subsection (a) to an individual for any taxable year may not exceed—

"(A) twice the amount paid to the account, for the annuity, or for the bond, established for the individual or for his spouse to or for which the lesser amount was paid for the taxable year,

"(B) an amount equal to 15 percent of the compensation includible in the individual's gross income for the taxable year, or

"(C) $1,750,

whichever is the smallest amount.

"(2) Alternative deduction. No deduction is allowed under subsection (a) for the taxable year if the individual claims the deduction allowed by section 219 for the taxable year.

"(3) Coverage under certain other plans. No deduction is allowed under subsection () for an individual for the taxable year if for any part of such year—

"(A) he or his spouse was an active participant in—

"(i) a plan described in section 401(a) which includes a trust exempt from tax under section 501(a),

"(ii) an annuity plan described in section 403(a),

"(iii) a qualified bond purchase plan described in section 405(a), or

"(iv) a plan established for its employees by the Untied States, by a State or political subdivision thereof, or by an agency or instrumentality of any of the foregoing, or

"(B) amounts were contributed by his employer, or his spouse's employer, for an annuity contract described in section 403(b) (whether or not his, or his spouse's rights in such contract are nonforfeitable.

"(4) Contributions after age 70½. No deduction is allowed under subsection (a) with respect to any payment described in subsection (a) which is made for a taxable year of an individual if either the individual or his spouse has attained age 70½ before the close of such taxable year.

"(5) Recontributed amounts. No deduction is allowed under this section with respect to a rollover contribution described in section 402(a)(5), 402(a)(7), 403(a)(4), 403(b)(8), 408(d)(3), or 409(b)(3)(C).

"(6) Amounts contributed under endowment contract. In the case of an endowment contract described in section 408(b), no deduction is allowed under subsection (a) for that portion of the amounts paid under the contract for the taxable year properly allocable, under regulations prescribed by the Secretary, to the cost of life insurance.

"(7) Employed spouses. No deduction is allowed under subsection (a) with respect to a payment described in subsection (a) made for any taxable year of the individual if the spouse of the individual has any compensation (determined without regard to section 911) for the taxable year of such spouse ending with or within such taxable year.

"(c) Definition and special rules.

"(1) Compensation. For purposes of this section, the term compensation includes earned income as defined in section 401(c)(2).

"(2) Married individuals. This section shall be applied without regard to any community property laws.

"(3) Determination of marital status. The determination of whether an individual is married for purposes of this section shall be made in accordance with the provisions of section 143(a).

"(4) Time when contributions deemed made. For purposes of this section, a taxpayer shall be deemed to have made a contribution on the last day of the preceding taxable year if the contribution is made on account for such taxable year and is made not later than the time prescribed by law for filing the return for such taxable year (including extensions thereof).

"(5) Participation in governmental plans by certain individuals. A member of a reserve component of the armed forces or a volunteer firefighter is not considered to be an active participant in a plan described in subsection (b)(3)(A)(iv) if, under section 219(c)(4), he is not considered to be an active participant in such a plan.

"(6) Excess contributions treated as contribution made during subsequent year for which there is an unused limitation.

"(A) In general. If for the taxable year the maximum amount allowable as a deduction under this section exceeds the amount contributed, then the taxpayer shall be treated as having made an additional contribution for the taxable year in an amount equal to the lesser of—
"(i) the amount of such excess, or
"(ii) the amount of the excess contributions for such taxable year (determined under section 4973(b)(2) without regard to subparagraph (C) thereof).
"(B) Amount contributed. For purposes of this paragraph, the amount contributed—
"(i) shall be determined without regard to this paragraph, and
"(ii) shall not include any rollover contribution.
"(C) Special rule where excess deduction was allowed for closed year. Proper reduction shall be made in the amount allowable as a deduction by reason of this paragraph for any amount allowed as a deduction under this section or section 219 for a prior taxable year for which the period for assessing a deficiency has expired if the amount so allowed exceeds the amount which should have been allowed for such prior taxable year.

In 1980, P.L. 96-222, Sec. 101(A)(13)(a), amended the effective date for changes made by Sec. 156(c) of P.L. 95-600 to distributions or transfers made after '77, in tax. yrs. begin. after 12/31/77 [see below].
— P.L. 96-222, Sec. 101(a)(14)(B), added '402(a)(7),' after 'section 402(a)(5)' in para. (b)(4), effective for distributions or transfers made after '77, in tax. yrs. begin after 12/31/77.
In 1978, P.L. 95-600, Sec. 156(c)(3), added '403(b)(8),' following '403(a)(4_' in para. (b)(5), effective for distributions or transfers after '77, in tax. yrs. begin. after 12/31/77.
— P.L. 95-600, Sec. 157(a)(2), substituted, 'not later than the time prescribed by law for filing the return for such taxable year (including extensions thereof)' for 'not alter than 45 days after the end of such taxable year' in para. (c)(4), effective for tax. yrs. begin. after '77.
— P.L. 95-600, Sec. 157(b)(2), added para. (c)(6), for determination of deductions for tax. yrs. begin after '75. Sec. 157(b)(4)(B) of this Act provides:
"(B) Transitional rule. If, but for this subparagraph, an amount would be allowable as a deduction by reason of section 219(c)(5) or 220(c)(6) of the Internal Revenue Code of 1954 for a taxable year beginning before January 1, 1978, such amount shall be allowable only for the taxpayer's first taxable year beginning in 1978"
— P.L. 95-600, Sec. 703(c)(2), substituted "amount paid to the account, for the annuity, or for the bond" for "amount paid to the acount or annuity, or for the bond" in subpara. (b)(1)(A) . . . Sec. 703(c)(3), added "described in subsection (a)" following "any payment" in para. (b)(4), for tax. yrs. begin after 1976.
In 1976, P.L. 94-455, Sec. 1501(a), added Code Sec. 220, for tax. yrs. begin after 1976.

⎡ • **Caution:** Code Sec. 221, following, was amended by P.L. 107-16, EGTRRA. These provisions generally sunset for tax years beginning after 12/31/2012. For specific sunset provisions, see Sec. 901, P.L. 107-16 (as amended) reproduced in history notes for this Code Sec. ⎦

Sec. 221. Interest on education loans.
(a) Allowance of deduction.
In the case of an individual, there shall be allowed as a deduction for the taxable year an amount equal to the interest paid by the taxpayer during the taxable year on any qualified education loan.
(b) Maximum deduction.
(1) **In general.** Except as provided in paragraph (2), the deduction allowed by subsection (a) for the taxable year shall not exceed the amount determined in accordance with the following table:

In the case of taxable years beginning in:	The dollar amount is:
1998	$1,000
1999	$1,500
2000	$2,000
2001 or thereafter	$2,500

(2) **Limitation based on modified adjusted gross income.**
(A) In general. The amount which would (but for this paragraph) be allowable as a deduction under this section shall be reduced (but not below zero) by the amount determined under subparagraph (B).
(B) Amount of reduction. The amount determined under this subparagraph is the amount which bears the same ratio to the amount which would be so taken into account as—
(i) the excess of—
(I) the taxpayer's modified adjusted gross income for such taxable year, over
(II) $50,000 ($100,000 in the case of a joint return), bears to
(ii) $15,000 ($30,000 in the case of a joint return).
(C) Modified adjusted gross income. The term "modified adjusted gross income" means adjusted gross income determined—
(i) without regard to this section and sections 199, 222, 911, 931, and 933, and
(ii) after application of sections 86, 135, 137, 219, and 469.
(c) Dependents not eligible for deduction.
No deduction shall be allowed by this section to an individual for the taxable year if a deduction under section 151 with respect to such individual is allowed to another taxpayer for the taxable year beginning in the calendar year in which such individual's taxable year begins.
(d) Definitions.
For purposes of this section—
(1) Qualified education loan. The term "qualified education loan" means any indebtedness incurred by the taxpayer solely to pay qualified higher education expenses—
(A) which are incurred on behalf of the taxpayer, the taxpayer's spouse, or any dependent of the taxpayer as of the time the indebtedness was incurred,
(B) which are paid or incurred within a reasonable period of time before or after the indebtedness is incurred, and
(C) which are attributable to education furnished during a period during which the recipient was an eligible student.
Such term includes indebtedness used to refinance indebtedness which qualifies as a qualified education loan. The term "qualified education loan" shall not include any indebtedness owed to a person who is related (within the meaning of section 267(b) or 707(b)(1)) to the taxpayer or to any person by reason of a loan under any qualified employer plan (as defined in section 72(p)(4)) or under any contract referred to in section 72(p)(5).
(2) Qualified higher education expenses. The term "qualified higher education expenses" means the cost of attendance (as defined in section 472 of the Higher Education Act of 1965, 20 U.S.C. 1087ll, as in effect on the day before the date of the enactment of the Taxpayer Relief Act of 1997) at an eligible educational institution, reduced by the sum of—
(A) the amount excluded from gross income under section 127, 135, 529, or 530 by reason of such expenses, and
(B) the amount of any scholarship, allowance, or payment described in section 25A(g)(2).
For purposes of the preceding sentence, the term "eligible educational institution" has the same meaning given such term by section 25A(f)(2), except that such term shall also include an institution conducting an internship or residency program leading to a degree or certificate awarded by an institution of higher education, a hospital, or a health care facility which offers postgraduate training.

(3) Eligible student. The term "eligible student" has the meaning given such term by section 25A(b)(3).

(4) Dependent. The term "dependent" has the meaning given such term by section 152 (determined without regard to subsections (b)(1), (b)(2), and (d)(1)(B) thereof).

(e) Special rules.

(1) Denial of double benefit. No deduction shall be allowed under this section for any amount for which a deduction is allowable under any other provision of this chapter.

(2) Married couples must file joint return. If the taxpayer is married at the close of the taxable year, the deduction shall be allowed under subsection (a) only if the taxpayer and the taxpayer's spouse file a joint return for the taxable year.

(3) Marital status. Marital status shall be determined in accordance with section 7703.

(f) Inflation adjustments.

(1) In general. In the case of a taxable year beginning after 2002, the $50,000 and $100,000 amounts in subsection (b)(2) shall each be increased by an amount equal to—

(A) such dollar amount, multiplied by

(B) the cost-of-living adjustment determined under section 1(f)(3) for the calendar year in which the taxable year begins, determined by substituting "calendar year 2001" for "calendar year 1992" in subparagraph (B) thereof.

(2) Rounding. If any amount as adjusted under paragraph (1) is not a multiple of $5,000, such amount shall be rounded to the next lowest multiple of $5,000.

In 2010, P.L. 111-312, Sec. 101(a)(1), substituted "December 31, 2012" for "December 31, 2010" both places it appeared in Sec. 901, P.L. 107-16 [see below], effective as if included in the enactment of P.L. 107-16, EGTRRA, 6/7/2001.

In 2006, P.L. 109-280, Sec. 1304(a), of this Act [relating to Sec. 901 of P.L. 107-16, see below], provides:

"(a) Permanent extension of modifications. Section 901 of the Economic Growth and Tax Relief Reconciliation Act of 2001 [P.L. 107-16] (relating to sunset provisions) shall not apply to section 402 of such Act (relating to modifications to qualified tuition programs)."

In 2005, P.L. 109-135, Sec. 403(a)(19), amended Sec. 102(e) of P.L. 108-357 [see below].

Prior to amendment, Sec. 102(e) of P.L. 108-357 [see below] read as follows:

"(e) Effective date. The amendments made by this section shall apply to taxable years beginning after December 31, 2004."

—P.L. 109-135, Sec. 412(t), substituted "the Taxpayer Relief Act of 1997" for "this Act" in para. (d)(2), effective 12/21/2005.

In 2004, P.L. 108-357, Sec. 102(e)(2), added "199," before "222" in clause (b)(2)(C)(i), effective as provided by Sec. 102(e) of this Act [as amended by Sec. 403(a)(19) of P.L. 109-135, see above], which reads as follows:

"(e) Effective date.

"(1) The amendments made by this section shall apply to taxable years beginning after December 31, 2004.

"(2) Application to pass-thru entities, etc. In determining the deduction under section 199 of the Internal Revenue Code of 1986 (as added by this section), items arising from a taxable year of a partnership, S corporation, estate, or trust beginning before January 1, 2005, shall not be taken into account for purposes of subsection (d)(1) of such section."

—P.L. 108-311, Sec. 207(20), added "(determined without regard to subsections (b)(1), (b)(2), and (d)(1)(B) thereof)" after "section 152" in para. (d)(4), effective for tax. yrs. begin. after 12/31/2004.

—P.L. 108-311, Sec. 408(b)(5), substituted "Section 221(f)(1)" for "Section 221(g)(1)" in Sec. 412(b)(2) of P.L . 107-16 [see below], enacted 10/4/2004.

In 2002, P.L. 107-358, Sec. 2, added subsec. (c) in Sec. 901 of P.L. 107-16 [see below], effective 12/17/2002.

In 2001, P.L. 107-16, Sec. 402(b)(2)(B), added "529," after "135," in subpara. (e)(2)(A), [prior to redesignation by Sec. 412(a)(1) of this Act, see below] effective for tax. yrs. begin. after 12/31/2001.

—P.L. 107-16, Sec. 412(a)(1), deleted subsec. (d) and redesignated subsecs. (e)-(g) as (d)-(f), effective for any loan interest paid after 12/31/2001, in tax. yrs. ending after 12/31/2001.

Prior to deletion, subsec. (d) read as follows:

"(d) Limit on period deduction allowed. A deduction shall be allowed under this section only with respect to interest paid on any qualified education loan during the first 60 months (whether or not consecutive) in which interest payments are required. For purposes of this paragraph, any loan and all refinancings of such loan shall be treated as 1 loan. Such 60 months shall be determined in the manner prescribed by the Secretary in the case of multiple loans which are refinanced by, or serviced as, a single loan and in the case of loans incurred before the date of the enactment of this section."

—P.L. 107-16, Sec. 412(b)(1), amended clauses (b)(2)(B)(i) and (ii) . . . Sec. 412(b)(2), substituted "$50,000 and $100,000 amounts" for "$40,000 and $60,000 amounts" in para. (f)(1) [as clarified by Sec. 408(b)(5) of P.L. 108-311, see above], [as redesignated by Sec. 412(a)(1) of this Act, see above] effective for tax. yrs. end. after 12/31/2001.

Prior to amendment, clauses (b)(2)(B)(i) and (ii) read as follows:

"(i) the excess of—

"(II) the taxpayer's modified adjusted gross income for such taxable year, over

"(II) $40,000 ($60,000 in the case of a joint return), bears to

"(ii) $15,000."

—P.L. 107-16, Sec. 431(c)(2), added "222," before "911," in clause (b)(2)(C)(i), effective for payments made in tax. yrs. begin. after 12/31/2001.

—P.L. 107-16, Sec. 901, of this Act [as amended by Sec. 2, P.L. 107-358 and Sec. 101(a)(1), P.L. 111-312, and as related to Sec. 1304(a) of P.L. 109-280, see above], reads as follows:

"SEC. 901. SUNSET OF PROVISIONS OF ACT.

"(a) In general. All provisions of, and amendments made by, this Act shall not apply—

"(1) to taxable, plan, or limitation years beginning after December 31, 2012, or

"(2) in the case of title V, to estates of decedents dying, gifts made, or generation-skipping transfers, after December 31, 2012.

"(b) Application of certain laws. The Internal Revenue Code of 1986 and the Employee Retirement Income Security Act of 1974 shall be applied and administered to years, estates, gifts, and transfers described in subsection (a) as if the provisions and amendments described in subsection (a) had never been enacted.

"(c) Exception. Subsection (a) shall not apply to section 803 (relating to no federal income tax on restitution received by victims of the Nazi regime or their heirs or estates)."

In 1998, P.L. 105-277, Sec. 4003(a)(2)(A)(i), deleted "135, 137," after "and sections" in clause (b)(2)(C)(i) . . . Sec. 4003(a)(2)(A)(ii), added "135, 137," after "sections 86," in clause (b)(2)(C)(ii) . . . Sec. 4003(a)(2)(A)(iii), deleted "For purposes of sections 86, 135, 137, 219, and 469, adjusted gross income shall be determined without regard to the deduction allowed under this section." at the end of subpara. (b)(2)(C) . . . Sec. 4003(a)(3), added "or to any person by reason of a loan under any qualified employer plan (as defined in section 72(p)(4)) or under any contract referred to in section 72(p)(5)" at the end of para. (e)(1), effective as provided in Sec. 202(e) of P.L. 105-34, which reads as follows:

"(e) Effective date. The amendments made by this section shall apply to any qualified education loan (as defined in section 221(e)(1) of the Internal Revenue Code of 1986, as added by this section) incurred on, before, or after the date of the enactment of this Act, but only with respect to—

"(1) any loan interest payment due and paid after December 31, 1997, and

"(2) the portion of the 60-month period referred to in section 221(d) of the Internal Revenue Code of 1986 (as added by this section) after December 31, 1997."

—P.L. 105-206, Sec. 6004(b)(1), added "by the taxpayer solely" after "incurred" in para. (e)(1) . . . Sec. 6004(b)(2), added a sentence at the end of subsec. (d), effective for any qualified education loan (as defined in Code Sec. 221(e)(1)) incurred on, before, or after 8/5/97, but only with respect to any loan interest payment due and paid after 12/31/97, and the portion of the 60-month period referred to in Code Sec. 221(d) after 12/31/97.

In 1997, P.L. 105-34, Sec. 202(a), added Code Sec. 221, effective for any qualified education loan (as defined in Code Sec. 221(e)(1) as added by this section) incurred on, before, or after 8/5/97, but only with respect to any loan interest payment due and paid after 12/31/97, and the portion of the 60-month period referred to in Code Sec. 221(d) (as added by this section) after 12/31/97.

Sec. 221. Repealed.

In 1986, P.L. 99-514, Sec. 131(a), repealed Code Sec. 221, effective for tax. yrs. begin. after 12/31/86.

Prior to repeal, Code Sec. 221 read as follows:

"SEC. 221. DEDUCTION FOR TWO-EARNER MARRIED COUPLES.

"(a) Deduction allowed.

"(1) In general. In the case of a joint return under section 6013 for the taxable year, there shall be allowed as a deduction an amount equal to 10 percent of the lesser of

"(A) $30,000, or

"(B) the qualified earned income of the spouse with the lower qualified earned income for such taxable year.

"(2) Special rule for 1982. In the case of a taxable year beginning during 1982, paragraph (1) shall be applied by substituting '5 percent' for '10 percent'.

"(b) Qualified earned income defined.

"(1) In general. For purposes of this section, the term 'qualified earned income' means an amount equal to the excess of

"(A) the earned income of the spouse for the taxable year, over

"(B) an amount equal to the sum of the deductions described in paragraphs (1), (2), (7), (10), and (15) of section 62 to the extent such deductions are properly allocable to or chargeable against earned income described in subparagraph (A).

The amount of qualified earned income shall be determined without regard to any community property laws.

Deductions Code Sec. 222

"(2) Earned income. For purposes of paragraph (1), the term 'earned income' means income which is earned income within the meaning of section 911(d)(2) or 401(c)(2)(C), except that

"(A) such term shall not include any amount

"(i) not includible in gross income,

"(ii) received as a pension or annuity,

"(iii) paid or distributed out of an individual retirement plan (within the meaning of section 7701(a)(37)),

"(iv) received as deferred compensation, or

"(v) received for services performed by an individual in the employ of his spouse (within the meaning of section 3121(b)(3)(A)), and

"(B) section 911(d)(2)(B) shall be applied without regard to the phrase 'not in excess of 30 percent of his share of net profits of such trade or business'.

"(c) Deduction disallowed for individual claiming benefits of section 911 or 931.

"No deduction shall be allowed under this section for any taxable year if either spouse claims the benefits of section 911 or 931 for such taxable years."

In 1983, P.L. 97-448, Sec. 305(d)(4), deleted "(9)" after "(7)" in subpara. (b)(1)(B), effective 10/19/82.

In 1981, P.L. 97-34, Sec. 103(a), added Code Sec. 221, effective for tax yrs. begin. after 12/31/81.

• **Caution:** Code Sec. 222, following, was added by P.L. 107-16, EGTRRA. These provisions generally sunset for tax years beginning after 12/31/2012. For specific sunset provisions, see Sec. 901, P.L. 107-16 (as amended), reproduced in history notes for this Code Sec.

Sec. 222. Qualified tuition and related expenses.
(a) Allowance of deduction.

In the case of an individual, there shall be allowed as a deduction an amount equal to the qualified tuition and related expenses paid by the taxpayer during the taxable year.

(b) Dollar limitations.

(1) In general. The amount allowed as a deduction under subsection (a) with respect to the taxpayer for any taxable year shall not exceed the applicable dollar limit.

(2) Applicable dollar limit.

(A) 2002 and 2003. In the case of a taxable year beginning in 2002 or 2003, the applicable dollar limit shall be equal to—

(i) in the case of a taxpayer whose adjusted gross income for the taxable year does not exceed $65,000 ($130,000 in the case of a joint return), $3,000, and—

(ii) in the case of any other taxpayer, zero.

(B) After 2003. In the case of any taxable year beginning after 2003, the applicable dollar amount shall be equal to—

(i) in the case of a taxpayer whose adjusted gross income for the taxable year does not exceed $65,000 ($130,000 in the case of a joint return), $4,000,

(ii) in the case of a taxpayer not described in clause (i) whose adjusted gross income for the taxable year does not exceed $80,000 ($160,000 in the case of a joint return), $2,000, and

(iii) in the case of any other taxpayer, zero.

(C) Adjusted gross income. For purposes of this paragraph, adjusted gross income shall be determined—

(i) without regard to this section and sections 199, 911, 931, and 933, and

(ii) after application of sections 86, 135, 137, 219, 221, and 469.

(c) No double benefit.

(1) In general. No deduction shall be allowed under subsection (a) for any expense for which a deduction is allowed to the taxpayer under any other provision of this chapter.

(2) Coordination with other education incentives.

(A) Denial of deduction if credit elected. No deduction shall be allowed under subsection (a) for a taxable year with respect to the qualified tuition and related expenses with respect to an individual if the taxpayer or any other person elects to have section 25A apply with respect to such individual for such year.

(B) Coordination with exclusions. The total amount of qualified tuition and related expenses shall be reduced by the amount of such expenses taken into account in determining any amount excluded under section 135, 529(c)(1), or 530(d)(2). For purposes of the preceding sentence, the amount taken into account in determining the amount excluded under section 529(c)(1) shall not include that portion of the distribution which represents a return of any contributions to the plan.

(3) Dependents. No deduction shall be allowed under subsection (a) to any individual with respect to whom a deduction under section 151 is allowable to another taxpayer for a taxable year beginning in the calendar year in which such individual's taxable year begins.

(d) Definitions and special rules.

For purposes of this section—

(1) Qualified tuition and related expenses. The term "qualified tuition and related expenses" has the meaning given such term by section 25A(f). Such expenses shall be reduced in the same manner as under section 25A(g)(2).

(2) Identification requirement. No deduction shall be allowed under subsection (a) to a taxpayer with respect to the qualified tuition and related expenses of an individual unless the taxpayer includes the name and taxpayer identification number of the individual on the return of tax for the taxable year.

(3) Limitation on taxable year of deduction.

(A) In general. A deduction shall be allowed under subsection (a) for qualified tuition and related expenses for any taxable year only to the extent such expenses are in connection with enrollment at an institution of higher education during the taxable year.

(B) Certain prepayments allowed. Subparagraph (A) shall not apply to qualified tuition and related expenses paid during a taxable year if such expenses are in connection with an academic term beginning during such taxable year or during the first 3 months of the next taxable year.

(4) No deduction for married individuals filing separate returns. If the taxpayer is a married individual (within the meaning of section 7703), this section shall apply only if the taxpayer and the taxpayer's spouse file a joint return for the taxable year.

(5) Nonresident aliens. If the taxpayer is a nonresident alien individual for any portion of the taxable year, this section shall apply only if such individual is treated as a resident alien of the United States for purposes of this chapter by reason of an election under subsection (g) or (h) of section 6013.

(6) Regulations. The Secretary may prescribe such regulations as may be necessary or appropriate to carry out this section, including regulations requiring recordkeeping and information reporting.

(e) Termination.

This section shall not apply to taxable years beginning after December 31, 2011.

In 2010, P.L. 111-312, Sec. 101(a)(1), substituted "December 31, 2012" for "December 31, 2010" both places it appeared in Sec. 901, P.L. 107-16 [see below], effective as if included in the enactment of P.L. 107-16, EGTRRA, 6/7/2001.

—P.L. 111-312, Sec. 724(a), substituted "December 31, 2011" for "December 31, 2009" in subsec. (e), effective for tax. yrs. begin. after 12/31/2009.

In 2008, P.L. 110-343, Sec. 202(a)DivC, substituted "December 31, 2009" for "December 31, 2007" in subsec. (e), effective for tax. yrs. begin. after 12/31/2007.

In 2006, P.L. 109-432, Sec. 101(a), substituted "2007" for "2005" in subsec. (e) ... Sec. 101(b)(1), substituted "any taxable year beginning after 2003" for "a taxable year beginning in 2004 or 2005" in subpara. (b)(2)(B) ... Sec. 101(b)(2), substituted "After 2003" for "2004 and 2005" in the heading of subpara. (b)(2)(B), effective for tax. yrs. begin. after 12/31/2005.

In 2005, P.L. 109-135, Sec. 403(a)(19), amended Sec. 102(e) of P.L. 108-357 [see below].

Prior to amendment, Sec. 102(e) of P.L. 108-357 [see below] read as follows:

"*(e) Effective date.* The amendments made by this section shall apply to taxable years beginning after December 31, 2004."

In 2004, P.L. 108-357, Sec. 102(d)(3), added "199," before "911" in clause (b)(2)(C)(i), effective as provided by Sec. 102(e) of this Act [as amended by Sec. 403(a)(19) of P.L. 109-135, see above], which reads as follows:

"*(e) Effective date.*

"(1) The amendments made by this section shall apply to taxable years beginning after December 31, 2004.

"(2) Application to pass-thru entities, etc. In determining the deduction under section 199 of the Internal Revenue Code of 1986 (as added by this section), items arising from a taxable year of a partnership, S corporation, estate, or trust beginning before January 1, 2005, shall not be taken into account for purposes of subsection (d)(1) of such section."

In 2002, P.L. 107-358, Sec. 2, added subsec. (c) in Sec. 901 of P.L. 107-16 [see below], effective 12/17/2002.

In 2001, P.L. 107-16, Sec. 431(a), added Code Sec. 222, effective for payments made in tax. yrs. begin. after 12/31/2001.

—P.L. 107-16, Sec. 901, of this Act [as amended by Sec. 2, P.L. 107-358, and Sec. 101(a)(1), P.L. 111-312, see above], reads as follows:

"Sec. 901. Sunset of provisions of Act.

"(a) In general. All provisions of, and amendments made by, this Act shall not apply—

"(1) to taxable, plan, or limitation years beginning after December 31, 2012, or

"(2) in the case of title V, to estates of decedents dying, gifts made, or generation skipping transfers, after December 31, 2012.

"(b) Application of certain laws. The Internal Revenue Code of 1986 and the Employee Retirement Income Security Act of 1974 shall be applied and administered to years, estates, gifts, and transfers described in subsection (a) as if the provisions and amendments described in subsection (a) had never been enacted.

"(c) Exception. Subsection (a) shall not apply to section 803 (relating to no federal income tax on restitution received by victims of the Nazi regime or their heirs or estates)."

Sec. 222. Repealed.

In 1986, P.L. 99-514, Sec. 135(a), repealed Code Sec. 222, effective for tax. yrs. begin. after 12/31/86.

Prior to repeal, Code Sec. 222 read as follows:

"SEC. 222. ADOPTION EXPENSES.

"*(a) Allowance of deduction.*

"In the case of an individual, there shall be allowed as a deduction for the taxable year the amount of the qualified adoption expenses paid or incurred by the taxpayer during such taxable year.

"*(b) Limitations.*

"(1) Maximum dollar amount. The aggregate amount of adoption expenses which may be taken into account under subsection (a) with respect to the adoption of a child shall not exceed $1,500.

"(2) Denial of double benefit.

"(A) In general. No deduction shall be allowable under subsection (a) for any expense for which a deduction or credit is allowable under any other provision of this chapter.

"(B) Grants. No deduction shall be allowable under subsection (a) for any expenses paid from any funds received under any Federal, State, or local program.

"*(c) Definitions.*

"For purposes of this section

"(1) Qualified adoption expenses. The term 'qualified adoption expenses' means reasonable and necessary adoption fees, court costs, attorney fees, and other expenses which are directly related to the legal adoption of a child with special needs by the taxpayer and which are not incurred in violation of State or Federal law.

"(2) Child with special needs. The term 'child with special needs' means any child determined by the State to be a child described in paragraphs (1) and (2) of section 473(c) of the Social Security Act."

In 1983, P.L. 97-448, Sec. 101(f), amended para. (c)(2), for tax. yrs. begin. after 12/31/80.

Prior to amendment, para. (c)(2) read as follows:

"(2) Child with special needs. The term 'child with special needs' means a child with respect to whom adoption assistance payments are made under section 473 of the Social Security Act"

In 1981, P.L. 97-34, Sec. 125(a), added Code Sec. 222, effective for tax. yrs. begin. after 12/31/80.

Sec. 223. Health savings accounts.

(a) Deduction allowed.

In the case of an individual who is an eligible individual for any month during the taxable year, there shall be allowed as a deduction for the taxable year an amount equal to the aggregate amount paid in cash during such taxable year by or on behalf of such individual to a health savings account of such individual.

(b) Limitations.

(1) In general. The amount allowable as a deduction under subsection (a) to an individual for the taxable year shall not exceed the sum of the monthly limitations for months during such taxable year that the individual is an eligible individual.

(2) Monthly limitation. The monthly limitation for any month is $1/12$ of—

(A) in the case of an eligible individual who has self-only coverage under a high deductible health plan as of the first day of such month, $2,250.

(B) in the case of an eligible individual who has family coverage under a high deductible health plan as of the first day of such month, $4,500.

(3) Additional contributions for individuals 55 or older.

(A) In general. In the case of an individual who has attained age 55 before the close of the taxable year, the applicable limitation under subparagraphs (A) and (B) of paragraph (2) shall be increased by the additional contribution amount.

(B) Additional contribution amount. For purposes of this section, the additional contribution amount is the amount determined in accordance with the following table:

For taxable years beginning in:	The additional contribution amount is:
2004	$500
2005	$600
2006	$700
2007	$800
2008	$900
2009 and thereafter	$1,000

(4) Coordination with other contributions. The limitation which would (but for this paragraph) apply under this subsection to an individual for any taxable year shall be reduced (but not below zero) by the sum of—

(A) the aggregate amount paid for such taxable year to Archer MSAs of such individual,

(B) the aggregate amount contributed to health savings accounts of such individual which is excludable from the taxpayer's gross income for such taxable year under section 106(d) (and such amount shall not be allowed as a deduction under subsection (a)), and

(C) the aggregate amount contributed to health savings accounts of such individual for such taxable year under section 408(d)(9) (and such amount shall not be allowed as a deduction under subsection (a)).

Subparagraph (A) shall not apply with respect to any individual to whom paragraph (5) applies.

(5) Special rule for married individuals. In the case of individuals who are married to each other, if either spouse has family coverage—

(A) both spouses shall be treated as having only such family coverage (and if such spouses each have family coverage under different plans, as having the family coverage with the lowest annual deductible), and

Deductions

Code Sec. 223(c)(3)

(B) the limitation under paragraph (1) (after the application of subparagraph (A) and without regard to any additional contribution amount under paragraph (3))—

(i) shall be reduced by the aggregate amount paid to Archer MSAs of such spouses for the taxable year, and

(ii) after such reduction, shall be divided equally between them unless they agree on a different division.

(6) Denial of deduction to dependents. No deduction shall be allowed under this section to any individual with respect to whom a deduction under section 151 is allowable to another taxpayer for a taxable year beginning in the calendar year in which such individual's taxable year begins.

(7) Medicare eligible individuals. The limitation under this subsection for any month with respect to an individual shall be zero for the first month such individual is entitled to benefits under title XVIII of the Social Security Act and for each month thereafter.

(8) Increase in limit for individuals becoming eligible individuals after the beginning of the year.

(A) In general. For purposes of computing the limitation under paragraph (1) for any taxable year, an individual who is an eligible individual during the last month of such taxable year shall be treated—

(i) as having been an eligible individual during each of the months in such taxable year, and

(ii) as having been enrolled, during each of the months such individual is treated as an eligible individual solely by reason of clause (i), in the same high deductible health plan in which the individual was enrolled for the last month of such taxable year.

(B) Failure to maintain high deductible health plan coverage.

(i) In general. If, at any time during the testing period, the individual is not an eligible individual, then—

(I) gross income of the individual for the taxable year in which occurs the first month in the testing period for which such individual is not an eligible individual is increased by the aggregate amount of all contributions to the health savings account of the individual which could not have been made but for subparagraph (A), and

(II) the tax imposed by this chapter for any taxable year on the individual shall be increased by 10 percent of the amount of such increase.

(ii) Exception for disability or death. Subclauses (I) and (II) of clause (i) shall not apply if the individual ceased to be an eligible individual by reason of the death of the individual or the individual becoming disabled (within the meaning of section 72(m)(7)).

(iii) Testing period. The term "testing period" means the period beginning with the last month of the taxable year referred to in subparagraph (A) and ending on the last day of the 12th month following such month.

(c) Definitions and special rules.

For purposes of this section—

(1) Eligible individual.

(A) In general. The term "eligible individual" means, with respect to any month, any individual if—

(i) such individual is covered under a high deductible health plan as of the 1st day of such month, and

(ii) such individual is not, while covered under a high deductible health plan, covered under any health plan—

(I) which is not a high deductible health plan, and

(II) which provides coverage for any benefit which is covered under the high deductible health plan.

(B) Certain coverage disregarded. Subparagraph (A)(ii) shall be applied without regard to—

(i) coverage for any benefit provided by permitted insurance,

(ii) coverage (whether through insurance or otherwise) for accidents, disability, dental care, vision care, or long-term care, and

(iii) for taxable years beginning after December 31, 2006, coverage under a health flexible spending arrangement during any period immediately following the end of a plan year of such arrangement during which unused benefits or contributions remaining at the end of such plan year may be paid or reimbursed to plan participants for qualified benefit expenses incurred during such period if—

(I) the balance in such arrangement at the end of such plan year is zero, or

(II) the individual is making a qualified HSA distribution (as defined in section 106(e)) in an amount equal to the remaining balance in such arrangement as of the end of such plan year, in accordance with rules prescribed by the Secretary.

(2) High deductible health plan.

(A) In general. The term "high deductible health plan" means a health plan—

(i) which has an annual deductible which is not less than—

(I) $1,000 for self-only coverage, and

(II) twice the dollar amount in subclause (I) for family coverage, and

(ii) the sum of the annual deductible and the other annual out-of-pocket expenses required to be paid under the plan (other than for premiums) for covered benefits does not exceed—

(I) $5,000 for self-only coverage, and

(II) twice the dollar amount in subclause (I) for family coverage.

(B) Exclusion of certain plans. Such term does not include a health plan if substantially all of its coverage is coverage described in paragraph (1)(B).

(C) Safe harbor for absence of preventive care deductible. A plan shall not fail to be treated as a high deductible health plan by reason of failing to have a deductible for preventive care (within the meaning of section 1871 of the Social Security Act, except as otherwise provided by the Secretary).

(D) Special rules for network plans. In the case of a plan using a network of providers—

(i) Annual out-of-pocket limitation. Such plan shall not fail to be treated as a high deductible health plan by reason of having an out-of-pocket limitation for services provided outside of such network which exceeds the applicable limitation under subparagraph (A)(ii).

(ii) Annual deductible. Such plan's annual deductible for services provided outside of such network shall not be taken into account for purposes of subsection (b)(2).

(3) Permitted insurance. The term "permitted insurance" means—

(A) insurance if substantially all of the coverage provided under such insurance relates to—
  (i) liabilities incurred under workers' compensation laws,
  (ii) tort liabilities,
  (iii) liabilities relating to ownership or use of property, or
  (iv) such other similar liabilities as the Secretary may specify by regulations,
(B) insurance for a specified disease or illness, and
(C) insurance paying a fixed amount per day (or other period) of hospitalization.

(4) Family coverage. The term "family coverage" means any coverage other than self-only coverage.

(5) Archer MSA. The term "Archer MSA" has the meaning given such term in section 220(d).

(d) Health savings account.
For purposes of this section—

(1) In general. The term "health savings account" means a trust created or organized in the United States as a health savings account exclusively for the purpose of paying the qualified medical expenses of the account beneficiary, but only if the written governing instrument creating the trust meets the following requirements:

(A) Except in the case of a rollover contribution described in subsection (f)(5) or section 220(f)(5), no contribution will be accepted—
  (i) unless it is in cash, or
  (ii) to the extent such contribution, when added to previous contributions to the trust for the calendar year, exceeds the sum of—
    (I) the dollar amount in effect under subsection (b)(2)(B), and
    (II) the dollar amount in effect under subsection (b)(3)(B).
(B) The trustee is a bank (as defined in section 408(n)), an insurance company (as defined in section 816), or another person who demonstrates to the satisfaction of the Secretary that the manner in which such person will administer the trust will be consistent with the requirements of this section.
(C) No part of the trust assets will be invested in life insurance contracts.
(D) The assets of the trust will not be commingled with other property except in a common trust fund or common investment fund.
(E) The interest of an individual in the balance in his account is nonforfeitable.

(2) Qualified medical expenses.
(A) In general. The term "qualified medical expenses" means, with respect to an account beneficiary, amounts paid by such beneficiary for medical care (as defined in section 213(d) for such individual, the spouse of such individual, and any dependent (as defined in section 152, determined without regard to subsections (b)(1), (b)(2), and (d)(1)(B) thereof) of such individual, but only to the extent such amounts are not compensated for by insurance or otherwise. Such term shall include an amount paid for medicine or a drug only if such medicine or drug is a prescribed drug (determined without regard to whether such drug is available without a prescription) or is insulin.
(B) Health insurance may not be purchased from account. Subparagraph (A) shall not apply to any payment for insurance.

(C) Exceptions. Subparagraph (B) shall not apply to any expense for coverage under—
  (i) a health plan during any period of continuation coverage required under any Federal law,
  (ii) a qualified long-term care insurance contract (as defined in section 7702B(b)),
  (iii) a health plan during a period in which the individual is receiving unemployment compensation under any Federal or State law, or
  (iv) in the case of an account beneficiary who has attained the age specified in section 1811 of the Social Security Act, any health insurance other than a medicare supplemental policy (as defined in section 1882 of the Social Security Act).

(3) Account beneficiary. The term "account beneficiary" means the individual on whose behalf the health savings account was established.

(4) Certain rules to apply. Rules similar to the following rules shall apply for purposes of this section:
(A) Section 219(d)(2) (relating to no deduction for rollovers).
(B) Section 219(f)(3) (relating to time when contributions deemed made).
(C) Except as provided in section 106(d), section 219(f)(5) (relating to employer payments).
(D) Section 408(g) (relating to community property laws).
(E) Section 408(h) (relating to custodial accounts).

(e) Tax treatment of accounts.
(1) In general. A health savings account is exempt from taxation under this subtitle unless such account has ceased to be a health savings account. Notwithstanding the preceding sentence, any such account is subject to the taxes imposed by section 511 (relating to imposition of tax on unrelated business income of charitable, etc. organizations).

(2) Account terminations. Rules similar to the rules of paragraphs (2) and (4) of section 408(e) shall apply to health savings accounts, and any amount treated as distributed under such rules shall be treated as not used to pay qualified medical expenses.

(f) Tax treatment of distributions.
(1) Amounts used for qualified medical expenses. Any amount paid or distributed out of a health savings account which is used exclusively to pay qualified medical expenses of any account beneficiary shall not be includible in gross income.

(2) Inclusion of amounts not used for qualified medical expenses. Any amount paid or distributed out of a health savings account which is not used exclusively to pay the qualified medical expenses of the account beneficiary shall be included in the gross income of such beneficiary.

(3) Excess contributions returned before due date of return.
(A) In general. If any excess contribution is contributed for a taxable year to any health savings account of an individual, paragraph (2) shall not apply to distributions from the health savings accounts of such individual (to the extent such distributions do not exceed the aggregate excess contributions to all such accounts of such individual for such year) if—
  (i) such distribution is received by the individual on or before the last day prescribed by law (including extensions of time) for filing such individual's return for such taxable year, and

(ii) such distribution is accompanied by the amount of net income attributable to such excess contribution.

Any net income described in clause (ii) shall be included in the gross income of the individual for the taxable year in which it is received.

(B) Excess contribution. For purposes of subparagraph (A), the term "excess contribution" means any contribution (other than a rollover contribution described in paragraph (5) or section 220(f)(5)) which is neither excludable from gross income under section 106(d) nor deductible under this section.

(4) Additional tax on distributions not used for qualified medical expenses.

(A) In general. The tax imposed by this chapter on the account beneficiary for any taxable year in which there is a payment or distribution from a health savings account of such beneficiary which is includible in gross income under paragraph (2) shall be increased by 20 percent of the amount which is so includible.

(B) Exception for disability or death. Subparagraph (A) shall not apply if the payment or distribution is made after the account beneficiary becomes disabled within the meaning of section 72(m)(7) or dies.

(C) Exception for distributions after medicare eligibility. Subparagraph (A) shall not apply to any payment or distribution after the date on which the account beneficiary attains the age specified in section 1811 of the Social Security Act.

(5) Rollover contribution. An amount is described in this paragraph as a rollover contribution if it meets the requirements of subparagraphs (A) and (B).

(A) In general. Paragraph (2) shall not apply to any amount paid or distributed from a health savings account to the account beneficiary to the extent the amount received is paid into a health savings account for the benefit of such beneficiary not later than the 60th day after the day on which the beneficiary receives the payment or distribution.

(B) Limitation. This paragraph shall not apply to any amount described in subparagraph (A) received by an individual from a health savings account if, at any time during the 1-year period ending on the day of such receipt, such individual received any other amount described in subparagraph (A) from a health savings account which was not includible in the individual's gross income because of the application of this paragraph.

(6) Coordination with medical expense deduction. For purposes of determining the amount of the deduction under section 213, any payment or distribution out of a health savings account for qualified medical expenses shall not be treated as an expense paid for medical care.

(7) Transfer of account incident to divorce. The transfer of an individual's interest in a health savings account to an individual's spouse or former spouse under a divorce or separation instrument described in subparagraph (A) of section 71(b)(2) shall not be considered a taxable transfer made by such individual notwithstanding any other provision of this subtitle, and such interest shall, after such transfer, be treated as a health savings account with respect to which such spouse is the account beneficiary.

(8) Treatment after death of account beneficiary.

(A) Treatment if designated beneficiary is spouse. If the account beneficiary's surviving spouse acquires such beneficiary's interest in a health savings account by reason of being the designated beneficiary of such account at the death of the account beneficiary, such health savings account shall be treated as if the spouse were the account beneficiary.

(B) Other cases.

(i) In general. If, by reason of the death of the account beneficiary, any person acquires the account beneficiary's interest in a health savings account in a case to which subparagraph (A) does not apply—

(I) such account shall cease to be a health savings account as of the date of death, and

(II) an amount equal to the fair market value of the assets in such account on such date shall be includible if such person is not the estate of such beneficiary, in such person's gross income for the taxable year which includes such date, or if such person is the estate of such beneficiary, in such beneficiary's gross income for the last taxable year of such beneficiary.

(ii) Special rules.

(I) Reduction of inclusion for predeath expenses. The amount includible in gross income under clause (i) by any person (other than the estate) shall be reduced by the amount of qualified medical expenses which were incurred by the decedent before the date of the decedent's death and paid by such person within 1 year after such date.

(II) Deduction for estate taxes. An appropriate deduction shall be allowed under section 691(c) to any person (other than the decedent or the decedent's spouse) with respect to amounts included in gross income under clause (i) by such person.

(g) Cost-of-living adjustment.

(1) In general. Each dollar amount in subsections (b)(2) and (c)(2)(A) shall be increased by an amount equal to—

(A) such dollar amount, multiplied by

(B) the cost-of-living adjustment determined under section 1(f)(3) for the calendar year in which such taxable year begins determined by substituting for "calendar year 1992" in subparagraph (B) thereof—

(i) except as provided in clause (ii), "calendar year 1997", and

(ii) in the case of each dollar amount in subsection (c)(2)(A), "calendar year 2003".

In the case of adjustments made for any taxable year beginning after 2007, section 1(f)(4) shall be applied for purposes of this paragraph by substituting "March 31" for "August 31", and the Secretary shall publish the adjusted amounts under subsections (b)(2) and (c)(2)(A) for taxable years beginning in any calendar year no later than June 1 of the preceding calendar year.

(2) Rounding. If any increase under paragraph (1) is not a multiple of $50, such increase shall be rounded to the nearest multiple of $50.

(h) Reports.

The Secretary may require—

(1) the trustee of a health savings account to make such reports regarding such account to the Secretary and to the account beneficiary with respect to contributions, distributions, the return of excess contributions, and such other matters as the Secretary determines appropriate, and

(2) any person who provides an individual with a high deductible health plan to make such reports to the Secretary and to the account beneficiary with respect to such plan as the Secretary determines appropriate.

The reports required by this subsection shall be filed at such time and in such manner and furnished to such individuals at

Code Sec. 223(h)(2)

such time and in such manner as may be required by the Secretary.

In 2010, P.L. 111-148, Sec. 9003(a), added "Such term shall include an amount paid for medicine or a drug only if such medicine or drug is a prescribed drug (determined without regard to whether such drug is available without a prescription) or is insulin." in subpara. (d)(2)(A), effective for amounts paid with respect to tax. yrs. begin. after 12/31/2010.

—P.L. 111-148, Sec. 9004(a), substituted "20 percent" for "15 percent" in subpara. (f)(4)(A), effective for distributions made after 12/31/2010.

In 2006, P.L. 109-432, Sec. 302(b), deleted "and" at the end of clause (c)(1)(B)(i), substituted ", and" for the period at the end of clause (c)(1)(B)(ii), and added clause (c)(1)(B)(iii), effective 12/20/2006.

—P.L. 109-432, Sec. 303(a)(1), substituted "$2,250." for "the lesser of—" and all that follows in subpara. (b)(2)(A) . . . Sec. 303(a)(2), substituted "$4,500." for "the lesser of—" and all that follows in subpara. (b)(2)(B), effective for tax. yrs. begin. after 12/31/2006.

—P.L. 109-432, Sec. 303(b), substituted "subsection (b)(2)(B)" for "subsection (b)(2)(B)(ii)" in subclause (d)(1)(A)(ii)(I), effective for tax. yrs. begin. after 12/31/2006.

—P.L. 109-432, Sec. 304, added "In the case of adjustments made for any taxable year beginning after 2007, section 1(f)(4) shall be applied for purposes of this paragraph by substituting 'March 31' for 'August 31', and the Secretary shall publish the adjusted amounts under subsections (b)(2) and (c)(2)(A) for taxable years beginning in any calendar year no later than June 1 of the preceding calendar year" as a flush sentence at the end of para. (g)(1), enacted 12/20/2006.

—P.L. 109-432, Sec. 305(a), added para. (b)(8), effective for tax. yrs. begin. after 12/31/2006.

—P.L. 109-432, Sec. 307(b), deleted "and" at the end of subpara. (b)(4)(A), substituted ", and" for the period at the end of subpara. (b)(4)(B), and added subpara. (b)(4)(C), effective for tax. yrs. begin. after 12/31/2006.

In 2005, P.L. 109-135, Sec. 404(c), added ", determined without regard to subsections (b)(1), (b)(2), and (d)(1)(B) thereof" after "section 152" in subpara. (d)(2)(A), effective for tax. yrs. begin. after 12/31/2004 as if included in Sec. 207 of the Working Families Tax Relief Act of 2004, P.L. 108-311.

In 2003, P.L. 108-173, Sec. 1201(a), added Code Sec. 223, effective for tax. yrs. begin. after 12/31/2003.

Sec. 224. Cross reference.

• **Caution:** Code Sec. 224, following, was redesignated by P.L. 107-16, EGTRRA and P.L. 108-173. These provisions generally sunset for tax years beginning after 12/31/2012. For specific sunset provisions, see Sec. 901, P.L. 107-16 (as amended) reproduced in history notes for this Code Sec.

For deductions in respect of a decedent, see section 691.

In 2010, P.L. 111-312, Sec. 101(a)(1), substituted "December 31, 2012" for "December 31, 2010" both places it appeared in Sec. 901 of P.L. 107-16 [see below], effective as if included in the enactment of P.L. 107-16, EGTRRA, 6/7/2001.

In 2003, P.L. 108-173, Sec. 1201(a), redesignated Code Sec. 223 as Code Sec. 224, effective for tax. yrs. begin. after 12/31/2003.

In 2002, P.L. 107-358, Sec. 2, added subsec. (c) in Sec. 901 of P.L. 107-16 [see below], effective 12/17/2002.

In 2001, P.L. 107-16, Sec. 431(a), redesignated Code Sec. 222 as Code Sec. 223, effective for payments made in tax. yrs. begin. after 12/31/2001.

—P.L. 107-16, Sec. 901, of this Act [as amended by Sec. 2 of P.L. 107-358, and Sec. 101(a)(1) of P.L. 111-312, see above], reads as follows:

"SEC. 901. SUNSET OF PROVISIONS OF ACT.

"(a) In general. All provisions of, and amendments made by, this Act shall not apply—

"(1) to taxable, plan, or limitation years beginning after December 31, 2012, or

"(2) in the case of title V, to estates of decedents dying, gifts made, or generation skipping transfers, after December 31, 2012.

"(b) Application of certain laws. The Internal Revenue Code of 1986 and the Employee Retirement Income Security Act of 1974 shall be applied and administered to years, estates, gifts, and transfers described in subsection (a) as if the provisions and amendments described in subsection (a) had never been enacted.

"(c) Exception. Subsection (a) shall not apply to section 803 (relating to no federal income tax on restitution received by victims of the Nazi regime or their heirs or estates)."

In 1997, P.L. 105-34, Sec. 202(a), redesignated Code Sec. 221 as Code Sec. 222, effective for any qualified education loan (as defined in Code Sec. 221(e)(1) as added by this section) incurred on, before, or after 8/5/97, but only with respect to any loan interest payment due and paid after 12/31/97, and the portion of the 60-

Deductions

month period referred to in Code Sec. 221(d) (as added by this section) after 12/31/97.

In 1996, P.L. 104-191, Sec. 301(a), redesignated Code Sec. 220 as Code Sec. 221, effective for tax. yrs. begin. after 12/31/96.

In 1990, P.L. 101-508, Sec. 11802(e)(2), redesignated Code Sec. 221 as Code Sec. 220, effective 11/5/90 except as provided in Sec. 11821(b) of this Act, which reads as follows:

"(b) Savings provision.

"If

"(1) any provision amended or repealed by this part applied to—

"(A) any transaction occurring before the date of the enactment of this Act [11/5/90],

"(B) any property acquired before such date of enactment [11/5/90], or

"(C) any item of income, loss, deduction, or credit taken into account before such date of enactment [11/5/90], and

"(2) the treatment of such transaction, property, or item under such provision would (without regard to the amendments made by this part) affect liability for tax for periods ending after such date of enactment [11/5/90],

nothing in the amendments made by this part shall be construed to affect the treatment of such transaction, property, or item for purposes of determining liability for tax for periods ending after such date of enactment [11/5/90]."

In 1988, P.L. 100-647, Sec. 6007(a), redesignated Code Sec. 220 as Code Sec. 221, effective for tax. yrs. begin. after 12/31/86.

In 1986, P.L. 99-514, Sec. 135(b)(1), redesignated Code Sec. 223 as Code Sec. 220 . . . Sec. 301(b)(5)(A), amended Code Sec. 223 [before redesignation by Sec. 135(b)(1) of this Act, see above] effective for tax. yrs. begin. after 12/31/86. Prior to amendment, Code Sec. 223 read as follows:

"SEC. 223. CROSS REFERENCES.

"(1) For deduction for long-term capital gains in the case of a taxpayer other than a corporation, see section 1202.

"(2) For deductions in respect of a decedent, see section 691."

In 1981, P.L. 97-34, Sec. 103(a), redesignated Code Sec. 221 as Code Sec. 222, effective for tax. yrs. begin. after 12/31/81.

—P.L. 97-34, Sec. 125(a), redesignated Code Sec. 222 [as redesignated by Sec. 103(a) of this Act, see above] as Code Sec. 223, effective for tax. yrs. begin. after 12/31/80.

In 1976, P.L. 94-455, Sec. 1501(a), redesignated Code Sec. 220 as Code Sec. 221, effective for tax. yrs. begin. after 12/31/76.

In 1974, P.L. 93-406, Sec. 2002(a)(1), redesignated Code Sec. 219 as Code Sec. 220, effective for tax. yrs. begin. after 12/31/74.

In 1971, P.L. 92-178, Sec. 702(a), redesignated Code Sec. 218 as Code Sec. 219, effective for tax. yrs. end. after 12/31/71, but only with respect to political contributions, payment of which is made after 12/31/71.

In 1964, P.L. 88-272, Sec. 213(a)(1), redesignated Code Sec. 217 as Code Sec. 218, effective for expenses incurred after 12/31/63, in tax. yrs. end. after 12/31/63.

PART VIII.—SPECIAL DEDUCTIONS FOR CORPORATIONS

Sec.
241. Allowance of special deductions.
242. Repealed. [Partially tax-exempt interest.]
243. Dividends received by corporations.
244. Dividends received on certain preferred stock.
245. Dividends received from certain foreign corporations.
246. Rules applying to deductions for dividends received.
246A. Dividends received deduction reduced where portfolio stock is debt financed.
247. Dividends paid on certain preferred stock of public utilities.
248. Organizational expenditures.
249. Limitation on deduction of bond premium on repurchase.
250. Repealed. [Certain payments to the national railroad passenger corporation.]

In 1990, P.L. 101-508, Sec. 11801(b)(4), repealed item 250.
Prior to repeal, item 250 read as follows:
"250. Certain payments to the national railroad passenger corporation."

In 1984, P.L. 98-369, Sec. 51(b), added item 246A.

In 1976, P.L. 94-455, Sec. 1901(b)(1)(AA), repealed item 242.
Prior to repeal, item 242 read as follows:
"Sec. 242. Partially tax-exempt interest."

In 1970, P.L. 91-518, Sec. 901, added item 250.

In 1969, P.L. 91-172, Sec. 414, added item 249.

Deductions

Sec. 241. Allowance of special deductions.

In addition to the deductions provided in part VI (sec. 161 and following), there shall be allowed as deductions in computing taxable income the items specified in this part.

Sec. 242. Repealed.

In 1976, P.L. 94-455, Sec. 1901(a)(33), repealed Code Sec. 242, effective for tax. yrs. begin. after '76.

Prior to amendment, Code Sec. 242 read as follows:

"SEC. 242. PARTIALLY TAX-EXEMPT INTEREST.

"(a) Allowance of deduction.

"There shall be allowed to a corporation as a deduction the amount received as interest on obligations of the United States or on obligations of corporations organized under Act of Congress which are instrumentalities of the United States, but only if—

"(1) such interest is included in gross income; and

"(2) such interest is exempt from normal tax under the act authorizing the issuance of such obligations. No deduction shall be allowed under this section for purposes of any surtax imposed by this subtitle.

"(b) Cross reference.

"For reduction of deduction under subsection (a) on account of amortizable bond premium, see section 171."

In 1964, P.L. 88-272, added the last sentence of subsec. (a), effective for tax. yrs. begin. after '63.

Sec. 243. Dividends received by corporations.

(a) General rule.

In the case of a corporation, there shall be allowed as a deduction an amount equal to the following percentages of the amount received as dividends from a domestic corporation which is subject to taxation under this chapter:

(1) 70 percent, in the case of dividends other than dividends described in paragraph (2) or (3);

(2) 100 percent, in the case of dividends received by a small business investment company operating under the Small Business Investment Act of 1958 (15 U.S.C. 661 and following); and

(3) 100 percent, in the case of qualifying dividends (as defined in subsection (b)(1)).

(b) Qualifying dividends.

(1) In general. For purposes of this section, the term "qualifying dividend" means any dividend received by a corporation—

(A) if at the close of the day on which such dividend is received, such corporation is a member of the same affiliated group as the corporation distributing such dividend, and

(B) if—

(i) such dividend is distributed out of the earnings and profits of a taxable year of the distributing corporation which ends after December 31, 1963, for which an election under section 1562 was not in effect, and on each day of which the distributing corporation and the corporation receiving the dividend were members of such affiliated group, or

(ii) such dividend is paid by a corporation with respect to which an election under section 936 is in effect for the taxable year in which such dividend is paid.

(2) Affiliated group. For purposes of this subsection:

(A) In general. The term "affiliated group" has the meaning given such term by section 1504(a), except that for such purposes sections 1504(b)(2), 1504(b)(4), and 1504(c) shall not apply.

(B) Group must be consistent in foreign tax treatment. The requirements of paragraph (1)(A) shall not be treated as being met with respect to any dividend received by a corporation if, for any taxable year which includes the day on which such dividend is received—

(i) 1 or more members of the affiliated group referred to in paragraph (1)(A) choose to any extent to take the benefits of section 901, and

(ii) 1 or more other members of such group claim to any extent a deduction for taxes otherwise creditable under section 901.

(3) Special rule for groups which include life insurance companies.

(A) In general. In the case of an affiliated group which includes 1 or more insurance companies under section 801, no dividend by any member of such group shall be treated as a qualifying dividend unless an election under this paragraph is in effect for the taxable year in which the dividend is received. The preceding sentence shall not apply in the case of a dividend described in paragraph (1)(B)(ii).

(B) Effect of election. If an election under this paragraph is in effect with respect to any affiliated group—

(i) part II of subchapter B of chapter 6 (relating to certain controlled corporations) shall be applied with respect to the members of such group without regard to sections 1563(a)(4) and 1563(b)(2)(D), and

(ii) for purposes of this subsection, a distribution by any member of such group which is subject to tax under section 801 shall not be treated as a qualifying dividend if such distribution is out of earnings and profits for a taxable year for which an election under this paragraph is not effective and for which such distributing corporation was not a component member of a controlled group of corporations within the meaning of section 1563 solely by reason of section 1563(b)(2)(D).

(C) Election. An election under this paragraph shall be made by the common parent of the affiliated group and at such time and in such manner as the Secretary shall by regulations prescribe. Any such election shall be binding on all members of such group and may be revoked only with the consent of the Secretary.

(c) Retention of 80-percent dividends received deduction for dividends from 20-percent owned corporations.

(1) In general. In the case of any dividend received from a 20-percent owned corporation—

(A) subsection (a)(1) of this section, and

(B) subsections (a)(3) and (b)(2) of section 244, shall be applied by substituting "80 percent" for "70 percent".

(2) 20-percent owned corporation. For purposes of this section, the term "20-percent owned corporation" means any corporation if 20 percent or more of the stock of such corporation (by vote and value) is owned by the taxpayer. For purposes of the preceding sentence, stock described in section 1504(a)(4) shall not be taken into account.

(d) Special rules for certain distributions.

For purposes of subsection (a)—

(1) Any amount allowed as a deduction under section 591 (relating to deduction for dividends paid by mutual savings banks, etc.) shall not be treated as a dividend.

(2) A dividend received from a regulated investment company shall be subject to the limitations prescribed in section 854.

(3) Any dividend received from a real estate investment trust which, for the taxable year of the trust in which the dividend is paid, qualifies under part II of subchapter M (section 856 and following) shall not be treated as a dividend.

Code Sec. 243(d)(4) — Deductions

(4) Any dividend received which is described in section 244 (relating to dividends received on preferred stock of a public utility) shall not be treated as a dividend.

(e) Certain dividends from foreign corporations.

For purposes of subsection (a) and for purposes of section 245, any dividend from a foreign corporation from earnings and profits accumulated by a domestic corporation during a period with respect to which such domestic corporation was subject to taxation under this chapter (or corresponding provisions of prior law) shall be treated as a dividend from a domestic corporation which is subject to taxation under this chapter.

In 1996, P.L. 104-188, Sec. 1702(h)(4), added "of" after "In the case" in subpara. (b)(3)(A) . . . Sec. 1702(h)(8), amended para. (b)(2), effective for tax. yrs. begin. after 12/31/90, except as provided in Sec. 11814(c)(2) of P.L. 101-508, reproduced below.

Prior to amendment, para. (b)(2) read as follows:

"(2) Affiliated group. For purposes of this subsection, the term 'affiliated group' has the meaning given such term by section 1504(a), except that for such purposes sections 1504(b)(2), 1504(b)(4), and 1504(c) shall not apply."

In 1990, P.L. 101-508, Sec. 11814(a), amended subsec. (b), effective for tax. yrs. begin. after 12/31/90, except as provided in Sec. 11814(c)(2) of this Act, which reads as follows:

"(2) Treatment of old elections. For purposes of section 243(b)(3) of the Internal Revenue Code of 1986 (as amended by subsection (a)), any reference to an election under such section shall be treated as including a reference to an election under section 243(b) of such Code (as in effect on the day before the date of the enactment of this Act [11/5/90])."

Prior to amendment, subsec. (b) read as follows:
"(b) Qualifying dividends.

"(1) Definitions. For purposes of subsection (a)(3), the term 'qualifying dividends' means dividends received by a corporation which, at the close of the day the dividends are received, is a member of the same affiliated group of corporations (as defined in paragraph (5)) as the corporation distributing the dividends, if—

"(A) such affiliated group has made an election under paragraph (2) which is effective for the taxable years of its members which include such day, and either

"(B) such dividends are distributed out of earnings and profits of a taxable year of the distributing corporation ending after December 31, 1963—

"(i) on each day of which the distributing corporation and the corporation receiving the dividends were members of such affiliated group, and

"(ii) for which an election under section 1562 (relating to election of multiple surtax exemptions) is not effective, or

"(C) such dividends are paid by a corporation with respect to which an election under section 936 is in effect for the taxable year in which such dividends are paid.

"(2) Election. An election under this paragraph shall be made for an affiliated group by the common parent corporation, at such time and in such manner as the Secretary by regulations prescribes. Such election may not be made for an affiliated group for any taxable year of the common parent corporation for which an election under section 1562 is effective. Each corporation which is a member of such group at any time during its taxable year which includes the last day of such taxable year of the common parent corporation must consent to such election at such time and in such manner as the Secretary by regulations prescribes. An election under this paragraph shall be effective—

"(A) for the taxable year of each member of such affiliated group which includes the last day of the taxable year of the common parent corporation with respect to which the election is made, and

"(B) for the taxable year of each member of such affiliated group which ends after the last day of such taxable year of the common parent corporation but which does not include such date, unless the election is terminated under paragraph (4).

"(3) Effect of election. If an election by an affiliated group is effective with respect to a taxable year of the common parent corporation, then under regulations prescribed by the Secretary—

"(A) no member of such affiliated group may consent to an election under section 1562 for such taxable year,

"(B) the members of such affiliated group shall be treated as one taxpayer for purposes of making the election under section 901(a) (relating to allowance of foreign tax credit), and

"(C) the members of such affiliated group shall be limited to one—

"(i) minimum accumulated earnings credit under section 535(c)(2) or (3), and

"(ii) surtax exemption, and one amount under sections 6154(c)(2) and section 6655(e)(2), for purposes of estimated tax payment requirements under section 6154 and the addition to the tax under section 6655 for failure to pay estimated tax.

"(4) Termination. An election by an affiliated group under paragraph (2) shall terminate with respect to the taxable year of the common parent corporation and with respect to the taxable years of the members of such affiliated group which include the last day of such taxable year of the common parent corporation if—

"(A) Consent of members. Such affiliated group files a termination of such election (at such time and in such manner as the Secretary by regulations prescribes) with respect to such taxable year of the common parent corporation, and each corporation which is a member of such affiliated group at any time during its taxable year which includes the last day of such taxable year of the common parent corporation consents to such termination, or

"(B) Refusal by new member to consent. During such taxable year of the common parent corporation such affiliated group includes a member which—

"(i) was not a member of such group during such common parent corporation's immediately preceding taxable year, and

"(ii) such member files a statement that it does not consent to the election at such time and in such manner as the Secretary by regulations prescribes.

"(5) Definition of affiliated group. For purposes of this subsection, the term 'affiliated group' has the meaning assigned to it by section 1504(a), except that for such purposes sections 1504(b)(2), 1504(b)(4), and 1504(c) shall not apply.

"(6) Special rules for insurance companies. If an election under this subsection is effective for the taxable year of an insurance company subject to taxation under section 801—

"(A) part II of subchapter B of chapter 6 (relating to certain controlled corporations) shall be applied without regard to section 1563(a)(4) (relating to certain insurance companies) and section 1563(b)(2)(D) (relating to certain excluded members) with respect to such company and the other corporations which are members of the controlled group of corporations (as determined under section 1563 without regard to subsections (a)(4) and (b)(2)(D)) of which such company is a member, and

"(B) for purposes of paragraph (1), a distribution by such company out of earnings and profits of a taxable year for which an election under this subsection was not effective, and for which such company was not a component member of a controlled group of corporations within the meaning of section 1563 solely by reason of section 1563(b)(2)(D), shall not be a qualifying dividend."

In 1988, P.L. 100-647, Sec. 1010(f)(4), deleted "or 821" after "801" in para. (b)(6), effective for tax. yrs. begin. after 12/31/86.

—P.L. 100-647, Sec. 2004(i)(1), changed the effective date for amendments made by Sec. 10221(b) of P.L. 100-203 from Sec. 10221(e)(1) of P.L. 100-203 to Sec. 10221(e)(1) of P.L. 100-203. The changes made by Sec. 10221(b) of P.L. 100-203 are now effective for dividends received or accrued after 12/31/87 in tax. yrs. begin. after 12/31/87.

Prior to the amendments made by Sec. 2004(i)(1) of this Act, the changes made by Sec. 10221(b) of P.L. 100-203 were effective for tax. yrs. begin. after 12/31/87.

In 1987, P.L. 100-203, Sec. 10221(a)(1), substituted "70 percent" for "80 percent" in para. (a)(1) . . . Sec. 10221(b), redesignated subsecs. (c) and (d) as subsecs. (d) and (e) and added new subsec. (c), effective [as amended by Sec. 2004(i)(1) of P.L. 100-647, see above] for dividends received or accrued after 12/31/87, in tax. yrs. end. after 12/31/87.

In 1986, P.L. 99-514, Sec. 411(b)(2)(C)(iv), added "and" at the end of clause (b)(3)(C)(i), deleted clause (b)(3)(C)(ii) and redesignated clause (b)(3)(C)(iii) as clause (b)(3)(C)(ii), effective for costs paid or incurred after 12/31/86 in tax. yrs. end. after 12/31/86. Sec. 411(c)(2) of this Act provides:

"(2) Transition rule.—The amendments made by this section shall not apply with respect to intangible drilling and development costs incurred by United States companies pursuant to a minority interest in a license for Netherlands or United Kingdom North Sea development if such interest was acquired on or before December 31, 1985."

Prior to deletion, clause (b)(3)(C)(ii) read as follows:

"(ii) $400,000 limitation for certain exploration expenditures under section 617(h)(1), and"

—P.L. 99-514, Sec. 611(a)(1), substituted "80 percent" for "85 percent" in para. (a)(1), effective for dividends received or accrued after 12/31/86, in tax. yrs. end. after 12/31/86.

In 1984, P.L. 98-369, Sec. 211(b)(3)(A), deleted clause (b)(3)(C)(iii), added "and" at the end of clause (b)(3)(C)(ii), and redesignated clause (b)(3)(C)(iv) as clause (b)(3)(C)(iii) . . . Sec. 211(b)(3)(B), substituted "section 801" for "section 802" in para. (b)(6), effective for tax. yrs. begin. after 12/31/83.

Prior to deletion, clause (b)(3)(C)(iii) read as follows:

"(iii) $25,000 limitation on small business deduction of life insurance companies under sections 804(a)(3) and 809(d)(10), and"

In 1981, P.L. 97-34, Sec. 232(b), deleted "$150,000" from clause (b)(3)(C)(i), effective for tax. yrs. begin. after 12/31/81.

In 1976, P.L. 94-455, Sec. 1031(b)(2), amended subpara. (b)(3)(B), for tax. yrs. begin. after 12/31/75, except as provided in Sec. 1031(c)(2)-(4) of this Act, which reads as follows:

"(2) Exception for certain mining operations.—In the case of a domestic corporation or includible corporation in an affiliated group (as define in section 1504 of the Internal Revenue Code of 1954) which has as of October 1, 1975—

"(A) been engaged in the active conduct of the trade or business of the extraction of minerals (of a character with respect to which a deduction for depletion is allowable under section 613 of such Code) outside the United States or its possessions for less than 5 years preceding the date of enactment of this Act,

"(B) had deductions properly apportioned or allocated to its gross income from such trade or business in excess of such gross income in at least 2 taxable years,

"(C) 80 percent of its gross receipts are from the sale of such minerals, and

"(D) made commitments for substantial expansion of such mineral extraction activities,

the amendments made by this section shall apply to taxable years beginning after December 31, 1978. In the case of losses sustained in taxable years beginning before January 1, 1979, by any corporation to which this paragraph applies, the

Deductions   Code Sec. 244

provisions of section 904(f) of such Code shall be applied with respect to such losses under the principles of section 904(a)(1) of such Code as in effect before the enactment of this Act.

"(3) Exception for income from possessions.—In the case of gross income from sources within a possession of the United States (and the deductions properly apportioned or allocated thereto), the amendments made by this section shall apply to taxable years beginning after December 31, 1978. In the case of losses sustained in a possession of the United States in taxable years beginning before January 1, 1979, the provisions of section 904(f) of such Code shall be applied with respect to such losses under the principles of section 904(a)(1) of such Code as in effect before the enactment of this Act.

"(4) Carrybacks and carryovers in the case of mining operations and income from a possession.—In the case of a taxpayer to whom paragraph (2) or (3) of this subsection applies, section 904(e) of such Code shall apply except that 'January 1, 1979' shall be substituted for 'January 1, 1976' each place it appears therein. If such a taxpayer elects the overall limitation for a taxable year beginning before January 1, 1979, such section 904(e) shall be applied by substituting 'the January 1, of the last year for which such taxpayer is on the per-country limitation' for 'January 1, 1976' each place it appears therein."

Prior to amendment, subpara. (b)(3)(B) read as follows:

"(B) the member of such affiliated group shall be treated as one taxpayer for purposes of making the elections under section 901(a) (relating to allowance of foreign credit) and section 904(b)(1) (relating to election of overall limitation), and"

—P.L. 94-455, Sec. 1051(f)(1), added "either" at the end of subpara. (b)(1)(A), substituted ", or" for the period at the end of clause (b)(1)(B)(ii), and added subpara. (b)(1)(C), effective for tax. yrs. begin. after 12/31/75. Sec. 1051(i)(1) of this Act provided the following exception to the effective date:

"(i) Effective Date.

"(1) Except as provided by paragraph (2), the amendments made by this section shall apply to taxable years beginning after December 31, 1975, except that 'qualified possession source investment income' as defined in section 936(d)(2) of the Internal Revenue Code of 1954 shall include income from any source outside the United States if the taxpayer establishes to the satisfaction of the Secretary of the Treasury or his delegate that the income from such sources was earned before October 1, 1976."

—P.L. 94-455, Sec. 1051(f)(2), added "1504(b)(4)," after "1504(b)(2)" in para. (b)(5), effective for tax. yrs. begin. after 12/31/75. Sec. 1051(i)(1) provided exceptions to the effective date (see the note for subpara. (b)(1)(C)).

—P.L. 94-455, Sec. 1901(a)(34)(A), added "(15 U.S.C. 661 and following)" after "Small Business Act of 1958" in para. (a)(2), effective for tax. yrs. begin. after 12/31/76.

—P.L. 94-455, Sec. 1901(a)(34)(B), deleted "(except that in the case of a taxable year of a member beginning in 1963 and ending in 1964, if the election is effective for the taxable year of the common parent corporation which includes the last day of such taxable year of such member, such election shall be effective for such taxable year of such member, if such member consents to such election with respect to such taxable year)" following "with respect to which the election is made" in subpara. (b)(2)(A), effective for tax. yrs. begin. after 12/31/76.

—P.L. 94-455, Sec. 1901(b)(21)(A)(i), amended clause (b)(3)(C)(ii), deleted clause (b)(3)(C)(iii), and redesignated clauses (b)(3)(C)(iv) and (v) as (b)(3)(C)(iii) and (iv), effective for tax. yrs. begin. after 12/31/76.

Prior to amendment, clauses (b)(3)(C)(ii) and (iii) read as follows:

"(ii) $100,000 limitation for exploration expenditures under section 615(a) and (b),

"(iii) $400,000 limitation for exploration expenditures under sections 615(c)(1) and 617(h)(1),"

—P.L. 94-455, Sec. 1901(b)(1)(J)(ii), substituted "sections 804(a)(3)" for "sections 804(a)(4)" in clause (b)(3)(C)(iii), as redesignated by this Act, effective for tax. yrs. begin. after 12/31/76.

—P.L. 94-455, Sec. 1906(b)(3)(C)(ii), substituted "section 6154(c)(2)" for "sections 6154(c)(2) and (3)" and substituted "section 6655(e)(2)" for "sections 6655(e)(2) and (3)" in clause (b)(3)(C)(iv) as redesignated by this Act, effective for tax. yrs. begin. after 2/1/77.

—P.L. 94-455, Sec. 1906(b)(13)(A), substituted "Secretary" for "Secretary or his delegate" each time it appears in subsec. (b), effective for tax. yrs. begin. after 12/31/76.

In 1975, P.L. 94-12, Sec. 304(b), substituted "$150,000" for "$100,000" in clause (b)(3)(C)(i), effective for tax. yrs. begin. after 12/31/74.

In 1969, P.L. 91-172, Sec. 504(c)(1), substituted "sections 615(c)(1) and 617(h)(1)" for "section 615(c)(1)" in clause (b)(3)(C)(iii), effective for exploration expenditures paid or incurred after 12/31/69.

In 1968, P.L. 90-364, Sec. 103(e)(2), amended clause (b)(3)(C)(v), effective for tax. yrs. begin. after 12/31/67. For special provision on effective date, see Sec. 104 of the P. L., reproduced after Code Sec. 6425.

Prior to amendment, subpara. (b)(3)(C)(v) read as follows:

"(v) $100,000 exemption for purposes of estimated tax filing requirements under section 6016 and the addition to tax under section 6655 for failure to pay estimated tax."

In 1964, P.L. 88-272, Sec. 214(a), amended subsecs. (a)-(d), effective for dividends received in tax. yrs. end. after 12/31/63.

Prior to amendment, subsecs. (a)-(d) read as follows:

"(a) General rule.

"In the case of a corporation (other than a small business investment company operating under the Small Business Investment Act of 1958) there shall be allowed as a deduction an amount equal to 85 percent of the amount received as dividends (other than dividends described in paragraph (1) of section 244, relating to dividends on the preferred stock of a public utility) from a domestic corporation which is subject to taxation under this chapter.

"(b) Small business investment companies.

"In the case of a small business investment company operating under the Small Business Investment Act of 1958, there shall be allowed as a deduction an amount equal to 100 percent of the amount received as dividends (other than dividends described in paragraph (1) of section 244, relating to dividends on preferred stock of a public utility) from a domestic corporation which is subject to taxation under this chapter.

"(c) Special rules for certain distributions.

"For purposes of subsections (a) and (b)—

"(1) Any amount allowed as a deduction under section 591 (relating to deduction for dividends paid by mutual savings banks, etc.) shall not be treated as a dividend.

"(2) A dividend received from a regulated investment company shall be subject to the limitations prescribed in section 854.

"(3) Any dividend received from a real estate investment trust which, for the taxable year of the trust in which the dividend is paid, qualifies under part II of subchapter M (Sec. 856 and following) shall not be treated as a dividend.

"(d) Certain dividends from foreign corporations.

"For purposes of subsections (a) and (b) of this section and for purposes of section 245, any dividend from a foreign corporation from earnings and profits accumulated by a domestic corporation during a period with respect to which such domestic corporation was subject to taxation under this chapter (or corresponding provisions of prior law) shall be treated as a dividend from a domestic corporation which is subject to taxation under this chapter."

In 1960, P.L. 86-779, Sec. 10, added para. (c)(3), effective for tax. yrs. of real estate investment trusts begin. after 12/31/60.

—P.L. 86-779, Sec. 3(a), added subsec. (d), effective for dividends received after '59 in tax. yrs. end. after '59.

In 1958, P.L. 85-866, Sec. 57, substituted "In the case of a corporation (other than a small business investment company operating under the Small Business Investment Act of 1958)" for "In the case of a corporation" in subsec. (a), redesignated subsec. (b) as (c) and added new subsec. (b), and substituted "subsections (a) and (b)" for "subsection (a)" in subsec. (c), effective for tax. yrs. begin. after 9/2/58.

Sec. 244. Dividends received on certain preferred stock.
(a) General rule.

In the case of a corporation, there shall be allowed as a deduction an amount computed as follows:

(1) First determine the amount received as dividends on the preferred stock of a public utility which is subject to taxation under this chapter and with respect to which the deduction provided in section 247 for dividends paid is allowable.

(2) Then multiply the amount determined under paragraph (1) by the fraction—

(A) the numerator of which is 14 percent, and

(B) the denominator of which is that percentage which equals the highest rate of tax specified in section 11(b).

(3) Finally ascertain the amount which is 70 percent of the excess of—

(A) the amount determined under paragraph (1), over

(B) the amount determined under paragraph (2).

(b) Exception.

If the dividends described in subsection (a)(1) are qualifying dividends (as defined in section 243(b)(1), but determined without regard to section 243(d)(4)) —

(1) subsection (a) shall be applied separately to such qualifying dividends, and

(2) for purposes of subsection (a)(3), the percentage applicable to such qualifying dividends shall be 100 percent in lieu of 70 percent.

In 1988, P.L. 100-647, Sec. 2004(i)(2), substituted "243(d)(4)" for "243(c)(4)" in subsec. (b), effective for tax. yrs. begin. after 12/31/87.

In 1987, P.L. 100-203, Sec. 10221(a)(2), substituted "70 percent" for "80 percent", in paras. (a)(3) and (b)(2), effective for dividends received or accrued after 12/31/87, in tax. yrs. end. after 12/31/87.

In 1986, P.L. 99-514, Sec. 611(a)(2), substituted "80 percent" for "85 percent" in paras. (a)(3) and (b)(2), effective for dividends received or accrued after 12/31/86, in tax. yrs. begin. after 12/31/86.

In 1978, P.L. 95-600, Sec. 301(b)(3), substituted "the highest rate of tax specified in section 11(b)" for "the sum of the normal tax rate and surtax rate for the taxable year specified in section 11" in subpara. (a)(2)(B), effective for tax. yrs. begin. after 12/31/78.

In 1964, P.L. 88-272, Sec. 214(b)(1), designated existing provisions as subsec. (a), and added subsec. (b), effective for dividends received in tax. yrs. end. after 12/31/63.

Sec. 245. Dividends received from certain foreign corporations.

(a) Dividends from 10-percent owned foreign corporations.

(1) **In general.** In the case of dividends received by a corporation from a qualified 10-percent owned foreign corporation, there shall be allowed as a deduction an amount equal to the percent (specified in section 243 for the taxable year) of the U.S.-source portion of such dividends.

(2) **Qualified 10-percent owned foreign corporation.** For purposes of this subsection, the term "qualified 10-percent owned foreign corporation" means any foreign corporation (other than a passive foreign investment company) if at least 10 percent of the stock of such corporation (by vote and value) is owned by the taxpayer.

(3) **U.S.-source portion.** For purposes of this subsection, the U.S.-source portion of any dividend is an amount which bears the same ratio to such dividend as—

(A) the post-1986 undistributed U.S. earnings, bears to

(B) the total post-1986 undistributed earnings.

(4) **Post-1986 undistributed earnings.** For purposes of this subsection, the term "post-1986 undistributed earnings" has the meaning given to such term by section 902(c)(1).

(5) **Post-1986 undistributed U.S. earnings.** For purposes of this subsection, the term "post-1986 undistributed U.S. earnings" means the portion of the post-1986 undistributed earnings which is attributable to—

(A) income of the qualified 10-percent owned foreign corporation which is effectively connected with the conduct of a trade or business within the United States and subject to tax under this chapter, or

(B) any dividend received (directly or through a wholly owned foreign corporation) from a domestic corporation at least 80 percent of the stock of which (by vote and value) is owned (directly or through such wholly owned foreign corporation) by the qualified 10-percent owned foreign corporation.

(6) **Special rule.** If the 1st day on which the requirements of paragraph (2) are met with respect to any foreign corporation is in a taxable year of such corporation beginning after December 31, 1986, the post-1986 undistributed earnings and the post-1986 undistributed U.S. earnings of such corporation shall be determined by only taking into account periods beginning on and after the 1st day of the 1st taxable year in which such requirements are met.

(7) **Coordination with subsection (b).** Earnings and profits of any qualified 10-percent owned foreign corporation for any taxable year shall not be taken into account under this subsection if the deduction provided by subsection (b) would be allowable with respect to dividends paid out of such earnings and profits.

(8) **Disallowance of foreign tax credit.** No credit shall be allowed under section 901 for any taxes paid or accrued (or treated as paid or accrued) with respect to the United States-source portion of any dividend received by a corporation from a qualified 10-percent-owned foreign corporation.

(9) **Coordination with section 904.** For purposes of section 904, the U.S.-source portion of any dividend received by a corporation from a qualified 10-percent owned foreign corporation shall be treated as from sources in the United States.

(10) **Coordination with treaties.** If—

(A) any portion of a dividend received by a corporation from a qualified 10-percent-owned foreign corporation would be treated as from sources in the United States under paragraph (9),

(B) under a treaty obligation of the United States (applied without regard to this subsection), such portion would be treated as arising from sources outside the United States, and

(C) the taxpayer chooses the benefits of this paragraph, this subsection shall not apply to such dividend (but subsections (a), (b), and (c) of section 904 and sections 902, 907, and 960 shall be applied separately with respect to such portion of such dividend).

(11) **Coordination with section 1248.** For purposes of this subsection, the term "dividend" does not include any amount treated as a dividend under section 1248.

(b) Certain dividends received from wholly owned foreign subsidiaries.

(1) **In general.** In the case of dividends described in paragraph (2) received from a foreign corporation by a domestic corporation which, for its taxable year in which such dividends are received, owns (directly or indirectly) all of the outstanding stock of such foreign corporation, there shall be allowed as a deduction (in lieu of the deduction provided by subsection (a)) an amount equal to 100 percent of such dividends.

(2) **Eligible dividends.** Paragraph (1) shall apply only to dividends which are paid out of the earnings and profits of a foreign corporation for a taxable year during which—

(A) all of its outstanding stock is owned (directly or indirectly) by the domestic corporation to which such dividends are paid; and

(B) all of its gross income from all sources is effectively connected with the conduct of a trade or business within the United States.

(3) **Exception.** Paragraph (1) shall not apply to any dividends if an election under section 1562 is effective for either—

(A) the taxable year of the domestic corporation in which such dividends are received, or

(B) the taxable year of the foreign corporation out of the earnings and profits of which such dividends are paid.

(c) Certain dividends received from FSC.

(1) **In general.** In the case of a domestic corporation, there shall be allowed as a deduction an amount equal to—

(A) 100 percent of any dividend received from another corporation which is distributed out of earnings and profits attributable to foreign trade income for a period during which such other corporation was a FSC, and

(B) 70 percent (80 percent in the case of dividends from a 20-percent owned corporation as defined in section 243(c)(2)) of any dividend received from another corporation which is distributed out of earnings and profits attributable to effectively connected income received or accrued by such other corporation while such other corporation was a FSC.

(2) **Exception for certain dividends.** Paragraph (1) shall not apply to any dividend which is distributed out of earnings and profits attributable to foreign trade income which—

(A) is section 923(a)(2) nonexempt income (within the meaning of section 927(d)(6)), or

(B) would not, but for section 923(a)(4), be treated as exempt foreign trade income.

(3) No deduction under subsection (a) or (b). No deduction shall be allowable under subsection (a) or (b) with respect to any dividend which is distributed out of earnings and profits of a corporation accumulated while such corporation was a FSC.

(4) Definitions. For purposes of this subsection—

(A) Foreign trade income; exempt foreign trade income. The terms "foreign trade income" and "exempt foreign trade income" have the respective meanings given such terms by section 923.

(B) Effectively connected income. The term "effectively connected income" means any income which is effectively connected (or treated as effectively connected) with the conduct of a trade or business in the United States and is subject to tax under this chapter. Such term shall not include any foreign trade income.

(C) FSC. The term "FSC" has the meaning given such term by section 922.

(5) References to prior law. Any reference in this subsection to section 922, 923, or 927 shall be treated as a reference to such section as in effect before its repeal by the FSC Repeal and Extraterritorial Income Exclusion Act of 2000.

In 2007, P.L. 110-172, Sec. 11(g)(3), added subpara. (c)(4)(C) . . . Sec. 11(g)(4), added para. (c)(5), enacted 12/29/2007.

—P.L. 108-357, Sec. 413(c)(3), deleted "foreign personal holding company or" after "other than a" in para. (a)(2), effective for tax. yrs. of foreign corporations begin. after 12/31/2004, and for tax. yrs. of United States shareholders with or within which such tax. yrs. of foreign corporations end.

In 1988, P.L. 100-647, Sec. 1006(b)(1)(A), provides:

"(1) In the case of dividends received or accrued during 1987—

"(A) subparagraph (B) of section 245(c)(1) of the 1986 Code shall be applied by substituting '80 percent' for the percentage specified therein, and"

—P.L. 100-647, Sec. 1006(e)(16), deleted subsec. (d), effective as provided in Sec. 633(a)(3) of P.L. 99-514, reproduced in note following Code Sec. 311.

Prior to deletion, subsec. (d) read as follows:

"(d) Property distributions. For purposes of this section, the amount of any distribution of property other than money shall be the amount determined by applying section 301(b)(1)(B)."

—P.L. 100-647, Sec. 1012(l)(2)(A), amended para. (a)(8) . . . Sec. 1012(l)(2)(B), added para. (a)(10) . . . Sec. 1012(l)(3), added para. (a)(11), effective for distributions out of earnings and profits for tax. yrs. begin. after 12/31/87.

Prior to amendment, para. (a)(8) read as follows:

"(8) Coordination with section 902. In the case of a dividend received by a corporation from a qualified 10-percent owned foreign corporation, no credit shall be allowed under section 901 for any taxes treated as paid under section 902 with respect to the U.S. source portion of such dividend."

—P.L. 100-647, Sec. 1012(bb)(9)(A), amended subsec. (c), effective for transactions after 12/31/84, in tax. yrs. end. after 12/31/84.

Prior to amendment, subsec. (c) read as follows:

"(c) Certain dividends received from FSC.

"(1) In general. In the case of a domestic corporation, there shall be allowed as a deduction an amount equal to—

"(A) 100 percent of any dividend received by such corporation from another corporation which is distributed out of earnings and profits attributable to foreign trade income for a period during which such corporation was a FSC, and

"(B) 70 percent (80 percent in the case of dividends from a 20-percent owned corporation as defined in section 243(c)(2)) of any dividend received by such corporation from another corporation which is distributed out of earnings and profits attributable to qualified interest and carrying charges received or accrued by such other corporation while such other corporation was a FSC.

The deduction allowable under the preceding sentence with respect to any dividend shall be in lieu of any deduction allowable under subsection (a) or (b) with respect to such dividend.

"(2) Exception for certain dividends. Paragraph (1) shall not apply to any dividend which is distributed out of earnings and profits attributable to foreign trade income which—

"(A) is section 923(a)(2) non-exempt income (within the meaning of section 927(d)(6)), or

"(B) would not, but for section 923(a)(4), be treated as exempt foreign trade income.

"(3) Coordination with subsections (a) and (b). The gross income giving rise to the earnings and profits described in subparagraph (A) or (B) of paragraph (1) (and not described in paragraph (2)) shall not be taken into account under subsections (a) and (b).

"(4) Definitions. For purposes of this subsection, the terms 'foreign trade income' and 'exempt foreign trade income' have the meaning given such terms by section 923. For purposes of this subsection, the term 'qualified interest and carrying charges' means any interest or carrying charges (as defined in section 927(d)(1)) derived from a transaction which results in foreign trade income."

In 1987, P.L. 100-203, Sec. 10221(d)(1), substituted "70 percent (80 percent in the case of dividends from a 20-percent owned corporation as defined in section 243(c)(2))" for "85 percent" in subpara. (c)(1)(B), effective for dividends received or accrued after 12/31/87, in tax. yrs. end. after 12/31/87.

In 1986, P.L. 99-514, Sec. 1226(a), amended subsec. (a), effective for distributions out of earnings and profits for tax. yrs. begin. after 12/31/86.

Prior to amendment, subsec. (a) read as follows:

"(a) General rule.

"In the case of dividends received from a foreign corporation (other than a foreign personal holding company) which is subject to taxation under this chapter, if, for an uninterrupted period of not less than 36 months ending with the close of such foreign corporation's taxable year in which such dividends are paid (or, if the corporation has not been in existence for 36 months at the close of such taxable year, for the period the foreign corporation has been in existence as of the close of such taxable year) such foreign corporation has been engaged in trade or business within the United States and if 50 percent or more of the gross income of such corporation from all sources for such period is effectively connected with the conduct of a trade or business within the United States, there shall be allowed as a deduction in the case of a corporation—

"(1) An amount equal to the percent (specified in section 243 for the taxable year) of the dividends received out of its earnings and profits specified in paragraph (2) of the first sentence of section 316(a), but such amount shall not exceed an amount which bears the same ratio to such percent of such dividends received out of such earnings and profits as the gross income of such foreign corporation for the taxable year which is effectively connected with the conduct of a trade or business within the United States bears to its gross income from all sources for such taxable year, and

"(2) An amount equal to the percent (specified in section 243 for the taxable year) of the dividends received out of that part of its earnings and profits specified in paragraph (1) of the first sentence of section 316(a) accumulated after the beginning of such uninterrupted period, but such amount shall not exceed an amount which bears the same ratio to such percent of such dividends received out of such accumulated earnings and profits as the gross income of such foreign corporation, which is effectively connected with the conduct of a trade or business within the United States, for the portion of such uninterrupted period ending at the beginning of such taxable year bears to its gross income from all sources for such portion of such uninterrupted period.

For purposes of this subsection, the gross income of the foreign corporation for any period before the first taxable year beginning after December 31, 1966, which is effectively connected with the conduct of a trade or business within the United States is an amount equal to the gross income for such period from sources within the United States. For purposes of paragraph (2), there shall not be taken into account any taxable year within such uninterrupted period if, with respect to dividends paid out of the earnings and profits of such year, the deduction provided by subsection (b) would be allowable."

—P.L. 99-514, Sec. 1876(d)(1)(A), amended para. (c)(1) . . . Sec. 1876(d)(1)(B), added the last sentence to para. (c)(3) [sic (c)(4)] . . . Sec. 1876(j), redesignated para. (c)(3) as para. (c)(4), and added new para. (c)(3), effective for transactions after 12/31/84, in tax. yrs. end. after 12/31/84.

Prior to amendment, para. (c)(1) read as follows:

"(1) In general. In the case of a domestic corporation, there shall be allowed as a deduction an amount equal to 100 percent of any dividend received by such corporation from another corporation which is distributed out of earnings and profits attributable to foreign trade income for a period during which such other corporation was a FSC. The deduction allowable under the preceding sentence with respect to any dividend shall be in lieu of any deduction allowable under subsection (a) or (b) with respect to such dividend."

In 1984, P.L. 98-369, Sec. 801(b)(1), redesignated subsec. (c) as subsec. (d), and added new subsec. (c) . . . Sec. 801(b)(2)(B), substituted "this section" for "subsections (a) and (b)" in subsec. (d), as redesignated by Sec. 801(b)(1), effective for transactions after 12/31/84, in tax. yrs. end. after 12/31/84.

In 1966, P.L. 89-809, Sec. 104(d), substituted "and if 50 percent or more of the gross income of such corporation from all sources for such period is effectively connected with the conduct of a trade or business within the United States" for "and has derived 50 percent or more of its gross income from sources within the United States" in the material preceding para. (a)(1), substituted "which is effectively connected with the conduct of a trade or business within the United States" for "from sources within the United States" in para. (a)(1), substituted ", which is effectively connected with the conduct of a trade or business within the United States" for "from sources within the United States" in para. (a)(2), and added the sentence at the end of subsec. (a) . . . Sec. 104(e)(1), redesignated subsec. (b) as subsec. (c) and added new subsec. (b) . . . Sec. 104(e)(2), added the sentence at the end of subsec. (a) . . . Sec. 104(e)(3), substituted "subsections (a) and (b)" for "subsection (a)" in subsec. (c) [as redesignated], effective for tax. yrs. begin. after 12/31/66.

In 1962, P.L. 87-834, designated existing provisions as subsec. (a), and added subsec. (b), effective for distributions made after 12/31/62.

Sec. 246. Rules applying to deductions for dividends received.

(a) Deduction not allowed for dividends from certain corporations.

(1) In general. The deductions allowed by sections 243, 244, and 245 shall not apply to any dividend from a corporation which, for the taxable year of the corporation in which the distribution is made, or for the next preceding taxable year of the corporation, is a corporation exempt from tax under section 501 (relating to certain charitable, etc., organizations) or section 521 (relating to farmers' cooperative associations).

(2) Subsection not to apply to certain dividends of federal home loan banks.

(A) Dividends out of current earnings and profits. In the case of any dividend paid by any FHLB out of earnings and profits of the FHLB for the taxable year in which such dividend was paid, paragraph (1) shall not apply to that portion of such dividend which bears the same ratio to the total dividend as—

(i) the dividends received by the FHLB from the FHLMC during such taxable year, bears to

(ii) the total earnings and profits of the FHLB for such taxable year.

(B) Dividends out of accumulated earnings and profits. In the case of any dividend which is paid out of any accumulated earnings and profits of any FHLB, paragraph (1) shall not apply to that portion of the dividend which bears the same ratio to the total dividend as —

(i) the amount of dividends received by such FHLB from the FHLMC which are out of earnings and profits of the FHLMC—

(I) for taxable years ending after December 31, 1984, and

(II) which were not previously treated as distributed under subparagraph (A) or this subparagraph, bears to

(ii) the total accumulated earnings and profits of the FHLB as of the time such dividend is paid.

For purposes of clause (ii), the accumulated earnings and profits of the FHLB as of January 1, 1985, shall be treated as equal to its retained earnings as of such date.

(C) Coordination with section 243. To the extent that paragraph (1) does not apply to any dividend by reason of subparagraph (A) or (B) of this paragraph, the requirement contained in section 243(a) that the corporation paying the dividend be subject to taxation under this chapter shall not apply.

(D) Definitions. For purposes of this paragraph—

(i) FHLB. The term "FHLB" means any Federal Home Loan Bank.

(ii) FHLMC. The term "FHLMC" means the Federal Home Loan Mortgage Corporation.

(iii) Taxable year of FHLB. The taxable year of an FHLB shall, except as provided in regulations prescribed by the Secretary, be treated as the calendar year.

(iv) Earnings and profits. The earnings and profits of any FHLB for any taxable year shall be treated as equal to the sum of—

(I) any dividends received by the FHLB from the FHLMC during such taxable year, and

(II) the total earnings and profits (determined without regard to dividends described in subclause (I)) of the FHLB as reported in its annual financial statement prepared in accordance with section 20 of the Federal Home Loan Bank Act (12 U.S.C. 1440).

(b) Limitation on aggregate amount of deductions.

(1) General rule. Except as provided in paragraph (2), the aggregate amount of the deductions allowed by sections 243(a)(1), 244(a), and subsection (a) or (b) of section 245 shall not exceed the percentage determined under paragraph (3) of the taxable income computed without regard to the deductions allowed by sections 172, 199, 243(a)(1), 244(a), subsection (a) or (b) of section 245, and 247, without regard to any adjustment under section 1059, and without regard to any capital loss carryback to the taxable year under section 1212(a)(1).

(2) Effect of net operating loss. Paragraph (1) shall not apply for any taxable year for which there is a net operating loss (as determined under section 172).

(3) Special rules. The provisions of paragraph (1) shall be applied—

(A) first separately with respect to dividends from 20-percent owned corporations (as defined in section 243(c)(2)) and the percentage determined under this paragraph shall be 80 percent, and

(B) then separately with respect to dividends not from 20-percent owned corporations and the percentage determined under this paragraph shall be 70 percent and the taxable income shall be reduced by the aggregate amount of dividends from 20-percent owned corporations (as so defined).

(c) Exclusion of certain dividends.

(1) In general. No deduction shall be allowed under section 243, 244, or 245, in respect of any dividend on any share of stock—

(A) which is held by the taxpayer for 45 days or less during the 91-day period beginning on the date which is 45 days before the date on which such share becomes ex-dividend with respect to such dividend, or

(B) to the extent that the taxpayer is under an obligation (whether pursuant to a short sale or otherwise) to make related payments with respect to positions in substantially similar or related property.

(2) 90-day rule in the case of certain preference dividends. In the case of stock having preference in dividends, if the taxpayer receives dividends with respect to such stock which are attributable to a period or periods aggregating in excess of 366 days, paragraph (1)(A) shall be applied—

(A) by substituting "90 days" for "45 days" each place it appears, and

(B) by substituting "181-day period" for "91-day period".

(3) Determination of holding periods. For purposes of this subsection, in determining the period for which the taxpayer has held any share of stock—

(A) the day of disposition, but not the day of acquisition, shall be taken into account, and

(B) paragraph (3) of section 1223 shall not apply.

(4) Holding period reduced for periods where risk of loss diminished. The holding periods determined for purposes of this subsection shall be appropriately reduced (in the manner provided in regulations prescribed by the Secretary) for any period (during such periods) in which—

(A) the taxpayer has an option to sell, is under a contractual obligation to sell, or has made (and not closed) a short sale of, substantially identical stock or securities,

Deductions Code Sec. 246

(B) the taxpayer is the grantor of an option to buy substantially identical stock or securities, or

(C) under regulations prescribed by the Secretary, a taxpayer has diminished his risk of loss by holding 1 or more other positions with respect to substantially similar or related property.

The preceding sentence shall not apply in the case of any qualified covered call (as defined in section 1092(c)(4) but without regard to the requirement that gain or loss with respect to the option not be ordinary income or loss), other than a qualified covered call option to which section 1092(f) applies.

(d) Dividends from a DISC or Former DISC.

No deduction shall be allowed under section 243 in respect of a dividend from a corporation which is a DISC or former DISC (as defined in section 992(a)) to the extent such dividend is paid out of the corporation's accumulated DISC income or previously taxed income, or is a deemed distribution pursuant to section 995(b)(1).

(e) Certain distributions to satisfy requirements.

No deduction shall be allowed under section 243(a) with respect to a dividend received pursuant to a distribution described in section 936(h)(4).

In 2005, P.L. 109-135, Sec. 402(a)(4), substituted "paragraph (3) of section 1223" for "paragraph (4) of section 1223" in subpara. (c)(3)(B), effective 8/8/2005 as if included in Sec. 1263 of the Energy Policy Act of 2005, P.L. 109-58. Sec. 402(m)(2) of this Act, reads as follows:

"(2) Repeal of Public Utility Holding Company Act of 1935. The amendments made by subsection (a) shall not apply with respect to any transaction ordered in compliance with the Public Utility Holding Company Act of 1935 before its repeal."

—P.L. 109-135, Sec. 403(a)(19), amended Sec. 102(e) of P.L. 108-357 [see below].

Prior to amendment, Sec. 102(e) of P.L. 108-357 [see below] read as follows:

"(e) Effective date. The amendments made by this section shall apply to taxable years beginning after December 31, 2004."

In 2004, P.L. 108-357, Sec. 102(d)(4), added "199," after "172," in para. (b)(1), effective as provided by Sec. 102(e) of this Act [as amended by Sec. 403(a)(19) of P.L. 109-135, see above], which reads as follows:

"(e) Effective date.

"(1) The amendments made by this section shall apply to taxable years beginning after December 31, 2004.

"(2) Application to pass-thru entities, etc. In determining the deduction under section 199 of the Internal Revenue Code of 1986 (as added by this section), items arising from a taxable year of a partnership, S corporation, estate, or trust beginning before January 1, 2005, shall not be taken into account for purposes of subsection (d)(1) of such section."

—P.L. 108-357, Sec. 888(d), added ", other than a qualified covered call option to which section 1092(f) applies" before the period at the end of subsec. (c), effective for positions established on or after 10/22/2004.

—P.L. 108-311, Sec. 406(f)(1), substituted "91-day period" for "90-day period" in subpara. (c)(1)(A) . . . Sec. 406(f)(2)(A), substituted "181-day period" for "180-day period" in subpara. (c)(2)(B) . . . Sec. 406(f)(2)(B), substituted "91-day period" for "90-day period" in subpara. (c)(2)(B), effective for dividends received or accrued after the 30th day after date of enactment of P.L. 105-34 [8/5/97] as if included in the amendments made by Sec. 1015 of such Act. For transitional rules, see Sec. 1015(c)(2) of P.L. 105-34, reproduced below.

In 1997, P.L. 105-34, Sec. 1015(a), amended subpara. (c)(1)(A) . . . Sec. 1015(b)(1), amended para. (c)(2) . . . Sec. 1015(b)(2), deleted "and" at the end of subpara. (c)(3)(A), deleted subpara. (c)(3)(B), and redesignated subpara. (c) (3)(C) as subpara. (c)(3)(B), effective for dividends received or accrued after the 30th day after date of enactment [8/5/1997]. For transitional rule, see Sec. 1015(c)(2) of this Act, which provides:

"(2) Transitional rule.—The amendments made by this section shall not apply to dividends received or accrued during the 2-year period beginning on the date of the enactment of this Act if—

"(A) the dividend is paid with respect to stock held by the taxpayer on June 8, 1997, and at all times thereafter until the dividend is received,

"(B) such stock is continuously subject to a position described in section 246(c)(4) of the Internal Revenue Code of 1986 on June 8, 1997, and all times thereafter until the dividend is received, and

"(C) such stock and position are clearly identified in the taxpayer's records within 30 days after the date of the enactment of this Act.

"Stock shall not be treated as meeting the requirement of subparagraph (B) if the position is sold, closed, or otherwise terminated and reestablished."

Prior to amendment, subpara. (c)(1)(A) read as follows:

"(A) which is held by the taxpayer for 45 days or less, or"

Prior to amendment, para. (c)(2) read as follows:

"(2) 90-day rule in the case of certain preference dividends. In the case of any stock having preference in dividends, the holding period specified in paragraph (1)(A) shall be 90 days in lieu of 45 days if the taxpayer receives dividends with respect to such stock which are attributable to a period or periods aggregating in excess of 366 days."

Prior to deletion, subpara. (c)(3)(B) read as follows:

"(B) there shall not be taken into account any day which is more than 45 days (or 90 days in the case of stock to which paragraph (2) applies) after the date on which such share becomes ex-dividend, and"

In 1996, P.L. 104-188, Sec. 1616(b)(4), deleted subsec. (f), effective for tax. yrs. begin. after 12/31/95.

Prior to deletion, subsec. (f) read as follows:

"(f) Cross reference. For special rule relating to mutual savings banks, etc., to which section 593 applies, see section 596."

In 1988, P.L. 100-647, Sec. 1018(u)(10), substituted "which" for "Which" in subpara. (c)(1)(A), effective for stock acquired after 3/1/86.

—P.L. 100-647, Sec. 2004(i)(1), changed the effective date for amendments made by Secs. 10221(c)(1)(A) and (B) of P.L. 100-203, from Sec. 10221(e)(1) of P.L. 100-203 to Sec. 10221(e)(2) of P.L. 100-203. The changes made by Secs. 10221(c)(1)(A) and (B) of P.L. 100-203 are now effective in tax. yrs. begin. after 12/31/87.

Prior to the amendments made by Sec. 2004(i)(1) of this Act, the changes made by Secs. 10221(c)(1)(A) and (B) of P.L. 100-203 were effective for dividends received or accrued after 12/31/87 in tax. yrs. end. after 12/31/87.

In 1987, P.L. 100-203, Sec. 10221(c)(1)(A), substituted "the percentage determined under paragraph (3)" for "80 percent" in para. (b)(1) . . . Sec. 10221(c)(1)(B), added para. (b)(3), effective for tax. yrs. begin. after 12/31/87 [as amended by Sec. 2004(i)(1) of P.L. 100-647 see above].

In 1986, P.L. 99-514, Sec. 611(a)(3), substituted "80 percent" for "85 percent" in para. (b)(1) . . . Sec. 1275(a)(2)(B), deleted "or 934(e)(3)" after "section 936(h)(4)" at the end of subsec. (e), effective for tax. yrs. begin. after 12/31/86.

—P.L. 99-514, Sec. 1804(b)(1)(A), amended subpara. (c)(1)(A) . . . Sec. 1804(b)(1)(B), substituted "determined for purposes of this subsection" for "determined under paragraph (3)" in para. (c)(4), effective for stock acquired after 3/1/86.

Prior to amendment, subpara. (c)(1)(A) read as follows:

"(A) which is sold or otherwise disposed of in any case in which the taxpayer has held such share for 45 days or less, or"

—P.L. 99-514, Sec. 1812(d)(1)(A)(i), substituted "In" for "For purposes of subparagraph (A), in" in the second sentence of subpara. (a)(2)(B) . . . Sec. 1812(d)(1)(A)(ii), amended clause (a)(2)(B)(i)(II) . . . Sec. 1812(d)(1)(B), redesignated subpara. (a)(2)(C) as subpara. (a)(2)(D) and added new subpara. (a)(2)(C) . . . Sec. 1812(d)(1)(C), added clause (a)(2)(D)(iv), effective 1/1/85 except as provided by Sec. 177(d)(2)-(7) of P.L. 98-369, reproduced below.

Prior to amendment, clause (a)(2)(B)(i)(II) read as follows:

"(II) which were not taken into account under subparagraph (A), bears to"

—P.L. 99-514, Sec. 1812(d)(2), amended Sec. 177(d)(4) of P.L. 98-369 [reproduced below], part of the effective date for changes made by Sec. 177 of P.L. 98-369, see below.

Prior to amendment, Sec. 177(d)(4) of P.L. 98-369 read as follows:

"(4) No accumulated earnings and profits on January 1, 1985. For purposes of the Internal Revenue Code of 1954, the accumulated profits of the Federal Home Loan Mortgage Corporation as of January 1, 1985, shall be treated as zero."

In 1984, P.L. 98-369, Sec. 53(b)(1), substituted "45" for "15" each place it appeared in subsec. (c) . . . Sec. 53(b)(2), added para. (c)(4) . . . Sec. 53(b)(3), amended subpara. (c)(1)(B) . . . Sec. 53(b)(4), deleted the last sentence of para. (c)(3), effective for stock acquired after 7/18/84 in tax. yrs. end. after 7/18/84.

Prior to amendment, subpara. (c)(1)(B) read as follows:

"(B) to the extent that the taxpayer is under an obligation (whether pursuant to a short sale or otherwise) to make corresponding payments with respect to substantially identical stock or securities."

Prior to deletion, the last sentence of para. (c)(3) read as follows:

"The holding periods determined under the preceding provisions of this paragraph shall be appropriately reduced (in the manner provided in regulations prescribed by the Secretary) for any period (during such holding periods) in which the taxpayer has an option to sell, is under a contractual obligation to sell, or has made (and not closed) a short sale of, substantially identical stock or securities."

—P.L. 98-369, Sec. 53(d)(2), substituted "without regard to any adjustment under section 1059, and without regard" for "and without regard", in para. (b)(1), effective for distributions after 3/1/84, in tax. yrs. end. after 3/1/84.

—P.L. 98-369, Sec. 177(b), amended subsec. (a), effective on 1/1/85. Sec. 177(d)(2) through (7) of this Act [as amended by Sec. 1812(d)(2) of P.L. 99-514, see above] provides:

"(2) Adjusted basis of assets.

"(A) In general. Except as otherwise provided in subparagraph (B), the adjusted basis of any asset of the Federal Home Loan Mortgage Corporation held on January 1, 1985, shall—

"(i) for purposes of determining any loss, be equal to the lesser of the adjusted basis of such asset or the fair market value of such asset as of such date, and

"(ii) for purposes of determining any gain, be equal to the higher of the adjusted basis of such asset or the fair market value of such asset as of such date.

"(B) Special rule for tangible depreciable property. In the case of any tangible property which—

"(i) is of a character subject to the allowance for depreciation provided by section 167 of the Internal Revenue Code of 1954, and

"(ii) is held by the Federal Home Loan Mortgage Corporation on January 1, 1985, the adjusted basis of such property shall be equal to the lesser of the basis of such property or the fair market value of such property as of such date.

"(3) Treatment of participation certificates.

"(A) In general. Paragraph (2) shall not apply to any right to receive income with respect to any mortgage pool participation certificate or other similar interest in any mortgage (not including any mortgage).

"(B) Treatment of certain sales after March 15, 1984, and before January 1, 1985. If any gain is realized on the sale or exchange of any right described in subparagraph (A) after March 15, 1984, and before January 1, 1985, the gain shall not be recognized when realized but shall be recognized on January 1, 1985.

"(4) Clarification of earnings and profits of federal home loan mortgage corporation.

"(A) Treatment of distribution of preferred stock, etc. For purposes of the Internal Revenue Code of 1954, the distribution of preferred stock by the Federal Home Loan Mortgage Corporation during December of 1984, and the other distributions of such stock by the Federal Home Loan Banks during January of 1985, shall be treated as if they were distributions of money equal to the fair market value of the stock on the date of the distribution by the Federal Home Loan Banks (and such stock shall be treated as if it were purchased with the money treated as so distributed). No deduction shall be allowed under section 243 of the Internal Revenue Code of 1954 with respect to any dividend paid by the Federal Home Loan Mortgage Corporation out of earnings and profits accumulated before January 1, 1985.

"(B) Section 246(a) not to apply to distributions out of earnings and profits accumulated during 1985. Subsection (a) of section 246 of the Internal Revenue Code of 1954 shall not apply to any dividend paid by the Federal Home Loan Mortgage Corporation during 1985 out of earnings and profits accumulated after December 31, 1984.

"(5) Adjusted basis. For purposes of this subsection, the adjusted basis of any asset shall be determined under part II of subchapter O of the Internal Revenue Code of 1954.

"(6) No carrybacks for years before 1985. No net operating loss, capital loss, or excess credit of the Federal Home Loan Mortgage Corporation for any taxable year beginning after December 31, 1984, shall be allowed as a carryback to any taxable year beginning before January 1, 1985.

"(7) No deduction allowed for interest on replacement obligations.

"(A) In general. The Federal Home Loan Mortgage Corporation shall not be allowed any deduction for interest accruing after December 31, 1984, on any replacement obligation.

"(B) Replacement obligation defined. For purposes of subparagraph (A), the term 'replacement obligation' means any obligation to any person created after March 15, 1984, which the Secretary of the Treasury or his delegate determines replaces any equity or debt interest of a Federal Home Loan Bank or any other person in the Federal Home Loan Mortgage Corporation existing on such date. The preceding sentence shall not apply to any obligation with respect to which the Federal Home Loan Mortgage Corporation establishes that there is no tax avoidance effect."

Prior to amendment, subsec. (a) read as follows:

"(a) Deduction not allowed for dividends from certain corporations.

"The deductions allowed by sections 243, 244, and 245 shall not apply to any dividend from a corporation which, for the taxable year of the corporation in which the distribution is made, or for the next preceding taxable year of the corporation, is a corporation exempt from tax under section 501 (relating to certain charitable, etc., organizations) or section 521 (relating to farmers' cooperative associations)."

—P.L. 98-369, Sec. 801(b)(2)(A), substituted "subsection (a) or (b) of section 245" for "245" each place it appeared in para. (b)(1), effective for transactions after 12/31/84, in tax. yrs. end. after 12/31/84.

In **1982**, P.L. 97-248, Sec. 213(c), redesignated subsec. (e) as subsec. (f) and added new subsec. (e), effective for tax. yrs. begin. after 12/31/82.

In **1976**, P.L. 94-455, Sec. 1051(f)(3), amended subsec. (a), effective for tax. yrs. begin. after 12/31/75. Sec. 1051(i)(1) of the Act provided exceptions to the effective date (see the note at Code Sec. 243).

Prior to amendment, subsec. (a) read as follows:

"(a) Deduction not allowed for dividends from certain corporations.

"The deductions allowed by sections 243, 244 and 245 shall not apply to any dividend from—

"(1) a corporation organized under the China Trade Act, 1922 (see Sec. 941); or

"(2) a corporation which, for the taxable year of the corporation in which the distribution is made, or for the next preceding taxable year of the corporation, is—

"(A) a corporation exempt from tax under section 501 (relating to certain charitable, etc., organizations) or section 521 (relating to farmers' cooperative associations); or

"(B) a corporation to which section 931 (relating to income from sources within possessions of the United States) applies."

—P.L. 94-455, Sec. 1906(b)(13)(A), substituted "Secretary" for "Secretary or his delegate" in Code Sec. 246, effective for tax. yrs. begin. after 12/31/76.

In **1971**, P.L. 92-178, Sec. 502(a), redesignated subsec. (d) as subsec. (e), and added new subsec. (d), effective for tax. yrs. end. after 12/31/71, except that a corporation may not be a DISC, for any tax. yr. begin. before 1/1/72.

In **1969**, P.L. 91-172, Sec. 434(b), added subsec. (d), effective for tax. yrs. begin. after 7/11/69.

—P.L. 91-172, Sec. 512(f)(3), added ", and without regard to any capital loss carryback to the taxable year under section 1212(a)(1)", after "and 247", effective for net capital losses sustained in tax. yr. end. after 12/31/69.

In **1964**, P.L. 88-272, Sec. 214(b)(2), substituted "243(a)(1), 244(a)" for "243(a), 244" each place it appeared in subsec. (b), effective for dividends received in tax. yrs. end. after 12/31/63.

In **1958**, P.L. 85-866, Sec. 57, substituted "243(a)" for "243" each place it appeared in para. (b)(1), effective for tax. yrs. begin. after 9/2/58

—P.L. 85-866, Sec. 18, added subsec. (c), effective for tax. yrs. end. after 12/31/57, but only with respect to shares of stock acquired or short sales made after 12/31/57.

Sec. 246A. Dividends received deduction reduced where portfolio stock is debt financed.

(a) General rule.

In the case of any dividend on debt-financed portfolio stock, there shall be substituted for the percentage which (but for this subsection) would be used in determining the amount of the deduction allowable under section 243, 244, or 245(a) a percentage equal to the product of—

(1) 70 percent (80 percent in the case of any dividend from a 20-percent owned corporation as defined in section 243(c)(2)), and

(2) 100 percent minus the average indebtedness percentage.

(b) Section not to apply to dividends for which 100 percent dividends received deduction allowable.

Subsection (a) shall not apply to—

(1) qualifying dividends (as defined in section 243(b) without regard to section 243(d)(4)), and

(2) dividends received by a small business investment company operating under the Small Business Investment Act of 1958.

(c) Debt financed portfolio stock.

For purposes of this section—

(1) In general. The term "debt financed portfolio stock" means any portfolio stock if at some time during the base period there is portfolio indebtedness with respect to such stock.

(2) Portfolio stock. The term "portfolio stock" means any stock of a corporation unless—

(A) as of the beginning of the ex-dividend date, the taxpayer owns stock of such corporation—

(i) possessing at least 50 percent of the total voting power of the stock of such corporation, and

(ii) having a value equal to at least 50 percent of the total value of the stock of such corporation, or

(B) as of the beginning of the ex-dividend date—

(i) the taxpayer owns stock of such corporation which would meet the requirements of subparagraph (A) if "20 percent" were substituted for "50 percent" each place it appears in such subparagraph, and

(ii) stock meeting the requirements of subparagraph (A) is owned by 5 or fewer corporate shareholders.

(3) Special rule for stock in a bank or bank holding company.

(A) In general. If, as of the beginning of the ex-dividend date, the taxpayer owns stock of any bank or bank holding company having a value equal to at least 80 percent of the total value of the stock of such bank or bank holding company, for purposes of paragraph (2)(A)(i), the taxpayer shall be treated as owning any stock of such bank or bank holding company which the taxpayer has an option to acquire.

(B) Definitions. For purposes of subparagraph (A)

(i) Bank. The term "bank" has the meaning given such term by section 581.

(ii) Bank holding company. The term "bank holding company" means a bank holding company (within the meaning of section 2(a) of the Bank Holding Company Act of 1956).

(4) Treatment of certain preferred stock. For purposes of determining whether the requirements of subparagraph (A) or (B) of paragraph (2) or of subparagraph (A) of paragraph (3) are met, stock described in section 1504(a)(4) shall not be taken into account.

(d) Average indebtedness percentage.

For purposes of this section—

(1) In general. Except as provided in paragraph (2), the term "average indebtedness percentage" means the percentage obtained by dividing—

(A) the average amount (determined under regulations prescribed by the Secretary) of the portfolio indebtedness with respect to the stock during the base period, by

(B) the average amount (determined under regulations prescribed by the Secretary) of the adjusted basis of the stock during the base period.

(2) Special rule where stock not held throughout base period. In the case of any stock which was not held by the taxpayer throughout the base period, paragraph (1) shall be applied as if the base period consisted only of that portion of the base period during which the stock was held by the taxpayer.

(3) Portfolio indebtedness.

(A) In general. The term "portfolio indebtedness" means any indebtedness directly attributable to investment in the portfolio stock.

(B) Certain amounts received from short sale treated as indebtedness. For purposes of subparagraph (A), any amount received from a short sale shall be treated as indebtedness for the period beginning on the day on which such amount is received and ending on the day the short sale is closed.

(4) Base period. The term "base period" means, with respect to any dividend, the shorter of—

(A) the period beginning on the ex-dividend date for the most recent previous dividend on the stock and ending on the day before the ex-dividend date for the dividend involved, or

(B) the 1-year period ending on the day before the ex-dividend date for the dividend involved.

(e) Reduction in dividends received deduction not to exceed allocable interest.

Under regulations prescribed by the Secretary, any reduction under this section in the amount allowable as a deduction under section 243, 244, or 245 with respect to any dividend shall not exceed the amount of any interest deduction (including any deductible short sale expense) allocable to such dividend.

(f) Regulations.

The regulations prescribed for purposes of this section under section 7701(f) shall include regulations providing for the disallowance of interest deductions or other appropriate treatment (in lieu of reducing the dividend received deduction) where the obligor of the indebtedness is a person other than the person receiving the dividend.

In **2004**, P.L. 108-311, Sec. 408(a)(9), substituted "section 243(d)(4)" for "section 243(c)(4)" in para. (b)(1), enacted 10/4/2004.

In **1988**, P.L. 100-647, Sec. 1012(1)(1), deleted the last sentence of subsec. (a), effective for distributions out of earnings and profits for tax. yrs. begin. after 12/31/86.

Prior to deletion the last sentence of subsec. (a) read as follows: "The preceding sentence shall be applied before any determination of a ratio under paragraph (1) or (2) of section 245(a).".

In **1987**, P.L. 100-203, Sec. 10221(d)(2), substituted "70 percent (80 percent in the case of any dividend from a 20-percent owned corporation as defined in section 243(c)(2))" for "80 percent" in para. (a)(1), effective for dividends received or accrued after 12/31/87, in tax. yrs. end. after 12/31/87.

In **1986**, P.L. 99-514, Sec. 611(a)(4), substituted "80 percent" for "85 percent" in para. (a)(1), effective for dividends received or accrued after 12/31/86, in tax. yrs. end. after 12/31/86.

—P.L. 99-514, Sec. 1804(a)(1), substituted "or 245(a)" for "or 245" in subsec. (a) . . . Sec. 1804(a)(2), added the last sentence to subsec. (a), effective for stock the holding period for which begins after 7/18/84 in tax. yrs. end. after 7/18/84.

In **1984**, P.L. 98-369, Sec. 51(a), added Code Sec. 246A, effective for stock the holding period for which begins after 7/18/84 in tax. yrs. ending after 7/18/84.

Sec. 247. Dividends paid on certain preferred stock of public utilities.

(a) Amount of deduction.

In the case of a public utility, there shall be allowed as a deduction an amount computed as follows:

(1) First determine the amount which is the lesser of—

(A) the amount of dividends paid during the taxable year on its preferred stock, or

(B) the taxable income for the taxable year (computed without the deduction allowed by this section).

(2) Then multiply the amount determined under paragraph (1) by the fraction—

(A) the numerator of which is 14 percent, and

(B) the denominator of which is that percentage which equals the highest rate of tax specified in section 11(b).

For purposes of the deduction provided in this section, the amount of dividends paid shall not include any amount distributed in the current taxable year with respect to dividends unpaid and accumulated in any taxable year ending before October 1, 1942. Amounts distributed in the current taxable year with respect to dividends unpaid and accumulated for a prior taxable year shall for purposes of this subsection be deemed to be distributed with respect to the earliest year or years for which there are dividends unpaid and accumulated.

(b) Definitions.

For purposes of this section and section 244—

(1) Public utility. The term "public utility" means a corporation engaged in the furnishing of telephone service or in the sale of electrical energy, gas, or water, if the rates for such furnishing or sale, as the case may be, have been established or approved by a State or political subdivision thereof or by an agency or instrumentality of the United States or by a public utility or public service commission or other similar body of the District of Columbia or of any State or political subdivision thereof.

(2) Preferred stock.

(A) In general. The term "preferred stock" means stock issued before October 1, 1942, which during the whole of the taxable year (or the part of the taxable year after its issue) was stock the dividends in respect of which were cumulative, limited to the same amount, and payable in preference to the payment of dividends on other stock.

(B) Certain stock issued on or after October 1, 1942. Stock issued on or after October 1, 1942, shall be deemed for purposes of this paragraph to have been issued before October 1, 1942, if it was issued to refund or replace bonds or debentures issued before October 1, 1942, or to refund or replace other preferred stock (including stock which is preferred stock by reason of this subparagraph or subparagraph (D)), but only to the extent that the par or stated value of the new stock does not exceed the par, stated, or face value of the bonds or debentures issued before October 1, 1942, or the other preferred stock, which such new stock is issued to refund or replace.

(C) Determination under regulations. The determination of whether stock was issued to refund or replace bonds or debentures issued before October 1, 1942, or to refund or replace other preferred stock, shall be made under regulations prescribed by the Secretary.

(D) Issuance of stock. For purposes of subparagraph (B), issuance of stock includes issuance either by the same or another corporation in a transaction which is a reorganization (as defined in section 368(a)) or a transaction subject to part VI of subchapter O as in effect before its repeal (relating to exchanges in SEC obedience orders), or the respectively corresponding provisions of the Internal Revenue Code of 1939.

In **2005**, P.L. 109-135, Sec. 402(a)(5), added "as in effect before its repeal" after "part VI of subchapter O" in subpara. (b)(2)(D), effective 8/8/2005 as if included in Sec. 1263 of the Energy Policy Act of 2005, P.L. 109-58. Sec. 402(m)(2) of this Act, provides:
"(2) Repeal of Public Utility Holding Company Act of 1935. The amendments made by subsection (a) shall not apply with respect to any transaction ordered in compliance with the Public Utility Holding Company Act of 1935 before its repeal."

In **1996**, P.L. 104-188, Sec. 1704(t)(49), amended Sec. 11801(c)(8)(C) of P.L. 101-508 by substituting "reorganizations" for "reorganization" in the material proposed to be stricken, see below.

In **1990**, P.L. 101-508, Sec. 11801(c)(8)(C), [as amended by Sec. 1704(t)(49) of P.L. 104-188, see above] deleted ", a transaction to which section 371 (relating to insolvency reorganizations) applies," after "(as defined in section 368(a))" in subpara. (b)(2)(D), effective 11/5/90 except as provided in Sec. 11821(b) of this Act, reproduced in note following Code Sec. 370.

In **1978**, P.L. 95-600, Sec. 301(b)(4), substituted "the highest rate of tax specified in section 11(b)" for "the sum of the normal tax rate and the surtax rate for the taxable year specified in section 11" in subpara. (a)(2)(B), effective for tax. yrs. begin. after 12/31/78.

In **1976**, P.L. 94-455, Sec. 1901(a)(35), amended para. (b)(2), effective for tax. yrs. begin. after 12/31/76.
Prior to amendment, para. (b)(2) read as follows:
"(2) Preferred stock. The term 'preferred stock' means stock issued before October 1, 1942, which during the whole of the taxable year (or the part of the taxable year after its issue) was stock the dividends in respect of which were cumulative, limited to the same amount, and payable in preference to the payment of dividends on other stock. Stock issued on or after October 1, 1942, shall be deemed for purposes of this paragraph to have been issued before October 1, 1942, if it was issued (including issuance either by the same or another corporation in a transaction which is a reorganization (as defined in section 368(a)), a transaction to which section 371 (relating to insolvency reorganizations) applies, or a transaction subject to part VI of subchapter O (relating to exchanges in SEC obedience orders), or the respectively corresponding provisions of the Internal Revenue Code of 1939 to refund or replace bonds or debentures issued before October 1, 1942, or to refund or replace other preferred stock (including stock which is preferred stock by reason of this sentence), but only to the extent that the par or stated value of the new stock does not exceed the par, stated, or face value of the bonds or debentures issued before October 1, 1942, or the other preferred stock, which such new stock is issued to refund or replace. The determination of whether stock was issued to refund or replace bonds or debentures issued before October 1, 1942, or to refund or replace other preferred stock, shall be made under regulations prescribed by the Secretary or his delegate."

Sec. 248. Organizational expenditures.
(a) Election to deduct.
If a corporation elects the application of this subsection (in accordance with regulations prescribed by the Secretary) with respect to any organizational expenditures—

(1) the corporation shall be allowed a deduction for the taxable year in which the corporation begins business in an amount equal to the lesser of—

(A) the amount of organizational expenditures with respect to the taxpayer, or

(B) $5,000, reduced (but not below zero) by the amount by which such organizational expenditures exceed $50,000, and

(2) the remainder of such organizational expenditures shall be allowed as a deduction ratably over the 180-month period beginning with the month in which the corporation begins business.

(b) Organizational expenditures defined.
The term "organizational expenditures" means any expenditure which—

(1) is incident to the creation of the corporation;

(2) is chargeable to capital account; and

(3) is of a character which, if expended incident to the creation of a corporation having a limited life, would be amortizable over such life.

(c) Time for and scope of election.
The election provided by subsection (a) may be made for any taxable year beginning after December 31, 1953, but only if made not later than the time prescribed by law for filing the return for such taxable year (including extensions thereof). The period so elected shall be adhered to in computing the taxable income of the corporation for the taxable year for which the election is made and all subsequent taxable years. The election shall apply only with respect to expenditures paid or incurred on or after August 16, 1954.

In **2004**, P.L. 108-357, Sec. 902(b), amended subsec. (a), effective for amounts paid or incurred after 10/22/2004.
Prior to amendment, subsec. (a) read as follows:
"(a) Election to amortize. The organizational expenditures of a corporation may, at the election of the corporation (made in accordance with regulations prescribed by the Secretary), be treated as deferred expenses. In computing taxable income, such deferred expenses shall be allowed as a deduction ratably over such period of not less than 60 months as may be selected by the corporation (beginning with the month in which the corporation begins business)."

In **1976**, P.L. 94-455, Sec. 1901(a)(36), substituted "August 16, 1954" for "the date of enactment of this title" in subsec. (c), effective for tax. yrs. begin. after 12/31/76.
—P.L. 94-455, Sec. 1906(b)(13)(A), substituted "Secretary" for "Secretary or his delegate" in subsec. (a), effective for tax. yrs. begin. after 12/31/76.

Sec. 249. Limitation on deduction of bond premium on repurchase.
(a) General rule.
No deduction shall be allowed to the issuing corporation for any premium paid or incurred upon the repurchase of a bond, debenture, note, or certificate or other evidence of indebtedness which is convertible into the stock of the issuing corporation, or a corporation in control of, or controlled by, the issuing corporation, to the extent the repurchase price exceeds an amount equal to the adjusted issue price plus a normal call premium on bonds or other evidences of indebtedness which are not convertible. The preceding sentence shall not apply to the extent that the corporation can demonstrate to the satisfaction of the Secretary that such excess is attributable to the cost of borrowing and is not attributable to the conversion feature.

(b) Special rules.
For purposes of subsection (a)—

(1) **Adjusted issue price.** The adjusted issue price is the issue price (as defined in sections 1273(b) and 1274) increased by any amount of discount deducted before repurchase, or, in the case of bonds or other evidences of indebtedness issued after February 28, 1913, decreased by any amount of premium included in gross income before repurchase by the issuing corporation.

(2) **Control.** The term "control" has the meaning assigned to such term by section 368(c).

In **1984**, P.L. 98-369, Sec. 42(a)(5), substituted "sections 1273(b) and 1274" for "section 1232(b)" in para. (b)(1), effective for tax. yrs. end. after 7/18/84.

In **1976**, P.L. 94-455, Sec. 1906(b)(13)(A), substituted "Secretary" for "Secretary or his delegate" in subsec. (a), effective for tax. yrs. begin. after 12/31/76.

In **1969**, P.L. 91-172, Sec. 414(a), added Code Sec. 249, effective for a convertible bond or other convertible evidence of indebtedness repurchased after 4/22/69, other than such a bond or other evidence of indebtedness repurchased pursuant to a binding obligation incurred on or before 4/22/69, to repurchase such bond or other evidence of indebtedness at a specified call premium, but no inference shall be drawn from the fact that section 249 of the Internal Revenue Code of 1954 does not apply to the repurchase of such convertible bond or other convertible evidence of indebtedness.

Deductions   Part IX

Sec. 250. Repealed.

In **1990**, P.L. 101-508, Sec. 11801(a)(15), repealed Code Sec. 250, effective 11/5/90, except as provided in Sec. 11821(b) of this Act which reads as follows:
"(b) Savings provision. If—
"(1) any provision amended or repealed by this part applied to—
"(A) any transaction occurring before the date of the enactment of this Act [11/5/90],
"(B) any property acquired before such date of enactment [11/5/90], or
"(C) any item of income, loss, deduction, or credit taken into account before such date of enactment [11/5/90], and
"(2) the treatment of such transaction, property, or item under such provision would (without regard to the amendments made by this part) affect liability for tax for periods ending after such date of enactment [11/5/90],
nothing in the amendments made by this part shall be construed to affect the treatment of such transaction, property, or item for purposes of determining liability for tax for periods ending after such date of enactment [11/5/90]."
Prior to repeal, Code Sec. 250 read as follows:
"SEC. 250. CERTAIN PAYMENTS TO THE NATIONAL RAILROAD PASSENGER CORPORATION.
"(a) General rule.
"If—
"(1) any corporation which is a rail carrier (as defined in section 10102(19) of title 49) makes a payment in cash, rail passenger equipment, or services to the National Railroad Passenger Corporation (hereinafter in this section referred to as the 'Passenger Corporation') pursuant to a contract entered into under section 401(a) of the Rail Passenger Service Act of 1970, and
"(2) no stock in the Passenger Corporation is issued at any time to such corporation in connection with any contract entered into under such section 401(a),
Then the amount of such payment shall (subject to subsection (c)) be allowed as a deduction for the taxable year in which it is made.
"(b) When payment is made.
"Under regulations prescribed by the Secretary, a payment in rail passenger equipment shall be treated as made when title to the equipment is transferred, and a payment in services shall be treated as made when the services are rendered.
"(c) Effect of certain subsequent acquisitions of stock.
"(1) Disallowance of deductions. If any deduction has been allowed under subsection (a) to a corporation and such corporation (or a successor corporation) acquires any stock in the Passenger Corporation (other than in a transaction described in section 374 or 381) before the close of the 36-month period which begins with the day on which the last payment is made to the Passenger Corporation pursuant to the contract entered into under such section 401(a), then such deduction shall be disallowed (as of the close of the taxable year for which it was allowed under subsection (a)).
"(2) Collection of deficiency. If any deduction is disallowed by reason of paragraph (1), then the periods of limitation provided in sections 6501 and 6502 on the making of an assessment and the collection by levy or a proceeding in court shall, with respect to any deficiency (including interest and additions to the tax) resulting from such a disallowance, include one year following the date on which the person acquiring the stock which results in the disallowance (in accordance with regulations prescribed by the Secretary) notifies the Secretary of such acquisition; and such assessment and collection may be made notwithstanding any provision of law or rule of law which otherwise would prevent such assessment and collection.
"(d) Members of controlled group.
"Under regulations prescribed by the Secretary, if a corporation is a member of a controlled group of corporations (within the meaning of section 1563), subsections (a)(2) and (c) shall be applied by treating all members of such controlled group as one corporation."
In **1982**, P.L. 97-261, Sec. 6(d)(3), substituted "10102(19)" for "10102(18)" in para. (a)(1), effective 11/19/82.
In **1980**, P.L. 96-454, Sec. 3(b)(1), substituted "10102(18)" for "10102(17)" in para. (a)(1), effective 10/15/80.
In **1978**, P.L. 95-473, Sec. 2(a)(2)(C), substituted "rail carrier (as defined in section 10102(17) of title 49)" for "common carrier by railroad (as defined in section 1(3) of the Interstate Commerce Act (49 U.S.C. 1(3))" in para. (a)(1), effective 10/17/78.
In **1976**, P.L. 94-455, Sec. 1906(b)(13)(A), substituted "Secretary" for "Secretary or his delegate" each place it appeared in Code Sec. 250, effective for tax. yrs. begin. after 12/31/76.
In **1970**, P.L. 91-518, Sec. 901, added Code Sec. 250, effective for tax. yrs. end. after 10/30/70.

PART IX.—ITEMS NOT DEDUCTIBLE

Sec.
261. General rule for disallowance of deductions.
262. Personal, living, and family expenses.
263. Capital expenditures.
263A. Capitalization and inclusion in inventory costs of certain expenses.
264. Certain amounts paid in connection with insurance contracts.
265. Expenses and interest relating to tax-exempt income.
266. Carrying charges.
267. Losses, expenses, and interest with respect to transactions between related taxpayers.
268. Sale of land with unharvested crop.
269. Acquisitions made to evade or avoid income tax.
269A. Personal service corporations formed or availed of to avoid or evade income tax.
269B. Stapled entities.
271. Debts owed by political parties, etc.
272. Disposal of coal or domestic iron ore.
273. Holders of life or terminable interest.
274. Disallowance of certain entertainment, etc., expenses.
275. Certain taxes.
276. Certain indirect contributions to political parties.
277. Deductions incurred by certain membership organizations in transactions with members.
279. Interest on indebtedness incurred by corporation to acquire stock or assets of another corporation.
280A. Disallowance of certain expenses in connection with business use of home, rental of vacation homes, etc.
280B. Demolition of structures.
280C. Certain expenses for which credits are allowable.
280E. Expenditures in connection with the illegal sale of drugs.
280F. Limitation on depreciation for luxury automobiles; limitation where certain property used for personal purposes.
280G. Golden parachute payments.
280H. Limitation on certain amounts paid to owner-employees by personal service corporations electing alternative taxable years.

In **1990**, P.L. 101-508, Sec. 11813(b)(13)(F), deleted "investment tax credit and" after "Limitation on", in item 280F.
In **1988**, P.L. 100-418, Sec. 1941(b)(4)(B), deleted item 280D.
Prior to deletion, item 280D read as follows:
"280D. Portion of chapter 45 taxes for which credit or refund is allowable under section 6429."
In **1987**, P.L. 100-203, Sec. 10206(c)(2), added item 280H.
In **1986**, P.L. 99-514, Sec. 803(c)(1), added item 263A and deleted items 278 and 280.
Prior to deletion, item 278 read as follows:
"278. Capital expenditures incurred in planting and developing groves; certain capital expenditures of farming syndicates."
Prior to deletion, item 280 read as follows:
"280. Certain expenditures incurred in production of films, books, records, or similar property."
In **1984**, P.L. 98-369, Sec. 67(d)(1), added item 280G . . . Sec. 136(b), added item 269B . . . Sec. 179(c), added item 280F . . . Sec. 1063(b)(2), deleted "certain historic" before "structures" in the item for Code Sec. 280B.
In **1983**, P.L. 97-414, Sec. 4(b)(2)(B), amended the item for Code Sec. 280C.
Prior to amendment, item 280C read as follows:
"280C. Portion of wages for which credit is claimed under section 44B."
In **1982**, P.L. 97-248, Sec. 250(b), added item 269A.
—P.L. 97-248, Sec. 351(b), added item 280E.
In **1980**, P.L. 96-499, Sec. 1131(d)(2), added item 280D.
In **1977**, P.L. 95-30, Sec. 202(c)(2), added the item for Code Sec. 280C.
In **1976**, P.L. 94-455, Sec. 210(b), added item 280.
—P.L. 94-455, Sec. 601(b), added item 280A.
—P.L. 94-455, Sec. 2124(b)(2), added item 280B.
In **1971**, added "and almond" to item 278.
In **1969**, P.L. 91-172, Sec. 213(c)(2), deleted item 270 which provided for limitation on deductions allowable to individuals in certain cases.
—P.L. 91-172, Sec. 121(b)(3), added item 277.
—P.L. 91-172, Sec. 216(b), added item 278.
—P.L. 91-172, Sec. 411(b), added item 279.
In **1965**, P.L. 89-368, Sec. 301, added item 276.
In **1964**, inserted "or domestic iron ore" in item 272, and added item 275.

In **1962,** added item 274.

Sec. 261. General rule for disallowance of deductions.

In computing taxable income no deduction shall in any case be allowed in respect of the items specified in this part.

Sec. 262. Personal, living, and family expenses.

(a) General rule.

Except as otherwise expressly provided in this chapter, no deduction shall be allowed for personal, living, or family expenses.

(b) Treatment of certain phone expenses.

For purposes of subsection (a), in the case of an individual, any charge (including taxes thereon) for basic local telephone service with respect to the 1st telephone line provided to any residence of the taxpayer shall be treated as a personal expense.

In **1988,** P.L. 100-647, Sec. 5073(a), amended Code Sec. 262, effective for tax. yrs. begin. after 12/31/88.
Prior to amendment, Code Sec. 262 read as follows:
"SEC. 262. PERSONAL, LIVING, AND FAMILY EXPENSES.
"Except as otherwise expressly provided in this chapter, no deduction shall be allowed for personal, living, or family expenses."

Sec. 263. Capital expenditures.

(a) General rule.

No deduction shall be allowed for—

(1) Any amount paid out for new buildings or for permanent improvements or betterments made to increase the value of any property or estate. This paragraph shall not apply to—

(A) expenditures for the development of mines or deposits deductible under section 616,

(B) research and experimental expenditures deductible under section 174,

(C) soil and water conservation expenditures deductible under section 175,

(D) expenditures by farmers for fertilizer, etc., deductible under section 180,

(E) expenditures for removal of architectural and transportation barriers to the handicapped and elderly which the taxpayer elects to deduct under section 190,

(F) expenditures for tertiary injectants with respect to which a deduction is allowed under section 193,

(G) expenditures for which a deduction is allowed under section 179,

(H) expenditures for which a deduction is allowed under section 179A,

(I) expenditures for which a deduction is allowed under section 179B,

(J) expenditures for which a deduction is allowed under section 179C,

(K) expenditures for which a deduction is allowed under section 179D, or

(L) expenditures for which a deduction is allowed under section 179E.

(2) Any amount expended in restoring property or in making good the exhaustion thereof for which an allowance is or has been made.

(b) Repealed.

(c) Intangible drilling and development costs in the case of oil and gas wells and geothermal wells.

Notwithstanding subsection (a), and except as provided in subsection (i), regulations shall be prescribed by the Secretary under this subtitle corresponding to the regulations which granted the option to deduct as expenses intangible drilling and development costs in the case of oil and gas wells and which were recognized and approved by the Congress in House Concurrent Resolution 50, Seventy-ninth Congress. Such regulations shall also grant the option to deduct as expenses intangible drilling and development costs in the case of wells drilled for any geothermal deposit (as defined in section 613(e)(2)) to the same extent and in the same manner as such expenses are deductible in the case of oil and gas wells. This subsection shall not apply with respect to any costs to which any deduction is allowed under section 59(e) or 291.

(d) Expenditures in connection with certain railroad rolling stock.

In the case of expenditures in connection with the rehabilitation of a unit of railroad rolling stock (except a locomotive) used by a domestic common carrier by railroad which would, but for this subsection, be properly chargeable to capital account, such expenditures, if during any 12-month period they do not exceed an amount equal to 20 percent of the basis of such unit in the hands of the taxpayer, shall, at the election of the taxpayer, be treated (notwithstanding subsection (a)) as deductible repairs under section 162 or 212. An election under this subsection shall be made for any taxable year at such time and in such manner as the Secretary prescribes by regulations. An election may not be made under this subsection for any taxable year to which an election under subsection (e) applies to railroad rolling stock (other than locomotives).

(e) Repealed.

(f) Railroad ties.

In the case of a domestic common carrier by rail (including a railroad switching or terminal company) which uses the retirement-replacement method of accounting for depreciation of its railroad track, expenditures for acquiring and installing replacement ties of any material (and fastenings related to such ties) shall be accorded the same tax accounting treatment as expenditures for replacement ties of wood (and fastenings related to such ties).

(g) Certain interest and carrying costs in the case of straddles.

(1) General rule. No deduction shall be allowed for interest and carrying charges properly allocable to personal property which is part of a straddle (as defined in section 1092(c)). Any amount not allowed as a deduction by reason of the preceding sentence shall be chargeable to the capital account with respect to the personal property to which such amount relates.

(2) Interest and carrying charges defined. For purposes of paragraph (1), the term "interest and carrying charges" means the excess of—

(A) the sum of—

(i) interest on indebtedness incurred or continued to purchase or carry the personal property, and

(ii) all other amounts (including charges to insure, store, or transport the personal property) paid or incurred to carry the personal property, over

(B) the sum of—

(i) the amount of interest (including original issue discount) includible in gross income for the taxable year with respect to the property described in subparagraph (A),

(ii) any amount treated as ordinary income under section 1271(a)(3)(A), 1276, or 1281(a) with respect to such property for the taxable year,

(iii) the excess of any dividends includible in gross income with respect to such property for the taxable year over the amount of any deduction allowable with respect to such dividends under section 243, 244, or 245, and

Limitations on deduction   **Code Sec. 263**

(iv) any amount which is a payment with respect to a security loan (within the meaning of section 512(a)(5)) includible in gross income with respect to such property for the taxable year.

For purposes of subparagraph (A), the term "interest" includes any amount paid or incurred in connection with personal property used in a short sale.

(3) Exception for hedging transactions. This subsection shall not apply in the case of any hedging transaction (as defined in section 1256(e)).

(4) Application with other provisions.

(A) Subsection (c). In the case of any short sale, this subsection shall be applied after subsection (h).

(B) Section 1277 or 1282. In the case of any obligation to which section 1277 or 1282 applies, this subsection shall be applied after section 1277 or 1282.

(h) Payments in lieu of dividends in connection with short sales.

(1) In general. If—

(A) a taxpayer makes any payment with respect to any stock used by such taxpayer in a short sale and such payment is in lieu of a dividend payment on such stock, and

(B) the closing of such short sale occurs on or before the 45th day after the date of such short sale,

then no deduction shall be allowed for such payment. The basis of the stock used to close the short sale shall be increased by the amount not allowed as a deduction by reason of the preceding sentence.

(2) Longer period in case of extraordinary dividends. If the payment described in paragraph (1)(A) is in respect of an extraordinary dividend, paragraph (1)(B) shall be applied by substituting "the day 1 year after the date of such short sale" for "the 45th day after the date of such short sale".

(3) Extraordinary dividend. For purposes of this subsection, the term "extraordinary dividend" has the meaning given to such term by section 1059(c); except that such section shall be applied by treating the amount realized by the taxpayer in the short sale as his adjusted basis in the stock.

(4) Special rule where risk of loss diminished. The running of any period of time applicable under paragraph (1)(B) (as modified by paragraph (2)) shall be suspended during any period in which—

(A) the taxpayer holds, has an option to buy, or is under a contractual obligation to buy, substantially identical stock or securities, or

(B) under regulations prescribed by the Secretary, a taxpayer has diminished his risk of loss by holding 1 or more other positions with respect to substantially similar or related property.

(5) Deduction allowable to extent of ordinary income from amounts paid by lending broker for use of collateral.

(A) In general. Paragraph (1) shall apply only to the extent that the payments or distributions with respect to any short sale exceed the amount which—

(i) is treated as ordinary income by the taxpayer, and

(ii) is received by the taxpayer as compensation for the use of any collateral with respect to any stock used in such short sale.

(B) Exception not to apply to extraordinary dividends. Subparagraph (A) shall not apply if one or more payments or distributions is in respect of an extraordinary dividend.

(6) Application of this subsection with subsection (g). In the case of any short sale, this subsection shall be applied before subsection (g).

(i) Special rules for intangible drilling and development costs incurred outside the United States.

In the case of intangible drilling and development costs paid or incurred with respect to an oil, gas, or geothermal well located outside the United States—

(1) subsection (c) shall not apply, and

(2) such costs shall—

(A) at the election of the taxpayer, be included in adjusted basis for purposes of computing the amount of any deduction allowable under section 611 (determined without regard to section 613), or

(B) if subparagraph (A) does not apply, be allowed as a deduction ratably over the 10-taxable year period beginning with the taxable year in which such costs were paid or incurred.

This subsection shall not apply to costs paid or incurred with respect to a nonproductive well.

In 2006, P.L. 109-432, Sec. 404(b)(1), deleted "or" at the end of subpara. (a)(1)(J), substituted ", or" for the period at the end of subpara. (a)(1)(K), and added subpara. (a)(1)(L), effective for costs paid or incurred after 12/20/2006.

In 2005, P.L. 109-58, Sec. 1323(b)(2), deleted "or" at the end of subpara. (a)(1)(H), substituted ", or" for the period at the end of subpara. (a)(1)(I), and added subpara. (a)(1)(J), effective for properties placed in service after 8/8/2005.

—P.L. 109-58, Sec. 1331(b)(4), deleted "or" at the end of subpara. (a)(1)(I) [as amended by Sec. 1323(b)(2) of this Act, see above], substituted ", or" for the period at the end of subpara. (a)(1)(J) [as added by Sec. 1323(b)(2) of this Act, see above], and added subpara. (a)(1)(K), effective for property placed in service after 12/31/2005.

In 2004, P.L. 108-357, Sec. 338(b)(1), deleted "or" at the end of subpara. (a)(1)(G), substituted ", or " for the period at the end of subpara. (a)(1)(H), and added subpara. (a)(1)(I), effective for expenses paid or incurred after 12/31/2002, in tax. yrs. end. after 12/31/2002.

—P.L. 108-311, Sec. 408(a)(10), substituted "1276" for "1278" in clause (g)(2)(B)(ii), enacted 10/4/2004.

In 1997, P.L. 105-34, Sec. 1604(a)(1), deleted "or" at the end of subpara. (a)(1)(F), substituted "; or" for the period at the end of subpara. (a)(1)(G), and added subpara. (a)(1)(H), effective for property placed in service after 6/30/93.

In 1990, P.L. 101-508, Sec. 11801(a)(16), repealed subsec. (b)... Sec. 11815(b)(3), substituted "section 613(e)(2)" for "section 613(e)(3)" in subsec. (c), effective 11/5/90 except as provided in Sec. 11821(b) of this Act, which reads as follows:

"(b) Savings provision.

"If—

"(1) any provision amended or repealed by this part applied to—

"(A) any transaction occurring before the date of the enactment of this Act [11/5/90],

"(B) any property acquired before such date of enactment [11/5/90], or

"(C) any item of income, loss, deduction, or credit taken into account before such date of enactment [11/5/90], and

"(2) the treatment of such transaction, property, or item under such provision would (without regard to the amendments made by this part) affect liability for tax for periods ending after such date of enactment [11/5/90], nothing in the amendments made by this part shall be construed to affect the treatment of such transaction, property, or item for purposes for determining liability for tax for periods ending after such date of enactment [11/5/90]."

Prior to repeal, subsec. (b) read as follows:

"(b) Expenditures for advertising and good will.

If a corporation has, for the purpose of computing its excess profits tax credit under chapter 2E or subchapter D of chapter 1 of the Internal Revenue Code of 1939 claimed the benefits of the election provided in section 733 or section 451 of such code, as the case may be, no deduction shall be allowable under section 162 to such corporation for expenditures for advertising or the promotion of good will which, under the rules and regulations prescribed under section 733 or section 451 of such code, as the case may be, may be regarded as capital investments."

In 1988, P.L. 100-647, Sec. 1007(g)(5), substituted "59(e)" for "59(d)" in subsec. (c), effective for tax. yrs. begin. after 12/31/86.

In 1986, P.L. 99-514, Sec. 402(b)(1), deleted subpara. (a)(1)(E) and redesignated subparas. (a)(1)(F), (G), and (H) as subparas. (a)(1)(E), (F), and (G), effective for amounts paid or incurred after 12/31/85, in tax. yrs. begin. after 12/31/85.

Prior to repeal, subpara. (a)(1)(E) read as follows:

"(E) expenditures by farmers for clearing land deductible under section 182,"

—P.L. 99-514, Sec. 411(b)(1)(A), added subsec. (i)... Sec. 411(b)(1)(B), added "and except as provided in subsection (i)," after "subsection (a)," in subsec. (c), effective for costs paid or incurred after 12/31/86, in tax. yrs. end. after 12/31/86. Sec. 411(c)(2) of this Act provides the following transitional rule:

1,727

"(2) Transition rule.—The amendments made by this section shall not apply with respect to intangible drilling and development costs incurred by United States companies pursuant to a minority interest in a license for Netherlands or United Kingdom North Sea development if such interest was acquired on or before December 31, 1985."

—P.L. 99-514, Sec. 701(e)(4)(D), substituted "59(d)" for "58(i)", in subsec. (c), effective for tax. yrs. begin. after 12/31/86.

—P.L. 99-514, Sec. 1808(b), deleted "and" at the end of clause (g)(2)(B)(ii), substituted ", and" for the period at the end of clause (g)(2)(B)(iii) and added clause (g)(2)(B)(iv), effective for positions established after 7/18/84, in tax. yrs. end. after 7/18/84. For special rules, see Sec. 102(g)-(i) of P.L. 98-369, reproduced in note following Code Sec. 1256.

In 1984, P.L. 98-369, Sec. 56(a), added subsec. (h), effective for short sales after 7/18/84 in tax. yrs. end. after 7/18/84.

—P.L. 98-369, Sec. 102(e)(7), amended para. (g)(2) . . . Sec. 102(e)(8), added new para. (g)(4), effective for positions established after 7/18/84, in tax. yrs. end. after 7/18/84. For special rules and elections see Sec. 102(g), (h) and (i) of this Act, reproduced in note following Code Sec. 1256.

Prior to amendment, para. (g)(2) read as follows:

"(2) Interest and carrying charges defined. For purposes of paragraph (l), the term 'interest and carrying charges' means the excess of—

"(A) the sum of—

"(i) interest on indebtedness incurred or continued to purchase or carry the personal property, and

"(ii) all other amounts (including charges for temporary use of the personal property in a short sale, or to insure, store, or transport the personal property) paid or incurred to carry the personal property, over

"(B) the sum of—

"(i) the amount of interest (including original issue discount) includible in gross income for the taxable year with respect to the property described in subparagraph (A), and

"(ii) any amount treated as ordinary income under section 1232(a)(3)(A) with respect to such property for the taxable year."

In 1983, P.L. 97-448, Sec. 105(b)(1), amended clause (g)(2)(A)(ii), effective for property acquired and positions established by the taxpayer after 9/22/82 in tax. yrs. end. after 9/22/82.

Prior to amendment, clause (g)(2)(A)(ii) read as follows:

"(ii) amounts paid or incurred to insure, store, or transport the personal property, over"

—P.L. 97-448, Sec. 306(a)(9)(A), substituted "section 1232(a)(3)(A)" for "section 1232(a)(4)(A)" in clause (g)(2)(B)(ii), effective 9/3/82.

In 1982, P.L. 97-248, Sec. 204(c)(1), added the last sentence to subsec. (c), effective for tax. yrs. begin. after 12/31/82. Sec. 204(d)(4) of this Act provides:

"(4) Drilling and mining costs.— Section 291(b) of such Code shall apply to expenditures after December 31, 1982, in taxable years ending after such date."

In 1981, P.L. 97-34, Sec. 201(c), repealed subsec. (e) . . . Sec. 202(d)(1), deleted "or" at the end of subpara (a)(1)(F), substituted "; or" for the period at the end of subpara. (a)(1)(G), and added subpara. (a)(1)(H), effective for property placed in service after 12/31/80 in tax. yrs. end. after 12/31/80.

Prior to deletion subsec. (e) read as follows:

"(e) Reasonable repair allowance.

"The Secretary may by regulations provide that the taxpayer may make an election under which amounts representing either repair expenses or specified repair, rehabilitation, or improvement expenditures for any class of depreciable property—

"(1) are allowable as a deduction under section 162(a) or 212 (whichever is appropriate) to the extent of the repair allowance for that class, and

"(2) to the extent such amounts exceed for the taxable year such repair allowance, are chargeable to capital account.

Any allowance prescribed under this subsection shall reasonably reflect the anticipated repair experience of the class of property in the industry or other group."

—P.L. 97-34, Sec. 502, added subsec. (g), effective for property acquired and positions established by the taxpayer after 6/23/81 in tax. yrs. end. after 6/23/81.

In 1980, P.L. 96-223, Sec. 251(a)(2)(B), deleted "or" at the end of subpara. (a)(1)(E) . . . substituted a comma and "or" for the period at the end of subpara. (a)(1)(F) . . . added subpara. (a)(1)(G), effective for tax. yrs. begin. after 12/31/79.

In 1979, P.L. 96-167, Sec. 9(d), extended the effective date of changes made by Sec. 2122(c) of P.L. 94-455 to tax. yrs. begin. after '76 and before '83. See below.

In 1978, P.L. 95-618, Sec. 402(a), added "and geothermal wells" to the heading of subsec. (c), added the last sentence of subsec. (c), effective with respect to wells commenced on or after 10/1/78, in tax. yrs. end. on or after 10/1/78. Sec. 402(e)(2) of the Act provides:

"(2) Election. The taxpayer may elect to capitalize or deduct any costs to which section 263(c) of the Internal Revenue Code of 1954 applies by reason of the amendments made by this section. Any such election shall be made before the expiration of the time for filing claim for credit or refund of any overpayment of tax imposed by chapter 1 of such Code with respect to the taxpayer's first taxable year to which the amendments made by this section apply and for which he pays or incurs costs to which such section 263(c) applies by reason of the amendments made by this section. Any election under this paragraph may be changed or revoked at any time before the expiration of the time referred to in the preceding sentence, but after the expiration of such time such election may not be changed or revoked."

In 1976, P.L. 94-455, Sec. 1701(a), added subsec. (g), effective 10/4/76.

—P.L. 94-455, Sec. 1904(b)(10)(A)(i), deleted para. (a)(3) and subsec. (d), and redesignated subsecs. (e), (f) and (g) as subsecs. (d), (e) and (f), respectively substituted "subsection (e)" for "subsection (f)" in redesignated subsec. (d), effective for acquisitions of stock or debt obligations made after 6/30/74.

Prior to amendment, para. (a)(3) read as follows:

"(3) Except as provided in subsection (d), any amount paid as tax under section 4911 (relating to imposition of interest equalization tax)."

Prior to amendment, subsec. (d) read as follows:

"(d) Reimbursement of interest equalization tax.

"The deduction allowed by section 162(a) or 212 (whichever is appropriate) shall include any amount paid or accrued in the taxable year or a preceding taxable year as tax under section 4911 (relating to imposition of interest equalization tax) to the extent that any amount attributable to the amount paid or accrued as tax is included in gross income for the taxable year. Under regulations prescribed by the Secretary or his delegate, the preceding sentence shall not apply with respect to any amount attributable to that part of the tax so paid or accrued which is attributable to an amount for which a deduction has been claimed for the taxable year or a preceding taxable year under section 171 (relating to amortization of bond premium)."

—P.L. 94-455, Sec. 1906(b)(13)(A), substituted "Secretary" for "Secretary or his delegate" each place it appeared in Code Sec. 263, for tax. yrs. begin. after '76.

—P.L. 94-455, Sec. 2119, covered the application of Code Sec. 263 to publishers' prepublication expenditures. See note to Code Sec. 174.

—P.L. 94-455, Sec. 2122(b)(2), deleted "or" at the end of subpara. (a)(1)(D), substituted a comma and "or" for the period at the end of subpara. (a)(1)(E), and added subpara. (a)(1)(F), effective for tax. yrs. begin. after 12/31/76 and before 1/1/80.

In 1971, P.L. 92-178, Sec. 109(b), added subsec. (f), for tax. yrs. end. after 12/31/70 . . . Sec. 109(c), substituted "shall, at the election of the taxpayer, be treated" for "shall be treated" in subsec. (e) added two sentences to the end of subsec. (e), effective for tax. yrs. begin. after 12/31/69.

In 1969, P.L. 91-172, Sec. 706(a), added subsec. (e), effective for tax. yrs. begin. after 12/31/69.

In 1965, P.L. 89-243, Sec. 4(p)(1), added subsec. (d) and amended para. (a)(3), for tax. yrs. end. after 9/2/64.

Prior to amendment, para. (a)(3) read as follows:

"(3) Any amount paid as tax under section 4911 (relating to imposition of interest equalization tax) except to the extent that any amount attributable to the amount paid as tax is included in gross income for the taxable year."

In 1964, P.L. 88-563, added para. (a)(3).

In 1962, P.L. 87-834, deleted "or" at the end of subpara. (a)(1)(C), substituted ", or" for the period at the end of subpara. (a)(1)(D), and added subpara. (a)(1)(E), effective for tax. yrs. begin. after 12/31/62.

In 1960, P.L. 86-779, added subpara. (a)(1)(D), for tax. yrs. begin. after '59.

Sec. 263A. Capitalization and inclusion in inventory costs of certain expenses.

(a) Nondeductibility of certain direct and indirect costs.

(1) In general. In the case of any property to which this section applies, any costs described in paragraph (2)—

(A) in the case of property which is inventory in the hands of the taxpayer, shall be included in inventory costs, and

(B) in the case of any other property, shall be capitalized.

(2) Allocable costs. The costs described in this paragraph with respect to any property are—

(A) the direct costs of such property, and

(B) such property's proper share of those indirect costs (including taxes) part or all of which are allocable to such property.

Any cost which (but for this subsection) could not be taken into account in computing taxable income for any taxable year shall not be treated as a cost described in this paragraph.

(b) Property to which section applies.

Except as otherwise provided in this section, this section shall apply to—

(1) Property produced by taxpayer. Real or tangible personal property produced by the taxpayer.

(2) Property acquired for resale.

(A) In general. Real or personal property described in section 1221(a)(1) which is acquired by the taxpayer for resale.

(B) Exception for taxpayer with gross receipts of $10,000,000 or less. Subparagraph (A) shall not apply

Limitations on deduction   Code Sec. 263A(e)(2)(A)

to any personal property acquired during any taxable year by the taxpayer for resale if the average annual gross receipts of the taxpayer (or any predecessor) for the 3-taxable year period ending with the taxable year preceding such taxable year do not exceed $10,000,000.

(C) Aggregation rules, etc. For purposes of subparagraph (B), rules similar to the rules of paragraphs (2) and (3) of section 448(c) shall apply.

For purposes of paragraph (1), the term "tangible personal property" shall include a film, sound recording, video tape, book, or similar property.

(c) General exceptions.

(1) Personal use property. This section shall not apply to any property produced by the taxpayer for use by the taxpayer other than in a trade or business or an activity conducted for profit.

(2) Research and experimental expenditures. This section shall not apply to any amount allowable as a deduction under section 174.

(3) Certain development and other costs of oil and gas wells or other mineral property. This section shall not apply to any cost allowable as a deduction under section 167(h), 179B, 263(c), 263(i), 291(b)(2), 616, or 617.

(4) Coordination with long-term contract rules. This section shall not apply to any property produced by the taxpayer pursuant to a long-term contract.

(5) Timber and certain ornamental trees. This section shall not apply to—

(A) trees raised, harvested, or grown by the taxpayer other than trees described in clause (ii) of subsection (e)(4)(B) (after application of the last sentence thereof), and

(B) any real property underlying such trees.

(6) Coordination with section 59(e). Paragraphs (2) and (3) shall apply to any amount allowable as a deduction under section 59(e) for qualified expenditures described in subparagraphs (B), (C), (D), and (E) of paragraph (2) thereof.

(d) Exception for farming businesses.

(1) Section not to apply to certain property.

(A) In general. This section shall not apply to any of the following which is produced by the taxpayer in a farming business:

(i) Any animal.

(ii) Any plant which has a preproductive period of 2 years or less.

(B) Exception for taxpayers required to use accrual method. Subparagraph (A) shall not apply to any corporation, partnership, or tax shelter required to use an accrual method of accounting under section 447 or 448(a)(3).

(2) Treatment of certain plants lost by reason of casualty.

(A) In general. If plants bearing an edible crop for human consumption were lost or damaged (while in the hands of the taxpayer) by reason of freezing temperatures, disease, drought, pests, or casualty, this section shall not apply to any costs of the taxpayer of replanting plants bearing the same type of crop (whether on the same parcel of land on which such lost or damaged plants were located or any other parcel of land of the same acreage in the United States).

(B) Special rule for person with minority interest who materially participates. Subparagraph (A) shall apply to amounts paid or incurred by a person (other than the taxpayer described in subparagraph (A)) if—

(i) the taxpayer described in subparagraph (A) has an equity interest of more than 50 percent in the plants described in subparagraph (A) at all times during the taxable year in which such amounts were paid or incurred, and

(ii) such other person holds any part of the remaining equity interest and materially participates in the planting, maintenance, cultivation, or development of the plants described in subparagraph (A) during the taxable year in which such amounts were paid or incurred.

The determination of whether an individual materially participates in any activity shall be made in a manner similar to the manner in which such determination is made under section 2032A(e)(6).

(3) Election to have this section not apply.

(A) In general. If a taxpayer makes an election under this paragraph, this section shall not apply to any plant produced in any farming business carried on by such taxpayer.

(B) Certain persons not eligible. No election may be made under this paragraph by a corporation, partnership, or tax shelter, if such corporation, partnership, or tax shelter is required to use an accrual method of accounting under section 447 or 448(a)(3).

(C) Special rule for citrus and almond growers. An election under this paragraph shall not apply with respect to any item which is attributable to the planting, cultivation, maintenance, or development of any citrus or almond grove (or part thereof) and which is incurred before the close of the 4th taxable year beginning with the taxable year in which the trees were planted. For purposes of the preceding sentence, the portion of a citrus or almond grove planted in 1 taxable year shall be treated separately from the portion of such grove planted in another taxable year.

(D) Election. Unless the Secretary otherwise consents, an election under this paragraph may be made only for the taxpayer's 1st taxable year which begins after December 31, 1986, and during which the taxpayer engages in a farming business. Any such election, once made, may be revoked only with the consent of the Secretary.

(e) Definitions and special rules for purposes of subsection (d).

(1) Recapture of expensed amounts on disposition.

(A) In general. In the case of any plant with respect to which amounts would have been capitalized under subsection (a) but for an election under subsection (d)(3)—

(i) such plant (if not otherwise section 1245 property) shall be treated as section 1245 property, and

(ii) for purposes of section 1245, the recapture amount shall be treated as a deduction allowed for depreciation with respect to such property.

(B) Recapture amount. For purposes of subparagraph (A), the term "recapture amount" means any amount allowable as a deduction to the taxpayer which, but for an election under subsection (d)(3), would have been capitalized with respect to the plant.

(2) Effects of election on depreciation.

(A) In general. If the taxpayer (or any related person) makes an election under subsection (d)(3), the provisions of section 168(g)(2) (relating to alternative depreciation) shall apply to all property of the taxpayer used predominantly in the farming business and placed in service in any taxable year during which any such election is in effect.

(B) **Related person.** For purposes of subparagraph (A), the term "related person" means—

(i) the taxpayer and members of the taxpayer's family,

(ii) any corporation (including an S corporation) if 50 percent or more (in value) of the stock of such corporation is owned (directly or through the application of section 318) by the taxpayer or members of the taxpayer's family,

(iii) a corporation and any other corporation which is a member of the same controlled group described in section 1563(a)(1), and

(iv) any partnership if 50 percent or more (in value) of the interests in such partnership is owned directly or indirectly by the taxpayer or members of the taxpayer's family.

(C) **Members of family.** For purposes of this paragraph, the term "family" means the taxpayer, the spouse of the taxpayer, and any of their children who have not attained age 18 before the close of the taxable year.

(3) **Preproductive period.**

(A) **In general.** For purposes of this section, the term "preproductive period" means—

(i) in the case of a plant which will have more than 1 crop or yield, the period before the 1st marketable crop or yield from such plant, or

(ii) in the case of any other plant, the period before such plant is reasonably expected to be disposed of.

For purposes of this subparagraph, use by the taxpayer in a farming business of any supply produced in such business shall be treated as a disposition.

(B) **Rule for determining period.** In the case of a plant grown in commercial quantities in the United States, the preproductive period for such plant if grown in the United States shall be based on the nationwide weighted average preproductive period for such plant.

(4) **Farming business.** For purposes of this section—

(A) **In general.** The term "farming business" means the trade or business of farming.

(B) **Certain trades and businesses included.** The term "farming business" shall include the trade or business of—

(i) operating a nursery or sod farm, or

(ii) the raising or harvesting of trees bearing fruit, nuts, or other crops, or ornamental trees.

For purposes of clause (ii), an evergreen tree which is more than 6 years old at the time severed from the roots shall not be treated as an ornamental tree.

(5) **Certain inventory valuation methods permitted.** The Secretary shall by regulations permit the taxpayer to use reasonable inventory valuation methods to compute the amount required to be capitalized under subsection (a) in the case of any plant.

(f) **Special rules for allocation of interest to property produced by the taxpayer.**

(1) **Interest capitalized only in certain cases.** Subsection (a) shall only apply to interest costs which are—

(A) paid or incurred during the production period, and

(B) allocable to property which is described in subsection (b)(1) and which has—

(i) a long useful life,

(ii) an estimated production period exceeding 2 years, or

(iii) an estimated production period exceeding 1 year and a cost exceeding $1,000,000.

(2) **Allocation rules.**

(A) **In general.** In determining the amount of interest required to be capitalized under subsection (a) with respect to any property—

(i) interest on any indebtedness directly attributable to production expenditures with respect to such property shall be assigned to such property, and

(ii) interest on any other indebtedness shall be assigned to such property to the extent that the taxpayer's interest costs could have been reduced if production expenditures (not attributable to indebtedness described in clause (i)) had not been incurred.

(B) **Exception for qualified residence interest.** Subparagraph (A) shall not apply to any qualified residence interest (within the meaning of section 163(h)).

(C) **Special rule for flow-through entities.** Except as provided in regulations, in the case of any flow-through entity, this paragraph shall be applied first at the entity level and then at the beneficiary level.

(3) **Interest relating to property used to produce property.** This subsection shall apply to any interest on indebtedness allocable (as determined under paragraph (2)) to property used to produce property to which this subsection applies to the extent such interest is allocable (as so determined) to the produced property.

(4) **Definitions.** For purposes of this subsection—

(A) **Long useful life.** Property has a long useful life if such property is—

(i) real property, or

(ii) property with a class life of 20 years or more (as determined under section 168).

(B) **Production period.** The term "production period" means, when used with respect to any property, the period—

(i) beginning on the date on which production of the property begins, and

(ii) ending on the date on which the property is ready to be placed in service or is ready to be held for sale.

(C) **Production expenditures.** The term "production expenditures" means the costs (whether or not incurred during the production period) required to be capitalized under subsection (a) with respect to the property.

(g) **Production.**

For purposes of this section—

(1) **In general.** The term "produce" includes construct, build, install, manufacture, develop, or improve.

(2) **Treatment of property produced under contract for the taxpayer.** The taxpayer shall be treated as producing any property produced for the taxpayer under a contract with the taxpayer; except that only costs paid or incurred by the taxpayer (whether under such contract or otherwise) shall be taken into account in applying subsection (a) to the taxpayer.

(h) **Exemption for free lance authors, photographers, and artists.**

(1) **In general.** Nothing in this section shall require the capitalization of any qualified creative expense.

(2) **Qualified creative expense.** For purposes of this subsection, the term "qualified creative expense" means any expense—

(A) which is paid or incurred by an individual in the trade or business of such individual (other than as an employee) of being a writer, photographer, or artist, and

(B) which, without regard to this section, would be allowable as a deduction for the taxable year.

Such term does not include any expense related to printing, photographic plates, motion picture films, video tapes, or similar items.

(3) **Definitions.** For purposes of this subsection—

(A) Writer. The term "writer" means any individual if the personal efforts of such individual create (or may reasonably be expected to create) a literary manuscript, musical composition (including any accompanying words), or dance score.

(B) Photographer. The term "photographer" means any individual if the personal efforts of such individual create (or may reasonably be expected to create) a photograph or photographic negative or transparency.

(C) Artist.—

(i) In general. The term "artist" means any individual if the personal efforts of such individual create (or may reasonably be expected to create) a picture, painting, sculpture, statue, etching, drawing, cartoon, graphic design, or original print edition.

(ii) Criteria. In determining whether any expense is paid or incurred in the trade or business of being an artist, the following criteria shall be taken into account:

(I) The originality and uniqueness of the item created (or to be created).

(II) The predominance of aesthetic value over utilitarian value of the item created (or to be created).

(D) Treatment of certain corporations.

(i) In general. If—

(I) substantially all of the stock of a corporation is owned by a qualified employee-owner and members of his family (as defined in section 267(c)(4)), and

(II) the principal activity of such corporation is performance of personal services directly related to the activities of the qualified employee-owner and such services are substantially performed by the qualified employee-owner,

this subsection shall apply to any expense of such corporation which directly relates to the activities of such employee-owner in the same manner as if such expense were incurred by such employee-owner.

(ii) Qualified employee-owner. For purposes of this subparagraph, the term "qualified employee-owner" means any individual who is an employee-owner of the corporation (as defined in section 269A(b)(2)) and who is a writer, photographer, or artist.

(i) **Regulations.**

The Secretary shall prescribe such regulations as may be necessary or appropriate to carry out the purposes of this section, including—

(1) regulations to prevent the use of related parties, pass-thru entities, or intermediaries to avoid the application of this section, and

(2) regulations providing for simplified procedures for the application of this section in the case of property described in subsection (b)(2).

In 2005, P.L. 109-58, Sec. 1329(b), added "167(h)," after "under section" in para. (c)(3), effective for amounts paid or incurred in tax. yrs. begin. after 8/8/2005.

In 2004, P.L. 108-357, Sec. 338(b)(2), added "179B," after "deduction under section" in para. (c)(3), effective for expenses paid or incurred after 12/31/2002, in tax. yrs. end. after 12/31/2002.

In 1999, P.L. 106-170, Sec. 532(c)(2)(B), substituted "section 1221(a)(1)" for "section 1221(1)" in subpara. (b)(2)(A), effective for any instrument held, acquired, or entered into, any transaction entered into, and supplies held or acquired on or after 12/17/99.

In 1989, P.L. 101-239, Sec. 7816(d)(1), amended subpara. (h)(3)(D), effective for costs incurred after 12/31/86, in tax. yrs. end. after 12/31/86, except as provided in Secs. 803(d)(2)-(7) of P.L. 99-514, reproduced below.

Prior to amendment subpara. (h)(3)(D) read as follows:

"(D) Treatment of certain personal service corporations.

"(i) In general. In the case of a personal service corporation, this subsection shall apply to any expense of such corporation which directly relates to the activities of the qualified employee-owner in the same manner as if such expense were incurred by such employee-owner.

"(ii) Qualified employee-owner. The term 'qualified employee-owner' means any individual who is an employee-owner of the personal service corporation and who is a writer, photographer, or artist, but only if substantially all of the stock of such corporation is owned by such individual and members of his family (as defined in section 267(c)(4)).

"(iii) Personal service corporation. For purposes of this subparagraph, the term 'personal service corporation' means any personal service corporation (as defined in section 269A(b))."

— P.L. 101-239, Sec. 7816(d)(2), amended Sec. 6026(d)(2)(B) of P.L. 100-647 [reproduced below], provisions relating to amendments made by Sec. 6026(b) of P.L. 100-647, by substituting "a taxpayer engaged in a farming business involving the production of animals having a preproductive period of more than 2 years made" for "the taxpayer made", see below.

— P.L. 101-239, Sec. 7831(d)(1), amended the part of Sec. 803(d)(4)(A) of P.L. 99-514 [reproduced below], part of the effective date for changes made by Sec. 803 of 99-514, see below. Sec. 7831(d)(2) of this Act provides:

"(2) If any interest costs incurred after December 31, 1986, are attributable to costs incurred before January 1, 1987, the amendments made by section 803 of the Tax Reform Act of 1986 shall apply to such interest costs only to the extent such interest costs are attributable to costs which were required to be capitalized under section 263 of the Internal Revenue Code of 1954 and which would have been taken into account in applying section 189 of the Internal Revenue Code of 1954 (as in effect before its repeal by section 803 of the Tax Reform Act of 1986) or, if applicable, section 266 of such Code."

Prior to amendment Sec. 803(a)(4)(A) of P.L. 99-514 read as follows:

"(A) Transition property exempted from interest capitalization. Section 263A(f) of the Internal Revenue Code of 1986 (as added by this section) and the amendment made by subsection (b)(1) shall not apply to any property—

"(i) to which the amendments made by section 201 do not apply by reason of sections 204(a)(1)(D) and (E) and 204(a)(5)(A), and

"(ii) to which the amendments made by section 251 do not apply by reason of section 251(d)(3)(M).

"(B) Interest and taxes. Section 263A of such Code shall not apply to property described in the matter following subparagraph (B) of section 207(e)(2) of the Tax Equity and Fiscal Responsibility Act of 1982 to the extent it would require the capitalization of interest and taxes paid or incurred in connection with such property which are not required to be capitalized under section 189 of such Code (as in effect before the amendment made by subsection (b)(1))."

In 1988, P.L. 100-647, Sec. 1008(b)(1), added the last sentence to para. (a)(2) . . . Sec. 1008(b)(2)(A), substituted "263(c), 263(i), 291(b)(2), 616 or 617" for "263(c), 616(a) or 617(a)" in para. (c)(3) . . . Sec. 1008(b)(2)(B), added para. (c)(6) . . . Sec. 1008(b)(3)(A), substituted "the plants described in subparagraph (A) at all times during the taxable year in which such amounts were paid or incurred" for "such grove, orchard, or vineyard" in clause (d)(2)(B)(i) . . . Sec. 1008(b)(3)(B), substituted "the plants described in subparagraph (A) during the taxable year in which such amounts were paid or incurred" for "such grove, orchard, or vineyard during the 4-taxable year period beginning with the taxable year in which the grove, orchard, or vineyard was lost or damaged" in clause (d)(2)(B)(ii) . . . Sec. 1008(b)(4)(A), and (B) substituted "allocable as determined under paragraph (2))" for "incurred or continued in connection with" and added "(as so determined)" after "allocable" in para. (f)(3), effective for costs incurred after 12/31/86 in tax. yrs. end. after 12/31/86, except as provided in Sec. 803(d)(2)-(7) of P.L. 99-514, reproduced below.

— P.L. 100-647, Sec. 1008(b)(7), amended Sec. 803(d)(4)(A)(i) [reproduced below] of P.L. 99-514, part of the effective date for changes made by Sec. 803(a) of P.L. 99-514, by substituting "204" for "203" each place it appeared, see below.

— P.L. 100-647, Sec. 1008(b)(8), provides:

"(8) The allocation used in the regulations prescribed under section 263A(h)(2) of the Internal Revenue Code of 1986 for apportioning storage costs and related handling costs shall be determined by dividing the amount of such costs by the beginning inventory balances and the purchases during the year and by multiplying the resulting allocation ratio by inventory amounts determined in accordance with the provisions of the joint explanatory statement of the committee of conference of the conference report accompanying H.R. 3838 (H.R. Rept. No. 99-841, Vol. II., 99th Cong., 2d Sess. II-306-307 (1986))."

— P.L. 100-647, Sec. 6026(a), redesignated subsec. (h) as subsec. (i) and added new subsec. (h), effective for costs incurred after 12/31/86, in tax. yrs. end. after 12/31/86, except as provided in Secs. 803(d)(2)-(7) of P.L. 99-514, reproduced below.

— P.L. 100-647, Sec. 6026(b)(1), amended subpara. (d)(1)(A) . . . Sec. 6026(b)(2)(A), substituted "(1) Section not to apply to certain property." for "(1) Section to apply only if preproductive period is more than 2 years." in the heading of para. (d)(1) . . . Sec. 6026(b)(2)(B), deleted "or animal" after "any plant" each place it appeared in para. (d)(3) and subsec. (e), effective for costs incurred after 12/31/88, in tax. yrs. end. after 12/31/88. Sec. 6026(d)(2)(B) of this Act [as amended by Sec. 7816(d)(2) of P.L. 101-239, see above] provides

"(B) Revocation of election.—If a taxpayer engaged in a farming business involving the production of animals having a preproductive period of more than 2 years made an election under section 263A(d)(3) of the 1986 Code for a taxable year beginning before January 1, 1989, such taxpayer may, without the consent of the Secretary of the Treasury or his delegate, revoke such election effective for the taxpayer's list taxable year beginning after December 31, 1988."

Prior to amendment, subpara. (d)(1)(A), read as follows:

"(A) In general. This section shall not apply to any plant or animal which is produced by the taxpayer in a farming business and which has a preproductive period of 2 years or less."

—P.L. 100-647, Sec. 6026(c), amended subpara. (d)(3)(B), effective for costs incurred after 12/31/86, in tax. yrs. end. after 12/31/86, except as provided in Secs 803(d)(2)-(7) of P.L. 99-514, reproduced below.

Prior to the amendment, subpara. (d)(3)(B) read as follows:

"(B) Exception for taxpayers required to use accrual method. Subparagraph (A) shall not apply to any corporation, partnership, or tax shelter required to use an accrual method of accounting under section 447 or 448(a)(3)."

In 1987, P.L. 100-203, Sec. 10204, provides as follows:

"SEC. 10204. AMORTIZATION OF PAST SERVICE PENSION COSTS.

"(a) In general.

"For purposes of sections 263A and 460 of the Internal Revenue Code of 1986, the allocable costs (within the meaning of section 263A(a)(2) or section 460(c) of such Code, whichever is applicable) with respect to any property shall include contributions paid to or under a pension or annuity plan whether or not such contributions represent past service costs.

"(b) Effective date.—

"(1) In general.—Except as provided in paragraph (2), subsection (a) shall apply to costs incurred after December 31, 1987, in taxable years ending after such date.

"(2) Special rule for inventory property.—In the case of any property which is inventory in the hands of the taxpayer—

"(A) In general.—Subsection (a) shall apply to taxable years beginning after December 31, 1987.

"(B) Change in method of accounting.—If the taxpayer is required by this section to change its method of accounting for any taxable year—

"(i) such change shall be treated as initiated by the taxpayer,

"(ii) such change shall be treated as made with the consent of the Secretary of the Treasury or his delegate, and

"(iii) the net amount of adjustments required by section 481 of the Internal Revenue Code of 1986 shall be taken into account over a period not longer than 4 taxable years."

In 1986, P.L. 99-514, Sec. 803(a), added Code Sec. 263A, effective for costs incurred after 12/31/86, in tax. yrs. end. after 12/31/86. Secs. 803(d)(2)-(7) [as amended by Sec. 1008(b)(7) of P.L. 100-647 and Sec. 7831(d)(1) of P.L. 101-239, see above] of this Act provide:

"(2) Special rule for inventory property. In the case of any property which is inventory in the hands of the taxpayer—

"(A) In general. The amendments made by this section shall apply to taxable years beginning after December 31, 1986.

"(B) Change in method of accounting. If the taxpayer is required by the amendments made by this section [Sec. 803] to change its method of accounting with respect to such property for any taxable year—

"(i) such change shall be treated as initiated by the taxpayer,

"(ii) such change shall be treated as made with the consent of the Secretary, and

"(iii) the period for taking into account the adjustments under section 481 by reason of such change shall not exceed 4 years.

"(3) Special rule for self-constructed property. The amendments made by this section shall not apply to any property which is produced by the taxpayer for use by the taxpayer if substantial construction had occurred before March 1, 1986.

"(4) Transitional rule for capitalization of interest and taxes.—

"(A) Transition property exempted from interest capitalization.—Section 263A of the Internal Revenue Code of 1986 (as added by this section) and the amendment made by subsection (b)(1) shall not apply to interest costs which are allocable to any property—

"(i) to which the amendments made by section 201 do not apply by reason of sections 204(a)(1)(D) and (E) and 204(a)(5)(A), and

"(ii) to which the amendments made by section 251 do not apply by reason of section 251(d)(3)(M).

"(B) Interest and taxes. Section 263A of such Code shall not apply to property described in the matter following subparagraph (B) of section 207(e)(2) of the Tax Equity and Fiscal Responsibility Act of 1982 to the extent it would require the capitalization of interest and taxes paid or incurred in connection with such property which are not required to be capitalized under section 189 of such Code (as in effect before the amendment made by subsection (b)(1)).

"(5) Transition rule concerning capitalization of inventory rules. In the case of a corporation which on the date of the enactment of this Act was a member of an affiliated group of corporations (within the meaning of section 1504(a) of the Internal Revenue Code of 1986), the parent of which—

"(A) was incorporated in California on April 15, 1925,

"(B) adopted LIFO accounting as of the close of the taxable year ended December 31, 1950, and

"(C) was, on May 22, 1986, merged into a Delaware corporation incorporated on March 12, 1986,

the amendment made by this section shall apply under a cutoff method whereby the uniform capitalization rules are applied only in costing layers of inventory acquired during taxable years beginning on or after January 1, 1987.

"(6) Treatment of certain rehabilitation project. The amendments made by this section shall not apply to interest and taxes paid or incurred with respect to the rehabilitation and conversion of a certified historic building which was formerly a factory into an apartment project with 155 units, 39 units of which are for low-income families, if the project was approved for annual interest assistance on June 10, 1986, by the housing authority of the State in which the project is located.

"(7) Special rule for casualty losses. Section 263A(d)(2) of the Internal Revenue Code of 1986 (as added by this section) shall apply to expenses incurred on or after the date of the enactment of this Act."

Sec. 264. Certain amounts paid in connection with insurance contracts.

(a) General rule.

No deduction shall be allowed for—

(1) Premiums on any life insurance policy, or endowment or annuity contract, if the taxpayer is directly or indirectly a beneficiary under the policy or contract.

(2) Any amount paid or accrued on indebtedness incurred or continued to purchase or carry a single premium life insurance, endowment, or annuity contract.

(3) Except as provided in subsection (d), any amount paid or accrued on indebtedness incurred or continued to purchase or carry a life insurance, endowment, or annuity contract (other than a single premium contract or a contract treated as a single premium contract) pursuant to a plan of purchase which contemplates the systematic direct or indirect borrowing of part or all of the increases in the cash value of such contract (either from the insurer or otherwise).

(4) Except as provided in subsection (e), any interest paid or accrued on any indebtedness with respect to 1 or more life insurance policies owned by the taxpayer covering the life of any individual, or any endowment or annuity contracts owned by the taxpayer covering any individual.

Paragraph (2) shall apply in respect of annuity contracts only as to contracts purchased after March 1, 1954. Paragraph (3) shall apply only in respect of contracts purchased after August 6, 1963. Paragraph (4) shall apply with respect to contracts purchased after June 20, 1986.

(b) Exceptions to subsection (a)(1).

Subsection (a)(1) shall not apply to—

(1) any annuity contract described in section 72(s)(5), and

(2) any annuity contract to which section 72(u) applies.

(c) Contracts treated as single premium contracts.

For purposes of subsection (a)(2), a contract shall be treated as a single premium contract—

(1) if substantially all the premiums on the contract are paid within a period of 4 years from the date on which the contract is purchased, or

(2) if an amount is deposited after March 1, 1954, with the insurer for payment of a substantial number of future premiums on the contract.

(d) Exceptions.

Subsection (a)(3) shall not apply to any amount paid or accrued by a person during a taxable year on indebtedness incurred or continued as part of a plan referred to in subsection (a)(3)—

(1) if no part of 4 of the annual premiums due during the 7-year period (beginning with the date the first premium on the contract to which such plan relates was paid) is paid under such plan by means of indebtedness,

(2) if the total of the amounts paid or accrued by such person during such taxable year for which (without regard to this paragraph) no deduction would be allowable by reason of subsection (a)(3) does not exceed $100,

(3) if such amount was paid or accrued on indebtedness incurred because of an unforeseen substantial loss of income or unforeseen substantial increase in his financial obligations, or

(4) if such indebtedness was incurred in connection with his trade or business.

For purposes of applying paragraph (1), if there is a substantial increase in the premiums on a contract, a new 7-year period described in such paragraph with respect to such contract shall commence on the date the first such increased premium is paid.

(e) Special rules for application of subsection (a)(4).

(1) Exception for key persons. Subsection (a)(4) shall not apply to any interest paid or accrued on any indebtedness with respect to policies or contracts covering an individual who is a key person to the extent that the aggregate amount of such indebtedness with respect to policies and contracts covering such individual does not exceed $50,000.

(2) Interest rate cap on key persons and pre-1986 contracts.

(A) In general. No deduction shall be allowed by reason of paragraph (1) or the last sentence of subsection (a) with respect to interest paid or accrued for any month beginning after December 31, 1995, to the extent the amount of such interest exceeds the amount which would have been determined if the applicable rate of interest were used for such month.

(B) Applicable rate of interest. For purposes of subparagraph (A)—

(i) In general. The applicable rate of interest for any month is the rate of interest described as Moody's Corporate Bond Yield Average-Monthly Average Corporates as published by Moody's Investors Service, Inc., or any successor thereto, for such month.

(ii) Pre-1986 contracts. In the case of indebtedness on a contract purchased on or before June 20, 1986—

(I) which is a contract providing a fixed rate of interest, the applicable rate of interest for any month shall be the Moody's rate described in clause (i) for the month in which the contract was purchased, or

(II) which is a contract providing a variable rate of interest, the applicable rate of interest for any month in an applicable period shall be such Moody's rate for the third month preceding the first month in such period.

For purposes of subclause (II), the term "applicable period" means the 12-month period beginning on the date the policy is issued (and each successive 12-month period thereafter) unless the taxpayer elects a number of months (not greater than 12) other than such 12-month period to be its applicable period. Such an election shall be made not later than the 90th day after the date of the enactment of this sentence and, if made, shall apply to the taxpayer's first taxable year ending on or after October 13, 1995, and all subsequent taxable years unless revoked with the consent of the Secretary.

(3) Key person. For purposes of paragraph (1), the term "key person" means an officer or 20-percent owner, except that the number of individuals who may be treated as key persons with respect to any taxpayer shall not exceed the greater of—

(A) 5 individuals, or

(B) the lesser of 5 percent of the total officers and employees of the taxpayer or 20 individuals.

(4) 20-percent owner. For purposes of this subsection, the term "20-percent owner" means—

(A) if the taxpayer is a corporation, any person who owns directly 20 percent or more of the outstanding stock of the corporation or stock possessing 20 percent or more of the total combined voting power of all stock of the corporation, or

(B) if the taxpayer is not a corporation, any person who owns 20 percent or more of the capital or profits interest in the taxpayer.

(5) Aggregation rules.

(A) In general. For purposes of paragraph (4)(A) and applying the $50,000 limitation in paragraph (1)—

(i) all members of a controlled group shall be treated as 1 taxpayer, and

(ii) such limitation shall be allocated among the members of such group in such manner as the Secretary may prescribe.

(B) Controlled group. For purposes of this paragraph, all persons treated as a single employer under subsection (a) or (b) of section 52 or subsection (m) or (o) of section 414 shall be treated as members of a controlled group.

(f) Pro rata allocation of interest expense to policy cash values.

(1) In general. No deduction shall be allowed for that portion of the taxpayer's interest expense which is allocable to unborrowed policy cash values.

(2) Allocation. For purposes of paragraph (1), the portion of the taxpayer's interest expense which is allocable to unborrowed policy cash values is an amount which bears the same ratio to such interest expense as—

(A) the taxpayer's average unborrowed policy cash values of life insurance policies, and annuity and endowment contracts, issued after June 8, 1997, bears to

(B) the sum of—

(i) in the case of assets of the taxpayer which are life insurance policies or annuity or endowment contracts, the average unborrowed policy cash values of such policies and contracts, and

(ii) in the case of assets of the taxpayer not described in clause (i), the average adjusted bases (within the meaning of section 1016) of such assets.

(3) Unborrowed policy cash value. For purposes of this subsection, the term "unborrowed policy cash value" means, with respect to any life insurance policy or annuity or endowment contract, the excess of—

(A) the cash surrender value of such policy or contract determined without regard to any surrender charge, over

(B) the amount of any loan in respect of such policy or contract.

If the amount described in subparagraph (A) with respect to any policy or contract does not reasonably approximate its actual value, the amount taken into account under subparagraph (A) shall be the greater of the amount of the insurance company liability or the insurance company reserve with respect to such policy or contract (as determined for purposes of the annual statement approved by the National Association of Insurance Commissioners) or shall be such other amount as is determined by the Secretary.

(4) Exception for certain policies and contracts.

(A) Policies and contracts covering 20-percent owners, officers, directors, and employees. Paragraph (1) shall not apply to any policy or contract owned by an entity engaged in a trade or business if such policy or contract covers only 1 individual and if such individual is (at the time first covered by the policy or contract)—

(i) a 20-percent owner of such entity, or

(ii) an individual (not described in clause (i)) who is an officer, director, or employee of such trade or business.

A policy or contract covering a 20-percent owner of such entity shall not be treated as failing to meet the requirements of the preceding sentence by reason of covering the joint lives of such owner and such owner's spouse.

(B) Contracts subject to current income inclusion. Paragraph (1) shall not apply to any annuity contract to which section 72(u) applies.

(C) Coordination with paragraph (2). Any policy or contract to which paragraph (1) does not apply by reason of this paragraph shall not be taken into account under paragraph (2).

(D) 20-percent owner. For purposes of subparagraph (A), the term "20-percent owner" has the meaning given such term by subsection (e)(4).

(E) Master contracts. If coverage for each insured under a master contract is treated as a separate contract for purposes of sections 817(h), 7702, and 7702A, coverage for each such insured shall be treated as a separate contract for purposes of subparagraph (A). For purposes of the preceding sentence, the term "master contract" shall not include any group life insurance contract (as defined in section 848(e)(2)).

(5) Exception for policies and contracts held by natural persons; treatment of partnerships and S corporations.

(A) Policies and contracts held by natural persons.

(i) In general. This subsection shall not apply to any policy or contract held by a natural person.

(ii) Exception where business is beneficiary. If a trade or business is directly or indirectly the beneficiary under any policy or contract, such policy or contract shall be treated as held by such trade or business and not by a natural person.

(iii) Special rules.

(I) Certain trades or businesses not taken into account. Clause (ii) shall not apply to any trade or business carried on as a sole proprietorship and to any trade or business performing services as an employee.

(II) Limitation on unborrowed cash value. The amount of the unborrowed cash value of any policy or contract which is taken into account by reason of clause (ii) shall not exceed the benefit to which the trade or business is directly or indirectly entitled under the policy or contract.

(iv) Reporting. The Secretary shall require such reporting from policyholders and issuers as is necessary to carry out clause (ii).

(B) Treatment of partnerships and S corporations. In the case of a partnership or S corporation, this subsection shall be applied at the partnership and corporate levels.

(6) Special rules.

(A) Coordination with subsection (a) and section 265. If interest on any indebtedness is disallowed under subsection (a) or section 265—

(i) such disallowed interest shall not be taken into account for purposes of applying this subsection, and

(ii) the amount otherwise taken into account under paragraph (2)(B) shall be reduced (but not below zero) by the amount of such indebtedness.

(B) Coordination with section 263A. This subsection shall be applied before the application of section 263A (relating to capitalization of certain expenses where taxpayer produces property).

(7) Interest expense. The term "interest expense" means the aggregate amount allowable to the taxpayer as a deduction for interest (within the meaning of section 265(b)(4)) for the taxable year (determined without regard to this subsection, section 265(b), and section 291).

(8) Aggregation rules.

(A) In general. All members of a controlled group (within the meaning of subsection (e)(5)(B)) shall be treated as 1 taxpayer for purposes of this subsection.

(B) Treatment of insurance companies. This subsection shall not apply to an insurance company subject to tax under subchapter L, and subparagraph (A) shall be applied without regard to any member of an affiliated group which is an insurance company.

In **1998**, P.L. 105-277, Sec. 4003(i), added a flush sentence at the end of para. (f)(3), effective as provided by Sec. 1084(d)[sic (f)] of P.L. 105-34 [see below]

—P.L. 105-206, Sec. 6010(o)(1), substituted "subsection (d)" for "subsection (c)" in para. (a)(3)... Sec. 6010(o)(2), substituted "subsection (e)" for "subsection (d)" in para. (a)(4)... Sec. 6010(o)(3)(A), added subpara. (f)(4)(E), effective as provided in Sec. 1084(d)[sic (f)] of P.L. 105-34 [reproduced below].

—P.L. 105-206, Sec. 6010(o)(3)(B), substituted "except that, in the case of a master contract (within the meaning of section 264(f)(4)(E) of the Internal Revenue Code of 1986), the addition of covered lives shall be treated as a new contract only with respect to such additional covered lives." for "but the addition of covered lives shall be treated as a new contract only with respect to such additional covered lives. For purposes of this subsection, an increase in the death benefit under a policy or contract issued in connection with a lapse described in section 501(d)(2) of the Health Insurance Portability and Accountability Act of 1996 [P.L. 104-191] shall not be treated as a new contract." in Sec. 1084(d) [sic (f)] of P.L. 105-34, the effective date for amendments made by Sec. 1084 [see below].

—P.L. 105-206, Sec. 6010(o)(4)(A), deleted "Any report required under the preceding sentence shall be treated as a statement referred to in section 6724(d)(1)." at the end of clause (f)(5)(A)(iv)... Sec. 6010(o)(5), substituted "subsection (e)(5)(B)" for "subsection (d)(5)(B)" in subpara. (f)(8)(A), effective as provided in Sec. 1084(d)[sic (f)] of P.L. 105-34 [reproduced below].

In **1997**, P.L. 105-34, Sec. 1084(a)(1), amended para. (a)(1)... Sec. 1084(a)(2), redesignated subsecs. (b), (c), and (d) as subsecs. (c), (d), and (e), and added new subsec. (b)... Sec. 1084(b)(1), amended para. (a)(4), as amended by Sec. 1602(f)(1) of this Act, see below.... Sec. 1084(c), added subsec. (f), effective as provided in Sec. 1084(d)[sic (f)] of this Act [as amended by Sec. 6010(o)(3)(A) of 105-206, see above], which reads:

"(d)[sic (f)] Effective date. The amendments made by this section shall apply to contracts issued after June 8, 1997, in taxable years ending after such date. For purposes of the preceding sentence, any material increase in the death benefit or other material change in the contract shall be treated as a new contract except that, in the case of a master contract (within the meaning of section 264(f)(4)(E) of the Internal Revenue Code of 1986), the addition of covered lives shall be treated as a new contract only with respect to such additional covered lives."

Prior to amendment, para. (a)(1) read as follows:

"(1) Premiums paid on any life insurance policy covering the life of any officer or employee, or of any person financially interested in any trade or business carried on by the taxpayer, when the taxpayer is directly or indirectly a beneficiary under such policy."

Prior to amendment, para. (a)(4), read as follows:

"(4) Except as provided in subsection (d), any interest paid or accrued on any indebtedness with respect to 1 or more life insurance policies owned by the taxpayer covering the life of any individual, or any endowment or annuity contracts own by the taxpayer covering any individual, who—

"(A) is or was an officer or employer, or

"(B) is or was financially interested in,

any trade or business carried on (currently or formerly) by the taxpayer."

—P.L. 105-34, Sec. 1602(f)(1), amended subparas. (a)(4)(A), (B) and the flush language that follows... Sec. 1602(f)(2), amended the last two sentences of clause (d)(2)(B)(ii)... Sec. 1602(f)(3), substituted "the taxpayer" for "the employer" in subpara. (d)(4)(B)... Sec. 1602(f)(4), deleted Sec. 501(c)(3) of P.L. 104-191... Sec. 1602(f)(5), substituted "a lapse occurring after October 13, 1995, by reason of no additional premiums being received under the contract." for "no additional premiums being received under the contract by reason of a lapse occurring after October 13, 1995." in Sec. 501(d)(2) of P.L. 104-191 [see below], effective for interest paid or accrued after 10/13/95. For other rules, see Secs. 501(c)(2) and (d), of P.L. 104-191 [as amended by Sec. 1602(f)(4) of P.L. 105-34 and (5)], reproduced below.

Prior to amendment, subparas. (a)(4)(A), (B) and the flush language that followed read as follows:

"(A) is an officer or employee of, or

"(B) is financially interested in,

any trade or business carried on by the taxpayer."

Prior to amendment, the last two sentences of clause (d)(2)(B)(ii) read as follows:

Limitations on deduction   **Code Sec. 265(b)(2)**

"For purposes of subclause (II), the taxpayer shall elect an applicable period for such contract on its return of tax imposed by this chapter for its first taxable year ending on or after October 13, 1995. Such applicable period shall be for any number of months (not greater than 12) specified in the election and may not be changed by the taxpayer without the consent of the Secretary."

Prior to deletion, Sec. 501(c)(3) of P.L. 104-19 read as follows:

"(3) Special rule for grandfathered contracts. This section shall not apply to any contract purchased on or before June 20, 1986, except that section 264(d)(2) of the Internal Revenue Code of 1986 shall apply to interest paid or accrued after October 13, 1995."

In **1996**, P.L. 104-191, Sec. 501(a)(1), added ", or any endowment or annuity contracts owned by the taxpayer covering an individual," after "the life of an individual" in para. (a)(4) ... Sec. 501(a)(2), substituted a period for "to the extent that the aggregate amount of such indebtedness with respect to policies covering such individual exceeds $50,000." at the end of para. (a)(4) ... Sec. 501(b)(1), substituted 'Except as provided in subsection (d), any' for 'Any' in para. (a)(4) ... Sec. 501(b)(2), added subsec. (d), effective for interest paid or accrued after 10/13/95. For other rules, see Sec. 501(c)(2) and (d), of this Act, [as amended by Sec. 1602(f)(4) of P.L. 105-34 and (5), see above] which reads as follows:

"(2) Transition rule for existing indebtedness.

"(A) In general. In the case of—

"(i) indebtedness incurred before January 1, 1996, or

"(ii) indebtedness incurred before January 1, 1997 with respect to any contract or policy entered into in 1994 or 1995,

the amendments made by this section shall not apply to qualified interest paid or accrued on such indebtedness after October 13, 1995, and before January 1, 1999.

"(B) Qualified interest. For purposes of subparagraph (A), the qualified interest with respect to any indebtedness for any month is the amount of interest (otherwise deductible) which would be paid or accrued for such month on such indebtedness if—

"(i) in the case of any interest paid or accrued after December 31, 1995, indebtedness with respect to no more than 20,000 insured individuals were taken into account, and

"(ii) the lesser of the following rates of interest were used for such month:

"(I) The rate of interest specified under the terms of the indebtedness as in effect on October 13, 1995 (and without regard to modification of such terms after such date).

"(II) The applicable percentage of the rate of interest described as Moody's Corporate Bond Yield Average-Monthly Average Corporates as published by Moody's Investors Service, Inc., or any successor thereto, for such month.

For purposes of clause (i), all persons treated as a single employer under subsection (a) or (b) of section 52 of the Internal Revenue Code of 1986 or subsection (m) or (o) of section 414 of such Code shall be treated as 1 person. Subclause (II) of clause (ii) shall not apply to any month before January 1, 1996.

"(C) Applicable percentage. For purposes of subparagraph (B), the applicable percentage is as follows:

For calendar year:	The percentage is:
1996	100 percent
1997	90 percent
1998	80 percent.

"(d) Spread of income inclusion on surrender, etc. of contracts.

"(1) In general. If any amount is received under any life insurance policy or endowment or annuity contract described in paragraph (4) of section 264(a) of the Internal Revenue Code of 1986—

"(A) on the complete surrender, redemption, or maturity of such policy or contract during calendar year 1996, 1997, or 1998, or

"(B) in full discharge during any such calendar year of the obligation under the policy or contract which is in the nature of a refund of the consideration paid for the policy or contract,

then (in lieu of any other inclusion in gross income) such amount shall be includible in gross income ratably over the 4-taxable year period beginning with the taxable year such amount would (but for this paragraph) be includible. The preceding sentence shall only apply to the extent the amount is includible in gross income for the taxable year in which the event described in subparagraph (A) or (B) occurs.

"(2) Special rules for applying section 264. A contract shall not be treated as—

"(A) failing to meet the requirement of section 264(c)(1) of the Internal Revenue Code of 1986, or

"(B) a single premium contract under section 264(b)(1) of such Code, solely by reason of an occurrence described in subparagraph (A) or (B) of paragraph (1) of this subsection or

solely by reason of a lapse occurring after October 13, 1995, by reason of no additional premiums being received under the contract.

"(3) Special rule for deferred acquisition costs. In the case of the occurrence of any event described in subparagraph (A) or (B) of paragraph (1) of this subsection with respect to any policy or contract—

"(A) section 848 of the Internal Revenue Code of 1986 shall not apply to the unamortized balance (if any) of the specified policy acquisition expenses attributable to such policy or contract immediately before the insurance company's taxable year in which such event occurs, and

"(B) there shall be allowed as a deduction to such company for such taxable year under chapter 1 of such Code an amount equal to such unamortized balance."

In **1986**, P.L. 99-514, Sec. 1003(a), added para. (a)(4) ... Sec. 1003(b), added the sentence to the end of subsec. (a), effective for contracts purchased after 6/20/86, in tax. yrs. ending after 6/20/86.

In **1964**, P.L. 88-272, Sec. 215(a)(1), added para. (a)(3) ... Sec. 215(a)(2), added the sentence to the end of subsec. (a) ... Sec. 215(b), added subsec. (c), effective for amounts paid or accrued in tax. yrs. begin. after 12/31/63.

Sec. 265. Expenses and interest relating to tax-exempt income.

(a) General rule.

No deduction shall be allowed for—

(1) Expenses. Any amount otherwise allowable as a deduction which is allocable to one or more classes of income other than interest (whether or not any amount of income of that class or classes is received or accrued) wholly exempt from the taxes imposed by this subtitle, or any amount otherwise allowable under section 212 (relating to expenses for production of income) which is allocable to interest (whether or not any amount of such interest is received or accrued) wholly exempt from the taxes imposed by this subtitle.

(2) Interest. Interest on indebtedness incurred or continued to purchase or carry obligations the interest on which is wholly exempt from the taxes imposed by this subtitle.

(3) Certain regulated investment companies. In the case of a regulated investment company which distributes during the taxable year an exempt-interest dividend (including exempt-interest dividends paid after the close of the taxable year as described in section 855), that portion of any amount otherwise allowable as a deduction which the amount of the income of such company wholly exempt from taxes under this subtitle bears to the total of such exempt income and its gross income (excluding from gross income, for this purpose, capital gain net income, as defined in section 1222(9)).

(4) Interest related to exempt-interest dividends. Interest on indebtedness incurred or continued to purchase or carry shares of stock of a regulated investment company which during the taxable year of the holder thereof distributes exempt-interest dividends.

(5) Special rules for application of paragraph (2) in the case of short sales. For purposes of paragraph (2)—

(A) In general. The term "interest" includes any amount paid or incurred—

(i) by any person making a short sale in connection with personal property used in such short sale, or

(ii) by any other person for the use of any collateral with respect to such short sale.

(B) Exception where no return on cash collateral. If—

(i) the taxpayer provides cash as collateral for any short sale, and

(ii) the taxpayer receives no material earnings on such cash during the period of the sale,

subparagraph (A)(i) shall not apply to such short sale.

(6) Section not to apply with respect to parsonage and military housing allowances. No deduction shall be denied under this section for interest on a mortgage on, or real property taxes on, the home of the taxpayer by reason of the receipt of an amount as—

(A) a military housing allowance, or

(B) a parsonage allowance excludable from gross income under section 107.

(b) Pro rata allocation of interest expense of financial institutions to tax-exempt interest.

(1) In general. In the case of a financial institution, no deduction shall be allowed for that portion of the taxpayer's interest expense which is allocable to tax-exempt interest.

(2) Allocation. For purposes of paragraph (1), the portion of the taxpayer's interest expense which is allocable to tax-exempt interest is an amount which bears the same ratio to such interest expense as—

(A) the taxpayer's average adjusted bases (within the meaning of section 1016) of tax-exempt obligations acquired after August 7, 1986, bears to

(B) such average adjusted bases for all assets of the taxpayer.

(3) Exception for certain tax-exempt obligations.

(A) In general. Any qualified tax-exempt obligation acquired after August 7, 1986, shall be treated for purposes of paragraph (2) and section 291(e)(1)(B) as if it were acquired on August 7, 1986.

(B) Qualified tax-exempt obligation.

(i) In general. For purposes of subparagraph (A), the term "qualified tax-exempt obligation" means a tax-exempt obligation—

(I) which is issued after August 7, 1986, by a qualified small issuer,

(II) which is not a private activity bond (as defined in section 141), and

(III) which is designated by the issuer for purposes of this paragraph.

(ii) Certain bonds not treated as private activity bonds. For purposes of clause (i)(II), there shall not be treated as a private activity bond—

(I) any qualified 501(c)(3) bond (as defined in section 145), or

(II) any obligation issued to refund (or which is part of a series of obligations issued to refund) an obligation issued before August 8, 1986, which was not an industrial development bond (as defined in section 103(b)(2) as in effect on the day before the date of the enactment [10/22/86] of the Tax Reform Act of 1986) or a private loan bond (as defined in section 103(o)(2)(A), as so in effect, but without regard to any exception from such definition other than section 103(o)(2)(A)).

(C) Qualified small issuer.

(i) In general. For purposes of subparagraph (B), the term "qualified small issuer" means, with respect to obligations issued during any calendar year, any issuer if the reasonably anticipated amount of tax-exempt obligations (other than obligations described in clause (ii)) which will be issued by such issuer during such calendar year does not exceed $10,000,000.

(ii) Obligations not taken into account in determining status as qualified small issuer. For purposes of clause (i), an obligation is described in this clause if such obligation is—

(I) a private activity bond (other than a qualified 501(c)(3) bond, as defined in section 145),

(II) an obligation to which section 141(a) does not apply by reason of section 1312, 1313, 1316(g), or 1317 of the Tax Reform Act of 1986 and which would (if issued on August 15, 1986) have been an industrial development bond (as defined in section 103(b)(2) as in effect on the day before the date of the enactment of such Act) or a private loan bond (as defined in section 103(o)(2)(A), as so in effect, but without regard to any exception from such definition other than section 103(o)(2)(A)), or

(III) an obligation issued to refund (other than to advance refund within the meaning of section 149(d)(5)) any obligation to the extent the amount of the refunding obligation does not exceed the outstanding amount of the refunded obligation.

(iii) Allocation of amount of issue in certain cases. In the case of an issue under which more than 1 governmental entity receives benefits, if—

(I) all governmental entities receiving benefits from such issue irrevocably agree (before the date of issuance of the issue) on an allocation of the amount of such issue for purposes of this subparagraph, and

(II) such allocation bears a reasonable relationship to the respective benefits received by such entities, then the amount of such issue so allocated to an entity (and only such amount with respect to such issue) shall be taken into account under clause (i) with respect to such entity.

(D) Limitation on amount of obligations which may be designated.

(i) In general. Not more than $10,000,000 of obligations issued by an issuer during any calendar year may be designated by such issuer for purposes of this paragraph.

(ii) Certain refundings of designated obligations deemed designated.—Except as provided in clause (iii), in the case of a refunding (or series of refundings) of a qualified tax-exempt obligation, the refunding obligation shall be treated as a qualified tax-exempt obligation (and shall not be taken into account under clause (i)) if—

(I) the refunding obligation was not taken into account under subparagraph (C) by reason of clause (ii)(III) thereof,

(II) the average maturity date of the refunding obligations issued as part of the issue of which such refunding obligation is a part is not later than the average maturity date of the obligations to be refunded by such issue, and

(III) the refunding obligation has a maturity date which is not later than the date which is 30 years after the date the original qualified tax-exempt obligation was issued.

Subclause (II) shall not apply if the average maturity of the issue of which the original qualified tax-exempt obligation was a part (and of the issue of which the obligations to be refunded are a part) is 3 years or less. For purposes of this clause, average maturity shall be determined in accordance with section 147(b)(2)(A).

(iii) Certain obligations may not be designated or deemed designated. No obligation issued as part of an issue may be designated under this paragraph (or may be treated as designated under clause (ii)) if—

(I) any obligation issued as part of such issue is issued to refund another obligation, and

(II) the aggregate face amount of such issue exceeds $10,000,000.

(E) Aggregation of issuers. For purposes of subparagraphs (C) and (D)—

(i) an issuer and all entities which issue obligations on behalf of such issuer shall be treated as 1 issuer,

(ii) all obligations issued by a subordinate entity shall, for purposes of applying subparagraphs (C) and (D) to each other entity to which such entity is subordinate, be treated as issued by such other entity, and

(iii) an entity formed (or, to the extent provided by the Secretary, availed of) to avoid the purposes of subparagraph (C) or (D) and all entities benefiting thereby shall be treated as 1 issuer.

(F) Treatment of composite issues. In the case of an obligation which is issued as part of a direct or indirect composite issue, such obligation shall not be treated as a qualified tax-exempt obligation unless—

(i) the requirements of this paragraph are met with respect to such composite issue (determined by treating such composite issue as a single issue), and

(ii) the requirements of this paragraph are met with respect to each separate lot of obligations which are part of the issue (determined by treating each such separate lot as a separate issue).

(G) Special rules for obligations issued during 2009 and 2010.

(i) Increase in limitation. In the case of obligations issued during 2009 or 2010, subparagraphs (C)(i), (D)(i), and (D)(iii)(II) shall each be applied by substituting "$30,000,000" for "$10,000,000".

(ii) Qualified 501(c)(3) bonds treated as issued by exempt organization. In the case of a qualified 501(c)(3) bond (as defined in section 145) issued during 2009 or 2010, this paragraph shall be applied by treating the 501(c)(3) organization for whose benefit such bond was issued as the issuer.

(iii) Special rule for qualified financings. In the case of a qualified financing issue issued during 2009 or 2010—

(I) subparagraph (F) shall not apply, and

(II) any obligation issued as a part of such issue shall be treated as a qualified tax-exempt obligation if the requirements of this paragraph are met with respect to each qualified portion of the issue (determined by treating each qualified portion as a separate issue which is issued by the qualified borrower with respect to which such portion relates).

(iv) Qualified financing issue. For purposes of this subparagraph, the term "qualified financing issue" means any composite, pooled, or other conduit financing issue the proceeds of which are used directly or indirectly to make or finance loans to 1 or more ultimate borrowers each of whom is a qualified borrower.

(v) Qualified portion. For purposes of this subparagraph, the term "qualified portion" means that portion of the proceeds which are used with respect to each qualified borrower under the issue.

(vi) Qualified borrower. For purposes of this subparagraph, the term "qualified borrower" means a borrower which is a State or political subdivision thereof or an organization described in section 501(c)(3) and exempt from taxation under section 501(a).

(4) **Definitions.** For purposes of this subsection—

(A) Interest expense. The term "interest expense" means the aggregate amount allowable to the taxpayer as a deduction for interest for the taxable year (determined without regard to this subsection, section 264, and section 291). For purposes of the preceding sentence, the term "interest" includes amounts (whether or not designated as interest) paid in respect of deposits, investment certificates, or withdrawable or repurchasable shares.

(B) Tax-exempt obligation. The term "tax-exempt obligation" means any obligation the interest on which is wholly exempt from taxes imposed by this subtitle. Such term includes shares of stock of a regulated investment company which during the taxable year of the holder thereof distributes exempt-interest dividends.

(5) **Financial institution.** For purposes of this subsection, the term "financial institution" means any person who—

(A) accepts deposits from the public in the ordinary course of such person's trade or business, and is subject to Federal or State supervision as a financial institution, or

(B) is a corporation described in section 585(a)(2).

(6) **Special rules.**

(A) Coordination with subsection (a). If interest on any indebtedness is disallowed under subsection (a) with respect to any tax-exempt obligation—

(i) such disallowed interest shall not be taken into account for purposes of applying this subsection, and

(ii) for purposes of applying paragraph (2), the adjusted basis of such tax-exempt obligation shall be reduced (but not below zero) by the amount of such indebtedness.

(B) Coordination with section 263A. This section shall be applied before the application of section 263A (relating to capitalization of certain expenses where taxpayer produces property).

(7) **De minimis exception for bonds issued during 2009 or 2010.**

(A) In general. In applying paragraph (2)(A), there shall not be taken into account tax-exempt obligations issued during 2009 or 2010.

(B) Limitation. The amount of tax-exempt obligations not taken into account by reason of subparagraph (A) shall not exceed 2 percent of the amount determined under paragraph (2)(B).

(C) Refundings. For purposes of this paragraph, a refunding bond (whether a current or advance refunding) shall be treated as issued on the date of the issuance of the refunded bond (or in the case of a series of refundings, the original bond).

In 2009, P.L. 111-5, Sec. 1501(a), added para. (b)(7), effective for obligations issued after 12/31/2008.
—P.L. 111-5, Sec. 1502(a), added subpara. (b)(3)(G), effective for obligations issued after 12/31/2008.
In 1998, P.L. 105-206, Sec. 6010(o)(3)(B), substituted "except that, in the case of a master contract (within the meaning of section 264(f)(4)(E) of the Internal Revenue Code of 1986), the addition of covered lives shall be treated as a new contract only with respect to such additional covered lives." for "but the addition of covered lives shall be treated as a new contract only with respect to such additional covered lives. For purposes of this subsection, an increase in the death benefit under a policy or contract issued in connection with a lapse described in section 501(d)(2) of the Health Insurance Portability and Accountability Act of 1996 [P.L.104-191] shall not be treated as a new contract." in Sec. 1084(d) [sic (f)], P.L. 105-34, the effective date for amendments made by Sec. 1084, see below.
In 1997, P.L. 105-34, Sec. 1084(c) [sic (e)], added ", section 264," before "and section 291" in subpara. (b)(4)(A), effective as provided in Sec. 1084(d)[sic (f)] of this Act [as amended by Sec. 6010(o)(3)(A), 105-206, see above], which reads:
"(d)[sic (f)] Effective date. The amendments made by this section shall apply to contracts issued after June 8, 1997, in taxable years ending after such date. For purposes of the preceding sentence, any material increase in the death benefit or other material change in the contract shall be treated as a new contract except that, in the case of a master contract (within the meaning of section 264(f)(4)(E) of the Internal Revenue Code of 1986), the addition of covered lives shall be treated as a new contract only with respect to such additional covered lives."
In 1990, P.L. 101-508, Sec. 11801(c)(4), amended para. (a)(2), effective 11/5/90 except as provided in Sec. 11821(b) of this Act, reproduced in note following Code Sec. 110.
Prior to amendment, para. (a)(2) read as follows:
"(2) Interest. Interest on indebtedness incurred or continued to purchase or carry obligations the interest on which is wholly exempt from the taxes imposed by this subtitle, or to purchase or carry any certificate to the extent the interest on such certificate is excludable under section 128."
In 1989, P.L. 101-239, Sec. 7811(f)(2), amended Sec. 1009(b)(3)(B) of P.L. 100-647, by substituting "section 265(b)(3)(B)(i)(III)" for "section 265(b)(3)(B)(iii)".
—P.L. 101-73, Sec. 1401(a)(3)(B), repealed Sec. 904(c)(2)(B) of P.L. 99-514, effective as provided in Sec. 1401(c)(3) of this Act, which reads as follows:
"(3) Subsection (a)(3) [Sec. 1401(a)(3)].—
"(A) In general.—The amendments made by subsection (a)(3) [Sec. 1401(a)(3)] shall apply to any amount received or accrued by the financial institution on or after May 10, 1989, except that such amendments shall not apply to

Code Sec. 265 — Limitations on deduction

transfers on or after such date pursuant to an acquisition to which the amendment made by subsection (a)(1) does not apply.

"(B) Interim rule.— In the case of any payment pursuant to a transaction on or after May 10, 1989, and before the date on which the Secretary of the Treasury (or his delegate) takes action in exercise of his regulatory authority under section 597 of the Internal Revenue Code of 1986 (as amended by subsection (a)(3) [Sec. 1401(a)(3)]), the taxpayer may rely on the legislative history for the amendments made by subsection (a)(3) [Sec. 1401(a)(3)] in determining the proper treatment of such payment."

Prior to repeal, Sec. 904(c)(2)(B) of P.L. 99-514 [as amended by Sec. 4012(c)(2) of P.L. 100-647, see below] read as follows:

"(B) Clarification of treatment of amounts excluded under section 597 — Section 265 of the Internal Revenue Code of 1986 (as amended by this title) shall not deny any deduction by reason of such deduction being allocable to amounts excluded from gross income under section 597 of the Internal Revenue Code of 1954 (as in effect on the day before the date of the enactment of this Act)."

In **1988**, P.L. 100-647, Sec. 1009(b)(1)(A)-(E), amended Sec. 902(f)(3) of P.L. 99-514 [reproduced below] part of the effective date for changes made by Secs. 902(a), (b) and (d) of P.L. 99-514, by substituting "distribution facility" for "distribution company" Sec. 902(f)(3)(F) of P.L. 99-514 substituting "2 Festival Market Place projects at Union Pier Terminal and 1 project at the Remount Road Container Yard, State Pier No. 15 at North Charleston Terminal" for "waterfront project" in Sec. 902(f)(3)(L) of P.L. 99-514 substituting "Pontalba" for "Pontabla" in Sec. 902(f)(3)(M) of P.L. 99-514 substituting "Homewood, Alabama, the" for "Birmingham, Alabama" Sec. 902(f)(3)(P) of P.L. 99-514 and by adding Secs. 902(f)(3)(T)-(V) of P.L. 99-514 [reproduced below] . . . Sec. 1009(b)(2), amended Sec. 902(f)(4) of P.L. 99-514 [reproduced below] by substituting "paragraph" for "subparagraph" . . . Sec. 1009(b)(7)(A), (B), amended Sec. 902(f)(4) of P.L. 99-514 [reproduced below] by adding "and qualified 501(c)(3) bonds designated by such Governor for purposes of this paragraph" after "1987)," and substituting "subparagraph" for "paragraph", see below

—P.L. 100-647, Sec. 1009(b)(3)(A), amended para. (b)(3), effective for tax. yrs. ending after 12/31/86. Prior to amendment see Secs. 902(f)(2)-(4) of P.L. 99-514, reproduced below.

Prior to amendment, para. (b)(3) read as follows:

"(3) Exception for certain tax-exempt obligations.

"(A) In general. Any qualified tax-exempt obligation acquired after August 7, 1986, shall be treated for purposes of paragraph (2) and section 291(e)(1)(B) as if it were acquired on August 7, 1986.

"(B) Qualified tax-exempt obligation. For purposes of subparagraph (A), the term 'qualified tax-exempt obligation' means a tax-exempt obligation which—

"(i) is not a private activity bond (as defined in section 141), and

"(ii) is designated by the issuer for purposes of this paragraph. For purposes of the preceding sentence and subparagraph (C), a qualified 501(c)(3) bond (as defined in section 145) shall not be treated as a private activity bond.

"(C) Limitation on issuer. An obligation issued by an issuer during any calendar year shall not be treated as a qualified tax-exempt obligation unless the reasonably anticipated amount of qualified tax-exempt obligations (other than private activity bonds) which will be issued by such issuer during such calendar year does not exceed $10,000,000.

"(D) Over all $10,000,000 limitation. Not more than $10,000,000 of obligations issued by an issuer during any calendar year may be designated by such issuer for purposes of this paragraph.

"(E) Aggregation of issuers. For purposes of subparagraphs (C) and (D), an issuer and all subordinate entities thereof shall be treated as 1 issuer."

—P.L. 100-647, Sec. 1009(b)(3)(B)-(D), [as amended by Sec. 7811(f)(2) of P.L. 101-239, see above] provide:

"(B) In the case of any obligation issued after August 7, 1986, and before January 1, 1987, the time for making a designation with respect to such obligation under section 265(b)(3)(B)(i)(III) of the 1986 Code shall not expire before January 1, 1989.

"(C) If—

"(i) an obligation is issued on or after January 1, 1986, and on or before August 7, 1986,

"(ii) when such obligation was issued, the issuer made a designation that it intended to qualify under section 802(e)(3) of H.R. 3838 of the 99th Congress as passed by the House of Representatives, and

"(iii) the issuer makes an election under this subparagraph with respect to such obligation,

for purposes of section 265(b)(3) of the 1986 Code, such obligation shall be treated as issued on August 8, 1986.

"(D)(i) Except as provided in clause (ii), the following provisions of section 265(b)(3) of the 1986 Code (as amended by this subparagraph (A)) shall apply to obligations issued after June 30, 1987:

"(I) subparagraph (C)(ii)(III),

"(II) clauses (ii) and (iii) of subparagraph (D), and

"(III) subparagraphs (E) and (F).

"(ii) At the election of an issuer (made at such time and in such manner as the Secretary of the Treasury or his delegate may prescribe), the provisions referred to in clause (i) shall apply to such issuer as if included in the amendments made by section 902(a) of the Tax Reform Act of 1986."

—P.L. 100-647, Sec. 4012(c)(2), amended Sec. 904(c)(2)(B) of P.L. 99-514 by substituting "Section 265" for "Section 265(a)(1)" [Sec. 904(c)(2)(B) of P.L. 99-514 repealed by Sec. 1401(a)(3)(B) of P.L. 101-73, see above]

In **1986**, P.L. 99-514, Sec. 144, added para. (a)(6), effective for tax. yrs. begin. before, on or after 12/31/86.

—P.L. 99-514, Sec. 902(a), added subsec. (b) . . . Sec. 902(b), deleted the second sentence from para. (a)(2) . . . Sec. 902(d), substituted "(a) General rule. No deduction shall be allowed for—" for "No deduction shall be allowed for—" at the beginning of subsec. (a), effective for tax. yrs. ending after 12/31/86. [see Secs. 1009(b)(3)(B)-(D) of P.L. 100-647, above] Secs. 902(f)(2)-(4) [as amended by Secs. 1009(b)(1)(A)-(E), (b)(2), (b)(7)(A), (B) of P.L. 100-647 see above] of this Act provide:

"(2) Obligations acquired pursuant to certain commitments. For purposes of sections 265(b) and 291(e)(1)(B) of the Internal Revenue Code of 1986, any tax-exempt obligation which is acquired after August 7, 1986, pursuant to a direct or indirect written commitment—

"(A) to purchase or repurchase such obligation, and

"(B) entered into on or before September 25, 1985,

shall be treated as an obligation acquired before August 8, 1986.

"(3) Transitional rules. For purposes of sections 265(b) and 291(e)(1)(B) of the Internal Revenue Code of 1986, obligations with respect to any of the following projects shall be treated as obligations acquired before August 8, 1986, in the hands of the first and any subsequent financial institution acquiring such obligations:

"(A) Park Forest, Illinois, redevelopment project.
"(B) Clinton, Tennessee, Carriage Trace project.
"(C) Savannah, Georgia, Mall Terrace Warehouse project.
"(D) Chattanooga, Tennessee, Warehouse Row project.
"(E) Dalton, Georgia, Towne Square project.
"(F) Milwaukee, Wisconsin, Standard Electric Supply Company — distribution facility.
"(G) Wausau, Wisconsin, urban renewal project.
"(H) Cassville, Missouri, UDAG project.
"(I) Outlook Envelope Company — plant expansion.
"(J) Woodstock, Connecticut, Crabtree Warehouse partnership.
"(K) Louisville, Kentucky, Speed Mansion renovation project.
"(L) Charleston, South Carolina
2 Festival Market Place projects at Union Pier Terminal and 1 project at the Remount Road Container Yard, State Pier No. 15 at North Charleston Terminal.
"(M) New Orleans, Louisiana, Upper Pontalba Building renovation.
"(N) Woodward Wight Building.
"(O) Minneapolis, Minnesota, Miller Milling Company — flour mill project.
"(P) Homewood, Alabama, the Club Apartments.
"(Q) Charlotte, North Carolina — qualified mortgage bonds acquired by NCNB bank ($5,250,000).
"(R) Grand Rapids, Michigan, Central Bank project.
"(S) Ruppman Marketing Services, Inc. — building project.
"(T) Bellows Falls, Vermont — building project.
"(U) East Broadway Project, Louisville, Kentucky.
"(V) O.K. Industries, Oklahoma.

"(4) Additional transitional rule. Obligations issued pursuant to an allocation of a State's volume limitation for private activity bonds, which allocation was made by Executive Order 25 signed by the Governor of the State on May 22, 1986 (as such order may be amended before January 1, and qualified 501(c)(3) bonds designated by such Governor for purposes of this paragraph, shall be treated as acquired on or before August 7, 1986, in the hands of the first and any subsequent financial institution acquiring such obligation. The aggregate face amount of obligations to which this paragraph applies shall not exceed $200,000,000."

Prior to amendment, the second sentence of para. (a)(2) read as follows:

"In applying the preceding sentence to a financial institution (other than a bank) which is a face-amount certificate company registered under the Investment Company Act of 1940 (15 U.S.C. 80a-1 and following) and which is subject to the banking laws of the State in which such institution is incorporated, interest on face-amount certificates (as defined in section 2(a)(15) of such Act) issued by such institution, and interest on amounts received for the purchase of such certificates to be issued by such institution, shall not be considered as interest on indebtedness incurred or continued to purchase or carry obligations the interest on which is wholly exempt from the taxes imposed by this subtitle, to the extent that the average amount of such obligations held by such institution during the taxable year (as determined under regulations prescribed by the Secretary) does not exceed 15 percent of the average of the total assets held by such institution during the taxable year (as so determined)."

—P.L. 99-514, Sec. 904(c)(2)(B), [as amended by Sec. 4012(c)(2) of P.L. 100-647, see above] dealing with Clarification of treatment of amounts excluded under Code Sec. 597 is repealed by Sec. 1401(a)(3)(B) of P.L. 101-73, see above.

In **1984**, P.L. 98-369, Sec. 16(a), repealed as if not enacted Sec. 302(c)(2) of P.L. 97-34 which substituted "or to purchase or carry obligations or shares, or to make other deposits or investments, the interest on which is described in section 128(c)(1) to the extent such interest is excludable from gross income under section 128" for "or to purchase or carry any certificate to the extent the interest on such certificate is excludable under section 128" [added by Sec. 301(b)(2) of P.L. 97-34] in para. (2), effective as if the amendment made by Sec. 302(c)(2) of P.L. 97-34 had not been enacted.

—P.L. 98-369, Sec. 56(c), added new para. (5), effective for short sales after 7/18/84 in tax. yrs. end. after 7/18/84.

—P.L. 98-369, Sec. 1052, provides:

"Sec. 1052. Allocation of expenses to parsonage allowances.

"With respect to any mortgage interest or real property tax costs paid or incurred before January 1, 1986, by any minister of the gospel who owned and occupied a home before January 3, 1983 (or had a contract to purchase a home before such date and subsequently owned and occupied such home), the application of section 265(1) of the Internal Revenue Code of 1954 to such costs shall be

1,738

Limitations on deduction — Code Sec. 267(c)

determined without regard to Revenue Ruling 83-3 (and without regard to any other regulation, ruling, or decision reaching the same result, or a result similar to the result, set forth in such Revenue Ruling)."

In 1981, P.L. 97-34, Sec. 301(b)(2), added ", or to purchase or carry any certificate to the extent the interest on such certificate is excludable under section 128" after "116" in para. (2), for tax. yrs. end. after 9/30/81.

— P.L. 97-34, Sec. 302(b)(1), amended the effective date for changes made by Sec. 404(b)(2) of P.L. 96-223 from tax. yrs. begin after 12/31/80 and before 1/1/83 to tax. yrs. begin. after 12/31/80 and before 1/1/82 [see below].

In 1980, P.L. 96-223, Sec. 404(b)(2), added ", or to purchase or carry obligations or shares, or to make deposits or other investments, the interest on which is described in section 116(c) to the extent such interest is excludable from gross income under section 116" after "subtitle," to the first sentence of subsec. (2), for tax. yrs. begin. after 12/31/80 and before 1/1/82.

In 1976, P.L. 94-455, Sec. 1901(a)(37), deleted "(other than obligations of the United States issued after September 24, 1917, and originally subscribed for by the taxpayer)", after "carry obligations" in the first sentence of para. (2), effective for tax. yrs. begin. after 12/31/76.

— P.L. 94-455, Sec. 1906(b)(13)(A), substituted "Secretary" for "Secretary or his delegate" in para. (2), effective for tax. yrs. begin. after 12/31/76.

— P.L. 94-455, Sec. 2137(e), added paras. (3) and (4), effective for tax. yrs. begin. after 12/31/75.

In 1964, P.L. 88-272, Sec. 216(a), added the last sentence in (2), effective for tax. yrs. end. after 2/21/64.

Sec. 266. Carrying charges.

No deduction shall be allowed for amounts paid or accrued for such taxes and carrying charges as, under regulations prescribed by the Secretary, are chargeable to capital account with respect to property, if the taxpayer elects, in accordance with such regulations, to treat such taxes or charges as so chargeable.

In 1976, P.L. 94-455, Sec. 1906(b)(13)(A), substituted "Secretary" for "Secretary or his delegate" in Code Sec. 266, effective for tax. yrs. begin. after 12/31/76.

Sec. 267. Losses, expenses, and interest with respect to transactions between related taxpayers.

(a) In general.

(1) Deduction for losses disallowed. No deduction shall be allowed in respect of any loss from the sale or exchange of property, directly or indirectly, between persons specified in any of the paragraphs of subsection (b). The preceding sentence shall not apply to any loss of the distributing corporation (or the distributee) in the case of a distribution in complete liquidation.

(2) Matching of deduction and payee income item in the case of expenses and interest. If—

(A) by reason of the method of accounting of the person to whom the payment is to be made, the amount thereof is not (unless paid) includible in the gross income of such person, and

(B) at the close of the taxable year of the taxpayer for which (but for this paragraph) the amount would be deductible under this chapter, both the taxpayer and the person to whom the payment is to be made are persons specified in any of the paragraphs of subsection (b),

then any deduction allowable under this chapter in respect of such amount shall be allowable as of the day as of which such amount is includible in the gross income of the person to whom the payment is made (or, if later, as of the day on which it would be so allowable but for this paragraph). For purposes of this paragraph, in the case of a personal service corporation (within the meaning of section 441(i)(2)), such corporation and any employee-owner (within the meaning of section 269A(b)(2), as modified by section 441(i)(2)) shall be treated as persons specified in subsection (b).

(3) Payments to foreign persons.

(A) In general. The Secretary shall by regulations apply the matching principle of paragraph (2) in cases in which the person to whom the payment is to be made is not a United States person.

(B) Special rule for certain foreign entities.

(i) In general. Notwithstanding subparagraph (A), in the case of any item payable to a controlled foreign corporation (as defined in section 957) or a passive foreign investment company (as defined in section 1297), a deduction shall be allowable to the payor with respect to such amount for any taxable year before the taxable year in which paid only to the extent that an amount attributable to such item is includible (determined without regard to properly allocable deductions and qualified deficits under section 952(c)(1)(B)) during such prior taxable year in the gross income of a United States person who owns (within the meaning of section 958(a)) stock in such corporation.

(ii) Secretarial authority. The Secretary may by regulation exempt transactions from the application of clause (i), including any transaction which is entered into by a payor in the ordinary course of a trade or business in which the payor is predominantly engaged and in which the payment of the accrued amounts occurs within 8½ months after accrual or within such other period as the Secretary may prescribe.

(b) Relationships.

The persons referred to in subsection (a) are:

(1) Members of a family, as defined in subsection (c)(4);

(2) An individual and a corporation more than 50 percent in value of the outstanding stock of which is owned, directly or indirectly, by or for such individual;

(3) Two corporations which are members of the same controlled group (as defined in subsection (f));

(4) A grantor and a fiduciary of any trust;

(5) A fiduciary of a trust and a fiduciary of another trust, if the same person is a grantor of both trusts;

(6) A fiduciary of a trust and a beneficiary of such trust;

(7) A fiduciary of a trust and a beneficiary of another trust, if the same person is a grantor of both trusts;

(8) A fiduciary of a trust and a corporation more than 50 percent in value of the outstanding stock of which is owned, directly or indirectly, by or for the trust or by or for a person who is a grantor of the trust;

(9) A person and an organization to which section 501 (relating to certain educational and charitable organizations which are exempt from tax) applies and which is controlled directly or indirectly by such person or (if such person is an individual) by members of the family of such individual;

(10) A corporation and a partnership if the same persons own—

(A) more than 50 percent in value of the outstanding stock of the corporation, and

(B) more than 50 percent of the capital interest, or the profits interest, in the partnership;

(11) An S corporation and another S corporation if the same persons own more than 50 percent in value of the outstanding stock of each corporation;

(12) An S corporation and a C corporation, if the same persons own more than 50 percent in value of the outstanding stock of each corporation; or

(13) Except in the case of a sale or exchange in satisfaction of a pecuniary bequest, an executor of an estate and a beneficiary of such estate.

(c) Constructive ownership of stock.

For purposes of determining, in applying subsection (b), the ownership of stock—

(1) Stock owned, directly or indirectly, by or for a corporation, partnership, estate, or trust shall be considered as being owned proportionately by or for its shareholders, partners, or beneficiaries;

(2) An individual shall be considered as owning the stock owned, directly or indirectly, by or for his family;

(3) An individual owning (otherwise than by the application of paragraph (2)) any stock in a corporation shall be considered as owning the stock owned, directly or indirectly, by or for his partner;

(4) The family of an individual shall include only his brothers and sisters (whether by the whole or half blood), spouse, ancestors, and lineal descendants; and

(5) Stock constructively owned by a person by reason of the application of paragraph (1) shall, for the purpose of applying paragraph (1), (2), or (3), be treated as actually owned by such person, but stock constructively owned by an individual by reason of the application of paragraph (2) or (3) shall not be treated as owned by him for the purpose of again applying either of such paragraphs in order to make another the constructive owner of such stock.

(d) **Amount of gain where loss previously disallowed.** If—

(1) in the case of a sale or exchange of property to the taxpayer a loss sustained by the transferor is not allowable to the transferor as a deduction by reason of subsection (a)(1) (or by reason of section 24(b) of the Internal Revenue Code of 1939); and

(2) after December 31, 1953, the taxpayer sells or otherwise disposes of such property (or of other property the basis of which in his hands is determined directly or indirectly by reference to such property) at a gain,

then such gain shall be recognized only to the extent that it exceeds so much of such loss as is properly allocable to the property sold or otherwise disposed of by the taxpayer. This subsection applies with respect to taxable years ending after December 31, 1953. This subsection shall not apply if the loss sustained by the transferor is not allowable to the transferor as a deduction by reason of section 1091 (relating to wash sales) or by reason of section 118 of the Internal Revenue Code of 1939.

(e) **Special rules for pass-thru entities.**

(1) **In general.** In the case of any amount paid or incurred by, to, or on behalf of, a pass-thru entity, for purposes of applying subsection (a)(2)—

(A) such entity,

(B) in the case of—

(i) a partnership, any person who owns (directly or indirectly) any capital interest or profits interest of such partnership, or

(ii) an S corporation, any person who owns (directly or indirectly) any of the stock of such corporation,

(C) any person who owns (directly or indirectly) any capital interest or profits interest of a partnership in which such entity owns (directly or indirectly) any capital interest or profits interest, and

(D) any person related (within the meaning of subsection (b) of this section or section 707(b)(1)) to a person described in subparagraph (B) or (C),

shall be treated as persons specified in a paragraph of subsection (b). Subparagraph (C) shall apply to a transaction only if such transaction is related either to the operations of the partnership described in such subparagraph or to an interest in such partnership.

(2) **Pass-thru entity.** For purposes of this section, the term "pass-thru entity" means—

(A) a partnership, and

(B) an S corporation.

(3) **Constructive ownership in the case of partnerships.** For purposes of determining ownership of a capital interest or profits interest of a partnership, the principles of subsection (c) shall apply, except that—

(A) paragraph (3) of subsection (c) shall not apply, and

(B) interests owned (directly or indirectly) by or for a C corporation shall be considered as owned by or for any shareholder only if such shareholder owns (directly or indirectly) 5 percent or more in value of the stock of such corporation.

(4) **Subsection (a)(2) not to apply to certain guaranteed payments of partnerships.** In the case of any amount paid or incurred by a partnership, subsection (a)(2) shall not apply to the extent that section 707(c) applies to such amount.

(5) **Exception for certain expenses and interest of partnerships owning low-income housing.**

(A) In general. This subsection shall not apply with respect to qualified expenses and interest paid or incurred by a partnership owning low-income housing to—

(i) any qualified 5-percent or less partner of such partnership, or

(ii) any person related (within the meaning of subsection (b) of this section or section 707(b)(1)) to any qualified 5-percent or less partner of such partnership.

(B) Qualified 5-percent or less partner. For purposes of this paragraph, the term "qualified 5-percent or less partner" means any partner who has (directly or indirectly) an interest of 5 percent or less in the aggregate capital and profits interests of the partnership but only if—

(i) such partner owned the low-income housing at all times during the 2-year period ending on the date such housing was transferred to the partnership, or

(ii) such partnership acquired the low-income housing pursuant to a purchase, assignment, or other transfer from the Department of Housing and Urban Development or any State or local housing authority.

For purposes of the preceding sentence, a partner shall be treated as holding any interest in the partnership which is held (directly or indirectly) by any person related (within the meaning of subsection (b) of this section or section 707(b)(1)) to such partner.

(C) Qualified expenses and interest. For purpose of this paragraph, the term "qualified expenses and interest" means any expense or interest incurred by the partnership with respect to low-income housing held by the partnership but—

(i) only if the amount of such expense or interest (as the case may be) is unconditionally required to be paid by the partnership not later than 10 years after the date such amount was incurred, and

(ii) in the case of such interest, only if such interest is incurred at an annual rate not in excess of 12 percent.

(D) Low-income housing. For purposes of this paragraph, the term "low-income housing" means—

(i) any interest in property described in clause (i), (ii), (iii), or (iv) of section 1250(a)(1)(B), and

(ii) any interest in a partnership owning such property.

(6) **Cross reference.** For additional rules relating to partnerships, see section 707(b).

Limitations on deduction Code Sec. 267

(f) **Controlled group defined; special rules applicable to controlled groups.**

(1) **Controlled group defined.** For purposes of this section, the term "controlled group" has the meaning given to such term by section 1563(a), except that—

(A) "more than 50 percent" shall be substituted for "at least 80 percent" each place it appears in section 1563(a), and

(B) the determination shall be made without regard to subsections (a)(4) and (e)(3)(C) of section 1563.

(2) **Deferral (rather than denial) of loss from sale or exchange between members.** In the case of any loss from the sale or exchange of property which is between members of the same controlled group and to which subsection (a)(1) applies (determined without regard to this paragraph but with regard to paragraph (3))—

(A) subsections (a)(1) and (d) shall not apply to such loss, but

(B) such loss shall be deferred until the property is transferred outside such controlled group and there would be recognition of loss under consolidated return principles or until such other time as may be prescribed in regulations.

(3) **Loss deferral rules not to apply in certain cases.**

(A) Transfer to DISC. For purposes of applying subsection (a)(1), the term "controlled group" shall not include a DISC.

(B) Certain sales of inventory. Except to the extent provided in regulations prescribed by the Secretary, subsection (a)(1) shall not apply to the sale or exchange of property between members of the same controlled group (or persons described in subsection (b)(10)) if—

(i) such property in the hands of the transferor is property described in section 1221(a)(1),

(ii) such sale or exchange is in the ordinary course of the transferor's trade or business,

(iii) such property in the hands of the transferee is property described in section 1221(a)(1), and

(iv) the transferee or the transferor is a foreign corporation.

(C) Certain foreign currency losses. To the extent provided in regulations, subsection (a)(1) shall not apply to any loss sustained by a member of a controlled group on the repayment of a loan made to another member of such group if such loan is payable in a foreign currency or is denominated in such a currency and such loss is attributable to a reduction in value of such foreign currency.

(D) Redemptions by fund-of-funds regulated investment companies. Except to the extent provided in regulations prescribed by the Secretary, subsection (a)(1) shall not apply to any distribution in redemption of stock of a regulated investment company if—

(i) such company issues only stock which is redeemable upon the demand of the stockholder, and

(ii) such redemption is upon the demand of another regulated investment company.

(4) **Determination of relationship resulting in disallowance of loss, for purposes of other provisions.** For purposes of any other section of this title which refers to a relationship which would result in a disallowance of losses under this section, deferral under paragraph (2) shall be treated as disallowance.

(g) **Coordination with section 1041.**

Subsection (a)(1) shall not apply to any transfer described in section 1041(a) (relating to transfers of property between spouses or incident to divorce).

In **2010**, P.L. 111-325, Sec. 306(b), added subpara. (f)(3)(D), effective for distributions after 12/22/2010.

In **2004**, P.L. 108-357, Sec. 841(b)(1), substituted "(A) In general. The Secretary" for "The Secretary" in para. (a)(3)... Sec. 841(b)(2), added subpara. (a)(3)(B), effective for payments accrued on or after 10/22/2004.

In **1999**, P.L. 106-170, Sec. 532(c)(2)(C), substituted "section 1221(a)(1)" for "section 1221(1)" in clauses (f)(3)(B)(i) and (iii), effective for any instrument held, acquired, or entered into, any transaction entered into, and supplies held or acquired on or after 12/17/99.

In **1997**, P.L. 105-34, Sec. 1308(a), deleted "or" at the end of para. (b)(11), substituted "; or" for the period at the end of para. (b)(12), and added para. (b)(13), effective for tax. yrs. begin. after 8/5/97.

—P.L. 105-34, Sec. 1604(e)(1), added para. (f)(4), effective for transactions after 12/31/83, in tax. yrs. end. 12/31/83, excepting property transferred to a foreign corporation on or before 3/1/84.

In **1988**, P.L. 100-647, Sec. 1006(e)(9)(A), deleted "(other than a loss in case of a distribution in corporate liquidation)" which followed "of property" in para. (a)(1)... Sec. 1006(e)(9)(B), added a sentence at the end of para. (a)(1), effective for any distribution in complete liquidation, and any sale or exchange made by a corporation after 7/31/86, unless such corporation is completely liquidated before 1/1/87.

—P.L. 100-647, Sec. 1008(e)(6), corrected Sec. 806(c)(2) of P.L. 99-514, by having it add the last sentence to para. (a)(2) instead of subsec. (a), see below.

—P.L. 100-647, Sec. 1008(e)(7)(A), deleted "(including such short taxable year)" after "first 4 taxable years" in Sec. 806(e)(2)(C) of P.L. 99-514 [reproduced below]... Sec. 1008(e)(7)(B), substituted "the partner's or shareholder's taxable year with or within which the partnership's or S corporation's short taxable year ends" for "short taxable year" the second place it appeared in Sec. 806(e)(2)(C) of P.L. 99-514 [reproduced below]... Sec. 1008(e)(8)(A), substituted "the taxpayer's first taxable year beginning after December 31, 1986" for "any taxable year" in Sec. 806(e)(2) of P.L. 99-514 [reproduced below]... Sec. 1008(e)(8)(B), substituted "partnership, S corporation, or personal service corporation" for "taxpayer" each place it appeared in Sec. 806(e)(2) of P.L. 99-514 [reproduced below], see below.

—P.L. 100-647, Sec. 1008(e)(9), provides:

"(9) Nothing in section 806 of the Reform Act or in any legislative history relating thereto shall be construed as requiring the Secretary to permit an automatic change of a taxable year."

—P.L. 100-647, Sec. 1008(e)(10), added Sec. 806(e)(3) of P.L. 99-514 [reproduced below] see below.

In **1986**, P.L. 99-514, Sec. 803(b)(5)(A), substituted "property described in clause (i), (ii), (iii), or (iv) of section 1250(a)(1)(B)" for "low-income housing (as defined in paragraph (5) of section 189(e))" in subpara. (e)(5)(D)... Sec. 803(b)(5)(B), substituted "such property" for "low-income housing (as so defined)" in subpara. (e)(5)(D), effective for costs incurred after 12/31/86, in tax. yrs. end. after 12/31/86.

—P.L. 99-514, Sec. 806(c)(2), [as amended by Sec. 1008(e)(6) of P.L. 100-647, see above], added the last sentence to para. (a)(2), effective for tax. yrs. begin. after 12/31/86 [see Sec. 1008(e)(9) of P.L. 100-647, reproduced above]. Sec. 806(e)(2) [as amended by P.L. 100-647 Secs. 1008(e)(7), (8) and (10), see above] of this Act provides:

"(2) Change in accounting period. — In the case of any partnership, S corporation, or personal service corporation required by the amendments made by this section to change its accounting period for the taxpayer's first taxable year beginning after December, 31, 1986 —

"(A) such change shall be treated as initiated by the partnership, S corporation, or personal service corporation

"(B) such change shall be treated as having been made with the consent of the Secretary, and

"(C) with respect to any partner or shareholder of an S corporation which is required to include the items from more than 1 taxable year of the partnership or S corporation in any 1 taxable year, income in excess of expenses of such partnership or corporation for the short taxable year required by such amendments shall be taken into account ratably in each of the first 4 taxable years beginning after December 31, 1986, unless such partner or shareholder elects to include all such income in the partner's or shareholder's taxable year with or within which the partnership's of S corporation's short taxable year ends.

Subparagraph (c) shall apply to a shareholder of an S corporation only if such corporation was an S corporation for a taxable year beginning in 1986.

"(3) Basis, etc, rules.—

"(A) Basis rule. The adjusted basis of any partner's interest in a partnership or shareholder's stock in an S corporation shall be determined as if all of the income to be taken into account ratably in the 4 taxable years referred to in paragraph (2)(C) were included in gross income for the 1st of such taxable years.

"(B) Treatment of dispositions. If any interest in a partnership or stock in an S corporation is disposed of before the last taxable year in the spread period, all amounts which would be included in the gross income of the partner or shareholder for subsequent taxable years in the spread period under paragraph (2)(C) and attributable to the interest or stock disposed of shall be included in gross income for the taxable year in which the disposition occurs. For purposes of the preceding sentence, the term 'spread period' means the period consisting of the 4 taxable years referred to in paragraph (2)(C)."

—P.L. 99-514, Sec. 1812(c)(1), added para. (a)(3)... Sec. 1812(c)(2), added "(or persons described in subsection (b)(10))" after "same controlled group" in subpara. (f)(3)(B)... Sec. 1812(c)(3)(C), added para. (e)(6)... Sec. 1812(c)(4)(A), substituted "own" for "owns" in para. (b)(12), effective for tax. yrs. begin. after

1,741

Code Sec. 267 — Limitations on deduction

12/31/83. Special rules are provided by Sec. 174(c)(1) and (c)(3) of P.L. 98-369, see below.

— P.L. 99-514, Sec. 1812(c)(5), provides:

"(5) Exception for certain indebtedness.— Clause (i) of section 174(c)(3)(A) of the Tax Reform Act of 1984 [P.L. 98-369, see below] shall be applied by substituting 'December 31, 1983' for 'September 29, 1983' in the case of indebtedness which matures on January 1, 1999, the payments on which from January 1989 through November 1993 equal U/L plus $77,600, the payments on which from December 1993 to maturity equal U/L plus $50,100, and which accrued interest at 13.75 percent through December 31, 1989."

— P.L. 99-514, Sec. 1842(a), added subsec. (g), effective for transfers after 7/18/84, in tax. yrs. end. after 7/18/84.

In 1984, P.L. 98-369, Sec. 174(a)(1), amended subsec. (a) . . . Sec. 174(a)(2), deleted subsec. (e) . . . Sec. 174(b)(1), deleted subsec. (f) and added new subsec. (e), effective for amounts allowable as deductions under chapter 1 of the Internal Revenue Code of 1954 for tax. yrs. begin. after 12/31/83. Sec. 174(c)(1) provides that: "For purposes of the preceding sentence, the allowability of a deduction shall be determined without regard to any disallowance or postponement of deductions under section 267 of such Code."

Sec. 174(c)(3) provides the following exceptions:

"(3) Exception for existing indebtedness, etc.—

"(A) In general.— The amendments made by this section shall not apply to any amount paid or incurred —

"(i) on indebtedness incurred on or before September 29, 1983[December 31, 1983 in the case of certain indebtedness, see Sec. 1812(c)(5) of P.L. 99-514, above], or

"(ii) pursuant to a contract which was binding on September 29, 1983, and at all times thereafter before the amount is paid or incurred.

"(B) Treatment of renegotiations, extensions, etc.— If any indebtedness (or contract described in subparagraph (A)) is renegotiated, extended, renewed, or revised after September 29, 1983, subparagraph (A) shall not apply to any amount paid or incurred on such indebtedness (or pursuant to such contract) after the date of such renegotiation, extension, renewal, or revision."

Prior to amendment, subsec. (a) read as follows:

"(a) Deductions disallowed—

"No deduction shall be allowed—

"(1) Losses. In respect of losses from sales or exchanges of property) other than losses in cases of distributions in corporate liquidations), directly or indirectly, between persons specified within any one of the paragraphs of subsection (b).

"(2) Unpaid expenses and interest. In respect of expenses, otherwise deductible under section 162 or 212, or of interest, otherwise deductible under section 163,—

"(A) If within the period consisting of the taxable year of the taxpayer and 2½ months after the close thereof (i) such expenses or interest are not paid, and (ii) the amount thereof is not includible in the gross income of the person to whom the payment is to be made; and

"(B) If, by reason of the method of accounting of the person to whom the payment is to be made, the amount thereof is not, unless paid, includible in the gross income of such person for the taxable year in which or with which the taxable year of the taxpayer ends; and

"(C) If, at the close of the taxable year of the taxpayer or at any time within 2½ months thereafter, both the taxpayer and the person to whom the payment is to be made are persons specified within any one of the paragraphs of subsection (b)."

Prior to deletion, subsecs. (e) and (f) read as follows:

"(e) Rule where last day of 2½ month period falls on Sunday, etc. For purposes of subsection (a)(2)—

"(1) where the last day of the 2½ month period falls on Saturday, Sunday, or a legal holiday, such last day shall be treated as falling on the next succeeding day which is not a Saturday, Sunday, or a legal holiday, and

"(2) the determination of what constitutes a legal holiday shall be made under section 7503 with respect to the payor's return of tax under this chapter for the preceding taxable year.

"(f) Special rules for unpaid expenses and interest of S corporations.

"(1) In general. In the case of any amount paid or incurred by an S corporation, if—

"(A) by reason of the method of accounting of the person to whom the payment is to be made, the amount thereof is not (unless paid) includible in the gross income of such person, and

"(B) at the close of the taxable year of the S corporation for which (but for this paragraph) the amount would be deductible under section 162, 212, or 163, both the S corporation and the person to whom the payment is to be paid are persons specified in one of the paragraphs of subsection (b),

then any deduction allowable under such sections in respect of such amount shall be allowable as of the day as of which such amount is includible in the gross income of the person to whom the payment is made (or, if later, as of the day on which it would be so allowable but for this paragraph).

"(2) Certain shareholders, etc., treated as related persons. For purposes of applying paragraph (1)—

"(A) an S corporation,

"(B) any person who owns, directly or indirectly, 2 percent or more in value of the outstanding stock of such corporation, and

"(C) any person related (within the meaning of subsection (b) of this section or section 707(b)(1)(A)) to a person described in subparagraph (B),

shall be treated as persons specified in a paragraph of subsection (b).

"(3) Subsection (a)(2) not to apply. Subsection (a)(2) shall not apply to any amount paid or incurred by an S corporation."

— P.L. 98-369, Sec. 174(b)(2)(A), amended para. (b)(3) . . . Sec. 174(b)(2)(B), added subsec. (f), effective for transactions after 12/31/83, in tax. yrs. end. after 12/31/83, excepting property transferred to a foreign corporation on or before 3/1/84.

Prior to amendment, para. (b)(3) read as follows:

"(3) Two corporations more than 50 percent in value of the outstanding stock of each of which is owned, directly or indirectly, by or for the same individual, if either one of such corporations, with respect to the taxable year of the corporation preceding the date of the sale or exchange was, under the law applicable to such taxable year, a personal holding company or a foreign personal holding company;"

— P.L. 98-369, Sec. 174(b)(3)(A), and (B), substituted "A corporation" for "An S corporation" and substituted "the corporation" for "the S corporation" in para. (b)(10) . . . Sec. 174(b)(4), substituted "same persons" for "same individual" in para. (b)(12), effective for transactions after 12/31/83, in tax. yrs. end. after 12/31/83.

— P.L. 98-369, Sec. 721(s), substituted

"then any deduction allowable under such sections in respect of such amount shall be allowable as of the day as of which such amount is includible in the gross income of the person to whom the payment is made (or, if later, as of the day on which it would be so allowable but for this paragraph)." for "then no deduction shall be allowed in respect of expenses otherwise deductible under section 162 or 212, or of interest otherwise deductible under section 163, before the day as of which the amount thereof is includible in the gross income of the person to whom the payment is made." after subpara. (f)(1)(B) (before deletion by Sec. 174(b)(1) of the Act), effective for tax. yrs. begin. after 12/31/82.

In 1982, P.L. 97-354, Sec. 3(h)(1), added paras. (b)(10), (11) and (12) . . . Sec. 3(h)(2), added subsec. (f) . . . Sec. 3(h)(3), deleted "or" from the end of para. (b)(8) and substituted a semicolon for a period at the end of para. (b)(9), effective for tax. yrs. begin. after 12/31/82.

In 1978, P.L. 95-628, Sec. 2(a), added subsec. (e), effective for payments made after 11/10/78.

Sec. 268. Sale of land with unharvested crop.

Where an unharvested crop sold by the taxpayer is considered under the provisions of section 1231 as "property used in the trade or business", in computing taxable income no deduction (whether or not for the taxable year of the sale and whether for expenses, depreciation, or otherwise) attributable to the production of such crop shall be allowed.

Sec. 269. Acquisitions made to evade or avoid income tax.

(a) In general.

If—

(1) any person or persons acquire, or acquired on or after October 8, 1940, directly or indirectly, control of a corporation, or

(2) any corporation acquires, or acquired on or after October 8, 1940, directly or indirectly, property of another corporation, not controlled, directly or indirectly, immediately before such acquisition, by such acquiring corporation or its stockholders, the basis of which property, in the hands of the acquiring corporation, is determined by reference to the basis in the hands of the transferor corporation,

and the principal purpose for which such acquisition was made is evasion or avoidance of Federal income tax by securing the benefit of a deduction, credit, or other allowance which such person or corporation would not otherwise enjoy, then the Secretary may disallow such deduction, credit, or other allowance. For purposes of paragraphs (1) and (2), control means the ownership of stock possessing at least 50 percent of the total combined voting power of all classes of stock entitled to vote or at least 50 percent of the total value of shares of all classes of stock of the corporation.

(b) Certain liquidations after qualified stock purchases.

(1) In general. If—

(A) there is a qualified stock purchase by a corporation of another corporation,

(B) an election is not made under section 338 with respect to such purchase,

(C) the acquired corporation is liquidated pursuant to a plan of liquidation adopted not more than 2 years after the acquisition date, and

(D) the principal purpose for such liquidation is the evasion or avoidance of Federal income tax by securing the benefit of a deduction, credit, or other allowance which the acquiring corporation would not otherwise enjoy,

then the Secretary may disallow such deduction, credit, or other allowance.

(2) Meaning of terms. For purposes of paragraph (1), the terms "qualified stock purchase" and "acquisition date" have the same respective meanings as when used in section 338.

(c) Power of Secretary to allow deduction, etc., in part.

In any case to which subsection (a) or (b) applies the Secretary is authorized—

(1) to allow as a deduction, credit, or allowance any part of any amount disallowed by such subsection, if he determines that such allowance will not result in the evasion or avoidance of Federal income tax for which the acquisition was made; or

(2) to distribute, apportion, or allocate gross income, and distribute, apportion, or allocate the deductions, credits, or allowances the benefit of which was sought to be secured, between or among the corporations, or properties, or parts thereof, involved, and to allow such deductions, credits, or allowances so distributed, apportioned, or allocated, but to give effect to such allowance only to such extent as he determines will not result in the evasion or avoidance of Federal income tax for which the acquisition was made; or

(3) to exercise his powers in part under paragraph (1) and in part under paragraph (2).

In 1984, P.L. 98-369, Sec. 712(k)(8)(A), redesignated subsec. (b) as subsec. (c) and added new subsec. (b)... Sec. 712(k)(8)(B), substituted "subsection (a) or (b)" for "subsection (a)" in subsec. (c) (as redesignated by Sec. 712(k)(8)(A) of the Act), effective for liquidations after 10/20/83, in tax. yrs. end. after 10/20/83.

In 1976, P.L. 94-455, Sec. 1901(a)(38), repealed subsec. (c), effective for tax. yrs. begin. after 12/31/76.

Prior to amendment, subsec. (c) read as follows:

"*(c) Presumption in case of disproportionate purchase price.*

"The fact that the consideration paid upon an acquisition by any person or corporation described in subsection (a) is substantially disproportionate to the aggregate—

"(1) of the adjusted basis of the property of the corporation (to the extent attributable to the interest acquired specified in paragraph (1) of subsection (a)), or of the property acquired specified in paragraph (2) of subsection (a); and

"(2) of the tax benefits (to the extent not reflected in the adjusted basis of the property) not available to such person or corporation otherwise than as a result of such acquisition,

shall be prima facie evidence of the principal purpose of evasion or avoidance of Federal income tax. This subsection shall apply only with respect to acquisitions after March 1, 1954."

—P.L. 94-455, Sec. 1906(b)(13)(A), substituted "Secretary" for "Secretary or his delegate" each place it appeared in Code Sec. 269, effective for tax. yrs. begin. after 12/31/76.

In 1964, P.L. 88-272, Sec. 235(c)(2), substituted "the Secretary or his delegate may disallow such deduction, credit, or other allowance" for "such deduction, credit or other allowance shall not be allowed" in subsec. (a), effective for tax. yrs. end. after 12/31/63.

Sec. 269A. Personal service corporations formed or availed of to avoid or evade income tax.

(a) General rule.

If—

(1) substantially all of the services of a personal service corporation are performed for (or on behalf of) 1 other corporation, partnership, or other entity, and

(2) the principal purpose for forming, or availing of, such personal service corporation is the avoidance or evasion of Federal income tax by reducing the income of, or securing the benefit of any expense, deduction, credit, exclusion, or other allowance for, any employee-owner which would not otherwise be available,

then the Secretary may allocate all income, deductions, credits, exclusions, and other allowances between such personal service corporation and its employee-owners, if such allocation is necessary to prevent avoidance or evasion of Federal income tax or clearly to reflect the income of the personal service corporation or any of its employee-owners.

(b) Definitions.

For purposes of this section—

(1) Personal service corporation. The term "personal service corporation" means a corporation the principal activity of which is the performance of personal services and such services are substantially performed by employee-owners.

(2) Employee-owner. The term "employee-owner" means any employee who owns, on any day during the taxable year, more than 10 percent of the outstanding stock of the personal service corporation. For purposes of the preceding sentence, section 318 shall apply, except that "5 percent" shall be substituted for "50 percent" in section 318(a)(2)(C).

(3) Related persons. All related persons (within the meaning of section 144(a)(3)) shall be treated as 1 entity.

In 1986, P.L. 99-514, Sec. 1301(j)(4), substituted "144(a)(3)" for "103(b)(6)(C)", effective for bonds issued after 8/15/86.

In 1982, P.L. 97-248, Sec. 250(a), added Code Sec. 269A, effective for tax. yrs. begin. after 12/31/82.

Sec. 269B. Stapled entities.

(a) General rule.

Except as otherwise provided by regulations, for purposes of this title—

(1) if a domestic corporation and a foreign corporation are stapled entities, the foreign corporation shall be treated as a domestic corporation.

(2) in applying section 1563, stock in a second corporation which constitutes a stapled interest with respect to stock of a first corporation shall be treated as owned by such first corporation, and

(3) in applying subchapter M for purposes of determining whether any stapled entity is a regulated investment company or a real estate investment trust, all entities which are stapled entities with respect to each other shall be treated as 1 entity.

(b) Secretary to prescribe regulations.

The Secretary shall prescribe such regulations as may be necessary to prevent avoidance or evasion of Federal income tax through the use of stapled entities. Such regulations may include (but shall not be limited to) regulations providing the extent to which 1 of such entities shall be treated as owning the other entity (to the extent of the stapled interest) and regulations providing that any tax imposed on the foreign corporation referred to in subsection (a)(1) may, if not paid by such corporation, be collected from the domestic corporation referred to in such subsection or the shareholders of such foreign corporation.

(c) Definitions.

For purposes of this section—

(1) Entity. The term "entity" means any corporation, partnership, trust, association, estate, or other form of carrying on a business or activity.

(2) Stapled entities. The term "stapled entities" means any group of 2 or more entities if more than 50 percent in value of the beneficial ownership in each of such entities consists of stapled interests.

(3) Stapled interests. Two or more interests are stapled interests if, by reason of form of ownership, restrictions on transfer, or other terms or conditions, in connection with the transfer of 1 of such interests the other such interests are also transferred or required to be transferred.

(d) Special rule for treaties.

Nothing in section 894 or 7852(d) or in any other provision of law shall be construed as permitting an exemption, by reason of any treaty obligation of the United States heretofore or hereafter entered into, from the provisions of this section.

(e) Subsection (a)(1) not to apply in certain cases.

(1) In general. Subsection (a)(1) shall not apply if it is established to the satisfaction of the Secretary that the domestic corporation and the foreign corporation referred to in such subsection are foreign owned.

(2) Foreign owned. For purposes of paragraph (1), a corporation is foreign owned if less than 50 percent of—

(A) the total combined voting power of all classes of stock of such corporation entitled to vote, and

(B) the total value of the stock of the corporation,

is held directly (or indirectly through applying paragraphs (2) and (3) of section 958(a) and paragraph (4) of section 318(a)) by United States persons (as defined in section 7701(a)(30)).

In 1998, P.L. 105-206, Sec. 7002, of this Act, reads as follows:

"SEC. 7002. TERMINATION OF EXCEPTION FOR CERTAIN REAL ESTATE INVESTMENT TRUSTS FROM THE TREATMENT OF STAPLED ENTITIES.

"(a) In general. Notwithstanding paragraph (3) of section 136(c) of the Tax Reform Act of 1984 (relating to stapled stock; stapled entities), the REIT gross income provisions shall be applied by treating the activities and gross income of members of the stapled REIT group properly allocable to any nonqualified real property interest held by the exempt REIT or any stapled entity which is a member of such group (or treated under subsection (c) as held by such REIT or stapled entity) as the activities and gross income of the exempt REIT in the same manner as if the exempt REIT and such group were one entity.

"(b) Nonqualified real property interest. For purposes of this section—

"(1) In general. The term 'nonqualified real property interest' means, with respect to any exempt REIT, any interest in real property acquired after March 26, 1998, by the exempt REIT or any stapled entity.

"(2) Exception for binding contracts, etc. Such term shall not include any interest in real property acquired after March 26, 1998, by the exempt REIT or any stapled entity if—

"(A) the acquisition is pursuant to a written agreement (including a put option, buy-sell agreement, and an agreement relating to a third party default) which was binding on such date and at all times thereafter on such REIT or stapled entity; or

"(B) the acquisition is described on or before such date in a public announcement or in a filing with the Securities and Exchange Commission.

"(3) Improvements and leases.

"(A) In general. Except as otherwise provided in this paragraph, the term 'nonqualified real property interest' shall not include—

"(i) any improvement to land owned or leased by the exempt REIT or any member of the stapled REIT group; and

"(ii) any repair to, or improvement of, any improvement owned or leased by the exempt REIT or any member of the stapled REIT group,

if such ownership or leasehold interest is a qualified real property interest.

"(B) Leases. The term 'nonqualified real property interest' shall not include—

"(i) any lease of a qualified real property interest if such lease is not otherwise such an interest; or

"(ii) any renewal of a lease which is a qualified real property interest,

but only if the rent on any lease referred to in clause (i) or any renewal referred to in clause (ii) does not exceed an arm's length rate.

"(C) Termination where change in use.

"(i) In general. Subparagraph (A) shall not apply to any improvement placed in service after December 31, 1999, which is part of a change in the use of the property to which such improvement relates unless the cost of such improvement does not exceed 200 percent of—

"(I) the cost of such property; or

"(II) if such property is substituted basis property (as defined in section 7701(a)(42) of the Internal Revenue Code of 1986, the fair market value of the property at the time of acquisition.

"(ii) Binding contracts. For purposes of clause (i), an improvement shall be treated as placed in service before January 1, 2000, if such improvement is placed in service before January 1, 2004, pursuant to a binding contract in effect on December 31, 1999, and at all times thereafter.

"(4) Exception for permitted transfers, etc. The term 'nonqualified real property interest' shall not include any interest in real property acquired solely as a result of a direct or indirect contribution, distribution, or other transfer of such interest from the exempt REIT or any member of the stapled REIT group to such REIT or any such member, but only to the extent the aggregate of the interests of the exempt REIT and all stapled entities in such interest in real property (determined in accordance with subsection (c)(1)) is not increased by reason of the transfer.

"(5) Treatment of entities which are not stapled, etc. on March 26, 1998. Notwithstanding any other provision of this section, all interests in real property held by an exempt REIT or any stapled entity with respect to such REIT (or treated under subsection (c) as held by such REIT or stapled entity) shall be treated as nonqualified real property interests unless—

"(A) such stapled entity was a stapled entity with respect to such REIT as of March 26, 1998, and at all times thereafter; and

"(B) as of March 26, 1998, and at all times thereafter, such REIT was a real estate investment trust.

"(6) Qualified real property interest. The term 'qualified real property interest' means any interest in real property other than a nonqualified real property interest.

"(c) Treatment of property held by 10-percent subsidiaries. For purposes of this section—

"(1) In general. Any exempt REIT and any stapled entity shall be treated as holding their proportionate shares of each interest in real property held by any 10-percent subsidiary entity of the exempt REIT or stapled entity, as the case may be.

"(2) Property held by 10-percent subsidiaries treated as nonqualified.

"(A) In general. Except as provided in subparagraph (B), any interest in real property held by a 10-percent subsidiary entity of an exempt REIT or stapled entity shall be treated as a nonqualified real property interest.

"(B) Exception for interests in real property held on March 26, 1998, etc. In the case of an entity which was a 10-percent subsidiary entity of an exempt REIT or stapled entity on March 26, 1998, and at all times thereafter, an interest in real property held by such subsidiary entity shall be treated as a qualified real property interest if such interest would be so treated if held or acquired directly by the exempt REIT or the stapled entity.

"(3) Reduction in qualified real property interests if increase in ownership of subsidiary. If, after March 26, 1998, an exempt REIT or stapled entity increases its ownership interest in a subsidiary entity to which paragraph (2)(B) applies above its ownership interest in such subsidiary entity as of such date, the additional portion of each interest in real property which is treated as held by the exempt REIT or stapled entity by reason of such increased ownership shall be treated as a nonqualified real property interest.

"(4) Special rules for determining ownership. For purposes of this subsection—

"(A) percentage ownership of an entity shall be determined in accordance with subsection (e)(4);

"(B) interests in the entity which are acquired by an exempt REIT or a member of the stapled REIT group in any acquisition described in an agreement, announcement, or filing described in subsection (b)(2) shall be treated as acquired on March 26, 1998; and

"(C) except as provided in guidance prescribed by the Secretary, any change in proportionate ownership which is attributable solely to fluctuations in the relative fair market values of different classes of stock shall not be taken into account.

"(5) Treatment of 60-percent partnerships.

"(A) In general. If, as of March 26, 1998—

"(i) an exempt REIT or stapled entity held directly or indirectly at least 60 percent of the capital or profits interest in a partnership; and

"(ii) 90 percent or more of the capital interests and 90 percent or more of the profits interests in such partnership (other than interests held directly or indirectly by the exempt REIT or stapled entity) are, or will be, redeemable or exchangeable for consideration the amount of which is determined by reference to the value of shares of stock in the exempt REIT or stapled entity (or both),

paragraph (3) shall not apply to such partnership, and such REIT or entity shall be treated for all purposes of this section as holding all of the capital and profits interests in such partnership.

"(B) Limitation to one partnership. If, as of January 1, 1999, more than one partnership owned by any exempt REIT or stapled entity meets the requirements of subparagraph (A), only the largest such partnership on such date (determined by aggregate asset bases) shall be treated as meeting such requirements.

"(C) Mirror entity. For purposes of subparagraph (A), an interest in a partnership formed after March 26, 1998, shall be treated as held by an exempt REIT or stapled entity on March 26, 1998, if such partnership is formed to mirror the stapling of an exempt REIT and a stapled entity in connection with an acquisition agreed to or announced on or before March 26, 1998.

"(d) Treatment of property secured by mortgage held by exempt REIT or member of stapled REIT group.

"(1) In general. In the case of any nonqualified obligation held by an exempt REIT or any member of the stapled REIT group, the REIT gross income provisions shall be applied by treating the exempt REIT as having impermissible tenant service income equal to—

"(A) the interest income from such obligation which is properly allocable to the property described in paragraph (2); and

"(B) the income of any member of the stapled REIT group from services described in paragraph (2) with respect to such property.

If the income referred to in subparagraph (A) or (B) is of a 10-percent subsidiary entity, only the portion of such income which is properly allocable to the exempt REIT's or the stapled entity's interest in the subsidiary entity shall be taken into account.

"(2) Nonqualified obligation. Except as otherwise provided in this subsection, the term 'nonqualified obligation' means any obligation secured by a mortgage on an interest in real property if the income of any member of the stapled REIT group for services furnished with respect to such property would be impermissible tenant service income were such property held by the exempt REIT and such services furnished by the exempt REIT.

"(3) Exception for certain market rate obligations. Such term shall not include any obligation—

"(A) payments under which would be treated as interest if received by a REIT; and

"(B) the rate of interest on which does not exceed an arm's length rate.

"(4) Exception for existing obligations. Such term shall not include any obligation —

"(A) which is secured on March 26, 1998, by an interest in real property; and

"(B) which is held on such date by the exempt REIT or any entity which is a member of the stapled REIT group on such date and at all times thereafter,

but only so long as such obligation is secured by such interest, and the interest payable on such obligation is not changed to a rate which exceeds an arm's length rate unless such change is pursuant to the terms of the obligation in effect on March 26, 1998. The preceding sentence shall not cease to apply by reason of the refinancing of the obligation if (immediately after the refinancing) the principal amount of the obligation resulting from the refinancing does not exceed the principal amount of the refinanced obligation (immediately before the refinancing) and the interest payable on such refinanced obligation does not exceed an arm's length rate.

"(5) Treatment of entities which are not stapled, etc. on March 26, 1998. A rule similar to the rule of subsection (b)(5) shall apply for purposes of this subsection.

"(6) Increase in amount of nonqualified obligations if increase in ownership of subsidiary. A rule similar to the rule of subsection (c)(3) shall apply for purposes of this subsection.

"(7) Coordination with subsection (a). This subsection shall not apply to the portion of any interest in real property that the exempt REIT or stapled entity holds or is treated as holding under this section without regard to this subsection.

"(e) Definitions. For purposes of this section —

"(1) REIT gross income provisions. The term 'REIT gross income provisions' means —

"(A) paragraphs (2), (3), and (6) of section 856(c) of the Internal Revenue Code of 1986; and

"(B) section 857(b)(5) of such Code.

"(2) Exempt REIT. The term 'exempt REIT' means a real estate investment trust to which section 269B of the Internal Revenue Code of 1986 does not apply by reason of paragraph (3) of section 136(c) of the Tax Reform Act of 1984.

"(3) Stapled REIT group. The term 'stapled REIT group' means, with respect to an exempt REIT, the group consisting of —

"(A) all entities which are stapled entities with respect to the exempt REIT; and

"(B) all entities which are 10-percent subsidiary entities of the exempt REIT or any such stapled entity.

"(4) 10-percent subsidiary entity.

"(A) In general. The term '10-percent subsidiary entity' means, with respect to any exempt REIT or stapled entity, any entity in which the exempt REIT or stapled entity (as the case may be) directly or indirectly holds at least a 10-percent interest.

"(B) Exception for certain C corporation subsidiaries of REITs. A corporation which would, but for this subparagraph, be treated as a 10-percent subsidiary of an exempt REIT shall not be so treated if such corporation is taxable under section 11 of the Internal Revenue Code of 1986.

"(C) 10-percent interest. The term '10-percent interest' means —

"(i) in the case of an interest in a corporation, ownership of 10 percent (by vote or value) of the stock in such corporation;

"(ii) in the case of an interest in a partnership, ownership of 10 percent of the capital or profits interest in the partnership; and

"(iii) in any other case, ownership of 10 percent of the beneficial interests in the entity.

"(5) Other definitions. Terms used in this section which are used in section 269B or section 856 of such Code shall have the respective meanings given such terms by such section.

"(f) Guidance. The Secretary may prescribe such guidance as may be necessary or appropriate to carry out the purposes of this section, including guidance to prevent the avoidance of such purposes and to prevent the double counting of income.

"(g) Effective date. This section shall apply to taxable years ending after March 26, 1998."

In 1986, P.L. 99-514, Sec. 1810(j)(1), added "and regulations providing that any tax imposed on the foreign corporation referred to in subsection (a)(1) may, if not paid by such corporation, be collected from the domestic corporation referred to in such subsection or the shareholders of such foreign corporation" before the period at the end of subsec. (b). . . . Sec. 1810(j)(2), added subsec. (e), effective 7/18/84 except as provided in Sec. 136(c)(2)-(c)(7) of P.L. 98-369, reproduced below.

In 1984, P.L. 98-369, Sec. 136(a), added Code Sec. 269B, effective 7/18/84 except as provided in Sec. 136 (c)(2) – (c)(7) of this Act, which read as follows:

"(2) Interests stapled as of June 30, 1983. Except as otherwise provided in this subsection, in the case of any interests which on June 30, 1983, were stapled interests (as defined in section 269B(c)(3) of the Internal Revenue Code of 1954 (as added by this section)), the amendments made by this section shall take effect on January 1, 1985 (January 1, 1987, in the case of stapled interests in a foreign corporation).

"(3) Certain stapled entities which include real estate investment trust. Paragraph (3) of section 269B(a) of such Code shall not apply in determining the application of the provisions of part II of subchapter M of chapter 1 of such Code to any real estate investment trust which is part of a group of stapled entities if —

"(A) all members of such group were stapled entities as of June 30, 1983, and

"(B) as of June 30, 1983, such group included one or more real estate investment trusts.

"(4) Certain stapled entities which include Puerto Rican corporations.

"(A) Paragraph (1) of section 269B(a) of such Code shall not apply to a domestic corporation and a qualified Puerto Rican corporation which, on June 30, 1983, were stapled entities.

"(B) For purposes of subparagraph (A), the term 'qualified Puerto Rican corporation' means any corporation organized in Puerto Rico —

"(i) which is described in section 957(c) of such Code or would be so described if any dividends it received from any other corporation described in such section 957(c) were treated as gross income of the type described in such section 957(c), and

"(ii) does not, at any time during the taxable year, own (within the meaning of section 958 of such Code but before applying paragraph (2) of section 269B(a) of such Code) any stock of any corporation which is not described in such section 957(c).

"(5) Treaty rule not to apply to stapled entities entitled to treaty benefits as of June 30, 1983. In the case of any entity which was a stapled entity as of June 30, 1983, subsection (d) of section 269B of such Code shall not apply to any treaty benefit to which such entity was entitled as of June 30, 1983.

"(6) Elections to treat stapled foreign entities as subsidiaries.

"(A) In general. In the case of any foreign corporation and domestic corporation which as of June 30, 1983, were stapled entities, such domestic corporation may elect (in lieu of applying paragraph (1) of section 269B(a) of such Code) to be treated as owning all interests in the foreign corporation which constitute stapled interests with respect to stock of the domestic corporation.

"(B) Election. Any election under subparagraph (A) shall be made not later than 180 days after the date of the enactment of this Act and shall be made in such manner as the Secretary of the Treasury or his delegate shall prescribe.

"(C) Election irrevocable. Any election under subparagraph (A), once made, may be revoked only with the consent of the Secretary of the Treasury or his delegate.

"(7) Other stapled entities which include real estate investment trust.

"(A) In general. Paragraph (3) of section 269B(a) of such Code shall not apply in determining the application of the provisions of part II of subchapter M of chapter 1 of such Code to any qualified real estate investment trust which is a part of a group of stapled entities —

"(i) which was created pursuant to a written board of directors resolution adopted on April 5, 1984, and

"(ii) all members of such group were stapled entities as of June 16, 1985.

"(B) Qualified real estate investment trust. The term 'qualified real estate investment trust' means any real estate trust —

"(i) at least 75 percent of the gross income of which is derived from interest on obligations secured by mortgages on real property (as defined in section 856 of such Code),

"(ii) with respect to which the interest on the obligations described in clause (i) made or acquired by such trust (other than to persons who are independent contractors, as defined in section 856(d)(3) of such Code) is at an arm's length rate or a rate not more than 1 percentage point greater than the associated borrowing cost of the trust, and

"(iii) with respect to which any real property held by the trust is not used in the trade or business of any other member of the group of stapled entities."

Sec. 270. Repealed.

In 1969, P.L. 91-172, Sec. 213(b), repealed Code Sec. 270, effective for tax. yrs. begin. after 12/31/69.

Prior to repeal, Code Sec. 270 read as follows:

"Sec. 270. Limitation on deductions allowable to individuals in certain cases.

"(a) Recomputation of taxable income.

"If the deductions allowed by this chapter or the corresponding provisions of prior revenue laws (other than specially treated deductions, as defined in subsection (b)) allowable to an individual (except for the provisions of this section or the corresponding provisions of prior revenue laws) and attributable to a trade or business carried on by him for 5 consecutive taxable years have, in each of such years (including at least one year to which this subtitle applies), exceeded by more than $50,000 the gross income derived from such trade or business, the taxable income (computed under section 63 or the corresponding provisions of prior revenue laws) of such individual for each of such years shall be recomputed. For the purpose of such recomputation in the case of any such taxable year, such deductions shall be allowed only to the extent of $50,000 plus the gross income attributable to such trade or business, except that the net operating loss deduction, to the extent attributable to such trade or business, shall not be allowed.

"(b) Specially treated deductions.

"For the purpose of subsection (a) the specially treated deductions shall be taxes, interest, casualty and abandonment losses connected with a trade or business deductible under section 165(c)(1), losses and expenses of the trade or business of farming which are directly attributable to drought, the net operating loss deduction allowed by section 172, and expenditures as to which taxpayers are given the option, under law or regulations, either (1) to deduct as expenses when incurred or (2) to defer or capitalize.

"(c) Redetermination of tax.

"On the basis of the taxable income computed under the provisions of subsection (a) for each of the 5 consecutive taxable years specified in such subsection, the tax imposed by this subtitle or the corresponding provisions of prior revenue laws shall be redetermined for each such taxable year. If for any such taxable year assessment of a deficiency is prevented (except for the provisions of section 1311 and following) by the operation of any law or rule of law (other than section 7122, relating to compromises), any increase in the tax previously determined for such taxable year shall be considered a deficiency for purposes of this section. For purposes of this section, the term 'tax previously determined' shall have the meaning assigned to such term by section 1314(a)(1).

"(d) Extension of statute of limitations.

"Notwithstanding any law or rule of law (other than section 7122, relating to compromises), any amount determined as a deficiency under subsection (c), or which would be so determined if assessment were prevented in the manner described in subsection (c), with respect to any taxable year may be assessed as if on the date of the expiration of the time prescribed by law for the assessment of a deficiency for the fifth taxable year of the 5 consecutive taxable years specified in subsection (a), 1 year remained before the expiration of the period of limitation upon assessment for any such taxable year."

Sec. 271. Debts owed by political parties, etc.
(a) General rule.

In the case of a taxpayer (other than a bank as defined in section 581) no deduction shall be allowed under section 166 (relating to bad debts) or under section 165(g) (relating to worthlessness of securities) by reason of the worthlessness of any debt owed by a political party.

(b) Definitions.

(1) **Political party.** For purposes of subsection (a), the term "political party" means—

(A) a political party;

(B) a national, State, or local committee of a political party; or

(C) a committee, association, or organization which accepts contributions or makes expenditures for the purpose of influencing or attempting to influence the election of presidential or vice-presidential electors or of any individual whose name is presented for election to any Federal, State, or local elective public office, whether or not such individual is elected.

(2) **Contributions.** For purposes of paragraph (1)(C), the term "contributions" includes a gift, subscription, loan, advance, or deposit, of money, or anything of value, and includes a contract, promise, or agreement to make a contribution, whether or not legally enforceable.

(3) **Expenditures.** For purposes of paragraph (1)(C), the term "expenditures" includes a payment, distribution, loan, advance, deposit, or gift, of money, or anything of value, and includes a contract, promise, or agreement to make an expenditure, whether or not legally enforceable.

(c) Exception.

In the case of a taxpayer who uses an accrual method of accounting, subsection (a) shall not apply to a debt which accrued as a receivable on a bona fide sale of goods or services in the ordinary course of the taxpayer's trade or business if—

(1) for the taxable year in which such receivable accrued, more than 30 percent of all receivables which accrued in the ordinary course of the trades and businesses of the taxpayer were due from political parties, and

(2) the taxpayer made substantial continuing efforts to collect on the debt.

In 1976, P.L. 94-455, Sec. 2104(c), added subsec. (c), effective for tax. yrs. begin. after 12/31/75.

Sec. 272. Disposal of coal or domestic iron ore.

Where the disposal of coal or iron ore is covered by section 631, no deduction shall be allowed for expenditures attributable to the making and administering of the contract under which such disposition occurs and to the preservation of the economic interest retained under such contract, except that if in any taxable year such expenditures plus the adjusted depletion basis of the coal or iron ore disposed of in such taxable year exceed the amount realized under such contract, such excess, to the extent not availed of as a reduction of gain under section 1231, shall be a loss deductible under section 165(a). This section shall not apply to any taxable year during which there is no income under the contract.

In 1964, P.L. 88-272, Sec. 227(a)(3), added "or iron ore" after "coal" each place it appeared in Code Sec. 272 . . . Sec. 227(b)(3), added "or domestic iron ore" after "coal" in the heading of Code Sec. 272, effective for amounts received or accrued in tax. yrs. begin. after 12/31/63, attributable to iron ore mined in tax. yrs. begin. after 12/31/63.

Sec. 273. Holders of life or terminable interest.

Amounts paid under the laws of a State, the District of Columbia, a possession of the United States, or a foreign country as income to the holder of a life or terminable interest acquired by gift, bequest, or inheritance shall not be reduced or diminished by any deduction for shrinkage (by whatever name called) in the value of such interest due to the lapse of time.

In 1976, P.L. 94-455, Sec. 1901(c)(2), deleted "a Territory," after "under the laws of a State," in Code Sec. 273, effective for tax. yrs. begin. after 12/31/76.

Sec. 274. Disallowance of certain entertainment, etc., expenses.

(a) Entertainment, amusement, or recreation.

(1) **In general.** No deduction otherwise allowable under this chapter shall be allowed for any item—

(A) **Activity.** With respect to an activity which is of a type generally considered to constitute entertainment, amusement, or recreation, unless the taxpayer establishes that the item was directly related to, or, in the case of an item directly preceding or following a substantial and bona fide business discussion (including business meetings at a convention or otherwise), that such item was associated with, the active conduct of the taxpayer's trade or business, or

(B) **Facility.** With respect to a facility used in connection with an activity referred to in subparagraph (A).

In the case of an item described in subparagraph (A), the deduction shall in no event exceed the portion of such item which meets the requirements of subparagraph (A).

(2) **Special rules.** For purposes of applying paragraph (1)—

(A) Dues or fees to any social, athletic, or sporting club or organization shall be treated as items with respect to facilities.

(B) An activity described in section 212 shall be treated as a trade or business.

(C) In the case of a club, paragraph (1)(B) shall apply unless the taxpayer establishes that the facility was used primarily for the furtherance of the taxpayer's trade or business and that the item was directly related to the active conduct of such trade or business.

(3) **Denial of deduction for club dues.** Notwithstanding the preceding provisions of this subsection, no deduction shall be allowed under this chapter for amounts paid or incurred for membership in any club organized for business, pleasure, recreation, or other social purpose.

(b) Gifts.

(1) **Limitation.** No deduction shall be allowed under section 162 or section 212 for any expense for gifts made directly or indirectly to any individual to the extent that such expense, when added to prior expenses of the taxpayer for gifts made to such individual during the same taxable year, exceeds $25. For purposes of this section, the term "gift" means any item excludable from gross income of the recipient under section 102 which is not excludable from his gross income under any other provision of this chapter, but such term does not include—

(A) an item having a cost to the taxpayer not in excess of $4.00 on which the name of the taxpayer is clearly and permanently imprinted and which is one of a number of identical items distributed generally by the taxpayer, or

(B) a sign, display rack, or other promotional material to be used on the business premises of the recipient.

(2) Special rules.

(A) In the case of a gift by a partnership, the limitation contained in paragraph (1) shall apply to the partnership as well as to each member thereof.

(B) For purposes of paragraph (1), a husband and wife shall be treated as one taxpayer.

(c) Certain foreign travel.

(1) In general. In the case of any individual who travels outside the United States away from home in pursuit of a trade or business or in pursuit of an activity described in section 212, no deduction shall be allowed under section 162 or section 212 for that portion of the expenses of such travel otherwise allowable under such section which, under regulations prescribed by the Secretary, is not allocable to such trade or business or to such activity.

(2) Exception. Paragraph (1) shall not apply to the expenses of any travel outside the United States away from home if—

(A) such travel does not exceed one week, or

(B) the portion of the time of travel outside the United States away from home which is not attributable to the pursuit of the taxpayer's trade or business or an activity described in section 212 is less than 25 percent of the total time on such travel.

(3) Domestic travel excluded. For purposes of this subsection, travel outside the United States does not include any travel from one point in the United States to another point in the United States.

(d) Substantiation required.

No deduction or credit shall be allowed—

(1) under section 162 or 212 for any traveling expense (including meals and lodging while away from home),

(2) for any item with respect to an activity which is of a type generally considered to constitute entertainment, amusement, or recreation, or with respect to a facility used in connection with such an activity,

(3) for any expense for gifts, or

(4) with respect to any listed property (as defined in section 280F(d)(4)),

unless the taxpayer substantiates by adequate records or by sufficient evidence corroborating the taxpayer's own statement (A) the amount of such expense or other item, (B) the time and place of the travel, entertainment, amusement, recreation, or use of the facility or property, or the date and description of the gift, (C) the business purpose of the expense or other item, and (D) the business relationship to the taxpayer of persons entertained, using the facility or property, or receiving the gift. The Secretary may by regulations provide that some or all of the requirements of the preceding sentence shall not apply in the case of an expense which does not exceed an amount prescribed pursuant to such regulations. This subsection shall not apply to any qualified nonpersonal use vehicle (as defined in subsection (i)).

(e) Specific exceptions to application of subsection (a).

Subsection (a) shall not apply to—

(1) Food and beverages for employees. Expenses for food and beverages (and facilities used in connection therewith) furnished on the business premises of the taxpayer primarily for his employees.

(2) Expenses treated as compensation.

(A) In general. Except as provided in subparagraph (B), expenses for goods, services, and facilities, to the extent that the expenses are treated by the taxpayer, with respect to the recipient of the entertainment, amusement, or recreation, as compensation to an employee on the taxpayer's return of tax under this chapter and as wages to such employee for purposes of chapter 24 (relating to withholding of income tax at source on wages).

(B) Specified individuals.

(i) In general. In the case of a recipient who is a specified individual, subparagraph (A) and paragraph (9) shall each be applied by substituting "to the extent that the expenses do not exceed the amount of the expenses which" for "to the extent that the expenses".

(ii) Specified individual. For purposes of clause (i), the term "specified individual" means any individual who—

(I) is subject to the requirements of section 16(a) of the Securities Exchange Act of 1934 with respect to the taxpayer or a related party to the taxpayer, or

(II) would be subject to such requirements if the taxpayer (or such related party) were an issuer of equity securities referred to in such section.

For purposes of this clause, a person is a related party with respect to another person if such person bears a relationship to such other person described in section 267(b) or 707(b).

(3) Reimbursed expenses. Expenses paid or incurred by the taxpayer, in connection with the performance by him of services for another person (whether or not such other person is his employer), under a reimbursement or other expense allowance arrangement with such other person, but this paragraph shall apply—

(A) where the services are performed for an employer, only if the employer has not treated such expenses in the manner provided in paragraph (2), or

(B) where the services are performed for a person other than an employer, only if the taxpayer accounts (to the extent provided by subsection (d)) to such person.

(4) Recreational, etc., expenses for employees. Expenses for recreational, social, or similar activities (including facilities therefor) primarily for the benefit of employees (other than employees who are highly compensated employees (within the meaning of section 414(q))). For purposes of this paragraph, an individual owning less than a 10-percent interest in the taxpayer's trade or business shall not be considered a shareholder or other owner, and for such purposes an individual shall be treated as owning any interest owned by a member of his family (within the meaning of section 267(c)(4)). This paragraph shall not apply for purposes of subsection (a)(3).

(5) Employee, stockholder, etc., business meetings. Expenses incurred by a taxpayer which are directly related to business meetings of his employees, stockholders, agents, or directors.

(6) Meetings of business leagues, etc. Expenses directly related and necessary to attendance at a business meeting or convention of any organization described in section 501(c)(6) (relating to business leagues, chambers of commerce, real estate boards, and boards of trade) and exempt from taxation under section 501(a).

(7) Items available to public. Expenses for goods, services, and facilities made available by the taxpayer to the general public.

(8) Entertainment sold to customers. Expenses for goods or services (including the use of facilities) which are sold by the taxpayer in a bona fide transaction for an adequate and full consideration in money or money's worth.

(9) Expenses includible in income of persons who are not employees. Expenses paid or incurred by the taxpayer for goods, services, and facilities to the extent that the expenses are includible in the gross income of a recipient of the entertainment, amusement, or recreation who is not an employee of the taxpayer as compensation for services rendered or as a prize or award under section 74. The preceding sentence shall not apply to any amount paid or incurred by the taxpayer if such amount is required to be included (or would be so required except that the amount is less than $600) in any information return filed by such taxpayer under part III of subchapter A of chapter 61 and is not so included.

For purposes of this subsection, any item referred to in subsection (a) shall be treated as an expense.

(f) Interest, taxes, casualty losses, etc.

This section shall not apply to any deduction allowable to the taxpayer without regard to its connection with his trade or business (or with his income-producing activity). In the case of a taxpayer which is not an individual, the preceding sentence shall be applied as if it were an individual.

(g) Treatment of entertainment, etc., type facility.

For purposes of this chapter, if deductions are disallowed under subsection (a) with respect to any portion of a facility, such portion shall be treated as an asset which is used for personal, living, and family purposes (and not as an asset used in the trade or business).

(h) Attendance at conventions, etc.

(1) In general. In the case of any individual who attends a convention, seminar, or similar meeting which is held outside the North American area, no deduction shall be allowed under section 162 for expenses allocable to such meeting unless the taxpayer establishes that the meeting is directly related to the active conduct of his trade or business and that, after taking into account in the manner provided by regulations prescribed by the Secretary—

(A) the purpose of such meeting and the activities taking place at such meeting,

(B) the purposes and activities of the sponsoring organizations or groups,

(C) the residences of the active members of the sponsoring organization and the places at which other meetings of the sponsoring organization or groups have been held or will be held, and

(D) such other relevant factors as the taxpayer may present,

it is as reasonable for the meeting to be held outside the North American area as within the North American area.

(2) Conventions on cruise ships. In the case of any individual who attends a convention, seminar, or other meeting which is held on any cruise ship, no deduction shall be allowed under section 162 for expenses allocable to such meeting, unless the taxpayer meets the requirements of paragraph (5) and establishes that the meeting is directly related to the active conduct of his trade or business and that—

(A) the cruise ship is a vessel registered in the United States; and

(B) all ports of call of such cruise ship are located in the United States or in possessions of the United States. With respect to cruises beginning in any calendar year, not more than $2,000 of the expenses attributable to an individual attending one or more meetings may be taken into account under section 162 by reason of the preceding sentence.

(3) Definitions. For purposes of this subsection—

(A) North American area. The term "North American area" means the United States, its possessions, and the Trust Territory of the Pacific Islands, and Canada and Mexico.

(B) Cruise ship. The term "cruise ship" means any vessel sailing within or without the territorial waters of the United States.

(4) Subsection to apply to employer as well as to traveler.

(A) Except as provided in subparagraph (B), this subsection shall apply to deductions otherwise allowable under section 162 to any person, whether or not such person is the individual attending the convention, seminar, or similar meeting.

(B) This subsection shall not deny a deduction to any person other than the individual attending the convention, seminar, or similar meeting with respect to any amount paid by such person to or on behalf of such individual if includible in the gross income of such individual. The preceding sentence shall not apply if the amount is required to be included in any information return filed by such person under part III of subchapter A of chapter 61 and is not so included.

(5) Reporting requirements. No deduction shall be allowed under section 162 for expenses allocable to attendance at a convention, seminar, or similar meeting on any cruise ship unless the taxpayer claiming the deduction attaches to the return of tax on which the deduction is claimed—

(A) a written statement signed by the individual attending the meeting which includes—

(i) information with respect to the total days of the trip, excluding the days of transportation to and from the cruise ship port, and the number of hours of each day of the trip which such individual devoted to scheduled business activities,

(ii) a program of the scheduled business activities of the meeting, and

(iii) such other information as may be required in regulations prescribed by the Secretary; and

(B) a written statement signed by an officer of the organization or group sponsoring the meeting which includes—

(i) a schedule of business activities of each day of the meeting,

(ii) the number of hours which the individual attending the meeting attended such scheduled business activities, and

(iii) such other information as may be required in regulations prescribed by the Secretary.

(6) Treatment of conventions in certain Caribbean countries.

(A) In general. For purposes of this subsection, the term "North American area" includes, with respect to any convention, seminar, or similar meeting, any beneficiary country if (as of the time such meeting begins)—

(i) there is in effect a bilateral or multilateral agreement described in subparagraph (C) between such country and the United States providing for the ex-

Limitations on deduction Code Sec. 274(j)(3)(B)(ii)

change of information between the United States and such country, and

(ii) there is not in effect a finding by the Secretary that the tax laws of such country discriminate against conventions held in the United States.

(B) Beneficiary country. For purposes of this paragraph, the term "beneficiary country" has the meaning given to such term by section 212(a)(1)(A) of the Caribbean Basin Economic Recovery Act; except that such term shall include Bermuda.

(C) Authority to conclude exchange of information agreements.

(i) In general. The Secretary is authorized to negotiate and conclude an agreement for the exchange of information with any beneficiary country. Except as provided in clause (ii), an exchange of information agreement shall provide for the exchange of such information (not limited to information concerning nationals or residents of the United States or the beneficiary country) as may be necessary or appropriate to carry out and enforce the tax laws of the United States and the beneficiary country (whether criminal or civil proceedings), including information which may otherwise be subject to nondisclosure provisions of the local law of the beneficiary country such as provisions respecting bank secrecy and bearer shares. The exchange of information agreement shall be terminable by either country on reasonable notice and shall provide that information received by either country will be disclosed only to persons or authorities (including courts and administrative bodies) involved in the administration or oversight of, or in the determination of appeals in respect of, taxes of the United States or the beneficiary country and will be used by such persons or authorities only for such purposes.

(ii) Nondisclosure of qualified confidential information sought for civil tax purposes. An exchange of information agreement need not provide for the exchange of qualified confidential information which is sought only for civil tax purposes if—

(I) the Secretary of the Treasury, after making all reasonable efforts to negotiate an agreement which includes the exchange of such information, determines that such an agreement cannot be negotiated but that the agreement which was negotiated will significantly assist in the administration and enforcement of the tax laws of the United States, and

(II) the President determines that the agreement as negotiated is in the national security interest of the United States.

(iii) Qualified confidential information defined. For purposes of this subparagraph, the term "qualified confidential information" means information which is subject to the nondisclosure provisions of any local law of the beneficiary country regarding bank secrecy or ownership of bearer shares.

(iv) Civil tax purposes. For purposes of this subparagraph, the determination of whether information is sought only for civil tax purposes shall be made by the requesting party.

(D) Coordination with other provisions. Any exchange of information agreement negotiated under subparagraph (C) shall be treated as an income tax convention for purposes of section 6103(k)(4). The Secretary may exercise his authority under subchapter A of chapter 78 to carry out any obligation of the United States under an agreement referred to in subparagraph (C).

(E) Determinations published in the Federal Register. The following shall be published in the Federal Register—

(i) any determination by the President under subparagraph (C)(ii) (including the reasons for such determination),

(ii) any determination by the Secretary under subparagraph (C)(ii) (including the reasons for such determination), and

(iii) any finding by the Secretary under subparagraph (A)(ii) (and any termination thereof).

(7) Seminars, etc. for section 212 purposes. No deduction shall be allowed under section 212 for expenses allocable to a convention, seminar, or similar meeting.

(i) Qualified nonpersonal use vehicle.

For purposes of subsection (d), the term "qualified nonpersonal use vehicle" means any vehicle which, by reason of its nature, is not likely to be used more than a de minimis amount for personal purposes.

(j) Employee achievement awards.

(1) General rule. No deduction shall be allowed under section 162 or section 212 for the cost of an employee achievement award except to the extent that such cost does not exceed the deduction limitations of paragraph (2).

(2) Deduction limitations. The deduction for the cost of an employee achievement award made by an employer to an employee—

(A) which is not a qualified plan award, when added to the cost to the employer for all other employee achievement awards made to such employee during the taxable year which are not qualified plan awards, shall not exceed $400, and

(B) which is a qualified plan award, when added to the cost to the employer for all other employee achievement awards made to such employee during the taxable year (including employee achievement awards which are not qualified plan awards), shall not exceed $1,600.

(3) Definitions. For purposes of this subsection—

(A) Employee achievement award. The term "employee achievement award" means an item of tangible personal property which is—

(i) transferred by an employer to an employee for length of service achievement or safety achievement,

(ii) awarded as part of a meaningful presentation, and

(iii) awarded under conditions and circumstances that do not create a significant likelihood of the payment of disguised compensation.

(B) Qualified plan award.

(i) In general. The term "qualified plan award" means an employee achievement award awarded as part of an established written plan or program of the taxpayer which does not discriminate in favor of highly compensated employees (within the meaning of section 414(q)) as to eligibility or benefits.

(ii) Limitation. An employee achievement award shall not be treated as a qualified plan award for any taxable year if the average cost of all employee achievement awards which are provided by the employer during the year, and which would be qualified plan awards but for this subparagraph, exceeds $400. For purposes of the preceding sentence, average cost shall be determined by including the entire cost of qualified plan awards, without taking into account employee achievement awards of nominal value.

(4) Special rules. For purposes of this subsection—

(A) Partnerships. In the case of an employee achievement award made by a partnership, the deduction limitations contained in paragraph (2) shall apply to the partnership as well as to each member thereof.

(B) Length of service awards. An item shall not be treated as having been provided for length of service achievement if the item is received during the recipient's 1st 5 years of employment or if the recipient received a length of service achievement award (other than an award excludable under section 132(e)(1)) during that year or any of the prior 4 years.

(C) Safety achievement awards. An item provided by an employer to an employee shall not be treated as having been provided for safety achievement if—

(i) during the taxable year, employee achievement awards (other than awards excludable under section 132(e)(1)) for safety achievement have previously been awarded by the employer to more than 10 percent of the employees of the employer (excluding employees described in clause (ii)), or

(ii) such item is awarded to a manager, administrator, clerical employee, or other professional employee.

(k) Business meals.

(1) In general. No deduction shall be allowed under this chapter for the expense of any food or beverages unless—

(A) such expense is not lavish or extravagant under the circumstances, and

(B) the taxpayer (or an employee of the taxpayer) is present at the furnishing of such food or beverages.

(2) Exceptions. Paragraph (1) shall not apply to—

(A) any expense described in paragraph (2), (3), (4), (7), (8), or (9) of subsection (e), and

(B) any other expense to the extent provided in regulations.

(l) Additional limitations on entertainment tickets.

(1) Entertainment tickets.

(A) In general. In determining the amount allowable as a deduction under this chapter for any ticket for any activity or facility described in subsection (d)(2), the amount taken into account shall not exceed the face value of such ticket.

(B) Exception for certain charitable sports events. Subparagraph (A) shall not apply to any ticket for any sports event—

(i) which is organized for the primary purpose of benefiting an organization which is described in section 501(c)(3) and exempt from tax under section 501(a),

(ii) all of the net proceeds of which are contributed to such organization, and

(iii) which utilizes volunteers for substantially all of the work performed in carrying out such event.

(2) Skyboxes, etc. In the case of a skybox or other private luxury box leased for more than 1 event, the amount allowable as a deduction under this chapter with respect to such events shall not exceed the sum of the face value of non-luxury box seat tickets for the seats in such box covered by the lease. For purposes of the preceding sentence, 2 or more related leases shall be treated as 1 lease.

(m) Additional limitations on travel expenses.

(1) Luxury water transportation.

(A) In general. No deduction shall be allowed under this chapter for expenses incurred for transportation by water to the extent such expenses exceed twice the aggregate per diem amounts for days of such transportation. For purposes of the preceding sentence, the term "per diem amounts" means the highest amount generally allowable with respect to a day to employees of the executive branch of the Federal Government for per diem while away from home but serving in the United States.

(B) Exceptions. Subparagraph (A) shall not apply to—

(i) any expense allocable to a convention, seminar, or other meeting which is held on any cruise ship, and

(ii) any expense described in paragraph (2), (3), (4), (7), (8), or (9) of subsection (e).

(2) Travel as form of education. No deduction shall be allowed under this chapter for expenses for travel as a form of education.

(3) Travel expenses of spouse, dependent, or others. No deduction shall be allowed under this chapter (other than section 217) for travel expenses paid or incurred with respect to a spouse, dependent, or other individual accompanying the taxpayer (or an officer or employee of the taxpayer) on business travel, unless—

(A) the spouse, dependent, or other individual is an employee of the taxpayer,

(B) the travel of the spouse, dependent, or other individual is for a bona fide business purpose, and

(C) such expenses would otherwise be deductible by the spouse, dependent, or other individual.

(n) Only 50 percent of meal and entertainment expenses allowed as deduction.

(1) In general. The amount allowable as a deduction under this chapter for—

(A) any expense for food or beverages, and

(B) any item with respect to an activity which is of a type generally considered to constitute entertainment, amusement, or recreation, or with respect to a facility used in connection with such activity,

shall not exceed 50 percent of the amount of such expense or item which would (but for this paragraph) be allowable as a deduction under this chapter.

(2) Exceptions. Paragraph (1) shall not apply to any expense if—

(A) such expense is described in paragraph (2), (3), (4), (7), (8), or (9) of subsection (e),

(B) in the case of an expense for food or beverages, such expense is excludable from the gross income of the recipient under section 132 by reason of subsection (e) thereof (relating to de minimis fringes),

(C) such expense is covered by a package involving a ticket described in subsection (l)(1)(B),

(D) in the case of an employer who pays or reimburses moving expenses of an employee, such expenses are includible in the income of the employee under section 82, or

(E) such expense is for food or beverages—

(i) required by any Federal law to be provided to crew members of a commercial vessel,

(ii) provided to crew members of a commercial vessel—

(I) which is operating on the Great Lakes, the Saint Lawrence Seaway, or any inland waterway of the United States, and

(II) which is of a kind which would be required by Federal law to provide food and beverages to crew members if it were operated at sea,

(iii) provided on an oil or gas platform or drilling rig if the platform or rig is located offshore, or

Limitations on deduction — Code Sec. 274

(iv) provided on an oil or gas platform or drilling rig, or at a support camp which is in proximity and integral to such platform or rig, if the platform or rig is located in the United States north of 54 degrees north latitude.

Clauses (i) and (ii) of subparagraph (E) shall not apply to vessels primarily engaged in providing luxury water transportation (determined under the principles of subsection (m)). In the case of the employee, the exception of subparagraph (A) shall not apply to expenses described in subparagraph (D).

(3) Special rule for individuals subject to federal hours of service.

(A) In general. In the case of any expenses for food or beverages consumed while away from home (within the meaning of section 162(a)(2)) by an individual during, or incident to, the period of duty subject to the hours of service limitations of the Department of Transportation, paragraph (1) shall be applied by substituting "the applicable percentage" for "50 percent".

(B) Applicable percentage. For purposes of this paragraph, the term "applicable percentage" means the percentage determined under the following table:

For taxable years beginning in calendar year—	The applicable percentage is—
1998 or 1999	55
2000 or 2001	60
2002 or 2003	65
2004 or 2005	70
2006 or 2007	75
2008 or thereafter	80

(o) Regulatory authority.

The Secretary shall prescribe such regulations as he may deem necessary to carry out the purposes of this section, including regulations prescribing whether subsection (a) or subsection (b) applies in cases where both such subsections would otherwise apply.

In 2008, P.L. 110-343, Sec. 702DivC, Sec. 702 Div C, P.L. 110-343, relating to tax relief for areas damaged by 2008 Midwestern storms, reads as follows:

"Sec. 702. Temporary tax relief for areas damaged by 2008 Midwestern severe storms, tornados, and flooding.

"(a) In general. Subject to the modifications described in this section, the following provisions of or relating to the Internal Revenue Code of 1986 shall apply to any Midwestern disaster area in addition to the areas to which such provisions otherwise apply:

"(1) Go Zone benefits.

"(A) Section 1400N (relating to tax benefits) other than subsections (b), (d), (e), (i), (j), (m), and (o) thereof.

"(B) Section 1400O (relating to education tax benefits).

"(C) Section 1400P (relating to housing tax benefits).

"(D) Section 1400Q (relating to special rules for use of retirement funds).

"(E) Section 1400R(a) (relating to employee retention credit for employers).

"(F) Section 1400S (relating to additional tax relief) other than subsection (d) thereof.

"(G) Section 1400T (relating to special rules for mortgage revenue bonds).

"(2) Other benefits included in Katrina Emergency Tax Relief Act of 2005. Sections 302, 303, 304, 401, and 405 of the Katrina Emergency Tax Relief Act of 2005.

"(b) Midwestern disaster area.

"(1) In general. For purposes of this section and for applying the substitutions described in subsections (d) and (e), the term 'Midwestern disaster area' means an area—

"(A) with respect to which a major disaster has been declared by the President on or after May 20, 2008, and before August 1, 2008, under section 401 of the Robert T. Stafford Disaster Relief and Emergency Assistance Act by reason of severe storms, tornados, or flooding occurring in any of the States of Arkansas, Illinois, Indiana, Iowa, Kansas, Michigan, Minnesota, Missouri, Nebraska, and Wisconsin, and

"(B) determined by the President to warrant individual or individual and public assistance from the Federal Government under such Act with respect to damages attributable to such severe storms, tornados, or flooding.

"(2) Certain benefits available to areas eligible only for public assistance. For purposes of applying this section to benefits under the following provisions, paragraph (1) shall be applied without regard to subparagraph (B):

"(A) Sections 1400Q, 1400S(b), and 1400S(d) of the Internal Revenue Code of 1986.

"(B) Sections 302, 401, and 405 of the Katrina Emergency Tax Relief Act of 2005.

"(c) References.

"(1) Area. Any reference in such provisions to the Hurricane Katrina disaster area or the Gulf Opportunity Zone shall be treated as a reference to any Midwestern disaster area and any reference to the Hurricane Katrina disaster area or the Gulf Opportunity Zone within a State shall be treated as a reference to all Midwestern disaster areas within the State.

"(2) Items attributable to disaster. Any reference in such provisions to any loss, damage, or other item attributable to Hurricane Katrina shall be treated as a reference to any loss, damage, or other item attributable to the severe storms, tornados, or flooding giving rise to any Presidential declaration described in subsection (b)(1)(A).

"(3) Applicable disaster date. For purposes of applying the substitutions described in subsections (d) and (e), the term 'applicable disaster date' means, with respect to any Midwestern disaster area, the date on which the severe storms, tornados, or flooding giving rise to the Presidential declaration described in subsection (b)(1)(A) occurred.

* * * * * * * * *

"(e) Modifications to Katrina Emergency Tax Relief Act of 2005. The following provisions of the Katrina Emergency Tax Relief Act of 2005 shall be applied with the following modifications:

* * * * * * * * *

"(3) Mileage reimbursement for charitable volunteers. Section 304—

"(A) by substituting 'beginning on the applicable disaster date and ending on December 31, 2008' for 'beginning on August 25, 2005, and ending on December 31, 2006' in subsection (a), and

"(B) by substituting 'the applicable disaster date' for 'August 25, 2005' in subsection (a).

* * * * * * * * *

In 2005, P.L. 109-135, Sec. 403(mm)(1), added 'or a related party to the taxpayer' after 'the taxpayer' in subclause (e)(2)(B)(ii)(I) . . . Sec. 403(mm)(2), added '(or such related party)' after 'the taxpayer' in subclause (e)(2)(B)(ii)(II) . . . Sec. 403(mm)(3), added 'For purposes of this clause, a person is a related party with respect to another person if such person bears a relationship to such other person described in section 267(b) or 707(b).' as a flush sentence at the end of clause (e)(2)(B)(ii), effective for expenses incurred after 10/22/2004 as if included in Sec. 907 of the American Jobs Creation Act of 2004, P.L. 108-357.

—P.L. 109-73, Sec. 304, of this Act, reads as follows:

"Sec. 304. Mileage reimbursements to charitable volunteers excluded from gross income.

"(a) In general. For purposes of the Internal Revenue Code of 1986, gross income of an individual for taxable years ending on or after August 25, 2005, does not include amounts received, from an organization described in section 170(c) of such Code, as reimbursement of operating expenses with respect to use of a passenger automobile for the benefit of such organization in connection with providing relief relating to Hurricane Katrina during the period beginning on August 25, 2005, and ending on December 31, 2006. The preceding sentence shall apply only to the extent that the expenses which are reimbursed would be deductible under chapter 1 of such Code if section 274(d) of such Code were applied—

"(1) by using the standard business mileage rate in effect under section 162(a) at the time of such use, and

"(2) as if the individual were an employee of an organization not described in section 170(c) of such Code.

"(b) Application to volunteer services only. Subsection (a) shall not apply with respect to any expenses relating to the performance of services for compensation.

"(c) No double benefit. No deduction or credit shall be allowed under any other provision of such Code with respect to the expenses excludable from gross income under subsection (a)."

In 2004, P.L. 108-357, Sec. 907(a), amended para. (e)(2), effective for expenses incurred after 10/22/2004.

Prior to amendment, para. (e)(2) read as follows:

"(2) Expenses treated as compensation. Expenses for goods, services, and facilities, to the extent that the expenses are treated by the taxpayer, with respect to the recipient of the entertainment, amusement, or recreation, as compensation to an employee on the taxpayer's return of tax under this chapter and as wages to such employee for purposes of chapter 24 (relating to withholding of income tax at source on wages)."

In 1997, P.L. 105-34, Sec. 969(a), added para. (n)(3), effective for tax. yrs. begin. after 12/31/97.

—P.L. 105-34, Sec. 1203(b), repealed Sec. 6008 of P.L. 100-647.

Prior to repeal, Sec. 6008 of P.L. 100-647 read as follows:

"Sec. 6008. Business use of automobiles by rural mail carriers.

"(a) General rule.

"In the case of any employee of the United States Postal Service who performs services involving the collection and delivery of mail on a rural route, such employee shall be permitted to compute the amount allowable as a deduction under chapter 1 of the Internal Revenue Code of 1986 for the use of an automobile in performing such services by using a standard mileage rate for all miles of such use equal to 150 percent of the basic standard rate.

"(b) Subsection (a) not to apply if employee claims depreciation deductions for automobile.

Code Sec. 274 — Limitations on deduction

"Subsection (a) shall not apply with respect to any automobile if, for any taxable year beginning after December 31, 1987, the taxpayer claimed depreciation deductions for such automobile.

"(c) Basic standard rate.

"For purposes of this section, the term 'basic standard rate' means the standard mileage rate which is prescribed by the Secretary of the Treasury or his delegate for computing the amount of the deduction for the business use of an automobile and which—

"(1) is in effect at the time of the use referred to in subsection (a),

"(2) applies to an automobile which is not fully depreciated, and

"(3) applies to the first 15,000 miles (or such other number as the Secretary of the Treasury or his delegate may hereafter prescribe of business use during the taxable year.

"(d) Effective date.

"The provisions of this section shall apply to taxable years beginning after December 31, 1987."

In 1993, P.L. 103-66, Sec. 13209(a), substituted "50 percent" for "80 percent" in para. (n)(1)...Sec. 13209(b), substituted "50" for "80" in the heading of subsec. (n), effective for tax. yrs. begin. after 12/31/93.

—P.L. 103-66, Sec. 13210(a), added para. (a)(3)...Sec. 13210(b), added the sentence at the end of para. (e)(4), effective for amounts paid or incurred after 12/31/93.

—P.L. 103-66, Sec. 13272(a), added para. (m)(3), effective for amounts paid or incurred after 12/31/93.

In 1990, P.L. 101-508, Sec. 11802(b)(1), amended para. (1)(2)...Sec. 11802(b)(2)(A)(i), deleted subpara. (n)(2)(D) and redesignated subparas. (n)(2)(E) and (n)(2)(F) as subparas. (n)(2)(D) and (n)(2)(E)...Sec. 11802(b)(2)(A)(ii), substituted "described in subparagraph (D)" for "described in subparagraph (E)" in the last sentence of para. (n)(2)...Sec. 11802(b)(2)(A)(iii), substituted "of subparagraph (E)" for "of subparagraph (F)" in para. (n)(2)...Sec. 11802(b)(2)(B), deleted para. (n)(3), effective 11/5/90, except as provided in Sec. 11821(b) of this Act, reproduced in note following Code Sec. 263.

Prior to amendment, para. (l)(2) read as follows:

"(2) Skyboxes, etc.

"(A) In general. In the case of a skybox or other private luxury box leased for more than 1 event, the amount allowable as a deduction under this chapter with respect to such events shall not exceed the sum of the face value of non-luxury box seat tickets for the seats in such box covered by the lease. For purposes of the preceding sentence, 2 or more related leases shall be treated as 1 lease.

"(B) Phase-in. In the case of—

"(i) a taxable year beginning in 1987, the amount disallowed under subparagraph (A) shall be ⅓ of the amount which would be disallowed without regard to this subparagraph, and

"(ii) in the case of a taxable year beginning in 1988, the amount disallowed under subparagraph (A) shall be ⅔ of the amount which would have been disallowed without regard to this subparagraph."

Prior to deletion, subpara. (n)(2)(D) read as follows:

"(D) in the case of an expense for food or beverages before January 1, 1989, such expense is an integral part of a qualified meeting."

Prior to deletion, para. (n)(3) read as follows:

"(3) Qualified meeting. For purposes of paragraph (2)(D), the term 'qualified meeting' means any convention, seminar, annual meeting, or similar business program with respect to which—

"(A) an expense for food or beverages is not separately stated,

"(B) more than 50 percent of the participants are away from home,

"(C) at least 40 individuals attend, and

"(D) such food and beverages are part of a program which includes a speaker."

In 1989, P.L. 101-239, Sec. 7816(a)(1), amended subpara. (n)(2)(E)...Sec. 7816(a)(2), added the sentence to the end of para. (n)(2), effective as provided in Sec. 6003(b) of P.L. 100-647, reproduced below.

Prior to amendment, subpara. (n)(2)(E) read as follows:

"(E) in the case of an employer who pays or reimburses moving expenses of an employee, such expenses are includible in the income of the employee under section 82, or"

—P.L. 101-239, Sec. 7841(d)(18), added "any" before "Federal" in clause (n)(2)(F)(i), effective 12/19/89.

In 1988, P.L. 100-647, Sec. 1001(g)(1), amended subpara. (n)(2)(A)...Sec. 1001(g)(2), amended para. (k)(2)...Sec. 1001(g)(3), amended clause (m)(1)(B)(ii)...Sec. 1001(g)(4)(A), deleted "or" from the end of subpara. (n)(2)(C), substituted "or" for the period at the end of subpara. (n)(2)(D), and added subpara. (n)(2)(E)...Sec. 1001(g)(5), substituted "trade or business and that" for "trade or business that" each time it appeared in paras. (h)(1) and (h)(2), effective for tax. yrs. begin. after 12/31/86.

Prior to amendment, para. (k)(2) read as follows:

"(2) Exceptions. Paragraph (1) shall not apply to any expense if subsection (a) does not apply to such expense by reason of paragraph (2), (3), (4), (7), (8), or (9) of subsection (e)."

Prior to amendment, clause (m)(1)(B)(ii) read as follows:

"(ii) any expense to which subsection (a) does not apply by reason of paragraph (2), (3), (4), (7), (8), or (9) of subsection (e)."

Prior to amendment, subpara. (n)(2)(A) read as follows:

"(A) subsection (a) does not apply to such expense by reason of paragraph (2), (3), (4), (7), (8), or (9) of subsection (e)."

—P.L. 100-647, Sec. 1018(u)(2), amended Sec. 122(c)(2) of P.L. 99-514, [see below] so it would also delete the comma at the end of subpara. (b)(1)(B).

—P.L. 100-647, Sec. 6003(a), deleted "or" from the end of subpara. (n)(2)(D), substituted "or" for the period at the end of subpara. (n)(2)(E) [as amended by Sec. 1001(g)(1) of this Act] and added subpara. (n)(2)(F), effective as provided in Sec. 6003(b) of this Act which reads:

"(b) Effective dates,;

"(1) Clauses (i) and (ii) of section 274(n)(2)(F) of the 1986 Code, as added by subsection (a), shall apply to taxable years beginning after December 31, 1988.

"(2) Clauses (iii) and (iv) of section 274(n)(2)(F) of the 1986 Code, as added by subsection (a), shall apply to taxable years beginning after December 31, 1987."

—P.L. 100-647, Sec. 6008, was repealed by Sec. 1203(b) of P.L. 105-34, see above.

In 1986, P.L. 99-514, Sec. 122(c)(1), added "or" at the end of subpara. (b)(1)(A)...Sec. 122(c)(2), [as amended by Sec. 1018(u)(2) of P.L. 100-647, see above] substituted a period for ", or," at the end of subpara. (b)(1)(B)...Sec. 122(c)(3), deleted subpara. (b)(1)(C)...Sec. 122(c)(4), deleted para. (b)(3)...Sec. 122(d), redesignated subsec. (j) as subsec. (k), and added new subsec. (j), effective for prizes and awards granted after 12/31/86.

Prior to deletion, subpara. (b)(1)(C) read as follows:

"(C) an item of tangible personal property which is awarded to an employee by reason of length of service, productivity, or safety achievement, but only to the extent that—

"(i) the cost of such item to the taxpayer does not exceed $400, or

"(ii) such item is a qualified plan award."

Prior to deletion, para. (b)(3) read as follows:

"(3) Qualified plan award. For purposes of this subsection—

"(A) In general. The term 'qualified plan award' means an item which is awarded as part of a permanent, written plan or program of the taxpayer which does not discriminate in favor of officers, shareholders, or highly compensated employees as to eligibility or benefits.

"(B) Average amount of awards. An item shall not be treated as a qualified plan award for any taxable year if the average cost of all items awarded under all plans described in subparagraph (A) of the taxpayer during the taxable year exceeds $400.

"(C) Maximum amount per item. An item shall not be treated as a qualified plan award under this paragraph to the extent that the cost of such item exceeds $1,600."

—P.L. 99-514, Sec. 142(a)(1), redesignated subsec. (k) [as redesignated by Sec. 122(d) of this Act, above], as subsec. (o), and added new subsec. (k)...Sec. 142(a)(2)(A), deleted para. (e)(1), and redesignated paras. (e)(2)-(10) as paras. (e)(1)-(9)...Sec. 142(a)(2)(B), substituted "paragraph (2)" for "paragraph (3)" in para. (e)(3) [as redesignated by Sec. 142(a)(2)(A), above]...Sec. 142(b), added subsecs. (l), (m), and (n)...Sec. 142(c)(1), added para. (h)(7)...Sec. 142(c)(2)(A), deleted "or 212" after "section 162" each place appeared in paras. (h)(1), (2), (4), and (5)...Sec. 142(c)(2)(B), deleted "or to an activity described in section 212 and" after "trade or business" each place it appeared in paras. (h)(1) and (2), effective for tax. yrs. begin. after 12/31/86.

Prior to deletion, para. (e)(1) read as follows:

"(1) Business meals. Expenses for food and beverages furnished to any individual under circumstances which (taking into account the surroundings in which furnished, the taxpayer's trade, business, or income-producing activity and the relationship to such trade, business, or activity of the persons to whom the food and beverages are furnished) are of a type generally considered to be conducive to a business discussion."

—P.L. 99-514, Sec. 1114(b)(6), substituted "highly compensated employees (within the meaning of section 414(q))" for "officers, shareholders or other owners, or highly compensated employees" in para. (e)(4) [as redesignated by Sec. 142(a)(2)(A) of this Act, above], effective for yrs. begin. after 12/31/86.

—P.L. 99-514, Sec. 1567, provides:

"SEC. 1567. CERTAIN RECORDKEEPING REQUIREMENTS.

"(a) In general.

"For purposes of sections 132 and 274 of the Internal Revenue Code of 1954, use of an automobile by a special agent of the Internal Revenue Service shall be treated in the same manner as use of an automobile by an officer of any other law enforcement agency.

"(b) Effective date.

"The provisions of this section shall take effect on January 1, 1985."

In 1985, P.L. 99-44, Sec. 6(b), provided that for tax. yrs. begin. in '85, subsec. (d) shall apply as it read before the amendments made by Sec. 179(b)(1) of P.L. 98-369 (see below).

—P.L. 99-44, Sec. 1(a), substituted "adequate records or by sufficient evidence corroborating the taxpayer's own statement" for "adequate contemporaneous records" in subsec. (d) to take effect as if included in Sec. 179(b) of P.L. 98-369 (see below). Sec. 1(a) also provides that "the Internal Revenue Code of 1954 shall be applied and administered as if the word 'contemporaneous' had not been added to such subsection (d)". Sec. 1(c) of this Act provides

"(c) Repeal of Regulations.

Regulations issued before the date of the enactment of this Act [5/24/85] to carry out the amendments made by paragraphs (1)(C), (2), and (3) of section 179(b) of the Tax Reform Act of 1984 [P.L. 98-369] shall have no force and effect."

—P.L. 99-44, Sec. 2(a), added the last sentence to subsec. (d)...Sec. 2(b), redesignated subsec. (i) as (j) and added new subsec. (i), effective for tax. yrs. begin. after 12/31/85.

In 1984, P.L. 98-369, Sec. 179(b)(1)(A), substituted "No deduction or credit" for "No deduction" in subsec. (d)...Sec. 179(b)(1)(B), deleted "or" at the end of para. (d)(2), added "or" at the end of para. (d)(3), and added para. (d)(4)...Sec.

179(b)(1)(C), substituted "adequate contemporaneous records" for "adequate records or by sufficient evidence corroborating his own statement" in subsec. (d) . . . Sec. 179(b)(1)(D), substituted "the facility or property" for "the facility" each place it appeared in subsec. (d), effective for tax. yrs. begin. after 12/31/84 (sic, but see Sec. 6(b) of P.L. 99-44, above, for the rule for tax years beginning in '85).

—P.L. 98-369, Sec. 801(c)(1), and (2), added the last sentence of subpara. (h)(6)(D) and substituted "Coordination with other provisions" for "Coordination with section 6103" as the heading for subpara. (h)(6)(D), for transactions after 12/31/84, in tax. yrs. end. after 12/31/84.

In 1983, P.L. 98-67, Sec. 222(a), added para. (h)(6), effective for conventions, seminars, or other meetings which begin after 6/30/83.

—P.L. 97-424, Sec. 543(a)(1), amended para. (h)(2) . . . Sec. 543(a)(2), added para. (h)(5), effective for tax. yrs. begin. after 12/31/82.

Prior to amendment, para. (h)(2) read as follows:

"(2) Conventions on cruise ships. In the case of any individual who attends a convention, seminar, or other meeting which is held on any cruise ship, no deduction shall be allowed under section 162 or 212 for expenses allocable to such meeting."

In 1981, P.L. 97-34, Sec. 265(a), amended subpara. (b)(1)(C) . . . Sec. 265(b), added para. (b)(3), effective for tax. yrs. end. on or after 8/13/81.

Prior to amendment, subpara. (b)(1)(C) read as follows:

"(C) an item of tangible personal property having a cost to the taxpayer not in excess of $100 which is awarded to an employee by reason of length of service or for safety achievement."

In 1980, P.L. 96-608, Sec. 4(a), amended subsec. (h), for conventions, seminars and meetings begin. after 12/31/80 except "that in the case of any convention, seminar, or meeting beginning after such date [12/31/80] which was scheduled on or before such date [12/31/80], a person, in such manner as the Secretary of the Treasury or his delegate may prescribe, may elect to have the provisions of section 274(h) of the Internal Revenue Code of 1954 be applied to such convention, seminar or meeting without regard to such amendment."

Prior to amendment, subsec. (h) read as follows:

"(h) Foreign conventions.

"(1) Deductions with respect to not more than 2 foreign conventions per year allowed. If any individual attends more than 2 foreign conventions during his taxable year—

"(A) he shall select not more than 2 of such conventions to be taken into account for purposes of this subsection, and

"(B) no deduction allocable to his attendance at any foreign convention during such taxable year (other than a foreign convention selected under subparagraph (A)) shall be allowed under section 162 or 212.

"(2) Deductible transportation cost cannot exceed cost of coach or economy air fare. In the case of any foreign convention, no deduction for the expenses of transportation outside the United States to and from the site of such convention shall be allowed under section 162 or 212 in an amount which exceeds the lowest coach or economy rate at the time of travel charged by a commercial airline for transportation to and from such site during the calendar month in which such convention begins. If there is no such coach or economy rate, the preceding sentence shall be applied by substituting 'first class' for 'coach or economy'.

"(3) Transportation costs deductible in full only if at least one-half of the days are devoted to business related activities. In the case of any foreign convention, a deduction for the full expenses of transportation (determined after the application of paragraph (2)) to and from the site of such convention shall be allowed only if at least one-half of the total days of the trip, excluding the days of transportation to and from the site of such convention, are devoted to business related activities. If less than one-half of the total days of the trip, excluding the days of transportation to and from the site of the convention, are devoted to business related activities, no deduction for the expenses of transportation shall be allowed which exceeds the percentage of the days of the trip devoted to business related activities.

"(4) Deductions for subsistence expenses not allowed unless the individual attends two-thirds of business activities. In the case of any foreign convention, no deduction for subsistence expenses shall be allowed except as follows:

"(A) a deduction for a full day of subsistence expenses while at the convention shall be allowed if there are at least 6 hours of scheduled business activities during such day and the individual attending the convention has attended at least two-thirds of these activities, and

"(B) a deduction for one-half day of subsistence expenses while at the convention shall be allowed if there are at least 3 hours of scheduled business activities during such day and the individual attending the convention has attended at least two-thirds of these activities.

Notwithstanding subparagraphs (A) and (B), a deduction for subsistence expenses for all of the days or half days, as the case may be, of the convention shall be allowed if the individual attending the convention has attended at least two-thirds of the scheduled business activities, and each such full day consists of at least 6 hours of scheduled business activities and each such half day consists of at least 3 hours of scheduled business activities.

"(5) Deductible subsistence costs cannot exceed per diem rate for United States civil servants. In the case of any foreign convention, no deduction for subsistence expenses while at the convention or traveling to or from such convention shall be allowed at a rate in excess of the dollar per diem rate for the site of the convention which has been established under section 5702(a) of title 5 of the United States Code and which is in effect for the calendar month in which the convention begins.

"(6) Definitions and special rules. For purposes of this subsection—

"(A) Foreign convention defined. The term 'foreign convention' means any convention, seminar, or similar meeting held outside the United States, its possessions, and the Trust Territory of the Pacific.

"(B) Subsistence expenses defined. The term 'subsistence expenses' means lodging, meals, and other necessary expenses for the personal sustenance and comfort of the traveler. Such term includes tips and taxi and other local transportation expenses.

"(C) Allocation of expenses in certain cases. In any case where the transportation expenses or the subsistence expenses are not separately stated, or where there is reason to believe that the stated charge for transportation expenses or subsistence expenses or both does not properly reflect the amounts properly allocable to such purposes, all amounts paid for transportation expenses and subsistence expenses shall be treated as having been paid solely for subsistence expenses.

"(D) Subsection to apply to employer as well as to traveler.

"(i) Except as provided in clause (ii), this subsection shall apply to deductions otherwise allowable under section 162 or 212 to any person, whether or not such person is the individual attending the foreign convention. For the purposes of the preceding sentence such person shall be treated, with respect to each individual, as having selected the same 2 foreign conventions as were selected by such individual.

"(ii) This subsection shall not deny a deduction to any person other than the individual attending the foreign convention with respect to any amount paid by such person to or on behalf of another person if includible in the gross income of such other person. The preceding sentence shall not apply if such amount is required to be included in any information return filed by such person under part III of subchapter A of chapter 61 and is not so included.

"(E) Individuals residing in foreign countries. For purposes of this subsection, in the case of an individual citizen of the United States who establishes to the satisfaction of the Secretary that he was a bona fide resident of a foreign country at the time that he attended a convention in such foreign country, such individual's attendance at such convention shall not be considered as attendance at a foreign convention.

"(7) Reporting requirements. No deduction shall be allowed under section 162 or 212 for transportation or subsistence expenses allocable to attendance at a foreign convention unless the taxpayer claiming the deduction attaches to the return of tax on which the deduction is claimed—

"(A) a written statement signed by the individual attending the convention which includes—

"(i) information with respect to the total days of the trip, excluding the days of transportation to and from the site of such convention, and the number of hours of each day of the trip which such individual devoted to scheduled business activities,

"(ii) a program of the scheduled business activities of the convention, and

"(iii) such other information as may be required in regulations prescribed by the Secretary; and

"(B) a written statement signed by an officer of the organization or group sponsoring the convention which includes—

"(i) a schedule of the business activities of each day of the convention,

"(ii) the number of hours which the individual attending the convention attended such scheduled business activities, and

"(iii) such other information as may be required in regulations prescribed by the Secretary."

—P.L. 96-605, Sec. 108(a), made the same amendment as Sec. 5(a) of P.L. 96-598, see below.

—P.L. 96-598, Sec. 5(a), added para. (e)(10), effective for any expenses paid or incurred after 12/31/80, in tax. yrs. ending after 12/31/80.

—P.L. 96-222, Sec. 103(a)(10)(A), deleted "country" in subpara. (a)(2)(C), effective for items paid or incurred after 12/31/78, in tax. yrs. end. after 12/31/78.

—P.L. 96-222, Sec. 103(a)(10)(B), amended Sec. 361(b) of P.L. 95-600 to amend subpara. (a)(2)(C) instead of (2)(C) [see below]. Sec. 103(a)(10)(C) provides:

"(i) In general. Subsection (a) of section 274 of the Internal Revenue Code of 1954 (relating to disallowance of certain entertainment, etc., expenses) shall not apply to expenses paid or incurred by the taxpayer for goods, services, and facilities to the extent that the expenses are includible in the gross income of a recipient of the entertainment, amusement, or recreation who is not an employee of the taxpayer as compensation for services rendered or as a prize or award under section 74 of such Code.

"(ii) Information return requirement. Clause (i) shall not apply to any amount paid or incurred by the taxpayer if such amount is required to be included in any information return filed by such taxpayer under part III of subchapter A of chapter 61 of such Code and is not so included.

"(iii) Application of subparagraph. This subparagraph shall only apply with respect to expenses paid or incurred during 1979 or 1980."

In 1978, P.L. 95-600, Sec. 361(a), amended so much of para. (a)(1) as followed subpara. (a)(1)(A) . . . Sec. 361(b), added subpara. (a)(2)(C), effective for items paid or incurred after 12/31/78, in tax. yrs. end. after 12/31/78.

Prior to amendment, so much of para. (a)(1) as followed subpara. (a)(1)(A) read as follows:

"(B) Facility. With respect to a facility used in connection with an activity referred to in subparagraph (A), unless the taxpayer establishes that the facility was used primarily for the furtherance of the taxpayer's trade or business and that the item was directly related to the active conduct of such trade or business,

and such deduction shall in no event exceed the portion of such item directly related to, or, in the case of an item described in subparagraph (A) directly preceding or following a substantial and bona fide business discussion (including business meetings at a convention or otherwise), the portion of such item associated with, the active conduct of the taxpayer's trade or business."

—P.L. 95-600, Sec. 701(g), amended subpara. (h)(6)(D), added subpara. (h)(6)(E), and substituted "at least one-half" for "more than one-half" in the first sentence of para. (h)(3), effective for conventions beginning after 12/31/76.

Prior to amendment, subpara. (h)(6)(D) read as follows:

"(D) Subsection to apply to employer as well as to traveler. This subsection shall apply to deductions otherwise allowable under section 162 or 212 to any person, whether or not such person is the individual attending the foreign convention. For purposes of the preceding sentence such person shall be treated, with respect to each individual, as having selected the same 2 foreign conventions as were selected by such individual."

In **1976**, P.L. 94-455, Sec. 602(a), redesignated subsec. (h) as (i), and added new subsec. (h), effective for conventions begin. after 12/31/76.

—P.L. 94-455, Sec. 1906(b)(13)(A), substituted "Secretary" for "Secretary or his delegate" each place it appeared in Code Sec. 274, effective for tax. yrs. begin. after 12/31/76.

In **1964**, P.L. 88-272, Sec. 217(a), amended subsec. (c), effective for tax. yrs. end. after 12/31/62, but only in respect of periods after 12/31/62.

Prior to amendment, subsec. (c) read as follows:

"(c) Traveling. In the case of any individual who is traveling away from home in pursuit of a trade or business or in pursuit of an activity described in section 212, no deduction shall be allowed under section 162 or section 212 for that portion of the expenses of such travel otherwise allowable under such section which, under regulations prescribed by the Secretary or his delegate, is not allocable to such trade or business or to such activity. This subsection shall not apply to the expenses of any travel away from home which does not exceed one week or where the portion of the time away from home which is not attributable to the pursuit of the taxpayer's trade or business or an activity described in section 212 is less than 25 percent of the total time away from home on such travel."

In **1962**, P.L. 87-834, Sec. 4, added Code Sec. 274 for tax. yrs. end. after 12/31/62, but only in respect of periods after 12/31/62.

Sec. 275. Certain taxes.
(a) General rule.

No deduction shall be allowed for the following taxes:

(1) Federal income taxes, including—

(A) the tax imposed by section 3101 (relating to the tax on employees under the Federal Insurance Contributions Act);

(B) the taxes imposed by sections 3201 and 3211 (relating to the taxes on railroad employees and railroad employee representatives); and

(C) the tax withheld at source on wages under section 3402.

(2) Federal war profits and excess profits taxes.

(3) Estate, inheritance, legacy, succession, and gift taxes.

(4) Income, war profits, and excess profits taxes imposed by the authority of any foreign country or possession of the United States if the taxpayer chooses to take to any extent the benefits of section 901.

(5) Taxes on real property, to the extent that section 164(d) requires such taxes to be treated as imposed on another taxpayer.

(6) Taxes imposed by chapters 41, 42, 43, 44, 45, 46, and 54.

Paragraph (1) shall not apply to any taxes to the extent such taxes are allowable as a deduction under section 164(f). Paragraph (1) shall not apply to the tax imposed by section 59A.

(b) Cross reference.

For disallowance of certain other taxes, see section 164(c).

In **2007**, P.L. 110-172, Sec. 11(g)(5), substituted "if the taxpayer chooses to take to any extent the benefits of section 901." for "if—" and the remainder of para. (a)(4), enacted 12/29/2007.

Prior to amendment, the remainder of para. (a)(4) read as follows:

"if—

"(A) the taxpayer chooses to take to any extent the benefits of section 901, or

"(B) such taxes are paid or accrued with respect to foreign trade income (within the meaning of section 923(b)) of a FSC."

In **2006**, P.L. 109-222, Sec. 513(a), amended Sec. 5(c)(1) of P.L. 106-519 [see below] . . . Sec. 513(b), repealed Sec. 101(f) of P.L. 108-357 [see below], effective for tax. yrs. begin. after 5/17/2006.

Prior to amendment, Sec. 5(c)(1) of P.L. 106-519 read as follows:

"(1) In general. In the case of a FSC (as so defined) in existence on September 30, 2000, and at all times thereafter, the amendments made by this Act shall not apply to any transaction in the ordinary course of trade or business involving a FSC which occurs—

"(A) before January 1, 2002; or

"(B) after December 31, 2001, pursuant to a binding contract—

"(i) which is between the FSC (or any related person) and any person which is not a related person; and

"(ii) which is in effect on September 30, 2000, and at all times thereafter.

For purposes of this paragraph, a binding contract shall include a purchase option, renewal option, or replacement option which is included in such contract and which is enforceable against the seller or lessor."

Prior to repeal, Sec. 101(f) of P.L. 108-357 read as follows:

"(f) Binding contracts. The amendments made by this section shall not apply to any transaction in the ordinary course of a trade or business which occurs pursuant to a binding contract—

"(1) which is between the taxpayer and a person who is not a related person (as defined in section 943(b)(3) of such Code, as in effect on the day before the date of the enactment of this Act), and

"(2) which is in effect on September 17, 2003, and at all times thereafter.

"For purposes of this subsection, a binding contract shall include a purchase option, renewal option, or replacement option which is included in such contract and which is enforceable against the seller or lessor."

In **2004**, P.L. 108-357, Sec. 101(b)(5)(A), added "or" at the end of subpara. (a)(4)(A), substituted a period for "or" at the end of subpara. (a)(4)(B), and deleted subpara. (a)(4)(C) . . . Sec. 101(b)(5)(B), deleted "A rule similar to the rule of section 943(d) shall apply for purposes of paragraph 4(C)." at the end of subsec. (a), effective for transactions after 12/31/2004. Sec. 101(d)-(f) [subsec. (f) was repealed by Sec. 513(b) of P.L. 109-222, see above] of this Act, reads as follows:

"(d) Transitional rule for 2005 and 2006.

"(1) In general. In the case of transactions during 2005 or 2006, the amount includible in gross income by reason of the amendments made by this section shall not exceed the applicable percentage of the amount which would have been so included but for this subsection.

"(2) Applicable percentage. For purposes of paragraph (1), the applicable percentage shall be as follows:

"(A) For 2005, the applicable percentage shall be 20 percent.

"(B) For 2006, the applicable percentage shall be 40 percent.

"(e) Revocation of election to be treated as domestic corporation. If, during the 1-year period beginning on the date of the enactment of this Act, a corporation for which an election is in effect under section 943(e) of the Internal Revenue Code of 1986 revokes such election, no gain or loss shall be recognized with respect to property treated as transferred under clause (ii) of section 943(e)(4)(B) of such Code to the extent such property—

"(1) was treated as transferred under clause (i) thereof, or

"(2) was acquired during a taxable year to which such election applies and before May 1, 2003, in the ordinary course of its trade or business.

The Secretary of the Treasury (or such Secretary's delegate) may prescribe such regulations as may be necessary to prevent the abuse of the purposes of this subsection."

"(f)" [Repealed by Sec. 513(b) of P.L. 109-222, see above]

—P.L. 108-357, Sec. 802(b)(1), added "45," before "46," in para. (a)(6), effective 3/4/2003; except that periods before such date shall not be taken into account in applying the periods in subsections (a) and (e)(1) of Code Sec. 4985, as added by this section.

In **2000**, P.L. 106-519, Sec. 4(2)(A), deleted "or" at the end of subpara. (a)(4)(A), substituted ", or" for the period at the end of subpara. (a)(4)(B), and added subpara. (a)(4)(C) . . . Sec. 4(2)(B), added "A rule similar to the rule of section 943(d) shall apply for purposes of paragraph 4(C)." at the end of subsec. (a), effective for transactions after 9/30/2000. Sec. 5(b)–(d) [para. (c)(1) as amended by Sec. 513(a) of P.L. 109-222, see above] of this Act, provides:

"(b) No new FSCs; termination of inactive FSCs—

"(1) No new FSCs. No corporation may elect after September 30, 2000, to be a FSC (as defined in section 922 of the Internal Revenue Code of 1986, as in effect before the amendments made by this Act).

"(2) Termination of inactive FSCs. If a FSC has no foreign trade income (as defined in section 923(b) of such Code, as so in effect) for any period of 5 consecutive taxable years beginning after December 31, 2001, such FSC shall cease to be treated as a FSC for purposes of such Code for any taxable year beginning after such period.

"(c) Transition period for existing Foreign Sales Corporations.

"(1) In general. In the case of a FSC (as so defined) in existence on September 30, 2000, and at all times thereafter, the amendments made by this Act shall not apply to any transaction in the ordinary course of trade or business involving a FSC which occurs before January 1, 2002.

"(2) Election to have amendments apply earlier. A taxpayer may elect to have the amendments made by this Act apply to any transaction by a FSC or any related person to which such amendments would apply but for the application of paragraph (1). Such election shall be effective for the taxable year for which made and all subsequent taxable years, and, once made, may be revoked only with the consent of the Secretary of the Treasury.

"(3) Exception for old earnings and profits of certain corporations.

"(A) In general. In the case of a foreign corporation to which this paragraph applies—

"(i) earnings and profits of such corporation accumulated in taxable years ending before October 1, 2000, shall not be included in the gross income of the persons holding stock in such corporation by reason of section 943(e)(4)(B)(i), and

Limitations on deduction — Code Sec. 276

"(ii) rules similar to the rules of clauses (ii), (iii), and (iv) of section 953(d)(4)(B) shall apply with respect to such earnings and profits.

The preceding sentence shall not apply to earnings and profits acquired in a transaction after September 30, 2000, to which section 381 applies unless the distributor or transferor corporation was immediately before the transaction a foreign corporation to which this paragraph applies.

"(B) Existing FSCs. This paragraph shall apply to any controlled foreign corporation (as defined in section 957) if—

"(i) such corporation is a FSC (as so defined) in existence on September 30, 2000,

"(ii) such corporation is eligible to make the election under section 943(e) by reason of being described in paragraph (2)(B) of such section, and

"(iii) such corporation makes such election not later than for its first taxable year beginning after December 31, 2001.

"(C) Other corporations. This paragraph shall apply to any controlled foreign corporation (as defined in section 957), and such corporation shall (notwithstanding any provision of section 943(e)) be treated as an applicable foreign corporation for purposes of section 943(e), if—

"(i) such corporation is in existence on September 30, 2000;

"(ii) as of such date, such corporation is wholly owned (directly or indirectly) by a domestic corporation (determined without regard to any election under section 943(e));

"(iii) for each of the 3 taxable years preceding the first taxable year to which the election under section 943(e) by such controlled foreign corporation applies—

"(I) all of the gross income of such corporation is subpart F income (as defined in section 952), including by reason of section 954(h)(3)(B); and

"(II) in the ordinary course of such corporation's trade or business, such corporation regularly sold (or paid commissions) to a FSC which on September 30, 2000, was a related person to such corporation;

"(iv) such corporation has never made an election under section 922(a)(2) (as in effect before the date of the enactment of this paragraph) to be treated as a FSC; and

"(v) such corporation makes the election under section 943(e) not later than for its first taxable year beginning after December 31, 2001.

The preceding sentence shall cease to apply as of the date that the domestic corporation referred to in clause (ii) ceases to wholly own (directly or indirectly) such controlled foreign corporation.

"(4) Related person. For purposes of this subsection, the term 'related person' has the meaning given to such term by section 943(b)(3).

"(5) Section references. Except as otherwise expressly provided, any reference in this subsection to a section or other provision shall be considered to be a reference to a section or other provision of the Internal Revenue Code of 1986, as amended by this Act.

"(d) Special rules relating to leasing transactions.

"(1) Sales income. If foreign trade income in connection with the lease or rental of property described in section 927(a)(1)(B) of such Code (as in effect before the amendments made by this Act) is treated as exempt foreign trade income for purposes of section 921(a) of such Code (as so in effect), such property shall be treated as property described in section 941(c)(1)(B) of such Code (as added by this Act) for purposes of applying section 941(c)(2) of such Code (as so added) to any subsequent transaction involving such property to which the amendments made by this Act apply.

"(2) Limitation on use of gross receipts method. If any person computed its foreign trade income from any transaction with respect to any property on the basis of a transfer price determined under the method described in section 925(a)(1) of such Code (as in effect before the amendments made by this Act), then the qualifying foreign trade income (as defined in section 941(a) of such Code, as in effect after such amendment) of such person (or any related person) with respect to any other transaction involving such property (and to which the amendments made by this Act apply) shall be zero."

In 1987, P.L. 100-203, Sec. 10228(b), substituted "46, and 54" for "and 46" in para. (a)(6), effective for consideration received after 12/22/87 in tax. yrs. end. after 12/22/87, except for any acquisition pursuant to a written binding contract in effect on 12/15/87, and at all times thereafter before the acquisition.

In 1986, P.L. 99-499, Sec. 516(b)(2)(B), added the sentence at the end of subsec. (a), effective for tax. yrs. begin. after 12/31/86.

In 1984, P.L. 98-369, Sec. 67(b)(2), substituted "44, and 46" for "and 44" in para. (a)(6), effective for payments under agreements entered into or renewed after 6/14/84, in tax. yrs. end. after 6/14/84. Sec. 67(e)(2) provides the following special rule:

"(2) Special rule for contract amendments. Any contract entered into before June 15, 1984, which is amended after June 14, 1984, in any significant relevant aspect shall be treated as a contract entered into after June 14, 1984."

—P.L. 98-369, Sec. 801(d)(5), amended para. (a)(4), effective for transactions after 12/31/84, in tax. yrs. end. after 12/31/84.

Prior to amendment, para. (a)(4) read as follows:

"(4) Income, war profits, and excess profits taxes imposed by the authority of any foreign country or possession of the United States, if the taxpayer chooses to take to any extent the benefits of section 901 (relating to the foreign tax credit)."

In 1983, P.L. 98-21, Sec. 124(c)(5), added the sentence to the end of subsec. (a), effective for tax. yrs. begin. after 12/31/89.

In 1978, P.L. 95-600, Sec. 701(t)(3)(B), repealed the amendment made by Sec. 1605(b)(1) of P.L. 94-455, effective 10/4/76.

In 1976, P.L. 94-455, Sec. 1307(d)(2)(A), amended para. (a)(6), effective for tax. yrs. begin. after 12/31/76.

Prior to amendment, para. (a)(6) read as follows:

"(6) Taxes imposed by chapter 42, chapter 43."

—P.L. 94-455, Sec. 1605(b)(1), [repealed by Sec. 701(f)(3)(B) of P.L. 95-600, see above] substituted ", chapter 43, and chapter 44." for "and chapter 43." in para. (a)(6), effective for tax. yrs. of real estate investment trusts begin. after 10/4/76.

—P.L. 94-455, Sec. 1901(a)(39), deleted ", and corresponding provisions of prior revenue laws" after "section 3402" in subpara. (a)(1)(C), effective for tax. yrs. begin. after 12/31/76.

In 1974, P.L. 93-406, Sec. 1016(a)(1), added para. (a)(6), effective 9/2/74 or other date as specified in Sec. 1017 of the Act (reproduced following Code Sec. 401).

In 1964, P.L. 88-272, Sec. 207, added Code Sec. 275, effective for tax. yrs. begin. after 12/31/63.

Sec. 276. Certain indirect contributions to political parties.

(a) Disallowance of deduction.

No deduction otherwise allowable under this chapter shall be allowed for any amount paid or incurred for—

(1) advertising in a convention program of a political party, or in any other publication if any part of the proceeds of such publication directly or indirectly inures (or is intended to inure) to or for the use of a political party or a political candidate,

(2) admission to any dinner or program, if any part of the proceeds of such dinner or program directly or indirectly inures (or is intended to inure) to or for the use of a political party or a political candidate, or

(3) admission to an inaugural ball, inaugural gala, inaugural parade, or inaugural concert, or to any similar event which is identified with a political party or a political candidate.

(b) Definitions.

For purposes of this section—

(1) Political Party. The term "political party" means—

(A) a political party;

(B) a National, State, or local committee of a political party; or

(C) a committee, association, or organization, whether incorporated or not, which directly or indirectly accepts contributions (as defined in section 271(b)(2)) or make [sic s] expenditures (as defined in section 271(b)(3)) for the purpose of influencing or attempting to influence the selection, nomination, or election of any individual to any Federal, State, or local elective public office, or the election of presidential and vice-presidential electors, whether or not such individual or electors are selected, nominated, or elected.

(2) Proceeds inuring to or for the use of political candidates. Proceeds shall be treated as inuring to or for the use of a political candidate only if—

(A) such proceeds may be used directly or indirectly for the purpose of furthering his candidacy for selection, nomination, or election to any elective public office, and

(B) such proceeds are not received by such candidate in the ordinary course of a trade or business (other than the trade or business of holding elective public office).

(c) Cross reference.

For disallowance of certain entertainment, etc., expenses, see section 274.

In 1975, P.L. 93-625, Sec. 10(g), repealed P.L. 90-346.

In 1974, P.L. 93-443, Sec. 406(d), deleted subsec. (c) and redesignated subsec. (d) as subsec. (c), effective for tax. yrs. begin. after 12/31/74.

Prior to deletion, subsec. (c) read as follows:

"(c) Advertising in a convention program of a national political convention.

"Subsection (a) shall not apply to any amount paid or incurred for advertising in a convention program of a political party distributed in connection with a convention held for the purpose of nominating candidates for the offices of President and Vice President of the United States, if the proceeds from such program are used solely to defray the costs of conducting such convention (or a subsequent convention of such party held for such purpose) and the amount paid or incurred for such advertising is reasonable in light of the business the taxpayer may expect to receive —

"(1) directly as a result of such advertising, or

"(2) as a result of the convention being held in an area in which the taxpayer has a principal place of business."

In **1968**, P.L. 90-364, [repealed by Sec. 10(g) of P.L. 93-625, see above] 6/28/68, Sec. 108(a), redesignated subsec. (c) as subsec. (d) and added new subsec. (c), effective for amounts paid or incurred on or after 1/1/68.

6/18/68, contained a similar provision as follows:

"Sec. 1. That subsection (a) of section 276 of the Internal Revenue Code of 1954 (relating to certain indirect contributions to political parties) shall not apply to any amount paid or incurred for advertising in a convention program of a political party distributed in connection with a convention held for the purpose of nominating candidates for the offices of President and Vice President of the United States, if the proceeds from such program are used solely to defray the costs of conducting such convention (or a subsequent convention of such party held for such purpose) and the amount paid or incurred for such advertising is reasonable in light of the business the taxpayer may expect to receive —

"(1) directly as a result of such advertising, or

"(2) as a result of the convention being held in an area in which the taxpayer has a principal place of business."

"Sec. 2. The first section of this Act shall apply with respect to amounts paid or incurred on or after January 1, 1968."

In **1966**, P.L. 89-368, Sec. 301(a), added Code Sec. 276, effective for tax. yrs. begin. after 12/31/65, but only for amounts paid or incurred after 3/15/66.

Sec. 277. Deductions incurred by certain membership organizations in transaction with members.

(a) General rule.

In the case of a social club or other membership organization which is operated primarily to furnish services or goods to members and which is not exempt from taxation, deductions for the taxable year attributable to furnishing services, insurance, goods, or other items of value to members shall be allowed only to the extent of income derived during such year from members or transactions with members (including income derived during such year from institutes and trade shows which are primarily for the education of members). If for any taxable year such deductions exceed such income, the excess shall be treated as a deduction attributable to furnishing services, insurance, goods, or other items of value to members paid or incurred in the succeeding taxable year. The deductions provided by sections 243, 244, and 245 (relating to dividends received by corporations) shall not be allowed to any organization to which this section applies for the taxable year.

(b) Exceptions.

Subsection (a) shall not apply to any organization—

(1) which for the taxable year is subject to taxation under subchapter H or L,

(2) which has made an election before October 9, 1969, under section 456(c) or which is affiliated with such an organization,

(3) which for each day of any taxable year is a national securities exchange subject to regulation under the Securities Exchange Act of 1934 or a contract market subject to regulation under the Commodity Exchange Act , or

(4) which is engaged primarily in the gathering and distribution of news to its members for publication.

In **1986**, P.L. 99-514, Sec. 1604(a)(1), deleted "or" from the end of para. (b)(2) ... Sec. 1604(a)(2), substituted ", or" for the period at the end of para. (b)(3) ... Sec. 1604(a)(3), added para. (b)(4), effective for tax. yrs. begin. after 10/22/86.

In **1976**, P.L. 94-568, Sec. 1(c), added the last sentence in subsec. (a), effective for tax. yrs. begin. after 10/20/76.

In **1969**, P.L. 91-172, Sec. 121(b)(3), added Code Sec. 277, effective for tax. yrs. begin. after 12/31/70.

Sec. 278. Repealed.

In **1986**, P.L. 99-514, Sec. 803(b)(6), repealed Code Sec. 278, effective for costs incurred after 12/31/86, in tax. yrs. end. after 12/31/86.

Prior to amendment, Code Sec. 278 read as follows:

"SEC. 278. CAPITAL EXPENDITURES INCURRED IN PLANTING AND DEVELOPING CITRUS AND ALMOND GROVES; CERTAIN CAPITAL EXPENDITURES OF FARMING SYNDICATES.

"(a) General rule.

"Except as provided in subsection (c), any amount (allowable as a deduction without regard to this section), which is attributable to the planting, cultivation, maintenance, or development of any citrus or almond grove (or part thereof), and which is incurred before the close of the fourth taxable year beginning with the taxable year in which the trees were planted, shall be charged to capital account. For purposes of the preceding sentence, the portion of a citrus or almond grove planted in one taxable year shall be treated separately from the portion of such grove planted in another taxable year.

"(b) Farming syndicates.

"Except as provided in subsection (c), in the case of any farming syndicate (as defined in section 464(c)) engaged in planting, cultivating, maintaining, or developing a grove, orchard, or vineyard in which fruit or nuts are grown, any amount —

"(1) which would be allowable as a deduction but for the provisions of this subsection,

"(2) which is attributable to the planting, cultivation, maintenance, or development of such grove, orchard, or vineyard, and

"(3) which is incurred in a taxable year before the first taxable year in which such grove, orchard, or vineyard bears a crop or yield in commercial quantities, shall be charged to capital account.

"(c) Exceptions.

"Subsections (a) and (b) shall not apply to amounts allowable as deductions (without regard to this section) attributable to a grove, orchard, or vineyard which was replanted after having been lost or damaged (while in the hands of the taxpayer) by reason of freezing temperatures, disease, drought, pests, or casualty."

In **1976**, P.L. 94-455, Sec. 207(b)(1), amended subsec. (b) ... added subsec. (c) ... Sec. 207(b)(2)(A), substituted "Sec. 278. Capital expenditures incurred in planting and developing citrus and almond groves; certain capital expenditures of farming syndicates." for "Sec. 278. Capital expenditures incurred in planting and developing citrus and almond groves." in the heading of Code Sec. 278 ... Sec. 207(b)(2)(B), substituted "subsection (c)" for "subsection (b)" in subsec. (a), for tax. yrs. begin. after 12/31/75.

Sec. 207(b)(3) of the Act provided the following exceptions to the effective date:

"(3) Effective date. — The amendments made by this subsection shall apply to taxable years beginning after December 31, 1975. The amendments made by this subsection shall not apply in the case of a grove, orchard, or vineyard referred to in the amendment made by subsection (b)(1) which was planted or replanted on or before December 31, 1975. For purposes of the preceding sentence, a tree or vine which, on or before December 31, 1975, was planted at a place other than the grove, orchard, or vineyard of the taxpayer but which, on such date, was owned by the taxpayer (or with respect to which the taxpayer had a binding contract to purchase) shall be treated as planted on December 31, 1975, in the grove, orchard, or vineyard of the taxpayer."

Prior to amendment, subsec. (b) read as follows:

"(b) Exceptions.

"Subsection (a) shall not apply to amounts allowable as deductions (without regard to this section), and attributable to a citrus or almond grove (or part thereof) which was:

"(1) replanted after having been lost or damaged (while in the hands of the taxpayer), by reason of freeze, disease, drought, pests or casualty, or

"(2) planted or replanted before —

"(A) December 30, 1969, in the case of a citrus grove, or

"(B) December 30, 1970, in the case of an almond grove."

In **1971**, P.L. 91-680, Sec. I, substituted "citrus or almond grove" for "citrus grove" each place it appeared in Code Sec. 278, added "and almond" to the heading and amended para. (b)(2), effective for tax. yrs. begin. after 1/12/71.

Prior to amendment, para. (b)(2) read as follows:

"(2) planted or replanted prior to the enactment of this section."

In **1969**, P.L. 91-172, Sec. 216(a), added Code Sec. 278, effective for tax. yrs. begin. after 12/31/69.

Sec. 279. Interest on indebtedness incurred by corporation to acquire stock or assets of another corporation.

(a) General rule.

No deduction shall be allowed for any interest paid or incurred by a corporation during the taxable year with respect to its corporate acquisition indebtedness to the extent that such interest exceeds—

(1) $5,000,000, reduced by

(2) the amount of interest paid or incurred by such corporation during such year on obligations (A) issued after December 31, 1967, to provide consideration for an acquisition described in paragraph (1) of subsection (b), but (B) which are not corporate acquisition indebtedness.

(b) Corporate acquisition indebtedness.

For purposes of this section, the term "corporate acquisition indebtedness" means any obligation evidenced by a bond, debenture, note, or certificate or other evidence of indebtedness issued after October 9, 1969, by a corporation

Limitations on deduction Code Sec. 279(d)(2)

(hereinafter in this section referred to as "issuing corporation") if—
  (1) such obligation is issued to provide consideration for the acquisition of—
    (A) stock in another corporation (hereinafter in this section referred to as "acquired corporation"), or
    (B) assets of another corporation (hereinafter in this section referred to as "acquired corporation") pursuant to a plan under which at least two-thirds (in value) of all the assets (excluding money) used in trades and businesses carried on by such corporation are acquired,
  (2) such obligation is either—
    (A) subordinated to the claims of trade creditors of the issuing corporation generally, or
    (B) expressly subordinated in right of payment to the payment of any substantial amount of unsecured indebtedness, whether outstanding or subsequently issued, of the issuing corporation,
  (3) the bond or other evidence of indebtedness is either—
    (A) convertible directly or indirectly into stock of the issuing corporation, or
    (B) part of an investment unit or other arrangement which includes, in addition to such bond or other evidence of indebtedness, an option to acquire, directly or indirectly, stock in the issuing corporation, and
  (4) as of a day determined under subsection (c)(1), either—
    (A) the ratio of debt to equity (as defined in subsection (c)(2)) of the issuing corporation exceeds 2 to 1, or
    (B) the projected earnings (as defined in subsection (c)(3)) do not exceed 3 times the annual interest to be paid or incurred (determined under subsection (c)(4)).

(c) Rules for application of subsection (b)(4).
For purposes of subsection (b)(4)—
  (1) Time of determination. Determinations are to be made as of the last day of any taxable year of the issuing corporation in which it issues any obligation to provide consideration for an acquisition described in subsection (b)(1) of stock in, or assets of, the acquired corporation.
  (2) Ratio of debt to equity. The term "ratio of debt to equity" means the ratio which the total indebtedness of the issuing corporation bears to the sum of its money and all its other assets (in an amount equal to their adjusted basis for determining gain) less such total indebtedness.
  (3) Projected earnings.
    (A) The term "projected earnings" means the "average annual earnings" (as defined in subparagraph (B)) of—
      (i) the issuing corporation only, if clause (ii) does not apply, or
      (ii) both the issuing corporation and the acquired corporation, in any case where the issuing corporation has acquired control (as defined in section 368(c)), or has acquired substantially all of the properties, of the acquired corporation.
    (B) The average annual earnings referred to in subparagraph (A) is, for any corporation, the amount of its earnings and profits for any 3-year period ending with the last day of a taxable year of the issuing corporation described in paragraph (1), computed without reduction for—
      (i) interest paid or incurred,
      (ii) depreciation or amortization allowed under this chapter,
      (iii) liability for tax under this chapter, and
      (iv) distributions to which section 301(c)(1) applies (other than such distributions from the acquired to the issuing corporation),
    and reduced to an annual average for such 3-year period pursuant to regulations prescribed by the Secretary. Such regulations shall include rules for cases where any corporation was not in existence for all of such 3-year period or such period includes only a portion of a taxable year of any corporation.
  (4) Annual interest to be paid or incurred. The term "annual interest to be paid or incurred" means—
    (A) if subparagraph (B) does not apply, the annual interest to be paid or incurred by the issuing corporation only, determined by reference to its total indebtedness outstanding, or
    (B) if projected earnings are determined under clause (ii) of paragraph (3)(A), the annual interest to be paid or incurred by both the issuing corporation and the acquired corporation, determined by reference to their combined total indebtedness outstanding.
  (5) Special rules for banks and lending or finance companies. With respect to any corporation which is a bank (as defined in section 581) or is primarily engaged in a lending or finance business—
    (A) in determining under paragraph (2) the ratio of debt to equity of such corporation (or of the affiliated group of which such corporation is a member), the total indebtedness of such corporation (and the assets of such corporation) shall be reduced by an amount equal to the total indebtedness owed to such corporation which arises out of the banking business of such corporation, or out of the lending or finance business of such corporation, as the case may be;
    (B) in determining under paragraph (4) the annual interest to be paid or incurred by such corporation (or by the issuing and acquired corporations referred to in paragraph (4)(B) or by the affiliated group of which such corporation is a member) the amount of such interest (determined without regard to this paragraph) shall be reduced by an amount which bears the same ratio to the amount of such interest as the amount of the reduction for the taxable year under subparagraph (A) bears to the total indebtedness of such corporation; and
    (C) in determining under paragraph (3)(B) the average annual earnings, the amount of the earnings and profits for the 3-year period shall be reduced by the sum of the reductions under subparagraph (B) for such period.
For purposes of this paragraph, the term "lending or finance business" means a business of making loans or purchasing or discounting accounts receivable, notes, or installment obligations.

(d) Taxable years to which applicable.
In applying this section—
  (1) First year of disallowance. The deduction of interest on any obligation shall not be disallowed under subsection (a) before the first taxable year of the issuing corporation as of the last day of which the application of either subparagraph (A) or subparagraph (B) of subsection (b)(4) results in such obligation being corporate acquisition indebtedness.
  (2) General rule for succeeding years. Except as provided in paragraphs (3), (4), and (5), if an obligation is determined to be corporate acquisition indebtedness as of the last day of any taxable year of the issuing corporation, it shall be corporate acquisition indebtedness for such taxable year and all subsequent taxable years.

(3) Redetermination where control, etc., is acquired. If an obligation is determined to be corporate acquisition indebtedness as of the close of a taxable year of the issuing corporation in which clause (i) of subsection (c)(3)(A) applied, but would not be corporate acquisition indebtedness if the determination were made as of the close of the first taxable year of such corporation thereafter in which clause (ii) of subsection (c)(3)(A) could apply, such obligation shall be considered not to be corporate acquisition indebtedness for such later taxable year and all taxable years thereafter.

(4) Special 3-year rule. If an obligation which has been determined to be corporate acquisition indebtedness for any taxable year would not be such indebtedness for each of any 3 consecutive taxable years thereafter if subsection (b)(4) were applied as of the close of each of such 3 years, then such obligation shall not be corporate acquisition indebtedness for all taxable years after such 3 consecutive taxable years.

(5) 5 percent stock rule. In the case of obligations issued to provide consideration for the acquisition of stock in another corporation, such obligations shall be corporate acquisition indebtedness for a taxable year only if at some time after October 9, 1969, and before the close of such year the issuing corporation owns 5 percent or more of the total combined voting power of all classes of stock entitled to vote of such other corporation.

(e) Certain nontaxable transactions.

An acquisition of stock of a corporation of which the issuing corporation is in control (as defined in section 368(c)) in a transaction in which gain or loss is not recognized shall be deemed an acquisition described in paragraph (1) of subsection (b) only if immediately before such transaction (1) the acquired corporation was in existence, and (2) the issuing corporation was not in control (as defined in section 368(c)) of such corporation.

(f) Exemption for certain acquisitions of foreign corporations.

For purposes of this section, the term "corporate acquisition indebtedness" does not include any indebtedness issued to any person to provide consideration for the acquisition of stock in, or assets of, any foreign corporation substantially all of the income of which, for the 3-year period ending with the date of such acquisition or for such part of such period as the foreign corporation was in existence, is from sources without the United States.

(g) Affiliated groups.

In any case in which the issuing corporation is a member of an affiliated group, the application of this section shall be determined, pursuant to regulations prescribed by the Secretary, by treating all of the members of the affiliated group in the aggregate as the issuing corporation, except that the ratio of debt to equity of, projected earnings of, and annual interest to be paid or incurred by any corporation (other than the issuing corporation determined without regard to this subsection) shall be included in the determinations required under subparagraphs (A) and (B) of subsection (b)(4) as of any day only if such corporation is a member of the affiliated group on such day, and, in determining projected earnings of such corporation under subsection (c)(3), there shall be taken into account only the earnings and profits of such corporation for the period during which it was a member of the affiliated group. For purposes of the preceding sentence, the term "affiliated group" has the meaning assigned to such term by section 1504(a), except that all corporations other than the acquired corporation shall be treated as includible corporations (without any exclusion under section 1504(b)) and the acquired corporation shall not be treated as an includible corporation.

(h) Changes in obligation.

For purposes of this section—

(1) Any extension, renewal, or refinancing of an obligation evidencing a preexisting indebtedness shall not be deemed to be the issuance of a new obligation.

(2) Any obligation which is corporate acquisition indebtedness of the issuing corporation is also corporate acquisition indebtedness of any corporation which becomes liable for such obligation as guarantor, endorser, or indemnitor or which assumes liability for such obligation in any transaction.

(i) Certain obligations issued after October 9, 1969.

For purposes of this section, an obligation shall not be corporate acquisition indebtedness if issued after October 9, 1969, to provide consideration for the acquisition of—

(1) stock or assets pursuant to a binding written contract which was in effect on October 9, 1969, and at all times thereafter before such acquisition, or

(2) stock in any corporation where the issuing corporation, on October 9, 1969, and at all times thereafter before such acquisition, owned at least 50 percent of the total combined voting power of all classes of stock entitled to vote of the acquired corporation.

(j) Effect on other provisions.

No inference shall be drawn from any provision in this section that any instrument designated as a bond, debenture, note, or certificate or other evidence of indebtedness by its issuer represents an obligation or indebtedness of such issuer in applying any other provision of this title.

In 1976, P.L. 94-514, Sec. 1(a), deleted the last sentence in subsec. (i), for tax. yrs. end. after 10/9/69, except if refund or credit of any overpayment of income tax resulting from this amendment of Code Sec. 279(i) is prevented on 10/15/76 or at any time within one year after 10/15/76 by the operation of any law or rule of law, refund or credit of such over payment may, nevertheless, be made or allowed if claim thereof is filed within one year of 10/15/76.

Prior to amendment, the last sentence in subsec. (i) read as follows:

"Paragraph (2) shall cease to apply when (at any time on or after October 9, 1969) the issuing corporation has acquired control (as defined in section 368(c)) of the acquired corporation."

—P.L. 94-455, Sec. 1906(b)(13)(A), substituted "Secretary" for "Secretary or his delegate" in para. (c)(3) and subsec. (8), effective for tax. yrs. begin. after 12/31/76.

In 1969, P.L. 91-172, Sec. 411(a), added Code Sec. 279, effective for the determination of the allowability of the deduction of interest paid or incurred with respect to indebtedness incurred after 10/9/69.

Sec. 280. Repealed.

In 1986, P.L. 99-514, Sec. 803(b)(2)(A), repealed Code Sec. 280, effective for costs incurred after 12/31/86, in tax. yrs. end. after 12/31/86.

Prior to amendment, Code Sec. 280 read as follows:

"SEC. 280. CERTAIN EXPENDITURES INCURRED IN PRODUCTION OF FILMS, BOOKS, RECORDS, OR SIMILAR PROPERTY.

"(a) General rule.

"In the case of an individual, except in the case of production costs which are charged to capital account, amounts attributable to the production of a film, sound recording, book, or similar property which are otherwise deductible under this chapter shall be allowed as deductions only in accordance with the provisions of subsection (b). For purposes of this section, an S corporation, a personal holding company (as defined in section 542), and a foreign personal holding company (as defined in section 552) shall be treated as an individual.

"(b) Proration of production cost over income period.

"Amounts referred to in subsection (a) are deductible only for those taxable years ending during the period during which the taxpayer reasonably may be expected to receive substantially all of the income he will receive from any such film, sound recording, book, or similar property. The amount deductible for any such taxable year is an amount which bears the same ratio to the sum of all such amounts (attributable to such film, sound recording, book, or similar property) as the income received from the property for that taxable year bears to the sum of the income the taxpayer may reasonably be expected to receive during such period.

"(c) Definitions.

"For purposes of this section—

Limitations on deduction   Code Sec. 280A(c)(6)

"(1) Film. The term 'film' means any motion picture film or video tape.

"(2) Sound recording. The term 'sound recording' means works that result from the fixation of a series of musical, spoken, or other sounds, regardless of the nature of the material objects, such as discs, tapes, or other phonorecordings, in which such sounds are embodied."

In 1982, P.L. 97-354, Sec. 5(a)(25), substituted "an S corporation," for "an electing small business corporation (as defined in section 1371(b))," in subsec. (a), effective for tax. yrs. begin. after 12/31/82.

In 1978, P.L. 95-600, Sec. 701(m)(2), substituted "In the case of an individual, except" for "Except in the case of a corporation (other than an electing small business corporation (as defined in section 1371(b)) or a personal holding company (as defined in section 542) and except" in the first sentence of subsec. (a), and added the last sentence in subsec. (a), effective for amounts paid or incurred after 12/31/75, with respect to property the principal production of which begins after 12/31/75.

In 1976, P.L. 94-455, Sec. 210(a), added Code Sec. 280, effective for amounts paid or incurred after 12/31/75, with respect to property the principal production of which begins after 12/31/75.

Sec. 280A. Disallowance of certain expenses in connection with business use of home, rental of vacation homes, etc.

(a) General rule.

Except as otherwise provided in this section, in the case of a taxpayer who is an individual or an S corporation, no deduction otherwise allowable under this chapter shall be allowed with respect to the use of a dwelling unit which is used by the taxpayer during the taxable year as a residence.

(b) Exception for interest, taxes, casualty losses, etc.

Subsection (a) shall not apply to any deduction allowable to the taxpayer without regard to its connection with his trade or business (or with his income-producing activity).

(c) Exceptions for certain business or rental use; limitation on deductions for such use.

(1) Certain business use. Subsection (a) shall not apply to any item to the extent such item is allocable to a portion of the dwelling unit which is exclusively used on a regular basis—

(A) as the principal place of business for any trade or business of the taxpayer,

(B) as a place of business which is used by patients, clients, or customers in meeting or dealing with the taxpayer in the normal course of his trade or business, or

(C) in the case of a separate structure which is not attached to the dwelling unit, in connection with the taxpayer's trade or business.

In the case of an employee, the preceding sentence shall apply only if the exclusive use referred to in the preceding sentence is for the convenience of his employer. For purposes of subparagraph (A), the term "principal place of business" includes a place of business which is used by the taxpayer for the administrative or management activities of any trade or business of the taxpayer if there is no other fixed location of such trade or business where the taxpayer conducts substantial administrative or management activities of such trade or business.

(2) Certain storage use. Subsection (a) shall not apply to any item to the extent such item is allocable to space within the dwelling unit which is used on a regular basis as a storage unit for the inventory or product samples of the taxpayer held for use in the taxpayer's trade or business of selling products at retail or wholesale, but only if the dwelling unit is the sole fixed location of such trade or business.

(3) Rental use. Subsection (a) shall not apply to any item which is attributable to the rental of the dwelling unit or portion thereof (determined after the application of subsection (e)).

(4) Use in providing day care services.

(A) In general. Subsection (a) shall not apply to any item to the extent that such item is allocable to the use of any portion of the dwelling unit on a regular basis in the taxpayer's trade or business of providing day care for children, for individuals who have attained age 65, or for individuals who are physically or mentally incapable of caring for themselves.

(B) Licensing, etc., requirement. Subparagraph (A) shall apply to items accruing for a period only if the owner or operator of the trade or business referred to in subparagraph (A)—

(i) has applied for (and such application has not been rejected),

(ii) has been granted (and such granting has not been revoked), or

(iii) is exempt from having,

a license, certification, registration, or approval as a day care center or as a family or group day care home under the provisions of any applicable State law. This subparagraph shall apply only to items accruing in periods beginning on or after the first day of the first month which begins more than 90 days after the date of the enactment [5/23/77] of the Tax Reduction and Simplification Act of 1977.

(C) Allocation formula. If a portion of the taxpayer's dwelling unit used for the purposes described in subparagraph (A) is not used exclusively for those purposes, the amount of the expenses attributable to that portion shall not exceed an amount which bears the same ratio to the total amount of the items allocable to such portion as the number of hours the portion is used for such purposes bears to the number of hours the portion is available for use.

(5) Limitation on deductions. In the case of a use described in paragraph (1), (2), or (4), and in the case of a use described in paragraph (3) where the dwelling unit is used by the taxpayer during the taxable year as a residence, the deductions allowed under this chapter for the taxable year by reason of being attributed to such use shall not exceed the excess of—

(A) the gross income derived from such use for the taxable year, over

(B) the sum of—

(i) the deductions allocable to such use which are allowable under this chapter for the taxable year whether or not such unit (or portion thereof) was so used, and

(ii) the deductions allocable to the trade or business (or rental activity) in which such use occurs (but which are not allocable to such use) for such taxable year.

Any amount not allowable as a deduction under this chapter by reason of the preceding sentence shall be taken into account as a deduction (allocable to such use) under this chapter for the succeeding taxable year. Any amount taken into account for any taxable year under the preceding sentence shall be subject to the limitation of the 1st sentence of this paragraph whether or not the dwelling unit is used as a residence during such taxable year.

(6) Treatment of rental to employer. Paragraphs (1) and (3) shall not apply to any item which is attributable to the rental of the dwelling unit (or any portion thereof) by the taxpayer to his employer during any period in which the taxpayer uses the dwelling unit (or portion) in performing services as an employee of the employer.

Code Sec. 280A(d)

(d) Use as residence.
(1) In general. For purposes of this section, a taxpayer uses a dwelling unit during the taxable year as a residence if he uses such unit (or portion thereof) for personal purposes for a number of days which exceeds the greater of—
(A) 14 days, or
(B) 10 percent of the number of days during such year for which such unit is rented at a fair rental.
For purposes of subparagraph (B), a unit shall not be treated as rented at a fair rental for any day for which it is used for personal purposes.
(2) Personal use of unit. For purposes of this section, the taxpayer shall be deemed to have used a dwelling unit for personal purposes for a day if, for any part of such day, the unit is used—
(A) for personal purposes by the taxpayer or any other person who has an interest in such unit, or by any member of the family (as defined in section 267(c)(4)) of the taxpayer or such other person;
(B) by any individual who uses the unit under an arrangement which enables the taxpayer to use some other dwelling unit (whether or not a rental is charged for the use of such other unit); or
(C) by any individual (other than an employee with respect to whose use section 119 applies), unless for such day the dwelling unit is rented for a rental which, under the facts and circumstances, is fair rental.
The Secretary shall prescribe regulations with respect to the circumstances under which use of the unit for repairs and annual maintenance will not constitute personal use under this paragraph, except that if the taxpayer is engaged in repair and maintenance on a substantially full time basis for any day, such authority shall not allow the Secretary to treat a dwelling unit as being used for personal use by the taxpayer on such day merely because other individuals who are on the premises on such day are not so engaged.
(3) Rental to family member, etc., for use as principal residence.
(A) In general. A taxpayer shall not be treated as using a dwelling unit for personal purposes by reason of a rental arrangement for any period if for such period such dwelling unit is rented, at a fair rental, to any person for use as such person's principal residence.
(B) Special rules for rental to person having interest in unit.
(i) Rental must be pursuant to shared equity financing agreement. Subparagraph (A) shall apply to a rental to a person who has an interest in the dwelling unit only if such rental is pursuant to a shared equity financing agreement.
(ii) Determination of fair rental. In the case of a rental pursuant to a shared equity financing agreement, fair rental shall be determined as of the time the agreement is entered into and by taking into account the occupant's qualified ownership interest.
(C) Shared equity financing agreement. For purposes of this paragraph, the term "shared equity financing agreement" means an agreement under which—
(i) 2 or more persons acquire qualified ownership interests in a dwelling unit, and
(ii) the person (or persons) holding 1 or more of such interests—
(I) is entitled to occupy the dwelling unit for use as a principal residence, and
(II) is required to pay rent to 1 or more other persons holding qualified ownership interests in the dwelling unit.
(D) Qualified ownership interest. For purposes of this paragraph, the term "qualified ownership interest" means an undivided interest for more than 50 years in the entire dwelling unit and appurtenant land being acquired in the transaction to which the shared equity financing agreement relates.
(4) Rental of principal residence.
(A) In general. For purposes of applying subsection (c)(5) to deductions allocable to a qualified rental period, a taxpayer shall not be considered to have used a dwelling unit for personal purposes for any day during the taxable year which occurs before or after a qualified rental period described in subparagraph (B)(i), or before a qualified rental period described in subparagraph (B)(ii), if with respect to such day such unit constitutes the principal residence (within the meaning of section 121) of the taxpayer.
(B) Qualified rental period. For purposes of subparagraph (A), the term "qualified rental period" means a consecutive period of—
(i) 12 or more months which begins or ends in such taxable year, or
(ii) less than 12 months which begins in such taxable year and at the end of which such dwelling unit is sold or exchanged, and
for which such unit is rented, or is held for rental, at a fair rental.
(e) Expenses attributable to rental.
(1) In general. In any case where a taxpayer who is an individual or an S corporation uses a dwelling unit for personal purposes on any day during the taxable year (whether or not he is treated under this section as using such unit as a residence), the amount deductible under this chapter with respect to expenses attributable to the rental of the unit (or portion thereof) for the taxable year shall not exceed an amount which bears the same relationship to such expenses as the number of days during each year that the unit (or portion thereof) is rented at a fair rental bears to the total number of days during such year that the unit (or portion thereof) is used.
(2) Exception for deductions otherwise allowable. This subsection shall not apply with respect to deductions which would be allowable under this chapter for the taxable year whether or not such unit (or portion thereof) was rented.
(f) Definitions and special rules.
(1) Dwelling unit defined. For purposes of this section—
(A) In general. The term "dwelling unit" includes a house, apartment, condominium, mobile home, boat, or similar property, and all structures or other property appurtenant to such dwelling unit.
(B) Exception. The term "dwelling unit" does not include that portion of a unit which is used exclusively as a hotel, motel, inn, or similar establishment.
(2) Personal use by shareholders of S corporation. In the case of an S corporation, subparagraphs (A) and (B) of subsection (d)(2) shall be applied by substituting "any shareholder of the S corporation" for "the taxpayer" each place it appears.
(3) Coordination with section 183. If subsection (a) applies with respect to any dwelling unit (or portion thereof) for the taxable year—

Limitations on deduction — Code Sec. 280B

(A) section 183 (relating to activities not engaged in for profit) shall not apply to such unit (or portion thereof) for such year, but

(B) such year shall be taken into account as a taxable year for purposes of applying subsection (d) of section 183 (relating to 5-year presumption).

(4) Coordination with Section 162(a)(2) Nothing in this section shall be construed to disallow any deduction allowable under section 162(a)(2) (or any deduction which meets the tests of section 162(a)(2) but is allowable under another provision of this title) by reason of the taxpayer's being away from home in the pursuit of a trade or business (other than the trade or business of renting dwelling units).

(g) Special rule for certain rental use.

Notwithstanding any other provision of this section or section 183, if a dwelling unit is used during the taxable year by the taxpayer as a residence and such dwelling unit is actually rented for less than 15 days during the taxable year, then—

(1) no deduction otherwise allowable under this chapter because of the rental use of such dwelling unit shall be allowed, and

(2) the income derived from such use for the taxable year shall not be included in the gross income of such taxpayer under section 61.

In 1998, P.L. 105-206, Sec. 6005(e)(3), added "on or" before "before" each place it appeared in the heading and text of Sec. 312(d)(2)[sic (e)] of P.L. 105-34, see below.

In 1997, P.L. 105-34, Sec. 312(d)(1), substituted "section 121" for "section 1034" in subpara. (d)(4)(A), effective for sales and exchanges after 5/6/97. Sec. 312(d)(2)-(4) [sic (e)(2)-(4)] of this Act [as amended by Sec. 6005(e)(3), 105-206, see above] provides:

"(2) Sales on or before date of enactment. At the election of the taxpayer, the amendments made by this section shall not apply to any sale or exchange on or before the date of the enactment of this Act.

"(3) Certain sales within 2 years after date of enactment. Section 121 of the Internal Revenue Code of 1986 (as amended by this section) shall be applied without regard to subsection (c)(2)(B) thereof in the case of any sale or exchange of property during the 2-year period beginning on the date of the enactment of this Act if the taxpayer held such property on the date of the enactment of this Act and fails to meet the ownership and use requirements of subsection (a) thereof with respect to such property.

"(4) Binding contracts. At the election of the taxpayer, the amendments made by this section shall not apply to a sale or exchange after the date of the enactment of this Act, if—

"(A) such sale or exchange is pursuant to a contract which was binding on such date, or

"(B) without regard to such amendments, gain would not be recognized under section 1034 of the Internal Revenue Code of 1986 (as in effect on the day before the date of the enactment of this Act) on such sale or exchange by reason of a new residence acquired on or before such date or with respect to the acquisition of which by the taxpayer a binding contract was in effect on such date.

This paragraph shall not apply to any sale or exchange by an individual if the treatment provided by section 877(a)(1) of the Internal Revenue Code of 1986 applies to such individual."

—P.L. 105-34, Sec. 932(a), added a sentence at the end of para. (c)(1), effective for tax. yrs. begin. after 12/31/98.

In 1996, P.L. 104-188, Sec. 1113(a), substituted "inventory or product samples" for "inventory" in para. (c)(2), effective for tax. yrs. begin. after 12/31/95.

—P.L. 104-188, Sec. 1704(t)(39), amended subpara. (c)(1)(A), effective 8/20/96. Prior to amendment, subpara. (c)(1)(A) read as follows:

"(A) [as] the principal place of business for any trade or business of the taxpayer."

In 1988, P.L. 100-647, Sec. 1001(h)(1), added a sentence to the end of para. (c)(5) . . . Sec. 1001(h)(2), substituted "trade or business(or rental activity)" for "trade or business" in clause (c)(5)(B)(ii), effective for tax yrs. begin. after 12/31/86.

In 1986, P.L. 99-514, Sec. 143(b), added para. (c)(6) . . . Sec. 143(c), amended subpara. (c)(5)(B), effective for tax. yrs. begin. after 12/31/86.

Prior to amendment, subpara. (c)(5)(B) read as follows:

"(B) the deductions allocable to such use which are allowable under this chapter for the taxable year whether or not such unit (or portion thereof) was so used."

In 1982, P.L. 97-354, Sec. 5(a)(26)(A), substituted "an S corporation," for "an electing small business corporation," in subsec. (a) . . . Sec. 5(a)(26)(B), substituted "an S corporation" for "an electing small business corporation" in para.

(e)(1) . . . Sec. 5(a)(26)(C), amended para. (f)(2), effective for tax. yrs. begin. after 12/31/82.

Prior to amendment, para. (f)(2) read as follows:

"(2) Personal use by electing small business corporation. In the case of an electing small business corporation, subparagraphs (A) and (B) of subsection (d)(2) shall be applied by substituting 'any shareholder of the electing small business corporation' for 'the taxpayer' each place it appears."

—P.L. 97-216, Sec. 215(b), amended para. (f)(4), effective for tax. yrs. begin. after 12/31/81.

Prior to amendment para. (f)(4) read as follows:

"(4) Coordination with section 162(a)(2), etc.

"(A) In general. Nothing in this section shall be construed to disallow any deduction allowable under section 162(a)(2) (or any deduction which meets the tests of section 162(a)(2) but is allowable under another provision of this title) by reason of the taxpayer's being away from home in the pursuit of a trade or business (other than the trade or business of renting dwelling units).

"(B) Limitation. The Secretary shall prescribe amounts deductible (without substantiation) pursuant to the last sentence of section 162(a), but nothing in subparagraph (A) or any other provision of this title shall permit such a deduction for any taxable year of amounts in excess of the amounts determined to be appropriate under the circumstances."

In 1981, P.L. 97-119, Sec. 113(a)(1), redesignated para. (d)(3) as para. (d)(4) and added new para. (d)(3) . . . Sec. 113(a)(2), deleted "to a person other than a member of the family (as defined in section 267(c)(4)) of the taxpayer" after "for which such unit is rented" in subpara. (d)(4)(B) (as redesignated) . . . Sec. 113(b), added para. (f)(4) . . . Sec. 113(c), amended subpara. (c)(1)(A) . . . Sec. 113(d), added ", except that if the taxpayer is engaged in repair and maintenance on a substantially full time basis for any day, such authority shall not allow the Secretary to treat a dwelling unit as being used for personal use by the taxpayer on such day merely because other individuals who are on the premises on such day are not so engaged" after "paragraph" in the last sentence of para. (d)(2), effective for tax. yrs. begin. after 12/31/75, except "that in the case of taxable years beginning after 12/31/75, and before 1/1/80, the amendment made by this section [Sec. 113] shall apply only to taxable years for which, on the date of the enactment of this Act [12/29/81], the making of a refund, or the assessment of a deficiency, was not barred by law or any rule of law."

Prior to amendment, subpara. (c)(1)(A) read as follows:

"(A) as the taxpayer's principal place of business,"

In 1980, P.L. 96-369, Sec. 123, provides that: No funds appropriated by this Act [making continuing appropriations for the fiscal year 1981, and for other purposes] may be used to implement or enforce provisions of any regulations or ruling with respect to section 280A of the Internal Revenue Code which relate to—

(1) the rental of a dwelling unit so a member of the family of a taxpayer,

(2) the determination of the principal place of business of the taxpayer, or

(3) the circumstances under which use of the dwelling unit for repairs and maintenance constitutes personal use by the taxpayer.

In 1978, P.L. 95-600, Sec. 701(h)(1), added para. (d)(3), effective for tax. yrs. begin. after 12/31/75.

In 1977, P.L. 95-30, Sec. 306, redesignated para. (c)(4) as para. (c)(5), added new para. (c)(4) and substituted "paragraph (1), (2), or (4)" for "paragraph (1) or (2)" in redesignated para. (c)(5), effective for tax. yrs. begin. after 12/31/75.

In 1976, P.L. 94-455, Sec. 601(a), added Code Sec. 280A, effective for tax. yrs. begin. after 12/31/75.

Sec. 280B. Demolition of structures.

In the case of the demolition of any structure—

(1) no deduction otherwise allowable under this chapter shall be allowed to the owner or lessee of such structure for—

(A) any amount expended for such demolition, or

(B) any loss sustained on account of such demolition; and

(2) amounts described in paragraph (1) shall be treated as properly chargeable to capital account with respect to the land on which the demolished structure was located.

In 1986, P.L. 99-514, Sec. 1878(h), amended Sec. 1063(c) of P.L. 98-369 [reproduced below], the effective date for changes made by Sec. 1063 of P.L. 98-369.

Prior to amendment, Sec. 1063(c) of P.L. 98-369 read as follows:

"(c) Effective date.

"The amendments made by this section shall apply to taxable years beginning after December 31, 1983."

In 1984, P.L. 98-369, Sec. 1063(a)(1), substituted "In the case of the demolition of any structure—" for the designation, name and first sentence of subsec (a) . . . Sec. 1063(a)(2), repealed subsecs. (b) and (c) . . . Sec. 1063(b)(1), substituted "structures" for "certain historic structures" in the heading of Code Sec. 280B, effective as provided in Sec. 1063(c) of this Act [as amended by Sec. 1878(h) of P.L. 99-514], which reads as follows:

"(c) Effective dates.

"(1) The amendments made by this section shall apply to taxable years ending after December 31, 1983, but shall not apply to any demolition (other than of a certified historic structure) commencing before July 19, 1984.

Code Sec. 280B   Limitations on deduction

"(2) For purposes of paragraph (1), if a demolition is delayed until the completion of the replacement structure on the same site, the demolition shall be treated as commencing when construction of the replacement structure commences.

"(3) The amendments made by this section shall not apply to any demolition commencing before September 1, 1984, pursuant to a bank headquarters building project if—

"(A) on April 1, 1984, a corporation was retained to advise the bank on the final completion of the project, and

"(B) on June 12, 1984, the Comptroller of the Currency approved the project.

"(4) The amendments made by this section shall not apply to the remaining adjusted basis at the time of demolition of any structure if—

"(A) such structure was used in the manufacture, storage, or distribution of lead alkyl antiknock products and intermediate and related products at facilities located in or near Baton Rouge, Louisiana, and Houston, Texas, owned by the same corporation, and

"(B) demolition of at least one such structure at the Baton Rouge facility commenced before January 1, 1984."

Prior to substitution, the name and first sentence of subsec. (a) read as follows:

"(a) General rule.

"In the case of the demolition of a certified historic structure (as defined in section 48(g)(3)(A))—"

Prior to deletion, subsecs. (b) and (c) read as follows:

"(b) Special rule for registered districts.

"For purposes of this section, any building or other structure located in a registered historic district (as defined in section 48(g)(3)(B)) shall be treated as a certified historic structure unless the Secretary of the Interior has certified that such structure is not a certified historic structure, and that such structure is not of historic significance to the district, and if such certification occurs after the beginning of the demolition of such structure, the taxpayer has certified to the Secretary that, at the time of such demolition, he in good faith was not aware of the certification requirements by the Secretary of the Interior.

"(c) Application of section.

"This section shall apply with respect to demolitions commencing after June 30, 1976, and before January 1, 1984."

In 1983, P.L. 97-448, Sec. 102(f)(1), amended Sec. 212(e)(2)(B) of P.L. 97-34, part of the effective date for changes made by Sec. 212(d)(2)(C) of P.L. 97-34, see below.

Prior to amendment, Sec. 212(e)(2)(B) of P.L. 97-34 read as follows:

"(B) such building meets the requirements of paragraph (1) of section 48(g) of the Internal Revenue Code of 1954 (as in effect on the day before the date of enactment of this Act) but does not meet the requirements of such paragraph (1) (as amended by this Act)."

In 1981, P.L. 97-34, Sec. 212(d)(2)(C)(i), substituted "section 48(g)(3)(A)" for "section 191(d)(1)" in subsec. (a) . . . Sec. 212(d)(2)(C)(ii), substituted "section 48(g)(3)(B)" for "section 191(d)(2)" in subsec. (b), effective for expenditures incurred after 12/31/81 in tax. yrs. end. after 12/31/81. Sec. 212(e)(2) [as amended by Sec. 102(f)(1) of P.L. 97-448, see above] of this Act provides:

"(2) Transitional rule. The amendments made by this section shall not apply with respect to any rehabilitation of a building if—

"(A) the physical work on such rehabilitation began before January 1, 1982, and

"(B) such building does not meet the requirements of paragraph (1) of section 48(g) of the Internal Revenue Code of 1954 (as amended by this Act)."

In 1980, P.L. 96-541, Sec. 2(b), added subsec. (c), effective 12/17/80.

—P.L. 96-541, Sec. 2(e)(2), deleted Sec. 2124(b)(3) of P.L. 94-455, the effective date for changes made by Sec. 2124(b)(1) of P.L. 94-455, see below.

Prior to deletion, Sec. 2124(b)(3) of P.L. 94-455 read as follows:

"(3) Effective date. The amendments made by this subsection shall apply with respect to demolitions commencing after June 30, 1976, and before January 1, 1981."

In 1978, P.L. 95-600, Sec. 701(f)(5), amended subsec. (b), effective for demolitions commencing after 6/30/76 and before '81.

Prior to amendment, subsec. (b) read as follows:

"(b) Special rule for registered historic districts.

"For purposes of this section, any building or other structure located in a Registered Historic District shall be treated as a certified historic structure unless the Secretary of the Interior has certified, prior to the demolition of such structure, that such structure is not of historic significance to the district."

In 1976, P.L. 94-455, Sec. 2124(b)(1), added Code Sec. 280B, effective for demolitions commencing after 6/30/76 and before 1/1/81.

Sec. 280C. Certain expenses for which credits are allowable.

(a) Rule for employment credits.

No deduction shall be allowed for that portion of the wages or salaries paid or incurred for the taxable year which is equal to the sum of the credits determined for the taxable year under sections 45A(a), 45P(a), 51(a), 1396(a), 1400P(b), and 1400R. In the case of a corporation which is a member of a controlled group of corporations (within the meaning of section 52(a)) or a trade or business which is treated as being under common control with other trades or businesses (within the meaning of section 52(b)), this subsection shall be applied under rules prescribed by the Secretary similar to the rules applicable under subsections (a) and (b) of section 52.

(b) Credit for qualified clinical testing expenses for certain drugs.

(1) In general. No deduction shall be allowed for that portion of the qualified clinical testing expenses (as defined in section 45C(b)) otherwise allowable as a deduction for the taxable year which is equal to the amount of the credit allowable for the taxable year under section 45C (determined without regard to section 38(c)).

(2) Similar rule where taxpayer capitalizes rather than deducts expenses. If—

(A) the amount of the credit allowable for the taxable year under section 45C (determined without regard to section 38(c)), exceeds

(B) the amount allowable as a deduction for the taxable year for qualified clinical testing expenses (determined without regard to paragraph (1)),

the amount chargeable to capital account for the taxable year for such expenses shall be reduced by the amount of such excess.

(3) Controlled groups. In the case of a corporation which is a member of a controlled group of corporations (within the meaning of section 41(f)(5)) or a trade or business which is treated as being under common control with other trades or business (within the meaning of section 41(f)(1)(B)), this subsection shall be applied under rules prescribed by the Secretary similar to the rules applicable under subparagraphs (A) and (B) of section 41(f)(1).

(c) Credit for increasing research activities.

(1) In general. No deduction shall be allowed for that portion of the qualified research expenses (as defined in section 41(b)) or basic research expenses (as defined in section 41(e)(2)) otherwise allowable as a deduction for the taxable year which is equal to the amount of the credit determined for such taxable year under section 41(a).

(2) Similar rule where taxpayer capitalizes rather than deducts expenses. If—

(A) the amount of the credit determined for the taxable year under section 41(a)(1), exceeds

(B) the amount allowable as a deduction for such taxable year for qualified research expenses or basic research expenses (determined without regard to paragraph (1)),

the amount chargeable to capital account for the taxable year for such expenses shall be reduced by the amount of such excess.

(3) Election of reduced credit.

(A) In general. In the case of any taxable year for which an election is made under this paragraph—

(i) paragraphs (1) and (2) shall not apply, and

(ii) the amount of the credit under section 41(a) shall be the amount determined under subparagraph (B).

(B) Amount of reduced credit. The amount of credit determined under this subparagraph for any taxable year shall be the amount equal to the excess of—

(i) the amount of credit determined under section 41(a) without regard to this paragraph, over

(ii) the product of—

(I) the amount described in clause (i), and

(II) the maximum rate of tax under section 11(b)(1).

(C) Election. An election under this paragraph for any taxable year shall be made not later than the time for filing the return of tax for such year (including exten-

Limitations on deduction Code Sec. 280C

sions), shall be made on such return, and shall be made in such manner as the Secretary may prescribe. Such an election, once made, shall be irrevocable.

(4) Controlled groups. Paragraph (3) of subsection (b) shall apply for purposes of this subsection.

(d) Credit for low sulfur diesel fuel production.

The deductions otherwise allowed under this chapter for the taxable year shall be reduced by the amount of the credit determined for the taxable year under section 45H(a).

(e) Mine rescue team training credit.

No deduction shall be allowed for that portion of the expenses otherwise allowable as a deduction for the taxable year which is equal to the amount of the credit determined for the taxable year under section 45N(a).

(f) Credit for security of agricultural chemicals.

No deduction shall be allowed for that portion of the expenses otherwise allowable as a deduction taken into account in determining the credit under section 45O for the taxable year which is equal to the amount of the credit determined for such taxable year under section 45O(a).

> • **Caution:** Code Sec. 280C(g) following is effective for tax. yrs. ending after 12/31/2013. For Code Sec. 280C(g) that applies to amounts paid or incurred after 12/31/2008, in the taxable years beginning after 12/31/08 see below.

(g) Credit for health insurance premiums.

No deduction shall be allowed for the portion of the premiums paid by the taxpayer for coverage of 1 or more individuals under a qualified health plan which is equal to the amount of the credit determined for the taxable year under section 36B(a) with respect to such premiums.

> • **Caution:** Code Sec. 280C(g) following applies to amounts paid or incurred after 12/31/2008, in taxable years beginning after 12/31/2008. For Code Sec. 280C(g) effective after tax. yrs. 12/31/2013 see above.

(g) Qualifying therapeutic discovery project credit.

(1) In general. No deduction shall be allowed for that portion of the qualified investment (as defined in section 48D(b)) otherwise allowable as a deduction for the taxable year which—

(A) would be qualified research expenses (as defined in section 41(b)), basic research expenses (as defined in section 41(e)(2)), or qualified clinical testing expenses (as defined in section 45C(b)) if the credit under section 41 or section 45C were allowed with respect to such expenses for such taxable year, and

(B) is equal to the amount of the credit determined for such taxable year under section 48D(a), reduced by—

(i) the amount disallowed as a deduction by reason of section 48D(e)(2)(B), and

(ii) the amount of any basis reduction under section 48D(e)(1).

(2) Similar rule where taxpayer capitalizes rather than deducts expenses. In the case of expenses described in paragraph (1)(A) taken into account in determining the credit under section 48D for the taxable year, if—

(A) the amount of the portion of the credit determined under such section with respect to such expenses, exceeds

(B) the amount allowable as a deduction for such taxable year for such expenses (determined without regard to paragraph (1)), the amount chargeable to capital account for the taxable year for such expenses shall be reduced by the amount of such excess.

(3) Controlled groups. Paragraph (3) of subsection (b) shall apply for purposes of this subsection.

(h) Credit for employee health insurance expenses of small employers.

No deduction shall be allowed for that portion of the premiums for qualified health plans (as defined in section 1301(a) of the Patient Protection and Affordable Care Act), or for health insurance coverage in the case of taxable years beginning in 2010, 2011, 2012, or 2013, paid by an employer which is equal to the amount of the credit determined under section 45R(a) with respect to the premiums.

In 2010, P.L. 111-148, Sec. 1401(b), added subsec (g), effective for tax. yrs. ending after 12/31/2013.... Sec. 1421(d)(1), added subsec. (h), effective for amounts paid or incurred in tax. yrs. begin. after 12/31/2010.... Sec. 9023(c)(2), added subsec. (g), effective for for amounts paid or incurred after 12/31/2008, in tax yrs. begin. after such date.... Sec. 10105(e)(3), substituted " 2010, 2011" for "2011" in subsec. (h) (as added by Sec. 1421(d)(1) of this Act), effective 3/23/2010.

In 2008, P.L. 110-246, Sec. 4, Repeals the duplicative enactment and provides effective date provisions of the Act entitled "An Act to provide for the continuation of agricultural programs through fiscal year 2012, and for other purposes" Sec. 4, P.L. 110-246 reads as follows:

"Sec. 4. Repeal of duplicative enactment.

"(a) In General- The Act entitled 'An Act to provide for the continuation of agricultural programs through fiscal year 2012, and for other purposes' (H.R. 2419 of the 110th Congress), and the amendments made by that Act, are repealed, effective on the date of enactment of that Act.

"(b) Effective Date- Except as otherwise provided in this Act, this Act and the amendments made by this Act shall take effect on the earlier of—

"(1) the date of enactment of this Act; or

"(2) the date of the enactment of the Act entitled 'An Act to provide for the continuation of agricultural programs through fiscal year 2012, and for other purposes' (H.R. 2419 of the 110th Congress)."

—P.L. 110-246, Sec. 15343(c), added subsec. (f), effective for amounts paid or incurred after 5/22/2008. [Ed. Note: May 22, 2008 was the date of enactment for H.R. 2419 (PL 110-234), which was repealed by (2008 Farm Act § 4(a)) (PL 110-246, 6/18/2008), in connection with the reenactment of the farm bill to correct a technical deficiency in its original passage.]

In 2007, P.L. 110-172, Sec. 7(a)(1)(B), amended subsec. (d), effective for expenses paid or incurred after 12/31/2002, in tax. yrs. end. after 12/31/2002.

Prior to amendment, subsec. (d) read as follows

"(d) Low sulfur diesel fuel production credit. No deduction shall be allowed for that portion of the expenses otherwise allowable as a deduction for the taxable year which is equal to the amount of the credit determined for the taxable year under section 45H(a)."

In 2006, P.L. 109-432, Sec. 405(c), added subsec. (e), effective for tax. yrs. end. after 12/31/2005.

—P.L. 109-432, Sec. 123, of this Act, reads as follows:

"Sec. 123. Special rule for elections under expired provisions.

"(a) Research credit elections. In the case of any taxable year ending after December 31, 2005, and before the date of the enactment of this Act, any election under section 41(c)(4) or section 280C(c)(3)(C) of the Internal Revenue Code of 1986 shall be treated as having been timely made for such taxable year if such election is made not later than the later of April 15, 2007, or such time as the Secretary of the Treasury, or his designee, may specify. Such election shall be made in the manner prescribed by such Secretary or designee.

"(b) Other elections. Except as otherwise provided by such Secretary or designee, a rule similar to the rule of subsection (a) shall apply with respect to elections under any other expired provision of the Internal Revenue Code of 1986 the applicability of which is extended by reason of the amendments made by this title."

In 2005, P.L. 109-135, Sec. 103(b)(2), substituted "1396(a), and 1400P(b)" for "and 1396(a)" in subsec. (a), effective 12/21/2005.

—P.L. 109-135, Sec. 201(b)(2), substituted "1400P(b), and 1400R" for "and 1400P(b)" [as added by Sec. 103(b)(2) of this Act, see above] in subsec. (a), effective 12/21/2005.

In 2004, P.L. 108-357, Sec. 339(c), added subsec. (d), effective for expenses paid or incurred after 12/31/2002, in tax. yrs. end. after 12/31/2002.

In 2000, P.L. 106-554, Sec. 1(a)(7), [which enacted into law Sec. 311(a)(1) of P.L. 106-554 deleted "or credit" after "deduction" each place it appeared in para. (c)(1), effective for amounts paid or incurred after 6/30/99.

In 1999, P.L. 106-170, Sec. 502(c)(2), added "or credit" after "deduction" each place it appeared in para. (c)(1), effective for amounts paid or incurred after 6/30/99.

In 1996, P.L. 104-188, Sec. 1205(d)(7)(A), substituted "section 45C(b)" for "section 28(b)" in para. (b)(1) ... Sec. 1205(d)(7)(B), substituted "section 45C" for "section 28" in para. (b)(1) and subpara. (b)(2)(A) ... Sec. 1205(d)(7)(C), substituted "section 38(c)" for "subsection (d)(2) thereof" in para. (b)(1) and subpara. (b)(2)(A), effective for amounts paid or incurred in tax. yrs. end. after 6/30/96.

Code Sec. 280C

In 1993, P.L. 103-66, Sec. 13302(b)(1)(A), substituted "the sum of the credits determined for the taxable year under sections 51(a) and 1396(a)" for "the amount of the credit determined for the taxable year under section 51(a)" in subsec. (a) ... Sec. 13302(b)(1)(B), substituted "employment credits" for "targeted jobs credit" in the heading of subsec. (a), effective 8/10/93.

—P.L. 103-66, Sec. 13322(c)(1), substituted "45A(a), 51(a), and" for "51(a)" in subsec. (a), effective for wages paid or incurred after 12/31/93.

In 1989, P.L. 101-239, Sec. 7110(c)(1), deleted "50 percent of" before "the amount of the credit" each place it appeared in subsec. (c), effective for tax. yrs. begin. after 12/31/89.

—P.L. 101-239, Sec. 7814(e)(2)(A), redesignated para. (c)(3) as para. (c)(4) and added new para. (c)(3), effective for tax. yrs. begin. after 12/31/88.

—P.L. 101-239, Sec. 7814(e)(2)(B), of this Act provides:

"(B) In the case of a taxable year for which the last date for making the election under section 280C(c)(3) of the Internal Revenue Code of 1986 (as added by subparagraph (A)) is on or before the date which is 75 days after the date of the enactment of this Act, [12/19/89] such an election for such year may be made—

"(i) at any time before the date which is 75 days after such date of enactment, [12/19/89] and

"(ii) in such form and manner as the Secretary of the Treasury or his delegate may prescribe."

In 1988, P.L. 100-647, Sec. 4008(a), added subsec. (c), effective for tax. yrs. begin. after 12/31/88.

In 1986, P.L. 99-514, Sec. 231(d)(3)(E)(i), substituted "section 41(f)(5)" for "section 30(f)(5)" in para. (b)(3) . . . Sec. 231(d)(3)(E)(ii), substituted "section 41(f)(1)(B)" for "section 30(f)(1)(B)" in para. (b)(3) . . . Sec. 231(d)(3)(E)(iii), substituted "section 41(f)(1)" for "section 30(f)(1)" in para. (b)(3), effective for tax. yrs. begin. after 12/31/85.

—P.L. 99-514, Sec. 1847(b)(8)(A), substituted "section 28" for "section 29" each place it appeared in subsec. (b) . . . Sec. 1847(b)(8)(B), substituted "section 28(b)" for "section 29(b)" in para. (b)(1), effective for tax. yrs. begin. after 12/31/83, and for carrybacks from tax. yrs. begin. after 12/31/83.

In 1984, P.L. 98-369, Sec. 474(r)(10)(A), deleted subsec. (a) and redesignated subsecs. (b) and (c) as subsecs. (a) and (b) . . . Sec. 474(r)(10)(B)(i), amended the first sentence in subsec. (a) (as redesignated by Sec. 474(r)(10)(A) of this Act) . . . Sec. 474(r)(10)(B)(ii), substituted "targeted jobs credit" for "section 44B credit" in the heading of subsec. (a) . . . Sec. 474(r)(10)(C), substituted "29" for "44H" each place it appeared in subsec. (b) (as redesignated by Sec. 474(r)(10)(A) of the Act) . . . Sec. 474(r)(10)(D), substituted "30(f)(5)" for "44F(f)(5)", substituted "30(f)(1)(B)" for "44F(f)(1)(B)" and substituted "30(f)(1)" for "44F(f)(1)" in para. (b)(3), effective for tax. yrs. begin. after 12/31/83, and for carrybacks from tax. yrs. begin. after 12/31/83.

Prior to deletion, subsec. (a) read as follows:

"(a) Rule for section 40 credit.

"No deduction shall be allowed for that portion of the work incentive program expenses paid or incurred for the taxable year which is equal to the amount of the credit allowable for the taxable year under section 40 (relating to credit for expenses of work incentive programs) determined without regard to the provisions of section 50A(a)(2) (relating to limitation based on amount of tax). In the case of a corporation which is a member of a controlled group of corporations (within the meaning of section 50B(g)(1)) or a trade or business which is treated as being under common control with other trades or businesses (within the meaning of section 50B(g)(2)), this subsection shall be applied under rules prescribed by the Secretary similar to the rules applicable under paragraphs (1) and (2) of section 50B(g)."

Prior to amendment, the first sentence in subsec. (b) (as redesignated) read as follows:

"No deduction shall be allowed for that portion of the wages or salaries paid or incurred for the taxable year which is equal to the amount of the credit allowable for the taxable year under section 44B (relating to credit for employment of certain new employees) determined without regard to the provisions of section 53 (relating to limitation based on amount of tax)."

In 1983, P.L. 97-414, Sec. 4(b)(1), added subsec. (c) . . . Sec. 4(b)(2)(A), amended the heading of Code Sec. 280C, effective for amounts paid or incurred after 12/31/82, in tax. yrs. end. after 12/31/82.

Prior to amendment, the heading of Code Sec. 280C read as follows:

"Sec. 280C. Portion of wages for which credit is claimed under section 40 or 44B."

In 1980, P.L. 96-222, Sec. 103(a)(7)(D)(iv), amended Sec. 322(d)(1)(A)[sic] of P.L. 95-600, by substituting "out" for "our"[see below].

In 1978, P.L. 95-600, Sec. 322(d)(1)(A), [sic], (as amended by P.L. 96-178, Sec. (c)(4)) struck out "section 44B" and inserted "section 40 or 44B" for "section 44B" in the heading of Code Sec. 280C . . . Sec. 322(d)(1)(B), [sic], inserted "(b) Rule for section 44B credit." before "No deduction" in the first sentence . . . Sec. 322(d)(1)(C), [sic], substituted "this subsection shall be applied" for "this section shall be applied" in the second sentence . . . Sec. 322(d)(1)(D), [sic], added subsec. (a) in Code Sec. 280C, for work incentive program expenses paid or incurred after 12/31/78, in tax. yrs. end. after 12/31/78.

In 1977, P.L. 95-30, Sec. 202(c)(1), added Code Sec. 280C, effective for tax. yrs. begin. after '76 and to credit carrybacks from such yrs.

Sec. 280D. Repealed

In 1988, P.L. 100-418, Sec. 1941(b)(4)(A), repealed Code Sec. 280D, effective for crude oil removed from the premises on or after 8/23/88.

Prior to repeal Code Sec. 280D read as follows:

Limitations on deduction

"Sec. 280D. Portion of chapter 45 taxes for which credit or refund is allowable under section 6429.

"No deduction shall be allowed for that portion of the tax imposed by section 4986 for which a credit or refund is allowable under section 6429."

In 1980, P.L. 96-499, Sec. 1131(d)(1), added Code Sec. 280D, effective for tax. yrs. ending after 2/29/80.

Sec. 280E. Expenditures in connection with the illegal sale of drugs.

No deduction or credit shall be allowed for any amount paid or incurred during the taxable year in carrying on any trade or business if such trade or business (or the activities which comprise such trade or business) consists of trafficking in controlled substances (within the meaning of schedule I and II of the Controlled Substances Act) which is prohibited by Federal law or the law of any State in which such trade or business is conducted.

In 1982, P.L. 97-248, Sec. 351(a), added Code Sec. 280E, effective for amounts paid or incurred after 9/3/82, in tax. yrs. ending after 9/3/82.

Sec. 280F. Limitation on depreciation for luxury automobiles; limitation where certain property used for personal purposes.

(a) **Limitation on amount of depreciation for luxury automobiles.**

(1) **Depreciation.**

(A) **Limitation.** The amount of the depreciation deduction for any taxable year for any passenger automobile shall not exceed—

(i) $2,560 for the 1st taxable year in the recovery period,

(ii) $4,100 for the 2nd taxable year in the recovery period,

(iii) $2,450 for the 3rd taxable year in the recovery period, and

(iv) $1,475 for each succeeding taxable year in the recovery period.

(B) **Disallowed deductions allowed for years after recovery period.**

(i) **In general.** Except as provided in clause (ii), the unrecovered basis of any passenger automobile shall be treated as an expense for the 1st taxable year after the recovery period. Any excess of the unrecovered basis over the limitation of clause (ii) shall be treated as an expense in the succeeding taxable year.

(ii) **$1,475 limitation.** The amount treated as an expense under clause (i) for any taxable year shall not exceed $1,475.

(iii) **Property must be depreciable.** No amount shall be allowable as a deduction by reason of this subparagraph with respect to any property for any taxable year unless a depreciation deduction would be allowable with respect to such property for such taxable year.

(iv) **Amount treated as depreciation deduction.** For purposes of this subtitle, any amount allowable as a deduction by reason of this subparagraph shall be treated as a depreciation deduction allowable under section 168.

(C) **Special rule for certain clean-fuel passenger automobiles.**

(i) **Modified automobiles.** In the case of a passenger automobile which is propelled by a fuel which is not a clean-burning fuel to which is installed qualified clean-fuel vehicle property (as defined in section 179A(c)(1)(A)) for purposes of permitting such vehicle to be propelled by a clean burning fuel (as defined in section 179A(e)(1)), subparagraph (A) shall

Limitations on deduction — Code Sec. 280F(d)(4)(C)

not apply to the cost of the installed qualified clean burning vehicle property.

(ii) **Purpose built passenger vehicles.** In the case of a purpose built passenger vehicle (as defined in section 4001(a)(2)(C)(ii)), each of the annual limitations specified in subparagraphs (A) and (B) shall be tripled.

(iii) **Application of subparagraph.** This subparagraph shall apply to property placed in service after August 5, 1997, and before January 1, 2007.

(2) **Coordination with reductions in amount allowable by reason of personal use, etc.** This subsection, shall be applied before—

(A) the application of subsection (b), and

(B) the application of any other reduction in the amount of any depreciation deduction allowable under section 168 by reason of any use not qualifying the property for such credit or depreciation deduction.

(b) **Limitation where business use of listed property not greater than 50 percent.**

(1) **Depreciation.** If any listed property is not predominantly used in a qualified business use for any taxable year, the deduction allowed under section 168 with respect to such property for such taxable year and any subsequent taxable year shall be determined under section 168(g) (relating to alternative depreciation system).

(2) **Recapture.**

(A) Where business use percentage does not exceed 50 percent. If—

(i) property is predominantly used in a qualified business use in a taxable year in which it is placed in service, and

(ii) such property is not predominantly used in a qualified business use for any subsequent taxable year,

then any excess depreciation shall be included in gross income for the taxable year referred to in clause (ii), and the depreciation deduction for the taxable year referred to in clause (ii) and any subsequent taxable years shall be determined under section 168(g) (relating to alternative depreciation system).

(B) Excess depreciation. For purposes of subparagraph (A), the term "excess depreciation" means the excess (if any) of—

(i) the amount of the depreciation deductions allowable with respect to the property for taxable years before the 1st taxable year in which the property was not predominantly used in a qualified business use, over

(ii) the amount which would have been so allowable if the property had not been predominantly used in a qualified business use for the taxable year in which it was placed in service.

(3) **Property predominantly used in qualified business use.** For purposes of this subsection, property shall be treated as predominantly used in a qualified business use for any taxable year if the business use percentage for such taxable year exceeds 50 percent.

(c) **Treatment of leases.**

(1) **Lessor's deductions not affected.** This section shall not apply to any listed property leased or held for leasing by any person regularly engaged in the business of leasing such property.

(2) **Lessee's deductions reduced.** For purposes of determining the amount allowable as a deduction under this chapter for rentals or other payments under a lease for a period of 30 days or more of listed property, only the allowable percentage of such payments shall be taken into account.

(3) **Allowable percentage.** For purposes of paragraph (2), the allowable percentage shall be determined under tables prescribed by the Secretary. Such tables shall be prescribed so that the reduction in the deduction under paragraph (2) is substantially equivalent to the applicable restrictions contained in subsections (a) and (b).

(4) **Lease term.** In determining the term of any lease for purposes of paragraph (2), the rules of section 168(i)(3)(A) shall apply.

(5) **Lessee recapture.** Under regulations prescribed by the Secretary, rules similar to the rules of subsection (b)(3) shall apply to any lessee to which paragraph (2) applies.

(d) **Definitions and special rules.**

For purposes of this section—

(1) **Coordination with section 179.** Any deduction allowable under section 179 with respect to any listed property shall be subject to the limitations of subsections (a) and (b), and the limitation of paragraph (3) of this subsection, in the same manner as if it were a depreciation deduction allowable under section 168.

(2) **Subsequent depreciation deductions reduced for deductions allocable to personal use.** Solely for purposes of determining the amount of the depreciation deduction for subsequent taxable years, if less than 100 percent of the use of any listed property during any taxable year is used in a trade or business (including the holding for the production of income), all of the use of such property during such taxable year shall be treated as use so described.

(3) **Deductions of employee.**

(A) In general. Any employee use of listed property shall not be treated as use in a trade or business for purposes of determining the amount of any depreciation deduction allowable to the employee (or the amount of any deduction allowable to the employee for rentals or other payments under a lease of listed property) unless such use is for the convenience of the employer and required as a condition of employment.

(B) Employee use. For purposes of subparagraph (A), the term "employee use" means any use in connection with the performance of services as an employee.

(4) **Listed property.**

(A) In general. Except as provided in subparagraph (B), the term "listed property" means—

(i) any passenger automobile,

(ii) any other property used as a means of transportation,

(iii) any property of a type generally used for purposes of entertainment, recreation, or amusement,

(iv) any computer or peripheral equipment (as defined in section 168(i)(2)(B)), and

(v) any other property of a type specified by the Secretary by regulations.

(B) Exception for certain computers. The term "listed property" shall not include any computer or peripheral equipment (as so defined) used exclusively at a regular business establishment and owned or leased by the person operating such establishment. For purposes of the preceding sentence, any portion of a dwelling unit shall be treated as a regular business establishment if (and only if) the requirements of section 280A(c)(1) are met with respect to such portion.

(C) Exception for property used in business of transporting persons or property. Except to the extent provided in regulations, clause (ii) of subparagraph (A) shall not apply to any property substantially all of the use of which is in a trade or business of providing to unrelated persons services consisting of the transportation of persons or property for compensation or hire.

(5) Passenger automobile.

(A) In general. Except as provided in subparagraph (B), the term "passenger automobile" means any 4-wheeled vehicle—

(i) which is manufactured primarily for use on public streets, roads, and highways, and

(ii) which is rated at 6,000 pounds unloaded gross vehicle weight or less.

In the case of a truck or van, clause (ii) shall be applied by substituting "gross vehicle weight" for "unloaded gross vehicle weight".

(B) Exception for certain vehicles. The term "passenger automobile" shall not include—

(i) any ambulance, hearse, or combination ambulance-hearse used by the taxpayer directly in a trade or business,

(ii) any vehicle used by the taxpayer directly in the trade or business of transporting persons or property for compensation or hire, and

(iii) under regulations, any truck or van.

(6) Business use percentage.

(A) In general. The term "business use percentage" means the percentage of the use of any listed property during any taxable year which is a qualified business use.

(B) Qualified business use. Except as provided in subparagraph (C), the term "qualified business use" means any use in a trade or business of the taxpayer.

(C) Exception for certain use by 5-percent owners and related persons.

(i) In general. The term "qualified business use" shall not include—

(I) leasing property to any 5-percent owner or related person,

(II) use of property provided as compensation for the performance of services by a 5-percent owner or related person, or

(III) use of property provided as compensation for the performance of services by any person not described in subclause (II) unless an amount is included in the gross income of such person with respect to such use, and, where required, there was withholding under chapter 24.

(ii) Special rule for aircraft. Clause (i) shall not apply with respect to any aircraft if at least 25 percent of the total use of the aircraft during the taxable year consists of qualified business use not described in clause (i).

(D) Definitions. For purposes of this paragraph—

(i) 5-percent owner. The term "5-percent owner" means any person who is a 5-percent owner with respect to the taxpayer (as defined in section 416(i)(1)(B)(i)).

(ii) Related person. The term "related person" means any person related to the taxpayer (within the meaning of section 267(b)).

(7) Automobile price inflation adjustment.

(A) In general. In the case of any passenger automobile placed in service after 1988, subsection (a) shall be applied by increasing each dollar amount contained in such subsection by the automobile price inflation adjustment for the calendar year in which such automobile is placed in service. Any increase under the preceding sentence shall be rounded to the nearest multiple of $100 (or if the increase is a multiple of $50, such increase shall be increased to the next higher multiple of $100).

(B) Automobile price inflation adjustment. For purposes of this paragraph—

(i) In general. The automobile price inflation adjustment for any calendar year is the percentage (if any) by which—

(I) the CPI automobile component for October of the preceding calendar year, exceeds

(II) the CPI automobile component for October of 1987.

(ii) CPI automobile component. The term "CPI automobile component" means the automobile component of the Consumer Price Index for All Urban Consumers published by the Department of Labor.

(8) Unrecovered basis. For purposes of subsection (a)(2), the term "unrecovered basis" means the adjusted basis of the passenger automobile determined after the application of subsection (a) and as if all use during the recovery period were use in a trade or business (including the holding of property for the production of income).

(9) All taxpayers holding interests in passenger automobile treated as 1 taxpayer. All taxpayers holding interests in any passenger automobile shall be treated as 1 taxpayer for purposes of applying subsection (a) to such automobile, and the limitations of subsection (a) shall be allocated among such taxpayers in proportion to their interests in such automobile.

(10) Special rule for property acquired in nonrecognition transactions. For purposes of subsection (a)(2), any property acquired in a nonrecognition transaction shall be treated as a single property originally placed in service in the taxable year in which it was placed in service after being so acquired.

(e) Regulations.

The Secretary shall prescribe such regulations as may be necessary or appropriate to carry out the purposes of this section, including regulations with respect to items properly included in, or excluded from, the adjusted basis of any listed property.

In **2010**, P.L. 111-240, Sec. 2043(a), added "and" at the end of clause (d)(4)(A)(iv), repealed clause (v), and redesignated clause (vi) as clause (v), effective for tax. yrs. begin. after 12/31/2009.

Prior to repeal, subpara. (d)(4)(A)(v) read as follows:

"(v) any cellular telephone (or other similar telecommunications equipment), and"

In **2002**, P.L. 107-147, Sec. 602(b)(1), added clause (a)(1)(C)(iii) . . . Sec. 602(b)(2), deleted "and before January 1, 2005" after "after 8/5/97" in Sec. 971(b) of P.L. 105-34, which provides the effective date for amendments made by Sec. 971(a) of P.L. 105-34 [see below], effective for property placed in service after 12/31/2001.

In **1998**, P.L. 105-206, Sec. 6009(c), substituted "subparagraphs (A) and (B)" for "subparagraph (A)" in clause (a)(1)(C)(ii), effective for property placed in service after 8/5/97 and before 1/1/2005.

In **1997**, P.L. 105-34, Sec. 971(a), added subpara. (a)(1)(C), effective [as amended by Sec. 602(b)(2) of P.L. 107-147, see above] for property placed in service after 8/5/97.

In **1996**, P.L. 104-188, Sec. 1702(h)(5), deleted "investment tax credit and" in the heading of subsec. (a), effective for property placed in service after 12/31/90, except as provided in Sec. 11813(c)(2) of P.L. 101-508, reproduced in note following Code Sec. 46.

In **1990**, P.L. 101-508, Sec. 11813(b)(13)(A)(i), deleted paras. (a)(1) and (a)(4) and redesignated paras. (a)(2) and (a)(3) as paras. (a)(1) and (a)(2), respectively . . . Sec. 11813(b)(13)(A)(ii), deleted "the credit determined under section 46(a) or" after "in the amount of" in subpara. (a)(2)(B) (as redesignated by Sec. 11813(b)(13)(A)(i)) . . . Sec. 11813(b)(13)(B), deleted para. (b)(1) and redesignated paras. (b)(2), (b)(3) and (b)(4) as paras. (b)(1), (b)(2) and (b)(3), respectively . . . Sec. 11813(b)(13)(C), deleted "credits and" after "Lessor's" in the

Limitations on deduction
Code Sec. 280G(b)(2)(A)(ii)

heading of para. (c)(1) . . . Sec. 11813(b)(13)(D), deleted "the amount of any credit allowable under section 38 to the employee or" after "for purposes of determining" in subpara. (d)(3)(A) . . . Sec. 11813(b)(13)(E), deleted "investment tax credit and" after "Limitation on" in the heading of Code Sec. 280F, effective for property placed in service after 12/31/90, except as provided in Sec. 11813(c)(2) of this Act, reproduced in note following Code Sec. 46.

Prior to deletion, para. (a)(1) read as follows:

"(1) Investment tax credit. The amount of the credit determined under section 46(a) for any passenger automobile shall not exceed $675."

Prior to deletion, para. (a)(4) read as follows:

"(4) Special rule where election of reduced credit in lieu of the basis adjustment. In the case of any election under section 48(q)(4) with respect to any passenger automobile, the limitation of paragraph (1) applicable to such passenger automobile shall be ⅔ of the amount which would be so applicable but for this paragraph."

Prior to deletion, para. (b)(1) read as follows:

"(1) Investment tax credit. For purposes of this subtitle, any listed property shall not be treated as section 38 property for any taxable year unless such property is predominantly used in a qualified business use for such taxable year."

In 1989, P.L. 101-239, Sec. 7643(a), deleted "and" at the end of clause (d)(4)(A)(iv), redesignated clause (d)(4)(A)(v) as (d)(4)(A)(vi), and added a new clause (d)(4)(A)(v), effective for property placed in service or leased in tax. yrs. begin. after 12/31/89.

In 1988, P.L. 100-647, Sec. 1002(a)(10), substituted "any depreciation deduction" for "any recovery deduction", in subpara. (d)(3)(A), effective for property placed in service after 12/31/86, in tax. yrs. end. after 12/31/86. For special rules see Secs. 203(b)-(e) and 204 reproduced in notes following Code Sec. 168, and in Secs. 251(d)(2)-(6) reproduced in notes following Code Sec. 46.

—P.L. 100-647, Sec. 1002(b)(2), substituted "subsections (a) and (b), and the limitation of paragraph (3) of this subsection," for "subsections (a) and (b)", in para. (d)(1) effective for property placed in service after 12/31/86, in tax. yrs. end. after such date. Sec. 1002(c)(3) of this Act provides:

"(3) Notwithstanding section 203 of the Reform Act, the amendments made by section 201 of the Reform Act shall apply to any real property which was acquired before January 1, 1987, and was converted on or after such date from personal use to a use for which depreciation is allowable."

—P.L. 100-647, Sec. 1018(u)(3), substituted "depreciation deductions" for "recovery deductions", in clause (b)(3)(B)(i), effective for property placed in service and for property leased after 6/18/84 in tax. yrs. end. after 6/18/84.

In 1986, P.L. 99-514, Sec. 201(d)(4)(A)(i), deleted clauses (a)(2)(A)(i) and (a)(2)(A)(ii) and added new clauses (a)(2)(A)(i), (a)(2)(A)(ii), (a)(2)(A)(iii), (a)(2)(A)(iv) . . . Sec. 201(d)(4)(A)(ii), substituted "1,475" for "4,800" each place it appeared in subpara. (a)(2)(B) . . . Sec. 201(d)(4)(B), substituted "section 168(g) (relating to alternative depreciation system)" for "the straight line method over the earnings and profits life" in subpara. (b)(3)(A) . . . Sec. 201(d)(4)(C), amended para. (b)(4) . . . Sec. 201(d)(4)(D), substituted "section 168(i)(3)(A)" for "section 168(j)(6)(B)" in para. (c)(4) . . . Sec. 201(d)(4)(E), substituted "depreciation deduction" for "recovery deduction" in para. (d)(1) . . . Sec. 201(d)(4)(F)(i), substituted "depreciation deduction" for "recovery deduction" in para. (d)(2) . . . Sec. 201(d)(4)(F)(ii), substituted "use in a trade or business (including the holding for the production of income)" for "use described in section 168(c)(1) (defining recovery property)" in para. (d)(2) . . . Sec. 201(d)(4)(G), substituted "section 168(i)(2)(B)" for "section 168(j)(5)(D)" in clause (d)(4)(A)(iv) . . . Sec. 201(d)(4)(H), amended para. (d)(8) . . . Sec. 201(d)(4)(I), deleted ", notwithstanding any regulations prescribed under section 168(f)(7)," after "subsection (a)(2)," in para. (d)(10) . . . Sec. 201(d)(4)(J), substituted "section 168(g) (relating to alternative depreciation system)" for "the straight line method over the earnings and profits life for such property" in para. (b)(2) . . . Sec. 201(d)(4)(K), substituted "depreciation deduction" for "recovery deduction" each place it appeared in subsec. (a) and (b), effective for property placed in service after 12/31/86, in tax. yrs. end. after 12/31/86. Special rules are provided in Secs. 203(b)-(e) and 204, reproduced in the notes following Code Sec. 168, and in Sec. 251(d)(2)-(6), reproduced in the notes following Code Sec. 46. [see Sec. 1002(c)(3) of P.L. 100-647, reproduced above.]

Prior to deletion, clauses (a)(2)(A)(i) and (a)(2)(A)(ii) read as follows:

"(i) $3,200 for the first taxable year in the recovery period, and

"(ii) $4,800 for each succeeding taxable year in the recovery period."

Prior to amendment, para. (b)(4) read as follows:

"(4) Definitions. For purposes of this subsection—

"(A) Property predominantly used in qualified business use. Property shall be treated as predominantly used in a qualified business use for any taxable year if the business use percentage for such taxable year exceeds 50 percent.

"(B) Straight line method over earnings and profits life. The amount determined under the straight line method over the earnings and profits life with respect to any property shall be the amount which would be determined with respect to such property under the principles of section 312(k)(3). If the recovery period applicable to any property under section 168 is longer than the recovery period applicable to such property under section 312(k)(3), such longer recovery period shall be used for purposes of the preceding sentence."

Prior to amendment, para. (d)(8) read as follows:

"(8) Unrecovered basis. For purposes of subsection (a)(2), the term 'unrecovered basis' means the excess (if any) of—

"(A) the unadjusted basis (as defined in section 168(d)(1)(A)) of the passenger automobile, over

"(B) the amount of the recovery deductions which would have been allowable for taxable years in the recovery period determined after the application of subsection (a) and as if all use during the recovery period were use described in section 168(c)(1)."

—P.L. 99-514, Sec. 1812(e)(1)(A), substituted "unloaded gross vehicle weight" for "gross vehicle weight" in clause (d)(5)(A)(ii) . . . Sec. 1812(e)(1)(C), added the last sentence to subpara. (d)(5)(A) . . . Sec. 1812(e)(2), substituted "recovery deduction allowable to the employee (or the amount of any deduction allowable to the employee for rentals or other payments under a lease of listed property)" for "recovery deduction allowable to the employee" in subpara. (d)(3)(A) . . . Sec. 1812(e)(3), substituted "at a regular business establishment and owned or leased by the person operating such establishment" for "at a regular business establishment" in subpara. (d)(4)(B) . . . Sec. 1812(e)(4), added subpara. (d)(4)(C) . . . Sec. 1812(e)(5), substituted "is use described in" for "is not use described in" in para. (d)(2) [before amendment by Sec. 201(d)(4)(F) of this Act, see above], effective for property placed in service and for property leased after 6/18/84, in tax. yrs. end. after 6/18/84.

In 1985, P.L. 99-44, Sec. 4(a)(1), substituted "$675" for "$1,000" in para. (a)(1) . . . Sec. 4(a)(2)(A), substituted "$3,200" for "$4,000" in clause (a)(2)(A)(i) . . . Sec. 4(a)(2)(B), substituted "$4,800" for "$6,000" each place it appeared in clauses (a)(2)(A)(ii) and (a)(2)(B)(ii) . . . Sec. 4(b)(1), substituted "passenger automobile placed in service after 1988" for "passenger automobile" in subpara. (d)(7)(A) . . . Sec. 4(b)(2), substituted "1987" for "1983" in subclause (d)(7)(B)(ii)(II) . . . Sec. 4(b)(3), deleted the last sentence of clause (d)(7)(B)(i), effective as provided in Sec. 6(e) of the Act, which reads as follows:

"(e) Reduction in Limitations on Investment Tax Credit and Depreciation.

"(1) Except as provided in paragraph (2), the amendments made by section 4 shall apply to—

"(A) property placed in service after April 2, 1985, in taxable years ending after such date, and

"(B) property leased after April 2, 1985, in taxable years ending after such date.

"(2) The amendments made by section 4 shall not apply to any property—

"(A) acquired by the taxpayer pursuant to a binding contract in effect on April 1, 1985, and at all times thereafter, but only if the property is placed in service before August 1, 1985, or

"(B) of which the taxpayer is the lessee, but only if the lease is pursuant to a binding contract in effect on April 1, 1985, and at all times thereafter, and only if the taxpayer first uses such property under the lease before August 1, 1985."

Prior to deletion the last sentence of clause (d)(7)(B)(i) read as follows:

"In the case of calendar year 1984, the automobile price inflation adjustment shall be zero."

In 1984, P.L. 98-369, Sec. 179(a), added Code Sec. 280F, effective for property placed in service and for property leased after 6/18/84 in tax. yrs. ending after 6/18/84 except as provided in Sec. 179(d)(1)(B) of the Act, which reads as follows:

"(B) The amendments made by subsections (a) and (c) shall not apply to any property—

"(i) acquired by the taxpayer pursuant to a binding contract in effect on June 18, 1984, and at all times thereafter (or under construction on such date) but only if the property is placed in service before January 1, 1985 (January 1, 1987, in the case of 15-year real property), or

"(ii) of which the taxpayer is the lessee but only if the lease is pursuant to a binding contract in effect on June 18, 1984, and at all times thereafter and only if the taxpayer first uses such property under the lease before January 1, 1985 (January 1, 1987, in the case of 15-year real property).

For purposes of the preceding sentence, the term '15-year real property' includes 18-year real property."

Sec. 280G. Golden parachute payments.
(a) General rule.

No deduction shall be allowed under this chapter for any excess parachute payment.

(b) Excess parachute payment.

For purposes of this section—

(1) In general. The term "excess parachute payment" means an amount equal to the excess of any parachute payment over the portion of the base amount allocated to such payment.

(2) Parachute payment defined.

(A) In general. The term "parachute payment" means any payment in the nature of compensation to (or for the benefit of) a disqualified individual if—

(i) such payment is contingent on a change—

(I) in the ownership or effective control of the corporation, or

(II) in the ownership of a substantial portion of the assets of the corporation, and

(ii) the aggregate present value of the payments in the nature of compensation to (or for the benefit of) such individual which are contingent on such change equals or exceeds an amount equal to 3 times the base amount.

1,767

For purposes of clause (ii), payments not treated as parachute payments under paragraph (4)(A), (5), or (6) shall not be taken into account.

(B) Agreements. The term "parachute payment" shall also include any payment in the nature of compensation to (or for the benefit of) a disqualified individual if such payment is made pursuant to an agreement which violates any generally enforced securities laws or regulations. In any proceeding involving the issue of whether any payment made to a disqualified individual is a parachute payment on account of a violation of any generally enforced securities laws or regulations, the burden of proof with respect to establishing the occurrence of a violation of such a law or regulation shall be upon the Secretary.

(C) Treatment of certain agreements entered into within 1 year before change of ownership. For purposes of subparagraph (A)(i), any payment pursuant to—

(i) an agreement entered into within 1 year before the change described in subparagraph (A)(i), or

(ii) an amendment made within such 1-year period of a previous agreement,

shall be presumed to be contingent on such change unless the contrary is established by clear and convincing evidence.

(3) Base amount.

(A) In general. The term "base amount" means the individual's annualized includible compensation for the base period.

(B) Allocation. The portion of the base amount allocated to any parachute payment shall be an amount which bears the same ratio to the base amount as—

(i) the present value of such payment, bears to

(ii) the aggregate present value of all such payments.

(4) Treatment of amounts which taxpayer establishes as reasonable compensation. In the case of any payment described in paragraph (2)(A)—

(A) the amount treated as a parachute payment shall not include the portion of such payment which the taxpayer establishes by clear and convincing evidence is reasonable compensation for personal services to be rendered on or after the date of the change described in paragraph (2)(A)(i), and

(B) the amount treated as an excess parachute payment shall be reduced by the portion of such payment which the taxpayer establishes by clear and convincing evidence is reasonable compensation for personal services actually rendered before the date of the change described in paragraph (2)(A)(i).

For purposes of subparagraph (B), reasonable compensation for services actually rendered before the date of the change described in paragraph (2)(A)(i) shall be first offset against the base amount.

(5) Exemption for small business corporations, etc.

(A) In general. Notwithstanding paragraph (2), the term "parachute payment" does not include—

(i) any payment to a disqualified individual with respect to a corporation which (immediately before the change described in paragraph (2)(A)(i)) was a small business corporation (as defined in section 1361(b), but without regard to paragraph (1)(C) thereof), or

(ii) any payment to a disqualified individual with respect to a corporation (other than a corporation described in clause (i)) if—

(I) immediately before the change described in paragraph (2)(A)(i), no stock in such corporation was readily tradeable on an established securities market or otherwise, and

(II) the shareholder approval requirements of subparagraph (B) are met with respect to such payment.

The Secretary may, by regulations, prescribe that the requirements of subclause (I) of clause (ii) are not met where a substantial portion of the assets of any entity consists (directly or indirectly) of stock in such corporation and interests in such other entity are readily tradeable on an established securities market, or otherwise. Stock described in section 1504(a)(4) shall not be taken into account under clause (ii)(I) if the payment does not adversely affect the shareholder's redemption and liquidation rights.

(B) Shareholder approval requirements. The shareholder approval requirements of this subparagraph are met with respect to any payment if—

(i) such payment was approved by a vote of the persons who owned, immediately before the change described in paragraph (2)(A)(i), more than 75 percent of the voting power of all outstanding stock of the corporation, and

(ii) there was adequate disclosure to shareholders of all material facts concerning all payments which (but for this paragraph) would be parachute payments with respect to a disqualified individual.

The regulations prescribed under subsection (e) shall include regulations providing for the application of this subparagraph in the case of shareholders which are not individuals (including the treatment of nonvoting interests in an entity which is a shareholder) and where an entity holds a de minimis amount of stock in the corporation.

(6) Exemption for payments under qualified plans. Notwithstanding paragraph (2), the term "parachute payment" shall not include any payment to or from—

(A) a plan described in section 401(a) which includes a trust exempt from tax under section 501(a),

(B) an annuity plan described in section 403(a),

(C) a simplified employee pension (as defined in section 408(k)), or

(D) a simple retirement account described in section 408(p).

(c) Disqualified individuals.

For purposes of this section, the term "disqualified individual" means any individual who is—

(1) an employee, independent contractor, or other person specified in regulations by the Secretary who performs personal services for any corporation, and

(2) is an officer, shareholder, or highly-compensated individual.

For purposes of this section, a personal service corporation (or similar entity) shall be treated as an individual. For purposes of paragraph (2), the term "highly-compensated individual" only includes an individual who is (or would be if the individual were an employee) a member of the group consisting of the highest paid 1 percent of the employees of the corporation or, if less, the highest paid 250 employees of the corporation.

(d) Other definitions and special rules.

For purposes of this section—

(1) Annualized includible compensation for base period. The term "annualized includible compensation for the base period" means the average annual compensation which—

Limitations on deduction Code Sec. 280G

(A) was payable by the corporation with respect to which the change in ownership or control described in paragraph (2)(A) of subsection (b) occurs, and

(B) was includible in the gross income of the disqualified individual for taxable years in the base period.

(2) Base period. The term "base period" means the period consisting of the most recent 5 taxable years ending before the date on which the change in ownership or control described in paragraph (2)(A) of subsection (b) occurs (or such portion of such period during which the disqualified individual performed personal services for the corporation).

(3) Property transfers. Any transfer of property—

(A) shall be treated as a payment, and

(B) shall be taken into account as its fair market value.

(4) Present value. Present value shall be determined by using a discount rate equal to 120 percent of the applicable Federal rate (determined under section 1274(d)), compounded semiannually.

(5) Treatment of affiliated groups. Except as otherwise provided in regulations, all members of the same affiliated group (as defined in section 1504, determined without regard to section 1504(b)) shall be treated as 1 corporation for purposes of this section. Any person who is an officer of any member of such group shall be treated as an officer of such 1 corporation.

(e) Special rule for application to employers participating in the troubled assets relief program.

(1) In general. In the case of the severance from employment of a covered executive of an applicable employer during the period during which the authorities under section 101(a) of the Emergency Economic Stabilization Act of 2008 are in effect (determined under section 120 of such Act), this section shall be applied to payments to such executive with the following modifications:

(A) Any reference to a disqualified individual (other than in subsection (c)) shall be treated as a reference to a covered executive.

(B) Any reference to a change described in subsection (b)(2)(A)(i) shall be treated as a reference to an applicable severance from employment of a covered executive, and any reference to a payment contingent on such a change shall be treated as a reference to any payment made during an applicable taxable year of the employer on account of such applicable severance from employment.

(C) Any reference to a corporation shall be treated as a reference to an applicable employer.

(D) The provisions of subsections (b)(2)(C), (b)(4), (b)(5), and (d)(5) shall not apply.

(2) Definitions and special rules. For purposes of this subsection:

(A) Definitions. Any term used in this subsection which is also used in section 162(m)(5) shall have the meaning given such term by such section.

(B) Applicable severance from employment. The term "applicable severance from employment" means any severance from employment of a covered executive—

(i) by reason of an involuntary termination of the executive by the employer, or

(ii) in connection with any bankruptcy, liquidation, or receivership of the employer.

(C) Coordination and other rules.

(i) In general. If a payment which is treated as a parachute payment by reason of this subsection is also a parachute payment determined without regard to this subsection, this subsection shall not apply to such payment.

(ii) Regulatory authority. The Secretary may prescribe such guidance, rules, or regulations as are necessary—

(I) to carry out the purposes of this subsection and the Emergency Economic Stabilization Act of 2008, including the extent to which this subsection applies in the case of any acquisition, merger, or reorganization of an applicable employer,

(II) to apply this section and section 4999 in cases where one or more payments with respect to any individual are treated as parachute payments by reason of this subsection, and other payments with respect to such individual are treated as parachute payments under this section without regard to this subsection, and

(III) to prevent the avoidance of the application of this section through the mischaracterization of a severance from employment as other than an applicable severance from employment.

(f) Regulations.

The Secretary shall prescribe such regulations as may be necessary or appropriate to carry out the purposes of this section (including regulations for the application of this section in the case of related corporations and in the case of personal service corporations).

In **2008**, P.L. 110-343, Sec. 111DivA, of this Act, provides:
"Sec. 111. Executive compensation and corporate governance.

"(a) Applicability. Any financial institution that sells troubled assets to the Secretary under this Act shall be subject to the executive compensation requirements of subsections (b) and (c) and the provisions under the Internal Revenue Code of 1986, as provided under the amendment by section 302, as applicable.

"(b) Direct purchases.

"(1) In general. Where the Secretary determines that the purposes of this Act are best met through direct purchases of troubled assets from an individual financial institution where no bidding process or market prices are available, and the Secretary receives a meaningful equity or debt position in the financial institution as a result of the transaction, the Secretary shall require that the financial institution meet appropriate standards for executive compensation and corporate governance. The standards required under this subsection shall be effective for the duration of the period that the Secretary holds an equity or debt position in the financial institution.

"(2) Criteria. The standards required under this subsection shall include—

"(A) limits on compensation that exclude incentives for senior executive officers of a financial institution to take unnecessary and excessive risks that threaten the value of the financial institution during the period that the Secretary holds an equity or debt position in the financial institution;

"(B) a provision for the recovery by the financial institution of any bonus or incentive compensation paid to a senior executive officer based on statements of earnings, gains, or other criteria that are later proven to be materially inaccurate; and

"(C) a prohibition on the financial institution making any golden parachute payment to its senior executive officer during the period that the Secretary holds an equity or debt position in the financial institution.

"(3) Definition. For purposes of this section, the term 'senior executive officer' means an individual who is one of the top 5 highly paid executives of a public company, whose compensation is required to be disclosed pursuant to the Securities Exchange Act of 1934, and any regulations issued thereunder, and non-public company counterparts.

"(c) Auction purchases. Where the Secretary determines that the purposes of this Act are best met through auction purchases of troubled assets, and only where such purchases per financial institution in the aggregate exceed $300,000,000 (including direct purchases), the Secretary shall prohibit, for such financial institution, any new employment contract with a senior executive officer that provides a golden parachute in the event of an involuntary termination, bankruptcy filing, insolvency, or receivership. The Secretary shall issue guidance to carry out this paragraph not later than 2 months after the date of enactment of this Act, and such guidance shall be effective upon issuance.

"(d) Sunset. The provisions of subsection (c) shall apply only to arrangements entered into during the period during which the authorities under section 101(a) are in effect, as determined under section 120."

—P.L. 110-343, Sec. 302(b)(1)DivA, redesignated subsec. (e) as subsec. (f) . . . Sec. 302(b)(2)DivA, added new subsec. (e), effective for payments with respect to severances occurring during the period during which the authorities under section 101(a) of this Act are in effect (determined under section 120 of this Act). Sec. 101(a), P.L. 110-343 and Sec. 120, P.L. 110-343 provide:

"Sec. 101. Purchases of troubled assets.

Code Sec. 280G — Limitations on deduction

"(a) Offices; authority.
"(1) Authority. The Secretary is authorized to establish the Troubled Asset Relief Program (or 'TARP') to purchase, and to make and fund commitments to purchase, troubled assets from any financial institution, on such terms and conditions as are determined by the Secretary, and in accordance with this Act and the policies and procedures developed and published by the Secretary.
"(2) Commencement of program. Establishment of the policies and procedures and other similar administrative requirements imposed on the Secretary by this Act are not intended to delay the commencement of the TARP.
"(3) Establishment of treasury office.
"(A) In general. The Secretary shall implement any program under paragraph (1) through an Office of Financial Stability, established for such purpose within the Office of Domestic Finance of the Department of the Treasury, which office shall be headed by an Assistant Secretary of the Treasury, appointed by the President, by and with the advice and consent of the Senate, except that an interim Assistant Secretary may be appointed by the Secretary.

* * * * * * * *

"SEC. 120. TERMINATION OF AUTHORITY.
"(a) Termination. The authorities provided under sections 101(a), excluding section 101(a)(3), and 102 shall terminate on December 31, 2009.
"(b) Extension upon certification. The Secretary, upon submission of a written certification to Congress, may extend the authority provided under this Act to expire not later than 2 years from the date of enactment of this Act. Such certification shall include a justification of why the extension is necessary to assist American families and stabilize financial markets, as well as the expected cost to the taxpayers for such an extension."

In **1996**, P.L. 104-188, Sec. 1421(b)(9)(A), deleted "or" at end of subpara. (b)(6)(B), substituted ", or" for the period at end of subpara. (b)(6)(C), and added subpara. (b)(6)(D), effective for tax. yrs. begin. after 12/31/96.

In **1988**, P.L. 100-647, Sec. 1018(d)(6)(A), substituted "section 1361(b) but without regard to paragraph (1)(C) thereof)" for "section 1361(b))" in clause (b)(5)(A)(i) . . . Sec. 1018(d)(6)(B), added a sentence at the end of subpara. (b)(5)(A) . . . Sec. 1018(d)(7), added a sentence at the end of subpara. (b)(5)(B) . . . Sec. 1018(d)(8), substituted "officer of any member" for "officer or any member" in para. (d)(5), effective for payments under agreements entered into or renewed after 6/14/84, in tax. years. end. after 6/18/84. For special rule, see Sec. 67(e)(2) of P.L. 98-369, reproduced below.

In **1986**, P.L. 99-514, Sec. 1804(j)(1), added para. (b)(5) . . . Sec. 1804(j)(2), amended para. (b)(4) . . . Sec. 1804(j)(3), added para. (b)(6) . . . Sec. 1804(j)(4), added para. (d)(5) . . . Sec. 1804(j)(5), added a sentence at the end of subsec. (c) . . . Sec. 1804(j)(6), added a sentence at the end of subpara. (b)(2)(A) . . . Sec. 1804(j)(7), amended subpara. (b)(2)(B) . . . Sec. 1804(j)(8), substituted "performed personal services for the corporation" for "was an employee of the corporation" in para. (d)(2), effective for payments under agreements entered into or renewed after 6/14/84, in tax. yrs. ending after 6/18/84. For special rule, see Sec. 67(e)(2) of P.L. 98-369, reproduced below.

Prior to amendment, para. (b)(4) read as follows:
"(4) Excess parachute payments reduced to extent taxpayer establishes reasonable compensation. In the case of any parachute payment described in paragraph (2)(A), the amount of any excess parachute payment shall be reduced by the portion of such payment which the taxpayer establishes by clear and convincing evidence is reasonable compensation for personal services actually rendered. For purposes of the preceding sentence, reasonable compensation shall be first offset against the base amount."

Prior to amendment, subpara. (b)(2)(B) read as follows:
"(B) Agreements. The term 'parachute payment' shall also include any payment in the nature of compensation to (or for the benefit of) a disqualified individual if such payment is pursuant to an agreement which violates any securities laws or regulations."

In **1985**, P.L. 99-121, Sec. 102(c)(4), substituted "by using a discount rate equal to 120 percent of the applicable Federal rate (determined under section 1274(d)), compounded semiannually" for "in accordance with section 1274(b)(2)" in para. (d)(4), effective for sales and exchanges after 6/30/85, in tax. yrs. end. after 6/30/85.

In **1984**, P.L. 98-369, Sec. 67, added Code Sec. 280G, effective for payments under agreements entered into or renewed after 6/14/84 in tax. yrs. ending after 6/14/84. Sec. 67(e)(2) of this Act provides:
"(2) Special rule for contract amendments. Any contract entered into before June 15, 1984, which is amended after June 14, 1984, in any significant relevant aspect shall be treated as a contract entered into after June 14, 1984."

Sec. 280H. Limitation on certain amounts paid to employee-owners by personal service corporations electing alternative taxable years.

(a) General rule.

If—

(1) an election by a personal service corporation under section 444 is in effect for a taxable year, and

(2) such corporation does not meet the minimum distribution requirements of subsection (c) for such taxable year,

then the deduction otherwise allowed under this chapter for applicable amounts paid or incurred by such corporation to employee-owners shall not exceed the maximum deductible amount. The preceding sentence shall not apply for purposes of subchapter G (relating to personal holding companies).

(b) Carryover of nondeductible amounts.

If any amount is not allowed as a deduction for a taxable year under subsection (a), such amount shall be treated as paid or incurred in the succeeding taxable year.

(c) Minimum distribution requirement.

For purposes of this section—

(1) In general. A personal service corporation meets the minimum distribution requirements of this subsection if the applicable amounts paid or incurred during the deferral period of the taxable year (determined without regard to subsection (b)) equal or exceed the lesser of—

(A) the product of—

(i) the applicable amounts paid during the preceding taxable year, divided by the number of months in such taxable year, multiplied by

(ii) the number of months in the deferral period of the preceding taxable year, or

(B) the applicable percentage of the adjusted taxable income for the deferral period of the taxable year.

(2) Applicable percentage. The term "applicable percentage" means the percentage (not in excess of 95 percent) determined by dividing—

(A) the applicable amounts paid or incurred during the 3 taxable years immediately preceding the taxable year, by

(B) the adjusted taxable income of such corporation for such 3 taxable years.

(d) Maximum deductible amount.

For purposes of this section, the term "maximum deductible amount" means the sum of—

(1) the applicable amounts paid during the deferral period, plus

(2) an amount equal to the product of—

(A) the amount determined under paragraph (1), divided by the number of months in the deferral period, multiplied by

(B) the number of months in the nondeferral period.

(e) Disallowance of net operating loss carrybacks.

No net operating loss carryback shall be allowed to (or from) any taxable year of a personal service corporation to which an election under section 444 applies.

(f) Other definitions and special rules.

For purposes of this section—

(1) Applicable amount. The term "applicable amount" means any amount paid to an employee-owner which is includible in the gross income of such employee, other than—

(A) any gain from the sale or exchange of property between the owner-employee and the corporation, or

(B) any dividend paid by the corporation.

(2) Employee-owner. The term "employee-owner" has the meaning given such term by section 269A(b)(2) (as modified by section 441(i)(2)).

(3) Nondeferral and deferral periods.

(A) Deferral period. The term "deferral period" has the meaning given to such term by section 444(b)(4).

(B) Nondeferral period. The term "nondeferral period" means the portion of the taxable year of the personal service corporation which occurs after the portion of such year constituting the deferral period.

(4) Adjusted taxable income. The term "adjusted taxable income" means taxable income determined without regard to—

Terminal railroad corporations

(A) any amount paid to an employee-owner which is includible in the gross income of such employee-owner, and

(B) any net operating loss carryover to the extent such carryover is attributable to amounts described in subparagraph (A).

(5) Personal service corporation. The term "personal service corporation" has the meaning given to such term by section 441(i)(2).

In 1988, P.L. 100-647, Sec. 2004(e)(2)(B), added para. (f)(5)... Sec. 2004(e)(3), substituted "section 269A(b)(2) (as modified by section 441(i)(2))" for "section 296A(b)(2)" in para. (f)(2)... Sec. 2004(e)(14)(A), amended para. (f)(4)... Sec. 2004(e)(14)(C), deleted "or incurred" after "paid" in clause (c)(1)(A)(i) and para. (d)(1), effective for tax. yrs. begin. after 12/31/86.

Prior to amendment, para. (f)(4) read as follows:

"(4) Adjusted taxable income. The term 'adjusted taxable income' means taxable income increased by any amount paid or incurred to an employee-owner which was includible in the gross income of such employee-owner."

In 1987, P.L. 100-203, Sec. 10206(c)(1), added Code Sec. 280H, effective for tax. yrs. begin. after 12/31/86. For special rules, see Sec. 10206(d)(3) and (4), reproduced in note following Code Sec. 444.

PART X.—TERMINAL RAILROAD CORPORATIONS AND THEIR SHAREHOLDERS

Sec.
281. Terminal railroad corporations and their shareholders.

In 1962, P.L. 87-870, Sec. 1, added Part X and item 281.

Sec. 281. Terminal railroad corporations and their shareholders.

(a) Computation of taxable income of terminal railroad corporations.

(1) In general. In computing the taxable income of a terminal railroad corporation—

(A) such corporation shall not be considered to have received or accrued—

(i) the portion of any liability of any railroad corporation, with respect to related terminal services provided by such corporation, which is discharged by crediting such liability with an amount of related terminal income, or

(ii) the portion of any charge which would be made by such corporation for related terminal services provided by it, but which is not made as a result of taking related terminal income into account in computing such charge; and

(B) no deduction otherwise allowable under this chapter shall be disallowed as a result of any discharge of liability described in subparagraph (A)(i) or as a result of any computation of charges in the manner described in subparagraph (A)(ii).

(2) Limitation. In the case of any taxable year ending after the date of the enactment of this section, paragraph (1) shall not apply to the extent that it would (but for this paragraph) operate to create (or increase) a net operating loss for the terminal railroad corporation for the taxable year.

(b) Computation of taxable income of shareholders.

Subject to the limitation in subsection (a)(2), in computing the taxable income of any shareholder of a terminal railroad corporation, no amount shall be considered to have been received or accrued or paid or incurred by such shareholder as a result of any discharge of liability described in subsection (a)(1)(A)(i) or as a result of any computation of charges in the manner described in subsection (a)(1)(A)(ii).

(c) Agreement required.

In the case of any taxable year, subsections (a) and (b) shall apply with respect to any discharge of liability described in subsection (a)(1)(A)(i), and to any computation of charges in the manner described in subsection (a)(1)(A)(ii), only if such discharge or computation (as the case may be) was provided for in a written agreement, to which all of the shareholders of the terminal railroad corporation were parties, entered into before the beginning of such taxable year.

(d) Definitions.

For purposes of this section—

(1) Terminal railroad corporation. The term "terminal railroad corporation" means a domestic railroad corporation which is not a member, other than as a common parent corporation, of an affiliated group (as defined in section 1504) and—

(A) all of the shareholders of which are rail carriers subject to part A of subtitle IV of title 49;

(B) the primary business of which is the providing of railroad terminal and switching facilities and services to rail carriers subject to part A of subtitle IV of title 49 and to the shippers and passengers of such railroad corporations;

(C) a substantial part of the services of which for the taxable year is rendered to one or more of its shareholders; and

(D) each shareholder of which computes its taxable income on the basis of a taxable year beginning or ending on the same day that the taxable year of the terminal railroad corporation begins or ends.

(2) Related terminal income. The term "related terminal income" means the income (determined in accordance with regulations prescribed by the Secretary) of a terminal railroad corporation derived—

(A) from services or facilities of a character ordinarily and regularly provided by terminal railroad corporations for railroad corporations or for the employees, passengers, or shippers of railroad corporations;

(B) from the use by persons other than railroad corporations of portions of a facility, or a service which is used primarily for railroad purposes;

(C) from any railroad corporation for services or facilities provided by such terminal railroad corporation in connection with railroad operations; and

(D) from the United States in payment for facilities or services in connection with mail handling.

For purposes of subparagraph (B), a substantial addition, constructed after the date of the enactment of this section, to a facility shall be treated as a separate facility.

(3) Related terminal services. The term "related terminal services" includes only services, and the use of facilities, taken into account in computing related terminal income.

(e) Regulations.

The Secretary shall prescribe such regulations as may be necessary to carry out the purposes of this section.

In 1995, P.L. 104-88, Sec. 304(b), substituted "rail carriers subject to part A of subtitle IV" for "domestic railroad corporations providing transportation subject to subchapter I of chapter 105" in subparas. (d)(1)(A) and (B), effective 12/29/95.

In 1978, P.L. 95-473, Sec. 2(a)(2)(D), substituted "providing transportation subject to subchapter I of chapter 105 of title 49" for "subject to part I of the Interstate Commerce Act (49 U.S.C. 1 and following)" in subpara. (d)(1)(A)... Sec. 2(a)(2)(E), substituted "providing transportation subject to subchapter I of chapter 105 of title 49" for "subject to part I of the Interstate Commerce Act" in subpara. (d)(1)(B), effective 10/17/78.

In 1976, P.L. 94-455, Sec. 1901(a)(40)(A), added "(49 U.S.C. 1 and following)" after "Interstate Commerce Act" in subpara. (d)(1)(A)... Sec. 1901(a)(40)(B), deleted subsec. (e), and redesignated subsec. (f) as subsec. (e), effective for tax. yrs. begin. after 12/31/76.

Prior to deletion, subsec. (e) read as follows:

"(e) Application to taxable years ending before the date of enactment. In the case of any taxable year ending before the date of the enactment of this section—

"(1) this section shall apply only to the extent that the taxpayer computed on its return, filed at or prior to the time (including extensions thereof) that the return for such taxable year was required to be filed, its taxable income in the manner described in subsection (a) in the case of a terminal railroad corporation, or in the manner described in subsection (b) in the case of a shareholder of a terminal railroad corporation; and

"(2) this section shall apply to a taxable year for which the assessment of any deficiency, or for which refund or credit of any overpayment, whichever is applicable, was prevented, on the date of the enactment of this section, by the operation of any law or rule of law (other than section 3760 of the Internal Revenue Code of 1939 or section 7121 of this title, relating to closing agreements, and section 3761 of the Internal Revenue Code of 1939 or section 7122 of this title, relating to compromises), only—

"(A) to the extent any overpayment of income tax would result from the recomputation of the taxable income of a terminal railroad corporation in the manner described in subsection (a),

"(B) if claim for credit or refund of such overpayment, based upon such recomputation, is filed prior to one year after the date of the enactment of this section,

"(C) to the extent that paragraph (1) applies, and

"(D) if each shareholder of such terminal railroad corporation consents in writing to the assessment, within such period as may be agreed upon with the Secretary or his delegate, of any deficiency for any year to the extent attributable to the recomputation of its taxable income in the manner described in subsection (b) correlative to its allocable share of the adjustment of taxable income made by the terminal railroad corporation in its recomputation under subparagraph (A)."

—P.L. 94-455, Sec. 1906(b)(13)(A), substituted "Secretary" for "Secretary or his delegate" in para. (d)(2) and subsec. (e), effective for tax. yrs. begin. after 12/31/76.

In **1962**, P.L. 87-870, Sec. 1, added Code Sec. 281, effective for tax. yrs. begin. after 12/31/53, and end. after 8/16/54.

—P.L. 87-870, Sec. 2, provided that: "Provisions having the same effect as section 281 of the Internal Revenue Code of 1954 (as added by the first section of this Act) shall be deemed to be included in the Internal Revenue Code of 1939, effective with respect to all taxable years to which such Code applies."

PART XI.—SPECIAL RULES RELATING TO CORPORATE PREFERENCE ITEMS

Sec.
291. Special rules relating to corporate preference items.

In **1982**, P.L. 97-248, Sec. 204(c)(2), added Part XI to Subchapter B of Chapter 1.

Sec. 291. Special rules relating to corporate preference items.

(a) Reduction in certain preference items, etc.

For purposes of this subtitle, in the case of a corporation—

(1) Section 1250 capital gain treatment. in the case of section 1250 property which is disposed of during the taxable year, 20 percent of the excess (if any) of—

(A) the amount which would be treated as ordinary income if such property was section 1245 property, over

(B) the amount treated as ordinary income under section 1250 (determined without regard to this paragraph), shall be treated as gain which is ordinary income under section 1250 and shall be recognized notwithstanding any other provision of this title. Under regulations prescribed by the Secretary, the provisions of this paragraph shall not apply to the disposition of any property to the extent section 1250(a) does not apply to such disposition by reason of section 1250(d).

(2) Reduction in percentage depletion. In the case of iron ore and coal (including lignite), the amount allowable as a deduction under section 613 with respect to any property (as defined in section 614) shall be reduced by 20 percent of the amount of the excess (if any) of —

(A) the amount of the deduction allowable under section 613 for the taxable year (determined without regard to this paragraph), over

(B) the adjusted basis of the property at the close of the taxable year (determined without regard to the depletion deduction for the taxable year).

(3) Certain financial institution preference items. The amount allowable as a deduction under this chapter (determined without regard to this section) with respect to any financial institution preference item shall be reduced by 20 percent.

(4) Amortization of pollution control facilities. If an election is made under section 169 with respect to any certified pollution control facility, the amortizable basis of such facility for purposes of such section shall be reduced by 20 percent.

(b) Special rules for treatment of intangible drilling costs and mineral exploration and development costs.

For purposes of this subtitle, in the case of a corporation—

(1) In general. The amount allowable as a deduction for any taxable year (determined without regard to this section)—

(A) under section 263(c) in the case of an integrated oil company, or

(B) under section 616(a) or 617(a),

shall be reduced by 30 percent.

(2) Amortization of amounts not allowable as deductions under paragraph (1). The amount not allowable as a deduction under section 263(c), 616(a), or 617(a) (as the case may be) for any taxable year by reason of paragraph (1) shall be allowable as a deduction ratably over the 60-month period beginning with the month in which the costs are paid or incurred.

(3) Dispositions. For purposes of section 1254, any deduction under paragraph (2) shall be treated as a deduction allowable under section 263(c), 616(a), or 617(a) (whichever is appropriate).

(4) Integrated oil company defined For purposes of this subsection, the term "integrated oil company" means, with respect to any taxable year, any producer of crude oil to whom subsection (c) of section 613A does not apply by reason of paragraph (2) or (4) of section 613A(d).

(5) Coordination with cost depletion. The portion of the adjusted basis of any property which is attributable to amounts to which paragraph (1) applied shall not be taken into account for purposes of determining depletion under section 611.

(c) Special rules relating to pollution control facilities.

For purposes of this subtitle—

(1) Accelerated cost recovery deduction. Section 168 shall apply with respect to that portion of the basis of any property not taken into account under section 169 by reason of subsection (a)(4).

(2) 1250 recapture. Subsection (a)(1) shall not apply to any section 1250 property which is part of a certified pollution control facility (within the meaning of section 169(d)(1)) with respect to which an election under section 169 was made.

(d) Special rule for real estate investment trusts.

In the case of a real estate investment trust (as defined in section 856), the difference between the amounts described in subparagraphs (A) and (B) of subsection (a)(1) shall be reduced to the extent that a capital gain dividend (as defined in section 857(b)(3)(C), applied without regard to this section) is treated as paid out of such difference. Any capital gain dividend treated as having been paid out of such difference to a shareholder which is an applicable corporation retains its character in the hands of the shareholder as gain from the disposition of section 1250 property for purposes of applying subsection (a)(1) to such shareholder.

Corporate distributions and adjustments

Code Sec. 291

(e) Definitions.
For purposes of this section—

(1) Financial institution preference item. The term "financial institution preference item" includes the following:

(A) Repealed.

(B) Interest on debt to carry tax-exempt obligations acquired after December 31, 1982, and before August 8, 1986.

(i) In general. In the case of a financial institution which is a bank (as defined in section 585(a)(2)), the amount of interest on indebtedness incurred or continued to purchase or carry obligations acquired after December 31, 1982, and before August 8, 1986, the interest on which is exempt from taxes for the taxable year, to the extent that a deduction would (but for this paragraph or section 265(b)) be allowable with respect to such interest for such taxable year.

(ii) Determination of interest allocable to indebtedness on tax-exempt obligations. Unless the taxpayer (under regulations prescribed by the Secretary) establishes otherwise, the amount determined under clause (i) shall be an amount which bears the same ratio to the aggregate amount allowable (determined without regard to this section and section 265(b)) to the taxpayer as a deduction for interest for the taxable year as—

(I) the taxpayer's average adjusted basis (within the meaning of section 1016) of obligations described in clause (i), bears to

(II) such average adjusted basis for all assets of the taxpayer.

(iii) Interest. For purposes of this subparagraph, the term "interest" includes amounts (whether or not designated as interest) paid in respect of deposits, investment certificates, or withdrawable or repurchasable shares.

(iv) Application of subparagraph to certain obligations issued after August 7, 1986. For application of this subparagraph to certain obligations issued after August 7, 1986, see section 265(b)(3). That portion of any obligation not taken into account under paragraph (2)(A) of section 265(b) by reason of paragraph (7) of such section shall be treated for purposes of this section as having been acquired on August 7, 1986.

(2) Section 1245 and 1250 property. The terms "section 1245 property" and "section 1250 property" have the meanings given such terms by sections 1245(a)(3) and 1250(c), respectively.

In 2009, P.L. 111-5, Sec. 1501(b), added "That portion of any obligation not taken into account under paragraph (2)(A) of section 265(b) by reason of paragraph (7) of such section shall be treated for purposes of this section as having been acquired on August 7, 1986." at the end of clause (e)(1)(B)(iv), effective for obligations issued after 12/31/2008.

In 2007, P.L. 110-172, Sec. 11(g)(6)(A), deleted para. (a)(4) and redesignated para. (a)(5) as (a)(4), enacted 12/29/2007.

Prior to deletion, para. (a)(4) read as follows:

"(4) Certain FSC income.

"In the case of taxable years beginning after December 31, 1984, section 923(a) shall be applied with respect to any FSC by substituting—

"(A) '30 percent' for '32 percent' in paragraph (2), and

"(B) '¹⁵⁄₂₃' for '¹⁶⁄₂₃' in paragraph (3).

"If all of the stock in the FSC is not held by 1 or more C corporations throughout the taxable year, under regulations, proper adjustments shall be made in the application of the preceding sentence to take into account stock held by persons other than C corporations."

—P.L. 110-172, Sec. 11(g)(6)(B), substituted "subsection (a)(4)" for "subsection (a)(5)" in para. (c)(1), enacted 12/29/2007.

In 1996, P.L. 104-188, Sec. 1602(b)(1), deleted clause (e)(1)(B)(iv) and redesignated clause (e)(1)(B)(v) as (iv), effective for loans made after 8/20/96. Sec. 1602(c)(2) and (3) of this Act provides:

"(2) Refinancings. The amendments made by this section shall not apply to loans made after the date of the enactment of this Act to refinance securities acquisition loans (determined without regard to section 133(b)(1)(B) of the Internal Revenue Code of 1986, as in effect on the day before the date of the enactment of this Act) made on or before such date or to refinance loans described in this paragraph if—

"(A) the refinancing loans meet the requirements of section 133 of such Code (as so in effect),

"(B) immediately after the refinancing the principal amount of the loan resulting from the refinancing does not exceed the principal amount of the refinanced loan (immediately before the refinancing), and

"(C) the term of such refinancing loan does not extend beyond the last day of the term of the original securities acquisition loan.

For purposes of this paragraph, the term 'securities acquisition loan' includes a loan from a corporation to an employee stock ownership plan described in section 133(b)(3) of such Code (as so in effect).

"(3) Exception. Any loan made pursuant to a binding written contract in effect before June 10, 1996, and at all times thereafter before such loan is made, shall be treated for purposes of paragraphs (1) and (2) as a loan made on or before the date of the enactment of this Act."

Prior to deletion, clause (e)(1)(B)(iv) read as follows:

"(iv) Special rules for obligations to which section 133 applies. In the case of an obligation to which section 133 applies, interest on such obligation shall not be treated as exempt from taxes for purposes of this subparagraph."

—P.L. 104-188, Sec. 1616(b)(5), deleted "or to which section 592 applies" after "section 585(a)(2))" in clause (e)(1)(B)(i), effective for tax. yrs. begin. after 12/31/95.

In 1990, P.L. 101-508, Sec. 11801(c)(12)(B), deleted subpara. (e)(1)(A), effective 11/5/90 except as provided in Sec. 11821(b) of this Act, reproduced in note following Code Sec. 585.

Prior to deletion, subpara. (e)(1)(A) read as follows:

"(A) Excess reserves for losses on bad debts of financial institutions. In the case of a financial institution to which section 585 applies, the excess of—

"(i) the amount which would, but for this section, be allowable as a deduction for the taxable year for a reasonable addition to a reserve for bad debts, over

"(ii) the amount which would have been allowable had such institution maintained its bad debt reserve for all taxable years on the basis of actual experience."

In 1988, P.L. 100-647, Sec. 1002(c)(3), provides:

"(3) Notwithstanding section 203 of the Reform Act, the amendments made by section 201 of the Reform Act shall apply to any real property which was acquired before January 1, 1987, and was converted on or after such date from personal use to a use for which depreciation is allowable."

—P.L. 100-647, Sec. 1009(b)(1)(A)-(E), amended Sec. 902(f)(3) of P.L. 99-514 [the effective date for changes made by Sec. 902(f) of P.L. 99-514, see below] by substituting "distribution facility" for "distribution company" in Sec. 902(f)(3)(F), by substituting "2 Festival Market Place projects at Union Pier Terminal and 1 project at the Remount Road Container Yard, State Pier No. 15 at North Charleston Terminal" for "waterfront project" in Sec. 902(f)(3)(L), by substituting "Pontalba" for "Pontalba" in Sec. 902(f)(3)(M), by substituting "Homewood, Alabama, the" for "Birmingham, Alabama," in Sec. 902(f)(3)(P), and by adding Secs. 902(f)(3)(T), (U) and (V)... Sec. 1009(b)(2), amended Sec. 902(f)(4) of P.L. '99-514 [the effective date for changes made by Sec. 902(c) of P.L. 99-514, see below], by substituting "paragraph" for "subparagraph",... Sec. 1009(b)(7)(A), and (B), amended Sec. 902(f)(4) of P.L. 99-514 [see below], by adding "and qualified 501(c)(3) bonds designated by such Governor for purposes of this paragraph" after "1987)," in para. (f)(4), and by substituting "paragraph" for "subparagraph" [same amendment as Sec. 1009(b)(2) of this Act].

—P.L. 100-647, Sec. 1009(b)(4), redesignated clause (e)(1)(B)(iv) [as added by Sec. 902(c)(2) of P.L. 99-514, see below] as (e)(1)(B)(v)... Sec. 1009(b)(5), substituted "section 585(a)(2)" for "section 582(a)(2)" in clause (e)(1)(B)(i), effective for tax. yrs. begin. after 12/31/86. Secs. 902(f)(2)-(f)(4) of P.L. 99-514, [as amended by Secs. 1009(b)(1), (b)(2) and (b)(7), see above] provides special rules, see below.

—P.L. 100-418, Sec. 1941(b)(5), amended para. (b)(4), effective for crude oil removed from the premises on or after 8/23/88.

Prior to amendment, para. (b)(4) read as follows:

"(4) Integrated oil company defined. For purposes of this subsection, the term 'integrated oil company' means, with respect to any taxable year, any producer (within the meaning of section 4996(a)(1)) of crude oil other than an independent producer (within the meaning of section 4992(b))."

In 1986, P.L. 99-514, Sec. 201(d)(5)(A), deleted "or section 1245 recovery property" after "section 1245 property" in subpara. (a)(1)(A)... Sec. 201(d)(5)(B), amended para. (c)(1)... Sec. 201(d)(5)(C), deleted ", 'section 1245 recovery property' after 'section 1245 property' and deleted ', 1245(a)(5),' after '1245(a)(3)', in para. (e)(2) effective for property placed in service after 12/31/86, in tax. yrs. end. after 12/31/86 [see Sec. 1002(c)(3) of P.L. 100-647, above]. For other rules, see Sec. 203(b)-(e), reproduced in note following Code Sec. 168. Sec 203(a)(1)(B) of this Act provides as follows:

"(B) Election to have amendments made by section 201 apply. 'A taxpayer may elect (at such time and in such manner as the Secretary of the Treasury or his delegate may prescribe) to have the amendments made by section 201 apply to any property placed in service after July 31, 1986, and before January 1, 1987."

Prior to amendment, para. (c)(1) read as follows:

1,773

Code Sec. 291 — Corporate distributions and adjustments

"(1) Accelerated cost recovery deduction. For purposes of subclause (I) of section 168(d)(1)(A)(ii), a taxpayer shall not be treated as electing the amortization deduction under section 169 with respect to that portion of the basis not taken into account under section 169 by reason of subsection (a)(5)."

— P.L. 99-514, Sec. 411(a)(1), substituted "30 percent" for "20 percent" in para. (b)(1)... Sec. 411(a)(2), deleted paras. (b)(2)-(6) and added new paras. (b)(2)-(5) ... Sec. 411(b)(2)(C)(ii), substituted "617(a)" for "617" in subpara. (b)(1)(B), effective for costs paid or incurred after 12/31/86, in tax. yrs. end. after 12/31/86. Sec. 411(c)(2) of this Act provides transitional rule as follows:

"(2) Transition rule. — The amendments made by this section shall not apply with respect to intangible drilling and development costs incurred by United States companies pursuant to a minority interest in a license for Netherlands or United Kingdom North Sea development if such interest was acquired on or before December 31, 1985."

Prior to deletion, paras. (b)(2)-(6) read as follows:

"(2) Special rule for amounts not allowable as deductions under paragraph (1).

"(A) Intangible drilling costs. The amount not allowable as a deduction under section 263(c) for any taxable year by reason of paragraph (1) shall be allowable as a deduction ratably over the 36-month period beginning with the month in which the costs are paid or incurred.

"(B) Mineral exploration and development costs. In the case of any amount not allowable as a deduction under section 616(a) or 617 for any taxable year by reason of paragraph (1) —

"(i) the applicable percentage of the amount not so allowable as a deduction shall be allowable as a deduction for the taxable year in which the costs are paid or incurred and in each of the 4 succeeding taxable years, and

"(ii) in the case of a deposit located in the United States, such costs shall be treated, for purposes of determining the amount of the credit allowable under section 38 for the taxable year in which paid or incurred, as qualified investment (within the meaning of subsections (c) and (d) of section 46) with respect to property placed in service during such year.

"(3) Applicable percentage. For purposes of paragraph (2)(B), the term 'applicable percentage' means the percentage determined in accordance with the following table:

"Taxable Year:	Applicable Percentage:
1.	15
2.	22
3.	21
4.	21
5.	21.

"(4) Dispositions.

"(A) Oil, gas, and geothermal property. In the case of any disposition of any oil, gas, or geothermal property to which section 1254 applies (determined without regard to this section) any deduction under paragraph (2)(A) with respect to intangible drilling and development costs under section 263(c) which are allocable to such property shall, for purposes of section 1254, be treated as a deduction allowable under section 263(c).

"(B) Application of section 617(d). In the case of any disposition of mining property to which section 617(d) applies (determined without regard to this section), any amount allowable as a deduction under paragraph (2)(B) which is allocable to such property shall, for purposes of section 617(d), be treated as a deduction allowable under section 617(a).

"(C) Recapture of investment credit. In the case of any disposition of any property to which the credit allowable under section 38 by reason of paragraph (2)(B) is allocable, such disposition shall, for purposes of section 47, be treated as a disposition of section 38 recovery property which is not 3-year property.

"(5) Integrated oil company defined. For purposes of this subsection, the term 'integrated oil company' means, with respect to any taxable year, any producer (within the meaning of section 4996(a)(1)) of crude oil other than an independent producer (within the meaning of section 4992(b)).

"(6) Coordination with cost depletion. The portion of the adjusted basis of any property which is attributable to amounts to which paragraph (1) applied shall not be taken into account for purposes of determining depletion under section 611."

— P.L. 99-514, Sec. 412(b)(1), substituted "20 percent" for "15 percent" in para. (a)(2), effective for tax. yrs. begin. after 12/31/86.

— P.L. 99-514, Sec. 901(b)(4), deleted "or 593" in subpara. (e)(1)(A) ... Sec. 901(d)(4)(C), substituted "which is a bank (as defined in section 582(a)(2)) or to which section 593 applies" for "to which section 585 or 593 applies" in clause (e)(1)(B)(i), effective for taxable years begin. after 12/31/86.

— P.L. 99-514, Sec. 902(c)(1), substituted "after December 31, 1982, and before August 8, 1986" for "after December 31, 1982" in clause (e)(1)(B)(i) ... Sec. 902(c)(2)(A), substituted "(but for this paragraph or section 265(b))" for "(but for this paragraph)" in clause (e)(1)(B)(i) ... Sec. 902(c)(2)(B), substituted "without regard to this section and section 265(b)" for "without regard to this section" in clause (e)(1)(B)(ii) ... Sec. 902(c)(2)(C), substituted "after December 31, 1982, and before August 8, 1986" for "after December 31, 1982" in the heading of subpara. (e)(1)(B) ... Sec. 902(c)(2)(D), added clause (e)(1)(B)(iv) [Sic (v), see Sec. 1009(b)(4) of P.L. 100-647, above], effective for tax. yrs. end. after 12/31/86. Secs. 902(f)(2)-(f)(4) of this Act [as amended by Sec. 1009(b)(1), (b)(2) and (b)(7) of P.L. 100-647, see above] provides as follows:

"(2) Obligations acquired pursuant to certain commitments. — For purposes of sections 265(b) and 291(e)(1)(B) of the Internal Revenue Code of 1986, any tax-exempt obligation which is acquired after August 7, 1986, pursuant to a direct or indirect written commitment —

"(A) to purchase or repurchase such obligation, and

"(B) entered into on or before September 25, 1985, shall be treated as an obligation acquired before August 8, 1986.

"(3) Transitional rules. — For purposes of sections 265(b) and 291(e)(1)(B) of the Internal Revenue Code of 1986, obligations with respect to any of the following projects shall be treated as obligations acquired before August 8, 1986, in the hands of the first and any subsequent financial institution acquiring such obligations:

"(A) Park Forest, Illinois, redevelopment project.
"(B) Clinton, Tennessee, Carriage Trace project.
"(C) Savannah, Georgia, Mall Terrace Warehouse project.
"(D) Chattanooga, Tennessee, Warehouse Row project.
"(E) Dalton, Georgia, Towne Square project.
"(F) Milwaukee, Wisconsin, Standard Electric Supply Company — distribution facility.
"(G) Wausau, Wisconsin, urban renewal project.
"(H) Cassville, Missouri, UDAG project.
"(I) Outlook Envelope Company — plant expansion.
"(J) Woodstock, Connecticut, Crabtree Warehouse partnership.
"(K) Louisville, Kentucky, Speed Mansion renovation project.
"(L) Charleston, South Carolina, 2 Festival Market Place projects at Union Pier Terminal and 1 project at the Remount Road Container Yard, State Pier No. 15 at North Charleston Terminal.
"(M) New Orleans, Louisiana, Upper Pontalba Building renovation.
"(N) Woodward Wight Building.
"(O) Minneapolis, Minnesota, Miller Milling Company — flour mill project.
"(P) Homewood, Alabama, the Club Apartments.
"(Q) Charlotte, North Carolina — qualified mortgage bonds acquired by NCNB bank ($5,250,000).
"(R) Grand Rapids, Michigan, Central Bank project.
"(S) Ruppman Marketing Services, Inc. — building project.
"(T) Bellows Falls, Vermont — building project.
"(U) East Broadway Project, Louisville, Kentucky.
"(V) O.K. Industries, Oklahoma.

"(4) Additional transitional rule. — Obligations issued pursuant to an allocation of a State's volume limitation for private activity bonds, which allocation was made by Executive Order 25 signed by the Governor of the State on May 22, 1986 (as such order may be amended before January 1, 1987), and qualified 501(c)(3) bonds designated by such Governor for purposes of this paragraph, shall be treated as acquired on or before August 7, 1986, in the hands of the first and any subsequent financial institution acquiring such obligation. The aggregate face amount of obligations to which this paragraph applies shall not exceed $200,000,000."

— P.L. 99-514, Sec. 1804(k)(1), substituted "a C corporation" for "a corporation" in para. (a)(4) (as in effect on the day before the date of enactment of P.L. 98-369 [7/18/84]), effective for tax. yrs. begin. after 12/31/82.

— P.L. 99-514, Sec. 1804(k)(2)(A), substituted "of the Internal Revenue Code of 1954, and the amendment made by subsection (c)(2) of this section," for "of the Internal Revenue Code of 1954" in Sec. 68(e)(2) of P.L. 98-369 [the effective date for amendments made by Secs. 68(a) and (b) of P.L. 98-369, see below] ... Sec. 1804(k)(2)(B), substituted "of such Code, and so much of the amendment made by subsection (c)(1) of this section as relates to pollution control facilities," for "of such Code" in Sec. 68(e)(3) [the effective date for amendments made by Secs. 68(a) and (b) of P.L. 98-369, see below].

— P.L. 99-514, Sec. 1804(k)(3)(A), deleted "20-percent" before "Reduction" in the heading of subsec. (a), effective for tax. yrs. begin. after 12/31/84. Secs. 68(e)(2)-(e)(4) of P.L. 98-369 [as amended by Secs. 1804(k)(2)(A) and (k)(2)(B) of this Act, see above] provides special rules and exceptions, see below.

— P.L. 99-514, Sec. 1854(c)(1), added clause (e)(1)(B)(iv), effective for loans used to acquire employer securities after 7/18/84.

— P.L. 99-514, Sec. 1876(b)(1), amended para. (a)(4), effective for tax. yrs. begin. after 12/31/84.

Prior to amendment, para. (a)(4) read as follows:

"(4) Certain deferred FSC income. If a corporation is a shareholder of the FSC, in the case of taxable years beginning after December 31, 1984, section 923(a) shall be applied with respect to such corporation by substituting —

"(A) '30 percent' for '32 percent' in paragraph (2), and
"(B) '15/23' for '16/23' in paragraph (3)."

In 1984, P.L. 98-369, Sec. 68(a), substituted "20 percent" for "15 percent" each place it appeared in Code Sec. 291 (except para. (a)(2)) ... Sec. 68(b), amended para. (a)(4), effective for tax. yrs. begin. after 12/31/84. Sec. 68(e)(2)–(4) of this Act [as amended by Sec. 1804(k)(2)(A) of P.L. 99-514 and (B), see above] provides as follows:

"(2) 1250 gain. — The amendments made by this section to section 291(a)(1) of the Internal Revenue Code of 1954, and the amendment made by subsection (c)(2) of this section [Code Sec. 57(b)(2)] shall apply to sales or other dispositions after December 31, 1984, in taxable years ending after such date.

"(3) Pollution control facilities. — The amendments made by this section to section 291(a)(5) of such Code, and so much of the amendment made by subsection (c)(1) [Code Sec. 57(b)(1)] of this section as relates to pollution control facilities, shall apply to property placed in service after December 31, 1984, in taxable years ending after such date.

"(4) Drilling and mining costs. — The amendments made by this section to section 291(b) of such Code shall apply to expenditures after December 31, 1984, in taxable years ending after such date."

Prior to amendment, para. (a)(4) [as amended by Sec. 1804(k)(1) of P.L. 99-514, see above] read as follows:

Corporate distributions and adjustments

"(4) Certain deferred disc income. If a C corporation is a shareholder of a DISC, in the case of taxable years beginning after December 31, 1982, section 995(b)(1)(F)(i) shall be applied with respect to such corporation by substituting '57.5 percent' for 'one-half'."

—P.L. 98-369, Sec. 712(a)(1)(A)(i), substituted "under section 1250 (determined without regard to this paragraph)" for "under section 1250" in subpara. (a)(1)(B) ... Sec. 712(a)(1)(A)(ii), substituted "which is ordinary income under section 1250" for "which is ordinary income" in subpara. (a)(1)(B) ... Sec. 712(a)(2), added "in the case of a deposit located in the United States" after "(ii)" of clause (b)(2)(B)(ii) ... Sec. 712(a)(3), amended para. (b)(6) ... Sec. 712(a)(4), added clause (e)(1)(B)(iii), effective for tax. yrs. begin. after 12/31/82.

Prior to amendment, para. (b)(6) read as follows:

"(6) Coordination with cost depletion. The portion of the adjusted basis of any property which is attributable to intangible drilling and development costs or mining exploration and development costs shall not be taken into account for purposes of determining depletion under section 611."

In **1983**, P.L. 97-448, Sec. 306(a)(2), added the sentence to the end of para. (a)(1), effective for tax. yrs. begin. after 12/31/82.

In **1982**, P.L. 97-354, Sec. 5(a)(27)(A), substituted "a corporation" for "an applicable corporation" in subsecs. (a) and (b) ... Sec. 5(a)(27)(B), deleted para. (e)(2) and redesignated para. (e)(3) as para. (e)(2), effective for tax. yrs. begin. after 12/31/82.

Prior to deletion, para. (e)(2) read as follows:

"(2) Applicable corporation. For purposes of this section, the term 'applicable corporation' means any corporation other than an electing small business corporation (as defined in section 1371(b))."

—P.L. 97-248, Sec. 204(a), added Code Sec. 291, effective for tax. yrs. begin. after 12/31/82. Secs. 204(d)(2)–(5) of this Act provide:

"(2) 1250 gain.— Section 291(a)(1) of the Internal Revenue Code of 1954 shall apply to sales or other dispositions after December 31, 1982, in taxable years ending after such date.

"(3) Pollution control facilities.— Section 291(a)(5) of such Code shall apply to property placed in service after December 31, 1982, in taxable years ending after such date.

"(4) Drilling and mining costs.— Section 291(b) of such Code shall apply to expenditures after December 31, 1982, in taxable years ending after such date.

"(5) Reduction in percentage depletion for coal and iron ore.— Section 291(a)(2) of such Code shall apply to taxable years beginning after December 31, 1983."

Subchapter C.— Corporate Distributions and Adjustments

Part
- I. Distributions by corporations.
- II. Corporate liquidations.
- III. Corporate organizations and reorganizations.
- IV. Repealed. [Insolvency reorganizations.]
- V. Carryovers.
- VI. Treatment of certain corporate interests as stock or indebtedness.
- VII. Miscellaneous corporate provisions. [Repealed.]

In **1990**, P.L. 101-508, Sec. 11801(b)(5), repealed the item for Part IV.

Prior to repeal, the item for Part IV read as follows:

"IV. Insolvency reorganizations."

In **1988**, P.L. 100-647, Sec. 1006(e)(8)(C), repealed Part VII. This Act did not amend the list of Parts in Subchapter C.

In **1984**, P.L. 98-369, Sec. 75(d), added the item for Part VII.

In **1976**, P.L. 94-455, Sec. 1901(b)(15), repealed the item for Part VII.

Prior to repeal, the item for Part VII read as follows:

"VII. Effective date of Subchapter C."

In **1969**, P.L. 91-172, Sec. 415(a), added Part VI. ... Sec. 415(b), redesignated old Part VI as Part VII.

PART I.— DISTRIBUTIONS BY CORPORATIONS

Subpart
A. Effects on recipients.
B. Effects on corporation.
C. Definitions; constructive ownership of stock.

SUBPART A.— EFFECTS ON RECIPIENTS

Sec.
301. Distributions of property.
302. Distributions in redemption of stock.
303. Distributions in redemption of stock to pay death taxes.
304. Redemption through use of related corporations.
305. Distributions of stock and stock rights.
306. Dispositions of certain stock.
307. Basis of stock and stock rights acquired in distributions.

Sec. 301.   Distributions of property.

(a) In general.

Except as otherwise provided in this chapter, a distribution of property (as defined in section 317(a)) made by a corporation to a shareholder with respect to its stock shall be treated in the manner provided in subsection (c).

(b) Amount distributed.

(1) General rule. For purposes of this section, the amount of any distribution shall be the amount of money received, plus the fair market value of the other property received.

(2) Reduction for liabilities. The amount of any distribution determined under paragraph (1) shall be reduced (but not below zero) by—

(A) the amount of any liability of the corporation assumed by the shareholder in connection with the distribution, and

(B) the amount of any liability to which the property received by the shareholder is subject immediately before, and immediately after, the distribution.

(3) Determination of fair market value. For purposes of this section, fair market value shall be determined as of the date of the distribution.

(c) Amount taxable.

In the case of a distribution to which subsection (a) applies—

(1) Amount constituting dividend. That portion of the distribution which is a dividend (as defined in section 316) shall be included in gross income.

(2) Amount applied against basis. That portion of the distribution which is not a dividend shall be applied against and reduce the adjusted basis of the stock.

(3) Amount in excess of basis.

(A) In general. Except as provided in subparagraph (B), that portion of the distribution which is not a dividend, to the extent that it exceeds the adjusted basis of the stock, shall be treated as gain from the sale or exchange of property.

(B) Distributions out of increase in value accrued before March 1, 1913. That portion of the distribution which is not a dividend, to the extent that it exceeds the adjusted basis of the stock and to the extent that it is out of increase in value accrued before March 1, 1913, shall be exempt from tax.

(d) Basis.

The basis of property received in a distribution to which subsection (a) applies shall be the fair market value of such property.

(e) Special rule for certain distributions received by 20 percent corporate shareholder.

(1) In general. Except to the extent otherwise provided in regulations, solely for purposes of determining the taxable income of any 20 percent corporate shareholder (and its adjusted basis in the stock of the distributing corporation), section 312 shall be applied with respect to the distributing corporation as if it did not contain subsections (k) and (n) thereof.

(2) 20 percent corporate shareholder. For purposes of this subsection, the term "20 percent corporate shareholder" means, with respect to any distribution, any corporation which owns (directly or through the application of section 318)—

(A) stock in the corporation making the distribution possessing at least 20 percent of the total combined voting power of all classes of stock entitled to vote, or

(B) at least 20 percent of the total value of all stock of the distributing corporation (except nonvoting stock which is limited and preferred as to dividends),

but only if, but for this subsection, the distributee corporation would be entitled to a deduction under section 243, 244, or 245 with respect to such distribution.

(3) Application of section 312(n)(7) not affected. The reference in paragraph (1) to subsection (n) of section 312 shall be treated as not including a reference to paragraph (7) of such subsection.

(4) Regulations. The Secretary shall prescribe such regulations as may be necessary or appropriate to carry out the purposes of this subsection.

(f) Special rules.

(1) For distributions in redemption of stock, see section 302.

(2) For distributions in complete liquidation, see part II (sec. 331 and following).

(3) For distributions in corporate organizations and reorganizations, see part III (sec. 351 and following).

• *Caution:* Code Sec. 301(f)(4), following, was amended by Sec. 302(e)(2), P.L. 108-27. These provisions generally sunset for tax years beginning after 12/31/2012. For specific sunset provisions see Sec. 303, P.L. 108-27 reproduced in history notes for this Code Sec.

(4) For taxation of dividends received by individuals at capital gain rates, see section 1(h)(11).

In 2010, P.L. 111-312, Sec. 102(a), substituted "December 31, 2012" for "December 31, 2010" in Sec. 303, P.L. 108-27 [see below], effective as if included in the enactment of P.L. 108-27, 5/28/2003.

In 2006, P.L. 109-222, Sec. 102, substituted "December 31, 2010" for "December 31, 2008" in Sec. 303 of P.L. 108-27 [see below], effective 5/17/2006.

In 2004, P.L. 108-311, Sec. 402(a)(6), of this Act [which amended Sec. 302(f)(2) of P.L. 108-27, see below], provides:

"(2) Pass-thru entities. In the case of a pass-thru entity described in subparagraph (A), (B), (C), (D), (E), or (F) of section 1(h)(10) of the Internal Revenue Code of 1986, as amended by this Act, the amendments made by this section shall apply to taxable years ending after December 31, 2002; except that dividends received by such an entity on or before such date shall not be treated as qualified dividend income (as defined in section 1(h)(11)(B) of such Code, as added by this Act)."

In 2003, P.L. 108-27, Sec. 302(f)(2), added para. (f)(4), effective for tax. yrs. begin. after 12/31/2002. Sec. 302(f)(2), of this Act [prior to amendment by Sec. 402(a)(6) of P.L. 108-311 see above] provides:

"(2) Regulated investment companies and real estate investment trusts. In the case of a regulated investment company or a real estate investment trust, the amendments made by this section shall apply to taxable years ending after December 31, 2002; except that dividends received by such a company or trust on or before such date shall not be treated as qualified dividend income (as defined in section 1(h)(11)(B) of the Internal Revenue Code of 1986, as added by this Act)."

—P.L. 108-27, Sec. 303, of this Act [as amended by Sec. 102 of P.L. 109-222, and Sec. 102(a), P.L. 111-312, see above], reads as follows:

"SEC. 303. SUNSET OF TITLE. All provisions of, and amendments made by, this title [Secs. 301 and 302] shall not apply to taxable years beginning after December 31, 2012, and the Internal Revenue Code of 1986 shall be applied and administered to such years as if such provisions and amendments had never been enacted."

In 1988, P.L. 100-647, Sec. 1006(e)(10), amended para. (b)(1) . . . Sec. 1006(e)(11), amended subsec. (d) . . . Sec. 1006(e)(12), deleted subsec. (e) and redesignated subsecs. (f) and (g) as (e) and (f), effective as provided in Sec. 633(a)(3) of P.L. 99-514 reproduced in note following Code Sec. 311. For transitional rule see Sec. 633(d)(9) of P.L. 99-514, reproduced in note following Code Sec. 311.

Prior to amendment, para. (b)(1) read as follows:

"(b) Amount distributed.

"(1) General rule. For purposes of this section, the amount of any distribution shall be—

"(A) Noncorporate distributees. If the shareholder is not a corporation, the amount of money received, plus the fair market value of the other property received.

"(B) Corporate distributees. If the shareholder is a corporation, unless subparagraph (D) applies, the amount of money received, plus whichever of the following is the lesser:

"(i) the fair market value of the other property received; or

"(ii) the adjusted basis (in the hands of the distributing corporation immediately before the distribution) of the other property received, increased in the amount of gain recognized to the distributing corporation on the distribution.

"(C) Certain corporate distributees of foreign corporation. Notwithstanding subparagraph (B), if the shareholder is a corporation and the distributing corporation is a foreign corporation, the amount taken into account with respect to property (other than money) shall be the fair market value of such property; except that if any deduction is allowable under section 245 with respect to such distribution, then the amount taken into account shall be the sum (determined under regulations prescribed by the Secretary) of—

"(i) the proportion of the adjusted basis of such property (or, if lower, its fair market value) properly attributable to gross income which is effectively connected with the conduct of a trade or business within the United States, and

"(ii) the proportion of the fair market value of such property properly attributable to gross income which is not effectively connected with the conduct of a trade or business within the United States.

For purposes of clause (i), the gross income of a foreign corporation for any period before its first taxable year beginning after December 31, 1966, which is effectively connected with the conduct of a trade or business within the United States is an amount equal to the gross income for such period from sources within the United States. For purposes of clause (ii), the gross income of a foreign corporation for any period before its first taxable year beginning after December 31, 1966, which is not effectively connected with the conduct of a trade or business within the United States is an amount equal to the gross income for such period from sources without the United States.

"(D) Foreign corporate distributees. In the case of a distribution to a shareholder which is a foreign corporation, if the amount received by the foreign corporation is not effectively connected with the conduct by it of a trade or business within the United States, the amount of the money received, plus the fair market value of the other property received."

Prior to amendment, subsec. (d) read as follows:

"(d) Basis. The basis of property received in a distribution to which subsection (a) applies shall be—

"(1) Noncorporate distributees. If the shareholder is not a corporation, the fair market value of such property.

"(2) Corporate distributees. If the shareholder is a corporation, unless paragraph (3) applies, whichever of the following is the lesser:

"(A) the fair market value of such property; or

"(B) the adjusted basis (in the hands of the distributing corporation immediately before the distribution) of such property, increased in the amount of gain recognized to the distributing corporation on the distribution.

"(3) Foreign corporate distributees. In the case of a distribution of property to a shareholder which is a foreign corporation, if the amount received by the foreign corporation is not effectively connected with the conduct by it of a trade or business within the United States, the fair market value of the property received.

"(4) Certain corporate distributees of foreign corporation. In the case of property described in subparagraph (C) of subsection (b)(1), the basis shall be determined by substituting the amount determined under such subparagraph (C) for the amount described in paragraph (2) of this subsection."

Prior to deletion, subsec. (e) read as follows:

"(e) Special rule for holding period of appreciated property distributed to corporation. For purposes of this subtitle—

"(1) Where gain recognized under section 311(d). If—

"(A) property is distributed to a corporation, and

"(B) gain is recognized on such distribution under paragraph (1) of section 311(d),

then such corporation's holding period in the distributed property shall begin on the date of such distribution.

"(2) Where gain not recognized under section 311(d). If—

"(A) property is distributed to a corporation,

"(B) gain is not recognized on such distribution under paragraph (1) of section 311(d), and

"(C) the basis of such property in the hands of such corporation is determined under subsection (d)(2)(B),

then (except for purposes of section 1248) such corporation shall not be treated as holding the distributed property during any period before the date on which such corporation's holding period in the stock began."

—P.L. 100-647, Sec. 2004(j)(3)(B), redesignated para. (e)(3) as (4) and added para. (e)(3), effective as provided in Sec. 10222(b)(2) of P.L. 100-203, reproduced below.

—P.L. 100-647, Sec. 2004(j)(4), amended Sec. 10222(b)(2)(B) of P.L. 100-203 [reproduced below], an exception to the effective date for changes made by Sec. 10222(b)(1) of P.L. 100-203, see below.

Prior to amendment, Sec. 10222(b)(2)(B) of P.L. 100-203 read as follows:

"(B) Exception. The amendment made by paragraph (1) shall not apply for purposes of determining gain or loss on any disposition described in subsection (a)(2)(B) of this section."

In 1987, P.L. 100-203, Sec. 10222(b)(1), substituted "subsections (k) and (n) thereof" for "subsection (n) thereof" in para. (f)(1), effective as provided in Sec.

Corporate distributions and adjustments — Code Sec. 302(a)

10222(b)(2) [as amended by Sec. 2004(j)(4) of P.L. 100-647, see above] of this Act which reads as follows:

"(2) Effective dates.

"(A) In general. The amendment made by paragraph (1) shall apply to distributions after December 15, 1987. For purposes of applying such amendment to any such distribution—

"(i) for purposes of determining earnings and profits, such amendment shall be deemed to be in effect for all periods whether before, on, or after December 15, 1987, but

"(ii) such amendment shall not affect the determination of whether any distribution on or before December 15, 1987, is a dividend and the amount of any reduction in accumulated earnings and profits on account of any such distribution.

"(B) Exception. The amendment made by paragraph (1) shall not apply for purposes of determining gain or loss on any disposition of stock after December 15, 1987, and before January 1, 1989, if such disposition is pursuant to a written binding contract, governmental order, letter of intend or preliminary agreement, or stock acquisition agreement, in effect on or before December 15, 1987."

In 1986, P.L. 99-514, Sec. 612(b)(1), deleted para. (g)(4), effective for tax. yrs. begin. after 12/31/86.

Prior to deletion, para. (g)(4) read as follows:

"(4) For partial exclusion from gross income of dividends received by individuals, see section 116."

—P.L. 99-514, Sec. 1804(f)(2)(B), substituted "this subsection" for "this section" in para. (f)(3), effective for distributions after 7/18/84 in tax. yrs. after 7/18/84.

In 1984, P.L. 98-369, Sec. 54(b), redesignated subsec. (e) as (f) and added subsec. (e), effective for distributions after 7/18/84 in tax. yrs. end. after 7/18/84. Sec. 54(d)(5) and (6) of this Act provides:

"(5) Exception for certain distributions.

"(A) In general. The amendments made by this section [] shall not apply to distributions before February 1, 1986, if—

"(i) the distribution consists of property held on March 7, 1984 (or property acquired thereafter in the ordinary course of a trade or business) by—

"(I) the controlled corporation, or

"(II) any subsidiary controlled corporation,

"(ii) a group of 1 or more shareholders (acting in concert)—

"(I) acquired, during the 1-year period ending on February 1, 1984, at least 10 percent of the outstanding stock of the controlled corporation,

"(II) held at least 10 percent of the outstanding stock of the common parent on February 1, 1984, and

"(III) submitted a proposal for distributions of interests in a royalty trust from the common parent or the controlled corporation, and

"(iii) the common parent acquired control of the controlled corporation during the 1-year period ending on February 1, 1984.

"(B) Definitions. For purposes of this paragraph—

"(i) The term 'common parent' has the meaning given such term by section 1504(a) of the Internal Revenue Code of 1954.

"(ii) The term 'controlled corporation' means a corporation with respect to which 50 percent or more of the outstanding stock of its common parent is tendered for pursuant to a tender offer outstanding on March 7, 1984.

"(iii) The term 'subsidiary controlled corporation' means any corporation with respect to which the controlled corporation has control (within the meaning of section 368(c) of such Code) on March 7, 1984.

"(6) Exception for certain distribution of partnership interests. The amendments made by this section [Sec. 54 of P.L. 98-369] shall not apply to any distribution before February 1, 1986, of an interest in a partnership the interests of which were being traded on a national securities exchange on March 7, 1984, if—

"(A) such interest was owned by the distributing corporation (or any member of an affiliated group within the meaning of section 1504(a) of such Code of which the distributing corporation was a member) on March 7, 1984,

"(B) the distributing corporation (or any such affiliated member) owned more than 80 percent of the interests in such partnership on March 7, 1984, and

"(C) more than 10 percent of the interests in such partnership was offered for sale to the public during the 1-year period ending on March 7, 1984."

—P.L. 98-369, Sec. 61(d), redesignated subsec. (f) (as redesignated by Sec. 54(b) of the Act) as subsec. (g) and added subsec. (f), effective for distributions after 7/18/84 in tax. yrs. end. after 7/18/84.

—P.L. 98-369, Sec. 712(i)(1), substituted "complete liquidation" for "partial or complete liquidation" in para. (e)(2) (prior to redesignation by Sec. 54(b), above), effective for distributions after 8/31/82.

In 1978, P.L. 95-628, Sec. 3(a), amended clause (b)(1)(B)(ii) . . . Sec. 3(b), amended subsec. (d)(2)(B), effective for distributions made after 11/10/78.

Prior to amendment, clause (b)(1)(B)(ii) read as follows:

"(ii) the adjusted basis (in the hands of the distributing corporation immediately before the distribution) of the other property received, increased in the amount of gain to the distributing corporation which is recognized under subsection (b), (c), or (d) of section 311, under section 341(f), or under section 617(d)(1), 1245(a), 1250(a), 1251(c), 1252(a), or 1254(a)."

Prior to amendment, subpara. (d)(2)(B) read as follows:

"(B) the adjusted basis (in the hands of the distributing corporation immediately before the distribution) of such property, increased in the amount of gain to the distributing corporation which is recognized under subsection (b), (c), or (d) of section 311, under section 341(f), or under section 617(d)(1), 1245(a), 1250(a), 1251(c), 1252(a), or 1254(a)."

In 1976, P.L. 94-455, Sec. 205(c)(1)(B), substituted "1252(a), or 1254(a)" for "or 1252(a)" in clause (b)(1)(B)(ii) . . . Sec. 205(c)(1)(C), substituted "1252(a), or

1254(a)" for "or 1252(a)" in subpara. (d)(2)(B), effective for tax. yrs. end. after 12/31/75.

—P.L. 94-455, Sec. 1901(a)(41), deleted subsec. (e), effective for tax. yrs. begin. after 12/31/76.

Prior to deletion, subsec. (e) read as follows:

"(e) Exception for certain distributions by personal service corporations. Any distribution made by a corporation, which was classified as a personal service corporation under the provisions of the Revenue Act of 1918 or the Revenue Act of 1921, out of its earnings or profits which were taxable in accordance with the provisions of section 218 of the Revenue Act of 1918 (40 Stat 1070), or section 218 of the Revenue Act of 1921 (42 Stat 245), shall be exempt from tax to the distributees."

—P.L. 94-455, Sec. 1901(b)(32)(A), deleted subsec. (f) and redesignated subsec. (g) as (e), for tax. yrs. begin. after 12/31/76.

Prior to deletion, subsec. (f) read as follows:

"(f) Special rules for distributions of antitrust stock to corporations.

"(1) Definition of antitrust stock. For purposes of this subsection, the term 'antitrust stock' means stock received, by a corporation which is a party to a suit described in section 1111(d) (relating to definition of antitrust order), in a distribution made after September 6, 1961, either pursuant to the terms of, or in anticipation of, an antitrust order (as defined in subsection (d) of section 1111).

"(2) Amount distributed. Notwithstanding subsection (b)(1) (but subject to subsection (b)(2)), for purposes of this section the amount of a distribution of antitrust stock received by a corporation shall be the fair market value of such stock.

"(3) Basis. Notwithstanding subsection (d), the basis of antitrust stock received by a corporation in a distribution to which subsection (a) applies shall be the fair market value of such stock decreased by so much of the deduction for dividends received under the provisions of section 243, 244, or 245 as is, under regulations prescribed by the Secretary or his delegate, attributable to the excess, if any, of—

"(A) the fair market value of the stock, over

"(B) the adjusted basis (in the hands of the distributing corporation immediately before the distribution) of the stock, increased by the amount of gain which is recognized to the distributing corporation by reason of the distribution."

—P.L. 94-455, Sec. 1906(b)(13)(A), substituted "Secretary" for "Secretary or his delegate" in subpara. (b)(1)(C), effective for tax. yrs. begin. after 12/31/76.

In 1971, P.L. 92-178, Sec. 312(a)(1), added ", unless subparagraph (D) applies" after "corporation" the first time it appeared in subpara. (b)(1)(B) . . . Sec. 312(a)(2), added subpara. (b)(1)(D) . . . Sec. 312(a)(3), added ", unless paragraph (3) applies" after "corporation" the first time it appears in para. (d)(2) . . . Sec. 312(a)(4), redesignated para. (d)(3) as (4) and added para. (d)(3), effective for distributions made after 11/8/71.

In 1969, P.L. 91-172, Sec. 211(b)(1), substituted "1250(a), 1251(c), or 1252(a)" for "or 1250(a)" in clause (b)(1)(B)(ii) . . . Sec. 211(b)(2), substituted "1250(a), 1251(c), or 1252(a)" for "or 1250(a)" in subpara. (d)(2)(B), effective for tax. yrs. begin. after 12/31/69.

—P.L. 91-172, Sec. 905(b)(2), substituted "subsection (b), (c), or (d)" for "subsection (b) or (c)", in clause (b)(1)(B)(ii) and subpara. (d)(2)(B), effective for distributions after 11/30/69. For special limitations on effective date, see note following Code Sec. 311.

In 1966, P.L. 89-809, Sec. 104, amended clauses (b)(1)(C)(i) and (ii), and added the last two sentences of subsec. (b)(1)(C), effective for tax. yrs. begin. after 12/31/66.

Prior to amendment, clauses (b)(1)(C)(i) and (ii) read as follows:

"(i) the proportion of the adjusted basis of such property (or, if lower, its fair market value) properly attributable to gross income from sources within the United States, and

"(ii) the proportion of the fair market value of such property properly attributable to gross income from sources without the United States."

—P.L. 89-570, Sec. [1](b)(2), substituted "section 617(d)(1), 1245(a)," for "section 1245(a)" in clause (b)(1)(B)(ii) and subpara. (d)(2)(B), effective for tax. yrs. end. after 9/12/66, but only for expenditures paid or incurred after 9/12/66.

In 1964, P.L. 88-484, Sec. [1](b)(1), added ", under section 341(f)," after "section 311" in subsecs. (b) and (d), effective for transactions after 8/22/64 in tax. yrs. end. after 8/22/64.

—P.L. 88-272, Sec. 231(b)(2), added "or 1250(a)", in subsecs. (b) and (d), effective for dispositions after 12/31/63, in tax. yrs. end. after 12/31/63.

In 1962, P.L. 87-834, Sec. 5, added subpara. (b)(1)(C) and para. (d)(3), effective for distributions made after 12/31/62.

—P.L. 87-834, Sec. 13(f)(2), substituted "subsection (b) or (c) of section 311 or under section 1245(a)" for "subsection (b) or (c) of section 311" in subsecs. (b) and (d), effective for tax. yrs. begin. after 12/31/62.

—P.L. 87-403, Sec. 2(a), redesignated subsec. (f) as (g) and added subsec. (f), effective for distributions after 2/2/62.

Sec. 302. Distributions in redemption of stock.

(a) General rule.

If a corporation redeems its stock (within the meaning of section 317(b)), and if paragraph (1), (2), (3), (4), or (5) of subsection (b) applies, such redemption shall be treated as a distribution in part or full payment in exchange for the stock.

1,777

(b) Redemptions treated as exchanges.
  (1) Redemptions not equivalent to dividends. Subsection (a) shall apply if the redemption is not essentially equivalent to a dividend.
  (2) Substantially disproportionate redemption of stock.
    (A) In general. Subsection (a) shall apply if the distribution is substantially disproportionate with respect to the shareholder.
    (B) Limitation. This paragraph shall not apply unless immediately after the redemption the shareholder owns less than 50 percent of the total combined voting power of all classes of stock entitled to vote.
    (C) Definitions. For purposes of this paragraph, the distribution is substantially disproportionate if—
      (i) the ratio which the voting stock of the corporation owned by the shareholder immediately after the redemption bears to all of the voting stock of the corporation at such time,
    is less than 80 percent of—
      (ii) the ratio which the voting stock of the corporation owned by the shareholder immediately before the redemption bears to all of the voting stock of the corporation at such time.
    For purposes of this paragraph, no distribution shall be treated as substantially disproportionate unless the shareholder's ownership of the common stock of the corporation (whether voting or nonvoting) after and before redemption also meets the 80 percent requirement of the preceding sentence. For purposes of the preceding sentence, if there is more than one class of common stock, the determinations shall be made by reference to fair market value.
    (D) Series of redemptions. This paragraph shall not apply to any redemption made pursuant to a plan the purpose or effect of which is a series of redemptions resulting in a distribution which (in the aggregate) is not substantially disproportionate with respect to the shareholder.
  (3) Termination of shareholder's interest. Subsection (a) shall apply if the redemption is in complete redemption of all of the stock of the corporation owned by the shareholder.
  (4) Redemption from noncorporate shareholder in partial liquidation. Subsection (a) shall apply to a distribution if such distribution is—
    (A) in redemption of stock held by a shareholder who is not a corporation, and
    (B) in partial liquidation of the distributing corporation.
  (5) Redemptions by certain regulated investment companies. Except to the extent provided in regulations prescribed by the Secretary, subsection (a) shall apply to any distribution in redemption of stock of a publicly offered regulated investment company (within the meaning of section 67(c)(2)(B)) if—
    (A) such redemption is upon the demand of the stockholder, and
    (B) such company issues only stock which is redeemable upon the demand of the stockholder.
  (6) Application of paragraphs. In determining whether a redemption meets the requirements of paragraph (1), the fact that such redemption fails to meet the requirements of paragraph (2), (3), or (4) shall not be taken into account. If a redemption meets the requirements of paragraph (3) and also the requirements of paragraph (1), (2), or (4), then so much of subsection (c)(2) as would (but for this sentence) apply in respect of the acquisition of an interest in the corporation within the 10-year period beginning on the date of the distribution shall not apply.

(c) Constructive ownership of stock.
  (1) In general. Except as provided in paragraph (2) of this subsection, section 318(a) shall apply in determining the ownership of stock for purposes of this section.
  (2) For determining termination of interest.
    (A) In the case of a distribution described in subsection (b)(3), section 318(a)(1) shall not apply if—
      (i) immediately after the distribution the distributee has no interest in the corporation (including an interest as officer, director, or employee), other than an interest as a creditor,
      (ii) the distributee does not acquire any such interest (other than stock acquired by bequest or inheritance) within 10 years from the date of such distribution, and
      (iii) the distributee, at such time and in such manner as the Secretary by regulations prescribes, files an agreement to notify the Secretary of any acquisition described in clause (ii) and to retain such records as may be necessary for the application of this paragraph.
    If the distributee acquires such an interest in the corporation (other than by bequest or inheritance) within 10 years from the date of the distribution, then the periods of limitation provided in sections 6501 and 6502 on the making of an assessment and the collection by levy or a proceeding in court shall, with respect to any deficiency (including interest and additions to the tax) resulting from such acquisition, include one year immediately following the date on which the distributee (in accordance with regulations prescribed by the Secretary) notifies the Secretary of such acquisition; and such assessment and collection may be made notwithstanding any provision of law or rule of law which otherwise would prevent such assessment and collection.
    (B) Subparagraph (A) of this paragraph shall not apply if—
      (i) any portion of the stock redeemed was acquired, directly or indirectly, within the 10-year period ending on the date of the distribution by the distributee from a person the ownership of whose stock would (at the time of distribution) be attributable to the distributee under section 318(a), or
      (ii) any person owns (at the time of the distribution) stock the ownership of which is attributable to the distributee under section 318(a) and such person acquired any stock in the corporation, directly or indirectly, from the distributee within the 10-year period ending on the date of the distribution, unless such stock so acquired from the distributee is redeemed in the same transaction.
    The preceding sentence shall not apply if the acquisition (or, in the case of clause (ii), the disposition) by the distributee did not have as one of its principal purposes the avoidance of Federal income tax.
    (C) Special rule for waivers by entities.
      (i) In general. Subparagraph (A) shall not apply to a distribution to any entity unless—
        (I) such entity and each related person meet the requirements of clauses (i), (ii), and (iii) of subparagraph (A), and
        (II) Each related person agrees to be jointly and severally liable for any deficiency (including interest and additions to tax) resulting from an acquisition described in clause (ii) of subparagraph (A).

Corporate distributions and adjustments   Code Sec. 302

In any case to which the preceding sentence applies, the second sentence of subparagraph (A) and subparagraph (B)(ii) shall be applied by substituting "distributee or any related person" for "distributee" each place it appears.

(ii) Definitions. For purposes of this subparagraph—

(I) the term "entity" means a partnership, estate, trust, or corporation; and

(II) the term "related person" means any person to whom ownership of stock in the corporation is (at the time of the distribution) attributable under section 318(a)(1) if such stock is further attributable to the entity under section 318(a)(3).

(d) Redemptions treated as distributions of property.

Except as otherwise provided in this subchapter, if a corporation redeems its stock (within the meaning of section 317(b)), and if subsection (a) of this section does not apply, such redemption shall be treated as a distribution of property to which section 301 applies.

(e) Partial liquidation defined.

(1) In general. For purposes of subsection (b)(4), a distribution shall be treated as in partial liquidation of a corporation if—

(A) the distribution is not essentially equivalent to a dividend (determined at the corporate level rather than at the shareholder level), and

(B) the distribution is pursuant to a plan and occurs within the taxable year in which the plan is adopted or within the succeeding taxable year.

(2) Termination of business. The distributions which meet the requirements of paragraph (1)(A) shall include (but shall not be limited to) a distribution which meets the requirements of subparagraphs (A) and (B) of this paragraph:

(A) The distribution is attributable to the distributing corporation's ceasing to conduct, or consists of the assets of, a qualified trade or business.

(B) Immediately after the distribution, the distributing corporation is actively engaged in the conduct of a qualified trade or business.

(3) Qualified trade or business. For purposes of paragraph (2), the term "qualified trade or business" means any trade or business which—

(A) was actively conducted throughout the 5-year period ending on the date of the redemption, and

(B) was not acquired by the corporation within such period in a transaction in which gain or loss was recognized in whole or in part.

(4) Redemption may be pro rata. Whether or not a redemption meets the requirements of subparagraphs (A) and (B) of paragraph (2) shall be determined without regard to whether or not the redemption is pro rata with respect to all of the shareholders of the corporation.

(5) Treatment of certain pass-thru entities. For purposes of determining under subsection (b)(4) whether any stock is held by a shareholder who is not a corporation, any stock held by a partnership, estate, or trust shall be treated as if it were actually held proportionately by its partners or beneficiaries.

(f) Cross references.

For special rules relating to redemption—

(1) Death taxes. Of stock to pay death taxes, see section 303.

(2) Section 306 stock. Of section 306 stock, see section 306.

(3) Liquidations. Of stock in complete liquidation, see section 331.

In 2010, P.L. 111-325, Sec. 306(a)(1), redesignated para. (b)(5) as para. (b)(6), and added para. (b)(5)... Sec. 306(a)(2), substituted "(4), or (5)" for "or (4)" in subsec. (a), effective for distributions after 12/22/2010.

In 1984, P.L. 98-369, Sec. 712(i)(1), substituted "complete liquidation" for "partial or complete liquidation" in para. (f)(3), effective for distributions after 8/31/82.

In 1983, P.L. 97-448, Sec. 306(a)(6)(A), added ", except that in applying such section both direct and indirect ownership of stock shall be taken into account" before the period at the end of Sec. 222(f)(2) of P.L. 97-248, the exception to the effective date of changes made by Sec. 222 of P.L. 97-248 [reproduced below].

In 1982, P.L. 97-248, Sec. 222(c)(1), redesignated para. (b)(4) as para. (b)(5) and added new para. (b)(4)... Sec. 222(c)(2), redesignated subsec. (e) as subsec. (f) and added new subsec. (e)... Sec. 222(c)(3), substituted "paragraph (1), (2), (3), or (4)" for "paragraph (1), (2), or (3)" in subsec. (a)... Sec. 222(c)(4)(A), substituted "paragraph (2), (3), or (4)" for "paragraph (2) or (3)" in para. (b)(5) [as redesignated by Sec. 222(c)(1) of this Act, see below]... Sec. 222(c)(4)(B), substituted "paragraph (1), (2), or (4)" for "paragraph (1) or (2)" in para. (b)(5) [as redesignated, see above] effective for distributions after 8/31/82. Secs. 222(f)(2)-(4) of this Act provide:

"(2) Exceptions.—

"(A) Ruling requests.—The amendments made by this section shall not apply to distributions made by any corporation if—

"(i)(I) on July 22, 1982, there was a ruling request by such corporation pending with the Internal Revenue Service as to whether such distributions would qualify as a partial liquidation, or

"(II) within the period beginning on July 12, 1981, and ending on July 22, 1982, the Internal Revenue Service granting a ruling to such corporation that the distributions would qualify as a partial liquidation, and

"(ii) such distributions are pursuant to a plan of partial liquidation adopted before October 1, 1982 (or, if later, 90 days after the date on which the Internal Revenue Service granted a ruling pursuant to the request described in clause (i)(I)).

"(B) Plans adopted before July 23, 1982.—The amendments made by this section shall not apply to distributions made pursuant to a plan of partial liquidation adopted before July 23, 1982.

"(C) Control acquired after 1981 and before July 23, 1982.—The amendments made by this section shall not apply to distributions made pursuant to a plan of partial liquidation adopted before October 1, 1982, where control of the corporation making the distributions was acquired after December 31, 1981, and before July 23, 1982.

"(D) Tender offer or binding contract outstanding on July 22, 1982.—

"(i) In general.—The amendments made by this section shall not apply to distributions made by a corporation if—

"(I) such distributions are pursuant to a plan of liquidation adopted before October 1, 1982, and

"(II) control of such corporation was acquired after July 22, 1982, pursuant to a tender offer or binding contract outstanding on such date.

"(ii) Extension of time for adopting plan where acquisition subject to federal regulatory approval.—If the acquisition described in clause (i)(II) is subject to approval by a Federal regulatory agency, clause (i) shall be applied by substituting for 'October 1, 1982' the date which is 90 days after the date on which approval by the Federal regulatory agency of such acquisition becomes final.

"(iii) Special rule where offer subject to approval by foreign regulatory body.—In any case where an offer to acquire stock in a corporation was subject to intervention by a foreign regulatory body and a public announcement of such an offer resulted in the intervention by such foreign regulatory body before July 23, 1982—

"(I) such public announcement shall be treated as a tender offer, and

"(II) clause (i) shall be applied by substituting for 'October 1, 1982' the date which is 90 days after the date on which such regulatory body approves a public offer to acquire stock in such corporation.

"(iv) Special rule where one-third of shares acquired during March and April 1982.—If—

"(I) one-third or more of the shares of a corporation were acquired by another corporation during March and April 1982, and

"(II) during March or April 1982, the acquiring corporation filed with the Federal Trade Commission notification of its intent to acquire control of the acquired corporation, subclause (II) of clause (i) shall not apply with respect to distributions made by the acquired corporation.

"(E) Insurance companies.—The amendments made by this section shall not apply to distributions made by an insurance company pursuant to a plan of partial liquidation adopted before October 1, 1982, where control was acquired by the distributee or its parent after December 31, 1980, and before July 23, 1982, and the conduct of the insurance business by the distributee is conditioned on approval by a State regulatory authority.

For purposes of this paragraph, the term 'control' has the meaning given to such term by section 368(c) of the Internal Revenue Code of 1954, except that in applying such section both direct and indirect ownership of stock shall be taken into account.

"(3) Approval of plan by board of directors.—For purposes of—

"(A) paragraph (2), and

"(B) applying section 346(a)(2) of the Internal Revenue Code of 1954 (as in effect on the day before the date of the enactment of this Act) to distributions to which (but for paragraph (2)) the amendments made by this section would apply, a plan for liquidation shall be treated and adopted when approved by the corporation's board of directors.

Code Sec. 302   **Corporate distributions and adjustments**

"(4) Coordination with amendments made by section 224.—For purposes of section 338(e)(2)(C) of the Internal Revenue Code of 1954 (as added by section 224), any property acquired in a distribution to which the amendments made by this section do not apply by reason of paragraph (2) shall be treated as acquired before September 1, 1982."

—P.L. 97-248, Sec. 228(a), added subpara. (c)(2)(C), effective for distributions after 8/31/82, in tax. yrs. ending after 8/31/82.

In **1980**, P.L. 96-589, Sec. 5(b)(1), deleted para. (b)(4) and redesignated para. (b)(5) as (b)(4) . . . Sec. 5(b)(2)(A), substituted "(2), or (3)" for "(2), (3), or (4)" in subsec. (a) . . . Sec. 5(b)(2)(B), substituted "(2) or (3)" for "(2), (3), or (4)" and substituted "(1) or (2)" for "(1), (2) or (4)" in para. (b)(4) [as redesignated by Sec. 5(b)(1) of this Act, see above] effective for stock issued after 12/31/80 (other than stock issued pursuant to a plan of reorganization approved on or before 12/31/80). Sec. 7(f) and (g) of this Act provides:

"(f) Election to substitute September 30, 1979, for December 31, 1980.—

"(1) In general. The debtor (or debtors) in a bankruptcy case or similar judicial proceeding may (with the approval of the court) elect to apply [subsection 7(d) of this Act] by substituting 'September 30, 1979' for 'December 31, 1980' each place it appears in such subsections.

"(2) Effect of election. Any election made under paragraph (1) with respect to any proceeding shall apply to all parties to the proceeding.

"(3) Revocation only with consent. Any election under this subsection may be revoked only with the consent of the Secretary of the Treasury or his delegate.

"(4) Time and manner of election. Any election under this subsection shall be made at such time, and in such manner, as the Secretary of the Treasury or his delegate may by regulations prescribe.

"(g) Definitions.

For purposes of this section—

"(1) Bankruptcy case. The term 'bankruptcy case' means any case under title 11 of the United States Code (as recodified by P.L. 95-598).

"(2) Similar judicial proceeding. The term 'similar judicial proceeding' means a receivership, foreclosure, or similar proceeding in a Federal or State court (as modified by section 368(a)(3)(D) of the Internal Revenue Code of 1954)."

Prior to deletion, para. (b)(4) read as follows:

"(4) Stock issued by railroad corporations in certain reorganizations. Subsection (a) shall apply if the redemption is of stock issued by a railroad corporation (as defined in section 77(m) of the Bankruptcy Act, as amended) pursuant to a plan of reorganization under section 77 of the Bankruptcy Act."

In **1976**, P.L. 94-455, Sec. 1906(b)(13)(A), substituted "Secretary" for "Secretary or his delegate" each place it appeared in subpara. (c)(2)(A), effective for tax. yrs. begin. after 12/31/76.

Sec. 303. Distributions in redemption of stock to pay death taxes.

(a) In general.

A distribution of property to a shareholder by a corporation in redemption of part or all of the stock of such corporation which (for Federal estate tax purposes) is included in determining the gross estate of a decedent, to the extent that the amount of such distribution does not exceed the sum of—

(1) the estate, inheritance, legacy, and succession taxes (including any interest collected as a part of such taxes) imposed because of such decedent's death, and

(2) the amount of funeral and administration expenses allowable as deductions to the estate under section 2053 (or under section 2106 in the case of the estate of a decedent nonresident, not a citizen of the United States),

shall be treated as a distribution in full payment in exchange for the stock so redeemed.

(b) Limitations on application of subsection (a).

(1) **Period for distribution.** Subsection (a) shall apply only to amounts distributed after the death of the decedent and—

(A) within the period of limitations provided in section 6501(a) for the assessment of the Federal estate tax (determined without the application of any provision other than section 6501(a)), or within 90 days after the expiration of such period,

(B) if a petition for redetermination of a deficiency in such estate tax has been filed with the Tax Court within the time prescribed in section 6213, at any time before the expiration of 60 days after the decision of the Tax Court becomes final, or

(C) If an election has been made under section 6166 and if the time prescribed by this subparagraph expires at a later date than the time prescribed by subparagraph (B) of this paragraph, within the time determined under section 6166 for the payment of the installments.

(2) **Relationship of stock to decedent's estate.**

(A) In general. Subsection (a) shall apply to a distribution by a corporation only if the value (for Federal estate tax purposes) of all of the stock of such corporation which is included in determining the value of the decedent's gross estate exceeds 35 percent of the excess of—

(i) the value of the gross estate of such decedent, over

(ii) the sum of the amounts allowable as a deduction under section 2053 or 2054.

(B) Special rule for stock in 2 or more corporations. For purposes of subparagraph (A), stock of 2 or more corporations, with respect to each of which there is included in determining the value of the decedent's gross estate 20 percent or more in value of the outstanding stock, shall be treated as the stock of a single corporation. For purposes of the 20-percent requirement of the preceding sentence, stock which, at the decedent's death, represents the surviving spouse's interest in property held by the decedent and the surviving spouse as community property or as joint tenants, tenants by the entirety, or tenants in common shall be treated as having been included in determining the value of the decedent's gross estate.

(3) **Relationship of shareholder to estate tax.** Subsection (a) shall apply to a distribution by a corporation only to the extent that the interest of the shareholder is reduced directly (or through a binding obligation to contribute) by any payment of an amount described in paragraph (1) or (2) of subsection (a).

(4) **Additional requirements for distributions made more than 4 years after decedent's death.** In the case of amounts distributed more than 4 years after the date of the decedent's death, subsection (a) shall apply to a distribution by a corporation only to the extent of the lesser of—

(A) the aggregate of the amounts referred to in paragraph (1) or (2) of subsection (a) which remained unpaid immediately before the distribution, or

(B) the aggregate of the amounts referred to in paragraph (1) or (2) of subsection (a) which are paid during the 1-year period beginning on the date of such distribution.

(c) Stock with substituted basis.

If—

(1) a shareholder owns stock of a corporation (referred to in this subsection as "new stock") the basis of which is determined by reference to the basis of stock of a corporation (referred to in this subsection as "old stock"),

(2) the old stock was included (for Federal estate tax purposes) in determining the gross estate of a decedent, and

(3) subsection (a) would apply to a distribution of property to such shareholder in redemption of the old stock,

then, subject to the limitations specified in subsection (b), subsection (a) shall apply in respect of a distribution in redemption of the new stock.

(d) Special rules for generation-skipping transfers.

Where stock in a corporation is the subject of a generation-skipping transfer (within the meaning of section 2611(a)) occurring at the same time as and as a result of the death of an individual—

(1) the stock shall be deemed to be included in the gross estate of such individual;

(2) taxes of the kind referred to in subsection (a)(1) which are imposed because of the generation-skipping transfer

shall be treated as imposed because of such individual's death (and for this purpose the tax imposed by section 2601 shall be treated as an estate tax);

(3) the period of distribution shall be measured from the date of the generation-skipping transfer; and

(4) the relationship of stock to the decedent's estate shall be measured with reference solely to the amount of the generation-skipping transfer.

In 1990, P.L. 101-508, Sec. 11703(c)(3), of this Act, provides:

"(3) Subparagraph (C) of section 1433(b)(2) of the Tax Reform Act of 1986 shall not exempt any generation-skipping transfer from the amendments made by subtitle D of title XVI of such Act to the extent such transfer is attributable to property transferred by gift or by reason of the death of another person to the decedent (or trust) referred to in such subparagraph after August 3, 1990."

In 1988, P.L. 100-647, Sec. 1014(h)(5), of this Act, provides:

"(5) Subparagraph (C) of section 1433(b)(2) of the Reform Act shall not exempt any direct skip from the amendments made by subtitle D of title XIV of the Reform Act if—

"(A) such direct skip results from the application of section 2044 of the 1986 Code, and

"(B) such direct skip is attributable to property transferred to the trust after October 21, 1988."

In 1986, P.L. 99-514, Sec. 1432(b), amended subsec. (d), effective for any generation-skipping transfer (within the meaning of section 2611 of the Internal Revenue Code of 1986) made after 10/22/86.

Prior to amendment, subsec. (d) read as follows:

"(d) Special rules for generation-skipping transfers. Under regulations prescribed by the Secretary, where stock in a corporation is subject to tax under section 2601 as a result of a generation-skipping transfer (within the meaning of section 2611(a)), which occurs at or after the death of the deemed transferor (within the meaning of section 2612)—

"(1) the stock shall be deemed to be included in the gross estate of the deemed transferor;

"(2) taxes of the kind referred to in subsection (a)(1) which are imposed because of the generation-skipping transfer shall be treated as imposed because of the deemed transferor's death (and for this purpose the tax imposed by section 2601 shall be treated as an estate tax);

"(3) the period of distribution shall be measured from the date of the generation-skipping transfer; and

"(4) the relationship of stock to the decedent's estate shall be measured with reference solely to the amount of the generation-skipping transfer."

— P.L. 99-514, Sec. 1433(b)-(d), of this Act [as amended by Sec. 1014(h)(1)-(4) of P.L. 100-647] provides:

"(b) *Special rules.*

"(1) Treatment of certain inter vivos transfers made after September 25, 1985. For purposes of subsection (a) and chapter 13 of the Internal Revenue Code of 1986 as amended by this part, any inter vivos transfer after September 25, 1985, and on or before the date of the enactment of this Act shall be treated as if it were made on the 1st day the date of enactment of this Act.

"(2) Exceptions. The amendments made by this subtitle shall not apply to—

"(A) any generation-skipping transfer under a trust which was irrevocable on September 25, 1985, but only to the extent that such transfer is not made out of corpus added to the trust after September 25, 1985 (or out of income attributable to corpus so added),

"(B) any generation-skipping transfer under a will or revocable trust executed before the date of the enactment of this Act if the decedent dies before January 1, 1987, and

"(C) any generation-skipping transfer—

"(i) under a trust to the extent such trust consists of property included in the gross estate of a decedent (other than property transferred by the decedent during his life after the date of the enactment of this Act), or reinvestments thereof, or

"(ii) which is a direct skip which occurs by reason of the death of any decedent;

but only if such decedent was, on the date of the enactment of this Act, under a mental disability to change the disposition of his property and did not regain his competence to dispose of such property before the date of his death.

"(3) Treatment of certain transfers to grandchildren.

"(A) In general. For purposes of chapter 13 of the Internal Revenue Code of 1986, the term 'direct skip' shall not include any transfer before January 1, 1990, from a transferor to a grandchild of the transferor to the extent the aggregate transfers from such transferor to such grandchild do not exceed $2,000,000.

"(B) Treatment of transfers in trust. For purposes of subparagraph (A), a transfer in trust for the benefit of a grandchild shall be treated as a transfer to such grandchild if (and only if)—

"(i) during the life of the grandchild, no portion of the corpus or income of the trust may be distributed to (or for the benefit of) any person other than such grandchild,

"(ii) the assets of the trust will be includible in the gross estate of the grandchild if the grandchild dies before the trust is terminated, and

"(iii) all of the income of the trust for periods after the grandchild has attained age 21 will be distributed to (or for the benefit of) such grandchild not less frequently than annually.

"(C) Coordination with section 2653(a) of the 1986 Code. In the case of any transfer which would be a generation-skipping transfer but for subparagraph (A), the rules of section 2653(a) of the Internal Revenue Code of 1986 shall apply as if such transfer were a generation-skipping transfer.

"(D) Coordination with taxable terminations and taxable distributions. For purposes of chapter 13 of the Internal Revenue Code of 1986, the terms 'taxable termination' and 'taxable distribution' shall not include any transfer which would be a direct skip but for subparagraph (A).

"(4) Definitions. Terms used in this section shall have the same respective meanings as when used in chapter 13 of the Internal Revenue Code of 1986; except that section 2612(c)(2) of such Code shall not apply in determining whether an individual is a grandchild of the transferor.

"(c) Repeal of existing tax on generation-skipping transfers.

"(1) In general. In the case of any tax imposed by chapter 13 of the Internal Revenue Code of 1954 (as in effect on the day before the date of the enactment of this Act), such tax (including interest, additions to tax, and additional amounts) shall not be assessed and if assessed, the assessment shall be abated, and if collected, shall be credited or refunded (with interest) as an overpayment.

"(2) Waiver of statute of limitations. If on the date of the enactment of this Act (or at any time within 1 year after such date of enactment) refund or credit of any overpayment of tax resulting from the application of paragraph (1) is barred by any law or rule of law, refund or credit of such overpayment shall, nevertheless, be made or allowed if claim therefore is filed before the date 1 year after the date of the enactment of this Act.

"(d) Election for certain transfers benefiting grandchild.

"(1) In general. For purposes of chapter 13 of the Internal Revenue Code of 1986 (as amended by this Act) and subsection (b) of this section, any transfer in trust for the benefit of a grandchild of a transferor shall be treated as a direct skip to such grandchild if—

"(A) the transfer occurs before the date of enactment of this Act,

"(B) the transfer would be a direct skip to a grandchild except for the fact that the trust instrument provides that, if the grandchild dies before vesting of the interest transferred, the interest is transferred to the grandchild's heir (rather than the grandchild's estate), and

"(C) an election under this subsection applies to such transfer.

"(2) Election. An election under paragraph (1) shall be made at such time and in such manner as the Secretary of the Treasury or his delegate may prescribe.

Any transfer treated as a direct skip by reason of the preceding sentence shall be subject to Federal estate tax on the grandchild's death in the same manner as if the contingent gift over had been to the grandchild's estate. Unless the grandchild otherwise directs by will, the estate of such grandchild shall be entitled to recover from the person receiving the property on the death of the grandchild any increase in Federal estate tax on the estate of the grandchild by reason of the preceding sentence."

In 1981, P.L. 97-34, Sec. 422(b)(1), substituted "35 percent" for "50 percent" in subpara. (b)(2)(A) . . . Sec. 422(b)(2), amended subpara. (b)(2)(B) . . . Sec. 422(e)(1), deleted "or 6166A" after "6166" each place it appeared in subpara. (b)(1)(C), effective for estates of decedents dying after 12/31/81.

Prior to amendment, subpara. (b)(2)(B) read as follows:

"(B) Special rule for stock of two or more corporations. For purposes of the 50 percent requirement of subparagraph (A), stock of two or more corporations, with respect to each of which there is included in the value of the decedent's gross estate more than 75 percent in value of the outstanding stock, shall be treated as the stock of a single corporation. For the purpose of the 75 percent requirement of the preceding sentence, stock which, at the decedent's death, represents the surviving spouse's interest in property held by the decedent and the surviving spouse as community property shall be treated as having been included in determining the value of the decedent's gross estate."

— P.L. 97-34, Sec. 428, amended Sec. 2006(c)(2)(B) of P.L. 94-455 (as amended by Sec. 702(n)(1) of P.L. 95-600) by substituting "January 1, 1983" for "January 1, 1982" [see below].

In 1978, P.L. 95-600, Sec. 702(n)(1), substituted "June 11, 1976" for "April 30, 1976" each place it appeared in Sec. 2006(c) of P.L. 94-455, [see below].

In 1976, P.L. 94-455, Sec. 2004(e), deleted "or" at the end of subpara. (b)(1)(A), substituted ", or" for the period at the end of subpara. (b)(1)(B), added subpara. (b)(1)(C), amended subpara. (b)(2)(A), substituted "the 50 percent requirement" for "the 35 percent and 50 percent requirements" in the first sentence of subpara. (b)(2)(B), added paras. (b)(3) and (4), and substituted "limitations specified in subsection (b)" for "limitation specified in subsection (b)(1)" in subsec. (c), effective for estates of decedents dying after 12/31/76.

Prior to amendment, subpara. (b)(2)(A) read as follows:

"(A) In general. Subsection (a) shall apply to a distribution by a corporation only if the value (for Federal estate tax purposes) of all the stock of such corporation which is included in determining the value of the decedent's gross estate is either—

"(i) more than 35 percent of the value of the gross estate of such decedent, or

"(ii) more than 50 percent of the taxable estate of such decedent."

— P.L. 94-455, Sec. 2006(b)(4), added subsec. (d). Sec. 2006(c) of the Act provided as follows:

"(c) Effective dates.—

"(1) In general.—Except as provided in paragraph (2), the amendments made by this section shall apply to any generation-skipping transfer (within the meaning of section 2611(a) of the Internal Revenue Code of 1954) made after June 11, 1976.

"(2) Exceptions.—The amendments made by this section shall not apply to any generation-skipping transfer—

"(A) under a trust which was irrevocable on June 11, 1976, but only to the extent that the transfer is not made out of corpus added to the trust after June 11, 1976, or

"(B) in the case of a decedent dying before January 1, 1983, pursuant to a will (or revocable trust) which was in existence on June 11, 1976, and was not amended at any time after that date in any respect which will result in the creation of, or increasing the amount of, any generation-skipping transfer.

For purposes of subparagraph (B), if the decedent on June 11, 1976, was under a mental disability to change the disposition of his property, the period set forth in such subparagraph shall not expire before the date which is 2 years after the date on which he first regains his competence to dispose of such property.

"(3) Trust equivalents.—For purposes of paragraph (2), in the case of a trust equivalent within the meaning of subsection (d) of section 2611 of the Internal Revenue Code of 1954, the provisions of such subsection (d) shall apply."

Sec. 304. Redemption through use of related corporations.

(a) Treatment of certain stock purchases.

(1) Acquisition by related corporation (other than subsidiary). For purposes of sections 302 and 303, if—

(A) one or more persons are in control of each of two corporations, and

(B) in return for property, one of the corporations acquires stock in the other corporation from the person (or persons) so in control,

then (unless paragraph (2) applies) such property shall be treated as a distribution in redemption of the stock of the corporation acquiring such stock. To the extent that such distribution is treated as a distribution to which section 301 applies, the transferor and the acquiring corporation shall be treated in the same manner as if the transferor had transferred the stock so acquired to the acquiring corporation in exchange for stock of the acquiring corporation in a transaction to which section 351(a) applies, and then the acquiring corporation had redeemed the stock it was treated as issuing in such transaction.

(2) Acquisition by subsidiary. For purposes of sections 302 and 303, if—

(A) in return for property, one corporation acquires from a shareholder of another corporation stock in such other corporation, and

(B) the issuing corporation controls the acquiring corporation,

then such property shall be treated as a distribution in redemption of the stock of the issuing corporation.

(b) Special rules for application of subsection (a).

(1) Rule for determinations under section 302(b). In the case of any acquisition of stock to which subsection (a) of this section applies, determinations as to whether the acquisition is, by reason of section 302(b), to be treated as a distribution in part or full payment in exchange for the stock shall be made by reference to the stock of the issuing corporation. In applying section 318(a) (relating to constructive ownership of stock) with respect to section 302(b) for purposes of this paragraph, sections 318(a)(2)(C) and 318(a)(3)(C) shall be applied without regard to the 50 percent limitation contained therein.

(2) Amount constituting dividend. In the case of any acquisition of stock to which subsection (a) applies, the determination of the amount which is a dividend (and the source thereof) shall be made as if the property were distributed—

(A) by the acquiring corporation to the extent of its earnings and profits, and

(B) then by the issuing corporation to the extent of its earnings and profits.

(3) Coordination with section 351.

(A) Property treated as received in redemption. Except as otherwise provided in this paragraph, subsection (a) (and not section 351 and not so much of sections 357 and 358 as relates to section 351) shall apply to any property received in a distribution described in subsection (a).

(B) Certain assumptions of liability, etc.

(i) In general. In the case of an acquisition described in section 351, subsection (a) shall not apply to any liability—

(I) assumed by the acquiring corporation, or

(II) to which the stock is subject,

if such liability was incurred by the transferor to acquire the stock. For purposes of the preceding sentence, the term "stock" means stock referred to in paragraph (1)(B) or (2)(A) of subsection (a).

(ii) Extension of obligations, etc. For purposes of clause (i), an extension, renewal, or refinancing of a liability which meets the requirements of clause (i) shall be treated as meeting such requirements.

(iii) Clause (i) does not apply to stock acquired from related person except where complete termination. Clause (i) shall apply only to stock acquired by the transferor from a person—

(I) none of whose stock is attributable to the transferor under section 318(a) (other than paragraph (4) thereof), or

(II) who satisfies rules similar to the rules of section 302(c)(2) with respect to both the acquiring and the issuing corporations (determined as if such person were a distributee of each such corporation).

(C) Distributions incident to formation of bank holding companies. If—

(i) pursuant to a plan, control of a bank is acquired and within 2 years after the date on which such control is acquired, stock constituting control of such bank is transferred to a BHC in connection with its formation,

(ii) incident to the formation of the BHC there is a distribution of property described in subsection (a), and

(iii) the shareholders of the BHC who receive distributions of such property do not have control of such BHC,

then, subsection (a) shall not apply to any securities received by a qualified minority shareholder incident to the formation of such BHC. For purposes of this subparagraph, any assumption of (or acquisition of stock subject to) a liability under subparagraph (B) shall not be treated as a distribution of property.

(D) Definitions and special rule. For purposes of subparagraph (C) and this subparagraph—

(i) Qualified minority shareholder. The term "qualified minority shareholder" means any shareholder who owns less than 10 percent (in value) of the stock of the BHC. For purposes of the preceding sentence, the rules of paragraph (3) of subsection (c) shall apply.

(ii) BHC. The term "BHC" means a bank holding company (within the meaning of section 2(a) of the Bank Holding Company Act of 1956).

(iii) Special rule in case of BHC's formed before 1985. In the case of a BHC which is formed before 1985, clause (i) of subparagraph (C) shall not apply.

(4) Treatment of certain intragroup transactions.

(A) In general. In the case of any transfer described in subsection (a) of stock from 1 member of an affiliated

group to another member of such group, proper adjustments shall be made to—
  (i) the adjusted basis of any intragroup stock, and
  (ii) the earnings and profits of any member of such group,
to the extent necessary to carry out the purposes of this section.
  (B) Definitions. For purposes of this paragraph—
    (i) Affiliated group. The term "affiliated group" has the meaning given such term by section 1504(a).
    (ii) Intragroup stock. The term "intragroup stock" means any stock which—
      (I) is in a corporation which is a member of an affiliated group, and
      (II) is held by another member of such group.

(5) Acquisitions by foreign corporations.
  (A) In general. In the case of any acquisition to which subsection (a) applies in which the acquiring corporation is a foreign corporation, the only earnings and profits taken into account under paragraph (2)(A) shall be those earnings and profits—
    (i) which are attributable (under regulations prescribed by the Secretary) to stock of the acquiring corporation owned (within the meaning of section 958(a)) by a corporation or individual which is—
      (I) a United States shareholder (within the meaning of section 951(b)) of the acquiring corporation, and
      (II) the transferor or a person who bears a relationship to the transferor described in section 267(b) or 707(b), and
    (ii) which were accumulated during the period or periods such stock was owned by such person while the acquiring corporation was a controlled foreign corporation.
  (B) Special rule in case of foreign acquiring corporation. In the case of any acquisition to which subsection (a) applies in which the acquiring corporation is a foreign corporation, no earnings and profits shall be taken into account under paragraph (2)(A)(and subparagraph (A) shall not apply) if more than 50 percent of the dividends arising from such acquisition (determined without regard to this subparagraph) would neither—
    (i) be subject to tax under this chapter for the taxable year in which the dividends arise, nor
    (ii) be includible in the earnings and profits of a controlled foreign corporation (as defined in section 957 and without regard to section 953(c)).
  (C) Regulations. The Secretary shall prescribe such regulations as are appropriate to carry out the purposes of this paragraph.

(6) Avoidance of multiple inclusions, etc. In the case of any acquisition to which subsection (a) applies in which the acquiring corporation or the issuing corporation is a foreign corporation, the Secretary shall prescribe such regulations as are appropriate in order to eliminate a multiple inclusion of any item in income by reason of this subpart and to provide appropriate basis adjustments (including modifications to the application of sections 959 and 961).

(c) Control.
  (1) In general. For purposes of this section, control means the ownership of stock possessing at least 50 percent of the total combined voting power of all classes of stock entitled to vote, or at least 50 percent of the total value of shares of all classes of stock. If a person (or persons) is in control (within the meaning of the preceding sentence) of a corporation which in turn owns at least 50 percent of the total combined voting power of all stock entitled to vote of another corporation, or owns at least 50 percent of the total value of the shares of all classes of stock of another corporation, then such person (or persons) shall be treated as in control of such other corporation.

  (2) Stock acquired in the transaction. For purposes of subsection (a)(1)—
    (A) General rule. Where 1 or more persons in control of the issuing corporation transfer stock of such corporation in exchange for stock of the acquiring corporation, the stock of the acquiring corporation received shall be taken into account in determining whether such person or persons are in control of the acquiring corporation.
    (B) Definition of control group. Where 2 or more persons in control of the issuing corporation transfer stock of such corporation to the acquiring corporation and, after the transfer, the transferors are in control of the acquiring corporation, the person or persons in control of each corporation shall include each of the persons who so transfer stock.

  (3) Constructive ownership.
    (A) In general. Section 318(a) (relating to constructive ownership of stock) shall apply for purposes of determining control under this section.
    (B) Modification of 50-percent limitations in section 318. For purposes of subparagraph (A)—
      (i) paragraph (2)(C) of section 318(a) shall be applied by substituting "5 percent" for "50 percent," and
      (ii) paragraph (3)(C) of section 318(a) shall be applied—
        (I) by substituting "5 percent" for "50 percent," and
        (II) in any case where such paragraph would not apply but for subclause (I), by considering a corporation as owning the stock (other than stock in such corporation) owned by or for any shareholder of such corporation in that proportion which the value of the stock which such shareholder owned in such corporation bears to the value of all stock in such corporation.

In 2010, P.L. 111-226, Sec. 215(a), redesignated subpara. (b)(5)(B) as subpara. (b)(5)(C), and added new subpara. (b)(5)(B), effective for acquisitions after 8/10/2010.

In 1998, P.L. 105-206, Sec. 6010(d)(1), deleted subpara. (b)(5)(B) and redesignated subpara. (b)(5)(C) as (B) . . . Sec. 6010(d)(2), added para. (b)(6), effective for distributions and acquisitions after 6/8/97. For transition rules, see Sec. (d)(2) of P.L. 105-34 [reproduced below].
Prior to deletion, subpara. (b)(5)(B) read as follows:
 "(B) Application of section 1248. For purposes of subparagraph (A), the rules of section 1248(d) shall apply except to the extent otherwise provided by the Secretary."

In 1997, P.L. 105-34, Sec. 1013(a), substituted "To the extent that such distribution is treated as a distribution to which section 301 applies, the transferor and the acquiring corporation shall be treated in the same manner as if the transferor had transferred the stock so acquired to the acquiring corporation in exchange for stock of the acquiring corporation in a transaction to which section 351(a) applies, and then the acquiring corporation had redeemed the stock it was treated as issuing in such transaction." for "To the extent that such distribution is treated as a distribution to which section 301 applies, the stock so acquired shall be treated as having been transferred by the person from whom acquired, and as having been received by the corporation acquiring it, as a contribution to the capital of such corporation." at the end of para. (a)(1) . . . Sec. 1013(c), added para. (b)(5), effective for distributions and acquisitions after 6/8/97. Sec. 1013(d)((2) of this Act provides:
 "(2) Transition rule. The amendments made by this section shall not apply to any distribution or acquisition after June 8, 1997, if such distribution or acquisition is—
 "(A) made pursuant to a written agreement which was binding on such date and at all times thereafter,
 "(B) described in a ruling request submitted to the Internal Revenue Service on or before such date, or

"(C) described in a public announcement or filing with the Securities and Exchange Commission on or before such date."

In **1988,** P.L. 100-647, Sec. 2004(k)(2), substituted "stock from 1 member" for "stock of 1 member" in subpara. (b)(4)(A) effective for distributions or transfers after 12/15/87, except as provided in Sec. 10223(d)(2)(A) through (d)(2)(D) [as amended by Sec. 2004(k)(3) of this Act, see below] of this Act, reproduced below.

—P.L. 100-647, Sec. 2004(k)(3), added Sec. 10223(d)(2)(D) to P.L. 100-203 [reproduced below], part of the effective date for changes made by Sec. 10223(c) of P.L. 100-203, see below... Sec. 2004(k)(4)(A), and (B), amended Sec. 10223(d)(2)(B) of P.L. 100-203 [reproduced below] by substituting "on or before March 31, 1988" for "before January 1, 1993" and by deleting "before January 1, 1989," after "affiliated group", see below.

In **1987,** P.L. 100-203, Sec. 10223(c), added para. (b)(4), effective for distributions or transfers after 12/15/87, except as provided in Sec. 10223(d)(2)(A) through (d)(2)(D) [as amended by Sec. 2004(k)(3) of P.L. 100-647, see above], which reads as follows:

"(2) Exceptions

"(A) Distributions. The amendments made by this section shall not apply to any distribution after December 15, 1987, and before January 1, 1993, if —

"(i) 80 percent or more of the stock of the distributing corporation was acquired by the distributee before December 15, 1987, or

"(ii) 80 percent or more of the stock of the distributing corporation was acquired by the distributee before January 1, 1989, pursuant to a binding written contract or tender offer in effect on December 15, 1987.

For purposes of the preceding sentence, stock described in section 1504(a)(4) of the Internal Revenue Code of 1986 shall not be taken into account.

"(B) Section 304 transfers. The amendment made by subsection (c) shall not apply to any transfer after December 15, 1987, and on or before March 31, 1988, if such transfer is —

"(i) between corporations which are members of the same affiliated group on December 15, 1987, or

"(ii) between corporations which become members of the same affiliated group pursuant to a binding written contract or tender offer in effect on December 15, 1987.

"(C) Distributions covered by prior transition rule. The amendments made by this section shall not apply to any distribution to which the amendments made by subtitle D of title VI of the Tax Reform Act of 1986 do not apply.

"(D) Treatment of certain members of affiliated group.

"(i) In general. For purposes of subparagraph (A), all corporations which were in existence on the designated date and were members of the same affiliated group which included the distributee on such date shall be treated as 1 distributee.

"(ii) Limitation to stock held on designated date. Clause (i) shall not exempt any distribution from the amendments made by this section if such distribution is with respect to stock not held by the distributee (determined without regard to clause (i)) on the designated date directly or indirectly through a corporation which goes out of existence in the transaction.

"(iii) Designated date. For purposes of this subparagraph, the term 'designated date' means the later of —

"(I) December 15, 1987, or

"(II) the date on which the acquisition meeting the requirements of subparagraph (A) occurred."

In **1986,** P.L. 99-514, Sec. 1875(b), substituted "To the extent that such distribution is treated as a distribution to which section 301 applies" for "In any such case" in para. (a)(1), effective for stock acquired after 6/18/84, in tax. yrs. end. after 6/18/84, except as provided in Sec. 712(l)(7)(B) and (C) of P.L. 98-369, reproduced below.

In **1984,** P.L. 98-369, Sec. 712(l)(1), amended para. (b)(2), effective for stock acquired after 6/18/84, in tax. yrs. ending after 6/18/84. Sec. 712(l)(7)(B) and (C) of this Act provides:

"(B) Election by taxpayer to have amendments apply earlier. Any taxpayer may elect, at such time and in such manner as the Secretary of the Treasury or his delegate may prescribe, to have the amendments made by paragraphs (1) and (3) apply as if included in section 226 of the Tax Equity and Fiscal Responsibility Act of 1982.

"(C) Special rule for certain transfers to form bank holding company. Except as provided in subparagraph (D), the amendments made by paragraphs (1) and (3) shall not apply to transfers pursuant to an application to form a BHC (as defined in section 3(a)(3)(D)(ii) of the Internal Revenue Code of 1954) filed with the Federal Reserve Board before June 18, 1984, if —

"(i) such BHC was formed not later than the 90th day after the date of the last required approval of any regulatory authority to form such BHC, and

"(ii) such BHC did not elect (at such time and in such manner as the Secretary of the Treasury or his delegate shall prescribe) not to have the provisions of this subparagraph apply."

Prior to amendment, para. (b)(2) read as follows:

"(2) Amount constituting dividend.

"(A) Where subsection (a)(1) applies. In the case of any acquisition of stock to which paragraph (1) (and not paragraph (2)) of subsection (a) of this section applies, the determination of the amount which is a dividend shall be made as if the property were distributed by the issuing corporation to the acquiring corporation and immediately thereafter distributed by the acquiring corporation.

"(B) Where subsection (a)(2) applies. In the case of any acquisition of stock to which subsection (a)(2) of this section applies, the determination of the amount which is a dividend shall be made as if the property were distributed by the acquiring corporation to the issuing corporation and immediately thereafter distributed by the issuing corporation."

—P.L. 98-369, Sec. 712(l)(2), substituted "(and not section 351 and not so much of sections 357 and 358 as relates to section 351)" for "(and not part III)" in subpara. (b)(3)(A), effective for transfers occurring after 8/31/82, in tax. yrs. ending after 8/31/82.

—P.L. 98-369, Sec. 712(l)(3)(A), substituted "In the case of an acquisition described in section 351, subsection (a)" for "Subsection (a)" in clause (b)(3)(B)(i), effective for acquisition of any stock to the extent the liability assumed, or to which such stock is subject, was incurred by the transferor after 10/20/83.

—P.L. 98-369, Sec. 712(l)(3)(B), added clause (b)(3)(B)(iii), effective for stock acquired after 6/18/84, in tax. yrs. ending after 6/18/84. For special rules, see Sec. 712(l)(7)(B) and (C) of this Act reproduced above.

—P.L. 98-369, Sec. 712(l)(4), added a sentence at the end of subpara. (b)(3)(C) ... Sec. 712(l)(5)(A), amended para. (c)(3), effective for transfers occurring after 8/31/82, in tax. yrs. ending after 8/31/82.

Prior to amendment, para. (c)(3) read as follows:

"(3) Constructive ownership. Section 318(a) (relating to the constructive ownership of stock) shall apply for purposes of determining control under this section. For purposes of the preceding sentence, sections 318(a)(2)(C) and 318(a)(3)(C) shall be applied without regard to the 50 percent limitation contained therein."

In **1982,** P.L. 97-248, Sec. 226(a)(1)(A), added para. (b)(3) ... Sec. 226(a)(2)(A), redesignated para. (c)(2) as (3) and added para. (c)(2) ... Sec. 226(a)(2)(B), substituted "this section" for "paragraph (1)" in para. (c)(3) [as redesignated by Sec. 226(a)(2)(A) of this Act, see above] ... Sec. 226(a)(3), amended subpara. (b)(2)(A), effective for transfers occurring after 8/31/82, in tax. yrs. ending after 8/31/82. Sec. 226(c)(2) of this Act provides:

"(2) Approval by federal reserve board. The amendments made by this section shall not apply to transfers pursuant to an application to form a BHC filed with the Federal Reserve Board before August 16, 1982, if the BHC was formed not later than the later of —

"(A) the 90th day after the date of the last required approval of any regulatory authority to form such BHC, or

"(B) January 1, 1983.

For purposes of this paragraph, the term 'BHC' means a bank holding company (within the meaning of section 2(a) of the Bank Holding Company Act of 1956)."

Prior to amendment, subpara. (b)(2)(A) read as follows

"(A) Where subsection (a)(1) applies. In the case of any acquisition of stock to which paragraph (1) (and not paragraph (2)) of subsection (a) of this section applies, the determination of the amount which is a dividend shall be made solely by reference to the earnings and profits of the acquiring corporation."

In **1964,** P.L. 88-554, Sec. 4(b)(1), substituted "sections 318(a)(2)(C) and 318(a)(3)(C)" for "section 318(a)(2)(C)" in paras. (b)(1) and (c)(2), effective 8/31/64 except for distributions in payment for stock acquisitions or redemptions, if such acquisitions or redemptions occurred before 8/31/64.

Sec. 305. Distributions of stock and stock rights.
(a) General rule.

Except as otherwise provided in this section, gross income does not include the amount of any distribution of the stock of a corporation made by such corporation to its shareholders with respect to its stock.

(b) Exceptions.

Subsection (a) shall not apply to a distribution by a corporation of its stock, and the distribution shall be treated as a distribution of property to which section 301 applies —

(1) Distributions in lieu of money. If the distribution is, at the election of any of the shareholders (whether exercised before or after the declaration thereof), payable either —

(A) in its stock, or

(B) in property.

(2) Disproportionate distributions. If the distribution (or a series of distributions of which such distribution is one) has the result of —

(A) the receipt of property by some shareholders, and

(B) an increase in the proportionate interests of other shareholders in the assets or earnings and profits of the corporation.

(3) Distributions of common and preferred stock. If the distribution (or a series of distributions of which such distribution is one) has the result of —

(A) the receipt of preferred stock by some common shareholders, and

(B) the receipt of common stock by other common shareholders.

(4) Distributions on preferred stock. If the distribution is with respect to preferred stock, other than an increase in the conversion ratio of convertible preferred stock made solely to take account of a stock dividend or stock split with respect to the stock into which such convertible stock is convertible.

(5) Distributions of convertible preferred stock. If the distribution is of convertible preferred stock, unless it is established to the satisfaction of the Secretary that such distribution will not have the result described in paragraph (2).

(c) Certain transactions treated as distributions.

For purposes of this section and section 301, the Secretary shall prescribe regulations under which a change in conversion ratio, a change in redemption price, a difference between redemption price and issue price, a redemption which is treated as a distribution to which section 301 applies, or any transaction (including a recapitalization) having a similar effect on the interest of any shareholder shall be treated as a distribution with respect to any shareholder whose proportionate interest in the earnings and profits or assets of the corporation is increased by such change, difference, redemption, or similar transaction. Regulations prescribed under the preceding sentence shall provide that—

(1) where the issuer of stock is required to redeem the stock at a specified time or the holder of stock has the option to require the issuer to redeem the stock, a redemption premium resulting from such requirement or option shall be treated as reasonable only if the amount of such premium does not exceed the amount determined under the principles of section 1273(a)(3);

(2) a redemption premium shall not fail to be treated as a distribution (or series of distributions) merely because the stock is callable, and

(3) in any case in which a redemption premium is treated as a distribution (or series of distributions), such premium shall be taken into account under principles similar to the principles of section 1272(a).

(d) Definitions.

(1) Rights to acquire stock. For purposes of this section, the term "stock" includes rights to acquire such stock.

(2) Shareholders. For purposes of subsections (b) and (c), the term "shareholder" includes a holder of rights or of convertible securities.

(e) Treatment of purchaser of stripped preferred stock.

(1) In general. If any person purchases after April 30, 1993, any stripped preferred stock, then such person, while holding such stock, shall include in gross income amounts equal to the amounts which would have been so includible if such stripped preferred stock were a bond issued on the purchase date and having original issue discount equal to the excess, if any, of—

(A) the redemption price for such stock, over

(B) the price at which such person purchased such stock.

The preceding sentence shall also apply in the case of any person whose basis in such stock is determined by reference to the basis in the hands of such purchaser.

(2) Basis adjustments. Appropriate adjustments to basis shall be made for amounts includible in gross income under paragraph (1).

(3) Tax treatment of person stripping stock. If any person strips the rights to 1 or more dividends from any stock described in paragraph (5)(B) and after April 30, 1993, disposes of such dividend rights, for purposes of paragraph (1), such person shall be treated as having purchased the stripped preferred stock on the date of such disposition for a purchase price equal to such person's adjusted basis in such stripped preferred stock.

(4) Amounts treated as ordinary income. Any amount included in gross income under paragraph (1) shall be treated as ordinary income.

(5) Stripped preferred stock. For purposes of this subsection—

(A) In general. The term "stripped preferred stock" means any stock described in subparagraph (B) if there has been a separation in ownership between such stock and any dividend on such stock which has not become payable.

(B) Description of stock. Stock is described in this subsection if such stock—

(i) is limited and preferred as to dividends and does not participate in corporate growth to any significant extent, and

(ii) has a fixed redemption price.

(6) Purchase. For purposes of this subsection, the term "purchase" means—

(A) any acquisition of stock, where

(B) the basis of such stock is not determined in whole or in part by the reference to the adjusted basis of such stock in the hands of the person from whom acquired.

(7) Cross reference. For treatment of stripped interests in certain accounts or entities holding preferred stock, see section 1286(f).

(f) Cross references.

For special rules—

(1) Relating to the receipt of stock and stock rights in corporate organizations and reorganizations, see part III (sec. 351 and following).

(2) In the case of a distribution which results in a gift, see section 2501 and following.

(3) In the case of a distribution which has the effect of the payment of compensation, see section 61(a)(1).

In 2004, P.L. 108-357, Sec. 831(b), added para. (e)(7), effective for purchases and dispositions after 10/22/2004.

In 1993, P.L. 103-66, Sec. 13206(c)(1), redesignated subsec. (e) as (f) and added subsec. (e), effective 4/30/93.

In 1990, P.L. 101-508, Sec. 11322(a), added the sentence at the end of subsec. (c), effective for stock issued after 10/9/90, except as provided in Sec. 11322(b)(2) of this Act, which reads as follows:

"(2) Exception. The amendment made by subsection (a) shall not apply to any stock issued after October 9, 1990, if—

"(A) such stock is issued pursuant to a written binding contract in effect on October 9, 1990, and at all times thereafter before such issuance,

"(B) such stock is issued pursuant to a registration or offering statement filed on or before October 9, 1990, with a Federal or State agency regulating the offering or sale of securities and such stock is issued before the date 90 days after the date of such filing, or

"(C) such stock is issued pursuant to a plan filed on or before October 9, 1990, in a title 11 or similar case (as defined in section 368(a)(3)(A) of the Internal Revenue Code of 1986)."

—P.L. 101-508, Sec. 11801(a)(17), deleted subsec. (e)... Sec. 11801(c)(7)(A), deleted "(other than subsection (e))" after "this section" in para. (d)(1)... Sec. 11801(c)(7)(B), redesignated subsec. (f) as (e), effective 11/5/90, except as provided in Sec. 11821(b) of this Act, which reads as follows:

"(b) Savings provision. If—

"(1) any provision amended or repealed by this part applied to—

"(A) any transaction occurring before the date of the enactment of this Act [11/5/90],

"(B) any property acquired before such date of enactment [11/5/90], or

"(C) any item of income, loss, deduction, or credit taken into account before such date of enactment [11/5/90], and

"(2) the treatment of such transaction, property, or item under such provision would (without regard to the amendments made by this part) affect liability for tax for periods ending after such date of enactment [11/5/90],

nothing in the amendments made by this part shall be construed to affect the treatment of such transaction, property, or item for purposes of determining liability for tax for periods ending after such date of enactment [11/5/90]."

Prior to deletion, subsec. (e) read as follows:

"(e) Dividend reinvestment in stock of public utilities.

"(1) In general. Subsection (b) shall not apply to any qualified reinvested dividend.

"(2) Qualified reinvested dividend defined. For purposes of this subsection, the term 'qualified reinvested dividend' means—

"(A) a distribution by a qualified public utility of shares of its qualified common stock to an individual with respect to the common or preferred stock of such corporation pursuant to a plan under which shareholders may elect to receive dividends in the form of stock instead of property, but

"(B) only if the shareholder elects to have this subsection apply to such shares.

"(3) Qualified public utility defined.

"(A) In general. For purposes of this subsection, the term 'qualified public utility' means, for any taxable year of the corporation, a domestic corporation which, for the 10-year period ending on the day before the beginning of the taxable year, placed in service qualified long-life public utility property having a cost equal to at least 60 percent of the aggregate cost of all tangible property described in subparagraph (A) or (B) of section 1245(a)(3) placed in service by the corporation during such period.

"(B) Special rules. For purposes of subparagraph (A)—

"(i) all members of an affiliated group shall be treated as one corporation,

"(ii) a successor corporation shall take into account the acquisitions of its predecessor, and

"(iii) a new corporation to which clause (ii) does not apply shall substitute its period of existence for the 10-year period set forth in subparagraph (A).

"(C) Definitions. For purposes of this paragraph—

"(i) Affiliated group. The term 'affiliated group' has the meaning given to such term by subsection (a) of section 1504 (determined without regard to subsection (b) of section 1504).

"(ii) Qualified long-life public utility property. The term 'qualified long-life public utility property' means any tangible property which—

"(I) is described in subparagraph (A) or (B) of section 1245(a)(3),

"(II) has a present class life (as defined in section 168(g)(2)) of more than 18 years, and

"(III) is public utility property (within the meaning of section 167(1)(3)(A)).

"(4) Qualified common stock defined.

"(A) In general. For purposes of this subsection, the term 'qualified common stock' means authorized but unissued common stock of the corporation—

"(i) which has been designated by the board of directors of the corporation as issued for purposes of this subsection, but

"(ii) only if the number of shares to be issued to a shareholder was determined by reference to a value which is not less than 95 percent and not more than 105 percent of the stock's fair market value during the period immediately before the distribution (determined under regulations prescribed by the Secretary).

"(B) Certain purchases by corporation of its own stock. Except as provided in subparagraph (D), if a corporation has purchased or purchases its common stock within a 2-year period beginning 1 year before the date of the distribution and ending 1 year after such date, such distribution shall be treated as not being a qualified reinvested dividend.

"(C) Members of affiliated group. For purposes of subparagraph (B), the purchase by any corporation which is a member of the same affiliated group (as defined in paragraph (3)(C)(i)) as the distributing corporation of common stock in any corporation which is a member of such group from any person (other than a member of such group) shall be treated as a purchase by the distributing corporation of its common stock.

"(D) Waiver of subparagraph (B) where there is business purpose. Under regulations prescribed by the Secretary, subparagraph (B) shall not apply where the distributing corporation establishes that there was a business purpose for the purchase of the stock and such purchase is not inconsistent with the purposes of this subsection.

"(5) Share includes fractional share. For purposes of this subsection, the term 'share' includes a fractional share.

"(6) Limitation.

"(A) In general. In the case of any individual, the aggregate amount of distributions to which this subsection applies for the taxable year shall not exceed $750 ($1,500 in the case of a joint return).

"(B) Application of ceiling. If, but for this subparagraph, a share of stock would, by reason of subparagraph (A), be treated as partly within this subsection and partly outside this subsection, such share shall be treated as outside this subsection.

"(7) Basis and holding period. In the case of stock received as a qualified reinvested dividend—

"(A) notwithstanding section 307, the basis shall be zero, and

"(B) the holding period shall begin on the date the dividend would (but for this subsection) be includible in income.

"(8) Election. An election under this subsection with respect to any share shall be made on the shareholder's return for the taxable year in which the dividend would (but for this subsection) be includible in income. Any such election, once made, shall be revocable only with the consent of the Secretary.

"(9) Dispositions within 1 year of distribution. Under regulations prescribed by the Secretary—

"(A) Disposition of other common stock. If—

"(i) a shareholder receives any qualified reinvested dividend from a corporation, and

"(ii) during the period which begins on the record date for the qualified reinvested dividend and ends 1 year after the date of the distribution of such dividend, the shareholder disposes of any common stock of such corporation,

"the shareholder shall be treated as having disposed of the stock received as a qualified reinvested dividend (to the extent there remains such stock to which this paragraph has not applied).

"(B) Ordinary income treatment. If any stock received as a qualified reinvested dividend is disposed of within 1 year after the date such stock is distributed, such disposition shall be treated as a disposition of property which is not a capital asset.

"(10) No reduction in earnings and profits for distribution of qualified common stock. The earnings and profits of any corporation shall not be reduced by reason of the distribution of any qualified common stock of such corporation pursuant to a plan under which shareholders may elect to receive dividends in the form of stock instead of property.

"(11) Certain individuals ineligible.

"(A) In general. This subsection shall not apply to any individual who is—

"(i) a trust or estate, or

"(ii) a nonresident alien individual.

"(B) 5 percent shareholders ineligible. Any distribution by a corporation to a 5 percent shareholder in such corporation shall not be treated as a qualified reinvested dividend.

"(C) 5 percent shareholder defined. For purposes of subparagraph (B), the term '5 percent shareholder' means any individual who, immediately before the distribution, owns (directly or through the application of section 318)—

"(i) stock possessing more than 5 percent of the total combined voting power of the distributing corporation, or

"(ii) more than 5 percent of the total value of all classes of stock of the distributing corporation.

"(12) Termination. This subsection shall not apply to distributions after December 31, 1985."

In 1983, P.L. 97-448, Sec. 103(f)(1), amended subpara. (e)(3)(A) . . . Sec. 103(f)(2), amended clause (e)(3)(C)(ii), effective for distributions after 12/31/81 in tax. yrs. end. after 12/31/81.

Prior to amendment, subpara. (e)(3)(A) read as follows:

"(A) In general. For purposes of this subsection, the term 'qualified public utility' means, for any taxable year of the corporation, a domestic corporation which, for the 10-year period ending on the day before the beginning of the taxable year, acquired public utility recovery property having a cost equal to at least 60 percent of the aggregate cost of all tangible property described in section 1245(a)(3) (other than subparagraph (C) and (D) thereof) acquired by the corporation during such period."

Prior to amendment, clause (e)(3)(C)(ii) read as follows:

"(ii) Public utility recovery property. The term 'public utility recovery property' means public utility property (within the meaning of section 167(1)(3)(A)) which is recovery property which is 10-year property or 15-year public utility property (within the meaning of section 168), except that any requirement that the property be placed in service after December 31, 1980, shall not apply."

In 1981, P.L. 97-34, Sec. 321(a), redesignated subsec. (e) as (f) and added subsec. (e) . . . Sec. 321(b), substituted "this section (other than subsection (e))" for "this section" in para. (d)(1), effective for distributions after 12/31/81, in tax. yrs. end. after 12/31/81.

In 1976, P.L. 94-455, Sec. 1906(b)(13)(A), substituted "Secretary" for "Secretary or his delegate" each place it appeared in Code Sec. 305, effective for tax. yrs. begin. after 12/31/76.

In 1969, P.L. 91-172, Sec. 421(a), amended Code Sec. 305. Sec. 421(b) of this Act provides:

"(1) Except as otherwise provided in this subsection, the amendment made shall apply with respect to distributions (or deemed distributions) made after January 10, 1969, in taxable years ending after such date.

"(2)(A) Section 305(b)(2) of the Internal Revenue Code of 1954 shall not apply to a distribution (or deemed distribution) of stock made before January 1, 1991, with respect to stock (i) outstanding on January 10, 1969, (ii) issued pursuant to a contract binding on January 10, 1969, on the distributing corporation, (iii) which is additional stock of that class of stock which (as of January 10, 1969) had the largest fair market value of stock of the corporation (taking into account all classes of stock of the corporation (taking into account only stock outstanding on January 10, 1969, or issued pursuant to a contract binding on January 10, 1969), (iv) described in subparagraph (C)(iii), or (v) issued in a prior distribution described in clause (i), (ii), (iii), or (v).

"(B) Subparagraph (A) shall apply only if—

"(i) the stock as to which there is a receipt of property was outstanding on January 10, 1969 (or was issued pursuant to a contract binding on January 10, 1969 on the distributing corporation), and

"(ii) if such stock and any stock described in subparagraph (A)(i) were also outstanding on January 10, 1968, a distribution of property was made on or before January 10, 1969, with respect to such stock, and a distribution of stock was made on or before January 10, 1969, with respect to such stock described in subparagraph (A)(i).

"(C) Subparagraph (A) shall cease to apply when at any time after October 9, 1969, the distributing corporation issues any of its stock (other than in a distribution of stock with respect to stock of the same class) which is not—

"(i) nonconvertible preferred stock,

"(ii) additional stock of that class of stock which meets the requirements of subparagraph (A)(iii), or

"(iii) preferred stock which is convertible into stock which meets the requirements of subparagraph (A)(iii) at a fixed conversion ratio which takes account of all stock dividends and stock splits with respect to the stock into which such convertible stock is convertible.

Corporate distributions and adjustments — Code Sec. 306(c)(1)(C)

"(D) For purposes of this paragraph, the term 'stock' includes rights to acquire such stock.

"(3) In cases to which Treasury Decision 6990 (promulgated January 10, 1969) would not have applied, in applying paragraphs (1) and (2) April 22, 1969, shall be substituted for January 10, 1969

"(4) Section 305(b)(4) of the Internal Revenue Code of 1954 (as added by subsection (a)) shall not apply to any distribution (or deemed distribution) with respect to preferred stock (including any increase in the conversion ratio of convertible stock) made before January 1, 1991, pursuant to the terms relating to the issuance of such stock which were in effect on January 10, 1969.

"(5) With respect to distributions made or considered as made after January 10, 1969, in taxable years ending after such date, to the extent that the amendment made by subsection (a) does not apply by reason of paragraph (2), (3), or (4) of this subsection, section 305 of the Internal Revenue Code of 1954 (as in effect before the amendment made by subsection (a)) shall continue to apply."

Prior to amendment Code Sec. 305 read as follows:

"(a) General rule. Except as provided in subsection (b), gross income does not include the amount of any distribution made by a corporation to its shareholders, with respect to the stock of such corporation, in its stock or in rights to acquire its stock.

"(b) Distributions in lieu of money. Subsection (a) shall not apply to a distribution by a corporation of its stock (or rights to acquire its stock), and the distribution shall be treated as a distribution of property to which section 301 applies—

"(1) to the extent that the distribution is made in discharge of preference dividends for the taxable year of the corporation in which the distribution is made or for the preceding taxable year; or

"(2) if the distribution is, at the election of any of the shareholders (whether exercised before or after the declaration thereof) payable either—

"(A) in its stock (or in rights to acquire its stock), or

"(B) in property.

"(c) Cross references. For special rules—

"(1) Relating to the receipt of stock and stock rights in corporate organizations and reorganizations, see part III (sec 351 and following).

"(2) In the case of a distribution which results in a gift, see section 2501 and following.

"(3) In the case of a distribution which has the effect of the payment of compensation, see section 61(a)(1)."

Sec. 306. Dispositions of certain stock.

(a) General rule.

If a shareholder sells or otherwise disposes of section 306 stock (as defined in subsection (c))—

(1) Dispositions other than redemptions. If such disposition is not a redemption (within the meaning of section 317(b))—

(A) The amount realized shall be treated as ordinary income. This subparagraph shall not apply to the extent that—

(i) the amount realized, exceeds

(ii) such stock's ratable share of the amount which would have been a dividend at the time of distribution if (in lieu of section 306 stock) the corporation had distributed money in an amount equal to the fair market value of the stock at the time of distribution.

(B) Any excess of the amount realized over the sum of—

(i) the amount treated under subparagraph (A) as ordinary income, plus

(ii) the adjusted basis of the stock,

shall be treated as gain from the sale of such stock.

(C) No loss shall be recognized.

> • **Caution:** Code Sec. 306(a)(1)(D), following, was added by Sec. 302(e)(3), P.L. 108-27. This provision generally sunsets for tax years beginning after 12/31/2012. For specific sunset provisions, see Sec. 303, P.L. 108-27, as amended by Sec. 102(a), P.L. 111-312, reproduced in history notes for this Code Sec.

(D) Treatment as dividend. For purposes of section 1(h)(11) and such other provisions as the Secretary may specify, any amount treated as ordinary income under this paragraph shall be treated as a dividend received from the corporation.

(2) Redemption. If the disposition is a redemption, the amount realized shall be treated as a distribution of property to which section 301 applies.

(b) Exceptions.

Subsection (a) shall not apply—

(1) Termination of shareholder's interest, etc.

(A) Not in redemption. If the disposition—

(i) is not a redemption;

(ii) is not, directly or indirectly, to a person the ownership of whose stock would (under section 318(a)) be attributable to the shareholder; and

(iii) terminates the entire stock interest of the shareholder in the corporation (and for purposes of this clause, section 318(a) shall apply).

(B) In redemption. If the disposition is a redemption and paragraph (3) or (4) of section 302(b) applies.

(2) Liquidations. If the section 306 stock is redeemed in a distribution in complete liquidation to which part II (sec. 331 and following) applies.

(3) Where gain or loss is not recognized. To the extent that, under any provision of this subtitle, gain or loss to the shareholder is not recognized with respect to the disposition of the section 306 stock.

(4) Transactions not in avoidance. If it is established to the satisfaction of the Secretary—

(A) that the distribution, and the disposition or redemption, or

(B) in the case of a prior or simultaneous disposition (or redemption) of the stock with respect to which the section 306 stock disposed of (or redeemed) was issued, that the disposition (or redemption) of the section 306 stock,

was not in pursuance of a plan having as one of its principal purposes the avoidance of Federal income tax.

(c) Section 306 stock defined.

(1) In general. For purposes of this subchapter, the term "section 306 stock" means stock which meets the requirements of subparagraph (A), (B), or (C) of this paragraph.

(A) Distributed to seller. Stock (other than common stock issued with respect to common stock) which was distributed to the shareholder selling or otherwise disposing of such stock if, by reason of section 305(a), any part of such distribution was not includible in the gross income of the shareholder.

(B) Received in a corporate reorganization or separation. Stock which is not common stock and—

(i) which was received, by the shareholder selling or otherwise disposing of such stock, in pursuance of a plan of reorganization (within the meaning of section 368(a)), or in a distribution or exchange to which section 355 (or so much of section 356 as relates to section 355) applied, and

(ii) with respect to the receipt of which gain or loss to the shareholder was to any extent not recognized by reason of part III, but only to the extent that either the effect of the transaction was substantially the same as the receipt of a stock dividend, or the stock was received in exchange for section 306 stock.

For purposes of this section, a receipt of stock to which the foregoing provisions of this subparagraph apply shall be treated as a distribution of stock.

(C) Stock having transferred or substituted basis. Except as otherwise provided in subparagraph (B), stock the basis of which (in the hands of the shareholder selling or otherwise disposing of such stock) is determined by reference to the basis (in the hands of such shareholder or any other person) of section 306 stock.

(2) Exception where no earnings and profits. For purposes of this section, the term "section 306 stock" does not include any stock, no part of the distribution of which would have been a dividend at the time of the distribution if money had been distributed in lieu of the stock.

(3) Certain stock acquired in section 351 exchange. The term "section 306 stock" also includes any stock which is not common stock acquired in an exchange to which section 351 applied if receipt of money (in lieu of the stock) would have been treated as a dividend to any extent. Rules similar to the rules of section 304(b)(2) shall apply—

(A) for purposes of the preceding sentence, and

(B) for purposes of determining the application of this section to any subsequent disposition of stock which is section 306 stock by reason of an exchange described in the preceding sentence.

(4) Application of attribution rules for certain purposes. For purposes of paragraphs (1)(B)(ii) and (3), section 318(a) shall apply. For purposes of applying the preceding sentence to paragraph (3), the rules of section 304(c)(3)(B) shall apply.

(d) Stock rights.

For purposes of this section—

(1) stock rights shall be treated as stock, and

(2) stock acquired through the exercise of stock rights shall be treated as stock distributed at the time of the distribution of the stock rights, to the extent of the fair market value of such rights at the time of the distribution.

(e) Convertible stock.

For purposes of subsection (c)—

(1) if section 306 stock was issued with respect to common stock and later such section 306 stock is exchanged for common stock in the same corporation (whether or not such exchange is pursuant to a conversion privilege contained in the section 306 stock), then (except as provided in paragraph (2)) the common stock so received shall not be treated as section 306 stock; and

(2) common stock with respect to which there is a privilege of converting into stock other than common stock (or into property), whether or not the conversion privilege is contained in such stock, shall not be treated as common stock.

(f) Source of gain.

The amount treated under subsection (a)(1)(A) as ordinary income shall, for purposes of part I of subchapter N (sec. 861 and following, relating to determination of sources of income), be treated as derived from the same source as would have been the source if money had been received from the corporation as a dividend at the time of the distribution of such stock. If under the preceding sentence such amount is determined to be derived from sources within the United States, such amount shall be considered to be fixed or determinable annual or periodical gains, profits, and income within the meaning of section 871(a) or section 881(a), as the case may be.

(g) Change in terms and conditions of stock.

If a substantial change is made in the terms and conditions of any stock, then, for purposes of this section—

(1) the fair market value of such stock shall be the fair market value at the time of the distribution or at the time of such change, whichever such value is higher;

(2) such stock's ratable share of the amount which would have been a dividend if money had been distributed in lieu of stock shall be determined as of the time of distribution or as of the time of such change, whichever such ratable share is higher; and

(3) subsection (c)(2) shall not apply unless the stock meets the requirements of such subsection both at the time of such distribution and at the time of such change.

In **2010,** P.L. 111-312, Sec. 102(a), substituted "December 31, 2012" for "December 31, 2010" in Sec. 303 of P.L. 108-27 [see below], effective as if included in the enactment of P.L. 108-27, 5/28/2003.

In **2006,** P.L. 109-222, Sec. 102, substituted "December 31, 2010" for "December 31, 2008" in Sec. 303 of P.L. 108-27 [see below], effective 5/17/2006.

In **2004,** P.L. 108-311, Sec. 402(a)(6), of this Act [which amended Sec. 302(f)(2) of P.L. 108-27, see below], provides:

"(2) Pass-thru entities. In the case of a pass-thru entity described in subparagraph (A), (B), (C), (D), (E), or (F) of section 1(h)(10) of the Internal Revenue Code of 1986, as amended by this Act, the amendments made by this section shall apply to taxable years ending after December 31, 2002; except that dividends received by such an entity on or before such date shall not be treated as qualified dividend income (as defined in section 1(h)(11)(B) of such Code, as added by this Act)."

In **2003,** P.L. 108-27, Sec. 302(e)(3), added subpara. (a)(1)(D), effective for tax. yrs. begin. after 12/31/2002. Sec. 302(f)(2), of this Act [prior to amendment by Sec. 402(a)(6) of P.L. 108-311 see above] provides:

"(2) Regulated investment companies and real estate investment trusts. In the case of a regulated investment company or a real estate investment trust, the amendments made by this section shall apply to taxable years ending after December 31, 2002; except that dividends received by such a company or trust on or before such date shall not be treated as qualified dividend income (as defined in section 1(h)(11)(B) of the Internal Revenue Code of 1986, as added by this Act)."

—P.L. 108-27, Sec. 303, of this Act [as amended by Sec. 102, P.L. 109-222, and Sec. 102(a), P.L. 111-312, see above], reads as follows:

"Sec. 303. Sunset of title. All provisions of, and amendments made by, this title [Secs. 301 and 302] shall not apply to taxable years beginning after December 31, 2012, and the Internal Revenue Code of 1986 shall be applied and administered to such years as if such provisions and amendments had never been enacted."

In **1990,** P.L. 101-508, Sec. 11801(a)(18), deleted subsec. (h), effective 11/5/90, except as provided in Sec. 11821(b) of this Act, reproduced in note following Code Sec. 305.

Prior to deletion, subsec. (h) read as follows:

"(h) Stock received in distributions and reorganizations to which 1939 Code applied. If stock—

"(1) was received in a distribution or reorganization to which the Internal Revenue Code of 1939 (or the corresponding provisions of prior law) applied,

"(2) such stock would have been section 306 stock if this Code applied to such distribution or reorganization, and

"(3) such stock is disposed of or redeemed on or after June 22, 1954,

then the foregoing subsections of this section shall not apply in respect of such disposition or redemption. The extent to which such disposition or redemption shall be treated as a dividend shall be determined as if the Internal Revenue Code of 1939 (as modified by the provisions of this Code other than the foregoing subsections of this section) continued to apply in respect of such disposition or redemption."

In **1984,** P.L. 98-369, Sec. 712(i)(2), substituted ", interest, etc." for "interest" in the heading for para. (b)(1), effective for distributions after 8/31/82.

—P.L. 98-369, Sec. 712(l)(5)(B), amended para. (c)(4) . . . Sec. 712(l)(6), amended para. (c)(3), effective for transfers occurring after 8/31/82, in tax. yrs. end. after 8/31/82, except as provided in Sec. 226(c)(2) of P.L. 97-248, reproduced in note following Code Sec. 304.

Prior to amendment, paras. (c)(3) and (c)(4) read as follows:

"(3) Certain stock acquired in section 351 exchange. The term 'section 306 stock' also includes any stock which is not common stock acquired in an exchange to which section 351 applied if receipt of money (in lieu of the stock) would have been treated as a dividend to any extent. In the case of such stock, rules similar to the rules of section 304(b)(2) shall apply for purposes of this section.

"(4) Application of attribution rules for certain purposes. For purposes of paragraphs (1)(B)(ii) and (3), section 318(a) shall apply. For purposes of applying the preceding sentence to paragraph (3), sections 318(a)(2)(C) and 318(a)(3)(C) shall be applied without regard to the 50 percent limitation contained therein."

In **1982,** P.L. 97-248, Sec. 222(e)(1)(A), substituted "complete liquidation" for "partial or complete liquidation" in para. (b)(2), . . . Sec. 222(e)(2), substituted "paragraph (3) or (4) of section 302(b)" for "section 302(b)(3)" in subpara. (b)(1)(B), effective for distributions after 8/31/82. For exceptions and special rules see Sec. 222(f)(2)–(4) of this Act reproduced in note following Code Sec. 302.

—P.L. 97-248, Sec. 226(b), added para. (c)(3), effective for transfers occurring after 8/31/82, in tax. yrs. ending after 8/31/82, except as provided in Sec. 226(c)(2) of this Act reproduced in note following Code Sec. 304.

—P.L. 97-248, Sec. 227(a), added para. (c)(4), effective for stock received after 8/31/82, in tax. yrs. ending after 8/31/82.

In **1980,** P.L. 96-223, Sec. 401(a), repealed Sec. 702(a)(1) of P.L. 95-600, which added para. (a)(3), repealed Sec. 702(a)(2) of P.L. 95-600 which added para. (b)(5), and repealed Sec. 702(a)(3), the effective date for changes made by Sec. 702(a)(1) and (2) of P.L. 95-600 effective for decedents dying after 12/31/76 [see below]. Sec. 401(b) of P.L. 96-223 provides as follows:

Corporate distributions and adjustments   Code Sec. 311

"(b) **Revival of prior law.** Except to the extent necessary to carry out subsection (d), the Internal Revenue Code of 1954 shall be applied and administered as if the provisions repealed by subsection (a), and the amendments made by those provisions, had not been enacted."

Prior to the repeal of Sec. 702(a)(1) of P.L. 95-600, which added para. (a)(3), para. (a)(3), read as follows:

"(3) Ordinary income from sale or redemption of section 306 stock which is carryover basis property adjusted for 1976 value.

"(A) In general. If any section 306 stock was distributed before January 1, 1977, and if the adjusted basis of such stock in the hands of the person disposing of it is determined under section 1023 (relating to carryover basis), then the amount treated as ordinary income under paragraph (1)(A) of this subsection (or the amount treated as a dividend under section 301(c)(1)) shall not exceed the excess of the amount realized over the sum of—

"(i) the adjusted basis of such stock on December 31, 1976, and

"(ii) any increase in basis under section 1023(h).

"(B) Redemption must be described in section 302(b). Subparagraph (A) shall apply to a redemption only if such redemption is described in paragraph (1), (2), or (4) of section 302(b)."

Prior to the repeal of Sec. 702(a)(2) of P.L. 95-600, which added para. (b)(5), para. (b)(5) read as follows:

"(5) Section 303 redemptions. To the extent that section 303 applies to a distribution in redemption of section 306 stock."

In 1978, P.L. 95-600, Sec. 702(a)(1), [repealed by Sec. 401(a) of P.L. 96-223, see above], added para. (a)(3) . . . Sec. 702(a)(2), [repealed by Sec. 401(a) of P.L. 96-223, see above], added para. (b)(5), effective [repealed by Sec. 401(a) of P.L. 96-223, see above] for estates of decedents dying after 12/31/79.

In 1976, P.L. 94-455, Sec. 1901(b)(3)(J), substituted "ordinary income" for "gain from the sale of property which is not a capital asset" in subparas. (a)(1)(A) and (B) and subsec. (f), effective for tax. yrs. begin. after 12/31/76.

—P.L. 94-455, Sec. 1906(b)(13)(A), substituted "Secretary" for "Secretary or his delegate" in para. (b)(4), effective for tax. yrs. begin. after 12/31/76.

Sec. 307. Basis of stock and stock rights acquired in distributions.
(a) General rule.

If a shareholder in a corporation receives its stock or rights to acquire its stock (referred to in this subsection as "new stock") in a distribution to which section 305(a) applies, then the basis of such new stock and of the stock with respect to which it is distributed (referred to in this section as "old stock"), respectively, shall, in the shareholder's hands, be determined by allocating between the old stock and the new stock the adjusted basis of the old stock. Such allocation shall be made under regulations prescribed by the Secretary.

(b) Exception for certain stock rights.
(1) In general. If—

(A) a corporation distributes rights to acquire its stock to a shareholder in a distribution to which section 305(a) applies, and

(B) the fair market value of such rights at the time of the distribution is less than 15 percent of the fair market value of the old stock at such time,

then subsection (a) shall not apply and the basis of such rights shall be zero, unless the taxpayer elects under paragraph (2) of this subsection to determine the basis of the old stock and of the stock rights under the method of allocation provided in subsection (a).

(2) **Election.** The election referred to in paragraph (1) shall be made in the return filed within the time prescribed by law (including extensions thereof) for the taxable year in which such rights were received. Such election shall be made in such manner as the Secretary may by regulations prescribe, and shall be irrevocable when made.

(c) Cross reference.

For basis of stock and stock rights distributed before June 22, 1954, see section 1052.

In 1976, P.L. 94-455, Sec. 1906(b)(13)(A), substituted "Secretary" for "Secretary or his delegate" each place it appeared in Code Sec. 307, effective for tax. yrs. begin. after 12/31/76.

SUBPART B.—EFFECTS ON CORPORATION

Sec.
311. Taxability of corporation on distribution.
312. Effect on earnings and profits.

Sec. 311. Taxability of corporation on distribution.
(a) General rule.

Except as provided in subsection (b), no gain or loss shall be recognized to a corporation on the distribution (not in complete liquidation) with respect to its stock of—

(1) its stock (or rights to acquire its stock), or

(2) property.

(b) Distributions of appreciated property.
(1) In general. If—

(A) a corporation distributes property (other than an obligation of such corporation) to a shareholder in a distribution to which subpart A applies, and

(B) the fair market value of such property exceeds its adjusted basis (in the hands of the distributing corporation),

then gain shall be recognized to the distributing corporation as if such property were sold to the distributee at its fair market value.

(2) **Treatment of liabilities.** Rules similar to the rules of section 336(b) shall apply for purposes of this subsection.

(3) **Special rule for certain distributions of partnership or trust interests.** If the property distributed consists of an interest in a partnership or trust, the Secretary may by regulations provide that the amount of the gain recognized under paragraph (1) shall be computed without regard to any loss attributable to property contributed to the partnership or trust for the principal purpose of recognizing such loss on the distribution.

In 1988, P.L. 100-647, Sec. 1006(e)(8)(B), added para. (b)(3) . . . Sec. 1006(e)(21)(B), deleted "in excess of basis" after "liabilities" in the heading of para. (b)(2), effective as provided in Sec. 633(a)(3) and (d)(9) of P.L. 99-514, reproduced below.

—P.L. 100-647, Sec. 1006(e)(3), added Sec. 633(d)(9) of P.L. p9-514 [reproduced below], transitional rules for changes made by Sec. 631(c) of P.L. 99-514, see below.

—P.L. 100-647, Sec. 1018(d)(1), corrected Sec. 1804(b)(3) of P.L. 99-514, to add Sec. 54(d)(3)(D) of P.L. 98-369 instead of Sec. 54(3)(D) of P.L. 98-369, see below.

—P.L. 100-647, Sec. 1018(d)(2), and (3), amended Sec. 54(d)(3)(D) of P.L. 98-369 [reproduced below], part of the effective date for changes made by Sec. 54(a) of P.L. 98-369, by substituting "subtitle D of title VI of the Tax Reform Act of 1986" for "subtitle D of title VI" in Sec. 54(d)(3)(D)(i) of P.L. 98-369, by substituting "December 10, 1968," for "December 9, 1968," each place it appeared in Sec. 54(d)(3)(D)(ii) of P.L. 98-369, and by substituting "March 2, 1978," for "October 5, 1981" in Sec. 54(d)(3)(D)(ii) of P.L. 98-369, see below.

—P.L. 100-647, Sec. 1018(d)(5)(E), substituted "distribution (not in complete liquidation) with respect to its stock" for "distribution, with respect to its stock" in subsec. (a), effective for distributions declared on or after 6/14/84, in tax. yrs. end. after 6/14/84. For exceptions see Sec. 54(d)(3) and (4) of P.L. 98-369, reproduced below.

In 1986, P.L. 99-514, Sec. 631(c), amended Code Sec. 311, effective as provided in Sec. 633(a)(3) and Sec. 633(d)(9) [added by Sec. 1006(g)(6) of P.L. 100-647, see above] of this Act which read as follows:

"(a) *General rule.*—

"Except as otherwise provided in this section, the amendments made by this subtitle shall apply to—
* * *

"(3) any distribution (not in complete liquidation) made after December 31, 1986."

Sec. 633(d)(9) of this Act [as added by Sec. 1006(g)(6) of P.L. 100-647] provides the following:

"(9) Application to nonliquidating distributions.—The provisions of this subsection shall also apply in the case of any distribution (not in complete liquidation) made by a qualified corporation before January 1, 1989, without regard to whether such corporation is completely liquidated."

For other transitional rules, see Sec. 633(d)(1)-(6) of this Act reproduced in the notes following Code Sec. 336.

Prior to amendment, Code Sec. 311 read as follows:

"SEC. 311. TAXABILITY OF CORPORATION ON DISTRIBUTION.

"(a) *General rule.*

1,789

"Except as provided in subsections (b), (c) and (d) of this section and section 453(B), no gain or loss shall be recognized to a corporation on the distribution, with respect to its stock, of—

"(1) its stock (or rights to acquire its stock), or

"(2) property.

"(b) LIFO inventory.

"(1) Recognition of gain. If a corporation inventorying goods under the method provided in section 472 (relating to last-in, first-out inventories) distributes inventory assets (as defined in paragraph (2)(A)), then the amount (if any) by which—

"(A) the inventory amount (as defined in paragraph (2)(B)) of such assets under a method authorized by section 471 (relating to general rule for inventories), exceeds

"(B) the inventory amount of such assets under the method provided in section 472,

shall be treated as gain to the corporation recognized from the sale of such inventory assets.

"(2) Definitions. For purposes of paragraph (1)—

"(A) Inventory assets. The term 'inventory assets' means stock in trade of the corporation, or other property of a kind which would properly be included in the inventory of the corporation if on hand at the close of the taxable year.

"(B) Inventory amount. The term 'inventory amount' means, in the case of inventory assets distributed during a taxable year, the amount of such inventory assets determined as of the time of such distribution.

"(3) Method of determining inventory amount. For purposes of this subsection, the inventory amount of assets under a method authorized by section 471 shall be determined—

"(A) if the corporation uses the retail method of valuing inventories under section 472, by using such method, or

"(B) if subparagraph (A) does not apply, by using cost or market, whichever is lower.

"(c) Liability in excess of basis.

"If—

"(1) a corporation distributes property to a shareholder with respect to its stock,

"(2) such property is subject to a liability, or the shareholder assumes a liability of the corporation in connection with the distribution, and

"(3) the amount of such liability exceeds the adjusted basis (in the hands of the distributing corporation) of such property,

then gain shall be recognized to the distributing corporation in an amount equal to such excess as if the property distributed had been sold at the time of the distribution. In the case of a distribution of property subject to a liability which is not assumed by the shareholder, the amount of gain to be recognized under the preceding sentence shall not exceed the excess, if any, of the fair market value of such property over its adjusted basis.

"(d) Distributions of appreciated property.

"(1) In general. If—

"(A) a corporation distributes property (other than an obligation of such corporation) to a shareholder in a distribution to which subpart A applies, and

"(B) the fair market value of such property exceeds its adjusted basis (in the hands of the distributing corporation),

then gain shall be recognized to the distributing corporation in an amount equal to such excess as if the property distributed had been sold at the time of the distribution. This subsection shall be applied after the application of subsections (b) and (c).

"(2) Exceptions and limitations.

"Paragraph (1) shall not apply to—

"(A) a distribution which is made with respect to qualified stock if—

"(i) section 302(b)(4) applies to such distribution, or

"(ii) such distribution is a qualified dividend;

"(B) a distribution of stock or an obligation of a corporation if the requirements of paragraph (2) of subsection (e) are met with respect to the distribution;

"(C) a distribution to the extent that section 303(a) (relating to distributions in redemption of stock to pay death taxes) applies to such distribution;

"(D) a distribution to a private foundation in redemption of stock which is described in section 537(b)(2)(A) and (B); and

"(E) a distribution by a corporation to which part I of subchapter M (relating to regulated investment companies) applies, if such distribution is in redemption of its stock upon the demand of the shareholder.

"(e) Definitions and special rules for subsection (d)(2).

"For purposes of subsection (d)(2) and this subsection—

"(1) Qualified stock.

"(A) In general. The term 'qualified stock' means stock held by a person (other than a corporation) who at all times during the lesser of—

"(i) the 5-year period ending on the date of distribution, or

"(ii) the period during which the distributing corporation (or a predecessor corporation) was in existence,

held at least 10 percent in value of the outstanding stock of the distributing corporation (or predecessor corporation).

"(B) Determination of stock held. Section 318 shall apply in determining ownership of stock under subparagraph (A); except that, in applying section 318(a)(1), the term 'family' includes any individual described in section 267(c)(4) and any spouse of any such individual.

"(C) Rules for passthru entities. In the case of an S corporation, partnership, trust, or estate—

"(i) the determination of whether subparagraph (A) is satisfied shall be made at the shareholder, partner, or beneficiary level (rather than at the entity level), and

"(ii) the distribution shall be treated as made directly to the shareholders, partners, or beneficiaries in proportion to their respective interests in the entity.

"(2) Distributions of stock or obligations of controlled corporations.

"(A) Requirements. A distribution of stock or an obligation of a corporation (hereinafter in this paragraph referred to as the 'controlled corporation' meets the requirements of this paragraph if—

"(i) such distribution is made with respect to qualified stock,

"(ii) substantially all of the assets of the controlled corporation consists of the assets of 1 or more qualified businesses,

"(iii) no substantial part of the controlled corporation's nonbusiness assets were acquired from the distributing corporation, in a transaction to which section 351 applied or as a contribution to capital, within the 5-year period ending on the date of the distribution, and

"(iv) more than 50 percent in value of the outstanding stock of the controlled corporation is distributed by the distributing corporation with respect to qualified stock.

"(B) Definitions. For purposes of subparagraph (A)—

"(i) Qualified business. The term 'qualified business' means any trade or business which—

"(I) was actively conducted throughout the 5-year period ending on the date of the distribution, and

"(II) was not acquired by any person within such period in a transaction in which gain or loss was recognized in whole or in part.

"(ii) Nonbusiness asset. The term 'nonbusiness asset' means any asset not used in the active conduct of a trade or business.

"(3) Qualified dividend. The term 'qualified dividend' means any distribution of property to a shareholder other than a corporation if—

"(A) such distribution is a dividend,

"(B) such property was used by the distributing corporation in the active conduct of a qualified business (as defined in paragraph (2)), and

"(C) such property is not property described in paragraph (1) or (4) of section 1221."

—P.L. 99-514, Sec. 1804(b)(3), [as amended by Sec. 1018(d)(1) of P.L. 100-647], added Sec. 54(d)(3)(D) to P.L. 98-369 [reproduced below], part of the exception to the effective date for amendments made by Sec. 54(a)(3) of P.L. 98-369, see below.

In 1984, P.L. 98-369, Sec. 54(a)(1), amended para. (d)(1) . . . Sec. 54(a)(2)(A), amended para. (d)(2)(A) and deleted subpara. (d)(2)(B)(B) . . . Sec. 54(a)(2)(B), redesignated paras. (d)(2)(C), (D), (E), and (F) as paras. (d)(2)(B), (C), (D), and (E) . . . Sec. 54(a)(2)(C), added new para. (e)(3) . . . Sec. 54(a)(3), substituted "Distributions of appreciation property." for "Appreciated property used to redeem stock.", in the heading for subsec. (d), effective for distributions declared on or after 6/14/84, in tax. yrs. end. after 6/14/84. Secs. 54(d)(3) and (4) of the Act [as amended by Secs. 1018(d)(2) and (3) of P.L. 100-647 and Sec. 1804(b)(3) of P.L. 99-514, see above] provide the following exceptions:

"(3) Exception for distributions before January 1, 1985, to 80-percent corporate shareholders.—

"(A) In general.—The amendments made by subsection (a) shall not apply to any distribution before January 1, 1985, to an 80-percent corporate shareholder if the basis of the property distributed is determined under section 301(d)(2) of the Internal Revenue Code of 1954.

"(B) 80-percent corporate shareholder.—The term '80-percent corporate shareholder' means, with respect to any distribution, any corporation which owns—

"(i) stock in the corporation making the distribution possessing at least 80 percent of the total combined voting power of all classes of stock entitled to vote, and

"(ii) at least 80 percent of the total number of shares of all other classes of stock of the distributing corporation (except nonvoting stock which is limited and preferred as to dividends).

"(C) Special rule for affiliated group filing consolidated return. — For purposes of this paragraph and paragraph (4), all members of the same affiliated group (as defined in section 1504 of the Internal Revenue Code of 1954) which file a consolidated return for the taxable year which includes the date of the distribution shall be treated as 1 corporation.

"(D) Special rule for certain distributions before January 1, 1988.—

"(i) In general.—In the case of a transaction to which this subparagraph applies, subparagraph (A) shall be applied by substituting '1988' for '1985' and the amendments made by subtitle D of title VI of the Tax Reform Act of 1986 shall not apply.

"(ii) Transaction to which subparagraph applies.—This subparagraph applies to a transaction in which a Delaware corporation which was incorporated on May 31, 1927, and which was acquired by the transferee on December 10, 1968, transfers to the transferee stock in a corporation—

"(I) with respect to which such Delaware corporation is a 100-percent corporate shareholder, and

"(II) which is a Tennessee corporation which was incorporated on March 2, 1978, and which is a successor to an Indiana corporation which was incorporated on June 28, 1946, and acquired by the transferee on December 10, 1968.

"(4) Exception for certain distributions where tender offer commenced on May 23, 1984.—

"(A) In general.—The amendments made by subsection (a) shall not apply to any distribution made before September 1, 1986, if—

"(i) such distribution consists of qualified stock held (directly or indirectly) on June 15, 1984, by the distributing corporation,

"(ii) control of the distributing corporation (as defined in section 368(c) of the Internal Revenue Code of 1954) is acquired other than in a tax-free transaction after January 1, 1984, but before January 1, 1985,

"(iii) a tender offer for the shares of the distributing corporation was commenced on May 23, 1984, and was amended on May 24, 1984, and "(iv) the distributing corporation and the distributee corporation are members of the same affiliated group (as defined in section 1504 of such Code) which filed a consolidated return for the taxable year which includes the date of the distribution. If the common parent of any affiliated group filing a consolidated return meets the requirements of clauses (ii) and (iii), each other member of such group shall be treated as meeting such requirements.

"(B) Qualified stock.—For purposes of subparagraph (A), the term 'qualified stock' means any stock in a corporation which on June 15, 1984, was a member of the same affiliated group as the distributing corporation and which filed a consolidated return with the distributing corporation for the taxable year which included June 15, 1984."

For further exceptions, see Secs. 54(d)(5) and (6) of this Act reproduced in the note following Code Sec. 301.

Prior to amendment, para. (d)(1) read as follows:

"(1) In general.

"If—

"(A) a corporation distributes property (other than an obligation of such corporation) to a shareholder in a redemption (to which subpart A applies) of part or all of his stock in such corporation, and

"(B) the fair market value of such property exceeds its adjusted basis (in the hands of the distributing corporation),

then a gain shall be recognized to the distributing corporation in an amount equal to such excess as if the property distributed had been sold at the time of the distribution. Subsections (b) and (c) shall not apply to any distribution to which this subsection applies."

Prior to amendment, subpara. (d)(2)(A) read as follows:

"(A) a distribution to a corporate shareholder if the basis of the property distributed is determined under section 301(d)(2);"

Prior to deletion, subpara. (d)(2)(B) read as follows:

"(B) a distribution to which section 302(b)(4) applies and which is made with respect to qualified stock; "

—P.L. 98-369, Sec. 712(j), added new subpara. (e)(1)(C), effective for distributions after 8/31/82.

In 1983, P.L. 97-448, Sec. 306(a)(7), amended Sec. 223(b)(2)(B) of P.L. 97-248, part of the effective date for changes made by Sec. 223 of P.L. 97-248 [reproduced below].

Prior to amendment, Sec. 223(b)(2)(B) of P.L. 97-248 read as follows:

"(B) within 90 days after the date of such ruling."

In 1982, P.L. 97-248, Sec. 223(a)(1), amended subparas. (d)(2)(A), (B) and (C) ... Sec. 223(a)(2), added subsec. (e) ... Sec. 223(a)(3)(A), added "and" at end of subpara. (d)(2)(E) ... Sec. 223(a)(3)(B), substituted a period for "; and" at end of subpara. (d)(2)(F) ... Sec. 223(a)(3)(C), deleted subpara. (d)(2)(G), effective for distributions after 8/31/82. Secs. 223(b)(2)–(4) of this Act provide:

"(2) Distributions pursuant to ruling requests before July 23, 1982.— In the case of a ruling request under section 311(d)(2)(A) of the Internal Revenue Code of 1954 (as in effect before the amendments made by this section) made before July 23, 1982, the amendments made by this section shall not apply to distributions made—

"(A) pursuant to a ruling granted pursuant to such request, and

"(B) either before October 21, 1982, or within 90 days after the date of such ruling.

"(3) Distributions pursuant to final judgments of court.— In the case of a final judgment described in section 311(d)(2)(C) of such Code (as in effect before the amendments made by this section) rendered before July 23, 1982, the amendments made by this section shall not apply to distributions made before January 1, 1986, pursuant to such judgment.

"(4) Certain distributions with respect to stock acquired before May 1982.— The amendments made by this section shall not apply to distributions—

"(A) which meet the requirements of section 311(d)(2)(A) of such Code (as in effect on the day before the date of the enactment of this Act),

"(B) which are made on or before August 31, 1983, and

"(C) which are made with respect to stock acquired after 1980 and before May 1982."

Prior to amendment, subparas. (d)(2)(A), (B) and (C) read as follows:

"(A) a distribution in complete redemption of all of the stock of a shareholder who, at all times within the 12-month period ending on the date of such distribution, owns at least 10 percent in value of the outstanding stock of the distributing corporation, but only if the redemption qualifies under section 302(b)(3) (determined without the application of section 302(c)(2)(A)(iii));

"(B) a distribution of stock or an obligation of a corporation—

"(i) which is engaged in at least one trade or business,

"(ii) which has not received property constituting a substantial part of its assets from the distributing corporation, in a transaction to which section 351 applied or as a contribution to capital, within the 5-year period ending on the date of the distribution, and

"(iii) at least 50 percent in value of the outstanding stock of which is owned by the distributing corporation at anytime within the 9-year period ending one year before the date of the distribution;

"(C) a distribution of stock or securities pursuant to the terms of a final judgment rendered by a court with respect to the distributing corporation in a court proceeding under the Sherman Act (15 U.S.C. 1-7) or the Clayton Act (15 U.S.C. 12-27), or both, to which the United States is a party, but only if the distribution of such stock or securities in redemption of the distributing corporation's stock is in furtherance of the purposes of the judgment;"

Prior to deletion, subpara. (d)(2)(G) read as follows:

"(G) a distribution of stock to a distributee which is not an organization exempt from tax under section 501(a), if with respect to such distributee, subsection (a)(1) or (b)(1) of section 1101 (relating to distributions pursuant to Bank Holding Company Act) applies to such distribution."

In 1980, P.L. 96-471, Sec. 2(b)(1), substituted "453B" for "453(d)" in subsec. (a), effective for dispositions made after 10/19/80 in tax. yrs. end. after 10/19/80 [date of enactment].

In 1978, P.L. 95-600, Sec. 703(j)(B), redesignated subpara. (d)(2)(H) as subpara. (d)(2)(G), effective 10/1/77, with respect to distributions after 12/31/75, in tax. yrs. ending after 12/31/75.

In 1976, P.L. 94-455, Sec. 1901(a)(42)(A), substituted "then a gain shall be recognized" for "then again shall be recognized" in para. (d)(1), for tax. yrs. begin. after '76.

— P.L. 94-455, Sec. 1901(a)(42)(B)(i), deleted subpara. (d)(2)(C) and redesignated subparas. (d)(2)(D), (E), (F) and (G) as subparas. (d)(2)(C), (D), (E) and (F), respectively, for distributions after 11/30/74.

Prior to amendment, subpara. (d)(2)(C) read as follows:

"(C) a distribution before December 1, 1974, of stock of a corporation substantially all of the assets of which the distributing corporation (or a corporation which is a member of the same affiliated group (as defined in section 1504(a)) as the distributing corporation) held on November 30, 1969, if such assets constitute a trade or business which has been actively conducted throughout the one-year period ending on the date of the distribution;"

— P.L. 94-455, Sec. 1901(a)(42)(C), deleted "26 Stat. 209;", which preceded "15 U.S.C. 1-7", and "38 Stat. 730;", which preceded "15 U.S.C. 12-27", in redesignated subpara. (d)(2)(C), for tax. yrs. begin. after '76.

— P.L. 94-452, Sec. 2(b), deleted "and" at the end of subpara. (d)(2)(F) ... substituted "; and" for the period at the end of subpara. (d)(2)(G) ... added subpara. (d)(2)(H), effective 10/1/77 for distributions after '75 in tax. yrs. end. after '75.

In 1971, P.L. 91-675, Sec. [1](a), substituted "(2), (3), (4) and (5)" for "(2) and (3)" in Sec. 905(c)(1) of P.L. 91-172 ... Sec. [1](b), added Secs. 905(c)(4) and (5) of P.L. 91-172, reproduced below.

In 1969, P.L. 91-172, Sec. 905(a), added subsec. (d) ... Sec. 905(b), substituted "(b), (c), and (d)" for "(b) and (c)", effective as provided in Sec. 905(c) of this Act as amended by P.L. 91-675 see above.

"(c) Effective date—

"(1) Except as provided in paragraphs (2), (3), (4) and (5), the amendments made by subsections (a) and (b) shall apply with respect to distributions after November 30, 1969.

"(2) The amendments made by subsections (a) and (b) shall not apply to a distribution before April 1, 1970, pursuant to the terms of—

"(A) a written contract which was binding on the distributing corporation on November 30, 1969, and at all times thereafter before the distribution,

"(B) an offer made by the distributing corporation before December 1, 1969,

"(C) an offer made in accordance with a request for a ruling filed by the distributing corporation with the Internal Revenue Service before December 1, 1969, or

"(D) an offer made in accordance with a registration statement filed with the Securities and Exchange Commission before December 1, 1969. For purposes of subparagraphs (B), (C), and (D), an offer shall be treated as an offer only if it was in writing and not revocable by its express terms.

"(3) The amendments made by subsections (a) and (b) shall not apply to a distribution by a corporation of specific property in redemption of stock outstanding on November 30, 1969, if—

"(A) every holder of such stock on such date had the right to demand redemption of his stock in such specific property, and

"(B) the corporation had such specific property on hand on such date in a quantity sufficient to redeem all of such stock.

For purposes of the preceding sentence, stock shall be considered to have been outstanding on November 30, 1969, if it could have been acquired on such date through the exercise of an existing right of conversion contained in other stock held on such date.

"(4) The amendments made by sections (a) and (b) shall not apply to a distribution by a corporation of property (held on December 1, 1969, by the distributing corporation or a corporation which was a wholly owned subsidiary of the distributing corporation on such date) in redemption of stock outstanding on November 30, 1969, which is redeemed and cancelled before July 31, 1971, if—

"(A) such redemption is pursuant to a resolution adopted before November 1, 1969, by the Board of Directors authorizing redemption of a specific amount of stock constituting more than 10 percent of the outstanding stock of the corporation at the time of the adoption of such resolution; and

"(B) more than 40 percent of the stock authorized to be redeemed pursuant to such resolution was redeemed before December 30, 1969, and more than one-half of the stock so redeemed was redeemed with property other than money.

"(5) The amendments made by subsections (a) and (b) shall not apply to a distribution of stock by a corporation organized prior to December 1, 1969, for the principal purpose of providing an equity participation plan for employees of the corporation whose stock is being distributed (hereinafter referred to as the 'employer corporation', if—

"(A) the stock being distributed was owned by the distributing corporation on November 30, 1969,

"(B) the stock being redeemed was acquired before January 1, 1973, pursuant to such equity participation plan by the shareholder presenting such stock for redemption (or by a predecessor of such shareholder),

"(C) the employment of the shareholder presenting the stock for redemption (or the predecessor of such shareholder) by the employer corporation commenced before January 1, 1971,

"(D) at least 90 percent in value of the assets of the distributing corporation on November 30, 1969, consisted of common stock of the employer corporation, and

"(E) at least 50 percent of the outstanding voting stock of the employer corporation is owned by the distributing corporation at any time within the nine-year period ending one year before the date of such distributions."

Sec. 312. Effect on earnings and profits.
(a) General rule.
  Except as otherwise provided in this section, on the distribution of property by a corporation with respect to its stock, the earnings and profits of the corporation (to the extent thereof) shall be decreased by the sum of—
  (1) the amount of money,
  (2) the principal amount of the obligations of such corporation (or, in the case of obligations having original issue discount, the aggregate issue price of such obligations), and
  (3) the adjusted basis of the other property,
so distributed.
(b) Distributions of appreciated property.
  On the distribution by a corporation, with respect to its stock, of any property (other than an obligation of such corporation) the fair market value of which exceeds the adjusted basis thereof—
  (1) the earnings and profits of the corporation shall be increased by the amount of such excess, and
  (2) subsection (a)(3) shall be applied by substituting "fair market value" for "adjusted basis".
For purposes of this subsection and subsection (a), the adjusted basis of any property is its adjusted basis as determined for purposes of computing earnings and profits.
(c) Adjustments for liabilities.
  In making the adjustments to the earnings and profits of a corporation under subsection (a) or (b), proper adjustment shall be made for—
  (1) the amount of any liability to which the property distributed is subject, and
  (2) the amount of any liability of the corporation assumed by a shareholder in connection with the distribution.
(d) Certain distributions of stock and securities.
  (1) **In general.** The distribution to a distributee by or on behalf of a corporation of its stock or securities, of stock or securities in another corporation, or of property, in a distribution to which this title applies, shall not be considered a distribution of the earnings and profits of any corporation—
    (A) if no gain to such distributee from the receipt of such stock or securities, or property, was recognized under this title, or
    (B) if the distribution was not subject to tax in the hands of such distributee by reason of section 305(a).
  (2) **Prior distributions.** In the case of a distribution of stock or securities, or property, to which section 115(h) of the Internal Revenue Code of 1939 (or the corresponding provision of prior law) applied, the effect on earnings and profits of such distribution shall be determined under such section 115(h), or the corresponding provision of prior law, as the case may be.
  (3) **Stock or securities.** For purposes of this subsection, the term "stock or securities" includes rights to acquire stock or securities.
(e) Repealed.
(f) Effect on earnings and profits of gain or loss and of receipt of tax-free distributions.
  (1) **Effect on earnings and profits of gain or loss.** The gain or loss realized from the sale or other disposition (after February 28, 1913) of property by a corporation—
    (A) for the purpose of the computation of the earnings and profits of the corporation, shall (except as provided in subparagraph (B)) be determined by using as the adjusted basis the adjusted basis (under the law applicable to the year in which the sale or other disposition was made) for determining gain, except that no regard shall be had to the value of the property as of March 1, 1913; but
    (B) for purposes of the computation of the earnings and profits of the corporation for any period beginning after February 28, 1913, shall be determined by using as the adjusted basis the adjusted basis (under the law applicable to the year in which the sale or other disposition was made) for determining gain.
Gain or loss so realized shall increase or decrease the earnings and profits to, but not beyond, the extent to which such a realized gain or loss was recognized in computing taxable income under the law applicable to the year in which such sale or disposition was made. Where, in determining the adjusted basis used in computing such realized gain or loss, the adjustment to the basis differs from the adjustment proper for the purpose of determining earnings and profits, then the latter adjustment shall be used in determining the increase or decrease above provided. For purposes of this subsection, a loss with respect to which a deduction is disallowed under section 1091 (relating to wash sales of stock or securities), or the corresponding provision of prior law, shall not be deemed to be recognized.
  (2) **Effect on earnings and profits of receipt of tax-free distributions.** Where a corporation receives (after February 28, 1913) a distribution from a second corporation which (under the law applicable to the year in which the distribution was made) was not a taxable dividend to the shareholders of the second corporation, the amount of such distribution shall not increase the earnings and profits of the first corporation in the following cases:
    (A) no such increase shall be made in respect of the part of such distribution which (under such law) is directly applied in reduction of the basis of the stock in respect of which the distribution was made; and
    (B) no such increase shall be made if (under such law) the distribution causes the basis of the stock in respect of which the distribution was made to be allocated between such stock and the property received (or such basis would, but for section 307(b), be so allocated).
(g) Earnings and profits—increase in value accrued before March 1, 1913.
  (1) If any increase or decrease in the earnings and profits for any period beginning after February 28, 1913, with respect to any matter would be different had the adjusted basis of the property involved been determined without regard to its March 1, 1913, value, then, except as provided in paragraph (2), an increase (properly reflecting such difference) shall be made in that part of the earnings and profits consisting of increase in value of property accrued before March 1, 1913.
  (2) If the application of subsection (f) to a sale or other disposition after February 28, 1913, results in a loss which is to be applied in decrease of earnings and profits for any period beginning after February 28, 1913, then, notwithstanding subsection (f) and in lieu of the rule provided in paragraph (1) of this subsection, the amount of such loss so to be applied shall be reduced by the amount, if any, by which the adjusted basis of the property used in determining the loss exceeds the adjusted basis computed without regard to the value of the property on March 1, 1913,

and if such amount so applied in reduction of the decrease exceeds such loss, the excess over such loss shall increase that part of the earnings and profits consisting of increase in value of property accrued before March 1, 1913.

(h) Allocation in certain corporate separations and reorganizations.

(1) Section 355. In the case of a distribution or exchange to which section 355 (or so much of section 356 as relates to section 355) applies, proper allocation with respect to the earnings and profits of the distributing corporation and the controlled corporation (or corporations) shall be made under regulations prescribed by the Secretary.

(2) Section 368(a)(1)(C) or (D). In the case of a reorganization described in subparagraph (C) or (D) of section 368(a)(1), proper allocation with respect to the earnings and profits of the acquired corporation shall, under regulations prescribed by the Secretary, be made between the acquiring corporation and the acquired corporation (or any corporation which had control of the acquired corporation before the reorganization).

(i) Distribution of proceeds of loan insured by the United States.

If a corporation distributes property with respect to its stock and if, at the time of distribution—

(1) there is outstanding a loan to such corporation which was made, guaranteed, or insured by the United States (or by any agency or instrumentality thereof), and

(2) the amount of such loan so outstanding exceeds the adjusted basis of the property constituting security for such loan,

then the earnings and profits of the corporation shall be increased by the amount of such excess, and (immediately after the distribution) shall be decreased by the amount of such excess. For purposes of paragraph (2), the adjusted basis of the property at the time of distribution shall be determined without regard to any adjustment under section 1016(a)(2) (relating to adjustment for depreciation, etc.). For purposes of this subsection, a commitment to make, guarantee, or insure a loan shall be treated as the making, guaranteeing, or insuring of a loan.

(j) Repealed.

(k) Effect of depreciation on earnings and profits.

(1) General rule. For purposes of computing the earnings and profits of a corporation for any taxable year beginning after June 30, 1972, the allowance for depreciation (and amortization, if any) shall be deemed to be the amount which would be allowable for such year if the straight line method of depreciation had been used for each taxable year beginning after June 30, 1972.

(2) Exception. If for any taxable year a method of depreciation was used by the taxpayer which the Secretary has determined results in a reasonable allowance under section 167(a) and which is the unit-of-production method or other method not expressed in a term of years, then the adjustment to earnings and profits for depreciation for such year shall be determined under the method so used (in lieu of the straight line method).

(3) Exception for tangible property.

(A) In general. Except as provided in subparagraph (B), in the case of tangible property to which section 168 applies, the adjustment to earnings and profits for depreciation for any taxable year shall be determined under the alternative depreciation system (within the meaning of section 168(g)(2)).

(B) Treatment of amounts deductible under section 179, 179A, 179B, 179C, 179D, or 179E. For purposes of computing the earnings and profits of a corporation, any amount deductible under section 179, 179A, 179B, 179C, 179D, or 179E shall be allowed as a deduction ratably over the period of 5 taxable years (beginning with the taxable year for which such amount is deductible under section 179, 179A, 179B, 179C, 179D, or 179E, as the case may be).

(4) Certain foreign corporations. The provisions of paragraph (1) shall not apply in computing the earnings and profits of a foreign corporation for any taxable year for which less than 20 percent of the gross income from all sources of such corporation is derived from sources within the United States.

(5) Basis adjustment not taken into account. In computing the earnings and profits of a corporation for any taxable year, the allowance for depreciation (and amortization, if any) shall be computed without regard to any basis adjustment under section 50(c).

(l) Discharge of indebtedness income.

(1) Does not increase earnings and profits if applied to reduce basis. The earnings and profits of a corporation shall not include income from the discharge of indebtedness to the extent of the amount applied to reduce basis under section 1017.

(2) Reduction of deficit in earnings and profits in certain cases. If—

(A) the interest of any shareholder of a corporation is terminated or extinguished in a title 11 or similar case (within the meaning of section 368(a)(3)(A)), and

(B) there is a deficit in the earnings and profits of the corporation,

then such deficit shall be reduced by an amount equal to the paid-in capital which is allocable to the interest of the shareholder which is so terminated or extinguished.

(m) No adjustment for interest paid on certain registration-required obligations not in registered form.

The earnings and profits of any corporation shall not be decreased by any interest with respect to which a deduction is not or would not be allowable by reason of section 163(f), unless at the time of issuance the issuer is a foreign corporation that is not a controlled foreign corporation (within the meaning of section 957) and the issuance did not have as a purpose the avoidance of section 163(f) or this subsection.

(n) Adjustments to earnings and profits to more accurately reflect economic gain and loss.

For purposes of computing the earnings and profits of a corporation, the following adjustments shall be made:

(1) Construction period carrying charges.

(A) In general. In the case of any amount paid or incurred for construction period carrying charges—

(i) no deduction shall be allowed with respect to such amount, and

(ii) the basis of the property with respect to which such charges are allocable shall be increased by such amount.

(B) Construction period carrying charges defined. For purposes of this paragraph, the term "construction period carrying charges" means all—

(i) interest paid or accrued on indebtedness incurred or continued to acquire, construct, or carry property,

(ii) property taxes, and

(iii) similar carrying charges,

to the extent such interest, taxes, or charges are attributable to the construction period for such property and would be allowable as a deduction in determining taxable income under this chapter for the taxable year in which paid or incurred.

(C) Construction period. The term "construction period" has the meaning given the term production period under section 263A(f)(4)(B).

(2) Intangible drilling costs and mineral exploration and development costs.

(A) Intangible drilling costs. Any amount allowable as a deduction under section 263(c) in determining taxable income (other than costs incurred in connection with a nonproductive well)—

(i) shall be capitalized, and

(ii) shall be allowed as a deduction ratably over the 60-month period beginning with the month in which such amount was paid or incurred.

(B) Mineral exploration and development costs. Any amount allowable as a deduction under section 616(a) or 617 in determining taxable income—

(i) shall be capitalized, and

(ii) shall be allowed as a deduction ratably over the 120-month period beginning with the later of—

(I) the month in which production from the deposit begins, or

(II) the month in which such amount was paid or incurred.

(3) Certain amortization provisions not to apply. Sections 173 and 248 shall not apply.

(4) LIFO inventory adjustments.

(A) In general. Earnings and profits shall be increased or decreased by the amount of any increase or decrease in the LIFO recapture amount as of the close of each taxable year; except that any decrease below the LIFO recapture amount as of the close of the taxable year preceding the 1st taxable year to which this paragraph applies to the taxpayer shall be taken into account only to the extent provided in regulations prescribed by the Secretary.

(B) LIFO recapture amount. For purposes of this paragraph, the term "LIFO recapture amount" means the amount (if any) by which—

(i) the inventory amount of the inventory assets under the first-in, first-out method authorized by section 471, exceeds

(ii) the inventory amount of such assets under the LIFO method.

(C) Definitions. For purposes of this paragraph—

(i) LIFO method. The term "LIFO method" means the method authorized by section 472 (relating to last-in, first-out inventories).

(ii) Inventory assets. The term "inventory assets" means stock in trade of the corporation, or other property of a kind which would properly be included in the inventory of the corporation if on hand at the close of the taxable year.

(iii) Inventory amount. The inventory amount of assets under the first-in, first-out method authorized by section 471 shall be determined—

(I) if the corporation uses the retail method of valuing inventories under section 472, by using such method, or

(II) if subclause (I) does not apply, by using cost or market, whichever is lower.

(5) Installment sales. In the case of any installment sale, earnings and profits shall be computed as if the corporation did not use the installment method.

(6) Completed contract method of accounting. In the case of a taxpayer who uses the completed contract method of accounting, earnings and profits shall be computed as if such taxpayer used the percentage of completion method of accounting.

(7) Redemptions. If a corporation distributes amounts in a redemption to which section 302(a) or 303 applies, the part of such distribution which is properly chargeable to earnings and profits shall be an amount which is not in excess of the ratable share of the earnings and profits of such corporation accumulated after February 28, 1913, attributable to the stock so redeemed.

(8) Special rule for certain foreign corporations. In the case of a foreign corporation described in subsection (k)(4)—

(A) paragraphs (4) and (6) shall apply only in the case of taxable years beginning after December 31, 1985, and

(B) paragraph (5) shall apply only in the case of taxable years beginning after December 31, 1987.

(o) Definition of original issue discount and issue price for purposes of subsection (a)(2).

For purposes of subsection (a)(2), the terms "original issue discount" and "issue price" have the same respective meanings as when used in subpart A of part V of subchapter P of this chapter.

In 2006, P.L. 109-432, Sec. 404(b)(2), substituted "179D, or 179E" for "or 179D" each place it appeared in the heading and text of subpara. (k)(3)(B), effective for costs paid or incurred after 12/20/2006.

In 2005, P.L. 109-58, Sec. 1323(b)(3), substituted "179, 179A, 179B, or 179C" for "179, 179A, or 179B" each place it appeared in subpara. (k)(3)(B), effective for properties placed in service after 8/8/2005.

—P.L. 109-58, Sec. 1331(b)(5), substituted "179, 179A, 179B, 179C, or 179D" for "179, 179A, 179B, or 179C" each place it appeared in subpara. (k)(3)(B) [as amended by Sec. 1323(b)(3) of this Act, see above], effective for property placed in service after 12/31/2005.

In 2004, P.L. 108-357, Sec. 338(b)(3), substituted "179A, or 179B" for "or 179A" each place it appeared in the heading and text of subpara. (k)(3)(B), effective for expenses paid or incurred after 12/31/2002, in tax. yrs. end. after 12/31/2002.

—P.L. 108-357, Sec. 413(c)(4), deleted subsec. (j) . . . Sec. 413(c)(5), deleted ", a foreign investment company (within the meaning of section 1246(b)), or a foreign personal holding company (within the meaning of section 552)" after "section 957)" in subsec. (m), effective for tax. yrs. of foreign corporations begin. after 12/31/2004, and for tax. yrs. of United States shareholders with or within which such tax. yrs. of foreign corporations end.

Prior to deletion, subsec. (j) read as follows:

"(j) Earnings and profits of foreign investment companies.

"(1) Allocation within affiliated group. In the case of a sale or exchange of stock in a foreign investment company (as defined in section 1246(b)) by a United States person (as defined in section 7701(a)(30)), if such company is a member of an affiliated group, then the accumulated earnings and profits of all members of such affiliated group shall be allocated, under regulations prescribed by the Secretary, in such manner as is proper to carry out the purposes of section 1246.

"(2) Affiliated group defined. For purposes of paragraph (1) of this subsection, the term 'affiliated group' has the meaning assigned to such term by section 1504(a); except that (A) 'more than 50 percent' shall be substituted for '80 percent or more', and (B) all corporations shall be treated as includible corporations (without regard to the provisions of section 1504(b))."

In 1997, P.L. 105-34, Sec. 1604(a)(2)(A), substituted "179 or 179A" for "179" in the heading and the first place it appeared in the text of subpara. (k)(3)(B) . . . Sec. 1604(a)(2)(B), substituted "179 or 179A, as the case may be" for "179" the last place it appeared in subpara. (k)(3)(B), effective for property placed in service after 6/30/93.

In 1990, P.L. 101-508, Sec. 11812(b)(5), amended para. (k)(2), effective for property placed in service after 11/5/90 except as provided in Sec. 11812(c)(2) of this Act, reproduced in note following Code Sec. 42.

Prior to amendment, para. (k)(2) read as follows:

"(2) Exception. If for any taxable year beginning after June 30, 1972, a method of depreciation was used by the taxpayer which the Secretary has determined results in a reasonable allowance under section 167(a), and which is not—

"(A) a declining balance method,

"(B) the sum of the years-digits method, or

"(C) any other method allowable solely by reason of the application of subsection (b)(4) or (j)(1)(C) of section 167,

then the adjustment to earnings and profits for depreciation for such year shall be determined under the method so used (in lieu of under the straight-line method)."

—P.L. 101-508, Sec. 11813(b)(14), substituted "section 50(c)" for "section 48(q)" in para. (k)(5), effective for property placed in service after 12/31/90 except as provided in Sec. 11813(c)(2) of this Act, reproduced in note following Code Sec. 46.

Corporate distributions and adjustments — Code Sec. 312

In 1989, P.L. 101-239, Sec. 7611(f)(5)(A), substituted "in which such amount was paid or incurred" for "in which the production from the well begins" in clause (n)(2)(A)(ii), effective for costs paid or incurred in tax. yrs. begin. after 12/31/89.

—P.L. 101-239, Sec. 7811(m)(2), corrected Sec. 1018(d)(4) of P.L. 100-647, to substitute "of any property (other than an obligation of such corporation" for "of any property" the first place it appeared in subsec. (b), see below.

In 1988, P.L. 100-647, Sec. 1002(a)(3), substituted "paragraph (1)" for "paragraphs (1) and (3)" in para. (k)(4), effective for property placed in service after 12/31/86, in tax. yrs. end. after 12/31/86. Sec. 1002(c)(3) of this Act provides:

"(3) Notwithstanding section 203 of the Reform Act, the amendments made by section 201 of the Reform Act shall apply to any real property which was acquired before January 1, 1987, and was converted on or after such date from personal use to a use for which depreciation is allowable."

—P.L. 100-647, Sec. 1018(d)(4), [as amended by Sec. 7811(m)(2) of P.L. 101-239, see above], substituted "of any property (other than an obligation of such corporation)" for "of any property" the first place it appeared in subsec. (b), effective as provided in Sec. 61(e)(1) of P.L. 98-369 reproduced below.

In 1986, P.L. 99-514, Sec. 201(b), amended para. (k)(3)... Sec. 201(d)(6), deleted the last sentence in para. (k)(4), effective for property placed in service after 12/31/86, in tax. yrs. end. after 12/31/86 [see Sec. 1002(c)(3) of P.L. 100-647, above]. Sec. 203(a)(1)(B) of this Act provides:

"(B) Election to have amendments made by section 201 apply. A taxpayer may elect (at such time and in such manner as the Secretary of the Treasury or his delegate may prescribe) to have the amendments made by section 201 apply to any property placed in service after July 31, 1986, and before January 1, 1987."
For special rules, see Sec. 203(b)-(e) and Sec. 204 of this Act reproduced in note following Code Sec. 168, and Sec. 251(d) of this Act reproduced in note following Code Sec. 46.

Prior to amendment, para. (k)(3) [as amended by Sec. 1809(a)(2)(C)(ii) of this Act] read as follows:

"(3) Exception for recovery and section 179 property.

"(A) Recovery property. Except as provided in subparagraphs (B) and (C), in the case of recovery property (within the meaning of section 168), the adjustment to earnings and profits for depreciation for any taxable year shall be the amount determined under the straight-line method (using a half year convention in the case of property other than the 19-year real property and low-income housing and without regard to salvage value) and using a recovery period determined in accordance with the following table:

In the case of:	The applicable recovery period is:
3-year property	5 years.
5-year property	12 years.
10-year property	25 years.
19-year real property and low-income housing	40 years.
15-year public utility property	35 years.

For purposes of this subparagraph, no adjustment shall be allowed in the year of disposition (except with respect to 19-year real property and low-income housing).

"(B) Treatment of amounts deductible under section 179. For purposes of computing the earnings and profits of a corporation, any amount deductible under section 179 shall be allowed as a deduction ratably over the period of 5 years (beginning with the year for which such amount is deductible under section 179).

"(C) Flexibility. In any case where a different recovery percentage is elected under section 168(b)(3) or (f)(2)(C) based on a recovery period longer than the recovery period provided in subparagraph (A), the adjustment to earnings and profits shall be based on such longer period under rules similar to those provided in subparagraph (A)."

Prior to deletion, the last sentence of para. (k)(4) read as follows:

"In determining the earnings and profits of such corporation in the case of recovery property (within the meaning of section 168), the rules of section 168(f)(2) shall apply."

—P.L. 99-514, Sec. 241(b)(1), deleted ", 177," after "173" in para. (n)(3), effective for expenditures paid or incurred after 12/31/86. For transitional rule see Sec. 241(c)(2) of this Act reproduced in note following Code Sec. 177.

—P.L. 99-514, Sec. 631(e)(1), amended para. (n)(4) [as redesignated by Sec. 1804(f)(1)(D) of this Act, see below], effective as provided in Sec. 633(a)(1) and (3) of this Act which read as follows:

"(a) General rule. Except as otherwise provided in this section [Sec. 633], the amendments made by this subtitle shall apply to—

"(1) any distribution in complete liquidation, and any sale or exchange, made by a corporation after July 31, 1986, unless such corporation is completely liquidated before January 1, 1987."

* * *

"(3) any distribution (not in complete liquidation) made after December 31, 1986."

Sec. 633(d) [sic (e)] of this Act provides:

"(d) [sic (e)] Complete liquidation defined. For purposes of this section, a corporation shall be treated as completely liquidated if all of the assets of such corporation are distributed in complete liquidation, less assets retained to meet claims."

Prior to amendment, para. (n)(4) [as redesignated by Sec. 1804(f)(1)(D) of this Act, see below] read as follows:

"(4) LIFO inventory adjustments. Earnings and profits shall be increased or decreased by the amount of any increase or decrease in the LIFO recapture amount (determined under section 336(b)(3)) as of the close of each taxable year; except that any decrease below the LIFO recapture amount as of the close of the taxable year preceding the first taxable year to which this paragraph applies to the taxpayer shall be taken into account only to the extent provided in regulations prescribed by the Secretary."

—P.L. 99-514, Sec. 803(b)(3)(A), deleted "(determined without regard to section 189)" before the period at the end of subpara. (n)(1)(B)... Sec. 803(b)(3)(B), amended subpara. (n)(1)(C), effective for costs incurred after 12/31/86, in tax. yrs. ending after 12/31/86. For special rules, see Sec. 803(d)(2)-(7) of this Act, reproduced in note following Code Sec. 263A.

Prior to amendment, subpara. (n)(1)(C) read as follows:

"(C) Construction period. The term 'construction period' has the meaning given such term by section 189(e)(2) (determined without regard to any real property limitation)."

—P.L. 99-514, Sec. 1804(f)(1)(A), amended subsec. (b)... Sec. 1804(f)(1)(B), added "and" at the end of para. (c)(1), substituted a period for ", and" at the end of para. (c)(2), and deleted para. (c)(3)... Sec. 1804(f)(1)(C), deleted ", etc" in the heading of subsec. (c)... Sec. 1804(f)(1)(D), deleted para. (n)(4) and redesignated paras. (n)(5)-(9) as paras. (n)(4)-(8)... Sec. 1804(f)(1)(E), amended para. (n)(8) (as redesignated), effective as provided in Sec. 61(e)(1) of P.L. 98-369 reproduced below. Secs. 1804(f)(1)(F) and (f)(3) of this Act provide:

"(F) Any reference in subsection (e) of section 61 of the Tax Reform Act of 1984 [reproduced below] to a paragraph of section 312(n) of the Internal Revenue Code of 1954 shall be treated as a reference to such paragraph as in effect before its redesignation by subparagraph (D)."

* * *

"(3) Effective date for treatment of redemptions.—Paragraph (7) of section 312(n) of the Internal Revenue Code of 1954 (as redesignated by paragraph (1)(D) of this subsection [Sec. 1804(f)]), and the amendments made by section 61(a)(2) of the Tax Reform Act of 1984, shall apply to distributions in taxable years beginning after September 30, 1984."

Prior to amendment, subsec. (b) read as follows:

"(b) Certain inventory assets.

"(1) In general. On the distribution by a corporation, with respect to its stock, of inventory assets (as defined in paragraph (2)(A)) the fair market value of which exceeds the adjusted basis thereof, the earnings and profits of the corporation—

"(A) shall be increased by the amount of such excess; and

"(B) shall be decreased by whichever of the following is the lesser:

"(i) the fair market value of the inventory assets distributed, or

"(ii) the earnings and profits (as increased under subparagraph (A)).

"(2) Definitions.

"(A) Inventory assets. For purposes of paragraph (1), the term 'inventory assets' means—

"(i) stock in trade of the corporation, or other property of a kind which would properly be included in the inventory of the corporation if on hand at the close of the taxable year;

"(ii) property held by the corporation primarily for sale to customers in the ordinary course of its trade or business; and

"(iii) unrealized receivables or fees, except receivables from sales or exchanges of assets other than assets described in this subparagraph.

"(B) Unrealized receivables or fees. For purposes of subparagraph (A)(iii), the term 'unrealized receivables or fees' means, to the extent not previously includible in income under the method of accounting used by the corporation, any rights (contractual or otherwise) to payment for—

"(i) goods delivered, or to be delivered, to the extent that the proceeds therefrom would be treated as amounts received from the sale or exchange of property other than a capital asset, or

"(ii) services rendered or to be rendered."

Prior to deletion, para. (c)(3) read as follows:

"(3) any gain recognized to the corporation on the distribution."

Prior to deletion, para. (n)(4) read as follows:

"(4) Certain untaxed appreciation of distributed property. In the case of any distribution of property by a corporation described in section 311(d), earnings and profits shall be increased by the amount of any gain which would be includible in gross income for any taxable year if section 311(d)(2) did not apply."

Prior to amendment, para. (n)(8) (as redesignated) read as follows:

"(8) Special rule for certain foreign corporations. In the case of a foreign corporation described in subsection (k)(4), paragraphs (5), (6), and (7) shall apply only in the case of taxable years beginning after December 31, 1985."

—P.L. 99-514, Sec. 1809(a)(2)(C)(ii), deleted ", and rules similar to the rules under the next to the last sentence of section 168(b)(2)(A) and section 168(b)(2)(B) shall apply" after "low-income housing)" at the end of subpara. (k)(3)(A), effective for property placed in service by the taxpayer after 3/15/84.

In 1985, P.L. 99-121, Sec. 103(b)(1)(C), substituted "19-year real property" for "18-year real property" each place it appeared in subpara. (k)(3)(A), effective for property placed in service by the taxpayer after 5/8/85, except as provided by Sec. 105(b)(2) and (3) of this Act reproduced in note following Code Sec. 168.

In 1984, P.L. 98-369, Sec. 61(a)(1), added subsec. (n), effective as provided in Sec. 61(e)(1) of the Act, following:

"(1) Adjustments to earnings and profits.—

"(A) Paragraphs (1), (2), and (3) of section 312(n).—The provisions of paragraphs (1), (2), and (3) of section 312(n) of the Internal Revenue Code of 1954 (as added by subsection (a)) shall apply to amounts paid or incurred in taxable years beginning after September 30, 1984.

"(B) Paragraph (4) of section 312(n).—The provisions of paragraph (4) of section 312(n) of such Code (as so added) shall apply to distributions after September 30, 1984; except that such provisions shall not apply to any distribution to which the amendments made by section 54(a) of this Act do not apply.

1,795

"(C) LIFO inventory.—The provisions of paragraph (5) of section 312(n) of such Code (as so added) shall apply to taxable years beginning after September 30, 1984.

"(D) Installment sales.—The provisions of paragraph (6) of section 312(n) of such Code (as so added) shall apply to sales after September 30, 1984, in taxable years ending after such date.

"(E) Completed contract method.—The provisions of paragraph (7) of section 312(n) of such Code (as so added) shall apply to contracts entered into after September 30, 1984, in taxable years ending after such date."

—P.L. 98-369, Sec. 61(a)(2)(A), deleted para. (j)(3) . . . Sec. 61(a)(2)(B), deleted subsec. (e), effective for distributions in tax. yrs. begin. after 9/30/84.

Prior to deletion, para. (j)(3) read as follows:

"(3) Redemptions. If a foreign investment company (as defined in section 1246) distributes amounts in a redemption to which section 302(a) or 303 applies, the part of such distribution which is properly chargeable to earnings and profits shall be an amount which is not in excess of the ratable share of the earnings and profits of the company accumulated after February 28, 1913, attributable to the stock so redeemed."

Prior to deletion, subsec. (e) read as follows:

"(e) Special rule for certain redemptions.

"In the case of amounts distributed in a redemption to which section 302(a) or 303 applies, the part of such distribution which is properly chargeable to capital account shall not be treated as a distribution of earnings and profits."

—P.L. 98-369, Sec. 61(b), substituted "40 years" for "35 years" in the item relating to 15-year real property and 20-year real property in the table in subpara. (k)(3)(A), effective for property placed in service in tax. yrs. begin. after 9/30/84.

—P.L. 98-369, Sec. 61(c)(1)(A), amended para. (a)(2) . . . Sec. 61(c)(1)(B), added new subsec. (o), effective with respect to distributions declared after 3/15/84, in tax. yrs. end. after 3/15/84.

Prior to amendment, para. (a)(2) read as follows:

"(2) the principal amount of the obligations of such corporation, and"

—P.L. 98-369, Sec. 63(b), amended subsec. (h), effective for transactions pursuant to plans adopted after 7/18/84.

Prior to amendment, subsec. (h) read as follows:

"(h) Allocation in certain corporate separations.

"In the case of a distribution or exchange to which section 355 (or so much of section 356 as relates to section 355) applies, proper allocation with respect to the earnings and profits of the distributing corporation and the controlled corporation (or corporations) shall be made under regulations prescribed by the Secretary."

—P.L. 98-369, Sec. 111(e)(5), substituted "18-year real property and low-income housing" for "15-year real property" each place it appeared in subpara. (k)(3)(A), effective for property placed in service by the taxpayer after 3/15/84.

In 1983, P.L. 97-448, Sec. 306(a)(6)(B)(i), deleted "in partial liquidation or" from after "distributes amounts" in para. (j)(3) . . . Sec. 306(a)(6)(B)(ii), amended the heading of para. (j)(3), effective for distributions after 8/31/82.

Prior to amendment, the heading of para. (j)(3) read as follows:

"(3) Partial liquidations and redemptions."

In 1982, P.L. 97-248, Sec. 205(a)(3), added para. (k)(5), effective for periods after 12/31/82, under rules similar to the rules of Code Sec. 48(m). For exceptions see Sec. 205(c)(1)(B)-(E) of this Act reproduced in note following Code Sec. 48.

—P.L. 97-248, Sec. 222(e)(3)(A), deleted "in partial liquidation (whether before, on or after June 22, 1954) or" after "amounts distributed" in subsec. (e) . . . Sec. 222(e)(3)(B), deleted, "partial liquidations and" after "Special rule for" in heading of subsec. (e), effective for distributions after 8/31/82. For exceptions and special rules see Sec. 222(f)(2)-(4) of this Act reproduced in note following Code Sec. 302.

—P.L. 97-248, Sec. 310(b)(3), added subsec. (m), effective for obligations issued after 12/31/82.

—P.L. 97-248, Sec. 310(d)(3), of this Act provides:

"(3) Exception for certain warrants, etc.—The amendments made by subsection (b) shall not apply to any obligations issued after December 31, 1982, on the exercise of a warrant or the conversion of a convertible obligation if such warrant or obligation was offered or sold outside the United States without registration under the Securities Act of 1933 and was issued before August 10, 1982. A rule similar to the rule of the preceding sentence shall also apply in the case of any regulations issued under section 163(f)(2)(C) of the Internal Revenue Code of 1954 (as added by this section) except that the date on which such regulations take effect shall be substituted for 'August 10, 1982'."

In 1981, P.L. 97-34, Sec. 206(a), redesignated para. (k)(3) as (k)(4) and added new para. (k)(3) . . . Sec. 206(b), substituted "paragraphs (1) and (3)" for "paragraph (1)" and added the last sentence to para. (k)(4) (as redesignated), effective for property placed in service after 12/31/80, in tax. yrs. end. after 12/30/80.

In 1980, P.L. 96-589, Sec. 5(f), added subsec. (l), effective for any transaction which occurs after 12/31/80, other than a transaction which occurs in a proceeding in a bankruptcy case or similar judicial proceeding (or in a proceeding under the Bankruptcy Act) commencing on or before 12/31/80.

Sec. 7(f) and (g) of this Act provides:

"(f) Election to substitute September 30, 1979, for December 31, 1980.

"(1) In general. The debtor (or debtors) in a bankruptcy case or similar judicial proceeding may (with the approval of the court) elect to apply [subsection 7(a) of this Act] by substituting 'September 30, 1979' for 'December 31, 1980' each place it appears in such subsections.

"(2) Effect of election. Any election made under paragraph (1) with respect to any proceeding shall apply to all parties to the proceeding.

"(3) Revocation only with consent. Any election under this subsection may be revoked only with the consent of the Secretary of the Treasury or his delegate.

"(4) Time and manner of election. Any election under this subsection shall be made at such time, and in such manner, as the Secretary of the Treasury or his delegate may by regulations prescribe.

"(g) Definitions. For purposes of this section—

"(1) Bankruptcy case. The term 'bankruptcy case' means any case under title 11 of the United States Code (as recodified by P.L. 95-598).

"(2) Similar judicial proceeding. The term 'similar judicial proceeding' means a receivership, foreclosure, or similar proceeding in a Federal or State court (as modified by section 368(a)(3)(D) of the Internal Revenue Code of 1954)."

In 1978, P.L. 95-628, Sec. 3(c), amended para. (c)(3), effective for distributions made after 11/10/78.

Prior to amendment, para. (c)(3) read as follows:

"(3) any gain to the corporation recognized under subsection (b), (c), or (d) of section 311, under section 341(f), or under section 617(d)(i), 1245(a), 1250(a), 1251(c), 1252(a) or 1254(a)."

In 1976, P.L. 94-455, Sec. 205(c)(1)(D), substituted "1252(a), or 1254(a)" for "or 1252(a)" in para. (c)(3), effective for tax. yrs. end. after 12/31/75.

—P.L. 94-455, Sec. 1901(a)(43), substituted "this title" for "this Code" each place it appeared in para. (d)(1), deleted subsec. (h) and redesignated subsecs. (i) and (j) as subsecs. (h) and (i), amended subsec. (i), as redesignated by this Act and amended para. (j)(3), as redesignated by this Act, effective for tax. yrs. begin. after 12/31/76.

Prior to deletion, subsec. (h) read as follows:

"(h) Earnings and profits of personal service corporations. In the case of a personal service corporation subject for any taxable year to supplement S of the Internal Revenue Code of 1939, an account equal to the undistributed supplement S net income of the personal service corporation for its taxable year shall be considered as paid in as of the close of such taxable year as paid-in surplus or as a contribution to capital, and the accumulated earnings and profits as of the close of such taxable year shall be correspondingly reduced, if such amount or any portion thereof is required to be included as a dividend in the gross income of the shareholders."

Prior to amendment, subsec. (i) read as follows:

"(i) Distribution of proceeds of loan insured by the United States.

"(1) In general. If a corporation distributes property with respect to its stock, and if, at the time of the distribution—

"(A) there is outstanding a loan to such corporation which was made, guaranteed, or insured by the United States (or by any agency or instrumentality thereof), and

"(B) the amount of such loan so outstanding exceeds the adjusted basis of the property constituting security for such loan,

then the earnings and profits of the corporation shall be increased by the amount of such excess, and (immediately after the distribution) shall be decreased by the amount of such excess. For purposes of subparagraph (B) of the preceding sentence, the adjusted basis of the property at the time of distribution shall be determined without regard to any adjustment under section 1016(a)(2) (relating to adjustment for depreciation, etc.). For purposes of this paragraph, a commitment to make, guarantee, or insure a loan shall be treated as the making, guaranteeing, or insuring of a loan.

"(2) Effective date. Paragraph (1) shall apply only with respect to distributions made on or after June 22, 1954."

Prior to amendment, para. (j)(3) read as follows:

"(3) Partial liquidations and redemptions.

"(A) In general. If a foreign investment company (as defined in section 1246) distributes amounts in partial liquidation or in a redemption to which section 302(a) or 303 applies, the part of such distribution which is properly chargeable to earnings and profits shall be an amount which is not in excess of the ratable share of the earnings and profits of the company accumulated after February 28, 1913, attributable to the stock so redeemed.

"(B) Effective date. Subparagraph (A) shall apply only with respect to distributions made after December 31, 1962."

—P.L. 94-455, Sec. 1901(b)(32)(B)(i), deleted subsec. (k) and redesignated subsecs. (l) and (m) as subsecs. (j) and (k), effective for tax. yrs. begin. after 12/31/76.

Prior to deletion, subsec. (k) read as follows:

"(k) Special adjustment on disposition of antitrust received as a dividend. If a corporation received antitrust stock (as defined in section 301(f)) in a distribution to which section 301 applied, and the amount of the distribution determined under section 301(f)(2) exceeded the basis of the stock determined under section 301(f)(3), then proper adjustment shall be made, under regulations prescribed by the Secretary or his delegate, to the earnings and profits of such corporation at the time such stock (or other property the basis of which is determined by reference to the basis of such stock) is disposed of by such corporation."

—P.L. 94-455, Sec. 1906(b)(13)(A), substituted "Secretary" for "Secretary or his delegate" each place it appeared in Code Sec. 312, effective for tax. yrs. begin. after 12/31/76.

In 1969, P.L. 91-172, Sec. 211(b)(3), substituted "1250(a), 1251(c), or 1252(a)" for "or 1250(a)" in para. (c)(3), effective for tax. yrs. begin. after 12/31/69.

—P.L. 91-172, Sec. 442(a), added subsec. (m), effective 12/30/69.

—P.L. 91-172, Sec. 905(b)(2), substituted "subsection (b), (c), or (d)" for "subsection (b) or (c)" in para. (c)(3), effective for distributions after 11/30/69. For special limitations see Sec. 905(c) of this Act reproduced in note following Code Sec. 311.

In 1966, P.L. 89-570, Sec. [1](b)(3), substituted "section 617(d)(1), 1245(a)," for "section 1245(a)" in para (c)(3), effective for tax. yrs. end. after 9/12/66, but only for expenditures paid or incurred after 9/12/66.

Corporate distributions and adjustments   Code Sec. 318(a)(1)(A)(i)

In 1964, P.L. 88-484, Sec. 1(b), substituted "section 311, under section 341(f)," for "section 311", effective for transactions after 8/22/64, in tax. yrs. end. after 8/22/64.

—P.L. 88-272, Sec. 231(b)(3), substituted "or under section 1245(a) or 1250(a)" for "or under section 1245(a)" in para. (c)(3), effective for dispositions after 12/31/63, in tax. yrs. end. after 12/31/63.

In 1962, P.L. 87-834, Sec. 13(f)(3), substituted "subsection (b) or (c) of section 311 or under section 1245(a)" for "subsection (b) or (c) of section 311" in para. (c)(3) . . . Sec. 14(b)(1), added subsec. (l), effective for tax. yrs. begin. after 12/31/62.

—P.L. 87-403, Sec. 3(a), added subsec. (k), effective for distributions made after 2/2/62.

SUBPART C.—DEFINITIONS; CONSTRUCTIVE OWNERSHIP OF STOCK

Sec.
316. Dividend defined.
317. Other definitions.
318. Constructive ownership of stock.

Sec. 316. Dividend defined.
(a) General rule.

For purposes of this subtitle, the term "dividend" means any distribution of property made by a corporation to its shareholders—

(1) out of its earnings and profits accumulated after February 28, 1913, or

(2) out of its earnings and profits of the taxable year (computed as of the close of the taxable year without diminution by reason of any distributions made during the taxable year), without regard to the amount of the earnings and profits at the time the distribution was made.

Except as otherwise provided in this subtitle, every distribution is made out of earnings and profits to the extent thereof, and from the most recently accumulated earnings and profits. To the extent that any distribution is, under any provision of this subchapter, treated as a distribution of property to which section 301 applies, such distribution shall be treated as a distribution of property for purposes of this subsection.

(b) Special rules.

(1) Certain insurance company dividends. The definition in subsection (a) shall not apply to the term "dividend" as used in subchapter L in any case where the reference is to dividends of insurance companies paid to policyholders as such.

(2) Distributions by personal holding companies.

(A) In the case of a corporation which—

(i) under the law applicable to the taxable year in which the distribution is made, is a personal holding company (as defined in section 542), or

(ii) for the taxable year in respect of which the distribution is made under section 563(b) (relating to dividends paid after the close of the taxable year), or section 547 (relating to deficiency dividends), or the corresponding provisions of prior law, is a personal holding company under the law applicable to such taxable year,

the term "dividend" also means any distribution of property (whether or not a dividend as defined in subsection (a)) made by the corporation to its shareholders, to the extent of its undistributed personal holding company income (determined under section 545 without regard to distributions under this paragraph) for such year.

(B) For purposes of subparagraph (A), the term "distribution of property" includes a distribution in complete liquidation occurring within 24 months after the adoption of a plan of liquidation, but—

(i) only to the extent of the amounts distributed to distributees other than corporate shareholders, and

(ii) only to the extent that the corporation designates such amounts as a dividend distribution and duly notifies such distributees of such designation, under regulations prescribed by the Secretary, but

(iii) not in excess of the sum of such distributees' allocable share of the undistributed personal holding company income for such year, computed without regard to this subparagraph or section 562(b).

(3) Deficiency dividend distributions by a regulated investment company or real estate investment trust. The term "dividend" also means any distribution of property (whether or not a dividend as defined in subsection (a)) which constitutes a "deficiency dividend" as defined in section 860(f).

(4) Certain distributions by regulated investment companies in excess of earnings and profits. In the case of a regulated investment company that has a taxable year other than a calendar year, if the distributions by the company with respect to any class of stock of such company for the taxable year exceed the company's current and accumulated earnings and profits which may be used for the payment of dividends on such class of stock, the company's current earnings and profits shall, for purposes of subsection (a), be allocated first to distributions with respect to such class of stock made during the portion of the taxable year which precedes January 1.

In 2010, P.L. 111-325, Sec. 305(a), added para. (b)(4), effective for distributions made in tax. yrs. begin. after 12/22/2010.

In 1980, P.L. 96-222, Sec. 103(a)(11)(A), amended Sec. 362(e) of P.L. 95-600, the effective date for changes made by Sec. 362 of P.L. 95-600, by substituting "860(e)" for "860(d)" [see below]

In 1978, P.L. 95-600, Sec. 362(d)(1), substituted "section 860(f)" for "section 859(d)" in para. (b)(3), and substituted "regulated investment company or real estate investment trust" for "real estate investment trust" in the heading of para. (b)(3), effective for determinations (as defined in Code Sec. 860(e)) after 11/6/78.

In 1976, P.L. 94-455, Sec. 1601(d), added para. (b)(3), effective for determinations (as defined in subsec. 859(c)) occurring after 10/4/76.

—P.L. 94-455, Sec. 1906(b)(13)(A), substituted "Secretary" for "Secretary or his delegate" in clause (b)(2)(B)(ii), effective for tax. yrs. begin. after 12/31/76.

In 1964, P.L. 88-272, Sec. 225(f)(1), added the definition of "distribution of property" in subsec. (b)(2), effective for distributions made in any tax. yr. of the distributing corporation begin. after 12/31/63.

In 1956, ch. 83, Sec. 5(1), substituted "subchapter L" for "sections 803(e), 821(a)(2), and 832(c)(11)", in para. (b)(1), effective for tax. yrs. begin. after 12/31/54.

Sec. 317. Other definitions.
(a) Property.

For purposes of this part, the term "property" means money, securities, and any other property; except that such term does not include stock in the corporation making the distribution (or rights to acquire such stock).

(b) Redemption of stock.

For purposes of this part, stock shall be treated as redeemed by a corporation if the corporation acquires its stock from a shareholder in exchange for property, whether or not the stock so acquired is cancelled, retired, or held as treasury stock.

Sec. 318. Constructive ownership of stock.
(a) General rule.

For purposes of those provisions of this subchapter to which the rules contained in this section are expressly made applicable—

(1) Members of family.

(A) In general. An individual shall be considered as owning the stock owned, directly or indirectly, by or for—

(i) his spouse (other than a spouse who is legally separated from the individual under a decree of divorce or separate maintenance), and

1,797

(ii) his children, grandchildren, and parents.

(B) Effect of adoption. For purposes of subparagraph (A)(ii), a legally adopted child of an individual shall be treated as a child of such individual by blood.

(2) Attribution from partnerships, estates, trusts, and corporations.

(A) From partnerships and estates. Stock owned, directly or indirectly, by or for a partnership or estate shall be considered as owned proportionately by its partners or beneficiaries.

(B) From trusts.

(i) Stock owned, directly or indirectly, by or for a trust (other than an employees' trust described in section 401(a) which is exempt from tax under section 501(a)) shall be considered as owned by its beneficiaries in proportion to the actuarial interest of such beneficiaries in such trust.

(ii) Stock owned, directly or indirectly, by or for any portion of a trust of which a person is considered the owner under subpart E of part I of subchapter J (relating to grantors and others treated as substantial owners) shall be considered as owned by such person.

(C) From corporations. If 50 percent or more in value of the stock in a corporation is owned, directly or indirectly, by or for any person, such person shall be considered as owning the stock owned, directly or indirectly, by or for such corporation, in that proportion which the value of the stock which such person so owns bears to the value of all the stock in such corporation.

(3) Attribution to partnerships, estates, trusts, and corporations.

(A) To partnerships and estates. Stock owned, directly or indirectly, by or for a partner or a beneficiary of an estate shall be considered as owned by the partnership or estate.

(B) To trusts.

(i) Stock owned directly or indirectly, by or for a beneficiary of a trust (other than an employees' trust described in section 401(a) which is exempt from tax under section 501(a)) shall be considered as owned by the trust, unless such beneficiary's interest in the trust is a remote contingent interest. For purposes of this clause, a contingent interest of a beneficiary in a trust shall be considered remote if, under the maximum exercise of discretion by the trustee in favor of such beneficiary, the value of such interest, computed actuarially, is 5 percent or less of the value of the trust property.

(ii) Stock owned, directly or indirectly, by or for a person who is considered the owner of any portion of a trust under subpart E of part I of subchapter J (relating to grantors and others treated as substantial owners) shall be considered as owned by the trust.

(C) To corporations. If 50 percent or more in value of the stock in a corporation is owned, directly or indirectly, by or for any person, such corporation shall be considered as owning the stock owned, directly or indirectly, by or for such person.

(4) Options. If any person has an option to acquire stock, such stock shall be considered as owned by such person. For purposes of this paragraph, an option to acquire such an option, and each one of a series of such options, shall be considered as an option to acquire such stock.

(5) Operating rules.

(A) In general. Except as provided in subparagraphs (B) and (C), stock constructively owned by a person by reason of the application of paragraph (1), (2), (3), or (4), shall, for purposes of applying paragraphs (1), (2), (3), and (4), be considered as actually owned by such person.

(B) Members of family. Stock constructively owned by an individual by reason of the application of paragraph (1) shall not be considered as owned by him for purposes of again applying paragraph (1) in order to make another the constructive owner of such stock.

(C) Partnerships, estates, trusts, and corporations. Stock constructively owned by a partnership, estate, trust, or corporation by reason of the application of paragraph (3) shall not be considered as owned by it for purposes of applying paragraph (2) in order to make another the constructive owner of such stock.

(D) Option rule in lieu of family rule. For purposes of this paragraph, if stock may be considered as owned by an individual under paragraph (1) or (4), it shall be considered as owned by him under paragraph (4).

(E) S Corporation treated as partnership. For purposes of this subsection—

(i) an S corporation shall be treated as a partnership, and

(ii) any shareholder of the S corporation shall be treated as a partner of such partnership.

The preceding sentence shall not apply for purposes of determining whether stock in the S corporation is constructively owned by any person.

(b) Cross references.

For provisions to which the rules contained in subsection (a) apply, see—

(1) section 302 (relating to redemption of stock);

(2) section 304 (relating to redemption by related corporations);

(3) section 306(b)(1)(A) (relating to disposition of section 306 stock);

(4) section 338(h)(3) (defining purchase);

(5) section 382(l)(3) (relating to special limitations on net operating loss carryovers);

(6) section 856(d) (relating to definition of rents from real property in the case of real estate investment trusts);

(7) section 958(b) (relating to constructive ownership rules with respect to controlled foreign corporations); and

(8) section 6038(e)(2) (relating to information with respect to certain foreign corporations).

In **2005**, P.L. 109-135, Sec. 412(u), substituted "section 6038(e)(2)" for "section 6038(d)(2)" in para. (b)(8), effective 12/21/2005.

In **1997**, P.L. 105-34, Sec. 1142(e)(3), substituted "6038(d)(2)" for "6038(d)(1)" in para. (b)(8), effective for annual accounting periods begin. after 8/5/97.

In **1988**, P.L. 100-647, Sec. 1006(d)(11), amended Sec. 621(f)(1) of P.L. 99-514 [reproduced below].

Prior to amendment Sec. 621(f)(1) of P.L. 99-514 read as follows:

"(1) In general. — The amendments made by subsection (a), (b) and (c) [Sec. 621] shall apply to any ownership change following —

"(A) an owner shift involving a 5-percent shareholder occurring after December 31, 1986, or

"(B) an equity structure shift occurring pursuant to a plan of reorganization adopted after December 31, 1986."

In **1986**, P.L. 99-514, Sec. 621(c)(1), substituted "section 382(l)(3)" for "section 382(a)(3)" in para. (b)(5), effective as provided in Sec. 621(f)(1) [as amended by Sec. 1006(d)(11) of P.L. 100-647, see above]. of this Act which reads:

"(1) Amendments made by subsections (a), (b), and (c). —

"(A) In general. —

"(i) Changes after 1986. The amendments made by subsections (a), (b), and (c) shall apply to any ownership change after December 31, 1986.

"(ii) Plans of reorganization adopted before 1987. For purposes of clause (i), any equity structure shift pursuant to a plan of reorganization adopted before January 1, 1987, shall be treated as occurring when such plan was adopted.

"(B) Termination of old section 382. Except in a case described in any of the following paragraphs—

"(i) section 382(a) of the Internal Revenue Code of 1954 (as in effect before the amendment made by subsection (a) and the amendments made by section 806 of the Tax Reform Act of 1976) shall not apply to any increase in percentage points occurring after December 31, 1988, and

"(ii) section 382(b) of such Code (as so in effect) shall not apply to any reorganization occurring pursuant to a plan of reorganization adopted after December 31, 1986.

In no event shall sections 382 (a) and (b) of such Code (as so in effect) apply to any ownership change described in subparagraph (A).

"(C) Coordination with section 382(i). For purposes of section 382(i) of the Internal Revenue Code of 1986 (as added by this section), any equity structure shift pursuant to a plan of reorganization adopted before January 1, 1987, shall be treated as occurring when such plan was adopted."

In 1984, P.L. 98-369, Sec. 712(k)(5)(E), amended para. (b)(4), effective for any target corporation whose acquisition date occurs after 8/31/82, with the following exceptions, as provided in Secs. 712(k)(9)(A) and (B) of this Act, following:

"(A) In general.—The amendments made by this subsection shall not apply to any qualified stock purchase (as defined in section 338(d)(3) of the Internal Revenue Code of 1954) where the acquisition date (as defined in section 338(h)(2) of such Code) is before September 1, 1982.

"(B) Extension of time for making election.—In the case of any qualified stock purchase described in subparagraph (A), the time for making an election under section 338 of such Code shall not expire before the close of the 60th day after the date of the enactment of this Act."

Prior to amendment, para. (b)(4) read as follows:

"(4) section 338(h)(3)(B) (relating to purchase of stock from subsidiaries, etc.);"

—P.L. 98-369, Sec. 721(j), added subpara. (a)(5)(E), effective for tax. yrs. begin. after 12/31/84.

In 1982, P.L. 97-248, Sec. 224(c)(3), amended para. (b)(4), effective for any target corporation (within the meaning of Code Sec. 338 as added by Sec. 224(a) of this Act) whose acquisition date (within the meaning of Code Sec. 338) occurs after 8/31/82.

Prior to amendment, para. (b)(4) read as follows:

"(4) section 334(b)(3)(C) (relating to basis of property received in certain liquidations of subsidiaries);"

In 1964, P.L. 88-554, Sec. 4(a), amended paras. (a)(2), (3) and (4) and added para. (a)(5) ... Sec. 4(b)(1), deleted "and" at the end of para. (b)(6), redesignated para. (b)(7) as para. (b)(8) and added new para. (b)(7), effective 8/31/64, except that, for purposes of Code Secs. 302 and 304, such amendments shall not apply for distributions in payment for stock acquisitions or redemptions, if such acquisitions or redemptions occurred before 8/31/64.

Prior to amendment, paras. (a)(2)-(4) read as follows:

"(2) Partnerships, estates, trusts, and corporations.

"(A) Partnerships and estates. Stock owned, directly or indirectly, by or for a partnership or estate shall be considered as being owned proportionably by its partners or beneficiaries. Stock owned, directly or indirectly, by or for a partner or a beneficiary of an estate shall be considered as being owned by the partnership or estate.

"(B) Trusts. Stock owned, directly or indirectly, by or for a trust shall be considered as being owned by its beneficiaries in proportion to the actuarial interest of such beneficiaries in such trust. Stock owned, directly or indirectly, by or for a beneficiary of a trust shall be considered as being owned by the trust, unless such beneficiary's interest in the trust is a remote contingent interest. For purposes of the preceding sentence, a contingent interest of a beneficiary in a trust shall be considered remote, if, under the maximum exercise of discretion by the trustee in favor of such beneficiary, the value of such interest, computed actuarially, is 5 percent or less of the value of the trust property. Stock owned, directly or indirectly, by or for any portion of a trust of which a person is considered the owner under subpart E of part I of subchapter J (relating to grantors and others treated as substantial owners) shall be considered as being owned by such person; and such trust shall be treated as owning the stock owned, directly or indirectly, by or for that person. This subparagraph shall not apply with respect to any employees' trust described in section 401(a) which is exempt from tax under section 501(a).

"(C) Corporations. If 50 percent or more in value of the stock in a corporation is owned, directly or indirectly, by or for any person, then—

"(i) such person shall be considered as owning the stock owned, directly or indirectly, by or for that corporation, in that proportion which the value of the stock which such person so owns bears to the value of all the stock in such corporation; and

"(ii) such corporation shall be considered as owning the stock owned, directly or indirectly, by or for that person.

"(3) Options. If any person has an option to acquire stock, such stock shall be considered as owned by such person. For purposes of this paragraph, an option to acquire such an option, and each one of a series of such options, shall be considered as an option to acquire such stock.

"(4) Constructive ownership as actual ownership.

"(A) In general. Except as provided in subparagraph (B), stock constructively owned by a person by reason of the application of paragraph (1), (2), or (3) shall, for purposes of applying paragraph (1), (2), or (3), be treated as actually owned by such person.

"(B) Members of family. Stock constructively owned by an individual by reason of the application of paragraph (1) shall not be treated as owned by him for purposes of again applying paragraph (1) in order to make another the constructive owner of such stock.

"(C) Option rule in lieu of family rule. For purposes of this paragraph, if stock may be considered as owned by an individual under paragraph (1) or (3), it shall be considered as owned by him under paragraph (3)."

In 1962, P.L. 87-834, Sec. 20(d), deleted "and" at the end of para. (b)(5), substituted "; and" for the period at the end of para. (b)(6), and added para. (b)(7).

In 1960, P.L. 86-779, Sec. 10(h), deleted "and" at the end of para. (b)(4), substituted "; and" for the period at the end of para. (b)(5), and added para. (b)(6), effective for tax yrs. of real estate investment trusts begin. after 12/31/60.

PART II.—CORPORATE LIQUIDATIONS

Subpart
A. Effects on recipients.
B. Effects on corporation.
C. Repealed. [Collapsible corporations.]
D. Definition and special rule.

In 2003, P.L. 108-27, Sec. 302(e)(4)(B)(iii), deleted the item for subpart C.

Prior to deletion, the item for subpart C read as follows:

"C. Collapsible corporations."

—P.L. 108-27, Sec. 303, of this Act [as amended by Sec. 102 of P.L. 109-222, and. Sec. 102(a), P.L. 111-312, see above], reads as follows:

"SEC. 303. SUNSET OF TITLE. All provisions of, and amendments made by, this title [Secs. 301 and 302] shall not apply to taxable years beginning after December 31, 2012, and the Internal Revenue Code of 1986 shall be applied and administered to such years as if such provisions and amendments had never been enacted."

In 1982, P.L. 97-248, Sec. 222(e)(8)(B), amended the item for Subpart D.

Prior to amendment, the item for Subpart D read as follows:

"D. Definition."

In 1976, P.L. 94-455, Sec. 1901(b)(12)(B), amended the item for Subpart C.

Prior to amendment, that item for Subpart C read as follows:

"C. Collapsible corporations; foreign personal holding companies."

SUBPART A.—EFFECTS ON RECIPIENTS

Sec.
331. Gain or loss to shareholders in corporate liquidations.
332. Complete liquidations of subsidiaries.
333. Repealed. [Election as to recognition of gain of certain liquidations.]
334. Basis of property received in liquidations.

In 1986, P.L. 99-514, Sec. 631(e)(16), repealed item 333.

Prior to repeal, item 333 read as follows:

"333. Election as to recognition of gain in certain liquidations."

Sec. 331. Gain or loss to shareholders in corporate liquidations.

(a) Distributions in complete liquidation treated as exchanges.

Amounts received by a shareholder in a distribution in complete liquidation of a corporation shall be treated as in full payment in exchange for the stock.

(b) Nonapplication of section 301.

Section 301 (relating to effects on shareholder of distributions of property) shall not apply to any distribution of property (other than a distribution referred to in paragraph (2)(B) of section 316(b)) in complete liquidation.

(c) Cross reference.

For general rule for determination of the amount of gain or loss recognized, see section 1001.

In 1982, P.L. 97-248, Sec. 222(a), amended subsec. (a) ... Sec. 222(e)(1)(B), substituted "complete liquidation" for "partial or complete liquidation" in subsec. (b), effective for distributions after 8/31/82. For exceptions and special rules see Sec. 222(f)(2)–(4) of this Act reproduced in note following Code Sec. 302.

Prior to amendment, subsec. (a) read as follows:

"(a) General rule.

"(1) Complete liquidations. Amounts distributed in complete liquidation of a corporation shall be treated as in full payment in exchange for the stock.

"(2) Partial liquidations. Amounts distributed in partial liquidation of a corporation (as defined in section 346) shall be treated as in part or full payment in exchange for the stock."

In 1976, P.L. 94-455, Sec. 1901(b)(28)(A), amended subsec. (c), effective for tax. yrs. begin. after 12/31/76.

Prior to amendment, subsec. (c) read as follows:
"(c) Cross references.
"(1) For general rule for determination of the amount of gain or loss to the distributee, see section 1001.
"(2) For general rule for determination of the amount of gain or loss recognized, see section 1002."

In 1964, P.L. 88-272, Sec. 225(f)(2), added "(other than a distribution referred to in paragraph (2)(B) of section 316(b))" after "any distribution of property" in subsec. (b), effective for distributions made in any tax. yr. of the distributing corporation begin. after 12/31/63.

Sec. 332. Complete liquidations of subsidiaries.

(a) General rule.

No gain or loss shall be recognized on the receipt by a corporation of property distributed in complete liquidation of another corporation.

(b) Liquidations to which section applies.

For purposes of this section, a distribution shall be considered to be in complete liquidation only if—

(1) the corporation receiving such property was, on the date of the adoption of the plan of liquidation, and has continued to be at all times until the receipt of the property, the owner of stock (in such other corporation) meeting the requirements of section 1504(a)(2); and either

(2) the distribution is by such other corporation in complete cancellation or redemption of all its stock, and the transfer of all the property occurs within the taxable year; in such case the adoption by the shareholders of the resolution under which is authorized the distribution of all the assets of such corporation in complete cancellation or redemption of all its stock shall be considered an adoption of a plan of liquidation, even though no time for the completion of the transfer of the property is specified in such resolution; or

(3) such distribution is one of a series of distributions by such other corporation in complete cancellation or redemption of all its stock in accordance with a plan of liquidation under which the transfer of all the property under the liquidation is to be completed within 3 years from the close of the taxable year during which is made the first of the series of distributions under the plan, except that if such transfer is not completed within such period, or if the taxpayer does not continue qualified under paragraph (1) until the completion of such transfer, no distribution under the plan shall be considered a distribution in complete liquidation.

If such transfer of all the property does not occur within the taxable year, the Secretary may require of the taxpayer such bond, or waiver of the statute of limitations on assessment and collection, or both, as he may deem necessary to insure, if the transfer of the property is not completed within such 3-year period, or if the taxpayer does not continue qualified under paragraph (1) until the completion of such transfer, the assessment and collection of all income taxes then imposed by law for such taxable year or subsequent taxable years, to the extent attributable to property so received. A distribution otherwise constituting a distribution in complete liquidation within the meaning of this subsection shall not be considered as not constituting such a distribution merely because it does not constitute a distribution or liquidation within the meaning of the corporate law under which the distribution is made; and for purposes of this subsection a transfer of property of such other corporation to the taxpayer shall not be considered as not constituting a distribution (or one of a series of distributions) in complete cancellation or redemption of all the stock of such other corporation, merely because the carrying out of the plan involves (A) the transfer under the plan to the taxpayer by such other corporation of property, not attributable to shares owned by the taxpayer, on an exchange described in section 361, and (B) the complete cancellation or redemption under the plan, as a result of exchanges described in section 354, of the shares not owned by the taxpayer.

(c) Deductible liquidating distributions of regulated investment companies and real estate investment trusts.

If a corporation receives a distribution from a regulated investment company or a real estate investment trust which is considered under subsection (b) as being in complete liquidation of such company or trust, then, notwithstanding any other provision of this chapter, such corporation shall recognize and treat as a dividend from such company or trust an amount equal to the deduction for dividends paid allowable to such company or trust by reason of such distribution.

(d) Recognition of gain on liquidation of certain holding companies.

(1) **In general.** In the case of any distribution to a foreign corporation in complete liquidation of an applicable holding company—

(A) subsection (a) and section 331 shall not apply to such distribution, and

(B) such distribution shall be treated as a distribution of property to which section 301 applies.

(2) **Applicable holding company.** For purposes of this subsection—

(A) In general. The term "applicable holding company" means any domestic corporation—

(i) which is a common parent of an affiliated group,

(ii) stock of which is directly owned by the distributee foreign corporation,

(iii) substantially all of the assets of which consist of stock in other members of such affiliated group, and

(iv) which has not been in existence at all times during the 5 years immediately preceding the date of the liquidation.

(B) Affiliated group. For purposes of this subsection, the term "affiliated group" has the meaning given such term by section 1504(a) (without regard to paragraphs (2) and (4) of section 1504(b)).

(3) **Coordination with subpart F.** If the distributee of a distribution described in paragraph (1) is a controlled foreign corporation (as defined in section 957), then notwithstanding paragraph (1) or subsection (a), such distribution shall be treated as a distribution to which section 331 applies.

(4) **Regulations.** The Secretary shall provide such regulations as appropriate to prevent the abuse of this subsection, including regulations which provide, for the purposes of clause (iv) of paragraph (2)(A), that a corporation is not in existence for any period unless it is engaged in the active conduct of a trade or business or owns a significant ownership interest in another corporation so engaged.

In 2005, P.L. 109-135, Sec. 412(v), substituted "distribution of property to which section 301 applies" for "distribution to which section 301 applies" in subpara. (d)(1)(B), effective 12/21/2005.

In 2004, P.L. 108-357, Sec. 893(a), added subsec. (d), effective for distributions in complete liquidation occurring on or after 10/22/2004.

In 2000, P.L. 106-554, Sec. 1(a)(7), [which enacted into law Sec. 311(c) of P.L. 106-554] of this Act, reads as follows:

"(c) Clarification related to section 538 of the Act. The reference to section 332(b)(1) of the Internal Revenue Code of 1986 in Treasury Regulation section 1.1502-34 shall be deemed to include a reference to section 732(f) of such Code."

In 1998, P.L. 105-277, Sec. 3001(a), added subsec. (c) . . . Sec. 3001(b)(1), substituted "this section" for "subsection (a)" in subsec. (b), effective for distributions after 5/21/98.

—P.L. 105-277, Sec. 3001(d), of this Act, reads as follows:

"(d) Assumptions. In making the estimate required for this Act by section 252(d)(2) of the Balanced Budget and Emergency Deficit Control Act of 1985,

Corporate distributions and adjustments   **Code Sec. 333**

that part of the estimate that measures the change in receipts resulting from the amendments made by this section shall be based on the economic and technical assumptions underlying the supplemental summary of the budget for fiscal year 1999, submitted on May 26, 1998, pursuant to section 1106 of title 31, United states Code, notwithstanding section 252(d)(2)(B). All other parts of such estimate required by such section 252(d)(2) shall be made pursuant to the requirements of such section 252(d)(2)(B)."

In 1988, P.L. 100-647, Sec. 1006(g)(2), amended Sec. 633(c)(1)(B) of P.L. 99-514, [reproduced below] by substituting "more than 50 percent" for "50 percent or more", effective as provided in Secs. 633(a)(1) and (c) of P.L. 99-514, see below.

In 1986, P.L. 99-514, Sec. 631(e)(2), deleted subsec. (c), effective as provided in Secs. 633(a)(1) and (c) [as amended by Sec. 1006(g)(2) of P.L. 100-647, see above] of this Act:

"*(a) General rule.*—

"Except as otherwise provided in this section, the amendments made by this subtitle shall apply to—

"(1) any distribution in complete liquidation, and any sale or exchange, made by a corporation after July 31, 1986, unless such corporation is completely liquidated before January 1, 1987,"

"*(c) Exception for certain plans of liquidation and binding contracts.*—

"(1) In general.—The amendments made by this subtitle shall not apply to—

"(A) any distribution or sale or exchange made pursuant to a plan of liquidation adopted before August 1, 1986, if the liquidating corporation is completely liquidated before January 1, 1988,

"(B) any distribution or sale or exchange made by any corporation if more than 50 percent of the voting stock (by value) of such corporation is acquired on or after August 1, 1986, pursuant to a written binding contract in effect before such date and if such corporation is completely liquidated before January 1, 1988,

"(C) any distribution or sale or exchange made by any corporation if substantially all of the assets of such corporation are sold on or after August 1, 1986, pursuant to 1 or more written binding contracts in effect before such date and if such corporation is completely liquidated before January 1, 1988, or

"(D) any transaction described in section 338 of the Internal Revenue Code of 1986 with respect to any target corporation if a qualified stock purchase of such target corporation is made on or after August 1, 1986, pursuant to a written binding contract in effect before such date and the acquisition date (within the meaning of such section 338) is before January 1, 1988.

"(2) Special rule for certain actions taken before November 20, 1985.—For purposes of paragraph (1), transactions shall be treated as pursuant to a plan of liquidation adopted before August 1, 1986, if—

"(A) before November 20, 1985—

"(i) the board of directors of the liquidating corporation adopted a resolution to solicit shareholder approval for a transaction of a kind described in section 336 or 337, or

"(ii) the shareholders or board of directors have approved such a transaction,

"(B) before November 20, 1985—

"(i) there has been an offer to purchase a majority of the voting stock of the liquidating corporation, or

"(ii) the board of directors of the liquidating corporation has adopted a resolution approving an acquisition or recommending the approval of an acquisition to the shareholders, or

"(C) before November 20, 1985, a ruling request was submitted to the Secretary of the Treasury or his delegate with respect to a transaction of a kind described in section 336 or 337 of the Internal Revenue Code of 1954 (as in effect before the amendments made by this subtitle).

For purposes of the preceding sentence, any action taken by the board of directors or shareholders of a corporation with respect to any subsidiary of such corporation shall be treated as taken by the board of directors or shareholders of such subsidiary."

Sec. 633(e) of this Act provides:

"*(e) Complete liquidation defined.*—

"For purposes of this section, a corporation shall be treated as completely liquidated if all of the assets of such corporation are distributed in complete liquidation, less assets retained to meet claims."

Prior to deletion, subsec. (c) read as follows:

"*(c) Special rule for indebtedness of subsidiary to parent.* If—

"(1) a corporation is liquidated and subsection (a) applies to such liquidation, and

"(2) on the date of the adoption of the plan of liquidation, such corporation was indebted to the corporation which meets the 80 percent stock ownership requirements specified in subsection (b),

then no gain or loss shall be recognized to the corporation so indebted because of the transfer of property in satisfaction of such indebtedness."

—P.L. 99-514, Sec. 1804(e)(6)(A), amended para. (b)(1), effective as provided in Sec. 1804(e)(6)(B) of this Act:

"(B) Effective date.—

"(i) In general.—Except as provided in clause (iii), the amendment made by subparagraph (A) [Sec. 1804(e)(6)(A)] shall apply with respect to plans of complete liquidation adopted after March 28, 1985.

"(ii) Certain distributions made after December 31, 1984.—Except as provided in clause (iii), the amendment made by subparagraph (A) [Sec. 1804(e)(6)(A)] shall also apply with respect to plans of complete liquidations adopted on or before March 28, 1985, pursuant to which any distribution is made in a taxable year beginning after December 31, 1984 (December 31, 1983, in the case of an affiliated group to which an election under section 60(b)(7) of the Tax Reform Act of 1984 [P.L. 98-369] applies), but only if the liquidating corporation and any corporation which receives a distribution in complete liquidation of such corporation are members of an affiliated group of corporations filing a consolidated return for the taxable year which includes the date of the distribution.

"(iii) Transitional rule for affiliated groups.—The amendment made by subparagraph (A) [Sec. 1804(e)(6)(A)] shall not apply with respect to plans of complete liquidation if the liquidating corporation is a member of an affiliated group of corporations under section 60(b)(2), (5), (6), or (8) of the Tax Reform Act of 1984 [P.L. 98-369], for all taxable years which include the date of any distribution pursuant to such plan."

Prior to amendment, para. (b)(1) read as follows:

"(1) the corporation receiving such property was, on the date of the adoption of the plan of liquidation, and has continued to be at all times until the receipt of the property, the owner of stock (in such other corporation) possessing at least 80 percent of the total combined voting power of all classes of stock entitled to vote and the owner of at least 80 percent of the total number of shares of all other classes of stock (except nonvoting stock which is limited and preferred as to dividends); and either"

In 1976, P.L. 94-455, Sec. 1906(b)(13)(A), substituted "Secretary" for "Secretary or his delegate" in Code Sec. 332, effective for tax. yrs. begin. after 12/31/76.

Sec. 333. Repealed.

In 1986, P.L. 99-514, Sec. 631(e)(3), repealed Code Sec. 333, effective as provided in Sec. 633(a)(1), (d) [sic (e)] and (c) of this Act which reads as follows:

"*(a) General rule.*—

"Except as otherwise provided in this section, the amendments made by this subtitle shall apply to—

"(1) any distribution in complete liquidation, and any sale or exchange, made by a corporation after July 31, 1986, unless such corporation is completely liquidated before January 1, 1987,"

Sec. 633(d)[sic (e)] of this Act provides:

"*(d) [sic (e)] Complete liquidation defined.*—

"For purposes of this section, a corporation shall be treated as completely liquidated if all of the assets of such corporation are distributed in complete liquidation, less assets retained to meet claims."

For exceptions see Sec. 633(c) of this Act reproduced in note following Code Sec. 336.

Prior to repeal, Code Sec. 333 read as follows:

"SEC. 333. ELECTION AS TO RECOGNITION OF GAIN IN CERTAIN LIQUIDATIONS.

"*(a) General rule*

"In the case of property distributed in complete liquidation of a domestic corporation (other than a collapsible corporation to which section 341(a) applies), if—

"(1) the liquidation is made in pursuance of a plan of liquidation adopted, and

"(2) the distribution is in complete cancellation or redemption of all the stock, and the transfer of all the property under the liquidation occurs within some one calendar month,

then in the case of each qualified electing shareholder (as defined in subsection (c)) gain on the shares owned by him at the time of the adoption of the plan of liquidation shall be recognized only to the extent provided in subsections (e) and (f).

"*(b) Excluded corporation.*

"For purposes of this section, the term 'excluded corporation' means a corporation which at any time between January 1, 1954, and the date of the adoption of the plan of liquidation, both dates inclusive, was the owner of stock possessing 50 percent or more of the total combined voting power of all classes of stock entitled to vote on the adoption of such plan.

"*(c) Qualified electing shareholders.*

"For purposes of this section, the term 'qualified electing shareholder' means a shareholder (other than an excluded corporation) of any class of stock (whether or not entitled to vote on the adoption of the plan of liquidation) who is a shareholder at the time of the adoption of such plan, and whose written election to have the benefits of subsection (a) has been made and filed in accordance with subsection (d), but—

"(1) in the case of a shareholder other than a corporation, only if written elections have been so filed by shareholders (other than corporations) who at the time of the adoption of the plan of liquidation are owners of stock possessing at least 80 percent of the total combined voting power (exclusive of voting power possessed by stock owned by corporations) of all classes of stock entitled to vote on the adoption of such plan of liquidation; or

"(2) in the case of a shareholder which is a corporation, only if written elections have been so filed by corporate shareholders (other than an excluded corporation) which at the time of the adoption of such plan of liquidation are owners of stock possessing at least 80 percent of the total combined voting power (exclusive of voting power possessed by stock owned by an excluded corporation and by shareholders who are not corporations) of all classes of stock entitled to vote on the adoption of such plan of liquidation.

"*(d) Making and filing of elections.*

"The written elections referred to in subsection (c) must be made and filed in such manner as to be not in contravention of regulations prescribed by the Secretary. The filing must be within 30 days after the date of the adoption of the plan of liquidation.

"*(e) Noncorporate shareholders.*

"In the case of a qualified electing shareholder other than a corporation—

"(1) there shall be recognized, and treated as a dividend, so much of the gain as is not in excess of his ratable share of the earnings and profits of the corporation accumulated after February 28, 1913, such earnings and profits to be determined as of the close of the month in which the transfer in liquidation occurred under

Code Sec. 333 — Corporate distributions and adjustments

subsection (a)(2), but without diminution by reason of distributions made during such month; but by including in the computation thereof all amounts accrued up to the date on which the transfer of all the property under the liquidation is completed; and

"(2) there shall be recognized, and treated as short-term or long-term capital gain, as the case may be, so much of the remainder of the gain as is not in excess of the amount by which the value of that portion of the assets received by him which consists of money, or of stock or securities acquired by the corporation after December 31, 1953, exceeds his ratable share of such earnings and profits.

"(f) Corporate shareholders.

"In the case of a qualified electing shareholder which is a corporation, the gain shall be recognized only to the extent of the greater of the two following —

"(1) the portion of the assets received by it which consists of money, or of stock or securities acquired by the liquidating corporation after December 31, 1953; or

"(2) its ratable share of the earnings and profits of the liquidating corporation accumulated after February 28, 1913, such earnings and profits to be determined as of the close of the month in which the transfer in liquidation occurred under subsection (a)(2), but without diminution by reason of distributions made during such month; but by including in the computation thereof all amounts accrued up to the date on which the transfer of all the property under the liquidation is completed."

In 1984, P.L. 98-369, Sec. 713(h), amended Sec. 247(a) of P.L. 97-348 [reproduced below], by adding "which is in existence on September 3, 1982," after "section 535(c)(2)(B) of the Internal Revenue Code of 1954)".

In 1983, P.L. 97-448, Sec. 305(d)(1)(B), provides:

"(B) If—

"(i) after September 30, 1982, and on or before the date of the enactment of this Act, stock or securities were transferred to a small business corporation (as defined in section 1361(b) of the Internal Revenue Code of 1954 as amended by the Subchapter S Revision Act of 1982) in a transaction to which section 351 of such Code applies, and

"(ii) such corporation is liquidated under section 333 of such Code before March 1, 1983,

then such stock or securities shall not be taken into account under section 333(e)(2) of such Code."

In 1982, P.L. 97-248, Sec. 247, [as amended by Sec. 713(h) of P.L. 97-384, see above] provides:

"SEC. 247. EXISTING PERSONAL SERVICE CORPORATIONS MAY LIQUIDATE UNDER SECTION 333 DURING 1983 OR 1984.

"(a) In general.—

"In the case of a complete liquidation of a personal service corporation (within the meaning of section 535(c)(2)(B) of the Internal Revenue Code of 1954) which is in existence on September 3, 1982 during 1983 or 1984, the following rules shall apply with respect to any shareholder other than a corporation:

"(1) The determination of whether section 333 of such Code applies shall be made without regard to whether the corporation is a collapsible corporation to which section 341(a) of such Code applies.

"(2) No gain or loss shall be recognized by the liquidating corporation on the distribution of any unrealized receivable in such liquidation.

"(3)(A) Except as provided in subparagraph (C), any disposition by a shareholder of any unrealized receivable received in the liquidation shall be treated as a sale at fair market value of such receivable and any gain or loss shall be treated as ordinary gain or loss.

"(B) For purposes of subparagraph (A), the term 'disposition' includes—

"(i) failing to hold the property in the trade or business which generated the receivables, and

"(ii) failing to hold a continuing interest in such trade or business.

"(C) For purposes of subparagraph (A), the term 'disposition' does not include transmission at death to the estate of the decedent or transfer to a person pursuant to the right of such person to receive such property by reason of the death of the decedent or by bequest, devise, or inheritance from the decedent.

"(4) Unrealized receivables distributed in the liquidation shall be treated as having a zero basis.

"(5) For purposes of computing earnings and profits, the liquidating corporation shall not treat unrealized receivables distributed in the liquidation as an item of income.

"(b) Unrealized receivables defined.—

"For purposes of this section, the term 'unrealized receivables' has the meaning given such term by the first sentence of section 751(c) of such Code."

In 1976, P.L. 94-455, Sec. 1901(a)(44), deleted "on or after June 22, 1954" following "liquidation adopted" in para. (a)(1), effective for tax. yrs. begin. after 12/31/76.

—P.L. 94-455, Sec. 1906(b)(13)(A), substituted "Secretary" for "Secretary or his delegate" in subsec. (d), effective for tax. yrs. begin. after 12/31/76.

—P.L. 94-455, Sec. 1951(b)(6)(A), repealed subsec. (g), effective for tax. yrs. begin. after 12/31/76, except as provided in Sec. 1951(b)(6)(B) and (b)(6)(C) of this Act, which read as follows:

"(B) Savings provisions. Notwithstanding subparagraph (A), if any corporation meets all the requirements of section 333(g)(2)(B), as in effect before its repeal by this Act, the liquidation of such corporation shall be treated as if paragraphs (2), (3), and (4) of section 333(g) had not been repealed.

"(C) Phase-in of 12-month holding period requirement.—For purposes of subparagraph (B), the period for holding of stock specified in section 333(g)(2)(A)(ii), as in effect before such repeal, shall—

"(i) in the case of taxable years beginning in 1977, be considered to be '9 months'; and

"(ii) in the case of taxable years beginning after December 31, 1977, be considered to be '1 year'."

Prior to repeal, subsec. (g) read as follows:

"(g) Special rule.

"(1) Liquidations before January 1, 1967. In the case of a liquidation occurring before January 1, 1967, of a corporation referred to in paragraph (3)—

"(A) the date 'December 31, 1953' referred to in subsection (e)(2) and (f)(1) shall be treated as if such date were 'December 31, 1962', and

"(B) in the case of stock in such corporation held for more than 6 months, the term 'a dividend' as used in subsection (e)(1) shall be treated as if such term were 'long-term capital gain'.

Subparagraph (B) shall not apply to any earnings and profits to which the corporation succeeds after December 31, 1963, pursuant to any corporate reorganization or pursuant to any liquidation to which section 332 applies, except earnings and profits which on December 31, 1963, constituted earnings and profits of a corporation referred to in paragraph (3), and except earnings and profits which were earned after such date by a corporation referred to in paragraph (3).

"(2) Liquidations after December 31, 1966.

"(A) In general. In the case of a liquidation occurring after December 31, 1966, of a corporation to which this subparagraph applies—

"(i) the date 'December 31, 1953' referred to in subsections (e)(2) and (f)(1) shall be treated as if such date were 'December 31, 1962', and

"(ii) so much of the gain recognized under subsection (e)(1) as is attributable to the earnings and profits accumulated after February 28, 1913, and before January 1, 1967, shall, in the case of stock in such corporation held for more than 6 months, be treated as long-term capital gain, and only the remainder of such gain shall be treated as a dividend.

Clause (ii) shall not apply to any earnings and profits to which the corporation succeeds after December 31, 1963, pursuant to any corporate reorganization or pursuant to any liquidation to which section 332 applies, except earnings and profits which on December 31, 1963, constituted earnings and profits of a corporation referred to in paragraph (3), and except earnings and profits which were earned after such date by a corporation referred to in paragraph (3).

"(B) Corporations to which applicable. Subparagraph (A) shall apply only with respect to a corporation which is referred to in paragraph (3) and which—

"(i) on January 1, 1964, owes qualified indebtedness (as defined in section 545(c)),

"(ii) before January 1, 1968, notifies the Secretary or his delegate that it may wish to have subparagraph (A) apply to it and submits such information as may be required by regulations prescribed by the Secretary or his delegate, and

"(iii) liquidates before the close of the taxable year in which such corporation ceases to owe such qualified indebtedness or (if earlier) the taxable year referred to in subparagraph (C).

"(C) Adjusted post-1963 earnings and profits exceed qualified indebtedness. In the case of any corporation, the taxable year referred to in this subparagraph is the first taxable year at the close of which its adjusted post-1963 earnings and profits equal or exceed the amount of such corporation's qualified indebtedness on January 1, 1964. For purposes of the preceding sentence, the term 'adjusted post-1963 earnings and profits' means the sum of—

"(i) the earnings and profits of such corporation for taxable years beginning after December 31, 1963, without diminution by reason of any distributions made out of such earnings and profits, and

"(ii) the deductions allowed for taxable years beginning after December 31, 1963, for exhaustion, wear and tear, obsolescence, amortization, or depletion.

"(3) Corporations referred to. For purposes of paragraphs (1) and (2), a corporation referred to in this paragraph is a corporation which for at least one of the two most recent taxable years ending before the date of the enactment of this subsection was not a personal holding company under section 542, but would have been a personal holding company under section 542 for such taxable year if the law applicable for the first taxable year beginning after December 31, 1963, had been applicable to such taxable year.

"(4) Mistake as to applicability of subsection. An election made under this section by a qualified electing shareholder of a corporation in which such shareholder states that such election is made on the assumption that such corporation is a corporation referred to in paragraph (3) shall have no force or effect if it is determined that the corporation is not a corporation referred to in paragraph (3)."

In 1969, P.L. 91-172, Sec. 917, provided:

"Sec. 917. Recognition of gain in certain liquidations.

For purposes of applying section 333(e) and (f) of the Internal Revenue Code of 1954 to a distribution in liquidation of a corporation during 1970, stock (including stock received in respect of such stock by reason of a stock dividend or stock split) or securities received by a qualified electing shareholder in exchange for his stock in the liquidating corporation shall be considered as having been acquired by the liquidating corporation before January 1, 1954, if—

"(1) such stock or securities were acquired by the liquidating corporation after December 31, 1953, from such qualified electing shareholder (or from a person from whom such qualified electing shareholder acquired such stock in the liquidating corporation by gift, bequest, or inheritance) solely in exchange for its stock in a transaction to which section 351 of such Code (or the corresponding provisions of prior law) applied, and

"(2) the holding period of such stock or securities in the hands of the liquidating corporation, determined under section 1223(2) of such Code, includes any period before January 1, 1954."

In 1964, P.L. 88-272, Sec. 225(g), added subsec. (g), effective for distributions made in any tax. yr. of the distributing corporation begin. after 12/31/63.

—P.L. 88-272, Sec. 225(h), provided that:

"(h) Exceptions for certain corporations

Corporate distributions and adjustments Code Sec. 334

"(1) General rule.—Except as provided in paragraph (2), in the case of a corporation referred to in section 333(g)(3) of the Internal Revenue Code of 1954 (as added by subsection (g) of this section), the amendments made by this section (other than subsections (f) and (g)) shall not apply if there is a complete liquidation of such corporation and if the distribution of all the property under such liquidation occurs before January 1, 1966.

"(2) Exception.—Paragraph (1) shall not apply to any liquidation to which section 332 of the Internal Revenue Code of 1954 applies unless—

"(A) the corporate distributee (referred to in subsection (b)(1) of such section 332) in such liquidation is liquidated in a complete liquidation to which such section 332 does not apply, and

"(B) the distribution of all the property under such liquidation occurs before the 91st day after the last distribution referred to in paragraph (1) and before January 1, 1966."

Sec. 334. Basis of property received in liquidations.
(a) General rule.

If property is received in a distribution in complete liquidation, and if gain or loss is recognized on receipt of such property, then the basis of the property in the hands of the distributee shall be the fair market value of such property at the time of the distribution.

(b) Liquidation of subsidiary.

(1) In general. If property is received by a corporate distributee in a distribution in a complete liquidation to which section 332 applies (or in a transfer described in section 337(b)(1)), the basis of such property in the hands of such distributee shall be the same as it would be in the hands of the transferor; except that, in the hands of such distributee—

(A) the basis of such property shall be the fair market value of the property at the time of the distribution in any case in which gain or loss is recognized by the liquidating corporation with respect to such property, and
(B) the basis of any property described in section 362(e)(1)(B) shall be the fair market value of the property at the time of the distribution in any case in which such distributee's aggregate adjusted basis of such property would (but for this subparagraph) exceed the fair market value of such property immediately after such liquidation.

(2) Corporate distributee. For purposes of this subsection, the term "corporate distributee" means only the corporation which meets the stock ownership requirements specified in section 332(b).

In 2005, P.L. 109-135, Sec. 403(dd)(1), substituted "except that, in the hands of such distributee—(A) the basis of such property shall be the fair market value of the property at the time of the distribution in any case in which gain or loss is recognized by the liquidating corporation with respect to such property, and (B) the basis of any property described in section 362(e)(1)(B) shall be the fair market value of the property at the time of the distribution in any case in which such distributee's aggregate adjusted basis of such property would (but for this subparagraph) exceed the fair market value of such property immediately after such liquidation." for "except that the basis of such property shall be the fair market value of the property at the time of the distribution—(A) in any case in which gain or loss is recognized by the liquidating corporation with respect to such property, or (B) in any case in which the liquidating corporation is a foreign corporation, the corporate distributee is a domestic corporation, and the corporate distributee's aggregate adjusted bases of property described in section 362(e)(1)(B) which is distributed in such liquidation would (but for this subparagraph) exceed the fair market value of such property immediately after such liquidation." in para. (b)(1), effective for liquidations after 10/22/2004 as if included in Sec. 836 of the American Jobs Creation Act of 2004, P.L. 108-357.

In 2004, P.L. 108-357, Sec. 836(b), amended para. (b)(1), effective for liquidations after 10/22/2004.
Prior to amendment, para. (b)(1) read as follows:

"(1) In general. If property is received by a corporate distributee in a distribution in a complete liquidation to which section 332 applies (or in a transfer described in section 337(b)(1)), the basis of such property in the hands of such distributee shall be the same as it would be in the hands of the transferor; except that, in any case in which gain or loss is recognized by the liquidating corporation with respect to such property, the basis of such property in the hands of such distributee shall be the fair market value of the property at the time of the distribution."

In 1998, P.L. 105-277, Sec. 3001(b)(2), substituted "section 332" for "section 332(a)" in para. (b)(1), effective for distributions after 5/21/98.

In 1988, P.L. 100-647, Sec. 1006(e)(6), amended subsec. (b), effective as provided in Sec. 633(a)(1) of P.L. 99-514 reproduced below.
Prior to amendment, subsec. (b) read as follows:
"(b) Liquidation of subsidiary.

"(1) Distribution in complete liquidation. If property is received by a corporation in a distribution in a complete liquidation to which section 332(a) applies, the basis of the property in the hands of the distributee shall be the same as it would be in the hands of the transferor.

"(2) Transfers to which section 332(c) applies. If property is received by a corporation in a transfer to which section 332(c) applies, the basis of the property in the hands of the transferee shall be the same as it would be in the hands of the transferor.

"(3) Distributee defined. For purposes of this subsection, the term 'distributee' means only the corporation which meets the 80-percent stock ownership requirements specified in section 332(b)."

—P.L. 100-647, Sec. 1006(g)(8), amended Sec. 633(e) of P.L. 99-514 [reproduced below], part of the effective date for changes made by Sec. 631(e)(4) of P.L. 99-514, by redesignating Sec. 633(d) of P.L. 99-514, dealing with complete liquidation, as Sec. 633(e) of P.L. 99-514, see below.

In 1986, P.L. 99-514, Sec. 631(e)(4)(A), deleted "(other than a distribution to which section 333 applies)" after "complete liquidation" in subsec. (a) . . . Sec. 631(e)(4)(B), deleted subsec. (c), effective as provided in Sec. 633(a)(1), and (e) [as amended by Sec. 1006(g)(8) of P.L. 100-647, see above] of this Act:
"(a) General rule.—

"Except as otherwise provided in this section, the amendments made by this subtitle shall apply to—

"(1) any distribution in complete liquidation, and any sale or exchange, made by a corporation after July 31, 1986, unless such corporation is completely liquidated before January 1, 1987,"

Sec. 633(e) of this Act [as redesignated by Sec. 1006(g)(8) of P.L. 100-647] provides:

"(e) Complete liquidation defined.—

"For purposes of this section, a corporation shall be treated as completely liquidated if all of the assets of such corporation are distributed in complete liquidation, less assets retained to meet claims."
For exceptions, see Sec. 633(c) of this Act reproduced in note following Code Sec. 336.
Prior to deletion, subsec. (c) read as follows:
"(c) Property received in liquidation under section 333. If—

"(1) property was acquired by a shareholder in the liquidation of a corporation in cancellation or redemption of stock, and

"(2) with respect to such acquisition—

"(A) gain was realized, but

"(B) as the result of an election made by the shareholder under section 333, the extent to which gain was recognized was determined under section 333,
then the basis shall be the same as the basis of such stock cancelled or redeemed in the liquidation, decreased in the amount of any money received by the shareholder, and increased in the amount of gain recognized to him."

In 1982, P.L. 97-248, Sec. 222(e)(1)(C), substituted "complete liquidation" for "partial or complete liquidation" in subsec. (a), effective for distributions after 8/31/82. For exceptions and special rules see Sec. 222(f)(2)-(4) of this Act reproduced in note following Code Sec. 302.

—P.L. 97-248, Sec. 224(b), amended subsec. (b). For effective date see Sec. 224(d) of this Act reproduced in note following Code Sec. 338.
Prior to amendment, subsec. (b) read as follows:
"(b) Liquidation of subsidiary.

"(1) In general. If property is received by a corporation in a distribution in complete liquidation of another corporation (within the meaning of section 332(b)), then, except as provided in paragraph (2), the basis of the property in the hands of the distributee shall be the same as it would be in the hands of the transferor. If property is received by a corporation in a transfer to which section 332(c) applies, and if paragraph (2) of this subsection does not apply, then the basis of the property in the hands of the transferee shall be the same as it would be in the hands of the transferor.

"(2) Exception. If property is received by a corporation in a distribution in complete liquidation of another corporation, within the meaning of section 332(b), and if—

"(A) the distribution is pursuant to a plan of liquidation adopted not more than 2 years after the date of the transaction described in subparagraph (B) (or, in the case of a series of transactions, the date of the last such transaction); and

"(B) stock of the distributing corporation possessing at least 80 percent of the total combined voting power of all classes of stock entitled to vote, and at least 80 percent of the total number of shares of all other classes of stock (except nonvoting stock which is limited and preferred as to dividends), was acquired by the distributee by purchase (as defined in paragraph (3)) during a 12-month period beginning with the earlier of—

"(i) the date of the first acquisition by purchase of such stock, or

"(ii) if any of such stock was acquired in an acquisition which is a purchase within the meaning of the second sentence of paragraph (3), the date on which the distributee is first considered under section 318(a) as owning stock owned by the corporation from which such acquisition was made;
then the basis of the property in the hands of the distributee shall be the adjusted basis of the stock with respect to which the distribution was made. For purposes of the preceding sentence, under regulations prescribed by the Secretary, proper adjustment in the adjusted basis of any stock shall be made for any distribution made to the distributee with respect to such stock before the adoption of the plan

1,803

Code Sec. 334 — Corporate distributions and adjustments

of liquidation, for any money received, for any liabilities assumed or subject to which the property was received, and for other items.

"(3) Purchase defined. For purposes of paragraph (2)(B), the term 'purchase' means any acquisition of stock, but only if—

"(A) the basis of the stock in the hands of the distributee is not determined (i) in whole or in part by reference to the adjusted basis of such stock in the hands of the person from whom acquired, or (ii) under section 1014(a) (relating to property acquired from a decedent),

"(B) the stock is not acquired in an exchange to which section 351 applies, and

"(C) the stock is not acquired from a person the ownership of whose stock would, under section 318(a), be attributed to the person acquiring such stock. Notwithstanding subparagraph (C) of this paragraph, for purposes of paragraph (2)(B), the term 'purchase' also means an acquisition of stock from a corporation when ownership of such stock would be attributed under section 318(a) to the person acquiring such stock, if the stock of such corporation by reason of which such ownership would be attributed was acquired by purchase (within the meaning of the preceding sentence).

"(4) Distributee defined. For purposes of this subsection, the term 'distributee' means only the corporation which meets the 80 percent stock ownership requirements specified in section 332(b)."

In 1976, P.L. 94-455, Sec. 1901(a)(45), amended subpara. (b)(2)(A), effective for tax. yrs. begin. after 12/31/76.
Prior to amendment, subpara. (b)(2)(A) read as follows:
"(A) the distribution is pursuant to a plan of liquidation adopted—
"(i) on or after June 22, 1954, and
"(ii) not more than 2 years after the date of the transaction described in subparagraph (B) (or, in the case of a series of transactions, the date of the last such transaction); and"
—P.L. 94-455, Sec. 1906(b)(13)(A), substituted "Secretary" for "Secretary or his delegate" in para. (b)(2), effective for tax. yrs. begin. after 12/31/76

In 1966, P.L. 89-809, Sec. 202(a), added the last sentence to para. (b)(3), effective for acquisitions of stock after 12/31/65.
—P.L. 89-809, Sec. 202(b), substituted "during a 12-month period beginning with the earlier of—" for "during a period of not more than 12 months," and added clauses (b)(2)(B)(i) and (b)(2)(B)(ii), effective for distributions made after 11/13/66.

SUBPART B.—EFFECTS ON CORPORATION

Sec.
336. Gain or loss recognized on property distributed in complete liquidation.
337. Nonrecognition for property distributed to parent in complete liquidation of subsidiary.
338. Certain stock purchases treated as asset acquisitions.

In 1986, P.L. 99-514, Sec. 631(e)(17), amended items 336 and 337.
Prior to amendment items 336 and 337 read as follows:
"336. Distributions of property in liquidations.
"337. Gain or loss on sales or exchanges in connection with certain liquidations."
In 1982, P.L. 97-248, Sec. 224(c)(9), amended item 338.
Prior to amendment, item 338 read as follows:
"338. Effect on earnings and profits."

Sec. 336. Gain or loss recognized on property distributed in complete liquidation.

(a) General rule.

Except as otherwise provided in this section or section 337, gain or loss shall be recognized to a liquidating corporation on the distribution of property in complete liquidation as if such property were sold to the distributee at its fair market value.

(b) Treatment of liabilities.

If any property distributed in the liquidation is subject to a liability or the shareholder assumes a liability of the liquidating corporation in connection with the distribution, for purposes of subsection (a) and section 337, the fair market value of such property shall be treated as not less than the amount of such liability.

(c) Exception for liquidations which are part of a reorganization.

For provision providing that this subpart does not apply to distributions in pursuance of a plan of reorganization, see section 361(c)(4).

(d) Limitations on recognition of loss.

(1) No loss recognized in certain distributions to related persons.

(A) In general. No loss shall be recognized to a liquidating corporation on the distribution of any property to a related person (within the meaning of section 267) if—

(i) such distribution is not pro rata, or

(ii) such property is disqualified property.

(B) Disqualified property. For purposes of subparagraph (A), the term "disqualified property" means any property which is acquired by the liquidating corporation in a transaction to which section 351 applied, or as a contribution to capital, during the 5-year period ending on the date of the distribution. Such term includes any property if the adjusted basis of such property is determined (in whole or in part) by reference to the adjusted basis of property described in the preceding sentence.

(2) Special rule for certain property acquired in certain carryover basis transactions.

(A) In general. For purposes of determining the amount of loss recognized by any liquidating corporation on any sale, exchange, or distribution of property described in subparagraph (B), the adjusted basis of such property shall be reduced (but not below zero) by the excess (if any) of—

(i) the adjusted basis of such property immediately after its acquisition by such corporation, over

(ii) the fair market value of such property as of such time.

(B) Description of property.

(i) In general. For purposes of subparagraph (A), property is described in this subparagraph if—

(I) such property is acquired by the liquidating corporation in a transaction to which section 351 applied or as a contribution to capital, and

(II) the acquisition of such property by the liquidating corporation was part of a plan a principal purpose of which was to recognize loss by the liquidating corporation with respect to such property in connection with the liquidation.

Other property shall be treated as so described if the adjusted basis of such other property is determined (in whole or in part) by reference to the adjusted basis of property described in the preceding sentence.

(ii) Certain acquisitions treated as part of plan. For purposes of clause (i), any property described in clause (i)(I) acquired by the liquidated corporation after the date 2 years before the date of the adoption of the plan of complete liquidation shall, except as provided in regulations, be treated as acquired as part of a plan described in clause (i)(II).

(C) Recapture in lieu of disallowance. The Secretary may prescribe regulations under which, in lieu of disallowing a loss under subparagraph (A) for a prior taxable year, the gross income of the liquidating corporation for the taxable year in which the plan of complete liquidation is adopted shall be increased by the amount of the disallowed loss.

(3) Special rule in case of liquidation to which section 332 applies. In the case of any liquidation to which section 332 applies, no loss shall be recognized to the liquidating corporation on any distribution in such liquidation. The preceding sentence shall apply to any distribution to the 80-percent distributee only if subsection (a) or (b)(1) of section 337 applies to such distribution.

(e) Certain stock sales and distributions may be treated as asset transfers.

Under regulations prescribed by the Secretary, if—

Corporate distributions and adjustments   **Code Sec. 336**

"(1) a corporation owns stock in another corporation meeting the requirements of section 1504(a)(2), and

"(2) such corporation sells, exchanges, or distributes all of such stock,

an election may be made to treat such sale, exchange, or distribution as a disposition of all of the assets of such other corporation, and no gain or loss shall be recognized on the sale, exchange, or distribution of such stock."

In 1988, P.L. 100-647, Sec. 1006(e)(1), amended clause (d)(2)(B)(ii)... Sec. 1006(e)(2), added a sentence to the end of para. (d)(3)... Sec. 1006(e)(3), substituted "an election may be made" for "such corporation may elect" in subsec. (e) ... Sec. 1006(e)(21)(A), deleted "in excess of basis" after "liabilities" in the heading of subsec. (b), effective as provided in Secs. 633(a)(1), (c), (d)(1)-(6), (e), (f), (g) of P.L. 99-514 [reproduced below].

Prior to amendment, clause (d)(2)(B)(ii) read as follows:

"(ii) Certain acquisitions treated as part of plan. For purposes of clause (i), any property described in clause (i)(I) acquired by the liquidating corporation during the 2-year period ending on the date of the adoption of the plan of complete liquidation shall, except as provided in regulations, be treated as part of a plan described in clause (i)(II)."

—P.L. 100-647, Sec. 1006(g)(2), amended Sec. 633(c)(1)(B) of P.L. 99-514 [reproduced below] part of the effective date for changes made by Sec. 631(a) of P.L. 99-514, by substituting "more than 50 percent" for "50 percent or more" ... Sec. 1006(g)(3), amended Sec. 633(d)(1) of P.L. 99-514 [reproduced below] by substituting "this subtitle" for "this section", by substituting "would be recognized by the liquidating corporation" for "would be recognized", and by adding the last sentence, see below ... Sec. 1006(g)(4), amended Sec. 633(d)(2)(C) of P.L. 99-514 [reproduced below], see below ... Sec. 1006(g)(5)(A), amended Sec. 633(d)(5)(A) of P.L. 99-514 [reproduced below] by substituting "a qualified group" for "10 or fewer qualified persons", see below ... Sec. 1006(g)(5)(B), amended Sec. 633(d)(6) of P.L. 99-514 [reproduced below], see below ... Sec. 1006(g)(8), amended Sec. 633 of P.L. 99-514 [reproduced below] by redesignating the subsecs. following the first subsec. (d) as (e), (f) and (g), see below ... Sec. 1006(g)(9), amended Sec. 633(f)(2) of P.L. 99-514 [as so redesignated by Sec. 1006(g)(8) of this Act] by substituting "May 9, 1929 (or any direct or indirect subsidiary of such corporation)" for "May 9, 1929", see below ... Sec. 1006(g)(10), amended Sec. 633(f)(2) of P.L. 99-514 [as so redesignated by Sec. 1006(g)(8) of this Act] by substituting "of such Code" for "of such Code)", see below ... Sec. 1006(g)(11), amended Sec. 633(f)(4)(A)(i)(I) of P.L. 99-514 [as so redesignated by Sec. 1006(g)(8) of this Act] by substituting, "to sell substantially all of the assets of a selling corporation under the laws of Massachusetts on October 20, 1976," for "binding on the selling corporation to sell substantially all of its assets", see below

"(C) any gain to the extent section 453B of such Code applies."

Prior to amendment, para. (d)(6) read as follows:

"(6) Definitions and special rules. For purposes of this subsection —

"(A) Qualified person. The term 'qualified person' means —

"(i) an individual,

"(ii) an estate, or

"(iii) any trust described in clause (ii) or (iii) of section 1361(c)(2)(A) of the Internal Revenue Code of 1986.

"(B) Attribution rules. —

"(i) Entities. Any stock held by a corporation, trust, or partnership shall be treated as owned proportionally by its shareholders, beneficiaries, or partners. Stock considered to be owned by a person by reason of the application of the preceding sentence shall, for purposes of applying such sentence, be treated as actually owned by such person.

"(ii) Family members. Stock owned (or treated as owned under clause (i)) by members of the same family (within the meaning of section 318(a)(1) of the Internal Revenue Code of 1986) shall be treated as owned by 1 person.

"(C) Controlled group of corporations. All members of the same controlled group (as defined in section 267(f)(1) of such Code) shall be treated as 1 corporation for purposes of this subsection."

Prior to amendment, subpara. (f)(5)(A) read as follows:

"(A) a voting trust established not later than December 31, 1987, for purposes of holding employees' shares of stock in such corporation, shall qualify as a trust permitted as a shareholder of an S corporation, and"

—P.L. 100-647, Sec. 1018(d)(5)(D), amended subsec. (c), effective for plans of reorganizations adopted after 10/22/86.

Prior to amendment, subsec. (c) read as follows:

"(c) Exception for certain liquidations to which part III applies.

"This section shall not apply with respect to any distribution of property to the extent there is nonrecognition of gain or loss with respect to such property to the recipient under part III."

In 1986, P.L. 99-514, Sec. 631(a), amended Code Sec. 336, effective as provided in Secs. 633(a)(1), (c), (d)(1)-(6), (e), (f), (g) [as amended by Sec. 1006(e) and (g) of P.L. 100-647] of this Act:

"(a) General rule. —

"Except as otherwise provided in this section [Sec. 633], the amendments made by this subtitle shall apply to —

"(1) any distribution in complete liquidation, and any sale or exchange, made by a corporation after July 31, 1986, unless such corporation is completely liquidated before January 1, 1987,

---

* * *

"(c) Exception for certain plans of liquidation and binding contracts. —

"(1) In general. — The amendments made by this subtitle [Subtitle D] shall not apply to —

"(A) any distribution or sale or exchange made pursuant to a plan of liquidation adopted before August 1, 1986, if the liquidating corporation is completely liquidated before January 1, 1988,

"(B) any distribution or sale or exchange made by any corporation if more than 50 percent of the voting stock (by value) of such corporation is acquired on or after August 1, 1986, pursuant to a written binding contract in effect before such date and if such corporation is completely liquidated before January 1, 1988.

"(C) any distribution or sale or exchange made by any corporation if substantially all of the assets of such corporation are sold on or after August 1, 1986, pursuant to 1 or more written binding contracts in effect before such date and if such corporation is completely liquidated before January 1, 1988, or

"(D) any transaction described in section 338 of the Internal Revenue Code of 1986 with respect to any target corporation if a qualified stock purchase of such target corporation is made on or after August 1, 1986, pursuant to a written binding contract in effect before such date and the acquisition date (within the meaning of such section 338) is before January 1, 1988.

"(2) Special rule for certain actions taken before November 20, 1985. — For purposes of paragraph (1), transactions shall be treated as pursuant to a plan of liquidation adopted before August 1, 1986, if —

"(A) before November 20, 1985 —

"(i) the board of directors of the liquidating corporation adopted a resolution to solicit shareholder approval for a transaction of a kind described in section 336 or 337, or

"(ii) the shareholders or board of directors have approved such a transaction,

"(B) before November 20, 1985 —

"(i) there has been an offer to purchase a majority of the voting stock of the liquidating corporation, or

"(ii) the board of directors of the liquidating corporation has adopted a resolution approving an acquisition or recommending the approval of an acquisition to the shareholders, or

"(C) before November 20, 1985, a ruling request was submitted to the Secretary of the Treasury or his delegate with respect to a transaction of a kind described in section 336 or 337 of the Internal Revenue Code of 1954 (as in effect before the amendments made by this subtitle).

For purposes of the preceding sentence, any action taken by the board of directors or shareholders of a corporation with respect to any subsidiary of such corporation shall be treated as taken by the board of directors or shareholders of such subsidiary.

"(d) Transitional rule for certain small corporations. —

"(1) In general. — In the case of the complete liquidation before January 1, 1989, of a qualified corporation, the amendments made by this subtitle [Sec. 633] shall not apply to the applicable percentage of each gain or loss which (but for this paragraph) would be recognized by the liquidating corporation by reason of the amendments made by this subtitle [Subtitle D]. Section 333 of the Internal Revenue Code of 1954 (as in effect on the day before the date of the enactment of this Act) shall continue to apply to any complete liquidation described in the preceding sentence.

"(2) Paragraph (1) not to apply to certain items. — Paragraph (1) shall not apply to —

"(A) any gain or loss which is an ordinary gain or loss (determined without regard to section 1239 of the Internal Revenue Code of 1986),

"(B) any gain or loss on a capital asset held for not more than 6 months, and

"(C) any gain on an asset acquired by the qualified corporation if —

"(i) the basis of such asset in the hands of the qualified corporation is determined (in whole or in part) by reference to the basis of such asset in the hands of the person from whom acquired, and

"(ii) a principal purpose for the transfer of such asset to the qualified corporation was to secure the benefits of this subsection.

"(3) Applicable percentage. — For purposes of this subsection, the term 'applicable percentage' means —

"(A) 100 percent if the applicable value of the qualified corporation is less than $5,000,000, or

"(B) 100 percent reduced by an amount which bears the same ratio to 100 percent as —

"(i) the excess of the applicable value of the corporation over $5,000,000, bears to

"(ii) $5,000,000.

"(4) Applicable value. — For purposes of this subsection, the applicable value is the fair market value of all of the stock of the corporation on the date of the adoption of the plan of complete liquidation (or if greater, on August 1, 1986).

"(5) Qualified corporation. — For purposes of this subsection, the term 'qualified corporation' means any corporation if —

"(A) on August 1, 1986, and at all times thereafter before the corporation is completely liquidated, more than 50 percent (by value) of the stock in such corporation is held by a qualified group, and

"(B) the applicable value of such corporation does not exceed $10,000,000.

"(6) Definitions and special rules. For purposes of this subsection —

"(A) Qualified group.

"(i) In general. Except as provided in clause (ii), the term 'qualified group' means any group of 10 or fewer qualified persons who at all times during the 5-year period ending on the date of the adoption of the plan of complete liquidation (or, if shorter, the period during which the corporation or any predecessor was in

1,805

existence) owned (or was treated as owning under the rules of subparagraph (C)) more than 50 percent (by value) of the stock in such corporation.

"(ii) 5-Year ownership requirement not to apply in certain cases. In the case of—

"(I) any complete liquidation pursuant to a plan of liquidation adopted before March 31, 1988,

"(II) any distribution not in liquidation made before March 31, 1988,

"(III) an election to be an S corporation filed before March 31, 1988, or

"(IV) a transaction described in section 338 of the Internal Revenue Code of 1986 where the acquisition date (within the meaning of such section 338) is before March 31, 1988, the term 'qualified group' means any group of 10 or fewer qualified persons.

"(B) Qualified person. The term 'qualified person' means—
"(i) an individual,
"(ii) an estate, or
"(iii) any trust described in clause (ii) or clause (iii) of section 1361(c)(2)(A) of the Internal Revenue Code of 1986.

"(C) Attribution rules.—

"(i) In general. Any stock owned by a corporation, trust (other than a trust referred to in subparagraph (B)(iii), or partnership shall be treated as owned proportionately by its shareholders, beneficiaries, or partners, and shall not be treated as owned by such corporation, trust, or partnership. Stock considered to be owned by a person by reason of the application of the preceding sentence shall, for purposes of applying such sentence, be treated as actually owned by such person.

"(ii) Family members. Stock owned (or treated as owned) by members of the same family (within the meaning of section 318(a)(1) of the Internal Revenue Code of 1986) shall be treated as owned by 1 person, and shall be treated as owned by such 1 person for any period during which it was owned (or treated as owned) by any such member.

"(iii) Treatment of certain trusts. Stock owned (or treated as owned) by the estate of any decedent or by any trust referred to in subparagraph (B)(iii) with respect to such decedent shall be treated as owned by 1 person and shall be treated as owned by such 1 person for the period during which it was owned (or treated as owned) by such estate or any such trust or by the decedent.

"(D) Special holding period rules. Any property acquired by reason of the death of an individual shall be treated as owned at all times during which such property was owned (or treated as owned) by the decedent.

"(E) Controlled group of corporations. All members of the same controlled group (as defined in section 267(f)(1) of such Code) shall be treated as 1 corporation for purposes of determining whether any of such corporations met the requirement of paragraph (5)(B) and for purposes of determining the applicable percentage with respect to any of such corporations. For purposes of the preceding sentence, an S corporation shall not be treated as a member of a controlled group unless such corporation was a C corporation for its taxable year which includes August 1, 1986, or it was not described for such taxable year in paragraph (1) or (2) of section 1374(c) of such Code (as in effect on the day before the date of the enactment of this Act)."

* * *

"(e) Complete liquidation defined.—

"For purposes of this section [Sec. 633] a corporation shall be treated as completely liquidated if all of the assets of such corporation are distributed in complete liquidation, less assets retained to meet claims.

"(f) Other transitional rules.—

"(1) The amendments made by this subtitle [Subtitle D] shall not apply to any liquidation of a corporation incorporated under the laws of Pennsylvania on August 3, 1970, if—

"(A) the board of directors of such corporation approved a plan of liquidation before January 1, 1986,

"(B) an agreement for the sale of a material portion of the assets of such corporation was signed on May 9, 1986 (whether or not the assets are sold in accordance with such agreement), and

"(C) the corporation is completely liquidated on or before December 31, 1988.

"(2) The amendments made by this subtitle [Subtitle D] shall not apply to any liquidation (or deemed liquidation under section 338 of the Internal Revenue Code of 1986) of a diversified financial services corporation incorporated under the laws of Delaware on May 9, 1929 (or any direct or indirect subsidiary of such corporation), pursuant to a binding written contract entered into on or before December 31, 1986; but only if the liquidation is completed (or in the case of a section 338 election, the acquisition date occurs) before January 1, 1988.

"(3) The amendments made by this subtitle [Subtitle D] shall not apply to any distribution, or sale, or exchange—

"(A) of the assets owned (directly or indirectly) by a testamentary trust established under the will of a decedent dying on June 15, 1956, or its beneficiaries,

"(B) made pursuant to a court order in an action filed on January 18, 1984, if such order—

"(i) is issued after July 31, 1986, and

"(ii) directs the disposition of the assets of such trust and the division of the trust corpus into 3 separate subtrusts.

For purposes of the preceding sentence, an election under section 338(g) of the Internal Revenue Code of 1986 (or an election under section 338(h)(10) of such Code qualifying as a section 337 liquidation pursuant to regulations prescribed by the Secretary under section 1.338(h)(10)-1T(j)) made in connection with a sale or exchange pursuant to a court order described in subparagraph (B) shall be treated as a sale of exchange.

"(4)(A) The amendments made by this subtitle [Subtitle D] shall not apply to any distribution, or sale, or exchange—

"(i) if—

"(I) an option agreement to sell substantially all of the assets of a selling corporation organized under the laws of Massachusetts on October 20, 1976, is executed before August 1, 1986, the corporation adopts (by approval of its shareholders) a conditional plan of liquidation before August 1, 1986 to become effective upon the exercise of such option agreement (or modification thereto), and the assets are sold pursuant to the exercise of the option (as originally executed or subsequently modified provided that the purchase price is not thereby increased), or

"(II) in the event that the optionee does not acquire substantially all the assets of the corporation, the optionor corporation sells substantially all its assets to another purchaser at a purchase price not greater than that contemplated by such option agreement pursuant to an effective plan of liquidation, and

"(ii) the complete liquidation of the corporation occurs within 12 months of the time the plan of liquidation becomes effective, but in no event later than December 31, 1989.

"(B) For purposes of subparagraph (A), a distribution, or sale, or exchange, of a distributee corporation (within the meaning of section 337(c)(3) of the Internal Revenue Code of 1986) shall be treated as satisfying the requirements of subparagraph (A) if its subsidiary satisfies the requirements of subparagraph (A).

"(C) For purposes of section 56 of the Internal Revenue Code of 1986 (as amended by this Act), any gain or loss not recognized by reason of this paragraph shall not be taken into account in determining the adjusted net book income of the corporation.

"(5) In the case of a corporation incorporated under the laws of Wisconsin on April 3, 1948—

"(A) a voting trust established not later than December 31, 1987, shall qualify as a trust permitted as a shareholder of an S corporation shall be treated as only 1 shareholder if the holders of beneficial interests in such voting trust are—

"(i) employees or retirees of such corporation, or

"(ii) in the case of stock or voting trust certificates acquired from an employee or retiree of such corporation, the spouse, child, or estate of such employee or retiree or a trust created by such employee or retiree which is described in section 1361(c)(2) of the Internal Revenue Code of 1986 (or treated as described in such section by reason of section 1361(d) of such Code), and

"(B) the amendment made by section 632 (other than subsection (b) thereof) shall not apply to such corporation if it elects to be an S corporation before January 1, 1989.

"(6) The amendments made by this subtitle [Subtitle D] shall not apply to the liquidation of a corporation incorporated on January 26, 1982, under the laws of the State of Alabama with a principal place of business in Colbert County, Alabama, but only if such corporation is completely liquidated on or before December 31, 1987.

"(7) The amendments made by this subtitle [Subtitle D] shall not apply to the acquisition by a Delaware bank holding company of all of the assets of an Iowa bank holding company pursuant to a written contract dated December 9, 1981.

"(8) The amendments made by this subtitle [Subtitle D] shall not apply to the liquidation of a corporation incorporated under the laws of Delaware on January 20, 1984, if more than 40 percent of the stock of such corporation was acquired by purchase on June 11, 1986, and there was a tender offer with respect to all additional outstanding shares of such corporation on July 29, 1986, but only if the corporation is completely liquidated on or before December 31, 1987.

"(g) Treatment of certain distributions in response to hostile tender offer.—

"(1) In general.— No gain or loss shall be recognized under the Internal Revenue Code of 1986 to a corporation (hereinafter in this subsection referred to as 'parent') on a qualified distribution.

"(2) Qualified distribution defined.— For purposes of paragraph (1)—

"(A) In general.— The term 'qualified distribution' means a distribution—

"(i) by parent of all of the stock of a qualified subsidiary in exchange for stock of parent which was acquired for purposes of such exchange pursuant to a tender offer dated February 16, 1982, and

"(ii) pursuant to a contract dated February 13, 1982, and

"(iii) which was made not more than 60 days after the board of directors of parent recommended rejection of an unsolicited tender offer to obtain control of parent.

"(B) Qualified subsidiary — The term 'qualified subsidiary' means a corporation created or organized under the laws of Delaware on September 7, 1976, all of the stock of which was owned by parent immediately before the qualified distribution."

Prior to amendment, Code Sec. 336 read as follows:

"SEC. 336. DISTRIBUTIONS OF PROPERTY IN LIQUIDATION.

"(a) General rule.

"Except as provided in subsection (b) of this section and in section 453(B) (relating to disposition of installment obligations), no gain or loss shall be recognized to a corporation on the distribution of property in complete liquidation.

"(b) LIFO inventory.

"(1) In general. If a corporation inventorying goods under the LIFO method distributes inventory assets in complete liquidation, then the LIFO recapture amount with respect to such assets shall be treated as gain to the corporation recognized from the sale of such inventory assets.

"(2) Exception where basis determined under section 334(b). Paragraph (1) shall not apply to any liquidation under section 332 for which the basis of property received is determined under section 334(b).

"(3) LIFO recapture amount. For purposes of this subsection, the term LIFO recapture amount means the amount (if any) by which

"(A) the inventory amount of the inventory assets under the first-in, first-out method authorized by section 471, exceeds

"(B) the inventory amount of such assets under the LIFO method.

"(4) Definitions. For purposes of this subsection—

Corporate distributions and adjustments   **Code Sec. 337**

"(A) LIFO method. The term LIFO method means the method authorized by section 472 (relating to last-in, first-out inventories).

"(B) Other definitions. The term 'inventory assets' has the meaning given to such term by subparagraph (A) of section 311(b)(2), and the term 'inventory amount' has the meaning given to such term by subparagraph (B) of section 311(b)(2) (as modified by paragraph (3) of section 311(b))."

In 1982, P.L. 97-248, Sec. 222(b), substituted "complete liquidation" for "partial or complete liquidation" in subsec. (a)... Sec. 222(e)(1)(D), substituted "complete liquidation" for "partial or complete liquidation" in para. (b)(1), effective for distributions after 8/31/82. For exceptions and special rules see Sec. 222(f)(2) – (4) of this Act reproduced in note following Code Sec 302.

—P.L. 97-248, Sec. 224(c)(4), substituted "334(b)" for "334(b)(1)" each place it appeared in para. (b)(2). For effective date see Sec. 224(d) of this Act reproduced in note following Code Sec. 338.

In 1980, P.L. 96-471, Sec. 2(b)(1), substituted "453B" for "453(d)" in Code Sec. 336, effective for distributions made after 10/19/80 in tax. yrs. ending after 10/19/80 [date of enactment].

—P.L. 96-471, Sec. 2(c)(1), substituted "453B" for "453(d)" in subsec. (a), effective for distributions and dispositions pursuant to plans of liquidation adopted after 12/31/81.

—P.L. 96-223, Sec. 403(b)(1), amended Sec. 336, effective for distributions and dispositions pursuant to plans of liquidation adopted after 12/31/81.

Sec. 337. Nonrecognition for property distributed to parent in complete liquidation of subsidiary.

(a) In general.

No gain or loss shall be recognized to the liquidating corporation on the distribution to the 80-percent distributee of any property in a complete liquidation to which section 332 applies.

(b) Treatment of indebtedness of subsidiary, etc.

(1) Indebtedness of subsidiary to parent. If—

(A) a corporation is liquidated in a liquidation to which section 332 applies, and

(B) on the date of the adoption of the plan of liquidation, such corporation was indebted to the 80-percent distributee,

for purposes of this section and section 336, any transfer of property to the 80-percent distributee in satisfaction of such indebtedness shall be treated as a distribution to such distributee in such liquidation.

(2) Treatment of tax-exempt distributee.

(A) In general. Except as provided in subparagraph (B), paragraph (1) and subsection (a) shall not apply where the 80-percent distributee is an organization (other than a cooperative described in section 521) which is exempt from the tax imposed by this chapter.

(B) Exception where property will be used in unrelated business.

(i) In general. Subparagraph (A) shall not apply to any distribution of property to an organization described in section 511(a)(2) if, immediately after such distribution, such organization uses such property in an activity the income from which is subject to tax under section 511(a).

(ii) Later disposition or change in use. If any property to which clause (i) applied is disposed of by the organization acquiring such property, notwithstanding any other provision of law, any gain (not in excess of the amount not recognized by reason of clause (i)) shall be included in such organization's unrelated business taxable income. For purposes of the preceding sentence, if such property ceases to be used in an activity referred to in clause (i), such organization shall be treated as having disposed of such property on the date of such cessation.

(c) 80-percent distributee.

For purposes of this section, the term "80-percent distributee" means only the corporation which meets the 80-percent stock ownership requirements specified in section 332(b). For purposes of this section, the determination of whether any corporation is an 80-percent distributee shall be made without regard to any consolidated return regulation.

(d) Regulations.

The Secretary shall prescribe such regulations as may be necessary or appropriate to carry out the purposes of the amendments made by subtitle D of title VI of the Tax Reform Act of 1986, including—

(1) regulations to ensure that such purposes may not be circumvented through the use of any provision of law or regulations (including the consolidated return regulations and part III of this subchapter) or through the use of a regulated investment company, real estate investment trust, or tax-exempt entity, and

(2) regulations providing for appropriate coordination of the provisions of this section with the provisions of this title relating to taxation of foreign corporations and their shareholders.

In 2005, P.L. 109-59, Sec. 11146, of this Act, reads as follows:
"Sec. 11146. Tax treatment of State ownership of railroad real estate investment trust.

"(a) In general. If a State owns all of the outstanding stock of a corporation—
"(1) which is a real estate investment trust on the date of the enactment of this Act,
"(2) which is a non-operating class III railroad, and
"(3) substantially all of the activities of which consist of the ownership, leasing, and operation by such corporation of facilities, equipment, and other property used by the corporation or other persons for railroad transportation and for economic development purposes for the benefit of the State and its citizens, then, to the extent such activities are of a type which are an essential governmental function within the meaning of section 115 of the Internal Revenue Code of 1986, income derived from such activities by the corporation shall be treated as accruing to the State for purposes of section 115 of such Code.

"(b) Gain or loss not recognized on conversion.
"Notwithstanding section 337(d) of the Internal Revenue Code of 1986—
"(1) no gain or loss shall be recognized under section 336 or 337 of such Code, and
"(2) no change in basis of the property of such corporation shall occur, because of any change of status of a corporation to a tax-exempt entity by reason of the application of subsection (a).

"(c) Tax-exempt financing.
"(1) In general. Any obligation issued by a corporation described in subsection (a) at least 95 percent of the net proceeds (as defined in section 150(a) of the Internal Revenue Code of 1986) of which are to be used to provide for the acquisition, construction, or improvement of railroad transportation infrastructure (including railroad terminal facilities)—
"(A) shall be treated as a State or local bond (within the meaning of section 103(c) of such Code), and
"(B) shall not be treated as a private activity bond (within the meaning of section 103(b)(1) of such Code) solely by reason of the ownership or use of such railroad transportation infrastructure by the corporation.

"(2) No inference. Except as provided in paragraph (1), nothing in this subsection shall be construed to affect the treatment of the private use of proceeds or property financed with obligations issued by the corporation for purposes of section 103 of the Internal Revenue Code of 1986 and part IV of subchapter B of such Code.

"(d) Definitions. For purposes of this section:
"(1) Real estate investment trust. The term 'real estate investment trust' has the meaning given such term by section 856(a) of the Internal Revenue Code of 1986.
"(2) Non-operating class III railroad. The term 'non-operating class III railroad' has the meaning given such term by part A of subtitle IV of title 49, United States Code (49 U.S.C. 10101 et seq.), and the regulations thereunder.
"(3) State. The term 'State' includes—
"(A) the District of Columbia and any possession of the United States, and
"(B) any authority, agency, or public corporation of a State.

"(e) Applicability.
"(1) In general. Except as provided in paragraph (2), this section shall apply on and after the date on which a State becomes the owner of all of the outstanding stock of a corporation described in subsection (a) through action of such corporation's board of directors.
"(2) Exception. This section shall not apply to any State which—
"(A) becomes the owner of all of the voting stock of a corporation described in subsection (a) after December 31, 2003, or
"(B) becomes the owner of all of the outstanding stock of a corporation described in subsection (a) after December 31, 2006."

In 1988, P.L. 100-647, Sec. 1006(e)(4)(A), deleted "or 511(b)(2)" before "if, immediately" in clause (b)(2)(B)(i)... Sec. 1006(e)(4)(B), substituted "in an activity the income from which is subject to tax under section 511(a)" for "in an unrelated trade or business (as defined in section 513)" in clause (b)(2)(B)(i)... Sec. 1006(e)(4)(C), substituted "an activity referred to in clause (i)" for "an unrelated trade or business of such organization" in clause (b)(2)(B)(ii), effective as provided in Sec. 633(a)(1) of P.L. 99-514, see below.

1,807

Code Sec. 337 — Corporate distributions and adjustments

—P.L. 100-647, Sec. 1006(e)(5)(A), substituted "made by subtitle D of title VI of the Tax Reform Act of 1986" for "made to this subpart of the Tax Reform Act of 1986" and added "or through the use of a regulated investment company, real estate investment trust, or tax-exempt entity" after "subchapter)" in subsec. (d), effective as provided in Sec. 1006(e)(5)(B) of this Act which reads:

"(B) The amendment made by subparagraph (A)(ii) shall not apply to any reorganization if before June 10, 1987—

"(i) the board of directors of a party to the reorganization adopted a resolution to solicit shareholder approval for the transaction, or

"(ii) the shareholders or the board of directors of a party to the reorganization approved the transaction."

—P.L. 100-647, Sec. 2004(k)(3), added Sec. 10223(d)(2)(D) pf P.L. 100-203, see below . . . Sec. 2004(k)(4)(A), substituted "on or before March 31, 1988" for "before January 1, 1993" in Sec. 10223(d)(2)(B) pf P.L. 100-203, see below . . . Sec. 2004(k)(4)(B), deleted "before January 1, 1989" after "affiliated group" in Sec. 10223(d)(2)(C) pf P.L. 100-203, see below.

In 1987, P.L. 100-203, Sec. 10223(a), added the last sentence to subsec. (c), effective for distributions or transfers after 12/15/87, except as provided in Sec. 10223(d)(2) [as amended by Sec. 2004(k)(3) and (4) of P.L. 100-647, see above] which reads as follows:

"(2) Exceptions.—

"(A) Distributions.— The amendments made by this section shall not apply to any distribution after December 15, 1987, and before January 1, 1993, if—

"(i) 80 percent or more of the stock of the distributing corporation was acquired by the distributee before December 15, 1987, or

"(ii) 80 percent or more of the stock of the distributing corporation was acquired by the distributee before January 1, 1989, pursuant to a binding written contract or tender offer in effect on December 15, 1987.

For purposes of the preceding sentence, stock described in section 1504(a)(4) of the Internal Revenue Code of 1986 shall not be taken into account.

"(B) Section 304 transfers.— The amendment made by subsection (c) shall not apply to any transfer after December 15, 1987, and on or before March 31, 1988, if such transfer is—

"(i) between corporations which are members of the same affiliated group on December 15, 1987, or

"(ii) between corporations which become members of the same affiliated group, pursuant to a binding written contract or tender offer in effect on December 15, 1987.

"(C) Distributions covered by prior transition rule.— The amendments made by this section shall not apply to any distribution to which the amendments made by subtitle D of title VI of the Tax Reform Act of 1986 do not apply."

"(D) Treatment of certain members of affiliated group.—

"(i) In general.— For purposes of subparagraph (A), all corporations which were in existence on the designated date and were members of the same affiliated group which included the distributees on such date shall be treated as 1 distributee.

"(ii) Limitation to stock held on designated date.— Clause (i) shall not exempt any distribution from the amendments made by this section if such distribution is with respect to stock not held by the distributee (determined without regard to clause (i)) on the designated date directly or indirectly through a corporation which goes out of existence in the transaction.

"(iii) Designated date.— For purposes of this subparagraph, the term 'designated date' means the later of—

"(I) December 15, 1987, or

"(II) the date on which the acquisition meeting the requirements of subparagraph (A) occurred."

In 1986, P.L. 99-514, Sec. 631(a), amended Code Sec. 337, effective as provided in Sec. 633(a)(1) of this Act reproduced in note following Code Sec. 336.

For exceptions and transitional rules, see Secs. 633(c), (e), (f) and (g) of this Act reproduced in note following Code Sec. 336.

Prior to amendment, Code Sec. 337 [as amended by Sec. 1804(e)(7)(A) of this Act, see below] read as follows:

"SEC. 337. GAIN OR LOSS ON SALES OR EXCHANGES IN CONNECTION WITH CERTAIN LIQUIDATIONS.

"(a) General rule.

"If, within the 12-month period beginning on the date on which a corporation adopts a plan of complete liquidation, all of the assets of the corporation are distributed in complete liquidation, less assets retained to meet claims, then no gain or loss shall be recognized to such corporation from the sale or exchange by it of property within such 12-month period.

"(b) Property defined.

"(1) In general. For purposes of subsection (a), the term 'property' does not include—

"(A) stock in trade of the corporation, or other property of a kind which would properly be included in the inventory of the corporation if on hand at the close of the taxable year, and property held by the corporation primarily for sale to customers in the ordinary course of its trade or business.

"(B) installment obligations acquired in respect of the sale or exchange (without regard to whether such sale or exchange occurred before, on, or after the date of the adoption of the plan referred to in subsection (a)) of stock in trade or other property described in subparagraph (A) of this paragraph, and

"(C) installment obligations acquired in respect of property (other than property described in subparagraph (A)) sold or exchanged before the date of the adoption of such plan of liquidation.

"(2) Nonrecognition with respect to inventory in certain cases. Notwithstanding paragraph (1) of this subsection, if substantially all of the property described in subparagraph (A) of such paragraph (1) which is attributable to a trade or business of the corporation is, in accordance with this section, sold or exchanged to one person in one transaction, then for purposes of subsection (a) the term 'property' includes—

"(A) such property so sold or exchanged, and

"(B) installment obligations acquired in respect of such sale or exchange.

"(c) Limitations.

"(1) Collapsible corporations and liquidations to which section 333 applies. This section shall not apply to any sale or exchange—

"(A) made by a collapsible corporation (as defined in section 341 (b)), or

"(B) following the adoption of a plan of complete liquidation, if section 333 applies with respect to such liquidation.

"(2) Liquidations to which section 332 applies. In the case of any sale or exchange following the adoption of a plan of complete liquidation, if section 332 applies with respect to such liquidation, this section shall not apply.

"(3) Special rule for affiliated group.

"(A) In general. Paragraph (2) shall not apply to a sale or exchange by a corporation (hereinafter in this paragraph referred to as the 'selling corporation') if—

"(i) within the 12-month period beginning on the date of the adoption of a plan of complete liquidation by the selling corporation, the selling corporation and each distributee corporation is completely liquidated, and

"(ii) none of the complete liquidations referred to in clause (i) is a liquidation with respect to which section 333 applies.

"(B) Distributee corporation. For purposes of subparagraph (A), the term 'distributee corporation' means any corporation which receives a distribution to which section 332 applies in a complete liquidation of the selling corporation. Such term also includes any other corporation which receives a distribution to which section 332 applies in a complete liquidation of a corporation which is a distributee corporation under the preceding sentence or prior application of this sentence.

"(d) Special rule for certain minority shareholders.

"If a corporation adopts a plan of complete liquidation, and if subsection (a) does not apply to sales or exchanges of property by such corporation, solely by reason of the application of subsection (c)(2), then for the first taxable year of any shareholder (other than a corporation which meets the 80 percent stock ownership requirement specified in section 332(b)(1)) in which he receives a distribution in complete liquidation—

"(1) the amount realized by such shareholder on the distribution shall be increased by his proportionate share of the amount by which the tax imposed by this subtitle on such corporation would have been reduced if subsection (c)(2) had not been applicable, and

"(2) for purposes of this title, such shareholder shall be deemed to have paid, on the last day prescribed by law for the payment of the tax imposed by this subtitle on such shareholder for such taxable year, an amount of tax equal to the amount of the increase described in paragraph (1).

"(e) Special rule for involuntary conversions.

"If—

"(1) there is an involuntary conversion (within the meaning of section 1033) of property of a distributing corporation and there is a complete liquidation of such corporation which qualifies under subsection (a),

"(2) the disposition of the converted property (within the meaning of clause (ii) of section 1033(a)(2)(E)) occurs during the 60-day period which ends on the day before the first day of the 12-month period, and

"(3) such corporation elects the application of this subsection at such manner as the Secretary may by regulations prescribe,

then for purposes of this section such disposition shall be treated as a sale or exchange occurring within the 12-month period.

"(f) Special rule for LIFO inventories.

"(1) In general. In the case of a corporation inventorying goods under the LIFO method, this section shall apply to gain from the sale or exchange of inventory assets (which under subsection (b)(2) constitute property) only to the extent that such gain exceeds the LIFO recapture amount with respect to such assets.

"(2) Definitions. The terms used in this subsection shall have the same meaning as when used in section 336(b).

"(3) Cross reference. For treatment of gain from the sale or exchange of an installment obligation as gain resulting from the sale or exchange of the property in respect of which the obligation was received, see the last sentence of section 453B(a).

"(g) Title 11 or similar cases.

"If a corporation completely liquidates pursuant to a plan of complete liquidation adopted in a title 11 or similar case (within the meaning of section 368(a)(3)(A))—

"(1) for purposes of subsection (a), the term 'property' shall not include any item acquired on or after the date of the adoption of the plan of liquidation if such item is not property within the meaning of subsection (b)(2), and

"(2) subsection (a) shall apply to sales and exchanges by corporation of property within the period beginning on the date of the adoption of the plan and ending on the date of the termination of the case."

—P.L. 99-514, Sec. 1804(e)(7)(A), amended subpara. (c)(3)(B), [before amendment by Sec. 631(a) of this Act, see above], effective as provided in Sec. 1804(e)(7)(B) of this Act:

"(B) Effective date.— The amendment made by subparagraph (A) [Sec. 1804(e)(7)(A)] shall apply in the case of plans of complete liquidation pursuant to which any distribution is made in a taxable year beginning after December 31, 1984 (December 31, 1983, in the case of an affiliated group to which an election under section 60(b)(7) of the Tax Reform Act of 1984 applies)."

Prior to amendment, subpara. (c)(3)(B) read as follows:

"(B) Definitions. For purposes of subparagraph (A)—

Corporate distributions and adjustments — Code Sec. 338(b)(5)

"(i) The term 'distributee corporation' means a corporation in the chain of includible corporations to which the selling corporation or a corporation above the selling corporation in such chain makes a distribution in complete liquidation within the 12-month period referred to in subparagraph (A)(i).

"(ii) The term 'chain of includible corporation' includes, in the case of any distribution, any corporation which (at the time of such distribution) is in a chain of includible corporations for purposes of section 1504(a) (determined without regard to the exceptions contained in section 1504(b)). Such term includes, where appropriate, the common parent corporation."

In 1982, P.L. 97-248, Sec. 224(c)(5), amended para. (c)(2), effective for any target corporation (within the meaning of Code Sec. 338 as added by Sec. 224(a) of this Act) for which the acquisition date occurs after 8/31/82.

Prior to amendment, para. (c)(2) read as follows:

"(2) Liquidations to which section 332 applies. In the case of a sale or exchange following the adoption of a plan of complete liquidation, if section 332 applies with respect to such liquidation, then—

"(A) if the basis of the property of the liquidating corporation in the hands of the distributee is determined under section 334(b)(1), this section shall not apply; or

"(B) if the basis of the property of the liquidating corporation in the hands of the distributee is determined under section 334(b)(2), this section shall apply only to that portion (if any) of the gain which is not greater than the excess of (i) that portion of the adjusted basis (adjusted for any adjustment required under the second sentence of section 334(b)(2)) of the stock of the liquidating corporation which is allocable, under regulations prescribed by the Secretary, to the property sold or exchanged, over (ii) the adjusted basis, in the hands of the liquidating corporation, of the property sold or exchanged."

—P.L. 97-248, Sec. 224(c)(6), substituted "subsection (c)(2)" for "subsection (c)(2)(A)" each place it appeared in subsec. (d). For effective date see Sec. 224(d) of this Act reproduced in note following Code Sec. 338.

In 1980, P.L. 96-589, Sec. 5(c), added subsec. (g) Sec. 7(d)(3) of this Act makes this amendment effective for any bankruptcy case or similar judicial proceeding commenced after 12/31/80.

Sec. 7(f) and (g) of this Act provides:

"(f) *Election to substitute September 30, 1979, for December 31, 1980.*—

"(1) In general. The debtor (or debtors) in a bankruptcy case or similar judicial proceeding may (with the approval of the court) elect to apply [subsection 7(d) of this Act] by substituting 'September 30, 1979' for 'December 31, 1980' each place it appears in subsections.

"(2) Effect of election. Any election made under paragraph (1) with respect to any proceeding shall apply to all parties to the proceeding.

"(3) Revocation only with consent. Any election under this subsection may be revoked only with the consent of the Secretary of the Treasury or his delegate.

"(4) Time and manner of election. Any election under this subsection shall be made at such time, and in such manner, as the Secretary of the Treasury or his delegate may by regulations prescribe.

"(g) *Definitions.*

"For purposes of this section—

"(1) Bankruptcy case. The term 'bankruptcy case' means any case under title 11 of the United States Code (as recodified by P.L. 95-598).

"(2) Similar judicial proceeding. The term 'similar judicial proceeding' means a receivership, foreclosure, or similar proceeding in a Federal or State court (as modified by section 368(a)(3)(D) of the Internal Revenue Code of 1954)."

—P.L. 96-471, Sec. 2(c)(2), substituted "453B(a)" for "453(d)(1)" in para. (f)(3), effective for distributions and dispositions pursuant to plans of liquidation adopted after 12/31/81.

—P.L. 96-223, Sec. 403(b)(2)(A), amended Sec. 337 by adding subsec. (f), effective for distributions and dispositions pursuant to plans of liquidation adopted after 12/31/81.

In 1978, P.L. 95-628, Sec. 4(a), added subsec. (e), effective for dispositions of the converted property (within the meaning of Code Sec. 1033(a)(2)(E)(ii)) occurring after 11/10/78 in tax. yrs. end. after 11/10/78.

—P.L. 95-600, Sec. 701(i)(1), deleted the last sentence of para. (c)(2) and added new para. (c)(3), effective for sales or exchanges made pursuant to a plan of complete liquidation adopted after 12/31/75.

Prior to amendment, the last sentence of para. (c)(2) read as follows:

"This paragraph shall not apply to a sale or exchange by a member of an affiliated group of corporations, as defined in section 1504(a) (but without regard to the exceptions contained in section 1504(b)), if each member of such group (including the common parent corporation) which receives, within the 12-month period beginning on the date of the adoption of a plan of complete liquidation by the corporation which made the sale or exchange, a distribution in complete liquidation from any other member of such group is itself completely liquidated within such 12-month period."

In 1976, P.L. 94-455, Sec. 1901(a)(46), amended subsec. (a) . . . deleted "on or after January 1, 1958", which followed "complete liquidation", in subsec. (d), effective for tax. yrs. begin. after 12/31/76.

Prior to amendment, subsec. (a) read as follows:

"(a) *General rule.*

"If—

"(1) a corporation adopts a plan of complete liquidation on or after June 22, 1954, and

"(2) within the 12-month period beginning on the date of the adoption of such plan, all of the assets of the corporation are distributed in complete liquidation, less assets retained to meet claims,

then no gain or loss shall be recognized to such corporation from the sale or exchange by it of property within such 12-month period."

—P.L. 94-455, Sec. 1906(b)(13)(A), substituted "Secretary" for "Secretary or his delegate" in subpara. (c)(2)(B), effective for tax. yrs. begin. after 12/31/76.

—P.L. 94-455, Sec. 2118(a), added the last sentence in para. (c)(2), effective for sales or exchanges made pursuant to a plan of complete liquidation adopted after 12/31/75.

In 1958, P.L. 85-866, Sec. 19, added subsec. (d), effective 1/1/54.

Sec. 338. Certain stock purchases treated as asset acquisitions.

(a) General rule.

For purposes of this subtitle, if a purchasing corporation makes an election under this section (or is treated under subsection (e) as having made such an election), then, in the case of any qualified stock purchase, the target corporation—

(1) shall be treated as having sold all of its assets at the close of the acquisition date at fair market value in a single transaction, and

(2) shall be treated as a new corporation which purchased all of the assets referred to in paragraph (1) as of the beginning of the day after the acquisition date.

(b) Basis of assets after deemed purchase.

(1) In general. For purposes of subsection (a), the assets of the target corporation shall be treated as purchased for an amount equal to the sum of—

(A) the grossed-up basis of the purchasing corporation's recently purchased stock, and

(B) the basis of the purchasing corporation's nonrecently purchased stock.

(2) Adjustment for liabilities and other relevant items. The amount described in paragraph (1) shall be adjusted under regulations prescribed by the Secretary for liabilities of the target corporation and other relevant items.

(3) Election to step-up the basis of certain target stock.

(A) In general. Under regulations prescribed by the Secretary, the basis of the purchasing corporation's nonrecently purchased stock shall be the basis amount determined under subparagraph (B) of this paragraph if the purchasing corporation makes an election to recognize gain as if such stock were sold on the acquisition date for an amount equal to the basis amount determined under subparagraph (B).

(B) Determination of basis amount. For purposes of subparagraph (A), the basis amount determined under this subparagraph shall be an amount equal to the grossed-up basis determined under subparagraph (A) of paragraph (1) multiplied by a fraction—

(i) the numerator of which is the percentage of stock (by value) in the target corporation attributable to the purchasing corporation's nonrecently purchased stock, and

(ii) the denominator of which is 100 percent minus the percentage referred to in clause (i).

(4) Grossed-up basis. For purposes of paragraph (1), the grossed-up basis shall be an amount equal to the basis of the corporation's recently purchased stock, multiplied by a fraction—

(A) the numerator of which is 100 percent, minus the percentage of stock (by value) in the target corporation attributable to the purchasing corporation's nonrecently purchased stock, and

(B) the denominator of which is the percentage of stock (by value) in the target corporation attributable to the purchasing corporation's recently purchased stock.

(5) Allocation among assets. The amount determined under paragraphs (1) and (2) shall be allocated among the assets of the target corporation under regulations prescribed by the Secretary.

(6) Definitions of recently purchased stock and nonrecently purchased stock. For purposes of this subsection—

(A) Recently purchased stock. The term "recently purchased stock" means any stock in the target corporation which is held by the purchasing corporation on the acquisition date and which was purchased by such corporation during the 12-month acquisition period.

(B) Nonrecently purchased stock. The term "nonrecently purchased stock" means any stock in the target corporation which is held by the purchasing corporation on the acquisition date and which is not recently purchased stock.

(c) Repealed.

(d) Purchasing corporation; target corporation; qualified stock purchase.

For purposes of this section—

(1) Purchasing corporation. The term "purchasing corporation" means any corporation which makes a qualified stock purchase of stock of another corporation.

(2) Target corporation. The term "target corporation" means any corporation the stock of which is acquired by another corporation in a qualified stock purchase.

(3) Qualified stock purchase. The term "qualified stock purchase" means any transaction or series of transactions in which stock (meeting the requirements of section 1504(a)(2)) of 1 corporation is acquired by another corporation by purchase during the 12-month acquisition period.

(e) Deemed election where purchasing corporation acquires asset of target corporation.

(1) In general. A purchasing corporation shall be treated as having made an election under this section with respect to any target corporation if, at any time during the consistency period, it acquires any asset of the target corporation (or a target affiliate).

(2) Exceptions. Paragraph (1) shall not apply with respect to any acquisition by the purchasing corporation if—

(A) such acquisition is pursuant to a sale by the target corporation (or the target affiliate) in the ordinary course of its trade or business,

(B) the basis of the property acquired is determined wholly by reference to the adjusted basis of such property in the hands of the person from whom acquired,

(C) such acquisition was before September 1, 1982, or

(D) such acquisition is described in regulations prescribed by the Secretary and meets such conditions as such regulations may provide.

(3) Anti-avoidance rule. Whenever necessary to carry out the purpose of this subsection and subsection (f), the Secretary may treat stock acquisitions which are pursuant to a plan and which meet the requirements of section 1504(a)(2) as qualified stock purchases.

(f) Consistency required for all stock acquisitions from same affiliated group.

If a purchasing corporation makes qualified stock purchases with respect to the target corporation and 1 or more target affiliates during any consistency period, then (except as otherwise provided in subsection (e))—

(1) any election under this section with respect to the first such purchase shall apply to each other such purchase, and

(2) no election may be made under this section with respect to the second or subsequent such purchase if such an election was not made with respect to the first such purchase.

(g) Election.

(1) When made. Except as otherwise provided in regulations, an election under this section shall be made not later than the 15th day of the 9th month beginning after the month in which the acquisition date occurs.

(2) Manner. An election by the purchasing corporation under this section shall be made in such manner as the Secretary shall by regulations prescribe.

(3) Election irrevocable. An election by a purchasing corporation under this section, once made, shall be irrevocable.

(h) Definitions and special rules.

For purposes of this section—

(1) 12-month acquisition period. The term "12-month acquisition period" means the 12-month period beginning with the date of the first acquisition by purchase of stock included in a qualified stock purchase (or, if any of such stock was acquired in an acquisition which is a purchase by reason of subparagraph (C) of paragraph (3), the date on which the acquiring corporation is first considered under section 318(a) (other than paragraph (4) thereof) as owning stock owned by the corporation from which such acquisition was made).

(2) Acquisition date. The term "acquisition date" means, with respect to any corporation, the first day on which there is a qualified stock purchase with respect to the stock of such corporation.

(3) Purchase.

(A) In general. The term "purchase" means any acquisition of stock, but only if—

(i) the basis of the stock in the hands of the purchasing corporation is not determined (I) in whole or in part by reference to the adjusted basis of such stock in the hands of the person from whom acquired, or (II) under section 1014(a) (relating to property acquired from a decedent),

(ii) the stock is not acquired in an exchange to which section 351, 354, 355, or 356 applies and is not acquired in any other transaction described in regulations in which the transferor does not recognize the entire amount of the gain or loss realized on the transaction, and

(iii) the stock is not acquired from a person the ownership of whose stock would, under section 318(a) (other than paragraph (4) thereof), be attributed to the person acquiring such stock.

(B) Deemed purchase under subsection (a). The term "purchase" includes any deemed purchase under subsection (a)(2). The acquisition date for a corporation which is deemed purchased under subsection (a)(2) shall be determined under regulations prescribed by the Secretary.

(C) Certain stock acquisitions from related corporations.

(i) In general. Clause (iii) of subparagraph (A) shall not apply to an acquisition of stock from a related corporation if at least 50 percent in value of the stock of such related corporation was acquired by purchase (within the meaning of subparagraphs (A) and (B)).

(ii) Certain distributions. Clause (i) of subparagraph (A) shall not apply to an acquisition of stock described in clause (i) of this subparagraph if the corporation acquiring such stock—

(I) made a qualified stock purchase of stock of the related corporation, and

(II) made an election under this section (or is treated under subsection (e) as having made such an election) with respect to such qualified stock purchase.

(iii) Related corporation defined. For purposes of this subparagraph, a corporation is a related corporation if stock owned by such corporation is treated (under section 318(a) other than paragraph (4) thereof) as owned by the corporation acquiring the stock.

(4) Consistency period.

(A) In general. Except as provided in subparagraph (B), the term "consistency period" means the period consisting of—

(i) the 1-year period before the beginning of the 12-month acquisition period for the target corporation,

(ii) such acquisition period (up to and including the acquisition date), and

(iii) the 1-year period beginning on the day after the acquisition date.

(B) Extension where there is plan. The period referred to in subparagraph (A) shall also include any period during which the Secretary determines that there was in effect a plan to make a qualified stock purchase plus 1 or more other qualified stock purchases (or asset acquisitions described in subsection (e)) with respect to the target corporation or any target affiliate.

(5) Affiliated group. The term "affiliated group" has the meaning given to such term by section 1504(a) (determined without regard to the exceptions contained in section 1504(b)).

(6) Target affiliate.

(A) In general. A corporation shall be treated as a target affiliate of the target corporation if each of such corporations was, at any time during so much of the consistency period as ends on the acquisition date of the target corporation, a member of an affiliated group which had the same common parent.

(B) Certain foreign corporations, etc. Except as otherwise provided in regulations and subject to such conditions as may be provided in regulations)—

(i) the term "target affiliate" does not include a foreign corporation, a DISC, or a corporation to which an election under section 936 applies, and

(ii) stock held by a target affiliate in a foreign corporation or a domestic corporation which is a DISC or described in section 1248(e) shall be excluded from the operation of this section.

(7) Repealed.

(8) Acquisitions by affiliated group treated as made by 1 corporation. Except as provided in regulations prescribed by the Secretary, stock and asset acquisitions made by members of the same affiliated group shall be treated as made by 1 corporation.

(9) Target not treated as member of affiliated group. Except as otherwise provided in paragraph (10) or in regulations prescribed under this paragraph, the target corporation shall not be treated as a member of an affiliated group with respect to the sale described in subsection (a)(1).

(10) Elective recognition of gain or loss by target corporation, together with nonrecognition of gain or loss on stock sold by selling consolidated group.

(A) In general. Under regulations prescribed by the Secretary, an election may be made under which if—

(i) the target corporation was, before the transaction, a member of the selling consolidated group, and

(ii) the target corporation recognizes gain or loss with respect to the transaction as if it sold all of its assets in a single transaction,

then the target corporation shall be treated as a member of the selling consolidated group with respect to such sale, and (to the extent provided in regulations) no gain or loss will be recognized on stock sold or exchanged in the transaction by members of the selling consolidated group.

(B) Selling consolidated group. For purposes of subparagraph (A), the term "selling consolidated group" means any group of corporations which (for the taxable period which includes the transaction)—

(i) includes the target corporation, and

(ii) files a consolidated return.

To the extent provided in regulations, such term also includes any affiliated group of corporations which includes the target corporation (whether or not such group files a consolidated return).

(C) Information required to be furnished to the Secretary. Under regulations, where an election is made under subparagraph (A), the purchasing corporation and the common parent of the selling consolidated group shall, at such times and in such manner as may be provided in regulations, furnish to the Secretary the following information:

(i) The amount allocated under subsection (b)(5) to goodwill or going concern value.

(ii) Any modification of the amount described in clause (i).

(iii) Any other information as the Secretary deems necessary to carry out the provisions of this paragraph.

(11) Elective formula for determining fair market value. For purposes of subsection (a)(1), fair market value may be determined on the basis of a formula provided in regulations prescribed by the Secretary which takes into account liabilities and other relevant items.

(12) Repealed.

(13) Tax on deemed sale not taken into account for estimated tax purposes. For purposes of section 6655, tax attributable to the sale described in subsection (a)(1) shall not be taken into account. The preceding sentence shall not apply with respect to a qualified stock purchase for which an election is made under paragraph (10).

> • **Caution:** Code Sec. 338(h)(14) was repealed by Sec. 302(e)(4)(B)(ii), P.L. 108-27. These provisions generally sunset for tax years beginning after 12/31/2012. For specific sunset provisions see Sec. 303, P.L. 108-27, as amended by Sec. 102(a), P.L. 111-312, reproduced in history notes for this Code Sec.

(14) Repealed.

(15) Combined deemed sale return. Under regulations prescribed by the Secretary, a combined deemed sale return may be filed by all target corporations acquired by a purchasing corporation on the same acquisition date if such target corporations were members of the same selling consolidated group (as defined in subparagraph (B) of paragraph (10)).

(16) Coordination with foreign tax credit provisions. Except as provided in regulations, this section shall not apply for purposes of determining the source or character of any item for purposes of subpart A of part III of subchapter N of this chapter (relating to foreign tax credit). The preceding sentence shall not apply to any gain to the extent such gain is includible in gross income as a dividend under section 1248 (determined without regard to any deemed sale under this section by a foreign corporation).

(i) Regulations.

The Secretary shall prescribe such regulations as may be necessary or appropriate to carry out the purposes of this section, including—

(1) regulations to ensure that the purpose of this section to require consistency of treatment of stock and asset sales and purchases may not be circumvented through the use of any provision of law or regulations (including the consolidated return regulations) and

(2) regulations providing for the coordination of the provisions of this section with the provision of this title relating to foreign corporations and their shareholders.

In **2010**, P.L. 111-312, Sec. 102(a), substituted "December 31, 2012" for "December 31, 2010" in Sec. 303 of P.L. 108-27 [see below], effective as if included in the enactment of the Jobs and Growth Tax Relief Reconciliation Act, P.L. 108-27, 5/28/2003.

In **2006**, P.L. 109-222, Sec. 102, substituted "December 31, 2010" for "December 31, 2008" in Sec. 303 of P.L. 108-27 [see below], effective 5/17/2006.

In **2004**, P.L. 108-357, Sec. 839(a), added "The preceding sentence shall not apply with respect to a qualified stock purchase for which an election is made under paragraph (10)." at the end of para. (h)(13), effective for transactions occurring after 10/22/2004.

—P.L. 108-311, Sec. 402(a)(6), of this Act [which amended Sec. 302(f)(2) of P.L. 108-27, see below], provides:

"(2) Pass-thru entities. In the case of a pass-thru entity described in subparagraph (A), (B), (C), (D), (E), or (F) of section 1(h)(10) of the Internal Revenue Code of 1986, as amended by this Act, the amendments made by this section shall apply to taxable years ending after December 31, 2002; except that dividends received by such an entity on or before such date shall not be treated as qualified dividend income (as defined in section 1(h)(11)(B) of such Code, as added by this Act)."

In **2003**, P.L. 108-27, Sec. 302(e)(4)(B)(i), deleted para. (h)(14), effective for tax. yrs. begin. after 12/31/2002. Sec. 302(f)(2), of this Act [prior to amendment by Sec. 402(a)(6) of P.L. 108-311, see above] provides:

"(2) Regulated investment companies and real estate investment trusts. In the case of a regulated investment company or a real estate investment trust, the amendments made by this section shall apply to taxable years ending after December 31, 2002; except that dividends received by such a company or trust on or before such date shall not be treated as qualified dividend income (as defined in section 1(h)(11)(B) of the Internal Revenue Code of 1986, as added by this Act)." Prior to deletion, para. (h)(14) read as follows:

"(14) Coordination with section 341. For purposes of determining whether section 341 applies to a disposition within 1 year after the acquisition date of stock by a shareholder (other than the acquiring corporation) who held stock in the target corporation on the acquisition date, section 341 shall be applied without regard to this section."

—P.L. 108-27, Sec. 303, of this Act [as amended by Sec. 102, P.L. 109-222 and Sec. 102(a), P.L. 111-312, see above], reads as follows:

"Sec. 303. Sunset of title. All provisions of, and amendments made by, this title [Secs. 301 and 302] shall not apply to taxable years beginning after December 31, 2012, and the Internal Revenue Code of 1986 shall be applied and administered to such years as if such provisions and amendments had never been enacted."

In **1990**, P.L. 101-508, Sec. 11323(c)(1), added subpara. (h)(10)(C), effective for acquisitions made after 10/9/90 except as provided in Sec. 11323(d)(2) of this Act, which reads as follows:

"(2) Binding contract exception. The amendments made by this section shall not apply to any acquisition pursuant to a written binding contract in effect on October 9, 1990, and at all times thereafter before such acquisition."

In **1988**, P.L. 100-647, Sec. 1006(e)(20), deleted para. (h)(7), effective as provided in Secs. 633(a)(2), (c)(1)(D) and (d)(7) of P.L. 99-514, see below. Prior to deletion, para. (h)(7) read as follows:

"(7) Additional percentage must be attributable to purchase, etc. For purposes of subsection (c)(1), any increase in the maximum percentage of stock taken into account over the percentage of stock (by value) of the target corporation held by the purchasing corporation on the acquisition date shall be taken into account only to the extent such increase is attributable to—

"(A) purchase, or

"(B) a redemption of stock of the target corporation—

"(i) to which a section 302(a) applies, or

"(ii) in the case of a shareholder who is not a corporation, to which section 301 applies."

—P.L. 100-647, Sec. 1012(bb)(5)(A), added para. (h)(16), effective for qualified stock purchases (as defined in Code Sec. 338(d)(3)) after 3/31/88, except that, in the case of an election under Code Sec. 338(h)(10), such amendment shall apply to qualified stock purchases (as so defined) after 6/10/87.

—P.L. 100-647, Sec. 1018(d)(9), substituted "which meet the requirements of section 1504(a)(2)" for "which meet the 80 percent requirements of subparagraphs (A) and (B) of subsection (d)(3)" in para. (e)(3), effective in cases where the 12-month acquisition period (as defined in Code Sec. 338(h)(1)) begins after 12/31/85.

In **1986**, P.L. 99-514, Sec. 631(b)(1), deleted "to which section 337 applies" after "single transaction" in para. (a)(1) . . . Sec. 631(b)(2), deleted subsec. (c) . . . Sec. 631(b)(3), added the sentence at the end of subpara. (h)(10)(B) . . . Sec. 631(e)(5), deleted para. (h)(12), effective as provided in Secs. 633(a)(2), (c)(1)(D) and (d)(7) of this Act:

"(a) General rule.—

"Except as otherwise provided in this section, the amendments made by this subtitle shall apply to—

* * *

"(2) any transaction described in section 338 of the Internal Revenue Code of 1986 for which the acquisition date occurs after December 31, 1986, and"

* * *

"(c) Exception for certain plans of liquidation and binding contracts.—

"(1) In general.— The amendments made by this subtitle shall not apply to—

* * *

"(D) any transaction described in section 338 of the Internal Revenue Code of 1986 with respect to any target corporation if a qualified stock purchase of such target corporation is made on or after August 1, 1986, pursuant to a written binding contract in effect before such date and the acquisition date (within the meaning of such section 338) is before January 1, 1988."

"(d) Transitional rule for certain small corporations.—

* * *

"(7) Section 338 transactions.— The provisions of this subsection shall also apply in the case of a transaction described in section 338 of the Internal Revenue Code of 1986 where the acquisition date (within the meaning of such section 338) is before January 1, 1989."

For other transitional rules, see Sec. 633(d)(1)-(6) and (f)(2) and (3) of this Act reproduced in note following Code Sec. 336.

Prior to deletion, subsec. (c) read as follows:

"(c) Special rules.

"(1) Coordination with section 337 where purchasing corporation holds less than 100 percent of stock. If during the 1-year period beginning on the acquisition date the maximum percentage (by value) of stock in the target corporation held by the purchasing corporation is less than 100 percent, then in applying section 337 for purposes of subsection (a)(1), the nonrecognition of gain or loss shall be limited to an amount determined by applying such maximum percentage to such gain or loss. The preceding sentence shall not apply if the target corporation is liquidated during such 1-year period and section 333 does not apply to such liquidation.

"(2) Certain redemptions where election made. If, in connection with a qualified stock purchase with respect to which an election is made under this section, the target corporation makes a distribution in complete redemption of all of the stock of a shareholder which qualifies under section 302(b)(3) (determined without regard to the application of section 302(c)(2)(A)(ii), section 336 shall apply to such distribution as if it were a distribution in complete liquidation."

Prior to deletion, para. (h)(12) read as follows:

"(12) Section 337 to apply where target had adopted plan for complete liquidation. If—

"(A) during the 12-month period ending on the acquisition date the target corporation adopted a plan of complete liquidation,

"(B) such plan was not rescinded before the close of the acquisition date, and

"(C) the purchasing corporation makes an election under this section (or is treated under subsection (e) as having made such an election) with respect to the target corporation,

then, subject to rules similar to the rules of subsection (c)(1), for purposes of section 337 (and other provisions which relate to section 337), the target corporation shall be treated as having distributed all of its assets as of the close of the acquisition date."

—P.L. 99-514, Sec. 1275(c)(6), deleted "a corporation described in section 934(b)," after "a DISC," in clause (h)(6)(B)(i), effective as provided in Secs. 1277(c)(1) and (d) of this Act:

"(c) Special rules for the Virgin Islands.—

"(1) In general.— The amendments made by section 1275(c) shall apply with respect to the Virgin Islands (and residents thereof and corporations created or organized therein) only if (and so long as) an implementing agreement is in effect between the United States and the Virgin Islands with respect to the establishment of rules under which the evasion or avoidance of United States income tax shall not be permitted or facilitated by such possession. Any such implementing agreement shall be executed on behalf of the United States by the Secretary of the Treasury, after consultation with the Secretary of the Interior."

"(d) Report on implementing agreements.—

"If, during the 1-year period beginning on the date of the enactment of this Act, any implementing agreement described in subsection (b) or (c) is not executed, the Secretary of the Treasury or his delegate shall report to the Committee on Finance of the United States Senate, the Committee on Ways and Means, and the Committee on Interior and Insular Affairs of the House of Representatives with respect to—

"(1) the status of such negotiations, and

"(2) the reason why such agreement has not been executed."

Corporate distributions and adjustments — Code Sec. 338

—P.L. 99-514, Sec. 1804(e)(8)(A), amended para. (d)(3), effective in cases where the 12-month acquisition period (as defined in Code Sec. 338(h)(1)) begins after 12/31/85.

Prior to amendment, para. (d)(3) read as follows:

"(3) Qualified stock purchase. The term 'qualified stock purchase' means any transaction or series of transactions in which stock of 1 corporation possessing—

"(A) at least 80 percent of total combined voting power of all classes of stock entitled to vote, and

"(B) at least 80 percent of the total number of shares of all other classes of stock (except nonvoting stock which is limited and preferred as to dividends), is acquired by another corporation by purchase during the 12-month acquisition period."

—P.L. 99-514, Sec. 1899A(7), substituted "subparagraphs (A) and (B)" for "subparagraph (A) and (B)" in clause (h)(3)(C)(i), effective 10/22/86.

—P.L. 99-509, Sec. 8021, of this Act provides:

"SEC. 8021. TAX TREATMENT OF CONRAIL PUBLIC SALE.

"(a) Treatment as new corporation.—

"(1) In general.—For periods after the public sale, for purposes of the Internal Revenue Code of 1954, Conrail shall be treated as a new corporation which purchased all of its assets as of the beginning of the day after the date of the public sale for an amount equal to the deemed purchase price.

"(2) Allocation among assets.—The deemed purchase price shall be allocated among the assets of Conrail in accordance with the temporary regulations prescribed under section 338 of the Internal Revenue Code of 1954 (as such regulations were in effect on the date of the enactment of this Act). The Secretary shall establish specific guidelines for carrying out the preceding sentence so that the basis of each asset will be clearly ascertainable. For purposes of applying the regulations referred to in the first sentence, accounts receivable and materials and supplies shall be treated as cash equivalents.

"(3) Deemed purchase price.—For purposes of this subsection, the deemed purchase price is an amount equal to the gross amount received pursuant to the public sale, multiplied by a fraction—

"(A) the numerator of which is 100 percent, and

"(B) the denominator of which is the percentage (by value) of the stock of Conrail sold in the public sale. The amount determined under the preceding sentence shall be adjusted under regulations prescribed by the Secretary for liabilities of Conrail and other relevant items.

"(b) No income from cancellation of debt or preferred stock.—

"No amount shall be included in the gross income of any person by reason of cancellation of any obligation (or preferred stock) of Conrail in connection with the public sale.

"(c) Disallowance of certain deductions.—

"No deduction shall be allowed to Conrail for any amount which is paid after the date of the public sale to employees of Conrail for services performed on or before the date of the public sale.

"(d) Waiver of certain employee stock ownership plan provisions.—

"For purposes of determining whether the employee stock ownership plans of Conrail meet the qualifications of sections 401 and 501 of the Internal Revenue Code of 1954—

"(1) the limits of section 415 of such Code (relating to limitations on benefits and contributions under qualified plans) shall not apply with respect to interests in stock transferred pursuant to this Act or a law heretofore enacted, and

"(2) the 2-year waiting period for withdrawals shall not apply to withdrawals of amounts (or shares) in participants accounts in connection with the public sale.

"(e) Definitions.—

"For purposes of this section—

"(1) Conrail.—The term 'Conrail' means the Consolidated Rail Corporation. Such term includes any corporation which was a subsidiary of Conrail immediately before the public sale.

"(2) Public sale.—The term 'public sale' means the sale of stock in Conrail pursuant to a public offering under the Conrail Privatization Act. If there is more than 1 public offering under such Act, such term means the sale pursuant to the initial public offering under such Act.

"(3) Secretary.—The term 'Secretary' means the Secretary of the Treasury or his delegate."

In 1984, P.L. 98-369, Sec. 712(k)(1)(A), added "at fair market value" after "acquisition date" in para. (a)(1)... Sec. 712(k)(1)(B), amended subsec. (b)... Sec. 712(k)(2), added "and section 333 does not apply to such liquidation" after "such 1-year period" in para. (c)(1)... Sec. 712(k)(3)(A), substituted "(wholly)" for "(in whole or in part)" in subpara. (e)(2)(B)... Sec. 712(k)(3)(B), added "or" at the end of subpara. (e)(2)(C)... Sec. 712(k)(3)(C), deleted subparas. (e)(2)(D) and (E) and added new subpara. (e)(2)(D)... Sec. 712(k)(4), amended para. (g)(1) ... Sec. 712(k)(5)(A), amended subpara. (h)(3)(B)... Sec. 712(k)(5)(B), added subpara. (h)(3)(C)... Sec. 712(k)(5)(C), amended para. (h)(1)... Sec. 712(k)(5)(D), amended clause (h)(3)(A)(ii)... Sec. 712(k)(6)(A), deleted para. (h)(7), redesignated paras. (h)(8) and (9) as paras. (h)(9) and (10), and added new paras. (h)(7) and (8)... Sec. 712(k)(6)(B), substituted "paragraph (10)" for "paragraph (9)" in para. (h)(9) (as redesignated by Sec. 712(k)(6)(A) of this Act)... Sec. 712(k)(6)(C), added paras. (h)(11)—(15)... Sec. 712(k)(7), amended subsec. (i), effective as provided in Sec 224(d) of P.L. 97-218 reproduced below, except as provided in Secs. 712(k)(9)(A) and (B) and 712(k)(10) which read as follows:

"(9) Amendments not to apply to acquisitions before September 1, 1982 —

"(A) In General.—The amendments made by this subsection shall not apply to any qualified stock purchase (as defined in section 338(d)(3) of the Internal Revenue Code of 1954) where the acquisition date (as defined in section 338(h)(2) of such Code) is before September 1, 1982.

"(B) Extension of time for making election.—In the case of any qualified stock purchase described in subparagraph (A), the time for making an election under section 338 of such Code shall not expire before the close of the 60th day after the date of the enactment of this Act."

Sec. 712(k)(10) provides:

"(10) Special rules for deemed purchases under prior law.—If, before October 20, 1983, a corporation was treated as making a qualified stock purchase (as defined in section 338(d)(3) of the Internal Revenue Code of 1954), but would not be so treated under the amendments made by paragraphs (5) and (6) of this subsection, the amendments made by such paragraphs shall not apply to such purchase unless such corporation elects (at such time and in such manner as the Secretary of the Treasury or his delegate may by regulations prescribe) to have the amendments made by such paragraphs apply."

Prior to amendment, subsec. (b) read as follows:

"(b) Price at which deemed sale made.—

"(1) In general. For purposes of subsection (a), the assets of the target corporation shall be treated as sold (and purchased) at an amount equal to—

"(A) the grossed-up basis of the purchasing corporation's stock in the target corporation on the acquisition date,

"(B) properly adjusted under regulations prescribed by the Secretary for liabilities of the target corporation and other relevant items.

"(2) Grossed-up basis. For purposes of paragraph (1), the grossed-up basis shall be an amount equal to the basis of the purchasing corporation's stock in the target corporation on the acquisition date multiplied by a fraction—

"(A) the numerator of which is 100 percent, and

"(B) the denominator of which is the percentage of stock (by value) of the target corporation held by the purchasing corporation on the acquisition date.

"(3) Allocation among assets. The amount determined under paragraph (1) shall be allocated among the assets of the target corporation under regulations prescribed by the Secretary"

Prior to deletion, subparas. (e)(2)(D) and (E) read as follows:

"(D) to the extent provided in regulations, the property acquired is located outside the United States, or

"(E) such acquisition is described in regulations prescribed by the Secretary."

Prior to amendment, para. (g)(1) read as follows:

"(1) When made. Except as otherwise provided in regulations, an election under this section shall be made not later than 75 days after the acquisition date."

Prior to amendment, subpara. (h)(3)(B) read as follows:

"(B) Deemed purchase of stock of subsidiaries. If stock in a corporation is acquired by purchase (within the meaning of subparagraph (A)) and, as a result of such acquisition, the corporation making such purchase is treated (by reason of section 318(a)) as owning stock in a 3rd corporation, the corporation making such purchase shall be treated as having purchased such stock in such 3rd corporation. The corporation making such purchase shall be treated as purchasing stock in the 3rd corporation by reason of the preceding sentence on the first day on which the purchasing corporation is considered under section 318(a) as owning such stock."

Prior to amendment, para. (h)(1) read as follows:

"(1) 12-month acquisition period. The term '12-month acquisition period' means the 12-month period beginning with the date of the first acquisition by purchase of stock included in a qualified stock purchase."

Prior to amendment, clause (h)(3)(A)(ii) read as follows:

"(ii) the stock is not acquired in an exchange to which section 351 applies, and"

Prior to deletion, para. (h)(7) read as follows:

"(7) Acquisitions by purchasing corporation include acquisitions by corporations affiliated with purchasing corporation. Except as otherwise provided in regulations, an acquisition of stock or assets by any member of an affiliated group which includes a purchasing corporation shall be treated as made by the purchasing corporation."

Prior to amendment, subsec. (i) read as follows:

"(i) Regulations.

"The Secretary shall prescribe such regulations as may be necessary to ensure that the purposes of this section to require consistency of treatment of stock and asset purchases with respect to a target corporation and its target affiliates (whether by treating all of them as stock purchases or as asset purchases) may not be circumvented through the use of any provision of law or regulations (including the consolidated return regulations)."

—P.L. 98-369, Sec. 722(a)(3), amended Sec. 306(a)(8)(A)(ii) of P.L. 97-448 (reproduced below), by substituting "September 1, 1982" for "the date of the enactment of the Tax Equity and Fiscal Responsibility Act of 1982".

In 1983, P.L. 97-448, Sec. 306(a)(8)(A)(i), added paras. (h)(8) and (h)(9), effective as provided in Sec. 224(d) of P.L. 97-248, reproduced below.

—P.L. 97-448, Sec. 306(a)(8)(A)(ii), [as amended by Sec. 722(a)(3) of P.L. 98-369, see above] of this Act provides:

"(ii) If—

"(I) any portion of a qualified stock purchase is pursuant to a binding contract entered into or after September 1, 1982, and on or before the date of the enactment of this Act, and

"(II) the purchasing corporation establishes by clear and convincing evidence that such contract was negotiated on the contemplation that, with respect to the deemed sale under section 338 of the Internal Revenue Code of 1954, the target corporation would be treated as a member of the affiliated group which includes the selling corporation,

then the amendment made by clause (i) shall not apply to such qualified stock purchase."

—P.L. 97-448, Sec. 306(a)(8)(B)(i), added paras. (4) and (5) to Sec. 224(d) of P.L. 97-248, the effective date for changes made by Sec. 224 of P.L. 97-248 [re-

Code Sec. 338 — Corporate distributions and adjustments

produced below]... Sec. 306(a)(8)(B)(ii), substituted "(within the meaning of section 338 of such Code without regard to paragraph (5) of this subsection)" for "under paragraph (1)" in Sec. 224(d)(2)(A) of P.L. 97-248 [reproduced below].

In 1982, P.L. 97-248, Sec. 222(e)(4), repealed Code Sec. 338, effective for distributions after 8/31/82. For exceptions and special rules see Sec. 222(f)(2)–(4) of this Act reproduced in note following Code Sec 302.

Prior to repeal, Code Sec. 338 read as follows:

"SEC. 338. EFFECT ON EARNINGS AND PROFITS.

"For special rule relating to the effect on earnings and profits of certain distributions in partial liquidation, see section 312(e)."

—P.L. 97-248, Sec. 224(a), added Code Sec. 338, effective as provided in Sec. 224(d) of this Act which reads as follows:

"(d) Effective dates.—

"(1) In general.—The amendments made by this section shall apply to any target corporation (within the meaning of section 338 of the Internal Revenue Code of 1954 as added by this section) with respect to which the acquisition date (within the meaning of such section) occurs after August 31, 1982.

"(2) Certain acquisitions before September 1, 1982.—If—

"(A) an acquisition date (within the meaning of section 338 of such Code without regard to paragraph (5) of this subsection) occurred after August 31, 1980, and before September 1, 1982,

"(B) the target corporation (within the meaning of section 338 of such Code) is not liquidated before September 1, 1982, and

"(C) the purchasing corporation (within the meaning of section 338 of such Code) makes, not later than November 15, 1982, an election under section 338 of such Code,

then the amendments made by this section shall apply to the acquisition of such target corporation.

"(3) Certain acquisitions of financial institutions.—In any case in which—

"(A) there is, on July 22, 1982, a binding contract to acquire control (within the meaning of section 368(c) of such Code) of any financial institution,

"(B) the approval of one or more regulatory authorities is required in order to complete such acquisition, and

"(C) within 90 days after the date of the final approval of the last such regulatory authority granting final approval, a plan of complete liquidation of such financial institution is adopted,

then the purchasing corporation may elect not to have the amendments made by this section apply to the acquisition pursuant to such contract.

"(4) Extension of time for making elections; revocation of elections.—

"(A) Extension.—The time for making an election under section 338 of such Code shall not expire before the close of February 28, 1983.

"(B) Revocation.—Any election made under section 338 of such Code may be revoked by the purchasing corporation if revoked before March 1, 1983.

"(5) Rules for acquisitions described in paragraph (2).—

"(A) In general.—For purposes of applying section 338 of such Code with respect to any acquisition described in paragraph (2)—

"(i) the date selected under subparagraph (B) of this paragraph shall be treated as the acquisition date,

"(ii) a rule similar to the last sentence of section 334(b)(2) of such Code (as in effect on August 31, 1982) shall apply, and

"(iii) subsections (e), (f), and (i) of such section 338, and paragraphs (4), (6), (8), and (9) of subsection (h) of such section 338, shall not apply.

"(B) Selection of acquisition date by purchasing corporation.—The purchasing corporation may select any date for purposes of subparagraph (A)(i) if such date—

"(i) is after the later of June 30, 1982, or the acquisition date (within the meaning of section 338 of such Code without regard to this paragraph), and

"(ii) is on or before the date on which the election described in paragraph (2)(C) is made."

SUBPART C.—COLLAPSIBLE CORPORATIONS [REPEALED]

Sec.

341. Repealed. [Collapsible corporations.]

342. Repealed. [Liquidation of certain foreign personal holding companies.]

In 2003, P.L. 108-27, Sec. 302(e)(4)(B)(iii), repealed item 341.

—P.L. 108-27, Sec. 303, of this Act [as amended by Sec. 102 of P.L. 109-222, and Sec. 102(a), P.L. 111-312, see above], reads as follows:

"SEC. 303. SUNSET OF TITLE. All provisions of, and amendments made by, this title [Secs. 301 and 302] shall not apply to taxable years beginning after December 31, 2012, and the Internal Revenue Code of 1986 shall be applied and administered to such years as if such provisions and amendments had never been enacted."

In 1976, P.L. 94-455, Sec. 1901(b)(12)(C), repealed item 342... Sec. 1901(b)(12)(D), amended the heading of Subpart C.

Prior to amendment, the heading of Subpart C read as follows:

"Subpart C. Collapsible corporations; foreign personal holding companies."

Prior to repeal, item 342 read as follows:

"342. Liquidation of certain foreign personal holding companies."

Sec. 341.

• **Caution:** Code Sec. 341, following, was repealed by Sec. 302(e)(4)(A) of P.L. 108-27, effective for tax. yrs. begin. after 12/31/2002. These provisions generally sunset for tax years beginning after 12/31/2012. For special rules, see Sec. 302(f)(2) of P.L. 108-27 and Sec. 402(a)(6) of P.L. 108-311. For sunset provision see Sec. 303, P.L. 108-27 as amended by Sec. 102(a), P.L. 111-312, reproduced in history notes for this Code Sec.

Repealed.

In 2010, P.L. 111-312, Sec. 102(a), substituted "December 31, 2012" for "December 31, 2010" in Sec. 303 of P.L. 108-27 [see below], effective as if included in the enactment of the Jobs and Growth Tax Relief Reconciliation Act, P.L. 108-27, 5/28/2003.

In 2006, P.L. 109-222, Sec. 102, substituted "December 31, 2010" for "December 31, 2008" in Sec. 303 of the Jobs and Growth Tax Relief Reconciliation Act of 2003 [P.L. 108-27, see below].

In 2004, P.L. 108-311, Sec. 402(a)(6), of this Act [which amended Sec. 302(f)(2) of P.L. 108-27, see below], provides:

"(2) Pass-thru entities. In the case of a pass-thru entity described in subparagraph (A), (B), (C), (D), (E), or (F) of section 1(h)(10) of the Internal Revenue Code of 1986, as amended by this Act, the amendments made by this section shall apply to taxable years ending after December 31, 2002; except that dividends received by such an entity on or before such date shall not be treated as qualified dividend income (as defined in section 1(h)(11)(B) of such Code, as added by this Act)."

In 2003, P.L. 108-27, Sec. 302(e)(4)(A), repealed Code Sec. 341 as part of repeal of subpart C of part II of subchapter C of chapter 1, effective for tax. yrs. begin. after 12/31/2002. Sec. 302(f)(2), of this Act [prior to amendment by Sec. 402(a)(6) of P.L. 108-311 see above] provides:

"(2) Regulated investment companies and real estate investment trusts. In the case of a regulated investment company or a real estate investment trust, the amendments made by this section shall apply to taxable years ending after December 31, 2002; except that dividends received by such a company or trust on or before such date shall not be treated as qualified dividend income (as defined in section 1(h)(11)(B) of the Internal Revenue Code of 1986, as added by this Act)."

Prior to repeal, Code Sec. 341 read as follows:

"SEC. 341. COLLAPSIBLE CORPORATIONS.

"(a) Treatment of gain to shareholders. Gain from—

"(1) the sale or exchange of stock of a collapsible corporation,

"(2) a distribution—

"(A) in complete liquidation of a collapsible corporation if such distribution is treated under this part as in part or full payment in exchange for stock, or

"(B) in partial liquidation (within the meaning of section 302(e)) of a collapsible corporation if such distribution is treated under section 302(b)(4) as in part or full payment in exchange for the stock, and

"(3) a distribution made by a collapsible corporation which, under section 301(c)(3)(A), is treated, to the extent it exceeds the basis of the stock, in the same manner as a gain from the sale or exchange of property,

to the extent that it would be considered (but for the provisions of this section) as gain from the sale or exchange of a capital asset shall, except as otherwise provided in this section, be considered as ordinary income.

"(b) Definitions.

"(1) Collapsible corporation. For purposes of this section, the term 'collapsible corporation' means a corporation formed or availed of principally for the manufacture, construction, or production of property, for the purchase of property which (in the hands of the corporation) is property described in paragraph (3), or for the holding of stock in a corporation so formed or availed of, with a view to—

"(A) the sale or exchange of stock by its shareholders (whether in liquidation or otherwise), or a distribution to its shareholders, before the realization by the corporation manufacturing, constructing, producing, or purchasing the property of ⅔ of the taxable income to be derived from such property, and

"(B) the realization by such shareholders of gain attributable to such property.

"(2) Production or purchase of property. For purposes of paragraph (1), a corporation shall be deemed to have manufactured, constructed, produced, or purchased property, if—

"(A) it engaged in the manufacture, construction, or production of such property to any extent,

"(B) it holds property having a basis determined, in whole or in part, by reference to the cost of such property in the hands of a person who manufactured, constructed, produced, or purchased the property, or

"(C) it holds property having a basis determined, in whole or in part, by reference to the cost of property manufactured, constructed, produced, or purchased by the corporation.

"(3) Section 341 assets. For purposes of this section, the term 'section 341 assets' means property held for a period of less than 3 years which is—

"(A) stock in trade of the corporation, or other property of a kind which would properly be included in the inventory of the corporation if on hand at the close of the taxable year;

"(B) property held by the corporation primarily for sale to customers in the ordinary course of its trade or business;

"(C) unrealized receivables or fees, except receivables from sales of property other than property described in this paragraph; or

"(D) property described in section 1231(b) (without regard to any holding period therein provided), except such property which is or has been used in connection with the manufacture, construction, production, or sale of property described in subparagraph (A) or (B).

In determining whether the 3-year holding period specified in this paragraph has been satisfied, section 1223 shall apply, but no such period shall be deemed to begin before the completion of the manufacture, construction, production, or purchase.

"(4) Unrealized receivables. For purposes of paragraph (3)(C), the term 'unrealized receivables or fees' means, to the extent not previously includible in income under the method of accounting used by the corporation, any rights (contractual or otherwise) to payment for—

"(A) goods delivered, or to be delivered, to the extent the proceeds therefrom would be treated as amounts received from the sale or exchange of property other than a capital asset, or

"(B) services rendered or to be rendered.

"(c) Presumption in certain cases.

"(1) In general. For purposes of this section, a corporation shall, unless shown to the contrary, be deemed to be a collapsible corporation if (at the time of the sale or exchange, or the distribution, described in subsection (a)) the fair market value of its section 341 assets (as defined in subsection (b)(3)) is—

"(A) 50 percent or more of the fair market value of its total assets, and

"(B) 120 percent or more of the adjusted basis of such section 341 assets.

Absence of the conditions described in subparagraphs (A) and (B) shall not give rise to a presumption that the corporation was not a collapsible corporation.

"(2) Determination of total assets. In determining the fair market value of the total assets of a corporation for purposes of paragraph (1)(A), there shall not be taken into account—

"(A) cash,

"(B) obligations which are capital assets in the hands of the corporation, and

"(C) stock in any other corporation.

"(d) Limitations on application of section. In the case of gain realized by a shareholder with respect to his stock in a collapsible corporation, this section shall not apply—

"(1) unless, at any time after the commencement of the manufacture, construction, or production of the property, or at the time of the purchase of the property described in subsection (b)(3) or at any time thereafter, such shareholder (A) owned (or was considered as owning) more than 5 percent in value of the outstanding stock of the corporation, or (B) owned stock which was considered as owned at such time by another shareholder who then owned (or was considered as owning) more than 5 percent in value of the outstanding stock of the corporation;

"(2) to the gain recognized during a taxable year, unless more than 70 percent of such gain is attributable to the property described in subsection (b)(1); and

"(3) to gain realized after the expiration of 3 years following the completion of such manufacture, construction, production, or purchase.

For purposes of paragraph (1), the ownership of stock shall be determined in accordance with the rules prescribed in paragraphs (1), (2), (3), (5), and (6) of section 544(a) (relating to personal holding companies); except that, in addition to the persons prescribed [sic] by paragraph (2) of that section, the family of an individual shall include the spouses of that individual's brothers and sisters (whether by the whole or half blood) and the spouses of that individual's lineal descendants. In determining whether property is described in subsection (b)(1) for purposes of applying paragraph (2), all property described in section 1221(a)(1) shall, to the extent provided in regulations prescribed by the Secretary, be treated as one item of property.

"(e) Exceptions to application of section.

"(1) Sales or exchanges of stock. For purposes of subsection (a)(1), a corporation shall not be considered to be a collapsible corporation with respect to any sale or exchange of stock of the corporation by a shareholder, if, at the time of such sale or exchange, the sum of—

"(A) the net unrealized appreciation in subsection (e) assets of the corporation (as defined in paragraph (5)(A)), plus

"(B) if the shareholder owns more than 5 percent in value of the outstanding stock of the corporation, the net unrealized appreciation in assets of the corporation (other than assets described in subparagraph (A)) which would be subsection (e) assets under clauses (i) and (iii) of paragraph (5)(A) if the shareholder owned more than 20 percent in value of such stock, plus

"(C) if the shareholder owns more than 20 percent in value of the outstanding stock of the corporation and owns, or at any time during the preceding 3-year period owned, more than 20 percent in value of the outstanding stock of any other corporation more than 70 percent in value of the assets of which are, or were at any time during which such shareholder owned during such 3-year period more than 20 percent in value of the outstanding stock, assets similar or related in service or use to assets comprising more than 70 percent in value of the assets of the corporation, the net unrealized appreciation in assets of the corporation (other than assets described in subparagraph (A)) which would be subsection (e) assets under clauses (i) and (iii) of paragraph (5)(A) if the determination whether the property, in the hands of such shareholder, would be property gain from the sale or exchange of which under any provision of this chapter be considered in whole or in part as ordinary income, were made—

"(i) by treating any sale or exchange by such shareholder of stock in such other corporation within the preceding 3-year period (but only if at the time of such sale or exchange the shareholder owned more than 20 percent in value of the outstand-

ing stock in such other corporation) as a sale or exchange by such shareholder of his proportionate share of the assets of such other corporation, and

"(ii) by treating any liquidating sale or exchange of property by such other corporation within such 3-year period (but only if at the time of such sale or exchange the shareholder owned more than 20 percent in value of the outstanding stock in such other corporation) as a sale or exchange by such shareholder of his proportionate share of the property sold or exchanged,

does not exceed an amount equal to 15 percent of the net worth of the corporation. This paragraph shall not apply to any sale or exchange of stock to the issuing corporation or, in the case of a shareholder who owns more than 20 percent in value of the outstanding stock of the corporation, to any sale or exchange of stock by such shareholder to any person related to him (within the meaning of paragraph (8)).

"(2) Repealed.

"(3) Repealed.

"(4) Repealed.

"(5) Subsection (e) asset defined.

"(A) For purposes of paragraph (1), the term 'subsection (e) asset' means, with respect to property held by any corporation—

"(i) property (except property used in the trade or business, as defined in paragraph (9)) which in the hands of the corporation is, or, in the hands of a shareholder who owns more than 20 percent in value of the outstanding stock of the corporation, would be, property gain from the sale or exchange of which would under any provision of this chapter be considered in whole or in part as ordinary income;

"(ii) property used in the trade or business (as defined in paragraph (9)), but only if the unrealized depreciation on all such property on which there is unrealized depreciation exceeds the unrealized appreciation on all such property on which there is unrealized appreciation;

"(iii) if there is net unrealized appreciation on all property used in the trade or business (as defined in paragraph (9)), property used in the trade or business (as defined in paragraph (9)) which, in the hands of a shareholder who owns more than 20 percent in value of the outstanding stock of the corporation, would be property gain from the sale or exchange of which would under any provision of this chapter be considered in whole or in part as ordinary income; and

"(iv) property (unless included under clause (i), (ii), or (iii)) which consists of a copyright, a literary, musical, or artistic composition, a letter or memorandum, or similar property, or any interest in any such property, if the property was created in whole or in part by the personal efforts of, or (in the case of a letter, memorandum, or similar property) was prepared, or produced in whole or in part for, any individual who owns more than 5 percent in value of the stock of the corporation. The determination as to whether property of the corporation in the hands of the corporation is, or in the hands of a shareholder would be, property gain from the sale or exchange of which would under any provision of this chapter be considered in whole or in part as ordinary income shall be made as if all property of the corporation had been sold or exchanged to one person in one transaction.

"(B) Repealed.

"(6) Net unrealized appreciation defined.

"(A) For purposes of this subsection, the term 'net unrealized appreciation' means, with respect to the assets of a corporation, the amount by which—

"(i) the unrealized appreciation in such assets on which there is unrealized appreciation, exceeds

"(ii) the unrealized depreciation in such assets on which there is unrealized depreciation.

"(B) For purposes of subparagraph (A) and paragraph (5)(A), the term 'unrealized appreciation' means, with respect to any asset, the amount by which—

"(i) the fair market value of such asset, exceeds

"(ii) the adjusted basis for determining gain from the sale or other disposition of such asset.

"(C) For purposes of subparagraph (A) and paragraph (5)(A), the term 'unrealized depreciation' means, with respect to any asset, the amount by which—

"(i) the adjusted basis for determining gain from the sale or other disposition of such asset, exceeds

"(ii) the fair market value of such asset.

"(D) For purposes of this paragraph (but not paragraph (5)(A)), in the case of any asset on the sale or exchange of which only a portion of the gain would under any provision of this chapter be considered as ordinary income, there shall be taken into account only an amount of the unrealized appreciation in such asset which is equal to such portion of the gain.

"(7) Net worth defined. For purposes of this subsection, the net worth of a corporation, as of any day, is the amount by which—

"(A)(i) the fair market value of all its assets at the close of such day, plus

"(ii) the amount of any distribution in complete liquidation made by it on or before such day, exceeds

"(B) all its liabilities at the close of such day. For purposes of this paragraph, the net worth of a corporation as of any day shall not take into account any increase in net worth during the one-year period ending on such day to the extent attributable to any amount received by it for stock, or as a contribution to capital or as paid-in surplus, if it appears that there was not a bona fide business purpose for the transaction in respect of which such amount was received.

"(8) Related person defined. For purposes of paragraphs (1) and (4), the following persons shall be considered to be related to a shareholder:

"(A) If the shareholder is an individual—

"(i) his spouse, ancestors, and lineal descendants, and

"(ii) a corporation which is controlled by such shareholder.

"(B) If the shareholder is a corporation—

"(i) a corporation which controls, or is controlled by, the shareholder, and "(ii) if more than 50 percent in value of the outstanding stock of the shareholder is owned by any person, a corporation more than 50 percent in value of the outstanding stock of which is owned by the same person.

For purposes of determining the ownership of stock in applying subparagraphs (A) and (B), the rules of section 267(c) shall apply, except that the family of an individual shall include only his spouse, ancestors, and lineal descendants. For purposes of this paragraph, control means the ownership of stock possessing at least 50 percent of the total combined voting power of all classes of stock entitled to vote or at least 50 percent of the total value of shares of all classes of stock of the corporation.

"(9) Property used in the trade or business. For purposes of this subsection the term 'property used in the trade or business' means property described in section 1231(b), without regard to any holding period therein provided.

"(10) Ownership of stock. For purposes of this subsection (other than paragraph (8)), the ownership of stock shall be determined in the manner prescribed in subsection (d).

"(11) Corporations and shareholders not meeting requirements. In determining whether or not any corporation is a collapsible corporation within the meaning of subsection (b), the fact that such corporation, or such corporation with respect to any of its shareholders, does not meet the requirements of paragraph (1), (2), (3), or (4) of this subsection shall not be taken into account, and such determination, in the case of a corporation which does not meet such requirements, shall be made as if this subsection had not been enacted.

"(12) Nonapplication of section 1245(a), etc. For purposes of this subsection, the determination of whether gain from the sale or exchange of property would under any provision of this chapter be considered as ordinary income shall be made without regard to the application of sections 617(d)(1), 1245(a), 1250(a), 1252(a), 1254(a), and 1276(a).

"(f) Certain sales of stock of consenting corporations.

"(1) In general. Subsection (a)(1) shall not apply to a sale of stock of a corporation (other than a sale to the issuing corporation) if such corporation (hereinafter in this subsection referred to as 'consenting corporation') consents (at such time and in such manner as the Secretary may by regulations prescribe) to have the provisions of paragraph (2) apply. Such consent shall apply with respect to each sale of stock of such corporation made within the 6-month period beginning with the date on which such consent is filed.

"(2) Recognition of gain. Except as provided in paragraph (3), if a subsection (f) asset (as defined in paragraph (4)) is disposed of at any time by a consenting corporation (or, if paragraph (3) applies, by a transferee corporation), then the amount by which—

"(A) in the case of a sale, exchange, or involuntary conversion, the amount realized, or

"(B) in the case of any other disposition, the fair market value of such asset, exceeds the adjusted basis of such asset shall be treated as gain from the sale or exchange of such asset. Such gain shall be recognized notwithstanding any other provision of this subtitle, but only to the extent such gain is not recognized under any other provision of this subtitle.

"(3) Exception for certain tax-free transactions. If the basis of a subsection (f) asset in the hands of a transferee is determined by reference to its basis in the hands of the transferor by reason of the application of section 332, 351, or 361, then the amount of gain taken into account by the transferor under paragraph (2) shall not exceed the amount of gain recognized to the transferor on the transfer of such asset (determined without regard to this subsection). This paragraph shall apply only if the transferee—

"(A) is not an organization which is exempt from tax imposed by this chapter, and

"(B) agrees (at such time and in such manner as the Secretary may by regulations prescribe) to have the provisions of paragraph (2) apply to any disposition by it of such subsection (f) asset.

"(4) Subsection (f) asset defined. For purposes of this subsection—

"(A) In general. The term 'subsection (f) asset' means any property which, as of the date of any sale of stock referred to in paragraph (1), is not a capital asset and is property owned by, or subject to an option to acquire held by, the consenting corporation. For purposes of this subparagraph, land or any interest in real property (other than a security interest), and unrealized receivables or fees (as defined in subsection (b)(4)), shall be treated as property which is not a capital asset.

"(B) Property under construction. If manufacture, construction, or production with respect to any property described in subparagraph (A) has commenced before any date of sale described therein, the term 'subsection (f) asset' includes the property resulting from such manufacture, construction, or production.

"(C) Special rule for land. In the case of land or any interest in real property (other than a security interest) described in subparagraph (A), the term 'subsection (f) asset' includes any improvements resulting from construction with respect to such property if such construction is commenced (by the consenting corporation or by a transferee corporation which has agreed to the application of paragraph (2)) within 2 years after the date of any sale described in subparagraph (A).

"(5) 5-year limitation as to shareholder. Paragraph (1) shall not apply to the sale of stock of a corporation by a shareholder if, during the 5-year period ending on the date of such sale, such shareholder (or any related person within the meaning of subsection (e)(8)(A)) sold any stock of another consenting corporation within any 6-month period beginning on a date on which a consent was filed under paragraph (1) by such other corporation.

"(6) Special rule for stock ownership in other corporations. If a corporation (hereinafter in this paragraph referred to as 'owning corporation') owns 5 percent or more in value of the outstanding stock of another corporation on the date of any sale of stock of the owning corporation during a 6-month period with respect to which a consent under paragraph (1) was filed by the owning corporation, such consent shall not be valid with respect to such sale unless such other corporation has (within the 6-month period ending on the date of such sale) filed a valid consent under paragraph (1) with respect to sales of its stock. For purposes of applying paragraph (4) to such other corporation, a sale of stock of the owning corporation to which paragraph (1) applies shall be treated as a sale of stock of such other corporation. In the case of a chain of corporations connected by the 5-percent ownership requirements of this paragraph, rules similar to the rules of the two preceding sentences shall be applied.

"(7) Adjustments to basis. The Secretary shall prescribe such regulations as he may deem necessary to provide for adjustments to the basis of property to reflect gain recognized under paragraph (2).

"(8) Special rule for foreign corporations. Except to the extent provided in regulations prescribed by the Secretary—

"(A) any consent given by a foreign corporation under paragraph (1) shall not be effective, and

"(B) paragraph (3) shall not apply if the transferee is a foreign corporation."

—P.L. 108-27, Sec. 303, of this Act, [as amended by Sec. 102, P.L. 109-222, and Sec. 102(a), P.L. 111-312, see above] reads as follows:

"Sec. 303. Sunset of title. All provisions of, and amendments made by, this title [Secs. 301 and 302] shall not apply to taxable years beginning after December 31, 2012 and the Internal Revenue Code of 1986 shall be applied and administered to such years as if such provisions and amendments had never been enacted."

In 1999, P.L. 106-170, Sec. 532(c)(2)(D), substituted "section 1221(a)(1)" for "section 1221(1)" in flush sentence following para. (d)(3) [Act directs to amend para. (d)(3). Amendment cannot be made as directed by Act], effective for any instrument held, acquired, or entered into, any transaction entered into, and supplies held or acquired on or after 12/17/99.

In 1996, P.L. 104-188, Sec. 1702(h)(7), substituted "351, or 361" for "351, 361, 371(a), or 374(a)" in para. (f)(3), effective 11/5/90, except as provided in Sec. 11821(b) of P.L. 101-508, reproduced in note following Code Sec. 370.

In 1988, P.L. 100-647, Sec. 1006(e)(18)(A), substituted "liquidating sale or exchange" for "sale or exchange" in clause (e)(1)(C)(ii) ... Sec. 1006(e)(18)(B), deleted ", gain or loss on which was not recognized to such other corporation under section 337(a)," after "in such other corporation)" in clause (e)(1)(C)(ii), effective as provided in Sec. 633(a)(1) of P.L. 99-514, reproduced below.

In 1986, P.L. 99-514, Sec. 631(e)(6)(A), deleted paras. (e)(2), (3) and (4) ... Sec. 631(e)(6)(B), substituted "paragraph (1)" for "paragraphs (1), (2), and (4)" in subpara. (e)(5)(A) and deleted subpara. (e)(5)(B), effective as provided in Sec. 633(a)(1) of this Act:

"(a) General rule.

"Except as otherwise provided in this section, the amendments made by this subtitle shall apply to—

"(1) any distribution in complete liquidation, and any sale or exchange, made by a corporation after July 31, 1986, unless such corporation is completely liquidated before January 1, 1987," . . .

Sec. 633(d) [sic (e)] of this Act provides:

"(d) [sic (e)] Complete liquidation defined.

"For purposes of this section, a corporation shall be treated as completely liquidated if all of the assets of such corporation are distributed in complete liquidation, less assets retained to meet claims."

For exceptions, see Sec. 633(c) of this Act reproduced in note following Code Sec. 336.

Prior to amendment, paras. (e)(2), (3) and (4) read as follows:

"(2) Distributions in liquidation. For purposes of subsection (a)(2), a corporation shall not be considered to be a collapsible corporation with respect to any distribution to a shareholder pursuant to a plan of complete liquidation if, by reason of the application of paragraph (4) of this subsection, section 337(a) applies to sales or exchanges of property by the corporation within the 12-month period beginning on the date of the adoption of such plan, and if, at all times after the adoption of the plan of liquidation, the sum of—

"(A) the net unrealized appreciation in subsection (e) assets of the corporation (as defined in paragraph (5)(A)), plus

"(B) if the shareholder owns more than 5 percent in value of the outstanding stock of the corporation, the net unrealized appreciation in assets of the corporation described in paragraph (1)(B) (other than assets described in subparagraph (A) of this paragraph), plus

"(C) if the shareholder owns more than 20 percent in value of the outstanding stock of the corporation and owns, or at any time during the preceding 3-year period owned more than 20 percent in value of the outstanding stock of any other corporation more than 70 percent in value of the assets of which are, or were at any time during which such shareholder owned during such 3-year period more than 20 percent in value of the outstanding stock, assets similar or related in service or use to assets comprising more than 70 percent in value of the assets of the corporation, the net unrealized appreciation in assets of the corporation described in paragraph (1)(C) (other than assets described in subparagraph (A) of this paragraph),

does not exceed an amount equal to 15 percent of the net worth of the corporation.

"(3) Recognition of gain in certain liquidations. For purposes of section 333, a corporation shall not be considered to be a collapsible corporation if at all times after the adoption of the plan of liquidation, the net unrealized appreciation in subsection (e) assets of the corporation (as defined in paragraph (5)(B)) does not exceed an amount equal to 15 percent of the net worth of the corporation.

"(4) Gain or loss on sales or exchanges in connection with certain liquidations. For purposes of section 337, a corporation shall not be considered to be a collapsible corporation with respect to any sale or exchange by it of property within the

12-month period beginning on the date of the adoption of a plan of complete liquidation, if—

"(A) at all times after the adoption of such plan, the net unrealized appreciation in subsection (e) assets of the corporation (as defined in paragraph (5)(A)) does not exceed an amount equal to 15 percent of the net worth of the corporation,

"(B) within the 12-month period beginning on the date of the adoption of such plan, the corporation sells substantially all of the properties held by it on such date, and

"(C) following the adoption of such plan, no distribution is made of any property which in the hands of the corporation or in the hands of the distributee is property in respect of which a deduction for exhaustion, wear and tear, obsolescence, amortization, or depletion is allowable.

This paragraph shall not apply with respect to any sale or exchange of property by the corporation to any shareholder who owns more than 20 percent in value of the outstanding stock of the corporation or to any person related to such shareholder (within the meaning of paragraph (8)) if such property in the hands of the corporation or in the hands of such shareholder or related person is property in respect of which a deduction for exhaustion, wear and tear, obsolescence, amortization, or depletion is allowable."

Prior to deletion, subpara. (e)(5)(B) read as follows:

"(B) For purposes of paragraph (3), the term 'subsection (e) asset' means, with respect to property held by any corporation, property described in clauses (i), (ii), (iii), and (iv) of subparagraph (A), except that clauses (i) and (iii) shall apply in respect to any shareholder who owns more than 5 percent in value of the outstanding stock of the corporation (in lieu of any shareholder who owns more than 20 percent in value of such stock)."

—P.L. 99-514, Sec. 1804(i)(1), deleted "held for more than 6 months" after "exchange of a capital asset" in subsec. (a), effective for sales, exchanges and distributions after 9/27/85.

—P.L. 99-514, Sec. 1899A(8), substituted "1245(a), etc." for "1245(a)" in the heading of para. (e)(12), effective 10/22/86.

In 1984, P.L. 98-369, Sec. 43(c)(1), substituted "1254(a), and 1276(a)" for "and 1254(a)" in para. (e)(12), effective for tax. yrs. ending after 7/18/84.

—P.L. 98-369, Sec. 65(a), substituted "2/3" for "a substantial part" in subpara. (b)(1)(A) . . . Sec. 65(b), added the last sentence of subsec. (d) . . . Sec. 65(c), substituted "described in subsection (b)(1)" for "so manufactured, constructed, produced, or purchased" in para. (d)(2), effective for sales, exchanges, and distributions made after 7/18/84.

—P.L. 98-369, Sec. 135(a), added para. (f)(8), effective 7/18/84.

—P.L. 98-369, Sec. 492(b)(2), deleted "1251(c)" in para. (e)(12), effective for tax. yrs. begin. after 12/31/83.

—P.L. 98-369, Sec. 1001(b)(2), substituted "6 months" for "1 year" each place it appeared in subsec. (a), effective for property acquired after 6/22/84, and before 1/1/88.

In 1982, P.L. 97-248, Sec. 222(e)(5), amended para. (a)(2), effective for distributions after 8/31/82. For exceptions and special rules see Sec. 222(f)(2)-(4) of this Act reproduced in note following Code Sec. 302.

Prior to amendment, para. (a)(2) read as follows:

"(2) a distribution in partial or complete liquidation of a collapsible corporation, which distribution is treated under this part as in part or full payment in exchange for stock, and"

In 1981, P.L. 97-34, Sec. 505(c)(2), deleted "(and governmental obligations described in section 1221(5)" after "corporations" and before ", and" in subpara. (c)(2)(B), effective for property acquired and positions established after 6/23/81, in tax. yrs. end. after 6/23/81.

In 1976, P.L. 94-455, Sec. 205(c)(2), substituted "1252(a), and 1254(a)" for "and 1252(a)" in para. (e)(12), effective for tax. yrs. end. after 12/31/75.

—P.L. 94-455, Sec. 1402(b)(1)(B), substituted "9 months" for "6 months" in subsec. (a) . . . Sec. 1402(b)(2), substituted "1 year" for "9 months" in subsec. (a), effective for tax. yrs. begin. after '77.

—P.L. 94-455, Sec. 1901(b)(3)(A), substituted "ordinary income" for "gain from the sale or exchange of property which is neither a capital asset nor property described in section 1231(b)" in subpars. (e)(1)(C), (e)(5)(A), (e)(6)(D) and para. (e)(12), effective for tax. yrs. begin. after 12/31/76.

—P.L. 94-455, Sec. 1901(b)(3)(I), substituted "ordinary income" for "gain from the sale or exchange of property which is not a capital asset" in subsec. (a), effective for tax. yrs. begin. after 12/31/76.

—P.L. 94-455, Sec. 1906(b)(13)(A), substituted "Secretary" for "Secretary or his delegate" each place it appeared in subsec. (f), effective for tax. yrs. begin. after 12/31/76.

In 1969, P.L. 91-172, Sec. 211(b)(4), substituted "1250(a), 1251(c), and 1252(a)" for "and 1250(a)" in para. (e)(12), effective for tax. yrs. begin. after 12/31/69.

—P.L. 91-172, Sec. 514(b)(1), amended clause (e)(5)(A)(iv), effective for sales and other dispositions occurring after 7/25/69.

Prior to amendment, clause (e)(5)(A)(iv) read as follows:

"(iv) property (unless included under clause (i), (ii), or (iii)) which consists of a copyright, a literary, musical, or artistic composition, or similar property, or any interest in any such property, if the property was created in whole or in part by the personal efforts of any individual who owns more than 5 percent in value of the stock of the corporation."

In 1966, P.L. 89-570, Sec. [1](b)(4), substituted "section 617(d)(1), 1245(a)," for "section 1245(a)" in para. (e)(12), effective for tax. yrs. end. after 9/12/66, but only in respect of expenditures paid or incurred after that date.

In 1964, P.L. 88-484, Sec. [1](a), substituted "except as otherwise provided in this section" for "except as provided in subsection (d)" in subsec. (a) and added subsec. (f), effective for transactions after 8/22/64, in tax. yrs. end. after such date.

—P.L. 88-272, Sec. 231(b)(4), substituted "sections 1245(a) and 1250(a)" for "section 1245(a)" in para. (e)(12), effective for dispositions after 12/31/63, in tax. yrs. end. after such date.

In 1962, P.L. 87-834, Sec. 13(f)(4), added para. (e)(12), effective for tax. yrs. begin. after 12/31/62.

In 1958, P.L. 85-866, Sec. 20(a), added subsec. (e), effective for tax. yrs. begin. after 12/31/57, but only with respect to sales, exchanges, and distributions after 9/2/58.

Sec. 342. Repealed.

In 1976, P.L. 94-455, Sec. 1901(a)(47), repealed Code Sec. 342, for tax. yrs. begin. after '76.

Prior to repeal, Code Sec. 342 read as follows:

"SEC. 342. LIQUIDATION OF CERTAIN FOREIGN PERSONAL HOLDING COMPANIES.

"(a) In general.

"If any distribution—

"(1) is, within the meaning of the Internal Revenue Code of 1939, a distribution in partial liquidation or in complete liquidation (including any one of a series of distributions made by the corporation in complete cancellation or redemption of all its stock) and

"(2) is made by a foreign corporation which, with respect to any taxable year beginning on or before, and ending after, August 26, 1937, was a foreign personal holding company, and with respect to which a United States group (as defined in section 552(a)(2)) existed after August 26, 1937, and before January 1, 1938,

then the distribution shall be treated as a distribution in full or part payment in exchange for the stock, and the amount of the gain recognized (determined under section 1002 without regard to this part) resulting from such distribution shall be considered as a gain from the sale or exchange of a capital asset held for not more than 6 months.

"(b) Special rule for certain liquidations before 1956.

"Subsection (a) shall not apply in the case of a series of distributions in complete liquidation described in subsection (a) if—

"(1) the first distribution is made on or after June 22, 1954, and

"(2) the final distribution is made before January 1, 1956;

and the amount of the gain recognized (determined under section 1002 without regard to this part) resulting from such distributions shall be considered as a gain from the sale or exchange of a capital asset, or of property which is not a capital asset, as the case may be."

SUBPART D.—DEFINITION AND SPECIAL RULE

Sec.

346. Definition and special rule.

In 1982, P.L. 97-248, Sec. 222(e)(8)(A), amended the heading of Subpart D and item 346.

Prior to amendment, the heading of Subpart D and item 346 read as follows:

"SUBPART D.—DEFINITION

"Sec.

"346. Partial liquidation defined."

Sec. 346. Definition and special rule.
(a) Complete liquidation.

For purposes of this subchapter, a distribution shall be treated as in complete liquidation of a corporation if the distribution is one of a series of distributions in redemption of all of the stock of the corporation pursuant to a plan.

(b) Transactions which might reach same result as partial liquidations.

The Secretary shall prescribe such regulations as may be necessary to ensure that the purposes of subsections (a) and (b) of section 222 of the Tax Equity and Fiscal Responsibility Act of 1982 (which repeal the special tax treatment for partial liquidations) may not be circumvented through the use of section 355, 351, or any other provision of law or regulations (including the consolidated return regulations).

In 1986, P.L. 99-514, Sec. 631(e)(7), deleted "337," following "section 355, 351," in subsec. (b), effective as provided in Sec. 633(a)(1) of this Act.

"(a) General rule.—

"Except as otherwise provided in this section, the amendments made by this subtitle shall apply to—

"(1) any distribution in complete liquidation, and any sale or exchange, made by a corporation after July 31, 1986, unless such corporation is completely liquidated before January 1, 1987,"

Sec. 633(d) [sic e] of this act provides:

"(d) [sic e] Complete liquidation defined.—

"For purposes of this section, a corporation shall be treated as completely liquidated if all of the assets of such corporation are distributed in complete liquidation, less assets retained to meet claims."

For exceptions, see Sec. 633(c) of this Act reproduced in note following Code Sec. 336.

In 1982, P.L. 97-248, Sec. 222(d), amended Code Sec. 346, effective for distributions after 8/31/82. For exceptions and special rules see Sec. 222(f)(2)-(4) of this Act reproduced in note following Code Sec. 302.

Prior to amendment, Code Sec. 346 read as follows:

"SEC. 346. PARTIAL LIQUIDATION DEFINED.

"(a) In general.

"For purposes of this subchapter, a distribution shall be treated as in partial liquidation of a corporation if—

"(1) the distribution is one of a series of distributions in redemption of all of the stock of the corporation pursuant to a plan; or

"(2) the distribution is not essentially equivalent to a dividend, is in redemption of a part of the stock of the corporation pursuant to a plan, and occurs within the taxable year in which the plan is adopted or within the succeeding taxable year, including (but not limited to) a distribution which meets the requirements of subsection (b).

For purposes of section 562(b) (relating to the dividends paid deduction) and section 6043 (relating to information returns), a partial liquidation includes a redemption of stock to which section 302 applies.

"(b) Termination of a business.

"A distribution shall be treated as a distribution described in subsection (a)(2) if the requirements of paragraphs (1) and (2) of this subsection are met.

"(1) The distribution is attributable to the corporation's ceasing to conduct, or consists of the assets of, a trade or business which has been actively conducted throughout the 5-year period immediately before the distribution, which trade or business was not acquired by the corporation within such period in a transaction in which gain or loss was recognized in whole or in part.

"(2) Immediately after the distribution the liquidating corporation is actively engaged in the conduct of a trade or business, which trade or business was actively conducted throughout the 5-year period ending on the date of the distribution and was not acquired by the corporation within such period in a transaction in which gain or loss was recognized in whole or in part.

Whether or not a distribution meets the requirements of paragraphs (1) and (2) of this subsection shall be determined without regard to whether or not the distribution is pro rata with respect to all of the shareholders of the corporation.

"(c) Treatment of certain redemptions.

"The fact that, with respect to a shareholder, a distribution qualifies under section 302(a) (relating to redemptions treated as distributions in part or full payment in exchange for stock) by reason of section 302(b) shall not be taken into account in determining whether the distribution, with respect to such shareholder, is also a distribution in partial liquidation of the corporation."

PART III.—CORPORATE ORGANIZATIONS AND REORGANIZATIONS

Subpart
A. Corporate organizations.
B. Effects on shareholders and security holders.
C. Effects on corporations.
D. Special rule; definitions.

SUBPART A.—CORPORATE ORGANIZATIONS

Sec.
351. Transfer to corporation controlled by transferor.

Sec. 351. Transfer to corporation controlled by transferor.

(a) General rule.

No gain or loss shall be recognized if property is transferred to a corporation by one or more persons solely in exchange for stock in such corporation and immediately after the exchange such person or persons are in control (as defined in section 368(c)) of the corporation.

(b) Receipt of property.

If subsection (a) would apply to an exchange but for the fact that there is received, in addition to the stock permitted to be received under subsection (a), other property or money, then—

(1) gain (if any) to such recipient shall be recognized, but not in excess of—

(A) the amount of money received, plus

(B) the fair market value of such other property received; and

(2) no loss to such recipient shall be recognized.

(c) Special rules where distribution to shareholders.

(1) In general. In determining control for purposes of this section, the fact that any corporate transferor distributes part or all of the stock in the corporation which it receives in the exchange to its shareholders shall not be taken into account.

(2) Special rule for section 355. If the requirements of section 355 (or so much of section 356 as relates to section 355) are met with respect to a distribution described in paragraph (1), then, solely for purposes of determining the tax treatment of the transfers of property to the controlled corporation by the distributing corporation, the fact that the shareholders of the distributing corporation dispose of part or all of the distributed stock, or the fact that the corporation whose stock was distributed issues additional stock, shall not be taken into account in determining control for purposes of this section.

(d) Services, certain indebtedness, and accrued interest not treated as property.

For purposes of this section, stock issued for—

(1) services,

(2) indebtedness of the transferee corporation which is not evidenced by a security, or

(3) interest on indebtedness of the transferee corporation which accrued on or after the beginning of the transferor's holding period for the debt,

shall not be considered as issued in return for property.

(e) Exceptions.

This section shall not apply to—

(1) Transfer of property to an investment company. A transfer of property to an investment company. For purposes of the preceding sentence, the determination of whether a company is an investment company shall be made—

(A) by taking into account all stock and securities held by the company, and

(B) by treating as stocks and securities:

(i) money,

(ii) stocks and other equity interests in a corporation, evidences of indebtedness, options, forward or futures contracts, notional principal contracts and derivatives,

(iii) any foreign currency,

(iv) any interest in a real estate investment trust, a common trust fund, a regulated investment company, a publicly-traded partnership (as defined in section 7704(b)) or any other equity interest (other than in a corporation) which pursuant to its terms or any other arrangement is readily convertible into, or exchangeable for, any asset described in any preceding clause, this clause or clause (v) or (viii),

(v) except to the extent provided in regulations prescribed by the Secretary, any interest in a precious metal, unless such metal is used or held in the active conduct of a trade or business after the contribution,

(vi) except as otherwise provided in regulations prescribed by the Secretary, interests in any entity if substantially all of the assets of such entity consist (directly or indirectly) of any assets described in any preceding clause or clause (viii),

(vii) to the extent provided in regulations prescribed by the Secretary, any interest in any entity not described in clause (vi), but only to the extent of the value of such interest that is attributable to assets listed in clauses (i) through (v) or clause (viii), or

(viii) any other asset specified in regulations prescribed by the Secretary.

The Secretary may prescribe regulations that, under appropriate circumstances, treat any asset described in clauses (i) through (v) as not so listed.

(2) Title 11 or similar case. A transfer of property of a debtor pursuant to a plan while the debtor is under the jurisdiction of a court in a title 11 or similar case (within the meaning of section 368(a)(3)(A)), to the extent that the stock received in the exchange is used to satisfy the indebtedness of such debtor.

(f) Treatment of controlled corporation.

If—

(1) property is transferred to a corporation (hereinafter in this subsection referred to as the "controlled corporation") in an exchange with respect to which gain or loss is not recognized (in whole or in part) to the transferor under this section, and

(2) such exchange is not in pursuance of a plan of reorganization,

section 311 shall apply to any transfer in such exchange by the controlled corporation in the same manner as if such transfer were a distribution to which subpart A of part I applies.

(g) Nonqualified preferred stock not treated as stock.

(1) **In general.** In the case of a person who transfers property to a corporation and receives nonqualified preferred stock—

(A) subsection (a) shall not apply to such transferor, and

(B) if (and only if) the transferor receives stock other than nonqualified preferred stock—

(i) subsection (b) shall apply to such transferor; and

(ii) such nonqualified preferred stock shall be treated as other property for purposes of applying subsection (b).

(2) **Nonqualified preferred stock.** For purposes of paragraph (1)—

(A) In general. The term "nonqualified preferred stock" means preferred stock if—

(i) the holder of such stock has the right to require the issuer or a related person to redeem or purchase the stock,

(ii) the issuer or a related person is required to redeem or purchase such stock,

(iii) the issuer or a related person has the right to redeem or purchase the stock and, as of the issue date, it is more likely than not that such right will be exercised, or

(iv) the dividend rate on such stock varies in whole or in part (directly or indirectly) with reference to interest rates, commodity prices, or other similar indices.

(B) Limitations. Clauses (i), (ii), and (iii) of subparagraph (A) shall apply only if the right or obligation referred to therein may be exercised within the 20-year period beginning on the issue date of such stock and such right or obligation is not subject to a contingency which, as of the issue date, makes remote the likelihood of the redemption or purchase.

(C) Exceptions for certain rights or obligations.

(i) In general. A right or obligation shall not be treated as described in clause (i), (ii), or (iii) of subparagraph (A) if—

(I) it may be exercised only upon the death, disability, or mental incompetency of the holder, or

(II) in the case of a right or obligation to redeem or purchase stock transferred in connection with the performance of services for the issuer or a related person (and which represents reasonable compensation), it may be exercised only upon the holder's separation from service from the issuer or a related person.

(ii) Exception. Clause (i)(I)shall not apply if the stock relinquished in the exchange, or the stock acquired in the exchange is in—

(I) a corporation if any class of stock in such corporation or a related party is readily tradable on an established securities market or otherwise, or

(II) any other corporation if such exchange is part of a transaction or series of transactions in which such corporation is to become a corporation described in subclause (I).

(3) **Definitions.** For purposes of this subsection—

(A) Preferred stock. The term "preferred stock" means stock which is limited and preferred as to dividends and does not participate in corporate growth to any significant extent. Stock shall not be treated as participating in corporate growth to any significant extent unless there is a real and meaningful likelihood of the shareholder actually participating in the earnings and growth of the corporation. If there is not a real and meaningful likelihood that dividends beyond any limitation or preference will actually be paid, the possibility of such payments will be disregarded in determining whether stock is limited and preferred as to dividends. If there is not a real and meaningful likelihood that dividends beyond any limitation or preference will actually be paid, the possibility of such payments will be disregarded in determining whether stock is limited and preferred as to dividends.

(B) Related person. A person shall be treated as related to another person if they bear a relationship to such other person described in section 267(b) or 707(b).

(4) **Regulations.** The Secretary may prescribe such regulations as may be necessary or appropriate to carry out the purposes of this subsection and sections 354(a)(2)(C), 355(a)(3)(D), and 356(e). The Secretary may also prescribe regulations, consistent with the treatment under this subsection and such sections, for the treatment of nonqualified preferred stock under other provisions of this title.

(h) Cross references.

(1) For special rule where another party to the exchange assumes a liability, see section 357.

(2) For the basis of stock or property received in an exchange to which this section applies, see sections 358 and 362.

(3) For special rule in the case of an exchange described in this section but which results in a gift, see section 2501 and following.

(4) For special rule in the case of an exchange described in this section but which has the effect of the payment of compensation by the corporation or by a transferor, see section 61(a)(1).

(5) For coordination of this section with section 304, see section 304(b)(3).

In 2005, P.L. 109-135, Sec. 403(kk), added "If there is not a real and meaningful likelihood that dividends beyond any limitation or preference will actually be paid, the possibility of such payments will be disregarded in determining whether stock is limited and preferred as to dividends." at the end of subpara. (g)(3)(A), effective for transactions after 5/14/2003 as if included in Sec. 899 of the American Jobs Creation Act of 2004, P.L. 108-357.

In 2004, P.L. 108-357, Sec. 899(a), added "Stock shall not be treated as participating in corporate growth to any significant extent unless there is a real and meaningful likelihood of the shareholder actually participating in the earnings and

Code Sec. 351 — Corporate distributions and adjustments

growth of the corporation." at the end of subpara. (g)(3)(A), effective for transactions after 5/14/2003.

In 2002, P.L. 107-147, Sec. 417(9), added "," after "liability" in para. (h)(1), effective 3/9/2002.

In 1999, P.L. 106-36, Sec. 3001(d)(1), deleted ", or acquires property subject to a liability," after "assumes a liability" in para. (h)(1), effective for transfers after 10/18/98.

In 1998, P.L. 105-277, Sec. 4003(f)(1), added ", or the fact that the corporation whose stock was distributed issues additional stock," after "dispose of part or all of the distributed stock" in para. (c)(2), effective for transfers after 8/5/97, except as provided in Sec. 1012(d)(3) of P.L. 105-34 [reproduced below].

—P.L. 105-206, Sec. 6010(c)(3)(A), amended subsec. (c), effective for transfers after 8/5/97, except as provided in Sec. 1012(d)(3) of P.L. 105-34 [reproduced below].

Prior to amendment, subsec. (c) read as follows:

"(c) Special rules where distribution to shareholders. In determining control for purposes of this section—

"(1) the fact that any corporate transferor distributes part or all of the stock in the corporation which it receives in the exchange to its shareholders shall not be taken into account, and

"(2) if the requirements of section 355 are met with respect to such distribution, the shareholders shall be treated as in control of such corporation immediately after the exchange if the shareholders own (immediately after the distribution) stock possessing—

"(A) more than 50 percent of the total combined voting power of all classes of stock of such corporation entitled to vote, and

"(B) more than 50 percent of the total value of shares of all classes of stock of such corporation."

—P.L. 105-206, Sec. 6010(e)(1), added "and" at the end of subpara. (g)(1)(A), deleted subparas. (g)(1)(B) and (C), and added new subpara. (g)(1)(B), effective for transactions after 6/8/97, except as provided in Sec. 1014(f)(2) of P.L. 105-34 [reproduced below].

Prior to deletion, subparas. (g)(1)(B) and (C) read as follows:

"(B) subsection (b) shall apply to such transferor, and

"(C) such nonqualified preferred stock shall be treated as other property for purposes of applying subsection (b)."

In 1997, P.L. 105-34, Sec. 1002(a), added a sentence and subparas. (e)(1)(A)-(B) after "A transfer of property to an investment company." in para. (e)(1), effective for transfers after 6/8/97, in tax. yrs. end. after 6/8/97, except as provided in Sec. 1002(b)(2) of this Act, which reads as follows:

"(2) Binding contracts. The amendment made by subsection (a) shall not apply to any transfer pursuant to a written binding contract in effect on June 8, 1997, and at all times thereafter before such transfer if such contract provides for the transfer of a fixed amount of property."

—P.L. 105-34, Sec. 1012(c)(1), amended subsec. (c), effective for transfers after 8/5/97, except as provided in Sec. 1012(d)(3) of this Act which reads as follows:

"(3) Transition rule. The amendments made by this section shall not apply to any distribution pursuant to a plan (or series of related transactions) which involves an acquisition described in section 355(e)(2)(A)(ii) of the Internal Revenue Code of 1986 (or, in the case of the amendments made by subsection (c), any transfer) occurring after April 16, 1997, if such acquisition or transfer is—

"(A) made pursuant to an agreement which was binding on such date and at all times thereafter,

"(B) described in a ruling request submitted to the Internal Revenue Service on or before such date, or

"(C) described on or before such date in a public announcement or in a filing with the Securities and Exchange Commission required solely by reason of the acquisition or transfer.

This paragraph shall not apply to any agreement, ruling request, or public announcement or filing unless it identifies the acquirer of the distributing corporation or any controlled corporation, or the transferee, whichever is applicable."

Prior to amendment, subsec. (c) read as follows:

"(c) Special rule. In determining control, for purposes of this section, the fact that any corporate transferor distributes part or all of the stock which it receives in the exchange to its shareholders shall not be taken into account."

—P.L. 105-34, Sec. 1014(a), redesignated subsec. (g) as subsec. (h) and added new subsec. (g), effective for transactions after 6/8/97, except as provided in Sec. 1014(f)(2) of this Act, which reads as follows:

"(2) Transition rule. The amendments made by this section shall not apply to any transaction after June 8, 1997, if such transaction is—

"(A) made pursuant to a written agreement which was binding on such date and at all times thereafter,

"(B) described in a ruling request submitted to the Internal Revenue Service on or before such date, or

"(C) described on or before such date in a public announcement or in a filing with the Securities and Exchange Commission required solely by reason of the transaction."

In 1990, P.L. 101-508, Sec. 11704(a)(3), substituted "is used" for "are used" in para. (e)(2), effective 11/5/90.

In 1989, P.L. 101-239, Sec. 7203(a), deleted "or securities" after "in exchange for stock" in subsec. (a) . . . Sec. 7203(b)(1), deleted "or securities" after "in addition to the stock" in subsec. (b), deleted "or securities" after "stock" in subsec. (d) and para. (e)(2) . . . Sec. 7203(b)(2), substituted "stock or property" for "stock, securities, or property" in para. (g)(2), effective for transfers after 10/2/89, in tax years ending after 10/2/89 except as provided by Sec. 7203(c)(2) and (3), which reads as follows:

"(2) Binding contract.—The amendments made by this section shall not apply to any transfer pursuant to a written binding contract in effect on October 2, 1989, and at all times thereafter before such transfer.

"(3) Corporate transfers.—In the case of property transferred (directly or indirectly through a partnership or otherwise) by a C corporation, paragraphs (1) and (2) shall be applied by substituting 'July 11, 1989' for 'October 2, 1989'. The preceding sentence shall not apply where the corporation meets the requirements of section 1504(a)(2) of the Internal Revenue Code of 1986 with respect to the transferee corporation (and where the transfer is not part of a plan pursuant to which the transferor subsequently fails to meet such requirements)."

In 1988, P.L. 100-647, Sec. 1018(d)(5)(G), redesignated subsec. (f) as subsec. (g) and added new subsec. (f), effective with respect to transfers on or after 6/21/88.

In 1982, P.L. 97-248, Sec. 226(a)(1)(B), added para. (f)(5), effective for transfers occurring after 8/31/82, in tax. yrs. ending after 8/31/82.

In 1980, P.L. 96-589, Sec. 5(e)(1), redesignated subsec. (e) as subsec. (f), deleted subsec. (d), and added new subsecs. (d) and (e) . . . Sec. 5(e)(2), deleted the last sentence of subsec. (a). Secs. 7(a)(5) and 7(a)(1) of this Act make this amendment effective for any transaction which occurs after 12/31/80, other than a transaction which occurs in a proceeding in a bankruptcy case or similar judicial proceeding (or in a proceeding under the Bankruptcy Act) commencing on or before 12/31/80.

Sec. 7(f) and (g) of this Act provides:

"(f) Election to substitute September 30, 1979, for December 31, 1980. —

"(1) In general. The debtor (or debtors) in a bankruptcy case or similar judicial proceeding may (with the approval of the court) elect to apply [Subsections 7(a) and (d) of this Act] by substituting 'September 20, 1979' for 'December 31, 1980' each place it appears in such subsections.

"(2) Effect of election. Any election made under paragraph (1) with respect to any proceeding shall apply to all parties to the proceeding.

"(3) Revocation only with consent. Any election under this subsection may be revoked only with the consent of the Secretary of the Treasury or his delegate.

"(4) Time and manner of election. Any election under this subsection shall be made at such time, and in such manner, as the Secretary of the Treasury or his delegate may by regulations prescribe.

"(g) Definitions.

"For purposes of this section—

"(1) Bankruptcy case. The term 'bankruptcy case' means any case under title 11 of the United States Code (as recodified by P.L. 95-598).

"(2) Similar judicial proceeding. The term 'similar judicial proceeding' means a receivership, foreclosure, or similar proceeding in a Federal or State court (as modified by section 368(a)(3)(D) of the Internal Revenue Code of 1954)."

Prior to amendment, subsec. (d) read as follows:

"(d) Exception.

"This section shall not apply to a transfer of property to an investment company."

Prior to amendment, the last sentence of subsec. (a) read as follows:

"For purposes of this section, stock or securities issued for services shall not be considered as issued in return for property."

In 1976, P.L. 94-455, Sec. 1901(a)(48)(A), deleted "(including, in the case of transfers made on or before June 30, 1967, an investment company)", after "transferred to a corporation", in subsec. (a) . . . Sec. 1901(a)(48)(B), amended subsec. (d), effective for transfers of property occurring after 10/4/76.

Prior to amendment, subsec. (d) read as follows:

"(d) Application of June 30, 1967, date.

"For purposes of this section, if, in connection with the transaction, a registration statement is required to be filed with the Securities and Exchange Commission, a transfer of property to an investment company shall be treated as made on or before June 30, 1967, only if—

"(1) such transfer is made on or before such date,

"(2) the registration statement was filed with the Securities and Exchange Commission before January 1, 1967, and the aggregate issue price of the stock and securities of the investment company which are issued in the transaction does not exceed the aggregate amount therefor specified in the registration statement as of the close of December 31, 1966, and

"(3) the transfer of property to the investment company in the transaction includes only property deposited before May 1, 1967."

In 1966, P.L. 89-809, Sec. 203(a), added "(including, in the case of transfers made on or before June 30, 1967, an investment company)" after "to a corporation" in the first sentence of subsec. (a) . . . Sec. 203(b), redesignated subsec. (d) as subsec. (e) and added new subsec. (d), effective for transfers of property to investment companies whether made before, on, or after 11/13/66.

SUBPART B.—EFFECTS ON SHAREHOLDERS AND SECURITY HOLDERS

Sec.

354. Exchanges of stock and securities in certain reorganizations.

355. Distribution of stock and securities of a controlled corporation.

356. Receipt of additional consideration.

357. Assumption of liability.

358. Basis to distributees.

Sec. 354. Exchanges of stock and securities in certain reorganizations.

(a) General rule.

(1) In general. No gain or loss shall be recognized if stock or securities in a corporation a party to a reorganization are, in pursuance of the plan of reorganization, exchanged solely for stock or securities in such corporation or in another corporation a party to the reorganization.

(2) Limitations.

(A) Excess principal amount. Paragraph (1) shall not apply if—

(i) the principal amount of any such securities received exceeds the principal amount of any such securities surrendered, or

(ii) any such securities are received and no such securities are surrendered.

(B) Property attributable to accrued interest. Neither paragraph (1) nor so much of section 356 as relates to paragraph (1) shall apply to the extent that any stock (including nonqualified preferred stock, as defined in section 351(g)(2), securities, or other property received is attributable to interest which has accrued on securities on or after the beginning of the holder's holding period.

(C) Nonqualified preferred stock.

(i) In general. Nonqualified preferred stock (as defined in section 351(g)(2) received in exchange for stock other than nonqualified preferred stock (as so defined) shall not be treated as stock or securities.

(ii) Recapitalizations of family-owned corporations.

(I) In general. Clause (i) shall not apply in the case of a recapitalization under section 368(a)(1)(E) of a family-owned corporation.

(II) Family-owned corporation. For purposes of this clause, except as provided in regulations, the term "family-owned corporation" means any corporation which is described in clause (i) of section 447(d)(2)(C) throughout the 8-year period beginning on the date which is 5 years before the date of the recapitalization. For purposes of the preceding sentence, stock shall not be treated as owned by a family member during any period described in section 355(d)(6)(B).

(III) Extension of statute of limitations. The statutory period for the assessment of any deficiency attributable to a corporation failing to be a family-owned corporation shall not expire before the expiration of 3 years after the date the Secretary is notified by the corporation (in such manner as the Secretary may prescribe) of such failure, and such deficiency may be assessed before the expiration of such 3-year period notwithstanding the provisions of any other law or rule of law which would otherwise prevent such assessment.

(3) Cross references.

(A) For treatment of the exchange if any property is received which is not permitted to be received under this subsection (including an excess principal amount of securities received over securities surrendered, but not including nonqualified preferred stock and property to which paragraph (2)(B) applies), see section 356.

(B) For treatment of accrued interest in the case of an exchange described in paragraph (2)(B), see section 61.

(b) Exception.

(1) In general. Subsection (a) shall not apply to an exchange in pursuance of a plan of reorganization within the meaning of subparagraph (D) or (G) of section 368(a)(1) unless—

(A) the corporation to which the assets are transferred acquires substantially all of the assets of the transferor of such assets; and

(B) the stock, securities, and other properties received by such transferor, as well as the other properties of such transferor, are distributed in pursuance of the plan of reorganization.

(2) Cross reference. For special rules for certain exchanges in pursuance of plans of reorganization within the meaning of subparagraph (D) or (G) of section 368(a)(1), see section 355.

(c) Certain railroad reorganizations.

Notwithstanding any other provision of this subchapter, subsection (a)(1) (and so much of section 356 as relates to this section) shall apply with respect to a plan of reorganization (whether or not a reorganization within the meaning of section 368(a)) for a railroad confirmed under section 1173 of title 11 of the United States Code, as being in the public interest.

In 1998, P.L. 105-206, Sec. 6010(e)(2), added subclause (a)(2)(C)(ii)(III), effective for transactions after 6/8/97, except as provided in Sec. 1014(f)(2) of P.L. 105-34 [reproduced below].

In 1997, P.L. 105-34, Sec. 1014(b), added subpara. (a)(2)(C) . . . Sec. 1014(e)(1), added "(including nonqualified preferred stock, as defined in section 351(g)(2))" after "any stock" in subpara. (a)(2)(B) . . . Sec. 1014(e)(2), added "nonqualified preferred stock and" after "but not including" in subpara. (a)(3)(A), effective for transactions after 6/8/97, except as provided in Sec. 1014(f)(2) of this Act, which reads as follows:

"(2) Transition rule. The amendments made by this section shall not apply to any transaction after June 8, 1997, if such transaction is—

"(A) made pursuant to a written agreement which was binding on such date and at all times thereafter,

"(B) described in a ruling request submitted to the Internal Revenue Service on or before such date, or

"(C) described on or before such date in a public announcement or in a filing with the Securities and Exchange Commission required solely by reason of the transaction."

In 1995, P.L. 104-88, Sec. 304(c), deleted "or approved by the Interstate Commerce under subchapter IV of chapter 113 of title 49," after "United States Code," in subsec. (c), effective 12/29/95.

In 1990, P.L. 101-508, Sec. 11801(c)(8)(D), repealed subsec. (d), effective 11/5/90 except as provided in Sec. 11821(b) of this Act, reproduced in note following Code Sec. 370.

Prior to repeal, subsec. (d) read as follows:

"(d) Exchanges under the final system plan for ConRail.

"No gain or loss shall be recognized if stock or securities in a corporation are, in pursuance of an exchange to which paragraph (1) or (2) of section 374(c) applies, exchanged solely for stock of the Consolidated Rail Corporation, securities of such Corporation, certificates of value of the United States Railway Association, or any combination thereof."

In 1980, P.L. 96-589, Sec. 4(e)(1), amended paras. (a)(2) and (a)(3) . . . Sec. 4(h)(1), substituted "subparagraph (D) or (G) of section 368(a)(1)" for "section 368(a)(1)(D)" in paras. (b)(1) and (2). Sec. 7(c)(1) of this Act makes these changes effective for any bankruptcy case or similar judicial proceeding begin. after 12/31/80.

Sec. 7(c)(2) of this Act provides:

"(2) Exchanges of property for accrued interest. The amendments made [by subsection (e) of section 4 of this Act] (relating to treatment of property attributable to accrued interest) shall also apply to any exchange—

"(A) which occurs after December 31, 1980, and

"(B) which does not occur in a bankruptcy case or similar judicial proceeding (or in a proceeding under the Bankruptcy Act) commenced on or before December 31, 1980."

Sec. 7(f) and (g) of this Act provides:

"(f) Election to substitute September 30, 1979, for December 31, 1980.—

"(1) In general. The debtor (or debtors) in a bankruptcy case or similar judicial proceeding may (with the approval of the court) elect to apply [subsection 7(c) of this Act] by substituting 'September 30, 1979' for 'December 31, 1980' each place it appears in such subsections.

"(2) Effect of election. Any election made under paragraph (1) with respect to any proceeding shall apply to all parties to the proceeding.

"(3) Revocation only with consent. Any election under this subsection may be revoked only with the consent of the Secretary of the Treasury or his delegate.

"(4) Time and manner of election. Any election under this subsection shall be made at such time, and in such manner, as the Secretary of the Treasury or his delegate may by regulations prescribe.

"(g) Definitions.

For purposes of this section—

"(1) Bankruptcy case. The term 'bankruptcy case' means any case under title 11 of the United States Code (as recodified by P.L. 95-598).

"(2) Similar judicial proceeding. The term 'similar judicial proceeding' means a receivership, foreclosure, or similar proceeding in a Federal or State court (as modified by section 368(a)(3)(D) of the Internal Revenue Code of 1954)."

Prior to amendment, paras. (a)(2) and (a)(3) read as follows:

"(2) Limitation. Paragraph (1) shall not apply if—

"(A) the principal amount of any such securities received exceeds the principal amount of any such securities surrendered, or

"(B) any such securities are received and no such securities are surrendered.

"(3) Cross reference. For treatment of the exchange if any property is received which is not permitted to be received under this subsection (including an excess principal amount of securities received over securities surrendered), see section 356."

—P.L. 96-589, Sec. 6(i)(2), substituted "confirmed under section 1173 of title 11 of the United States Code, or approved by the Interstate Commerce Commission" for "approved by the Interstate Commerce Commission under section 77 of the Bankruptcy Act, or" in subsec. (c), effective 10/1/79, except for any proceeding under the Bankruptcy Act begun before 10/1/79.

See Sec. 7(g) of this Act, reproduced above.

In 1978, P.L. 95-473, Sec. 2(a)(2)(F), substituted "subchapter IV of chapter 113 of title 49" for "section 20b of the Interstate Commerce Act" in subsec. (c), effective 10/17/78.

In 1976, P.L. 94-253, Sec. 1(c), added subsec. (d), effective for tax. yrs. end. after 3/31/76.

Sec. 355. Distribution of stock and securities of a controlled corporation.

(a) Effect on distributees.

(1) General rule. If—

(A) a corporation (referred to in this section as the "distributing corporation")—

(i) distributes to a shareholder, with respect to its stock, or

(ii) distributes to a security holder, in exchange for its securities,

solely stock or securities of a corporation (referred to in this section as "controlled corporation") which it controls immediately before the distribution,

(B) the transaction was not used principally as a device for the distribution of the earnings and profits of the distributing corporation or the controlled corporation or both (but the mere fact that subsequent to the distribution stock or securities in one or more of such corporations are sold or exchanged by all or some of the distributees (other than pursuant to an arrangement negotiated or agreed upon prior to such distribution) shall not be construed to mean that the transaction was used principally as such a device),

(C) the requirements of subsection (b) (relating to active businesses) are satisfied, and

(D) as part of the distribution, the distributing corporation distributes—

(i) all of the stock and securities in the controlled corporation held by it immediately before the distribution, or

(ii) an amount of stock in the controlled corporation constituting control within the meaning of section 368(c), and it is established to the satisfaction of the Secretary that the retention by the distributing corporation of stock (or stock and securities) in the controlled corporation was not in pursuance of a plan having as one of its principal purposes the avoidance of Federal income tax,

then no gain or loss shall be recognized to (and no amount shall be includible in the income of) such shareholder or security holder on the receipt of such stock or securities.

(2) Non pro rata distributions, etc. Paragraph (1) shall be applied without regard to the following:

(A) whether or not the distribution is pro rata with respect to all of the shareholders of the distributing corporation,

(B) whether or not the shareholder surrenders stock in the distributing corporation, and

(C) whether or not the distribution is in pursuance of a plan of reorganization (within the meaning of section 368(a)(1)(D)).

(3) Limitations.

(A) Excess principal amount. Paragraph (1) shall not apply if—

(i) the principal amount of the securities in the controlled corporation which are received exceeds the principal amount of the securities which are surrendered in connection with such distribution, or

(ii) securities in the controlled corporation are received and no securities are surrendered in connection with such distribution.

(B) Stock acquired in taxable transactions within 5 years treated as boot. For purposes of this section (other than paragraph (1)(D) of this subsection) and so much of section 356 as relates to this section, stock of a controlled corporation acquired by the distributing corporation by reason of any transaction—

(i) which occurs within 5 years of the distribution of such stock, and

(ii) in which gain or loss was recognized in whole or in part,

shall not be treated as stock of such controlled corporation, but as other property.

(C) Property attributable to accrued interest. Neither paragraph (1) nor so much of section 356 as relates to paragraph (1) shall apply to the extent that any stock (including nonqualified preferred stock, as defined in section 351(g)(2)), securities, or other property received is attributable to interest which has accrued on securities on or after the beginning of the holder's holding period.

(D) Nonqualified preferred stock. Nonqualified preferred stock (as defined in section 351(g)(2)) received in a distribution with respect to stock other than nonqualified preferred stock (as so defined) shall not be treated as stock or securities.

(4) Cross references.

(A) For treatment of the exchange if any property is received which is not permitted to be received under this subsection (including nonqualified preferred stock and an excess principal amount of securities received over securities surrendered, but not including property to which paragraph (3)(C) applies), see section 356.

(B) For treatment of accrued interest in the case of an exchange described in paragraph (3)(C), see section 61.

(b) Requirements as to active business.

(1) In general. Subsection (a) shall apply only if either—

(A) the distributing corporation, and the controlled corporation (or, if stock of more than one controlled corporation is distributed, each of such corporations), is engaged immediately after the distribution in the active conduct of a trade or business, or

(B) immediately before the distribution, the distributing corporation had no assets other than stock or securities in the controlled corporations and each of the controlled corporations is engaged immediately after the distribution in the active conduct of a trade or business.

(2) Definition. For purposes of paragraph (1), a corporation shall be treated as engaged in the active conduct of a trade or business if and only if—

(A) it is engaged in the active conduct of a trade or business,
(B) such trade or business has been actively conducted throughout the 5-year period ending on the date of the distribution,
(C) such trade or business was not acquired within the period described in subparagraph (B) in a transaction in which gain or loss was recognized in whole or in part, and
(D) control of a corporation which (at the time of acquisition of control) was conducting such trade or business—
　(i) was not acquired by any distributee corporation directly (or through 1 or more corporations, whether through the distributing corporation or otherwise) within the period described in subparagraph (B) and was not acquired by the distributing corporation directly (or through 1 or more corporations) within such period, or
　(ii) was so acquired by any such corporation within such period, but, in each case in which such control was so acquired, it was so acquired, only by reason of transactions in which gain or loss was not recognized in whole or in part, or only by reason of such transactions combined with acquisitions before the beginning of such period.
For purposes of subparagraph (D), all distributee corporations which are members of the same affiliated group (as defined in section 1504(a) without regard to section 1504(b)) shall be treated as 1 distributee corporation.

(3) Special rules for determining active conduct in the case of affiliated groups.
(A) In general. For purposes of determining whether a corporation meets the requirements of paragraph (2)(A), all members of such corporation's separate affiliated group shall be treated as one corporation.
(B) Separate affiliated group. For purposes of this paragraph, the term "separate affiliated group" means, with respect to any corporation, the affiliated group which would be determined under section 1504(a) if such corporation were the common parent and section 1504(b) did not apply.
(C) Treatment of trade or business conducted by acquired member. If a corporation became a member of a separate affiliated group as a result of one or more transactions in which gain or loss was recognized in whole or in part, any trade or business conducted by such corporation (at the time that such corporation became such a member) shall be treated for purposes of paragraph (2) as acquired in a transaction in which gain or loss was recognized in whole or in part.
(D) Regulations. The Secretary shall prescribe such regulations as are necessary or appropriate to carry out the purposes of this paragraph, including regulations which provide for the proper application of subparagraphs (B), (C), and (D) of paragraph (2), and modify the application of subsection (a)(3)(B), in connection with the application of this paragraph.

(c) Taxability of corporation on distribution.
(1) In general. Except as provided in paragraph (2), no gain or loss shall be recognized to a corporation on any distribution to which this section (or so much of section 356 as relates to this section) applies and which is not in pursuance of a plan of reorganization.
(2) Distribution of appreciated property.
(A) In general. If—
　(i) in a distribution referred to in paragraph (1), the corporation distributes property other than qualified property, and
　(ii) the fair market value of such property exceeds its adjusted basis (in the hands of the distributing corporation),
then gain shall be recognized to the distributing corporation as if such property were sold to the distributee at its fair market value.
(B) Qualified property. For purposes of subparagraph (A), the term "qualified property" means any stock or securities in the controlled corporation.
(C) Treatment of liabilities. If any property distributed in the distribution referred to in paragraph (1) is subject to a liability or the shareholder assumes a liability of the distributing corporation in connection with the distribution, then, for purposes of subparagraph (A), the fair market value of such property shall be treated as not less than the amount of such liability.
(3) **Coordination with sections 311 and 336(a).** Sections 311 and 336(a) shall not apply to any distribution referred to in paragraph (1).

(d) Recognition of gain on certain distributions of stock or securities in controlled corporation.
(1) In general. In the case of a disqualified distribution, any stock or securities in the controlled corporation shall not be treated as qualified property for purposes of subsection (c)(2) of this section or section 361(c)(2).
(2) Disqualified distribution. For purposes of this subsection, the term "disqualified distribution" means any distribution to which this section (or so much of section 356 as relates to this section) applies if, immediately after the distribution—
(A) any person holds disqualified stock in the distributing corporation which constitutes a 50-percent or greater interest in such corporation, or
(B) any person holds disqualified stock in the controlled corporation (or, if stock of more than 1 controlled corporation is distributed, in any controlled corporation) which constitutes a 50-percent or greater interest in such corporation.
(3) **Disqualified stock.** For purposes of this subsection, the term "disqualified stock" means—
(A) any stock in the distributing corporation acquired by purchase after October 9, 1990, and during the 5-year period ending on the date of the distribution, and
(B) any stock in any controlled corporation—
　(i) acquired by purchase after October 9, 1990, and during the 5-year period ending on the date of the distribution, or
　(ii) received in the distribution to the extent attributable to distributions on—
　　(I) stock described in subparagraph (A), or
　　(II) any securities in the distributing corporation acquired by purchase after October 9, 1990, and during the 5-year period ending on the date of the distribution.
(4) **50-percent or greater interest.** For purposes of this subsection, the term "50-percent or greater interest" means stock possessing at least 50 percent of the total combined voting power of all classes of stock entitled to vote or at least 50 percent of the total value of shares of all classes of stock.
(5) **Purchase.** For purposes of this subsection—
(A) In general. Except as otherwise provided in this paragraph, the term "purchase" means any acquisition but only if—

(i) the basis of the property acquired in the hands of the acquirer is not determined (I) in whole or in part by reference to the adjusted basis of such property in the hands of the person from whom acquired, or (II) under section 1014(a), and

(ii) the property is not acquired in an exchange to which section 351, 354, 355, or 356 applies.

(B) Certain section 351 exchanges treated as purchases. The term "purchase" includes any acquisition of property in an exchange to which section 351 applies to the extent such property is acquired in exchange for—

(i) any cash or cash item,

(ii) any marketable stock or security, or

(iii) any debt of the transferor.

(C) Carryover basis transactions. If—

(i) any person acquires property from another person who acquired such property by purchase (as determined under this paragraph with regard to this subparagraph), and

(ii) the adjusted basis of such property in the hands of such acquirer is determined in whole or in part by reference to the adjusted basis of such property in the hands of such other person,

such acquirer shall be treated as having acquired such property by purchase on the date it was so acquired by such other person.

(6) Special rule where substantial diminution of risk.

(A) In general. If this paragraph applies to any stock or securities for any period, the running of any 5-year period set forth in subparagraph (A) or (B) of paragraph (3) (whichever applies) shall be suspended during such period.

(B) Property to which suspension applies. This paragraph applies to any stock or securities for any period during which the holder's risk of loss with respect to such stock or securities, or with respect to any portion of the activities of the corporation, is (directly or indirectly) substantially diminished by—

(i) an option,

(ii) a short sale,

(iii) any special class of stock, or

(iv) any other device or transaction.

(7) Aggregation rules.

(A) In general. For purposes of this subsection, a person and all persons related to such person (within the meaning of section 267(b) or 707(b)(1)) shall be treated as one person.

(B) Persons acting pursuant to plans or arrangements. If two or more persons act pursuant to a plan or arrangement with respect to acquisitions of stock or securities in the distributing corporation or controlled corporation, such persons shall be treated as one person for purposes of this subsection.

(8) Attribution from entities.

(A) In general. Paragraph (2) of section 318(a) shall apply in determining whether a person holds stock or securities in any corporation (determined by substituting "10 percent" for "50 percent" in subparagraph (C) of such paragraph (2) and by treating any reference to stock as including a reference to securities).

(B) Deemed purchase rule. If—

(i) any person acquires by purchase an interest in any entity, and

(ii) such person is treated under subparagraph (A) as holding any stock or securities by reason of holding such interest,

such stock or securities shall be treated as acquired by purchase by such person on the later of the date of the purchase of the interest in such entity or the date such stock or securities are acquired by purchase by such entity.

(9) Regulations. The Secretary shall prescribe such regulations as may be necessary to carry out the purposes of this subsection, including—

(A) regulations to prevent the avoidance of the purposes of this subsection through the use of related persons, intermediaries, pass-thru entities, options, or other arrangements, and

(B) regulations modifying the definition of the term "purchase."

(e) Recognition of gain on certain distributions of stock or securities in connection with acquisition.

(1) General rule. If there is a distribution to which this subsection applies, any stock or securities in the controlled corporation shall not be treated as qualified property for purposes of subsection (c)(2) of this section or section 361(c)(2).

(2) Distributions to which subsection applies.

(A) In general. This subsection shall apply to any distribution—

(i) to which this section (or so much of section 356 as relates to this section) applies, and

(ii) which is part of a plan (or series of related transactions) pursuant to which 1 or more persons acquire directly or indirectly stock representing a 50-percent or greater interest in the distributing corporation or any controlled corporation.

(B) Plan presumed to exist in certain cases. If 1 or more persons acquire directly or indirectly stock representing a 50-percent or greater interest in the distributing corporation or any controlled corporation during the 4-year period beginning on the date which is 2 years before the date of the distribution, such acquisition shall be treated as pursuant to a plan described in subparagraph (A)(ii) unless it is established that the distribution and the acquisition are not pursuant to a plan or series of related transactions.

(C) Certain plans disregarded. A plan (or series of related transactions) shall not be treated as described in subparagraph (A)(ii) if, immediately after the completion of such plan or transactions, the distributing corporation and all controlled corporations are members of a single affiliated group (as defined in section 1504 without regard to subsection (b) thereof).

(D) Coordination with subsection (d). This subsection shall not apply to any distribution to which subsection (d) applies.

(3) Special rules relating to acquisitions.

(A) Certain acquisitions not taken into account. Except as provided in regulations, the following acquisitions shall not be taken into account in applying paragraph (2)(A)(ii):

(i) The acquisition of stock in any controlled corporation by the distributing corporation.

(ii) The acquisition by a person of stock in any controlled corporation by reason of holding stock or securities in the distributing corporation.

(iii) The acquisition by a person of stock or securities in any successor corporation of the distributing corporation or any controlled corporation by reason of holding stock or securities in such distributing or controlled corporation.

(iv) The acquisition of stock in the distributing corporation or any controlled corporation to the extent that the percentage of stock owned directly or indirectly in such corporation by each person owning stock in such corporation immediately before the acquisition does not decrease.

This subparagraph shall not apply to any acquisition if the stock held before the acquisition was acquired pursuant to a plan (or series of related transactions) described in paragraph (2)(A)(ii).

(B) Asset acquisitions. Except as provided in regulations, for purposes of this subsection, if the assets of the distributing corporation or any controlled corporation are acquired by a successor corporation in a transaction described in subparagraph (A), (C), or (D) of section 368(a)(1) or any other transaction specified in regulations by the Secretary, the shareholders (immediately before the acquisition) of the corporation acquiring such assets shall be treated as acquiring stock in the corporation from which the assets were acquired.

(4) Definition and special rules. For purposes of this subsection—

(A) 50-percent or greater interest. The term "50-percent or greater interest" has the meaning given such term by subsection (d)(4).

(B) Distributions in title 11 or similar case. Paragraph (1) shall not apply to any distribution made in a title 11 or similar case (as defined in section 368(a)(3)).

(C) Aggregation and attribution rules.

(i) Aggregation. The rules of paragraph (7)(A) of subsection (d) shall apply.

(ii) Attribution. Section 318(a)(2) shall apply in determining whether a person holds stock or securities in any corporation. Except as provided in regulations, section 318(a)(2)(C) shall be applied without regard to the phrase "50 percent or more in value" for purposes of the preceding sentence.

(D) Successors and predecessors. For purposes of this subsection, any reference to a controlled corporation or a distributing corporation shall include a reference to any predecessor or successor of such corporation.

(E) Statute of limitations. If there is a distribution to which paragraph (1) applies—

(i) the statutory period for the assessment of any deficiency attributable to any part of the gain recognized under this subsection by reason of such distribution shall not expire before the expiration of 3 years from the date the Secretary is notified by the taxpayer (in such manner as the Secretary may by regulations prescribe) that such distribution occurred, and

(ii) such deficiency may be assessed before the expiration of such 3-year period notwithstanding the provisions of any other law or rule of law which would otherwise prevent such assessment.

(5) Regulations. The Secretary shall prescribe such regulations as may be necessary to carry out the purposes of this subsection, including regulations—

(A) providing for the application of this subsection where there is more than 1 controlled corporation,

(B) treating 2 or more distributions as 1 distribution where necessary to prevent the avoidance of such purposes, and

(C) providing for the application of rules similar to the rules of subsection (d)(6) where appropriate for purposes of paragraph (2)(B).

(f) Section not to apply to certain intragroup transactions.

Except as provided in regulations, this section (or so much of section 356 as relates to this section) shall not apply to the distribution of stock from 1 member of an affiliated group (as defined in section 1504(a)) to another member of such group if such distribution is part of a plan (or series of related transactions) described in subsection (e)(2)(A)(ii) (determined after the application of subsection (e)).

(g) Section not to apply to distributions involving disqualified investment corporations.

(1) In general. This section (and so much of section 356 as relates to this section) shall not apply to any distribution which is part of a transaction if—

(A) either the distributing corporation or controlled corporation is, immediately after the transaction, a disqualified investment corporation, and

(B) any person holds, immediately after the transaction, a 50-percent or greater interest in any disqualified investment corporation, but only if such person did not hold such an interest in such corporation immediately before the transaction.

(2) Disqualified investment corporation. For purposes of this subsection—

(A) In general. The term "disqualified investment corporation" means any distributing or controlled corporation if the fair market value of the investment assets of the corporation is—

(i) in the case of distributions after the end of the 1-year period beginning on the date of the enactment of this subsection, ⅔ or more of the fair market value of all assets of the corporation, and

(ii) in the case of distributions during such 1-year period, ¾ or more of the fair market value of all assets of the corporation.

(B) Investment assets.

(i) In general. Except as otherwise provided in this subparagraph, the term "investment assets" means—

(I) cash,

(II) any stock or securities in a corporation,

(III) any interest in a partnership,

(IV) any debt instrument or other evidence of indebtedness,

(V) any option, forward or futures contract, notional principal contract, or derivative,

(VI) foreign currency, or

(VII) any similar asset.

(ii) Exception for assets used in active conduct of certain financial trades or businesses. Such term shall not include any asset which is held for use in the active and regular conduct of—

(I) a lending or finance business (within the meaning of section 954(h)(4)),

(II) a banking business through a bank (as defined in section 581), a domestic building and loan association (within the meaning of section 7701(a)(19)), or any similar institution specified by the Secretary, or

(III) an insurance business if the conduct of the business is licensed, authorized, or regulated by an applicable insurance regulatory body.

This clause shall only apply with respect to any business if substantially all of the income of the business is derived from persons who are not related (within the meaning of section 267(b) or 707(b)(1)) to the person conducting the business.

(iii) Exception for securities marked to market. Such term shall not include any security (as defined in section 475(c)(2)) which is held by a dealer in securities and to which section 475(a) applies.

(iv) Stock or securities in a 20-percent controlled entity.

(I) In general. Such term shall not include any stock and securities in, or any asset described in subclause (IV) or (V) of clause (i) issued by, a corporation which is a 20-percent controlled entity with respect to the distributing or controlled corporation.

(II) Look-thru rule. The distributing or controlled corporation shall, for purposes of applying this subsection, be treated as owning its ratable share of the assets of any 20-percent controlled entity.

(III) 20-percent controlled entity. For purposes of this clause, the term "20-percent controlled entity" means, with respect to any distributing or controlled corporation, any corporation with respect to which the distributing or controlled corporation owns directly or indirectly stock meeting the requirements of section 1504(a)(2), except that such section shall be applied by substituting "20-percent" for "80-percent" and without regard to stock described in section 1504(a)(4).

(v) Interests in certain partnerships.

(I) In general. Such term shall not include any interest in a partnership, or any debt instrument or other evidence of indebtedness, issued by the partnership, if 1 or more of the trades or businesses of the partnership are (or, without regard to the 5-year requirement under subsection (b)(2)(B), would be) taken into account by the distributing or controlled corporation, as the case may be, in determining whether the requirements of subsection (b) are met with respect to the distribution.

(II) Look-thru rule. The distributing or controlled corporation shall, for purposes of applying this subsection, be treated as owning its ratable share of the assets of any partnership described in subclause (I).

(3) 50-Percent or greater interest. For purposes of this subsection—

(A) In general. The term "50-percent or greater interest" has the meaning given such term by subsection (d)(4).

(B) Attribution rules. The rules of section 318 shall apply for purposes of determining ownership of stock for purposes of this paragraph.

(4) Transaction. For purposes of this subsection, the term "transaction" includes a series of transactions.

(5) Regulations. The Secretary shall prescribe such regulations as may be necessary to carry out, or prevent the avoidance of, the purposes of this subsection, including regulations—

(A) to carry out, or prevent the avoidance of, the purposes of this subsection in cases involving—

(i) the use of related persons, intermediaries, pass-thru entities, options, or other arrangements, and

(ii) the treatment of assets unrelated to the trade or business of a corporation as investment assets if, prior to the distribution, investment assets were used to acquire such unrelated assets,

(B) which in appropriate cases exclude from the application of this subsection a distribution which does not have the character of a redemption which would be treated as a sale or exchange under section 302, and

(C) which modify the application of the attribution rules applied for purposes of this subsection.

In **2007,** P.L. 110-172, Sec. 4(b)(1), amended subpara. (b)(2)(A) . . . Sec. 4(b)(2), amended para. (b)(3), effective for distributions made after 5/17/2006, except as provided in Sec. 4(d)(2)(B)-(D) of this Act, which reads as follows:

"(B) Transition rule. The amendments made by subsection (b) shall not apply to any distribution pursuant to a transaction which is--

"(i) made pursuant to an agreement which was binding on May 17, 2006, and at all times thereafter,

"(ii) described in a ruling request submitted to the Internal Revenue Service on or before such date, or

"(iii) described on or before such date in a public announcement or in a filing with the Securities and Exchange Commission.

"(C) Election out of transition rule. Subparagraph (B) shall not apply if the distributing corporation elects not to have such subparagraph apply to distributions of such corporation. Any such election, once made, shall be irrevocable.

"(D) Special rule for certain pre-enactment distributions. For purposes of determining the continued qualification under section 355(b)(2)(A) of the Internal Revenue Code of 1986 of distributions made on or before May 17, 2006, as a result of an acquisition, disposition, or other restructuring after such date, such distribution shall be treated as made on the date of such acquisition, disposition, or restructuring for purposes of applying subparagraphs (A) through (C) of this paragraph. The preceding sentence shall only apply with respect to the corporation that undertakes such acquisition, disposition, or other restructuring, and only if such application results in continued qualification under section 355(b)(2)(A) of such Code."

Prior to amendment, subpara. (b)(2)(A) read as follows:

"(A) it is engaged in the active conduct of a trade or business, or substantially all of its assets consist of stock and securities of a corporation controlled by it (immediately after the distribution) which is so engaged,"

Prior to amendment, para. (b)(3) [as amended by Sec. 202, P.L. 109-222, and Sec. 410(a), P.L. 109-432, see below and as affected by Sec. 4(b)(3) of this Act] see below, read as follows:

"(3) Special rule relating to active business requirement.

"(A) In general. In the case of any distribution made after the date of the enactment of this paragraph and on or before December 31, 2010, a corporation shall be treated as meeting the requirement of paragraph (2)(A) if and only if such corporation is engaged in the active conduct of a trade or business.

"(B) Affiliated group rule. For purposes of subparagraph (A), all members of such corporation's separate affiliated group shall be treated as one corporation. For purposes of the preceding sentence, a corporation's separate affiliated group is the affiliated group which would be determined under section 1504(a) if such corporation were the common parent and section 1504(b) did not apply.

"(C) Transition rule. Subparagraph (A) shall not apply to any distribution pursuant to a transaction which is—

"(i) made pursuant to an agreement which was binding on the date of the enactment of this paragraph and at all times thereafter,

"(ii) described in a ruling request submitted to the Internal Revenue Service on or before such date, or

"(iii) described on or before such date in a public announcement or in a filing with the Securities and Exchange Commission.

The preceding sentence shall not apply if the distributing corporation elects not to have such sentence apply to distributions of such corporation. Any such election, once made, shall be irrevocable.

"(D) Special rule for certain pre-enactment distributions. For purposes of determining the continued qualification under paragraph (2)(A) of distributions made on or before the date of the enactment of this paragraph and on or before December 31, 2010 as a result of an acquisition, disposition, or other restructuring after such date, such distribution shall be treated as made on the date of such acquisition, disposition, or restructuring for purposes of applying subparagraphs (A) through (C) of this paragraph."

—P.L. 110-172, Sec. 4(b)(3), provides that the amendments made by Sec. 202, P.L. 109-222, and Sec. 410(a), P.L. 109-432 (enacting and amending para. (b)(3)) [see below] shall be applied and administered as never enacted.

In **2006,** P.L. 109-432, Sec. 410(a), [deleted by 110-172, Sec. 4(b)(3), see above] deleted "and on or before December 31, 2010" after "enactment of this paragraph" in subpara. (b)(3)(A) and after "restructuring after such date" in subpara. (b)(3)(D), effective 5/17/2006.

—P.L. 109-222, Sec. 202, added para. (b)(3), enacted 5/17/2006.

—P.L. 109-222, Sec. 507(a), added subsec. (g), effective for distributions after 5/17/2006. Sec. 507(b)(2), of this Act, provides:

"(2) Transition rule. The amendments made by this section shall not apply to any distribution pursuant to a transaction which is—

"(A) made pursuant to an agreement which was binding on such date of enactment and at all times thereafter,

"(B) described in a ruling request submitted to the Internal Revenue Service on or before such date, or

"(C) described on or before such date in a public announcement or in a filing with the Securities and Exchange Commission."

In **1998,** P.L. 105-206, Sec. 6010(c)(1), substituted "1997; except that the amendment made by subsection (a) shall apply to such distributions only if pursuant" for "1997, pursuant" in Sec. 1012(d)(1) of P.L. 105-34, the effective date for amendments made by Sec. 1012 [see below].

—P.L. 105-206, Sec. 6010(c)(2)(A), substituted "shall not be taken into account in applying" for "shall not be treated as described in" in subpara. (e)(3)(A)... Sec. 6010(c)(2)(B), amended clause (e)(3)(A)(iv), effective for distributions after 4/16/97 if pursuant to a plan (or series of related transactions) which involves an acquisition described in Code Sec. 355(e)(2)(A)(ii) occurring after 4/16/97. [as amended by Sec. 6010(c)(1) of 105-206, see above] For transition rules, see Sec. 1012(d)(3) of P.L. 105-34, reproduced below.

Prior to amendment, clause (e)(3)(A)(iv) read as follows:

"(iv) The acquisition of stock in a corporation if shareholders owning directly or indirectly stock possessing—

"(I) more than 50 percent of the total combined voting power of all classes of stock entitled to vote, and

"(II) more than 50 percent of the total value of shares of all classes of stock, in the distributing corporation or any controlled corporation before such acquisition own directly or indirectly stock possessing such vote and value in such distributing or controlled corporation after such acquisition."

In 1997, P.L. 105-34, Sec. 1012(a), added subsec. (e)... Sec. 1012(b)(1), added subsec. (f), effective for distributions after 4/16/97 if pursuant to a plan (or series of related transactions) which involves an acquisition described in Code Sec. 355(e)(2)(A)(ii) occurring after 4/16/97. [as amended by Sec. 6010(c)(1) of 105-206, see above] Sec. 1012(d)(3) of this Act, provides:

"(3) Transition rule. The amendments made by this section shall not apply to any distribution pursuant to a plan (or series of related transactions) which involves an acquisition described in section 355(e)(2)(A)(ii) of the Internal Revenue Code of 1986 (or, in the case of the amendments made by subsection (c), any transfer) occurring after April 16, 1997, if such acquisition or transfer is—

"(A) made pursuant to an agreement which was binding on such date and at all times thereafter,

"(B) described in a ruling request submitted to the Internal Revenue Service on or before such date, or

"(C) described on or before such date in a public announcement or in a filing with the Securities and Exchange Commission required solely by reason of the acquisition or transfer.

This paragraph shall not apply to any agreement, ruling request, or public announcement or filing unless it identifies the acquirer of the distributing corporation or any controlled corporation, or the transferee, whichever is applicable."

—P.L. 105-34, Sec. 1014(c), added subpara. (a)(3)(D)... Sec. 1014(e)(1), added "(including nonqualified preferred stock, as defined in section 351(g)(2))" after "that any stock" in subpara. (a)(3)(C)... Sec. 1014(e)(2), added "nonqualified preferred stock and" after "but not including" in subpara. (a)(4)(A), effective for transactions after 6/8/97, except as provided in Sec. 1014(f)(2) of this Act which reads as follows:

"(2) Transition rule. The amendments made by this section shall not apply to any transaction after June 8, 1997, if such transaction is—

"(A) made pursuant to a written agreement which was binding on such date and at all times thereafter,

"(B) described in a ruling request submitted to the Internal Revenue Service on or before such date, or

"(C) described on or before such date in a public announcement or in a filing with the Securities and Exchange Commission required solely by reason of the transaction."

In 1996, P.L. 104-188, Sec. 1704(t)(31), added "section" before "267(b)" in subpara. (d)(7)(A), effective 8/20/96.

In 1990, P.L. 101-508, Sec. 11321(a), amended subsec. (c) [as amended by Sec. 11702(e)(2) of this Act, see below] and added subsec. (d), effective for distributions after 10/9/90 except as provided in Sec. 11321(c)(2) and (3) of this Act, which read as follows:

"(2) Binding contract exception.—The amendments made by this section shall not apply to any distribution pursuant to a written binding contract in effect on October 9, 1990, and at all times thereafter before such distribution.

"(3) Transitional rules.—For purposes of subparagraphs (A) and (B) of section 355(d)(3) of the Internal Revenue Code of 1986 (as amended by subsection (a)), an acquisition shall be treated as occurring on or before October 9, 1990, if—

"(A) such acquisition is pursuant to a written binding contract in effect on October 9, 1990, and at all times thereafter before such acquisition,

"(B) such acquisition is pursuant to a transaction which was described in documents filed with the Securities and Exchange Commission on or before October 9, 1990, or

"(C) such acquisition is pursuant to a transaction—

"(i) the material terms of which were described in a written public announcement on or before October 9, 1990,

"(ii) which was the subject of a prior filing with the Securities and Exchange Commission, and

"(iii) which is the subject of a subsequent filing with the Securities and Exchange Commission before January 1, 1991." Prior to amendment, subsec. (c) [as amended by Sec. 11702(e)(2) of this Act, see below] read as follows:

"(c) Taxability of corporation on distribution.

"(1) In general. Except as provided in paragraph (2), no gain or loss shall be recognized to a corporation on any distribution to which this section (or so much of section 356 as relates to this section) applies and which is not in pursuance of a plan of reorganization.

"(2) Distribution of appreciated property.

"(A) In general. If—

"(i) in a distribution referred to in paragraph (1), the corporation distributes property other than stock or securities in the controlled corporation, and

"(ii) the fair market value of such property exceeds its adjusted basis (in the hands of the distributing corporation),

then gain shall be recognized to the distributing corporation as if such property were sold to the distributee at its fair market value.

"(B) Treatment of liabilities. If any property distributed in the distribution referred to in paragraph (1) is subject to a liability or the shareholder assumes a liability of the distributing corporation in connection with the distribution, then, for purposes of subparagraph (A), the fair market value of such property shall be treated as not less than the amount of such liability.

"(3) Coordination with sections 311 and 336(a). Sections 311 and 336(a) shall not apply to any distribution referred to in paragraph (1)."

—P.L. 101-508, Sec. 11702(e)(2), amended subsec. (c) [before amended by Sec. 11321(a) of this Act, see above], effective for distributions declared on or after 6/14/84, in tax. yrs. end. after 6/14/84 except as provided in Sec. 54(d)(3) and (d)(4) of P.L. 98-369 reproduced in note following Code Sec. 311.

Prior to amendment, subsec. (c) read as follows:

"(c) Taxability of corporation on distribution.

"Section 311 shall apply to any distribution—

"(1) to which this section (or so much of section 356 as relates to this section) applies, and

"(2) which is not in pursuance of a plan of reorganization,

in the same manner as if such distribution were a distribution to which subpart A of part I applies; except that subsection (b) of section 311 shall not apply to any distribution of stock or securities in the controlled corporation."

In 1988, P.L. 100-647, Sec. 1018(d)(5)(C), added subsec. (c), effective for distributions declared on or after 6/14/84, in tax. yrs. end. after 6/14/84 except as provided in Sec. 54(d)(3) and (d)(4) of P.L. 98-369 reproduced in note following Code Sec. 311.

—P.L. 100-647, Sec. 2004(k)(1), amended clauses (b)(2)(D)(i) and (b)(2)(D)(ii), effective for distributions or transfers after 12/15/87, except as provided in Sec. 10223(d)(2)(A) and (d)(2)(C) of P.L. 100-203 reproduced below.

Prior to amendment, clauses (b)(2)(D)(i) and (b)(2)(D)(ii) read as follows:

"(i) was not acquired by any distributee corporation directly (or through 1 or more corporations, whether through the distributing corporation or otherwise) within the period described in subparagraph (B), or

"(ii) was so acquired by such distributee corporation within such period, but such control was so acquired only by reason of transactions in which gain or loss was not recognized in whole or in part, or only by reason of such transactions combined with acquisitions before the beginning of such period."

In 1987, P.L. 100-203, Sec. 10223(b)(1), amended clause (b)(2)(D)(i)... Sec. 10223(b)(2), substituted "such distributee corporation" for "by another corporation", in clause (b)(2)(D)(ii)... Sec. 10223(b)(3), added the last sentence to clause (b)(2)(D)(ii), effective for distributions or transfers after 12/15/87, except as provided in Sec. 10223(d)(2)(A) and (d)(2)(C) which reads:

"(2) Exceptions.—

"(A) Distributions.—The amendments made by this section shall not apply to any distribution after December 15, 1987, and before January 1, 1993, if—

"(i) 80 percent or more of the stock of the distributing corporation was acquired by the distributee before December 15, 1987, or

"(ii) 80 percent or more of the stock of the distributing corporation was acquired by the distributee before January 1, 1989, pursuant to a binding written contract or tender offer in effect on December 15, 1987.

For purposes of the preceding sentence, stock described in section 1504(a)(4) of the Internal Revenue Code of 1986 shall not be taken into account."

* * *

"(C) Distributions covered by prior transition rule.—The amendments made by this section shall not apply to any distribution to which the amendments made by subtitle D of title VI of the Tax Reform Act of 1986 do not apply."

Prior to amendment, clause (b)(2)(D)(i) read as follows:

"(i) was not acquired directly (or through one or more corporations) by another corporation within the period described in subparagraph (B), or"

In 1980, P.L. 96-589, Sec. 4(e)(2), amended paras. (a)(3) and (a)(4), effective for any bankruptcy case or similar judicial proceeding begin. after 12/31/80. Secs. 7(c)(2), 7(f) and 7(g) of this Act provide as follows:

"(2) Exchanges of property for accrued interest. The amendments made by subsection (e) of section 4 of this Act] (relating to treatment of property attributable to accrued interest) shall also apply to any exchange—

"(A) which occurs after December 31, 1980, and

"(B) which does not occur in a bankruptcy case or similar judicial proceeding (or in a proceeding under the Bankruptcy Act) commenced on or before December 31, 1980."

* * *

"(f) Election to substitute September 30, 1979, for December 31, 1980.

"(1) In general. The debtor (or debtors) in a bankruptcy case or similar judicial proceeding may (with the approval of the court) elect to apply [subsection 7(c) of this Act] by substituting 'September 30, 1979' for 'December 31, 1980' each place it appears in such subsections.

"(2) Effect of election. Any election made under paragraph (1) with respect to any proceeding shall apply to all parties to the proceeding.

"(3) Revocation only with consent. Any election under this subsection may be revoked only with the consent of the Secretary of the Treasury or his delegate.

"(4) Time and manner of election. Any election under this subsection shall be made at such time, and in such manner, as the Secretary of the Treasury or his delegate may by regulations prescribe.

"(g) Definitions.

"For purposes of this section—

"(1) Bankruptcy case. The term 'bankruptcy case' means any case under title 11 of the United States Code (as recodified by P.L. 95-598).

Code Sec. 355 — Corporate distributions and adjustments

"(2) Similar judicial proceeding. The term 'similar judicial proceeding' means a receivership, foreclosure, or similar proceeding in a Federal or State court (as modified by section 368(a)(3)(D) of the Internal Revenue Code of 1954)."

Prior to amendment, paras. (a)(3) and (a)(4) read as follows:

"(3) Limitation. Paragraph (1) shall not apply if—

"(A) the principal amount of the securities in the controlled corporation which are received exceeds the principal amount of the securities which are surrendered in connection with such distribution, or

"(B) securities in the controlled corporation are received and no securities are surrendered in connection with such distribution.

"For purposes of this section (other than paragraph (1)(D) of this subsection) and so much of section 356 as relates to this section, stock of a controlled corporation acquired by the distributing corporation by reason of any transaction which occurs within 5 years of the distribution of such stock and in which gain or loss was recognized in whole or in part, shall not be treated as stock of such controlled corporation, but as other property.

"(4) Cross reference. For treatment of the distribution if any property is received which is not permitted to be received under this subsection (including an excess principal amount of securities received over securities surrendered), see section 356."

In 1976, P.L. 94-455, Sec. 1906(b)(13)(A), substituted "Secretary" for "Secretary or his delegate" in Code Sec. 355, effective for tax. yrs. begin. after 12/31/76.

Sec. 356. Receipt of additional consideration.

(a) Gain on exchanges.

(1) Recognition of gain. If—

(A) Section 354 or 355 would apply to an exchange but for the fact that

(B) the property received in the exchange consists not only of property permitted by section 354 or 355 to be received without the recognition of gain but also of other property or money,

then the gain, if any, to the recipient shall be recognized, but in an amount not in excess of the sum of such money and the fair market value of such other property.

(2) Treatment as dividend. If an exchange is described in paragraph (1) but has the effect of the distribution of a dividend (determined with the application of section 318(a)), then there shall be treated as a dividend to each distributee such an amount of the gain recognized under paragraph (1) as is not in excess of his ratable share of the undistributed earnings and profits of the corporation accumulated after February 28, 1913. The remainder, if any, of the gain recognized under paragraph (1) shall be treated as gain from the exchange of property.

(b) Additional consideration received in certain distributions.

If—

(1) section 355 would apply to a distribution but for the fact that

(2) the property received in the distribution consists not only of property permitted by section 355 to be received without the recognition of gain, but also of other property or money,

then an amount equal to the sum of such money and the fair market value of such other property shall be treated as a distribution of property to which section 301 applies.

(c) Loss.

If—

(1) section 354 would apply to an exchange, or section 355 would apply to an exchange or distribution, but for the fact that

(2) the property received in the exchange or distribution consists not only of property permitted by section 354 or 355 to be received without the recognition of gain or loss, but also of other property or money,

then no loss from the exchange or distribution shall be recognized.

(d) Securities as other property.

For purposes of this section—

(1) In general. Except as provided in paragraph (2), the term "other property" includes securities.

(2) Exceptions.

(A) Securities with respect to which nonrecognition of gain would be permitted. The term "other property" does not include securities to the extent that, under section 354 or 355, such securities would be permitted to be received without the recognition of gain.

(B) Greater principal amount in section 354 exchange. If—

(i) in an exchange described in section 354 (other than subsection (c) thereof), securities of a corporation a party to the reorganization are surrendered and securities of any corporation a party to the reorganization are received, and

(ii) the principal amount of such securities received exceeds the principal amount of such securities surrendered,

then, with respect to such securities received, the term "other property" means only the fair market value of such excess. For purposes of this subparagraph and subparagraph (C), if no securities are surrendered, the excess shall be the entire principal amount of the securities received.

(C) Greater principal amount in section 355 transaction. If, in an exchange or distribution described in section 355, the principal amount of the securities in the controlled corporation which are received exceeds the principal amount of the securities in the distributing corporation which are surrendered, then, with respect to such securities received, the term "other property" means only the fair market value of such excess.

(e) Nonqualified preferred stock treated as other property.

For purposes of this section—

(1) In general. Except as provided in paragraph (2), the term "other property" includes nonqualified preferred stock (as defined in section 351(g)(2)).

(2) Exception. The term "other property" does not include nonqualified preferred stock (as so defined) to the extent that, under section 354 or 355, such preferred stock would be permitted to be received without the recognition of gain.

(f) Exchanges for section 306 stock.

Notwithstanding any other provision of this section, to the extent that any of the other property (or money) is received in exchange for section 306 stock, an amount equal to the fair market value of such other property (or the amount of such money) shall be treated as a distribution of property to which section 301 applies.

(g) Transactions involving gift or compensation.

For special rules for a transaction described in section 354, 355, or this section, but which—

(1) results in a gift, see section 2501 and following, or

(2) has the effect of the payment of compensation, see section 61(a)(1).

In 1997, P.L. 105-34, Sec. 1014(d), redesignated subsecs. (e) and (f) as (f) and (g) and added new subsec. (e), effective for transactions after 6/8/97, except as provided in Sec. 1022(f)(2) of this Act, which reads as follows:

"(2) Transition rule. The amendments made by this section shall not apply to any transaction after June 8, 1997, if such transaction is—

"(A) made pursuant to a written agreement which was binding on such date and at all times thereafter,

"(B) described in a ruling request submitted to the Internal Revenue Service on or before such date, or

"(C) described on or before such date in a public announcement or in a filing with the Securities and Exchange Commission required solely by reason of the transaction."

In 1990, P.L. 101-508, Sec. 11801(c)(8)(E), deleted "or (d)" after "subsection (c)" in clause (d)(2)(B)(i), effective 11/5/90 except as provided in Sec. 11821(b) of this Act, reproduced in note following Code Sec. 358.

Corporate distributions and adjustments — Code Sec. 357

In 1982, P.L. 97-248, Sec. 227(b), added "(determined with the application of section 318(a))" after "distribution of a dividend" in para. (a)(2), effective for distributions after 8/31/82, in tax. yrs. end. after 8/31/82.

In 1976, P.L. 94-253, Sec. 1(c), substituted "subsection (c) or (d) thereof" for "subsection (c) thereof" in clause (d)(2)(B)(i), effective for tax. yrs. end. after 3/31/76.

Sec. 357. Assumption of liability.

(a) General rule.

Except as provided in subsections (b) and (c), if—

(1) the taxpayer receives property which would be permitted to be received under section 351 or 361 without the recognition of gain if it were the sole consideration, and

(2) as part of the consideration, another party to the exchange assumes a liability of the taxpayer,

then such assumption shall not be treated as money or other property, and shall not prevent the exchange from being within the provisions of section 351 or 361 as the case may be.

(b) Tax avoidance purpose.

(1) **In general.** If, taking into consideration the nature of the liability and the circumstances in the light of which the arrangement for the assumption was made, it appears that the principal purpose of the taxpayer with respect to the assumption described in subsection (a)—

(A) was a purpose to avoid Federal income tax on the exchange, or

(B) if not such purpose, was not a bona fide business purpose,

then such assumption (in the total amount of the liability assumed pursuant to such exchange) shall, for purposes of section 351 or 361 (as the case may be), be considered as money received by the taxpayer on the exchange.

(2) **Burden of proof.** In any suit or proceeding where the burden is on the taxpayer to prove such assumption is not to be treated as money received by the taxpayer, such burden shall not be considered as sustained unless the taxpayer sustains such burden by the clear preponderance of the evidence.

(c) Liabilities in excess of basis.

(1) **In general.** In the case of an exchange—

(A) to which section 351 applies, or

(B) to which section 361 applies by reason of a plan of reorganization within the meaning of section 368(a)(1)(D) with respect to which stock or securities of the corporation to which the assets are transferred are distributed in a transaction which qualifies under section 355,

if the sum of the amount of the liabilities assumed exceeds the total of the adjusted basis of the property transferred pursuant to such exchange, then such excess shall be considered as a gain from the sale or exchange of a capital asset or of property which is not a capital asset, as the case may be.

(2) **Exceptions.** Paragraph (1) shall not apply to any exchange—

(A) to which subsection (b)(1) of this section applies, or

(B) which is pursuant to a plan of reorganization within the meaning of section 368(a)(1)(G) where no former shareholder of the transferor corporation receives any consideration for his stock.

(3) **Certain liabilities excluded.**

(A) In general. If a taxpayer transfers, in an exchange to which section 351 applies, a liability the payment of which either—

(i) would give rise to a deduction, or

(ii) would be described in section 736(a),

then, for purposes of paragraph (1), the amount of such liability shall be excluded in determining the amount of liabilities assumed.

(B) Exception. Subparagraph (A) shall not apply to any liability to the extent that the incurrence of the liability resulted in the creation of, or an increase in, the basis of any property.

(d) Determination of amount of liability assumed.

(1) **In general.** For purposes of this section, section 358(d), section 358(h), section 361(b)(3), section 362(d), section 368(a)(1)(C), and section 368(a)(2)(B), except as provided in regulations—

(A) a recourse liability (or portion thereof) shall be treated as having been assumed if, as determined on the basis of all facts and circumstances, the transferee has agreed to, and is expected to, satisfy such liability (or portion), whether or not the transferor has been relieved of such liability; and

(B) except to the extent provided in paragraph (2), a nonrecourse liability shall be treated as having been assumed by the transferee of any asset subject to such liability.

(2) **Exception for nonrecourse liability.** The amount of the nonrecourse liability treated as described in paragraph (1)(B) shall be reduced by the lesser of—

(A) the amount of such liability which an owner of other assets not transferred to the transferee and also subject to such liability has agreed with the transferee to, and is expected to, satisfy; or

(B) the fair market value of such other assets (determined without regard to section 7701(g)).

(3) **Regulations.** The Secretary shall prescribe such regulations as may be necessary to carry out the purposes of this subsection and section 362(d). The Secretary may also prescribe regulations which provide that the manner in which a liability is treated as assumed under this subsection is applied, where appropriate, elsewhere in this title.

In 2005, P.L. 109-135, Sec. 403(jj)(2), added "section 361(b)(3)," after "section 358(h)," in para. (d)(1), effective for transfers of money or other property, or liabilities assumed, in connection with a reorganization occurring on or after 10/22/2004, as if included in Sec. 898 of the American Jobs Creation Act of 2004, P.L. 108-357.

In 2004, P.L. 108-357, Sec. 898(b), added "with respect to which stock or securities of the corporation to which the assets are transferred are distributed in a transaction which qualifies under section 355" after "section 368(a)(1)(D)" in subpara. (c)(1)(B), effective for transfers of money or other property, or liabilities assumed, in connection with a reorganization occurring on or after 10/22/2004.

In 2000, P.L. 106-554, Sec. 1(a)(7), [which enacted into law Sec. 309(b) of P.L. 106-554] added "section 358(h)," after "section 358(d)," in para. (d)(1), effective for assumptions of liability after 10/18/99. For special rules, see Sec. 309(c)–(d) of this Act, which reads as follows:

"(c) Application of comparable rules to partnerships and S corporations. The Secretary of the Treasury or his delegate—

"(1) shall prescribe rules which provide appropriate adjustments under subchapter K of chapter 1 of the Internal Revenue Code of 1986 to prevent the acceleration or duplication of losses through the assumption of (or transfer of assets subject to) liabilities described in section 358(h)(3) of such Code (as added by subsection (a)) in transactions involving partnerships, and

"(2) may prescribe rules which provide appropriate adjustments under subchapter S of chapter 1 of such Code in transactions described in paragraph (1) involving S corporations rather than partnerships.

"(d) Effective dates.

"(1) In general. The amendments made by this section shall apply to assumptions of liability after October 18, 1999.

"(2) Rules. The rules prescribed under subsection (c) shall apply to assumptions of liability after October 18, 1999, or such later date as may be prescribed in such rules."

In 1999, P.L. 106-36, Sec. 3001(a)(1), deleted ", or acquires from the taxpayer property subject to a liability" after "taxpayer" at the end of para. (a)(2) . . . Sec. 3001(b)(1), added subsec. (d) . . . Sec. 3001(d)(2), deleted "or acquisition" after "assumption" each place it appeared in subsec. (a) and (b) . . . Sec. 3001(d)(3), deleted "or acquired" after "assumed" in para. (b)(1) . . . Sec. 3001(d)(4), deleted ", plus the amount of the liabilities to which the property is subject," after "liabilities assumed" in para. (c)(1) . . . Sec. 3001(d)(5), deleted "or to which the

Code Sec. 357 — Corporate distributions and adjustments

property transferred is subject" after "liabilities assumed" in subpara. (c)(3)(A), effective for transfers after 10/18/98.

In 1990, P.L. 101-508, Sec. 11801(c)(8)(F)(i), substituted "351 or 361" for "351, 361, 371, or 374" each place it appeared in subsecs. (a) and (b) . . . Sec. 11801(c)(8)(F)(ii), added "or" at the end of subpara. (c)(2)(A), deleted subpara. (c)(2)(B) and redesignated subpara. (c)(2)(C) as subpara. (c)(2)(B), effective 11/5/90, except as provided in Sec. 11821(b) of this Act, reproduced in note following Code Sec. 358.

Prior to deletion, subpara. (c)(2)(B) read as follows:

"(B) to which section 371 or 374 applies, or"

In 1980, P.L. 96-589, Sec. 4(h)(2), amended para. (c)(2), effective for any bankruptcy case or similar judicial proceeding begin. after 12/31/80.

Sec. 7(f) and (g) of this Act provides:

"(f) Election to substitute September 30, 1979, for December 31, 1980.

"(1) In general. The debtor (or debtors) in a bankruptcy case or similar judicial proceeding may (with the approval of the court) elect to apply [subsection 7(c) of this Act] by substituting 'September 30, 1979' for 'December 31, 1980' each place it appears in such subsections.

"(2) Effect of election. Any election made under paragraph (1) with respect to any proceeding shall apply to all parties to the proceeding.

"(3) Revocation only with consent. Any election under this subsection may be revoked only with the consent of the Secretary of the Treasury or his delegate.

"(4) Time and manner of election. Any election under this subsection shall be made at such time, and in such manner, as the Secretary of the Treasury or his delegate may by regulations prescribe.

"(g) Definitions.

"For purposes of this section—

"(1) Bankruptcy case. The term 'bankruptcy case' means any case under title 11 of the United States Code (as recodified by P.L. 95-598).

"(2) Similar judicial proceeding. The term 'similar judicial proceeding' means a receivership, foreclosure, or similar proceeding in a Federal or State court (as modified by section 368(a)(3)(D) of the Internal Revenue Code of 1954)."

Prior to amendment, para. (c)(2) read as follows:

"(2) Exceptions. Paragraph (1) shall not apply to any exchange to which—

"(A) subsection (b)(1) of this section applies, or

"(B) section 371 or 374 applies."

—P.L. 96-222, Sec. 103(a)(12), amended Sec. 357(c)(3)(A), effective for transfers made after 11/6/78.

Prior to amendment, subpara. (c)(3)(A) read as follows:

"(A) In general. If—

"(i) the taxpayer's taxable income is computed under the cash receipts and disbursements method of accounting, and

"(ii) such taxpayer transfers, in an exchange to which section 351 applies, a liability which is either—

"(I) an account payable payment of which would give rise to a deduction, or

"(II) an amount payable which is described in section 736(a),

then, for purposes of paragraph (1), the amount of such liability shall be excluded in determining the amount of liabilities assumed or to which the property transferred is subject."

In 1978, P.L. 95-600, Sec. 365(a), added new para. (c)(3), for transfers occurring on or after 11/6/78.

In 1956, ch. 463, Sec. 2, substituted "371, or 374" for "or 371" in subsecs. (a), (b) and subpara. (c)(2)(B).

Sec. 358. Basis to distributees.

(a) General rule.

In the case of an exchange to which section 351, 354, 355, 356, or 361 applies—

(1) Nonrecognition property. The basis of the property permitted to be received under such section without the recognition of gain or loss shall be the same as that of the property exchanged—

(A) decreased by—

(i) the fair market value of any other property (except money) received by the taxpayer,

(ii) the amount of any money received by the taxpayer, and

(iii) the amount of loss to the taxpayer which was recognized on such exchange, and

(B) increased by—

(i) the amount which was treated as a dividend, and

(ii) the amount of gain to the taxpayer which was recognized on such exchange (not including any portion of such gain which was treated as a dividend).

(2) Other property. The basis of any other property (except money) received by the taxpayer shall be its fair market value.

(b) Allocation of basis.

(1) In general. Under regulations prescribed by the Secretary, the basis determined under subsection (a)(1) shall be allocated among the properties permitted to be received without the recognition of gain or loss.

(2) Special rule for section 355. In the case of an exchange to which section 355 (or so much of section 356 as relates to section 355) applies, then in making the allocation under paragraph (1) of this subsection, there shall be taken into account not only the property so permitted to be received without the recognition of gain or loss, but also the stock or securities (if any) of the distributing corporation which are retained, and the allocation of basis shall be made among all such properties.

(c) Section 355 transactions which are not exchanges.

For purposes of this section, a distribution to which section 355 (or so much of section 356 as relates to section 355) applies shall be treated as an exchange, and for such purposes the stock and securities of the distributing corporation which are retained shall be treated as surrendered, and received back, in the exchange.

(d) Assumption of liability.

(1) In general. Where, as part of the consideration to the taxpayer, another party to the exchange assumed a liability of the taxpayer, such assumption shall, for purposes of this section, be treated as money received by the taxpayer on the exchange.

(2) Exception. Paragraph (1) shall not apply to the amount of any liability excluded under section 357(c)(3).

(e) Exception.

This section shall not apply to property acquired by a corporation by the exchange of its stock or securities (or the stock or securities of a corporation which is in control of the acquiring corporation) as consideration in whole or in part for the transfer of the property to it.

(f) Definition of nonrecognition property in case of section 361 exchange.

For purposes of this section, the property permitted to be received under section 361 without the recognition of gain or loss shall be treated as consisting only of stock or securities in another corporation a party to the reorganization.

(g) Adjustments in intragroup transactions involving section 355.

In the case of a distribution to which section 355 (or so much of section 356 as relates to section 355) applies and which involves the distribution of stock from 1 member of an affiliated group (as defined in section 1504(a) without regard to subsection (b) thereof) to another member of such group, the Secretary may, notwithstanding any other provision of this section, provide adjustments to the adjusted basis of any stock which—

(1) is in a corporation which is a member of such group, and

(2) is held by another member of such group,

to appropriately reflect the proper treatment of such distribution.

(h) Special rules for assumption of liabilities to which subsection (d) does not apply.

(1) In general. If, after application of the other provisions of this section to an exchange or series of exchanges, the basis of property to which subsection (a)(1) applies exceeds the fair market value of such property, then such basis shall be reduced (but not below such fair market value) by the amount (determined as of the date of the exchange) of any liability—

(A) which is assumed by another person as part of the exchange, and

1,830

Corporate distributions and adjustments Code Sec. 361(b)(1)(B)

(B) with respect to which subsection (d)(1) does not apply to the assumption.

(2) Exceptions. Except as provided by the Secretary, paragraph (1) shall not apply to any liability if—

(A) the trade or business with which the liability is associated is transferred to the person assuming the liability as part of the exchange, or

(B) substantially all of the assets with which the liability is associated are transferred to the person assuming the liability as part of the exchange.

(3) Liability. For purposes of this subsection, the term "liability" shall include any fixed or contingent obligation to make payment, without regard to whether the obligation is otherwise taken into account for purposes of this title.

In 2002, P.L. 107-147, Sec. 412(c), amended subpara. (h)(1)(A), effective as provided in Sec. 309(d)(1) of P.L. 106-554 [as enacted into law by P.L. 106-554, 12/21/2000], reproduced below.
Prior to amendment, subpara. (h)(1)(A) read as follows:
"(A) which is assumed in exchange for such property, and"
In 2000, P.L. 106-554, Sec. 1(a)(7), [which enacted into law Sec. 309(a) of P.L. 106-554] added subsec. (h), effective for assumptions of liability after 10/18/99. For special rules, see Sec. 309(c) – (d) of this Act, which reads as follows:
"(c) Application of comparable rules to partnerships and S corporations. The Secretary of the Treasury or his delegate—
"(1) shall prescribe rules which provide appropriate adjustments under subchapter K of chapter 1 of the Internal Revenue Code of 1986 to prevent the acceleration or duplication of losses through the assumption of (or transfer of assets subject to) liabilities described in section 358(h)(3) of such Code (as added by subsection (a)) in transactions involving partnerships, and
"(2) may prescribe rules which provide appropriate adjustments under subchapter S of chapter 1 of such Code in transactions described in paragraph (1) involving S corporations rather than partnerships.
"(d) Effective dates.
"(1) In general. The amendments made by this section shall apply to assumptions of liability after October 18, 1999.
"(2) Rules. The rules prescribed under subsection (c) shall apply to assumptions of liability after October 18, 1999, or such later date as may be prescribed in such rules."
In 1999, P.L. 106-36, Sec. 3001(a)(2), deleted "or acquired from the taxpayer property subject to a liability" after "liability of the taxpayer" in para. (d)(1) . . . Sec. 3001(d)(6), deleted "or acquisition (in the amount of the liability)" after "such assumption" in para. (d)(1), effective for transfers after 10/18/98.
In 1997, P.L. 105-34, Sec. 1012(b)(2), added subsec. (g), effective for distributions after 4/16/97 pursuant to a plan (or series of related transactions) which involves an acquisition described in Code Sec. 355(e)(2)(A)(ii) occurring after 4/16/97, except as provided in Sec. 1012(d)(3) of this Act, which reads as follows:
"(3) Transition rule.— The amendments made by this section shall not apply to any distribution pursuant to a plan (or series of related transactions) which involves an acquisition described in section 355(e)(2)(A)(ii) of the Internal Revenue Code of 1986 (or, in the case of the amendments made by subsection (c), any transfer) occurring after April 16, 1997, if such acquisition or transfer is —
"(A) made pursuant to an agreement which was binding on such date and at all times thereafter,
"(B) described in a ruling request submitted to the Internal Revenue Service on or before such date, or
"(C) described on or before such date in a public announcement or in a filing with the Securities and Exchange Commission required solely by reason of the acquisition or transfer.
This paragraph shall not apply to any agreement, ruling request, or public announcement or filing unless it identifies the acquirer of the distributing corporation or any controlled corporation, or the transferee, whichever is applicable."
In 1990, P.L. 101-508, Sec. 11801(c)(8)(G)(i), substituted "or 361" for "361, 371(b), or 374" in subsec. (a) . . . Sec. 11801(c)(8)(G)(ii), deleted para. (b)(3), effective 11/5/90 except as provided in Sec. 11821(b) of this Act, which reads as follows:
"(b) Savings provision.
"If—
"(1) any provision amended or repealed by this part applied to—
"(A) any transaction occurring before the date of the enactment of this Act [11/5/90],
"(B) any property acquired before such date of enactment [11/5/90], or
"(C) any item of income, loss, deduction, or credit taken into account before such date of enactment [11/5/90], and
"(2) the treatment of such transaction, property, or item under such provision would (without regard to the amendments made by this part) affect liability for tax for periods ending after such date of enactment [11/5/90],
nothing in the amendments made by this part shall be construed to affect the treatment of such transaction, property, or item for purposes of determining liability for tax for periods ending after such date of enactment [11/5/90]."
Prior to deletion, para. (b)(3) read as follows:

"(3) Certain exchanges involving Conrail. To the extent provided in regulations prescribed by the Secretary, in the case of an exchange to which section 354(d) (or so much of section 356 as relates to section 354(d)) or section 374(c) applies, for purposes of allocating basis under paragraph (1), stock of the Consolidated Rail Corporation and the certificate of value of the United States Railway Association which relates to such stock shall, so long as they are held by the same person, be treated as one property."
In 1988, P.L. 100-647, Sec. 1018(d)(5)(B), added subsec. (f), effective for plans of reorganizations adopted after 10/22/86.
In 1978, P.L. 95-600, Sec. 365(b), amended subsec. (d), effective for transfers occurring on or after 11/6/78.
Prior to amendment, subsec. (d) read as follows:
"(d) Assumption of liability.
W"here, as part of the consideration to the taxpayer, another party to the exchange assumed a liability of the taxpayer or acquired from the taxpayer property subject to a liability, such assumption or acquisition (in the amount of the liability) shall, for purposes of this section, be treated as money received by the taxpayer on the exchange."
In 1976, P.L. 94-455, Sec. 1906(b)(13)(A), substituted "Secretary" for "Secretary or his delegate" in Code Sec. 358, effective for tax. yrs. begin. after 12/31/76.
—P.L. 94-253, Sec. 1(b)(1), substituted "371(b), or 374" for "or 371(b)" in subsec. (a) . . . Sec. 1(b)(2), added para. (b)(3), effective for tax. yrs. end. after 3/31/76.
In 1968, P.L. 90-621, Sec. 2(a), amended subsec. (e), effective only in respect to plans of reorganization adopted after 10/22/68.
Prior to amendment, subsec. (e) read as follows:
"(e) Exception. This section shall not apply to property acquired by a corporation by the issuance of its stock or securities as consideration in whole or in part for the transfer of the property to it."
In 1958, P.L. 85-866, Sec. 21(a), added clause (a)(1)(A)(iii), effective as provided in Code Sec. 393 as if clause (iii) had been included in the 1954 Code at the time of its enactment.

SUBPART C.— EFFECTS ON CORPORATIONS

Sec.
361. Nonrecognition of gain or loss to corporations; treatment of distributions.
362. Basis to corporations.
363. Repealed.

In 1988, P.L. 100-647, Sec. 1018(d)(5)(F), amended item 361.
Prior to amendment, item 361 read as follows:
"361. Nonrecognition of gain or loss to transfer or corporation; other treatment of transferor corporation; etc."
In 1986, P.L. 99-514, Sec. 1804(g)(3), amended item 361.
Prior to amendment, item 361 read as follows:
"361. Nonrecognition of gain or loss to corporations."
In 1976, P.L. 94-455, Sec. 1901(b)(13), repealed item 363.
Prior to repeal, item 363 read as follows:
"363. Effect on earnings and profits."

Sec. 361. Nonrecognition of gain or loss to corporations; treatment of distributions.

(a) General rule.

No gain or loss shall be recognized to a corporation if such corporation is a party to a reorganization and exchanges property, in pursuance of the plan of reorganization, solely for stock or securities in another corporation a party to the reorganization.

(b) Exchanges not solely in kind.

(1) Gain. If subsection (a) would apply to an exchange but for the fact that the property received in exchange consists not only of stock or securities permitted by subsection (a) to be received without the recognition of gain, but also of other property or money, then—

(A) Property distributed. If the corporation receiving such other property or money distributes it in pursuance of the plan of reorganization, no gain to the corporation shall be recognized from the exchange, but

(B) Property not distributed. If the corporation receiving such other property or money does not distribute it in pursuance of the plan of reorganization, the gain, if any, to the corporation shall be recognized.

The amount of gain recognized under subparagraph (B) shall not exceed the sum of the money and the fair market value of the other property so received which is not so distributed.

(2) Loss. If subsection (a) would apply to an exchange but for the fact that the property received in exchange consists not only of property permitted by subsection (a) to be received without the recognition of gain or loss, but also of other property or money, then no loss from the exchange shall be recognized.

(3) Treatment of transfers to creditors. For purposes of paragraph (1), any transfer of the other property or money received in the exchange by the corporation to its creditors in connection with the reorganization shall be treated as a distribution in pursuance of the plan of reorganization. The Secretary may prescribe such regulations as may be necessary to prevent avoidance of tax through abuse of the preceding sentence or subsection (c)(3). In the case of a reorganization described in section 368(a)(1)(D) with respect to which stock or securities of the corporation to which the assets are transferred are distributed in a transaction which qualifies under section 355, this paragraph shall apply only to the extent that the sum of the money and the fair market value of other property transferred to such creditors does not exceed the adjusted bases of such assets transferred (reduced by the amount of the liabilities assumed (within the meaning of section 357(c))).

(c) Treatment of distributions.

(1) In general. Except as provided in paragraph (2), no gain or loss shall be recognized to a corporation a party to a reorganization on the distribution to its shareholders of property in pursuance of the plan of reorganization.

(2) Distributions of appreciated property.

(A) In general. If—

(i) in a distribution referred to in paragraph (1), the corporation distributes property other than qualified property, and

(ii) the fair market value of such property exceeds its adjusted basis (in the hands of the distributing corporation),

then gain shall be recognized to the distributing corporation as if such property were sold to the distributee at its fair market value.

(B) Qualified property. For purposes of this subsection, the term "qualified property" means—

(i) any stock in (or right to acquire stock in) the distributing corporation or obligation of the distributing corporation, or

(ii) any stock in (or right to acquire stock in) another corporation which is a party to the reorganization or obligation of another corporation which is such a party if such stock (or right) or obligation is received by the distributing corporation in the exchange.

(C) Treatment of liabilities. If any property distributed in the distribution referred to in paragraph (1) is subject to a liability or the shareholder assumes a liability of the distributing corporation in connection with the distribution, then, for purposes of subparagraph (A), the fair market value of such property shall be treated as not less than the amount of such liability.

(3) Treatment of certain transfers to creditors. For purposes of this subsection, any transfer of qualified property by the corporation to its creditors in connection with the reorganization shall be treated as a distribution to its shareholders pursuant to the plan of reorganization.

(4) Coordination with other provisions. Section 311 and subpart B of part II of this subchapter shall not apply to any distribution referred to in paragraph (1).

(5) Cross reference. For provision providing for recognition of gain in certain distributions, see section 355(d).

In 2005, P.L. 109-135, Sec. 403(jj)(1), added "(reduced by the amount of the liabilities assumed (within the meaning of section 357(c)))" before the period at the end of para. (b)(3), effective for transfers of money or other property, or liabilities assumed, in connection with a reorganization occurring on or after 10/22/2004, as if included in Sec. 898 of the American Jobs Creation Act of 2004, P.L. 108-357.

In 2004, P.L. 108-357, Sec. 898(a), added "In the case of a reorganization described in section 368(a)(1)(D) with respect to which stock or securities of the corporation to which the assets are transferred are distributed in a transaction which qualifies under section 355, this paragraph shall apply only to the extent that the sum of the money and the fair market value of other property transferred to such creditors does not exceed the adjusted bases of such assets transferred." at the end of para. (b)(3), effective for transfers of money or other property, or liabilities assumed, in connection with a reorganization occurring on or after 10/22/2004.

In 1988, P.L. 100-647, Sec. 1018(d)(5)(A), amended Code Sec. 361, effective for plans of reorganizations adopted after 10/22/86.

Prior to amendment, Code Sec. 361 read as follows:

"SEC. 361. NONRECOGNITION OF GAIN OR LOSS TO TRANSFEROR CORPORATION; OTHER TREATMENT OF TRANSFEROR CORPORATION; ETC.

"(a) General rule.

"No gain or loss shall be recognized to a transferor corporation which is a party to a reorganization on any exchange of property pursuant to the plan of reorganization.

"(b) Other treatment of transferor corporation.

"In the case of a transferor corporation which is a party to a reorganization—

"(1) sections 336 and 337 shall not apply with respect to any liquidation of such corporation pursuant to the plan of reorganization,

"(2) the basis of the property (other than stock and securities described in paragraph (3)) received by the corporation pursuant to such plan of reorganization shall be the same as it would be in the hands of the transferor of such property, adjusted by the amount of gain or loss recognized to such transferor on such transfer, and

"(3) no gain or loss shall be recognized by such corporation on any disposition (pursuant to the plan of reorganization) of stock or securities which were received pursuant to such plan and which are in another corporation which is a party to such reorganization.

For purposes of paragraph (3), if the transferor corporation is merged, consolidated, or liquidated pursuant to the plan of reorganization, or if a transaction meets the requirements of section 368(a)(1)(C) pursuant to a waiver granted by the Secretary under section 368(a)(2)(G)(ii), any distribution of such stock or securities by the transferor corporation to its creditors in connection with such transaction shall be treated as pursuant to such plan of reorganization.

"(c) Treatment of distributions of appreciated property.

"Notwithstanding any other provision of this subtitle, gain shall be recognized on the distribution of property (other than property permitted by section 354, 355, or 356 to be received without the recognition of gain) pursuant to a plan of reorganization in the same manner as if such property had been sold to the distributee at its fair market value."

In 1986, P.L. 99-514, Sec. 1804(g)(1), amended Code Sec. 361, effective for plans of reorganizations adopted after 10/22/86.

Prior to amendment, Code Sec. 361 read as follows:

"SEC. 361. NONRECOGNITION OF GAIN OR LOSS TO CORPORATIONS.

"(a) General rule.

"No gain or loss shall be recognized if a corporation a party to a reorganization exchanges property, in pursuance of the plan of reorganization, solely for stock or securities in another corporation a party to the reorganization.

"(b) Exchanges not solely in kind.

"(1) Gain. If subsection (a) would apply to an exchange but for the fact that the property received in exchange consists not only of stock or securities permitted by subsection (a) to be received without the recognition of gain, but also of other property or money, then—

"(A) if the corporation receiving such other property or money distributes it in pursuance of the plan of reorganization, no gain to the corporation shall be recognized from the exchange, but

"(B) if the corporation receiving such other property or money does not distribute it in pursuance of the plan of reorganization, the gain, if any, to the corporation shall be recognized, but in an amount not in excess of the sum of such money and the fair market value of such other property so received, which is not so distributed.

"(2) Loss. If subsection (a) would apply to an exchange but for the fact that the property received in exchange consists not only of property permitted by subsection (a) to be received without the recognition of gain or loss, but also of other property or money, then no loss from the exchange shall be recognized."

Sec. 362. Basis to corporations.

(a) Property acquired by issuance of stock or as paid-in surplus.

If property was acquired on or after June 22, 1954, by a corporation—

(1) in connection with a transaction to which section 351 (relating to transfer of property to corporation controlled by transferor) applies, or

(2) as paid-in surplus or as a contribution to capital,

then the basis shall be the same as it would be in the hands of the transferor, increased in the amount of gain recognized to the transferor on such transfer.

(b) Transfers to corporations.

If property was acquired by a corporation in connection with a reorganization to which this part applies, then the basis shall be the same as it would be in the hands of the transferor, increased in the amount of gain recognized to the transferor on such transfer. This subsection shall not apply if the property acquired consists of stock or securities in a corporation a party to the reorganization, unless acquired by the exchange of stock or securities of the transferee (or of a corporation which is in control of the transferee) as the consideration in whole or in part for the transfer.

(c) Special rule for certain contributions to capital.

(1) Property other than money. Notwithstanding subsection (a)(2), if property other than money—

(A) is acquired by a corporation, on or after June 22, 1954, as a contribution to capital, and

(B) is not contributed by a shareholder as such, then the basis of such property shall be zero.

(2) Money. Notwithstanding subsection (a)(2), if money—

(A) is received by a corporation, on or after June 22, 1954, as a contribution to capital, and

(B) is not contributed by a shareholder as such, then the basis of any property acquired with such money during the 12-month period beginning on the day the contribution is received shall be reduced by the amount of such contribution. The excess (if any) of the amount of such contribution over the amount of the reduction under the preceding sentence shall be applied to the reduction (as of the last day of the period specified in the preceding sentence) of the basis of any other property held by the taxpayer. The particular properties to which the reductions required by this paragraph shall be allocated shall be determined under regulations prescribed by the Secretary.

(d) Limitation on basis increase attributable to assumption of liability.

(1) In general. In no event shall the basis of any property be increased under subsection (a) or (b) above the fair market value of such property (determined without regard to section 7701(g)) by reason of any gain recognized to the transferor as a result of the assumption of a liability.

(2) Treatment of gain not subject to tax. Except as provided in regulations, if—

(A) gain is recognized to the transferor as a result of an assumption of a nonrecourse liability by a transferee which is also secured by assets not transferred to such transferee; and

(B) no person is subject to tax under this title on such gain,

then, for purposes of determining basis under subsections (a) and (b), the amount of gain recognized by the transferor as a result of the assumption of the liability shall be determined as if the liability assumed by the transferee equaled such transferee's ratable portion of such liability determined on the basis of the relative fair market values (determined without regard to section 7701(g)) of all of the assets subject to such liability.

(e) Limitations on built-in losses.

(1) Limitation on importation of built-in losses.

(A) In general. If in any transaction described in subsection (a) or (b) there would (but for this subsection) be an importation of a net built-in loss, the basis of each property described in subparagraph (B) which is acquired in such transaction shall (notwithstanding subsections (a) and (b)) be its fair market value immediately after such transaction.

(B) Property described. For purposes of subparagraph (A), property is described in this subparagraph if—

(i) gain or loss with respect to such property is not subject to tax under this subtitle in the hands of the transferor immediately before the transfer, and

(ii) gain or loss with respect to such property is subject to such tax in the hands of the transferee immediately after such transfer.

In any case in which the transferor is a partnership, the preceding sentence shall be applied by treating each partner in such partnership as holding such partner's proportionate share of the property of such partnership.

(C) Importation of net built-in loss. For purposes of subparagraph (A), there is an importation of a net built-in loss in a transaction if the transferee's aggregate adjusted bases of property described in subparagraph (B) which is transferred in such transaction would (but for this paragraph) exceed the fair market value of such property immediately after such transaction.

(2) Limitation on transfer of built-in losses in section 351 transactions.

(A) In general. If—

(i) property is transferred by a transferor in any transaction which is described in subsection (a) and which is not described in paragraph (1) of this subsection, and

(ii) the transferee's aggregate adjusted bases of such property so transferred would (but for this paragraph) exceed the fair market value of such property immediately after such transaction,

then, notwithstanding subsection (a), the transferee's aggregate adjusted bases of the property so transferred shall not exceed the fair market value of such property immediately after such transaction.

(B) Allocation of basis reduction. The aggregate reduction in basis by reason of subparagraph (A) shall be allocated among the property so transferred in proportion to their respective built-in losses immediately before the transaction.

(C) Election to apply limitation to transferor's stock basis.

(i) In general. If the transferor and transferee of a transaction described in subparagraph (A) both elect the application of this subparagraph—

(I) subparagraph (A) shall not apply, and

(II) the transferor's basis in the stock received for property to which subparagraph (A) does not apply by reason of the election shall not exceed its fair market value immediately after the transfer.

(ii) Election. Any election under clause (i) shall be made at such time and in such form and manner as the Secretary may prescribe, and, once made, shall be irrevocable.

In 2005, P.L. 109-135, Sec. 403(dd)(2), amended clause (e)(2)(C)(ii), effective for transactions after 10/22/2004 as if included in the amendments made by Sec. 836 of the American Jobs Creation Act of 2004, P.L. 108-357 [see below].
Prior to amendment, clause (e)(2)(C)(ii) read as follows:

Code Sec. 362 — Corporate distributions and adjustments

"(ii) Election. An election under clause (i) shall be included with the return of tax for the taxable year in which the transaction occurred, shall be in such form and manner as the Secretary may prescribe, and, once made, shall be irrevocable."

In 2004, P.L. 108-357, Sec. 836(a), added subsec. (e), effective for transactions after 10/22/2004.

In 1999, P.L. 106-36, Sec. 3001(b)(2), added subsec. (d), effective for transfers after 10/18/98.

In 1986, P.L. 99-514, Sec. 824(b), deleted para. (c)(3), effective for amounts received after 12/31/86, in tax. yrs. end. after 12/31/86.

Prior to amendment, para. (c)(3), read as follows:

"(3) Exception for contributions in aid of construction. The provisions of this subsection shall not apply to contributions in aid of construction to which section 118(b) applies."

In 1976, P.L. 94-455, Sec. 1906(b)(13)(A), substituted "Secretary" for "Secretary or his delegate" in para. (c)(2), effective for tax. yrs. begin. after 12/31/76.

—P.L. 94-455, Sec. 2120(b), added para. (c)(3), effective for contributions made after 1/31/76.

In 1968, P.L. 90-621, Sec. 2(b), amended the last sentence of subsec. (b), effective only with respect to plans of reorganization adopted after 10/22/86.

Prior to amendment, the last sentence of subsec. (b) sentence read as follows:

"This subsection shall not apply if the property acquired consists of stock or securities in a corporation a party to the reorganization, unless acquired by the issuance of stock or securities of the transferee as the consideration in whole or in part for the transfer."

Sec. 363. Repealed.

In 1976, P.L. 94-455, Sec. 1901(a)(49), repealed Code Sec. 363, effective for tax. yrs. begin. after '76.

Prior to repeal, Code Sec. 363 read as follows:

"SEC. 363. EFFECT ON EARNINGS AND PROFITS.

"For rules relating to the effect on earnings and profits of transactions to which this part applies, see sections 312 and 381."

SUBPART D.—SPECIAL RULE; DEFINITIONS

Sec.
367. Foreign corporations.
368. Definitions relating to corporate reorganizations.

Sec. 367. Foreign corporations.

(a) Transfers of property from the United States.

(1) General rule. If, in connection with any exchange described in section 332, 351, 354, 356, or 361, a United States person transfers property to a foreign corporation, such foreign corporation shall not, for purposes of determining the extent to which gain shall be recognized on such transfer, be considered to be a corporation.

(2) Exception for certain stock or securities. Except to the extent provided in regulations, paragraph (1) shall not apply to the transfer of stock or securities of a foreign corporation which is a party to the exchange or a party to the reorganization.

(3) Exception for transfers of certain property used in the active conduct of a trade or business.

(A) In general. Except as provided in regulations prescribed by the Secretary, paragraph (1) shall not apply to any property transferred to a foreign corporation for use by such foreign corporation in the active conduct of a trade or business outside of the United States.

(B) Paragraph not to apply to certain property. Except as provided in regulations prescribed by the Secretary, subparagraph (A) shall not apply to any—

(i) property described in paragraph (1) or (3) of section 1221(a) (relating to inventory and copyrights, etc.),

(ii) installment obligations, accounts receivable, or similar property,

(iii) foreign currency or other property denominated in foreign currency,

(iv) intangible property (within the meaning of section 936(h)(3)(B)), or

(v) property with respect to which the transferor is a lessor at the time of the transfer, except that this clause shall not apply if the transferee was the lessee.

(C) Transfer of foreign branch with previously deducted losses. Except as provided in regulations prescribed by the Secretary, subparagraph (A) shall not apply to gain realized on the transfer of the assets of a foreign branch of a United States person to a foreign corporation in an exchange described in paragraph (1) to the extent that—

(i) the sum of losses—

(I) which were incurred by the foreign branch before the transfer, and

(II) with respect to which a deduction was allowed to the taxpayer, exceeds

(ii) the sum of—

(I) any taxable income of such branch for a taxable year after the taxable year in which the loss was incurred and through the close of the taxable year of the transfer, and

(II) the amount which is recognized under section 904(f)(3) on account of the transfer.

Any gain recognized by reason of the preceding sentence shall be treated for purposes of this chapter as income from sources outside the United States having the same character as such losses had.

(4) Special rule for transfer of partnership interests. Except as provided in regulations prescribed by the Secretary, a transfer by a United States person of an interest in a partnership to a foreign corporation in an exchange described in paragraph (1) shall, for purposes of this subsection, be treated as a transfer to such corporation of such person's pro rata share of the assets of the partnership.

(5) Paragraphs (2) and (3) not to apply to certain section 361 transactions. Paragraphs (2) and (3) shall not apply in the case of an exchange described in subsection (a) or (b) of section 361. Subject to such basis adjustments and such other conditions as shall be provided in regulations, the preceding sentence shall not apply if the transferor corporation is controlled (within the meaning of section 368(c)), by 5 or fewer domestic corporations. For purposes of the preceding sentence, all members of the same affiliated group (within the meaning of section 1504) shall be treated as 1 corporation.

(6) Secretary may exempt certain transactions from application of this subsection. Paragraph (1) shall not apply to the transfer of any property which the Secretary, in order to carry out the purposes of this subsection, designates by regulation.

(b) Other transfers.

(1) Effect of section to be determined under regulations. In the case of any exchange described in section 332, 351, 354, 355, 356, or 361 in connection with which there is no transfer of property described in subsection (a)(1), a foreign corporation shall be considered to be a corporation except to the extent provided in regulations prescribed by the Secretary which are necessary or appropriate to prevent the avoidance of Federal income taxes.

(2) Regulations relating to sale or exchange of stock in foreign corporations. The regulations prescribed pursuant to paragraph (1) shall include (but shall not be limited to) regulations dealing with the sale or exchange of stock or securities in a foreign corporation by a United States person, including regulations providing—

(A) the circumstances under which—

(i) gain shall be recognized currently, or amounts included in gross income currently as a dividend, or both, or

Corporate distributions and adjustments Code Sec. 367

(ii) gain or other amounts may be deferred for inclusion in the gross income of a shareholder (or his successor in interest) at a later date, and

(B) the extent to which adjustments shall be made to earnings and profits, basis of stock or securities, and basis of assets.

(c) Transactions to be treated as exchanges.

(1) Section 355 distribution. For purposes of this section, any distribution described in section 355 (or so much of section 356 as relates to section 355) shall be treated as an exchange whether or not it is an exchange.

(2) Contribution of capital to controlled corporations. For purposes of this chapter, any transfer of property to a foreign corporation as a contribution to the capital of such corporation by one or more persons who, immediately after the transfer, own (within the meaning of section 318) stock possessing at least 80 percent of the total combined voting power of all classes of stock of such corporation entitled to vote shall be treated as an exchange of such property for stock of the foreign corporation equal in value to the fair market value of the property transferred.

(d) Special rules relating to transfers of intangibles.

(1) In general. Except as provided in regulations prescribed by the Secretary, if a United States person transfers any intangible property (within the meaning of section 936(h)(3)(B)) to a foreign corporation in an exchange described in section 351 or 361—

(A) subsection (a) shall not apply to the transfer of such property, and

(B) the provisions of this subsection shall apply to such transfer.

(2) Transfer of intangibles treated as transfer pursuant to sale of contingent payments.

(A) In general. If paragraph (1) applies to any transfer, the United States person transferring such property shall be treated as—

(i) having sold such property in exchange for payments which are contingent upon the productivity, use, or disposition of such property, and

(ii) receiving amounts which reasonably reflect the amounts which would have been received—

(I) annually in the form of such payments over the useful life of such property, or

(II) in the case of a disposition following such transfer (whether direct or indirect), at the time of the disposition.

The amounts taken into account under clause (ii) shall be commensurate with the income attributable to the intangible.

(B) Effect on earnings and profits. For purposes of this chapter, the earnings and profits of a foreign corporation to which the intangible property was transferred shall be reduced by the amount required to be included in the income of the transferor of the intangible property under subparagraph (A)(ii).

(C) Amounts received treated as ordinary income. For purposes of this chapter, any amount included in gross income by reason of this subsection shall be treated as ordinary income. For purposes of applying section 904(d), any such amount shall be treated in the same manner as if such amount were a royalty.

(3) Regulations relating to transfers of intangibles to partnerships. The Secretary may provide by regulations that the rules of paragraph (2) also apply to the transfer of intangible property by a United States person to a partnership in circumstances consistent with the purposes of this subsection.

(e) Treatment of distributions described in section 355 or liquidations under section 332.

(1) Distributions described in section 355. In the case of any distribution described in section 355 (or so much of section 356 as relates to section 355) by a domestic corporation to a person who is not a United States person, to the extent provided in regulations, gain shall be recognized under principles similar to the principles of this section.

(2) Liquidations under section 332. In the case of any liquidation to which section 332 applies, except as provided in regulations, subsections (a) and (b)(1) of section 337 shall not apply where the 80-percent distributee (as defined in section 337(c)) is a foreign corporation.

(f) Other transfers.

To the extent provided in regulations, if a United States person transfers property to a foreign corporation as paid-in surplus or as a contribution to capital (in a transaction not otherwise described in this section), such transfer shall be treated as a sale or exchange for an amount equal to the fair market value of the property transferred, and the transferor shall recognize as gain the excess of—

(1) the fair market value of the property so transferred, over

(2) the adjusted basis (for purposes of determining gain) of such property in the hands of the transferor.

In **2004,** P.L. 108-357, Sec. 406(a), added "For purposes of applying section 904(d), any such amount shall be treated in the same manner as if such amount were a royalty." at the end of subpara. (d)(2)(C), effective for amounts treated as received pursuant to Code Sec. 367(d)(2) on or after 8/5/97.

In **1999,** P.L. 106-170, Sec. 532(c)(1)(C), substituted "section 1221(a)" for "section 1221" in clause (a)(3)(B)(i), effective for any instrument held, acquired, or entered into, any transaction entered into, and supplies held or acquired on or after 12/17/99.

In **1997,** P.L. 105-34, Sec. 1131(b)(2) [sic (c)(2)], added subsec. (f) . . . Sec. 1131(b)(4) [sic (c)(4)], amended subpara. (d)(2)(C) . . . Sec. 1131(b)(5)(A) [sic (c)(5)(A)], added para. (d)(3), effective 8/5/97.

Prior to amendment, subpara. (d)(2)(C) read as follows:

"(C) Amounts received treated as United States source ordinary income. For purposes of this chapter, any amount included in gross income by reason of this subsection shall be treated as ordinary income from sources within the United States."

In **1990,** P.L. 101-508, Sec. 11702(a)(1), substituted "subsection (a) or (b) of section 361" for "section 361" in para. (a)(5), effective for exchanges on or after 6/21/88, except that para. (a)(5) shall not apply to any exchange pursuant to any reorganization for which a plan of reorganization was adopted before 6/21/88. For special provisions, see Sec. 1006(e)(13)(C) of P.L. 100-647 reproduced below.

In **1988,** P.L. 100-647, Sec. 1006(e)(13)(A), redesignated para. (a)(5) as (a)(6) and added new para. (a)(5), effective for exchanges on or after 6/21/88, except that para. (a)(5) shall not apply to any exchange pursuant to any reorganization for which a plan of reorganization was adopted before 6/21/88. Sec. 1006(e)(13)(C) of this Act provides:

"(C) Section 367(e)(2) of the 1986 Code (as amended by the Reform Act [Sec. 631(d)(1) of P.L. 99-514]) shall not apply in the case of any corporation completely liquidated before June 10, 1987, into a corporation organized in a country which has an income tax treaty with the United States."

— P.L. 100-647, Sec. 1012(n)(1), added the last sentence to Sec. 1231(g)(2)(A) of P.L. 99-514, special rules for changes made by Sec. 1231(e)(1) of P.L. 99-514, see below.

In **1986,** P.L. 99-514, Sec. 631(d)(1), amended subsec. (e) [as amended by Sec. 1810(g)(4)(B) of this Act, see below], effective as provided in Secs. 633(a)(1) and (3) of this Act:

"(a) General rule. Except as otherwise provided in this section, the amendments made by this subtitle shall apply to—

"(1) any distribution in complete liquidation, and any sale or exchange, made by a corporation after July 31, 1986, unless such corporation is completely liquidated before January 1, 1987,

* * *

"(3) any distribution (not in complete liquidation) made after December 31, 1986."

Sec. 633(d) [sic (e)] of this Act provides:

"(d)[sic (e)] Complete liquidation defined. For purposes of this section, a corporation shall be treated as completely liquidated if all of the assets of such corporation are distributed in complete liquidation, less assets retained to meet claims."

Prior to amendment, subsec. (e) [as amended by Sec. 1810(g)(4)(B) of this Act] read as follows:

1,835

Code Sec. 367 — Corporate distributions and adjustments

"(e) Treatment of distributions described in section 336 or 355. In the case of any distribution described in section 336 or 355 (or so much of section 356 as relates to section 355) by a domestic corporation which is made to a person who is not a United States person, to the extent provided in regulations, gain shall be recognized under principles similar to the principles of this section."

—P.L. 99-514, Sec. 1231(e)(2), added the sentence at the end of subpara. (d)(2)(A), effective as provided in Sec. 1231(g)(2) of this Act [as amended by Sec. 1012(n)(1) of P.L. 100-647]:

"(2) Special rule for transfer of intangibles.

"(A) In general. The amendments made by subsection (e) shall apply to taxable years beginning after December 31, 1986, but only with respect to transfers after November 16, 1985, or licenses granted after such date (or before such date with respect to property not in existence or owned by the taxpayer on such date). In the case of any transfer (or license) which is not to a foreign person, the preceding sentence shall be applied by substituting 'August 16, 1986' for 'November 16, 1985'.

"(B) Special rule under section 936. For purposes of section 936(h)(5)(C) of the Internal Revenue Code of 1986 the amendments made by subsection (e) shall apply to taxable years beginning after December 31, 1986, without regard to when the transfer (or license) was made."

—P.L. 99-514, Sec. 1810(g)(1), repealed subsec. (f), . . . Sec. 1810(g)(4)(A), deleted "355," following "section 332, 351, 354," in para. (a)(1) . . . Sec. 1810(g)(4)(B)(i), substituted "described in section 336 or 355 (or so much of section 356 as relates to section 355)" for "described in section 336" in subsec. (e) [before amendment by Sec. 631(d)(1) of this Act, see above] . . . Sec. 1810(g)(4)(B)(ii), substituted "distributions described in section 336 or 355" for "liquidations under section 366" in the heading of subsec. (e) [before amendment by Sec. 631(d)(1) of this Act, see above], effective for transfers and exchanges after 12/31/84, in tax. yrs. end. after 12/31/84. For special rules, see Secs. 131(g)(2) and (g)(3) of P.L. 98-369 reproduced below.

Prior to repeal, subsec. (f) read as follows:

"(f) Transitional rule. In the case of any exchange beginning before January 1, 1978—

"(1) subsection (a) shall be applied without regard to whether or not there is a transfer of property described in subsection (a)(1), and

"(2) subsection (b) shall not apply."

In 1984, P.L. 98-369, Sec. 131(a), amended subsec. (a) . . . Sec. 131(b), amended subsec. (d) . . . Sec. 131(c), redesignated subsec. (e) as subsec. (f) and added new subsec. (e), effective for transfers or exchanges after 12/31/84, in tax. yrs. ending after 12/31/84. Secs. 131(g)(2) and (g)(3) of the Act also provide:

"(2) Special rule for certain transfers of intangibles.

"(A) In general. If, after June 6, 1984, and before January 1, 1985, a United States person transfers any intangible property (within the meaning of section 936(h)(3)(B) of the Internal Revenue Code of 1954) to a foreign corporation or in a transfer described in section 1491, such transfer shall be treated for purposes of sections 367(a), 1492(2), and 1494(b) of such Code as pursuant to a plan having as 1 of its principal purposes the avoidance of Federal income tax.

"(B) Waiver. Subject to such terms and conditions as the Secretary of the Treasury or his delegate may prescribe, the Secretary may waive the application of subparagraph (A) with respect to any transfer.

"(3) Ruling request before March 1, 1984. The amendments made by this section [Se. 131 of P.L. 98-369] (and the provisions of paragraph (2) of this subsection) shall not apply to any transfer or exchange of property described in a request filed before March 1, 1984, under section 367(a), 1492(2), or 1494(b) of the Internal Revenue Code of 1954 (as in effect before such amendments)."

Prior to amendment, subsec. (a) read as follows:

"(a) Transfers of property from the United States.

"(1) General rule. If, in connection with any exchange described in section 332, 351, 354, 355, 356, or 361, there is a transfer of property (other than stock or securities of a foreign corporation which is a party to the exchange or a party to the reorganization) by a United States person to a foreign corporation, for purposes of determining the extent to which gain shall be recognized on such transfer, a foreign corporation shall not be considered to be a corporation unless, pursuant to a request filed not later than the close of the 183d day after the beginning of such transfer (and filed in such form and manner as may be prescribed by regulations by the Secretary), it is established to the satisfaction of the Secretary that such exchange is not in pursuance of a plan having as one of it principal purposes the avoidance of Federal income taxes.

"(2) Exception for transactions designated by the secretary. Paragraph (1) shall not apply to any exchange (otherwise within paragraph (1)), or to any type of property, which the Secretary by regulation designates as not requiring the filing of a request."

Prior to amendment, subsec. (d) read as follows:

"(d) Special rule relating to transfer of intangibles by possession corporations.

"(1) In general. If, after August 14, 1982, any possession corporation transfers, directly or indirectly, any intangible property (within the meaning of section 936(h)(3)(B)) to any foreign corporation, such transfer shall be treated for purposes of subsection (a) as pursuant to a plan having as one of its principal purposes the avoidance of Federal income taxes.

"(2) Possession corporation.

"(A) In general. The term 'possession corporation' means any corporation—

"(i) to which an election under section 936 applies, or

"(ii) which is described in subsection (b) of section 934 and which is an inhabitant of the Virgin Islands (within the meaning of section 28(a) of the Revised Organic Act of the Virgin Islands).

"(B) Former possession corporation. A corporation shall be treated as a possession corporation with respect to any transfer if such corporation was a possession corporation (within the meaning of subparagraph (A)) at any time during the 5-year period ending on the date of such transfer.

"(3) Transfer by United States affiliates. A rule similar to the rule of paragraph (1) shall apply in the case of a direct or indirect transfer by a United States affiliate to a foreign person of intangible property which, after August 14, 1982, was being used (or held for use) by a possession corporation under an arrangement with a United States affiliate. For purposes of the preceding sentence, the term 'United States affiliate' means any United States person who is a member of an affiliated group (within the meaning of section 936(h)(5)(C)(i)(I)(b)) which includes the possession corporation.

"(4) Waiver authority. Subject to such terms and conditions as the Secretary may provide, paragraph (1) or (3) shall not apply to any case where the Secretary is satisfied that the transfer will not result in the reduction of current or future Federal income taxes."

In 1982, P.L. 97-248, Sec. 213(d), redesignated subsec. (d) as subsec. (e) and added new subsec. (d), effective for tax. yrs. ending after 8/14/82.

In 1976, P.L. 94-455, Sec. 1042(a), amended Code Sec. 367, effective for transfers begin. after 10/9/75 and for sales, exchanges and distributions taking place after 10/9/75, except as provided by Sec. 1042(e)(2) of the Act, which reads as follows:

"(2) In the case of any exchange described in section 367 of the Internal Revenue Code of 1954 (as in effect on December 31, 1974) in any taxable year beginning after December 31, 1962, and before the date of the enactment of this Act, which does not involve the transfer of property to or from a United States person, a taxpayer shall have for purposes of such section until 183 days after the date of the enactment of this Act to file a request with the Secretary of the Treasury or his delegate seeking to establish to the satisfaction of the Secretary of the Treasury or his delegate that such exchange was not in pursuance of a plan having as one of its principal purposes the avoidance of Federal income taxes and that for purposes of such section a foreign corporation is to be treated as a foreign corporation."

Prior to amendment, Code Sec. 367 read as follows:

"SEC. 367. FOREIGN CORPORATIONS.

"(a) General rule. In determining the extent to which gain shall be recognized in the case of any of the exchanges described in section 332, 351, 354, 355, 356, or 361, a foreign corporation shall not be considered as a corporation unless—

"(1) before such exchange, or

"(2) in the case of an exchange described in subsection (b), either before or after such exchange,

it has been established to the satisfaction of the Secretary or his delegate that such exchange is not in pursuance of a plan having as one of its principal purposes the avoidance of Federal income taxes.

"(b) Application of subsection (a)(2). Subsection (a)(2) shall apply in the case of a mere change in form in which there is an exchange by a foreign corporation of—

"(1) stock in one foreign corporation for,

"(2) stock in another foreign corporation,

if the corporations referred to in paragraphs (1) and (2) differ only in their form of organization, and if the ownership of the corporation referred to in paragraph (1) immediately before such exchange is identical to the ownership of the corporation referred to in paragraph (2) immediately after such exchange.

"(c) Section 355 distributions treated as exchanges. For purposes of this section, any distribution in section 355 (or so much of section 356 as relates to section 355) shall be treated as an exchange whether or not it is an exchange.

"(d) Contributions of capital to controlled corporations. For purposes of this chapter, any transfer of property to a foreign corporation as a contribution to the capital of such corporation by one or more persons who, immediately after the transfer, own (within the meaning of section 318) stock possessing at least 80 percent of the total combined voting power of all classes of stock of such corporation entitled to vote shall be treated as an exchange of such property for stock of the foreign corporation equal in value to the fair market value of the property transferred unless, before such transfer, it has been established to the satisfaction of the Secretary or his delegate that such transfer is not in pursuance of a plan having as one of its principal purposes the avoidance of Federal income taxes."

In 1971, P.L. 91-681, Sec. 1(a), amended Code Sec. 367, effective for transfers made after 12/31/67; except that subsec. (d) shall apply only with respect to transfers made after 12/31/70.

Prior to amendment, Code Sec. 367 read as follows:

"SEC. 367. FOREIGN CORPORATIONS.

"In determining the extent to which gain shall be recognized in the case of any of the exchanges described in section 332, 351, 354, 355, 356, or 361, a foreign corporation shall not be considered as a corporation unless, before such exchange, it has been established to the satisfaction of the Secretary or his delegate that such exchange is not in pursuance of a plan having as one of its principal purposes the avoidance of Federal income taxes. For purposes of this section, any distribution described in section 355 (or so much of section 355) shall be treated as an exchange whether or not it is an exchange."

Sec. 368. Definitions relating to corporate reorganizations.

(a) Reorganization.

(1) In general. For purposes of parts I and II and this part, the term "reorganization" means—

(A) a statutory merger or consolidation;

(B) the acquisition by one corporation, in exchange solely for all or a part of its voting stock (or in exchange solely for all or a part of the voting stock of a corporation which is in control of the acquiring corporation, of stock of another corporation if, immediately after the acquisition, the acquiring corporation has control of such other corporation (whether or not such acquiring corporation had control immediately before the acquisition);

(C) the acquisition by one corporation, in exchange solely for all or a part of its voting stock (or in exchange solely for all or a part of the voting stock of a corporation which is in control of the acquiring corporation), of substantially all of the properties of another corporation, but in determining whether the exchange is solely for stock the assumption by the acquiring corporation of a liability of the other shall be disregarded;

(D) a transfer by a corporation of all or a part of its assets to another corporation if immediately after the transfer the transferor, or one or more of its shareholders (including persons who were shareholders immediately before the transfer), or any combination thereof, is in control of the corporation to which the assets are transferred; but only if, in pursuance of the plan, stock or securities of the corporation to which the assets are transferred are distributed in a transaction which qualifies under section 354, 355, or 356;

(E) a recapitalization;

(F) a mere change in identity, form, or place of organization of one corporation, however effected; or

(G) a transfer by a corporation of all or part of its assets to another corporation in a title 11 or similar case; but only if, in pursuance of the plan, stock or securities of the corporation to which the assets are transferred are distributed in a transaction which qualifies under section 354, 355, or 356.

(2) Special rules relating to paragraph (1).

(A) Reorganizations described in both paragraph (1)(C) and paragraph (1)(D). If a transaction is described in both paragraph (1)(C) and paragraph (1)(D), then, for purposes of this subchapter (other than for purposes of subparagraph (C)), such transaction shall be treated as described only in paragraph (1)(D).

(B) Additional consideration in certain paragraph (1)(C) cases. If—

(i) one corporation acquires substantially all of the properties of another corporation,

(ii) the acquisition would qualify under paragraph (1)(C) but for the fact that the acquiring corporation exchanges money or other property in addition to voting stock, and

(iii) the acquiring corporation acquires, solely for voting stock described in paragraph (1)(C), property of the other corporation having a fair market value which is at least 80 percent of the fair market value of all of the property of the other corporation,

then such acquisition shall (subject to subparagraph (A) of this paragraph) be treated as qualifying under paragraph (1)(C). Solely for the purpose of determining whether clause (iii) of the preceding sentence applies, the amount of any liability assumed by the acquiring corporation shall be treated as money paid for the property.

(C) Transfers of assets or stock to subsidiaries in certain paragraph (1)(A), (1)(B), (1)(C), and (1)(G) cases. A transaction otherwise qualifying under paragraph (1)(A), (1)(B), or (1)(C) shall not be disqualified by reason of the fact that part or all of the assets or stock which were acquired in the transaction are transferred to a corporation controlled by the corporation acquiring such assets or stock. A similar rule shall apply to a transaction otherwise qualifying under paragraph (1)(G) where the requirements of subparagraphs (A) and (B) of section 354(b)(1) are met with respect to the acquisition of the assets.

(D) Use of stock of controlling corporation in paragraph (1)(A) and (1)(G) cases. The acquisition by one corporation, in exchange for stock of a corporation (referred to in this subparagraph as "controlling corporation") which is in control of the acquiring corporation, of substantially all of the properties of another corporation shall not disqualify a transaction under paragraph (1)(A) or (1)(G) if—

(i) no stock of the acquiring corporation is used in the transaction, and

(ii) in the case of a transaction under paragraph (1)(A), such transaction would have qualified under paragraph (1)(A) had the merger been into the controlling corporation.

(E) Statutory merger using voting stock of corporation controlling merged corporation. A transaction otherwise qualifying under paragraph (1)(A) shall not be disqualified by reason of the fact that stock of a corporation (referred to in this subparagraph as the "controlling corporation") which before the merger was in control of the merged corporation is used in the transaction, if—

(i) after the transaction, the corporation surviving the merger holds substantially all of its properties and of the properties of the merged corporation (other than stock of the controlling corporation distributed in the transaction); and

(ii) in the transaction, former shareholders of the surviving corporation exchanged, for an amount of voting stock of the controlling corporation, an amount of stock in the surviving corporation which constitutes control of such corporation.

(F) Certain transactions involving 2 or more investment companies.

(i) If immediately before a transaction described in paragraph (1) (other than subparagraph (E) thereof), 2 or more parties to the transaction were investment companies, then the transaction shall not be considered to be a reorganization with respect to any such investment company (and its shareholders and security holders) unless it was a regulated investment company, a real estate investment trust, or a corporation which meets the requirements of clause (ii).

(ii) A corporation meets the requirements of this clause if not more than 25 percent of the value of its total assets is invested in the stock and securities of any one issuer and not more than 50 percent of the value of its total assets is invested in the stock and securities of 5 or fewer issuers. For purposes of this clause, all members of a controlled group of corporations (within the meaning of section 1563(a)) shall be treated as one issuer. For purposes of this clause, a person holding stock in a regulated investment company, a real estate investment trust, or an investment company which meets the requirements of this clause shall, except as provided in regulations, be treated as holding its proportionate share of the assets held by such company or trust.

(iii) For purposes of this subparagraph the term "investment company" means a regulated investment company, a real estate investment trust, or a corporation 50 percent or more of the value of whose total assets are stock and securities and 80 percent or more of the value of whose total assets are assets held for investment. In making the 50-percent and 80-percent determinations under the preceding sentence, stock and securities in any subsidiary corporation shall be disregarded and the parent corporation shall be deemed to own its ratable share of the subsidiary's assets, and a corporation shall be considered a subsidiary if the parent owns 50 percent or more of the combined voting power of all classes of stock entitled to vote, or 50 percent or more of the total value of shares of all classes of stock outstanding.

(iv) For purposes of this subparagraph, in determining total assets there shall be excluded cash and cash items (including receivables). Government securities, and, under regulations prescribed by the Secretary, assets acquired (through incurring indebtedness or otherwise) for purposes of meeting the requirements of clause (ii) or ceasing to be an investment company.

(v) This subparagraph shall not apply if the stock of each investment company is owned substantially by the same persons in the same proportions.

(vi) If an investment company which does not meet the requirements of clause (ii) acquires assets of another corporation, clause (i) shall be applied to such investment company and its shareholders and security holders as though its assets had been acquired by such other corporation. If such investment company acquires stock of another corporation in a reorganization described in section 368(a)(1)(B), clause (i) shall be applied to the shareholders of such investment company as though they had exchanged with such other corporation all of their stock in such company for stock having a fair market value equal to the fair market value of their stock of such investment company immediately after the exchange. For purposes of section 1001, the deemed acquisition or exchange referred to in the two preceding sentences shall be treated as a sale or exchange of property by the corporation and by the shareholders and security holders to which clause (i) is applied.

(vii) For purposes of clauses (ii) and (iii), the term "securities" includes obligations of State and local governments, commodity futures contracts, shares of regulated investment companies and real estate investment trusts, and other investments constituting a security within the meaning of the Investment Company Act of 1940 (15 U.S.C. 80a-2(36)).

(G) Distribution requirement for paragraph (1)(C).

(i) In general. A transaction shall fail to meet the requirements of paragraph (1)(C) unless the acquired corporation distributes the stock, securities, and other properties it receives, as well as its other properties, in pursuance of the plan of reorganization. For purposes of the preceding sentence, if the acquired corporation is liquidated pursuant to the plan of reorganization, any distribution to its creditors in connection with such liquidation shall be treated as pursuant to the plan of reorganization.

(ii) Exception. The Secretary may waive the application of clause (i) to any transaction subject to any conditions the Secretary may prescribe.

(H) Special rules for determining whether certain transactions are qualified under paragraph (1)(D). For purposes of determining whether a transaction qualifies under paragraph (1)(D)—

(i) in the case of a transaction with respect to which the requirements of subparagraphs (A) and (B) of section 354(b)(1) are met, the term "control" has the meaning given such term by section 304(c), and

(ii) in the case of a transaction with respect to which the requirements of section 355 (or so much of section 356 as relates to section 355) are met, the fact that the shareholders of the distributing corporation dispose of part or all of the distributed stock, or the fact that the corporation whose stock was distributed issues additional stock, shall not be taken into account.

(3) Additional rules relating to title 11 and similar cases.

(A) Title 11 or similar case defined. For purposes of this part, the term "title 11 or similar case" means—

(i) a case under title 11 of the United States Code, or

(ii) a receivership, foreclosure, or similar proceeding in a Federal or State court.

(B) Transfer of assets in a title 11 or similar case. In applying paragraph (1)(G), a transfer of the assets of a corporation shall be treated as made in a title 11 or similar case if and only if—

(i) any party to the reorganization is under the jurisdiction of the court in such case, and

(ii) the transfer is pursuant to a plan of reorganization approved by the court.

(C) Reorganizations qualifying under paragraph (1)(G) and another provision. If a transaction would (but for this subparagraph) qualify both—

(i) under subparagraph (G) of paragraph (1), and

(ii) under any other subparagraph of paragraph (1) or under section 332 or 351,

then, for purposes of this subchapter (other than section 357(c)(1)), such transaction shall be treated as qualifying only under subparagraph (G) of paragraph (1).

(D) Agency receivership proceedings which involve financial institutions. For purposes of subparagraphs (A) and (B), in the case of a receivership, foreclosure, or similar proceeding before a Federal or State agency involving a financial institution referred to in section 581 or 591, the agency shall be treated as a court.

(E) Application of paragraph (2)(E)(ii). In the case of a title 11 or similar case, the requirement of clause (ii) of paragraph (2)(E) shall be treated as met if—

(i) no former shareholder of the surviving corporation received any consideration for his stock, and

(ii) the former creditors of the surviving corporation exchanged, for an amount of voting stock of the controlling corporation, debt of the surviving corporation which had a fair market value equal to 80 percent or more of the total fair market value of the debt of the surviving corporation.

(b) Party to a reorganization.

For purposes of this part, the term "a party to a reorganization" includes—

(1) a corporation resulting from a reorganization, and

(2) both corporations, in the case of a reorganization resulting from the acquisition by one corporation of stock or properties of another.

In the case of a reorganization qualifying under paragraph (1)(B) or (1)(C) of subsection (a), if the stock exchanged for the stock or properties is stock of a corporation which is in control of the acquiring corporation, the term "a party to a reorganization" includes the corporation so controlling the acquiring corporation. In the case of a reorganization quali-

Corporate distributions and adjustments   Code Sec. 368

fying under paragraph (1)(A), (1)(B), (1)(C), or (1)(G) of subsection (a) by reason of paragraph (2)(C) of subsection (a), the term "a party to a reorganization" includes the corporation controlling the corporation to which the acquired assets or stock are transferred. In the case of a reorganization qualifying under paragraph (1)(A) or (1)(G) of subsection (a) by reason of paragraph (2)(D) of that subsection, the term "a party to a reorganization" includes the controlling corporation referred to in such paragraph (2)(D). In the case of a reorganization qualifying under subsection (a)(1)(A) by reason of subsection (a)(2)(E), the term "party to a reorganization" includes the controlling corporation referred to in subsection (a)(2)(E).

(c) Control defined.

For purposes of part I (other than section 304), part II, this part, and part V, the term "control" means the ownership of stock possessing at least 80 percent of the total combined voting power of all classes of stock entitled to vote and at least 80 percent of the total number of shares of all other classes of stock of the corporation.

In 1999, P.L. 106-36, Sec. 3001(a)(3)(A), deleted ", or the fact that property acquired is subject to a liability," after "liability of the other" in subpara. (a)(1)(C) ... Sec. 3001(a)(3)(B), deleted ", and the amount of any liability to which any property acquired from the acquiring corporation is subject," after "acquiring corporation" in subpara. (a)(2)(B), effective for transfers after 10/18/98.

In 1998, P.L. 105-277, Sec. 4003(f)(2), added ", or the fact that the corporation whose stock was distributed issues additional stock," after "dispose of part or all of the distributed stock" in clause (a)(2)(H)(ii), effective for transfers after 8/5/97, except as provided in Sec. 1012(d)(3) of P.L. 105-34 [reproduced below].

—P.L. 105-206, Sec. 6010(c)(3)(B), amended clause (a)(2)(H)(ii), effective for transfers after 8/5/97, except as provided in Sec. 1012(d)(3) of P.L. 105-34 [reproduced below].

Prior to amendment, clause (a)(2)(H)(ii) read as follows:

"(ii) in the case of a transaction with respect to which the requirements of section 355 are met, the shareholders described in paragraph (1)(D) shall be treated as having control of the corporation to which the assets are transferred if such shareholders own (immediately after the distribution) stock possessing—

"(I) more than 50 percent of the total combined voting power of all classes of stock of such corporation entitled to vote, and

"(II) more than 50 percent of the total value of shares of all classes of stock of such corporation."

In 1997, P.L. 105-34, Sec. 1012(c)(2), amended subpara. (a)(2)(H), effective for transfers after 8/5/97, except as provided in Sec. 1012(d)(3) of this Act which reads as follows:

"(3) Transition rule. The amendments made by this section shall not apply to any distribution pursuant to a plan (or series of related transactions) which involves an acquisition described in section 355(e)(2)(A)(ii) of the Internal Revenue Code of 1986 (or, in the case of the amendments made by subsection (c), any transfer) occurring after April 16, 1997, if such acquisition or transfer is—

"(A) made pursuant to an agreement which was binding on such date and at all times thereafter,

"(B) described in a ruling request submitted to the Internal Revenue Service on or before such date, or

"(C) described on or before such date in a public announcement or in a filing with the Securities and Exchange Commission required solely by reason of the acquisition or transfer.

This paragraph shall not apply to any agreement, ruling request, or public announcement or filing unless it identifies the acquirer of the distributing corporation or any controlled corporation, or the transferee, whichever is applicable."

Prior to amendment, subpara. (a)(2)(H) read as follows:

"(H) Special rule for determining whether certain transactions are qualified under paragraph (1)(D). In the case of any transaction with respect to which the requirements of subparagraphs (A) and (B) of section 354(b)(1) are met, for purposes of determining whether such transaction qualifies under subparagraph (D) of paragraph (1), the term 'control' has the meaning given to such term by section 304(c)."

In 1989, P.L. 101-73, Sec. 1401(a)(1), amended subpara. (a)(3)(D), effective for acquisitions on or after 5/10/89.

Prior to amendment, subpara. (a)(3)(D) read as follows:

"(D) Agency proceedings which involve financial institutions.

"(i) For purpose of subparagraphs (A) and (B)—

"(I) In the case of a receivership, foreclosure, or similar proceeding before a Federal or State agency involving a financial institution to which section 585 applies, the agency shall be treated as a court, and

"(II) In the case of a financial institution to which section 593 applies, the term 'title 11 or similar case' means only a case in which the Board (which will be treated as the court in such case) makes the certification described in clause (ii).

"(ii) A transaction otherwise meeting the requirements of subparagraph (G) of paragraph (1), in which the transferor corporation is a financial institution to which section 593 applies, will not be disqualified as a reorganization if no stock or securities of the corporation to which the assets are transferred (transferee) are received or distributed, but only if all of the following conditions are met:

"(I) the requirements of subparagraphs (A) and (B) of section 354(b)(1) are met with respect to the acquisition of the assets,

"(II) substantially all of the liabilities of the transferor immediately before the transfer become, as a result of the transfer, liabilities of the transferee, and

"(III) the Board certifies that the grounds set forth in section 1464(d)(6)(A)(i), (ii), or (iii) of title 12, United States Code, exist with respect to the transferor or will exist in the near future in the absence of action by the Board.

"(iii) For purposes of this subparagraph, the 'Board' means the Federal Home Loan Bank Board or the Federal Savings and Loan Insurance Corporation or, if neither has supervisory authority with respect to the transferor, the equivalent State authority.

"(iv) In the case of a financial institution to which section 585 applies—

"(I) the term 'title 11 or similar case' means only a case in which the applicable authority (which shall be treated as the court in such case) makes the certification described in subclause (II), and

"(II) clause (ii) shall apply to such institution, except that for purposes of clause (ii)(III), the applicable authority must certify that the grounds set forth in such clause (modified in such manner as the Secretary determines necessary because such institution is not an institution to which section 593 applies) exist with respect to such transferor or will exist in the near future in the absence of action by the applicable authority.

For purposes of this clause, the term 'applicable authority' means the Comptroller of the Currency or the Federal Deposit Insurance Corporation, or if neither has the supervisory authority with respect to the transfer, the equivalent State authority.

"(v) For purposes of this subparagraph, in applying section 593, the determination as to whether a corporation is a domestic building and loan association shall be made without regard to section 7701(a)(19)(C)."

—P.L. 101-73, Sec. 1401(b)(1), repealed as if not enacted Sec. 904 of P.L. 99-514 (except Sec. 904(c)(2)(B) of P.L. 99-514), effective 10/22/86, see below.

In 1988, P.L. 100-647, Sec. 1018(q)(5)(A), deleted the two parenthetical phrases in the first sentence of clause (a)(2)(F)(ii) ... Sec. 1018(q)(5)(B), added the last sentence to clause (a)(2)(F)(ii), effective for transfers made after 2/1/76 in tax. yrs. end. after 2/1/76 but not for transfers made in accordance with a ruling issued by the Internal Revenue Service before 2/18/76, which held that a proposed transaction would be a reorganization described in para. 368(a)(1).

Prior to deletion, clause (a)(2)(F)(ii) read as follows:

"(ii) A corporation meets the requirements of this clause if not more than 25 percent of the value of its total assets is invested in the stock and securities of any one issuer (other than stock in a regulated investment company, a real estate investment trust, or an investment company which meets the requirements of this clause (ii)), and not more than 50 percent of the value of its total assets is invested in the stock and securities of 5 or fewer issuers (other than stock in a regulated investment company, a real estate investment trust, or an investment company which meets the requirements of this clause (ii)). For purposes of this clause, all members of a controlled group of corporations (within the meaning of section 1563(a)) shall be treated as one issuer."

—P.L. 100-647, Sec. 4012(a)(1), amended Sec. 904(c)(1) of P.L. 99-514 the effective date for changes made by Sec. 904(a) of P.L. 99-514 [see below]. Sec. 904 of P.L. 99-514 repealed as if not enacted by Sec. 1401(b)(1) of P.L. 101-73, see above.]

—P.L. 100-647, Sec. 4012(b)(1)(A), added clauses (a)(3)(D)(iv) and (v), effective for acquisitions after 11/10/88 and before 1/1/90.

—P.L. 100-647, Sec. 6126, of this Act, reads as follows:

"SEC. 6126. DUAL RESIDENT COMPANIES.

"(a) General rule. In the case of a transaction which—

"(1) involves the transfer after the date of the enactment of this Act by a domestic corporation, with respect to which there is a qualified excess loss account, of its assets and liabilities to a foreign corporation in exchange for all of the stock of such foreign corporation, followed by the complete liquidation of the domestic corporation into the common parent, and

"(2) qualifies, pursuant to Revenue Ruling 87-27, as a reorganization which is described in section 368(a)(1)(F) of the 1986 Code,

then, solely for purposes of applying Treasury Regulation section 1.1502-19 to such qualified excess loss account, such foreign corporation shall be treated as a domestic corporation in determining whether such foreign corporation is a member of the affiliated group of the common parent.

"(b) Treatment of income of new foreign corporation.

"(1) In general. In any case to which subsection (a) applies, for purposes of the 1986 Code—

"(A) the source and character of any item of income of the foreign corporation referred to in subsection (a) shall be determined as if such foreign corporation were a domestic corporation,

"(B) the net amount of any such income shall be treated as subpart F income (without regard to section 952(c) of the 1986 Code), and

"(C) the amount in the qualified excess loss account referred to in subsection (a) shall—

"(i) be reduced by the net amount of any such income, and

"(ii) be increased by the amount of any such income distributed directly or indirectly to the common parent described in subsection (a).

"(2) Limitation. Paragraph (1) shall apply to any item of income only to the extent that the net amount of such income does not exceed the amount in the qualified excess loss account after being reduced under paragraph (1)(C) for prior income.

"(3) Basis adjustments not applicable. To the extent paragraph (1) applies to any item of income, there shall be no increase in basis under section 961(a) of

1,839

such Code on account of such income (and there shall be no reduction in basis under section 961(b) of such Code on account of an exclusion attributable to the inclusion of such income).

"(4) Recognition of gain. For purposes of paragraph (1), if the foreign corporation referred to in subsection (a) transfers any property acquired by such foreign corporation in the transaction referred to in subsection (a) (or transfers any other property the basis of which is determined in whole or in part by reference to the basis of property so acquired) and (but for this paragraph) there is not full recognition of gain on such transfer, the excess (if any) of—

"(A) the fair market value of the property transferred, over

"(B) its adjusted basis,

shall be treated as gain from the sale or exchange of such property and shall be recognized notwithstanding any other provision of law. Proper adjustment shall be made to the basis of any such property for gain recognized under the preceding sentence.

"(c) Definitions. For purposes of this section—

"(1) Common parent. The term 'common parent' means the common parent of the affiliated group which included the domestic corporation referred to in subsection (a)(1).

"(2) Qualified excess loss account. The term 'qualified excess loss account' means any excess loss account (within the meaning of the consolidated return regulations) to the extent such account is attributable—

"(A) to taxable years beginning before January 1, 1988, and

"(B) to periods during which the domestic corporation was subject to an income tax of a foreign country on its income on a residence basis or without regard to whether such income is from sources in or outside of such foreign country.

The amount of such account shall be determined as of immediately after the transaction referred to in subsection (a) and without, except as provided in subsection (b), diminution for any future adjustment.

"(3) Net amount. The net amount of any item of income is the amount of such income reduced by allocable deductions as determined under the rules of section 954(b)(5) of the 1986 Code.

"(4) Second same country corporation may be treated as domestic corporation i certain cases. If—

"(A) another foreign corporation acquires from the common parent stock of the foreign corporation referred to in subsection (a) after the transaction referred to in subsection (a),

"(B) both of such foreign corporations are subject to the income tax of the same foreign country on a residence basis, and

"(C) such common parent complies with such reporting requirements as the Secretary of the Treasury or his delegate may prescribe for purposes of this paragraph,

such other foreign corporation shall be treated as a domestic corporation in determining whether the foreign corporation referred to in subsection (a) is a member of the affiliated group referred to in subsection (a) (and the rules of subsection (b) shall apply (i) to any gain of such other foreign corporation on any disposition of such stock, and (ii) to any other income of such other foreign corporation except to the extent it establishes to the satisfaction of the Secretary of the Treasury or his delegate that such income is not attributable to property acquired from the foreign corporation referred to in subsection (a))."

In 1986, P.L. 99-514, Sec. 621(e)(1), repealed Sec. 806(f)(1) of P.L. 94-455 [see below] which amended subsec. (c), effective 1/1/86.

—P.L. 99-514, Sec. 904(a), [repealed as if not enacted by Sec. 1401(b)(1) of P.L. 101-73, see above] amended subpara. (a)(3)(D).

—P.L. 99-514, Sec. 1804(g)(2), added the sentence at the end of clause (a)(2)(G)(i), effective for plans of reorganizations adopted after 10/22/86.

—P.L. 99-514, Sec. 1804(h)(1), amended subsec. (c) . . . Sec. 1804(h)(2), added subpara. (a)(2)(H) . . . Sec. 1804(h)(3), added "(other than for purposes of subparagraph (C))" after "subchapter" in subpara. (a)(2)(A), effective for transactions pursuant to plans adopted after 7/18/84.

Prior to amendment, subsec. (c) read as follows:

"(c) Control defined.

"(1) In general. For purposes of part I (other than section 304), part II, this part, and part V, the term 'control' means the ownership of stock possessing at least 80 percent of the total combined voting power of all classes of stock entitled to vote and at least 80 percent of the total number of shares of all other classes of stock of the corporation.

"(2) Special rule for determining whether certain transactions are described in subsection (a)(1)(D). In the case of any transaction with respect to which the requirements of subparagraphs (A) and (B) of section 354(b)(1) are met, for purposes of determining whether such transaction is described in subparagraph (D) of subsection (a)(1), the term 'control' has the meaning given to such term by section 304(c)."

—P.L. 99-514, Sec. 1879(l)(1), amended clause (a)(2)(F)(ii), effective for transfers made after 2/1/76 in tax. yrs. end. after 2/1/76, but not for transfers made in accordance with a ruling issued by the Internal Revenue Service before 2/18/76, which held that a proposed transaction would be a reorganization described in para. 368(a)(1).

Prior to amendment, clause (a)(2)(F)(ii), read as follows:

"(ii) A corporation meets the requirements of this clause if not more than 25 percent of the value of its total assets is invested in the stock and securities of any one issuer, and not more than 50 percent of the value of its total assets is invested in the stock and securities of 5 or fewer issuers. For purposes of this clause, all members of a controlled group of corporations (within the meaning of section 1563(a)) shall be treated as one issuer."

In 1984, P.L. 98-369, Sec. 63(a), added subpara. (a)(2)(G) . . . Sec. 64(a), amended subsec. (c), effective for transactions pursuant to plans adopted after 7/18/84.

Prior to amendment, subsec. (c) [after the repeal of Sec. 806(f)(1) of P.L. 94-455, see below, by Sec. 621(e)(1) of P.L. 99-514, see above] read as follows:

"(c) Control. For purposes of part I (other than section 304), part II, this part, the term 'control' means the ownership of stock possessing at least 80 percent of the total combined voting power of all classes of stock entitled to vote and at least 80 percent of the total number of shares of all other classes of stock of the corporation."

—P.L. 98-369, Sec. 174(b)(5)(D), deleted clause (a)(2)(F)(viii), effective for transactions after 12/31/83, in tax. yrs. end. after 12/31/83.

Prior to deletion, clause (a)(2)(F)(viii) read as follows:

"(viii) In applying paragraph (3) of section 267(b) in respect of any transaction to which this subparagraph applies, the reference to a personal holding company in such paragraph (3) shall be treated as including a reference to an investment company and the determination of whether a corporation is an investment company shall be made as of the time immediately before the transaction instead of with respect to the taxable year referred to in such paragraph (3)."

In 1983, P.L. 97-448, Sec. 304(b), deleted "or stock" after "assets" from the last sentence of subpara. (a)(2)(C), effective for any bankruptcy case or similar judicial proceeding begin. after 12/31/80.

—P.L. 97-448, Sec. 304(c), substituted "any party to the reorganization" for "such corporation" in clause (a)(3)(B)(i), effective 1/12/83.

In 1982, P.L. 97-248, Sec. 225(a), added "of one corporation" after "place of organization" in subpara. (a)(1)(F), effective for transactions occurring after 8/31/82. Sec. 225(b)(2) of this Act provides:

"(2) Plans adopted on or before August 31, 1982. The amendment made by subsection (a) shall not apply with respect to plans of reorganization adopted on or before August 31, 1982, but only if the transaction occurs before January 1, 1983."

In 1981, P.L. 97-34, Sec. 241, amended subpara. (a)(3)(D), effective for transfers made on or after 1/1/81.

Prior to amendment, subpara. (a)(3)(D) read as follows:

"(D) Agency receivership proceedings which involve financial institutions. For purposes of subparagraphs (A) and (B), in the case of a receivership, foreclosure, or similar proceeding before a Federal or State agency involving a financial institution to which section 585 or 593 applies, the agency shall be treated as a court."

In 1980, P.L. 96-589, Sec. 4(a), added subpara. (a)(1)(G) . . . Sec. 4(b), added para. (a)(3) . . . Sec. 4(c), amended subpara. (a)(2)(C) . . . Sec. 4(d), amended subpara. (a)(2)(D) . . . Sec. 4(h)(3)(A), deleted "or" at the end of subpara. (a)(1)(E) . . . Sec. 4(h)(3)(B), substituted "; or" for the period at the end of subpara. (a)(1)(F) . . . Sec. 4(h)(4)(A), substituted "(1)(C), or (1)(G)" for "or (1)(C)" in subsec. (b) . . . Sec. 4(h)(4)(B), substituted "paragraph (1)(A) or (1)(G)" for "paragraph (1)(A)" in subsec. (b), effective for any bankruptcy case or similar judicial proceeding begin. after 12/31/80.

Sec. 7(f) and (g) of this Act provides:

"(f) Election to substitute September 30, 1979, for December 31, 1980.

"(1) In general. The debtor (or debtors) in a bankruptcy case or similar judicial proceeding may (with the approval of the court) elect to apply [subsection 7(c) of this Act] by substituting 'September 30, 1979' for 'December 31, 1980' each place it appears in such subsections.

"(2) Effect of election. Any election made under paragraph (1) with respect to any proceeding shall apply to all parties to the proceeding.

"(3) Revocation only with consent. Any election under this subsection may be revoked only with the consent of the Secretary of the Treasury or his delegate.

"(4) Time and manner of election. Any election under this subsection shall be made at such time, and in such manner, as the Secretary of the Treasury or his delegate may by regulations prescribe.

"(g) Definitions. For purposes of this section—

"(1) Bankruptcy case. The term 'bankruptcy case' means any case under title 11 of the United States Code (as recodified by P.L. 95-598).

"(2) Similar judicial proceeding. The term 'similar judicial proceeding' means a receivership, foreclosure, or similar proceeding in a Federal or State court (as modified by section 368(a)(3)(D) of the Internal Revenue Code of 1954)."

Prior to amendment, subparas. (a)(2)(C) and (D) read as follows:

"(C) Transfers of assets or stock to subsidiaries in certain paragraph (1)(A), (1)(B), and (1)(C) cases. A transaction otherwise qualifying under paragraph (1)(A), (1)(B), or (1)(C) shall not be disqualified by reason of the fact that part or all of the assets or stock which were acquired in the transaction are transferred to a corporation controlled by the corporation acquiring such assets or stock.

"(D) Statutory merger using stock of controlling corporation. The acquisition by one corporation, in exchange for stock of a corporation (referred to in this subparagraph as 'controlling corporation') which is in control of the acquiring corporation, of substantially all of the properties of another corporation which in the transaction is merged into the acquiring corporation shall not disqualify a transaction under paragraph (1)(A) if (i) such transaction would have qualified under paragraph (1)(A) if the merger had been into the controlling corporation, and (ii) no stock of the acquiring corporation is used in the transaction."

In 1978, P.L. 95-600, Sec. 701(j)(1)(A)(i), substituted "50 percent or more" for "more than 50 percent" in clause (a)(2)(F)(iii) . . . Sec. 701(j)(1)(A)(ii), substituted "80 percent or more" for "more than 80 percent" in clause (a)(2)(F)(iii) . . . Sec. 701(j)(1)(B), substituted "does not meet the requirements" for "is not diversified within the meaning" in clause (a)(2)(F)(vi) . . . Sec. 701(j)(1)(C), amended the second sentence of clause (a)(2)(F)(vi), effective for transfers made after 2/17/76 in tax. yrs. end. after 2/17/76, but not for transfers made in accordance

with a ruling issued by the Internal Revenue Service before 2/18/76, which held that a proposed transaction would be a reorganization described in para. (a)(1).
Prior to amendment, the second sentence of clause (a)(2)(F)(vi) read as follows:

"If such investment company acquires stock of another corporation in a reorganization described in section 368(a)(1)(B) (hereafter referred to as the 'actual acquisition'), clause (i) shall be applied to the shareholders and security holders of such investment company as though they had exchanged with such other corporation all of their stock in such investment company for a percentage of the value of the total outstanding stock of the other corporation equal to the percentage of the value of the total outstanding stock of such investment company which such shareholders own immediately after the actual acquisition."

—P.L. 95-600, Sec. 701(j)(1)(D), added new clauses (a)(2)(F)(vii) and (viii). Sec. 701(j)(2)(B) and (C) of this Act provided the following with respect to the effective dates of amendment made by 701(j)(1)(D):

"(B) Clause (viii) of section 368(a)(2)(F) of the Internal Revenue Code of 1954 (as added by paragraph (1)) shall apply only with respect to losses sustained after September 26, 1977.

"(C) Clause (vii) of section 368(a)(2)(F) of the Internal Revenue Code of 1954 (as added by paragraph (1)) shall apply only with respect to transfers made after September 26, 1977."

In 1976, P.L. 94-455, Sec. 806(f)(1), substituted "this part, and part V," for "and this part," in subsec. (c), effective for tax yrs. begin. after 6/30/78. [Repealed by Sec. 621(e)(1) of P.L. 99-514, see above.]

—P.L. 94-455, Sec. 2131(a), added subpara. (a)(2)(F), effective for transfers made after 2/17/76 in tax. yrs. end. after 2/17/76, but not for transfers made in accordance with a ruling issued by the Internal Revenue Service before 2/18/76, which held that a proposed transaction would be a reorganization described in para. (a)(1).

In 1971, P.L. 91-693, Sec. 1(a), added subpara. (a)(2)(E) . . . Sec. 1(b), added the last sentence of subsec. (b), effective for statutory mergers occurring after 12/31/70.

In 1968, P.L. 90-621, Sec. 1(a), added subpara. (a)(2)(D) . . . Sec. 1(b), added the last sentence of subsec. (b), effective for statutory mergers occurring after 10/22/68.

In 1964, P.L. 88-272, Sec. 218(a), added "(or in exchange solely for all or a part of the voting stock of a corporation which is in control of the acquiring corporation)" after "voting stock" in subpara. (a)(1)(B) . . . Sec. 218(b)(1), amended subpara. (a)(2)(C) . . . Sec. 218(b)(2), amended the last two sentences in subsec. (b), effective for transactions after 12/31/63 in tax. yrs. end. after 12/31/63.

Prior to amendment, subpara. (a)(2)(C) read as follows:

"(C) Transfers of assets to subsidiaries in certain paragraph (1)(A) and (1)(C) cases. A transaction otherwise qualifying under paragraph (1)(A) or paragraph (1)(C) shall not be disqualified by reason of the fact that part or all of the assets which were acquired in the transaction are transferred to a corporation controlled by the corporation acquiring such assets."

Prior to amendment, the last two sentences of subsec. (b) read as follows:

"In the case of a reorganization qualifying under paragraph (1)(C) of subsection (a), if the stock exchanged for the properties is stock of a corporation which is in control of the acquiring corporation, the term 'a party to a reorganization' includes the corporation so controlling the acquiring corporation. In the case of a reorganization qualifying under paragraph (1)(A) or (1)(C) of subsection (a) by reason of paragraph (2)(C) of subsection (a), the term 'a party to a reorganization' includes the corporation controlling the corporation to which the acquired assets are transferred."

PART IV.—INSOLVENCY REORGANIZATIONS [REPEALED]

Sec.
370. Repealed [Termination of part].
371. Repealed [Reorganization in certain receivership and bankruptcy proceedings].
372. Repealed [Basis in connection with certain receivership and bankruptcy proceedings].
373. Repealed. [Loss not recognized in certain railroad reorganizations.]
374. Repealed [Gain or loss not recognized in certain railroad reorganizations].

In 1990, P.L. 101-508, Sec. 11801(a)(19), repealed Part IV of Subchapter C of Chapter 1.
In 1980, P.L. 96-589, Sec. 4(h)(5), added item 370.
In 1976, P.L. 94-455, Sec. 1901(b)(14)(E), repealed item 373.
Prior to repeal, item 373 read as follows:
"373. Loss not recognized in certain railroad reorganizations."
In 1956, P.L. 628, Sec. 4, added item 374.

Sec. 370. Repealed.

In 1990, P.L. 101-508, Sec. 11801(a)(19), repealed Code Sec. 370 as part of the repeal of part IV of subchapter C of chapter 1, effective 11/5/90 except as provided in Sec. 11821(b) of this Act which reads as follows:
"(b) Savings provision.

"If—
"(1) any provision amended or repealed by this part applied to—
"(A) any transactions occurring before the date of the enactment of this Act [11/5/90],
"(B) any property acquired before such date of enactment, [11/5/90], or
"(C) any item of income, loss, deduction, or credit taken into account before such date of enactment, [11/5/90], and
"(2) the treatment of such transaction, property, or item under such provision would (without regard to the amendments made by this part) affect liability for tax for periods ending after such date of enactment, [11/5/90],
nothing in the amendments made by this part shall be construed to affect the treatment of such transaction, property, or item for purposes of determining liability for tax for periods ending after such date of enactment [11/5/90]."
Prior to repeal, Code Sec. 370 read as follows:
"Sec. 370. Termination of Part.
"(a) General rule.
"Except as provided in subsection (b), this part shall not apply to any proceeding which is begun after September 30, 1979.
"(b) Exceptions.
"Subsection (a) shall not apply to subsections (c) and (e) of section 374."
In 1980, P.L. 96-589, Sec. 4(f), added Code Sec. 370. Sec. 7(c) of this Act makes this amendment effective for any bankruptcy case or similar judicial proceeding begin. after 12/31/80.
Sec. 7(f) and (g) of this Act provides:
"(f) Election to substitute September 30, 1979, for December 31, 1980.—
"(1) In general. The debtor (or debtors) in a bankruptcy case or similar judicial proceeding may (with the approval of the court) elect to apply [subsection 7(c) of this Act] by substituting 'September 30, 1979' for 'December 31, 1980' each place it appears in such subsections.
"(2) Effect of election. Any election made under paragraph (1) with respect to any proceeding shall apply to all parties to the proceeding.
"(3) Revocation only with consent. Any election under this subsection may be revoked only with the consent of the Secretary of the Treasury or his delegate.
"(4) Time and manner of election. Any election under this subsection shall be made at such time, and in such manner, as the Secretary of the Treasury or his delegate may by regulations prescribe.
"(g) Definitions.
"For purposes of this section—
"(1) Bankruptcy case. The term 'bankruptcy case' means any case under title 11 of the United States Code (as recodified by P.L. 95-598).
"(2) Similar judicial proceeding. The term 'similar judicial proceeding' means a receivership, foreclosure, or similar proceeding in a Federal or State court (as modified by section 368(a)(3)(D) of the Internal Revenue Code of 1954)."

Sec. 371. Repealed.

In 1990, P.L. 101-508, Sec. 11801(a)(19), repealed Code Sec. 371, as part of the repeal of part IV of subchapter C of chapter 1, effective 11/5/90 except as provided in Sec. 11821(b) of this Act, reproduced in note following Code Sec. 370.
Prior to repeal, Code Sec. 371 read as follows:
"Sec. 371. Reorganization in certain receivership and bankruptcy proceedings.
"(a) Exchanges by corporations.
"(1) In general. No gain or loss shall be recognized if property of a corporation (other than a railroad corporation, as defined in section 77(m) of the Bankruptcy Act (11 U.S.C. 205)) is transferred in pursuance of an order of the court having jurisdiction of such corporation—
"(A) in a receivership, foreclosure, or similar proceeding, or
"(B) in a proceeding under chapter X of the Bankruptcy Act (11 U.S.C. 501 and following),
to another corporation organized or made use of to effectuate a plan of reorganization approved by the court in such proceeding, in exchange solely for stock or securities in such other corporation.
"(2) Gain from exchanges not solely in kind. If an exchange would be within the provisions of paragraph (1) if it were not for the fact that the property received in exchange consists not only of stock or securities permitted by paragraph (1) to be received without the recognition of gain, but also of other property or money, then—
"(A) if the corporation receiving such other property or money distributes it in pursuance of the plan of reorganization, no gain to the corporation shall be recognized from the exchange, but
"(B) if the corporation receiving such other property or money does not distribute it in pursuance of the plan of reorganization, the gain, if any, to the corporation shall be recognized, but in an amount not in excess of the sum of such money and the fair market value of such other property so received, which is not so distributed.
"(b) Exchanges by security holders.
"(1) In general. No gain or loss shall be recognized on an exchange consisting of the relinquishment or extinguishment of stock or securities in a corporation the plan of reorganization of which is approved by the court in a proceeding described in subsection (a), in consideration of the acquisition solely of stock or securities in a corporation organized or made use of to effectuate such plan of reorganization.
"(2) Gain from exchanges not solely in kind. If an exchange would be within the provisions of paragraph (1) if it were not for the fact that the property received in exchange consists not only of property permitted by paragraph (1) to be

received without the recognition of gain, but also of other property or money, then the gain, if any, to the recipient shall be recognized, but in an amount not in excess of the sum of such money and the fair market value of such other property.

"*(c) Loss from exchanges not solely in kind.*

"If an exchange would be within the provisions of subsection (a)(1) or (b)(1) if it were not for the fact that the property received in exchange consists not only of property permitted by subsection (a)(1) or (b)(1) to be received without the recognition of gain or loss, but also of other property or money, then no loss from the exchange shall be recognized.

"*(d) Assumption of liabilities.*

"In the case of a transaction involving an assumption of a liability or the acquisition of property subject to a liability, the rules provided in section 357 shall apply."

In **1976**, P.L. 94-455, Sec. 1901(a)(50), deleted "49 Stat. 922;", after "section 77(m) of the Bankruptcy Act", and substituted "(11 U.S.C. 501 and following)" for "(52 Stat. 883-905; 11 U.S.C., chapter 10) or the corresponding provisions of prior law" , in para. (a)(1), effective for tax. yrs. begin. after 12/31/76.

Sec. 372. Repealed.

In **1990**, P.L. 101-508, Sec. 11801(a)(19), repealed Code Sec. 372, as part of the repeal of part IV of subchapter C of chapter 1, effective 11/5/90 except as provided in Sec. 11821(b) of this Act reproduced in note following Code Sec. 370.
Prior to repeal, Code Sec. 372 read as follows:
"SEC. 372. BASIS IN CONNECTION WITH CERTAIN RECEIVERSHIP AND BANKRUPTCY PROCEEDINGS.

"*(a) Corporation.*

If property was acquired by a corporation in a transfer to which—

"(1) section 371(a) applies,

"(2) so much of section 371(c) as relates to section 371(a)(1) applies, or

"(3) the corresponding provisions of prior law apply,

then notwithstanding the provisions of section 270 of the Bankruptcy Act (11 U.S.C. 670), the basis in the hands of the acquiring corporation shall be the same as it would be in the hands of the corporation whose property was so acquired, increased in the amount of gain recognized to the corporation whose property was so acquired under the law applicable to the year in which the acquisition occurred, and such basis shall not be adjusted under section 1017 by reason of a discharge of indebtedness in pursuance of the plan of reorganization under which such transfer was made.

"*(b) Adjustment for depreciation sustained before March 1, 1913, in certain cases of property acquired from retirement method corporations.*

"(1) In general. If the taxpayer has acquired property in a transaction described in section 374(b), and if any such property constitutes retirement-straight line property, then, in determining the adjusted basis of all retirement-straight line property held by the taxpayer on his adjustment date, adjustment shall be made (in lieu of the adjustment provided in section 1016(a)(3)(A)) for depreciation sustained before March 1, 1913, on retirement-straight line property which was held on such date for which cost was or is claimed as basis, and which either—

"(A) Retired before acquisition by taxpayer. Was retired before the acquisition of the retirement-straight line property by the taxpayer, but only if a deduction was allowed in computing net income by reason of such retirement, and such deduction was computed on the basis of cost without adjustment for depreciation sustained before March 1, 1913. In the case of any such property retired during any taxable year beginning after December 31, 1929, the adjustment under this subparagraph shall not exceed that portion of the amount attributable to depreciation sustained before March 1, 1913, which resulted (by reason of the deduction so allowed) in a reduction in taxes under this subtitle or prior income, war-profits, or excess-profits tax laws.

"(B) Acquired by taxpayer. Was acquired by the taxpayer.

"The adjustment determined under this paragraph shall be allocated (in the manner prescribed by the Secretary) among all retirement-straight line property held by the taxpayer on his adjustment date. Such adjustment shall apply to all periods on and after the adjustment date.

"(2) Retirement-straight line property defined. For purposes of this subsection, the term 'retirement-straight line property' means any property of a kind or class with respect to which (A) the corporation transferring such property to the taxpayer was using (at the time of transfer) the retirement method of computing the allowance of deductions for depreciation, and (B) the acquiring corporation has adopted any other method of computing such allowance.

"(3) Other definitions. For purposes of this subsection:

"(A) Depreciation. The term 'depreciation' means exhaustion, wear and tear, and obsolescence.

"(B) Adjustment date. In the case of any kind or class of property, the term 'adjustment date' means whichever of the following is the later:

"(i) the first day of the taxpayer's first taxable year beginning after December 31, 1955, or

"(ii) the first day of the first taxable year in which the taxpayer uses a method of computing the allowance of deductions for depreciation other than the retirement method.

"*(c) Stock or security holder.*

For basis of stock or securities acquired under section 371(b), see section 358."

In **1976**, P.L. 94-455, Sec. 1901(a)(51), deleted "54 Stat. 709;", before "11 U.S.C. 670", in subsec. (a), effective for tax. yrs. begin. after 12/31/76.

—P.L. 94-455, Sec. 1901(b)(14)(A), deleted "373(b) or", before "374(b),", in para. (b)(1), effective for tax. yrs. begin. after 12/31/76.

—P.L. 94-455, Sec. 1906(b)(13)(A), substituted "Secretary" for "Secretary or his delegate" in para. (b)(1), effective for tax. yrs. begin. after 12/31/76.

In **1958**, P.L. 85-866, Sec. 95(a), redesignated subsec. (b) as subsec. (c) and added a new subsec. (b), effective for tax. yrs. begin. after 12/31/55, except as provided in Sec. 95(b)(2) of this Act which reads as follows:

"(2) Exception. The amendments made by subsection (a) shall not apply with respect to any taxpayer if, before the date of the enactment of this Act [9/2/58], there has been a determination for any taxable year, of the adjusted basis of retirement-straight line property of the taxpayer of the type described in section 372(b) of the Internal Revenue Code of 1954 (as added by subsection (a) by the Tax Court of the United States, or by any other court of competent jurisdiction, in any proceeding in which the decision of the court became final after December 31, 1955, and which established the right of the taxpayer to use the straight line depreciation method of computing the annual depreciation allowance with respect to such property for Federal tax purposes for any year."

Sec. 373. Repealed.

In **1976**, P.L. 94-455, Sec. 1901(a)(52), repealed Code Sec. 373, effective for tax. yrs. begin. after 12/31/76.
Prior to repeal, Code Sec. 373 read as follows:
"SEC. 373. LOSS NOT RECOGNIZED IN CERTAIN RAILROAD REORGANIZATIONS.

"*(a) Nonrecognition of loss.*

"No loss shall be recognized if property of a railroad corporation, as defined in section 77(m) of the Bankruptcy Act (49 Stat. 922; 11 U.S.C. 205), is transferred before August 1, 1955, in pursuance of an order of the court having jurisdiction of such corporation—

"(1) in a receivership proceeding, or

"(2) in a proceeding under section 77 of the Bankruptcy Act,

to a railroad corporation (as defined in section 77(m) of the Bankruptcy Act) organized or made use of to effectuate a plan of reorganization approved by the court in such proceeding.

"*(b) Basis.*

"(1) Railroad corporations. If the property of a railroad corporation (as defined in section 77(m) of the Bankruptcy Act) was acquired after December 31, 1938, and before August 1, 1955, in pursuance of an order of the court having jurisdiction of such corporation—

"(A) in a receivership proceeding, or

"(B) in a proceeding under section 77 of the Bankruptcy Act,

and the acquiring corporation is a railroad corporation (as defined in section 77(m) of the Bankruptcy Act) organized or made use of to effectuate a plan of reorganization approved by the court in such proceeding, the basis shall be the same as it would be in the hands of the railroad corporation whose property was so acquired.

"(2) Property acquired by street, suburban, or interurban electric railway corporation. If the property of any street, suburban, or interurban electric railway corporation engaged as a common carrier in the transportation of persons or property in interstate commerce was acquired after December 31, 1934, in pursuance of an order of the court having jurisdiction of such corporation in a proceeding under section 77B of the Bankruptcy Act (48 Stat. 912), and the acquiring corporation is a street, suburban, or interurban electric railway engaged as a common carrier in the transportation of persons or property in interstate commerce, organized or made use of to effectuate a plan of reorganization approved by the court in such proceeding, then, notwithstanding the provisions of section 270 of the Bankruptcy Act (52 Stat. 904; 11 U.S.C. 670), the basis shall be the same as it would be in the hands of the corporation whose property was so acquired."

In **1956**, P.L. 628, Sec. 3(1), substituted "transferred before August 1, 1955, in pursuance" for "transferred in pursuance" in subsec. (a) . . . Sec. 3(2), substituted "December 31, 1938, and before August 1, 1955," for "December 31, 1938" in subsec. (b)(1).

Sec. 374. Repealed.

In **1990**, P.L. 101-508, Sec. 11801(a)(19), repealed Code Sec. 374, as part of the repeal of Part IV of Subchapter C of Chapter 1, effective 11/5/90 except as provided in Sec. 11821(b) of this Act reproduced in note following Code Sec. 370.
Prior to repeal, Code Sec. 374 read as follows:
"SEC. 374. GAIN OR LOSS NOT RECOGNIZED IN CERTAIN RAILROAD REORGANIZATIONS.

"*(a) Exchanges by corporations.*

"(1) Nonrecognition of gain or loss. No gain or loss shall be recognized if property of a railroad corporation, as defined in section 77(m) of the Bankruptcy Act (11 U.S.C. 205), is transferred after July 31, 1955, in pursuance of an order of the court having jurisdiction of such corporation—

"(A) in a receivership proceeding, or

"(B) in a proceeding under section 77 of the Bankruptcy Act,

to another railroad corporation (as defined in section 77(m) of the Bankruptcy Act) organized or made use of to effectuate a plan of reorganization approved by the court in such proceeding, in exchange solely for stock or securities in such other railroad corporation.

"(2) Gain from exchanges not solely in kind. If an exchange would be within the provisions of paragraph (1) if it were not for the fact that the property received in exchange consists not only of stock or securities permitted by paragraph (1) to be received without the recognition of gain, but also of other property or money, then—

"(A) if the corporation receiving such other property or money distributes it in pursuance of the plan of reorganization, no gain to the corporation shall be recognized from the exchange, but

"(B) if the corporation receiving such other property or money does not distribute it in pursuance of the plan of reorganization, the gain, if any, to the corporation shall be recognized, but in an amount not in excess of the sum of such money and the fair market value of such other property so received, which is not so distributed.

"(3) Loss from exchanges not solely in kind. If an exchange would be within the provisions of paragraph (1) if it were not for the fact that the property received in exchange consists not only of property permitted by such paragraph to be received without the recognition of gain or loss, but also of other property or money, then no loss from the exchange shall be recognized.

"(b) Basis.

"(1) Railroad corporations. If the property of a railroad corporation, as defined in section 77(m) of the Bankruptcy Act (11 U.S.C. 205(m)), was acquired before December 31, 1938, in pursuance of an order of the court having jurisdiction of such corporation—

"(A) in a receivership proceeding, or

"(B) in a proceeding under section 77 of the Bankruptcy Act,

and the acquiring corporation is a railroad corporation (as defined in section 77(m) of the Bankruptcy Act) organized or made use of to effectuate a plan of reorganization approved by the court in such proceeding, the basis shall be the same as it would be in the hands of the railroad corporation whose property was so acquired, increased in the amount of gain recognized under subsection (a)(2) to the transferor on such transfer.

"(2) Property acquired by street, suburban, or interurban electric railway corporation. If the property of a street, suburban, or interurban electric railway corporation engaged as a common carrier in the transportation of persons or property in interstate commerce was acquired after December 31, 1934, in pursuance of an order of the court having jurisdiction of such corporation in a proceeding under section 77 of the Bankruptcy Act (11 U.S.C. 501 and following), and the acquiring corporation is a street, suburban, or interurban electric railway engaged as a common carrier in the transportation of persons or property in interstate commerce, organized or made use of to effectuate a plan of reorganization approved by the court in such proceeding, then, notwithstanding the provisions of section 270 of the Bankruptcy Act (11 U.S.C. 670), the basis shall be the same as it would be in the hands of the corporation whose property was so acquired.

"(c) Exchanges under the final system plan for ConRail.

"(1) In general. No gain or loss shall be recognized if, in order to carry out the final system plan, rail properties of a transferor railroad corporation are transferred to the Consolidated Rail Corporation (or any subsidiary thereof) pursuant to an order of the special court under section 303 or 305(d) of the Regional Rail Reorganization Act of 1973 in exchange solely for stock of the Consolidated Rail Corporation, securities of such Corporation, certificates of value of the United States Railway Association, or any combination thereof.

"(2) Exchanges not solely in kind. If paragraph (1) would apply to an exchange if it were not for the fact that the property received in exchange consists not only of property permitted by paragraph (1) to be received without the recognition of gain or loss, but also of other property or money, then rules similar to the rules set forth in paragraph (2) or (3) of subsection (a) (whichever is appropriate) shall be applied.

"(3) Basis. The basis of the property transferred to the Consolidated Rail Corporation (or any subsidiary thereof) in an exchange to which paragraph (1) or (2) applies shall be determined under rules similar to the rules set forth in subsection (b)(1).

"(4) Denial of net operating loss carryovers to ConRail. Neither the Consolidated Rail Corporation nor any subsidiary thereof shall succeed to any net operating loss carryover of any transferor railroad corporation.

"(5) Definitions. For purposes of this subsection—

"(A) Rail properties. The term 'rail properties' means rail properties within the meaning of paragraph (12) of section 102 of the Regional Rail Reorganization Act of 1973.

"(B) Transferor railroad corporation. The term 'transferor railroad corporation' means a corporation which, on March 11, 1976, was—

"(i) a railroad in reorganization (within the meaning of paragraph (14) of section 102 of the Regional Rail Reorganization Act of 1973) in the region (within the meaning of paragraph (15) of such section 102), or

"(ii) a corporation leased, operated, or controlled by such a railroad in reorganization.

"(C) Final system plan. The term 'final system plan' means the final system plan (within the meaning of paragraph (6) of section 102 of such Act). Such term includes supplemental transactions under section 305 of such Act.

"(D) Subsidiary. The term 'subsidiary' means any corporation 100 percent of whose total combined voting shares are, directly or indirectly, owned or controlled by the Consolidated Rail Corporation.

"(d) Assumption of liabilities.

In the case of a transaction involving an assumption of a liability or the acquisition of property subject to a liability, the rules provided in section 357 shall apply.

"(e) Use of expired net operating loss carryovers to offset income arising from certain railroad reorganization proceedings.

"(1) In general. If—

"(A) any corporation receives or accrues any amount pursuant to—

"(i) an award in (or settlement of) a proceeding under section 77 of the Bankruptcy Act,

"(ii) an award in (or settlement of) a proceeding before the special court to carry out section 303(c), 305, or 306 of the Regional Rail Reorganization Act of 1973,

"(iii) an award in (or settlement of) a proceeding in the United States Claims Court under section 1491 of title 28 of the United States Code, to the extent such proceeding involves a claim arising under the Regional Rail Reorganization Act of 1973, or

"(iv) a redemption of a certificate of value of the United States Railway Association issued under section 306 of such act to such corporation (or issued to another member of the same affiliated group (within the meaning of section 1504) as such corporation for their taxable years which included March 31, 1976),

"(B) any portion of such amount is includible in the gross income of such corporation for the taxable year in which such portion is received or accrued, and such taxable year begins not more than 5 years after the date of such award, settlement, or redemption, and

"(C) the net operating loss of such corporation for any taxable year—

"(i) was a net operating loss carryover to, or arose in, the first taxable year of such corporation ending after March 31, 1976 (or, in the case of a proceeding referred to in subparagraph (A)(i) which began after March 31, 1976, ending after the beginning of such proceeding), but

"(ii) solely by reason of the lapse of time, is not a net operating loss carryover to the taxable year referred to in subparagraph (B),

then such net operating loss shall be a net operating loss carryover to the taxable year described in subparagraph (B) but only for use (to the extent not theretofore used under this subsection to offset other amounts) to offset the portion referred to in subparagraph (B).

"(2) Special rule. For purposes of paragraph (1)(C)(i), a corporation which was a regulated transportation corporation (within the meaning of 172(g)) for its last taxable year ending on or before March 31, 1976, shall be treated as such a regulated transportation corporation for its first taxable year ending after such date."

In 1986, P.L. 99-514, Sec. 1899A(9), substituted "United States Claims Court" for "Court of Claims" in clause (e)(1)(A)(iii), effective 10/22/86.

In 1980, P.L. 96-613, Sec. 4, provides:

"SEC. 4. RESTORATION OF CERTAIN NET OPERATING LOSS CARRYOVERS TO RAILROADS IN CONRAIL PROCEEDINGS WHERE OTHER MEMBERS OF CONSOLIDATED GROUP HAD INCOME BECAUSE OF STOCK DISPOSITION.

"(a) In general.

For purposes of subsection (e) of section 374 of the Internal Revenue Code of 1954 (relating to use of expired net operating loss carryovers to offset income arising from certain railroad reorganization proceedings), if—

"(1) subparagraphs (A) and (B) of paragraph (1) of such subsection are satisfied with respect to a corporation,

"(2) such corporation had a net operating loss for a taxable year which would have satisfied the requirements of clause (i) of subparagraph (C) of such paragraph (1) but for the fact that such net operating loss was used to reduce the income of an affiliated group of corporations which filed a consolidated return, and

"(3) any portion of the amount so used was included in an excess loss account which was required to be restored to the income of a member or members of the affiliated group, (or would be required to be so restored but for an election under Regulation § 1.1502-19(a)(6)),

then an amount equal to the restoration amount shall be treated as meeting the requirements of subparagraph (C) of such paragraph (1).

"(b) Restoration amount defined.—

"(1) In general. For purposes of subsection (a), the term 'restoration amount' means, with respect to the net operating loss for any taxable year, an amount equal to the sum of—

"(A) so much of the portion referred to in subsection (a)(3) as was required to be treated as ordinary income, and

"(B) an amount equal to so much of such portion as was required to be treated as long-term capital gain, multiplied by the capital gain conversion fraction.

"(2) Capital gain conversion fraction. For purposes of paragraph (1), the capital gain conversion fraction is a fraction—

"(A) the numerator of which is the rate of tax set forth in section 1201(a)(2) of such Code for the taxable year the portion was required to be included in income, and

"(B) the denominator of which is the highest rate of tax set forth in section 11(b) of such Code for such taxable year.

"(3) FIFO rule for additions to excess loss account. For purposes of this subsection, the amount in any excess loss account at the time of restoration (and the ordinary income portion of the restoration) shall be treated as attributable to net operating losses in the order of the years in which the respective net operating losses arose.

"(4) Capital gain treatment. For purposes of paragraph (1), any amount to which an election under Regulation § 1.1502-19(a)(6) applies shall be treated as long-term capital gain.

"(c) Effective date.

This section shall apply to restorations occurring after March 31, 1976."

—P.L. 96-222, Sec. 103(a)(14), substituted "March 31, 1976" for "March 31, 1967" in clause (e)(1)(A)(iv), effective for tax. yrs. ending after 3/31/76.

In 1978, P.L. 95-600, Sec. 369(a), amended clause (e)(1)(A)(iv), effective for tax. yrs. ending after 3/31/76.

Prior to amendment, clause (e)(1)(A)(iv) read as follows:

"(iv) a redemption of a certificate of value of the United States Railway Association issued to such corporation under section 306 of such Act,"

In 1976, P.L. 94-455, Sec. 1901(a)(53), deleted "49 Stat. 922" before "11 U.S.C. 205" in para. (a)(1) ... Sec. 1901(b)(14)(B), designated subsec. (b) as para. (b)(1),

1,843

added para. (b)(2) and substituted "December 31, 1938" for "July 31, 1955" in para. (b)(1), as redesignated, effective for tax. yrs. begin. after 12/31/76.
—P.L. 94-455, Sec. 1901(b)(10)(A), substituted "172(g)" for "section 172(j)" in para. (e)(2), for tax. yrs. end. after 10/4/76.
—P.L. 94-253, Sec. 1(a), redesignated subsec. (c) as subsec. (d) and added new subsec. (c) . . . Sec. 1(d), added subsec. (e), effective for tax. yrs. end. after 3/31/76.
In 1956, ch. 463, Sec. 1, added Code Sec. 374.

PART V.—CARRYOVERS

Sec.
381. Carryovers in certain corporate acquisitions.
382. Limitation on net operating loss carryforwards and certain built-in losses following ownership change.
383. Special limitations on certain excess credits, etc.
384. Limitation on use of preacquisition losses to offset built-in gains.

In 1987, P.L. 100-203, Sec. 10226(b), added item 384.
In 1986, P.L. 99-514, Sec. 621(c)(2)(A), amended item 382 . . . Sec. 621(c)(2)(B), amended item 383.
Prior to amendment, item 382 read as follows:
"382. Special limitations on net operating loss carryovers."
Prior to amendment, item 383 read as follows:
"383. Special limitations on unused business credits, research credits, foreign taxes, and capital losses."
In 1984, P.L. 98-369, Sec. 474(r)(12)(C), amended item 383.
Prior to amendment, item 383 read as follows:
"383. Special limitations on carryovers of unused investment credits, work incentive program credits, new employee credits, alcohol fuel credits, research credits, employee stock ownership credits, foreign taxes, and capital losses."
In 1981, P.L. 97-34, Sec. 221(b)(1)(E), added "alcohol fuel credits, research credits," after "new employee credits," in item 383 . . . Sec. 331(d)(1)(E), added "employee stock ownership credits," after "research credits," in item 383.
In 1977, P.L. 95-30, Sec. 202(d)(3)(D), substituted "work incentive program credits, new employee credits," for "work incentive program credits," in item 383.
In 1971, P.L. 92-178, Sec. 302(b), added item 383.

Sec. 381. Carryovers in certain corporate acquisitions.
(a) General rule.
In the case of the acquisition of assets of a corporation by another corporation—
(1) in a distribution to such other corporation to which section 332 (relating to liquidations of subsidiaries) applies; or
(2) in a transfer to which section 361 (relating to nonrecognition of gain or loss to corporations) applies, but only if the transfer is in connection with a reorganization described in subparagraph (A), (C), (D), (F), or (G) of section 368(a)(1),
the acquiring corporation shall succeed to and take into account, as of the close of the day of distribution or transfer, the items described in subsection (c) of the distributor or transferor corporation, subject to the conditions and limitations specified in subsections (b) and (c). For purposes of the preceding sentence, a reorganization shall be treated as meeting the requirements of subparagraph (D) or (G) of section 368(a)(1) only if the requirements of subparagraphs (A) and (B) of section 354(b)(1) are met.

(b) Operating rules.
Except in the case of an acquisition in connection with a reorganization described in subparagraph (F) of section 368(a)(1)—
(1) The taxable year of the distributor or transferor corporation shall end on the date of distribution or transfer.
(2) For purposes of this section, the date of distribution or transfer shall be the day on which the distribution or transfer is completed; except that, under regulations prescribed by the Secretary, the date when substantially all of the property has been distributed or transferred may be used if the distributor or transferor corporation ceases all operations, other than liquidating activities, after such date.
(3) The corporation acquiring property in a distribution or transfer described in subsection (a) shall not be entitled to carry back a net operating loss or a net capital loss for a taxable year ending after the date of distribution or transfer to a taxable year of the distributor or transferor corporation.

(c) Items of the distributor or transferor corporation.
The items referred to in subsection (a) are:
(1) Net operating loss carryovers. The net operating loss carryovers determined under section 172, subject to the following conditions and limitations:
(A) The taxable year of the acquiring corporation to which the net operating loss carryovers of the distributor or transferor corporation are first carried shall be the first taxable year ending after the date of distribution or transfer.
(B) In determining the net operating loss deduction, the portion of such deduction attributable to the net operating loss carryovers of the distributor or transferor corporation to the first taxable year of the acquiring corporation ending after the date of distribution or transfer shall be limited to an amount which bears the same ratio to the taxable income (determined without regard to a net operating loss deduction) of the acquiring corporation in such taxable year as the number of days in the taxable year after the date of distribution or transfer bears to the total number of days in the taxable year.
(C) For the purpose of determining the amount of the net operating loss carryovers under section 172(b)(2), a net operating loss for a taxable year (hereinafter in this subparagraph referred to as the "loss year") of a distributor or transferor corporation which ends on or before the end of a loss year of the acquiring corporation shall be considered to be a net operating loss for a year prior to such loss year of the acquiring corporation. For the same purpose, the taxable income for a "prior taxable year" (as the term is used in section 172(b)(2)) shall be computed as provided in such section; except that, if the date of distribution or transfer is on a day other than the last day of a taxable year of the acquiring corporation—
(i) such taxable year shall (for the purpose of this subparagraph only) be considered to be 2 taxable years (hereinafter in this subparagraph referred to as the "pre-acquisition part year" and the "post-acquisition part year");
(ii) the pre-acquisition part year shall begin on the same day as such taxable year begins and shall end on the date of distribution or transfer;
(iii) the post-acquisition part year shall begin on the day following the date of distribution or transfer and shall end on the same day as the end of such taxable year;
(iv) the taxable income for such taxable year (computed with the modifications specified in section 172(b)(2)(A) but without a net operating loss deduction) shall be divided between the pre-acquisition part year and the post-acquisition part year in proportion to the number of days in each;
(v) the net operating loss deduction for the pre-acquisition part year shall be determined as provided in section 172(b)(2)(B), but without regard to a net operating loss year of the distributor or transferor corporation; and

(vi) the net operating loss deduction for the post-acquisition part year shall be determined as provided in section 172(b)(2)(B).

(2) Earnings and profits. In the case of a distribution or transfer described in subsection (a)—

(A) the earnings and profits or deficit in earnings and profits, as the case may be, of the distributor or transferor corporation shall, subject to subparagraph (B), be deemed to have been received or incurred by the acquiring corporation as of the close of the date of the distribution or transfer; and

(B) a deficit in earnings and profits of the distributor, transferor, or acquiring corporation shall be used only to offset earnings and profits accumulated after the date of transfer. For this purpose, the earnings and profits for the taxable year of the acquiring corporation in which the distribution or transfer occurs shall be deemed to have been accumulated after such distribution or transfer in an amount which bears the same ratio to the undistributed earnings and profits of the acquiring corporation for such taxable year (computed without regard to any earnings and profits received from the distributor or transferor corporation, as described in subparagraph (A) of this paragraph) as the number of days in the taxable year after the date of distribution or transfer bears to the total number of days in the taxable year.

(3) Capital loss carryover. The capital loss carryover determined under section 1212, subject to the following conditions and limitations:

(A) The taxable year of the acquiring corporation to which the capital loss carryover of the distributor or transferor corporation is first carried shall be the first taxable year ending after the date of distribution or transfer.

(B) The capital loss carryover shall be a short-term capital loss in the taxable year determined under subparagraph (A) but shall be limited to an amount which bears the same ratio to the capital gain net income (determined without regard to a short-term capital loss attributable to capital loss carryover), if any, of the acquiring corporation in such taxable year as the number of days in the taxable year after the date of distribution or transfer bears to the total number of days in the taxable year.

(C) For purposes of determining the amount of such capital loss carryover to taxable years following the taxable year determined under subparagraph (A), the capital gain net income in the taxable year determined under subparagraph (A) shall be considered to be an amount equal to the amount determined under subparagraph (B).

(4) Method of accounting. The acquiring corporation shall use the method of accounting used by the distributor or transferor corporation on the date of distribution or transfer unless different methods were used by several distributor or transferor corporations or by a distributor or transferor corporation and the acquiring corporation. If different methods were used, the acquiring corporation shall use the method or combination of methods of computing taxable income adopted pursuant to regulations prescribed by the Secretary.

(5) Inventories. In any case in which inventories are received by the acquiring corporation, such inventories shall be taken by such corporation (in determining its income) on the same basis on which such inventories were taken by the distributor or transferor corporation, unless different methods were used by several distributor or transferor corporations or by a distributor or transferor corporation and the acquiring corporation. If different methods were used, the acquiring corporation shall use the method or combination of methods of taking inventory adopted pursuant to regulations prescribed by the Secretary.

(6) Method of computing depreciation allowance. The acquiring corporation shall be treated as the distributor or transferor corporation for purposes of computing the depreciation allowance under sections 167 and 168 on property acquired in a distribution or transfer with respect to so much of the basis in the hands of the acquiring corporation as does not exceed the adjusted basis in the hands of the distributor or transferor corporation.

(7) Repealed.

(8) Installment method. If the acquiring corporation acquires installment obligations (the income from which the distributor or transferor corporation reports on the installment basis under section 453) the acquiring corporation shall, for purposes of section 453, be treated as if it were the distributor or transferor corporation.

(9) Amortization of bond discount or premium. If the acquiring corporation assumes liability for bonds of the distributor or transferor corporation issued at a discount or premium, the acquiring corporation shall be treated as the distributor or transferor corporation after the date of distribution or transfer for purposes of determining the amount of amortization allowable or includible with respect to such discount or premium.

(10) Treatment of certain mining development and exploration expenses of distributor or transferor corporation. The acquiring corporation shall be entitled to deduct, as if it were the distributor or transferor corporation, expenses deferred under section 616 (relating to certain development expenditures) if the distributor or transferor corporation has so elected.

(11) Contributions to pension plans, employees' annuity plans, and stock bonus and profit-sharing plans. The acquiring corporation shall be considered to be the distributor or transferor corporation after the date of distribution or transfer for the purpose of determining the amounts deductible under section 404 with respect to pension plans, employees' annuity plans, and stock bonus and profit-sharing plans.

(12) Recovery of tax benefit items. If the acquiring corporation is entitled to the recovery of any amounts previously deducted by (or allowable as credits to) the distributor or transferor corporation, the acquiring corporation shall succeed to the treatment under section 111 which would apply to such amounts in the hands of the distributor or transferor corporation.

(13) Involuntary conversions under section 1033. The acquiring corporation shall be treated as the distributor or transferor corporation after the date of distribution or transfer for purposes of applying section 1033.

(14) Dividend carryover to personal holding company. The dividend carryover (described in section 564) to taxable years ending after the date of distribution or transfer.

(15) Repealed.

(16) Certain obligations of distributor or transferor corporation. If the acquiring corporation—

(A) assumes an obligation of the distributor or transferor corporation which, after the date of the distribution or transfer, gives rise to a liability, and

(B) such liability, if paid or accrued by the distributor or transferor corporation, would have been deductible in computing its taxable income, the acquiring corporation shall be entitled to deduct such items when paid or accrued, as the case may be, as if such corporation were the distributor or transferor corporation. A corporation which would have been an acquiring corporation under this section if the date of distribution or transfer had occurred on or after the effective date of the provisions of this subchapter applicable to a liquidation or reorganization, as the case may be, shall be entitled, even though the date of distribution or transfer occurred before such effective date, to apply this paragraph with respect to amounts paid or accrued in taxable years beginning after December 31, 1953, on account of such obligations of the distributor or transferor corporation. This paragraph shall not apply if such obligations are reflected in the amount of stock, securities, or property transferred by the acquiring corporation to the transferor corporation for the property of the transferor corporation.

(17) Deficiency dividend of personal holding company. If the acquiring corporation pays a deficiency dividend (as defined in section 547(d)) with respect to the distributor or transferor corporation, such distributor or transferor corporation shall, with respect to such payments, be entitled to the deficiency dividend deduction provided in section 547.

(18) Percentage depletion on extraction of ores or minerals from the waste or residue of prior mining. The acquiring corporation shall be considered to be the distributor or transferor corporation for the purpose of determining the applicability of section 613(c)(3) (relating to extraction of ores or minerals from the ground).

(19) Charitable contributions in excess of prior years' limitation. Contributions made in the taxable year ending on the date of distribution or transfer and the 4 prior taxable years by the distributor or transferor corporation in excess of the amount deductible under section 170(b)(2) for such taxable years shall be deductible by the acquiring corporation for its taxable years which begin after the date of distribution or transfer, subject to the limitations imposed in section 170(b)(2). In applying the preceding sentence, each taxable year of the distributor or transferor corporation beginning on or before the date of distribution or transfer shall be treated as a prior taxable year with reference to the acquiring corporation's taxable years beginning after such date.

(20) Repealed.

(21) Repealed.

(22) Successor insurance company. If the acquiring corporation is an insurance company taxable under subchapter L, there shall be taken into account (to the extent proper to carry out the purposes of this section and of subchapter L, and under such regulations as may be prescribed by the Secretary) the items required to be taken into account for purposes of subchapter L in respect of the distributor or transferor corporation.

(23) Deficiency dividend of regulated investment company or real estate investment trust. If the acquiring corporation pays a deficiency dividend (as defined in section 860(f)) with respect to the distributor or transferor corporation, such distributor or transferor corporation shall, with respect to such payments, be entitled to the deficiency dividend deduction provided in section 860.

(24) Credit under section 38. The acquiring corporation shall take into account (to the extent proper to carry out the purposes of this section and section 38, and under such regulations as may be prescribed by the Secretary) the items required to be taken into account for purposes of section 38 in respect of the distributor or transferor corporation.

(25) Credit under section 53. The acquiring corporation shall take into account (to the extent proper to carry out the purposes of this section and section 53, and under such regulations as may be prescribed by the Secretary) the items required to be taken into account for purposes of section 53 in respect of the distributor or transferor corporation.

(26) Enterprise zone provisions. The acquiring corporation shall take into account (to the extent proper to carry out the purposes of this section and subchapter U, and under such regulations as may be prescribed by the Secretary) the items required to be taken into account for purposes of subchapter U in respect of the distributor or transferor corporation.

(d) Operations loss carrybacks and carryovers of life insurance companies.

For application of this part to operations loss carrybacks and carryovers of life insurance companies, see section 810.

In 1996, P.L. 104-188, Sec. 1704(t)(26), amended Sec. 7841(d)(10) of P.L. 101-239, by substituting "section 381(c)" for "section 381(a)", see below.
In 1993, P.L. 103-66, Sec. 13302(e), added para. (c)(26), effective 8/10/93.
In 1990, P.L. 101-508, Sec. 11801(c)(10)(A), repealed para. (c)(15), effective 11/5/90, except as provided in Sec. 11821(b) of this Act, reproduced in note following Code Sec. 545.
Prior to repeal, para. (c)(15) read as follows:
"(15) Indebtedness of certain personal holding companies. The acquiring corporation shall be considered to be the distributor or transferor corporation for the purpose of determining the applicability of subsection (c) of section 545, relating to deduction with respect to payment of certain indebtedness."
—P.L. 101-508, Sec. 11812(b)(6)(A), substituted "sections 167 and 168" for "subsections (b), (j), and (k) of section 167" in para. (c)(6)... Sec. 11812(b)(6)(B), deleted para. (c)(24) and redesignated paras. (c)(25) and (c)(26) as paras. (c)(24) and (c)(25), effective for property placed in service after 11/5/90, except as provided in Sec. 11812(c)(2) of this Act, reproduced in note following Code Sec. 42.
Prior to repeal, para. (c)(24) read as follows:
"(24) Method of computing depreciation deduction. The acquiring corporation shall be treated as the distributor or transferor corporation for purposes of computing the deduction allowable under section 168(a) on property acquired in a distribution or transfer with respect to so much of the basis in the hands of the acquiring corporation as does not exceed the adjusted basis in the hands of the distributor or transferor corporation."
In 1989, P.L. 101-239, Sec. 7841(d)(10), [as amended by Sec. 1704(t)(26) of P.L. 104-188, see above] redesignated para. (c)(27) as para. (c)(26), effective 12/19/89.
In 1988, P.L. 100-647, Sec. 1002(a)(13), substituted "depreciation deduction" for "recovery allowance for recovery property", in the heading of para. (c)(24), effective for property placed in service after 12/31/86 in tax. yrs. end. after 12/31/86. For special provisions, see Sec. 203(a)(1)(B) of P.L. 99-514, reproduced at Code Sec. 168.
In 1987, P.L. 100-203, Sec. 10202(c)(3), deleted "or 453A" after "453", each place it appeared in para. (c)(8), effective for dispositions in tax. yrs. begin. after 12/31/87, except as provided by Sec. 10202(e)(3)(A) which reads:
"(3) Special rule for nondealers.—
"(A) Election.— A taxpayer may elect, at such time and in such manner as the Secretary of the Treasury or his delegate may prescribe, to have the amendments made by subsections (a) and (c) apply to taxable years ending after December 31, 1986, with respect to dispositions and pledges occurring after August 16, 1986."
In 1986, P.L. 99-514, Sec. 221(d)(2), amended Sec. 221(d) of P.L. 97-34, the effective date for changes made by Sec. 221(b)(1)(A) of P.L. 97-34, by substituting "amounts paid or incurred after June 30, 1981" for "amounts paid or incurred after June 30, 1981 and before January 1, 1986" [see below].
—P.L. 99-514, Sec. 231(d)(3)(F), deleted para. (c)(25) and redesignated paras. (c)(26) as (c)(25), effective for tax. yrs. begin. after 12/31/85.
Prior to deletion, para. (c)(25) read as follows:
"(25) Credit under section 30. The acquiring corporation shall take into account (to the extent proper to carry out the purposes of this section and section 30, and under such regulations as may be prescribed by the Secretary) the items required to be taken into account for purposes of section 30 in respect of the distributor or transferor corporation."
—P.L. 99-514, Sec. 411(b)(2)(C)(iii), deleted the last sentence of para. (c)(10), effective for costs paid or incurred after 12/31/86, in tax. yrs. end. after 12/31/86
Prior to deletion, the last sentence of para. (c)(10) read as follows:
"For the purpose of applying the limitation provided in section 617(h), if, for any taxable year, the distributor or transferor corporation was allowed a deduction under section 617(a), the acquiring corporation shall be deemed to have been allowed such deduction."
—P.L. 99-514, Sec. 701(e)(1), added para. (c)(27) [sic (c)(26)], effective for tax. yrs. begin. after 12/31/86.
—P.L. 99-514, Sec. 1812(a)(3), amended para. (c)(12), effective for amounts recovered after 12/31/83, in tax. yrs. end. after 12/31/83.

Prior to amendment, para. (c)(12) read as follows:

"(12) Recovery of bad debts, prior taxes, or delinquency amounts. If the acquiring corporation is entitled to the recovery of bad debts, prior taxes, or delinquency amounts previously deducted or credited by the distributor or transferor corporation, the acquiring corporation shall include in its income such amounts as would have been includible by the distributor or transferor corporation in accordance with section 111 (relating to the recovery of bad debts, prior taxes, and delinquency amounts)."

In 1984, P.L. 98-369, Sec. 211(b)(4), substituted "section 810" for "section 812(f)" in subsec. (d), effective for tax. yrs. begin. after 12/31/83.

—P.L. 98-369, Sec. 474(r)(11)(A), deleted paras. (c)(23), (c)(24), (c)(26), (c)(27), and (c)(30) . . . Sec. 474(r)(11)(B), redesignated paras. (c)(25), (c)(28), and (c)(29) as paras. (c)(23), (c)(24) and (c)(25) . . . Sec. 474(r)(11)(C), substituted "30" for "44F" each place it appeared in para. (c)(25) (as redesignated by Sec. 474(r)(11)(B) of this Act) . . . Sec. 474(r)(11)(D), added para. (c)(26), effective for tax. yrs. begin. after 12/31/83, and to carrybacks from tax. yrs. begin. after 12/31/83.

Prior to deletion, paras. (c)(23), (c)(24), (c)(26), (c)(27), and (c)(30) read as follows:

"(23) Credit under section 38 for investment in certain depreciable property. The acquiring corporation shall take into account (to the extent proper to carry out the purposes of this section and section 38, and under such regulations as may be prescribed by the Secretary) the items required to be taken into account for purposes of section 38 in respect of the distributor or transferor corporation.

"(24) Credit under section 40 for work incentive program expenses. The acquiring corporation shall take into account (to the extent proper to carry out the purposes of this section and section 40, and under such regulations as may be prescribed by the Secretary) the items required to be taken into account for purposes of section 40 in respect of the distributor or transferor corporation.

"(26) Credit under section 44B for employment of certain new employees. The acquiring corporation shall take into account (to the extent proper to carry out the purposes of this section and section 44B, and under such regulations as may be prescribed by the Secretary) the items required to be taken into account for purposes of section 44B in respect of the distributor or transferor corporation.

"(27) Credit under section 44E for alcohol used as fuel. The acquiring corporation shall take into account (to the extent proper to carry out the purposes of this section and section 44E, and under such regulations as may be prescribed by the Secretary) the items required to be taken into account for purposes of section 44E in respect of the distributor or transferor corporation.

"(30) Credit under section 44G. The acquiring corporation shall take into account (to the extent proper to carry out the purposes of this section and section 44G, and under such regulations as may be prescribed by the Secretary) the items required to be taken into account for purposes of section 44G in respect of the distributor or transferor corporation."

In 1983, P.L. 97-448, Sec. 102(h)(3), redesignated para. (c)(28) [as added by Sec. 221(b)(1)(B) of P.L. 97-34, see below] as (c)(29), effective for amounts paid or incurred after 6/30/81.

—P.L. 97-448, Sec. 103(g)(2)(F), redesignated para. (c)(29) as (c)(30), effective for tax yrs. end. after 12/31/81.

In 1982, P.L. 97-248, Sec. 224(c)(7), deleted ", except in a case in which the basis of the assets distributed is determined under section 334(b)(2)" after "applies" in para. (a)(1). For effective date see Sec. 224(d) of this Act reproduced in note following Code Sec. 338.

In 1981, P.L. 97-34, Sec. 208, added para. (c)(28), effective for property placed in service after 12/31/80, in tax. yrs. end. after 12/31/80.

—P.L. 97-34, Sec. 221(b)(1)(B), added para. (c)(28), effective for amounts paid or incurred after 6/30/81 [as amended by Sec. 231(a)(2) of P.L. 99-514, see above]. For transitional rule, see Sec. 221(d)(2) of this Act reproduced in note following Code Sec. 30.

—P.L. 97-34, Sec. 331(d)(1)(B), added para. (c)(29), effective for tax. yrs. end. after 12/31/81.

In 1980, P.L. 96-589, Sec. 4(g), substituted "subparagraph (A), (C), (D), (F), or (G) of section 368(a)(1)" for "subparagraph (A), (C), (D) (but only if the requirements of subparagraphs (A) and (B) of section 354(b)(1) are met), or (F) of section 368(a)(1)" in para. (a)(2), and added a sentence at the end of subsec. (a). Sec. 7(c)(1) of this Act makes these amendments effective for any bankruptcy case or similar judicial proceeding begin. after 12/31/80.

Sec. 7(f) and (g) of this Act provides:

"(f) Election to substitute September 30, 1979, for December 31, 1980.

"(1) In general. The debtor (or debtors) in a bankruptcy case or similar judicial proceeding may (with the approval of the court) elect to apply [subsection 7(c) of this Act] by substituting 'September 30, 1979' for 'December 31, 1980' each place it appears in such subsections.

"(2) Effect of election. Any election made under paragraph (1) with respect to any proceeding shall apply to all parties to the proceeding.

"(3) Revocation only with consent. Any election under this subsection may be revoked only with the consent of the Secretary of the Treasury or his delegate.

"(4) Time and manner of election. Any election under this subsection shall be made at such time, and in such manner, as the Secretary of the Treasury or his delegate may by regulations prescribe.

"(g) Definitions.

"For purposes of the section—

"(1) Bankruptcy case. The term 'bankruptcy case' means any case under title 11 of the United States Code (as recodified by P.L. 95-598).

"(2) Similar judicial proceeding. The term 'similar judicial proceeding' means a receivership, foreclosure, or similar proceeding in a Federal or State court (as modified by section 368(a)(3)(D) of the Internal Revenue Code of 1954)."

—P.L. 96-471, Sec. 2(b)(2), substituted "reports on the installment basis under section 453 or 453A" for "has elected, under section 453, to report on the installment basis", and substituted "for purposes of section 453 or 453A" for "for purposes of section 453" in para. (c)(8), effective for dispositions made after 10/19/80 in tax. yrs. end. after 10/19/80.

—P.L. 96-223, Sec. 232(b)(2)(B), added para. (c)(27), effective for sales or uses after 9/30/80, in tax. yrs. end. after 9/30/80.

—P.L. 96-222, Sec. 103(a)(11)(A), amended Sec. 362(e) of P.L. 95-600, the effective date for changes made by Sec. 362 of P.L. 95-600, by substituting "860(e)" for "860(d)" [see below].

In 1978, P.L. 95-600, Sec. 362(d)(2)(A), substituted "section 860(f)" for "section 859(d)" in para. (c)(25) . . . Sec. 362(d)(2)(B), substituted "section 860" for "section 859" in para. (c)(25) . . . Sec. 362(d)(2)(C), substituted "regulated investment company or real estate investment trust" for "real estate investment trust" in the heading of para. (c)(25), effective for determinations (as defined in section 860(e) of the Internal Revenue Code of 1954) after 11/6/78.

In 1977, P.L. 95-30, Sec. 202(d)(3)(A), added para. (c)(26), effective for tax. yrs. begin. after '76 and to credit carrybacks from such yrs.

In 1976, P.L. 94-455, Sec. 1601(e), added para. (c)(25), effective for determinations as defined in Code Sec. 859(c) occurring after 10/4/76.

—P.L. 94-455, Sec. 1901(a)(54), deleted para. (c)(20), effective for tax. yrs. begin. after 12/31/76.

Prior to deletion, para. (c)(20) read as follows:

"(20) Carry-over of unused pension trust deduction in certain cases. Notwithstanding the other provisions of this section, or section 394(a), a corporation which has acquired the properties and assumed the liabilities of a wholly owned subsidiary shall be considered to have succeeded to and to be entitled to take into account contributions of the subsidiary to a pension plan, and shall be considered to be the distributor or transferor corporation after the date of distribution or transfer (but not for taxable years with respect to which this paragraph does not apply) for the purpose of determining the amounts deductible under section 404 with respect to contributions to a pension plan if—

"(A) the corporate laws of the State of incorporation of the subsidiary required the surviving corporation in the case of merger to be incorporated under the laws of the State of incorporation of the subsidiary; and

"(B) the properties were acquired in a liquidation of the subsidiary in a transaction subject to section 112(b)(6) of the Internal Revenue Code of 1939."

—P.L. 94-455, Sec. 1901(b)(16), deleted para. (c)(21), effective for tax. yrs. begin. after 12/31/76.

Prior to deletion, para. (c)(21) read as follows:

"(21) Pre-1954 adjustments resulting from change in method of accounting. The acquiring corporation shall take into account any net amount of any adjustment described in section 481(b)(4) of the distributor or transferor corporation—

"(A) to the extent such net amount of such adjustment has not been taken into account by the distributor or transferor corporation, and

"(B) in the same manner and at the same time as such net amount would have been taken into account by the distributor or transferor corporation."

—P.L. 94-455, Sec. 1901(b)(17), substituted "subsection (c)" for "subsections (b)(7) and (c)", in para. (c)(15), effective for tax. yrs. begin. after 12/31/76.

—P.L. 94-455, Sec. 1901(b)(21)(B), amended para. (c)(10), effective for tax. yrs. begin. after 12/31/76.

Prior to amendment, para. (c)(10) read as follows:

"(10) Treatment of certain mining exploration and development expenses of distributor or transferor corporation. The acquiring corporation shall be entitled to deduct, as if it were the distributor or transferor corporation, expenses deferred under sections 615 and 616 (relating to pre-1970 exploration expenditures and development expenditures, respectively) if the distributor or transferor corporation has so elected. For the purpose of applying the limitation provided in section 615, if, for any taxable year, the distributor or transferor corporation was allowed the deduction in section 615(a) or made the election in section 615(b), the acquiring corporation shall be deemed to have been allowed such deduction or to have made such election, as the case may be. For the purpose of applying the limitation provided in section 617, if, for any taxable year, the distributor or transferor corporation was allowed the deduction in section 615(a) or section 617(a) or made the election provided in section 615(b), the acquiring corporation shall be deemed to have been allowed such deduction or deductions or to have made such election, as the case may be."

—P.L. 94-455, Sec. 1901(b)(33)(N), substituted "capital gain net income" for "net capital gain" in subparas. (c)(3)(B) and (C), effective for tax. yrs. begin. after 12/31/76.

—P.L. 94-455, Sec. 1906(b)(13)(A), substituted "Secretary" for "Secretary or his delegate" in Code Sec. 381, effective for tax. yrs. begin. after 12/31/76.

In 1971, P.L. 92-178, Sec. 601(c)(3), added para. (c)(24), effective for tax. yrs. begin. after 12/31/71.

In 1969, P.L. 91-172, Sec. 521(f), amended para. (c)(6), effective for tax. yrs. end. after 7/24/69.

Prior to amendment, para. (c)(6) read as follows:

"(6) Method of computing depreciation allowance. The acquiring corporation shall be treated as the distributor or transferor corporation for purposes of computing the depreciation allowance under paragraphs (2), (3), and (4) of section 167(b) on property acquired in a distribution or transfer with respect to that part or all of the basis in the hands of the acquiring corporation as does not exceed the basis in the hands of the distributor or transferor corporation."

—P.L. 91-172, Sec. 512(c), substituted "a net operating loss or a net capital loss" for "a net operating loss" in para. (b)(3), effective for net capital losses sustained in tax. yrs. begin. after 12/31/69.

—P.L. 91-172, Sec. 504(c)(2), amended para. (c)(10), effective for exploration expenditures paid or incurred after 12/31/69.

Prior to amendment, para. (c)(10) read as follows:

"(10) Treatment of certain expenses deferred by the election of distributor or transferor corporation. The acquiring corporation shall be entitled to deduct, as if it were the distributor or transferor corporation, expenses deferred under sections 615 and 616 (relating to exploration and development expenditures, respectively) if the distributor or transferor corporation has so elected. For the purpose of applying the limitation provided in section 615, if, for any taxable year, the distributor or transferor corporation was allowed the deduction in section 615(a) or made the election in section 615(b), the acquiring corporation shall be deemed to have been allowed such deduction or to have made such election, as the case may be."

In 1968, P.L. 90-240, Sec. 5(d), deleted "life" before "insurance company" in the heading and text of para. (c)(22), substituted "taxable under subchapter L" for "(as defined in section 801(a))" deleted "and part I" in references to subchap. L, and deleted "(relating to life insurance companies)" before the last phrase, beginning "in respect of the distributor", in para. (c)(22), effective for tax. yrs. begin. after 12/31/66.

In 1964, P.L. 88-272, Sec. 209(d)(2), amended para. (c)(19), effective for tax. yrs. begin. 12/31/63, for contributions which are paid (or treated as paid under section 170(a)(2)) in tax. yrs. begin. after 12/31/61.

Prior to amendment, para. (c)(19) read as follows:

"(19) Charitable contributions in excess of prior years' limitation.—Contributions made in the taxable year ending on the date of distribution or transfer and the prior taxable year by the distributor or transferor corporation in excess of the amount deductible under section 170(b)(2) in such taxable years shall be deductible by the acquiring corporation in its first two taxable years which begin after the date of distribution or transfer, subject to the limitations imposed in section 170(b)(2)."

—P.L. 88-272, Sec. 225(i)(3), amended para. (c)(15), effective for tax. yrs. begin. after 12/31/63.

Prior to amendment, para. (c)(15) read as follows:

"(15) Indebtedness of certain personal holding companies.—The acquiring corporation shall be considered to be the distributor or transferor corporation for the purpose of determining the applicability of section 545(b)(7), relating to a deduction for payment of certain indebtedness incurred before January 1, 1934."

In 1962, P.L. 87-834, Sec. 2, added para. (c)(23), effective for tax. yrs. end. after 12/31/61.

In 1959, P.L. 86-69, Sec. 3(c)(1), added para. (c)(22); . . . Sec. 3(c)(2), added subsec. (d), effective for tax. yrs. begin. after 12/31/57.

In 1958, P.L. 85-866, Sec. 29(c), added para. (c)(21), effective as provided in Sec. 29(d) of this Act which reads as follows:

"(1) In general.—The amendments made by this section shall apply with respect to any change in a method of accounting where the year of the change (within the meaning of section 481 of the Internal Revenue Code of 1954) is a taxable year beginning after December 31, 1953, and ending after August 16, 1954.

"(2) Exception for certain agreements.—The amendments made by subsections (a), (b)(1), and (c) shall not apply if before the date of the enactment of this Act [9/2/58]—

"(A) the taxpayer applied for a change in the method of accounting in the manner provided by regulations prescribed by the Secretary of the Treasury or his delegate, and

"(B) the taxpayer and the Secretary of the Treasury or his delegate agreed to the terms and conditions for making the change."

In 1956, ch. 15, Sec. 1, added para. (c)(20), effective for tax. yrs. begin after 12/31/53 and end after 12/6/54.

In 1955, ch. 143, Sec. 2(1), deleted para. (c)(7), effective for tax. yrs. begin after 12/31/53, and end after 8/16/54.

Prior to deletion, para. (c)(7) read as follows:

"(7) Prepaid income. If the acquiring corporation assumes the liability described in section 452(e)(2) with respect to prepaid income of a distributor or transferor corporation which had elected, under section 452(d), to report such income as provided in section 452, the acquiring corporation shall be treated, for this purpose, as if it were the distributor or transferor corporation, unless the acquiring corporation, after the date of distribution or transfer, uses the cash receipts and disbursements method of accounting. In the latter case, the acquiring corporation shall include in gross income for the first taxable year ending after the date of distribution or transfer, so much of such prepaid income as was not includible in gross income of the distributor or transferor corporation under section 452 for preceding taxable years."

Sec. 382. Limitation on net operating loss carryforwards and certain built-in losses following ownership change.

(a) General rule.

The amount of the taxable income of any new loss corporation for any post-change year which may be offset by pre-change losses shall not exceed the section 382 limitation for such year.

(b) Section 382 limitation.

For purposes of this section—

(1) In general. Except as otherwise provided in this section, the section 382 limitation for any post-change year is an amount equal to—

(A) the value of the old loss corporation, multiplied by

(B) the long-term tax-exempt rate.

(2) Carryforward of unused limitation. If the section 382 limitation for any post-change year exceeds the taxable income of the new loss corporation for such year which was offset by pre-change losses, the section 382 limitation for the next post-change year shall be increased by the amount of such excess.

(3) Special rule for post-change year which includes change date. In the case of any post-change year which includes the change date—

(A) Limitation does not apply to taxable income before change. Subsection (a) shall not apply to the portion of the taxable income for such year which is allocable to the period in such year on or before the change date. Except as provided in subsection (h)(5) and in regulations, taxable income shall be allocated ratably to each day in the year.

(B) Limitation for period after change. For purposes of applying the limitation of subsection (a) to the remainder of the taxable income for such year, the section 382 limitation shall be an amount which bears the same ratio to such limitation (determined without regard to this paragraph) as—

(i) the number of days in such year after the change date, bears to

(ii) the total number of days in such year.

(c) Carryforwards disallowed if continuity of business requirements not met.

(1) In general. Except as provided in paragraph (2), if the new loss corporation does not continue the business enterprise of the old loss corporation at all times during the 2-year period beginning on the change date, the section 382 limitation for any post-change year shall be zero.

(2) Exception for certain gains. The section 382 limitation for any post-change year shall not be less than the sum of—

(A) any increase in such limitation under—

(i) subsection (h)(1)(A) for recognized built-in gains for such year, and

(ii) subsection (h)(1)(C) for gain recognized by reason of an election under section 338, plus

(B) any increase in such limitation under subsection (b)(2) for amounts described in subparagraph (A) which are carried forward to such year.

(d) Pre-change loss and post-change year.

For purposes of this section—

(1) Pre-change loss. The term "pre-change loss" means—

(A) any net operating loss carryforward of the old loss corporation to the taxable year ending with the ownership change or in which the change date occurs, and

(B) the net operating loss of the old loss corporation for the taxable year in which the ownership change occurs to the extent such loss is allocable to the period in such year on or before the change date.

Except as provided in subsection (h)(5) and in regulations, the net operating loss shall, for purposes of subparagraph (B), be allocated ratably to each day in the year.

(2) Post-change year. The term "post-change year" means any taxable year ending after the change date.

Corporate distributions and adjustments — Code Sec. 382(h)(1)(B)(i)

(e) Value of old loss corporation.
For purposes of this section—
(1) In general. Except as otherwise provided in this subsection, the value of the old loss corporation is the value of the stock of such corporation (including any stock described in section 1504(a)(4)) immediately before the ownership change.
(2) Special rule in the case of redemption or other corporate contraction. If a redemption or other corporate contraction occurs in connection with an ownership change, the value under paragraph (1) shall be determined after taking such redemption or other corporate contraction into account.
(3) Treatment of foreign corporations. Except as otherwise provided in regulations, in determining the value of any old loss corporation which is a foreign corporation, there shall be taken into account only items treated as connected with the conduct of a trade or business in the United States.

(f) Long-term tax-exempt rate.
For purposes of this section—
(1) In general. The long-term tax-exempt rate shall be the highest of the adjusted Federal long-term rates in effect for any month in the 3-calendar-month period ending with the calendar month in which the change date occurs.
(2) Adjusted federal long-term rate. For purposes of paragraph (1), the term "adjusted Federal long-term rate" means the Federal long-term rate determined under section 1274(d), except that—
  (A) paragraphs (2) and (3) thereof shall not apply, and
  (B) such rate shall be properly adjusted for differences between rates on long-term taxable and tax-exempt obligations.

(g) Ownership change.
For purposes of this section—
(1) In general. There is an ownership change if, immediately after any owner shift involving a 5-percent shareholder or any equity structure shift—
  (A) the percentage of the stock of the loss corporation owned by 1 or more 5-percent shareholders has increased by more than 50 percentage points, over
  (B) the lowest percentage of stock of the loss corporation (or any predecessor corporation) owned by such shareholders at any time during the testing period.
(2) Owner shift involving 5-percent shareholder. There is an owner shift involving a 5-percent shareholder if—
  (A) there is any change in the respective ownership of stock of a corporation, and
  (B) such change affects the percentage of stock of such corporation owned by any person who is a 5-percent shareholder before or after such change.
(3) Equity structure shift defined.
  (A) In general. The term "equity structure shift" means any reorganization (within the meaning of section 368). Such term shall not include—
    (i) any reorganization described in subparagraph (D) or (G) of section 368(a)(1) unless the requirements of section 354(b)(1) are met, and
    (ii) any reorganization described in subparagraph (F) of section 368(a)(1).
  (B) Taxable reorganization-type transactions, etc. To the extent provided in regulations, the term "equity structure shift" includes taxable reorganization-type transactions, public offerings, and similar transactions.

(4) Special rules for application of subsection.
  (A) Treatment of less than 5-percent shareholders. Except as provided in subparagraphs (B)(i) and (C), in determining whether an ownership change has occurred, all stock owned by shareholders of a corporation who are not 5-percent shareholders of such corporation shall be treated as stock owned by 1 5-percent shareholder of such corporation.
  (B) Coordination with equity structure shifts. For purposes of determining whether an equity structure shift (or subsequent transaction) is an ownership change—
    (i) Less than 5-percent shareholders. Subparagraph (A) shall be applied separately with respect to each group of shareholders (immediately before such equity structure shift) of each corporation which was a party to the reorganization involved in such equity structure shift.
    (ii) Acquisitions of stock. Unless a different proportion is established, acquisitions of stock after such equity structure shift shall be treated as being made proportionately from all shareholders immediately before such acquisition.
  (C) Coordination with other owner shifts. Except as provided in regulations, rules similar to the rules of subparagraph (B) shall apply in determining whether there has been an owner shift involving a 5-percent shareholder and whether such shift (or subsequent transaction) results in an ownership change.
  (D) Treatment of worthless stock. If any stock held by a 50-percent shareholder is treated by such shareholder as becoming worthless during any taxable year of such shareholder and such stock is held by such shareholder as of the close of such taxable year, for purposes of determining whether an ownership change occurs after the close of such taxable year, such shareholder—
    (i) shall be treated as having acquired such stock on the 1st day of his 1st succeeding taxable year, and
    (ii) shall not be treated as having owned such stock during any prior period.
  For purposes of the preceding sentence, the term "50-percent shareholder" means any person owning 50 percent or more of the stock of the corporation at any time during the 3-year period ending on the last day of the taxable year with respect to which the stock was so treated.

(h) Special rules for built-in gains and losses and section 338 gains.
For purposes of this section—
(1) In general.
  (A) Net unrealized built-in gain.
    (i) In general. If the old loss corporation has a net unrealized built-in gain, the section 382 limitation for any recognition period taxable year shall be increased by the recognized built-in gains for such taxable year.
    (ii) Limitation. The increase under clause (i) for any recognition period taxable year shall not exceed—
      (I) the net unrealized built-in gain, reduced by
      (II) recognized built-in gains for prior years ending in the recognition period.
  (B) Net unrealized built-in loss.
    (i) In general. If the old loss corporation has a net unrealized built-in loss, the recognized built-in loss for any recognition period taxable year shall be subject to limitation under this section in the same manner as if such loss were a pre-change loss.

1,849

(ii) Limitation. Clause (i) shall apply to recognized built-in losses for any recognition period taxable year only to the extent such losses do not exceed—
  (I) the net unrealized built-in loss, reduced by
  (II) recognized built-in losses for prior taxable years ending in the recognition period.
(C) Special rules for certain section 338 gains. If an election under section 338 is made in connection with an ownership change and the net unrealized built-in gain is zero by reason of paragraph (3)(B), then, with respect to such change, the section 382 limitation for the post-change year in which gain is recognized by reason of such election shall be increased by the lesser of—
  (i) the recognized built-in gains by reason of such election, or
  (ii) the net unrealized built-in gain (determined without regard to paragraph (3)(B)).
(2) **Recognized built-in gain and loss.**
  (A) Recognized built-in gain. The term "recognized built-in gain" means any gain recognized during the recognition period on the disposition of any asset to the extent the new loss corporation establishes that—
    (i) such asset was held by the old loss corporation immediately before the change date, and
    (ii) such gain does not exceed the excess of—
      (I) the fair market value of such asset on the change date, over
      (II) the adjusted basis of such asset on such date.
  (B) Recognized built-in loss. The term "recognized built-in loss" means any loss recognized during the recognition period on the disposition of any asset except to the extent the new loss corporation establishes that—
    (i) such asset was not held by the old loss corporation immediately before the change date, or
    (ii) such loss exceeds the excess of—
      (I) the adjusted basis of such asset on the change date, over
      (II) the fair market value of such asset on such date.
  Such term includes any amount allowable as depreciation, amortization, or depletion for any period within the recognition period except to the extent the new loss corporation establishes that the amount so allowable is not attributable to the excess described in clause (ii).
(3) **Net unrealized built-in gain and loss defined.**
  (A) Net unrealized built-in gain and loss.
    (i) In general. The terms "net unrealized built-in gain" and "net unrealized built-in loss" mean, with respect to any old loss corporation, the amount by which—
      (I) the fair market value of the assets of such corporation immediately before an ownership change is more or less, respectively, than
      (II) the aggregate adjusted basis of such assets at such time.
    (ii) Special rule for redemptions or other corporate contractions. If a redemption or other corporate contraction occurs in connection with an ownership change, to the extent provided in regulations, determinations under clause (i) shall be made after taking such redemption or other corporate contraction into account.
  (B) Threshold requirement.
    (i) In general. If the amount of the net unrealized built-in gain or net unrealized built-in loss (determined without regard to this subparagraph) of any old loss corporation is not greater than the lesser of—
      (I) 15 percent of the amount determined for purposes of subparagraph (A)(i)(I), or
      (II) $10,000,000,
    the net unrealized built-in gain or net unrealized built-in loss shall be zero.
    (ii) Cash and cash items not taken into account. In computing any net unrealized built-in gain or net unrealized built-in loss under clause (i), except as provided in regulations, there shall not be taken into account—
      (I) any cash or cash item, or
      (II) any marketable security which has a value which does not substantially differ from adjusted basis.
(4) **Disallowed loss allowed as a carryforward.** If a deduction for any portion of a recognized built-in loss is disallowed for any post-change year, such portion—
  (A) shall be carried forward to subsequent taxable years under rules similar to the rules for the carrying forward of net operating losses (or to the extent the amount so disallowed is attributable to capital losses, under rules similar to the rules for the carrying forward of net capital losses), but
  (B) shall be subject to limitation under this section in the same manner as a pre-change loss.
(5) **Special rules for post-change year which includes change date.** For purposes of subsection (b)(3)—
  (A) in applying subparagraph (A) thereof, taxable income shall be computed without regard to recognized built-in gains to the extent such gains increased the section 382 limitation for the year (or recognized built-in losses to the extent such losses are treated as pre-change losses), and gain described in paragraph (1)(C), for the year, and
  (B) in applying subparagraph (B) thereof, the section 382 limitation shall be computed without regard to recognized built-in gains, and gain described in paragraph (1)(C), for the year.
(6) **Treatment of certain built-in items.**
  (A) Income items. Any item of income which is properly taken into account during the recognition period but which is attributable to periods before the change date shall be treated as a recognized built-in gain for the taxable year in which it is properly taken into account.
  (B) Deduction items. Any amount which is allowable as a deduction during the recognition period (determined without regard to any carryover) but which is attributable to periods before the change date shall be treated as a recognized built-in loss for the taxable year for which it is allowable as a deduction.
  (C) Adjustments. The amount of the net unrealized built-in gain or loss shall be properly adjusted for amounts which would be treated as recognized built-in gains or losses under this paragraph if such amounts were properly taken into account (or allowable as a deduction) during the recognition period.
(7) **Recognition period, etc.**
  (A) Recognition period. The term "recognition period" means, with respect to any ownership change, the 5-year period beginning on the change date.
  (B) Recognition period taxable year. The term "recognition period taxable year" means any taxable year any portion of which is in the recognition period.

(8) Determination of fair market value in certain cases. If 80 percent or more in value of the stock of a corporation is acquired in 1 transaction (or in a series of related transactions during any 12-month period), for purposes of determining the net unrealized built-in loss, the fair market value of the assets of such corporation shall not exceed the grossed up amount paid for such stock properly adjusted for indebtedness of the corporation and other relevant items.

(9) Tax-free exchanges or transfers. The Secretary shall prescribe such regulations as may be necessary to carry out the purposes of this subsection where property held on the change date was acquired (or is subsequently transferred) in a transaction where gain or loss is not recognized (in whole or in part).

(i) Testing period.
For purposes of this section—

(1) 3-year period. Except as otherwise provided in this section, the testing period is the 3-year period ending on the day of any owner shift involving a 5-percent shareholder or equity structure shift.

(2) Shorter period where there has been recent ownership change. If there has been an ownership change under this section, the testing period for determining whether a 2nd ownership change has occurred shall not begin before the 1st day following the change date for such earlier ownership change.

(3) Shorter period where all losses arise after 3-year period begins. The testing period shall not begin before the earlier of the 1st day of the 1st taxable year from which there is a carryforward of a loss or of an excess credit to the 1st post-change year or the taxable year in which the transaction being tested occurs. Except as provided in regulations, this paragraph shall not apply to any loss corporation which has a net unrealized built-in loss (determined after application of subsection (h)(3)(B)).

(j) Change date.
For purposes of this section, the change date is—

(1) in the case where the last component of an ownership change is an owner shift involving a 5-percent shareholder, the date on which such shift occurs, and

(2) in the case where the last component of an ownership change is an equity structure shift, the date of the reorganization.

(k) Definitions and special rules.
For purposes of this section—

(1) Loss corporation. The term "loss corporation" means a corporation entitled to use a net operating loss carryover or having a net operating loss for the taxable year in which the ownership change occurs. Except to the extent provided in regulations, such term includes any corporation with a net unrealized built-in loss.

(2) Old loss corporation. The term "old loss corporation" means any corporation—

(A) with respect to which there is an ownership change, and

(B) which (before the ownership change) was a loss corporation.

(3) New loss corporation. The term "new loss corporation" means a corporation which (after an ownership change) is a loss corporation. Nothing in this section shall be treated as implying that the same corporation may not be both the old loss corporation and the new loss corporation.

(4) Taxable income. Taxable income shall be computed with the modifications set forth in section 172(d).

(5) Value. The term "value" means fair market value.

(6) Rules relating to stock.

(A) Preferred stock. Except as provided in regulations and subsection (e), the term "stock" means stock other than stock described in section 1504(a)(4).

(B) Treatment of certain rights, etc. The Secretary shall prescribe such regulations as may be necessary—

(i) to treat warrants, options, contracts to acquire stock, convertible debt interests, and other similar interests as stock, and

(ii) to treat stock as not stock.

(C) Determinations on basis of value. Determinations of the percentage of stock of any corporation held by any person shall be made on the basis of value.

(7) 5-percent shareholder. The term "5-percent shareholder" means any person holding 5 percent or more of the stock of the corporation at any time during the testing period.

(l) Certain additional operating rules.
For purposes of this section—

(1) Certain capital contributions not taken into account.

(A) In general. Any capital contribution received by an old loss corporation as part of a plan a principal purpose of which is to avoid or increase any limitation under this section shall not be taken into account for purposes of this section.

(B) Certain contributions treated as part of plan. For purposes of subparagraph (A), any capital contribution made during the 2-year period ending on the change date shall, except as provided in regulations, be treated as part of a plan described in subparagraph (A).

(2) Ordering rules for application of section.

(A) Coordination with section 172(b) carryover rules. In the case of any pre-change loss for any taxable year (hereinafter in this subparagraph referred to as the "loss year") subject to limitation under this section, for purposes of determining under the 2nd sentence of section 172(b)(2) the amount of such loss which may be carried to any taxable year, taxable income for any taxable year shall be treated as not greater than—

(i) the section 382 limitation for such taxable year, reduced by

(ii) the unused pre-change losses for taxable years preceding the loss year.

Similar rules shall apply in the case of any credit or loss subject to limitation under section 383.

(B) Ordering rule for losses carried from same taxable year. In any case in which—

(i) a pre-change loss of a loss corporation for any taxable year is subject to a section 382 limitation, and

(ii) a net operating loss of such corporation from such taxable year is not subject to such limitation,

taxable income shall be treated as having been offset first by the loss subject to such limitation.

(3) Operating rules relating to ownership of stock.

(A) Constructive ownership. Section 318 (relating to constructive ownership of stock) shall apply in determining ownership of stock, except that—

(i) paragraphs (1) and (5)(B) of section 318(a) shall not apply and an individual and all members of his family described in paragraph (1) of section 318(a) shall be treated as 1 individual for purposes of applying this section,

(ii) paragraph (2) of section 318(a) shall be applied—
  (I) without regard to the 50-percent limitation contained in subparagraph (C) thereof, and
  (II) except as provided in regulations, by treating stock attributed thereunder as no longer being held by the entity from which attributed,
(iii) paragraph (3) of section 318(a) shall be applied only to the extent provided in regulations,
(iv) except to the extent provided in regulations, an option to acquire stock shall be treated as exercised if such exercise results in an ownership change, and
(v) in attributing stock from an entity under paragraph (2) of section 318(a), there shall not be taken into account—
  (I) in the case of attribution from a corporation, stock which is not treated as stock for purposes of this section, or
  (II) in the case of attribution from another entity, an interest in such entity similar to stock described in subclause (I).
A rule similar to the rule of clause (iv) shall apply in the case of any contingent purchase, warrant, convertible debt, put, stock subject to a risk of forfeiture, contract to acquire stock, or similar interests.
(B) Stock acquired by reason of death, gift, divorce, separation, etc. If—
  (i) the basis of any stock in the hands of any person is determined—
    (I) under section 1014 (relating to property acquired from a decedent),
    (II) section 1015 (relating to property acquired by a gift or transfer in trust), or
    (III) section 1041(b)(2) (relating to transfers of property between spouses or incident to divorce),
  (ii) stock is received by any person in satisfaction of a right to receive a pecuniary bequest, or
  (iii) stock is acquired by a person pursuant to any divorce or separation instrument (within the meaning of section 71(b)(2)),
such person shall be treated as owning such stock during the period such stock was owned by the person from whom it was acquired.
(C) Certain changes in percentage ownership which are attributable to fluctuations in value not taken into account. Except as provided in regulations, any change in proportionate ownership which is attributable solely to fluctuations in the relative fair market values of different classes of stock shall not be taken into account.
(4) Reduction in value where substantial nonbusiness assets.
(A) In general. If, immediately after an ownership change, the new loss corporation has substantial nonbusiness assets, the value of the old loss corporation shall be reduced by the excess (if any) of—
  (i) the fair market value of the nonbusiness assets of the old loss corporation, over
  (ii) the nonbusiness asset share of indebtedness for which such corporation is liable.
(B) Corporation having substantial nonbusiness assets. For purposes of subparagraph (A)—
  (i) In general. The old loss corporation shall be treated as having substantial nonbusiness assets if at least 1/3 of the value of the total assets of such corporation consists of nonbusiness assets.

(ii) Exception for certain investment entities. A regulated investment company to which part I of subchapter M applies, a real estate investment trust to which part II of subchapter M applies, or a REMIC to which part IV of subchapter M applies, shall not be treated as a new loss corporation having substantial nonbusiness assets.
(C) Nonbusiness assets. For purposes of this paragraph, the term "nonbusiness assets" means assets held for investment.
(D) Nonbusiness asset share. For purposes of this paragraph, the nonbusiness asset share of the indebtedness of the corporation is an amount which bears the same ratio to such indebtedness as—
  (i) the fair market value of the nonbusiness assets of the corporation, bears to
  (ii) the fair market value of all assets of such corporation.
(E) Treatment of subsidiaries. For purposes of this paragraph, stock and securities in any subsidiary corporation shall be disregarded and the parent corporation shall be deemed to own its ratable share of the subsidiary's assets. For purposes of the preceding sentence, a corporation shall be treated as a subsidiary if the parent owns 50 percent or more of the combined voting power of all classes of stock entitled to vote, and 50 percent or more of the total value of shares of all classes of stock.
(5) Title 11 or similar case.
(A) In general. Subsection (a) shall not apply to any ownership change if—
  (i) the old loss corporation is (immediately before such ownership change) under the jurisdiction of the court in a title 11 or similar case, and
  (ii) the shareholders and creditors of the old loss corporation (determined immediately before such ownership change) own (after such ownership change and as a result of being shareholders or creditors immediately before such change) stock of the new loss corporation (or stock of a controlling corporation if also in bankruptcy) which meets the requirements of section 1504(a)(2) (determined by substituting "50 percent" for "80 percent" each place it appears).
(B) Reduction for interest payments to creditors becoming shareholders. In any case to which subparagraph (A) applies, the pre-change losses and excess credits (within the meaning of section 383(a)(2)) which may be carried to a post-change year shall be computed as if no deduction was allowable under this chapter for the interest paid or accrued by the old loss corporation on indebtedness which was converted into stock pursuant to title 11 or similar case during—
  (i) any taxable year ending during the 3-year period preceding the taxable year in which the ownership change occurs, and
  (ii) the period of the taxable year in which the ownership change occurs on or before the change date.
(C) Coordination with section 108. In applying section 108(e)(8) to any case to which subparagraph (A) applies, there shall not be taken into account any indebtedness for interest described in subparagraph (B).
(D) Section 382 limitation zero if another change within 2 years. If, during the 2-year period immediately following an ownership change to which this paragraph applies, an ownership change of the new loss corporation occurs, this paragraph shall not apply and the section 382 limitation with respect to the 2nd ownership

change for any post-change year ending after the change date of the 2nd ownership change shall be zero.

(E) Only certain stock taken into account. For purposes of subparagraph (A)(ii), stock transferred to a creditor shall be taken into account only to the extent such stock is transferred in satisfaction of indebtedness and only if such indebtedness—

(i) was held by the creditor at least 18 months before the date of the filing of the title 11 or similar case, or

(ii) arose in the ordinary course of the trade or business of the old loss corporation and is held by the person who at all times held the beneficial interest in such indebtedness.

(F) Special rule for certain financial institutions.

(i) In general. In the case of any ownership change to which this subparagraph applies, this paragraph shall be applied—

(I) by substituting "1504(a)(2)(B)" for "1504(a)(2)" and "20 percent" for "50 percent" in subparagraph (A)(ii), and

(II) without regard to subparagraphs (B) and (C).

(ii) Special rule for depositors. For purposes of applying this paragraph to an ownership change to which this subparagraph applies—

(I) a depositor in the old loss corporation shall be treated as a stockholder in such loss corporation immediately before the change,

(II) deposits which, after the change, become deposits of the new loss corporation shall be treated as stock of the new loss corporation, and

(III) the fair market value of the outstanding stock of the new loss corporation shall include the amount of deposits in the new loss corporation immediately after the change.

(iii) Changes to which subparagraph applies. This subparagraph shall apply to—

(I) an equity structure shift which is a reorganization described in section 368(a)(3)(D)(ii) (as modified by section 368(a)(3)(D)(iv)), or

(II) any other equity structure shift (or transaction to which section 351 applies) which occurs as an integral part of a transaction involving a change to which subclause (I) applies.

This subparagraph shall not apply to any equity structure shift or transaction occurring on or after May 10, 1989.

(G) Title 11 or similar case. For purposes of this paragraph, the term "title 11 or similar case" has the meaning given such term by section 368(a)(3)(A).

(H) Election not to have paragraph apply. A new loss corporation may elect, subject to such terms and conditions as the Secretary may prescribe, not to have the provisions of this paragraph apply.

(6) Special rule for insolvency transactions. If paragraph (5) does not apply to any reorganization described in subparagraph (G) of section 368(a)(1) or any exchange of debt for stock in a title 11 or similar case (as defined in section 368(a)(3)(A)), the value under subsection (e) shall reflect the increase (if any) in value of the old loss corporation resulting from any surrender or cancellation of creditors' claims in the transaction.

(7) Coordination with alternative minimum tax. The Secretary shall by regulation provide for the application of this section to the alternative tax net operating loss deduction under section 56(d).

(8) Predecessor and successor entities. Except as provided in regulations, any entity and any predecessor or successor entities of such entity shall be treated as 1 entity.

(m) Regulations.

The Secretary shall prescribe such regulations as may be necessary or appropriate to carry out the purposes of this section and section 383, including (but not limited to) regulations—

(1) providing for the application of this section and section 383 where an ownership change with respect to the old loss corporation is followed by an ownership change with respect to the new loss corporation, and

(2) providing for the application of this section and section 383 in the case of a short taxable year,

(3) providing for such adjustments to the application of this section and section 383 as is necessary to prevent the avoidance of the purposes of this section and section 383, including the avoidance of such purposes through the use of related persons, pass-thru entities, or other intermediaries,

(4) providing for the application of subsection (g)(4) where there is only 1 corporation involved, and

(5) providing, in the case of any group of corporations described in section 1563(a) (determined by substituting "50 percent" for "80 percent" each place it appears and determined without regard to paragraph (4) thereof), appropriate adjustments to value, built-in gain or loss, and other items so that items are not omitted or taken into account more than once.

(n) Special rule for certain ownership changes.

(1) In general. The limitation contained in subsection (a) shall not apply in the case of an ownership change which is pursuant to a restructuring plan of a taxpayer which—

(A) is required under a loan agreement or a commitment for a line of credit entered into with the Department of the Treasury under the Emergency Economic Stabilization Act of 2008, and

(B) is intended to result in a rationalization of the costs, capitalization, and capacity with respect to the manufacturing workforce of, and suppliers to, the taxpayer and its subsidiaries.

(2) Subsequent acquisitions. Paragraph (1) shall not apply in the case of any subsequent ownership change unless such ownership change is described in such paragraph.

(3) Limitation based on control in corporation.

(A) In general. Paragraph (1) shall not apply in the case of any ownership change if, immediately after such ownership change, any person (other than a voluntary employees' beneficiary association under section 501(c)(9)) owns stock of the new loss corporation possessing 50 percent or more of the total combined voting power of all classes of stock entitled to vote, or of the total value of the stock of such corporation.

(B) Treatment of related persons.

(i) In general. Related persons shall be treated as a single person for purposes of this paragraph.

(ii) Related persons. For purposes of clause (i), a person shall be treated as related to another person if—

(I) such person bears a relationship to such other person described in section 267(b) or 707(b), or

(II) such persons are members of a group of persons acting in concert.

In 2009, P.L. 111-5, Sec. 1261, of this Act, reads as follows:

"Sec. 1261. Clarification of regulations related to limitations on certain built-in losses following an ownership change.

"(a) Findings. Congress finds as follows:
"(1) The delegation of authority to the Secretary of the Treasury under section 382(m) of the Internal Revenue Code of 1986 does not authorize the Secretary to provide exemptions or special rules that are restricted to particular industries or classes of taxpayers.
"(2) Internal Revenue Service Notice 2008-83 is inconsistent with the congressional intent in enacting such section 382(m).
"(3) The legal authority to prescribe Internal Revenue Service Notice 2008-83 is doubtful.
"(4) However, as taxpayers should generally be able to rely on guidance issued by the Secretary of the Treasury legislation is necessary to clarify the force and effect of Internal Revenue Service Notice 2008-83 and restore the proper application under the Internal Revenue Code of 1986 of the limitation on built-in losses following an ownership change of a bank.
"(b) Determination of force and effect of internal revenue service notice 2008-83 exempting banks from limitation on certain built-in losses following ownership change.
"(1) In general. Internal Revenue Service Notice 2008-83—
"(A) shall be deemed to have the force and effect of law with respect to any ownership change (as defined in section 382(g) of the Internal Revenue Code of 1986) occurring on or before January 16, 2009, and
"(B) shall have no force or effect with respect to any ownership change after such date.
"(2) Binding contracts. Notwithstanding paragraph (1), Internal Revenue Service Notice 2008-83 shall have the force and effect of law with respect to any ownership change (as so defined) which occurs after January 16, 2009, if such change—
"(A) is pursuant to a written binding contract entered into on or before such date, or
"(B) is pursuant to a written agreement entered into on or before such date and such agreement was described on or before such date in a public announcement or in a filing with the Securities and Exchange Commission required by reason of such ownership change."
—P.L. 111-5, Sec. 1262(a), added subsec. (n), effective for ownership changes after 2/17/2009.
In 2004, P.L. 108-357, Sec. 835(b)(2), substituted "or a REMIC to which part IV of subchapter M applies," for "a REMIC to which part IV of subchapter M applies, or a FASIT to which part V of subchapter M applies," in clause (l)(4)(B)(ii), effective 1/1/2005, except as provided in Sec. 835(c)(2) of this Act, which reads as follows:
"(2) Exception for existing FASITs. Paragraph (1) shall not apply to any FASIT in existence on the date of the enactment of this Act to the extent that regular interests issued by the FASIT before such date continue to remain outstanding in accordance with the original terms of issuance."
In 1996, P.L. 104-188, Sec. 1621(b)(3), substituted "a REMIC to which part IV of subchapter M applies, or a FASIT to which part V of subchapter M applies" for "or a REMIC to which part IV of subchapter M applies" in clause (l)(4)(B)(ii), effective 9/1/97.
In 1993, P.L. 103-66, Sec. 13226(a)(2)(A), amended subpara. (l)(5)(C), effective for stock transferred after 12/31/94, in satisfaction of any indebtedness, except as provided in Sec. 13226(a)(3) of this Act, which read as follows:
"(B) Exception for title 11 cases. The amendments made by this subsection shall not apply to stock transferred in satisfaction of any indebtedness if such transfer is in a title 11 or similar case (as defined in section 368(a)(3)(A) of the Internal Revenue Code of 1986) which was filed on or before December 31, 1993."
Prior to amendment, subpara. (l)(5)(C) read as follows:
"(C) Reduction of tax attributes where discharge of indebtedness.
"(i) In general. In any case to which subparagraph (A) applies, 50 percent of the amount which, but for the application of section 108(e)(10)(B), would have been applied to reduce tax attributes under section 108(b) shall be so applied.
"(ii) Clarification with subparagraph (B). In applying clause (i), there shall not be taken into account any indebtedness for interest described in subparagraph (B)."
In 1989, P.L. 101-239, Sec. 7205(a), amended clause (h)(3)(B)(i), effective for ownership changes and acquisitions after 10/2/89, in tax. yrs. end. after 10/2/89, except as otherwise provided by Secs. 7205(c)(2)-(4) of this Act, which read as follows:
"(2) Binding contract.—The amendments made by this section shall not apply to any ownership change or acquisition pursuant to a written binding contract in effect on October 2, 1989, and at all times thereafter before such change or acquisition.
"(3) Bankruptcy proceedings.—In the case of a reorganization described in section 368(a)(1)(G) of the Internal Revenue Code of 1986, or an exchange of debt for stock in a title 11 or similar case (as defined in section 368(a)(3) of such Code), the amendments made by this section shall not apply to any ownership change resulting from such a reorganization or proceeding if a petition in such case was filed with the court before October 3, 1989.
"(4) Subsidiaries of bankrupt parent.—The amendments made by this section shall not apply to any built-in loss of a corporation which is a member (on October 2, 1989) of an affiliated group the common parent of which (on such date) was subject to title 11 or similar case (as defined in section 368(a)(3) of such Code). The preceding sentence shall apply only if the ownership change or acquisition is pursuant to the plan approved in such proceeding and is before the date 2 years after the date on which the petition which commenced such proceeding was filed."
Prior to amendment, clause (h)(3)(B)(i) read as follows:

"(i) If the amount of the net unrealized built-in gain or net unrealized built-in loss (determined without regard to this subparagraph) of any old loss corporation is not greater than 25 percent of the amount determined for purposes of subparagraph (A)(i)(I), the net unrealized built-in gain or net unrealized built-in loss shall be zero."
—P.L. 101-239, Sec. 7304(d)(1), deleted subpara. (l)(3)(C) and redesignated subpara. (l)(3)(D) as (l)(3)(C), effective for acquisitions of employer securities after 7/12/89, except for acquisitions after 7/12/89, pursuant to a written binding contract in effect on 7/12/89, and at all times thereafter before such acquisition.
Prior to deletion, subpara (l)(3)(C) read as follows:
"(C) Special rule for employee stock ownership plans.
"(i) In general. Except as provided in clause (ii), the acquisition of employer securities (within the meaning of section 409(l)) by—
"(I) a tax credit employee stock ownership plan or an employee stock ownership plan (within the meaning of section 4975(e)(7)), or
"(II) a participant of any such plan pursuant to the requirements of section 409(h),
shall not be taken into account in determining whether an ownership change has occurred.
"(ii) Ownership and allocation requirements. Subclause (I) of clause (i) shall not apply to any acquisition unless—
"(I) immediately after such acquisition the plan holds stock meeting the requirements of section 1042(b)(2), except that such section shall be applied by substituting '50 percent' for '30 percent',
"(II) the plan meets requirements similar to the requirements of section 409(n), and,
"(III) immediately after the acquisition the plan has a number of participants which is not less than 50 percent of the average number of employees of the loss corporation during the 3-year period ending with such acquisition.
For purposes of subclause (III), except as provided in regulations, all members of an affiliated group which includes the loss corporation and which files a consolidated return shall be treated as 1 loss corporation."
—P.L. 101-239, Sec. 7811(c)(5)(A)(i), substituted "during the recognition period (determined without regard to any carryover)" for "during the recognition period" in subpara. (h)(6)(B)... Sec. 7811(c)(5)(A)(ii), substituted "which would be treated as recognized built-in gains or losses under this paragraph if such amounts were properly taken into account (or allowable as a deduction) during the recognition period" for "treated as recognized built-in gains or losses under this paragraph" in subpara. (h)(6)(C), effective as provided in Secs. 621(f)(1) and (f)(3) of P.L. 99-514, [reproduced in note following Code Sec. 383] and Secs. 621(f)(4)-(9) of P.L. 99-514, reproduced below.
—P.L. 101-239, Sec. 7815(h), substituted "For purposes of subclause (III)" for "for purposes of subclause (III)," in clause (l)(3)(C)(ii) (prior to amendment by Sec. 7304(d)(1) of this Act see above), effective as provided in Secs. 621(f)(1) and (f)(3) of P.L. 99-514, reproduced in note following Code Sec. 383 and Secs. 621(f)(4)-(9) of P.L. 99-514, reproduced below.
—P.L. 101-239, Sec. 7841(d)(11), substituted "divorce)," for "divorce," in subclause (l)(3)(B)(i)(III), effective 12/19/89.
—P.L. 101-73, Sec. 1401(a)(2), substituted "on or after May 10, 1989" for "after December 31, 1989" in the last sentence of subpara. (l)(5)(F), effective for transactions on or after 5/10/89.
In 1988, P.L. 100-647, Sec. 1006(d)(1)(A), added "or other corporate contraction" after "redemption" each place it appeared in para. (e)(2)... Sec. 1006(d)(1)(B)(i), added "or other corporate contraction" after "redemption" each place it appeared in clause (h)(3)(A)(ii)... Sec. 1006(d)(1)(B)(ii), added "or other corporate contractions" after "redemptions" in the heading of clause (h)(3)(A)(ii)... Sec. 1006(d)(1)(C), added "and" at the end of para. (m)(3), deleted para. (m)(4) and redesignated para. (m)(5) as para. (m)(4), effective for ownership changes after 6/10/87.
Prior to deletion, para. (m)(4) read as follows:
"(4) providing for the treatment of corporate contractions as redemptions for purposes of subsections (e)(2) and (h)(3)(A), and"
—P.L. 100-647, Sec. 1006(d)(2), added "rules similar to" before "the rules" in subpara. (g)(4)(C)... Sec. 1006(d)(3)(A), amended subpara. (h)(1)(C)... Sec. 1006(d)(3)(B), substituted "recognized built-in gains to the extent such gains increased the section 382 limitation for the year (or recognized built-in losses to the extent such losses are treated as pre-change losses)" for "recognized built-in gains and losses" in para. (h)(5)... Sec. 1006(d)(4)(A), added "the earlier of" before "the first day" in para. (i)(3)... Sec. 1006(d)(4)(B), added "or the taxable year in which the transaction being tested occurs" after "1st post-change year" in para. (i)(3)... Sec. 1006(d)(5)(A), added "or having a net operating loss for the taxable year in which the ownership change occurs" after "carryover" in para. (k)(1)... Sec. 1006(d)(5)(B), amended para. (k)(2)... Sec. 1006(d)(6), deleted "and" at the end of clause (l)(3)(A)(iii), deleted clause (l)(3)(A)(iv) and added clauses (l)(3)(A)(iv) and (v)... Sec. 1006(d)(7), substituted "after such ownership change and as a result of being shareholders or creditors immediately before such change" for "immediately after such ownership change" in clause (l)(5)(A)(ii)... Sec. 1006(d)(8)(A), added "1504(a)(2)(B)" for "1504(a)(2) and" after "substituting" in subclause (1)(5)(F)(i)(I)... Sec. 1006(d)(8)(B), substituted "the amount of deposits in the new loss corporation immediately after the change" for "deposits described in subclause (II)" in subclause (1)(5)(F)(ii)(III)... Sec. 1006(d)(9), substituted "shall reflect the increase (if any) in value of the old loss corporation resulting from any surrender or cancellation of creditors' claims in the transaction" for "shall be the value of the new loss corporation immediately after the ownership change" in para. (l)(6)... Sec. 1006(d)(10), added para. (l)(8)... Sec. 1006(d)(18), amended subpara. (l)(5)(C)... Sec. 1006(d)(19), amended subpara. (l)(5)(E)... Sec. 1006(d)(20)(A), added "(or to the extent the amount so disallowed is attributable to capital loss, under rules similar to the rules for the carry-

ing forward of net capital losses)" after "net operating losses" in subpara. (h)(4)(A) . . . Sec. 1006(d)(20)(B), substituted "allowed as a carryforward" for "treated as a net operating loss" in the heading of para. (h)(4) . . . Sec. 1006(d)(21)(A), substituted "loss corporation" for "new loss corporation" in para. (g)(1) . . . Sec. 1006(d)(21)(B), substituted "loss corporation" for "old loss corporation" in para. (g)(1) . . . Sec. 1006(d)(22), amended para. (h)(6) . . . Sec. 1006(d)(23), substituted "was acquired (or is subsequently transferred)" for "is transferred" in para. (h)(9) . . . Sec. 1006(d)(24), deleted "and" at the end of para. (m)(3) [as amended by Sec. 1006(d)(1)(C) of this Act], substituted ", and" for the period at the end of para. (m)(4) [as so redesignated by Sec. 1006(d)(1)(C) of this Act], and added para. (m)(5) . . . Sec. 1006(d)(25), substituted "stock of a controlling corporation" for "stock of controlling corporation" in clause (l)(5)(A)(ii) . . . Sec. 1006(d)(26), substituted "except as provided in regulations, there shall not" for "there shall not" in clause (h)(3)(B)(ii) . . . Sec. 1006(d)(27), substituted "the pre-change losses and excess credits (within the meaning of section 383(a)(2)) which may be carried to a post-change year shall be computed" for "the net operating loss deduction under section 172(a) for any post-change year shall be determined" in subpara. (l)(5)(B) . . . Sec. 1006(d)(29), substituted "section 368(a)(3)(D)(ii)" for "section 368(a)(D)(ii)" in clause (l)(5)(F)(iii)(I), effective as provided in Secs. 621(f)(1) and (f)(3) of P.L. 99-514 [reproduced in Note following Code Sec. 383] and Secs. 621(f)(4)-(9) of P.L. 99-514, reproduced below.

Prior to amendment, subpara. (h)(1)(C) read as follows:

"(C) Section 338 gain. The section 382 limitation for any taxable year in which gain is recognized by reason of an election under section 338 shall be increased by the excess of—

"(i) the amount of such gain, over

"(ii) the portion of such gain taken into account in computing recognized built-in gains for such taxable year."

Prior to amendment, para. (k)(2) read as follows:

"(2) Old loss corporation. The term 'old loss corporation' means any corporation with respect to which there is an ownership change—

"(A) which (before the ownership change) was a loss corporation, or

"(B) with respect to which there is a pre-change loss described in subsection (d)(1)(B)."

Prior to amendment, clause (l)(3)(A)(iv) read as follows:

"(iv) except to the extent provided in regulations, paragraph (4) of section 318(a) shall apply to an option if such application results in an ownership change."

Prior to amendment, subpara. (l)(5)(C) read as follows:

"(C) Reduction of carryforwards where discharge of indebtedness. In any case to which subparagraph (A) applies, the pre-change losses and excess credits (within the meaning of section 383(a)(2)) which may be carried to a post-change year shall be computed as if 50 percent of the amount which, but for the application of section 108(e)(10)(B), would have been includible in gross income for any taxable year had been so included."

Prior to amendment, subpara. (l)(5)(E) read as follows:

"(E) Only certain stock of creditors taken into account. For purposes of subparagraph (A)(ii), stock transferred to a creditor in satisfaction of indebtedness shall be taken into account only if such indebtedness—

"(i) was held by the creditor at least 18 months before the date of the filing of the title 11 or similar case, or

"(ii) arose in the ordinary course of the trade or business of the old loss corporation and is held by the person who at all times held the beneficial interest in such indebtedness."

Prior to amendment, para. (h)(6) read as follows:

"(6) Secretary may treat certain deductions as built-in losses. The Secretary may by regulation treat amounts which accrue on or before the change date but which are allowable as a deduction after such date as recognized built-in losses."

—P.L. 100-647, Sec. 1006(d)(12)(A), amended Sec. 621(f)(2)(C) of P.L. 99-514 [reproduced below] by adding "and reincorporated in Delaware in 1987" after "1924", see below . . . Sec. 1006(d)(12)(B), amended Sec. 621(f)(2)(C)(ii) of P.L. 99-514 [reproduced below], see below . . . Sec. 1006(d)(13), amended Sec. 621(f)(2)(D) of P.L. 99-514 [reproduced below] by deleting "or reorganization" which followed "such restructuring" , and by adding the last sentence, see below:

Prior to amendment, Sec. 621(f)(2)(C)(ii) of P.L. 99-514 read as follows:

"(ii) the amendments made by subsections (e) and (f) of section 806 of the Tax Reform Act of 1976 (including the amendment treated as part of such subsections under section 59(b) of the Tax Reform Act of 1984) shall apply to such debt restructuring."

—P.L. 100-647, Sec. 1006(d)(15), replaced the last sentence of Sec. 621(f)(4) of P.L. 99-514, [part of the effective date for changes made by Sec. 621(a) of P.L. 99-514] reproduced below, with two sentences.

Prior to amendment, the last sentence of Sec. 621(f)(4) of P.L. 99-514, read as follows:

"Any regulations prescribed under section 382(g)(3)(B) of the Internal Revenue Code of 1986 (as amended by subsection (a)) shall not apply with respect to domestic building and loan transactions for any period before January 1, 1989."

—P.L. 100-647, Sec. 1006(d)(16), substituted "a parent corporation incorporated in March 1980 under the laws of Delaware" for "the parent corporation referred to in section 203(d)(13)(B)" in Sec. 621(f)(7)(A) of P.L. 99-514 [part of the effective date for changes made by Sec. 621(a) of P.L. 99-514] reproduced below.

—P.L. 100-647, Sec. 1006(d)(17)(A), added para. (e)(3) effective as provided in Sec. 1006(d)(17)(B) of this Act which reads as follows:

"(B) The amendment made by subparagraph (A) [Sec. 1006(d)(17)(A)] shall apply to any ownership change after June 10, 1987. For purposes of the preceding sentence, any equity structure shift pursuant to a plan of reorganization adopted on or before June 10, 1987, shall be treated as occurring when such plan was adopted."

—P.L. 100-647, Sec. 1006(d)(28)(A), substituted "to the extent provided in regulations, determinations under clause (i)" for "determinations under clause (i)" in clause (h)(3)(A)(ii), effective in the case of ownership changes on or after 6/21/88.

—P.L. 100-647, Sec. 1006(t)(22), substituted "REMIC" for "real estate mortgage pool" in clause (l)(4)(B)(ii), effective for tax. yrs. begin. after 12/31/86.

—P.L. 100-647, Sec. 4012(a)(3), substituted "December 31, 1989" for "December 31, 1988" in the last sentence of subpara. (l)(5)(F), effective 11/10/88.

—P.L. 100-647, Sec. 4012(b)(1)(B), added "(as modified by section 368(a)(3)(D)(iv))" after "section 368(a)(3)(D)(ii)" in clause (l)(5)(F)(iii)(I), effective for any ownership change occurring after 11/10/88 and before 1/1/90.

—P.L. 100-647, Sec. 5077(a), deleted "and" at the end of subclause (l)(3)(C)(ii)(I), substituted ", and" for the period at the end of subclause (l)(3)(C)(ii)(II), and added subclause (l)(3)(C)(ii)(III), effective for acquisition after 12/31/88, except as provided in Sec. 5077(b)(2) of P.L. 100-647, as follows:

"(2) Exception. The amendment made by subsection (a) shall not apply to acquisitions after December 31, 1988, pursuant to a binding written contract entered into on or before October 21, 1988."

—P.L. 100-647, Sec. 6277(a), added the last sentence to Sec. 621(f)(5) of P.L. 99-514 [reproduced below] part of the effective date for changes made by Sec. 621(a) of P.L. 99-514 . . . Sec. 6277(b), substituted "Unless the taxpayer elects not to have the provisions of this paragraph apply, in" for "In" in Sec. 621(f)(5) of P.L. 99-514, see below:

In 1987, P.L. 100-203, Sec. 10225(a), added subpara. (g)(4)(D), effective for stock treated as becoming worthless in tax. yrs. begin. after 12/31/87.

—P.L. 100-203, Sec. 10225(b), added the last sentence to subpara. (h)(2)(B), effective for ownership changes (as defined in Code Sec. 382, as amended by Sec. 10225(a) of this Act, after 12/15/87; except for any ownership change pursuant to a binding written contract which was in effect on 12/15/87, and at all times thereafter before such ownership change.

In 1986, P.L. 99-514, Sec. 621(a), amended Code Sec. 382, effective as provided in Secs. 621(f)(1) and (f)(3) [reproduced in Note following Code Sec. 383] and (f)(4)-(9) [as amended by Secs. 1006(d)(15) and (16) of P.L. 100-647, see above] of this Act which read as follows

"(4) Special transition rules.—The amendments made by subsections (a), (b), and (c) shall not apply to any—

"(A) stock-for-debt exchanges and stock sales made pursuant to a plan of reorganization with respect to a petition for reorganization filed by a corporation under chapter 11 of title 11, United States Code, on August 26, 1982, and which filed with a United States district court a first amended and related plan of reorganization before March 1, 1986, or

"(B) ownership change of a Delaware corporation incorporated in August 1983, which may result from the exercise of put or call option under an agreement entered into on September 14, 1983, but only with respect to taxable years beginning after 1991 regardless of when such ownership change takes place.

Any regulations prescribed under section 382 of the Internal Revenue Code of 1986 (as added by subsection (a)) which have the effect of treating a group of shareholders as a separate 5-percent shareholder by reason of a public offering shall not apply to any public offering before January 1, 1989, for the benefit of institutions described in section 591 of such Code. Unless the corporation otherwise elects, an underwriter of any offering of stock in a corporation before September 19, 1986 (January 1, 1989, in the case of an offering for the benefit of an institution described in the preceding sentence), shall not be treated as acquiring any stock of such corporation by reason of a firm commitment underwriting to the extent the stock is disposed of pursuant to the offering (but in no event later than 60 days after the initial offering).

"(5) Bankruptcy proceedings.—Unless the taxpayer elects not to have the provisions of this paragraph apply, in the case of a reorganization described in subparagraph (G) of section 368(a)(1) of the Internal Revenue Code of 1986 or an exchange of debt for stock in a title 11 or similar case, as defined in section 368(a)(3) of such Code, the amendments made by subsections (a), (b), and (c) shall not apply to any ownership change resulting from such a reorganization or proceeding if a petition in such case was filed with the court before August 14, 1986. The determination as to whether an ownership change has occurred during the period beginning January 1, 1987, and ending on the final settlement of any reorganization or proceeding described in the preceding sentence shall be redetermined as of the time of such final settlement.

"(6) Certain plans.—The amendments made by subsections (a), (b), and (c) shall not apply to any ownership change with respect to—

"(A) the acquisition of a corporation the stock of which is acquired pursuant to a plan of divestiture which identified such corporation and its assets, and was agreed to by the board of directors of such corporation's parent corporation on May 17, 1985,

"(B) a merger which occurs pursuant to a merger agreement (entered into before September 24, 1985) and an application for approval by the Federal Home Loan Bank Board was filed on October 4, 1985,

"(C) a reorganization involving a party to a reorganization of a group of corporations engaged in enhanced oil recovery operations in California, merged in furtherance of a plan of reorganization adopted by a board of directors vote on September 24, 1985, and a Delaware corporation whose principal oil and gas producing fields are located in California, or

"(D) the conversion of a mutual savings and loan association holding a Federal charter dated March 22, 1985, to a stock savings and loan association pursuant to the rules and regulations of the Federal Home Loan Bank Board.

"(7) Ownership change of regulated air carrier.—The amendments made by subsections (a), (b), and (c) shall not apply to an ownership change of a regulated air carrier if—

"(A) on July 16, 1986, at least 40 percent of the outstanding common stock (excluding all preferred stock, whether or not convertible) of such carrier had been acquired by a parent corporation incorporated in March 1980 under the laws of Delaware, and

"(B) the acquisition (by or for such parent corporation) or retirement of the remaining common stock of such carrier is completed before the later of March 31, 1987, or 90 days after the requisite governmental approvals are finally granted, but only if the ownership change occurs on or before the later of March 31, 1987, or such 90th day. The aggregate reduction in tax for any taxable year by reason of this paragraph shall not exceed $10,000,000. The testing period for determining whether a subsequent ownership change has occurred shall not begin before the 1st day following an ownership change to which this paragraph applies.

"(8) The amendments made by subsections (a), (b), and (c) [Sec. 621] shall not apply to any ownership change resulting from the conversion of a Minnesota mutual savings bank holding a Federal charter dated December 31, 1985, to a stock savings bank pursuant to the rules and regulations of the Federal Home Loan Bank Board, and from the issuance of stock pursuant to that conversion to a holding company incorporated in Delaware on February 21, 1984. For purposes of determining whether any ownership change occurs with respect to the holding company or any subsidiary thereof (whether resulting from the transaction described in the preceding sentence or otherwise), any issuance of stock made by such holding company in connection with the transaction described in the preceding sentence shall not be taken into account.

"(9) Definitions.—Except as otherwise provided, terms used in this subsection shall have the same meaning as when used in section 382 of the Internal Revenue Code of 1986 (as amended by this section [Sec. 621])."

Prior to amendment, Code Sec. 382 read as follows:

"Sec. 382. Special limitations on net operating loss carryovers.

"(a) Purchase of a corporation and change in its trade or business.

"(1) In general. If, at the end of a taxable year of a corporation—

"(A) any one or more of those persons described in paragraph (2) own a percentage of the total fair market value of the outstanding stock of such corporation which is at least 50 percentage points more than such person or persons owned at—

"(i) the beginning of such taxable year, or

"(ii) the beginning of the prior taxable year,

"(B) the increase in percentage points at the end of such taxable year is attributable to—

"(i) a purchase by such person or persons of such stock, the stock of another corporation owning stock in such corporation, or an interest in a partnership or trust owning stock in such corporation, or

"(ii) a decrease in the amount of such stock outstanding or the amount of stock outstanding of another corporation owning stock in such corporation, except a decrease resulting from a redemption to pay death taxes to which section 303 applies, and

"(C) such corporation has not continued to carry on a trade or business substantially the same as that conducted before any change in the percentage ownership of the fair market value of such stock,

the net operating loss carryovers, if any, from prior taxable years of such corporation to such taxable year and subsequent taxable years shall not be included in the net operating loss deduction for such taxable year and subsequent taxable years.

"(2) Description of person or persons. The person or persons referred to in paragraph (1) shall be the 10 persons (or such lesser number as there are persons owning the outstanding stock at the end of such taxable year) who own the greatest percentage of the fair market value of such stock at the end of such taxable year; except that, if any other person owns the same percentage of such stock at such time as is owned by one of the 10 persons, such person shall also be included. If any of the persons are so related that such stock owned by one is attributed to the other under the rules specified in paragraph (3), such persons shall be considered as only one person solely for the purpose of selecting the 10 persons (more or less) who own the greatest percentage of the fair market value of such outstanding stock.

"(3) Attribution of ownership. Section 318 (relating to constructive ownership of stock) shall apply in determining the ownership of stock, except that sections 318(a)(2)(C) and 318(a)(3)(C) shall be applied without regard to the 50 percent limitation contained therein.

"(4) Definition of purchase. For purposes of this subsection, the term 'purchase' means the acquisition of stock, the basis of which is determined solely by reference to its cost to the holder thereof, in a transaction from a person or persons other than the person or persons the ownership of whose stock would be attributed to the holder by application of paragraph (3).

"(b) Change of ownership as the result of a reorganization.

"(1) In general. If, in the case of a reorganization specified in paragraph (2) of section 381(a), the transferor corporation or the acquiring corporation—

"(A) has a net operating loss which is a net operating loss carryover to the first taxable year of the acquiring corporation ending after the date of transfer, and

"(B) the stockholders (immediately before the reorganization) of such corporation (hereinafter in this subsection referred to as the 'loss corporation'), as the result of owning stock of the loss corporation, own (immediately after the reorganization) less than 20 percent of the fair market value of the outstanding stock of the acquiring corporation,

the total net operating loss carryover from prior taxable years of the loss corporation to the first taxable year of the acquiring corporation ending after the date of transfer shall be reduced by the percentage determined under paragraph (2).

"(2) Reduction of net operating loss carryover. The reduction applicable under paragraph (1) shall be the percentage determined by subtracting from 100 percent—

"(A) in the percent of the fair market value of the outstanding stock of the acquiring corporation owned (immediately after the reorganization) by the stockholders (immediately before the reorganization) of the loss corporation, as the result of owning stock of the loss corporation, multiplied by

"(B) five.

"(3) Exception to limitation in this subsection. The limitation in this subsection shall not apply if the transferor corporation and the acquiring corporation are owned substantially by the same persons in the same proportion.

"(4) Net operating loss carryovers to subsequent years. In computing the net operating loss carryovers to taxable years subsequent to a taxable year in which there was a limitation applicable to a net operating loss carryover by operation of this subsection, the income in such taxable year, as computed under section 172(b)(2), shall be increased by the amount of the reduction of the total net operating loss carryover determined under paragraph (2).

"(5) attribution of ownership. If the transferor corporation or the acquiring corporation owns (immediately before the reorganization) any of the outstanding stock of the loss corporation, such transferor corporation or acquiring corporation shall, for purposes of this subsection, be treated as owning (immediately after the reorganization) a percentage of the fair market value of the acquiring corporation's outstanding stock which bears the same ratio to the percentage of the fair market value of the outstanding stock of the loss corporation (immediately before the reorganization) owned by such transferor corporation or acquiring corporation as the fair market value of the total outstanding stock of the loss corporation (immediately before the reorganization) bears to the fair market value of the total outstanding stock of the acquiring corporation (immediately after the reorganization).

"(6) Stock of corporation controlling acquiring corporation. If the stockholders of the loss corporation (immediately before the reorganization) own, as a result of the reorganization, stock in a corporation controlling the acquiring corporation, such stock of the controlling corporation shall, for purposes of this subsection, be treated as stock of the acquiring corporation in an amount valued at an equivalent fair market value.

"(7) Special rule for reorganizations in title 11 or similar cases.

For purposes of this subsection.

"(A) a creditor who receives stock in a reorganization in a title 11 or similar case (within the meaning of section 368(a)(3)(A)) shall be treated as a stockholder immediately before the reorganization, and

"(B) in a transaction qualifying under section 368(a)(3)(D)(ii)—

"(i) a depositor in the transferor shall be treated as a stockholder immediately before the reorganization of the loss corporation,

"(ii) deposits in the transferor which become, as a result of the transfer, deposits in the transferee shall be treated as stock of the acquiring corporation owned as a result of owning stock of the loss corporation, and

"(iii) the fair market value of the outstanding stock of the acquiring corporation shall include the amount of deposits in the acquiring corporation immediately after the reorganization.

"(c) Definition of stock.

"For purposes of this section, 'stock' means all shares except nonvoting stock which is limited and preferred as to dividends."

—P.L. 99-514, Sec. 621(e)(1), repealed Sec. 806(e) of P.L. 94-455 which amended Code Sec. 382, effective as provided in Sec. 621(f)(2) [as amended by P.L. 100-647, Secs. 1006(d)(12)(A) and (B) and Sec. 1006(d)(13)] of this Act:

"(2) For amendments to tax reform act of 1976.—

"(A) In general.—The repeals made by subsection (e)(1) [Sec. 621] and the amendment made by subsection (e)(2) shall take effect on January 1, 1986.

"(B) Election to have amendments apply.—

"(i) If a taxpayer described in clause (ii) elects to have the provisions of this subparagraph apply, the amendments made by subsections (e) and (f) of section 806 of the Tax Reform Act of 1976 shall apply to the reorganization described in clause (ii).

"(ii) A taxpayer is described in this clause if the taxpayer filed a title 11 or similar case on December 8, 1981, filed a plan of reorganization on February 5, 1986, filed an amended plan on March 14, 1986, and received court approval for the amended plan and disclosure statement on April 16, 1986.

"(C) Application of old rules to certain debt.— In the case of debt of a corporation incorporated in Colorado on November 8, 1924, and reincorporated in Delaware in 1987 with headquarters in Denver, Colorado—

"(i) the amendments made by subsections (a), (b), and (c) shall not apply to any debt restructuring of such debt which was approved by the debtor's Board of Directors and the lenders in 1986, and

"(ii) the amendments made by subsections (e) and (f) of section 806 of the Tax Reform Act of 1976 shall not apply to such debt restructuring, except that the amendment treated as part of such subsections under section 59(b) of the Tax Reform Act of 1984 (relating to qualified workouts) shall apply to such debt restructuring.

"(D) Special rule for oil and gas well drilling business.—In the case of a Texas corporation incorporated on July 23, 1935, in applying section 382 of the Internal Revenue Code of 1986 (as in effect before and after the amendments made by subsections (a), (b), and (c) [Sec. 621]) to a loan restructuring agreement during 1985, section 382(a)(5)(C) of the Internal Revenue Code of 1954 (as added by the amendments made by subsections (e) and (f) of section 806 of the Tax Reform Act of 1976) shall be applied as if it were in effect with respect to such restructuring. For purposes of the preceding sentence, in applying section 382 (as so in effect), if a person has a warrant to acquire stock, such stock shall be considered as owned by such person."

Prior to repeal of Sec. 806(e) of P.L. 94-455, Code Sec. 382 [as amended by Sec. 806(e) of P.L. 94-455] read as follows:

"Sec. 382. Special limitations on net operating loss carryover.

Corporate distributions and adjustments Code Sec. 382

"(a) Certain acquisitions of stock of a corporation.

"(1) In general. If—

"(A) on the last day of a taxable year of a corporation,

"(B) any one or more of the persons described in paragraph (4)(B) own, directly or indirectly, a percentage of the total fair market value of the participating stock or of all the stock of the corporation which exceeds by more than 60 percentage points the percentage of such stock owned by such person or persons at—

"(i) the beginning of such taxable year, or

"(ii) the beginning of the first or second preceding taxable year, and

"(C) such increase in percentage points is attributable to—

"(i) a purchase by such person or persons of such stock, or of the stock of another corporation owning stock in such corporation, or of an interest in a partnership or trust owning stock in such corporation,

"(ii) an acquisition (by contribution, merger, or consolidation) of an interest in a partnership owning stock in such corporation, or an acquisition (by contribution, merger, or consolidation) by a partnership of such stock,

"(iii) an exchange to which section 351 (relating to transfer to corporation controlled by transferor) applies, or an acquisition by a corporation of such stock in an exchange in which section 351 applies to the transferor,

"(iv) a contribution to the capital of such corporation,

"(v) a decrease in the amount of such stock outstanding or in the amount of stock outstanding of another corporation owning stock in such corporation (except a decrease resulting from a redemption to pay death taxes to which section 303 applies),

"(vi) a liquidation of the interest of a partner in a partnership owning stock in such corporation, or

"(vii) any combination of the transactions described in clauses (i) through (vi), then the net operating loss carryover, if any, from such taxable year and the net operating loss carryovers, if any, from prior taxable years to such taxable year and subsequent taxable years of such corporation shall be reduced by the percentage determined under paragraph (2),

"(2) Reduction of net operating loss carryover. The reduction applicable under paragraph (1) shall be the sum of the percentages determined by multiplying—

"(A) by three and one-half the increase in percentage points (including fractions thereof) in excess of 60 and up to and including 80, and

"(B) by one and one-half the increase in percentage points (including fractions thereof) in excess of 80.

The reduction under this paragraph shall be determined by reference to the increase in percentage points of the total fair market value of the participating stock or of all the stock, whichever increase is greater.

"(3) Minimum ownership rule. Notwithstanding the provisions of paragraph (1), a net operating loss carryover from a taxable year shall not be reduced under this subsection if, at all times during the last half of such taxable year, and of the persons described in paragraph (4)(B) (determined on the last day of the taxable year referred to in paragraph (1)(A)) owned at least 40 percent of the total fair market value of the participating stock and of all the stock of the corporation. For purposes of the preceding sentence, persons owning stock of a corporation on the last day of its first taxable year shall be considered to have owned such stock at all times during the last half of such first taxable year.

"(4) Operating rules. For purposes of this subsection—

"(A) Definition of purchase. The term 'purchase' means an acquisition of stock the basis of which is determined by reference to its cost to the holder thereof.

"(B) Description of person or persons. The person or persons referred to in paragraph (1)(B) shall be the 15 persons (or such lesser number as there are persons owning the stock on the last day of the taxable year) who own the greatest percentage of the total fair market value of all the stock on the last day of that year, except that if any other person owns the same percentage of such stock at such time as is owned by one of the 15 persons, that other person shall also be included. If any of the persons are so related that the stock owned by one is attributed to the other under the rules specified in subparagraph (C), such persons shall be considered as only one person solely for the purpose of selecting the 15 persons (more or less) who own the greatest percentage of the total fair market value of all the stock.

"(C) Constructive ownership. Section 318 (relating to constructive ownership of stock) shall apply in determining the ownership of stock, except that section 318(a)(2)(C) and 318(a)(3)(C) shall be applied without regard to the 50 percent limitation contained therein.

"(D) Short taxable years. If one of the taxable years of the corporation referred to in paragraph (i)(B) is a short taxable year, then such paragraph and paragraph (6) shall be applied by substituting 'first, second, or third' for 'first or second' each time such phrase occurs.

"(5) Exceptions. This subsection shall not apply to a purchase or other acquisition of stock (or of an interest in a partnership or trust owning stock in the corporation)—

"(A) from a person whose ownership of stock would be attributed to the holder by application of paragraph (4)(C) to the extent that such stock would be so attributed;

"(B) if (and to the extent) the basis thereof is determined under section 1014 or 1023 (relating to property acquired from a decedent), or section 1015(a) or (b) (relating to property acquired by gift or transfers in trust);

"(C) by a security holder or creditor in exchange for the relinquishment or extinguishment in whole or part of a claim against the corporation, unless the claim was acquired for the purpose of acquiring such stock;

"(D) by one or more persons who were full-time employees of the corporation at all times during the period of 36 months ending on the last day of the taxable year of the corporation (or at all times during the period of the corporation's existence, if shorter);

"(E) by a trust described in section 401(a) which is exempt from tax under section 501(a) and which benefits exclusively the employees (or their beneficiaries) of the corporation, including a member of a controlled group of corporations (within the meaning of section 1563(a) determined without regard to Section 1563(a)(4) and (e)(3)(C)) which includes such corporation;

"(F) by an employee stock ownership plan meeting the requirements of section 301(d) of the Tax Reduction Act of 1975; or

"(G) in a recapitalization described in section 368(a)(1)(E).

"(6) Successive applications of subsection. If—

"(A) a net operating loss carryover is reduced under this subsection at the end of a taxable year of a corporation, and

"(B) any person described in paragraph (4)(B) who owns stock of the corporation on the last day of such taxable year does not own, on the last day of the first or second succeeding taxable year of the corporation, a greater percentage of the total fair market value of the participating stock or of all the stock of the corporation than such person owned on the last day of such taxable year,

then, for purposes of applying this subsection as of the end of the first or second succeeding taxable year (as the case may be), stock owned by such person at the end of such succeeding taxable year shall be considered owned by such person at the beginning of the first or second preceding taxable year. Other rules relating to the manner and extent of successive applications of this section in the case of increases in ownership and transfers of stock by the persons described in paragraph (4)(B) shall be prescribed by regulations issued by the Secretary.

"(b) Reorganizations.

"(1) In general. If one corporation acquires the stock or assets of another corporation in a reorganization described in subparagraph (A), (B), (C), or (F) of section 368(a)(1) or subparagraph (D) or (G) of section 368(a)(1) (but only if the requirements of section 354(b)(1) are met), and if—

"(A) the acquiring or acquired corporation has a net operating loss for the taxable year which includes the date of the acquisition, or a net operating loss carryover from a prior taxable year to such taxable year, and

"(B) the shareholders (immediately before the reorganization) of such corporation (the 'loss corporation'), as the result of owning stock of the loss corporation, own (immediately after the reorganization) less than 40 percent of the total fair market value of the participating stock or of all the stock of the acquiring corporation,

then the net operating loss carryover (if any) of the loss corporation from the taxable year which includes the date of the acquisition, and the net operating loss carryovers (if any) of the loss corporation from prior taxable years to such taxable year and subsequent taxable years, shall be reduced by the percentage determined under paragraph (2).

"(2) Reduction of net operating loss carryover.

"(A) Ownership of 20 percent or more. If such shareholders own less than 40 percent, but not less than 20 percent, of the total fair market value of the participating stock or of all the stock of the acquiring corporation, the reduction applicable under paragraph (1) shall be the percentage equal to the number of percentage points (including fractions thereof) less than 40 percent, multiplied by three and one-half.

"(B) Ownership of less than 20 percent. If such shareholders own less than 20 percent of the total fair market value of the participating stock or of all the stock of the acquiring corporation, the reduction applicable under paragraph (1) shall be the sum of—

"(i) the percentage that would be determined under subparagraph (A) if the shareholders owned 20 percent of such stock, plus

"(ii) the percentage equal to the number of percentage points (including fractions thereof) of such stock less than 20 percent, multiplied by one and one-half.

The reduction under this paragraph shall be determined by reference to the lesser of the percentage of the total fair market value of the participating stock or of all the stock of the acquiring corporation owned by such shareholders.

"(3) Losses of controlled corporations. For purposes of this subsection—

"(A) Holding companies. If, immediately before the reorganization, the acquiring or acquired corporation controls a corporation which has a net operating loss for the taxable year which includes the date of the acquisition, or a net operating loss carryover from a prior taxable year to such taxable year, the acquiring or acquired corporation, as the case may be, shall be treated as the loss corporation (whether or not such corporation is a loss corporation). The reduction, if any, so determined under paragraph (2) shall be applied to the losses of such controlled corporation.

"(B) Triangular reorganizations. Except as otherwise provided in paragraph (5), if the shareholders of the loss corporation (immediately before the reorganization) own, as a result of the reorganization, stock in a corporation controlling the acquiring corporation, such shareholders shall be treated as owning (immediately after the reorganization) a percentage of the total fair market value of the participating stock and of all the stock of the acquiring corporation owned by the controlling corporation equal to the percentage of the total fair market value of the participating stock and of all the stock, respectively, of the controlling corporation owned by such shareholders.

"(4) Special rules. For purposes of applying paragraph (1)(B)—

"(A) Certain related transactions. If, immediately before the reorganization—

"(i) one or more shareholders of the loss corporation own stock of such corporation which such shareholder acquired during the 36-month period ending on the date of the acquisition in a transaction described in paragraph (1) or in subsection (a)(1)(C) (unless excepted by subsection (a)(5)), and

"(ii) such shareholders own more than 50 percent of the total fair market value of the stock of another corporation a party to the reorganization, or any such shareholder is a corporation controlled by another corporation a party to the reorganization, then such shareholders shall not be treated as shareholders of the loss corporation with respect to such stock.

"(B) Certain prior ownership of loss corporation. If, immediately before the reorganization, the acquiring or acquired corporation owns stock of the loss corporation, then paragraph (1)(B) shall be applied by treating the shareholders of the loss corporation as owning an additional amount of the total fair market value of the participating stock and of all the stock of the acquiring corporation, as a result of owning stock in the loss corporation, equal to the total fair market value of the participating stock and of all the stock, respectively, of the loss corporation owned (immediately before the reorganization) by the acquiring or acquired corporation. This subparagraph shall not apply to stock of the loss corporation owned by the acquiring or acquired corporation if such stock was acquired by such corporation within the 36-month period ending on the date of the reorganization in a transaction described in subsection (a)(1)(C) (unless excepted by subsection (a)(5)); or to a reorganization described in section 368(a)(1)(B) or (C) to the extent the acquired corporation does not distribute the stock received by it to its own shareholders.

"(C) Certain asset acquisitions. If a loss corporation receives stock of the acquiring corporation in a reorganization described in section 368(a)(1)(C) and does not distribute such stock to its shareholders, paragraph (1)(B) shall be applied by treating the shareholders of the loss corporation as owning (immediately after the reorganization) such undistributed stock in proportion to the fair market value of the stock which such shareholders own in the loss corporation.

"(5) Certain stock-for-stock reorganizations. In the case of a reorganization described in section 368(a)(1)(B) in which the acquired corporation is a loss corporation—

"(A) Stock which is exchanged. Paragraphs (1)(B) and (2) shall be applied by reference to the ownership of stock of the loss corporation (rather than the acquiring corporation) immediately after the reorganization. Shareholders of the loss corporation who exchange stock of the loss corporation shall be treated as owning (immediately after the reorganization) a percentage of the total fair market value of the participating stock and of all the stock of the loss corporation acquired in the exchange by the acquiring corporation which is equal to the percentage of the total fair market value of the participating stock and of all the stock, respectively, of the acquiring corporation owned (immediately after the reorganization) by such shareholders.

"(B) Stock which is not exchanged. Stock of the loss corporation owned by shareholders immediately before the reorganization which was not exchanged in the reorganization shall be taken into account in applying paragraph (1)(B). For purposes of the preceding sentence, the acquiring corporation (or a corporation controlled by the acquiring corporation) shall not be treated as a shareholder of the loss corporation with respect to stock of the loss corporation acquired in a transaction described in paragraph (1), or in subsection (a)(1)(C) (unless excepted by subsection (a)(5)), during the 36-month period ending on the date of the exchange.

"(C) Triangular exchanges. For purposes of applying the rules in this paragraph, if the shareholders of the loss corporation receive stock of a corporation controlling the acquiring corporation, such shareholders shall be treated as owning a percentage of the participating stock and of all the stock of the acquiring corporation owned by the controlling corporation equal to the percentage of the total fair market value of the participating stock and of all the stock, respectively, which such shareholders own of the controlling corporation immediately after the reorganization.

"(6) Exceptions. The limitations in this subsection shall not apply—

"(A) if the same persons own substantially all the stock of the acquiring corporation and of the other corporation in substantially the same proportions; or

"(B) to a net operating loss carryover from a taxable year if the acquiring or acquired corporation owned at least 40 percent of the total fair market value of the participating stock and of all the stock of the loss corporation at all times during the last half of such taxable year.

For purposes of subparagraph (A), if the acquiring or acquired corporation is controlled by another corporation, the shareholders of the controlling corporation shall be considered as also owning the stock owned by the controlling corporation in that proportion which the total fair market value of the stock which each shareholder owns in the controlling corporation bears to the total fair market value of all the stock in the controlling corporation.

"(c) Rules relating to stock.

"For purposes of this section—

"(1) The term 'stock' means all shares of stock, except stock which—

"(A) is not entitled to vote,

"(B) is fixed and preferred as to dividends and does not participate in corporate growth to any significant extent,

"(C) has redemption and liquidation rights which do not exceed the paid-in capital or par value represented by such stock (except for a reasonable redemption premium in excess of such paid-in capital or par value), and

"(D) is not convertible into another class of stock.

"(2) The term 'participating stock' means stock (including common stock) which represents an interest in the earnings and assets of the issuing corporation which is not limited to a stated amount of money or property or percentage of paid-in capital or par value, or by any similar formula.

"(3) The Secretary shall prescribe regulations under which—

"(A) stock or convertible securities shall be treated as stock or participating stock, or

"(B) stock (however denoted) shall not be treated as stock or participating stock,

by reason of conversion and call rights, rights in earnings and assets, priorities and preferences as to distributions of earnings or assets, and similar factors."

—P.L. 99-514, Sec. 621(e)(2), repealed Secs. 806(g)(2) and (3) of P.L. 94-455 [reproduced below], the effective dates for changes made by Sec. 806(e) of P.L. 94-455, effective as provided in Sec. 621(f)(2) of this Act reproduced above.

In 1984, P.L. 98-369, Sec. 62(a), amended Sec. 806(g)(2) and (3) [reproduced below] of P.L. 94-455, the effective date for changes made by Sec. 806(e) of P.L. 94-455, by substituting "December 31, 1985" for "June 30, 1984" in Sec. 806(g)(2) and by substituting "January 1, 1986" for "January 1, 1984" in Secs. 806(g)(2)(B) and (3).

—P.L. 98-369, Sec. 62(b)(1), substituted "subparagraph (A), (B), (C), or (F) of section 368(a)(1) or subparagraph (D) or (G) of section 368(a)(1) (but only if the requirements of section 354(b)(1) are met)" for "section 368(a)(1)(A), (B), (C), (D) (but only if the requirements of section 354(b)(1) are met), or (F)" in para. (b)(1), effective generally for any bankruptcy case or similar judicial proceeding commencing after 12/31/80.

In 1981, P.L. 97-119, Sec. 111, substituted "1984" for "1982" each place it appeared in Sec. 806(g)(2) and (3) of P.L. 94-455, the effective date for changes made by Sec. 806(e) of P.L. 94-455, see below.

—P.L. 97-34, Sec. 242, amended para. (b)(7), effective for transfers made on or after 1/1/81.

Prior to amendment, para. (b)(7) read as follows:

"(7) Special rule for reorganizations in title 11 or similar cases. For purposes of this subsection, a creditor who receives stock in a reorganization in a title 11 or similar case (within the meaning of section 368(a)(3)(A)) shall be treated as a stockholder immediately before the reorganization."

In 1980, P.L. 96-589, Sec. 2(d), added para. (b)(7). Sec. 7(a) of this Act makes this amendment effective for any transaction which occurs after 12/31/80, other than a transaction which occurs in a proceeding in a bankruptcy case or similar judicial proceeding (or in a proceeding under the Bankruptcy Act) beginning on or before 12/31/80. Sec. 7(f) and (g) of this Act provide:

"(f) Election to substitute September 30, 1979, for December 31, 1980.

"(1) In general. The debtor (or debtors) in a bankruptcy case or similar judicial proceeding may (with the approval of the court) elect to apply [subsection 7(a) of this Act] by substituting 'September 30, 1979' for 'December 31, 1980' each place it appears in such subsections.

"(2) Effect of election. Any election made under paragraph (1) with respect to any proceeding shall apply to all parties to the proceeding.

"(3) Revocation only with consent. Any election under this subsection may be revoked only with the consent of the Secretary of the Treasury or his delegate.

"(4) Time and manner of election. Any election under this subsection shall be made at such time, and in such manner, as the Secretary of the Treasury or his delegate may by regulations prescribe.

"(g) Definitions.

"For purposes of this section—

"(1) Bankruptcy case. The term 'bankruptcy case' means any case under title 11 of the United States Code (as recodified by P.L. 95-598).

"(2) Similar judicial proceeding. The term 'similar judicial proceeding' means a receivership, foreclosure, or similar proceeding in a Federal or State court (as modified by section 368(a)(3)(D) of the Internal Revenue Code of 1954)."

In 1979, P.L. 96-167, Sec. 9(e), extended the effective date of Sec. 806(g)(2) and (3) of P.L. 95-455, by substituting "1982" for "1980" each place it appears. See below.

In 1978, P.L. 95-600, Sec. 368(a), extended the effective date of Sec. 806(g)(2) and (3) of P.L. 95-455, by substituting "1980" for "1978" each place it appeared. See below. Sec. 368(b) of the Act provides as follows:

"(b) Election of prior law.

"(1) A taxpayer may elect not to have the amendment made by subsection (a) apply with respect to any acquisition or reorganization occurring before the end of the taxpayer's first taxable year beginning after June 30, 1978, where such acquisition or reorganization occurs pursuant to a written binding contract or option to acquire stock or assets which was entered into before September 27, 1978.

"(2) An election under this subsection shall be filed with a taxpayer's timely filed return for the first taxable year in which a reorganization or acquisition described in paragraph (1) occurs, or, if later, within 90 days after the date of enactment of this Act. Such election shall apply to all acquisitions and reorganizations to which, but for such election, subsection (a) would apply."

In 1976, P.L. 94-455, Sec. 806(e), [repealed by Sec. 621(e)(1) of P.L. 99-514, see above] amended Code Sec. 382. Sec. 806(g)(2) and (3) [repealed by Sec. 621(e)(2) of P.L. 99-514, see above] of the Act provides:

"(2) For purposes of applying sections 382(a) and 383 (as it relates to section 382(a)) of the Internal Revenue Code of 1954, as amended by subsections (e) and (f), the amendments made by subsections (e) and (f) shall take effect for taxable years beginning after December 31, 1985, except that the beginning of the taxable years specified in clause (ii) of section 382(a)(1)(B) of such Code, as so amended, shall be considered to be the later of:

"(A) the beginning of such taxable years, or

"(B) January 1, 1986.

"(3) Sections 382(b) and 383 (as it relates to section 382(b)) of the Internal Revenue Code of 1954, as amended by subsections (e) and (f), shall apply (and such sections as in effect prior to such amendment shall not apply) to reorganizations pursuant to a plan of reorganization adopted by one or more of the parties thereto on or after January 1, 1986. For purposes of the preceding sentence, a corporation shall be considered to have adopted a plan of reorganization on the date on which a resolution of the board of directors is passed adopting the plan or recommending its adoption to the shareholders, or on the date on which the shareholders approve the plan of reorganization, whichever is earlier."

In 1964, P.L. 88-554, Sec. 4(b)(3), substituted "sections 318(a)(2) and 318(a)(3)" for "section 318(a)(2)" in para. (a)(3), effective 8/31/64, except that for purposes

Corporate distributions and adjustments — Code Sec. 383

Sec. 383. Special limitations on certain excess credits, etc.

(a) Excess credits.

(1) In general. Under regulations, if an ownership change occurs with respect to a corporation, the amount of any excess credit for any taxable year which may be used in any post-change year shall be limited to an amount determined on the basis of the tax liability which is attributable to so much of the taxable income as does not exceed the section 382 limitation for such post-change year to the extent available after the application of section 382 and subsections (b) and (c) of this section.

(2) Excess credit. For purposes of paragraph (1), the term "excess credit" means—

(A) any unused general business credit of the corporation under section 39, and

(B) any unused minimum tax credit of the corporation under section 53.

(b) Limitation on net capital loss.

If an ownership change occurs with respect to a corporation, the amount of any net capital loss under section 1212 for any taxable year before the 1st post-change year which may be used in any post-change year shall be limited under regulations which shall be based on the principles applicable under section 382. Such regulations shall provide that any such net capital loss used in a post-change year shall reduce the section 382 limitation which is applied to pre-change losses under section 382 for such year.

(c) Foreign tax credits.

If an ownership change occurs with respect to a corporation, the amount of any excess foreign taxes under section 904(c) for any taxable year before the 1st post-change taxable year shall be limited under regulations which shall be consistent with purposes of this section and section 382.

(d) Pro ration rules for year which includes change.

For purposes of this section, rules similar to the rules of subsections (b)(3) and (d)(1)(B) of section 382 shall apply.

(e) Definitions.

Terms used in this section shall have the same respective meanings as when used in section 382, except that appropriate adjustments shall be made to take into account that the limitations of this section apply to credits and net capital losses.

In 1988, P.L. 100-647, Sec. 1006(d)(11), amended Sec. 621(f)(1) [reproduced below] of P.L. 99-514, part of the effective date for changes made by Sec. 621(b) of P.L. 99-514 . . . Sec. 1006(d)(14), deleted " after December 31, 1986" after "ownership change" in Sec. 621(f)(3) [reproduced below] of P.L. 99-514, part of the effective date for changes made by Sec. 621(b) at P.L. 99-514, see below.

Prior to amendment, Sec. 621(f)(1) of P.L. 99-514 read as follows:

"(1) In general. The amendments made by subsections (a), (b), and (c) [Sec. 621] shall apply to any ownership change following

"(A) an owner shift involving a 5-percent shareholder occurring after December 31, 1986, or

"(B) an equity structure shift occurring pursuant to a plan of reorganization adopted after December 31, 1986."

In 1986, P.L. 99-514, Sec. 231(a)(2), amended Sec. 221(d) of P.L. 97-34, the effective date for changes made by Sec. 221(b)(1)(A) of P.L. 97-34, by substituting "amounts paid or incurred after June 30, 1981" for "amounts paid or incurred after June 30, 1981 and before January 1, 1986" [see below].

—P.L. 99-514, Sec. 621(b), amended Code Sec. 383, effective as provided in Secs. 621(f)(1) and (3) [as amended by P.L. 100-647, Secs. 1006(d)(11) and (d)(14), see above] of this Act:

"(1) Amendments made by subsections (a), (b), and (c).—

"(A) In general.—

"(i) Changes after 1986.—The amendments made by subsections (a), (b), and (c) shall apply to any ownership change after December 31, 1986.

"(ii) Plans of reorganization adopted before 1987.—For purposes of clause (i), any equity structure shift pursuant to a plan of reorganization adopted before January 1, 1987, shall be treated as occurring when such plan was adopted.

"(B) Termination of old section 382.—Except in a case described in any of the following paragraphs—

"(i) section 382(a) of the Internal Revenue Code of 1954 (as in effect before the amendment made by subsection (a) and the amendments made by section 806 of the Tax Reform Act of 1976) shall not apply to any increase in percentage points occurring after December 31, 1988, and

"(ii) section 382(b) of such Code (as so in effect) shall not apply to any reorganization occurring pursuant to a plan of reorganization adopted after December 31, 1986.

In no event shall sections 382(a) and (b) of such Code (as so in effect) apply to any ownership change described in subparagraph (A).

"(C) Coordination with section 382(i).—For purposes of section 382(i) of the Internal Revenue Code of 1986 (as added by this section), any equity structure shift pursuant to a plan of reorganization adopted before January 1, 1987, shall be treated as occurring when such plan was adopted."

* * *

"(3) Testing period.—For purposes of determining whether there is an ownership change the testing period shall not begin before the later of—

"(A) May 6, 1986, or

"(B) in the case of an ownership change which occurs after May 5, 1986, and to which the amendments made by subsections (a), (b), and (c) do not apply, the first day following the date on which such ownership change occurs."

For special transitional rules, see Secs. 621(f)(4)-(9) of this Act reproduced in note following Code Sec. 382.

Prior to amendment, Code Sec. 383 read as follows:

"SEC. 383. SPECIAL LIMITATIONS ON UNUSED BUSINESS CREDITS, RESEARCH CREDITS, FOREIGN TAXES, AND CAPITAL LOSSES.

"If—

"(1) the ownership and business of a corporation are changed in the manner described in section 382(a)(1), or

"(2) in the case of a reorganization specified in paragraph (2) of section 381(a), there is a change in ownership described in section 382(b)(1)(B),

then the limitations provided in section 382 in such cases with respect to the carryover of net operating losses shall apply in the same manner, as provided under regulations prescribed by the Secretary, with respect to any unused business credit of the corporation which can otherwise be carried forward under section 39, to any unused credit of the corporation which could otherwise be carried forward under section 30(g)(2), to any excess foreign taxes of the corporation which could otherwise be carried forward under section 904(c), and to any net capital loss of the corporation which can otherwise be carried forward under section 1212."

—P.L. 99-514, Sec. 621(e)(1), repealed Sec. 806(f)(2) of P.L. 94-455 which amended Code Sec. 383, effective as provided in Sec. 621(f)(2) of this Act reproduced in the note following Code Sec. 382.

Prior to repeal of Sec. 806(f) of P.L. 94-455, Code Sec. 383, [as amended by Sec. 806(f)(2) of P.L. 94-455] read as follows:

"SEC. 383. SPECIAL LIMITATIONS ON UNUSED BUSINESS CREDITS, RESEARCH CREDITS, FOREIGN TAXES, AND CAPITAL LOSSES.

"In the case of a change of ownership of a corporation in the manner described in section 382(a) or (b), the limitations provided in section 382 in such cases with respect to net operating losses shall apply in the same manner, as provided under regulations prescribed by the Secretary, with respect to any unused business credit of the corporation under section 39, to any unused credit of the corporation under section 30(g)(2), to any excess foreign taxes of the corporation under section 904(c), and to any net capital loss of the corporation under section 1212."

—P.L. 99-514, Sec. 621(e)(2), repealed Secs. 806(g)(2) and (3), [reproduced below], of P.L. 94-455, the effective dates for changes made by Sec. 806(e) of P.L. 94-455, effective as provided in Sec. 621(f)(2) of this Act, reproduced in note following Code Sec. 382.

In 1984, P.L. 98-369, Sec. 62(a), amended Secs. 806(g)(2) and (3) [reproduced below] of P.L. 94-455, the effective date for changes made by Sec. 806(f) of P.L. 94-455, by substituting "December 31, 1985" for "June 30, 1984" in Sec. 806(g)(2) and by substituting "January 1, 1986" for "January 1, 1984" in Secs. 806(g)(2)(B) and (3).

—P.L. 98-369, Sec. 474(r)(12)(A), substituted "with respect to any unused business credit of the corporation which can otherwise be carried forward under section 39, to any unused credit of the corporation which could otherwise be carried forward under section 30(g)(2), to any excess foreign taxes of the corporation which could otherwise be carried forward under section 904(c), and to any net capital loss of the corporation which can otherwise be carried forward under section 1212." for "with respect to any unused investment credit of the corporation which can otherwise be carried forward under section 46(b), to any unused work incentive program credit of the corporation which can otherwise be carried forward under section 50A(b), to any unused new employee credit of the corporation which could otherwise be carried forward under section 53(b), to any unused credit of the corporation under section 44E(e)(2), to any unused credit of the corporation which could otherwise be carried forward under section 44F(g)(2), to any unused credit of the corporation which could otherwise be carried forward under section 44G(b)(2), to any excess foreign taxes of the corporation which can otherwise be carried forward under section 904(c), and to any net capital loss of the corporation which can otherwise be carried forward under section 1212." in Code Sec. 383, as in effect on the day before the enactment of P.L. 94-455, effective for tax. yrs. begin. after 12/31/83, and to carrybacks from such years.

Prior to amendment, the section heading read as follows:

"SEC. 383. SPECIAL LIMITATIONS ON CARRYOVERS OF UNUSED INVESTMENT CREDITS, WORK INCENTIVE PROGRAM CREDITS, NEW EMPLOYEE CREDITS, ALCOHOL FUEL CREDITS, RESEARCH CREDITS, EMPLOYEE STOCK OWNERSHIP CREDITS, FOREIGN TAXES, AND CAPITAL LOSSES."

Code Sec. 383   Corporate distributions and adjustments

—P.L. 98-369, Sec. 474(r)(12)(B), substituted "with respect to any unused business credit of the corporation under section 39, to any unused credit of the corporation under section 30(g)(2), to any excess foreign taxes of the corporation under section 904(c), and to any net capital loss of the corporation under section 1212." for "with respect to any unused investment credit of the corporation under section 46(b), to any unused work incentive program credit of the corporation under section 50A(b), to any unused new employee credit of the corporation under section 53(b), to any unused credit of the corporation under section 44E(e)(2), to any unused credit of the corporation under section 44F(g)(2), to any unused credit of the corporation under section 44G(b)(2), to any excess foreign taxes of the corporation under section 904(c), and to any net capital loss of the corporation under section 1212." in Code Sec. 383, as amended by P.L. 94-455, and amended the section heading, effective for tax. yrs. begin. after 12/31/83, and for carrybacks from such yrs.

Prior to amendment, the section heading read as follows:

"Special limitations on unused investment credits, work incentive program credits, new employee credits, alcohol fuel credits, research credits, employee stock ownership credits, foreign taxes, and capital losses."

In **1981**, P.L. 97-119, Sec. 111, substituted "1984" for "1982" each place it appears in Sec. 806(g)(2) and (3) of P.L. 94-455, the effective date for changes made by Sec. 806(f)(2) of P.L. 94-455, see below.

—P.L. 97-34, Sec. 221(b)(1)(C), added "to any unused credit of the corporation under section 44F(g)(2)," after "44E(e)(2)," to Code Sec. 383 as in effect for tax. yrs. begin. after 6/30/82 and added "research credits," after "alcohol fuel credits," to the heading of Code Sec. 383 as in effect for tax. yrs. begin. after 6/30/82 . . . Sec. 221(b)(1)(D), added "to any unused credit of the corporation which could otherwise be carried forward under section 44F(g)(2)," after "44E(e)(2)," to Code Sec. 383 as in effect for tax. yrs. begin. before 7/1/82 and added "research credits," after "alcohol fuel credits," to the heading of Code Sec. 383 as in effect for tax. yrs. begin. before 7/1/82, effective for amounts paid or incurred after 6/30/81 [as amended by Sec. 2311(a) of P.L. 99-514, see above]. For transitional rule, see Sec. 221(d)(2) of this Act reproduced in note following Code Sec. 30.

—P.L. 97-34, Sec. 331(d)(1)(C), added "to any unused credit of the corporation under section 44G(b)(2)," after "44F(g)(2)," in Code Sec. 383 as in effect for tax. yrs. begin. after 6/30/82 and added "employee stock ownership credits," after "research credits," to the heading of Code Sec. 383 as in effect for tax. yrs. begin. after 6/30/82 . . . Sec. 331(d)(1)(D), added "to any unused credit of the corporation which could otherwise be carried forward under section 44G(b)(2)," after "44F(g)(2)," in Code Sec. 383 as in effect for tax. yrs. begin. before 7/1/82 and added "employee stock ownership credits," after "research credits," to the heading of Code Sec. 383 as in effect for tax. yrs. begin. before 7/1/82, effective for tax. yrs. begin. after 12/31/81.

In **1980**, P.L. 96-223, Sec. 232(b)(2)(C)(i), added "to any unused credit of the corporation under section 44E(e)(2)," after "section 53(c)," in Code Sec. 383 . . . Sec. 232(b)(2)(C)(ii), substituted "new employee credits, alcohol fuel credits" for "new employee credits" in heading of Code Sec. 383 effective for sales or uses after 9/30/80 in tax. yrs. end. after 9/30/80.

—P.L. 96-223, Sec. 232(b)(2)(D)(i), added "to any unused credit of the corporation under section 44E(e)(2)," after "section 53(c)," in Code Sec. 383 . . . Sec. 232(b)(2)(D)(ii), substituted "new employee credits, alcohol fuel credits" for "new employee credits" in the section heading, effective for sales or uses after 9/30/80 in tax. yrs. end. after 9/30/80.

—P.L. 96-222, Sec. 103(a)(6)(G)(xiii), substituted "section 53(b)" for "section 53(c)" in Code Sec. 383, effective for tax. yrs. begin. after '78.

In **1979**, P.L. 96-167, Sec. 9(e), extended the effective date of Sec. 806(g)(2) and (3) of P.L. 95-455, by substituting "1982" for "1980" each place it appears. See below.

In **1978**, P.L. 95-600, Sec. 368(a), extended the effective date of Sec. 806(g)(2) and (3) of P.L. 95-455, by substituting "1980" for "1978" each place it appears. See below. Sec. 368(b) of the Act provides as follows:

"*(b) Election of prior law.*

"(1) A taxpayer may elect not to have the amendment made by subsection (a) apply with respect to any acquisition or reorganization occurring before the end of the taxpayer's first taxable year beginning after June 30, 1978, where such acquisition or reorganization occurs pursuant to a written binding contract or option to acquire stock or assets which was entered into before September 27, 1978.

"(2) An election under this subsection shall be filed with a taxpayer's timely filed return for the first taxable year in which a reorganization or acquisition described in paragraph (1) occurs, or, if later, within 90 days after the date of enactment of this Act. Such election shall apply to all acquisitions and reorganizations to which, but for such election, subsection (a) would apply."

In **1977**, P.L. 95-30, Sec. 202(d)(3)(B), added "to any unused new employee credit of the corporation under section 53(c)" after "section 50A(b)" in Code Sec. 383, and added "new employee credits," after "work incentive program credits," in the heading for Code Sec. 383, as in effect for tax. yrs. begin. after 6/30/78, effective for tax. yrs. begin. after 12/31/76 and to credit carrybacks from such yrs.

—P.L. 95-30, Sec. 202(d)(3)(C), added "to any unused new employee credit of the corporation which could otherwise be carried forward under section 53(c)" after "section 50A(b)," . . . added "new employee credits," after "work incentive program credits," in the heading for Code Sec. 383, as in effect on the day before the date of enactment of the Tax Reform Act of '76 (10/4/76), effective for tax. yrs. begin. after '76 and to credit carrybacks from such yrs.

In **1976**, P.L. 94-455, Sec. 806(f)(2), [repealed by Sec. 621(e)(1) of P.L. 99-514, see above] amended Code Sec. 383. Sec. 806(g)(2) and (3) [repealed by Sec. 621(e)(2) of P.L. 99-514, see above] of the Act provides as follows:

"(2) For purposes of applying sections 382(a) and 383 (as it relates to section 382(a)) of the Internal Revenue Code of 1954, as amended by subsections (e) and (f), the amendments made by subsections (e) and (f) shall take effect for taxable years beginning after December 31, 1985, except that the beginning of the taxable years specified in clause (ii) of section 382(a)(1)(B) of such Code, as so amended, shall be considered to be the later of:

"(A) the beginning of such taxable years, or

"(B) January 1, 1986.

"(3) Sections 382(b) and 383 (as it relates to section 382(b)) of the Internal Revenue Code of 1954, as amended by subsections (e) and (f), shall apply (and such sections as in effect prior to such amendment shall not apply) to reorganizations pursuant to a plan of reorganization adopted by one or more of the parties thereto on or after January 1, 1986. For purposes of the preceding sentence, a corporation shall be considered to have adopted a plan of reorganization on the date on which a resolution of the board of directors is passed adopting the plan or recommending its adoption to the shareholders, or on the date on which the shareholders approve the plan of reorganization, whichever is earlier."

—P.L. 94-455, Sec. 1031(b)(5), substituted "section 904(c)" for "section 904(d)" in Code Sec. 383, effective for tax. yrs. begin. after 12/31/75.

—P.L. 94-455, Sec. 1906(b)(13)(A), substituted "Secretary" for "Secretary or his delegate" in Code Sec. 383, effective for tax. yrs. begin. after 12/31/76.

In **1971**, P.L. 92-178, Sec. 302(a), added Code Sec. 383, effective for reorganizations and other changes in ownership occurring after 12/10/71 pursuant to a plan of reorganization or contract entered into on or after 9/29/71.

Sec. 384. Limitation on use of preacquisition losses to offset built-in gains.

(a) General rule.

If—

(1) (A) a corporation acquires directly (or through 1 or more other corporations) control of another corporation, or

(B) the assets of a corporation are acquired by another corporation in a reorganization described in subparagraph (A), (C), or (D) of section 368(a)(1), and

(2) either of such corporations is a gain corporation, income for any recognition period taxable year (to the extent attributable to recognized built-in gains) shall not be offset by any preacquisition loss (other than a preacquisition loss of the gain corporation).

(b) Exception where corporations under common control.

(1) In general. Subsection (a) shall not apply to the preacquisition loss of any corporation if such corporation and the gain corporation were members of the same controlled group at all times during the 5-year period ending on the acquisition date.

(2) Controlled group. For purposes of this subsection, the term "controlled group" means a controlled group of corporations (as defined in section 1563(a)); except that—

(A) "more than 50 percent" shall be substituted for "at least 80 percent" each place it appears,

(B) the ownership requirements of section 1563(a) must be met both with respect to voting power and value, and

(C) the determination shall be made without regard to subsection (a)(4) of section 1563.

(3) Shorter period where corporations not in existence for 5 years. If either of the corporations referred to in paragraph (1) was not in existence throughout the 5-year period referred to in paragraph (1), the period during which such corporation was in existence (or if both, the shorter of such periods) shall be substituted for such 5-year period.

(c) Definitions.

For purposes of this section—

(1) Recognized built-in gain.

(A) In general. The term "recognized built-in gain" means any gain recognized during the recognition period on the disposition of any asset except to the extent the gain corporation (or, in any case described in subsection (a)(1)(B), the acquiring corporation) establishes that—

(i) such asset was not held by the gain corporation on the acquisition date, or

(ii) such gain exceeds the excess (if any) of—

(I) the fair market value of such asset on the acquisition date, over

(II) the adjusted basis of such asset on such date.

(B) Treatment of certain income items. Any item of income which is properly taken into account for any recognition period taxable year but which is attributable to periods before the acquisition date shall be treated as a recognized built-in gain for the taxable year in which it is properly taken into account and shall be taken into account in determining the amount of the net unrealized built-in gain.

(C) Limitation. The amount of the recognized built-in gains for any recognition period taxable year shall not exceed—

(i) the net unrealized built-in gain, reduced by

(ii) the recognized built-in gains for prior years ending in the recognition period which (but for this section) would have been offset by preacquisition losses.

(2) Acquisition date. The term "acquisition date" means

(A) in any case described in subsection (a)(1)(A), the date on which the acquisition of control occurs, or

(B) in any case described in subsection (a)(1)(B), the date of the transfer in the reorganization.

(3) Preacquisition loss.

(A) In general. The term "preacquisition loss" means—

(i) any net operating loss carryforward to the taxable year in which the acquisition date occurs, and

(ii) any net operating loss for the taxable year in which the acquisition date occurs to the extent such loss is allocable to the period in such year on or before the acquisition date.

Except as provided in regulations, the net operating loss shall, for purposes of clause (ii), be allocated ratably to each day in the year.

(B) Treatment of recognized built-in loss. In the case of a corporation with a net unrealized built-in loss, the term "preacquisition loss" includes any recognized built-in loss.

(4) **Gain corporation.** The term "gain corporation" means any corporation with a net unrealized built-in gain.

(5) **Control.** The term "control" means ownership of stock in a corporation which meets the requirements of section 1504(a)(2).

(6) **Treatment of members of same group.** Except as provided in regulations and except for purposes of subsection (b), all corporations which are members of the same affiliated group immediately before the acquisition date shall be treated as 1 corporation. To the extent provided in regulations, section 1504 shall be applied without regard to subsection (b) thereof for purposes of the preceding sentence.

(7) **Treatment of predecessors and successors.** Any reference in this section to a corporation shall include a reference to any predecessor or successor thereof.

(8) **Other definitions.** Except as provided in regulations, the terms "net unrealized built-in gain", "net unrealized built-in loss", "recognized built-in loss", "recognition period", and "recognition period taxable year", have the same respective meanings as when used in section 382(h), except that the acquisition date shall be taken into account in lieu of the change date.

(d) **Limitation also to apply to excess credits or net capital losses.**

Rules similar to the rules of subsection (a) shall also apply in the case of any excess credit (as defined in section 383(a)(2)) or net capital loss.

(e) **Ordering rules for net operating losses, etc.**

(1) **Carryover rules.** If any preacquisition loss may not offset a recognized built-in gain by reason of this section, such gain shall not be taken into account in determining under section 172(b)(2) the amount of such loss which may be carried to other taxable years. A similar rule shall apply in the case of any excess credit or net capital loss limited by reason of subsection (d).

(2) **Ordering rule for losses carried from same taxable year.** In any case in which—

(A) a preacquisition loss for any taxable year is subject to limitation under subsection (a), and

(B) a net operating loss from such taxable year is not subject to such limitation, taxable income shall be treated as having been offset 1st by the loss subject to such limitation.

(f) **Regulations.**

The Secretary shall prescribe such regulations as may be necessary to carry out the purposes of this section, including regulations to ensure that the purposes of this section may not be circumvented through—

(1) the use of any provision of law or regulations (including subchapter K of this chapter), or

(2) contributions of property to a corporation.

In 1989, P.L. 101-239, Sec. 7812(c)(1), substituted "built-in gain" for "build-in gain" in para. (e)(1), effective as provided in Sec. 10226(c) of P.L. 100-203 and Sec. 2004(m)(5) of P.L. 100-647, reproduced below.

In 1988, P.L. 100-647, Sec. 2004(m)(1)(A), amended subsec. (a)...Sec. 2003(m)(1)(B), redesignated para. (c)(4) as para. (c)(8) and added new paras. (c)(4)-(c)(7)...Sec. 2004(m)(1)(C), amended para. (c)(2)...Sec. 2004(m)(1)(D), substituted "subsection (a)(1)(B)" for "subsection (a)(2)" in para. (c)(1)...Sec. 2004(m)(2), substituted "a corporation" for "the gain corporation" in para. (e)(2) ...Sec. 2004(m)(3), amended subsec. (b)...Sec. 2004(m)(4), redesignated subsec. (e) as subsec. (f) and added new subsec. (e), effective as provided in Sec. 10226(c) of P.L. 100-203, reproduced below. Sec. 2004(m)(5) of this Act provides:

"(5) In any case where the acquisition date (as defined in section 384(c)(2) of the 1986 Code as amended by this subsection [Sec. 2004(m)]) is before March 31, 1988, the acquiring corporation may elect to have the amendments made by this subsection not apply. Such an election shall be made in such manner as the Secretary of the Treasury or his delegate shall prescribe and shall be made not later than the later of the due date (including extensions) for filing the return for the taxable year of the acquiring corporation in which the acquisition date occurs or the date 120 days after the date of the enactment of this Act [11/10/88]. Such an election, once made, shall be irrevocable.

Prior to amendment subsec. (a) read as follows:

"(a) General rule.

"(1) Stock acquisitions, etc. If—

"(A) a corporation (hereinafter in this section referred to as the 'gain corporation') becomes a member of an affiliated group, and

"(B) such corporation has a net unrealized built-in gain, the income of such corporation for any recognition period taxable year (to the extent attributable to recognized built-in gains) shall not be offset by any preacquisition loss of any other member of such group.

"(2) Asset acquisitions. If—

"(A) the assets of a corporation (hereinafter in this section referred to as the 'gain corporation') are acquired by another corporation—

"(i) in a liquidation to which section 332 applies, or

"(ii) in a reorganization described in subparagraph (A), (C), or (D) of section 368(a)(1), and

"(B) the gain corporation has a net unrealized built-in gain,

the income of the acquiring corporation for any recognition period taxable year (to the extent attributable to recognized built-in gains of the gain corporation) shall not be offset by any preacquisition loss of any corporation (other than the gain corporation)."

Prior to amendment para. (c)(2) read as follows:

"(2) Acquisition date. The term 'acquisition date' means the date on which the gain corporation becomes a member of the affiliated group or, in any case described in subsection(a)(2), the date of the distribution or transfer in the liquidation or reorganization."

Prior to amendment subsec. (b) read as follows:

"(b) Exception where 50 percent of gain corporation held.

"Subsection (a) shall not apply if more than 50 percent of the stock (by vote and value) of the gain corporation was held throughout the 5-year period ending on the acquisition date—

"(1) in any case described in subsection (a)(1), by members of the affiliated group referred to in subsection (a)(1), or

"(2) in any case described in subsection (a)(2), by the acquiring corporation or members of such acquiring corporation's affiliated group.

For purposes of the preceding sentence, stock described in section 1504(a)(4) shall not be taken into account."

In 1987, P.L. 100-203, Sec. 10226(a), added new Code Sec. 384, effective as provided in Sec. 10226(c) of this Act which read as follows:

"(c) Effective date.

The amendments made by this section shall apply in cases where the acquisition date (as defined in section 384(c)(2) of the Internal Revenue Code of 1986 as added by this section) is after December 15, 1987; except that such amendments shall not apply in case of any transaction pursuant to—

"(1) a binding written contract in effect on or before December 15, 1987, or

"(2) a letter of intent or agreement of merger signed on or before December 15, 1987."

PART VI.—TREATMENT OF CERTAIN CORPORATE INTERESTS AS STOCK OR INDEBTEDNESS

Sec.

385. Treatment of certain interests in corporations as stock or indebtedness.

In 1969, P.L. 91-172, Sec. 415(a), added Part VI.

Sec. 385. Treatment of certain interests in corporations as stock or indebtedness.

(a) Authority to prescribe regulations.

The Secretary is authorized to prescribe such regulations as may be necessary or appropriate to determine whether an interest in a corporation is to be treated for purposes of this title as stock or indebtedness (or as in part stock and in part indebtedness).

(b) Factors.

The regulations prescribed under this section shall set forth factors which are to be taken into account in determining with respect to a particular factual situation whether a debtor-creditor relationship exists or a corporation-shareholder relationship exists. The factors so set forth in the regulations may include among other factors:

(1) whether there is a written unconditional promise to pay on demand or on a specified date a sum certain in money in return for an adequate consideration in money or money's worth, and to pay a fixed rate of interest,

(2) whether there is subordination to or preference over any indebtedness of the corporation,

(3) the ratio of debt to equity of the corporation,

(4) whether there is convertibility into the stock of the corporation, and

(5) the relationship between holdings of stock in the corporation and holdings of the interest in question.

(c) Effect of classification by issuer.

(1) In general. The characterization (as of the time of issuance) by the issuer as to whether an interest in a corporation is stock or indebtedness shall be binding on such issuer and on all holders of such interest (but shall not be binding on the Secretary).

(2) Notification of inconsistent treatment. Except as provided in regulations, paragraph (1) shall not apply to any holder of an interest if such holder on his return discloses that he is treating such interest in a manner inconsistent with the characterization referred to in paragraph (1).

(3) Regulations. The Secretary is authorized to require such information as the Secretary determines to be necessary to carry out the provisions of this subsection.

In 1992, P.L. 102-486, Sec. 1936(a), added subsec. (c), effective for instruments issued after 10/24/92.

In 1989, P.L. 101-239, Sec. 7208(a)(1), added "(or as in part stock and in part indebtedness)" before the period at the end of subsec. (a), effective 12/19/89.

—P.L. 101-239, Sec. 7208(a)(2), of this Act provides:

"(2) Regulations not to be applied retroactively.—Any regulations issued pursuant to the authority granted by the amendment made by paragraph (1) shall only apply with respect to instruments issued after the date on which the Secretary of the Treasury or his delegate provides public guidance as to the characterization of such instruments whether by regulation, ruling, or otherwise."

In 1976, P.L. 94-455, Sec. 1906(b)(13)(A), substituted "Secretary" and "Secretary or his delegate" in subsec. (a), effective for tax. yrs. begin. after 12/31/76.

In 1969, P.L. 91-172, Sec. 415(a), added Code Sec. 385.

PART VII.—MISCELLANEOUS CORPORATE PROVISIONS [REPEALED]

Sec.

386. Repealed. [Transfers of partnership and trust interests by corporations.]

In 1988, P.L. 100-647, Sec. 1006(e)(8)(C), repealed Part VII.
Prior to repeal, Part VII read as follows:

"PART VII.—MISCELLANEOUS CORPORATE PROVISIONS

"Sec.

"386. Transfers of partnership and trust interests by corporations."

In 1984, P.L. 98-369, Sec. 75(a), added the heading for part VII and the item for Code Sec. 386.

In 1976, P.L. 94-455, Sec. 1901(b)(15), repealed Part VII.
Prior to repeal, Part VII read as follows:

"PART VII.—EFFECTIVE DATE OF SUBCHAPTER C

"Sec.

"391. Effective date of part I.

"392. Effective date of part II.

"393. Effective date of parts III and IV.

"394. Effective date of part V.

"395. Special rules for application of this subchapter."

In 1969, P.L. 91-172, Sec. 415(b), redesignated Part VI as Part VII.

Sec. 386. Repealed.

In 1988, P.L. 100-647, Sec. 1006(e)(8)(A), repealed Code Sec. 386, effective as provided in Secs. 633(a)(1), (c), (d)(1)-(6), (e), (f), (g) of P.L. 99-514, reproduced in note following Code Sec 336, and as provided in Sec. 633(a)(3) of P.L. 99-514, reproduced in note following Code Sec. 311.

Prior to repeal Code Sec. 386 read as follows:

"SEC. 386. TRANSFERS OF PARTNERSHIP AND TRUST INTERESTS BY CORPORATIONS.

"(a) Corporate distributions.

"For purposes of determining the amount (and character) of gain recognized by a corporation on any distribution of an interest in a partnership, the distribution shall be treated in the same manner as if it included a property distribution consisting of the corporation's proportionate share of the recognition property of such partnership.

"(b) Sales or exchange to which section 337 applies.

"For purposes of determining the amount (and character) of gain recognized on a sale or exchange described in section 337, any sale or exchange by a corporation of an interest in a partnership shall be treated as a sale or exchange of the corporation's proportionate share of the recognition property of such partnership.

"(c) Recognition property.

"For purposes of this section, the term 'recognition property' means any property with respect to which gain would be recognized to the corporation if such property—

"(1) were distributed by the corporation in a distribution described in section 311 or 336, or

"(2) were sold in a sale described in section 337,

whichever is appropriate. In determining whether property of a partnership is recognition property, such partnership shall be treated as owning its proportionate share of the property of any other partnership in which it is a partner.

"(d) Limitation on amount of gain recognized in case of non-liquidating distributions.

"In the case of any distribution by a corporation to which section 311 applies, the amount of any gain recognized by reason of subsection (a) shall not exceed the amount of the gain which would have been recognized if the partnership interest had been sold. The Secretary may by regulations provide that the amount of such gain shall be computed without regard to any loss attributable to property contributed to the partnership for the principal purpose of recognizing such loss on the distribution.

"(e) Extension to trusts.

"Under regulations, rules similar to the rules of this section shall also apply in the case of the distribution or sale or exchange by a corporation of an interest in a trust."

In 1986, P.L. 99-514, Sec. 1805(c)(1), redesignated subsec. (d) as subsec. (e), and added new subsec. (d), effective for distributions, sales and exchanges made after 3/31/84, in tax. yrs. end. after 3/31/84.

In 1984, P.L. 98-369, Sec. 75(a), added Code Sec. 386, effective for distributions, sales and exchanges made after 3/31/84 in tax. yrs. ending after 3/31/84.

Employee benefit plans

Subchapter D.—Deferred Compensation, Etc.
Part
  I. Pension, profit-sharing, stock bonus plans, etc.
  II. Certain stock options.
  III. Rules relating to minimum funding standards and benefit limitations.

In 1964, P.L. 88-272, Sec. 221(a), amended the heading of Part II. Prior to amendment, the heading of Part II read as follows: "Miscellaneous provisions"

PART I.—PENSION, PROFIT-SHARING, STOCK BONUS PLANS, ETC.
Subpart
A. General rules.
B. Special rules.
C. Special rules for multiemployer plans.
D. Treatment of welfare benefit funds.
[E. Treatment of transfers to retiree health accounts.]

In 1990, P.L. 101-508, Sec. 12011(a), added Subpart E. This Act did not amend the list of Subparts in Part I, but Congress presumably intended to do so.
In 1984, P.L. 98-369, Sec. 511(d), added the item for subpart D.
In 1980, P.L. 96-364, Sec. 202(b), added Subpart C.
In 1974, P.L. 93-406, Sec. 1016(b)(1), added the items for Subparts A and B.

SUBPART A.—GENERAL RULES
Sec.
401. Qualified pension, profit-sharing, and stock bonus plans.
402. Taxability of beneficiary of employees' trust.
402A. Optional treatment of elective deferrals as Roth contributions.
403. Taxation of employee annuities.
404. Deduction for contributions of an employer to an employees' trust or annuity plan and compensation under a deferred-payment plan.
404A. Deduction for certain foreign deferred compensation plans.
405. Repealed. [Qualified bond purchase plans.]
406. Employees of foreign affiliates covered by section 3121(l) agreements.
407. Certain employees of domestic subsidiaries engaged in business outside the United States.
408. Individual retirement accounts.
408A. Roth IRAs.
409. Qualifications for tax credit employee stock ownership plans.
409A. Inclusion in gross income of deferred compensation under nonqualified deferred compensation plans.

In 2004, P.L. 108-357, Sec. 885(c), added item 409A.
In 2001, P.L. 107-16, Sec. 617(e)(2), added item 402A.
In 1997, P.L. 105-34, Sec. 302(e), added item 408A.
In 1986, P.L. 99-514, Sec. 1899A(70), substituted "Qualifications" for "Qualification" in item 409.
In 1984, P.L. 98-369, Sec. 491(d)(54), repealed items 405 and 409 ... Sec. 491(e)(10), redesignated item 409A as 409.
Prior to repeal, item 405 read as follows:
"405. Qualified bond purchase plans."
Prior to repeal, item 409 read as follows:
"409. Retirement bonds."
In 1983, P.L. 98-21, Sec. 321(e)(2)(D)(ii), amended item 406.
Prior to amendment, item 406 read as follows:
"406. Certain employees of foreign subsidiaries."
In 1980, P.L. 96-603, Sec. 2(d)(1), added item 404A.
  —P.L. 96-222, Sec. 101(a)(7)(L)(v)(VIII), substituted "tax credit employee stock ownership plans" for "ESOP's" in item 409A.
In 1978, P.L. 95-600, Sec. 141(f)(8), added item 409A.

In 1974, P.L. 93-406, Sec. 1016(b)(1), established Subparts A and B, Subpart A to include sections 401 through 407
  —P.L. 93-406, Sec. 2002(h)(1), added sections 408 and 409 to Subpart A.

Sec. 401. Qualified pension, profit-sharing, and stock bonus plans.
(a) Requirements for qualification.
A trust created or organized in the United States and forming part of a stock bonus, pension, or profit-sharing plan of an employer for the exclusive benefit of his employees or their beneficiaries shall constitute a qualified trust under this section—
(1) if contributions are made to the trust by such employer, or employees, or both, or by another employer who is entitled to deduct his contributions under section 404(a)(3)(B) (relating to deduction for contributions to profit-sharing and stock bonus plans), or by a charitable remainder trust pursuant to a qualified gratuitous transfer (as defined in section 664(g)(1)), for the purpose of distributing to such employees or their beneficiaries the corpus and income of the fund accumulated by the trust in accordance with such plan;
(2) if under the trust instrument it is impossible, at any time prior to the satisfaction of all liabilities with respect to employees and their beneficiaries under the trust, for any part of the corpus or income to be (within the taxable year or thereafter) used for, or diverted to, purposes other than for the exclusive benefit of his employees or their beneficiaries (but this paragraph shall not be construed, in the case of a multiemployer plan, to prohibit the return of a contribution within 6 months after the plan administrator determines that the contribution was made by a mistake of fact or law (other than a mistake relating to whether the plan is described in section 401(a) or the trust which is part of such plan is exempt from taxation under section 501(a), or the return of any withdrawal liability payment determined to be an overpayment within 6 months of such determination);
(3) if the plan of which such trust is a part satisfies the requirements of section 410 (relating to minimum participation standards); and
(4) if the contributions or benefits provided under the plan do not discriminate in favor of highly compensated employees (within the meaning of section 414(q)). For purposes of this paragraph, there shall be excluded from consideration employees described in section 410(b)(3)(A) and (C).

(5) Special rules relating to nondiscrimination requirements.
(A) Salaried or clerical employees. A classification shall not be considered discriminatory within the meaning of paragraph (4) or section 410(b)(2)(A)(i) merely because it is limited to salaried or clerical employees.
(B) Contributions and benefits may bear uniform relationship to compensation. A plan shall not be considered discriminatory within the meaning of paragraph (4) merely because the contributions or benefits of, or on behalf of, the employees under the plan bear a uniform relationship to the compensation (within the meaning of section 414(s)) of such employees.
(C) Certain disparity permitted. A plan shall not be considered discriminatory within the meaning of paragraph (4) merely because the contributions or benefits of, or on behalf of, the employees under the plan favor highly compensated employees (as defined in section 414(q)) in the manner permitted under subsection (l).
(D) Integrated defined benefit plan.

(i) In general. A defined benefit plan shall not be considered discriminatory within the meaning of paragraph (4) merely because the plan provides that the employer-derived accrued retirement benefit for any participant under the plan may not exceed the excess (if any) of—
   (I) the participant's final pay with the employer, over
   (II) the employer-derived retirement benefit created under Federal law attributable to service by the participant with the employer.
For purposes of this clause, the employer-derived retirement benefit created under Federal law shall be treated as accruing ratably over 35 years.
   (ii) Final pay. For purposes of this subparagraph, the participant's final pay is the compensation (as defined in section 414(q)(4)) paid to the participant by the employer for any year—
      (I) which ends during the 5-year period ending with the year in which the participant separated from service for the employer, and
      (II) for which the participant's total compensation from the employer was highest.
(E) 2 or more plans treated as single plan. For purposes of determining whether 2 or more plans of an employer satisfy the requirements of paragraph (4) when considered as a single plan—
   (i) Contributions. If the amount of contributions on behalf of the employees allowed as a deduction under section 404 for the taxable year with respect to such plans, taken together, bears a uniform relationship to the compensation (within the meaning of section 414(s)) of such employees, the plans shall not be considered discriminatory merely because the rights of employees to, or derived from, the employer contributions under the separate plans do not become nonforfeitable at the same rate.
   (ii) Benefits. If the employees' rights to benefits under the separate plans do not become nonforfeitable at the same rate, but the levels of benefits provided by the separate plans satisfy the requirements of regulations prescribed by the Secretary to take account of the differences in such rates, the plans shall not be considered discriminatory merely because of the difference in such rates.
(F) Social security retirement age. For purposes of testing for discrimination under paragraph (4)—
   (i) the social security retirement age (as defined in section 415(b)(8)) shall be treated as a uniform retirement age, and
   (ii) subsidized early retirement benefits and joint and survivor annuities shall not be treated as being unavailable to employees on the same terms merely because such benefits or annuities are based in whole or in part on an employee's social security retirement age (as so defined).
(G) Governmental plans. Paragraphs (3) and (4) shall not apply to a governmental plan (within the meaning of section 414(d)).
(6) A plan shall be considered as meeting the requirements of paragraph (3) during the whole of any taxable year of the plan if on one day in each quarter it satisfied such requirements.
(7) A trust shall not constitute a qualified trust under this section unless the plan of which such trust is a part satisfies the requirements of section 411 (relating to minimum vesting standards).

(8) A trust forming part of a defined benefit plan shall not constitute a qualified trust under this section unless the plan provides that forfeitures must not be applied to increase the benefits any employee would otherwise receive under the plan.

(9) Required distributions.
(A) In general. A trust shall not constitute a qualified trust under this subsection unless the plan provides that the entire interest of each employee—
   (i) will be distributed to such employee not later than the required beginning date, or
   (ii) will be distributed, beginning not later than the required beginning date, in accordance with regulations, over the life of such employee or over the lives of such employee and a designated beneficiary (or over a period not extending beyond the life expectancy of such employee or the life expectancy of such employee and a designated beneficiary).
(B) Required distribution where employee dies before entire interest is distributed.
   (i) Where distributions have begun under subparagraph (A)(ii). A trust shall not constitute a qualified trust under this section unless the plan provides that if—
      (I) the distribution of the employee's interest has begun in accordance with subparagraph (A)(ii), and
      (II) the employee dies before his entire interest has been distributed to him,
   the remaining portion of such interest will be distributed at least as rapidly as under the method of distributions being used under subparagraph (A)(ii) as of the date of his death.
   (ii) 5-year rule for other cases. A trust shall not constitute a qualified trust under this section unless the plan provides that, if an employee dies before the distribution of the employee's interest has begun in accordance with subparagraph (A)(ii), the entire interest of the employee will be distributed within 5 years after the death of such employee.
   (iii) Exception to 5-year rule for certain amounts payable over life of beneficiary. If—
      (I) any portion of the employee's interest is payable to (or for the benefit of) a designated beneficiary,
      (II) such portion will be distributed (in accordance with regulations) over the life of such designated beneficiary (or over a period not extending beyond the life expectancy of such beneficiary), and
      (III) such distributions begin not later than 1 year after the date of the employee's death or such later date as the Secretary may by regulations prescribe,
   for purposes of clause (ii), the portion referred to in subclause (I) shall be treated as distributed on the date on which such distributions begin.
   (iv) Special rule for surviving spouse of employee. If the designated beneficiary referred to in clause (iii)(I) is the surviving spouse of the employee—
      (I) the date on which the distributions are required to begin under clause (iii)(III) shall not be earlier than the date on which the employee would have attained age 70 ½, and
      (II) if the surviving spouse dies before the distributions to such spouse begin, this subparagraph shall be applied as if the surviving spouse were the employee.
(C) Required beginning date. For purposes of this paragraph—

(i) In general. The term "required beginning date" means April 1 of the calendar year following the later of—

(I) the calendar year in which the employee attains age 70 ½, or

(II) the calendar year in which the employee retires.

(ii) Exception. Subclause (II) of clause (i) shall not apply—

(I) except as provided in section 409(d), in the case of an employee who is a 5-percent owner (as defined in section 416) with respect to the plan year ending in the calendar year in which the employee attains age 70 ½, or

(II) for purposes of section 408(a)(6) or (b)(3).

(iii) Actuarial adjustment. In the case of an employee to whom clause (i)(II) applies who retires in a calendar year after the calendar year in which the employee attains age 70 ½, the employee's accrued benefit shall be actuarially increased to take into account the period after age 70 ½ in which the employee was not receiving any benefits under the plan.

(iv) Exception for governmental and church plans. Clauses (ii) and (iii) shall not apply in the case of a governmental plan or church plan. For purposes of this clause, the term "church plan" means a plan maintained by a church for church employees, and the term "church" means any church (as defined in section 3121(w)(3)(A)) or qualified church-controlled organization (as defined in section 3121(w)(3)(B)).

(D) Life expectancy. For purposes of this paragraph, the life expectancy of an employee and the employee's spouse (other than in the case of a life annuity) may be redetermined but not more frequently than annually.

(E) Designated beneficiary. For purposes of this paragraph, the term "designated beneficiary" means any individual designated as a beneficiary by the employee.

(F) Treatment of payments to children. Under regulations prescribed by the Secretary, for purposes of this paragraph, any amount paid to a child shall be treated as if it had been paid to the surviving spouse if such amount will become payable to the surviving spouse upon such child reaching majority (or other designated event permitted under regulations).

(G) Treatment of incidental death benefit distributions. For purposes of this title, any distribution required under the incidental death benefit requirements of this subsection shall be treated as a distribution required under this paragraph.

(H) Temporary waiver of minimum required distribution.

(i) In general. The requirements of this paragraph shall not apply for calendar year 2009 to—

(I) a defined contribution plan which is described in this subsection or in section 403(a) or 403(b),

(II) a defined contribution plan which is an eligible deferred compensation plan described in section 457(b) but only if such plan is maintained by an employer described in section 457(e)(1)(A), or

(III) an individual retirement plan.

(ii) Special rules regarding waiver period. For purposes of this paragraph—

(I) the required beginning date with respect to any individual shall be determined without regard to this subparagraph for purposes of applying this paragraph for calendar years after 2009, and

(II) if clause (ii) of subparagraph (B) applies, the 5-year period described in such clause shall be determined without regard to calendar year 2009.

(10) Other requirements.

(A) Plans benefiting owner-employees. In the case of any plan which provides contributions or benefits for employees some or all of whom are owner-employees (as defined in subsection (c)(3)), a trust forming part of such plan shall constitute a qualified trust under this section only if the requirements of subsection (d) are also met.

(B) Top-heavy plans.

(i) In general. In the case of any top-heavy plan, a trust forming part of such plan shall constitute a qualified trust under this section only if the requirements of section 416 are met.

(ii) Plans which may become top-heavy. Except to the extent provided in regulations, a trust forming part of a plan (whether or not a top-heavy plan) shall constitute a qualified trust under this section only if such plan contains provisions—

(I) which will take effect if such plan becomes a top-heavy plan, and

(II) which meet the requirements of section 416.

(iii) Exemption for governmental plans. This subparagraph shall not apply to any governmental plan.

(11) Requirement of joint and survivor annuity and preretirement survivor annuity.

(A) In general. In the case of any plan to which this paragraph applies, except as provided in section 417, a trust forming part of such plan shall not constitute a qualified trust under this section unless—

(i) in the case of a vested participant who does not die before the annuity starting date, the accrued benefit payable to such participant is provided in the form of a qualified joint and survivor annuity, and

(ii) in the case of a vested participant who dies before the annuity starting date and who has a surviving spouse, a qualified preretirement survivor annuity is provided to the surviving spouse of such participant.

(B) Plans to which paragraph applies. This paragraph shall apply to—

(i) any defined benefit plan,

(ii) any defined contribution plan which is subject to the funding standards of section 412, and

(iii) any participant under any other defined contribution plan unless—

(I) such plan provides that the participant's nonforfeitable accrued benefit (reduced by any security interest held by the plan by reason of a loan outstanding to such participant) is payable in full, on the death of the participant, to the participant's surviving spouse (or, if there is no surviving spouse or the surviving spouse consents in the manner required under section 417(a)(2), to a designated beneficiary),

(II) such participant does not elect a payment of benefits in the form of a life annuity, and

(III) with respect to such participant, such plan is not a direct or indirect transferee (in a transfer after December 31, 1984) of a plan which is described in clause (i) or (ii) or to which this clause applied with respect to the participant.

Clause (iii)(III) shall apply only with respect to the transferred assets (and income therefrom) if the plan separately accounts for such assets and any income therefrom.

(C) Exception for certain ESOP benefits.

(i) In general. In the case of—

(I) a tax credit employee stock ownership plan (as defined in section 409(a)), or

(II) an employee stock ownership plan (as defined in section 4975(e)(7)),

subparagraph (A) shall not apply to that portion of the employee's accrued benefit to which the requirements of section 409(h) apply.

(ii) Nonforfeitable benefit must be paid in full, etc. In the case of any participant, clause (i) shall apply only if the requirements of subclauses (I), (II), and (III) of subparagraph (B)(iii) are met with respect to such participant.

(D) Special rule where participant and spouse married less than 1 year. A plan shall not be treated as failing to meet the requirements of subparagraphs (B)(iii) or (C) merely because the plan provides that benefits will not be payable to the surviving spouse of the participant unless the participant and such spouse had been married throughout the 1-year period ending on the earlier of the participant's annuity starting date or the date of the participant's death.

(E) Exception for plans described in section 404(c). This paragraph shall not apply to a plan which the Secretary has determined is a plan described in section 404(c) (or a continuation thereof) in which participation is substantially limited to individuals who, before January 1, 1976, ceased employment covered by the plan.

(F) Cross reference. For—

(i) provisions under which participants may elect to waive the requirements of this paragraph, and

(ii) other definitions and special rules for purposes of this paragraph,

see section 417.

(12) A trust shall not constitute a qualified trust under this section unless the plan of which such trust is a part provides that in the case of any merger or consolidation with, or transfer of assets or liabilities to, any other plan after September 2, 1974, each participant in the plan would (if the plan then terminated) receive a benefit immediately after the merger, consolidation, or transfer which is equal to or greater than the benefit he would have been entitled to receive immediately before the merger, consolidation, or transfer (if the plan had then terminated). The preceding sentence does not apply to any multiemployer plan with respect to any transaction to the extent that participants either before or after the transaction are covered under a multiemployer plan to which title IV of the Employee Retirement Income Security Act of 1974 applies.

(13) Assignment and alienation.

(A) In general. A trust shall not constitute a qualified trust under this section unless the plan of which such trust is a part provides that benefits provided under the plan may not be assigned or alienated. For purposes of the preceding sentence, there shall not be taken into account any voluntary and revocable assignment of not to exceed 10 percent of any benefit payment made by any participant who is receiving benefits under the plan unless the assignment or alienation is made for purposes of defraying plan administration costs. For purposes of this paragraph a loan made to a participant or beneficiary shall not be treated as an assignment or alienation if such loan is secured by the participant's accrued nonforfeitable benefit and is exempt from the tax imposed by section 4975 (relating to tax on prohibited transactions) by reason of section 4975(d)(1). This paragraph shall take effect on January 1, 1976 and shall not apply to assignments which were irrevocable on September 2, 1974.

(B) Special rules for domestic relations orders. Subparagraph (A) shall apply to the creation, assignment, or recognition of a right to any benefit payable with respect to a participant pursuant to a domestic relations order, except that subparagraph (A) shall not apply if the order is determined to be a qualified domestic relations order.

(C) Special rule for certain judgments and settlements. Subparagraph (A) shall not apply to any offset of a participant's benefits provided under a plan against an amount that the participant is ordered or required to pay to the plan if—

(i) the order or requirement to pay arises—

(I) under a judgment of conviction for a crime involving such plan,

(II) under a civil judgment (including a consent order or decree) entered by a court in an action brought in connection with a violation (or alleged violation) of part 4 of subtitle B of title I of the Employee Retirement Income Security Act of 1974, or

(III) pursuant to a settlement agreement between the Secretary of Labor and the participant, or a settlement agreement between the Pension Benefit Guaranty Corporation and the participant, in connection with a violation (or alleged violation) of part 4 of such subtitle by a fiduciary or any other person,

(ii) the judgment, order, decree, or settlement agreement expressly provides for the offset of all or part of the amount ordered or required to be paid to the plan against the participant's benefits provided under the plan, and

(iii) in a case in which the survivor annuity requirements of section 401(a)(11) apply with respect to distributions from the plan to the participant, if the participant has a spouse at the time at which the offset is to be made—

(I) either such spouse has consented in writing to such offset and such consent is witnessed by a notary public or representative of the plan (or it is established to the satisfaction of a plan representative that such consent may not be obtained by reason of circumstances described in section 417(a)(2)(B)), or an election to waive the right of the spouse to either a qualified joint and survivor annuity or a qualified preretirement survivor annuity is in effect in accordance with the requirements of section 417(a),

(II) such spouse is ordered or required in such judgment, order, decree, or settlement to pay an amount to the plan in connection with a violation of part 4 of such subtitle, or

(III) in such judgment, order, decree, or settlement, such spouse retains the right to receive the survivor annuity under a qualified joint and survivor annuity provided pursuant to section 401(a)(11)(A)(i) and under a qualified preretirement survivor annuity provided pursuant to section 401(a)(11)(A)(ii), determined in accordance with subparagraph (D).

A plan shall not be treated as failing to meet the requirements of this subsection, subsection (k), section

403(b), or section 409(d) solely by reason of an offset described in this subparagraph.
(D) Survivor annuity.
   (i) In general. The survivor annuity described in subparagraph (C)(iii)(III) shall be determined as if—
      (I) the participant terminated employment on the date of the offset,
      (II) there was no offset,
      (III) the plan permitted commencement of benefits only on or after normal retirement age,
      (IV) the plan provided only the minimum-required qualified joint and survivor annuity, and
      (V) the amount of the qualified preretirement survivor annuity under the plan is equal to the amount of the survivor annuity payable under the minimum-required qualified joint and survivor annuity.
   (ii) Definition. For purposes of this subparagraph, the term "minimum-required qualified joint and survivor annuity" means the qualified joint and survivor annuity which is the actuarial equivalent of the participant's accrued benefit (within the meaning of section 411(a)(7)) and under which the survivor annuity is 50 percent of the amount of the annuity which is payable during the joint lives of the participant and the spouse.

(14) A trust shall not constitute a qualified trust under this section unless the plan of which such trust is a part provides that, unless the participant otherwise elects, the payment of benefits under the plan to the participant will begin not later than the 60th day after the latest of the close of the plan year in which—
   (A) the date on which the participant attains the earlier of age 65 or the normal retirement age specified under the plan,
   (B) occurs the 10th anniversary of the year in which the participant commenced participation in the plan, or
   (C) the participant terminates his service with the employer.
In the case of a plan which provides for the payment of an early retirement benefit, a trust forming a part of such plan shall not constitute a qualified trust under this section unless a participant who satisfied the service requirements for such early retirement benefit, but separated from the service (with any nonforfeitable right to an accrued benefit) before satisfying the age requirement for such early retirement benefit, is entitled upon satisfaction of such age requirement to receive a benefit not less than the benefit to which he would be entitled at the normal retirement age, actuarially, reduced under regulations prescribed by the Secretary.

(15) a trust shall not constitute a qualified trust under this section unless under the plan of which such trust is a part—
   (A) in the case of a participant or beneficiary who is receiving benefits under such plan, or
   (B) in the case of a participant who is separated from the service and who has nonforfeitable rights to benefits,
such benefits are not decreased by reason of any increase in the benefit levels payable under title II of the Social Security Act or any increase in the wage base under such title II, if such increase takes place after September 2, 1974, or (if later) the earlier of the date of first receipt of such benefits or the date of such separation, as the case may be.

(16) A trust shall not constitute a qualified trust under this section if the plan of which such trust is a part provides for benefits or contributions which exceed the limitations of section 415.

(17) **Compensation limit.**
   (A) In general. A trust shall not constitute a qualified trust under this section unless, under the plan of which such trust is a part, the annual compensation of each employee taken into account under the plan for any year does not exceed $200,000.
   (B) Cost-of-living adjustment. The Secretary shall adjust annually the $200,000 amount in subparagraph (A) for increases in the cost-of-living at the same time and in the same manner as adjustments under section 415(d); except that the base period shall be the calendar quarter beginning July 1, 2001, and any increase which is not a multiple of $5,000 shall be rounded to the next lowest multiple of $5,000.

(18) **Repealed.**

(19) A trust shall not constitute a qualified trust under this section if under the plan of which such trust is a part any part of a participant's accrued benefit derived from employer contributions (whether or not otherwise nonforfeitable), is forfeitable solely because of withdrawal by such participant of any amount attributable to the benefit derived from contributions made by such participant. The preceding sentence shall not apply to the accrued benefit of any participant unless, at the time of such withdrawal, such participant has a nonforfeitable right to at least 50 percent of such accrued benefit (as determined under section 411). The first sentence of this paragraph shall not apply to the extent that an accrued benefit is permitted to be forfeited in accordance with section 411(a)(3)(D)(iii) (relating to proportional forfeitures of benefits accrued before September 2, 1974, in the event of withdrawal of certain mandatory contributions).

(20) A trust forming part of a pension plan shall not be treated as failing to constitute a qualified trust under this section merely because the pension plan of which such trust is a part makes 1 or more distributions within 1 taxable year to a distributee on account of a termination of the plan of which the trust is a part, or in the case of a profit-sharing or stock bonus plan, a complete discontinuance of contributions under such plan. This paragraph shall not apply to a defined benefit plan unless the employer maintaining such plan files a notice with the Pension Benefit Guaranty Corporation (at the time and in the manner prescribed by the Pension Benefit Guaranty Corporation) notifying the Corporation of such payment or distribution and the Corporation has approved such payment or distribution or, within 90 days after the date on which such notice was filed, has failed to disapprove such payment or distribution. For purposes of this paragraph, rules similar to the rules of section 402(a)(6)(B) (as in effect before its repeal by section 521 of the Unemployment Compensation Amendments of 1992) shall apply.

(21) **Repealed.**

(22) If a defined contribution plan (other than a profit-sharing plan)—
   (A) is established by an employer whose stock is not readily tradable on an established market, and
   (B) after acquiring securities of the employer, more than 10 percent of the total assets of the plan are securities of the employer,
any trust forming part of such plan shall not constitute a qualified trust under this section unless the plan meets the requirements of subsection (e) of section 409. The requirements of subsection (e) of section 409 shall not apply to any employees of an employer who are participants in any

defined contribution plan established and maintained by such employer if the stock of such employer is not readily tradable on an established market and the trade or business of such employer consists of publishing on a regular basis a newspaper for general circulation. For purposes of the preceding sentence, subsections (b), (c), (m), and (o) of section 414 shall not apply except for determining whether stock of the employer is not readily tradable on an established market.

(23) A stock bonus plan shall not be treated as meeting the requirements of this section unless such plan meets the requirements of subsections (h) and (o) of section 409, except that in applying section 409(h) for purposes of this paragraph, the term "employer securities" shall include any securities of the employer held by the plan.

(24) Any group trust which otherwise meets the requirements of this section shall not be treated as not meeting such requirements on account of the participation or inclusion in such trust of the moneys of any plan or governmental unit described in section 818(a)(6).

(25) **Requirement that actuarial assumptions be specified.** A defined benefit plan shall not be treated as providing definitely determinable benefits unless, whenever the amount of any benefit is to be determined on the basis of actuarial assumptions, such assumptions are specified in the plan in a way which precludes employer discretion.

(26) **Additional participation requirements.**
   (A) In general. In the case of a trust which is part of a defined benefit plan, such trust shall not constitute a qualified trust under this subsection unless on each day of the plan year such trust benefits at least the lesser of—
      (i) 50 employees of the employer, or
      (ii) the greater of—
         (I) 40 percent of all employees of the employer, or
         (II) 2 employees (or if there is only 1 employee, such employee).
   (B) Treatment of excludable employees.
      (i) In general. A plan may exclude from consideration under this paragraph employees described in paragraphs (3) and (4)(A) of section 410(b).
      (ii) Separate application for certain excludable employees. If employees described in section 410(b)(4)(B) are covered under a plan which meets the requirements of subparagraph (A) separately with respect to such employees, such employees may be excluded from consideration in determining whether any plan of the employer meets such requirements if—
         (I) the benefits for such employees are provided under the same plan as benefits for other employees,
         (II) the benefits provided to such employees are not greater than comparable benefits provided to other employees under the plan, and
         (III) no highly compensated employee (within the meaning of section 414(q)) is included in the group of such employees for more than 1 year.
   (C) Special rule for collective bargaining units. Except to the extent provided in regulations, a plan covering only employees described in section 410(b)(3)(A) may exclude from consideration any employees who are not included in the unit or units in which the covered employees are included.
   (D) Paragraph not to apply to multiemployer plans. Except to the extent provided in regulations, this paragraph shall not apply to employees in a multiemployer plan (within the meaning of section 414(f)) who are covered by collective bargaining agreements.
   (E) Special rule for certain dispositions or acquisitions. Rules similar to the rules of section 410(b)(6)(C) shall apply for purposes of this paragraph.
   (F) Separate lines of business. At the election of the employer and with the consent of the Secretary, this paragraph may be applied separately with respect to each separate line of business of the employer. For purposes of this paragraph, the term "separate line of business" has the meaning given such term by section 414(r) (without regard to paragraph (2)(A) or (7) thereof).
   (G) Exception for governmental plans. This paragraph shall not apply to a governmental plan (within the meaning of section 414(d)).
   (H) Regulations. The Secretary may by regulation provide that any separate benefit structure, any separate trust, or any other separate arrangement is to be treated as a separate plan for purposes of applying this paragraph.

(27) **Determinations as to profit-sharing plans.**
   (A) Contributions need not be based on profits. The determination of whether the plan under which any contributions are made is a profit-sharing plan shall be made without regard to current or accumulated profits of the employer and without regard to whether the employer is a tax-exempt organization.
   (B) Plan must designate type. In the case of a plan which is intended to be a money purchase pension plan or a profit-sharing plan, a trust forming part of such plan shall not constitute a qualified trust under this subsection unless the plan designates such intent at such time and in such manner as the Secretary may prescribe.

(28) **Additional requirements relating to employee stock ownership plans.**
   (A) In general. In the case of a trust which is part of an employee stock ownership plan (within the meaning of section 4975(e)(7)) or a plan which meets the requirements of section 409(a), such trust shall not constitute a qualified trust under this section unless such plan meets the requirements of subparagraphs (B) and (C).
   (B) Diversification of investments.
      (i) In general. A plan meets the requirements of this subparagraph if each qualified participant in the plan may elect within 90 days after the close of each plan year in the qualified election period to direct the plan as to the investment of at least 25 percent of the participant's account in the plan (to the extent such portion exceeds the amount to which a prior election under this subparagraph applies). In the case of the election year in which the participant can make his last election, the preceding sentence shall be applied by substituting "50 percent" for "25 percent".
      (ii) Method of meeting requirements. A plan shall be treated as meeting the requirements of clause (i) if—
         (I) the portion of the participant's account covered by the election under clause (i) is distributed within 90 days after the period during which the election may be made, or
         (II) the plan offers at least 3 investment options (not inconsistent with regulations prescribed by the Secretary) to each participant making an election under clause (i) and within 90 days after the period during which the election may be made, the plan invests the portion of the participant's account cov-

ered by the election in accordance with such election.

(iii) Qualified participant. For purposes of this subparagraph, the term "qualified participant" means any employee who has completed at least 10 years of participation under the plan and has attained age 55.

(iv) Qualified election period. For purposes of this subparagraph, the term "qualified election period" means the 6-plan-year period beginning with the later of—

(I) the 1st plan year in which the individual first became a qualified participant, or

(II) the 1st plan year beginning after December 31, 1986.

For purposes of the preceding sentence, an employer may elect to treat an individual first becoming a qualified participant in the 1st plan year beginning in 1987 as having become a participant in the 1st plan year beginning in 1988.

(v) Exception. This subparagraph shall not apply to an applicable defined contribution plan (as defined in paragraph (35)(E)).

(C) Use of independent appraiser. A plan meets the requirements of this subparagraph if all valuations of employer securities which are not readily tradable on an established securities market with respect to activities carried on by the plan are by an independent appraiser. For purposes of the preceding sentence, the term "independent appraiser" means any appraiser meeting requirements similar to the requirements of the regulations prescribed under section 170(a)(1).

(29) Benefit limitations. In the case of a defined benefit plan (other than a multiemployer plan) to which the requirements of section 412 apply, the trust of which the plan is a part shall not constitute a qualified trust under this subsection unless the plan meets the requirements of section 436.

(30) Limitations on elective deferrals. In the case of a trust which is part of a plan under which elective deferrals (within the meaning of section 402(g)(3)) may be made with respect to any individual during a calendar year, such trust shall not constitute a qualified trust under this subsection unless the plan provides that the amount of such deferrals under such plan and all other plans, contracts, or arrangements of an employer maintaining such plan may not exceed the amount of the limitation in effect under section 402(g)(1)(A) for taxable years beginning in such calendar year.

(31) Direct transfer of eligible rollover distributions.

(A) In general. A trust shall not constitute a qualified trust under this section unless the plan of which such trust is a part provides that if the distributee of any eligible rollover distribution—

(i) elects to have such distribution paid directly to an eligible retirement plan, and

(ii) specifies the eligible retirement plan to which such distribution is to be paid (in such form and at such time as the plan administrator may prescribe),

such distribution shall be made in the form of a direct trustee-to-trustee transfer to the eligible retirement plan so specified.

(B) Certain mandatory distributions.

(i) In general. In case of a trust which is part of an eligible plan, such trust shall not constitute a qualified trust under this section unless the plan of which such trust is a part provides that if—

(I) a distribution described in clause (ii) in excess of $1,000 is made, and

(II) the distributee does not make an election under subparagraph (A) and does not elect to receive the distribution directly,

the plan administrator shall make such transfer to an individual retirement plan of a designated trustee or issuer and shall notify the distributee in writing (either separately or as part of the notice under section 402(f)) that the distribution may be transferred to another individual retirement plan.

(ii) Eligible plan. For purposes of clause (i) the term "eligible plan" means a plan which provides that any nonforfeitable accrued benefit for which the present value (as determined under section 411(a)(11)) does not exceed $5,000 shall be immediately distributed to the participant.

(C) Limitation. Subparagraphs (A) and (B) shall apply only to the extent that the eligible rollover distribution would be includible in gross income if not transferred as provided in subparagraph (A) (determined without regard to sections 402(c), 403(a)(4), 403(b)(8), and 457(e)(16)). The preceding sentence shall not apply to such distribution if the plan to which such distribution is transferred—

(i) is a qualified trust which is part of a plan which is a defined contribution plan and agrees to separately account for amounts so transferred, including separately accounting for the portion of such distribution which is includible in gross income and the portion of such distribution which is not so includible, or

(ii) is an eligible retirement plan described in clause (i) or (ii) of section 402(c)(8)(B).

(D) Eligible rollover distribution. For purposes of this paragraph, the term "eligible rollover distribution" has the meaning given such term by section 402(f)(2)(A).

(E) Eligible retirement plan. For purposes of this paragraph, the term "eligible retirement plan" has the meaning given such term by section 402(c)(8)(B), except that a qualified trust shall be considered an eligible retirement plan only if it is a defined contribution plan, the terms of which permit the acceptance of rollover distributions.

(32) Treatment of failure to make certain payments if plan has liquidity shortfall.

(A) In general. A trust forming part of a pension plan to which section 430(j)(4) applies shall not be treated as failing to constitute a qualified trust under this section merely because such plan ceases to make any payment described in subparagraph (B) during any period that such plan has a liquidity shortfall (as defined in section 430(j)(4)).

(B) Payments described. A payment is described in this subparagraph if such payment is—

(i) any payment, in excess of the monthly amount paid under a single life annuity (plus any social security supplements described in the last sentence of section 411(a)(9)), to a participant or beneficiary whose annuity starting date (as defined in section 417(f)(2)) occurs during the period referred to in subparagraph (A),

(ii) any payment for the purchase of an irrevocable commitment from an insurer to pay benefits, and

(iii) any other payment specified by the Secretary by regulations.

(C) Period of shortfall. For purposes of this paragraph, a plan has a liquidity shortfall during the period that there is an underpayment of an installment under section 430(j)(3) by reason of section 430(j)(4)(A) thereof.

(33) Prohibition on benefit increases while sponsor is in bankruptcy.

(A) In general. A trust which is part of a plan to which this paragraph applies shall not constitute a qualified trust under this section if an amendment to such plan is adopted while the employer is a debtor in a case under title 11, United States Code, or similar Federal or State law, if such amendment increases liabilities of the plan by reason of—

(i) any increase in benefits,

(ii) any change in the accrual of benefits, or

(iii) any change in the rate at which benefits become nonforfeitable under the plan,

with respect to employees of the debtor, and such amendment is effective prior to the effective date of such employer's plan of reorganization.

(B) Exceptions. This paragraph shall not apply to any plan amendment if—

(i) the plan, were such amendment to take effect, would have a funding target attainment percentage (as defined in section 430(d)(2)) of 100 percent or more,

(ii) the Secretary determines that such amendment is reasonable and provides for only de minimis increases in the liabilities of the plan with respect to employees of the debtor,

(iii) such amendment only repeals an amendment described in section 412(d)(2), or

(iv) such amendment is required as a condition of qualification under this part.

(C) Plans to which this paragraph applies. This paragraph shall apply only to plans (other than multiemployer plans) covered under section 4021 of the Employee Retirement Income Security Act of 1974.

(D) Employer. For purposes of this paragraph, the term "employer" means the employer referred to in section 412(b)(1), without regard to section 412(b)(2).

(34) Benefits of missing participants on plan termination. In the case of a plan covered by title IV of the Employee Retirement Income Security Act of 1974, a trust forming part of such plan shall not be treated as failing to constitute a qualified trust under this section merely because the pension plan of which such trust is a part, upon its termination, transfers benefits of missing participants to the Pension Benefit Guaranty Corporation in accordance with section 4050 of such Act.

(35) Diversification requirements for certain defined contribution plans.

(A) In general. A trust which is part of an applicable defined contribution plan shall not be treated as a qualified trust unless the plan meets the diversification requirements of subparagraphs (B), (C), and (D).

(B) Employee contributions and elective deferrals invested in employer securities. In the case of the portion of an applicable individual's account attributable to employee contributions and elective deferrals which is invested in employer securities, a plan meets the requirements of this subparagraph if the applicable individual may elect to direct the plan to divest any such securities and to reinvest an equivalent amount in other investment options meeting the requirements of subparagraph (D).

(C) Employer contributions invested in employer securities. In the case of the portion of the account attributable to employer contributions other than elective deferrals which is invested in employer securities, a plan meets the requirements of this subparagraph if each applicable individual who—

(i) is a participant who has completed at least 3 years of service, or

(ii) is a beneficiary of a participant described in clause (i) or of a deceased participant,

may elect to direct the plan to divest any such securities and to reinvest an equivalent amount in other investment options meeting the requirements of subparagraph (D).

(D) Investment options.

(i) In general. The requirements of this subparagraph are met if the plan offers not less than 3 investment options, other than employer securities, to which an applicable individual may direct the proceeds from the divestment of employer securities pursuant to this paragraph, each of which is diversified and has materially different risk and return characteristics.

(ii) Treatment of certain restrictions and conditions.

(I) Time for making investment choices. A plan shall not be treated as failing to meet the requirements of this subparagraph merely because the plan limits the time for divestment and reinvestment to periodic, reasonable opportunities occurring no less frequently than quarterly.

(II) Certain restrictions and conditions not allowed. Except as provided in regulations, a plan shall not meet the requirements of this subparagraph if the plan imposes restrictions or conditions with respect to the investment of employer securities which are not imposed on the investment of other assets of the plan. This subclause shall not apply to any restrictions or conditions imposed by reason of the application of securities laws.

(E) Applicable defined contribution plan. For purposes of this paragraph—

(i) In general. The term "applicable defined contribution plan" means any defined contribution plan which holds any publicly traded employer securities.

(ii) Exception for certain ESOPs. Such term does not include an employee stock ownership plan if—

(I) there are no contributions to such plan (or earnings thereunder) which are held within such plan and are subject to subsection (k) or (m), and

(II) such plan is a separate plan for purposes of section 414(l) with respect to any other defined benefit plan or defined contribution plan maintained by the same employer or employers.

(iii) Exception for one participant plans. Such term does not include a one-participant retirement plan.

(iv) One-participant retirement plan. For purposes of clause (iii), the term "one-participant retirement plan" means a retirement plan that on the first day of the plan year—

(I) covered only one individual (or the individual and the individual's spouse) and the individual (or the individual and the individual's spouse) owned 100 percent of the plan sponsor (whether or not incorporated), or

(II) covered only one or more partners (or partners and their spouses) in the plan sponsor.

(F) Certain plans treated as holding publicly traded employer securities.

(i) In general. Except as provided in regulations or in clause (ii), a plan holding employer securities which are not publicly traded employer securities shall be

Employee benefit plans   Code Sec. 401(c)(1)(B)(i)

treated as holding publicly traded employer securities if any employer corporation, or any member of a controlled group of corporations which includes such employer corporation, has issued a class of stock which is a publicly traded employer security.

(ii) Exception for certain controlled groups with publicly traded securities. Clause (i) shall not apply to a plan if—

(I) no employer corporation, or parent corporation of an employer corporation, has issued any publicly traded employer security, and

(II) no employer corporation, or parent corporation of an employer corporation, has issued any special class of stock which grants particular rights to, or bears particular risks for, the holder or issuer with respect to any corporation described in clause (i) which has issued any publicly traded employer security.

(iii) Definitions. For purposes of this subparagraph, the term—

(I) "controlled group of corporations" has the meaning given such term by section 1563(a), except that "50 percent" shall be substituted for "80 percent" each place it appears,

(II) "employer corporation" means a corporation which is an employer maintaining the plan, and

(III) "parent corporation" has the meaning given such term by section 424(e).

(G) Other definitions. For purposes of this paragraph—

(i) Applicable individual. The term "applicable individual" means—

(I) any participant in the plan, and

(II) any beneficiary who has an account under the plan with respect to which the beneficiary is entitled to exercise the rights of a participant.

(ii) Elective deferral. The term "elective deferral" means an employer contribution described in section 402(g)(3)(A).

(iii) Employer security. The term "employer security" has the meaning given such term by section 407(d)(1) of the Employee Retirement Income Security Act of 1974.

(iv) Employee stock ownership plan. The term "employee stock ownership plan" has the meaning given such term by section 4975(e)(7).

(v) Publicly traded employer securities. The term "publicly traded employer securities" means employer securities which are readily tradable on an established securities market.

(vi) Year of service. The term "year of service" has the meaning given such term by section 411(a)(5).

(H) Transition rule for securities attributable to employer contributions.

(i) Rules phased in over 3 years.

(I) In general. In the case of the portion of an account to which subparagraph (C) applies and which consists of employer securities acquired in a plan year beginning before January 1, 2007, subparagraph (C) shall only apply to the applicable percentage of such securities. This subparagraph shall be applied separately with respect to each class of securities.

(II) Exception for certain participants aged 55 or over. Subclause (I) shall not apply to an applicable individual who is a participant who has attained age 55 and completed at least 3 years of service before the first plan year beginning after December 31, 2005.

(ii) Applicable percentage. For purposes of clause (i), the applicable percentage shall be determined as follows:

Plan year to which subparagraph (C) applies:	The applicable percentage is:
1st	33
2d	66
3d and following	100.

(36) Distributions during working retirement. A trust forming part of a pension plan shall not be treated as failing to constitute a qualified trust under this section solely because the plan provides that a distribution may be made from such trust to an employee who has attained age 62 and who is not separated from employment at the time of such distribution.

(37) Death benefits under USERRA-qualified active military service. A trust shall not constitute a qualified trust unless the plan provides that, in the case of a participant who dies while performing qualified military service (as defined in section 414(u)), the survivors of the participant are entitled to any additional benefits (other than benefit accruals relating to the period of qualified military service) provided under the plan had the participant resumed and then terminated employment on account of death.

Paragraphs (11), (12), (13), (14), (15), (19), and (20) shall apply only in the case of a plan to which section 411 (relating to minimum vesting standards) applies without regard to subsection (e)(2) of such section.

(b) Certain retroactive changes in plan.

A stock bonus, pension, profit-sharing, or annuity plan shall be considered as satisfying the requirements of subsection (a) for the period beginning with the date on which it was put into effect, or for the period beginning with the earlier of the date on which there was adopted or put into effect any amendment which caused the plan to fail to satisfy such requirements, and ending with the time prescribed by law for filing the return of the employer for his taxable year in which such plan or amendment was adopted (including extensions thereof) or such later time as the Secretary may designate, if all provisions of the plan which are necessary to satisfy such requirements are in effect by the end of such period and have been made effective for all purposes for the whole of such period.

(c) Definitions and rules relating to self-employed individuals and owner-employees.

For purposes of this section—

(1) Self-employed individual treated as employee.

(A) In general. The term "employee" includes, for any taxable year, an individual who is a self-employed individual for such taxable year.

(B) Self-employed individual. The term "self-employed individual" means, with respect to any taxable year, an individual who has earned income (as defined in paragraph (2)) for such taxable year. To the extent provided in regulations prescribed by the Secretary, such term also includes, for any taxable year—

(i) an individual who would be a self-employed individual within the meaning of the preceding sentence but for the fact that the trade or business carried on by such individual did not have net profits for the taxable year, and

(ii) an individual who has been a self-employed individual within the meaning of the preceding sentence for any prior taxable year.

(2) Earned income.

(A) In general. The term "earned income" means the net earnings from self-employment (as defined in section 1402(a)), but such net earnings shall be determined—

(i) only with respect to a trade or business in which personal services of the taxpayer are a material income-producing factor,

(ii) without regard to paragraphs (4) and (5) of section 1402(c),

(iii) in the case of any individual who is treated as an employee under sections 3121(d)(3)(A), (C), or (D), without regard to paragraph (2) of section 1402(c),

(iv) without regard to items which are not included in gross income for purposes of this chapter, and the deductions properly allocable to or chargeable against such items,

(v) with regard to the deductions allowed by section 404 to the taxpayer, and

(vi) with regard to the deduction allowed to the taxpayer by section 164(f).

For purposes of this subparagraph, section 1402, as in effect for a taxable year ending on December 31, 1962, shall be treated as having been in effect for all taxable years ending before such date. For purposes of this part only (other than sections 419 and 419A), this subparagraph shall be applied as if the term "trade or business" for purposes of section 1402 included service described in section 1402(c)(6).

(B) Repealed.

(C) Income from disposition of certain property. For purposes of this section, the term "earned income" includes gains (other than any gain which is treated under any provision of this chapter as gain from the sale or exchange of a capital asset) and net earnings derived from the sale or other disposition of, the transfer of any interest in, or the licensing of the use of property (other than good will) by an individual whose personal efforts created such property.

(3) Owner-employee. The term "owner-employee" means an employee who—

(A) owns the entire interest in an unincorporated trade or business, or

(B) in the case of a partnership, is a partner who owns more than 10 percent of either the capital interest or the profits interest in such partnership.

To the extent provided in regulations prescribed by the Secretary, such term also means an individual who has been an owner-employee within the meaning of the preceding sentence.

(4) Employer. An individual who owns the entire interest in an unincorporated trade or business shall be treated as his own employer. A partnership shall be treated as the employer of each partner who is an employee within the meaning of paragraph (1).

(5) Contributions on behalf of owner-employees. The term "contribution on behalf of an owner-employee" includes, except as the context otherwise requires, a contribution under a plan—

(A) by the employer for an owner-employee, and

(B) by an owner-employee as an employee.

(6) Special rule for certain fishermen. For purposes of this subsection, the term "self-employed individual" includes an individual described in section 3121(b)(20) (relating to certain fishermen).

(d) Contribution limit on owner-employees.

A trust forming part of a pension or profit-sharing plan which provides contributions or benefits for employees some or all of whom are owner-employees shall constitute a qualified trust under this section only if, in addition to meeting the requirements of subsection (a), the plan provides that contributions on behalf of any owner-employee may be made only with respect to the earned income of such owner-employee which is derived from the trade or business with respect to which such plan is established.

(e) Repealed.

(f) Certain custodial accounts and contracts.

For purposes of this title, a custodial account, an annuity contract, or a contract (other than a life, health or accident, property, casualty, or liability insurance contract) issued by an insurance company qualified to do business in a State shall be treated as a qualified trust under this section if—

(1) the custodial account or contract would, except for the fact that it is not a trust, constitute a qualified trust under this section, and

(2) in the case of a custodial account the assets thereof are held by a bank (as defined in section 408(n)) or another person who demonstrates, to the satisfaction of the Secretary, that the manner in which he will hold the assets will be consistent with the requirements of this section.

For purposes of this title, in the case of a custodial account or contract treated as a qualified trust under this section by reason of this subsection, the person holding the assets of such account or holding such contract shall be treated as the trustee thereof.

(g) Annuity defined.

For purposes of this section and sections 402, 403, and 404, the term "annuity" includes a face-amount certificate, as defined in section 2(a)(15) of the Investment Company Act of 1940 (15 U.S.C., sec. 80a-2); but does not include any contract or certificate issued after December 31, 1962, which is transferable, if any person other than the trustee of a trust described in section 401(a) which is exempt from tax under section 501(a) is the owner of such contract or certificate.

(h) Medical, etc., benefits for retired employees and their spouses and dependents.

Under regulations prescribed by the Secretary, and subject to the provisions of section 420, a pension or annuity plan may provide for the payment of benefits for sickness, accident, hospitalization, and medical expenses of retired employees, their spouses and their dependents, but only if—

(1) such benefits are subordinate to the retirement benefits provided by the plan,

(2) a separate account is established and maintained for such benefits,

(3) the employer's contributions to such separate account are reasonable and ascertainable,

(4) it is impossible, at any time prior to the satisfaction of all liabilities under the plan to provide such benefits, for any part of the corpus or income of such separate account to be (within the taxable year or thereafter) used for, or diverted to, any purpose other than the providing of such benefits,

(5) notwithstanding the provisions of subsection (a)(2), upon the satisfaction of all liabilities under the plan to provide such benefits, any amount remaining in such separate account must, under the terms of the plan, be returned to the employer, and

(6) in the case of an employee who is a key employee, a separate account is established and maintained for such benefits payable to such employee (and his spouse and dependents) and such benefits (to the extent attributable to plan years beginning after March 31, 1984, for which the employee is a key employee) are only payable to such employee (and his spouse and dependents) from such separate account.

For purposes of paragraph (6), the term "key employee" means any employee, who at any time during the plan year or any preceding plan year during which contributions were made on behalf of such employee, is or was a key employee as defined in section 416(i). In no event shall the requirements of paragraph (1) be treated as met if the aggregate actual contributions for medical benefits, when added to actual contributions for life insurance protection under the plan, exceed 25 percent of the total actual contributions to the plan (other than contributions to fund past service credits) after the date on which the account is established. For purposes of this subsection, the term "dependent" shall include any individual who is a child (as defined in section 152(f)(1)) of a retired employee who as of the end of the calendar year has not attained age 27.

(i) Certain union-negotiated pension plans.

In the case of a trust forming part of a pension plan which has been determined by the Secretary to constitute a qualified trust under subsection (a) and to be exempt from taxation under section 501(a) for a period beginning after contributions were first made to or for such trust, if it is shown to the satisfaction of the Secretary that—

(1) such trust was created pursuant to a collective bargaining agreement between employee representatives and one or more employers,

(2) any disbursements of contributions, made to or for such trust before the time as of which the Secretary determined that the trust constituted a qualified trust, substantially complied with the terms of the trust, and the plan of which the trust is a part, as subsequently qualified, and

(3) before the time as of which the Secretary determined that the trust constitutes a qualified trust, the contributions to or for such trust were not used in a manner which would jeopardize the interests of its beneficiaries,

then such trust shall be considered as having constituted a qualified trust under subsection (a) and as having been exempt from taxation under section 501(a) for the period beginning on the date on which contributions were first made to or for such trust and ending on the date such trust first constituted (without regard to this subsection) a qualified trust under subsection (a).

(j) Repealed.

(k) Cash or deferred arrangements.

(1) General rule. A profit-sharing or stock bonus plan, a pre-ERISA money purchase plan, or a rural cooperative plan shall not be considered as not satisfying the requirements of subsection (a) merely because the plan includes a qualified cash or deferred arrangement.

(2) Qualified cash or deferred arrangement. A qualified cash or deferred arrangement is any arrangement which is part of a profit-sharing or stock bonus plan, a pre-ERISA money purchase plan, or a rural cooperative plan which meets the requirements of subsection (a)—

(A) under which a covered employee may elect to have the employer make payments as contributions to a trust under the plan on behalf of the employee, or to the employee directly in cash;

(B) under which amounts held by the trust which are attributable to employer contributions made pursuant to the employee's election—

(i) may not be distributable to participants or other beneficiaries earlier than—

(I) severance from employment, death, or disability,

(II) an event described in paragraph (10),

(III) in the case of a profit-sharing or stock bonus plan, the attainment of age 59 ½,

(IV) in the case of contributions to a profit-sharing or stock bonus plan to which section 402(e)(3) applies, upon hardship of the employee, or

(V) in the case of a qualified reservist distribution (as defined in section 72(t)(2)(G)(iii)), the date on which a period referred to in subclause (III) of such section begins, and

(ii) will not be distributable merely by reason of the completion of a stated period of participation or the lapse of a fixed number of years;

(C) which provides that an employee's right to his accrued benefit derived from employer contributions made to the trust pursuant to his election is nonforfeitable, and

(D) which does not require, as a condition of participation in the arrangement, that an employee complete a period of service with the employer (or employers) maintaining the plan extending beyond the period permitted under section 410(a)(1) (determined without regard to subparagraph (B)(i) thereof).

(3) Application of participation and discrimination standards.

(A) A cash or deferred arrangement shall not be treated as a qualified cash or deferred arrangement unless—

(i) those employees eligible to benefit under the arrangement satisfy the provisions of section 410(b)(1), and

(ii) the actual deferral percentage for eligible highly compensated employees (as defined in paragraph (5)) for the plan year bears a relationship to the actual deferral percentage for all other eligible employees for the preceding plan year which meets either of the following tests:

(I) The actual deferral percentage for the group of eligible highly compensated employees is not more than the actual deferral percentage of all other eligible employees multiplied by 1.25.

(II) The excess of the actual deferral percentage for the group of eligible highly compensated employees over that of all other eligible employees is not more than 2 percentage points, and the actual deferral percentage for the group of eligible highly compensated employees is not more than the actual deferral percentage of all other eligible employees multiplied by 2.

If 2 or more plans which include cash or deferred arrangements are considered as 1 plan for purposes of section 401(a)(4) or 410(b), the cash or deferred arrangements included in such plans shall be treated as 1 arrangement for purposes of this subparagraph.

If any highly compensated employee is a participant under 2 or more cash or deferred arrangements of the employer, for purposes of determining the deferral percentage with respect to such employee, all such cash or deferred arrangements shall be treated as 1 cash or deferred arrangement. An arrangement may apply clause

(ii) by using the plan year rather than the preceding plan year if the employer so elects, except that if such an election is made, it may not be changed except as provided by the Secretary.

(B) For purposes of subparagraph (A), the actual deferral percentage for a specified group of employees for a plan year shall be the average of the ratios (calculated separately for each employee in such group) of—

(i) the amount of employer contributions actually paid over to the trust on behalf of each such employee for such plan year, to

(ii) the employee's compensation for such plan year.

(C) A cash or deferred arrangement shall be treated as meeting the requirements of subsection (a)(4) with respect to contributions if the requirements of subparagraph (A)(ii) are met.

(D) For purposes of subparagraph (B), the employer contributions on behalf of any employee—

(i) shall include any employer contributions made pursuant to the employee's election under paragraph (2), and

(ii) under such rules as the Secretary may prescribe, may, at the election of the employer, include—

(I) matching contributions (as defined in 401(m)(4)(A)) which meet the requirements of paragraph (2)(B) and (C), and

(II) qualified nonelective contributions (within the meaning of section 401(m)(4)(C)).

(E) For purposes of this paragraph, in the case of the first plan year of any plan (other than a successor plan), the amount taken into account as the actual deferral percentage of nonhighly compensated employees for the preceding plan year shall be—

(i) 3 percent, or

(ii) if the employer makes an election under this subclause, the actual deferral percentage of nonhighly compensated employees determined for such first plan year.

(F) Special rule for early participation. If an employer elects to apply section 410(b)(4)(B) in determining whether a cash or deferred arrangement meets the requirements of subparagraph (A)(i), the employer may, in determining whether the arrangement meets the requirements of subparagraph (A)(ii), exclude from consideration all eligible employees (other than highly compensated employees) who have not met the minimum age and service requirements of section 410(a)(1)(A).

(G) Governmental plan. A governmental plan (within the meaning of section 414(d)) shall be treated as meeting the requirements of this paragraph.

(4) Other requirements.

(A) Benefits (other than matching contributions) must not be contingent on election to defer. A cash or deferred arrangement of any employer shall not be treated as a qualified cash or deferred arrangement if any other benefit is conditioned (directly or indirectly) on the employee electing to have the employer make or not make contributions under the arrangement in lieu of receiving cash. The preceding sentence shall not apply to any matching contribution (as defined in section 401(m)) made by reason of such an election.

(B) Eligibility of state and local governments and tax-exempt organizations.

(i) Tax-exempts eligible. Except as provided in clause (ii), any organization exempt from tax under this subtitle may include a qualified cash or deferred arrangement as part of a plan maintained by it.

(ii) Governments ineligible. A cash or deferred arrangement shall not be treated as a qualified cash or deferred arrangement if it is part of a plan maintained by a State or local government or political subdivision thereof, or any agency or instrumentality thereof. This clause shall not apply to a rural cooperative plan or to a plan of an employer described in clause (iii).

(iii) Treatment of Indian tribal governments. An employer which is an Indian tribal government (as defined in section 7701(a)(40)), a subdivision of an Indian tribal government (determined in accordance with section 7871(d)), an agency or instrumentality of an Indian tribal government or subdivision thereof, or a corporation chartered under Federal, State, or tribal law which is owned in whole or in part by any of the foregoing may include a qualified cash or deferred arrangement as part of a plan maintained by the employer.

(C) Coordination with other plans. Except as provided in section 401(m), any employer contribution made pursuant to an employee's election under a qualified cash or deferred arrangement shall not be taken into account for purposes of determining whether any other plan meets the requirements of section 401(a) or 410(b). This subparagraph shall not apply for purposes of determining whether a plan meets the average benefit requirement of section 410(b)(2)(A)(ii).

(5) Highly compensated employee. For purposes of this subsection, the term "highly compensated employee" has the meaning given such term by section 414(q).

(6) Pre-ERISA money purchase plan. For purposes of this subsection, the term "pre-ERISA money purchase plan" means a pension plan—

(A) which is a defined contribution plan (as defined in section 414(i)),

(B) which was in existence on June 27, 1974, and which, on such date, included a salary reduction arrangement, and

(C) under which neither the employee contributions nor the employer contributions may exceed the levels provided for by the contribution formula in effect under the plan on such date.

(7) Rural cooperative plan. For purposes of this subsection—

(A) In general. The term "rural cooperative plan" means any pension plan—

(i) which is a defined contribution plan (as defined in section 414(i)), and

(ii) which is established and maintained by a rural cooperative.

(B) Rural cooperative defined. For purposes of subparagraph (A), the term "rural cooperative" means—

(i) any organization which—

(I) is engaged primarily in providing electric service on a mutual or cooperative basis, or

(II) is engaged primarily in providing electric service to the public in its area of service and which is exempt from tax under this subtitle or which is a State or local government (or an agency or instrumentality thereof), other than a municipality (or an agency or instrumentality thereof),

(ii) any organization described in paragraph (4) or (6) of section 501(c) and at least 80 percent of the members of which are organizations described in clause (i),

(iii) a cooperative telephone company described in section 501(c)(12),

(iv) any organization which—

(I) is a mutual irrigation or ditch company described in section 501(c)(12) (without regard to the 85 percent requirement thereof), or

(II) is a district organized under the laws of a State as a municipal corporation for the purpose of irrigation, water conservation, or drainage, and

(v) an organization which is a national association of organizations described in clause (i), (ii), (iii), or (iv).

(C) Special rule for certain distributions. A rural cooperative plan which includes a qualified cash or deferred arrangement shall not be treated as violating the requirements of section 401(a) or of paragraph (2) merely by reason of a hardship distribution or a distribution to a participant after attainment of age 59 ½. For purposes of this section, the term "hardship distribution" means a distribution described in paragraph (2)(B)(i)(IV) (without regard to the limitation of its application to profit-sharing or stock bonus plans).

(8) Arrangement not disqualified if excess contributions distributed.

(A) In general. A cash or deferred arrangement shall not be treated as failing to meet the requirements of clause (ii) of paragraph (3)(A) for any plan year if, before the close of the following plan year—

(i) the amount of the excess contributions for such plan year (and any income allocable to such contributions through the end of such year) is distributed, or

(ii) to the extent provided in regulations, the employee elects to treat the amount of the excess contributions as an amount distributed to the employee and then contributed by the employee to the plan.

Any distribution of excess contributions (and income) may be made without regard to any other provision of law.

(B) Excess contributions. For purposes of subparagraph (A), the term "excess contributions" means, with respect to any plan year, the excess of—

(i) the aggregate amount of employer contributions actually paid over to the trust on behalf of highly compensated employees for such plan year, over

(ii) the maximum amount of such contributions permitted under the limitations of clause (ii) of paragraph (3)(A) (determined by reducing contributions made on behalf of highly compensated employees in order of the actual deferral percentages beginning with the highest of such percentages).

(C) Method of distributing excess contributions. Any distribution of the excess contributions for any plan year shall be made to highly compensated employees on the basis of the amount of contributions by, or on behalf of, each of such employees.

(D) Additional tax under section 72(t) not to apply. No tax shall be imposed under section 72(t) on any amount required to be distributed under this paragraph.

(E) Treatment of matching contributions forfeited by reason of excess deferral or contribution or permissible withdrawal. For purposes of paragraph (2)(C), a matching contribution (within the meaning of subsection (m)) shall not be treated as forfeitable merely because such contribution is forfeitable if the contribution to which the matching contribution relates is treated as an excess contribution under subparagraph (B), an excess deferral under section 402(g)(2)(A), a permissible withdrawal under section 414(w), or an excess aggregate contribution under section 401(m)(6)(B).

(F) Cross reference. For excise tax on certain excess contributions, see section 4979.

(9) Compensation. For purposes of this subsection, the term "compensation" has the meaning given such term by section 414(s).

(10) Distributions upon termination of plan.

(A) In general. An event described in this subparagraph is the termination of the plan without establishment or maintenance of another defined contribution plan (other than an employee stock ownership plan as defined in section 4975(e)(7)).

(B) Distributions must be lump sum distributions.

(i) In general. A termination shall not be treated as described in subparagraph (A) with respect to any employee unless the employee receives a lump sum distribution by reason of the termination.

(ii) Lump-sum distribution. For purposes of this subparagraph, the term "lump-sum distribution" has the meaning given such term by section 402(e)(4)(D) (without regard to subclauses (I), (II), (III), and (IV) of clause (i) thereof). Such term includes a distribution of an annuity contract from—

(I) a trust which forms a part of a plan described in section 401(a) and which is exempt from tax under section 501(a), or

(II) an annuity plan described in section 403(a).

(11) Adoption of simple plan to meet nondiscrimination tests.

(A) In general. A cash or deferred arrangement maintained by an eligible employer shall be treated as meeting the requirements of paragraph (3)(A)(ii) if such arrangement meets—

(i) the contribution requirements of subparagraph (B),

(ii) the exclusive plan requirements of subparagraph (C), and

(iii) the vesting requirements of section 408(p)(3).

(B) Contribution requirements.

(i) In general. The requirements of this subparagraph are met if, under the arrangement—

(I) an employee may elect to have the employer make elective contributions for the year on behalf of the employee to a trust under the plan in an amount which is expressed as a percentage of compensation of the employee but which in no event exceeds the amount in effect under section 408(p)(2)(A)(ii),

(II) the employer is required to make a matching contribution to the trust for the year in an amount equal to so much of the amount the employee elects under subclause (I) as does not exceed 3 percent of compensation for the year, and

(III) no other contributions may be made other than contributions described in subclause (I) or (II).

(ii) Employer may elect 2-percent nonelective contribution. An employer shall be treated as meeting the requirements of clause (i)(II) for any year if, in lieu of the contributions described in such clause, the employer elects (pursuant to the terms of the arrangement) to make nonelective contributions of 2 percent of compensation for each employee who is eligible to participate in the arrangement and who has at least

$5,000 of compensation from the employer for the year. If an employer makes an election under this subparagraph for any year, the employer shall notify employees of such election within a reasonable period of time before the 60th day before the beginning of such year.

(iii) Administrative requirements.

(I) In general. Rules similar to the rules of subparagraphs (B) and (C) of section 408(p)(5) shall apply for purposes of this subparagraph.

(II) Notice of election period. The requirements of this subparagraph shall not be treated as met with respect to any year unless the employer notifies each employee eligible to participate, within a reasonable period of time before the 60th day before the beginning of such year (and, for the first year the employee is so eligible, the 60th day before the first day such employee is so eligible), of the rules similar to the rules of section 408(p)(5)(C) which apply by reason of subclause (I).

(C) Exclusive plan requirement. The requirements of this subparagraph are met for any year to which this paragraph applies if no contributions were made, or benefits were accrued, for services during such year under any qualified plan of the employer on behalf of any employee eligible to participate in the cash or deferred arrangement, other than contributions described in subparagraph (B).

(D) Definitions and special rule.

(i) Definitions. For purposes of this paragraph, any term used in this paragraph which is also used in section 408(p) shall have the meaning given such term by such section.

(ii) Coordination with top-heavy rules. A plan meeting the requirements of this paragraph for any year shall not be treated as a top-heavy plan under section 416 for such year if such plan allows only contributions required under this paragraph.

(12) Alternative methods of meeting nondiscrimination requirements.

(A) In general. A cash or deferred arrangement shall be treated as meeting the requirements of paragraph (3)(A)(ii) if such arrangement—

(i) meets the contribution requirements of subparagraph (B) or (C), and

(ii) meets the notice requirements of subparagraph (D).

(B) Matching contributions.

(i) In general. The requirements of this subparagraph are met if, under the arrangement, the employer makes matching contributions on behalf of each employee who is not a highly compensated employee in an amount equal to—

(I) 100 percent of the elective contributions of the employee to the extent such elective contributions do not exceed 3 percent of the employee's compensation, and

(II) 50 percent of the elective contributions of the employee to the extent that such elective contributions exceed 3 percent but do not exceed 5 percent of the employee's compensation.

(ii) Rate for highly compensated employees. The requirements of this subparagraph are not met if, under the arrangement, the rate of matching contribution with respect to any elective contribution of a highly compensated employee at any rate of elective contribution is greater than that with respect to an employee who is not a highly compensated employee.

(iii) Alternative plan designs. If the rate of any matching contribution with respect to any rate of elective contribution is not equal to the percentage required under clause (i), an arrangement shall not be treated as failing to meet the requirements of clause (i) if—

(I) the rate of an employer's matching contribution does not increase as an employee's rate of elective contributions increase, and

(II) the aggregate amount of matching contributions at such rate of elective contribution is at least equal to the aggregate amount of matching contributions which would be made if matching contributions were made on the basis of the percentages described in clause (i).

(C) Nonelective contributions. The requirements of this subparagraph are met if, under the arrangement, the employer is required, without regard to whether the employee makes an elective contribution or employee contribution, to make a contribution to a defined contribution plan on behalf of each employee who is not a highly compensated employee and who is eligible to participate in the arrangement in an amount equal to at least 3 percent of the employee's compensation.

(D) Notice requirement. An arrangement meets the requirements of this paragraph if, under the arrangement, each employee eligible to participate is, within a reasonable period before any year, given written notice of the employee's rights and obligations under the arrangement which—

(i) is sufficiently accurate and comprehensive to appraise the employee of such rights and obligations, and

(ii) is written in a manner calculated to be understood by the average employee eligible to participate.

(E) Other requirements.

(i) Withdrawal and vesting restrictions. An arrangement shall not be treated as meeting the requirements of subparagraph (B) or (C) of this paragraph unless the requirements of subparagraphs (B) and (C) of paragraph (2) are met with respect to all employer contributions (including matching contributions) taken into account in determining whether the requirements of subparagraphs (B) and (C) of this paragraph are met.

(ii) Social security and similar contributions not taken into account. An arrangement shall not be treated as meeting the requirements of subparagraph (B) or (C) unless such requirements are met without regard to subsection (l), and, for purposes of subsection (l), employer contributions under subparagraph (B) or (C) shall not be taken into account.

(F) Other plans. An arrangement shall be treated as meeting the requirements under subparagraph (A)(i) if any other plan maintained by the employer meets such requirements with respect to employees eligible under the arrangement.

(13) Alternative method for automatic contribution arrangements to meet nondiscrimination requirements.

(A) In general. A qualified automatic contribution arrangement shall be treated as meeting the requirements of paragraph (3)(A)(ii).

(B) Qualified automatic contribution arrangement. For purposes of this paragraph, the term "qualified auto-

Employee benefit plans   Code Sec. 401(l)(2)(A)(ii)(II)

matic contribution arrangement" means any cash or deferred arrangement which meets the requirements of subparagraphs (C) through (E).

(C) Automatic deferral.

(i) In general. The requirements of this subparagraph are met if, under the arrangement, each employee eligible to participate in the arrangement is treated as having elected to have the employer make elective contributions in an amount equal to a qualified percentage of compensation.

(ii) Election out. The election treated as having been made under clause (i) shall cease to apply with respect to any employee if such employee makes an affirmative election—

(I) to not have such contributions made, or

(II) to make elective contributions at a level specified in such affirmative election.

(iii) Qualified percentage. For purposes of this subparagraph, the term "qualified percentage" means, with respect to any employee, any percentage determined under the arrangement if such percentage is applied uniformly, does not exceed 10 percent, and is at least—

(I) 3 percent during the period ending on the last day of the first plan year which begins after the date on which the first elective contribution described in clause (i) is made with respect to such employee,

(II) 4 percent during the first plan year following the plan year described in subclause (I),

(III) 5 percent during the second plan year following the plan year described in subclause (I), and

(IV) 6 percent during any subsequent plan year.

(iv) Automatic deferral for current employees not required. Clause (i) may be applied without taking into account any employee who—

(I) was eligible to participate in the arrangement (or a predecessor arrangement) immediately before the date on which such arrangement becomes a qualified automatic contribution arrangement (determined after application of this clause), and

(II) had an election in effect on such date either to participate in the arrangement or to not participate in the arrangement.

(D) Matching or nonelective contributions.

(i) In general. The requirements of this subparagraph are met if, under the arrangement, the employer—

(I) makes matching contributions on behalf of each employee who is not a highly compensated employee in an amount equal to the sum of 100 percent of the elective contributions of the employee to the extent that such contributions do not exceed 1 percent of compensation plus 50 percent of so much of such contributions as exceed 1 percent but do not exceed 6 percent of compensation, or

(II) is required, without regard to whether the employee makes an elective contribution or employee contribution, to make a contribution to a defined contribution plan on behalf of each employee who is not a highly compensated employee and who is eligible to participate in the arrangement in an amount equal to at least 3 percent of the employee's compensation.

(ii) Application of rules for matching contributions. The rules of clauses (ii) and (iii) of paragraph (12)(B) shall apply for purposes of clause (i)(I).

(iii) Withdrawal and vesting restrictions. An arrangement shall not be treated as meeting the requirements of clause (i) unless, with respect to employer contributions (including matching contributions) taken into account in determining whether the requirements of clause (i) are met—

(I) any employee who has completed at least 2 years of service (within the meaning of section 411(a)) has a nonforfeitable right to 100 percent of the employee's accrued benefit derived from such employer contributions, and

(II) the requirements of subparagraph (B) of paragraph (2) are met with respect to all such employer contributions.

(iv) Application of certain other rules. The rules of subparagraphs (E)(ii) and (F) of paragraph (12) shall apply for purposes of subclauses (I) and (II) of clause (i).

(E) Notice requirements.

(i) In general. The requirements of this subparagraph are met if, within a reasonable period before each plan year, each employee eligible to participate in the arrangement for such year receives written notice of the employee's rights and obligations under the arrangement which—

(I) is sufficiently accurate and comprehensive to apprise the employee of such rights and obligations, and

(II) is written in a manner calculated to be understood by the average employee to whom the arrangement applies.

(ii) Timing and content requirements. A notice shall not be treated as meeting the requirements of clause (i) with respect to an employee unless—

(I) the notice explains the employee's right under the arrangement to elect not to have elective contributions made on the employee's behalf (or to elect to have such contributions made at a different percentage),

(II) in the case of an arrangement under which the employee may elect among 2 or more investment options, the notice explains how contributions made under the arrangement will be invested in the absence of any investment election by the employee, and

(III) the employee has a reasonable period of time after receipt of the notice described in subclauses (I) and (II) and before the first elective contribution is made to make either such election.

(l) Permitted disparity in plan contributions or benefits.

(1) In general. The requirements of this subsection are met with respect to a plan if—

(A) in the case of a defined contribution plan, the requirements of paragraph (2) are met, and

(B) in the case of a defined benefit plan, the requirements of paragraph (3) are met.

(2) Defined contribution plan.

(A) In general. A defined contribution plan meets the requirements of this paragraph if the excess contribution percentage does not exceed the base contribution percentage by more than the lesser of—

(i) the base contribution percentage, or

(ii) the greater of—

(I) 5.7 percentage points, or

(II) the percentage equal to the portion of the rate of tax under section 3111(a) (in effect as of the be-

1,877

ginning of the year) which is attributable to old-age insurance.

(B) Contribution percentages. For purposes of this paragraph—

(i) Excess contribution percentage. The term "excess contribution percentage" means the percentage of compensation which is contributed by the employer under the plan with respect to that portion of each participant's compensation in excess of the integration level.

(ii) Base contribution percentage. The term "base contribution percentage" means the percentage of compensation contributed by the employer under the plan with respect to that portion of each participant's compensation not in excess of the integration level.

(3) Defined benefit plan. A defined benefit plan meets the requirements of this paragraph if—

(A) Excess plans.

(i) In general. In the case of a plan other than an offset plan—

(I) the excess benefit percentage does not exceed the base benefit percentage by more than the maximum excess allowance,

(II) any optional form of benefit, preretirement benefit, actuarial factor, or other benefit or feature provided with respect to compensation in excess of the integration level is provided with respect to compensation not in excess of such level, and

(III) benefits are based on average annual compensation.

(ii) Benefit percentages. For purposes of this subparagraph, the excess and base benefit percentages shall be computed in the same manner as the excess and base contribution percentages under paragraph (2)(B), except that such determination shall be made on the basis of benefits attributable to employer contributions rather than contributions.

(B) Offset plans. In the case of an offset plan, the plan provides that—

(i) a participant's accrued benefit attributable to employer contributions (within the meaning of section 411(c)(1)) may not be reduced (by reason of the offset) by more than the maximum offset allowance, and

(ii) benefits are based on average annual compensation.

(4) Definitions relating to paragraph (3). For purposes of paragraph (3)—

(A) Maximum excess allowance. The maximum excess allowance is equal to—

(i) in the case of benefits attributable to any year of service with the employer taken into account under the plan, ¾ of a percentage point, and

(ii) in the case of total benefits, ¾ of a percentage point, multiplied by the participant's years of service (not in excess of 35) with the employer taken into account under the plan.

In no event shall the maximum excess allowance exceed the base benefit percentage.

(B) Maximum offset allowance. The maximum offset allowance is equal to—

(i) in the case of benefits attributable to any year of service with the employer taken into account under the plan, ¾ percent of the participant's final average compensation, and

(ii) in the case of total benefits, ¾ percent of the participant's final average compensation, multiplied by the participant's years of service (not in excess of 35) with the employer taken into account under the plan.

In no event shall the maximum offset allowance exceed 50 percent of the benefit which would have accrued without regard to the offset reduction.

(C) Reductions.

(i) In general. The Secretary shall prescribe regulations requiring the reduction of the ¾ percentage factor under subparagraph (A) or (B)—

(I) in the case of a plan other than an offset plan which has an integration level in excess of covered compensation, or

(II) with respect to any participant in an offset plan who has final average compensation in excess of covered compensation.

(ii) Basis of reductions. Any reductions under clause (i) shall be based on the percentages of compensation replaced by the employer-derived portions of primary insurance amounts under the Social Security Act for participants with compensation in excess of covered compensation.

(D) Offset plan. The term "offset plan" means any plan with respect to which the benefit attributable to employer contributions for each participant is reduced by an amount specified in the plan.

(5) Other definitions and special rules. For purposes of this subsection—

(A) Integration level.

(i) In general. The term "integration level" means the amount of compensation specified under the plan (by dollar amount or formula) at or below which the rate at which contributions or benefits are provided (expressed as a percentage) is less than such rate above such amount.

(ii) Limitation. The integration level for any year may not exceed the contribution and benefit base in effect under section 230 of the Social Security Act for such year.

(iii) Level to apply to all participants. A plan's integration level shall apply with respect to all participants in the plan.

(iv) Multiple integration levels. Under rules prescribed by the Secretary, a defined benefit plan may specify multiple integration levels.

(B) Compensation. The term "compensation" has the meaning given such term by section 414(s).

(C) Average annual compensation. The term "average annual compensation" means the participant's highest average annual compensation for—

(i) any period of at least 3 consecutive years, or

(ii) if shorter, the participant's full period of service.

(D) Final average compensation.

(i) In general. The term "final average compensation" means the participant's average annual compensation for—

(I) the 3-consecutive year period ending with the current year, or

(II) if shorter, the participant's full period of service.

(ii) Limitation. A participant's final average compensation shall be determined by not taking into account in any year compensation in excess of the contribution and benefit base in effect under section 230 of the Social Security Act for such year.

(E) Covered compensation.

Employee benefit plans Code Sec. 401(m)(5)(B)

(i) In general. The term "covered compensation" means, with respect to an employee, the average of the contribution and benefit bases in effect under section 230 of the Social Security Act for each year in the 35-year period ending with the year in which the employee attains the social security retirement age.

(ii) Computation for any year. For purposes of clause (i), the determination for any year preceding the year in which the employee attains the social security retirement age shall be made by assuming that there is no increase in the bases described in clause (i) after the determination year and before the employee attains the social security retirement age.

(iii) Social security retirement age. For purposes of this subparagraph, the term "social security retirement age" has the meaning given such term by section 415(b)(8).

(F) Regulations. The Secretary shall prescribe such regulations as are necessary or appropriate to carry out the purposes of this subsection, including—

(i) in the case of a defined benefit plan which provides for unreduced benefits commencing before the social security retirement age (as defined in section 415(b)(8)), rules providing for the reduction of the maximum excess allowance and the maximum offset allowance, and

(ii) in the case of an employee covered by 2 or more plans of the employer which fail to meet the requirements of subsection (a)(4) (without regard to this subsection), rules preventing the multiple use of the disparity permitted under this subsection with respect to any employee.

For purposes of clause (i), unreduced benefits shall not include benefits for disability (within the meaning of section 223(d) of the Social Security Act).

(6) Special rule for plan maintained by railroads. In determining whether a plan which includes employees of a railroad employer who are entitled to benefits under the Railroad Retirement Act of 1974 meets the requirements of this subsection, rules similar to the rules set forth in this subsection shall apply. Such rules shall take into account the employer-derived portion of the employees' tier 2 railroad retirement benefits and any supplemental annuity under the Railroad Retirement Act of 1974.

(m) Nondiscrimination test for matching contributions and employee contributions.

(1) In general. A defined contribution plan shall be treated as meeting the requirements of subsection (a)(4) with respect to the amount of any matching contribution or employee contribution for any plan year only if the contribution percentage requirement of paragraph (2) of this subsection is met for such plan year.

(2) Requirements.

(A) Contribution percentage requirement. A plan meets the contribution percentage requirement of this paragraph for any plan year only if the contribution percentage for eligible highly compensated employees for such plan year does not exceed the greater of—

(i) 125 percent of such percentage for all other eligible employees for the preceding plan year, or

(ii) the lesser of 200 percent of such percentage for all other eligible employees for the preceding plan year, or such percentage for all other eligible employees for the preceding plan year plus 2 percentage points.

This subparagraph may be applied by using the plan year rather than the preceding plan year if the employer so elects, except that if such an election is made, it may not be changed except as provided the Secretary.

(B) Multiple plans treated as a single plan. If two or more plans of an employer to which matching contributions, employee contributions, or elective deferrals are made are treated as one plan for purposes of section 410(b), such plans shall be treated as one plan for purposes of this subsection. If a highly compensated employee participates in two or more plans of an employer to which contributions to which this subsection applies are made, all such contributions shall be aggregated for purposes of this subsection.

(3) Contribution percentage. For purposes of paragraph (2), the contribution percentage for a specified group of employees for a plan year shall be the average of the ratios (calculated separately for each employee in such group) of—

(A) the sum of the matching contributions and employee contributions paid under the plan on behalf of each such employee for such plan year, to

(B) the employee's compensation (within the meaning of section 414(s)) for such plan year.

Under regulations, an employer may elect to take into account (in computing the contribution percentage) elective deferrals and qualified nonelective contributions under the plan or any other plan of the employer. If matching contributions are taken into account for purposes of subsection (k)(3)(A)(ii) for any plan year, such contributions shall not be taken into account under subparagraph (A) for such year. Rules similar to the rules of subsection (k)(3)(E) shall apply for purposes of this subsection.

(4) Definitions. For purposes of this subsection—

(A) Matching contribution. The term "matching contribution" means—

(i) any employer contribution made to a defined contribution plan on behalf of an employee on account of an employee contribution made by such employee, and

(ii) any employer contribution made to a defined contribution plan on behalf of an employee on account of an employee's elective deferral.

(B) Elective deferral. The term "elective deferral" means any employer contribution described in section 402(g)(3).

(C) Qualified nonelective contributions. The term "qualified nonelective contribution" means any employer contribution (other than a matching contribution) with respect to which—

(i) the employee may not elect to have the contribution paid to the employee in cash instead of being contributed to the plan, and

(ii) the requirements of subparagraphs (B) and (C) of subsection (k)(2) are met.

(5) Employees taken into consideration.

(A) In general. Any employee who is eligible to make an employee contribution (or, if the employer takes elective contributions into account, elective contributions) or to receive a matching contribution under the plan being tested under paragraph (1) shall be considered an eligible employee for purposes of this subsection.

(B) Certain nonparticipants. If an employee contribution is required as a condition of participation in the plan, any employee who would be a participant in the plan if

1,879

such employee made such a contribution shall be treated as an eligible employee on behalf of whom no employer contributions are made.

(C) Special rule for early participation. If an employer elects to apply section 410(b)(4)(B) in determining whether a plan meets the requirements of section 410(b), the employer may, in determining whether the plan meets the requirements of paragraph (2), exclude from consideration all eligible employees (other than highly compensated employees) who have not met the minimum age and service requirements of section 410(a)(1)(A).

(6) **Plan not disqualified if excess aggregate contributions distributed before end of following plan year.**

(A) In general. A plan shall not be treated as failing to meet the requirements of paragraph (1) for any plan year if, before the close of the following plan year, the amount of the excess aggregate contributions for such plan year (and any income allocable to such contributions through the end of such year) is distributed (or, if forfeitable, is forfeited). Such contributions (and such income) may be distributed without regard to any other provision of law.

(B) Excess aggregate contributions. For purposes of subparagraph (A), the term "excess aggregate contributions" means, with respect to any plan year, the excess of—

(i) the aggregate amount of the matching contributions and employee contributions (and any qualified nonelective contribution or elective contribution taken into account in computing the contribution percentage) actually made on behalf of highly compensated employees for such plan year, over

(ii) the maximum amount of such contributions permitted under the limitations of paragraph (2)(A) (determined by reducing contributions made on behalf of highly compensated employees in order of their contribution percentages beginning with the highest of such percentages).

(C) Method of distributing excess aggregate contributions. Any distribution of the excess aggregate contributions for any plan year shall be made to highly compensated employees on the basis of the amount of contributions on behalf of, or by, each such employee. Forfeitures of excess aggregate contributions may not be allocated to participants whose contributions are reduced under this paragraph.

(D) Coordination with subsection (k) and 402(g). The determination of the amount of excess aggregate contributions with respect to a plan shall be made after—

(i) first determining the excess deferrals (within the meaning of section 402(g)), and

(ii) then determining the excess contributions under subsection (k).

(7) **Treatment of distributions.**

(A) Additional tax of section 72(t) not applicable. No tax shall be imposed under section 72(t) on any amount required to be distributed under paragraph (6).

(B) Exclusion of employee contributions. Any distribution attributable to employee contributions shall not be included in gross income except to the extent attributable to income on such contributions.

(8) **Highly compensated employee.** For purposes of this subsection, the term "highly compensated employee" has the meaning given to such term by section 414(q).

(9) **Regulations.** The Secretary shall prescribe such regulations as may be necessary to carry out the purposes of this subsection and subsection (k), including regulations permitting appropriate aggregation of plans and contributions.

(10) **Alternative method of satisfying tests.** A defined contribution plan shall be treated as meeting the requirements of paragraph (2) with respect to matching contributions if the plan—

(A) meets the contribution requirements of subparagraph (B) of subsection (k)(11),

(B) meets the exclusive plan requirements of subsection (k)(11)(C), and

(C) meets the vesting requirements of section 408(p)(3).

(11) **Additional alternative method of satisfying tests.**

(A) In general. A defined contribution plan shall be treated as meeting the requirements of paragraph (2) with respect to matching contributions if the plan—

(i) meets the contribution requirements of subparagraph (B) or (C) of subsection (k)(12),

(ii) meets the notice requirements of subsection (k)(12)(D), and

(iii) meets the requirements of subparagraph (B).

(B) Limitation on matching contributions. The requirements of this subparagraph are met if—

(i) matching contributions on behalf of any employee may not be made with respect to an employee's contributions or elective deferrals in excess of 6 percent of the employee's compensation,

(ii) the rate of an employer's matching contribution does not increase as the rate of an employee's contributions or elective deferrals increase, and

(iii) the matching contribution with respect to any highly compensated employee at any rate of an employee contribution or rate of elective deferral is not greater than that with respect to an employee who is not a highly compensated employee.

(12) **Alternative method for automatic contribution arrangements.** A defined contribution plan shall be treated as meeting the requirements of paragraph (2) with respect to matching contributions if the plan—

(A) is a qualified automatic contribution arrangement (as defined in subsection (k)(13)), and

(B) meets the requirements of paragraph (11)(B).

(13) **Cross reference.** For excise tax on certain excess contributions, see section 4979.

(n) **Coordination with qualified domestic relations orders.**

The Secretary shall prescribe such rules or regulations as may be necessary to coordinate the requirements of subsection (a)(13)(B) and section 414(p) (and the regulations issued by the Secretary of Labor thereunder) with the other provisions of this chapter.

(o) **Cross reference.**

For exemption from tax of a trust qualified under this section, see section 501(a).

In 2010, P.L. 111-312, Sec. 101(a)(1), substituted "December 31, 2012" for "December 31, 2010" both places it appeared in Sec. 901 of P.L. 107-16 [see below], effective as if included in the enactment of P.L. 107-16, EGTRRA, 6/7/2001.

—P.L. 111-192, Sec. 202(b)(1), substituted "eligible cooperative plan or an eligible charity plan" for "eligible cooperative plan" wherever it appeared in Sec. 104(a)-(b) of P.L. 109-280 [see below]

—P.L. 111-192, Sec. 202(b)(2), added subsec. (d) to Sec. 104 of P.L. 109-280 [see below], effective for plan yrs. begin. after 12/31/2007, except that a plan sponsor may elect to apply such amendments to plan yrs. begin. after 12/31/2008. Any such election shall be made at such time, and in such form and manner, as shall be prescribed by the Secretary of the Treasury, and may be revoked only with the consent of the Secretary of the Treasury.

Employee benefit plans Code Sec. 401

—P.L. 111-152, Sec. 1004(d)(5), added "For purposes of this subsection, the term 'dependent' shall include any individual who is a child (as defined in section 152(f)(1) of a retired employee who as of the end of the calendar year has not attained age 27." at the end of subsec. (h), effective 3/30/2010.

In **2008**, P.L. 110-458, Sec. 101(d)(2)(A), deleted "on plans in at-risk status" in the heading of para. (a)(29)... Sec. 101(d)(2)(B)(i), substituted "section 430(j)(3)" for "section 430(j)" in subpara. (a)(32)(C)... Sec. 101(d)(2)(B)(ii), substituted "section 430(j)(4)(A)" for "paragraph (5)(A)" in subpara. (a)(32)(C) ... Sec. 101(d)(2)(C)(i), substituted "section 412(d)(2)" for "section 412(c)(2)" in clause (a)(33)(B)(iii)... Sec. 101(d)(2)(C), substituted "section 412(b)(1), without regard to section 412(b)(2)" for "section 412(b)(2) (without regard to subparagraph (B) thereof)" in clause (a)(33)(D), effective for plan yrs. begin. after 2007, as if included in the provisions of Sec. 114 of the Pension Protection Act of 2006, P.L. 109-280.

—P.L. 110-458, Sec. 101(d)(3), added Sec. 114(g), P.L. 109-280, providing the effective dates for amendments made by Sec. 114, P.L. 109-280, see below. Sec. 114(g), P.L. 109-280, as added by this Act, provides:

"'(g) Effective dates.

"'(1) In general. The amendments made by this section shall apply to plan years beginning after 2007.

"'(2) Excise tax. The amendments made by subsection (e) shall apply to taxable years beginning after 2007, but only with respect to plan years described in paragraph (1) which end with or within any such taxable year.'"

—P.L. 110-458, Sec. 109(a), amended clause (a)(35)(E)(iv), effective for plan yrs. begin. after 12/31/2006, (as if included in Sec. 901, P.L. 109-280) For special rules, see Sec. 901(c)(2)-(3), P.L. 109-280 reproduced below.

Prior to amendment, clause (a)(35)(E)(iv) read as follows:

"(iv) One-participant retirement plan. For purposes of clause (iii), the term 'one-participant retirement plan' means a retirement plan that—

"(I) on the first day of the plan year covered only one individual (or the individual and the individual's spouse) and the individual owned 100 percent of the plan sponsor (whether or not incorporated), or covered only one or more partners (or partners and their spouses) in the plan sponsor,

"(II) meets the minimum coverage requirements of section 410(b) without being combined with any other plan of the business that covers the employees of the business,

"(III) does not provide benefits to anyone except the individual (and the individual's spouse) or the partners (and their spouses),

"(IV) does not cover a business that is a member of an affiliated service group, a controlled group of corporations, or a group of businesses under common control, and

"(V) does not cover a business that uses the services of leased employees (within the meaning of section 414(n)).

"For purposes of this clause, the term 'partner' includes a 2-percent shareholder (as defined in section 1372(b)) of an S corporation."

—P.L. 110-458, Sec. 109(b)(1), substituted "such contributions as exceed 1 percent but do not" for "such compensation as exceeds 1 percent but does not" in subclause (k)(13)(D)(i)(I)... Sec. 109(b)(2)(A), substituted "a permissible withdrawal" for "an erroneous automatic contribution" in subpara. (k)(8)(E)... Sec. 109(b)(2)(B), substituted "permissible withdrawal" for "erroneous automatic contribution" in the heading of subpara. (k)(8)(E), effective for plan yrs. begin. after 12/31/2007, as if included in the provisions of Sec. 902, P.L. 109-280.

—P.L. 110-458, Sec. 201(a), added subpara. (a)(9)(H), effective for calendar yrs. begin. after 12/31/2008. Sec. 201(c)(2) of this Act provides:

"(2) Provisions relating to plan or contract amendments.

"(A) In general. If this paragraph applies to any pension plan or contract amendment, such pension plan or contract shall not fail to be treated as being operated in accordance with the terms of the plan during the period described in subparagraph (B)(ii) solely because the plan operates in accordance with this section.

"(B) Amendments to which paragraph applies.

"(i) In general. This paragraph shall apply to any amendment to any pension plan or annuity contract which—

"(I) is made pursuant to the amendments made by this section, and

"(II) is made on or before the last day of the first plan year beginning on or after January 1, 2011.

"In the case of a governmental plan, subclause (II) shall be applied by substituting '2012' for '2011'.

"(ii) Conditions. This paragraph shall not apply to any amendment unless during the period beginning on the effective date of the amendment and ending on December 31, 2009, the plan or contract is operated as if such plan or contract amendment were in effect."

—P.L. 110-245, Sec. 104(a), added para. (a)(37), effective for deaths and disabilities occurring on or after 1/1/2007. Sec. 104(d)(2) of this Act provides:

"(2) Provisions relating to plan amendments.

"(A) In general. If this subparagraph applies to any plan or contract amendment, such plan or contract shall be treated as being operated in accordance with the terms of the plan during the period described in subparagraph (B)(iii).

"(B) Amendments to which subparagraph (A) applies.

"(i) In general. Subparagraph (A) shall apply to any amendment to any plan or annuity contract which is made—

"(I) pursuant to the amendments made by subsection (a) or pursuant to any regulation issued by the Secretary of the Treasury under subsection (a), and

"(II) on or before the last day of the first plan year beginning on or after January 1, 2010.

In the case of a governmental plan (as defined in section 414(d) of the Internal Revenue Code of 1986), this clause shall be applied by substituting '2012' for '2010' in subclause (II).

"(ii) Conditions. This paragraph shall not apply to any amendment unless--

"(I) the plan or contract is operated as if such plan or contract amendment were in effect for the period described in clause (iii), and

"(II) such plan or contract amendment applies retroactively for such period.

"(iii) Period described. The period described in this clause is the period--

"(I) beginning on the effective date specified by the plan, and

"(II) ending on the date described in clause (i)(II) (or, if earlier, the date the plan or contract amendment is adopted)."

In **2007**, P.L. 110-142, Sec. 10, of this Act provides:

"The percentage under subparagraph (B) of section 401(l) of the Tax Increase Prevention and Reconciliation Act of 2005 in effect on the date of the enactment of this Act is increased by 1.50 percentage points."

In **2006**, P.L. 109-280, Sec. 104, [as amended by Sec. 202(b)(1)-(2) of P.L. 111-192 see above] of this Act, reads as follows:

"SEC. 104. SPECIAL RULES FOR MULTIPLE EMPLOYER PLANS OF CERTAIN COOPERATIVES.

"(a) General rule. Except as provided in this section, if a plan in existence on July 26, 2005, was an eligible cooperative plan or an eligible charity plan for its plan year which includes such date, the amendments made by this subtitle and subtitle B shall not apply to plan years beginning before the earlier of—

"(1) the first plan year for which the plan ceases to be an eligible cooperative plan or an eligible charity plan, or

"(2) January 1, 2017.

"(b) Interest rate. In applying section 302(b)(5)(B) of the Employee Retirement Income Security Act of 1974 and section 412(b)(5)(B) of the Internal Revenue Code of 1986 (as in effect before the amendments made by this subtitle and subtitle B) to an eligible cooperative plan or an eligible charity plan for plan years beginning after December 31, 2007, and before the first plan year to which such amendments apply, the third segment rate determined under section 303(h)(2)(C)(iii) of such Act and section 430(h)(2)(C)(iii) of such Code (as added by such amendments) shall be used in lieu of the interest rate otherwise used.

"(c) eligible cooperative plan or an eligible charity plan defined. For purposes of this section, a plan shall be treated as an eligible cooperative plan or an eligible charity plan for a plan year if the plan is maintained by more than 1 employer and at least 85 percent of the employers are—

"(1) rural cooperatives (as defined in section 401(k)(7)(B) of such Code without regard to clause (iv) thereof), or

"(2) organizations which are—

"(A) cooperative organizations described in section 1381(a) of such Code which are more than 50-percent owned by agricultural producers or by cooperatives owned by agricultural producers, or

"(B) more than 50-percent owned, or controlled by, one or more cooperative organizations described in subparagraph (A).

A plan shall also be treated as an eligible cooperative plan or an eligible charity plan for any plan year for which it is described in section 210(a) of the Employee Retirement Income Security Act of 1974 and is maintained by a rural telephone cooperative association described in section 3(40)(B)(v) of such Act.

"(d) Eligible charity plan defined. For purposes of this section, a plan shall be treated as an eligible charity plan for a plan year if the plan is maintained by more than one employer (determined without regard to section 414(c) of the Internal Revenue Code) and 100 percent of the employers are described in section 501(c)(3) of such Code."

—P.L. 109-280, Sec. 114(a)(1), amended para. (a)(29)... Sec. 114(a)(2)(A), substituted "section 430(j)(4)" for "412(m)(5)" each place it appeared in subpara. (a)(32)(A)... Sec. 114(a)(2)(B), substituted "section 430(j)" for "section 412(m)" in subpara. (a)(32)(C)... Sec. 114(a)(3)(A), substituted "funding target attainment percentage (as defined in section 430(d)(2))" for "funded current liability percentage (within the meaning of section 412(l)(8))" in clause (a)(33)(B)(i) ... Sec. 114(a)(3)(B), substituted "section 412(c)(2)" for "subsection 412(c)(8)" in clause (a)(33)(B)(iii)... Sec. 114(a)(3)(C), substituted "section 412(b)(2) (without regard to subparagraph (B) thereof)" for "section 412(c)(11) (without regard to subparagraph (B) thereof)" in subpara. (a)(33)(D), effective for plan yrs. begin. after 2007 [as provided in Sec. 114(g) of this Act as added by Sec. 101(d)(3), P.L. 110-458, see above].

Prior to amendment, para. (a)(29) read as follows:

"(29) Security required upon adoption of plan amendment resulting in significant underfunding.

"(A) In general. If—

"(i) a defined benefit plan (other than a multiemployer plan) to which the requirements of section 412 apply adopts an amendment an effect of which is to increase current liability under the plan for a plan year, and

"(ii) the funded current liability percentage of the plan for the plan year in which the amendment takes effect is less than 60 percent, including the amount of the unfunded current liability under the plan attributable to the plan amendment, the trust of which such plan is a part shall not constitute a qualified trust under this subsection unless such amendment does not take effect until the contributing sponsor (or any member of the controlled group of the contributing sponsor) provides security to the plan.

"(B) Form of security. The security required under subparagraph (A) shall consist of—

"(i) a bond issued by a corporate surety company that is an acceptable surety for purposes of section 412 of the Employee Retirement Income Security Act of 1974,

1,881

"(ii) cash, or United States obligations which mature in 3 years or less, held in escrow by a bank or similar financial institution, or

"(iii) such other form of security as is satisfactory to the Secretary and the parties involved.

"(C) Amount of security. The security shall be in an amount equal to the excess of—

"(i) the lesser of—

"(I) the amount of additional plan assets which would be necessary to increase the funded current liability percentage under the plan to 60 percent, including the amount of the unfunded current liability under the plan attributable to the plan amendment, or

"(II) the amount of the increase in current liability under the plan attributable to the plan amendment and any other plan amendments adopted after December 22, 1987, and before such plan amendment, over

"(ii) $10,000,000.

"(D) Release of security. The security shall be released (and any amounts thereunder shall be refunded together with any interest accrued thereon) at the end of the first plan year which ends after the provision of the security and for which the funded current liability percentage under the plan is not less than 60 percent. The Secretary may prescribe regulations for partial releases of the security by reason of increases in the funded current liability percentage.

"(E) Definitions. For purposes of this paragraph, the terms 'current liability', 'funded current liability percentage', and 'unfunded current liability' shall have the meanings given such terms by section 412(l), except that in computing unfunded current liability there shall not be taken into account any unamortized portion of the unfunded old liability amount as of the close of the plan year."

—P.L. 109-280, Sec. 811, of this Act [relating to P.L. 107-16, Sec. 901, , see below] provides:

"SEC. 811. PENSIONS AND INDIVIDUAL RETIREMENT ARRANGEMENT PROVISIONS OF ECONOMIC GROWTH AND TAX RELIEF RECONCILIATION ACT OF 2001 MADE PERMANENT.

"Title IX of the Economic Growth and Tax Relief Reconciliation Act of 2001 shall not apply to the provisions of, and amendments made by, subtitles A through F of title VI of such Act (relating to pension and individual retirement arrangement provisions)."

—P.L. 109-280, Sec. 823, of this Act, reads as follows:

"SEC. 823. CLARIFICATION OF MINIMUM DISTRIBUTION RULES FOR GOVERNMENTAL PLANS.

"The Secretary of the Treasury shall issue regulations under which a governmental plan (as defined in section 414(d) of the Internal Revenue Code of 1986) shall, for all years to which section 401(a)(9) of such Code applies to such plan, be treated as having complied with such section 401(a)(9) if such plan complies with a reasonable good faith interpretation of such section 401(a)(9)."

—P.L. 109-280, Sec. 826, of this Act, reads as follows:

"SEC. 826. MODIFICATIONS OF RULES GOVERNING HARDSHIPS AND UNFORESEEN FINANCIAL EMERGENCIES.

"Within 180 days after the date of the enactment of this Act, the Secretary of the Treasury shall modify the rules for determining whether a participant has had a hardship for purposes of section 401(k)(2)(B)(i)(IV) of the Internal Revenue Code of 1986 to provide that if an event (including the occurrence of a medical expense) would constitute a hardship under the plan if it occurred with respect to the participant's spouse or dependent (as defined in section 152 of such Code), such event shall, to the extent permitted under a plan, constitute a hardship if it occurs with respect to a person who is a beneficiary under the plan with respect to the participant. The Secretary of the Treasury shall issue similar rules for purposes of determining whether a participant has had—

"(1) a hardship for purposes of section 403(b)(11)(B) of such Code; or

"(2) an unforeseen financial emergency for purposes of sections 409A(a)(2)(A)(vi), 409A(a)(2)(B)(ii), and 457(d)(1)(A)(iii) of such Code."

—P.L. 109-280, Sec. 827(b)(1), deleted "or" at the end of subclause (k)(2)(B)(i)(III), substituted "or" for "and" at the end of subclause (k)(2)(B)(i)(IV) and added subclause (k)(2)(B)(i)(V), effective for distributions after 9/11/2001. Sec. 827(c)(2) of this Act, reads as follows:

"(2) Waiver of limitations. If refund or credit of any overpayment of tax resulting from the amendments made by this section is prevented at any time before the close of the 1-year period beginning on the date of the enactment of this Act by the operation of any law or rule of law (including res judicata), such refund or credit may nevertheless be made or allowed if claim therefor is filed before the close of such period."

—P.L. 109-280, Sec. 861(a)(1), substituted "section 414(d))." for "section 414(d) maintained by a State or local government or political subdivision thereof (or agency or instrumentality thereof)." in subpara. (a)(5)(G) and subpara. (a)(26)(G) . . . Sec. 861(a)(2), deleted "maintained by a State or local government or political subdivision thereof (or agency or instrumentality thereof)" after "section 414(d))" in subpara. (k)(3)(G) and after "Internal Revenue Code of 1986)" in P.L. 105-34, Sec. 1505(d)(2), [see below] . . . Sec. 861(b)(1), substituted "Governmental" for "State and local governmental" in the heading of subpara. (a)(5)(G) . . . Sec. 861(b)(2), substituted "Exception for" for "Exception for State and local" in the heading of subpara. (a)(26)(G) . . . Sec. 861(b)(3), added "Governmental plan." after "(G)" in subpara. (k)(3)(G), effective for any year begin. after 8/17/2006.

—P.L. 109-280, Sec. 865, of this Act, reads as follows:

"SEC. 865. GRANDFATHER RULE FOR CHURCH PLANS WHICH SELF-ANNUITIZE.

"(a) In general. In the case of any plan year ending after the date of the enactment of this Act, annuity payments provided with respect to any account maintained for a participant or beneficiary under a qualified church plan shall not fail to satisfy the requirements of section 401(a)(9) of the Internal Revenue Code of 1986 merely because the payments are not made under an annuity contract purchased from an insurance company if such payments would not fail such requirements if provided with respect to a retirement income account described in section 403(b)(9) of such Code."

"(b) Qualified church plan. For purposes of this section, the term 'qualified church plan' means any money purchase pension plan described in section 401(a) of such Code which—

'(1) is a church plan (as defined in section 414(e) of such Code) with respect to which the election provided by section 410(d) of such Code has not been made, and

"(2) was in existence on April 17, 2002."

— P.L. 109-280, Sec. 901(a)(1), added para. (a)(35) . . . Sec. 901(a)(2)(A), added clause (a)(28)(B)(v), effective for plan yrs. begin. after 12/31/2006. Sec. 901(c)(2) and (3) of this Act reads as follows:

"(2) Special rule for collectively bargained agreements. In the case of a plan maintained pursuant to 1 or more collective bargaining agreements between employee representatives and 1 or more employers ratified on or before the date of the enactment of this Act, paragraph (1) shall be applied to benefits pursuant to, and individuals covered by, any such agreement by substituting for 'December 31, 2006' the earlier of—

"(A) the later of—

"(i) December 31, 2007, or

"(ii) the date on which the last of such collective bargaining agreements terminates (determined without regard to any extension thereof after such date of enactment), or

"(B) December 31, 2008.

"(3) Special rule for certain employer securities held in an ESOP.

"(A) In general. In the case of employer securities to which this paragraph applies, the amendments made by this section shall apply to plan years beginning after the earlier of—

"(i) December 31, 2007, or

"(ii) the first date on which the fair market value of such securities exceeds the guaranteed minimum value described in subparagraph (B)(ii).

"(B) Applicable securities. This paragraph shall apply to employer securities which are attributable to employer contributions other than elective deferrals, and which, on September 17, 2003—

"(i) consist of preferred stock, and

"(ii) are within an employee stock ownership plan (as defined in section 4975(e)(7) of the Internal Revenue Code of 1986), the terms of which provide that the value of the securities cannot be less than the guaranteed minimum value specified by the plan on such date.

"(C) Coordination with transition rule. In applying section 401(a)(35)(H) of the Internal Revenue Code of 1986 and section 204(j)(7) of the Employee Retirement Income Security Act of 1974 (as added by this section) to employer securities to which this paragraph applies, the applicable percentage shall be determined without regard to this paragraph."

—P.L. 109-280, Sec. 902(a), added para. (k)(13) . . . Sec. 902(b), redesignated para. (m)(12) as (13) and added para. (m)(12) . . . Sec. 902(d)(2)(C), added "an erroneous automatic contribution under section 414(w)," after "402(g)(2)(A)," in subpara. (k)(8)(E) . . . Sec. 902(d)(2)(D), added "or erroneous automatic contribution" before the period at the end of the heading of subpara. (k)(8)(E) . . . Sec. 902(e)(3)(B)(i), added "through the end of such year" after "such contributions" in clause (k)(8)(A)(i) . . . Sec. 902(e)(3)(B)(ii), added "through the end of such year" after "to such contributions" in subpara. (m)(6)(A), effective for plan yrs. begin. after 12/31/2007.

—P.L. 109-280, Sec. 905(b), added para. (a)(36), effective for distributions in plan yrs. begin. after 12/31/2006.

In 2005, P.L. 109-135, Sec. 201(b)(4)(A), repealed Secs. 101, 102, and 104 of P.L. 109-73, effective 12/21/2005.

Prior to repeal, Sec. 101 of P.L. 109-73 read as follows:

"SEC. 101. TAX-FAVORED WITHDRAWALS FROM RETIREMENT PLANS FOR RELIEF RELATING TO HURRICANE KATRINA.

"(a) In general. Section 72(t) of the Internal Revenue Code of 1986 shall not apply to any qualified Hurricane Katrina distribution.

"(b) Aggregate dollar limitation.

"(1) In general. For purposes of this section, the aggregate amount of distributions received by an individual which may be treated as qualified Hurricane Katrina distributions for any taxable year shall not exceed the excess (if any) of—

"(A) $100,000, over

"(B) the aggregate amounts treated as qualified Hurricane Katrina distributions received by such individual for all prior taxable years.

"(2) Treatment of plan distributions. If a distribution to an individual would (without regard to paragraph (1)) be a qualified Hurricane Katrina distribution, a plan shall not be treated as violating any requirement of the Internal Revenue Code of 1986 merely because the plan treats such distribution as a qualified Hurricane Katrina distribution, unless the aggregate amount of such distributions from all plans maintained by the employer (and any member of any controlled group which includes the employer) to such individual exceeds $100,000.

"(3) Controlled group. For purposes of paragraph (2), the term 'controlled group' means any group treated as a single employer under subsection (b), (c), (m), or (o) of section 414 of such Code.

"(c) Amount distributed may be repaid.

"(1) In general. Any individual who receives a qualified Hurricane Katrina distribution may, at any time during the 3-year period beginning on the day after the date on which such distribution was received, make one or more contributions in an aggregate amount not to exceed the amount of such distribution to an eligible retirement plan of which such individual is a beneficiary and to which a rollover contribution of such distribution could be made under section 402(c), 403(a)(4), 403(b)(8), 408(d)(3), or 457(e)(16) of such Code, as the case may be.

"(2) Treatment of repayments of distributions from eligible retirement plans other than IRAs. For purposes of such Code, if a contribution is made pursuant to paragraph (1) with respect to a qualified Hurricane Katrina distribution from an eligible retirement plan other than an individual retirement plan, then the taxpayer shall, to the extent of the amount of the contribution, be treated as having received the qualified Hurricane Katrina distribution in an eligible rollover distribution (as defined in section 402(c)(4) of such Code) and as having transferred the amount to the eligible retirement plan in a direct trustee to trustee transfer within 60 days of the distribution.

"(3) Treatment of repayments for distributions from IRAs. For purposes of such Code, if a contribution is made pursuant to paragraph (1) with respect to a qualified Hurricane Katrina distribution from an individual retirement plan (as defined by section 7701(a)(37) of such Code), then, to the extent of the amount of the contribution, the qualified Hurricane Katrina distribution shall be treated as a distribution described in section 408(d)(3) of such Code and as having been transferred to the eligible retirement plan in a direct trustee to trustee transfer within 60 days of the distribution.

"(d) Definitions. For purposes of this section—

"(1) Qualified Hurricane Katrina distribution. Except as provided in subsection (b), the term 'qualified Hurricane Katrina distribution' means any distribution from an eligible retirement plan made on or after August 25, 2005, and before January 1, 2007, to an individual whose principal place of abode on August 28, 2005, is located in the Hurricane Katrina disaster area and who has sustained an economic loss by reason of Hurricane Katrina.

"(2) Eligible retirement plan. The term 'eligible retirement plan' shall have the meaning given such term by section 402(c)(8)(B) of such Code.

"(e) Income inclusion spread over 3 year period for qualified Hurricane Katrina distributions.

"(1) In general. In the case of any qualified Hurricane Katrina distribution, unless the taxpayer elects not to have this subsection apply for any taxable year, any amount required to be included in gross income for such taxable year shall be so included ratably over the 3-taxable year period beginning with such taxable year.

"(2) Special rule. For purposes of paragraph (1), rules similar to the rules of subparagraph (E) of section 408A(d)(3) of such Code shall apply.

"(f) Special rules.

"(1) Exemption of distributions from trustee to trustee transfer and withholding rules. For purposes of sections 401(a)(31), 402(f), and 3405 of such Code, qualified Hurricane Katrina distributions shall not be treated as eligible rollover distributions.

"(2) Qualified Hurricane Katrina distributions treated as meeting plan distribution requirements. For purposes of such Code, a qualified Hurricane Katrina distribution shall be treated as meeting the requirements of sections 401(k)(2)(B)(i), 403(b)(7)(A)(ii), 403(b)(11), and 457(d)(1)(A) of such Code."

Prior to repeal, Sec. 102 of P.L. 109-73 read as follows:

"SEC. 102. RECONTRIBUTIONS OF WITHDRAWALS FOR HOME PURCHASES CANCELLED DUE TO HURRICANE KATRINA.

"(a) Recontributions.

"(1) In general. Any individual who received a qualified distribution may, during the period beginning on August 25, 2005, and ending on February 28, 2006, make one or more contributions in an aggregate amount not to exceed the amount of such qualified distribution to an eligible retirement plan (as defined in section 402(c)(8)(B) of the Internal Revenue Code of 1986) of which such individual is a beneficiary and to which a rollover contribution of such distribution could be made under section 402(c), 403(a)(4), 403(b)(8), or 408(d)(3) of such Code, as the case may be.

"(2) Treatment of repayments. Rules similar to the rules of paragraphs (2) and (3) of section 101(c) of this Act shall apply for purposes of this section.

"(b) Qualified distribution defined. For purposes of this section, the term 'qualified distribution' means any distribution—

"(1) described in section 401(k)(2)(B)(i)(IV), 403(b)(7)(A)(ii) (but only to the extent such distribution relates to financial hardship), 403(b)(11)(B), or 72(t)(2)(F) of such Code,

"(2) received after February 28, 2005, and before August 29, 2005, and

"(3) which was to be used to purchase or construct a principal residence in the Hurricane Katrina disaster area, but which was not so purchased or constructed on account of Hurricane Katrina."

Prior to repeal, Sec. 104 of P.L. 109-73 read as follows:

"SEC. 104. PROVISIONS RELATING TO PLAN AMENDMENTS.

"(a) In general. If this section applies to any amendment to any plan or annuity contract, such plan or contract shall be treated as being operated in accordance with the terms of the plan during the period described in subsection (b)(2)(A).

"(b) Amendments to which section applies.

"(1) In general. This section shall apply to any amendment to any plan or annuity contract which is made—

"(A) pursuant to any amendment made by this title, or pursuant to any regulation issued by the Secretary of the Treasury or the Secretary of Labor under this title, and

"(B) on or before the last day of the first plan year beginning on or after January 1, 2007, or such later date as the Secretary of the Treasury may prescribe.

In the case of a governmental plan (as defined in section 414(d) of the Internal Revenue Code of 1986), subparagraph (B) shall be applied by substituting the date which is 2 years after the date otherwise applied under subparagraph (B).

"(2) Conditions. This section shall not apply to any amendment unless—

"(A) during the period—

"(i) beginning on the date the legislative or regulatory amendment described in paragraph (1)(A) takes effect (or in the case of a plan or contract amendment not required by such legislative or regulatory amendment, the effective date specified by the plan), and

"(ii) ending on the date described in paragraph (1)(B) (or, if earlier, the date the plan or contract amendment is adopted),

the plan or contract is operated as if such plan or contract amendment were in effect; and

"(B) such plan or contract amendment applies retroactively for such period."

In 2004, P.L. 108-476, Sec. 1, of this Act, provides:

"SECTION 1. CERTAIN ARRANGEMENTS MAINTAINED BY THE YMCA RETIREMENT FUND TREATED AS CHURCH PLANS.

"(a) Retirement plans.

"(1) In general. For purposes of sections 401(a) and 403(b) of the Internal Revenue Code of 1986, any retirement plan maintained by the YMCA Retirement Fund as of January 1, 2003, shall be treated as a church plan (within the meaning of section 414(e) of such Code) which is maintained by an organization described in section 414(e)(3)(A) of such Code.

"(2) Tax-deferred retirement plan. In the case of a retirement plan described in paragraph (1) which allows contributions to be made under a salary reduction agreement—

"(A) such treatment shall not apply for purposes of section 415(c)(7) of such Code, and

"(B) any account maintained for a participant or beneficiary of such plan shall be treated for purposes of such Code as a retirement income account described in section 403(b)(9) of such Code, except that such account shall not, for purposes of section 403(b)(12) of such Code, be treated as a contract purchased by a church for purposes of section 403(b)(1)(D) of such Code.

"(3) Money purchase pension plan. In the case of a retirement plan described in paragraph (1) which is subject to the requirements of section 401(a) of such Code—

"(A) such plan (but not any reserves held by the YMCA Retirement Fund)—

"(i) shall be treated for purposes of such Code as a defined contribution plan which is a money purchase pension plan, and

"(ii) shall be treated as having made an election under section 410(d) of such Code for plan years beginning after December 31, 2005, except that notwithstanding the election—

"(I) nothing in the Employee Retirement Income Security Act of 1974 or such Code shall prohibit the YMCA Retirement Fund from commingling for investment purposes the assets of the electing plan with the assets of such Fund and with the assets of any employee benefit plan maintained by such Fund, and

"(II) nothing in this section shall be construed as subjecting any assets described in subclause (I), other than the assets of the electing plan, to any provision of such Act,

"(B) notwithstanding section 401(a)(11) or 417 of such Code or section 205 of such Act, such plan may offer a lump-sum distribution option to participants who have not attained age 55 without offering such participants an annuity option, and

"(C) any account maintained for a participant or beneficiary of such plan shall, for purposes of section 401(a)(9) of such Code, be treated as a retirement income account described in section 403(b)(9) of such Code.

"(4) Self-funded death benefit plan. For purposes of section 7702(j) of such Code, a retirement plan described in paragraph (1) shall be treated as an arrangement described in section 7702(j)(2).

"(b) YMCA retirement fund. For purposes of this section, the term 'YMCA Retirement Fund' means the Young Men's Christian Association Retirement Fund, a corporation created by an Act of the State of New York which became law on April 30, 1921.

"(c) Effective date. This section shall apply to plan years beginning after December 31, 2003."

—P.L. 108-311, Sec. 407(b), deleted subpara. (a)(26)(C) and redesignated subparas. (a)(26)(D)-(I) as (a)(26)(C)-(H), effective for yrs. begin. after 12/31/96 as if included in Sec. 1432 of the Small Business Job Protection Act of 1996, P.L. 104-188.

Prior to deletion, subpara. (a)(26)(C) read as follows:

"(C) Eligibility to participate. In the case of contributions under section 401(k) or 401(m), employees who are eligible to contribute (or may elect to have contributions made on their behalf) shall be treated as benefiting under the plan."

In 2002, P.L. 107-358, Sec. 2, added subsec. (c) in Sec. 901 of P.L. 107-16 [see below], effective 12/17/2002.

—P.L. 107-147, Sec. 411(o)(2), substituted "402(g)(1)(A)" for "402(g)(1)" in para. (a)(30), effective for contributions in tax. yrs. begin. after 12/31/2001.

—P.L. 107-147, Sec. 411(q)(1), added "is a qualified trust which is part of a plan which is a defined contribution plan" before "agrees" in clause (a)(31)(C)(i), effective for distributions made after 12/31/2001.

In 2001, P.L. 107-16, Sec. 611(c)(1), substituted "$200,000" for "$150,000" each place it appeared in para. (a)(17) ... Sec. 611(c)(2)(A), substituted "July 1, 2001" for "October 1, 1993" in subpara. (a)(17)(B) ... Sec. 611(c)(2)(B), substituted "$5,000" for "$10,000" each place it appeared in subpara. (a)(17)(B) ... Sec. 611(f)(3)(A), substituted "the amount in effect under section 408(p)(2)(A)(ii)" for "$6,000" in subclause (k)(11)(B)(i)(I) ... Sec. 611(f)(3)(B), deleted subpara. (k)(11)(E) ... Sec. 611(g)(1), added a sentence at the end of subpara. (c)(2)(A), effective for yrs. begin. after 12/31/2001.

Prior to deletion, subpara. (k)(11)(E) read as follows:

"(E) Cost-of-living adjustment. The Secretary shall adjust the $6,000 amount under subparagraph (B)(i)(I) at the same time and in the same manner as under section 408(p)(2)(E)."

—P.L. 107-16, Sec. 634, of this Act, provides:

"SEC. 634. MODIFICATION TO MINIMUM DISTRIBUTION RULES.

"The Secretary of the Treasury shall modify the life expectancy tables under the regulations relating to minimum distribution requirements under sections 401(a)(9), 408(a)(6) and (b)(3), 403(b)(10), and 457(d)(2) of the Internal Revenue Code to reflect current life expectancy."

—P.L. 107-16, Sec. 636(a)(1), of this Act, provides:

"(1) In general. The Secretary of the Treasury shall revise the regulations relating to hardship distributions under section 401(k)(2)(B)(i)(IV) of the Internal Revenue Code of 1986 to provide that the period an employee is prohibited from making elective and employee contributions in order for a distribution to be deemed necessary to satisfy financial need shall be equal to 6 months."

—P.L. 107-16, Sec. 641(e)(3), substituted ", 403(a)(4), 403(b)(8), and 457(e)(16)" for "and 403(a)(4)" in subpara. (a)(31)(B) [as redesignated by Sec. 657(a)(1) of this Act, see below], effective for distributions after 12/31/2001. Sec. 641(f)(2) and (3) of this Act, provide:

"(2) Reasonable notice. No penalty shall be imposed on a plan for the failure to provide the information required by the amendment made by subsection (c) with respect to any distribution made before the date that is 90 days after the date on which the Secretary of the Treasury issues a safe harbor rollover notice after the date of the enactment of this Act, if the administrator of such plan makes a reasonable attempt to comply with such requirement.

"(3) Special rule. Notwithstanding any other provision of law, subsections (h)(3) and (h)(5) of section 1122 of the Tax Reform Act of 1986 shall not apply to any distribution from an eligible retirement plan (as defined in clause (iii) or (iv) of section 402(c)(8)(B) of the Internal Revenue Code of 1986) on behalf of an individual if there was a rollover to such plan on behalf of such individual which is permitted solely by reason of any amendment made by this section."

—P.L. 107-16, Sec. 643(b), added the second sentence in subpara. (a)(31)(B) and clauses (a)(31)(B)(i) and (ii) [as redesignated by Sec. 657(a)(1) of this Act, see below], effective for distributions made after 12/31/2001.

—P.L. 107-16, Sec. 646(a)(1)(A), substituted "severance from employment" for "separation from service" in subclause (k)(2)(B)(i)(I) . . . Sec. 646(a)(1)(B), amended subpara. (k)(10)(A) . . . Sec. 646(a)(1)(C)(i)(I), substituted "A termination" for "An event" in subpara. (k)(10)(B) . . . Sec. 646(a)(1)(C)(i)(II), substituted "the termination" for "the event" in clause (k)(10)(B)(i) . . . Sec. 646(a)(1)(C)(ii), deleted subpara. (k)(10)(C) . . . Sec. 646(a)(1)(C)(iii), deleted "or disposition of assets or subsidiary" after "termination of plan" in the heading of para. (k)(10), effective for distributions after 12/31/2001.

Prior to amendment, subpara. (k)(10)(A) read as follows:

"(A) In general. The following events are described in this paragraph:

"(i) Termination. The termination of the plan without establishment or maintenance of another defined contribution plan (other than an employee stock ownership plan as defined in section 4975(e)(7)).

"(ii) Disposition of assets. The disposition by a corporation of substantially all of the assets (within the meaning of section 409(d)(2)) used by such corporation in a trade or business of such corporation, but only with respect to an employee who continues employment with the corporation acquiring such assets.

"(iii) Disposition of subsidiary. The disposition by a corporation of such corporation's interest in a subsidiary (within the meaning of section 409(d)(3)), but only with respect to an employee who continues employment with such subsidiary."

Prior to deletion, subpara. (k)(10)(C) read as follows:

"(C) Transferor corporation must maintain plan. An event shall not be treated as described in clause (ii) or (iii) of subparagraph (A) unless the transferor corporation continues to maintain the plan after the disposition."

—P.L. 107-16, Sec. 657(a)(1), redesignated subparas. (a)(31)(B) [as amended by Secs. 641(e)(3) and 643(b) of this Act, see above], (C) and (D) as subparas. (a)(31)(C), (D) and (E) respectively, and added new subpara. (a)(31)(B) . . . Sec. 657(a)(2)(A), substituted "Direct" for "Optional direct" in the heading of para. (a)(31) . . . Sec. 657(a)(2)(B), substituted "Subparagraphs (A) and (B)" for "Subparagraph (A)" in subpara. (a)(31)(C) [as redes. by Sec. 657(a)(1) of this Act, see above], effective for distributions made after final regulations implementing Sec. 657(c)(2)(A) of this Act are prescribed. Sec. 657(c)(2) of this Act, provides:

"(2) Regulations.

"(A) Automatic rollover safe harbor. Not later than 3 years after the date of enactment of this Act, the Secretary of Labor shall prescribe regulations providing for safe harbors under which the designation of an institution and investment of funds in accordance with section 401(a)(31)(B) of the Internal Revenue Code of 1986 is deemed to satisfy the fiduciary requirements of section 404(a) of the Employee Retirement Income Security Act of 1974 (29 U.S.C. 1104(a)).

"(B) Use of low-cost individual retirement plans. The Secretary of the Treasury and the Secretary of Labor may provide, and shall give consideration to providing, special relief with respect to the use of low-cost individual retirement plans for purposes of transfers under section 401(a)(31)(B) of the Internal Revenue Code of 1986 and for other uses that promote the preservation of assets for retirement income purposes."

—P.L. 107-16, Sec. 663(a), repealed Sec. 1114(c)(4) of P.L. 99-514 [reproduced below], effective for plan yrs. begin. after 12/31/2001.

—P.L. 107-16, Sec. 664, of this Act, provides:

"SEC. 664. EMPLOYEES OF TAX-EXEMPT ENTITIES.

"(a) In general. The Secretary of the Treasury shall modify Treasury Regulations section 1.410(b)-6(g) to provide that employees of an organization described in section 403(b)(1)(A)(i) of the Internal Revenue Code of 1986 who are eligible to make contributions under section 403(b) of such Code pursuant to a salary reduction agreement may be treated as excludable with respect to a plan under section 401(k) or (m) of such Code that is provided under the same general arrangement as a plan under such section 401(k), if—

"(1) no employee of an organization described in section 403(b)(1)(A)(i) of such Code is eligible to participate in such section 401(k) plan or section 401(m) plan; and

"(2) 95 percent of the employees who are not employees of an organization described in section 403(b)(1)(A)(i) of such Code are eligible to participate in such plan under such section 401(k) or (m).

"(b) Effective date. The modification required by subsection (a) shall apply as of the same date set forth in section 1426(b) of the Small Business Job Protection Act of 1996."

—P.L. 107-16, Sec. 666(a), amended para. (m)(9), effective for yrs. begin. after 12/31/2001.

Prior to amendment, para. (m)(9) read as follows:

"(9) Regulations. The Secretary shall prescribe such regulations as may be necessary to carry out the purposes of this subsection and subsection (k) including—

"(A) such regulations as may be necessary to prevent the multiple use of the alternative limitation with respect to any highly compensated employee, and

"(B) regulations permitting appropriate aggregation of plans and contributions. For purposes of the preceding sentence, the term 'alternative limitation' means the limitation of section 401(k)(3)(A)(ii)(II) and the limitation of paragraph (2)(A)(ii) of this subsection."

—P.L. 107-16, Sec. 901, of this Act [as amended by Sec. 2 of P.L. 107-358, and Sec. 101(a)(1) of P.L. 111-312, and as related to Sec. 811 of P.L. 109-280, see above], reads as follows:

"SEC. 901. SUNSET OF PROVISIONS OF ACT.

"(a) In general. All provisions of, and amendments made by, this Act shall not apply—

"(1) to taxable, plan, or limitation years beginning after December 31, 2012, or

"(2) in the case of title V, to estates of decedents dying, gifts made, or generation skipping transfers, after December 31, 2012.

"(b) Application of certain laws. The Internal Revenue Code of 1986 and the Employee Retirement Income Security Act of 1974 shall be applied and administered to years, estates, gifts, and transfers described in subsection (a) as if the provisions and amendments described in subsection (a) had never been enacted.

"(c) Exception. Subsection (a) shall not apply to section 803 (relating to no federal income tax on restitution received by victims of the Nazi regime or their heirs or estates)."

In 2000, P.L. 106-554, Sec. 1(a)(7), [which enacted into law Sec. 316(c) of P.L. 106-554] added "Such term includes a distribution of an annuity contract from— (I) a trust which forms a part of a plan described in section 401(a) and which is exempt from tax under section 501(a), or (II) an annuity plan described in section 403(a)." at the end of clause (k)(10)(B)(ii), effective for tax. yrs. begin. after 12/31/99. For transition rules, see Sec. 1401(c)(2) of P.L. 104-188, reproduced below.

In 1998, P.L. 105-206, Sec. 6015(b), substituted "(b)(12)(A)(i)" for "(b)(12)" in Sec. 1505(d)(2) of P.L. 105-34, see below.

In 1997, P.L. 105-34, Sec. 1502(b), added subparas. (a)(13)(C) and (D), effective for judgments, orders, and decrees issued, and settlement agreements entered into, on or after 8/5/97.

—P.L. 105-34, Sec. 1505(a)(1), added subpara. (a)(5)(G) . . . Sec. 1505(a)(2), amended subpara. (a)(26)(H) . . . Sec. 1505(b), added subpara. (k)(3)(G), effective for tax. yrs. begin. on or after 8/5/97. Sec. 1505(d)(2) of this Act [as amended by Sec. 6015(b) of 105-206 and Sec. 861(a)(2) of P.L. 109-280, see above] provides:

"(2) Treatment for years beginning before date of enactment. A governmental plan (within the meaning of section 414(d) of the Internal Revenue Code of 1986) shall be treated as satisfying the requirements of sections 401(a)(3), 401(a)(4), 401(a)(26), 401(k), 401(m), 403(b)(1)(D) and (b)(12)(A)(i), and 410 of such Code for all taxable years beginning before the date of enactment of this Act. [8/5/97]"

Prior to amendment, subpara. (a)(26)(H) read as follows:

"(H) Special rule for certain police or firefighters.

"(i) In general. An employer may elect to have this paragraph applied separately with respect to any classification of qualified public safety employees for whom a separate plan is maintained.

"(ii) Qualified public safety employee. For purposes of this subparagraph, the term 'qualified public safety employee' means any employee of any police department or fire department organized and operated by a State or political subdivision if the employee provides police protection, firefighting services, or emergency medical services for any area within the jurisdiction of such State or political subdivision."

—P.L. 105-34, Sec. 1509, of this Act, relating to the clarification of disqualification rules relating to acceptance of rollover contributions, provides:

"SEC. 1509. CLARIFICATION OF DISQUALIFICATION RULES RELATING TO ACCEPTANCE OF ROLLOVER CONTRIBUTIONS. The Secretary of the Treasury or his delegate shall clarify that, under the Internal Revenue Service regulations protecting pension plans from disqualification by reason of the receipt of invalid rollover contributions under section 402(c) of the Internal Revenue Code of 1986, in order for the administrator of the plan receiving any such contribution to reasonably conclude that the contribution is a valid rollover contribution it is not necessary for the distributing plan to have a determination letter with respect to its status as a qualified plan under section 401 of such Code."

—P.L. 105-34, Sec. 1525(a)(1), deleted "and" at the end of clause (k)(7)(B)(iii), redesignated clause (k)(7)(B)(iv) as (v) and added new clause (k)(7)(B)(iv) . . . Sec. 1525(a)(2), substituted ", (iii), or (iv)" for "or (iii)" in clause (k)(7)(B)(v) as redesignated, effective for yrs. begin. after 12/31/97.

—P.L. 105-34, Sec. 1530(c)(1), added "or by a charitable remainder trust pursuant to a qualified gratuitous transfer (as defined in section 664(g)(1))" after "stock bonus plan)," in para. (a)(1), effective for transfers made by trusts to, or for the use of, an employee stock ownership plan after 8/5/97.

—P.L. 105-34, Sec. 1601(d)(2)(A), substituted "if such plan allows only contributions required under this paragraph." for the period in clause (k)(11)(D)(ii) . . . Sec. 1601(d)(2)(B), added subpara. (k)(11)(E), effective for plan yrs. begin. after 12/31/96.

—P.L. 105-34, Sec. 1601(d)(2)(D), added clause (k)(11)(B)(iii), effective for calendar yrs. begin. after 8/5/97.

—P.L. 105-34, Sec. 1601(d)(3), substituted "Additional alternative" for "Alternative" in the heading of para. (m)(11), effective for yrs. begin. after 12/31/98.

In 1996, P.L. 104-188, Sec. 1401(b)(5), deleted clause (a)(28)(B)(v) . . . Sec. 1401(b)(6), amended clause (k)(10)(B)(ii), effective for tax. yrs. begin. after 12/31/99. For transitional rules, see Sec. 1401(c)(2), of this Act, which reads as follows:

"(2) Retention of certain transition rules. The amendments made by this section shall not apply to any distribution for which the taxpayer is eligible to elect the benefits of section 1122(h)(3) or (5) of the Tax Reform Act of 1986. Notwithstanding the preceding sentence, individuals who elect such benefits after December 31, 1999, shall not be eligible for 5-year averaging under section 402(d) of the Internal Revenue Code of 1986 (as in effect immediately before such amendments)."

Prior to deletion, clause (a)(28)(B)(v) read as follows:

"(v) Coordination with distribution rules. Any distribution required by this subparagraph shall not be taken into account in determining whether a subsequent distribution is a lump sum distribution under section 402(d)(4)(A) or in determining whether section 402(c)(10) applies."

Prior to amendment, clause (k)(10)(B)(ii) read as follows;

"(ii) Lump sum distribution. For purposes of this subparagraph, the term 'lump sum distribution' has the meaning given such term by section 402(d)(4), without regard to clauses (i), (ii), (iii), and (iv) of subparagraph (A), subparagraph (B), or subparagraph (F) thereof."

—P.L. 104-188, Sec. 1404(a), amended subpara. (a)(9)(C), effective for yrs. begin. after 12/31/96.

Prior to amendment, subpara. (a)(9)(C) read as follows:

"(C) Required beginning date. For purposes of this paragraph, the term 'required beginning date' means April 1 of the calendar year following the calendar year in which the employee attains age 70½. In the case of a governmental plan or church plan, the required beginning date shall be the later of the date determined under the preceding sentence or April 1 of the calendar year following the calendar year in which the employee retires. For purposes of this subparagraph, the term 'church plan' means a plan maintained by a church for church employees, and the term 'church' means any church (as defined in section 3121(w)(3)(A)) or qualified church-controlled organization (as defined in section 3121(w)(3)(B))."

—P.L. 104-188, Sec. 1422(a), added para. (k)(11) . . . Sec. 1422(b), redesignated para. (m)(10) as (11) and added para. (m)(10), effective for plan yrs. begin. after 12/31/96.

—P.L. 104-188, Sec. 1426(a), amended subpara. (k)(4)(B), effective for plan yrs begin. after 12/31/96, but shall not apply to any cash or deferred arrangement to which clause (i) of section 1116(f)(2)(B) of the Tax Reform Act of 1986 applies.

Prior to amendment, subpara. (k)(4)(B) read as follows:

"(B) State and local governments and tax-exempt organizations not eligible. A cash or deferred arrangement shall not be treated as a qualified cash or deferred arrangement if it is part of a plan maintained by—

"(i) a State or local government or political subdivision thereof, or any agency or instrumentality thereof, or

"(ii) any organization exempt from tax under this subtitle.

This subparagraph shall not apply to a rural cooperative plan."

—P.L. 104-188, Sec. 1431(b)(2), deleted "In determining the compensation of an employee, the rules of section 414(q)(6) shall apply, except that in applying such rules, the term 'family' shall include only the spouse of the employee and any lineal descendants of the employee who have not attained age 19 before the close of the year." at the end of subpara. (a)(17)(A), effective for yrs. begin. after 12/31/96.

—P.L. 104-188, Sec. 1431(c)(1)(B), substituted "section 414(q)(4)" for "section 414(q)(7)" in clause (a)(5)(D)(ii), effective for yrs. begin. after 12/31/96, except that in determining whether an employee is a highly compensated employee for yrs. begin. in 1997, such amendments shall be treated as having been in effect for yrs. begin. in 1996.

—P.L. 104-188, Sec. 1431(c)(2), added "Any reference in this paragraph to section 414(q) shall be treated as a reference to such section as in effect on the day before the date of the enactment of the Small Business Job Protection Act of 1996." to the end of Sec. 1114(c)(4) of P.L. 99-514, reproduced below.

—P.L. 104-188, Sec. 1432(a), amended subpara. (a)(26)(A) . . . Sec. 1432(b), substituted "paragraph (2)(A) or (7)" for "paragraph (7)" in subpara. (a)(26)(G), effective for yrs. begin. after 12/31/96.

Prior to amendment, subpara. (a)(26)(A) read as follows:

"(A) In general. A trust shall not constitute a qualified trust under this subsection unless such trust is part of a plan which on each day of the plan year benefits the lesser of—

"(i) 50 employees of the employer, or

"(ii) 40 percent or more of all employees of the employer."

—P.L. 104-188, Sec. 1433(a), added para. (k)(12) . . . Sec. 1433(b), redesignated para. (m)(11) [as redesignated by Sec. 1422(b) of this Act, see above] as para. (m)(12) and added new para. (m)(11), effective for yrs. begin. after 12/31/98.

—P.L. 104-188, Sec. 1433(c)(1)(A), substituted "the plan year" for "such year" in clause (k)(3)(A)(ii) . . . Sec. 1433(c)(1)(B), substituted "for the preceding plan year" for "for such plan year" in clause (k)(3)(A)(ii) . . . Sec. 1433(c)(1)(C), added the sentence to the end of subpara. (k)(3)(A) . . . Sec. 1433(c)(2)(A), added "for such plan year" after "highly compensated employees" in subpara. (m)(2)(A) . . . Sec. 1433(c)(2)(B), added "for the preceding plan year" after "eligible employees" each place it appeared in clauses (m)(2)(A)(i) and (ii) . . . Sec. 1433(c)(2)(C), added the sentence to the end of subpara. (m)(2)(A) . . . Sec. 1433(d)(1), added subpara. (k)(3)(E) . . . Sec. 1433(d)(2), added the sentence to the end of para. (m)(3) . . . Sec. 1433(e)(1), substituted "on the basis of the amount of contributions by, or on behalf of, each of such employees" for "on the basis of the respective portions of the excess contributions attributable to each of such employees" in subpara. (k)(8)(C) . . . Sec. 1433(e)(2), substituted "on the basis of the amount of contributions on behalf of, or by, each such employee" for "on the basis of the respective portions of such amounts attributable to each of such employees" in subpara. (m)(6)(C), effective for yrs. begin. after 12/31/96.

—P.L. 104-188, Sec. 1441(a), amended subsec. (d), effective for yrs. begin. after 12/31/96.

Prior to amendment, subsec. (d) read as follows:

"(d) Additional requirements for qualification of trusts and plans benefiting owner-employees. A trust forming part of a pension or profit-sharing plan which provides contributions or benefits for employees some or all of whom are owner-employees shall constitute a qualified trust under this section only if, in addition to meeting the requirements of subsection (a), the following requirements of this subsection are met by the trust and by the plan of which such trust is a part:

"(1)(A) If the plan provides contributions or benefits for an owner-employee who controls, or for two or more owner-employees who together control, the trade or business with respect to which the plan is established, and who also control as an owner-employee or as owner-employees one or more other trades or businesses, such plan and the plans established with respect to such other trades or businesses, when coalesced, constitute a single plan which meets the requirements of subsection (a) (including paragraph (10) thereof) and of this subsection with respect to the employees of all such trades or businesses (including the trade or business with respect to which the plan intended to qualify under this section is established).

"(B) For purposes of subparagraph (A), an owner-employee, or two or more owner-employees, shall be considered to control a trade or business if such owner-employee, or such two or more owner-employees together—

"(i) own the entire interest in an unincorporated trade or business, or

"(ii) in the case of a partnership, own more than 50 percent of either the capital interest or the profits interest in such partnership.

For purposes of the preceding sentence, an owner-employee, or two or more owner-employees, shall be treated as owning any interest in a partnership which is owned, directly or indirectly, by a partnership which such owner-employee, or such two or more owner-employees, are considered to control within the meaning of the preceding sentence.

"(2) The plan does not provide contributions or benefits for any owner-employee who controls (within the meaning of paragraph (1)(B)), or for two or more owner-employees who together control, as an owner-employee or as owner-employees, any other trade or business, unless the employees of each trade or business which such owner-employee or such owner-employees control are included under a plan which meets the requirements of subsection (a) (including paragraph (10) thereof) and of this subsection, and provides contributions and benefits for employees which are not less favorable than contributions and benefits provided for owner-employees under the plan.

"(3) Under the plan, contributions on behalf of any owner-employee may be made only with respect to the earned income of such owner-employee which is derived from the trade or business with respect to which such plan is established."

—P.L. 104-188, Sec. 1443(a), added subpara. (k)(7)(C), effective for distributions after 8/20/96.

—P.L. 104-188, Sec. 1443(b), amended clause (k)(7)(B)(i), effective for plan yrs. begin. after 12/31/96.

Prior to amendment, clause (k)(7)(B)(i) read as follows:

"(i) any organization which—

"(I) is exempt from tax under this subtitle or which is a State or local government or political subdivision thereof (or agency or instrumentality thereof), and

"(II) is engaged primarily in providing electric service on a mutual or cooperative basis,"

—P.L. 104-188, Sec. 1445(a), added subpara. (a)(5)(F), effective for yrs. begin. after 12/31/96.

—P.L. 104-188, Sec. 1459(a), added subpara. (k)(3)(F) . . . Sec. 1459(b), added subpara. (m)(5)(C), effective for plan yrs. begin. after 12/31/98.

—P.L. 104-188, Sec. 1465, of this Act, provides:

"SEC. 1465. DATE FOR ADOPTION OF PLAN AMENDMENTS.

"If any amendment made by this subtitle requires an amendment to any plan or annuity contract, such amendment shall not be required to be made before the first day of the first plan year beginning on or after January 1, 1998, if—

"(1) during the period after such amendment takes effect and before such first plan year, the plan or contract is operated in accordance with the requirements of such amendment, and

"(2) such amendment applies retroactively to such period.

In the case of a a governmental plan (as defined in section 414(d) of the Internal Revenue Code of 1986), this section shall be applied by substituting '2000' for '1998'."

—P.L. 104-188, Sec. 1704(t)(27), amended Sec. 7861(c)(2) of P.L. 101-239 [which amended Sec. 1140(c) of P.L. 99-514, see below], by adding "the second place it appears" before "and inserting", see below. . . . Sec. 1704(t)(67), substituted "section 521" for "section 211" in para. (a)(20), effective 8/20/96.

In 1994, P.L. 103-465, Sec. 732(a), amended subpara. (a)(17)(B), effective for yrs. begin. after 12/31/94, except as provided in Sec. 732(e)(2) of this Act, which reads as follows:

"(2) Rounding not to result in decreases. The amendments made by this section providing for the rounding of indexed amounts shall not apply to any year to the extent the rounding would require the indexed amount to be reduced below the amount in effect for years beginning in 1994."

Prior to amendment, subpara. (a)(17)(B) read as follows:

"(B) Cost-of-living adjustment.

"(i) In general. If, for any calendar year after 1994, the excess (if any) of—

"(I) $150,000, increased by the cost-of-living adjustment for the calendar year, over

"(II) the dollar amount in effect under subparagraph (A) for taxable years beginning in the calendar year, is equal to or greater than $10,000, then the $150,000 amount under subparagraph (A) (as previously adjusted under this subparagraph) for any taxable year beginning in any subsequent calendar year shall be increased by the amount of such excess, rounded to the next lowest multiple of $10,000.

"(III) Cost-of-living adjustment. The cost-of-living adjustment for any calendar year shall be the adjustment made under section 415(d) for such calendar year, except that the base period for purposes of section 415(d)(1)(A) shall be the calendar quarter beginning October 1, 1993."

—P.L. 103-465, Sec. 751(a)(9)(C), added para. (a)(32), effective for plan yrs. begin. after 12/31/94.

—P.L. 103-465, Sec. 766(b), added para. (a)(33), effective for plan amendments adopted on or after 12/8/94.

—P.L. 103-465, Sec. 776(d), added para. (a)(34), effective for distributions that occur in plan years commencing after final regulations implementing these provisions are prescribed by the Pension Benefit Guaranty Corporation.

In 1993, P.L. 103-66, Sec. 13212(a)(1)(A), substituted "$150,000" for "$200,000" in the first sentence of para. (a)(17) . . . Sec. 13212(a)(1)(B), deleted the second sentence of para. (a)(17) . . . Sec. 13212(a)(1)(C), added subpara. (a)(17)(B) . . . Sec. 13212(a)(2), substituted "Compensation limit. (A) In general. A trust" for "A trust" in para. (a)(17), effective for benefits accruing in plan yrs. begin. after 12/31/93, except as provided in Sec. 13212(d)(2) and (3) of this Act, which reads as follows:

"(2) Collectively bargained plans. In the case of a plan maintained pursuant to 1 or more collective bargaining agreements between employee representatives and 1 or more employers ratified before the date of the enactment of this Act, the amendments made by this section shall not apply to contributions or benefits pursuant to such agreements for plan years beginning before the earlier of—

"(A) the latest of—

"(i) January 1, 1994

"(ii) the date on which the last of such collective bargaining agreements terminates (without regard to any extension, amendment, or modification of such agreements on or after such date of enactment), or

"(iii) in the case of a plan maintained pursuant to collective bargaining under the Railway Labor Act, the date of execution of an extension or replacement of the last of such collective bargaining agreements in effect on such date of enactment, or

"(B) January 1, 1997.

"(3) Transition rule for state and local plans.

"(A) In general. In the case of an eligible participant in a governmental plan (within the meaning of section 414(d) of the Internal Revenue Code of 1986), the dollar limitation under section 401(a)(17) of such Code shall not apply to the extent the amount of compensation which is allowed to be taken into account under the plan would be reduced below the amount which was allowed to be taken into account under the plan as in effect on July 1, 1993.

"(B) Eligible participant. For purposes of subparagraph (A), an eligible participant is an individual who first became a participant in the plan during a plan year beginning before the 1st plan year beginning after the earlier of—

"(i) the plan year in which the plan is amended to reflect the amendments made by this section, or

"(ii) December 31, 1995.

"(C) Plan must be amended to incorporate limits. This paragraph shall not apply to any eligible participant of a plan unless the plan is amended so that the plan incorporates by reference the dollar limitation under section 401(a)(17) of the Internal Revenue Code of 1986, effective with respect to noneligible participants for plan years beginning after December 31, 1995 (or earlier if the plan amendment so provides)."

Prior to deletion, the second sentence of para. (a)(17) read as follows:

"The Secretary shall adjust the $200,000 amount at the same time and in the same manner as under section 415(d)."

In 1992, P.L. 102-318, Sec. 521(b)(5)(A), substituted "1 or more distributions within 1 taxable year to a distributee on account of a termination of the plan of which the trust is a part, or in the case of a profit-sharing or stock bonus plan, a complete discontinuance of contributions under such plan" for "a qualified total distribution described in section 402(a)(5)(E)(i)(I)" in para. (a)(20) . . . Sec. 521(b)(5)(B), added a new sentence at the end of para. (a)(20) . . . Sec. 521(b)(6), amended clause (a)(28)(B)(v) . . . Sec. 521(b)(7), substituted "section 402(e)(3)" for "section 402(a)(8)" in subclause (k)(2)(B)(i)(IV) . . . Sec. 521(b)(8)(A), substituted "section 402(d)(4)" for "section 402(e)(4)" in clause (k)(10)(B)(ii) . . . Sec. 521(b)(8)(B), substituted "subparagraph (F)" for "subparagraph (H)" in clause (k)(10)(B)(ii), effective for distributions after 12/31/92. For special rule, see Sec. 521(e)(2) of this Act which reads as follows:

"(2) Special rule for partial distributions. For purposes of section 402(a)(5)(D)(i)(II) of the Internal Revenue Code of 1986 (as in effect before the amendments made by this section), a distribution before January 1, 1993, which is made before or at the same time as a series of periodic payments shall not be treated as one of such series if it is not substantially equal in amount to other payments in such series."

Prior to amendment, clause (a)(28)(B)(v) read as follows:

"(v) Coordination with distribution rules. Any distribution required by this subparagraph shall not be taken into account in determining whether—

"(I) a subsequent distribution is a lump-sum distribution under section 402(e)(4)(A), or

"(II) section 402(a)(5)(D)(iii) applies to a subsequent distribution."

—P.L. 102-318, Sec. 522(a)(1), added para. (a)(31), effective for distributions after 12/31/92, except as provided in Sec. 522(d)(2) of this Act which reads as follows:

"(2) Transition rule for certain annuity contracts. If, as of July 1, 1992, a State law prohibits a direct trustee-to-trustee transfer from an annuity contract described in section 403(b) of the Internal Revenue Code of 1986 which was purchased for an employee by an employer which is a State or a political subdivision thereof (or an agency or instrumentality of any 1 or more of either), the amendments made by this section shall not apply to distributions before the earlier of—

"(A) 90 days after the first day after July 1, 1992, on which such transfer is allowed under State law, or

"(B) January 1, 1994."

—P.L. 102-318, Sec. 523, of this Act provides:

"SEC. 523. DATE FOR ADOPTION OF PLAN AMENDMENTS.

"If any amendment made by this subtitle requires an amendment to any plan, such plan amendment shall not be required to be made before the first plan year beginning on or after January 1, 1994, if—

"(1) during the period after such amendment takes effect and before such first plan year, the plan is operated in accordance with the requirements of such amendment, and

"(2) such plan amendment applies retroactively to such period."

In 1990, P.L. 101-508, Sec. 12011(b), added ", and subject to the provisions of section 420" after "Secretary" in subsec. (h), effective for transfers in tax. yrs. begin. after 12/31/90 except as provided in Sec. 12011(c)(2) of this Act, which reads as follows:

"(2) Waiver of estimated tax penalties. No addition to tax shall be made under section 6654 or section 6655 of the Internal Revenue Code of 1986 for the taxable year preceding the taxpayer's 1st taxable year beginning after December 31, 1990, with respect to any underpayment to the extent such underpayment was created or increased by reason of section 420(b)(4)(B) of such Code (as added by subsection (a))."

In 1989, P.L. 101-239, Sec. 7311(a), added the last sentence to subsec. (h), effective for contributions after 10/3/89, except as provided in Sec. 7311(b)(2) of this Act which reads as follows:

"(2) Transition. The amendment made by this section shall not apply to contributions made before January 1, 1990, if—

"(A) the employer requested before October 3, 1989, a private letter ruling or determination letter with respect to the qualification of the plan maintaining the account under section 401(h) of the Internal Revenue Code of 1986,

"(B) the request sets forth a method under which the amount of contributions to the account are to be determined on the basis of cost,

"(C) such method is permissible under section 401(h) of such Code under the provisions of General Counsel Memorandum 39785, and

"(D) the Internal Revenue Service issued before October 4, 1989, a private letter ruling, determination letter, or other letter providing that the specific plan involved qualifies under section 401(a) of such Code when such method is used, that contributions to the account are deductible, or acknowledging that the account would not adversely affect the qualified status of the plan (contingent on all phases of the particular plan being approved)."

—P.L. 101-239, Sec. 7811(g)(1), moved para. (a)(30) from the end of subsec. (a) and inserted para. (a)(30) after para. (a)(29), effective for plan yrs. begin. after 12/31/87, except as provided in Sec. 1011(c)(7)(E)(ii) of P.L. 100-647 reproduced below.

—P.L. 101-239, Sec. 7811(h)(3), corrected Sec. 1011B(j)(l) of P.L. 100-647 to amend clause (a)(28)(B)(ii)(II) instead of clause (a)(28)(B)(II), see below.

—P.L. 101-239, Sec. 7816(l), corrected Sec. 6071(b)(2) of P.L. 100-647 to substitute "rural cooperative plan" for "rural electric cooperative plan" instead of substituting "rural cooperative plan" for "rural electric plan" in subpara. (k)(4)(B), see below.

—P.L. 101-239, Sec. 7861(c)(1), amended Sec. 1140(a) of P.L. 99-514, provisions for plan amendments, [reproduced below] by substituting ", subtitle C, or title XVIII of this Act" for "or subtitle C" . . . Sec. 7861(c)(2), [as amended by Sec. 1704(t)(27) of P.L. 104-188, see above] amended Sec. 1140(c) of P.L. 99-514, reproduced below . . . Sec. 7861(c)(3), added the last sentence to Sec. 1140(c) of P.L. 99-514, reproduced below.

Prior to amendment, Sec. 1140(c) of P.L. 99-514 read as follows:

"(c) Special rule for collectively bargained plans.

"In the case of a plan maintained pursuant to 1 or more collective bargaining agreements between employee representatives and 1 or more employers ratified before March 1, 1986, subsection (a) shall be applied by substituting for the first plan year beginning on or after January 1, 1989, the first plan year beginning after the earlier of—

"(1) the later of—

"(A) January 1, 1989, or

"(B) the date on which the last of such collective bargaining agreements terminate (determined without regard to any extension thereof after February 28, 1986), or

"(2) January 1, 1991.".

—P.L. 101-239, Sec. 7861(d)(1), amended Sec. 303(f) of P.L. 98-397 [reproduced below] relating to transitional rules, by substituting "July 17, 1984" for "July 24, 1984", see below.

—P.L. 101-239, Sec. 7881(i)(1)(A), added "and any other plan amendments adopted after December 22, 1987, and before such plan amendment" after "amendment" in subclause (a)(29)(C)(i)(II) . . . Sec. 7881(i)(4)(A), added "to which the requirements of section 412 apply" after "multiemployer plan)" in clause (a)(29)(A)(i), effective for plan amendments adopted after 12/22/87, except as provided in Sec. 9341(c)(2) of P.L. 100-203 reproduced below.

—P.L. 101-239, Sec. 7881(i)(5), amended Sec. 9341(c)(2) of P.L. 100-203 [reproduced below], part of the effective date for changes made by Sec. 9341(a) of P.L. 100-203, see below, by adding "(without regard to any extension, amendment, or modification of such agreements on or after such date of enactment)" after "ratified before the date of enactment", see below.

—P.L. 101-140, Sec. 203(a)(5)(A), deleted "(as defined in section 89(i)(4))" after "church plan" in subpara. (a)(9)(C) . . . Sec. 203(a)(5)(B), added the last sentence of subpara. (a)(9)(C), effective as provided in Sec. 1151(k)(1) and (4) of P.L. 99-514, reproduced in note following Code Sec. 414.

In 1988, P.L. 100-647, Sec. 1011(c)(7)(A), added para. (a)(30), effective for plan yrs. begin. after 12/31/87, except as provided in Sec. 1011(c)(7)(E)(ii) of this Act which reads as follows:

"(ii) In the case of a plan described in section 1105(c)(2) of the Reform Act, the amendments made by this paragraph shall not apply to contributions made pursuant to an agreement described in such section for plan years beginning before the earlier of—

"(I) the later of January 1, 1988, or the date on which the last of such agreements terminates (determined without regard to any extension thereof after February 28, 1986), or

"(II) January 1, 1989."

—P.L. 100-647, Sec. 1011(d)(4), added the last sentence to para. (a)(17), effective for benefits accruing in yrs. begin. after 12/31/88. For special rules see Sec. 1106(i)(5)(B) of P.L. 99-514, reproduced below.

—P.L. 100-647, Sec. 1011(e)(3), amended para. (k)(7), effective for tax. yrs. begin. after 12/31/88, except as provided in Sec. 1107(c)(2)-(5) of P.L. 99-514, reproduced in note following Code Sec. 457.

Prior to amendment, para. (k)(7) read as follows:

"(7) Rural electric cooperative plan. For purposes of this subsection, the term 'rural electric cooperative plan' means any pension plan—

"(A) which is a defined contribution plan (as defined in section 414(i)), and

"(B) which is established and maintained by a rural electric cooperative (as defined in section 457(d)(9)(B)) or a national association of such rural electric cooperatives."

—P.L. 100-647, Sec. 1011(g)(1)(A), added "by the employer" after "contributed" each place it appeared in subpara. (l)(2)(B). . . . Sec. 1011(g)(1)(B), added "attributable to employer contributions" after "benefits" in clause (l)(3)(A)(ii) . . . Sec. 1011(g)(2), amended subpara. (l)(5)(C) . . . Sec. 1011(g)(3)(A), substituted "the social security retirement age" for "age 65" each place it appeared in subpara. (l)(5)(E) . . . Sec. 1011(g)(3)(B), added clause (l)(5)(E)(iii), effective for benefits attributable to plan yrs. begin. after 12/31/88. For special rules, see Sec. 1111(c)(3) of P.L. 99-514, reproduced below.

Prior to amendment, para. (l)(5)(C) read as follows:

"(C) Average annual compensation. The term 'average annual compensation' means the greater of—

"(i) the participant's final average compensation (determined without regard to subparagraph (D)(ii)), or

"(ii) the participant's highest average annual compensation for any other period of at least 3 consecutive years."

—P.L. 100-647, Sec. 1011(g)(4), amended Sec. 1111(c)(3) of P.L. 99-514 [reproduced below], special rule for amendments made by Sec. 1111(a) of P.L. 99-514, by deleting "benefits pursuant to, and individuals covered by, any such agreement in" after "shall not apply to" see below.

—P.L. 100-647, Sec. 1011(h)(3), redesignated subpara. (a)(26)(F) as subpara. (a)(26)(H) and added subparas. (a)(26)(F) and (G), effective for plan yrs. begin. after 12/31/88. For special rules see Sec. 1112(e)(2) of P.L. 99-514, reproduced below.

—P.L. 100-647, Sec. 1011(h)(7), amended Sec. 1112(e)(2) of P.L. 99-514 [reproduced below] by deleting "employees covered by such agreement" after "shall not apply to", see below

—P.L. 100-647, Sec. 1011(k)(1)(A), deleted subclauses (k)(2)(B)(i)(II)-(IV), added new subclause (k)(2)(B)(i)(II) and redesignated subclauses (k)(2)(B)(i)(V) and (VI) as subclauses (k)(2)(B)(i)(III) and (VI), effective for distributions after 12/31/84.

Prior to amendment, subclauses (k)(2)(B)(i)(II)-(IV) read as follows:

"(II) termination of the plan without establishment of a successor plan,

"(III) the date of the sale by a corporation of substantially all of the assets (within the meaning of section 409(d)(2)) used by such corporation in a trade or business of such corporation with respect to an employee who continues employment with the corporation acquiring such assets,

"(IV) the date of the sale by a corporation of such corporation's interest in a subsidiary (within the meaning of section 409(d)(3)) with respect to an employee who continues employment with such subsidiary,"

—P.L. 100-647, Sec. 1011(k)(1)(B), added para. (k)(10), effective for yrs. begin. after 12/31/88, except as provided in Sec. 1011(k)(1)(C) of this Act, which read as follows:

"(C)(i) Subparagraph (A)(i) of section 401(k)(10) of the 1986 Code (as added by subparagraph (B) [Sec. 1011(k)(1)]) shall apply to distributions after October 16, 1987.

"(ii) Subparagraph (B) of section 401(k)(10) of the 1986 Code (as added by subparagraph (B) [Sec. 1011(k)(1)]) shall apply to distributions after March 31, 1988."

—P.L. 100-647, Sec. 1011(k)(2)(A), added "amounts held by the trust which are attributable to employer contributions made pursuant to the employee's election" after "under which" in subpara. (k)(2)(B) . . . Sec. 1011(k)(2)(B), deleted "amounts held by the trust which are attributable to employer contributions made pursuant to the employee's election" before "may not" in clause (k)(2)(B)(i) . . . Sec. 1011(k)(2)(C), deleted "amounts" before "will not" in clause (k)(2)(B)(ii), effective for yrs. begin. after 12/31/88.

—P.L. 100-647, Sec. 1011(k)(3)(A), added "eligible" before "highly compensated employees" each place it appeared in clause (k)(3)(A)(ii), effective for yrs. begin. after 12/31/86.

—P.L. 100-647, Sec. 1011(k)(3)(B), corrected Sec. 1116(b)(4) of P.L. 99-514 by substituting "any highly compensated employee" for "an employee" instead of "any employee" in the last sentence of subpara. (k)(3)(A), see below.

—P.L. 100-647, Sec. 1011(k)(4), redesignated subpara. (k)(3)(C) (as added by Sec. 1116(e) of P.L. 99-514) as subpara. (k)(3)(D) . . . Sec. 1011(k)(5), substituted "meet" for "meets" in subclause (k)(3)(D)(ii)(I), as redesignated by Sec. 1011(k)(4) of this Act, effective for yrs. begin. after 12/31/86.

—P.L. 100-647, Sec. 1011(k)(6), deleted "provided by such employer" after "if any other benefit" in subpara. (k)(4)(A), effective for yrs. begin. after 12/31/88, except as provided in Sec. 1116(f)(2)(B) of P.L. 99-514, reproduced below.

—P.L. 100-647, Sec. 1011(k)(7), redesignated subpara. (k)(8)(E) as subpara. (k)(8)(F) and added new subpara. (k)(8)(E), effective for yrs. begin. after 12/31/86.

—P.L. 100-647, Sec. 1011(k)(8), amended Sec. 1116(f)(2)(B) of P.L. 99-514 [reproduced below], transitional rules for amendments made by Sec. 1116(b)(3) of P.L. 99-514, by adding the last sentence, see below.

—P.L. 100-647, Sec. 1011(k)(9), added the last sentence to subpara. (k)(4)(B), effective for yrs. begin. after 12/31/88, for yrs. begin. after 12/31/86, except as provided in Sec. 1116(f)(2)(B) of P.L. 99-514, reproduced below.

—P.L. 100-647, Sec. 1011(k)(10), amended Sec. 1116(f)(2)(B)(i) of P.L. 99-514 [reproduced below], transitional rules for amendments made by Sec. 1116(b)(3) of P.L. 99-514 by substituting "or political subdivision thereof, or any agency or instrumentality thereof," for "(or political subdivision thereof)", see below.

—P.L. 100-647, Sec. 1011(l)(1), substituted "A defined contribution plan" for "A plan" in para. (m)(1) . . . Sec. 1011(l)(2), added the last sentence to para. (m)(3) . . . Sec. 1011(l)(3), substituted "contributions to which this subsection applies" for "such contributions" the first place it appeared in the last sentence of subpara. (m)(2)(B) . . . Sec. 1011(l)(4), substituted "a defined contribution plan" for "the plan" each place it appeared in subpara. (m)(4)(A), effective for plan yrs. begin. after 12/31/86. For special rules see Sec. 1117(d)(2) of P.L. 99-514, reproduced below.

—P.L. 100-647, Sec. 1011(l)(5)(A), substituted "section 402(g)(3)" for "402(g)(3)(A)" in subpara. (m)(4)(B), effective for yrs. begin. after 12/31/88.

—P.L. 100-647, Sec. 1011(l)(6), substituted "excess aggregate" for "excess" in the heading of subpara. (m)(6)(C) . . . Sec. 1011(l)(7), substituted "paragraph (6)" for "paragraph (8)" in subpara. (m)(7)(A), effective for plan yrs. begin. after 12/31/86. For special rules see Sec. 1117(d)(2) of P.L. 99-514, reproduced below.

—P.L. 100-647, Sec. 1011(l)(12), added Sec. 1117(d)(4) of P.L. 99-514, [reproduced below] part of the effective date for amendments made by Sec. 1121(b) of P.L. 99-514, see below.

—P.L. 100-647, Sec. 1011A(a)(3), added Sec. 1121(d)(5) [reproduced below] of P.L. 99-514, see below . . . Sec. 1011A(a)(4), amended Sec. 1121(d)(3) of P.L. 99-514, [reproduced below] by substituting "years" for "plan years", see below.

—P.L. 100-647, Sec. 1011A(j)(1), added subpara. (a)(27)(B) . . . Sec. 1011A(j)(2), substituted "(27) Determinations as to profit-sharing plans. (A) Contributions need not be based on profits." for "(27)" in subpara. (a)(27), effective for yrs. begin. after 12/31/85.

—P.L. 100-647, Sec. 1011A(1), redesignated subpara. (a)(11)(E), (relating to cross references), as subpara. (a)(11)(F), effective for plan yrs. begin. after 12/31/84.

—P.L. 100-647, Sec. 1011B(j)(1), [as amended by Sec. 7811(h)(3) of P.L. 101-239, see above], added "and within 90 days after the period during which the election may be made, the plan invests the portion of the participant's account covered by the election in accordance with such election" after "clause (i)" in subclause (a)(28)(B)(ii)(II) . . . Sec. 1011B(j)(2), amended clause (a)(28)(B)(iv), . . . Sec. 1011B(j)(6), added clause (a)(28)(B)(v), effective for stock acquired after 12/31/86.

Prior to amendment, clause (a)(28)(B)(iv) read as follows:

"(iv) Qualified election period. For purposes of this subparagraph, the term 'qualified election period' means the 5-plan-year period beginning with the plan year after the plan year in which the participant attains age 55 (or, if later, beginning with the plan year after the 1st plan year in which the individual 1st became a qualified participant)."

—P.L. 100-647, Sec. 1011B(k)(1), substituted "is not readily tradable on an established market" for "is not publicly traded" each place it appeared in para. (a)(22) . . . Sec. 1011B(k)(2), added the last sentence to para. (a)(22), effective 12/31/86.

—P.L. 100-647, Sec. 1011B(l)(1), and (l)(2), amended Sec. 1177(b) of P.L. 99-514 [reproduced below], part of transitional rules relating to changes made by Subtitle C of Title XI of P.L. 99-514, [Secs. 1171-1177] by substituting "section 146(d)(3)(C)" for "section 143(d)(3)(C)" in Sec. 1177(b)(2) of P.L. 99-514, and by substituting "made by section 1175" for "made by this subtitle" in Sec. 1177(b) of P.L. 99-514, see below. Sec. 1011B(l)(3) of this Act provides:

"(3) If any newspaper corporation described in section 1177(b) of the Reform Act, as amended by this subsection, pays in cash a dividend within 60 days after

Code Sec. 401 — Employee benefit plans

the date of the enactment of this Act to the corporation's employee stock ownership plans and if a corporate resolution declaring such dividend was adopted before November 30, 1987, and such resolution specifies that such dividend shall be contingent upon passage by the Congress of technical corrections, then such dividend (to the extent the aggregate amount so paid does not exceed $3,500,000) shall be treated as if it had been declared and paid in 1987 for all purposes of the Internal Revenue Code of 1986."

—P.L. 100-647, Sec. 1018(t)(3)(A), added Sec. 1852(a)(4)(C) [reproduced below] of P.L. 99-514, part of the effective date for changes made by Sec. 1852(a)(4)(A), see below.

—P.L. 100-647, Sec. 1018(t)(3)(C), amended the effective date for changes made by Sec. 1852(h)(1) of P.L. 99-514 from tax. yrs. begin. after 3/31/84 to tax. yrs. begin. after 12/31/85, see below.

—P.L. 100-647, Sec. 6053(a), added the last sentence to subpara. (a)(9)(C), effective for yrs. begin. after 12/31/88. For special rules see Secs. 1121(d)(3), (d)(4) and (d)(5) of P.L. 99-514, reproduced below.

—P.L. 100-647, Sec. 6055(a), redesignated subpara. (a)(26)(H), (as redesignated by Sec. 1011(h)(3) of this Act), as subpara. (a)(26)(I) and added new subpara. (a)(26)(H), effective for plan yrs. begin. after 12/31/88. For special rules, see Sec. 1112(e)(2) of P.L. 99-514 reproduced below and Sec. 1112(e)(3) reproduced in note following Code Sec. 4980.

—P.L. 100-647, Sec. 6056, of this Act provides:

"SEC. 6056. STUDY OF EFFECT OF MINIMUM PARTICIPATION RULE ON EMPLOYERS REQUIRED TO PROVIDE CERTAIN RETIREMENT BENEFITS.

"(a) Study.

"The Secretary of the Treasury or his delegate shall conduct a study on the application of section 401(a)(26) of the Internal Revenue Code of 1986 to Government contractors who—

"(1) are required by Federal law to provide certain employees specified retirement benefits, and

"(2) establish a separate plan for such employees while maintaining a separate plan for employees who are not entitled to such benefits.

Such study shall consider the Federal requirements with respect to employee benefits for employees of Government contractors, whether a special minimum participation rule should apply to such employees, and methods by which plans may be modified to satisfy minimum participation requirements.

"(b) Report. The Secretary of the Treasury or his delegate shall report the results of the study under subsection (a) to the Committee on Finance of the Senate and the Committee on Ways and Means of the House of Representatives not later than September 1, 1989."

—P.L. 100-647, Sec. 6065, of this Act provides:

"SEC. 6065 EXCEPTION FOR GOVERNMENTAL PLANS.

"In the case of plan years beginning before January 1, 1993, section 401(a)(26) of the 1986 Code shall not apply to any governmental plan (within the meaning of section 414(d) of such Code) with respect to employees who were participants in such plan on July 14, 1988."

—P.L. 100-647, Sec. 6071(a), substituted "or a rural cooperative plan" for "or a rural electric cooperative plan" in paras. (k)(1) and (k)(2) . . . Sec. 6071(b)(1), amended para. (k)(7) (as amended by Sec. 1011(e)(3) of this Act) . . . Sec. 6071(b)(2), [as amended by Sec. 7816(l) of P.L. 101-239, see above], amended subpara. (k)(4)(B) (as amended by Sec. 1011(k)(9) of this Act) by substituting "rural cooperative plan" for "rural electric cooperative plan", effective for tax. yrs. begin. after 11/10/88.

Prior to amendment, para. (k)(7) read as follows:

"(7) Rural electric cooperative plan. For purposes of this subsection—

"(A) In general. The term 'rural electric cooperative plan' means any pension plan—

"(i) which is a defined contribution plan (as defined in section 414(i)), and

"(ii) which is established and maintained by a rural electric cooperative.

"(B) Rural electric cooperative defined. For purposes of subparagraph (A), the term 'rural electric cooperative' means—

"(i) any organization which—

"(I) is exempt from tax under this subtitle or which is a State or local government or political subdivision thereof (or agency or instrumentality thereof), and

"(II) is engaged primarily in providing electric service on a mutual or cooperative basis,

"(ii) any organization described in paragraph (4) or (6) of section 501(c) and at least 80 percent of the members of which are organizations described in clause (i), and

"(iii) an organization in which is a national association of organizations described in clause (i) or (ii)."

In 1987, P.L. 100-203, Sec. 9341(a), added para. (a)(29), effective for plan amendments adopted after 12/22/87, except as provided in Sec. 9341(c)(2) [as amended by Sec. 7881(i)(5) of P.L. 101-239, see above], which reads as follows:

"(2) Collective bargaining agreements. In the case of a plan maintained pursuant to 1 or more collective bargaining agreements between employee representatives and 1 or more employers ratified before the date of the enactment of this Act, the amendments made by this section shall not apply to plan amendments adopted pursuant to collective bargaining agreements ratified before the date of enactment (without regard to any extension, amendment, or modification of such agreements on or after such date of enactment)."

In 1986, P.L. 99-514, Sec. 1106(d)(1), added para. (a)(17), effective for benefits accruing in years. begin. after 12/31/88. Sec. 1106(i)(5)(B) of this Act provides:

"(B) Collective bargaining agreements. In the case of a plan [maintained pursuant to 1 or more collective bargaining agreements between employee representatives and 1 or more employers ratified before March 1, 1986], the amendments made by subsection (d) shall apply to benefits accruing in years beginning on or after the earlier of—

"(i) the later of—

"(I) the date determined under [Sec. 1106(i)(2)(A) of P.L. 99-514] or

"(II) January 1, 1989, or

"(ii) January 1, 1991."

—P.L. 99-514, Sec. 1111(a), amended subsec. (l), effective for benefits attributable to plan yrs. begin. after 12/31/88. Sec. 1111(c)(3) [as amended by Sec. 1011(g)(4) of P.L. 100-647, see above] of this Act provides:

"(3) Special rule for collective bargaining agreements. In the case of a plan maintained pursuant to 1 or more collective bargaining agreements between employee representatives and 1 or more employers ratified before March 1, 1986, the amendments made by this section shall not apply to plan years beginning before the earlier of—

"(A) the later of—

"(i) January 1, 1989, or

"(ii) the date on which the last of such collective bargaining agreements terminates (determined without regard to any extension thereof after February 28, 1986), or

"(B) January 1, 1991."

Prior to amendment, subsec. (l) read as follows:

"(l) Nondiscriminatory coordination of defined contribution plans with OASDI.

"(1) In general. Notwithstanding subsection (a)(5), the coordination of a defined contribution plan with OASDI meets the requirements of subsection (a)(4) only if the total contributions with respect to each participant, when increased by the OASDI contributions, bear a uniform relationship—

"(A) to the total compensation of such employee, or

"(B) to the basic or regular rate of compensation of such employee.

"(2) Definitions. For purposes of paragraph (1)—

"(A) OASDI contributions. The term 'OASDI contributions' means the product of—

"(i) so much of the remuneration paid by the employer to the employee during the plan year as—

"(I) constitutes wages (within the meaning of section 3121(a) without regard to paragraph (1) thereof), and

"(II) does not exceed the contribution and benefit base applicable under OASDI at the beginning of the plan year, multiplied by

"(ii) the rate of tax applicable under section 3111(a) (relating to employer's OASDI tax) at the beginning of the plan year.

In the case of an individual who is an employee within the meaning of subsection (c)(1), the preceding sentence shall be applied by taking into account his earned income (as defined in subsection (c)(2)).

"(B) OASDI. The term 'OASDI' means the system of old-age, survivors, and disability insurance established under title II of the Social Security Act and the Federal Insurance Contributions Act.

"(C) Remuneration. The term 'remuneration' means—

"(i) total compensation, or

"(ii) basic or regular rate of compensation,

whichever is used in determining contributions or benefits under the plan.

"(3) Determination of compensation, etc., of self-employed individuals. For purposes of this subsection, in the case of an individual who is an employee within the meaning of subsection (c)(1)—

"(A) his total compensation shall include his earned income (as defined in subsection (c)(2)), and

"(B) his basic or regular rate of compensation shall be determined (under regulations prescribed by the Secretary) with respect to that portion of his earned income which bears the same ratio to his earned income as the basic or regular compensation of the employees under the plan (other than employees within the meaning of subsection (c)(1)) bears to the total compensation of such employees."

—P.L. 99-514, Sec. 1111(b), amended para. (a)(5), effective for yrs. begin. after 12/31/88. For special rules for collective bargaining agreements, see Sec. 1111(c)(3) of this Act, reproduced above.

Prior to amendment, para. (a)(5) read as follows:

"(5) A classification shall not be considered discriminatory within the meaning of paragraph (4) or section 410(b) (without regard to paragraph (1)(A) thereof) merely because it excludes employees the whole of whose remuneration constitutes 'wages' under section 3121(a)(1) (relating to the Federal Insurance Contribution Act) or merely because it is limited to salaried or clerical employees. Neither shall a plan be considered discriminatory within the meaning of such provisions merely because the contributions or benefits of or on behalf of the employees under the plan bear a uniform relationship to the total compensation, or the basic or regular rate of compensation, of such employees, or merely because the contributions or benefits based on that part of an employee's remuneration which is excluded from 'wages' by section 3121(a)(1) differ from the contributions or benefits based on employee's remuneration not so excluded, or differ because of any retirement benefits created under State or Federal law. For purposes of this paragraph and paragraph (10), the total compensation of an individual who is an employee within the meaning of subsection (c)(1) means such individual's earned income (as defined in subsection (c)(2)), and the basic or regular rate of compensation of such an individual shall be determined, under regulations prescribed by the Secretary, with respect to that portion of his earned income which bears the same ratio to his earned income as the basic or regular compensation of the employees under the plan bears to the total compensation of such employees. For purposes of determining whether two or more plans of an employer satisfy the requirements of paragraph (4) when considered as a single plan, if the amount of contributions on behalf of the employees allowed as a deduction under section 404 for the taxable year with respect to such plans, taken together, bears a uni-

Employee benefit plans — Code Sec. 401

form relationship to the total compensation, or the basic or regular rate of compensation, of such employees, the plans shall not be considered discriminatory merely because the rights of employees to, or derived from the employer contributions under the separate plans do not become nonforfeitable at the same rate. For the purposes of determining whether two or more plans of an employer satisfy the requirements of paragraph (4) when considered as a single plan, if the employees' rights to benefits under the separate plans do not become nonforfeitable at the same rate, but the levels of benefits provided by the separate plans satisfy the requirements of regulations prescribed by the Secretary to take account of the differences in such rates, the plans shall not be considered discriminatory merely because of the difference in such rates. For purposes of determining whether one or more plans of an employer satisfy the requirements of paragraph (4) and of section 410(b), an employer may take into account all simplified employee pensions to which only the employer contributes."

—P.L. 99-514, Sec. 1112(b), added para. (a)(26)... Sec. 1112(d)(1), deleted "of subparagraph (A) and (B)" before "of section 410(b)(1)" in clause (k)(3)(A)(i), effective for plan yrs. begin. after 12/31/88. Sec. 1112(e)(2) [as amended by Sec. 1011(h)(7) of P.L. 100-647, see above] and Sec. 1112(e)(4) [as added by Sec. 1011(h)(8) of P.L. 100-647] of this Act provide:

"(2) Special rule for collective bargaining agreements. In the case of a plan maintained pursuant to 1 or more collective bargaining agreements between employee representatives and 1 or more employers ratified before March 1, 1986, the amendments made by this section shall not apply to plan years beginning before the earlier of—

"(A) the later of—
"(i) January 1, 1989, or
"(ii) the date on which the last of such collective bargaining agreement terminates (determined without regard to any extension thereof after February 28, 1986), or
"(B) January 1, 1991."

* * * * *

"(4) Special rule for plans which may not terminate. To the extent provided in regulations prescribed by the Secretary of the Treasury or his delegate, if a plan is prohibited from terminating under title IV of the Employee Retirement Income Security Act of 1974 before the 1st year to which the amendment made by subsection (b) [Sec. 1112(b) of this Act] would apply, the amendment made by subsection (b) shall only apply to years after the 1st year in which the plan is able to terminate."

For waiver of excise tax on reversions, see Sec. 1112(e)(3) of this Act reproduced in note following Code Sec. 4980."

—P.L. 99-514, Sec. 1114(b)(7), amended para. (a)(4), effective for yrs. begin. after 12/31/88. Sec. 1114(c)(4) [as amended by Sec. 1431(c)(2) of P.L. 104-188, see above] of this Act provides:

Caution. Sec. 663(a) of P.L. 107-16, repealed Sec. 1114(c)(4), effective for plan yrs. begin. after 12/31/2001.

"(4) Special rule for determining highly compensated employees. For purposes of sections 401(k) and 401(m) of the Internal Revenue Code of 1986, in the case of an employer incorporated on December 15, 1924, if more than 50 percent of its employees in the top-paid group (within the meaning of section 414(q)(4) of such Code) earn less than $25,000 (indexed at the same time and in the same manner as under section 415(d) of such Code), then the highly compensated employees shall include employees described in section 414(q)(1)(C) of such Code determined without regard to the level of compensation of such employees. Any reference in this paragraph to section 414(q) shall be treated as a reference to such section as in effect on the day before the date of the enactment of the Small Business Job Protection Act of 1996."

Prior to amendment, para. (a)(4) read as follows:

"(4) If the contributions or the benefits provided under the plan do not discriminate in favor of employees who are—
"(A) officers,
"(B) shareholders, or
"(C) highly compensated.

For purposes of this paragraph, there shall be excluded from consideration employees described in section 410(b)(3)(A) and (C)."

—P.L. 99-514, Sec. 1116(a)(1), substituted "1.25" for "1.5" in subclause (k)(3)(A)(ii)(I)... Sec. 1116(a)(2), substituted "2 percentage points" for "3 percentage points" in subclause (k)(3)(A)(ii)(II)... Sec. 1116(a)(3), substituted "2" for "2.5" in subclause (k)(3)(A)(ii)(II)... Sec. 1116(b)(1), amended subpara. (k)(2)(B)... Sec. 1116(b)(2), deleted "and" at the end of subpara. (k)(2)(B), substituted ", and" for the period at the end of subpara. (k)(2)(C), and added subpara. (k)(2)(D)... Sec. 1116(b)(3), redesignated paras. (k)(4), (5) and (6) as paras. (k)(5), (6) and (7), and added new para. (k)(4)... Sec. 1116(b)(4), [as amended by Sec. 1011(k)(3)(B) of P.L. 100-647, see above] substituted "any highly compensated employee" for "an employee" in the last sentence of subpara. (k)(3)(A)... Sec. 1116(c)(1), added para. (k)(8)... Sec. 1116(c)(2), substituted "paragraph (5)" for "paragraph (4)" in clause (k)(3)(A)(ii)... Sec. 1116(d)(1), amended para. (k)(5)... Sec. 1116(d)(2), added para. (k)(9)... Sec. 1116(d)(3), deleted the last sentence of subpara. (k)(3)(B)... Sec. 1116(e), added subpara. (k)(3)(C)[(D)], effective as provided in Sec. 1116(f) [as amended by Sec. 1011(k)(8) and (10) of P.L. 100-647, see above] of this Act, which reads as follows:

"(f) Effective dates.

"(1) In general. Except as provided in this subsection, the amendments made by this section shall apply to years beginning after December 31, 1988.

"(2) Nondiscrimination rules.

"(A) In general. Except as provided in subparagraph (B), the amendments made by subsections (a), (b)(4), and (d), and the provisions of section 401(k)(3)(B) of

the Internal Revenue Code of 1986 (as added by this section), shall apply to years beginning after December 31, 1986.

"(B) Transition rules for certain governmental and tax-exempt plans. Subparagraph (B) of section 401(k)(4) of the Internal Revenue Code of 1986 (relating to governments and tax-exempt organizations not eligible for cash or deferred arrangements), as added by this section, shall not apply to any cash or deferred arrangement adopted by—

"(i) a State or local government or political subdivision thereof, or any agency or instrumentality thereof, before May 6, 1986, or
"(ii) a tax-exempt organization before July 2, 1986.

In the case of an arrangement described in clause (i), the amendments made by subsections (a), (b)(4), and (d) shall apply to years beginning after December 31, 1988. If clause (i) or (ii) applies to any arrangement adopted by a governmental unit, then any cash or deferred arrangement adopted by such unit on or after the date referred to in the applicable clause shall be treated as adopted before such date.

"(3) Aggregation and excess contributions. The amendments made by subsections (c) and (e) shall apply to years beginning after December 31, 1986.

"(4) Collective bargaining agreements.

"(A) In general. In the case of a plan maintained pursuant to 1 or more collective bargaining agreements between employee representatives and 1 or more employers ratified before March 1, 1986, the amendments made by this section shall not apply to years beginning before the earlier of—

"(i) the later of—
"(I) January 1, 1989, or
"(II) the date on which the last of such collective bargaining agreements terminates (determined without regard to any extension thereof after February 28, 1986), or
"(ii) January 1, 1991.

"(B) Special rule for nondiscrimination rules. In the case of a plan described in subparagraph (A), the amendments and provisions described in paragraph (2) shall not apply to years beginning before the earlier of—

"(i) the date determined under subparagraph (A)(i)(II), or
"(ii) January 1, 1989.

"(5) Special rule for qualified offset arrangements.

"(A) In general. A cash or deferred arrangement shall not be treated as failing to meet the requirements of section 401(k)(4) of the Internal Revenue Code of 1986 (as added by this section) to the extent such arrangement is part of a qualified offset arrangement consisting of such cash or deferred arrangement and a defined benefit plan.

"(B) Qualified offset arrangement. For purposes of subparagraph (A), a cash or deferred arrangement is part of a qualified offset arrangement with a defined benefit plan to the extent such offset arrangement satisfies each of the following conditions with respect to the employer maintaining the arrangement on April 16, 1986, and at all times thereafter:

"(i) The benefit under the defined benefit plan is directly and uniformly conditioned on the initial elective deferrals (up to 4 percent of compensation).
"(ii) The benefit provided under the defined benefit plan (before the offset) is at least 60 percent of an employee's cumulative elective deferrals (up to 4 percent of compensation).
"(iii) The benefit under the defined benefit plan is reduced by the benefit attributable to the employee's elective deferrals under the plan (up to 4 percent of compensation) and the income allocable thereto. The interest rate used to calculate the reduction shall not exceed the greater of the rate under section 411(a)(11)(B)(ii) of such Code or the interest rate applicable under section 411(c)(2)(C)(iii) of such Code, taking into account section 411(c)(2)(D) of such Code.

For purposes of applying section 401(k)(3) of such Code to the cash or deferred arrangement, the benefits under the defined benefit plan conditioned on initial elective deferrals may be treated as matching contributions under such rules as the Secretary of the Treasury or his delegate may prescribe. The Secretary shall provide rules for the application of this paragraph in the case of successor plans.

"(C) Definition of employer. For purposes of this paragraph, the term 'employer' includes any research and development center which is federally funded and engaged in cancer research, but only with respect to employees of contractor-operators whose salaries are reimbursed as direct costs against the operator's contract to perform work at such center.

"(6) Withdrawals on sale of assets. Subclauses (II), (III), and (IV) of section 401(k)(2)(B)(i) of the Internal Revenue Code of 1986 (as added by subsection (b)(1)) shall apply to distributions after December 31, 1984.

"(7) Distributions before plan amendment.

"(A) In general. If a plan amendment is required to allow a plan to make any distribution described in section 401(k)(8) of the Internal Revenue Code of 1986, any such distribution which is made before the close of the 1st plan year for which such amendment is required to be in effect under section 1140, shall be treated as made in accordance with the provisions of such plan.

"(B) Distributions pursuant to model amendment.

"(i) Secretary to prescribe amendment. The Secretary of the Treasury or his delegate shall prescribe an amendment which allows a plan to make any distribution described in section 401(k)(8) of such Code.

"(ii) Adoption by plan. If a plan adopts the amendment prescribed under clause (i) and makes a distribution in accordance with such amendment, such distribution shall be treated as made in accordance with the provisions of the plan."

Prior to amendment, subpara. (k)(2)(B) read as follows:

"(B) under which amounts held by the trust which are attributable to employer contributions made pursuant to the employee's election may not be distributable to participants or other beneficiaries earlier than upon retirement, death, disability, or separation from service (or in the case of a profit sharing or stock bonus plan,

1,889

hardship or the attainment of age 59½), and will not be distributable merely by reason of the completion of a stated period of participation or the lapse of a fixed number of years;"

Prior to amendment, para. (k)(5) read as follows:

"(5) Highly compensated employee. For purposes of this subsection, the term 'highly compensated employee' means any employee who is more highly compensated than two-thirds of all eligible employees, taking into account only compensation which is considered in applying paragraph (3)."

Prior to deletion, the last sentence of subpara. (k)(3)(B) read as follows:

For purposes of the preceding sentence, the compensation of any employee for a plan year shall be the amount of his compensation which is taken into account under the plan in calculating the contribution which may be made on his behalf for such plan year."

—P.L. 99-514, Sec. 1117(a), redesignated subsecs. (m) and (n) (as designated by Sec. 1898(c)(3) of this Act, see below) as subsecs. (n) and (o) and added new subsec. (m), effective for plan yrs. begin. after 12/31/86. Sec. 1117(b)(2)-(4) of this Act [as amended by Sec. 1011(l)(12) of P.L. 100-647, see above] provide:

"(2) Collective bargaining agreements. In the case of a plan maintained pursuant to 1 or more collective bargaining agreements between employee representatives and 1 or more employers ratified before March 1, 1986, the amendments made by this section shall not apply to plan years beginning before the earlier of—

"(A) January 1, 1989, or

"(B) the date on which the last of such collective bargaining agreements terminates (determined without regard to any extension thereof after February 28, 1986)."

"(3) Annuity contracts. In the case of an annuity contract under section 403(b) of the Internal Revenue Code of 1986—

"(A) the amendments made by this section shall apply to plan years beginning after December 31, 1988, and

"(B) in the case of a collective bargaining agreement described in paragraph (2), the amendments made by this section shall not apply to years beginning before the earlier of—

"(i) the later of—

"(I) January 1, 1989, or

"(II) the date determined under paragraph (2)(B), or

"(ii) January 1, 1991."

"(4) Distributions before plan amendment.

"(A) In general. If a plan amendment is required to allow a plan to make any distribution described in section 401(m)(6) of the Internal Revenue Code of 1986, any such distribution which is made before the close of the 1st plan year for which such amendment is required to be in effect under section 1140 shall be treated as made in accordance with the provisions of the plan.

"(B) Distributions pursuant to model amendment.

"(i) Secretary to prescribe amendment. The Secretary of the Treasury or his delegate shall prescribe an amendment which allows a plan to make any distribution described in section 401(m)(6) of the Internal Revenue Code of 1986.

"(ii) Adoption by plan. If a plan adopts the amendment prescribed under clause (i) and makes a distribution in accordance with such amendment, such distribution shall be treated as made in accordance with the provisions of the plan."

—P.L. 99-514, Sec. 1119(a), substituted "defined benefit plan" for "pension plan" in para. (a)(8), effective for plan yrs. begin. after 12/31/85.

—P.L. 99-514, Sec. 1121(b), amended subpara. (a)(9)(C), effective for yrs. begin. after 12/31/88. Sec. 1121(d)(3)-(5) [as amended by P.L. 100-647, Secs. 1011A(a)(3) and (a)(4), see above] of this Act provide:

"(3) Collective bargaining agreements. In the case of a plan maintained pursuant to 1 or more collective bargaining agreements between employee representatives and 1 or more employers ratified before March 1, 1986, the amendments made by this section shall not apply to distributions to individuals covered by such agreements in years beginning before the earlier of—

"(A) the later of—

"(i) the date on which the last of such collective bargaining agreements terminates (determined without regard to any extension thereof after February 28, 1986), or

"(ii) January 1, 1989, or

"(B) January 1, 1991.

"(4) Transition rules.

"(A) The amendments made by subsections (a) and (b) shall not apply with respect to any benefits with respect to which a designation is in effect under section 242(b)(2) of the Tax Equity and Fiscal Responsibility Act of 1982.

"(B)(i) Except as provided in clause (ii), the amendment made by subsection (b) shall not apply in the case of any individual who has attained age 70½ before January 1, 1988.

"(ii) Clause (i) shall not apply to any individual who is a 5-percent owner (as defined in section 416(i) of the Internal Revenue Code of 1986), at any time during—

"(I) the plan year ending with or within the calendar year in which such owner attains age 66½, and

"(II) any subsequent plan year."

Prior to amendment, subpara. (a)(9)(C) read as follows:

"(C) Required beginning date. For purposes of this paragraph, the term 'required beginning date' means April 1 of the calendar year following the later of—

"(i) the calendar year in which the employee attains age 70½, or

"(ii) the calendar year in which the employee retires.

Clause (ii) shall not apply in the case of an employee who is a 5-percent owner (as defined in section 416(i)(1)(B)) at any time during the 5-plan-year period ending in the calendar year in which the employee attains age 70½. If the employee becomes a 5-percent owner during any subsequent plan year, the required beginning date shall be April 1 of the calendar year following the calendar year in which such subsequent plan year ends.

"(5) Plans may incorporate section 401(a)(9) requirements by reference. Notwithstanding any other provision of law, except as provided in regulations prescribed by the Secretary of the Treasury or his delegate, a plan may incorporate by reference the requirements of section 401(a)(9) of the Internal Revenue Code of 1986."

—P.L. 99-514, Sec. 1136(a), added para. (a)(27), effective for yrs. begin. after 12/31/85.

—P.L. 99-514, Sec. 1140, [as amended by Sec. 7861(c)(1)-(3) of P.L. 101-239 and Sec. 1704(t)(27) of P.L. 104-188, see above] of this Act provides:

"SEC. 1140. PLAN AMENDMENTS NOT REQUIRED UNTIL JANUARY 1, 1989.

"(a) In general. If any amendment made by this subtitle, subtitle C, or title XVIII of this Act requires an amendment to any plan, such plan amendment shall not be required to be made before the first plan year beginning on or after January 1, 1989, if—

"(1) during the period after such amendment takes effect and before such first plan year, the plan is operated in accordance with the requirements of such amendment or in accordance with an amendment prescribed by the Secretary and adopted by the plan, and

"(2) such plan amendment applies retroactively to the period after such amendment takes effect and such first plan year.

A pension plan shall not be treated as failing to provide definitely determinable benefits or contributions, or to be operated in accordance with the provisions of the plan, merely because it operates in accordance with this provision.

"(b) Model amendment.

"(1) Secretary to prescribe amendment. The Secretary of the Treasury or his delegate shall prescribe an amendment or amendments which allow a plan to meet the requirements of any amendment made by this subtitle or subtitle C—

"(A) which requires an amendment to such plan, and

"(B) is effective before the first plan year beginning after December 31, 1988.

"(2) Adoption by plan. If a plan adopts the amendment or amendments prescribed under paragraph (1) and operates in accordance with such amendment or amendments, such plan shall not be treated as failing to provide definitely determinable benefits or contributions or to be operated in accordance with the provisions of the plan.

"(c) Special rule for collectively bargained plans. In the case of a plan maintained pursuant to 1 or more collective bargaining agreements between employee representatives and 1 or more employers ratified before March 1, 1986, subsection (a) shall be applied by substituting for the first plan year beginning on or after January 1, 1989, the first plan year beginning after the later of—

"(1) December 31, 1988, or

"(2) the earlier of—

"(A) December 31, 1990, or

"(B) the date on which the last of such collective bargaining agreements terminate (without regard to any extension thereof after February 28, 1986)."

For purposes of paragraph (1)(B) and any other provision of this title, an agreement shall not be treated as terminated merely because the plan is amended pursuant to such agreement to meet the requirements of any amendment made by this title or title XVIII of this Act."

—P.L. 99-514, Sec. 1143(a), added para. (c)(6), effective for tax. yrs. begin. after 12/31/86.

—P.L. 99-514, Sec. 1145(a), redesignated subpara. (a)(11)(D) [before redesignation by Sec. 1898(b)(14)(A) of the Act] as subpara. (a)(11)(E) and added new subpara. (a)(11)(E) [sic (D)], effective for plan yrs. begin. after 12/31/84.

—P.L. 99-514, Sec. 1145(c), amended Sec. 303 of P.L. 98-397, transitional rules for changes made by Secs. 203 and 301 of P.L. 98-397, by adding subsec. (f), see below.

—P.L. 99-514, Sec. 1171(b)(5), deleted para. (a)(21), effective for compensation paid or accrued after 12/31/86, in tax. yrs. end. after 12/31/86. Sec. 1177(a) of this Act provides the following transitional rules:

"(a) Section 1171. The amendments made by section 1171 shall not apply in the case of a tax credit employee stock ownership plan if—

"(1) such plan was favorably approved on September 23, 1983, by employees, and

"(2) not later than January 11, 1984, the employer of such employees was 100 percent owned by such plan."

Prior to deletion, para. (a)(21) read as follows:

"(21) A trust forming part of a tax credit employee stock ownership plan shall not fail to be considered a permanent program merely because employer contributions under the plan are determined solely by reference to the amount of credit which would be allowable under section 41 if the employer made the transfer described in section 41(c)(1)(B)."

—P.L. 99-514, Sec. 1174(c)(2)(A), amended para. (a)(23), effective for distributions attributable to stock acquired after 12/31/86.

Prior to amendment, para. (a)(23) read as follows:

"(23) A stock bonus plan which otherwise meets the requirements of this section shall not be considered to fail to meet the requirements of this section because it provides a cash distribution option to participants if that option meets the requirements of section 409(h), except that in applying section 409(h) for purposes of this paragraph, the term 'employer securities' shall include any securities of the employer held by the plan."

—P.L. 99-514, Sec. 1175(a)(1), added para. (a)(28), effective for stock acquired after 12/31/86.

—P.L. 99-514, Sec. 1176(a), added the last sentence to para. (a)(22), effective 12/31/86.

—P.L. 99-514, Sec. 1177(b), [as amended by Sec. 1011B(l) of P.L. 100-647, see above] provides the following transitional rules for changes made by Subtitle C of Title XI (Secs. 1171-1177) of the Act:

"(b) Subtitle not to apply to certain newspaper.

"The amendments made by section 1175 shall not apply to any daily newspaper—

"(1) which was first published on December 17, 1855, and which began publication under its current name in 1954, and

"(2) which is published in a constitutional home rule city (within the meaning of section 146(d)(3)(C) of the Internal Revenue Code of 1986) which has a population of less than 2,500,000."

—P.L. 99-514, Sec. 1848(b), substituted "section 404" for "sections 404 and 405(c)" in clause (c)(2)(A)(v), effective for obligations issued after 12/31/83.

—P.L. 99-514, Sec. 1852(a)(4)(A), amended the material following clause (a)(9)(C)(ii) [as in effect before amendment by Sec. 1121(b) of this Act] effective for tax. yrs. begin. after 12/31/84. Sec. 1852(a)(4)(C) of this Act [as added by Sec. 1018(t)(3) of P.L. 100-647, see above] provides:

"(C) An individual whose required beginning date would, but for the amendment made by subparagraph (A), occur after December 31, 1986, but whose required beginning date after such amendment occurs before January 1, 1987, shall be treated as if such individual had become a 5-percent owner during the plan year ending in 1986."

Prior to amendment, the material following clause (a)(9)(c)(ii) read as follows:

"Except as provided in section 409(d), clause (ii) shall not apply in the case of an employee who is a 5-percent owner (as defined in section 416) with respect to the plan year ending in the calendar year in which the employee attains 70½."

—P.L. 99-514, Sec. 1852(a)(6), added subpara. (a)(9)(G), effective for yrs. begin. after 12/31/84.

—P.L. 99-514, Sec. 1852(b)(8), substituted "qualified total distribution described in section 402(a)(5)(E)(i)(I)" for "qualifying rollover distribution (determined as if section 402(a)(5)(D)(i) did not contain subclause (II) thereof) described in section 402(a)(5)(A)(i) or 403(a)(4)(A)(i)" in para. (a)(20), effective for distributions made after 7/18/84, in tax. yrs. end. after 7/18/84.

—P.L. 99-514, Sec. 1852(g)(1), added subpara. (k)(3)(C) . . . Sec. 1852(g)(2), amended the last sentence of subpara. (k)(3)(A) . . . Sec. 1852(g)(3), substituted "is nonforfeitable" for "are nonforfeitable" in subpara. (k)(2)(C), effective for plan yrs. begin. after 12/31/84, with exceptions provided by Sec. 527(b)(1)(B) of P.L. 98-369, reproduced in the note following Sec. 527(a) of P.L. 98-369, see below.

Prior to amendment, the last sentence of subpara. (k)(3)(A) read as follows:

"The deferral percentage taken into account under this subparagraph for any highly compensated employee who is a participant under 2 or more cash or deferred arrangements of the employer shall be the sum of the deferral percentages for such employee under each of such arrangements."

—P.L. 99-514, Sec. 1852(h)(1)(A), substituted "key employee" for "5-percent owner" each place it appeared in para. (h)(6) . . . Sec. 1852(h)(1)(B), amended the last sentence of subsec. (h), effective [as amended by Sec. 1018(t)(3)(C) of P.L. 100-647, see above] for yrs. begin. after 12/31/85.

Prior to amendment, the last sentence of subsec. (h) read as follows:

"For purposes of paragraph (6), the term '5-percent owner' means any employee who, at any time during the plan year or any preceding plan year during which contributions were made on behalf of such employee, is or was a 5-percent owner (as defined in section 416(i)(1)(B))."

—P.L. 99-514, Sec. 1879(g)(1), substituted ", a pre-ERISA money purchase plan, or a rural electric cooperative plan" for "(or a pre-ERISA money purchase plan)" in paras. (k)(1) and (k)(2) . . . Sec. 1879(g)(2), added para. (k)(6) [as so designated before the amendment made by Sec. 1116(b)(3) of this Act], effective for plan yrs. begin. after 12/31/84.

—P.L. 99-514, Sec. 1898(b)(2)(A)(i), substituted "indirect transferee (in a transfer after December 31, 1984)" for "indirect transferee" in subclause (a)(11)(B)(iii)(III) . . . Sec. 1898(b)(2)(A)(ii), added the last sentence of subpara. (a)(11)(B) . . . Sec. 1898(b)(3)(A), substituted "who does not die before the annuity starting date" for "who retires under the plan" in clause (a)(11)(A)(i) . . . Sec. 1898(b)(7)(A), substituted "the participant's nonforfeitable accrued benefit (reduced by any security interest held by the plan by reason of a loan outstanding to such participant)" for "the participant's nonforfeitable accrued benefit" in subclause (a)(11)(B)(iii)(I) . . . Sec. 1898(b)(13)(A), substituted "section 417(a)(2)" for "section 417(a)(2)(A)" in subclause (a)(11)(B)(iii)(I) . . . Sec. 1898(b)(14)(A), redesignated subpara. (a)(11)(D) as (a)(11)(E) and added new subpara. (a)(11)(D), effective for plan yrs. begin. after 12/31/84. For exceptions and special rules, see P.L. 98-397, Secs. 302(b) and 303, reproduced below.

—P.L. 99-514, Sec. 1898(c)(3), redesignated subsec. (o) as (n) and added subsec. (m), effective for plan yrs. begin. after 12/31/84, except as provided in Secs. 302(b) and 303 of P.L. 98-397, reproduced below.

—P.L. 99-514, Sec. 1898(g), amended Sec. 302(b) of P.L. 98-397, exceptions to and special rules for changes made by Sec. 203 of P.L. 98-397, by substituting "July 1, 1988" for "January 1, 1987", see below.

—P.L. 99-514, Sec. 1898(h)(1)(A), amended Sec. 303 of P.L. 98-397, transitional rules for changes made by Secs. 203 and 301 of P.L. 98-397, by adding para. (c)(4), see below.

—P.L. 99-514, Sec. 1898(h)(2), amended Sec. 303(e)(2)(A) of P.L. 98-397, transitional rules for changes made by P.L. 98-397, Secs. 203 and 301, by substituting "in any plan year" for "in the first plan year", see below.

—P.L. 99-514, Sec. 1898(h)(3), amended Sec. 303(c)(2) of P.L. 98-397, transitional rules for changes made by Secs. 203 and 301 of P.L. 98-397, by adding the last sentence, see below.

—P.L. 99-514, Sec. 1899A(10), substituted "If" for "if" as the first word in para. (a)(22), effective 10/22/86.

—P.L. 99-509, Sec. 8021(d), and (e), reproduced in note following Code Sec. 338, provides tax treatment of Conrail public sale.

In 1984, P.L. 98-397, Sec. 203(a), amended para. (a)(11), effective for plan yrs. begin. after 12/31/84, except as provided in Sec. 302(b) of this Act, following, and Sec. 303 of this Act, reproduced below. Sec. 302(b) of this Act [as amended by Sec. 1898(g) of P.L. 99-514, see above] provides:

"(b) Special rule for collective bargaining agreements. In the case of a plan maintained pursuant to 1 or more collective bargaining agreements between employee representatives and 1 or more employers ratified before the date of the enactment of this Act, except as provided in subsection (d) or section 303, the amendments made by this Act shall not apply to plan years beginning before the earlier of—

"(1) the date on which the last of the collective bargaining agreements relating to the plan terminates (determined without regard to any extension thereof agreed to after the date of the enactment of this Act), or

"(2) July 1, 1988.

For purposes of paragraph (1), any plan amendment made pursuant to a collective bargaining agreement relating to the plan which amends the plan solely to conform to any requirement added by title I or II shall not be treated as a termination of such collective bargaining agreement."

Prior to amendment, para. (a)(11) read as follows:

"(11)(A) A trust shall not constitute a qualified trust under this section if the plan of which such trust is a part provides for the payment of benefits in the form of an annuity unless such plan provides for the payment of annuity benefits of a form having the effect of a qualified joint and survivor annuity.

"(B) Notwithstanding the provisions of subparagraph (A), in the case of a plan which provides for the payments of benefits before the normal retirement age (as defined in section 411(a)(8)), the plan is not required to provide for the payment of annuity benefits in a form having the effect of a qualified joint and survivor annuity during the period beginning on the date on which the employee enters into the plan as a participant and ending on the later of—

"(i) the date the employee reaches the earliest retirement age under the plan, or

"(ii) the first day of the 120th month beginning before the date on which the employee reaches normal retirement age.

"(C) A plan described in subparagraph (B) does not meet the requirements of subparagraph (A) unless, under the plan, a participant has a reasonable period during which he may elect the qualified joint and survivor annuity form with respect to the period beginning on the date on which the period described in subparagraph (B) ends and ending on the date on which he reaches normal retirement age (as defined in section 411(a)(8)) if he continues his employment during that period. A plan does not meet the requirements of this subparagraph unless, in the case of such an election, the payments under the survivor annuity are not less than the payments which would have been made under the joint annuity to which the participant would have been entitled if he made an election described in this subparagraph immediately prior to his retirement and if his retirement had occurred on the day before his death and within the period within which an election can be made.

"(D) A plan shall not be treated as not satisfying the requirements of this paragraph solely because the spouse of the participant is not entitled to receive a survivor annuity (whether or not an election described in subparagraph (C) has been made under subparagraph (C)) unless the participant and his spouse have been married throughout the 1-year period ending on the date of such participant's death.

"(E) A plan shall not be treated as satisfying the requirements of this paragraph unless, under the plan, each participant has a reasonable period (as described by the Secretary by regulations) before the annuity starting date during which he may elect in writing (after having received a written explanation of the terms and conditions of the joint and survivor annuity and the effect of an election under this subparagraph) not to take such joint and survivor annuity.

"(F) A plan shall not be treated as not satisfying the requirements of this paragraph solely because under the plan there is a provision that any election described in subparagraph (C) or (E), and any revocation of any such election, does not become effective (or ceases to be effective) if the participant dies within a period (not in excess of 2 years) beginning on the date of such election or revocation, as the case may be. The preceding sentence does not apply unless the plan provision described in the preceding sentence also provides that such an election or revocation will be given effect in any case in which—

"(i) the participant dies from accidental causes,

"(ii) a failure to give effect to the election or revocation would deprive the participant's survivor of a survivor annuity, and

"(iii) such election or revocation is made before such accident occurred.

"(G) For purposes of this paragraph—

"(i) the term 'annuity starting date' means the first day of the first period for which an amount is received as an annuity (whether by reason of retirement or by reason of disability),

"(ii) the term 'earliest retirement age' means the earliest date on which, under the plan, the participant could elect to receive retirement benefits, and

"(iii) the term 'qualified joint and survivor annuity' means an annuity for the life of the participant with a survivor annuity for the life of his spouse which is not less than one-half of, or greater than, the amount of the annuity payable during the joint lives of the participant and his spouse and which is the actuarial equivalent of a single life annuity for the life of the participant.

For purposes of this paragraph, a plan may take into account in any equitable manner (as determined by the Secretary) any increased costs resulting from providing joint and survivor annuity benefits.

"(H) This paragraph shall apply only if—

"(i) the annuity starting date did not occur before the effective date of this paragraph, and

"(ii) the participant was an active participant in the plan on or after such effective date."

—P.L. 98-397, Sec. 204(a), amended para. (a)(13), effective as provided in Sec. 303(d) of this Act, which reads as follows:

"(d) Amendments relating to assignments in divorce, etc., proceedings. The amendments made by sections 104 and 204 shall take effect on January 1, 1985, except that in the case of a domestic relations order entered before such date, the plan administrator—

"(1) shall treat such order as a qualified domestic relations order if such administrator is paying benefits pursuant to such order on such date, and

"(2) may treat any other such order entered before such date as a qualified domestic relations order even if such order does not meet the requirements of such amendments."

Prior to amendment, para. (a)(13) read as follows:

"(13) A trust shall not constitute a qualified trust under this section unless the plan of which such trust is a part provides that benefits provided under the plan may not be assigned or alienated. For purposes of the preceding sentence, there shall not be taken into account any voluntary and revocable assignment of not to exceed 10 percent of any benefit payment made by any participant who is receiving benefits under the plan unless the assignment or alienation is made for purposes of defraying plan administration costs. For purposes of this paragraph a loan made to a participant or beneficiary shall not be treated as an assignment or alienation if such loan is secured by the participant's accrued nonforfeitable benefit and is exempt from the tax imposed by section 4975 (relating to tax on prohibited transactions) by reason of section 4975(d)(1). This paragraph shall take effect on January 1, 1976 and shall not apply to assignments which were irrevocable on September 2, 1974."

—P.L. 98-397, Sec. 301(b), added para. (a)(25), effective for plan amendments made after 7/30/84, except as provided in Sec. 302(d)(2) of this Act, following and Sec. 303 of this Act reproduced below. Sec. 302(d)(2) of this Act provides:

"(2) Special rule for collective bargaining agreements. In the case of a plan maintained pursuant to 1 or more collective bargaining agreements entered into before January 1, 1985, which are—

"(A) between employee representatives and 1 or more employers, and

"(B) successor agreements to 1 or more collective bargaining agreements which terminate after July 30, 1984, and before January 1, 1985,

the amendments made by section 301 shall not apply to plan amendments adopted before April 1, 1985, pursuant to such successor agreements (without regard to any modification or reopening after December 31, 1984)."

—P.L. 98-397, Sec. 303, [as amended by P.L. 99-514, Secs. 1145(c), 1898(h)(1)(A), 1898(h)(2), and 1898(h)(3), and Sec. 7861(d)(1) of P.L. 101-239 see above] provides the following transitional rules:

"SEC. 303. TRANSITIONAL RULES.

"(a) Amendments relating to vesting rules; breaks in service; maternity or paternity leave.

"(1) Minimum age for vesting. The amendments made by sections 102(b) and 202(b) shall apply in the case of participants who have at least 1 hour of service under the plan on or after the first day of the first plan year to which the amendments made by this Act apply.

"(2) Break in service rules. If, as of the day before the first day of the first plan year to which the amendments made by this Act apply, section 202(a) or (b) or 203(b) of the Employee Retirement Income Security Act of 1974 or section 410(a) or 411(a) of the Internal Revenue Code of 1954 (as in effect on the day before the date of the enactment of this Act) would not require any service to be taken into account, nothing in the amendments made by subsections (c) and (d) of section 102 of this Act and subsections (c) and (d) of section 202 of this Act shall be construed as requiring such service to be taken into account under such section 202(a) or (b), 203(b), 410(a), or 411(a); as the case may be.

"(3) Maternity or paternity leave. The amendments made by sections 102(e) and 202(e) shall apply in the case of absences from work which begin on or after the first day of the first plan year to which the amendments made by this Act apply.

"(b) Special rule for amendments relating to maternity or paternity absences. If a plan is administered in a manner which would meet the amendments made by sections 102(e) and 202(e) (relating to certain maternity or paternity absences not treated as breaks in service), such plan need not be amended to meet such requirements until the earlier of—

"(1) the date on which such plan is first otherwise amended after the date of the enactment of this Act, or

"(2) the beginning of the first plan year beginning after December 31, 1986.

"(c) Requirement of joint and survivor annuity and preretirement survivor annuity.

"(1) Requirement that participant have at least 1 hour of service or paid leave on or after date of enactment. The amendments made by sections 103 and 203 shall apply only in the case of participants who have at least 1 hour of service under the plan on or after the date of the enactment of this Act or have at least 1 hour of paid leave on or after such date of enactment.

"(2) Requirement that preretirement survivor annuity be provided in case of certain participants dying on or after date of enactment. In the case of any participant—

"(A) who has at least 1 hour of service under the plan on or after the date of the enactment of this Act or has at least 1 hour of paid leave on or after such date of enactment,

"(B) who dies before the annuity starting date, and

"(C) who dies on or after the date of the enactment of this Act and before the first day of the first plan year to which the amendments made by this Act apply,

the amendments made by sections 103 and 203 shall be treated as in effect as of the time of such participant's death. In the case of a profit-sharing or stock bonus plan to which this paragraph applies, the plan shall be treated as meeting the requirements of the amendments made by sections 103 and 203 with respect to any participant if the plan made a distribution in a form other than a life annuity to the surviving spouse of the participant of such participant's nonforfeitable benefit.

"(3) Spousal consent required for certain elections after December 31, 1984. Any election after December 31, 1984, and before the first day of the first plan year to which the amendments made by this Act apply not to take a joint and survivor annuity shall not be effective unless the requirements of section 205(c)(2) of the Employee Retirement Income Security Act of 1974 (as amended by section 103 of this Act) and section 417(a)(2) of the Internal Revenue Code of 1954 (as added by section 203 of this Act) are met with respect to such election.

"(4) Elimination of double death benefits.

"(A) In general. In the case of a participant described in paragraph (2), death benefits (other than a qualified joint and survivor annuity or a qualified preretirement survivor annuity) payable to any beneficiary shall be reduced by the amount payable to the surviving spouse of such participant by reason of paragraph (2). The reduction under the preceding sentence shall be made on the basis of the respective present values (as of the date of the participant's death) of such death benefits and the amount so payable to the surviving spouse.

"(B) Spouse may waive provisions of paragraph (2). In the case of any participant described in paragraph (2), the surviving spouse of such participant may waive the provisions of paragraph (2). Such waiver shall be made on or before the close of the second plan year to which the amendments made by section 103 of this Act apply. Such a waiver shall not be treated as a transfer of property for purposes of chapter 12 of the Internal Revenue Code of 1954 and shall not be treated as an assignment or alienation for purposes of section 401(a)(13) of the Internal Revenue Code of 1954 or section 206(d) of the Employee Retirement Income Security Act of 1974.

"(d) Amendments relating to assignments in divorce, etc., proceedings. The amendments made by sections 104 and 204 shall take effect on January 1, 1985, except that in the case of a domestic relations order entered before such date, the plan administrator—

"(1) shall treat such order as a qualified domestic relations order if such administrator is paying benefits pursuant to such order on such date, and

"(2) may treat any other such order entered before such date as a qualified domestic relations order even if such order does not meet the requirements of such amendments.

"(e) Treatment of certain participants who separate from service before date of enactment.

"(1) Joint and survivor annuity provisions of employee retirement income security act of 1974 apply to certain participants. If—

"(A) a participant had at least 1 hour of service under the plan on or after September 2, 1974,

"(B) section 205 of the Employee Retirement Income Security Act of 1974 and section 401(a)(11) of the Internal Revenue Code of 1954 (as in effect on the day before the date of the enactment of this Act) would not (but for this paragraph) apply to such participant,

"(C) the amendments made by sections 103 and 203 of this Act do not apply to such participant, and

"(D) as of the date of the enactment of this Act, the participant's annuity starting date has not occurred and the participant is alive,

then such participant may elect to have section 205 of the Employee Retirement Income Security Act of 1974 and section 401(a)(11) of the Internal Revenue Code of 1954 (as in effect on the day before the date of the enactment of this Act) apply.

"(2) Treatment of certain participants who perform service on or after January 1, 1976. If—

"(A) a participant had at least 1 hour of service in any plan year beginning on or after January 1, 1976,

"(B) the amendments made by sections 103 and 203 would not (but for this paragraph) apply to such participant,

"(C) when such participant separated from service, such participant had at least 10 years of service under the plan and had a nonforfeitable right to all (or any portion) of such participant's accrued benefit derived from employer contributions, and

"(D) as of the date of the enactment of this Act, such participant's annuity starting date has not occurred and such participant is alive,

then such participant may elect to have the qualified preretirement survivor annuity requirements of the amendments made by sections 103 and 203 apply.

"(3) Period during which election may be made. An election under paragraph (1) or (2) may be made by any participant during the period—

"(A) beginning on the date of the enactment of this Act, and

"(B) ending on the earlier of the participant's annuity starting date or the date of the participant's death.

"(4) Requirement of notice.

"(A) In general.

"(i) Time and manner. Every plan shall give notice of the provisions of this subsection at such time or times and in such manner or manners as the Secretary of the Treasury may prescribe.

"(ii) Penalty. If any plan fails to meet the requirements of clause (i), such plan shall pay a civil penalty to the Secretary of the Treasury equal to $1 per participant for each day during the period beginning with the first day on which such failure occurs and ending on the day before notice is given by the plan; except that the amount of such penalty imposed on any plan shall not exceed $2,500.

"(B) Responsibilities of Secretary of Labor. The Secretary of Labor shall take such steps (by public announcements and otherwise) as may be necessary or appropriate to bring to public attention the provisions of this subsection.

"(f) The amendments made by section 301 of this Act shall not apply to the termination of a defined benefit plan if such termination—

"(1) is pursuant to a resolution directing the termination of such plan which was adopted by the Board of Directors of a corporation on July 17, 1984, and

"(2) occurred on November 30, 1984."

—P.L. 98-369, Sec. 211(b)(5), substituted "section 818(a)(6)" for "section 805(d)(6)" in para. (a)(24), effective for tax. yrs. begin. after 12/31/83.

—P.L. 98-369, Sec. 474(r)(13), substituted "allowable under section 41 if the employer made the transfer described in section 41(c)(1)(B)" for "allowable—

"(A) under section 46(a) if the employer made the transfer described in section 48(n)(1), or

"(B) under section 44G if the employer made the transfer described in section 44G(c)(1)(B)"

in para. (a)(21), effective for tax. yrs. begin. after 12/31/83, and for carrybacks from tax. yrs. begin. after 12/31/83.

—P.L. 98-369, Sec. 491(e)(4), substituted "section 409" for "section 409A" in para. (a)(22) . . . Sec. 491(e)(5), substituted "section 409(h)" for "section 409A(h)" each place it appeared in para. (a)(23), effective 1/1/84.

—P.L. 98-369, Sec. 521(a)(1), amended para. (a)(9), as in effect before amend. by , effective for yrs. begin. after 12/31/84. For special rules, see Sec. 521(e)(3)-(5) of this Act, reproduced in note following Code Sec. 408.

Prior to amendment, para. (a)(9) read as follows:

"(9) In the case of a plan which provides contributions or benefits for employees some or all of whom are employees within the meaning of subsection (c)(1), a trust forming part of such plan shall not constitute a qualified trust under this section unless, under the plan, the entire interest of each employee—

"(A) either will be distributed to him not later than his taxable year in which he attains the age of 70½ years, or, in the case of an employee other than an owner-employee (as defined in subsection (c)(3)), in which he retires, whichever is the later, or

"(B) will be distributed, commencing not later than such taxable year, (i) in accordance with regulations prescribed by the Secretary, over the life of such employee or over the lives of such employee and his spouse, or (ii) in accordance with such regulations, over a period not extending beyond the life expectancy of such employee or the life expectancy of such employee and his spouse.

A trust shall not be disqualified under this paragraph by reason of distributions under a designation, prior to the date of the enactment of this paragraph, by any employee under the plan of which such trust is a part, of a method of distribution which does not meet the terms of the preceding sentence."

—P.L. 98-369, Sec. 521(a)(2), repealed Sec. 242 of P.L. 97-248 [see below] which amended para. (a)(9) and provided the effective date and transitional rules for the amendment.

Prior to the repeal of Sec. 242 of P.L. 97-248, para. (a)(9) read as follows:

"(9) Required distributions.

"(A) Before death. A trust forming part of a plan shall not constitute a qualified trust under this section unless the plan provides that the entire interest of each employee—

"(i) either will be distributed to him not later than his taxable year in which he attains age 70½ or, in the case of an employee other than a key employee who is a participant in a top-heavy plan, in which he retires, whichever is the later, or

"(ii) will be distributed, commencing not later than such taxable year—

"(I) in accordance with regulations prescribed by the Secretary, over the life of such employee or over the lives of such employee and his spouse, or

"(II) in accordance with such regulations, over a period not extending beyond the life expectancy of such employee or the life expectancy of such employee and his spouse.

"(B) After death. A trust forming part of a plan shall not constitute a qualified trust under this section unless the plan provides that if—

"(i) an employee dies before his entire interest has been distributed to him, or

"(ii) distribution has been commenced in accordance with subparagraph (A)(ii) to his surviving spouse and such surviving spouse dies before his entire interest has been distributed to such surviving spouse,

his entire interest (or the remaining part of such interest if distribution thereof has commenced) will be distributed within 5 years after his death (or the death of his surviving spouse). The preceding sentence shall not apply if the distribution of the interest of the employee has commenced and such distribution is for a term certain over a period permitted under subparagraph (A)(ii)(II)."

Prior to repeal, Sec. 242(b) of P.L. 97-248 read as follows:

"(b) Effective date.

"(1) In general. The amendment made by subsection (a) shall apply to plan years beginning after December 31, 1983.

"(2) Transition rule. A trust forming part of a plan shall not be disqualified under paragraph (9) of section 401(a) of the Internal Revenue Code of 1954, as amended by subsection (a), by reason of distributions under a designation (before January 1, 1984) by any employee of a method of distribution—

"(A) which does not meet the requirements of such paragraph (9), but

"(B) which would not have disqualified such trust under paragraph (9) of section 401(a) of such Code as in effect before the amendment made by subsection (a)."

—P.L. 98-369, Sec. 524(d)(1), added clause (a)(10)(B)(iii), effective for plan yrs. begin. after 12/31/83.

—P.L. 98-369, Sec. 524(e), for qualification requirements modified if regulations not issued, is reproduced in note following Code Sec. 416.

—P.L. 98-369, Sec. 527(a), amended subpara. (k)(3)(A), effective for plan yrs. begin. after 12/31/84. Sec. 527(c)(1)(B) of this Act provides:

"(B) exception for certain existing plans. The amendment made by subsection (a) shall not apply to any plan—

"(i) which was maintained by a State on June 8, 1984, and

"(ii) with respect to which a determination letter had been issued by the Secretary on December 6, 1982."

Prior to amendment, subpara. (k)(3)(A) read as follows:

"(A) A qualified cash or deferred arrangement shall be considered to satisfy the requirements of subsection (a)(4), with respect to the amount of contributions, and of subparagraph (B) of section 410(b)(1) for a plan year if those employees eligible to benefit under the plan satisfy the provisions of subparagraph (A) or (B) of section 410(b)(1) and if the actual deferral percentage for highly compensated employees (as defined in paragraph (4)) for such plan year bears a relationship to the actual deferral percentage for all other eligible employees for such plan year which meets either of the following tests:

"(i) The actual deferral percentage for the group of highly compensated employees is not more than the actual deferral percentage of all other eligible employees multiplied by 1.5.

"(ii) The excess of the actual deferral percentage for the group of highly compensated employees over that of all other eligible employees is not more than 3 percentage points, and the actual deferral percentage for the group of highly compensated employees is not more than the actual deferral percentage of all other eligible employees multiplied by 2.5."

—P.L. 98-369, Sec. 527(b)(1), added "(or a pre-ERISA money purchase plan)" after "stock bonus plan" in paragraphs (k)(1) and (2) . . . Sec. 527(b)(2), para. (k)(5) . . . Sec. 527(b)(3), substituted "(or in the case of a profit sharing or stock bonus plan, hardship or the attainment of age 59½)" for "hardship or the attainment of age 59½" in subpara. (k)(2)(B), effective for plan yrs. begin. after 7/18/84. Sec. 527(c)(2)(B) of the Act also provides:

"(B) Transitional rule. Rules similar to the rules under section 135(c)(2) of the Revenue Act of 1978 shall apply with respect to any pre-ERISA money purchase plan (as defined in section 401(k)(5) of the Internal Revenue Code of 1954) for plan years beginning after December 31, 1979, and on or before the date of the enactment of this Act."

—P.L. 98-369, Sec. 528(b), deleted "and" at the end of para. (h)(4), substituted ", and" for the period at the end of para. (h)(5), and added para. (h)(6), effective for yrs. begin. after 3/31/84.

—P.L. 98-369, Sec. 558(a), and (d) provide:

"(a) In general.

"(1) Liability. Any withdrawal liability incurred by an employer pursuant to part 1 of subtitle E of title IV of the Employee Retirement Income Security Act of 1974 (29 U.S.C. 1381 et seq.) as a result of the complete or partial withdrawal of such employer from a multiemployer plan before September 26, 1980, shall be void.

"(2) Refunds. Any amounts paid by an employer to a plan sponsor as a result of such withdrawal liability shall be refunded by the plan sponsor to the employer with interest (in accordance with section 401(a)(2)), less a reasonable amount for administrative expenses incurred by the plan sponsor (other than legal expenses incurred with respect to the plan) in calculating, assessing, and refunding such amounts."

* * *

"(d) Special rule for certain binding agreements. In the case of an employer who, on September 26, 1980, has a binding agreement to withdraw from a multiemployer plan, subsection (a)(1) shall be applied by substituting 'December 31, 1980' for 'September 26, 1980'."

—P.L. 98-369, Sec. 713(c)(2)(A), substituted "(as defined in section 408(n))" for "(as defined in subsection (d)(1))" in subsec. (f) . . . Sec. 713(d)(3), deleted subsec. (e), effective for yrs. begin. after 12/31/83.

Prior to deletion, subsec. (e) read as follows:

"(e) Contributions for premiums on annuity, etc., contracts.

"A contribution by the employer on behalf of an owner-employee is described in this subsection if—

"(1) under the plan such contribution is required to be applied (directly or through a trustee) to pay premiums or other consideration for one or more annuity, endowment, or life insurance contracts on the life of such owner-employee issued under the plan,

"(2) the amount of such contribution exceeds the amount deductible under section 404 with respect to contributions made by the employer on behalf of such owner-employee under the plan, and

"(3) the amount of such contribution does not exceed the average of the amounts which were deductible under section 404 with respect to contributions made by the employer on behalf of such owner-employee under the plan (or which would have been deductible if such section had been in effect) for the first three taxable years (A) preceding the year in which the last such annuity, endowment, or life insurance contract was issued under the plan, and (B) in which such owner-employee derived earned income from the trade or business with respect to which the plan is established, or for so many of such taxable years as such owner-employee was engaged in such trade or business and derived earned income therefrom.

In the case of any individual on whose behalf contributions described in paragraph (1) are made under more than one plan as an owner-employee during any taxable year, the preceding sentence does not apply if the amount of such contributions under all such plans for such taxable year exceeds $15,000. Any contribution which is described in this subsection shall, for purposes of section 4972(b), be taken into account as a contribution made by such owner-employee as an employee to the extent that the amount of such contribution is not deductible under section 404 for the taxable year, but only for the purpose of applying section 4972(b) to other contributions made by such owner-employee as an employee."

In 1983, P.L. 98-21, Sec. 124(c)(4)(A), deleted "and" from the end of clause (c)(2)(A)(iv), substituted ", and" for the period at the end of clause (c)(2)(A)(v), and added new clause (c)(2)(A)(vi), effective for tax. yrs. begin. after 12/31/89.

—P.L. 97-448, Sec. 103(c)(10)(A), amended the second sentence of para. (d)(5) ... Sec. 103(d)(2)(A), substituted "paragraph (2)" for "subsection (j)(2)" in the last sentence of para. (j)(3) ... Sec. 103(d)(2)(B), added "with respect only to such change" after "participation" in the last sentence of para. (j)(3), effective for tax yrs. begin. after 12/31/81.

Prior to amendment, the second sentence of para. (d)(5) read as follows: "Subparagraphs (A) and (B) do not apply to contributions described in subsection (e)."

—P.L. 97-448, Sec. 103(d)(3), corrected Sec. 312(f)(1) of P.L. 97-34, the effective date for changes made by Sec. 312 of P.L. 97-34 to "taxable years beginning after December 31, 1981" from "to plans which include employees within the meaning of section 401(c)(1) with respect to taxable years beginning after 12/31/81' [see below].

—P.L. 97-448, Sec. 103(g)(2)(A), substituted "which would be allowable —" and subparas (a)(21)(A) and (B) for "which would be allowable under section 46(a) if the employer made the transfer described in section 48(n)(1).", in para. (a)(21), effective for tax. yrs. end. after 12/31/82.

—P.L. 97-448, Sec. 306(a)(12), substituted "paragraph (1)(B)" for "paragraph (9)(B)" in para. (d)(2) (as redesignated by Sec. 237(a)(2) of P.L. 97-248, [see below], effective for yrs. begin. after 12/31/83.

In 1982, P.L. 97-248, Sec. 237(a)(1), deleted paras. (d)(1) through (7) ... Sec. 237(a)(2), redesignated paras. (d)(9), (10) and (11) as (d)(1), (2) and (3), ... Sec. 237(b), deleted paras. (a)(17) and (18) ... Sec. 237(e)(1), amended para. (a)(10) ... Sec. 238(b), deleted subsec. (j). ... Sec. 238(d)(1), amended para. (c)(1) ... Sec. 238(d)(2), deleted "and" at end of clause (c)(2)(A)(iii), substituted ", and", for the period at end of clause (c)(2)(A)(iv) and added new clause (c)(2)(A)(v) ... Sec. 240(b), added subpara. (a)(10)(B), effective for yrs. begin. after 12/31/83.

Prior to deletion, paras. (d)(1) through (d)(7) read as follows:

"(1) In the case of a trust which is created on or after October 10, 1962, or which was created before such date but is not exempt from tax under section 501(a) as an organization described in subsection (a) on the day before such date, the assets thereof are held by a bank or other person who demonstrates to the satisfaction of the Secretary that the manner in which he will administer the trust will be consistent with the requirements of this section. A trust shall not be disqualified under this paragraph merely because a person (including the employer) other than the trustee or custodian so administering the trust may be granted, under the trust instrument, the power to control the investment of the trust funds either by directing investments (including reinvestments, disposals, and exchanges) or by disapproving proposed investments (including reinvestments, disposals, or exchanges). this paragraph shall not apply to a trust created or organized outside the United States before October 10, 1962, if, under section 402(c), it is treated as exempt from tax under section 501(a) on the day before such date; or, to the extent provided under regulations prescribed by the Secretary, to a trust which uses annuity, endowment, or life insurance contracts of a life insurance company exclusively to fund the benefits prescribed by the trust, if the life insurance company supplies annually such information about trust transactions affecting owner-employees as the Secretary, shall by forms or regulations prescribe. For purposes of this paragraph, the term 'bank' means a bank as defined in section 581, an insured credit union (within the meaning of section 101(6) of the Federal Credit Union Act), a corporation which under the laws of the State of its incorporation is subject to supervision and examination by the commissioner of banking or other officer of such State in charge of the administration of the banking laws of such State, and, in the case of a trust created or organized outside the United States, a bank or trust company, wherever incorporated, exercising fiduciary powers and subject to supervision and examination by governmental authority.

"(2) Under the plan—

"(A) the employees' rights to or derived from the contributions under the plan are nonforfeitable at the time the contributions are paid to or under the plan; and

"(B) in the case of a profit-sharing plan, there is a definite formula for determining the contributions to be made by the employer on behalf of employees (other than owner-employees).

Subparagraph (A) shall not apply to contributions which, under provisions of the plan adopted pursuant to regulations prescribed by the Secretary to preclude the discrimination prohibited by subsection (a)(4), may not be used to provide benefits for designated employees in the event of early termination of the plan.

"(3)(A) The plan benefits each employee having 3 or more years of service (within the meaning of section 410(a)(3)).

"(B) For purposes of subparagraph (A), the term 'employee' does not include—

"(i) any employee included in a unit of employees covered by a collective-bargaining agreement described in section 410(b)(3)(A), and

"(ii) any employee who is a nonresident alien individual described in section 410(b)(3)(C).

"(4) Under the plan—

"(A) contributions or benefits are not provided for any owner-employee unless such owner-employee has consented to being included under the plan; and

"(B) no benefits in excess of contributions made by an owner-employee as an employee may be paid to any owner-employee, except in the case of his becoming disabled (within the meaning of section 72(m)(7)), prior to his attaining the age of 59½ years.

Subparagraph (B) shall not apply to any distribution to which section 72(m)(9) applies.

"(5) The plan does not permit—

"(A) contributions to be made by the employer on behalf of any owner-employee in excess of the amounts which may be deducted under section 404 for the taxable year;

"(B) in the case of a plan which provides contributions or benefits only for owner-employees, contributions to be made on behalf of any owner-employee in excess of the amounts which may be deducted under section 404 for the taxable year; and

"(C) if a distribution under the plan is made to any employee and if any portion of such distribution is an amount described in section 72(m)(5)(A)(i), contributions to be made on behalf of such employee for the 5 taxable years succeeding the taxable year in which such distribution is made.

Subparagraphs (A) and (B) do not apply to contributions described in subsection (e). Subparagraph (C) shall not apply to a distribution on account of the termination of the plan.

"(6) Except as provided in this paragraph, the plan meets the requirements of subsection (a)(4) without taking into account for any purpose contributions or benefits under chapter 2 (relating to tax on self-employment income), chapter 21 (relating to Federal Insurance Contributions Act), title II of the Social Security Act, as amended, or any other Federal or State law. If—

"(A) of the contributions deductible under section 404, not more than one-third is deductible by reason of contributions by the employer on behalf of owner-employees, and

"(B) taxes paid by the owner-employees under chapter 2 (relating to tax on self-employment income), and the taxes which would be payable under such chapter 2 by the owner-employees but for paragraphs (4) and (5) of section 1402(c), are taken into account as contributions by the employer on behalf of such owner-employees,

then taxes paid under section 3111 (relating to tax on employers) with respect to an employee may, for purposes of subsection (a)(4), be taken into account as contributions by the employer for such employee under the plan.

"(7) Under the plan, if an owner-employee dies before his entire interest has been distributed to him, or if distribution has been commenced in accordance with subsection (a)(9)(B) to his surviving spouse and such surviving spouse dies before his entire interest has been distributed to such surviving spouse, his entire interest (or the remaining part of such interest if distribution thereof has commenced) will, within 5 years after his death (or the death of his surviving spouse), be distributed, or applied to the purchase of an immediate annuity for his beneficiary or beneficiaries (or the beneficiary or beneficiaries of his surviving spouse) which will be payable for the life of such beneficiary or beneficiaries (or for a term certain not extending beyond the life expectancy of such beneficiary or beneficiaries) and which will be immediately distributed to such beneficiary or beneficiaries. The preceding sentence shall not apply if distribution of the interest of an owner-employee has commenced and such distribution is for a term certain over a period permitted under subsection (a)(9)(B)(ii)."

Prior to deletion, paras. (a)(17) and (18) read as follows:

"(17) In the case of a plan which provides contributions or benefits for employees some or all of whom are employees within the meaning of subsection (c)(1), or are shareholder-employees within the meaning of section 1379(d), only if—

"(A) the annual compensation of each employee taken into account under the plan does not exceed the first $200,000 of compensation, and

"(B) in the case of—

"(i) a defined contribution plan with respect to which compensation in excess of $100,000 is taken into account, contributions on behalf of each employee (other than an employee within the meaning of section 401(c)(1)) to the plan or plans are at a rate (expressed as a percentage of compensation) not less than 7.5 percent, or

"(ii) a defined benefit plan with respect to which compensation in excess of $100,000 is taken into account, the annual benefit accrual for each employee (other than an employee within the meaning of section 401(c)(1)) is a percentage of compensation which is not less than one-half of the applicable percentage provided by subsection (j)(3).

"(18) In the case of a trust which is part of a plan providing a defined benefit for employees some or all of whom are employees within the meaning of subsection (c)(1), or are shareholder-employees within the meaning of section 1379(d), only if such plan satisfies the requirements of subsection (j)."

Prior to amendment, para. (a)(10) read as follows:

"(10) In the case of a plan which provides contributions or benefits for employees some or all of whom are owner-employees (as defined in subsection (c)(3))—

"(A) paragraph (3), the first and second sentences of paragraph (5), and section 410 shall not apply, but—

"(i) such plan shall not be considered discriminatory within the meaning of paragraph (4) merely because the contributions or benefits of or on behalf of employees under the plan bear a uniform relationship to the total compensation, or the basic or regular rate of compensation, of such employees, and

"(ii) such plan shall not be considered discriminatory within the meaning of paragraph (4) solely because under the plan contributions described in subsection (e) which are in excess of the amounts which may be deducted under section 404 for the taxable year may be made on behalf of any owner-employee; and

"(B) a trust forming a part of such plan shall constitute a qualified trust under this section only if the requirements in subsection (d) are also met."

Prior to deletion, subsec. (j) read as follows:

"(j) Defined benefit plans providing benefits for self-employed individuals and shareholder-employees.

"(1) In general. A defined benefit plan satisfies the requirements of this subsection only if the basic benefit accruing under the plan for each plan year of participation by an employee within the meaning of subsection (c)(1) (or a shareholder-employee) is permissible under regulations prescribed by the Secretary under this

Employee benefit plans — Code Sec. 401

subsection to insure that there will be reasonable comparability (assuming level funding) between the maximum retirement benefits which may be provided with favorable tax treatment under this title for such employees under—

"(A) defined contribution plans,

"(B) defined benefit plans, and

"(C) a combination of defined contribution plans and defined benefit plans.

"(2) Guidelines for regulations. The regulations prescribed under this subsection shall provide that a plan does not satisfy the requirements of this subsection if, under the plan, the basic benefit of any employee within the meaning of subsection (c)(1) (or a shareholder-employee) may exceed the sum of the products for each plan year of participation of—

"(A) his annual compensation (not in excess of $100,000) for such year, and

"(B) the applicable percentage determined under paragraph (3).

"(3) Applicable percentage.

"(A) Table. For purposes of paragraph (2), the applicable percentage for any individual for any plan year shall be based on the percentage shown on the following table opposite his age when his current period of participation in the plan began.

Age when participation began:	Applicable percentage
30 or less	6.5
35	5.4
40	4.4
45	3.6
50	3.0
55	2.5
60 or over	2.0

"(B) Additional requirements. The regulations prescribed under this subsection shall include provisions—

"(i) for applicable percentages for ages between any two ages shown on the table,

"(ii) for adjusting the applicable percentages in the case of plans providing benefits other than a basic benefit,

"(iii) that any increase in the rate of accrual, and any increase in the compensation base which may be taken into account, shall, with respect only to such increase, begin a new period of participation in the plan, and

"(iv) when appropriate, in the case of periods beginning after December 31, 1977, for adjustments in the applicable percentages based on changes in prevailing interest and mortality rates occurring after 1973. For purposes of this paragraph, a change in the annual compensation taken into account under subparagraph (A) of subsection (j)(2) shall be treated as beginning a new period of plan participation.

"(4) Certain contributions and benefits may not be taken into account. A defined benefit plan which provides contributions or benefits for owner-employees does not satisfy the requirements of this subsection unless such plan meets the requirements of subsection (a)(4) without taking into account contributions or benefits under chapter 2 (relating to tax on self-employment income), chapter 21 (relating to Federal Insurance Contributions Act), title II of the Social Security Act, or any other Federal or State law.

"(5) Definitions. For purposes of this subsection—

"(A) Basic benefit. The term 'basic benefit' means a benefit in the form of a straight life annuity commencing at the later of—

"(i) age 65, or

"(ii) the day 5 years after the day the participant's current period of participation began

under a plan which provides no ancillary benefits and to which employees do not contribute.

"(B) Shareholder-employee. The term 'shareholder-employee' has the same meaning as when used in section 1379(d).

"(C) Compensation. The term 'compensation' means—

"(i) in the case of an employee within the meaning of subsection (c)(1), the earned income of such individual, or

"(ii) in the case of a shareholder-employee, the compensation received or accrued by the individual from the electing small business corporation.

"(6) Special rules. Section 404(e) (relating to special limitations for self-employed individuals) and section 1379(b) (relating to taxability of shareholder-employee beneficiaries) do not apply to a trust to which this subsection applies."

Prior to amendment, para. (c)(1) read as follows:

"(1) Employee. The term 'employee' includes, for any taxable year, an individual who has earned income (as defined in paragraph (2)) for the taxable year. To the extent provided in regulations prescribed by the Secretary, such term also includes, for any taxable year—

"(A) an individual who would be an employee within the meaning of the preceding sentence but for the fact that the trade or business carried on by such individual did not have net profits for the taxable year, and

"(B) an individual who has been an employee within the meaning of the preceding sentence for any prior taxable year."

—P.L. 97-248, Sec. 242, [Repealed by Sec. 521(a)(2) of P.L. 98-369, see above] amended para. (a)(9) and provided the effective date and transitional rules for the amendment, see above.

—P.L. 97-248, Sec. 249(a), redesignated subsec. (l) as subsec. (o) and added new subsec. (l), effective for plan yrs. begin. after 12/31/83.

—P.L. 97-248, Sec. 251(d), provides:

"(d) Correction period for church plans. A church plan (within the meaning of section 414(e) of the Internal Revenue Code of 1954) shall not be treated as not meeting the requirements of section 401 or 403 of such Code if—

"(1) by reason of any change in any law, regulation, ruling, or otherwise such plan is required to be amended to meet such requirements, and

"(2) such plan is so amended at the next earliest church convention or such other time as the Secretary of the Treasury or his delegate may prescribe."

—P.L. 97-248, Sec. 254(a), added para. (a)(24), effective for tax. yrs. begin. after 12/31/81.

In 1981, P.L. 97-34, Sec. 312(b), amended para. (a)(17) . . . Sec. 312(c)(2), substituted "for such taxable year exceeds $15,000" for "for all such years exceeds $7,500" in subsec. (e) . . . Sec. 312(c)(3), substituted "$100,000" for "$50,000" in subpara. (j)(2)(A) . . . Sec. 312(c)(4), added the sentence to the end of para. (j)(3) . . . Sec. 312(e)(2), added the last sentence of para. (d)(4), effective for tax. yrs. begin. after 12/31/81.

Prior to amendment, para. (a)(17) read as follows:

"(17) In the case of a plan which provides contributions or benefits for employees some or all of whom are employees within the meaning of subsection (c)(1), or are shareholder-employees within the meaning of section 1379(d), only if the annual compensation of each employee taken into account under the plan does not exceed the first $100,000 of such compensation."

—P.L. 97-34, Sec. 314(a)(1), added the last sentence of para. (d)(5), effective for distributions after 12/31/80 in tax. yrs. end. after 12/31/80.

—P.L. 97-34, Sec. 335, substituted "409A(h), except that in applying section 409A(h) for purposes of this paragraph, the term 'employer securities' shall include any securities of the employer held by the plan" for "409A(h)(2)" in para. (a)(23), effective for tax. yrs. begin. after 12/31/81.

—P.L. 97-34, Sec. 338(a), amended para. (a)(22), effective for acquisitions of securities after 12/31/79.

Prior to amendment, para. (a)(22) read as follows:

"(22) If a defined contributions plan—

"(A) is established by an employer whose stock is not publicly traded, and

"(B) after acquiring securities of the employer, more than 10 percent of the total assets of the plan are securities of the employer,

any trust forming part of said plan shall not constitute a qualified trust under this section unless the plan meets the requirements of subsection (e) of section 409A."

In 1980, P.L. 96-605, Sec. 221(a), added para. (a)(23) . . . Sec. 225(b)(1), substituted "section 410(b)(3)(A)" for "section 410(b)(2)(A)" in the last sentence of para. (a)(4) . . . Sec. 225(b)(2), substituted "section 410(b)(3)(A)" for "section 410(b)(2)(A)" and substituted "section 410(b)(3)(C)" for "section 410(b)(2)(C)" in subpara. (d)(3)(B), effective for plan yrs. begin. after 12/31/80.

—P.L. 96-364, Sec. 208(a), amended the last sentence of para. (a)(12) . . . Sec. 208(e), added ", or the return of any withdrawal liability payment determined to be an overpayment within 6 months of such determination" after "501(a)" in para. (a)(2) as amended by "Sec. 411(b)" [sic , Sec. 410(b)] of this Act [see below], effective 9/26/80.

Prior to amendment, the last sentence of para. (a)(12) read as follows:

"This paragraph shall apply in the case of a multiemployer plan only to the extent determined by the Pension Benefit Guaranty Corporation."

—P.L. 96-364, Sec. 410(b), added "(but this paragraph shall not be construed, in the case of a multiemployer plan, to prohibit the return of a contribution within 6 months after the plan administrator determines that the contribution was made by a mistake of fact or law after a mistake relating to whether the plan is described in section 401(a) or the trust which is part of such plan is exempt from taxation under section 501(a))." before the semicolon at the end of para. (a)(2), effective as provided in Sec. 410(c), which reads as follows:

"(c) The amendment made by this section shall take effect January 1, 1975, except that in the case of contributions received by a collectively bargained plan maintained by more than one employer before the date of enactment of this Act [9/26/80], any determination by the plan administrator that any such contribution was made by mistake of fact or law before such date [9/26/80] shall be deemed to have been made on such date of enactment [9/26/80]."

—P.L. 96-222, Sec. 101(a)(7)(B), corrected Sec. 141(g) of P.L. 95-600 [see below].

Prior to corrections, Sec. 141(g) of P.L. 95-600 read as follows:

"(g) Effective dates.

"(1) In general. The amendments made by this section (other than by subsection (f)(3)) shall apply with respect to qualified investment for taxable years beginning after December 31, 1978. The amendment made by subsection (f)(7) shall apply to years beginning after December 31, 1978."

—P.L. 96-222, Sec. 101(a)(7)(L)(i)(V), substituted "a tax credit employee stock ownership plan" for "an ESOP" in para. (a)(21), presumably intended by Congress to be effective 11/6/78 [Sec. 101(b)(2)] although technically effective with respect to decedents dying after 4/1/80 [Sec. 101(b)(1)(D)] .

—P.L. 96-222, Sec. 101(a)(9), substituted "are securities" for "as securities" in subpara. (a)(22)(B), effective for acquisitions of securities after '79.

—P.L. 96-222, Sec. 101(a)(14)(E)(iii), substituted "makes a qualifying rollover distribution (determined as if section 402(a)(5)(D)(i) did not contain subclause (II) thereof) described in section 402(a)(5)(A)(i) or 403(a)(4)(A)(i)" for "makes a payment or distribution described in section 402(a)(5)(A)(i) or 403(a)(4)(A)(i)", effective for payments made in tax. yrs. begin. after 12/31/77.

In 1978, P.L. 95-600, Sec. 135(a), redesignated subsec. (k) as subsec. (l) and added new subsec. (k), effective for plan yrs. begin. after 12/31/79. Sec. 135(c)(2) of the Act provides:

"(2) Transitional rule. In the case of cash or deferred arrangements in existence on June 27, 1974—

"(A) the qualification of the plan and the trust under section 401 of the Internal Revenue Code of 1954;

"(B) the exemption of the trust under section 501(a) of such Code;

"(C) the taxable year of inclusion in gross income of the employee of any amount so contributed by the employer to the trust; and

"(D) the excludability of the interest of the employee in the trust under sections 2039 and 2517 of such Code,
shall be determined for plan years beginning before January 1, 1980 in a manner consistent with Revenue Ruling 56-497 (1956-2 C.B. 284), Revenue Ruling 63-180 (1963-2 C.B. 189), and Revenue Ruling 68-89 (1968-1 C.B. 402)."

—P.L. 95-600, Sec. 141(f)(3), amended para. (a)(21), effective 11/6/78.

—P.L. 95-600, Sec. 141(g)(2), of this Act provides:

"(2) Election to have amendments apply during 1978. At the election of the taxpayer, paragraph (1) shall be applied by substituting 'December 31, 1977' for 'December 31, 1978'; except that in the case of a plan in existence before December 31, 1978, any such election shall not affect the required allocation of employer securities attributable to qualified investment for taxable years beginning before January 1, 1979. An election under the preceding sentence shall be made at such time and in such manner as the Secretary of the Treasury or his delegate shall prescribe. Such an election, once made, shall be irrevocable."

Prior to amendment, para. (a)(21) read as follows:

"(21) A trust forming part of an employee stock ownership plan which satisfies the requirements of section 301(d) of the Tax Reduction Act of 1975 shall not fail to be considered a permanent program merely because employer contributions under the plan are determined solely by reference to the amount of credit which would be allowable under section 46(a) if the employer made the transfer described in subsection (d)(6) or (e)(3) of section 301 of the Tax Reduction Act of 1975."

—P.L. 95-600, Sec. 143(a), added para. (a)(22), effective for acquisitions of securities after '79.

—P.L. 95-600, Sec. 152(e), added the last sentence in para. (a)(5), effective for tax. yrs. begin. after '78.

In 1976, P.L. 94-455, Sec. 803(b)(2), added para. (a)(21), effective for tax. yrs. begin. after 12/31/74.

—P.L. 94-455, Sec. 1505(b), amended subsec. (f), effective for tax. yrs. begin. after 12/31/75.

Prior to amendment, subsec. (f) read as follows:

"(f) Certain custodial accounts and annuity contracts.

"For purposes of this title, a custodial account or an annuity contract shall be treated as a qualified trust under this section if—

"(1) the custodial account or annuity contract would, except for the fact that it is not a trust, constitute a qualified trust under this section, and

"(2) in the case of a custodial account the assets thereof are held by a bank (as defined in subsection (d)(1)) or another person who demonstrates, to the satisfaction of the Secretary or his delegate, that the manner in which he will hold the assets will be consistent with the requirements of this section.

"For purposes of this title, in the case of a custodial account or annuity contract treated as a qualified trust under this section by reason of this subsection, the person holding the assets of such account or holding such contract shall be treated as the trustee thereof."

—P.L. 94-455, Sec. 1901(a)(56), substituted "September 2, 1974" for "the date of the enactment of the Employee Retirement Income Security Act of 1974" in paras. (a)(12), (a)(13) and (a)(15), substituted "September 2, 1974" for "enactment of the Employee Retirement Income Security Act of 1974" in para. (a)(19), and amended the last sentence of subsec. (a), effective for tax. yrs. begin. after 12/31/76.

Prior to amendment, the last sentence of subsec. (a) read as follows:

"Paragraphs (11), (12), (13), (14), (15), (19) shall apply only in the case of a plan to which section 411 (relating to minimum vesting standards) applies without regard to subsection (e)(2) of such section."

—P.L. 94-455, Sec. 1906(b)(13)(A), substituted "Secretary" for "Secretary or his delegate" each place it appeared in Code Sec. 401, effective for tax. yrs. begin. after 12/31/76.

—P.L. 94-267, Sec. 1(c)(1), added new para. (a)(20) . . . Sec. 1(c)(2), substituted "19, and 20" for "and 19" in the last sentence of subsec. (a), effective for payments made to an employee on or after 7/4/74.

In 1975, P.L. 94-12, Sec. 402, amended Sec. 1017 of P.L. 93-406[see below] by substituting "(c) through (i)" for "(c) through (h)" in subsec. (b) and by adding new subsec. (i), effective 3/29/75.

In 1974, P.L. 93-406, Sec. 1012(b), added the last two sentences of para. (a)(5) . . . Sec. 1016(a)(2)(A), amended para. (a)(3) . . . Sec. 1016(a)(2)(B), substituted "paragraph (4) or section 410(b) (without regard to paragraph (1)(A) thereof)" for "paragraph (3)(B) or (4)" in para. (a)(5) . . . Sec. 1016(a)(2)(C), amended para. (a)(7), effective 9/2/74 for plans not in existence on 1/1/74 and effective for plan yrs. begin. after 12/31/75 for plans in existence on 1/1/74, subject to special rules in Sec. 1017 of this Act [see below].

Prior to amendment, para. (a)(3) read as follows:

"(3) if the trust, or two or more trusts, or the trust or trusts and annuity plan or plans are designated by the employer as constituting parts of a plan intended to qualify under this subsection which benefits either—

"(A) 70 percent or more of all the employees, or 80 percent or more of all the employees who are eligible to benefit under the plan if 70 percent or more of all the employees are eligible to benefit under the plan, excluding in each case employees who have been employed not more than a minimum period prescribed by the plan, not exceeding 5 years, employees whose customary employment is for not more than 20 hours in any one week, and employees whose customary employment is for not more than 5 months in any calendar year, or

"(B) such employees as qualify under a classification set up by the employer and found by the Secretary or his delegate not to be discriminatory in favor of employees who are officers, shareholders, persons whose principal duties consist in supervising the work of other employees, or highly compensated employees; and"

Prior to amendment, para. (a)(7) read as follows:

"(7) A trust shall not constitute a qualified trust under this section unless the plan of which such trust is a part provides that, upon its termination or upon complete discontinuance of contributions under the plan, the right of all employees to benefits accrued to the date of such termination or discontinuance, to the extent then funded, or the amounts credited to the employees' accounts are nonforfeitable. This paragraph shall not apply to benefits or contributions which, under provisions of the plan adopted pursuant to regulations prescribed by the Secretary or his delegate to preclude the discrimination prohibited by paragraph (4), may not be used for designated employees in the event of early termination of the plan."

—P.L. 93-406, Sec. 1021(a)(1), added para. (a)(11), effective for plan yrs. begin. after 12/31/75.

—P.L. 93-406, Sec. 1021(a)(2), added the last sentence of subsec. (a), effective 9/2/74 for plans not in existence on 1/1/74 and effective for plan yrs. begin. after 12/31/75 for plans not in existence on 1/1/74, subject to special rules in Sec. 1017 of this Act, [see below].

—P.L. 93-406, Sec. 1021(b), added para. (a)(12), effective for plan yrs. begin. after 1975.

—P.L. 93-406, Sec. 1021(c), added para. (a)(13), effective 1/1/76, not applicable to assignments which were revocable on 9/2/74.

—P.L. 93-406, Sec. 1021(d), added para. (a)(14), effective 9/2/74 for plans not in existence on 1/1/74 and effective for plan yrs. be gin. after 12/31/75 for plans in existence on 1/1/74, subject to special rules in Sec. 1017 of this Act [see below].

—P.L. 93-406, Sec. 1021(e), added para. (a)(15), effective for plan yrs. begin. after 12/31/75 for plans in existence on 1/1/74, subject to special rules in Sec. 1017 of this Act [see below], but only with respect to increases in social security benefits or wage bases occurring after 9/2/74 or (if later) the earlier of the date of first receipt of plan benefits or separation from service.

—P.L. 93-406, Sec. 1021(f), added para. (a)(19) . . . Sec. 1022(a), amended para. (a)(4) . . . Sec. 1022(b)(1), substituted "(A) paragraph (3), the first and second sentences of paragraph (5), and section 410 shall not apply but—" for "(A) paragraph (3) and the first and second sentences of paragraph (5) shall not apply, but—" in subpara. (a)(10)(A) . . . Sec. 1022(b)(2), amended para. (d)(3) . . . Sec. 1022(c)(1), amended the first sentence and added the second sentence of para. (d)(1) . . . Sec. 1022(c)(2), substituted "October 10, 1962," for "the date of enactment of this subsection" in the third sentence of para. (d)(1) [as amended by Sec. 1022(c)(1) of P.L. 93-406], effective 9/2/74 for plans not in existence on 1/1/74 and effective for plan yrs. begin. after 12/31/75 for plans not in existence on 1/1/74, subject to special rules in Sec. 1017 of this Act [see below].

Prior to amendment, para. (a)(4) read as follows:

"(4) if the contributions or benefits provided under the plan do not discriminate in favor of employees who are officers, shareholders, persons whose principal duties consist in supervising the work of other employees, or highly compensated employees."

Prior to amendment, para. (d)(3) read as follows:

"(3) The plan benefits each employee having a period of employment of 3 years or more. For purposes of the preceding sentence, the term 'employee' does not include any employee whose customary employment is for not more than 20 hours in any one week or is for not more than 5 months in any calendar year."

Prior to amendment, the first sentence of para. (d)(1) read as follows: in the case of a trust which is created on or after the date of the enactment of this subsection, or which was created before such date but is not exempt from tax under section 501(a) as an organization described in subsection (a) on the day before such date, the trustee is a bank, but a person (including the employer) other than a bank may be granted, under the trust instrument, the power to control the investment of the trust funds either by directing investments (including reinvestments, disposals, and exchanges) or by disapproving proposed investments (including reinvestments, disposals, and exchanges)."

—P.L. 93-406, Sec. 1022(d), amended subsec. (f), effective 1/1/74.

Prior to amendment, subsec. (f) read as follows:

"(f) Certain custodial accounts.

"(1) Treatment as qualified trust. For purposes of this title, a custodial account shall be treated as a qualified trust under this section, if—

"(A) such custodial account would, except for the fact that it is not a trust, constitute a qualified trust under this section;

"(B) the custodian is a bank (as defined in subsection (d)(1));

"(C) the investment of the funds in such account (including all earnings) is to be made—

"(i) solely in regulated investment company stock with respect to which an employee is the beneficial owner, or

"(ii) solely in annuity, endowment, or life insurance contracts issued by an insurance company;

"(D) the shareholder of record of any such stock described in subparagraph (C)(i) is the custodian or its nominee; and

"(E) the contracts described in subparagraph (C)(ii) are held by the custodian until distributed under the plan.

for purposes of this title, in the case of a custodial account treated as a qualified trust under this section by reason of the preceding sentence, the custodian of such account shall be treated as the trustee thereof.

"(2) Definition. For purposes of paragraph (1), the term 'regulated investment company' means a domestic corporation which—

"(A) is a regulated investment company within the meaning of section 851(a), and

"(B) issues only redeemable stock."

—P.L. 93-406, Sec. 1022(f), substituted "section 581, an insured credit union (within the meaning of section 101(6) of the Federal Credit Union Act)" for "section 581" in the last sentence of para. (d)(1), effective 1/1/74.

—P.L. 93-406, Sec. 1023, amended subsec. (b), effective 9/2/74.

Employee benefit plans

Code Sec. 401

Prior to amendment, subsec. (b) read as follows:
"(b) Certain retroactive changes in plan. A stock bonus, pension, profit-sharing, or annuity plan shall be considered as satisfying the requirements of paragraphs (3), (4), (5), and (6) of subsection (a) for the period beginning with the date on which it was put into effect and ending with the 15th day of the third month following the close of the taxable year of the employer in which the plan was put in effect, if all provisions of the plan which are necessary to satisfy such requirements are in effect by the end of such period and have been made effective for all purposes with respect to the whole of such period."
—P.L. 93-406, Sec. 2001(c), added para. (a)(17), effective as provided in Sec. 2001(i)(2) of this Act, which reads as follows:
"(2) The amendments made by subsection (c) apply to—
"(A) taxable years beginning after December 31, 1975, and
"(B) any other taxable years beginning after December 31, 1973, for which contributions were made under the plan in excess of the amounts permitted to be made under sections 404(e) and 1379(b) as in effect on the day before the date of the enactment of this Act. [9/2/74]"
—P.L. 93-406, Sec. 2001(d)(1), added para. (a)(18)... Sec. 2001(d)(2), redesignated subsec. (j) as (k) and added new subsec. (j), effective for tax. yrs. begin. after 12/31/75.
—P.L. 93-406, Sec. 2001(e)(1), amended the last sentence of para. (d)(5)... Sec. 2001(e)(2), deleted para. (d)(8)... Sec. 2001(e)(3), amended subsec. (e)... Sec. 2001(e)(4), substituted "subsection (e)" for "subsection (e)(3)(A)" in clause (a)(10)(A)(ii), effective for contributions made in tax. years begin. after 12/31/75.
Prior to amendment, the last sentence of para. (d)(5) read as follows:
"Subparagraphs (A) and (B) shall not apply to any contribution which is not considered to be an excess contribution (as defined in subsection (e)(1)) by reason of the application of subsection (e)(3)."
Prior to deletion, para. (d)(8) read as follows:
"(8) Under the plan—
"(A) any contribution which is an excess contribution, together with the income attributable to such excess contribution, is (unless subsection (e)(2)(E) applies) to be repaid to the owner-employee on whose behalf such excess contribution is made;
"(B) if for any taxable year the plan does not, by reason of subsection (e)(2)(A), meet (for purposes of section 404) the requirements of this subsection with respect to an owner-employee, the income for the taxable year attributable to the interest of such owner-employee under the plan is to be paid to such owner-employee; and
"(C) the entire interest of an owner-employee is to be repaid to him when required by the provisions of subsection (e)(2)(E)."
Prior to amendment, subsec. (e) read as follows:
"(e) Excess contributions on behalf of owner-employees.
"(1) Excess contribution defined. For purposes of this section, the term 'excess contribution' means, except as provided in paragraph (3)—
"(A) if, in the taxable year, contributions are made under the plan only on behalf of owner-employees, the amount of any contribution made on behalf of any owner-employee which (without regard to this subsection) is not deductible under section 404 for the taxable year; or
"(B) if, in the taxable year, contributions are made under the plan on behalf of employees other than owner-employees—
"(i) the amount of any contribution made by the employer on be half of any owner-employee which (without regard to this subsection) is not deductible under section 404 for the taxable year;
"(ii) the amount of any contribution made by any owner-employee (as an employee) at a rate which exceeds the rate of contributions permitted to be made by employees other than owner-employees;
"(iii) the amount of any contribution made by any owner-employee (as an employee) which exceeds the lesser of $2,500 or 10 percent of the earned income for such taxable year derived by such owner-employee from the trade or business with respect to which the plan is established; and
"(iv) in the case of any individual on whose behalf contributions are made under more than one plan as an owner-employee, the amount of any contribution made by such owner-employee (as an employee) under all such plans which exceeds $2,500; and
"(C) the amount of any contribution made on behalf of an owner-employee in any taxable year for which, under paragraph (2)(A) or (E), the plan does not (for purposes of section 404) meet the requirements of subsection (d) with respect to such owner-employee.
For purposes of this subsection, the amount of any contribution which is allocable (determined in accordance with regulations prescribed by the Secretary or his delegate) to the purchase of life, accident, health, or other insurance shall not be taken into account.
"(2) Effect of excess contribution.
"(A) In general. If an excess contribution (other than an excess contribution to which subparagraph (E) applies) is made on behalf of an owner-employee in any taxable year, the plan with respect to which such excess contribution is made shall, except as provided in subparagraphs (C) and (D), be considered, for purposes of section 404, as not meeting the requirements of subsection (d) with respect to such owner-employee for the taxable year and for all succeeding taxable years.
"(B) Inclusion of amounts in gross income of owner-employees. For any taxable year for which any plan does not meet the requirements of subsection (d) with respect to an owner-employee by reason of subparagraph (A), the gross income of such owner-employee shall, for purposes of this chapter, include the amount of net income for such taxable year attributable to the interest of such owner-employee under such plan.

"(C) Repayment within prescribed period. Subparagraph (A) shall not apply to an excess contribution with respect to any taxable year, if, on or before the close of the 6-month period beginning on the day on which the Secretary or his delegate sends notice (by certified or registered mail) to the person to whom such excess contribution was paid on the amount of such excess contribution, the amount of such excess contribution, and the net income attributable thereto, is repaid to the owner-employee on whose behalf such excess contribution was made. If the excess contribution is an excess contribution as defined in paragraph (1)(A) or (B)(i), or is an excess contribution as defined in paragraph (1)(C) with respect to which a deduction has been claimed under section 404, the notice required by the preceding sentence shall not be mailed prior to the time that the amount of the tax under this chapter of such owner-employee for the taxable year in which such excess contribution was made has been finally determined.
"(D) Repayment after prescribed period. If an excess contribution, together with the net income attributable thereto, is not repaid within the 6-month period referred to in subparagraph (C), subparagraph (A) shall not apply to an excess contribution with respect to any taxable year beginning with the taxable year in which the person to whom such excess contribution was paid repays the amount of such excess contribution to the owner-employee on whose behalf such excess contribution was made, and pays to such owner-employee the amount of net income attributable to the interest of such owner-employee which, under subparagraph (B), has been included in the gross income of such owner-employee for any prior taxable year.
"(E) Special rule if excess contribution was willfully made. If an excess contribution made on behalf of an owner-employee is determined to have been willfully made, then—
"(i) subparagraphs (A), (B), (C), and (D) shall not apply with respect to such excess contribution;
"(ii) there shall be distributed to the owner-employee on whose behalf such excess contribution was willfully made his entire interest in all plans with respect to which he is an owner-employee; and
"(iii) no plan shall, for purposes of section 404, be considered as meeting the requirements of subsection (d) with respect to such owner-employee for the taxable year in which it is determined that such excess contribution was willfully made and for the 5 taxable years following such taxable year.
"(F) Statute of limitations. In any case in which subparagraph (A) applies, the period for assessing any deficiency arising by reason of—
"(i) the disallowance of any deduction under section 404 on account of a plan not meeting the requirements of subsection (d) with respect to the owner-employee on whose behalf an excess contribution was made, or
"(ii) the inclusion, under subparagraph (B), in gross income of such owner-employee of income attributable to the interest of such owner-employee under a plan, for the taxable year in which such excess contribution was made or for any succeeding taxable year shall not expire prior to one year after the close of the 6-month period referred to in subparagraph (C).
"(3) Contributions for premiums on annuity, etc., contracts. A contribution by the employer on behalf of an owner-employee shall not be considered to be an excess contribution within the meaning of paragraph (1), if—
"(A) under the plan such contribution is required to be applied (directly or through a trustee) to pay premiums or other consideration for one or more annuity, endowment, or life insurance contracts on the life of such owner-employee issued under the plan,
"(B) the amount of such contribution exceeds the amount deductible under section 404 with respect to contributions made by the employer on behalf of such owner-employee under the plan, and
"(C) the amount of such contribution does not exceed the average of the amounts which were deductible under section 404 with respect to contributions made by the employer on behalf of such owner-employee under the plan (or which would have been deductible under such section if such section had been in effect) for the first 3 taxable years (i) preceding the year in which the last such annuity, endowment, or life insurance contract was issued under the plan and (ii) in which such owner-employee derived earned income from the trade or business with respect to which the plan is established, or for so many of such taxable years as such owner-employee was engaged in such trade or business and derived earned income therefrom.
In the case of any individual on whose behalf contributions described in subparagraph (A) are made under more than one plan as an owner-employee during any taxable year, the preceding sentence shall not apply if the amount of such contributions under all such plans for such taxable year exceeds $2,500. Any contribution which is not considered to be an excess contribution by reason of the application of this paragraph shall, for purposes of subparagraphs (B)(ii), (iii), and (iv) of paragraph (1), be taken into account as a contribution made by such owner-employee as an employee to the extent that the amount of such contribution is not deductible under section 404 for the taxable year, but only for the purpose of applying such subparagraphs to other contributions made by such owner-employee as an employee."
—P.L. 93-406, Sec. 2001(h)(1), added "in excess of contributions made by an owner-employee as an employee" after "benefits" in subpara. (d)(4)(B), effective for tax. yrs. end. after 9/2/74.
—P.L. 93-406, Sec. 2004(a)(1), added para. (a)(16), effective for yrs. begin. after 12/31/72.
—P.L. 93-406, Sec. 1017, of the Employee Retirement Income Security Act of 1974 [as amended by Sec. 402 of P.L. 94-12, see above] provided the following effective dates and transitional rules:
"SEC. 1017. EFFECTIVE DATES AND TRANSITIONAL RULES.
"(a) General Rule. Except as otherwise provided in this section, the amendments made by this part shall apply for plan years beginning after the date of the enactment of this Act.

1,897

"(b) Existing plans. Except as otherwise provided in subsections (c) through (i), in the case of a plan in existence on January 1, 1974, the amendments made by this part shall apply for plan years beginning after December 31, 1975.

"(c) Existing plans under collective bargaining agreements.

"(1) Application of vesting rules to certain plan provisions.

"(A) Waiver of application. In the case of a plan maintained on January 1, 1974, pursuant to the one or more agreements which the Secretary of Labor finds to be collective bargaining agreements between employee representatives and one or more employers, during the special temporary waiver period the plan shall not be treated as not meeting the requirements of section 411(b) (1) or (2) of the Internal Revenue Code of 1954 solely by reason of a supplementary or special plan provision (within the meaning of subparagraph (D)).

"(B) Special temporary waiver period. For purposes of this paragraph, the term 'special temporary waiver period' means plan years beginning after December 31, 1975, and before the earlier of—

"(i) the date on which the last of the collective bargaining agreements relating to the plan terminates (determined without regard to any extension thereof agreed to after the date of the enactment of this Act), or

"(ii) January 1, 1981.

For purposes of clause (i), any plan amendment made pursuant to a collective bargaining agreement relating to the plan which amends the plan solely to conform to any requirement contained in this Act shall not be treated as a termination of such collective bargaining agreement.

"(C) Determination by Secretary of Labor required. Subparagraph (A) shall not apply unless the Secretary of Labor determines that the participation and vesting rules in effect on the date of the enactment of this Act are not less favorable to the employees, in the aggregate, than the rules provided under sections 410 and 411 of the Internal Revenue Code of 1954.

"(D) Supplementary or special plan provisions. For purposes of this paragraph, the term 'supplementary or special plan provision' means any plan provision which—

"(i) provides supplementary benefits, not in excess of one-third of the basic benefit, in the form of an annuity for the life of the participant, or

"(ii) provides that, under a contractual agreement based on medical evidence as to the effects of working in an adverse environment for an extended period of time, a participant having 25 years of service is to be treated as having 30 years of service.

"(2) Application of funding rules.

"(A) In general. In the case of a plan maintained on January 1, 1974, pursuant to one or more agreements which the Secretary of Labor finds to be collective bargaining agreements between employee representatives and one or more employers, section 412 of the Internal Revenue Code of 1954, and other amendments made by this part to the extent such amendments relate to such section 412, shall not apply during the special temporary waiver period (as defined in paragraph (1)(B)).

"(B) Waiver of underfunding. In the case of a plan maintained on January 1, 1974, pursuant to one or more agreements which the Secretary of Labor finds to be collective bargaining agreements between employee representatives and one or more employers, if by reason of subparagraph (A) the requirements of section 401 (a)(7) of the Internal Revenue Code of 1954 apply without regard to the amendment of such section 401(a)(7) by section 1016(a)(2)(C) of this Act, the plan shall not be treated as not meeting such requirements solely by reason of the application of the amendments made by sections 1011 and 1012 of this Act or related amendments made by this part.

"(C) Labor organization conventions. In the case of a plan maintained by a labor organization, which is exempt from tax under section 501(c)(5) of the Internal Revenue Code of 1954, exclusively for the benefit of its employees and their beneficiaries, section 412 of such Code and other amendments made by this part to the extent such amendments relate to such section 412, shall be applied by substituting for the term 'December 31, 1975' in subsection (b), the earlier of—

"(i) the date on which the second convention of such labor organization held after the date of the enactment of this Act ends, or

"(ii) December 31, 1980,

but in no event shall a date earlier than the later of December 31, 1975, or the date determined under subparagraph (A) or (B) be substituted.

"(d) Existing plans may elect new provisions. In the case of a plan in existence on January 1, 1974, the provisions of the Internal Revenue Code of 1954 relating to participation, vesting, funding, and form of benefit (as in effect from time to time) shall apply in the case of the plan year (which begins after the date of the enactment of this Act but before the applicable effective date determined under subsection (b) or (c)) selected by the plan administrator and to all subsequent plan years, if the plan administrator elects (in such manner and at such time as the Secretary of the Treasury or his delegate shall by regulations prescribe) to have such provisions so apply. Any election made under this subsection, once made, shall be irrevocable.

"(e) Certain definitions and special rules. Section 414 of the Internal Revenue Code of 1954 (other than subsections (b) and (c) of such section 414), as added by section 1015(a) of this Act, shall take effect on the date of the enactment of this Act.

"(f) Transitional rules with respect to breaks in service.

"(1) Participation. In the case of a plan to which section 410 of the Internal Revenue Code of 1954 applies, if any plan amendment with respect to breaks in service (which amendment is made or becomes effective after January 1, 1974, and before the date on which such section 410 first becomes effective with respect to such plan) provides that any employee's participation in the plan would commence at any date later than the later of—

"(A) the date on which his participation would commence under the break in service rules of section 410(a)(5) of such Code, or

"(B) the date on which his participation would commence under the plan as in effect on January 1, 1974,

such plan shall not constitute a plan described in section 403(a) or 405(a) of such Code and a trust forming a part of such plan shall not constitute a qualified trust under section 401(a) of such Code.

"(2) Vesting. In the case of a plan to which section 411 of the Internal Revenue Code of 1954 applies, if any plan amendment with respect to breaks in service (which amendment is made or becomes effective after January 1, 1974, and before the date on which such section 411 first becomes effective with respect to such plan) provides that the nonforfeitable benefit derived from employer contributions to which any employee would be entitled is less than the lesser of the nonforfeitable benefit derived from employer contributions to which he would be entitled under—

"(A) the break in service rules of section 411(a)(6) of such Code, or

"(B) the plan as in effect on January 1, 1974,

such plan shall not constitute a plan described in section 403(a) or 405(a) of such Code and a trust forming a part of such plan shall not constitute a qualified trust under section 401(a) of such Code. Subparagraph (B) shall not apply if the break in service rules under the plan would have been in violation of any law or rule of law in effect on January 1, 1974.

"(g) 3-Year delay for certain provisions. Subparagraphs (B) and (C) of section 404(a)(1) shall apply only in the case of plan years beginning on or after 3 years after the date of the enactment of this Act.

"(h)(1) Except as provided in paragraph (2), section 413 of the Internal Revenue Code of 1954 shall apply to plan years beginning after December 31, 1953.

"(2)(A) For plan years beginning before the applicable effective date of section 410 of such Code, the provisions of paragraphs (1) and (8) of subsection (b) of such section 413 shall be applied by substituting '401(a)(3)' for '410'.

"(B) For plan years beginning before the applicable effective date of section 411 of such Code, the provisions of subsection (b)(2) of such section 413 shall be applied by substituting '401(a)(7)' for '411(d)(3)'.

"(C)(i) The provisions of subsection (b)(4) of such section 413 shall not apply to plan years beginning before the applicable effective date of section 411 of such Code.

"(ii) The provisions of subsection (b)(5) (other than the second sentence thereof) [sic] of such section 413 shall not apply to plan years beginning before the applicable effective date of section 412 of such Code.

"(i) Contributions to H.R. 10 plans. Notwithstanding subsections (b) and (c)(2), in the case of a plan in existence on January 1, 1974, the amendment made by section 1013(c)(2) of this Act shall apply, with respect to a plan which provides contributions or benefits for employees some or all of whom are employees within the meaning of section 401(c)(1) of the Internal Revenue Code of 1954, for plan years beginning after December 31, 1974, but only if the employer (within the meaning of section 401(c)(4) of such Code) elects in such manner and at such time as the Secretary of the Treasury or his delegate shall by regulations prescribe, to have such amendment so apply. Any election made under this subsection, once made, shall be irrevocable."

In 1971, P.L. 91-691, Sec. 1(a), deleted "multiemployer" after "union-negotiated" in the heading of subsec. (i) and amended para. (i)(1), effective for tax. yrs. begin. after 12/31/53, and end. after 8/16/54, but only with respect to contributions made after 12/31/54.

Prior to amendment para. (i)(1) read as follows:

"(1) such trust was created pursuant to a collective bargaining agreement between employee representatives and two or more employers who are not related (determined under regulations prescribed by the Secretary or his delegate),"

In 1968, P.L. 90-607, amended Sec. 204(d) of P.L. 89-809 [see below] by adding the effective date for para. (c)(2) as follows:

"The amendment made by subsection (c) shall apply with respect to taxable years beginning after December 31, 1967, and in the case of a taxpayer who applies the averaging provisions of section 401(e)(3) of the Internal Revenue Code of 1954 for a taxable year beginning after December 31, 1967, the computation of the amount deductible under section 404 of such Code for any prior taxable year which began before January 1, 1968, shall be made, for purposes of such averaging provisions, as if the amendment made by subsection (c) were applicable to such prior taxable year."

In 1966, P.L. 89-809, Sec. 204(b), deleted "(determined without regard to section 404 (a)(10))" following "section 404" from the following subsecs. of Code Sec. 401(a)(10)(A)(ii), (d)(5)(A), (d)(5)(B), (d)(6)(A), (e)(1)(A) & (B)(i), and (e)(3)(B) & (C) and the last sentence thereof, effective for tax. yrs. begin. after 12/31/67.

—P.L. 89-809, Sec. 204(c), deleted subparas. (c)(2)(A) and (B) and added (c)(2)(A).

Prior to deletion, subparas. (c)(2)(A) and (b) read as follows:

"(A) In general. The term 'earned income' means the net earnings from self-employment (as defined in section 1402(a)) [to the extent that such net earnings constitute earned income (as defined in section 911(b) but determined with the application of subparagraph (B)),] but such net earnings shall be determined—

"(i) without regard to paragraphs (4) and (5) of section 1402(c),

"(ii) in the case of any individual who is treated as an employee under sections 3121(d)(3)(A), (C), or (D), without regard to paragraph (2) of section 1402(c), and

"(iii) without regard to items which are not included in gross income for purposes of this chapter, and the deductions properly allocable to or chargeable against such items.

"For purposes of this subparagraph, sections 911(b) and 1402, as in effect for a taxable year ending on December 31, 1962, and subparagraph (B), as in effect for a taxable year beginning on January 1, 1963, shall be treated as having been in effect for all taxable years ending before such date.

Employee benefit plans

Code Sec. 402(c)(3)(A)

"(B) Earned income when both personal services and capital are material income-producing factors. In applying section 911(b) for purposes of subparagraph (A), in the case of an individual who is an employee within the meaning of paragraph (1) and who is engaged in a trade or business in which both personal services and capital are material income-producing factors and with respect to which the individual actually renders personal services on a full-time, or substantially full-time, basis, so much of his share of the net profits of such trade or business as does not exceed $2,500 shall be considered as earned income. In the case of any such individual who is engaged in more than one trade or business with respect to which he actually renders substantial personal services, if with respect to all such trades or businesses he actually renders personal services on a full-time, or substantially full-time, basis, there shall be considered as earned income with respect to the trades or businesses in which both personal services and capital are material income-producing factors—

"(i) so much of his share of the net profits of such trades or businesses as does not exceed $2,500, reduced by

"(ii) his share of the net profits of any trade or business in which only personal services is a material income-producing factor.

"The preceding sentences shall not be construed to reduce the share of net profits of any trade or business which under the second sentence of section 911(b) would be considered as earned income of any such individual." . . . Sec. 204(d), of this Act [as amended by P.L. 90-607 and P.L. 99-514, Sec. 2], provides:

"The amendments made by subsections (a) and (b) shall apply with respect to taxable years beginning after December 31, 1967. The amendment made by subsection (c) shall apply with respect to taxable years beginning after December 31, 1967, and in the case of a taxpayer who applies the averaging provisions of section 401(e)(3) of the Internal Revenue Code of 1986 for a taxable year beginning after December 31, 1967, the computation of the amount deductible under section 404 of such Code for any prior taxable year which began before January 1, 1968, shall be made, for purposes of such averaging provisions, as if the amendment made by subsection (c) were applicable to such prior taxable year."

—P.L. 89-809, Sec. 205(a), added subpara. (c)(2)(C), effective for tax. yrs. ending after 11/13/66.

In 1965, P.L. 89-97, Sec. 106(d), substituted "section 72(m)(7)" for "section 213(g)(3)" in subpara. (d)(4)(B), effective for tax. yrs. begin. after 12/31/66.

In 1964, P.L. 88-272, Sec. 219(a), redesignated subsec. (i) as (j) and added subsec. (i), effective for tax. yrs. begin. after 12/31/53, and end. after 8/16/54, but only with respect to contributions made after 12/31/54.

In 1962, P.L. 87-863, Sec. 2(a), redesignated subsec. (h) as (i) and added subsec. (h), effective for tax. yrs. begin. after 10/23/62.

—P.L. 87-792, Sec. 2(1), added a sentence at the end of para. (a)(5) . . . Sec. 2(2), added paras. (a)(7)–(10) . . . Sec. 2(3), redesignated subsec. (c) as (h) and added subsecs. (c)-(g), effective for tax. yrs. begin. after 12/31/62.

Sec. 402. Taxability of beneficiary of employees' trust.
(a) Taxability of beneficiary of exempt trust.

Except as otherwise provided in this section, any amount actually distributed to any distributee by any employees' trust described in section 401(a) which is exempt from tax under section 501(a) shall be taxable to the distributee, in the taxable year of the distributee in which distributed, under section 72 (relating to annuities).

(b) Taxability of beneficiary of nonexempt trust.

(1) Contributions. Contributions to an employees' trust made by an employer during a taxable year of the employer which ends with or within a taxable year of the trust for which the trust is not exempt from tax under section 501(a) shall be included in the gross income of the employee in accordance with section 83 (relating to property transferred in connection with performance of services), except that the value of the employee's interest in the trust shall be substituted for the fair market value of the property for purposes of applying such section.

(2) Distributions. The amount actually distributed or made available to any distributee by any trust described in paragraph (1) shall be taxable to the distributee, in the taxable year in which so distributed or made available, under section 72 (relating to annuities), except that distributions of income of such trust before the annuity starting date (as defined in section 72(c)(4)) shall be included in the gross income of the employee without regard to section 72(e)(5) (relating to amounts not received as annuities).

(3) Grantor trusts. A beneficiary of any trust described in paragraph (1) shall not be considered the owner of any portion of such trust under subpart E of part I of subchapter J (relating to grantors and others treated as substantial owners).

(4) Failure to meet requirements of section 410(b).

(A) Highly compensated employees. If 1 of the reasons a trust is not exempt from tax under section 501(a) is the failure of the plan of which it is a part to meet the requirements of section 401(a)(26) or 410(b), then a highly compensated employee shall, in lieu of the amount determined under paragraph (1) or (2) include in gross income for the taxable year with or within which the taxable year of the trust ends an amount equal to the vested accrued benefit of such employee (other than the employee's investment in the contract) as of the close of such taxable year of the trust.

(B) Failure to meet coverage tests. If a trust is not exempt from tax under section 501(a) for any taxable year solely because such trust is part of a plan which fails to meet the requirements of section 401(a)(26) or 410(b), paragraphs (1) and (2) shall not apply by reason of such failure to any employee who was not a highly compensated employee during—

(i) such taxable year, or

(ii) any preceding period for which service was creditable to such employee under the plan.

(C) Highly compensated employee. For purposes of this paragraph, the term "highly compensated employee" has the meaning given such term by section 414(q).

(c) Rules applicable to rollovers from exempt trusts.

(1) Exclusion from income. If—

(A) any portion of the balance to the credit of an employee in a qualified trust is paid to the employee in an eligible rollover distribution,

(B) the distributee transfers any portion of the property received in such distribution to an eligible retirement plan, and

(C) in the case of a distribution of property other than money, the amount so transferred consists of the property distributed,

then such distribution (to the extent so transferred) shall not be includible in gross income for the taxable year in which paid.

(2) Maximum amount which may be rolled over. In the case of any eligible rollover distribution, the maximum amount transferred to which paragraph (1) applies shall not exceed the portion of such distribution which is includible in gross income (determined without regard to paragraph (1)). The preceding sentence shall not apply to such distribution to the extent—

(A) such portion is transferred in a direct trustee-to-trustee transfer to a qualified trust or to an annuity contract described in section 403(b) and such trust or contract provides for separate accounting for amounts so transferred (and earnings thereon), including separately accounting for the portion of such distribution which is includible in gross income and the portion of such distribution which is not so includible, or

(B) such portion is transferred to an eligible retirement plan described in clause (i) or (ii) of paragraph (8)(B).

In the case of a transfer described in subparagraph (A) or (B), the amount transferred shall be treated as consisting first of the portion of such distribution that is includible in gross income (determined without regard to paragraph (1)).

(3) Transfer must be made within 60 days of receipt.

(A) In general. Except as provided in subparagraph (B), paragraph (1) shall not apply to any transfer of a distri-

1,899

bution made after the 60th day following the day on which the distributee received the property distributed.

(B) Hardship exception. The Secretary may waive the 60-day requirement under subparagraph (A) where the failure to waive such requirement would be against equity or good conscience, including casualty, disaster, or other events beyond the reasonable control of the individual subject to such requirement.

(4) Eligible rollover distribution. For purposes of this subsection, the term "eligible rollover distribution" means any distribution to an employee of all or any portion of the balance to the credit of the employee in a qualified trust; except that such term shall not include —

(A) any distribution which is one of a series of substantially equal periodic payments (not less frequently than annually) made —

(i) for the life (or life expectancy) of the employee or the joint lives (or joint life expectancies) of the employee and the employee's designated beneficiary, or

(ii) for a specified period of 10 years or more,

(B) any distribution to the extent such distribution is required under section 401(a)(9),

(C) any distribution which is made upon hardship of the employee.

If all or any portion of a distribution during 2009 is treated as an eligible rollover distribution but would not be so treated if the minimum distribution requirements under section 401(a)(9) had applied during 2009, such distribution shall not be treated as an eligible rollover distribution for purposes of section 401(a)(31) or 3405(c) or subsection (f) of this section.

(5) Transfer treated as rollover contribution under section 408. For purposes of this title, a transfer to an eligible retirement plan described in clause (i) or (ii) of paragraph (8)(B) resulting in any portion of a distribution being excluded from gross income under paragraph (1) shall be treated as a rollover contribution described in section 408(d)(3).

(6) Sales of distributed property. For purposes of this subsection —

(A) Transfer of proceeds from sale of distributed property treated as transfer of distributed property. The transfer of an amount equal to any portion of the proceeds from the sale of property received in the distribution shall be treated as the transfer of property received in the distribution.

(B) Proceeds attributable to increase in value. The excess of fair market value of property on sale over its fair market value on distribution shall be treated as property received in the distribution.

(C) Designation where amount of distribution exceeds rollover contribution. In any case where part or all of the distribution consists of property other than money —

(i) the portion of the money or other property which is to be treated as attributable to amounts not included in gross income, and

(ii) the portion of the money or other property which is to be treated as included in the rollover contribution,

shall be determined on a ratable basis unless the taxpayer designates otherwise. Any designation under this subparagraph for a taxable year shall be made not later than the time prescribed by law for filing the return for such taxable year (including extensions thereof). Any such designation, once made, shall be irrevocable.

(D) Nonrecognition of gain or loss. No gain or loss shall be recognized on any sale described in subparagraph (A) to the extent that an amount equal to the proceeds is transferred pursuant to paragraph (1).

(7) Special rule for frozen deposits.

(A) In general. The 60-day period described in paragraph (3) shall not —

(i) include any period during which the amount transferred to the employee is a frozen deposit, or

(ii) end earlier than 10 days after such amount ceases to be a frozen deposit.

(B) Frozen deposits. For purposes of this subparagraph, the term "frozen deposit" means any deposit which may not be withdrawn because of —

(i) the bankruptcy or insolvency of any financial institution, or

(ii) any requirement imposed by the State in which such institution is located by reason of the bankruptcy or insolvency (or threat thereof) of 1 or more financial institutions in such State.

A deposit shall not be treated as a frozen deposit unless on at least 1 day during the 60-day period described in paragraph (3) (without regard to this paragraph) such deposit is described in the preceding sentence.

(8) Definitions. For purposes of this subsection —

(A) Qualified trust. The term "qualified trust" means an employees' trust described in section 401(a) which is exempt from tax under section 501(a).

(B) Eligible retirement plan. The term "eligible retirement plan" means —

(i) an individual retirement account described in section 408(a),

(ii) an individual retirement annuity described in section 408(b) (other than an endowment contract),

(iii) a qualified trust,

(iv) an annuity plan described in section 403(a),

(v) an eligible deferred compensation plan described in section 457(b) which is maintained by an eligible employer described in section 457(e)(1)(A), and

(vi) an annuity contract described in section 403(b).

If any portion of an eligible rollover distribution is attributable to payments or distributions from a designated Roth account (as defined in section 402A), an eligible retirement plan with respect to such portion shall include only another designated Roth account and a Roth IRA.

(9) Rollover where spouse receives distribution after death of employee. If any distribution attributable to an employee is paid to the spouse of the employee after the employee's death, the preceding provisions of this subsection shall apply to such distribution in the same manner as if the spouse were the employee.

(10) Separate accounting. Unless a plan described in clause (v) of paragraph (8)(B) agrees to separately account for amounts rolled into such plan from eligible retirement plans not described in such clause, the plan described in such clause may not accept transfers or rollovers from such retirement plans.

(11) Distributions to inherited individual retirement plan of nonspouse beneficiary.

(A) In general. If, with respect to any portion of a distribution from an eligible retirement plan described in paragraph (8)(B)(iii) of a deceased employee, a direct trustee-to-trustee transfer is made to an individual retirement plan described in clause (i) or (ii) of paragraph (8)(B) established for the purposes of receiving the distribution on behalf of an individual who is a designated beneficiary (as defined by section 401(a)(9)(E)) of the employee and who is not the surviving spouse of the employee—

(i) the transfer shall be treated as an eligible rollover distribution,

(ii) the individual retirement plan shall be treated as an inherited individual retirement account or individual retirement annuity (within the meaning of section 408(d)(3)(C)) for purposes of this title, and

(iii) section 401(a)(9)(B) (other than clause (iv) thereof) shall apply to such plan.

(B) Certain trusts treated as beneficiaries. For purposes of this paragraph, to the extent provided in rules prescribed by the Secretary, a trust maintained for the benefit of one or more designated beneficiaries shall be treated in the same manner as a designated beneficiary.

(d) Taxability of beneficiary of certain foreign situs trusts.

For purposes of subsections (a), (b), and (c), a stock bonus, pension, or profit-sharing trust which would qualify for exemption from tax under section 501(a) except for the fact that it is a trust created or organized outside the United States shall be treated as if it were a trust exempt from tax under section 501(a).

(e) Other rules applicable to exempt trusts.

(1) Alternate payees.

(A) Alternate payee treated as distributee. For purposes of subsection (a) and section 72, an alternate payee who is the spouse or former spouse of the participant shall be treated as the distributee of any distribution or payment made to the alternate payee under a qualified domestic relations order (as defined in section 414(p)).

(B) Rollovers. If any amount is paid or distributed to an alternate payee who is the spouse or former spouse of the participant by reason of any qualified domestic relations order (within the meaning of section 414(p)), subsection (c) shall apply to such distribution in the same manner as if such alternate payee were the employee.

(2) Distributions by United States to nonresident aliens. The amount includible under subsection (a) in the gross income of a nonresident alien with respect to a distribution made by the United States in respect of services performed by an employee of the United States shall not exceed an amount which bears the same ratio to the amount includible in gross income without regard to this paragraph as—

(A) the aggregate basic pay paid by the United States to such employee for such services, reduced by the amount of such basic pay which was not includible in gross income by reason of being from sources without the United States, bears to

(B) the aggregate basic pay paid by the United States to such employee for such services.

In the case of distributions under the civil service retirement laws, the term "basic pay" shall have the meaning provided in section 8331(3) of title 5, United States Code.

(3) Cash or deferred arrangements. For purposes of this title, contributions made by an employer on behalf of an employee to a trust which is a part of a qualified cash or deferred arrangement (as defined in section 401(k)(2)) or which is part of a salary reduction agreement under section 403(b) shall not be treated as distributed or made available to the employee nor as contributions made to the trust by the employee merely because the arrangement includes provisions under which the employee has an election whether the contribution will be made to the trust or received by the employee in cash.

(4) Net unrealized appreciation.

(A) Amounts attributable to employee contributions. For purposes of subsection (a) and section 72, in the case of a distribution other than a lump sum distribution, the amount actually distributed to any distributee from a trust described in subsection (a) shall not include any net unrealized appreciation in securities of the employer corporation attributable to amounts contributed by the employee (other than deductible employee contributions within the meaning of section 72(o)(5)). This subparagraph shall not apply to a distribution to which subsection (c) applies.

(B) Amounts attributable to employer contributions. For purposes of subsection (a) and section 72, in the case of any lump sum distribution which includes securities of the employer corporation, there shall be excluded from gross income the net unrealized appreciation attributable to that part of the distribution which consists of securities of the employer corporation. In accordance with rules prescribed by the Secretary, a taxpayer may elect, on the return of tax on which a lump sum distribution is required to be included, not to have this subparagraph apply to such distribution.

(C) Determination of amounts and adjustments. For purposes of subparagraphs (A) and (B), net unrealized appreciation and the resulting adjustments to basis shall be determined in accordance with regulations prescribed by the Secretary.

(D) Lump-sum distribution. For purposes of this paragraph—

(i) In general. The term "lump sum distribution" means the distribution or payment within one taxable year of the recipient of the balance to the credit of an employee which becomes payable to the recipient—

(I) on account of the employee's death,

(II) after the employee attains age 59 ½,

(III) on account of the employee's separation from service, or

(IV) after the employee has become disabled (within the meaning of section 72(m)(7)),

from a trust which forms a part of a plan described in section 401(a) and which is exempt from tax under section 501 or from a plan described in section 403(a). Subclause (III) of this clause shall be applied only with respect to an individual who is an employee without regard to section 401(c)(1), and subclause (IV) shall be applied only with respect to an employee within the meaning of section 401(c)(1). For purposes of this clause, a distribution to two or more trusts shall be treated as a distribution to one recipient. For purposes of this paragraph, the balance to the credit of the employee does not include the accumulated deductible employee contributions under the plan (within the meaning of section 72(o)(5)).

(ii) Aggregation of certain trusts and plans. For purposes of determining the balance to the credit of an employee under clause (i)—

(I) all trusts which are part of a plan shall be treated as a single trust, all pension plans maintained by the employer shall be treated as a single plan, all profit-sharing plans maintained by the employer shall be treated as a single plan, and all stock bonus plans maintained by the employer shall be treated as a single plan, and

(II) trusts which are not qualified trusts under section 401(a) and annuity contracts which do not satisfy the requirements of section 404(a)(2) shall not be taken into account.

(iii) Community property laws. The provisions of this paragraph shall be applied without regard to community property laws.

(iv) Amounts subject to penalty. This paragraph shall not apply to amounts described in subparagraph (A) of section 72(m)(5) to the extent that section 72(m)(5) applies to such amounts.

(v) Balance to credit of employee not to include amounts payable under qualified domestic relations order. For purposes of this paragraph, the balance to the credit of an employee shall not include any amount payable to an alternate payee under a qualified domestic relations order (within the meaning of section 414(p)).

(vi) Transfers to cost-of-living arrangement not treated as distribution. For purposes of this paragraph, the balance to the credit of an employee under a defined contribution plan shall not include any amount transferred from such defined contribution plan to a qualified cost-of-living arrangement (within the meaning of section 415(k)(2)) under a defined benefit plan.

(vii) Lump-sum distributions of alternate payees. If any distribution or payment of the balance to the credit of an employee would be treated as a lump-sum distribution, then, for purposes of this paragraph, the payment under a qualified domestic relations order (within the meaning of section 414(p)) of the balance to the credit of an alternate payee who is the spouse or former spouse of the employee shall be treated as a lump-sum distribution. For purposes of this clause, the balance to the credit of the alternate payee shall not include any amount payable to the employee.

(E) Definitions relating to securities. For purposes of this paragraph—

(i) Securities. The term "securities" means only shares of stock and bonds or debentures issued by a corporation with interest coupons or in registered form.

(ii) Securities of the employer. The term "securities of the employer corporation" includes securities of a parent or subsidiary corporation (as defined in subsections (e) and (f) of section 424) of the employer corporation.

(5) Repealed.

(6) Direct trustee-to-trustee transfers. Any amount transferred in a direct trustee-to-trustee transfer in accordance with section 401(a)(31) shall not be includible in gross income for the taxable year of such transfer.

(f) Written explanation to recipients of distributions eligible for rollover treatment.

(1) In general. The plan administrator of any plan shall, within a reasonable period of time before making an eligible rollover distribution, provide a written explanation to the recipient—

(A) of the provisions under which the recipient may have the distribution directly transferred to an eligible retirement plan and that the automatic distribution by direct transfer applies to certain distributions in accordance with section 401(a)(31)(B),

(B) of the provision which requires the withholding of tax on the distribution if it is not directly transferred to an eligible retirement plan,

(C) of the provisions under which the distribution will not be subject to tax if transferred to an eligible retirement plan within 60 days after the date on which the recipient received the distribution,

(D) if applicable, of the provisions of subsections (d) and (e) of this section, and

(E) of the provisions under which distributions from the eligible retirement plan receiving the distribution may be subject to restrictions and tax consequences which are different from those applicable to distributions from the plan making such distribution.

(2) Definitions. For purposes of this subsection—

(A) Eligible rollover distribution. The term "eligible rollover distribution" has the same meaning as when used in subsection (c) of this section, paragraph (4) of section 403(a), subparagraph (A) of section 403(b)(8), or subparagraph (A) of section 457(e)(16). Such term shall include any distribution to a designated beneficiary which would be treated as an eligible rollover distribution by reason of subsection (c)(11), or section 403(a)(4)(B), 403(b)(8)(B), or 457(e)(16)(B), if the requirements of subsection (c)(11) were satisfied.

(B) Eligible retirement plan. The term "eligible retirement plan" has the meaning given such term by subsection (c)(8)(B).

(g) Limitation on exclusion for elective deferrals.

(1) In general.

(A) Limitation. Notwithstanding subsections (e)(3) and (h)(1)(B), the elective deferrals of any individual for any taxable year shall be included in such individual's gross income to the extent the amount of such deferrals for the taxable year exceeds the applicable dollar amount. The preceding sentence shall not apply to the portion of such excess as does not exceed the designated Roth contributions of the individual for the taxable year.

(B) Applicable dollar amount. For purposes of subparagraph (A), the applicable dollar amount shall be the amount determined in accordance with the following table:

For taxable years beginning in calendar year:	The applicable dollar amount:
2002	$11,000
2003	$12,000
2004	$13,000
2005	$14,000
2006 or thereafter	$15,000

(C) Catch-up contributions. In addition to subparagraph (A), in the case of an eligible participant (as defined in section 414(v)), gross income shall not include elective deferrals in excess of the applicable dollar amount under subparagraph (B) to the extent that the amount of such elective deferrals does not exceed the applicable dollar amount under section 414(v)(2)(B)(i) for the taxable year (without regard to the treatment of the elective deferrals by an applicable employer plan under section 414(v)).

(2) Distribution of excess deferrals.

(A) In general. If any amount (hereinafter in this paragraph referred to as "excess deferrals") is included in the gross income of an individual under paragraph (1) (or would be included but for the last sentence thereof) for any taxable year—

(i) not later than the 1st March 1 following the close of the taxable year, the individual may allocate the amount of such excess deferrals among the plans under which the deferrals were made and may notify each such plan of the portion allocated to it, and

(ii) not later than the 1st April 15 following the close of the taxable year, each such plan may distribute to the individual the amount allocated to it under clause (i) (and any income allocable to such amount through the end of such taxable year).

The distribution described in clause (ii) may be made notwithstanding any other provision of law.

(B) Treatment of distribution under section 401(k). Except to the extent provided under rules prescribed by the Secretary, notwithstanding the distribution of any portion of an excess deferral from a plan under subparagraph (A)(ii), such portion shall, for purposes of applying section 401(k)(3)(A)(ii), be treated as an employer contribution.

(C) Taxation of distribution. In the case of a distribution to which subparagraph (A) applies—

(i) except as provided in clause (ii), such distribution shall not be included in gross income, and

(ii) any income on the excess deferral shall, for purposes of this chapter, be treated as earned and received in the taxable year in which such income is distributed.

No tax shall be imposed under section 72(t) on any distribution described in the preceding sentence.

(D) Partial distributions. If a plan distributes only a portion of any excess deferral and income allocable thereto, such portion shall be treated as having been distributed ratably from the excess deferral and the income.

(3) Elective deferrals. For purposes of this subsection, the term "elective deferrals" means, with respect to any taxable year, the sum of—

(A) any employer contribution under a qualified cash or deferred arrangement (as defined in section 401(k)) to the extent not includible in gross income for the taxable year under subsection (e)(3) (determined without regard to this subsection),

(B) any employer contribution to the extent not includible in gross income for the taxable year under subsection (h)(1)(B) (determined without regard to this subsection),

(C) any employer contribution to purchase an annuity contract under section 403(b) under a salary reduction agreement (within the meaning of section 3121(a)(5)(D)), and

(D) any elective employer contribution under section 408(p)(2)(A)(i).

An employer contribution shall not be treated as an elective deferral described in subparagraph (C) if under the salary reduction agreement such contribution is made pursuant to a one-time irrevocable election made by the employee at the time of initial eligibility to participate in the agreement or is made pursuant to a similar arrangement involving a one-time irrevocable election specified in regulations.

(4) Cost-of-living adjustment. In the case of taxable years beginning after December 31, 2006, the Secretary shall adjust the $15,000 amount under paragraph (1)(B) at the same time and in the same manner as under section 415(d), except that the base period shall be the calendar quarter beginning July 1, 2005, and any increase under this paragraph which is not a multiple of $500 shall be rounded to the next lowest multiple of $500.

(5) Disregard of community property laws. This subsection shall be applied without regard to community property laws.

(6) Coordination with section 72. For purposes of applying section 72, any amount includible in gross income for any taxable year under this subsection but which is not distributed from the plan during such taxable year shall not be treated as investment in the contract.

(7) Special rule for certain organizations.

(A) In general. In the case of a qualified employee of a qualified organization, with respect to employer contributions described in paragraph (3)(C) made by such organization, the limitation of paragraph (1) for any taxable year shall be increased by whichever of the following is the least:

(i) $3,000,

(ii) $15,000 reduced by the sum of—

(I) the amounts not included in gross income for prior taxable years by reason of this paragraph, plus

(II) the aggregate amount of designated Roth contributions (as defined in section 402A(c)) permitted for prior taxable years by reason of this paragraph, or

(iii) the excess of $5,000 multiplied by the number of years of service of the employee with the qualified organization over the employer contributions described in paragraph (3) made by the organization on behalf of such employee for prior taxable years (determined in the manner prescribed by the Secretary).

(B) Qualified organization. For purposes of this paragraph, the term "qualified organization" means any educational organization, hospital, home health service agency, health and welfare service agency, church, or convention or association of churches. Such term includes any organization described in section 414(e)(3)(B)(ii). Terms used in this subparagraph shall have the same meaning as when used in section 415(c)(4) (as in effect before the enactment of the Economic Growth and Tax Relief Reconciliation Act of 2001).

(C) Qualified employee. For purposes of this paragraph, the term "qualified employee" means any employee who has completed 15 years of service with the qualified organization.

(D) Years of service. For purposes of this paragraph, the term "years of service" has the meaning given such term by section 403(b).

(8) Matching contributions on behalf of self-employed individuals not treated as elective employer contributions. Except as provided in section 401(k)(3)(D)(ii), any matching contribution described in section 401(m)(4)(A) which is made on behalf of a self-employed individual (as defined in section 401(c)) shall not be treated as an elective employer contribution under a qualified cash or deferred arrangement (as defined in section 401(k)) for purposes of this title.

(h) Special rules for simplified employee pensions.

For purposes of this chapter—

(1) In general. Except as provided in paragraph (2), contributions made by an employer on behalf of an employee to an individual retirement plan pursuant to a simplified employee pension (as defined in section 408(k))—

(A) shall not be treated as distributed or made available to the employee or as contributions made by the employee, and

(B) if such contributions are made pursuant to an arrangement under section 408(k)(6) under which an employee may elect to have the employer make contributions to the simplified employee pension on behalf of the employee, shall not be treated as distributed or made available or as contributions made by the employee merely because the simplified employee pension includes provisions for such election.

(2) Limitations on employer contributions. Contributions made by an employer to a simplified employee pension with respect to an employee for any year shall be treated as distributed or made available to such employee and as contributions made by the employee to the extent such contributions exceed the lesser of—

(A) 25 percent of the compensation (within the meaning of section 414(s)) from such employer includible in the employee's gross income for the year (determined without regard to the employer contributions to the simplified employee pension), or

(B) the limitation in effect under section 415(c)(1)(A), reduced in the case of any highly compensated employee (within the meaning of section 414(q)) by the amount taken into account with respect to such employee under section 408(k)(3)(D).

(3) Distributions. Any amount paid or distributed out of an individual retirement plan pursuant to a simplified employee pension shall be included in gross income by the payee or distributee, as the case may be, in accordance with the provisions of section 408(d).

(i) Treatment of self-employed individuals.

For purposes of this section, except as otherwise provided in subparagraph (A) of subsection (d)(4), the term "employee" includes a self-employed individual (as defined in section 401(c)(1)(B)) and the employer of such individual shall be the person treated as his employer under section 401(c)(4).

(j) Effect of disposition of stock by plan on net unrealized appreciation.

(1) In general. For purposes of subsection (e)(4), in the case of any transaction to which this subsection applies, the determination of net unrealized appreciation shall be made without regard to such transaction.

(2) Transaction to which subsection applies. This subsection shall apply to any transaction in which—

(A) the plan trustee exchanges the plan's securities of the employer corporation for other such securities, or

(B) the plan trustee disposes of securities of the employer corporation and uses the proceeds of such disposition to acquire securities of the employer corporation within 90 days (or such longer period as the Secretary may prescribe), except that this subparagraph shall not apply to any employee with respect to whom a distribution of money was made during the period after such disposition and before such acquisition.

(k) Treatment of simple retirement accounts.

Rules similar to the rules of paragraphs (1) and (3) of subsection (h) shall apply to contributions and distributions with respect to a simple retirement account under section 408(p).

(l) Distributions from governmental plans for health and long-term care insurance.

(1) In general. In the case of an employee who is an eligible retired public safety officer who makes the election described in paragraph (6) with respect to any taxable year of such employee, gross income of such employee for such taxable year does not include any distribution from an eligible retirement plan maintained by the employer described in paragraph (4)(B) to the extent that the aggregate amount of such distributions does not exceed the amount paid by such employee for qualified health insurance premiums for such taxable year.

(2) Limitation. The amount which may be excluded from gross income for the taxable year by reason of paragraph (1) shall not exceed $3,000.

(3) Distributions must otherwise be includible.

(A) In general. An amount shall be treated as a distribution for purposes of paragraph (1) only to the extent that such amount would be includible in gross income without regard to paragraph (1).

(B) Application of section 72. Notwithstanding section 72, in determining the extent to which an amount is treated as a distribution for purposes of subparagraph (A), the aggregate amounts distributed from an eligible retirement plan in a taxable year (up to the amount excluded under paragraph (1)) shall be treated as includible in gross income (without regard to subparagraph (A)) to the extent that such amount does not exceed the aggregate amount which would have been so includible if all amounts to the credit of the eligible public safety officer in all eligible retirement plans maintained by the employer described in paragraph (4)(B) were distributed during such taxable year and all such plans were treated as 1 contract for purposes of determining under section 72 the aggregate amount which would have been so includible. Proper adjustments shall be made in applying section 72 to other distributions in such taxable year and subsequent taxable years.

(4) Definitions. For purposes of this subsection—

(A) Eligible retirement plan. For purposes of paragraph (1), the term "eligible retirement plan" means a governmental plan (within the meaning of section 414(d)) which is described in clause (iii), (iv), (v), or (vi) of subsection (c)(8)(B).

(B) Eligible retired public safety officer. The term "eligible retired public safety officer" means an individual who, by reason of disability or attainment of normal retirement age, is separated from service as a public safety officer with the employer who maintains the eligible retirement plan from which distributions subject to paragraph (1) are made.

(C) Public safety officer. The term "public safety officer" shall have the same meaning given such term by section 1204(9)(A) of the Omnibus Crime Control and Safe Streets Act of 1968 (42 U.S.C. 3796b(9)(A)).

(D) Qualified health insurance premiums. The term "qualified health insurance premiums" means premiums for coverage for the eligible retired public safety officer, his spouse, and dependents (as defined in section 152), by an accident or health plan or qualified long-term care insurance contract (as defined in section 7702B(b)).

(5) Special rules. For purposes of this subsection—

(A) Direct payment to insurer required. Paragraph (1) shall only apply to a distribution if payment of the premiums is made directly to the provider of the accident or health plan or qualified long-term care insurance contract by deduction from a distribution from the eligible retirement plan.

(B) Related plans treated as 1. All eligible retirement plans of an employer shall be treated as a single plan.

(6) Election described.

(A) In general. For purposes of paragraph (1), an election is described in this paragraph if the election is made by an employee after separation from service with respect to amounts not distributed from an eligible retirement plan to have amounts from such plan distributed in order to pay for qualified health insurance premiums.

(B) Special rule. A plan shall not be treated as violating the requirements of section 401, or as engaging in a prohibited transaction for purposes of section 503(b), merely because it provides for an election with respect to amounts that are otherwise distributable under the plan or merely because of a distribution made pursuant to an election described in subparagraph (A).

(7) Coordination with medical expense deduction. The amounts excluded from gross income under paragraph (1) shall not be taken into account under section 213.

(8) Coordination with deduction for health insurance costs of self-employed individuals. The amounts excluded from gross income under paragraph (1) shall not be taken into account under section 162(l).

In 2010, P.L. 111-312, Sec. 101(a)(1), substituted "December 31, 2012" for "December 31, 2010" both places it appeared in Sec. 901 of P.L. 107-16 [see below], effective as if included in the enactment of P.L. 107-16, EGTRRA, 6/7/2001.

In 2008, P.L. 110-458, Sec. 108(f)(1)(A), added "described in paragraph (8)(B)(iii)" after "eligible retirement plan" in subpara. (c)(11)(A) . . . Sec. 108(f)(1)(B), deleted "trust" before "designated beneficiary" in subpara. (c)(11)(B), effective for distributions after 12/31/2006, as if included in the provisions of Sec. 829, P.L. 109-280.

—P.L. 110-458, Sec. 108(f)(2)(A), added a sentence at the end of subpara. (f)(2)(A) . . . Sec. 108(f)(2)(B), deleted "for purposes of this subsection" in clause (c)(11)(A)(i), effective for plan yrs. begin. after 12/31/2009.

—P.L. 110-458, Sec. 108(j)(1)(A)(i), added "maintained by the employer described in paragraph (4)(B)" after "an eligible retirement plan" in para. (l)(1) . . . Sec. 108(j)(1)(A)(ii), deleted "of the employee, his spouse, or dependents (as defined in section 152)" in para. (l)(1) . . . Sec. 108(j)(1)(B)(i), added "(as defined in section 152)" after "dependents" in subpara. (l)(4)(D) . . . Sec. 108(j)(1)(B)(ii), substituted "health plan" for "health insurance plan" in subpara. (l)(4)(D) . . . Sec. 108(j)(1)(C), substituted "health plan" for "health insurance plan" in subpara. (l)(5)(A) . . . Sec. 108(j)(2), substituted "all amounts to the credit of the eligible public safety officer in all eligible retirement plans maintained by the employer described in paragraph (4)(B) were distributed during such taxable year and all such plans were treated as 1 contract for purposes of determining under section 72 the aggregate amount which would have been so includible" for "all amounts distributed from all eligible retirement plans were treated as 1 contract for purposes of determining the inclusion of such distribution under section 72" in subpara. (l)(3)(B), effective for distributions in tax. yrs. begin. after 12/31/2006, as if included in the provisions of Sec. 845, P.L. 109-280.

—P.L. 110-458, Sec. 109(b)(3), added "through the end of such taxable year" after "such amount" in clause (g)(2)(A)(ii), effective for plan yrs. begin. after 12/31/2007, as if included in the provisions of Sec. 902, P.L. 109-280.

—P.L. 110-458, Sec. 201(b), added flush language at the end of para. (c)(4), effective for calendar yrs. begin. after 12/31/2008. Sec. 201(c)(2) of this Act provides:

"(2) Provisions relating to plan or contract amendments.

"(A) In general. If this paragraph applies to any pension plan or contract amendment, such pension plan or contract shall not fail to be treated as being operated in accordance with the terms of the plan during the period described in subparagraph (B)(ii) solely because the plan operates in accordance with this section.

"(B) Amendments to which paragraph applies.

"(i) In general. This paragraph shall apply to any amendment to any pension plan or annuity contract which—

"(I) is made pursuant to the amendments made by this section, and

"(II) is made on or before the last day of the first plan year beginning on or after January 1, 2011. In the case of a governmental plan, subclause (II) shall be applied by substituting '2012' for '2011'.

"(ii) Conditions. This paragraph shall not apply to any amendment unless during the period beginning on the effective date of the amendment and ending on December 31, 2009, the plan or contract is operated as if such plan or contract amendment were in effect.

In 2007, P.L. 110-172, Sec. 8(a)(1), substituted 'permitted for prior taxable years by reason of this paragraph' for 'for prior taxable years' in subclause (g)(7)(A)(ii)(II), effective for tax. yrs. begin. after 12/31/2005.

In 2006, P.L. 109-280, Sec. 811, of this Act [relating to Sec. 901 of P.L. 107-16, see below], provides:

"Sec. 811. Pensions and individual retirement arrangement provisions of Economic Growth and Tax Relief Reconciliation Act of 2001 made permanent.

"Title IX of the Economic Growth and Tax Relief Reconciliation Act of 2001 shall not apply to the provisions of, and amendments made by, subtitles A through F of title VI of such Act (relating to pension and individual retirement arrangement provisions)."

—P.L. 109-280, Sec. 822(a)(1), substituted "or to an annuity contract described in section 403(b) and such trust or contract provides for separate accounting" for "which is part of a plan which is a defined contribution plan and which agrees to separately account" in subpara. (c)(2)(A) . . . Sec. 822(a)(2), added "(and earnings thereon)" after "so transferred" in subpara. (c)(2)(A), effective for tax. yrs. begin. after 12/31/2006.

—P.L. 109-280, Sec. 829(a)(1), added para. (c)(11), effective for distributions after 12/31/2006.

—P.L. 109-280, Sec. 845(a), added subsec. (l), effective for distributions in tax. yrs. begin. after 12/31/2006.

—P.L. 109-280, Sec. 1102(a)(1)(B), of this Act, reads as follows:

"(B) Modification of regulations. The Secretary of the Treasury shall modify the regulations under sections 402(f), 411(a)(11), and 417 of the Internal Revenue Code of 1986 by substituting '180 days' for '90 days' each place it appears in Treasury Regulations sections 1.402(f)-1, 1.411(a)-11(c), and 1.417(e)-1(b)."

In 2005, P.L. 109-135, Sec. 201(b)(4)(A), repealed Secs. 101 and 102 of P.L. 109-73, effective 12/21/2005.

Prior to repeal, Sec. 101 of P.L. 109-73 read as follows:

"Sec. 101. Tax-favored withdrawals from retirement plans for relief relating to Hurricane Katrina.

"(a) In general. Section 72(t) of the Internal Revenue Code of 1986 shall not apply to any qualified Hurricane Katrina distribution.

"(b) Aggregate dollar limitation.

"(1) In general. For purposes of this section, the aggregate amount of distributions received by an individual which may be treated as qualified Hurricane Katrina distributions for any taxable year shall not exceed the excess (if any) of—

"(A) $100,000, over

"(B) the aggregate amounts treated as qualified Hurricane Katrina distributions received by such individual for all prior taxable years.

"(2) Treatment of plan distributions. If a distribution to an individual would (without regard to paragraph (1)) be a qualified Hurricane Katrina distribution, a plan shall not be treated as violating any requirement of the Internal Revenue Code of 1986 merely because the plan treats such distribution as a qualified Hurricane Katrina distribution, unless the aggregate amount of such distributions from all plans maintained by the employer (and any member of any controlled group which includes the employer) to such individual exceeds $100,000.

"(3) Controlled group. For purposes of paragraph (2), the term 'controlled group' means any group treated as a single employer under subsection (b), (c), (m), or (o) of section 414 of such Code.

"(c) Amount distributed may be repaid.

"(1) In general. Any individual who receives a qualified Hurricane Katrina distribution may, at any time during the 3-year period beginning on the day after the date on which such distribution was received, make one or more contributions in an aggregate amount not to exceed the amount of such distribution to an eligible retirement plan of which such individual is a beneficiary and to which a rollover contribution of such distribution could be made under section 402(c), 403(a)(4), 403(b)(8), 408(d)(3), or 457(e)(16) of such Code, as the case may be.

"(2) Treatment of repayments of distributions from eligible retirement plans other than IRAs. For purposes of such Code, if a contribution is made pursuant to paragraph (1) with respect to a qualified Hurricane Katrina distribution from an eligible retirement plan other than an individual retirement plan, then the taxpayer shall, to the extent of the amount of the contribution, be treated as having received the qualified Hurricane Katrina distribution in an eligible rollover distribution (as defined in section 402(c)(4) of such Code) and as having transferred the amount to the eligible retirement plan in a direct trustee to trustee transfer within 60 days of the distribution.

"(3) Treatment of repayments for distributions from IRAs. For purposes of such Code, if a contribution is made pursuant to paragraph (1) with respect to a qualified Hurricane Katrina distribution from an individual retirement plan (as defined by section 7701(a)(37) of such Code), then, to the extent of the amount of the contribution, the qualified Hurricane Katrina distribution shall be treated as a distribution described in section 408(d)(3) of such Code and as having been transferred to the eligible retirement plan in a direct trustee to trustee transfer within 60 days of the distribution.

"(d) Definitions. For purposes of this section—

"(1) Qualified Hurricane Katrina distribution. Except as provided in subsection (b), the term 'qualified Hurricane Katrina distribution' means any distribution from an eligible retirement plan made on or after August 25, 2005, and before January 1, 2007, to an individual whose principal place of abode on August 28, 2005, is located in the Hurricane Katrina disaster area and who has sustained an economic loss by reason of Hurricane Katrina.

"(2) Eligible retirement plan. The term 'eligible retirement plan' shall have the meaning given such term by section 402(c)(8)(B) of such Code.

"(e) Income inclusion spread over 3 year period for qualified Hurricane Katrina distributions.

"(1) In general. In the case of any qualified Hurricane Katrina distribution, unless the taxpayer elects not to have this subsection apply for any taxable year, any amount required to be included in gross income for such taxable year shall be so included ratably over the 3-taxable year period beginning with such taxable year.

"(2) Special rule. For purposes of paragraph (1), rules similar to the rules of subparagraph (E) of section 408A(d)(3) of such Code shall apply.

"(f) Special rules.

"(1) Exemption of distributions from trustee to trustee transfer and withholding rules. For purposes of sections 401(a)(31), 402(f), and 3405 of such Code, qualified Hurricane Katrina distributions shall not be treated as eligible rollover distributions.

"(2) Qualified Hurricane Katrina distributions treated as meeting plan distribution requirements. For purposes of such Code, a qualified Hurricane Katrina distribution shall be treated as meeting the requirements of sections 401(k)(2)(B)(i), 403(b)(7)(A)(ii), 403(b)(11), and 457(d)(1)(A) of such Code."

Prior to repeal, Sec. 102 of P.L. 109-73 read as follows:

"SEC. 102. RECONTRIBUTIONS OF WITHDRAWALS FOR HOME PURCHASES CANCELLED DUE TO HURRICANE KATRINA.

"(a) Recontributions.

"(1) In general. Any individual who received a qualified distribution may, during the period beginning on August 25, 2005, and ending on February 28, 2006, make one or more contributions in an aggregate amount not to exceed the amount of such qualified distribution to an eligible retirement plan (as defined in section 402(c)(8)(B) of the Internal Revenue Code of 1986) of which such individual is a beneficiary and to which a rollover contribution of such distribution could be made under section 402(c), 403(a)(4), 403(b)(8), or 408(d)(3) of such Code, as the case may be.

"(2) Treatment of repayments. Rules similar to the rules of paragraphs (2) and (3) of section 101(c) of this Act shall apply for purposes of this section.

"(b) Qualified distribution defined. For purposes of this section, the term 'qualified distribution' means any distribution—

"(1) described in section 401(k)(2)(B)(i)(IV), 403(b)(7)(A)(ii) (but only to the extent such distribution relates to financial hardship), 403(b)(11)(B), or 72(t)(2)(F) of such Code,

"(2) received after February 28, 2005, and before August 29, 2005, and

"(3) which was to be used to purchase or construct a principal residence in the Hurricane Katrina disaster area, but which was not so purchased or constructed on account of Hurricane Katrina."

—P.L. 109-135, Sec. 407(a)(1), amended clause (g)(7)(A)(ii) . . . Sec. 407(a)(2), added "to" after "shall not apply" in subpara. (g)(1)(A), effective for tax. yrs. begin. after 12/31/2005 as if included in Sec. 617 of the Economic Growth and Tax Relief Reconciliation Act of 2001, P.L. 107-16.

Prior to amendment, clause (g)(7)(A)(ii) read as follows:

"(ii) $15,000 reduced by amounts not included in gross income for prior taxable years by reason of this paragraph, or"

In 2002, P.L. 107-358, Sec. 2, added subsec. (c) in Sec. 901 of P.L. 107-16 [see below], effective 12/17/2002.

—P.L. 107-147, Sec. 411(l)(3), substituted "25 percent" for "15 percent" in subpara. (h)(2)(A), effective for yrs. begin. after 12/31/2001.

—P.L. 107-147, Sec. 411(o)(1), added subpara. (g)(1)(C), effective for contributions in tax. yrs. begin. after 12/31/2001.

—P.L. 107-147, Sec. 411(p)(6), substituted "2001)." for "2001." in subpara. (g)(7)(B), effective for yrs. begin. after 12/31/2001.

—P.L. 107-147, Sec. 411(q)(2), added a flush sentence at the end of para. (c)(2), effective for distributions made after 12/31/2001.

In 2001, P.L. 107-16, Sec. 611(d)(1), amended para. (g)(1) . . . Sec. 611(d)(2), amended para. (g)(5) . . . Sec. 611(d)(3)(A), deleted para. (g)(4) and redesignated paras. (g)(5)-(9) as (4)-(8), effective for yrs. begin. after 12/31/2001. Sec. 611(i)(3) of this Act, provides:

"(3) Special rule. In the case of plan that, on June 7, 2001, incorporated by reference the limitation of section 415(b)(1)(A) of the Internal Revenue Code of 1986, section 411(d)(6) of such Code and section 204(g)(1) of the Employee Retirement Income Security Act of 1974 do not apply to a plan amendment that—

"(A) is adopted on or before June 30, 2002,

"(B) reduces benefits to the level that would have applied without regard to the amendments made by subsection (a) of this section, and

"(C) is effective no earlier than the years described in paragraph (2)."

Prior to amendment, para. (g)(1) read as follows:

"(1) In general. Notwithstanding subsections (e)(3) and (h)(1)(B), the elective deferrals of any individual for any taxable year shall be included in such individual's gross income to the extent the amount of such deferrals for the taxable year exceeds $7,000."

Prior to amendment, para. (g)(5) read as follows:

"(5) Cost-of-living adjustment. The Secretary shall adjust the $7,000 amount under paragraph (1) at the same time and in the same manner as under section 415(d); except that any increase under this paragraph which is not a multiple of $500 shall be rounded to the next lowest multiple of $500."

Prior to deletion, para. (g)(4) read as follows:

"(4) Increase in limit for amounts contributed under section 403(b) contracts. The limitation under paragraph (1) shall be increased (but not to an amount in excess of $9,500) by the amount of any employer contributions for the taxable year described in paragraph (3)(C)."

—P.L. 107-16, Sec. 617(b)(1), added "The preceding sentence shall not apply the portion of such excess as does not exceed the designated Roth contributions of the individual for the taxable year." at the end of subpara. (g)(1)(A) [as added by Sec. 611(d)(1) of this Act, see above] . . . Sec. 617(b)(2), added "(or would be included but for the last sentence thereof)" after "paragraph (1)" in subpara. (g)(2)(A) . . . Sec. 617(c), added "If any portion of an eligible rollover distribution is attributable to payments or distributions from a designated Roth account (as defined in section 402A), an eligible retirement plan with respect to such portion shall include only another designated Roth account and a Roth IRA." at the end of subpara. (c)(8)(B), effective for tax. yrs. begin. after 12/31/2005.

—P.L. 107-16, Sec. 632(a)(3)(G), added "(as in effect before the enactment of the Economic Growth and Tax Relief Reconciliation Act of 2001" before the period at the end of subpara. (g)(7)(B) [as redesignated by Sec. 611(d)(3)(A) of this Act, see above], effective for yrs. begin. after 12/31/2001.

—P.L. 107-16, Sec. 636(b)(1), amended subpara. (c)(4)(C), effective for distributions made after 12/31/2001.

Prior to amendment, subpara. (c)(4)(C) read as follows:

"(C) any hardship distribution described in section 401(k)(2)(B)(i)(IV)."

—P.L. 107-16, Sec. 641(a)(2)(A), deleted "and" at the end of clause (c)(8)(B)(iii), substituted ", and" for the period at the end of clause (c)(8)(B)(iv), and added clause (c)(8)(B)(v) . . . Sec. 641(a)(2)(B), added para. (c)(10) . . . Sec. 641(b)(2), deleted "and" at the end of clause (c)(8)(B)(iv) [as amended by Sec. 641(a)(2)(A) of this Act, see above], substituted ", and" for the period at the end of clause (c)(8)(B)(v), and added clause (c)(8)(B)(vi) . . . Sec. 641(c), deleted "and" at the end of subpara. (f)(1)(C), substituted ", and" for the period at the end of subpara. (f)(1)(D), and added subpara. (f)(1)(E) . . . Sec. 641(d), deleted "; except that a trust or plan described in clause (iii) or (iv) of paragraph (8)(B) shall not be treated as an eligible retirement plan with respect to such distribution" after "were the employee" in para. (c)(9) . . . Sec. 641(e)(4), substituted ", paragraph (4) of section 403(a), subparagraph (A) of section 403(b)(8), or subparagraph (A) of section 457(e)(16)" for "or paragraph (4) of section 403(a)" in subpara. (f)(2)(A) . . . Sec. 641(e)(5), deleted "from an eligible retirement plan" after "rollover distribution" in para. (f)(1) . . . Sec. 641(e)(6), substituted "an eligible retirement plan" for "another eligible retirement plan" in subparas. (f)(1)(A) and (B), effective for distributions after 12/31/2001. Sec. 641(f)(2) and (3) of this Act, provides:

"(2) Reasonable notice. No penalty shall be imposed on a plan for the failure to provide the information required by the amendment made by subsection (c) with respect to any distribution made before the date that is 90 days after the date on which the Secretary of the Treasury issues a safe harbor rollover notice after the date of the enactment of this Act, if the administrator of such plan makes a reasonable attempt to comply with such requirement.

"(3) Special rule. Notwithstanding any other provision of law, subsections (h)(3) and (h)(5) of section 1122 of the Tax Reform Act of 1986 shall not apply to any distribution from an eligible retirement plan (as defined in clause (iii) or (iv) of section 402(c)(8)(B) of the Internal Revenue Code of 1986) on behalf of an individual if there was a rollover to such plan on behalf of such individual which is permitted solely by reason of any amendment made by this section."

—P.L. 107-16, Sec. 643(a), amended para. (c)(2), effective for distributions made after 12/31/2001.

Prior to amendment, para. (c)(2) read as follows:

"(2) Maximum amount which may be rolled over. In the case of any eligible rollover distribution, the maximum amount transferred to which paragraph (1) applies shall not exceed the portion of such distribution which is includible in gross income (determined without regard to paragraph (1))."

—P.L. 107-16, Sec. 644(a), amended para. (c)(3), effective for distributions after 12/31/2001.

Prior to amendment, para. (c)(3) read as follows:

"(3) Transfer must be made within 60 days of receipt. Paragraph (1) shall not apply to any transfer of a distribution made after the 60th day following the day on which the distributee received the property distributed."

—P.L. 107-16, Sec. 657(b), added "and that the automatic distribution by direct transfer applies to certain distributions in accordance with section 401(a)(31)(B)" before the comma at the end of subpara. (f)(1)(A), effective for distributions made after final regulations implementing Sec. 657(c)(2)(A) of this Act are prescribed. Sec. 657(c)(2)(A) of this Act, reads as follows:

"(A) Automatic rollover safe harbor. Not later than 3 years after the date of enactment of this Act, the Secretary of Labor shall prescribe regulations providing for safe harbors under which the designation of an institution and investment of funds in accordance with section 401(a)(31)(B) of the Internal Revenue Code of 1986 is deemed to satisfy the fiduciary requirements of section 404(a) of the Employee Retirement Income Security Act of 1974 (29 U.S.C. 1104(a))."

—P.L. 107-16, Sec. 901, of this Act [as amended by Sec. 2 of P.L. 107-358, and Sec. 101(a)(1) of P.L. 111-312, and as related to Sec. 811 of P.L. 109-280, see above], reads as follows:

"SEC. 901. SUNSET OF PROVISIONS OF ACT.

"(a) In general. All provisions of, and amendments made by, this Act shall not apply—

"(1) to taxable, plan, or limitation years beginning after December 31, 2012, or

"(2) in the case of title V, to estates of decedents dying, gifts made, or generation skipping transfers, after December 31, 2012.

"(b) Application of certain laws. The Internal Revenue Code of 1986 and the Employee Retirement Income Security Act of 1974 shall be applied and administered to years, estates, gifts, and transfers described in subsection (a) as if the provisions and amendments described in subsection (a) had never been enacted.

"(c) Exception. Subsection (a) shall not apply to section 803 (relating to no federal income tax on restitution received by victims of the Nazi regime or their heirs or estates)."

In 1998, P.L. 105-206, Sec. 6005(c)(2)(A), deleted "and" at the end of subpara. (c)(4)(A), substituted ", and" for the period at the end of subpara. (c)(4)(B) and added subpara. (c)(4)(C), effective for distributions after 12/31/98.

In 1997, P.L. 105-34, Sec. 1501(a), added para. (g)(9), effective for yrs. begin. after 12/31/97.

—P.L. 105-34, Sec. 1509, of this Act, relating to the clarification of disqualification rules relating to acceptance of rollover contributions is reproduced in notes following Code Sec. 401.

In 1996, P.L. 104-188, Sec. 1401(a), amended subsec. (d) . . . Sec. 1401(b)(1), amended subpara. (e)(4)(D) . . . Sec. 1401(b)(2), deleted para. (c)(10) . . . Sec. 1401(b)(13), deleted para. (e)(5), effective for tax. yrs. begin. after 12/31/99. For transitional rules, see Sec. 1401(c)(2), of this Act, which reads as follows:

"(2) Retention of certain transition rules. The amendments made by this section shall not apply to any distribution for which the taxpayer is eligible to elect the benefits of section 1122(h)(3) or (5) of the Tax Reform Act of 1986. Notwithstanding the preceding sentence, individuals who elect such benefits after December 31, 1999, shall not be eligible for 5-year averaging under section 402(d) of the Internal Revenue Code of 1986 (as in effect immediately before such amendments).''

Prior to amendment, subsec. (d) read as follows:

"(d) Tax on lump sum distributions.

"(1) Imposition of separate tax on lump sum distributions.

"(A) Separate tax. There is hereby imposed a tax (in the amount determined under subparagraph (B)) on a lump sum distribution.

"(B) Amount of tax. The amount of tax imposed by subparagraph (A) for any taxable year is an amount equal to 5 times the tax which would be imposed by subsection (c) of section 1 if the recipient were an individual referred to in such subsection and the taxable income were an amount equal to ⅕ of the excess of—

"(i) the total taxable amount of the lump sum distribution for the taxable year, over

"(ii) the minimum distribution allowance.

"(C) Minimum distribution allowance. For purposes of this paragraph, the minimum distribution allowance for any taxable year is an amount equal to—

"(i) the lesser of $10,000 or one-half of the total taxable amount of the lump sum distribution for the taxable year, reduced (but not below zero) by

"(ii) 20 percent of the amount (if any) by which such total taxable amount exceeds $20,000.

"(D) Liability for tax. The recipient shall be liable for the tax imposed by this paragraph.

"(2) Distributions of annuity contracts.

"(A) In general. In the case of any recipient of a lump sum distribution for any taxable year, if the distribution (or any part thereof) is an annuity contract, the total taxable amount of the distribution shall be aggregated for purposes of computing the tax imposed by paragraph (1)(A), except that the amount of tax so computed shall be reduced (but not below zero) by that portion of the tax on the aggregate total taxable amount which is attributable to annuity contracts.

"(B) Beneficiaries. For purposes of this paragraph, a beneficiary of a trust to which a lump sum distribution is made shall be treated as the recipient of such distribution if the beneficiary is an employee (including an employee within the meaning of section 401(c)(1)) with respect to the plan under which the distribution is made or if the beneficiary is treated as the owner of such trust for purposes of subpart E of part I of subchapter J.

"(C) Annuity contracts. For purposes of this paragraph, in the case of the distribution of an annuity contract, the taxable amount of such distribution shall be deemed to be the current actuarial value of the contract, determined on the date of such distribution.

"(D) Trusts. In the case of a lump sum distribution with respect to any individual which is made only to 2 or more trusts, the tax imposed by paragraph (1)(A) shall be computed as if such distribution was made to a single trust, but the liability for such tax shall be apportioned among such trusts according to the relative amounts received by each.

"(E) Regulations. The Secretary shall prescribe such regulations as may be necessary to carry out the purposes of this paragraph.

"(3) Allowance of deduction. The total taxable amount of a lump sum distribution for any taxable year shall be allowed as a deduction from gross income for such taxable year, but only to the extent included in the taxpayer's gross income for such taxable year.

"(4) Definitions and special rules.

"(A) Lump sum distribution. For purposes of this section and section 403, the term 'lump sum distribution' means the distribution or payment within 1 taxable year of the recipient of the balance to the credit of an employee which becomes payable to the recipient—

"(i) on account of the employee's death,

"(ii) after the employee attains age 59½,

"(iii) on account of the employee's separation from the service, or

"(iv) after the employee has become disabled (within the meaning of section 72(m)(7)),

from a trust which forms a part of a plan described in section 401(a) and which is exempt from tax under section 501 or from a plan described in section 403(a). Clause (iii) of this subparagraph shall be applied only with respect to an individual who is an employee without regard to section 401(c)(1), and clause (iv) shall be applied only with respect to an employee within the meaning of section 401(c)(1). A distribution of an annuity contract from a trust or annuity plan referred to in the first sentence of this subparagraph shall be treated as a lump sum distribution. For purposes of this subparagraph, a distribution to 2 or more trusts shall be treated as a distribution to 1 recipient. For purposes of this subsection, the balance to the credit of the employee does not include the accumulated deductible employee contributions under the plan (within the meaning of section 72(o)(5)).

"(B) Averaging to apply to 1 lump sum distribution after age 59½. Paragraph (1) shall apply to a lump sum distribution with respect to an employee under subparagraph (A) only if—

"(i) such amount is received on or after the date on which the employee has attained age 59 ½, and

"(ii) the taxpayer elects for the taxable year to have all such amounts received during such taxable year so treated.

Not more than 1 election may be made under this subparagraph by any taxpayer with respect to any employee. No election may be made under this subparagraph by any taxpayer other than an individual, an estate, or a trust. In the case of a lump sum distribution made with respect to an employee to 2 or more trusts, the election under this subparagraph shall be made by the personal representative of the taxpayer.

"(C) Aggregation of certain trusts and plans. For purposes of determining the balance to the credit of an employee under subparagraph (A)—

"(i) all trusts which are part of a plan shall be treated as a single trust, all pension plans maintained by the employer shall be treated as a single plan, all profit-sharing plans maintained by the employer shall be treated as a single plan, and all stock bonus plans maintained by the employer shall be treated as a single plan, and

"(ii) trusts which are not qualified trusts under section 401(a) and annuity contracts which do not satisfy the requirements of section 404(a)(2) shall not be taken into account.

"(D) Total taxable amount. For purposes of this section and section 403, the term 'total taxable amount' means, with respect to a lump sum distribution, the amount of such distribution which exceeds the sum of—

"(i) the amounts considered contributed by the employee (determined by applying section 72(f)), reduced by any amounts previously distributed which were not includible in gross income, and

"(ii) the net unrealized appreciation attributable to that part of the distribution which consists of the securities of the employer corporation so distributed.

"(E) Community property laws. The provisions of this subsection, other than paragraph (3), shall be applied without regard to community property laws.

"(F) Minimum period of service. For purposes of this subsection, no amount distributed to an employee from or under a plan may be treated as a lump sum distribution under subparagraph (A) unless the employee has been a participant in the plan for 5 or more taxable years before the taxable year in which such amounts are distributed.

"(G) Amounts subject to penalty. This subsection shall not apply to amounts described in subparagraph (A) of section 72(m)(5) to the extent that section 72(m)(5) applies to such amounts.

"(H) Balance to credit of employee not to include amounts payable under qualified domestic relations order. For purposes of this subsection, the balance to the credit of an employee shall not include any amount payable to an alternate payee under a qualified domestic relations order (within the meaning of section 414(p)).

"(I) Transfers to cost-of-living arrangement not treated as distribution. For purposes of this subsection, the balance to the credit of an employee under a defined contribution plan shall not include any amount transferred from such defined contribution plan to a qualified cost-of-living arrangement (within the meaning of section 415(k)(2)) under a defined benefit plan.

"(J) Lump sum distributions of alternate payees. If any distribution or payment of the balance to the credit of an employee would be treated as a lump sum distribution, then, for purposes of this subsection, the payment under a qualified domestic relations order (within the meaning of section 414(p)) of the balance to the credit of an alternate payee who is the spouse or former spouse of the employee shall be treated as a lump sum distribution. For purposes of this subparagraph, the balance to the credit of the alternate payee shall not include any amount payable to the employee.

"(K) Treatment of portion not rolled over. If any portion of a lump sum distribution is transferred in a transfer to which subsection (c) applies, paragraphs (1) and (3) shall not apply with respect to the distribution.

"(L) Securities. For purposes of this subsection, the terms 'securities' and 'securities of the employer corporation' have the respective meanings provided by subsection (e)(4)(E).

"(5) Special rule where portions of lump sum distribution attributable to rollover of bond purchased under qualified bond purchase plan. If any portion of a lump sum distribution is attributable to a transfer described in section 405(d)(3)(A)(ii) (as in effect before its repeal by the Tax Reform Act of 1984), paragraphs (1) and (3) of this subsection shall not apply to such portion.

"(6) Treatment of potential future vesting.

"(A) In general. For purposes of determining whether any distribution which becomes payable to the recipient on account of the employee's separation from service is a lump sum distribution, the balance to the credit of the employee shall be determined without regard to any increase in vesting which may occur if the employee is reemployed by the employer.

"(B) Recapture in certain cases. If—

"(i) an amount is treated as a lump sum distribution by reason of subparagraph (A),

"(ii) special lump sum treatment applies to such distribution,

"(iii) the employee is subsequently reemployed by the employer, and

"(iv) as a result of services performed after being so reemployed, there is an increase in the employee's vesting for benefits accrued before the separation referred to in subparagraph (A),

under regulations prescribed by the Secretary, the tax imposed by this chapter for the taxable year (in which the increase in vesting first occurs) shall be increased by the reduction in tax which resulted from the special lump sum treatment (and any election under paragraph (4)(B) shall not be taken into account for purposes of determining whether the employee may make another election under paragraph (4)(B)).

"(C) Special lump sum treatment. For purposes of this paragraph, special lump sum treatment applies to any distribution if any portion of such distribution is taxed under the subsection by reason of an election under paragraph (4)(B).

"(D) Vesting. For purposes of this paragraph, the term 'vesting' means the portion of the accrued benefits derived from employer contributions to which the participant has a nonforfeitable right.

"(7) Coordination with foreign tax credit limitations. Subsections (a), (b), and (c) of section 904 shall be applied separately with respect to any lump sum distribution on which tax is imposed under paragraph (1), and the amount of such distribution shall be treated as the taxable income for purposes of such separate application."

Code Sec. 402 — Employee benefit plans

Prior to amendment, subpara. (e)(4)(D) read as follows:

"(D) Lump sum distribution. For purposes of this paragraph, the term 'lump sum distribution' has the meaning given such term by subsection (d)(4)(A) (without regard to subsection (d)(4)(F))."

Prior to deletion, para. (c)(10) read as follows:

"(10) Denial of averaging for subsequent distributions. If paragraph (1) applies to any distribution paid to any employee, paragraphs (1) and (3) of subsection (d) shall not apply to any distribution (paid after such distribution) of the balance to the credit of the employee under the plan under which the preceding distribution was made (or under any other plan which, under subsection (d) (4)(C), would be aggregated with such plan)."

Prior to deletion, para. (e)(5) read as follows:

"(5) Taxability of beneficiary of certain foreign situs trusts. For purposes of subsections (a), (b), and (c), a stock bonus, pension, or profit-sharing trust which would qualify for exemption from tax under section 501(a) except for the fact that it is a trust created or organized outside the United States shall be treated as if it were a trust exempt from tax under section 501(a)."

—P.L. 104-188, Sec. 1421(b)(3)(A), added subsec. (k) . . . Sec. 1421(b)(9)(B), deleted "and" at the end of subpara. (g)(3)(B), substituted ", and" for the period at the end of subpara. (g)(3)(C), and added subpara. (g)(3)(D), effective for tax. yrs. begin. after 12/31/96.

—P.L. 104-188, Sec. 1450(a)(2), added "or which is part of a salary reduction agreement under section 403(b)" after "section 401(k)(2))" in para. (e)(3), effective for tax. yrs. begin. after 12/31/95.

—P.L. 104-188, Sec. 1704(t)(68), substituted "subsection (e)(3)" for "subsection (a)(8)" in subpara. (g)(3)(A), effective 8/20/96.

In 1994, P.L. 103-465, Sec. 732(c), added "; except that any increase under this paragraph which is not a multiple of $500 shall be rounded to the next lowest multiple of $500" before the period at the end of para. (g)(5), effective for yrs. begin. after 12/31/94, except as provided in Sec. 732(e)(2) of this Act, which reads as follows:

"(2) Rounding not to result in decreases. The amendments made by this section providing for the rounding of indexed amounts shall not apply to any year to the extent the rounding would require the indexed amount to be reduced below the amount in effect for years beginning in 1994."

In 1992, P.L. 102-318, Sec. 521(a), amended so much of Code Sec. 402 as preceded subsec. (g) . . . Sec. 521(b)(9), substituted "subsections (e)(3)" for "subsections (a)(8)" in para. (g)(1) . . . Sec. 521(b)(10), substituted "subsection (d)(4)" for "subsection (e)(4)" in subsec. (i) . . . Sec. 521(b)(11), substituted "(e)(4)" for "(a)(1) or (e)(4)(J)" in para. (j)(1), effective for distributions after 12/31/92. For special rule, see Sec. 521(e)(2) of this Act which reads as follows:

"(2) Special rule for partial distributions. For purposes of section 402(a)(5)(D)(i)(II) of the Internal Revenue Code of 1986 (as in effect before the amendments made by this section), a distribution before January 1, 1993, which is made before or at the same time as a series of periodic payments shall not be treated as one of such series if it is not substantially equal in amount to other payments in such series."

Prior to amendment, so much of Code Sec. 402 as preceded subsec. (g) read as follows:

"SEC. 402. TAXABILITY OF BENEFICIARY OF EMPLOYEES' TRUST.

"(a) Taxability of beneficiary of exempt trust.

"(1) General rule. Except as provided in paragraph (4), the amount actually distributed to any distributee by any employees' trust described in section 401(a) which is exempt from tax under section 501(a) shall be taxable to him, in the year in which so distributed, under section 72 (relating to annuities). The amount actually distributed to any distributee shall not include net unrealized appreciation in securities of the employer corporation attributable to the amount contributed by the employee (other than deductible employee contributions within the meaning of section 72(o)(5)). Such net unrealized appreciation and the resulting adjustments to basis of such securities shall be determined in accordance with regulations prescribed by the Secretary.

"(2) [Repealed].

"(3) Definitions. For purposes of this subsection—

"(A) The term 'securities' means only shares of stock and bonds or debentures issued by a corporation with interest coupons or in registered form.

"(B) The term 'securities of the employer corporation' includes securities of a parent or subsidiary corporation (as defined in subsections (e) and (f) of section 424) of the employer corporation.

"(4) Distributions by United States to nonresident aliens. The amount includible under paragraph (1) of this subsection in the gross income of a nonresident alien individual with respect to a distribution made by the United States in respect of services performed by an employee of the United States shall not exceed an amount which bears the same ratio to the amount includible in gross income without regard to this paragraph as—

"(A) the aggregate basic pay paid by the United States to such employee for such services, reduced by the amount of such basic pay which was not includible in gross income by reason of being from sources without the United States, bears to

"(B) the aggregate basic pay paid by the United States to such employee for such services.

In the case of distributions under the civil service retirement laws, the term 'basic pay' shall have the meaning provided in section 8331(3) of title 5, United States Code.

"(5) Rollover amounts.

"(A) General rule. If—

"(i) any portion of the balance to the credit of an employee in a qualified trust is paid to him,

"(ii) the employee transfers any portion of the property he receives in such distribution to an eligible retirement plan, and

"(iii) in the case of a distribution of property other than money, the amount so transferred consists of the property distributed,

then such distribution (to the extent so transferred) shall not be includible in gross income for the taxable year in which paid.

"(B) Maximum amount which may be rolled over. In the case of any qualified total distribution, the maximum amount transferred to which subparagraph (A) applies shall not exceed the fair market value of all the property the employee receives in the distribution, reduced by the employee contributions (other than accumulated deductible employee contributions within the meaning of section 72(o)(5)). In the case of any partial distribution, the maximum amount transferred to which subparagraph (A) applies shall not exceed the portion of such distribution which is includible in gross income (determined without regard to subparagraph (A)).

"(C) Transfer must be made within 60 days of receipt. Subparagraph (A) shall not apply to any transfer of a distribution made after the 60th day following the day on which the employee received the property distributed.

"(D) Special rules for partial distributions.

"(i) Requirements. Subparagraph (A) shall apply to a partial distribution only if—

"(I) such distribution is payable as provided in clause (i), (iii), or (iv) of subsection (e)(4)(A) (without regard to the second sentence thereof) and is of an amount equal to at least 50 percent of the balance to the credit of the employee in a qualified trust (determined immediately before such distribution and without regard to subsection (e)(4)(C)),

"(II) such distribution is not one of a series of periodic payments, and

"(III) the employee elects (at such time and in such manner as the Secretary shall by regulations prescribe) to have subparagraph (A) apply to such partial distribution.

For purposes of subclause (I), the balance to the credit of the employee shall not include any accumulated deductible employee contributions (within the meaning of section 72(o)(5)). Any distribution described in section 401(a)(28)(B)(ii) shall be treated as meeting the requirements of subclauses (I) and (II).

"(ii) Partial distributions may be transferred only to individual retirement plans. In the case of a partial distribution, a trust or plan described in subclause (III) or (IV) of subparagraph (E)(iv) shall not be treated as an eligible retirement plan.

"(iii) Denial of averaging for subsequent distributions. If an election under clause (i) is made with respect to any partial distribution paid to any employee, paragraphs (1) and (3) of subsection (e) shall not apply to any distribution (paid after such partial distribution) of the balance to the credit of such employee under the plan under which such partial distribution was made (or under any other plan which, under subsection (e)(4)(C), would be aggregated with such plan).

"(iv) Special rule for unrealized appreciation. If an election under clause (i) is made with respect to any partial distribution, the second and third sentences of paragraph (1) shall not apply to such distribution.

"(E) Definitions. For purposes of this paragraph—

"(i) Qualified total distribution. The term 'qualified total distribution' means 1 or more distributions—

"(I) within 1 taxable year of the employee on account of a termination of the plan of which the trust is a part or, in the case of a profit-sharing or stock bonus plan, a complete discontinuance of contributions under such plan,

"(II) which constitute a lump sum distribution within the meaning of subsection (e)(4)(A) (determined without reference to subparagraphs (B) and (H) of subsection (e)(4)), or

"(III) which constitute a distribution of accumulated deductible employee contributions (within the meaning of section 72(o)(5)).

"(ii) Employee contributions. The term 'employee contributions' means—

"(I) the excess of the amounts considered contributed by the employee (determined by applying section 72(F)), over

"(II) any amounts theretofore distributed to the employee which were not includible in gross income (determined without regard to this paragraph).

"(iii) Qualified trust. The term 'qualified trust' means an employees' trust described in section 401(a) which is exempt from tax under section 501(a).

"(iv) Eligible retirement plan. The term 'eligible retirement plan' means—

"(I) an individual retirement account described in section 408(a),

"(II) an individual retirement annuity described in section 408(b) (other than an endowment contract),

"(III) a qualified trust, and

"(IV) an annuity plan described in section 403(a).

"(v) Partial distribution. The term 'partial distribution' means any distribution to an employee of all or any portion of the balance to the credit of such employee in a qualified trust; except that such term shall not include any distribution which is a qualified total distribution.

"(F) Transfer treated as rollover contribution under section 408. For purposes of this title, a transfer resulting in any portion of a distribution being excluded from gross income under subparagraph (A) to an eligible retirement plan described in subclause (I) or (II) of subparagraph (E)(iv) shall be treated as a rollover contribution described in section 408(d)(3).

"(G) Required distributions not eligible for rollover treatment. Subparagraph (A) shall not apply to any distribution to the extent such distribution is required under section 401(a)(9).

"(6) Special rollover rules.

"(A) Time of termination. For purposes of paragraph (5)(E)(i), a complete discontinuance of contributions under a profit-sharing or stock bonus plan shall be deemed to occur on the day the plan administrator notifies the Secretary (in accordance with regulations prescribed by the Secretary) that all contributions to the plan have been completely discontinued. For purposes of section 411(d)(3), the plan shall be considered to be terminated no later than the day such notice is filed with the Secretary.

"(B) Sale of subsidiary or assets. For purposes of paragraph (5)(E)(i)—

"(i) A payment of the balance to the credit of an employee of a corporation (hereinafter referred to as the employer corporation) which is a subsidiary corporation (within the meaning of section 424(f)) or which is a member of a controlled group of corporations (within the meaning of section 1563(a), determined by substituting '50 percent' for '80 percent' each place it appears therein) in connection with the liquidation, sale, or other means of terminating the parent-subsidiary or controlled group relationship of the employer corporation with the parent corporation or controlled group, or

"(ii) a payment of the balance to the credit of an employee of a corporation (hereinafter referred to as the acquiring corporation) in connection with the sale or other transfer to the acquiring corporation of all or substantially all of the assets used by the previous employer of the employee (hereinafter referred to as the selling corporation) in a trade or business conducted by the selling corporation,

shall be treated as a payment or distribution on account of the termination of the plan with respect to such employee if the employees of the employer corporation or the acquiring corporation (whichever applies) are not active participants in such plan at the time of such payment or distribution. For purposes of this subparagraph, in no event shall a payment or distribution be deemed to be in connection with a sale or other transfer of assets, or a liquidation, sale, or other means of terminating such parent-subsidiary or controlled group relationship, if such payment or distribution is made later than the end of the second calendar year after the calendar year in which occurs such sale or other transfer of assets, or such liquidation, sale, or other means of terminating such parent-subsidiary or controlled group relationship.

"(C) Treatment of portion not rolled over. If any portion of a lump sum distribution is transferred in a transfer to which paragraph (5)(A) applies, paragraphs (1) and (3) of subsection (e) shall not apply with respect to such lump sum distribution.

"(D) Sales of distributed property. For purposes of subparagraphs (5) and (7)—

"(i) Transfer of proceeds from sale of distributed property treated as transfer of distributed property. The transfer of an amount equal to any portion of the proceeds from the sale of property received in the distribution shall be treated as the transfer of property received in the distribution.

"(ii) Proceeds attributable to increase in value. The excess of fair market value of property on sale over its fair market value on distribution shall be treated as property received in the distribution.

"(iii) Designation where amount of distribution exceeds rollover contribution. In any case where part or all of the distribution consists of property other than money, the taxpayer may designate—

"(I) the portion of the money or other property which is to be treated as attributable to employee contributions (or, in the case of a partial distribution, the amount not includible in gross income), and

"(II) the portion of the money or other property which is to be treated as included in the rollover contribution.

Any designation under this clause for a taxable year shall be made not later than the time prescribed by law for filing the return for such taxable year (including extensions thereof). Any such designation, once made, shall be irrevocable.

"(iv) Treatment where no designation. In any case where part or all of the distribution consists of property other than money and the taxpayer fails to make a designation under clause (iii) within the time provided therein, then—

"(I) the portion of the money or other property which is to be treated as attributable to employee contributions (or, in the case of a partial distribution, the amount not includible in gross income), and

"(II) the portion of the money or other property which is to be treated as included in the rollover contribution

shall be determined on a ratable basis.

"(v) Nonrecognition of gain or loss. In the case of any sale described in clause (i), to the extent that an amount equal to the proceeds is transferred pursuant to paragraph (5)(B) or (7) (as the case by [may] be), neither gain nor loss on such sale shall be recognized.

"(E) Special rule where employer maintains money purchase pension plan and other pension plan.

"(i) In general. In the case of any distribution from a money purchase pension plan which is maintained by an employer, for purposes of paragraph (5)(D) or (5)(E)(i)(II), subsection (e)(4)(C) shall be applied by not taking into account any pension plan maintained by such employer which is not a money purchase pension plan. The preceding sentence shall not apply to any distribution which is a qualified total distribution without regard to this subparagraph.

"(ii) Treatment of subsequent distributions. If—

"(I) any distribution of the balance to the credit of an employee from a money purchase pension plan maintained by an employer is treated as a qualifying rollover distribution by reason of clause (i), and

"(II) any portion of such distribution is transferred in a transfer to which paragraph (5)(A) applies,

then paragraphs (1) and (3) of subsection (e) shall not apply to any distribution (after the taxable year in which the distribution described in subparagraph (A) of paragraph (5) is made) of the balance to the credit of such employee from any other pension plan maintained by such employer.

"(F) Qualified domestic relations orders. If—

"(i) within 1 taxable year of the recipient, the balance to the credit of the recipient by reason of any qualified domestic relations order (within the meaning of section 414(p)) is distributed or paid to the recipient,

"(ii) the recipient transfers any portion of the property the recipient receives in such distributions to an eligible retirement plan described in subclause (I) or (II) of paragraph (5)(E)(iv), and

"(iii) in the case of a distribution of property other than money, the amount so transferred consists of the property distributed,

then the portion of the distribution so transferred shall be treated as a distribution described in paragraph (5).

"(G) Payments from certain pension plan termination trusts. If—

"(i) any amount is paid or distributed to a recipient from a trust described in section 501(c)(24),

"(ii) the recipient transfers any portion of the property received in such distribution to an eligible retirement plan described in subclause (I) or (II) of paragraph (5)(E)(iv), and

"(iii) in the case of a distribution of property other than money, the amount so transferred consists of the property distributed,

then the portion of the distribution so transferred shall be treated as a distribution described in paragraph (5)(A).

"(H) Special rule for frozen deposits.

"(i) In general. The 60-day period described in paragraph (5)(C) shall not—

"(I) include any period during which the amount transferred to the employee is a frozen deposit, or

"(II) end earlier than 10 days after such amount ceases to be a frozen deposit.

"(ii) Frozen deposit. For purposes of this subparagraph, the term 'frozen deposit' means any deposit which may not be withdrawn because of—

"(I) the bankruptcy or insolvency of any financial institution, or

"(II) any requirement imposed by the State in which such institution is located by reason of the bankruptcy or insolvency (or threat thereof) of 1 or more financial institutions in such State.

A deposit shall not be treated as a frozen deposit unless on at least 1 day during the 60-day period described in paragraph (5)(C) (without regard to this subparagraph) such deposit is described in the preceding sentence.

"(I) Treatment of potential future vesting.

"(i) In general. For purposes of paragraph (5), in determining whether any portion of a distribution on account of the employee's separation from service may be transferred in a transfer to which paragraph (5)(A) applies, the balance to the credit of the employee shall be determined without regard to any increase in vesting which may occur if the employee is re-employed by the employer.

"(ii) Treatment of subsequent distributions. If—

"(I) any portion of a distribution is transferred in a transfer to which paragraph (5)(A) applies by reason of clause (i),

"(II) the employee is subsequently re-employed by the employer, and

"(III) as a result of service performed after being so re-employed, there is an increase in the employee's vesting for benefits accrued before the separation referred to in clause (i),

then the provisions of paragraph (5)(D)(iii) shall apply to any distribution from the plan after the distribution referred to in clause (i). The preceding sentence shall not apply if the distribution referred to in subclause (I) is made without the consent of the participant.

"(7) Rollover where spouse receives distributions after death of employee. If any distribution attributable to an employee is paid to the spouse of the employee after the employee's death, paragraph (5) shall apply to such distribution in the same manner as if the spouse were the employee; except that a trust or plan described in subclause (III) or (IV) of paragraph (5)(E)(iv) shall not be treated as an eligible retirement plan with respect to such distribution.

"(8) Cash or deferred arrangements. For purposes of this title, contributions made by an employer on behalf of an employee to a trust which is a part of a qualified cash or deferred arrangement (as defined in section 401(k)(2)) shall not be treated as distributed or made available to the employee nor as contributions made to the trust by the employee merely because the arrangement includes provisions under which the employee has an election whether the contribution will be made to the trust or received by the employee in cash.

"(9) Alternate payee under qualified domestic relations order treated as distributee. For purposes of subsection (a)(1) and section 72, any alternate payee who is the spouse or former spouse of the participant shall be treated as the distributee of any distribution or payment made to the alternate payee under a qualified domestic relations order (as defined in section 414(p)).

"(b) Taxability of beneficiary of nonexempt trust.

"(1) In general. Contributions to an employees trust made by an employer during a taxable year of the employer which ends within or with a taxable year of the trust for which the trust is not exempt from tax under section 501(a) shall be included in the gross income of the employee in accordance with section 83 (relating to property transferred in connection with performance of services), except that the value of the employee's interest in the trust shall be substituted for the fair market value of the property for purposes of applying such section. The amount actually distributed or made available to any distributee by any such trust shall be taxable to him in the year in which so distributed or made available, under section 72 (relating to annuities), except that distributions of income of such trust before the annuity starting date (as defined in section 72(c)(4)) shall be included in the gross income of the employee without regard to section 72(e)(5) (relating to amount not received as annuities). A beneficiary of any such trust shall not be considered the owner of any portion of such trust under subpart E of part I of subchapter J (relating to grantors and others treated as substantial owners).

"(2) Failure to meet requirements of section 410(b).

"(A) Highly compensated employees. If 1 of the reasons a trust is not exempt from tax under section 501(a) is the failure of the plan of which it is a part to meet the requirements of section 401(a)(26) or 410(b), then a highly compensated employee shall, in lieu of the amount determined under paragraph (1), include in gross income for the taxable year with or within which the taxable year of the trust ends an amount equal to the vested accrued benefit of such employee (other than the employee's investment in the contract) as of the close of such taxable year of the trust.

"(B) Failure to meet coverage tests. If a trust is not exempt from tax under section 501(a) for any taxable year solely because such trust is part of a plan which fails to meet the requirements of section 401(a)(26) or 410(b), paragraph (1) shall not apply by reason of such failure to any employee who was not a highly compensated employee during—

"(i) such taxable year, or

"(ii) any preceding period for which service was creditable to such employee under the plan.

"(C) Highly compensated employee. For purposes of this paragraph, the term 'highly compensated employee' has the meaning given such term by section 414(q).

"(c) Taxability of beneficiary of certain foreign situs trusts. For purposes of subsections (a) and (b), a stock bonus, pension, or profit-sharing trust which would qualify for exemption from tax under section 501(a) except for the fact that it is a trust created or organized outside the United States shall be treated as if it were a trust exempt from tax under section 501(a).

"(d) [Repealed].

"(e) Tax on lump sum distributions.

"(1) Imposition of separate tax on lump sum distributions.

"(A) Separate tax. There is hereby imposed a tax (in the amount determined under subparagraph (B)) on the lump sum distribution.

"(B) Amount of tax. The amount of tax imposed by subparagraph (A) for any taxable year is an amount equal to 5 times the tax which would be imposed by subsection (c) of section 1 if the recipient were an individual referred to in such subsection and the taxable income were an amount equal to ⅕ of the excess of—

"(i) the total taxable amount of the lump sum distribution for the taxable year, over

"(ii) the minimum distribution allowance.

For purposes of the preceding sentence, in determining the amount of tax under section 1(c), section 1(g) shall be applied without regard to paragraph (2)(B) thereof.

"(C) Minimum distribution allowance. For purposes of this paragraph, the minimum distribution allowance for the taxable year is an amount equal to—

"(i) the lesser of $10,000 or one-half of the total taxable amount of the lump sum distribution for the taxable year, reduced (but not below zero) by

"(ii) 20 percent of the amount (if any) by which such total taxable amount exceeds $20,000.

"(D) Liability for tax. The recipient shall be liable for the tax imposed by this paragraph.

"(2) Multiple distributions and distributions of annuity contracts. In the case of any recipient of a lump sum distribution for the taxable year with respect to whom during the 6-taxable-year period ending on the last day of the taxable year there has been one or more other lump sum distributions after December 31, 1973, or if the distribution (or any part thereof) is an annuity contract, in computing the tax imposed by paragraph (1)(A), the total taxable amounts of all such distributions during such 6-taxable-year period shall be aggregated, but the amount of tax so computed shall be reduced (but not below zero) by the sum of—

"(A) the amount of the tax imposed by paragraph (1)(A) paid with respect to such other distributions, plus

"(B) that portion of the tax on the aggregated total taxable amounts which is attributable to annuity contracts.

For purposes of this paragraph, a beneficiary of a trust to which a lump sum distribution is made shall be treated as the recipient of such distribution if the beneficiary is an employee (including an employee within the meaning of section 401(c)(1)) with respect to the plan under which the distribution is made or if the beneficiary is treated as the owner of such trust for purposes of subpart E of part I of subchapter J. In the case of the distribution of an annuity contract, the taxable amount of such distribution shall be deemed to be the current actuarial value of the contract, determined on the date of such distribution. In the case of a lump sum distribution with respect to any individual which is made only to two or more trusts, the tax imposed by paragraph (1)(A) shall be computed as if such distribution was made to a single trust, but the liability for such tax shall be apportioned among such trusts according to the relative amounts received by each. The Secretary shall prescribe such regulations as may be necessary to carry out the purposes of this paragraph.

"(3) Allowance of deduction. The total taxable amount of a lump sum distribution for the taxable year shall be allowed as a deduction from gross income for such taxable year, but only to the extent included in the taxpayer's gross income for such taxable year.

"(4) Definitions and special rules.

"(A) Lump sum distribution. For purposes of this section and section 403, the term 'lump sum distribution' means the distribution or payment within one taxable year of the recipient of the balance to the credit of an employee which becomes payable to the recipient—

"(i) on account of the employee's death,

"(ii) after the employee attains age 59½,

"(iii) on account of the employee's separation from the service, or

"(iv) after the employee has become disabled (within the meaning of section 72(m)(7))

from a trust which forms a part of a plan described in section 401(a) and which is exempt from tax under section 501 or from a plan described in section 403(a). Clause (iii) of this subparagraph shall be applied only with respect to an individual who is an employee without regard to section 401(c)(1), and clause (iv) shall

be applied only with respect to an employee within the meaning of section 401(c)(1). A distribution of an annuity contract from a trust or annuity plan referred to in the first sentence of this subparagraph shall be treated as a lump sum distribution. For purposes of this subparagraph, a distribution to two or more trusts shall be treated as a distribution to one recipient. For purposes of this subsection, the balance to the credit of the employee does not include the accumulated deductible employee contributions under the plan (within the meaning of section 72(o)(5)).

"(B) Averaging to apply to 1 lump sum distribution after age 59½. Paragraph (1) shall apply to a lump sum distribution with respect to an employee under subparagraph (A) only if—

"(i) such amount is received on or after the employee has attained age 59½, and

"(ii) the taxpayer elects for the taxable year to have all such amounts received during such taxable year so treated.

Not more than 1 election may be made under this subparagraph by any taxpayer with respect to any employee. No election may be made under this subparagraph by any taxpayer other than an individual, an estate, or a trust. In the case of a lump sum distribution made with respect to an employee to 2 or more trusts, the election under this subparagraph shall be made by the personal representative of the taxpayer.

"(C) Aggregation of certain trusts and plans. For purposes of determining the balance to the credit of an employee under subparagraph (A)—

"(i) all trusts which are part of a plan shall be treated as a single trust, all pension plans maintained by the employer shall be treated as a single plan, all profit-sharing plans maintained by the employer shall be treated as a single plan, and all stock bonus plans maintained by the employer shall be treated as a single plan, and

"(ii) trusts which are not qualified trusts under section 401(a) and annuity contracts which do not satisfy the requirements of section 404(a)(2) shall not be taken into account.

"(D) Total taxable amount. For purposes of this section and section 403, the term 'total taxable amount' means, with respect to a lump sum distribution, the amount of such distribution which exceeds the sum of—

"(i) the amounts considered contributed by the employee (determined by applying section 72(f)), which employee contributions shall be reduced by any amounts theretofore distributed to him which were not includible in gross income, and

"(ii) the net unrealized appreciation attributable to that part of the distribution which consists of the securities of the employer corporation so distributed.

"(E) [Repealed].

"(F) [Repealed].

"(G) Community property laws. The provisions of this subsection, other than paragraph (3), shall be applied without regard to community property laws.

"(H) Minimum period of service. For purposes of this subsection, no amount distributed to an employee from or under a plan may be treated as a lump sum distributed under subparagraph (A) unless he has been a participant in the plan for 5 or more taxable years before the taxable year in which such amounts are distributed.

"(I) Amounts subject to penalty. This subsection shall not apply to amounts described in subparagraph (A) of section 72(m)(5) to the extent that section 72(m)(5) applies to such amounts.

"(J) Unrealized appreciation of employer securities. In the case of any distribution including securities of the employer corporation which, without regard to the requirement of subparagraph (H), would be treated as a lump sum distribution under subparagraph (A), there shall be excluded from gross income the net unrealized appreciation attributable to that part of the distribution which consists of securities of the employer corporation so distributed. In the case of any such distribution or any lump sum distribution including securities of the employer corporation, the amount of net unrealized appreciation of such securities and the resulting adjustments to the basis of such securities shall be determined under regulations prescribed by the Secretary. This subparagraph shall not apply to distributions of accumulated deductible employee contributions (within the meaning of section 72(o)(5)). In accordance with rules prescribed by the Secretary, a taxpayer may elect, on the return of tax on which a distribution is required to be included, not to have this subparagraph apply with respect to such distribution.

"(K) Securities. For purposes of this subsection, the terms 'securities' and 'securities of the employer corporation' have the respective meanings provided by subsection (a)(3).

"(L) [Repealed].

"(M) Balance to credit of employee not to include amounts payable under qualified domestic relations order. For purposes of this subsection, the balance to the credit of an employee shall not include any amount payable to an alternate payee under a qualified domestic relations order (within the meaning of section 414(p)).

"(N) Transfers to cost-of-living arrangement not treated as distribution. For purposes of this subsection, the balance to the credit of an employee under a defined contribution plan shall not include any amount transferred from such defined contribution plan to a qualified cost-of-living arrangement (within the meaning of section 415(k)(2)) under a defined benefit plan.

"(O) Lump-sum distributions of alternate payees. If any distribution or payment of the balance to the credit of an employee would be treated as a lump-sum distribution, then, for purposes of this subsection, the payment under a qualified domestic relations order (within the meaning of section 414(p)) of the balance to the credit of an alternate payee who is the spouse or former spouse of the employee shall be treated as a lump-sum distribution. For purposes of this subparagraph, the balance to the credit of the alternate payee shall not include any amount payable to the employee.

"(5) Special rule where portion of lump-sum distribution attributable to rollover of bond purchased under qualified bond purchase plan. If any portion of a lump-sum distribution is attributable to a transfer described in section 405(d)(3)(A)(ii)

Employee benefit plans — Code Sec. 402

(as in effect before its repeal by the Tax Reform Act of 1984), paragraphs (1) and (3) of this subsection shall not apply to such portion.

"(6) Treatment of potential future vesting.

"(A) In general. For purposes of determining whether any distribution which becomes payable to the recipient on account of the employee's separation from service is a lump sum distribution, the balance to the credit of the employee shall be determined without regard to any increase in vesting which may occur if the employee is re-employed by the employer.

"(B) Recapture in certain cases. If—

"(i) an amount is treated as a lump sum distribution by reason of subparagraph (A),

"(ii) special lump sum treatment applies to such distribution,

"(iii) the employee is subsequently re-employed by the employer; and

"(iv) as a result of services performed after being so re-employed, there is an increase in the employee's vesting for benefits accrued before the separation referred to in subparagraph (A),

under regulations prescribed by the Secretary, the tax imposed by this chapter for the taxable year (in which the increase in vesting first occurs) shall be increased by the reduction in tax which resulted from the special lump sum treatment (and any election under paragraph (4)(B) shall not be taken into account for purposes of determining whether the employee may make another election under paragraph (4)(B)).

"(C) Special lump-sum treatment. For purposes of this paragraph, special lump sum treatment applies to any distribution if any portion of such distribution is taxed under this subsection by reason of an election under paragraph (4)(B).

"(D) Vesting. For purposes of this paragraph the term 'vesting' means the portion of the accrued benefits derived from employer contributions to which the participant has a nonforfeitable right.

"(7) Coordination with foreign tax credit limitations. Subsections (a), (b), and (c) of section 904 shall be applied separately with respect to any lump sum distribution on which tax is imposed under paragraph (1), and the amount of such distribution shall be treated as the taxable income for purposes of such separate application.

"(f) Written explanation to recipients of distributions eligible for rollover treatment.

"(1) In general. The plan administrator of any plan shall, when making an eligible rollover distribution, provide a written explanation to the recipient—

"(A) of the provisions under which such distribution will not be subject to tax if transferred to an eligible retirement plan within 60 days after the date on which the recipient received the distribution, and

"(B) if applicable, the provisions of subsections (a)(2) and (e) of this section.

"(2) Definitions. For purposes of this subsection—

"(A) Eligible rollover distribution. The term 'eligible rollover distribution' means any distribution any portion of which may be excluded from gross income under subsection (a)(5) of this section or subsection (a)(4) of section 403 if transferred to an eligible retirement plan in accordance with the requirements of such subsection.

"(B) Eligible retirement plan. The term 'eligible retirement plan' has the meaning given such term by subsection (a)(5)(E)(iv)."

— P.L. 102-318, Sec. 521(d), of this Act provides:

"(d) Model explanation. The Secretary of the Treasury or his delegate shall develop a model explanation which a plan administrator may provide to a recipient in order to meet the requirements of section 402(f) of the Internal Revenue Code of 1986."

— P.L. 102-318, Sec. 522(c)(1), added para. (e)(6), effective for distributions after 12/31/92, except as provided in Sec. 522(d)(2) of this Act which reads as follows:

"(2) Transition rule for certain annuity contracts. If, as of July 1, 1992, a State law prohibits a direct trustee-to-trustee transfer from an annuity contract described in section 403(b) of the Internal Revenue Code of 1986 which was purchased for an employee by an employer which is a State or a political subdivision thereof (or an agency or instrumentality of any 1 or more of either), the amendments made by this section shall not apply to distributions before the earlier of—

"(A) 90 days after the first day after July 1, 1992, on which such transfer is allowed under State law, or

(B) January 1, 1994."

In 1990, P.L. 101-508, Sec. 11801(c)(9)(I)(i), substituted "section 424" for "section 425" in subpara. (a)(3)(B)... Sec. 11801(c)(9)(I)(ii), substituted "section 424(f)" for "section 425(f)" in clause (a)(6)(B)(i), effective 11/5/90 except as provided in Sec. 11821(b) of this Act, reproduced in note following Code Sec. 424.

In 1989, P.L. 101-239, Sec. 7811(g)(2), added "involving a one-time irrevocable election" after "similar arrangement" in the last sentence of para. (g)(3), effective for tax. yrs. begin. after 12/31/86, except as provided in Secs. 1105(c)(2)-(5) of P.L. 99-514, reproduced below.

— P.L. 101-239, Sec. 7811(i)(13), added para. (e)(7), effective for tax. yrs. end. after 12/19/89 (or, at the election of the taxpayer, begin. after 12/31/86).

In 1988, P.L. 100-647, Sec. 1011(c)(1)(A), deleted "(and no tax shall be imposed under section 72(t))" after "in gross income" in clause (g)(2)(C)(i)... Sec. 1011(c)(1)(B), substituted "such income is distributed" for "such excess deferral is made" in subpara. (g)(2)(C)... Sec. 1011(c)(2), added a sentence at the end of subpara. (g)(2)(C)... Sec. 1011(c)(2), substituted "distribution" for "required distribution" in the heading of para. (g)(2)... Sec. 1011(c)(3), added subpara. (g)(2)(D)... Sec. 1011(c)(4), substituted "subsection" for "paragraph" in para. (g)(3)... Sec. 1011(c)(5)(A), added "(determined in the manner prescribed by the Secretary)" after "taxable years" in clause (g)(8)(A)(iii)... Sec. 1011(c)(5)(B), added subpara. (g)(8)(D)... Sec. 1011(c)(6)(A), redesignated subsec. (g), [as added by Sec. 1852(b)(3)(A) of P.L. 99-514], as subsec. (i)... Sec. 1011(c)(6)(B), redesignated subsec. (g), as added by Sec. 1854(f)(2) of P.L. 99-514, as subsec. (j)) effective for tax. yrs. begin. after 12/31/86, except as provided in Secs. 1105(c)(2)-(5) of P.L. 99-514, reproduced below.

— P.L. 100-647, Sec. 1011(c)(6)(C), substituted "section 402(j)" for "section 402(g)" in Sec. 1854(f)(4)(C) [reproduced below] of P.L. 99-514, part of the effective date for changes made by Sec. 1854(f)(2) of P.L. 99-514, see below ... Sec. 1011(c)(8), substituted "such agreement" for "the last of such collective bargaining agreements" in Sec. 1105(c)(2)(A) [reproduced below] of P.L. 99-514, part of the effective date for changes made by Sec. 1105(a) of P.L. 99-514, see below.

— P.L. 100-647, Sec. 1011(c)(10), provides:

"(10) Notwithstanding any other provision of law, a plan may incorporate by reference the dollar limitations under section 402(g) of the Internal Revenue Code of 1986."

— P.L. 100-647, Sec. 1011(c)(11), added a sentence at the end of para. (g)(3), effective for tax. yrs. begin. after 12/31/86, except as provided in Secs. 1105(c)(2)-(5) of P.L. 99-514, reproduced below.

— P.L. 100-647, Sec. 1011(h)(4), amended subparas. (b)(2)(A) and (B), effective for plan yrs. begin. after 12/31/88. For special rules, see Sec. 1112(e)(2) of P.L. 99-514 reproduced below and Sec. 1112(e)(3) reproduced in note following Code Sec. 4980.

Prior to amendment, subparas. (b)(2)(A) and (B) read as follows:

"(A) In general. In the case of a trust which is not exempt from tax under section 501(a) solely because such trust is part of a plan which fails to meet the requirements of section 410(b)—

"(i) such trust shall be treated as exempt from tax under section 501(a) for purposes of applying paragraph (1) to employees who are not highly compensated employees, and

"(ii) paragraph (1) shall be applied to the vested accrued benefit (other than employee contributions) of any highly compensated employee as of the close of the employer's taxable year described in paragraph (1) (rather than contributions made during such year).

"(B) Failure in more than 1 year. If a plan fails to meet the requirements of section 410(b) for more than 1 taxable year, any portion of the vested accrued benefit to which subparagraph (A) applies shall be included in gross income only once."

— P.L. 100-647, Sec. 1011A(a)(1), substituted "resulting in any portion of a distribution being excluded from gross income under subparagraph (A)" for "described in subparagraph (A)" in subpara. (a)(5)(F), effective for yrs. begin. after 12/31/86. For special rules, see Sec. 1121(d)(3) of P.L. 99-514, reproduced below.

— P.L. 100-647, Sec. 1011A(a)(5), of this Act, provides:

"(5) Section 402(a)(5)(F)(ii) of the Internal Revenue Code of 1954 shall not apply to distributions after October 22, 1986, and before the 1st taxable year beginning after 1986 which are attributable to benefits which accrued before January 1, 1985."

— P.L. 100-647, Sec. 1011A(b)(4)(A), repealed Sec. 1122(e)(1) of P.L. 99-514, which amended Code Sec. 402(a)(5)(D)(i). Sec. 1011A(b)(4)(E) of this Act provides:

"(E) Section 402(a)(5)(D)(i)(II) of the 1986 Code (as in effect after the amendment made by subparagraph (A)) shall not apply to distributions after December 31, 1986, and before March 31, 1988."

Prior to the repeal of Sec. 1122(e)(1) of P.L. 99-514, clause (a)(5)(D)(i) (as amended by Sec. 1122(e)(1) of P.L. 99-514) read as follows:

"(i) Requirements. Subparagraph (A) shall apply to a partial distribution only if the employee elects to have subparagraph (A) apply to such distribution and such distribution would be a lump sum distribution if subsection (e)(4)(A) were applied—

"(I) by substituting '50 percent of the balance to the credit of an employee' for 'the balance to the credit of an employee',

"(II) without regard to clause (ii) thereof, the second sentence thereof, and subparagraph (B) of subsection (e)(4).

Any distribution described in section 401(a)(28)(B)(ii) shall be treated as meeting the requirements of this clause. For purposes of subclause (I), the balance to the credit of the employee shall not include any accumulated deductible employee contributions (within the meaning of section 72(o)(5))."

— P.L. 100-647, Sec. 1011A(b)(4)(B), added "is payable as provided in clause (i), (iii) or (iv) of subsection (e)(4)(A) (without regard to the second sentence thereof) and" after "such distribution" the first place it appeared in subclause (a)(5)(D)(i)(I)... Sec. 1011A(b)(4)(C), added a new sentence at the end of clause (a)(5)(D)(i)... Sec. 1011A(b)(4)(D), deleted "10-year" before "averaging" in the heading of clause (a)(5)(D)(iii), effective for amounts distributed after 12/31/86, in tax. yrs. end. after 12/31/86. For special rules see Sec. 1122(h)(3)-(6) of P.L. 99-514, reproduced below.

— P.L. 100-647, Sec. 1011A(b)(5), added a flush sentence at the end of clause (a)(6)(H)(ii), effective as provided in Sec. 1122(h)(8) of P.L. 99-514, reproduced below.

— P.L. 100-647, Sec. 1011A(b)(6), substituted "employee" for "taxpayer" in clause (e)(4)(B)(i), effective as provided in Sec. 1122(h)(8) of P.L. 99-514, reproduced below.

— P.L. 100-647, Sec. 1011A(b)(7), amended the last sentence of subpara. (e)(4)(J), effective for amounts distributed after 12/31/86.

Prior to amendment, the last sentence of subpara. (e)(4)(J) read as follows:

"To the extent provided by the Secretary, a taxpayer may elect before any distribution not to have this paragraph apply with respect to such distribution."

— P.L. 100-647, Sec. 1011A(b)(8)(A), substituted "paragraph (4)" for "paragraphs (2) and (4)" in para. (a)(1)... Sec. 1011A(b)(8)(B), deleted "or (2)" before "of this" in para. (a)(4)... Sec. 1011A(b)(8)(C), deleted "paragraph (2) of subsection (a), and" before "paragraphs (1)" in subpara. (a)(6)(C)... Sec. 1011A(b)(8)(D), deleted "paragraph (2) of subsection (a), and" before "paragraphs (1)" and deleted the comma after "subsection (e)" in clause (a)(6)(E)(ii)... Sec. 1011A(b)(8)(E), deleted "ordinary income portion of a" before "lump sum" in subpara. (e)(1)(A)... Sec. 1011A(b)(8)(F)(i), substituted "A" for "Except for purposes of subsection (a)(2) and section 403(a)(2), a" in subpara. (e)(4)(A)... Sec. 1011A(b)(8)(F)(ii), deleted "subsection (a)(2) of this section, and subsection (a)(2) of section 403," before "the balance" in subpara. (e)(4)(L)... Sec. 1011A(b)(8)(G), repealed subpara. (e)(4)(L)... Sec. 1011A(b)(8)(H), deleted ", subsection (a)(2) of this section, and section 403(a)(2)" after "of this subsection" in subpara. (e)(4)(M)... Sec. 1011A(b)(8)(I), deleted "an paragraph (2) of subsection (a)" before "shall not" in para. (e)(5)... Sec. 1011A(b)(8)(J), amended subpara. (e)(6)(C)... Sec. 1011A(b)(10), added the last sentence to subpara. (e)(1)(B), effective for amounts distributed after 12/31/86, in tax. yrs. end. after 12/31/86. For special rules see Secs. 1112(h)(3)-(6) of P.L. 99-514, reproduced below.

Prior to repeal, subpara. (e)(4)(L) read as follows:

"(L) Election to treat pre-1974 participation as post-1973 participation. For purposes of subparagraph (E), subsection (a)(2), and section 403(a)(2), if a taxpayer elects (at the time and in the manner provided under regulations prescribed by the Secretary), all calendar years of an employee's active participation in all plans in which the employee has been an active participant shall be considered years of active participation by such employee after December 31, 1973. An election made under this subparagraph, once made, shall be irrevocable and shall apply to all lump-sum distributions received by the taxpayer with respect to the employee. This subparagraph shall not apply if the taxpayer received a lump-sum distribution in a previous taxable year of the employee beginning after December 31, 1975, unless no portion of such lump-sum distribution was treated under subsection (a)(2) or section 403(a)(2) as gain from the sale or exchange of a capital asset held for more than 1 year."

Prior to amendment, subpara. (e)(6)(C) read as follows:

"(C) Special lump sum treatment. For purposes of this paragraph, special lump sum treatment applies to any distribution if any portion of such distribution—

"(i) is taxed under this subsection by reason of an election under paragraph (4)(B), or

"(ii) is treated as long-term capital gain under subsection (a)(2) of this section or section 403(a)(2)."

— P.L. 100-647, Sec. 1011A(b)(13), amended Secs. 1122(h)(3)(C) and (h)(4)(C) [reproduced below] of P.L. 99-514, part of the effective date for changes made by Sec. 1122(a)(1), (a)(2), (b)(1)(A), (b)(2)(A), (b)(2)(B)(i)-(iii), (b)(2)(C), (b)(2)(D), (b)(3)(E), and (e)(1) of P.L. 99-514, by substituting, "for purposes of such Code" for "with respect to any other lump sum distribution", see below.

— P.L. 100-647, Sec. 1011A(b)(14)(A), (B), substituted "employee" for "individual" and added "or by an individual, estate, or trust with respect to such an employee" after "1986" in Sec. 1122(h)(3)(C)(i) [reproduced below] of P.L. 99-514, part of the effective date for changes made by Sec. 1122(e)(1) of P.L. 99-514... Sec. 1011A(b)(15), amended Sec. 1122(h)(5) [reproduced below] of P.L. 99-514, by substituting "employee" for "individual", inserting "and by including in gross income the zero bracket amount in effect under section 63(d) of such Code for such years" after "1986" in what was the last sentence before the addition of the following new last sentence "This paragraph shall also apply to an individual, estate, or trust which receives a distribution with respect to an employee described in this paragraph", see below.

— P.L. 100-647, Sec. 1011A(c)(9), deleted "clause (ii) of" before "subparagraph A" in subpara. (e)(4)(I), effective for tax. yrs. begin. after 12/31/86.

— P.L. 100-647, Sec. 1011A(d)(1)-(d)(3), amended Sec. 1124 [reproduced below] of P.L. 99-514, part of special rules relating to lump sum distributions, by amending Sec. 1124(a) [reproduced below] of P.L. 99-514, by substituting "individual, estate or trust" for "employee" each place it appeared in Sec. 1124(b) [reproduced below] of P.L. 99-514, by inserting "with respect to an employee" after "receives" in Sec. 1124(b) of P.L. 99-514, and by adding Sec. 1124(c) [reproduced below] of P.L. 99-514, see below.

Prior to amendment, Sec. 1124(a) of P.L. 99-514 read as follows:

"(a) In general.

"If an employee separates from service during 1986 and receives a lump sum distribution (within the meaning of section 402(e)(4)(A) of such Code) after December 31, 1986, and before March 16, 1987, on account of such separation from service, then, for purposes of the Internal Revenue Code of 1986, such employee may elect to treat such lump sum distribution as if it were received when such employee separated from service."

— P.L. 100-647, Sec. 1018(t)(8)(A), redesignated subpara. (a)(6)(G) as added by Sec. 1898(a)(3) of P.L. 99-514 as subpara. (a)(6)(I), effective for plan yrs. begin. after 12/31/84, except as provided by Sec. 302(b) of P.L. 98-397 [reproduced below] and subject to the transitional rules in Sec. 303 of P.L. 98-397, reproduced in the note following Code Sec. 401.

— P.L. 100-647, Sec. 1018(t)(8)(C), substituted "an eligible" for "a eligible" in para. (f)(1), effective for distributions after 12/31/84.

— P.L. 100-647, Sec. 1018(u)(6), amended Sec. 1122(b)(2)(B)(iii) of P.L. 99-514, by applying it as if it struck out "Initial Separate Tax" instead of "Initial Tax" in the heading of Code Sec. 402(e)(1)(B).

— P.L. 100-647, Sec. 1018(u)(7), amended Sec. 1122(b)(2)(C) of P.L. 99-514, by having it substitute "total taxable amount" for "ordinary income portion" instead of "total taxable amount" for "the ordinary income portion" in Code Sec. 402(e)(3).

— P.L. 100-647, Sec. 6068(a), added new subpara. (e)(4)(O), effective for tax. yrs. end. after 12/31/84.

In 1986, P.L. 99-514, Sec. 104(b)(5), deleted "the zero bracket amount applicable to such individual for the taxable year plus" after "equal to" in subpara. (e)(1)(B) (as redesignated by Sec. 1122(b) of this Act), effective for tax. yrs. begin. after 12/31/86.

— P.L. 99-514, Sec. 1105(a), added subsec. (g)[sic (i)], effective for tax. yrs. begin. after 12/31/86. Sec. 1105(c)(2)-(c)(5) of this Act provide:

"(2) Deferrals under collective bargaining agreements.—In the case of a plan maintained pursuant to 1 or more collective bargaining agreements between employee representatives and 1 or more employers ratified before March 1, 1986, the amendment made by subsection (a) shall not apply to contributions made pursuant to such an agreement for taxable years beginning before the earlier of—

"(A) the date on which such agreement terminates (determined without regard to any extension thereof after February 28, 1986), or

"(B) January 1, 1989.

Such contributions shall be taken into account for purposes of applying the amendment made by this section to other plans.

"(3) Distributions made before plan amendment.—

"(A) In general.—If a plan amendment is required to allow the plan to make any distribution described in section 402(g)(2)(A)(ii) of the Internal Revenue Code of 1986, any such distribution which is made before the close of the 1st plan year for which such amendment is required to be in effect under section 1140 shall be treated as made in accordance with the provisions of such plan.

"(B) Distributions pursuant to model amendment.—

"(i) Secretary to prescribe amendment.—The Secretary of the Treasury or his delegate shall prescribe an amendment which allows a plan to make any distribution described in section 402(g)(2)(A)(ii) of such Code.

"(ii) Adoption by plan.—If a plan adopts the amendment prescribed under clause (i) and makes a distribution in accordance with such amendment, such distribution shall be treated as made in accordance with the provisions of the plan.

"(4) Special rule for taxable years or partnerships which include January 1, 1987.—In the case of the taxable year of any partnership which begins before January 1, 1987, and ends after January 1, 1987, elective deferrals (within the meaning of section 402(g)(3) of the Internal Revenue Code of 1986) made on behalf of a partner for such taxable year shall, for purposes of section 402(g)(3) of such Code, be treated as having been made ratably during such taxable year.

"(5) Cash or deferred arrangements.—The amendments made by this section shall not apply to employer contributions made during 1987 and attributable to services performed during 1986 under a qualified cash or deferred arrangement (as defined in section 401(k) of the Internal Revenue Code of 1986), if, under the terms of such arrangement as in effect on August 16, 1986—

"(A) the employee makes an election with respect to such contribution before January 1, 1987, and

"(B) the employer identifies the amount of such contribution before January 1, 1987."

— P.L. 99-514, Sec. 1106(c)(2), added subpara. (e)(4)(N), effective for yrs. begin. after 12/31/86. Sec. 1106(i)(2) of this Act provides:

"(2) Collective bargaining agreements.—In the case of a plan maintained pursuant to 1 or more collective bargaining agreements between employee representatives and 1 or more employers ratified before March 1, 1986, the amendments made by this section (other than subsection (d)) shall not apply to contributions or benefits pursuant to such agreement in years beginning before the earlier of—

"(A) the date on which the last of such collective bargaining agreements terminates (determined without regard to any extension thereof after February 28, 1986), or

"(B) January 1, 1989."

— P.L. 99-514, Sec. 1108(b), added subsec. (h) (as amended by Sec. 1105(a) of this Act), effective for yrs. begin. after 12/31/86.

— P.L. 99-514, Sec. 1112(c)(1), added para. (b)(2)... Sec. 1112(c)(2), added "(1) In general—" after the heading of subsec. (b), effective for plan yrs. begin. after 12/31/88. Sec. 1112(e)(2) of this Act provides:

"(2) Special rule for collective bargaining agreements.—In the case of a plan maintained pursuant to 1 or more collective bargaining agreements between employee representatives and 1 or more employers ratified before March 1, 1986, the amendments made by this section shall not apply to employees covered by any such agreement in plan years beginning before the earlier of—

"(A) the later of—

"(i) January 1, 1989, or

"(ii) the date on which the last of such collective bargaining agreement terminates (determined without regard to any extension thereof after February 28, 1986), or

"(B) January 1, 1991."

For special rules, see Sec. 1112(e)(3) of this Act reproduced in note following Code Sec. 4980.

— P.L. 99-514, Sec. 1121(c)(1), amended subpara. (a)(5)(F), effective for yrs. begins. after 12/31/86. Sec. 1121(d)(3) of this Act provide:

"(3) Collective bargaining agreements.—In the case of a plan maintained pursuant to 1 or more collective bargaining agreements between employee representatives and 1 or more employers ratified before March 1, 1986, the amendments made by this section shall not apply to distributions to individuals covered by such agreements in plan years beginning before the earlier of—

"(A) the later of—

"(i) the date on which the last of such collective bargaining agreements terminates (determined without regard to any extension thereof after February 28, 1986), or

"(ii) January 1, 1989, or

"(B) January 1, 1991."

Prior to amendment, subpara. (a)(5)(F) [see Sec. 1011A(a)(5) of P.L. 100-647, reproduced above] read as follows:

"(F) Special rules.

Employee benefit plans — Code Sec. 402

"(i) Transfer treated as rollover contribution under Section 408. For purposes of this title, a transfer resulting in any portion of a distribution being excluded from gross income under subparagraph (A) to an eligible retirement plan described in subclause (I), or (II) of subparagraph (E)(iv) shall be treated as a rollover contribution described in section 408(d)(3).

"(ii) 5-percent owners. An eligible retirement plan described in subclause (III) or (IV) of subparagraph (E)(iv) shall not be treated as an eligible retirement plan for the transfer of a distribution if the employee is a 5-percent owner at the time such distribution is made. For purposes of the preceding sentence, the term '5-percent owner' means any individual who is a 5-percent owner (as defined in section 416(i)(1)(B)) at any time during the 5 plan years preceding the plan year in which the distribution is made."

—P.L. 99-514, Sec. 1122(a)(1), amended subpara. (e)(4)(B) ... Sec. 1122(a)(2), substituted "5 times" for "10 times" and "⅕" for "one-tenth" in subpara. (e)(1)(C) [before redesignation by this section] ... Sec. 1122(b)(1)(A), deleted para. (a)(2) ... Sec. 1122(b)(2)(A), amended clause (a)(5)(D)(iii) ... Sec. 1122(b)(2)(B)(i), deleted subpara. (e)(1)(B) and redesignated subparas. (e)(1)(C), (D), and (E) as subparas. (e)(1)(B), (C), and (D), respectively ... Sec. 1122(b)(2)(B)(ii), substituted "The amount of tax imposed by subparagraph (A)" for "The initial separate tax" in subpara. (e)(1)(B) [as redesignated by this section] ... Sec. 1122(b)(2)(B)(iii), [as amended by Sec. 1018(u)(6) of P.L. 100-647], substituted "Amount of tax" for "Initial separate tax" in the heading of subpara. (e)(1)(B) [as redesignated by this section] ... Sec. 1122(b)(2)(C), [as amended by Sec. 1018(u)(7) of P.L. 100-647, see above], substituted "total taxable income" for "total ordinary income" in para. (e)(3) ... Sec. 1122(b)(2)(D), deleted subpara. (e)(4)(E) ... Sec. 1122(b)(2)(E), deleted "(but not for purposes of subsection (a)(2) or section 403(a)(2)(A))" after "of this subsection" in subpara. (e)(4)(H) ... Sec. 1122(e)(1), [repealed by Sec. 1011A(b)(4)(A) of P.L. 100-647, see above], amended clause (a)(5)(D)(i), effective for amounts distributed after 12/31/86, in tax. yrs. end. after 12/31/86. Secs. 1122(b)(3)-(h)(6) [as amended by Sec. 1011A(b)(13) of P.L. 100-647, and Sec. 1011A(b)(15), see above] of this Act provide:

"(3) Special rule for individuals who attained age 50 before January 1, 1986.—

"(A) In general.—In the case of a lump sum distribution to which this paragraph applies—

"(i) the existing capital gains provisions shall continue to apply, and

"(ii) the requirement of subparagraph (B) of section 402(e)(4) of the Internal Revenue Code of 1986 (as amended by subsection (a)) that the distribution be received after attaining age 59½ shall not apply.

"(B) Computation of tax.—If subparagraph (A) applies to any lump sum distribution of any taxpayer for any taxable year, the tax imposed by section 1 of the Internal Revenue Code of 1986 on such taxpayer for such taxable year shall be equal to the sum of—

"(i) the tax imposed by such section 1 on the taxable income of the taxpayer (reduced by the portion of such lump sum distribution to which clause (ii) applies), plus

"(ii) 20 percent of the portion of such lump sum distribution to which the existing capital gains provisions continue to apply by reason of this paragraph.

"(C) Lump sum distributions to which paragraph applies.—This paragraph shall apply to any lump sum distribution if—

"(i) such lump sum distribution is received by an employee who has attained age 50 before January 1, 1986 or by an individual, estate, or trust with respect to such an employee, and

"(ii) the taxpayer makes an election under this paragraph.

Not more than 1 election may be made under this paragraph with respect to an employee. An election under this subparagraph shall be treated as an election under section 402(e)(4)(B) of such Code for purposes of such Code.

"(4) 5-year phase-out of capital gains treatment.—

"(A) Notwithstanding the amendment made by subsection (b), if the taxpayer elects the application of this paragraph with respect to any distribution after December 31, 1986, and before January 1, 1992, the phase-out percentage of the amount which would have been treated, without regard to this subparagraph, as long-term capital gain under the existing capital gains provisions shall be treated as long-term capital gain.

"(B) For purposes of this paragraph—

In the case of distributions during calendar year:	The phase-out percentage is:
1987	100
1988	95
1989	75
1990	50
1991	25

"(C) No more than 1 election may be made under this paragraph with respect to an employee. An election under this paragraph shall be treated as an election under section 402(e)(4)(B) of the Internal Revenue Code of 1986 for purposes of such Code.

"(5) Election of 10-year averaging.—An employee who has attained age 50 before January 1, 1986, and elects the application of paragraph (3) or section 402(e)(1) of the Internal Revenue Code of 1986 (as amended by this Act) may elect to have such section applied by substituting '10 times' for '5 times' and '⅒' for '⅕' in subparagraph (B) thereof. For purposes of the preceding sentence, section 402(e)(1) of such Code shall be applied by using the rate of tax in effect under section 1 of the Internal Revenue Code of 1954 for taxable years beginning during 1986 and by including in gross income the zero bracket amount in effect under section 63(d) of such Code for such years.

This paragraph shall also apply to an individual, estate, or trust which receives a distribution with respect to an employee described in this paragraph.

"(6) Existing capital gain provisions.—For purposes of paragraphs (3) and (4), the term 'existing capital gains provisions' means the provisions of paragraph (2) of section 402(a) of the Internal Revenue Code of 1954 (as in effect on the date before the date of the enactment of this Act) and paragraph (2) of section 403(a) of such Code (as so in effect)."

Prior to amendment, subpara. (e)(4)(B) read as follows:

"(B) Election of lump sum treatment. For purposes of this section and section 403, no amount which is not an annuity contract may be treated as a lump sum distribution under subparagraph (A) unless the taxpayer elects for the taxable year to have all such amounts received during such year so treated at the time and in the manner provided under regulations prescribed by the Secretary. Not more than one election may be made under this subparagraph with respect to any individual after such individual has attained age 59½. No election may be made under this subparagraph by any taxpayer other than an individual, an estate, or a trust. In the case of a lump sum distribution made with respect to an employee to two or more trusts, the election under this subparagraph shall be made by the personal representative of the employee."

Prior to deletion, para. (a)(2) [as in effect for property acquired after 6/22/84 and before 1/1/88; see Sec. 1001(b)(3) of P.L. 98-369, below] read as follows:

"(2) Capital gains treatment for portion of lump sum distributions. In the case of an employee trust described in section 401(a), which is exempt from tax under section 501(a), so much of the total taxable amount (as defined in subparagraph (D) of subsection (e)(4)) of a lump sum distribution as is equal to the product of such total taxable amount multiplied by a fraction—

"(A) the numerator of which is the number of calendar years of active participation by the employee in such plan before January 1, 1974, and

"(B) the denominator of which is the number of calendar years of active participation by the employee in such plan,

shall be treated as a gain from the sale or exchange of a capital asset held for more than 6 months. For purposes of computing the fraction described in this paragraph and the fraction under subsection (e)(4)(E), the Secretary may prescribe regulations under which plan years may be used in lieu of calendar years. For purposes of this paragraph, in the case of an individual who is an employee without regard to section 401(c)(1), determination of whether or not any distribution is a lump sum distribution shall be made without regard to the requirement that an election be made under subsection (e)(4)(B), but no distribution to any taxpayer other than an individual, estate, or trust may be treated as a lump sum distribution under this paragraph."

Prior to amendment, clause (a)(5)(D)(iii) read as follows:

"(iii) Denial of 10-year averaging and capital gains treatment for subsequent distributions. If an election under clause (i) is made with respect to any partial distribution paid to any employee—

"(I) paragraph (2) of this subsection,

"(II) paragraphs (1) and (3) of subsection (e), and

"(III) paragraph (2) of section 403(a).

shall not apply to any distribution (paid after such partial distribution) of the balance to the credit of such employee under the plan under which such partial distribution was made (or under any other plan which, under subsection (e)(4)(C), would be aggregated with such plan)."

Prior to deletion, subpara. (e)(1)(B) read as follows:

"(B) Amount of tax. The amount of tax imposed by subparagraph (A) for any taxable year shall be an amount equal to the amount of the initial separate tax for such taxable year multiplied by a fraction, the numerator of which is the ordinary income portion of the lump sum distribution for the taxable year and the denominator of which is the total taxable amount of such distribution for such year."

Prior to deletion, subpara. (e)(4)(E) read as follows:

"(E) Ordinary income portion. For purposes of this section, the term 'ordinary income portion' means, with respect to a lump sum distribution, so much of the total taxable amount of such distribution as is equal to the product of such total taxable amount multiplied by a fraction—

"(i) the numerator of which is the number of calendar years of active participation by the employee in such plan after December 31, 1973, and

"(ii) the denominator of which is the number of calendar years of active participation by the employee in such plan."

Prior to amendment, clause (a)(5)(D)(i) read as follows:

"(i) Requirements. Subparagraph (A) shall apply to a partial distribution only if—

"(I) such distribution is of an amount equal to at least 50 percent of the balance to the credit of the employee in a qualified trust (determined immediately before such distribution and without regard to subsection (e)(4)(C)),

"(II) such distribution is not one of a series of periodic payments, and

"(III) the employee elects (at such time and in such manner as the Secretary shall by regulations prescribe) to have subparagraph (A) apply to such partial distribution."

—P.L. 99-514, Sec. 1122(e)(2)(A), added subpara. (a)(6)(H) [sic (I)], effective as provided in Sec. 1122(h)(8) of this Act, which reads as follows:

"(8) Frozen deposits.—The amendments made by subsection (e)(2) shall apply to amounts transferred to an employee before, on, or after the date of the enactment of this Act [10/22/86], except that in the case of an amount transferred on or before such date, the 60-day period referred to in section 402(a)(5)(C) of the Internal Revenue Code of 1986 shall not expire before the 60th day after the date of the enactment of this Act."

—P.L. 99-514, Sec. 1122(g), added the last sentence of subpara. (e)(4)(J), effective for amounts distributed after 12/31/86, in tax. yrs. end. after 12/31/86.

—P.L. 99-514, Sec. 1124, [as amended by Sec. 1011(d)(1) of P.L. 100-647-(d)(B), see above], provides:

"SEC. 1124. ELECTION TO TREAT CERTAIN LUMP SUM DISTRIBUTIONS RECEIVED DURING 1987 AS RECEIVED DURING 1986.

"(a) In general. If an employee dies, separates from service, or becomes disabled before 1987 and an individual, trust, or estate receives a lump-sum distribution with respect to such employee after December 31, 1986, and before March 16, 1987, on account of such death, separation from service, or disability, then, for purposes of the Internal Revenue Code of 1986, such individual, estate, or trust may treat such distribution as if it were received in 1986.

"(b) Special rule for terminated plan. —

"In the case of an individual, estate or trust who receives with respect to an employee a distribution from a terminated plan which was maintained by a corporation organized under the laws of the State of Nevada, the principal place of business of which is Denver, Colorado, and which filed for relief from creditors under the United States Bankruptcy Code on August 28, 1986, the individual, estate or trust may treat a lump sum distribution received from such plan before June 30, 1987, as if it were received in 1986.

"(c) Lump sum distribution. For purposes of this section, the term 'lump sum distribution' has the meaning given such term by section 402(e)(4)(A) of the Internal Revenue Code of 1986, without regard to subparagraph (B) or (H) of section 402(e)(4) of such Code."

— P.L. 99-514, Sec. 1852(a)(5)(A), added subpara. (a)(5)(G) . . . Sec. 1852(b)(1), substituted "of all or any portion of" for "of any portion of" in clause (a)(5)(E)(v) . . . Sec. 1852(b)(2), added the last sentence of clause (a)(5)(D)(i) . . . Sec. 1852(b)(3)(A), added subsec. (g) . . . Sec. 1852(b)(3)(B), deleted subpara. (e)(4)(F) . . . Sec. 1852(b)(4), substituted "the spouse were the employee; except that a trust or plan described in subclause (III) or (IV) of paragraph (5)(E)(iv) shall not be treated as an eligible retirement plan with respect to such distribution" for "the spouse were the employee" in para. (a)(7) . . . Sec. 1852(b)(5), substituted "a trust or plan described in subclause (III) or (IV)" for "a plan described in subclause (IV) or (V)" in clause (a)(5)(D)(ii) . . . Sec. 1852(b)(6), substituted "a transfer resulting in any portion of a distribution being excluded from gross income under subparagraph (A)" for "a transfer described in subparagraph (A)" in clause (a)(5)(F)(i) (as in effect before amendment by Sec. 1121(c)(1) of this Act) . . . Sec. 1852(b)(7), substituted "(7)" for "(7)(B)" in clause (a)(6)(D)(v), effective for distributions made after 7/18/84 in tax. yrs. end. after 7/18/84.

Prior to deletion, subpara. (e)(4)(F) read as follows:

"(F) Employee. For purposes of this subsection and subsection (a)(2), except as otherwise provided in subparagraph (A), the term 'employee' includes an individual who is an employee within the meaning of section 401(c)(1) and the employer of such individual is the person treated as his employer under section 401(c)(4)."

— P.L. 99-514, Sec. 1852(c)(5), substituted "section 72(e)(5)" for "section 72(e)(1)" in subsec. (b), effective for amounts received and loans made after the 90th day after 7/18/84 [10/16/84].

— P.L. 99-514, Sec. 1854(f)(2), added subsec. (g) [sic (h)], effective as provided by Sec. 1854(f)(4)(C) [as amended by Sec. 1011(c)(6)(C) of P.L. 100-647 see above] of this Act, which reads:

"(C) The amendments made by paragraph (2) shall apply to any transaction occurring after December 31, 1984, except that in the case of any transaction occurring before the date of the enactment of this Act [10/22/86], the period under which proceeds are required to be invested under section 402(j) of the Internal Revenue Code of 1954 (as added by paragraph (2)) shall not end before the earlier of 1 year after the date of such transaction or 180 days after the date of the enactment of this Act."

— P.L. 99-514, Sec. 1875(c)(1)(A), amended clause (a)(5)(F)(ii), effective as provided by Sec. 1875(c)(1)(B) of this Act, which reads:

"(B) The amendments made by subparagraph (A) shall apply to distributions after the date of the enactment of this Act [10/22/86]. Such amendments shall apply also to distributions after 1983 and on or before the date of the enactment of this Act to individuals who are not 5-percent owners (as defined in section 402(a)(5)(F)(ii) of the Internal Revenue Code of 1954 (as amended by this paragraph))."

Prior to amendment, clause (a)(5)(F)(ii) read as follows:

"(ii) Key employees. An eligible retirement plan described in subclause (III) or (IV) of subparagraph (E)(iv) shall not be treated as an eligible retirement plan for the transfer of a distribution if any part of the distribution is attributable to contributions made on behalf of the employee while he was a key employee in a top-heavy plan. For purposes of the preceding sentence, the terms 'key employee' and 'top-heavy plan' have the same respective meanings as when used in section 416."

— P.L. 99-514, Sec. 1875(c)(2), added Sec. 713(c)(4) to P.L. 98-369, the effective date for changes made by Sec. 713(c)(3) of P.L. 98-369, see below.

— P.L. 99-514, Sec. 1898(a)(2), added para. (e)(6) . . . Sec. 1898(a)(3), added subpara. (a)(6)(G) [sic (H)], effective for plan yrs. begin. after 12/31/84, except as provided by Sec. 302(b) of P.L. 98-397 [reproduced below] and subject to the transitional rules in Sec. 303 of P.L. 98-397, reproduced in the note following Code Sec. 401.

— P.L. 99-514, Sec. 1898(c)(1)(A), substituted "any alternate payee who is the spouse or former spouse of the participant shall be treated" for "the alternate payee shall be treated" in para. (a)(9), effective for payments made after 10/22/86.

— P.L. 99-514, Sec. 1898(c)(7)(A)(i), substituted "paragraph (5)" for "paragraph (5)(A)" in subpara. (a)(6)(F), effective as provided in Sec. 303(d) of P.L. 98-397, which reads as follows:

"(d) Amendments relating to assignments in divorce, etc., proceedings. The amendments made by sections 104 and 204 shall take effect on January 1, 1985, except that in the case of a domestic relations order entered before such date, the plan administrator.—

"(1) shall treat such order as a qualified domestic relations order if such administrator is paying benefits pursuant to such order on such date, and

"(2) may treat any other such order entered before such date as a qualified domestic relations order even if such order does not meet the requirements of such amendments."

— P.L. 99-514, Sec. 1898(e)(1), substituted "eligible rollover distribution" for "qualifying rollover distribution" in para. (f)(1) . . . Sec. 1898(e)(2), amended para. (f)(2), effective for distributions after 12/31/84. For transitional rules, see Sec. 303 of P.L. 98-369 at note following Code Sec. 401.

Prior to amendment, para. (f)(2) read as follows:

"(2) Definitions. For purposes of this subsection, the terms 'qualifying rollover distribution' and 'eligible retirement plan' have the respective meanings given such terms by subsection (a)(5)(E)."

— P.L. 99-272, Sec. 11012(c), added subpara. (a)(6)(G), effective 1/1/86.

In 1984, P.L. 98-397, Sec. 204(c)(1), added para. (a)(9) . . . Sec. 204(c)(3), added subpara. (a)(6)(F) . . . Sec. 204(c)(4), added subpara. (e)(4)(M), effective for plan years begin. after 12/31/84, except as provided in Sec. 302(b) of this Act, following, and subject to transitional rules in Sec. 303 of this Act, reproduced in note following Code Sec. 401.

"(b) Special rule for collective bargaining agreements. In the case of a plan maintained pursuant to 1 or more collective bargaining agreements between employee representatives and 1 or more employers ratified before the date of the enactment of this Act, except as provided in subsection (d) of section 303, the amendments made by this Act shall not apply to plan years beginning before the earlier of—

"(1) the date on which the last of the collective bargaining agreements relating to the plan terminates (determined without regard to any extension thereof agreed to after the date of enactment of this Act), or

"(2) January 1, 1987

For purposes of paragraph (1), any plan amendment made pursuant to a collective bargaining agreement relating to the plan which amends the plan solely to conform to any requirement added by title I or II shall not be treated as a termination of such collective bargaining agreement."

— P.L. 98-397, Sec. 207(a), added subsec. (f), effective for distributions after 12/31/84. For transitional rules see Sec. 303 of this Act reproduced in note following Code Sec. 401.

— P.L. 98-369, Sec. 491(c)(2), added para. (e)(5), effective for redemptions after 7/18/84 in tax. yrs. end. after 7/18/84.

— P.L. 98-369, Sec. 491(d)(9), deleted subclause (a)(5)(D)(iv)(III) and redesignated subclauses (a)(5)(D)(iv)(IV) and (V) as subclauses (a)(5)(D)(iv)(III) and (IV), respectively . . . Sec. 491(d)(10), substituted "or (II)" for ", (II), or (III)" in clause (a)(5)(F)(i) (as redesignated by Sec. 522(b)) . . . Sec. 491(d)(11), substituted "(III) or (IV)" for "(IV) or (V)" in clause (a)(5)(F)(ii) (as redesignated by Sec. 522(b)), effective for obligations issued after 12/31/83.

Prior to deletion, subclause (a)(5)(D)(iv)(III) read as follows:

"(III) a retirement bond described in section 409,"

— P.L. 98-369, Sec. 522(a)(1), amended clause (a)(5)(A)(i) . . . Sec. 522(b), redesignated subparas. (a)(5)(D) and (E) as subparas. (a)(5)(E) and (F), and added new subpara. (a)(5)(D) . . . Sec. 522(c), amended para. (a)(7) . . . Sec. 522(d)(1)(A)-(C), substituted "qualified total distribution" for "qualifying rollover distribution" in subpara. (a)(5)(B), clause (a)(5)(E)(i), and clause (a)(6)(E)(i) . . . Sec. 522(d)(2), added "In the case of any partial distribution, the maximum amount transferred to which subparagraph (A) applies shall not exceed the portion of such distribution which is includible in gross income (determined without regard to subparagraph (A))." at the end of subpara. (a)(5)(B) . . . Sec. 522(d)(3), added "(determined without regard to this paragraph)" after "gross income" in clause (a)(5)(E)(ii) . . . Sec. 522(d)(4), amended clause (a)(5)(E)(v) . . . Sec. 522(d)(5), substituted "subparagraph (E)(iv)" for "subparagraph (D)(iv)" each place it appeared in subpara. (a)(5)(F) . . . Sec. 522(d)(6), substituted "paragraph (5)(E)(i)" for "paragraph (5)(D)(i)" each place it appeared in para. (a)(6) . . . Sec. 522(d)(7), added "(or, in the case of a partial distribution, the amount not includible in gross income)" after "employee contributions" in clauses (a)(6)(D)(iii) and (iv) . . . Sec. 522(d)(8), substituted "paragraph (5)(D) or (5)(E)(i)(II)" for "paragraph (5)(D)(i)(II)" in clause (a)(6)(E)(i), effective for distributions made after 7/18/84, in tax. yrs. end. after 7/18/84.

Prior to amendment, clause (a)(5)(A)(i) read as follows:

"(i) the balance to the credit of an employee in a qualified trust is paid to him in qualifying rollover distribution,"

Prior to amendment, para. (a)(7) read as follows:

"(7) Rollover where spouse receives lump-sum distribution at death of employee.

"(A) General rule. If—

"(i) any portion of a qualifying rollover distribution attributable to an employee is paid to the spouse of the employee after the employee's death,

"(ii) the spouse transfers any portion of the property which the spouse receives in such distribution to an individual retirement plan, and

"(iii) in the case of a distribution of property other than money, the amount so transferred consists of the property distributed,

then such distribution (to the extent so transferred) shall not be includible in gross income for the taxable year in which paid.

"(B) Certain rules made applicable. Rules similar to the rules of subparagraphs (B) through (E) of paragraph (5) and of paragraph (6) shall apply for purposes of this paragraph."

Prior to amendment, clause (a)(5)(E)(v) read as follows:

"(v) Rollover of partial distributions of deductible employee contributions permitted. In the case of any qualifying rollover distribution described in subclause (III) of clause (i), clause (i) of subparagraph (A) shall be applied by substituting 'any portion of the balance' for 'the balance'."

—P.L. 98-369, Sec. 713(c)(3), amended clause (a)(5)(E)(ii) (before redesignation by Sec. 522(b)), effective for distributions after 7/18/84 [as provided by Sec. 1875(c)(2) of P.L. 99-514, see above].

Prior to amendment and redesignation, clause (a)(5)(E)(ii) read as follows:

"(ii) Self-employed individuals and owner-employees. An eligible retirement plan described in subclause (III) or (IV) of subparagraph (E)(iv) shall not be treated as an eligible retirement plan for the transfer of a distribution if any part of the distribution is attributable to a trust forming part of a plan under which the employee was an employee within the meaning of section 401(c)(1) at the time contributions were made on his behalf under the plan."

—P.L. 98-369, Sec. 1001(b)(3), substituted "6 months" for "1 year" each time it appeared in para. (a)(2) and subpara. (e)(4)(L), effective for property acquired after 6/22/84 and before 1/1/88.

In 1983, P.L. 97-448, Sec. 101(b), substituted "the zero bracket amount applicable to such an individual for the taxable year" for "$2,300" in subpara. (e)(1)(C) . . . Sec. 103(c)(7), substituted "this subsection, subsection (a)(2) of this section, and subsection (a)(2) of section 403" for "this section and section 403" in subpara. (e)(4)(A) . . . Sec. 103(c)(8)(A), added clause (a)(5)(D)(v), effective for tax. yrs. begin. after 12/31/81. For transitional note, see Sec. 311(i)(2) of this Act reproduced in note following Code Sec. 219.

—P.L. 97-448, Sec. 103(c)(12)(D), corrected Sec. 311(c)(2) of P.L. 97-34 to amend subpara. (e)(4)(J) instead of (e)(J) [see below] and substituted "section 72(o)(5)" for "section 77(o)(5)" in the last sentence of para. (e)(4)(J)[as added by Sec. 311(c)(2) of P.L. 97-34].

In 1981, P.L. 97-34, Sec. 311(b)(2), added the last sentence to the end of subpara. (e)(4)(A) . . . Sec. 311(b)(3)(A), added "(other than accumulated deductible employee contributions within the meaning of section 72(o)(5))" after "contributions" at the end of subpara. (a)(5)(B), deleted "or" at the end of clause (a)(5)(D)(i)(I), substituted ", or" for the period at the end of clause (a)(5)(D)(i)(II), and added clause (a)(5)(D)(i)(III) . . . Sec. 311(c)(1), substituted "by the employee (other than deductible employee contributions within the meaning of section 72(o)(5))" for "by the employee" in para. (a)(1) . . . Sec. 311(c)(2), [as amended by Sec. 103(c)(12)(D) of P.L. 97-448, see above], added the last sentence to the end of subpara. (e)(4)(J), effective for tax. yrs. begin. after 12/31/81. For transitional rule see Sec. 311(i)(2) of this Act reproduced in note following Code Sec. 219.

—P.L. 97-34, Sec. 314(c)(1), deleted "or made available" after "distributed" each place it appeared in para. (a)(1), effective for tax. yrs. begin. after 12/31/81.

In 1980, P.L. 96-608, Sec. 2(a), added subpara. (a)(6)(E), for payments made in tax. yrs. begin. after 12/31/78. Sec. 2(b)(2) of this Act provides:

"(2) Transitional rule. In the case of any payment made before January 1, 1982, in a taxable year beginning after December 31, 1978, which is treated as a qualifying rollover distribution (as defined in section 402(a)(5)(D)(i) of the Internal Revenue Code of 1954) by reason of the amendment made by subsection (a), the applicable period specified in section 402(a)(5)(C) of such Code shall not expire before the close of December 31, 1981."

—P.L. 96-222, Sec. 101(a)(13)(A), amended the effective date for changes made Secs. 156(a) and (b) of P.L. 95-600 to distributions or transfers made after '77, in tax. yrs. begin. after 12/31/77 [see below]. Sec. 101(a)(13)(B) of P.L. 96-222 provides:

"(B) Transitional rule for making section 403(b)(8) rollover in the case of payments during 1978. In the case of any payment made during 1978 in a qualifying distribution described in section 403(b)(8) of the Internal Revenue Code of 1954, the applicable period specified in section 402(a)(5)(C) of such Code shall not expire before the close of December 31, 1980."

—P.L. 96-222, Sec. 101(a)(14)(A), substituted "subsection" for "section" each place it appeared in Sec. 157(h)(3) of P.L. 95-600 [see below] . . . Sec. 101(a)(14)(D), substituted "any payment made during 1978" for "any payment" and substituted "December 31, 1980" for "December 31, 1798" in Sec. 157(h)(3)(B) of P.L. 95-600 [see below].

—P.L. 96-222, Sec. 101(a)(14)(C), amended clause (a)(7)(A)(i), effective for lump-sum distributions completed after 12/31/78 in tax yrs. end. after 12/31/78.

Prior to amendment, clause (a)(7)(A)(i) read as follows:

"(i) any portion of a lump-sum distribution from a qualified trust is paid to the spouse of the employee on account of the employee's death,"

—P.L. 96-222, Sec. 101(a)(14)(E)(i), substituted "may designate" for "many designate" in clause (a)(6)(D)(iii), effective for qualifying rollover distributions (as defined in Code Sec. 402(a)(5)(D)(i)) completed after 12/31/78 in tax. yrs. end. after 12/31/78.

In 1978, P.L. 95-600, Sec. 101(d)(1), substituted "$2,300" for "$2,200" in subpara. (e)(1)(C), effective for tax. yrs. begin. after 12/31/78.

—P.L. 95-600, Sec. 135(b), added para. (a)(8), effective for plan yrs. begin. after '79. Sec. 135(c)(2) of the Act provides:

"(2) Transitional rule. In the case of cash or deferred arrangements in existence on June 27, 1974—

"(A) the qualification of the plan and the trust under section 401 of the Internal Revenue Code of 1954;

"(B) the exemption of the trust under section 501(a) of such Code;

"(C) the taxable year of inclusion in gross income of the employee of any amount so contributed by the employer to the trust; and

"(D) the excludability of the interest of the employee in the trust under sections 2039 and 2517 of such Code,

shall be determined for plan years beginning before January 1, 1980 in a manner consistent with Revenue Ruling 56-497 (1956-2 C.B. 284), Revenue Ruling 63-180 (1963-2 C.B. 189), and Revenue Ruling 68-89 (1968-1 C.B. 402)."

—P.L. 95-600, Sec. 157(f)(1), added subpara. (a)(6)(D), effective for qualifying rollover distributions (as defined in Code Sec. 402(a)(5)(D)(i)) completed after 12/31/78 in tax. yrs. end. after 12/31/78.

—P.L. 95-600, Sec. 157(g)(1), added para. (a)(7), effective for lump-sum distributions completed after 12/31/78 in tax. yrs. end. after 12/31/78.

—P.L. 95-600, Sec. 157(h)(1), substituted "subparagraphs (B) and (H) of subsection (e)(4)" for "subsection (e)(4)(B)" in subclause (a)(5)(D)(i)(II), effective for payments made in tax. yrs. begin. after 12/31/77. Sec. 157(h)(3)(B) [as amended by Sec. 101(a)(14)(D) of P.L. 96-222, see above] of this Act provides:

"(B) Transitional rule. In the case of any payment made during 1978 which is described in section 402(a)(5)(A) or 403(a)(4)(A) of the Internal Revenue Code of 1954 by reason of the amendments made by this section, the applicable period specified in section 402(a)(5)(C) of such Code (or in the case of an individual retirement annuity, such section as made applicable by section 403(a)(4)(B) of such Code) shall not expire before the close of December 31, 1980."

—P.L. 95-458, Sec. 4(a), amended para. (a)(5), effective for tax. yrs. begin. after 12/31/74. Sec. 4(d)(2) of this Act provides as follows:

"(2) Validation of certain attempted rollovers. If the taxpayer—

"(A) attempted to comply with the requirements of section 402(a)(5) or 403(a)(4) of the Internal Revenue Code of 1954 for a taxable year beginning before the date of the enactment of this Act, and

"(B) failed to meet the requirements of such section that all property received in the distribution be transferred,

such section (as amended by this section) shall be applied by treating any transfer of property made on or before December 31, 1978, as if it were made on or before the 60th day after the day on which the taxpayer received such property. For purposes of the preceding sentence, a transfer of money shall be treated as transfer of property received in a distribution to the extent that the amount of the money transferred does not exceed the highest fair market value of the property distributed during the 60-day period beginning on the date on which the taxpayer received such property."

Prior to amendment, para. (a)(5) read as follows:

"(5) Rollover amounts. In the case of an employees' trust described in section 401(a) which is exempt from tax under section 501(a), if—

"(A) the balance to the credit of an employee is paid to him—

"(i) within one taxable year of the employee on account of a termination of the plan of which the trust is a part or, in the case of a profit-sharing or stock bonus plan, a complete discontinuance of contributions under such plan, or

"(ii) in one or more distributions which constitute a lump-sum distribution within the meaning of subsection (e)(4)(A) (determined without reference to subsection (e)(4)(B)),

"(B)(i) the employee transfers all the property he receives in such distribution to an individual retirement account described in section 408(a), an individual retirement annuity described in section 408(b) (other than an endowment contract), or a retirement bond described in section 409, on or before the 60th day after the day on which he received such property, to the extent the fair market value of such property exceeds the amount referred to in subsection (e)(4)(D)(i), or

"(ii) the employee transfers all the property he receives in such distribution to an employees' trust described in section 401(a) which is exempt from tax under section 501(a), or to an annuity plan described in section 403(a) on or before the 60th day after the day on which he received such property, to the extent the fair market value of such property exceeds the amount referred to in subsection (e)(4)(D)(i), and

"(C) the amount so transferred consists of the property (other than money) distributed, to the extent that the fair market value of such property does not exceed the amount required to be transferred pursuant to subparagraph (B),

then such distributions are not includible in gross income for the year in which paid. For purposes of this title, a transfer described in subparagraph (B)(i) shall be treated as a rollover contribution as described in section 408(d)(3). Subparagraph (B)(ii) does not apply in the case of a transfer to an employees' trust, or annuity plan if any part of a payment described in subparagraph (A) is attributable to a trust forming part of a plan under which the employee was an employee within the meaning of section 401(c)(1) at the time contributions were made on his behalf under the plan."

—P.L. 95-458, Sec. 4(c), added new subpara. (a)(6)(C), deleted "For purposes of paragraph (5)(A)(i)" after the heading of para. (a)(6), substituted "For purposes of paragraph (5)(D)(i), a complete" for "A complete" in subpara. (a)(6)(A), and added "For purposes of paragraph (5)(D)(i)—" after "Assets", in subpara (a)(6)(B), effective for tax. yrs. begin. after 12/31/74. Sec. 4(d)(2) of this Act provides as follows:

"(2) Validation of certain attempted rollovers. If the taxpayer—

"(A) attempted to comply with the requirements of section 402(a)(5) or 403(a)(4) of the Internal Revenue Code of 1954 for a taxable year beginning before the date of the enactment of this Act, and

"(B) failed to meet the requirements of such section that all property received in the distribution be transferred,

such section (as amended by this section) shall be applied by treating any transfer of property made on or before December 31, 1978, as if it were made on or before the 60th day after the day on which the taxpayer received such property. For purposes of the preceding sentence, a transfer of money shall be treated as transfer of property received in a distribution to the extent that the amount of the money transferred does not exceed the highest fair market value of the property distributed during the 60-day period beginning on the date on which the taxpayer received such property."

In 1977, P.L. 95-30, Sec. 102(b)(4), substituted "amount equal to $2,200 plus one-tenth of the excess of" for "amount equal to one-tenth of the excess of" in subpara. (e)(1)(C), effective for tax. yrs. begin. after 12/31/76.

In 1976, P.L. 94-455, Sec. 1402(b)(1)(C), substituted "9 months" for "6 months" in para. (a)(2) and subpara. (e)(4)(L), . . . Sec. 1402(b)(2), substituted "1 year" for "9 months" in para. (a)(2) and subpara. (e)(4)(L), effective for tax. yrs. begin. after 12/31/77.

—P.L. 94-455, Sec. 1512(a), added subpara. (e)(4)(L), effective for distributions and payments made after 12/31/75, in tax. yrs. begin. after 12/31/75.

—P.L. 94-455, Sec. 1901(a)(57)(A), substituted "basic pay" for "basic salary" each place it appeared in para. (a)(4), and amended the last sentence of para. (a)(4) . . . Sec. 1901(a)(57)(B), deleted subsec. (d), effective for tax. yrs. begin. after 12/31/76.

Prior to amendment, the last sentence of para. (a)(4) read as follows:

"In the case of distributions under the Civil Service Retirement Act (5 U.S.C. 2251), the term 'basic salary' shall have the meaning provided in section 1(d) of such Act."

Prior to deletion, subsec. (d) read as follows:

"(d) Certain employees' annuities. Notwithstanding subsection (b) or any other provision of this subtitle, a contribution to a trust by an employer shall not be included in the gross income of the employee in the year in which the contribution is made if—

"(1) such contribution is to be applied by the trustee for the purchase of annuity contracts for the benefit of such employee;

"(2) such contribution is made to the trustee pursuant to a written agreement entered into prior to October 21, 1942, between the employer and the trustee, or between the employer and the employee; and

"(3) under the terms of the trust agreement the employee is not entitled during his lifetime, except with the consent of the trustee, to any payments under annuity contracts purchased by the trustee other than annuity payments.

The employee shall include in his gross income the amounts received under such contracts for the year received as provided in section 72 (relating to annuities). This subsection shall have no application with respect to amounts contributed to a trust after June 1, 1949, if the trust on such date was exempt under section 165(a) of the Internal Revenue Code of 1939. For purposes of this subsection, amounts paid by an employer for the purchase of annuity contracts which are transferred to the trustee shall be deemed to be contributions made to a trust or trustee and contributions applied by the trustee for the purchase of annuity contracts; the term 'annuity contracts purchased by the trustee' shall include annuity contracts so purchased by the employer and transferred to the trustee; and the term 'employee' shall include only a person who was in the employ of the employer, and was covered by the agreement referred to in paragraph (2), prior to October 21, 1942."

—P.L. 94-455, Sec. 1901(a)(57)(C), substituted "Except for purposes of subsection (a)(2) and section 403(a)(2)," for "For purposes of this subparagraph," in the third sentence of subpara. (e)(4)(A), effective for distributions or payments made after 12/31/73, in tax. yrs. begin. after 12/31/73.

—P.L. 94-455, Sec. 1906(b)(13)(A), substituted "Secretary" for "Secretary or his delegate" each place it appeared in subsecs. (a) and (e), effective for tax. yrs. begin. after 12/31/76.

—P.L. 94-267, Sec. 1(a), amended subpara. (a)(5)(A), effective for payments made to an employee on or after 7/4/74, subject to Sec. 1(d) of this Act, which reads as follows:

"(d) Transitional rules.

"(1) In general.

"(A) Period for rollover contribution. In the case of a payment described in section 402(a)(5)(A) (other than a payment described in section 402(a)(5)(A) as in effect on the day before the date of the enactment of this Act) or section 403(a)(4)(A) (other than a payment described in section 403(a)(4)(A) as in effect on the day before the date of the enactment of this Act) of the Internal Revenue Code of 1954 (relating to distributions of the balance to the credit of the employee) which is contributed by an employee after the date of the enactment of this Act to a trust, plan, account, annuity, or bond described in section 402(a)(5)(B) or 403(a)(4)(B) of such Code, the applicable period specified in section 402(a)(5)(B) or 403(a)(4)(B) of such Code (relating to rollover distributions to another plan or retirement account) shall not expire before December 31, 1976.

"(B) Time of contribution.

"(i) General rule. If the initial portion of a payment the applicable period for which is determined under subparagraph (A) is contributed before December 31, 1976, by an individual to a trust, plan, account, annuity, or bond described in subparagraph (A) and the remaining portion of such payment is contributed by such individual to such a trust, plan, account, annuity, or bond not later than 30 days after the date a credit or refund is allowed by the Secretary of the Treasury or his delegate under section 6402 of the Internal Revenue Code of 1954 with respect to the contribution, then, for purposes of subparagraph (A) and sections 402(a)(5) and 403(a)(4) of such Code, at the election of the individual (made in accordance with regulations prescribed by the Secretary or his delegate), such remaining portion shall be considered to have been contributed on the date the initial portion of the payment was contributed. For purposes of this subparagraph, the initial portion of a payment is the amount by which such payment exceeds the amount of the tax imposed on such payment by chapter 1 of such Code (determined without regard to this subparagraph).

"(ii) Regulations. For purposes of this subparagraph, the tax imposed on a payment by chapter 1 of the Internal Revenue Code of 1954, and the date a credit or refund is allowed by the Secretary of the Treasury or his delegate under section 6402 with respect to a contribution, shall be determined under regulations prescribed by the Secretary of the Treasury or his delegate.

"(C) Period of limitations. If an individual has made the election provided by subparagraph (B), then—

"(i) the period provided by the Internal Revenue Code of 1954 for the assessment of any deficiency for the taxable year in which the payment described in subparagraph (A) was made and each subsequent taxable year for which tax is determined by reference to the treatment of such payment under such Code or the status under such Code of any trust, plan, account, annuity, or bond described in subparagraph (A) shall, to the extent attributable to such treatment, not expire before the expiration of 3 years from the date the Secretary of the Treasury or his delegate is notified by the individual (in such manner as the Secretary of the Treasury or his delegate may prescribe) that such individual has made (or failed to make) the contribution of the remaining portion of the payment within the period specified in subparagraph (B)(i), and

"(ii) such deficiency may be assessed before the expiration of such 3-year period notwithstanding the provisions of section 6212(c) of such Code or the provisions of any other law or rule of law which would otherwise prevent such assessment.

"(2) Rollover contribution for certain property sold. Sections 402(a)(5)(C) and 403(a)(4)(C) of the Internal Revenue Code of 1954 (relating to the requirement that rollover amount must consist of property received in a distribution) shall not apply with respect to that portion of the property received in a payment described in section 402(a)(5)(A) (other than a payment described in section 402(a)(5)(A) as in effect on the day before the date of the enactment of this Act) or 403(a)(4)(A) (other than a payment described in section 403(a)(4)(A) as in effect on the day before the date of the enactment of this Act) of such Code which is sold or exchanged by the employee on or before the date of the enactment of this Act, if the employee transfers an amount of cash equal to the proceeds received from the sale or exchange of such property in excess of the amount considered contributed by the employee (within the meaning of section 402(a)(4)(D)(i) of such Code).

"(3) Nonrecognition of gain or loss. For purposes of the Internal Revenue Code of 1954, no gain or loss shall be recognized with respect to the sale or exchange of property described in paragraph (2) if the proceeds of such sale or exchange are transferred by an employee in accordance with this subsection and the applicable provisions of section 402(a)(5) or 403(a)(4) of such Code."

Prior to amendment, subpara. (a)(5)(A) read as follows:

"(A) the balance to the credit of an employee is paid to him on one or more distributions which constitute a lump sum distribution within the meaning of subsection (e)(4)(A) (determined without reference to subsection (e)(4)(B)),"

—P.L. 94-267, Sec. 1(a)(2), substituted "a payment" for "the lump-sum distribution" in para. (a)(5) . . . Sec. 1(a)(3), added para. (a)(6), effective for payments made to an employee on or after 7/4/74.

In 1974, P.L. 93-406, Sec. 2005(a), amended subsec. (e), effective for distributions or payments made after 12/31/73, in tax. yrs. begin. 12/31/73.

Prior to amendment, subsec. (e) read as follows:

"(e) Certain plan terminations. For purposes of subsection (a)(2), distributions made after December 31, 1953, and before January 1, 1955, as a result of the complete termination of a stock bonus, pension, or profit-sharing plan of an employer which is a corporation, if the termination of the plan is incident to the complete liquidation occurring before the date of enactment of this title, of the corporation, whether or not such liquidation is incident to a reorganization as defined in section 368(a), shall be considered to be distributions on account of separation from service."

—P.L. 93-406, Sec. 2005(b)(1), amended para. (a)(2), effective for distributions or payments made after 12/31/73, in tax. yrs. begin. after such date.

Prior to amendment, para. (a)(2) read as follows:

"(2) Capital gains treatment for certain distributions. In the case of an employees' trust described in section 401(a), which is exempt from tax under section 501(a), if the total distributions payable with respect to any employee are paid to the distributee within 1 taxable year of the distributee on account of the employee's death or other separation from the service, or on account of the death of the employee after his separation from the service, the amount of such distribution, to the extent exceeding the amounts contributed by the employee (determined by applying section 72(f)), which employee contributions shall be reduced by any amounts theretofore distributed to him which were not includible in gross income, shall be considered a gain from the sale or exchange of a capital asset held for more than 6 months. Where such total distributions include securities of the employer corporation, there shall be excluded from such excess the net unrealized appreciation attributable to that part of the total distributions which consists of the securities of the employer corporation so distributed. The amount of such net unrealized appreciation and the resulting adjustments to basis of the securities of the employer corporation so distributed shall be determined in accordance with regulations prescribed by the Secretary or his delegate. This paragraph shall not apply to distributions paid to any distributee to the extent such distributions are attributable to contributions made on behalf of the employee while he was an employee within the meaning of section 401(c)(1)."

—P.L. 93-406, Sec. 2005(c)(1), deleted subpara. (a)(3)(C), effective for distributions or payments made after 12/31/73, in tax. yrs. begin. after 12/31/73.

Prior to deletion, subpara. (a)(3)(C) read as follows:

"(C) The term 'total distributions payable' means the balance to the credit of an employee which becomes payable to a distributee on account of the employee's death or other separation from the service, or on account of his death after separation from the service."

—P.L. 93-406, Sec. 2005(c)(2), deleted para. (a)(5), effective for distributions or payments made after 12/31/73, in tax. yrs. begin. after 12/31/73.

Prior to deletion, para. (a)(5) read as follows:

"(5) Limitation on capital gains treatment. The first sentence of paragraph (2) shall apply to a distribution paid after December 31, 1969, only to the extent that it does not exceed the sum of—

"(A) the benefits accrued by the employee on behalf of whom it is paid during plan years beginning before January 1, 1970, and

"(B) the portion of the benefits accrued by such employee during plan years beginning after December 31, 1969, which the distributee establishes does not consist of the employee's allocable share of employer contributions to the trust by which such distribution is paid.

The Secretary or his delegate shall prescribe such regulations as may be necessary to carry out the purposes of this paragraph."

—P.L. 93-406, Sec. 2002(g)(5), added para. (a)(5), effective on or after 9/2/74 for contributions to an employees' trust described in Code Sec. 401(a) which is exempt from tax under Code Sec. 501(a) or an annuity described in Code Sec. 403(a).

In 1969, P.L. 91-172, Sec. 321(b)(1), amended subsec. (b), effective for contributions made and premiums paid after 8/1/69.

Prior to amendment, subsec. (b) read as follows:

"(b) Taxability of beneficiary of non-exempt trust. Contributions to an employees' trust made by an employer during a taxable year of the employer which ends within or with a taxable year of the trust for which the trust is not exempt from tax under section 501(a) shall be included in the gross income of an employee for the taxable year in which the contribution is made to the trust in the case of an employee whose beneficial interest in such contribution is nonforfeitable at the time the contribution is made. The amount actually distributed or made available to any distributee by any such trust shall be taxable to him, in the year in which so distributed or made available under section 72 (relating to annuities)."

—P.L. 91-172, Sec. 515(a)(1), added para. (a)(5), effective for tax. yrs. end. after 12/31/69.

In 1964, P.L. 88-272, Sec. 221(c)(1), substituted "subsections (e) and (f) of section 425" for "section 421(d)(2) and (3)" in subpara. (a)(3)(B), effective for tax. yrs. end. after 12/31/63.

—P.L. 88-272, Sec. 232(e)(1), deleted "except that section 72(e)(3) shall not apply" following "(relating to annuities)" in subsecs. (a)(1), (b) and (d), effective for tax. yrs. begin. after 12/31/63.

In 1962, P.L. 87-792, Sec. 4, added the last sentence of para. (a)(2), effective for tax. yrs. begin. after 12/31/62.

In 1960, P.L. 86-437, Sec. 1, added para. (a)(4)... Sec. 2(a), substituted "paragraphs (2) and (4)" for "paragraph (2)" in para. (a)(1), effective for tax. yrs. begin. after 12/31/59.

Sec. 402A. Optional treatment of elective deferrals as Roth contributions.

(a) General rule.

If an applicable retirement plan includes a qualified Roth contribution program—

(1) any designated Roth contribution made by an employee pursuant to the program shall be treated as an elective deferral for purposes of this chapter, except that such contribution shall not be excludable from gross income, and

(2) such plan (and any arrangement which is part of such plan) shall not be treated as failing to meet any requirement of this chapter solely by reason of including such program.

(b) Qualified Roth contribution program.

For purposes of this section—

(1) **In general.** The term "qualified Roth contribution program" means a program under which an employee may elect to make designated Roth contributions in lieu of all or a portion of elective deferrals the employee is otherwise eligible to make under the applicable retirement plan.

(2) **Separate accounting required.** A program shall not be treated as a qualified Roth contribution program unless the applicable retirement plan—

(A) establishes separate accounts ("designated Roth accounts") for the designated Roth contributions of each employee and any earnings properly allocable to the contributions, and

(B) maintains separate recordkeeping with respect to each account.

(c) Definitions and rules relating to designated Roth contributions.

For purposes of this section—

(1) **Designated Roth contribution.** The term "designated Roth contribution" means any elective deferral which—

(A) is excludable from gross income of an employee without regard to this section, and

(B) the employee designates (at such time and in such manner as the Secretary may prescribe) as not being so excludable.

(2) **Designation limits.** The amount of elective deferrals which an employee may designate under paragraph (1) shall not exceed the excess (if any) of—

(A) the maximum amount of elective deferrals excludable from gross income of the employee for the taxable year (without regard to this section), over

(B) the aggregate amount of elective deferrals of the employee for the taxable year which the employee does not designate under paragraph (1).

(3) **Rollover contributions.**

(A) In general. A rollover contribution of any payment or distribution from a designated Roth account which is otherwise allowable under this chapter may be made only if the contribution is to—

(i) another designated Roth account of the individual from whose account the payment or distribution was made, or

(ii) a Roth IRA of such individual.

(B) Coordination with limit. Any rollover contribution to a designated Roth account under subparagraph (A) shall not be taken into account for purposes of paragraph (1).

(4) **Taxable rollovers to designated Roth accounts.**

(A) In general. Notwithstanding sections 402(c), 403(b)(8), and 457(e)(16), in the case of any distribution to which this paragraph applies—

(i) there shall be included in gross income any amount which would be includible were it not part of a qualified rollover contribution,

(ii) section 72(t) shall not apply, and

(iii) unless the taxpayer elects not to have this clause apply, any amount required to be included in gross income for any taxable year beginning in 2010 by reason of this paragraph shall be so included ratably over the 2-taxable-year period beginning with the first taxable year beginning in 2011.

Any election under clause (iii) for any distributions during a taxable year may not be changed after the due date for such taxable year.

(B) Distributions to which paragraph applies. In the case of an applicable retirement plan which includes a qualified Roth contribution program, this paragraph shall apply to a distribution from such plan other than from a designated Roth account which is contributed in a qualified rollover contribution (within the meaning of section 408A(e)) to the designated Roth account maintained under such plan for the benefit of the individual to whom the distribution is made.

(C) Coordination with limit. Any distribution to which this paragraph applies shall not be taken into account for purposes of paragraph (1).

(D) Other rules. The rules of subparagraphs (D), (E), and (F) of section 408A(d)(3) (as in effect for taxable years beginning after 2009) shall apply for purposes of this paragraph.

(d) Distribution rules.

For purposes of this title—

(1) **Exclusion.** Any qualified distribution from a designated Roth account shall not be includible in gross income.

(2) **Qualified distribution.** For purposes of this subsection—

(A) In general. The term "qualified distribution" has the meaning given such term by section 408A(d)(2)(A) (without regard to clause (iv) thereof).

(B) **Distributions within nonexclusion period.** A payment or distribution from a designated Roth account shall not be treated as a qualified distribution if such payment or distribution is made within the 5-taxable-year period beginning with the earlier of—

(i) the first taxable year for which the individual made a designated Roth contribution to any designated Roth account established for such individual under the same applicable retirement plan, or

(ii) if a rollover contribution was made to such designated Roth account from a designated Roth account previously established for such individual under another applicable retirement plan, the first taxable year for which the individual made a designated Roth contribution to such previously established account.

(C) **Distributions of excess deferrals and contributions and earnings thereon.** The term "qualified distribution" shall not include any distribution of any excess deferral under section 402(g)(2) or any excess contribution under section 401(k)(8), and any income on the excess deferral or contribution.

(3) **Treatment of distributions of certain excess deferrals.** Notwithstanding section 72, if any excess deferral under section 402(g)(2) attributable to a designated Roth contribution is not distributed on or before the 1st April 15 following the close of the taxable year in which such excess deferral is made, the amount of such excess deferral shall—

(A) not be treated as investment in the contract, and

(B) be included in gross income for the taxable year in which such excess is distributed.

(4) **Aggregation rules.** Section 72 shall be applied separately with respect to distributions and payments from a designated Roth account and other distributions and payments from the plan.

(e) **Other definitions.**

For purposes of this section—

(1) **Applicable retirement plan.** The term "applicable retirement plan" means—

(A) an employees' trust described in section 401(a) which is exempt from tax under section 501(a),

(B) a plan under which amounts are contributed by an individual's employer for an annuity contract described in section 403(b), and

(C) an eligible deferred compensation plan (as defined in section 457(b)) of an eligible employer described in section 457(e)(1)(A).

(2) **Elective deferral.** The term "elective deferral" means—

(A) any elective deferral described in subparagraph (A) or (C) of section 402(g)(3), and

(B) any elective deferral of compensation by an individual under an eligible deferred compensation plan (as defined in section 457(b)) of an eligible employer described in section 457(e)(1)(A).

In **2010**, P.L. 111-312, Sec. 101(a)(1), substituted "December 31, 2012" for "December 31, 2010" both places it appeared in Sec. 901 of P.L. 107-16 [see below], effective as if included in the enactment of P.L. 107-16, EGTRRA, 6/7/2001.

—P.L. 111-240, Sec. 2111(a), deleted "and" at the end of subpara. (e)(1)(A), substituted ", and" for the period at the end of subpara. (e)(1)(B), and added subpara. (e)(1)(C) . . . Sec. 2111(b), amended para. (e)(2), effective for tax. yrs. begin. after 12/31/2010.

Prior to amendment, para. (e)(2) read as follows:

"(2) Elective deferral. The term 'elective deferral' means any elective deferral described in subparagraph (A) or (C) of section 402(g)(3)."

—P.L. 111-240, Sec. 2112(a), added para. (c)(4), effective for distributions after 9/27/2010.

In **2006**, P.L. 109-280, Sec. 811, of this Act [relating to Sec. 901 of P.L. 107-16, see below], provides:

"SEC. 811. PENSIONS AND INDIVIDUAL RETIREMENT ARRANGEMENT PROVISIONS OF ECONOMIC GROWTH AND TAX RELIEF RECONCILIATION ACT OF 2001 MADE PERMANENT.

"Title IX of the Economic Growth and Tax Relief Reconciliation Act of 2001 shall not apply to the provisions of, and amendments made by, subtitles A through F of title VI of such Act (relating to pension and individual retirement arrangement provisions)."

In **2002**, P.L. 107-358, Sec. 2, added subsec. (c) in Sec. 901 of P.L. 107-16 [see below], effective 12/17/2002.

In **2001**, P.L. 107-16, Sec. 617(a), added Code Sec. 402A, effective for tax. yrs. begin. after 12/31/2005.

—P.L. 107-16, Sec. 901, of this Act [as amended by Sec. 2 of P.L. 107-358, and Sec. 101(a)(1) of P.L. 111-312, and as related to Sec. 811 of P.L. 109-280, see above], reads as follows:

"SEC. 901. SUNSET OF PROVISIONS OF ACT.

"(a) In general. All provisions of, and amendments made by, this Act shall not apply—

"(1) to taxable, plan, or limitation years beginning after December 31, 2012, or

"(2) in the case of title V, to estates of decedents dying, gifts made, or generation skipping transfers, after December 31, 2012.

"(b) Application of certain laws. The Internal Revenue Code of 1986 and the Employee Retirement Income Security Act of 1974 shall be applied and administered to years, estates, gifts, and transfers described in subsection (a) as if the provisions and amendments described in subsection (a) had never been enacted.

"(c) Exception. Subsection (a) shall not apply to section 803 (relating to no federal income tax on restitution received by victims of the Nazi regime or their heirs or estates)."

Sec. 403. Taxation of employee annuities.

(a) **Taxability of beneficiary under a qualified annuity plan.**

(1) **Distributee taxable under section 72.** If an annuity contract is purchased by an employer for an employee under a plan which meets the requirements of section 404(a)(2) (whether or not the employer deducts the amounts paid for the contract under such section), the amount actually distributed to any distributee under the contract shall be taxable to the distributee (in the year in which so distributed) under section 72 (relating to annuities).

(2) **Special rule for health and long-term care insurance.** To the extent provided in section 402(l), paragraph (1) shall not apply to the amount distributed under the contract which is otherwise includible in gross income under this subsection.

(3) **Self-employed individuals.** For purposes of this subsection, the term "employee" includes an individual who is an employee within the meaning of section 401(c)(1), and the employer of such individual is the person treated as his employer under section 401(c)(4).

(4) **Rollover amounts.**

(A) General rule. If—

(i) any portion of the balance to the credit of an employee in an employee annuity described in paragraph (1) is paid to him in an eligible rollover distribution (within the meaning of section 402(c)(4)),

(ii) the employee transfers any portion of the property he receives in such distribution to an eligible retirement plan, and

(iii) in the case of a distribution of property other than money, the amount so transferred consists of the property distributed,

then such distribution (to the extent so transferred) shall not be includible in gross income for the taxable year in which paid.

(B) Certain rules made applicable. The rules of paragraphs (2) through (7) and (11) and (9) of section 402(c) and section 402(f) shall apply for purposes of subparagraph (A).

(5) **Direct trustee-to-trustee transfer.** Any amount transferred in a direct trustee-to-trustee transfer in accordance with section 401(a)(31) shall not be includible in gross income for the taxable year of such transfer.

Employee benefit plans   Code Sec. 403(b)(8)(B)

(b) Taxability of beneficiary under annuity purchased by section 501(c)(3) organization or public school.

(1) General rule. If—

(A) an annuity contract is purchased—

(i) for an employee by an employer described in section 501(c)(3) which is exempt from tax under section 501(a),

(ii) for an employee (other than an employee described in clause (i)), who performs services for an educational organization described in section 170(b)(1)(A)(ii), by an employer which is a State, a political subdivision of a State, or an agency or instrumentality of any one or more of the foregoing, or

(iii) for the minister described in section 414(e)(5)(A) by the minister or by an employer,

(B) such annuity contract is not subject to subsection (a),

(C) the employee's rights under the contract are nonforfeitable, except for failure to pay future premiums,

(D) except in the case of a contract purchased by a church, such contract is purchased under a plan which meets the nondiscrimination requirements of paragraph (12), and

(E) in the case of a contract purchased under a salary reduction agreement, the contract meets the requirements of section 401(a)(30),

then contributions and other additions by such employer for such annuity contract shall be excluded from the gross income of the employee for the taxable year to the extent that the aggregate of such contributions and additions (when expressed as an annual addition (within the meaning of section 415(c)(2))) does not exceed the applicable limit under section 415. The amount actually distributed to any distributee under such contract shall be taxable to the distributee (in the year in which so distributed) under section 72 (relating to annuities). For purposes of applying the rules of this subsection to contributions and other additions by an employer for a taxable year, amounts transferred to a contract described in this paragraph by reason of a rollover contribution described in paragraph (8) of this subsection or section 408(d)(3)(A)(ii) shall not be considered contributed by such employer.

(2) Special rule for health and long-term care insurance. To the extent provided in section 402(l), paragraph (1) shall not apply to the amount distributed under the contract which is otherwise includible in gross income under this subsection.

(3) Includible compensation. For purposes of this subsection, the term "includible compensation" means, in the case of any employee, the amount of compensation which is received from the employer described in paragraph (1)(A), and which is includible in gross income (computed without regard to section 911) for the most recent period (ending not later than the close of the taxable year) which under paragraph (4) may be counted as one year of service, and which precedes the taxable year by no more than five years. Such term does not include any amount contributed by the employer for any annuity contract to which this subsection applies. Such term includes—

(A) any elective deferral (as defined in section 402(g)(3)), and

(B) any amount which is contributed or deferred by the employer at the election of the employee and which is not includible in the gross income of the employee by reason of section 125, 132(f)(4), or 457.

(4) Years of service. In determining the number of years of service for purposes of this subsection, there shall be included—

(A) one year for each full year during which the individual was a full-time employee of the organization purchasing the annuity for him, and

(B) a fraction of a year (determined in accordance with regulations prescribed by the Secretary) for each full year during which such individual was a part-time employee of such organization and for each part of a year during which such individual was a full-time or part-time employee of such organization.

In no case shall the number of years of service be less than one.

(5) Application to more than one annuity contract. If for any taxable year of the employee this subsection applies to 2 or more annuity contracts purchased by the employer, such contracts shall be treated as one contract.

(6) Repealed.

(7) Custodial accounts for regulated investment company stock.

(A) Amounts paid treated as contributions. For purposes of this title, amounts paid by an employer described in paragraph (1)(A) to a custodial account which satisfies the requirements of section 401(f)(2) shall be treated as amounts contributed by him for an annuity contract for his employee if—

(i) the amounts are to be invested in regulated investment company stock to be held in that custodial account, and

(ii) under the custodial account no such amounts may be paid or made available to any distributee (unless such amount is a distribution to which section 72(t)(2)(G) applies) before the employee dies, attains age 59½, has a severance from employment, becomes disabled (within the meaning of section 72(m)(7)), or in the case of contributions made pursuant to a salary reduction agreement (within the meaning of section 3121(a)(5)(D)), encounters financial hardship.

(B) Account treated as plan. For purposes of this title, a custodial account which satisfies the requirements of section 401(f)(2) shall be treated as an organization described in section 401(a) solely for purposes of subchapter F and subtitle F with respect to amounts received by it (and income from investment thereof).

(C) Regulated investment company. For purposes of this paragraph, the term "regulated investment company" means a domestic corporation which is a regulated investment company within the meaning of section 851(a).

(8) Rollover amounts.

(A) General rule. If—

(i) any portion of the balance to the credit of an employee in an annuity contract described in paragraph (1) is paid to him in an eligible rollover distribution (within the meaning of section 402(c)(4)),

(ii) the employee transfers any portion of the property he receives in such distribution to an eligible retirement plan described in section 402(c)(8)(B), and

(iii) in the case of a distribution of property other than money, the property so transferred consists of the property distributed,

then such distribution (to the extent so transferred) shall not be includible in gross income for the taxable year in which paid.

(B) Certain rules made applicable. The rules of paragraphs (2) through (7) , (9), and (11) of section

1,919

402(c) and section 402(f) shall apply for purposes of subparagraph (A), except that section 402(f) shall be applied to the payor in lieu of the plan administrator.

(9) Retirement income accounts provided by churches, etc.

(A) Amounts paid treated as contributions. For purposes of this title—

(i) a retirement income account shall be treated as an annuity contract described in this subsection, and

(ii) amounts paid by an employer described in paragraph (1)(A) to a retirement income account shall be treated as amounts contributed by the employer for an annuity contract for the employee on whose behalf such account is maintained.

(B) Retirement income account. For purposes of this paragraph, the term "retirement income account" means a defined contribution program established or maintained by a church, or a convention or association of churches, including an organization described in section 414(e)(3)(A), to provide benefits under section 403(b) for an employee described in paragraph (1) or his beneficiaries.

(10) Distribution requirements. Under regulations prescribed by the Secretary, this subsection shall not apply to any annuity contract (or to any custodial account described in paragraph (7) or retirement income account described in paragraph (9)) unless requirements similar to the requirements of sections 401(a)(9) and 401(a)(31) are met (and requirements similar to the incidental death benefit requirements of section 401(a) are met) with respect to such annuity contract (or custodial account or retirement income account). Any amount transferred in a direct trustee-to-trustee transfer in accordance with section 401(a)(31) shall not be includible in gross income for the taxable year of the transfer.

(11) Requirement that distributions not begin before age 59½, severance from employment, death, or disability. This subsection shall not apply to any annuity contract unless under such contract distributions attributable to contributions made pursuant to a salary reduction agreement (within the meaning of section 402(g)(3)(C)) may be paid only—

(A) when the employee attains age 59½, has a severance from employment, dies, or becomes disabled (within the meaning of section 72(m)(7)),

(B) in the case of hardship, or

(C) for distributions to which section 72(t)(2)(G) applies.

Such contract may not provide for the distribution of any income attributable to such contributions in the case of hardship.

(12) Nondiscrimination requirements.

(A) In general. For purposes of paragraph (1)(D), a plan meets the nondiscrimination requirements of this paragraph if—

(i) with respect to contributions not made pursuant to a salary reduction agreement, such plan meets the requirements of paragraphs (4), (5), (17), and (26) of section 401(a), section 401(m), and section 410(b) in the same manner as if such plan were described in section 401(a), and

(ii) all employees of the organization may elect to have the employer make contributions of more than $200 pursuant to a salary reduction agreement if any employee of the organization may elect to have the organization make contributions for such contracts pursuant to such agreement.

For purposes of clause (i), a contribution shall be treated as not made pursuant to a salary reduction agreement if under the agreement it is made pursuant to a 1-time irrevocable election made by the employee at the time of initial eligibility to participate in the agreement or is made pursuant to a similar arrangement involving a one-time irrevocable election specified in regulations. For purposes of clause (ii), there may be excluded any employee who is a participant in an eligible deferred compensation plan (within the meaning of section 457) or a qualified cash or deferred arrangement of the organization or another annuity contract described in this subsection. Any nonresident alien described in section 410(b)(3)(C) may also be excluded. Subject to the conditions applicable under section 410(b)(4), there may be excluded for purposes of this subparagraph employees who are students performing services described in section 3121(b)(10) and employees who normally work less than 20 hours per week.

(B) Church. For purposes of paragraph (1)(D), the term "church" has the meaning given to such term by section 3121(w)(3)(A). Such term shall include any qualified church-controlled organization (as defined in section 3121(w)(3)(B)).

(C) State and local governmental plans. For purposes of paragraph (1)(D), the requirements of subparagraph (A)(i) (other than those relating to section 401(a)(17)) shall not apply to a governmental plan (within the meaning of section 414(d)) maintained by a State or local government or political subdivision thereof (or agency or instrumentality thereof).

(13) Trustee-to-trustee transfers to purchase permissive service credit. No amount shall be includible in gross income by reason of a direct trustee-to-trustee transfer to a defined benefit governmental plan (as defined in section 414(d)) if such transfer is—

(A) for the purchase of permissive service credit (as defined in section 415(n)(3)(A)) under such plan, or

(B) a repayment to which section 415 does not apply by reason of subsection (k)(3) thereof.

(14) Death benefits under USERRA-qualified active military service. This subsection shall not apply to an annuity contract unless such contract meets the requirements of section 401(a)(37).

(c) Taxability of beneficiary under nonqualified annuities or under annuities purchased by exempt organizations.

Premiums paid by an employer for an annuity contract which is not subject to subsection (a) shall be included in the gross income of the employee in accordance with section 83 (relating to property transferred in connection with performance of services), except that the value of such contract shall be substituted for the fair market value of the property for purposes of applying such section. The preceding sentence shall not apply to that portion of the premiums paid which is excluded from gross income under subsection (b). In the case of any portion of any contract which is attributable to premiums to which this subsection applies, the amount actually paid or made available under such contract to any beneficiary which is attributable to such premiums shall be taxable to the beneficiary (in the year in which so paid or made available) under section 72 (relating to annuities).

In 2010, P.L. 111-312, Sec. 101(a)(1), substituted "December 31, 2012" for "December 31, 2010" both places it appeared in Sec. 901 of P.L. 107-16 [see below], effective as if included in the enactment of P.L. 107-16, EGTRRA, 6/7/2001.

Employee benefit plans   Code Sec. 403

In 2008, P.L. 110-245, Sec. 104(c)(2), added para. (b)(14), effective for deaths and disabilities occurring on or after 1/1/2007. Sec. 104(d)(2), of this Act, provides:

"(2) Provisions relating to plan amendments.

"(A) In general. If this subparagraph applies to any plan or contract amendment, such plan or contract shall be treated as being operated in accordance with the terms of the plan during the period described in subparagraph (B)(iii).

"(B) Amendments to which subparagraph (A) applies.

"(i) In general. Subparagraph (A) shall apply to any amendment to any plan or annuity contract which is made —

"(I) pursuant to the amendments made by subsection (a) or pursuant to any regulation issued by the Secretary of the Treasury under subsection (a), and

"(II) on or before the last day of the first plan year beginning on or after January 1, 2010.

"In the case of a governmental plan (as defined in section 414(d) of the Internal Revenue Code of 1986), this clause shall be applied by substituting '2012' for '2010' in subclause (II).

"(ii) Conditions. This paragraph shall not apply to any amendment unless —

"(I) the plan or contract is operated as if such plan or contract amendment were in effect for the period described in clause (iii), and

"(II) such plan or contract amendment applies retroactively for such period.

"(iii) Period described. The period described in this clause is the period —

"(I) beginning on the effective date specified by the plan, and

"(II) ending on the date described in clause (i)(II) (or, if earlier, the date the plan or contract amendment is adopted)."

In 2006, P.L. 109-280, Sec. 811, of this Act [relating to Sec. 901 of P.L. 107-16, see below], provides:

"SEC. 811. PENSIONS AND INDIVIDUAL RETIREMENT ARRANGEMENT PROVISIONS OF ECONOMIC GROWTH AND TAX RELIEF RECONCILIATION ACT OF 2001 MADE PERMANENT.

"Title IX of the Economic Growth and Tax Relief Reconciliation Act of 2001 shall not apply to the provisions of, and amendments made by, subtitles A through F of title VI of such Act (relating to pension and individual retirement arrangement provisions)."

— P.L. 109-280, Sec. 826, of this Act, reads as follows:

"SEC. 826. MODIFICATIONS OF RULES GOVERNING HARDSHIPS AND UNFORSEEN FINANCIAL EMERGENCIES.

"Within 180 days after the date of the enactment of this Act, the Secretary of the Treasury shall modify the rules for determining whether a participant has had a hardship for purposes of section 401(k)(2)(B)(i)(IV) of the Internal Revenue Code of 1986 to provide that if an event (including the occurrence of a medical expense) would constitute a hardship under the plan if it occurred with respect to the participant's spouse or dependent (as defined in section 152 of such Code), such event shall, to the extent permitted under a plan, constitute a hardship if it occurs with respect to a person who is a beneficiary under the plan with respect to the participant. The Secretary of the Treasury shall issue similar rules for purposes of determining whether a participant has had —

"(1) a hardship for purposes of section 403(b)(11)(B) of such Code; or

"(2) an unforeseen financial emergency for purposes of sections 409A(a)(2)(A)(vi), 409A(a)(2)(B)(ii), and 457(d)(1)(A)(iii) of such Code."

— P.L. 109-280, Sec. 827(b)(2), added "(unless such amount is a distribution to which section 72(t)(2)(G) applies)" after "distributee" in clause (b)(7)(A)(ii) . . . Sec. 827(b)(3), deleted "or" at the end of subpara. (b)(11)(A), substituted ", or" for the period at the end of subpara. (b)(11)(B) and added subpara. (b)(11)(C), effective for distributions after 9/11/2001. Sec. 827(c)(2) of this Act reads as follows:

"(2) Waiver of limitations. If refund or credit of any overpayment of tax resulting from the amendments made by this section is prevented at any time before the close of the 1-year period beginning on the date of the enactment of this Act by the operation of any law or rule of law (including res judicata), such refund or credit may nevertheless be made or allowed if claim therefor is filed before the close of such period."

— P.L. 109-280, Sec. 829(a)(2), added "and (11)" after "(7)" in subpara. (a)(4)(B) . . . Sec. 829(a)(3), substituted ", (9), and (11)" for "and (9)" in subpara. (b)(8)(B), effective for distributions after 12/31/2006.

— P.L. 109-280, Sec. 845(b)(1), added para. (a)(2) . . . Sec. 845(b)(2), added para. (b)(2), effective for distributions in tax. yrs. begin. after 12/31/2006.

— P.L. 109-280, Sec. 861(a)(2), deleted "maintained by a State or local government or political subdivision thereof (or agency or instrumentality thereof)" after "Internal Revenue Code of 1986)" in Sec. 1505(d)(2) of P.L. 105-34 [see below], effective for any yr. begin. after 8/17/2006.

In 2005, P.L. 109-135, Sec. 201(b)(4)(A), repealed Secs. 101 and 102 of P.L. 109-73, effective 12/21/2005.

Prior to repeal, Sec. 101 of P.L. 109-73 read as follows:

"SEC. 101. TAX-FAVORED WITHDRAWALS FROM RETIREMENT PLANS FOR RELIEF RELATING TO HURRICANE KATRINA.

"(a) In general. Section 72(t) of the Internal Revenue Code of 1986 shall not apply to any qualified Hurricane Katrina distribution.

"(b) Aggregate dollar limitation.

"(1) In general. For purposes of this section, the aggregate amount of distributions received by an individual which may be treated as qualified Hurricane Katrina distributions for any taxable year shall not exceed the excess (if any) of —

"(A) $100,000, over

"(B) the aggregate amounts treated as qualified Hurricane Katrina distributions received by such individual for all prior taxable years.

"(2) Treatment of plan distributions. If a distribution to an individual would (without regard to paragraph (1)) be a qualified Hurricane Katrina distribution, a plan shall not be treated as violating any requirement of the Internal Revenue Code of 1986 merely because the plan treats such distribution as a qualified Hurricane Katrina distribution, unless the aggregate amount of such distributions from all plans maintained by the employer (and any member of any controlled group which includes the employer) to such individual exceeds $100,000.

"(3) Controlled group. For purposes of paragraph (2), the term 'controlled group' means any group treated as a single employer under subsection (b), (c), (m), or (o) of section 414 of such Code.

"(c) Amount distributed may be repaid.

"(1) In general. Any individual who receives a qualified Hurricane Katrina distribution may, at any time during the 3-year period beginning on the day after the date on which such distribution was received, make one or more contributions in an aggregate amount not to exceed the amount of such distribution to an eligible retirement plan of which such individual is a beneficiary and to which a rollover contribution of such distribution could be made under section 402(c), 403(a)(4), 403(b)(8), 408(d)(3), or 457(e)(16) of such Code, as the case may be.

"(2) Treatment of repayments of distributions from eligible retirement plans other than IRAs. For purposes of such Code, if a contribution is made pursuant to paragraph (1) with respect to a qualified Hurricane Katrina distribution from an eligible retirement plan other than an individual retirement plan, then the taxpayer shall, to the extent of the amount of the contribution, be treated as having received the qualified Hurricane Katrina distribution in an eligible rollover distribution (as defined in section 402(c)(4) of such Code) and as having transferred the amount to the eligible retirement plan in a direct trustee to trustee transfer within 60 days of the distribution.

"(3) Treatment of repayments for distributions from IRAs. For purposes of such Code, if a contribution is made pursuant to paragraph (1) with respect to a qualified Hurricane Katrina distribution from an individual retirement plan (as defined by section 7701(a)(37) of such Code), then, to the extent of the amount of the contribution, the qualified Hurricane Katrina distribution shall be treated as a distribution described in section 408(d)(3) of such Code and as having been transferred to the eligible retirement plan in a direct trustee to trustee transfer within 60 days of the distribution.

"(d) Definitions. For purposes of this section —

"(1) Qualified Hurricane Katrina distribution. Except as provided in subsection (b), the term 'qualified Hurricane Katrina distribution' means any distribution from an eligible retirement plan made on or after August 25, 2005, and before January 1, 2007, to an individual whose principal place of abode on August 28, 2005, is located in the Hurricane Katrina disaster area and who has sustained an economic loss by reason of Hurricane Katrina.

"(2) Eligible retirement plan. The term 'eligible retirement plan' shall have the meaning given such term by section 402(c)(8)(B) of such Code.

"(e) Income inclusion spread over 3 year period for qualified Hurricane Katrina distributions.

"(1) In general. In the case of any qualified Hurricane Katrina distribution, unless the taxpayer elects not to have this subsection apply for any taxable year, any amount required to be included in gross income for such taxable year shall be so included ratably over the 3-taxable year period beginning with such taxable year.

"(2) Special rule. For purposes of paragraph (1), rules similar to the rules of subparagraph (E) of section 408A(d)(3) of such Code shall apply.

"(f) Special rules.

"(1) Exemption of distributions from trustee to trustee transfer and withholding rules. For purposes of sections 401(a)(31), 402(f), and 3405 of such Code, qualified Hurricane Katrina distributions shall not be treated as eligible rollover distributions.

"(2) Qualified Hurricane Katrina distributions treated as meeting plan distribution requirements. For purposes of such Code, a qualified Hurricane Katrina distribution shall be treated as meeting the requirements of sections 401(k)(2)(B)(i), 403(b)(7)(A)(ii), 403(b)(11), and 457(d)(1)(A) of such Code."

Prior to repeal, Sec. 102 of P.L. 109-73 read as follows:

"SEC. 102. RECONTRIBUTIONS OF WITHDRAWALS FOR HOME PURCHASES CANCELLED DUE TO HURRICANE KATRINA.

"(a) Recontributions.

"(1) In general. Any individual who received a qualified distribution may, during the period beginning on August 25, 2005, and ending on February 28, 2006, make one or more contributions in an aggregate amount not to exceed the amount of such qualified distribution to an eligible retirement plan (as defined in section 402(c)(8)(B) of the Internal Revenue Code of 1986) of which such individual is a beneficiary and to which a rollover contribution of such distribution could be made under section 402(c), 403(a)(4), 403(b)(8), or 408(d)(3) of such Code, as the case may be.

"(2) Treatment of repayments. Rules similar to the rules of paragraphs (2) and (3) of section 101(c) of this Act shall apply for purposes of this section.

"(b) Qualified distribution defined. For purposes of this section, the term 'qualified distribution' means any distribution —

"(1) described in section 401(k)(2)(B)(i)(IV), 403(b)(7)(A)(ii) (but only to the extent such distribution relates to financial hardship), 403(b)(11)(B), or 72(t)(2)(F) of such Code,

"(2) received after February 28, 2005, and before August 29, 2005, and

"(3) which was to be used to purchase or construct a principal residence in the Hurricane Katrina disaster area, but which was not so purchased or constructed on account of Hurricane Katrina."

— P.L. 109-135, Sec. 412(w), added "or" before "a convention" in subpara. (b)(9)(B), effective 12/21/2005.

In 2004, P.L. 108-476, Sec. 1, of this Act, provides:

"SECTION 1. CERTAIN ARRANGEMENTS MAINTAINED BY THE YMCA RETIREMENT FUND TREATED AS CHURCH PLANS.

"(a) Retirement plans.

"(1) In general. For purposes of sections 401(a) and 403(b) of the Internal Revenue Code of 1986, any retirement plan maintained by the YMCA Retirement Fund as of January 1, 2003, shall be treated as a church plan (within the meaning of section 414(e) of such Code) which is maintained by an organization described in section 414(e)(3)(A) of such Code.

"(2) Tax-deferred retirement plan. In the case of a retirement plan described in paragraph (1) which allows contributions to be made under a salary reduction agreement—

"(A) such treatment shall not apply for purposes of section 415(c)(7) of such Code, and

"(B) any account maintained for a participant or beneficiary of such plan shall be treated for purposes of such Code as a retirement income account described in section 403(b)(9) of such Code, except that such account shall not, for purposes of section 403(b)(12) of such Code, be treated as a contract purchased by a church for purposes of section 403(b)(1)(D) of such Code.

"(3) Money purchase pension plan. In the case of a retirement plan described in paragraph (1) which is subject to the requirements of section 401(a) of such Code—

"(A) such plan (but not any reserves held by the YMCA Retirement Fund)—

"(i) shall be treated for purposes of such Code as a defined contribution plan which is a money purchase pension plan, and

"(ii) shall be treated as having made an election under section 410(d) of such Code for plan years beginning after December 31, 2005, except that notwithstanding the election—

"(I) nothing in the Employee Retirement Income Security Act of 1974 or such Code shall prohibit the YMCA Retirement Fund from commingling for investment purposes the assets of the electing plan with the assets of such Fund and with the assets of any employee benefit plan maintained by such Fund, and

"(II) nothing in this section shall be construed as subjecting any assets described in subclause (I), other than the assets of the electing plan, to any provision of such Act,

"(B) notwithstanding section 401(a)(11) or 417 of such Code or section 205 of such Act, such plan may offer a lump-sum distribution option to participants who have not attained age 55 without offering such participants an annuity option, and

"(C) any account maintained for a participant or beneficiary of such plan shall, for purposes of section 401(a)(9) of such Code, be treated as a retirement income account described in section 403(b)(9) of such Code.

"(4) Self-funded death benefit plan. For purposes of section 7702(j) of such Code, a retirement plan described in paragraph (1) shall be treated as an arrangement described in section 7702(j)(2).

"(b) YMCA retirement fund. For purposes of this section, the term 'YMCA Retirement Fund' means the Young Men's Christian Association Retirement Fund, a corporation created by an Act of the State of New York which became law on April 30, 1921.

"(c) Effective date. This section shall apply to plan years beginning after December 31, 2003."

—P.L. 108-311, Sec. 404(e), amended subpara. (a)(4)(B), effective for distributions after 12/31/2001 as if included in Sec. 641 of the Economic Growth and Tax Relief Reconciliation Act of 2001, P.L. 107-16.

Prior to amendment, subpara. (a)(4)(B) read as follows:

"(B) Certain rules made applicable. Rules similar to the rules of paragraphs (2) through (7) of section 402(c) shall apply for purposes of subparagraph (A)."

—P.L. 108-311, Sec. 408(a)(11), substituted "section 3121(a)(5)(D)" for "section 3121(a)(1)(D)" in clause (b)(7)(A)(ii), enacted 10/4/2004.

In 2002, P.L. 107-358, Sec. 2, added subsec. (c) in Sec. 901 of P.L. 107-16 [see below], effective 12/17/2002.

—P.L. 107-147, Sec. 411(p)(1), amended flush language at the end of subpara. (b)(1)(E) . . . Sec. 411(p)(2), deleted para. (b)(6) . . . Sec. 411(p)(3)(A), added ", and which precedes the taxable year by no more than five years" after "year of service" in para. (b)(3) . . . Sec. 411(p)(3)(B), deleted "or any amount received by a former employee after the fifth taxable year following the taxable year in which such employee was terminated" after "subsection applies" in para. (b)(3), effective for yrs. begin. after 12/31/2001.

Prior to amendment, the flush language at the end of subpara. (b)(1)(E) read as follows:

"then amounts contributed by such employer for such annuity contract on or after such rights become nonforfeitable shall be excluded from the gross income of the employee for the taxable year to the extent that the aggregate of such amounts does not exceed the applicable limit under section 415. The amount actually distributed to any distributee under such contract shall be taxable to the distributee (in the year in which so distributed) under section 72 (relating to annuities). For purposes of applying the rules of this subsection to amounts contributed by an employer for a taxable year, amounts transferred to a contract described in this paragraph by reason of a rollover contribution described in paragraph (8) of this subsection or section 408(d)(3)(A)(ii) shall not be considered contributed by such employer."

Prior to deletion, para. (b)(6) read as follows:

"(6) Forfeitable rights which become nonforfeitable. For purposes of this subsection and section 72(f) (relating to special rules for computing employees' contributions to annuity contracts), if rights of the employee under an annuity contract described in subparagraphs (A) and (B) of paragraph (1) change from forfeitable to nonforfeitable rights, then the amount (determined without regard to this subsection) includible in gross income by reason of such change shall be treated as an amount contributed by the employer for such annuity contract as of the time such rights become nonforfeitable."

In 2001, P.L. 107-16, Sec. 632(a)(2)(A), substituted "the applicable limit under section 415" for "the exclusion allowance for such taxable year" in para. (b)(1) . . . Sec. 632(a)(2)(B), deleted para. (b)(2) . . . Sec. 632(a)(2)(C), added "or any

amount received by a former employee after the fifth taxable year following the taxable year in which such employee was terminated" after "to which this subsection applies" in para. (b)(3), effective for yrs. begin. after 12/31/2001.

Prior to deletion, para. (b)(2) read as follows:

"(2) Exclusion allowance.

"(A) In general. For purposes of this subsection, the exclusion allowance for any employee for the taxable year is an amount equal to the excess, if any, of—

"(i) the amount determined by multiplying 20 percent of his includible compensation by the number of years of service, over

"(ii) the aggregate of the amounts contributed by the employer for annuity contracts and excludible from the gross income of the employee for any prior taxable year.

"(B) Election to have allowance determined under section 415 rules. In the case of an employee who makes an election under section 415(c)(4)(D) to have the provisions of section 415(c)(4)(C) (relating to special rule for section 403(b) contracts purchased by educational institutions, hospitals, home health service agencies, and certain churches, etc.) apply, the exclusion allowance for any such employee for the taxable year is the amount which could be contributed (under section 415 without regard to section 415(c)(8)(7) by his employer under a plan described in section 403(a) if the annuity contract for the benefit of such employee were treated as a defined contribution plan maintained by the employer.

"(C) Number of years of service for duly ordained, commissioned, or licensed ministers or lay employees. For purposes of this subsection and section 415(c)(4)(A)—

"(i) all years of service by—

"(I) a duly ordained, commissioned, or licensed minister of a church, or

"(II) a lay person,

as an employee of a church, a convention or association of churches, including an organization described in section 414(e)(3)(B)(ii), shall be considered as years of service for 1 employer, and

"(ii) all amounts contributed for annuity contracts by each such church (or convention or association of churches) or such organization during such years for such minister or lay person shall be considered to have been contributed by 1 employer.

For purposes of the preceding sentence, the terms 'church' and 'convention or association of churches' have the same meaning as when used in section 414(e).

"(D) Alternative exclusion allowance.

"(i) In general. In the case of any individual described in subparagraph (C), the amount determined under subparagraph (A) shall not be less than the lesser of—

"(I) $3,000, or

"(II) the includible compensation of such individual.

"(ii) Subparagraph not to apply to individuals with adjusted gross income over $17,000. This subparagraph shall not apply with respect to any taxable year to any individual whose adjusted gross income for such taxable year (determined separately and without regard to any community property laws) exceeds $17,000.

"(iii) Special rule for foreign missionaries. In the case of an individual described in subparagraph (C)(i) performing services outside the United States, there shall be included as includible compensation for any year under clause (i)(II) any amount contributed during such year by a church (or convention or association of churches) for an annuity contract with respect to such individual."

—P.L. 107-16, Sec. 632(b)(3), of this Act, reads as follows:

"(3) Election to modify section 403(b) exclusion allowance to conform to section 415 modification. In the case of taxable years beginning after December 31, 1999, and before January 1, 2002, a plan may disregard the requirement in the regulations regarding the exclusion allowance under section 403(b)(2) of the Internal Revenue Code of 1986 that contributions to a defined benefit pension plan be treated as previously excluded amounts for purposes of the exclusion allowance."

—P.L. 107-16, Sec. 634, of this Act, reads as follows:

"SEC. 634. MODIFICATION TO MINIMUM DISTRIBUTION RULES. The Secretary of the Treasury shall modify the life expectancy tables under the regulations relating to minimum distribution requirements under sections 401(a)(9), 408(a)(6) and (b)(3), 403(b)(10), and 457(d)(2) of the Internal Revenue Code to reflect current life expectancy."

—P.L. 107-16, Sec. 641(b)(1), substituted "such distribution to an eligible retirement plan described in section 402(c)(8)(B), and" for "such distributions to an individual retirement plan or to an annuity contract described in paragraph (1), and" in clause (b)(8)(A)(ii) . . . Sec. 641(e)(7), amended subpara. (b)(8)(B), effective for distributions after 12/31/2001. Sec. 641(f)(2) and (3) of this Act, provides:

"(2) Reasonable notice. No penalty shall be imposed on a plan for the failure to provide the information required by the amendment made by subsection (c) with respect to any distribution made before the date that is 90 days after the date on which the Secretary of the Treasury issues a safe harbor rollover notice after the date of the enactment of this Act, if the administrator of such plan makes a reasonable attempt to comply with such requirement.

"(3) Special rule. Notwithstanding any other provision of law, subsections (h)(3) and (h)(5) of section 1122 of the Tax Reform Act of 1986 shall not apply to any distribution from an eligible retirement plan (as defined in clause (iii) or (iv) of section 402(c)(8)(B) of the Internal Revenue Code of 1986) on behalf of an individual if there was a rollover to such plan on behalf of such individual which is permitted solely by reason of any amendment made by this section."

Prior to amendment, subpara. (b)(8)(B) read as follows:

"(B) Certain rules made applicable. Rules similar to the rules of paragraphs (2) through (7) of section 402(c) (including paragraph (4)(C) thereof) shall apply for purposes of subparagraph A."

—P.L. 107-16, Sec. 642(b)(1), substituted "section 408(d)(3)(A)(ii)" for "section 408(d)(3)(A)(iii)" in para. (b)(1), effective for distributions after 12/31/2001. Sec. 642(c)(2) of this Act, provides:

Employee benefit plans — Code Sec. 403

"(2) Special rule. Notwithstanding any other provision of law, subsections (h)(3) and (h)(5) of section 1122 of the Tax Reform Act of 1986 shall not apply to any distribution from an eligible retirement plan (as defined in clause (iii) or (iv) of section 402(c)(8)(B) of the Internal Revenue Code of 1986) on behalf of an individual if there was a rollover to such plan on behalf of such individual which is permitted solely by reason of the amendments made by this section."

—P.L. 107-16, Sec. 646(a)(2)(A), substituted "has a severance from employment" for "separates from service" in clause (b)(7)(A)(ii) and subpara. (b)(11)(A) . . . Sec. 646(a)(2)(B), substituted "severance from employment" for "separation from service" in the heading of para. (b)(11), effective for distributions after 12/31/2001.

—P.L. 107-16, Sec. 647(a), added para. (b)(13), effective for trustee-to-trustee transfers after 12/31/2001.

—P.L. 107-16, Sec. 664, of this Act, reads as follows:

"SEC. 664. EMPLOYEES OF TAX-EXEMPT ENTITIES.

"(a) In general. The Secretary of the Treasury shall modify Treasury Regulations section 1.410(b)-6(g) to provide that employees of an organization described in section 403(b)(1)(A)(i) of the Internal Revenue Code of 1986 who are eligible to make contributions under section 403(b) of such Code pursuant to a salary reduction agreement may be treated as excludable with respect to a plan under section 401(k) or (m) of such Code that is provided under the same general arrangement as a plan under such section 401(k), if—

"(1) no employee of an organization described in section 403(b)(1)(A)(i) of such Code is eligible to participate in such section 401(k) plan or section 401(m) plan; and

"(2) 95 percent of the employees who are not employees of an organization described in section 403(b)(1)(A)(i) of such Code are eligible to participate in such plan under such section 401(k) or (m).

"(b) Effective date. The modification required by subsection (a) shall apply as of the same date set forth in section 1426(b) of the Small Business Job Protection Act of 1996."

—P.L. 107-16, Sec. 901, of this Act [as amended by Sec. 2 of P.L. 107-358, and Sec. 101(a)(1) of P.L. 111-312, and as related to Sec. 811 of P.L. 109-280, see above], reads as follows:

"SEC. 901. SUNSET OF PROVISIONS OF ACT.

"(a) In general. All provisions of, and amendments made by, this Act shall not apply—

"(1) to taxable, plan, or limitation years beginning after December 31, 2012, or

"(2) in the case of title V, to estates of decedents dying, gifts made, or generation skipping transfers, after December 31, 2012.

"(b) Application of certain laws. The Internal Revenue Code of 1986 and the Employee Retirement Income Security Act of 1974 shall be applied and administered to years, estates, gifts, and transfers described in subsection (a) as if the provisions and amendments described in subsection (a) had never been enacted.

"(c) Exception. Subsection (a) shall not apply to section 803 (relating to no federal income tax on restitution received by victims of the Nazi regime or their heirs or estates)."

In 2000, P.L. 106-554, Sec. 1(a)(7), [which enacted into law Sec. 314(e)(1) of P.L. 106-554] substituted "section 125, 132(f)(4), or" for "section 125 or" in subpara. (b)(3)(B), effective for tax. yrs. begin. after 12/31/97.

In 1998, P.L. 105-206, Sec. 6005(c)(2)(B), added "(including paragraph (4)(C) thereof)" after "section 402(c)" in subpara. (b)(8)(B), effective for distributions after 12/31/98.

—P.L. 105-206, Sec. 6015(b), substituted "(b)(12)(A)(i)" for "(b)(12)" in Sec. 1505(d)(2) of P.L. 105-34, see below.

—P.L. 105-206, Sec. 6016(a)(2)(A), substituted "Paragraphs (7)(A)(ii) and (11) of section 403(b)" for "Section 403(b)(11)" in Sec. 1601(d)(4)(A) of P.L. 105-34, see below . . . Sec. 6016(a)(2)(B), substituted "403(b)(10)" for "403(b)(1)" in Sec. 1601(d)(4)(A)(ii) of P.L. 105-34, see below.

In 1997, P.L. 105-34, Sec. 1504(a)(1), added the last sentence to para. (b)(3) which included subparas. (b)(3)(A) and (B), effective for yrs. begin. after 12/31/97.

—P.L. 105-34, Sec. 1504(b), of this Act relating to repeal of rules in Code Sec. 415(e), reads as follows:

"(b) Repeal of rules in section 415(e).—The Secretary of the Treasury shall modify the regulations regarding the exclusion allowance under section 403(b)(2) of the Internal Revenue Code of 1986 to reflect the amendment made by section 1452(a) of the Small Business Job Protection Act of 1996. Such modification shall take effect for years beginning after December 31, 1999."

—P.L. 105-34, Sec. 1505(c), added subpara. (b)(12)(C), effective for tax. yrs. begin. on or after 8/5/97. Sec. 1505(d)(2) of this Act [as amended by Sec. 6015(b) of P.L. 105-206 and Sec. 861(a)(2) of P.L. 109-280, see above] provides:

"(2) Treatment for years beginning before date of enactment. A governmental plan (within the meaning of section 414(d) of the Internal Revenue Code of 1986) shall be treated as satisfying the requirements of sections 401(a)(3), 401(a)(4), 401(a)(26), 401(k), 401(m), 403(b)(1)(D) and (b)(12)(A)(i), and 410 of such Code for all taxable years beginning before the date of enactment of this Act."

—P.L. 105-34, Sec. 1601(d)(4), of this Act [as amended by Sec. 6016(a)(2)(A) and (B) of 105-206, see above], provides:

"(4) Clarification of section 1450.

"(A) Paragraphs (7)(A)(ii) and (11) of section 403(b) of the Internal Revenue Code of 1986 shall not apply with respect to a distribution from a contract described in section 1450(b)(1) of such Act to the extent that such distribution is not includible in income by reason of—

"(i) in the case of distributions before January 1, 1998, section 403(b)(8) or (b)(10) of such Code (determined after the application of section 1450(b)(2) of such Act), and

"(ii) in the case of distributions on and after such date, such section 403(b)(10).

"(B) This paragraph shall apply as if included in section 1450 of the Small Business Job Protection Act of 1996."

—P.L. 105-34, Sec. 1601(d)(6)(B), deleted "or" at the end of clause (b)(1)(A)(i), added "or" at the end of clause (b)(1)(A)(ii), and added clause (b)(1)(A)(iii), effective for yrs. begin. after 12/31/96.

In 1996, P.L. 104-188, Sec. 1450(a)(1), of this Act, effective for tax. yrs. begin. after 12/31/95, provides:

"(1) General rule. For purposes of section 403(b) of the Internal Revenue Code of 1986, the frequency that an employee is permitted to enter into a salary reduction agreement, the salary to which such an agreement may apply, and the ability to revoke such an agreement shall be determined under the rules applicable to cash or deferred elections under section 401(k) of such Code."

—P.L. 104-188, Sec. 1450(b), of this Act, provides:

"(b) Treatment of Indian tribal governments.

"(1) In general. In the case of any contract purchased in a plan year beginning before January 1, 1995, section 403(b) of the Internal Revenue Code of 1986 shall be applied as if any reference to an employer described in section 501(c)(3) of such Code included a reference to an employer which is an Indian tribal government (as defined by section 7701(a)(40) of such Code), a subdivision of an Indian tribal government (determined in accordance with section 7871(d) of such Code), an agency or instrumentality of an Indian tribal government or subdivision thereof, or a corporation chartered under Federal, State, or tribal law which is owned in whole or in part by any of the foregoing.

"(2) Rollovers. Solely for purposes of applying section 403(b)(8) of such Code to a contract to which paragraph (1) applies, a qualified cash or deferred arrangement under section 401(k) of such Code shall be treated as if it were a plan or contract described in clause (ii) of section 403(b)(8)(A) of such Code."

—P.L. 104-188, Sec. 1450(c)(1), amended subpara. (b)(1)(E), effective for yrs. begin. after 12/31/95, except a contract shall not be required to meet any change in requirement by reason of such amendment before the 90th day after 8/20/96.

Prior to amendment, subpara. (b)(1)(E) read as follows:

"(E) in the case of a contract purchased under a plan which provides a salary reduction agreement, the plan meets the requirements of section 401(a)(30),"

—P.L. 104-188, Sec. 1704(t)(69), substituted "a direct" for "an direct" in para. (b)(10), effective 8/20/96.

In 1992, P.L. 102-318, Sec. 521(b)(12)(A), added "in an eligible rollover distribution (within the meaning of section 402(c)(4))" before the comma at the end of clause (a)(4)(A)(i) . . . Sec. 521(b)(12)(B), amended subpara. (a)(4)(B) . . . Sec. 521(b)(13)(A), added "in an eligible rollover distribution (within the meaning of section 402(c)(4))" before the comma at the end of clause (b)(8)(A)(i) . . . Sec. 521(b)(13)(B), deleted subparas. (b)(8)(B), (C) and (D) and added new subpara. (b)(8)(B), effective for distributions after 12/31/92. For special rule, see Sec. 521(e)(2) of this Act which reads as follows:

"(2) Special rule for partial distributions. For purposes of section 402(a)(5)(D)(i)(II) of the Internal Revenue Code of 1986 (as in effect before the amendments made by this section), a distribution before January 1, 1993, which is made before or at the same time as a series of periodic payments shall not be treated as one of such series if it is not substantially equal in amount to other payments in such series."

Prior to amendment, subpara. (a)(4)(B) read as follows:

"(B) Certain rules made applicable. Rules similar to the rules of subparagraphs (B) through (G) of section 402(a)(5) and of paragraphs (6) and (7) of section 402(a) shall apply for purposes of subparagraph (A)."

Prior to deletion, subparas. (b)(8)(B), (C) and (D) read as follows:

"(B) Special rules for partial distributions.

"(i) In general. In the case of any distribution other than a total distribution, rules similar to the rules of clauses (i) and (ii) of section 402(a)(5)(D) shall apply.

"(ii) Total distribution. For purposes of subparagraph (A), the term 'total distribution' means one or more distributions from an annuity contract described in paragraph (1) which would constitute a lump-sum distribution within the meaning of section 402(e)(4)(A) (determined without regard to subparagraphs (B) and (H) of section 402(e)(4)) if such annuity contract were described in subsection (a), or 1 or more distributions of accumulated deductible employee contributions (within the meaning of section 72(o)(5)).

"(C) Certain rules made applicable. Rules similar to the rules of subparagraphs (B), (C), and (F)(i) of section 402(a)(5) and of paragraphs (6) and (7) of section 402(a) shall apply for purposes of subparagraph (A).

"(D) Required distributions not eligible for rollover treatment. Subparagraph (A) shall not apply to any distribution to the extent such distribution is required under paragraph (10)."

—P.L. 102-318, Sec. 522(a)(3), substituted "sections 401(a)(9) and 401(a)(31)" for "section 401(a)(9)" in para. (b)(10) . . . Sec. 522(c)(2), added para. (a)(5) . . . Sec. 522(c)(3), added a new sentence at the end of para. (b)(10), effective for distributions after 12/31/92, except as provided in Sec. 522(d)(2) of this Act which reads as follows:

"(2) Transition rule for certain annuity contracts. If, as of July 1, 1992, a State law prohibits a direct trustee-to-trustee transfer from an annuity contract described in section 403(b) of the Internal Revenue Code of 1986 which was purchased for an employee by an employer which is a State or a political subdivision thereof (or an agency or instrumentality of any 1 or more of either), the amendments made by this section shall not apply to distributions before the earlier of—

"(A) 90 days after the first day after July 1, 1992, on which such transfer is allowed under State law, or

"(B) January 1, 1994."

In 1990, P.L. 101-508, Sec. 11701(k), added "involving a one-time irrevocable election" after "similar arrangement" in second sentence of subpara. (b)(12)(A), effective for tax. yrs. begin. after 12/31/86, except as provided in Sec. 1105(c)(2) and (5) of P.L. 99-514, reproduced in note following Code Sec. 402.

In 1988, P.L. 100-647, Sec. 1011(c)(7)(B), deleted "and" at the end of subpara. (b)(1)(C), added "and" at the end of subpara. (b)(1)(D), and added subpara. (b)(1)(E), effective for plan yrs. begin. after 12/31/87, Sec. 1011(c)(7)(E)(ii) of this Act provides:

"(ii) In the case of a plan described in section 1105(c)(2) of the Reform Act, the amendments made by this paragraph shall not apply to contributions made pursuant to an agreement described in such section for plan years beginning before the earlier of—

"(I) the later of January 1, 1988, or the date on which the last of such agreements terminates (determined without regard to any extension thereof after February 28, 1986), or

"(II) January 1, 1989."

—P.L. 100-647, Sec. 1011(c)(12), added "For purposes of clause (i), a contribution shall be treated as not made pursuant to a salary reduction agreement if under the agreement it is made pursuant to a 1-time irrevocable election made by the employee at the time of initial eligibility to participate in the agreement or is made pursuant to a similar arrangement specified in regulations." after clause (b)(12)(A)(ii) [as redesignated by Sec. 1011(m)(1)(A), of this Act], effective for tax. yrs. begin. after 12/31/86, except as provided in Secs. 1105(c)(2) and (5) of P.L. 99-514, reproduced in note following Code Sec. 402.

see Sec. 1011(h)(9) of this Act reproduced in note following Code Sec. 4980.

—P.L. 100-647, Sec. 1011(m)(1)(A), redesignated para. (b)(10) as added by Sec. 1120(b) of P.L. 99-514, as para. (b)(12) . . . Sec. 1011(m)(1)(B), substituted "paragraph (12)" for "paragraph (10)" in subpara. (b)(1)(D) . . . Sec. 1011(m)(2)(A), added "(17)" after "(5)", in clause (b)(12)(A)(i) . . . Sec. 1011(m)(2)(B), added ", section 401(m)," after "section 401(a)" the first place it appeared in clause (b)(12)(A)(i), effective for tax. yrs. begin. after 12/31/88.

—P.L. 100-647, Sec. 1011(m)(3), added Sec. 1120(c)(2) of P.L. 99-514 [reproduced below], part of the effective date for changes made by Sec. 1120 of P.L. 99-514, see below.

—P.L. 100-647, Sec. 1011A(c)(11)(A), amended Sec. 1123(e)(2) of P.L. 99-514, part of the effective date for changes made by Sec. 1123(c) of P.L. 99-514, see below.

Prior to amendment, Sec. 1123(e)(2) of P.L. 99-514 read as follows:

"(2) Subsection (c).—The amendments made by subsection (c) shall apply to taxable years beginning after December 31, 1988."

—P.L. 100-647, Sec. 6052(a)(1), amended the last sentence of subpara. (b)(12)(A), effective for tax. yrs. begin. after 12/31/88, except as provided in Sec. 1120(c)(2) of P.L. 99-514, reproduced below.

Prior to amendment, the last sentence of subpara. (b)(12)(A) read as follows:

"For purposes of this subparagraph, students who normally work less than 20 hours per week may (subject to the conditions applicable under section 410(b)(4)) be excluded."

—P.L. 100-647, Sec. 6052(b)(1), and (2) of this Act provide:

"(b) Sampling. In the case of plan years beginning in 1989, 1990, or 1991, determinations as to whether a plan meets the requirements of section 403(b)(12) of the 1986 Code may be made on the basis of a statistically valid random sample. The preceding sentence shall apply only if—

"(1) the sampling is conducted by an independent person in a manner not inconsistent with regulations prescribed by the Secretary, and

"(2) the statistical method and sample size result in a 95 percent probability that the results will have a margin of error not greater than 3 percent."

In 1986, P.L. 99-514, Sec. 1120(a), deleted "and" at the end of subpara. (b)(1)(B), added "and" to the end of subpara. (b)(1)(C), and added subpara. (b)(1)(D) . . . Sec. 1120(b), added para. (b)(10), effective for yrs. begin. after 12/31/88, Sec. 1120(c)(2) of this Act [as added by Sec. 1011(m)(3) of P.L. 100-647, see above] provides:

"(2) Collective bargaining agreements. In the case of a plan maintained pursuant to 1 or more collective bargaining agreements between employee representatives and 1 or more employers ratified before March 1, 1986, the amendments made by this section shall not apply to plan years beginning before the earlier of—

"(A) January 1, 1991, or

"(B) the later of—

"(i) January 1, 1989, or

"(ii) the date on which the last of such collective bargaining agreements terminates (determined without regard to any extension thereof after February 28, 1986)."

—P.L. 99-514, Sec. 1122(b)(1)(B), deleted para. (a)(2), effective for amounts distributed after 12/31/86, in tax. yrs. end. after 12/31/86. For special and transitional rules see Sec. 1123(h)(3)-(6) reproduced in note following Code Sec. 402.

Prior to deletion, para. (a)(2) read as follows:

"(2) Capital gains treatment for certain distributions.

"(A) General rule. If—

"(i) an annuity contract is purchased by an employer for an employee under a plan described in paragraph (1);

"(ii) such plan requires that refunds of contributions with respect to annuity contracts purchased under such plan be used to reduce subsequent premiums on the contracts under the plan; and

"(iii) a lump sum distribution (as defined in section 402(e)(4)(A)) is paid to the recipient,

so much of the total taxable amount (as defined in section 402(e)(4)(D)) of such distribution as is equal to the product of such total taxable amount multiplied by the fraction described in section 402(a)(2) shall be treated as a gain from the sale or exchange of a capital asset held for more than 6 months. For purposes of this paragraph, in the case of an individual who is an employee without regard to section 401(c)(1), determination of whether or not any distribution is a lump sum distribution shall be made without regard to the requirement that an election be made under subsection (e)(4)(B) of section 402, but no distribution to any taxpayer other than an individual, estate, or trust may be treated as a lump sum distribution under this paragraph.

"(B) Cross reference. For imposition of separate tax on ordinary income portion of lump sum distribution, see section 402(e)."

—P.L. 99-514, Sec. 1122(d)(1), amended para. (a)(1) . . . Sec. 1122(d)(2), amended the second sentence of para. (b)(1) . . . Sec. 1122(d)(3), amended the last sentence of subsec. (c), effective for tax. yrs. begin. after 12/31/85.

Prior to amendment, para. (a)(1) read as follows:

"(1) General rule. Except as provided in paragraph (2), if an annuity contract is purchased by an employer for an employee under a plan which meets the requirements of section 404(a)(2) (whether or not the employer deducts the amounts paid for the contract under such section), the employee shall include in his gross income the amounts received under such contract for the year received as provided in section 72 (relating to annuities)."

Prior to amendment, the second sentence of para. (b)(1) read as follows:

"The employee shall include in his gross income the amounts received under such contract for the year received as provided in section 72 (relating to annuities)."

Prior to amendment, the last sentence of subsec. (c) read as follows:

"The amount actually paid or made available to any beneficiary under such contract shall be taxable to him in the year in which so paid or made available under section 72 (relating to annuities)."

—P.L. 99-514, Sec. 1123(c)(1), added para. (b)(11) [sic . (b)(12)] . . . Sec. 1123(c)(2), added "in the case of contributions made pursuant to a salary reduction agreement (within the meaning of section 3121(a)(1)(D))," before "encounters" in clause (b)(7)(ii) [sic , (b)(7)(A)(ii)]. Sec. 1123(e)(2) of this Act [as amended by Secs. 1011A(c)(11)(A) and (B) of P.L. 100-647, see above] provides:

"(2) Subsection (c).—The amendments made by subsection (c) shall apply to years beginning after December 31, 1988, but only with respect to distributions from contracts described in section 403(b) of the Internal Revenue Code of 1986 which are attributable to assets other than assets held as of the close of the last year beginning before January 1, 1989."

—P.L. 99-514, Sec. 1852(a)(3)(A), added para. (b)(10) . . . Sec. 1852(a)(3)(B), deleted subpara. (b)(7)(D), effective for benefits accruing after 12/31/86, in tax. yrs. end. after 12/31/86.

Prior to deletion, subpara. (b)(7)(D) read as follows:

"(D) Distribution requirements. For purposes of determining when the interest of an employee in a custodial account must be distributed, such account shall be treated in the same manner as an annuity contract."

—P.L. 99-514, Sec. 1852(a)(5)(B)(i), substituted "through (G)" for "through (F)" in subpara. (a)(4)(B) . . . Sec. 1852(a)(5)(B)(ii), added subpara. (b)(8)(D), effective for yrs. begin. after 12/31/84. For transitional and special rules, see Sec. 521(e)(3)-(5) of P.L. 98-369 reproduced in note following Code Sec. 408.

—P.L. 99-514, Sec. 1852(b)(10), substituted "and (F)(i)" for "(F)(i)" in subpara. (b)(8)(C), effective for distributions made after 7/18/84, in tax. yrs. end. after 7/18/84.

In 1984, P.L. 98-369, Sec. 491(d)(12), deleted "or 409(b)(3)(C)" after "or section 408(d)(3)(A)(iii)" at the end of para. (b)(1), effective for obligations issued after 12/31/83.

—P.L. 98-369, Sec. 521(c), added subpara. (b)(7)(D), effective for yrs. begin. after 12/31/84. For transitional and special rules, see Secs. 521(e)(3)-(5) of this Act reproduced in note following Code Sec. 408.

—P.L. 98-369, Sec. 522(a)(2), amended clause (a)(4)(A)(i) . . . Sec. 522(a)(3), amended clause (b)(8)(A)(i) . . . Sec. 522(d)(9), substituted "B through F" for "B through E" in subpara. (a)(4)(B) . . . Sec. 522(d)(10), amended subpara. (b)(8)(B) . . . Sec. 522(d)(11), substituted "F(i)" for "D(v) and E(i)" in subpara. (b)(8)(C), effective for distributions made after 7/18/84, in tax. yrs. end. after 7/18/84.

Prior to amendment, clause (a)(4)(A)(i) read as follows:

"(i) the balance to the credit of an employee in an employee annuity described in paragraph (1) is paid to him in a qualifying rollover distribution."

Prior to amendment, clause (b)(8)(A)(i) read as follows:

"(i) the balance to the credit of an employee is paid to him in a qualifying distribution,"

Prior to amendment, subpara. (b)(8)(B) read as follows:

"(B) Qualifying distribution defined.

"(i) In general. For purposes of subparagraph (A), the term 'qualifying distribution' means 1 or more distributions from an annuity contract described in paragraph (1) which would constitute a lump sum distribution within the meaning of section 402(e)(4)(A) (determined without regard to subparagraphs (B) and (H) of section 402(e)(4)) if such annuity contract were described in subsection (a), or 1 or more distributions of accumulated deductible employee contributions (within the meaning of section 72(o)(5)).

"(ii) Aggregation of annuity contracts. For purposes of this paragraph, all annuity contracts described in paragraph (1) purchased by an employer shall be treated as a single contract, and section 402(e)(4)(C) shall not apply."

—P.L. 98-369, Sec. 1001(b)(4), substituted "6 months" for "1 year" each place it appeared in subpara. (a)(2)(A), effective for property acquired after 6/22/84, and before 1/1/88.

In 1983, P.L. 98-21, Sec. 122(c)(4), substituted "section 911" for "sections 105(d) and 911" in para. (b)(3), effective for tax. yrs. begin. after 12/31/83.

—P.L. 97-448, Sec. 103(c)(8)(B), substituted "subparagraphs (B), (C), (D)(v)" for "subparagraphs (B), (C)" in subpara. (b)(8)(C), effective for tax. yrs. begin. after 12/31/81.

In 1982, P.L. 97-248, Sec. 251(a)(1), substituted "(under section 415 without regard to section 415(c)(8))" for "(under section 415)" in subpara. (b)(2)(B) . . . Sec. 251(a)(2), added subparas. (b)(2)(C) and (D), effective for tax. yrs. begin. after 12/31/81.

—P.L. 97-248, Sec. 251(b), added para. (b)(9), effective for tax. yrs. begin. after 12/31/74.

—P.L. 97-248, Sec. 251(c)(3), substituted "home health service agencies, and certain churches, etc." for "and home health service agencies" in subpara. (b)(2)(B), effective for yrs. begin. after 12/31/81.

—P.L. 97-248, Sec. 251(d), provides as follows:

"(d) Correction period for church plans. —A church plan (within the meaning of section 414(e) of the Internal Revenue Code of 1954) shall not be treated as not meeting the requirements of section 401 or 403 of such Code if—

"(1) by reason of any change in any law, regulation, ruling, or otherwise such plan is required to be amended to meet such requirements, and

"(2) such plan is so amended at the next earliest church convention or such other time as the Secretary of the Treasury or his delegate may prescribe."

—P.L. 97-248, Sec. 251(e)(5), provides:

"Any defined benefit arrangement which is established by a church or a convention or association of churches (including an organization described in section 414(e)(3)(B)(ii) of the Internal Revenue Code of 1954) and which is in effect on the date of the enactment of this Act shall not be treated as failing to meet the requirements of section 403(b)(2) of such Code merely because it is a defined benefit arrangement."

In 1981, P.L. 97-34, Sec. 311(b)(3)(B), added ", or 1 or more distributions of accumulated deductible employee contributions (within the meaning of section 72(o)(5))" after "subsection (a)" in clause (b)(8)(B)(i), effective for tax. yrs. begin. after 12/31/81. For transitional rule see Sec. 311(i)(2) of this Act reproduced in note following Code Sec. 219.

In 1980, P.L. 96-613, Sec. 1, provides:

"SECTION 1. ANNUITY CONTRACTS PURCHASED BY THE UNIFORMED SERVICES UNIVERSITY OF THE HEALTH SCIENCES.

"(a) In general.

"An annuity contract purchased by the Uniformed Services University of the Health Sciences for any employee who is a member of the civilian faculty or staff of such university shall, for purposes of section 403(b) of the Internal Revenue Code of 1954, be treated as an annuity contract purchased for an employee by an employer described in section 501(c)(3) of such Code which is exempt from tax under section 501(a) of such Code.

"(b) Effective date.

"Subsection (a) shall apply to service after December 31, 1979, in taxable years ending after such date."

—P.L. 96-222, Sec. 101(a)(13)(A), amended Sec. 156(d) of P.L. 95-600, the effective date for amendments made by Sec. 156(a) and (b) of P.L. 95-600, so that the amendments are effective for distributions or transfers made after 12/31/77, in tax yrs. begin. after 12/31/77 rather than effective for distributions or transfers made after 12/31/78 in tax yrs. begin. after 12/31/77, see below, provides:

"(B) Transitional rule for making section 403(b)(8) rollover in the case of payments during 1978. In the case of any payment made during 1978 in a qualifying distribution described in section 403(b)(8) of the Internal Revenue Code of 1954, the applicable period specified in section 402(a)(5)(C) of such Code shall not expire before the close of December 31, 1980."

—P.L. 96-222, Sec. 101(a)(12), substituted "which satisfies" for "which satisfied" in subpara. (b)(7)(A), effective for tax. yrs. begin. after 12/31/78.

—P.L. 96-222, Sec. 101(a)(13)(C), substituted "409(b)(3)(C)" for "409(d)(3)(C) in para. (b)(1), effective for distributions or transfers made after 12/31/77, in tax. yrs. begin. after 12/31/77.

In 1978, P.L. 95-600, Sec. 154(a), amended subpara. (b)(7)(A), effective for tax. yrs. begin. after 12/31/78.

Prior to amendment, subpara. (b)(7)(A) read as follows:

"(A) Amounts paid treated as contributions. For purposes of this title, amounts paid by an employer described in paragraph (1)(A) to a custodial account which satisfies the requirements of section 401(f)(2) shall be treated as amounts contributed by him for an annuity contract for his employee if the amounts are paid to provide a retirement benefit for that employee and are to be invested in regulated investment company stock to be held in that custodial account."

—P.L. 95-600, Sec. 156(a)(1), added para. (b)(8) . . . Sec. 156(b), added the last sentence in para. (b)(1), effective [as amended by Sec. 101(a)(13)(A) of P.L. 96-222, see above] for distributions or transfers made after 12/31/77, in tax. yrs. begin. after 12/31/77.

—P.L. 95-600, Sec. 157(g)(2), substituted "paragraphs (6) and (7)" for "paragraph (6)" in subpara. (a)(4)(B), effective for lump-sum distributions completed after 12/31/78, in tax. yrs. end. after 12/31/78.

—P.L. 95-458, Sec. 4(b), deleted paras. (a)(4) and (a)(5) and added new para. (a)(4), effective for tax. yrs. begin. after 12/31/74. Sec. 4(d)(2) of the Act provides as follows:

"(2) Validation of certain attempted rollovers. If the taxpayer—

"(A) attempted to comply with the requirements of section 402(a)(5) or 403(a)(4) of the Internal Revenue Code of 1954 for a taxable year beginning before the date of the enactment of this Act, and

"(B) failed to meet the requirements of such section that all property received in the distribution be transferred,

such section (as amended by this section) shall be applied by treating any transfer of property made on or before December 31, 1978, as if it were made on or before the 60th day after the day on which the taxpayer received such property. For purposes of the preceding sentence, a transfer of money shall be treated as transfer of property received in a distribution to the extent that the amount of the money transferred does not exceed the highest fair market value of the property distributed during the 60-day period beginning on the date on which the taxpayer received such property."

Prior to amendment, paras. (a)(4) and (a)(5) read as follows:

"(4) Rollover amounts. In the case of an employee annuity described in 403(a), if—

"(A) the balance to the credit of an employee is paid to him—

"(i) within one taxable year of the employee on account of a termination of the plan of which such trust is a part or, in the case of a profit-sharing plan, a complete discontinuance of contributions under such plan, or

"(ii) in one or more distributions which constitutes a lump-sum distribution within the meaning of section 402(e)(4)(A) (determined without reference to section 402(e)(4)(B)).

"(B)(i) the employee transfers all the property he receives in such distribution to an individual account described in section 408(a) an individual retirement annuity described in section 408(b) (other than an endowment contract), or a retirement bond described in section 409, on or before the 60th day after the day on which he received such property to the extent the fair market value of such property exceeds the amount referred to in section 402(e)(4)(D)(i), or

"(ii) the employee transfers all the property he receives in such distribution to an employees' trust described in section 401(a) which is exempt from tax under section 501(a), or to an annuity plan described in subsection (a) on or before the 60th day after the day on which he received such property to the extent the fair market value of such property exceeds the amount referred to in section 402(e)(4)(D)(i), and

"(C) the amount so transferred consists of the property distributed to the extent that the fair market value of such property does not exceed the amount required to be transferred pursuant to subparagraph (B),

then such distribution is not includible in gross income for the year in which paid. For purposes of this title, a transfer described in subparagraph (B)(i) shall be treated as a rollover contribution described in section 408(d)(3). Subparagraph (B)(ii) does not apply in the case of a transfer to an employees' trust, or annuity plan if any part of a payment described in subparagraph (A) is attributable to an annuity plan under which the employee was an employee within the meaning of section 401(c)(1) at the time contributions were made on his behalf under the plan.

"(5) Special rollover rules. For purposes of paragraph (4)(A)(i)—

"(A) Time of termination. A complete discontinuance of contributions under a profit-sharing plan shall be deemed to occur on the day the plan administrator notifies the Secretary or his delegate (in accordance with regulations prescribed by the Secretary) that all contributions to the plan have been completely discontinued. For purposes of section 411(d)(3), the plan shall be considered to be terminated no later than the day such notice is filed with the Secretary.

"(B) Sale of subsidiary or assets.—

"(i) A payment of the balance to the credit of an employee of a corporation (hereinafter referred to as the employer corporation) which is a subsidiary corporation (within the meaning of section 425(f) or which is a member of a controlled group of corporations (within the meaning of section 1563(a), determined by substituting '50 percent' for '80 percent' each place it appears therein) in connection with the liquidation, sale, or other means of terminating the parent-subsidiary or controlled group relationship of the employer corporation with the parent corporation or controlled group, or

"(ii) A payment of the balance to the credit of an employee of a corporation (hereinafter referred to as the acquiring corporation) in connection with the sale or other transfer to the acquiring corporation of all or substantially all of the assets used by the previous employer of the employee (hereinafter referred to as the selling corporation) in a trade or business conducted by the selling corporation,

shall be treated as a payment or distribution on account of the termination of the plan with respect to such employee if the employees of the employer corporation or the acquiring corporation (whichever applies) are not active participants in such plan at the time of such payment or distribution. For purposes of this subparagraph, in no event shall a payment or distribution be deemed to be in accordance with a sale or other transfer of assets, or a liquidation, sale, or other means of terminating such parent-subsidiary or controlled group relationship, if such payment or distribution is made later than the end of the second calendar year after the calendar year in which occurs such sale or other transfer of assets, or such liquidation, sale, or other means of terminating such parent-subsidiary or controlled group relationship."

In 1976, P.L. 94-455, Sec. 1402(b)(1)(D), substituted "9 months" for "6 months" in subpara. (a)(2)(A), effective for tax. yrs. begin. in 1977.

—P.L. 94-455, Sec. 1402(b)(2), substituted "1 year" for "9 months" each place it appeared in subpara. (a)(2)(A), effective for tax. yrs. begin. after 12/31/77.

—P.L. 94-455, Sec. 1504(a), deleted ", and which issues only redeemable stock" from the end of the last sentence of subpara. (b)(7)(C), effective for tax. yrs. begin. after 12/31/75.

—P.L. 94-455, Sec. 1901(a)(58), amended the last two sentences of para. (a)(4), effective for tax. yrs. begin. after '76.

Prior to amendment, the last two sentences of para. (a)(4) read as follows:

"For purposes of this title, a transfer described in subparagraph (B)(i) shall be treated as a rollover contribution described in section 408(d)(3).

"Subparagraph (B)(ii) does not apply in the case of a transfer to an employees' trust, or annuity plan if any part of a payment described in subparagraph (A) is attributable to an annuity plan under which the employee was an employee within the meaning of section 401(c)(1) at the time contributions were made on his behalf under the plan."

—P.L. 94-455, Sec. 1901(b)(8)(A), substituted "educational organization described in section 170(b)(2)(A)(ii)" for "educational institution (as defined in section 151(e)(4))" in clause (b)(1)(A)(ii), effective for tax. yrs. begin. after 12/31/76.

—P.L. 94-455, Sec. 1906(b)(13)(A), substituted "Secretary" for "Secretary or his delegate" in para. (a)(5) and subpara. (b)(4)(B), effective for tax. yrs. begin. after 12/31/76.

—P.L. 94-267, Sec. 1(b)(1), substituted new material for subpara. (a)(4)(A), effective for payments made to an employee on or after 7/4/74, subject Sec. (d) of the Act (reproduced following Code Sec. 402).

Prior to amendment, subpara. (a)(4)(A) read as follows:

"(A) the balance to the credit of an employee is paid to him in one or more distributions which constitute a lump sum distribution within the meaning of section 402(e)(4)(A) determined without reference to section 402(e)(4)(B),"

—P.L. 94-267, Sec. 1(b)(2), substituted "a payment" for "the lump-sum distribution" in the last sentence of para. (a)(4) . . . Sec. 1(b)(3), added para. (a)(5), effective for payments made to an employee on or after 7/4/74.

In **1974**, P.L. 93-406, Sec. 2005(b)(2), amended that portion of para. (2) which followed clause (ii) of subpara. (A), effective for distributions or payments made after 12/31/73, in tax. yrs. begin. after such date.

Prior to amendment, this material read as follows:

"(iii) the total amounts payable by reason of an employee's death or other separation from the service, or by reason of the death of an employee after the employee's separation from the service, are paid to the payee within one taxable year of the payee,

then the amount of such payments, to the extent exceeding the amount contributed by the employee (determined by applying section 72(f)), which employee contributions shall be reduced by any amounts theretofore paid to him which were not includible in gross income, shall be considered a gain from the sale or exchange of a capital asset held for more than 6 months. This subparagraph shall not apply to amounts paid to any payee to the extent such amounts are attributable to contributions made on behalf of the employee while he was an employee within the meaning of section 401(c)(1).

"(B) Definition. For purposes of subparagraph (A), the term 'total amounts' means the balance to the credit of an employee which becomes payable to the payee by reason of the employee's death or other separation from the service, or by reason of his death after separation from the service.

"(C) Limitation on capital gains treatment. Subparagraph (A) shall apply to a payment paid after December 31, 1969, only to the extent it does not exceed the sum of—

"(i) the benefits accrued by the employee on behalf of whom it is paid during plan years beginning before January 1, 1970, and

"(ii) the portion of the benefits accrued by such employee during plan years beginning after December 31, 1969, which the payee establishes does not consist of the employee's allocable share of employer contributions under the plan under which the annuity contract is purchased.

"The Secretary or his delegate shall prescribe such regulations as may be necessary to carry out the purposes of this subparagraph."

—P.L. 93-406, Sec. 2002(g)(6), added para. (a)(4), effective on or after 9/2/74 for contributions to an employees' trust described in Code Sec. 401(a) which is exempt from tax under Code Sec. 501(a) or an annuity plan described in Code Sec. 403(a).

—P.L. 93-406, Sec. 2004(c)(4), amended para. (b)(2), effective for yrs. begin. after 12/31/75.

Prior to amendment, para. (b)(2) read as follows:

"(2) Exclusion allowance. For purposes of this subsection, the exclusion allowance for any employee for the taxable year is an amount equal to the excess, if any, of—

"(A) the amount determined by multiplying (i) 20 percent of his includible compensation, by (ii) the number of years of service, over

"(B) the aggregate of the amounts contributed by the employer for annuity contracts and excludable from the gross income of the employee for any prior taxable year."

—P.L. 93-406, Sec. 1022(e), added para. (b)(7), effective 1/1/74.

In **1969**, P.L. 91-172, Sec. 321(b)(2), deleted subsecs. (c) and (d) and added new subsec. (c), effective for contributions made and premiums paid after 8/1/69.

Prior to amendment, subsecs. (c) and (d) read as follows:

"(c) Taxability of beneficiary under a nonqualified annuity.

"If an annuity contract purchased by an employer for an employee is not subject to subsection (a) and the employee's rights under the contract are nonforfeitable, except for failure to pay future premiums, the amount contributed by the employer for such annuity contract on or after such rights become nonforfeitable shall be included in the gross income of the employee in the year in which the amount is contributed. The employee shall include in his gross income the amounts received under such contract for the year received as provided in section 72 (relating to annuities).

"(d) Taxability of beneficiary under certain forfeitable contracts purchased by exempt organizations.

"Notwithstanding the first sentence of subsection (c), if rights of an employee under an annuity contract purchased by an employer which is exempt from tax under section 501(a) or 521(a) change from forfeitable to nonforfeitable rights, the value of such contract on the date of such change (to the extent attributable to amounts contributed by the employer after December 31, 1957) shall, except as provided in subsection (b), be included in the gross income of the employee in the year of such change."

—P.L. 91-172, Sec. 515(a)(2), added subpara. (a)(2)(C), effective for tax. yrs. end. after 12/31/69.

In **1964**, P.L. 88-272, Sec. 232(e)(4), deleted "except that section 72(e)(3) shall not apply" after "(relating to annuities)" in paras. (a)(1), (b)(1) and subsec. (c), effective for tax. yrs. begin. after 12/31/63.

In **1962**, P.L. 87-792, Sec. 4, substituted "described in paragraph (1)" for "which meets the requirements of section 401(a) (3), (4), (5), and (6)" in clause (a)(2)(A)(i) and added last sentence of subpara. (a)(2)(A); and added para. (a)(3), effective for tax. yrs. begin. after 12/31/62.

In **1961**, P.L. 87-370, Sec. 3(a)(1), amended subpara. (b)(1)(A) . . . Sec. 3(a)(2), substituted "the employer described in paragraph (1)(A)," for "the employer described in section 501(c)(3) and exempt from tax under section 501(a)," in para. (b)(3) . . . Sec. 3(a)(3), added "or public school" before the period in the heading of subsec. (b), effective for tax. yrs. begin. after 12/31/57.

Prior to amendment, subpara. (b)(1)(A) read as follows:

"(A) an annuity contract is purchased for an employee by an employer described in section 501(c)(3) which is exempt from tax under section 501(a)."

In **1958**, P.L. 85-866, Sec. 23, substituted "which meets the requirements of section 404(a)(2) (whether or not the employer deducts the amounts paid for the contract under such section)," for "with respect to which the employer's contribution is deductible under section 404(a)(2), or if an annuity contract is purchased for an employee by an employer described in section 501(c)(3) which is exempt from tax under section 501(a)" in subsec. (a)(1); added subsec. (b) and redesignated former subsec. (b) as (c) and, added subsec. (d), for tax. yrs. begin. after '57.

Sec. 404. Deduction for contributions of an employer to an employees' trust or annuity plan and compensation under a deferred-payment plan.

(a) General rule.

If contributions are paid by an employer to or under a stock bonus, pension, profit-sharing, or annuity plan, or if compensation is paid or accrued on account of any employee under a plan deferring the receipt of such compensation, such contributions or compensation shall not be deductible under this chapter; but, if they would otherwise be deductible, they shall be deductible under this section, subject, however, to the following limitations as to the amounts deductible in any year:

(1) Pension trusts.

(A) In general. In the taxable year when paid, if the contributions are paid into a pension trust (other than a trust to which paragraph (3) applies), and if such taxable year ends within or with a taxable year of the trust for which the trust is exempt under section 501(a), in the case of a defined benefit plan other than a multiemployer plan, in an amount determined under subsection (o), and in the case of any other plan in an amount determined as follows:

(i) the amount necessary to satisfy the minimum funding standard provided by section 412(a) for plan years ending within or with such taxable year (or for any prior plan year), if such amount is greater than the amount determined under clause (ii) or (iii) (whichever is applicable with respect to the plan),

(ii) the amount necessary to provide with respect to all of the employees under the trust the remaining unfunded cost of their past and current service credits distributed as a level amount, or a level percentage of compensation, over the remaining future service of each such employee, as determined under regulations prescribed by the Secretary, but if such remaining unfunded cost with respect to any 3 individuals is more than 50 percent of such remaining unfunded cost, the amount of such unfunded cost attributable to such individuals shall be distributed over a period of at least 5 taxable years.

(iii) an amount equal to the normal cost of the plan, as determined under regulations prescribed by the Secretary, plus, if past service or other supplementary pension or annuity credits are provided by the plan, an amount necessary to amortize the unfunded costs attributable to such credits in equal annual payments (until fully amortized) over 10 years, as determined under regulations prescribed by the Secretary.

Employee benefit plans Code Sec. 404(a)(3)(A)(v)

In determining the amount deductible in such year under the foregoing limitations the funding method and the actuarial assumptions used shall be those used for such year under section 431, and the maximum amount deductible for such year shall be an amount equal to the full funding limitation for such year determined under section 431.

(B) Special rule in case of certain amendments. In the case of a multiemployer plan which the Secretary of Labor finds to be collectively bargained which makes an election under this subparagraph (in such manner and at such time as may be provided under regulations prescribed by the Secretary), if the full funding limitation determined under section 431(c)(6) for such year is zero, if as a result of any plan amendment applying to such plan year, the amount determined under section 431(c)(6)(A)(ii) exceeds the amount determined under section 431(c)(6)(A)(i), and if the funding method and the actuarial assumptions used are those used for such year under section 431, the maximum amount deductible in such year under the limitations of this paragraph shall be an amount equal to the lesser of—

  (i) the full funding limitation for such year determined by applying section 431(c)(6) but increasing the amount referred to in subparagraph (A) thereof by the decrease in the present value of all unamortized liabilities resulting from such amendment, or

  (ii) the normal cost under the plan reduced by the amount necessary to amortize in equal annual installments over 10 years (until fully amortized) the decrease described in clause (i).

In the case of any election under this subparagraph, the amount deductible under the limitations of this paragraph with respect to any of the plan years following the plan year for which such election was made shall be determined as provided under such regulations as may be prescribed by the Secretary to carry out the purposes of this subparagraph.

(C) Certain collectively-bargained plans. In the case of a plan which the Secretary of Labor finds to be collectively bargained, established or maintained by an employer doing business in not less than 40 States and engaged in the trade or business of furnishing or selling services described in section 168(i)(10)(C), with respect to which the rates have been established or approved by a State or political subdivision thereof, by any agency or instrumentality of the United States, or by a public service or public utility commission or other similar body of any State or political subdivision thereof, and in the case of any employer which is a member of a controlled group with such employer, subparagraph (B) shall be applied by substituting for the words "plan amendment" the words "plan amendment or increase in benefits payable under title II of the Social Security Act". For purposes of this subparagraph, the term "controlled group" has the meaning provided by section 1563(a), determined without regard to section 1563(a)(4) and (e)(3)(C).

(D) Amount determined on basis of unfunded current liability. In the case of a defined benefit plan which is a multiemployer plan, except as provided in regulations, the maximum amount deductible under the limitations of this paragraph shall not be less than the excess (if any) of—

  (i) 140 percent of the current liability of the plan determined under section 431(c)(6)(D), over

  (ii) the value of the plan's assets determined under section 431(c)(2).

(E) Carryover. Any amount paid in a taxable year in excess of the amount deductible in such year under the foregoing limitations shall be deductible in the succeeding taxable years in order of time to the extent of the difference between the amount paid and deductible in each such succeeding year and the maximum amount deductible for such year under the foregoing limitations.

(F) Repealed.

(2) Employees' annuities. In the taxable year when paid, in an amount determined in accordance with paragraph (1), if the contributions are paid toward the purchase of retirement annuities, or retirement annuities and medical benefits as described in section 401(h), and such purchase is part of a plan which meets the requirements of section 401(a)(3), (4), (5), (6), (7), (8), (9), (11), (12), (13), (14), (15), (16), (17), (19), (20), (22), (26), (27), (31), and (37) and, if applicable, the requirements of section 401(a)(10) and of section 401(d), and if refunds of premiums, if any, are applied within the current taxable year or next succeeding taxable year towards the purchase of such retirement annuities, or such retirement annuities and medical benefits.

(3) Stock bonus and profit-sharing trusts.

(A) Limits on deductible contributions.

  (i) In general. In the taxable year when paid, if the contributions are paid into a stock bonus or profit-sharing trust, and if such taxable year ends within or with a taxable year of the trust with respect to which the trust is exempt under section 501(a), in an amount not in excess of the greater of—

    (I) 25 percent of the compensation otherwise paid or accrued during the taxable year to the beneficiaries under the stock bonus or profit-sharing plan, or

    (II) the amount such employer is required to contribute to such trust under section 401(k)(11) for such year.

  (ii) Carryover of excess contributions. Any amount paid into the trust in any taxable year in excess of the limitation of clause (i) (or the corresponding provision of prior law) shall be deductible in the succeeding taxable years in order of time, but the amount so deductible under this clause in any 1 such succeeding taxable year together with the amount allowable under clause (i) shall not exceed the amount described in subclause (I) or (II) of clause (i), whichever is greater, with respect to such taxable year.

  (iii) Certain retirement plans excluded. For purposes of this subparagraph, the term "stock bonus or profit-sharing trust" shall not include any trust designed to provide benefits upon retirement and covering a period of years, if under the plan the amounts to be contributed by the employer can be determined actuarially as provided in paragraph (1).

  (iv) 2 or more trusts treated as 1 trust. If the contributions are made to 2 or more stock bonus or profit-sharing trusts, such trusts shall be considered a single trust for purposes of applying the limitations in this subparagraph.

  (v) Defined contribution plans subject to the funding standards. Except as provided by the Secretary, a defined contribution plan which is subject to the funding standards of section 412 shall be treated in the same manner as a stock bonus or profit-sharing plan for purposes of this subparagraph.

(B) Profit-sharing plan of affiliated group. In the case of a profit-sharing plan, or a stock bonus plan in which contributions are determined with reference to profits, of a group of corporations which is an affiliated group within the meaning of section 1504, if any member of such affiliated group is prevented from making a contribution which it would otherwise have made under the plan, by reason of having no current or accumulated earnings or profits or because such earnings or profits are less than the contributions which it would otherwise have made, then so much of the contribution which such member was so prevented from making may be made, for the benefit of the employees of such member, by the other members of the group, to the extent of current or accumulated earnings or profits, except that such contribution by each such other member shall be limited, where the group does not file a consolidated return, to that proportion of its total current and accumulated earnings or profits remaining after adjustment for its contribution deductible without regard to this subparagraph which the total prevented contribution bears to the total current and accumulated earnings or profits of all the members of the group remaining after adjustment for all contributions deductible without regard to this subparagraph. Contributions made under the preceding sentence shall be deductible under subparagraph (A) of this paragraph by the employer making such contribution, and, for the purpose of determining amounts which may be carried forward and deducted under the second sentence of subparagraph (A) of this paragraph in succeeding taxable years, shall be deemed to have been made by the employer on behalf of whose employees such contributions were made.

(4) Trusts created or organized outside the United States. If a stock bonus, pension, or profit-sharing trust would qualify for exemption under section 501(a) except for the fact that it is a trust created or organized outside the United States, contributions to such a trust by an employer which is a resident, or corporation, or other entity of the United States, shall be deductible under the preceding paragraphs.

(5) Other plans. If the plan is not one included in paragraph (1), (2), or (3), in the taxable year in which an amount attributable to the contribution is includible in the gross income of employees participating in the plan, but, in the case of a plan in which more than one employee participates only if separate accounts are maintained for each employee. For purposes of this section, any vacation pay which is treated as deferred compensation shall be deductible for the taxable year of the employer in which paid to the employee.

(6) Time when contributions deemed made. For purposes of paragraphs (1), (2), and (3), a taxpayer shall be deemed to have made a payment on the last day of the preceding taxable year if the payment is on account of such taxable year and is made not later than the time prescribed by law for filing the return for such taxable year (including extensions thereof).

(7) Limitation on deductions where combination of defined contribution plan and defined benefit plan.
(A) In general. If amounts are deductible under the foregoing paragraphs of this subsection (other than paragraph (5)) in connection with 1 or more defined contribution plans and 1 or more defined benefit plans or in connection with trusts or plans described in 2 or more of such paragraphs, the total amount deductible in a taxable year under such plans shall not exceed the greater of—
(i) 25 percent of the compensation otherwise paid or accrued during the taxable year to the beneficiaries under such plans, or
(ii) the amount of contributions made to or under the defined benefit plans to the extent such contributions do not exceed the amount of employer contributions necessary to satisfy the minimum funding standard provided by section 412 with respect to any such defined benefit plans for the plan year which ends with or within such taxable year (or for any prior plan year).

A defined contribution plan which is a pension plan shall not be treated as failing to provide definitely determinable benefits merely by limiting employer contributions to amounts deductible under this section. In the case of a defined benefit plan which is a single employer plan, the amount necessary to satisfy the minimum funding standard provided by section 412 shall not be less than the excess (if any) of the plan's funding target (as defined in section 430(d)(1)) over the the value of the plan's assets (as determined under section 430(g)(3)).

(B) Carryover of contribution in excess of the deductible limit. Any amount paid under the plans in any taxable year in excess of the limitation of subparagraph (A) shall be deductible in the succeeding taxable years in order of time, but the amount so deductible under this subparagraph in any 1 such succeeding taxable year together with the amount allowable under subparagraph (A) shall not exceed 25 percent of the compensation otherwise paid or accrued during such taxable year to the beneficiaries under the plans.

(C) Paragraph not to apply in certain cases.
(i) Beneficiary test. This paragraph shall not have the effect of reducing the amount otherwise deductible under paragraphs (1), (2), and (3), if no employee is a beneficiary under more than 1 trust or under a trust and an annuity plan.
(ii) Elective deferrals. If, in connection with 1 or more defined contribution plans and 1 or more defined benefit plans, no amounts (other than elective deferrals (as defined in section 402(g)(3))) are contributed to any of the defined contribution plans for the taxable year, then subparagraph (A) shall not apply with respect to any of such defined contribution plans and defined benefit plans.
(iii) Limitation. In the case of employer contributions to 1 or more defined contribution plans—
(I) if such contributions do not exceed 6 percent of the compensation otherwise paid or accrued during the taxable year to the beneficiaries under such plans, this paragraph shall not apply to such contributions or to employer contributions to the defined benefit plans to which this paragraph would otherwise apply by reason of contributions to the defined contribution plans, and
(II) if such contributions exceed 6 percent of such compensation, this paragraph shall be applied by only taking into account such contributions to the extent of such excess.

For purposes of this clause, amounts carried over from preceding taxable years under subparagraph (B) shall be treated as employer contributions to 1 or more defined contributions plans to the extent attribu-

Employee benefit plans Code Sec. 404(b)(2)(B)

table to employer contributions to such plans in such preceding taxable years.

(iv) Guaranteed plans. In applying this paragraph, any single-employer plan covered under section 4021 of the Employee Retirement Income Security Act of 1974 shall not be taken into account.

(v) Multiemployer plans. In applying this paragraph, any multiemployer plan shall not be taken into account.

(D) Insurance contract plans. For purposes of this paragraph, a plan described in section 412(e)(3) shall be treated as a defined benefit plan.

(8) Self-employed individuals. In the case of a plan included in paragraph (1), (2), or (3) which provides contributions or benefits for employees some or all of whom are employees within the meaning of section 401(c)(1), for purposes of this section—

(A) the term "employee" includes an individual who is an employee within the meaning of section 401(c)(1), and the employer of such individual is the person treated as his employer under section 401(c)(4);

(B) the term "earned income" has the meaning assigned to it by section 401(c)(2);

(C) the contributions to such plan on behalf of an individual who is an employee within the meaning of section 401(c)(1) shall be considered to satisfy the conditions of section 162 or 212 to the extent that such contributions do not exceed the earned income of such individual (determined without regard to the deductions allowed by this section) derived from the trade or business with respect to which such plan is established, and to the extent that such contributions are not allocable (determined in accordance with regulations prescribed by the Secretary) to the purchase of life, accident, health, or other insurance; and

(D) any reference to compensation shall, in the case of an individual who is an employee within the meaning of section 401(c)(1), be considered to be a reference to the earned income of such individual derived from the trade or business with respect to which the plan is established.

(9) Certain contributions to employee stock ownership plans.

(A) Principal payments. Notwithstanding the provisions of paragraphs (3) and (7), if contributions are paid into a trust which forms a part of an employee stock ownership plan (as described in section 4975(e)(7)), and such contributions are, on or before the time prescribed in paragraph (6), applied by the plan to the repayment of the principal of a loan incurred for the purpose of acquiring qualifying employer securities (as described in section 4975(e)(8)), such contributions shall be deductible under this paragraph for the taxable year determined under paragraph (6). The amount deductible under this paragraph shall not, however, exceed 25 percent of the compensation otherwise paid or accrued during the taxable year to the employees under such employee stock ownership plan. Any amount paid into such trust in any taxable year in excess of the amount deductible under this paragraph shall be deductible in the succeeding taxable years in order of time to the extent of the difference between the amount paid and deductible in each such succeeding year and the maximum amount deductible for such year under the preceding sentence.

(B) Interest payment. Notwithstanding the provisions of paragraphs (3) and (7), if contributions are made to an employee stock ownership plan (described in subparagraph (A)) and such contributions are applied by the plan to the repayment of interest on a loan incurred for the purpose of acquiring qualifying employer securities (as described in subparagraph (A)), such contributions shall be deductible for the taxable year with respect to which such contributions are made as determined under paragraph (6).

(C) S corporations. This paragraph shall not apply to an S corporation.

(D) Qualified gratuitous transfers. A qualified gratuitous transfer (as defined in section 664(g)(1)) shall have no effect on the amount or amounts otherwise deductible under paragraph (3) or (7) or under this paragraph.

(10) Contributions by certain ministers to retirement income accounts. In the case of contributions made by a minister described in section 414(e)(5) to a retirement income account described in section 403(b)(9) and not by a person other than such minister, such contributions—

(A) shall be treated as made to a trust which is exempt from tax under section 501(a) and which is part of a plan which is described in section 401(a), and

(B) shall be deductible under this subsection to the extent such contributions do not exceed the limit on elective deferrals under section 402(g) or the limit on annual additions under section 415.

For purposes of this paragraph, all plans in which the minister is a participant shall be treated as one plan.

(11) Determinations relating to deferred compensation. For purposes of determining under this section—

(A) whether compensation of an employee is deferred compensation; and

(B) when deferred compensation is paid,

no amount shall be treated as received by the employee, or paid, until it is actually received by the employee.

(12) Definition of compensation. For purposes of paragraphs (3), (7), (8), and (9) and subsection (h)(1)(C), the term "compensation" shall include amounts treated as "participant's compensation" under subparagraph (C) or (D) of section 415(c)(3).

(b) Method of contributions, etc., having the effect of a plan; certain deferred benefits.

(1) Method of contributions, etc., having the effect of a plan. If—

(A) there is no plan, but

(B) there is a method or arrangement of employer contributions or compensation which has the effect of a stock bonus, pension, profit-sharing, or annuity plan, or other plan deferring the receipt of compensation (including a plan described in paragraph (2)),

subsection (a) shall apply as if there were such a plan.

(2) Plans providing certain deferred benefits.

(A) In general. For purposes of this section, any plan providing for deferred benefits (other than compensation) for employees, their spouses, or their dependents shall be treated as a plan deferring the receipt of compensation. In the case of such a plan, for purposes of this section, the determination of when an amount is includible in gross income shall be made without regard to any provisions of this chapter excluding such benefits from gross income.

(B) Exception. Subparagraph (A) shall not apply to any benefit provided through a welfare benefit fund (as defined in section 419(e)).

(c) Certain negotiated plans.
If contributions are paid by an employer—

(1) under a plan under which such contributions are held in trust for the purpose of paying (either from principal or income or both) for the benefit of employees and their families and dependents at least medical or hospital care, or pensions on retirement or death of employees; and

(2) such plan was established prior to January 1, 1954, as a result of an agreement between employee representatives and the Government of the United States during a period of Government operation, under seizure powers, of a major part of the productive facilities of the industry in which such employer is engaged,

such contributions shall not be deductible under this section nor be made nondeductible by this section, but the deductibility thereof shall be governed solely by section 162 (relating to trade or business expenses). For purposes of this chapter and subtitle B, in the case of any individual who before July 1, 1974, was a participant in a plan described in the preceding sentence—

(A) such individual, if he is or was an employee within the meaning of section 401(c)(1), shall be treated (with respect to service covered by the plan) as being an employee other than an employee within the meaning of section 401(c)(1) and as being an employee of a participating employer under the plan,

(B) earnings derived from service covered by the plan shall be treated as not being earned income within the meaning of section 401(c)(2), and

(C) such individual shall be treated as an employee of a participating employer under the plan with respect to service before July 1, 1975, covered by the plan.

Section 277 (relating to deductions incurred by certain membership organizations in transactions with members) does not apply to any trust described in this subsection. The first and third sentences of this subsection shall have no application with respect to amounts contributed to a trust on or after any date on which such trust is qualified for exemption from tax under section 501(a).

(d) Deductibility of payments of deferred compensation, etc., to independent contractors.
If a plan would be described in so much of subsection (a) as precedes paragraph (1) thereof (as modified by subsection (b)) but for the fact that there is no employer-employee relationship, the contributions or compensation—

(1) shall not be deductible by the payor thereof under this chapter, but

(2) shall (if they would be deductible under this chapter but for paragraph (1)) be deductible under this subsection for the taxable year in which an amount attributable to the contribution or compensation is includible in the gross income of the persons participating in the plan.

(e) Contributions allocable to life insurance protection for self-employed individuals.
In the case of a self-employed individual described in section 401(c)(1), contributions which are allocable (determined under regulations prescribed by the Secretary) to the purchase of life, accident, health, or other insurance shall not be taken into account under paragraph (1), (2), or (3) of subsection (a).

(f) Repealed.

(g) Certain employer liability payments considered as contributions.

(1) **In general.** For purposes of this section, any amount paid by an employer under section 4041(b), 4062, 4063, or 4064, or part 1 of subtitle E of title IV of the Employee Retirement Income Security Act of 1974 shall be treated as a contribution to which this section applies by such employer to or under a stock bonus, pension, profit-sharing, or annuity plan.

(2) **Controlled group deductions.** In the case of a payment described in paragraph (1) made by an entity which is liable because it is a member of a commonly controlled group of corporations, trades, or businesses, within the meaning of subsection (b) or (c) of section 414, the fact that the entity did not directly employ participants of the plan with respect to which the liability payment was made shall not affect the deductibility of a payment which otherwise satisfies the conditions of section 162 (relating to trade or business expenses) or section 212 (relating to expenses for the production of income).

(3) **Timing of deduction of contributions.**

(A) In general. Except as otherwise provided in this paragraph, any payment described in paragraph (1) shall (subject to the last sentence of subsection (a)(1)(A)) be deductible under this section when paid.

(B) Contributions under standard terminations. Subparagraph (A) shall not apply (and subsection (a)(1)(A) shall apply) to any payments described in paragraph (1) which are paid to terminate a plan under section 4041(b) of the Employee Retirement Income Security Act of 1974 to the extent such payments result in the assets of the plan being in excess of the total amount of benefits under such plan which are guaranteed by the Pension Benefit Guaranty Corporation under section 4022 of such Act.

(C) Contributions to certain trusts. Subparagraph (A) shall not apply to any payment described in paragraph (1) which is made under section 4062(c) of such Act and such payment shall be deductible at such time as may be prescribed in regulations which are based on principles similar to the principles of subsection (a)(1)(A).

(4) **References to Employee Retirement Income Security Act of 1974.** For purposes of this subsection, any reference to a section of the Employee Retirement Income Security Act of 1974 shall be treated as a reference to such section as in effect on the date of the enactment of the Retirement Protection Act of 1994.

(h) Special rules for simplified employee pensions.

(1) **In general.** Employer contributions to a simplified employee pension shall be treated as if they are made to a plan subject to the requirements of this section. Employer contributions to a simplified employee pension are subject to the following limitations:

(A) Contributions made for a year are deductible—

(i) in the case of a simplified employee pension maintained on a calendar year basis, for the taxable year with or within which the calendar year ends, or

(ii) in the case of a simplified employee pension which is maintained on the basis of the taxable year of the employer, for such taxable year.

(B) Contributions shall be treated for purposes of this subsection as if they were made for a taxable year if such contributions are made on account of such taxable year and are made not later than the time prescribed by law for filing the return for such taxable year (including extensions thereof).

(C) The amount deductible in a taxable year for a simplified employee pension shall not exceed 25 percent of the compensation paid to the employees during the calendar year ending with or within the taxable year (or during the taxable year in the case of a taxable year described in subparagraph (A)(ii)). The excess of the amount contributed over the amount deductible for a taxable year shall be deductible in the succeeding taxable years in order of time, subject to the 25 percent limit of the preceding sentence.

(2) Effect on certain trusts. For any taxable year for which the employer has a deduction under subparagraph (1), the otherwise applicable limitations in subsection (a)(3)(A) shall be reduced by the amount of the allowable deductions under paragraph (1) with respect to participants in the trust subject to subsection (a)(3)(A).

(3) Coordination with subsection (a)(7). For purposes of subsection (a)(7), a simplified employee pension shall be treated as if it were a separate stock bonus or profit-sharing trust.

(i) Repealed.

(j) Special rules relating to application with section 415.

(1) No deduction in excess of section 415 limitation. In computing the amount of any deduction allowable under paragraph (1), (2), (3), (4), (7), or (9) of subsection (a) for any year—

(A) in the case of a defined benefit plan, there shall not be taken into account any benefits for any year in excess of any limitation on such benefits under section 415 for such year, or

(B) in the case of a defined contribution plan, the amount of any contributions otherwise taken into account shall be reduced by any annual additions in excess of the limitation under section 415 for such year.

(2) No advance funding of cost-of-living adjustments. For purposes of clause (i), (ii) or (iii) of subsection (a)(1)(A), and in computing the full funding limitation, there shall not be taken into account any adjustments under section 415(d)(1) for any year before the year for which such adjustment first takes effect.

(k) Deduction for dividends paid on certain employer securities.

(1) General rule. In the case of a C corporation, there shall be allowed as a deduction for a taxable year the amount of any applicable dividend paid in cash by such corporation with respect to applicable employer securities. Such deduction shall be in addition to the deductions allowed under subsection (a).

(2) Applicable dividend. For purposes of this subsection—

(A) In general. The term "applicable dividend" means any dividend which, in accordance with the plan provisions—

(i) is paid in cash to the participants in the plan or their beneficiaries,

(ii) is paid to the plan and is distributed in cash to participants in the plan or their beneficiaries not later than 90 days after the close of the plan year in which paid,

(iii) is, at the election of such participants or their beneficiaries—

(I) payable as provided in clause (i) or (ii), or

(II) paid to the plan and reinvested in qualifying employer securities, or

(iv) is used to make payments on a loan described in subsection (a)(9) the proceeds of which were used to acquire the employer securities (whether or not allocated to participants) with respect to which the dividend is paid.

(B) Limitation on certain dividends. A dividend described in subparagraph (A)(iv) which is paid with respect to any employer security which is allocated to a participant shall not be treated as an applicable dividend unless the plan provides that employer securities with a fair market value of not less than the amount of such dividend are allocated to such participant for the year which (but for subparagraph (A)) such dividend would have been allocated to such participant.

(3) Applicable employer securities. For purposes of this subsection, the term "applicable employer securities" means, with respect to any dividend, employer securities which are held on the record date for such dividend by an employee stock ownership plan which is maintained by—

(A) the corporation paying such dividend, or

(B) any other corporation which is a member of a controlled group of corporations (within the meaning of section 409(l)(4)) which includes such corporation.

(4) Time for deduction.

(A) In general. The deduction under paragraph (1) shall be allowable in the taxable year of the corporation in which the dividend is paid or distributed to a participant or his beneficiary.

(B) Reinvestment dividends. For purposes of subparagraph (A), an applicable dividend reinvested pursuant to clause (iii)(II) of paragraph (2)(A) shall be treated as paid in the taxable year of the corporation in which such dividend is reinvested in qualifying employer securities or in which the election under clause (iii) of paragraph (2)(A) is made, whichever is later.

(C) Repayment of loans. In the case of an applicable dividend described in clause (iv) of paragraph (2)(A), the deduction under paragraph (1) shall be allowable in the taxable year of the corporation in which such dividend is used to repay the loan described in such clause.

(5) Other rules. For purposes of this subsection—

(A) Disallowance of deduction. The Secretary may disallow the deduction under paragraph (1) for any dividend if the Secretary determines that such dividend constitutes, in substance, an avoidance or evasion of taxation.

(B) Plan qualification. A plan shall not be treated as violating the requirements of section 401, 409, or 4975(e)(7), or as engaging in a prohibited transaction for purposes of section 4975(d)(3), merely by reason of any payment or distribution described in paragraph (2)(A).

(6) Definitions. For purposes of this subsection—

(A) Employer securities. The term "employer securities" has the meaning given such term by section 409(l).

(B) Employee stock ownership plan. The term "employee stock ownership plan" has the meaning given such term by section 4975(e)(7). Such term includes a tax credit employee stock ownership plan (as defined in section 409).

(7) Full vesting. In accordance with section 411, an applicable dividend described in clause (iii)(II) of paragraph (2)(A) shall be subject to the requirements of section 411(a)(1).

(l) Limitation on amount of annual compensation taken into account.

For purposes of applying the limitations of this section, the amount of annual compensation of each employee taken into account under the plan for any year shall not exceed $200,000. The Secretary shall adjust the $200,000 amount at the same time, and by the same amount, as any adjustment under section 401(a)(17)(B). For purposes of clause (i), (ii), or (iii) of subsection (a)(1)(A), and in computing the full funding limitation, any adjustment under the preceding sentence shall not be taken into account for any year before the year for which such adjustment first takes effect.

(m) Special rules for simple retirement accounts.

(1) **In general.** Employer contributions to a simple retirement account shall be treated as if they are made to a plan subject to the requirements of this section.

(2) **Timing.**

(A) Deduction. Contributions described in paragraph (1) shall be deductible in the taxable year of the employer with or within which the calendar year for which the contributions were made ends.

(B) Contributions after end of year. For purposes of this subsection, contributions shall be treated as made for a taxable year if they are made on account of the taxable year and are made not later than the time prescribed by law for filing the return for the taxable year (including extensions thereof).

(n) Elective deferrals not taken into account for purposes of deduction limits.

Elective deferrals (as defined in section 402(g)(3)) shall not be subject to any limitation contained in paragraph (3), (7), or (9) of subsection (a) or paragraph (1)(C) of subsection (h) and such elective deferrals shall not be taken into account in applying any such limitation to any other contributions.

(o) Deduction limit for single-employer plans.

For purposes of subsection (a)(1)(A)—

(1) **In general.** In the case of a defined benefit plan to which subsection (a)(1)(A) applies (other than a multiemployer plan), the amount determined under this subsection for any taxable year shall be equal to the greater of—

(A) the sum of the amounts determined under paragraph (2) with respect to each plan year ending with or within the taxable year, or

(B) the sum of the minimum required contributions under section 430 for such plan years.

(2) **Determination of amount.**

(A) In general. The amount determined under this paragraph for any plan year shall be equal to the excess (if any) of—

(i) the sum of—

(I) the funding target for the plan year,

(II) the target normal cost for the plan year, and

(III) the cushion amount for the plan year, over

(ii) the value (determined under section 430(g)(3)) of the assets of the plan which are held by the plan as of the valuation date for the plan year.

(B) Special rule for certain employers. If section 430(i) does not apply to a plan for a plan year, the amount determined under subparagraph (A)(i) for the plan year shall in no event be less than the sum of—

(i) the funding target for the plan year (determined as if section 430(i) applied to the plan), plus

(ii) the target normal cost for the plan year (as so determined).

(3) **Cushion amount.** For purposes of paragraph (2)(A)(i)(III)—

(A) In general. The cushion amount for any plan year is the sum of—

(i) 50 percent of the funding target for the plan year, and

(ii) the amount by which the funding target for the plan year would increase if the plan were to take into account—

(I) increases in compensation which are expected to occur in succeeding plan years, or

(II) if the plan does not base benefits for service to date on compensation, increases in benefits which are expected to occur in succeeding plan years (determined on the basis of the average annual increase in benefits over the 6 immediately preceding plan years).

(B) Limitations.

(i) In general. In making the computation under subparagraph (A)(ii), the plan's actuary shall assume that the limitations under subsection (l) and section 415(b) shall apply.

(ii) Expected increases. In the case of a plan year during which a plan is covered under section 4021 of the Employee Retirement Income Security Act of 1974, the plan's actuary may, notwithstanding subsection (l), take into account increases in the limitations which are expected to occur in succeeding plan years.

(4) **Special rules for plans with 100 or fewer participants.**

(A) In general. For purposes of determining the amount under paragraph (3) for any plan year, in the case of a plan which has 100 or fewer participants for the plan year, the liability of the plan attributable to benefit increases for highly compensated employees (as defined in section 414(q)) resulting from a plan amendment which is made or becomes effective, whichever is later, within the last 2 years shall not be taken into account in determining the target liability.

(B) Rule for determining number of participants. For purposes of determining the number of plan participants, all defined benefit plans maintained by the same employer (or any member of such employer's controlled group (within the meaning of section 412(d)(3))) shall be treated as one plan, but only participants of such member or employer shall be taken into account.

(5) **Special rule for terminating plans.** In the case of a plan which, subject to section 4041 of the Employee Retirement Income Security Act of 1974, terminates during the plan year, the amount determined under paragraph (2) shall in no event be less than the amount required to make the plan sufficient for benefit liabilities (within the meaning of section 4041(d) of such Act).

(6) **Actuarial assumptions.** Any computation under this subsection for any plan year shall use the same actuarial assumptions which are used for the plan year under section 430.

(7) **Definitions.** Any term used in this subsection which is also used in section 430 shall have the same meaning given such term by section 430.

In 2010, P.L. 111-312, Sec. 101(a)(1), substituted "December 31, 2012" for "December 31, 2010" both places it appeared in Sec. 901 of P.L. 107-16 [see below], effective as if included in the enactment of P.L. 107-16, EGTRRA, 6/7/2001.

In 2008, P.L. 110-458, Sec. 103(a), substituted "2009" for "2008" in Sec. 101(c)(2)(A)(ii), P.L. 108-218, pertaining to provisions relating to plan amendments, see below.

—P.L. 110-458, Sec. 108(a)(1)(A), substituted "430(g)(3)" for "430(g)(2)" in clause (o)(2)(A)(ii) . . . Sec. 108(a)(1)(B), substituted "412(d)(3)" for "412(f)(4)" in para. (o)(4)(B) . . . Sec. 108(a)(2)(A), deleted " For purposes of clause (ii) , if paragraph (1)(D) applies to a defined benefit plan for any plan year, the amount necessary to satisfy the minimum funding standard provided by section 412 with respect to such plan for such plan year shall not be less than the unfunded current liability of such plan under section 412(l) ." after "this section." in subpara. (a)(7)(A) . . . Sec. 108(a)(2)(B), substituted "the excess (if any) of the plan's funding target (as defined in section 430(d)(1)) over the value of the plan's assets (as determined under section 430(g)(3))' for "the plan's funding shortfall determined under section 430" in subpara. (a)(7)(A), effective for yrs. begin. after 12/31/2007, as if included in the amendments made by Sec. 801, P.L. 109-280, see below.

—P.L. 110-458, Sec. 108(b), substituted "431(c)(6)(D)" for "431(c)(6)(C)" in clause (a)(1)(D)(i), effective for yrs. begin. after 12/31/2007 [effective as included in the amendments made by Sec. 802, P.L. 109-280, see below]

—P.L. 110-458, Sec. 108(c), amended clause (a)(7)(C)(iii), effective for contributions for tax yrs. begin. after 12/31/2005 [effective as included in the amendments made by Sec. 803, P.L. 109-280, see below]

Prior to amendment clause (a)(7)(C)(iii) read as follows

"(iii) Limitation. In the case of employer contributions to 1 or more defined contribution plans, this paragraph shall only apply to the extent that such contributions exceed 6 percent of the compensation otherwise paid or accrued during the taxable year to the beneficiaries under such plans. For purposes of this clause, amounts carried over from preceding taxable years under subparagraph (B) shall be treated as employer contributions to 1 or more defined contributions to the extent attributable to employer contributions to such plans in such preceding taxable years.

—P.L. 110-245, Sec. 401(c)(1), substituted '(31), and (37)' for 'and (31)' in para. (a)(2), effective for deaths and disabilities occurring on or after 1/1/2007. Sec. 104(d)(2) of this Act provides:

"(2) Provisions relating to plan amendments.

"(A) In general. If this subparagraph applies to any plan or contract amendment, such plan or contract shall be treated as being operated in accordance with the terms of the plan during the period described in subparagraph (B)(iii).

"(B) Amendments to which subparagraph (A) applies.

"(i) In general. Subparagraph (A) shall apply to any amendment to any plan or annuity contract which is made—

"(I) pursuant to the amendments made by subsection (a) or pursuant to any regulation issued by the Secretary of the Treasury under subsection (a), and

"(II) on or before the last day of the first plan year beginning on or after January 1, 2010.

In the case of a governmental plan (as defined in section 414(d) of the Internal Revenue Code of 1986), this clause shall be applied by substituting '2012' for '2010' in subclause (II).

"(ii) Conditions. This paragraph shall not apply to any amendment unless--

"(I) the plan or contract is operated as if such plan or contract amendment were in effect for the period described in clause (iii), and

"(II) such plan or contract amendment applies retroactively for such period.

"(iii) Period described. The period described in this clause is the period--

"(I) beginning on the effective date specified by the plan, and

"(II) ending on the date described in clause (i)(II) (or, if earlier, the date the plan or contract amendment is adopted).

In 2006, P.L. 109-280, Sec. 301(c), substituted '2008' for '2006' in Sec. 101(c)(2)(A)(ii) of P.L. 108-218 [see below].

—P.L. 109-280, Sec. 402(g)(3), of this Act, reads as follows:

"(3) Limitation on deductions under certain plans. Section 404(a)(7)(C)(iv) of the Internal Revenue Code of 1986, as added by this Act, shall not apply with respect to any taxable year of a plan sponsor of an eligible plan if any applicable plan year with respect to such plan ends with or within such taxable year."

—P.L. 109-280, Sec. 801(a)(1), added "in the case of a defined benefit plan other than a multiemployer plan, in an amount determined under subsection (o), and in the case of any other plan" after "section 501(a)," in subpara. (a)(1)(A) . . . Sec. 801(a)(2), added subsec. (o) . . . Sec. 801(b), added clause (a)(7)(C)(iv) . . . Sec. 801(c)(1), substituted "section 431" for "section 412" each place it appeared in subpara. (a)(1)(A) . . . Sec. 801(c)(2)(A), substituted "In the case of a multiemployer plan" for "In the case of a plan" in subpara. (a)(1)(B) . . . Sec. 801(c)(2)(B), substituted "section 431(c)(6)" for "section 412(c)(7)" each place it appeared in subpara. (a)(1)(B) . . . Sec. 801(c)(2)(C), substituted "section 431(c)(6)(A)(ii)" for "section 412(c)(7)(B)" in subpara. (a)(1)(B) . . . Sec. 801(c)(2)(D), substituted "section 431(c)(6)(A)(i)" for "section 412(c)(7)(A)" in subpara. (a)(1)(B) . . . Sec. 801(c)(2)(E), substituted "section 431" for "section 412" in subpara. (a)(1)(B) . . . Sec. 801(c)(3)(A), added "In the case of a defined benefit plan which is a single employer plan, the amount necessary to satisfy the minimum funding standard provided by section 412 shall not be less than the plans funding shortfall determined under section 430." at the end of subpara. (a)(7)(A) . . . Sec. 801(c)(3)(B), amended subpara. (a)(7)(D), effective for yrs. begin. after 12/31/2007.

Prior to amendment, subpara. (a)(7)(D) read as follows:

"(D) Section 412(i) plans. For purposes of this paragraph, any plan described in section 412(i) shall be treated as a defined benefit plan."

—P.L. 109-280, Sec. 801(d)(1), substituted "section 412(l)(8)(A), except that section 412(l)(8)(A) shall be applied for purposes of this clause by substituting '150 percent (140 percent in the case of a multiemployer plan) of current liability' for 'the current liability' in clause (i)." in clause (a)(1)(D)(i) . . . Sec. 801(d)(2), deleted subpara. (a)(1)(F), effective for yrs. begin. after 12/31/2005.

Prior to deletion, subpara. (a)(1)(F) read as follows:

"(F) Election to disregard modified interest rate. An employer may elect to disregard subsections (b)(5)(B)(ii)(II) and (l)(7)(C)(i)(IV) of section 412 solely for purposes of determining the interest rate used in calculating the maximum amount of the deduction allowable under this paragraph."

—P.L. 109-280, Sec. 802(a), amended subpara. (a)(1)(D) [as amended by Sec. 801(d)(1) of this Act, see above], effective for yrs. begin. after 12/31/2007.

Prior to amendment, subpara. (a)(1)(D) [as amended by Sec. 801(d)(1) of this Act, see above] read as follows:

"(D) Special rule in case of certain plans.

"(i) In general. In the case of any defined benefit plan, except as provided in regulations, the maximum amount deductible under the limitations of this paragraph shall not be less than the unfunded current liability determined under section 412(l)(8)(A), except that section 412(l)(8)(A) shall be applied for purposes of this clause by substituting '150 percent (140 percent in the case of a multiemployer plan) of current liability' for 'the current liability' in clause (i). . [sic]

"(ii) Plans with 100 or less participants. For purposes of this subparagraph, in the case of a plan which has 100 or less participants for the plan year, unfunded current liability shall not include the liability attributable to benefit increases for highly compensated employees (as defined in section 414(q)) resulting from a plan amendment which is made or becomes effective, whichever is later, within the last 2 years.

"(iii) Rule for determining number of participants. For purposes of determining the number of plan participants, all defined benefit plans maintained by the same employer (or any member of such employer's controlled group (within the meaning of section 412(l)(8)(C))) shall be treated as one plan, but only employees of such member or employer shall be taken into account.

"(iv) Special rule for terminating plans. In the case of a plan which, subject to section 4041 of the Employee Retirement Income Security Act of 1974, terminates during the plan year, clause (i) shall be applied by substituting for unfunded current liability the amount required to make the plan sufficient for benefit liabilities (within the meaning of section 4041(d) of such Act)."

—P.L. 109-280, Sec. 803(a), added clause (a)(7)(C)(iii) . . . Sec. 803(b), added clause (a)(7)(C)(v), effective for contributions for tax. yrs. begin. after 12/31/2005.

—P.L. 109-280, Sec. 811, of this Act [relating to Sec. 901 of P.L. 107-16, see below], provides:

"SEC. 811. PENSIONS AND INDIVIDUAL RETIREMENT ARRANGEMENT PROVISIONS OF ECONOMIC GROWTH AND TAX RELIEF RECONCILIATION ACT OF 2001 MADE PERMANENT.

"Title IX of the Economic Growth and Tax Relief Reconciliation Act of 2001 shall not apply to the provisions of, and amendments made by, subtitles A through F of title VI of such Act (relating to pension and individual retirement arrangement provisions)."

In 2004, P.L. 108-218, Sec. 101(b)(5), added subpara. (a)(1)(F), effective for plan yrs. begin. after 12/31/2003. Sec. 101(d)(2) and (3) of this Act, provides:

"(2) Lookback rules. For purposes of applying subsections (d)(9)(B)(ii) and (e)(1) of section 302 of the Employee Retirement Income Security Act of 1974 and subsections (l)(9)(B)(ii) and (m)(1) of section 412 of the Internal Revenue Code of 1986 to plan years beginning after December 31, 2003, the amendments made by this section may be applied as if such amendments had been in effect for all prior plan years. The Secretary of the Treasury may prescribe simplified assumptions which may be used in applying the amendments made by this section to such prior plan years.

"(3) Transition rule for section 415 limitation. In the case of any participant or beneficiary receiving a distribution after December 31, 2003 and before January 1, 2005, the amount payable under any form of benefit subject to section 417(e)(3) of the Internal Revenue Code of 1986 and subject to adjustment under section 415(b)(2)(B) of such Code shall not, solely by reason of the amendment made by subsection (b)(4), be less than the amount that would have been so payable had the amount payable been determined using the applicable interest rate in effect as of the last day of the last plan year beginning before January 1, 2004."

—P.L. 108-218, Sec. 101(c), of this Act [as amended by Sec. 301(c), P.L. 108-280 and Sec. 103(a), P.L. 110-458, see above], reads as follows:

"(c) Provisions relating to plan amendments.

"(1) In general. If this subsection applies to any plan or annuity contract amendment—

"(A) such plan or contract shall be treated as being operated in accordance with the terms of the plan or contract during the period described in paragraph (2)(B)(i), and

"(B) except as provided by the Secretary of the Treasury, such plan shall not fail to meet the requirements of section 411(d)(6) of the Internal Revenue Code of 1986 and section 204(g) of the Employee Retirement Income Security Act of 1974 by reason of such amendment.

"(2) Amendments to which section applies.

"(A) In general. This subsection shall apply to any amendment to any plan or annuity contract which is made—

"(i) pursuant to any amendment made by this section, and

"(ii) on or before the last day of the first plan year beginning on or after January 1, 2009.

"(B) Conditions. This subsection shall not apply to any plan or annuity contract amendment unless—

"(i) during the period beginning on the date the amendment described in subparagraph (A)(i) takes effect and ending on the date described in subparagraph (A)(ii) (or, if earlier, the date the plan or contract amendment is adopted), the plan or contract is operated as if such plan or contract amendment were in effect; and

"(ii) such plan or contract amendment applies retroactively for such period."

In 2002, P.L. 107-358, Sec. 2, added subsec. (c) in Sec. 901 of P.L. 107-16 [see below], effective 12/17/2002.

—P.L. 107-147, Sec. 411(l)(1), substituted "(9) and subsection (h)(1)(C)," for "(9)," in para. (a)(12) . . . Sec. 411(l)(2), substituted "subsection (a) or paragraph (1)(C) of subsection (h)" for "subsection (a)," in subsec. (n) . . . Sec. 411(l)(4), amended subpara. (a)(7)(C), effective for yrs. begin. after 12/31/2001.

Prior to amendment, subpara. (a)(7)(C) read as follows:

"(C) Paragraph not to apply in certain cases. This paragraph shall not have the effect of reducing the amount otherwise deductible under paragraphs (1), (2), and (3), if no employee is a beneficiary under more than 1 trust or under a trust and an annuity plan."

—P.L. 107-147, Sec. 411(s), substituted "Special rule for terminating plans" for "Plans maintained by professional service employers" in the heading of clause (a)(1)(D)(iv), effective for plan yrs. begin. after 12/31/2001.

—P.L. 107-147, Sec. 411(w)(1)(A), deleted "during the taxable year" after "such corporation" in para. (k)(1)... Sec. 411(w)(1)(B), substituted "(A)(iv)" for "(A)(iii)" in subpara. (k)(2)(B)... Sec. 411(w)(1)(C), substituted "(iv)" for "(iii)" in subpara. (k)(4)(B)... Sec. 411(w)(1)(D), redesignated subpara. (k)(4)(B) [as amended by Sec. 411(w)(1)(C) of this Act, see above] as subpara. (k)(4)(B) and added subpara. (k)(4)(B)... Sec. 411(w)(2), added para. (k)(7), effective for tax. yrs. begin. after 12/31/2001.

In 2001, P.L. 107-16, Sec. 611(c)(1), substituted "$200,000" for "$150,000" each place it appeared in subsec. (l), effective for yrs. begin. after 12/31/2001.

—P.L. 107-16, Sec. 614(a), added subsec. (n), effective for yrs. begin. after 12/31/2001.

—P.L. 107-16, Sec. 616(a)(1)(A), substituted "25 percent" for "15 percent" in subclause (a)(3)(A)(i)(I)... Sec. 616(a)(1)(B), substituted "25 percent" for "15 percent" each place it appeared in subpara. (h)(1)(C)... Sec. 616(a)(2)(A), amended clause (a)(3)(A)(v)... Sec. 616(a)(2)(B)(i), added "(other than a trust to which paragraph (3) applies)" after "pension trust" in subpara. (a)(1)(A)... Sec. 616(a)(2)(B)(ii), substituted "trust subject to subsection (a)(3)(A)" for "stock bonus or profit-sharing trust" in para. (h)(2)... Sec. 616(a)(2)(B)(iii), substituted "certain trusts" for "stock bonus and profit-sharing trust" in the heading of para. (h)(2)... Sec. 616(b)(1), added para. (a)(12)... Sec. 616(b)(2)(A), deleted "The term "compensation otherwise paid or accrued during the taxable year to all employees" shall include any amount with respect to which an election under section 415(c)(3)(C) is in effect, but only to the extent that any contribution with respect to such amount is nonforfeitable." at the end of subpara. (a)(3)(B), effective for yrs. begin. after 12/31/2001.

Prior to amendment, clause (a)(3)(A)(v) read as follows:

"(v) Pre-87 limitation carryforwards.

"(I) In general. The limitation of clause (i) for any taxable year shall be increased by the unused pre-87 limitation carryforwards (but not to an amount in excess of 25 percent of the compensation described in clause (i)).

"(II) Unused pre-87 limitation carryforwards. For purposes of subclause (I), the term 'unused pre-87 limitation carryforwards' means the amount by which the limitation of the first sentence of this subparagraph (as in effect on the day before the date of the enactment of the Tax Reform Act of 1986) for any taxable year beginning before January 1, 1987, exceeded the amount paid to the trust for such taxable year (to the extent such excess was not taken into account in prior taxable years)."

—P.L. 107-16, Sec. 632(a)(3)(B), deleted ", the exclusion allowance under section 403(b)(2)," after "elective deferrals under section 402(g)," in subpara. (a)(10)(B), effective for yrs. begin. after 12/31/2001.

—P.L. 107-16, Sec. 652(a), amended subpara. (a)(1)(D), effective for plan yrs. begin. after 12/31/2001.

Prior to amendment, subpara. (a)(1)(D) read as follows:

"(D) Special rule in case of certain plans. In the case of any defined benefit plan (other than a multiemployer plan) which has more than 100 participants for the plan year, except as provided in regulations, the maximum amount deductible under the limitations of this paragraph shall not be less than the unfunded current liability determined under section 412(l). For purposes of determining whether a plan has more than 100 participants, all defined benefit plans maintained by the same employer (or any member of such employer's controlled group (within the meaning of section 412(l)(8)(c))) shall be treated as 1 plan, but only employees of such member or employer shall be taken into account."

—P.L. 107-16, Sec. 658, of this Act provides:

"SEC. 658. CLARIFICATION OF TREATMENT OF CONTRIBUTIONS TO MULTIEMPLOYER PLAN.

"(a) Not considered method of accounting. For purposes of section 446 of the Internal Revenue Code of 1986, a determination under section 404(a)(6) of such Code regarding the taxable year with respect to which a contribution to a multiemployer pension plan is deemed made shall not be treated as a method of accounting of the taxpayer. No deduction shall be allowed for any taxable year for any contribution to a multiemployer pension plan with respect to which a deduction was previously allowed.

"(b) Regulations. The Secretary of the Treasury shall promulgate such regulations as necessary to clarify that a taxpayer shall not be allowed an aggregate amount of deductions for contributions to a multiemployer pension plan which exceeds the amount of such contributions made or deemed made under section 404(a)(6) of the Internal Revenue Code of 1986 to such plan.

"(c) Effective date. Subsection (a), and any regulations promulgated under subsection (b), shall be effective for years ending after the date of the enactment of this Act."

—P.L. 107-16, Sec. 662(a), deleted "or" at the end of clause (k)(2)(A)(ii), redesignated clause (k)(2)(A)(iii) as (iv), and added clause (k)(2)(A)(iii) ... Sec. 662(b), added "avoidance or" before "evasion" in subpara. (k)(5)(A), effective for tax. yrs. begin. after 12/31/2001.

—P.L. 107-16, Sec. 901, of this Act [as amended by Sec. 2 of P.L. 107-358, and Sec. 101(a)(1) of P.L. 111-312, and as related to Sec. 811 of P.L. 109-280, see above], reads as follows:

"SEC. 901. SUNSET OF PROVISIONS OF ACT.

"(a) In general. All provisions of, and amendments made by, this Act shall not apply—

"(1) to taxable, plan, or limitation years beginning after December 31, 2012, or

"(2) in the case of title V, to estates of decedents dying, gifts made, or generation skipping transfers, after December 31, 2012.

"(b) Application of certain laws. The Internal Revenue Code of 1986 and the Employee Retirement Income Security Act of 1974 shall be applied and administered to years, estates, gifts, and transfers described in subsection (a) as if the provisions and amendments described in subsection (a) had never been enacted.

"(c) Exception. Subsection (a) shall not apply to section 803 (relating to no federal income tax on restitution received by victims of the Nazi regime or their heirs or estates)."

In 1998, P.L. 105-206, Sec. 6015(d), redesignated subpara. (a)(9)(C) [sic (D)] as subpara. (a)(9)(D) and substituted "Qualified gratuitous transfers. A qualified" for "A qualified" in subpara. (a)(9)(D), effective for transfers made by trusts to, or for the use of, an employee stock ownership plan after 8/5/97.

—P.L. 105-206, Sec. 7001(a), added para. (a)(11), effective for tax. yrs. end. after 7/22/98. Sec. 7001(b)(2), of this Act, provides:

"(2) Change in method of accounting. In the case of any taxpayer required by the amendment made by subsection (a) to change its method of accounting for its first taxable year ending after the date of the enactment of this Act—

"(A) such change shall be treated as initiated by the taxpayer,

"(B) such change shall be treated as made with the consent of the Secretary of the Treasury; and

"(C) the net amount of the adjustments required to be taken into account by the taxpayer under section 481 of the Internal Revenue Code of 1986 shall be taken into account ratably over the 3-taxable year period beginning with such first taxable year."

In 1997, P.L. 105-34, Sec. 1530(c)(2), added subpara. (a)(9)(C)[sic (D)], effective for transfers made by trusts to, or for the use of, an employee stock ownership plan after 8/5/97.

—P.L. 105-34, Sec. 1601(d)(2)(C)(i), amended clause (a)(3)(A)(i) ... Sec. 1601(d)(2)(C)(ii), substituted "the amount described in subclause (I) or (II) of clause (i), whichever is greater, with respect to such taxable year." for "15 percent of the compensation otherwise paid or accrued during such taxable year to the beneficiaries under the plan." in clause (a)(3)(A)(ii), effective for plan yrs. begin. after 12/31/96.

Prior to amendment, clause (a)(3)(A)(i) read as follows:

"(i) In general. In the taxable year when paid, if the contributions are paid into a stock bonus or profit-sharing trust, and if such taxable year ends within or with a taxable year of the trust with respect to which the trust is exempt under section 501(a), in an amount not in excess of 15 percent of the compensation otherwise paid or accrued during the taxable year to the beneficiaries under the stock bonus or profit-sharing plan."

In 1996, P.L. 104-188, Sec. 1316(d)(1), added subpara. (a)(9)(C) ... Sec. 1316(d)(2), substituted "a C corporation" for "a corporation" in para. (k)(1), effective for tax. yrs. begin. after 12/31/97.

—P.L. 104-188, Sec. 1421(b)(2), added subsec. (m), effective for tax. yrs. begin. after 12/31/96.

—P.L. 104-188, Sec. 1431(b)(3), deleted "In determining the compensation of an employee, the rules of section 414(q)(6) shall apply, except that in applying such rules, the term 'family' shall include only the spouse of the employee and any lineal descendants of the employee who have not attained age 19 before the close of the year." at the end of subsec. (l), effective for yrs. begin. after 12/31/96.

—P.L. 104-188, Sec. 1461(b), added para. (a)(10), effective for yrs. begin. after 12/31/96.

—P.L. 104-188, Sec. 1704(q)(1), substituted "(9)" for "(10)" in para. (j)(1), effective for yrs. begin. after 12/31/83.

—P.L. 104-188, Sec. 1704(t)(76), deleted "(18)," after "(17)," in para. (a)(2), effective 8/20/96.

In 1994, P.L. 103-465, Sec. 751(a)(11), substituted "the Retirement Protection Act of 1994" for "the Single-Employer Pension Plan Amendments Act of 1986" in para. (g)(4), effective 12/8/94.

In 1993, P.L. 103-66, Sec. 13212(c)(1)(A), substituted "$150,000" for "$200,000" in subsec. (l) ... Sec. 13212(c)(1)(B), substituted "The Secretary shall adjust the $150,000 amount at the same time, and by the same amount, as any adjustment under section 401(a)(17)(B)." for "The Secretary shall adjust the $200,000 amount at the same time and in the same manner as under section 415(d)." in subsec. (l), effective for benefits accruing in plan yrs. begin. after 12/31/93, except as provided in Sec. 13212(d)(2) and (3) of this Act, which reads as follows:

"(2) Collectively bargained plans. In the case of a plan maintained pursuant to 1 or more collective bargaining agreements between employee representatives and 1 or more employers ratified before the date of the enactment of this Act, the amendments made by this section shall not apply to contributions or benefits pursuant to such agreements for plan years beginning before the earlier of—

"(A) the latest of—

"(i) January 1, 1994,

"(ii) the date on which the last of such collective bargaining agreements terminates (without regard to any extension, amendment, or modification of such agreements on or after such date of enactment), or

"(iii) in the case of a plan maintained pursuant to collective bargaining under the Railway Labor Act, the date of execution of an extension or replacement of the last of such collective bargaining agreements in effect on such date of enactment, or

"(B) January 1, 1997.

"(3) Transition rule for State and local plans.—

"(A) In general. In the case of an eligible participant in a governmental plan (within the meaning of section 414(d) of the Internal Revenue Code of 1986), the dollar limitation under section 401(a)(17) of such Code shall not apply to the extent the amount of compensation which is allowed to be taken into account under the plan would be reduced below the amount which was allowed to be taken into account under the plan as in effect on July 1, 1993.

"(B) Eligible participant. For purposes of subparagraph (A), an eligible participant is an individual who first became a participant in the plan during a plan year beginning before the 1st plan year beginning after the earlier of—

Employee benefit plans Code Sec. 404

"(i) the plan year in which the plan is amended to reflect the amendments made by this section, or

"(ii) December 31, 1995.

"(C) Plan must be amended to incorporate limits. This paragraph shall not apply to any eligible participant of a plan unless the plan is amended so that the plan incorporates by reference the dollar limitation under section 401(a)(17) of the Internal Revenue Code of 1986, effective with respect to noneligible participants for plan years beginning after December 31, 1995 (or earlier if the plan amendment so provides)."

In **1992**, P.L. 102-318, Sec. 522(a)(2), substituted "(27), and (31)" for "and (27)" in para. (a)(2), effective for distributions after 12/31/92, except as provided in Sec. 522(d)(2) of this Act which reads as follows:

"(2) Transition rule for certain annuity contracts. If, as of July 1, 1992, a State law prohibits a direct trustee-to-trustee transfer from an annuity contract described in section 403(b) of the Internal Revenue Code of 1986 which was purchased for an employee by an employer which is a State or a political subdivision thereof (or an agency or instrumentality of any 1 or more of either), the amendments made by this section shall not apply to distributions before the earlier of—

"(A) 90 days after the first day after July 1, 1992, on which such transfer is allowed under State law, or

"(B) January 1, 1994."

In **1990**, P.L. 101-508, Sec. 11812(b)(7), substituted "section 168(i)(10)(C)" for "section 167(1)(3)(A)(iii)" in subpara. (a)(1)(C), effective for property placed in service after 11/5/90 except as provided in Sec. 11812(c)(2) of this Act, reproduced in note following Code Sec. 42.

In **1989**, P.L. 101-239, Sec. 7302(a), amended subsec. (k), effective for employer securities acquired after 8/4/89, except as provided in Sec. 7302(b)(2) of this Act which reads as follows:

"(2) Securities acquired with certain loans. The amendment made by this section shall not apply to employer securities acquired after August 4, 1989, which are acquired—

"(A) with the proceeds of any loan which was made pursuant to a binding written commitment in effect on August 4, 1989, and at all times thereafter before such loan is made, and

"(B) pursuant to a written binding contract (or tender offer registered with the Securities and Exchange Commission) in effect on August 4, 1989, and at all times thereafter before such securities are acquired."

Prior to amendment, subsec. (k) read as follows:

"(k) Dividends paid deductions. In addition to the deductions provided under subsection (a), there shall be allowed as a deduction to a corporation the amount of any dividend paid in cash by such corporation with respect to the stock of such corporation if—

"(1) such stock is held on the record date for the dividend by a tax credit employee stock ownership plan (as defined in section 409) or an employee stock ownership plan (as defined in section 4975(e)(7)) which is maintained by such corporation or by any other corporation that is a member of a controlled group of corporations (within the meaning of section 409(1)(4)) that includes such corporation, and

"(2) in accordance with the plan provisions—

"(A) the dividend is paid in cash to the participants in the plan or their beneficiaries,

"(B) the dividend is paid to the plan and is distributed in cash to participants in the plan or their beneficiaries not later than 90 days after the close of the plan year in which paid, or

"(C) the dividend with respect to employer securities (whether or not allocated to participants) is used to make payments on a loan described in section 404(a)(9). Any deduction under subparagraph (A) or (B) of paragraph (2) shall be allowed in the taxable year of the corporation in which the dividend is paid or distributed to the participant under paragraph (2). A plan to which this subsection applies shall not be treated as violating the requirements of section 401, 409, or 4975(e)(7) or as engaging in a prohibited transaction for purposes of section 4975(d)(3) merely by reason of any distribution or payment described in paragraph (2). The Secretary may disallow the deduction under this subsection for any dividend if the Secretary determines that such dividend constitutes, in substance, an evasion of taxation. Any deduction under paragraph (2)(C) shall be allowable in the taxable year of the corporation in which the dividend is used to repay the loan described in such paragraph.

Paragraph (2)(C) shall not apply to dividends from employer securities which are allocated to any participant unless the plan provides that employer securities with a fair market value not less than the amount of such dividends are allocated to such participant for the year which (but for paragraph (2)(C)) such dividends would have been allocated to such participant."

—P.L. 101-239, Sec. 7841(b)(1), added "4041(b)," before "4062" in para. (g)(1), effective for payments made after 1/1/86, in tax. yrs. end. after 1/1/86.

In **1988**, P.L. 100-647, Sec. 1011(d)(1), added "For purposes of clause (i), (ii), or (iii) of subsection (a)(1)(A), and in computing the full funding limitation, any adjustment under the preceding sentence shall not be taken into account for any year before the year for which such adjustment first takes effect." at the end of subsec. (l)... Sec. 1011(d)(4), added "In determining the compensation of an employee, the rules of section 414(q)(6) shall apply, except that in applying such rules, the term 'family' shall include only the spouse of the employee and any lineal descendants of the employee who have not attained age 19 before the close of the year." to the end of subsec. (l), effective for benefits accruing in yrs. begin. after 12/31/88, except as provided in Sec. 1106(d)(5)(B) of P.L. 99-514, reproduced in the note following Code Sec. 401.

—P.L. 100-647, Sec. 1011(f)(6), added "(or during the taxable year in the case of a taxable year described in subparagraph (A)(ii))" after "taxable year" the second place it appeared in subpara. (h)(1)(C), effective for yrs. begin. after 12/31/86.

—P.L. 100-647, Sec. 1011A(e)(3), added Sec. 1131(d)(2) of P.L. 99-514, [part of the effective date for changes made by Secs. 1131(a) and (b) of P.L. 99-514, see below.]

—P.L. 100-647, Sec. 1011A(e)(4)(A)(i), substituted "paragraphs" for "provisions" in subpara. (a)(7)(A)... Sec. 1011A(e)(4)(A)(ii), added "or in connection with trusts or plans described in 2 or more of such paragraphs" after "1 or more defined benefit plans" in subpara. (a)(7)(A)... Sec. 1011A(e)(4)(B), amended para. (h)(3), effective for tax. yrs. begin. after 12/31/86.

Prior to amendment, para. (h)(3) read as follows:

"(3) Effect on limit on deductions. For any taxable year for which the employer has a deduction under paragraph (1), the otherwise applicable 25 percent limitations in subsection (a)(7) shall be reduced by the amount of the allowable deductions under paragraph (1) with respect to participants in the stock bonus or profit-sharing trust."

—P.L. 100-647, Sec. 1011B(h)(3)(A), added "(whether or not allocated to participants)" after "employer securities" in subpara. (k)(2)(C)... Sec. 1011B(h)(3)(B), added the sentence at the end of subsec. (k)... Sec. 1011B(h)(6), substituted "or as engaging in a prohibited transaction for purposes of section 4975(d)(3) merely by reason of any distribution or payment" for "merely by reason of any distribution" in the third sentence of subsec (k), effective for dividends paid in tax. yrs. begin. after 12/31/86.

—P.L. 100-647, Sec. 1018(t)(4)(A), substituted "evasion" for "avoidance" in the fourth sentence of subsec. (k), effective for tax. yrs. begin. after 7/18/84, except as provided in Sec. 1854(b)(6) of P.L. 99-514 reproduced below.

—P.L. 100-647, Sec. 1018(t)(5), amended Sec. 1875(c)(7)(B) of P.L. 99-514 by deleting "and section 405(c)", see below.

—P.L. 100-647, Sec. 2005(b)(1), substituted "For purposes of determining whether a plan has more than 100 participants" for "For purposes of this subparagraph" in subpara. (a)(1)(D)... Sec. 2005(b)(2), added the sentence at the end of subpara. (a)(7)(A)... Sec. 2005(b)(3), deleted "(without regard to any reduction by the credit balance in the funding standard account)" after "section 412(1))" in subpara. (a)(1)(D), effective for yrs. begin. after 12/31/87.

In **1987**, P.L. 100-203, Sec. 9307(c), redesignated subpara. (a)(1)(D) as (E), and added subpara. (a)(1)(D)... Sec. 9307(d), substituted "to amortize the unfunded costs attributable to such credits" for "to amortize such credits" in clause (a)(1)(A)(iii), effective for yrs. begin. after 12/31/87.

—P.L. 100-203, Sec. 10201(b)(2), amended subpara. (b)(2)(B)... Sec. 10201(b)(3), added the sentence at the end of para. (a)(5), effective for tax. yrs. begin. after 12/31/87.

Prior to amendment, subpara. (b)(2)(B) read as follows:

"(B) Exception for certain benefits. Subparagraph (A) shall not apply to—

"(i) any benefit provided through a welfare benefit fund (as defined in section 419(e)), or

"(ii) any benefit with respect to which an election under section 463 applies.".

—P.L. 100-203, Sec. 10201(c)(2), of this Act provides:

"(2) Change in method of accounting. In the case of any taxpayer who elected to have section 463 of the Internal Revenue Code of 1986 apply for such taxpayer's last taxable year beginning before January 1, 1988, and who is required to change his method of accounting by reason of the amendments made by this section—

"(A) such change shall be treated as initiated by the taxpayer,

"(B) such change shall be treated as having been made with the consent of the Secretary, and

"(C) the net amount of adjustments required by section 481 of such Code to be taken into account by the taxpayer—

"(i) shall be reduced by the balance in the suspense account under section 463(c) of such Code as of the close of such last taxable year, and

"(ii) shall be taken into account over the 4-taxable year period beginning with the taxable year following such last taxable year as follows:

"In the case of the: The percentage taken into account is:
"1st year 25
"2nd year 5
"3rd year 35
"4th year .... 35.

"Notwithstanding subparagraph (C)(ii), if the period the adjustments are required to be taken into account under section 481 of such Code is less than 4 years, such adjustments shall be taken into account ratably over such shorter period."

In **1986**, P.L. 99-514, Sec. 1106(d)(2), added subsec. (l), effective for benefits accruing in yrs. begin. after 12/31/88, except as provided in Sec. 1106(i)(5)(B) of this Act, reproduced in the note following Code Sec. 401.

—P.L. 99-514, Sec. 1108(c), amended subparas. (h)(1)(A) and (B), effective for yrs. begin. after 12/31/86.

Prior to amendment, subparas. (h)(1)(A) and (B) read as follows:

"(A) Contributions made for a calendar year are deductible for the taxable year with which or within which the calendar year ends.

"(B) Contributions made within 3½ months after the close of a calendar year are treated as if they were made on the last day of such calendar year if they are made on account of such calendar year."

—P.L. 99-514, Sec. 1112(d)(2), substituted "(22), and (26)" for "and (22)" in para. (a)(2), effective for plan yrs. begin. after 12/31/88. For special rules, see Sec. 1112(e)(2) and (4) of this Act reproduced in note following Code Sec. 401, and Sec. 1112(e)(3) of this Act reproduced in note following Code Sec. 4980.

—P.L. 99-514, Sec. 1131(a), amended subpara. (a)(3)(A)... Sec. 1131(b), amended para. (a)(7), effective for tax. yrs. begin. after 12/31/86. Sec. 1131(d)(2)

1,935

[as added by Sec. 1011A(e)(3) of P.L. 100-647, see above] of this Act provides as follows:

"(2) Special rules for collective bargaining agreements. In the case of a plan maintained pursuant to 1 or more collective bargaining agreements between employee representatives and 1 or more employers ratified before March 1, 1986, the amendments made by this section shall not apply to contributions pursuant to any such agreement for taxable years beginning before the earlier of—

"(A) January 1, 1989, or

"(B) the date on which the last of such collective bargaining agreements terminates (determined without regard to any extension thereof after February 28, 1986)."

Prior to amendment, subpara. (a)(3)(A) read as follows:

"(A) Limits on deductible contributions. In the taxable year when paid, if the contributions are paid into a stock bonus or profit-sharing trust, and if such taxable year ends within or with a taxable year of the trust with respect to which the trust is exempt under section 501(a), in an amount not in excess of 15 percent of the compensation otherwise paid or accrued during the taxable year to all employees under the stock bonus or profit-sharing plan. If in any taxable year there is paid into the trust, or a similar trust then in effect, amounts less than the amounts deductible under the preceding sentence, the excess, or if no amount is paid, the amounts deductible, shall be carried forward and be deductible when paid in the succeeding taxable years in order of time, but the amount so deductible under this sentence in any such succeeding taxable year shall not exceed 15 percent of the compensation otherwise paid or accrued during such succeeding taxable year to the beneficiaries under the plan, but the amount so deductible under this sentence in any one succeeding taxable year together with the amount so deductible under the first sentence of this subparagraph shall not exceed 25 percent of the compensation otherwise paid or accrued during such taxable year to the beneficiaries under the plan. In addition, any amount paid into the trust in any taxable year in excess of the amount allowable with respect to such year under the preceding provisions of this subparagraph shall be deductible in the succeeding taxable years in order of time, but the amount so deductible under this sentence in any one such succeeding taxable year together with the amount allowable under the first sentence of this subparagraph shall not exceed 15 percent of the compensation otherwise paid or accrued during such taxable year to the beneficiaries under the plan. The term 'stock bonus or profit-sharing trust', as used in this subparagraph, shall not include any trust designed to provide benefits upon retirement and covering a period of years, if under the plan the amounts to be contributed by the employer can be determined actuarially as provided in paragraph (1). If the contributions are made to 2 or more stock bonus or profit-sharing trusts, such trusts shall be considered a single trust for purposes of applying the limitations in this subparagraph."

Prior to amendment, para. (a)(7) read as follows:

"(7) Limit on deductions. If amounts are deductible under paragraphs (1) and (3), or (2) and (3), or (1), (2), and (3), in connection with two or more trusts, or one or more trusts and an annuity plan, the total amount deductible in a taxable year under such trusts and plans shall not exceed the greater of 25 percent of the compensation otherwise paid or accrued during the taxable year to the beneficiaries of the trusts or plans, or the amount of contributions made to or under the trusts or plans to the extent such contributions do not exceed the amount of employer contributions necessary to satisfy the minimum funding standard provided by section 412 for the plan year which ends with or within such taxable year (or for any prior plan year). In addition, any amount paid into such trust or under such annuity plans in any taxable year in excess of the amount allowable with respect to such year under the preceding provisions of this paragraph shall be deductible in the succeeding taxable years in order of time, but the amount so deductible under this sentence in any one such succeeding taxable year together with the amount allowable under the first sentence of this paragraph shall not exceed 25 percent of the compensation otherwise paid or accrued during such taxable years to the beneficiaries under the trusts or plans. This paragraph shall not have the effect of reducing the amount otherwise deductible under paragraphs (1), (2), and (3), if no employee is a beneficiary under more than one trust or a trust and an annuity plan."

—P.L. 99-514, Sec. 1136(b), substituted "(26), and (27)" for "and (26)" in para. (a)(2) [as amended by Sec. 1131(b) of this Act, see above] effective 10/22/86.

—P.L. 99-514, Sec. 1171(b)(6), deleted subsec. (i), effective for compensation paid or accrued after 12/31/86 in tax. yrs. end. after 12/31/86. Sec. 1171(c)(2) of this Act provides exception as follows:

"(2) Sections 404(i) and 6699 to continue to apply to pre-1987 credits.—The provisions of sections 404(i) and 6699 of the Internal Revenue Code of 1986 shall continue to apply with respect to credits under section 41 of such Code attributable to compensation paid or accrued before January 1, 1987 (or under section 38 of such Code with respect to qualified investment before January 1, 1983)."

Prior to deletion, subsec. (i) read as follows:

"(i) Deductibility of unused portions of employee stock ownership credit.

"(1) Unused credit carryovers. If any portion of the employee stock ownership credit determined under section 41 for any taxable year has not, after the application of section 38(c), been allowed under section 38 for any taxable year, such portion shall be allowed as a deduction (without regard to any limitations provided under this section) for the last taxable year to which such portion could have been allowed as a credit under section 39.

"(2) Reductions in credit. There shall be allowed as a deduction (subject to the limitations provided under this section) an amount equal to any reduction of the credit allowed under section 41 resulting from a final determination of such credit to the extent such reduction is not taken into account under section 41(c)(3)."

—P.L. 99-514, Sec. 1173(a)(1), deleted "or" at the end of subpara. (k)(2)(A), substituted ", or" for the period at the end of subpara. (k)(2)(B), and added subpara. (k)(2)(C) . . . Sec. 1173(a)(2), added the sentence at the end of subsec. (k)

[after amendment by Sec. 1854 of this Act, see below], effective for dividends paid in tax. yrs. begin. after 10/22/86.

—P.L. 99-514, Sec. 1848(c), substituted "the deduction allowed by this section" for "the deductions allowed by this section and section 405(c)" in subpara. (a)(8)(D), effective for obligations issued after 12/31/83.

—P.L. 99-514, Sec. 1851(b)(2)(A), substituted "any benefit" for "to any benefit" in clause (b)(2)(B)(ii) . . . Sec. 1851(b)(2)(B)(i), substituted "certain" for "unfunded" in the heading of subsec. (b) . . . Sec. 1851(b)(2)(B)(ii), substituted "certain" for "unfunded" in the heading of para. (b)(2) . . . Sec. 1851(b)(2)(C)(i), substituted "this chapter; but, if they would otherwise be deductible," for "section 162 (relating to trade or business expenses) or section 212 (relating to expenses for the production of income); but, if they satisfy the conditions of either of such sections," in subsec. (a) . . . Sec. 1851(b)(2)(C)(ii), substituted "under this chapter" for "under section 162 or 212" after "payor thereof" and after "would be deductible" each place it appeared in paras. (d)(1) and (d)(2), effective for amounts paid or incurred after 7/18/84, in tax. yrs. end. after 7/18/84. For exceptions, see Sec. 512(c) of P.L. 98-369, reproduced in the note following Code Sec. 162.

—P.L. 99-514, Sec. 1854(b)(2)(A), added the flush sentence at the end of subsec. (k) [before amendment Sec. 1173(a)(2) of this Act, see above] . . . Sec. 1854(b)(2)(B), deleted "during the taxable year" after "by such corporation" in the matter preceding para. (k)(1) . . . Sec. 1854(b)(3), added the sentence at the end of subsec. (k) [before amendment by Sec. 1173(a)(2) of this Act, see above] . . . Sec. 1854(b)(4), added the sentence at the end of subsec. (k) [before amendment by Sec. 1173(a)(2) of this Act, see above] . . . Sec. 1854(b)(5), substituted "participants in the plan or their beneficiaries" for "participants in the plan" each place it appeared in para. (k)(2), effective for tax. yrs. begin. after 7/18/84, except as provided in Sec. 1854(b)(6), which reads as follows:

"(6) The amendments made by paragraphs (1) and (2) of this Act shall not apply to dividends paid before January 1, 1986, if the taxpayer treated such dividends in a manner inconsistent with such amendments on a return filed with the Secretary before the date of the enactment of this Act [10/22/86]."

—P.L. 99-514, Sec. 1875(c)(7)(A), substituted "the earned income of such individual (determined without regard to the deductions allowed by this section)" for "the earned income of such individual" in subpara. (a)(8)(C), effective for yrs. begin. after 12/31/83.

—P.L. 99-514, Sec. 1875(c)(7)(B), [as amended by Sec. 1018(t)(5) of P.L. 100-647, see above] deleted "(determined without regard to the deductions allowed by this section)" after "of such individual" in subpara. (a)(8)(D), [as amended by Sec. 1848(c) of this Act, see above] effective for tax. yrs. begin. after 12/31/84.

—P.L. 99-272, Sec. 11011(c)(1), amended para. (g)(3) . . . Sec. 11011(c)(2), added para. (g)(4), effective for payments made after 1/1/86 in tax. yrs. end. after 1/1/86.

Prior to amendment, para. (g)(3) read as follows:

"(3) Coordination with subsection (a). Any payment described in paragraph (1) shall (subject to the last sentence of subsection (a)(1)(A)) be deductible under this section when paid."

In 1984, P.L. 98-369, Sec. 474(r)(14), amended subsec. (i), effective for tax. yrs. begin. after 12/31/83 and for carrybacks from tax. yrs. begin after 12/31/83.

Prior to amendment, subsec. (i) read as follows:

"(i) Deductibility of unused portions of employee stock ownership credit.

"(1) Unused credit carryovers. There shall be allowed as a deduction (without regard to any limitations provided under this section) for the last taxable year to which an unused employee stock ownership credit carryover (within the meaning of section 44G(b)(2)(A)) may be carried, an amount equal to the portion of such unused credit carryover which expires at the close of such taxable year.

"(2) Reductions in credit. There shall be allowed as a deduction (subject to the limitations provided under this section) an amount equal to any reduction of the credit allowed under section 44G resulting from a final determination of such credit to the extent such reduction is not taken into account in section 44G(c)(3)."

—P.L. 98-369, Sec. 512(a), amended subsec. (b), effective for amounts paid or incurred after 7/18/84 in tax. yrs. end. after 7/18/84. For exceptions, see Sec. 512(c)(2) of this Act, reproduced in the note following Code Sec. 162.

Prior to amendment, subsec. (b) read as follows:

"(b) Method of contributions, etc., having the effect of a plan. If there is no plan but a method of employer contributions or compensation has the effect of a stock bonus, pension, profit-sharing, or annuity plan, or other plan deferring the receipt of compensation, subsection (a) shall apply as if there were such a plan."

—P.L. 98-369, Sec. 542(a), added subsec. (k), effective for tax. yrs. begin. after 7/18/84.

—P.L. 98-369, Sec. 713(b)(3), deleted subsec. (f), effective for loans, assignments, and pledges made after 8/13/82. For purposes of the preceding sentence, the outstanding balance of any loan which is renegotiated, extended, renewed or revised after 1/13/82 shall be treated as an amount received as a loan on the date of such renegotiation, extension, renewal or revision.

Prior to deletion, subsec. (f) read as follows:

"(f) Certain loan repayments considered as contributions. For purposes of this section, any amount paid, directly or indirectly, by an owner-employee (within the meaning of section 401(c)(3)) in repayment of any loan which under section 72(m)(4)(B) was treated as an amount received under a contract purchased by a trust described in section 401(a) which is exempt from tax under section 501(a) or purchased as a part of a plan described in section 403(a) shall be treated as a contribution to which this section applies on behalf of such owner-employee to such trust or to or under such plan."

—P.L. 98-369, Sec. 713(d)(4)(A), deleted para. (a)(9) and redesignated para. (a)(10) as (a)(9) . . . Sec. 713(d)(5), deleted para. (h)(4) . . . Sec. 713(d)(6), substituted "the earned income of such individual (determined without regard to the de-

ductions allowed by this section and section 405(c))" for "the earned income of such individual" in subpara. (a)(8)(D), effective for yrs. begin. after 12/31/83.
Prior to deletion, para. (a)(9) read as follows:

"(9) Plans benefiting self-employed individuals. In the case of a plan included in paragraph (1), (2), or (3) which provides contributions or benefits for employees some or all of whom are employees within the meaning of section 401(c)(1)—

"(A) the limitations provided by paragraphs (1), (2), (3), and (7) on the amounts deductible for any taxable year shall be computed, with respect to contributions on behalf of employees (other than employees within the meaning of section 401(c)(1)), as if such employees were the only employees for whom contributions and benefits are provided under the plan;

"(B) the limitations provided by paragraphs (1), (2), (3), and (7) on the amounts deductible for any taxable year shall be computed, with respect to contributions on behalf of employees within the meaning of section 401(c)(1)—

"(i) as if such employees were the only employees for whom contributions and benefits are provided under the plan, and

"(ii) without regard to the second sentence of paragraph (3); and

"(C) the amounts deductible under paragraphs (1), (2), (3), and (7), with respect to contributions on behalf of any employee within the meaning of section 401(c)(1), shall not exceed the applicable limitation provided in subsection (e)."
Prior to deletion, para. (h)(4) read as follows:

"(4) Effect on self-employed individuals or shareholder employees. The limitations described in paragraphs (1), (2)(a), and (4) of subsection (e) or described in section 1379(b)(1) for any taxable year shall be reduced by the amount of the allowable deductions under paragraph (1) with respect to an employee within the meaning of section 401(c)(1) or a shareholder-employee (as defined in section 1379(d))."

—P.L. 98-369, Sec. 713(d)(9), substituted "under paragraph (1), (2), or (3) of subsection (a)" for "under this section" in subsec. (e), effective for years begin. after 12/31/83. Sec. 713(d)(9) of this Act provides as follows:

"(8) Coordination of repeals of certain sections. Sections 404(e) and 1379(b) of the Internal Revenue Code of 1954 (as in effect on the day before the date of the enactment of the Tax Equity and Fiscal Responsibility Act of 1982) shall not apply to any plan to which section 401(j) of such Code applies (or would apply but for its repeal)."

In 1983, P.L. 97-448, Sec. 103(d)(3), deleted "plans which include employees within the meaning of section 401(c)(1) with respect to" in Sec. 312(f)(1) of P.L. 97-34 [the effective date for amendments made by Sec. 312(a) of P.L. 97-34, see below].

In 1982, P.L. 97-248, Sec. 235(f), added subsec. (j), effective as provided in Sec. 235(g) of this Act reproduced in note following Code Sec. 415.

—P.L. 97-248, Sec. 237(e)(2)(A), substituted "(8), (9), (11)" for "(8), (11)" in para. (a)(2)... Sec. 237(e)(2)(B), substituted "section 401(a)(10) and of section 401(d)" for "section 401(a)(9), (10), (17), and (18), and of section 401(d) (other than paragraph (1))" in para. (a)(2), effective for yrs. begin. after 12/31/83.

—P.L. 97-248, Sec. 238(a), amended subsec. (e), effective for yrs. begin. after 12/31/82.
Prior to amendment, subsec. (e) read as follows:
"(e) Special limitations for self-employed individuals.

"(1) In general. In the case of a plan included in subsection (a) (1), (2), or (3), which provides contributions or benefits for employees some or all of whom are employees within the meaning of section 401(c)(1), the amounts deductible under subsection (a) (determined without regard to paragraph (10) thereof) in any taxable year with respect to contributions on behalf of any employees within the meaning of section 401(c)(1) shall, subject to paragraphs (2) and (4), not exceed $15,000, or 15 percent of the earned income derived by such employees from the trade or business with respect to which the plan is established, whichever is the lesser.

"(2) Contributions made under more than one plan.

"(A) Overall limitation. In any taxable year in which amounts are deductible with respect to contributions under two or more plans on behalf of an individual who is an employee within the meaning of section 401(c)(1) with respect to such plans, the aggregate amount deductible for such taxable year under all such plans with respect to contributions on behalf of such employee (determined without regard to subsection (a)(10)) shall (subject to paragraph (4)) not exceed $15,000, or 15 percent of the earned income derived by such employee from the trades or businesses with respect to which the plans are established, whichever is the lesser.

"(B) Allocation of amounts deductible. In any case in which the amounts deductible under subsection (a) (with the application of the limitations of this subsection) with respect to contributions made on behalf of an employee within the meaning of section 401(c)(1) under two or more plans are, by reason of subparagraph (A), less than the amounts deductible under such subsection determined without regard to such subparagraph, the amount deductible under subsection (a) (determined without regard to paragraph (10) thereof) with respect to such contributions under each such plan shall be determined in accordance with regulations prescribed by the Secretary.

"(3) Contributions allocable to insurance protection. For purposes of this subsection, contributions which are allocable (determined under regulations prescribed by the Secretary) to the purchase of life, accident, health, or other insurance shall not be taken into account.

"(4) Limitations cannot be lower than $750 or 100 percent of earned income. The limitations under paragraphs (1) and (2)(A) for any employee shall not be less than the lesser of—.

"(A) $750, or

"(B) 100 percent of the earned income derived by such employee from the trades or businesses taken into account for purposes of paragraph (1) or (2)(A) as the case may be.

This paragraph does not apply for any taxable year to any employee whose adjusted gross income for such taxable year (determined separately for each individual, without regard to any community property laws, and without regard to the deduction allowable under subsection (a)) exceeds $15,000."

—P.L. 97-248, Sec. 253(b), added the sentence at the end of subpara. (a)(3)(B), effective for tax. yrs. begin. after 12/31/81.

In 1981, P.L. 97-34, Sec. 312(a), substituted "$15,000" for "$7,500" in paras. (e)(1) and (e)(2), effective [as amended by Sec. 103(d)(3) of P.L. 97-448, see above] for tax. yrs. begin. after 12/31/81.

—P.L. 97-34, Sec. 331(b), added subsec. (i), effective for tax. yrs. end. after 12/31/82.

—P.L. 97-34, Sec. 333(a), added para. (a)(10), effective for tax. yrs. begin. after 12/31/81.

In 1980, P.L. 96-364, Sec. 205, amended subsec. (g), effective 9/26/80. Sec. 408 of this Act provides as follows:

"SEC. 408. DEDUCTIBILITY OF PAYMENTS TO PLAN BY A CORPORATION OPERATING PUBLIC TRANSPORTATION SYSTEM ACQUIRED BY A STATE.

"(a) For purposes of subsection (g) of section 404 of the Internal Revenue Code of 1954 (relating to certain employer liability payments considered as contributions), as amended by section 205 of this Act, any payment made to a plan covering employees of a corporation operating a public transportation system shall be treated as a payment described in paragraph (1) of such subsection if—

"(1) such payment is made to fund accrued benefits under the plan in conjunction with an acquisition by a State (or agency or instrumentality thereof) of the stock or assets of such corporation, and

"(2) such acquisition is pursuant to a State public transportation law enacted after June 30, 1979, and before January 1, 1980.

"(b) The provisions of this section shall apply to payments made after June 29, 1980."
Prior to amendment, subsec. (g) read as follows:

"(g) Certain employer liability payments considered as contributions.

"For purposes of this section any amount paid by an employer under section 4062, 4063, or 4064 of the Employee Retirement Income Security Act of 1974 shall be treated as a contribution to which this section applies by such employer to or under a stock bonus, pension, profit-sharing, or annuity plan."

—P.L. 96-222, Sec. 101(a)(5), amended Sec. 133(c) of P.L. 95-600, [the effective date for changes made by Secs. 133(a) and (b) of P.L. 95-600, by adding subpara. (c)(2), a special rule for certain life insurance companies, see below].

—P.L. 96-222, Sec. 101(a)(7)(B), amended Sec. 141(g) of P.L. 95-600 [the effective date for amendments made by Sec. 141(f)(9), see below].
Prior to amendment, Sec. 141(g)(1) of P.L. 95-600 read as follows:
"(g) Effective dates.

"(1) In general. The amendments made by this section (other than by subsection (f)(3)) shall apply with respect to qualified investment for taxable years beginning after December 31, 1978. The amendment made by subsection (f)(7) shall apply to years beginning after December 31, 1978."

—P.L. 96-222, Sec. 101(a)(10)(E)(i), added "or described in section 1379(b)(1)" after "of subsection (e)" in para. (h)(4)... Sec. 101(a)(10)(E)(ii), added "or a shareholder-employee (as defined in section 1379(d))" after "(section 401(c)(1)" in para (h)(4)... Sec. 101(a)(10)(E)(iii), substituted "self-employed individuals or shareholder employees" for "self employed individuals" in the heading of para. (h)(4)... Sec. 101(a)(10)(J)(ii), substituted "paragraph (1)" for "subparagraph (1)" each place it appeared in paras. (h)(2), (h)(3) and (h)(4) effective for tax. yrs. begin. after 12/31/78.

In 1978, P.L. 95-600, Sec. 133(a), added subsec. (d)... Sec. 133(b), substituted "other plan" for "similar plan" in subsec. (b), effective [as amended by Sec. 101(a)(5) of P.L. 96-222, see above] for deductions for tax. yrs. begin. after 12/31/78. Sec. 133(c)(2) of this Act [as amended by Sec. 101(a)(5) of P.L. 96-222, see above] provides special rules as follows:

"(2) Special rule for certain title insurance companies.

"(A) In general. In the case of a qualified title insurance company plan, the amendment made by subsection (a) shall apply to deductions for taxable years beginning after December 31, 1979.

"(B) Qualified title insurance company plan. For purposes of subparagraph (A), the term 'qualified title insurance company plan' means a plan of a qualified title insurance company

"(i) which defers the payment of amounts credited by such company to separate accounts for members of such company in consideration of their issuance of policies of title insurance, and

"(ii) under which no part of such amounts is payable to or withdrawable by the members until after the period for the adverse possession of real property under applicable State law.

"(C) Qualified title insurance company. For purposes of subparagraph (B), the term 'qualified title insurance company' means an unincorporated title insurance company organized as a business trust.

"(i) which is engaged in the business of providing title insurance coverage on interests in and liens upon real property obtained by clients of the members of such company, and

"(ii) which is subject to tax under section 831 of the Internal Revenue Code of 1954."

—P.L. 95-600, Sec. 141(f)(9), substituted "(20), and (22)" for "and (20)" in para. (a)(2), effective [as amended by Sec. 101(a)(7)(B) of P.L. 96-222, see above] for qualified investment for tax. yrs. begin. after 12/31/78. Sec. 141(g)(2) of this Act [as amended by Sec. 101(a)(7)(B) of P.L. 96-222, see above] provides:

"(2) Election to have amendments apply during 1978. At the election of the taxpayer, paragraph (1) shall be applied by substituting 'December 31, 1977' for 'December 31, 1978'; except that in the case of a plan in existence before December 31, 1978, any such election shall not affect the required allocation of employer securities attributable to qualified investment for taxable years beginning before January 1, 1979. An election under the preceding sentence shall be made at such time and in such manner as the Secretary of the Treasury or his delegate shall prescribe. Such an election, once made, shall be irrevocable."

—P.L. 95-600, Sec. 152(f), added subsec. (h), effective for tax. yrs. begin. after 12/31/78.

In 1976, P.L. 94-455, Sec. 1502(a)(2), added the sentence at the end of para. (e)(4), effective for tax. yrs. begin. after 12/31/75.

—P.L. 94-455, Sec. 1901(a)(59), deleted subsec. (d), effective for tax. yrs. begin. after 12/31/76.

Prior to deletion, subsec. (d) read as follows:

"(d) Carryover of unused deductions. The amount of any unused deductions or contributions in excess of the deductible amounts for taxable years to which this part does not apply which under section 23(p) of the Internal Revenue Code of 1939 would be allowable as deductions in later years had such section 23(p) remained in effect, shall be allowable as deductions in taxable years to which this part applies as if such section 23(p) were continued in effect for such years. However, the deduction under the preceding sentence shall not exceed an amount which, when added to the deduction allowable under subsection (a) for contributions made in taxable years to which this part applies, is not greater than the amount which would be deductible under subsection (a) if the contributions which give rise to the deduction under the preceding sentence were made in a taxable year to which this part applies."

—P.L. 94-455, Sec. 1906(b)(13)(A), substituted "Secretary" for "Secretary or his delegate" each place it appeared in paras. (a)(1), (e)(2) and (3), effective for tax. yrs. begin. after 12/31/76.

—P.L. 94-267, Sec. (c)(3), substituted ", (19), and (20)" for "and (19)" in para. (a)(2), effective for payments made to an employee on or after 7/4/74.

In 1975, P.L. 94-12, Sec. 402(1), substituted "(c) through (i)," for "(c) through (h)," in Sec. 1017(b) of P.L. 93-406 . . . Sec. 402(2), added subsec. 1017(i) to P.L. 93-406 [the effective date for amendments made by Secs. 1013(c)(1), 1013(c)(2), 1013(c)(3) and 1016(a)(3) of P.L. 93-406, see below].

In 1974, P.L. 93-406, Sec. 1013(c)(1), amended para. (a)(1) . . . Sec. 1013(c)(2), amended para. (a)(6) . . . Sec. 1013(c)(3), amended para. (a)(7) . . . Sec. 1016(a)(3), substituted "(8), (11), (12), (13), (14), and (15)" for "and (8)," in para. (a)(2), effective for plan yrs. begin. after 9/2/74, and as provided in Sec. 1017 of this Act reproduced in note following Code Sec. 401.

Prior to amendment, para. (a)(1) read as follows:

"(1) Pension trusts. In the taxable year when paid, if the contributions are paid into a pension trust, and if such taxable year ends within or with a taxable year of the trust for which the trust is exempt under section 501(a), in an amount determined as follows:

"(A) an amount not in excess of 5 percent of the compensation otherwise paid or accrued during the taxable year to all the employees under the trust, but such amount may be reduced for future years if found by the Secretary or his delegate upon periodical examinations at not less than 5-year intervals to be more than the amount reasonably necessary to provide the remaining unfunded cost of past and current service credits of all employees under the plan, plus

"(B) any excess over the amount allowable under subparagraph (A) necessary to provide with respect to all of the employees under the trust the remaining unfunded cost of their past and current service credits distributed as a level amount or a level percentage of compensation, over the remaining future service of each such employee, as determined under regulations prescribed by the Secretary or his delegate, but if such remaining unfunded cost with respect to any 3 individuals is more than 50 percent of such remaining unfunded cost, the amount of such unfunded cost attributable to such individuals shall be distributed over a period of at least 5 taxable years, or

"(C) in lieu of the amounts allowable under subparagraphs (A) and (B) above, an amount equal to the normal cost of the plan, as determined under regulations prescribed by the Secretary or his delegate, plus, if past service or other supplementary pension or annuity credits are provided by the plan, an amount not in excess of 10 percent of the cost which would be required to completely fund or purchase such pension or annuity credits as of the date when they are included in the plan, as determined under regulations prescribed by the Secretary or his delegate, except that in no case shall a deduction be allowed for any amount (other than the normal cost) paid in after such pension or annuity credits are completely funded or purchased.

"(D) Any amount paid in a taxable year in excess of the amount deductible in such year under the foregoing limitations shall be deductible in the succeeding taxable years in order of time to the extent of the difference between the amount paid and deductible in each such succeeding year and the maximum amount deductible for such year in accordance with the foregoing limitations."

Prior to amendment, para. (a)(6) read as follows:

"(6) Taxpayers on accrual basis. For purposes of paragraphs (1), (2), and (3), a taxpayer on the accrual basis shall be deemed to have made a payment on the last day of the year of accrual if the payment is on account of such taxable year and is made not later than the time prescribed by law for filing the return for such taxable year (including extensions thereof)."

Prior to amendment, para. (a)(7) read as follows:

"(7) Limit of deduction. If amounts are deductible under paragraphs (1) and (3), or (2) and (3), or (1), (2), and (3), in connection with 2 or more trusts or one or more trusts and an annuity plan, the total amount deductible in a taxable year under such trusts and plans shall not exceed 25 percent of the compensation otherwise paid or accrued during the taxable year to the persons who are the beneficiaries of the trust or plans. In addition, any amount paid into such trust or under such annuity plans in any taxable year in excess of the amount allowable with respect to such year under the preceding provisions of this paragraph shall be deductible in the succeeding taxable years in order of time, but the amount so deductible under this sentence in any one such succeeding taxable year together with the amount allowable under the first sentence of this paragraph shall not exceed 30 percent of the compensation otherwise paid or accrued during such taxable years to the beneficiaries under the trusts or plans. This paragraph shall not have the effect of reducing the amount otherwise deductible under paragraphs (1), (2), and (3), if no employee is a beneficiary under more than one trust, or a trust and an annuity plan."

P.L. 93-406, Secs. 1022(i) and (j) provide as follows:

"(i) Certain Puerto Rican pension, etc., plans to be exempt from tax under section 501(a).

"(1) General rule. Effective for taxable years beginning after December 31, 1973, for purposes of section 501(a) of the Internal Revenue Code of 1954 (relating to exemption from tax), any trust forming part of a pension, profit-sharing, or stock bonus plan all of the participants of which are residents of the Commonwealth of Puerto Rico shall be treated as an organization described in section 401(a) of such Code if such trust—

"(A) forms part of a pension, profit-sharing, or stock bonus plan, and

"(B) is exempt from income tax under the laws of the Commonwealth of Puerto Rico.

"(2) Election to have provisions of, and amendments made by, title II of this act apply.

"(A) If the administrator of a pension, profit-sharing, or stock bonus plan which is created or organized in Puerto Rico elects, at such time and in such manner as the Secretary of the Treasury may require, to have the provisions of this paragraph apply, for plan years beginning after the date of election any trust forming a part of such plan shall be treated as a trust created or organized in the United States for purposes of section 401(a) of the Internal Revenue Code of 1954.

"(B) An election under subparagraph (A), once made, is irrevocable.

"(C) This paragraph applies to plan years beginning after the date of enactment of this Act.

"(D) The source of any distributions made under a plan which makes an election under this paragraph to participants and beneficiaries residing outside of the United States shall be determined, for purposes of subchapter N of chapter 1 of the Internal Revenue Code of 1954, by the Secretary of the Treasury in accordance with regulations prescribed by him. For purposes of this subparagraph the United States means the United States as defined in section 7701(a)(9) of the Internal Revenue Code of 1954.

"(j) Year of deduction for certain employer contributions for severance payments required by foreign law. Effective for taxable years beginning after December 31, 1973, if—

"(1) an employer is engaged in a trade or business in a foreign country,

"(2) such employer is required by the laws of that country to make payments, based on periods of service, to its employees or their beneficiaries after the employees' retirement, death, or other separation from the service, and

"(3) such employer establishes a trust (whether organized within or outside the United States) for the purpose of funding the payments required by such law, then, in determining for purposes of paragraph (5) of section 404(a) of the Internal Revenue Code of 1954 the taxable year in which any contribution to or under the plan is includible in the gross income of the nonresident alien employees of such employer, such paragraph (5) shall be treated as not requiring that separate accounts be maintained for such nonresident alien employees."

—P.L. 93-406, Sec. 2001(a)(1)(A), substituted "$7,500, or 15 percent" for "$2,500, or 10 percent" in para. (e)(1) . . . Sec. 2001(a)(1)(B), substituted "subject to paragraphs (2) and (4)" for "subject to the provisions of paragraph (2)" in para. (e)(1) . . . Sec. 2001(a)(2), substituted "shall (subject to paragraph (4)) not exceed $7,500, or 15 percent" for "shall not exceed $2,500, or 10 percent" in subpara. (e)(2)(A) . . . Sec. 2001(a)(3), added para. (e)(4), effective for tax. yrs. begin. after 12/31/73.

—P.L. 93-406, Sec. 2001(g)(2)(E), substituted "(16), (17), (18)" for "(16)" in para. (a)(2) . . . Sec. 2001(g)(2)(F), amended clause (a)(9)(B)(ii), effective for distributions made in tax. yrs. begin. after 12/31/75.

Prior to amendment, clause (a)(9)(B)(ii) read as follows:

"(ii) without regard to paragraph (1)(D), the second and third sentences of paragraph (3), and the second sentence of paragraph (7); and"

—P.L. 93-406, Sec. 2004(b), substituted "beneficiaries under the plan, but the amount so deductible under this sentence in any one succeeding taxable year together with the amount so deductible under the first sentence of this subparagraph shall not exceed 25 percent of the compensation otherwise paid or accrued during such taxable year to the beneficiaries under the plan." for "beneficiaries under the plan." in subpara. (a)(3)(A) . . . Sec. 2004(c)(1), substituted "(15), (16), and (19)" for "(15)" and substituted "(a)(9), (10), (17), and (18)" for "(a)(9) and (10)" in para. (a)(2), effective for yrs. begin. after 12/31/75. Sec. 2004(d)(2) of this Act provides transitional rules as follows:

"(2) Transition rule for defined benefit plans. In the case of an individual who was an active participant in a defined benefit plan before October 3, 1973, if—

"(A) the annual benefit (within the meaning of section 415(b)(2) of the Internal Revenue Code of 1954) payable to such participant on retirement does not exceed 100 percent of his annual rate of compensation on the earlier of (i) October 2, 1973, or (ii) the date on which he separated from the service of the employer,

"(B) such annual benefit is no greater than the annual benefit which would have been payable to such participant on retirement if (i) all the terms and conditions of such plan in existence on such date had remained in existence until such retirement, and (ii) his compensation taken into account for any period after October 2, 1973, had not exceeded his annual rate of compensation on such date, and

"(C) in the case of a participant who separated from the service of the employer prior to October 2, 1973, such annual benefit is no greater than his vested accrued benefit as of the date he separated from the service,

Employee benefit plans

then such annual benefit shall be treated as not exceeding the limitation of subsection (b) of section 415 of the Internal Revenue Code of 1954."
—P.L. 93-406, Sec. 2007(a), added "For purposes of this chapter and subtitle B, in the case of any individual who before July 1, 1974, was a participant in a plan described in the preceding sentence—" following the first sentence in subsec. (c), added subparas. (c)(2)(A), (B) and (C), and added "Section 277 (relating to deductions incurred by certain membership organizations in transactions with members) does not apply to any trust described in this subsection." before the sentence at the end of subsec. (c) . . . Sec. 2007(b)(1), substituted "or pensions" for "and pensions" in the first sentence of para. (c)(1) . . . Sec. 2007(b)(2), substituted "The first and third sentences of this subsection" for "This subsection" in subsec. (c), effective for tax. yrs. end. on or after 6/30/72.
—P.L. 93-406, Sec. 4081(a), added subsec. (g), effective 9/2/74. Sec. 4082(b)-(c) of this Act provides special rules as follows:
"(b) Notwithstanding the provisions of subsection (a), the corporation shall pay benefits guaranteed under this title with respect to any plan—
"(1) which is not a multiemployer plan,
"(2) which terminates after June 30, 1974, and before the date of enactment of this Act,
"(3) to which section 4021 would apply if that section were effective beginning on July 1, 1974, and
"(4) with respect to which a notice is filed with the Secretary of Labor and received by him not later than 10 days after the date of enactment of this Act, except that, for reasonable cause shown, such notice may be filed with the Secretary of Labor and received by him not later than October 31, 1974, stating that the plan is a plan described in paragraphs (1), (2), and (3).
The corporation shall not pay benefits guaranteed under this title with respect to a plan described in the preceding sentence unless the corporation finds substantial evidence that the plan was terminated for a reasonable business purpose and not for the purpose of obtaining the payment of benefits by the corporation under this title or for the purpose of avoiding the liability which might be imposed under subtitle D if the plan terminated on or after the date of enactment of this Act. The provisions of subtitle D do not apply in the case of such a plan which terminates before the date of enactment of this Act. For purposes of determining whether a plan is a plan described in paragraph (2), the provisions of section 4048 shall not apply, but the corporation shall make the determination on the basis of the date on which benefits ceased to accrue or on any other reasonable basis consistent with the purposes of this subsection.
"(c)(1) Except as provided in paragraphs (2),(3), and (4), the corporation shall not pay benefits guaranteed under this title with respect to a multiemployer plan which terminates before January 1, 1978. Whenever the corporation exercises the authority granted under paragraph (2) or (3), the corporation shall notify the Committee on Education and Labor and the Committee on Ways and Means of the House of Representatives, and the Committee on Labor and Public Welfare and the Committee on Finance of the Senate.
"(2) The corporation may, in its discretion, pay benefits guaranteed under this title with respect to a multiemployer plan which terminates after the date of enactment of this Act and before January 1, 1978, if—
"(A) the plan was maintained during the 60 months immediately preceding the date on which the plan terminates, and
"(B) the corporation determines that the payment by the corporation of benefits guaranteed under this title with respect to that plan will not jeopardize the payments the corporation anticipates it may be required to make in connection with benefits guaranteed under this title with respect to multiemployer plans which terminate after December 31, 1977.
"(3) Notwithstanding any provision of section 4021 or 4022 which would prevent such payments, the corporation, in carrying out its authority under paragraph (2), may pay benefits guaranteed under this title with respect to a multiemployer plan described in paragraph (2) in any case in which those benefits would otherwise not be payable if—
"(A) the plan has been in effect for at least 5 years,
"(B) the plan has been in substantial compliance with the funding requirements for a qualified plan with respect to the employees and former employees in those employment units on the basis of which the participating employers have contributed to the plan for the preceding 5 years, and
"(C) the participating employers and employee organization or organizations had no reasonable recourse other than termination.
"(4) If the corporation determines, under paragraph (2) or (3), that it will pay benefits guaranteed under this title with respect to a multiemployer plan which terminates before January 1, 1978, the corporation—
"(A) may establish requirements for the continuation of payments which commenced before January 2, 1974, with respect to retired participants under the plan,
"(B) may not, notwithstanding any other provision of this title, make payments with respect to any participant under such a plan who, on January 1, 1974, was receiving payment of retirement benefits, in excess of the amounts and rates payable with respect to such participant on that date,
"(C) may not make any payments with respect to benefits guaranteed under this title in connection with such a plan which are derived, directly or indirectly, from amounts borrowed under section 4005(c), and
"(D) shall review from time to time payments made under the authority granted to it by paragraphs (2) and (3), and reduce or terminate such payments to the extent necessary to avoid jeopardizing the ability of the corporation to make payments of benefits guaranteed under this title in connection with multiemployer plans which terminate after December 31, 1977, without increasing premium rates for such plans."
In 1969, P.L. 91-172, Sec. 321(b)(3), amended para. (a)(5), effective for contributions made and premiums paid after 8/1/69.

Code Sec. 404A(b)(3)(A)(i)

Prior to amendment subsec. (a)(5) read as follows:
"(5) Other plans. In the taxable year when paid, if the plan is not one included in paragraph (1), (2), or (3), if the employees' rights to or derived from such employer's contribution or such compensation are nonforfeitable at the time the contribution or compensation is paid."
In 1966, P.L. 89-809, Sec. 204(a), deleted para. (a)(10) . . . Sec. 204(b)(1)(A), deleted "(determined without regard to section 404(a)(10))" in clause (a)(10)(A)(ii) . . . Sec. 204(b)(1)(B), deleted "(determined without regard to section 404(a)(10))" in subparas. (d)(5)(A) and (B) . . . Sec. 204(b)(1)(C), deleted "(determined without regard to section 404(a)(10))" in subpara. (d)(6)(A) . . . Sec. 204(b)(1)(D), deleted "(determined without regard to section 404(a)(10))" in subpara. (e)(1)(A), and clause (e)(1)(B)(i) . . . Sec. 204(b)(1)(E), deleted "(determined without regard to section 404(a)(10))" in subparas. (e)(3)(B) and (C), and in the sentence at the end of para. (e)(3) . . . Sec. 204(b)(2), deleted "(determined without regard to subsection (a)(10)" in subpara. (e)(2)(A) . . . Sec. 204(b)(3), deleted "(determined without regard to paragraph (10) thereof," in para. (e)(1) and subpara. (e)(2)(B), effective for tax. yrs. begin. after 12/31/67.
Prior to deletion, para. (a)(10) read as follows:
"(10) Special limitation on amount allowed as deduction for self-employed individuals. Notwithstanding any other provision of this section, the amount allowable as a deduction under paragraphs (1), (2), (3), and (7) in any taxable year with respect to contributions made on behalf of an individual who is an employee within the meaning of section 401(c)(1) shall be an amount equal to one-half of the contributions made on behalf of such individual in such taxable year which are deductible under such paragraphs determined with the application of paragraph (9) and of subsection (e) but without regard to this paragraph). For purposes of section 401, the amount which may be deducted, or the amount deductible, under this section with respect to contributions made on behalf of such individual shall be determined without regard to the preceding sentence."
In 1962, P.L. 87-863, Sec. 2(b)(1), added ", or retirement annuities and medical benefits as described in section 401(h)," after "purchase of retirement annuities" in para. (a)(2) . . . Sec. 2(b)(2), added ", or such retirement annuities and medical benefits" after "such retirement annuities" in para. (a)(2), effective for tax. yrs. begin. after 10/23/62.
—P.L. 87-792, Sec. 3(a)(1), substituted "(6), (7), and (8), and, if applicable, the requirements of section 401(a)(9) and (10) and of section 401(d) (other than paragraph (1)," for "and (6)," in para. (a)(2) . . . Sec. 3(a)(2), added paras. (a)(8), (9) and (10) . . . Sec. 3(b), added subsecs. (e) and (f), effective for tax.yrs. begin. after 12/31/62.
In 1958, P.L. 85-866, Sec. 24, substituted "income); but, if" for "income) but if" in the matter preceding para. (a)(1) in subsec. (a), effective 1/1/54.

Sec. 404A. Deduction for certain foreign deferred compensation plans.

(a) General rule.
Amounts paid or accrued by an employer under a qualified foreign plan—

(1) shall not be allowable as a deduction under this chapter, but

(2) if they would otherwise be deductible, shall be allowed as a deduction under this section for the taxable year for which such amounts are properly taken into account under this section.

(b) Rules for qualified funded plans.
For purposes of this section—

(1) In general. Except as otherwise provided in this section, in the case of a qualified funded plan contributions are properly taken into account for the taxable year in which paid.

(2) Payment after close of taxable year. For purposes of paragraph (1), a payment made after the close of a taxable year shall be treated as made on the last day of such year if the payment is made—

(A) on account of such year, and

(B) not later than the time prescribed by law for filing the return for such year (including extensions thereof).

(3) Limitations. In the case of a qualified funded plan, the amount allowable as a deduction for the taxable year shall be subject to—

(A) in the case of—

(i) a plan under which the benefits are fixed or determinable, limitations similar to those contained in clauses (ii) and (iii) of subparagraph (A) of section 404(a)(1) (determined without regard to the last sentence of such subparagraph (A)), or

(ii) any other plan, limitations similar to the limitations contained in paragraph (3) of section 404(a), and

(B) limitations similar to those contained in paragraph (7) of section 404(a).

(4) Carryover. If—

(A) the aggregate of the contributions paid during the taxable year reduced by any contributions not allowable as a deduction under paragraphs (1) and (2) of subsection (g), exceeds

(B) the amount allowable as a deduction under subsection (a) (determined without regard to subsection (d)),

such excess shall be treated as an amount paid in the succeeding taxable year.

(5) Amounts must be paid to qualified trust, etc. In the case of a qualified funded plan, a contribution shall be taken into account only if it is paid—

(A) to a trust (or the equivalent of a trust) which meets the requirements of section 401(a)(2),

(B) for a retirement annuity, or

(C) to a participant or beneficiary.

(c) Rules relating to qualified reserve plans.

For purposes of this section—

(1) In general. In the case of a qualified reserve plan, the amount properly taken into account for the taxable year is the reasonable addition for such year to a reserve for the taxpayer's liability under the plan. Unless otherwise required or permitted in regulations prescribed by the Secretary, the reserve for the taxpayer's liability shall be determined under the unit credit method modified to reflect the requirements of paragraphs (3) and (4). All benefits paid under the plan shall be charged to the reserve.

(2) Income item. In the case of a plan which is or has been a qualified reserve plan, an amount equal to that portion of any decrease for the taxable year in the reserve which is not attributable to the payment of benefits shall be included in gross income.

(3) Rights must be nonforfeitable, etc. In the case of a qualified reserve plan, an item shall be taken into account for a taxable year only if—

(A) there is no substantial risk that the rights of the employee will be forfeited, and

(B) such item meets such additional requirements as the Secretary may by regulations prescribe as necessary or appropriate to ensure that the liability will be satisfied.

(4) Spreading of certain increases and decreases in reserves. There shall be amortized over a 10-year period any increase or decrease to the reserve on account of—

(A) the adoption of the plan or a plan amendment,

(B) experience gains and losses, and

(C) any change in actuarial assumptions,

(D) changes in the interest rate under subsection (g)(3)(B), and

(E) such other factors as may be prescribed by regulations.

(d) Amounts taken into account must be consistent with amounts allowed under foreign law.

(1) General rule. In the case of any plan, the amount allowed as a deduction under subsection (a) for any taxable year shall equal—

(A) the lesser of —

(i) the cumulative United States amount, or

(ii) the cumulative foreign amount, reduced by

(B) the aggregate amount determined under this section for all prior taxable years.

(2) Cumulative amounts defined. For purposes of paragraph (1)—

(A) Cumulative United States amount. The term "cumulative United States amount" means the aggregate amount determined with respect to the plan under this section for the taxable year and for all prior taxable years to which this section applies. Such determination shall be made for each taxable year without regard to the application of paragraph (1).

(B) Cumulative foreign amount. The term "cumulative foreign amount" means the aggregate amount allowed as a deduction under the appropriate foreign tax laws for the taxable year and all prior taxable years to which this section applies.

(3) Effect on earnings and profits, etc. In determining the earnings and profits and accumulated profits of any foreign corporation with respect to a qualified foreign plan, except as provided in regulations, the amount determined under paragraph (1) with respect to any plan for any taxable year shall in no event exceed the amount allowed as a deduction under the appropriate foreign tax laws for such taxable year.

(e) Qualified foreign plan.

For purposes of this section, the term "qualified foreign plan" means any written plan of an employer for deferring the receipt of compensation but only if—

(1) such plan is for the exclusive benefit of the employer's employees or their beneficiaries,

(2) 90 percent or more of the amounts taken into account for the taxable year under the plan are attributable to services—

(A) performed by nonresident aliens, and

(B) the compensation for which is not subject to tax under this chapter, and

(3) the employer elects (at such time and in such manner as the Secretary shall by regulations prescribe) to have this section apply to such plan.

(f) Funded and reserve plans.

For purposes of this section—

(1) Qualified funded plan. The term "qualified funded plan" means a qualified foreign plan which is not a qualified reserve plan.

(2) Qualified reserve plan. The term "qualified reserve plan" means a qualified foreign plan with respect to which an election made by the taxpayer is in effect for the taxable year. An election under the preceding sentence shall be made in such manner and form as the Secretary may by regulations prescribe and, once made, may be revoked only with the consent of the Secretary.

(g) Other special rules.

(1) No deduction for certain amounts. Except as provided in section 404(a)(5), no deduction shall be allowed under this section for any item to the extent such item is attributable to services—

(A) performed by a citizen or resident of the United States who is a highly compensated employee (within the meaning of section 414(q)), or

(B) performed in the United States the compensation for which is subject to tax under this chapter.

(2) Taxpayer must furnish information.

(A) In general. No deduction shall be allowed under this section with respect to any plan for any taxable year unless the taxpayer furnishes to the Secretary with respect to such plan (at such time as the Secretary may by regulations prescribe)—

(i) a statement from the foreign tax authorities specifying the amount of the deduction allowed in computing taxable income under foreign law for such year with respect to such plan,

(ii) if the return under foreign tax law shows the deduction for plan contributions or reserves as a separate, identifiable item, a copy of the foreign tax return for the taxable year, or

(iii) such other statement, return, or other evidence as the Secretary prescribes by regulation as being sufficient to establish the amount of the deduction under foreign law.

(B) Redetermination where foreign tax deduction is adjusted. If the deduction under foreign tax law is adjusted, the taxpayer shall notify the Secretary of such adjustment on or before the date prescribed by regulations, and the Secretary shall redetermine the amount of the tax for the year or years affected. In any case described in the preceding sentence, rules similar to the rules of subsection (c) of section 905 shall apply.

(3) Actuarial assumptions must be reasonable; full funding.

(A) In general. Except as provided in subparagraph (B), principles similar to those set forth in paragraphs (3) and (6) of section 431(c) shall apply for purposes of this section.

(B) Interest rate for reserve plan.

(i) In general. In the case of a qualified reserve plan, in lieu of taking rates of interest into account under subparagraph (A), the rate of interest for the plan shall be the rate selected by the taxpayer which is within the permissible range.

(ii) Rate remains in effect so long as it falls within permissible range. Any rate selected by the taxpayer for the plan under this subparagraph shall remain in effect for such plan until the first taxable year for which such rate is no longer within the permissible range. At such time, the taxpayer shall select a new rate of interest which is within the permissible range applicable at such time.

(iii) Permissible range. For purposes of this subparagraph, the term "permissible range" means a rate of interest which is not more than 20 percent above, and not more than 20 percent below, the average rate of interest for long-term corporate bonds in the appropriate country for the 15-year period ending on the last day before the beginning of the taxable year.

(4) Accounting method. Any change in the method (but not the actuarial assumptions) used to determine the amount allowed as a deduction under subsection (a) shall be treated as a change in accounting method under section 446(e).

(5) Section 481 applies to election. For purposes of section 481, any election under this section shall be treated as a change in the taxpayer's method of accounting. In applying section 481 with respect to any such election, the period for taking into account any increase or decrease in accumulated profits, earnings and profits or taxable income resulting from the application of section 481(a)(2) shall be the year for which the election is made and the fourteen succeeding years.

(h) Regulations.

The Secretary shall prescribe such regulations as may be necessary to carry out the purposes of this section (including regulations providing for the coordination of the provisions of this section with section 404 in the case of a plan which has been subject to both of such sections).

In 2006, P.L. 109-280, Sec. 801(c)(4), substituted "paragraphs (3) and (6) of section 431(c)" for "paragraphs (3) and (7) of section 412(c)" in subpara. (g)(3)(A), effective for yrs. begin. after 12/31/2007.

In 1988, P.L. 100-647, Sec. 1012(b)(4), substituted "except as provided in regulations, the amount determined" for "the amount determined" in para. (d)(3), effective for distributions by foreign corporations out of, and to inclusions under Code Sec. 951(a) attributable to, earnings and profits for tax. yrs. begin after 12/31/86.

In 1986, P.L. 99-514, Sec. 1114(b)(8), substituted "a highly compensated employee (within the meaning of section 414(q))" for "an officer, shareholder, or highly compensated" in subpara. (g)(1)(A), effective for yrs. begin. after 12/31/88. — P.L. 99-514, Sec. 1851(b)(2)(C)(iii)(I), substituted "under this chapter" for "under section 162, 212, or 404" in subsec. (a) . . . Sec. 1851(b)(2)(C)(iii)(II), substituted "they would otherwise be deductible" for "they satisfy the conditions of section 162" in subsec. (a), effective for amounts paid or incurred after 7/18/84 in tax. yrs. end. after 7/18/84, except as provided in Sec. 512(c) of P.L. 98-369, reproduced in note following Code Sec. 162.

In 1980, P.L. 96-603, Sec. 2(a), added Code Sec. 404A, effective for employer contributions or accruals for tax yrs. begin. after 12/31/79. Sec. 2(e)(2), (3) and (4) of this Act provides:

"(2) Election to apply amendments retroactively with respect to foreign subsidiaries.—

"(A) In general. The taxpayer may elect to have the amendments made by this section apply retroactively with respect to its foreign subsidiaries.

"(B) Scope of retroactive application. Any election made under this paragraph shall apply with respect to all foreign subsidiaries of the taxpayer for the taxpayer's open period.

"(C) Distributions by foreign subsidiary must be out of post-1971 earnings and profits. The election under this paragraph shall apply to distributions made by a foreign subsidiary only if made out of accumulated profits (or earnings and profits) earned after December 31, 1970.

"(D) Revocation only with consent. An election under this paragraph may be revoked only with the consent of the Secretary of the Treasury or his delegate.

"(E) Open period. For purposes of this subsection, the term 'open period' means, with respect to any taxpayer, all taxable years which begin before January 1, 1980, and which begin after December 31, 1971, and for which, on December 31, 1980, the making of a refund, or the assessment of a deficiency, was barred by any law or rule of law.

"(3) Allowance or prior deductions in case of certain funded branch plans.—

"(A) In general. If—

"(i) the taxpayer elects to have this paragraph apply, and

"(ii) the taxpayer agrees to the assessment of all deficiencies (including interest thereon) arising from all erroneous deductions,

then an amount equal to 1/15th of the aggregate of the prior deductions which would have been allowable if the amendments made by this section applied to taxable years beginning before January 1, 1980, shall be allowed as a deduction for the taxpayer's first taxable year beginning in 1980, and an equal amount shall be allowed for each of the succeeding 14 taxable years.

"(B) Prior deduction. For purposes of subparagraph (A), the term 'prior deduction' means a deduction with respect to a qualified funded plan (within the meaning of section 404A(f)(1) of the Internal Revenue Code of 1954) of the taxpayer—

"(i) which the taxpayer claimed for a taxable year (or could have claimed if the amendments made by this section applied to taxable years beginning before January 1, 1980) beginning before January 1, 1980,

"(ii) which was not allowable, and

"(iii) with respect to which, on December 1, 1980, the assessment of a deficiency was not barred by any law or rule of law.

"(4) Time and manner for making elections.—

"(A) Time. An election under paragraph (2) or (3) may be made only on or before the due date (including extensions) for filing the taxpayer's return of tax under chapter 1 of the Internal Revenue Code of 1954 for its first taxable year ending on or after December 31, 1980.

"(B) Manner. An election under paragraph (2) may be made only by a statement attached to the taxpayer's return for its first taxable year ending on or after December 31, 1980. An election under paragraph (3) may be made only if the taxpayer, on or before the last day for making the election, files with the Secretary of the Treasury or his delegate such amended return and such other information as the Secretary of the Treasury or his delegate may require, and agrees to the assessment of a deficiency for any closed year falling within the open period, to the extent such deficiency is attributable to the operation of such election."

Sec. 405. Repealed.

In 1984, P.L. 98-369, Sec. 42(a)(6), amended para. (d)(1), effective for tax. yrs. end. after 7/18/84.

Prior to amendment, para. (d)(1) read as follows:

"(1) Gross income not to include bonds at time of distribution. For purposes of this chapter, in the case of a distributee of a bond described in subsection (b) under a qualified bond purchase plan, or from a trust described in section 401(a) which is exempt from tax under section 501(a), gross income does not include any amount attributable to the receipt of such bond. Upon redemption of such bond, except as provided in paragraph (3), the proceeds shall be subject to taxation under this chapter, but the provisions of section 72 (relating to annuities, etc.) and section 1232 (relating to bonds and other evidences of indebtedness) shall not apply."

Code Sec. 405 — Employee benefit plans

—P.L. 98-369, Sec. 491(a), repealed Code Sec. 405, effective for obligations issued after 12/31/83.

Prior to repeal, Code Sec. 405 read as follows:

"Sec. 405. Qualified bond purchase plans.

"(a) Requirements for qualification.

"A plan of an employer for the purchase for and distribution to his employees or their beneficiaries of United States bonds described in subsection (b) shall constitute a qualified bond purchase plan under this section if—

"(1) the plan meets the requirements of section 401(a)(3), (4), (5), (6), (7), (8), (16), and (19) and, if applicable, the requirements of section 401(a)(9) and (10) and of section 401(d) (other than paragraphs (1), (5), (B), and (8)); and

"(2) contributions under the plan are used solely to purchase for employees or their beneficiaries United States bonds described in subsection (b).

"(b) Bonds to which applicable.

"(1) Characteristics of bonds. This section shall apply only to a bond issued under chapter 31 of title 31 which by its terms, or by regulations prescribed by the Secretary under such chapter—

"(A) provides for payment of interest, or investment yield, only upon redemption;

"(B) may be purchased only in the name of an individual;

"(C) ceases to bear interest, or provide investment yield, not later than 5 years after the death of the individual in whose name it is purchased;

"(D) may be redeemed before the death of the individual in whose name it is purchased only if such individual—

(i) has attained the age of 59½ years, or

(ii) has become disabled (within the meaning of section 72(m)(7)); and

"(E) is nontransferable.

"(2) Must be purchased in name of employee. This section shall apply to a bond described in paragraph (1) only if it is purchased in the name of the employee.

"(c) Deduction for contributions to bond purchase plans.

"Contributions paid by an employer to or under a qualified bond purchase plan shall be allowed as a deduction in an amount determined under section 404 in the same manner and to the same extent as if such contributions were made to a trust described in section 401(a) which is exempt from tax under section 501(a).

"(d) Taxability of beneficiary of qualified bond purchase plan.

"(1) Gross income not to include bonds at time of distribution. For purposes of this chapter, in the case of a distributee of a bond described in subsection (b) under a qualified bond purchase plan, or from a trust described in section 401(a) which is exempt from tax under section 501(a), gross income does not include any amount attributable to the receipt of such bond. Upon redemption of such bond, except as provided in paragraph (3), the proceeds shall be subject to taxation under this chapter, but the provisions of section 72 (relating to annuities, etc.) and section 1271 (relating to treatment of amounts received on retirement or sale or exchange of debt instruments) shall not apply.

"(2) Basis. The basis of any bond received by a distributee under a qualified bond purchase plan—

"(A) if such bond is distributed to an employee, or with respect to an employee, who at the time of purchase of the bond, was an employee other than an employee within the meaning of section 401(c)(1), shall be the amount of the contributions by the employee which were used to purchase the bond, and

"(B) if such bond is distributed to an employee, or with respect to an employee, who, at the time of purchase of the bond, was an employee within the meaning of section 401(c)(1), shall be the amount of the contributions used to purchase the bond which were made on behalf of such employee and were not allowed as a deduction under subsection (c).

The basis of any bond described in subsection (b) received by a distributee from a trust described in section 401(a) which is exempt from tax under section 501(a) shall be determined under regulations prescribed by the Secretary.

"(3) Rollover into an individual retirement account or annuity.

"(A) In general. If—

"(i) any qualified bond is redeemed,

"(ii) any portion of the excess of the proceeds from such redemption over the basis of such bond is transferred to an individual retirement plan which is maintained for the benefit of the individual redeeming such bond, or to a qualified trust (as defined in section 402(a)(5)(D)(iii)) for the benefit of such individual, and

"(iii) such transfer is made on or before the 60th day after the individual received the proceeds of such redemption,

then gross income shall not include the proceeds to the extent so transferred and the transfer shall be treated as a rollover contribution described in section 408(d)(3).

"(B) Qualified bond. For purposes of this paragraph, the term 'qualified bond' means any bond described in subsection (b) which is distributed under a qualified bond purchase plan or from a trust described in section 401(a) which is exempt from tax under section 501(a).

"(e) Capital gains treatment and limitation of tax not to apply to bonds distributed by trusts.

"Subsections (a)(2) and (e) of section 402 shall not apply to any bond described in subsection (b) distributed to any distributee and, for purposes of applying such sections, any such bond distributed to any distributee and any such bond to the credit of any employee shall not be taken into account.

"(f) Employee defined.

"For purposes of this section, the term 'employee' includes an individual who is an employee within the meaning of section 401(c)(1), and the employer of such individual shall be the person treated as his employer under section 401(c)(4).

"(g) Proof of purchase.

"At the time of purchase of any bond to which this section applies, proof of such purchase shall be furnished in such form as will enable the purchaser, and the employee in whose name such bond is purchased, to comply with the provisions of this section."

"(h) Regulations.

"The Secretary shall prescribe such regulations as may be necessary to carry out the provisions of this section."

—P.L. 98-369, Sec. 491(c)(1), amended subpara. (d)(3)(A) (as in effect before its repeal by Sec. 491(a)), effective for redemptions after 7/18/84 in tax. yrs. end. after 7/18/84.

Sec. 491(f)(4) of this Act provides:

"(4) Bonds under qualified bond purchase plans may be redeemed at any time. Notwithstanding—

"(A) subparagraph (D) of section 405(d)(1) of the Internal Revenue Code of 1954 (as in effect before its repeal by this section), and

"(B) the terms of any bond described in subsection (b) of such section 405, such a bond may be redeemed at any time after the date of the enactment of this Act in the same manner as if the individual redeeming the bond had attained age 59½."

Prior to amendment, subpara. (d)(3)(A) read as follows:

"(A) In general. If

"(i) any qualified bond is redeemed,

"(ii) any portion of the excess of the proceeds from such redemption over the basis of such bond is transferred to an individual retirement plan which is maintained for the benefit of the individual redeeming such bond, and

"(iii) such transfer is made on or before the 60th day after the day on which the individual received the proceeds of such redemption,

then, gross income shall not include the proceeds to the extent so transferred and the transfer shall be treated as a rollover contribution described in section 408(d)(3)."

In **1983**, P.L. 97-452, Sec. 2(c)(1), substituted "chapter 31 of title 31" for "the Second Liberty Bond Act, as amended", and substituted "chapter" for "Act" in para. (b)(1).

In **1981**, P.L. 97-34, Sec. 313(a), added para. (d)(3) . . . Sec. 313(b)(1), substituted "except as provided in paragraph (3), the proceeds" for "the proceeds" in para. (d)(1), effective for redemptions occurring after 8/13/81 in tax. yrs. end. after 8/13/81.

In **1976**, P.L. 94-455, Sec. 1906(b)(13)(A), substituted "Secretary" for "Secretary or his delegate" in para. (d)(2) and subsec. (h), effective for tax. yrs. begin. after 12/31/76.

In **1974**, P.L. 93-406, Sec. 2004(c)(2), substituted "(8), (16), and (19)" for "and (8)" in para. (a)(1), effective for tax. yrs. begin. after 12/31/75.

—P.L. 93-406, Sec. 2005(c)(11), substituted "Subsections (a)(2) and (e) of section 402" for "Section 72(n) and section 402(a)(2)" in subsec. (e), effective for distributions and payments made after 12/31/73 in tax. yrs. begin. after 12/31/73.

In **1969**, P.L. 91-172, Sec. 515(c)(1), added "and limitation of tax" to heading of subsec. (e), substituted "Section 72(n) and section 402(a)(2)" for "Section 402(a)(2)" and substituted "sections" for "section" in subsec. (e), effective for tax. yrs. end. after 12/31/69.

In **1965**, P.L. 89-97, Sec. 106(d), substituted "section 72(m)(7)" for "section 213(g)(3)" in subsec. (b)(1)(D)(ii), effective for tax. yrs. begin. after 12/31/66.

In **1962**, P.L. 87-792, Sec. 5(a), added Code Sec. 405, effective for tax. yrs. begin. after 12/31/62.

Sec. 406. Employees of foreign affiliates covered by section 3121(l) agreements.

(a) Treatment as employees of American employer.

For purposes of applying this part with respect to a pension, profit-sharing, or stock bonus plan described in section 401(a) or an annuity plan described in section 403(a), of an American employer (as defined in section 3121(h)), an individual who is a citizen or resident of the United States and who is an employee of a foreign affiliate (as defined in section 3121(l)(6)) of such American employer shall be treated as an employee of such American employer, if—

(1) such American employer has entered into an agreement under section 3121(l) which applies to the foreign affiliate of which such individual is an employee;

(2) the plan of such American employer expressly provides for contributions or benefits for individuals who are citizens or residents of the United States and who are employees of its foreign affiliates to which an agreement entered into by such American employer under section 3121(l) applies; and

(3) contributions under a funded plan of deferred compensation (whether or not a plan described in section 401(a) or 403(a)) are not provided by any other person with respect to the remuneration paid to such individual by the foreign affiliate.

Employee benefit plans Code Sec. 406

(b) Special rules for application of section 401(a).

(1) Nondiscrimination requirements. For purposes of applying section 401(a)(4) and section 410(b) with respect to an individual who is treated as an employee of an American employer under subsection (a)—

(A) if such individual is a highly compensated employee (within the meaning of section 414(q)), he shall be treated as having such capacity with respect to such American employer; and

(B) the determination of whether such individual is a highly compensated employee (as so defined) shall be made by treating such individual's total compensation (determined with the application of paragraph (2) of this subsection) as compensation paid by such American employer and by determining such individual's status with regard to such American employer.

(2) Determination of compensation. For purposes of applying paragraph (5) of section 401(a) with respect to an individual who is treated as an employee of an American employer under subsection (a)—

(A) the total compensation of such individual shall be the remuneration paid to such individual by the foreign affiliate which would constitute his total compensation if his services had been performed for such American employer, and the basic or regular rate of compensation of such individual shall be determined under regulations prescribed by the Secretary; and

(B) such individual shall be treated as having paid the amount paid by such American employer which is equivalent to the tax imposed by section 3101.

(c) Repealed.

(d) Deductibility of contributions.

For purposes of applying section 404 with respect to contributions made to or under a pension, profit-sharing, stock bonus, or annuity plan by an American employer, or by another taxpayer which is entitled to deduct its contributions under section 404(a)(3)(B), on behalf of an individual who is treated as an employee of such American employer under subsection (a)—

(1) except as provided in paragraph (2), no deduction shall be allowed to such American employer or to any other taxpayer which is entitled to deduct its contributions under such sections,

(2) there shall be allowed as a deduction to the foreign affiliate of which such individual is an employee an amount equal to the amount which (but for paragraph (1)) would be deductible under section 404 by the American employer if he were an employee of the American employer, and

(3) any reference to compensation shall be considered to be a reference to the total compensation of such individual (determined with the application of subsection (b)(2)).

Any amount deductible by a foreign affiliate under this subsection shall be deductible for its taxable year with or within which the taxable year of such American employer ends.

(e) Treatment as employee under related provisions.

An individual who is treated as an employee of an American employer under subsection (a) shall also be treated as an employee of such American employer, with respect to the plan described in subsection (a)(2), for purposes of applying the following provisions of this title:

(1) Section 72(f) (relating to special rules for computing employees' contributions).

(2) Section 2039 (relating to annuities).

In 1996, P.L. 104-188, Sec. 1401(b)(7), deleted subsec. (c), effective for tax. yrs. begin. after 12/31/99. For transitional rules, see Sec. 1401(c)(2), of this Act, which reads as follows:

"(2) Retention of certain transition rules. The amendments made by this section shall not apply to any distribution for which the taxpayer is eligible to elect the benefits of section 1122(h)(3) or (5) of the Tax Reform Act of 1986. Notwithstanding the preceding sentence, individuals who elect such benefits after December 31, 1999, shall not be eligible for 5-year averaging under section 402(d) of the Internal Revenue Code of 1986 (as in effect immediately before such amendments)."

Prior to deletion, subsec. (c) read as follows:

"(c) Termination of status as deemed employee not to be treated as separation from service for purpose of limitation of tax. For purposes of applying section 402(d) with respect to an individual who is treated as an employee of an American employer under subsection (a), such individual shall not be considered as separated from the service of such American employer solely by reason of the fact that—

"(1) the agreement entered into by such American employer under section 3121(l) which covers the employment of such individual is terminated under the provisions of such section,

"(2) such individual becomes an employee of a foreign affiliate with respect to which such agreement does not apply,

"(3) such individual ceases to be an employee of the foreign affiliate by reason of which he is treated as an employee of such American employer, if he becomes an employee of another entity in which such American employer has not less than a 10-percent interest (within the meaning of section 3121(l)(6)(B)), or

"(4) the provision of the plan described in subsection (a)(2) is terminated."

—P.L. 104-188, Sec. 1402(b)(2), deleted para. (e)(2) and redesignated para. (e)(3) as para. (e)(2), effective for decedents dying after 8/20/96.

Prior to deletion, para. (e)(2) read as follows:

"(2) Section 101(b) (relating to employees' death benefits)."

In 1992, P.L. 102-318, Sec. 521(b)(14), substituted "section 402(d)" for "section 402(e)" in subsec. (c), effective for distributions after 12/31/92. For special rule, see Sec. 521(e)(2) of this Act which reads as follows:

"(2) Special rule for partial distributions. For purposes of section 402(a)(5)(D)(i)(II) of the Internal Revenue Code of 1986 (as in effect before the amendments made by this section), a distribution before January 1, 1993, which is made before or at the same time as a series of periodic payments shall not be treated as one of such series if it is not substantially equal in amount to other payments in such series."

In 1989, P.L. 101-239, Sec. 7811(g)(3), substituted "purposes of limitation" for "purposes limitation" in the heading of subsec. (c), effective for amounts distributed after 12/31/86 in tax. yrs. end. after 12/31/86.

—P.L. 101-239, Sec. 7831(f), substituted "consist in supervising" for "consist of supervising" in Sec. 1114(b)(9)(A) of P.L. 99-514, see below.

—P.L. 101-239, Sec. 10201(b)(1), substituted "section 3121(l)(6)" for "section 3121(l)(8)" in subsec. (a)... Sec. 10201(b)(2), substituted "section 3121(l)(6)(B)" for "section 3121(l)(8)(B)" in para. (c)(3), effective for any agreement in effect under section 3121(l) of the '86 Code on or after 6/15/89, for which no notice of termination is in effect on 6/15/89.

In 1988, P.L. 100-647, Sec. 1011A(b)(1)(C), deleted para. (e)(1) and redesignated paras. (e)(2), (3) and (4) as paras. (e)(1), (2) and (3), effective for individuals whose annuities start after 7/1/86.

Prior to deletion, para. (e)(1) read as follows:

"(1) Section 72(d) (relating to employees' annuities)."

—P.L. 100-647, Sec. 1011A(b)(16)(A), substituted "section 402(e)" for "subsections (a)(2) and (e) of section 402, and section 402(a)(2)" in subsec. (c)... Sec. 1011A(b)(16)(B), deleted "of capital gain provisions and" after "service for purposes" in the heading of subsec. (c), effective for amounts distributed after 12/31/86, in tax. yrs. end. after 12/31/86.

In 1986, P.L. 99-514, Sec. 1112(d)(3), deleted "(without regard to paragraph (1)(A) thereof)" after "section 410(b)" in para. (b)(1), effective for plan yrs. begin. after 12/31/88.

—P.L. 99-514, Sec. 1114(b)(9)(A), [as amended by Sec. 7831(f) of P.L. 101-239, see above] substituted "a highly compensated employee (within the meaning of section 414(q))" for "an officer, shareholder, or person whose principal duties consist in supervising the work of other employees of a foreign affiliate of such American employer" in subpara. (b)(1)(A)... Sec. 1114(b)(9)(C), added "(as so defined)" after "employee" in subpara. (b)(1)(B), effective for yrs. begin. after 12/31/88.

—P.L. 99-514, Sec. 1852(e)(2)(C), deleted para. (e)(5), effective for transfers after 10/22/86.

Prior to deletion, para. (e)(5) read as follows:

"(5) Section 2517 (relating to certain annuities under qualified plans)."

In 1984, P.L. 98-369, Sec. 491(d)(13), substituted "or an annuity plan described in section 403(a)" for ", an annuity plan described in section 403(a), or a bond purchase plan described in section 405(a)" in subsec. (a)... Sec. 491(d)(14), substituted "or 403(a)" for ", 403(a), or 405(a)" in para. (a)(3)... Sec. 491(d)(15)(A), substituted "section 404" for "sections 404 and 405(c)" in subsec. (d)... Sec. 491(d)(15)(B), substituted "or annuity" for "annuity, or bond purchase" in subsec. (d)... Sec. 491(d)(15)(C), deleted "(or section 405(c))" in para. (d)(2), effective for obligations issued after 12/31/83.

In 1983, P.L. 98-21, Sec. 321(c), amended subsec. (a)... Sec. 321(e)(2)(A), substituted "American employer" for "domestic corporation" and substituted "affiliate" for "subsidiary" and substituted "an" for "a" where it appeared before "domestic" each place they appeared in Code Sec. 406, with the exception of subsec.

1,943

Code Sec. 406   Employee benefit plans

(a) ... Sec. 321(e)(2)(B), substituted "another entity in which such American employer has not less than a 10-percent interest (within the meaning of section 3121(1)(8)(B))" for "another corporation controlled by such domestic corporation" in para. (c)(3) [prior to amendment by Sec. 321(e)(2)(A), see above] ... Sec. 321(e)(2)(C)(i), substituted "another taxpayer" for "another corporation" in the material preceding para. (d)(1) ... Sec. 321(e)(2)(C)(ii), substituted "any other taxpayer" for "any other corporation" in para. (d)(1) ... Sec. 321(e)(2)(D)(i), amended the heading of Code Sec. 406, effective for agreements entered into after 4/20/83. Sec. 321(f)(1)(B) of this Act provides special rules as follows:

"(B) At the election of any American employer, the amendments made by this section (other than subsection (d)) shall also apply to any agreement entered into on or before the date of the enactment of this Act [4/20/83]. Any such election shall be made at such time and in such manner as the Secretary may by regulations prescribe."

Prior to amendment, subsec. (a) read as follows:

"(a) Treatment as employees of domestic corporation.

"For purposes of applying this part with respect to a pension, profit-sharing, or stock bonus plan described in section 401(a), an annuity plan described in section 403(a), or a bond purchase plan described in section 405(a), of a domestic corporation, an individual who is a citizen of the United States and who is an employee of a foreign subsidiary (as defined in section 3121(*l*)(8)) of such domestic corporation shall be treated as an employee of such domestic corporation, if—

"(1) such domestic corporation has entered into an agreement under section 3121(*l*) which applies to the foreign subsidiary of which such individual is an employee;

"(2) the plan of such domestic corporation expressly provides for contributions or benefits for individuals who are citizens of the United States and who are employees of its foreign subsidiaries to which an agreement entered into by such domestic corporation under section 3121(*l*) applies; and

"(3) contributions under a funded plan of deferred compensation (whether or not a plan described in section 401(a), 403(a), or 405(a)) are not provided by any other person with respect to the remuneration paid to such individual by the foreign subsidiary."

Prior to amendment, the heading of Code Sec. 406 read as follows:

"SEC. 406. CERTAIN EMPLOYEES OF FOREIGN SUBSIDIARIES."

In **1976**, P.L. 94-455, Sec. 1906(b)(13)(A), substituted "Secretary" for "Secretary or his delegate" in subpara. (b)(2)(A), effective for tax. yrs. begin. after 12/31/76.

In **1974**, P.L. 93-406, Sec. 1016(a)(4), substituted "section 401(a)(4) and section 410(b) (without regard to paragraph (1)(A) thereof)" for "paragraphs (3)(B) and (4) of section 401(a)" in para. (b)(1), effective 9/2/74 and as provided in Sec. 1017 of this Act reproduced following Code Sec. 401.

—P.L. 93-406, Sec. 2005(c)(12), substituted "subsections (a)(2) and (e) of section 402" for "section 72(n), section 402(a)(2)" in subsec. (c), effective for distributions and payments made after 12/31/73 in tax. years begin. after 12/31/73.

In **1969**, P.L. 91-172, Sec. 515(c)(2)(A), substituted "provisions and limitation of tax." for "provisions." in the heading of subsec. (c) ... Sec. 515(c)(2)(B), substituted "section 72(n), section 402(a)(2)," for "section 402(a)(2)" in subsec. (c), effective for tax. yrs. end. after 12/31/69.

In **1964**, P.L. 88-272, Sec. 220(a), added Code Sec. 406, effective for tax. yrs. end. after 12/31/63.

Sec. 407. Certain employees of domestic subsidiaries engaged in business outside the United States.

(a) Treatment as employees of domestic parent corporation.

(1) In general. For purposes of applying this part with respect to a pension, profit-sharing, or stock bonus plan described in section 401(a) or an annuity plan described in section 403(a), of a domestic parent corporation, an individual who is a citizen or resident of the United States and who is an employee of a domestic subsidiary (within the meaning of paragraph (2)) of such domestic parent corporation shall be treated as an employee of such domestic parent corporation, if—

(A) the plan of such domestic parent corporation expressly provides for contributions or benefits for individuals who are citizens or residents of the United States and who are employees of its domestic subsidiaries; and

(B) contributions under a funded plan of deferred compensation (whether or not a plan described in section 401(a) or 403(a)) are not provided by any other person with respect to the remuneration paid to such individual by the domestic subsidiary.

(2) Definitions. For purposes of this section—

(A) Domestic subsidiary. A corporation shall be treated as a domestic subsidiary for any taxable year only if—

(i) such corporation is a domestic corporation 80 percent or more of the outstanding voting stock of which is owned by another domestic corporation;

(ii) 95 percent or more of its gross income for the three-year period immediately preceding the close of its taxable year which ends on or before the close of the taxable year of such other domestic corporation (or for such part of such period during which the corporation was in existence) was derived from sources without the United States; and

(iii) 90 percent or more of its gross income for such period (or such part) was derived from the active conduct of a trade or business.

If for the period (or part thereof) referred to in clauses (ii) and (iii) such corporation has no gross income, the provisions of clauses (ii) and (iii) shall be treated as satisfied if it is reasonable to anticipate that, with respect to the first taxable year thereafter for which such corporation has gross income, the provisions of such clauses will be satisfied.

(B) Domestic parent corporation. The domestic parent corporation of any domestic subsidiary is the domestic corporation which owns 80 percent or more of the outstanding voting stock of such domestic subsidiary.

(b) Special rules for application of section 401(a).

(1) Nondiscrimination requirements. For purposes of applying section 401(a)(4) and section 410(b) with respect to an individual who is treated as an employee of a domestic parent corporation under subsection (a)—

(A) if such individual is a highly compensated employee (within meaning of section 414(q)), he shall be treated as having such capacity with respect to such domestic parent corporation; and

(B) the determination of whether such individual is a highly compensated employee (as so defined) shall be made by treating such individual's total compensation (determined with the application of paragraph (2) of this subsection) as compensation paid by such domestic parent corporation and by determining such individual's status with regard to such domestic parent corporation.

(2) Determination of compensation. For purposes of applying paragraph (5) of section 401(a) with respect to an individual who is treated as an employee of a domestic parent corporation under subsection (a), the total compensation of such individual shall be the remuneration paid to such individual by the domestic subsidiary which would constitute his total compensation if his services had been performed for such domestic parent corporation, and the basic or regular rate of compensation of such individual shall be determined under regulations prescribed by the Secretary.

(c) Repealed.

(d) Deductibility of contributions.

For purposes of applying section 404 with respect to contributions made to or under a pension, profit-sharing, stock bonus, or annuity plan by a domestic parent corporation, or by another corporation which is entitled to deduct its contributions under section 404(a)(3)(B), on behalf of an individual who is treated as an employee of such domestic corporation under subsection (a)—

(1) except as provided in paragraph (2), no deduction shall be allowed to such domestic parent corporation or to any other corporation which is entitled to deduct its contributions under such sections;

(2) there shall be allowed as a deduction to the domestic subsidiary of which such individual is an employee an amount equal to the amount which (but for paragraph (1)) would be deductible under section 404 by the domestic parent corporation if he were an employee of the domestic parent corporation, and

(3) any reference to compensation shall be considered to be a reference to the total compensation of such individual (determined with the application of subsection (b)(2)).

Any amount deductible by a domestic subsidiary under this subsection shall be deductible for its taxable year with or within which the taxable year of such domestic parent corporation ends.

(e) Treatment as employee under related provisions.

An individual who is treated as an employee of a domestic parent corporation under subsection (a) shall also be treated as an employee of such domestic parent corporation, with respect to the plan described in subsection (a)(1)(A), for purposes of applying the following provisions of this title:

(1) Section 72(f) (relating to special rules for computing employees' contributions).

(2) Section 2039 (relating to annuities).

In 1996, P.L. 104-188, Sec. 1401(b)(8), deleted subsec. (c), effective for tax. yrs. begin. after 12/31/99. For transitional rules, see Sec. 1401(c)(2), of this Act, which reads as follows:

"(2) Retention of certain transition rules. The amendments made by this section shall not apply to any distribution for which the taxpayer is eligible to elect the benefits of section 1122(h)(3) or (5) of the Tax Reform Act of 1986. Notwithstanding the preceding sentence, individuals who elect such benefits after December 31, 1999, shall not be eligible for 5-year averaging under section 402(d) of the Internal Revenue Code of 1986 (as in effect immediately before such amendments)."

Prior to deletion, subsec. (c) read as follows:

"(c) Termination of status as deemed employee not to be treated as separation from service for purposes of limitation of tax. For purposes of applying section 402(d) with respect to an individual who is treated as an employee of a domestic parent corporation under subsection (a), such individual shall not be considered as separated from the service of such domestic parent corporation solely by reason of the fact that—

"(1) the corporation of which such individual is an employee ceases, for any taxable year, to be a domestic subsidiary within the meaning of subsection (a)(2)(A),

"(2) such individual ceases to be an employee of a domestic subsidiary of such domestic parent corporation, if he becomes an employee of another corporation controlled by such domestic parent corporation, or

"(3) the provision of the plan described in subsection (a)(1)(A) is terminated."

—P.L. 104-188, Sec. 1402(b)(2), deleted para. (e)(2) and redesignated para. (e)(3) as para. (e)(2), effective for decedents dying after 8/20/96.

Prior to deletion, para. (e)(2) read as follows:

"(2) Section 101(b) (relating to employees' death benefits)."

In 1992, P.L. 102-318, Sec. 521(b)(15), substituted "section 402(d)" for "section 402(e)" in subsec. (c), effective for distributions after 12/31/92. For special rule, see Sec. 521(e)(2) of this Act which reads as follows:

"(2) Special rule for partial distributions. For purposes of section 402(a)(5)(D)(i)(II) of the Internal Revenue Code of 1986 (as in effect before the amendments made by this section), a distribution before January 1, 1993, which is made before or at the same time as a series of periodic payments shall not be treated as one of such series if it is not substantially equal in amount to other payments in such series."

In 1989, P.L. 101-239, Sec. 7811(g)(3), substituted "purposes of limitation" for "purposes limitation" in the heading of subsec. (c), effective for amounts distributed after 12/31/86 in tax. yrs. end. after 12/31/86.

—P.L. 101-239, Sec. 7831(f), substituted "consist in supervising" for "consist of supervising" in Sec. 1114(b)(9)(B) of P.L. 99-514, see below.

In 1988, P.L. 100-647, Sec. 1011A(b)(1)(C), deleted para. (e)(1), and redesignated paras. (e)(2), (3) and (4) as paras. (e)(1), (2) and (3), effective for individuals whose annuities start after 7/1/86.

Prior to deletion, para. (e)(1) read as follows:

"(1) Section 72(d) (relating to employees' annuities)."

—P.L. 100-647, Sec. 1011A(b)(16)(A), substituted "section 402(e)" for "subsections (a)(2) and (e) of section 402, and section 403(a)(2)" in subsec. (c) . . . Sec. 1011A(b)(16)(B), deleted "of capital gain provisions and" after "service for purposes" in the heading of subsec. (c), effective for amounts distributed after 12/31/86, in tax. yrs. end. after 12/31/86.

In 1986, P.L. 99-514, Sec. 1112(d)(3), deleted "(without regard to paragraph (1)(A) thereof)" after "and section 410(b)" in para. (b)(1), effective for plan yrs. begin. after 12/31/88, except as provided in Secs. 1112(e)(2) and (3) of P.L. 99-514, which reads as follows:

"(2) Special rule for collective bargaining agreements.—In the case of a plan maintained pursuant to 1 or more collective bargaining agreements between employee representatives and 1 or more employers ratified before March 1, 1986, the amendments made by [Sec. 1112 of P.L. 99-514] shall not apply to employees covered by any such agreement in plan years beginning before the earlier of—

"(A) the later of—

"(i) January 1, 1989, or

"(ii) the date on which the last of such collective bargaining agreement terminates (determined without regard to any extension thereof after February 28, 1986), or

"(B) January 1, 1991.

"(3) Waiver of excise tax on reversions.

"(A) In general. If—

"(i) a plan is in existence on August 16, 1986,

"(ii) such plan would fail to meet the requirements of section 401(a)(26) of the Internal Revenue Code of 1986 (as added by subsection (b)) if such section were in effect for the plan year including August 16, 1986, and

"(iii) there is no transfer of assets to or liabilities from a plan or merger or spinoff or merger involving such plan after August 16, 1986,

then no tax shall be imposed under section 4980 of such Code on any employer reversion by reason of the termination or merger of such plan before the 1st year to which the amendment made by subsection (b) applies.

"(B) Determination of amount of reversion. For purposes of the Internal Revenue Code of 1986, in determining the present value of the accrued benefit of any highly compensated employee (within the meaning of section 414(q) of such Code) on the termination or merger of any plan to which subparagraph (A) applies, the plan shall use the highest interest rate which may be used for calculating present value under section 411(a)(11)(B) of such Code.

"(C) Special rule for plans which may not terminate. To the extent provided in regulations prescribed by the Secretary of the Treasury or his delegate, if a plan is prohibited from terminating under title IV of the Employee Retirement Income Security Act of 1974 then for the 1st year to which the amendment made by subsection (b) applies, subparagraph (A) shall be applied by substituting 'the 1st year in which the plan is able to terminate' for 'the 1st year to which the amendment made by subsection (b) applies'."

—P.L. 99-514, Sec. 1114(b)(9)(B), [as amended by Sec. 7831(f) of P.L. 101-239, see above] substituted "a highly compensated employee (within the meaning of section 414(q))" for "an officer, shareholder, or person whose principal duties consist in supervising the work of other employees of a domestic subsidiary" in subpara (b)(1)(A) . . . Sec. 1114(b)(9)(C), added "(as so defined)" after "employee" in subpara. (b)(1)(B), effective for tax. yrs. begin. after 12/31/88.

—P.L. 99-514, Sec. 1852(e)(2)(D), deleted para. (e)(5), effective for transfers made after 10/22/86.

Prior to deletion, para. (e)(5) read as follows:

"(5) Section 2517 (relating to certain annuities under qualified plans)."

In 1984, P.L. 98-369, Sec. 491(d)(16), substituted "or an annuity plan described in section 403(a)" for ", an annuity plan described in section 403(a), or a bond purchase plan described in section 405(a)" in para. (a)(1) . . . Sec. 491(d)(17), substituted "or 403(a)" for ", 403(a), or 405(a)" in subpara. (a)(1)(B) . . . Sec. 491(d)(18)(A), substituted "section 404" for "sections 404 and 405(c)" in subsec. (c) . . . Sec. 491(d)(18)(B), substituted "or annuity" for "annuity, or bond purchase" in subsec. (d) . . . Sec. 491(d)(18)(C), deleted "(c or section 405(c))" after "section 404" in para. (d)(2), effective for obligations issued after 12/31/83.

In 1983, P.L. 98-21, Sec. 321(d)(1), substituted "citizen or resident of the Untied States" for "citizen of the United States" in para. (a)(1) . . . Sec. 321(d)(2), substituted "citizens or residents of the United States" for "citizens of the United States" in para. (a)(1), effective for plans established after 4/20/83. Sec. 321(f)(2)(B) of the Act provides as follows:

"(B) At the election of any domestic parent corporation the amendments made by subsection (d) shall also apply to any plan established on or before the date of the enactment of this Act. Any such election shall be made at such time and in such manner as the Secretary may by regulations prescribe."

In 1976, P.L. 94-455, Sec. 1906(b)(13)(A), substituted "Secretary" for "Secretary or his delegate" in para. (b)(2), effective for tax. yrs. begin. after 12/31/76.

In 1974, P.L. 93-406, Sec. 1016(a)(5), substituted "section 401(a)(4) and section 410(b) (without regard to paragraph (1)(A) thereof)" for "paragraphs (3)(B) and (4) of section 401(a)", effective 9/2/74 or other date as specified in Sec. 1017 of this Act, reproduced in note following Code Sec. 401.

—P.L. 93-406, Sec. 2005(c)(13), substituted "subsections (a)(2) and (e) of section 402" for "section 72(n), section 402(a)(2)" in subsec. (c), effective for distributions and payments made after 12/31/73, in tax. yrs. begin. after 12/31/73.

In 1969, P.L. 91-172, Sec. 515(c)(3)(A), substituted "Provisions and limitations of tax," for "Provisions." in the heading of subsec. (c) . . . Sec. 515(c)(3)(B), substituted "section 72(n), section 402(a)(2)," for "section 402(a)(2)" in subsec. (c), effective for tax. yrs. end. after 12/31/69.

In 1964, P.L. 88-272, Sec. 220(b), added Code Sec. 407, effective for tax. yrs. end. after 12/31/63.

Sec. 408. Individual retirement accounts.
(a) Individual retirement account.

For purposes of this section, the term "individual retirement account" means a trust created or organized in the United States for the exclusive benefit of an individual or his beneficiaries, but only if the written governing instrument creating the trust meets the following requirements:

(1) Except in the case of a rollover contribution described in subsection (d)(3) in section 402(c), 403(a)(4),

403(b)(8), or 457(e)(16), no contribution will be accepted unless it is in cash, and contributions will not be accepted for the taxable year on behalf of any individual in excess of the amount in effect for such taxable year under section 219(b)(1)(A).

(2) The trustee is a bank (as defined in subsection (n)) or such other person who demonstrates to the satisfaction of the Secretary that the manner in which such other person will administer the trust will be consistent with the requirements of this section.

(3) No part of the trust funds will be invested in life insurance contracts.

(4) The interest of an individual in the balance in his account is nonforfeitable.

(5) The assets of the trust will not be commingled with other property except in a common trust fund or common investment fund.

(6) Under regulations prescribed by the Secretary, rules similar to the rules of section 401(a)(9) and the incidental death benefit requirements of section 401(a) shall apply to the distribution of the entire interest of an individual for whose benefit the trust is maintained.

(b) Individual retirement annuity.

For purposes of this section, the term "individual retirement annuity" means an annuity contract, or an endowment contract (as determined under regulations prescribed by the Secretary), issued by an insurance company which meets the following requirements:

(1) The contract is not transferable by the owner.

(2) Under the contract—
 (A) the premiums are not fixed,
 (B) the annual premium on behalf of any individual will not exceed the dollar amount in effect under section 219(b)(1)(A), and
 (C) any refund of premiums will be applied before the close of the calendar year following the year of the refund toward the payment of future premiums or the purchase of additional benefits.

(3) Under regulations prescribed by the Secretary, rules similar to the rules of section 401(a)(9) and the incidental death benefit requirements of section 401(a) shall apply to the distribution of the entire interest of the owner.

(4) The entire interest of the owner is nonforfeitable.

Such term does not include such an annuity contract for any taxable year of the owner in which it is disqualified on the application of subsection (e) or for any subsequent taxable year. For purposes of this subsection, no contract shall be treated as an endowment contract if it matures later than the taxable year in which the individual in whose name such contract is purchased attains age 70½; if it is not for the exclusive benefit of the individual in whose name it is purchased or his beneficiaries; or if the aggregate annual premiums under all such contracts purchased in the name of such individual for any taxable year exceed the dollar amount in effect under section 219(b)(1)(A).

(c) Accounts established by employers and certain associations of employees.

A trust created or organized in the United States by an employer for the exclusive benefit of his employees or their beneficiaries, or by an association of employees (which may include employees within the meaning of section 401(c)(1)) for the exclusive benefit of its members or their beneficiaries, shall be treated as an individual retirement account (described in subsection (a)), but only if the written governing instrument creating the trust meets the following requirements:

(1) The trust satisfies the requirements of paragraphs (1) through (6) of subsection (a).

(2) There is a separate accounting for the interest of each employee or member (or spouse of an employee or member).

The assets of the trust may be held in a common fund for the account of all individuals who have an interest in the trust.

(d) Tax treatment of distributions.

(1) **In general.** Except as otherwise provided in this subsection, any amount paid or distributed out of an individual retirement plan shall be included in gross income by the payee or distributee, as the case may be, in the manner provided under section 72.

(2) **Special rules for applying section 72.** For purposes of applying section 72 to any amount described in paragraph (1)—
 (A) all individual retirement plans shall be treated as 1 contract,
 (B) all distributions during any taxable year shall be treated as 1 distribution, and
 (C) the value of the contract, income on the contract, and investment in the contract shall be computed as of the close of the calendar year in which the taxable year begins.

For purposes of subparagraph (C), the value of the contract shall be increased by the amount of any distributions during the calendar year.

(3) **Rollover contribution.** An amount is described in this paragraph as a rollover contribution if it meets the requirements of subparagraphs (A) and (B).

 (A) In general. Paragraph (1) does not apply to any amount paid or distributed out of an individual retirement account or individual retirement annuity to the individual for whose benefit the account or annuity is maintained if—
  (i) the entire amount received (including money and any other property) is paid into an individual retirement account or individual retirement annuity (other than an endowment contract) for the benefit of such individual not later than the 60th day after the day on which he receives the payment or distribution; or
  (ii) the entire amount received (including money and any other property) is paid into an eligible retirement plan for the benefit of such individual not later than the 60th day after the date on which the payment or distribution is received, except that the maximum amount which may be paid into such plan may not exceed the portion of the amount received which is includible in gross income (determined without regard to this paragraph).

For purposes of clause (ii), the term "eligible retirement plan" means an eligible retirement plan described in clause (iii), (iv), (v), or (vi) of section 402(c)(8)(B).

 (B) Limitation. This paragraph does not apply to any amount described in subparagraph (A)(i) received by an individual from an individual retirement account or individual retirement annuity if at any time during the 1-year period ending on the day of such receipt such individual received any other amount described in that subparagraph from an individual retirement account or an individual retirement annuity which was not includible in his gross income because of the application of this paragraph.

 (C) Denial of rollover treatment for inherited accounts, etc.

(i) In general. In the case of an inherited individual retirement account or individual retirement annuity—

(I) this paragraph shall not apply to any amount received by an individual from such an account or annuity (and no amount transferred from such account or annuity to another individual retirement account or annuity shall be excluded from gross income by reason of such transfer), and

(II) such inherited account or annuity shall not be treated as an individual retirement account or annuity for purposes of determining whether any other amount is a rollover contribution.

(ii) Inherited individual retirement account or annuity. An individual retirement account or individual retirement annuity shall be treated as inherited if—

(I) the individual for whose benefit the account or annuity is maintained acquired such account by reason of the death of another individual, and

(II) such individual was not the surviving spouse of such other individual.

(D) Partial rollovers permitted.

(i) In general. If any amount paid or distributed out of an individual retirement account or individual retirement annuity would meet the requirements of subparagraph (A) but for the fact that the entire amount was not paid into an eligible plan as required by clause (i) or (ii) of subparagraph (A), such amount shall be treated as meeting the requirements of subparagraph (A) to the extent it is paid into an eligible plan referred to in such clause not later than the 60th day referred to in such clause.

(ii) Eligible plan. For purposes of clause (i), the term "eligible plan" means any account, annuity, contract, or plan referred to in subparagraph (A).

(E) Denial of rollover treatment for required distributions. This paragraph shall not apply to any amount to the extent such amount is required to be distributed under subsection (a)(6) or (b)(3).

(F) Frozen deposits. For purposes of this paragraph, rules similar to the rules of section 402(c)(7) (relating to frozen deposits) shall apply.

(G) Simple retirement accounts. In the case of any payment or distribution out of a simple retirement account (as defined in subsection (p)) to which section 72(t)(6) applies, this paragraph shall not apply unless such payment or distribution is paid into another simple retirement account.

(H) Application of section 72.

(i) In general. If—

(I) a distribution is made from an individual retirement plan, and

(II) a rollover contribution is made to an eligible retirement plan described in section 402(c)(8)(B)(iii), (iv), (v), or (vi) with respect to all or part of such distribution,

then, notwithstanding paragraph (2), the rules of clause (ii) shall apply for purposes of applying section 72.

(ii) Applicable rules. In the case of a distribution described in clause (i)—

(I) section 72 shall be applied separately to such distribution,

(II) notwithstanding the pro rata allocation of income on, and investment in, the contract to distributions under section 72, the portion of such distribution rolled over to an eligible retirement plan described in clause (i) shall be treated as from income on the contract (to the extent of the aggregate income on the contract from all individual retirement plans of the distributee), and

(III) appropriate adjustments shall be made in applying section 72 to other distributions in such taxable year and subsequent taxable years.

(I) Waiver of 60-day requirement. The Secretary may waive the 60-day requirement under subparagraphs (A) and (D) where the failure to waive such requirement would be against equity or good conscience, including casualty, disaster, or other events beyond the reasonable control of the individual subject to such requirement.

(4) Contributions returned before due date of return. Paragraph (1) does not apply to the distribution of any contribution paid during a taxable year to an individual retirement account or for an individual retirement annuity if—

(A) such distribution is received on or before the day prescribed by law (including extensions of time) for filing such individual's return for such taxable year,

(B) no deduction is allowed under section 219 with respect to such contribution, and

(C) such distribution is accompanied by the amount of net income attributable to such contribution.

In the case of such a distribution, for purposes of section 61, any net income described in subparagraph (C) shall be deemed to have been earned and receivable in the taxable year in which such contribution is made.

(5) Distributions of excess contributions after due date for taxable year and certain excess rollover contributions.

(A) In general. In the case of any individual, if the aggregate contributions (other than rollover contributions) paid for any taxable year to an individual retirement account or for an individual retirement annuity do not exceed the dollar amount in effect under section 219(b)(1)(A), paragraph (1) shall not apply to the distribution of any such contribution to the extent that such contribution exceeds the amount allowable as a deduction under section 219 for the taxable year for which the contribution was paid—

(i) if such distribution is received after the date described in paragraph (4),

(ii) but only to the extent that no deduction has been allowed under section 219 with respect to such excess contribution.

If employer contributions on behalf of the individual are paid for the taxable year to a simplified employee pension, the dollar limitation of the preceding sentence shall be increased by the lesser of the amount of such contributions or the dollar limitation in effect under section 415(c)(1)(A) for such taxable year.

(B) Excess rollover contributions attributable to erroneous information. If—

(i) the taxpayer reasonably relies on information supplied pursuant to subtitle F for determining the amount of a rollover contribution, but

(ii) the information was erroneous,

subparagraph (A) shall be applied by increasing the dollar limit set forth therein by that portion of the excess contribution which was attributable to such information.

For purposes of this paragraph, the amount allowable as a deduction under section 219 shall be computed without regard to section 219(g).

(6) Transfer of account incident to divorce. The transfer of an individual's interest in an individual retirement account or an individual retirement annuity to his spouse or former spouse under a divorce or separation instrument described in subparagraph (A) of section 71(b)(2) is not to be considered a taxable transfer made by such individual notwithstanding any other provision of this subtitle, and such interest at the time of the transfer is to be treated as an individual retirement account of such spouse, and not of such individual. Thereafter such account or annuity for purposes of this subtitle is to be treated as maintained for the benefit of such spouse.

(7) **Special rules for simplified employee pensions or simple retirement accounts.**

(A) Transfer or rollover of contributions prohibited until deferral test met. Notwithstanding any other provision of this subsection or section 72(t), paragraph (1) and section 72(t)(1) shall apply to the transfer or distribution from a simplified employee pension of any contribution under a salary reduction arrangement described in subsection (k)(6) (or any income allocable thereto) before a determination as to whether the requirements of subsection (k)(6)(A)(iii) are met with respect to such contribution.

(B) Certain exclusions treated as deductions. For purposes of paragraphs (4) and (5) and section 4973, any amount excludable or excluded from gross income under section 402(h) or 402(k) shall be treated as an amount allowable or allowed as a deduction under section 219.

(8) **Distributions for charitable purposes.**

(A) In general. So much of the aggregate amount of qualified charitable distributions with respect to a taxpayer made during any taxable year which does not exceed $100,000 shall not be includible in gross income of such taxpayer for such taxable year.

(B) Qualified charitable distribution. For purposes of this paragraph, the term "qualified charitable distribution" means any distribution from an individual retirement plan (other than a plan described in subsection (k) or (p))—

(i) which is made directly by the trustee to an organization described in section 170(b)(1)(A) (other than any organization described in section 509(a)(3) or any fund or account described in section 4966(d)(2)), and

(ii) which is made on or after the date that the individual for whose benefit the plan is maintained has attained age 70 ½.

A distribution shall be treated as a qualified charitable distribution only to the extent that the distribution would be includible in gross income without regard to subparagraph (A).

(C) Contributions must be otherwise deductible. For purposes of this paragraph, a distribution to an organization described in subparagraph (B)(i) shall be treated as a qualified charitable distribution only if a deduction for the entire distribution would be allowable under section 170 (determined without regard to subsection (b) thereof and this paragraph).

(D) Application of section 72. Notwithstanding section 72, in determining the extent to which a distribution is a qualified charitable distribution, the entire amount of the distribution shall be treated as includible in gross income without regard to subparagraph (A) to the extent that such amount does not exceed the aggregate amount which would have been so includible if all amounts in all individual retirement plans of the individual were distributed during such taxable year and all such plans were treated as 1 contract for purposes of determining under section 72 the aggregate amount which would have been so includible. Proper adjustments shall be made in applying section 72 to other distributions in such taxable year and subsequent taxable years.

(E) Denial of deduction. Qualified charitable distributions which are not includible in gross income pursuant to subparagraph (A) shall not be taken into account in determining the deduction under section 170.

(F) Termination. This paragraph shall not apply to distributions made in taxable years beginning after December 31, 2011.

(9) **Distribution for health savings account funding.**

(A) In general. In the case of an individual who is an eligible individual (as defined in section 223(c)) and who elects the application of this paragraph for a taxable year, gross income of the individual for the taxable year does not include a qualified HSA funding distribution to the extent such distribution is otherwise includible in gross income.

(B) Qualified HSA funding distribution. For purposes of this paragraph, the term "qualified HSA funding distribution" means a distribution from an individual retirement plan (other than a plan described in subsection (k) or (p)) of the employee to the extent that such distribution is contributed to the health savings account of the individual in a direct trustee-to-trustee transfer.

(C) Limitations.

(i) Maximum dollar limitation. The amount excluded from gross income by subparagraph (A) shall not exceed the excess of—

(I) the annual limitation under section 223(b) computed on the basis of the type of coverage under the high deductible health plan covering the individual at the time of the qualified HSA funding distribution, over

(II) in the case of a distribution described in clause (ii)(II), the amount of the earlier qualified HSA funding distribution.

(ii) One-time transfer.

(I) In general. Except as provided in subclause (II), an individual may make an election under subparagraph (A) only for one qualified HSA funding distribution during the lifetime of the individual. Such an election, once made, shall be irrevocable.

(II) Conversion from self-only to family coverage. If a qualified HSA funding distribution is made during a month in a taxable year during which an individual has self-only coverage under a high deductible health plan as of the first day of the month, the individual may elect to make an additional qualified HSA funding distribution during a subsequent month in such taxable year during which the individual has family coverage under a high deductible health plan as of the first day of the subsequent month.

(D) Failure to maintain high deductible health plan coverage.

(i) In general. If, at any time during the testing period, the individual is not an eligible individual, then the aggregate amount of all contributions to the health savings account of the individual made under subparagraph (A)—

(I) shall be includible in the gross income of the individual for the taxable year in which occurs the first month in the testing period for which such individual is not an eligible individual, and

(II) the tax imposed by this chapter for any taxable year on the individual shall be increased by 10 percent of the amount which is so includible.

(ii) Exception for disability or death. Subclauses (I) and (II) of clause (i) shall not apply if the individual ceased to be an eligible individual by reason of the death of the individual or the individual becoming disabled (within the meaning of section 72(m)(7)).

(iii) Testing period. The term "testing period" means the period beginning with the month in which the qualified HSA funding distribution is contributed to a health savings account and ending on the last day of the 12th month following such month.

(E) Application of section 72. Notwithstanding section 72, in determining the extent to which an amount is treated as otherwise includible in gross income for purposes of subparagraph (A), the aggregate amount distributed from an individual retirement plan shall be treated as includible in gross income to the extent that such amount does not exceed the aggregate amount which would have been so includible if all amounts from all individual retirement plans were distributed. Proper adjustments shall be made in applying section 72 to other distributions in such taxable year and subsequent taxable years.

(e) Tax treatment of accounts and annuities.

(1) Exemption from tax. Any individual retirement account is exempt from taxation under this subtitle unless such account has ceased to be an individual retirement account by reason of paragraph (2) or (3). Notwithstanding the preceding sentence, any such account is subject to the taxes imposed by section 511 (relating to imposition of tax on unrelated business income of charitable, etc. organizations).

(2) Loss of exemption of account where employee engages in prohibited transaction.

(A) In general. If, during any taxable year of the individual for whose benefit any individual retirement account is established, that individual or his beneficiary engages in any transaction prohibited by section 4975 with respect to such account, such account ceases to be an individual retirement account as of the first day of such taxable year. For purposes of this paragraph—

(i) the individual for whose benefit any account was established is treated as the creator of such account, and

(ii) the separate account for any individual within an individual retirement account maintained by an employer or association of employees is treated as a separate individual retirement account.

(B) Account treated as distributing all its assets. In any case in which any account ceases to be an individual retirement account by reason of subparagraph (A) as of the first day of any taxable year, paragraph (1) of subsection (d) applies as if there were a distribution on such first day in an amount equal to the fair market value (on such first day) of all assets in the account (on such first day).

(3) Effect of borrowing on annuity contract. If during any taxable year the owner of an individual retirement annuity borrows any money under or by use of such contract, the contract ceases to be an individual retirement annuity as of the first day of such taxable year. Such owner shall include in gross income for such year an amount equal to the fair market value of such contract as of such first day.

(4) Effect of pledging account as security. If, during any taxable year of the individual for whose benefit an individual retirement account is established, that individual uses the account or any portion thereof as security for a loan, the portion so used is treated as distributed to that individual.

(5) Purchase of endowment contract by individual retirement account. If the assets of an individual retirement account or any part of such assets are used to purchase an endowment contract for the benefit of the individual for whose benefit the account is established—

(A) to the extent that the amount of the assets involved in the purchase are not attributable to the purchase of life insurance, the purchase is treated as a rollover contribution described in subsection (d)(3), and

(B) to the extent that the amount of the assets involved in the purchase are attributable to the purchase of life, health, accident, or other insurance, such amounts are treated as distributed to that individual (but the provisions of subsection (f) do not apply).

(6) Commingling individual retirement account amounts in certain common trust funds and common investment funds. Any common trust fund or common investment fund of individual retirement account assets which is exempt from taxation under this subtitle does not cease to be exempt on account of the participation or inclusion of assets of a trust exempt from taxation under section 501(a) which is described in section 401(a).

(f) Repealed.

(g) Community property laws.

This section shall be applied without regard to any community property laws.

(h) Custodial accounts.

For purposes of this section, a custodial account shall be treated as a trust if the assets of such account are held by a bank (as defined in subsection (n)) or another person who demonstrates, to the satisfaction of the Secretary, that the manner in which he will administer the account will be consistent with the requirements of this section, and if the custodial account would, except for the fact that it is not a trust, constitute an individual retirement account described in subsection (a). For purposes of this title, in the case of a custodial account treated as a trust by reason of the preceding sentence, the custodian of such account shall be treated as the trustee thereof.

(i) Reports.

The trustee of an individual retirement account and the issuer of an endowment contract described in subsection (b) or an individual retirement annuity shall make such reports regarding such account, contract, or annuity to the Secretary and to the individuals for whom the account, contract, or annuity is, or is to be, maintained with respect to contributions (and the years to which they relate), distributions aggregating $10 or more in any calendar year and such other matters as the Secretary may require. The reports required by this subsection—

(1) shall be filed at such time and in such manner as the Secretary prescribes, and

(2) shall be furnished to individuals—

(A) not later than January 31 of the calendar year following the calendar year to which such reports relate, and

(B) in such manner as the Secretary prescribes.

In the case of a simple retirement account under subsection (p), only one report under this subsection shall be required to be submitted each calendar year to the Secretary (at the time provided under paragraph (2)) but, in addition to the report under this subsection, there shall be furnished, within 31 days after each calendar year, to the individual on whose behalf the account is maintained a statement with respect to the account balance as of the close of, and the account activity during, such calendar year.

(j) Increase in maximum limitations for simplified employee pensions.

In the case of any simplified employee pension, subsections (a)(1) and (b)(2) of this section shall be applied by increasing the amounts contained therein by the amount of the limitation in effect under section 415(c)(1)(A).

(k) Simplified employee pension defined.

　(1) **In general.** For purposes of this title, the term "simplified employee pension" means an individual retirement account or individual retirement annuity—

　　(A) with respect to which the requirements of paragraphs (2), (3), (4), and (5) of this subsection are met, and

　　(B) if such account or annuity is part of a top-heavy plan (as defined in section 416), with respect to which the requirements of section 416(c)(2) are met.

　(2) **Participation requirements.** This paragraph is satisfied with respect to a simplified employee pension for a year only if for such year the employer contributes to the simplified employee pension of each employee who—

　　(A) has attained age 21,

　　(B) has performed service for the employer during at least 3 of the immediately preceding 5 years, and

　　(C) received at least $450 in compensation (within the meaning of section 414(q)(4)) from the employer for the year.

For purposes of this paragraph, there shall be excluded from consideration employees described in subparagraph (A) or (C) of section 410(b)(3). For purposes of any arrangement described in subsection (k)(6), any employee who is eligible to have employer contributions made on the employee's behalf under such arrangement shall be treated as if such a contribution was made.

　(3) **Contributions may not discriminate in favor of the highly compensated, etc.**

　　(A) **In general.** The requirements of this paragraph are met with respect to a simplified employee pension for a year if for such year the contributions made by the employer to simplified employee pensions for his employees do not discriminate in favor of any highly compensated employee (within the meaning of section 414(q)).

　　(B) **Special rules.** For purposes of subparagraph (A), there shall be excluded from consideration employees described in subparagraph (A) or (C) of section 410(b)(3).

　　(C) Contributions must bear uniform relationship to total compensation. For purposes of subparagraph (A), and except as provided in subparagraph (D), employer contributions to simplified employee pensions (other than contributions under an arrangement described in paragraph (6)) shall be considered discriminatory unless contributions thereto bear a uniform relationship to the compensation (not in excess of the first $200,000) of each employee maintaining a simplified employee pension.

　　(D) **Permitted disparity.** For purposes of subparagraph (C), the rules of section 401(l)(2) shall apply to contributions to simplified employee pensions (other than contributions under an arrangement described in paragraph (6)).

　(4) **Withdrawals must be permitted.** A simplified employee pension meets the requirements of this paragraph only if—

　　(A) employer contributions thereto are not conditioned on the retention in such pension of any portion of the amount contributed, and

　　(B) there is no prohibition imposed by the employer on withdrawals from the simplified employee pension.

　(5) **Contributions must be made under written allocation formula.** The requirements of this paragraph are met with respect to a simplified employee pension only if employer contributions to such pension are determined under a definite written allocation formula which specifies—

　　(A) the requirements which an employee must satisfy to share in an allocation, and

　　(B) the manner in which the amount allocated is computed.

　(6) **Employee may elect salary reduction arrangement.**

　　(A) Arrangements which qualify.

　　　(i) In general. A simplified employee pension shall not fail to meet the requirements of this subsection for a year merely because, under the terms of the pension, an employee may elect to have the employer make payments—

　　　　(I) as elective employer contributions to the simplified employee pension on behalf of the employee, or

　　　　(II) to the employee directly in cash.

　　　(ii) 50 percent of eligible employees must elect. Clause (i) shall not apply to a simplified employee pension unless an election described in clause (i)(I) is made or is in effect with respect to not less than 50 percent of the employees of the employer eligible to participate.

　　　(iii) Requirements relating to deferral percentage. Clause (i) shall not apply to a simplified employee pension for any year unless the deferral percentage for such year of each highly compensated employee eligible to participate is not more than the product of—

　　　　(I) the average of the deferral percentages for such year of all employees (other than highly compensated employees) eligible to participate, multiplied by

　　　　(II) 1.25.

　　　(iv) Limitations on elective deferrals. Clause (i) shall not apply to a simplified employee pension unless the requirements of section 401(a)(30) are met.

　　(B) Exception where more than 25 employees. This paragraph shall not apply with respect to any year in the case of a simplified employee pension maintained by an employer with more than 25 employees who were eligible to participate (or would have been required to be eligible to participate if a pension was maintained) at any time during the preceding year.

　　(C) Distributions of excess contributions.

　　　(i) In general. Rules similar to the rules of section 401(k)(8) shall apply to any excess contribution under this paragraph. Any excess contribution under a simplified employee pension shall be treated as an excess contribution for purposes of section 4979.

　　　(ii) Excess contribution. For purposes of clause (i), the term "excess contribution" means, with respect to a highly compensated employee, the excess of elective employer contributions under this paragraph over the maximum amount of such contributions allowable under subparagraph (A)(iii).

(D) Deferral percentage. For purposes of this paragraph, the deferral percentage for an employee for a year shall be the ratio of—
  (i) the amount of elective employer contributions actually paid over to the simplified employee pension on behalf of the employee for the year, to
  (ii) the employee's compensation (not in excess of the first $200,000) for the year.
(E) Exception for State and local and tax-exempt pensions. This paragraph shall not apply to a simplified employee pension maintained by—
  (i) a State or local government or political subdivision thereof, or any agency or instrumentality thereof, or
  (ii) an organization exempt from tax under this title.
(F) Exception where pension does not meet requirements necessary to insure distribution of excess contributions. This paragraph shall not apply with respect to any year for which the simplified employee pension does not meet such requirements as the Secretary may prescribe as are necessary to insure that excess contributions are distributed in accordance with subparagraph (C), including—
  (i) reporting requirements, and
  (ii) requirements which, notwithstanding paragraph (4), provide that contributions (and any income allocable thereto) may not be withdrawn from a simplified employee pension until a determination has been made that the requirements of subparagraph (A)(iii) have been met with respect to such contributions.
(G) Highly compensated employee. For purposes of this paragraph, the term "highly compensated employee" has the meaning given such term by section 414(q).
(H) Termination. This paragraph shall not apply to years beginning after December 31, 1996. The preceding sentence shall not apply to a simplified employee pension of an employer if the terms of simplified employee pensions of such employer, as in effect on December 31, 1996, provide that an employee may make the election described in subparagraph (A).

(7) **Definitions.** For purposes of this subsection and subsection (1)—
(A) Employee, employer, or owner-employee. The terms "employee", "employer", and "owner-employee" shall have the respective meanings given such terms by section 401(c).
(B) Compensation. Except as provided in paragraph (2)(C), the term "compensation" has the meaning given such term by section 414(s).
(C) Year. The term "year" means—
  (i) the calendar year, or
  (ii) if the employer elects, subject to such terms and conditions as the Secretary may prescribe, to maintain the simplified employee pension on the basis of the employer's taxable year.

(8) **Cost-of-living adjustment.** The Secretary shall adjust the $450 amount in paragraph (2)(C) at the same time and in the same manner as under section 415(d) and shall adjust the $200,000 amount in paragraphs (3)(C) and (6)(D)(ii) at the same time, and by the same amount, as any adjustment under section 401(a)(17)(B); except that any increase in the $450 amount which is not a multiple of $50 shall be rounded to the next lowest multiple of $50.

(9) **Cross reference.** For excise tax on certain excess contributions, see section 4979.

(l) **Simplified employer reports.**
(1) **In general.** An employer who makes a contribution on behalf of an employee to a simplified employee pension shall provide such simplified reports with respect to such contributions as the Secretary may require by regulations. The reports required by this subsection shall be filed at such time and in such manner, and information with respect to such contributions shall be furnished to the employee at such time and in such manner, as may be required by regulations.
(2) **Simple retirement accounts.**
  (A) No employer reports. Except as provided in this paragraph, no report shall be required under this section by an employer maintaining a qualified salary reduction arrangement under subsection (p).
  (B) Summary description. The trustee of any simple retirement account established pursuant to a qualified salary reduction arrangement under subsection (p) and the issuer of an annuity established under such an arrangement shall provide to the employer maintaining the arrangement, each year a description containing the following information:
    (i) The name and address of the employer and the trustee or issuer.
    (ii) The requirements for eligibility for participation.
    (iii) The benefits provided with respect to the arrangement.
    (iv) The time and method of making elections with respect to the arrangement.
    (v) The procedures for, and effects of, withdrawals (including rollovers) from the arrangement.
  (C) Employee notification. The employer shall notify each employee immediately before the period for which an election described in subsection (p)(5)(C) may be made of the employee's opportunity to make such election. Such notice shall include a copy of the description described in subparagraph (B).

(m) **Investment in collectibles treated as distributions.**
(1) **In general.** The acquisition by an individual retirement account or by an individually-directed account under a plan described in section 401(a) of any collectible shall be treated (for purposes of this section and section 402) as a distribution from such account in an amount equal to the cost to such account of such collectible.
(2) **Collectible defined.** For purposes of this subsection, the term "collectible" means—
  (A) any work of art,
  (B) any rug or antique,
  (C) any metal or gem,
  (D) any stamp or coin,
  (E) any alcoholic beverage, or
  (F) any other tangible personal property specified by the Secretary for purposes of this subsection.
(3) **Exception for certain coins and bullion.** For purposes of this subsection, the term "collectible" shall not include—
  (A) any coin which is—
    (i) a gold coin described in paragraph (7), (8), (9), or (10) of section 5112(a) of title 31, United States Code,
    (ii) a silver coin described in section 5112(e) of title 31, United States Code,
    (iii) a platinum coin described in section 5112(k) of title 31, United States Code, or
    (iv) a coin issued under the laws of any State, or

(B) any gold, silver, platinum, or palladium bullion of a fineness equal to or exceeding the minimum fineness that a contract market (as described in section 7 of the Commodity Exchange Act, 7 U.S.C. 7) requires for metals which may be delivered in satisfaction of a regulated futures contract,

if such bullion is in the physical possession of a trustee described under subsection (a) of this section.

(n) Bank.

For purposes of subsection (a)(2), the term "bank" means—

(1) any bank (as defined in section 581),

(2) an insured credit union (within the meaning of paragraph (6) or (7) of section 101 of the Federal Credit Union Act), and

(3) a corporation which, under the laws of the State of its incorporation, is subject to supervision and examination by the Commissioner of Banking or other officer of such State in charge of the administration of the banking laws of such State.

(o) Definitions and rules relating to nondeductible contributions to individual retirement plans.

(1) In general. Subject to the provisions of this subsection, designated nondeductible contributions may be made on behalf of an individual to an individual retirement plan.

(2) Limits on amounts which may be contributed.

(A) In general. The amount of the designated nondeductible contributions made on behalf of any individual for any taxable year shall not exceed the nondeductible limit for such taxable year.

(B) Nondeductible limit. For purposes of this paragraph—

(i) In general. The term "nondeductible limit" means the excess of—

(I) the amount allowable as a deduction under section 219 (determined without regard to section 219(g)), over

(II) the amount allowable as a deduction under section 219 (determined with regard to section 219(g)).

(ii) Taxpayer may elect to treat deductible contributions as nondeductible. If a taxpayer elects not to deduct an amount which (without regard to this clause) is allowable as a deduction under section 219 for any taxable year, the nondeductible limit for such taxable year shall be increased by such amount.

(C) Designated nondeductible contributions.

(i) In general. For purposes of this paragraph, the term "designated nondeductible contribution" means any contribution to an individual retirement plan for the taxable year which is designated (in such manner as the Secretary may prescribe) as a contribution for which a deduction is not allowable under section 219.

(ii) Designation. Any designation under clause (i) shall be made on the return of tax imposed by chapter 1 for the taxable year.

(3) Time when contributions made. In determining for which taxable year a designated nondeductible contribution is made, the rule of section 219(f)(3) shall apply.

(4) Individual required to report amount of designated nondeductible contributions.

(A) In general. Any individual who—

(i) makes a designated nondeductible contribution to any individual retirement plan for any taxable year, or

(ii) receives any amount from any individual retirement plan for any taxable year,

shall include on his return of the tax imposed by chapter 1 for such taxable year and any succeeding taxable year (or on such other form as the Secretary may prescribe for any such taxable year) information described in subparagraph (B).

(B) Information required to be supplied. The following information is described in this subparagraph:

(i) The amount of designated nondeductible contributions for the taxable year.

(ii) The amount of distributions from individual retirement plans for the taxable year.

(iii) The excess (if any) of—

(I) the aggregate amount of designated nondeductible contributions for all preceding taxable years, over

(II) the aggregate amount of distributions from individual retirement plans which was excludable from gross income for such taxable years.

(iv) The aggregate balance of all individual retirement plans of the individual as of the close of the calendar year in which the taxable year begins.

(v) Such other information as the Secretary may prescribe.

(C) Penalty for reporting contributions not made. For penalty where individual reports designated nondeductible contributions not made, see section 6693(b).

(p) Simple retirement accounts.

(1) In general. For purposes of this title, the term "simple retirement account" means an individual retirement plan (as defined in section 7701(a)(37))—

(A) with respect to which the requirements of paragraphs (3), (4), and (5) are met; and

(B) with respect to which the only contributions allowed are contributions under a qualified salary reduction arrangement.

(2) Qualified salary reduction arrangement.

(A) In general. For purposes of this subsection, the term "qualified salary reduction arrangement" means a written arrangement of an eligible employer under which—

(i) an employee eligible to participate in the arrangement may elect to have the employer make payments—

(I) as elective employer contributions to a simple retirement account on behalf of the employee, or

(II) to the employee directly in cash,

(ii) the amount which an employee may elect under clause (i) for any year is required to be expressed as a percentage of compensation and may not exceed a total of the applicable dollar amount for any year,

(iii) the employer is required to make a matching contribution to the simple retirement account for any year in an amount equal to so much of the amount the employee elects under clause (i)(I) as does not exceed the applicable percentage of compensation for the year, and

(iv) no contributions may be made other than contributions described in clause (i) or (iii).

(B) Employer may elect 2-percent nonelective contribution.

(i) In general. An employer shall be treated as meeting the requirements of subparagraph (A)(iii) for any year if, in lieu of the contributions described in such clause, the employer elects to make nonelective contributions of 2 percent of compensation for each employee who is eligible to participate in the arrangement and who has at least $5,000 of compensation from the employer for the year. If an employer makes an election under this subparagraph for any year, the employer shall notify employees of such election within a reasonable period of time before the 60-day period for such year under paragraph (5)(C).

(ii) Compensation limitation. The compensation taken into account under clause (i) for any year shall not exceed the limitation in effect for such year under section 401(a)(17).

(C) Definitions. For purposes of this subsection—

(i) Eligible employer—

(I) In general. The term "eligible employer" means, with respect to any year, an employer which had no more than 100 employees who received at least $5,000 of compensation from the employer for the preceding year.

(II) 2-year grace period. An eligible employer who establishes and maintains a plan under this subsection for 1 or more years and who fails to be an eligible employer for any subsequent year shall be treated as an eligible employer for the 2 years following the last year the employer was an eligible employer. If such failure is due to any acquisition, disposition, or similar transaction involving an eligible employer, the preceding sentence shall not apply.

(ii) Applicable percentage.

(I) In general. The term "applicable percentage" means 3 percent.

(II) Election of lower percentage. An employer may elect to apply a lower percentage (not less than 1 percent) for any year for all employees eligible to participate in the plan for such year if the employer notifies the employees of such lower percentage within a reasonable period of time before the 60-day election period for such year under paragraph (5)(C). An employer may not elect a lower percentage under this subclause for any year if that election would result in the applicable percentage being lower than 3 percent in more than 2 of the years in the 5-year period ending with such year.

(III) Special rule for years arrangement not in effect. If any year in the 5-year period described in subclause (II) is a year prior to the first year for which any qualified salary reduction arrangement is in effect with respect to the employer (or any predecessor), the employer shall be treated as if the level of the employer matching contribution was at 3 percent of compensation for such prior year.

(D) Arrangement may be only plan of employer.

(i) In general. An arrangement shall not be treated as a qualified salary reduction arrangement for any year if the employer (or any predecessor employer) maintained a qualified plan with respect to which contributions were made, or benefits were accrued, for service in any year in the period beginning with the year such arrangement became effective and ending with the year for which the determination is being made. If only individuals other than employees described in subparagraph (A) of section 410(b)(3) are eligible to participate in such arrangement, then the preceding sentence shall be applied without regard to any qualified plan in which only employees so described are eligible to participate.

(ii) Qualified plan. For purposes of this subparagraph, the term "qualified plan" means a plan, contract, pension, or trust described in subparagraph (A) or (B) of section 219(g)(5).

(E) Applicable dollar amount; cost-of-living adjustment.

(i) In general. For purposes of subparagraph (A)(ii), the applicable dollar amount shall be the amount determined in accordance with the following table:

For years beginning in calendar year:	The applicable dollar amount:
2002	$7,000
2003	$8,000
2004	$9,000
2005 or thereafter	$10,000.

(ii) Cost-of-living adjustment. In the case of a year beginning after December 31, 2005, the Secretary shall adjust the $10,000 amount under clause (i) at the same time and in the same manner as under section 415(d), except that the base period taken into account shall be the calendar quarter beginning July 1, 2004, and any increase under this subparagraph which is not a multiple of $500 shall be rounded to the next lower multiple of $500.

(3) Vesting requirements. The requirements of this paragraph are met with respect to a simple retirement account if the employee's rights to any contribution to the simple retirement account are nonforfeitable. For purposes of this paragraph, rules similar to the rules of subsection (k)(4) shall apply.

(4) Participation requirements.

(A) In general. The requirements of this paragraph are met with respect to any simple retirement account for a year only if, under the qualified salary reduction arrangement, all employees of the employer who—

(i) received at least $5,000 in compensation from the employer during any 2 preceding years, and

(ii) are reasonably expected to receive at least $5,000 in compensation during the year,

are eligible to make the election under paragraph (2)(A)(i) or receive the nonelective contribution described in paragraph (2)(B).

(B) Excludable employees. An employer may elect to exclude from the requirement under subparagraph (A) employees described in section 410(b)(3).

(5) Administrative requirements. The requirements of this paragraph are met with respect to any simple retirement account if, under the qualified salary reduction arrangement—

(A) an employer must—

(i) make the elective employer contributions under paragraph (2)(A)(i) not later than the close of the 30-day period following the last day of the month with respect to which the contributions are to be made, and

(ii) make the matching contributions under paragraph (2)(A)(iii) or the nonelective contributions under paragraph (2)(B) not later than the date described in section 404(m)(2)(B),

(B) an employee may elect to terminate participation in such arrangement at any time during the year, except that if an employee so terminates, the arrangement may provide that the employee may not elect to resume participation until the beginning of the next year, and

(C) each employee eligible to participate may elect, during the 60-day period before the beginning of any year (and the 60-day period before the first day such employee is eligible to participate), to participate in the arrangement, or to modify the amounts subject to such arrangement, for such year.

(6) Definitions. For purposes of this subsection—

(A) Compensation.

(i) In general. The term "compensation" means amounts described in paragraphs (3) and (8) of section 6051(a). For purposes of the preceding sentence, amounts described in section 6051(a)(3) shall be determined without regard to section 3401(a)(3).

(ii) Self-employed. In the case of an employee described in subparagraph (B), the term "compensation" means net earnings from self-employment determined under section 1402(a) without regard to any contribution under this subsection. The preceding sentence shall be applied as if the term "trade or business" for purposes of section 1402 included service described in section 1402(c)(6).

(B) Employee. The term "employee" includes an employee as defined in section 401(c)(1).

(C) Year. The term "year" means the calendar year.

(7) Use of designated financial institution. A plan shall not be treated as failing to satisfy the requirements of this subsection or any other provision of this title merely because the employer makes all contributions to the individual retirement accounts or annuities of a designated trustee or issuer. The preceding sentence shall not apply unless each plan participant is notified in writing (either separately or as part of the notice under subsection (l)(2)(C)) that the participant's balance may be transferred without cost or penalty to another individual account or annuity in accordance with subsection (d)(3)(G).

(8) Coordination with maximum limitation under subsection (a). In the case of any simple retirement account, subsections (a)(1) and (b)(2) shall be applied by substituting "the sum of the dollar amount in effect under paragraph (2)(A)(ii) of this subsection and the employer contribution required under subparagraph (A)(iii) or (B)(i) of paragraph (2) of this subsection, whichever is applicable" for "the dollar amount in effect under section 219(b)(1)(A)".

(9) Matching contributions on behalf of self-employed individuals not treated as elective employer contributions. Any matching contribution described in paragraph (2)(A)(iii) which is made on behalf of a self-employed individual (as defined in section 401(c)) shall not be treated as an elective employer contribution to a simple retirement account for purposes of this title.

(10) Special rules for acquisitions, dispositions, and similar transactions.

(A) In general. An employer which fails to meet any applicable requirement by reason of an acquisition, disposition, or similar transaction shall not be treated as failing to meet such requirement during the transition period if—

(i) the employer satisfies requirements similar to the requirements of section 410(b)(6)(C)(i)(II); and

(ii) the qualified salary reduction arrangement maintained by the employer would satisfy the requirements of this subsection after the transaction if the employer which maintained the arrangement before the transaction had remained a separate employer.

(B) Applicable requirement. For purposes of this paragraph, the term "applicable requirement" means—

(i) the requirement under paragraph (2)(A)(i) that an employer be an eligible employer;

(ii) the requirement under paragraph (2)(D) that an arrangement be the only plan of an employer; and

(iii) the participation requirements under paragraph (4).

(C) Transition period. For purposes of this paragraph, the term "transition period" means the period beginning on the date of any transaction described in subparagraph (A) and ending on the last day of the second calendar year following the calendar year in which such transaction occurs.

(q) Deemed IRAs under qualified employer plans.

(1) General rule. If—

(A) a qualified employer plan elects to allow employees to make voluntary employee contributions to a separate account or annuity established under the plan, and

(B) under the terms of the qualified employer plan, such account or annuity meets the applicable requirements of this section or section 408A for an individual retirement account or annuity,

then such account or annuity shall be treated for purposes of this title in the same manner as an individual retirement plan and not as a qualified employer plan (and contributions to such account or annuity as contributions to an individual retirement plan and not to the qualified employer plan). For purposes of subparagraph (B), the requirements of subsection (a)(5) shall not apply.

(2) Special rules for qualified employer plans. For purposes of this title, a qualified employer plan shall not fail to meet any requirement of this title solely by reason of establishing and maintaining a program described in paragraph (1).

(3) Definitions. For purposes of this subsection—

(A) Qualified employer plan. The term "qualified employer plan" has the meaning given such term by section 72(p)(4)(A)(i); except that such term shall also include an eligible deferred compensation plan (as defined in section 457(b)) of an eligible employer described in section 457(e)(1)(A).

(B) Voluntary employee contribution. The term "voluntary employee contribution" means any contribution (other than a mandatory contribution within the meaning of section 411(c)(2)(C))—

(i) which is made by an individual as an employee under a qualified employer plan which allows employees to elect to make contributions described in paragraph (1), and

(ii) with respect to which the individual has designated the contribution as a contribution to which this subsection applies.

(r) Cross references.

(1) For tax on excess contributions in individual retirement accounts or annuities, see section 4973.

(2) For tax on certain accumulations in individual retirement accounts or annuities, see section 4974.

In 2010, P.L. 111-312, Sec. 101(a)(1), substituted "December 31, 2012" for "December 31, 2010" both places it appeared in Sec. 901, P.L. 107-16 [see below], effective as if included in the enactment of P.L. 107-16, EGTRRA, 6/7/2001.

—P.L. 111-312, Sec. 725(a), substituted "December 31, 2011" for "December 31, 2009" in subpara. (d)(8)(F), effective for distributions made in tax. yrs. begin. after 12/31/2009.

—P.L. 111-312, Sec. 725(b)(2), reads as follows:

"(2) Special rule. For purposes of subsections (a)(6), (b)(3), and (d)(8) of section 408 of the Internal Revenue Code of 1986, at the election of the taxpayer (at such time and in such manner as prescribed by the Secretary of the Treasury) any qualified charitable distribution made after December 31, 2010, and before February 1, 2011, shall be deemed to have been made on December 31, 2010.

In 2008, P.L. 110-343, Sec. 205(a)DivC, substituted 'December 31, 2009' for 'December 31, 2007' in subpara. (d)(8)(F), effective for distributions made in tax. yrs. begin. after 12/31/2007.

In 2007, P.L. 110-172, Sec. 3(a), substituted 'all amounts in all individual retirement plans of the individual were distributed during such taxable year and all such plans were treated as contract for purposes of determining under section 72 the aggregate amount which would have been so includible' for 'all amounts distributed from all individual retirement plans were treated as contract under paragraph (2)(A) for purposes of determining the inclusion of such distribution under section 72' in subpara. (d)(8)(D), effective for distributions made in tax. yrs. begin. after 12/31/2005.

In 2006, P.L. 109-432, Sec. 307(a), added para. (d)(9), effective for tax. yrs. begin. after 12/31/2006.

—P.L. 109-280, Sec. 811, of this Act [relating to Sec. 901 of P.L. 107-16, see below], provides:

"SEC. 811. PENSIONS AND INDIVIDUAL RETIREMENT ARRANGEMENT PROVISIONS OF ECONOMIC GROWTH AND TAX RELIEF RECONCILIATION ACT OF 2001 MADE PERMANENT.

"Title IX of the Economic Growth and Tax Relief Reconciliation Act of 2001 shall not apply to the provisions of, and amendments made by, subtitles A through F of title VI of such Act (relating to pension and individual retirement arrangement provisions)."

—P.L. 109-280, Sec. 1201(a), added para. (d)(8), effective for distributions made in tax. yrs. begin. after 12/31/2005.

In 2005, P.L. 109-135, Sec. 201(b)(4)(A), repealed Secs. 101 and 102 of P.L. 109-73.

Prior to repeal, Sec. 101 of P.L. 109-73 read as follows:

"SEC. 101. TAX-FAVORED WITHDRAWALS FROM RETIREMENT PLANS FOR RELIEF RELATING TO HURRICANE KATRINA.

"(a) In general. Section 72(t) of the Internal Revenue Code of 1986 shall not apply to any qualified Hurricane Katrina distribution.

"(b) Aggregate dollar limitation.

"(1) In general. For purposes of this section, the aggregate amount of distributions received by an individual which may be treated as qualified Hurricane Katrina distributions for any taxable year shall not exceed the excess (if any) of—

"(A) $100,000, over

"(B) the aggregate amounts treated as qualified Hurricane Katrina distributions received by such individual for all prior taxable years.

"(2) Treatment of plan distributions. If a distribution to an individual would (without regard to paragraph (1)) be a qualified Hurricane Katrina distribution, a plan shall not be treated as violating any requirement of the Internal Revenue Code of 1986 merely because the plan treats such distribution as a qualified Hurricane Katrina distribution, unless the aggregate amount of such distributions from all plans maintained by the employer (and any member of any controlled group which includes the employer) to such individual exceeds $100,000.

"(3) Controlled group. For purposes of paragraph (2), the term 'controlled group' means any group treated as a single employer under subsection (b), (c), (m), or (o) of section 414 of such Code.

"(c) Amount distributed may be repaid.

"(1) In general. Any individual who receives a qualified Hurricane Katrina distribution may, at any time during the 3-year period beginning on the day after the date on which such distribution was received, make one or more contributions in an aggregate amount not to exceed the amount of such distribution to an eligible retirement plan of which such individual is a beneficiary and to which a rollover contribution of such distribution could be made under section 402(c), 403(a)(4), 403(b)(8), 408(d)(3), or 457(e)(16) of such Code, as the case may be.

"(2) Treatment of repayments of distributions from eligible retirement plans other than IRAs. For purposes of such Code, if a contribution is made pursuant to paragraph (1) with respect to a qualified Hurricane Katrina distribution from an eligible retirement plan other than an individual retirement plan, then the taxpayer shall, to the extent of the amount of the contribution, be treated as having received the qualified Hurricane Katrina distribution in an eligible rollover distribution (as defined in section 402(c)(4) of such Code) and as having transferred the amount to the eligible retirement plan in a direct trustee to trustee transfer within 60 days of the distribution.

"(3) Treatment of repayments for distributions from IRAs. For purposes of such Code, if a contribution is made pursuant to paragraph (1) with respect to a qualified Hurricane Katrina distribution from an individual retirement plan (as defined by section 7701(a)(37) of such Code), then, to the extent of the amount of the contribution, the qualified Hurricane Katrina distribution shall be treated as a distribution described in section 408(d)(3) of such Code and as having been transferred to the eligible retirement plan in a direct trustee to trustee transfer within 60 days of the distribution.

"(d) Definitions. For purposes of this section—

"(1) Qualified Hurricane Katrina distribution. Except as provided in subsection (b), the term 'qualified Hurricane Katrina distribution' means any distribution from an eligible retirement plan made on or after August 25, 2005, and before January 1, 2007, to an individual whose principal place of abode on August 28, 2005, is located in the Hurricane Katrina disaster area and who has sustained an economic loss by reason of Hurricane Katrina.

"(2) Eligible retirement plan. The term 'eligible retirement plan' shall have the meaning given such term by section 402(c)(8)(B) of such Code.

"(e) Income inclusion spread over 3 year period for qualified Hurricane Katrina distributions.

"(1) In general. In the case of any qualified Hurricane Katrina distribution, unless the taxpayer elects not to have this subsection apply for any taxable year, any amount required to be included in gross income for such taxable year shall be so included ratably over the 3-taxable year period beginning with such taxable year.

"(2) Special rule. For purposes of paragraph (1), rules similar to the rules of subparagraph (E) of section 408A(d)(3) of such Code shall apply.

"(f) Special rules.

"(1) Exemption of distributions from trustee to trustee transfer and withholding rules. For purposes of sections 401(a)(31), 402(f), and 3405 of such Code, qualified Hurricane Katrina distributions shall not be treated as eligible rollover distributions.

"(2) Qualified Hurricane Katrina distributions treated as meeting plan distribution requirements. For purposes of such Code, a qualified Hurricane Katrina distribution shall be treated as meeting the requirements of sections 401(k)(2)(B)(i), 403(b)(7)(A)(ii), 403(b)(11), and 457(d)(1)(A) of such Code."

Prior to repeal, Sec. 102 of P.L. 109-73 read as follows:

"SEC. 102. RECONTRIBUTIONS OF WITHDRAWALS FOR HOME PURCHASES CANCELLED DUE TO HURRICANE KATRINA.

"(a) Recontributions.

"(1) In general. Any individual who received a qualified distribution may, during the period beginning on August 25, 2005, and ending on February 28, 2006, make one or more contributions in an aggregate amount not to exceed the amount of such qualified distribution to an eligible retirement plan (as defined in section 402(c)(8)(B) of the Internal Revenue Code of 1986) of which such individual is a beneficiary and to which a rollover contribution of such distribution could be made under section 402(c), 403(a)(4), 403(b)(8), or 408(d)(3) of such Code, as the case may be.

"(2) Treatment of repayments. Rules similar to the rules of paragraphs (2) and (3) of section 101(c) of this Act shall apply for purposes of this section.

"(b) Qualified distribution defined. For purposes of this section, the term 'qualified distribution' means any distribution—

"(1) described in section 401(k)(2)(B)(i)(IV), 403(b)(7)(A)(ii) (but only to the extent such distribution relates to financial hardship), 403(b)(11)(B), or 72(t)(2)(F) of such Code,

"(2) received after February 28, 2005, and before August 29, 2005, and

"(3) which was to be used to purchase or construct a principal residence in the Hurricane Katrina disaster area, but which was not so purchased or constructed on account of Hurricane Katrina."

In 2004, P.L. 108-311, Sec. 404(d), added "For purposes of the preceding sentence, amounts described in section 6051(a)(3) shall be determined without regard to section 3401(a)(3)." at the end of clause (p)(6)(A)(i), effective for tax. yrs. begin. after 12/31/2001 as if included in Sec. 637 of the Economic Growth and Tax Relief Reconciliation Act of 2001, P.L. 107-16.

—P.L. 108-311, Sec. 408(a)(12), substituted "457(e)(16)," for "457(e)(16)" in para. (a)(1) . . . Sec. 408(a)(13), substituted "paragraph (6) or (7) of section 101" for "section 101(6)" in para. (n)(2), enacted 10/4/2004.

In 2002, P.L. 107-358, Sec. 2, added subsec. (c) in Sec. 901 of P.L. 107-16 [see below], effective 12/17/2002.

—P.L. 107-147, Sec. 411(i)(1), amended subpara. (q)(3)(A), effective for plan yrs. begin. after 12/31/2002.

Prior to amendment, subpara. (q)(3)(A) read as follows:

"(A) Qualified employer plan. The term 'qualified employer plan' has the meaning given such term by section 72(p)(4); except such term shall not include a government plan which is not a qualified plan unless the plan is an eligible deferred compensation plan (as defined in section 457(b))."

—P.L. 107-147, Sec. 411(j)(1)(A), substituted "$450" for "$300" in subpara. (k)(2)(C) . . . Sec. 411(j)(1)(B), substituted "$450" for "$300" each place it appeared in para. (k)(8), effective for yrs. begin. after 12/31/2001.

In 2001, P.L. 107-16, Sec. 601(b)(1), substituted "on behalf of any individual in excess of the amount in effect for such taxable year under section 219(b)(1)(A)" for "in excess of $2,000 on behalf of any individual" in para. (a)(1) . . . Sec. 601(b)(2), substituted "the dollar amount in effect under section 219(b)(1)(A)" for "$2,000" in subpara. (b)(2)(B) . . . Sec. 601(b)(3), substituted "the dollar amount in effect under section 219(b)(1)(A)" for "$2,000" in subsec. (b) . . . Sec. 601(b)(4), deleted "$2,000" after "increasing the" in subsec. (j) . . . Sec. 601(b)(5), substituted "the dollar amount in effect under section 219(b)(1)(A)" for "$2,000" in para. (p)(8), effective for tax. yrs. begin. after 12/31/2001.

—P.L. 107-16, Sec. 602(a), redesignated subsec. (q) as (r) and added subsec. (q), effective for plan yrs. begin. after 12/31/2002.

—P.L. 107-16, Sec. 611(c)(1), substituted "$200,000" for "$150,000" each place it appeared in subsec. (k), . . . Sec. 611(f)(1), substituted "the applicable dollar amount" for "$6,000" in clause (p)(2)(A)(ii) . . . Sec. 611(f)(2), amended subpara. (p)(2)(E) . . . Sec. 611(g)(2), added "The preceding sentence shall be applied as if the term 'trade or business' for purposes of section 1402 included service described in section 1402(c)(6)." at the end of clause (p)(6)(A)(ii), effective for yrs. begin. after 12/31/2001.

Prior to amendment, subpara. (p)(2)(E) read as follows:

"(E) Cost-of-living adjustment. The Secretary shall adjust the $6,000 amount under subparagraph (A)(ii) at the same time and in the same manner as under section 415(d), except that the base period taken into account shall be the calendar quarter ending September 30, 1996, and any increase under this subparagraph which is not a multiple of $500 shall be rounded to the next lower multiple of $500."

—P.L. 107-16, Sec. 634, of this Act, reads as follows:

"SEC. 634. MODIFICATION TO MINIMUM DISTRIBUTION RULES.

"The Secretary of the Treasury shall modify the life expectancy tables under the regulations relating to minimum distribution requirements under sections 401(a)(9), 408(a)(6) and (b)(3), 403(b)(10), and 457(d)(2) of the Internal Revenue Code to reflect current life expectancy."

—P.L. 107-16, Sec. 641(e)(8), substituted "403(b)(8), or 457(e)(16)" for "or 403(b)(8)," in para. (a)(1), effective for distributions after 12/31/2001. Sec. 641(f)(2) and (3) of this Act, provides:

"(2) Reasonable notice. No penalty shall be imposed on a plan for the failure to provide the information required by the amendment made by subsection (c) with respect to any distribution made before the date that is 90 days after the date on which the Secretary of the Treasury issues a safe harbor rollover notice after the date of the enactment of this Act, if the administrator of such plan makes a reasonable attempt to comply with such requirement.

"(3) Special rule. Notwithstanding any other provision of law, subsections (h)(3) and (h)(5) of section 1122 of the Tax Reform Act of 1986 shall not apply to any distribution from an eligible retirement plan (as defined in clause (iii) or (iv) of section 402(c)(8)(B) of the Internal Revenue Code of 1986) on behalf of an individual if there was a rollover to such plan on behalf of such individual which is permitted solely by reason of any amendment made by this section."

—P.L. 107-16, Sec. 642(a), added "or" at the end of clause (d)(3)(A)(i), deleted clauses (d)(3)(A)(ii) and (iii), and added clause (d)(3)(A)(ii) . . . Sec. 642(b)(2), substituted "(i) or (ii)" for "(i), (ii), or (iii)" in clause (d)(3)(D)(i) . . . Sec. 642(b)(3), amended subpara. (d)(3)(G), effective for distributions after 12/31/2001. Sec. 642(c)(2) of this Act, provides:

"(2) Special rule. Notwithstanding any other provision of law, subsections (h)(3) and (h)(5) of section 1122 of the Tax Reform Act of 1986 shall not apply to any distribution from an eligible retirement plan (as defined in clause (iii) or (iv) of section 402(c)(8)(B) of the Internal Revenue Code of 1986) on behalf of an individual if there was a rollover to such plan on behalf of such individual which is permitted solely by reason of the amendments made by this section."

Prior to deletion, clauses (d)(3)(A)(ii) and (iii) read as follows:

"(ii) no amount in the account and no part of the value of the annuity is attributable to any source other than a rollover contribution (as defined in section 402) from an employee's trust described in section 401(a) which is exempt from tax under section 501(a) or from an annuity plan described in section 403(a) (and any earnings on such contribution), and the entire amount received (including property and other money) is paid (for the benefit of such individual) into another such trust or annuity plan not later than the 60th day on which the individual receives the payment or the distribution; or

"(iii)(I) the entire amount received (including money and other property) represents the entire interest in the account or the entire value of the annuity,

"(II) no amount in the account and no part of the value of the annuity is attributable to any source other than a rollover contribution from an annuity contract described in section 403(b) and any earnings on such rollover, and

"(III) the entire amount thereof is paid into another annuity contract described in section 403(b) (for the benefit of such individual) not later than the 60th day after he receives the payment or distribution."

Prior to amendment, subpara. (d)(3)(G) read as follows:

"(G) Simple retirement accounts. This paragraph shall not apply to any amount paid or distributed out of a simple retirement account (as defined in subsection (p)) unless—

"(i) it is paid into another simple retirement account, or

"(ii) in the case of any payment or distribution to which section 72(t)(6) does not apply, it is paid into an individual retirement plan."

—P.L. 107-16, Sec. 643(c), added subpara. (d)(3)(H), effective for distributions made after 12/31/2001.

—P.L. 107-16, Sec. 644(b), added subpara. (d)(3)(I), effective for distributions after 12/31/2001.

—P.L. 107-16, Sec. 901, of this Act [as amended by Sec. 2 of P.L. 107-358, and Sec. 101(a)(1), P.L. 111-312, and as related to Sec. 811 of P.L. 109-280, see above], reads as follows:

"SEC. 901. SUNSET OF PROVISIONS OF ACT.

"(a) In general. All provisions of, and amendments made by, this Act shall not apply—

"(1) to taxable, plan, or limitation years beginning after December 31, 2012, or

"(2) in the case of title V, to estates of decedents dying, gifts made, or generation skipping transfers, after December 31, 2012.

"(b) Application of certain laws. The Internal Revenue Code of 1986 and the Employee Retirement Income Security Act of 1974 shall be applied and administered to years, estates, gifts, and transfers described in subsection (a) as if the provisions and amendments described in subsection (a) had never been enacted.

"(c) Exception. Subsection (a) shall not apply to section 803 (relating to no federal income tax on restitution received by victims of the Nazi regime or their heirs or estates)."

In 2000, P.L. 106-554, Sec. 1(a)(7), [which enacted into law Sec. 319(3) of P.L. 106-554] substituted "(5) Distributions of excess contributions after due date for taxable year and certain excess rollover contributions." for "(5) Certain distributions of excess contributions after due date for taxable year." in the heading of para. (d)(5), effective 12/21/2000.

In 1998, P.L. 105-206, Sec. 6015(a), redesignated para. (p)(8) [sic (9)] as (9), effective for yrs. begin. after 12/31/96.

—P.L. 105-206, Sec. 6016(a)(1)(A), deleted "or (B)" after "subparagraph (A)" in clause (p)(2)(D)(i) . . . Sec. 6016(a)(1)(B), added para. (p)(10) . . . Sec. 6016(a)(1)(C)(i), substituted "the preceding sentence shall not apply" for "the preceding sentence shall apply only in accordance with rules similar to the rules of section 410(b)(6)(C)(i)" in subclause (p)(2)(C)(i)(II) . . . Sec. 6016(a)(1)(C)(ii), deleted clause (p)(2)(D)(iii), effective for tax. yrs. begin. after 12/31/96.

Prior to deletion, clause (p)(2)(D)(iii) read as follows:

"(iii) Grace period. In the case of an employer who establishes and maintains a plan under this subsection for 1 or more years and who fails to meet any requirement of this subsection for any subsequent year due to any acquisition, disposition, or similar transaction involving another such employer, rules similar to the rules of section 410(b)(6)(C) shall apply for purposes of this subsection."

—P.L. 105-206, Sec. 6018(b)(1), added "or 402(k)" after "section 402(h)" in subpara. (d)(7)(B) . . . Sec. 6018(b)(2), added "or simple retirement accounts" after "pensions" in the heading of para. (d)(7), effective for tax. yrs. begin. after 12/31/96.

In 1997, P.L. 105-34, Sec. 302(d)(1), deleted "under regulations" after "Secretary may require" in subsec. (i) . . . Sec. 302(d)(2), deleted "in such regulations" after "Secretary prescribes" in para. (i)(1) and subpara. (i)(2)(B), effective for tax. yrs. begin. after 12/31/97.

—P.L. 105-34, Sec. 304(a), amended para. (m)(3), effective for tax. yrs. begin. after 12/31/97.

Prior to amendment, para. (m)(3) read as follows:

"(3) Exception for certain coins. In the case of an individual retirement account, paragraph (2) shall not apply to—

"(A) any gold coin described in paragraph (7), (8), (9), or (10) of section 5112(a) of title 31,

"(B) any silver coin described in section 5112(e) of title 31, or

"(C) any coin issued under the laws of any State."

—P.L. 105-34, Sec. 1501(b), added para. (a)(8)[sic (9)], effective for yrs. begin. after 12/31/96.

—P.L. 105-34, Sec. 1601(d)(1)(A), substituted "31 days" for "30 days" in subsec. (i) . . . Sec. 1601(d)(1)(B), substituted "of an employer if the terms of simplified employee pensions of such employer" for "if the terms of such pension" in subpara. (k)(6)(H) . . . Sec. 1601(d)(1)(C)(i)(I), added "and the issuer of an annuity established under such an arrangement" after "under subsection (p)" in subpara. (l)(2)(B) . . . Sec. 1601(d)(1)(C)(i)(II), added "or issuer" after "trustee" in clause (l)(2)(B)(i) . . . Sec. 1601(d)(1)(D), added para. (p)(8) . . . Sec. 1601(d)(1)(E), added a sentence at the end of clause (p)(2)(D)(i) . . . Sec. 1601(d)(1)(F), added clause (p)(2)(D)(iii) . . . Sec. 1601(d)(1)(G), substituted "simple" for "simplified" in the text preceding subpara. (p)(5)(A), effective for tax. yrs. begin. after 12/31/96.

In 1996, P.L. 104-188, Sec. 1421(a), redesignated subsec. (p) as (q) and added subsec. (p) . . . Sec. 1421(b)(3)(B), added subpara. (d)(3)(G) . . . Sec. 1421(b)(5)(A), added para. (l)(2) . . . Sec. 1421(b)(5)(B), substituted "(1) In general. An employer" for "An employer" in subsec. (l) . . . Sec. 1421(b)(6), added a flush sentence to the end of subsec. (i) . . . Sec. 1421(c), added subpara. (k)(6)(H), effective for tax. yrs. begin. after 12/31/96.

—P.L. 104-188, Sec. 1427(b)(3), substituted "the dollar amount in effect under section 219(b)(1)(A)" for "$2,250" in para. (d)(5), effective for tax. yrs. begin. after 12/31/96.

—P.L. 104-188, Sec. 1431(c)(1)(B), substituted "section 414(q)(4)" for "section 414(q)(7)" in subpara. (k)(2)(C), effective for yrs. begin. after 12/31/96, except that in determining whether an employee is a highly compensated employee for yrs. begin. in 1997, such amendments shall be treated as having been in effect for yrs. begin. in 1996.

—P.L. 104-188, Sec. 1455(b)(1), added "aggregating $10 or more in any calendar year" after "distributions" in subsec. (i), effective for returns, reports, and other statements the due date for which (determined without regard to extension) is after 12/31/96.

In 1994, P.L. 103-465, Sec. 732(d), added "; except that any increase in the $300 amount which is not a multiple of $50 shall be rounded to the next lowest multiple of $50" before the period at the end of para. (k)(8), effective for yrs. begin. after 12/31/94, except as provided in Sec. 732(e)(2) of this Act, which reads as follows:

"(2) Rounding not to result in decreases. The amendments made by this section providing for the rounding of indexed amounts shall not apply to any year to the extent the rounding would require the indexed amount to be reduced below the amount in effect for years beginning in 1994."

In 1993, P.L. 103-66, Sec. 13212(b)(1), substituted "$150,000" for "$200,000" in subpara. (k)(3)(C) and clause (k)(6)(D)(ii) . . . Sec. 13212(b)(2), amended para. (k)(8), effective for benefits accruing in plan yrs. begin. after 12/31/93, except as provided in Sec. 13212(d)(2) and (3) of this Act [reproduced following Code Sec. 401].

Prior to amendment, para. (k)(8) read as follows:

"(8) Cost-of-living adjustment. The Secretary shall adjust the $300 amount in paragraph (2)(C) and the $200,000 amount in paragraphs (3)(C) and (6)(D)(ii) at the same time and in the same manner as under section 415(d), except that in the case of years beginning after 1988, the $200,000 amount (as so adjusted) shall not exceed the amount in effect under section 401(a)(17)."

In 1992, P.L. 102-318, Sec. 521(b)(16), substituted "section 402(c)" for "section 402(a)(5), 402(a)(7)" in para. (a)(1) . . . Sec. 521(b)(17), amended clause (d)(3)(A)(ii) . . . Sec. 521(b)(18), deleted the second sentence of subpara. (d)(3)(B) . . . Sec. 521(b)(19), substituted "section 402(c)(7)" for "section 402(a)(6)(H)" in subpara. (d)(3)(F), effective for distributions after 12/31/92. For special rule, see Sec. 521(e)(2) of this Act which reads as follows:

"(2) Special rule for partial distributions. For purposes of section 402(a)(5)(D)(i)(II) of the Internal Revenue Code of 1986 (as in effect before the amendments made by this section), a distribution before January 1, 1993, which is made before or at the same time as a series of periodic payments shall not be treated as one of such series if it is not substantially equal in amount to other payments in such series."

Prior to amendment, clause (d)(3)(A)(ii) read as follows:

"(ii) the entire amount received (including money and any other property) represents the entire amount in the account or the entire value of the annuity and no amount in the account and no part of the value of the annuity is attributable to any source other than a rollover contribution of a qualified total distribution (as

Employee benefit plans Code Sec. 408

defined in section 402(a)(5)(E)(i)) from an employee's trust described in section 401(a) which is exempt from tax under section 501(a), or an annuity plan described in section 501(a), or an annuity plan described in section 403(a) and any earnings on such sums and the entire amount thereof is paid into another such trust (for the benefit of such individual) or annuity plan not later than the 60th day on which he receives the payment or distribution; or"
Prior to deletion, the second sentence of subpara. (d)(3)(B) read as follows:
"Clause (ii) of subparagraph (A) shall not apply to any amount paid or distributed out of an individual retirement account or an individual retirement annuity to which an amount was contributed which was treated as a rollover contribution by section 402(a)(7) (or in the case of an individual retirement annuity, such section as made applicable by section 403(a)(4)(B))."

In 1989, P.L. 101-239, Sec. 7811(m)(7), deleted "(without regard to subparagraph (C)(ii) thereof)" after "section 401(a)(9)" in paras. (a)(6) and (b)(3), effective for yrs. begin. after 12/31/84.

—P.L. 101-239, Sec. 7841(a)(1), substituted "his spouse or former spouse under a divorce or separation instrument described in subparagraph (A) of section 71(b)(2)" for "his former spouse under a divorce decree or under a written instrument incident to such divorce" in para. (d)(6), effective for transfers after 12/19/89 in tax. yrs. end. after 12/19/89.

In 1988, P.L. 100-647, Sec. 1011(b)(1), substituted "in which the taxable year begins" for "with or within which the taxable year ends" in subpara. (d)(2)(C) and clause (o)(4)(B)(iv) . . . Sec. 1011(b)(2)(A), deleted "to the extent that such contribution exceeds the amount allowable as a deduction under section 219" before "if—" in para. (d)(4) . . . Sec. 1101(b)(2)(B)(i), deleted "excess" before "contribution" each place it appeared in para. (d)(4) . . . Sec. 1101(b)(2)(B)(ii), substituted "contributions" for "excess contributions" in the heading of para. (d)(4) . . . Sec. 1011(b)(3), substituted "shall be computed without regard to section 219(g)." for "(after application of section 408(o)(2)(B)(ii)) shall be increased by the nondeductible limit under section 408(o)(2)(B)." in subpara. (d)(5)(B), effective for contributions and distributions made for tax. yrs. begin. after 12/31/86.

—P.L. 100-647, Sec. 1011(c)(7)(C), added clause (k)(6)(A)(iv), effective for plan yrs. begin. 12/31/87, except as provided in Sec. 1011(c)(7)(E)(ii) of this Act, which reads as follows:

"(ii) In the case of a plan described in section 1105(c)(2) of the Reform Act [P.L. 99-514], the amendments made by this paragraph [Sec. 1011(c)(7)] shall not apply to contributions made pursuant to an agreement described in such section for plan years beginning before the earlier of—

"(I) the later of January 1, 1988, or the date on which the last of such agreements terminates (determined without regard to any extension thereof after February 28, 1986), or

"(II) January 1, 1989."

—P.L. 100-647, Sec. 1011(f)(1), amended subpara. (k)(6)(A) . . . Sec. 1011(f)(2), added "who were eligible to participate (or would have been required to be eligible to participate if a pension was maintained)" after "25 employees" in subpara. (k)(6)(B) . . . Sec. 1011(f)(3)(A), substituted "(not in excess of the first $200,000)" for "(within the meaning of section 414(s))" in clause (k)(6)(D)(ii) . . . Sec. 1011(f)(3)(B), amended subpara. (k)(7)(B) . . . Sec. 1011(f)(3)(C), deleted "total" before "compensation" in subpara. (k)(3)(C) . . . Sec. 1011(f)(3)(D), substituted "paragraphs (3)(C) and (6)(D)(ii)" for "paragraph (3)(C)" in para. (k)(8) . . . Sec. 1011(f)(4), redesignated subpara. (k)(6)(F) as (k)(6)(G) and added subpara. (k)(6)(F) . . . Sec. 1011(f)(5), added para. (d)(7) . . . Sec. 1011(f)(7), added Sec. 1108(h)(2) of P.L. 99-514 [reproduced below], exceptions to the effective date for changes made by Sec. 1108 of P.L. 99-514, see below . . . Sec. 1011(f)(10), added ", except that in the case of years beginning after 1988, the $200,000 amount (as so adjusted) shall not exceed the amount in effect under section 401(a)(17)" after "section 415(d)" in para. (k)(8), effective for tax yrs. begin. after 12/31/86 except as provided in Sec. 1108(h)(2) of P.L. 99-514, see below.
Prior to amendment, subpara. (k)(6)(A) read as follows:

"(A) In general. A simplified employee pension shall not fail to meet the requirements of this subsection for a year merely because, under the terms of the pension—

"(i) an employee may elect to have the employer make payments—

"(I) as elective employer contributions to the simplified employee pension on behalf of the employee, or

"(II) to the employee directly in cash,

"(ii) an election described in clause (i)(I) is made or is in effect with respect to not less than 50 percent of the employees of the employer, and

"(iii) the deferral percentage for such year of each highly compensated employee eligible to participate is not more than the product derived by multiplying the average of the deferral percentages for such year of all employees (other than highly compensated employees) eligible to participate by 1.25."
Prior to amendment, subpara. (k)(7)(B) read as follows:

"(B) Compensation. The term 'compensation' means, in the case of an employee within the meaning of section 401(c)(1), earned income within the meaning of section 401(c)(2)."

—P.L. 100-647, Sec. 1011(i)(5), amended subpara. (k)(3)(B), effective for yrs. begin. after 12/31/86.
Prior to amendment, subpara. (k)(3)(B) read as follows:

"(B) Special rules. For purposes of subparagraph (A)—

"(i) there shall be excluded from consideration employees described in subparagraph (A) or (C) of section 410(b)(3), and

"(ii) an individual shall be considered a shareholder if he owns (with the application of section 318) more than 10 percent of the value of the stock of the employer."

—P.L. 100-647, Sec. 1011A(a)(2)(A), deleted the last sentence in subpara. (d)(3)(A), effective for rollover contributions made in tax yrs. begin. after 12/31/86.
Prior to deletion, the last sentence of subpara. (d)(3)(A) read as follows:

"Clause (ii) shall not apply during the 5-year period beginning on the date of the qualified total distribution referred to in such clause if the individual was treated as a 5-percent owner with respect to such distribution under section 402(a)(5)(F)(ii)."

—P.L. 100-647, Sec. 1018(t)(3)(D), substituted "paragraph" for "subparagraph" in subpara. (d)(3)(E), effective for yrs. begin. after 12/31/84.

—P.L. 100-647, Sec. 6057(a), amended para. (m)(3), effective for acquisitions after 11/10/88.
Prior to amendment, para. (m)(3) read as follows:

"(3) Exception for certain coins. In the case of an individual retirement account, paragraph (2) shall not apply to any gold coin described in paragraph (7), (8), (9), or (10) of section 5112(a) of title 31 or any silver coin described in section 5112(e) of title 31."

In 1986, P.L. 99-514, Sec. 1102(a), redesignated subsec. (o) as (p), and added subsec. (o) . . . Sec. 1102(b)(2), added the sentence at the end of para. (d)(5) . . . Sec. 1102(c), amended paras. (d)(1) and (2) . . . Sec. 1102(e)(2), amended the last sentence of subsec. (i), effective for contributions and distributions made for tax. yrs. begin. after 12/31/86.
Prior to amendment, paras. (d)(1) and (2) read as follows:

"(1) In general. Except as otherwise provided in this subsection, any amount paid or distributed out of an individual retirement account or under an individual retirement annuity shall be included in gross income by the payee or distributee, as the case may be, for the taxable year in which the payment or distribution is received. Notwithstanding any other provision of this title (including chapters 11 and 12), the basis any person in such an account or annuity is zero.

"(2) Distributions of annuity contracts. Paragraph (1) does not apply to any annuity contract which meets the requirements of paragraphs (1), (3), (4), and (5) of subsection (b) and which is distributed from an individual retirement account. Section 72 applies to any such annuity contract, and for purposes of section 72 the investment in such contract is zero."
Prior to amendment, the last sentence of subsec. (i) read as follows:

"The reports required by this subsection shall be filed at such time and in such manner and furnished to such individuals at such time and in such manner as may be required by those regulations."

—P.L. 99-514, Sec. 1108(a), added para. (k)(6) . . . Sec. 1108(d), amended para. (k)(2) [as amended by Sec. 1898(a)(5) of this Act, see below] . . . Sec. 1108(e), added para. (k)(8) . . . Sec. 1108(f), added subpara. (k)(7)(C) . . . Sec. 1108(g)(1)(A), substituted "any highly compensated employee (within the meaning of section 414(q))." for "of any employee who is—

"(i) an officer,

"(ii) a shareholder,

"(iii) a self-employed individual, or

"(iv) highly compensated."

in subpara. (k)(3)(A) . . . Sec. 1108(g)(1)(B)(i), added "and except as provided in subparagraph (D)" after "subparagraph (A)" in subpara. (k)(3)(C) . . . Sec. 1108(g)(1)(B)(ii), added "(other than contributions under an arrangement described in paragraph (b))" after "employer contributions to simplified employee pensions" in subpara. (k)(3)(C) . . . Sec. 1108(g)(1)(B)(iii), deleted the last sentence of subpara. (k)(3)(C) . . . Sec. 1108(g)(1)(C), deleted subparas. (k)(3)(D) and (k)(3)(E) and added subpara. (k)(3)(D) . . . Sec. 1108(g)(4), deleted "calendar" after "pension for a" in subpara. (k)(3)(A) . . . Sec. 1108(g)(6), added para. (k)(9), effective for yrs. begin. after 12/31/86, except as provided by Sec. 1108(h)(2) of this Act [as added by Sec. 1011(f)(7) of P.L. 100-647] which reads as follows:

"(2) Integration rules. Subparagraphs (D) and (E) of section 408(k)(3) of the Internal Revenue Code of 1954 (as in effect before the amendments made by this section) shall continue to apply for years beginning after December 31, 1986, and before January 1, 1989, except that employer contributions under an arrangement under section 408(k)(6) of the Internal Revenue Code of 1986 (as added by this section) may not be integrated under such subparagraphs."
Prior to amendment, para. (k)(2) read as follows:

"(2) Participation requirements. This paragraph is satisfied with respect to a simplified employee pension for a calendar year only if for such year the employer contributes to the simplified employee pension of each employee who—

"(A) has attained age 21, and

"(B) has performed service for the employer during at least 3 of the immediately preceding 5 calendar years.

For purposes of this paragraph, there shall be excluded from consideration employees described in subparagraph (A) or (C) of section 410(b)(3)."
Prior to deletion, the last sentence of subpara. (k)(3)(C) read as follows:
"The Secretary shall annually adjust the $200,000 amount contained in the preceding sentence at the same time and in the same manner as he adjusts the dollar amount contained in section 415(c)(1)(A)."
Prior to deletion, subparas. (k)(3)(D) and (k)(3)(E) read as follows:

"(D) Treatment of certain contributions and taxes. Except as provided in this subparagraph, employer contributions do not meet the requirements of this paragraph unless such contributions meet the requirements of this paragraph without taking into account contributions or benefits under chapter 2 (relating to tax on self-employment income), chapter 21 (relating to Federal Insurance Contribution Act), title II of the Social Security Act, or any other Federal or State law. If the employer does not maintain an integrated plan at any time during the taxable year, OASDI contributions (as defined in section 401(1)(2)) may, for purposes of this paragraph, be taken into account as contributions by the employer to the employee's simplified employee pension, but only if such contributions are so taken into account with respect to each employee maintaining a simplified employee pension.

"(E) Integrated plan defined. For purposes of subparagraph (D), the term 'integrated plan' means a plan which meets the requirements of section 401(a) or 403(a) but would not meet such requirements if contributions or benefits under chapter 2 (relating to tax on self-employment income), chapter 21 (relating to Federal Insurance Contributions Act), title II of the Social Security Act, or any other Federal or State law were not taken into account."

—P.L. 99-514, Sec. 1121(c)(2), deleted the third and fourth parenthetical phrases in clause (d)(3)(A)(ii), effective for yrs. begin. after 12/31/86. This amendment was rendered inoperable by Sec. 1875(c)(8)(A) and (B) of this Act, see below.

—P.L. 99-514, Sec. 1122(e)(2)(B), added subpara. (d)(3)(F), effective for amounts transferred to an employee before, on, or after 10/22/86, except that in the case of an amount transferred before 10/23/86, the 60-day period referred to in Code Sec. 402(a)(5)(C) shall not expire before 12/20/86.

—P.L. 99-514, Sec. 1123(d)(2), deleted subsec. (f), effective for tax yrs. begin. after 12/31/86, except as provided in Sec. 1123(e)(3) and (4) of this Act which reads as follows:

"(3) Exception where distribution commences. The amendments made by this section shall not apply to distributions to any employee from a plan maintained by any employer if—

"(A) as of March 1, 1986, the employee separated from service with the employer,

"(B) as of March 1, 1986, the accrued benefit of the employee was in pay status pursuant to a written election providing a specific schedule for the distribution of the entire accrued benefit of the employee, and

"(C) such distribution is made pursuant to such written election."

"(4) Transition rule. The amendments made by this section shall not apply with respect to any benefits with respect to which a designation is in effect under section 242(b)(2) of the Tax Equity and Fiscal Responsibility Act of 1982."

Prior to deletion, subsec. (f) read as follows:

"(f) Additional tax on certain amounts included in gross income before age 59½.

"(1) Early distributions from an individual retirement account, etc. If a distribution from an individual retirement account or under an individual retirement annuity to the individual for whose benefit such account or annuity was established is made before such individual attains age 59½ his tax under this chapter for the taxable year in which such distribution is received shall be increased by an amount equal to 10 percent of the amount of the distribution which is includible in his gross income for such taxable year.

"(2) Disqualification cases. If an amount is includible in gross income for a taxable year under subsection (e) and the taxpayer has not attained age 59½ before the beginning of such taxable year, his tax under this chapter for such taxable year shall be increased by an amount equal to 10 percent of such amount so required to be included in his gross income.

"(3) Disability cases. Paragraphs (1) and (2) do not apply if the amount paid or distributed, or the disqualification of the account or annuity under subsection (e), is attributable to the taxpayer becoming disabled within the meaning of section 72(m)(7)."

—P.L. 99-514, Sec. 1144(a), added para. (m)(3), effective for acquisitions after 12/31/86.

—P.L. 99-514, Sec. 1852(a)(1)(A), substituted "(without regard to subparagraph (C)(ii) thereof) and the incidental death benefit requirements of section 401(a)" for "(relating to required distributions)" in para. (a)(6) . . . Sec. 1852(a)(1)(B), substituted "(without regard to subpara. (C)(ii) thereof) and the incidental death benefit requirements of section 401(a)" for "(relating to required distributions)" in para. (b)(3) . . . Sec. 1852(a)(5)(C), added subpara. (d)(3)(E) . . . Sec. 1852(a)(7)(A), substituted "paragraphs (1) through (6)" for "paragraphs (1) through (7)" in para (c)(1), effective for yrs. begin. after 12/31/84. For transitional rules, see Sec. 521(e)(3)-(5) of P.L. 98-369, reproduced below.

—P.L. 99-514, Sec. 1875(c)(6)(A), substituted "the dollar limitation in effect under section 415(c)(1)(A) for such taxable year" for "$15,000" in para. (d)(5) . . . Sec. 1875(c)(8)(A), deleted "(other than a trust forming part of a plan under which the individual was an employee within the meaning of section 401(c)(1) at the time contributions were made on his behalf under the plan)" after "section 501(a)" in clause (d)(3)(A)(ii) . . . Sec. 1875(c)(8)(B), deleted "(other than a plan under which the individual was an employee within the meaning of section 401(c)(1) at the time contributions were made on his behalf under the plan)" after "section 403(a)" in clause (d)(3)(A)(ii) . . . Sec. 1875(c)(8)(C), added the sentence at the end of subpara. (d)(3)(A), effective for individuals dying after 12/31/83.

—P.L. 99-514, Sec. 1898(a)(5), substituted "age 21" for "age 25" in subpara. (k)(2)(A) (as in effect before amendment by Sec. 1108(d) of this Act, see above), effective for plan yrs. begin. after 10/22/86.

In 1984, P.L. 98-369, Sec. 147(a), added "(and the years to which they relate)" after "contributions" in subsec. (i), effective for contributions made after 12/31/84.

—P.L. 98-369, Sec. 491(d)(19), substituted "or 403(b)(8)" for "403(b)(8), 405(d)(3), or 409(b)(3)(C)" in para. (a)(1) . . . Sec. 491(d)(20), deleted "or retirement bond" after "(other than an endowment contract)" in clause (d)(3)(A)(i) . . . Sec. 491(d)(21), substituted "or an individual retirement annuity" for ", individual retirement annuity, or a retirement bond" in subpara. (d)(3)(B) . . . Sec. 491(d)(22), deleted "bond," after "annuity," in clause (d)(3)(D)(ii) . . . Sec. 491(d)(23), amended para. (d)(6) . . . Sec. 491(d)(24), substituted "or 403(a)" for ", 403(a), or 405(a)" in subpara. (k)(3)(E), *effective for obligations issued after 12/31/83.*

Prior to amendment, para. (d)(6) read as follows:

"(6) Transfer of account incident to divorce. The transfer of an individual's interest in an individual retirement account, individual retirement annuity, or retirement bond to his former spouse under a divorce decree or under a written instrument incident to such divorce is not to be considered a taxable transfer made by such individual notwithstanding any other provision of this subtitle, and such interest at the time of the transfer is to be treated as an individual retirement account of such spouse, and not of such individual. Thereafter such account, annuity, or bond for purposes of this subtitle is to be treated as maintained for the benefit of such spouse."

—P.L. 98-369, Sec. 521(b)(1), deleted paras. (a)(6) and (7) and added para. (a)(6) . . . Sec. 521(b)(2), deleted paras. (b)(3) and (4), added new para. (b)(3), and redesignated para. (b)(5) as para. (b)(4), effective for yrs. begin. after 12/31/84. Sec. 521(e)(3)-(5) of this Act provides:

"(3) Transition rule. A trust forming part of a plan shall not be disqualified under paragraph (9) of section 401(a) of the Internal Revenue Code of 1954, as amended by subsection (a)(1), by reason of distributions under a designation (before January 1, 1984) by any employee in accordance with a designation described in section 242(b)(2) of the Tax Equity and Fiscal Responsibility Act of 1982 (as in effect before the amendments made by this Act).

"(4) Special rule for governmental plans. In the case of a governmental plan (within the meaning of section 414(d) of the Internal Revenue Code of 1954), paragraph (1) shall be applied by substituting '1986' for '1984'.

"(5) Special rule for collective bargaining agreements. In the case of a plan maintained pursuant to one or more collective bargaining agreements ratified on or before the date of the enactment of this Act between employee representatives and one or more employers, the amendments made by this section shall not apply to years beginning before the earlier of—

"(A) the date on which the last of the collective bargaining agreements relating to the plan terminates (determined without regard to any extension thereof agreed to after the date of the enactment of this Act), or

"(B) January 1, 1988.

For purposes of subparagraph (A), any plan amendment made pursuant to a collective bargaining agreement relating to the plan which amends the plan solely to conform to any requirement added by this section shall not be treated as a termination of such collective bargaining agreement."

Prior to deletion, paras. (a)(6) and (7) read as follows:

"(6) The entire interest of an individual for whose benefit the trust is maintained will be distributed to him not later than the close of his taxable year in which he attains age 70½, or will be distributed, commencing before the close of such taxable year, in accordance with regulations prescribed by the Secretary, over—

"(A) the life of such individual or the lives of such individual and his spouse, or

"(B) a period not extending beyond the life expectancy of such individual or the life expectancy of such individual and his spouse.

"(7) If—

"(A) an individual for whose benefit the trust is maintained dies before his entire interest has been distributed to him, or

"(B) distribution has been commenced as provided in paragraph (6) to his surviving spouse and such surviving spouse dies before the entire interest has been distributed to such spouse,

the entire interest (or the remaining part of such interest if distribution thereof has commenced) will be distributed within 5 years after his death (or the death of the surviving spouse). The preceding sentence shall not apply if distributions over a term certain commenced before the death of the individual for whose benefit the trust was maintained and the term certain is for a period permitted under paragraph (6)."

Prior to deletion, paras. (b)(3) and (4) read as follows:

"(3) The entire interest of the owner will be distributed to him not later than the close of his taxable year in which he attains age 70½, or will be distributed, in accordance with regulations prescribed by the Secretary, over—

"(A) the life of such owner or the lives of such owner and his spouse, or

"(B) a period not extending beyond the life expectancy of such owner or the life expectancy of such owner and his spouse.

"(4) If—

"(A) the owner dies before his entire interest has been distributed to him, or

"(B) distribution has been commenced as provided in paragraph (3) to his surviving spouse and such surviving spouse dies before the entire interest has been distributed to such spouse,

the entire interest (or the remaining part of such interest if distribution thereof has commenced) will be distributed within 5 years after his death (or the death of his surviving spouse). The preceding sentence shall not apply if distributions over a term certain commenced before the death of the owner and the term certain is for a period permitted under paragraph (3)."

—P.L. 98-369, Sec. 522(d)(12), substituted "rollover contribution of a qualified total distribution (as defined in section 402(a)(5)(E)(i)) from an employee's trust" for "rollover contribution from an employee's trust" in clause (d)(3)(A)(ii), effective for distributions made after 7/18/84, in tax. yrs. end. after 7/18/84.

—P.L. 98-369, Sec. 713(c)(2)(B), substituted "(as defined in subsection (n))" for "(as defined in section 401(d)(1))" in subsec. (h) . . . Sec. 713(f)(2), amended para. (k)(1) . . . Sec. 713(f)(5)(B), added the sentence "The Secretary shall annually adjust the $200,000 amount contained in the preceding sentence at the same time and in the same manner as he adjusts the dollar amount contained in section 415(c)(1)(A)." at the end of subpara. (k)(3)(C), effective for yrs. begin. after 12/31/83.

Prior to amendment, para. (k)(1) read as follows:

"(1) In general. For purposes of this title, the term 'simplified employee pension' means an individual retirement account or individual retirement annuity with respect to which the requirements of paragraphs (2), (3), (4), and (5) of this subsection are met."

—P.L. 98-369, Sec. 713(g)(1), amended Sec. 243(c) of P.L. 97-248, the effective date for changes made by Sec. 243(b)(1)(A), to apply to "individuals dying after December 31, 1983" rather than to "taxable years beginning after December 31, 1983" (see below).
—P.L. 98-369, Sec. 713(g)(2), redesignated subpara. (d)(3)(C)[sic (D)] as subpara. (d)(3)(D), effective for individuals dying after 12/31/83.
—P.L. 98-369, Sec. 713(j), amended subpara. (k)(3)(D), effective for yrs. begin. after 12/31/83.
Prior to amendment, subpara. (k)(3)(D) read as follows:
"(D) Treatment of certain contributions and taxes. Except as provided in this subparagraph, employer contributions do not meet the requirements of this paragraph unless such contributions meet the requirements of this paragraph without taking into account contributions or benefits under chapter 2 (relating to tax on self-employment income), chapter 21 (relating to Federal Insurance Contribution Act), title II of the Social Security Act, or any other Federal or State law. If the employer does not maintain an integrated plan at any time during the taxable year, taxes paid under section 3111 (relating to tax on employers) with respect to an employee may, for purposes of this paragraph, be taken into account as a contribution by the employer to an employee's simplified employee pension. If contributions are made to the simplified employee pension of an owner-employee, the preceding sentence shall not apply unless taxes paid by all such owner-employees under chapter 2, and the taxes which would be payable under chapter 2 by such owner-employees but for paragraphs (4) and (5) of section 1402(c), are taken into account as contributions by the employer on behalf of such owner-employees."
In 1983, P.L. 97-448, Sec. 103(d)(1)(A), substituted "on behalf of each employee (other than an employee within the meaning of section 401(c)(1))" for "on behalf of each employee" in clause (k)(3)(C)(ii) . . . Sec. 103(d)(1)(B), substituted "$17,000" for "$15,000" in subsec. (j), effective for tax. yrs. begin. after 12/31/81.
—P.L. 97-448, Sec. 103(d)(3), amended Sec. 312(f)(1) of P.L. 97-34, the effective date for changes made by Sec. 312 of P.L. 97-34 to "taxable years beginning after December 31, 1981" from "to plans which include employees within the meaning of section 401(c)(1) with respect to taxable years beginning after 12/31/81" [see below].
—P.L. 97-448, Sec. 103(e)(1), corrected Sec. 314(b)(1) of P.L. 97-34 to redesignate subsec. (m) as subsec. (n) and insert new subsec. (n) following subsec. (l) instead of redesignating subsec. (n) as subsec. (o) and inserting new subsec. (n) after subsec. (m), [see below] . . . Sec. 103(e)(2), redesignated subsec. (n) as added by Sec. 314(b)(1) of P.L. 97-34 as subsec. (m), effective for tax. yrs. begin. after 12/31/81.
In 1982, P.L. 97-248, Sec. 237(e)(3)(A), substituted "as defined in subsection (n)" for "as defined in section 401(d)(1)" in para. (a)(2) . . . Sec. 237(e)(3)(B), redesignated the subsec. relating to cross references as subsec. (o) and added new subsec. (n) effective for yrs. begin. after 12/31/83.
—P.L. 97-248, Sec. 238(d)(3), amended subsec. (j) . . . Sec. 238(d)(4)(A), deleted para. (k)(6) . . . Sec. 238(d)(4)(B), substituted "and (5)" for "(5), and (6)" in para. (k)(1) . . . Sec. 238(d)(4)(C), amended subpara. (k)(3)(C), effective for yrs. begin. after 12/31/83.
Prior to amendment, subsec. (j) read as follows:
"(j) Increase in maximum limitations for simplified employee pensions.
"In the case of a simplified employee pension, this section shall be applied by substituting '$15,000' for '$2000' in the following provisions:
"(1) paragraph (1) of subsection (a), and
"(2) paragraph (2) of subsection (b)."
Prior to deletion, para. (k)(6) read as follows:
"(6) Employer may not maintain plan to which section 401(j) applies. The requirements of this paragraph are met with respect to a simplified employee pension for a calendar year unless the employer maintains during any part of such year a plan—
"(A) some or all of the active participants in which are employees (within the meaning of section 401(c)(1)) or shareholder-employees (as defined in section 1379(d)), and
"(B) to which section 401(j) applies."
Prior to amendment, subpara. (k)(3)(C) read as follows:
"(C) Contributions must bear a uniform relationship to total compensation. For purposes of subparagraph (A), employer contributions to simplified employee pensions shall be considered discriminatory unless
"(i) contributions thereto bear a uniform relationship to the total compensation (not in excess of the first $200,000) of each employee maintaining a simplified employee pension, and
"(ii) if compensation in excess of $100,000 is taken into account under a simplified employee pension for an employee, contributions to a simplified employee pension on behalf of each employee for whom a contribution is required are at a rate (expressed as a percentage of compensation) not less than 7.5 percent."
—P.L. 97-248, Sec. 243(a)(1), amended para. (a)(7) . . . Sec. 243(a)(2), amended para. (b)(4), effective for individuals dying after 12/31/83.
Prior to amendment, para. (a)(7) read as follows:
"(7) If an individual for whose benefit the trust is maintained dies before his entire interest has been distributed to him, or if distribution has been commenced as provided in paragraph (6) to his surviving spouse and such surviving spouse dies before the entire interest has been distributed to such spouse, the entire interest (or the remaining part of such interest if distribution thereof has commenced) will, within 5 years after his death (or the death of the surviving spouse), be distributed, or applied to the purchase of an immediate annuity for his beneficiary or beneficiaries (or the beneficiary or beneficiaries of his surviving spouse) which will be payable for the life of such beneficiary or beneficiaries (or for a term certain not extending beyond the life expectancy of such beneficiary or beneficiaries) and which annuity will be immediately distributed to such beneficiary or beneficiaries. The preceding sentence does not apply if distributions over a term certain commenced before the death of the individual for whose benefit the trust was maintained and the term certain is for a period permitted under paragraph (6)."
Prior to amendment, para. (b)(4) read as follows:
"(4) If the owner dies before his entire interest has been distributed to him, or if distribution has been commenced as provided in paragraph (3) to his surviving spouse and such surviving spouse dies before the entire interest has been distributed to such spouse, the entire interest (or the remaining part of such interest if distribution thereof has commenced) will, within 5 years after his death (or the death of the surviving spouse), be distributed, or applied to the purchase of an immediate annuity for his beneficiary or beneficiaries (or the beneficiary or beneficiaries of his surviving spouse) which will be payable for the life of such beneficiary or beneficiaries (or for a term certain not extending beyond the life expectancy of such beneficiary or beneficiaries) and which annuity will be immediately distributed to such beneficiary or beneficiaries. The preceding sentence shall have no application if distributions over a term certain commenced before the death of the owner and the term certain is for a period permitted under paragraph (3)."
—P.L. 97-248, Sec. 243(b)(1)(A), added subpara. (d)(3)(C), effective [as amended by Sec. 713(g)(1) of P.L. 98-369, see above] for individuals dying after 12/31/83.
—P.L. 97-248, Sec. 355(a)(1), added subpara. (d)(3)(C) [sic (D)], effective for distributions made after 12/31/82, in tax. yrs. ending after 12/31/82.
In 1981, P.L. 97-34, Sec. 311(g)(1)(A), (B), and (C), substituted "$2,000" for "$1,500" in para. (a)(1), subsecs. (b) and (j) . . . Sec. 311(g)(2), substituted "$2,500" for "$1,750" in subpara. (d)(5)(A) . . . Sec. 311(h)(2), substituted "section 219" for "section 219 or 220" in paras. (d)(4) and (5), effective for tax. yrs. begin. after 12/31/81. Sec. 311(i)(2) of this Act provides:
"(2) Transitional rule. For purposes of the Internal Revenue Code of 1954, any amount allowed as a deduction under section 220 of such Code (as in effect before its repeal by this Act) shall be treated as if it were allowed by section 219 of such Code."
—P.L. 97-34, Sec. 312(b)(2), amended subpara. (k)(3)(C) . . . Sec. 312(c)(5), substituted "$15,000" for "$7,500" in para. (d)(5) and subsec. (j), effective for tax. yrs. begin. after 12/31/81.
Prior to amendment, subpara. (k)(3)(C) read as follows:
"(C) Contributions must bear a uniform relationship to total compensation. For purposes of subparagraph (A), employer contributions to simplified employee pensions shall be considered discriminatory unless contributions thereto bear a uniform relationship to the total compensation (not in excess of the first $100,000) of each employee maintaining a simplified employee pension."
—P.L. 97-34, Sec. 313(b)(2), added "405(d)(3)" after "403(b)(8)" in para. (a)(1), effective for redemptions in tax. yrs. end. after 8/13/81.
—P.L. 97-34, Sec. 314(b)(1), redesignated subsec. (n) as (o) and added subsec. (n) effective for property acquired after 12/31/81, in tax. yrs. end. after 12/31/81.
In 1980, P.L. 96-605, Sec. 225(b)(3), substituted "section 410(b)(3)" for "section 410(b)(2)" in para. (k)(2) . . . Sec. 225(b)(4), substituted "section 410(b)(3)" for "section 410(b)(2)", in clause (k)(3)(B)(i), effective for plan yrs. begin. after 12/31/80.
—P.L. 96-222, Sec. 101(a)(10)(A), added "For purposes of this paragraph, there shall be excluded from consideration employees described in subparagraph (A) or (C) of section 410(b)(2)." at the end of para. (k)(2), effective for tax. yrs. begin. after 12/31/78.
—P.L. 96-222, Sec. 101(a)(10)(C), added "If employer contributions on behalf of the individual are paid for the taxable year to a simplified employee pension, the dollar limitation of the preceding sentence shall be increased by the lesser of the amount of such contributions or $7,500." to the end of subpara. (d)(5)(A), effective for distributions in tax. yrs. begin. after 12/31/75. For transitional rules, see Sec. 157(c)(2)(B) of P.L. 95-600 reproduced below.
—P.L. 96-222, Sec. 101(a)(10)(F)(i), substituted "(5), and (6)" for "and (5)" in para. (k)(1) . . . Sec. 101(a)(10)(F)(ii), redesignated para. (k)(6) as para. (k)(7) . . . Sec. 101(a)(10)(F)(iii), added para. (k)(6) . . . Sec. 101(a)(10)(G)(i), substituted "If the employer does not maintain an integrated plan at any time during the taxable year, taxes paid" for "Taxes paid" in subpara. (k)(3)(D) . . . Sec. 101(a)(10)(G)(ii), added new subpara. (k)(3)(E) . . . Sec. 101(a)(10)(J)(i), added "and" at the end of para. (j)(1), substituted a period for ", and" at the end of para. (j)(2) and deleted para. (j)(3), effective for tax. yrs. begin. after 12/31/78.
Prior to deletion, para. (j)(3) read as follows:
"(3) paragraph (5) of subsection (b)."
—P.L. 96-222, Sec. 101(a)(13)(A), amended Sec. 156(d) the effective date for changes made by Sec. 156 of P.L. 95-600 so that amendments made by Sec. 156(c) are effective for distributions or transfers made after 12/31/77, in tax. yrs. begin after 12/31/77 rather than effective for distributions or transfers made after 12/31/78, in tax. yrs. begin. after 12/31/78 [see below].
—P.L. 96-222, Sec. 101(a)(14)(A), substituted "subsection" for "section" each place it appeared in Sec. 157(h)(3) of P.L. 95-600 [see below] . . . Sec. 101(a)(14)(D), substituted "any payment made during 78" for "any payment" and substituted "December 31, 1980" for "December 31, 1978" in Sec. 157(h)(3)(B) of P.L. 95-600 [see below].
—P.L. 96-222, Sec. 101(a)(14)(B), added "402(a)(7)" after "402(a)(5)," in para. (a)(1), effective [as amended by Sec. 101(a)(13)(A) of this Act, see above] for distributions or transfers made after '78, in tax. yrs. begin. after 12/31/77.
—P.L. 96-222, Sec. 101(a)(14)(E)(ii), amended subpara. (d)(5)(B), effective for distributions in tax. yrs. begin. after 12/31/75. For transitional rules see Sec. 157(c)(2)(B) of P.L. 95-600 reproduced below.
Prior to amendment, subpara. (d)(5)(B) read as follows:

"(B) Excess rollover contributions attributable to erroneous information. If—
"(i) the taxpayer reasonably relies on information supplied pursuant to subtitle F for determining the amount of a rollover contribution, but
"(ii) such information was erroneous, subparagraph (A) shall be applied by increasing the dollar limit set forth therein by that portion of the excess contribution which was attributable to such information."

In 1978, P.L. 95-600, Sec. 152(a), redesignated subsec. (j) as subsec. (m) and added subsec. (j) . . . Sec. 152(b), added subsecs. (k) and (l), effective for tax. yrs. begin. after 12/31/78.

—P.L. 95-600, Sec. 156(c)(1), deleted "or" at the end of clause (d)(3)(A)(i), substituted "; or" for the period at the end of clause (d)(3)(A)(ii), and added clause (d)(3)(A)(iii) . . . Sec. 156(c)(3), added "403(b)(8)," after "403(a)(4)," in para. (a)(1), effective [as amended by Sec. 101(a)(13)(A) of P.L. 96-222, see above] for distributions or transfers made after 12/31/77, in tax. yrs. begin. after 12/31/77.

—P.L. 95-600, Sec. 157(c)(1), redesignated para. (d)(5) as (d)(6) and added new para. (d)(5), effective for distributions in tax. yrs. begin. after 12/31/75. Sec. 157(c)(2)(B) of the Act provides:

"(B) Transitional rule. In the case of contributions for taxable years beginning before January 1, 1978, paragraph (5) of section 408(d) of the Internal Revenue Code of 1954 shall be applied as if such paragraph did not contain any dollar limitation."

—P.L. 95-600, Sec. 157(d)(1), amended para. (b)(2), effective for contracts issued after 11/6/78. Sec. 157(d)(3) of the Act, provides:

"(3) Tax relief for fixed premium contracts heretofore issued. In the case of any annuity or endowment contract issued on or before the date of the enactment of this Act which would be an individual retirement annuity within the meaning of section 408(b) of the Internal Revenue Code of 1954 (as amended by paragraph (1)) but for the fact that the premiums under the contract are fixed, at the election of the taxpayer an exchange before January, 1, 1981, of that contract for an individual retirement annuity within the meaning of such section 408(b) (as amended by paragraph (1)) shall be treated as a nontaxable exchange which does not constitute a distribution."

Prior to amendment, para. (b)(2) read as follows:

"(2) The annual premium under the contract will not exceed $1,500 and any refund of premiums will be applied before the close of the calendar year following the year of the refund toward the payment of future premiums or the purchase of additional benefits."

—P.L. 95-600, Sec. 157(e)(1)(A), added "on behalf of any individual" following "annual premium" in subpara. (b)(2)(B), as amended by Sec. 157(d)(1) of this Act, effective for tax. yrs. begin. after 12/31/76.

—P.L. 95-600, Sec. 157(g)(3), added the sentence at the end of subpara. (d)(3)(B), effective for lump-sum distributions completed after 12/31/78, in tax. yrs. end. after 12/31/78.

—P.L. 95-600, Sec. 157(h)(2), substituted "1-year period" for "3-year period" in the first sentence of subpara. (d)(3)(B), effective [as amended by Sec. 101(a)(14)(D) of P.L. 96-222. See above] for payments made in tax. yrs. begin. after '77. Sec. 157(h)(3)(B) of the Act provides as follows:

"(B) Transitional rule. In the case of any payment which is described in section 402(a)(5)(A) or 403(a)(4)(A) of the Internal Revenue Code of 1954 by reason of the amendments made by this section, the applicable period specified in section 402(a)(5)(C) of such Code (or in the case of an individual retirement annuity, such section as made applicable by section 403(a)(4)(B) of such Code) shall not expire before the close of December 31, 1978."

—P.L. 95-600, Sec. 703(c)(4), amended Sec. 1501(b)(5)(A) of P.L. 94-455, to insert "or 220" after "219" each place it appeared in para. (d)(4), effective for tax. yrs. begin. after 12/31/76. See below.

In 1976, P.L. 94-455, Sec. 1501(b)(2), added "(or spouse of an employee or member)" after "member" in para. (c)(2), effective for tax. yrs. begin. after 12/31/76.

—P.L. 94-455, Sec. 1501(b)(5), added "or 220" after "219" in para. (d)(4) and amended the last sentence of para. (d)(4), effective for tax. yrs. begin. after 12/31/76.

Prior to amendment, the last sentence of para. (d)(4) read as follows:

"Any net income described in subparagraph (c) shall be included in the gross income of the individual for the taxable year in which received."

—P.L. 94-455, Sec. 1501(b)(10), amended the second sentence of para. (d)(1), effective for tax. yrs. begin. after 12/31/76.

Prior to amendment, the second sentence of para. (d)(1) read as follows:

"The basis of any person in such an account or annuity is zero."

—P.L. 94-455, Sec. 1906(b)(13)(A), substituted "Secretary" for "Secretary or his delegate" each place it appeared in subsecs. (a), (b), (h), and (i), effective for tax. yrs. begin. after 12/31/76.

In 1974, P.L. 93-406, Sec. 2002(b), added Code Sec. 408, effective for tax. yrs. begin. after 12/31/74.

Sec. 408A. Roth IRAs.
(a) General rule.

Except as provided in this section, a Roth IRA shall be treated for purposes of this title in the same manner as an individual retirement plan.

(b) Roth IRA.

For purposes of this title, the term "Roth IRA" means an individual retirement plan (as defined in section 7701(a)(37)) which is designated (in such manner as the Secretary may prescribe) at the time of the establishment of the plan as a Roth IRA. Such designation shall be made in such manner as the Secretary may prescribe.

(c) Treatment of contributions.

(1) No deduction allowed. No deduction shall be allowed under section 219 for a contribution to a Roth IRA.

(2) Contribution limit. The aggregate amount of contributions for any taxable year to all Roth IRAs maintained for the benefit of an individual shall not exceed the excess (if any) of—

(A) the maximum amount allowable as a deduction under section 219 with respect to such individual for such taxable year (computed without regard to subsection (d)(1) or (g) of such section), over

(B) the aggregate amount of contributions for such taxable year to all other individual retirement plans (other than Roth IRAs) maintained for the benefit of the individual.

(3) Limits based on modified adjusted gross income.

(A) Dollar limit. The amount determined under paragraph (2) for any taxable year shall not exceed an amount equal to the amount determined under paragraph (2)(A) for such taxable year, reduced (but not below zero) by the amount which bears the same ratio to such amount as—

(i) the excess of—

(I) the taxpayer's adjusted gross income for such taxable year, over

(II) the applicable dollar amount, bears to

(ii) $15,000 ($10,000 in the case of a joint return or a married individual filing a separate return).

The rules of subparagraphs (B) and (C) of section 219(g)(2) shall apply to any reduction under this subparagraph.

(B) Definitions. For purposes of this paragraph—

(i) adjusted gross income shall be determined in the same manner as under section 219(g)(3), except that any amount included in gross income under subsection (d)(3) shall not be taken into account, and

(ii) the applicable dollar amount is—

(I) in the case of a taxpayer filing a joint return, $150,000,

(II) in the case of any other taxpayer (other than a married individual filing a separate return), $95,000, and

(III) in the case of a married individual filing a separate return, zero.

(C) Marital status. Section 219(g)(4) shall apply for purposes of this paragraph.

(D) Inflation adjustment. In the case of any taxable year beginning in a calendar year after 2006, the dollar amounts in subclauses (I) and (II) of subparagraph (B)(ii) shall each be increased by an amount equal to—

(i) such dollar amount, multiplied by

(ii) the cost-of-living adjustment determined under section 1(f)(3) for the calendar year in which the taxable year begins, determined by substituting "calendar year 2005" for "calendar year 1992" in subparagraph (B) thereof.

Any increase determined under the preceding sentence shall be rounded to the nearest multiple of $1,000.

(4) Contributions permitted after age 70½. Contributions to a Roth IRA may be made even after the individual for whom the account is maintained has attained age 70½.

Employee benefit plans

(5) Mandatory distribution rules not to apply before death. Notwithstanding subsections (a)(6) and (b)(3) of section 408 (relating to required distributions), the following provisions shall not apply to any Roth IRA:

(A) Section 401(a)(9)(A).

(B) The incidental death benefit requirements of section 401(a).

(6) Rollover contributions.

(A) In general. No rollover contribution may be made to a Roth IRA unless it is a qualified rollover contribution.

(B) Coordination with limit. A qualified rollover contribution shall not be taken into account for purposes of paragraph (2).

(7) Time when contributions made. For purposes of this section, the rule of section 219(f)(3) shall apply.

(d) Distribution rules.

For purposes of this title—

(1) Exclusion. Any qualified distribution from a Roth IRA shall not be includible in gross income.

(2) Qualified distribution. For purposes of this subsection—

(A) In general. The term "qualified distribution" means any payment or distribution—

(i) made on or after the date on which the individual attains age 59½,

(ii) made to a beneficiary (or to the estate of the individual) on or after the death of the individual,

(iii) attributable to the individual's being disabled (within the meaning of section 72(m)(7)), or

(iv) which is a qualified special purchase distribution.

(B) Distributions within nonexclusion period. A payment or distribution from a Roth IRA shall not be treated as a qualified distribution under subparagraph (A) if such payment or distribution is made within the 5-taxable year period beginning with the first taxable year for which the individual made a contribution to a Roth IRA (or such individual's spouse made a contribution to a Roth IRA) established for such individual.

(C) Distributions of excess contributions and earnings. The term "qualified distribution" shall not include any distribution of any contribution described in section 408(d)(4) and any net income allocable to the contribution.

(3) Rollovers from an eligible retirement plan other than a Roth IRA.

(A) In general. Notwithstanding sections 402(c), 403(b)(8), 408(d)(3), and 457(e)(16), in the case of any distribution to which this paragraph applies—

(i) there shall be included in gross income any amount which would be includible were it not part of a qualified rollover contribution,

(ii) section 72(t) shall not apply, and

(iii) unless the taxpayer elects not to have this clause apply, any amount required to be included in gross income for any taxable year beginning in 2010 by reason of this paragraph shall be so included ratably over the 2-taxable-year period beginning with the first taxable year beginning in 2011.

Any election under clause (iii) for any distributions during a taxable year may not be changed after the due date for such taxable year.

(B) Distributions to which paragraph applies. This paragraph shall apply to a distribution from an eligible retirement plan (as defined by section 402(c)(8)(B)) This paragraph shall not apply to a distribution which is a qualified rollover contribution from a Roth IRA or a qualified rollover contribution from a designated Roth account which is a rollover contribution described in section 402A(c)(3)(A) maintained for the benefit of an individual which is contributed to a Roth IRA maintained for the benefit of such individual in a qualified rollover contribution.

(C) Conversions. The conversion of an individual retirement plan (other than a Roth IRA) to a Roth IRA shall be treated for purposes of this paragraph as a distribution to which this paragraph applies.

(D) Additional reporting requirements. Trustees of Roth IRAs, trustees of individual retirement plans, persons subject to section 6047(d)(1), or all of the foregoing persons, whichever is appropriate, shall include such additional information in reports required under section 408(i) or 6047 as the Secretary may require to ensure that amounts required to be included in gross income under subparagraph (A) are so included.

(E) Special rules for contributions to which 2-year averaging applies. In the case of a qualified rollover contribution to a Roth IRA of a distribution to which subparagraph (A)(iii) applied, the following rules shall apply:

(i) Acceleration of inclusion.

(I) In general. The amount otherwise required to be included in gross income for any taxable year beginning in 2010 or the first taxable year in the 2-year period under subparagraph (A)(iii) shall be increased by the aggregate distributions from Roth IRAs for such taxable year which are allocable under paragraph (4) to the portion of such qualified rollover contribution required to be included in gross income under subparagraph (A)(i).

(II) Limitation on aggregate amount included. The amount required to be included in gross income for any taxable year under subparagraph (A)(iii) shall not exceed the aggregate amount required to be included in gross income under subparagraph (A)(iii) for all taxable years in the 2-year period (without regard to subclause (I)) reduced by amounts included for all preceding taxable years.

(ii) Death of distributee.

(I) In general. If the individual required to include amounts in gross income under such subparagraph dies before all of such amounts are included, all remaining amounts shall be included in gross income for the taxable year which includes the date of death.

(II) Special rule for surviving spouse. If the spouse of the individual described in subclause (I) acquires the individual's entire interest in any Roth IRA to which such qualified rollover contribution is properly allocable, the spouse may elect to treat the remaining amounts described in subclause (I) as includible in the spouse's gross income in the taxable years of the spouse ending with or within the taxable years of such individual in which such amounts would otherwise have been includible. Any such election may not be made or changed after the due date for the spouse's taxable year which includes the date of death.

(F) Special rule for applying section 72.

(i) In general. If—

(I) any portion of a distribution from a Roth IRA is properly allocable to a qualified rollover contribution described in this paragraph; and

(II) such distribution is made within the 5-taxable year period beginning with the taxable year in which such contribution was made,

then section 72(t) shall be applied as if such portion were includible in gross income.

(ii) **Limitation.** Clause (i) shall apply only to the extent of the amount of the qualified rollover contribution includible in gross income under subparagraph (A)(i).

(4) Aggregation and ordering rules.

(A) Aggregation rules. Section 408(d)(2) shall be applied separately with respect to Roth IRAs and other individual retirement plans.

(B) Ordering rules. For purposes of applying this section and section 72 to any distribution from a Roth IRA, such distribution shall be treated as made—

(i) from contributions to the extent that the amount of such distribution, when added to all previous distributions from the Roth IRA, does not exceed the aggregate contributions to the Roth IRA; and

(ii) from such contributions in the following order:

(I) Contributions other than qualified rollover contributions to which paragraph (3) applies.

(II) Qualified rollover contributions to which paragraph (3) applies on a first-in, first-out basis.

Any distribution allocated to a qualified rollover contribution under clause (ii)(II) shall be allocated first to the portion of such contribution required to be included in gross income.

(5) Qualified special purpose distribution. For purposes of this section, the term "qualified special purpose distribution" means any distribution to which subparagraph (F) of section 72(t)(2) applies.

(6) Taxpayer may make adjustments before due date.

(A) In general. Except as provided by the Secretary, if, on or before the due date for any taxable year, a taxpayer transfers in a trustee-to-trustee transfer any contribution to an individual retirement plan made during such taxable year from such plan to any other individual retirement plan, then, for purposes of this chapter, such contribution shall be treated as having been made to the transferee plan (and not the transferor plan).

(B) Special rules.

(i) Transfer of earnings. Subparagraph (A) shall not apply to the transfer of any contribution unless such transfer is accompanied by any net income allocable to such contribution.

(ii) No deduction. Subparagraph (A) shall apply to the transfer of any contribution only to the extent no deduction was allowed with respect to the contribution to the transferor plan.

(7) Due date. For purposes of this subsection, the due date for any taxable year is the date prescribed by law (including extensions of time) for filing the taxpayer's return for such taxable year.

(e) Qualified rollover contribution.

For purposes of this section—

(1) In general. The term "qualified rollover contribution" means a rollover contribution—

(A) to a Roth IRA from another such account,

(B) from an eligible retirement plan, but only if—

(i) in the case of an individual retirement plan, such rollover contribution meets the requirements of section 408(d)(3), and

(ii) in the case of any eligible retirement plan (as defined in section 402(c)(8)(B) other than clauses (i) and (ii) thereof), such rollover contribution meets the requirements of section 402(c), 403(b)(8), or 457(e)(16), as applicable.

For purposes of section 408(d)(3)(B), there shall be disregarded any qualified rollover contribution from an individual retirement plan (other than a Roth IRA) to a Roth IRA.

(2) Military death gratuity.

(A) In general. The term "qualified rollover contribution" includes a contribution to a Roth IRA maintained for the benefit of an individual made before the end of the 1-year period beginning on the date on which such individual receives an amount under section 1477 of title 10, United States Code, or section 1967 of title 38 of such Code, with respect to a person, to the extent that such contribution does not exceed—

(i) the sum of the amounts received during such period by such individual under such sections with respect to such person, reduced by

(ii) the amounts so received which were contributed to a Coverdell education savings account under section 530(d)(9).

(B) Annual limit on number of rollovers not to apply. Section 408(d)(3)(B) shall not apply with respect to amounts treated as a rollover by the subparagraph (A).

(C) Application of section 72. For purposes of applying section 72 in the case of a distribution which is not a qualified distribution, the amount treated as a rollover by reason of subparagraph (A) shall be treated as investment in the contract.

(f) Individual retirement plan.

For purposes of this section—

(1) a simplified employee pension or a simple retirement account may not be designated as a Roth IRA; and

(2) contributions to any such pension or account shall not be taken into account for purposes of subsection (c)(2)(B).

In 2010, P.L. 111-312, Sec. 101(a)(1), substituted "December 31, 2012" for "December 31, 2010" both places it appeared in Sec. 901 of P.L. 107-16 [see below], effective as if included in the enactment of P.L. 107-16, EGTRRA, 6/7/2001.

In 2008, P.L. 110-458, Sec. 108(d)(1)(A), deleted the second "an" preceding "eligible" in subpara. (b)(3)(B), as in effect after the amendments made by Sec. 824, P.L. 109-280 . . . Sec. 108(d)(1)(B), deleted "other than a Roth IRA" before "during any taxable year" in subpara. (b)(3)(B), as in effect after the amendments made by Sec. 824, P.L. 109-280 . . . Sec. 108(d)(1)(C), added a flush sentence at the end of subpara. (b)(3)(B), as in effect after the amendments made by Sec. 824, P.L. 109-280 . . . Sec. 108(d)(2), substituted "This paragraph shall not apply to a distribution which is a qualified rollover contribution from a Roth IRA or a qualified rollover contribution from a designated Roth account which is a rollover contribution described in section 402A(c)(3)(A)" for "(other than a Roth IRA)" in subpara. (d)(3)(B), effective for distributions after 12/31/2007 (as if included in the provisions of Sec. 824, P.L. 109-280, see below).

— P.L. 110-458, Sec. 108(h)(1), subpara. (c)(3)(C), as added by Sec. 833(c), P.L. 109-280, is redesignated as subpara. (c)(3)(E), effective for tax. yrs. begin. after 2006 (as if included in the provisions of Sec. 833, P.L. 109-280, see below)

— P.L. 110-458, Sec. 108(h)(2)(A), subpara. (c)(3)(E) [as redesignated by Sec. 108(h)(1) of this Act] is redesignated as subpara. (c)(3)(D) . . . Sec. 108(h)(2)(B), substituted "subparagraph (B)(ii)" for "subparagraph (c)(ii)" in the case of taxable years beginning after 12/31/2009 (as provided in Sec. 108(h)(2) of this Act.

— P.L. 110-458, Sec. 125, of this Act read as follows:

"SEC. 125. ROLLOVER OF AMOUNTS RECEIVED IN AIRLINE CARRIER BANKRUPTCY TO ROTH IRAS.

"(a) General rule. If a qualified airline employee receives any airline payment amount and transfers any portion of such amount to a Roth IRA within 180 days of receipt of such amount (or, if later, within 180 days of the date of the enactment of this Act), then such amount (to the extent so transferred) shall be treated as a qualified rollover contribution described in section 408A(e) of the Internal Revenue Code of 1986, and the limitations described in section 408A(c)(3) of such Code shall not apply to any such transfer.

"(b) Definitions and special rules. For purposes of this section—

"(1) Airline payment amount.

"(A) In general. The term 'airline payment amount' means any payment of any money or other property which is payable by a commercial passenger airline carrier to a qualified airline employee—

"(i) under the approval of an order of a Federal bankruptcy court in a case filed after September 11, 2001, and before January 1, 2007, and "(ii) in respect of the qualified airline employee's interest in a bankruptcy claim against the carrier, any note of the carrier (or amount paid in lieu of a note being issued), or any other fixed obligation of the carrier to pay a lump sum amount.

"The amount of such payment shall be determined without regard to any requirement to deduct and withhold tax from such payment under sections 3102(a) and 3402(a).

"(B) Exception. An airline payment amount shall not include any amount payable on the basis of the carrier's future earnings or profits.

"(2) Qualified airline employee. The term 'qualified airline employee' means an employee or former employee of a commercial passenger airline carrier who was a participant in a defined benefit plan maintained by the carrier which—

"(A) is a plan described in section 401(a) of the Internal Revenue Code of 1986 which includes a trust exempt from tax under section 501(a) of such Code, and

"(B) was terminated or became subject to the restrictions contained in paragraphs (2) and (3) of section 402(b) of the Pension Protection Act of 2006.

"(3) Reporting requirements. If a commercial passenger airline carrier pays 1 or more airline payment amounts, the carrier shall, within 90 days of such payment (or, if later, within 90 days of the date of the enactment of this Act), report—

"(A) to the Secretary of the Treasury, the names of the qualified airline employees to whom such amounts were paid, and

"(B) to the Secretary and to such employees, the years and the amounts of the payments. Such reports shall be in such form, and contain such additional information, as the Secretary may prescribe.

"(c) Effective date. This section shall apply to transfers made after the date of the enactment of this Act with respect to airline payment amounts paid before, on, or after such date.

—P.L. 110-245, Sec. 109(a), amended subsec. (e), as in effective prior to amendment by Sec. 824(a), P.L. 109-280 . . . Sec. 109(b), amended subsec. (e), as in effect after the amendments made by Sec. 824(a), P.L. 109-280, effective as provided in Sec. 109(d) of this Act which reads as follows:

"(d) Effective dates.

"(1) In general. Except as provided by paragraphs (2) and (3), the amendments made by this section shall apply with respect to deaths from injuries occurring on or after the date of the enactment of this Act.

"(2) Application of amendments to deaths from injuries occurring on or after october 7, 2001, and before enactment. The amendments made by this section shall apply to any contribution made pursuant to section 408A(e)(2) or 530(d)(5) of the Internal Revenue Code of 1986, as amended by this Act, with respect to amounts received under section 1477 of title 10, United States Code, or under section 1967 of title 38 of such Code, for deaths from injuries occurring on or after October 7, 2001, and before the date of the enactment of this Act if such contribution is made not later than 1 year after the date of the enactment of this Act.

"(3) Pension Protection Act changes. Section 408A(e)(1) of the Internal Revenue Code of 1986 (as in effect after the amendments made by subsection (b)) shall apply to taxable years beginning after December 31, 2007."

Prior to amendment, subsec. (e) as in effect prior to amendment made by Sec. 824(a), P.L. 109-280, read as follows:

"(e) Qualified rollover contribution.

"For purposes of this section, the term 'qualified rollover contribution' means a rollover contribution to a Roth IRA from another such account, or from an individual retirement plan, but only if such rollover contribution meets the requirements of section 408(d)(3). Such term includes a rollover contribution described in section 402A(c)(3)(A). For purposes of section 408(d)(3)(B), there shall be disregarded any qualified rollover contribution from an individual retirement plan (other than a Roth IRA) to a Roth IRA."

Prior to amendment, subsec. (e) as in effect after the amendments made by Sec. 824(a), P.L. 109-280, read as follows:

"(e) Qualified rollover contribution.

"For purposes of this section, the term 'qualified rollover contribution' means a rollover contribution—

"(1) to a Roth IRA from another such account,

"(2) from an eligible retirement plan, but only if—

"(A) in the case of an individual retirement plan, such rollover contribution meets the requirements of section 408(d)(3), and

"(B) in the case of any eligible retirement plan (as defined in section 402(c)(8)(B) other than clauses (i) and (ii) thereof), such rollover contribution meets the requirements of section 402(c), 403(b)(8), or 457(e)(16), as applicable. For purposes of section 408(d)(3)(B), there shall be disregarded any qualified rollover contribution from an individual retirement plan (other than a Roth IRA) to a Roth IRA."

In 2006, P.L. 109-280, Sec. 811, of this Act [relating to Sec. 901 of P.L. 107-16, see below], provides:

"Sec. 811. Pensions and Individual Retirement Arrangement Provisions of Economic Growth and Tax Relief Reconciliation Act of 2001 made permanent.

"Title IX of the Economic Growth and Tax Relief Reconciliation Act of 2001 shall not apply to the provisions of, and amendments made by, subtitles A through F of title VI of such Act (relating to pension and individual retirement arrangement provisions)."

—P.L. 109-280, Sec. 824(a), amended subsec. (e). Sec. 109(a), P.L. 110-245, amended subsec. (e), effective prior to the the amendments made by Sec. 824(a) of this Act. For effective dates and amendments of Sec. 109(a), P.L. 110-245, see above. . . . Sec. 824(b)(1)(A), substituted "an eligible retirement plan (as defined by section 402(c)(8)(B))" for "individual retirement plan" in subpara. (c)(3)(B) [prior to deletion by Sec. 512(a)(1) of P.L. 109-222, see below] . . . Sec. 824(b)(1)(B), substituted "eligible retirement plan" for "IRA" in the heading of subpara. (c)(3)(B) [prior to deletion by Sec. 512(a)(1) of P.L. 109-222, see below] . . . Sec. 824(b)(2)(A), substituted "sections 402(c), 403(b)(8), 408(d)(3), and 457(e)(16)" for "section 408(d)(3)" in subpara. (d)(3)(A) . . . Sec. 824(b)(2)(B), substituted "eligible retirement plan (as defined by section 402(c)(8)(B))" for "individual retirement plan" in subpara. (d)(3)(B) . . . Sec. 824(b)(2)(C), added "or 6047" after "408(i)" in subpara. (d)(3)(D) . . . Sec. 824(b)(2)(D), substituted "persons subject to section 6047(d)(1), or all of the foregoing persons" for "or both" in subpara. (d)(3)(D) . . . Sec. 824(b)(2)(E), substituted "eligible retirement plan" for "IRA" in the heading of para. (d)(3), effective for distributions after 12/31/2007.

Subsec. (e) as amended by Sec. 109(a), P.L. 110-245, see above, read as follows:

" (e) Qualified rollover contribution. For purposes of this section

" (1) In general. The term 'qualified rollover contribution' means a rollover contribution to a Roth IRA from another such account, or from an individual retirement plan, but only if such rollover contribution meets the requirements of section 408(d)(3). Such term includes a rollover contribution described in section 402A(c)(3)(A). For purposes of section 408(d)(3)(B), there shall be disregarded any qualified rollover contribution from an individual retirement plan (other than a Roth IRA) to a Roth IRA.

" (2) Military death gratuity.

" (A) In general. The term 'qualified rollover contribution' includes a contribution to a Roth IRA maintained for the benefit of an individual made before the end of the 1-year period beginning on the date on which such individual receives an amount under section 1477 of title 10, United States Code, or section 1967 of title 38 of such Code, with respect to a person, to the extent that such contribution does not exceed

" (i) the sum of the amounts received during such period by such individual under such sections with respect to such person, reduced by

" (ii) the amounts so received which were contributed to a Coverdell education savings account under section 530(d)(9).

" (B) Annual limit on number of rollovers not to apply. Section 408(d)(3)(B) shall not apply with respect to amounts treated as a rollover by subparagraph (A).

" (C) Application of section 72. For purposes of applying section 72 in the case of a distribution which is not a qualified distribution, the amount treated as a rollover by reason of subparagraph (A) shall be treated as investment in the contract."

—P.L. 109-280, Sec. 833(c), added subpara. (c)(3)(C) [sic (D)], effective for tax. yrs. begin. after 2006.

—P.L. 109-222, Sec. 512(a)(1), deleted subpara. (c)(3)(B) [as amended by Sec. 824(b)(1)(A) and (B) of P.L. 109-280, see above] and redesignated subparas. (c)(3)(C) and (D) as (c)(3)(B) and (C) . . . Sec. 512(a)(2), substituted "except that any amount included in gross income under subsection (d)(3) shall not be taken into account, and" for "except that—(I) any amount included in gross income under subsection (d)(3) shall not be taken into account; and (II) any amount included in gross income by reason of a required distribution under a provision described in paragraph (5) shall not be taken into account for purposes of subparagraph (B)(i), and" in clause (c)(3)(B)(i) [as redesignated by Sec. 512(a)(1) of this Act, see above] . . . Sec. 512(b)(1), amended clause (d)(3)(A)(iii) . . . Sec. 512(b)(2)(A), amended clause (d)(3)(E)(i) . . . Sec. 512(b)(2)(B), substituted "2-year" for "4-year" in the heading of subpara. (d)(3)(E), effective for tax. yrs. begin. after 12/31/2009.

Prior to deletion, subpara. (c)(3)(B) [as amended by Sec. 824(b)(1)(A)-(B) of P.L. 109-280, see above] read as follows:

"(B) Rollover from eligible retirement plan. A taxpayer shall not be allowed to make a qualified rollover contribution to a Roth IRA from an an [sic] eligible retirement plan (as defined by section 402(c)(8)(B)) other than a Roth IRA during any taxable year if, for the taxable year of the distribution to which such contribution relates—

"(i) the taxpayer's adjusted gross income exceeds $100,000, or

"(ii) the taxpayer is a married individual filing a separate return."

Prior to amendment, clause (d)(3)(A)(iii) read as follows:

"(iii) unless the taxpayer elects not to have this clause apply for any taxable year, any amount required to be included in gross income for such taxable year by reason of this paragraph for any distribution before January 1, 1999, shall be so included ratably over the 4-taxable year period beginning with such taxable year."

Prior to amendment, clause (d)(3)(E)(i) read as follows:

"(i) Acceleration of inclusion.

"(I) In general. The amount required to be included in gross income for each of the first 3 taxable years in the 4-year period under subparagraph (A)(iii) shall be increased by the aggregate distributions from Roth IRAs for such taxable year which are allocable under paragraph (4) to the portion of such qualified rollover contribution required to be included in gross income under subparagraph (A)(i).

"(II) Limitation on aggregate amount included. The amount required to be included in gross income for any taxable year under subparagraph (A)(iii) shall not exceed the aggregate amount required to be included in gross income under subparagraph (A)(iii) for all taxable years in the 4-year period (without regard to subclause (I)) reduced by amounts included for all preceding taxable years."

In 2002, P.L. 107-358, Sec. 2, added subsec. (c) in Sec. 901 of P.L. 107-16 [see below], effective 12/17/2002.

In 2001, P.L. 107-16, Sec. 617(e)(1), added "Such term includes a rollover contribution described in section 402A(c)(3)(A)." after "section 408(d)(3)." in subsec. (e), effective for tax. yrs. begin. after 12/31/2005.

—P.L. 107-16, Sec. 901, of this Act [as amended by Sec. 2 of P.L. 107-358, and Sec. 101(a)(1) of P.L. 111-312, and as related to Sec. 811 of P.L. 109-280, see above], reads as follows:

"SEC. 901. SUNSET OF PROVISIONS OF ACT.

"(a) In general. All provisions of, and amendments made by, this Act shall not apply—

"(1) to taxable, plan, or limitation years beginning after December 31, 2012, or

"(2) in the case of title V, to estates of decedents dying, gifts made, or generation skipping transfers, after December 31, 2012.

"(b) Application of certain laws. The Internal Revenue Code of 1986 and the Employee Retirement Income Security Act of 1974 shall be applied and administered to years, estates, gifts, and transfers described in subsection (a) as if the provisions and amendments described in subsection (a) had never been enacted.

"(c) Exception. Subsection (a) shall not apply to section 803 (relating to no federal income tax on restitution received by victims of the Nazi regime or their heirs or estates)."

In 1998, P.L. 105-277, Sec. 4002(j), substituted ", and" for the period at the end of subclause (c)(3)(C)(i)(II), effective for tax. yrs. begin. after 12/31/2004.

—P.L. 105-206, Sec. 6005(b)(1), substituted "shall not exceed an amount equal to the amount determined under paragraph (2)(A) for such taxable year, reduced" for "shall be reduced" in subpara. (c)(3)(A) . . . Sec. 6005(b)(2)(A), added "or a married individual filing a separate return" after "joint return" in clause (c)(3)(A)(ii) . . . Sec. 6005(b)(2)(B)(i), added ", for the taxable year of the distribution to which such contribution relates" after "taxable year if" in subpara. (c)(3)(B) . . . Sec. 6005(b)(2)(B)(ii), deleted "for such taxable year" after "gross income" in clause (c)(3)(B)(i) . . . Sec. 6005(b)(2)(C), deleted "and the deduction under section 219 shall be taken into account" after "subsection (d)(3) shall not be taken into account" in clause (c)(3)(C)(i) . . . Sec. 6005(b)(3)(A), amended subpara. (d)(2)(B) . . . Sec. 6005(b)(3)(B), added subpara. (d)(2)(C) . . . Sec. 6005(b)(4)(A), amended clause (d)(3)(A)(iii) and added a flush sentence at the end of subpara. (d)(3)(A) . . . Sec. 6005(b)(4)(B), added subparas. (d)(3)(F) and (G) . . . Sec. 6005(b)(5)(A), amended para. (d)(4) . . . Sec. 6005(b)(5)(B), amended para. (d)(1) . . . Sec. 6005(b)(6)(A), added para. (d)(6) . . . Sec. 6005(b)(6)(B), deleted subpara. (d)(3)(D) and redesignated subparas. (d)(3)(E)-(G) as subparas. (d)(3)(D)-(F) . . . Sec. 6005(b)(7), added para. (d)(7) . . . Sec. 6005(b)(9), added subsec. (f), effective for tax. yrs. begin. after 12/31/97.

Prior to amendment, para. (d)(1) read as follows:

"(1) General rules.

"(A) Exclusions from gross income. Any qualified distribution from a Roth IRA shall not be includible in gross income.

"(B) Nonqualified distributions. In applying section 72 to any distribution from a Roth IRA which is not a qualified distribution, such distribution shall be treated as made from contributions to the Roth IRA to the extent that such distribution, when added to all previous distributions from the Roth IRA, does not exceed the aggregate amount of contributions to the Roth IRA."

Prior to amendment, subpara. (d)(2)(B) read as follows:

"(B) Certain distributions within 5 years. A payment or distribution shall not be treated as a qualified distribution under subparagraph (A) if—

"(i) it is made within the 5-taxable year period beginning with the 1st taxable year for which the individual made a contribution to a Roth IRA (or such individual's spouse made a contribution to a Roth IRA) established for such individual, or

"(ii) in the case of a payment or distribution properly allocable (as determined in the manner prescribed by the Secretary) to a qualified rollover contribution from an individual retirement plan other than a Roth IRA (or income allocable thereto), it is made within the 5-taxable year period beginning with the taxable year in which the rollover contribution was made."

Prior to amendment, clause (d)(3)(A)(iii) read as follows:

"(iii) in the case of a distribution before January 1, 1999, any amount required to be included in gross income by reason of this paragraph shall be so included ratably over the 4-taxable year period beginning with the taxable year in which the payment or distribution is made."

Prior to deletion, subpara. (d)(3)(D) read as follows:

"(D) Conversion of excess contributions. If, no later than the due date for filing the return of tax for any taxable year (without regard to extensions), an individual transfers, from an individual retirement plan (other than a Roth IRA), contributions for such taxable year (and any earnings allocable thereto) to a Roth IRA, no such amount shall be includible in gross income to the extent no deduction was allowed with respect to such amount."

Prior to amendment, para. (d)(4) read as follows:

"(4) Coordination with individual retirement accounts. Section 408(d)(2) shall be applied separately with respect to Roth IRAs and other individual retirement plans."

—P.L. 105-206, Sec. 7004(a), amended clause (c)(3)(C)(i), effective for tax. yrs. begin. after 12/31/2004.

Prior to amendment, clause (c)(3)(C)(i) read as follows:

"(i) adjusted gross income shall be determined in the same manner as under section 219(g)(3), except that any amount included in gross income under subsection (d)(3) shall not be taken into account, and"

In 1997, P.L. 105-34, Sec. 302(a), added Code Sec. 408A, effective for tax. yrs. begin. after 12/31/97.

Sec. 409. Qualifications for tax credit employee stock ownership plans.

(a) **Tax credit employee stock ownership plan defined.** Except as otherwise provided in this title, for purposes of this title, the term "tax credit employee stock ownership plan" means a defined contribution plan which—

(1) meets the requirements of section 401(a),

(2) is designed to invest primarily in employer securities, and

(3) meets the requirements of subsections (b), (c), (d), (e), (f), (g), (h), and (o) of this section.

(b) **Required allocation of employer securities.**

(1) **In general.** A plan meets the requirements of this subsection if—

(A) the plan provides for the allocation for the plan year of all employer securities transferred to it or purchased by it (because of the requirements of section 41(c)(1)(B)) to the accounts of all participants who are entitled to share in such allocation, and

(B) for the plan year the allocation to each participant so entitled is an amount which bears substantially the same proportion to the amount of all such securities allocated to all such participants in the plan for that year as the amount of compensation paid to such participant during that year bears to the compensation paid to all such participants during that year.

(2) **Compensation in excess of $100,000 disregarded.** For purposes of paragraph (1), compensation of any participant in excess of the first $100,000 per year shall be disregarded.

(3) **Determination of compensation.** For purposes of this subsection, the amount of compensation paid to a participant for any period is the amount of such participant's compensation (within the meaning of section 415(c)(3)) for such period.

(4) **Suspension of allocation in certain cases.** Notwithstanding paragraph (1), the allocation to the account of any participant which is attributable to the basic employee plan credit or the credit allowed under section 41 (relating to the employee stock ownership credit) may be extended over whatever period may be necessary to comply with the requirements of section 415.

(c) **Participants must have nonforfeitable rights.**

A plan meets the requirements of this subsection only if it provides that each participant has a nonforfeitable right to any employer security allocated to his account.

(d) **Employer securities must stay in the plan.**

A plan meets the requirements of this subsection only if it provides that no employer security allocated to a participant's account under subsection (b) (or allocated to a participant's account in connection with matched employer and employee contributions) may be distributed from that account before the end of the 84th month beginning after the month in which the security is allocated to the account. To the extent provided in the plan, the preceding sentence shall not apply in the case of—

(1) death, disability, separation from service, or termination of the plan;

(2) a transfer of a participant to the employment of an acquiring employer from the employment of the selling corporation in the case of a sale to the acquiring corporation of substantially all of the assets used by the selling corporation in a trade or business conducted by the selling corporation, or

(3) with respect to the stock of a selling corporation, a disposition of such selling corporation's interest in a subsidiary when the participant continues employment with such subsidiary.

This subsection shall not apply to any distribution required under section 401(a)(9) or to any distribution or reinvestment required under section 401(a)(28).

(e) **Voting rights.**

(1) **In general.** A plan meets the requirements of this subsection if it meets the requirements of paragraph (2) or (3), whichever is applicable.

Employee benefit plans — Code Sec. 409(h)(5)(B)

(2) Requirements where employer has a registration-type class of securities. If the employer has a registration-type class of securities, the plan meets the requirements of this paragraph only if each participant or beneficiary in the plan is entitled to direct the plan as to the manner in which securities of the employer which are entitled to vote and are allocated to the account of such participant or beneficiary are to be voted.

(3) Requirement for other employers. If the employer does not have a registration-type class of securities, the plan meets the requirements of this paragraph only if each participant or beneficiary in the plan is entitled to direct the plan as to the manner in which voting rights under securities of the employer which are allocated to the account of such participant or beneficiary are to be exercised with respect to any corporate matter which involves the voting of such shares with respect to the approval or disapproval of any corporate merger or consolidation, recapitalization, reclassification, liquidation, dissolution, sale of substantially all assets of a trade or business, or such similar transaction as the Secretary may prescribe in regulations.

(4) Registration-type class of securities defined. For purposes of this subsection, the term, "registration-type class of securities" means—

(A) a class of securities required to be registered under section 12 of the Securities Exchange Act of 1934, and

(B) a class of securities which would be required to be so registered except for the exemption from registration provided in subsection (g)(2)(H) of such section 12.

(5) 1 vote per participant. A plan meets the requirements of paragraph (3) with respect to an issue if—

(A) the plan permits each participant 1 vote with respect to such issue, and

(B) the trustee votes the shares held by the plan in the proportion determined after application of subparagraph (A).

(f) Plan must be established before employer's due date.

(1) In general. A plan meets the requirements of this subsection only if it is established on or before the due date (including any extension of such date) for the filing of the employer's tax return for the first taxable year of the employer for which an employee plan credit is claimed by the employer with respect to the plan.

(2) Special rule for first year. A plan which otherwise meets the requirements of this section shall not be considered to have failed to meet the requirements of section 401(a) merely because it was not established by the close of the first taxable year of the employer for which an employee plan credit is claimed by the employer with respect to the plan.

(g) Transferred amounts must stay in plan even though investment credit is redetermined or recaptured.

A plan meets the requirement of this subsection only if it provides that amounts which are transferred to the plan (because of the requirements of section 48(n)(1) or 41(c)(1)(B)) shall remain in the plan (and, if allocated under the plan, shall remain so allocated) even though part or all of the employee plan credit or the credit allowed under section 41 (relating to employee stock ownership credit) is recaptured or redetermined. For purposes of the preceding sentence, the references to section 48(n)(1) and the employee plan credit shall refer to such section and credit as in effect before the enactment of the Tax Reform Act of 1984.

(h) Right to demand employer securities; put option.

(1) In general. A plan meets the requirements of this subsection if a participant who is entitled to a distribution from the plan—

(A) has a right to demand that his benefits be distributed in the form of employer securities, and

(B) if the employer securities are not readily tradable on an established market, has a right to require that the employer repurchase employer securities under a fair valuation formula.

(2) Plan may distribute cash in certain cases.

(A) In general. A plan which otherwise meets the requirements of this subsection or of section 4975(e)(7) shall not be considered to have failed to meet the requirements of section 401(a) merely because under the plan the benefits may be distributed in cash or in the form of employer securities.

(B) Exception for certain plans restricted from distributing securities.

(i) In general. A plan to which this subparagraph applies shall not be treated as failing to meet the requirements of this subsection or section 401(a) merely because it does not permit a participant to exercise the right described in paragraph (1)(A) if such plan provides that the participant entitled to a distribution has a right to receive the distribution in cash, except that such plan may distribute employer securities subject to a requirement that such securities may be resold to the employer under terms which meet the requirements of paragraph (1)(B).

(ii) Applicable plans. This subparagraph shall apply to a plan which otherwise meets the requirements of this subsection or section 4975(e)(7) and which is established and maintained by—

(I) an employer whose charter or bylaws restrict the ownership of substantially all outstanding employer securities to employees or to a trust described in section 401(a), or

(II) an S corporation.

(3) Special rule for banks. In the case of a plan established and maintained by a bank (as defined in section 581) which is prohibited by law from redeeming or purchasing its own securities, the requirements of paragraph (1)(B) shall not apply if the plan provides that participants entitled to a distribution from the plan shall have a right to receive a distribution in cash.

(4) Put option period. An employer shall be deemed to satisfy the requirements of paragraph (1)(B) if it provides a put option for a period of at least 60 days following the date of distribution of stock of the employer and, if the put option is not exercised within such 60-day period, for an additional period of at least 60 days in the following plan year (as provided in regulations promulgated by the Secretary).

(5) Payment requirement for total distribution. If an employer is required to repurchase employer securities which are distributed to the employee as part of a total distribution, the requirements of paragraph (1)(B) shall be treated as met if—

(A) the amount to be paid for the employer securities is paid in substantially equal periodic payments (not less frequently than annually) over a period beginning not later than 30 days after the exercise of the put option described in paragraph (4) and not exceeding 5 years, and

(B) there is adequate security provided and reasonable interest paid on the unpaid amounts referred to in subparagraph (A).

For purposes of this paragraph, the term "total distribution" means the distribution within 1 taxable year to the recipient of the balance to the credit of the recipient's account.

(6) Payment requirement for installment distributions. If an employer is required to repurchase employer securities as part of an installment distribution, the requirements of paragraph (1)(B) shall be treated as met if the amount to be paid for the employer securities is paid not later than 30 days after the exercise of the put option described in paragraph (4).

(7) Exception where employee elected diversification. Paragraph (1)(A) shall not apply with respect to the portion of the participant's account which the employee elected to have reinvested under section 401(a)(28)(B) or subparagraph (B) or (C) of section 401(a)(35).

(i) Reimbursement for expenses of establishing and administering plan.

A plan which otherwise meets the requirements of this section shall not be treated as failing to meet such requirements merely because it provides that—

(1) Expenses of establishing plan. As reimbursement for the expenses of establishing the plan, the employer may withhold from amounts due the plan for the taxable year for which the plan is established (or the plan may pay) so much of the amounts paid or incurred in connection with the establishment of the plan as does not exceed the sum of—

(A) 10 percent of the first $100,000 which the employer is required to transfer to the plan for that taxable year under section 41(c)(1)(B), and

(B) 5 percent of any amount so required to be transferred in excess of the first $100,000; and

(2) Administrative expenses. As reimbursement for the expenses of administering the plan, the employer may withhold from amounts due the plan (or the plan may pay) so much of the amounts paid or incurred during the taxable year as expenses of administering the plan as does not exceed the lesser of—

(A) the sum of—

(i) 10 percent of the first $100,000 of the dividends paid to the plan with respect to stock of the employer during the plan year ending with or within the employer's taxable year, and

(ii) 5 percent of the amount of such dividends in excess of $100,000 or

(B) $100,000.

(j) Conditional contributions to the plan.

A plan which otherwise meets the requirements of this section shall not be treated as failing to satisfy such requirements (or as failing to satisfy the requirements of section 401(a) of this title or of section 403(c)(1) of the Employee Retirement Income Security Act of 1974) merely because of the return of a contribution (or a provision permitting such a return) if—

(1) the contribution to the plan is conditioned on a determination by the Secretary that such plan meets the requirements of this section,

(2) The application for a determination described in paragraph (1) is filed with the Secretary not later than 90 days after the date on which an employee plan credit is claimed, and

(3) the contribution is returned within 1 year after the date on which the Secretary issues notice to the employer that such plan does not satisfy the requirements of this section.

(k) Requirements relating to certain withdrawals.

Notwithstanding any other law or rule of law—

(1) the withdrawal from a plan which otherwise meets the requirements of this section by the employer of an amount contributed for purposes of the matching employee plan credit shall not be considered to make the benefits forfeitable, and

(2) the plan shall not, by reason of such withdrawal, fail to be for the exclusive benefit of participants or their beneficiaries,

if the withdrawn amounts were not matched by employee contributions or were in excess of the limitations of section 415. Any withdrawal described in the preceding sentence shall not be considered to violate the provisions of section 403(c)(1) of the Employee Retirement Income Security Act of 1974. For purposes of this subsection, the reference to the matching employee plan credit shall refer to such credit as in effect before the enactment of the Tax Reform Act of 1984.

(l) Employer securities defined.

For purposes of this section—

(1) In general. The term "employer securities" means common stock issued by the employer (or by a corporation which is a member of the same controlled group) which is readily tradable on an established securities market.

(2) Special rule where there is no readily tradable common stock. If there is no common stock which meets the requirements of paragraph (1), the term "employer securities" means common stock issued by the employer (or by a corporation which is a member of the same controlled group) having a combination of voting power and dividend rights equal to or in excess of—

(A) that class of common stock of the employer (or of any other such corporation) having the greatest voting power, and

(B) that class of common stock of the employer (or of any other such corporation) having the greatest dividend rights.

(3) Preferred stock may be issued in certain cases. Noncallable preferred stock shall be treated as employer securities if such stock is convertible at any time into stock which meets the requirements of paragraph (1) or (2) (whichever is applicable) and if such conversion is at a conversion price which (as of the date of the acquisition by the tax credit employee stock ownership plan) is reasonable. For purposes of the preceding sentence, under regulations prescribed by the Secretary, preferred stock shall be treated as noncallable if after the call there will be a reasonable opportunity for a conversion which meets the requirements of the preceding sentence.

(4) Application to controlled group of corporations.

(A) In general. For purposes of this subsection, the term "controlled group of corporations" has the meaning given to such term by section 1563(a) (determined without regard to subsections (a)(4) and (e)(3)(C) of section 1563).

(B) Where common parent owns at least 50 percent of first tier subsidiary. For purposes of subparagraph (A), if the common parent owns directly stock possessing at least 50 percent of the voting power of all classes of stock and at least 50 percent of each class of nonvoting stock in a first tier subsidiary, such subsidiary (and all other corporations below it in the chain which would meet the 80 percent test of section 1563(a) if the first tier subsidiary were the common parent) shall be treated as includible corporations.

Employee benefit plans Code Sec. 409(o)(1)(C)

(C) Where common parent owns 100 percent of first-tier subsidiary. For purposes of subparagraph (A), if the common parent owns directly stock possessing all of the voting power of all classes of stock and all of the nonvoting stock, in a first tier subsidiary, and if the first tier subsidiary owns directly stock possessing at least 50 percent of the voting power of all classes of stock, and at least 50 percent of each class of nonvoting stock, in a second-tier subsidiary of the common parent, such second-tier subsidiary (and all other corporations below it in the chain which would meet the 80 percent test of section 1563(a) if the second-tier subsidiary were the common parent) shall be treated as includible corporations.

(5) **Nonvoting common stock may be acquired in certain cases.** Nonvoting common stock of an employer described in the second sentence of section 401(a)(22) shall be treated as employer securities if an employer has a class of nonvoting common stock outstanding and the specific shares that the plan acquires have been issued and outstanding for at least 24 months.

(m) **Nonrecognition of gain or loss on contribution of employer securities to tax credit employee stock ownership plan.**

No gain or loss shall be recognized to the taxpayer with respect to the transfer of employer securities to a tax credit employee stock ownership plan maintained by the taxpayer to the extent that such transfer is required under section 41(c)(1)(B), or subparagraph (A) or (B) of section 48(n)(1).

(n) **Securities received in certain transactions.**

(1) **In general.** A plan to which section 1042 applies and an eligible worker-owned cooperative (within the meaning of section 1042(c)) shall provide that no portion of the assets of the plan or cooperative attributable to (or allocable in lieu of) employer securities acquired by the plan or cooperative in a sale to which section 1042 applies may accrue (or be allocated directly or indirectly under any plan of the employer meeting the requirements of section 401(a))—

(A) during the nonallocation period, for the benefit of—

(i) any taxpayer who makes an election under section 1042(a) with respect to employer securities,

(ii) any individual who is related to the taxpayer (within the meaning of section 267(b)), or

(B) for the benefit of any other person who owns (after application of section 318(a)) more than 25 percent of—

(i) any class of outstanding stock of the corporation which issued such employer securities or of any corporation which is a member of the same controlled group of corporations (within the meaning of subsection (l)(4) as such corporation, or

(ii) the total value of any class of outstanding stock of any such corporation.

For purposes of subparagraph (B), section 318(a) shall be applied without regard to the employee trust exception in paragraph (2)(B)(i).

(2) **Failure to meet requirements.** If a plan fails to meet the requirements of paragraph (1)—

(A) the plan shall be treated as having distributed to the person described in paragraph (1) the amount allocated to the account of such person in violation of paragraph (1) at the time of such allocation,

(B) the provisions of section 4979A shall apply, and

(C) the statutory period for the assessment of any tax imposed by section 4979A shall not expire before the date which is 3 years from the later of—

(i) the 1st allocation of employer securities in connection with a sale to the plan to which section 1042 applies, or

(ii) the date on which the Secretary is notified of such failure.

(3) **Definitions and special rules.** For purposes of this subsection—

(A) Lineal descendants. Paragraph (1)(A)(ii) shall not apply to any individual if—

(i) such individual is a lineal descendant of the taxpayer, and

(ii) the aggregate amount allocated to the benefit of all such lineal descendants during the nonallocation period does not exceed more than 5 percent of the employer securities (or amounts allocated in lieu thereof) held by the plan which are attributable to a sale to the plan by any person related to such descendants (within the meaning of section 267(c)(4)) in a transaction to which section 1042 applied.

(B) 25-percent shareholders. A person shall be treated as failing to meet the stock ownership limitation under paragraph (1)(B) if such person fails such limitation—

(i) at any time during the 1-year period ending on the date of sale of qualified securities to the plan or cooperative, or

(ii) on the date as of which qualified securities are allocated to participants in the plan or cooperative.

(C) Nonallocation period. The term "nonallocation period" means the period beginning on the date of the sale of the qualified securities and ending on the later of—

(i) the date which is 10 years after the date of sale, or

(ii) the date of the plan allocation attributable to the final payment of acquisition indebtedness incurred in connection with such sale.

(o) **Distribution and payment requirements.**

A plan meets the requirements of this subsection if—

(1) **Distribution requirement.**

(A) In general. The plan provides that, if the participant and, if applicable pursuant to sections 401(a)(11) and 417, with the consent of the participant's spouse elects, the distribution of the participant's account balance in the plan will commence not later than 1 year after the close of the plan year—

(i) in which the participant separates from service by reason of the attainment of normal retirement age under the plan, disability, or death, or

(ii) which is the 5th plan year following the plan year in which the participant otherwise separates from service, except that this clause shall not apply if the participant is reemployed by the employer before distribution is required to begin under this clause.

(B) Exception for certain financed securities. For purposes of this subsection, the account balance of a participant shall not include any employer securities acquired with the proceeds of the loan described in section 404(a)(9) until the close of the plan year in which such loan is repaid in full.

(C) Limited distribution period. The plan provides that, unless the participant elects otherwise, the distribution of the participant's account balance will be in substan-

tially equal periodic payments (not less frequently than annually) over a period not longer than the greater of—
(i) 5 years, or
(ii) in the case of a participant with an account balance in excess of $800,000, 5 years plus 1 additional year (but not more than 5 additional years) for each $160,000 or fraction thereof by which such balance exceeds $800,000.

(2) Cost-of-living adjustment. The Secretary shall adjust the dollar amounts under paragraph (1)(C) at the same time and in the same manner as under section 415(d).

(p) Prohibited allocations of securities in an S corporation.

(1) In general. An employee stock ownership plan holding employer securities consisting of stock in an S corporation shall provide that no portion of the assets of the plan attributable to (or allocable in lieu of) such employer securities may, during a nonallocation year, accrue (or be allocated directly or indirectly under any plan of the employer meeting the requirements of section 401(a)) for the benefit of any disqualified person.

(2) Failure to meet requirements.

(A) In general. If a plan fails to meet the requirements of paragraph (1), the plan shall be treated as having distributed to any disqualified person the amount allocated to the account of such person in violation of paragraph (1) at the time of such allocation.

(B) Cross reference. For excise tax relating to violations of paragraph (1) and ownership of synthetic equity, see section 4979A.

(3) Nonallocation year. For purposes of this subsection—
(A) In general. The term "nonallocation year" means any plan year of an employee stock ownership plan if, at any time during such plan year—
(i) such plan holds employer securities consisting of stock in an S corporation, and
(ii) disqualified persons own at least 50 percent of the number of shares of stock in the S corporation.
(B) Attribution rules. For purposes of subparagraph (A)—
(i) In general. The rules of section 318(a) shall apply for purposes of determining ownership, except that—
(I) in applying paragraph (1) thereof, the members of an individual's family shall include members of the family described in paragraph (4)(D), and
(II) paragraph (4) thereof shall not apply.
(ii) Deemed-owned shares. Notwithstanding the employee trust exception in section 318(a)(2)(B)(i), an individual shall be treated as owning deemed-owned shares of the individual.

Solely for purposes of applying paragraph (5), this subparagraph shall be applied after the attribution rules of paragraph (5) have been applied.

(4) Disqualified person. For purposes of this subsection—
(A) In general. The term "disqualified person" means any person if—
(i) the aggregate number of deemed-owned shares of such person and the members of such person's family is at least 20 percent of the number of deemed-owned shares of stock in the S corporation, or
(ii) in the case of a person not described in clause (i), the number of deemed-owned shares of such person is at least 10 percent of the number of deemed-owned shares of stock in such corporation.

(B) Treatment of family members. In the case of a disqualified person described in subparagraph (A)(i), any member of such person's family with deemed-owned shares shall be treated as a disqualified person if not otherwise treated as a disqualified person under subparagraph (A).

(C) Deemed-owned shares.
(i) In general. The term "deemed-owned shares" means, with respect to any person—
(I) the stock in the S corporation constituting employer securities of an employee stock ownership plan which is allocated to such person under the plan, and
(II) such person's share of the stock in such corporation which is held by such plan but which is not allocated under the plan to participants.
(ii) Person's share of unallocated stock. For purposes of clause (i)(II), a person's share of unallocated S corporation stock held by such plan is the amount of the unallocated stock which would be allocated to such person if the unallocated stock were allocated to all participants in the same proportions as the most recent stock allocation under the plan.

(D) Member of family. For purposes of this paragraph, the term "member of the family" means, with respect to any individual—
(i) the spouse of the individual,
(ii) an ancestor or lineal descendant of the individual or the individual's spouse,
(iii) a brother or sister of the individual or the individual's spouse and any lineal descendant of the brother or sister, and
(iv) the spouse of any individual described in clause (ii) or (iii).

A spouse of an individual who is legally separated from such individual under a decree of divorce or separate maintenance shall not be treated as such individual's spouse for purposes of this subparagraph.

(5) Treatment of synthetic equity. For purposes of paragraphs (3) and (4), in the case of a person who owns synthetic equity in the S corporation, except to the extent provided in regulations, the shares of stock in such corporation on which such synthetic equity is based shall be treated as outstanding stock in such corporation and deemed-owned shares of such person if such treatment of synthetic equity of 1 or more such persons results in—
(A) the treatment of any person as a disqualified person, or
(B) the treatment of any year as a nonallocation year.

For purposes of this paragraph, synthetic equity shall be treated as owned by a person in the same manner as stock is treated as owned by a person under the rules of paragraphs (2) and (3) of section 318(a). If, without regard to this paragraph, a person is treated as a disqualified person or a year is treated as a nonallocation year, this paragraph shall not be construed to result in the person or year not being so treated.

(6) Definitions. For purposes of this subsection—
(A) Employee stock ownership plan. The term "employee stock ownership plan" has the meaning given such term by section 4975(e)(7).
(B) Employer securities. The term "employer security" has the meaning given such term by section 409(l).
(C) Synthetic equity. The term "synthetic equity" means any stock option, warrant, restricted stock, deferred issuance stock right, or similar interest or right

Employee benefit plans Code Sec. 409

that gives the holder the right to acquire or receive stock of the S corporation in the future. Except to the extent provided in regulations, synthetic equity also includes a stock appreciation right, phantom stock unit, or similar right to a future cash payment based on the value of such stock or appreciation in such value.

(7) Regulations and guidance.

(A) In general. The Secretary shall prescribe such regulations as may be necessary to carry out the purposes of this subsection.

(B) Avoidance or evasion. The Secretary may, by regulation or other guidance of general applicability, provide that a nonallocation year occurs in any case in which the principal purpose of the ownership structure of an S corporation constitutes an avoidance or evasion of this subsection.

(q) Cross references.

(1) For requirements for allowance of employee plan credit, see section 48(n).

(2) For assessable penalties for failure to meet requirements of this section, or for failure to make contributions required with respect to the allowance of an employee plan credit or employee stock ownership credit, see section 6699.

(3) For requirements for allowance of an employee stock ownership credit, see section 41.

In 2010, P.L. 111-312, Sec. 101(a)(1), substituted "December 31, 2012" for "December 31, 2010" both places it appeared in Sec. 901 of P.L. 107-16, [see below] effective as if included in the enactment of P.L. 107-16, EGTRRA, 6/7/2001.

In 2006, P.L. 109-280, Sec. 811, of this Act [relating to Sec. 901 of P.L. 107-16, see below], provides:

"SEC. 811. PENSIONS AND INDIVIDUAL RETIREMENT ARRANGEMENT PROVISIONS OF ECONOMIC GROWTH AND TAX RELIEF RECONCILIATION ACT OF 2001 MADE PERMANENT.

"Title IX of the Economic Growth and Tax Relief Reconciliation Act of 2001 shall not apply to the provisions of, and amendments made by, subtitles A through F of title VI of such Act (relating to pension and individual retirement arrangement provisions)."

—P.L. 109-280, Sec. 901(a)(2)(B), added "or subparagraph (B) or (C) of section 401(a)(35)" before the period at the end of para. (h)(7), effective for plan. yrs. begin. after 12/31/2006, except as provided in Sec. 901(c)(2) and (3), of this Act, which read as follows:

"(2) Special rule for collectively bargained agreements. In the case of a plan maintained pursuant to 1 or more collective bargaining agreements between employee representatives and 1 or more employers ratified on or before the date of the enactment of this Act, paragraph (1) shall be applied to benefits pursuant to, and individuals covered by, any such agreement by substituting for 'December 31, 2006' the earlier of—

"(A) the later of—

"(i) December 31, 2007, or

"(ii) the date on which the last of such collective bargaining agreements terminates (determined without regard to any extension thereof after such date of enactment), or

"(B) December 31, 2008.

"(3) Special rule for certain employer securities held in an ESOP.

"(A) In general. In the case of employer securities to which this paragraph applies, the amendments made by this section shall apply to plan years beginning after the earlier of—

"(i) December 31, 2007, or

"(ii) the first date on which the fair market value of such securities exceeds the guaranteed minimum value described in subparagraph (B)(ii).

"(B) Applicable securities. This paragraph shall apply to employer securities which are attributable to employer contributions other than elective deferrals, and which, on September 17, 2003—

"(i) consist of preferred stock, and

"(ii) are within an employee stock ownership plan (as defined in section 4975(e)(7) of the Internal Revenue Code of 1986), the terms of which provide that the value of the securities cannot be less than the guaranteed minimum value specified by the plan on such date.

"(C) Coordination with transition rule. In applying section 401(a)(35)(H) of the Internal Revenue Code of 1986 and section 204(j)(7) of the Employee Retirement Income Security Act of 1974 (as added by this section) to employer securities to which this paragraph applies, the applicable percentage shall be determined without regard to this paragraph."

In 2002, P.L. 107-358, Sec. 2, added subsec. (c) in Sec. 901 of P.L. 107-16 [see below], effective 12/17/2002.

—P.L. 107-147, Sec. 411(j)(2)(A), substituted "$800,000" for "$500,000" each place it appeared in clause (o)(1)(C)(ii)... Sec. 411(j)(2)(B), substituted "$160,000" for "$100,000" in clause (o)(1)(C)(ii), effective for yrs. begin. after 12/31/2001.

In 2001, P.L. 107-16, Sec. 656(a), redesignated subsec. (p) as (q) and added subsec. (p), effective for plan yrs. begin. after 12/31/2004. Sec. 656(d)(2) of this Act, provides:

"(2) Exception for certain plans. In the case of any—

"(A) employee stock ownership plan established after March 14, 2001, or

"(B) employee stock ownership plan established on or before such date if employer securities held by the plan consist of stock in a corporation with respect to which an election under section 1362(a) of the Internal Revenue Code of 1986 is not in effect on such date,

the amendments made by this section shall apply to plan years ending after March 14, 2001."

—P.L. 107-16, Sec. 901, of this Act [as amended by Sec. 2 of P.L. 107-358, and Sec. 101(a)(1) of P.L. 111-312, see above], reads as follows:

"SEC. 901. SUNSET OF PROVISIONS OF ACT.

"(a) In general. All provisions of, and amendments made by, this Act shall not apply—

"(1) to taxable, plan, or limitation years beginning after December 31, 2012, or

"(2) in the case of title V, to estates of decedents dying, gifts made, or generation skipping transfers, after December 31, 2012.

"(b) Application of certain laws. The Internal Revenue Code of 1986 and the Employee Retirement Income Security Act of 1974 shall be applied and administered to years, estates, gifts, and transfers described in subsection (a) as if the provisions and amendments described in subsection (a) had never been enacted.

"(c) Exception. Subsection (a) shall not apply to section 803 (relating to no federal income tax on restitution received by victims of the Nazi regime or their heirs or estates)."

In 1997, P.L. 105-34, Sec. 1506(a)(1), added subpara. (h)(2)(B)... Sec. 1506(a)(2)(A), designated the text of para. (h)(2) preceding subpara. (h)(2)(B) [as added by Sec. 1506(a)(1) of this Act] as subpara. (h)(2)(A), and added the heading of subpara. (h)(2)(A).... Sec. 1506(a)(2)(B), deleted "In the case of an employer whose charter or bylaws restrict the ownership of substantially all outstanding employer securities to employees or to a trust described in section 401(a), a plan which otherwise meets the requirements of this subsection or section 4975(e)(7) shall not be considered to have failed to meet the requirements of this subsection or of section 401(a) merely because it does not permit a participant to exercise the right described in paragraph (1)(A) if such plan provides that participants entitled to a distribution from the plan shall have a right to receive such distribution in cash, except that such plan may distribute employer securities subject to a requirement that such securities may be resold to the employer under terms which meet the requirements of paragraph (1)(B)." at the end of subpara. (h)(2)(A) [as designated by Sec. 1506(a)(2)(A) of this Act], effective for tax. yrs. begin. after 12/31/97.

In 1989, P.L. 101-239, Sec. 7304(a)(2)(A)(i), deleted "or section 2057" after "1042" each place it appeared in para. (n)(1)... Sec. 7304(a)(2)(A)(ii), deleted "or any decedent if the executor of the estate of such decedent makes a qualified sale to which section 2057 applies" after "employer securities," in clause (n)(1)(A)(i)... Sec. 7304(a)(2)(A)(iii), deleted "or the decedent" after "the taxpayer" in clause (n)(1)(A)(ii)... Sec. 7304(a)(2)(B), deleted "or section 2057" after "1042 applies" in clause (n)(2)(C)(i) and after "section 1042" in clause (n)(3)(A)(ii), effective for the estates of decedents dying after 12/19/89.

—P.L. 101-239, Sec. 7811(h)(1), substituted "the second sentence" for "the last sentence" in para. (1)(5), effective for acquisitions of securities after 12/31/86.

In 1988, P.L. 100-647, Sec. 1011B(g)(1), amended Sec. 1172(b)(1)(A) of P.L. 99-514, by adding "each place it appears" after the comma, thereby inserting "or section 2057" after "a plan to which section 1042" in para. (n)(1)... Sec. 1011B(g)(2), inserted "or section 2057" after "section 1042" each place it appeared in paras. (n)(2) and (n)(3), effective for sales after 10/22/86 for which an election is made by the executor of an estate who is required to file the return of the tax imposed by the Internal Revenue Code of 1986 on a date (including extensions) after 10/22/86.

—P.L. 100-647, Sec. 1011B(i)(1), substituted "distribution is required to begin under this clause" for "such year" in clause (o)(1)(A)(ii), effective for distributions attributable to stock acquired after 12/31/86.

—P.L. 100-647, Sec. 1011B(i)(2), amended Sec. 1174(a)(2) of P.L. 99-514, the effective date for changes made by Sec. 1174(a)(1) of P.L. 99-514, by substituting "distributions" for "plan terminations", effective for distributions after 12/31/84.

—P.L. 100-647, Sec. 1011B(i)(3), substituted "if the participant and, if applicable pursuant to sections 401(a)(11) and 417, with the consent of the participant's spouse elects" for "unless the participant otherwise elects" in subpara. (o)(1)(A), effective for distributions attributable to stock acquired after 12/31/86.

—P.L. 100-647, Sec. 1011B(j)(3), added "or to any distribution or reinvestment required under section 401(a)(28)" after "section 401(a)(9)" in subsec. (d)... Sec. 1011B(j)(5), added para. (h)(7), effective for stock acquired after 12/31/86.

—P.L. 100-647, Sec. 1011B(k)(3), redesignated para. (1)(4) [sic (5)], relating to nonvoting common stock may be acquired in certain cases, as (1)(5), effective for acquisitions of securities after 12/31/86.

—P.L. 100-647, Sec. 1018(t)(4)(B), substituted "paragraph (1)(B)" for "section 409(o)", in para. (h)(2), effective 10/22/86.

—P.L. 100-647, Sec. 1018(t)(4)(C), amended subpara. (n)(3)(C), effective for sales of securities after 10/22/86.

Prior to amendment, subpara. (n)(3)(C) read as follows:

"(C) Nonallocation period. The term 'nonallocation period' means the 10-year period beginning on the later of—

"(i) the date of the sale of the qualified securities, or

"(ii) the date of the plan allocation attributable to the final payment of acquisition indebtedness incurred in connection with such sale."

—P.L. 100-647, Sec. 1018(t)(4)(G), amended Sec. 1854(a)(3)(C) [reproduced below] of P.L. 99-514, the effective date for changes made by Sec. 1854(a)(3)(A), by adding Sec. 1854(a)(3)(C)(ii) of P.L. 99-514, exception to the effective date. Sec. 1854(a)(3)(C)(ii) of the Act [as added by Sec. 1018(t)(4)(G) of P.L. 100-647], provides:

"(ii) A taxpayer or executor may elect to have section 1042(b)(3) of the Internal Revenue Code of 1954 (as in effect before the amendment made by subparagraph (B)) apply to sales before the date of the enactment of this Act as if such section included the last sentence of section 409(n)(1) of the Internal Revenue Code of 1986 (as added by subparagraph (A))."

—P.L. 100-647, Sec. 1018(t)(4)(H), deleted "(2) or" after "paragraph" in para. (e)(5), effective 10/22/86.

In 1986, P.L. 99-514, Sec. 1172(b)(1)(A), added "or section 2057" after "section 1042" in para. (n)(1) [as added by Sec. 1854(a)(3)(A) of this Act, below] . . . Sec. 1172(b)(1)(B), added "or any decedent if the executor of the estate of such decedent makes a qualified sale to which section 2057 applies," after "securities" in clause (n)(1)(A)(i) . . . Sec. 1172(b)(1)(C), added "or the decedent" after "taxpayer" in clause (n)(1)(A)(ii), effective for sales after 10/22/86 for which an election is made by the executor of an estate who is required to file the return of the tax imposed by the Internal Revenue Code of 1986 on a date (including extensions) after 10/22/86.

—P.L. 99-514, Sec. 1174(a)(1), substituted "separation from service, or termination of the plan" for "or separation from service" in para. (d)(1), effective [as amended by Sec. 1011B(i)(2) of P.L. 100-647] for distributions after 12/31/84.

—P.L. 99-514, Sec. 1174(b)(1), redesignated subsec. (o) as (p), and added new subsec. (o) . . . Sec. 1174(b)(2), substituted "(h), and (o)" for "and (h)" in para. (a)(3), effective for distributions attributable to stock acquired after 12/31/86.

—P.L. 99-514, Sec. 1174(c)(1)(A), added paras. (h)(5) and (6), effective for distributions attributable to stock acquired after 12/31/86, except that a plan may elect to have such amendment apply to all distributions after 10/22/86.

—P.L. 99-514, Sec. 1176(b), added para. (1)(4) [sic (5)], effective for acquisitions of securities after 12/31/86.

—P.L. 99-514, Sec. 1852(a)(4)(B), added the last sentence to subsec. (d), effective for yrs. begin. after 12/31/84.

—P.L. 99-514, Sec. 1854(a)(3)(A), redesignated subsec. (n) as subsec. (o), and added new subsec. (n), effective for sales of securities after 10/22/86.

—P.L. 99-514, Sec. 1854(f)(1)(A), added para. (e)(5), effective 10/22/86.

—P.L. 99-514, Sec. 1854(f)(1)(B), substituted "any corporate matter which involves the voting of such shares with respect to the approval or disapproval of any corporate merger or consolidation, recapitalization, reclassification, liquidation, dissolution, sale of substantially all assets of a trade or business, or such similar transaction as the Secretary may prescribe in regulations" for "a corporate matter which (by law or charter) must be decided by more than a majority vote of outstanding common shares voted" in para. (e)(3) . . . Sec. 1854(f)(1)(C), substituted "securities of the employer" for "employer securities" in paras. (e)(2) and (3) . . . Sec. 1854(f)(1)(D), added "or beneficiary" after "participant" each place it appeared in paras. (e)(2) and (3), effective after 12/31/86, to stock acquired after 12/31/79.

—P.L. 99-514, Sec. 1854(f)(3)(C), substituted "in cash, except that such plan may distribute employer securities subject to a requirement that such securities may be resold to the employer under terms which meet the requirements of section 409(o)" for "in cash" in the second sentence of para. (h)(2), effective 10/22/86.

—P.L. 99-514, Sec. 1899A(11), substituted "participant's" for "participants's" in subsec. (d), effective 10/22/86.

In 1984, P.L. 98-369, Sec. 474(r)(15)(A), substituted "41" for "44G" each place it appeared in subsecs. (b), (g), (i), (m), and (n) . . . Sec. 474(r)(15)(B), deleted "48(n)(1)(A) or" after "the requirements of section" in para. (b)(1) . . . Sec. 474(r)(15)(C), added a sentence at the end of subsec. (g) . . . Sec. 474(r)(15)(D), deleted "48(n)(1) or" after "taxable year under section" in subpara. (i)(1)(A) . . . Sec. 474(r)(15)(E), added a sentence at the end of subsec. (k), effective for tax. yrs. begin. after 12/31/83, and for carrybacks from such yrs.

—P.L. 98-369, Sec. 491(e)(1), redesignated Code Sec. 409A as Code Sec. 409, effective 1/1/84.

In 1983, P.L. 97-448, Sec. 103(h), substituted "the requirements of this subsection or of section 401(a)" for "the requirements of section 401(a)" in para. (h)(2) . . . Sec. 103(i), amended para. (d)(2), effective for tax. yrs. begin. after 12/31/81. Prior to amendment, para. (d)(2) read as follows:

"(2) a transfer of a participant to the employment of an acquiring employer from the employment of the selling corporation in the case of

"(A) a sale to the acquiring employer of substantially all of the assets used by the selling corporation in a trade or business conducted by the selling corporation, or

"(B) the sale of substantially all of the stock of a subsidiary of the employer, or"

In 1981, P.L. 97-34, Sec. 331(c)(1)(A), added "or 44G(c)(1)(B)" after "section 48(n)(1)(A)" in subpara. (b)(1)(A) . . . Sec. 331(c)(1)(B), added "or the credit allowed under section 44G (relating to the employee stock ownership credit)" after "basic employee plan credit" in para. (b)(4) . . . Sec. 331(c)(1)(C), added "or 44G(c)(1)(B)" after "section 48(n)(1)" in subsec. (g) . . . Sec. 331(c)(1)(D), added "or the credit allowed under section 44G (relating to employee stock ownership credit)" after "employee credit plan" in subsec. (g) . . . Sec. 331(c)(1)(E), added "or 44G(c)(1)(B)" after "section 48(n)(1)" in subpara. (i)(1)(A) . . . Sec. 331(c)(1)(F), added "section 44G(c)(1)(B), or" after "required under" in subsec. (m) . . . Sec. 331(c)(1)(G), added "or employee stock ownership credit" after "employee credit plan" in para. (n)(2) . . . Sec. 331(c)(1)(H), added para. (n)(3), effective for tax. yrs. end. after 12/31/82.

—P.L. 97-34, Sec. 334, added the last sentence to para. (h)(2) and substituted "this subsection" for "this section" in the first sentence of para. (h)(2), effective for tax. yrs. begin. after 12/31/81.

—P.L. 97-34, Sec. 336, added paras. (h)(3) and (h)(4), effective for tax. yrs. begin. after 12/31/81.

—P.L. 97-34, Sec. 337(a), amended the last sentence of subsec. (d), effective for distributions described in Code Sec. 409A(d) (or any corresponding provision of prior law made after 3/29/75.

Prior to amendment, the last sentence of subsec. (d) read as follows:

"To the extent provided in the plan, the preceding sentence shall not apply in the case of separation from service, death, or disability."

In 1980, P.L. 96-605, Sec. 224(a), substituted "Application to controlled group of corporations." for "Controlled group of corporations defined." in the heading of para. (1)(4), substituted "Where common parent owns at least" for "Common parent may own only" in the first sentence of subpara. (1)(4)(B), and added subpara. (1)(4)(C), effective for qualified investment for tax. yrs. begin. after 12/31/78.

—P.L. 96-222, Sec. 101(a)(7)(B), corrected Sec. 141(g) of P.L. 95-600 [see below].

Prior to corrections Sec. 141(g) of P.L. 95-600 read as follows:

"(g) Effective dates.

"(1) In general. The amendments made by this section (other than by subsection (f)(3)) shall apply with respect to qualified investment for taxable years beginning after December 31, 1978."

—P.L. 96-222, Sec. 101(a)(7)(D), amended subsec. (m) . . . Sec. 101(a)(7)(E), added "or of section 4975(e)(7)" after "the requirements of this section" in para. (h)(2) . . . Sec. 101(a)(7)(F), added "(or allocated to a participant's account in connection with matched employer and employee contributions)" after "under subsection (b)" in subsec. (d) . . . Sec. 101(a)(7)(I)(i), amended para. (f)(1) . . . Sec. 101(a)(7)(I)(ii), added "with respect to the plan" before the period at the end of para. (f)(2) . . . Sec. 101(a)(7)(J)(i), substituted "class of common stock" for "class of stock" in subpara. (l)(2)(B) . . . Sec. 101(a)(7)(J)(ii), amended para. (l)(3) . . . Sec. 101(a)(7)(L)(i)(VI), substituted "a credit employee stock ownership plan" for "an ESOP" each time it appeared in subsec. (m) [inoperative, see changes made by Sec. 101(a)(7)(D), above) . . . Sec. 101(a)(7)(L)(ii)(I), substituted "tax credit employee stock ownership plan" for "ESOP" each place it appeared in subsec. (a) other than the subsec. heading . . . Sec. 101(a)(7)(L)(ii)(II), substituted "tax credit employee stock ownership plan" for "ESOP" each place it appeared in para. (l)(3) . . . Sec. 101(a)(7)(L)(iii)(V), substituted "employee plan" for "ESOP" each place it appeared (other than in a heading) in sec. 409A . . . Sec. 101(a)(7)(L)(v)(VI), substituted "tax credit employee stock ownership plan" for "ESOPS" in the heading of subsec. (a) . . . Sec. 101(a)(7)(L)(v)(VII), substituted "tax credit employee stock ownership plans" for "ESOPS" in the heading for sec. 409A . . . Sec. 101(a)(7)(L)(v)(VIII), substituted "tax credit employee stock ownership plans" for "ESOPS" in sec. 409A of the table of sections for subpart A, part I, subchapter D, chapter 1, presumably intended by Congress to be effective for qualified investments for tax. yrs. begin. after '78 [Sec. 101(b)(2)] although technically effective with respect to decedents dying after 4/1/80 [Sec. 101(b)(1)(D)].

Prior to amendment, subsec. (m) read as follows:

"(m) Contributions of stock of controlling corporation.

"If the stock of a corporation which controls another corporation or which controls a corporation controlled by such other corporation is contributed to an ESOP of the controlled corporation, then no gain or loss shall be recognized, because of that contribution, to the controlled corporation. For purposes of this subsection, the term 'control' has the same meaning as that term has in section 368(c)."

Prior to amendment, para. (f)(1) read as follows:

"(1) In general. A plan meets the requirements of this subsection for a plan year only if it is established on or before the due date for the filing of the employer's tax return for the taxable year (including any extensions of such date) in which or with which the plan year ends."

Prior to amendment, para. (l)(3) read as follows:

"(3) Preferred stock may be issued in certain cases. Noncallable preferred stock shall be treated as meeting the requirements of paragraph (l) if such stock is convertible at any time into stock which meets the requirements of paragraph (l) and if such conversion is at a conversion price which (as of the date of the acquisition by the ESOP) is reasonable."

In 1978, P.L. 95-600, Sec. 141(a), added Code Sec. 409A, effective [as amended by Sec. 101(a)(7)(B) of P.L. 96-222, see above] for qualified investment for tax. yrs. begin. after 12/31/78, except as provided in Sec. 141(g)(2)-(4) which reads as follows:

"(2) Election to have amendments apply during 1978. At the election of the taxpayer, paragraph (l) shall be applied by substituting 'December 31, 1977' for 'December 31, 1978'; except that in the case of a plan in existence before December 31, 1978, any such election shall not affect the required allocation of employer securities attributable to qualified investment for taxable years beginning before January 1, 1979. An election under the preceding sentence shall be made at such time and in such manner as the Secretary of the Treasury or his delegate shall prescribe. Such an election, once made, shall be irrevocable.

"(3) Voting right provisions. Section 409A(e) of the Internal Revenue Code of 1954 (as added by subsection (a)) shall apply to plans to which section 409A of such Code applies, beginning with the first day of such application.

"(4) Right to demand employer securities, etc. Paragraphs (1)(A) and (2) of section 409A(h) of the Internal Revenue Code of 1954 (as added by subsection (a)) shall apply to distributions after December 31, 1978, made by a plan to which section 409A of such Code applies."

Sec. 409. Repealed.

In 1984, P.L. 98-369, Sec. 42(a)(7), substituted "section 1271 (relating to treatment of amounts received on retirement or sale or exchange of debt instruments)" for "section 1232 (relating to bonds and other evidences of indebtedness)" in para. (b)(1), effective for tax. yrs. end. after 7/18/84.

—P.L. 98-369, Sec. 491(b), repealed Code Sec. 409, effective for obligations issued after 12/31/83.

Sec. 491(f)(5) of this Act provides:

"(5) Treatment of tax imposed under section 409(c).—For purposes of section 26(b) of the Internal Revenue Code of 1954 (as amended by this Act), any tax imposed by section 409(c) of such Code (as in effect before its repeal by this section) shall be treated as a tax imposed by section 408(f) of such Code."

Prior to repeal, Code Sec. 409 read as follows:

"SEC. 409. RETIREMENT BONDS.

"(a) Retirement bond.

"For purposes of this section and section 219(a), the term 'retirement bond' means a bond issued under chapter 31 of title 31, which by its terms, or by regulations prescribed by the Secretary under such chapter—

"(1) provides for payment of interest, or investment yield, only on redemption;

"(2) provides that no interest, or investment yield, is payable if the bond is redeemed within 12 months after the date of its issuance;

"(3) provides that it ceases to bear interest, or provide investment yield on the earlier of—

"(A) the date on which the individual in whose name it is purchased (hereinafter in this section referred to as the 'registered owner') attains age 70½; or

"(B) 5 years after the date on which the registered owner dies, but not later than the date on which he would have attained the age 70½ had he lived;

"(4) provides that, except in the case of a rollover contribution described in subsection (b)(3)(C) or in section 402(a)(5), 402(a)(7), 403(a)(4), 403(b)(8), or 408(d)(3) the registered owner may not contribute on behalf of any individual for the purchase of such bonds in excess of $2,000 for any taxable year; and

"(5) is not transferable.

"(b) Income tax treatment of bonds.

"(1) In general. Except as otherwise provided in this subsection, on the redemption of a retirement bond the entire proceeds shall be included in the gross income of the taxpayer entitled to the proceeds on redemption. If the registered owner has not tendered it for redemption before the close of the taxable year in which he attains age 70½, such individual shall include in his gross income for such taxable year the amount of proceeds he would have received if the bond had been redeemed at age 70½. The provisions of section 72 (relating to annuities) and section 1271 (relating to treatment of amounts received on retirement or sale or exchange of debt instruments).

"(2) Basis. The basis of a retirement bond is zero.

"(3) Exceptions.

"(A) Redemption within 12 months. If a retirement bond is redeemed within 12 months after the date of its issuance, the proceeds are excluded from gross income if no deduction is allowed under section 219 on account of the purchase of such bond. The preceding sentence shall not apply to the extent that the bond was purchased with a rollover contribution described in subparagraph (C) of this paragraph or in section 402(a)(5), 402(a)(7), 403(a)(4), 403(b)(8), 405(b)(3), or 408(d)(3).

"(B) Redemption after age 70½. If a retirement bond is redeemed after the close of the taxable year in which the registered owner attains age 70½, the proceeds from the redemption of the bond are excluded from the gross income of the registered owner to the extent that such proceeds were includible in his gross income for such taxable year.

"(C) Rollover into an individual retirement account or annuity or a qualified plan. If a retirement bond is redeemed at any time before the close of the taxable year in which the registered owner attains age 70½, and the registered owner transfers the entire amount of the proceeds from the redemption of the bond to an individual retirement account described in section 408(a) or to an individual retirement annuity described in section 408(b) (other than an endowment contract) which is maintained for the benefit of the registered owner of the bond, or to an employees' trust described in section 401(a) which is exempt from tax under section 501(a), an annuity plan described in section 403(a), or annuity contract described in section 403(b) for the benefit of the registered owner, on or before the 60th day after the day on which he received the proceeds of such redemption, then the proceeds shall be excluded from gross income and the transfer shall be treated as a rollover contribution described in section 408(d)(3). This subparagraph does not apply in the case of a transfer to such an employee's trust or such an annuity unless no part of the value of such proceeds is attributable to any source other than a qualified rollover contribution. For purposes of the preceding sentence, the term 'qualified rollover contribution' means any rollover contribution of a qualified total distribution (as defined in section 402(a)(5)(E)(i)) which is from such an employee's trust or annuity plan (other than an annuity plan or a trust forming part of a plan under which the individual was an employee within the meaning of section 401(c)(1) at the time contributions were made on his behalf under such plan), and which did not qualify as a rollover contribution by reason of section 402(a)(7). This subparagraph does not apply in the case of a transfer to such an employees' trust or such an annuity plan unless no part of the value of such proceeds is attributable to any source other than a rollover contribution from such an employees' trust or annuity plan (other than an annuity plan or a trust forming part of a plan under which the individual was an employee within the meaning of section 401(c)(1) at the time contributions were made on his behalf under the plan). This subparagraph does not apply in the case of a transfer to an annuity contract described in section 403(b) unless no part of the value of such proceeds is attributable to any source other than a rollover contribution from such an annuity contract. This subparagraph shall not apply to any retirement bond if such bond is acquired by the owner by reason of the death of another individual and the owner was not the surviving spouse of such other individual.

"(D) Partial rollovers permitted. Rules similar to the rules of section 408(d)(3)(C) shall apply for purposes of subparagraph (C).

"(c) Additional tax on certain redemptions before age 59½.

"(1) Early redemption of bond. If a retirement bond is redeemed by the registered owner before he attains age 59½, his tax under this chapter for the taxable year in which the bond is redeemed shall be increased by an amount equal to 10 percent of the amount of the proceeds of the redemption includible in his gross income for the taxable year.

"(2) Disability cases. Paragraph (1) does not apply for any taxable year during which the retirement bond is redeemed if, for that taxable year, the registered owner is disabled within the meaning of section 72(m)(7).

"(3) Redemption within one year. Paragraph (1) does not apply if the registered owner tenders the bond for redemption within 12 months after the date of its issuance."

—P.L. 98-369, Sec. 522(d)(13), amended subpara. (b)(3)(C), effective for distributions made after 7/18/84, in tax. yrs. end. after 7/18/84.

Prior to amendment, subpara. (b)(3)(C) read as follows:

"(C) Rollover into an individual retirement account or annuity or a qualified plan. If a retirement bond is redeemed at any time before the close of the taxable year in which the registered owner attains age 70½, and the registered owner transfers the entire amount of the proceeds from the redemption of the bond to an individual retirement account described in section 408(a) or to an individual retirement annuity described in section 408(b) (other than an endowment contract) which is maintained for the benefit of the registered owner of the bond, or to an employees' trust described in section 401(a) which is exempt from tax under section 501(a), an annuity plan described in section 403(a), or annuity contract described in section 403(b) for the benefit of the registered owner, on or before the 60th day after the day on which he received the proceeds of such redemption, then the proceeds shall be excluded from gross income and the transfer shall be treated as a rollover contribution described in section 408(d)(3). This subparagraph does not apply in the case of a transfer to such an employees' trust or such an annuity plan unless no part of the value of such proceeds is attributable to any source other than a rollover contribution from such an employees' trust or annuity plan (other than an annuity plan or a trust forming part of a plan under which the individual was an employee within the meaning of section 401(c)(1) at the time contributions were made on his behalf under the plan). This subparagraph does not apply in the case of a transfer to an annuity contract described in section 403(b) unless no part of the value of such proceeds is attributable to any source other than a rollover contribution from such an annuity contract. This subparagraph shall not apply to any retirement bond if such bond is acquired by the owner by reason of the death of another individual and the owner was not the surviving spouse of such other individual."

—P.L. 98-369, Sec. 713(g)(1), corrected Sec. 243(c) of P.L. 97-248, the effective date for changes made by Sec. 243(b)(1)(B), to apply to "individuals dying after December 31, 1983" rather than to "taxable years beginning after December 31, 1983" (see below).

In 1983, P.L. 97-452, Sec. 2(c)(1), substituted "chapter 31 of title 31" for "the Second Liberty Bond Act, as amended" in subsec. (a) and substituted "chapter" for "Act" in subsec. (a).

In 1982, P.L. 97-248, Sec. 243(b)(1)(B), added the last sentence to subpara. (b)(3)(C), for individuals dying after 12/31/83 [as amended by Sec. 713(g)(1) of P.L. 98-369, see above].

—P.L. 97-248, Sec. 335(a)(2), added new subpara. (b)(3)(D), for distributions made after 12/31/82.

In 1981, P.L. 97-34, Sec. 311(g)(1)(D), substituted "$2,000" for "$1,500" in para. (a)(4), for tax. yrs. begin after 12/31/81. For transitional rule, see Sec. 311(i)(2) of this Act reproduced in note following Code Sec. 219.

Sec. 311(g)(3) of P.L. 97-34, added the last sentence to the end of subpara. (b)(3)(A), for tax. yrs. begin. after 12/31/74.

In 1980, P.L. 96-222, Sec. 101(a)(13)(A), amended the effective date for changes made by Sec. 156 of P.L. 95-600 to distributions or transfers made after '77, in tax. yrs. begin. after 12/31/77 [see below] . . . Sec. 101(a)(14)(B), added "402(a)(7)," after "402(a)(5)" in para. (a)(4), for tax. yrs. begin. after '76.

In 1978, P.L. 95-600, Sec. 156(c)(2), substituted "an annuity plan described in section 403(a), or an annuity contract described in section 403(b)" for "or an annuity plan described in section 403(a)" in subpara. (b)(3)(C) . . . added the last sentence in subpara. (b)(3)(C) . . . Sec. 156(c)(3), inserted "403(b)(8)." following "403(a)(4)," in para. (a)(4), for distributions or transfers made after '77, in tax. yrs. begin. after 12/31/77.

—P.L. 95-600, Sec. 157(e)(1)(B), inserted "on behalf of any individual" after "may not contribute" in para. (a)(4), for tax. yrs. begin. after '76.

In 1976, P.L. 94-455, Sec. 1501(b)(6), substituted "for any taxable year" for "in any taxable year" in para. (a)(4), for tax. yrs. begin. after '76.

—P.L. 94-455, Sec. 1901(a)(60), substituted "section 408(d)(3)" for "section 403(d)(3)" in subpara. (b)(3)(C), for tax. yrs. begin. after '76.

—P.L. 94-455, Sec. 1906(b)(13)(A), substituted "Secretary" for "Secretary or his delegate" in subsec. (a), for tax. yrs. begin. after '76.

In 1974, P.L. 93-406, Sec. 2002(c), added Code Sec. 409, effective with respect to taxable years beginning after 12/31/74.

Sec. 409A. Inclusion in gross income of deferred compensation under nonqualified deferred compensation plans.

(a) **Rules relating to constructive receipt.**

(1) **Plan failures.**

(A) Gross income inclusion.

(i) In general. If at any time during a taxable year a nonqualified deferred compensation plan—

(I) fails to meet the requirements of paragraphs (2), (3), and (4), or

(II) is not operated in accordance with such requirements,

all compensation deferred under the plan for the taxable year and all preceding taxable years shall be includible in gross income for the taxable year to the extent not subject to a substantial risk of forfeiture and not previously included in gross income.

(ii) Application only to affected participants. Clause (i) shall only apply with respect to all compensation deferred under the plan for participants with respect to whom the failure relates.

(B) Interest and additional tax payable with respect to previously deferred compensation.

(i) In general. If compensation is required to be included in gross income under subparagraph (A) for a taxable year, the tax imposed by this chapter for the taxable year shall be increased by the sum of—

(I) the amount of interest determined under clause (ii), and

(II) an amount equal to 20 percent of the compensation which is required to be included in gross income.

(ii) Interest. For purposes of clause (i), the interest determined under this clause for any taxable year is the amount of interest at the underpayment rate plus 1 percentage point on the underpayments that would have occurred had the deferred compensation been includible in gross income for the taxable year in which first deferred or, if later, the first taxable year in which such deferred compensation is not subject to a substantial risk of forfeiture.

(2) **Distributions.**

(A) In general. The requirements of this paragraph are met if the plan provides that compensation deferred under the plan may not be distributed earlier than—

(i) separation from service as determined by the Secretary (except as provided in subparagraph (B)(i)),

(ii) the date the participant becomes disabled (within the meaning of subparagraph (C)),

(iii) death,

(iv) a specified time (or pursuant to a fixed schedule) specified under the plan at the date of the deferral of such compensation,

(v) to the extent provided by the Secretary, a change in the ownership or effective control of the corporation, or in the ownership of a substantial portion of the assets of the corporation, or

(vi) the occurrence of an unforeseeable emergency.

(B) Special rules.

(i) Specified employees. In the case of any specified employee, the requirement of subparagraph (A)(i) is met only if distributions may not be made before the date which is 6 months after the date of separation from service (or, if earlier, the date of death of the employee). For purposes of the preceding sentence, a specified employee is a key employee (as defined in section 416(i) without regard to paragraph (5) thereof) of a corporation any stock in which is publicly traded on an established securities market or otherwise.

(ii) Unforeseeable emergency. For purposes of subparagraph (A)(vi)—

(I) In general. The term "unforeseeable emergency" means a severe financial hardship to the participant resulting from an illness or accident of the participant, the participant's spouse, or a dependent (as defined in section 152(a)) of the participant, loss of the participant's property due to casualty, or other similar extraordinary and unforeseeable circumstances arising as a result of events beyond the control of the participant.

(II) Limitation on distributions. The requirement of subparagraph (A)(vi) is met only if, as determined under regulations of the Secretary, the amounts distributed with respect to an emergency do not exceed the amounts necessary to satisfy such emergency plus amounts necessary to pay taxes reasonably anticipated as a result of the distribution, after taking into account the extent to which such hardship is or may be relieved through reimbursement or compensation by insurance or otherwise or by liquidation of the participant's assets (to the extent the liquidation of such assets would not itself cause severe financial hardship).

(C) Disabled. For purposes of subparagraph (A)(ii), a participant shall be considered disabled if the participant—

(i) is unable to engage in any substantial gainful activity by reason of any medically determinable physical or mental impairment which can be expected to result in death or can be expected to last for a continuous period of not less than 12 months, or

(ii) is, by reason of any medically determinable physical or mental impairment which can be expected to result in death or can be expected to last for a continuous period of not less than 12 months, receiving income replacement benefits for a period of not less than 3 months under an accident and health plan covering employees of the participant's employer.

(3) **Acceleration of benefits.** The requirements of this paragraph are met if the plan does not permit the acceleration of the time or schedule of any payment under the plan, except as provided in regulations by the Secretary.

(4) **Elections.**

(A) In general. The requirements of this paragraph are met if the requirements of subparagraphs (B) and (C) are met.

(B) Initial deferral decision.

(i) In general. The requirements of this subparagraph are met if the plan provides that compensation for services performed during a taxable year may be deferred at the participant's election only if the election to defer such compensation is made not later than the close of the preceding taxable year or at such other time as provided in regulations.

(ii) First year of eligibility. In the case of the first year in which a participant becomes eligible to participate in the plan, such election may be made with respect to services to be performed subsequent to the election within 30 days after the date the participant becomes eligible to participate in such plan.

(iii) Performance-based compensation. In the case of any performance-based compensation based on services performed over a period of at least 12 months, such election may be made no later than 6 months before the end of the period.

(C) Changes in time and form of distribution. The requirements of this subparagraph are met if, in the case of a plan which permits under a subsequent election a delay in a payment or a change in the form of payment—

(i) the plan requires that such election may not take effect until at least 12 months after the date on which the election is made,

(ii) in the case of an election related to a payment not described in clause (ii), (iii), or (vi) of paragraph (2)(A), the plan requires that the payment with respect to which such election is made be deferred for a period of not less than 5 years from the date such payment would otherwise have been made, and

(iii) the plan requires that any election related to a payment described in paragraph (2)(A)(iv) may not be made less than 12 months prior to the date of the first scheduled payment under such paragraph.

(b) Rules relating to funding.

(1) Offshore property in a trust. In the case of assets set aside (directly or indirectly) in a trust (or other arrangement determined by the Secretary) for purposes of paying deferred compensation under a nonqualified deferred compensation plan, for purposes of section 83 such assets shall be treated as property transferred in connection with the performance of services whether or not such assets are available to satisfy claims of general creditors—

(A) at the time set aside if such assets (or such trust or other arrangement) are located outside of the United States, or

(B) at the time transferred if such assets (or such trust or other arrangement) are subsequently transferred outside of the United States.

This paragraph shall not apply to assets located in a foreign jurisdiction if substantially all of the services to which the nonqualified deferred compensation relates are performed in such jurisdiction.

(2) Employer's financial health. In the case of compensation deferred under a nonqualified deferred compensation plan, there is a transfer of property within the meaning of section 83 with respect to such compensation as of the earlier of—

(A) the date on which the plan first provides that assets will become restricted to the provision of benefits under the plan in connection with a change in the employer's financial health, or

(B) the date on which assets are so restricted,

whether or not such assets are available to satisfy claims of general creditors.

(3) Treatment of employer's defined benefit plan during restricted period.

(A) In general. If—

(i) during any restricted period with respect to a single-employer defined benefit plan, assets are set aside or reserved (directly or indirectly) in a trust (or other arrangement as determined by the Secretary) or transferred to such a trust or other arrangement for purposes of paying deferred compensation of an applicable covered employee under a nonqualified deferred compensation plan of the plan sponsor or member of a controlled group which includes the plan sponsor, or

(ii) a nonqualified deferred compensation plan of the plan sponsor or member of a controlled group which includes the plan sponsor provides that assets will become restricted to the provision of benefits under the plan to an applicable covered employee in connection with such restricted period (or other similar financial measure determined by the Secretary) with respect to the defined benefit plan, or assets are so restricted,

such assets shall, for purposes of section 83, be treated as property transferred in connection with the performance of services whether or not such assets are available to satisfy claims of general creditors. Clause (i) shall not apply with respect to any assets which are so set aside before the restricted period with respect to the defined benefit plan.

(B) Restricted period. For purposes of this section, the term "restricted period" means, with respect to any plan described in subparagraph (A)—

(i) any period during which the plan is in at-risk status (as defined in section 430(i));

(ii) any period the plan sponsor is a debtor in a case under title 11, United States Code, or similar Federal or State law, and

(iii) the 12-month period beginning on the date which is 6 months before the termination date of the plan if, as of the termination date, the plan is not sufficient for benefit liabilities (within the meaning of section 4041 of the Employee Retirement Income Security Act of 1974).

(C) Special rule for payment of taxes on deferred compensation included in income. If an employer provides directly or indirectly for the payment of any Federal, State, or local income taxes with respect to any compensation required to be included in gross income by reason of this paragraph—

(i) interest shall be imposed under subsection (a)(1)(B)(i)(I) on the amount of such payment in the same manner as if such payment was part of the deferred compensation to which it relates,

(ii) such payment shall be taken into account in determining the amount of the additional tax under subsection (a)(1)(B)(i)(II) in the same manner as if such payment was part of the deferred compensation to which it relates, and

(iii) no deduction shall be allowed under this title with respect to such payment.

(D) Other definitions. For purposes of this section—

(i) Applicable covered employee. The term "applicable covered employee" means any—

(I) covered employee of a plan sponsor,

(II) covered employee of a member of a controlled group which includes the plan sponsor, and

(III) former employee who was a covered employee at the time of termination of employment with the plan sponsor or a member of a controlled group which includes the plan sponsor.

(ii) Covered employee. The term "covered employee" means an individual described in section 162(m)(3) or an individual subject to the requirements of section 16(a) of the Securities Exchange Act of 1934.

(4) Income inclusion for offshore trusts and employer's financial health. For each taxable year that assets treated as transferred under this subsection remain set aside in a trust or other arrangement subject to paragraph (1), (2), or (3), any increase in value in, or earnings with respect to, such assets shall be treated as an additional transfer of property under this subsection (to the extent not previously included in income).

(5) Interest on tax liability payable with respect to transferred property.

(A) In general. If amounts are required to be included in gross income by reason of paragraph (1), (2), or (3) for a taxable year, the tax imposed by this chapter for such taxable year shall be increased by the sum of—

(i) the amount of interest determined under subparagraph (B), and

(ii) an amount equal to 20 percent of the amounts required to be included in gross income.

(B) Interest. For purposes of subparagraph (A), the interest determined under this subparagraph for any taxable year is the amount of interest at the underpayment rate plus 1 percentage point on the underpayments that would have occurred had the amounts so required to be included in gross income by paragraph (1), (2), or (3) been includible in gross income for the taxable year in which first deferred or, if later, the first taxable year in which such amounts are not subject to a substantial risk of forfeiture.

(c) No inference on earlier income inclusion or requirement of later inclusion.

Nothing in this section shall be construed to prevent the inclusion of amounts in gross income under any other provision of this chapter or any other rule of law earlier than the time provided in this section. Any amount included in gross income under this section shall not be required to be included in gross income under any other provision of this chapter or any other rule of law later than the time provided in this section.

(d) Other definitions and special rules.

For purposes of this section—

(1) Nonqualified deferred compensation plan. The term "nonqualified deferred compensation plan" means any plan that provides for the deferral of compensation, other than—

(A) a qualified employer plan, and

(B) any bona fide vacation leave, sick leave, compensatory time, disability pay, or death benefit plan.

(2) Qualified employer plan. The term "qualified employer plan" means—

(A) any plan, contract, pension, account, or trust described in subparagraph (A) or (B) of section 219(g)(5) (without regard to subparagraph (A)(iii)),

(B) any eligible deferred compensation plan (within the meaning of section 457(b)), and

(C) any plan described in section 415(m).

(3) Plan includes arrangements, etc. The term "plan" includes any agreement or arrangement, including an agreement or arrangement that includes one person.

(4) Substantial risk of forfeiture. The rights of a person to compensation are subject to a substantial risk of forfeiture if such person's rights to such compensation are conditioned upon the future performance of substantial services by any individual.

(5) Treatment of earnings. References to deferred compensation shall be treated as including references to income (whether actual or notional) attributable to such compensation or such income.

(6) Aggregation rules. Except as provided by the Secretary, rules similar to the rules of subsections (b) and (c) of section 414 shall apply.

(e) Regulations.

The Secretary shall prescribe such regulations as may be necessary or appropriate to carry out the purposes of this section, including regulations—

(1) providing for the determination of amounts of deferral in the case of a nonqualified deferred compensation plan which is a defined benefit plan,

(2) relating to changes in the ownership and control of a corporation or assets of a corporation for purposes of subsection (a)(2)(A)(v),

(3) exempting arrangements from the application of subsection (b) if such arrangements will not result in an improper deferral of United States tax and will not result in assets being effectively beyond the reach of creditors,

(4) defining financial health for purposes of subsection (b)(2), and

(5) disregarding a substantial risk of forfeiture in cases where necessary to carry out the purposes of this section.

In **2008,** P.L. 110-458, Sec. 101(e), added "to an applicable covered employee" after "under the plan" in clause (b)(3)(A)(ii), effective for transfers or other reservation of assets after 8/17/2006, [effective as if included in the amendments made by Sec. 116, P.L. 109-280, see below]

In **2006,** P.L. 109-280, Sec. 116(a), redesignated paras. (b)(3) and (4) as paras. (b)(4) and (5) respectively and added para. (b)(3) . . . Sec. 116(b), substituted "paragraph (1), (2), or (3)" for "paragraph (1) or (2)" each place it appeared in paras. (b)(4) and (5) [as redes. by Sec. 116(a) of this Act, see above], effective for transfers or other reservation of assets after 8/17/2006.

—P.L. 109-280, Sec. 826, of this Act, provides:

"Sec. 826. Modifications of rules governing hardships and unforseen financial emergencies.

"Within 180 days after the date of the enactment of this Act, the Secretary of the Treasury shall modify the rules for determining whether a participant has had a hardship for purposes of section 401(k)(2)(B)(i)(IV) of the Internal Revenue Code of 1986 to provide that if an event (including the occurrence of a medical expense) would constitute a hardship under the plan if it occurred with respect to the participant's spouse or dependent (as defined in section 152 of such Code), such event shall, to the extent permitted under a plan, constitute a hardship if it occurs with respect to a person who is a beneficiary under the plan with respect to the participant. The Secretary of the Treasury shall issue similar rules for purposes of determining whether a participant has had—

"(1) a hardship for purposes of section 403(b)(11)(B) of such Code; or

"(2) an unforeseen financial emergency for purposes of sections 409A(a)(2)(A)(vi), 409A(a)(2)(B)(ii), and 457(d)(1)(A)(iii) of such Code."

In **2005,** P.L. 109-135, Sec. 403(hh)(2), deleted "first" after "requires that the" in clause (a)(4)(C)(ii), effective for amounts deferred after 12/31/2004, except as provided in Sec. 885(d)(2) and (3) of P.L. 108-357 [see below].

—P.L. 109-135, Sec. 403(hh)(3), of this Act, reads as follows:

"(3)(A) Notwithstanding section 885(d)(1) of the American Jobs Creation Act of 2004, subsection (b) of section 409A of the Internal Revenue Code of 1986 shall take effect on January 1, 2005.

"(B) Not later than 90 days after the date of the enactment of this Act, the Secretary of the Treasury shall issue guidance under which a nonqualified deferred compensation plan which is in violation of the requirements of section 409A(b) of such Code shall be treated as not having violated such requirements if such plan comes into conformance with such requirements during such limited period as the Secretary may specify in such guidance."

—P.L. 109-135, Sec. 403(hh)(4), substituted "January 1, 2005" for "December 31, 2004" the first place it appeared in Sec. 885(f) of P.L. 108-357 [see below], enacted 12/21/2005.

In **2004,** P.L. 108-357, Sec. 885(a), added Code Sec. 409A, effective for amounts deferred after 12/31/2004, except as provided in Sec. 885(d)(2) and (3) of this Act, which read as follows:

"(2) Special rules.

"(A) Earnings. The amendments made by this section shall apply to earnings on deferred compensation only to the extent that such amendments apply to such compensation.

"(B) Material modifications. For purposes of this subsection, amounts deferred in taxable years beginning before January 1, 2005, shall be treated as amounts deferred in a taxable year beginning on or after such date if the plan under which the deferral is made is materially modified after October 3, 2004, unless such modification is pursuant to the guidance issued under subsection (f).

"(3) Exception for nonelective deferred compensation. The amendments made by this section shall not apply to any nonelective deferred compensation to which section 457 of the Internal Revenue Code of 1986 does not apply by reason of section 457(e)(12) of such Code, but only if such compensation is provided under a nonqualified deferred compensation plan—

Employee benefit plans Code Sec. 410(a)(5)(B)

"(A) which was in existence on May 1, 2004,
"(B) which was providing nonelective deferred compensation described in such section 457(e)(12) on such date, and
"(C) which is established or maintained by an organization incorporated on July 2, 1974.
"If, after May 1, 2004, a plan described in the preceding sentence adopts a plan amendment which provides a material change in the classes of individuals eligible to participate in the plan, this paragraph shall not apply to any nonelective deferred compensation provided under the plan on or after the date of the adoption of the amendment."

Sec. 885(e) and (f) [as amended by Sec. 403(hh)(4) of P.L. 109-135, see above] of this Act, provide:

"(e) Guidance relating to change of ownership or control. Not later than 90 days after the date of the enactment of this Act, the Secretary of the Treasury shall issue guidance on what constitutes a change in ownership or effective control for purposes of section 409A of the Internal Revenue Code of 1986, as added by this section.

"(f) Guidance relating to termination of certain existing arrangements. Not later than 60 days after the date of the enactment of this Act, the Secretary of the Treasury shall issue guidance providing a limited period during which a nonqualified deferred compensation plan adopted before January 1, 2005, may, without violating the requirements of paragraphs (2), (3), and (4) of section 409A(a) of the Internal Revenue Code of 1986 (as added by this section), be amended—

"(1) to provide that a participant may terminate participation in the plan, or cancel an outstanding deferral election with regard to amounts deferred after December 31, 2004, but only if amounts subject to the termination or cancellation are includible in income of the participant as earned (or, if later, when no longer subject to substantial risk of forfeiture), and

"(2) to conform to the requirements of such section 409A with regard to amounts deferred after December 31, 2004."

SUBPART B.—SPECIAL RULES

Sec.
410. Minimum participation standards.
411. Minimum vesting standards.
412. Minimum funding standards.
413. Collectively bargained plans.
414. Definitions and special rules.
415. Limitations on benefits and contributions under qualified plans.
416. Special rules for top-heavy plans.
417. Definitions and special rules for purposes of minimum survivor annuity requirements.

In **1984,** P.L. 98-397, Sec. 203(c), added item 417.
In **1982,** P.L. 97-248, Sec. 240(d), added item 416.
In **1974,** P.L. 93-406, Sec. 1011(a), added the table of sections for Subpart B, to include new sections 410 through 415.

Sec. 410. Minimum participation standards.
(a) Participation.
(1) Minimum age and service conditions.

(A) General rule. A trust shall not constitute a qualified trust under section 401(a) if the plan of which it is a part requires, as a condition of participation in the plan, that an employee complete a period of service with the employer or employers maintaining the plan extending beyond the later of the following dates—

(i) the date on which the employee attains the age of 21; or

(ii) the date on which he completes 1 year of service.

(B) Special rules for certain plans.

(i) In the case of any plan which provides that after not more than 2 years of service each participant has a right to 100 percent of his accrued benefit under the plan which is nonforfeitable (within the meaning of section 411) at the time such benefit accrues, clause (ii) of subparagraph (A) shall be applied by substituting "2 years of service" for "1 year of service".

(ii) In the case of any plan maintained exclusively for employees of an educational institution (as defined in section 170(b)(1)(A)(ii)) by an employer which is exempt from tax under section 501(a) which provides that each participant having at least 1 year of service has a right to 100 percent of his accrued benefit under the plan which is nonforfeitable (within the meaning of section 411) at the time such benefit accrues, clause (i) of subparagraph (A) shall be applied by substituting "26" for "21". This clause shall not apply to any plan to which clause (i) applies.

(2) Maximum age conditions. A trust shall not constitute a qualified trust under section 401(a) if the plan of which it is a part excludes from participation (on the basis of age) employees who have attained a specified age.

(3) Definition of year of service.

(A) General rule. For purposes of this subsection, the term "year of service" means a 12-month period during which the employee has not less than 1,000 hours of service. For purposes of this paragraph, computation of any 12-month period shall be made with reference to the date on which the employee's employment commenced, except that, under regulations prescribed by the Secretary of Labor, such computation may be made by reference to the first day of a plan year in the case of an employee who does not complete 1,000 hours of service during the 12-month period beginning on the date his employment commenced.

(B) Seasonal industries. In the case of any seasonal industry where the customary period of employment is less than 1,000 hours during a calendar year, the term "year of service" shall be such period as may be determined under regulations prescribed by the Secretary of Labor.

(C) Hours of service. For purposes of this subsection, the term "hour of service" means a time of service determined under regulations prescribed by the Secretary of Labor.

(D) Maritime industries. For purposes of this subsection, in the case of any maritime industry, 125 days of service shall be treated as 1,000 hours of service. The Secretary of Labor may prescribe regulations to carry out this subparagraph.

(4) Time of participation. A plan shall be treated as not meeting the requirements of paragraph (1) unless it provides that any employee who has satisfied the minimum age and service requirements specified in such paragraph, and who is otherwise entitled to participate in the plan, commences participation in the plan no later than the earlier of—

(A) the first day of the first plan year beginning after the date on which such employee satisfied such requirements, or

(B) the date 6 months after the date on which he satisfied such requirements,

unless such employee was separated from the service before the date referred to in subparagraph (A) or (B), whichever is applicable.

(5) Breaks in service.

(A) General rule. Except as otherwise provided in subparagraphs (B), (C), and (D), all years of service with the employer or employers maintaining the plan shall be taken into account in computing the period of service for purposes of paragraph (1).

(B) Employees under 2-year 100 percent vesting. In the case of any employee who has any 1-year break in service (as defined in section 411(a)(6)(A)) under a plan to which the service requirements of clause (i) of paragraph (1)(B) apply, if such employee has not satisfied

1,975

such requirements, service before such break shall not be required to be taken into account.

(C) 1-year break in service. In computing an employee's period of service for purposes of paragraph (1) in the case of any participant who has any 1-year break in service (as defined in section 411(a)(6)(A)), service before such break shall not be required to be taken into account under the plan until he has completed a year of service (as defined in paragraph (3)) after his return.

(D) Nonvested participants.

(i) In general. For purposes of paragraph (1), in the case of a nonvested participant, years of service with the employer or employers maintaining the plan before any period of consecutive 1-year breaks in service shall not be required to be taken into account in computing the period of service if the number of consecutive 1-year breaks in service within such period equals or exceeds the greater of—

(I) 5, or

(II) the aggregate number of years of service before such period.

(ii) Years of service not taken into account. If any years of service are not required to be taken into account by reason of a period of breaks in service to which clause (i) applies, such years of service shall not be taken into account in applying clause (i) to a subsequent period of breaks in service.

(iii) Nonvested participant defined. For purposes of clause (i), the term "nonvested participant" means a participant who does not have any nonforfeitable right under the plan to an accrued benefit derived from employer contributions.

(E) Special rule for maternity or paternity absences.—

(i) General rule. In the case of each individual who is absent from work for any period—

(I) by reason of the pregnancy of the individual,

(II) by reason of the birth of a child of the individual,

(III) by reason of the placement of a child with the individual in connection with the adoption of such child by such individual, or

(IV) for purposes of caring for such child for a period beginning immediately following such birth or placement,

the plan shall treat as hours of service, solely for purposes of determining under this paragraph whether a 1-year break in service (as defined in section 411(a)(6)(A)) has occurred, the hours described in clause (ii).

(ii) Hours treated as hours of service. The hours described in this clause are—

(I) the hours of service which otherwise would normally have been credited to such individual but for such absence, or

(II) in any case in which the plan is unable to determine the hours described in subclause (I), 8 hours of service per day of such absence,

except that the total number of hours treated as hours of service under this clause by reason of any such pregnancy or placement shall not exceed 501 hours.

(iii) Year to which hours are credited. The hours described in clause (ii) shall be treated as hours of service as provided in this subparagraph—

(I) only in the year in which the absence from work begins, if a participant would be prevented from incurring a 1-year break in service in such year solely because the period of absence is treated as hours of service as provided in clause (i); or

(II) in any other case, in the immediately following year.

(iv) Year defined. For purposes of this subparagraph, the term "year" means the period used in computations pursuant to paragraph (3).

(v) Information required to be filed. A plan shall not fail to satisfy the requirements of this subparagraph solely because it provides that no credit will be given pursuant to this subparagraph unless the individual furnishes to the plan administrator such timely information as the plan may reasonably require to establish—

(I) that the absence from work is for reasons referred to in clause (i), and

(II) the number of days for which there was such an absence.

(b) **Minimum coverage requirements.**

(1) **In general.** A trust shall not constitute a qualified trust under section 401(a) unless such trust is designated by the employer as part of a plan which meets 1 of the following requirements:

(A) The plan benefits at least 70 percent of employees who are not highly compensated employees.

(B) The plan benefits—

(i) a percentage of employees who are not highly compensated employees which is at least 70 percent of

(ii) the percentage of highly compensated employees benefiting under the plan.

(C) The plan meets the requirements of paragraph (2).

(2) **Average benefit percentage test.**

(A) In general. A plan shall be treated as meeting the requirements of this paragraph if—

(i) the plan benefits such employees as qualify under a classification set up by the employer and found by the Secretary not to be discriminatory in favor of highly compensated employees, and

(ii) the average benefit percentage for employees who are not highly compensated employees is at least 70 percent of the average benefit percentage for highly compensated employees.

(B) Average benefit percentage. For purposes of this paragraph, the term "average benefit percentage" means, with respect to any group, the average of the benefit percentages calculated separately with respect to each employee in such group (whether or not a participant in any plan).

(C) Benefit percentage. For purposes of this paragraph—

(i) In general. The term "benefit percentage" means the employer-provided contribution or benefit of an employee under all qualified plans maintained by the employer, expressed as a percentage of such employee's compensation (within the meaning of section 414(s)).

(ii) Period for computing percentage. At the election of an employer, the benefit percentage for any plan year shall be computed on the basis of contributions or benefits for—

(I) such plan year, or

(II) any consecutive plan year period (not greater than 3 years) which ends with such plan year and which is specified in such election.

Employee benefit plans

An election under this clause, once made, may be revoked or modified only with the consent of the Secretary.

(D) Employees taken into account. For purposes of determining who is an employee for purposes of determining the average benefit percentage under subparagraph (B)—

(i) except as provided in clause (ii), paragraph (4)(A) shall not apply, or

(ii) if the employer elects, paragraph (4)(A) shall be applied by using the lowest age and service requirements of all qualified plans maintained by the employer.

(E) Qualified plan. For purposes of this paragraph, the term "qualified plan" means any plan which (without regard to this subsection) meets the requirements of section 401(a).

(3) Exclusion of certain employees. For purposes of this subsection, there shall be excluded from consideration—

(A) employees who are included in a unit of employees covered by an agreement which the Secretary of Labor finds to be a collective bargaining agreement between employee representatives and one or more employers, if there is evidence that retirement benefits were the subject of good faith bargaining between such employee representatives and such employer or employers,

(B) in the case of a trust established or maintained pursuant to an agreement which the Secretary of Labor finds to be a collective bargaining agreement between air pilots represented in accordance with title II of the Railway Labor Act and one or more employers, all employees not covered by such agreement, and

(C) employees who are nonresident aliens and who receive no earned income (within the meaning of section 911(d)(2)) from the employer which constitutes income from sources within the United States (within the meaning of section 861(a)(3)).

Subparagraph (A) shall not apply with respect to coverage of employees under a plan pursuant to an agreement under such subparagraph. For purposes of subparagraph (B), management pilots who are not represented in accordance with title II of the Railway Labor Act shall be treated as covered by a collective bargaining agreement described in such subparagraph if the management pilots manage the flight operations of air pilots who are so represented and the management pilots are, pursuant to the terms of the agreement, included in the group of employees benefitting under the trust described in such subparagraph. Subparagraph (B) shall not apply in the case of a plan which provides contributions or benefits for employees whose principal duties are not customarily performed aboard an aircraft in flight (other than management pilots described in the preceding sentence).

(4) Exclusion of employees not meeting age and service requirements.

(A) In general. If a plan—

(i) prescribes minimum age and service requirements as a condition of participation, and

(ii) excludes all employees not meeting such requirements from participation,

then such employees shall be excluded from consideration for purposes of this subsection.

(B) Requirements may be met separately with respect to excluded group. If employees not meeting the minimum age or service requirements of subsection (a)(1) (without regard to subparagraph (B) thereof) are covered under a plan of the employer which meets the requirements of paragraph (1) separately with respect to such employees, such employees may be excluded from consideration in determining whether any plan of the employer meets the requirements of paragraph (1).

(C) Requirements not treated as being met before entry date. An employee shall not be treated as meeting the age and service requirements described in this paragraph until the first date on which, under the plan, any employee with the same age and service would be eligible to commence participation in the plan.

(5) Line of business exception.

(A) In general. If, under section 414(r), an employer is treated as operating separate lines of business for a year, the employer may apply the requirements of this subsection for such year separately with respect to employees in each separate line of business.

(B) Plan must be nondiscriminatory. Subparagraph (A) shall not apply with respect to any plan maintained by an employer unless such plan benefits such employees as qualify under a classification set up by the employer and found by the Secretary not to be discriminatory in favor of highly compensated employees.

(6) Definitions and special rules. For purposes of this subsection—

(A) Highly compensated employee. The term "highly compensated employee" has the meaning given such term by section 414(q).

(B) Aggregation rules. An employer may elect to designate—

(i) 2 or more trusts,

(ii) 1 or more trusts and 1 or more annuity plans, or

(iii) 2 or more annuity plans,

as part of 1 plan intended to qualify under section 401(a) to determine whether the requirements of this subsection are met with respect to such trusts or annuity plans. If an employer elects to treat any trusts or annuity plans as 1 plan under this subparagraph, such trusts or annuity plans shall be treated as 1 plan for purposes of section 401(a)(4).

(C) Special rules for certain dispositions or acquisitions.

(i) In general. If a person becomes, or ceases to be, a member of a group described in subsection (b), (c), (m), or (o) of section 414, then the requirements of this subsection shall be treated as having been met during the transition period with respect to any plan covering employees of such person or any other member of such group if—

(I) such requirements were met immediately before each such change, and

(II) the coverage under such plan is not significantly changed during the transition period (other than by reason of the change in members of a group) or such plan meets such other requirements as the Secretary may prescribe by regulation.

(ii) Transition period. For purposes of clause (i), the term "transition period" means the period—

(I) beginning on the date of the change in members of a group, and

(II) ending on the last day of the 1st plan year beginning after the date of such change.

(D) Special rule for certain employee stock ownership plans. A trust which is part of a tax credit employee stock ownership plan which is the only plan of an employer intended to qualify under section 401(a) shall not be treated as not a qualified trust under section 401(a) solely because it fails to meet the requirements of this subsection if—

(i) such plan benefits 50 percent or more of all the employees who are eligible under a nondiscriminatory classification under the plan, and

(ii) the sum of the amounts allocated to each participant's account for the year does not exceed 2 percent of the compensation of that participant for the year.

(E) Eligibility to contribute. In the case of contributions which are subject to section 401(k) or 401(m), employees who are eligible to contribute (or elect to have contributions made on their behalf) shall be treated as benefiting under the plan (other than for purposes of paragraph (2)(A)(ii)).

(F) Employers with only highly compensated employees. A plan maintained by an employer which has no employees other than highly compensated employees for any year shall be treated as meeting the requirements of this subsection for such year.

(G) Regulations. The Secretary shall prescribe such regulations as may be necessary or appropriate to carry out the purposes of this subsection.

(c) **Application of participation standards to certain plans.**

(1) The provisions of this section (other than paragraph (2) of this subsection) shall not apply to—

(A) a governmental plan (within the meaning of section 414(d)),

(B) a church plan (within the meaning of section 414(e)) with respect to which the election provided by subsection (d) of this section has not been made,

(C) a plan which has not at any time after September 2, 1974, provided for employer contributions, and

(D) a plan established and maintained by a society, order, or association described in section 501(c)(8) or (9) if no part of the contributions to or under such plan are made by employers of participants in such plan.

(2) A plan described in paragraph (1) shall be treated as meeting the requirements of this section for purposes of section 401(a), except that in the case of a plan described in subparagraph (B), (C), or (D) of paragraph (1), this paragraph shall apply only if such plan meets the requirements of section 401(a)(3) (as in effect on September 1, 1974).

(d) **Election by church to have participation, vesting, funding, etc., provisions apply.**

(1) **In general.** If the church or convention or association of churches which maintains any church plan makes an election under this subsection (in such form and manner as the Secretary may by regulations prescribe), then the provisions of this title relating to participation, vesting, funding, etc. (as in effect from time to time) shall apply to such church plan as if such provisions did not contain an exclusion for church plans.

(2) **Election irrevocable.** An election under this subsection with respect to any church plan shall be binding with respect to such plan, and, once made, shall be irrevocable.

In 2006, P.L. 109-280, Sec. 402(h)(1), substituted "For purposes of subparagraph (B), management pilots who are not represented in accordance with title II of the Railway Labor Act shall be treated as covered by a collective bargaining agreement described in such subparagraph if the management pilots manage the flight operations of air pilots who are so represented and the management pilots are, pursuant to the terms of the agreement, included in the group of employees benefitting under the trust described in such subparagraph. Subparagraph (B) shall not apply in the case of a plan which provides contributions or benefits for employees whose principal duties are not customarily performed aboard an aircraft in flight (other than management pilots described in the preceding sentence)." for "Subparagraph (B) shall not apply in the case of a plan which provides contributions or benefits for employees whose principal duties are not customarily performed aboard aircraft in flight." at the end of para. (b)(3), effective for yrs. begin. before, on, or after 8/17/2006.

—P.L. 109-280, Sec. 861(a)(2), deleted "maintained by a State or local government or political subdivision thereof (or agency or instrumentality thereof)" after "Internal Revenue Code of 1986)" in , see below, effective for any year begin. after 8/17/2006.

—P.L. 109-280, Sec. 865, of this Act, provides:

"SEC. 865. GRANDFATHER RULE FOR CHURCH PLANS WHICH SELF-ANNUITIZE.

"(a) In general. In the case of any plan year ending after the date of the enactment of this Act, annuity payments provided with respect to any account maintained for a participant or beneficiary under a qualified church plan shall not fail to satisfy the requirements of section 401(a)(9) of the Internal Revenue Code of 1986 merely because the payments are not made under an annuity contract purchased from an insurance company if such payments would not fail such requirements if provided with respect to a retirement income account described in section 403(b)(9) of such Code.

"(b) Qualified church plan. For purposes of this section, the term 'qualified church plan' means any money purchase pension plan described in section 401(a) of such Code which—

"(1) is a church plan (as defined in section 414(e) of such Code) with respect to which the election provided by section 410(d) of such Code has not been made, and

"(2) was in existence on April 17, 2002."

—P.L. 109-280, Sec. 1103, of this Act, provides:

"SEC. 1103. REPORTING SIMPLIFICATION.

"(a) Simplified annual filing requirement for owners and their spouses.

"(1) In general. The Secretary of the Treasury shall modify the requirements for filing annual returns with respect to one-participant retirement plans to ensure that such plans with assets of $250,000 or less as of the close of the plan year need not file a return for that year.

"(2) One-participant retirement plan defined. For purposes of this subsection, the term 'one-participant retirement plan' means a retirement plan with respect to which the following requirements are met:

"(A) on the first day of the plan year—

"(i) the plan covered only one individual (or the individual and the individual's spouse) and the individual owned 100 percent of the plan sponsor (whether or not incorporated), or

"(ii) the plan covered only one or more partners (or partners and their spouses) in the plan sponsor;

"(B) the plan meets the minimum coverage requirements of section 410(b) of the Internal Revenue Code of 1986 without being combined with any other plan of the business that covers the employees of the business;

"(C) the plan does not provide benefits to anyone except the individual (and the individual's spouse) or the partners (and their spouses);

"(D) the plan does not cover a business that is a member of an affiliated service group, a controlled group of corporations, or a group of businesses under common control; and

"(E) the plan does not cover a business that uses the services of leased employees (within the meaning of section 414(n) of such Code).

For purposes of this paragraph, the term 'partner' includes a 2-percent shareholder (as defined in section 1372(b) of such Code) of an S corporation.

"(3) Other definitions. Terms used in paragraph (2) which are also used in section 414 of the Internal Revenue Code of 1986 shall have the respective meanings given such terms by such section.

"(4) Effective date. The provisions of this subsection shall apply to plan years beginning on or after January 1, 2007.

"(b) Simplified annual filing requirement for plans with fewer than 25 participants. In the case of plan years beginning after December 31, 2006, the Secretary of the Treasury and the Secretary of Labor shall provide for the filing of a simplified annual return for any retirement plan which covers less than 25 participants on the first day of a plan year and which meets the requirements described in subparagraphs (B), (D), and (E) of subsection (a)(2)."

In 2004, P.L. 108-476, Sec. 1, of this Act, provides:

"SECTION 1. CERTAIN ARRANGEMENTS MAINTAINED BY THE YMCA RETIREMENT FUND TREATED AS CHURCH PLANS.

"(a) Retirement plans.

"(1) In general. For purposes of sections 401(a) and 403(b) of the Internal Revenue Code of 1986, any retirement plan maintained by the YMCA Retirement Fund as of January 1, 2003, shall be treated as a church plan (within the meaning of section 414(e) of such Code) which is maintained by an organization described in section 414(e)(3)(A) of such Code.

"(2) Tax-deferred retirement plan. In the case of a retirement plan described in paragraph (1) which allows contributions to be made under a salary reduction agreement—

"(A) such treatment shall not apply for purposes of section 415(c)(7) of such Code, and

"(B) any account maintained for a participant or beneficiary of such plan shall be treated for purposes of such Code as a retirement income account described in section 403(b)(9) of such Code, except that such account shall not, for purposes of section 403(b)(12) of such Code, be treated as a contract purchased by a church for purposes of section 403(b)(1)(D) of such Code.

"(3) Money purchase pension plan. In the case of a retirement plan described in paragraph (1) which is subject to the requirements of section 401(a) of such Code—

"(A) such plan (but not any reserves held by the YMCA Retirement Fund)—

"(i) shall be treated for purposes of such Code as a defined contribution plan which is a money purchase pension plan, and

"(ii) shall be treated as having made an election under section 410(d) of such Code for plan years beginning after December 31, 2005, except that notwithstanding the election—

"(I) nothing in the Employee Retirement Income Security Act of 1974 or such Code shall prohibit the YMCA Retirement Fund from commingling for investment purposes the assets of the electing plan with the assets of such Fund and with the assets of any employee benefit plan maintained by such Fund, and

"(II) nothing in this section shall be construed as subjecting any assets described in subclause (I), other than the assets of the electing plan, to any provision of such Act,

"(B) notwithstanding section 401(a)(11) or 417 of such Code or section 205 of such Act, such plan may offer a lump-sum distribution option to participants who have not attained age 55 without offering such participants an annuity option, and

"(C) any account maintained for an accountant or beneficiary of such plan shall, for purposes of section 401(a)(9) of such Code, be treated as a retirement income account described in section 403(b)(9) of such Code.

"(4) Self-funded death benefit plan. For purposes of section 7702(j) of such Code, a retirement plan described in paragraph (1) shall be treated as an arrangement described in section 7702(j)(2).

"(b) YMCA retirement fund. For purposes of this section, the term 'YMCA Retirement Fund' means the Young Men's Christian Association Retirement Fund, a corporation created by an Act of the State of New York which became law on April 30, 1921.

"(c) Effective date. This section shall apply to plan years beginning after December 31, 2003."

In **2001**, P.L. 107-16, Sec. 664, of this Act, reads as follows:
"SEC. 664. EMPLOYEES OF TAX-EXEMPT ENTITIES.
"(a) In general. The Secretary of the Treasury shall modify Treasury Regulations section 1.410(b)-6(g) to provide that employees of an organization described in section 403(b)(1)(A)(i) of the Internal Revenue Code of 1986 who are eligible to make contributions under section 403(b) of such Code pursuant to a salary reduction agreement may be treated as excludable with respect to a plan under section 401(k) or (m) of such Code that is provided under the same general arrangement as a plan under such section 401(k), if—

"(1) no employee of an organization described in section 403(b)(1)(A)(i) of such Code is eligible to participate in such section 401(k) plan or section 401(m) plan; and

"(2) 95 percent of the employees who are not employees of an organization described in section 403(b)(1)(A)(i) of such Code are eligible to participate in such plan under such section 401(k) or (m).

"(b) Effective date. The modification required by subsection (a) shall apply as of the same date set forth in section 1426(b) of the Small Business Job Protection Act of 1996."

In **1998**, P.L. 105-206, Sec. 6015(b), substituted "(b)(12)(A)(i)" for "(b)(12)" in Sec. 1505(d)(2) of P.L. 105-34, see below.

In **1997**, P.L. 105-34, Sec. 1505(a)(3), amended para. (c)(2), effective for tax. yrs. begin. after 8/5/97. Sec. 1505(d)(2) of this Act [as amended by Sec. 6015(b) of P.L. 105-206, and Sec. 861(a)(2) of P.L. 109-280, see above] provides:

"(2) Treatment for years beginning before date of enactment. A governmental plan (within the meaning of section 414(d) of the Internal Revenue Code of 1986) shall be treated as satisfying the requirements of sections 401(a)(3), 401(a)(4), 401(a)(26), 401(k), 401(m), 403(b)(1)(D) and (b)(12)(A)(i), and 410 of such Code for all taxable years beginning before the date of enactment of this Act."

Prior to amendment, para. (c)(2) read as follows:
"(2) A plan described in paragraph (1) shall be treated as meeting the requirements of this section, for purposes of section 401(a), if such plan meets the requirements of section 401(a)(3) as in effect on September 1, 1974."

In **1989**, P.L. 101-239, Sec. 7841(d)(6), deleted the comma before the period at the end of para. (a)(2), effective 12/19/89.

—P.L. 101-239, Sec. 7861(a)(3), redesignated the second Sec. 1113(e) of P.L. 99-514, special rules for amendments made by Sec. 1113(c) and (d)(A) of P.L. 99-514, as Sec. 1113(f) of P.L. 99-514, reproduced below... Sec. 7861(a)(4), added Sec. 1113(f)(4) [as redesignated] of P.L. 99-514, reproduced below.

In **1988**, P.L. 100-647, Sec. 1011(h)(1)(A), substituted "not meeting" for "do not meet" in subpara. (b)(4)(B)... Sec. 1011(h)(1)(B), deleted "and" before "are covered" in subpara. (b)(4)(B)... Sec. 1011(h)(2), redesignated subpara. (b)(6)(F) as (b)(6)(G), and added new subpara. (b)(6)(F)... Sec. 1011(h)(11), added subpara. (b)(4)(C), effective for plan yrs. begin. after 12/31/88.

—P.L. 100-647, Sec. 3021(a)(13)(B), added "or such plan meets such other requirements as the Secretary may prescribe by regulation" before the period at the end of subclause (b)(6)(C)(i)(II), effective as provided in Secs. 1151(k)(1)-(4) of P.L. 99-514, reproduced in note following Code Sec. 414.

In **1986**, P.L. 99-514, Sec. 1112(a), amended subsec. (b), effective for plan years begin. after 12/31/88. Sec. 1112(e)(2) of this Act provides the following special rule:

"(2) Special rule for collective bargaining agreements. — In the case of a plan maintained pursuant to 1 or more collective bargaining agreements between employee representatives and 1 or more employers ratified before March 1, 1986, the amendments made by this section shall not apply to employees covered by any such agreement in plan years beginning before the earlier of—

"(A) the later of—
"(i) January 1, 1989, or
"(ii) the date on which the last of such collective bargaining agreement terminates (determined without regard to any extension thereof after February 28, 1986), or

"(B) January 1, 1991."

Prior to amendment, subsec. (b) read as follows:
"(b) Eligibility.

"(1) In general. A trust shall not constitute a qualified trust under section 401(a) unless the trust, or two or more trusts, or the trust or trusts and annuity plan or plans are designated by the employer as constituting parts of a plan intended to qualify under section 401(a) which benefits either—

"(A) 70 percent or more of all employees, or 80 percent or more of all the employees who are eligible to benefit under the plan if 70 percent or more of all the employees are eligible to benefit under the plan, excluding in each case employees who have not satisfied the minimum age and service requirements, if any, prescribed by the plan as a condition of participation, or

"(B) such employees as qualify under a classification set up by the employer and found by the Secretary not to be discriminatory in favor of employees who are officers, shareholders, or highly compensated.

"(2) Special rule for certain plans. A trust which is part of a tax credit employees stock ownership plan which is the only plan of an employer intended to qualify under section 401(a) shall not be treated as not a qualified trust under section 401(a) solely because it fails to meet the requirements of paragraph (1) if—

"(A) it benefits 50 percent or more of all the employees who are eligible under the plan (excluding employees who have not satisfied the minimum age and service requirements, if any, prescribed by the plan as a condition of participation), and

"(B) the sum of the amounts allocated to each participant's account for the year does not exceed 2 percent of the compensation of that participant for the year.

"(3) Exclusion of certain employees. For purposes of paragraphs (1) and (2) there shall be excluded from consideration—

"(A) employees not included in the plan who are included in a unit of employees covered by an agreement which the Secretary of Labor finds to be a collective bargaining agreement between employee representatives and one or more employers, if there is evidence that retirement benefits were the subject of good faith bargaining between such employee representatives and such employer or employers,

"(B) in the case of a trust established or maintained pursuant to an agreement which the Secretary of Labor finds to be a collective bargaining agreement between air pilots represented in accordance with title II of the Railway Labor Act and one or more employers, all employees not covered by such agreement, and

"(C) employees who are nonresident aliens and who receive no earned income (within the meaning of section 911(d)(2)) from the employer which constitutes income from sources within the United States (within the meaning of section 861(a)(3)).

Subparagraph (B) shall not apply in the case of a plan which provides contributions or benefits for employees whose principal duties are not customarily performed aboard aircraft in flight."

—P.L. 99-514, Sec. 1113(c), substituted "2 years" for "3 years" each place it appeared in clause (a)(1)(B)(i)... Sec. 1113(d)(A), substituted "2-year" for "3-year" in the heading of subpara. (a)(5)(B), effective for plan yrs. begin. after 12/31/88. Sec. 1113(f)(2), (3) and (4) of this Act [as amended by Sec. 7861(a)(3) of P.L. 101-239 and (4), see above] provides:

"(2) Special rule for collective bargaining agreements. — In the case of a plan maintained pursuant to 1 or more collective bargaining agreements between employee representatives and 1 or more employers ratified before March 1, 1986, the amendments made by this section shall not apply to employees covered by any such agreement in plan years beginning before the earlier of—

"(A) the later of—
"(i) January 1, 1989, or
"(ii) the date on which the last of such collective bargaining agreements terminates (determined without regard to any extension thereof after February 28, 1986), or

"(B) January 1, 1991.

"(3) Participation required. — The amendments made by this section shall not apply to any employee who does not have 1 hour of service in any plan year to which the amendments made by this section apply.

"(4) Repeal of class year vesting. — If a plan amendment repealing class year vesting is adopted after October 22, 1986, such amendment shall not apply to any employee for the 1st plan year to which the amendments made by subsections (b) and (e)(2) apply (and any subsequent plan year) if—

"(A) such plan amendment would reduce the nonforfeitable right of such employee for such year, and

"(B) such employee has at least 1 hour of service before the adoption of such plan amendment and after the beginning of such 1st plan year.

This paragraph shall not apply to an employee who has 5 consecutive 1-year breaks in service (as defined in section 411(a)(6)(A) of the Internal Revenue Code of 1986) which include the 1st day of the 1st plan year to which the amendments made by subsection (b) and (e)(2) apply. A plan shall not be treated as failing to meet the requirements of section 401(a)(26) of such Code by reason of complying with the provisions of this paragraph."

—P.L. 99-509, Sec. 9203(a)(2), amended para. (a)(2), effective for plan yrs. begin. on or after 1/1/88, and only for service performed on or after 1/1/88 Sec. 9204(c) of this Act provides:

"(c) Plan amendments.—

"If any amendment made by this subtitle requires an amendment to any plan, such plan amendment shall not be required to be made before the first plan year beginning on or after January 1, 1989, if—

"(1) during the period after such amendment takes effect and before such first plan year, the plan is operated in accordance with the requirements of such amendment, and

"(2) such plan amendment applies retroactively to the period after such amendment takes effect and such first plan year.

A pension plan shall not be treated as failing to provide definitely determinable benefits or contributions, or to be operated in accordance with the provisions of the plan, merely because it operates in accordance with this subsection."

Prior to amendment, para. (a)(2) read as follows:

"(2) Maximum age conditions. A trust shall not constitute a qualified trust under section 401(a) if the plan of which it is a part excludes from participation (on the basis of age) employees who have attained a specified age, unless—

"(A) the plan is a—
"(i) defined benefit plan, or
"(ii) target benefit plan (as defined under regulations prescribed by the Secretary, and

"(B) such employees begin employment with the employer after they have attained a specified age which is not more than 5 years before the normal retirement age under the plan."

In 1984, P.L. 98-397, Sec. 202(a)(1), substituted "21" for "25" in clause (a)(1)(A)(i)... Sec. 202(a)(2), substituted "'26' for '21'" for "'30' for '25'" in clause (a)(1)(B)(ii)... Sec. 202(d)(1), amended subpara. (a)(5)(D)... Sec. 202(e)(1), added subpara. (a)(5)(E), effective for plan yrs. begin. after 12/31/84. Sec. 302(b) of this Act provides the following special rule:

"(b) Special rule for collective bargaining agreements.—In the case of a plan maintained pursuant to 1 or more collective bargaining agreements between employee representatives and 1 or more employers ratified before the date of the enactment of this Act, except as provided in subsection (d) or section 303, the amendments made by this Act shall not apply to plan years beginning before the earlier of—

"(1) the date on which the last of the collective bargaining agreements relating to the plan terminates (determined without regard to any extension thereof agreed to after the date of the enactment of this Act), or

"(2) January 1, 1987.

For purposes of paragraph (1), any plan amendment made pursuant to a collective bargaining agreement relating to the plan which amends the plan solely to conform to any requirement added by title I or II shall not be treated as a termination of such collective bargaining agreement."

For transitional rules see Sec. 303 of this Act reproduced at note following Code Sec. 401.

Prior to amendment, subpara. (a)(5)(D) read as follows:

"(D) Nonvested participants. In the case of a participant who does not have any nonforfeitable right to an accrued benefit derived from employer contributions, years of service with the employer or employers maintaining the plan before a break in service shall not be required to be taken into account in computing the period of service for purposes of paragraph (1) if the number of consecutive 1-year breaks in service equals or exceeds the aggregate number of such years of service before such break. Such aggregate number of years of service before such break shall be deemed not to include any years of service not required to be taken into account under this subparagraph by reason of any prior break in service."

In 1981, P.L. 97-34, Sec. 111(b)(4), substituted "section 911(d)(2)" for "section 911(b)" in subpara. (b)(3)(C), effective for tax. yrs. begin. after 12/31/81.

In 1980, P.L. 96-605, Sec. 225(a), redesignated para. (b)(2) as (b)(3), substituted "paragraphs (1) and (2)" for "paragraph (1)" in para. (b)(3) (as redesignated), and added new para. (b)(2), effective for plan yrs. begin. after 12/31/80.

In 1976, P.L. 94-455, Sec. 1901(a)(61), substituted "purposes of paragraph (1)" for "purposes of subsection (a)(1)" in subparas. (a)(5)(C) and (D), substituted "September 2, 1974," for "the date of the enactment of the Employee Retirement Income Security Act of 1974" in subpara. (c)(1)(C), and substituted "September 1, 1974" for "the day before the date of the enactment of this section" in para. (c)(2), effective for tax. yrs. begin. after 12/31/76.

—P.L. 94-455, Sec. 1906(b)(13)(A), substituted "Secretary" for "Secretary or his delegate" each place it appeared in subsecs. (a), (b), and (d) effective for tax. yrs. begin. after 12/31/76.

In 1974, P.L. 93-406, Sec. 1011, added Code Sec. 410, effective 9/2/74 or other date as specified in Sec. 1017 of the Act (reproduced following Code Sec. 401).

Sec. 411. Minimum vesting standards.

(a) General rule.

A trust shall not constitute a qualified trust under section 401(a) unless the plan of which such trust is a part provides that an employee's right to his normal retirement benefit is nonforfeitable upon the attainment of normal retirement age (as defined in paragraph (8)) and in addition satisfies the requirements of paragraphs (1), (2), and (11) of this subsection and the requirements of subsection (b)(3), and also satisfies, in the case of a defined benefit plan, the requirements of subsection (b)(1) and, in the case of a defined contribution plan, the requirements of subsection (b)(2).

(1) **Employee contributions.** A plan satisfies the requirements of this paragraph if an employee's rights in his accrued benefit derived from his own contributions are nonforfeitable.

(2) **Employer contributions.**

(A) Defined benefit plans.

(i) In general. In the case of a defined benefit plan, a plan satisfies the requirements of this paragraph if it satisfies the requirements of clause (ii) or (iii).

(ii) 5-year vesting. A plan satisfies the requirements of this clause if an employee who has completed at least 5 years of service has a nonforfeitable right to 100 percent of the employee's accrued benefit derived from employer contributions.

(iii) 3 to 7 year vesting. A plan satisfies the requirements of this clause if an employee has a nonforfeitable right to a percentage of the employee's accrued benefit derived from employer contributions determined under the following table:

Years of service:	The nonforfeitable percentage is:
3	20
4	40
5	60
6	80
7 or more	100

(B) Defined contribution plans.

(i) In general. In the case of a defined contribution plan, a plan satisfies the requirements of this paragraph if it satisfies the requirements of clause (ii) or (iii).

(ii) 3-year vesting. A plan satisfies the requirements of this clause if an employee who has completed at least 3 years of service has a nonforfeitable right to 100 percent of the employee's accrued benefit derived from employer contributions.

(iii) 2 to 6 year vesting. A plan satisfies the requirements of this clause if an employee has a nonforfeitable right to a percentage of the employee's accrued benefit derived from employer contributions determined under the following table:

Years of service:	The nonforfeitable percentage is:
2	20
3	40
4	60
5	80
6 or more	100

(3) **Certain permitted forfeitures, suspensions, etc.** For purposes of this subsection—

(A) Forfeiture on account of death. A right to an accrued benefit derived from employer contributions shall not be treated as forfeitable solely because the plan provides that it is not payable if the participant dies (except in the case of a survivor annuity which is payable as provided in section 401(a)(11)).

(B) Suspension of benefits upon reemployment of retiree. A right to an accrued benefit derived from employer contributions shall not be treated as forfeitable solely because the plan provides that the payment of benefits is suspended for such period as the employee is employed, subsequent to the commencement of payment of such benefits—

(i) in the case of a plan other than a multiemployer plan, by the employer who maintains the plan under which such benefits were being paid; and

(ii) in the case of a multiemployer plan, in the same industry, the same trade or craft, and the same geographic area covered by the plan as when such benefits commenced.

The Secretary of Labor shall prescribe such regulations as may be necessary to carry out the purposes of this subparagraph, including regulations with respect to the meaning of the term "employed".

(C) Effect of retroactive plan amendments. A right to an accrued benefit derived from employer contributions shall not be treated as forfeitable solely because plan amendments may be given retroactive application as provided in section 412(d)(2).

(D) Withdrawal of mandatory contribution.

(i) A right to an accrued benefit derived from employer contributions shall not be treated as forfeitable solely because the plan provides that, in the case of a participant who does not have a nonforfeitable right to at least 50 percent of his accrued benefit derived from employer contributions, such accrued benefit may be forfeited on account of the withdrawal by the participant of any amount attributable to the benefit derived from mandatory contributions (as defined in subsection (c)(2)(C)) made by such participant.

(ii) Clause (i) shall not apply to a plan unless the plan provides that any accrued benefit forfeited under a plan provision described in such clause shall be restored upon repayment by the participant of the full amount of the withdrawal described in such clause plus, in the case of a defined benefit plan, interest. Such interest shall be computed on such amount at the rate determined for purposes of subsection (c)(2)(C) on the date of such repayment (computed annually from the date of such withdrawal). The plan provision required under this clause may provide that such repayment must be made (I) in the case of a withdrawal on account of separation from service, before the earlier of 5 years after the first date on which the participant is subsequently re-employed by the employer, or the close of the first period of 5 consecutive 1-year breaks in service commencing after the withdrawal; or (II) in the case of any other withdrawal, 5 years after the date of the withdrawal.

(iii) In the case of accrued benefits derived from employer contributions which accrued before September 2, 1974, a right to such accrued benefit derived from employer contributions shall not be treated as forfeitable solely because the plan provides that an amount of such accrued benefit may be forfeited on account of the withdrawal by the participant of an amount attributable to the benefit derived from mandatory contributions (as defined in subsection (c)(2)(C)) made by such participant before September 2, 1974, if such amount forfeited is proportional to such amount withdrawn. This clause shall not apply to any plan to which any mandatory contribution is made after September 2, 1974. The Secretary shall prescribe such regulations as may be necessary to carry out the purposes of this clause.

(iv) For purposes of this subparagraph, in the case of any class-year plan, a withdrawal of employee contributions shall be treated as a withdrawal of employee contributions on a plan year by plan year basis in succeeding order of time.

(v) For nonforfeitability where the employee has a nonforfeitable right to at least 50 percent of his accrued benefit, see section 401(a)(19).

(E) Cessation of contributions under a multiemployer plan. A right to an accrued benefit derived from employer contributions under a multiemployer plan shall not be treated as forfeitable solely because the plan provides that benefits accrued as a result of service with the participant's employer before the employer had an obligation to contribute under the plan may not be payable if the employer ceases contributions to the multiemployer plan.

(F) Reduction and suspension of benefits by a multiemployer plan. A participant's right to an accrued benefit derived from employer contributions under a multiemployer plan shall not be treated as forfeitable solely because—

(i) the plan is amended to reduce benefits under section 418D or under section 4281 of the Employee Retirement Income Security Act of 1974, or

(ii) benefit payments under the plan may be suspended under section 418E or under section 4281 of the Employee Retirement Income Security Act of 1974.

(G) Treatment of matching contributions forfeited by reason of excess deferral or contribution or permissible withdrawal. A matching contribution (within the meaning of section 401(m)) shall not be treated as forfeitable merely because such contribution is forfeitable if the contribution to which the matching contribution relates is treated as an excess contribution under section 401(k)(8)(B), an excess deferral under section 402(g)(2)(A) a permissible withdrawal under section 414(w), or an excess aggregate contribution under section 401(m)(6)(B).

(4) Service included in determination of nonforfeitable percentage. In computing the period of service under the plan for purposes of determining the nonforfeitable percentage under paragraph (2), all of an employee's years of service with the employer or employers maintaining the plan shall be taken into account, except that the following may be disregarded:

(A) years of service before age 18, [sic ;]

(B) years of service during a period for which the employee declined to contribute to a plan requiring employee contributions;

(C) years of service with an employer during any period for which the employer did not maintain the plan or a predecessor plan (as defined under regulations prescribed by the Secretary);

(D) service not required to be taken into account under paragraph (6);

(E) years of service before January 1, 1971, unless the employee has had at least 3 years of service after December 31, 1970;

(F) years of service before the first plan year to which this section applies, if such service would have been disregarded under the rules of the plan with regard to breaks in service as in effect on the applicable date; and

(G) in the case of a multiemployer plan, years of service—

(i) with an employer after—

(I) a complete withdrawal of that employer from the plan (within the meaning of section 4203 of the Employee Retirement Income Security Act of 1974), or

(II) to the extent permitted in regulations prescribed by the Secretary, a partial withdrawal described in section 4205(b)(2)(A)(i) of such Act in conjunction with the decertification of the collective bargaining representative, and

(ii) with any employer under the plan after the termination date of the plan under section 4048 of such Act.

(5) Year of service.

(A) General rule. For purposes of this subsection, except as provided in subparagraph (C), the term "year of service" means a calendar year, plan year, or other 12-consecutive month period designated by the plan (and not prohibited under regulations prescribed by the Secretary of Labor) during which the participant has completed 1,000 hours of service.

(B) Hours of service. For purposes of this subsection, the term "hours of service" has the meaning provided by section 410(a)(3)(C).

(C) Seasonal industries. In the case of any seasonal industry where the customary period of employment is less than 1,000 hours during a calendar year, the term "year of service" shall be such period as may be determined under regulations prescribed by the Secretary of Labor.

(D) Maritime industries. For purposes of this subsection, in the case of any maritime industry, 125 days of service shall be treated as 1,000 hours of service. The Secretary of Labor may prescribe regulations to carry out the purposes of this subparagraph.

(6) Breaks in service.

(A) Definition of 1-year break in service. For purposes of this paragraph, the term "1-year break in service" means a calendar year, plan year, or other 12-consecutive-month period designated by the plan (and not prohibited under regulations prescribed by the Secretary of Labor) during which the participant has not completed more than 500 hours of service.

(B) 1 year of service after 1-year break in service. For purposes of paragraph (4), in the case of any employee who has any 1-year break in service, years of service before such break shall not be required to be taken into account until he has completed a year of service after his return.

(C) 5 consecutive 1-year breaks in service under defined contribution plan. For purposes of paragraph (4), in the case of any participant in a defined contribution plan, or an insured defined benefit plan which satisfies the requirements of subsection (b)(1)(F), who has 5 consecutive 1-year breaks in service, years of service after such 5-year period shall not be required to be taken into account for purposes of determining the nonforfeitable percentage of his accrued benefit derived from employer contributions which accrued before such 5-year period.

(D) Nonvested participants.

(i) In general. For purposes of paragraph (4), in the case of a nonvested participant, years of service with the employer or employers maintaining the plan before any period of consecutive 1-year breaks in service shall not be required to be taken into account if the number of consecutive 1-year breaks in service within such period equals or exceeds the greater of—

(I) 5, or

(II) the aggregate number of years of service before such period.

(ii) Years of service not taken into account. If any years of service are not required to be taken into account by reason of a period of breaks in service to which clause (i) applies, such years of service shall not be taken into account in applying clause (i) to a subsequent period of breaks in service.

(iii) Nonvested participant defined. For purposes of clause (i), the term "nonvested participant" means a participant who does not have any nonforfeitable right under the plan to an accrued benefit derived from employer contributions.

(E) Special rule for maternity or paternity absences.

(i) General rule. In the case of each individual who is absent from work for any period—

(I) by reason of the pregnancy of the individual,

(II) by reason of the birth of a child of the individual,

(III) by reason of the placement of a child with the individual in connection with the adoption of such child by such individual, or

(IV) for purposes of caring for such child for a period beginning immediately following such birth or placement,

the plan shall treat as hours of service, solely for purposes of determining under this paragraph whether a 1-year break in service has occurred, the hours described in clause (ii).

(ii) Hours treated as hours of service. The hours described in this clause are—

(I) the hours of service which otherwise would normally have been credited to such individual but for such absence, or

(II) in any case in which the plan is unable to determine the hours described in subclause (I), 8 hours of service per day of absence,

except that the total number of hours treated as hours of service under this clause by reason of any such pregnancy or placement shall not exceed 501 hours.

(iii) Year to which hours are credited. The hours described in clause (ii) shall be treated as hours of service as provided in this subparagraph—

(I) only in the year in which the absence from work begins, if a participant would be prevented from incurring a 1-year break in service in such year solely because the period of absence is treated as hours of service as provided in clause (i); or

(II) in any other case, in the immediately following year.

(iv) Year defined. For purposes of this subparagraph, the term "year" means the period used in computations pursuant to paragraph (5).

(v) Information required to be filed. A plan shall not fail to satisfy the requirements of this subparagraph solely because it provides that no credit will be given pursuant to this subparagraph unless the individual furnishes to the plan administrator such timely information as the plan may reasonably require to establish—

(I) that the absence from work is for reasons referred to in clause (i), and

(II) the number of days for which there was such an absence.

(7) Accrued benefit.

(A) In general. For purposes of this section, the term "accrued benefit" means—

(i) in the case of a defined benefit plan, the employee's accrued benefit determined under the plan and, except as provided in subsection (c)(3), expressed in the form of an annual benefit commencing at normal retirement age, or

(ii) in the case of a plan which is not a defined benefit plan, the balance of the employee's account.

(B) Effect of certain distributions. Notwithstanding paragraph (4), for purposes of determining the employee's accrued benefit under the plan, the plan may disregard service performed by the employee with respect to which he has received—

(i) a distribution of the present value of his entire nonforfeitable benefit if such distribution was in an amount (not more than the dollar limit under section 411(a)(11)(A)) permitted under regulations prescribed by the Secretary, or

(ii) a distribution of the present value of his nonforfeitable benefit attributable to such service which he elected to receive.

Clause (i) of this subparagraph shall apply only if such distribution was made on termination of the employee's participation in the plan. Clause (ii) of this subparagraph shall apply only if such distribution was made on termination of the employee's participation in the plan or under such other circumstances as may be provided under regulations prescribed by the Secretary.

(C) Repayment of subparagraph (B) distributions. For purposes of determining the employee's accrued benefit under a plan, the plan may not disregard service as provided in subparagraph (B) unless the plan provides an opportunity for the participant to repay the full amount of the distribution described in such subparagraph (B) with, in the case of a defined benefit plan, interest at the rate determined for purposes of subsection (c)(2)(C) and provides that upon such repayment the employee's accrued benefit shall be recomputed by taking into account service so disregarded. This subparagraph shall apply only in the case of a participant who—

(i) received such a distribution in any plan year to which this section applies, which distribution was less than the present value of his accrued benefit,

(ii) resumes employment covered under the plan, and

(iii) repays the full amount of such distribution with, in the case of a defined benefit plan, interest at the rate determined for purposes of subsection (c)(2)(C).

The plan provision required under this subparagraph may provide that such repayment must be made (I) in the case of a withdrawal on account of separation from service, before the earlier of 5 years after the first date on which the participant is subsequently re-employed by the employer, or the close of the first period of 5 consecutive 1-year breaks in service commencing after the withdrawal; or (II) in the case of any other withdrawal, 5 years after the date of the withdrawal.

(D) Accrued benefit attributable to employee contributions. The accrued benefit of an employee shall not be less than the amount determined under subsection (c)(2)(B) with respect to the employee's accumulated contributions.

(8) Normal retirement age. For purposes of this section, the term "normal retirement age" means the earlier of—

(A) the time a plan participant attains normal retirement age under the plan, or

(B) the later of—

(i) the time a plan participant attains age 65, or

(ii) the 5th anniversary of the time a plan participant commenced participation in the plan.

(9) Normal retirement benefit. For purposes of this section, the term "normal retirement benefit" means the greater of the early retirement benefit under the plan, or the benefit under the plan commencing at normal retirement age. The normal retirement benefit shall be determined without regard to—

(A) medical benefits, and

(B) disability benefits not in excess of the qualified disability benefit.

For purposes of this paragraph, a qualified disability benefit is a disability benefit provided by a plan which does not exceed the benefit which would be provided for the participant if he separated from the service at normal retirement age. For purposes of this paragraph, the early retirement benefit under a plan shall be determined without regard to any benefits commencing before benefits payable under title II of the Social Security Act become payable which—

(i) do not exceed such social security benefits, and

(ii) terminate when such social security benefits commence.

(10) Changes in vesting schedule.

(A) General rule. A plan amendment changing any vesting schedule under the plan shall be treated as not satisfying the requirements of paragraph (2) if the nonforfeitable percentage of the accrued benefit derived from employer contributions (determined as of the later of the date such amendment is adopted, or the date such amendment becomes effective) of any employee who is a participant in the plan is less than such nonforfeitable percentage computed under the plan without regard to such amendment.

(B) Election of former schedule. A plan amendment changing any vesting schedule under the plan shall be treated as not satisfying the requirements of paragraph (2) unless each participant having not less than 3 years of service is permitted to elect, within a reasonable period after the adoption of such amendment, to have his nonforfeitable percentage computed under the plan without regard to such amendment.

(11) Restrictions on certain mandatory distributions.

(A) In general. If the present value of any nonforfeitable accrued benefit exceeds $5,000, a plan meets the requirements of this paragraph only if such plan provides that such benefit may not be immediately distributed without the consent of the participant.

(B) Determination of present value. For purposes of subparagraph (A), the present value shall be calculated in accordance with section 417(e)(3).

(C) Dividend distributions of ESOPs arrangement. This paragraph shall not apply to any distribution of dividends to which section 404(k) applies.

(D) Special rule for rollover contributions. A plan shall not fail to meet the requirements of this paragraph if, under the terms of the plan, the present value of the nonforfeitable accrued benefit is determined without regard to that portion of such benefit which is attributable to rollover contributions (and earnings allocable thereto). For purposes of this subparagraph, the term "rollover contributions" means any rollover contribution under sections 402(c), 403(a)(4), 403(b)(8), 408(d)(3)(A)(ii), and 457(e)(16).

(12) Repealed.

(13) Special rules for plans computing accrued benefits by reference to hypothetical account balance or equivalent amounts.

(A) In general. An applicable defined benefit plan shall not be treated as failing to meet—
(i) subject to subparagraph (B), the requirements of subsection (a)(2), or
(ii) the requirements of subsection (a)(11) or (c), or the requirements of section 417(e), with respect to accrued benefits derived from employer contributions, solely because the present value of the accrued benefit (or any portion thereof) of any participant is, under the terms of the plan, equal to the amount expressed as the balance in the hypothetical account described in subparagraph (C) or as an accumulated percentage of the participant's final average compensation.
(B) 3-year vesting. In the case of an applicable defined benefit plan, such plan shall be treated as meeting the requirements of subsection (a)(2) only if an employee who has completed at least 3 years of service has a nonforfeitable right to 100 percent of the employee's accrued benefit derived from employer contributions.
(C) Applicable defined benefit plan and related rules. For purposes of this subsection—
(i) In general. The term "applicable defined benefit plan" means a defined benefit plan under which the accrued benefit (or any portion thereof) is calculated as the balance of a hypothetical account maintained for the participant or as an accumulated percentage of the participant's final average compensation.
(ii) Regulations to include similar plans. The Secretary shall issue regulations which include in the definition of an applicable defined benefit plan any defined benefit plan (or any portion of such a plan) which has an effect similar to an applicable defined benefit plan.

(b) Accrued benefit requirements.
(1) Defined benefit plans.
(A) 3-percent method. A defined benefit plan satisfies the requirements of this paragraph if the accrued benefit to which each participant is entitled upon his separation from the service is not less than—
(i) 3 percent of the normal retirement benefit to which he would be entitled if he commenced participation at the earliest possible entry age under the plan and served continuously until the earlier of age 65 or the normal retirement age specified under the plan, multiplied by
(ii) the number of years (not in excess of 33⅓) of his participation in the plan.
In the case of a plan providing retirement benefits based on compensation during any period, the normal retirement benefit to which a participant would be entitled shall be determined as if he continued to earn annually the average rate of compensation which he earned during consecutive years of service, not in excess of 10, for which his compensation was the highest. For purposes of this subparagraph, social security benefits and all other relevant factors used to compute benefits shall be treated as remaining constant as of the current year for all years after such current year.
(B) 133⅓ percent rule. A defined benefit plan satisfies the requirements of this paragraph for a particular plan year if under the plan the accrued benefit payable at the normal retirement age is equal to the normal retirement benefit and the annual rate at which any individual who is or could be a participant can accrue the retirement benefits payable at normal retirement age under the plan for any later plan year is not more than 133⅓ percent of the annual rate at which he can accrue benefits for any plan year beginning on or after such particular plan year and before such later plan year. For purposes of this subparagraph—
(i) any amendment to the plan which is in effect for the current year shall be treated as in effect for all other plan years;
(ii) any change in an accrual rate which does not apply to any individual who is or could be a participant in the current year shall be disregarded;
(iii) the fact that benefits under the plan may be payable to certain employees before normal retirement age shall be disregarded; and
(iv) social security benefits and all other relevant factors used to compute benefits shall be treated as remaining constant as of the current year for all years after the current year.
(C) Fractional rule. A defined benefit plan satisfies the requirements of this paragraph if the accrued benefit to which any participant is entitled upon his separation from the service is not less than a fraction of the annual benefit commencing at normal retirement age to which he would be entitled under the plan as in effect on the date of his separation if he continued to earn annually until normal retirement age the same rate of compensation upon which his normal retirement benefit would be computed under the plan, determined as if he had attained normal retirement age on the date on which any such determination is made (but taking into account no more than the 10 years of service immediately preceding his separation from service). Such fraction shall be a fraction, not exceeding 1, the numerator of which is the total number of his years of participation in the plan (as of the date of his separation from the service) and the denominator of which is the total number of years he would have participated in the plan if he separated from the service at the normal retirement age. For purposes of this subparagraph, social security benefits and all other relevant factors used to compute benefits shall be treated as remaining constant as of the current year for all years after such current year.
(D) Accrual for service before effective date. Subparagraphs (A), (B), and (C) shall not apply with respect to years of participation before the first plan year to which this section applies, but a defined benefit plan satisfies the requirements of this subparagraph with respect to such years of participation only if the accrued benefit of any participant with respect to such years of participation is not less than the greater of—
(i) his accrued benefit determined under the plan, as in effect from time to time prior to September 2, 1974 or
(ii) an accrued benefit which is not less than one-half of the accrued benefit to which such participant would have been entitled if subparagraph (A), (B), or (C) applied with respect to such years of participation.
(E) First two years of service. Notwithstanding subparagraphs (A), (B), and (C) of this paragraph, a plan shall not be treated as not satisfying the requirements of this paragraph solely because the accrual of benefits under the plan does not become effective until the employee has two continuous years of service. For purposes of this subparagraph, the term "years of service" has the meaning provided by section 410(a)(3)(A).
(F) Certain insured defined benefit plans. Notwithstanding subparagraphs (A), (B), and (C), a defined benefit

plan satisfies the requirements of this paragraph if such plan—
(i) is funded exclusively by the purchase of insurance contracts, and
(ii) satisfies the requirements of subparagraphs (B) and (C) of section 412(e)(3) (relating to certain insurance contract plans),

but only if an employee's accrued benefit as of any applicable date is not less than the cash surrender value his insurance contracts would have on such applicable date if the requirements of subparagraphs (D), (E), and (F) of section 412(e)(3) were satisfied.

(G) Accrued benefit may not decrease on account of increasing age or service. Notwithstanding the preceding subparagraphs, a defined benefit plan shall be treated as not satisfying the requirements of this paragraph if the participant's accrued benefit is reduced on account of any increase in his age or service. The preceding sentence shall not apply to benefits under the plan commencing before entitlement to benefits payable under title II of the Social Security Act which benefits under the plan—
(i) do not exceed such social security benefits, and
(ii) terminate when such social security benefits commence.

(H) Continued accrual beyond normal retirement age.
(i) In general. Notwithstanding the preceding subparagraphs, a defined benefit plan shall be treated as not satisfying the requirements of this paragraph if, under the plan, an employee's benefit accrual is ceased, or the rate of an employee's benefit accrual is reduced, because of the attainment of any age.
(ii) Certain limitations permitted. A plan shall not be treated as failing to meet the requirements of this subparagraph solely because the plan imposes (without regard to age) a limitation on the amount of benefits that the plan provides or a limitation on the number of years of service or years of participation which are taken into account for purposes of determining benefit accrual under the plan.
(iii) Adjustments under plan for delayed retirement taken into account. In the case of any employee who, as of the end of any plan year under a defined benefit plan, has attained normal retirement age under such plan—
(I) if distribution of benefits under such plan with respect to such employee has commenced as of the end of such plan year, then any requirement of this subparagraph for continued accrual of benefits under such plan with respect to such employee during such plan year shall be treated as satisfied to the extent of the actuarial equivalent of in-service distribution of benefits, and
(II) if distribution of benefits under such plan with respect to such employee has not commenced as of the end of such year in accordance with section 401(a)(14)(C), and the payment of benefits under such plan with respect to such employee is not suspended during such plan year pursuant to subsection (a)(3)(B), then any requirement of this subparagraph for continued accrual of benefits under such plan with respect to such employee during such plan year shall be treated as satisfied to the extent of any adjustment in the benefit payable under the plan during such plan year attributable to the delay in the distribution of benefits after the attainment of normal retirement age.

The preceding provisions of this clause shall apply in accordance with regulations of the Secretary. Such regulations may provide for the application of the preceding provisions of this clause, in the case of any such employee, with respect to any period of time within a plan year.
(iv) Disregard of subsidized portion of early retirement benefit. A plan shall not be treated as failing to meet the requirements of clause (i) solely because the subsidized portion of any early retirement benefit is disregarded in determining benefit accruals.
(v) Coordination with other requirements. The Secretary shall provide by regulation for the coordination of the requirements of this subparagraph with the requirements of subsection (a), sections 404, 410, and 415, and the provisions of this subchapter precluding discrimination in favor of highly compensated employees.

(2) **Defined contribution plans.**
(A) In general. A defined contribution plan satisfies the requirements of this paragraph if, under the plan, allocations to the employee's account are not ceased, and the rate at which amounts are allocated to the employee's account is not reduced, because of the attainment of any age.
(B) Application to target benefit plans. The Secretary shall provide by regulation for the application of the requirements of this paragraph to target benefit plans.
(C) Coordination with other requirements. The Secretary may provide by regulation for the coordination of the requirements of this paragraph with the requirements of subsection (a), sections 404, 410, and 415, and the provisions of this subchapter precluding discrimination in favor of highly compensated employees.

(3) **Separate accounting required in certain cases.** A plan satisfies the requirements of this paragraph if—
(A) in the case of a defined benefit plan, the plan requires separate accounting for the portion of each employee's accrued benefit derived from any voluntary employee contributions permitted under the plan; and
(B) in the case of any plan which is not a defined benefit plan, the plan requires separate accounting for each employee's accrued benefit.

(4) **Year of participation.**
(A) Definition. For purposes of determining an employee's accrued benefit, the term "year of participation" means a period of service (beginning at the earliest date on which the employee is a participant in the plan and which is included in a period of service required to be taken into account under section 410(a)(5), determined without regard to section 410(a)(5)(E)) as determined under regulations prescribed by the Secretary of Labor which provide for the calculation of such period on any reasonable and consistent basis.
(B) Less than full time service. For purposes of this paragraph, except as provided in subparagraph (C), in the case of any employee whose customary employment is less than full time, the calculation of such employee's service on any basis which provides less than a ratable portion of the accrued benefit to which he would be entitled under the plan if his customary employment were full time shall not be treated as made on a reasonable and consistent basis.
(C) Less than 1,000 hours of service during year. For purposes of this paragraph, in the case of any employee whose service is less than 1,000 hours during any cal-

endar year, plan year or other 12-consecutive month period designated by the plan (and not prohibited under regulations prescribed by the Secretary of Labor) the calculation of his period of service shall not be treated as not made on a reasonable and consistent basis solely because such service is not taken into account.

(D) Seasonal industries. In the case of any seasonal industry where the customary period of employment is less than 1,000 hours during a calendar year, the term "year of participation" shall be such period as determined under regulations prescribed by the Secretary of Labor.

(E) Maritime industries. For purposes of this subsection, in the case of any maritime industry, 125 days of service shall be treated as a year of participation. The Secretary of Labor may prescribe regulations to carry out the purposes of this subparagraph.

(5) Special rules relating to age.

(A) Comparison to similarly situated younger individual.

(i) In general. A plan shall not be treated as failing to meet the requirements of paragraph (1)(H)(i) if a participant's accrued benefit, as determined as of any date under the terms of the plan, would be equal to or greater than that of any similarly situated, younger individual who is or could be a participant.

(ii) Similarly situated. For purposes of this subparagraph, a participant is similarly situated to any other individual if such participant is identical to such other individual in every respect (including period of service, compensation, position, date of hire, work history, and any other respect) except for age.

(iii) Disregard of subsidized early retirement benefits. In determining the accrued benefit as of any date for purposes of this subparagraph, the subsidized portion of any early retirement benefit or retirement-type subsidy shall be disregarded.

(iv) Accrued benefit. For purposes of this subparagraph, the accrued benefit may, under the terms of the plan, be expressed as an annuity payable at normal retirement age, the balance of a hypothetical account, or the current value of the accumulated percentage of the employee's final average compensation.

(B) Applicable defined benefit plans.

(i) Interest credits.

(I) In general. An applicable defined benefit plan shall be treated as failing to meet the requirements of paragraph (1)(H) unless the terms of the plan provide that any interest credit (or an equivalent amount) for any plan year shall be at a rate which is not greater than a market rate of return. A plan shall not be treated as failing to meet the requirements of this subclause merely because the plan provides for a reasonable minimum guaranteed rate of return or for a rate of return that is equal to the greater of a fixed or variable rate of return.

(II) Preservation of capital. An applicable defined benefit plan shall be treated as failing to meet the requirements of paragraph (1)(H) unless the plan provides that an interest credit (or equivalent amount) of less than zero shall in no event result in the account balance or similar amount being less than the aggregate amount of contributions credited to the account.

(III) Market rate of return. The Secretary may provide by regulation for rules governing the calculation of a market rate of return for purposes of subclause (I) and for permissible methods of crediting interest to the account (including fixed or variable interest rates) resulting in effective rates of return meeting the requirements of subclause (I).

(ii) Special rule for plan conversions. If, after June 29, 2005, an applicable plan amendment is adopted, the plan shall be treated as failing to meet the requirements of paragraph (1)(H) unless the requirements of clause (iii) are met with respect to each individual who was a participant in the plan immediately before the adoption of the amendment.

(iii) Rate of benefit accrual. Subject to clause (iv), the requirements of this clause are met with respect to any participant if the accrued benefit of the participant under the terms of the plan as in effect after the amendment is not less than the sum of—

(I) the participant's accrued benefit for years of service before the effective date of the amendment, determined under the terms of the plan as in effect before the amendment, plus

(II) the participant's accrued benefit for years of service after the effective date of the amendment, determined under the terms of the plan as in effect after the amendment.

(iv) Special rules for early retirement subsidies. For purposes of clause (iii)(I), the plan shall credit the accumulation account or similar amount with the amount of any early retirement benefit or retirement-type subsidy for the plan year in which the participant retires if, as of such time, the participant has met the age, years of service, and other requirements under the plan for entitlement to such benefit or subsidy.

(v) Applicable plan amendment. For purposes of this subparagraph—

(I) In general. The term "applicable plan amendment" means an amendment to a defined benefit plan which has the effect of converting the plan to an applicable defined benefit plan.

(II) Special rule for coordinated benefits. If the benefits of 2 or more defined benefit plans established or maintained by an employer are coordinated in such a manner as to have the effect of the adoption of an amendment described in subclause (I), the sponsor of the defined benefit plan or plans providing for such coordination shall be treated as having adopted such a plan amendment as of the date such coordination begins.

(III) Multiple amendments. The Secretary shall issue regulations to prevent the avoidance of the purposes of this subparagraph through the use of 2 or more plan amendments rather than a single amendment.

(IV) Applicable defined benefit plan. For purposes of this subparagraph, the term "applicable defined benefit plan" has the meaning given such term by section 411(a)(13).

(vi) Termination requirements. An applicable defined benefit plan shall not be treated as meeting the requirements of clause (i) unless the plan provides that, upon the termination of the plan—

(I) if the interest credit rate (or an equivalent amount) under the plan is a variable rate, the rate of interest used to determine accrued benefits under the plan shall be equal to the average of the rates of interest used under the plan during the 5-year period ending on the termination date, and

(II) the interest rate and mortality table used to determine the amount of any benefit under the plan payable in the form of an annuity payable at normal retirement age shall be the rate and table specified under the plan for such purpose as of the termination date, except that if such interest rate is a variable rate, the interest rate shall be determined under the rules of subclause (I).

(C) Certain offsets permitted. A plan shall not be treated as failing to meet the requirements of paragraph (1)(H)(i) solely because the plan provides offsets against benefits under the plan to the extent such offsets are otherwise allowable in applying the requirements of section 401(a).

(D) Permitted disparities in plan contributions or benefits. A plan shall not be treated as failing to meet the requirements of paragraph (1)(H) solely because the plan provides a disparity in contributions or benefits with respect to which the requirements of section 401(l) are met.

(E) Indexing permitted.

(i) In general. A plan shall not be treated as failing to meet the requirements of paragraph (1)(H) solely because the plan provides for indexing of accrued benefits under the plan.

(ii) Protection against loss. Except in the case of any benefit provided in the form of a variable annuity, clause (i) shall not apply with respect to any indexing which results in an accrued benefit less than the accrued benefit determined without regard to such indexing.

(iii) Indexing. For purposes of this subparagraph, the term "indexing" means, in connection with an accrued benefit, the periodic adjustment of the accrued benefit by means of the application of a recognized investment index or methodology.

(F) Early retirement benefit or retirement-type subsidy. For purposes of this paragraph, the terms "early retirement benefit" and "retirement-type subsidy" have the meaning given such terms in subsection (d)(6)(B)(i).

(G) Benefit accrued to date. For purposes of this paragraph, any reference to the accrued benefit shall be a reference to such benefit accrued to date.

(c) Allocation of accrued benefits between employer and employee contributions.

(1) Accrued benefit derived from employer contributions. For purposes of this section, an employee's accrued benefit derived from employer contributions as of any applicable date is the excess, if any, of the accrued benefit for such employee as of such applicable date over the accrued benefit derived from contributions made by such employee as of such date.

(2) Accrued benefit derived from employee contributions.

(A) Plans other than defined benefit plans. In the case of a plan other than a defined benefit plan, the accrued benefit derived from contributions made by an employee as of any applicable date is—

(i) except as provided in clause (ii), the balance of the employee's separate account consisting only of his contributions and the income, expenses, gains, and losses attributable thereto, or

(ii) if a separate account is not maintained with respect to an employee's contributions under such a plan, the amount which bears the same ratio to his total accrued benefit as the total amount of the employee's contributions (less withdrawals) bears to the sum of such contributions and the contributions made on his behalf by the employer (less withdrawals).

(B) Defined benefit plans. In the case of a defined benefit plan, the accrued benefit derived from contributions made by an employee as of any applicable date is the amount equal to the employee's accumulated contributions expressed as an annual benefit commencing at normal retirement age, using an interest rate which would be used under the plan under section 417(e)(3) (as of the determination date).

(C) Definition of accumulated contributions. For purposes of this subsection, the term "accumulated contributions" means the total of—

(i) all mandatory contributions made by the employee,

(ii) interest (if any) under the plan to the end of the last plan year to which subsection (a)(2) does not apply (by reason of the applicable effective date), and

(iii) interest on the sum of the amounts determined under clauses (i) and (ii) compounded annually—

(I) at the rate of 120 percent of the Federal mid-term rate (as in effect under section 1274 for the 1st month of a plan year) for the period beginning with the 1st plan year to which subsection (a)(2) applies (by reason of the applicable effective date) and ending with the date on which the determination is being made, and

(II) at the interest rate which would be used under the plan under section 417(e)(3) (as of the determination date) for the period beginning with the determination date and ending on the date on which the employee attains normal retirement age.

For purposes of this subparagraph, the term "mandatory contributions" means amounts contributed to the plan by the employee which are required as a condition of employment, as a condition of participation in such plan, or as a condition of obtaining benefits under the plan attributable to employer contributions.

(D) Adjustments. The Secretary is authorized to adjust by regulation the conversion factor described in subparagraph (B) from time to time as he may deem necessary. No such adjustment shall be effective for a plan year beginning before the expiration of 1 year after such adjustment is determined and published.

(3) Actuarial adjustment. For purposes of this section, in the case of any defined benefit plan, if an employee's accrued benefit is to be determined as an amount other than an annual benefit commencing at normal retirement age, or if the accrued benefit derived from contributions made by an employee is to be determined with respect to a benefit other than an annual benefit in the form of a single life annuity (without ancillary benefits) commencing at normal retirement age, the employee's accrued benefit, or the accrued benefits derived from contributions made by an employee, as the case may be, shall be the actuarial equivalent of such benefit or amount determined under paragraph (1) or (2).

(d) Special rules.

(1) Coordination with section 401(a)(4). A plan which satisfies the requirements of this section shall be treated as satisfying any vesting requirements resulting from the application of section 401(a)(4) unless—

(A) there has been a pattern of abuse under the plan (such as a dismissal of employees before their accrued benefits become nonforfeitable) tending to discriminate in favor of employees who are highly compensated employees (within the meaning of section 414(q)), or

(B) there have been, or there is reason to believe there will be, an accrual of benefits or forfeitures tending to discriminate in favor of employees who are highly compensated employees (within the meaning of section 414(q)).

(2) Prohibited discrimination. Subsection (a) shall not apply to benefits which may not be provided for designated employees in the event of early termination of the plan under provisions of the plan adopted pursuant to regulations prescribed by the Secretary to preclude the discrimination prohibited by section 401(a)(4).

(3) Termination or partial termination; discontinuance of contributions. Notwithstanding the provisions of subsection (a), a trust shall not constitute a qualified trust under section 401(a) unless the plan of which such trust is a part provides that—

(A) upon its termination or partial termination, or

(B) in the case of a plan to which section 412 does not apply, upon complete discontinuance of contributions under the plan,

the rights of all affected employees to benefits accrued to the date of such termination, partial termination, or discontinuance, to the extent funded as of such date, or the amounts credited to the employees' accounts, are nonforfeitable. This paragraph shall not apply to benefits or contributions which, under provisions of the plan adopted pursuant to regulations prescribed by the Secretary to preclude the discrimination prohibited by section 401(a)(4), may not be used for designated employees in the event of early termination of the plan. For purposes of this paragraph, in the case of the complete discontinuance of contributions under a profit-sharing or stock bonus plan, such plan shall be treated as having terminated on the day on which the plan administrator notifies the Secretary (in accordance with regulations) of the discontinuance.

(4) Repealed.

(5) Treatment of voluntary employee contributions. In the case of a defined benefit plan which permits voluntary employee contributions, the portion of an employee's accrued benefit derived from such contributions shall be treated as an accrued benefit derived from employee contributions under a plan other than a defined benefit plan.

(6) Accrued benefit not to be decreased by amendment.

(A) In general. A plan shall be treated as not satisfying the requirements of this section if the accrued benefit of a participant is decreased by an amendment of the plan, other than an amendment described in section 412(d)(2), or section 4281 of the Employee Retirement Income Security Act of 1974.

(B) Treatment of certain plan amendments. For purposes of subparagraph (A), a plan amendment which has the effect of—

(i) eliminating or reducing an early retirement benefit or a retirement-type subsidy (as defined in regulations), or

(ii) eliminating an optional form of benefit,

with respect to benefits attributable to service before the amendment shall be treated as reducing accrued benefits. In the case of a retirement-type subsidy, the preceding sentence shall apply only with respect to a participant who satisfies (either before or after the amendment) the preamendment conditions for the subsidy. The Secretary shall by regulations provide that this subparagraph shall not apply to any plan amendment which reduces or eliminates benefits or subsidies which create significant burdens or complexities for the plan and plan participants, unless such amendment adversely affects the rights of any participant in a more than de minimis manner. The Secretary may by regulations provide that this subparagraph shall not apply to a plan amendment described in clause (ii) (other than a plan amendment having an effect described in clause (i)).

(C) Special rule for ESOPs. For purposes of this paragraph, any—

(i) tax credit employee stock ownership plan (as defined in section 409(a)), or

(ii) employee stock ownership plan (as defined in section 4975(e)(7)),

shall not be treated as failing to meet the requirements of this paragraph merely because it modifies distribution options in a nondiscriminatory manner.

(D) Plan transfers.

(i) In general. A defined contribution plan (in this subparagraph referred to as the "transferee plan") shall not be treated as failing to meet the requirements of this subsection merely because the transferee plan does not provide some or all of the forms of distribution previously available under another defined contribution plan (in this subparagraph referred to as the "transferor plan") to the extent that—

(I) the forms of distribution previously available under the transferor plan applied to the account of a participant or beneficiary under the transferor plan that was transferred from the transferor plan to the transferee plan pursuant to a direct transfer rather than pursuant to a distribution from the transferor plan,

(II) the terms of both the transferor plan and the transferee plan authorize the transfer described in subclause (I),

(III) the transfer described in subclause (I) was made pursuant to a voluntary election by the participant or beneficiary whose account was transferred to the transferee plan,

(IV) the election described in subclause (III) was made after the participant or beneficiary received a notice describing the consequences of making the election, and

(V) the transferee plan allows the participant or beneficiary described in subclause (III) to receive any distribution to which the participant or beneficiary is entitled under the transferee plan in the form of a single sum distribution.

(ii) Special rule for mergers, etc. Clause (i) shall apply to plan mergers and other transactions having the effect of a direct transfer, including consolidations of benefits attributable to different employers within a multiple employer plan.

(E) Elimination of form of distribution. Except to the extent provided in regulations, a defined contribution plan shall not be treated as failing to meet requirements of this section merely because of the elimination of a form of distribution previously available thereunder. This subparagraph shall not apply to the elimination of a form of distribution with respect to any participant unless—

Employee benefit plans — Code Sec. 411

(i) a single sum payment is available to such participant at the same time or times as the form of distribution being eliminated, and

(ii) such single sum payment is based on the same or greater portion of the participant's account as the form of distribution being eliminated.

(e) Application of vesting standards to certain plans.

(1) The provisions of this section (other than paragraph (2)) shall not apply to—

(A) a governmental plan (within the meaning of section 414(d)),

(B) a church plan (within the meaning of section 414(e)) with respect to which the election provided by section 410(d) has not been made,

(C) a plan which has not, at any time after September 2, 1974, provided for employer contributions, and

(D) a plan established and maintained by a society, order, or association described in section 501(c)(8) or (9), if no part of the contributions to or under such plan are made by employers of participants in such plan.

(2) A plan described in paragraph (1) shall be treated as meeting the requirements of this section, for purposes of section 401(a), if such plan meets the vesting requirements resulting from the application of sections 401(a)(4) and 401(a)(7) as in effect on September 1, 1974.

In 2010, P.L. 111-312, Sec. 101(a)(1), substituted "December 31, 2012" for "December 31, 2010" both places it appeared in Sec. 901 of P.L. 107-16 [see below], effective as if included in the enactment of P.L. 107-16, EGTRRA, 6/7/2001.

In 2008, P.L. 110-458, Sec. 101(d)(2)(D)(i), substituted "section 412(d)(2)" for "section 412(c)(2)" in subpara. (a)(3)(C) . . . Sec. 101(d)(2)(D)(ii), substituted "section 412(d)(2)" for "section 412(c)(2)" in subpara. (d)(6)(A), effective for plan yrs. begin. after 2007 [as if included in the provisions of Sec. 114, P.L. 109-280).

—P.L. 110-458, Sec. 101(d)(3), . . . Sec. 101(d)(3), added Sec. 114(g), P.L. 109-280, providing effective dates for amendments made by Sec. 114, P.L. 109-280, see below. Sec. 114(g), P.L. 109-280, as added by this Act, provides:

"'(g) Effective dates.

"'(1) In general. The amendments made by this section shall apply to plan years beginning after 2007.

"'(2) Excise tax. The amendments made by subsection (e) shall apply to taxable years beginning after 2007, but only with respect to plan years described in paragraph (1) which end with or within any such taxable year."'

— P.L. 110-458, Sec. 104(b), substituted "commercial" for "commercial airline" in Sec. 401(c)(1)(A), P.L. 109-280, see below. . . . Sec. 107(b)(1)(A), substituted "subparagraph" for "clause" in clause (b)(5)(A)(iii) . . . Sec. 107(b)(1)(B), added "otherwise" before "allowable" in subpara. (b)(5)(C) . . . Sec. 107(b)(2)(A), substituted "subparagraph (B)" for "paragraph (2)" in subpara. (a)(3)(G) . . . Sec. 107(b)(2)(B), added new clause (a)(13)(A)(ii) . . . Sec. 107(b)(2)(C), substituted "subparagraph (C)" for "paragraph (3)" in the matter following clause (a)(3)(A)(ii) . . . Sec. 107(b)(3), amended subclause (b)(5)(B)(i)(II), effective as provided by Sec. 701(e), P.L. 109-280 [as amended by this Act, reproduced below]

—P.L. 110-458, Sec. 107(c)(1), substitute "205(g)" for "204(g)", effective for plan yrs. begin. after 12/31/2007.

—P.L. 110-458, Sec. 109(b)(2)(A), substituted "a permissible withdrawal" for "an erroneous automatic contribution" in subpara. (a)(3)(G) . . . Sec. 109(b)(2)(B), substituted "permissible withdrawal" for "erroneous automatic contribution" in the heading of subpara. (a)(3)(G), effective as if included in the provisions of the 2006 Act to which the amendments relate.

Prior to deletion, clause (a)(13)(A)(ii) read as follows:

"(ii) the requirements of subsection (c) or section 417(e) with respect to contributions other than employee contributions,"

Prior to amendment, subclause (b)(5)(B)(i)(II) read as follows:

"(II) Preservation of capital. An interest credit (or an equivalent amount) of less than zero shall in no event result in the account balance or similar amount being less than the aggregate amount of contributions credited to the account."

—P.L. 110-458, Sec. 126(a), amended Sec. 402(e)(4)(C), P.L. 109-280, reproduced below, effective for plan yrs. begin. afer 12/31/2007.

Prior to amendment, Sec. 402(e)(4)(C), P.L. 109-280, read as follows:

"(C) the value of plan assets shall be equal to their fair market value."

In 2006, P.L. 109-280, Sec. 114(b)(1), substituted "section 412(c)(2)" for "section 412(c)(8)" in subpara. (a)(3)(C) . . . Sec. 114(b)(2)(A), substituted "subparagraphs (B) and (C) of section 412(e)(3)" for "paragraphs (2) and (3) of section 412(i)" in clause (b)(1)(F)(ii) . . . Sec. 114(b)(2)(B), substituted "subparagraphs (D), (E), and (F) of section 412(e)(3)" for "paragraphs (4), (5), and (6) of section 412(i)" in subpara. (b)(1)(F) . . . Sec. 114(b)(3), substituted "section 412(e)(2)" for "section 412(c)(8)" in subpara. (d)(6)(A), effective for plan yrs. begin. after 2007 [as provided in Sec. 114(g) of this Act as added by Sec. 101(d)(3), P.L. 110-458, see above]

—P.L. 109-280, Sec. 402(a)-(g)(1), of this Act, [as amended by Sec. 104(b), P.L. 110-458, and Sec. 126(a), P.L. 110-458, see above] reads as follows:

"(a) In general. The plan sponsor of an eligible plan may elect to either—

"(1) have the rules of subsection (b) apply, or

"(2) have section 303 of the Employee Retirement Income Security Act of 1974 and section 430 of the Internal Revenue Code of 1986 applied to its first taxable year beginning in 2008 by amortizing the shortfall amortization base for such taxable year over a period of 10 plan years (rather than 7 plan years) beginning with such plan year.

"(b) Alternative funding schedule.

"In general. If an election is made under subsection (a)(1) to have this subsection apply to an eligible plan and the requirements of paragraphs (2) and (3) are met with respect to the plan—

"(A) in the case of any applicable plan year beginning before January 1, 2008, the plan shall not have an accumulated funding deficiency for purposes of section 302 of the Employee Retirement Income Security Act of 1974 and sections 412 and 4971 of the Internal Revenue Code of 1986 if contributions to the plan for the plan year are not less than the minimum required contribution determined under subsection (e) for the plan for the plan year, and

"(B) in the case of any applicable plan year beginning on or after January 1, 2008, the minimum required contribution determined under sections 303 of such Act and 430 of such Code shall, for purposes of sections 302 and 303 of such Act and sections 412, 430, and 4971 of such Code, be equal to the minimum required contribution determined under subsection (e) for the plan for the plan year.

"(2) Accrual restrictions.

"(A) In general. The requirements of this paragraph are met if, effective as of the first day of the first applicable plan year and at all times thereafter while an election under this section is in effect, the plan provides that—

"(i) the accrued benefit, any death or disability benefit, and any social security supplement described in the last sentence of section 411(a)(9) of such Code and section 204(b)(1)(G) of such Act, of each participant are frozen at the amount of such benefit or supplement immediately before such first day, and

"(ii) all other benefits under the plan are eliminated,

"but only to the extent the freezing or elimination of such benefits would have been permitted under section 411(d)(6) of such Code and section 204(g) of such Act if they had been implemented by a plan amendment adopted immediately before such first day.

"(B) Increases in section 415 limits. If a plan provides that an accrued benefit of a participant which has been subject to any limitation under section 415 of such Code will be increased if such limitation is increased, the plan shall not be treated as meeting the requirements of this section, effective as of the first day of the first applicable plan year (or, if later, the date of the enactment of this Act) and at all times thereafter while an election under this section is in effect, the plan provides that any such increase shall not take effect. A plan shall not fail to meet the requirements of section 411(d)(6) of such Code and section 204(g) of such Act solely because the plan is amended to meet the requirements of this subparagraph.

"(3) Restriction on applicable benefit increases.

"(A) In general. The requirements of this paragraph are met if no applicable benefit increase takes effect at any time during the period beginning on July 26, 2005, and ending on the day before the first day of the first applicable plan year.

"(B) Applicable benefit increase. For purposes of this paragraph, the term 'applicable benefit increase' means, with respect to any plan year, any increase in liabilities of the plan by plan amendment (or otherwise provided in regulations provided by the Secretary) which, but for this paragraph, would occur during the plan year by reason of—

"(i) any increase in benefits,

"(ii) any change in the accrual of benefits, or

"(iii) any change in the rate at which benefits become nonforfeitable under the plan.

"(4) Exception for imputed disability service. Paragraphs (2) and (3) shall not apply to any accrual or increase with respect to imputed service provided to a participant during any period of the participant's disability occurring on or after the effective date of the plan amendment providing the restrictions under paragraph (2) (or on or after July 26, 2005, in the case of the restrictions under paragraph (3)) if the participant—

"(A) was receiving disability benefits as of such date, or

"(B) was receiving sick pay and subsequently determined to be eligible for disability benefits as of such date.

"(c) Definitions. For purposes of this section—

"(1) Eligible plan. The term 'eligible plan' means a defined benefit plan (other than a multiemployer plan) to which sections 302 of such Act and 412 of such Code applies which is sponsored by an employer—

"(A) which is a commercial passenger airline, or

"(B) the principal business of which is providing catering services to a commercial passenger airline.

"(2) Applicable plan year. The term 'applicable plan year' means each plan year to which the election under subsection (a)(1) applies under subsection (d)(1)(A).

"(d) Elections and related terms.

"(1) Years for which election made.

"(A) Alternative funding schedule. If an election under subsection (a)(1) was made with respect to an eligible plan, the plan sponsor may select either a plan year beginning in 2006 or a plan year beginning in 2007 as the first plan year to which such election applies. The election shall apply to such plan year and all subsequent years. The election shall be made—

"(i) not later than December 31, 2006, in the case of an election for a plan year beginning in 2006, or

"(ii) not later than December 31, 2007, in the case of an election for a plan year beginning in 2007.

"(B) 10 year amortization. An election under subsection (a)(2) shall be made not later than December 31, 2007.

"(C) Election of new plan year for alternative funding schedule. In the case of an election under subsection (a)(1), the plan sponsor may specify a new plan year in such election and the plan year of the plan may be changed to such new plan year without the approval of the Secretary of the Treasury.

"(2) Manner of election. A plan sponsor shall make any election under subsection (a) in such manner as the Secretary of the Treasury may prescribe. Such election, once made, may be revoked only with the consent of such Secretary.

"(e) Minimum required contribution. In the case of an eligible plan with respect to which an election is made under subsection (a)(1)—

"(1) In general. In the case of any applicable plan year during the amortization period, the minimum required contribution shall be the amount necessary to amortize the unfunded liability of the plan, determined as of the first day of the plan year, in equal annual installments (until fully amortized) over the remainder of the amortization period. Such amount shall be separately determined for each applicable plan year.

"(2) Years after amortization period. In the case of any plan year beginning after the end of the amortization period, section 302(a)(2)(A) of such Act and section 412(a)(2)(A) of such Code shall apply to such plan, but the prefunding balance and funding standard carryover balance as of the first day of the first of such years under section 303(f) of such Act and section 430(f) of such Code shall be zero.

"(3) Definitions. For purposes of this section—

"(A) Unfunded liability. The term 'unfunded liability' means the unfunded accrued liability under the plan, determined under the unit credit funding method.

"(B) Amortization period. The term 'amortization period' means the 17-plan year period beginning with the first applicable plan year.

"(4) Other rules. In determining the minimum required contribution and amortization amount under this subsection—

"(A) the provisions of section 302(c)(3) of such Act and section 412(c)(3) of such Code, as in effect before the date of enactment of this section, shall apply,

"(B) a rate of interest of 8.85 percent shall be used for all calculations requiring an interest rate, and

"(C) the value of plan assets shall be determined under sections 303(g)(3) of such Act and 430(g)(3) of such Code.

"(5) Special rule for certain plan spin-offs. For purposes of subsection (b), if, with respect to any eligible plan to which this subsection applies—

"(A) any applicable plan year includes the date of the enactment of this Act,

"(B) a plan was spun off from the eligible plan during the plan year but before such date of enactment,

"the minimum required contribution under paragraph (1) for the eligible plan for such applicable plan year shall be an aggregate amount determined as if the plans were a single plan for that plan year (based on the full 12-month plan year in effect prior to the spin-off). The employer shall designate the allocation of such aggregate amount between such plans for the applicable plan year.

"(f) Special rules for certain balances and waivers. In the case of an eligible plan with respect to which an election is made under subsection (a)(1)—

"(1) Funding standard account and credit balances. Any charge or credit in the funding standard account under section 302 of such Act or section 412 of such Code, and any prefunding balance or funding standard carryover balance under section 303 of such Act or section 430 of such Code, as of the day before the first day of the first applicable plan year, shall be reduced to zero.

"(2) Waived funding deficiencies. Any waived funding deficiency under sections 302 and 303 of such Act or section 412 of such Code, as in effect before the date of enactment of this section, shall be deemed satisfied as of the first day of the first applicable plan year and the amount of such waived funding deficiency shall be taken into account in determining the plan's unfunded liability under subsection (e)(3)(A). In the case of a plan amendment adopted to satisfy the requirements of subsection (b)(2), the plan shall not be deemed to violate section 304(b) of such Act or section 412(f) of such Code, as so in effect, by reason of such amendment or any increase in benefits provided to such plan's participants under a separate plan that is a defined contribution plan or a multiemployer plan.

"(g) Other rules for plans making election under this section.

"(1) Successor plans to certain plans. If—

"(A) an election under paragraph (1) or (2) of subsection (a) is in effect with respect to any eligible plan, and

"(B) the eligible plan is maintained by an employer that establishes or maintains 1 or more other defined benefit plans (other than any multiemployer plan), and such other plans in combination provide benefit accruals to any substantial number of successor employees,

"the Secretary of the Treasury may, in the Secretary's discretion, determine that any trust of which any other such plan is a part does not constitute a qualified trust under section 401(a) of the Internal Revenue Code of 1986 unless all benefit obligations of the eligible plan have been satisfied. For purposes of this paragraph, the term 'successor employee' means any employee who is or was covered by the eligible plan and any employees who perform substantially the same type of work with respect to the same business operations as an employee covered by such eligible plan."

—P.L. 109-280, Sec. 701(b)(1), added para. (b)(5) . . . Sec. 701(b)(2), added para. (a)(13), effective as provided by Sec. 701(e) of this Act [as amended by Sec. 107(c)(2), P.L. 110-458, see above], which reads as follows:

"(e) Effective date.

"(1) In general. The amendments made by this section shall apply to periods beginning on or after June 29, 2005.

"(2) Present value of accrued benefit. The amendments made by subsections (a)(2) and (b)(2) shall apply to distributions made after the date of enactment of this Act.

"(3) Vesting and interest credit requirements. In the case of a plan in existence on June 29, 2005, the requirements of clause (i) of section 411(b)(5)(B) of the Internal Revenue Code of 1986, clause (i) of section 204(b)(5)(B) of the Employee Retirement Income Security Act of 1974, and clause (i) of section 4(i)(10)(B) of the Age Discrimination in Employment Act of 1967 (as added by this Act) and the requirements of 203(f)(2) of the Employee Retirement Income Security Act of 1974 and section 411(a)(13)(B) of the Internal Revenue Code of 1986 (as so added) shall, for purposes of applying the amendments made by subsections (a) and (b), apply to years beginning after December 31, 2007, unless the plan sponsor elects the application of such requirements for any period on or after June 29, 2005, and before the first year beginning after December 31, 2007.

"(4) Special rule for collectively bargained plans. In the case of a plan maintained pursuant to 1 or more collective bargaining agreements between employee representatives and 1 or more employers ratified on or before the earlier of the date of the enactment of this Act, the requirements described in paragraph (3) shall, for purposes of applying the amendments made by subsections (a) and (b), not apply to plan years beginning before—

"(A) the later of—

"(i) the date on which the last of such collective bargaining agreements terminates (determined without regard to any extension thereof on or after such date of enactment), or

"(ii) January 1, 2008, or (B) January 1, 2010.

"(5) Conversions. The requirements of clause (ii) of section 411(b)(5)(B) of the Internal Revenue Code of 1986, clause (ii) of section 204(b)(5)(B) of the Employee Retirement Income Security Act of 1974, and clause (ii) of section 4(i)(10)(B) of the Age Discrimination in Employment Act of 1967 (as added by this Act), shall apply to plan amendments adopted on or after, and taking effect on or after, June 29, 2005, except that the plan sponsor may elect to have such amendments apply to plan amendments adopted before, and taking effect on or after, such date.

"(6) Special rule for vesting requirements. The requirements of section 203(f)(2) of the Employee Retirement Income Security Act of 1974 and section 411(a)(13)(B) of the Internal Revenue Code of 1986 (as added by this Act)—

"(A) shall not apply to a participant who does not have an hour of service after the effective date of such requirements (as otherwise determined under this subsection); and

"(B) in the case of a plan other than a plan described in paragraph (3) or (4), shall apply to plan years ending on or after June 29, 2005."

—P.L. 109-280, Sec. 701(d), of this Act, [as amended by Sec. 107(c)(1), P.L. 110-458, see above] reads as follows:

"(d) No Inference. Nothing in the amendments made by this section shall be construed to create an inference with respect to—

"(1) the treatment of applicable defined benefit plans or conversions to applicable defined benefit plans under sections 204(b)(1)(H) of the Employee Retirement Income Security Act of 1974, 4(i)(1) of the Age Discrimination in Employment Act of 1967, and 411(b)(1)(H) of the Internal Revenue Code of 1986, as in effect before such amendments, or

"(2) the determination of whether an applicable defined benefit plan fails to meet the requirements of sections 203(a)(2), 204(c), or 205(g) of the Employee Retirement Income Security Act of 1974 or sections 411(a)(2), 411(c), or 417(e) of such Code, as in effect before such amendments, solely because the present value of the accrued benefit (or any portion thereof) of any participant is, under the terms of the plan, equal to the amount expressed as the balance in a hypothetical account or as an accumulated percentage of the participant's final average compensation.

For purposes of this subsection, the term 'applicable defined benefit plan' has the meaning given such term by section 203(f)(3) of the Employee Retirement Income Security Act of 1974 and section 411(a)(13)(C) of such Code, as in effect after such amendments."

—P.L. 109-280, Sec. 811, of this Act [relating to sec. 901 of P.L. 107-16, see below], provides:

"SEC. 811. PENSIONS AND INDIVIDUAL RETIREMENT ARRANGEMENT PROVISIONS OF ECONOMIC GROWTH AND TAX RELIEF RECONCILIATION ACT OF 2001 MADE PERMANENT.

"Title IX of the Economic Growth and Tax Relief Reconciliation Act of 2001 shall not apply to the provisions of, and amendments made by, subtitles A through F of title VI of such Act (relating to pension and individual retirement arrangement provisions)."

—P.L. 109-280, Sec. 902(d)(2)(A), added "an erroneous automatic contribution under section 414(w)" after "402(g)(2)(A)" in subpara. (a)(3)(G) . . . Sec. 902(d)(2)(B), added "or erroneous automatic contribution" before the period at the end of the heading of subpara. (a)(3)(G), effective for plan yrs. begin. after 12/31/2007.

—P.L. 109-280, Sec. 904(a)(1), amended para. (a)(2) . . . Sec. 904(a)(2), deleted para. (a)(12), effective for contributions for plan yrs. begin. after 12/31/2006. Sec. 902(c)(2)-(4), of this Act, reads as follows:

"(2) Collective bargaining agreements. In the case of a plan maintained pursuant to one or more collective bargaining agreements between employee representatives and one or more employers ratified before the date of the enactment of this

Act, the amendments made by this section shall not apply to contributions on behalf of employees covered by any such agreement for plan years beginning before the earlier of—

"(A) the later of—

"(i) the date on which the last of such collective bargaining agreements terminates (determined without regard to any extension thereof on or after such date of the enactment); or

"(ii) January 1, 2007; or

"(B) January 1, 2009.

"(3) Service required. With respect to any plan, the amendments made by this section shall not apply to any employee before the date that such employee has 1 hour of service under such plan in any plan year to which the amendments made by this section apply.

"(4) Special rule for stock ownership plans. Notwithstanding paragraph (1) or (2), in the case of an employee stock ownership plan (as defined in section 4975(e)(7) of the Internal Revenue Code of 1986) which had outstanding on September 26, 2005, a loan incurred for the purpose of acquiring qualifying employer securities (as defined in section 4975(e)(8) of such Code), the amendments made by this section shall not apply to any plan year beginning before the earlier of—

"(A) the date on which the loan is fully repaid, or

"(B) the date on which the loan was, as of September 26, 2005, scheduled to be fully repaid."

Prior to amendment, para. (a)(2) read as follows:

"(2) Employer contributions. Except as provided in paragraph (12), a plan satisfies the requirements of this paragraph if it satisfies the requirements of subparagraph (A) or (B).

"(A) 5-year vesting. A plan satisfies the requirements of this subparagraph if an employee who has completed at least 5 years of service has a nonforfeitable right to 100 percent of the employee's accrued benefit derived from employer contributions.

"(B) 3 to 7 year vesting. A plan satisfies the requirements of this subparagraph if an employee has a nonforfeitable right to a percentage of the employee's accrued benefit derived from employer contributions determined under the following table:

Years of service:	The nonforfeitable percentage is:
3	20
4	40
5	60
6	80
7 or more	100."

Prior to deletion, para. (a)(12) read as follows:

"(12) Faster vesting for matching contributions. In the case of matching contributions (as defined in section 401(m)(4)(A)), paragraph (2) shall be applied—

"(A) by substituting '3 years' for '5 years' in subparagraph (A), and

"(B) by substituting the following table for the table contained in subparagraph (B):

Years of service:	The nonforfeitable percentage is:
2	20
3	40
4	60
5	80
6 or more	100."

—P.L. 109-280, Sec. 1102(a)(1)(B), of this Act, reads as follows:

"(B) Modification of regulations. The Secretary of the Treasury shall modify the regulations under sections 402(f), 411(a)(11), and 417 of the Internal Revenue Code of 1986 by substituting '180 days' for '90 days' each place it appears in Treasury Regulations sections 1.402(f)-1, 1.411(a)-11(c), and 1.417(e)-1(b)."

—P.L. 109-280, Sec. 1102(b), of this Act, reads as follows:

"(b) Notification of right to defer.

"(1) In general. The Secretary of the Treasury shall modify the regulations under section 411(a)(11) of the Internal Revenue Code of 1986 and under section 205 of the Employee Retirement Income Security Act of 1974 to provide that the description of a participant's right, if any, to defer receipt of a distribution shall also describe the consequences of failing to defer such receipt.

"(2) Effective date.

"(A) In general. The modifications required by paragraph (1) shall apply to years beginning after December 31, 2006.

"(B) Reasonable notice. A plan shall not be treated as failing to meet the requirements of section 411(a)(11) of such Code or section 205 of such Act with respect to any description of consequences described in paragraph (1) made within 90 days after the Secretary of the Treasury issues the modifications required by paragraph (1) if the plan administrator makes a reasonable attempt to comply with such requirements."

—P.L. 109-280, Sec. 1107, of this Act, reads as follows:

"SEC. 1107. PROVISIONS RELATING TO PLAN AMENDMENTS.

"(a) In general. If this section applies to any pension plan or contract amendment—

"(1) such pension plan or contract shall be treated as being operated in accordance with the terms of the plan during the period described in subsection (b)(2)(A), and

"(2) except as provided by the Secretary of the Treasury, such pension plan shall not fail to meet the requirements of section 411(d)(6) of the Internal Revenue Code of 1986 and section 204(g) of the Employee Retirement Income Security Act of 1974 by reason of such amendment.

"(b) Amendments to which section applies.

"(1) In general. This section shall apply to any amendment to any pension plan or annuity contract which is made—

"(A) pursuant to any amendment made by this Act or pursuant to any regulation issued by the Secretary of the Treasury or the Secretary of Labor under this Act, and

"(B) on or before the last day of the first plan year beginning on or after January 1, 2009.

In the case of a governmental plan (as defined in section 414(d) of the Internal Revenue Code of 1986), this paragraph shall be applied by substituting '2011' for '2009'.

"(2) Conditions. This section shall not apply to any amendment unless—

"(A) during the period—

"(i) beginning on the date the legislative or regulatory amendment described in paragraph (1)(A) takes effect (or in the case of a plan or contract amendment not required by such legislative or regulatory amendment, the effective date specified by the plan), and

"(ii) ending on the date described in paragraph (1)(B) (or, if earlier, the date the plan or contract amendment is adopted), the plan or contract is operated as if such plan or contract amendment were in effect; and

"(B) such plan or contract amendment applies retroactively for such period."

In 2004, P.L. 108-311, Sec. 408(a)(14), substituted "6 or more ... 100." for "6 ... 100." in the last line of the table in subpara. (a)(12)(B), effective 10/4/2004.

In 2002, P.L. 107-358, Sec. 2, added subsec. (c) in Sec. 901 of P.L. 107-16 [see below], effective 12/17/2002.

—P.L. 107-147, Sec. 411(j)(3), added Sec. 611(i)(3) of P.L. 107-16 [see below], effective for yrs. begin. after 12/31/2001.

In 2001, P.L. 107-16, Sec. 611(i)(3), of this Act, reads as follows:

"(3) Special rule. In the case of plan that, on June 7, 2001, incorporated by reference the limitation of section 415(b)(1)(A) of the Internal Revenue Code of 1986, section 411(d)(6) of such Code and section 204(g)(1) of the Employee Retirement Income Security Act of 1974 do not apply to a plan amendment that—

"(A) is adopted on or before June 30, 2002,

"(B) reduces benefits to the level that would have applied without regard to the amendments made by subsection (a) of this section, and

"(C) is effective no earlier than the years described in paragraph (2)."

—P.L. 107-16, Sec. 633(a)(1), substituted "Except as provided in paragraph (12), a plan" for "A plan" in para. (a)(2) . . . Sec. 633(a)(2), added para. (a)(12), effective for contributions for plan yrs. begin. after 12/31/2001. Sec. 633(c)(2) and (3) of this Act, provides:

"(2) Collective bargaining agreements. In the case of a plan maintained pursuant to one or more collective bargaining agreements between employee representatives and one or more employers ratified by the date of the enactment of this Act, the amendments made by this section shall not apply to contributions on behalf of employees covered by any such agreement for plan years beginning before the earlier of—

"(A) the later of—

"(i) the date on which the last of such collective bargaining agreements terminates (determined without regard to any extension thereof on or after such date of the enactment); or

"(ii) January 1, 2002; or

"(B) January 1, 2006.

"(3) Service required. With respect to any plan, the amendments made by this section shall not apply to any employee before the date that such employee has 1 hour of service under such plan in any plan year to which the amendments made by this section apply."

—P.L. 107-16, Sec. 645(a)(1), added subparas. (d)(6)(D) and (d)(6)(E), effective for yrs. begin. after 12/31/2001.

—P.L. 107-16, Sec. 645(b)(1), added "The Secretary shall by regulations provide that this subparagraph shall not apply to any plan amendment which reduces or eliminates benefits or subsidies which create significant burdens or complexities for the plan and plan participants, unless such amendment adversely affects the rights of any participant in a more than de minimis manner." after "conditions for the subsidy." in subpara. (d)(6)(B), effective 6/7/2001.

—P.L. 107-16, Sec. 645(b)(3), of this Act, reads as follows:

"(3) Secretary directed. Not later than December 31, 2003, the Secretary of the Treasury is directed to issue regulations under section 411(d)(6) of the Internal Revenue Code of 1986 and section 204(g) of the Employee Retirement Income Security Act of 1974, including the regulations required by the amendment made by this subsection. Such regulations shall apply to plan years beginning after December 31, 2003, or such earlier date as is specified by the Secretary of the Treasury."

—P.L. 107-16, Sec. 648(a)(1), added subpara. (a)(11)(D), effective for distributions after 12/31/2001.

—P.L. 107-16, Sec. 901, of this Act [as amended by Sec. 2 of P.L. 107-358, and Sec. 101(a)(1) of P.L. 111-312, and as related to Sec. 811 of P.L. 109-280, see above], reads as follows:

"SEC. 901. SUNSET OF PROVISIONS OF ACT.

"(a) In general. All provisions of, and amendments made by, this Act shall not apply—

"(1) to taxable, plan, or limitation years beginning after December 31, 2012, or

"(2) in the case of title V, to estates of decedents dying, gifts made, or generation skipping transfers, after December 31, 2012.

"(b) Application of certain laws. The Internal Revenue Code of 1986 and the Employee Retirement Income Security Act of 1974 shall be applied and adminis-

Code Sec. 411 — Employee benefit plans

tered to years, estates, gifts, and transfers described in subsection (a) as if the provisions and amendments described in subsection (a) had never been enacted.

"(c) Exception. Subsection (a) shall not apply to section 803 (relating to no federal income tax on restitution received by victims of the Nazi regime or their heirs or estates)."

In 1997, P.L. 105-34, Sec. 1071(a)(1), substituted "$5,000" for "$3,500" in subpara. (a)(11)(A) ... Sec. 1071(a)(2)(A), substituted "the dollar limit under section 411(a)(11)(A)" for "$3,500" in clause (a)(7)(B)(i), effective for plan yrs. begin. after 8/5/97.

In 1996, P.L. 104-188, Sec. 1442(a)(1), substituted "subparagraph (A) or (B)" for "subparagraph (A), (B), or (C)" in para. (a)(2) ... Sec. 1442(a)(2), deleted subpara. (a)(2)(C), effective as provided in Sec. 1442(c) of this Act, which reads as follows:

"(c) Effective date. The amendments made by this section shall apply to plan years beginning on or after the earlier of—
"(1) the later of—
"(A) January 1, 1997, or
"(B) the date on which the last of the collective bargaining agreements pursuant to which the plan is maintained terminates (determined without regard to any extension thereof after the date of the enactment of this Act), or
"(2) January 1, 1999.
Such amendments shall not apply to any individual who does not have more than 1 hour of service under the plan on or after the 1st day of the 1st plan year to which such amendments apply."
Prior to deletion, subpara. (a)(2)(C) read as follows:
"(C) Multiemployer plans. A plan satisfies the requirements of this subparagraph if—
"(i) the plan is a multiemployer plan (within the meaning of section 414(f)), and
"(ii) under the plan—
"(I) an employee who is covered pursuant to a collective bargaining agreement described in section 414(f)(1)(B) and who has completed at least 10 years of service has a nonforfeitable right to 100 percent of the employee's accrued benefit derived from employer contributions, and
"(II) the requirements of subparagraph (A) or (B) are met with respect to employees not described in subclause (I)."
—P.L. 104-188, Sec. 1449(a), amended Sec. 767(d)(3)(A) of P.L. 103-465, see below.
Prior to amendment, Sec. 767(d)(3)(A) read as follows:
"(A) No reduction required. — An accrued benefit shall not be required to be reduced below the accrued benefit as of the last day of the last plan year beginning before January 1, 1995, merely because of the amendments made by subsection (b)."

In 1994, P.L. 103-465, Sec. 767(a)(1), amended subpara. (a)(11)(B), effective for plan yrs. and limitation yrs. begin. after 12/31/94; except that an employer may elect to treat the amendments made by this section as being effective on or after date of enactment. Sec. 767 (d)(2) and (3) [as amended by Sec. 1449(a) of P.L. 104-188, see above] of this Act provides:
"(2) No reduction in accrued benefits. — A participant's accrued benefit shall not be considered to be reduced in violation of section 411(d)(6) of the Internal Revenue Code of 1986 or section 204(g) of the Employee Retirement Income Security Act of 1974 merely because (A) the benefit is determined in accordance with section 417(e)(3)(A) of such Code, as amended by this Act, or section 205(g)(3) of the Employee Retirement Income Security Act of 1974, as amended by this Act, or (B) the plan applies section 415(b)(2)(E) of such Code, as amended by this Act.
"(3) Section 415.—
"(A) Exception. A plan that was adopted and in effect before December 8, 1994, shall not be required to apply the amendments made by subsection 9b) with respect to benefits accrued before the earlier of—
"(i) the later of the date a plan amendment applying the amendments made by subsection (b) is adopted or made effective, or
"(ii) the first day of the first limitation year beginning on December 31, 1999. Determinations under section 415(b)(2)(E) of the Internal Revenue Code of 1986 before such earlier date shall be made with respect to such benefits on the basis of such section as in effect on December 7, 1994 (except that the modification made by section 1449(b) of the Small Business Job Protection Act of 1996 shall be taken into account), and the provisions of the plan as in effect on December 7, 1994, but only if such provisions by the plan meet the requirements of such section (as so in effect).
"(B) Timing of plan amendment. — A plan that operates in accordance with the amendments made by subsection (b) shall not be treated as failing to satisfy section 401(a) of the Internal Revenue Code of 1986 or as not being operated in accordance with the provisions of the plan until such date as the Secretary of the Treasury provides merely because the plan has not been amended to include the amendments made by subsection (b)."
Prior to amendment, subpara. (a)(11)(B) read as follows:
"(B) Determination of present value.
"(i) In general. For purposes of subparagraph (A), the present value shall be calculated —
"(I) by using an interest rate no greater than the applicable interest rate if the vested accrued benefit (using such rate) is not in excess of $25,000, and
"(II) by using an interest rate no greater than 120 percent of the applicable interest rate if the vested accrued benefit exceeds $25,000 (as determined under subclause (I)).
In no event shall the present value determined under subclause (II) be less than $25,000.

"(ii) Applicable interest rate. For purposes of clause (i), the term 'applicable interest rate' means the interest rate which would be used (as of the date of the distribution) by the Pension Benefit Guaranty Corporation for purposes of determining the present value of a lump sum distribution on plan termination."

In 1992, P.L. 102-318, Sec. 521(b)(44), added a sentence to the end of para. (d)(3), effective for distributions after 12/31/92. For special rule, see Sec. 521(e)(2) of this Act which reads as follows:
"(2) Special rule for partial distributions. For purposes of section 402(a)(5)(D)(i)(II) of the Internal Revenue Code of 1986 (as in effect before the amendments made by this section), a distribution before January 1, 1993, which is made before or at the same time as a series of periodic payments shall not be treated as one of such series if it is not substantially equal in amount to other payments in such series."

In 1989, P.L. 101-239, Sec. 7861(a)(3), redesignated the second Sec. 1113(e) of P.L. 99-514, special rules for amendments made by Sec. 1113(a), (b) and (d)(B) of P.L. 99-514, as Sec. 1113(f) of P.L. 99-514, reproduced below... Sec. 7861(a)(4), added Sec. 1113(f)(4) [as redesignated] of P.L. 99-514, reproduced below.
—P.L. 101-239, Sec. 7861(a)(5)(A), added subpara. (a)(3)(G) ... Sec. 7861(a)(6)(A), amended subpara. (a)(4)(A), effective for plan yrs. begin. after 12/31/88, except as provided by Secs. 1113(f)(2), (3) and (4) of P.L. 99-514 reproduced below.
Prior to amendment, subpara. (a)(4)(A) read as follows:
"(A) years of service before age 18, except that in the case of a plan which does not satisfy subparagraph (A) or (B) of paragraph (2), the plan may not disregard any such year of service during which the employee was a participant; "
—P.L. 101-239, Sec. 7871(a)(1), deleted subpara. (b)(2)(B) and redesignated subparas. (b)(2)(C) and (D) as subparas. (b)(2)(B) and (C) ... Sec. 7871(a)(2), substituted "paragraph" for "subparagraph" in subpara. (b)(2)(C) [as redesignated], generally effective [as provided by Sec. 9204(a)(1) of P.L. 99-509] for plan yrs. begin. on or after 1/1/88, and only for employees who have 1 hour of service in any plan year to which the above amendments apply. For special rules, see Sec. 9204(a)(2) and (c) of P.L. 99-509 reproduced below.
Prior to deletion, subpara. (b)(2)(B) read as follows:
"(B) Disregard of subsidized portion of early retirement benefit. A plan shall not be treated as failing to meet the requirements of subparagraph (A) solely because the subsidized portion of any early retirement benefit is disregarded in determining benefit accruals."
—P.L. 101-239, Sec. 7871(b)(1), amended subpara. (a)(8)(B), effective for plan yrs. begin. on or after 1/1/88, and only for service performed on or after 1/1/88. For special rules concerning plan amendments, see Sec. 9204(c) of P.L. 99-509 reproduced below.
Prior to amendment, subpara. (a)(8)(B) read as follows:
"(B) the latest of—
"(i) the time a plan participant attains age 65,
"(ii) in the case of a plan participant who commences participation in the plan within 5 years before attaining normal retirement age under the plan, the 5th anniversary of the time the plan participant commences participation in the plan, or
"(iii) in the case of a plan participant not described in clause (ii), the 10th anniversary of the time the plan participant commences participation in the plan."
—P.L. 101-239, Sec. 7881(m)(1)(A), amended clause (c)(2)(C)(iii) ... Sec. 7881(m)(1)(B), amended subpara. (c)(2)(B) ... Sec. 7881(m)(1)(C), deleted subpara. (c)(2)(E) ... Sec. 7881(m)(1)(D), added subpara. (a)(7)(D), effective for plan yrs. begin. after 12/31/87 except as provided in Sec. 9346(c)(2) of P.L. 100-203 reproduced below. Sec. 7881(m)(3) of this Act provides:
"(3) If—
"(A) during the period beginning December 22, 1987, and ending June 21, 1988, a plan was amended to reflect the amendments made by section 9346 of the Pension Protection Act [P.L. 100-203], and
"(B) such plan is amended to reflect the amendments made by this subsection [Sec. 7881(m)],
any plan amendment described in subparagraph (B) shall not be treated as reducing accrued benefits for purposes of section 411(d)(6) of the Internal Revenue Code of 1986 or section 204(g) of ERISA."
Prior to amendment, clause (c)(2)(C)(iii) read as follows:
"(iii) interest on the sum of the amounts determined under clauses (i) and (ii) compounded annually at the rate of 120 percent of the Federal mid-term rate (as in effect under section 1274 for the 1st month of a plan year) from the beginning of the first plan year to which subsection (a)(2) applies (by reason of the applicable effective date) to the date upon which the employee would attain normal retirement age."
Prior to amendment, subpara. (c)(2)(B) read as follows:
"(B) Defined benefit plans.
"(i) In general. In the case of a defined benefit plan providing an annual benefit in the form of a single life annuity (without ancillary benefits) commencing at normal retirement age, the accrued benefit derived from contributions made by an employee as of any applicable date is the annual benefit equal to the employee's accumulated contributions multiplied by the appropriate conversion factor.
"(ii) Appropriate conversion factor. For purposes of clause (i), the term 'appropriate conversion factor' means the factor necessary to convert an amount equal to the accumulated contributions to a single life annuity (without ancillary benefits) commencing at normal retirement age and shall be 10 percent for a normal retirement age of 65 years. For other normal retirement ages the conversion factor shall be determined in accordance with regulations prescribed by the Secretary or his delegate."
Prior to deletion subpara. (c)(2)(E) read as follows:

Employee benefit plans — Code Sec. 411

"(E) Limitation. The accrued benefit derived from employee contributions shall not exceed the greater of—
"(i) the employee's accrued benefit under the plan, or
"(ii) the accrued benefit derived from employee contributions determined as though the amounts calculated under clauses (ii) and (iii) of subparagraph (C) were zero."

In **1988**, P.L. 100-647, Sec. 1011A(k), amended Sec. 1139(d)(2)(A)(i) of P.L. 99-514 [reproduced below], part of the effective date for changes made by Sec. 1139(d) of P.L. 99-514 by substituting "after January" for "before January", see below.

—P.L. 100-647, Sec. 1018(t)(8)(B), amended subsec. (a)(11)(A) by substituting "nonforfeitable" for "vested", effective for plan yrs. begin. after 12/31/84, with special rules provided by Sec. 302(b) of P.L. 98-397 [reproduced below].

In **1987**, P.L. 100-203, Sec. 9346(b)(1), substituted "120 percent of the Federal mid-term rate (as in effect under section 1274 for the 1st month of a plan year)" for "5 percent per annum" in clause (c)(2)(C)(iii) ... Sec. 9346(b)(2)(A), deleted ", the rate of interest described in clause (iii) of subparagraph (C), or both," in the first sentence of subpara. (c)(2)(D) ... Sec. 9346(b)(2)(B), deleted the second sentence of subpara. (c)(2)(D), effective for plan yrs. begin. after 12/31/87. Sec. 9346(c)(2) of this Act also provides:

"Plan amendments not required until January 1, 1989. If any amendment made by this section requires an amendment to any plan, such plan amendment shall not be required to be made before the first plan year beginning on or after January 1, 1989, if—
"(A) during the period after such amendments made by this section take effect and before such first plan year, the plan is operated in accordance with the requirements of such amendments or in accordance with an amendment prescribed by the Secretary of the Treasury and adopted by the plan, and
"(B) such plan amendment applies retroactively to the period after such amendments take effect and such first plan year.
A plan shall not be treated as failing to provide definitely determinable benefits or contributions, or to be operated in accordance with the provisions of the plan, merely because it operates in accordance with this subsection.".

Prior to deletion, the second sentence of subpara. (c)(2)(D) read as follows:
"The rate of interest shall bear the relationship to 5 percent which the Secretary determines to be comparable to the relationship which the long-term money rates and investment yields for the last period of 10 calendar years ending at least 12 months before the beginning of the plan year bear to the long-term money rates and investment yields for the 10-calendar year period 1964 through 1973."

In **1986**, P.L. 99-514, Sec. 1113(a), amended para. (a)(2) ... Sec. 1113(b), repealed para. (d)(4) ... Sec. 1113(d)(B), substituted "3 years" for "5 years" in subpara. (a)(10)(B), effective for plan yrs. begin. after 12/31/88. Sec. 1113(f)(2), (3), and (4) [as amended by Sec. 7861(a)(3) of P.L. 101-239 and (4), see above] provides:

"(2) Special rule for collective bargaining agreements.—In the case of a plan maintained pursuant to 1 or more collective bargaining agreements between employee representatives and 1 or more employers ratified before March 1, 1986, the amendments made by this section shall not apply to employees covered by any such agreement in plan years beginning before the earlier of—
"(A) the later of—
"(i) January 1, 1989, or
"(ii) the date on which the last of such collective bargaining agreements terminates (determined without regard to any extension thereof after February 28, 1986), or
"(B) January 1, 1991.
"(3) Participation required.—The amendments made by this section shall not apply to any employee who does not have 1 hour of service in any plan year to which the amendments made by this section apply.
"(4) Repeal of class year vesting.—If a plan amendment repealing class year vesting is adopted after October 22, 1986, such amendment shall not apply to any employee for the 1st plan year to which the amendments made by subsections (b) and (e)(2) apply (and any subsequent plan year) if—
"(A) such plan amendment would reduce the nonforfeitable right of such employee for such year, and
"(B) such employee has at least 1 hour of service before the adoption of such plan amendment and after the beginning of such 1st plan year.
This paragraph shall not apply to an employee who has 5 consecutive 1-year breaks in service (as defined in section 411(a)(6)(A) of the Internal Revenue Code of 1986) which include the 1st day of the 1st plan year to which the amendments made by subsection (b) and (e)(2) apply. A plan shall not be treated as failing to meet the requirements of section 401(a)(26) of such Code by reason of complying with the provisions of this paragraph."

Prior to amendment, para. (a)(2) read as follows:
"(2) Employer contributions. A plan satisfies the requirements of this paragraph if it satisfies the requirements of subparagraph (A), (B), or (C).
"(A) 10-year vesting. A plan satisfies the requirements of this subparagraph if an employee who has at least 10 years of service has a nonforfeitable right to 100 percent of his accrued benefit derived from employer contributions.
"(B) 5- to 15-year vesting. A plan satisfies the requirements of this subparagraph if an employee who has completed at least 5 years of service has a nonforfeitable right to a percentage of his accrued benefit derived from employer contributions which percentage is not less than the percentage determined under the following table:

"Years of service:	Nonforfeitable percentage
5	25
6	30
7	35
8	40
9	45
10	50
11	60
12	70
13	80
14	90
15 or more	100

"(C) Rule of 45.
"(i) A plan satisfies the requirements of this subparagraph if an employee who is not separated from the service, who has completed at least 5 years of service, and with respect to whom the sum of his age and years of service equals or exceeds 45, has a nonforfeitable right to a percentage of his accrued benefit derived from employer contributions determined under the following table:

"If years of service equal or exceed—	and sum of age and service equals or exceeds—	then the non-forfeitable percentage is—
5	45	50
6	47	60
7	49	70
8	51	80
9	53	90
10	55	100.

"(ii) Notwithstanding clause (i), a plan shall not be treated as satisfying the requirements of this subparagraph unless any employee who has completed at least 10 years of service has a nonforfeitable right to not less than 50 percent of his accrued benefit derived from employer contributions and to not less than an additional 10 percent for each additional year of service thereafter."

Prior to repeal, para. (d)(4) [as amended by Sec. 1898(a)(1)(A) of P.L. 99-514, see below] read as follows:
"(4) Class-year plans.
"(A) In general. The requirements of subsection (a)(2) shall be treated as satisfied in the case of a class-year plan if such plan provides that 100 percent of each employee's right to or derived from the contributions of the employer on the employee's behalf with respect to any plan year is nonforfeitable not later than when such participant was performing services for the employer as of the close of each of 5 plan years (whether or not consecutive) after the plan year for which the contributions were made.
"(B) 5-year break in service. For purposes of subparagraph (A) if—
"(i) any contributions are made on behalf of a participant with respect to any plan year, and
"(ii) before such participant meets the requirements of subparagraph (A), such participant was not performing services for the employer as of the close of each of any 5 consecutive plan years after such plan year,
then the plan may provide that the participant forfeits any right to or derived from the contributions made with respect to such plan year.
"(C) Class-year plan. For purposes of this section, the term 'class-year plan' means a profit-sharing, stock bonus, or money purchase plan which provides for the separate nonforfeitability of employees' rights to or derived from the contributions for each plan year."

—P.L. 99-514, Sec. 1114(b)(10), substituted "highly compensated employees (within the meaning of section 414(q))" for "officers, shareholders, or highly compensated" in subparas. (d)(1)(A) and (B), effective for yrs. begin. after 12/31/88.

—P.L. 99-514, Sec. 1139(a), amended subpara. (a)(11)(B), effective for distributions in plan yrs. begin. after 12/31/84, except for distributions in plan yrs. begin. after 12/31/84 and before 1/1/87, if such distributions were made in accordance with the requirements of the regulations issued under the Retirement Equity Act of 1984 [P.L. 98-397]. Sec. 1139(d)(2) [as amended by Sec. 1011A(k) of P.L. 100-647, see above] of this Act provides:

"(2) Reduction in accrued benefits.—
"(A) In general.—If a plan—
"(i) adopts a plan amendment before the close of the first plan year beginning on or after January 1, 1989, which provides for the calculation of the present value of the accrued benefits in the manner provided by the amendments made by this section, and
"(ii) the plan reduces the accrued benefits for any plan year to which such plan amendment applies in accordance with such plan amendment,
such reduction shall not be treated as a violation of section 411(d)(6) of the Internal Revenue Code of 1986 or section 204(g) of the Employee Retirement Income Security Act of 1974 (29 U.S.C. 1054(g)).
"(B) Special rule.—In the case of a plan maintained by a corporation incorporated on April 11, 1934, which is headquartered in Tarrant County, Texas—
"(i) such plan may be amended to remove the option of an employee to receive a lump sum distribution (within the meaning of section 402(e)(5) of such Code) if such amendment—
"(I) is adopted within 1 year of the date of the enactment of this Act, and
"(II) is not effective until 2 years after the employees are notified of such amendment, and
"(ii) the present value of any vested accrued benefit of such plan determined during the 3-year period beginning on the date of the enactment of this Act shall be determined under the applicable interest rate (within the meaning of section 411(a)(11)(B)(ii) of such Code), except that if such value (as so determined) ex-

ceeds $50,000, then the value of any excess over $50,000 shall be determined by using the interest rate specified in the plan as of August 16, 1986."

Prior to amendment, subpara. (a)(11)(B) read as follows:

"(B) Determination of present value. For purposes of subparagraph (A), the present value shall be calculated by using an interest rate not greater than the interest rate which would be used (as of the date of the distribution) by the Pension Benefit Guaranty Corporation for purposes of determining the present value of a lump sum distribution on plan termination."

—P.L. 99-514, Sec. 1898(a)(1)(A), amended para. (d)(4) [before repeal by Sec. 1113(b) of this Act, see above], effective as provided in Sec. 1898(a)(1)(C) of P.L. 99-514, which reads:

"(C) Effective date.—The amendments made by [Sec. 1898(a)(1) of P.L. 99-514] shall apply to contributions made for plan years beginning after the date of the enactment of this Act [10/22/86]; except that, in the case of a plan described in section 302(b) of the Retirement Equity Act of 1984 [P.L. 98-397], such amendments shall not apply to any plan year to which the amendments made by such Act do not apply by reason of such section 302(b)."

Prior to amendment, para. (d)(4) read as follows:

"(4) Class year plans. The requirements of subsection (a)(2) shall be deemed to be satisfied in the case of a class year plan if such plan provides that 100 percent of each employee's right to or derived from the contributions of the employer on his behalf with respect to any plan year are nonforfeitable not later than the end of the 5th plan year following the plan year for which such contributions were made. For purposes of this section, the term 'class year plan' means a profit-sharing, stock bonus, or money purchase plan which provides for the separate nonforfeitability of employees' rights to or derived from the contributions for each plan year."

—P.L. 99-514, Sec. 1898(a)(4)(A)(i), amended the last sentence of clause (a)(3)(D)(ii)... Sec. 1898(a)(4)(A)(ii), amended the last sentence of subpara. (a)(7)(C)... Sec. 1898(d)(1)(A)(i), amended subpara. (a)(11)(A)... Sec. 1898(d)(2)(A)(ii), substituted "paragraphs (1), (2), and (11)" for "paragraphs (1) and (2)" in subsec. (a)... Sec. 1898(d)(2)(A), added subpara. (a)(11)(C), effective for plan yrs. begin. after 12/31/84, with special rules provided by Sec. 302(b) of P.L. 98-397 [reproduced below].

Prior to amendment, the last sentence of clause (a)(3)(D)(ii) read as follows:

"In the case of a defined contribution plan, the plan provision required under this clause may provide that such repayment must be made before the participant has any one-year break in service commencing after the withdrawal."

Prior to amendment, the last sentence of subpara. (a)(7)(C) read as follows:

"In the case of a defined contribution plan, the plan provision required under this subparagraph may provide that such repayment must be made before the participant has 5 consecutive 1-year breaks in service commencing after such withdrawal."

Prior to amendment, subpara. (a)(11)(A) read as follows:

"(A) In general. If the present value of any accrued benefit exceeds $3,500, such benefit shall not be treated as nonforfeitable if the plan provides that the present value of such benefit could be immediately distributed without the consent of the participant."

—P.L. 99-514, Sec. 1898(f)(1)(A), added subpara. (d)(6)(C), effective for plan amendments made after 7/30/84, except as provided by Sec. 302(d)(2) of P.L. 98-397 [reproduced below].

—P.L. 99-509, Sec. 9202(b)(1)(A), amended the heading of para. (b)(1)... Sec. 9202(b)(1)(B), added subpara. (b)(1)(H)... Sec. 9202(b)(2), redesignated paras. (b)(2) and (b)(3) as paras. (b)(3) and (b)(4), and added new para. (b)(2)... Sec. 9202(b)(3), amended the first sentence of subsec. (a), generally effective [as provided by Sec. 9204(a)(1) of this Act] for plan yrs. begin. on or after 1/1/88, and only for employees who have 1 hour of service in any plan year to which the above amendments apply. Secs. 9204(a)(2) and (c)-(e) provide:

"(2) Special rule for collectively bargained plans.—In the case of a plan maintained pursuant to 1 or more collective bargaining agreements between employee representatives and 1 or more employers ratified before March 1, 1986, (1) [Sec. 9204(a)(1)] shall be applied to benefits pursuant to, and individuals covered by, any such agreement by substituting for 'January 1, 1988' the date of the commencement of the first plan year beginning on or after the earlier of—

"(A) the later of—

"(i) January 1, 1988, or

"(ii) the date on which the last of such collective bargaining agreements terminate (determined without regard to any extension thereof after February 28, 1986), or

"(B) January 1, 1990. [. . .]

"(c) Plan amendments. If any amendment made by this subtitle [Subtitle C, Title IX, P.L. 99-509] requires an amendment to any plan, such plan amendment shall not be required to be made before the first plan year beginning on or after January 1, 1989, if—

"(1) during the period after such amendment takes effect and before such first plan year, the plan is operated in accordance with the requirements of such amendment, and

"(2) such plan amendment applies retroactively to the period after such amendment takes effect and such first plan year.

A pension plan shall not be treated as failing to provide definitely determinable benefits or contributions, or to be operated in accordance with the provisions of the plan, merely because it operates in accordance with this subsection.

"(d) Interagency coordination. The regulations and rulings issued by the Secretary of Labor, the regulations and rulings issued by the Secretary of the Treasury, and the regulations and rulings issued by the Equal Employment Opportunity Commission pursuant to the amendments made by this subtitle shall each be consistent with the others. The Secretary of Labor, the Secretary of the Treasury, and the Equal Employment Opportunity Commission shall each consult with the others to the extent necessary to meet the requirements of the preceding sentence.

"(e) Final regulations. The Secretary of Labor, the Secretary of the Treasury, and the Equal Employment Opportunity Commission shall each issue before February 1, 1988, such final regulations as may be necessary to carry out the amendments made by this subtitle."

Prior to amendment, the heading for para. (b)(1) read as follows:

"(1) General rules."

Prior to amendment, the first sentence of subsec. (a) read as follows:

"A trust shall not constitute a qualified trust under section 401(a) unless the plan of which such trust is a part provides that an employee's right to his normal retirement benefit is nonforfeitable upon the attainment of normal retirement age (as defined in paragraph (8)) and in addition satisfies the requirements of paragraphs (1) and (2) of this subsection and the requirements of paragraph (2) of subsection (b), and in the case of a defined benefit plan, also satisfies the requirements of paragraph (1) of subsection (b)."

—P.L. 99-509, Sec. 9203(b)(2), amended subpara. (a)(8)(B), effective for plan yrs. begin. on or after 1/1/88, and only with respect to service performed on or after 1/1/88. For special rules concerning plan amendments, see Sec. 9204(c) of this Act, above.

Prior to amendment, subpara. (a)(8)(B) read as follows:

"(B) the latter of—

"(i) the time a plan participant attains age 65, or

"(ii) the 10th anniversary of the time a plan participant commenced participation in the plan."

In **1984**, P.L. 98-397, Sec. 202(b), substituted "18" for "22" in subpara. (a)(4)(A)... Sec. 202(c), substituted "5 consecutive 1-year breaks in service" for "1-year break in service" each place it appeared and substituted "such 5-year period" for "such break" in subpara. (a)(6)(C)... Sec. 202(d)(2), amended subpara. (a)(6)(D)... Sec. 202(e)(2), added subpara. (a)(6)(E)... Sec. 202(e)(3), added ", determined without regard to section 410(a)(5)(E)" after "section 410(a)(5)" in subpara. (b)(3)(A)... Sec. 202(f), substituted "5 consecutive 1-year breaks in service" for "any one-year break in service" in subpara. (a)(7)(C)... Sec. 205(a), added para. (a)(11)... Sec. 205(b), substituted "3,500" for "1,750" in subpara. (a)(7)(B), effective for plan yrs. begin. after 12/31/84. Sec. 302(b) of this Act provides the following special rule:

"(b) Special rule for collective bargaining agreements. In the case of a plan maintained pursuant to 1 or more collective bargaining agreements between employee representatives and 1 or more employers ratified before the date of the enactment of this Act, except as provided in subsection (d) or section 303, the amendments made by this Act shall not apply to plan years beginning before the earlier of—

"(1) the date on which the last of the collective bargaining agreements relating to the plan terminates (determined without regard to any extension thereof agreed to after the date of the enactment of this Act), or

"(2) January 1, 1987.

For purposes of paragraph (1), any plan amendment made pursuant to a collective bargaining agreement relating to the plan which amends the plan solely to conform to any requirement added by title I or II shall not be treated as a termination of such collective bargaining agreement."

For transitional rules see Sec. 303 of this Act reproduced at note following Code Sec. 401.

Prior to amendment, para. (a)(6)(D) read as follows:

"(D) Nonvested participants. For purposes of paragraph (4), in the case of a participant who, under the plan, does not have any nonforfeitable right to an accrued benefit derived from employer contributions, years of service before any 1-year break in service shall not be required to be taken into account if the number of consecutive 1-year breaks in service equals or exceeds the aggregate number of such years of service prior to such break. Such aggregate number of years of service before such break shall be deemed not to include any years of service not required to be taken into account under this subparagraph by reason of any prior break in service."

—P.L. 98-397, Sec. 301(a), amended para. (d)(6), effective for plan amendments made after 7/30/84, except as provided in Sec. 302(d)(2) of this Act which reads as follows:

"(2) Special rule for collective bargaining agreements.—In the case of a plan maintained pursuant to 1 or more collective bargaining agreements entered into before January 1, 1985, which are—

"(A) between employee representatives and 1 or more employers, and

"(B) successor agreements to 1 or more collective bargaining agreements which terminate after July 30, 1984, and before January 1, 1985,

the amendments made by section 301 shall not apply to plan amendments adopted before April 1, 1985, pursuant to such successor agreements (without regard to any modification or reopening after December 31, 1984)."

Prior to amendment, para. (d)(6) read as follows:

"(6) Accrued benefit not to be decreased by amendment. A plan shall be treated as not satisfying the requirements of this section if the accrued benefit of a participant is decreased by an amendment of the plan, other than an amendment described in section 412(c)(8), or section 4281 of the Employee Retirement Income Security Act of 1974."

In **1980**, P.L. 96-364, Sec. 206, added subparas. (a)(3)(E) and (F), deleted "and" at the end of subpara. (a)(4)(E), substituted "; and" for the period at the end of subpara. (a)(4)(F), added subpara. (a)(4)(G), substituted "section 412(c)(8), or section 4281 of the Employee Retirement Income Security Act of 1974" for "section 412(c)(8)" in subsec. (d)(6), effective 9/26/80.

In **1976**, P.L. 94-455, Sec. 1901(a)(62), substituted "paragraph (8)" for "subsection (a)(8)" in subsec. (a), substituted "September 2, 1974" for "the date of the enactment of the Employee Retirement Income Security Act of 1974" and substi-

Employee benefit plans Code Sec. 412(c)(4)(B)

tuted "September 2, 1974," for "the date of the enactment of the Act" in clause (a)(3)(D)(iii), amended the heading for subpara. (a)(7)(C), substituted "September 2, 1974" for "the date of the enactment of the Employee Retirement Income Security Act of 1974" in clause (b)(1)(D)(i) and subpara. (e)(1)(C), substituted "September 1, 1974" for "the date before the date of the enactment of the Employee Retirement Income Security Act of 1974" in para. (e)(2), effective for tax. yrs. begin. after 12/31/76.

Prior to amendment, the heading of subpara. (a)(7)(C) read as follows:

"(C) Repayment of subparagraph (b) distributions."

—P.L. 94-455, Sec. 1906(b)(13)(A), substituted "Secretary" for "Secretary or his delegate" each place it appeared in subsecs. (a) and (c), effective for tax. yrs. begin. after 12/31/76.

In **1974**, P.L. 93-406, Sec. 1012(a), added Code Sec. 411, effective 9/2/74 or other date as specified in Sec. 1017 of the Act (reproduced following Code Sec. 401).

Sec. 412. Minimum funding standards.

(a) Requirement to meet minimum funding standard.

(1) **In general.** A plan to which this section applies shall satisfy the minimum funding standard applicable to the plan for any plan year.

(2) **Minimum funding standard.** For purposes of paragraph (1), a plan shall be treated as satisfying the minimum funding standard for a plan year if—

(A) in the case of a defined benefit plan which is not a multiemployer plan, the employer makes contributions to or under the plan for the plan year which, in the aggregate, are not less than the minimum required contribution determined under section 430 for the plan for the plan year,

(B) in the case of a money purchase plan which is not a multiemployer plan, the employer makes contributions to or under the plan for the plan year which are required under the terms of the plan, and

(C) in the case of a multiemployer plan, the employers make contributions to or under the plan for any plan year which, in the aggregate, are sufficient to ensure that the plan does not have an accumulated funding deficiency under section 431 as of the end of the plan year.

(b) Liability for contributions.

(1) **In general.** Except as provided in paragraph (2), the amount of any contribution required by this section (including any required installments under paragraphs (3) and (4) of section 430(j)) shall be paid by the employer responsible for making contributions to or under the plan.

(2) **Joint and several liability where employer member of controlled group.** If the employer referred to in paragraph (1) is a member of a controlled group, each member of such group shall be jointly and severally liable for payment of such contributions.

(3) **Multiemployer plans in critical status.** Paragraph (1) shall not apply in the case of a multiemployer plan for any plan year in which the plan is in critical status pursuant to section 432. This paragraph shall only apply if the plan sponsor adopts a rehabilitation plan in accordance with section 432(e) and complies with such rehabilitation plan (and any modifications of the plan).

(c) Variance from minimum funding standards.

(1) **Waiver in case of business hardship.**

(A) In general. If—

(i) an employer is (or in the case of a multiemployer plan, 10 percent or more of the number of employers contributing to or under the plan are) unable to satisfy the minimum funding standard for a plan year without temporary substantial business hardship (substantial business hardship in the case of a multiemployer plan), and

(ii) application of the standard would be adverse to the interests of plan participants in the aggregate,

the Secretary may, subject to subparagraph (C), waive the requirements of subsection (a) for such year with respect to all or any portion of the minimum funding standard. The Secretary shall not waive the minimum funding standard with respect to a plan for more than 3 of any 15 (5 of any 15 in the case of a multiemployer plan) consecutive plan years

(B) Effects of waiver. If a waiver is granted under subparagraph (A) for any plan year—

(i) in the case of a defined benefit plan which is not a multiemployer plan, the minimum required contribution under section 430 for the plan year shall be reduced by the amount of the waived funding deficiency and such amount shall be amortized as required under section 430(e), and

(ii) in the case of a multiemployer plan, the funding standard account shall be credited under section 431(b)(3)(C) with the amount of the waived funding deficiency and such amount shall be amortized as required under section 431(b)(2)(C).

(C) Waiver of amortized portion not allowed. The Secretary may not waive under subparagraph (A) any portion of the minimum funding standard under subsection (a) for a plan year which is attributable to any waived funding deficiency for any preceding plan year.

(2) **Determination of business hardship.** For purposes of this subsection, the factors taken into account in determining temporary substantial business hardship (substantial business hardship in the case of a multiemployer plan) shall include (but shall not be limited to) whether or not—

(A) the employer is operating at an economic loss,

(B) there is substantial unemployment or underemployment in the trade or business and in the industry concerned,

(C) the sales and profits of the industry concerned are depressed or declining, and

(D) it is reasonable to expect that the plan will be continued only if the waiver is granted.

(3) **Waived funding deficiency.** For purposes of this section and part III of this subchapter, the term "waived funding deficiency" means the portion of the minimum funding standard under subsection (a) (determined without regard to the waiver) for a plan year waived by the Secretary and not satisfied by employer contributions.

(4) **Security for waivers for single-employer plans, consultations.**

(A) Security may be required.

(i) In general. Except as provided in subparagraph (C), the Secretary may require an employer maintaining a defined benefit plan which is a single-employer plan (within the meaning of section 4001(a)(15) of the Employee Retirement Income Security Act of 1974) to provide security to such plan as a condition for granting or modifying a waiver under paragraph (1).

(ii) Special rules. Any security provided under clause (i) may be perfected and enforced only by the Pension Benefit Guaranty Corporation, or at the direction of the Corporation, by a contributing sponsor (within the meaning of section 4001(a)(13) of the Employee Retirement Income Security Act of 1974), or a member of such sponsor's controlled group (within the meaning of section 4001(a)(14) of such Act).

(B) Consultation with the Pension Benefit Guaranty Corporation. Except as provided in subparagraph (C), the Secretary shall, before granting or modifying a waiver under this subsection with respect to a plan described in subparagraph (A)(i)—

(i) provide the Pension Benefit Guaranty Corporation with—

(I) notice of the completed application for any waiver or modification, and

(II) an opportunity to comment on such application within 30 days after receipt of such notice, and

(ii) consider—

(I) any comments of the Corporation under clause (i)(II), and

(II) any views of any employee organization (within the meaning of section 3(4) of the Employee Retirement Income Security Act of 1974) representing participants in the plan which are submitted in writing to the Secretary in connection with such application.

Information provided to the Corporation under this subparagraph shall be considered tax return information and subject to the safeguarding and reporting requirements of section 6103(p).

(C) Exception for certain waivers.

(i) In general. The preceding provisions of this paragraph shall not apply to any plan with respect to which the sum of—

(I) the aggregate unpaid minimum required contributions (within the meaning of section 4971(c)(4)) for the plan year and all preceding plan years, and

(II) the present value of all waiver amortization installments determined for the plan year and succeeding plan years under section 430(e)(2),

is less than $1,000,000.

(ii) Treatment of waivers for which applications are pending. The amount described in clause (i)(I) shall include any increase in such amount which would result if all applications for waivers of the minimum funding standard under this subsection which are pending with respect to such plan were denied.

(5) Special rules for single-employer plans.

(A) Application must be submitted before date 2½ months after close of year. In the case of a defined benefit plan which is not a multiemployer plan, no waiver may be granted under this subsection with respect to any plan for any plan year unless an application therefor is submitted to the Secretary not later than the 15th day of the 3rd month beginning after the close of such plan year.

(B) Special rule if employer is member of controlled group. In the case of a defined benefit plan which is not a multiemployer plan, if an employer is a member of a controlled group, the temporary substantial business hardship requirements of paragraph (1) shall be treated as met only if such requirements are met—

(i) with respect to such employer, and

(ii) with respect to the controlled group of which such employer is a member (determined by treating all members of such group as a single employer).

The Secretary may provide that an analysis of a trade or business or industry of a member need not be conducted if the Secretary determines such analysis is not necessary because the taking into account of such member would not significantly affect the determination under this paragraph.

(6) Advance notice.

(A) In general. The Secretary shall, before granting a waiver under this subsection, require each applicant to provide evidence satisfactory to the Secretary that the applicant has provided notice of the filing of the application for such waiver to each affected party (as defined in section 4001(a)(21) of the Employee Retirement Income Security Act of 1974). Such notice shall include a description of the extent to which the plan is funded for benefits which are guaranteed under title IV of the Employee Retirement Income Security Act of 1974 and for benefit liabilities.

(B) Consideration of relevant information. The Secretary shall consider any relevant information provided by a person to whom notice was given under subparagraph (A).

(7) Restriction on plan amendments.

(A) In general. No amendment of a plan which increases the liabilities of the plan by reason of any increase in benefits, any change in the accrual of benefits, or any change in the rate at which benefits become nonforfeitable under the plan shall be adopted if a waiver under this subsection or an extension of time under section 431(d) is in effect with respect to the plan, or if a plan amendment described in subsection (d)(2) which reduces the accrued benefit of any participant has been made at any time in the preceding 12 months (24 months in the case of a multiemployer plan). If a plan is amended in violation of the preceding sentence, any such waiver, or extension of time, shall not apply to any plan year ending on or after the date on which such amendment is adopted.

(B) Exception. Subparagraph (A) shall not apply to any plan amendment which—

(i) the Secretary determines to be reasonable and which provides for only de minimis increases in the liabilities of the plan,

(ii) only repeals an amendment described in subsection (d)(2), or

(iii) is required as a condition of qualification under part I of subchapter D, of chapter 1.

(d) Miscellaneous rules.

(1) Change in method or year. If the funding method or a plan year for a plan is changed, the change shall take effect only if approved by the Secretary.

(2) Certain retroactive plan amendments. For purposes of this section, any amendment applying to a plan year which—

(A) is adopted after the close of such plan year but no later than 2½ months after the close of the plan year (or, in the case of a multiemployer plan, no later than 2 years after the close of such plan year),

(B) does not reduce the accrued benefit of any participant determined as of the beginning of the first plan year to which the amendment applies, and

(C) does not reduce the accrued benefit of any participant determined as of the time of adoption except to the extent required by the circumstances,

shall, at the election of the plan administrator, be deemed to have been made on the first day of such plan year. No amendment described in this paragraph which reduces the accrued benefits of any participant shall take effect unless the plan administrator files a notice with the Secretary notifying him of such amendment and the Secretary has approved such amendment, or within 90 days after the date on which such notice was filed, failed to disapprove such amendment. No amendment described in this subsection shall be approved by the Secretary unless the Secretary determines that such amendment is necessary because of a temporary substantial business hardship (as determined

Employee benefit plans   Code Sec. 412

under subsection (c)(2)) or a substantial business hardship (as so determined) in the case of a multiemployer plan and that a waiver under subsection (c) (or, in the case of a multiemployer plan, any extension of the amortization period under section 431(d)) is unavailable or inadequate.

(3) **Controlled group.** For purposes of this section, the term "controlled group" means any group treated as a single employer under subsection (b), (c), (m), or (o) of section 414.

(e) **Plans to which section applies.**

(1) **In general.** Except as provided in paragraphs (2) and (4), this section applies to a plan if, for any plan year beginning on or after the effective date of this section for such plan under the Employee Retirement Income Security Act of 1974—

(A) such plan included a trust which qualified (or was determined by the Secretary to have qualified) under section 401(a), or

(B) such plan satisfied (or was determined by the Secretary to have satisfied) the requirements of section 403(a).

(2) **Exceptions.** This section shall not apply to—

(A) any profit-sharing or stock bonus plan,

(B) any insurance contract plan described in paragraph (3),

(C) any governmental plan (within the meaning of section 414(d)),

(D) any church plan (within the meaning of section 414(e)) with respect to which the election provided by section 410(d) has not been made,

(E) any plan which has not, at any time after September 2, 1974, provided for employer contributions, or

(F) any plan established and maintained by a society, order, or association described in section 501(c)(8) or (9), if no part of the contributions to or under such plan are made by employers of participants in such plan.

No plan described in subparagraph (C), (D), or (F) shall be treated as a qualified plan for purposes of section 401(a) unless such plan meets the requirements of section 401(a)(7) as in effect on September 1, 1974.

(3) **Certain insurance contract plans.** A plan is described in this paragraph if—

(A) the plan is funded exclusively by the purchase of individual insurance contracts,

(B) such contracts provide for level annual premium payments to be paid extending not later than the retirement age for each individual participating in the plan, and commencing with the date the individual became a participant in the plan (or, in the case of an increase in benefits, commencing at the time such increase becomes effective),

(C) benefits provided by the plan are equal to the benefits provided under each contract at normal retirement age under the plan and are guaranteed by an insurance carrier (licensed under the laws of a State to do business with the plan) to the extent premiums have been paid,

(D) premiums payable for the plan year, and all prior plan years, under such contracts have been paid before lapse or there is reinstatement of the policy,

(E) no rights under such contracts have been subject to a security interest at any time during the plan year, and

(F) no policy loans are outstanding at any time during the plan year.

A plan funded exclusively by the purchase of group insurance contracts which is determined under regulations prescribed by the Secretary to have the same characteristics as contracts described in the preceding sentence shall be treated as a plan described in this paragraph.

(4) **Certain terminated multiemployer plans.** This section applies with respect to a terminated multiemployer plan to which section 4021 of the Employee Retirement Income Security Act of 1974 applies until the last day of the plan year in which the plan terminates (within the meaning of section 4041A(a)(2) of such Act).

In **2010**, P.L. 111-312, Sec. 101(a)(1), substituted "December 31, 2012" for "December 31, 2010" both places it appeared in Sec. 901 of P.L. 107-16 [see below], effective as if included in the enactment of P.L. 107-16, EGTRRA, 6/7/2001.

—P.L. 111-192, Sec. 202(b)(1), substituted "eligible cooperative plan or an eligible charity plan" for "eligible cooperative plan" wherever it appeared in Sec. 104(a)-(b) of P.L. 109-280 [see below]

—P.L. 111-192, Sec. 202(b)(2), added subsec. (d) to Sec. 104 of P.L. 109-280 [see below], effective for plan yrs. begin. after 12/31/2007, except that a plan sponsor may elect to apply such amendments to plan yrs. begin. after 12/31/2008. Any such election shall be made at such time, and in such form and manner, as shall be prescribed by the Secretary of the Treasury, and may be revoked only with the consent of the Secretary of the Treasury.

In **2008**, P.L. 110-458, Sec. 101(a)(2)(A), substituted "the plan are" for the "the plan is" in clause (c)(1)(A)(i) . . . Sec. 101(a)(2)(B), inserted "which reduces the accrued benefit of any participant" after "subsection (d)(2)" in subparagraph (c)(7)(A) . . . Sec. 101(a)(2)(C), deleted ", the valuation date," before "or a plan year" in para. (d)(1), effective for plan yrs. begin. after 12/31/2007, as if included in Sec. 111 of the Pension Protection Act of 2006, P.L. 109-280.

—P.L. 110-458, Sec. 102(a), substituted "has not adopted, or ceased using," for "has not used" in Sec. 201(b)(2)(A), P.L. 109-280, see below.

—P.L. 110-458, Sec. 102(b)(2)(H), substituted "the plan sponsor adopts" for "the plan adopts" in para. (b)(3), effective for yrs. begin. after 2007, as if included in Sec. 212 of the Pension Protection Act of 2006, P.L. 109-280. For special rules see Sec. 212(e)(2) and (3), P.L. 109-280, [as amended by Sec. 102(b)(3)(C) of this Act] reproduced below.

—P.L. 110-458, Sec. 102(b)(3)(C), substituted "section 432(b)(3) of the Internal Revenue Code of 1986" for "section 305(b)(3) of the Employee Retirement Income Security Act of 1974" in Sec. 212(e)(2), P.L. 109-280, see below.

—P.L. 110-458, Sec. 103(a), substituted "2009" for "2008" in Sec. 101(c)(2)(A)(ii), P.L. 108-218, see below.

—P.L. 110-458, Sec. 104(b), substituted "commercial" for "commercial airline" in Sec. 402(c)(1)(A), P.L. 109-280, see below.

—P.L. 110-458, Sec. 126(a), amended Sec. 402(e)(4)(C), P.L. 109-280, reproduced below, effective for plan yrs. begin. afer 12/31/2007.

Prior to amendment, Sec. 402(e)(4)(C), P.L. 109-280, read as follows:

"(C) the value of plan assets shall be equal to their fair market value."

In **2006**, P.L. 109-280, Sec. 104, [as amended by Sec. 202(b)(1)-(2) of P.L. 111-192 see above] of this Act, reads as follows:

"SEC. 104. SPECIAL RULES FOR MULTIPLE EMPLOYER PLANS OF CERTAIN COOPERATIVES.

"*(a) General rule.* Except as provided in this section, if a plan in existence on July 26, 2005, was an eligible cooperative plan or an eligible charity plan for its plan year which includes such date, the amendments made by this subtitle and subtitle B shall not apply to plan years beginning before the earlier of—

"(1) the first plan year for which the plan ceases to be an eligible cooperative plan or an eligible charity plan, or

"(2) January 1, 2017.

"*(b) Interest rate.* In applying section 302(b)(5)(B) of the Employee Retirement Income Security Act of 1974 and section 412(b)(5)(B) of the Internal Revenue Code of 1986 (as in effect before the amendments made by this subtitle and subtitle B) to an eligible cooperative plan or an eligible charity plan for plan years beginning after December 31, 2007, and before the first plan year to which such amendments apply, the third segment rate determined under section 303(h)(2)(C)(iii) of such Act and section 430(h)(2)(C)(iii) of such Code (as added by such amendments) shall be used in lieu of the interest rate otherwise used.

"*(c) Eligible cooperative plan defined.* For purposes of this section, a plan shall be treated as an eligible cooperative plan for a plan year if the plan is maintained by more than 1 employer and at least 85 percent of the employers are—

"(1) rural cooperatives (as defined in section 401(k)(7)(B) of such Code without regard to clause (iv) thereof), or

"(2) organizations which are—

"(A) cooperative organizations described in section 1381(a) of such Code which are more than 50-percent owned by agricultural producers or by cooperatives owned by agricultural producers, or

"(B) more than 50-percent owned, or controlled by, one or more cooperative organizations described in subparagraph (A). A plan shall also be treated as an eligible cooperative plan for any plan year for which it is described in section 210(a) of the Employee Retirement Income Security Act of 1974 and is maintained by a rural telephone cooperative association described in section 3(40)(B)(v) of such Act.

"*(d) Eligible charity plan defined.* For purposes of this section, a plan shall be treated as an eligible charity plan for a plan year if the plan is maintained by more than one employer (determined without regard to section 414(c) of the Inter-

Code Sec. 412

nal Revenue Code) and 100 percent of the employers are described in section 501(c)(3) of such Code."
—P.L. 109-280, Sec. 105, of this Act, reads as follows:
"SEC. 105. TEMPORARY RELIEF FOR CERTAIN PBGC SETTLEMENT PLANS.
"(a) General rule. Except as provided in this section, if a plan in existence on July 26, 2005, was a PBGC settlement plan as of such date, the amendments made by this subtitle and subtitle B shall not apply to plan years beginning before January 1, 2014.
"(b) Interest rate. In applying section 302(b)(5)(B) of the Employee Retirement Income Security Act of 1974 and section 412(b)(5)(B) of the Internal Revenue Code of 1986 (as in effect before the amendments made by this subtitle and subtitle B), to a PBGC settlement plan for plan years beginning after December 31, 2007, and before January 1, 2014, the third segment rate determined under section 303(h)(2)(C)(iii) of such Act and section 430(h)(2)(C)(iii) of such Code (as added by such amendments) shall be used in lieu of the interest rate otherwise used.
"(c) PBGC settlement plan. For purposes of this section, the term 'PBGC settlement plan' means a defined benefit plan (other than a multiemployer plan) to which section 302 of such Act and section 412 of such Code apply and—
"(1) which was sponsored by an employer which was in bankruptcy, giving rise to a claim by the Pension Benefit Guaranty Corporation of not greater than $150,000,000, and the sponsorship of which was assumed by another employer that was not a member of the same controlled group as the bankrupt sponsor and the claim of the Pension Benefit Guaranty Corporation was settled or withdrawn in connection with the assumption of the sponsorship, or
"(2) which, by agreement with the Pension Benefit Guaranty Corporation, was spun off from a plan subsequently terminated by such Corporation under section 4042 of the Employee Retirement Income Security Act of 1974."
—P.L. 109-280, Sec. 106, of this Act, reads as follows:
"SEC. 106. SPECIAL RULES FOR PLANS OF CERTAIN GOVERNMENT CONTRACTORS.
"(a) General rule. Except as provided in this section, if a plan is an eligible government contractor plan, this subtitle and subtitle B shall not apply to plan years beginning before the earliest of—
"(1) the first plan year for which the plan ceases to be an eligible government contractor plan,
"(2) the effective date of the Cost Accounting Standards Pension Harmonization Rule, or
"(3) January 1, 2011.
"(b) Interest rate. In applying section 302(b)(5)(B) of the Employee Retirement Income Security Act of 1974 and section 412(b)(5)(B) of the Internal Revenue Code of 1986 (as in effect before the amendments made by this subtitle and subtitle B) to an eligible government contractor plan for plan years beginning after December 31, 2007, and before the first plan year to which such amendments apply, the third segment rate determined under section 303(h)(2)(C)(iii) of such Act and section 430(h)(2)(C)(iii) of such Code (as added by such amendments) shall be used in lieu of the interest rate otherwise used.
"(c) Eligible government contractor plan defined. For purposes of this section, a plan shall be treated as an eligible government contractor plan if it is maintained by a corporation or a member of the same affiliated group (as defined by section 1504(a) of the Internal Revenue Code of 1986), whose primary source of revenue is derived from business performed under contracts with the United States that are subject to the Federal Acquisition Regulations (Chapter 1 of Title 48, C.F.R.) and that are also subject to the Defense Federal Acquisition Regulation Supplement (Chapter 2 of Title 48, C.F.R.), and whose revenue derived from such business in the previous fiscal year exceeded $5,000,000,000, and whose pension plan costs that are assignable under those contracts are subject to sections 412 and 413 of the Cost Accounting Standards (48 C.F.R. 9904.412 and 9904.413).
"(d) Cost Accounting Standards pension harmonization rule. The Cost Accounting Standards Board shall review and revise sections 412 and 413 of the Cost Accounting Standards (48 C.F.R. 9904.412 and 9904.413) to harmonize the minimum required contribution under the Employee Retirement Income Security Act of 1974 of eligible government contractor plans and government reimbursable pension plan costs not later than January 1, 2010. Any final rule adopted by the Cost Accounting Standards Board shall be deemed the Cost Accounting Standards Pension Harmonization Rule."
—P.L. 109-280, Sec. 111(a), amended Code Sec. 412, effective for plan. yrs. begin. after 12/31/2007.
Prior to amendment, Code Sec. 412 read as follows:
"SEC. 412. MINIMUM FUNDING STANDARDS.
"(a) General rule. Except as provided in subsection (h), this section applies to a plan if, for any plan year beginning on or after the effective date of this section for such plan—
"(1) such plan included a trust which qualified (or was determined by the Secretary to have qualified) under section 401(a), or
"(2) such plan satisfied (or was determined by the Secretary to have satisfied) the requirements of section 403(a).
A plan to which this section applies shall have satisfied the minimum funding standard for such plan for a plan year if as of the end of such plan year, the plan does not have an accumulated funding deficiency. For purposes of this section and section 4971, the term 'accumulated funding deficiency' means for any plan the excess of the total charges to the funding standard account for all plan years (beginning with the first plan year to which this section applies) over the total credits to such account for such years or, if less, the excess of the total charges to the alternative minimum funding standard account for such plan years over the total credits to such account for such years. In any plan year in which a multiemployer plan is in reorganization, the accumulated funding deficiency of the plan shall be determined under section 418B.
"(b) Funding standard account.

"(1) Account required. Each plan to which this section applies shall establish and maintain a funding standard account. Such account shall be credited and charged solely as provided in this section.
"(2) Charges to account. For a plan year, the funding standard account shall be charged with the sum of—
"(A) the normal cost of the plan for the plan year,
"(B) the amounts necessary to amortize in equal annual installments (until fully amortized)—
"(i) in the case of a plan in existence on January 1, 1974, the unfunded past service liability under the plan on the first day of the first plan year to which this section applies, over a period of 40 plan years,
"(ii) in the case of a plan which comes into existence after January 1, 1974, the unfunded past service liability under the plan on the first day of the first plan year to which this section applies, over a period of 30 plan years,
"(iii) separately, with respect to each plan year, the net increase (if any) in unfunded past service liability under the plan arising from plan amendments adopted in such year, over a period of 30 plan years,
"(iv) separately, with respect to each plan year, the net experience loss (if any) under the plan, over a period of 5 plan years (15 plan years in the case of a multiemployer plan), and
"(v) separately, with respect to each plan year, the net loss (if any) resulting from changes in actuarial assumptions used under the plan, over a period of 10 plan years (30 plan years in the case of a multiemployer plan),
"(C) the amount necessary to amortize each waived funding deficiency (within the meaning of subsection (d)(3)) for each prior plan year in equal annual installments (until fully amortized) over a period of 5 plan years (15 plan years in the case of a multiemployer plan),
"(D) the amount necessary to amortize in equal annual installments (until fully amortized) over a period of 5 plan years any amount credited to the funding standard account under paragraph (3)(D), and
"(E) the amount necessary to amortize in equal annual installments (until fully amortized) over a period of 20 years the contributions which would be required to be made under the plan but for the provisions of subsection (c)(7)(A)(i)(I).
For additional requirements in the case of plans other than multiemployer plans, see subsection (l).
"(3) Credits to account. For a plan year, the funding standard account shall be credited with the sum of—
"(A) the amount considered contributed by the employer to or under the plan for the plan year,
"(B) the amount necessary to amortize in equal annual installments (until fully amortized)—
"(i) separately, with respect to each plan year, the net decrease (if any) in unfunded past service liability under the plan arising from plan amendments adopted in such year, over a period of 30 plan years,
"(ii) separately, with respect to each plan year, the net experience gain (if any) under the plan, over a period of 5 plan years (15 plan years in the case of a multiemployer plan), and
"(iii) separately, with respect to each plan year, the net gain (if any) resulting from changes in actuarial assumptions used under the plan, over a period of 10 plan years (30 plan years in the case of a multiemployer plan),
"(C) the amount of the waived funding deficiency (within the meaning of subsection (d)(3)) for the plan year, and
"(D) in the case of a plan year for which the accumulated funding deficiency is determined under the funding standard account if such plan year follows a plan year for which such deficiency was determined under the alternative minimum funding standard, the excess (if any) of any debit balance in the funding standard account (determined without regard to this subparagraph) over any debit balance in the alternative minimum funding standard account.
"(4) Combining and offsetting amounts to be amortized. Under regulations prescribed by the Secretary, amounts required to be amortized under paragraph (2) or paragraph (3), as the case may be—
"(A) may be combined into one amount under such paragraph to be amortized over a period determined on the basis of the remaining amortization period for all items entering into such combined amount, and
"(B) may be offset against amounts required to be amortized under the other such paragraph, with the resulting amount to be amortized over a period determined on the basis of the remaining amortization periods for all items entering into whichever of the two amounts being offset is the greater.
"(5) Interest.
"(A) In general. The funding standard account (and items therein) shall be charged or credited (as determined under regulations prescribed by the Secretary) with interest at the appropriate rate consistent with the rate or rates of interest used under the plan to determine costs.
"(B) Required change of interest rate. For purposes of determining a plan's current liability and for purposes of determining a plan's required contribution under section 412(l) for any plan year—
"(i) In general. If any rate of interest used under the plan to determine cost is not within the permissible range, the plan shall establish a new rate of interest within the permissible range.
"(ii) Permissible range. For purposes of this subparagraph—
"(I) In general. Except as provided in subclause (II) or (III), the term 'permissible range' means a rate of interest which is not more than 10 percent above, and not more than 10 percent below, the weighted average of the rates of interest on 30-year Treasury securities during the 4-year period ending on the last day before the beginning of the plan year.
"(II) Special rule for years 2004, 2005, 2006, and 2007. In the case of plan years beginning after December 31, 2003, and before January 1, 2008, the term 'permissible range' means a rate of interest which is not above, and not more than

10 percent below, the weighted average of the rates of interest on amounts invested conservatively in long-term investment grade corporate bonds during the 4-year period ending on the last day before the beginning of the plan year. Such rates shall be determined by the Secretary on the basis of 2 or more indices that are selected periodically by the Secretary and that are in the top 3 quality levels available. The Secretary shall make the permissible range, and the indices and methodology used to determine the average rate, publicly available.

"(III) Secretarial authority. If the Secretary finds that the lowest rate of interest permissible under subclause (I) or (II) is unreasonably high, the Secretary may prescribe a lower rate of interest, except that such rate may not be less than 80 percent of the average rate determined under such subclause.

"(iii) Assumptions. Notwithstanding subsection (c)(3)(A)(i), the interest rate used under the plan shall be—

"(I) determined without taking into account the experience of the plan and reasonable expectations, but

"(II) consistent with the assumptions which reflect the purchase rates which would be used by insurance companies to satisfy the liabilities under the plan.

"(6) Certain amortization charges and credits. In the case of a plan which, immediately before the date of the enactment of the Multiemployer Pension Plan Amendments Act of 1980, was a multiemployer plan (within the meaning of section 414(f) as in effect immediately before such date)—

"(A) any amount described in paragraph (2)(B)(ii), (2)(B)(iii), or (3)(B)(i) of this subsection which arose in a plan year beginning before such date shall be amortized in equal annual installments (until fully amortized) over 40 plan years, beginning with the plan year in which the amount arose;

"(B) any amount described in paragraph (2)(B)(iv) or (3)(B)(ii) of this subsection which arose in a plan year beginning before such date shall be amortized in equal annual installments (until fully amortized) over 20 plan years, beginning with the plan year in which the amount arose;

"(C) any change in past service liability which arises during the period of 3 plan years beginning on or after such date, and results from a plan amendment adopted before such date, shall be amortized in equal annual installments (until fully amortized) over 40 plan years, beginning with the plan year in which the change arises; and

"(D) any change in past service liability which arises during the period of 2 plan years beginning on or after such date, and results from the changing of a group of participants from one benefit level to another benefit level under a schedule of plan benefits which—

"(i) was adopted before such date, and

"(ii) was effective for any plan participant before the beginning of the first plan year beginning on or after such date,

shall be amortized in equal annual installments (until fully amortized) over 40 plan years, beginning with the plan year in which the change arises.

"(7) Special rules for multiemployer plans. For purposes of this section—

"(A) Withdrawal liability. Any amount received by a multiemployer plan in payment of all or part of an employer's withdrawal liability under part 1 of subtitle E of title IV of the Employee Retirement Income Security Act of 1974 shall be considered an amount contributed by the employer to or under the plan. The Secretary may prescribe by regulation additional charges and credits to a multiemployer plan's funding standard account to the extent necessary to prevent withdrawal liability payments from being unduly reflected as advance funding for plan liabilities.

"(B) Adjustments when a multiemployer plan leaves reorganization. If a multiemployer plan is not in reorganization in the plan year but was in reorganization in the immediately preceding plan year, any balance in the funding standard account at the close of such immediately preceding plan year—

"(i) shall be eliminated by an offsetting credit or charge (as the case may be), but

"(ii) shall be taken into account in subsequent plan years by being amortized in equal annual installments (until fully amortized) over 30 plan years.

The preceding sentence shall not apply to the extent of any accumulated funding deficiency under section 418B(a) as of the end of the last plan year that the plan was in reorganization.

"(C) Plan payments to supplemental program or withdrawal liability payment fund. Any amount paid by a plan during a plan year to the Pension Benefit Guaranty Corporation pursuant to section 4222 of such Act or to a fund exempt under section 501(c)(22) pursuant to section 4223 of such Act shall reduce the amount of contributions considered received by the plan for the plan year.

"(D) Interim withdrawal liability payments. Any amount paid by an employer pending a final determination of the employer's withdrawal liability under part 1 of subtitle E of title IV of such Act and subsequently refunded to the employer by the plan shall be charged to the funding standard account in accordance with regulations prescribed by the Secretary.

"(E) For purposes of the full funding limitation under subsection (c)(7), unless otherwise provided by the plan, the accrued liability under a multiemployer plan shall not include benefits which are not nonforfeitable under the plan after the termination of the plan (taking into consideration section 411(d)(3)).

"(F) Election for deferral of charge for portion of net experience loss.

"(i) In general. With respect to the net experience loss of an eligible multiemployer plan for the first plan year beginning after December 31, 2001, the plan sponsor may elect to defer up to 80 percent of the amount otherwise required to be charged under paragraph (2)(B)(iv) for any plan year beginning after June 30, 2003, and before July 1, 2005, to any plan year selected by the plan from either of the 2 immediately succeeding plan years.

"(ii) Interest. For the plan year to which a charge is deferred pursuant to an election under clause (i), the funding standard account shall be charged with interest on the deferred charge for the period of deferral at the rate determined under subsection (d) for multiemployer plans.

"(iii) Restrictions on benefit increases. No amendment which increases the liabilities of the plan by reason of any increase in benefits, any change in the accrual of benefits, or any change in the rate at which benefits become nonforfeitable under the plan shall be adopted during any period for which a charge is deferred pursuant to an election under clause (i), unless—

"(I) the plan's enrolled actuary certifies (in such form and manner prescribed by the Secretary) that the amendment provides for an increase in annual contributions which will exceed the increase in annual charges to the funding standard account attributable to such amendment, or

"(II) the amendment is required by a collective bargaining agreement which is in effect on the date of enactment of this subparagraph.

If a plan is amended during any such plan year in violation of the preceding sentence, any election under this paragraph shall not apply to any such plan year ending on or after the date on which such amendment is adopted.

"(iv) Eligible multiemployer plan. For purposes of this subparagraph, the term 'eligible multiemployer plan' means a multiemployer plan—

"(I) which had a net investment loss for the first plan year beginning after December 31, 2001, of at least 10 percent of the average fair market value of the plan assets during the plan year, and

"(II) with respect to which the plan's enrolled actuary certifies (not taking into account the application of this subparagraph), on the basis of the acutuarial assumptions used for the last plan year ending before the date of the enactment of this subparagraph, that the plan is projected to have an accumulated funding deficiency (within the meaning of subsection (a)) for any plan year beginning after June 30, 2003, and before July 1, 2006.

For purposes of subclause (I), a plan's net investment loss shall be determined on the basis of the actual loss and not under any actuarial method used under subsection (c)(2).

"(v) Exception to treatment of eligible multiemployer plan. In no event shall a plan be treated as an eligible multiemployer plan under clause (iv) if—

"(I) for any taxable year beginning during the 10-year period preceding the first plan year for which an election is made under clause (i), any employer required to contribute to the plan failed to timely pay any excise tax imposed under section 4971 with respect to the plan,

"(II) for any plan year beginning after June 30, 1993, and before the first plan year for which an election is made under clause (i), the average contribution required to be made by all employers to the plan does not exceed 10 cents per hour or no employer is required to make contributions to the plan, or

"(III) with respect to any of the plan years beginning after June 30, 1993, and before the first plan year for which an election is made under clause (i), a waiver was granted under section 412(d) or section 303 of the Employee Retirement Income Security Act of 1974 with respect to the plan or an extension of an amortization period was granted under subsection (e) or section 304 of such Act with respect to the plan.

"(vi) Election. An election under this subparagraph shall be made at such time and in such manner as the Secretary may prescribe.

"*(c) Special rules.*

"(1) Determinations to be made under funding method. For purposes of this section, normal costs, accrued liability, past service liabilities, and experience gains and losses shall be determined under the funding method used to determine costs under the plan.

"(2) Valuation of assets.

"(A) In general. For purposes of this section, the value of the plan's assets shall be determined on the basis of any reasonable actuarial method of valuation which takes into account fair market value and which is permitted under regulations prescribed by the Secretary.

"(B) Election with respect to bonds. The value of a bond or other evidence of indebtedness which is not in default as to principal or interest may, at the election of the plan administrator, be determined on an amortized basis running from initial cost at purchase to par value at maturity or earliest call date. Any election under this subparagraph shall be made at such time and in such manner as the Secretary shall by regulations provide, shall apply to all such evidences of indebtedness, and may be revoked only with the consent of the Secretary. In the case of a plan other than a multiemployer plan, this subparagraph shall not apply, but the Secretary may by regulations provide that the value of any dedicated bond portfolio of such plan shall be determined by using the interest rate under subsection (b)(5).

"(3) Actuarial assumptions must be reasonable. For purposes of this section, all costs, liabilities, rates of interest, and other factors under the plan shall be determined on the basis of actuarial assumptions and methods—

"(A) in the case of—

"(i) a plan other than a multiemployer plan, each of which is reasonable (taking into account the experience of the plan and reasonable expectations) or which, in the aggregate, result in a total contribution equivalent to that which would be determined if each such assumption and method were reasonable, or

"(ii) a multiemployer plan, which, in the aggregate, are reasonable (taking into account the experiences of the plan and reasonable expectations), and

"(B) which, in combination, offer the actuary's best estimate of anticipated experience under the plan.

"(4) Treatment of certain changes as experience gain or loss. For purposes of this section, if—

"(A) a change in benefits under the Social Security Act or in other retirement benefits created under Federal or State law, or

"(B) a change in the definition of the term 'wages' under section 3121 or a change in the amount of such wages taken into account under regulations prescribed for purposes of section 401(a)(5),

results in an increase or decrease in accrued liability under a plan, such increase or decrease shall be treated as an experience loss or gain.

Code Sec. 412 — Employee benefit plans

"(5) Change in funding method or in plan year requires approval.

"(A) In general. If the funding method for a plan is changed, the new funding method shall become the funding method used to determine costs and liabilities under the plan only if the change is approved by the Secretary. If the plan year for a plan is changed, the new plan year shall become the plan year for the plan only if the change is approved by the Secretary.

"(B) Approval required for certain changes in assumptions by certain single-employer plans subject to additional funding requirement.

"(i) In general. No actuarial assumption (other than the assumptions described in subsection (l)(7)(C)) used to determine the current liability for a plan to which this subparagraph applies may be changed without the approval of the Secretary.

"(ii) Plans to which subparagraph applies. This subparagraph shall apply to a plan only if—

"(I) the plan is a defined benefit plan (other than a multiemployer plan) to which title IV of the Employee Retirement Income Security Act of 1974 applies;

"(II) the aggregate unfunded vested benefits as of the close of the preceding plan year (as determined under section 4006(a)(3)(E)(iii) of the Employee Retirement Income Security Act of 1974) of such plan and all other plans maintained by the contributing sponsors (as defined in section 4001(a)(13) of such Act) and members of such sponsors' controlled groups (as defined in section 4001(a)(14) of such Act) which are covered by title IV of such Act (disregarding plans with no unfunded vested benefits) exceed $50,000,000; and

"(III) the change in assumptions (determined after taking into account any changes in interest rate and mortality table) results in a decrease in the unfunded current liability of the plan for the current plan year that exceeds $50,000,000, or that exceeds $5,000,000 and that is 5 percent or more of the current liability of the plan before such change.

"(6) Full funding. If, as of the close of a plan year, a plan would (without regard to this paragraph) have an accumulated funding deficiency (determined without regard to the alternative minimum funding standard account permitted under subsection (g)) in excess of the full funding limitation—

"(A) the funding standard account shall be credited with the amount of such excess, and

"(B) all amounts described in paragraphs (2)(B), (C), and (D) and (3)(B) of subsection (b) which are required to be amortized shall be considered fully amortized for purposes of such paragraphs.

"(7) Full-funding limitation.

"(A) In general. For purposes of paragraph (6), the term 'full-funding limitation' means the excess (if any) of—

"(i) the lesser of (I) in the case of plan years beginning before January 1, 2004, the applicable percentage of current liability (including the expected increase in current liability due to benefits accruing during the plan year), or (II) the accrued liability (including normal cost) under the plan (determined under the entry age normal funding method if such accrued liability cannot be directly calculated under the funding method used for the plan), over

"(ii) the lesser of—

"(I) the fair market value of the plan's assets, or

"(II) the value of such assets determined under paragraph (2).

"(B) Current liability. For purposes of subparagraph (D) and subclause (I) of subparagraph (A)(i), the term 'current liability' has the meaning given such term by subsection (l)(7) (without regard to subparagraphs (C) and (D) thereof) and using the rate of interest used under subsection (b)(5)(B).

"(C) Special rule for paragraph (6)(B). For purposes of paragraph (6)(B), subparagraph (A)(i) shall be applied without regard to subclause (I) thereof.

"(D) Regulatory authority. The Secretary may by regulations provide—

"(i) for adjustments to the percentage contained in subparagraph (A)(i) to take into account the respective ages or lengths of service of the participants, and

"(ii) alternative methods based on factors other than current liability for the determination of the amount taken into account under subparagraph (A)(i).

"(E) Minimum amount.

"(i) In general. In no event shall the full-funding limitation determined under subparagraph (A) be less than the excess (if any) of—

"(I) 90 percent of the current liability of the plan (including the expected increase in current liability due to benefits accruing during the plan year), over

"(II) the value of the plan's assets determined under paragraph (2).

"(ii) Current liability; assets. For purposes of clause (i)—

"(I) the term 'current liability' has the meaning given such term by subsection (l)(7) (without regard to subparagraph (D) thereof, and

"(II) assets shall not be reduced by any credit balance in the funding standard account.

"(F) Applicable percentage. For purposes of subparagraph (A)(i)(I), the applicable percentage shall be determined in accordance with the following table:

In the case of any plan year beginning in—	The applicable percentage is—
2002	165
2003	170

"(8) Certain retroactive plan amendments. For purposes of this section, any amendment applying to a plan year which—

"(A) is adopted after the close of such plan year but no later than 2 and one-half months after the close of the plan year (or, in the case of a multiemployer plan, no later than 2 years after the close of such plan year),

"(B) does not reduce the accrued benefit of any participant determined as of the beginning of the first plan year to which the amendment applies, and

"(C) does not reduce the accrued benefit of any participant determined as of the time of adoption except to the extent required by the circumstances,

shall, at the election of the plan administrator, be deemed to have been made on the first day of such plan year. No amendment described in this paragraph which reduces the accrued benefits of any participant shall take effect unless the plan administrator files a notice with the Secretary of Labor notifying him of such amendment and the Secretary of Labor has approved such amendment, or within 90 days after the date on which such notice was filed, failed to disapprove such amendment. No amendment described in this subsection shall be approved by the Secretary of Labor unless he determines that such amendment is necessary because of a substantial business hardship (as determined under subsection (d)(2)) and that a waiver under subsection (d)(1) is unavailable or inadequate.

"(9) Annual valuation.

"(A) In general. For purposes of this section, a determination of experience gains and losses and a valuation of the plan's liability shall be made not less frequently than once every year, except that such determination shall be made more frequently to the extent required in particular cases under regulations prescribed by the Secretary.

"(B) Valuation date.

"(i) Current year. Except as provided in clause (ii), the valuation referred to in subparagraph (A) shall be made as of a date within the plan year to which the valuation refers or within one month prior to the beginning of such year.

"(ii) Use of prior year valuation. The valuation referred to in subparagraph (A) may be made as of a date within the plan year prior to the year to which the valuation refers if, as of such date, the value of the assets of the plan are not less than 100 percent of the plan's current liability (as defined in paragraph (7)(B)).

"(iii) Adjustments. Information under clause (ii) shall, in accordance with regulations, be actuarially adjusted to reflect significant differences in participants.

"(iv) Limitation. A change in funding method to use a prior year valuation, as provided in clause (ii), may not be made unless as of the valuation date within the prior plan year, the value of the assets of the plan are not less than 125 percent of the plan's current liability (as defined in paragraph (7)(B)).

"(10) Time when certain contributions deemed made. For purposes of this section—

"(A) Defined benefit plans other than multiemployer plans. In the case of a defined benefit plan other than a multiemployer plan, any contributions for a plan year made by an employer during the period—

"(i) beginning on the day after the last day of such plan year, and

"(ii) ending on the day which is 8½ months after the close of the plan year, shall be deemed to have been made on such last day.

"(B) Other plans. In the case of a plan not described in subparagraph (A), any contributions for a plan year made by an employer after the last day of such plan year, but not later than two and one-half months after such day, shall be deemed to have been made on such last day. For purposes of this subparagraph, such two and one-half month period may be extended for not more than six months under regulations prescribed by the Secretary.

"(11) Liability for contributions.

"(A) In general. Except as provided in subparagraph (B), the amount of any contribution required by this section and any required installments under subsection (m) shall be paid by the employer responsible for contributing to or under the plan the amount described in subsection (b)(3)(A).

"(B) Joint and several liability where employer member of controlled group.

"(i) In general. In the case of a plan other than a multiemployer plan, if the employer referred to in subparagraph (A) is a member of a controlled group, each member of such group shall be jointly and severally liable for payment of such contribution or required installment.

"(ii) Controlled group. For purposes of clause (i), the term 'controlled group' means any group treated as a single employer under subsection (b), (c), (m), or (o) of section 414.

"(12) Anticipation of benefit increases effective in the future. In determining projected benefits, the funding method of a collectively bargained plan described in section 413(a) (other than a multiemployer plan) shall anticipate benefit increases scheduled to take effect during the term of the collective bargaining agreement applicable to the plan.

"(d) Variance from minimum funding standard.

"(1) Waiver in case of business hardship. If an employer or in the case of a multiemployer plan, 10 percent or more of the number of employers contributing to or under the plan, are unable to satisfy the minimum funding standard for a plan year without temporary substantial business hardship (substantial business hardship in the case of a multiemployer plan) and if application of the standard would be adverse to the interests of plan participants in the aggregate, the Secretary may waive the requirements of subsection (a) for such year with respect to all or any portion of the minimum funding standard other than the portion thereof determined under subsection (b)(2)(C). The Secretary shall not waive the minimum funding standard with respect to a plan for more than 3 of any 15 (5 of any 15 in the case of a multiemployer plan consecutive plan years. The interest rate used for purposes of computing the amortization charge described in subsection (b)(2)(C) for any plan year shall be—

"(A) in the case of a plan other than a multiemployer plan, the greater of (i) 150 percent of the Federal mid-term rate (as in effect under section 1274 for the 1st month of such plan year), or (ii) the rate of interest used under the plan in determining costs (including adjustments under subsection (b)(5)(B)), and

"(B) in the case of a multiemployer plan, the rate determined under section 6621(b).

"(2) Determination of business hardship. For purposes of this section, the factors taken into account in determining temporary substantial business hardship (substantial business hardship in the case of a multiemployer plan) shall include (but shall not be limited to) whether or not—

"(A) the employer is operating at an economic loss,

Employee benefit plans — Code Sec. 412

"(B) there is substantial unemployment or underemployment in the trade or business and in the industry concerned,

"(C) the sales and profits of the industry concerned are depressed or declining, and

"(D) it is reasonable to expect that the plan will be continued only if the waiver is granted.

"(3) Waived funding deficiency. For purposes of this section, the term 'waived funding deficiency' means the portion of the minimum funding standard (determined without regard to subsection (b)(3)(C)) for a plan year waived by the Secretary and not satisfied by employer contributions.

"(4) Application must be submitted before date 2½ months after close of year. In the case of a plan other than a multiemployer plan, no waiver may be granted under this subsection with respect to any plan for any plan year unless an application therefor is submitted to the Secretary not later than the 15th day of the 3rd month beginning after the close of such plan year.

"(5) Special rule if employer is member of controlled group.

"(A) In general. In the case of a plan other than a multiemployer plan, if an employer is a member of a controlled group, the temporary substantial business hardship requirements of paragraph (1) shall be treated as met only if such requirements are met—

"(i) with respect to such employer, and

"(ii) with respect to the controlled group of which such employer is a member (determined by treating all members of such group as a single employer).

The Secretary may provide that an analysis of a trade or business or industry of a member need not be conducted if the Secretary determines such analysis is not necessary because the taking into account of such member would not significantly affect the determination under this subsection.

"(B) Controlled group. For purposes of subparagraph (A), the term 'controlled group' means any group treated as a single employer under subsection (b), (c), (m), or (o) of section 414.

"(e) Extension of amortization periods. The period of years required to amortize any unfunded liability (described in any clause of subsection (b)(2)(B)) of any plan may be extended by the Secretary of Labor for a period of time (not in excess of 10 years) if he determines that such extension would carry out the purposes of the Employee Retirement Income Security Act of 1974 and would provide adequate protection for participants under the plan and their beneficiaries and if he determines that the failure to permit such extension would—

"(1) result in—

"(A) a substantial risk to the voluntary continuation of the plan, or

"(B) a substantial curtailment of pension benefit levels or employee compensation, and

"(2) be adverse to the interests of plan participants in the aggregate.

In the case of a plan other than a multiemployer plan, the interest rate applicable for any plan year under any arrangement entered into by the Secretary in connection with an extension granted under this subsection shall be the greater of (A) 150 percent of the Federal mid-term rate (as in effect under section 1274 for the 1st month of such plan year), or (B) the rate of interest used under the plan in determining costs. In the case of a multiemployer plan, such rate shall be the rate determined under section 6621(b).

"Requirements relating to waivers and extensions.

"(1) Benefits may not be increased during waiver or extension period. No amendment of the plan which increases the liabilities of the plan by reason of any increase in benefits, any change in the accrual of benefits, or any change in the rate at which benefits become nonforfeitable under the plan shall be adopted if a waiver under subsection (d)(1) or an extension of time under subsection (e) is in effect with respect to the plan, or if a plan amendment described in subsection (c)(8) has been made at any time in the preceding 12 months (24 months for multiemployer plans). If a plan is amended in violation of the preceding sentence, any such waiver or extension of time shall not apply to any plan year ending on or after the date on which such amendment is adopted.

"(2) Exception. Paragraph (1) shall not apply to any plan amendment which—

"(A) the Secretary of Labor determines to be reasonable and which provides for only de minimis increases in the liabilities of the plan,

"(B) only repeals an amendment described in subsection (c)(8), or

"(C) is required as a condition of qualification under this part.

"(3) Security for waivers and extensions; consultations.

"(A) Security may be required.

"(i) In general. Except as provided in subparagraph (C), the Secretary may require an employer maintaining a defined benefit plan which is a single-employer plan (within the meaning of section 4001(a)(15) of the Employee Retirement Income Security Act of 1974) to provide security to such plan as a condition for granting or modifying a waiver under subsection (d) or an extension under subsection (e).

"(ii) Special rules. Any security provided under clause (i) may be perfected and enforced only by the Pension Benefit Guaranty Corporation, or at the direction of the Corporation, by a contributing sponsor (within the meaning of section 4001(a)(13) of such Act), or a member of such sponsor's controlled group (within the meaning of section 4001(a)(14) of such Act).

"(B) Consultation with the Pension Benefit Guaranty Corporation. Except as provided in subparagraph (C), the Secretary shall, before granting or modifying a waiver under subsection (d) or an extension under subsection (e) with respect to a plan described in subparagraph (A)(i)—

"(i) provide the Pension Benefit Guaranty Corporation with—

"(I) notice of the completed application for any waiver, extension, or modification, and

"(II) an opportunity to comment on such application within 30 days after receipt of such notice, and

"(ii) consider—

"(I) any comments of the Corporation under clause (i)(II), and

"(II) any views of any employee organization (within the meaning of section 3(4) of the Employee Retirement Income Security Act of 1974) representing participants in the plan which are submitted in writing to the Secretary in connection with such application.

Information provided to the corporation under this subparagraph shall be considered tax return information and subject to the safeguarding and reporting requirements of section 6103(p).

"(C) Exception for certain waivers and extensions.

"(i) In general. The preceding provisions of this paragraph shall not apply to any plan with respect to which the sum of—

"(I) the outstanding balance of the accumulated funding deficiencies (within the meaning of subsection (a) and section 302(a) of such Act) of the plan,

"(II) the outstanding balance of the amount of waived funding deficiencies of the plan waived under subsection (d) or section 303 of such Act, and

"(III) the outstanding balance of the amount of decreases in the minimum funding standard allowed under subsection (e) or section 304 of such Act,

is less than $1,000,000.

"(ii) Accumulated funding deficiencies. For purposes of clause (i)(I), accumulated funding deficiencies shall include any increase in such amount which would result if all applications for waivers of the minimum funding standard under subsection (d) or section 303 of such Act and for extensions of the amortization period under subsection (e) or section 304 of such Act which are pending with respect to such plan were denied.

"(4) Additional requirements.

"(A) Advance notice. The Secretary shall, before granting a waiver under subsection (d) or an extension under subsection (e), require each applicant to provide evidence satisfactory to the Secretary that the applicant has provided notice of the filing of the application for such waiver or extension to each employee organization representing employees covered by the affected plan, and each participant, beneficiary, and alternate payee (within the meaning of section 414(p)(8)). Such notice shall include a description of the extent to which the plan is funded for benefits which are guaranteed under title IV of such Act and for benefit liabilities.

"(B) Consideration of relevant information. The Secretary shall consider any relevant information provided by a person to whom notice was given under subparagraph (A).

"(g) Alternative minimum funding standard.

"(1) In general. A plan which uses a funding method that requires contributions in all years not less than those required under the entry age normal funding method may maintain an alternative minimum funding standard account for any plan year. Such account shall be credited and charged solely as provided in this subsection.

"(2) Charges and credits to account. For a plan year the alternative minimum funding standard account shall be—

"(A) charged with the sum of—

"(i) the lesser of normal cost under the funding method used under the plan or normal cost determined under the unit credit method,

"(ii) the excess, if any, of the present value of accrued benefits under the plan over the fair market value of the assets, and

"(iii) an amount equal to the excess (if any) of credits to the alternative minimum standard account for all prior plan years over charges to such account for all such years, and

"(B) credited with the amount considered contributed by the employer to or under the plan for the plan year.

"(3) Special rules. The alternative minimum funding standard account (and items therein) shall be charged or credited with interest in the manner provided under subsection (b)(5) with respect to the funding standard account.

"(h) Exceptions. This section shall not apply to—

"(1) any profit-sharing or stock bonus plan,

"(2) any insurance contract plan described in subsection (i),

"(3) any governmental plan (within the meaning of section 414(d)),

"(4) any church plan (within the meaning of section 414(e)) with respect to which the election provided by section 410(d) has not been made,

"(5) any plan which has not, at any time after September 2, 1974, provided for employer contributions, or

"(6) any plan established and maintained by a society, order, or association described in section 501(c)(8) or (9), if no part of the contributions to or under such plan are made by employers of participants in such plan.

No plan described in paragraph (3), (4), or (6) shall be treated as a qualified plan for purposes of section 401(a) unless such plan meets the requirements of section 401(a)(7) as in effect on September 1, 1974.

"(i) Certain insurance contract plans. A plan is described in this subsection if—

"(1) the plan is funded exclusively by the purchase of individual insurance contracts,

"(2) such contracts provide for level annual premium payments to be paid extending not later than the retirement age for each individual participating in the plan, and commencing with the date the individual became a participant in the plan (or, in the case of an increase in benefits, commencing at the time such increase becomes effective),

"(3) benefits provided by the plan are equal to the benefits provided under each contract at normal retirement age under the plan and are guaranteed by an insurance carrier (licensed under the laws of a State to do business with the plan) to the extent premiums have been paid,

"(4) premiums payable for the plan year, and all prior plan years, under such contracts have been paid before lapse or there is reinstatement of the policy,

"(5) no rights under such contracts have been subject to a security interest at any time during the plan year, and

"(6) no policy loans are outstanding at any time during the plan year.

A plan funded exclusively by the purchase of group insurance contracts which is determined under regulations prescribed by the Secretary to have the same characteristics as contracts described in the preceding sentence shall be treated as a plan described in this subsection.

"(j) *Certain terminated multiemployer plans.* This section applies with respect to a terminated multiemployer plan to which section 4021 of the Employee Retirement Income Security Act of 1974 applies, until the last day of the plan year in which the plan terminates, within the meaning of section 4041A(a)(2) of that Act.

"(k) *Financial assistance.* Any amount of any financial assistance from the Pension Benefit Guaranty Corporation to any plan, and any repayment of such amount, shall be taken into account under this section in such manner as determined by the Secretary.

"(l) *Additional funding requirements for plans which are not multiemployer plans.*

"(1) In general. In the case of a defined benefit plan (other than a multiemployer plan) to which this subsection applies under paragraph (9) for any plan year, the amount charged to the funding standard account for such plan year shall be increased by the sum of—

"(A) the excess (if any) of—

"(i) the deficit reduction contribution determined under paragraph (2) for such plan year, over

"(ii) the sum of the charges for such plan year under subsection (b)(2), reduced by the sum of the credits for such plan year under subparagraph (B) of subsection (b)(3), plus

"(B) the unpredictable contingent event amount (if any) for such plan year.

Such increase shall not exceed the amount which, after taking into account charges (other than the additional charge under this subsection) and credits under subsection (b), is necessary to increase the funded current liability percentage (taking into account the expected increase in current liability due to benefits accruing during the plan year) to 100 percent.

"(2) *Deficit reduction contribution.* For purposes of paragraph (1), the deficit reduction contribution determined under this paragraph for any plan year is the sum of—

"(A) the unfunded old liability amount,

"(B) the unfunded new liability amount,

"(C) the expected increase in current liability due to benefits accruing during the plan year, and

"(D) the aggregate of the unfunded mortality increase amounts.

"(3) *Unfunded old liability amount.* For purposes of this subsection—

"(A) In general. The unfunded old liability amount with respect to any plan for any plan year is the amount necessary to amortize the unfunded old liability under the plan in equal annual installments over a period of 18 plan years (beginning with the 1st plan year beginning after December 31, 1988).

"(B) Unfunded old liability. The term 'unfunded old liability' means the unfunded current liability of the plan as of the beginning of the 1st plan year beginning after December 31, 1987 (determined without regard to any plan amendment increasing liabilities adopted after October 16, 1987).

"(C) Special rules for benefit increases under existing collective bargaining agreements.

"(i) In general. In the case of a plan maintained pursuant to 1 or more collective bargaining agreements between employee representatives and the employer ratified before October 29, 1987, the unfunded old liability amount with respect to such plan for any plan year shall be increased by the amount necessary to amortize the unfunded existing benefit increase liability in equal annual installments over a period of 18 plan years beginning with—

"(I) the plan year in which the benefit increase with respect to such liability occurs, or

"(II) if the taxpayer elects, the 1st plan year beginning after December 31, 1988.

"(ii) Unfunded existing benefit increase liabilities. For purposes of clause (i), the unfunded existing benefit increase liability means, with respect to any benefit increase under the agreements described in clause (i) which takes effect during or after the 1st plan year beginning after December 31, 1987, the unfunded current liability determined—

"(I) by taking into account only liabilities attributable to such benefit increase, and

"(II) by reducing (but not below zero) the amount determined under paragraph (8)(A)(ii) by the current liability determined without regard to such benefit increase.

"(iii) Extensions, modifications, etc. not taken into account. For purposes of this subparagraph, any extension, amendment, or other modification of an agreement after October 28, 1987, shall not be taken into account.

"(D) Special rule for required changes in actuarial assumptions.

"(i) In general. The unfunded old liability amount with respect to any plan for any plan year shall be increased by the amount necessary to amortize the amount of additional unfunded old liability under the plan in equal annual installments over a period of 12 plan years (beginning with the first plan year beginning after December 31, 1994).

"(ii) Additional unfunded old liability. For purposes of clause (i), the term 'additional unfunded old liability' means the amount (if any) by which—

"(I) the current liability of the plan as of the beginning of the first plan year beginning after December 31, 1994, valued using the assumptions required by paragraph (7)(C) as in effect for plan years beginning after December 31, 1994, exceeds

"(II) the current liability of the plan as of the beginning of such first plan year, valued using the same assumptions used under subclause (I) (other than the assumptions required by paragraph (7)(C)), using the prior interest rate, and using such mortality assumptions as were used to determine current liability for the first plan year beginning after December 31, 1992.

"(iii) Prior interest rate. For purposes of clause (ii), the term 'prior interest rate' means the rate of interest that is the same percentage of the weighted average under subsection (b)(5)(B)(ii)(I) for the first plan year beginning after December 31, 1994, as the rate of interest used by the plan to determine current liability for the first plan year beginning after December 31, 1992, is of the weighted average under subsection (b)(5)(B)(ii)(I)for such first plan year beginning after December 31, 1992.

"(E) Optional rule for additional unfunded old liability.

"(i) In general. If an employer makes an election under clause (ii), the additional unfunded old liability for purposes of subparagraph (D) shall be the amount (if any) by which—

"(I) the unfunded current liability of the plan as of the beginning of the first plan year beginning after December 31, 1994, valued using the assumptions required by paragraph (7)(C) as in effect for plan years beginning after December 31, 1994, exceeds

"(II) the unamortized portion of the unfunded old liability under the plan as of the beginning of the first plan year beginning after December 31, 1994.

"(ii) Election.

"(I) An employer may irrevocably elect to apply the provisions of this subparagraph as of the beginning of the first plan year beginning after December 31, 1994.

"(II) If an election is made under this clause, the increase under paragraph (1) for any plan year beginning after December 31, 1994, and before January 1, 2002, to which this subsection applies (without regard to this subclause) shall not be less than the increase that would be required under paragraph (1) if the provisions of this title as in effect for the last plan year beginning before January 1, 1995, had remained in effect.

"(4) Unfunded new liability amount. For purposes of this subsection—

"(A) In general. The unfunded new liability amount with respect to any plan for any plan year is the applicable percentage of the unfunded new liability.

"(B) Unfunded new liability. The term 'unfunded new liability' means the unfunded current liability of the plan for the plan year determined without regard to—

"(i) the unamortized portion of the unfunded old liability, the unamortized portion of the additional unfunded old liability, the unamortized portion of each unfunded mortality increase, and the unamortized portion of the unfunded existing benefit increase liability, and

"(ii) the liability with respect to any unpredictable contingent event benefits (without regard to whether the event has occurred).

"(C) Applicable percentage. The term 'applicable percentage' means, with respect to any plan year, 30 percent, reduced by the product of—

"(i) .40 multiplied by

"(ii) the number of percentage points (if any) by which the funded current liability percentage exceeds 60 percent.

"(5) Unpredictable contingent event amount.

"(A) In general. The unpredictable contingent event amount with respect to a plan for any plan year is an amount equal to the greatest of—

"(i) the applicable percentage of the product of—

"(I) 100 percent, reduced (but not below zero) by the funded current liability percentage for the plan year, multiplied by

"(II) the amount of unpredictable contingent event benefits paid during the plan year, including (except as provided by the Secretary) any payment for the purchase of an annuity contract for a participant or beneficiary with respect to such benefits,

"(ii) the amount which would be determined for the plan year if the unpredictable contingent event benefit liabilities were amortized in equal annual installments over 7 plan years (beginning with the plan year in which such event occurs), or

"(iii) the additional amount that would be determined under paragraph (4)(A) if the unpredictable contingent event benefit liabilities were included in unfunded new liability notwithstanding paragraph (4)(B)(ii).

"(B) Applicable percentage.

In the case of plan years beginning in:	The applicable percentage is:
1989 and 1990	5
1991	10
1992	15
1993	20
1994	30
1995	40
1996	50
1997	60
1998	70
1999	80
2000	90
2001 and thereafter	100

"(C) Paragraph not to apply to existing benefits. This paragraph shall not apply to unpredictable contingent event benefits (and liabilities attributable thereto) for which the event occurred before the first plan year beginning after December 31, 1988.

"(D) Special rule for first year of amortization. Unless the employer elects otherwise, the amount determined under subparagraph (A) for the plan year in which the event occurs shall be equal to 150 percent of the amount determined under subparagraph (A)(i). The amount under subparagraph (A)(ii) for subsequent plan

Employee benefit plans   Code Sec. 412

years in the amortization period shall be adjusted in the manner provided by the Secretary to reflect the application of this subparagraph.

"(E) Limitation. The present value of the amounts described in subparagraph (A) with respect to any one event shall not exceed the unpredictable contingent event benefit liabilities attributable to that event.

"(6) Special rules for small plans.

"(A) Plans with 100 or fewer participants. This subsection shall not apply to any plan for any plan year if on each day during the preceding plan year such plan had no more than 100 participants.

"(B) Plans with more than 100 but not more than 150 participants. In the case of a plan to which subparagraph (A) does not apply and which on each day during the preceding plan year had no more than 150 participants, the amount of the increase under paragraph (1) for such plan year shall be equal to the product of—

"(i) such increase determined without regard to this subparagraph, multiplied by

"(ii) 2 percent for the highest number of participants in excess of 100 on any such day.

"(C) Aggregation of plans. For purposes of this paragraph, all defined benefit plans maintained by the same employer (or any member of such employer's controlled group) shall be treated as 1 plan, but only employees of such employer or member shall be taken into account.

"(7) Current liability. For purposes of this subsection—

"(A) In general. The term 'current liability' means all liabilities to employees and their beneficiaries under the plan.

"(B) Treatment of unpredictable contingent event benefits.

"(i) In general. For purposes of subparagraph (A), any unpredictable contingent event benefit shall not be taken into account until the event on which the benefit is contingent occurs.

"(ii) Unpredictable contingent event benefit. The term 'unpredictable contingent event benefit' means any benefit contingent on an event other than—

"(I) age, service, compensation, death, or disability, or

"(II) an event which is reasonably and reliably predictable (as determined by the Secretary).

"(C) Interest rate and mortality assumptions used. Effective for plan years beginning after December 31, 1994—

"(i) Interest rate.

"(I) In general. The rate of interest used to determine current liability under this subsection shall be the rate of interest used under subsection (b)(5), except that the highest rate in the permissible range under subparagraph (B)(ii) thereof shall not exceed the specified percentage under subclause (II) of the weighted average referred to in such subparagraph.

"(II) Specified percentage. For purposes of subclause (I), the specified percentage shall be determined as follows:

In the case of plan years beginning in calendar year:	The specified percentage is:
1995	109
1996	108
1997	107
1998	106
1999 and thereafter	105

"(III) Special rule for 2002 and 2003. For a plan year beginning in 2002 or 2003, notwithstanding subclause (I), in the case that the rate of interest used under subsection (b)(5) exceeds the highest rate permitted under subclause (I), the rate of interest used to determine current liability under this subsection may exceed the rate of interest otherwise permitted under subclause (I); except that such rate of interest shall not exceed 120 percent of the weighted average referred to in subsection (b)(5)(B)(ii).

"(IV) Special rule for 2004, 2005, 2006, and 2007. For plan years beginning in 2004, 2005, 2006, or 2007 notwithstanding subclause (I), the rate of interest used to determine current liability under this subsection shall be the rate of interest under subsection (b)(5).

"(ii) Mortality tables.

"(I) Commissioners' standard table. In the case of plan years beginning before the first plan year to which the first tables prescribed under subclause (II) apply, the mortality table used in determining current liability under this subsection shall be the table prescribed by the Secretary which is based on the prevailing commissioners' standard table (described in section 807(d)(5)(A)) used to determine reserves for group annuity contracts issued on January 1, 1993.

"(II) Secretarial authority. The Secretary may by regulation prescribe for plan years beginning after December 31, 1999, mortality tables to be used in determining current liability under this subsection. Such tables shall be based upon the actual experience of pension plans and projected trends in such experience. In prescribing such tables, the Secretary shall take into account results of available independent studies of mortality of individuals covered by pension plans.

"(III) Periodic review. The Secretary shall periodically (at least every 5 years) review any tables in effect under this subsection and shall, to the extent the Secretary determines necessary, by regulation update the tables to reflect the actual experience of pension plans and projected trends in such experience.

"(iii) Separate mortality tables for the disabled. Notwithstanding clause (ii)—

"(I) In general. In the case of plan years beginning after December 31, 1995, the Secretary shall establish mortality tables which may be used (in lieu of the tables under clause (ii)) to determine current liability under this subsection for individuals who are entitled to benefits under the plan on account of disability. The Secretary shall establish separate tables for individuals whose disabilities occur in plan years beginning before January 1, 1995, and for individuals whose disabilities occur in plan years beginning on or after such date.

"(II) Special rule for disabilities occurring after 1994. In the case of disabilities occurring in plan years beginning after December 31, 1994, the tables under subclause (I) shall apply only with respect to individuals described in such subclause who are disabled within the meaning of title II of the Social Security Act and the regulations thereunder.

"(III) Plan years beginning in 1995. In the case of any plan year beginning in 1995, a plan may use its own mortality assumptions for individuals who are entitled to benefits under the plan on account of disability.

"(D) Certain service disregarded.

"(i) In general. In the case of a participant to whom this subparagraph applies, only the applicable percentage of the years of service before such individual became a participant shall be taken into account in computing the current liability of the plan.

"(ii) Applicable percentage. For purposes of this subparagraph, the applicable percentage shall be determined as follows:

If the years of participation are:	The applicable percentage is:
1	20
2	40
3	60
4	80
5 or more	100

"(iii) Participants to whom subparagraph applies. This subparagraph shall apply to any participant who, at the time of becoming a participant—

"(I) has not accrued any other benefit under any defined benefit plan (whether or not terminated) maintained by the employer or a member of the same controlled group of which the employer is a member,

"(II) who first becomes a participant under the plan in a plan year beginning after December 31, 1987, and

"(III) has years of service greater than the minimum years of service necessary for eligibility to participate in the plan.

"(iv) Election. An employer may elect not to have this subparagraph apply. Such an election, once made, may be revoked only with the consent of the Secretary.

"(8) Other definitions. For purposes of this subsection—

"(A) Unfunded current liability. The term 'unfunded current liability' means, with respect to any plan year, the excess (if any) of—

"(i) the current liability under the plan, over

"(ii) value of the plan's assets determined under subsection (c)(2).

"(B) Funded current liability percentage. The term 'funded current liability percentage' means, with respect to any plan year, the percentage which—

"(i) the amount determined under subparagraph (A)(ii), is of

"(ii) the current liability under the plan.

"(C) Controlled group. The term 'controlled group' means any group treated as a single employer under subsection (b), (c), (m), and (o) of section 414.

"(D) Adjustments to prevent omissions and duplications. The Secretary shall provide such adjustments in the unfunded old liability amount, the unfunded new liability amount, the unpredictable contingent event amount, the current payment amount, and any other charges or credits under this section as are necessary to avoid duplication or omission of any factors in the determination of such amounts, charges, or credits.

"(E) Deduction for credit balances. For purposes of this subsection, the amount determined under subparagraph (A)(ii) shall be reduced by any credit balance in the funding standard account. The Secretary may provide for such reduction for purposes of any other provision which references this subsection.

"(9) Applicability of subsection.

"(A) In general. Except as provided in paragraph (6)(A), this subsection shall apply to a plan for any plan year if its funded current liability percentage for such year is less than 90 percent.

"(B) Exception for certain plans at least 80 percent funded. Sbparagraph (A) shall not apply to a plan for a plan year if—

"(i) the funded current liability percentage for the plan year is at least 80 percent, and

"(ii) such percentage for each of the 2 immediately preceding plan years (or each of the 2d and 3d immediately preceding plan years) is at least 90 percent.

"(C) Funded current liability percentage. For purposes of subparagraphs (A) and (B), the term 'funded current liability percentage' has the meaning given such term by paragraph (8)(B), except that such percentage shall be determined for any plan year—

"(i) without regard to paragraph (8)(E), and

"(ii) by using the rate of interest which is the highest rate allowable for the plan year under paragraph (7)(C).

"(D) Transition rules. For purposes of this paragraph:

"(i) Funded percentage for years before 1995. The funded current liability percentage for any plan year beginning before January 1, 1995, shall be treated as not less than 90 percent only if for such plan year the plan met one of the following requirements (as in effect for such year):

"(I) The full-funding limitation under subsection (c)(7) for the plan was zero.

"(II) The plan had no additional funding requirement under this subsection (or would have had no such requirement if its funded current liability percentage had been determined under subparagraph (C)).

"(III) The plan's additional funding requirement under this subsection did not exceed the lesser of 0.5 percent of current liability or $5,000,000.

"(ii) Special rule for 1995 and 1996. For purposes of determining whether subparagraph (B) applies to any plan year beginning in 1995 or 1996, a plan shall be treated as meeting the requirements of subparagraph (B)(ii) if the plan met the requirements of clause (i) of this subparagraph for any two of the plan years beginning in 1992, 1993, and 1994 (whether or not consecutive).

"(10) Unfunded mortality increase amount.

"(A) In general. The unfunded mortality increase amount with respect to each unfunded mortality increase is the amount necessary to amortize such increase in equal annual installments over a period of 10 plan years (beginning with the first plan year for which a plan uses any new mortality table issued under paragraph (7)(C)(ii)(II) or (III)).

"(B) Unfunded mortality increase. For purposes of subparagraph (A), the term 'unfunded mortality increase' means an amount equal to the excess of—

"(i) the current liability of the plan for the first plan year for which a plan uses any new mortality table issued under paragraph (7)(C)(ii)(II) or (III), over

"(ii) the current liability of the plan for such plan year which would have been determined if the mortality table in effect for the preceding plan year had been used.

"(11) Phase-in of increases in funding required by Retirement Protection Act of 1994.

"(A) In general. For any applicable plan year, at the election of the employer, the increase under paragraph (1) shall not exceed the greater of—

"(i) the increase that would be required under paragraph (1) if the provisions of this title as in effect for plan years beginning before January 1, 1995, had remained in effect, or

"(ii) the amount which, after taking into account charges (other than the additional charge under this subsection) and credits under subsection (b), is necessary to increase the funded current liability percentage (taking into account the expected increase in current liability due to benefits accruing during the plan year) for the applicable plan year to a percentage equal to the sum of the initial funded current liability percentage of the plan plus the applicable number of percentage points for such applicable plan year.

"(B) Applicable number of percentage points.

"(i) Initial funded current liability percentage of 75 percent or less. Except as provided in clause (ii), for plans with an initial funded current liability percentage of 75 percent or less, the applicable number of percentage points for the applicable plan year is:

In the case of applicable plan years beginning in:	The applicable number of percentage points is:
1995	3
1996	6
1997	9
1998	12
1999	15
2000	19
2001	24

"(ii) Other cases. In the case of a plan to which this clause applies, the applicable number of percentage points for any such applicable plan year is the sum of—

"(I) 2 percentage points;

"(II) the applicable number of percentage points (if any) under this clause for the preceding applicable plan year;

"(III) the product of .10 multiplied by the excess (if any) of (a) 85 percentage points over (b) the sum of the initial funded current liability percentage and the number determined under subclause (II);

"(IV) for applicable plan years beginning in 2000, 1 percentage point; and

"(V) for applicable plan years beginning in 2001, 2 percentage points.

"(iii) Plans to which clause (ii) applies.

"(I) In general. Clause (ii) shall apply to a plan for an applicable plan year if the initial funded current liability percentage of such plan is more than 75 percent.

"(II) Plans initially under clause (i). In the case of a plan which (but for this subclause) has an initial funded current liability percentage of 75 percent or less, clause (ii) (and not clause (i)) shall apply to such plan with respect to applicable plan years beginning after the first applicable plan year for which the sum of the initial funded current liability percentage and the applicable number of percentage points (determined under clause (i)) exceeds 75 percent. For purposes of applying clause (ii) to such a plan, the initial funded current liability percentage of such plan shall be treated as being the sum referred to in the preceding sentence.

"(C) Definitions. For purposes of this paragraph—

"(i) The term 'applicable plan year' means a plan year beginning after December 31, 1994, and before January 1, 2002.

"(ii) The term 'initial funded current liability percentage' means the funded current liability percentage as of the first day of the first plan year beginning after December 31, 1994.

"(12) Election for certain plans.

"(A) In general. In the case of a defined benefit plan established and maintained by an applicable employer, if this subsection did not apply to the plan for the plan year beginning in 2000 (determined without regard to paragraph (6)), then, at the election of the employer, the increased amount under paragraph (1) for any applicable plan year shall be the greater of—

"(i) 20 percent of the increased amount under paragraph (1) determined without regard to this paragraph or

"(ii) the increased amount which would be determined under paragraph (1) if the deficit reduction contribution under paragraph (2) for the applicable plan year were determined without regard to subparagraphs (A), (B), and (D) of paragraph (2).

"(B) Restrictions on benefit increases. No amendment which increases the liabilities of the plan by reason of any increase in benefits, any change in the accrual of benefits, or any change in the rate at which benefits become nonforfeitable under the plan shall be adopted during any applicable plan year, unless—

"(i) the plan's enrolled actuary certifies (in such form and manner prescribed by the Secretary) that the amendment provides for an increase in annual contributions which will exceed the increase in annual charges to the funding standard account attributable to such amendment, or

"(ii) the amendment is required by a collective bargaining agreement which is in effect on the date of enactment of this subparagraph.

If a plan is amended during any applicable plan year in violation of the preceding sentence, any election under this paragraph shall not apply to any applicable plan year ending on or after the date on which such amendment is adopted.

"(C) Applicable employer. For purposes of this paragraph, the term 'applicable employer' means an employer which is—

"(i) a commercial passenger airline,

"(ii) primarily engaged in the production or manufacture of a steel mill product or the processing of iron ore pellets, or

"(iii) an organization described in section 501(c)(5) and which established the plan to which this paragraph applies on June 30, 1955.

"(D) Applicable plan year. For purposes of this paragraph—

"(i) In general. The term 'applicable plan year' means any plan year beginning after December 27, 2003, and before December 28, 2005, for which the employer elects the application of this paragraph.

"(ii) Limitation on number of years which may be elected. An election may not be made under this paragraph with respect to more than 2 plan years.

"(E) Election. An election under this paragraph shall be made at such time and in such manner as the Secretary may prescribe.

"(m) Quarterly contributions required.

"(1) In general. If a defined benefit plan (other than a multiemployer plan) which has a funded current liability percentage (as defined in subsection (l)(8)) for the preceding plan year of less than 100 percent fails to pay the full amount of a required installment for the plan year, then the rate of interest charged to the funding standard account under subsection (b)(5) with respect to the amount of the underpayment for the period of the underpayment shall be equal to the greater of—

"(A) 175 percent of the Federal mid-term rate (as in effect under section 1274 for the 1st month of such plan year), or

"(B) the rate of interest used under the plan in determining costs (including adjustments under subsection (b)(5)(B)).

"(2) Amount of underpayment, period of underpayment. For purposes of paragraph (1)—

"(A) Amount. The amount of the underpayment shall be the excess of—

"(i) the required installment, over

"(ii) the amount (if any) of the installment contributed to or under the plan on or before the due date for the installment.

"(B) Period of underpayment. The period for which interest is charged under this subsection with regard to any portion of the underpayment shall run from the due date for the installment to the date on which such portion is contributed to or under the plan (determined without regard to subsection (c)(10)).

"(C) Order of crediting contributions. For purposes of subparagraph (A)(ii), contributions shall be credited against unpaid required installments in the order in which such installments are required to be paid.

"(3) Number of required installments; due dates. For purposes of this subsection—

"(A) Payable in 4 installments. There shall be 4 required installments for each plan year.

"(B) Time for payment of installments.

In the case of the following required installments:	The due date is:
1st	April 15
2nd	July 15
3rd	October 15
4th	January 15 of the following year

"(4) Amount of required installment. For purposes of this subsection—

"(A) In general. The amount of any required installment shall be the applicable percentage of the required annual payment.

"(B) Required annual payment. For purposes of subparagraph (A), the term 'required annual payment' means the lesser of—

"(i) 90 percent of the amount required to be contributed to or under the plan by the employer for the plan year under section 412 (without regard to any waiver under subsection (d) thereof), or

"(ii) 100 percent of the amount so required for the preceding plan year.

Clause (ii) shall not apply if the preceding plan year was not a year of 12 months.

"(C) Applicable percentage. For purposes of subparagraph (A), the applicable percentage shall be determined in accordance with the following table:

2,004

Employee benefit plans Code Sec. 412

For plan years beginning in:	The applicable percentage is:
1989	6.25
1990	12.5
1991	18.75
1992 and thereafter	25

"(D) Special rules for unpredictable contingent event benefits. In the case of a plan to which subsection (l) applies for any calendar year and which has any unpredictable contingent event benefit liabilities—

"(i) Liabilities not taken into account. Such liabilities shall not be taken into account in computing the required annual payment under subparagraph (B).

"(ii) Increase in installments. Each required installment shall be increased by the greatest of—

"(I) the unfunded percentage of the amount of benefits described in subsection (l)(5)(A)(i) paid during the 3-month period preceding the month in which the due date for such installment occurs,

"(II) 25 percent of the amount determined under subsection (l)(5)(A)(ii) for the plan year, or

"(III) 25 percent of the amount determined under subsection (l)(5)(A)(iii) for the plan year.

"(iii) Unfunded percentage. For purposes of clause (ii)(I), the term 'unfunded percentage' means the percentage determined under subsection (l)(5)(A)(i)(I) for the plan year.

"(iv) Limitation on increase. In no event shall the increases under clause (ii) exceed the amount necessary to increase the funded current liability percentage (within the meaning of subsection (l)(8)(B)) for the plan year to 100 percent.

"(5) Liquidity requirement.

"(A) In general. A plan to which this paragraph applies shall be treated as failing to pay the full amount of any required installment to the extent that the value of the liquid assets paid in such installment is less than the liquidity shortfall (whether or not such liquidity shortfall exceeds the amount of such installment required to be paid but for this paragraph).

"(B) Plans to which paragraph applies. This paragraph shall apply to a defined benefit plan (other than a multiemployer plan or a plan described in subsection (l)(6)(A)) which—

"(i) is required to pay installments under this subsection for a plan year, and

"(ii) has a liquidity shortfall for any quarter during such plan year.

"(C) Period of underpayment. For purposes of paragraph (A), any portion of an installment that is treated as not paid under subparagraph (A) shall continue to be treated as unpaid until the close of the quarter in which the due date for such installment occurs.

"(D) Limitation on increase. If the amount of any required installment is increased by reason of subparagraph (A), in no event shall such increase exceed the amount which, when added to prior installments for the plan year, is necessary to increase the funded current liability percentage (taking into account the expected increase in current liability due to benefits accruing during the plan year) to 100 percent.

"(E) Definitions. For purposes of this paragraph:

"(i) Liquidity shortfall. The term 'liquidity shortfall' means, with respect to any required installment, an amount equal to the excess (as of the last day of the quarter for which such installment is made) of the base amount with respect to such quarter over the value (as of such last day) of the plan's liquid assets.

"(ii) Base amount.

"(I) In general. The term 'base amount' means, with respect to any quarter, an amount equal to 3 times the sum of the adjusted disbursements from the plan for the 12 months ending on the last day of such quarter.

"(II) Special rule. If the amount determined under subclause (I) exceeds an amount equal to 2 times the sum of the adjusted disbursements from the plan for the 36 months ending on the last day of the quarter and an enrolled actuary certifies to the satisfaction of the Secretary that such excess is the result of nonrecurring circumstances, the base amount with respect to such quarter shall be determined without regard to amounts related to those nonrecurring circumstances.

"(iii) Disbursements from the plan. The term 'disbursements from the plan' means all disbursements from the trust, including purchases of annuities, payments of single sums and other benefits, and administrative expenses.

"(iv) Adjusted disbursements. The term 'adjusted disbursements' means disbursements from the plan reduced by the product of—

"(I) the plan's funded current liability percentage (as defined in subsection (l)(8)) for the plan year, and

"(II) he sum of the purchases of annuities, payments of single sums, and such other disbursements as the Secretary shall provide in regulations.

"(v) Liquid assets. The term 'liquid assets' means cash, marketable securities and such other assets as specified by the Secretary in regulations.

"(vi) Quarter. The term 'quarter' means, with respect to any required installment, the 3-month period preceding the month in which the due date for such installment occurs.

"(F) Regulations. The Secretary may prescribe such regulations as are necessary to carry out this paragraph.

"(6) Fiscal years and short years.

"(A) Fiscal years. In applying this subsection to a plan year beginning on any date other than January 1, there shall be substituted for the months specified in this subsection, the months which correspond thereto.

"(B) Short plan year. This subsection shall be applied to plan years of less than 12 months in accordance with regulations prescribed by the Secretary.

"(7) Special rule for 2002. In any case in which the interest rate used to determine current liability is determined under subsection (l)(7)(C)(i)(III), for purposes of applying paragraphs (1) and (4)(B)(ii) for plan years beginning in 2002, the current liability for the preceding plan year shall be redetermined using 120 percent as the specified percentage determined under subsection (l)(7)(C)(i)(II).

"(n) Imposition of lien where failure to make required contributions.

"(1) In general. In the case of a plan to which this section applies, if—

"(A) any person fails to make a required installment under subsection (m) or any other payment required under this section before the due date for such installment or other payment, and

"(B) the unpaid balance of such installment or other payment (including interest), when added to the aggregate unpaid balance of all preceding such installments or other payments for which payment was not made before the due date (including interest), exceeds $1,000,000,

then there shall be a lien in favor of the plan in the amount determined under paragraph (3) upon all property and rights to property, whether real or personal, belonging to such person and any other person who is a member of the same controlled group of which such person is a member.

"(2) Plans to which subsection applies. This subsection shall apply to a defined benefit plan (other than a multiemployer plan) for any plan year for which the funded current liability percentage (within the meaning of subsection (1)(8)(B)) of such plan is less than 100 percent. This subsection shall not apply to any plan to which section 4021 of the Employee Retirement Income Security Act of 1974 does not apply (as such section is in effect on the date of the enactment of the Retirement Protection Act of 1994).

"(3) Amount of lien. For purposes of paragraph (1), the amount of the lien shall be equal to the aggregate unpaid balance of required installments and other payments required under this section (including interest)—

"(A) for plan years beginning after 1987, and

"(B) for which payment has not been made before the due date.

"(4) Notice of failure; lien.

"(A) Notice of failure. A person committing a failure described in paragraph (1) shall notify the Pension Benefit Guaranty Corporation of such failure within 10 days of the due date for the required installment or other payment.

"(B) Period of lien. The lien imposed by paragraph (1) shall arise on the due date for the required installment or other payment and shall continue until the last day of the first plan year in which the plan ceases to be described in paragraph (1)(B). Such lien shall continue to run without regard to whether such plan continues to be described in paragraph (2) during the period referred to in the preceding sentence.

"(C) Certain rules to apply. Any amount with respect to which a lien is imposed under paragraph (1) shall be treated as taxes due and owing the United States and rules similar to the rules of subsections (c), (d), and (e) of section 4068 of the Employee Retirement Income Security Act of 1974 shall apply with respect to a lien imposed by subsection (a) and the amount with respect to such lien.

"(5) Enforcement. Any lien created under paragraph (1) may be perfected and enforced only by the Pension Benefit Guaranty Corporation, or at the direction of the Pension Benefit Guaranty Corporation, by the contributing sponsor (or any member of the controlled group of the contributing sponsor).

"(6) Definitions. For purposes of this subsection—

"(A) Due date; required installment. The terms 'due date' and 'required installment' have the meanings given such terms by subsection (m), except that in the case of a payment other than a required installment, the due date shall be the date such payment is required to be made under this section.

"(B) Controlled group. The term 'controlled group' means any group treated as a single employer under subsections (b), (c), (m), and (o) of section 414."

—P.L. 109-280, Sec. 115(a)-(c), of this Act, reads as follows:

"(a) In general. In the case of a plan that—

"(1) was not required to pay a variable rate premium for the plan year beginning in 1996,

"(2) has not, in any plan year beginning after 1995, merged with another plan (other than a plan sponsored by an employer that was in 1996 within the controlled group of the plan sponsor); and

"(3) is sponsored by a company that is engaged primarily in the interurban or interstate passenger bus service,

the rules described in subsection (b) shall apply for any plan year beginning after December 31, 2007.

"(b) Modified rules. The rules described in this subsection are as follows:

"(1) For purposes of section 430(j)(3) of the Internal Revenue Code of 1986 and section 303(j)(3) of the Employee Retirement Income Security Act of 1974, the plan shall be treated as not having a funding shortfall for any plan year.

"(2) For purposes of—

"(A) determining unfunded vested benefits under section 4006(a)(3)(E)(iii) of such Act, and

"(B) determining any present value or making any computation under section 412 of such Code or section 302 of such Act,

the mortality table shall be the mortality table used by the plan.

"(3) Section 430(c)(5)(B) of such Code and section 303(c)(5)(B) of such Act (relating to phase-in of funding target for exemption from new shortfall amortization base) shall each be applied by substituting '2012' for '2011' therein and by substituting for the table therein the following:

In the case of a plan year beginning in calendar year:	The applicable percentage is:
2008	90 percent
2009	92 percent
2010	94 percent
2011	96 percent.

"(c) *Definitions.* Any term used in this section which is also used in section 430 of such Code or section 303 of such Act shall have the meaning provided such term in such section. If the same term has a different meaning in such Code and such Act, such term shall, for purposes of this section, have the meaning provided by such Code when applied with respect to such Code and the meaning provided by such Act when applied with respect to such Act."

—P.L. 109-280, Sec. 115(d)(1), substituted ", 2005, 2006, and 2007" for "and 2005" in Sec. 769(c)(3) of P.L. 103-465 [see below] effective for plan yrs. begin. after 12/31/2005.

—P.L. 109-280, Sec. 115(e)(1), deleted Sec. 769(c) of P.L. 103-465, effective 12/31/2007, and for plan yrs. begin. after 12/31/2007.

Prior to deletion, Sec. 769(c) of P.L. 103-465 read as follows:

"(c) Transition rules for certain plans.

"(1) In general. In the case of a plan that—

"(A) was not required to pay a variable rate premium for the plan year beginning in 1996;

"(B) has not, in any plan year beginning after 1995 and before 2009, merged with another plan (other than a plan sponsored by an employer that was in 1996 within the controlled group of the plan sponsor); and

"(C) is sponsored by a company that is engaged primarily in the interurban or interstate passenger bus service,

except as provided in paragraph (3), the transition rules described in paragraph (2) shall apply for any plan year beginning after 1996 and before 2010.

"(2) Transition rules. Except as provided in paragraph (3), the transition rules described in this paragraph are as follows:

"(A) For purposes of section 412(l)(9)(A) of the Internal Revenue Code of 1986 and section 302(d)(9)(A) of the Employee Retirement Income Security Act of 1974—

"(i) the funded current liability percentage for any plan year beginning after 1996 and before 2005 shall be treated as not less than 90 percent if for such plan year the funded current liability percentage is at least 85 percent, and

"(ii) the funded current liability percentage for any plan year beginning after 2004 and before 2010 shall be treated as not less than 90 percent if for such plan year the funded current liability percentage satisfies the minimum percentage determined according to the following table:

"In the case of a plan year beginning in:	The minimum percentage is:
2005	86 percent
2006	87 percent
2007	88 percent
2008	89 percent
2009 and thereafter	90 percent.

"(B) Sections 412(c)(7)(E)(i)(I) of such Code and 302(c)(7)(E)(i)(I) of such Act shall be applied—

"(i) by substituting '85 percent' for '90 percent' for plan years beginning after 1996 and before 2005, and

"(ii) by substituting the minimum percentage specified in the table contained in subparagraph (A)(ii) for '90 percent' for plan years beginning after 2004 and before 2010.

"(C) In the event the funded current liability percentage of a plan is less than 85 percent for any plan year beginning after 1996 and before 2005, except as provided in paragraph (3), the transition rules under subparagraphs (A) and (B) shall continue to apply to the plan if contributions for such a plan year are made to the plan in an amount equal to the lesser of—

"(i) the amount necessary to result in a funded current liability percentage of 85 percent, or

"(ii) the greater of—

"(I) 2 percent of the plan's current liability as of the beginning of such plan year, or

"(II) the amount necessary to result in a funded current liability percentage of 80 percent as of the end of such plan year.

For the plan year beginning in 2005 and for each of the 3 succeeding plan years, except as provided in paragraph (3), the transition rules under subparagraphs (A) and (B) shall continue to apply to the plan for such plan year only if contributions to the plan for such plan year equal at least the expected increase in current liability due to benefits accruing during such plan year.

"(3) Special rules. In the case of plan years beginning in 2004, 2005, 2006, and 2007 the following transition rules shall apply in lieu of the transition rules described in paragraph (2):

"(A) For purposes of section 412(l)(9)(A) of the Internal Revenue Code of 1986 and section 302(d)(9)(A) of the Employee Retirement Income Security Act of 1974, the funded current liability percentage for any plan year shall be treated as not less than 90 percent.

"(B) For purposes of section 412(m) of the Internal Revenue Code of 1986 and section 302(e) of the Employee Retirement Income Security Act of 1974, the funded current liability percentage for any plan year shall be treated as not less than 100 percent.

"(C) For purposes of determining unfunded vested benefits under section 4006(a)(3)(E)(iii) of the Employee Retirement Income Security Act of 1974, the mortality table shall be the mortality table used by the plan."

—P.L. 109-280, Sec. 201(b), as amended by Sec. 102(a), P.L. 110-458, [see above] of this Act, reads as follows:

"*(b) Shortfall Funding Method.*

"(1) In general. A multiemployer plan meeting the criteria of paragraph (2) may adopt, use, or cease using, the shortfall funding method and such adoption, use, or cessation of use of such method, shall be deemed approved by the Secretary of the Treasury under section 302(d)(1) of the Employee Retirement Income Security Act of 1974 and section 412(d)(1) of the Internal Revenue Code of 1986.

"(2) Criteria. A multiemployer pension plan meets the criteria of this clause if—

"(A) the plan has not adopted or ceased using the shortfall funding method during the 5-year period ending on the day before the date the plan is to use the method under paragraph (1); and

"(B) the plan is not operating under an amortization period extension under section 304(d) of such Act and did not operate under such an extension during such 5-year period.

"(3) Shortfall funding method defined. For purposes of this subsection, the term 'shortfall funding method' means the shortfall funding method described in Treasury Regulations section 1.412(c)(1)-2 (26 C.F.R. 1.412(c)(1)-2).

"(4) Benefit restrictions to apply. The benefit restrictions under section 302(c)(7) of such Act and section 412(c)(7) of such Code shall apply during any period a multiemployer plan is on the shortfall funding method pursuant to this subsection.

"(5) Use of shortfall method not to preclude other options. Nothing in this subsection shall be construed to affect a multiemployer plan's ability to adopt the shortfall funding method with the Secretary's permission under otherwise applicable regulations or to affect a multiemployer plan's right to change funding methods, with or without the Secretary's consent, as provided in applicable rules and regulations."

—P.L. 109-280, Sec. 206, of this Act, reads as follows:

"SEC. 206. SPECIAL RULE FOR CERTAIN BENEFITS FUNDED UNDER AN AGREEMENT APPROVED BY THE PENSION BENEFIT GUARANTY CORPORATION.

"In the case of a multiemployer plan that is a party to an agreement that was approved by the Pension Benefit Guaranty Corporation prior to June 30, 2005, and that—

"(1) increases benefits, and

"(2) provides for special withdrawal liability rules under section 4203(f) of the Employee Retirement Income Security Act of 1974 (29 U.S.C. 1383),

the amendments made by sections 201, 202, 211, and 212 of this Act shall not apply to the benefit increases under any plan amendment adopted prior to June 30, 2005, that are funded pursuant to such agreement if the plan is funded in compliance with such agreement (and any amendments thereto)."

—P.L. 109-280, Sec. 212(c), added para. (b)(3), effective for plan yrs. begin. after 2007. Sec. 212(e)(2) and (3), [as amended by Sec. 102(b)(3)(C), P.L. 110-458, see above] of this Act, read as follows:

"(2) Special rule for certain notices. In any case in which a plan's actuary certifies that it is reasonably expected that a multiemployer plan will be in critical status under section 432(b)(3) of the Internal Revenue Code of 1986, as added by this section, with respect to the first plan year beginning after 2007, the notice required under subparagraph (D) of such section may be provided at any time after the date of enactment, so long as it is provided on or before the last date for providing the notice under such subparagraph.

"(3) Special rule for certain restored benefits. In the case of a multiemployer plan—

"(A) with respect to which benefits were reduced pursuant to a plan amendment adopted on or after January 1, 2002, and before June 30, 2005, and

"(B) which, pursuant to the plan document, the trust agreement, or a formal written communication from the plan sponsor to participants provided before June 30, 2005, provided for the restoration of such benefits,

the amendments made by this section shall not apply to such benefit restorations to the extent that any restriction on the providing or accrual of such benefits would otherwise apply by reason of such amendments."

—P.L. 109-280, Sec. 221, of this Act, reads as follows:

"SEC. 221. SUNSET OF ADDITIONAL FUNDING RULES.

"*(a) Report.* Not later than December 31, 2011, the Secretary of Labor, the Secretary of the Treasury, and the Executive Director of the Pension Benefit Guaranty Corporation shall conduct a study of the effect of the amendments made by this subtitle on the operation and funding status of multiemployer plans and shall report the results of such study, including any recommendations for legislation, to the Congress.

"*(b) Matters included in study.* The study required under subsection (a) shall include—

"(1) the effect of funding difficulties, funding rules in effect before the date of the enactment of this Act, and the amendments made by this subtitle on small businesses participating in multiemployer plans,

"(2) the effect on the financial status of small employers of—

"(A) funding targets set in funding improvement and rehabilitation plans and associated contribution increases,

"(B) funding deficiencies,

"(C) excise taxes,

"(D) withdrawal liability,

"(E) the possibility of alternatives schedules and procedures for financially-troubled employers, and

"(F) other aspects of the multiemployer system, and

"(3) the role of the multiemployer pension plan system in helping small employers to offer pension benefits.

"(c) Sunset.

"(1) In general. Except as provided in this subsection, notwithstanding any other provision of this Act, the provisions of, and the amendments made by, sections 201(b), 202, and 212 shall not apply to plan years beginning after December 31, 2014.

"(2) Funding improvement and rehabilitation plans. If a plan is operating under a funding improvement or rehabilitation plan under section 305 of such Act or 432 of such Code for its last year beginning before January 1, 2015, such plan shall continue to operate under such funding improvement or rehabilitation plan during any period after December 31, 2014, such funding or rehabilitation plan is in effect and all provisions of such Act or Code relating to the operation of such funding improvement or rehabilitation plan shall continue in effect during such period."

—P.L. 109-280, Sec. 301(b)(1)(A), substituted "2008" for "2006" in subclause (b)(5)(B)(ii)(II) ... Sec. 301(b)(1)(B), substituted ", 2005, 2006, and 2007" for "and 2005" in the heading of subclause (b)(5)(B)(ii)(II), enacted 8/17/2006.

—P.L. 109-280, Sec. 301(c), substituted "2008" for "2006" in Sec. 101(c)(2)(A)(ii) of P.L. 108-218 [see below].

—P.L. 109-280, Sec. 301(b)(2)(A), substituted ", 2005, 2006, or 2007" for "or 2005" in clause (l)(7)(C)(i)(IV) ... Sec. 301(b)(2)(B), substituted ", 2005, 2006, and 2007" for "and 2005" in the heading of clause (l)(7)(C)(i)(IV), effective 8/17/2006.

—P.L. 109-280, Sec. 402(a)-(g)(1), of this Act [as amended by Sec. 104(b), P.L. 110-458, and Sec. 126(a), P.L. 110-458, see above] reads as follows:

"(a) In general. The plan sponsor of an eligible plan may elect to either—

"(1) have the rules of subsection (b) apply, or

"(2) have section 303 of the Employee Retirement Income Security Act of 1974 and section 430 of the Internal Revenue Code of 1986 applied to its first taxable year beginning in 2008 by amortizing the shortfall amortization base for such taxable year over a period of 10 plan years (rather than 7 plan years) beginning with such plan year.

"(b) Alternative funding schedule.

"In general. If an election is made under subsection (a)(1) to have this subsection apply to an eligible plan and the requirements of paragraphs (2) and (3) are met with respect to the plan—

"(A) in the case of any applicable plan year beginning before January 1, 2008, the plan shall not have an accumulated funding deficiency for purposes of section 302 of the Employee Retirement Income Security Act of 1974 and sections 412 and 4971 of the Internal Revenue Code of 1986 if contributions to the plan for the plan year are not less than the minimum required contribution determined under subsection (e) for the plan for the plan year, and

"(B) in the case of any applicable plan year beginning on or after January 1, 2008, the minimum required contribution determined under sections 303 of such Act and 430 of such Code shall, for purposes of sections 302 and 303 of such Act and sections 412, 430, and 4971 of such Code, be equal to the minimum required contribution determined under subsection (e) for the plan for the plan year.

"(2) Accrual restrictions.

"(A) In general. The requirements of this paragraph are met if, effective as of the first day of the first applicable plan year and at all times thereafter while an election under this section is in effect, the plan provides that—

"(i) the accrued benefit, any death or disability benefit, and any social security supplement described in the last sentence of section 411(a)(9) of such Code and section 204(b)(1)(G) of such Act, of each participant are frozen at the amount of such benefit or supplement immediately before such first day, and

"(ii) all other benefits under the plan are eliminated,

but only to the extent the freezing or elimination of such benefits would have been permitted under section 411(d)(6) of such Code and section 204(g) of such Act if they had been implemented by a plan amendment adopted immediately before such first day.

"(B) Increases in section 415 limits. If a plan provides that an accrued benefit of a participant which has been subject to any limitation under section 415 of such Code will be increased if such limitation is increased, the plan shall not be treated as meeting the requirements of this section unless, effective as of the first day of the first applicable plan year (or, if later, the date of the enactment of this Act) and at all times thereafter while an election under this section is in effect, the plan provides that any such increase shall not take effect. A plan shall not fail to meet the requirements of section 411(d)(6) of such Code and section 204(g) of such Act solely because the plan is amended to meet the requirements of this subparagraph.

"(3) Restriction on applicable benefit increases.

"(A) In general. The requirements of this paragraph are met if no applicable benefit increase takes effect at any time during the period beginning on July 26, 2005, and ending on the day before the first day of the first applicable plan year.

"(B) Applicable benefit increase. For purposes of this paragraph, the term 'applicable benefit increase' means, with respect to any plan year, any increase in liabilities of the plan by plan amendment (or otherwise provided in regulations provided by the Secretary) which, but for this paragraph, would occur during the plan year by reason of—

"(i) any increase in benefits,

"(ii) any change in the accrual of benefits, or

"(iii) any change in the rate at which benefits become nonforfeitable under the plan.

"(4) Exception for imputed disability service. Paragraphs (2) and (3) shall not apply to any accrual or increase with respect to imputed service provided to a participant during any period of the participant's disability occurring on or after the effective date of the plan amendment providing the restrictions under paragraph (2) (or on or after July 26, 2005, in the case of the restrictions under paragraph (3)) if the participant—

"(A) was receiving disability benefits as of such date, or

"(B) was receiving sick pay and subsequently determined to be eligible for disability benefits as of such date.

"(c) Definitions. For purposes of this section—

"(1) Eligible plan. The term 'eligible plan' means a defined benefit plan (other than a multiemployer plan) to which sections 302 of such Act and 412 of such Code applies which is sponsored by an employer—

"(A) which is a commercial passenger airline, or

"(B) the principal business of which is providing catering services to a commercial passenger airline.

"(2) Applicable plan year. The term 'applicable plan year' means each plan year to which the election under subsection (a)(1) applies under subsection (d)(1)(A).

"(d) Elections and related terms.

"(1) Years for which election made.

"(A) Alternative funding schedule. If an election under subsection (a)(1) was made with respect to an eligible plan, the plan sponsor may select either a plan year beginning in 2006 or a plan year beginning in 2007 as the first plan year to which such election applies. The election shall apply to such plan year and all subsequent years. The election shall be made—

"(i) not later than December 31, 2006, in the case of an election for a plan year beginning in 2006, or

"(ii) not later than December 31, 2007, in the case of an election for a plan year beginning in 2007.

"(B) 10 year amortization. An election under subsection (a)(2) shall be made not later than December 31, 2007.

"(C) Election of new plan year for alternative funding schedule. In the case of an election under subsection (a)(1), the plan sponsor may specify a new plan year in such election and the plan year of the plan may be changed to such new plan year without the approval of the Secretary of the Treasury.

"(2) Manner of election. A plan sponsor shall make any election under subsection (a) in such manner as the Secretary of the Treasury may prescribe. Such election, once made, may be revoked only with the consent of such Secretary.

"(e) Minimum required contribution. In the case of an eligible plan with respect to which an election is made under subsection (a)(1)—

"(1) In general. In the case of any applicable plan year during the amortization period, the minimum required contribution shall be the amount necessary to amortize the unfunded liability of the plan, determined as of the first day of the plan year, in equal annual installments (until fully amortized) over the remainder of the amortization period. Such amount shall be separately determined for each applicable plan year.

"(2) Years after amortization period. In the case of any plan year beginning after the end of the amortization period, section 302(a)(2)(A) of such Act and section 412(a)(2)(A) of such Code shall apply to such plan, but the prefunding balance and funding standard carryover balance as of the first day of the first of such years under section 303(f) of such Act and section 430(f) of such Code shall be zero.

"(3) Definitions. For purposes of this section—

"(A) Unfunded liability. The term 'unfunded liability' means the unfunded accrued liability under the plan, determined under the unit credit funding method.

"(B) Amortization period. The term 'amortization period' means the 17-plan year period beginning with the first applicable plan year.

"(4) Other rules. In determining the minimum required contribution and amortization amount under this subsection—

"(A) the provisions of section 302(c)(3) of such Act and section 412(c)(3) of such Code, as in effect before the date of enactment of this section, shall apply,

"(B) a rate of interest of 8.85 percent shall be used for all calculations requiring an interest rate, and

"(C) the value of plan assets shall be determined under sections 303(g)(3) of such Act and 430(g)(3) of such Code."

"(5) Special rule for certain plan spin-offs. For purposes of subsection (b), if, with respect to any eligible plan to which this subsection applies—

"(A) any applicable plan year includes the date of the enactment of this Act,

"(B) a plan was spun off from the eligible plan during the plan year but before such date of enactment,

the minimum required contribution under paragraph (1) for the eligible plan for such applicable plan year shall be an aggregate amount determined as if the plans were a single plan for that plan year (based on the full 12-month plan year in effect prior to the spin-off). The employer shall designate the allocation of such aggregate amount between such plans for the applicable plan year.

"(f) Special rules for certain balances and waivers. In the case of an eligible plan with respect to which an election is made under subsection (a)(1)—

"(1) Funding standard account and credit balances. Any charge or credit in the funding standard account under section 302 of such Act or section 412 of such Code, and any prefunding balance or funding standard carryover balance under section 303 of such Act or section 430 of such Code, as of the day before the first day of the first applicable plan year, shall be reduced to zero.

"(2) Waived funding deficiencies. Any waived funding deficiency under sections 302 and 303 of such Act or section 412 of such Code, as in effect before the date of enactment of this section, shall be deemed satisfied as of the first day of the first applicable plan year and the amount of such waived funding deficiency shall be taken into account in determining the plan's unfunded liability under subsection (e)(3)(A). In the case of a plan amendment adopted to satisfy the requirements of subsection (b)(2), the plan shall not be deemed to violate section 304(b) of such Act or section 412(f) of such Code, as so in effect, by reason of such amendment or any increase in benefits provided to such plan's participants under a separate plan that is a defined contribution plan or a multiemployer plan.

"(g) *Other rules for plans making election under this section.*

"(1) Successor plans to certain plans. If—

"(A) an election under paragraph (1) or (2) of subsection (a) is in effect with respect to any eligible plan, and

"(B) the eligible plan is maintained by an employer that establishes or maintains 1 or more other defined benefit plans (other than any multiemployer plan), and such other plans in combination provide benefit accruals to any substantial number of successor employees,

the Secretary of the Treasury may, in the Secretary's discretion, determine that any trust of which any other such plan is a part does not constitute a qualified trust under section 401(a) of the Internal Revenue Code of 1986 unless all benefit obligations of the eligible plan have been satisfied. For purposes of this paragraph, the term 'successor employee' means any employee who is or was covered by the eligible plan and any employees who perform substantially the same type of work with respect to the same business operations as an employee covered by such eligible plan."

—P.L. 109-280, Sec. 402(i), of this Act, reads as follows:

"*(i) Extension of special rule for additional funding requirements.* In the case of an employer which is a commercial passenger airline, section 302(d)(12) of the Employee Retirement Income Security Act of 1974 and section 412(l)(12) of the Internal Revenue Code of 1986, as in effect before the date of the enactment of this Act, shall each be applied—

"(1) by substituting 'December 28, 2007' for 'December 28, 2005' in subparagraph (D)(i) thereof, and

"(2) without regard to subparagraph (D)(ii)."

—P.L. 109-280, Sec. 811, of this Act [relating to Sec. 901 of P.L. 107-16, see below], provides:

"SEC. 811. PENSIONS AND INDIVIDUAL RETIREMENT ARRANGEMENT PROVISIONS OF ECONOMIC GROWTH AND TAX RELIEF RECONCILIATION ACT OF 2001 MADE PERMANENT.

"Title IX of the Economic Growth and Tax Relief Reconciliation Act of 2001 shall not apply to the provisions of, and amendments made by, subtitles A through F of title VI of such Act (relating to pension and individual retirement arrangement provisions)."

In 2005, P.L. 109-135, Sec. 412(x)(1), substituted "subsection (d)" for "subsection (c)" in clause (m)(4)(B)(i), effective 12/21/2005.

In 2004, P.L. 108-218, Sec. 101(b)(1)(A), redesignated subclause (b)(5)(B)(ii)(II) as subclause (b)(5)(B)(ii)(III) and added subclause (b)(5)(B)(ii)(II)... Sec. 101(b)(1)(B)(i), added "or (II)" after "subclause (I)" the first place it appeared in subclause (b)(5)(B)(ii)(III) [as redesignated by Sec. 101(b)(1)(A) of this Act, see above]... Sec. 101(b)(1)(B)(ii), substituted "such subclause" for "subclause (I)" the second place it appeared in subclause (b)(5)(B)(ii)(III) [as redesignated by Sec. 101(b)(1)(A) of this Act, see above]... Sec. 101(b)(1)(C), added "or (III)" after "subclause (II)" in subclause (b)(5)(B)(ii)(I)... Sec. 101(b)(2), added subclause (l)(7)(C)(i)(IV)... Sec. 101(b)(3), amended para. (m)(7), effective for plan yrs. begin. after 12/31/2003. Sec. 101(d)(2) and (3) of this Act, provides:

"(2) Lookback rules. For purposes of applying subsections (d)(9)(B)(ii) and (e)(1) of section 302 of the Employee Retirement Income Security Act of 1974 and subsections (l)(9)(B)(ii) and (m)(1) of section 412 of the Internal Revenue Code of 1986 to plan years beginning after December 31, 2003, the amendments made by this section may be applied as if such amendments had been in effect for all prior plan years. The Secretary of the Treasury may prescribe simplified assumptions which may be used in applying the amendments made by this section to such prior plan years.

"(3) Transition rule for section 415 limitation. In the case of any participant or beneficiary receiving a distribution after December 31, 2003 and before January 1, 2005, the amount payable under any form of benefit subject to section 417(e)(3) of the Internal Revenue Code of 1986 and subject to adjustment under section 415(b)(2)(B) of such Code shall not, solely by reason of the amendment made by subsection (b)(4), be less than the amount that would have been so payable had the amount payable been determined using the applicable interest rate in effect as of the last day of the last plan year beginning before January 1, 2004."

Prior to amendment, para. (m)(7) read as follows:

"(7) Special rules for 2002 and 2004. In any case in which the interest rate used to determine current liability is determined under subsection (l)(7)(C)(i)(III)—

"(A) 2002. For purposes of applying paragraphs (1) and (4)(B)(ii) for plan years beginning in 2002, the current liability for the preceding plan year shall be redetermined using 120 percent as the specified percentage determined under subsection (l)(7)(C)(i)(II).

"(B) 2004. For purposes of applying paragraphs (1) and (4)(B)(ii) for plan years beginning in 2004, the current liability for the preceding plan year shall be redetermined using 105 percent as the specified percentage determined under subsection (l)(7)(C)(i)(II)."

—P.L. 108-218, Sec. 101(c), of this Act [as amended by Sec. 301(c) of P.L. 109-280, and Sec. 103(a), P.L. 110-458, see above], reads as follows:

"(c) Provisions relating to plan amendments.

"(1) In general. If this subsection applies to any plan or annuity contract amendment—

"(A) such plan or contract shall be treated as being operated in accordance with the terms of the plan or contract during the period described in paragraph (2)(B)(i), and

"(B) except as provided by the Secretary of the Treasury, such plan shall not fail to meet the requirements of section 411(d)(6) of the Internal Revenue Code of 1986 and section 204(g) of the Employee Retirement Income Security Act of 1974 by reason of such amendment.

"(2) Amendments to which section applies.

"(A) In general. This subsection shall apply to any amendment to any plan or annuity contract which is made—

"(i) pursuant to any amendment made by this section, and

"(ii) on or before the last day of the first plan year beginning on or after January 1, 2009.

"(B) Conditions. This subsection shall not apply to any plan or annuity contract amendment unless—

"(i) during the period beginning on the date the amendment described in subparagraph (A)(i) takes effect and ending on the date described in subparagraph (A)(ii) (or, if earlier, the date the plan or contract amendment is adopted), the plan or contract is operated as if such plan or contract amendment were in effect; and

"(ii) such plan or contract amendment applies retroactively for such period."

—P.L. 108-218, Sec. 102(b), added para. (l)(12), effective 4/10/2004. Sec. 102(c) of this Act, provides:

"(c) Effect of election. An election under section 302(d)(12) of the Employee Retirement Income Security Act of 1974 or section 412(l)(12) of the Internal Revenue Code of 1986 (as added by this section) with respect to a plan shall not invalidate any obligation (pursuant to a collective bargaining agreement in effect on the date of the election) to provide benefits, to change the accrual of benefits, or to change the rate at which benefits become nonforfeitable under the plan."

—P.L. 108-218, Sec. 104(b), added subpara. (b)(7)(F), effective 4/10/2004.

—P.L. 108-218, Sec. 201(a)(1), added "except as provided in paragraph (3)," before "the transition rules" in Sec. 769(c) of P.L. 103-465 [as added by Sec. 1508 of P.L. 105-34], see below... Sec. 201(a)(2), added para. (c)(3) in Sec. 769 of P.L. 103-465 [as added by Sec. 1508 of P.L. 105-34 and amended by Sec. 201(a)(1) of this Act, see above], effective for plan yrs. begin. after 12/31/2003.

In 2002, P.L. 107-358, Sec. 2, added subsec. (c) in Sec. 901 of P.L. 107-16 [see below], effective 12/17/2002.

—P.L. 107-147, Sec. 405(a)(1), added subclause (l)(7)(C)(i)(III)... Sec. 405(a)(2), added para. (m)(7), effective 3/9/2002.

—P.L. 107-147, Sec. 411(v)(1)(A), substituted "100 percent" for "125 percent" in clause (c)(9)(B)(ii)... Sec. 411(v)(1)(B), added clause (c)(9)(B)(iv), effective for plan yrs. begin. after 12/31/2001.

In 2001, P.L. 107-16, Sec. 651(a)(1), substituted "in the case of plan years beginning before January 1, 2004, the applicable percentage" for "the applicable percentage" in clause (c)(7)(A)(i)... Sec. 651(a)(2), amended subpara. (c)(7)(F), effective for plan yrs. begin. after 12/31/2001.

Prior to amendment, subpara. (c)(7)(F) read as follows:

"(F) Applicable percentage. For purposes of subparagraph (A)(i)(I), the applicable percentage shall be determined in accordance with the following table:

In the case of any plan year beginning in—	The applicable percentage is—
1999 or 2000	155
2001 or 2002	160
2003 or 2004	165
2005 and succeeding years	170."

—P.L. 107-16, Sec. 661(a), amended para. (c)(9), effective for plan yrs. begin. after 12/31/2001.

Prior to amendment, para. (c)(9) read as follows:

"(9) Annual valuation. For purposes of this section, a determination of experience gains and losses and a valuation of the plan's liability shall be made not less frequently than once every year, except that such determination shall be made more frequently to the extent required in particular cases under regulations prescribed by the Secretary."

—P.L. 107-16, Sec. 901, of this Act [as amended by Sec. 2 of P.L. 107-358, and Sec. 101(a)(1) of P.L. 111-312, and as related to Sec. 811 of P.L. 109-280, see above], reads as follows:

"SEC. 901. SUNSET OF PROVISIONS OF ACT.

"(a) In general. All provisions of, and amendments made by, this Act shall not apply—

"(1) to taxable, plan, or limitation years beginning after December 31, 2012, or

"(2) in the case of title V, to estates of decedents dying, gifts made, or generation-skipping transfers, after December 31, 2012.

"(b) Application of certain laws. The Internal Revenue Code of 1986 and the Employee Retirement Income Security Act of 1974 shall be applied and administered to years, estates, gifts, and transfers described in subsection (a) as if the provisions and amendments described in subsection (a) had never been enacted.

"(c) Exception. Subsection (a) shall not apply to section 803 (relating to no federal income tax on restitution received by victims of the Nazi regime or their heirs or estates)."

In 1997, P.L. 105-34, Sec. 1508(a), added subsec (c) to Sec. 769 of P.L. 103-465[reproduced below], effective for plan yrs. begin. after 12/31/96.

—P.L. 105-34, Sec. 1521(a)(A) [sic (a)(1)], substituted "the applicable percentage" for "150 percent" in subclause (c)(7)(A)(i)(I)... Sec. 1521(a)(B) [sic (a)(2)], added subpara. (c)(7)(F)... Sec. 1521(c)(1), deleted "and" at the end of subpara. (b)(2)(C), substituted ", and" for the period at the end of subpara. (b)(2)(D), and added subpara. (b)(2)(E)... Sec. 1521(c)(3)(A), added "and" at the end of clause (c)(7)(D)(i), substituted a period for ", and" at the end of clause (c)(7)(D)(ii), and deleted clause (c)(7)(D)(iii), effective for plan yrs. begin. after 12/31/98. Sec. 1521(d)(2) of this Act provides:

"(2) Special rule for unamortized balances under existing law. The unamortized balance (as of the close of the plan year preceding the plan's first year beginning in 1999) of any amortization base established under section 412(c)(7)(D)(iii) of such Code and section 302(c)(7)(D)(iii) of such Act (as repealed by subsection (c)(3)) for any plan year beginning before 1999 shall be amortized in equal annual installments (until fully amortized) over a period of years equal to the excess of—

"(A) 20 years, over

"(B) the number of years since the amortization base was established."

Prior to deletion, clause (c)(7)(D)(iii) read as follows:

"(iii) for the treatment under this section of contributions which would be required to be made under the plan but for the provisions of subparagraph (A)(i)(I)."

—P.L. 105-34, Sec. 1604(b)(2)(A), substituted "subclause (I)" for "clause (i)" in subclause (m)(5)(E)(ii)(II), effective for plan yrs. begin. after 12/31/94.

In 1994, P.L. 103-465, Sec. 751(a)(1)(A), substituted "to which this subsection applies under paragraph (9)" for "which has an unfunded current liability" in para. (l)(1) . . . Sec. 751(a)(1)(B), added para. (l)(9) . . . Sec. 751(a)(2)(A), amended clause (l)(1)(A)(ii) . . . Sec. 751(a)(2)(B), amended the last sentence of para. (l)(1) . . . Sec. 751(a)(3)(A), deleted "plus" from the end of subpara. (l)(2)(A) . . . Sec. 751(a)(3)(B), substituted ", plus" for the period at the end of subpara. (l)(2)(B) . . . Sec. 751(a)(3)(C), added subpara. (l)(2)(C) . . . Sec. 751(a)(4)(A), added subparas. (l)(3)(D) and (E) . . . Sec. 751(a)(4)(B), added ", the unamortized portion of the additional unfunded old liability," after "old liability" in clause (l)(4)(B)(i) . . . Sec. 751(a)(5)(A), substituted ".40" for ".25' in clause (l)(4)(C)(i) . . . Sec. 751(a)(5)(B), substituted "60" for "35' in clause (l)(4)(C)(ii) . . . Sec. 751(a)(6)(A)(i), substituted "greatest of" for "greater of' in material preceding clause (l)(5)(A)(i) . . . Sec. 751(a)(6)(A)(ii), deleted "or" at the end of subclause (l)(5)(A)(i)(II) . . . Sec. 751(a)(6)(A)(iii), substituted ", or" for the period at the end of clause (l)(5)(A)(ii) . . . Sec. 751(a)(6)(A)(iv), added clause (l)(5)(A)(iii) . . . Sec. 751(a)(6)(B), added subpara. (l)(5)(E) . . . Sec. 751(a)(6)(C)(i), substituted "greatest of" for "greater of" in material preceding subclause (m)(4)(D)(ii)(I) . . . Sec. 751(a)(6)(C)(ii), deleted "or" from the end of subclause (m)(4)(D)(ii)(I) . . . Sec. 751(a)(6)(C)(iii), substituted ", or" for the period at the end of subclause (m)(4)(D)(ii)(II) . . . Sec. 751(a)(6)(C)(iv), added subclause (m)(4)(D)(ii)(III) . . . Sec. 751(a)(7)(A), amended subpara. (l)(7)(C) . . . Sec. 751(a)(7)(B)(i), deleted "plus" from the end of subpara. (l)(2)(B) [as amended by Sec. 751(a)(3)(B) of this Act, see above], substituted ", and" for the period at the end of subpara. (l)(2)(C) [as added by Sec. 751(a)(3)(C) of this Act, see above], and added subpara. (l)(2)(D) . . . Sec. 751(a)(7)(B)(ii), added para. (l)(10) . . . Sec. 751(a)(7)(B)(iii), added "the unamortized portion of each unfunded mortality increase," after "additional unfunded old liability," in clause (l)(4)(B)(i) [as amended by Sec. 751(a)(4)(B) of this Act, see above] . . . Sec. 751(a)(8), added para. (l)(11) . . . Sec. 751(a)(9)(A), redesignated para. (m)(5) as (m)(6) and added new para. (m)(5) . . . Sec. 751(a)(10)(A), added "(including the expected increase in current liability due to benefits accruing during the plan year)' after "current liability" in clause (c)(7)(A)(i) . . . Sec. 751(a)(10)(B), added subpara. (c)(7)(E) . . . Sec. 751(a)(10)(C), amended subpara. (c)(7)(B), effective for plan yrs. begin. after 12/31/94.

Prior to amendment, clause (l)(1)(A)(ii) read as follows:

"(ii) the sum of the charges for such plan year under subparagraphs (B) (other than clauses (iv) and (v) thereof), (C), and (D) of subsection (b)(2), reduced by the sum of the credits for such plan year under subparagraph (B)(i) of subsection (b)(3), plus"

Prior to amendment, the last sentence of para. (l)(1) read as follows:

"Such increase shall not exceed the amount necessary to increase the funded current liability percentage to 100 percent."

Prior to amendment, subpara. (c)(7)(B) read as follows:

"(B) Current liability. For purposes of subparagraphs (A) and (D), the term 'current liability' has the meaning given such term by subsection (l)(7) (without regard to subparagraph (D) thereof)."

Prior to amendment, subpara. (l)(7)(C) read as follows:

"(C) Interest rates used. The rate of interest used to determine current liability shall be the rate of interest used under subsection (b)(5)."

—P.L. 103-465, Sec. 752(a)(1), substituted "(A) In general. If the funding method" for "If the funding method" in para. (c)(5) . . . Sec. 752(a)(2), added subpara. (c)(5)(B), effective for changes in assumptions for plan yrs. begin. after 10/28/93, except as provided in Sec. 752(b)(2) of this Act which reads as follows:

"(2) Certain changes cease to be effective. In the case of changes in assumptions for plan years beginning after December 31, 1992, and on or before October 28, 1993, such changes shall cease to be effective for plan years beginning after December 31, 1994, if—

"(A) such change would have required the approval of the Secretary of the Treasury had such amendment applied to such change, and

"(B) such change is not so approved."

—P.L. 103-465, Sec. 753(a), added para. (c)(12), effective for plan yrs. begin. after 12/31/94, with respect to collective bargaining agreements in effect on or after 1/1/95.

—P.L. 103-465, Sec. 754(a)(1), added "which has a funded current liability percentage (as defined in subsection (l)(8)) for the preceding plan year of less than 100 percent" before "fails to pay the full amount" in para. (m)(1) . . . Sec. 754(a)(2), substituted "the plan year" for "any plan year" in para. (m)(1), effective for plan yrs. begin. after 12/8/94.

—P.L. 103-465, Sec. 768(a)(1), added the last sentence at the end of para. (n)(2) . . . Sec. 768(a)(2), amended para. (n)(3) . . . Sec. 768(a)(3), deleted "60th day following the" before "due date" in subpara. (n)(4)(B), effective for installments and other payments required under section 412 of the Internal Revenue Code of 1986 or under part 3 of subtitle B of the Employee Retirement Income Security Act of 1974 that become due on or after 12/8/94.

Prior to amendment, para. (n)(3) read as follows:

"(3) Amount of lien. For purposes of paragraph (1), the amount of the lien shall be equal to the lesser of—

"(A) the amount by which the unpaid balances described in paragraph (1)(B) (including interest) exceed $1,000,000, or

"(B) the aggregate unpaid balance of required installments and other payments required under this section (including interest)—

"(i) for plan years beginning after 1987, and

"(ii) for which payment has not been made before the due date."

—P.L. 103-465, Sec. 769, [as amended by Sec. 1508(a) of P.L. 105-34, Sec. 201(a)(1)-(2) of P.L. 108-218, and Sec. 115(d)(1) and (e)(1) of P.L. 109-280, see above] provides:

"Sec. 769. Special funding rules for certain plans.

"(a) Funding rules not to apply to certain plans. Any changes made by this Act to section 412 of the Internal Revenue Code of 1986 or to part 3 of subtitle B of title I of the Employee Retirement Income Security Act of 1974 shall not apply to—

"(1) a plan which is, on the date of enactment of this Act, subject to a restoration payment schedule order issued by the Pension Benefit Guaranty Corporation that meets the requirements of section 1.412(c)(1)-3 of the Treasury Regulations, or

"(2) a plan established by an affected air carrier (as defined under section 4001(a)(14)(C)(ii)(I) of such Act) and assumed by a new plan sponsor pursuant to the terms of a written agreement with the Pension Benefit Guaranty Corporation dated January 5, 1993, and approved by the United States Bankruptcy Court for the District of Delaware on December 30, 1992.

"(b) Change in actuarial method. Any amortization installments for bases established under section 412(b) of the Internal Revenue Code of 1986 and section 302(b) of the Employee Retirement Income Security Act of 1974 for plan years beginning after December 31, 1987, and before January 1, 1993, by reason of nonelective changes under the frozen entry age actuarial cost method shall not be included in the calculation of offsets under section 412(l)(1)(A)(ii) of such Code and section 302(d)(1)(A)(ii) of such Act for the 1st 5 plan years beginning after December 31, 1994.

In 1989, P.L. 101-239, Sec. 7881(a)(1)(A), added '(but not below zero)' after 'reducing' in subclause (l)(3)(C)(ii)(II) . . . Sec. 7881(a)(2)(A), added 'and the unamortized portion of the unfunded existing benefit increase liability' after 'liability' in clause (l)(4)(B)(i) . . . Sec. 7881(a)(3)(A), substituted 'the first plan year beginning after December 31, 1988' for 'October 17, 1987' in subpara. (l)(5)(C) . . . Sec. 7881(a)(4)(A), deleted 'and' at the end of subclause (l)(7)(D)(iii)(I), substituted ', and' for the period at the end of subclause (l)(7)(D)(iii)(II), added subclause (l)(7)(D)(iii)(III) and added clause (l)(7)(D)(iv) . . . Sec. 7881(a)(5)(A)(i), deleted 'reduced by any credit balance in the funding standard account' before the period at the end of clause (l)(8)(A)(ii) . . . Sec. 7881(a)(5)(A)(ii), added subpara. (l)(8)(E), effective for plan yrs. begin. after 12/31/88, except as provided in Sec. 9303(e)(3) of P.L. 100-203 reproduced below.

—P.L. 101-239, Sec. 7881(a)(6)(A)(i), substituted 'year' for '3 years' in para. (c)(9) . . . Sec. 7881(a)(6)(A)(ii), substituted 'Annual' for '3-year' in the heading of para. (c)(9), effective for plan yrs. begin. after 12/31/87.

—P.L. 101-239, Sec. 7881(a)(7), amended Sec. 9303(e)(3)(C)(ii)(II) of P.L. 100-203 [reproduced below], part of the effective date for changes made by Sec. 9303(a)(1) and (2) of P.L. 100-203, by adding '(and any income allocable to such amount)' after 'clause (i)', see below.

—P.L. 101-239, Sec. 7881(b)(1)(A)(i), added 'defined benefit' before 'plan other' in subpara. (c)(10)(A) . . . Sec. 7881(b)(1)(A)(ii), substituted 'Defined benefit plans' for 'Plans' in the heading of subpara. (c)(10)(A) . . . Sec. 7881(b)(2)(A)(i), substituted 'plan not described in subparagraph (A)' for 'multiemployer plan' in subpara. (c)(10)(B) . . . Sec. 7881(b)(2)(A)(ii), substituted 'Other' for 'Multiemployer' in the heading of subpara. (c)(10)(B), effective for plan yrs. begin. after 12/31/87.

—P.L. 101-239, Sec. 7881(b)(3)(A), added 'defined benefit' before 'plan (other' in para. (m)(1) . . . Sec. 7881(b)(4)(A), amended subpara. (m)(4)(D) . . . Sec. 7881(b)(6)(A)(i), amended subpara. (m)(1)(B) . . . Sec. 7881(b)(6)(A)(ii), added '(including adjustments under subsection (b)(5)(B))' after 'costs' in clause (d)(1)(A)(ii), effective for plan yrs. begin. after 1988.

Prior to amendment, subpara. (m)(4)(D) read as follows:

"(D) Special rules for unpredictable contingent event benefits. In the case of a plan with any unpredictable contingent event benefit liabilities—

"(i) such liabilities shall not be taken into account in computing the required annual payment under subparagraph (B), and

"(ii) each required installment shall be increased by the greater of—

"(I) the amount of benefits described in subsection (l)(5)(A)(i) paid during the 3-month period preceding the month in which the due date for such installment occurs, or

"(II) 25 percent of the amount determined under subsection (l)(5)(A)(ii) for the plan year."

Prior to amendment, subpara. (m)(1)(B) read as follows:

"(B) the rate under subsection (b)(5)."

—P.L. 101-239, Sec. 7881(c)(1), substituted "for benefit liabilities" for "the benefit liabilities" in the last sentence of subpara. (f)(4)(A), effective for applications submitted after 3/21/88.

—P.L. 101-239, Sec. 7881(c)(3), amended Sec. 9306(f)(3) of P.L. 100-203 [reproduced below], the effective date for changes made by Sec. 9306(b) of P.L. 100-203, see below.

Prior to amendment, Sec. 9306(f)(3) of P.L. 100-203 read as follows:

"(3) Frequency of waivers.—In applying the second sentence of section 412(d) of the 1986 Code and section 303(a) of ERISA to plans other than multiemployer plans, the number of waivers which may be granted pursuant to applications submitted after December 17, 1987, shall be determined without regard to waivers granted with respect to plan years beginning before January 1, 1988."

—P.L. 101-239, Sec. 7881(d)(1)(A), deleted "for purposes of this section and for purposes of determining current liability," before "the interest rate" in clause (b)(5)(B)(iii), effective for yrs. begin. 12/21/87, except as provided in Sec. 9307(f)(2) of P.L. 100-203, see below.

—P.L. 101-239, Sec. 7881(d)(3), added Sec. 9307(f)(2) [reproduced below] of P.L. 100-203, exceptions to the effective date for amendments made by Sec. 9307 of P.L. 100-203, see below.

In 1988, P.L. 100-647, Sec. 2005(a)(2)(A)(i), substituted "October 29, 1987" for "October 17, 1987" in clause (l)(3)(C)(i)... Sec. 2005(a)(2)(A)(ii), substituted "October 28, 1987" for "October 16, 1987" in clause (l)(3)(C)(iii), effective for plan yrs. begin. after 12/31/88. See Sec. 9303(c)(3) of P.L. 100-203 [reproduced below] for special rule for steel companies.

—P.L. 100-647, Sec. 2005(c)(1)(A), and (B), made the same amendments to clauses (I)(3)(C)(i) and (iii) as Sec. 2005(a)(2)(A)(i) and (ii) of this Act, see above.

In 1987, P.L. 100-203, Sec. 9301(a), amended para. (c)(7), effective for tax. yrs. begin. after 12/31/87. Sec. 9301(c)(2) of the Act provides:

"(2) Regulations.— The Secretary of the Treasury or his delegate shall prescribe such regulations as are necessary to carry out the amendments made by this section no later than August 15, 1988."

Prior to amendment, para. (c)(7) read as follows:

"(7) Full funding limitation. For purposes of paragraph (6), the term 'full funding limitation' means the excess (if any) of—

"(A) the accrued liability (including normal cost) under the plan (determined under the entry age normal funding method if such accrued liability cannot be directly calculated under the funding method used for the plan), over

"(B) the lesser of the fair market value of the plan's assets or the value of such assets determined under paragraph (2)."

—P.L. 100-203, Sec. 9303(a)(1), added subsec. (l)... Sec. 9303(a)(2), added the last sentence to para. (b)(2), effective for plan yrs. begin. after 12/31/88. Sec. 9303(e)(3) of this Act [as amended by Sec. 7881(a)(7) of P.L. 101-239, see above] provides:

"(3) Special rule for steel companies.—

"(A) In general.— For any plan year beginning before January 1, 1994, any increase in the funding standard account under section 412(l) of the 1986 Code or section 302(d) of ERISA (as added by this section) with respect to any steel employee plan shall not exceed the sum of—

"(i) the required percentage of the current liability under such plan, plus

"(ii) the amount determined under subparagraph (C)(i) for such plan year.

"(B) Required percentage.— For purposes of subparagraph (A), the term 'required percentage' means, with respect to any plan year, the excess (if any) of—

"(i) the sum of—

"(I) the funded current liability percentage as of the beginning of the 1st plan year beginning after December 31, 1988 (determined without regard to any plan amendment adopted after June 30, 1987), plus

"(II) 1 percentage point for the plan year for which the determination under this paragraph is being made and for each prior plan year beginning after December 31, 1988, over

"(ii) the funded current liability percentage as of the beginning of the plan year for which such determination is being made.

"(C) Special rules for contingent events.— In the case of any unpredictable contingent event benefit with respect to which the event on which such benefits are contingent occurs after December 17, 1987—

"(i) Amortization amount.— For purposes of subparagraph (A)(ii), the amount determined under this clause for any plan year is the amount which would be determined if the unpredictable contingent event benefit liability were amortized in equal annual installments over 10 plan years (beginning with the plan year in which such event occurs).

"(ii) Benefit and contributions not taken into account.— For purposes of subparagraph (B), in determining the funded current liability percentage for any plan year, there shall not be taken into account—

"(I) the unpredictable contingent event benefit liability, or

"(II) any amount contributed to the plan which is attributable to clause (i) (and any income allocable to such amount).

"(D) Steel employee plan.— For purposes of this paragraph, the term 'steel employee plan' means any plan if—

"(i) such plan is maintained by a steel company, and

"(ii) substantially all of the employees covered by such plan are employees of such company.

"(E) Other definitions.— For purposes of this paragraph—

"(i) Steel company.— The term 'steel company' means any corporation described in section 806(b) of the Steel Import Stabilization Act.

"(ii) Other definitions.— The terms 'current liability', 'funded current liability percentage', and 'unpredictable contingent event benefit' have the meanings given such terms by section 412(l) of the 1986 Code (as added by this section).

"(F) Special rule.— The provisions of this paragraph shall apply in the case of a company which was originally incorporated on April 25, 1927, in Michigan and reincorporated on June 3, 1968, in Delaware in the same manner as if such company were a steel company."

—P.L. 100-203, Sec. 9303(c), of this Act provides:

"(c) Revision of valuation regulations. Effective with respect to plan years beginning after December 31, 1987, the provisions of the regulations prescribed under section 412(c)(2) of the 1986 Code which permit asset valuations to be based on a range between 85 percent and 115 percent of average value shall have no force and effect with respect to plans other than multiemployer plans (as defined in section 414(f) of the 1986 Code). The Secretary of the Treasury or his delegate shall amend such regulations to carry out the purposes of the preceding sentence."

—P.L. 100-203, Sec. 9303(d)(1), added the last sentence to subpara. (c)(2)(B), effective for yrs. begin. after 12/31/87.

—P.L. 100-203, Sec. 9304(a)(1), amended para. (c)(10), effective for plan yrs. begin. after 12/31/87.

Prior to amendment, para. (c)(10) read as follows:

"(10) Time when certain contributions deemed made. For purposes of this section, any contributions for a plan year made by an employer after the last day of such plan year, but not later than two and one-half months after such day, shall be deemed to have been made on such last day. For purposes of this paragraph, such two and one-half month period may be extended for not more than six months under regulations prescribed by the Secretary."

—P.L. 100-203, Sec. 9304(b)(1), added subsec. (m), effective for plan yrs. begin. after 1988.

—P.L. 100-203, Sec. 9304(e)(1), added subsec. (n) [sic (l)]... Sec. 9305(b)(1), added para. (c)(11), effective for plan yrs. begin. after 12/31/87.

—P.L. 100-203, Sec. 9305(b)(1), added para. (c)(11), effective for plan yrs. begin. after 12/31/87.

—P.L. 100-203, Sec. 9306(a)(1)(A), added para. (d)(4), effective for plan yrs. begin. after 12/31/87. Sec. 9306(f)(2)(B) of the Act provides:

"(B) Transitional rule for years beginning in 1988. In the case of any plan year beginning during calendar 1988, section 412(d)(4) of the 1986 Code and section 303(d)(1) of ERISA (as added by subsection (a)(1)) shall be applied by substituting '6th month' for '3rd month'."

—P.L. 100-203, Sec. 9306(a)(1)(B)(i), substituted "temporary substantial business hardship (substantial business hardship in the case of a multiemployer plan)" for "substantial business hardship" in paras. (d)(1) and (d)(2)... Sec. 9306(a)(1)(B)(ii), deleted "substantial" before "business hardship" in the headings of paras. (d)(1) and (d)(2)... Sec. 9306(a)(1)(C), added para. (d)(5), effective for any application submitted after 12/17/87, and any waiver granted pursuant to such an application.

—P.L. 100-203, Sec. 9306(b)(1), substituted "more than 3 of any 15 (5 of any 15 in the case of a multiemployer plan)" for "more than 5 of any 15" in para. (d)(1), effective as provided in Sec. 9306(f)(3) of this Act [as amended by Sec. 7881(c)(3) of P.L. 101-239, see above] which reads as follows:

"(3) Subsection (b). The amendments made by subsection (b) [Sec. 9306(b)] shall apply to waivers for plan years beginning after December 31, 1987. For purposes of applying such amendments, the number of waivers which may be granted for plan years after December 31, 1987, shall be determined without regard to any waivers granted for plan years beginning before January 1, 1988."

—P.L. 100-203, Sec. 9306(c)(1)(A), amended the last sentence of para. (d)(1)... Sec. 9306(c)(1)(B), amended the last sentence of subsec. (e), effective for any application submitted after 12/17/87, and any waiver granted pursuant to such an application.

Prior to amendment, the last sentence of para. (d)(1) read as follows:

"The Secretary shall not waive the minimum funding standard with respect to a plan for more than 5 of any 15 consecutive plan years."

Prior to amendment, the last sentence of subsec. (e) read as follows:

"The interest rate applicable under any arrangement entered into by the Secretary in connection with an extension granted under this subsection shall be the rate determined under section 6621(b)."

—P.L. 100-203, Sec. 9306(d)(1), substituted "plan, and each participant, beneficiary, and alternate payee (within the meaning of section 414(p)(8)). Such notice shall include a description of the extent to which the plan is funded for benefits which are guaranteed under title IV of such Act and the benefit liabilities." for "plan." in subpara. (f)(4)(A), effective for applications submitted after 3/21/88.

—P.L. 100-203, Sec. 9306(e)(1), substituted "$1,000,000" for "$2,000,000" in clause (f)(3)(C)(i), effective for any application submitted after 12/17/87, and any waiver granted pursuant to such an application.

—P.L. 100-203, Sec. 9307(a)(1)(A), substituted "5 plan years (15 plan years in the case of a multiemployer plan)" for "15 plan years" in clause (b)(2)(B)(iv), subpara. (b)(2)(C) and clause (b)(3)(B)(ii)... Sec. 9307(a)(1)(B), substituted "10 plan years (30 plan years in the case of a multiemployer plan)" for "30 plan years" in clause (b)(2)(B)(v) and clause (b)(3)(B)(iii)... Sec. 9307(b)(1), amended para. (c)(3)... Sec. 9307(e)(1), amended para. (b)(5), effective for years begin. after 12/31/87, except as provided in Sec. 9307(f)(2) of this Act [as added by Sec. 7881(d)(3) of P.L. 101-239, see above] which reads as follows:

"(2) Amortization of gains and losses.— Sections 412(B)(2)(B)(iv) and 412(b)(3)(B)(ii) of the Internal Revenue Code of 1986 and sections 302(b)(2)(B)(iv) and 302(b)(3)(B)(ii) of the Employee Retirement Income Security Act of 1974 (as amended by paragraphs (1)(A) and (2)(A) of subsection (a)) shall apply to gains and losses established in years beginning after December 31, 1987. For purposes of the preceding sentence, any gain or loss determined by a valuation occurring as of January 1, 1988, shall be treated as established in years beginning before 1988, or at the election of the employer, shall be amortized in accordance with Internal Revenue Service Notice 89-52."

Prior to amendment, para. (c)(3) read as follows:

"(3) Actuarial assumptions must be reasonable. For purposes of this section, all costs, liabilities, rates of interest, and other factors under the plan shall be determined on the basis of actuarial assumptions and methods which, in the aggregate, are reasonable (taking into account the experience of the plan and reasonable expectations) and which, in combination, offer the actuary's best estimate of anticipated experience under the plan."

Prior to amendment, para. (b)(5) read as follows:

"(5) Interest. The funding standard account (and items therein) shall be charged or credited (as determined under regulations prescribed by the Secretary) with interest at the appropriate rate consistent with the rate or rates of interest used under the plan to determine costs."

In 1986, P.L. 99-272, Sec. 11015(a)(2)(A), added para. (f)(3) ... Sec. 11015(a)(2)(B), substituted "(f) Requirements relating to waivers and extensions." for "(f) Benefits may not be increased during waiver or extension period." in the heading of subsec. (f), and substituted "(1) Benefits may not be increased during waiver or extension period." for "(1) In general." in the heading of para. (f)(1), effective for applications for waivers, extensions, and modifications filed on or after 4/7/86 [date of enactment].

—P.L. 99-272, Sec. 11015(b)(2)(A), added the last sentence to para. (d)(1) ... Sec. 11015(b)(2)(B), added the last sentence to subsec. (e), effective 1/1/86.

—P.L. 99-272, Sec. 11016(c)(4), added para. (f)(4), effective 1/1/86.

In 1984, P.L. 98-369, Sec. 491(d)(25), deleted "or 405(a)" after "section 403(a)" in para. (a)(2), effective for obligations issued after 12/31/83.

In 1980, P.L. 96-364, Sec. 203(1), deleted "(40 plan years in the case of a multiemployer plan)" and "(20 plan years in the case of a multiemployer plan)" each place it appeared in subsec. (b) ... Sec. 203(2), added paras. (b)(6) and (b)(7) ... Sec. 203(3), added subsecs. (j) and (k), effective 9/26/80.

—P.L. 96-364, Sec. 208(c), added the last sentence to subsec. (a), effective 9/26/80.

In 1976, P.L. 94-455, Sec. 1901(a)(63), substituted "September 1, 1974" for "the day before the date of the enactment of the Employee Retirement Income Security Act of 1974" in subsec. (h), and substituted "September 2, 1974" for "the date of the enactment of the Employee Retirement Income Security Act of 1974" in para. (h)(5), effective for tax. yrs. begin. after 12/31/76.

—P.L. 94-455, Sec. 1906(b)(13)(A), substituted "Secretary" for "Secretary or his delegate" each place it appeared in Code Sec. 412, effective for tax. yrs. begin. after 12/31/76.

In 1974, P.L. 93-406, Sec. 1013(a), added Code Sec. 412, effective 9/2/74 or other date as specified in Sec. 1017 of the Act (reproduced following Code Sec. 401).

"Sec. 1013(d) of the Employee Retirement Income Security Act of 1974 provides as follows:

"(d) Alternative Amortization Method for Certain Multiemployer Plans.

"(1) General rule.—In the case of any multiemployer plan (as defined in section 414(f) of the Internal Revenue Code of 1954) to which section 412 of such Code applies, if—

"(A) on January 1, 1974, the contributions under the plan were based on a percentage of pay,

"(B) the actuarial assumptions with respect to pay are reasonably related to past and projected experience, and

"(C) the rates of interest under the plan are determined on the basis of reasonable actuarial assumptions,

the plan may elect (in such manner and at such time as may be provided under regulations prescribed by the Secretary of the Treasury or his delegate) to fund the unfunded past service liability under the plan existing as of the date 12 months following the first date on which such section 412 first applies to the plan by charging the funding standard account with an equal annual percentage of the aggregate pay of all participants in the plan in lieu of the level dollar charges to such account required under clauses (i), (ii), and (iii) of section 412(b)(2)(B) of such Code and section 302(b)(2)(B)(i), (ii), and (iii) of this Act.

"(2) Limitation. In the case of a plan which makes an election under paragraph (1), the aggregate of the charges required under such paragraph for a plan year shall not be less than the interest on the unfunded past service liabilities described in clauses (i), (ii), and (iii) of section 412(b)(2)(B) of the Internal Revenue Code of 1954."

Sec. 413. Collectively bargained plans, etc.
(a) Application of subsection (b).

Subsection (b) applies to—

(1) a plan maintained pursuant to an agreement which the Secretary of Labor finds to be a collective-bargaining agreement between employee representatives and one or more employers, and

(2) each trust which is a part of such plan.

(b) General rule.

If this subsection applies to a plan, notwithstanding any other provision of this title—

(1) **Participation.** Section 410 shall be applied as if all employees of each of the employers who are parties to the collective-bargaining agreement and who are subject to the same benefit computation formula under the plan were employed by a single employer.

(2) **Discrimination, etc.** Sections 401(a)(4) and 411(d)(3) shall be applied as if all participants who are subject to the same benefit computation formula and who are employed by employers who are parties to the collective bargaining agreement were employed by a single employer.

(3) **Exclusive benefit.** For purposes of section 401(a), in determining whether the plan of an employer is for the exclusive benefit of his employees and their beneficiaries, all plan participants shall be considered to be his employees.

(4) **Vesting.** Section 411 (other than subsection (d)(3)) shall be applied as if all employers who have been parties to the collective-bargaining agreement constituted a single employer, except that the application of any rules with respect to breaks in service shall be made under regulations prescribed by the Secretary of Labor.

(5) **Funding.** The minimum funding standard provided by section 412 shall be determined as if all participants in the plan were employed by a single employer.

(6) **Liability for funding tax.** For a plan year the liability under section 4971 of each employer who is a party to the collective bargaining agreement shall be determined in a reasonable manner not inconsistent with regulations prescribed by the Secretary—

(A) first on the basis of their respective delinquencies in meeting required employer contributions under the plan, and

(B) then on the basis of their respective liabilities for contributions under the plan.

For purposes of this subsection and the last sentence of section 4971(a), an employer's withdrawal liability under part 1 of subtitle E of title IV of the Employee Retirement Income Security Act of 1974 shall not be treated as a liability for contributions under the plan.

(7) **Deduction limitations.** Each applicable limitation provided by section 404(a) shall be determined as if all participants in the plan were employed by a single employer. The amounts contributed to or under the plan by each employer who is a party to the agreement, for the portion of his taxable year which is included within such a plan year, shall be considered not to exceed such a limitation if the anticipated employer contributions for such plan year (determined in a manner consistent with the manner in which actual employer contributions for such plan year are determined) do not exceed such limitation. If such anticipated contributions exceed such a limitation, the portion of each such employer's contributions which is not deductible under section 404 shall be determined in accordance with regulations prescribed by the Secretary.

(8) **Employees of labor unions.** For purposes of this subsection, employees of employee representatives shall be treated as employees of an employer described in subsection (a)(1) if such representatives meet the requirements of sections 401(a)(4) and 410 with respect to such employees.

(9) **Plans covering a professional employee.** Notwithstanding subsection (a), in the case of a plan (and trust forming part thereof) which covers any professional employee, paragraph (1) shall be applied by substituting "section 410(a)" for "section 410", and paragraph (2) shall not apply.

(c) Plans maintained by more than one employer.

In the case of a plan maintained by more than one employer—

(1) **Participation.** Section 410(a) shall be applied as if all employees of each of the employers who maintain the plan were employed by a single employer.

(2) **Exclusive benefit.** For purposes of section 401(a), in determining whether the plan of an employer is for the exclusive benefit of his employees and their beneficiaries all plan participants shall be considered to be his employees.

(3) **Vesting.** Section 411 shall be applied as if all employers who maintain the plan constituted a single employer, except that the application of any rules with respect to

breaks in service shall be made under regulations prescribed by the Secretary of Labor.

(4) Funding.

(A) In general. In the case of a plan established after December 31, 1988, each employer shall be treated as maintaining a separate plan for purposes of section 412 unless such plan uses a method for determining required contributions which provides that any employer contributes not less than the amount which would be required if such employer maintained a separate plan.

(B) Other plans. In the case of a plan not described in subparagraph (A), the requirements of section 412 shall be determined as if all participants in the plan were employed by a single employer unless the plan administrator elects not later than the close of the first plan year of the plan beginning after the date of enactment of the Technical and Miscellaneous Revenue Act of 1988 to have the provisions of subparagraph (A) apply. An election under the preceding sentence shall take effect for the plan year in which made and, once made, may be revoked only with the consent of the Secretary.

(5) Liability for funding tax. For a plan year the liability under section 4971 of each employer who maintains the plan shall be determined in a reasonable manner not inconsistent with regulations prescribed by the Secretary—

(A) first on the basis of their respective delinquencies in meeting required employer contributions under the plan, and

(B) then on the basis of their respective liabilities for contributions under the plan.

(6) Deduction limitations.

(A) In general. In the case of a plan established after December 31, 1988, each applicable limitation provided by section 404(a) shall be determined as if each employer were maintaining a separate plan.

(B) Other plans.

(i) In general. In the case of a plan not described in subparagraph (A), each applicable limitation provided by section 404(a) shall be determined as if all participants in the plan were employed by a single employer, except that if an election is made under paragraph (4)(B), subparagraph (A) shall apply to such plan.

(ii) Special rule. If this subparagraph applies, the amounts contributed to or under the plan by each employer who maintains the plan (for the portion of the taxable year included within a plan year) shall be considered not to exceed any such limitation if the anticipated employer contributions for such plan year (determined in a reasonable manner not inconsistent with regulations prescribed by the Secretary) do not exceed such limitation. If such anticipated contributions exceed such a limitation, the portion of each such employer's contributions which is not deductible under section 404 shall be determined in accordance with regulations prescribed by the Secretary.

(7) Allocations.

(A) In general. Except as provided in subparagraph (B), allocations of amounts under paragraphs (4), (5), and (6) among the employers maintaining the plan shall not be inconsistent with regulations prescribed for this purpose by the Secretary.

(B) Assets and liabilities of plan. For purposes of applying paragraphs (4)(A) and (6)(A), the assets and liabilities of each plan shall be treated as the assets and liabilities which would be allocated to a plan maintained by the employer if the employer withdrew from the multiple employer plan.

In **1996**, P.L. 104-188, Sec. 1704(k), of this Act provides:

"(k) Treatment of qualified football coaches plan.

"(1) In general. For purposes of the Internal Revenue Code of 1986, a qualified football coaches plan—

"(A) shall be treated as a multiemployer collectively bargained plan, and

"(B) notwithstanding section 401(k)(4)(B) of such Code, may include a qualified cash and deferred arrangement under section 401(k) of such Code.

"(2) Qualified football coaches plan. For purposes of this subsection, the term 'qualified football coaches plan' means any defined contribution plan which is established and maintained by an organization—

"(A) which is described in section 501(c) of such Code,

"(B) the membership of which consists entirely of individuals who primarily coach football as full-time employees of 4-year colleges or universities described in section 170(b)(1)(A)(ii) of such Code, and

"(C) which was in existence on September 18, 1986.

"(3) Effective date. This subsection shall apply to years beginning after December 22, 1987."

In **1990**, P.L. 101-508, Sec. 11704(a)(4), substituted "Assets" for "Asset" in the heading of subpara. (c)(7)(B), effective 11/5/90.

In **1988**, P.L. 100-647, Sec. 1011(h)(10), added para. (b)(9), effective for plan yrs. begin. after 12/31/88 except as provided by Sec. 1112(e)(2) of P.L. 99-514, reproduced in the notes following Code Sec. 410.

—P.L. 100-647, Sec. 6058(a), amended para. (c)(4)... Sec. 6058(b), amended para. (c)(6)... Sec. 6058(c), deleted the last sentence of subsec. (c) and added para. (c)(7), effective for plan yrs. begin. after 11/5/90.

Prior to amendment, para. (c)(4) read as follows:

"(4) Funding. The minimum funding standard provided by section 412 shall be determined as if all participants in the plan were employed by a single employer."

Prior to amendment, para. (c)(6) read as follows:

"(6) Deduction limitations. Each applicable limitation provided by section 404(a) shall be determined as if all participants in the plan were employed by a single employer. The amounts contributed to or under the plan by each employer who maintains the plan, for the portion of this taxable year which is included within such a plan year, shall be considered not to exceed such a limitation if the anticipated employer contributions for such plan year (determined in a reasonable manner not inconsistent with regulations prescribed by the Secretary) do not exceed such limitation. If such anticipated contributions exceed such a limitation, the portion of each such employer's contributions which is not deductible under section 404 shall be determined in accordance with regulations prescribed by the Secretary."

Prior to deletion, the last sentence of subsec. (c) read as follows:

"Allocations of amounts under paragraphs (4), (5), and (6), among the employers maintaining the plan, shall not be inconsistent with regulations prescribed for this purpose by the Secretary."

In **1980**, P.L. 96-364, Sec. 208(d), added the sentence at the end of para. (b)(6), effective 9/26/80.

In **1976**, P.L. 94-455, Sec. 1906(b)(13)(A), substituted "Secretary" for "Secretary or his delegate" each place it appeared in subsecs. (b) and (c), effective for tax. yrs. begin. after 12/31/76.

In **1974**, P.L. 93-406, Sec. 1014, added Code Sec. 413, effective for plan yrs. begin. after '53 subject to special rules in Sec. 1017 of the Act (reproduced following Code Sec. 401).

Sec. 414. Definitions and special rules.

(a) Service for predecessor employer.

For purposes of this part—

(1) in any case in which the employer maintains a plan of a predecessor employer, service for such predecessor shall be treated as service for the employer, and

(2) in any case in which the employer maintains a plan which is not the plan maintained by a predecessor employer, service for such predecessor shall, to the extent provided in regulations prescribed by the Secretary, be treated as service for the employer.

(b) Employees of controlled group of corporations.

For purposes of sections 401, 408(k), 408(p), 410, 411, 415, and 416, all employees of all corporations which are members of a controlled group of corporations (within the meaning of section 1563(a), determined without regard to section 1563(a)(4) and (e)(3)(C)) shall be treated as employed by a single employer. With respect to a plan adopted by more than one such corporation, the applicable limitations provided by section 404(a) shall be determined as if all such employers were a single employer, and allocated to each employer in accordance with regulations prescribed by the Secretary.

(c) Employees of partnerships, proprietorships, etc., which are under common control.

For purposes of sections 401, 408(k), 408(p), 410, 411, 415, and 416, under regulations prescribed by the Secretary, all employees of trades or businesses (whether or not incorporated) which are under common control shall be treated as employed by a single employer. The regulations prescribed under this subsection shall be based on principles similar to the principles which apply in the case of subsection (b).

(d) Governmental plan.

For purposes of this part, the term "governmental plan" means a plan established and maintained for its employees by the Government of the United States, by the government of any State or political subdivision thereof, or by any agency or instrumentality of any of the foregoing. The term "governmental plan" also includes any plan to which the Railroad Retirement Act of 1935 or 1937 applies and which is financed by contributions required under that Act and any plan of an international organization which is exempt from taxation by reason of the International Organizations Immunities Act (59 Stat. 669). The term "governmental plan" includes a plan which is established and maintained by an Indian tribal government (as defined in section 7701(a)(40)), a subdivision of an Indian tribal government (determined in accordance with section 7871(d)), or an agency or instrumentality of either, and all of the participants of which are employees of such entity substantially all of whose services as such an employee are in the performance of essential governmental functions but not in the performance of commercial activities (whether or not an essential government function).

(e) Church plan.

(1) In general. For purposes of this part, the term "church plan" means a plan established and maintained (to the extent required in paragraph (2)(B)) for its employees (or their beneficiaries) by a church or by a convention or association of churches which is exempt from tax under section 501.

(2) Certain plans excluded. The term "church plan" does not include a plan—

(A) which is established and maintained primarily for the benefit of employees (or their beneficiaries) of such church or convention or association of churches who are employed in connection with one or more unrelated trades or businesses (within the meaning of section 513); or

(B) if less than substantially all of the individuals included in the plan are individuals described in paragraph (1) or (3)(B) (or their beneficiaries).

(3) Definitions and other provisions. For purposes of this subsection—

(A) Treatment as church plan. A plan established and maintained for its employees (or their beneficiaries) by a church or by a convention or association of churches includes a plan maintained by an organization, whether a civil law corporation or otherwise, the principal purpose or function of which is the administration or funding of a plan or program for the provision of retirement benefits or welfare benefits, or both, for the employees of a church or a convention or association of churches, if such organization is controlled by or associated with a church or a convention or association of churches.

(B) Employee defined. The term employee of a church or a convention or association of churches shall include—

(i) a duly ordained, commissioned, or licensed minister of a church in the exercise of his ministry, regardless of the source of his compensation;

(ii) an employee of an organization, whether a civil law corporation or otherwise, which is exempt from tax under section 501 and which is controlled by or associated with a church or a convention or association of churches; and

(iii) an individual described in subparagraph (E).

(C) Church treated as employer. A church or a convention or association of churches which is exempt from tax under section 501 shall be deemed the employer of any individual included as an employee under subparagraph (B).

(D) Association with church. An organization, whether a civil law corporation or otherwise, is associated with a church or a convention or association of churches if it shares common religious bonds and convictions with that church or convention or association of churches.

(E) Special rule in case of separation from plan. If an employee who is included in a church plan separates from the service of a church or a convention or association of churches or an organization described in clause (ii) of paragraph (3)(B), the church plan shall not fail to meet the requirements of this subsection merely because the plan—

(i) retains the employee's accrued benefit or account for the payment of benefits to the employee or his beneficiaries pursuant to the terms of the plan; or

(ii) receives contributions on the employee's behalf after the employee's separation from such service, but only for a period of 5 years after such separation, unless the employee is disabled (within the meaning of the disability provisions of the church plan or, if there are no such provisions in the church plan, within the meaning of section 72(m)(7)) at the time of such separation from service.

(4) Correction of failure to meet church plan requirements.

(A) In general. If a plan established and maintained for its employees (or their beneficiaries) by a church or by a convention or association of churches which is exempt from tax under section 501 fails to meet one or more of the requirements of this subsection and corrects its failure to meet such requirements within the correction period, the plan shall be deemed to meet the requirements of this subsection for the year in which the correction was made and for all prior years.

(B) Failure to correct. If a correction is not made within the correction period, the plan shall be deemed not to meet the requirements of this subsection beginning with the date on which the earliest failure to meet one or more of such requirements occurred.

(C) Correction period defined. The term "correction period" means—

(i) the period ending 270 days after the date of mailing by the Secretary of a notice of default with respect to the plan's failure to meet one or more of the requirements of this subsection;

(ii) any period set by a court of competent jurisdiction after a final determination that the plan fails to meet such requirements, or, if the court does not specify such period, any reasonable period determined by the Secretary on the basis of all the facts and circumstances, but in any event not less than 270 days after the determination has become final; or

(iii) any additional period which the Secretary determines is reasonable or necessary for the correction of the default,

whichever has the latest ending date.

(5) Special rules for chaplains and self-employed ministers.

(A) Certain ministers may participate. For purposes of this part—

(i) In general. A duly ordained, commissioned, or licensed minister of a church is described in paragraph (3)(B) if, in connection with the exercise of their ministry, the minister—

(I) is a self-employed individual (within the meaning of section 401(c)(1)(B), or

(II) is employed by an organization other than an organization which is described in section 501(c)(3) and with respect to which the minister shares common religious bonds.

(ii) Treatment as employer and employee. For purposes of sections 403(b)(1)(A) and 404(a)(10), a minister described in clause (i)(I) shall be treated as employed by the minister's own employer which is an organization described in section 501(c)(3) and exempt from tax under section 501(a).

(B) Special rules for applying section 403(b) to self-employed ministers. In the case of a minister described in subparagraph (A)(i)(I)—

(i) the minister's includible compensation under section 403(b)(3) shall be determined by reference to the minister's earned income (within the meaning of section 401(c)(2)) from such ministry rather than the amount of compensation which is received from an employer, and

(ii) the years (and portions of years) in which such minister was a self-employed individual (within the meaning of section 401(c)(1)(B)) with respect to such ministry shall be included for purposes of section 403(b)(4).

(C) Effect on non-denominational plans. If a duly ordained, commissioned, or licensed minister of a church in the exercise of his or her ministry participates in a church plan (within the meaning of this section) and in the exercise of such ministry is employed by an employer not otherwise participating in such church plan, then such employer may exclude such minister from being treated as an employee of such employer for purposes of applying sections 401(a)(3), 401(a)(4), and 401(a)(5), as in effect on September 1, 1974, and sections 401(a)(4), 401(a)(5), 401(a)(26), 401(k)(3), 401(m), 403(b)(1)(D) (including section 403(b)(12)), and 410 to any stock bonus, pension, profit-sharing, or annuity plan (including an annuity described in section 403(b) or a retirement income account described in section 403(b)(9)). The Secretary shall prescribe such regulations as may be necessary or appropriate to carry out the purpose of, and prevent the abuse of, this subparagraph.

(D) Compensation taken into account only once. If any compensation is taken into account in determining the amount of any contributions made to, or benefits to be provided under, any church plan, such compensation shall not also be taken into account in determining the amount of any contributions made to, or benefits to be provided under, any other stock bonus, pension, profit-sharing, or annuity plan which is not a church plan.

(E) Exclusion. In the case of a contribution to a church plan made on behalf of a minister described in subparagraph (A)(i)(II), such contribution shall not be included in the gross income of the minister to the extent that such contribution would not be so included if the minister was an employee of a church.

(f) Multiemployer plan.

(1) Definition. For purposes of this part, the term "multiemployer plan" means a plan—

(A) to which more than one employer is required to contribute,

(B) which is maintained pursuant to one or more collective bargaining agreements between one or more employee organizations and more than one employer, and

(C) which satisfies such other requirements as the Secretary of Labor may prescribe by regulation.

(2) Cases of common control. For purposes of this subsection, all trades or businesses (whether or not incorporated) which are under common control within the meaning of subsection (c) are considered a single employer.

(3) Continuation of status after termination. Notwithstanding paragraph (1), a plan is a multiemployer plan on and after its termination date under title IV of the Employee Retirement Income Security Act of 1974 if the plan was a multiemployer plan under this subsection for the plan year preceding its termination date.

(4) Transitional rule. For any plan year which began before the date of the enactment [9/26/80] of the Multiemployer Pension Plan Amendments Act of 1980, the term "multiemployer plan" means a plan described in this subsection as in effect immediately before that date.

(5) Special election. Within one year after the date of the enactment [9/26/80] of the Multiemployer Pension Plan Amendments Act of 1980, a multiemployer plan may irrevocably elect, pursuant to procedures established by the Pension Benefit Guaranty Corporation and subject to the provisions of section 4403(b) and (c) of the Employee Retirement Income Security Act of 1974, that the plan shall not be treated as a multiemployer plan for any purpose under such Act or this title, if for each of the last 3 plan years ending prior to the effective date of the Multiemployer Pension Plan Amendments Act of 1980—

(A) the plan was not a multiemployer plan because the plan was not a plan described in section 3(37)(A)(iii) of the Employee Retirement Income Security Act of 1974 and section 414(f)(1)(C) (as such provisions were in effect on the day before the date of the enactment [9/26/80] of the Multiemployer Pension Plan Amendments Act of 1980); and

(B) the plan had been identified as a plan that was not a multiemployer plan in substantially all its filings with the Pension Benefit Guaranty Corporation, the Secretary of Labor and the Secretary.

(6) Election with regard to multiemployer status.

(A) Within 1 year after the enactment of the Pension Protection Act of 2006—

(i) An election under paragraph (5) may be revoked, pursuant to procedures prescribed by the Pension Benefit Guaranty Corporation, if, for each of the 3 plan years prior to the date of the enactment of that Act, the plan would have been a multiemployer but for the election under paragraph (5), and

(ii) a plan that meets the criteria in subparagraph (A) and (B) of paragraph (1) of this subsection or that is described in subparagraph (E) may, pursuant to procedures prescribed by the Pension Benefit Guaranty Corporation, elect to be a multiemployer plan, if—

(I) for each of the 3 plan years immediately preceding the first plan year for which the election under this paragraph is effective with respect to the plan, the plan has met those criteria or is so described,

(II) substantially all of the plan's employer contributions for each of those plan years were made or required to be made by organizations that were exempt from tax under section 501, and

(III) the plan was established prior to September 2, 1974.

(B) An election under this paragraph shall be effective for all purposes under this Act and under the Employee Retirement Income Security Act of 1974, starting with any plan year beginning on or after January 1, 1999, and ending before January 1, 2008, as designated by the plan in the election made under subparagraph (A)(ii).

(C) Once made, an election under this paragraph shall be irrevocable, except that a plan described in subparagraph (A)(ii) shall cease to be a multiemployer plan as of the plan year beginning immediately after the first plan year for which the majority of its employer contributions were made or required to be made by organizations that were not exempt from tax under section 501.

(D) The fact that a plan makes an election under subparagraph (A)(ii) does not imply that the plan was not a multiemployer plan prior to the date of the election or would not be a multiemployer plan without regard to the election.

(E) A plan is described in this subparagraph if it is a plan sponsored by an organization which is described in section 501(c)(5) and exempt from tax under section 501(a) and which was established in Chicago, Illinois, on August 12, 1881.

(F) Maintenance under collective bargaining agreement. For purposes of this title and the Employee Retirement Income Security Act of 1974, a plan making an election under this paragraph shall be treated as maintained pursuant to a collective bargaining agreement if a collective bargaining agreement, expressly or otherwise, provides for or permits employer contributions to the plan by one or more employers that are signatory to such agreement, or participation in the plan by one or more employees of an employer that is signatory to such agreement, regardless of whether the plan was created, established, or maintained for such employees by virtue of another document that is not a collective bargaining agreement.

(g) Plan administrator.

For purposes of this part, the term "plan administrator" means—

(1) the person specifically so designated by the terms of the instrument under which the plan is operated;

(2) in the absence of a designation referred to in paragraph (1)—

(A) in the case of a plan maintained by a single employer, such employer,

(B) in the case of a plan maintained by two or more employers or jointly by one or more employers and one or more employee organizations, the association, committee, joint board of trustees, or other similar group of representatives of the parties who maintained the plan, or

(C) in any case to which subparagraph (A) or (B) does not apply, such other person as the Secretary may by regulation, prescribe.

(h) Tax treatment of certain contributions.

(1) In general. Effective with respect to taxable years beginning after December 31, 1973, for purposes of this title, any amount contributed—

(A) to an employees' trust described in section 401(a), or

(B) under a plan described in section 403(a), shall not be treated as having been made by the employer if it is designated as an employee contribution.

(2) Designation by units of government. For purposes of paragraph (1), in the case of any plan established by the government of any State or political subdivision thereof, or by any agency or instrumentality of any of the foregoing, or a governmental plan described in the last sentence of section 414(d) (relating to plans of Indian tribal governments), where the contributions of employing units are designated as employee contributions but where any employing unit picks up the contributions, the contributions so picked up shall be treated as employer contributions.

(i) Defined contribution plan.

For purposes of this part, the term "defined contribution plan" means a plan which provides for an individual account for each participant and for benefits based solely on the amount contributed to the participant's account, and any income, expenses, gains and losses, and any forfeitures of accounts of other participants which may be allocated to such participant's account.

(j) Defined benefit plan.

For purposes of this part, the term "defined benefit plan" means any plan which is not a defined contribution plan.

(k) Certain plans.

A defined benefit plan which provides a benefit derived from employer contributions which is based partly on the balance of the separate account of a participant shall—

(1) for purposes of section 410 (relating to minimum participation standards), be treated as a defined contribution plan,

(2) for purposes of sections 72(d) (relating to treatment of employee contributions as separate contract), 411(a)(7)(A) (relating to minimum vesting standards), 415 (relating to limitations on benefits and contributions under qualified plans), and 401(m) (relating to nondiscrimination tests for matching requirements and employee contributions), be treated as consisting of a defined contribution plan to the extent benefits are based on the separate account of a participant and as a defined benefit plan with respect to the remaining portion of benefits under the plan, and

(3) for purposes of section 4975 (relating to tax on prohibited transactions), be treated as a defined benefit plan.

(l) Merger and consolidations of plans or transfers of plan assets.

(1) In general. A trust which forms a part of a plan shall not constitute a qualified trust under section 401 and a plan shall be treated as not described in section 403(a) unless in the case of any merger or consolidation of the plan with, or in the case of any transfer of assets or liabilities of such plan to, any other trust plan after September 2, 1974, each participant in the plan would (if the plan then terminated) receive a benefit immediately after the merger, consolidation, or transfer which is equal to or greater than the benefit he would have been entitled to receive immediately before the merger, consolidation, or transfer (if the plan had then terminated). The preceding sentence does not apply to any multiemployer plan with respect to any transaction to the extent that participants either before or after the transaction are covered under a multiemployer plan to which Title IV of the Employee Retirement Income Security Act of 1974 applies.

(2) Allocation of assets in plan spin-offs, etc.

(A) In general. In the case of a plan spin-off of a defined benefit plan, a trust which forms part of—

(i) the original plan, or

(ii) any plan spun off from such plan,

shall not constitute a qualified trust under this section unless the applicable percentage of excess assets are allocated to each of such plans.

(B) Applicable percentage. For purposes of subparagraph (A), the term "applicable percentage" means, with respect to each of the plans described in clauses (i) and (ii) of subparagraph (A), the percentage determined by dividing—

(i) the excess (if any) of—

(I) the sum of the funding target and target normal cost determined under section 430, over

(II) the amount of the assets required to be allocated to the plan after the spin-off (without regard to this paragraph), by

(ii) the sum of the excess amounts determined separately under clause (i) for all such plans.

(C) Excess assets. For purposes of subparagraph (A), the term "excess assets" means an amount equal to the excess (if any) of—

(i) the fair market value of the assets of the original plan immediately before the spin-off, over

(ii) the amount of assets required to be allocated after the spin-off to all plans (determined without regard to this paragraph).

(D) Certain spun-off plans not taken into account.

(i) In general. A plan involved in a spin-off which is described in clause (ii), (iii), or (iv) shall not be taken into account for purposes of this paragraph, except that the amount determined under subparagraph (C)(ii) shall be increased by the amount of assets allocated to such plan.

(ii) Plans transferred out of controlled groups. A plan is described in this clause if, after such spin-off, such plan is maintained by an employer who is not a member of the same controlled group as the employer maintaining the original plan.

(iii) Plans transferred out of multiple employer plans. A plan as described in this clause if, after the spin-off, any employer maintaining such plan (and any member of the same controlled group as such employer) does not maintain any other plan remaining after the spin-off which is also maintained by another employer (or member of the same controlled group as such other employer) which maintained the plan in existence before the spin-off.

(iv) Terminated plans. A plan is described in this clause if, pursuant to the transaction involving the spin-off, the plan is terminated.

(v) Controlled group. For purposes of this subparagraph, the term "controlled group" means any group treated as a single employer under subsection (b), (c), (m), or (o).

(E) Paragraph not to apply to multiemployer plans. This paragraph does not apply to any multiemployer plan with respect to any spin-off to the extent that participants either before or after the spin-off are covered under a multiemployer plan to which title IV of the Employee Retirement Income Security Act of 1974 applies.

(F) Application to similar transaction. Except as provided by the Secretary, rules similar to the rules of this paragraph shall apply to transactions similar to spin-offs.

(G) Special rules for bridge banks. For purposes of this paragraph, in the case of a bridge depository institution established under section 11(i) of the Federal Deposit Insurance Act (12 U.S.C. 1821(i))—

(i) such bank shall be treated as a member of any controlled group which includes any insured bank (as defined in section 3(h) of such Act (12 U.S.C. 1813(h))—

(I) which maintains a defined benefit plan,

(II) which is closed by the appropriate bank regulatory authorities, and

(III) any asset and liabilities of which are received by the bridge depository institution, and

(ii) the requirements of this paragraph shall not be treated as met with respect to such plan unless during the 180-day period beginning on the date such insured bank is closed—

(I) the bridge depository institution has the right to require the plan to transfer (subject to the provisions of this paragraph) not more than 50 percent of the excess assets (as defined in subparagraph (C)) to a defined benefit plan maintained by the bridge depository institution with respect to participants or former participants (including retirees and beneficiaries) in the original plan employed by the bridge depository institution or formerly employed by the closed bank, and

(II) no other merger, spin-off, termination, or similar transaction involving the portion of the excess assets described in subclause (I) may occur without the prior written consent of the bridge depository institution.

(m) Employees of an affiliated service group.

(1) In general. For purposes of the employee benefit requirements listed in paragraph (4), except to the extent otherwise provided in regulations, all employees of the members of an affiliated service group shall be treated as employed by a single employer.

(2) Affiliated service group. For purposes of this subsection, the term "affiliated service group" means a group consisting of a service organization (hereinafter in this paragraph referred to as the "first organization") and one or more of the following:

(A) any service organization which—

(i) is a shareholder or partner in the first organization, and

(ii) regularly performs services for the first organization or is regularly associated with the first organization in performing services for third persons, and

(B) any other organization if—

(i) a significant portion of the business of such organization is the performance of services (for the first organization, for organizations described in subparagraph (A), or for both) of a type historically performed in such service field by employees, and

(ii) 10 percent or more of the interests in such organization is held by persons who are highly compensated employees (within the meaning of section 414(q)) of the first organization or an organization described in subparagraph (A).

(3) Service organizations. For purposes of this subsection, the term "service organization" means an organiza-

Employee benefit plans — Code Sec. 414(n)(5)(C)(iii)(III)

tion the principal business of which is the performance of services.

(4) Employee benefit requirements. For purposes of this subsection, the employee benefit requirements listed in this paragraph are—

(A) paragraphs (3), (4), (7), (16), (17), and (26) of section 401(a), and

(B) sections 408(k), 408(p), 410, 411, 415, and 416.

(5) Certain organizations performing management functions. For purposes of this subsection, the term "affiliated service group" also includes a group consisting of—

(A) an organization the principal business of which is performing, on a regular and continuing basis, management functions for 1 organization (or for 1 organization and other organizations related to such 1 organization), and

(B) the organization (and related organizations) for which such functions are so performed by the organization described in subparagraph (A).

For purposes of this paragraph, the term "related organizations" has the same meaning as the term "related persons" when used in section 144(a)(3).

(6) Other definitions. For purposes of this subsection—

(A) Organization defined. The term "organization" means a corporation, partnership, or other organization.

(B) Ownership. In determining ownership, the principles of section 318(a) shall apply.

(n) Employee leasing.

(1) In general. For purposes of the requirements listed in paragraph (3), with respect to any person (hereinafter in this subsection referred to as the "recipient") for whom a leased employee performs services—

(A) the leased employee shall be treated as an employee of the recipient, but

(B) contributions or benefits provided by the leasing organization which are attributable to services performed for the recipient shall be treated as provided by the recipient.

(2) Leased employee. For purposes of paragraph (1), the term "leased employee" means any person who is not an employee of the recipient and who provides services to the recipient if—

(A) such services are provided pursuant to an agreement between the recipient and any other person (in this subsection referred to as the "leasing organization"),

(B) such person has performed such services for the recipient (or for the recipient and related persons) on a substantially full-time basis for a period of at least 1 year, and

(C) such services are performed under primary direction or control by the recipient.

(3) Requirements. For purposes of this subsection, the requirements listed in this paragraph are—

(A) paragraphs (3), (4), (7), (16), (17), and (26) of section 401(a),

(B) sections 408(k), 408(p), 410, 411, 415, and 416, and

(C) sections 79, 106, 117(d), 120, 125, 127, 129, 132, 137, 274(j), 505, and 4980B.

(4) Time when first considered as employee.

(A) In general. In the case of any leased employee, paragraph (1) shall apply only for purposes of determining whether the requirements listed in paragraph (3) are met for periods after the close of the period referred to in paragraph (2)(B).

(B) Years of service. In the case of a person who is an employee of the recipient (whether by reason of this subsection or otherwise), for purposes of the requirements listed in paragraph (3), years of service for the recipient shall be determined by taking into account any period for which such employee would have been a leased employee but for the requirements of paragraph (2)(B).

(5) Safe harbor.

(A) In general. In the case of requirements described in subparagraphs (A) and (B) of paragraph (3), this subsection shall not apply to any leased employee with respect to services performed for a recipient if—

(i) such employee is covered by a plan which is maintained by the leasing organization and meets the requirements of subparagraph (B), and

(ii) leased employees (determined without regard to this paragraph) do not constitute more than 20 percent of the recipient's nonhighly compensated work force.

(B) Plan requirements. A plan meets the requirements of this subparagraph if—

(i) such plan is a money purchase pension plan with a nonintegrated employer contribution rate for each participant of at least 10 percent of compensation,

(ii) such plan provides for full and immediate vesting, and

(iii) each employee of the leasing organization (other than employees who perform substantially all of their services for the leasing organization) immediately participates in such plan.

Clause (iii) shall not apply to any individual whose compensation from the leasing organization in each plan year during the 4-year period ending with the plan year is less than $1,000.

(C) Definitions. For purposes of this paragraph—

(i) Highly compensated employee. The term "highly compensated employee" has the meaning given such term by section 414(q).

(ii) Nonhighly compensated work force. The term "nonhighly compensated work force" means the aggregate number of individuals (other than highly compensated employees)—

(I) who are employees of the recipient (without regard to this subsection) and have performed services for the recipient (or for the recipient and related persons) on a substantially full-time basis for a period of at least 1 year, or

(II) who are leased employees with respect to the recipient (determined without regard to this paragraph).

(iii) Compensation. The term "compensation" has the same meaning as when used in section 415; except that such term shall include—

(I) any employer contribution under a qualified cash or deferred arrangement to the extent not included in gross income under section 402(e)(3) or 402(h)(1)(B),

(II) any amount which the employee would have received in cash but for an election under a cafeteria plan (within the meaning of section 125), and

(III) any amount contributed to an annuity contract described in section 403(b) pursuant to a salary reduction agreement (within the meaning of section 3121(a)(5)(D)).

(6) Other rules. For purposes of this subsection—
  (A) Related persons. The term "related persons" has the same meaning as when used in section 144(a)(3).
  (B) Employees of entities under common control. The rules of subsections (b), (c), (m), and (o) shall apply.

(o) Regulations.
The Secretary shall prescribe such regulations (which may provide rules in addition to the rules contained in subsections (m) and (n)) as may be necessary to prevent the avoidance of any employee benefit requirement listed in subsection (m)(4) or (n)(3) or any requirement under section 457 through the use of—
  (1) separate organizations,
  (2) employee leasing, or
  (3) other arrangements.
The regulations prescribed under subsection (n) shall include provisions to minimize the recordkeeping requirements of subsection (n) in the case of an employer which has no top-heavy plans (within the meaning of section 416(g)) and which uses the services of persons (other than employees) for an insignificant percentage of the employer's total workload.

(p) Qualified domestic relations order defined.
For purposes of this subsection and section 401(a)(13)—
  (1) In general.
    (A) Qualified domestic relations order. The term "qualified domestic relations order" means a domestic relations order—
      (i) which creates or recognizes the existence of an alternate payee's right to, or assigns to an alternate payee the right to, receive all or a portion of the benefits payable with respect to a participant under a plan, and
      (ii) with respect to which the requirements of paragraphs (2) and (3) are met.
    (B) Domestic relations order. The term "domestic relations order" means any judgment, decree, or order (including approval of a property settlement agreement) which—
      (i) relates to the provision of child support, alimony payments, or marital property rights to a spouse, former spouse, child, or other dependent of a participant, and
      (ii) is made pursuant to a State domestic relations law (including a community property law).
  (2) Order must clearly specify certain facts. A domestic relations order meets the requirements of this paragraph only if such order clearly specifies—
    (A) the name and the last known mailing address (if any) of the participant and the name and mailing address of each alternate payee covered by the order,
    (B) the amount or percentage of the participant's benefits to be paid by the plan to each such alternate payee, or the manner in which such amount or percentage is to be determined,
    (C) the number of payments or period to which such order applies, and
    (D) each plan to which such order applies.
  (3) Order may not alter amount, form, etc., of benefits. A domestic relations order meets the requirements of this paragraph only if such order—
    (A) does not require a plan to provide any type or form of benefit, or any option, not otherwise provided under the plan,
    (B) does not require the plan to provide increased benefits (determined on the basis of actuarial value), and
    (C) does not require the payment of benefits to an alternate payee which are required to be paid to another alternate payee under another order previously determined to be a qualified domestic relations order.
  (4) Exception for certain payments made after earliest retirement age.
    (A) In general. A domestic relations order shall not be treated as failing to meet the requirements of subparagraph (A) of paragraph (3) solely because such order requires that payment of benefits be made to an alternate payee—
      (i) in the case of any payment before a participant has separated from service, on or after the date on which the participant attains (or would have attained) the earliest retirement age,
      (ii) as if the participant had retired on the date on which such payment is to begin under such order (but taking into account only the present value of the benefits actually accrued and not taking into account the present value of any employer subsidy for early retirement), and
      (iii) in any form in which such benefits may be paid under the plan to the participant (other than in the form of a joint and survivor annuity with respect to the alternate payee and his or her subsequent spouse).
    For purposes of clause (ii), the interest rate assumption used in determining the present value shall be the interest rate specified in the plan or, if no rate is specified, 5 percent.
    (B) Earliest retirement age. For purposes of this paragraph, the term "earliest retirement age" means the earlier of—
      (i) the date on which the participant is entitled to a distribution under the plan, or
      (ii) the later of—
        (I) the date the participant attains age 50, or
        (II) the earliest date on which the participant could begin receiving benefits under the plan if the participant separated from service.
  (5) Treatment of former spouse as surviving spouse for purposes of determining survivor benefits. To the extent provided in any qualified domestic relations order—
    (A) the former spouse of a participant shall be treated as a surviving spouse of such participant for purposes of sections 401(a)(11) and 417 (and any spouse of the participant shall not be treated as a spouse of the participant for such purposes), and
    (B) if married for at least 1 year, the surviving former spouse shall be treated as meeting the requirements of section 417(d).
  (6) Plan procedures with respect to orders.
    (A) Notice and determination by administrator. In the case of any domestic relations order received by a plan—
      (i) the plan administrator shall promptly notify the participant and each alternate payee of the receipt of such order and the plan's procedures for determining the qualified status of domestic relations orders, and
      (ii) within a reasonable period after receipt of such order, the plan administrator shall determine whether such order is a qualified domestic relations order and notify the participant and each alternate payee of such determination.
    (B) Plan to establish reasonable procedures. Each plan shall establish reasonable procedures to determine the qualified status of domestic relations orders and to administer distributions under such qualified orders.

(7) Procedures for period during which determination is being made.
(A) In general. During any period in which the issue of whether a domestic relations order is a qualified domestic relations order is being determined (by the plan administrator, by a court of competent jurisdiction, or otherwise), the plan administrator shall separately account for the amounts (hereinafter in this paragraph referred to as the "segregated amounts") which would have been payable to the alternate payee during such period if the order had been determined to be a qualified domestic relations order.
(B) Payment to alternate payee if order determined to be qualified domestic relations order. If within the 18-month period described in subparagraph (E) the order (or modification thereof) is determined to be a qualified domestic relations order, the plan administrator shall pay the segregated amounts (including any interest thereon) to the person or persons entitled thereto.
(C) Payment to plan participant in certain cases. If within the 18-month period described in subparagraph (E)—
  (i) it is determined that the order is not a qualified domestic relations order, or
  (ii) the issue as to whether such order is a qualified domestic relations order is not resolved,
then the plan administrator shall pay the segregated amounts (including any interest thereon) to the person or persons who would have been entitled to such amounts if there had been no order.
(D) Subsequent determination or order to be applied prospectively only. Any determination that an order is a qualified domestic relations order which is made after the close of the 18-month period described in subparagraph (E) shall be applied prospectively only.
(E) Determination of 18-month period. For purposes of this paragraph, the 18-month period described in this subparagraph is the 18-month period beginning with the date on which the first payment would be required to be made under the domestic relations order.

(8) Alternate payee defined. The term "alternate payee" means any spouse, former spouse, child or other dependent of a participant who is recognized by a domestic relations order as having a right to receive all, or a portion of, the benefits payable under a plan with respect to such participant.

(9) Subsection not to apply to plans to which section 401(a)(13) does not apply. This subsection shall not apply to any plan to which section 401(a)(13) does not apply. For purposes of this title, except as provided in regulations, any distribution from an annuity contract under section 403(b) pursuant to a qualified domestic relations order shall be treated in the same manner as a distribution from a plan to which section 401(a)(13) applies.

(10) Waiver of certain distribution requirements. With respect to the requirements of subsections (a) and (k) of section 401, section 403(b), section 409(d), and section 457(d), a plan shall not be treated as failing to meet such requirements solely by reason of payments to an alternative payee pursuant to a qualified domestic relations order.

(11) Application of rules to certain other plans. For purposes of this title, a distribution or payment from a governmental plan (as defined in subsection (d)) or a church plan (as described in subsection (e)) or an eligible deferred compensation plan (within the meaning of section 457(b)) shall be treated as made pursuant to a qualified domestic relations order if it is made pursuant to a domestic relations order which meets the requirement of clause (i) of paragraph (1)(A).

(12) Tax treatment of payments from a section 457 plan. If a distribution or payment from an eligible deferred compensation plan described in section 457(b) is made pursuant to a qualified domestic relations order, rules similar to the rules of section 402(e)(1)(A) shall apply to such distribution or payment.

(13) Consultation with the Secretary. In prescribing regulations under this subsection and section 401(a)(13), the Secretary of Labor shall consult with the Secretary.

(q) Highly compensated employee.
  (1) In general. The term "highly compensated employee" means any employee who—
    (A) was a 5-percent owner at any time during the year or the preceding year, or
    (B) for the preceding year—
      (i) had compensation from the employer in excess of $80,000, and
      (ii) if the employer elects the application of this clause for such preceding year, was in the top-paid group of employees for such preceding year.
  The Secretary shall adjust the $80,000 amount under subparagraph (B) at the same time and in the same manner as under section 415(d), except that the base period shall be the calendar quarter ending September 30, 1996.

  (2) 5-percent owner. An employee shall be treated as a 5-percent owner for any year if at any time during such year such employee was a 5-percent owner (as defined in section 416(i)(1)) of the employer.

  (3) Top-paid group. An employee is in the top-paid group of employees for any year if such employee is in the group consisting of the top 20 percent of the employees when ranked on the basis of compensation paid during such year.

  (4) Compensation. For purposes of this subsection, the term "compensation" has the meaning given such term by section 415(c)(3).

  (5) Excluded employees. For purposes of subsection (r) and for purposes of determining the number of employees in the top-paid group, the following employees shall be excluded—
    (A) employees who have not completed 6 months of service,
    (B) employees who normally work less than 17 ½ hours per week,
    (C) employees who normally work during not more than 6 months during any year,
    (D) employees who have not attained age 21, and
    (E) except to the extent provided in regulations, employees who are included in a unit of employees covered by an agreement which the Secretary of Labor finds to be a collective bargaining agreement between employee representatives and the employer.
  Except as provided by the Secretary, the employer may elect to apply subparagraph (A), (B), (C), or (D) by substituting a shorter period of service, smaller number of hours or months, or lower age for the period of service, number of hours or months, or age (as the case may be) than that specified in such subparagraph.

  (6) Former employees. A former employee shall be treated as a highly compensated employee if—
    (A) such employee was a highly compensated employee when such employee separated from service, or
    (B) such employee was a highly compensated employee at any time after attaining age 55.

(7) Coordination with other provisions. Subsections (b), (c), (m), (n), and (o) shall be applied before the application of this subsection.

(8) Special rule for nonresident aliens. For purposes of this subsection and subsection (r), employees who are nonresident aliens and who receive no earned income (within the meaning of section 911(d)(2)) from the employer which constitutes income from sources within the United States (within the meaning of section 861(a)(3)) shall not be treated as employees.

(9) Certain employees not considered highly compensated and excluded employees under pre-ERISA rules for church plans. In the case of a church plan (as defined in subsection (e)), no employee shall be considered an officer, a person whose principal duties consist of supervising the work of other employees, or a highly compensated employee for any year unless such employee is a highly compensated employee under paragraph (1) for such year.

(r) Special rules for separate line of business.

(1) In general. For purposes of sections 129(d)(8) and 410(b), an employer shall be treated as operating separate lines of business during any year if the employer for bona fide business reasons operates separate lines of business.

(2) Line of business must have 50 employees, etc. A line of business shall not be treated as separate under paragraph (1) unless—

(A) such line of business has at least 50 employees who are not excluded under subsection (q)(5),

(B) the employer notifies the Secretary that such line of business is being treated as separate for purpose of paragraph (1), and

(C) such line of business meets guidelines prescribed by the Secretary or the employer receives a determination from the Secretary that such line of business may be treated as separate for purposes of paragraph (1).

(3) Safe harbor rule.

(A) In general. The requirements of subparagraph (C) of paragraph (2) shall not apply to any line of business if the highly compensated employee percentage with respect to such line of business is—

(i) not less than one-half, and

(ii) not more than twice,

the percentage which highly compensated employees are of all employees of the employer. An employer shall be treated as meeting the requirements of clause (i) if at least 10 percent of all highly compensated employees of the employer perform services solely for such line of business.

(B) Determination may be based on preceding year. The requirements of subparagraph (A) shall be treated as met with respect to any line of business if such requirements were met with respect to such line of business for the preceding year and if—

(i) no more than a de minimis number of employees were shifted to or from the line of business after the close of the preceding year, or

(ii) the employees shifted to or from the line of business after the close of the preceding year contained a substantially proportional number of highly compensated employees.

(4) Highly compensated employee percentage defined. For purposes of this subsection, the term "highly compensated employee percentage" means the percentage which highly compensated employees performing services for the line of business are of all employees performing services for the line of business.

(5) Allocation of benefits to line of business. For purposes of this subsection, benefits which are attributable to services provided to a line of business shall be treated as provided by such line of business.

(6) Headquarters personnel, etc. The Secretary shall prescribe rules providing for—

(A) the allocation of headquarters personnel among the lines of business of the employer, and

(B) the treatment of other employees providing services for more than 1 line of business of the employer or not in lines of business meeting the requirements of paragraph (2).

(7) Separate operating units. For purposes of this subsection, the term "separate line of business" includes an operating unit in a separate geographic area separately operated for a bona fide business reason.

(8) Affiliated service groups. This subsection shall not apply in the case of any affiliated service group (within the meaning of section 414(m)).

(s) Compensation.

For purposes of any applicable provision—

(1) In general. Except as provided in this subsection, the term "compensation" has the meaning given such term by section 415(c)(3).

(2) Employer may elect not to treat certain deferrals as compensation. An employer may elect not to include as compensation any amount which is contributed by the employer pursuant to a salary reduction agreement and which is not includible in the gross income of an employee under section 125, 132(f)(4), 402(e)(3), 402(h), or 403(b).

(3) Alternative determination of compensation. The Secretary shall by regulation provide for alternative methods of determining compensation which may be used by an employer, except that such regulations shall provide that an employer may not use an alternative method if the use of such method discriminates in favor of highly compensated employees (within the meaning of subsection (q)).

(4) Applicable provision. For purposes of this subsection, the term "applicable provision" means any provision which specifically refers to this subsection.

(t) Application of controlled group rules to certain employee benefits.

(1) In general. All employees who are treated as employed by a single employer under subsection (b), (c), or (m) shall be treated as employed by a single employer for purposes of an applicable section. The provisions of subsection (o) shall apply with respect to the requirements of an applicable section.

(2) Applicable section. For purposes of this subsection, the term "applicable section" means section 79, 106, 117(d), 120, 125, 127, 129, 132, 137, 274(j), 505, or 4980B.

(u) Special rules relating to veterans' reemployment rights under USERRA and to differential wage payments to members on active duty.

(1) Treatment of certain contributions made pursuant to veterans' reemployment rights. If any contribution is made by an employer or an employee under an individual account plan with respect to an employee, or by an employee to a defined benefit plan that provides for employee contributions, and such contribution is required by reason of such employee's rights under chapter 43 of title 38, United States Code, resulting from qualified military service, then—

(A) such contribution shall not be subject to any otherwise applicable limitation contained in section 402(g),

402(h), 403(b), 404(a), 404(h), 408, 415, or 457, and shall not be taken into account in applying such limitations to other contributions or benefits under such plan or any other plan, with respect to the year in which the contribution is made,

(B) such contribution shall be subject to the limitations referred to in subparagraph (A) with respect to the year to which the contribution relates (in accordance with rules prescribed by the Secretary), and

(C) such plan shall not be treated as failing to meet the requirements of section 401(a)(4), 401(a)(26), 401(k)(3), 401(k)(11), 401(k)(12), 401(m), 403(b)(12), 408(k)(3), 408(k)(6), 408(p), 410(b), or 416 by reason of the making of (or the right to make) such contribution.

For purposes of the preceding sentence, any elective deferral or employee contribution made under paragraph (2) shall be treated as required by reason of the employee's rights under such chapter 43.

(2) Reemployment rights under USERRA with respect to elective deferrals.

(A) In general. For purposes of this subchapter and section 457, if an employee is entitled to the benefits of chapter 43 of title 38, United States Code, with respect to any plan which provides for elective deferrals, the employer sponsoring the plan shall be treated as meeting the requirements of such chapter 43 with respect to such elective deferrals only if such employer—

(i) permits such employee to make additional elective deferrals under such plan (in the amount determined under subparagraph (B) or such lesser amount as is elected by the employee) during the period which begins on the date of the reemployment of such employee with such employer and has the same length as the lesser of—

(I) the product of 3 and the period of qualified military service which resulted in such rights, and

(II) 5 years, and

(ii) makes a matching contribution with respect to any additional elective deferral made pursuant to clause (i) which would have been required had such deferral actually been made during the period of such qualified military service.

(B) Amount of makeup required. The amount determined under this subparagraph with respect to any plan is the maximum amount of the elective deferrals that the individual would have been permitted to make under the plan in accordance with the limitations referred to in paragraph (1)(A) during the period of qualified military service if the individual had continued to be employed by the employer during such period and received compensation as determined under paragraph (7). Proper adjustment shall be made to the amount determined under the preceding sentence for any elective deferrals actually made during the period of such qualified military service.

(C) Elective deferral. For purposes of this paragraph, the term "elective deferral" has the meaning given such term by section 402(g)(3); except that such term shall include any deferral of compensation under an eligible deferred compensation plan (as defined in section 457(b)).

(D) After-tax employee contributions. References in subparagraphs (A) and (B) to elective deferrals shall be treated as including references to employee contributions.

(3) Certain retroactive adjustments not required. For purposes of this subchapter and subchapter E, no provision of chapter 43 of title 38, United States Code, shall be construed as requiring—

(A) any crediting of earnings to an employee with respect to any contribution before such contribution is actually made, or

(B) any allocation of any forfeiture with respect to the period of qualified military service.

(4) Loan repayment suspensions permitted. If any plan suspends the obligation to repay any loan made to an employee from such plan for any part of any period during which such employee is performing service in the uniformed services (as defined in chapter 43 of title 38, United States Code), whether or not qualified military service, such suspension shall not be taken into account for purposes of section 72(p), 401(a), or 4975(d)(1).

(5) Qualified military service. For purposes of this subsection, the term "qualified military service" means any service in the uniformed services (as defined in chapter 43 of title 38, United States Code) by any individual if such individual is entitled to reemployment rights under such chapter with respect to such service.

(6) Individual account plan. For purposes of this subsection, the term "individual account plan" means any defined contribution plan (including any tax-sheltered annuity plan under section 403(b), any simplified employee pension under section 408(k), any qualified salary reduction arrangement under section 408(p), and any eligible deferred compensation plan (as defined in section 457(b)).

(7) Compensation. For purposes of sections 403(b)(3), 415(c)(3), and 457(e)(5), an employee who is in qualified military service shall be treated as receiving compensation from the employer during such period of qualified military service equal to—

(A) the compensation the employee would have received during such period if the employee were not in qualified military service, determined based on the rate of pay the employee would have received from the employer but for absence during the period of qualified military service, or

(B) if the compensation the employee would have received during such period was not reasonably certain, the employee's average compensation from the employer during the 12-month period immediately preceding the qualified military service (or, if shorter, the period of employment immediately preceding the qualified military service).

(8) USERRA requirements for qualified retirement plans. For purposes of this subchapter and section 457, an employer sponsoring a retirement plan shall be treated as meeting the requirements of chapter 43 of title 38, United States Code, only if each of the following requirements is met:

(A) An individual reemployed under such chapter is treated with respect to such plan as not having incurred a break in service with the employer maintaining the plan by reason of such individual's period of qualified military service.

(B) Each period of qualified military service served by an individual is, upon reemployment under such chapter, deemed with respect to such plan to constitute service with the employer maintaining the plan for the purpose of determining the nonforfeitability of the individual's accrued benefits under such plan and for the purpose of determining the accrual of benefits under such plan.

(C) An individual reemployed under such chapter is entitled to accrued benefits that are contingent on the making of, or derived from, employee contributions or elective deferrals only to the extent the individual makes payment to the plan with respect to such contributions or deferrals. No such payment may exceed the amount the individual would have been permitted or required to contribute had the individual remained continuously employed by the employer throughout the period of qualified military service. Any payment to such plan shall be made during the period beginning with the date of reemployment and whose duration is 3 times the period of the qualified military service (but not greater than 5 years).

(9) Treatment in the case of death or disability resulting from active military service.

(A) In general. For benefit accrual purposes, an employer sponsoring a retirement plan may treat an individual who dies or becomes disabled (as defined under the terms of the plan) while performing qualified military service with respect to the employer maintaining the plan as if the individual has resumed employment in accordance with the individual's reemployment rights under chapter 43 of title 38, United States Code, on the day preceding death or disability (as the case may be) and terminated employment on the actual date of death or disability. In the case of any such treatment, and subject to subparagraphs (B) and (C), any full or partial compliance by such plan with respect to the benefit accrual requirements of paragraph (8) with respect to such individual shall be treated for purposes of paragraph (1) as if such compliance were required under such chapter 43.

(B) Nondiscrimination requirement. Subparagraph (A) shall apply only if all individuals performing qualified military service with respect to the employer maintaining the plan (as determined under subsections (b), (c), (m), and (o)) who die or became disabled as a result of performing qualified military service prior to reemployment by the employer are credited with service and benefits on reasonably equivalent terms.

(C) Determination of benefits. The amount of employee contributions and the amount of elective deferrals of an individual treated as reemployed under subparagraph (A) for purposes of applying paragraph (8)(C) shall be determined on the basis of the individual's average actual employee contributions or elective deferrals for the lesser of—

(i) the 12-month period of service with the employer immediately prior to qualified military service, or

(ii) if service with the employer is less than such 12-month period, the actual length of continuous service with the employer.

(10) Plans not subject to title 38. This subsection shall not apply to any retirement plan to which chapter 43 of title 38, United States Code, does not apply.

(11) References. For purposes of this section, any reference to chapter 43 of title 38, United States Code, shall be treated as a reference to such chapter as in effect on December 12, 1994 (without regard to any subsequent amendment).

(12) Treatment of differential wage payments.

(A) In general. Except as provided in this paragraph, for purposes of applying this title to a retirement plan to which this subsection applies—

(i) an individual receiving a differential wage payment shall be treated as an employee of the employer making the payment,

(ii) the differential wage payment shall be treated as compensation, and

(iii) the plan shall not be treated as failing to meet the requirements of any provision described in paragraph (1)(C) by reason of any contribution or benefit which is based on the differential wage payment.

(B) Special rule for distributions.

(i) In general. Notwithstanding subparagraph (A)(i), for purposes of section 401(k)(2)(B)(i)(I), 403(b)(7)(A)(ii), 403(b)(11)(A), or 457(d)(1)(A)(ii), an individual shall be treated as having been severed from employment during any period the individual is performing service in the uniformed services described in section 3401(h)(2)(A).

(ii) Limitation. If an individual elects to receive a distribution by reason of clause (i), the plan shall provide that the individual may not make an elective deferral or employee contribution during the 6-month period beginning on the date of the distribution.

(C) Nondiscrimination requirement. Subparagraph (A)(iii) shall apply only if all employees of an employer (as determined under subsections (b), (c), (m), and (o)) performing service in the uniformed services described in section 3401(h)(2)(A) are entitled to receive differential wage payments on reasonably equivalent terms and, if eligible to participate in a retirement plan maintained by the employer, to make contributions based on the payments on reasonably equivalent terms. For purposes of applying this subparagraph, the provisions of paragraphs (3), (4), and (5) of section 410(b) shall apply.

(D) Differential wage payment. For purposes of this paragraph, the term "differential wage payment" has the meaning given such term by section 3401(h)(2).

(v) Catch-up contributions for individuals age 50 or over.

(1) In general. An applicable employer plan shall not be treated as failing to meet any requirement of this title solely because the plan permits an eligible participant to make additional elective deferrals in any plan year.

(2) Limitation on amount of additional deferrals.

(A) In general. A plan shall not permit additional elective deferrals under paragraph (1) for any year in an amount greater than the lesser of—

(i) the applicable dollar amount, or

(ii) the excess (if any) of—

(I) the participant's compensation (as defined in section 415(c)(3)) for the year, over

(II) any other elective deferrals of the participant for such year which are made without regard to this subsection.

(B) Applicable dollar amount. For purposes of this paragraph—

(i) In the case of an applicable employer plan other than a plan described in section 401(k)(11) or 408(p), the applicable dollar amount shall be determined in accordance with the following table:

For taxable years beginning in:	The applicable dollar amount is:
2002	$ 1,000
2003	$ 2,000
2004	$ 3,000
2005	$ 4,000
2006 and thereafter	$ 5,000.

(ii) In the case of an applicable employer plan described in section 401(k)(11) or 408(p), the applicable dollar amount shall be determined in accordance with the following table:

For taxable years beginning in:	The applicable dollar amount is:
2002	$ 500
2003	$ 1,000
2004	$ 1,500
2005	$ 2,000
2006 and thereafter	$ 2,500.

(C) Cost-of-living adjustment. In the case of a year beginning after December 31, 2006, the Secretary shall adjust annually the $5,000 amount in subparagraph (B)(i) and the $2,500 amount in subparagraph (B)(ii) for increases in the cost-of-living at the same time and in the same manner as adjustments under section 415(d); except that the base period taken into account shall be the calendar quarter beginning July 1, 2005, and any increase under this subparagraph which is not a multiple of $500 shall be rounded to the next lower multiple of $500.

(D) Aggregation of plans. For purposes of this paragraph, plans described in clauses (i), (ii), and (iv) of paragraph (6)(A) that are maintained by the same employer (as determined under subsection (b), (c), (m) or (o)) shall be treated as a single plan, and plans described in clause (iii) of paragraph (6)(A) that are maintained by the same employer shall be treated as a single plan.

(3) Treatment of contributions. In the case of any contribution to a plan under paragraph (1)—

(A) such contribution shall not, with respect to the year in which the contribution is made—

(i) be subject to any otherwise applicable limitation contained in sections 401(a)(30), 402(h), 403(b), 408, 415(c), and 457(b)(2) (determined without regard to section 457(b)(3)), or

(ii) be taken into account in applying such limitations to other contributions or benefits under such plan or any other such plan, and

(B) except as provided in paragraph (4), such plan shall not be treated as failing to meet the requirements of section 401(a)(4), 401(k)(3), 401(k)(11), 403(b)(12), 408(k), 410(b), or 416 by reason of the making of (or the right to make) such contribution.

(4) Application of nondiscrimination rules.

(A) In general. An applicable employer plan shall be treated as failing to meet the nondiscrimination requirements under section 401(a)(4) with respect to benefits, rights, and features unless the plan allows all eligible participants to make the same election with respect to the additional elective deferrals under this subsection.

(B) Aggregation. For purposes of subparagraph (A), all plans maintained by employers who are treated as a single employer under subsection (b), (c), (m), or (o) of section 414 shall be treated as 1 plan, except that a plan described in clause (i) of section 410(b)(6)(C) shall not be treated as a plan of the employer until the expiration of the transition period with respect to such plan (as determined under clause (ii) of such section).

(5) Eligible participant. For purposes of this subsection, the term "eligible participant" means a participant in a plan—

(A) who would attain age 50 by the end of the taxable year,

(B) with respect to whom no other elective deferrals may (without regard to this subsection) be made to the plan for the plan (or other applicable) year by reason of the application of any limitation or other restriction described in paragraph (3) or comparable limitation or restriction contained in the terms of the plan.

(6) Other definitions and rules. For purposes of this subsection—

(A) Applicable employer plan. The term "applicable employer plan" means—

(i) an employees' trust described in section 401(a) which is exempt from tax under section 501(a),

(ii) a plan under which amounts are contributed by an individual's employer for an annuity contract described in section 403(b),

(iii) an eligible deferred compensation plan under section 457 of an eligible employer described in section 457(e)(1)(A), and

(iv) an arrangement meeting the requirements of section 408(k) or (p).

(B) Elective deferral. The term "elective deferral" has the meaning given such term by subsection (u)(2)(C).

(C) Exception for section 457 plans. This subsection shall not apply to a participant for any year for which a higher limitation applies to the participant under section 457(b)(3).

(w) Special rules for certain withdrawals from eligible automatic contribution arrangements.

(1) In general. If an eligible automatic contribution arrangement allows an employee to elect to make permissible withdrawals—

(A) the amount of any such withdrawal shall be includible in the gross income of the employee for the taxable year of the employee in which the distribution is made,

(B) no tax shall be imposed under section 72(t) with respect to the distribution, and

(C) the arrangement shall not be treated as violating any restriction on distributions under this title solely by reason of allowing the withdrawal.

In the case of any distribution to an employee by reason of an election under this paragraph, employer matching contributions shall be forfeited or subject to such other treatment as the Secretary may prescribe.

(2) Permissible withdrawal. For purposes of this subsection—

(A) In general. The term "permissible withdrawal" means any withdrawal from an eligible automatic contribution arrangement meeting the requirements of this paragraph which—

(i) is made pursuant to an election by an employee, and

(ii) consists of elective contributions described in paragraph (3)(B) (and earnings attributable thereto).

(B) Time for making election. Subparagraph (A) shall not apply to an election by an employee unless the election is made no later than the date which is 90 days after the date of the first elective contribution with respect to the employee under the arrangement.

(C) Amount of distribution. Subparagraph (A) shall not apply to any election by an employee unless the amount of any distribution by reason of the election is equal to the amount of elective contributions made with respect to the first payroll period to which the eligible automatic contribution arrangement applies to the employee and any succeeding payroll period beginning before the effective date of the election (and earnings attributable thereto).

(3) Eligible automatic contribution arrangement. For purposes of this subsection, the term "eligible automatic contribution arrangement" means an arrangement under an applicable employer plan—

(A) under which a participant may elect to have the employer make payments as contributions under the plan on behalf of the participant, or to the participant directly in cash,

(B) under which the participant is treated as having elected to have the employer make such contributions in an amount equal to a uniform percentage of compensation provided under the plan until the participant specifically elects not to have such contributions made (or specifically elects to have such contributions made at a different percentage), and

(C) which meets the requirements of paragraph (4).

(4) Notice requirements.

(A) In general. The administrator of a plan containing an arrangement described in paragraph (3) shall, within a reasonable period before each plan year, give to each employee to whom an arrangement described in paragraph (3) applies for such plan year notice of the employee's rights and obligations under the arrangement which—

(i) is sufficiently accurate and comprehensive to apprise the employee of such rights and obligations, and

(ii) is written in a manner calculated to be understood by the average employee to whom the arrangement applies.

(B) Time and form of notice. A notice shall not be treated as meeting the requirements of subparagraph (A) with respect to an employee unless—

(i) the notice includes an explanation of the employee's right under the arrangement to elect not to have elective contributions made on the employee's behalf (or to elect to have such contributions made at a different percentage),

(ii) the employee has a reasonable period of time after receipt of the notice described in clause (i) and before the first elective contribution is made to make such election, and

(iii) the notice explains how contributions made under the arrangement will be invested in the absence of any investment election by the employee.

(5) Applicable employer plan. For purposes of this subsection, the term "applicable employer plan" means—

(A) an employees' trust described in section 401(a) which is exempt from tax under section 501(a),

(B) a plan under which amounts are contributed by an individual's employer for an annuity contract described in section 403(b),

(C) an eligible deferred compensation plan described in section 457(b) which is maintained by an eligible employer described in section 457(e)(1)(A),

(D) a simplified employee pension the terms of which provide for a salary reduction arrangement described in section 408(k)(6), and

(E) a simple retirement account (as defined in section 408(p)).

(6) Special rule. A withdrawal described in paragraph (1) (subject to the limitation of paragraph (2)(C)) shall not be taken into account for purposes of section 401(k)(3) or for purposes of applying the limitation under section 402(g)(1).

(x) Special rules for eligible combined defined benefit plans and qualified cash or deferred arrangements.

(1) General rule. Except as provided in this subsection, the requirements of this title shall be applied to any defined benefit plan or applicable defined contribution plan which are part of an eligible combined plan in the same manner as if each such plan were not a part of the eligible combined plan. In the case of a termination of the defined benefit plan and the applicable defined contribution plan forming part of an eligible combined plan, the plan administrator shall terminate each such plan separately.

(2) Eligible combined plan. For purposes of this subsection—

(A) In general. The term "eligible combined plan" means a plan—

(i) which is maintained by an employer which, at the time the plan is established, is a small employer,

(ii) which consists of a defined benefit plan and an applicable defined contribution plan,

(iii) the assets of which are held in a single trust forming part of the plan and are clearly identified and allocated to the defined benefit plan and the applicable defined contribution plan to the extent necessary for the separate application of this title under paragraph (1), and

(iv) with respect to which the benefit, contribution, vesting, and nondiscrimination requirements of subparagraphs (B), (C), (D), (E), and (F) are met.

For purposes of this subparagraph, the term "small employer" has the meaning given such term by section 4980D(d)(2), except that such section shall be applied by substituting "500" for "50" each place it appears.

(B) Benefit requirements.

(i) In general. The benefit requirements of this subparagraph are met with respect to the defined benefit plan forming part of the eligible combined plan if the accrued benefit of each participant derived from employer contributions, when expressed as an annual retirement benefit, is not less than the applicable percentage of the participant's final average pay. For purposes of this clause, final average pay shall be determined using the period of consecutive years (not exceeding 5) during which the participant had the greatest aggregate compensation from the employer.

(ii) Applicable percentage. For purposes of clause (i), the applicable percentage is the lesser of—

(I) 1 percent multiplied by the number of years of service with the employer, or

(II) 20 percent.

(iii) Special rule for applicable defined benefit plans. If the defined benefit plan under clause (i) is an applicable defined benefit plan as defined in section 411(a)(13)(B) which meets the interest credit requirements of section 411(b)(5)(B)(i), the plan shall be treated as meeting the requirements of clause (i) with respect to any plan year if each participant receives a pay credit for the year which is not less than the percentage of compensation determined in accordance with the following table:

Employee benefit plans Code Sec. 414(x)(5)(B)(i)

If the participant's age as of the beginning of the year is—	The percentage is—
30 or less	2
Over 30 but less than 40	4
40 or over but less than 50	6
50 or over	8.

(iv) Years of service. For purposes of this subparagraph, years of service shall be determined under the rules of paragraphs (4), (5), and (6) of section 411(a), except that the plan may not disregard any year of service because of a participant making, or failing to make, any elective deferral with respect to the qualified cash or deferred arrangement to which subparagraph (C) applies.

(C) Contribution requirements.

(i) In general. The contribution requirements of this subparagraph with respect to any applicable defined contribution plan forming part of an eligible combined plan are met if—

(I) the qualified cash or deferred arrangement included in such plan constitutes an automatic contribution arrangement, and

(II) the employer is required to make matching contributions on behalf of each employee eligible to participate in the arrangement in an amount equal to 50 percent of the elective contributions of the employee to the extent such elective contributions do not exceed 4 percent of compensation.

Rules similar to the rules of clauses (ii) and (iii) of section 401(k)(12)(B) shall apply for purposes of this clause.

(ii) Nonelective contributions. An applicable defined contribution plan shall not be treated as failing to meet the requirements of clause (i) because the employer makes nonelective contributions under the plan but such contributions shall not be taken into account in determining whether the requirements of clause (i)(II) are met.

(D) Vesting requirements. The vesting requirements of this subparagraph are met if—

(i) in the case of a defined benefit plan forming part of an eligible combined plan an employee who has completed at least 3 years of service has a nonforfeitable right to 100 percent of the employee's accrued benefit under the plan derived from employer contributions, and

(ii) in the case of an applicable defined contribution plan forming part of an eligible combined plan—

(I) an employee has a nonforfeitable right to any matching contribution made under the qualified cash or deferred arrangement included in such plan by an employer with respect to any elective contribution, including matching contributions in excess of the contributions required under subparagraph (C)(i)(II), and

(II) an employee who has completed at least 3 years of service has a nonforfeitable right to 100 percent of the employee's accrued benefit derived under the arrangement from nonelective contributions of the employer.

For purposes of this subparagraph, the rules of section 411 shall apply to the extent not inconsistent with this subparagraph.

(E) Uniform provision of contributions and benefits. In the case of a defined benefit plan or applicable defined contribution plan forming part of an eligible combined plan, the requirements of this subparagraph are met if all contributions and benefits under each such plan, and all rights and features under each such plan, must be provided uniformly to all participants.

(F) Requirements must be met without taking into account social security and similar contributions and benefits or other plans.

(i) In general. The requirements of this subparagraph are met if the requirements of clauses (ii) and (iii) are met.

(ii) Social security and similar contributions. The requirements of this clause are met if—

(I) the requirements of subparagraphs (B) and (C) are met without regard to section 401(l), and

(II) the requirements of sections 401(a)(4) and 410(b) are met with respect to both the applicable defined contribution plan and defined benefit plan forming part of an eligible combined plan without regard to section 401(l).

(iii) Other plans and arrangements. The requirements of this clause are met if the applicable defined contribution plan and defined benefit plan forming part of an eligible combined plan meet the requirements of sections 401(a)(4) and 410(b) without being combined with any other plan.

(3) Nondiscrimination requirements for qualified cash or deferred arrangement.

(A) In general. A qualified cash or deferred arrangement which is included in an applicable defined contribution plan forming part of an eligible combined plan shall be treated as meeting the requirements of section 401(k)(3)(A)(ii) if the requirements of paragraph (2)(C) are met with respect to such arrangement.

(B) Matching contributions. In applying section 401(m)(11) to any matching contribution with respect to a contribution to which paragraph (2)(C) applies, the contribution requirement of paragraph (2)(C) and the notice requirements of paragraph (5)(B) shall be substituted for the requirements otherwise applicable under clauses (i) and (ii) of section 401(m)(11)(A).

(4) Satisfaction of top-heavy rules. A defined benefit plan and applicable defined contribution plan forming part of an eligible combined plan for any plan year shall be treated as meeting the requirements of section 416 for the plan year.

(5) Automatic contribution arrangement. For purposes of this subsection—

(A) In general. A qualified cash or deferred arrangement shall be treated as an automatic contribution arrangement if the arrangement—

(i) provides that each employee eligible to participate in the arrangement is treated as having elected to have the employer make elective contributions in an amount equal to 4 percent of the employee's compensation unless the employee specifically elects not to have such contributions made or to have such contributions made at a different rate, and

(ii) meets the notice requirements under subparagraph (B).

(B) Notice requirements.

(i) In general. The requirements of this subparagraph are met if the requirements of clauses (ii) and (iii) are met.

(ii) Reasonable period to make election. The requirements of this clause are met if each employee to whom subparagraph (A)(i) applies—

(I) receives a notice explaining the employee's right under the arrangement to elect not to have elective contributions made on the employee's behalf or to have the contributions made at a different rate, and

(II) has a reasonable period of time after receipt of such notice and before the first elective contribution is made to make such election.

(iii) Annual notice of rights and obligations. The requirements of this clause are met if each employee eligible to participate in the arrangement is, within a reasonable period before any year, given notice of the employee's rights and obligations under the arrangement.

The requirements of clauses (i) and (ii) of section 401(k)(12)(D) shall be met with respect to the notices described in clauses (ii) and (iii) of this subparagraph.

(6) Coordination with other requirements.

(A) Treatment of separate plans. Section 414(k) shall not apply to an eligible combined plan.

(B) Reporting. An eligible combined plan shall be treated as a single plan for purposes of sections 6058 and 6059.

(7) Applicable defined contribution plan. For purposes of this subsection—

(A) In general. The term "applicable defined contribution plan" means a defined contribution plan which includes a qualified cash or deferred arrangement.

(B) Qualified cash or deferred arrangement. The term "qualified cash or deferred arrangement" has the meaning given such term by section 401(k)(2).

In 2010, P.L. 111-312, Sec. 101(a)(1), substituted "December 31, 2012" for "December 31, 2010" both places it appeared in Sec. 901 of P.L. 107-16 [see below], effective as if included in the enactment of P.L. 107-16, EGTRRA, 6/7/2001.

In 2008, P.L. 110-458, Sec. 101(d)(2)(E), amended subclause (l)(2)(B)(i)(I), effective for plan yrs. begin. after 2007, [effective as if included in the amendments made by Sec. 114, P.L.109-280, see below]

Prior to amendment, subcl. (l)(2)(B)(i)(I) read as follows:

"(I) the amount determined under section 431(c)(6)(A)(i) in the case of a multiemployer plan (and the sum of the funding shortfall and target normal cost determined under section 430 in the case of any other plan), over"

—P.L. 110-458, Sec. 101(d)(3), added Sec. 114(g), P.L. 109-280, providing effective dates for amendments made by Sec. 114, P.L. 109-280, see below. Sec. 114(g), P.L. 109-280, as added by this Act, provides:

"(g) Effective dates.

"(1) In general. The amendments made by this section shall apply to plan years beginning after 2007.

"(2) Excise tax. The amendments made by subsection (e) shall apply to taxable years beginning after 2007, but only with respect to plan years described in paragraph (1) which end with or within any such taxable year."

—P.L. 110-458, Sec. 109(b)(4)(A), added "and" after the comma at the end of subpara. (w)(3)(B) . . . Sec. 109(b)(4)(B), deleted subpara. (w)(3)(C) . . . Sec. 109(b)(4)(C), redesignated subpara. (w)(3)(D) as subpara. (w)(3)(C) . . . Sec. 109(b)(5), deleted "and" at the end of subpara. (w)(5)(B), substituted a comma for the period at the end of subpara. (w)(5)(C), and added subparas. (w)(5)(D) and (E) . . . Sec. 109(b)(6), added "or for purposes of applying the limitation under section 402(g)(1)" before the period at the end of para. (w)(6), effective for plan yrs. begin. after 12/31/2007, as if included in the provisions of Sec. 902 of the Pension Protection Act of 2006, P.L. 109-280, see below.

—P.L. 110-458, Sec. 109(c)(1), added the last sentence at the end of para. (x)(1), effective for plan yrs. begin. after 12/31/2009, effective as if included in the amendments made by Sec. 903, P.L.109-280, see below.

Prior to deletion, subpara. (w)(3)(C) read as follows:

"(C) under which, in the absence of an investment election by the participant, contributions described in subparagraph (B) are invested in accordance with regulations prescribed by the Secretary of Labor under section 404(c)(5) of the Employee Retirement Income Security Act of 1974, and"

—P.L. 110-289, Sec. 1604(b)(4), substituted "bridge depository institution" for "bridge bank" in subpara. (l)(2)(G), enacted 7/30/2008.

—P.L. 110-245, Sec. 104(b), redesignated paras. (u)(9) and (u)(10) as paras. (u)(10) and (u)(11) and added para. (u)(9), effective for deaths and disabilities occurring on or after 1/1/2007. Sec. 104(d)(2) of this Act provides:

"(2) Provisions relating to plan amendments.

"(A) In general. If this subparagraph applies to any plan or contract amendment, such plan or contract shall be treated as being operated in accordance with the terms of the plan during the period described in subparagraph (B)(iii).

"(B) Amendments to which subparagraph (a) applies.

"(i) In general. Subparagraph (A) shall apply to any amendment to any plan or annuity contract which is made—

"(I) pursuant to the amendments made by subsection (a) or pursuant to any regulation issued by the Secretary of the Treasury under subsection (a), and

"(II) on or before the last day of the first plan year beginning on or after January 1, 2010.

"In the case of a governmental plan (as defined in section 414(d) of the Internal Revenue Code of 1986), this clause shall be applied by substituting '2012' for '2010' in subclause (II).

"(ii) Conditions. This paragraph shall not apply to any amendment unless—

"(I) the plan or contract is operated as if such plan or contract amendment were in effect for the period described in clause (iii), and

"(II) such plan or contract amendment applies retroactively for such period.

"(iii) Period described. The period described in this clause is the period—

"(I) beginning on the effective date specified by the plan, and

"(II) ending on the date described in clause (i)(II) (or, if earlier, the date the plan or contract amendment is adopted)."

—P.L. 110-245, Sec. 105(b)(1)(A), added para. (u)(12) . . . Sec. 105(b)(1)(B), added "and to differential wage payments to members on active duty" after "USERRA" in the heading of subsec. (u), effective for yrs. begin. after 12/31/2008.

—P.L. 110-245, Sec. 105(c), of this Act provides:

"(c) Provisions Relating to Plan Amendments.

"(1) In general. If this subsection applies to any plan or annuity contract amendment, such plan or contract shall be treated as being operated in accordance with the terms of the plan or contract during the period described in paragraph (2)(B)(i).

"(2) Amendments to which section applies.

"(A) In general. This subsection shall apply to any amendment to any plan or annuity contract which is made—

"(i) pursuant to any amendment made by subsection (b)(1), and

"(ii) on or before the last day of the first plan year beginning on or after January 1, 2010.

"In the case of a governmental plan (as defined in section 414(d) of the Internal Revenue Code of 1986), this subparagraph shall be applied by substituting '2012' for '2010' in clause (ii).

"(B) Conditions. This subsection shall not apply to any plan or annuity contract amendment unless—

"(i) during the period beginning on the date the amendment described in subparagraph (A)(i) takes effect and ending on the date described in subparagraph (A)(ii) (or, if earlier, the date the plan or contract amendment is adopted), the plan or contract is operated as if such plan or contract amendment were in effect, and

"(ii) such plan or contract amendment applies retroactively for such period."

In 2007, P.L. 110-28, Sec. 6611(a)(2)(A), substituted "for each of the 3 plan years immediately preceding the first plan year for which the election under this paragraph is effective with respect to the plan," for "for each of the 3 plan years immediately before the date of enactment of the Pension Protection Act of 2006," in subclause (f)(6)(A)(ii)(I) . . . Sec. 6611(a)(2)(B), substituted "starting with any plan year beginning on or after January 1, 1999, and ending before January 1, 2008, as designated by the plan in the election made under subparagraph (A)(ii)" for "starting with the first plan year ending after the date of the enactment of the Pension Protection Act of 2006" in subpara. (f)(6)(B) . . . Sec. 6611(a)(2)(C), added subpara. (f)(6)(F) . . . Sec. 6611(b)(2), substituted "if it is a plan sponsored by an organization which is described in section 501(c)(5) and exempt from tax under section 501(a) and which was established in Chicago, Illinois, on August 12, 1881." for "if it is a plan—" and all that follows in subpara. (f)(6)(E)

In 2006, P.L. 109-280, Sec. 114(c), amended subclause. (l)(2)(B)(i)(I), effective for plan yrs. begin. after 2007 [as provided in Sec. 114(g) of this Act as added by Sec. 101(d)(3), P.L. 110-458, see above].

Prior to amendment, subclause (l)(2)(B)(i)(I) read as follows:

"(I) the amount determined under section 412(c)(7)(A)(i) with respect to the plan, over"

—P.L. 109-280, Sec. 811, of this Act [relating to Sec. 901 of P.L. 107-16, see below], provides:

"SEC. 811. PENSIONS AND INDIVIDUAL RETIREMENT ARRANGEMENT PROVISIONS OF ECONOMIC GROWTH AND TAX RELIEF RECONCILIATION ACT OF 2001 MADE PERMANENT.

"Title IX of the Economic Growth and Tax Relief Reconciliation Act of 2001 shall not apply to the provisions of, and amendments made by, subtitles A through F of title VI of such Act (relating to pension and individual retirement arrangement provisions)."

—P.L. 109-280, Sec. 902(d)(1), added subsec. (w), effective for plan yrs. begin. after 12/31/2007.

—P.L. 109-280, Sec. 903(a), added subsec. (x), effective for plan yrs. begin. after 12/31/2009.

—P.L. 109-280, Sec. 906(a)(1), added "The term 'governmental plan' includes a plan which is established and maintained by an Indian tribal government (as defined in section 7701(a)(40)), a subdivision of an Indian tribal government (determined in accordance with section 7871(d)), or an agency or instrumentality of either, and all of the participants of which are employees of such entity substantially all of whose services as such an employee are in the performance of essential governmental functions but not in the performance of commercial activities (whether or not an essential government function))." at the end of subsec. (d) ... Sec. 906(b)(1)(C), added 'or a governmental plan described in the last sentence of section 414(d) (relating to plans of Indian tribal governments),' after 'foregoing,' in para. (h)(2), effective for any yr. begin. on or after 8/17/2006.

—P.L. 109-280, Sec. 1001, of this Act, provides:

"SEC. 1001. REGULATIONS ON TIME AND ORDER OF ISSUANCE OF DOMESTIC RELATIONS ORDERS.

"Not later than 1 year after the date of the enactment of this Act, the Secretary of Labor shall issue regulations under section 206(d)(3) of the Employee Retirement Security Act of 1974 and section 414(p) of the Internal Revenue Code of 1986 which clarify that—

"(1) a domestic relations order otherwise meeting the requirements to be a qualified domestic relations order, including the requirements of section 206(d)(3)(D) of such Act and section 414(p)(3) of such Code, shall not fail to be treated as a qualified domestic relations order solely because—

"(A) the order is issued after, or revises, another domestic relations order or qualified domestic relations order; or

"(B) of the time at which it is issued; and

"(2) any order described in paragraph (1) shall be subject to the same requirements and protections which apply to qualified domestic relations orders, including the provisions of section 206(d)(3)(H) of such Act and section 414(p)(7) of such Code."

—P.L. 109-280, Sec. 1103, of this Act, provides:

"SEC. 1103. REPORTING SIMPLIFICATION.

"(a) Simplified annual filing requirement for owners and their spouses.

"(1) In general. The Secretary of the Treasury shall modify the requirements for filing annual returns with respect to one-participant retirement plans to ensure that such plans with assets of $250,000 or less as of the close of the plan year need not file a return for that year.

"(2) One-participant retirement plan defined. For purposes of this subsection, the term 'one-participant retirement plan' means a retirement plan with respect to which the following requirements are met:

"(A) on the first day of the plan year—

"(i) the plan covered only one individual (or the individual and the individual's spouse) and the individual owned 100 percent of the plan sponsor (whether or not incorporated), or

"(ii) the plan covered only one or more partners (or partners and their spouses) in the plan sponsor;

"(B) the plan meets the minimum coverage requirements of section 410(b) of the Internal Revenue Code of 1986 without being combined with any other plan of the business that covers the employees of the business;

"(C) the plan does not provide benefits to anyone except the individual (and the individual's spouse) or the partners (and their spouses);

"(D) the plan does not cover a business that is a member of an affiliated service group, a controlled group of corporations, or a group of businesses under common control; and

"(E) the plan does not cover a business that uses the services of leased employees (within the meaning of section 414(n) of such Code).

"For purposes of this paragraph, the term 'partner' includes a 2-percent shareholder (as defined in section 1372(b) of such Code) of an S corporation.

"(3) Other definitions. Terms used in paragraph (2) which are also used in section 414 of the Internal Revenue Code of 1986 shall have the respective meanings given such terms by such section.

"(4) Effective date. The provisions of this subsection shall apply to plan years beginning on or after January 1, 2007.

"(b) Simplified annual filing requirement for plans with fewer than 25 participants. In the case of plan years beginning after December 31, 2006, the Secretary of the Treasury and the Secretary of Labor shall provide for the filing of a simplified annual return for any retirement plan which covers less than 25 participants on the first day of a plan year and which meets the requirements described in subparagraphs (B), (D), and (E) of subsection (a)(2)."

—P.L. 109-280, Sec. 1106(b), added para. (f)(6), enacted 8/17/2006
—P.L. 109-280, Sec. 1107, of this Act, provides:

"SEC. 1107. PROVISIONS RELATING TO PLAN AMENDMENTS.

"(a) In general. If this section applies to any pension plan or contract amendment—

"(1) such pension plan or contract shall be treated as being operated in accordance with the terms of the plan during the period described in subsection (b)(2)(A), and

"(2) except as provided by the Secretary of the Treasury, such pension plan shall not fail to meet the requirements of section 411(d)(6) of the Internal Revenue Code of 1986 and section 204(g) of the Employee Retirement Income Security Act of 1974 by reason of such amendment.

"(b) Amendments to which section applies.

"(1) In general. This section shall apply to any amendment to any pension plan or annuity contract which is made—

"(A) pursuant to any amendment made by this Act or pursuant to any regulation issued by the Secretary of the Treasury or the Secretary of Labor under this Act, and

"(B) on or before the last day of the first plan year beginning on or after January 1, 2009.

In the case of a governmental plan (as defined in section 414(d) of the Internal Revenue Code of 1986), this paragraph shall be applied by substituting '2011' for '2009'.

"(2) Conditions. This section shall not apply to any amendment unless—

"(A) during the period—

"(i) beginning on the date the legislative or regulatory amendment described in paragraph (1)(A) takes effect (or in the case of a plan or contract amendment not required by such legislative or regulatory amendment, the effective date specified by the plan), and

"(ii) ending on the date described in paragraph (1)(B) (or, if earlier, the date the plan or contract amendment is adopted), the plan or contract is operated as if such plan or contract amendment were in effect; and

"(B) such plan or contract amendment applies retroactively for such period."

In 2005, P.L. 109-135, Sec. 201(b)(4)(A), Repealed Sec. 104 of P.L. 109-73. Prior to repeal, Sec. 104 of P.L. 109-73 read as follows:

"SEC. 104. PROVISIONS RELATING TO PLAN AMENDMENTS.

"(a) In general. If this section applies to any amendment to any plan or annuity contract, such plan or contract shall be treated as being operated in accordance with the terms of the plan during the period described in subsection (b)(2)(A).

"(b) Amendments to which section applies.

"(1) In general. This section shall apply to any amendment to any plan or annuity contract which is made—

"(A) pursuant to any amendment made by this title, or pursuant to any regulation issued by the Secretary of the Treasury or the Secretary of Labor under this title, and

"(B) on or before the last day of the first plan year beginning on or after January 1, 2007, or such later date as the Secretary of the Treasury may prescribe.

In the case of a governmental plan (as defined in section 414(d) of the Internal Revenue Code of 1986), subparagraph (B) shall be applied by substituting the date which is 2 years after the date otherwise applied under subparagraph (B).

"(2) Conditions. This section shall not apply to any amendment unless—

"(A) during the period—

"(i) beginning on the date the legislative or regulatory amendment described in paragraph (1)(A) takes effect (or in the case of a plan or contract amendment not required by such legislative or regulatory amendment, the effective date specified by the plan), and

"(ii) ending on the date described in paragraph (1)(B) (or, if earlier, the date the plan or contract amendment is adopted),

the plan or contract is operated as if such plan or contract amendment were in effect; and

"(B) such plan or contract amendment applies retroactively for such period."

In 2004, P.L. 108-476, Sec. 1, of this Act, provides:

"SECTION 1. CERTAIN ARRANGEMENTS MAINTAINED BY THE YMCA RETIREMENT FUND TREATED AS CHURCH PLANS.

"(a) Retirement plans.

"(1) In general. For purposes of sections 401(a) and 403(b) of the Internal Revenue Code of 1986, any retirement plan maintained by the YMCA Retirement Fund as of January 1, 2003, shall be treated as a church plan (within the meaning of section 414(e) of such Code) which is maintained by an organization described in section 414(e)(3)(A) of such Code.

"(2) Tax-deferred retirement plan. In the case of a retirement plan described in paragraph (1) which allows contributions to be made under a salary reduction agreement—

"(A) such treatment shall not apply for purposes of section 415(c)(7) of such Code, and

"(B) any account maintained for a participant or beneficiary of such plan shall be treated for purposes of such Code as a retirement income account described in section 403(b)(9) of such Code, except that such account shall not, for purposes of section 403(b)(12) of such Code, be treated as a contract purchased by a church for purposes of section 403(b)(1)(D) of such Code.

"(3) Money purchase pension plan. In the case of a retirement plan described in paragraph (1) which is subject to the requirements of section 401(a) of such Code—

"(A) such plan (but not any reserves held by the YMCA Retirement Fund)—

"(i) shall be treated for purposes of such Code as a defined contribution plan which is a money purchase pension plan, and

"(ii) shall be treated as having made an election under section 410(d) of such Code for plan years beginning after December 31, 2005, except that notwithstanding the election—

"(I) nothing in the Employee Retirement Income Security Act of 1974 or such Code shall prohibit the YMCA Retirement Fund from commingling for investment purposes the assets of the electing plan with the assets of such Fund and with the assets of any employee benefit plan maintained by such Fund, and

"(II) nothing in this section shall be construed as subjecting any assets described in subclause (I), other than the assets of the electing plan, to any provision of such Act,

"(B) notwithstanding section 401(a)(11) or 417 of such Code or section 205 of such Act, such plan may offer a lump-sum distribution option to participants who have not attained age 55 without offering such participants an annuity option, and

"(C) any account maintained for a participant or beneficiary of such plan shall, for purposes of section 401(a)(9) of such Code, be treated as a retirement income account described in section 403(b)(9) of such Code.

"(4) Self-funded death benefit plan. For purposes of section 7702(j) of such Code, a retirement plan described in paragraph (1) shall be treated as an arrangement described in section 7702(j)(2).

"(b) YMCA retirement fund. For purposes of this section, the term 'YMCA Retirement Fund' means the Young Men's Christian Association Retirement Fund, a corporation created by an Act of the State of New York which became law on April 30, 1921.

"(c) Effective date. This section shall apply to plan years beginning after December 31, 2003."

Code Sec. 414 — Employee benefit plans

—P.L. 108-311, Sec. 408(a)(15), substituted "subsection" for "section" in para. (q)(7), enacted 10/4/2004.

In 2002, P.L. 107-358, Sec. 2, added subsec. (c) in Sec. 901 of P.L. 107-16 [see below], effective 12/17/2002.

—P.L. 107-147, Sec. 411(o)(3), added subpara. (v)(2)(D) . . . Sec. 411(o)(4), substituted "sections 401(a)(30), 402(h), 403(b), 408, 415(c), and 457(b)(2) (determined without regard to section 457(b)(3))" for "section 402(g), 402(h), 403(b), 404(a), 404(h), 408(k), 408(p), 415, or 457" in clause (v)(3)(A)(i) . . . Sec. 411(o)(5), substituted "section 401(a)(4), 401(k)(3), 401(k)(11), 403(b)(12), 408(k), 410(b), or 416" for "section 401(a)(4), 401(a)(26), 401(k)(3), 401(k)(11), 401(k)(12), 403(b)(12), 408(k), 408(p), 408B, 410(b), or 416" in subpara. (v)(3)(B) . . . Sec. 411(o)(6), added ", except that a plan described in clause (i) of section 410(b)(6)(C) shall not be treated as a plan of the employer until the expiration of the transition period with respect to such plan (as determined under clause (ii) of such section)" after "treated as 1 plan" at the end of subpara. (v)(4)(B) . . . Sec. 411(o)(7)(A), deleted ", with respect to any plan year," after "means" in para. (v)(5) . . . Sec. 411(o)(7)(B), amended subpara. (v)(5)(A) . . . Sec. 411(o)(7)(C), substituted "plan (or other applicable) year" for "plan year" in subpara. (v)(5)(B) . . . Sec. 411(o)(8), amended subpara. (v)(6)(C), effective for contributions in tax. yrs. begin. after 12/31/2001.

Prior to amendment, subpara. (v)(5)(A) read as follows:

"(A) who has attained the age of 50 before the close of the plan year, and"

Prior to amendment, subpara. (v)(6)(C) read as follows:

"(C) Exception for section 457 plans. This subsection shall not apply to an applicable employer plan described in subparagraph (A)(iii) for any year to which section 457(b)(3) applies."

In 2001, P.L. 107-16, Sec. 631(a), added subsec. (v), effective for contributions in tax. yrs. begin. after 12/31/2001.

—P.L. 107-16, Sec. 635(a)(1), added "or an eligible deferred compensation plan (within the meaning of section 457(b))" after "subsection (e))" in para. (p)(11) . . . Sec. 635(a)(2), substituted "certain other plans" for "governmental and church plans" in the heading of para. (p)(11) . . . Sec. 635(b), substituted "section 409(d), and section 457(d)" for "and section 409(d)" in para. (p)(10) . . . Sec. 635(c), redesignated para. (p)(12) as (13) and added para. (p)(12), effective for transfers, distributions, and payments made after 12/31/2001.

—P.L. 107-16, Sec. 663(a), deleted Sec. 1114(c)(4) of P.L. 99-514 [reproduced following Code Sec. 401].

—P.L. 107-16, Sec. 901, of this Act [as amended by Sec. 2 of P.L. 107-358, and Sec. 101(a)(1) of P.L. 111-312, and as related to Sec. 811 of P.L. 109-280, see above], reads as follows:

"SEC. 901. SUNSET OF PROVISIONS OF ACT.

"(a) In general. All provisions of, and amendments made by, this Act shall not apply—

"(1) to taxable, plan, or limitation years beginning after December 31, 2012, or

"(2) in the case of title V, to estates of decedents dying, gifts made, or generation skipping transfers, after December 31, 2012.

"(b) Application of certain laws. The Internal Revenue Code of 1986 and the Employee Retirement Income Security Act of 1974 shall be applied and administered to years, estates, gifts, and transfers described in subsection (a) as if the provisions and amendments described in subsection (a) had never been enacted.

"(c) Exception. Subsection (a) shall not apply to section 803 (relating to no federal income tax on restitution received by victims of the Nazi regime or their heirs or estates)."

In 2000, P.L. 106-554, Sec. 1(a)(7), [which enacted into law Sec. 314(e)(2) of P.L. 106-554] substituted "section 125, 132(f)(4), 402(e)(3)" for "section 125, 402(e)(3)" in para. (s)(2), effective for tax. yrs. begin. after 12/31/97.

In 1998, P.L. 105-206, Sec. 6018(c), amended Sec. 1431(c)(1)(E) of P.L. 104-188 by removing the comma after "paragraph (4)" in the material to be deleted, see below.

In 1997, P.L. 105-34, Sec. 1522(a)(1), substituted "not otherwise participating" for "not eligible to participate" in subpara. (e)(5)(C) . . . Sec. 1522(a)(2), added subpara. (e)(5)(E), effective for yrs. begin. after 12/31/97.

—P.L. 105-34, Sec. 1601(d)(6)(A), amended subpara. (e)(5)(A), effective for yrs. begin. after 12/31/96.

Prior to amendment, subpara. (e)(5)(A) read as follows:

"(A) Certain ministers may participate. For purposes of this part—

"(i) In general. An employee of a church or a convention or association of churches shall include a duly ordained, commissioned, or licensed minister of a church who, in connection with the exercise of his or her ministry—

"(I) is a self-employed individual (within the meaning of section 401(c)(1)(B)), or

"(II) is employed by an organization other than an organization described in section 501(c)(3).

"(ii) Treatment of employer and employee.

"(I) Self-employed. A minister described in clause (i)(I) shall be treated as his or her own employer which is an organization described in section 501(c)(3) and which is exempt from tax under section 501(a).

"(II) Others. A minister described in clause (i)(II) shall be treated as employed by an organization described in section 501(c)(3) and exempt from tax under section 501(a)."

—P.L. 105-34, Sec. 1601(d)(7), redesignated para. (q)(7) [sic (9)] as para. (q)(9), effective for yrs. begin. after 12/31/96.

—P.L. 105-34, Sec. 1601(h)(2)(D)(i), added "137," after "132," in subpara. (n)(3)(C) . . . Sec. 1601(h)(2)(D)(ii), added "137," after "132," in para. (t)(2), effective for tax. yrs. begin. after 12/31/96.

In 1996, P.L. 104-188, Sec. 1421(b)(9)(C), added "408(p)," after "408(k)," in subsecs. (b) and (c), and subparas. (m)(4)(B) and (n)(3)(B), effective for tax. yrs. begin. after 12/31/96.

—P.L. 104-188, Sec. 1431(a), amended para. (q)(1), effective for yrs. begin. after 12/31/96, except that in determining whether an employee is a highly compensated employee for yrs. begin. in 1997, such amendments shall be treated as having been in effect for yrs. begin. in 1996.

Prior to amendment, para. (q)(1) read as follows:

"(1) In general. The term 'highly compensated employee' means any employee who, during the year or the preceding year—

"(A) was at any time a 5-percent owner,

"(B) received compensation from the employer in excess of $75,000,

"(C) received compensation from the employer in excess of $50,000 and was in the top-paid group of employees for such year, or

"(D) was at any time an officer and received compensation greater than 50 percent of the amount in effect under section 415(b)(1)(A) for such year.

The Secretary shall adjust the $75,000 and $50,000 amounts under this paragraph at the same time and in the same manner as under section 415(d)."

—P.L. 104-188, Sec. 1431(b)(1), deleted para. (q)(6), effective for yrs. begin. after 12/31/96.

Prior to deletion, para. (q)(6) read as follows:

"(6) Treatment of certain family members.

"(A) In general. If any individual is a member of the family of a 5-percent owner or of a highly compensated employee in the group consisting of the 10 highly compensated employees paid the greatest compensation during the year, then—

"(i) such individual shall not be considered a separate employee, and

"(ii) any compensation paid to such individual (and any applicable contribution or benefit on behalf of such individual) shall be treated as if it were paid to (or on behalf of) the 5-percent owner or highly compensated employee.

"(B) Family. For purposes of subparagraph (A), the term 'family' means, with respect to any employee, such employee's spouse and lineal ascendants or descendants and the spouses of such lineal ascendants or descendants.

"(C) Rules to apply to other provisions.

"(i) In general. Except as provided in regulations and in clause (ii), the rules of subparagraph (A) shall be applied in determining the compensation of (or any contributions or benefits on behalf of) any employee for purposes of any section with respect to which a highly compensated employee is defined by reference to this subsection.

"(ii) Exception for determining integration levels. Clause (i) shall not apply in determining the portion of the compensation of a participant which is under the integration level for purposes of section 401(l)."

—P.L. 104-188, Sec. 1431(c)(1)(A), deleted paras. (q)(2), (5), and (12) and redesignated paras. (q)(3), (4), (7)–(11) as paras. (q)(2)–(8) . . . Sec. 1431(c)(1)(D), substituted "subsection (q)(5)" for "subsection (q)(8)" in subpara. (r)(2)(A) . . . Sec. 1431(c)(1)(E), deleted "under paragraph (4) or the number of officers taken into account under paragraph (5)" in para. (q)(5) [as redesignated by Sec. 1431(c)(1)(A) of this Act, see above], effective for yrs. begin. after 12/31/96, except that in determining whether an employee is a highly compensated employee for yrs. begin. in 1997, such amendments shall be treated as having been in effect for yrs. begin. in 1996.

Prior to deletion, para. (q)(2) read as follows:

"(2) Special rule for current year. In the case of the year for which the relevant determination is being made, an employee not described in subparagraph (B), (C), or (D) of paragraph (1) for the preceding year (without regard to this paragraph) shall not be treated as described in subparagraph (B), (C), or (D) of paragraph (1) unless such employee is a member of the group consisting of the 100 employees paid the greatest compensation during the year for which such determination is being made."

Prior to deletion, para. (q)(5) read as follows:

"(5) Special rules for treatment of officers.

"(A) Not more than 50 officers taken into account. For purposes of paragraph (1)(D), no more than 50 employees (or, if lesser, the greater of 3 employees or 10 percent of the employees) shall be treated as officers.

"(B) At least 1 officer taken into account. If for any year no officer of the employer is described in paragraph (1)(D), the highest paid officer of the employer for such year shall be treated as described in such paragraph."

Prior to deletion, para. (q)(12) read as follows:

"(12) Simplified method for determining highly compensated employees.

"(A) In general. If an election by the employer under this paragraph applies to any year, in determining whether an employee is a highly compensated employee for such year—

"(i) subparagraph (B) of paragraph (l) shall be applied by substituting '$50,000' for '$75,000', and

"(ii) subparagraph (C) of paragraph (l) shall not apply.

"(B) Requirement for election. An election under this paragraph shall not apply to any year unless—

"(i) at all times during such year, the employer maintained significant business activities (and employed employees) in at least 2 significantly separate geographic areas, and

"(ii) the employer satisfies such other conditions as the Secretary may prescribe."

—P.L. 104-188, Sec. 1434(b)(1), amended para. (q)(4) [as redesignated by Sec. 1431(c)(1)(A) of this Act, see above] . . . Sec. 1434(b)(2), added "not" after "elect" in the heading and text of para. (s)(2), effective for yrs. begin. after 12/31/97.

Employee benefit plans   Code Sec. 414

Prior to amendment, para. (q)(4) [as redesignated by Sec. 1431(c)(1)(A) of this Act, see above] read as follows:
"(4) Compensation. For purposes of this subsection—
"(A) In general. The term 'compensation' means compensation within the meaning of section 415(c)(3).
"(B) Certain provisions not taken into account. The determination under subparagraph (A) shall be made—
"(i) without regard to sections 125, 402(e)(3), and 402(h)(1)(B), and
"(ii) in the case of employer contributions made pursuant to a salary reduction agreement, without regard to section 403(b)."
—P.L. 104-188, Sec. 1454(a), amended subpara. (n)(2)(C), effective for yrs. begin. after 12/31/96, but shall not apply to any relationship determined under an Internal Revenue Service ruling issued before the date of the enactment of this Act [8/20/96] pursuant to section 414(n)(2)(C) of the Internal Revenue Code of 1986 (as in effect on the day before such date) not to involve a leased employee.
Prior to amendment, subpara. (n)(2)(C) read as follows:
"(C) such services are of a type historically performed, in the business field of the recipient, by employees."
—P.L. 104-188, Sec. 1457, of this Act, provides:
"Sec. 1457. Sample language for spousal consent and qualified domestic relations forms.
"(a) Development of sample language. Not later than January 1, 1997, the Secretary of the Treasury shall develop—
"(1) sample language for inclusion in a form for the spousal consent required under section 417(a)(2) of the Internal Revenue Code of 1986 and section 205(c)(2) of the Employee Retirement Income Security Act of 1974 which—
"(A) is written in a manner calculated to be understood by the average person, and
"(B) discloses in plain form—
"(i) whether the waiver to which the spouse consents is irrevocable, and
"(ii) whether such waiver may be revoked by a qualified domestic relations order, and
"(2) sample language for inclusion in a form for a qualified domestic relations order described in section 414(p)(1)(A) of such Code and section 206(d)(3)(B)(i) of such Act which—
"(A) meets the requirements contained in such sections, and
"(B) the provisions of which focus attention on the need to consider the treatment of any lump sum payment, qualified joint and survivor annuity, or qualified preretirement survivor annuity.
"(b) Publicity. The Secretary of the Treasury shall include publicity for the sample language developed under subsection (a) in the pension outreach efforts undertaken by the Secretary."
—P.L. 104-188, Sec. 1461(a), added para. (e)(5), effective for yrs. begin. after 12/31/96.
—P.L. 104-188, Sec. 1462(a), added para. (q)(7)[sic (9)], effective for yrs. begin. after 12/31/96.
—P.L. 104-188, Sec. 1462(b), of this Act, provides:
"(b) Safeharbor authority. The Secretary of the Treasury may design discrimination and coverage safe harbors for church plans."
—P.L. 104-188, Sec. 1704(n)(1), added subsec. (u), effective 12/12/94.
In 1992, P.L. 102-318, Sec. 521(b)(20), substituted "section 402(e)(3)" for "section 402(a)(8)" in subclause (n)(5)(C)(iii)(I) ... Sec. 521(b)(21), substituted "402(e)(3)" for "402(a)(8)" in clause (q)(7)(B)(i) ... Sec. 521(b)(22), substituted "402(e)(3)" for "402(a)(8)" in para. (s)(2), effective for distributions after 12/31/92. For special rule, see Sec. 521(e)(2) of this Act which reads as follows:
"(2) Special rule for partial distributions. For purposes of section 402(a)(5)(D)(i)(II) of the Internal Revenue Code of 1986 (as in effect before the amendments made by this section), a distribution before January 1, 1993, which is made before or at the same time as a series of periodic payments shall not be treated as one of such series if it is not substantially equal in amount to other payments in such series."
In 1990, P.L. 101-508, Sec. 11703(b)(1), deleted "(6 months in the case of core health benefits)" after "at least 1 year," in subpara. (n)(2)(B), effective as provided in Secs. 1151(k)(1) and (4) of P.L. 99-514, reproduced below.
In 1989, P.L. 101-239, Sec. 7811(m)(5), added "section" before "403(b)" in para. (p)(10), effective 12/31/84.
—P.L. 101-239, Sec. 7813(b), corrected Secs. 3011(b)(4) and (5) of P.L. 100-647 which amended subpara. (n)(3)(C) and para. (t)(2) to read "as amended by section 1011B(a) of this Act" instead of "as amended by section 111B(a) of this Act" and to strike out "162(k)" instead of "162(k)(2)", see below.
—P.L. 101-239, Sec. 7841(a)(2), redesignated para. (p)(11) as (12) and added para. (p)(11), effective for transfers after 12/19/89 in tax. yrs. end. after 12/19/89.
—P.L. 101-140, Sec. 203(a)(6)(A), deleted "89," after "79," in subpara. (n)(3)(C) ... Sec. 203(a)(6)(B), substituted "section" for "sections 89 and" in para. (r)(1) ... Sec. 203(a)(6)(C), deleted "89," after "79," in para. (t)(2), effective as provided in Sec. 1151(k)(1) and (4) of P.L. 99-514, reproduced below.
—P.L. 101-140, Sec. 204(b)(1), of this Act, effective for yrs. begin. after 12/31/86, provides:
"(1) Application of line of business test for period before guidelines issued.— In the case of any plan year beginning on or before the date the Secretary of the Treasury or his delegate issues guidelines and begins issuing determinations under section 414(r)(2)(C) of the Internal Revenue Code of 1986, an employer shall be treated as operating separate lines of business if the employer reasonably determines that it meets the requirements of section 414(r) (other than paragraph (2)(C) thereof) of such Code."

—P.L. 101-140, Sec. 204(b)(2), substituted "sections 129(d)(8) and 410(b)" for "section 410(b)" in para. (r)(1) [as amended by Sec. 203(a)(6)(B) of this Act, see above], effective for yrs. begin. after 12/31/88.
—P.L. 101-136, Sec. 528, provides:
"Sec. 528. No monies appropriated by this Act may be used to implement or enforce section 1151 of the Tax Reform Act of '86 or the amendments made by such section."
In 1988, P.L. 100-647, Sec. 1011(d)(8), substituted "50 percent of the amount in effect under section 415(b)(1)(A)" for "150 percent of the amount in effect under section 415(c)(1)(A)", effective for tax. yrs. begin. after 12/31/86.
—P.L. 100-647, Sec. 1011(e)(4), added "or any requirement under section 457" after "(n)(3)" in subsec. (o), effective for tax. yrs. begin. after 12/31/88.
—P.L. 100-647, Sec. 1011(h)(5), substituted "(16), (17), and (26)" for "and (16)" in subparas. (m)(4)(A) and (n)(3)(A), effective for plan yrs. begin. after 12/31/88.
—P.L. 100-647, Sec. 1011(i)(1), added the sentence at the end of para. (q)(1) ... Sec. 1011(i)(2), added subpara. (q)(6)(C) ... Sec. 1011(i)(3)(A), added "and" at the end of subpara. (q)(8)(D), substituted a period for ", and" at the end of subpara. (q)(8)(E), deleted subpara. (q)(8)(F) and substituted "Except as provided by the Secretary, the" for "The" in the last sentence of para. (q)(8) ... Sec. 1011(i)(3)(B), added para. (q)(11) ... Sec. 1011(i)(4)(A), added "or the number of officers taken into account under paragraph (5)" after "paragraph (4)" in para. (q)(8) ... Sec. 1011(j)(1), amended para. (s)(1) ... Sec. 1011(j)(2), deleted para. (s)(2), redesignated paras. (s)(3) and (s)(4) as paras. (s)(2) and (s)(3) and added para. (s)(4), effective for yrs. begin. after 12/31/86.
Prior to deletion, subpara. (q)(8)(F) read as follows:
"(F) employees who are nonresident aliens and who receive no earned income (within the meaning of section 911(d)(2)) from the employer which constitutes income from sources within the United States (within the meaning of section 861(a)(3))."
Prior to amendment, para. (s)(1) read as follows:
"(1) In general. The term 'compensation' means compensation for service performed for an employer which (taking into account the provisions of this chapter) is currently includible in gross income."
Prior to deletion, para. (s)(2) read as follows:
"(2) Self-employed individuals. The Secretary shall prescribe regulations for the determination of the compensation of an employee who is a self-employed individual (within the meaning of section 401(c)(1)) which are based on the principles of paragraph (1)."
—P.L. 100-647, Sec. 1011(l)(12), amended Sec. 1117 [reproduced below] of P.L. 99-514, by adding new para. 1117(d)(4), see below.
—P.L. 100-647, Sec. 1011A(b)(3), added "72(d) (relating to treatment of employee contributions as separate contract)," before "411(a)(7)(A)" in para. (k)(2), effective for amounts distributed after 12/31/86, in tax. yrs. end. after 12/31/86.
—P.L. 100-647, Sec. 1011B(a)(16), added "and" at the end of subpara. (m)(4)(A), substituted a period for a comma at the end of subpara. (m)(4)(B) and deleted subparas. (m)(4)(C) and (m)(4)(D) ... Sec. 1011B(a)(17), substituted "132, 162(i)(2), 162(k)," for "132," in para. (t)(2) ... Sec. 1011B(a)(19), substituted "132, 162(i)(2), 162(k)," for "132," in subpara. (n)(3)(C) ... Sec. 1011B(a)(20), deleted "of section 414" each place it appeared in para. (t)(1), effective as provided in Secs. 1115(k)(1) and (4) of P.L. 99-514 [reproduced below].
Prior to deletion, subparas. (m)(4)(C) and (D) read as follows:
"(C) section 105(h), and
"(D) section 125."
—P.L. 100-647, Sec. 1011B(a)(25), added the last sentence to Sec. 1151(k)(1) of P.L. 99-514 [reproduced below], part of the effective date for changes made by Sec. 1151(e)(1) and (i) of P.L. 99-514, see below
—P.L. 100-647, Sec. 1018(t)(8)(E), substituted "means the earlier of" for "means earlier of" and deleted "in" each place it appeared in para. (p)(4)(B) ... Sec. 1018(t)(8)(F), added ", 403(b)," after "401" in para. (p)(10) ... Sec. 1018(t)(8)(G), added the sentence at the end of para. (p)(9), effective 12/31/84.
—P.L. 100-647, Sec. 2005(c)(1), added para. (l)(2) ... Sec. 2005(c)(2), amended the heading of subsec. (l), effective for transactions occurring after 7/26/88. Sec. 2005(c)(3)(B) of this Act provides:
"(B) The amendments made by this subsection shall not apply to any transaction occurring after July 26, 1988, if on or before such date the board of directors of the employer, approves such transaction or the employer took similar binding action."
Prior to amendment, the heading of subsec. (l) read as follows:
"(l) Mergers and consolidations of plans or transfers of plan assets."
—P.L. 100-647, Sec. 3011(b)(4), [as amended by , see above] deleted "162(i)(2), 162(k)" before "247(j)" and substituted "505, and 4980B" for "and 505" in subpara. (n)(3)(C) [as amended by section 1011B(a) of this Act] ... Sec. 3011(b)(5), [as amended by Sec. 7813(b) of P.L. 101-239, see above] deleted "162(i)(2), 162(k)(2), " before "274(j)" and substituted "505, or 4980B" for "or 505" in para. (t)(2) [as amended by section 1011B(a) of this Act], effective for tax. yrs. begin. after 12/31/88, but shall not apply to any plan for any plan year to which '86 Code Sec. 162(k) (as in effect on 11/9/88) did not apply by reason of Sec. 10001(e)(2) of P.L. 99-272.
—P.L. 100-647, Sec. 3021(b)(1), added para. (q)(12) ... Sec. 3021(b)(2)(A), amended para. (r)(3), effective for yrs. begin. after 12/31/86.
Prior to amendment, para. (r)(3) read as follows:
"(3) Safe harbor rule. The requirements of subparagraph (C) of paragraph (2) shall not apply to any line of business if the highly compensated employee percentage with respect to such line of business is—
"(A) not less than one-half, and

2,029

"(B) not more than twice,
the percentage which highly compensated employees are of all employees of the employer. An employer shall be treated as meeting the requirements of subparagraph (A) if at least 10 percent of all highly compensated employees of the employer perform services solely for such line of business."
— P.L. 100-647, Sec. 6067(a), added subpara. (l)(2)(G), effective for transactions occurring after 7/26/88. For special rules, see Sec. 2005(c)(3)(B) reproduced above. Sec. 6067(b) of this Act provides:
"(b) Study. The Secretary of the Treasury or his delegate, in consultation with the Federal Deposit Insurance Corporation, shall conduct a study with respect to the proper method of allocating assets in the case of a transaction to which the amendment made by this subsection applies. The Secretary of the Treasury shall not later than January 1, 1990, report the results of such study to the Committee on Ways and Means of the House of Representatives and to the Committee on Finance of the Senate."

In 1987, P.L. 100-203, Sec. 9305(c), deleted "the minimum funding standard of section 412, the tax imposed by section 4971, and" after "more than one such corporation," in subsec. (b), effective for plan yrs. begin. after 12/31/87.

In 1986, P.L. 99-514, Sec. 1114(a), added subsec. (q), effective for yrs. begin. after 12/31/86.
— P.L. 99-514, Sec. 1114(b)(11), substituted "highly compensated employees (within the meaning of section 414(q))" for "officers, highly compensated employees, or owners" in clause (m)(2)(B)(ii), effective for yrs. begin. after 12/31/88.
— P.L. 99-514, Sec. 1115(a), added subsecs. (r) and (s), effective for yrs. begin. after 12/31/86.
— P.L. 99-514, Sec. 1117(c), substituted ", 415 (relating to limitations on benefits and contributions under qualified plans), and 401(m) (relating to nondiscrimination tests for matching requirements and employee contributions)" for "and 415 (relating to limitations on benefits and contributions under qualified plans)" in para. (k)(2), effective for plan yrs. begin. after 12/31/86. For special rules, see Sec. 1117(d)(2)-(4) of P.L. 99-514 [as added by Sec. 1011(l)(12) of P.L. 100-647] reproduced in note following Code Sec. 401.
— P.L. 99-514, Sec. 1146(a)(1), amended para. (n)(5), effective for services performed after 12/31/86.
Prior to amendment, para (n)(5) read as follows:
"(5) Safe harbor. This subsection shall not apply to any leased employee if such employee is covered by a plan which is maintained by the leasing organization if, with respect to such employee, such plan—
"(A) is a money purchase pension plan with a nonintegrated employer contribution rate of at least 7½ percent, and
"(B) provides for immediate participation and for full and immediate vesting."
— P.L. 99-514, Sec. 1146(a)(2), amended para. (n)(4) . . . Sec. 1146(a)(3), amended para. (n)(6) . . . Sec. 1146(b)(1), added the sentence at the end of subsec. (o) . . . Sec. 1146(b)(2), deleted "except to the extent otherwise provided in regulations," following "listed in paragraph (3)," in para. (n)(1), effective for tax. yrs. begin after 12/31/83. Sec. 1146(c)(3) of this Act provides:
"(3) Recordkeeping requirements. In the case of years beginning before the date of the enactment of this Act, the last sentence of section 414(o) shall be applied without regard to the requirement that an insignificant percentage of the workload be performed by persons other than employees."
Prior to amendment, para. (n)(4) read as follows:
"(4) Time when leased employee is first considered as employee. In the case of any leased employee, paragraph (1) shall apply only for purposes of determining whether the pension requirements listed in paragraph (3) are met for periods after the close of the 1-year period referred to in paragraph (2); except that years of service for the recipient shall be determined by taking into account the entire period for which the leased employee performed services for the recipient (or related persons)."
Prior to amendment, para. (n)(6) read as follows:
"(6) Related persons. For purposes of this subsection, the term 'related persons' has the same meaning as when used in section 103(b)(6)(C)."
— P.L. 99-514, Sec. 1151(e)(1), added subsec. (t) . . . Sec. 1151(i)(1), substituted "requirements" for "pension requirements" in para. (n)(1) . . . Sec. 1151(i)(2), added "(6 months in the case of core health benefits)" after "1 year" in subpara. (n)(2)(B) . . . Sec. 1151(i)(3), substituted "Requirements" for "Pension requirements" in the heading of para. (n)(3), substituted "requirements" for "pension requirements" in para. (n)(3), deleted "and" at the end of subpara. (n)(3)(A), substituted "and" for the period at the end of subpara. (n)(3)(B), and added subpara. (n)(3)(C), effective as provided in Secs. 1151(k)(1) [as amended by Sec. 1011B(a)(25) of P.L. 100-647, see above] and (4) of this Act which read as follows:
"(1) In general.—The amendments made by this section shall apply to years beginning after the later of—
"(A) December 31, 1987, or
"(B) the earlier of —
"(i) the date which is 3 months after the date on which the Secretary of the Treasury or his delegate issues such regulations as are necessary to carry out the provisions of section 89 of the Internal Revenue Code of 1986 (as added by this section), or
"(ii) December 31, 1988.
Notwithstanding the preceding sentence, the amendments made by subsections (e)(1) and (i)(3)(C) shall, to the extent they relate to sections 106, 162(i)(2), and 162(k) of the Internal Revenue Code of 1986, apply to years beginning after 1986."
* * *

"(4) Special rule for church plans. In the case of a church plan (within the meaning of section 414(e)(3) of the Internal Revenue Code of 1986) maintaining an insured accident and health plan, the amendments made by this section shall apply to years beginning after December 31, 1988."
— P.L. 99-514, Sec. 1301(j)(4), substituted "section 144(a)(3)" for "section 103(b)(6)(C)" in paras. (m)(5) and (n)(6), effective for bonds issued after 8/15/86. For transitional rules, see Secs. 1312-1318 of P.L. 99-514 at note following Code Sec. 103.
— P.L. 99-514, Sec. 1852(f), amended Sec. 526(d)(2) of P.L. 98-369 by deleting para. (m)(7) instead of para. (m)(6), see below, effective 7/18/84.
— P.L. 99-514, Sec. 1898(c)(2)(A)(i), substituted "shall separately account for the amounts (hereinafter in this paragraph referred to as the 'segregated amounts')" for "shall segregate in a separate account in the plan or in an escrow account the amounts" in subpara. (p)(7)(A) . . . Sec. 1898(c)(2)(A)(ii), substituted "the 18-month period described in subparagraph (E)" for "18 months" and substituted "including any interest" for "plus any interest" in subpara. (p)(7)(B) . . . Sec. 1898(c)(2)(A)(iii), substituted "the 18-month period described in subparagraph (E)" for "18 months" and substituted "including any interest" for "plus any interest" in subpara. (p)(7)(C) . . . Sec. 1898(c)(2)(A)(iv), substituted "the 18-month period described in subparagraph (E)" for "the 18-month period" in subpara. (p)(7)(D) . . . Sec. 1898(c)(2)(A)(v), added subpara. (p)(7)(E) . . . Sec. 1898(c)(4)(A), redesignated para. (p)(9) as para. (p)(11) and added para. (p)(9) . . . Sec. 1898(c)(6)(A), substituted "sections 401(a)(11) and 417 (and any spouse of the participant shall not be treated as a spouse of the participant for such purposes)" for "sections 401(a)(11) and 417" in subpara. (p)(5)(A) . . . Sec. 1898(c)(7)(A)(ii), substituted "to a spouse, former spouse," for "to a spouse," in clause (p)(1)(B)(i) . . . Sec. 1898(c)(7)(A)(iii), substituted "each alternate payee" for "any other alternate payee" in clause (p)(6)(A)(i) . . . Sec. 1898(c)(7)(A)(iv), substituted "the surviving former spouse" for "the surviving spouse" in subpara. (p)(5)(B) . . . Sec. 1898(c)(7)(A)(v), deleted the last sentence of para. (p)(5) and added para. (p)(10) . . . Sec. 1898(c)(7)(A)(vi), substituted "A" for "In the case of any payment before a participant has separated from service, a" in subpara. (p)(4)(A) . . . Sec. 1898(c)(7)(A)(vi), added "in the case of any payment before a participant has separated from service," before "on or" in clause (p)(4)(A)(i) . . . Sec. 1898(c)(7)(A)(vii), amended subpara. (p)(4)(B), effective 12/31/84 except as provided in Sec. 303 of P.L. 98-397 at note following Code Sec. 401.
Prior to amendment, subpara. (p)(4)(B) read as follows:
"(B) Earliest retirement age. For purposes of this paragraph, the term 'earliest retirement age' has the meaning given such term by section 417(f)(3), except that in the case of any defined contribution plan, the earliest retirement age shall be the date which is 10 years before the normal retirement age (within the meaning of section 411(a)(8))."
Prior to deletion, the last sentence of para. (p)(5) read as follows:
"A plan shall not be treated as failing to meet the requirements of subsection (a) or (k) of section 401 which prohibit payment of benefits before termination of employment solely by reason of payments to an alternate payee pursuant to a qualified domestic relations order."
— P.L. 99-514, Sec. 1899A(12), deleted the comma after "benefits" in subpara. (p)(3)(B), effective 10/22/86.

In 1984, P.L. 98-397, Sec. 204(b), added subsec. (p), effective for plan years begin. after 12/31/84, except as provided in Sec. 302(b) of this Act reproduced in note following Code Sec. 402. For transitional rules see Sec. 303 of this Act, reproduced in note following Code Sec. 401.
— P.L. 98-369, Sec. 491(d)(26), deleted "or 405(a)" after "section 403(a)" in subpara. (h)(1)(B) . . . Sec. 491(d)(27), deleted "or 405" after "section 403(a)" in subsec. (l), effective for obligations issued after 12/31/83.
— P.L. 98-369, Sec. 526(a)(1), substituted "section 318(a)" for "section 267(c)" in subpara. (m)(6)(B), effective for tax. yrs. begin. after 12/31/84.
— P.L. 98-369, Sec. 526(b)(1), substituted "any person who is not an employee of the recipient and " for "any person" in para. (n)(2), effective for tax. yrs. begin. after 12/31/83.
— P.L. 98-369, Sec. 526(d)(1), added subsec. (o) . . . Sec. 526(d)(2), [as amended by Sec. 1852(f) of P.L. 99-514, see above], deleted para. (m)(7), effective 7/18/84.
Prior to deletion, para. (m)(7) read as follows:
"(7) Prevention of avoidance. The Secretary shall prescribe such regulations as may be necessary to prevent the avoidance with respect to service organizations, through the use of separate organizations, of any employee benefit requirement listed in paragraph (4)."
— P.L. 98-369, Sec. 713(i), substituted "any person who is not an employee of the recipient and" for "any person" in para. (n)(2), effective for tax. yrs. begin. after 12/31/83.

In 1982, P.L. 97-248, Sec. 240(c)(1), substituted "415, and 416" for "and 415" in subsecs. (b) and (c) . . . Sec. 240(c)(2), substituted "415, and 416" for "and 415" in para. (m)(4), effective for yrs. begin. after 12/31/83.
— P.L. 97-248, Sec. 246(a), redesignated paras. (m)(5) and (m)(6) as paras. (m)(6) and (m)(7), and added para. (m)(5), effective for tax. yrs. begin. after 12/31/83.
— P.L. 97-248, Sec. 248(a), added subsec. (n), effective for tax. yrs. begin. after 12/31/83.

In 1980, P.L. 96-613, Sec. 5(a), added subsec. (m), the same amendment as Sec. 201(a) of P.L. 96-605, see below.
— P.L. 96-605, Sec. 201(a), added subsec. (m), effective for plan yrs. ending after 11/30/80 except as provided by Sec. 201(c)(2) of the Act which reads as follows:

be applied separately with respect to each change in the benefit structure of a plan.

(6) Computation of benefits and contributions. The computation of—

(A) benefits under a defined contribution plan, for purposes of section 401(a)(4),

(B) contributions made on behalf of a participant in a defined benefit plan, for purposes of section 401(a)(4), and

(C) contributions and benefits provided for a participant in a plan described in section 414(k), for purposes of this section

shall not be made on a basis inconsistent with regulations prescribed by the Secretary.

(7) Benefits under certain collectively bargained plans. For a year, the limitation referred to in paragraph (1)(B) shall not apply to benefits with respect to a participant under a defined benefit plan (other than a multiemployer plan)—

(A) which is maintained for such year pursuant to a collective bargaining agreement between employee representatives and one or more employers,

(B) which, at all times during such year, has at least 100 participants,

(C) under which benefits are determined solely by reference to length of service, the particular years during which service was rendered, age at retirement, and date of retirement,

(D) which provides that an employee who has at least 4 years of service has a nonforfeitable right to 100 percent of his accrued benefit derived from employer contributions, and

(E) which requires, as a condition of participation in the plan, that an employee complete a period of not more than 60 consecutive days of service with the employer or employers maintaining the plan.

This paragraph shall not apply to a participant whose compensation for any 3 years during the 10-year period immediately preceding the year in which he separates from service exceeded the average compensation for such 3 years of all participants in such plan. This paragraph shall not apply to a participant for any period for which he is a participant under another plan to which this section applies which is maintained by an employer maintaining this plan. For any year for which the paragraph applies to benefits with respect to a participant, paragraph (1)(A) and subsection (d)(1)(A) shall be applied with respect to such participant by substituting one-half the amount otherwise applicable for such year under paragraph (1)(A) for "$160,000".

(8) Social security retirement age defined. For purposes of this subsection, the term "social security retirement age" means the age used as the retirement age under section 216(l) of the Social Security Act, except that such section shall be applied—

(A) without regard to the age increase factor, and

(B) as if the early retirement age under section 216(l)(2) of such Act were 62.

(9) Special rule for commercial airline pilots.

(A) In general. Except as provided in subparagraph (B), in the case of any participant who is a commercial airline pilot, if, as of the time of the participant's retirement, regulations prescribed by the Federal Aviation Administration require an individual to separate from service as a commercial airline pilot after attaining any age occurring on or after age 60 and before age 62, paragraph (2)(C) shall be applied by substituting such age for age 62.

(B) Individuals who separate from service before age 60. If a participant described in subparagraph (A) separates from service before age 60, the rules of paragraph (2)(C) shall apply.

(10) Special rule for State, Indian tribal, and local government plans.

(A) Limitation to equal accrued benefit. In the case of a plan maintained for its employees by any State or political subdivision thereof, or by any agency or instrumentality of the foregoing, or a governmental plan described in the last sentence of section 414(d) (relating to plans of Indian tribal governments), the limitation with respect to a qualified participant under this subsection shall not be less than the accrued benefit of the participant under the plan (determined without regard to any amendment of the plan made after October 14, 1987).

(B) Qualified participant. For purposes of this paragraph, the term "qualified participant" means a participant who first became a participant in the plan maintained by the employer before January 1, 1990.

(C) Election.

(i) In general. This paragraph shall not apply to any plan unless each employer maintaining the plan elects before the close of the 1st plan year beginning after December 31, 1989, to have this subsection (other than paragraph (2)(G)).

(ii) Revocation of election. An election under clause (i) may be revoked not later than the last day of the third plan year beginning after the date of the enactment of this clause. The revocation shall apply to all plan years to which the election applied and to all subsequent plan years. Any amount paid by a plan in a taxable year ending after the revocation shall be includible in income in such taxable year under the rules of this chapter in effect for such taxable year, except that, for purposes of applying the limitations imposed by this section, any portion of such amount which is attributable to any taxable year during which the election was in effect shall be treated as received in such taxable year.

(11) Special limitation rule for governmental and multiemployer plans. In the case of a governmental plan (as defined in section 414(d)) or a multiemployer plan (as defined in section 414(f)), subparagraph (B) of paragraph (1) shall not apply. Subparagraph (B) of paragraph (1) shall not apply to a plan maintained by an organization described in section 3121(w)(3)(A) except with respect to highly compensated benefits. For purposes of this paragraph, the term "highly compensated benefits" means any benefits accrued for an employee in any year on or after the first year in which such employee is a highly compensated employee (as defined in section 414(q)) of the organization described in section 3121(w)(3)(A). For purposes of applying paragraph (1)(B) to highly compensated benefits, all benefits of the employee otherwise taken into account (without regard to this paragraph) shall be taken into account.

(c) Limitation for defined contribution plans.

(1) In general. Contributions and other additions with respect to a participant exceed the limitation of this subsection if, when expressed as an annual addition (within the meaning of paragraph (2)) to the participant's account, such annual addition is greater than the lesser of—

(A) $40,000, or

(B) 100 percent of the participant's compensation.

(2) **Annual addition.** For purposes of paragraph (1), the term "annual addition" means the sum for any year of—
  (A) employer contributions,
  (B) the employee contributions, and
  (C) forfeitures.
For the purposes of this paragraph, employee contributions under subparagraph (B) are determined without regard to any rollover contributions (as defined in sections 402(c), 403(a)(4), 403(b)(8), 408(d)(3), and 457(e)(16)) without regard to employee contributions to a simplified employee pension which are excludable from gross income under section 408(k)(6). Subparagraph (B) of paragraph (1) shall not apply to any contribution for medical benefits (within the meaning of section 419A(f)(2)) after separation from service which is treated as an annual addition.

(3) **Participant's compensation.** For purposes of paragraph (1)—
  (A) In general. The term "participant's compensation" means the compensation of the participant from the employer for the year.
  (B) Special rule for self-employed individuals. In the case of an employee within the meaning of section 401(c)(1), subparagraph (A) shall be applied by substituting "the participant's earned income (within the meaning of section 401(c)(2) but determined without regard to any exclusion under section 911)" for "compensation of the participant from the employer".
  (C) Special rules for permanent and total disability. In the case of a participant in any defined contribution plan—
    (i) who is permanently and totally disabled (as defined in section 22(e)(3)),
    (ii) who is not a highly compensated employee (within the meaning of section 414(q)), and
    (iii) with respect to whom the employer elects, at such time and in such manner as the Secretary may prescribe, to have this subparagraph apply,
  the term "participant's compensation" means the compensation the participant would have received for the year if the participant was paid at the rate of compensation paid immediately before becoming permanently and totally disabled. This subparagraph shall apply only if contributions made with respect to amounts treated as compensation under this subparagraph are nonforfeitable when made. If a defined contribution plan provides for the continuation of contributions on behalf of all participants described in clause (i) for a fixed or determinable period, this subparagraph shall be applied without regard to clauses (ii) and (iii).
  (D) Certain deferrals included. The term "participant's compensation" shall include—
    (i) any elective deferral (as defined in section 402(g)(3)), and
    (ii) any amount which is contributed or deferred by the employer at the election of the employee and which is not includible in the gross income of the employee by reason of section 125, 132(f)(4), or 457.
  (E) Annuity contracts. In the case of an annuity contract described in section 403(b), the term "participant's compensation" means the participant's includible compensation determined under section 403(b)(3).

(4) **Repealed.**
(5) **Repealed.**
(6) **Special rule for employee stock ownership plans.** If no more than one-third of the employer contributions to an employee stock ownership plan (as described in section 4975(e)(7)) for a year which are deductible under paragraph (9) of section 404(a) are allocated to highly compensated employees (within the meaning of section 414(q)), the limitations imposed by this section shall not apply to—
  (A) forfeitures of employer securities (within the meaning of section 409) under such an employee stock ownership plan if such securities were acquired with the proceeds of a loan (as described in section 404(a)(9)(A)), or
  (B) employer contributions to such an employee stock ownership plan which are deductible under section 404(a)(9)(B) and charged against the participant's account.
The amount of any qualified gratuitous transfer (as defined in section 664(g)(1)) allocated to a participant for any limitation year shall not exceed the limitations imposed by this section, but such amount shall not be taken into account in determining whether any other amount exceeds the limitations imposed by this section.

(7) **Special rules relating to church plans.**
  (A) Alternative contribution limitation.
    (i) In general. Notwithstanding any other provision of this subsection, at the election of a participant who is an employee of a church or a convention or association of churches, including an organization described in section 414(e)(3)(B)(ii), contributions and other additions for an annuity contract or retirement income account described in section 403(b) with respect to such participant, when expressed as an annual addition to such participant's account, shall be treated as not exceeding the limitation of paragraph (1) if such annual addition is not in excess of $10,000.
    (ii) $40,000 aggregate limitation. The total amount of additions with respect to any participant which may be taken into account for purposes of this subparagraph for all years may not exceed $40,000.
  (B) Number of years of service for duly ordained, commissioned, or licensed ministers or lay employees. For purposes of this paragraph—
    (i) all years of service by—
      (I) a duly ordained, commissioned, or licensed minister of a church, or
      (II) a lay person,
    as an employee of a church, a convention or association of churches, including an organization described in section 414(e)(3)(B)(ii), shall be considered as years of service for 1 employer, and
    (ii) all amounts contributed for annuity contracts by each such church (or convention or association of churches) or such organization during such years for such minister or lay person shall be considered to have been contributed by 1 employer.
  (C) Foreign missionaries. In the case of any individual described in subparagraph (B) performing services outside the United States, contributions and other additions for an annuity contract or retirement income account described in section 403(b) with respect to such employee, when expressed as an annual addition to such employee's account, shall not be treated as exceeding the limitation of paragraph (1) if such annual addition is not in excess of $3,000. This subparagraph shall not apply with respect to any taxable year to any individual whose adjusted gross income for such taxa-

ble year (determined separately and without regard to community property laws) exceeds $17,000.

(D) **Annual addition.** For purposes of this paragraph, the term "annual addition" has the meaning given such term by paragraph (2).

(E) **Church, convention or association of churches.** For purposes of this paragraph, the terms "church" and "convention or association of churches" have the same meaning as when used in section 414(e).

(d) Cost-of-living adjustments.

(1) **In general.** The Secretary shall adjust annually—

(A) the $160,000 amount in subsection (b)(1)(A),

(B) in the case of a participant who separated from service, the amount taken into account under subsection (b)(1)(B), and

(C) the $40,000 amount in subsection (c)(1)(A),

for increases in the cost-of-living in accordance with regulations prescribed by the Secretary.

(2) **Method.** The regulations prescribed under paragraph (1) shall provide for—

(A) an adjustment with respect to any calendar year based on the increase in the applicable index for the calendar quarter ending September 30 of the preceding calendar year over such index for the base period, and

(B) adjustment procedures which are similar to the procedures used to adjust benefit amounts under section 215(i)(2)(A) of the Social Security Act.

(3) **Base period.** For purposes of paragraph (2)—

(A) $160,000 amount. The base period taken into account for purposes of paragraph (1)(A) is the calendar quarter beginning July 1, 2001.

(B) Separations after December 31, 1994. The base period taken into account for purposes of paragraph (1)(B) with respect to individuals separating from service with the employer after December 31, 1994, is the calendar quarter beginning July 1 of the calendar year preceding the calendar year in which such separation occurs.

(C) Separations before January 1, 1995. The base period taken into account for purposes of paragraph (1)(B) with respect to individuals separating from service with the employer before January 1, 1995, is the calendar quarter beginning October 1 of the calendar year preceding the calendar year in which such separation occurs.

(D) $40,000 amount. The base period taken into account for purposes of paragraph (1)(C) is the calendar quarter beginning July 1, 2001.

(4) **Rounding.**

(A) $160,000 amount. Any increase under subparagraph (A) of paragraph (1) which is not a multiple of $5,000 shall be rounded to the next lowest multiple of $5,000. This subparagraph shall also apply for purposes of any provision of this title that provides for adjustments in accordance with the method contained in this subsection, except to the extent provided in such provision.

(B) $40,000 amount. Any increase under subparagraph (C) of paragraph (1) which is not a multiple of $1,000 shall be rounded to the next lowest multiple of $1,000.

(e) Repealed.

(f) Combining of plans.

(1) **In general.** For purposes of applying the limitations of subsections (b) and (c)—

(A) all defined benefit plans (whether or not terminated) of an employer are to be treated as one defined benefit plan, and

(B) all defined contribution plans (whether or not terminated) of an employer are to be treated as one defined contribution plan.

(2) **Exception for multiemployer plans.** Notwithstanding paragraph (1) and subsection (g), a multiemployer plan (as defined in section 414(f)) shall not be combined or aggregated—

(A) with any other plan which is not a multiemployer plan for purposes of applying subsection (b)(1)(B) to such other plan, or

(B) with any other multiemployer plan for purposes of applying the limitations established in this section.

(g) Aggregation of plans.

Except as provided in subsection (f)(3), the Secretary, in applying the provisions of this section to benefits or contributions under more than one plan maintained by the same employer, and to any trusts, contracts, accounts, or bonds referred to in subsection (a)(2), with respect to which the participant has the control required under section 414(b) or (c), as modified by subsection (h), shall, under regulations prescribed by the Secretary, disqualify one or more trusts, plans, contracts, accounts, or bonds, or any combination thereof until such benefits or contributions do not exceed the limitations contained in this section. In addition to taking into account such other factors as may be necessary to carry out the purposes of subsection (f), the regulations prescribed under this paragraph shall provide that no plan which has been terminated shall be disqualified until all other trusts, plans, contracts, accounts, or bonds have been disqualified.

(h) 50 percent control.

For purposes of applying subsections (b) and (c) of section 414 to this section, the phrase "more than 50 percent" shall be substituted for the phrase "at least 80 percent" each place it appears in section 1563(a)(1).

(i) Records not available for past periods.

Where for the period before January 1, 1976, or (if later) the first day of the first plan year of the plan, the records necessary for the application of this section are not available, the Secretary may by regulations prescribe alternative methods for determining the amounts to be taken into account for such period.

(j) Regulations; definition of year.

The Secretary shall prescribe such regulations as may be necessary to carry out the purposes of this section, including, but not limited to, regulations defining the term "year" for purposes of any provision of this section.

(k) Special rules.

(1) **Defined benefit plan and defined contribution plan.** For purposes of this title, the term "defined contribution plan" or "defined benefit plan" means a defined contribution plan (within the meaning of section 414(i)) or a defined benefit plan (within the meaning of section 414(j)), whichever applies, which is—

(A) a plan described in section 401(a) which includes a trust which is exempt from tax under section 501(a),

(B) an annuity plan described in section 403(a),

(C) an annuity contract described in section 403(b), or

(D) a simplified employee pension.

(2) **Contributions to provide cost-of-living protection under defined benefit plans.**

(A) In general. In the case of a defined benefit plan which maintains a qualified cost-of-living arrangement—

(i) any contribution made directly by an employee under such an arrangement shall not be treated as an annual addition for purposes of subsection (c), and

(ii) any benefit under such arrangement which is allocable to an employer contribution which was transferred from a defined contribution plan and to which the requirements of subsection (c) were applied shall, for purposes of subsection (b), be treated as a benefit derived from an employee contribution (and subsection (c) shall not again apply to such contribution by reason of such transfer).

(B) **Qualified cost-of-living arrangement defined.** For purposes of this paragraph, the term "qualified cost-of-living arrangement" means an arrangement under a defined benefit plan which—

(i) provides a cost-of-living adjustment to a benefit provided under such plan or a separate plan subject to the requirements of section 412, and

(ii) meets the requirements of subparagraphs (C), (D), (E), and (F) and such other requirements as the Secretary may prescribe.

(C) **Determination of amount of benefit.** An arrangement meets the requirement of this subparagraph only if the cost-of-living adjustment of participants is based—

(i) on increases in the cost-of-living after the annuity starting date, and

(ii) on average cost-of-living increases determined by reference to 1 or more indexes prescribed by the Secretary, except that the arrangement may provide that the increase for any year will not be less than 3 percent of the retirement benefit (determined without regard to such increase).

(D) **Arrangement elective; time for election.** An arrangement meets the requirements of this subparagraph only if it is elective, it is available under the same terms to all participants, and it provides that such election may at least be made in the year in which the participant—

(i) attains the earliest retirement age under the defined benefit plan (determined without regard to any requirement of separation from service), or

(ii) separates from service.

(E) **Nondiscrimination requirements.** An arrangement shall not meet the requirements of this subparagraph if the Secretary finds that a pattern of discrimination exists with respect to participation.

(F) **Special rules for key employees.**

(i) **In general.** An arrangement shall not meet the requirements of this paragraph if any key employee is eligible to participate.

(ii) **Key employee.** For purposes of this subparagraph, the term "key employee" has the meaning given such term by section 416(i)(1), except that in the case of a plan other than a top-heavy plan (within the meaning of section 416(g)), such term shall not include an individual who is a key employee solely by reason of section 416(i)(1)(A)(i).

(3) **Repayments of cashouts under governmental plans.** In the case of any repayment of contributions (including interest thereon) to the governmental plan with respect to an amount previously refunded upon a forfeiture of service credit under the plan or under another governmental plan maintained by a State or local government employer within the same State, any such repayment shall not be taken into account for purposes of this section.

(4) **Special rules for sections 403(b) and 408.** For purposes of this section, any annuity contract described in section 403(b) for the benefit of a participant shall be treated as a defined contribution plan maintained by each employer with respect to which the participant has the control required under subsection (b) or (c) of section 414 (as modified by subsection (h)). For purposes of this section, any contribution by an employer to a simplified employee pension plan for an individual for a taxable year shall be treated as an employer contribution to a defined contribution plan for such individual for such year.

(l) **Treatment of certain medical benefits.**

(1) **In general.** For purposes of this section, contributions allocated to any individual medical benefit account which is part of a pension or annuity plan shall be treated as an annual addition to a defined contribution plan for purposes of subsection (c). Subparagraph (B) of subsection (c)(1) shall not apply to any amount treated as an annual addition under the preceding sentence.

(2) **Individual medical benefit account.** For purposes of paragraph (1), the term "individual medical benefit account" means any separate account—

(A) which is established for a participant under a pension or annuity plan, and

(B) from which benefits described in section 401(h) are payable solely to such participant, his spouse, or his dependents.

(m) **Treatment of qualified governmental excess benefit arrangements.**

(1) **Governmental plan not affected.** In determining whether a governmental plan (as defined in section 414(d)) meets the requirements of this section, benefits provided under a qualified governmental excess benefit arrangement shall not be taken into account. Income accruing to a governmental plan (or to a trust that is maintained solely for the purpose of providing benefits under a qualified governmental excess benefit arrangement) in respect of a qualified governmental excess benefit arrangement shall constitute income derived from the exercise of an essential governmental function upon which such governmental plan (or trust) shall be exempt from tax under section 115.

(2) **Taxation of participant.** For purposes of this chapter—

(A) the taxable year or years for which amounts in respect of a qualified governmental excess benefit arrangement are includible in gross income by a participant, and

(B) the treatment of such amounts when so includible by the participant,

shall be determined as if such qualified governmental excess benefit arrangement were treated as a plan for the deferral of compensation which is maintained by a corporation not exempt from tax under this chapter and which does not meet the requirements for qualification under section 401.

(3) **Qualified governmental excess benefit arrangement.** For purposes of this subsection, the term "qualified governmental excess benefit arrangement" means a portion of a governmental plan if—

(A) such portion is maintained solely for the purpose of providing to participants in the plan that part of the participant's annual benefit otherwise payable under the terms of the plan that exceeds the limitations on benefits imposed by this section,

(B) under such portion no election is provided at any time to the participant (directly or indirectly) to defer compensation, and

(C) benefits described in subparagraph (A) are not paid from a trust forming a part of such governmental plan

Employee benefit plans Code Sec. 415

unless such trust is maintained solely for the purpose of providing such benefits.

(n) Special rules relating to purchase of permissive service credit.

(1) In general. If a participant makes 1 or more contributions to a defined benefit governmental plan (within the meaning of section 414(d)) to purchase permissive service credit under such plan, then the requirements of this section shall be treated as met only if—

(A) the requirements of subsection (b) are met, determined by treating the accrued benefit derived from all such contributions as an annual benefit for purposes of subsection (b), or

(B) the requirements of subsection (c) are met, determined by treating all such contributions as annual additions for purposes of subsection (c).

(2) Application of limit. For purposes of—

(A) applying paragraph (1)(A), the plan shall not fail to meet the reduced limit under subsection (b)(2)(C) solely by reason of this subsection, and

(B) applying paragraph (1)(B), the plan shall not fail to meet the percentage limitation under subsection (c)(1)(B) solely by reason of this subsection.

(3) Permissive service credit. For purposes of this subsection—

(A) In general. The term "permissive service credit" means service credit—

(i) recognized by the governmental plan for purposes of calculating a participant's benefit under the plan,

(ii) which such participant has not received under such governmental plan, and

(iii) which such participant may receive only by making a voluntary additional contribution, in an amount determined under such governmental plan, which does not exceed the amount necessary to fund the benefit attributable to such service credit.

Such term may include service credit for periods for which there is no performance of service, and, notwithstanding clause (ii), may include service credited in order to provide an increased benefit for service credit which a participant is receiving under the plan.

(B) Limitation on nonqualified service credit. A plan shall fail to meet the requirements of this section if—

(i) more than 5 years of nonqualified service credit are taken into account for purposes of this subsection, or

(ii) any nonqualified service credit is taken into account under this subsection before the employee has at least 5 years of participation under the plan.

(C) Nonqualified service credit. For purposes of subparagraph (B), the term "nonqualified service credit" means permissive service credit other than that allowed with respect to—

(i) service (including parental, medical, sabbatical, and similar leave) as an employee of the Government of the United States, any State or political subdivision thereof, or any agency or instrumentality of any of the foregoing (other than military service or service for credit which was obtained as a result of a repayment described in subsection (k)(3)),

(ii) service (including parental, medical, sabbatical, and similar leave) as an employee (other than as an employee described in clause (i)) of an educational organization described in section 170(b)(1)(A)(ii) which is a public, private, or sectarian school which provides elementary or secondary education (through grade 12), or a comparable level of education, as determined under the applicable law of the jurisdiction in which the service was performed,

(iii) service as an employee of an association of employees who are described in clause (i), or

(iv) military service (other than qualified military service under section 414(u)) recognized by such governmental plan.

In the case of service described in clause (i), (ii), or (iii), such service will be nonqualified service if recognition of such service would cause a participant to receive a retirement benefit for the same service under more than one plan.

(D) Special rules for trustee-to-trustee transfers. In the case of a trustee-to-trustee transfer to which section 403(b)(13)(A) or 457(e)(17)(A) applies (without regard to whether the transfer is made between plans maintained by the same employer)—

(i) the limitations of subparagraph (B) shall not apply in determining whether the transfer is for the purchase of permissive service credit, and

(ii) the distribution rules applicable under this title to the defined benefit governmental plan to which any amounts are so transferred shall apply to such amounts and any benefits attributable to such amounts.

In 2010, P.L. 111-312, Sec. 101(a)(1), substituted "December 31, 2012" for "December 31, 2010" both places it appeared in Sec. 901 of P.L. 107-16 [see below], effective as if included in the enactment of P.L. 107-16, EGTRRA, 6/7/2001.

In 2008, P.L. 110-458, Sec. 103(a), substituted "2009" for "2008" in Sec. 101(c)(2)(A)(ii), P.L. 108-218, see below

—P.L. 110-458, Sec. 103(b)(2)(B)(i), amended clause (b)(2)(E)(v), effective for yrs. begin. after 12/31/2008, except as provided in Sec. 103(b)(2)(B)(ii)(II), which reads as follows:

"(II) A plan sponsor may elect to have the amendment made by clause (i) apply to any year beginning after December 31, 2007, and before January 1, 2009, or to any portion of any such year.."

Prior to amendment, clause (b)(2)(E)(v) read as follows:

"(v) For purposes of adjusting any benefit or limitation under subparagraph (B), (C), or (D), the mortality table used shall be the table prescribed by the Secretary. Such table shall be based on the prevailing commissioners' standard table (described in section 807(d)(5)(A)) used to determine reserves for group annuity contracts issued on the date the adjustment is being made (without regard to any other subparagraph of section 807(d)(5))."

—P.L. 110-458, Sec. 103(b)(2)(B)(ii), of this Act, reads as follows:

"(ii)(I) Except as provided in subclause (II), the amendment made by clause (i) shall apply to years beginning after December 31, 2008.

"(II) A plan sponsor may elect to have the amendment made by clause (i) apply to any year beginning after December 31, 2007, and before January 1, 2009, or to any portion of any such year."

—P.L. 110-458, Sec. 104(b), substituted "commercial" for "commercial airline" in Sec. 402(c)(1)(A), P.L. 109-280, reproduced below.

—P.L. 110-458, Sec. 108(g), repealed para. (f)(2), and redesignated para. (f)(3) as para. (f)(2), effective for yrs. begin. after 12/31/2005, as if included in Sec. 832 of the Pension Protection Act of 2006 [P.L. 109-280].

Prior to repeal, para. (f)(2) read as follows:

"*(2) Annual compensation taken into account for defined benefit plans.* If the employer has more than one defined benefit plan—

"(A) subsection (b)(1)(B) shall be applied separately with respect to each such plan, but

"(B) subsection (b)(1)(B) to the aggregate of such defined benefit plans for purposes of this subsection, the high 3 years of compensation taken into account shall be the period of consecutive calendar years (not more than 3) during which the individual had the greatest aggregate compensation from the employer."

—P.L. 110-458, Sec. 109(d)(1), substituted "paragraph (10)" for "paragraph (1)", in Sec. 906(b)(1)(B)(ii), P.L. 109-280, correcting Sec. 906(b)(1)(B)(ii) so it amended para. (b)(10) instead of para. (b)(1), see below.

—P.L. 110-458, Sec. 122(a), added clause (b)(2)(E)(vi), effective for yrs. begin. after 12/31/2008.

—P.L. 110-458, Sec. 126(a), amended Sec. 402(e)(4)(C), P.L. 109-280, reproduced below, effective for plan yrs. begin. after 12/31/2007.

Prior to amendment, Sec. 402(e)(4)(C), P.L. 109-280, read as follows:

"(C) the value of plan assets shall be equal to their fair market value."

In 2006, P.L. 109-280, Sec. 301(c), substituted "2008" for "2006" in Sec. 101(a)(2)(A)(ii) of P.L. 108-218 [see below].

—P.L. 109-280, Sec. 303(a), amended clause (b)(2)(E)(ii), effective for distributions made in yrs. begin. after 12/31/2005.

Prior to amendment, clause (b)(2)(E)(ii) read as follows:

"(ii) For purposes of adjusting any benefit under subparagraph (B) for any form of benefit subject to section 417(e)(3), the applicable interest rate (as defined in section 417(e)(3)) shall be substituted for '5 percent' in clause (i), except that in the case of plan years beginning in 2004 or 2005, '5.5 percent' shall be substituted for '5 percent' in clause (i)."

— P.L. 109-280, Sec. 402(a)-(g)(1), of this Act, [as amended by Sec. 104(b), 110-458, and Sec. 126(a), 110-458, see above]reads as follows:

"(a) In general. The plan sponsor of an eligible plan may elect to either—

"(1) have the rules of subsection (b) apply, or

"(2) have section 303 of the Employee Retirement Income Security Act of 1974 and section 430 of the Internal Revenue Code of 1986 applied to its first taxable year beginning in 2008 by amortizing the shortfall amortization base for such taxable year over a period of 10 plan years (rather than 7 plan years) beginning with such plan year.

"(b) Alternative funding schedule.

"In general. If an election is made under subsection (a)(1) to have this subsection apply to an eligible plan and the requirements of paragraphs (2) and (3) are met with respect to the plan—

"(A) in the case of any applicable plan year beginning before January 1, 2008, the plan shall not have an accumulated funding deficiency for purposes of section 302 of the Employee Retirement Income Security Act of 1974 and sections 412 and 4971 of the Internal Revenue Code of 1986 if contributions to the plan for the plan year are not less than the minimum required contribution determined under subsection (e) for the plan for the plan year, and

"(B) in the case of any applicable plan year beginning on or after January 1, 2008, the minimum required contribution determined under sections 303 of such Act and 430 of such Code shall, for purposes of sections 302 and 303 of such Act and sections 412, 430, and 4971 of such Code, be equal to the minimum required contribution determined under subsection (e) for the plan for the plan year.

"(2) Accrual restrictions.

"(A) In general. The requirements of this paragraph are met if, effective as of the first day of the first applicable plan year and at all times thereafter while an election under this section is in effect, the plan provides that—

"(i) the accrued benefit, any death or disability benefit, and any social security supplement described in the last sentence of section 411(a)(9) of such Code and section 204(b)(1)(G) of such Act, of each participant are frozen at the amount of such benefit or supplement immediately before such first day, and

"(ii) all other benefits under the plan are eliminated, but only to the extent the freezing or elimination of such benefits would have been permitted under section 411(d)(6) of such Code and section 204(g) of such Act if they had been implemented by a plan amendment adopted immediately before such first day.

"(B) Increases in section 415 limits. If a plan provides that an accrued benefit of a participant which has been subject to any limitation under section 415 of such Code will be increased if such limitation is increased, the plan shall not be treated as meeting the requirements of this subsection unless, effective as of the first day of the first applicable plan year (or, if later, the date of the enactment of this Act) and at all times thereafter while an election under this section is in effect, the plan provides that any such increase shall not take effect. A plan shall not fail to meet the requirements of section 411(d)(6) of such Code and section 204(g) of such Act solely because the plan is amended to meet the requirements of this subparagraph.

"(3) Restriction on applicable benefit increases.

"(A) In general. The requirements of this paragraph are met if no applicable benefit increase takes effect at any time during the period beginning on July 26, 2005, and ending on the day before the first day of the first applicable plan year.

"(B) Applicable benefit increase. For purposes of this paragraph, the term 'applicable benefit increase' means, with respect to any plan year, any increase in liabilities of the plan by plan amendment (or otherwise provided in regulations provided by the Secretary) which, but for this paragraph, would occur during the plan year by reason of—

"(i) any increase in benefits,

"(ii) any change in the accrual of benefits, or

"(iii) any change in the rate at which benefits become nonforfeitable under the plan.

"(4) Exception for imputed disability service. Paragraphs (2) and (3) shall not apply to any accrual or increase with respect to imputed service provided to a participant during any period of the participant's disability occurring on or after the effective date of the plan amendment providing the restrictions under paragraph (2) (or on or after July 26, 2005, in the case of the restrictions under paragraph (3)) if the participant—

"(A) was receiving disability benefits as of such date, or

"(B) was receiving sick pay and subsequently determined to be eligible for disability benefits as of such date.

"(c) Definitions. For purposes of this section—

"(1) Eligible plan. The term 'eligible plan' means a defined benefit plan (other than a multiemployer plan) to which sections 302 of such Act and 412 of such Code applies which is sponsored by an employer—

"(A) which is a commercial passenger airline, or

"(B) the principal business of which is providing catering services to a commercial passenger airline.

"(2) Applicable plan year. The term 'applicable plan year' means each plan year to which the election under subsection (a)(1) applies under subsection (d)(1)(A).

"(d) Elections and related terms.

"(1) Years for which election made.

"(A) Alternative funding schedule. If an election under subsection (a)(1) was made with respect to an eligible plan, the plan sponsor may select either a plan year beginning in 2006 or a plan year beginning in 2007 as the first plan year to which such election applies. The election shall apply to such plan year and all subsequent years. The election shall be made—

"(i) not later than December 31, 2006, in the case of an election for a plan year beginning in 2006, or

"(ii) not later than December 31, 2007, in the case of an election for a plan year beginning in 2007.

"(B) 10 year amortization. An election under subsection (a)(2) shall be made not later than December 31, 2007.

"(C) Election of new plan year for alternative funding schedule. In the case of an election under subsection (a)(1), the plan sponsor may specify a new plan year in such election and the plan year of the plan may be changed to such new plan year without the approval of the Secretary of the Treasury.

"(2) Manner of election. A plan sponsor shall make any election under subsection (a) in such manner as the Secretary of the Treasury may prescribe. Such election, once made, may be revoked only with the consent of such Secretary.

"(e) Minimum required contribution. In the case of an eligible plan with respect to which an election is made under subsection (a)(1)—

"(1) In general. In the case of any applicable plan year during the amortization period, the minimum required contribution shall be the amount necessary to amortize the unfunded liability of the plan, determined as of the first day of the plan year, in equal annual installments (until fully amortized) over the remainder of the amortization period. Such amount shall be separately determined for each applicable plan year.

"(2) Years after amortization period. In the case of any plan year beginning after the end of the amortization period, section 302(a)(2)(A) of such Act and section 412(a)(2)(A) of such Code shall apply to such plan, but the prefunding balance and funding standard carryover balance as of the first day of the first of such years under section 303(f) of such Act and section 430(f) of such Code shall be zero.

"(3) Definitions. For purposes of this section—

"(A) Unfunded liability. The term 'unfunded liability' means the unfunded accrued liability under the plan, determined under the unit credit funding method.

"Amortization period. The term 'amortization period' means the 17-plan year period beginning with the first applicable plan year.

"(4) Other rules. In determining the minimum required contribution and amortization amount under this subsection—

"(A) the provisions of section 302(c)(3) of such Act and section 412(c)(3) of such Code, as in effect before the date of enactment of this section, shall apply,

"(B) a rate of interest of 8.85 percent shall be used for all calculations requiring an interest rate, and

"(C) the value of plan assets shall be determined under sections 303(g)(3) of such Act and 430(g)(3) of such Code.

"(5) Special rule for certain plan spin-offs. For purposes of subsection (b), if, with respect to any eligible plan to which this subsection applies—

"(A) any applicable plan year includes the date of the enactment of this Act,

"(B) a plan was spun off from the eligible plan during the plan year but before such date of enactment, the minimum required contribution under paragraph (1) for the eligible plan for such applicable plan year shall be an aggregate amount determined as if the plans were a single plan for that plan year (based on the full 12-month plan year in effect prior to the spin-off). The employer shall designate the allocation of such aggregate amount between such plans for the applicable plan year.

"Special rules for certain balances and waivers. In the case of an eligible plan with respect to which an election is made under subsection (a)(1)—

"(1) Funding standard account and credit balances. Any charge or credit in the funding standard account under section 302 of such Act or section 412 of such Code, and any prefunding balance or funding standard carryover balance under section 303 of such Act or section 430 of such Code, as of the day before the first day of the first applicable plan year, shall be reduced to zero.

"(2) Waived funding deficiencies. Any waived funding deficiency under sections 302 and 303 of such Act or section 412 of such Code, as in effect before the date of enactment of this section, shall be deemed satisfied as of the first day of the first applicable plan year and the amount of such waived funding deficiency shall be taken into account in determining the plan's unfunded liability under subsection (e)(3)(A). In the case of a plan amendment adopted to satisfy the requirements of subsection (b)(2), the plan shall not be deemed to violate section 304(b) of such Act or section 412(f) of such Code, as so in effect, by reason of such amendment or any increase in benefits provided to such plan's participants under a separate plan that is a defined contribution plan or a multiemployer plan.

"(g) Other rules for plans making election under this section.

"(1) Successor plans to certain plans. If—

"(A) an election under paragraph (1) or (2) of subsection (a) is in effect with respect to any eligible plan, and

"(B) the eligible plan is maintained by an employer that establishes or maintains 1 or more other defined benefit plans (other than any multiemployer plan), and such other plans in combination provide benefit accruals to any substantial number of successor employees, the Secretary of the Treasury may, in the Secretary's discretion, determine that any trust of which any other such plan is a part does not constitute a qualified trust under section 401(a) of the Internal Revenue Code of 1986 unless all benefit obligations of the eligible plan have been satisfied. For purposes of this paragraph, the term 'successor employee' means any employee who is or was covered by the eligible plan and any employees who perform substantially the same type of work with respect to the same business operations as an employee covered by such eligible plan."

—P.L. 109-280, Sec. 811, of this Act [relating to Sec. 901 of P.L. 107-16, see below], provides:

"SEC. 811. PENSIONS AND INDIVIDUAL RETIREMENT ARRANGEMENT PROVISIONS OF ECONOMIC GROWTH AND TAX RELIEF RECONCILIATION ACT OF 2001 MADE PERMANENT.

"Title IX of the Economic Growth and Tax Relief Reconciliation Act of 2001 shall not apply to the provisions of, and amendments made by, subtitles A through F of title VI of such Act (relating to pension and individual retirement arrangement provisions)."

—P.L. 109-280, Sec. 821(a)(1), substituted "a participant" for "an employee" in para. (n)(1) . . . Sec. 821(a)(2), added "Such term may include service credit for periods for which there is no performance of service, and, notwithstanding clause (ii), may include service credited in order to provide an increased benefit for service credit which a participant is receiving under the plan." at the end of subpara. (n)(3)(A), effective for permissive service credit contributions made in yrs. begin. after 12/31/97 [as if included in the amendments made by Sec. 1526 of P.L. 105-34] For Sec. 1526(c)(2) of P.L. 105-34, see below.

—P.L. 109-280, Sec. 821(b), added subpara. (n)(3)(D), effective for to trustee-to-trustee transfers after 12/31/2001 [as if included in the amendments made by Sec. 647 of P.L. 107-16].

—P.L. 109-280, Sec. 821(c)(1), substituted "nonqualified service credit" for "permissive service credit attributable to nonqualified service" each place it appeared in subpara. (n)(3)(B) . . . Sec. 821(c)(2), substituted "(C) Nonqualified service credit. For purposes of subparagraph (B), the term 'nonqualified service credit' means permissive service credit other than that allowed with respect to—" for "(C) Nonqualified service. For purposes of subparagraph (B), the term 'nonqualified service' means service for which permissive service credit is allowed other than—" in subpara. (n)(3)(C) . . . Sec. 821(c)(3), substituted "elementary or secondary education (through grade 12), or a comparable level of education, as determined under the applicable law of the jurisdiction in which the service was performed" for "elementary or secondary education (through grade 12), as determined under State law" in clause (n)(3)(C)(ii), effective for permissive service credit contributions made in yrs. begin. after 12/31/97 [as if included in the amendments made by Sec. 1526 of P.L. 105-34]. For Sec. 1526(c)(2) of P.L. 105-34, see below.

—P.L. 109-280, Sec. 832(a), deleted "both was an active participant in the plan and" after "during which the participant" in para. (b)(3), effective for yrs. begin. after 12/31/2005.

—P.L. 109-280, Sec. 867(a), added "Subparagraph (B) of paragraph (1) shall not apply to a plan maintained by an organization described in section 3121(w)(3)(A) except with respect to highly compensated benefits. For purposes of this paragraph, the term 'highly compensated benefits' means any benefits accrued for an employee in any year on or after the first year in which such employee is a highly compensated employee (as defined in section 414(q)) of the organization described in section 3121(w)(3)(A). For purposes of applying paragraph (1)(B) to highly compensated benefits, all benefits of the employee otherwise taken into account (without regard to this paragraph) shall be taken into account." at the end of para. (b)(11), effective for yrs. begin. after 12/31/2006.

—P.L. 109-280, Sec. 906(b)(1)(A)(i), substituted "State, Indian tribal government (as defined in section 7701(a)(40)), or any political subdivision" for "State or political subdivision" in clause (b)(2)(H)(i) . . . Sec. 906(b)(1)(A)(ii), substituted "State, Indian tribal government (as so defined), or any political subdivision" for "State or political subdivision" each place it appeared in subclause (b)(2)(H)(ii)(I) . . . Sec. 906(b)(1)(B)(i), added "or a governmental plan described in the last sentence of section 414(d) (relating to plans of Indian tribal governments)," after "foregoing," in subpara. (b)(10)(A) . . . Sec. 906(b)(1)(B)(ii), [as corrected by Sec. 109(d)(1), 110-458, see above] substituted "Special rule for State, Indian tribal, and" for "Special rule for State and" in the heading of para. (b)(10), effective for any yr. begin. on or after 8/17/2006.

In 2005, P.L. 109-135, Sec. 407(b), substituted "$3,000. This subparagraph shall not apply with respect to any taxable year to any individual whose adjusted gross income for such taxable year (determined separately and without regard to community property laws) exceeds $17,000." for "the greater of $3,000 or the employee's includible compensation determined under section 403(b)(3)." in subpara. (c)(7)(C), effective for yrs. begin. after 12/31/2001 as if included in Sec. 632 of the Economic Growth and Tax Relief Reconciliation Act of 2001, P.L. 107-16.

—P.L. 109-135, Sec. 412(y), substituted "individual medical benefit account" for "individual medical account" in para. (l)(1) . . . Sec. 412(z), substituted "clause" for "clauses" in subpara. (n)(3)(C), effective 12/21/2005.

In 2004, P.L. 108-476, Sec. 1, of this Act, provides:

"SECTION 1. CERTAIN ARRANGEMENTS MAINTAINED BY THE YMCA RETIREMENT FUND TREATED AS CHURCH PLANS.

"(a) Retirement plans.

"(1) In general. For purposes of sections 401(a) and 403(b) of the Internal Revenue Code of 1986, any retirement plan maintained by the YMCA Retirement Fund as of January 1, 2003, shall be treated as a church plan (within the meaning of section 414(e) of such Code) which is maintained by an organization described in section 414(e)(3)(A) of such Code.

"(2) Tax-deferred retirement plan. In the case of a retirement plan described in paragraph (1) which allows contributions to be made under a salary reduction agreement—

"(A) such treatment shall not apply for purposes of section 415(c)(7) of such Code, and

"(B) any account maintained for a participant or beneficiary of such plan shall be treated for purposes of such Code as a retirement income account described in section 403(b)(9) of such Code, except that such account shall not, for purposes of section 403(b)(12) of such Code, be treated as a contract purchased by a church for purposes of section 403(b)(1)(D) of such Code.

"(3) Money purchase pension plan. In the case of a retirement plan described in paragraph (1) which is subject to the requirements of section 401(a) of such Code—

"(A) such plan (but not any reserves held by the YMCA Retirement Fund)—

"(i) shall be treated for purposes of such Code as a defined contribution plan which is a money purchase pension plan, and

"(ii) shall be treated as having made an election under section 410(d) of such Code for plan years beginning after December 31, 2005, except that notwithstanding the election—

"(I) nothing in the Employee Retirement Income Security Act of 1974 or such Code shall prohibit the YMCA Retirement Fund from commingling for investment purposes the assets of the electing plan with the assets of such Fund and with the assets of any employee benefit plan maintained by such Fund, and

"(II) nothing in this section shall be construed as subjecting any assets described in subclause (I), other than the assets of the electing plan, to any provision of such Act,

"(B) notwithstanding section 401(a)(11) or 417 of such Code or section 205 of such Act, such plan may offer a lump-sum distribution option to participants who have not attained age 55 without offering such participants an annuity option, and

"(C) any account maintained for a participant or beneficiary of such plan shall, for purposes of section 401(a)(9) of such Code, be treated as a retirement income account described in section 403(b)(9) of such Code.

"(4) Self-funded death benefit plan. For purposes of section 7702(j) of such Code, a retirement plan described in paragraph (1) shall be treated as an arrangement described in section 7702(j)(2).

"(b) YMCA retirement fund. For purposes of this section, the term 'YMCA Retirement Fund' means the Young Men's Christian Association Retirement Fund, a corporation created by an Act of the State of New York which became law on April 30, 1921.

"(c) Effective date. This section shall apply to plan years beginning after December 31, 2003."

—P.L. 108-311, Sec. 404(b)(2), added "This subparagraph shall also apply for purposes of any provision of this title that provides for adjustments in accordance with the method contained in this subsection, except to the extent provided in such provision." at the end of subpara. (d)(4)(A), effective for yrs. begin. after 12/31/2001 as if included in Sec. 611 of the Economic Growth and Tax Relief Reconciliation Act of 2001, P.L. 107-16.

—P.L. 108-311, Sec. 408(a)(17), substituted "subparagraph (B)" for "subparagraph (D)" in subpara. (c)(7)(C), enacted 10/4/2004.

—P.L. 108-218, Sec. 101(b)(4), added ", except that in the case of plan years beginning in 2004 or 2005, '5.5 percent' shall be substituted for '5 percent' in clause (i)" before the period at the end of clause (b)(2)(E)(ii), effective for plan yrs. begin. after 12/31/2003. Sec. 101(d)(2) and (3) of this Act, provides:

"(2) Lookback rules. For purposes of applying subsections (d)(9)(B)(ii) and (e)(1) of section 302 of the Employee Retirement Income Security Act of 1974 and subsections (l)(9)(B)(ii) and (m)(1) of section 412 of the Internal Revenue Code of 1986 to plan years beginning after December 31, 2003, the amendments made by this section may be applied as if such amendments had been in effect for all prior plan years. The Secretary of the Treasury may prescribe simplified assumptions which may be used in applying the amendments made by this section to such prior plan years.

"(3) Transition rule for section 415 limitation. In the case of any participant or beneficiary receiving a distribution after December 31, 2003 and before January 1, 2005, the amount payable under any form of benefit subject to section 417(e)(3) of the Internal Revenue Code of 1986 and subject to adjustment under section 415(b)(2)(B) of such Code shall not, solely by reason of the amendment made by subsection (b)(4), be less than the amount that would have been so payable had the amount payable been determined using the applicable interest rate in effect as of the last day of the last plan year beginning before January 1, 2004."

—P.L. 108-218, Sec. 101(c), of this Act [as amended by Sec. 301(c) of P.L. 109-280, and Sec. 103(a), 110-458, see above], reads as follows:

"(c) Provisions relating to plan amendments.

"(1) In general. If this subsection applies to any plan or annuity contract amendment—

"(A) such plan or contract shall be treated as being operated in accordance with the terms of the plan or contract during the period described in paragraph (2)(B)(i), and

"(B) except as provided by the Secretary of the Treasury, such plan shall not fail to meet the requirements of section 411(d)(6) of the Internal Revenue Code of 1986 and section 204(g) of the Employee Retirement Income Security Act of 1974 by reason of such amendment.

"(2) Amendments to which section applies.

"(A) In general. This subsection shall apply to any amendment to any plan or annuity contract which is made—

"(i) pursuant to any amendment made by this section, and

"(ii) on or before the last day of the first plan year beginning on or after January 1, 2009.

"(B) Conditions. This subsection shall not apply to any plan or annuity contract amendment unless—

"(i) during the period beginning on the date the amendment described in subparagraph (A)(i) takes effect and ending on the date described in subparagraph (A)(ii) (or, if earlier, the date the plan or contract amendment is adopted), the plan or contract is operated as if such plan or contract amendment were in effect; and

"(ii) such plan or contract amendment applies retroactively for such period."

In 2002, P.L. 107-358, Sec. 2, added subsec. (c) in Sec. 901 of P.L. 107-16 [see below], effective 12/17/2002.

— P.L. 107-147, Sec. 411(j)(3), added Sec. 611(i)(3) of P.L. 107-16, reproduced below.
— P.L. 107-147, Sec. 411(p)(4), amended para. (c)(7), effective for yrs. begin. after 12/31/2001.

Prior to amendment, para. (c)(7) read as follows:

"(7) Certain contributions by church plans not treated as exceeding limit.

"(A) In general. Notwithstanding any other provision of this subsection, at the election of a participant who is an employee of a church or a convention or association of churches, including an organization described in section 414(e)(3)(B)(ii), contributions and other additions for an annuity contract or retirement income account described in section 403(b) with respect to such participant, when expressed as an annual addition to such participant's account, shall be treated as not exceeding the limitation of paragraph (1) if such annual addition is not in excess of $10,000.

"(B) $40,000 aggregate limitation. The total amount of additions with respect to any participant which may be taken into account for purposes of this subparagraph for all years may not exceed $40,000.

"(C) Annual addition. For purposes of this paragraph, the term 'annual addition' has the meaning given such term by paragraph (2)."

In 2001, P.L. 107-16, Sec. 611(a)(1)(A), substituted "$160,000" for "$90,000" in subpara. (b)(1)(A) ... Sec. 611(a)(1)(B), substituted "$160,000" for "$90,000" each place it appeared in subparas. (b)(2)(C) and (D) ... Sec. 611(a)(1)(C), substituted "one-half the amount otherwise applicable for such year under paragraph (1)(A) for '$160,000'" for "the greater of $68,212 or one-half the amount otherwise applicable for such year under paragraph (1)(A) for '$90,000'" in para. (b)(7) ... Sec. 611(a)(2), substituted "age 62" for "the social security retirement age" each place it appeared in subpara. (b)(2)(C) and deleted the second sentence. ... Sec. 611(a)(3), substituted "age 65" for "the social security retirement age" each place it appeared in subpara. (b)(2)(D) ... Sec. 611(a)(4)(A), substituted "$160,000" for "$90,000" in subpara. (d)(1)(A) ... Sec. 611(a)(4)(B)(i), substituted "$160,000" for "$90,000" in the heading of subpara. (d)(3)(A) ... Sec. 611(a)(4)(B)(ii), substituted "July 1, 2001" for "October 1, 1986" in subpara. (d)(3)(A) ... Sec. 611(a)(5)(A), deleted subpara. (b)(2)(F) ... Sec. 611(a)(5)(B), amended para. (b)(9) ... Sec. 611(a)(5)(C), deleted "applied without regard to paragraph (2)(F)" after "paragraph (2)(G))" in clause (b)(10)(C)(i), effective for yrs. end. after 12/31/2001. Sec. 611(i)(3) of this Act [as added by Sec. 411(j)(3) of P.L. 107-147, see above] provides:

"(3) Special rule. In the case of plan that, on June 7, 2001, incorporated by reference the limitation of section 415(b)(1)(A) of the Internal Revenue Code of 1986, section 411(d)(6) of such Code and section 204(g)(1) of the Employee Retirement Income Security Act of 1974 do not apply to a plan amendment that—

"(A) is adopted on or before June 30, 2002,

"(B) reduces benefits to the level that would have applied without regard to the amendments made by subsection (a) of this section, and

"(C) is effective no earlier than the years described in paragraph (2)."

Prior to deletion, subpara. (b)(2)(F) read as follows:

"(F) Plans maintained by governments and tax-exempt organizations. In the case of a governmental plan (within the meaning of section 414(d)), a plan maintained by an organization (other than a governmental unit) exempt from tax under this subtitle, or a qualified merchant marine plan—

"(i) subparagraph (C) shall be applied—

"(I) by substituting 'age 62' for 'social security retirement age' each place it appears, and

"(II) as if the last sentence thereof read as follows: 'The reduction under this subparagraph shall not reduce the limitation of paragraph (1)(A) below (i) $75,000 if the benefit begins at or after age 55, or (ii) if the benefit begins before age 55, the equivalent of the $75,000 limitation for age 55.', and

"(ii) subparagraph (D) shall be applied by substituting 'age 65' for 'social security retirement age' each place it appears.

For purposes of this subparagraph, the term 'qualified merchant marine plan' means a plan in existence on January 1, 1986, the participants in which are merchant marine officers holding licenses issued by the Secretary of Transportation under title 46, United States Code."

Prior to amendment, para. (b)(9) read as follows:

"(9) Special rule for commercial airline pilots.

"(A) In general. Except as provided in subparagraph (B), in the case of any participant who is a commercial airline pilot—

"(i) the rule of paragraph (2)(F)(i)(II) shall apply, and

"(ii) if, as of the time of the participant's retirement, regulations prescribed by the Federal Aviation Administration require an individual to separate from service as a commercial airline pilot after attaining any age occurring on or after age 60 and before the social security retirement age, paragraph (2)(C) (after application of clause (i)) shall be applied by substituting such age for the social security retirement age.

"(B) Individuals who separate from service before age 60. If a participant described in subparagraph (A) separates from service before age 60, the rules of paragraph (2)(F) shall apply."

— P.L. 107-16, Sec. 611(b)(1), substituted "$40,000" for "$30,000" in subpara. (c)(1)(A) ... Sec. 611(b)(2)(A), substituted "$40,000" for "$30,000" in subpara. (d)(1)(C) ... Sec. 611(b)(2)(B)(i), substituted "$40,000" for "$30,000" in the heading of subpara. (d)(3)(D) ... Sec. 611(b)(2)(B)(ii), substituted "July 1, 2001" for "October 1, 1993" in subpara. (d)(3)(D) ... Sec. 611(h), amended para. (d)(4), effective for yrs. begin. after 12/31/2001.

Prior to amendment, para. (d)(4) read as follows:

"(4) Rounding. Any increase under subparagraph (A) or (C) of paragraph (1) which is not a multiple of $5,000 shall be rounded to the next lowest multiple of $5,000."

— P.L. 107-16, Sec. 632(a)(1), substituted "100 percent" for "25 percent" in subpara. (c)(1)(B) ... Sec. 632(a)(3)(C), deleted ", and the amount of the contribution for such portion shall reduce the exclusion allowance as provided in section 403(b)(2)" after "whichever is appropriate" in para. (a)(2) ... Sec. 632(a)(3)(D), added subpara. (c)(3)(E) ... Sec. 632(a)(3)(E), deleted para. (c)(4) ... Sec. 632(a)(3)(F), amended para. (c)(7), effective for yrs. begin. after 12/31/2001.

Prior to deletion, para. (c)(4) read as follows:

"(4) Special election for section 403(b) contracts purchased by educational organizations, hospitals, home health service agencies, and certain churches, etc.

"(A) In the case of amounts contributed for an annuity contract described in section 403(b) for the year in which occurs a participant's separation from the service with an educational organization, a hospital, a home health service agency, a health and welfare service agency, or a church, convention or association of churches, or an organization described in section 414(e)(3)(B)(ii), at the election of the participant there is substituted for the amount specified in paragraph (1)(B) the amount of the exclusion allowance which would be determined under section 403(b)(2) (without regard to this section) for the participant's taxable year in which such separation occurs if the participant's years of service were computed only by taking into account his service for the employer (as determined for purposes of section 403(b)(2)) during the period of years (not exceeding ten) ending on the date of such separation.

"(B) In the case of amounts contributed for an annuity contract described in section 403(b) for any year in the case of a participant who is an employee of an educational organization, a hospital, a home health service agency, a health and welfare service agency, or a church, convention or association of churches, or an organization described in section 414(e)(3)(B)(ii), at the election of the participant there is substituted for the amount specified in paragraph (1)(B) the least of—

"(i) 25 percent of the participant's includible compensation (as defined in section 403(b)(3)) plus $4,000,

"(ii) the amount of the exclusion allowance determined for the year under section 403(b)(2), or

"(iii) $15,000.

"(C) In the case of amounts contributed for an annuity contract described in section 403(b) for any year for a participant who is an employee of an educational organization, a hospital, a home health service agency, a health and welfare service agency, or a church, convention or association of churches, or an organization described in section 414(e)(3)(B)(ii), at the election of the participant the provisions of section 403(b)(2)(A) shall not apply.

"(D)(i) The provisions of this paragraph apply only if the participant elects its application at the time and in the manner provided under regulations prescribed by the Secretary. Not more than one election may be made under subparagraph (A) by any participant. A participant who elects to have the provisions of subparagraph (A), (B), or (C) of this paragraph apply to him may not elect to have any other subparagraph of this paragraph apply to him. Any election made under this paragraph is irrevocable.

"(ii) For purposes of this paragraph the term 'educational organization' means an educational organization described in section 170(b)(1)(A)(ii).

"(iii) For purposes of this paragraph the term 'home health service agency' means an organization described in subsection 501(c)(3) which is exempt from tax under section 501(a) and which has been determined by the Secretary of Health, Education, and Welfare to be a home health agency (as defined in section 1861(o) of the Social Security Act).

"(iv) For purposes of this paragraph, the terms 'church' and 'convention or association of churches' have the same meaning as when used in section 414(e)."

Prior to amendment, para. (c)(7) read as follows:

"(7) Certain contributions by church plans not treated as exceeding limits.

"(A) Alternative exclusion allowance. Any contribution or addition with respect to any participant, when expressed as an annual addition, which is allocable to the application of section 403(b)(2)(D) to such participant for such year, shall be treated as not exceeding the limitations of paragraph (1).

"(B) Contributions not in excess of $40,000 ($10,000 per year).

"(i) In general. Notwithstanding any other provision of this subsection, at the election of a participant who is an employee of a church, a convention or association of churches, including an organization described in section 414(e)(3)(B)(ii), contributions and other additions for an annuity contract or retirement income account described in section 403(b) with respect to such participant, when expressed as an annual addition to such participant's account, shall be treated as not exceeding the limitation of paragraph (1) if such annual addition is not in excess of $10,000.

"(ii) $40,000 aggregate limitation. The total amount of additions with respect to any participant which may be taken into account for purposes of this subparagraph for all years may not exceed $40,000.

"(iii) No election if paragraph (4)(A) election made. No election my [sic may] be made under this subparagraph for any year if an election is made under paragraph (4)(A) for such year.

"(C) Annual addition. For purposes of this paragraph, the term 'annual addition' has the meaning given such term by paragraph (2)."

— P.L. 107-16, Sec. 632(b)(1), added para. (k)(4), effective for limitation yrs. begin. after 12/31/99. Sec. 632(b)(2)(B) of this Act, provides:

"(B) Exclusion allowance. Effective for limitation years beginning in 2000, in the case of any annuity contract described in section 403(b) of the Internal Revenue Code of 1986, the amount of the contribution disqualified by reason of section 415(g) of such Code shall reduce the exclusion allowance as provided in section 403(b)(2) of such Code."

— P.L. 107-16, Sec. 641(e)(9), substituted "403(b)(8), 408(d)(3), and 457(e)(16)" for "and 408(d)(3)" in subparas. (b)(2)(A) and (B) ... Sec. 641(e)(10), substituted

"408(d)(3), and 457(e)(16)" for "and 408(d)(3)" in para. (c)(2), effective for distributions after 12/31/2001. Sec. 641(f)(2) and (3) of this Act, provides:

"(2) Reasonable notice. No penalty shall be imposed on a plan for the failure to provide the information required by the amendment made by subsection (c) with respect to any distribution made before the date that is 90 days after the date on which the Secretary of the Treasury issues a safe harbor rollover notice after the date of the enactment of this Act, if the administrator of such plan makes a reasonable attempt to comply with such requirement.

"(3) Special rule. Notwithstanding any other provision of law, subsections (h)(3) and (h)(5) of section 1122 of the Tax Reform Act of 1986 shall not apply to any distribution from an eligible retirement plan (as defined in clause (iii) or (iv) of section 402(c)(8)(B) of the Internal Revenue Code of 1986) on behalf of an individual if there was a rollover to such plan on behalf of such individual which is permitted solely by reason of any amendment made by this section."

—P.L. 107-16, Sec. 654(a)(1), amended para. (b)(11) . . . Sec. 654(a)(2), added "(other than a multiemployer plan)" after "defined benefit plan" in para. (b)(7) . . . Sec. 654(b)(1), added para. (f)(3) . . . Sec. 654(b)(2), substituted "Except as provided in subsection (f)(3), the Secretary" for "The Secretary" in subsec. (g), effective for yrs. begin. after 12/31/2001.
Prior to amendment, para. (b)(11) read as follows:

"(11) Special limitation rule for governmental plans. In the case of a governmental plan (as defined in section 414(d)), subparagraph (B) of paragraph (1) shall not apply."

—P.L. 107-16, Sec. 901, of this Act [as amended by Sec. 2 of P.L. 107-358, and Sec. 101(a)(1) of P.L. 111-312, and as related to Sec. 811 of P.L. 109-280, see above], reads as follows:

"SEC. 901. SUNSET OF PROVISIONS OF ACT.

"(a) In general. All provisions of, and amendments made by, this Act shall not apply—

"(1) to taxable, plan, or limitation years beginning after December 31, 2012, or

"(2) in the case of title V, to estates of decedents dying, gifts made, or generation skipping transfers, after December 31, 2012.

"(b) Application of certain laws. The Internal Revenue Code of 1986 and the Employee Retirement Income Security Act of 1974 shall be applied and administered to years, estates, gifts, and transfers described in subsection (a) as if the provisions and amendments described in subsection (a) had never been enacted.

"(c) Exception. Subsection (a) shall not apply to section 803 (relating to no federal income tax on restitution received by victims of the Nazi regime or their heirs or estates)."

In 2000, P.L. 106-554, Sec. 1(a)(7), [which enacted into law Sec. 314(c)(1) of P.L. 106-554] substituted "section 125, 132(f)(4), or" for "section 125 or" in clause (c)(3)(D)(ii), effective for tax. yrs. begin. after 12/31/97.

In 1997, P.L. 105-34, Sec. 1526(a), added subsec. (n) . . . Sec. 1526(b), added para. (k)(3), effective for permissive service credit contributions made in yrs. begin. after 12/31/97. Sec. 1526(c)(2) of this Act provides:

"(2) Transition rule.

"(A) In general. In the case of an eligible participant in a governmental plan (within the meaning of section 414(d) of the Internal Revenue Code of 1986), the limitations of section 415(c)(1) of such Code shall not be applied to reduce the amount of permissive service credit which may be purchased to an amount less than the amount which was allowed to be purchased under the terms of the plan as in effect on the date of the enactment of this Act.

"(B) Eligible participant. For purposes of subparagraph (A), an eligible participant is an individual who first became a participant in the plan before the first plan year beginning after the last day of the calendar year in which the next regular session (following the date of the enactment of this Act) of the governing body with authority to amend the plan ends."

—P.L. 105-34, Sec. 1527(a), amended subpara. (b)(2)(G), effective for yrs. begin. after 12/31/96.
Prior to amendment, subpara. (b)(2)(G) read as follows:

"(G) Special limitation for qualified police or firefighters. In the case of a qualified participant—

"(i) subparagraph (C) shall not reduce the limitation of paragraph (1)(A) to an amount less than $50,000, and

"(ii) the rules of subparagraph (F) shall apply.
The Secretary shall adjust the $50,000 amount in clause (i) at the same time and in the same manner as under section 415(d)."

—P.L. 105-34, Sec. 1530(c)(3), added a sentence at the end of para. (c)(6) . . . Sec. 1530(c)(4)(A), redesignated para. (e)(6) as para. (e)(7) . . . Sec. 1530(c)(4)(B), added a new para. (e)(6), effective for transfers made by trusts to, or for the use of, an employee stock ownership plan after 8/5/97.

In 1996, P.L. 104-188, Sec. 1434(a), added subpara. (c)(3)(D), effective for yrs begin. after 12/31/97.

—P.L. 104-188, Sec. 1444(a), added para. (b)(11) . . . Sec. 1444(b)(1), added subsec. (m) . . . Sec. 1444(c), added subpara. (b)(2)(I), effective for yrs. begin. after 12/31/94. Sec. 1444(e)(2) of this Act provides:

"(2) Treatment for years beginning before January 1, 1995. Nothing in the amendments made by this section shall be construed to imply that a governmental plan (as defined in section 414(d) of the Internal Revenue Code of 1986) fails to satisfy the requirements of section 415 of such Code for any taxable year beginning before January 1, 1995."

—P.L. 104-188, Sec. 1444(d)(1), added clause (b)(10)(C)(ii) . . . Sec. 1444(d)(2), substituted "(i) In general. This" for "This" in subpara. (b)(10)(C), effective for revocations adopted after 8/20/96. Sec. 1444(e)(2) of this Act of this Act, provides special rules. See above.

—P.L. 104-188, Sec. 1446(a), added the sentence at the end of subpara. (c)(3)(C), effective for yrs. begin. after 12/31/96.

—P.L. 104-188, Sec. 1449(a), amended Sec. 767(d)(3)(A) of P.L. 103-465, see below.
Prior to amendment, Sec. 767(d)(3)(A) read as follows:

"(A) No reduction required. — An accrued benefit shall not be required to be reduced below the accrued benefit as of the last day of the last plan year beginning before January 1, 1995, merely because of the amendments made by subsection (b)."

—P.L. 104-188, Sec. 1449(b)(1), substituted "For purposes of adjusting any limitation under subparagraph (C) and, except as provided in clause (ii), for purposes of adjusting any benefit under subparagraph (B)," for "Except as provided in clause (ii), for purposes of adjusting any benefit of limitation under subparagraph (B) or (C)," in clause (b)(2)(E)(i) . . . Sec. 1449(b)(2), substituted "For purposes of adjusting any benefit under subparagraph (B) for any form of benefit subject to section 417(e)(3)," for "For purposes of adjusting the benefit or limitation of any form of benefit subject to section 417(e)(3)," in clause (b)(2)(E)(ii), effective for plan years and limitation years begin. after 12/31/94; except that an employer may elect to treat the amendments made by this section as being effective on or after 12/8/94. For special rules, see Sec. 767(d)(2) and (3) of P.L. 103-465, reproduced below.

—P.L. 104-188, Sec. 1449(d), of this Act provides:

"(d) Transitional rule. In the case of a plan that was adopted and in effect before December 8, 1994, if—

"(1) a plan amendment was adopted or made effective on or before the date of the enactment of this Act applying the amendments made by section 767 of the Uruguay Round Agreements Act, and

"(2) within 1 year after the date of the enactment of this Act, a plan amendment is adopted which repeals the amendment referred to in paragraph (1),
the amendment referred to in paragraph (1) shall not be taken into account in applying section 767(d)(3)(A) of the Uruguay Round Agreements Acts as amended by subsection (a)."

—P.L. 104-188, Sec. 1452(a), repealed subsec. (e) . . . Sec. 1452(c)(1)(A), added "or" at the end of subpara. (a)(1)(A), deleted ", or" at the end of subpara. (a)(1)(B), and deleted subpara. (a)(1)(C) . . . Sec. 1452(c)(2), deleted "and subsection (e)" after "and (4)" in subpara. (b)(5)(B) . . . Sec. 1452(c)(3), substituted "sections (b and (c)" for "sections (b), (c), and (e)" in para. (f)(1) . . . Sec. 1452(c)(4), substituted "subsection (f)" for "subsections (e) and (f)" in subsec. (g) . . . Sec. 1452(c)(5), amended clause (k)(2)(A)(i) . . . Sec. 1452(c)(6), substituted "subsection (c)" for "subsections (c) and (e)" in clause (k)(2)(A)(ii), effective for limitation yrs. begin. after 12/31/99.
Prior to repeal, subsec. (e) read as follows:

"(e) Limitation in case of defined benefit plan and defined contribution plan for same employee.

"(1) In general. In any case in which an individual is a participant in both a defined benefit plan and a defined contribution plan maintained by the same employer, the sum of the defined benefit plan fraction and the defined contribution plan fraction for any year may not exceed 1.0.

"(2) Defined benefit plan fraction. For purposes of this subsection, the defined benefit plan fraction for any year is a fraction—

"(A) the numerator of which is the projected annual benefit of the participant under the plan (determined as of the close of the year), and

"(B) the denominator of which is the lesser of—

"(i) the product of 1.25, multiplied by the dollar limitation in effect under subsection (b)(1)(A) for such year, or

"(ii) the product of—

"(I) 1.4, multiplied by

"(II) the amount which may be taken into account under subsection (b)(1)(B) with respect to such individual under the plan for such year.

"(3) Defined contribution plan fraction. For purposes of this subsection, the defined contribution plan fraction for any year is a fraction—

"(A) the numerator of which is the sum of the annual additions to the participant's account as of the close of the year, and

"(B) the denominator of which is the sum of the lesser of the following amounts determined for such year and for each prior year of service with the employer:

"(i) the product of 1.25, multiplied by the dollar limitation in effect under subsection (c)(1)(A) for such year (determined without regard to subsection (c)(6)), or

"(ii) the product of—

"(I) 1.4, multiplied by—

"(II) the amount which may be taken into account under subsection (c)(1)(B) (or subsection (c)(7), if applicable) with respect to such individual under such plan for such year.

"(4) Special transition rules for defined contribution fraction. In applying paragraph (3) with respect to years beginning before January 1, 1976—

"(A) the aggregate amount taken into account under paragraph (3)(A) may not exceed the aggregate amount taken into account under paragraph (3)(B), and

"(B) the amount taken into account under subsection (c)(2)(B)(i) for any year concerned is an amount equal to—

"(i) the excess of the aggregate amount of employee contributions for all years beginning before January 1, 1976, during which the employee was an active participant of the plan, over 10 percent of the employee's aggregate compensation for all such years, multiplied by

"(ii) a fraction the numerator of which is 1 and the denominator of which is the number of years beginning before January 1, 1976, during which the employee was an active participant in the plan.
Employee contributions made on or after October 2, 1973, shall be taken into account under subparagraph (B) of the preceding sentence only to the extent that the

amount of such contributions does not exceed the maximum amount of contributions permissible under the plan as in effect on October 2, 1973.

"(5) Special rules for sections 403(b) and 408. For purposes of this section, any annuity contract described in section 403(b) (except in the case of a participant who has elected subsection (c)(4)(D) to have the provisions of subsection (c)(4)(C) apply) for the benefit of a participant shall be treated as a defined contribution plan maintained by each employer with respect to which the participant has the control required under subsection (b) or (c) of section 414 (as modified by subsection (h)). For purposes of this section, any contribution by an employer to a simplified employee pension for an individual for a taxable year shall be treated as an employer contribution to a defined contribution plan for such individual for such year. In the case of any annuity contract described in section 403(b), the amount of the contribution disqualified by reason of subsection (g) shall reduce the exclusion allowance as provided in section 403(b)(2).

"(6) Special transition rule for defined contribution fraction for years ending after December 31, 1982.

"(A) In general. At the election of the plan administrator, in applying paragraph (3) with respect to any year ending after December 31, 1982, the amount taken into account under paragraph (3)(B) with respect to each participant for all years ending before January 1, 1983, shall be an amount equal to the product of —

"(i) the amount determined under paragraph (3)(B) (as in effect for the year ending in 1982) for the year ending in 1982, multiplied by

"(ii) the transition fraction.

"(B) Transition fraction. The term 'transition fraction' means a fraction—

"(i) the numerator of which is the lesser of—

"(I) $51,875, or

"(I) 1.4, multiplied by 25 percent of the compensation of the participant for the year ending in 1981, and

"(ii) the denominator of which is the lesser of—

"(I) $41,500, or

"(II) 25 percent of the compensation of the participant for the year ending in 1981.

"(C) Plan must have been in existence on or before July 1, 1982. This paragraph shall apply only to plans which were in existence on or before July 1, 1982."

Prior to deletion, subpara. (a)(1)(C) read as follows:

"(C) in any case in which an individual is a participant in both a defined benefit plan and a defined contribution plan maintained by the employer, the trust has been disqualified under subsection (g)."

Prior to amendment, clause (k)(2)(A)(i) read as follows:

"(i) any contribution made directly by an employee under such arrangement—

"(I) shall not be treated as an annual addition for purposes of subsection (c), but

"(II) shall be so treated for purposes of subsection (e), and"

—P.L. 104-188, Sec. 1704(t)(75), added "or" to the end of subpara. (k)(1)(C), deleted subparas. (k)(1)(D) and (E), and redesignated subpara. (k)(1)(F) as subpara. (k)(1)(D), effective 8/20/96.

Prior to deletion, subparas. (k)(1)(D) and (E) read as follows:

"(D) an individual retirement account described in section 408(a),

"(E) an individual retirement annuity described in section 408(b), or"

In 1994, P.L. 103-465, Sec. 732(b)(1), amended subsec. (d) . . . Sec. 732(b)(2), deleted "(or, if greater, ¼ of the dollar limitation in effect under subsection (b)(1)(A))" after "$30,000" in subpara. (c)(1)(A), effective for years begin. after 12/31/94, except as provided in 732(e)(2) of this Act, which reads as follows:

"(2) Rounding not to result in decreases. — The amendments made by this section providing for the rounding of indexed amounts shall not apply to any year to the extent the rounding would require the indexed amount to be reduced below the amount in effect for years beginning in 1994."

Prior to amendment, subsec. (d) read as follows:

"(d) Cost-of-living adjustments.

"(1) In general. The Secretary shall adjust annually—

"(A) the $90,000 amount in subsection (b)(1)(A), and

"(B) in the case of a participant who is separated from service, the amount taken into account under subsection (b)(1)(B),

for increases in the cost of living in accordance with regulations prescribed by the Secretary. Such regulations shall provide for adjustment procedures which are similar to the procedures used to adjust benefit amounts under section 215(i)(2)(A) of the Social Security Act.

"(2) Base periods. The base period taken into account—

"(A) for purposes of subparagraph (A) of paragraph (1) is the calendar quarter beginning October 1, 1986, and

"(B) for purposes of subparagraph (B) of paragraph (1) is the last calendar quarter of the calendar year before the calendar year in which the participant is separated from service.

"(3) Freeze on adjustment to defined contribution and benefit limits. The Secretary shall not make any adjustment under subparagraph (A) of paragraph (1) with respect to any year beginning after December 31, 1982, and before January 1, 1988."

—P.L. 103-465, Sec. 767(b)(1), redesignated clauses (b)(2)(E)(ii) and (iii) as clauses (b)(2)(E)(iii) and (iv) . . . Sec. 767(b)(2), deleted clause (b)(2)(E)(i) and added new clauses (b)(2)(E)(i) and (ii) . . . Sec. 767(b)(3), added clause (b)(2)(E)(v), effective for plan years and limitation years begin. after 12/31/94; except that an employer may elect to treat the amendments made by this section as being effective on or after 12/8/94. Sec. 767(d)(2) and (d)(3) [as amended by Sec. 1449(a) of P.L. 104-188, see above] of this Act reads as follows:

"(2) No reduction in accrued benefits. — A participant's accrued benefit shall not be considered to be reduced in violation of section 411(d)(6) of the Internal Revenue Code of 1986 or section 204(g) of the Employee Retirement Income Security Act of 1974 merely because (A) the benefit is determined in accordance with section 417(e)(3)(A) of such Code, as amended by this Act, or section 205(g)(3) of the Employee Retirement Income Security Act of 1974, as amended by this Act, or (B) the plan applies section 415(b)(2)(E) of such Code, as amended by this Act.

"(3) Section 415. —

"(A) Exception. A plan that was adopted and in effect before December 8, 1994, shall not be required to apply the amendments made by subsection (b) with respect to benefits accrued before the earlier of—

"(i) the later of the date a plan amendment applying the amendments made by subsection (b) is adopted or made effective, or

"(ii) the first day of the first limitation year beginning on December 31, 1999. Determinations under section 415(b)(2)(E) of the Internal Revenue Code of 1986 before such earlier date shall be made with respect to such benefits on the basis of such section as in effect on December 7, 1994 (except that the modification made by section 1449(b) of the Small Business Job Protection Act of 1996 shall be taken into account), and the provisions of the plan as in effect on December 7, 1994, but only if such provisions by the plan meet the requirements of such section (as so in effect).

"(B) Timing of plan amendment. — A plan that operates in accordance with the amendments made by subsection (b) shall not be treated as failing to satisfy section 401(a) of the Internal Revenue Code of 1986 or as not being operated in accordance with the provisions of the plan until such date as the Secretary of the Treasury provides merely because the plan has not been amended to include the amendments made by subsection (b)."

Prior to deletion, clause (b)(2)(E)(i) read as follows:

"(i) For purposes of adjusting any benefit or limitation under subparagraph (B) or (C), the interest rate assumption shall not be less than the greater of 5 percent or the rate specified in the plan."

In 1992, P.L. 102-318, Sec. 521(b)(23), substituted "sections 402(c)" for "sections 402(a)(5)" in subpara. (b)(2)(A) . . . Sec. 521(b)(24), substituted "sections 402(c)" for "sections 402(a)(5)" in subpara. (b)(2)(B) . . . Sec. 521(b)(25), substituted "sections 402(c)" for "sections 402(a)(5)" in para. (c)(2), effective for distributions after 12/31/92. For special rule, see Sec. 521(e)(2) of this Act which reads as follows:

"(2) Special rule for partial distributions. For purposes of section 402(a)(5)(D)(i)(II) of the Internal Revenue Code of 1986 (as in effect before the amendments made by this section), a distribution before January 1, 1993, which is made before or at the same time as a series of periodic payments shall not be treated as one of such series if it is not substantially equal in amount to other payments in such series."

In 1989, P.L. 101-239, Sec. 7304(c)(1), amended para. (c)(6), effective for yrs. begin. after 7/12/89.

Prior to amendment, para. (c)(6) read as follows:

"(6) Special limitation for employee stock ownership plan.

"(A) In the case of an employee stock ownership plan (as defined in subparagraph (B)), under which no more than one-third of the employer contributions for a year are allocated to highly compensated employees (within the meaning of section 414(q)), the amount described in paragraph (1)(A) for a year with respect to any participant shall be equal to the sum of (i) the amount described in paragraph (1)(A) determined without regard to this paragraph and (ii) the lesser of the amount determined under clause (i) or the amount of employer securities contributed, or purchased with cash contributed, to the employee stock ownership plan.

"(B) For purposes of this paragraph—

"(i) the term 'employee stock ownership plan' means an employee stock ownership plan (within the meaning of section 4975(e)(7)) or a tax credit employee stock ownership plan,

"(ii) the term 'employer securities' has the meaning given to such term by section 409.

"(C) In the case of an employee stock ownership plan (as described in section 4975(e)(7)), under which no more than one-third of the employer contributions for a year which are deductible under paragraph (9) of section 404(a) are allocated to highly compensated employees (within the meaning of section 414(q)), the limitations imposed by this section shall not apply to

"(i) forfeitures of employer securities under an employee stock ownership plan (as described in section 4975(e)(7)) if such securities were acquired with the proceeds of a loan (as described in section 404(a)(9)(A)), or

"(ii) employer contributions to such an employee stock ownership plan which are deductible under section 404(a)(9)(B) and charged against the participant's account."

In 1988, P.L. 100-647, Sec. 1011(d)(2), substituted "subparagraph (A)" for "this paragraph" in subpara. (b)(5)(D) . . . Sec. 1011(d)(3)(A), substituted "to such increase" for "to the arrangement" in clause (k)(2)(C)(ii) . . . Sec. 1011(d)(3)(B), amended subpara. (k)(2)(D) . . . Sec. 1011(d)(6), added "and subsection (e)" after "paragraphs (1)(B) and (4)" in subpara. (b)(5)(B) . . . Sec. 1011(d)(7)(A), substituted "paragraph (1)(A)" for "paragraph (c)(1)(A) (as adjusted for such year pursuant to subsection (d)(1))" in subpara. (c)(6)(A) . . . Sec. 1011(d)(7)(B), substituted "paragraph (1)(A)" for "paragraph (c)(1)(A) (as so adjusted)" in subpara. (c)(6)(A), effective for yrs. begin. after 12/31/86, except as provided in Secs. 1106(i)(2)-(4) [as amended by Sec. 1011(d)(5) of P.L. 100-647] and (6) of P.L. 99-514 [reproduced below].

Prior to amendment, subpara. (k)(2)(D) read as follows:

"(D) Arrangement elective; time for election. An arrangement meets the requirements of this subparagraph only if it is elective, it is available under the same terms to all participants, and it provides that such election may be made in—

"(i) the year in which the participant—
"(I) attains the earliest retirement age under the defined plan (determined without regard to any requirement of separation from service), or
"(II) separates from service, or
"(ii) both such years."

—P.L. 100-647, Sec. 1011(d)(5), amended Sec. 1105(i)(4) of P.L. 99-514, [reproduced below], part of the effective date for changes made by Sec. 1106 of P.L. 99-514, by inserting before the last period "(determined as if the amendments made by this section were in effect for such year)".

—P.L. 100-647, Sec. 1018(t)(8)(D), deleted Sec. 1899A(13) of P.L. 99-514, which amended Code Sec. 415(k). Code Sec. 415(k) as amended by 1899A(13) of P.L. 99-514 read as follows:

"(k) Definitions of defined contribution plan and defined benefit plan.

"For purposes of this title, the term 'defined contribution plan' or 'defined benefit plan' means a defined contribution plan (within the meaning of section 414(i)) or a defined benefit plan (within the meaning of section 414(j)), whichever applies, which is—

"(1) a plan described in section 401(a) which includes a trust which is exempt from tax under section 501(a),
"(2) an annuity plan described in section 403(a),
"(3) an annuity plan described in section 403(b),
"(4) an individual retirement account described in section 408(a),
"(5) an individual retirement annuity described in section 408(b), or
"(6) a simplified employee pension."

—P.L. 100-647, Sec. 6054(a), added para. (b)(10), effective for yrs. begin. after 12/31/82, except as provided in Sec. 6054(b)(2) of this Act which reads:

"(2) Election.—Section 415(b)(10)(C) of the 1986 Code (as added by subsection (a)) shall not apply to any year beginning before January 1, 1990."

—P.L. 100-647, Sec. 6059(a), substituted "15 years" for "20 years" in clause (b)(2)(H)(ii), effective for yrs. begin. after 12/31/86, except as provided in Secs. 1106(c)(1)-4) [as amended by Sec. 1101(d)(5) of P.L. 100-647] and (6) of P.L. 99-514 [reproduced below].

—P.L. 100-647, Sec. 6062(a), amended Sec. 1106(i)(2) of P.L. 99-514 [reproduced below], part of the effective date for changes made by Sec. 1106 of P.L. 99-514, effective for yrs. begin. after 12/31/86, see below.

Prior to amendment, Sec. 1106(i)(2) of P.L. 99-514 read as follows:

"(2) Collective Bargaining Agreements. In the case of a plan maintained pursuant to 1 or more collective bargaining agreements between employee representatives and 1 or more employers ratified before March 1, 1986, the amendments made by this section (other than subsection (d)) shall not apply to contributions or benefits pursuant to such agreement in years beginning before the earlier of

"(A) the date on which the last of such collective bargaining agreements terminates (determined without regard to any extension thereof after February 28, 1986), or
"(B) January 1, 1989."

In **1986**, P.L. 99-514, Sec. 1106(a), amended subpara. (c)(1)(A)...Sec. 1106(b)(1)(A)(i), substituted "the social security retirement age" for "age 62" and "age 65" each place it appeared in subparas. (b)(2)(C) and (D)...Sec. 1106(b)(1)(A)(ii), amended the last sentence of subpara. (b)(2)(C)...Sec. 1106(b)(1)(B), added para. (b)(8)...Sec. 1106(b)(2), added subparas. (b)(2)(F), (G), and (H)...Sec. 1106(b)(3), added para. (b)(9)...Sec. 1106(b)(4), added "a health and welfare service agency," after "a home health service agency," each place it appeared in subpara. (c)(4)(A), (B) and (C)...Sec. 1106(c)(1), added para. (k)(2)...Sec. 1106(e)(1), amended subpara. (c)(2)(B)...Sec. 1106(e)(2), added the sentence at the end of para. (c)(2)...Sec. 1106(f), amended para. (b)(5)...Sec. 1106(g)(1), added "and" at the end of subpara. (d)(1)(A), deleted subpara. (d)(1)(B) and redesignated subpara. (d)(1)(C) as subpara. (d)(1)(B)...Sec. 1106(g)(2)(A), substituted "subparagraph (A)" for "subparagraphs (A) and (B)" in subpara. (d)(2)(A)...Sec. 1106(g)(2)(B), substituted "subparagraph (B)" for "subparagraph (C)" in subpara. (d)(2)(B)...Sec. 1106(g)(3), substituted "subparagraph (A)" for "subparagraph (A) or (B)" in para. (d)(3), effective for yrs. begin. after 12/31/86, except as provided in Secs. 1106(i)(2)-(4) [as amended by Sec. 1011(d)(5) of P.L. 100-647 and Sec. 6062(a), see above] and (6) of this Act which reads as follows:

"(2) Collective bargaining agreements.— In the case of a plan in effect before March 1, 1986, pursuant to 1 or more collective bargaining agreements between employee representatives and 1 or more employers, the amendments made by this section (other than subsection (d)) shall not apply to contributions or benefits pursuant to such agreement in years beginning before October 1, 1991.

"(3) Right to higher accrued defined benefit preserved.—

"(A) In general.— In the case of an individual who is a participant (as of the 1st day of the 1st year to which the amendments made by this section apply) in a defined benefit plan which is in existence on May 6, 1986, and with respect to which the requirements of section 415 of the Internal Revenue Code of 1986 have been met for all plan years, if such individual's current accrued benefit under the plan exceeds the limitation of subsection (b) of section 415 of such Code (as amended by this section), then (in the case of such plan), for purposes of subsections (b) and (e) of such section, the limitation of such subsection (b)(1)(A) with respect to such individual shall be equal to such current accrued benefit.

"(B) Current accrued benefit defined.—

"(i) In general.— For purposes of this paragraph, the term 'current accrued benefit' means the individual's accrued benefit (at the close of the last year to which the amendments made by this section do not apply) when expressed as an annual benefit (within the meaning of section 415(b)(2) of such Code).

"(ii) Special rule.— For purposes of determining the amount of any individual's current accrued benefit—

"(I) no change in the terms and conditions of the plan after May 5, 1986, and

"(II) no cost-of-living adjustment occurring after May 5, 1986, shall be taken into account. For purposes of subclause (I), any change in the terms and conditions of the plan pursuant to a collective bargaining agreement ratified before May 6, 1986, shall be treated as a change made before May 6, 1986.

"(4) Transition rule where the sum of defined contribution and defined benefit plan fractions exceeds 1.0.— In the case of a plan which satisfied the requirements of section 415 of the Internal Revenue Code of 1986 for its last year beginning before January 1, 1987, the Secretary of the Treasury or his delegate shall prescribe regulations under which an amount is subtracted from the numerator of the defined contribution plan fraction (not exceeding such numerator) so that the sum of the defined benefit plan fraction and the defined contribution plan fraction computed under section 415(e)(1) of such Code does not exceed 1.0 for such year (determined as if the amendments made by this section were in effect for such year)."

* * *—

"(6) Special rule for amendment made by subsection (e) [Sec. 1106].— The amendment made by subsection (e) [Sec. 1106] shall not require the recomputation for purposes of section 415(e) of the Internal Revenue Code of 1986 of the annual addition for any year beginning before 1987."

—P.L. 99-514, Sec. 1106(h), provides:

"(h) Plans may incorporate section 415 limitations by reference.

"Notwithstanding any other provision of law, except as provided in regulations prescribed by the Secretary of the Treasury or his delegate, a plan may incorporate by reference the limitations under section 415 of the Internal Revenue Code of 1986."

Prior to amendment, subpara. (c)(1)(A) read as follows:
"(A) $30,000, or"

Prior to amendment, the last sentence of subpara. (b)(2)(C) read as follows:
"The reduction under this subparagraph shall not reduce the limitation of paragraph (1)(A) below—
"(i) if the benefit begins at or after age 55, $75,000, or
"(ii) if the benefit begins before age 55, the amount which is the equivalent of the $75,000 limitation for age 55."

Prior to amendment, subpara. (c)(2)(B) read as follows:
"(B) the lesser of—
"(i) the amount of the employee contributions in excess of 6 percent of his compensation, or
"(ii) one-half of the employee contributions, and"

Prior to amendment, para. (b)(5) read as follows:
"(5) Reduction for service less than 10 years. In the case of an employee who has less than 10 years of service with the employer, the limitation referred to in paragraph (1), and the limitation referred to in paragraph (4), shall be the limitation determined under such paragraph (without regard to this paragraph), multiplied by a fraction, the numerator of which is the number of years (or part thereof) of service with the employer and the denominator of which is 10."

Prior to deletion, subpara. (d)(1)(B) read as follows:
"(B) the $30,000 amount in subsection (c)(1)(A), and"

—P.L. 99-514, Sec. 1108(g)(5), substituted "which are excludable from gross income under section 408(k)(6)" for "allowable as a deduction under section 219(a), and without regard to deductible employee contributions within the meaning of section 72(o)(5)", in para. (c)(2), effective for yrs. begin. after 12/31/86.

—P.L. 99-514, Sec. 1114(b)(12), substituted "a highly compensated employee (within the meaning of section 414(q))" for "an officer, owner or highly compensated" in clause (c)(3)(C)(ii), effective for yrs. begin. after 12/31/88.

—P.L. 99-514, Sec. 1174(d)(1), substituted "highly compensated employees (within the meaning of section 414(q))" for "the group of employees consisting of officers, shareholders owning more than 10 percent of the employer's stock (determined under subparagraph (B)(iv)), or employees described in subparagraph (B)(iii)" in subpara. (c)(6)(A)...Sec. 1174(d)(2)(A), deleted clauses (c)(6)(B)(iii) and (iv)...Sec. 1174(d)(2)(B), substituted "highly compensated employees (within the meaning of section 414(q))" for "the group of employees consisting of officers, shareholders owning more than 10 percent of the employer's stock (determined under subparagraph (B)(iv)), or employees described in subparagraph (B)(iii)" in subpara. (c)(6)(C), effective for yrs. begin. after 12/31/86.

Prior to deletion, clauses (c)(6)(B)(iii) and (iv) read as follows:

"(iii) an employee described in this clause is any participant whose compensation for a year exceeds an amount equal to twice the amount described in paragraph (1)(A) for such year (as adjusted for such year pursuant to subsection (d)(1)), determined without regard to subparagraph (A) of this paragraph, and

"(iv) an individual shall be considered to own more than 10 percent of the employer's stock if, without regard to stock held under the employee stock ownership plan, he owns (after application of section 1563(e)) more than 10 percent of the total combined voting power of all classes of stock entitled to vote or more than 10 percent of the total value of shares of all classes of stock."

—P.L. 99-514, Sec. 1847(b)(4), substituted "section 22(e)(3)" for "section 37(e)(3)" in clause (c)(3)(C)(i), effective for tax. yrs. begin. after 12/31/83 and for carrybacks from 12/31/83.

—P.L. 99-514, Sec. 1852(h)(2), added the sentence at the end of para. (l)(1)...Sec. 1852(h)(3), substituted "a pension or annuity plan" for " a defined benefit plan", in each placed it appeared in subsec. (l), effective for yrs. begin. after 3/31/84.

—P.L. 99-514, Sec. 1875(c)(9), substituted "this subsection" for "adjusting any benefit or limitation under subparagraph (B), (C), or (D)", in clause (b)(2)(E)(iii), effective as provided in Sec. 235(g) of P.L. 97-248, reproduced below.

—P.L. 99-514, Sec. 1875(c)(11), substituted "any defined contribution plan" for "a profit-sharing or stock bonus plan" in subpara. (c)(3)(C), effective for tax. yrs. begin. after 12/31/81.

—P.L. 99-514, Sec. 1898(b)(15)(C), substituted "as defined in section 417" for "as defined in section 401(a)(11)(G)(iii), in subpara. (b)(2)(B), effective for plan yrs. begin. after 12/31/84 and as provided in Sec. 302(b) of P.L. 98-397, reproduced in note following Code Sec. 417. For transitional rules, see Sec. 303 of P.L. 98-397 reproduced in note following Code Sec. 401.

—P.L. 99-514, Sec. 1899A(13), amended subsec. (k), effective 10/22/86.

Prior to amendment, subsec. (k) read as follows:

"(k) Special rules.

"(1) Defined benefit plan and defined contribution plan.— For purposes of this title, the term 'defined contribution plan' or 'defined benefit plan' means a defined contribution plan (within the meaning of section 414(i) or a defined benefit plan (within the meaning of section 414(j)), whichever applies, which is—

"(A) a plan described in section 401(a) which includes a trust which is exempt from tax under section 501(a),

"(B) an annuity plan described in section 403(a),

"(C) an annuity contract described in section 403(b),

"(D) an individual retirement account described in section 408(a),

"(E) an individual retirement annuity described in section 408(b), or

"(F) a simplified employee pension."

In 1984, P.L. 98-369, Sec. 15(a), substituted "January 1, 1988" for "January 1, 1986" in para. (d)(3) . . . Sec. 15(b), substituted "October 1, 1986" for "October 1, 1984" in subpara. (d)(2)(A), (as amended by Sec. 235(b)(2)(B) of P.L. 97-248) effective for tax. yrs. end. after 12/31/83.

—P.L. 98-369, Sec. 491(d)(28), deleted subpara. (a)(2)(D), deleted "or" at the end of subpara. (a)(2)(C), added "or" at the end of subpara. (a)(2)(B), and deleted "405(a)," after "403(b)," in para. (a)(2) . . . Sec. 491(d)(29), substituted "and 408(d)(3)" for "408(d)(3) and 409(b)(3)(C)" in subpara. (b)(2)(A) . . . Sec. 491(d)(30), substituted "and 408(d)(3)" for "408(d)(3) and 409(b)(3)(C)" in subpara. (b)(2)(B) . . . Sec. 491(d)(31), substituted "and 408(d)(3)" for "405(d)(3), 408(d)(3), and 409(b)(3)(C)" in para. (c)(2) . . . Sec. 491(d)(32), deleted subparas. (k)(1)(C) and (H), redesignated subparas. (k)(1)(D), (E), (F) and (G) as subparas. (k)(1)(C), (D), (E) and (F), respectively, substituted a period for ", or" at the end of subpara. (k)(1)(F) (as redesignated), and added "or" at the end of subpara. (k)(1)(E) (as redesignated), effective for obligations issued after 12/31/83.

Prior to deletion, subpara. (a)(2)(D) read as follows:

"(D) a plan described in section 405(a),"

Prior to deletion, subpara. (k)(1)(C) read as follows:

"(C) a qualified bond purchase plan described in section 405(a),"

Prior to deletion, subpara. (k)(1)(H) read as follows:

"(H) an individual retirement bond described in section 409."

—P.L. 98-369, Sec. 491(e)(6), substituted "section 409" for "section 409A" in clause (c)(6)(B)(ii), effective on 1/1/84.

—P.L. 98-369, Sec. 528(a), added subsec. (1), effective for yrs. begin. after 3/31/84.

—P.L. 98-369, Sec. 713(a)(1)(A), amended the material preceding clause (i) in subpara. (b)(2)(C) . . . Sec. 713(a)(1)(B), amended subpara. (b)(2)(D) . . . Sec. 713(a)(1)(C)(i), substituted "any benefit or limitation" for "any benefit" in clauses (b)(2)(E)(i) and (iii) . . . Sec. 713(a)(1)(C)(ii), substituted "any limitation" for "any benefit" in clause (b)(2)(E)(ii), effective as provided in Sec. 235(g) of P.L. 97-248, reproduced below.

Prior to amendment, the material preceding clause (i) in subpara. (b)(2)(C) read as follows:

"(C) Adjustment to $90,000 limit where benefit begins before age 62. If the retirement income benefit under the plan begins before age 62, the determination as to whether the $90,000 limitation set forth in paragraph (1)(A) has been satisfied shall be made, in accordance with regulations prescribed by the Secretary, by adjusting such benefit so that it is equivalent to such a benefit beginning at age 62. The reduction under this subparagraph shall not reduce the limitation of paragraph (1)(A) below—"

Prior to amendment, subpara. (b)(2)(D) read as follows:

"(D) Adjustment to $90,000 limitation where benefit begins after age 65. If the retirement income benefit under the plan begins after age 65, the determination as to whether the $90,000 limitation set forth in paragraph (1)(A) has been satisfied shall be made, in accordance with regulations prescribed by the Secretary, by adjusting such benefit so that it is equivalent to such a benefit beginning at age 65."

—P.L. 98-369, Sec. 713(a)(2), and (4), amended Sec. 235(g)(4)(B) of P.L. 97-248, part of the effective date for changes made by Sec. 235 of P.L. 97-248 (reproduced below), by adding the last sentences to clauses (g)(4)(B)(i) and (ii) of Sec. 235.

—P.L. 98-369, Sec. 713(a)(3), added subpara. (e)(6)(C), effective as provided in Sec. 235(g) of P.L. 97-248, reproduced below.

—P.L. 98-369, Sec. 713(d)(4)(B)(i), substituted "paragraph (9) of section 404(a)" for "paragraph (10) of section 404(a)" in subpara. (c)(6)(C) . . . Sec. 713(d)(4)(B)(ii), substituted "section 404(a)(9)(A)" for "section 404(a)(10)(A)" in subpara. (c)(6)(C) . . . Sec. 713(d)(4)(B)(iii), substituted "section 404(a)(9)(B)" for "section 404(a)(10)(B)" in subpara. (c)(6)(C) . . . Sec. 713(d)(7)(A), deleted para. (c)(7) and redesignated para. (c)(8) as new para. (c)(7) . . . Sec. 713(d)(7)(B), substituted "subsection (c)(7)" for "subsection (c)(7) or (8)" in subclause (e)(3)(B)(ii)(II), effective for yrs. begin. after 12/31/83.

Prior to deletion, para. (c)(7) read as follows:

"(7) Certain level premium annuity contracts under plans benefiting owner-employees. Paragraph (1)(B) shall not apply to a contribution described in section 401(e) which is made on behalf of a participant for a year to a plan which benefits an owner-employee (within the meaning of section 401(c)(3)), if—

"(A) the annual addition determined under this section with respect to the participant for such year consists solely of such contribution, and

"(B) the participant is not an active participant at any time during such year in a defined benefit plan maintained by the employer.

For purposes of this section and section 401(e), in the case of a plan which provides contributions or benefits for employees who are not owner-employees, such plan will not be treated as failing to satisfy section 401(a)(4) merely because contributions made on behalf of employees who are not owner-employees are not permitted to exceed the limitations of paragraph (1)(B)."

—P.L. 98-369, Sec. 713(f)(3), amended Sec. 235(g)(3) of P.L. 97-248, part of the effective date for changes made by Sec. 235 of P.L. 97-248 (reproduced below), by adding the last sentence.

—P.L. 98-369, Sec. 713(k)(1), substituted "In the case of a participant in a profit-sharing or stock bonus plan" for "In the case of a participant" in subpara. (c)(3)(C) . . . Sec. 713(k)(2), substituted "This subparagraph shall apply only if contributions made with respect to amounts treated as compensation under this subparagraph are nonforfeitable when made." for "This subparagraph shall only apply if contributions made with respect to such participant are nonforfeitable when made." at the end of subpara. (c)(3)(C), effective for tax. yrs. begin. after 12/31/81.

In 1983, P.L. 98-21, Sec. 122(c)(5), substituted "section 37(e)(3)" for "section 105(d)(4)" in clause (c)(3)(C)(i), effective for tax. yrs. begin. after 12/31/83.

—P.L. 97-448, Sec. 306(a)(10), substituted "section 242" for "section 253" in Sec. 235(g)(5) of P.L. 97-248, the effective date for changes made by Sec. 235 of P.L. 97-248 [reproduced below].

In 1982, P.L. 97-248, Sec. 235(a)(1), substituted "$90,000" for "$75,000" in subpara. (b)(1)(A) . . . Sec. 235(a)(2), substituted "$30,000" for "25,000" in subpara. (c)(1)(A) . . . Sec. 235(a)(3)(A), substituted "$90,000" for "$75,000" each place it appeared in subpara. (b)(2)(C) . . . Sec. 235(a)(3)(B), substituted "by substituting the greater of $68,212 or one-half the amount otherwise applicable for such year under paragraph (1)(A) for '$90,000'" for "by substituting '$37,500' for '$75,000'" in the last sentence of para. (b)(7) . . . Sec. 235(b)(1), substituted "benefit amounts" for "primary insurance amounts" in para. (d)(1) . . . Sec. 235(b)(2)(A), added para. (d)(3) . . . Sec. 235(b)(2)(B), substituted "1984" for "1974" in para. (d)(2) . . . Sec. 235(b)(3)(A), substituted "$90,000" for "$75,000" in subpara. (d)(1)(A) . . . Sec. 235(b)(3)(B), substituted "$30,000" for "$25,000" in subpara. (d)(1)(B) . . . Sec. 235(c)(1), substituted "1.0" for "1.4" in para. (e)(1) . . . Sec. 235(c)(2)(A), amended subpara. (e)(2)(B) . . . Sec. 235(c)(2)(B), amended subpara. (e)(3)(B) . . . Sec. 235(d), added para. (e)(6) . . . Sec. 235(e)(1), substituted "62" for "55" each place it appeared in subpara. (b)(2)(C) . . . Sec. 235(e)(2), added the sentence at the end of subpara. (b)(2)(C) . . . Sec. 235(e)(3), added subpara. (b)(2)(D) . . . Sec. 235(e)(4), added subpara. (b)(2)(E), effective as provided in Sec. 235(g) of this Act which reads as follows:

"(g) Effective dates.

"(1) In general.—

"(A) New plans.—In the case of any plan which is not in existence on July 1, 1982, the amendments made by this section [Sec. 235] shall apply to years ending after July 1, 1982.

"(B) Existing plans.—

"(i) In the case of any plan which is in existence on July 1, 1982, the amendments made by this section shall apply to years beginning after December 31, 1982.

"(ii) Plan requirements.—A plan shall not be treated as failing to meet the requirements of section 401(a)(16) of the Internal Revenue Code of 1954 for any year beginning before January 1, 1984, merely because such plan provides for benefit or contribution limits which are in excess of the limitations under section 415 of such Code, as amended by this section. The preceding sentence shall not apply to any plan which provides such limits in excess of the limitation under section 415 of such Code before such amendments.

"(2) Amendments related to cost-of-living adjustments.—

"(A) In general.—Except as provided in subparagraph (B), the amendments made by subsection (b) [Sec. 235(b) of this Act] shall apply to adjustments for years beginning after December 31, 1982.

"(B) Adjustment procedures.—The amendments made by subsections (b)(1) and (b)(2)(B) [Sec. 235(b)(1) and (b)(2)(A) of this Act] shall apply to adjustments for years beginning after December 31, 1985.

"(3) Transition rule where the sum of defined contribution and defined benefit plan fractions exceeds 1.0.—In the case of a plan which satisfied the requirements of section 415 of the Internal Revenue Code of 1954 for the last year beginning before January 1, 1983, the Secretary of the Treasury or his delegate shall prescribe regulations under which an amount is subtracted from the numerator of the defined contribution plan fraction (not exceeding such numerator) so that the sum of the defined benefit plan fraction and the defined contribution plan fraction computed under section 415(e)(1) of the Internal Revenue Code of 1954 (as amended by the Tax Equity and Fiscal Responsibility Act of 1982) does not exceed 1.0 for such year. A similar rule shall apply with respect to the last plan year beginning before January 1, 1984, for purposes of applying section 416(h) of the Internal Revenue Code of 1954.

"(4) Right to higher accrued defined benefit preserved.—

"(A) In general.—In the case of an individual who is a participant before January 1, 1983, in a defined benefit plan which is in existence on July 1, 1982, and with respect to which the requirements of section 415 of such Code have been met for all years, if such individual's current accrued benefit under such plan exceeds the limitation of subsection (b) of section 415 of the Internal Revenue Code of 1954 (as amended by this section), then (in the case of such plan) for purposes of subsections (b) and (e) of such section, the limitation of such subsection (b) with respect to such individual shall be equal to such current accrued benefit.

"(B) Current accrued benefit defined.—

"(i) In general.—For purposes of this paragraph, the term 'current accrued benefit' means the individual's accrued benefit (at the close of the last year beginning

Employee benefit plans Code Sec. 415

before January 1, 1983) when expressed as an annual benefit (within the meaning of section 415(b)(2) of such Code as in effect before the amendments made by this Act). In the case of any plan described in the first sentence of paragraph (5), the preceding sentence shall be applied by substituting for 'January 1, 1983' the applicable date determined under paragraph (5).

"(ii) Special rule.— For purposes of determining the amount of any individual's current accrued benefit—

"(I) no change in the terms and conditions of the plan after July 1, 1982, and

"(II) no cost-of-living adjustment occurring after July 1, 1982,

shall be taken into account. For purposes of subclause (I), any change in the terms and conditions of the plan pursuant to a collective bargaining agreement entered into before July 1, 1982, and ratified before September 3, 1982, shall be treated as a change made before July 1, 1982.

"(5) Special rule for collective bargaining agreements.— In the case of a plan maintained on the date of the enactment of this Act pursuant to 1 or more collective bargaining agreements between employee representatives and 1 or more employers, the amendments made by this section and section 242 [of this Act] (relating to age 70½ shall not apply to years beginning before the earlier of—

"(A) the date on which the last of the collective bargaining agreements relating to the plan terminates (determined without regard to any extension thereof agreed to after the date of the enactment of this Act [9/3/82]), or

"(B) January 1, 1986.

For purposes of subparagraph (A), any plan amendment made pursuant to a collective bargaining agreement relating to the plan which amends the plan solely to conform to any requirement added by this section and section 253 [of this Act] shall not be treated as a termination of such collective bargaining agreement."

Prior to amendment, subpara. (e)(2)(B) read as follows:

"(B) the denominator of which is the projected annual benefit of the participant under the plan (determined as of the close of the year) if the plan provided the maximum benefit allowable under subsection (b),"

Prior to amendment, subpara. (c)(3)(B) read as follows:

"(B) the denominator of which is the sum of the maximum amount of annual additions to such account which could have been made under subsection (c) for such year and for each prior year of service with employer determined without regard to paragraph (6) of such subsection) [sic]. "

—P.L. 97-248, Sec. 238(d)(5), deleted para. (c)(5), effective for yrs. begin. after 12/31/83.

Prior to deletion, para. (d)(5) read as follows:

"(5) Application with section 404(e)(4). In the case of a plan which provides contributions or benefits for employees some or all of whom are employees within the meaning of section 401(c)(1), the amount determined under paragraph (1)(B) with respect to any participant shall not be less than the amount deductible under section 404(e) with respect to any individual who is an employee within the meaning of section 401(c)(1)."

—P.L. 97-248, Sec. 251(c)(1)(A), substituted "a home health service agency, or a church, convention or association of churches, or an organization described in section 414(e)(3)(B)(ii)" for "or a home health service agency" each place it appeared in para. (c)(4) . . . Sec. 251(c)(1)(B), added "(as determined for purposes of section 403(b)(2))" after "service for the employer" in subpara. (c)(4)(A) . . . Sec. 251(c)(1)(C), added clause (c)(4)(D)(iv) . . . Sec. 251(c)(1)(D), substituted ", home health service agencies, and certain churches, etc." for "and home health service agencies" in the heading of para. (c)(4) . . . Sec. 251(c)(2), added para. (c)(8), effective for yrs. begin. after 12/31/81.

—P.L. 97-248, Sec. 253(a), amended para. (c)(3), effective for tax. yrs. begin. after 12/31/81.

Prior to amendment, para. (c)(3) read as follows:

"(3) Participant's compensation. For purposes of paragraph (1), the term 'participant's compensation' means the compensation of the participant from the employer for the year. In the case of an employee within the meaning of section 401(c)(1), the preceding sentence shall be applied by substituting for the following: 'the participant's earned income (within the meaning of section 401(c)(2) but determined without regard to any exclusion under section 911)."

In 1981, P.L. 97-34, Sec. 311(g)(4)(A), amended para. (a)(2) . . . Sec. 311(g)(4)(B), amended the last sentence of para. (c)(2) . . . Sec. 311(g)(4)(C), amended para. (e)(5) . . . Sec. 311(h)(3), deleted para. (a)(3), effective for tax. yrs. after 12/31/81.

Prior to amendment, para. (a)(2) read as follows:

"(2) Section applies to certain annuities and accounts. Except as provided in paragraph (3), in the case of—

"(A) an employee annuity plan described in section 403(a),

"(B) an annuity contract described in section 403(b),

"(C) an individual retirement account described in section 408(a),

"(D) an individual retirement annuity described in section 408(b),

"(E) a simplified employee pension,

"(F) a plan described in section 405(a), or

"(G) a retirement bond described in section 409,

such contract, annuity plan, account, annuity, plan, or bond shall not be considered to be described in sections 403(a), 403(b), 405(a), 408(a), 408(b), 408(k), or 409, as the case may be, unless it satisfies the requirements of subparagraph (A) or subparagraph (B) of paragraph (1), whichever is appropriate, and has not been disqualified under subsection (g). In the case of an annuity contract described in section 403(b), the preceding sentence shall apply only to the portion of the annuity contract which exceeds the limitation of subsection (b) or the limitation of subsection (c), whichever is appropriate, and the amount of the contribution for such portion shall reduce the exclusion allowance as provided in section 403(b)'(2)."

Prior to amendment, para. (c)(2) read as follows:

"(2) Annual addition. For purposes of paragraph (1), the term 'annual addition' means the sum for any year of—

"(A) employer contributions,

"(B) the lessor of—

"(i) the amount of the employee contributions in excess of 6 percent of his compensation, or

"(ii) one-half of the employee contributions, and

"(C) forfeitures.

For the purposes of this paragraph, employee contributions under subparagraph (B) are determined without regard to any rollover contributions (as defined in sections 402(a)(5), 403(a)(4), 408(d)(3), and 409(b)(3)(C))."

Prior to amendment, para. (e)(5) read as follows:

"(5) Special rules for sections 403(b) and 408. For purposes of this section, any annuity contract described in section 403(b) (except in the case of a participant who has elected under subsection (c)(4)(D) to have the provisions of subsection (c)(4)(C) apply), any individual retirement account described in section 408(a), any individual retirement annuity described in section 408(b), and any retirement bond described in section 409, for the benefit of a participant shall be treated as a defined contribution plan maintained by each employer with respect to which the participant has the control required under subsection (b) or (c) of section 414 (as modified by subsection (h)). For purposes of this section, any contribution by an employer to a simplified employee pension for an individual for a taxable year shall be treated as an employer contribution to a defined contribution plan for such individual for such year. In the case of any annuity contract described in section 403(b), the amount of the contribution disqualified by reason of subsection (g) shall reduce the exclusion allowance as provided in section 403(b)(2)."

Prior to deletion, para. (a)(3) read as follows:

"(3) Accounts, etc., established for non-employed spouse. Paragraph (2) shall not apply for any year to an account, annuity, or bond described in section 408(a), 408(b), or 409, respectively, established for the benefit of the spouse of the individual contributing to such account, or for such annuity or bond, if a deduction is allowed under section 220 to such individual with respect to such contribution for such year."

—P.L. 97-34, Sec. 333(b)(1), added subpara. (c)(6)(C), effective for tax. begin. after 12/31/81.

In 1980, P.L. 96-605, Sec. 222(a), added ", or purchased with cash contributed," after "contributed" in subpara. (c)(6)(A), effective for yrs. begin. after 12/31/80.

—P.L. 96-222, Sec. 101(a)(7)(B), redesignated the effective date of changes made by Sec. 141(f)(7) of P.L. 95-600 from Sec. 141(g)(1) to Sec. 141(g)(5).

—P.L. 96-222, Sec. 101(a)(7)(L)(i)(VII), substituted "a tax credit employee stock ownership plan" for "an ESOP" in clause (c)(6)(B)(i) . . . Sec. 101(a)(7)(L)(iv)(I), substituted "employee" for "leveraged employee" in clause (c)(6)(B)(i), presumably intended by Congress to be effective for tax. yrs. begin. after 12/31/78 [Sec. 101(b)(2)] although technically effective for decedents dying after 4/1/80 [Sec. 101(b)(1)(D)].

—P.L. 96-222, Sec. 101(a)(10)(I)(i), deleted "any simplified employee pension" from para. (e)(5) . . . Sec. 101(a)(10)(I)(ii), added "For purposes of this section, any contribution by an employer to a simplified employee pension for an individual for a taxable year shall be treated as an employer contribution to a defined contribution plan for such individual for such year." after the first sentence in para. (e)(5), effective for tax. yrs. begin. after 4/1/80.

—P.L. 96-222, Sec. 101(a)(10)(J)(iii), amended Sec. 152(g)(2) of P.L. 95-600 to amend para. (a)(2) instead of (b)(2) [see below].

—P.L. 96-222, Sec. 101(a)(11)(A), added "This paragraph shall not apply to a participant for any period for which he is a participant under another plan to which this section applies which is maintained by an employer maintaining this plan." after the second sentence in para. (b)(7) . . . Sec. 101(a)(11)(B), amended subpara. (b)(7)(C), effective for yrs. begin. after 12/31/78.

Prior to amendment, subpara. (b)(7)(C) read as follows:

"(C) benefits under which are determined by multiplying a specified amount (which is the same amount for each participant) by the number of the participant's years of service,"

In 1978, P.L. 95-600, Sec. 141(f)(7), amended clauses (c)(6)(B)(i) and (ii), effective for tax. yrs. begin. after 12/31/78.

Prior to amendment, clauses (c)(6)(B)(i) and (ii) read as follows:

"(i) the term 'employee stock ownership plan' means a plan which meets the requirements of section 4975(e)(7) or section 301(d) of the Tax Reduction Act of 1975,

"(ii) the term 'employer securities' means, in the case of an employee stock ownership plan within the meaning of section 4975(e)(7), qualifying employer securities within the meaning of section 4975(e)(8), but only if they are described in section 301(d)(9)(A) of the Tax Reduction Act of 1975, or, in the case of an employee stock ownership plan described in section 301(d)(2) of the Tax Reduction Act of 1975, employer securities within the meaning of section 301(d)(9)(A) of such Act."

—P.L. 95-600, Sec. 152(g)(1), redesignated subparas. (a)(2)(E) and (F) as subparas. (a)(2)(F) and (G) and added new subpara. (a)(2)(E) . . . Sec. 152(g)(2), inserted "408(k)," after "408(b)," in the material following subpara. (a)(2)(G) . . . Sec. 152(g)(3), inserted "any simplified employee pension" after "section 408(b)," in para. (e)(5) . . . Sec. 152(g)(4), deleted "or" at the end of subpara. (k)(1)(F), redesignated subpara. (k)(1)(G) as (H), and added new subpara. (k)(1)(G), effective for tax. yrs. begin. after 12/31/78.

—P.L. 95-600, Sec. 153(a), added para. (b)(7), effective for yrs. begin. after 12/31/78.

2,045

Code Sec. 415 — Employee benefit plans

In 1976, P.L. 94-455, Sec. 803(b)(4), substituted "For purposes of this section," for "For purposes of this subsection," in para. (e)(5), effective for yrs. begin. after 12/31/75.
—P.L. 94-455, Sec. 803(f), added para. (c)(6) and added "determined without regard to paragraph (6) of such subsection [sic]" after "employer" in subpara. (e)(3)(B), effective for yrs. begin. after 12/31/75.
—P.L. 94-455, Sec. 1501(b)(3)(A), substituted "Except as provided in paragraph (3), in the case" for "In the case" in para. (a)(2) . . . Sec. 1501(b)(3)(B), added para. (a)(3), effective for yrs. begin. after 12/31/76.
—P.L. 94-455, Sec. 1502(a)(1), added para. (c)(5), effective for yrs. begin. after 12/31/75.
—P.L. 94-455, Sec. 1511(a), added para. (c)(7), effective for yrs. begin. after 12/31/75.
—P.L. 94-455, Sec. 1901(a)(65), substituted "and 409(b)(3)(C))" for "and 409(b)(3)(C)" in subpara. (b)(2)(A) and substituted "(as defined in section 401(a)(11)(G)(iii))" for "(as defined in section 401(a)(11)(H)(iii))" in subpara. (b)(2)(B), effective for tax. yrs. begin. after 12/31/76.
—P.L. 94-455, Sec. 1901(b)(8)(D)(i), substituted "educational organization" for "educational institution" each place it appeared in subparas. (c)(4)(A), (B) and (C), effective for tax. yrs. begin. after 12/31/76.
Prior to amendment, clause (c)(4)(D)(ii) read as follows:
"(ii) For purposes of this paragraph the term 'educational institution' means an educational institution as defined in section 151(e)(4)."
—P.L. 94-455, Sec. 1906(b)(13)(A), substituted "Secretary" for "Secretary or his delegate" each place it appeared in Code Sec. 415, effective for tax. yrs. begin. after 12/31/76.

In 1974, P.L. 93-406, Sec. 2004(a)(2), added Code Sec. 415, effective for yrs. begin. after 12/31/75. Sec. 2004(d) of the Employee Retirement Income Security Act of 1974 provides as follows:
"(d) Effective date.
"(1) General rule. The amendments made by this section shall apply to years beginning after December 31, 1975. The Secretary of the Treasury shall prescribe such regulations as may be necessary to carry out the provisions of this paragraph.
"(2) Transition rule for defined benefit plans. In the case of an individual who was an active participant in a defined benefit plan before October 3, 1973, if—
"(A) the annual benefit (within the meaning of section 415(b)(2) of the Internal Revenue Code of 1954) payable to such participant on retirement does not exceed 100 percent of his annual rate of compensation on the earlier of (i) October 2, 1973, or (ii) the date on which he separated from the service of the employer,
"(B) such annual benefit is no greater than the annual benefit which would have been payable to such participant on retirement if (i) all the terms and conditions of such plan in existence on such date had remained in existence until such retirement, and (ii) his compensation taken into account for any period after October 2, 1973, had not exceeded his annual rate of compensation on such date, and
"(C) in the case of a participant who separated from the service of the employer prior to October 2, 1973, such annual benefit is no greater than his vested accrued benefit as of the date he separated from the service,
then such annual benefit shall be treated as not exceeding the limitation of subsection (b) of section 415 of the Internal Revenue Code of 1954."
Sec. 2004(a)(3) of the Employee Retirement Income Security Act of 1974 provides as follows:
"(3) Special rule for certain plans in effect on date of enactment. In any case in which, on the date of enactment of this Act, an individual is a participant in both a defined benefit plan and a defined contribution plan maintained by the same employer, and the sum of the defined benefit plan fraction and the defined contribution plan fraction for the year during which such date occurs exceeds 1.4, the sum of such fractions may continue to exceed 1.4 if—
"(A) the defined benefit plan fraction is not increased, by amendment of the plan or otherwise, after the date of enactment of this Act, and
"(B) no contributions are made under the defined contribution plan after such date.
A trust which is part of a pension, profit-sharing, or stock bonus plan described in the preceding sentence shall not be treated as not constituting a qualified trust under section 401(a) of the Internal Revenue Code of 1954 on account of the provisions of section 415(e) of such Code, as long as it is described in the preceding sentence of this subsection."

Sec. 416. Special rules for top-heavy plans.
(a) General rule.

A trust shall not constitute a qualified trust under section 401(a) for any plan year if the plan of which it is a part is a top-heavy plan for such plan year unless such plan meets—

(1) the vesting requirements of subsection (b), and

(2) the minimum benefit requirements of subsection (c).

(b) Vesting requirements.

(1) **In general.** A plan satisfies the requirements of this subsection if it satisfies the requirements of either of the following subparagraphs:

(A) 3-year vesting. A plan satisfies the requirements of this subparagraph if an employee who has completed at least 3 years of service with the employer or employers maintaining the plan has a nonforfeitable right to 100 percent of his accrued benefit derived from employer contributions.

(B) 6-year graded vesting. A plan satisfies the requirements of this subparagraph if an employee has a nonforfeitable right to a percentage of his accrued benefit derived from employer contributions determined under the following table:

Years of service	The nonforfeitable percentage is:
2	20
3	40
4	60
5	80
6 or more	100

(2) **Certain rules made applicable.** Except to the extent inconsistent with the provisions of this subsection, the rules of section 411 shall apply for purposes of this subsection.

(c) Plan must provide minimum benefits.

(1) **Defined benefit plans.**

(A) In general. A defined benefit plan meets the requirements of this subsection if the accrued benefit derived from employer contributions of each participant who is a non-key employee, when expressed as an annual retirement benefit, is not less than the applicable percentage of the participant's average compensation for years in the testing period.

(B) Applicable percentage. For purposes of subparagraph (A), the term "applicable percentage" means the lesser of—

(i) 2 percent multiplied by the number of years of service with the employer, or

(ii) 20 percent.

(C) Years of service. For purposes of this paragraph—

(i) In general. Except as provided in clause (ii) or (iii), years of service shall be determined under the rules of paragraphs (4), (5), and (6) of section 411(a).

(ii) Exception for years during which plan was not top-heavy. A year of service with the employer shall not be taken into account under this paragraph if—

(I) the plan was not a top-heavy plan for any plan year ending during such year of service, or

(II) such year of service was completed in a plan year beginning before January 1, 1984.

(iii) Exception for plan under which no key employee (or former key employee) benefits for plan year. For purposes of determining an employee's years of service with the employer, any service with the employer shall be disregarded to the extent that such service occurs during a plan year when the plan benefits (within the meaning of section 410(b)) no key employee or former key employee.

(D) Average compensation for high 5 years. For purposes of this paragraph—

(i) In general. A participant's testing period shall be the period of consecutive years (not exceeding 5) during which the participant had the greatest aggregate compensation from the employer.

(ii) Year must be included in year of service. The years taken into account under clause (i) shall be properly adjusted for years not included in a year of service.

(iii) Certain years not taken into account. Except to the extent provided in the plan, a year shall not be taken into account under clause (i) if—

(I) such year ends in a plan year beginning before January 1, 1984, or

(II) such year begins after the close of the last year in which the plan was a top-heavy plan.

(E) Annual retirement benefit. For purposes of this paragraph, the term "annual retirement benefit" means a benefit payable annually in the form of a single life annuity (with no ancillary benefits) beginning at the normal retirement age under the plan.

(2) Defined contribution plans.

(A) In general. A defined contribution plan meets the requirements of the subsection if the employer contribution for the year for each participant who is a non-key employee is not less than 3 percent of such participant's compensation (within the meaning of section 415). Employer matching contributions (as defined in section 401(m)(4)(A)) shall be taken into account for purposes of this subparagraph (and any reduction under this sentence shall not be taken into account in determining whether section 401(k)(4)(A) applies).

(B) Special rule where maximum contribution less than 3 percent.

(i) In general. The percentage referred to in subparagraph (A) for any year shall not exceed the percentage at which contributions are made (or required to be made) under the plan for the year for the key employee for whom such percentage is the highest for the year.

(ii) Treatment of aggregation groups.

(I) For purposes of this subparagraph, all defined contribution plans required to be included in an aggregation group under subsection (g)(2)(A)(i) shall be treated as one plan.

(II) This subparagraph shall not apply to any plan required to be included in an aggregation group if such plan enables a defined benefit plan required to be included in such group to meet the requirements of section 401(a)(4) or 410.

(d) Repealed.

(e) Plan must meet requirements without taking into account social security and similar contributions and benefits.

A top-heavy plan shall not be treated as meeting the requirement of subsection (b) or (c) unless such plan meets such requirement without taking into account contributions or benefits under chapter 2 (relating to tax on self-employment income), chapter 21 (relating to Federal Insurance Contributions Act), title II of the Social Security Act, or any other Federal or State law.

(f) Coordination where employer has 2 or more plans.

The Secretary shall prescribe such regulations as may be necessary or appropriate to carry out the purposes of this section where the employer has 2 or more plans including (but not limited to) regulations to prevent inappropriate omissions or required duplication of minimum benefits or contributions.

(g) Top-heavy plan defined.

For purposes of this section—

(1) In general.

(A) Plans not required to be aggregated. Except as provided in subparagraph (B), the term "top-heavy plan" means, with respect to any plan year—

(i) any defined benefit plan if, as of the determination date, the present value of the cumulative accrued benefits under the plan for key employees exceeds 60 percent of the present value of the cumulative accrued benefits under the plan for all employees, and

(ii) any defined contribution plan if, as of the determination date, the aggregate of the accounts of key employees under the plan exceeds 60 percent of the aggregate of the accounts of all employees under such plan.

(B) Aggregated plans. Each plan of an employer required to be included in an aggregation group shall be treated as a top-heavy plan if such group is a top-heavy group.

(2) Aggregation. For purposes of this subsection—

(A) Aggregation group.

(i) Required aggregation. The term "aggregation group" means—

(I) each plan of the employer in which a key employee is a participant, and

(II) each other plan of the employer which enables any plan described in subclause (I) to meet the requirements of section 401(a)(4) or 410.

(ii) Permissive aggregation. The employer may treat any plan not required to be included in an aggregation group under clause (i) as being part of such group if such group would continue to meet the requirements of sections 401(a)(4) and 410 with such plan being taken into account.

(B) Top-heavy group. The term "top-heavy group" means any aggregation group if—

(i) the sum (as of the determination date) of—

(I) the present value of the cumulative accrued benefits for key employees under all defined benefit plans included in such group, and

(II) the aggregate of the accounts of key employees under all defined contribution plans included in such group,

(ii) exceeds 60 percent of a similar sum determined for all employees.

(3) Distributions during last year before determination date taken into account.

(A) In general. For purposes of determining—

(i) the present value of the cumulative accrued benefit for any employee, or

(ii) the amount of the account of any employee,

such present value or amount shall be increased by the aggregate distributions made with respect to such employee under the plan during the 1-year period ending on the determination date. The preceding sentence shall also apply to distributions under a terminated plan which if it had not been terminated would have been required to be included in an aggregation group.

(B) 5-year period in case of in-service distribution. In the case of any distribution made for a reason other than severance from employment, death, or disability, subparagraph (A) shall be applied by substituting "5-year period" for "1-year period."

(4) Other special rules. For purposes of this subsection—

(A) Rollover contributions to plan not taken into account. Except to the extent provided in regulations, any rollover contribution (or similar transfer) initiated by the employee and made after December 31, 1983, to a plan shall not be taken into account with respect to the transferee plan for purposes of determining whether such plan is a top-heavy plan (or whether any aggregation group which includes such plan is a top-heavy group).

(B) Benefits not taken into account if employee ceases to be key employee. If any individual is a non-key employee with respect to any plan for any plan year, but such individual was a key employee with respect to such plan for any prior plan year, any accrued benefit for such employee (and the account of such employee) shall not be taken into account.
(C) Determination date. The term "determination date" means, with respect to any plan year—
 (i) the last day of the preceding plan year, or
 (ii) in the case of the first plan year of any plan, the last day of such plan year.
(D) Years. To the extent provided in regulations, this section shall be applied on the basis of any year specified in such regulations in lieu of plan years.
(E) Benefits not taken into account if employee not employed for last year before determination date. If any individual has not performed services for the employer maintaining the plan at any time during the 1-year period ending on the determination date, any accrued benefit for such individual (and the account of such individual) shall not be taken into account.
(F) Accrued benefits treated as accruing ratably. The accrued benefit of any employee (other than a key employee) shall be determined—
 (i) under the method which is used for accrual purposes for all plans of the employer, or
 (ii) if there is no method described in clause (i), as if such benefit accrued not more rapidly than the slowest accrual rate permitted under section 411(b)(1)(C).
(G) Simple retirement accounts. The term "top-heavy plan" shall not include a simple retirement account under section 408(p).
(H) Cash or deferred arrangements using alternative methods of meeting nondiscrimination requirements. The term "top-heavy plan" shall not include a plan which consists solely of—
 (i) a cash or deferred arrangement which meets the requirements of section 401(k)(12) or 401(k)(13), and
 (ii) matching contributions with respect to which the requirements of section 401(m)(11) or 401(m)(12) are met.
If, but for this subparagraph, a plan would be treated as a top-heavy plan because it is a member of an aggregation group which is a top-heavy group, contributions under the plan may be taken into account in determining whether any other plan in the group meets the requirements of subsection (c)(2).
(h) Repealed.
(i) Definitions.
For purposes of this section—
 (1) Key employee.
  (A) In general. The term "key employee" means an employee who, at any time during the plan year, is—
   (i) an officer of the employer having an annual compensation greater than $130,000,
   (ii) a 5-percent owner of the employer, or
   (iii) a 1-percent owner of the employer having an annual compensation from the employer of more than $150,000.
  For purposes of clause (i), no more than 50 employees (or, if lesser, the greater of 3 or 10 percent of the employees) shall be treated as officers. In the case of plan years beginning after December 31, 2002, the $130,000 amount in clause (i) shall be adjusted at the same time and in the same manner as under section 415(d), except that the base period shall be the calendar quarter beginning July 1, 2001, and any increase under this sentence which is not a multiple of $5,000 shall be rounded to the next lower multiple of $5,000. Such term shall not include any officer or employee of an entity referred to in section 414(d) (relating to governmental plans). For purposes of determining the number of officers taken into account under clause (i), employees described in section 414(q)(5) shall be excluded.
  (B) Percentage owners.
   (i) 5-percent owner. For purposes of this paragraph, the term "5-percent owner" means—
    (I) if the employer is a corporation, any person who owns (or is considered as owning within the meaning of section 318) more than 5 percent of the outstanding stock of the corporation or stock possessing more than 5 percent of the total combined voting power of all stock of the corporation, or
    (II) if the employer is not a corporation, any person who owns more than 5 percent of the capital or profits interest in the employer.
   (ii) 1-percent owner. For purposes of this paragraph, the term "1-percent owner" means any person who would be described in clause (i) if "1 percent" were substituted for "5 percent" each place it appears in clause (i).
   (iii) Constructive ownership rules. For purposes of this subparagraph—
    (I) subparagraph (C) of section 318(a)(2) shall be applied by substituting "5 percent" for "50 percent", and
    (II) in the case of any employer which is not a corporation, ownership in such employer shall be determined in accordance with regulations prescribed by the Secretary which shall be based on principles similar to the principles of section 318 (as modified by subclause (I)).
  (C) Aggregation rules do not apply for purposes of determining ownership in the employer. The rules of subsections (b), (c), and (m) of section 414 shall not apply for purposes of determining ownership in the employer.
  (D) Compensation. For purposes of this paragraph, the term "compensation" has the meaning given such term by section 414(q)(4).
 (2) Non-key employee. The term "non-key employee" means any employee who is not a key employee.
 (3) Self-employed individuals. In the case of a self-employed individual described in section 401(c)(1)—
  (A) such individual shall be treated as an employee, and
  (B) such individual's earned income (within the meaning of section 401(c)(2)) shall be treated as compensation.
 (4) Treatment of employees covered by collective bargaining agreements. The requirements of subsections (b), (c), and (d) shall not apply with respect to any employee included in a unit of employees covered by an agreement which the Secretary of Labor finds to be a collective bargaining agreement between employee representatives and 1 or more employers if there is evidence that retirement benefits were the subject of good faith bargaining between such employee representatives and such employer or employers.
 (5) Treatment of beneficiaries. The terms "employee" and "key employee" include their beneficiaries.

(6) Treatment of simplified employee pensions.

(A) Treatment as defined contribution plans. A simplified employee pension shall be treated as a defined contribution plan.

(B) Election to have determinations based on employer contributions. In the case of a simplified employee pension, at the election of the employer, paragraphs (1)(A)(ii) and (2)(B) of subsection (g) shall be applied by taking into account aggregate employer contributions in lieu of the aggregate of the accounts of employees.

In 2010, P.L. 111-312, Sec. 101(a)(1), substituted "December 31, 2012" for "December 31, 2010" both places it appeared in Sec. 901 of P.L. 107-16 [see below], effective as if included in the enactment of P.L. 107-16, EGTRRA, 6/7/2001.

In 2006, P.L. 109-280, Sec. 811, of this Act [relating to Sec. 901 of P.L. 107-16, see below], provides:

"SEC. 811. PENSIONS AND INDIVIDUAL RETIREMENT ARRANGEMENT PROVISIONS OF ECONOMIC GROWTH AND TAX RELIEF RECONCILIATION ACT OF 2001 MADE PERMANENT.

"Title IX of the Economic Growth and Tax Relief Reconciliation Act of 2001 shall not apply to the provisions of, and amendments made by, subtitles A through F of title VI of such Act (relating to pension and individual retirement arrangement provisions)."

—P.L. 109-280, Sec. 902(c)(1), added "or 401(k)(13)" after "section 401(k)(12)" in clause (g)(4)(H)(i) . . . Sec. 902(c)(2), added "or 401(m)(12)" after "section 401(m)(11)" in clause (g)(4)(H)(ii), effective for plan yrs. begin. after 12/31/2007.

In 2004, P.L. 108-311, Sec. 408(a)(16), substituted "In the case of plan years" for "in the case of plan years" in subpara. (i)(1)(A), enacted 10/4/2004.

In 2002, P.L. 107-358, Sec. 2, added subsec. (c) in Sec. 901 of P.L. 107-16 [see below], effective 12/17/2002.

—P.L. 107-147, Sec. 411(k)(1), substituted "Exception for plan under which no key employee (or former key employee) benefits for plan year" for "Exception for frozen plan" in the heading of clause (c)(1)(C)(iii) . . . Sec. 411(k)(2), substituted "severance from employment" for "separation from service" in subpara. (g)(3)(B), effective for yrs. begin. after 12/31/2001.

In 2001, P.L. 107-16, Sec. 613(a)(1)(A), deleted "or any of the 4 preceding plan years" after "at any time during the plan year" in subpara. (i)(1)(A) . . . Sec. 613(a)(1)(B), amended clause (i)(1)(A)(i) . . . Sec. 613(a)(1)(C), deleted clause (i)(1)(A)(ii) and redesignated clauses (i)(1)(A)(iii) and (iv) as clauses (i)(1)(A)(ii) and (iii) . . . Sec. 613(a)(1)(D), substituted "[sic In] the case of plan years beginning after December 31, 2002, the $130,000 amount in clause (i) shall be adjusted at the same time and in the same manner as under section 415(d), except that the base period shall be the calendar quarter beginning July 1, 2001, and any increase under this sentence which is not a multiple of $5,000 shall be rounded to the next lower multiple of $5,000." for "For purposes of clause (ii), if 2 employees have the same interest in the employer, the employee having greater annual compensation from the employer shall be treated as having a larger interest." in subpara. (i)(1)(A) . . . Sec. 613(a)(2), deleted "and subparagraph (A)(ii)" after "this subparagraph" in clause (i)(1)(B)(iii) . . . Sec. 613(b), added a sentence at the end of subpara. (c)(2)(A) . . . Sec. 613(c)(1), amended para. (g)(3) . . . Sec. 613(c)(2)(A), substituted "last year before determination date" for "last 5 years" in the heading of subpara. (g)(4)(E) . . . Sec. 613(c)(2)(B), substituted "1-year period" for "5-year period" in subpara. (g)(4)(E) . . . Sec. 613(d), added subpara. (g)(4)(H) . . . Sec. 613(e)(A) [sic (1)], substituted "clause (ii) or (iii)" for "clause (ii)" in clause (c)(1)(C)(i) . . . Sec. 613(e)(B) [sic (2)], added clause (c)(1)(C)(iii), effective for yrs. begin. after 12/31/2001.

Prior to amendment, para. (g)(3) read as follows:

"(3) Distributions during last 5 years taken into account. For purposes of determining—

"(A) the present value of the cumulative accrued benefit for any employee, or

"(B) the amount of the account of any employee,

such present value or amount shall be increased by the aggregate distributions made with respect to such employee under the plan during the 5-year period ending on the determination date. The preceding sentence shall also apply to distributions under a terminated plan which if it had not been terminated would have been required to be included in an aggregation group."

Prior to amendment, clause (i)(1)(A)(i) read as follows:

"(i) an officer of the employer having an annual compensation greater than 50 percent of the amount in effect under section 415(b)(1)(A) for any such plan year,"

Prior to deletion, clause (i)(1)(A)(ii) read as follows:

"(ii) 1 of the 10 employees having annual compensation from the employer of more than the limitation in effect under section 415(c)(1)(A) and owning (or considered as owning within the meaning of section 318) the largest interests in the employer,"

—P.L. 107-16, Sec. 663(a), deleted Sec. 1114(c)(4) of P.L. 99-514 [reproduced in notes following Code Sec. 401], effective for plan yrs. begin. after 12/31/2001.

—P.L. 107-16, Sec. 901, of this Act [as amended by Sec. 2 of P.L. 107-358, and Sec. 101(a)(1) of P.L. 111-312, and as related to Sec. 811 of P.L. 109-280, see above], reads as follows:

"SEC. 901. SUNSET OF PROVISIONS OF ACT.

"(a) In general. All provisions of, and amendments made by, this Act shall not apply—

"(1) to taxable, plan, or limitation years beginning after December 31, 2012, or

"(2) in the case of title V, to estates of decedents dying, gifts made, or generation skipping transfers, after December 31, 2012.

"(b) Application of certain laws. The Internal Revenue Code of 1986 and the Employee Retirement Income Security Act of 1974 shall be applied and administered to years, estates, gifts, and transfers described in subsection (a) as if the provisions and amendments described in subsection (a) had never been enacted.

"(c) Exception. Subsection (a) shall not apply to section 803 (relating to no federal income tax on restitution received by victims of the Nazi regime or their heirs or estates)."

In 1996, P.L. 104-188, Sec. 1421(b)(7), added subpara. (g)(4)(G), effective for tax. yrs. begin. after 12/31/96.

—P.L. 104-188, Sec. 1431(c)(1)(B), substituted "section 414(q)(4)" for "section 414(q)(7)" in subpara. (i)(1)(D). . . . Sec. 1431(c)(1)(C), substituted "section 414(q)(5)" for "section 414(q)(8)" in subpara. (i)(1)(A), effective for yrs. begin. after 12/31/96, except that in determining whether an employee is a highly compensated employee for yrs. begin. in 1997, such amendments shall be treated as having been in effect for yrs. begin. in 1996.

—P.L. 104-188, Sec. 1452(c)(7), deleted subsec. (h), effective for limitation yrs. begin. after 12/31/99.

Prior to deletion, subsec. (h) read as follows:

"(h) Adjustments in section 415 limits for top-heavy plans.

"(1) In general. In the case of any top-heavy plan, paragraphs (2)(B) and (3)(B) of section 415(e) shall be applied by substituting '1.0' for '1.25'.

"(2) Exception where benefits for key employees do not exceed 90 percent of total benefits and additional contributions are made for non-key employees.

"Paragraph (1) shall not apply with respect to any top-heavy plan if the requirements of subparagraphs (A) and (B) of this paragraph are met with respect to such plan.

"(A) Minimum benefit requirements.

"(i) In general. The requirements of this subparagraph are met with respect to any top-heavy plan if such plan (and any plan required to be included in an aggregation group with such plan) meets the requirements of subsection (c) as modified by clause (ii).

"(ii) Modifications. For purposes of clause (i)—

"(I) paragraph (1)(B) of subsection (c) shall be applied by substituting '3 percent' for '2 percent', and by increasing (but not by more than 10 percentage points) 20 percent by 1 percentage point for each year for which such plan was taken into account under this subsection, and

"(II) paragraph (2)(A) shall be applied by substituting '4 percent' for '3 percent'.

"(B) Benefits for key employees cannot exceed 90 percent of total benefits. A plan meets the requirements of this subparagraph if such plan would not be a top-heavy plan if '90 percent' were substituted for '60 percent' each place it appears in paragraphs (1)(A) and (2)(B) of subsection (g).

"(3) Transition rule. If, but for this paragraph, paragraph (1) would begin to apply with respect to any top-heavy plan, the application of paragraph (1) shall be suspended with respect to any individual so long as there are no—

"(A) employer contributions, forfeitures, or voluntary nondeductible contributions allocated to such individual, or

"(B) accruals for such individual under the defined benefit plan.

"(4) Coordination with transitional rule under section 415. In the case of any top-heavy plan to which paragraph (1) applies, section 415(e)(6)(B)(i) shall be applied by substituting '$41,500' for '$51,875'".

In 1988, P.L. 100-647, Sec. 1011(d)(8), substituted "50 percent of the amount in effect under section 415(b)(1)(A)" for "150 percent of the amount in effect under section 415(c)(1)(A)" in clause (i)(1)(A)(i), effective for yrs. begin. after 12/31/86, except as provided in Sec. 1106(i)(2)-(4) and (6) of P.L. 99-514, reproduced in notes following.

—P.L. 100-647, Sec. 1011(i)(4)(B), added the sentence at the end of subpara. (i)(1)(A), effective for yrs. begin. after 12/31/86 except as provided in Sec. 1114(c)(4) of P.L. 99-514 as amended by 2000 Act [deleted by Sec. 663(a) of P.L. 107-16, see above], reproduced in notes following Code Sec. 414.

—P.L. 100-647, Sec. 1011(j)(3)(A), added subpara. (i)(1)(D), effective for yrs. begin. after 12/31/88.

In 1986, P.L. 99-514, Sec. 1106(d)(3)(A), added "and" at the end of para. (a)(1), substituted a period for ", and" at the end of para. (a)(2) and deleted para. (a)(3) . . . Sec. 1106(d)(3)(B)(i), deleted subsec. (d) . . . Sec. 1106(d)(3)(B)(ii), deleted clause (c)(2)(B)(ii) and redesignated clause (c)(2)(B)(iii) as clause (ii), effective for benefits accruing in yrs. begin. after 12/31/88, except as provided in Sec. 1106(i)(5)(B) of this Act which reads as follows:

"(B) Collective bargaining agreements.—In the case of a plan described in paragraph (2) [Sec. 1106(i)(2) of P.L. 99-514, reproduced in note following Code Sec. 415], the amendments made by subsection (d) shall apply to benefits accruing in years beginning on or after the earlier of—

"(i) the later of—

"(I) the date determined under paragraph (2)(A), or

"(II) January 1, 1989, or

"(ii) January 1, 1991."

Prior to deletion, para. (a)(3) read as follows:

"(3) the limitation on compensation requirement of subsection (d)."

Prior to deletion, subsec. (d) read as follows:

"(d) Not more than $200,000 in annual compensation taken into account.

"(1) In general. A plan meets the requirements of this subsection if the annual compensation of each employee taken into account under the plan does not exceed the first $200,000.

Code Sec. 416 — Employee benefit plans

"(2) Cost-of-living adjustments. The Secretary shall annually adjust the $200,000 amount contained in paragraph (1) of this subsection and in clause (ii) of subsection (c)(2)(B) at the same time and in the same manner as he adjusts the dollar amount contained in section 415(c)(1)(A)."

Prior to deletion, clause (c)(2)(B)(ii) read as follows:

"(ii) Determination of percentage. The determination referred to in clause (i) shall be determined for each key employee by dividing the contributions for such employee by so much of his total compensation for the year as does not exceed $200,000."

—P.L. 99-514, Sec. 1118(a), added subpara. (g)(4)(F), effective for plan yrs. begin after 12/31/86.

—P.L. 99-514, Sec. 1852(d)(1), added the sentence at the end of subpara. (i)(1)(A), effective for plan yrs. begin. after 12/31/83.

—P.L. 99-514, Sec. 1852(d)(2), amended subpara. (g)(4)(E), effective for plan yrs. begin. after 12/31/84. For exceptions see Sec. 524(e) of P.L. 98-369, reproduced below.

Prior to amendment, subpara. (g)(4)(E) read as follows:

"(E) Benefits not taken into account if employee not employed for last 5 years. If any individual has not received any compensation from any employer maintaining the plan (other than benefits under the plan) at any time during the 5-year period ending on the determination date, any accrued benefit for such individual (and the account of such individual) shall not be taken into account."

In 1984, P.L. 98-369, Sec. 524(a)(1), added "having an annual compensation greater than 150 percent of the amount in effect under section 415(c)(1)(A) for any such plan year." after "employer" in clause (i)(1)(A)(i), effective for plan yrs. begin. after 12/31/83.

—P.L. 98-369, Sec. 524(b)(1), added subpara. (g)(4)(E) ... Sec. 524(c)(1), deleted subpara. (c)(2)(C), effective for plan yrs. begin. after 12/31/84. Sec. 524(e) of this Act provides:

"(e) Qualification requirements modified if regulations not issued.

"(1) In general. — If the Secretary of the Treasury or his delegate does not publish final regulations under section 416 of the Internal Revenue Code of 1954 (as in effect on the day before the date of the enactment of this Act) before January 1, 1985, the Secretary shall publish before such date plan amendment provisions which may be incorporated in a plan to meet the requirements of section 401(a)(10)(B)(ii) of such Code.

"(2) Effect of incorporation. — If a plan is amended to incorporate the plan amendment provisions described in paragraph (1), such plan shall be treated as meeting the requirements of section 401(a)(10)(B)(ii) of the Internal Revenue Code of 1954 during the period such amendment is in effect but not later than 6 months after the final regulations described in paragraph (1) are published.

"(3) Failure by secretary to publish. — If the Secretary of the Treasury or his delegate does not publish plan amendment provisions described in paragraph (1), the plan shall be treated as meeting the requirements of section 401(a)(10)(B) of the Internal Revenue Code of 1954 if —

"(A) such plan is amended to incorporate such requirements by reference, except that

"(B) in the case of any optional requirement under section 416 of such Code, if such amendment does not specify the manner in which such requirement will be met, the employer shall be treated as having elected the requirement with respect to each employee which provides the maximum vested accrued benefit for such employee."

Prior to deletion, subpara. (c)(2)(C) read as follows:

"(C) Certain amounts not taken into account. For purposes of this paragraph, any employer contribution attributable to a salary reduction or similar arrangement shall not be taken into account."

—P.L. 98-369, Sec. 713(f)(1)(A), substituted "an employee" for "any participant in an employer plan" in subpara. (i)(1)(A) ... Sec. 713(f)(1)(B), amended clause (i)(1)(A)(ii) ... Sec. 713(f)(1)(C), added the sentence at the end of subpara. (i)(1)(A) ... Sec. 713(f)(1)(D), substituted "determining ownership in the employer" for "determining 5-percent or 1-percent owners" in the heading of subpara. (i)(1)(C) ... Sec. 713(f)(4), added the sentence at the end of para. (g)(3) ... Sec. 713(f)(5)(A), substituted "at the same time and" for "in the same manner" in para. (d)(2) ... Sec. 713(f)(6)(A), substituted "required" for "require" in subsec. (f) ... Sec. 713(f)(6)(B), substituted "subparagraph (A)(ii)" for "subparagraph (A)(ii)(II)" in clause (i)(1)(B)(iii), effective for yrs. begin. after 12/31/83.

Prior to amendment, clause (i)(1)(A)(ii) read as follows:

"(ii) 1 of the 10 employees owning (or considered as owning within the meaning of section 318) the largest interests in the employer,"

In 1982, P.L. 97-248, Sec. 240(a), added Code Sec. 416, effective for yrs. begin. after 12/31/83.

Sec. 417. Definitions and special rules for purposes of minimum survivor annuity requirements.

(a) Election to waive qualified joint and survivor annuity or qualified preretirement survivor annuity.

(1) In general. A plan meets the requirements of section 401(a)(11) only if —

(A) under the plan, each participant —

(i) may elect at any time during the applicable election period to waive the qualified joint and survivor annuity form of benefit or the qualified preretirement survivor annuity form of benefit (or both),

(ii) if the participant elects a waiver under clause (i), may elect the qualified optional survivor annuity at any time during the applicable election period, and

(iii) may revoke any such election at any time during the applicable election period, and

(B) the plan meets the requirements of paragraphs (2), (3), and (4) of this subsection.

(2) Spouse must consent to election. Each plan shall provide that an election under paragraph (1)(A)(i) shall not take effect unless —

(A)(i) the spouse of the participant consents in writing to such election,

(ii) such election designates a beneficiary (or a form of benefits) which may not be changed without spousal consent (or the consent of the spouse expressly permits designations by the participant without any requirement of further consent by the spouse), and

(iii) the spouse's consent acknowledges the effect of such election and is witnessed by a plan representative or a notary public, or

(B) it is established to the satisfaction of a plan representative that the consent required under subparagraph (A) may not be obtained because there is no spouse, because the spouse cannot be located, or because of such other circumstances as the Secretary may by regulations prescribe.

Any consent by a spouse (or establishment that the consent of a spouse may not be obtained) under the preceding sentence shall be effective only with respect to such spouse.

(3) Plan to provide written explanations.

(A) Explanation of joint and survivor annuity. Each plan shall provide to each participant, within a reasonable period of time before the annuity starting date (and consistent with such regulations as the Secretary may prescribe), a written explanation of —

(i) the terms and conditions of the qualified joint and survivor annuity and of the qualified optional survivor annuity,

(ii) the participant's right to make, and the effect of, an election under paragraph (1) to waive the joint and survivor annuity form of benefit,

(iii) the rights of the participant's spouse under paragraph (2), and

(iv) the right to make, and the effect of, a revocation of an election under paragraph (1).

(B) Explanation of qualified preretirement survivor annuity.

(i) In general. Each plan shall provide to each participant, within the applicable period with respect to such participant (and consistent with such regulations as the Secretary may prescribe), a written explanation with respect to the qualified preretirement survivor annuity comparable to that required under subparagraph (A).

(ii) Applicable period. For purposes of clause (i), the term "applicable period" means, with respect to a participant, whichever of the following periods ends last:

(I) The period beginning with the first day of the plan year in which the participant attains age 32 and ending with the close of the plan year preceding the plan year in which the participant attains age 35.

(II) a reasonable period after the individual becomes a participant.
(III) A reasonable period ending after paragraph (5) ceases to apply to the participant.
(IV) A reasonable period ending after section 401(a)(11) applies to the participant.

In the case of a participant who separates from service before attaining age 35, the applicable period shall be a reasonable period after separation.

(4) Requirement of spousal consent for using plan assets as security for loans. Each plan shall provide that, if section 401(a)(11) applies to a participant when part or all of the participant's accrued benefit is to be used as security for a loan, no portion of the participant's accrued benefit may be used as security for such loan unless—
(A) the spouse of the participant (if any) consents in writing to such use during the 90-day period ending on the date on which the loan is to be so secured, and
(B) requirements comparable to the requirements of paragraph (2) are met with respect to such consent.

(5) Special rules where plan fully subsidizes costs.
(A) In general. The requirements of this subsection shall not apply with respect to the qualified joint and survivor annuity form of benefit or the qualified preretirement survivor annuity form of benefit, as the case may be, if such benefit may not be waived (or another beneficiary selected) and if the plan fully subsidizes the costs of such benefit.
(B) Definition. For purposes of subparagraph (A), a plan fully subsidizes the costs of a benefit if under the plan the failure to waive such benefit by a participant would not result in a decrease in any plan benefits with respect to such participant and would not result in increased contributions from such participant.

(6) Applicable election period defined. For purposes of this subsection, the term "applicable election period" means—
(A) in the case of an election to waive the qualified joint and survivor annuity form of benefit, the 180-day period ending on the annuity starting date, or
(B) in the case of an election to waive the qualified preretirement survivor annuity, the period which begins on the first day of the plan year in which the participant attains age 35 and ends on the date of the participant's death.

In the case of a participant who is separated from service, the applicable election period under subparagraph (B) with respect to benefits accrued before the date of such separation from service shall not begin later than such date.

(7) Special rules relating to time for written explanation. Not withstanding any other provision of this subsection—
(A) Explanation may be provided after annuity starting date.
(i) In general. A plan may provide the written explanation described in paragraph (3)(A) after the annuity starting date. In any case to which this subparagraph applies, the applicable election period under paragraph (6) shall not end before the 30th day after the date on which such explanation is provided.
(ii) Regulatory authority. The Secretary may by regulations limit the application of clause (i), except that such regulations may not limit the period of time by which the annuity starting date precedes the provision of the written explanation other than by providing that the annuity starting date may not be earlier than termination of employment.
(B) Waiver of 30-day period. A plan may permit a participant to elect (with any applicable spousal consent) to waive any requirement that the written explanation be provided at least 30 days before the annuity starting date (or to waive the 30-day requirement under subparagraph (A)) if the distribution commences more than 7 days after such explanation is provided.

(b) Definition of qualified joint and survivor annuity.
For purposes of this section and section 401(a)(11), the term "qualified joint and survivor annuity" means an annuity—
(1) for the life of the participant with a survivor annuity for the life of the spouse which is not less than 50 percent of (and is not greater than 100 percent of) the amount of the annuity which is payable during the joint lives of the participant and the spouse, and
(2) which is the actuarial equivalent of a single annuity for the life of the participant.

Such term also includes any annuity in a form having the effect of an annuity described in the preceding sentence.

(c) Definition of qualified preretirement survivor annuity.
For purposes of this section and section 401(a)(11)—
(1) In general. Except as provided in paragraph (2), the term "qualified preretirement survivor annuity" means a survivor annuity for the life of the surviving spouse of the participant if—
(A) the payments to the surviving spouse under such annuity are not less than the amounts which would be payable as a survivor annuity under the qualified joint and survivor annuity under the plan (or the actuarial equivalent thereof) if—
(i) in the case of a participant who dies after the date on which the participant attained the earliest retirement age, such participant had retired with an immediate qualified joint and survivor annuity on the day before the participant's date of death, or
(ii) in the case of a participant who dies on or before the date on which the participant would have attained the earliest retirement age, such participant had—
(I) separated from service on the date of death,
(II) survived to the earliest retirement age,
(III) retired with an immediate qualified joint and survivor annuity at the earliest retirement age, and
(IV) died on the day after the day on which such participant would have attained the earliest retirement age, and
(B) under the plan, the earliest period for which the surviving spouse may receive a payment under such annuity is not later than the month in which the participant would have attained the earliest retirement age under the plan.

In the case of an individual who separated from service before the date of such individual's death, subparagraph (A)(ii)(I) shall not apply.

(2) Special rule for defined contribution plans. In the case of any defined contribution plan or participant described in clause (ii) or (iii) of section 401(a)(11)(B), the term "qualified preretirement survivor annuity" means an annuity for the life of the surviving spouse the actuarial equivalent of which is not less than 50 percent of the portion of the account balance of the participant (as of the date of death) to which the participant had a nonforfeitable right (within the meaning of section 411(a)).

(3) Security interests taken into account. For purposes of paragraphs (1) and (2), any security interest held by the plan by reason of a loan outstanding to the participant shall be taken into account in determining the amount of the qualified preretirement survivor annuity.

(d) Survivor annuities need not be provided if participant and spouse married less than 1 year.

(1) In general. Except as provided in paragraph (2), a plan shall not be treated as failing to meet the requirements of section 401(a)(11) merely because the plan provides that a qualified joint and survivor annuity (or a qualified preretirement survivor annuity) will not be provided unless the participant and spouse had been married throughout the 1-year period ending on the earlier of—

(A) the participant's annuity starting date, or

(B) the date of the participant's death.

(2) Treatment of certain marriages within 1 year of annuity starting date for purposes of qualified joint and survivor annuities. For purposes of paragraph (1), if—

(A) a participant marries within 1 year before the annuity starting date, and

(B) the participant and the participant's spouse in such marriage have been married for at least a 1-year period ending on or before the date of the participant's death,

such participant and such spouse shall be treated as having been married throughout the 1-year period ending on the participant's annuity starting date.

(e) Restrictions on cash-outs.

(1) Plan may require distribution if present value not in excess of dollar limit. A plan may provide that the present value of a qualified joint and survivor annuity or a qualified preretirement survivor annuity will be immediately distributed if such value does not exceed the amount that can be distributed without the participant's consent under section 411(a)(11). No distribution may be made under the preceding sentence after the annuity starting date unless the participant and the spouse of the participant (or where the participant has died, the surviving spouse) consents in writing to such distribution.

(2) Plan may distribute benefit in excess of dollar limit only with consent. If—

(A) the present value of the qualified joint and survivor annuity or the qualified preretirement survivor annuity exceeds the amount that can be distributed without the participant's consent under section 411(a)(11), and

(B) the participant and the spouse of the participant (or where the participant has died, the surviving spouse) consent in writing to the distribution,

the plan may immediately distribute the present value of such annuity.

(3) Determination of present value.

(A) In general. For purposes of paragraphs (1) and (2), the present value shall not be less than the present value calculated by using the applicable mortality table and the applicable interest rate.

(B) Applicable mortality table. For purposes of subparagraph (A), the term "applicable mortality table" means a mortality table, modified as appropriate by the Secretary, based on the mortality table specified for the plan year under subparagraph (A) of section 430(h)(3) (without regard to subparagraph (C) or (D) of such section).

(C) Applicable interest rate. For purposes of subparagraph (A), the term "applicable interest rate" means the adjusted first, second, and third segment rates applied under rules similar to the rules of section 430(h)(2)(C) for the month before the date of the distribution or such other time as the Secretary may by regulations prescribe.

(D) Applicable segment rates. For purposes of subparagraph (C), the adjusted first, second, and third segment rates are the first, second, and third segment rates which would be determined under section 430(h)(2)(C) if—

(i) section 430(h)(2)(D) were applied by substituting the average yields for the month described in subparagraph (C) for the average yields for the 24-month period described in such section,

(ii) section 430(h)(2)(G)(i)(II) were applied by substituting "section 417(e)(3)(A)(ii)(II)" for "section 412(b)(5)(B)(ii)(II)", and

(iii) the applicable percentage under section 430(h)(2)(G) were determined in accordance with the following table:

In the case of plan years beginning in:	The applicable percentage is:
2008	20 percent
2009	40 percent
2010	60 percent
2011	80 percent.

(f) Other definitions and special rules.

For purposes of this section and section 401(a)(11)—

(1) Vested participant. The term "vested participant" means any participant who has a nonforfeitable right (within the meaning of section 411(a)) to any portion of such participant's accrued benefit.

(2) Annuity starting date.

(A) In general. The term "annuity starting date" means—

(i) the first day of the first period for which an amount is payable as an annuity, or

(ii) in the case of a benefit not payable in the form of an annuity, the first day on which all events have occurred which entitle the participant to such benefit.

(B) Special rule for disability benefits. For purposes of subparagraph (A), the first day of the first period for which a benefit is to be received by reason of disability shall be treated as the annuity starting date only if such benefit is not an auxiliary benefit.

(3) Earliest retirement age. The term "earliest retirement age" means the earliest date on which, under the plan, the participant could elect to receive retirement benefits.

(4) Plan may take into account increased costs. A plan may take into account in any equitable manner (as determined by the Secretary) any increased costs resulting from providing a qualified joint or survivor annuity or a qualified preretirement survivor annuity.

(5) Distributions by reason of security interests. If the use of any participant's accrued benefit (or any portion thereof) as security for a loan meets the requirements of subsection (a)(4), nothing in this section or section 411(a)(11) shall prevent any distribution required by reason of a failure to comply with the terms of such loan.

(6) Requirements for certain spousal consents. No consent of a spouse shall be effective for purposes of subsection (e)(1) or (e)(2) (as the case may be) unless requirements comparable to the requirements for spousal consent to an election under subsection (a)(1)(A) are met.

(7) Consultation with the secretary of labor. In prescribing regulations under this section and section 401(a)(11), the Secretary shall consult with the Secretary of Labor.

(g) Definition of qualified optional survivor annuity.
   (1) In general. For purposes of this section, the term "qualified optional survivor annuity" means an annuity—
   (A) for the life of the participant with a survivor annuity for the life of the spouse which is equal to the applicable percentage of the amount of the annuity which is payable during the joint lives of the participant and the spouse, and
   (B) which is the actuarial equivalent of a single annuity for the life of the participant.
Such term also includes any annuity in a form having the effect of an annuity described in the preceding sentence.
   (2) Applicable percentage.
      (A) In general. For purposes of paragraph (1), if the survivor annuity percentage—
         (i) is less than 75 percent, the applicable percentage is 75 percent, and
         (ii) is greater than or equal to 75 percent, the applicable percentage is 50 percent.
      (B) Survivor annuity percentage. For purposes of subparagraph (A), the term "survivor annuity percentage" means the percentage which the survivor annuity under the plan's qualified joint and survivor annuity bears to the annuity payable during the joint lives of the participant and the spouse.

In 2008, P.L. 110-458, Sec. 103(b)(2)(A), substituted "subparagraph (C)" for "clause (ii)" in clause (e)(3)(D)(i), effective for plan yrs. begin. after 12/31/2007, as if included in the provisions of Sec. 302 of the Pension Protection Act of 2006 [P.L. 109-280, see below].
   —P.L. 110-458, Sec. 107(c)(1), substituted "205(g)" for "204(g)" in Sec. 701(d)(2) of P.L. 109-280, [see below]
In 2006, P.L. 109-280, Sec. 302(b), amended para. (e)(3), effective for plan yrs. begin. after 12/31/2007.
Prior to amendment, para. (e)(3) read as follows:
"(3) Determination of present value.
"(A) In general.
"(i) Present value. Except as provided in subparagraph (B), for purposes of paragraphs (1) and (2), the present value shall not be less than the present value calculated by using the applicable mortality table and the applicable interest rate.
"(ii) Definitions. For purposes of clause (i)—
"(I) Applicable mortality table. The term 'applicable mortality table' means the table prescribed by the Secretary. Such table shall be based on the prevailing commissioners' standard table (described in section 807(d)(5)(A)) used to determine reserves for group annuity contracts issued on the date as of which present value is being determined (without regard to any other subparagraph of section 807(d)(5)).
"(II) Applicable interest rate. The term 'applicable interest rate' means the annual rate of interest on 30-year Treasury securities for the month before the date of distribution or such other time as the Secretary may by regulations prescribe.
"(B) Exception. In the case of a distribution from a plan that was adopted and in effect before the date of the enactment of the Retirement Protection Act of 1994, the present value of any distribution made before the earlier of—
"(i) the later of the date a plan amendment applying subparagraph (A) is adopted or made effective, or
"(ii) the first day of the first plan year beginning after December 31, 1999, shall be calculated, for purposes of paragraphs (1) and (2), using the interest rate determined under the regulations of the Pension Benefit Guaranty Corporation for determining the present value of a lump sum distribution on plan termination that were in effect on September 1, 1993, and using the provisions of the plan as in effect on the day before such date of enactment; but only if such provisions of the plan met the requirements of section 417(e)(3) as in effect on the day before such date of enactment."
   —P.L. 109-280, Sec. 701(d), of this Act [as amended by Sec. 107(c)(1), P.L. 110-458, see above], reads as follows:
"(d) No inference. Nothing in the amendments made by this section shall be construed to create an inference with respect to—
"(1) the treatment of applicable defined benefit plans or conversions to applicable defined benefit plans under sections 204(b)(1)(H) of the Employee Retirement Income Security Act of 1974, 4(i)(1) of the Age Discrimination in Employment Act of 1967, and 411(b)(1)(H) of the Internal Revenue Code of 1986, as in effect before such amendments, or
"(2) the determination of whether an applicable defined benefit plan fails to meet the requirements of sections 203(a)(2), 204(c), or 205(g) of the Employee Retirement Income Security Act of 1974 or sections 411(a)(2), 411(c), or 417(e) of such Code, as in effect before such amendments, solely because the present value of the accrued benefit (or any portion thereof) of any participant is, under the terms of the plan, equal to the amount expressed as the balance in a hypothetical account or as an accumulated percentage of the participant's final average compensation.
For purposes of this subsection, the term 'applicable defined benefit plan' has the meaning given such term by section 203(f)(3) of the Employee Retirement Income Security Act of 1974 and section 411(a)(13)(C) of such Code, as in effect after such amendments."
   —P.L. 109-280, Sec. 1004(a)(1)(A), substituted a comma for ", and" at the end of clause (a)(1)(A)(i) . . . Sec. 1004(a)(1)(B), redesignated clause (a)(1)(A)(ii) as (iii) . . . Sec. 1004(a)(1)(C), added clause (a)(1)(A)(ii) . . . Sec. 1004(a)(2), added subsec. (g) . . . Sec. 1004(a)(3), added "and of the qualified optional survivor annuity" after "annuity" in clause (a)(3)(A)(i), effective for plan yrs. begin. after 12/31/2007. Sec. 1004(c)(2), of this Act, reads as follows:
"(2) Special rule for collectively bargained plans. In the case of a plan maintained pursuant to 1 or more collective bargaining agreements between employee representatives and 1 or more employers ratified on or before the date of the enactment of this Act, the amendments made by this section shall not apply to plan years beginning before the earlier of—
"(A) the later of—
"(i) January 1, 2008, or
"(ii) the date on which the last collective bargaining agreement related to the plan terminates (determined without regard to any extension thereof after the date of enactment of this Act), or
"(B) January 1, 2009."
   —P.L. 109-280, Sec. 1102(a)(1)(A), substituted "180-day" for "90-day" in subpara. (a)(6)(A), effective for yrs. begin. after 12/31/2006.
   —P.L. 109-280, Sec. 1102(a)(1)(B), of this Act, reads as follows:
"(B) Modification of regulations. The Secretary of the Treasury shall modify the regulations under sections 402(f), 411(a)(11), and 417 of the Internal Revenue Code of 1986 by substituting '180 days' for '90 days' each place it appears in Treasury Regulations sections 1.402(f)-1, 1.411(a)-11(c), and 1.417(e)-1(b)."
In 2004, P.L. 108-476, Sec. 1, of this Act, provides:
"SECTION 1. CERTAIN ARRANGEMENTS MAINTAINED BY THE YMCA RETIREMENT FUND TREATED AS CHURCH PLANS.
"(a) Retirement plans.
"(1) In general. For purposes of sections 401(a) and 403(b) of the Internal Revenue Code of 1986, any retirement plan maintained by the YMCA Retirement Fund as of January 1, 2003, shall be treated as a church plan (within the meaning of section 414(e) of such Code) which is maintained by an organization described in section 414(e)(3)(A) of such Code.
"(2) Tax-deferred retirement plan. In the case of a retirement plan described in paragraph (1) which allows contributions to be made under a salary reduction agreement—
"(A) such treatment shall not apply for purposes of section 415(c)(7) of such Code, and
"(B) any account maintained for a participant or beneficiary of such plan shall be treated for purposes of such Code as a retirement income account described in section 403(b)(9) of such Code, except that such account shall not, for purposes of section 403(b)(12) of such Code, be treated as a contract purchased by a church for purposes of section 403(b)(1)(D) of such Code.
"(3) Money purchase pension plan. In the case of a retirement plan described in paragraph (1) which is subject to the requirements of section 401(a) of such Code—
"(A) such plan (but not any reserves held by the YMCA Retirement Fund)—
"(i) shall be treated for purposes of such Code as a defined contribution plan which is a money purchase pension plan, and
"(ii) shall be treated as having made an election under section 410(d) of such Code for plan years beginning after December 31, 2005, except that notwithstanding the election—
"(I) nothing in the Employee Retirement Income Security Act of 1974 or such Code shall prohibit the YMCA Retirement Fund from commingling for investment purposes the assets of the electing plan with the assets of such Fund and with the assets of any employee benefit plan maintained by such Fund, and
"(II) nothing in this section shall be construed as subjecting any assets described in subclause (I), other than the assets of the electing plan, to any provision of such Act,
"(B) notwithstanding section 401(a)(11) or 417 of such Code or section 205 of such Act, such plan may offer a lump-sum distribution option to participants who have not attained age 55 without offering such participants an annuity option, and
"(C) any account maintained for a participant or beneficiary of such plan shall, for purposes of section 401(a)(9) of such Code, be treated as a retirement income account described in section 403(b)(9) of such Code.
"(4) Self-funded death benefit plan. For purposes of section 7702(j) of such Code, a retirement plan described in paragraph (1) shall be treated as an arrangement described in section 7702(j)(2).
"(b) YMCA retirement fund. For purposes of this section, the term 'YMCA Retirement Fund' means the Young Men's Christian Association Retirement Fund, a corporation created by an Act of the State of New York which became law on April 30, 1921.
"(c) Effective date. This section shall apply to plan years beginning after December 31, 2003."
In 2002, P.L. 107-147, Sec. 411(r)(1)(A), substituted "exceed the amount that can be distributed without the participant's consent under section 411(a)(11)" for "exceed the dollar limit under section 411(a)(11)(A)" in para. (e)(1) . . . Sec. 411(r)(1)(B), substituted "exceeds the amount that can be distributed without the participant's consent under section 411(a)(11)" for "exceeds the dollar limit under section 411(a)(11)(A)" in subpara. (e)(2)(A), effective for distributions after 12/31/2001.

In 1997, P.L. 105-34, Sec. 1071(a)(2)(A), substituted "the dollar limit under section 411(a)(11)(A)" for "$3,500" each place it appeared in paras. (e)(1) and (2). ... Sec. 1071(a)(2)(B), substituted "dollar limit" for "$3,500" in the headings of paras. (e)(1) and (2), effective for plan yrs. begin. after date of enactment.

In 1996, P.L. 104-188, Sec. 1449(a), amended Sec. 767(d)(3)(A) of P.L. 103-465, see below.

Prior to amendment, Sec. 767(d)(3)(A) read as follows:

"(A) No reduction required. — An accrued benefit shall not be required to be reduced below the accrued benefit as of the last day of the last plan year beginning before January 1, 1995, merely because of the amendments made by subsection (b)."

—P.L. 104-188, Sec. 1451(a), added para. (a)(7), effective for plan yrs. begin. after 12/31/96.

—P.L. 104-188, Sec. 1457, of this Act provides:

"Sec. 1457. Sample language for spousal consent and qualified domestic relations forms.

"(a) Development of sample language. Not later than January 1, 1997, the Secretary of the Treasury shall develop—

"(1) sample language for inclusion in a form for the spousal consent required under section 417(a)(2) of the Internal Revenue Code of 1986 and section 205(c)(2) of the Employee Retirement Income Security Act of 1974 which—

"(A) is written in a manner calculated to be understood by the average person, and

"(B) discloses in plain form—

"(i) whether the waiver to which the spouse consents is irrevocable, and

"(ii) whether such waiver may be revoked by a qualified domestic relations order, and

"(2) sample language for inclusion in a form for a qualified domestic relations order described in section 414(p)(1)(A) of such Code and section 206(d)(3)(B)(i) of such Act which—

"(A) meets the requirements contained in such sections, and

"(B) the provisions of which focus attention on the need to consider the treatment of any lump sum payment, qualified joint and survivor annuity, or qualified preretirement survivor annuity.

"(b) Publicity. The Secretary of the Treasury shall include publicity for the sample language developed under subsection (a) in the pension outreach efforts undertaken by the Secretary."

In 1994, P.L. 103-465, Sec. 767(a)(2), amended para. (e)(3), effective for plan yrs. and limitation yrs. begin. after 12/31/94; except that an employer may elect to treat the amendments made by this section as being effective on or after 12/8/94. Sec. 767(d)(2) and (3) [as amended by Sec. 1449(a) of P.L. 104-188, see above] of this Act, provides:

"(2) No reduction in accrued benefits. — A participant's accrued benefit shall not be considered to be reduced in violation of section 411(d)(6) of the Internal Revenue Code of 1986 or section 204(g) of the Employee Retirement Income Security Act of 1974 merely because (A) the benefit is determined in accordance with section 417(e)(3)(A) of such Code, as amended by this Act, or section 205(g)(3) of the Employee Retirement Income Security Act of 1974, as amended by this Act, or (B) the plan applies section 415(b)(2)(E) of such Code, as amended by this Act.

"(3) Section 415.—

"(A) Exception. A plan that was adopted and in effect before December 8, 1994, shall not be required to apply the amendments made by subsection 9b) with respect to benefits accrued before the earlier of—

"(i) the later of the date a plan amendment applying the amendments made by subsection (b) is adopted or made effective, or

"(ii) the first day of the first limitation year beginning on December 31, 1999. Determinations under section 415(b)(2)(E) of the Internal Revenue Code of 1986 before such earlier date shall be made with respect to such benefits on the basis of such section as in effect on December 7, 1994 (except that the modification made by section 1449(b) of the Small Business Job Protection Act of 1996 shall be taken into account), and the provisions of the plan as in effect on December 7, 1994, but only if such provisions by the plan meet the requirements of such section (as so in effect).

"(B) Timing of plan amendment. — A plan that operates in accordance with the amendments made by subsection (b) shall not be treated as failing to satisfy section 401(a) of the Internal Revenue Code of 1986 or as not being operated in accordance with the provisions of the plan until such date as the Secretary of the Treasury provides merely because the plan has not been amended to include the amendments made by subsection (b)."

Prior to amendment, para. (e)(3) read as follows:

"(3) Determination of present value.

"(A) In general. For purposes of paragraphs (1) and (2), the present value shall be calculated—

"(i) by using an interest rate no greater than the applicable interest rate if the vested accrued benefit (using such rate) is not in excess of $25,000, and

"(ii) by using an interest rate no greater than 120 percent of the applicable interest rate if the vested accrued benefit exceeds $25,000 (as determined under clause (i)).

In no event shall the present value determined under clause (ii) be less than $25,000.

"(B) Applicable interest rate. For purposes of subparagraph (A), the term 'applicable interest rate' means the interest rate which would be used (as of the date of the distribution) by the Pension Benefit Guaranty Corporation for purposes of determining the present value of a lump sum distribution on plan termination."

In 1989, P.L. 101-239, Sec. 7862(d)(1)(A), deleted subclause (a)(3)(B)(ii)(V) and inserted the sentence at the end of clause (a)(3)(B)(ii), effective for plan yrs. begin. after 12/31/84. For special rules, see Sec. 302(b) of P.L. 98-397, reproduced below.

Prior to deletion, subclause (a)(3)(B)(ii)(V) read as follows:

"(V) A reasonable period after separation from service in case of a participant who separates before attaining age 35."

—P.L. 101-239, Sec. 7862(d)(2), added Sec. 1898(b)(8)(C) of P.L. 99-514, the effective date for amendments made by Sec. 1891(b)(8) of P.L. 99-514, see below.

In 1988, P.L. 100-647, Sec. 1011A(k), amended Sec. 1139(d)(2)(A)(i) of P.L. 99-514 [reproduced below], part of the effective date for changes made by Sec. 1139(a) of P.L. 99-514, by substituting "after January" for "before January", see below.

—P.L. 100-647, Sec. 1018(u)(9), substituted "clause (ii)" for "subclause II" in subpara. (e)(3)(A), effective for distributions in plan yrs. begin. after 12/31/84, except not effective for any distributions in plan yrs. begin. after 12/31/84 and before 1/1/87, if such distributions were made in accordance with the requirements of the regulation issued under the Retirement Equity Act of 1984 [P.L. 98-397]. For special rules see Sec. 1139(d)(2) of P.L. 99-514 [as amended by Sec. 1011A(k) of P.L. 100-647, see above] reproduced below.

In 1986, P.L. 99-514, Sec. 1139(b), amended para. (e)(3), effective for distributions in plan yrs. begin. after 12/31/84, except not effective for any distributions in plan yrs. begin. after 12/31/84, and before 1/1/87, if such distributions were made in accordance with the requirements of the regulation issued under the Retirement Equity Act of 1984. See Sec. 1139(d)(2) [as amended by Sec. 1011A(k) of P.L. 100-647] of this Act provides:

"(2) Reduction in accrued benefits.—

"(A) in general. — If a plan—

"(i) adopts a plan amendment before the close of the first plan year beginning on or after January 1, 1989, which provides for the calculation of the present value of the accrued benefits in the manner provided by the amendments made by this section, and

"(ii) the plan reduces the accrued benefits for any plan year to which such plan amendment applies in accordance with such plan amendment,

such reduction shall not be treated as a violation of section 411(d)(6) of the Internal Revenue Code of 1986 or section 204(g) of the Employee Retirement Income Security Act of 1974 (29 U.S.C. 1054(g)).

"(B) Special rule. — In the case of a plan maintained by a corporation incorporated on April 11, 1934, which is headquartered in Tarrant County, Texas —

"(i) such plan may be amended to remove the option of an employee to receive a lump sum distribution (within the meaning of section 402(e)(5) of such Code) if such amendment —

"(I) is adopted within 1 year of the date of the enactment of this Act, and

"(II) is not effective until 2 years after the employees are notified of such amendment, and

"(ii) the present value of any vested accrued benefit of such plan determined during the 3-year period beginning on the date of the enactment of this Act shall be determined under the applicable interest rate (within the meaning of section 411(a)(11)(B)(ii) of such Code), except that if such value (as so determined) exceeds $50,000, then the value of any excess over $50,000 shall be determined by using the interest rate specified in the plan as of August 16, 1986."

Prior to amendment, para. (e)(3) read as follows:

"(3) Determination of present value. For purposes of paragraphs (1) and (2), the present value of a qualified joint and survivor annuity or a qualified preretirement survivor annuity shall be determined as of the date of the distribution and by using an interest rate not greater than the interest rate which would be used (as of the date of the distribution) by the Pension Benefit Guaranty Corporation for purposes of determining the present value of a lump sum distribution on plan termination."

—P.L. 99-514, Sec. 1898(b)(1)(A), added the sentence at the end of para. (c)(1), effective for plan yrs. begin. after 12/31/84. For special rules see Sec. 302(b) of P.L. 98-397, reproduced below.

—P.L. 99-514, Sec. 1898(b)(4)(A)(i), substituted "paragraphs (2), (3), and (4)" for "paragraphs (2) and (3) in subpara. (a)(1)(B) ... Sec. 1898(b)(4)(A)(ii), redesignated paras. (a)(4) and (5) as (a)(5) and (6), and added new para. (a)(4) . . . Sec. 1898(b)(4)(A)(iii), redesignated para. (f)(5) as (6) and added new para. (f)(5), effective for loans made after 8/18/85. Sec. 1852(b)(4)(C)(ii) and (iii) of this Act provide:

"(ii) In the case of any loan which was made on or before August 18, 1985, and which is secured by a portion of the participant's accrued benefit, nothing in the amendments made by sections 103 and 203 of the Retirement Equity Act of 1984 shall prevent any distribution required by reason of a failure to comply with the terms of such loan.

"(iii) For purposes of this subparagraph, any loan which is revised, extended, renewed, or renegotiated after August 18, 1985, shall be treated as made after August 18, 1985."

—P.L. 99-514, Sec. 1898(b)(5)(A), amended subpara. (a)(3)(B), effective for plan yrs. begin. after 12/31/84. For special rules see Sec. 302(b) of P.L. 98-397, reproduced below.

Prior to amendment, subpara. (a)(3)(B) read as follows:

"(B) Explanation of qualified preretirement survivor annuity. Each plan shall provide to each participant, within the period beginning with the first day of the plan year in which the participant attains age 32 and ending with the close of the plan year preceding the plan year in which the participant attains age 35 (and consistent with such regulations as the Secretary may prescribe), a written explanation with respect to the qualified preretirement survivor annuity comparable to that required under subparagraph (A)."

Employee benefit plans   Code Sec. 418(b)(5)(A)

—P.L. 99-514, Sec. 1898(b)(6)(A), amended subpara. (a)(2)(A), effective for plan yrs. begin. after 10/22/86.
Prior to amendment, subpara. (a)(2)(A) read as follows:
"(A) the spouse of the participant consents in writing to such election, and, the spouse's consent acknowledges the effect of such election and is witnessed by a plan representative or a notary public, or"
—P.L. 99-514, Sec. 1898(b)(8)(A), substituted "such participants accrued benefit" for "the accrued benefit derived from employer contributions" in para. (f)(1), effective for distributions after 10/22/86 [as amended by Sec. 7862(d)(2) of P.L. 101-239, see above].
—P.L. 99-514, Sec. 1898(b)(9)(A)(i), substituted "the portion of the account balance of the participant (as of the date of death) to which the participant had a nonforfeitable right (within the meaning of section 411(a))" for "the account balance of the participant as of the date of death" in para. (c)(2) . . . Sec. 1898(b)(9)(A)(ii), added para. (c)(3) . . . Sec. 1898(b)(10)(A), redesignated para. (f)(6) (as redesignated by Sec. 1898(b)(4)(A)(iii) of this Act) as (f)(7) and added new para. (f)(6) . . . Sec. 1898(b)(11)(A), substituted "if such benefit may not be waived (or another beneficiary selected) and if the plan" for "if the plan" in subpara. (a)(5)(A) (as redesignated by Sec. 1898(b)(4)(A) of this Act) . . . Sec. 1898(b)(12)(A), amended para. (f)(2) . . . Sec. 1898(b)(15)(A), substituted "section 401(a)(11)" for "section 401(a)(ii)" in para. (a)(1) . . . Sec. 1898(b)(15)(B), substituted "survivor annuity for the life of" for "survivor annuity or the life of" in para. (c)(1), effective for plan yrs. begin. after 12/31/84. For special rules see Sec. 302(b) of P.L. 98-397 reproduced below.
Prior to amendment, para. (f)(2) read as follows:
"(2) Annuity starting date. The term 'annuity starting day' means the first day of the first period for which an amount is received as an annuity (whether by reason of retirement or disability)."

In 1984, P.L. 98-397, Sec. 203(b), added Code Sec. 417, effective for plan yrs. begin. after 12/31/84. Sec. 302(b) of this Act provides the following special rule:
"(b) Special rule for collective bargaining agreements. In the case of a plan maintained pursuant to 1 or more collective bargaining agreements between employee representatives and 1 or more employers ratified before the date of the enactment of this Act, except as provided in subsection (d) or section 303, the amendments made by this Act shall not apply to plan years beginning before the earlier of—
"(1) the date on which the last of the collective bargaining agreements relating to the plan terminates (determined without regard to any extension thereof agreed to after the date of the enactment of this Act), or
"(2) January 1, 1987.
For purposes of paragraph (1), any plan amendment made pursuant to a collective bargaining agreement relating to the plan which amends the plan solely to conform to any requirement added by title I or II shall not be treated as a termination of such collective bargaining agreement."
For transitional rules see Sec. 303 of this Act reproduced in note following Code Sec. 401.

SUBPART C.—SPECIAL RULES FOR MULTIEMPLOYER PLANS
Sec.
418. Reorganization status.
418A. Notice of reorganization and funding requirements.
418B. Minimum contribution requirement.
418C. Overburden credit against minimum contribution requirement.
418D. Adjustments in accrued benefits.
418E. Insolvent plans.

In 1980, P.L. 96-364, Sec. 202(a), added Subpart C.

Sec. 418. Reorganization status.
(a) General rule.
A multiemployer plan is in reorganization for a plan year if the plan's reorganization index for that year is greater than zero.
(b) Reorganization index.
For purposes of this subpart—
(1) **In general.** A plan's reorganization index for any plan year is the excess of—
(A) the vested benefits charge for such year, over
(B) the net charge to the funding standard account for such year.
(2) **Net charge to funding standard account.** The net charge to the funding standard account for any plan year is the excess (if any) of—
(A) the charges to the funding standard account for such year under section 412(b)(2), over
(B) the credits to the funding standard account under section 412(b)(3)(B).

(3) **Vested benefits charge.** The vested benefits charge for any plan year is the amount which would be necessary to amortize the plan's unfunded vested benefits as of the end of the base plan year in equal annual installments—
(A) over 10 years, to the extent such benefits are attributable to persons in pay status, and
(B) over 25 years, to the extent such benefits are attributable to other participants.
(4) **Determination of vested benefits charge.**
(A) In general. The vested benefits charge for a plan year shall be based on an actuarial valuation of the plan as of the end of the base plan year, adjusted to reflect—
(i) any—
(I) decrease of 5 percent or more in the value of plan assets, or increase of 5 percent or more in the number of persons in pay status, during the period beginning on the first day of the plan year following the base plan year and ending on the adjustment date, or
(II) at the election of the plan sponsor, actuarial valuation of the plan as of the adjustment date or any later date not later than the last day of the plan year for which the determination is being made,
(ii) any change in benefits under the plan which is not otherwise taken into account under this subparagraph and which is pursuant to any amendment—
(I) adopted before the end of the plan year for which the determination is being made, and
(II) effective after the end of the base plan year and on or before the end of the plan year referred to in subclause (I), and
(iii) any other event (including an event described in subparagraph (B)(i)(I)) which, as determined in accordance with regulations prescribed by the Secretary, would substantially increase the plan's vested benefit charge.
(B) Certain changes in benefit levels.
(i) In general. In determining the vested benefits charge for a plan year following a plan year in which the plan was not in reorganization, any change in benefits which—
(I) results from the changing of a group of participants from one benefit level to another benefit level under a schedule of plan benefits as a result of changes in a collective bargaining agreement, or
(II) results from any other change in a collective bargaining agreement,
shall not be taken into account except to the extent provided in regulations prescribed by the Secretary.
(ii) Plan in reorganization. Except as otherwise determined by the Secretary, in determining the vested benefits charge for any plan year following any plan year in which the plan was in reorganization, any change in benefits—
(I) described in clause (i)(I), or
(II) described in clause (i)(II) as determined under regulations prescribed by the Secretary,
shall, for purposes of subparagraph (A)(ii), be treated as a change in benefits pursuant to an amendment to a plan.
(5) **Base plan year.**
(A) In general. The base plan year for any plan year is—

(i) if there is a relevant collective bargaining agreement, the last plan year ending at least 6 months before the relevant effective date, or

(ii) if there is no relevant collective bargaining agreement, the last plan year ending at least 12 months before the beginning of the plan year.

(B) Relevant collective bargaining agreement. A relevant collective bargaining agreement is a collective bargaining agreement—

(i) which is in effect for at least 6 months during the plan year, and

(ii) which has not been in effect for more than 36 months as of the end of the plan year.

(C) Relevant effective date. The relevant effective date is the earliest of the effective dates for the relevant collective bargaining agreements.

(D) Adjustment date. The adjustment date is the date which is—

(i) 90 days before the relevant effective date, or

(ii) if there is no relevant effective date, 90 days before the beginning of the plan year.

(6) Person in pay status. The term "person in pay status" means—

(A) a participant or beneficiary on the last day of the base plan year who, at any time during such year, was paid an early, late, normal, or disability retirement benefit (or a death benefit related to a retirement benefit), and

(B) to the extent provided in regulations prescribed by the Secretary, any other person who is entitled to such a benefit under the plan.

(7) Other definitions and special rules.

(A) Unfunded vested benefits. The term "unfunded vested benefits" means, in connection with a plan, an amount (determined in accordance with regulations prescribed by the Secretary) equal to—

(i) the value of vested benefits under the plan, less

(ii) the value of the assets of the plan.

(B) Vested benefits. The term "vested benefits" means any nonforfeitable benefit (within the meaning of section 4001(a)(8) of the Employee Retirement Income Security act of 1974.

(C) Allocation of assets. In determining the plan's unfunded vested benefits, plan assets shall first be allocated to the vested benefits attributable to persons in pay status.

(D) Treatment of certain benefit reductions. The vested benefits charge shall be determined without regard to reductions in accrued benefits under section 418D which are first effective in the plan year.

(E) Withdrawal liability. For purposes of this part, any outstanding claim for withdrawal liability shall not be considered a plan asset, except as otherwise provided in regulations prescribed by the Secretary.

(c) Prohibition of nonannuity payments.

Except as provided in regulations prescribed by the Pension Benefit Guaranty Corporation, while a plan is in reorganization a benefit with respect to a participant (other than a death benefit) which is attributable to employer contributions and which has a value of more than $1,750 may not be paid in a form other than an annuity which (by itself or in combination with social security, railroad retirement, or workers' compensation benefits) provides substantially level payments over the life of the participant.

(d) Terminated plans.

Any multiemployer plan which terminates under section 4041A(a)(2) of the Employee Retirement Income Security Act of 1974 shall not be considered in reorganization after the last day of the plan year in which the plan is treated as having terminated.

In 1980, P.L. 96-364, Sec. 202(a), added Code Sec. 418, effective with respect to each plan, on the first day of the first plan year beginning on or after the earlier of

"(1) the date on which the last collective-bargaining agreement providing for employer contributions under the plan, which was in effect on the date of the enactment of this Act [9/26/80], expires, without regard to extensions agreed to after such date of enactment [9/26/80], or

"(2) 3 years after the date of the enactment of this Act [9/26/80]."

Sec. 418A. Notice of reorganization and funding requirements.

(a) Notice requirement.

(1) In general. If—

(A) a multiemployer plan is in reorganization for a plan year, and

(B) section 418B would require an increase in contributions for such plan year,

the plan sponsor shall notify the persons described in paragraph (2) that the plan is in reorganization and that, if contributions to the plan are not increased, accrued benefits under the plan may be reduced or an excise tax may be imposed (or both such reduction and imposition may occur).

(2) Persons to whom notice is to be given. The persons described in this paragraph are—

(A) each employer who has an obligation to contribute under the plan (within the meaning of section 4212(a) of the Employee Retirement Income Security Act of 1974), and

(B) each employee organization which, for purposes of collective bargaining, represents plan participants employed by such an employer.

(3) Overburden credit not taken into account. The determination under paragraph (1)(B) shall be made without regard to the overburden credit provided by section 418C.

(b) Additional requirements.

The Pension Benefit Guaranty Corporation may prescribe additional or alternative requirements for assuring, in the case of a plan with respect to which notice is required by subsection (a)(1), that the persons described in subsection (a)(2)—

(1) receive appropriate notice that the plan is in reorganization,

(2) are adequately informed of the implications of reorganization status, and

(3) have reasonable access to information relevant to the plan's reorganization status.

In 1980, P.L. 96-364, Sec. 202(a), added Code Sec. 418A, effective with respect to each plan, on the first day of the first plan year beginning on or after the earlier of

"(1) the date on which the last collective-bargaining agreement providing for employer contributions under the plan, which was in effect on the date of the enactment of this Act [9/26/80], expires, without regard to extensions agreed to after such date of enactment [9/26/80], or

"(2) 3 years after the date of the enactment of this Act [9/26/80]."

Sec. 418B. Minimum contribution requirement.

(a) Accumulated funding deficiency in reorganization.

(1) In general. For any plan year in which a multiemployer plan is in reorganization—

(A) the plan shall continue to maintain its funding standard account, and

(B) the plan's accumulated funding deficiency under section 412(a) for such plan year shall be equal to the excess (if any) of—
  (i) the sum of the minimum contribution requirement for such plan year (taking into account any overburden credit under section 418C(a)) plus the plan's accumulated funding deficiency for the preceding plan year (determined under this section if the plan was in reorganization during such plan year or under section 412(a) if the plan was not in reorganization), over
  (ii) amounts considered contributed by employers to or under the plan for the plan year (increased by any amount waived under subsection (f) for the plan year).

(2) Treatment of withdrawal liability payments. For purposes of paragraph (1), withdrawal liability payments (whether or not received) which are due with respect to withdrawals before the end of the base plan year shall be considered amounts contributed by the employer to or under the plan if, as of the adjustment date, it was reasonable for the plan sponsor to anticipate that such payments would be made during the plan year.

(b) Minimum contribution requirement.

(1) In general. Except as otherwise provided in this section for purposes of this subpart the minimum contribution requirement for a plan year in which a plan is in reorganization is an amount equal to the excess of—
  (A) the sum of—
    (i) the plan's vested benefits charge for the plan year; and
    (ii) the increase in normal cost for the plan year determined under the entry age normal funding method which is attributable to plan amendments adopted while the plan was in reorganization, over
  (B) the amount of the overburden credit (if any) determined under section 418C for the plan year.

(2) Adjustment for reductions in contribution base units. If the plan's current contribution base for the plan year is less than the plan's valuation contribution base for the plan year, the minimum contribution requirement for such plan year shall be equal to the product of the amount determined under paragraph (1) (after any adjustment required by this subpart other than this paragraph) multiplied by a fraction—
  (A) the numerator of which is the plan's current contribution base for the plan year, and
  (B) the denominator of which is the plan's valuation contribution base for the plan year.

(3) Special rule where cash-flow amount exceeds vested benefits charge.
  (A) In general. If the vested benefits charge for a plan year of a plan in reorganization is less than the plan's cash-flow amount for the plan year, the plan's minimum contribution requirement for the plan year is the amount determined under paragraph (1) (determined before the application of paragraph (2)) after substituting the term "cash-flow amount" for the term "vested benefits charge" in paragraph (1)(A).
  (B) Cash-flow amount. For purposes of subparagraph (A), a plan's cash-flow amount for a plan year is an amount equal to—
    (i) the amount of the benefits payable under the plan for the base plan year, plus the amount of the plan's administrative expenses for the base plan year, reduced by
    (ii) the value of the available plan assets for the base plan year determined under regulations prescribed by the Secretary,
adjusted in a manner consistent with section 418(b)(4).

(c) Current contribution base; valuation contribution base.

(1) Current contribution base. For purposes of this subpart, a plan's current contribution base for a plan year is the number of contribution base units with respect to which contributions are required to be made under the plan for that plan year, determined in accordance with regulations prescribed by the Secretary.

(2) Valuation contribution base.
  (A) In general. Except as provided in subparagraph (B), for purposes of this subpart a plan's valuation contribution base is the number of contribution base units for which contributions were received for the base plan year—
    (i) adjusted to reflect declines in the contribution base which have occurred (or could reasonably be anticipated) as of the adjustment date for the plan year referred to in paragraph (1),
    (ii) adjusted upward (in accordance with regulations prescribed by the Secretary) for any contribution base reduction in the base plan year caused by a strike or lockout or by unusual events, such as fire, earthquake, or severe weather conditions, and
    (iii) adjusted (in accordance with regulations prescribed by the Secretary) for reductions in the contribution base resulting from transfers of liabilities.
  (B) Insolvent plans. For any plan year—
    (i) in which the plan is insolvent (within the meaning of section 418E(b)(1)), and
    (ii) beginning with the first plan year beginning after the expiration of all relevant collective bargaining agreements which were in effect in the plan year in which the plan became insolvent,
the plan's valuation contribution base is the greater of the number of contribution base units for which contributions were received for the first or second plan year preceding the first plan year in which the plan is insolvent, adjusted as provided in clause (ii) or (iii) of subparagraph (A).

(3) Contribution base unit. For purposes of this subpart, the term "contribution base unit" means a unit with respect to which an employer has an obligation to contribute under a multiemployer plan (as defined in regulations prescribed by the Secretary).

(d) Limitation on required increases in rate of employer contributions.

(1) In general. Under regulations prescribed by the Secretary, the minimum contribution requirement applicable to any plan for any plan year which is determined under subsection (b) (without regard to subsection (b)(2)) shall not exceed an amount which is equal to the sum of —
  (A) the greater of—
    (i) the funding standard requirement for such plan year, or
    (ii) 107 percent of—
      (I) if the plan was not in reorganization in the preceding plan year, the funding standard requirement for such preceding plan year, or
      (II) if the plan was in reorganization in the preceding plan year, the sum of the amount determined under this subparagraph for the preceding plan

year and the amount (if any) determined under subparagraph (B) for the preceding plan year, plus
(B) if for the plan year a change in benefits is first required to be considered in computing the charges under section 412(b)(2)(A) or (B), the sum of—

(i) the increase in normal cost for a plan year determined under the entry age normal funding method due to increases in benefits described in section 418(b)(4)(A)(ii) (determined without regard to section 418(b)(4)(B)(ii)), and

(ii) the amount necessary to amortize in equal annual installments the increase in the value of vested benefits under the plan due to increases in benefits described in clause (i) over—

(I) 10 years, to the extent such increase in value is attributable to persons in pay status, or

(II) 25 years, to the extent such increase in value is attributable to other participants.

(2) Funding standard requirement. For purposes of paragraph (1), the funding standard requirement for any plan year is an amount equal to the net charge to the funding standard account for such plan year (as defined in section 418(b)(2)).

(3) Special rule for certain plans.

(A) In general. In the case of a plan described in section 4216(b) of the Employee Retirement Income Security Act of 1974, if a plan amendment which increases benefits is adopted after January 1, 1980—

(i) paragraph (1) shall apply only if the plan is a plan described in subparagraph (B), and

(ii) the amount under paragraph (1) shall be determined without regard to subparagraph (1)(B).

(B) Eligible plans. A plan is described in this subparagraph if—

(i) the rate of employer contributions under the plan for the first plan year beginning on or after the date on which an amendment increasing benefits is adopted, multiplied by the valuation contribution base for that plan year, equals or exceeds the sum of—

(I) the amount that would be necessary to amortize fully, in equal annual installments, by July 1, 1986, the unfunded vested benefits attributable to plan provisions in effect on July 1, 1977 (determined as of the last day of the base plan year); and

(II) the amount that would be necessary to amortize fully, in equal annual installments, over the period described in subparagraph (C), beginning with the first day of the first plan year beginning on or after the date on which the amendment is adopted, the unfunded vested benefits (determined as of the last day of the base plan year) attributable to each plan amendment after July 1, 1977; and

(ii) the rate of employer contributions for each subsequent plan year is not less than the lesser of—

(I) the rate which when multiplied by the valuation contribution base for that subsequent plan year produces the annual amount that would be necessary to complete the amortization schedule described in clause (i), or

(II) the rate for the plan year immediately preceding such subsequent plan year, plus 5 percent of such rate.

(C) Period. The period determined under this subparagraph is the lesser of—

(i) 12 years, or

(ii) a period equal in length to the average of the remaining expected lives of all persons receiving benefits under the plan.

(4) Exception in case of certain benefit increases. Paragraph (1) shall not apply with respect to a plan, other than a plan described in paragraph (3), for the period of consecutive plan years in each of which the plan is in reorganization, beginning with a plan year in which occurs the earlier of the date of the adoption or the effective date of any amendment of the plan which increases benefits with respect to service performed before the plan year in which the adoption of the amendment occurred.

(e) Certain retroactive plan amendments.

In determining the minimum contribution requirement with respect to a plan for a plan year under subsection (b), the vested benefits charge may be adjusted to reflect a plan amendment reducing benefits under section 412(c)(8).

(f) Waiver of accumulated funding deficiency.

(1) In general. The Secretary may waive any accumulated funding deficiency under this section in accordance with the provisions of section 412(d)(1).

(2) Treatment of waiver. Any waiver under paragraph (1) shall not be treated as a waived funding deficiency (within the meaning of section 412(d)(3)).

(g) Actuarial assumptions must be reasonable.

For purposes of making any determination under this subpart, the requirements of section 412(c)(3) shall apply.

In 1980, P.L. 96-364, Sec. 202(a), added Code Sec. 418B, effective with respect to each plan, on the first day of the first plan year beginning on or after the earlier of "(1) the date on which the last collective-bargaining agreement providing for employer contributions under the plan, which was in effect on the date of the enactment of this Act [9/26/80], expires, without regard to extensions agreed to after such date of enactment [9/26/80], or
"(2) 3 years after the date of the enactment of this Act [9/26/80]."

Sec. 418C. Overburden credit against minimum contribution requirement.

(a) General rule.

For purposes of determining the contribution under section 418B (before the application of section 418B(b)(2) or (d)), the plan sponsor of a plan which is overburdened for the plan year shall apply an overburden credit against the plan's minimum contribution requirement for the plan year (determined without regard to section 418B(b)(2) or (d) and without regard to this section).

(b) Definition of overburdened plan.

A plan is overburdened for a plan year if—

(1) the average number of pay status participants under the plan in the base plan year exceeds the average of the number of active participants in the base plan year and the 2 plan years preceding the base plan year, and

(2) the rate of employer contributions under the plan equals or exceeds the greater of—

(A) such rate for the preceding plan year, or

(B) such rate for the plan year preceding the first year in which the plan is in reorganization.

(c) Amount of overburden credit.

The amount of the overburden credit for a plan year is the product of—

(1) one-half of the average guaranteed benefit paid for the base plan year, and

(2) the overburden factor for the plan year.

The amount of the overburden credit for a plan year shall not exceed the amount of the minimum contribution requirement for such year (determined without regard to this section).

Employee benefit plans Code Sec. 418D(b)(1)(A)(ii)

(d) Overburden factor.
For purposes of this section, the overburden factor of a plan for the plan year is an amount equal to—
(1) the average number of pay status participants for the base plan year, reduced by
(2) the average of the number of active participants for the base plan year and for each of the 2 plan years preceding the base plan year.

(e) Definitions.
For purposes of this section—
(1) Pay status participant. The term "pay status participant" means, with respect to a plan, a participant receiving retirement benefits under the plan.
(2) Number of active participants. The number of active participants for a plan year shall be the sum of—
(A) the number of active employees who are participants in the plan and on whose behalf contributions are required to be made during the plan year;
(B) the number of active employees who are not participants in the plan but who are in an employment unit covered by a collective bargaining agreement which requires the employees' employer to contribute to the plan unless service in such employment unit was never covered under the plan or a predecessor thereof, and
(C) the total number of active employees attributed to employers who made payments to the plan for the plan year of withdrawal liability pursuant to part 1 of subtitle E of title IV of the Employee Retirement Income Security Act of 1974, determined by dividing—
(i) the total amount of such payments, by
(ii) the amount equal to the total contributions received by the plan during the plan year divided by the average number of active employees who were participants in the plan during the plan year.

The Secretary shall by regulations provide alternative methods of determining active participants where (by reason of irregular employment, contributions on a unit basis, or otherwise) this paragraph does not yield a representative basis for determining the credit.

(3) Average number. The term "average number" means, with respect to pay status participants for a plan year, a number equal to one-half the sum of—
(A) the number with respect to the plan as of the beginning of the plan year, and
(B) the number with respect to the plan as of the end of the plan year.

(4) Average guaranteed benefit. The average guaranteed benefit paid is 12 times the average monthly pension payment guaranteed under section 4022A(c)(1) of the Employee Retirement Income Security Act of 1974 determined under the provisions of the plan in effect at the beginning of the first plan year in which the plan is in reorganization and without regard to section 4022A(c)(2).

(5) First year in reorganization. The first year in which the plan is in reorganization is the first of a period of 1 or more consecutive plan years in which the plan has been in reorganization not taking into account any plan years the plan was in reorganization prior to any period of 3 or more consecutive plan years in which the plan was not in reorganization.

(f) No overburden credit in case of certain reductions in contributions.
(1) In general. Notwithstanding any other provision of this section, a plan is not eligible for an overburden credit for a plan year if the Secretary finds that the plan's current contribution base for any plan year was reduced, without a corresponding reduction in the plan's unfunded vested benefits attributable to pay status participants, as a result of a change in an agreement providing for employer contributions under the plan.

(2) Treatment of certain withdrawals. For purposes of paragraph (1), a complete or partial withdrawal of an employer (within the meaning of part 1 of subtitle E of title IV of the Employee Retirement Income Security Act of 1974) does not impair a plan's eligibility for an overburden credit, unless the Secretary finds that a contribution base reduction described in paragraph (1) resulted from a transfer of liabilities to another plan in connection with the withdrawal.

(g) Mergers.
Notwithstanding any other provision of this section, if 2 or more multiemployer plans merge, the amount of the overburden credit which may be applied under this section with respect to the plan resulting from the merger for any of the 3 plan years ending after the effective date of the merger shall not exceed the sum of the used overburden credit for each of the merging plans for its last plan year ending before the effective date of the merger. For purposes of the preceding sentence, the used overburden credit is that portion of the credit which does not exceed the excess of the minimum contribution requirement determined without regard to any overburden credit under this section over the employer contributions required under the plan.

In 1980, P.L. 96-364, Sec. 202(a), added Code Sec. 418C, effective with respect to each plan, on the first day of the first plan year beginning on or after the earlier of

"(1) the date on which the last collective-bargaining agreement providing for employer contributions under the plan, which was in effect on the date of the enactment of this Act [9/26/80], expires, without regard to extensions agreed to after such date of enactment [9/26/80], or

"(2) 3 years after the date of the enactment of this Act [9/26/80]."

Sec. 418D. Adjustments in accrued benefits.
(a) Adjustments in accrued benefits.
(1) In general. Notwithstanding section 411, a multiemployer plan in reorganization may be amended, in accordance with this section, to reduce or eliminate accrued benefits attributable to employer contributions which, under section 4022A(b) of the Employee Retirement Income Security Act of 1974, are not eligible for the Pension Benefit Guaranty Corporation's guarantee. The preceding sentence shall only apply to accrued benefits under plan amendments (or plans) adopted after March 26, 1980, or under collective bargaining agreement entered into after March 26, 1980.

(2) Adjustment of vested benefits charge. In determining the minimum contribution requirement with respect to a plan for a plan year under section 418B(b), the vested benefits charge may be adjusted to reflect a plan amendment reducing benefits under this section or section 412(c)(8), but only if the amendment is adopted and effective no later than 2½ months after the end of the plan year, or within such extended period as the Secretary may prescribe by regulations under section 412(c)(10).

(b) Limitation on reduction.
(1) In general. Accrued benefits may not be reduced under this section unless—
(A) notice has been given, at least 6 months before the first day of the plan year in which the amendment reducing benefits is adopted, to—
(i) plan participants and beneficiaries,
(ii) each employer who has an obligation to contribute (within the meaning of section 4212(a) of the

Employee Retirement Income Security Act of 1974) under the plan, and

(iii) each employee organization which, for purposes of collective bargaining, represents plan participants employed by such an employer,

that the plan is in reorganization and that, if contributions under the plan are not increased, accrued benefits under the plan will be reduced or an excise tax will be imposed on employers;

(B) in accordance with regulations prescribed by the Secretary—

(i) any category of accrued benefits is not reduced with respect to inactive participants to a greater extent proportionally that such category of accrued benefits is reduced with respect to active participants,

(ii) benefits attributable to employer contributions other than accrued benefits and the rate of future benefit accruals are reduced at least to an extent equal to the reduction in accrued benefits of inactive participants, and

(iii) in any case in which the accrued benefit of a participant or beneficiary is reduced by changing the benefit form or the requirements which the participant or beneficiary must satisfy to be entitled to the benefit, such reduction is not applicable to—

(I) any participant or beneficiary in pay status on the effective date of the amendment, or the beneficiary of such a participant, or

(II) any participant who has attained normal retirement age, or who is within 5 years of attaining normal retirement age, on the effective date of the amendment, or the beneficiary of any such participant; and

(C) the rate of employer contributions for the plan year in which the amendment becomes effective and for all succeeding plan years in which the plan is in reorganization equals or exceeds the greater of—

(i) the rate of employer contributions, calculated without regard to the amendment, for the plan year in which the amendment becomes effective, or

(ii) the rate of employer contributions for the plan year preceding the plan year in which the amendment becomes effective.

(2) Information required to be included in notice. The plan sponsors shall include in any notice required to be sent to plan participants and beneficiaries under paragraph (1) information as to the rights and remedies of plan participants and beneficiaries as well as how to contact the Department of Labor for further information and assistance where appropriate.

(c) No recoupment.

A plan may not recoup a benefit payment which is in excess of the amount payable under the plan because of an amendment retroactively reducing accrued benefits under this section.

(d) Benefit increases under multiemployer plan in reorganization.

(1) Restoration of previously reduced benefits.

(A) In general. A plan which has been amended to reduce accrued benefits under this section may be amended to increase or restore accrued benefits, or the rate of future benefit accruals, only if the plan is amended to restore levels of previously reduced accrued benefits of inactive participants and of participants who are within 5 years of attaining normal retirement age to at least the same extent as any such increase in accrued benefits or in the rate of future benefit accruals.

(B) Benefit increases and benefit restorations. For purposes of this subsection, in the case of a plan which has been amended under this section to reduce accrued benefits—

(i) an increase in a benefit, or in the rate of future benefit accruals, shall be considered a benefit increase to the extent that the benefit, or the accrual rate, is thereby increased above the highest benefit level, or accrual rate, which was in effect under the terms of the plan before the effective date of the amendment reducing accrued benefits, and

(ii) an increase in a benefit, or in the rate of future benefit accruals, shall be considered a benefit restoration to the extent that the benefit, or the accrual rate, is not thereby increased above the highest benefit level, or accrual rate, which was in effect under the terms of the plan immediately before the effective date of the amendment reducing accrued benefits.

(2) Uniformity in benefit restoration. If a plan is amended to partially restore previously reduced accrued benefit levels, or the rate of future benefit accruals, the benefits of inactive participants shall be restored in at least the same proportions as other accrued benefits which are restored.

(3) No benefit increases in year of benefit reduction. No benefit increase under a plan may take effect in a plan year in which an amendment reducing accrued benefits under the plan, in accordance with this section, is adopted or first becomes effective.

(4) Retroactive payments. A plan is not required to make retroactive benefit payments with respect to that portion of an accrued benefit which was reduced and subsequently restored under this section.

(e) Inactive participant.

For purposes of this section, the term "inactive participant" means a person not in covered service under the plan who is in pay status under the plan or who has a nonforfeitable benefit under the plan.

(f) Regulations.

The Secretary may prescribe rules under which, notwithstanding any other provision of this section, accrued benefit reductions or benefit increases for different participant groups may be varied equitably to reflect variations in contribution rates and other relevant factors reflecting differences in negotiated levels of financial support for plan benefit obligations.

In 1980, P.L. 96-364, Sec. 202(a), added Code Sec. 418D, effective with respect to each plan, on the first day of the first plan year beginning on or after the earlier of

"(1) the date on which the last collective-bargaining agreement providing for employer contributions under the plan, which was in effect on the date of the enactment of this act [9/26/80], expires, without regard to extensions agreed to after such date of enactment [9/26/80], or

"(2) 3 years after the date of the enactment of this Act [9/26/80]."

Sec. 418E. Insolvent plans.
(a) Suspension of certain benefit payments.

Notwithstanding section 411, in any case in which benefit payments under an insolvent multiemployer plan exceed the resource benefit level, any such payments of benefits which are not basic benefits shall be suspended, in accordance with this section, to the extent necessary to reduce the sum of such payments and the payments of such basic benefits to the greater of the resource benefit level or the level of basic benefits, unless an alternative procedure is prescribed by the Pension Benefit Guaranty Corporation under section

Employee benefit plans   Code Sec. 418E(e)(4)

4022A(g)(5) of the Employee Retirement Income Security Act of 1974.

(b) Definitions.

For purposes of this section, for a plan year—

(1) Insolvency. A multiemployer plan is insolvent if the plan's available resources are not sufficient to pay benefits under the plan when due for the plan year, or if the plan is determined to be insolvent under subsection (d).

(2) Resource benefit level. The term "resource benefit level" means the level of monthly benefits determined under subsections (c)(1) and (3) and (d)(3) to be the highest level which can be paid out of the plan's available resources.

(3) Available resources. The term "available resources" means the plan's cash, marketable assets, contributions, withdrawal liability payments, and earnings, less reasonable administrative expenses and amounts owed for such plan year to the Pension Benefit Guaranty Corporation under section 4261(b)(2) of the Employee Retirement Income Security Act of 1974.

(4) Insolvency year. The term "insolvency year" means a plan year in which a plan is insolvent.

(c) Benefit payments under insolvent plans.

(1) Determination of resource benefit level. The plan sponsor of a plan in reorganization shall determine in writing the plan's resource benefit level for each insolvency year, based on the plan sponsor's reasonable projection of the plan's available resources and the benefits payable under the plan.

(2) Uniformity of the benefit suspension. The suspension of benefit payments under this section shall, in accordance with regulations prescribed by the Secretary, apply in substantially uniform proportions to the benefits of all persons in pay status (within the meaning of section 418(b)(6)) under the plan, except that the Secretary may prescribe rules under which benefit suspensions for different participant groups may be varied equitably to reflect variations in contribution rates and other relevant factors including differences in negotiated levels of financial support for plan benefit obligations.

(3) Resource benefit level below level of basic benefits. Notwithstanding paragraph (2), if a plan sponsor determines in writing a resource benefit level for a plan year which is below the level of basic benefits, the payment of all benefits other than basic benefits shall be suspended for that plan year.

(4) Excess resources.

(A) In general. If, by the end of an insolvency year, the plan sponsor determines in writing that the plan's available resources in that insolvency year could have supported benefit payments above the resource benefit level for that insolvency year, the plan sponsor shall distribute the excess resources to the participants and beneficiaries who received benefit payments from the plan in that insolvency year, in accordance with regulations prescribed by the Secretary.

(B) Excess resources. For purposes of this paragraph, the term "excess resources" means available resources above the amount necessary to support the resource benefit level, but no greater than the amount necessary to pay benefits for the plan year at the benefit levels under the plan.

(5) Unpaid benefits. If, by the end of an insolvency year, any benefit has not been paid at the resource benefit level, amounts up to the resource benefit level which were unpaid shall be distributed to the participants and beneficiaries, in accordance with regulations prescribed by the Secretary, to the extent possible taking into account the plan's total available resources in that insolvency year.

(6) Retroactive payments. Except as provided in paragraph (4) or (5), a plan is not required to make retroactive benefit payments with respect to that portion of a benefit which was suspended under this section.

(d) Plan sponsor determination.

(1) Triennial test. As of the end of the first plan year in which a plan is in reorganization, and at least every 3 plan years thereafter (unless the plan is no longer in reorganization), the plan sponsor shall compare the value of plan assets (determined in accordance with section 418B(b)(3)(B)(ii)) for that plan year with the total amount of benefit payments made under the plan for that plan year. Unless the plan sponsor determines that the value of plan assets exceeds 3 times the total amount of benefit payments, the plan sponsor shall determine whether the plan will be insolvent in any of the next 5 plan years. If the plan sponsor makes such a determination that the plan will be insolvent in any of the next 5 plan years, the plan sponsor shall make the comparison under this paragraph at least annually until the plan sponsor makes a determination that the plan will not be insolvent in any of the next 5 plan years.

(2) Determination of insolvency. If, at any time, the plan sponsor of a plan in reorganization reasonably determines, taking into account the plan's recent and anticipated financial experience, that the plan's available resources are not sufficient to pay benefits under the plan when due for the next plan year, the plan sponsor shall make such determination available to interested parties.

(3) Determination of resource benefit level. The plan sponsor of a plan in reorganization shall determine in writing for each insolvency year the resource benefit level and the level of basic benefits no later than 3 months before the insolvency year.

(e) Notice requirements.

(1) Impending insolvency. If the plan sponsor of a plan in reorganization determines under subsection (d)(1) or (2) that the plan may become insolvent (within the meaning of subsection (b)(1)), the plan sponsor shall—

(A) notify the Secretary, the Pension Benefit Guaranty Corporation, the parties described in section 418A(a)(2), and the plan participants and beneficiaries of that determination, and

(B) inform the parties described in section 418A(a)(2) and the plan participants and beneficiaries that if insolvency occurs certain benefit payments will be suspended, but that basic benefits will continue to be paid.

(2) Resource benefit level. No later than 2 months before the first day of each insolvency year, the plan sponsor of a plan in reorganization shall notify the Secretary, the Pension Benefit Guaranty Corporation, the parties described in section 418A(a)(2), and the plan participants and beneficiaries of the resource benefit level determined in writing for that insolvency year.

(3) Potential need for financial assistance. In any case in which the plan sponsor anticipates that the resource benefit level for an insolvency year may not exceed the level of basic benefits, the plan sponsor shall notify the Pension Benefit Guaranty Corporation.

(4) Regulations. Notice required by this subsection shall be given in accordance with regulations prescribed by the Pension Benefit Guaranty Corporation, except that notice to the Secretary shall be given in accordance with regulations prescribed by the Secretary.

(5) Corporation may prescribe time. The Pension Benefit Guaranty Corporation may prescribe a time other than the time prescribed by this section for the making of a determination or the filing of a notice under this section.

(f) Financial assistance.

(1) **Permissive application.** If the plan sponsor of an insolvent plan for which the resource benefit level is above the level of basic benefits anticipates that, for any month in an insolvency year, the plan will not have funds sufficient to pay basic benefits, the plan sponsor may apply for financial assistance from the Pension Benefit Guaranty Corporation under section 4261 of the Employee Retirement Income Security Act of 1974.

(2) **Mandatory application.** A plan sponsor who has determined a resource benefit level for an insolvency year which is below the level of basic benefits shall apply for financial assistance from the Pension Benefit Guaranty Corporation under section 4261 of the Employee Retirement Income Security Act of 1974.

(g) Financial Assistance.

Any amount of any financial assistance from the Pension Benefit Guaranty Corporation to any plan, and any repayment of such amount, shall be taken into account under this subpart in such manner as determined by the Secretary.

In 2006, P.L. 109-280, Sec. 213(a)(1), substituted "5 plans years" for "3 plan years" the second place it appeared in para. (d)(1) . . . Sec. 213(a)(2), added "If the plan sponsor makes such a determination that the plan will be insolvent in any of the next 5 plan years, the plan sponsor shall make the comparison under this paragraph at least annually until the plan sponsor makes a determination that the plan will not be insolvent in any of the next 5 plan years." at the end of para. (d)(1), effective for determinations made in plan yrs. begin. after 12/31/2007.

In 1980, P.L. 96-364, Sec. 202(a), added Code Sec. 418E, effective with respect to each plan, on the first day of the first plan year beginning on or after the earlier of

"(1) the date on which the last collective-bargaining agreement providing for employer contributions under the plan, which was in effect on the date of the enactment of this Act [9/26/80], expires, without regard to extensions agreed to after such date of enactment [9/26/80], or

"(2) 3 years after the date of the enactment of this Act [9/26/80]."

SUBPART D.—TREATMENT OF WELFARE BENEFIT FUNDS

Sec.
419. Treatment of funded welfare benefit plans.
419A. Qualified asset account; limitation on additions to account.

In 1984, P.L. 98-369, Sec. 511(a), added subpart D and the items for Code Secs. 419 and 419A.

Sec. 419. Treatment of funded welfare benefit plans.

(a) General rule.

Contributions paid or accrued by an employer to a welfare benefit fund—

(1) shall not be deductible under this chapter, but

(2) if they would otherwise be deductible, shall (subject to the limitation of subsection (b)) be deductible under this section for the taxable year in which paid.

(b) Limitation.

The amount of the deduction allowable under subsection (a)(2) for any taxable year shall not exceed the welfare benefit fund's qualified cost for the taxable year.

(c) Qualified cost.

For purposes of this section—

(1) **In general.** Except as otherwise provided in this subsection, the term "qualified cost" means, with respect to any taxable year, the sum of—

(A) the qualified direct cost for such taxable year, and

(B) subject to the limitation of section 419A(b), any addition to a qualified asset account for the taxable year.

(2) **Reduction for funds after-tax income.** In the case of any welfare benefit fund, the qualified cost for any taxable year shall be reduced by such fund's after-tax income for such taxable year.

(3) **Qualified direct cost.**

(A) In general. The term "qualified direct cost" means, with respect to any taxable year, the aggregate amount (including administrative expenses) which would have been allowable as a deduction to the employer with respect to the benefits provided during the taxable year, if—

(i) such benefits were provided directly by the employer, and

(ii) the employer used the cash receipts and disbursements method of accounting.

(B) Time when benefits provided. For purposes of subparagraph (A), a benefit shall be treated as provided when such benefit would be includible in the gross income of the employee if provided directly by the employer (or would be so includible but for any provision of this chapter excluding such benefit from gross income).

(C) 60-month amortization of child care facilities.

(i) In general. In determining qualified direct costs with respect to any child care facility for purposes of subparagraph (A), in lieu of depreciation the adjusted basis of such facility shall be allowable as a deduction ratably over a period of 60 months beginning with the month in which the facility is placed in service.

(ii) Child care facility. The term "child care facility" means any tangible property which qualifies under regulations prescribed by the Secretary as a child care center primarily for children of employees of the employer; except that such term shall not include any property—

(I) not of a character subject to depreciation; or

(II) located outside the United States.

(4) **After-tax income.**

(A) In general. The term "after-tax income" means, with respect to any taxable year, the gross income of the welfare benefit fund reduced by the sum of—

(i) the deductions allowed by this chapter which are directly connected with the production of such gross income, and

(ii) the tax imposed by this chapter on the fund for the taxable year.

(B) Treatment of certain amounts. In determining the gross income of any welfare benefit fund—

(i) contributions and other amounts received from employees shall be taken into account, but

(ii) contributions from the employer shall not be taken into account.

(5) **Item only taken into account once.** No item may be taken into account more than once in determining the qualified cost of any welfare benefit fund.

(d) Carryover of excess contributions.

If—

(1) the amount of the contributions paid (or deemed paid under this subsection) by the employer during any taxable year to a welfare benefit fund, exceeds

(2) the limitation of subsection (b),

such excess shall be treated as an amount paid by the employer to such fund during the succeeding taxable year.

Employee benefit plans — Code Sec. 419A(b)

(e) Welfare benefit fund.
For purposes of this section—
(1) In general. The term "welfare benefit fund" means any fund—
(A) which is part of a plan of an employer, and
(B) through which the employer provides welfare benefits to employees or their beneficiaries.
(2) Welfare benefit. The term "welfare benefit" means any benefit other than a benefit with respect to which—
(A) section 83(h) applies,
(B) section 404 applies (determined without regard to section 404(b)(2)), or
(C) section 404A applies.
(3) Fund. The term "fund" means—
(A) any organization described in paragraph (7), (9), (17), or (20) of section 501(c),
(B) any trust, corporation, or other organization not exempt from the tax imposed by this chapter, and
(C) to the extent provided in regulations, any account held for an employer by any person.
(4) Treatment of amounts held pursuant to certain insurance contracts.
(A) In general. Notwithstanding paragraph (3)(C), the term "fund" shall not include amounts held by an insurance company pursuant to an insurance contract if—
(i) such contract is a life insurance contract described in section 264(a)(1), or
(ii) such contract is a qualified nonguaranteed contract.
(B) Qualified nonguaranteed contract.
(i) In general. For purposes of this paragraph, the term "qualified nonguaranteed contract" means any insurance contract (including a reasonable premium stabilization reserve held thereunder) if—
(I) there is no guarantee of a renewal of such contract, and
(II) other than insurance protection, the only payments to which the employer or employees are entitled are experience rated refunds or policy dividends which are not guaranteed and which are determined by factors other than the amount of welfare benefits paid to (or on behalf of) the employees of the employer or their beneficiaries.
(ii) Limitation. In the case of any qualified nonguaranteed contract, subparagraph (A) shall not apply unless the amount of any experience rated refund or policy dividend payable to an employer with respect to a policy year is treated by the employer as received or accrued in the taxable year in which the policy year ends.

(f) Method of contributions, etc., having the effect of a plan.
If—
(1) there is no plan, but
(2) there is a method or arrangement of employer contributions or benefits which has the effect of a plan,
this section shall apply as if there were a plan.

(g) Extension to plans for independent contractors.
If any fund would be a welfare benefit fund (as modified by subsection (f)) but for the fact that there is no employee-employer relationship—
(1) this section shall apply as if there were such a relationship, and
(2) any reference in this section to the employer shall be treated as a reference to the person for whom services are provided, and any reference in this section to an employee shall be treated as a reference to the person providing the services.

In 1988, P.L. 100-647, Sec. 1018(t)(2)(C), substituted "chapter" for "subchapter" in para. (a)(1), effective for contributions paid or accrued after 12/31/85 in tax. yrs. end. after 12/31/85 except as provided in Secs. 511(e)(2)-(5) of P.L. 98-369, see below.
In 1987, P.L. 100-203, Sec. 10201(b)(4), added "or" at the end of subpara. (e)(2)(B), substituted a period for "or" at the end of subpara. (e)(2)(C) and deleted subpara. (e)(2)(D), effective for tax. yrs. begin. after 12/31/87, except as provided in Sec. 10201(c)(2) [reproduced in note at Code Sec. 463].
Prior to deletion, subpara. (e)(2)(D) read as follows:
"(D) an election under section 463 applies."
In 1986, P.L. 99-514, Sec. 1851(a)(1), substituted "such a relationship" for "such a plan" in para. (g)(1)... Sec. 1851(a)(8)(A), added para. (e)(4), effective for contributions paid or accrued after 12/31/85 in tax. yrs. end. after 12/31/85 except as provided in Secs. 511(e)(2)-(5) of P.L. 98-369, reproduced below. Sec. 1851(a)(8)(B) of this Act provides:
"(B) Effective date of regulations.—Except in the case of a reserve for post-retirement medical or life insurance benefits and any other arrangement between an insurance company and an employer under which the employer has a contractual right to a refund or dividend based solely on the experience of such employer, any account held for an employer by any person and defined as a fund in regulations issued pursuant to section 419(e)(3)(C) of the Internal Revenue Code of 1954 shall be considered a 'fund' no earlier than 6 months following the date such regulations are published in final form."
—P.L. 99-514, Sec. 1851(a)(14), deleted "and section 514" which followed "made by this section" in of Sec. 511(e)(2) of P.L. 98-369 [reproduced below], special rules for amendments made by Sec. 511(a) of P.L. 98-369, see below.
—P.L. 99-514, Sec. 1851(b)(2)(C)(iv), substituted "under this subchapter" for "under section 162 or 212" in para. (a)(1), and substituted "they would otherwise be deductible" for "they satisfy the requirements of either of such sections" in para. (a)(2), effective for amounts paid or incurred after 7/18/84, in tax. yrs. end. after 7/18/84. For exceptions see Sec. 512(c) of P.L. 98-369, reproduced in note following Code Sec. 162.
In 1984, P.L. 98-369, Sec. 511(a), added Code Sec. 419, effective for contributions paid or accrued after 12/31/85 in tax. yrs. end. after 12/31/85 except as provided in Secs. 511(e)(2)-(5) [as amended by Sec. 1851(a)(14) of P.L. 99-514, see above] of the Act, which reads as follows:
"(2) Special rule for collective bargaining agreements.—In the case of plan maintained pursuant to 1 or more collective bargaining agreements—
"(A) between employee representatives and 1 or more employers, and
"(B) in effect on July 1, 1985 (or ratified on or before such date),
the amendments made by this section shall not apply to years beginning before the date on which the last of the collective bargaining agreements relating to the plan terminates (determined without regard to any extension thereof agreed to after July 1, 1985).
"(3) Special rule for paragraph (2).—For purposes of paragraph (2), any plan amendment made pursuant to a collective bargaining agreement relating to the plan which amends the plan solely to conform to any requirement added by this section shall not be treated as a termination of such collective bargaining agreement.
"(4) Special effective date for contributions of facilities.—Notwithstanding paragraphs (1) and (2), the amendments made by this section shall apply in the case of—
"(A) any contribution after June 22, 1984, of a facility to a welfare benefit fund, and
"(B) any other contribution after June 22, 1984, to a welfare benefit fund to be used to acquire or improve a facility.
"(5) Binding contract exceptions to paragraph (4).—Paragraph (4) shall not apply to any facility placed in service before January 1, 1987—
"(A) which is acquired or improved by the fund (or contributed to the fund) pursuant to a binding contract in effect on June 22, 1984, and at all times thereafter, or
"(B) the construction of which by or for the fund began before June 22, 1984."

Sec. 419A. Qualified asset account; limitation on additions to account.

(a) General rule.
For purposes of this subpart and section 512, the term "qualified asset account" means any account consisting of assets set aside to provide for the payment of—
(1) disability benefits,
(2) medical benefits,
(3) SUB or severance pay benefits, or
(4) life insurance benefits.

(b) Limitation on additions to account.
No addition to any qualified asset account may be taken into account under section 419(c)(1)(B) to the extent such addition results in the amount in such account exceeding the account limit.

2,063

(c) Account limit.
For purposes of this section—
(1) In general. Except as otherwise provided in this subsection, the account limit for any qualified asset account for any taxable year is the amount reasonably and actuarially necessary to fund—
(A) claims incurred but unpaid (as of the close of such taxable year) for benefits referred to in subsection (a), and
(B) administrative costs with respect to such claims.
(2) Additional reserve for post-retirement medical and life insurance benefits. The account limit for any taxable year may include a reserve funded over the working lives of the covered employees and actuarially determined on a level basis (using assumptions that are reasonable in the aggregate) as necessary for—
(A) post-retirement medical benefits to be provided to covered employees (determined on the basis of current medical costs), or
(B) post-retirement life insurance benefits to be provided to covered employees.
(3) Amount taken into account for SUB or severance pay benefits.
(A) In general. The account limit for any taxable year with respect to SUB or severance pay benefits is 75 percent of the average annual qualified direct costs for SUB or severance pay benefits for any 2 of the immediately preceding 7 taxable years (as selected by the fund).
(B) Special rule for certain new plans. In the case of any new plan for which SUB or severance pay benefits are not available to any key employee, the Secretary shall, by regulations, provide for an interim amount to be taken into account under paragraph (1).
(4) Limitation on amounts to be taken into account.
(A) Disability benefits. For purposes of paragraph (1), disability benefits payable to any individual shall not be taken into account to the extent such benefits are payable at an annual rate in excess of the lower of—
(i) 75 percent of such individual's average compensation for his high 3 years (within the meaning of section 415(b)(3)), or
(ii) the limitation in effect under section 415(b)(1)(A).
(B) Limitation on SUB or severance pay benefits. For purposes of paragraph (3), any SUB or severance pay benefit payable to any individual shall not be taken into account to the extent such benefit is payable at an annual rate in excess of 150 percent of the limitation in effect under section 415(c)(1)(A).
(5) Special limitation where no actuarial certification.
(A) In general. Unless there is an actuarial certification of the account limit determined under this subsection for any taxable year, the account limit for such taxable year shall not exceed the sum of the safe harbor limits for such taxable year.
(B) Safe harbor limits.
(i) Short-term disability benefits. In the case of short-term disability benefits, the safe harbor limit for any taxable year is 17.5 percent of the qualified direct costs (other than insurance premiums) for the immediately preceding taxable year with respect to such benefits.
(ii) Medical benefits. In the case of medical benefits, the safe harbor limit for any taxable year is 35 percent of the qualified direct costs (other than insurance premiums) for the immediately preceding taxable year with respect to medical benefits.
(iii) SUB or severance pay benefits. In the case of SUB or severance pay benefits, the safe harbor limit for any taxable year is the amount determined under paragraph (3).
(iv) Long-term disability or life insurance benefits. In the case of any long-term disability benefit or life insurance benefit, the safe harbor limit for any taxable year shall be the amount prescribed by regulations.
(6) Additional reserve for medical benefits of bona fide association plans.
(A) In general. An applicable account limit for any taxable year may include a reserve in an amount not to exceed 35 percent of the sum of—
(i) the qualified direct costs, and
(ii) the change in claims incurred but unpaid,
for such taxable year with respect to medical benefits (other than post-retirement medical benefits).
(B) Applicable account limit. For purposes of this subsection, the term "applicable account limit" means an account limit for a qualified asset account with respect to medical benefits provided through a plan maintained by a bona fide association (as defined in section 2791(d)(3) of the Public Health Service Act (42 U.S.C. 300gg-91(d)(3)).
(d) Requirement of separate accounts for post-retirement medical or life insurance benefits provided to key employees.
(1) In general. In the case of any employee who is a key employee—
(A) a separate account shall be established for any medical benefits or life insurance benefits provided with respect to such employee after retirement, and
(B) medical benefits and life insurance benefits provided with respect to such employee after retirement may only be paid from such separate account.
The requirements of this paragraph shall apply to the first taxable year for which a reserve is taken into account under subsection (c)(2) and to all subsequent taxable years.
(2) Coordination with section 415. For purposes of section 415, any amount attributable to medical benefits allocated to an account established under paragraph (1) shall be treated as an annual addition to a defined contribution plan for purposes of section 415(c). Subparagraph (B) of section 415(c)(1) shall not apply to any amount treated as an annual addition under the preceding sentence.
(3) Key employee. For purposes of this section, the term "key employee" means any employee who, at any time during the plan year or any preceding plan year, is or was a key employee as defined in section 416(i).
(e) Special limitations on reserves for medical benefits or life insurance benefits provided to retired employees.
(1) Reserve must be nondiscriminatory. No reserve may be taken into account under subsection (c)(2) for post-retirement medical benefits or life insurance benefits to be provided to covered employees unless the plan meets the requirements of section 505(b) with respect to such benefits (whether or not such requirements apply to such plan). The preceding sentence shall not apply to any plan maintained pursuant to an agreement between employee representatives and 1 or more employers if the Secretary finds that such agreement is a collective bargaining agreement and that post-retirement medical benefits or life insurance

Employee benefit plans — Code Sec. 419A(i)

benefits were the subject of good faith bargaining between such employee representatives and such employer or employers.

(2) Limitation on amount of life insurance benefits. Life insurance benefits shall not be taken into account under subsection (c)(2) to the extent the aggregate amount of such benefits to be provided with respect to the employee exceeds $50,000.

(f) Definitions and other special rules.
For purposes of this section—

(1) SUB or severance pay benefit. The term "SUB or severance pay benefit" means—
  (A) any supplemental unemployment compensation benefit (as defined in section 501(c)(17)(D)), and
  (B) any severance pay benefit.

(2) Medical benefit. The term "medical benefit" means a benefit which consists of the providing (directly or through insurance) of medical care (as defined in section 213(d)).

(3) Life insurance benefit. The term "life insurance benefit" includes any other death benefit.

(4) Valuation. For purposes of this section, the amount of the qualified asset account shall be the value of the assets in such account (as determined under regulations).

(5) Special rule for collective bargained and employee pay-all plans. No account limits shall apply in the case of any qualified asset account under a separate welfare benefit fund—
  (A) under a collective bargaining agreement, or
  (B) an employee pay-all plan under section 501(c)(9) if—
    (i) such plan has at least 50 employees (determined without regard to subsection (h)(1)), and
    (ii) no employee is entitled to a refund with respect to amounts in the fund, other than a refund based on the experience of the entire fund.

(6) Exception for 10-or-more employer plans.
  (A) In general. This subpart shall not apply in the case of any welfare benefit fund which is part of a 10 or more employer plan. The preceding sentence shall not apply to any plan which maintains experience-rating arrangements with respect to individual employers.
  (B) 10 or more employer plan. For purposes of subparagraph (A), the term "10 or more employer plan" means a plan—
    (i) to which more than 1 employer contributes, and
    (ii) to which no employer normally contributes more than 10 percent of the total contributions contributed under the plan by all employers.

(7) Adjustments for existing excess reserves.
  (A) Increase in account limit. The account limit for any of the first 4 taxable years to which this section applies shall be increased by the applicable percentage of any existing excess reserves.
  (B) Applicable percentage. For purposes of subparagraph (A)—

In the case of:	The applicable percentage is:
The first taxable year to which this section applies	80
The second taxable year to which this section applies	60
The third taxable year to which this section applies	40
The fourth taxable year to which this section applies	20

  (C) Existing excess reserve. For purposes of computing the increase under subparagraph (A) for any taxable year, the term "existing excess reserve" means the excess (if any) of—
    (i) the amount of assets set aside at the close of the first taxable year ending after July 18, 1984, for purposes described in subsection (a), over
    (ii) the account limit determined under this section (without regard to this paragraph) for the taxable year for which such increase is being computed.
  (D) Funds to which paragraph applies. This paragraph shall apply only to a welfare benefit fund which, as of July 18, 1984, had assets set aside for purposes described in subsection (a).

(g) Employer taxed on income of welfare benefit fund in certain cases.

(1) In general. In the case of any welfare benefit fund which is not an organization described in paragraph (7), (9), (17), or (20) of section 501(c), the employer shall include in gross income for any taxable year an amount equal to such fund's deemed unrelated income for the fund's taxable year ending within the employer's taxable year.

(2) Deemed unrelated income. For purposes of paragraph (1), the deemed unrelated income of any welfare benefit fund shall be the amount which would have been its unrelated business taxable income under section 512(a)(3) if such fund were an organization described in paragraph (7), (9), (17), or (20) of section 501(c).

(3) Coordination with section 419. If any amount is included in the gross income of an employer for any taxable year under paragraph (1) with respect to any welfare benefit fund—
  (A) the amount of the tax imposed by this chapter which is attributable to the amount so included shall be treated as a contribution paid to such welfare benefit fund on the last day of such taxable year, and
  (B) the tax so attributable shall be treated as imposed on the fund for purposes of section 419(c)(4)(A).

(h) Aggregation rules.
For purposes of this subpart—

(1) Aggregation of funds.
  (A) Mandatory aggregation. For purposes of subsections (c)(4), (d)(2), and (e)(2), all welfare benefit funds of an employer shall be treated as 1 fund.
  (B) Permissive aggregation for purposes not specified in subparagraph (A). For purposes of this section (other than the provisions specified in subparagraph (A)), at the election of the employer, 2 or more welfare benefit funds of such employer may (to the extent not inconsistent with the purposes of this subpart and section 512) be treated as 1 fund.

(2) Treatment of related employers. Rules similar to the rules of subsections (b), (c), (m), and (n) of section 414 shall apply.

(i) Regulations.
The Secretary shall prescribe such regulations as may be appropriate to carry out the purposes of this subpart. Such regulations may provide that the plan administrator of any welfare benefit fund which is part of a plan to which more than 1 employer contributes shall submit such information to the employers contributing to the fund as may be necessary to enable the employers to comply with the provisions of this section.

Code Sec. 419A — Employee benefit plans

In 2006, P.L. 109-280, Sec. 843(a), added para. (c)(6), effective for tax. yrs. begin. after 12/31/2006.

In 1996, P.L. 104-188, Sec. 1704(t)(60), substituted "severance" for "severence" in the heading of para. (c)(3), effective 8/20/96.

In 1988, P.L. 100-647, Sec. 1018(t)(1)(C), substituted "account" for "accounts" in para. (f)(5), effective for contributions paid or accrued after 12/31/85 in tax. yrs. end. after 12/31/85, except as provided in Secs. 511(e)(2)-(5) of P.L. 98-369, reproduced in note following Code Sec. 419.

— P.L. 100-647, Sec. 1018(t)(2)(A), repealed Sec. 1851(a)(4) of P.L. 99-514, which amended para. (f)(5).

— P.L. 100-647, Sec. 1018(t)(2)(D), added ", section 505 and section 4976(b)(1)(B)" after "section 419A" in Sec. 1851(a)(3)(B) of P.L. 99-514, see below.

— P.L. 100-647, Sec. 1018(u)(12), corrected Sec. 1851(a)(6)(B) of P.L. 99-514 to amend subsec. (a) instead of subsec. (b), see below.

In 1986, P.L. 99-514, Sec. 1851(a)(2)(A), added the sentence at the end of para. (d)(2) . . . Sec. 1851(a)(2)(B), added the flush sentence at the end of para. (d)(1) . . . Sec. 1851(a)(3)(A), amended subsec. (e) . . . Sec. 1851(a)(4), [repealed by Sec. 1018(t)(2)(A) of P.L. 100-647, see above] substituted "maintained pursuant to" for "established under" in para. (f)(5) . . . Sec. 1851(a)(5), substituted "this subsection" for "paragraph (1)" in subpara. (c)(5)(A) . . . Sec. 1851(a)(6)(A), amended para. (h)(1) . . . Sec. 1851(a)(6)(B), [as amended by Sec. 1018(u)(12) of P.L. 100-647, see above] added "and section 512" after "this subpart" in subsec. (a) . . . Sec. 1851(a)(7), amended subpara. (f)(7)(C) and added subpara. (f)(7)(D) . . . Sec. 1851(a)(9), added para. (g)(3), effective for contributions paid or accrued after 12/31/85 in tax. yrs. end. after 12/31/85, except as provided in Secs. 511(e)(2)-(5) of P.L. 98-369, reproduced in the note following Code Sec. 419.

— P.L. 99-514, Sec. 1851(a)(3)(B), [as amended by Sec. 1018(t)(2)(D) of P.L. 100-647, see above] of this act provides the following special rule for the change made by Sec 1851(a)(3)(A) (see above):

"(B) Subsection (e) of section 419A, section 505, and section 4976(b)(1)(B) of the Internal Revenue Code of 1954 (as amended by subparagraph [(a)(3)(A)]) shall not apply to any group-term life insurance to the extent that the amendments made by section 223(a) of the Tax Reform Act of 1984 do not apply to such insurance by reason of paragraph (2) of section 223(d) of such Act."

Prior to amendment, subsec. (e) read as follows:

"(e) Special limitations on reserves for medical benefits or life insurance benefits provided to retired employees.

"(1) Benefits must be nondiscriminatory. No reserve may be taken into account under subsection (c)(2) for post-retirement medical benefits or life insurance benefits to be provided to covered employees unless the plan meets the requirements of section 505(b)(1) with respect to such benefits.

"(2) Taxable life insurance benefits not taken into account. No life insurance benefit may be taken into account under subsection (c)(2) to the extent—

"(A) such benefit is includible in gross income under section 79, or

"(B) such benefit would be includible in gross income under section 101(b) (determined by substituting '$50,000' for '$5,000')."

Prior to amendment, para. (h)(1) read as follows:

"(1) Aggregation of funds. At the election of the employer, 2 or more welfare benefit funds of such employer may be treated as 1 fund."

Prior to amendment, para. (f)(7)(C) read as follows:

"(C) Existing excess reserve. For purposes of this paragraph, the term 'existing excess reserve' means the excess (if any) of—

"(i) the amount of assets set aside for purposes described in subsection (a) as of the close of the first taxable year ending after the date of the enactment of the Tax Reform Act of 1984, over

"(ii) the account limit which would have applied under this section to such taxable year if this section had applied to such taxable year."

— P.L. 99-514, Sec. 1851(a)(12), added paras. (6) and (7) to Sec. 511(e) of P.L. 98-369, exceptions to the effective date for additions made by Sec. 511(a) of P.L. 98-369, reproduced in the note for P.L. 98-369 following Code Sec. 419.

— P.L. 99-514, Sec. 1851(a)(13), amended para. (f)(5), effective for contributions paid or accrued after 12/31/85 in tax. yrs. end. after 12/31/85, except as provided in Secs. 511(e)(2)-(7) of P.L. 98-369, reproduced in the note following Code Sec. 419.

Prior to amendment, para. (f)(5) read as follows:

"(5) Higher limit in case of collectively bargained plans. Not later than July 1, 1985, the Secretary shall by regulations provide for special account limits in the case of any qualified asset account under a welfare benefit fund established under a collective bargaining agreement."

In 1984, P.L. 98-369, Sec. 511(a), added Code Sec. 419A, effective for contributions paid or accrued after 12/31/85 in tax. yrs. end. after 12/31/85 except as provided in Secs. 511(e)(2)-(5) of the Act, reproduced in note following Code Sec. 419.

SUBPART E.—TREATMENT OF TRANSFERS TO RETIREE HEALTH ACCOUNTS

Sec.
420. Transfers of excess pension assets to retiree health accounts.

In 1990, P.L. 101-508, Sec. 12011(a), added subpart E and item 420.

Sec. 420. Transfers of excess pension assets to retiree health accounts.

(a) General rule.

If there is a qualified transfer of any excess pension assets of a defined benefit plan to a health benefits account which is part of such plan—

(1) a trust which is part of such plan shall not be treated as failing to meet the requirements of subsection (a) or (h) of section 401 solely by reason of such transfer (or any other action authorized under this section),

(2) no amount shall be includible in the gross income of the employer maintaining the plan solely by reason of such transfer,

(3) such transfer shall not be treated—

(A) as an employer reversion for purposes of section 4980, or

(B) as a prohibited transaction for purposes of section 4975, and

(4) the limitations of subsection (d) shall apply to such employer.

(b) Qualified transfer.

For purposes of this section

(1) In general. The term "qualified transfer" means a transfer

(A) of excess pension assets of a defined benefit plan to a health benefits account which is part of such plan in a taxable year beginning after December 31, 1990,

(B) which does not contravene any other provision of law, and

(C) with respect to which the following requirements are met in connection with the plan—

(i) the use requirements of subsection (c)(1),

(ii) the vesting requirements of subsection (c)(2), and

(iii) the minimum cost requirements of subsection (c)(3).

(2) Only 1 transfer per year.

(A) In general. No more than 1 transfer with respect to any plan during a taxable year may be treated as a qualified transfer for purposes of this section.

(B) Exception. A transfer described in paragraph (4) shall not be taken into account for purposes of subparagraph (A).

(3) Limitation on amount transferred. The amount of excess pension assets which may be transferred in a qualified transfer shall not exceed the amount which is reasonably estimated to be the amount the employer maintaining the plan will pay (whether directly or through reimbursement) out of such account during the taxable year of the transfer for qualified current retiree health liabilities.

(4) Special rule for 1990.

(A) In general. Subject to the provisions of subsection (c), a transfer shall be treated as a qualified transfer if such transfer—

(i) is made after the close of the taxable year preceding the employer's first taxable year beginning after December 31, 1990, and before the earlier of—

(I) the due date (including extensions) for the filing of the return of tax for such preceding taxable year, or

(II) the date such return is filed, and

(ii) does not exceed the expenditures of the employer for qualified current retiree health liabilities for such preceding taxable year.

(B) Deduction reduced. The amount of the deductions otherwise allowable under this chapter to an employer for the taxable year preceding the employer's first taxable year beginning after December 31, 1990, shall be reduced by the amount of any qualified transfer to which this paragraph applies.

(C) Coordination with reduction rule. Subsection (e)(1)(B) shall not apply to a transfer described in subparagraph (A).

(5) Expiration. No transfer made after December 31, 2013, shall be treated as a qualified transfer.

(c) Requirements of plans transferring assets.

(1) Use of transferred assets.

(A) In general. Any assets transferred to a health benefits account in a qualified transfer (and any income allocable thereto) shall be used only to pay qualified current retiree health liabilities (other than liabilities of key employees not taken into account under subsection (e)(1)(D)) for the taxable year of the transfer (whether directly or through reimbursement). In the case of a qualified future transfer or collectively bargained transfer to which subsection (f) applies, any assets so transferred may also be used to pay liabilities described in subsection (f)(2)(C).

(B) Amounts not used to pay for health benefits.

(i) In general. Any assets transferred to a health benefits account in a qualified transfer (and any income allocable thereto) which are not used as provided in subparagraph (A) shall be transferred out of the account to the transferor plan.

(ii) Tax treatment of amounts. Any amount transferred out of an account under clause (i)—

(I) shall not be includible in the gross income of the employer for such taxable year, but

(II) shall be treated as an employer reversion for purposes of section 4980 (without regard to subsection (d) thereof).

(C) Ordering rule. For purposes of this section, any amount paid out of a health benefits account shall be treated as paid first out of the assets and income described in subparagraph (A).

(2) Requirements relating to pension benefits accruing before transfer.

(A) In general. The requirements of this paragraph are met if the plan provides that the accrued pension benefits of any participant or beneficiary under the plan become nonforfeitable in the same manner which would be required if the plan had terminated immediately before the qualified transfer (or in the case of a participant who separated during the 1-year period ending on the date of the transfer, immediately before such separation).

(B) Special rule for 1990. In the case of a qualified transfer described in subsection (b)(4), the requirements of this paragraph are met with respect to any participant who separated from service during the taxable year to which such transfer relates by recomputing such participant's benefits as if subparagraph (A) had applied immediately before such separation.

(3) Minimum cost requirements.

(A) In general. The requirements of this paragraph are met if each group health plan or arrangement under which applicable health benefits are provided provides that the applicable employer cost for each taxable year during the cost maintenance period shall not be less than the higher of the applicable employer costs for each of the 2 taxable years immediately preceding the taxable year of the qualified transfer or, in the case of a transfer which involves a plan maintained by an employer described in subsection (f)(2)(E)(i)(III), if the plan meets the requirements of subsection (f)(2)(D)(i)(II).

(B) Applicable employer cost. For purposes of this paragraph, the term "applicable employer cost" means, with respect to any taxable year, the amount determined by dividing—

(i) the qualified current retiree health liabilities of the employer for such taxable year determined—

(I) without regard to any reduction under subsection (e)(1)(B), and

(II) in the case of a taxable year in which there was no qualified transfer, in the same manner as if there had been such a transfer at the end of the taxable year, by

(ii) the number of individuals to whom coverage for applicable health benefits was provided during such taxable year.

(C) Election to compute cost separately. An employer may elect to have this paragraph applied separately with respect to individuals eligible for benefits under title XVIII of the Social Security Act at any time during the taxable year and with respect to individuals not so eligible.

(D) Cost maintenance period. For purposes of this paragraph, the term "cost maintenance period" means the period of 5 taxable years beginning with the taxable year in which the qualified transfer occurs. If a taxable year is in two or more overlapping cost maintenance periods, this paragraph shall be applied by taking into account the highest applicable employer cost required to be provided under subparagraph (A) for such taxable year.

(E) Regulations.

(i) In general. The Secretary shall prescribe such regulations as may be necessary to prevent an employer who significantly reduces retiree health coverage during the cost maintenance period from being treated as satisfying the minimum cost requirement of this subsection.

(ii) Insignificant cost reductions permitted.

(I) In general. An eligible employer shall not be treated as failing to meet the requirements of this paragraph for any taxable year if, in lieu of any reduction of retiree health coverage permitted under the regulations prescribed under clause (i), the employer reduces applicable employer cost by an amount not in excess of the reduction in costs which would have occurred if the employer had made the maximum permissible reduction in retiree health coverage under such regulations. In applying such regulations to any subsequent taxable year, any reduction in applicable employer cost under this clause shall be treated as if it were an equivalent reduction in retiree health coverage.

(II) Eligible employer. For purposes of subclause (I), an employer shall be treated as an eligible employer for any taxable year if, for the preceding taxable year, the qualified current retiree health liabilities of the employer were at least 5 percent of the gross receipts of the employer. For purposes of this subclause, the rules of paragraphs (2), (3)(B), and (3)(C) of section 448(c) shall apply in determining the amount of an employer's gross receipts.

(d) Limitations on employer.
For purposes of this title—
(1) Deduction limitations. No deduction shall be allowed—
(A) for the transfer of any amount to a health benefits account in a qualified transfer (or any retransfer to the plan under subsection (c)(1)(B)),
(B) for qualified current retiree health liabilities paid out of the assets (and income) described in subsection (c)(1), or
(C) for any amounts to which subparagraph (B) does not apply and which are paid for qualified current retiree health liabilities for the taxable year to the extent such amounts are not greater than the excess (if any) of—
(i) the amount determined under subparagraph (A) (and income allocable thereto), over
(ii) the amount determined under subparagraph (B).
(2) No contributions allowed. An employer may not contribute after December 31, 1990, any amount to a health benefits account or welfare benefit fund (as defined in section 419(e)(1)) with respect to qualified current retiree health liabilities for which transferred assets are required to be used under subsection (c)(1).

(e) Definition and special rules.
For purposes of this section—
(1) Qualified current retiree health liabilities. For purposes of this section—
(A) In general. The term "qualified current retiree health liabilities" means, with respect to any taxable year, the aggregate amounts (including administrative expenses) which would have been allowable as a deduction to the employer for such taxable year with respect to applicable health benefits provided during such taxable year if—
(i) such benefits were provided directly by the employer, and
(ii) the employer used the cash receipts and disbursements method of accounting.
For purposes of the preceding sentence, the rule of section 419(c)(3)(B) shall apply.
(B) Reductions for amounts previously set aside. The amount determined under subparagraph (A) shall be reduced by the amount which bears the same ratio to such amount as—
(i) the value (as of the close of the plan year preceding the year of the qualified transfer) of the assets in all health benefits accounts or welfare benefit funds (as defined in section 419(e)(1)) set aside to pay for the qualified current retiree health liability, bears to
(ii) the present value of the qualified current retiree health liabilities for all plan years (determined without regard to this subparagraph).
(C) Applicable health benefits. The term "applicable health benefits" means health benefits or coverage which are provided to—
(i) retired employees who, immediately before the qualified transfer, are entitled to receive such benefits upon retirement and who are entitled to pension benefits under the plan, and
(ii) their spouses and dependents.
(D) Key employees excluded. If an employee is a key employee (within the meaning of section 416(i)(1)) with respect to any plan year ending in a taxable year, such employee shall not be taken into account in computing qualified current retiree health liabilities for such taxable year or in calculating applicable employer cost under subsection (c)(3)(B).
(2) Excess pension assets. The term "excess pension assets" means the excess (if any) of—
(A) the lesser of—
(i) the fair market value of the plan's assets (reduced by the prefunding balance and funding standard carryover balance determined under section 430(f)), or
(ii) the value of plan assets as determined under section 430(g)(3) after reduction under section 430(f), over
(B) 125 percent of the sum of the funding target and the target normal cost determined under section 430 for such plan year.
(3) Health benefits account. The term "health benefits account" means an account established and maintained under section 401(h).
(4) Coordination with section 430. In the case of a qualified transfer, any assets so transferred shall not, for purposes of this section and section 430, be treated as assets in the plan.
(5) Application to multiemployer plans. In the case of a multiemployer plan, this section shall be applied to any such plan—
(A) by treating any reference in this section to an employer as a reference to all employers maintaining the plan (or, if appropriate, the plan sponsor), and
(B) in accordance with such modifications of this section (and the provisions of this title relating to this section) as the Secretary determines appropriate to reflect the fact the plan is not maintained by a single employer.

(f) Qualified transfers to cover future retiree health costs and collectively bargained retiree health benefits.
(1) In general. An employer maintaining a defined benefit plan (other than a multiemployer plan) may, in lieu of a qualified transfer, elect for any taxable year to have the plan make—
(A) a qualified future transfer, or
(B) a collectively bargained transfer.
Except as provided in this subsection, a qualified future transfer and a collectively bargained transfer shall be treated for purposes of this title and the Employee Retirement Income Security Act of 1974 as if it were a qualified transfer.
(2) Qualified future and collectively bargained transfers. For purposes of this subsection—
(A) In general. The terms "qualified future transfer" and "collectively bargained transfer" mean a transfer which meets all of the requirements for a qualified transfer, except that—
(i) the determination of excess pension assets shall be made under subparagraph (B),
(ii) the limitation on the amount transferred shall be determined under subparagraph (C),
(iii) the minimum cost requirements of subsection (c)(3) shall be modified as provided under subparagraph (D), and
(iv) in the case of a collectively bargained transfer, the requirements of subparagraph (E) shall be met with respect to the transfer.
(B) Excess pension assets.
(i) In general. In determining excess pension assets for purposes of this subsection, subsection (e)(2) shall be applied by substituting "120 percent" for "125 percent".

(ii) Requirement to maintain funded status. If, as of any valuation date of any plan year in the transfer period, the amount determined under subsection (e)(2)(B) (after application of clause (i)) exceeds the amount determined under subsection (e)(2)(A), either—

(I) the employer maintaining the plan shall make contributions to the plan in an amount not less than the amount required to reduce such excess to zero as of such date, or

(II) there is transferred from the health benefits account to the plan an amount not less than the amount required to reduce such excess to zero as of such date.

(C) Limitation on amount transferred. Notwithstanding subsection (b)(3), the amount of the excess pension assets which may be transferred—

(i) in the case of a qualified future transfer shall be equal to the sum of—

(I) if the transfer period includes the taxable year of the transfer, the amount determined under subsection (b)(3) for such taxable year, plus

(II) in the case of all other taxable years in the transfer period, the sum of the qualified current retiree health liabilities which the plan reasonably estimates, in accordance with guidance issued by the Secretary, will be incurred for each of such years, and

(ii) in the case of a collectively bargained transfer, shall not exceed the amount which is reasonably estimated, in accordance with the provisions of the collective bargaining agreement and generally accepted accounting principles, to be the amount the employer maintaining the plan will pay (whether directly or through reimbursement) out of such account during the collectively bargained cost maintenance period for collectively bargained retiree health liabilities.

(D) Minimum cost requirements.

(i) In general. The requirements of subsection (c)(3) shall be treated as met if—

(I) in the case of a qualified future transfer, each group health plan or arrangement under which applicable health benefits are provided provides applicable health benefits during the period beginning with the first year of the transfer period and ending with the last day of the 4th year following the transfer period such that the annual average amount of the applicable employer cost during such period is not less than the applicable employer cost determined under subsection (c)(3)(A) with respect to the transfer, and

(II) in the case of a collectively bargained transfer, each collectively bargained group health plan under which collectively bargained health benefits are provided provides that the collectively bargained employer cost for each taxable year during the collectively bargained cost maintenance period shall not be less than the amount specified by the collective bargaining agreement.

(ii) Election to maintain benefits for future transfers. An employer may elect, in lieu of the requirements of clause (i)(I), to meet the requirements of subsection (c)(3) by meeting the requirements of such subsection (as in effect before the amendments made by section 535 of the Tax Relief Extension Act of 1999) for each of the years described in the period under clause (i)(I).

(iii) Collectively bargained employer cost. For purposes of this subparagraph, the term "collectively bargained employer cost" means the average cost per covered individual of providing collectively bargained retiree health benefits as determined in accordance with the applicable collective bargaining agreement. Such agreement may provide for an appropriate reduction in the collectively bargained employer cost to take into account any portion of the collectively bargained retiree health benefits that is provided or financed by a government program or other source.

(E) Special rules for collectively bargained transfers.

(i) In general. A collectively bargained transfer shall only include a transfer which—

(I) is made in accordance with a collective bargaining agreement,

(II) before the transfer, the employer designates, in a written notice delivered to each employee organization that is a party to the collective bargaining agreement, as a collectively bargained transfer in accordance with this section, and

(III) involves a plan maintained by an employer which, in its taxable year ending in 2005, provided health benefits or coverage to retirees and their spouses and dependents under all of the benefit plans maintained by the employer, but only if the aggregate cost (including administrative expenses) of such benefits or coverage which would have been allowable as a deduction to the employer (if such benefits or coverage had been provided directly by the employer and the employer used the cash receipts and disbursements method of accounting) is at least 5 percent of the gross receipts of the employer (determined in accordance with the last sentence of subsection (c)(3)(E)(ii)(II)) for such taxable year, or a plan maintained by a successor to such employer.

(ii) Use of assets. Any assets transferred to a health benefits account in a collectively bargained transfer (and any income allocable thereto) shall be used only to pay collectively bargained retiree health liabilities (other than liabilities of key employees not taken into account under paragraph (6)(B)(iii)) for the taxable year of the transfer or for any subsequent taxable year during the collectively bargained cost maintenance period (whether directly or through reimbursement).

(3) Coordination with other transfers. In applying subsection (b)(3) to any subsequent transfer during a taxable year in a transfer period or collectively bargained cost maintenance period, qualified current retiree health liabilities shall be reduced by any such liabilities taken into account with respect to the qualified future transfer or collectively bargained transfer to which such period relates.

(4) Special deduction rules for collectively bargained transfers. In the case of a collectively bargained transfer—

(A) the limitation under subsection (d)(1)(C) shall not apply, and

(B) notwithstanding subsection (d)(2), an employer may contribute an amount to a health benefits account or welfare benefit fund (as defined in section 419(e)(1)) with respect to collectively bargained retiree health liabilities for which transferred assets are required to be used under subsection (c)(1)(B), and the deductibility of any such contribution shall be governed by the limits applicable to the deductibility of contributions to a welfare benefit fund under a collective bargaining agreement (as determined under section 419A(f)(5)(A)) without regard to whether such contributions are made to a health benefits account or welfare benefit fund and without regard to the provisions of section 404 or the other provisions of this section.

The Secretary shall provide rules to ensure that the application of this paragraph does not result in a deduction being allowed more than once for the same contribution or for 2 or more contributions or expenditures relating to the same collectively bargained retiree health liabilities.

(5) Transfer period. For purposes of this subsection, the term "transfer period" means, with respect to any transfer, a period of consecutive taxable years (not less than 2) specified in the election under paragraph (1) which begins and ends during the 10-taxable-year period beginning with the taxable year of the transfer.

(6) Terms relating to collectively bargained transfers. For purposes of this subsection—

(A) Collectively bargained cost maintenance period. The term "collectively bargained cost maintenance period" means, with respect to each covered retiree and his covered spouse and dependents, the shorter of—

(i) the remaining lifetime of such covered retiree and his covered spouse and dependents, or

(ii) the period of coverage provided by the collectively bargained health plan (determined as of the date of the collectively bargained transfer) with respect to such covered retiree and his covered spouse and dependents.

(B) Collectively bargained retiree health liabilities.

(i) In general. The term "collectively bargained retiree health liabilities" means the present value, as of the beginning of a taxable year and determined in accordance with the applicable collective bargaining agreement, of all collectively bargained health benefits (including administrative expenses) for such taxable year and all subsequent taxable years during the collectively bargained cost maintenance period.

(ii) Reduction for amounts previously set aside. The amount determined under clause (i) shall be reduced by the value (as of the close of the plan year preceding the year of the collectively bargained transfer) of the assets in all health benefits accounts or welfare benefit funds (as defined in section 419(e)(1)) set aside to pay for the collectively bargained retiree health liabilities.

(iii) Key employees excluded. If an employee is a key employee (within the meaning of section 416(I)(1)) with respect to any plan year ending in a taxable year, such employee shall not be taken into account in computing collectively bargained retiree health liabilities for such taxable year or in calculating collectively bargained employer cost under subsection (c)(3)(C).

(C) Collectively bargained health benefits. The term "collectively bargained health benefits" means health benefits or coverage which are provided to—

(i) retired employees who, immediately before the collectively bargained transfer, are entitled to receive such benefits upon retirement and who are entitled to pension benefits under the plan, and their spouses and dependents, and

(ii) if specified by the provisions of the collective bargaining agreement governing the collectively bargained transfer, active employees who, following their retirement, are entitled to receive such benefits and who are entitled to pension benefits under the plan, and their spouses and dependents.

(D) Collectively bargained health plan. The term "collectively bargained health plan" means a group health plan or arrangement for retired employees and their spouses and dependents that is maintained pursuant to 1 or more collective bargaining agreements.

In 2008, P.L. 110-458, Sec. 101(d)(3), added Sec. 114(g), P.L. 109-280, providing the effective dates for amendments made by Sec. 114, P.L. 109-280, see below. Sec. 114(g), P.L. 109-280, as added by this Act, provides:

"'(g) Effective dates.

"'(1) In general. The amendments made by this section shall apply to plan years beginning after 2007.

"'(2) Excise tax. The amendments made by subsection (e) shall apply to taxable years beginning after 2007, but only with respect to plan years described in paragraph (1) which end with or within any such taxable year.'"

—P.L. 110-458, Sec. 108(i)(1), added "In the case of a qualified future transfer or collectively bargained transfer to which subsection (f) applies, any assets so transferred may also be used to pay liabilities described in subsection (f)(2)(C)." at the end of subpara. (c)(1)(A). . . . Sec. 108(i)(2), deleted "such" before "the applicable" in subclause (f)(2)(D)(i)(I), effective for transfers after 8/17/2006 as if included in provisions of Sec. 841 of the Pension Protection Act of 2006 [P. L. 109-280].

In 2007, P.L. 110-28, Sec. 6612(a), substituted "subsection (c)(3)(E)(ii)(II)" for "subsection (c)(2)(E)(ii)(II)" in subpara. (e)(2)(B) . . . Sec. 6612(b), substituted "funding target" for "funding shortfall" in subclause (f)(2)(e)(i)(III), effective as if included in the provisions of the Pension Protection Act of 2006 to which they relate.

—P.L. 110-28, Sec. 6613(a), substituted "transfer or, in the case of a transfer which involves a plan maintained by an employer described in subsection (f)(2)(E)(i)(III), if the plan meets the requirements of subsection (f)(2)(D)(i)(II)." for "subsection (c)(2)(E)(ii)(II)" for "transfer." in subpara. (c)(3)(A), effective for transfers after 5/25/2007.

In 2006, P.L. 109-280, Sec. 114(d)(1), amended para. (e)(2) . . . Sec. 114(d)(2), amended para. (e)(4), effective for plan yrs. begin. after 2007 [as provided in Sec. 114(g) of this Act as added by Sec. 101(d)(3), P.L. 110-458, see above].

"(g) Effective dates.

"(1) In general. The amendments made by this section shall apply to plan years beginning after 2007."

Prior to amendment, para. (e)(2) read as follows:

"(2) Excess pension assets. The term 'excess pension assets' means the excess (if any) of—

"(A) the amount determined under section 412(c)(7)(A)(ii), over

"(B) the greater of—

"(i) the amount determined under section 412(c)(7)(A)(i), or

"(ii) 125 percent of current liability (as defined in section 412(c)(7)(B)).

The determination under this paragraph shall be made as of the most recent valuation date of the plan preceding the qualified transfer.'

Prior to amendment, para. (e)(4) read as follows:

"(4) Coordination with section 412. In the case of a qualified transfer to a health benefits account—

"(A) any assets transferred in a plan year on or before the valuation date for such year (and any income allocable thereto) shall, for purposes of section 412, be treated as assets in the plan as of the valuation date for such year, and

"(B) the plan shall be treated as having a net experience loss under section 412(b)(2)(B)(iv) in an amount equal to the amount of such transfer (reduced by any amounts transferred back to the pension plan under subsection (c)(1)(B)) and for which amortization charges begin for the first plan year after the plan year in which such transfer occurs, except that such section shall be applied to such amount by substituting '10 plan years' for '5 plan years'."

—P.L. 109-280, Sec. 841(a), added subsec. (f), effective for transfers after 8/17/2006.

—P.L. 109-280, Sec. 842(a)(1), deleted "(other than a multiemployer plan)" after "defined benefit plan" in subsec. (a) . . . Sec. 842(a)(2), added para. (e)(5), effective for transfers made in tax. yrs. begin. after 12/31/2006.

In 2004, P.L. 108-357, Sec. 709(b)(1), added clause (c)(3)(E)(ii) . . . Sec. 709(b)(2), substituted "(i) In general. The Secretary" for "The Secretary" in subpara. (c)(3)(E), effective for tax. yrs. end. after 10/22/2004.

—P.L. 108-218, Sec. 204(a), substituted "December 31, 2013" for "December 31, 2005" in para. (b)(5), effective 4/10/2004.

In 1999, P.L. 106-170, Sec. 535(a)(1), substituted "made after December 31, 2005" for "in any taxable year beginning after December 31, 2000" in para. (b)(5) . . . Sec. 535(b)(1), amended para. (c)(3) . . . Sec. 535(b)(2)(A), substituted "cost" for "benefits" in clause (b)(1)(C)(iii) . . . Sec. 535(b)(2)(B), substituted "or in calculating applicable employer cost under subsection (c)(3)(B)" for "and shall not be subject to the minimum benefit requirements of subsection (c)(3)" in subpara. (e)(1)(D), effective for qualified transfers occurring after 12/17/99, except as provided in Sec. 535(c)(2), of this Act, which reads as follows:

"(2) Transition rule. If the cost maintenance period for any qualified transfer after the date of the enactment of this Act includes any portion of a benefit maintenance period for any qualified transfer on or before such date, the amendments

made by subsection (b) shall not apply to such portion of the cost maintenance period (and such portion shall be treated as a benefit maintenance period)".
Prior to amendment, para. (c)(3) read as follows:

"(3) Maintenance of benefit requirements.

"(A) In general. The requirements of this paragraph are met if each group health plan or arrangement under which applicable health benefits are provided provides that the applicable health benefits provided by the employer during each taxable year during the benefit maintenance period are substantially the same as the applicable health benefits provided by the employer during the taxable year immediately preceding the taxable year of the qualified transfer.

"(B) Election to apply separately. An employer may elect to have this paragraph applied separately with respect to individuals eligible for benefits under title XVIII of the Social Security Act at any time during the taxable year and with respect to individuals not so eligible.

"(C) Benefit maintenance period. For purposes of this paragraph, the term 'benefit maintenance period' means the period of 5 taxable years beginning with the taxable year in which the qualified transfer occurs. If a taxable year is in 2 or more benefit maintenance periods, this paragraph shall be applied by taking into account the highest level of benefits required to be provided under subparagraph (A) for such taxable year."

In 1996, P.L. 104-188, Sec. 1704(t)(32), substituted "means" for "mean" in subpara. (e)(1)(C), effective 8/20/96.

In 1994, P.L. 103-465, Sec. 731(a), substituted "2000" for "1995" in para. (b)(5), effective for tax. yrs. begin. after 12/31/95.

—P.L. 103-465, Sec. 731(b), amended para. (c)(3)... Sec. 731(c)(1), substituted "benefits" for "cost" in clause (b)(1)(C)(iii)... Sec. 731(c)(2), amended subpara. (e)(1)(B), effective for qualified transfers occurring after 12/8/94.

Prior to amendment, para. (c)(3) read as follows:

"(3) Minimum cost requirements.

"(A) In general. The requirements of this paragraph are met if each group health plan or arrangement under which applicable health benefits are provided provides that the applicable employer cost for each taxable year during the cost maintenance period shall not be less than the higher of the applicable employer costs for each of the 2 taxable years immediately preceding the taxable year of the qualified transfer.

"(B) Applicable employer cost. For purposes of this paragraph, the term 'applicable employer cost' means, with respect to any taxable year, the amount determined by dividing—

"(i) the qualified current retiree health liabilities of the employer for such taxable year determined—

"(I) without regard to any reduction under subsection (e)(1)(B), and

"(II) in the case of a taxable year in which there was no qualified transfer, in the same manner as if there had been such a transfer at the end of the taxable year, by

"(ii) the number of individuals to whom coverage for applicable health benefits was provided during such taxable year.

"(C) Election to compute cost separately. An employer may elect to have this paragraph applied separately with respect to individuals eligible for benefits under title XVIII of the Social Security Act at any time during the taxable year and with respect to individuals not so eligible.

"(D) Cost maintenance period. For purposes of this paragraph, the term 'cost maintenance period' means the period of 5 taxable years beginning with the taxable year in which the qualified transfer occurs. If a taxable year is in 2 or more overlapping cost maintenance periods, this paragraph shall be applied by taking into account the highest applicable employer cost required to be provided under subparagraph (A) for such taxable year."

Prior to amendment, subpara. (e)(1)(B) read as follows:

"(B) Reductions for amounts previously set aside. The amount determined under subparagraph (A) shall be reduced by any amount previously contributed to a health benefits account or welfare benefit fund (as defined in section 419(e)(1)) to pay for the qualified current retiree health liabilities. The portion of any reserves remaining as of the close of December 31, 1990, shall be allocated on a pro rata basis to qualified current retiree health liabilities."

—P.L. 103-465, Sec. 731(c)(3), substituted "and shall not be subject to the minimum benefit requirements of subsection (c)(3)" for "or in calculating applicable employer cost under subsection (c)(3)(B)" in subpara. (e)(1)(D), effective for tax. yrs. begin. after 12/31/94.

In 1990, P.L. 101-508, Sec. 12011(a), added Code Sec. 420 as part of subpart E of Part I of subchapter D of chapter 1, effective for transfers in tax. yrs. begin. after 12/31/90, except as provided in Sec. 12011(c)(2) of this Act, which reads as follows:

"(2) Waiver of estimated tax penalties.—No addition to tax shall be made under section 6654 or section 6655 of the Internal Revenue Code of 1986 for the taxable year preceding the taxpayer's 1st taxable year beginning after December 31, 1990, with respect to any underpayment to the extent such underpayment was created or increased by reason of section 420(b)(4)(B) of such Code (as added by subsection (a) [Sec. 12011(a)])."

PART II.—CERTAIN STOCK OPTIONS
Sec.
421. General rules.
422. Incentive stock options.
423. Employee stock purchase plans.
424. Definitions and special rules.

In 1990, P.L. 101-508, Sec. 11801(b)(6), repealed items 422 and 424... Sec. 11801(c)(9)(A)(ii), redesignated item 422A as item 422 and redesignated item 425 as 424.

Prior to repeal, item 422 read as follows:
"422. Qualified stock options."
Prior to repeal, item 424 read as follows:
"424. Restricted stock options."

In 1981, P.L. 97-34, Sec. 251(b)(6), added item 422A.

In 1964, P.L. 88-272, Sec. 221(d)(1), amended Part II.
Prior to amendment, the table for Part II read as follows:
"PART II—MISCELLANEOUS PROVISIONS
"Sec.
"421. Employee stock options."

Sec. 421. General rules.
(a) Effect of qualifying transfer.

If a share of stock is transferred to an individual in a transfer in respect of which the requirements of section 422(a) or 423(a) are met—

(1) no income shall result at the time of the transfer of such share to the individual upon his exercise of the option with respect to such share;

(2) no deduction under section 162 (relating to trade or business expenses) shall be allowable at any time to the employer corporation, a parent or subsidiary corporation of such corporation, or a corporation issuing or assuming a stock option in a transaction to which section 424(a) applies, with respect to the share so transferred; and

(3) no amount other than the price paid under the option shall be considered as received by any of such corporations for the share so transferred.

(b) Effect of disqualifying disposition.

If the transfer of a share of stock to an individual pursuant to his exercise of an option would otherwise meet the requirements of section 422(a) or 423(a) except that there is a failure to meet any of the holding period requirements of section 422(a)(1) or 423(a)(1), then any increase in the income of such individual or deduction from the income of his employer corporation for the taxable year in which such exercise occurred attributable to such disposition, shall be treated as an increase in income or a deduction from income in the taxable year of such individual or of such employer corporation in which such disposition occurred. No amount shall be required to be deducted and withheld under chapter 24 with respect to any increase in income attributable to a disposition described in the preceding sentence.

(c) Exercise by estate.

(1) In general. If an option to which this part applies is exercised after the death of the employee by the estate of the decedent, or by a person who acquired the right to exercise such option by bequest or inheritance or by reason of the death of the decedent, the provisions of subsection (a) shall apply to the same extent as if the option had been exercised by the decedent, except that—

(A) the holding period and employment requirements of sections 422(a) and 423(a) shall not apply, and

(B) any transfer by the estate of stock acquired shall be considered a disposition of such stock for purposes of section 423(c).

(2) Deduction for estate tax. If an amount is required to be included under section 423(c) in gross income of the estate of the deceased employee or of a person described in paragraph (1), there shall be allowed to the estate or such person a deduction with respect to the estate tax attributable to the inclusion in the taxable estate of the deceased employee of the net value for estate tax purposes of the option. For this purpose, the deduction shall be determined under section 691(c) as if the option acquired

Code Sec. 421(c)(2) — Stock options

from the deceased employee were an item of gross income in respect of the decedent under section 691 and as if the amount includible in gross income under section 423(c) were an amount included in gross income under section 691 in respect of such item of gross income.

(3) Basis of shares acquired. In the case of a share of stock acquired by the exercise of an option to which paragraph (1) applies—

(A) the basis of such share shall include so much of the basis of the option as is attributable to such share; except that the basis of such share shall be reduced by the excess (if any) of (i) the amount which would have been includible in gross income under section 423(c) if the employee had exercised the option on the date of his death and had held the share acquired pursuant to such exercise at the time of his death, over (ii) the amount which is includible in gross income under such section; and

(B) the last sentence of section 423(c) shall apply only to the extent that the amount includible in gross income under such section exceeds so much of the basis of the option as is attributable to such share.

(d) Certain sales to comply with conflict-of-interest requirements.

If—

(1) a share of stock is transferred to an eligible person (as defined in section 1043(b)(1)) pursuant to such person's exercise of an option to which this part applies, and

(2) such share is disposed of by such person pursuant to a certificate of divestiture (as defined in section 1043(b)(2)), such disposition shall be treated as meeting the requirements of section 422(a)(1) or 423(a)(1), whichever is applicable.

In 2004, P.L. 108-357, Sec. 251(b), added "No amount shall be required to be deducted and withheld under chapter 24 with respect to any increase in income attributable to a disposition described in the preceding sentence." at the end of subsec. (b), effective for stock acquired pursuant to options exercised after 10/22/2004.

—P.L. 108-357, Sec. 905(a), added subsec. (d), effective for sales after 10/22/2004.

In 1990, P.L. 101-508, Sec. 11801(c)(9)(B)(i)(I), substituted "422(a) or 423(a)" for "422(a), 422A(a), 423(a), or 424(a)" in subsec. (a)... Sec. 11801(c)(9)(B)(i)(II), deleted "except as provided in section 422(c)(1)," before "no income" in para. (a)(1)... Sec. 11801(c)(9)(B)(i)(III), substituted "424(a)" for "425(a)" in para. (a)(2)... Sec. 11801(c)(9)(B)(ii)(I), substituted "422(a) or 423(a)" for "422(a), 422A(a), 423(a), or 424(a)" in subsec. (b)... Sec. 11801(c)(9)(B)(ii)(II), substituted "422(a)(1) or 423(a)(1)," for "422(a)(1), 422(A)(a)(1), 423(a)(1), or 424(a)(1)," in subsec. (b)... Sec. 11801(c)(9)(B)(iii)(I), substituted "422(a) and 423(a)" for "422(a), 422A(a), 423(a), and 424(a)" in subpara. (c)(1)(A)... Sec. 11801(c)(9)(B)(iii)(II), substituted "section 423(c)" for "sections 423(c) and 424(c)(1)" in subpara. (c)(1)(B) ... Sec. 11801(c)(9)(B)(iii)(III), substituted "423(c)" for "422(c)(1), 423(c), or 424(c)(1)" each place it appeared in para. (c)(2) and subpara. (c)(3)(A)... Sec. 11801(c)(9)(B)(iii)(IV), substituted "section 423(c)" for "sections 422(c)(1), 423(c), and 424(c)(1)" in subpara. (c)(3)(B)... Sec. 11801(c)(9)(iii)(V), substituted "such section" for "such sections" in subpara. (c)(3)(B), effective 11/5/90, except as provided in Sec. 11821(b) of this Act, which reads as follows:

"(b) Savings provision.—If—

"(1) any provision amended or repealed by this part applied to—

"(A) any transaction occurring before the date of the enactment of this Act [11/5/90],

"(B) any property acquired before such date of enactment [11/5/90], or

"(C) any item of income, loss, deduction, or credit taken into account before such date of enactment [11/5/90], and

"(2) the treatment of such transaction, property, or item under such provision would (without regard to the amendments made by this part) affect liability for tax for periods ending after such date of enactment [11/5/90], nothing in the amendments made by this part shall be construed to affect the treatment of such transaction, property, or item for purposes of determining liability for tax for periods ending after such date of enactment [11/5/90]."

In 1981, P.L. 97-34, Sec. 251(b)(1)(A), added "422A(a)" after "422(a)" in subsecs. (a), (b), and subpara. (c)(1)(A)... Sec. 251(b)(1)(B), added "422A(a)(1)" after "422(a)(1)" in subsec. (b), effective for options granted on or after 1/1/76, and exercised on or after 1/1/81. For election and designation of options and changes in terms of options, see Secs. 251(c)(1)(B) and (c)(2) of this Act reproduced in note following Code Sec. 422A.

In 1964, P.L. 88-272, Sec. 221, amended Code Sec. 421, effective as provided in Sec. 221(e) of this Act which reads as follows:

"(e) Effective dates and transition rules.—

"(1) Except as provided in paragraphs (2) and (3), the amendments made by this section shall apply to taxable years ending after December 31, 1963.

"(2) The amendments made by paragraphs (1) and (3) of subsection (b), and paragraph (2) of subsection (c) of section 6652(a) of the Internal Revenue Code of 1954 (as amended by paragraph (2) of subsection (b)), shall apply to stock transferred pursuant to options exercised on or after January 1, 1964.

"(3) In the case of an option granted after December 31, 1963, and before January 1, 1965—

"(A) paragraphs (1) and (2) of section 422(b) of the Internal Revenue Code of 1954 (as added by subsection (a)) shall not apply, and

"(B) paragraph (1) of section 425(h) of such Code (as added by subsection (a)) shall not apply to any change in the terms of such option made before January 1, 1965, to permit such option to qualify under paragraphs (3), (4), and (5) of such section 422(b)."

Prior to amendment, Code Sec. 421 read as follows:

"SEC. 421. EMPLOYEE STOCK OPTIONS.

"(a) Treatment of restricted stock options.

"If a share of stock is transferred to an individual pursuant to his exercise after 1949 of a restricted stock option, and no disposition of such share is made by him within 2 years from the date of the granting of the option nor within 6 months after the transfer of such share to him—

"(1) no income shall result at the time of the transfer of such share to the individual upon his exercise of the option with respect to such share;

"(2) no deduction under section 162 (relating to trade or business expenses) shall be allowable at any time to the employer corporation, a parent or subsidiary corporation of such corporation, or a corporation issuing or assuming a stock option in a transaction to which subsection (g) is applicable, with respect to the share so transferred; and

"(3) no amount other than the price paid under the option shall be considered as received by any of such corporations for the share so transferred. This subsection and subsection (b) shall not apply unless (A) the individual, at the time he exercises the restricted stock option, is an employee of either the corporation granting such option, a parent or subsidiary corporation of such corporation, or a corporation or a parent or subsidiary of such corporation issuing or assuming a stock option in a transaction to which subsection (g) is applicable, or (B) the option is exercised by him within 3 months after the date he ceases to be an employee of such corporations.

In applying paragraphs (2) and (3) of subsection (d) for purposes of the preceding sentence, there shall be substituted for the term 'employer corporation' wherever it appears in such paragraphs the term 'grantor corporation', or the term 'corporation issuing or assuming a stock option in a transaction to which subsection (g) is applicable', as the case may be.

"(b) Special rule where option price is between 85 percent and 95 percent of value of stock.

"If no disposition of a share of stock acquired by an individual on his exercise after 1949 of a restricted stock option is made by him within 2 years from the date of the granting of the option nor within 6 months after the transfer of such share to him, but, at the time the restricted stock option was granted, the option price (computed under subparagraph (d)(1)(A)) was less than 95 percent of the fair market value at such time of such share, then, in the event of any disposition of such share by him, or in the event of his death (whenever occurring) while owning such share, there shall be included as compensation (and not as gain upon the sale or exchange of a capital asset) in his gross income, for the taxable year in which falls the date of such disposition or for the taxable year closing with his death, whichever applies—

"(1) in the case of a share of stock acquired under an option qualifying under clause (i) of subparagraph (d)(1)(A), an amount equal to the amount (if any) by which the option price is exceeded by the lesser of—

"(A) the fair market value of the share at the time of such disposition or death, or

"(B) the fair market value of the share at the time the option was granted; or

"(2) in the case of stock acquired under an option qualifying under clause (ii) of subparagraph (d)(1)(A), an amount equal to the lesser of—

"(A) the excess of the fair market value of the share at the time of such disposition or death over the price paid under the option, or

"(B) the excess of the fair market value of the share at the time the option was granted over the option price (computed as if the option had been exercised at such time).

In the case of the disposition of such share by the individual, the basis of the share in his hands at the time of such disposition shall be increased by an amount equal to the amount so includible in his gross income.

"(c) Acquisition of new stock.

"If stock is received by an individual in a distribution to which section 305, 354, 355, 356, or 1036, or so much of section 1031 as relates to section 1036, applies and such distribution was made with respect to stock transferred to him upon his exercise of the option, such stock shall be considered as having been transferred to him on his exercise of such option. A similar rule shall be applied in the case of a series of such distributions.

"(d) Definitions.

"For purposes of this section—

"(1) Restricted stock option. The term 'restricted stock option' means an option granted after February 26, 1945, to an individual, for any reason connected with his employment by a corporation, if granted by the employer corporation or its

Stock options   Code Sec. 422(a)

parent or subsidiary corporation, to purchase stock of any of such corporations, but only if—

"(A) at the time such option is granted—

"(i) the option price is at least 85 percent of the fair market value at such time of the stock subject to the option, or

"(ii) in the case of a variable price option, the option price (computed as if the option had been exercised when granted) is at least 85 percent of the fair market value of the stock at the time such option is granted; and

"(B) such option by its terms is not transferable by such individual otherwise than by will or the laws of descent and distribution, and is exercisable, during his lifetime, only by him; and

"(C) such individual, at the time the option is granted, does not own stock possessing more than 10 percent of the total combined voting power of all classes of stock of the employer corporation or of its parent or subsidiary corporation. This subparagraph shall not apply if at the time such option is granted the option price is at least 110 percent of the fair market value of the stock subject to the option and such option either by its terms is not exercisable after the expiration of 5 years from the date such option is granted or is exercised within one year after the date of enactment of this title. For purposes of this subparagraph—

"(i) such individual shall be considered as owning the stock owned, directly or indirectly, by or for his brothers and sisters (whether by the whole or half blood), spouse, ancestors, and lineal descendants; and

"(ii) stock owned, directly or indirectly, by or for a corporation, partnership, estate, or trust, shall be considered as being owned proportionately by or for its shareholders, partners, or beneficiaries; and

"(D) such option by its terms is not exercisable after the expiration of 10 years from the date such option is granted, if such option has been granted on or after June 22, 1954.

"(2) Parent corporation. The term 'parent corporation' means any corporation (other than the employer corporation) in an unbroken chain of corporations ending with the employer corporation if, at the time of the granting of the option, each of the corporations other than the employer corporation owns stock possessing 50 percent or more of the total combined voting power of all classes of stock in one of the other corporations in such chain.

"(3) Subsidiary corporation. The term 'subsidiary corporation' means any corporation (other than the employer corporation) in an unbroken chain of corporations beginning with the employer corporation if, at the time of the granting of the option each of the corporations other than the last corporation in the unbroken chain owns stock possessing 50 percent or more of the total combined voting power of all classes of stock in one of the other corporations in such chain.

"(4) Disposition.—

"(A) General rule. Except as provided in subparagraph (B), the term 'disposition' includes a sale, exchange, gift, or a transfer of legal title, but does not include—

"(i) a transfer from a decedent to an estate or a transfer by bequest or inheritance;

"(ii) an exchange to which section 354, 355, 356, or 1036 (or so much of section 1031 as relates to section 1036) applies; or

"(iii) a mere pledge or hypothecation.

"(B) Joint tenancy. The acquisition of a share of stock in the name of the employee and another jointly with the right of survivorship or a subsequent transfer of a share of stock into such joint ownership shall not be deemed a disposition, but a termination of such joint tenancy (except to the extent such employee acquires ownership of such stock) shall be treated as a disposition by him occurring at the time such joint tenancy is terminated.

"(5) Stockholder approval. If the grant of an option is subject to approval by stockholders, the date of grant of the option shall be determined as if the option had not been subject to such approval.

"(6) Exercise by estate.—

"(A) In general. If a restricted stock option is exercised subsequent to the death of the employee by the estate of the decedent, or by a person who acquired the right to exercise such option by bequest or inheritance or by reason of the death of the decedent, the provisions of this section shall apply to the same extent as if the option had been exercised by the decedent, except that—

"(i) the holding period and employment requirements of subsection (a) shall not apply, and

"(ii) any transfer by the estate of stock acquired shall be considered a disposition of such stock for purposes of subsection (b).

"(B) Deduction for estate tax. If an amount is required to be included under subsection (b) in gross income of the estate of the deceased employee or of a person described in subparagraph (A), there shall be allowed to the estate or such person a deduction with respect to the estate tax attributable to the inclusion in the taxable estate of the deceased employee of the net value for estate tax purposes of the restricted stock option. For this purpose, the deduction shall be determined under section 691 (c) as if the option acquired from the deceased employee were an item of gross income in respect of the decedent under section 691 and as if the amount includible in gross income under subsection (b) of this section were an amount included in gross income under section 691 in respect of such item of gross income.

"(C) Basis of shares acquired. In the case of a share of stock acquired by the exercise of an option to which subparagraph (A) applies—

"(i) the basis of such share shall include so much of the basis of the option as is attributable to such share; except that the basis of such share shall be reduced by the excess (if any) of the amount, which would have been includible in gross income under subsection (b) if the employee had exercised the option and held such share at the time of his death, over the amount which is includible in gross income under subsection (b); and

"(ii) the last sentence of subsection (b) shall apply only to the extent that the amount includible in gross income under such subsection exceeds so much of the basis of the option as is attributable to such share.

"(7) Variable price option. The term 'variable price option' means an option under which the purchase price of the stock is fixed or determinable under a formula in which the only variable is the fair market value of the stock at any time during a period of 6 months which includes the time the option is exercised; except that in the case of options granted after September 30, 1958, such term does not include any such option in which such formula provides for determining such price by reference to the fair market value of the stock at any time before the option is exercised if such value may be greater than the average fair market value of the stock during the calendar month in which the option is exercised.

"(e) Modification, extension, or renewal of option.—

"(1) Rules of application. For purposes of subsection (d), if the terms of any option to purchase stock are modified, extended, or renewed, the following rules shall be applied with respect to transfers of stock made on the exercise of the option after the making of such modification, extension, or renewal—

"(A) such modification, extension, or renewal shall be considered as the granting of a new option,

"(B) the fair market value of such stock at the time of the granting of such option shall be considered as—

"(i) the fair market value of such stock on the date of the original granting of the option,

"(ii) the fair market value of such stock on the date of the making of such modification, extension, or renewal, or

"(iii) the fair market value of such stock at the time of the making of any intervening modification, extension, or renewal,

whichever is the highest.

Subparagraph (B) shall not apply if the aggregate of the monthly average fair market values of the stock subject to the option for the 12 consecutive calendar months before the date of the modification, extension, or renewal, divided by 12, is an amount less than 80 percent of the fair market value of such stock on the date of the original granting of the option or the date of the making of any intervening modification, extension, or renewal, whichever is the highest.

"(2) Definition of modification. The term 'modification' means any change in the terms of the option which gives the employee additional benefits under the option, but such term shall not include a change in the terms of the option—

"(A) attributable to the issuance or assumption of an option under subsection (g); or

"(B) to permit the option to qualify under subsection (d)(1)(B).

If an option is exercisable after the expiration of 10 years from the date such option is granted, subparagraph (B) shall not apply unless the terms of the option are also changed to make it not exercisable after the expiration of such period.

"(f) Effect of disqualifying disposition.

"If a share of stock, acquired by an individual pursuant to his exercise of a restricted stock option, is disposed of by him within 2 years from the date of the granting of the option or within 6 months after the transfer of such share to him, then any increase in the income of such individual or deduction from the income of his employer corporation for the taxable year in which such exercise occurred attributable to such disposition, shall be treated as an increase in income or a deduction from income in the taxable year of such individual or of such employer corporation in which such disposition occurred.

"(g) Corporate reorganizations, liquidations, etc.

"For purposes of this section, the term 'issuing or assuming a stock option in a transaction to which subsection (g) is applicable' means a substitution of a new option for the old option, or an assumption of the old option, by an employer corporation, or a parent or subsidiary of such corporation, by reason of a corporate merger, consolidation, acquisition of property or stock, separation, reorganization, or liquidation, if—

"(1) the excess of the aggregate fair market value of the shares subject to the option immediately after the substitution or assumption over the aggregate option price of such shares is not more than the excess of the aggregate fair market value of all shares subject to the option immediately before such substitution or assumption over the aggregate option price of such shares, and

"(2) the new option or the assumption of the old option does not give the employee additional benefits which he did not have under the old option. For purposes of this subsection, the parent-subsidiary relationship shall be determined at the time of any such transaction under this subsection."

In 1958, P.L. 85-866, Sec. 25, had added the last sentence in subsec. (a) of former Code Sec. 421, for all '54 Code yrs. . . . Sec. 26, had added subsec. (d)(7) and substituted, in subsec. (d)(1)(A)(ii), "in the case of a variable price option" for "in case the purchase price of the stock under the option is fixed or determinable under a formula in which the only variable is the value of the stock at any time during a period of 6 months which includes the time the option is exercised" and inserted "fair" preceding "market value", for tax. yrs. end. after 9/30/58.

—P.L. 85-320, had added subpara. (d)(6)(C) to former Code Sec. 421, for tax. yrs. end. after '56 but only in case of employees dying after that date.

Sec. 422. Incentive stock options.
(a) In general.

Section 421(a) shall apply with respect to the transfer of a share of stock to an individual pursuant to his exercise of an incentive stock option if—

(1) no disposition of such share is made by him within 2 years from the date of the granting of the option nor within 1 year after the transfer of such share to him, and

(2) at all times during the period beginning on the date of the granting of the option and ending on the day 3 months before the date of such exercise, such individual was an employee of either the corporation granting such option, a parent or subsidiary corporation of such corporation, or a corporation or a parent or subsidiary corporation of such corporation issuing or assuming a stock option in a transaction to which section 424(a) applies.

(b) Incentive stock option.

For purposes of this part, the term "incentive stock option" means an option granted to an individual for any reason connected with his employment by a corporation, if granted by the employer corporation or its parent or subsidiary corporation, to purchase stock of any of such corporations, but only if—

(1) the option is granted pursuant to a plan which includes the aggregate number of shares which may be issued under options and the employees (or class of employees) eligible to receive options, and which is approved by the stockholders of the granting corporation within 12 months before or after the date such plan is adopted;

(2) such option is granted within 10 years from the date such plan is adopted, or the date such plan is approved by the stockholders, whichever is earlier;

(3) such option by its terms is not exercisable after the expiration of 10 years from the date such option is granted;

(4) the option price is not less than the fair market value of the stock at the time such option is granted;

(5) such option by its terms is not transferable by such individual otherwise than by will or the laws of descent and distribution, and is exercisable, during his lifetime, only by him; and

(6) such individual, at the time the option is granted, does not own stock possessing more than 10 percent of the total combined voting power of all classes of stock of the employer corporation or of its parent or subsidiary corporation.

Such term shall not include any option if (as of the time the option is granted) the terms of such option provide that it will not be treated as an incentive stock option.

(c) Special rules.

(1) Good faith efforts to value stock. If a share of stock is transferred pursuant to the exercise by an individual of an option which would fail to qualify as an incentive stock option under subsection (b) because there was a failure in an attempt, made in good faith, to meet the requirement of subsection (b)(4), the requirement of subsection (b)(4) shall be considered to have been met. To the extent provided in regulations by the Secretary, a similar rule shall apply for purposes of subsection (d).

(2) Certain disqualifying dispositions where amount realized is less than value at exercise. If—

(A) an individual who has acquired a share of stock by the exercise of an incentive stock option makes a disposition of such share within either of the periods described in subsection (a)(1), and

(B) such disposition is a sale or exchange with respect to which a loss (if sustained) would be recognized to such individual,

then the amount which is includible in the gross income of such individual, and the amount which is deductible from the income of his employer corporation, as compensation attributable to the exercise of such option shall not exceed the excess (if any) of the amount realized on such sale or exchange over the adjusted basis of such share.

(3) Certain transfers by insolvent individuals. If an insolvent individual holds a share of stock acquired pursuant to his exercise of an incentive stock option, and if such share is transferred to a trustee, receiver, or other similar fiduciary in any proceeding under title 11 or any other similar insolvency proceeding, neither such transfer, nor any other transfer of such share for the benefit of his creditors in such proceeding, shall constitute a disposition of such share for purposes of subsection (a)(1).

(4) Permissible provisions. An option which meets the requirements of subsection (b) shall be treated as an incentive stock option even if—

(A) the employee may pay for the stock with stock of the corporation granting the option,

(B) the employee has a right to receive property at the time of exercise of the option, or

(C) the option is subject to any condition not inconsistent with the provisions of subsection (b).

Subparagraph (B) shall apply to a transfer of property (other than cash) only if section 83 applies to the property so transferred.

(5) 10-percent shareholder rule. Subsection (b)(6) shall not apply if at the time such option is granted the option price is at least 110 percent of the fair market value of the stock subject to the option and such option by its terms is not exercisable after the expiration of 5 years from the date such option is granted.

(6) Special rule when disabled. For purposes of subsection (a)(2), in the case of an employee who is disabled (within the meaning of section 22(e)(3)), the 3-month period of subsection (a)(2) shall be 1 year.

(7) Fair market value. For purposes of this section, the fair market value of stock shall be determined without regard to any restriction other than a restriction which, by its terms, will never lapse.

(d) $100,000 per year limitation.

(1) In general. To the extent that the aggregate fair market value of stock with respect to which incentive stock options (determined without regard to this subsection) are exercisable for the 1st time by any individual during any calendar year (under all plans of the individual's employer corporation and its parent and subsidiary corporations) exceeds $100,000, such options shall be treated as options which are not incentive stock options.

(2) Ordering rule. Paragraph (1) shall be applied by taking options into account in the order in which they were granted.

(3) Determination of fair market value. For purposes of paragraph (1), the fair market value of any stock shall be determined as of the time the option with respect to such stock is granted.

In **1990**, P.L. 101-508, Sec. 11801(c)(9)(A)(i), redesignated Code Sec. 422A as Code Sec. 422 . . . Sec. 11801(c)(9)(C)(ii), substituted "424(a)" for "425(a)" in para. (a)(2) . . . Sec. 11801(c)(9)(C)(ii), deleted para. (c)(5) and redesignated paras. (c)(6), (c)(7) and (c)(8) as paras. (c)(5), (c)(6) and (c)(7), effective 11/5/90, except as provided in Sec. 11821(b) of this Act which reads as follows:

"*(b) Savings provision.*

"If—

"(1) any provision amended or repealed by this part applied to—

"(A) any transaction occurring before the date of the enactment of this Act [11/5/90],

"(B) any property acquired before such date of enactment [11/5/90], or

"(C) any item of income, loss, deduction, or credit taken into account before such date of enactment [11/5/90], and

"(2) the treatment of such transaction, property, or item under such provision would (without regard to the amendments made by this part) affect liability for tax for periods ending after such date of enactment [11/5/90], nothing in the amendments made by this part shall be construed to affect the treatment of such transaction, property, or item for purposes of determining liability for tax for periods ending after such date of enactment [11/5/90]."

Prior to deletion, para. (c)(5) read as follows:

"(5) Coordination with sections 422 and 424. Sections 422 and 424 shall not apply to an incentive stock option."

In 1988, P.L. 100-647, Sec. 1003(d)(1)(A), added a sentence to the end of subsec. (b), effective for options granted after 12/31/86.

—P.L. 100-647, Sec. 1003(d)(1)(B), of this Act provides:

"(B) In the case of an option granted after December 31, 1986, and on or before the date of the enactment of this Act, such option shall not be treated as an incentive stock option if the terms of such option are amended before the date 90 days after such date of enactment to provide that such option will not be treated as an incentive stock option."

—P.L. 100-647, Sec. 1003(d)(2)(A), added subsec. (d) . . . Sec. 1003(d)(2)(B), added "and" at the end of para. (b)(5) and substituted a period for "; and" at the end of para. (b)(6) and deleted para. (b)(7) . . . Sec. 1003(d)(2)(C), substituted "subsection (d)" for "paragraph (7) of subsection (b)" in para. (c)(1), effective for options granted after 12/31/86.

Prior to deletion, para. (b)(7) read as follows:

"(7) under the terms of the plan, the aggregate fair market value (determined at the time the option is granted) of the stock with respect to which incentive stock options are exercisable for the 1st time by such individual during any calendar year (under all such plans of the individual's employer corporation and its parent and subsidiary corporations) shall not exceed $100,000."

In 1986, P.L. 99-514, Sec. 321(a), added "and" to the end of para. (b)(6), deleted paras. (b)(7) and (8), and added new para. (b)(7) . . . Sec. 321(b)(1), deleted, paras. (c)(4) and (7) and redesignated paras. (c)(5), (6), (8), (9), and (10) as paras. (c)(4), (5), (6), (7), and (8) . . . Sec. 321(b)(2), substituted "paragraph (7) of subsection (b)" for "paragraph (8) of subsection (b) and paragraph (4) of this subsection" in the last sentence of para. (c)(1), effective for options granted after 12/31/86.

Prior to amendment, paras. (b)(7) and (8) read as follows:

"(7) such option by its terms is not exercisable while there is outstanding (within the meaning of subsection (c)(7)) any incentive stock option which was granted, before the granting of such option, to such individual to purchase stock in his employer corporation or in a corporation which (at the time of the granting of such option) is a parent or subsidiary corporation of the employer corporation, or in a predecessor corporation of any of such corporations; and

"(8) in the case of an option granted after December 31, 1980, under the terms of the plan the aggregate fair market value (determined as of the time the option is granted) of the stock for which any employee may be granted incentive stock options in any calendar year (under all such plans of his employer corporation and its parent and subsidiary corporation) shall not exceed $100,000 plus any unused limit carryover to such year."

Prior to deletion, para. (c)(4) read as follows:

"(4) Carryover of unused limit.

"(A) In general. If—

"(i) $100,000 exceeds,

"(ii) the aggregate fair market value (determined as of the time the option is granted) of the stock for which an employee was granted incentive stock options in any calendar year after 1980 (under all plans described in subsection (b) of his employer corporation and its parent and subsidiary corporations),

one-half of such excess shall be unused limit carry-over to each of the 3 succeeding calendar years.

"(B) Amount carried to each year. The amount of the unused limit carryover from any calendar year which may be taken into account in any succeeding calendar year shall be the amount of such carryover reduced by the amount of such carryover which was used in prior calendar years.

"(C) Special rules. For purposes of subparagraph (B)

"(i) the amount of options granted during any calendar year shall be treated as first using up the $100,000 limitation of subsection (b)(8), and

"(ii) then shall be treated as using up unused limit carryovers to such year in the order of the calendar years in which the carryovers arose."

Prior to deletion, para. (c)(7) read as follows:

"(7) Options outstanding. For purposes of subsection (b)(7), any incentive stock option shall be treated as outstanding until such option is exercised in full or expires by reason of lapse of time."

—P.L. 99-514, Sec. 1847(b)(5), substituted "section 22(e)(3)" for "section 37(e)(3)" in para. (c)(9) [redesignated as para. (c)(7) by Sec. 321(b)(1)(B) of this Act, above], effective for tax. yrs. begin. after 12/31/83, and to carryback from tax yrs. begin. after 12/31/83.

In 1984, P.L. 98-369, Sec. 555(a)(1), added para. (c)(10), effective for options granted after 3/20/84, except (as provided in Sec. 555(c)(1) of the Act) that such para. (c)(10) shall not apply to 9/20/84 pursuant to a plan adopted or corporate action taken by the board of directors of the grantor corporation before 5/15/84.

—P.L. 98-369, Sec. 2662(f)(1), substituted "section 37(e)(3)" for "section 105(d)(4)" in para. (c)(9), effective generally for tax. yrs. begin. after 12/31/83.

In 1983, P.L. 97-448, Sec. 102(j)(1), substituted "granted incentive stock options" for "granted options" in para. (b)(8) . . . Sec. 102(j)(2)(A), added the last sentence to para. (c)(1) . . . Sec. 102(j)(2)(B), amended the heading for para. (c)(1) . . . Sec. 102(j)(3), substituted "either of the periods" for "the 2-year period" in subpara. (c)(2)(A) . . . Sec. 102(j)(4), substituted "granted incentive stock options" for "granted options" in clause (c)(4)(A)(ii), effective for options granted on or after 1/1/76, and exercised on or after 1/1/81.

Prior to amendment, the heading for para. (c)(1) read as follows:

"(1) Exercise of option when price is less than value of stock."

In 1981, P.L. 97-34, Sec. 251(a), added Code Sec. 422A, effective for options granted on or after 1/1/76, and exercised on or after 1/1/81, or outstanding on 1/1/81. Secs. 251(c)(1)(B) and (c)(2) of this Act provide:

"(B) Election and designation of options. In the case of an option granted before January 1, 1981, the amendments made by this section shall apply only if the corporation granting such option elects (in the manner and at the time prescribed by the Secretary of the Treasury or his delegate) to have the amendments made by this section apply to such option. The aggregate fair market value (determined at the time the option is granted) of the stock for which any employee was granted options (under all plans of his employer corporation and its parent and subsidiary corporations) to which the amendments made by this section apply by reason of this subparagraph shall not exceed $50,000 per calendar year and shall not exceed $200,000 in the aggregate.

"(2) Changes in terms of options. In the case of an option granted on or after January 1, 1976, and outstanding on the date of the enactment of this Act, paragraph (1) of section 425(h) of the Internal Revenue Code of 1954 shall not apply to any change in the terms of such option (or the terms of the plan under which granted, including shareholder approval) made within 1 year after such date of enactment to permit such option to qualify as a incentive stock option."

Sec. 422. Repealed.

In 1990, P.L. 101-508, Sec. 11801(a)(20), repealed Code Sec. 422, effective 11/5/90, except as provided in Sec. 11821(b) of this Act which reads as follows:

"(b) Savings provision.

"If—

"(1) any provision amended or repealed by this part applied to—

"(A) any transaction occurring before the date of the enactment of this Act [11/5/90],

"(B) any property acquired before such date of enactment [11/5/90], or

"(C) any item of income, loss, deduction, or credit taken into account before such date of enactment [11/5/90], and

"(2) the treament of such transaction, property, or item under such provision would (without regard to the amendments made by this part [11/5/90] affect liability for tax for periods ending after such date of enactment [11/5/90],

nothing in the amendments made by this part shall be construed to affect the treatment of such transaction, property, or item for purposes of determining liability for tax for periods ending after such date of enactment [11/5/90]."

Prior to repeal Code Sec. 422 read as follows:

"SEC. 422. QUALIFIED STOCK OPTIONS.

"(a) In general.

"Subject to the provisions of subsection (c)(1), section 421 (a) shall apply with respect to the transfer of a share of stock to an individual pursuant to his exercise of a qualified stock option if—

"(1) no disposition of such share is made by such individual within the 3-year period beginning on the day after the day of the transfer of such share, and

"(2) at all times during the period beginning with the date of the granting of the option and ending on the day 3 months before the date of such exercise, such individual was an employee of either the corporation granting such option, a parent or subsidiary corporation of such corporation, or a corporation or a parent or subsidiary corporation of such corporation issuing or assuming a stock option in a transaction to which section 425(a) applies.

"(b) Qualified stock option.

"For purposes of this part, the term 'qualified stock option' means an option granted to an individual after December 31, 1963 (other than a restricted stock option granted pursuant to a contract described in section 424(c)(3)(A)), and before May 21, 1976 (or, if it meets the requirements of subsection (c)(7), granted to an individual after May 20, 1976), for any reason connected with his employment by a corporation, if granted by the employer corporation or its parent or subsidiary corporation, to purchase stock of any of such corporations, but only if—

"(1) the option is granted pursuant to a plan which includes the aggregate number of shares which may be issued under options, and the employees (or class of employees) eligible to receive options, and which is approved by the stockholders of the granting corporation within 12 months before or after the date such plan is adopted;

"(2) such option is granted within 10 years from the date such plan is adopted, or the date such plan is approved by the stockholders whichever is earlier;

"(3) such option by its terms is not exercisable after the expiration of 5 years from the date such option is granted;

"(4) except as provided in subsection (c)(1), the option price is not less than the fair market value of the stock at the time such option is granted;

"(5) such option by its terms is not exercisable while there is outstanding (within the meaning of subsection (c)(2)) any qualified stock option (or restricted stock option) which was granted, before the granting of such option, to such individual to purchase stock in his employer corporation or in a corporation which (at the time of the granting of such option) is a parent or subsidiary corporation of the employer corporation, or in a predecessor corporation of any of such corporations;

"(6) such option by its terms is not transferable by such individual otherwise than by will or the laws of descent and distribution, and is exercisable, during his lifetime, only by him; and

"(7) such individual, immediately after such option is granted, does not own stock possessing more than 5 percent of the total combined voting power or value of all classes of stock of the employer corporation or of its parent or subsidiary corporation; except that if the equity capital of such corporation or corporations (determined at the time the option is granted) is less than $2,000,000, then, for purposes of applying the limitation of this paragraph, there shall be added to such

Code Sec. 422 — Stock options

5 percent the percentage (not higher than 5 percent) which bears the same ratio to 5 percent as the difference between such equity capital and $2,000,000 bears to $1,000,000.

"(c) *Special rules.*

"(1) Exercise of option when price is less than value of stock. If a share of stock is transferred pursuant to the exercise by an individual of an option which fails to qualify as a qualified stock option under subsection (b) because there was a failure in an attempt, made in good faith, to meet the requirement of subsection (b)(4), the requirement of subsection (b)(4) shall be considered to have been met, but there shall be included as compensation (and not as gain upon the sale or exchange of a capital asset) in his gross income for the taxable year in which such option is exercised, an amount equal to the lesser of—

(A) 150 percent of the difference between the option price and the fair market value of the share at the time the option was granted, or

(B) the difference between the option price and the fair market value of the share at the time of such exercise.

"The basis of the share acquired shall be increased by an amount equal to the amount included in his gross income under this paragraph in the taxable year in which the exercise occurred.

"(2) Certain options treated as outstanding. For purposes of subsection (b)(5)—

(A) any restricted stock option which is not terminated before January 1, 1965, and

(B) any qualified stock option granted after December 31, 1963,

"shall be treated as outstanding until such option is exercised in full or expires by reason of the lapse of time. For purposes of the preceding sentence, a restricted stock option granted before January 1, 1964, shall not be treated as outstanding for any period before the first day on which (under the terms of such option) it may be exercised.

"(3) Options granted to certain shareholders.

"For purposes of subsection (b)(7)—

(A) the term 'equity capital' means—

"(i) in the case of one corporation, the sum of its money and other property (in an amount equal to the adjusted basis of such property for determining gain), less the amount of its indebtedness (other than indebtedness to shareholders), and

"(ii) in the case of a group of corporations consisting of a parent and its subsidiary corporations, the sum of the equity capital of each of such corporations adjusted, under regulations prescribed by the Secretary, to eliminate the effect of intercorporate ownership and transactions among such corporations;

(B) the rules of section 425(d) shall apply in determining the stock ownership of the individual; and

(C) stock which the individual may purchase under outstanding options shall be treated as stock owned by such individual.

"If an individual is granted an option which permits him to purchase stock in excess of the limitation of subsection (b)(7) (determined by applying the rules of this paragraph), such option shall be treated as meeting the requirement of subsection (b)(7) to the extent that such individual could, if the option were fully exercised at the time of grant, purchase stock under such option without exceeding such limitation. The portion of such option which is treated as meeting the requirement of subsection (b) (7) shall be deemed to be that portion of the option which is first exercised.

"(4) Certain disqualifying dispositions where amount realized is less than value at exercise.

" If —

"(A) an individual who has acquired a share of stock by the exercise of a qualified stock option makes a disposition of such share within the 3-year period described in subsection (a)(1), and

"(B) such disposition is a sale or exchange with respect to which a loss (if sustained) would be recognized to such individual,

then the amount which is includible in the gross income of such individual, and the amount which is deductible from the income of his employer corporation, as compensation attributable to the exercise of such option shall not exceed the excess (if any) of the amount realized on such sale or exchange over the adjusted basis of such share.

"(5) Certain transfers by insolvent individuals. If an insolvent individual holds a share of stock acquired pursuant to his exercise of a qualified stock option, and if such share is transferred to a trustee, receiver, or other similar fiduciary, in any proceeding under title 11 of the United States Code or any other similar insolvency proceeding, neither such transfer, nor any other transfer of such share for the benefit of his creditors in such proceeding, shall constitute a 'disposition of such share' for purposes of subsection (a)(1).

"(6) Application of subsection (b)(5) where options are for stock of same class in same corporation. The requirement of subsection (b)(5) shall be considered to have been met in the case of any option (referred to in this paragraph as 'new option') granted to an individual if—

"(A) the new option and all outstanding options referred to in subsection (b)(5) are to purchase stock of the same class in the same corporation, and

"(B) the new option by its terms is not exercisable while there is outstanding (within the meaning of paragraph (2)) any qualified stock option (or restricted stock option) which was granted, before the granting of the new option, to such individual to purchase stock in such corporation at a price (determined as of the date of grant of the new option) higher than the option price of the new option.

"(7) Certain options granted after May 20, 1976. For purposes of subsection (b), an option granted after May 20, 1976, meets the requirements of this paragraph —

"(A) if such option is granted to an individual pursuant to a written plan adopted before May 21, 1976, or

(B) if such option is a new option substituted, in a transaction to which section 425(a) applies, for an old option which was granted before May 21, 1976, or which met the requirements of subparagraph (A).

"An option described in the preceding sentence shall be treated as ceasing to meet the requirements of this paragraph if it is not exercised before May 21, 1981."

In **1980**, P.L. 96-589, Sec. 6(i)(3), substituted "under title 11 of the United States Code" for "under the Bankruptcy Act" in para. (c)(5), effective on 10/1/79, except for any proceeding under the Bankruptcy Act begun before 10/1/79. Sec. 7(g) of this Act provides:

"(g) *Definitions.*

"For purposes of this section—

"(1) Bankruptcy case. The term 'bankruptcy case' means any case under title 11 of the United States Code (as recodified by P.L. 95-598).

"(2) Similar judicial proceeding. The term 'similar judicial proceeding' means a receivership, foreclosure, or similar proceeding in a Federal or State court (as modified by section 368(a)(3)(D) of the Internal Revenue Code of 1954)."

In **1976**, P.L. 94-455, Sec. 603(a), added "and before May 21, 1976 (or, if it meets the requirements of subsection (c)(7), granted to an individual after May 20, 1976)," after "section 424(c)(3)(A))," in subsec. (b) . . . Sec. 603(b), added para. (c)(7), effective for tax. yrs. end. after 12/31/75.

— P.L. 94-455, Sec. 1906(b)(13)(A), substituted "Secretary" for "Secretary or his delegate" in Code Sec. 422, effective for tax. yrs. begin. after 12/31/76.

In **1964**, P.L. 88-272, Sec. 221(a), added Code Sec. 422. See note at end of Code Sec. 421.

Sec. 423. Employee stock purchase plans.

(a) General rule.

Section 421(a) shall apply with respect to the transfer of a share of stock to an individual pursuant to his exercise of an option granted after December 31, 1963, under an employee stock purchase plan (as defined in subsection (b)) if—

(1) no disposition of such share is made by him within 2 years after the date of the granting of the option nor within 1 year after the transfer of such share to him; and

(2) at all times during the period beginning with the date of the granting of the option and ending on the day 3 months before the date of such exercise, he is an employee of the corporation granting such option, a parent or subsidiary corporation of such corporation, or a corporation or a parent or subsidiary corporation of such corporation issuing or assuming a stock option in a transaction to which section 424(a) applies.

(b) Employee stock purchase plan.

For purposes of this part, the term "employee stock purchase plan" means a plan which meets the following requirements:

(1) the plan provides that options are to be granted only to employees of the employer corporation or of its parent or subsidiary corporation to purchase stock in any such corporation;

(2) such plan is approved by the stockholders of the granting corporation within 12 months before or after the date such plan is adopted;

(3) under the terms of the plan, no employee can be granted an option if such employee, immediately after the option is granted, owns stock possessing 5 percent or more of the total combined voting power or value of all classes of stock of the employer corporation or of its parent or subsidiary corporation. For purposes of this paragraph, the rules of section 424(d) shall apply in determining the stock ownership of an individual, and stock which the employee may purchase under outstanding options shall be treated as stock owned by the employee;

(4) under the terms of the plan, options are to be granted to all employees of any corporation whose employees are granted any of such options by reason of their employment by such corporation, except that there may be excluded—

(A) employees who have been employed less than 2 years,

(B) employees whose customary employment is 20 hours or less per week,
(C) employees whose customary employment is for not more than 5 months in any calendar year, and
(D) highly compensated employees (within the meaning of section 414(q));

(5) under the terms of the plan, all employees granted such options shall have the same rights and privileges, except that the amount of stock which may be purchased by any employee under such option may bear a uniform relationship to the total compensation, or the basic or regular rate of compensation, of employees, and the plan may provide that no employee may purchase more than a maximum amount of stock fixed under the plan;

(6) under the terms of the plan, the option price is not less than the lesser of—
(A) an amount equal to 85 percent of the fair market value of the stock at the time such option is granted, or
(B) an amount which under the terms of the option may not be less than 85 percent of the fair market value of the stock at the time such option is exercised;

(7) under the terms of the plan, such option cannot be exercised after the expiration of—
(A) 5 years from the date such option is granted if, under the terms of such plan, the option price is to be not less than 85 percent of the fair market value of such stock at the time of the exercise of the option, or
(B) 27 months from the date such option is granted, if the option price is not determinable in the manner described in subparagraph (A);

(8) under the terms of the plan, no employee may be granted an option which permits his rights to purchase stock under all such plans of his employer corporation and its parent and subsidiary corporations to accrue at a rate which exceeds $25,000 of fair market value of such stock (determined at the time such option is granted) for each calendar year in which such option is outstanding at any time. For purposes of this paragraph—
(A) the right to purchase stock under an option accrues when the option (or any portion thereof) first becomes exercisable during the calendar year;
(B) the right to purchase stock under an option accrues at the rate provided in the option, but in no case may such rate exceed $25,000 of fair market value of such stock (determined at the time such option is granted) for any one calendar year; and
(C) a right to purchase stock which has accrued under one option granted pursuant to the plan may not be carried over to any other option; and

(9) under the terms of the plan, such option is not transferable by such individual otherwise than by will or the laws of descent and distribution, and is exercisable, during his lifetime, only by him.

For purposes of paragraphs (3) to (9), inclusive, where additional terms are contained in an offering made under a plan, such additional terms shall, with respect to options exercised under such offering, be treated as a part of the terms of such plan.

(c) Special rule where option price is between 85 percent and 100 percent of value of stock.

If the option price of a share of stock acquired by an individual pursuant to a transfer to which subsection (a) applies was less than 100 percent of the fair market value of such share at the time such option was granted, then, in the event of any disposition of such share by him which meets the holding period requirements of subsection (a), or in the event of his death (whenever occurring) while owning such share, there shall be included as compensation (and not as gain upon the sale or exchange of a capital asset) in his gross income, for the taxable year in which falls the date of such disposition or for the taxable year closing with his death, whichever applies, an amount equal to the lesser of—

(1) the excess of the fair market value of the share at the time of such disposition or death over the amount paid for the share under the option, or
(2) the excess of the fair market value of the share at the time the option was granted over the option price.

If the option price is not fixed or determinable at the time the option is granted, then for purposes of this subsection, the option price shall be determined as if the option were exercised at such time. In the case of the disposition of such share by the individual, the basis of the share in his hands at the time of such disposition shall be increased by an amount equal to the amount so includible in his gross income. No amount shall be required to be deducted and withheld under chapter 24 with respect to any amount treated as compensation under this subsection.

In 2004, P.L. 108-357, Sec. 251(c), added "No amount shall be required to be deducted and withheld under chapter 24 with respect to any amount treated as compensation under this subsection." at the end of subsec. (c), effective for stock acquired pursuant to options exercised after 10/22/2004.

In 1990, P.L. 101-508, Sec. 11801(c)(9)(D)(i), deleted "(other than a restricted stock option granted pursuant to a plan described in section 424(c)(3)(B))" after "December 31, 1963" in subsec. (a)... Sec. 11801(c)(9)(D)(ii), substituted "424(a)" for "425(a)" in para. (a)(2)... Sec. 11801(c)(9)(E), substituted "424(d)" for "425(d)" in para. (b)(3), effective 11/5/90 except as provided in Sec. 11821(b) of this Act, reproduced in note following Code Sec. 422.

In 1986, P.L. 99-514, Sec. 1114(b)(13), substituted "highly compensated employees (within the meaning of section 414(q))" for "officers, persons whose principal duties consist of supervising the work of other employees, or highly compensated employees" in subsec. (b)(4)(D), effective for yrs. begin. after 12/31/86.

In 1984, P.L. 98-369, Sec. 1001(b)(5), substituted "6 months" for "1 year" in para. (a)(I), effective for property acquired after 6/22/84 and before 1/1/88.

In 1976, P.L. 94-455, Sec. 1402(b)(1)(E), substituted "9 months" for "6 months" in subsec. (a)... Sec. 1402(b)(2), substituted "1 year" for "9 months" in subsec. (a), effective for tax. yrs. begin. after '77.

In 1964, P.L. 88-272, Sec. 221(a), added Code Sec. 423, effective for tax yrs. after 12/31/63. See note following Code Sec. 421.

Sec. 424. Definitions and special rules.
(a) Corporate reorganizations, liquidations, etc.

For purposes of this part, the term "issuing or assuming a stock option in a transaction to which section 424(a) applies" means a substitution of a new option for the old option, or an assumption of the old option, by an employer corporation, or a parent or subsidiary of such corporation, by reason of a corporate merger, consolidation, acquisition of property or stock, separation, reorganization, or liquidation, if—

(1) the excess of the aggregate fair market value of the shares subject to the option immediately after the substitution or assumption over the aggregate option price of such shares is not more than the excess of the aggregate fair market value of all shares subject to the option immediately before such substitution or assumption over the aggregate option price of such shares, and
(2) the new option or the assumption of the old option does not give the employee additional benefits which he did not have under the old option.

For purposes of this subsection, the parent-subsidiary relationship shall be determined at the time of any such transaction under this subsection.

(b) Acquisition of new stock.

For purposes of this part, if stock is received by an individual in a distribution to which section 305, 354, 355, 356, or 1036 (or so much of section 1031 as relates to section

1036) applies, and such distribution was made with respect to stock transferred to him upon his exercise of the option, such stock shall be considered as having been transferred to him on his exercise of such option. A similar rule shall be applied in the case of a series of such distributions.

(c) Disposition.

(1) In general. Except as provided in paragraphs (2), (3), and (4), for purposes of this part, the term "disposition" includes a sale, exchange, gift, or a transfer of legal title, but does not include—

(A) a transfer from a decedent to an estate or a transfer by bequest or inheritance;

(B) an exchange to which section 354, 355, 356, or 1036 (or so much of section 1031 as relates to section 1036) applies; or

(C) a mere pledge or hypothecation.

(2) Joint tenancy. The acquisition of a share of stock in the name of the employee and another jointly with the right of survivorship or a subsequent transfer of a share of stock into such joint ownership shall not be deemed a disposition, but a termination of such joint tenancy (except to the extent such employee acquires ownership of such stock) shall be treated as a disposition by him occurring at the time such joint tenancy is terminated.

(3) Special rule where incentive stock is acquired through use of other statutory option stock.

(A) Nonrecognition sections not to apply. If—

(i) there is a transfer of statutory option stock in connection with the exercise of any incentive stock option, and

(ii) the applicable holding period requirements (under section 422(a)(1) or 423(a)(1)) are not met before such transfer,

then no section referred to in subparagraph (B) of paragraph (1) shall apply to such transfer.

(B) Statutory option stock. For purpose of subparagraph (A), the term "statutory option stock" means any stock acquired through the exercise of an incentive stock option or an option granted under an employee stock purchase plan.

(4) Transfers between spouses or incident to divorce. In the case of any transfer described in subsection (a) of section 1041—

(A) such transfer shall not be treated as a disposition for purposes of this part, and

(B) the same tax treatment under this part with respect to the transferred property shall apply to the transferee as would have applied to the transferor.

(d) Attribution of stock ownership.

For purposes of this part, in applying the percentage limitations of sections 422(b)(6) and 423(b)(3)—

(1) the individual with respect to whom such limitation is being determined shall be considered as owning the stock owned, directly or indirectly, by or for his brothers and sisters (whether by the whole or half blood), spouse, ancestors, and lineal descendants; and

(2) stock owned, directly or indirectly, by or for a corporation, partnership, estate, or trust, shall be considered as being owned proportionately by or for its shareholders, partners, or beneficiaries.

(e) Parent corporation.

For purposes of this part, the term "parent corporation" means any corporation (other than the employer corporation) in an unbroken chain of corporations ending with the employer corporation if, at the time of the granting of the option, each of the corporations other than the employer corporation owns stock possessing 50 percent or more of the total combined voting power of all classes of stock in one of the other corporations in such chain.

(f) Subsidiary corporation.

For purposes of this part, the term "subsidiary corporation" means any corporation (other than the employer corporation) in an unbroken chain of corporations beginning with the employer corporation if, at the time of the granting of the option, each of the corporations other than the last corporation in the unbroken chain owns stock possessing 50 percent or more of the total combined voting power of all classes of stock in one of the other corporations in such chain.

(g) Special rule for applying subsections (e) and (f).

In applying subsections (e) and (f) for purposes of section 422(a)(2) and 423(a)(2), there shall be substituted for the term "employer corporation" wherever it appears in subsections (e) and (f) the term "grantor corporation", or the term "corporation issuing or assuming a stock option in a transaction to which section 424(a) applies", as the case may be.

(h) Modification, extension, or renewal of option.

(1) In general. For purposes of this part, if the terms of any option to purchase stock are modified, extended, or renewed, such modification, extension, or renewal shall be considered as the granting of a new option.

(2) Special rule for section 423 options. In the case of the transfer of stock pursuant to the exercise of an option to which section 423 applies and which has been so modified, extended, or renewed, the fair market value of such stock at the time of the granting of the option shall be considered as whichever of the following is the highest—

(A) the fair market value of such stock on the date of the original granting of the option,

(B) the fair market value of such stock on the date of the making of such modification, extension, or renewal, or

(C) the fair market value of such stock at the time of the making of any intervening modification, extension, or renewal.

(3) Definition of modification. The term "modification" means any change in the terms of the option which gives the employee additional benefits under the option, but such term shall not include a change in the terms of the option—

(A) attributable to the issuance or assumption of an option under subsection (a);

(B) to permit the option to qualify under section 423(b)(9); or

(C) in the case of an option not immediately exercisable in full, to accelerate the time at which the option may be exercised.

(i) Stockholder approval.

For purposes of this part, if the grant of an option is subject to approval by stockholders, the date of grant of the option shall be determined as if the option had not been subject to such approval.

(j) Cross references.

For provisions requiring the reporting of certain acts with respect to a qualified stock option, an incentive stock option, options granted under employer stock purchase plans, or a restricted stock option, see section 6039.

In 1996, P.L. 104-188, Sec. 1702(h)(13), substituted "an incentive stock option or an option granted under an employee stock purchase plan" for "a qualified stock option, an incentive stock option, an option granted under an employee stock purchase plan, or a restricted stock option", in subpara. (c)(3)(B), effective 11/5/90, except as provided in Sec. 11821(b) of the Revenue Reconciliation Act of 1990, reproduced in note following Code Sec. 422.

Stock options Code Sec. 424

In 1990, P.L. 101-508, Sec. 11801(c)(9)(A)(i), redesignated Code Sec. 425 as Code Sec. 424... Sec. 11801(c)(9)(F)(i), substituted "424(a)" for "425(a)" in subsec. (a)... Sec. 11801(c)(9)(F)(ii), substituted "422(a)(1) or 423(a)(1)" for "422(a)(1), 422A(a)(1), 423(a)(1), or 424(a)(1)" in clause (c)(3)(A)(ii)... Sec. 11801(c)(9)(F)(iii), substituted "422(b)(6) and 423(b)(3)" for "422(b)(7), 422A(b)(6), 423(b)(3), and 424(b)(3)" in subsec. (d)... Sec. 11801(c)(9)(F)(iv)(I), substituted "422(a)(2) and 423(a)(2)" for "422(a)(2), 422A(a)(2), 423(a)(2), and 424(a)(2)" in subsec. (g)... Sec. 11801(c)(9)(F)(iv)(II), substituted "424(a)" for "425(a)" in subsec. (g)... Sec. 11801(c)(9)(F)(v)(I), amended para. (h)(2)... Sec. 11801(c)(9)(F)(v)(II), substituted "section 423(b)(9)" for "sections 422(b)(6), 423(b)(9), and 424(b)(2)" in subpara. (h)(3)(B)... Sec. 11801(c)(9)(F)(v)(III), deleted the last sentence of para. (h)(3), effective 11/5/90, except as provided in Sec. 11821(b) of this Act reproduced in note following Code Sec. 422.

Prior to amendment, para. (h)(2) read as follows:

"(2) Special rules for sections 423 and 424 options.

"(A) In the case of the transfer of stock pursuant to the exercise of an option to which section 423 or 424 applies and which has been so modified, extended, or renewed, then, except as provided in subparagraph (B), the fair market value of such stock at the time of the granting of such option shall be considered as whichever of the following is the highest:

"(i) the fair market value of such stock on the date of the original granting of the option,

"(ii) the fair market value of such stock on the date of the making of such modification, extension, or renewal, or

"(iii) the fair market value of such stock at the time of the making of any intervening modification, extension, or renewal.

"(B) Subparagraph (A) shall not apply with respect to a modification, extension, or renewal of a restricted stock option before January 1, 1964 (or after December 31, 1963, if made pursuant to a binding written contract entered into before January 1, 1964), if the aggregate of the monthly average fair market values of the stock subject to the option for the 12 consecutive calendar months before the date of the modification, extension, or renewal, divided by 12, is an amount less than 80 percent of the fair market value of such stock on the date of the original granting of the option or the date of the making of any intervening modification, extension, or renewal, whichever is the highest."

Prior to deletion, the last sentence of para. (h)(3) read as follows:

"If a restricted stock option is exercisable after the expiration of 10 years from the date such option is granted, subparagraph (B) shall not apply unless the terms of the option are also changed to make it not exercisable after the expiration of such period."

In 1988, P.L. 100-647, Sec. 1018(l)(1), added para. (c)(4)... Sec. 1018(l)(2), substituted "paragraphs (2), (3), and (4)" for "paragraphs (2) and (3)" in para. (c)(1), effective for transfers after 7/18/84, in tax. yrs. end. after 7/18/84, except as provided by Sec. 421(d)(2)-(4) of P.L. 98-369, reproduced in note following Code Sec. 1041.

In 1986, P.L. 99-514, Sec. 1855(a)(4), corrected the effective date for changes made by Sec. 555(b) of P.L. 98-369, from Sec. 555(c)(2) of P.L. 98-369 to Sec. 555(c)(3) of P.L. 98-369, see below.

In 1984, P.L. 98-369, Sec. 555(b), deleted "422A(b)(5)" after "sections 422(b)(6)," in subpara. (h)(3)(B), effective [as provided in Sec. 555(c)(3) of this Act] for modifications of options after 3/20/84.

In 1983, P.L. 97-448, Sec. 102(j)(5), added "an incentive stock option," after "qualified stock option" in subsec. (j), effective for options granted on or after 1/1/76, and exercised on or after 1/1/81, or outstanding on 1/1/81.

—P.L. 97-448, Sec. 102(j)(6)(A), added para. (c)(3)... Sec. 102(j)(6)(B), substituted "paragraphs (2) and (3)" for "paragraph (2)" in para. (c)(1), effective only for transfers after 3/15/82.

In 1981, P.L. 97-34, Sec. 251(b)(2), added "422A(b)(6)" after "422(b)(7)" in subsec. (d)... Sec. 251(b)(3), added "422A(a)(2)" after "422(a)(2)" in subsec. (g)... Sec. 251(b)(4), added "422A(b)(5)" after "422(b)(6)" in subpara. (h)(3)(B), effective for options granted on or after 1/1/76, and exercised on or after 1/1/81, or outstanding on 1/1/81. For election and designation of options and changes in terms of options, see Secs. 251(c)(1)(B) and (c)(2) of this Act reproduced in note following Code Sec. 422A.

In 1964, P.L. 88-272, Sec. 221(a), added Code Sec. 425. See note at end of Code Sec. 421.

Sec. 424. Repealed.

In 1990, P.L. 101-508, Sec. 11801(a)(21), repealed Code Sec. 424, effective 11/5/90, except as provided in Sec. 11821(b) of this Act reproduced in note following Code Sec. 422.

Prior to repeal, Code Sec. 424 read as follows:

"Sec. 424. Restricted stock options.

"(a) In general.

"Section 421(a) shall apply with respect to the transfer of a share of stock to an individual pursuant to his exercise after 1949 of a restricted stock option, if—

"(1) no disposition of such share is made by him within 2 years from the date of the granting of the option nor within 1 year after the transfer of such share to him, and

"(2) at the time he exercises such option—

"(A) he is an employee of either the corporation granting such option, a parent or subsidiary corporation of such corporation, or a corporation or a parent or subsidiary corporation of such corporation issuing or assuming a stock option in a transaction to which section 425(a) applies, or

"(B) he ceased to be an employee of such corporations within the 3-month period preceding the time of exercise.

"(b) Restricted stock option.

"For the purposes of this part, the term 'restricted stock option' means an option granted after February 26, 1945, and before January 1, 1964 (or, if it meets the requirements of subsection (c)(3), an option granted after December 31, 1963), to an individual, for any reason connected with his employment by a corporation, if granted by the employer corporation or its parent or subsidiaries corporation, to purchase stock of any of such corporations but only if—

"(1) at the time such option is granted—

"(A) the option price is at least 85 percent of the fair market value at such time of the stock subject to the option, or

"(B) in the case of a variable price option, the option price (computed as if the option had been exercised when granted) is at least 85 percent of the fair market value of the stock at the time such option is granted;

"(2) such option by its terms is not transferable by such individual otherwise than by will or the laws of descent and distribution, and is exercisable, during his lifetime, only by him;

"(3) such individual, at the time the option is granted, does not own stock possessing more than 10 percent of the total combined voting power of all classes of stock of the employer corporation or of its parent or subsidiary corporation. This paragraph shall not apply if at the time such option is granted the option price is at least 110 percent of the fair market value of the stock subject to the option, and such option either by its terms is not exercisable after the expiration of 5 years from the date such option is granted or is exercised within one year after August 16, 1954. For purposes of this paragraph, the provisions of section 425(d) shall apply in determining the stock ownership of an individual; and

"(4) such option by its terms is not exercisable after the expiration of 10 years from the date such option is granted, if such option has been granted on or after June 22, 1954.

"(c) Special rules.

"(1) Options under which option price is between 85 percent and 95 percent of value of stock. If no disposition of a share of stock acquired by an individual on his exercise after 1949 of a restricted stock option is made by him within 2 years from the date of the granting of the option nor within 1 year after the transfer of such share to him, but, at the time the restricted stock option was granted, the option price (computed under subsection (b)(1)) was less than 95 percent of the fair market value at such time of such share, then, in the event of any disposition of such share by him, or in the event of his death (whenever occurring) while owning such share, there shall be included as compensation (and not as gain upon the sale or exchange of a capital asset) in his gross income, for the taxable year in which falls the date of such disposition or for the taxable year closing with his death, whichever applies—

"(A) in the case of a share of stock acquired under an option qualifying under subsection (b)(1)(A), an amount equal to the amount (if any) by which the option price is exceeded by the lesser of—

"(i) if the fair market value of the share at the time of such disposition or death, or

"(ii) the fair market value of the share at the time the option was granted; or

"(B) in the case of stock acquired under an option qualifying under subsection (b)(1)(B), an amount equal to the lesser of—

"(i) the excess of the fair market value of the share at the time of such disposition or death over the price paid under the option, or

"(ii) the excess of the fair market value of the share at the time the option was granted over the option price (computed as if the option had been exercised at such time).

In the case of a disposition of such share by the individual, the basis of the share in his hands at the time of such disposition shall be increased by an amount equal to the amount so includible in his gross income.

"(2) Variable price option. For purposes of subsection (b)(1), the term 'variable price option' means an option under which the purchase price of the stock is fixed or determinable under a formula in which the only variable is the fair market value of the stock at any time during a period of 9 months [1 year for tax. yrs. begin. after '77] which includes the time the option is exercised; except that in the case of options granted after September 30, 1958, such term does not include any such option in which such formula provides for determining such price by reference to the fair market value of the stock at any time before the option is exercised if such value may be greater than the average fair market value of the stock during the calendar month in which the option is exercised.

"(3) Certain options granted after December 31, 1963. For purposes of subsection (b), an option granted after December 31, 1963, meets the requirements of this paragraph if granted pursuant to—

"(A) a binding written contract entered into before January 1, 1964, or

"(B) a written plan adopted and approved before January 1, 1964, which (as of January 1, 1964, and as of the date of the granting of the option)—

"(i) met the requirements of paragraphs (4) and (5) of section 423(b), or

"(ii) was being administered in a way which did not discriminate in favor of officers, persons whose principal duties consist of supervising the work of other employees, or highly compensated employees.

An option described in the preceding sentence shall be treated as ceasing to meet the requirements of this paragraph if it is not exercised before May 21, 1981."

In 1976, P.L. 94-455, Sec. 603(c), added the last sentence of para. (c)(3), effective for tax. yrs. end. after 12/31/75.

—P.L. 94-455, Sec. 1402(b)(1)(F), substituted "9 months" for "6 months" in paras. (a)(1), (c)(1) and (c)(2), for tax. yrs. begin. in 1977.

—P.L. 94-455, Sec. 1402(b)(2), substituted "1 year" for "9 months" in paras. (a)(1), (c)(1), and (c)(2), effective for tax. yrs. begin. after 12/31/77.

Code Sec. 424 — Stock options

In 1964, P.L. 88-272, Sec. 221(a), added Code Sec. 424. See note at end of Code Sec. 421.

PART III.—RULES RELATING TO MINIMUM FUNDING STANDARDS AND BENEFIT LIMITATIONS

Subpart
A. Minimum funding standards for pension plans.
B. Benefit limitations under single-employer plans.

In 2006, P.L. 109-280, Sec. 112(a), added Part III
— P.L. 109-280, Sec. 113(a), amended Part III
Prior to amendment Part III read as follows: "PART III. Minimum funding standards for single-employer defined benefit pension plans."

SUBPART A.— MINIMUM FUNDING STANDARDS FOR PENSION PLANS.

Sec.
430. Minimum funding standards for single-employer defined benefit pension plans.
431. Minimum funding standards for multiemployer plans.
432. Additional funding rules for multiemployer plans in endangered status or critical status.

In 2006, P.L. 109-280, Sec. 112(a), added item 430
— P.L. 109-280, Sec. 211(a), added item 431
— P.L. 109-280, Sec. 212(a), added item 432

Sec. 430. Minimum funding standards for single-employer defined benefit pension plans.

(a) Minimum required contribution.

For purposes of this section and section 412(a)(2)(A), except as provided in subsection (f), the term "minimum required contribution" means, with respect to any plan year of a defined benefit plan which is not a multiemployer plan—

(1) in any case in which the value of plan assets of the plan (as reduced under subsection (f)(4)(B)) is less than the funding target of the plan for the plan year, the sum of—

  (A) the target normal cost of the plan for the plan year,
  (B) the shortfall amortization charge (if any) for the plan for the plan year determined under subsection (c), and
  (C) the waiver amortization charge (if any) for the plan for the plan year as determined under subsection (e).

(2) in any case in which the value of plan assets of the plan (as reduced under subsection (f)(4)(B)) equals or exceeds the funding target of the plan for the plan year, the target normal cost of the plan for the plan year reduced (but not below zero) by such excess.

(b) Target normal cost.

For purposes of this section:

(1) In general. Except as provided in subsection (i)(2) with respect to plans in at-risk status, the term "target normal cost" means, for any plan year, the excess of—

  (A) the sum of—
    (i) the present value of all benefits which are expected to accrue or to be earned under the plan during the plan year, plus
    (ii) the amount of plan-related expenses expected to be paid from plan assets during the plan year, over
  (B) the amount of mandatory employee contributions expected to be made during the plan year.

(2) Special rule for increase in compensation. For purposes of this subsection, if any benefit attributable to services performed in a preceding plan year is increased by reason of any increase in compensation during the current plan year, the increase in such benefit shall be treated as having accrued during the current plan year.

(c) Shortfall amortization charge.

(1) In general. For purposes of this section, the shortfall amortization charge for a plan for any plan year is the aggregate total (not less than zero) of the shortfall amortization installments for such plan year with respect to any shortfall amortization base which has not been fully amortized under this subsection.

(2) Shortfall amortization installment. For purposes of paragraph (1)—

  (A) Determination. The shortfall amortization installments are the amounts necessary to amortize the shortfall amortization base of the plan for any plan year in level annual installments over the 7-plan-year period beginning with such plan year.
  (B) Shortfall installment. The shortfall amortization installment for any plan year in the 7-plan-year period under subparagraph (A) with respect to any shortfall amortization base is the annual installment determined under subparagraph (A) for that year for that base.
  (C) Segment rates. In determining any shortfall amortization installment under this paragraph, the plan sponsor shall use the segment rates determined under subparagraph (C) of subsection (h)(2), applied under rules similar to the rules of subparagraph (B) of subsection (h)(2).
  (D) Special election for eligible plan years.
    (i) In general. If a plan sponsor elects to apply this subparagraph with respect to the shortfall amortization base of a plan for any eligible plan year (in this subparagraph and paragraph (7) referred to as an "election year"), then, notwithstanding subparagraphs (A) and (B)—
      (I) the shortfall amortization installments with respect to such base shall be determined under clause (ii) or (iii), whichever is specified in the election, and
      (II) the shortfall amortization installment for any plan year in the 9-plan-year period described in clause (ii) or the 15-plan-year period described in clause (iii), respectively, with respect to such shortfall amortization base is the annual installment determined under the applicable clause for that year for that base.
    (ii) 2 plus 7 amortization schedule. The shortfall amortization installments determined under this clause are—
      (I) in the case of the first 2 plan years in the 9-plan-year period beginning with the election year, interest on the shortfall amortization base of the plan for the election year (determined using the effective interest rate for the plan for the election year), and
      (II) in the case of the last 7 plan years in such 9-plan-year period, the amounts necessary to amortize the remaining balance of the shortfall amortization base of the plan for the election year in level annual installments over such last 7 plan years (using the segment rates under subparagraph (C) for the election year).
    (iii) 15-year amortization. The shortfall amortization installments determined under this subparagraph are the amounts necessary to amortize the shortfall amortization base of the plan for the election year in level annual installments over the 15-plan-year period beginning with the election year (using the segment rates under subparagraph (C) for the election year).

2,080

(iv) Election.

(I) In general. The plan sponsor of a plan may elect to have this subparagraph apply to not more than 2 eligible plan years with respect to the plan, except that in the case of a plan described in section 106 of the Pension Protection Act of 2006, the plan sponsor may only elect to have this subparagraph apply to a plan year beginning in 2011.

(II) Amortization schedule. Such election shall specify whether the amortization schedule under clause (ii) or (iii) shall apply to an election year, except that if a plan sponsor elects to have this subparagraph apply to 2 eligible plan years, the plan sponsor must elect the same schedule for both years.

(III) Other rules. Such election shall be made at such time, and in such form and manner, as shall be prescribed by the Secretary, and may be revoked only with the consent of the Secretary. The Secretary shall, before granting a revocation request, provide the Pension Benefit Guaranty Corporation an opportunity to comment on the conditions applicable to the treatment of any portion of the election year shortfall amortization base that remains unamortized as of the revocation date.

(v) Eligible plan year. For purposes of this subparagraph, the term "eligible plan year" means any plan year beginning in 2008, 2009, 2010, or 2011, except that a plan year shall only be treated as an eligible plan year if the due date under subsection (j)(1) for the payment of the minimum required contribution for such plan year occurs on or after the date of the enactment of this subparagraph.

(vi) Reporting. A plan sponsor of a plan who makes an election under clause (i) shall—

(I) give notice of the election to participants and beneficiaries of the plan, and

(II) inform the Pension Benefit Guaranty Corporation of such election in such form and manner as the Director of the Pension Benefit Guaranty Corporation may prescribe.

(vii) Increases in required installments in certain cases. For increases in required contributions in cases of excess compensation or extraordinary dividends or stock redemptions, see paragraph (7).

(3) Shortfall amortization base. For purposes of this section, the shortfall amortization base of a plan for a plan year is—

(A) the funding shortfall of such plan for such plan year, minus

(B) the present value (determined using the segment rates determined under subparagraph (C) of subsection (h)(2), applied under rules similar to the rules of subparagraph (B) of subsection (h)(2)) of the aggregate total of the shortfall amortization installments and waiver amortization installments which have been determined for such plan year and any succeeding plan year with respect to the shortfall amortization bases and waiver amortization bases of the plan for any plan year preceding such plan year.

(4) Funding shortfall. For purposes of this section, the funding shortfall of a plan for any plan year is the excess (if any) of—

(A) the funding target of the plan for the plan year, over

(B) the value of plan assets of the plan (as reduced under subsection (f)(4)(B)) for the plan year which are held by the plan on the valuation date.

(5) Exemption from new shortfall amortization base.

(A) In general. In any case in which the value of plan assets of the plan (as reduced under subsection (f)(4)(A)) is equal to or greater than the funding target of the plan for the plan year, the shortfall amortization base of the plan for such plan year shall be zero.

(B) Transition rule.

(i) In general. Except as provided in clause (iii), in the case of plan years beginning after 2007 and before 2011, only the applicable percentage of the funding target shall be taken into account under paragraph (3)(A) in determining the funding shortfall for purposes of paragraph (3)(A) and subparagraph (A).

(ii) Applicable percentage. For purposes of subparagraph (A), the applicable percentage shall be determined in accordance with the following table:

In the case of a plan year beginning in calendar year:	The applicable percentage is
2008	92
2009	94
2010	96

(iii) Transition relief not available for new or deficit reduction plans. Clause (i) shall not apply to a plan—

(I) which was not in effect for a plan year beginning in 2007, or

(II) which was in effect for a plan year beginning in 2007 and which was subject to section 412(l) (as in effect for plan years beginning in 2007) for such year, determined after the application of paragraphs (6) and (9) thereof.

(6) Early deemed amortization upon attainment of funding target. In any case in which the funding shortfall of a plan for a plan year is zero, for purposes of determining the shortfall amortization charge for such plan year and succeeding plan years, the shortfall amortization bases for all preceding plan years (and all shortfall amortization installments determined with respect to such bases) shall be reduced to zero.

(7) Increases in alternate required installments in cases of excess compensation or extraordinary dividends or stock redemptions.

(A) In general. If there is an installment acceleration amount with respect to a plan for any plan year in the restriction period with respect to an election year under paragraph (2)(D), then the shortfall amortization installment otherwise determined and payable under such paragraph for such plan year shall, subject to the limitation under subparagraph (B), be increased by such amount.

(B) Total installments limited to shortfall base. Subject to rules prescribed by the Secretary, if a shortfall amortization installment with respect to any shortfall amortization base for an election year is required to be increased for any plan year under subparagraph (A)—

(i) such increase shall not result in the amount of such installment exceeding the present value of such installment and all succeeding installments with respect to such base (determined without regard to such increase but after application of clause (ii)), and

(ii) subsequent shortfall amortization installments with respect to such base shall, in reverse order of the otherwise required installments, be reduced to the extent necessary to limit the present value of such subsequent shortfall amortization installments (after application of this paragraph) to the present value of the remaining unamortized shortfall amortization base.

(C) Installment acceleration amount. For purposes of this paragraph—

(i) In general. The term "installment acceleration amount" means, with respect to any plan year in a restriction period with respect to an election year, the sum of—

(I) the aggregate amount of excess employee compensation determined under subparagraph (D) with respect to all employees for the plan year, plus

(II) the aggregate amount of extraordinary dividends and redemptions determined under subparagraph (E) for the plan year.

(ii) Annual limitation. The installment acceleration amount for any plan year shall not exceed the excess (if any) of—

(I) the sum of the shortfall amortization installments for the plan year and all preceding plan years in the amortization period elected under paragraph (2)(D) with respect to the shortfall amortization base with respect to an election year, determined without regard to paragraph (2)(D) and this paragraph, over

(II) the sum of the shortfall amortization installments for such plan year and all such preceding plan years, determined after application of paragraph (2)(D) (and in the case of any preceding plan year, after application of this paragraph).

(iii) Carryover of excess installment acceleration amounts.

(I) In general. If the installment acceleration amount for any plan year (determined without regard to clause (ii)) exceeds the limitation under clause (ii), then, subject to subclause (II), such excess shall be treated as an installment acceleration amount with respect to the succeeding plan year.

(II) Cap to apply. If any amount treated as an installment acceleration amount under subclause (I) or this subclause with respect any succeeding plan year, when added to other installment acceleration amounts (determined without regard to clause (ii)) with respect to the plan year, exceeds the limitation under clause (ii), the portion of such amount representing such excess shall be treated as an installment acceleration amount with respect to the next succeeding plan year.

(III) Limitation on years to which amounts carried for. No amount shall be carried under subclause (I) or (II) to a plan year which begins after the first plan year following the last plan year in the restriction period (or after the second plan year following such last plan year in the case of an election year with respect to which 15-year amortization was elected under paragraph (2)(D)).

(IV) Ordering rules. For purposes of applying subclause (II), installment acceleration amounts for the plan year (determined without regard to any carryover under this clause) shall be applied first against the limitation under clause (ii) and then carryovers to such plan year shall be applied against such limitation on a first-in, first-out basis.

(D) Excess employee compensation. For purposes of this paragraph—

(i) In general. The term "excess employee compensation" means, with respect to any employee for any plan year, the excess (if any) of—

(I) the aggregate amount includible in income under this chapter for remuneration during the calendar year in which such plan year begins for services performed by the employee for the plan sponsor (whether or not performed during such calendar year), over

(I) $1,000,000.

(ii) Amounts set aside for nonqualified deferred compensation. If during any calendar year assets are set aside or reserved (directly or indirectly) in a trust (or other arrangement as determined by the Secretary), or transferred to such a trust or other arrangement, by a plan sponsor for purposes of paying deferred compensation of an employee under a nonqualified deferred compensation plan (as defined in section 409A) of the plan sponsor, then, for purposes of clause (i), the amount of such assets shall be treated as remuneration of the employee includible in income for the calendar year unless such amount is otherwise includible in income for such year. An amount to which the preceding sentence applies shall not be taken into account under this paragraph for any subsequent calendar year.

(iii) Only remuneration for certain post-2009 services counted. Remuneration shall be taken into account under clause (i) only to the extent attributable to services performed by the employee for the plan sponsor after February 28, 2010.

(iv) Exception for certain equity payments.

(I) In general. There shall not be taken into account under clause (i)(I) any amount includible in income with respect to the granting after February 28, 2010, of service recipient stock (within the meaning of section 409A) that, upon such grant, is subject to a substantial risk of forfeiture (as defined under section 83(c)(1)) for at least 5 years from the date of such grant.

(II) Secretarial authority. The Secretary may by regulation provide for the application of this clause in the case of a person other than a corporation.

(v) Other exceptions. The following amounts includible in income shall not be taken into account under clause (i)(I):

(I) Commissions. Any remuneration payable on a commission basis solely on account of income directly generated by the individual performance of the individual to whom such remuneration is payable.

(II) Certain payments under existing contracts. Any remuneration consisting of nonqualified deferred compensation, restricted stock, stock options, or stock appreciation rights payable or granted under a written binding contract that was in effect on March 1, 2010, and which was not modified in any material respect before such remuneration is paid.

(vi) Self-employed individual treated as employee. The term "employee" includes, with respect to a calendar year, a self-employed individual who is treated as an employee under section 401(c) for the taxable year ending during such calendar year, and the term "compensation" shall include earned income of such individual with respect to such self-employment.

(vii) Indexing of amount. In the case of any calendar year beginning after 2010, the dollar amount under clause (i)(II) shall be increased by an amount equal to—
  (I) such dollar amount, multiplied by
  (II) the cost-of-living adjustment determined under section 1(f)(3) for the calendar year, determined by substituting "calendar year 2009" for "calendar year 1992" in subparagraph (B) thereof.
If the amount of any increase under clause (i) is not a multiple of $1,000, such increase shall be rounded to the next lowest multiple of $1,000.
(E) Extraordinary dividends and redemptions.
  (i) In general. The amount determined under this subparagraph for any plan year is the excess (if any) of the sum of the dividends declared during the plan year by the plan sponsor plus the aggregate amount paid for the redemption of stock of the plan sponsor redeemed during the plan year over the greater of—
    (I) the adjusted net income (within the meaning of section 4043 of the Employee Retirement Income Security Act of 1974) of the plan sponsor for the preceding plan year, determined without regard to any reduction by reason of interest, taxes, depreciation, or amortization, or
    (II) in the case of a plan sponsor that determined and declared dividends in the same manner for at least 5 consecutive years immediately preceding such plan year, the aggregate amount of dividends determined and declared for such plan year using such manner.
  (ii) Only certain post-2009 dividends and redemptions counted. For purposes of clause (i), there shall only be taken into account dividends declared, and redemptions occurring, after February 28, 2010.
  (iii) Exception for intra-group dividends. Dividends paid by one member of a controlled group (as defined in section 412(d)(3)) to another member of such group shall not be taken into account under clause (i).
  (iv) Exception for certain redemptions. Redemptions that are made pursuant to a plan maintained with respect to employees, or that are made on account of the death, disability, or termination of employment of an employee or shareholder, shall not be taken into account under clause (i).
  (v) Exception for certain preferred stock.
    (I) In general. Dividends and redemptions with respect to applicable preferred stock shall not be taken into account under clause (i) to the extent that dividends accrue with respect to such stock at a specified rate in all events and without regard to the plan sponsor's income, and interest accrues on any unpaid dividends with respect to such stock.
    (II) Applicable preferred stock. For purposes of subclause (I), the term "applicable preferred stock" means preferred stock which was issued before March 1, 2010 (or which was issued after such date and is held by an employee benefit plan subject to the provisions of title I of Employee Retirement Income Security Act of 1974).
(F) Other definitions and rules. For purposes of this paragraph—
  (i) Plan sponsor. The term "plan sponsor" includes any member of the plan sponsor's controlled group (as defined in section 412(d)(3)).

(ii) Restriction period. The term "restriction period" means, with respect to any election year—
  (I) except as provided in subclause (II), the 3-year period beginning with the election year (or, if later, the first plan year beginning after December 31, 2009), and
  (II) if the plan sponsor elects 15-year amortization for the shortfall amortization base for the election year, the 5-year period beginning with the election year (or, if later, the first plan year beginning after December 31, 2009).
(iii) Elections for multiple plans. If a plan sponsor makes elections under paragraph (2)(D) with respect to 2 or more plans, the Secretary shall provide rules for the application of this paragraph to such plans, including rules for the ratable allocation of any installment acceleration amount among such plans on the basis of each plan's relative reduction in the plan's shortfall amortization installment for the first plan year in the amortization period described in subparagraph (A) (determined without regard to this paragraph).
(iv) Mergers and acquisitions. The Secretary shall prescribe rules for the application of paragraph (2)(D) and this paragraph in any case where there is a merger or acquisition involving a plan sponsor making the election under paragraph (2)(D).

(d) Rules relating to funding target.
For purposes of this section—
(1) Funding target. Except as provided in subsection (i)(1) with respect to plans in at-risk status, the funding target of a plan for a plan year is the present value of all benefits accrued or earned under the plan as of the beginning of the plan year.
(2) Funding target attainment percentage. The "funding target attainment percentage" of a plan for a plan year is the ratio (expressed as a percentage) which—
  (A) the value of plan assets for the plan year (as reduced under subsection (f)(4)(B)), bears to
  (B) the funding target of the plan for the plan year (determined without regard to subsection (i)(1)).

(e) Waiver amortization charge.
(1) Determination of waiver amortization charge. The waiver amortization charge (if any) for a plan for any plan year is the aggregate total of the waiver amortization installments for such plan year with respect to the waiver amortization bases for each of the 5 preceding plan years.
(2) Waiver amortization installment. For purposes of paragraph (1)—
  (A) Determination. The waiver amortization installments are the amounts necessary to amortize the waiver amortization base of the plan for any plan year in level annual installments over a period of 5 plan years beginning with the succeeding plan year.
  (B) Waiver installment. The waiver amortization installment for any plan year in the 5-year period under subparagraph (A) with respect to any waiver amortization base is the annual installment determined under subparagraph (A) for that year for that base.
(3) Interest rate. In determining any waiver amortization installment under this subsection, the plan sponsor shall use the segment rates determined under subparagraph (C) of subsection (h)(2), applied under rules similar to the rules of subparagraph (B) of subsection (h)(2).
(4) Waiver amortization base. The waiver amortization base of a plan for a plan year is the amount of the waived

funding deficiency (if any) for such plan year under section 412(c).

(5) Early deemed amortization upon attainment of funding target. In any case in which the funding shortfall of a plan for a plan year is zero, for purposes of determining the waiver amortization charge for such plan year and succeeding plan years, the waiver amortization bases for all preceding plan years (and all waiver amortization installments determined with respect to such bases) shall be reduced to zero.

(f) Reduction of minimum required contribution by prefunding balance and funding standard carryover balance.

(1) Election to maintain balances.

(A) Prefunding balance. The plan sponsor of a defined benefit plan which is not a multiemployer plan may elect to maintain a prefunding balance.

(B) Funding standard carryover balance.

(i) In general. In the case of a defined benefit plan (other than a multiemployer plan) described in clause (ii), the plan sponsor may elect to maintain a funding standard carryover balance, until such balance is reduced to zero.

(ii) Plans maintaining funding standard account in 2007. A plan is described in this clause if the plan—

(I) was in effect for a plan year beginning in 2007, and

(II) had a positive balance in the funding standard account under section 412(b) as in effect for such plan year and determined as of the end of such plan year.

(2) Application of balances. A prefunding balance and a funding standard carryover balance maintained pursuant to this paragraph—

(A) shall be available for crediting against the minimum required contribution, pursuant to an election under paragraph (3),

(B) shall be applied as a reduction in the amount treated as the value of plan assets for purposes of this section, to the extent provided in paragraph (4), and

(C) may be reduced at any time, pursuant to an election under paragraph (5).

(3) Election to apply balances against minimum required contribution.

(A) In general. Except as provided in subparagraphs (B) and (C), in the case of any plan year in which the plan sponsor elects to credit against the minimum required contribution for the current plan year all or a portion of the prefunding balance or the funding standard carryover balance for the current plan year (not in excess of such minimum required contribution), the minimum required contribution for the plan year shall be reduced as of the first day of the plan year by the amount so credited by the plan sponsor. For purposes of the preceding sentence, the minimum required contribution shall be determined after taking into account any waiver under section 412(c).

(B) Coordination with funding standard carryover balance. To the extent that any plan has a funding standard carryover balance greater than zero, no amount of the prefunding balance of such plan may be credited under this paragraph in reducing the minimum required contribution.

(C) Limitation for underfunded plans. The preceding provisions of this paragraph shall not apply for any plan year if the ratio (expressed as a percentage) which—

(i) the value of plan assets for the preceding plan year (as reduced under paragraph (4)(C)), bears to

(ii) the funding target of the plan for the preceding plan year (determined without regard to subsection (i)(1)),

is less than 80 percent. In the case of plan years beginning in 2008, the ratio under this subparagraph may be determined using such methods of estimation as the Secretary may prescribe.

(D) Special rule for certain years of plans maintained by charities.

(i) In general. For purposes of applying subparagraph (C) for plan years beginning after August 31, 2009, and before September 1, 2011, the ratio determined under such subparagraph for the preceding plan year of a plan shall be the greater of—

(I) such ratio, as determined without regard to this subsection, or

(II) the ratio for such plan for the plan year beginning after August 31, 2007 and before September 1, 2008, as determined under rules prescribed by the Secretary.

(ii) Special rule. In the case of a plan for which the valuation date is not the first day of the plan year—

(I) clause (i) shall apply to plan years beginning after December 31, 2007, and before January 1, 2010, and

(II) clause (i)(II) shall apply based on the last plan year beginning before September 1, 2007, as determined under rules prescribed by the Secretary.

(iii) Limitation to charities. This subparagraph shall not apply to any plan unless such plan is maintained exclusively by one or more organizations described in section 501(c)(3).

(4) Effect of balances on amounts treated as value of plan assets. In the case of any plan maintaining a prefunding balance or a funding standard carryover balance pursuant to this subsection, the amount treated as the value of plan assets shall be deemed to be such amount, reduced as provided in the following subparagraphs:

(A) Applicability of shortfall amortization base. For purposes of subsection (c)(5), the value of plan assets is deemed to be such amount, reduced by the amount of the prefunding balance, but only if an election under paragraph (3) applying any portion of the prefunding balance in reducing the minimum required contribution is in effect for the plan year.

(B) Determination of excess assets, funding shortfall, and funding target attainment percentage.

(i) In general. For purposes of subsections (a), (c)(4)(B), and (d)(2)(A), the value of plan assets is deemed to be such amount, reduced by the amount of the prefunding balance and the funding standard carryover balance.

(ii) Special rule for certain binding agreements with PBGC. For purposes of subsection (c)(4)(B), the value of plan assets shall not be deemed to be reduced for a plan year by the amount of the specified balance if, with respect to such balance, there is in effect for a plan year a binding written agreement with the Pension Benefit Guaranty Corporation which provides that such balance is not available to reduce the minimum required contribution for the plan year. For purposes of the preceding sentence, the term "specified balance" means the prefunding balance or the funding standard carryover balance, as the case may be.

(C) Availability of balances in plan year for crediting against minimum required contribution. For purposes of paragraph (3)(C)(i) of this subsection, the value of plan assets is deemed to be such amount, reduced by the amount of the prefunding balance.

(5) Election to reduce balance prior to determinations of value of plan assets and crediting against minimum required contribution.

(A) In general. The plan sponsor may elect to reduce by any amount the balance of the prefunding balance and the funding standard carryover balance for any plan year (but not below zero). Such reduction shall be effective prior to any determination of the value of plan assets for such plan year under this section and application of the balance in reducing the minimum required contribution for such plan for such plan year pursuant to an election under paragraph (2).

(B) Coordination between prefunding balance and funding standard carryover balance. To the extent that any plan has a funding standard carryover balance greater than zero, no election may be made under subparagraph (A) with respect to the prefunding balance.

(6) Prefunding balance.

(A) In general. A prefunding balance maintained by a plan shall consist of a beginning balance of zero, increased and decreased to the extent provided in subparagraphs (B) and (C), and adjusted further as provided in paragraph (8).

(B) Increases.

(i) In general. As of the first day of each plan year beginning after 2008, the prefunding balance of a plan shall be increased by the amount elected by the plan sponsor for the plan year. Such amount shall not exceed the excess (if any) of—

(I) the aggregate total of employer contributions to the plan for the preceding plan year, over—

(II) the minimum required contribution for such preceding plan year.

(ii) Adjustments for interest. Any excess contributions under clause (i) shall be properly adjusted for interest accruing for the periods between the first day of the current plan year and the dates on which the excess contributions were made, determined by using the effective interest rate for the preceding plan year and by treating contributions as being first used to satisfy the minimum required contribution.

(iii) Certain contributions necessary to avoid benefit limitations disregarded. The excess described in clause (i) with respect to any preceding plan year shall be reduced (but not below zero) by the amount of contributions an employer would be required to make under subsection (b), (c), or (e) of section 436 to avoid a benefit limitation which would otherwise be imposed under such paragraph for the preceding plan year. Any contribution which may be taken into account in satisfying the requirements of more than 1 of such paragraphs shall be taken into account only once for purposes of this clause.

(C) Decreases. The prefunding balance of a plan shall be decreased (but not below zero) by—

(i) as of the first day of each plan year after 2008, the amount of such balance credited under paragraph (2) (if any) in reducing the minimum required contribution of the plan for the preceding plan year, and

(ii) as of the time specified in paragraph (5)(A), any reduction in such balance elected under paragraph (5).

(7) Funding standard carryover balance.

(A) In general. A funding standard carryover balance maintained by a plan shall consist of a beginning balance determined under subparagraph (B), decreased to the extent provided in subparagraph (C), and adjusted further as provided in paragraph (8).

(B) Beginning balance. The beginning balance of the funding standard carryover balance shall be the positive balance described in paragraph (1)(B)(ii)(II).

(C) Decreases. The funding standard carryover balance of a plan shall be decreased (but not below zero) by—

(i) as of the first day of each plan year after 2008, the amount of such balance credited under paragraph (2) (if any) in reducing the minimum required contribution of the plan for the preceding plan year, and

(ii) as of the time specified in paragraph (5)(A), any reduction in such balance elected under paragraph (5).

(8) Adjustments for investment experience. In determining the prefunding balance or the funding standard carryover balance of a plan as of the first day of the plan year, the plan sponsor shall, in accordance with regulations prescribed by the Secretary, adjust such balance to reflect the rate of return on plan assets for the preceding plan year. Notwithstanding subsection (g)(3), such rate of return shall be determined on the basis of fair market value and shall properly take into account, in accordance with such regulations, all contributions, distributions, and other plan payments made during such period.

(9) Elections. Elections under this subsection shall be made at such times, and in such form and manner, as shall be prescribed in regulations of the Secretary.

(g) Valuation of plan assets and liabilities.

(1) Timing of determinations. Except as otherwise provided under this subsection, all determinations under this section for a plan year shall be made as of the valuation date of the plan for such plan year.

(2) Valuation date. For purposes of this section—

(A) In general. Except as provided in subparagraph (B), the valuation date of a plan for any plan year shall be the first day of the plan year.

(B) Exception for small plans. If, on each day during the preceding plan year, a plan had 100 or fewer participants, the plan may designate any day during the plan year as its valuation date for such plan year and succeeding plan years. For purposes of this subparagraph, all defined benefit plans (other than multiemployer plans) maintained by the same employer (or any member of such employer's controlled group) shall be treated as 1 plan, but only participants with respect to such employer or member shall be taken into account.

(C) Application of certain rules in determination of plan size. For purposes of this paragraph—

(i) Plans not in existence in preceding year. In the case of the first plan year of any plan, subparagraph (B) shall apply to such plan by taking into account the number of participants that the plan is reasonably expected to have on days during such first plan year.

(ii) Predecessors. Any reference in subparagraph (B) to an employer shall include a reference to any predecessor of such employer.

(3) Determination of value of plan assets. For purposes of this section—

(A) In general. Except as provided in subparagraph (B), the value of plan assets shall be the fair market value of the assets.

(B) Averaging allowed. A plan may determine the value of plan assets on the basis of the averaging of fair market values, but only if such method—

(i) is permitted under regulations prescribed by the Secretary,

(ii) does not provide for averaging of such values over more than the period beginning on the last day of the 25th month preceding the month in which the valuation date occurs and ending on the valuation date (or a similar period in the case of a valuation date which is not the 1st day of a month), and

(iii) does not result in a determination of the value of plan assets which, at any time, is lower than 90 percent or greater than 110 percent of the fair market value of such assets at such time.

Any such averaging shall be adjusted for contributions, distributions, and expected earnings (as determined by the plan's actuary on the basis of an assumed earnings rate specified by the actuary but not in excess of the third segment rate applicable under subsection (h)(2)(C)(iii)), as specified by the Secretary.

(4) Accounting for contribution receipts. For purposes of determining the value of assets under paragraph (3)—

(A) Prior year contributions. If—

(i) an employer makes any contribution to the plan after the valuation date for the plan year in which the contribution is made, and

(ii) the contribution is for a preceding plan year,

the contribution shall be taken into account as an asset of the plan as of the valuation date, except that in the case of any plan year beginning after 2008, only the present value (determined as of the valuation date) of such contribution may be taken into account. For purposes of the preceding sentence, present value shall be determined using the effective interest rate for the preceding plan year to which the contribution is properly allocable.

(B) Special rule for current year contributions made before valuation date. If any contributions for any plan year are made to or under the plan during the plan year but before the valuation date for the plan year, the assets of the plan as of the valuation date shall not include—

(i) such contributions, and

(ii) interest on such contributions for the period between the date of the contributions and the valuation date, determined by using the effective interest rate for the plan year.

(h) Actuarial assumptions and methods.

(1) In general. Subject to this subsection, the determination of any present value or other computation under this section shall be made on the basis of actuarial assumptions and methods—

(A) each of which is reasonable (taking into account the experience of the plan and reasonable expectations), and

(B) which, in combination, offer the actuary's best estimate of anticipated experience under the plan.

(2) Interest rates.

(A) Effective interest rate. For purposes of this section, the term "effective interest rate" means, with respect to any plan for any plan year, the single rate of interest which, if used to determine the present value of the plan's accrued or earned benefits referred to in subsection (d)(1), would result in an amount equal to the funding target of the plan for such plan year.

(B) Interest rates for determining funding target. For purposes of determining the funding target and target normal cost of a plan for any plan year, the interest rate used in determining the present value of the benefits of the plan shall be—

(i) in the case of benefits reasonably determined to be payable during the 5-year period beginning on the first day of the plan year, the first segment rate with respect to the applicable month,

(ii) in the case of benefits reasonably determined to be payable during the 15-year period beginning at the end of the period described in clause (i), the second segment rate with respect to the applicable month, and

(iii) in the case of benefits reasonably determined to be payable after the period described in clause (ii), the third segment rate with respect to the applicable month.

(C) Segment rates. For purposes of this paragraph—

(i) First segment rate. The term "first segment rate" means, with respect to any month, the single rate of interest which shall be determined by the Secretary for such month on the basis of the corporate bond yield curve for such month, taking into account only that portion of such yield curve which is based on bonds maturing during the 5-year period commencing with such month.

(ii) Second segment rate. The term "second segment rate" means, with respect to any month, the single rate of interest which shall be determined by the Secretary for such month on the basis of the corporate bond yield curve for such month, taking into account only that portion of such yield curve which is based on bonds maturing during the 15-year period beginning at the end of the period described in clause (i).

(iii) Third segment rate. The term "third segment rate" means, with respect to any month, the single rate of interest which shall be determined by the Secretary for such month on the basis of the corporate bond yield curve for such month, taking into account only that portion of such yield curve which is based on bonds maturing during periods beginning after the period described in clause (ii).

(D) Corporate bond yield curve. For purposes of this paragraph—

(i) In general. The term "corporate bond yield curve" means, with respect to any month, a yield curve which is prescribed by the Secretary for such month and which reflects the average, for the 24-month period ending with the month preceding such month, of monthly yields on investment grade corporate bonds with varying maturities and that are in the top 3 quality levels available.

(ii) Election to use yield curve. Solely for purposes of determining the minimum required contribution under this section, the plan sponsor may, in lieu of the segment rates determined under subparagraph (C), elect to use interest rates under the corporate bond yield curve. For purposes of the preceding sentence such curve shall be determined without regard to the 24-month averaging described in clause (i). Such election, once made, may be revoked only with the consent of the Secretary.

(E) Applicable month. For purposes of this paragraph, the term "applicable month" means, with respect to any plan for any plan year, the month which includes the valuation date of such plan for such plan year or, at the election of the plan sponsor, any of the 4 months which precede such month. Any election made under this subparagraph shall apply to the plan year for which the election is made and all succeeding plan years, unless the election is revoked with the consent of the Secretary.

(F) Publication requirements. The Secretary shall publish for each month the corporate bond yield curve (and the corporate bond yield curve reflecting the modification described in section 417(e)(3)(D)(i) for such month) and each of the rates determined under subparagraph (C) for such month. The Secretary shall also publish a description of the methodology used to determine such yield curve and such rates which is sufficiently detailed to enable plans to make reasonable projections regarding the yield curve and such rates for future months based on the plan's projection of future interest rates.

(G) Transition rule.

(i) In general. Notwithstanding the preceding provisions of this paragraph, for plan years beginning in 2008 or 2009, the first, second, or third segment rate for a plan with respect to any month shall be equal to the sum of—

(I) the product of such rate for such month determined without regard to this subparagraph, multiplied by the applicable percentage, and

(II) the product of the rate determined under the rules of section 412(b)(5)(B)(ii)(II) (as in effect for plan years beginning in 2007), multiplied by a percentage equal to 100 percent minus the applicable percentage.

(ii) Applicable percentage. For purposes of clause (i), the applicable percentage is 33⅓ percent for plan years beginning in 2008 and 66⅔ percent for plan years beginning in 2009.

(iii) New plans ineligible. Clause (i) shall not apply to any plan if the first plan year of the plan begins after December 31, 2007.

(iv) Election. The plan sponsor may elect not to have this subparagraph apply. Such election, once made, may be revoked only with the consent of the Secretary.

(3) Mortality tables.

(A) In general. Except as provided in subparagraph (C) or (D), the Secretary shall by regulation prescribe mortality tables to be used in determining any present value or making any computation under this section. Such tables shall be based on the actual experience of pension plans and projected trends in such experience. In prescribing such tables, the Secretary shall take into account results of available independent studies of mortality of individuals covered by pension plans.

(B) Periodic revision. The Secretary shall (at least every 10 years) make revisions in any table in effect under subparagraph (A) to reflect the actual experience of pension plans and projected trends in such experience.

(C) Substitute mortality table.

(i) In general. Upon request by the plan sponsor and approval by the Secretary, a mortality table which meets the requirements of clause (iii) shall be used in determining any present value or making any computation under this section during the period of consecutive plan years (not to exceed 10) specified in the request.

(ii) Early termination of period. Notwithstanding clause (i), a mortality table described in clause (i) shall cease to be in effect as of the earliest of—

(I) the date on which there is a significant change in the participants in the plan by reason of a plan spinoff or merger or otherwise, or

(II) the date on which the plan actuary determines that such table does not meet the requirements of clause (iii).

(iii) Requirements. A mortality table meets the requirements of this clause if—

(I) there is a sufficient number of plan participants, and the pension plans have been maintained for a sufficient period of time, to have credible information necessary for purposes of subclause (II), and

(II) such table reflects the actual experience of the pension plans maintained by the sponsor and projected trends in general mortality experience.

(iv) All plans in controlled group must use separate table. Except as provided by the Secretary, a plan sponsor may not use a mortality table under this subparagraph for any plan maintained by the plan sponsor unless—

(I) a separate mortality table is established and used under this subparagraph for each other plan maintained by the plan sponsor and if the plan sponsor is a member of a controlled group, each member of the controlled group, and

(II) the requirements of clause (iii) are met separately with respect to the table so established for each such plan, determined by only taking into account the participants of such plan, the time such plan has been in existence, and the actual experience of such plan.

(v) Deadline for submission and disposition of application.

(I) Submission. The plan sponsor shall submit a mortality table to the Secretary for approval under this subparagraph at least 7 months before the 1st day of the period described in clause (i).

(II) Disposition. Any mortality table submitted to the Secretary for approval under this subparagraph shall be treated as in effect as of the 1st day of the period described in clause (i) unless the Secretary, during the 180-day period beginning on the date of such submission, disapproves of such table and provides the reasons that such table fails to meet the requirements of clause (iii). The 180-day period shall be extended upon mutual agreement of the Secretary and the plan sponsor.

(D) Separate mortality tables for the disabled. Notwithstanding subparagraph (A)—

(i) In general. The Secretary shall establish mortality tables which may be used (in lieu of the tables under subparagraph (A)) under this subsection for individuals who are entitled to benefits under the plan on account of disability. The Secretary shall establish separate tables for individuals whose disabilities occur in plan years beginning before January 1, 1995, and for individuals whose disabilities occur in plan years beginning on or after such date.

(ii) Special rule for disabilities occurring after 1994. In the case of disabilities occurring in plan years beginning after December 31, 1994, the tables under clause (i) shall apply only with respect to individuals described in such subclause who are disabled within the meaning of title II of the Social Security Act and the regulations thereunder.

(iii) Periodic revision. The Secretary shall (at least every 10 years) make revisions in any table in effect under clause (i) to reflect the actual experience of pension plans and projected trends in such experience.

(4) Probability of benefit payments in the form of lump sums or other optional forms. For purposes of determining any present value or making any computation under this section, there shall be taken into account—

(A) the probability that future benefit payments under the plan will be made in the form of optional forms of benefits provided under the plan (including lump sum distributions, determined on the basis of the plan's experience and other related assumptions), and

(B) any difference in the present value of such future benefit payments resulting from the use of actuarial assumptions, in determining benefit payments in any such optional form of benefits, which are different from those specified in this subsection.

(5) Approval of large changes in actuarial assumptions.

(A) In general. No actuarial assumption used to determine the funding target for a plan to which this paragraph applies may be changed without the approval of the Secretary.

(B) Plans to which paragraph applies. This paragraph shall apply to a plan only if—

(i) the plan is a defined benefit plan (other than a multiemployer plan) to which title IV of the Employee Retirement Income Security Act of 1974 applies,

(ii) the aggregate unfunded vested benefits as of the close of the preceding plan year (as determined under section 4006(a)(3)(E)(iii) of the Employee Retirement Income Security Act of 1974) of such plan and all other plans maintained by the contributing sponsors (as defined in section 4001(a)(13) of such Act) and members of such sponsors' controlled groups (as defined in section 4001(a)(14) of such Act) which are covered by title IV (disregarding plans with no unfunded vested benefits) exceed $50,000,000, and

(iii) the change in assumptions (determined after taking into account any changes in interest rate and mortality table) results in a decrease in the funding shortfall of the plan for the current plan year that exceeds $50,000,000, or that exceeds $5,000,000 and that is 5 percent or more of the funding target of the plan before such change.

(i) Special rules for at-risk plans.

(1) Funding target for plans in at-risk status.

(A) In general. In the case of a plan which is in at-risk status for a plan year, the funding target of the plan for the plan year shall be equal to the sum of—

(i) the present value of all benefits accrued or earned under the plan as of the beginning of the plan year, as determined by using the additional actuarial assumptions described in subparagraph (B), and

(ii) in the case of a plan which also has been in at-risk status for at least 2 of the 4 preceding plan years, a loading factor determined under subparagraph (C).

(B) Additional actuarial assumptions. The actuarial assumptions described in this subparagraph are as follows:

(i) All employees who are not otherwise assumed to retire as of the valuation date but who will be eligible to elect benefits during the plan year and the 10 succeeding plan years shall be assumed to retire at the earliest retirement date under the plan but not before the end of the plan year for which the at-risk funding target and at-risk target normal cost are being determined.

(ii) All employees shall be assumed to elect the retirement benefit available under the plan at the assumed retirement age (determined after application of clause (i)) which would result in the highest present value of benefits.

(C) Loading factor. The loading factor applied with respect to a plan under this paragraph for any plan year is the sum of—

(i) $700, times the number of participants in the plan, plus

(ii) 4 percent of the funding target (determined without regard to this paragraph) of the plan for the plan year.

(2) Target normal cost of at-risk plans. In the case of a plan which is in at-risk status for a plan year, the target normal cost of the plan for such plan year shall be equal to the sum of—

(A) the excess of—

(i) the sum of—

(I) the present value of all benefits which are expected to accrue or to be earned under the plan during the plan year, determined using the additional actuarial assumptions described in paragraph (1)(B), plus

(II) the amount of plan-related expenses expected to be paid from plan assets during the plan year, over

(ii) the amount of mandatory employee contributions expected to be made during the plan year, plus

(B) in the case of a plan which also has been in at-risk status for at least 2 of the 4 preceding plan years, a loading factor equal to 4 percent of the amount determined under subsection (b)(1)(A)(i) with respect to the plan for the plan year.

(3) Minimum amount. In no event shall—

(A) the at-risk funding target be less than the funding target, as determined without regard to this subsection, or

(B) the at-risk target normal cost be less than the target normal cost, as determined without regard to this subsection.

(4) Determination of at-risk status. For purposes of this subsection—

(A) In general. A plan is in at-risk status for a plan year if—

(i) the funding target attainment percentage for the preceding plan year (determined under this section without regard to this subsection) is less than 80 percent, and

(ii) the funding target attainment percentage for the preceding plan year (determined under this section by using the additional actuarial assumptions described in paragraph (1)(B) in computing the funding target) is less than 70 percent.

(B) Transition rule. In the case of plan years beginning in 2008, 2009, and 2010, subparagraph (A)(i) shall be applied by substituting the following percentages for "80 percent":

(i) 65 percent in the case of 2008.
(ii) 70 percent in the case of 2009.
(iii) 75 percent in the case of 2010.

In the case of plan years beginning in 2008, the funding target attainment percentage for the preceding plan year under subparagraph (A) may be determined using such methods of estimation as the Secretary may provide.

(C) Special rule for employees offered early retirement in 2006.

(i) In general. For purposes of subparagraph (A)(ii), the additional actuarial assumptions described in paragraph (1)(B) shall not be taken into account with respect to any employee if—

(I) such employee is employed by a specified automobile manufacturer,

(II) such employee is offered a substantial amount of additional cash compensation, substantially enhanced retirement benefits under the plan, or materially reduced employment duties on the condition that by a specified date (not later than December 31, 2010) the employee retires (as defined under the terms of the plan),

(III) such offer is made during 2006 and pursuant to a bona fide retirement incentive program and requires, by the terms of the offer, that such offer can be accepted not later than a specified date (not later than December 31, 2006), and

(IV) such employee does not elect to accept such offer before the specified date on which the offer expires.

(ii) Specified automobile manufacturer. For purposes of clause (i), the term "specified automobile manufacturer" means—

(I) any manufacturer of automobiles, and

(II) any manufacturer of automobile parts which supplies such parts directly to a manufacturer of automobiles and which, after a transaction or series of transactions ending in 1999, ceased to be a member of a controlled group which included such manufacturer of automobiles.

(5) Transition between applicable funding targets and between applicable target normal costs.

(A) In general. In any case in which a plan which is in at-risk status for a plan year has been in such status for a consecutive period of fewer than 5 plan years, the applicable amount of the funding target and of the target normal cost shall be, in lieu of the amount determined without regard to this paragraph, the sum of—

(i) the amount determined under this section without regard to this subsection, plus

(ii) the transition percentage for such plan year of the excess of the amount determined under this subsection (without regard to this paragraph) over the amount determined under this section without regard to this subsection.

(B) Transition percentage. For purposes of subparagraph (A), the transition percentage shall be determined in accordance with the following table:

If the consecutive number of years (including the plan year) the plan is in at-risk status is—	The transition percentage is—
1	20
2	40
3	60
4	80

(C) Years before effective date. For purposes of this paragraph, plan years beginning before 2008 shall not be taken into account.

(6) Small plan exception. If, on each day during the preceding plan year, a plan had 500 or fewer participants, the plan shall not be treated as in at-risk status for the plan year. For purposes of this paragraph, all defined benefit plans (other than multiemployer plans) maintained by the same employer (or any member of such employer's controlled group) shall be treated as 1 plan, but only participants with respect to such employer or member shall be taken into account and the rules of subsection (g)(2)(C) shall apply.

(j) Payment of minimum required contributions.

(1) In general. For purposes of this section, the due date for any payment of any minimum required contribution for any plan year shall be 8½ months after the close of the plan year.

(2) Interest. Any payment required under paragraph (1) for a plan year that is made on a date other than the valuation date for such plan year shall be adjusted for interest accruing for the period between the valuation date and the payment date, at the effective rate of interest for the plan for such plan year.

(3) Accelerated quarterly contribution schedule for underfunded plans.

(A) Failure to timely make required installment. In any case in which the plan has a funding shortfall for the preceding plan year, the employer maintaining the plan shall make the required installments under this paragraph and if the employer fails to pay the full amount of a required installment for the plan year, then the amount of interest charged under paragraph (2) on the underpayment for the period of underpayment shall be determined by using a rate of interest equal to the rate otherwise used under paragraph (2) plus 5 percentage points. In the case of plan years beginning in 2008, the funding shortfall for the preceding plan year may be determined using such methods of estimation as the Secretary may provide.

(B) Amount of underpayment, period of underpayment. For purposes of subparagraph (A)—

(i) Amount. The amount of the underpayment shall be the excess of—

(I) the required installment, over

(II) the amount (if any) of the installment contributed to or under the plan on or before the due date for the installment.

(ii) Period of underpayment. The period for which any interest is charged under this paragraph with respect to any portion of the underpayment shall run from the due date for the installment to the date on which such portion is contributed to or under the plan.

(iii) Order of crediting contributions. For purposes of clause (i)(II), contributions shall be credited against unpaid required installments in the order in which such installments are required to be paid.

(C) Number of required installments; due dates. For purposes of this paragraph—

(i) Payable in 4 installments. There shall be 4 required installments for each plan year.

(ii) Time for payment of installments. The due dates for required installments are set forth in the following table:

In the case of the following required installment:	The due date is:
1st	April 15
2nd	July 15
3rd	October 15
4th	January 15 of the following year.

(D) Amount of required installment. For purposes of this paragraph—
(i) In general. The amount of any required installment shall be 25 percent of the required annual payment.
(ii) Required annual payment. For purposes of clause (i), the term "required annual payment" means the lesser of—
(I) 90 percent of the minimum required contribution (determined without regard to this subsection) to the plan for the plan year under this section, or
(II) 100 percent of the minimum required contribution (determined without regard to this subsection or to any waiver under section 412(c)) to the plan for the preceding plan year.

Subclause (II) shall not apply if the preceding plan year referred to in such clause was not a year of 12 months.
(E) Fiscal years, short years, and years with alternate valuation date.
(i) Fiscal years. In applying this paragraph to a plan year beginning on any date other than January 1, there shall be substituted for the months specified in this paragraph, the months which correspond thereto.
(ii) Short plan year. This subparagraph shall be applied to plan years of less than 12 months in accordance with regulations prescribed by the Secretary.
(iii) Plan with alternate valuation date. The Secretary shall prescribe regulations for the application of this paragraph in the case of a plan which has a valuation date other than the first day of the plan year.
(F) Quarterly contributions not to include certain increased contributions. Subparagraph (D) shall be applied without regard to any increase under subsection (c)(7).

(4) Liquidity requirement in connection with quarterly contributions.
(A) In general. A plan to which this paragraph applies shall be treated as failing to pay the full amount of any required installment under paragraph (3) to the extent that the value of the liquid assets paid in such installment is less than the liquidity shortfall (whether or not such liquidity shortfall exceeds the amount of such installment required to be paid but for this paragraph).
(B) Plans to which paragraph applies. This paragraph shall apply to a plan (other than a plan described in subsection (g)(2)(B)) which—
(i) is required to pay installments under paragraph (3) for a plan year, and
(ii) has a liquidity shortfall for any quarter during such plan year.
(C) Period of underpayment. For purposes of paragraph (3)(A), any portion of an installment that is treated as not paid under subparagraph (A) shall continue to be treated as unpaid until the close of the quarter in which the due date for such installment occurs.

(D) Limitation on increase. If the amount of any required installment is increased by reason of subparagraph (A), in no event shall such increase exceed the amount which, when added to prior installments for the plan year, is necessary to increase the funding target attainment percentage of the plan for the plan year (taking into account the expected increase in funding target due to benefits accruing or earned during the plan year) to 100 percent.
(E) Definitions. For purposes of this paragraph—
(i) Liquidity shortfall. The term "liquidity shortfall" means, with respect to any required installment, an amount equal to the excess (as of the last day of the quarter for which such installment is made) of—
(I) the base amount with respect to such quarter, over
(II) the value (as of such last day) of the plan's liquid assets.
(ii) Base amount.
(I) In general. The term "base amount" means, with respect to any quarter, an amount equal to 3 times the sum of the adjusted disbursements from the plan for the 12 months ending on the last day of such quarter.
(II) Special rule. If the amount determined under subclause (I) exceeds an amount equal to 2 times the sum of the adjusted disbursements from the plan for the 36 months ending on the last day of the quarter and an enrolled actuary certifies to the satisfaction of the Secretary that such excess is the result of nonrecurring circumstances, the base amount with respect to such quarter shall be determined without regard to amounts related to those nonrecurring circumstances.
(iii) Disbursements from the plan. The term "disbursements from the plan" means all disbursements from the trust, including purchases of annuities, payments of single sums and other benefits, and administrative expenses.
(iv) Adjusted disbursements. The term "adjusted disbursements" means disbursements from the plan reduced by the product of—
(I) the plan's funding target attainment percentage for the plan year, and
(II) the sum of the purchases of annuities, payments of single sums, and such other disbursements as the Secretary shall provide in regulations.
(v) Liquid assets. The term "liquid assets" means cash, marketable securities, and such other assets as specified by the Secretary in regulations.
(vi) Quarter. The term "quarter" means, with respect to any required installment, the 3-month period preceding the month in which the due date for such installment occurs.
(F) Regulations. The Secretary may prescribe such regulations as are necessary to carry out this paragraph.

(k) Imposition of lien where failure to make required contributions.
(1) In general. In the case of a plan to which this subsection applies (as provided under paragraph (2)), if—
(A) any person fails to make a contribution payment required by section 412 and this section before the due date for such payment, and
(B) the unpaid balance of such payment (including interest), when added to the aggregate unpaid balance of all preceding such payments for which payment was not

Stock options — Code Sec. 430

made before the due date (including interest), exceeds $1,000,000,
then there shall be a lien in favor of the plan in the amount determined under paragraph (3) upon all property and rights to property, whether real or personal, belonging to such person and any other person who is a member of the same controlled group of which such person is a member.

(2) Plans to which subsection applies. This subsection shall apply to a defined benefit plan (other than a multiemployer plan) covered under section 4021 of the Employee Retirement Income Security Act of 1974 for any plan year for which the funding target attainment percentage (as defined in subsection (d)(2)) of such plan is less than 100 percent.

(3) Amount of lien. For purposes of paragraph (1), the amount of the lien shall be equal to the aggregate unpaid balance of contribution payments required under this section and section 412 for which payment has not been made before the due date.

(4) Notice of failure; lien.

(A) Notice of failure. A person committing a failure described in paragraph (1) shall notify the Pension Benefit Guaranty Corporation of such failure within 10 days of the due date for the required contribution payment.

(B) Period of lien. The lien imposed by paragraph (1) shall arise on the due date for the required contribution payment and shall continue until the last day of the first plan year in which the plan ceases to be described in paragraph (1)(B). Such lien shall continue to run without regard to whether such plan continues to be described in paragraph (2) during the period referred to in the preceding sentence.

(C) Certain rules to apply. Any amount with respect to which a lien is imposed under paragraph (1) shall be treated as taxes due and owing the United States and rules similar to the rules of subsections (c), (d), and (e) of section 4068 of the Employee Retirement Income Security Act of 1974 shall apply with respect to a lien imposed by subsection (a) and the amount with respect to such lien.

(5) Enforcement. Any lien created under paragraph (1) may be perfected and enforced only by the Pension Benefit Guaranty Corporation, or at the direction of the Pension Benefit Guaranty Corporation, by the contributing sponsor (or any member of the controlled group of the contributing sponsor).

(6) Definitions. For purposes of this subsection—

(A) Contribution payment. The term "contribution payment" means, in connection with a plan, a contribution payment required to be made to the plan, including any required installment under paragraphs (3) and (4) of subsection (j).

(B) Due date; required installment. The terms "due date" and "required installment" have the meanings given such terms by subsection (j).

(C) Controlled group. The term "controlled group" means any group treated as a single employer under subsections (b), (c), (m), and (o) of section 414.

(l) Qualified transfers to health benefit accounts.

In the case of a qualified transfer (as defined in section 420), any assets so transferred shall not, for purposes of this section, be treated as assets in the plan.

In 2010, P.L. 111-192, Sec. 201(b)(3)(A), substituted "any shortfall amortization base which has not been fully amortized under this subsection" for "the shortfall amortization bases for such plan year and each of the 6 preceding plan years" in subsec. (c)(1)... Sec. 201(b)(1), addded subpara. (c)(2)(D)... Sec. 201(b)(2), added para. (c)(7)... Sec. 201(b)(3)(B), added subpara. (j)(3)(F), effective for plan yrs. begin. after 12/31/2007... Sec. 204(b), added subpara. (f)(3)(D), effective for plan yrs. begin. after 8/31/2009. Sec. 204(c)(2) of this Act, reads as follows:

"(2) Special rule. In the case of a plan for which the valuation date is not the first day of the plan year, the amendments made by this section shall apply to plan years beginning after December 31, 2008."

In 2008, P.L. 110-458, Sec. 101(b)(2)(A), amended subsec. (b), effective for plan years beginning after 12/31/2008. Sec. 101(b)(3)(B), P.L. 110-458, provides:

"(B) Election for earlier application. The amendments made by such paragraphs shall apply to a plan for the first plan year beginning after December 31, 2007, if the plan sponsor makes the election under this subparagraph. An election under this subparagraph shall be made at such time and in such manner as the Secretary of the Treasury or the Secretary's delegate may prescribe, and, once made, may be revoked only with the consent of the Secretary."

Prior to amendment, subsec. (b) read as follows:

"(b) Target normal cost. For purposes of this section, except as provided in subsection (i)(2) with respect to plans in at-risk status, the term 'target normal cost' means, for any plan year, the present value of all benefits which are expected to accrue or to be earned under the plan during the plan year. For purposes of this subsection, if any benefit attributable to services performed in a preceding plan year is increased by reason of any increase in compensation during the current plan year, the increase in such benefit shall be treated as having accrued during the current plan year."

—P.L. 110-458, Sec. 101(b)(2)(B), inserted "beginning" before "after 2008" in clause (c)(5)(B)(iii) [Act Sec. 202(b)(1) repealed clause (c)(5)(B)(iii), see below] ... Sec. 101(b)(2)(C), added "for such year" after "beginning in 2007" in subclause (c)(5)(B)(iii)(II) [Sec. 202(b)(1) of this Act redesignated clause (c)(5)(B)(iv) as clause (c)(5)(B)(iii), see below] ... Sec. 101(b)(2)(D)(i), deleted "as of the first day of the plan year" after "by the plan sponsor" subpara. (f)(3)(A) ... Sec. 101(b)(2)(D)(ii), substituted "paragraph (3)" for "paragraph (2)" in subpara. (f)(4)(A) ... Sec. 101(b)(2)(D)(iii), substituted "subsection (b), (c), or (e) of section 436" for "paragraph (1), (2), or (4) of section 206(g)" in clause (f)(6)(B)(iii) ... Sec. 101(b)(2)(D)(iv), deleted "the sum of" after "(but not below zero) by" in subpara. (f)(6)(C) ... Sec. 101(b)(2)(D)(v), deleted "of the Treasury" after "Secretary" in para. (f)(8) ... Sec. 101(b)(2)(E)(i), inserted "and target normal cost" after "funding target" in subpara. (h)(2)(B) ... Sec. 101(b)(2)(E)(ii), substituted "benefits" for "liabilities" in subpara. (h)(2)(B) ... Sec. 101(b)(2)(E)(iii), substituted "section 417(e)(3)(D)(i) for such month" for "section 417(e)(3)(D)(i)) for such month" in subpara. (h)(2)(F) ... Sec. 101(b)(2)(E)(iv), substituted "subparagraph (C)" for "subparagraph (B)" in subpara. (h)(2)(F), effective for plan yrs. begin. after 12/31/2007 [as if included in Sec. 112, P.L. 109-280].

—P.L. 110-458, Sec. 101(b)(2)(F)(i)(I), amended subpara. (i)(2)(A).

Prior to amendment, subpara. (i)(2)(A) read as follows:

"(A) the present value of all benefits which are expected to accrue or be earned under the plan during the plan year, determined using the additional actuarial assumptions described in paragraph (1)(B), plus" ... Sec. 101(b)(2)(F)(i)(II), substituted "the amount determined under subsection (b)(1)(A)(i) with respect to the plan for the plan year" for "the target normal cost (determined without regard to this paragraph) of the plan for the plan year" in subpara. (i)(2)(B), effective for plan years beginning after 12/31/2008 and as provided in Sec. 101(b)(3)(B), P.L. 110-458, see above.... Sec. 101(b)(2)(F)(ii), substituted "subparagraph (A)" for "subparagraph (A)(ii)" in the last sentence of subpara. (i)(4)(B)... Sec. 101(b)(2)(G)(i), added a sentence at the end of subpara. (j)(3)(A)... Sec. 101(b)(2)(G)(ii), substituted "section 412(c)" for "section 302(c)" in subclause (j)(3)(D)(ii)(II)... Sec. 101(b)(2)(G)(iii), added clause (j)(3)(E)(iii)... Sec. 101(b)(2)(G)(iv), substituted ", short years, and years with alternate valuation date" for "and short years" in the heading of subpara. (j)(3)(E)... Sec. 101(b)(2)(H)(i), inserted "(as provided under paragraph (2))" after "applies" in para. (k)(1)... Sec. 101(b)(2)(H)(ii), substituted a period for ", except that in the case of a payment other than a required installment, the due date shall be the date such payment is required to be made under section 430." in subpara. (k)(6)(B), effective for plan yrs. begin. after 12/31/2007 [as if included in Sec. 112, P.L. 109-280].

—P.L. 110-458, Sec. 104(b), substituted "commercial" for "commercial airline" in Sec. 402(c)(1)(A), P.L. 109-280 [reproduced below] see below.

—P.L. 110-458, Sec. 121(b), amended the last sentence of subpara. (g)(3)(B), effective for plan yrs. begin. after 12/31/2007, as if included in Sec. 112 of the Pension Protection Act of 2006, P.L. 109-280.

Prior to amendment, the last sentence of subpara. (g)(3)(B) read as follows:

"Any such averaging shall be adjusted for contributions and distributions (as provided by the Secretary)."

—P.L. 110-458, Sec. 126(a), amended Sec. 402(e)(4)(C), P.L. 109-280, reproduced below, effective for plan yrs. begin. afer 12/31/2007.

Prior to amendment, Sec. 402(e)(4)(C), P.L. 109-280, read as follows:

"(C) the value of plan assets shall be equal to their fair market value."

—P.L. 110-458, Sec. 202(b)(1), repealed clause (c)(5)(B)(iii), and redesignated clause (c)(5)(B)(iv) as clause (c)(5)(B)(iii).... Sec. 202(b)(2), amended clause (c)(5)(B)(i), effective for plan yrs. begin. after 12/31/2007, as if included in Sec. 112 of the Pension Protection Act of 2006, P.L. 109-280.

Prior to repeal, clause (c)(5)(B)(iii) read as follows:

"(iii) Limitation. Clause (i) shall not apply with respect to any plan year beginning after 2008 unless the shortfall amortization base for each of the preceding years beginning after 2007 was zero (determined after application of this subparagraph).".

Prior to amendment, clause (c)(5)(B)(i) read as follows:

"(i) In general. Except as provided in clauses (iii) and (iv), in the case of plan years beginning after 2007 and before 2011, only the applicable percentage of the funding target shall be taken into account under paragraph (3)(A) in determining the funding shortfall for the plan year for purposes of subparagraph (A).".

In 2006, P.L. 109-280, Sec. 104, of this Act, reads as follows:

"Sec. 104. SPECIAL RULES FOR MULTIPLE EMPLOYER PLANS OF CERTAIN COOPERATIVES.

"(a) General Rule. Except as provided in this section, if a plan in existence on July 26, 2005, was an eligible cooperative plan for its plan year which includes such date, the amendments made by this subtitle and subtitle B shall not apply to plan years beginning before the earlier of—

"(1) the first plan year for which the plan ceases to be an eligible cooperative plan, or

"(2) January 1, 2017.

"(b) Interest Rate. In applying section 302(b)(5)(B) of the Employee Retirement Income Security Act of 1974 and section 412(b)(5)(B) of the Internal Revenue Code of 1986 (as in effect before the amendments made by this subtitle and subtitle B) to an eligible cooperative plan for plan years beginning after December 31, 2007, and before the first plan year to which such amendments apply, the third segment rate determined under section 303(h)(2)(C)(iii) of such Act and section 430(h)(2)(C)(iii) of such Code (as added by such amendments) shall be used in lieu of the interest rate otherwise used.

"(c) Eligible Cooperative Plan Defined. For purposes of this section, a plan shall be treated as an eligible cooperative plan for a plan year if the plan is maintained by more than 1 employer and at least 85 percent of the employers are—

"(1) rural cooperatives (as defined in section 401(k)(7)(B) of such Code without regard to clause (iv) thereof), or

"(2) organizations which are—

"(A) cooperative organizations described in section 1381(a) of such Code which are more than 50-percent owned by agricultural producers or by cooperatives owned by agricultural producers, or

"(B) more than 50-percent owned, or controlled by, one or more cooperative organizations described in subparagraph (A).

"A plan shall also be treated as an eligible cooperative plan for any plan year for which it is described in section 210(a) of the Employee Retirement Income Security Act of 1974 and is maintained by a rural telephone cooperative association described in section 3(40)(B)(v) of such Act."

—P.L. 109-280, Sec. 105, of this Act, reads as follows:

"Sec. 105. TEMPORARY RELIEF FOR CERTAIN PBGC SETTLEMENT PLANS.

"(a) General Rule. Except as provided in this section, if a plan in existence on July 26, 2005, was a PBGC settlement plan as of such date, the amendments made by this subtitle and subtitle B shall not apply to plan years beginning before January 1, 2014.

"(b) Interest Rate. In applying section 302(b)(5)(B) of the Employee Retirement Income Security Act of 1974 and section 412(b)(5)(B) of the Internal Revenue Code of 1986 (as in effect before the amendments made by this subtitle and subtitle B) to a PBGC settlement plan for plan years beginning after December 31, 2007, and before January 1, 2014, the third segment rate determined under section 303(h)(2)(C)(iii) of such Act and 430(h)(2)(C)(iii) of such Code (as added by such amendments) shall be used in lieu of the interest rate otherwise used.

"(c) PBGC Settlement Plan. For purposes of this section, the term 'PBGC settlement plan' means a defined benefit plan (other than a multiemployer plan) to which section 302 of such Act and section 412 of such Code apply and—

"(1) which was sponsored by an employer which was in bankruptcy, giving rise to a claim by the Pension Benefit Guaranty Corporation of not greater than $150,000,000, and the sponsorship of which was assumed by another employer that was not a member of the same controlled group as the bankrupt sponsor and the claim of the Pension Benefit Guaranty Corporation was settled or withdrawn in connection with the assumption of the sponsorship, or

"(2) which, by agreement with the Pension Benefit Guaranty Corporation, was spun off from a plan subsequently terminated by such Corporation under section 4042 of the Employee Retirement Income Security Act of 1974."

—P.L. 109-280, Sec. 106, of this Act, reads as follows:

"Sec. 106. SPECIAL RULES FOR PLANS OF CERTAIN GOVERNMENT CONTRACTORS.

"(a) General Rule. Except as provided in this section, if a plan is an eligible government contractor plan, this subtitle and subtitle B shall not apply to plan years beginning before the earliest of—

"(1) the first plan year for which the plan ceases to be an eligible government contractor plan,

"(2) the effective date of the Cost Accounting Standards Pension Harmonization Rule, or

"(3) January 1, 2011.

"(b) Interest Rate. In applying section 302(b)(5)(B) of the Employee Retirement Income Security Act of 1974 and section 412(b)(5)(B) of the Internal Revenue Code of 1986 (as in effect before the amendments made by this subtitle and subtitle B) to an eligible government contractor plan for plan years beginning after December 31, 2007, and before the first plan year to which such amendments apply, the third segment rate determined under section 303(h)(2)(C)(iii) of such Act and section 430(h)(2)(C)(iii) of such Code (as added by such amendments) shall be used in lieu of the interest rate otherwise used.

"(c) Eligible Government Contractor Plan Defined. For purposes of this section, a plan shall be treated as an eligible government contractor plan if it is maintained by a corporation or a member of the same affiliated group (as defined by section 1504(a) of the Internal Revenue Code of 1986), whose primary source of revenue is derived from business performed under contracts with the United States that are subject to the Federal Acquisition Regulations (Chapter 1 of Title 48, C.F.R.) and that are also subject to the Defense Federal Acquisition Regulation Supplement (Chapter 2 of Title 48, C.F.R.), and whose revenue derived from such business in the previous fiscal year exceeded $5,000,000,000, and whose pension plan costs that are assignable under those contracts are subject to sections 412 and 413 of the Cost Accounting Standards (48 C.F.R. 9904.412 and 9904.413).

"(d) Cost Accounting Standards Pension Harmonization Rule. The Cost Accounting Standards Board shall review and revise sections 412 and 413 of the Cost Accounting Standards (48 C.F.R. 9904.412 and 9904.413) to harmonize the minimum required contribution under the Employee Retirement Income Security Act of 1974 of eligible government contractor plans and government reimbursable pension plan costs not later than January 1, 2010. Any final rule adopted by the Cost Accounting Standards Board shall be deemed the Cost Accounting Standards Pension Harmonization Rule."

—P.L. 109-280, Sec. 112(a), added Code Sec. 430, effective for plan yrs. begin. after 12/31/2007.

—P.L. 109-280, Sec. 115, (a)-(c) of this Act, reads as follows:

"Sec. 115. MODIFICATION OF TRANSITION RULE TO PENSION FUNDING REQUIREMENTS.

"(a) In General. In the case of a plan that—

"(1) was not required to pay a variable rate premium for the plan year beginning in 1996,

"(2) has not, in any plan year beginning after 1995, merged with another plan (other than a plan sponsored by an employer that was in 1996 within the controlled group of the plan sponsor); and

"(3) is sponsored by a company that is engaged primarily in the interurban or interstate passenger bus service,

"the rules described in subsection (b) shall apply for any plan year beginning after December 31, 2007.

"(b) Modified Rules. The rules described in this subsection are as follows:

"(1) For purposes of section 430(j)(3) of the Internal Revenue Code of 1986 and section 303(j)(3) of the Employee Retirement Income Security Act of 1974, the plan shall be treated as not having a funding shortfall for any plan year.

"(2) For purposes of —

"(A) determining unfunded vested benefits under section 4006(a)(3)(E)(iii) of such Act, and

"(B) determining any present value or making any computation under section 412 of such Code or section 302 of such Act,

"the mortality table shall be the mortality table used by the plan.

"(3) Section 430(c)(5)(B) of such Code and section 303(c)(5)(B) of such Act (relating to phase-in of funding target for exemption from new shortfall amortization base) shall each be applied by substituting '2012' for '2011' therein and by substituting for the table therein the following:

In the case of a plan year beginning in calendar year:	The applicable percentage is
2008	90 percent
2009	92 percent
2010	94 percent
2011	96 percent

"(c) Definitions. Any term used in this section which is also used in section 430 of such Code or section 303 of such Act shall have the meaning provided such term in such section. If the same term has a different meaning in such Code and such Act, such term shall, for purposes of this section, have the meaning provided by such Code when applied with respect to such Code and the meaning provided by such Act when applied with respect to such Act."

—P.L. 109-280, Sec. 402, (a)-(g)(1) [as amended by Sec. 104(b), 126(a), P.L. 110-458, see above] of this Act, reads as follows:

"Sec. 402. SPECIAL FUNDING RULES FOR CERTAIN PLANS MAINTAINED BY COMMERCIAL AIRLINES. (a) In General. The plan sponsor of an eligible plan may elect to either—

"(1) have the rules of subsection (b) apply, or

"(2) have section 303 of the Employee Retirement Income Security Act of 1974 and section 430 of the Internal Revenue Code of 1986 applied to its first taxable year beginning in 2008 by amortizing the shortfall amortization base for such taxable year over a period of 10 plan years (rather than 7 plan years) beginning with such plan year.

"(b) Alternative Funding Schedule—

"(1) In general. If an election is made under subsection (a)(1) to have this subsection apply to an eligible plan and the requirements of paragraphs (2) and (3) are met with respect to the plan—

"(A) in the case of any applicable plan year beginning before January 1, 2008, the plan shall not have an accumulated funding deficiency for purposes of section 302 of the Employee Retirement Income Security Act of 1974 and sections 412 and 4971 of the Internal Revenue Code of 1986 if contributions to the plan for the plan year are not less than the minimum required contribution determined under subsection (e) for the plan for the plan year, and

"(B) in the case of any applicable plan year beginning on or after January 1, 2008, the minimum required contribution determined under sections 303 of such Act and 430 of such Code shall, for purposes of sections 302 and 303 of such Act and sections 412, 430, and 4971 of such Code, be equal to the minimum required contribution determined under subsection (e) for the plan for the plan year.

"(2) Accrual restrictions—

"(A) In general. The requirements of this paragraph are met if, effective as of the first day of the first applicable plan year and at all times thereafter while an election under this section is in effect, the plan provides that—

"(i) the accrued benefit, any death or disability benefit, and any social security supplement described in the last sentence of section 411(a)(9) of such Code and section 204(b)(1)(G) of such Act, of each participant are frozen at the amount of such benefit or supplement immediately before such first day, and

"(ii) all other benefits under the plan are eliminated,

"but only to the extent the freezing or elimination of such benefits would have been permitted under section 411(d)(6) of such Code and section 204(g) of such Act if they had been implemented by a plan amendment adopted immediately before such first day.

"(B) Increases in section 415 limits. If a plan provides that an accrued benefit of a participant which has been subject to any limitation under section 415 of such Code will be increased if such limitation is increased, the plan shall not be treated as meeting the requirements of this section unless, effective as of the first day of the first applicable plan year (or, if later, the date of the enactment of this Act) and at all times thereafter while an election under this section is in effect, the plan provides that any such increase shall not take effect. A plan shall not fail to meet the requirements of section 411(d)(6) of such Code and section 204(g) of such Act solely because the plan is amended to meet the requirements of this subparagraph.

"(3) Restriction on applicable benefit increases—

"(A) In general. The requirements of this paragraph are met if no applicable benefit increase takes effect at any time during the period beginning on July 26, 2005, and ending on the day before the first day of the first applicable plan year.

"(B) Applicable benefit increase. For purposes of this paragraph, the term 'applicable benefit increase' means, with respect to any plan year, any increase in liabilities of the plan by plan amendment (or otherwise provided in regulations provided by the Secretary) which, but for this paragraph, would occur during the plan year by reason of—

"(i) any increase in benefits,

"(ii) any change in the accrual of benefits, or

"(iii) any change in the rate at which benefits become nonforfeitable under the plan.

"(4) Exception for imputed disability service. Paragraphs (2) and (3) shall not apply to any accrual or increase with respect to imputed service provided to a participant during any period of the participant's disability occurring on or after the effective date of the plan amendment providing the restrictions under paragraph (2) (or on or after July 26, 2005, in the case of the restrictions under paragraph (3)) if the participant—

"(A) was receiving disability benefits as of such date, or

"(B) was receiving sick pay and subsequently determined to be eligible for disability benefits as of such date.

"(c) Definitions. For purposes of this section—

"(1) Eligible plan. The term 'eligible plan' means a defined benefit plan (other than a multiemployer plan) to which sections 302 of such Act and 412 of such Code applies which is sponsored by an employer—

"(A) which is a commercial passenger airline, or

"(B) the principal business of which is providing catering services to a commercial passenger airline.

"(2) Applicable plan year. The term 'applicable plan year' means each plan year to which the election under subsection (a)(1) applies under subsection (d)(1)(A).

"(d) Elections and Related Terms—

"(1) Years for which election made—

"(A) Alternative funding schedule. If an election under subsection (a)(1) was made with respect to an eligible plan, the plan sponsor may select either a plan year beginning in 2006 or a plan year beginning in 2007 as the first plan year to which such election applies. The election shall apply to such plan year and all subsequent years. The election shall be made—

"(i) not later than December 31, 2006, in the case of an election for a plan year beginning in 2006, or

"(ii) not later than December 31, 2007, in the case of an election for a plan year beginning in 2007.

"(B) 10 year amortization. An election under subsection (a)(2) shall be made not later than December 31, 2007.

"(C) Election of new plan year for alternative funding schedule. In the case of an election under subsection (a)(1), the plan sponsor may specify a new plan year in such election and the plan year of the plan may be changed to such new plan year without the approval of the Secretary of the Treasury.

"(2) Manner of election. A plan sponsor shall make any election under subsection (a) in such manner as the Secretary of the Treasury may prescribe. Such election, once made, may be revoked only with the consent of such Secretary.

"(e) Minimum Required Contribution. In the case of an eligible plan with respect to which an election is made under subsection (a)(1)—

"(1) In general. In the case of any applicable plan year during the amortization period, the minimum required contribution shall be the amount necessary to amortize the unfunded liability of the plan, determined as of the first day of the plan year, in equal annual installments (until fully amortized) over the remainder of the amortization period. Such amount shall be separately determined for each applicable plan year.

"(2) Years after amortization period. In the case of any plan year beginning after the end of the amortization period, section 302(a)(2)(A) of such Act and section 412(a)(2)(A) of such Code shall apply to such plan, but the prefunding balance and funding standard carryover balance as of the first day of the first of such years under section 303(f) of such Act and section 430(f) of such Code shall be zero.

"(3) Definitions. For purposes of this section—

"(A) Unfunded liability. The term 'unfunded liability' means the unfunded accrued liability under the plan, determined under the unit credit funding method.

"(B) Amortization period. The term 'amortization period' means the 17-plan year period beginning with the first applicable plan year.

"(4) Other rules. In determining the minimum required contribution and amortization amount under this subsection—

"(A) the provisions of section 302(c)(3) of such Act and section 412(c)(3) of such Code, as in effect before the date of enactment of this section, shall apply,

"(B) a rate of interest of 8.85 percent shall be used for all calculations requiring an interest rate, and

"(C) the value of plan assets shall be determined under sections 303(g)(3) of such Act and 430(g)(3) of such Code."

"(5) Special rule for certain plan spinoffs. For purposes of subsection (b), if, with respect to any eligible plan to which this subsection applies—

"(A) any applicable plan year includes the date of the enactment of this Act,

"(B) a plan was spun off from the eligible plan during the plan year but before such date of enactment,

"the minimum required contribution under paragraph (1) for the eligible plan for such applicable plan year shall be an aggregate amount determined as if the plans were a single plan for that plan year (based on the full 12-month plan year in effect prior to the spin-off). The employer shall designate the allocation of such aggregate amount between such plans for the applicable plan year.

"(f) Special Rules for Certain Balances and Waivers. In the case of an eligible plan with respect to which an election is made under subsection (a)(1)—

"(1) Funding standard account and credit balances. Any charge or credit in the funding standard account under section 302 of such Act or section 412 of such Code, and any prefunding balance or funding standard carryover balance under section 303 of such Act or section 430 of such Code, as of the day before the first day of the first applicable plan year, shall be reduced to zero.

"(2) Waived funding deficiencies. Any waived funding deficiency under sections 302 and 303 of such Act or section 412 of such Code, as in effect before the date of enactment of this section, shall be deemed satisfied as of the first day of the first applicable plan year and the amount of such waived funding deficiency shall be taken into account in determining the plan's unfunded liability under subsection (e)(3)(A). In the case of a plan amendment adopted to satisfy the requirements of subsection (b)(2), the plan shall not be deemed to violate section 304(b) of such Act or section 412(f) of such Code, as so in effect, by reason of such amendment or any increase in benefits provided to such plan's participants under a separate plan that is a defined contribution plan or a multiemployer plan.

"(g) Other Rules for Plans Making Election Under This Section—

"(1) Successor plans to certain plans. If—

"(A) an election under paragraph (1) or (2) of subsection (a) is in effect with respect to any eligible plan, and

"(B) the eligible plan is maintained by an employer that establishes or maintains 1 or more other defined benefit plans (other than any multiemployer plan), and such other plans in combination provide benefit accruals to any substantial number of successor employees,

"the Secretary of the Treasury may, in the Secretary's discretion, determine that any trust of which any other such plan is a part does not constitute a qualified trust under section 401(a) of the Internal Revenue Code of 1986 unless all benefit obligations of the eligible plan have been satisfied. For purposes of this paragraph, the term 'successor employee' means any employee who is or was covered by the eligible plan and any employees who perform substantially the same type of work with respect to the same business operations as an employee covered by such eligible plan."

Sec. 431. Minimum funding standards for multiemployer plans.

(a) In general.

For purposes of section 412, the accumulated funding deficiency of a multiemployer plan for any plan year is—

(1) except as provided in paragraph (2), the amount, determined as of the end of the plan year, equal to the excess (if any) of the total charges to the funding standard account of the plan for all plan years (beginning with the first plan year for which this part applies to the plan) over the total credits to such account for such years, and

(2) if the multiemployer plan is in reorganization for any plan year, the accumulated funding deficiency of the plan determined under section 4243 of the Employee Retirement Income Security Act of 1974.

(b) Funding standard account.

(1) Account required. Each multiemployer plan to which this part applies shall establish and maintain a funding standard account. Such account shall be credited and charged solely as provided in this section.

(2) Charges to account. For a plan year, the funding standard account shall be charged with the sum of—

(A) the normal cost of the plan for the plan year,

(B) the amounts necessary to amortize in equal annual installments (until fully amortized)—
  (i) in the case of a plan which comes into existence on or after January 1, 2008, the unfunded past service liability under the plan on the first day of the first plan year to which this section applies, over a period of 15 plan years,
  (ii) separately, with respect to each plan year, the net increase (if any) in unfunded past service liability under the plan arising from plan amendments adopted in such year, over a period of 15 plan years,
  (iii) separately, with respect to each plan year, the net experience loss (if any) under the plan, over a period of 15 plan years, and
  (iv) separately, with respect to each plan year, the net loss (if any) resulting from changes in actuarial assumptions used under the plan, over a period of 15 plan years,
(C) the amount necessary to amortize each waived funding deficiency (within the meaning of section 412(c)(3)) for each prior plan year in equal annual installments (until fully amortized) over a period of 15 plan years,
(D) the amount necessary to amortize in equal annual installments (until fully amortized) over a period of 5 plan years any amount credited to the funding standard account under section 412(b)(3)(D) (as in effect on the day before the date of the enactment of the Pension Protection Act of 2006), and
(E) the amount necessary to amortize in equal annual installments (until fully amortized) over a period of 20 years the contributions which would be required to be made under the plan but for the provisions of section 412(c)(7)(A)(i)(I) (as in effect on the day before the date of the enactment of the Pension Protection Act of 2006).

(3) Credits to account. For a plan year, the funding standard account shall be credited with the sum of—
(A) the amount considered contributed by the employer to or under the plan for the plan year,
(B) the amount necessary to amortize in equal annual installments (until fully amortized)—
  (i) separately, with respect to each plan year, the net decrease (if any) in unfunded past service liability under the plan arising from plan amendments adopted in such year, over a period of 15 plan years,
  (ii) separately, with respect to each plan year, the net experience gain (if any) under the plan, over a period of 15 plan years, and
  (iii) separately, with respect to each plan year, the net gain (if any) resulting from changes in actuarial assumptions used under the plan, over a period of 15 plan years,
(C) the amount of the waived funding deficiency (within the meaning of section 412(c)(3)) for the plan year, and
(D) in the case of a plan year for which the accumulated funding deficiency is determined under the funding standard account if such plan year follows a plan year for which such deficiency was determined under the alternative minimum funding standard under section 412(g) (as in effect on the day before the date of the enactment of the Pension Protection Act of 2006), the excess (if any) of any debit balance in the funding standard account (determined without regard to this subparagraph) over any debit balance in the alternative minimum funding standard account.

(4) Special rule for amounts first amortized in plan years before 2008. In the case of any amount amortized under section 412(b) (as in effect on the day before the date of the enactment of the Pension Protection Act of 2006) over any period beginning with a plan year beginning before 2008 in lieu of the amortization described in paragraphs (2)(B) and (3)(B), such amount shall continue to be amortized under such section as so in effect.

(5) Combining and offsetting amounts to be amortized. Under regulations prescribed by the Secretary, amounts required to be amortized under paragraph (2) or paragraph (3), as the case may be—
(A) may be combined into one amount under such paragraph to be amortized over a period determined on the basis of the remaining amortization period for all items entering into such combined amount, and
(B) may be offset against amounts required to be amortized under the other such paragraph, with the resulting amount to be amortized over a period determined on the basis of the remaining amortization periods for all items entering into whichever of the two amounts being offset is the greater.

(6) Interest. The funding standard account (and items therein) shall be charged or credited (as determined under regulations prescribed by the Secretary of the Treasury) with interest at the appropriate rate consistent with the rate or rates of interest used under the plan to determine costs.

(7) Special rules relating to charges and credits to funding standard account. For purposes of this part—
(A) Withdrawal liability. Any amount received by a multiemployer plan in payment of all or part of an employer's withdrawal liability under part 1 of subtitle E of title IV of the Employee Retirement Income Security Act of 1974 shall be considered an amount contributed by the employer to or under the plan. The Secretary may prescribe by regulation additional charges and credits to a multiemployer plan's funding standard account to the extent necessary to prevent withdrawal liability payments from being unduly reflected as advance funding for plan liabilities.
(B) Adjustments when a multiemployer plan leaves reorganization. If a multiemployer plan is not in reorganization in the plan year but was in reorganization in the immediately preceding plan year, any balance in the funding standard account at the close of such immediately preceding plan year—
  (i) shall be eliminated by an offsetting credit or charge (as the case may be), but
  (ii) shall be taken into account in subsequent plan years by being amortized in equal annual installments (until fully amortized) over 30 plan years.
The preceding sentence shall not apply to the extent of any accumulated funding deficiency under section 4243(a) of such Act as of the end of the last plan year that the plan was in reorganization.
(C) Plan payments to supplemental program or withdrawal liability payment fund. Any amount paid by a plan during a plan year to the Pension Benefit Guaranty Corporation pursuant to section 4222 of such Act or to a fund exempt under section 501(c)(22) pursuant to section 4223 of such Act shall reduce the amount of contributions considered received by the plan for the plan year.
(D) Interim withdrawal liability payments. Any amount paid by an employer pending a final determination of the employer's withdrawal liability under part 1 of subtitle E of title IV of such Act and subsequently re-

funded to the employer by the plan shall be charged to the funding standard account in accordance with regulations prescribed by the Secretary.

(E) Election for deferral of charge for portion of net experience loss. If an election is in effect under section 412(b)(7)(F) (as in effect on the day before the date of the enactment of the Pension Protection Act of 2006) for any plan year, the funding standard account shall be charged in the plan year to which the portion of the net experience loss deferred by such election was deferred with the amount so deferred (and paragraph (2)(B)(iii) shall not apply to the amount so charged).

(F) Financial assistance. Any amount of any financial assistance from the Pension Benefit Guaranty Corporation to any plan, and any repayment of such amount, shall be taken into account under this section and section 412 in such manner as is determined by the Secretary.

(G) Short-term benefits. To the extent that any plan amendment increases the unfunded past service liability under the plan by reason of an increase in benefits which are not payable as a life annuity but are payable under the terms of the plan for a period that does not exceed 14 years from the effective date of the amendment, paragraph (2)(B)(ii) shall be applied separately with respect to such increase in unfunded past service liability by substituting the number of years of the period during which such benefits are payable for "15".

(8) **Special relief rules.** Notwithstanding any other provision of this subsection—

(A) Amortization of net investment losses.

(i) In general. A multiemployer plan with respect to which the solvency test under subparagraph (C) is met may treat the portion of any experience loss or gain attributable to net investment losses incurred in either or both of the first two plan years ending after August 31, 2008, as an item separate from other experience losses, to be amortized in equal annual installments (until fully amortized) over the period —

(I) beginning with the plan year in which such portion is first recognized in the actuarial value of assets, and

(I) ending with the last plan year in the 30-plan year period beginning with the plan year in which such net investment loss was incurred.

(ii) Coordination with extensions. If this subparagraph applies for any plan year—

(I) no extension of the amortization period under clause (i) shall be allowed under subsection (d), and

(II) if an extension was granted under subsection (d) for any plan year before the election to have this subparagraph apply to the plan year, such extension shall not result in such amortization period exceeding 30 years.

(iii) Net investment losses. For purposes of this subparagraph—

(I) In general. Net investment losses shall be determined in the manner prescribed by the Secretary on the basis of the difference between actual and expected returns (including any difference attributable to any criminally fraudulent investment arrangement).

(II) Criminally fraudulent investment arrangements. The determination as to whether an arrangement is a criminally fraudulent investment arrangement shall be made under rules substantially similar to the rules prescribed by the Secretary for purposes of section 165.

(B) Expanded smoothing period.

(i) In general. A multiemployer plan with respect to which the solvency test under subparagraph (C) is met may change its asset valuation method in a manner which—

(I) spreads the difference between expected and actual returns for either or both of the first 2 plan years ending after August 31, 2008, over a period of not more than 10 years,

(II) provides that for either or both of the first 2 plan years beginning after August 31, 2008, the value of plan assets at any time shall not be less than 80 percent or greater than 130 percent of the fair market value of such assets at such time, or

(III) makes both changes described in subclauses (I) and (II) to such method.

(ii) Asset valuation methods. If this subparagraph applies for any plan year—

(I) the Secretary shall not treat the asset valuation method of the plan as unreasonable solely because of the changes in such method described in clause (i), and

(II) such changes shall be deemed approved by the Secretary under section 302(d)(1) of the Employee Retirement Income Security Act of 1974 and section 412(d)(1).

(iii) Amortization of reduction in unfunded accrued liability. If this subparagraph and subparagraph (A) both apply for any plan year, the plan shall treat any reduction in unfunded accrued liability resulting from the application of this subparagraph as a separate experience amortization base, to be amortized in equal annual installments (until fully amortized) over a period of 30 plan years rather than the period such liability would otherwise be amortized over.

(C) Solvency test. The solvency test under this paragraph is met only if the plan actuary certifies that the plan is projected to have sufficient assets to timely pay expected benefits and anticipated expenditures over the amortization period, taking into account the changes in the funding standard account under this paragraph.

(D) Restriction on benefit increases. If subparagraph (A) or (B) apply to a multiemployer plan for any plan year, then, in addition to any other applicable restrictions on benefit increases, a plan amendment increasing benefits may not go into effect during either of the 2 plan years immediately following such plan year unless—

(i) the plan actuary certifies that—

(I) any such increase is paid for out of additional contributions not allocated to the plan immediately before the application of this paragraph to the plan, and

(II) the plan's funded percentage and projected credit balances for such 2 plan years are reasonably expected to be at least as high as such percentage and balances would have been if the benefit increase had not been adopted, or

(ii) the amendment is required as a condition of qualification under part I of subchapter D or to comply with other applicable law.

(E) Reporting. A plan sponsor of a plan to which this paragraph applies shall—

(i) give notice of such application to participants and beneficiaries of the plan, and

(ii) inform the Pension Benefit Guaranty Corporation of such application in such form and manner as the Director of the Pension Benefit Guaranty Corporation may prescribe.

(c) **Additional rules.**

(1) **Determinations to be made under funding method.** For purposes of this part, normal costs, accrued liability, past service liabilities, and experience gains and losses shall be determined under the funding method used to determine costs under the plan.

(2) **Valuation of assets.**

(A) In general. For purposes of this part, the value of the plan's assets shall be determined on the basis of any reasonable actuarial method of valuation which takes into account fair market value and which is permitted under regulations prescribed by the Secretary.

(B) Election with respect to bonds. The value of a bond or other evidence of indebtedness which is not in default as to principal or interest may, at the election of the plan administrator, be determined on an amortized basis running from initial cost at purchase to par value at maturity or earliest call date. Any election under this subparagraph shall be made at such time and in such manner as the Secretary shall by regulations provide, shall apply to all such evidences of indebtedness, and may be revoked only with the consent of the Secretary.

(3) **Actuarial assumptions must be reasonable.** For purposes of this section, all costs, liabilities, rates of interest, and other factors under the plan shall be determined on the basis of actuarial assumptions and methods—

(A) each of which is reasonable (taking into account the experience of the plan and reasonable expectations), and

(B) which, in combination, offer the actuary's best estimate of anticipated experience under the plan.

(4) **Treatment of certain changes as experience gain or loss.** For purposes of this section, if—

(A) a change in benefits under the Social Security Act or in other retirement benefits created under Federal or State law, or

(B) a change in the definition of the term "wages" under section 3121, or a change in the amount of such wages taken into account under regulations prescribed for purposes of section 401(a)(5),

results in an increase or decrease in accrued liability under a plan, such increase or decrease shall be treated as an experience loss or gain.

(5) **Full funding.** If, as of the close of a plan year, a plan would (without regard to this paragraph) have an accumulated funding deficiency in excess of the full funding limitation—

(A) the funding standard account shall be credited with the amount of such excess, and

(B) all amounts described in subparagraphs (B), (C), and (D) of subsection (b) (2) and subparagraph (B) of subsection (b)(3) which are required to be amortized shall be considered fully amortized for purposes of such subparagraphs.

(6) **Full-funding limitation.**

(A) In general. For purposes of paragraph (5), the term "full-funding limitation" means the excess (if any) of—

(i) the accrued liability (including normal cost) under the plan (determined under the entry age normal funding method if such accrued liability cannot be directly calculated under the funding method used for the plan), over

(ii) the lesser of—

(I) the fair market value of the plan's assets, or

(II) the value of such assets determined under paragraph (2).

(B) Minimum amount.

(i) In general. In no event shall the full-funding limitation determined under subparagraph (A) be less than the excess (if any) of—

(I) 90 percent of the current liability of the plan (including the expected increase in current liability due to benefits accruing during the plan year), over

(II) the value of the plan's assets determined under paragraph (2).

(ii) Assets. For purposes of clause (i), assets shall not be reduced by any credit balance in the funding standard account.

(C) Full funding limitation. For purposes of this paragraph, unless otherwise provided by the plan, the accrued liability under a multiemployer plan shall not include benefits which are not nonforfeitable under the plan after the termination of the plan (taking into consideration section 411(d)(3)).

(D) Current liability. For purposes of this paragraph—

(i) In general. The term "current liability" means all liabilities to employees and their beneficiaries under the plan.

(ii) Treatment of unpredictable contingent event benefits. For purposes of clause (i), any benefit contingent on an event other than—

(I) age, service, compensation, death, or disability, or

(II) an event which is reasonably and reliably predictable (as determined by the Secretary),

shall not be taken into account until the event on which the benefit is contingent occurs.

(iii) Interest rate used. The rate of interest used to determine current liability under this paragraph shall be the rate of interest determined under subparagraph (E).

(iv) Mortality tables.

(I) Commissioners' standard table. In the case of plan years beginning before the first plan year to which the first tables prescribed under subclause (II) apply, the mortality table used in determining current liability under this paragraph shall be the table prescribed by the Secretary which is based on the prevailing commissioners' standard table (described in section 807(d)(5)(A)) used to determine reserves for group annuity contracts issued on January 1, 1993.

(II) Secretarial authority. The Secretary may by regulation prescribe for plan years beginning after December 31, 1999, mortality tables to be used in determining current liability under this subsection. Such tables shall be based upon the actual experience of pension plans and projected trends in such experience. In prescribing such tables, the Secretary shall take into account results of available independent studies of mortality of individuals covered by pension plans.

(v) Separate mortality tables for the disabled. Notwithstanding clause (iv)—

(I) In general. The Secretary shall establish mortality tables which may be used (in lieu of the tables under clause (iv)) to determine current liability under this subsection for individuals who are entitled to benefits under the plan on account of disability. The Secretary shall establish separate tables for individuals whose disabilities occur in plan years beginning before January 1, 1995, and for individuals whose disabilities occur in plan years beginning on or after such date.

(II) Special rule for disabilities occurring after 1994. In the case of disabilities occurring in plan years beginning after December 31, 1994, the tables under subclause (I) shall apply only with respect to individuals described in such subclause who are disabled within the meaning of title II of the Social Security Act and the regulations thereunder.

(vi) Periodic review. The Secretary shall periodically (at least every 5 years) review any tables in effect under this subparagraph and shall, to the extent such Secretary determines necessary, by regulation update the tables to reflect the actual experience of pension plans and projected trends in such experience.

(E) Required change of interest rate. For purposes of determining a plan's current liability for purposes of this paragraph—

(i) In general. If any rate of interest used under the plan under subsection (b)(6) to determine cost is not within the permissible range, the plan shall establish a new rate of interest within the permissible range.

(ii) Permissible range. For purposes of this subparagraph—

(I) In general. Except as provided in subclause (II), the term "permissible range" means a rate of interest which is not more than 5 percent above, and not more than 10 percent below, the weighted average of the rates of interest on 30-year Treasury securities during the 4-year period ending on the last day before the beginning of the plan year.

(II) Secretarial authority. If the Secretary finds that the lowest rate of interest permissible under subclause (I) is unreasonably high, the Secretary may prescribe a lower rate of interest, except that such rate may not be less than 80 percent of the average rate determined under such subclause.

(iii) Assumptions. Notwithstanding paragraph (3)(A), the interest rate used under the plan shall be—

(I) determined without taking into account the experience of the plan and reasonable expectations, but

(II) consistent with the assumptions which reflect the purchase rates which would be used by insurance companies to satisfy the liabilities under the plan.

(7) Annual valuation.

(A) In general. For purposes of this section, a determination of experience gains and losses and a valuation of the plan's liability shall be made not less frequently than once every year, except that such determination shall be made more frequently to the extent provided in particular cases under regulations prescribed by the Secretary.

(B) Valuation date.

(i) Current year. Except as provided in clause (ii), the valuation referred to in subparagraph (A) shall be made as of a date within the plan year to which the valuation refers or within one month prior to the beginning of such year.

(ii) Use of prior year valuation. The valuation referred to in subparagraph (A) may be made as of a date within the plan year prior to the year to which the valuation refers if, as of such date, the value of the assets of the plan are not less than 100 percent of the plan's current liability (as defined in paragraph (6)(D) without regard to clause (iv) thereof).

(iii) Adjustments. Information under clause (ii) shall, in accordance with regulations, be actuarially adjusted to reflect significant differences in participants.

(iv) Limitation. A change in funding method to use a prior year valuation, as provided in clause (ii), may not be made unless as of the valuation date within the prior plan year, the value of the assets of the plan are not less than 125 percent of the plan's current liability (as defined in paragraph (6)(D) without regard to clause (iv) thereof).

(8) Time when certain contributions deemed made. For purposes of this section, any contributions for a plan year made by an employer after the last day of such plan year, but not later than two and one-half months after such day, shall be deemed to have been made on such last day. For purposes of this subparagraph, such two and one half month period may be extended for not more than six months under regulations prescribed by the Secretary.

(d) Extension of amortization periods for multiemployer plans.

(1) Automatic extension upon application by certain plans.

(A) In general. If the plan sponsor of a multiemployer plan—

(i) submits to the Secretary an application for an extension of the period of years required to amortize any unfunded liability described in any clause of subsection (b)(2)(B) or described in subsection (b)(4), and

(ii) includes with the application a certification by the plan's actuary described in subparagraph (B),

the Secretary shall extend the amortization period for the period of time (not in excess of 5 years) specified in the application. Such extension shall be in addition to any extension under paragraph (2).

(B) Criteria. A certification with respect to a multiemployer plan is described in this subparagraph if the plan's actuary certifies that, based on reasonable assumptions—

(i) absent the extension under subparagraph (A), the plan would have an accumulated funding deficiency in the current plan year or any of the 9 succeeding plan years,

(ii) the plan sponsor has adopted a plan to improve the plan's funding status,

(iii) the plan is projected to have sufficient assets to timely pay expected benefits and anticipated expenditures over the amortization period as extended, and

(iv) the notice required under paragraph (3)(A) has been provided.

(C) Termination. The preceding provisions of this paragraph shall not apply with respect to any application submitted after December 31, 2014.

(2) Alternative extension.

(A) In general. If the plan sponsor of a multiemployer plan submits to the Secretary an application for an extension of the period of years required to amortize any unfunded liability described in any clause of subsection (b)(2)(B) or described in subsection (b)(4), the Secretary may extend the amortization period for a period of time (not in excess of 10 years reduced by the number of years of any extension under paragraph (1) with respect to such unfunded liability) if the Secretary makes the determination described in subparagraph (B). Such extension shall be in addition to any extension under paragraph (1).

(B) Determination. The Secretary may grant an extension under subparagraph (A) if the Secretary determines that—

(i) such extension would carry out the purposes of this Act and would provide adequate protection for participants under the plan and their beneficiaries, and

(ii) the failure to permit such extension would—

(I) result in a substantial risk to the voluntary continuation of the plan, or a substantial curtailment of pension benefit levels or employee compensation, and

(II) be adverse to the interests of plan participants in the aggregate.

(C) Action by secretary. The Secretary shall act upon any application for an extension under this paragraph within 180 days of the submission of such application. If the Secretary rejects the application for an extension under this paragraph, the Secretary shall provide notice to the plan detailing the specific reasons for the rejection, including references to the criteria set forth above.

(3) **Advance notice.**

(A) In general. The Secretary shall, before granting an extension under this subsection, require each applicant to provide evidence satisfactory to such Secretary that the applicant has provided notice of the filing of the application for such extension to each affected party (as defined in section 4001(a)(21) of the Employee Retirement Income Security Act of 1974) with respect to the affected plan. Such notice shall include a description of the extent to which the plan is funded for benefits which are guaranteed under title IV of such Act and for benefit liabilities.

(B) Consideration of relevant information. The Secretary shall consider any relevant information provided by a person to whom notice was given under paragraph (1).

In 2010, P.L. 111-192, Sec. 211(a)(2), added para. (b)(8), effective as of the first day of the first plan year ending after August 31, 2008, except that any election a plan makes pursuant to this section that affects the plan's funding standard account for the first plan year beginning after August 31, 2008, shall be disregarded for purposes of applying the provisions of section 305 of the Employee Retirement Income Security Act of 1974 and section 432 of the Internal Revenue Code of 1986 to such plan year.... Sec. 211(b)(2), of this Act read as follows:

"(2) RESTRICTIONS ON BENEFIT INCREASES- Notwithstanding paragraph (1), the restrictions on plan amendments increasing benefits in sections 304(b)(8)(D) of such Act and 431(b)(8)(D) of such Code, as added by this section, shall take effect on the date of enactment of this Act."

In 2006, P.L. 109-280, Sec. 206, of this Act, reads as follows:

"Sec. 206. SPECIAL RULE FOR CERTAIN BENEFITS FUNDED UNDER AN AGREEMENT APPROVED BY THE PENSION BENEFIT GUARANTY CORPORATION. In the case of a multiemployer plan that is a party to an agreement that was approved by the Pension Benefit Guaranty Corporation prior to June 30, 2005, and that—

"(1) increases benefits, and

"(2) provides for special withdrawal liability rules under section 4203(f) of the Employee Retirement Income Security Act of 1974 (29 U.S.C. 1383),

"the amendments made by sections 201, 202, 211, and 212 of this Act shall not apply to the benefit increases under any plan amendment adopted prior to June 30, 2005, that are funded pursuant to such agreement if the plan is funded in compliance with such agreement (and any amendments thereto)."

—P.L. 109-280, Sec. 211(a), added Code Sec. 431, effective for plan yrs. begin. after 2007, except as provided in Sec. 211(b)(2) of P.L. 109-280 which reads as follows:

"(2) Special rule for certain amortization extensions. If the Secretary of the Treasury grants an extension under section 304 of the Employee Retirement Income Security Act of 1974 and section 412(e) of the Internal Revenue Code of 1986 with respect to any application filed with the Secretary of the Treasury on or before June 30, 2005, the extension (and any modification thereof) shall be applied and administered under the rules of such sections as in effect before the enactment of this Act, including the use of the rate of interest determined under section 6621(b) of such Code.

Sec. 432. Additional funding rules for multiemployer plans in endangered status or critical status.

(a) General rule.

For purposes of this part, in the case of a multiemployer plan in effect on July 16, 2006—

(1) if the plan is in endangered status—

(A) the plan sponsor shall adopt and implement a funding improvement plan in accordance with the requirements of subsection (c), and

(B) the requirements of subsection (d) shall apply during the funding plan adoption period and the funding improvement period, and

(2) if the plan is in critical status—

(A) the plan sponsor shall adopt and implement a rehabilitation plan in accordance with the requirements of subsection (e), and

(B) the requirements of subsection (f) shall apply during the rehabilitation plan adoption period and the rehabilitation period.

(b) Determination of endangered and critical status.

For purposes of this section—

(1) **Endangered status.** A multiemployer plan is in endangered status for a plan year if, as determined by the plan actuary under paragraph (3), the plan is not in critical status for the plan year and, as of the beginning of the plan year, either—

(A) the plan's funded percentage for such plan year is less than 80 percent, or

(B) the plan has an accumulated funding deficiency for such plan year, or is projected to have such an accumulated funding deficiency for any of the 6 succeeding plan years, taking into account any extension of amortization periods under section 431(d).

For purposes of this section, a plan shall be treated as in seriously endangered status for a plan year if the plan is described in both subparagraphs (A) and (B).

(2) **Critical status.** A multiemployer plan is in critical status for a plan year if, as determined by the plan actuary under paragraph (3), the plan is described in 1 or more of the following subparagraphs as of the beginning of the plan year:

(A) A plan is described in this subparagraph if—

(i) the funded percentage of the plan is less than 65 percent, and

(ii) the sum of—

(I) the fair market value of plan assets, plus

(II) the present value of the reasonably anticipated employer contributions for the current plan year and each of the 6 succeeding plan years, assuming that the terms of all collective bargaining agreements pursuant to which the plan is maintained for the current plan year continue in effect for succeeding plan years,

is less than the present value of all nonforfeitable benefits projected to be payable under the plan during the current plan year and each of the 6 succeeding plan years (plus administrative expenses for such plan years).

(B) A plan is described in this subparagraph if—

(i) the plan has an accumulated funding deficiency for the current plan year, not taking into account any extension of amortization periods under section 431(d), or

(ii) the plan is projected to have an accumulated funding deficiency for any of the 3 succeeding plan years (4 succeeding plan years if the funded percentage of the plan is 65 percent or less), not taking into account any extension of amortization periods under section 431(d).

(C) A plan is described in this subparagraph if—

(i) (I) the plan's normal cost for the current plan year, plus interest (determined at the rate used for determining costs under the plan) for the current plan year on the amount of unfunded benefit liabilities under the plan as of the last date of the preceding plan year, exceeds

(II) the present value of the reasonably anticipated employer and employee contributions for the current plan year,

(ii) the present value, as of the beginning of the current plan year, of nonforfeitable benefits of inactive participants is greater than the present value of nonforfeitable benefits of active participants, and

(iii) the plan has an accumulated funding deficiency for the current plan year, or is projected to have such a deficiency for any of the 4 succeeding plan years, not taking into account any extension of amortization periods under section 431(d).

(D) A plan is described in this subparagraph if the sum of—

(i) the fair market value of plan assets, plus

(ii) the present value of the reasonably anticipated employer contributions for the current plan year and each of the 4 succeeding plan years, assuming that the terms of all collective bargaining agreements pursuant to which the plan is maintained for the current plan year continue in effect for succeeding plan years,

is less than the present value of all benefits projected to be payable under the plan during the current plan year and each of the 4 succeeding plan years (plus administrative expenses for such plan years).

(3) Annual certification by plan actuary.

(A) In general. Not later than the 90th day of each plan year of a multiemployer plan, the plan actuary shall certify to the Secretary and to the plan sponsor—

(i) whether or not the plan is in endangered status for such plan year and whether or not the plan is or will be in critical status for such plan year, and

(ii) in the case of a plan which is in a funding improvement or rehabilitation period, whether or not the plan is making the scheduled progress in meeting the requirements of its funding improvement or rehabilitation plan.

(B) Actuarial projections of assets and liabilities.

(i) In general. In making the determinations and projections under this subsection, the plan actuary shall make projections required for the current and succeeding plan years of the current value of the assets of the plan and the present value of all liabilities to participants and beneficiaries under the plan for the current plan year as of the beginning of such year. The actuary's projections shall be based on reasonable actuarial estimates, assumptions, and methods that, except as provided in clause (iii), offer the actuary's best estimate of anticipated experience under the plan. The projected present value of liabilities as of the beginning of such year shall be determined based on the most recent of either—

(I) the actuarial statement required under section 103(d) of the Employee Retirement Income Security Act of 1974 with respect to the most recently filed annual report, or

(II) the actuarial valuation for the preceding plan year.

(ii) Determinations of future contributions. Any actuarial projection of plan assets shall assume—

(I) reasonably anticipated employer contributions for the current and succeeding plan years, assuming that the terms of the one or more collective bargaining agreements pursuant to which the plan is maintained for the current plan year continue in effect for succeeding plan years, or

(II) that employer contributions for the most recent plan year will continue indefinitely, but only if the plan actuary determines there have been no significant demographic changes that would make such assumption unreasonable.

(iii) Projected industry activity. Any projection of activity in the industry or industries covered by the plan, including future covered employment and contribution levels, shall be based on information provided by the plan sponsor, which shall act reasonably and in good faith.

(C) Penalty for failure to secure timely actuarial certification. Any failure of the plan's actuary to certify the plan's status under this subsection by the date specified in subparagraph (A) shall be treated for purposes of section 502(c)(2) of the Employee Retirement Income Security Act of 1974 as a failure or refusal by the plan administrator to file the annual report required to be filed with the Secretary under section 101(b)(1) of such Act.

(D) Notice.

(i) In general. In any case in which it is certified under subparagraph (A) that a multiemployer plan is or will be in endangered or critical status for a plan year, the plan sponsor shall, not later than 30 days after the date of the certification, provide notification of the endangered or critical status to the participants and beneficiaries, the bargaining parties, the Pension Benefit Guaranty Corporation, and the Secretary of Labor.

(ii) Plans in critical status. If it is certified under subparagraph (A) that a multiemployer plan is or will be in critical status, the plan sponsor shall include in the notice under clause (i) an explanation of the possibility that—

(I) adjustable benefits (as defined in subsection (e)(8)) may be reduced, and

(II) such reductions may apply to participants and beneficiaries whose benefit commencement date is on or after the date such notice is provided for the first plan year in which the plan is in critical status.

(iii) Model notice. The Secretary, in consultation with the Secretary of Labor shall prescribe a model notice that a multiemployer plan may use to satisfy the requirements under clause (ii).

(c) Funding improvement plan must be adopted for multiemployer plans in endangered status.

(1) In general. In any case in which a multiemployer plan is in endangered status for a plan year, the plan sponsor, in accordance with this subsection—

(A) shall adopt a funding improvement plan not later than 240 days following the required date for the actuarial certification of endangered status under subsection (b)(3)(A), and

(B) within 30 days after the adoption of the funding improvement plan—

(i) shall provide to the bargaining parties 1 or more schedules showing revised benefit structures, revised contribution structures, or both, which, if adopted, may reasonably be expected to enable the multiemployer plan to meet the applicable benchmarks in accordance with the funding improvement plan, including—

(I) one proposal for reductions in the amount of future benefit accruals necessary to achieve the applicable benchmarks, assuming no amendments increasing contributions under the plan (other than amendments increasing contributions necessary to achieve the applicable benchmarks after amendments have reduced future benefit accruals to the maximum extent permitted by law), and

(II) one proposal for increases in contributions under the plan necessary to achieve the applicable benchmarks, assuming no amendments reducing future benefit accruals under the plan, and

(ii) may, if the plan sponsor deems appropriate, prepare and provide the bargaining parties with additional information relating to contribution rates or benefit reductions, alternative schedules, or other information relevant to achieving the applicable benchmarks in accordance with the funding improvement plan.

For purposes of this section, the term 'applicable benchmarks' means the requirements applicable to the multiemployer plan under paragraph (3) (as modified by paragraph (5)).

(2) Exception for years after process begins. Paragraph (1) shall not apply to a plan year if such year is in a funding plan adoption period or funding improvement period by reason of the plan being in endangered status for a preceding plan year. For purposes of this section, such preceding plan year shall be the initial determination year with respect to the funding improvement plan to which it relates.

(3) Funding improvement plan. For purposes of this section—

(A) In general. A funding improvement plan is a plan which consists of the actions, including options or a range of options to be proposed to the bargaining parties, formulated to provide, based on reasonably anticipated experience and reasonable actuarial assumptions, for the attainment by the plan during the funding improvement period of the following requirements:

(i) Increase in plan's funding percentage. The plan's funded percentage as of the close of the funding improvement period equals or exceeds a percentage equal to the sum of—

(I) such percentage as of the beginning of such period, plus

(II) 33 percent of the difference between 100 percent and the percentage under subclause (I).

(ii) Avoidance of accumulated funding deficiencies. No accumulated funding deficiency for any plan year during the funding improvement period (taking into account any extension of amortization periods under section 431(d)).

(B) Seriously endangered plans. In the case of a plan in seriously endangered status, except as provided in paragraph (5), subparagraph (A)(i)(II) shall be applied by substituting '20 percent' for '33 percent'.

(4) Funding improvement period. For purposes of this section—

(A) In general. The funding improvement period for any funding improvement plan adopted pursuant to this subsection is the 10-year period beginning on the first day of the first plan year of the multiemployer plan beginning after the earlier of—

(i) the second anniversary of the date of the adoption of the funding improvement plan, or

(ii) the expiration of the collective bargaining agreements in effect on the due date for the actuarial certification of endangered status for the initial determination year under subsection (b)(3)(A) and covering, as of such due date, at least 75 percent of the active participants in such multiemployer plan.

(B) Seriously endangered plans. In the case of a plan in seriously endangered status, except as provided in paragraph (5), subparagraph (A) shall be applied by substituting '15-year period' for '10-year period'.

(C) Coordination with changes in status.

(i) Plans no longer in endangered status. If the plan's actuary certifies under subsection (b)(3)(A) for a plan year in any funding plan adoption period or funding improvement period that the plan is no longer in endangered status and is not in critical status, the funding plan adoption period or funding improvement period, whichever is applicable, shall end as of the close of the preceding plan year.

(ii) Plans in critical status. If the plan's actuary certifies under subsection (b)(3)(A) for a plan year in any funding plan adoption period or funding improvement period that the plan is in critical status, the funding plan adoption period or funding improvement period, whichever is applicable, shall end as of the close of the plan year preceding the first plan year in the rehabilitation period with respect to such status.

(D) Plans in endangered status at end of period. If the plan's actuary certifies under subsection (b)(3)(A) for the first plan year following the close of the period described in subparagraph (A) that the plan is in endangered status, the provisions of this subsection and subsection (d) shall be applied as if such first plan year were an initial determination year, except that the plan may not be amended in a manner inconsistent with the funding improvement plan in effect for the preceding plan year until a new funding improvement plan is adopted.

(5) Special rules for seriously endangered plans more than 70 percent funded.

(A) In general. If the funded percentage of a plan in seriously endangered status was more than 70 percent as of the beginning of the initial determination year—

(i) paragraphs (3)(B) and (4)(B) shall apply only if the plan's actuary certifies, within 30 days after the certification under subsection (b)(3)(A) for the initial determination year, that, based on the terms of the plan and the collective bargaining agreements in effect at the time of such certification, the plan is not projected to meet the requirements of paragraph (3)(A) (without regard to paragraphs (3)(B) and (4)(B)), and

(ii) if there is a certification under clause (i), the plan may, in formulating its funding improvement plan, only take into account the rules of paragraph (3)(B) and (4)(B) for plan years in the funding improvement period beginning on or before the date on which the last of the collective bargaining agreements described in paragraph (4)(A)(ii) expires.

(B) Special rule after expiration of agreements. Notwithstanding subparagraph (A)(ii), if, for any plan year ending after the date described in subparagraph (A)(ii), the plan actuary certifies (at the time of the annual certification under subsection (b)(3)(A) for such plan year) that, based on the terms of the plan and collective bargaining agreements in effect at the time of that annual certification, the plan is not projected to be able to meet the requirements of paragraph (3)(A) (without regard to paragraphs (3)(B) and (4)(B)), paragraphs (3)(B) and (4)(B) shall continue to apply for such year.

(6) Updates to funding improvement plans and schedules.

(A) Funding improvement plan. The plan sponsor shall annually update the funding improvement plan and shall file the update with the plan's annual report under section 104 of the Employee Retirement Income Security Act of 1974.

(B) Schedules. The plan sponsor shall annually update any schedule of contribution rates provided under this subsection to reflect the experience of the plan.

(C) Duration of schedule. A schedule of contribution rates provided by the plan sponsor and relied upon by bargaining parties in negotiating a collective bargaining agreement shall remain in effect for the duration of that collective bargaining agreement.

(7) Imposition of default schedule where failure to adopt funding improvement plan.

(A) In general. If—

(i) a collective bargaining agreement providing for contributions under a multiemployer plan that was in effect at the time the plan entered endangered status expires, and

(ii) after receiving one or more schedules from the plan sponsor under paragraph (1)(B), the bargaining parties with respect to such agreement fail to adopt a contribution schedule with terms consistent with the funding improvement plan and a schedule from the plan sponsor,

the plan sponsor shall implement the schedule described in paragraph (1)(B)(i)(I) beginning on the date specified in subparagraph (B).

(B) Date of implementation. The date specified in this subparagraph is the date which is 180 days after the date on which the collective bargaining agreement described in subparagraph (A) expires.

(8) Funding plan adoption period. For purposes of this section, the term 'funding plan adoption period' means the period beginning on the date of the certification under subsection (b)(3)(A) for the initial determination year and ending on the day before the first day of the funding improvement period.

(d) Rules for operation of plan during adoption and improvement periods.

(1) Special rules for plan adoption period. During the funding plan adoption period—

(A) the plan sponsor may not accept a collective bargaining agreement or participation agreement with respect to the multiemployer plan that provides for—

(i) a reduction in the level of contributions for any participants,

(ii) a suspension of contributions with respect to any period of service, or

(iii) any new direct or indirect exclusion of younger or newly hired employees from plan participation,

(B) no amendment of the plan which increases the liabilities of the plan by reason of any increase in benefits, any change in the accrual of benefits, or any change in the rate at which benefits become nonforfeitable under the plan may be adopted unless the amendment is required as a condition of qualification under part I of subchapter D of chapter 1 or to comply with other applicable law, and

(C) in the case of a plan in seriously endangered status, the plan sponsor shall take all reasonable actions which are consistent with the terms of the plan and applicable law and which are expected, based on reasonable assumptions, to achieve—

(i) an increase in the plan's funded percentage, and

(ii) postponement of an accumulated funding deficiency for at least 1 additional plan year.

Actions under subparagraph (C) include applications for extensions of amortization periods under section 431(d), use of the shortfall funding method in making funding standard account computations, amendments to the plan's benefit structure, reductions in future benefit accruals, and other reasonable actions consistent with the terms of the plan and applicable law.

(2) Compliance with funding improvement plan.

(A) In general. A plan may not be amended after the date of the adoption of a funding improvement plan so as to be inconsistent with the funding improvement plan.

(B) No reduction in contributions. A plan sponsor may not during any funding improvement period accept a collective bargaining agreement or participation agreement with respect to the multiemployer plan that provides for—

(i) a reduction in the level of contributions for any participants,

(ii) a suspension of contributions with respect to any period of service, or

(iii) any new direct or indirect exclusion of younger or newly hired employees from plan participation.

(C) Special rules for benefit increases. A plan may not be amended after the date of the adoption of a funding improvement plan so as to increase benefits, including future benefit accruals, unless the plan actuary certifies that the benefit increase is consistent with the funding improvement plan and is paid for out of contributions not required by the funding improvement plan to meet the applicable benchmark in accordance with the schedule contemplated in the funding improvement plan.

(e) Rehabilitation plan must be adopted for multiemployer plans in critical status.

(1) In general. In any case in which a multiemployer plan is in critical status for a plan year, the plan sponsor, in accordance with this subsection—

(A) shall adopt a rehabilitation plan not later than 240 days following the required date for the actuarial certification of critical status under subsection (b)(3)(A), and

(B) within 30 days after the adoption of the rehabilitation plan—

(i) shall provide to the bargaining parties 1 or more schedules showing revised benefit structures, revised contribution structures, or both, which, if adopted, may reasonably be expected to enable the multiemployer plan to emerge from critical status in accordance with the rehabilitation plan, and

(ii) may, if the plan sponsor deems appropriate, prepare and provide the bargaining parties with additional information relating to contribution rates or benefit reductions, alternative schedules, or other information relevant to emerging from critical status in accordance with the rehabilitation plan.

The schedule or schedules described in subparagraph (B)(i) shall reflect reductions in future benefit accruals and adjustable benefits, and increases in contributions, that the plan sponsor determines are reasonably necessary to emerge from critical status. One schedule shall be designated as the default schedule and such schedule shall assume that there are no increases in contributions under the plan other than the increases necessary to emerge from critical status after future benefit accruals and other benefits (other than benefits the reduction or elimination of which are not permitted under section 411(d)(6)) have been reduced to the maximum extent permitted by law.

(2) **Exception for years after process begins.** Paragraph (1) shall not apply to a plan year if such year is in a rehabilitation plan adoption period or rehabilitation period by reason of the plan being in critical status for a preceding plan year. For purposes of this section, such preceding plan year shall be the initial critical year with respect to the rehabilitation plan to which it relates.

(3) **Rehabilitation plan.** For purposes of this section—
(A) In general. A rehabilitation plan is a plan which consists of—
(i) actions, including options or a range of options to be proposed to the bargaining parties, formulated, based on reasonably anticipated experience and reasonable actuarial assumptions, to enable the plan to cease to be in critical status by the end of the rehabilitation period and may include reductions in plan expenditures (including plan mergers and consolidations), reductions in future benefit accruals or increases in contributions, if agreed to by the bargaining parties, or any combination of such actions, or
(ii) if the plan sponsor determines that, based on reasonable actuarial assumptions and upon exhaustion of all reasonable measures, the plan can not reasonably be expected to emerge from critical status by the end of the rehabilitation period, reasonable measures to emerge from critical status at a later time or to forestall possible insolvency (within the meaning of section 4245 of the Employee Retirement Income Security Act of 1974).

A rehabilitation plan must provide annual standards for meeting the requirements of such rehabilitation plan. Such plan shall also include the schedules required to be provided under paragraph (1)(B)(i) and if clause (ii) applies, shall set forth the alternatives considered, explain why the plan is not reasonably expected to emerge from critical status by the end of the rehabilitation period, and specify when, if ever, the plan is expected to emerge from critical status in accordance with the rehabilitation plan.

(B) Updates to rehabilitation plan and schedules.
(i) Rehabilitation plan. The plan sponsor shall annually update the rehabilitation plan and shall file the update with the plan's annual report under section 104 of the Employee Retirement Income Security Act of 1974.
(ii) Schedules. The plan sponsor shall annually update any schedule of contribution rates provided under this subsection to reflect the experience of the plan.
(iii) Duration of schedule. A schedule of contribution rates provided by the plan sponsor and relied upon by bargaining parties in negotiating a collective bargaining agreement shall remain in effect for the duration of that collective bargaining agreement.
(C) Imposition of default schedule where failure to adopt rehabilitation plan.
(i) In general. If—
(I) a collective bargaining agreement providing for contributions under a multiemployer plan that was in effect at the time the plan entered critical status expires, and
(II) after receiving one or more schedules from the plan sponsor under paragraph (1)(B)(i), the bargaining parties with respect to such agreement fail to adopt a contribution schedule with terms consistent with the rehabilitation plan and a schedule from the plan sponsor under paragraph (1)(B)(i), the plan sponsor shall implement the default schedule described in the last sentence of paragraph (1) beginning on the date specified in clause (ii).
(ii) Date of implementation. The date specified in this clause is the date which is 180 days after the date on which the collective bargaining agreement described in clause (i) expires.

(4) **Rehabilitation period.** For purposes of this section—
(A) In general. The rehabilitation period for a plan in critical status is the 10-year period beginning on the first day of the first plan year of the multiemployer plan following the earlier of—
(i) the second anniversary of the date of the adoption of the rehabilitation plan, or
(ii) the expiration of the collective bargaining agreements in effect on the due date for the actuarial certification of critical status for the initial critical year under subsection (a)(1) and covering, as of such date at least 75 percent of the active participants in such multiemployer plan.

If a plan emerges from critical status as provided under subparagraph (B) before the end of such 10-year period, the rehabilitation period shall end with the plan year preceding the plan year for which the determination under subparagraph (B) is made.
(B) Emergence. A plan in critical status shall remain in such status until a plan year for which the plan actuary certifies, in accordance with subsection (b)(3)(A), that the plan is not projected to have an accumulated funding deficiency for the plan year or any of the 9 succeeding plan years, without regard to the use of the shortfall method but taking into account any extension of amortization periods under section 431(d).

(5) **Rehabilitation plan adoption period.** For purposes of this section, the term 'rehabilitation plan adoption period' means the period beginning on the date of the certification under subsection (b)(3)(A) for the initial critical year and ending on the day before the first day of the rehabilitation period.

(6) **Limitation on reduction in rates of future accruals.** Any reduction in the rate of future accruals under the default schedule described in the last sentence of paragraph (1) shall not reduce the rate of future accruals below—
(A) a monthly benefit (payable as a single life annuity commencing at the participant's normal retirement age) equal to 1 percent of the contributions required to be made with respect to a participant, or the equivalent

standard accrual rate for a participant or group of participants under the collective bargaining agreements in effect as of the first day of the initial critical year, or

(B) if lower, the accrual rate under the plan on such first day.

The equivalent standard accrual rate shall be determined by the plan sponsor based on the standard or average contribution base units which the plan sponsor determines to be representative for active participants and such other factors as the plan sponsor determines to be relevant. Nothing in this paragraph shall be construed as limiting the ability of the plan sponsor to prepare and provide the bargaining parties with alternative schedules to the default schedule that establish lower or higher accrual and contribution rates than the rates otherwise described in this paragraph.

(7) Automatic employer surcharge.

(A) Imposition of surcharge. Each employer otherwise obligated to make a contribution for the initial critical year shall be obligated to pay to the plan for such year a surcharge equal to 5 percent of the contribution otherwise required under the applicable collective bargaining agreement (or other agreement pursuant to which the employer contributes). For each succeeding plan year in which the plan is in critical status for a consecutive period of years beginning with the initial critical year, the surcharge shall be 10 percent of the contribution otherwise so required.

(B) Enforcement of surcharge. The surcharges under subparagraph (A) shall be due and payable on the same schedule as the contributions on which the surcharges are based. Any failure to make a surcharge payment shall be treated as a delinquent contribution under section 515 of the Employee Retirement Income Security Act of 1974 and shall be enforceable as such.

(C) Surcharge to terminate upon collective bargaining agreement renegotiation. The surcharge under this paragraph shall cease to be effective with respect to employees covered by a collective bargaining agreement (or other agreement pursuant to which the employer contributes), beginning on the effective date of a collective bargaining agreement (or other such agreement) that includes terms consistent with a schedule presented by the plan sponsor under paragraph (1)(B)(i), as modified under subparagraph (B) of paragraph (3).

(D) Surcharge not to apply until employer receives notice. The surcharge under this paragraph shall not apply to an employer until 30 days after the employer has been notified by the plan sponsor that the plan is in critical status and that the surcharge is in effect.

(E) Surcharge not to generate increased benefit accruals. Notwithstanding any provision of a plan to the contrary, the amount of any surcharge under this paragraph shall not be the basis for any benefit accrual under the plan.

(8) Benefit adjustments.

(A) Adjustable benefits.

(i) In general. Notwithstanding section 411(d)(6), the plan sponsor shall, subject to the notice requirement under subparagraph (C), make any reductions to adjustable benefits which the plan sponsor deems appropriate, based upon the outcome of collective bargaining over the schedule or schedules provided under paragraph (1)(B)(i).

(ii) Exception for retirees. Except in the case of adjustable benefits described in clause (iv)(III), the plan sponsor of a plan in critical status shall not reduce adjustable benefits of any participant or beneficiary whose benefit commencement date is before the date on which the plan provides notice to the participant or beneficiary under subsection (b)(3)(D) for the initial critical year.

(iii) Plan sponsor flexibility. The plan sponsor shall include in the schedules provided to the bargaining parties an allowance for funding the benefits of participants with respect to whom contributions are not currently required to be made, and shall reduce their benefits to the extent permitted under this title and considered appropriate by the plan sponsor based on the plan's then current overall funding status.

(iv) Adjustable benefit defined. For purposes of this paragraph, the term 'adjustable benefit' means—

(I) benefits, rights, and features under the plan, including post-retirement death benefits, 60-month guarantees, disability benefits not yet in pay status, and similar benefits,

(II) any early retirement benefit or retirement-type subsidy (within the meaning of section 411(d)(6)(B)(i) and any benefit payment option (other than the qualified joint-and survivor annuity), and

(III) benefit increases that would not be eligible for a guarantee under section 4022A of the Employee Retirement Income Security Act of 1974 on the first day of initial critical year because the increases were adopted (or, if later, took effect) less than 60 months before such first day.

(B) Normal retirement benefits protected. Except as provided in subparagraph (A)(iv)(III), nothing in this paragraph shall be construed to permit a plan to reduce the level of a participant's accrued benefit payable at normal retirement age.

(C) Notice requirements.

(i) In general. No reduction may be made to adjustable benefits under subparagraph (A) unless notice of such reduction has been given at least 30 days before the general effective date of such reduction for all participants and beneficiaries to—

(I) plan participants and beneficiaries,

(II) each employer who has an obligation to contribute (within the meaning of section 4212(a) of the Employee Retirement Income Security Act of 1974) under the plan, and

(III) each employee organization which, for purposes of collective bargaining, represents plan participants employed by such an employer.

(ii) Content of notice. The notice under clause (i) shall contain—

(I) sufficient information to enable participants and beneficiaries to understand the effect of any reduction on their benefits, including an estimate (on an annual or monthly basis) of any affected adjustable benefit that a participant or beneficiary would otherwise have been eligible for as of the general effective date described in clause (i), and

(II) information as to the rights and remedies of plan participants and beneficiaries as well as how to contact the Department of Labor for further information and assistance where appropriate.

(iii) Form and manner. Any notice under clause (i)—

(I) shall be provided in a form and manner prescribed in regulations of the Secretary, in consultation with the Secretary of Labor,

(II) shall be written in a manner so as to be understood by the average plan participant, and

(III) may be provided in written, electronic, or other appropriate form to the extent such form is reasonably accessible to persons to whom the notice is required to be provided.

the Secretary shall in the regulations prescribed under subclause (I) establish a model notice that a plan sponsor may use to meet the requirements of this subparagraph.

(9) Adjustments disregarded in withdrawal liability determination.

(A) Benefit reductions. Any benefit reductions under this subsection shall be disregarded in determining a plan's unfunded vested benefits for purposes of determining an employer's withdrawal liability under section 4201 of the Employee Retirement Income Security Act of 1974.

(B) Surcharges. Any surcharges under paragraph (7) shall be disregarded in determining the allocation of unfunded vested benefits to an employer under section 4211 of such Act, except for purposes of determining the unfunded vested benefits attributable to an employer under section 4211(c)(4) of such Act or a comparable method approved under section 4211(c)(5) of such Act.

(C) Simplified calculations. The Pension Benefit Guaranty Corporation shall prescribe simplified methods for the application of this paragraph in determining withdrawal liability.

(f) Rules for operation of plan during adoption and rehabilitation period.

(1) Compliance with rehabilitation plan.

(A) In general. A plan may not be amended after the date of the adoption of a rehabilitation plan under subsection (e) so as to be inconsistent with the rehabilitation plan.

(B) Special rules for benefit increases. A plan may not be amended after the date of the adoption of a rehabilitation plan under subsection (e) so as to increase benefits, including future benefit accruals, unless the plan actuary certifies that such increase is paid for out of additional contributions not contemplated by the rehabilitation plan, and, after taking into account the benefit increase, the multiemployer plan still is reasonably expected to emerge from critical status by the end of the rehabilitation period on the schedule contemplated in the rehabilitation plan.

(2) Restriction on lump sums and similar benefits.

(A) In general. Effective on the date the notice of certification of the plan's critical status for the initial critical year under subsection (b)(3)(D) is sent, and notwithstanding section 411(d)(6), the plan shall not pay—

(i) any payment, in excess of the monthly amount paid under a single life annuity (plus any social security supplements described in the last sentence of section 411(a)(9)), to a participant or beneficiary whose annuity starting date (as defined in section 417(f)(2)) occurs after the date such notice is sent,

(ii) any payment for the purchase of an irrevocable commitment from an insurer to pay benefits, and

(iii) any other payment specified by the Secretary by regulations.

(B) Exception. Subparagraph (A) shall not apply to a benefit which under section 411(a)(11) may be immediately distributed without the consent of the participant or to any makeup payment in the case of a retroactive annuity starting date or any similar payment of benefits owed with respect to a prior period.

(3) **Adjustments disregarded in withdrawal liability determination.** Any benefit reductions under this subsection shall be disregarded in determining a plan's unfunded vested benefits for purposes of determining an employer's withdrawal liability under section 4201 of the Employee Retirement Income Security Act of 1974.

(4) **Special rules for plan adoption period.** During the rehabilitation plan adoption period—

(A) the plan sponsor may not accept a collective bargaining agreement or participation agreement with respect to the multiemployer plan that provides for—

(i) a reduction in the level of contributions for any participants,

(ii) a suspension of contributions with respect to any period of service, or

(iii) any new direct or indirect exclusion of younger or newly hired employees from plan participation, and

(B) no amendment of the plan which increases the liabilities of the plan by reason of any increase in benefits, any change in the accrual of benefits, or any change in the rate at which benefits become nonforfeitable under the plan may be adopted unless the amendment is required as a condition of qualification under part I of subchapter D of chapter 1 or to comply with other applicable law.

(g) Expedited resolution of plan sponsor decisions.

If, within 60 days of the due date for adoption of a funding improvement plan under subsection (c) or a rehabilitation plan under subsection (e), the plan sponsor of a plan in endangered status or a plan in critical status has not agreed on a funding improvement plan or rehabilitation plan, then any member of the board or group that constitutes the plan sponsor may require that the plan sponsor enter into an expedited dispute resolution procedure for the development and adoption of a funding improvement plan or rehabilitation plan.

(h) Nonbargained participation.

(1) Both bargained and nonbargained employee-participants. In the case of an employer that contributes to a multiemployer plan with respect to both employees who are covered by one or more collective bargaining agreements and employees who are not so covered, if the plan is in endangered status or in critical status, benefits of and contributions for the nonbargained employees, including surcharges on those contributions, shall be determined as if those nonbargained employees were covered under the first to expire of the employer's collective bargaining agreements in effect when the plan entered endangered or critical status.

(2) Nonbargained employees only. In the case of an employer that contributes to a multiemployer plan only with respect to employees who are not covered by a collective bargaining agreement, this section shall be applied as if the employer were the bargaining party, and its participation agreement with the plan were a collective bargaining agreement with a term ending on the first day of the plan year beginning after the employer is provided the schedule or schedules described in subsections (c) and (e).

(i) Definitions; actuarial method.

For purposes of this section—

(1) Bargaining party. The term 'bargaining party' means—

(A) (i) except as provided in clause (ii), an employer who has an obligation to contribute under the plan; or

(ii) in the case of a plan described under section 404(c), or a continuation of such a plan, the association of employers that is the employer settlor of the plan; and

(B) an employee organization which, for purposes of collective bargaining, represents plan participants employed by an employer who has an obligation to contribute under the plan.

(2) Funded percentage. The term 'funded percentage' means the percentage equal to a fraction—

(A) the numerator of which is the value of the plan's assets, as determined under section 431(c)(2), and

(B) the denominator of which is the accrued liability of the plan, determined using actuarial assumptions described in section 431(c)(3).

(3) Accumulated funding deficiency. The term 'accumulated funding deficiency' has the meaning given such term in section 431(a).

(4) Active participant. The term 'active participant' means, in connection with a multiemployer plan, a participant who is in covered service under the plan.

(5) Inactive participant. The term 'inactive participant' means, in connection with a multiemployer plan, a participant, or the beneficiary or alternate payee of a participant, who—

(A) is not in covered service under the plan, and

(B) is in pay status under the plan or has a nonforfeitable right to benefits under the plan.

(6) Pay status. A person is in pay status under a multiemployer plan if—

(A) at any time during the current plan year, such person is a participant or beneficiary under the plan and is paid an early, late, normal, or disability retirement benefit under the plan (or a death benefit under the plan related to a retirement benefit), or

(B) to the extent provided in regulations of the Secretary, such person is entitled to such a benefit under the plan.

(7) Obligation to contribute. The term 'obligation to contribute' has the meaning given such term under section 4212(a) of the Employee Retirement Income Security Act of 1974.

(8) Actuarial method. Notwithstanding any other provision of this section, the actuary's determinations with respect to a plan's normal cost, actuarial accrued liability, and improvements in a plan's funded percentage under this section shall be based upon the unit credit funding method (whether or not that method is used for the plan's actuarial valuation).

(9) Plan sponsor. For purposes of this section, section 431, and section 4971(g):

(A) In general. The term 'plan sponsor' means, with respect to any multiemployer plan, the association, committee, joint board of trustees, or other similar group of representatives of the parties who establish or maintain the plan.

(B) Special rule for section 404(c) plans. In the case of a plan described in section 404(c) (or a continuation of such plan), such term means the bargaining parties described in paragraph (1).

(10) Benefit commencement date. The term 'benefit commencement date' means the annuity starting date (or in the case of a retroactive annuity starting date, the date on which benefit payments begin).

In **2008,** P.L. 110-458, Sec. 102(b)(2)(A), substituted 'section 101(b)(1)' for 'section 101(b)(4)' in subpara. (b)(3)(C) . . . Sec. 102(b)(2)(B), substituted 'The Secretary, in consultation with the Secretary of Labor' for 'The Secretary of Labor' in clause (b)(3)(D)(iii) . . . Sec. 102(b)(2)(C)(i), substituted 'section 431(d)' for 'section 304(d)' in clause (c)(3)(A)(ii) . . . Sec. 102(b)(2)(C)(ii)(I), substituted 'to adopt a contribution schedule with terms consistent with the funding improvement plan and a schedule from the plan sponsor,' for "to agree on changes to contribution or benefit schedules necessary to meet the applicable benchmarks in accordance with the funding improvement plan," in clause (c)(7)(A)(ii) . . . Sec. 102(b)(2)(C)(ii)(II), amended subpara. (c)(7)(B) . . . Sec. 102(b)(2)(D)(i)(I), substituted "to adopt a contribution schedule with terms consistent with the rehabilitation plan and a schedule from the plan sponsor under paragraph (1)(B)(i)," for "to adopt a contribution or benefit schedules with terms consistent with the rehabilitation plan and the schedule from the plan sponsor under paragraph (1)(B)(i)," in subcl. (e)(3)(C)(i)(II) . . . Sec. 102(b)(2)(D)(i)(II), amended clause (e)(3)(C)(ii) . . . Sec. 102(b)(2)(D)(ii)(I), deleted "the date of" after "agreements in effect on" in clause (e)(4)(A)(ii) . . . Sec. 102(b)(2)(D)(ii)(II), substituted "but taking" for "and taking" in subpara. (e)(4)(B) . . . Sec. 102(b)(2)(D)(iii)(I), substituted "the last sentence of paragraph (1)" for "paragraph (1)(B)(i)" in para. (e)(6) . . . Sec. 102(b)(2)(D)(iii)(II), substituted "establish" for "established" in para. (e)(6) . . . Sec. 102(b)(2)(D)(iv)(I), substituted "section 411(d)(6)" for "section 204(g)" in clause (e)(8)(A)(i) . . . Sec. 102(b)(2)(D)(iv)(II), added "of the Employee Retirement Income Security Act of 1974" after "4212(a)" in subcl. (e)(8)(C)(i)(II) . . . Sec. 102(b)(2)(D)(iv)(III), substituted "the Secretary, in consultation with the Secretary of Labor" for "the Secretary of Labor" in subcl. (e)(8)(C)(iii)(I) . . . Sec. 102(b)(2)(D)(iv)(IV), substituted "the Secretary" for "the Secretary of of Labor" in the last sentence of clause (e)(8)(C)(iii) . . . Sec. 102(b)(2)(D)(v), substituted "the allocation of unfunded vested benefits to an employer" for "an employer's withdrawal liability" in subpara. (e)(9)(B) . . . Sec. 102(b)(2)(E)(i), substituted "section 411(a)(9)" for "section 411(b)(1)(A)" in clause (f)(2)(A)(i) . . . Sec. 102(b)(2)(E)(ii), added "to a participant or beneficiary whose annuity starting date (as defined in section 417(f)(2)) occurs after the date such notice is sent," at the end of clause (f)(2)(A)(i) . . . Sec. 102(b)(2)(F), added "under subsection (c)" after "funding improvement plan" the first place it appears in subsec. (g) . . . Sec. 102(b)(2)(G)(i), substituted "section 431(a)" for "section 412(a)" in para. (i)(3) . . . Sec. 102(b)(2)(G)(ii), amended para. (i)(9), effective with respect to plan yrs. begin. after 2007, as if included in the provisions of Sec. 212 of the Pension Protection Act of 2006 [as amended by Sec. 102(b)(2) of this Act, see above] [see below for the provisions of Sec. 212 of P.L. 109-280]

—P.L. 110-458, Sec. 102(b)(3)(C), substituted "section 432(b)(3) of the Internal Revenue Code of 1986" for "section 305(b)(3) of the Employee Retirement Income Security Act of 1974" in Sec. 212(e)(2) of the Pension Protection Act of 2006 [P.L. 109-280, see below]

Prior to amendment, subpara. (c)(7)(B) read as follows:

"(B) Date of implementation. The date specified in this subparagraph is the earlier of the date—

"(i) on which the Secretary of Labor certifies that the parties are at an impasse, or

"(ii) which is 180 days after the date on which the collective bargaining agreement described in subparagraph (A) expires."

Prior to amendment, clause (e)(3)(C)(ii) read as follows:

"(ii) Date of implementation. The date specified in this clause is the earlier of the date—

"(I) on which the Secretary of Labor certifies that the parties are at an impasse, or

"(II) which is 180 days after the date on which the collective bargaining agreement described in clause (i) expires."

Prior to amendment, para. (i)(9) read as follows:

"(9) Plan sponsor. In the case of a plan described under section 404(c), or a continuation of such a plan, the term 'plan sponsor' means the bargaining parties described under paragraph (1)."

—P.L. 110-458, Sec. 204, of this Act, which reads as follows:

"Sec. 204. Temporary Delay of Designation of Multiemployer Plans as in Endangered or Critical Status.

"(a) In general. Notwithstanding the actuarial certification under section 305(b)(3) of the Employee Retirement Income Security Act of 1974 and section 432(b)(3) of the Internal Revenue Code of 1986, if a plan sponsor of a multiemployer plan elects the application of this section, then, for purposes of section 305 of such Act and section 432 of such Code—

"(1) the status of the plan for its first plan year beginning during the period beginning on October 1, 2008, and ending on September 30, 2009, shall be the same as the status of such plan under such sections for the plan year preceding such plan year, and

"(2) in the case of a plan which was in endangered or critical status for the preceding plan year described in paragraph (1), the plan shall not be required to update its plan or schedules under section 305(c)(6) of such Act and section 432(c)(6) of such Code, or section 305(e)(3)(B) of such Act and section 432(e)(3)(B) of such Code, whichever is applicable, until the plan year following the first plan year described in paragraph (1).

"If section 305 of the Employee Retirement Income Security Act of 1974 and section 432 of the Internal Revenue Code of 1986 did not apply to the preceding plan year described in paragraph (1), the plan actuary shall make a certification of the status of the plan under section 305(b)(3) of such Act and section 432(b)(3) of such Code for the preceding plan year in the same manner as if such sections had applied to such preceding plan year.

"(b) Exception for plans becoming critical during election. If—

"(1) an election was made under subsection (a) with respect to a multiemployer plan, and

"(2) such plan has, without regard to such election, been certified by the plan actuary under section 305(b)(3) of such Act and section 432(b)(3) of such Code to be in critical status for the first plan year described in subsection (a)(1),

"then such plan shall be treated as a plan in critical status for such plan year for purposes of applying section 4971(g)(1)(A) of such Code, section 302(b)(3) of such Act, and section 412(b)(3) of such Code.

"(c) Election and notice.

"(1) Election. An election under subsection (a) shall—

"(A) be made at such time and in such manner as the Secretary of the Treasury or the Secretary's delegate may prescribe and, once made, may be revoked only with the consent of the Secretary, and

"(B) if the election is made—

"(i) before the date the annual certification is submitted to the Secretary or the Secretary's delegate under section 305(b)(3) of such Act and section 432(b)(3) of such Code, be included with such annual certification, and

"(ii) after such date, be submitted to the Secretary or the Secretary's delegate not later than 30 days after the date of the election.

"(2) Notice to participants.

"(A) In general. Notwithstanding section 305(b)(3)(D) of such Act and section 431(b)(3)(D) of such Code, if the plan is neither in endangered nor critical status by reason of an election made under subsection (a)—

"(i) the plan sponsor of a multiemployer plan shall not be required to provide notice under such sections, and

"(ii) the plan sponsor shall provide to the participants and beneficiaries, the bargaining parties, the Pension Benefit Guaranty Corporation, and the Secretary of Labor a notice of the election and such other information as the Secretary of Labor may require—

"(I) if the election is made before the date the annual certification is submitted to the Secretary or the Secretary's delegate under section 305(b)(3) of such Act and section 432(b)(3) of such Code, not later than 30 days after the date of the certification, and

"(II) if the election is made after such date, not later than 30 days after the date of the election.

"(B) Notice of endangered status. Notwithstanding section 305(b)(3)(D) of such Act and section 431(b)(3)(D) of such Code, if the plan is certified to be in critical status for any plan year but is in endangered status by reason of an election made under subsection (a), the notice provided under such sections shall be the notice which would have been provided if the plan had been certified to be in endangered status."

—P.L. 110-458, Sec. 205, of this Act, which reads as follows:

"SEC. 205. TEMPORARY EXTENSION OF THE FUNDING IMPROVEMENT AND REHABILITATION PERIODS FOR MULTIEMPLOYER PENSION PLANS IN CRITICAL AND ENDANGERED STATUS FOR 2008 OR 2009.

"(a) In general. If the plan sponsor of a multiemployer plan which is in endangered or critical status for a plan year beginning in 2008 or 2009 (determined after application of section 204) elects the application of this section, then, for purposes of section 305 of the Employee Retirement Income Security Act of 1974 and section 432 of the Internal Revenue Code of 1986—

"(1) except as provided in paragraph (2), the plan's funding improvement period or rehabilitation period, whichever is applicable, shall be 13 years rather than 10 years, and

"(2) in the case of a plan in seriously endangered status, the plan's funding improvement period shall be 18 years rather than 15 years.

"(b) Definitions and special rules. For purposes of this section—

"(1) Election. An election under this section shall be made at such time, and in such manner and form, as the Secretary of Labor or the Secretary's delegate may prescribe.

"(2) Definitions. Any term which is used in this section which is also used in section 305 of the Employee Retirement Income Security Act of 1974 and section 432 of the Internal Revenue Code of 1986 shall have the same meaning as when used in such sections.

"(c) Effective date. This section shall apply to plan years beginning after December 31, 2007."

In 2006, P.L. 109-280, Sec. 206, of this Act, which reads as follows:

"Sec. 206. SPECIAL RULE FOR CERTAIN BENEFITS FUNDED UNDER AN AGREEMENT APPROVED BY THE PENSION BENEFIT GUARANTY CORPORATION. In the case of a multiemployer plan that is a party to an agreement that was approved by the Pension Benefit Guaranty Corporation prior to June 30, 2005, and that—

"(1) increases benefits, and

"(2) provides for special withdrawal liability rules under section 4203(f) of the Employee Retirement Income Security Act of 1974 (29 U.S.C. 1383),

"the amendments made by sections 201, 202, 211, and 212 of this Act shall not apply to the benefit increases under any plan amendment adopted prior to June 30, 2005, that are funded pursuant to such agreement if the plan is funded in compliance with such agreement (and any amendments thereto)."

—P.L. 109-280, Sec. 212(a), added Code Sec. 432, effective for plan yrs. begin. after 2007, except as provided in Secs. 212(e)(2) and (3) of P.L. 109-280 [as amended by Sec. 102(b)(3)(C) of P.L. 110-458, see above] which reads as follows:

"(2) special rule for certain notices. In any case in which a plan's actuary certifies that it is reasonably expected that a multiemployer plan will be in critical status under section 432(b)(3) of the Internal Revenue Code of 1986, as added by this section, with respect to the first plan year beginning after 2007, the notice required under subparagraph (D) of such section may be provided at any time after

the date of enactment, so long as it is provided on or before the last date for providing the notice under such subparagraph.

"(3) Special rule for certain restored benefits. In the case of a multiemployer plan—

"(A) with respect to which benefits were reduced pursuant to a plan amendment adopted on or after January 1, 2002, and before June 30, 2005, and

"(B) which, pursuant to the plan document, the trust agreement, or a formal written communication from the plan sponsor to participants provided before June 30, 2005, provided for the restoration of such benefits,

"the amendments made by this section shall not apply to such benefit restorations to the extent that any restriction on the providing or accrual of such benefits would otherwise apply by reason of such amendments."

—P.L. 109-280, Sec. 214, of this Act, which reads as follows:

"Sec. 214. EXEMPTION FROM EXCISE TAXES FOR CERTAIN MULTIEMPLOYER PENSION PLANS. (a) In General- Notwithstanding any other provision of law, no tax shall be imposed under subsection (a) or (b) of section 4971 of the Internal Revenue Code of 1986 with respect to any accumulated funding deficiency of a plan described in subsection (b) of this section for any taxable year beginning before the earlier of—

"(1) the taxable year in which the plan sponsor adopts a rehabilitation plan under section 305(e) of the Employee Retirement Income Security Act of 1974 and section 432(e) of such Code (as added by this Act); or

"(2) the taxable year that contains January 1, 2009.

"(b) Plan Described- A plan described under this subsection is a multiemployer pension plan—

"(1) with less than 100 participants;

"(2) with respect to which the contributing employers participated in a Federal fishery capacity reduction program;

"(3) with respect to which employers under the plan participated in the Northeast Fisheries Assistance Program; and

"(4) with respect to which the annual normal cost is less than $100,000 and the plan is experiencing a funding deficiency on the date of enactment of this Act."

—P.L. 109-432, Sec. 221, of this Act, which reads as follows:

"Sec. 221. SUNSET OF ADDITIONAL FUNDING RULES.

"(a) Report. Not later than December 31, 2011, the Secretary of Labor, the Secretary of the Treasury, and the Executive Director of the Pension Benefit Guaranty Corporation shall conduct a study of the effect of the amendments made by this subtitle on the operation and funding status of multiemployer plans and shall report the results of such study, including any recommendations for legislation, to the Congress.

"(b) Matters Included in Study. The study required under subsection (a) shall include—

"(1) the effect of funding difficulties, funding rules in effect before the date of the enactment of this Act, and the amendments made by this subtitle on small businesses participating in multiemployer plans,

"(2) the effect on the financial status of small employers of—

"(A) funding targets set in funding improvement and rehabilitation plans and associated contribution increases,

"(B) funding deficiencies,

"(C) excise taxes,

"(D) withdrawal liability,

"(E) the possibility of alternatives schedules and procedures for financially-troubled employers, and

"(F) other aspects of the multiemployer system, and

"(3) the role of the multiemployer pension plan system in helping small employers to offer pension benefits.

"(c) Sunset—

"(1) IN GENERAL. Except as provided in this subsection, notwithstanding any other provision of this Act, the provisions of, and the amendments made by, sections 201(b), 202, and 212 shall not apply to plan years beginning after December 31, 2014.

"(2) FUNDING IMPROVEMENT AND REHABILITATION PLANS- If a plan is operating under a funding improvement or rehabilitation plan under section 305 of such Act or 432 of such Code for its last year beginning before January 1, 2015, such plan shall continue to operate under such funding improvement or rehabilitation plan during any period after December 31, 2014, such funding improvement or rehabilitation plan is in effect and all provisions of such Act or Code relating to the operation of such funding improvement or rehabilitation plan shall continue in effect during such period."

SUBPART B.—BENEFIT LIMITATIONS UNDER SINGLE-EMPLOYER PLANS.

Sec.

436. Funding-based limitation on shutdown benefits and other unpredictable contingent event benefits under single-employer plans.

In 2006, P.L. 109-280, Sec. 113(a)(1)(B), added item 436

Sec. 436. Funding-based limits on benefits and benefit accruals under single-employer plans.

(a) General rule.

For purposes of section 401(a)(29), a defined benefit plan which is a single-employer plan shall be treated as meeting the requirements of this section if the plan meets the requirements of subsections (b), (c), (d), and (e).

(b) Funding-based limitation on shutdown benefits and other unpredictable contingent event benefits under single-employer plans.

(1) In general. If a participant of a defined benefit plan which is a single-employer plan is entitled to an unpredictable contingent event benefit payable with respect to any event occurring during any plan year, the plan shall provide that such benefit may not be provided if the adjusted funding target attainment percentage for such plan year—

(A) is less than 60 percent, or

(B) would be less than 60 percent taking into account such occurrence.

(2) Exemption. Paragraph (1) shall cease to apply with respect to any plan year, effective as of the first day of the plan year, upon payment by the plan sponsor of a contribution (in addition to any minimum required contribution under section 430) equal to—

(A) in the case of paragraph (1)(A), the amount of the increase in the funding target of the plan (under section 430) for the plan year attributable to the occurrence referred to in paragraph (1), and

(B) in the case of paragraph (1)(B), the amount sufficient to result in an adjusted funding target attainment percentage of 60 percent.

(3) Unpredictable contingent event benefit. For purposes of this subsection, the term "unpredictable contingent event benefit" means any benefit payable solely by reason of—

(A) a plant shutdown (or similar event, as determined by the Secretary), or

(B) an event other than the attainment of any age, performance of any service, receipt or derivation of any compensation, or occurrence of death or disability.

(c) Limitations on plan amendments increasing liability for benefits.

(1) In general. No amendment to a defined benefit plan which is a single-employer plan which has the effect of increasing liabilities of the plan by reason of increases in benefits, establishment of new benefits, changing the rate of benefit accrual, or changing the rate at which benefits become nonforfeitable may take effect during any plan year if the adjusted funding target attainment percentage for such plan year is—

(A) less than 80 percent, or

(B) would be less than 80 percent taking into account such amendment.

(2) Exemption. Paragraph (1) shall cease to apply with respect to any plan year, effective as of the first day of the plan year (or if later, the effective date of the amendment), upon payment by the plan sponsor of a contribution (in addition to any minimum required contribution under section 430) equal to—

(A) in the case of paragraph (1)(A), the amount of the increase in the funding target of the plan (under section 430) for the plan year attributable to the amendment, and

(B) in the case of paragraph (1)(B), the amount sufficient to result in an adjusted funding target attainment percentage of 80 percent.

(3) Exception for certain benefit increases. Paragraph (1) shall not apply to any amendment which provides for an increase in benefits under a formula which is not based on a participant's compensation, but only if the rate of such increase is not in excess of the contemporaneous rate of increase in average wages of participants covered by the amendment.

(d) Limitations on accelerated benefit distributions.

(1) Funding percentage less than 60 percent. A defined benefit plan which is a single employer plan shall provide that, in any case in which the plan's adjusted funding target attainment percentage for a plan year is less than 60 percent, the plan may not pay any prohibited payment after the valuation date for the plan year.

(2) Bankruptcy. A defined benefit plan which is a single-employer plan shall provide that, during any period in which the plan sponsor is a debtor in a case under title 11, United States Code, or similar Federal or State law, the plan may not pay any prohibited payment. The preceding sentence shall not apply on or after the date on which the enrolled actuary of the plan certifies that the adjusted funding target attainment percentage of such plan is not less than 100 percent.

(3) Limited payment if percentage at least 60 percent but less than 80 percent.

(A) In general. A defined benefit plan which is a single-employer plan shall provide that, in any case in which the plan's adjusted funding target attainment percentage for a plan year is 60 percent or greater but less than 80 percent, the plan may not pay any prohibited payment after the valuation date for the plan year to the extent the amount of the payment exceeds the lesser of—

(i) 50 percent of the amount of the payment which could be made without regard to this section, or

(ii) the present value (determined under guidance prescribed by the Pension Benefit Guaranty Corporation, using the interest and mortality assumptions under section 417(e)) of the maximum guarantee with respect to the participant under section 4022 of the Employee Retirement Income Security Act of 1974.

(B) One-time application.

(i) In general. The plan shall also provide that only 1 prohibited payment meeting the requirements of subparagraph (A) may be made with respect to any participant during any period of consecutive plan years to which the limitations under either paragraph (1) or (2) or this paragraph applies.

(ii) Treatment of beneficiaries. For purposes of this subparagraph, a participant and any beneficiary on his behalf (including an alternate payee, as defined in section 414(p)(8)) shall be treated as 1 participant. If the accrued benefit of a participant is allocated to such an alternate payee and 1 or more other persons, the amount under subparagraph (A) shall be allocated among such persons in the same manner as the accrued benefit is allocated unless the qualified domestic relations order (as defined in section 414(p)(1)(A)) provides otherwise.

(4) Exception. This subsection shall not apply to any plan for any plan year if the terms of such plan (as in effect for the period beginning on September 1, 2005, and ending with such plan year) provide for no benefit accruals with respect to any participant during such period.

(5) Prohibited payment. For purpose of this subsection, the term "prohibited payment" means—

(A) any payment, in excess of the monthly amount paid under a single life annuity (plus any social security supplements described in the last sentence of section 411(a)(9), to a participant or beneficiary whose annuity starting date (as defined in section 417(f)(2)) occurs during any period a limitation under paragraph (1) or (2) is in effect,

(B) any payment for the purchase of an irrevocable commitment from an insurer to pay benefits, and

(C) any other payment specified by the Secretary by regulations.

Such term shall not include the payment of a benefit which under section 411(a)(11) may be immediately distributed without the consent of the participant.

(e) Limitation on benefit accruals for plans with severe funding shortfalls.

(1) In general. A defined benefit plan which is a single-employer plan shall provide that, in any case in which the plan's adjusted funding target attainment percentage for a plan year is less than 60 percent, benefit accruals under the plan shall cease as of the valuation date for the plan year.

(2) Exemption. Paragraph (1) shall cease to apply with respect to any plan year, effective as of the first day of the plan year, upon payment by the plan sponsor of a contribution (in addition to any minimum required contribution under section 430) equal to the amount sufficient to result in an adjusted funding target attainment percentage of 60 percent.

(f) Rules relating to contributions required to avoid benefit limitations.

(1) Security may be provided.

(A) In general. For purposes of this section, the adjusted funding target attainment percentage shall be determined by treating as an asset of the plan any security provided by a plan sponsor in a form meeting the requirements of subparagraph (B).

(B) Form of security. The security required under subparagraph (A) shall consist of—

(i) a bond issued by a corporate surety company that is an acceptable surety for purposes of section 412 of the Employee Retirement Income Security Act of 1974,

(ii) cash, or United States obligations which mature in 3 years or less, held in escrow by a bank or similar financial institution, or

(iii) such other form of security as is satisfactory to the Secretary and the parties involved.

(C) Enforcement. Any security provided under subparagraph (A) may be perfected and enforced at any time after the earlier of—

(i) the date on which the plan terminates,

(ii) if there is a failure to make a payment of the minimum required contribution for any plan year beginning after the security is provided, the due date for the payment under section 430(j), or

(iii) if the adjusted funding target attainment percentage is less than 60 percent for a consecutive period of 7 years, the valuation date for the last year in the period.

(D) Release of security. The security shall be released (and any amounts thereunder shall be refunded together with any interest accrued thereon) at such time as the Secretary may prescribe in regulations, including regulations for partial releases of the security by reason of increases in the adjusted funding target attainment percentage.

(2) Prefunding balance or funding standard carryover balance may not be used. No prefunding balance or funding standard carryover balance under section 430(f) may be used under subsection (b), (c), or (e) to satisfy any payment an employer may make under any such subsection to avoid or terminate the application of any limitation under such subsection.

(3) Deemed reduction of funding balances.

(A) In general. Subject to subparagraph (C), in any case in which a benefit limitation under subsection (b), (c), (d), or (e) would (but for this subparagraph and determined without regard to subsection (b)(2), (c)(2), or (e)(2)) apply to such plan for the plan year, the plan sponsor of such plan shall be treated for purposes of this title as having made an election under section 430(f) to reduce the prefunding balance or funding standard carryover balance by such amount as is necessary for such benefit limitation to not apply to the plan for such plan year.

(B) Exception for insufficient funding balances. Subparagraph (A) shall not apply with respect to a benefit limitation for any plan year if the application of subparagraph (A) would not result in the benefit limitation not applying for such plan year.

(C) Restrictions of certain rules to collectively bargained plans. With respect to any benefit limitation under subsection (b), (c), or (e), subparagraph (A) shall only apply in the case of a plan maintained pursuant to 1 or more collective bargaining agreements between employee representatives and 1 or more employers.

(g) New plans.

Subsections (b), (c), and (e) shall not apply to a plan for the first 5 plan years of the plan. For purposes of this subsection, the reference in this subsection to a plan shall include a reference to any predecessor plan.

(h) Presumed underfunding for purposes of benefit limitations.

(1) Presumption of continued underfunding. In any case in which a benefit limitation under subsection (b), (c), (d), or (e) has been applied to a plan with respect to the plan year preceding the current plan year, the adjusted funding target attainment percentage of the plan for the current plan year shall be presumed to be equal to the adjusted funding target attainment percentage of the plan for the preceding plan year until the enrolled actuary of the plan certifies the actual adjusted funding target attainment percentage of the plan for the current plan year.

(2) Presumption of underfunding after 10th month. In any case in which no certification of the adjusted funding target attainment percentage for the current plan year is made with respect to the plan before the first day of the 10th month of such year, for purposes of subsections (b), (c), (d), and (e), such first day shall be deemed, for purposes of such subsection, to be the valuation date of the plan for the current plan year and the plan's adjusted funding target attainment percentage shall be conclusively presumed to be less than 60 percent as of such first day.

(3) Presumption of underfunding after 4th month for nearly underfunded plans. In any case in which—

(A) a benefit limitation under subsection (b), (c), (d), or (e) did not apply to a plan with respect to the plan year preceding the current plan year, but the adjusted funding target attainment percentage of the plan for such preceding plan year was not more than 10 percentage points greater than the percentage which would have caused such subsection to apply to the plan with respect to such preceding plan year, and

(B) as of the first day of the 4th month of the current plan year, the enrolled actuary of the plan has not certified the actual adjusted funding target attainment percentage of the plan for the current plan year, until the enrolled actuary so certifies, such first day shall be deemed, for purposes of such subsection, to be the valuation date of the plan for the current plan year and the adjusted funding target attainment percentage of the plan as of such first day shall, for purposes of such subsection, be presumed to be equal to 10 percentage points less than the adjusted funding target attainment percentage of the plan for such preceding plan year.

(i) Treatment of plan as of close of prohibited or cessation period.
For purposes of applying this title—
(1) Operation of plan after period. Unless the plan provides otherwise, payments and accruals will resume effective as of the day following the close of the period for which any limitation of payment or accrual of benefits under subsection (d) or (e) applies.
(2) Treatment of affected benefits. Nothing in this subsection shall be construed as affecting the plan's treatment of benefits which would have been paid or accrued but for this section.

(j) Terms relating to funding target attainment percentage.
For purposes of this section—
(1) In general. The term "funding target attainment percentage" has the same meaning given such term by section 430(d)(2).
(2) Adjusted funding target attainment percentage. The term "adjusted funding target attainment percentage" means the funding target attainment percentage which is determined under paragraph (1) by increasing each of the amounts under subparagraphs (A) and (B) of section 430(d)(2) by the aggregate amount of purchases of annuities for employees other than highly compensated employees (as defined in section 414(q)) which were made by the plan during the preceding 2 plan years.
(3) Application to plans which are fully funded without regard to reductions for funding balances.
(A) In general. In the case of a plan for any plan year, if the funding target attainment percentage is 100 percent or more (determined without regard to the reduction in the value of assets under section 430(f)(4)), the funding target attainment percentage for purposes of paragraphs (1) and (2) shall be determined without regard to such reduction.
(B) Transition rule. Subparagraph (A) shall be applied to plan years beginning after 2007 and before 2011 by substituting for "100 percent" the applicable percentage determined in accordance with the following table:

In the case of a plan year beginning in calendar year:	The applicable percentage is
2008	92
2009	94
2010	96

(C) Limitation. Subparagraph (B) shall not apply with respect to any plan year beginning after 2008 unless the funding target attainment percentage (determined without regard to the reduction in the value of assets under section 430(f)(4)) of the plan for each preceding plan year beginning after 2007 was not less than the applicable percentage with respect to such preceding plan year determined under subparagraph (B).
(3 [sic 4]) Special rule for certain years. Solely for purposes of any applicable provision—
(A) In general. For plan years beginning on or after October 1, 2008, and before October 1, 2010, the adjusted funding target attainment percentage of a plan shall be the greater of—
(i) such percentage, as determined without regard to this paragraph, or
(ii) the adjusted funding target attainment percentage for such plan for the plan year beginning after October 1, 2007, and before October 1, 2008, as determined under rules prescribed by the Secretary.
(B) Special rule. In the case of a plan for which the valuation date is not the first day of the plan year—
(i) subparagraph (A) shall apply to plan years beginning after December 31, 2007, and before January 1, 2010, and
(ii) subparagraph (A)(ii) shall apply based on the last plan year beginning before November 1, 2007, as determined under rules prescribed by the Secretary.
(C) Applicable provision. For purposes of this paragraph, the term 'applicable provision' means—
(i) subsection (d), but only for purposes of applying such paragraph to a payment which, as determined under rules prescribed by the Secretary, is a payment under a social security leveling option which accelerates payments under the plan before, and reduces payments after, a participant starts receiving social security benefits in order to provide substantially similar aggregate payments both before and after such benefits are received, and
(ii) subsection (e).

(k) Secretarial authority for plans with alternate valuation date.
In the case of a plan which has designated a valuation date other than the first day of the plan year, the Secretary may prescribe rules for the application of this section which are necessary to reflect the alternate valuation date.
(l) Single-employer plan.
For purposes of this section, the term "single employer plan" means a plan which is not a multiemployer plan.
(m) Special rule for 2008.
For purposes of this section, in the case of plan years beginning in 2008, the funding target attainment percentage for the preceding plan year may be determined using such methods of estimation as the Secretary may provide.

In 2010, P.L. 111-192, Sec. 203(a)(2), added para. (j)(3) [sic (4)], effective for plan yrs. begin. on or after 10/1/2008.
Special rule. In the case of a plan for which the valuation date is not the first day of the plan year, the amendments made by this section shall apply to plan years beginning after December 31, 2007.... Sec. 203(b), of this Act read as follows:
"Interaction With WRERA Rule. Section 203 of the Worker, Retiree, and Employer Recovery Act of 2008 shall apply to a plan for any plan year in lieu of the amendments made by this section applying to section 206(g)(4) of the Employee Retirement Income Security Act of 1974 and 436(e) of the Internal Revenue Code of 1986 only to the extent that such section produces a higher adjusted funding target attainment percentage for such plan for such year."
In 2008, P.L. 110-458, Sec. 101(c)(2)(A)(i), substituted "section 430" for "section 303" in the matter preceding subpara. (b)(2)(A)... Sec. 101(c)(2)(A)(ii), substituted "an adjusted funding" for "a funding" in subpara. (b)(2)(B)... Sec. 101(c)(2)(B)(i), added "benefit" after "event" in the heading of para. (b)(3)... Sec. 101(c)(2)(B)(ii), substituted "an event" for "any event" in subpara. (b)(3)(B) ... Sec. 101(c)(2)(C), added flush sentence "Such term shall not include the payment of a benefit which under section 411(a)(11) may be immediately distributed without the consent of the participant." at the end of para. (d)(5)... Sec. 101(c)(2)(D)(i), added "adjusted" before "funding" in subpara. (f)(1)(D)... Sec. 101(c)(2)(D)(ii), substituted "prefunding balance or funding standard carryover balance under section 430(f)" for "prefunding balance under section 430(f) or funding standard carryover balance" in para. (f)(2)... Sec. 101(c)(2)(E)(i)(I), deleted "without regard to this paragraph" after "(determined" in subpara. (j)(3)(A)... Sec. 101(c)(2)(E)(i)(II), substituted "section 430(f)(4)" for "section 430(f)(4)(A)" in subpara. (j)(3)(A)... Sec. 101(c)(2)(E)(i)(III), substituted "paragraphs (1) and (2)" for "paragraph (1)" in subpara. (j)(3)(A)... Sec. 101(c)(2)(E)(ii)(I), substituted "without regard to the reduction in the value of assets under section 430(f)(4)" for "without regard to this paragraph" in subpara. (j)(3)(C)... Sec. 101(c)(2)(E)(ii)(II), added "beginning" before "after" each place

it appears in subpara. (j)(3)(C)... Sec. 101(c)(2)(F), redesignated subsec. (k) as (m), and added subsec. (k) and (l), effective for plan yrs. begin. after 12/31/2007 [effective as if included in the amendments made by Sec. 113, P.L.109-280, see below]

—P.L. 110-458, Sec. 101(c)(3)(A), substituted "section" for "subsection" in Sec. 113(b)(2)(A)(ii), P.L. 109-280, relating to collective bargaining exception, [see below]

—P.L. 110-458, Sec. 101(c)(3)(B), substituted "paragraph" for "subparagraph" in Sec. 113(b)(2)(A)(ii), P.L. 109-280, relating to collective bargaining exception, [see below]

—P.L. 110-458, Sec. 203, of this Act provides:

"SEC. 203. TEMPORARY MODIFICATION OF APPLICATION OF LIMITATION ON BENEFIT ACCRUALS.

"In the case of the first plan year beginning during the period beginning on October 1, 2008, and ending on September 30, 2009, sections 206(g)(4)(A) of the Employee Retirement Income Security Act of 1974 (29 U.S.C. 1056(g)(4)(A)) and 436(e)(1) of the Internal Revenue Code of 1986 shall be applied by substituting the plan's adjusted funding target attainment percentage for the preceding plan year for such percentage for such plan year."

In 2006, P.L. 109-280, Sec. 113(a)(1)(B), added Code Sec. 436, effective for plan yrs. begin. after 12/31/2007, except as provided in Sec. 113(b)(2) [as amended by Sec. 101(c)(3)(A)- (B), P.L. 110-458, see above] of this Act, which reads as follows:

"(2) Collective bargaining exception. In the case of a plan maintained pursuant to 1 or more collective bargaining agreements between employee representatives and 1 or more employers ratified before January 1, 2008, the amendments made by this section shall not apply to plan years beginning before the earlier of—

"(A) the later of—

"(i) the date on which the last collective bargaining agreement relating to the plan terminates (determined without regard to any extension thereof agreed to after the date of the enactment of this Act), or

"(ii) the first day of the first plan year to which the amendments made by this section would (but for this paragraph) apply, or

"(B) January 1, 2010.

For purposes of subparagraph (A)(i), any plan amendment made pursuant to a collective bargaining agreement relating to the plan which amends the plan solely to conform to any requirement added by this section shall not be treated as a termination of such collective bargaining agreement."

Subchapter E.—Accounting Periods and Methods of Accounting

Part
   I. Accounting periods.
   II. Methods of accounting.
   III. Adjustments.

PART I.—ACCOUNTING PERIODS

Sec.
441. Period for computation of taxable income.
442. Change of annual accounting period.
443. Returns for a period of less than 12 months.
444. Election of taxable year other than required taxable year.

In 1987, P.L. 100-203, Sec. 10206(a)(2), added item 444.

Sec. 441. Period for computation of taxable income.
(a) Computation of taxable income.

Taxable income shall be computed on the basis of the taxpayer's taxable year.
(b) Taxable year.

For purposes of this subtitle, the term "taxable year" means—

(1) the taxpayer's annual accounting period, if it is a calendar year or a fiscal year;

(2) the calendar year, if subsection (g) applies;

(3) the period for which the return is made, if a return is made for a period of less than 12 months; or

(4) in the case of a DISC filing a return for a period of at least 12 months, the period determined under subsection (h).

(c) Annual accounting period.

For purposes of this subtitle, the term "annual accounting period" means the annual period on the basis of which the taxpayer regularly computes his income in keeping his books.

(d) Calendar year.

For purposes of this subtitle, the term "calendar year" means a period of 12 months ending on December 31.

(e) Fiscal year.

For purposes of this subtitle, the term "fiscal year" means a period of 12 months ending on the last day of any month other than December. In the case of any taxpayer who has made the election provided by subsection (f), the term means the annual period (varying from 52 to 53 weeks) so elected.

(f) Election of year consisting of 52–53 weeks.

(1) General rule. A taxpayer who, in keeping his books, regularly computes his income on the basis of an annual period which varies from 52 to 53 weeks and ends always on the same day of the week and ends always—

(A) on whatever date such same day of the week last occurs in a calendar month, or

(B) on whatever date such same day of the week falls which is nearest to the last day of a calendar month,

may (in accordance with the regulations prescribed under paragraph (3)) elect to compute his taxable income for purposes of this subtitle on the basis of such annual period. This paragraph shall apply to taxable years ending after the date of the enactment of this title.

(2) Special rules for 52–53-week year.

(A) Effective dates. In any case in which the effective date or the applicability of any provision of this title is expressed in terms of taxable years beginning, including, or ending with reference to a specified date which is the first or last day of a month, a taxable year described in paragraph (1) shall (except for purposes of the computation under section 15) be treated—

(i) as beginning with the first day of the calendar month beginning nearest to the first day of such taxable year, or

(ii) as ending with the last day of the calendar month ending nearest to the last day of such taxable year,

as the case may be.

(B) Change in accounting period. In the case of a change from or to a taxable year described in paragraph (1)—

(i) if such change results in a short period (within the meaning of section 443) of 359 days or more, or of less than 7 days, section 443(b) (relating to alternative tax computation) shall not apply;

(ii) if such change results in a short period of less than 7 days, such short period shall, for purposes of this subtitle, be added to and deemed a part of the following taxable year; and

(iii) if such change results in a short period to which subsection (b) of section 443 applies, the taxable income for such short period shall be placed on an annual basis for purposes of such subsection by multiplying the gross income for such short period (minus the deductions allowed by this chapter for the short period, but only the adjusted amount of the deductions for personal exemptions as described in section 443(c)) by 365, by dividing the result by the number of days in the short period, and the tax shall be the same part of the tax computed on the annual basis as the number of days in the short period is of 365 days.

(3) Special rule for partnerships, S corporations, and personal service corporations. The Secretary may by regulation provide terms and conditions for the application

2,110

of this subsection to a partnership, S corporation, or personal service corporation (within the meaning of section 441(i)(2)).

(4) Regulations. The Secretary shall prescribe such regulations as he deems necessary for the application of this subsection.

(g) No books kept; no accounting period.

Except as provided in section 443 (relating to returns for periods of less than 12 months), the taxpayer's taxable year shall be the calendar year if—

(1) the taxpayer keeps no books;

(2) the taxpayer does not have an annual accounting period; or

(3) the taxpayer has an annual accounting period, but such period does not qualify as a fiscal year.

(h) Taxable year of DISC's.

(1) In general. For purposes of this subtitle, the taxable year of any DISC shall be the taxable year of that shareholder (or group of shareholders with the same 12-month taxable year) who has the highest percentage of voting power.

(2) Special rule where more than one shareholder (or group) has highest percentage. If 2 or more shareholders (or groups) have the highest percentage of voting power under paragraph (1), the taxable year of the DISC shall be the same 12-month period as that of any such shareholder (or group).

(3) Subsequent changes of ownership. The Secretary shall prescribe regulations under which paragraphs (1) and (2) shall apply to a change of ownership of a corporation after the taxable year of the corporation has been determined under paragraph (1) or (2) only if such change is a substantial change of ownership.

(4) Voting power determined. For purposes of this subsection, voting power shall be determined on the basis of total combined voting power of all classes of stock of the corporation entitled to vote.

(i) Taxable year of personal service corporations.

(1) In general. For purposes of this subtitle, the taxable year of any personal service corporation shall be the calendar year unless the corporation establishes, to the satisfaction of the Secretary, a business purpose for having a different period for its taxable year. For purposes of this paragraph, any deferral of income to shareholders shall not be treated as a business purpose.

(2) Personal service corporation. For purposes of this subsection, the term "personal service corporation" has the meaning given such term by section 269A(b)(1), except that section 269A(b)(2) shall be applied—

(A) by substituting "any" for "more than 10 percent", and

(B) by substituting "any" for "50 percent or more in value" in section 318(a)(2)(C).

A corporation shall not be treated as a personal service corporation unless more than 10 percent of the stock (by value) in such corporation is held by employee-owners (within the meaning of section 269A(b)(2), as modified by the preceding sentence). If a corporation is a member of an affiliated group filing a consolidated return, all members of such group shall be taken into account in determining whether such corporation is a personal service corporation.

In 2007, P.L. 110-172, Sec. 11(g)(7)(A), deleted "FSC or" before "DISC filing" in para. (b)(4) . . . Sec. 11(g)(7)(B)(i), deleted "FSC or" before "DISC" in paras. (h)(1) and (2) . . . Sec. 11(g)(7)(B)(ii), deleted "FSC's and" before "DISC's" in the heading of subsec. (h), effective 12/29/2007.

In 1988, P.L. 100-647, Sec. 1008(e)(4), added two sentences at the end of para. (i)(2), effective for tax. yrs. begin. after 12/31/86.

—P.L. 100-647, Sec. 1008(e)(7)(A), and (B), amended Sec. 806(e)(2)(C) of P.L. 99-514, [reproduced below] part of the special rules for Code Sec. 441, by deleting "(including such short taxable year)" after "first 4 taxable years", and substituting "the partner's or shareholder's taxable year with or within which the partnership's or S corporation's short taxable year ends", see below.

—P.L. 100-647, Sec. 1008(e)(8)(A), and (B), amended Sec. 806(e)(2) [reproduced below] of P.L. 99-514, part of the special rules for Code Sec. 441, by substituting "the taxpayer's first taxable year beginning after December 31, 1986" for "any taxable year", and substituting "partnership, S corporation, or personal service corporation" for "taxpayer" throughout, see below.

—P.L. 100-647, Sec. 1008(e)(9), provides:

"(9) Nothing in section 806 of the Reform Act or in any legislative history relating thereto shall be construed as requiring the Secretary of the Treasury or his delegate to permit an automatic change of a taxable year."

—P.L. 100-647, Sec. 1008(e)(10), amended Sec. 806(e) of P.L. 99-514 [reproduced below] part of the special rules for Code Sec. 441, by adding new para. (e)(3), see below.

In 1986, P.L. 99-514, Sec. 104(b)(6), deleted "and by adding the zero bracket amount" after "and the tax shall be the same part" in clause (f)(2)(B)(iii) . . . Sec. 806(c)(1), added subsec. (i) . . . Sec. 806(d), redesignated para. (f)(3) as para. (f)(4) and added new para. (f)(3), effective for tax. yrs. begin. after 12/31/86. Sec. 806(e)(2) of this Act [as amended by Sec. 1008(e)(7)(A) and (B), Sec. 1008(e)(8)(A) and (B), and Sec. 1008(e)(10) of P.L. 100-647, see above.] provides:

"(2) Change in accounting period.—In the case of any partnership, S corporation, or personal service corporation required by the amendments made by this section to change its accounting period for the taxpayer's first taxable year beginning after 12/31/86

"(A) such change shall be treated as initiated by the partnership, S corporation, or personal service corporation

"(B) such change shall be treated as having been made with the consent of the Secretary, and

"(C) with respect to any partner or shareholder of an S corporation which is required to include the items from more than 1 taxable year of the partnership or S corporation in any 1 taxable year, income in excess of expenses of such partnership or corporation for the short taxable year required by such amendments shall be taken into account ratably in each of the first 4 taxable years beginning after December 31, 1986, unless such partner or shareholder elects to include all such income in the partner's or shareholder's taxable year with or within which the partnership's or S corporation's short taxable year ends.

Subparagraph (C) shall apply to a shareholder of an S corporation only if such corporation was an S corporation for a taxable year beginning in 1986.

"(3) Basis, etc. rules.

"(A) Basis rule. The adjusted basis of any partner's interest in a partnership or shareholder's stock in an S corporation shall be determined as if all of the income to be taken into account ratably in the 4 taxable years referred to in paragraph (2)(C) where included in gross income for the 1st of such taxable years.

"(B) Treatment of dispositions. If any interest in a partnership or stock in an S corporation is disposed of before the last taxable year in the spread period, all amounts which would be included in the gross income of the partner or shareholder for subsequent taxable years in the spread period under paragraph (2)(C) and attributable to the interest or stock disposed of shall be included in gross income for the taxable year in which the disposition occurs. For purposes of the preceding sentence, the term 'spread period' means the period consisting of the 4 taxable years referred to in paragraph (2)(C)."

—P.L. 99-514, Sec. 1876(i), amended Sec. 805(a)(4) of P.L. 98-369, the effective date of changes made by Sec. 803 of P.L. 98-369, by substituting "taxable years beginning after Dec. 31, '84" for "any DISC established after, March 21, '84," see below.

In 1984, P.L. 98-369, Sec. 474(b)(2), substituted "15" for "21" in subpara. (f)(2)(A), effective for tax. yrs. begin. after 12/31/83, and to carrybacks from tax. yrs. begin. after 12/31/84.

—P.L. 98-369, Sec. 803(a), deleted "or" at the end of para. (b)(2), substituted "; or" for the period at the end of para. (b)(3), and added para. (b)(4) . . . Sec. 803(b), added subsec. (h), effective for tax. yrs. begin. after 12/31/84 [as amended by Sec. 1876(i) of P.L. 99-514, see above].

In 1977, P.L. 95-30, Sec. 102(b)(5), amended clause (f)(2)(B)(iii), effective for tax. yrs. begin. after 12/31/76.

Prior to amendment, clause (f)(2)(B)(iii) read as follows:

"(iii) if such change results in a short period to which subsection (b) of section 443 applies, the taxable income for such short period shall be placed on an annual basis for purposes of such subsection by multiplying such income by 365 and dividing the result by the number of days in the short period, and the tax shall be the same part of the tax computed on the annual basis as the number of days in the short period is of 365 days."

In 1976, P.L. 94-455, Sec. 1906(b)(13)(A), substituted "Secretary" for "Secretary or his delegate" in Code Sec. 441, effective for tax. yrs. begin. after 12/31/76.

In 1964, P.L. 88-272, Sec. 235(c)(3), added ", including," before "or ending with reference to." in subpara. (f)(2)(A), effective for tax. yrs. end. after 12/31/63.

Sec. 442. Change of annual accounting period.

If a taxpayer changes his annual accounting period, the new accounting period shall become the taxpayer's taxable year only if the change is approved by the Secretary. For purposes of this subtitle, if a taxpayer to whom section

441(g) applies adopts an annual accounting period (as defined in section 441(c)) other than a calendar year, the taxpayer shall be treated as having changed his annual accounting period.

In 1976, P.L. 94-455, Sec. 1906(b)(13)(A), substituted "Secretary" for "Secretary or his delegate" in Code Sec. 442, effective for tax. yrs. begin. after 12/31/76.

Sec. 443. Returns for a period of less than 12 months.
(a) Returns for short period.
A return for a period of less than 12 months (referred to in this section as "short period") shall be made under any of the following circumstances:

(1) Change of annual accounting period. When the taxpayer, with the approval of the Secretary, changes his annual accounting period. In such a case, the return shall be made for the short period beginning on the day after the close of the former taxable year and ending at the close of the day before the day designated as the first day of the new taxable year.

(2) Taxpayer not in existence for entire taxable year. When the taxpayer is in existence during only part of what would otherwise be his taxable year.

(b) Computation of tax on change of annual accounting period.

(1) General rule. If a return is made under paragraph (1) of subsection (a), the taxable income for the short period shall be placed on an annual basis by multiplying the modified taxable income for such short period by 12, dividing the result by the number of months in the short period. The tax shall be the same part of the tax computed on the annual basis as the number of months in the short period is of 12 months.

(2) Exception.
(A) Computation based on 12-month period. If the taxpayer applies for the benefits of this paragraph and establishes the amount of his taxable income for the 12-month period described in subparagraph (B), computed as if that period were a taxable year and under the law applicable to that year, then the tax for the short period, computed under paragraph (1), shall be reduced to the greater of the following:

(i) an amount which bears the same ratio to the tax computed on the taxable income for the 12-month period as the modified taxable income computed on the basis of the short period bears to the modified taxable income for the 12-month period; or

(ii) the tax computed on the modified taxable income for the short period.

The taxpayer (other than a taxpayer to whom subparagraph (B)(ii) applies) shall compute the tax and file his return without the application of this paragraph.

(B) 12-month period. The 12-month period referred to in subparagraph (A) shall be—

(i) the period of 12 months beginning on the first day of the short period, or

(ii) the period of 12 months ending at the close of the last day of the short period, if at the end of the 12 months referred to in clause (i) the taxpayer is not in existence or (if a corporation) has theretofore disposed of substantially all of its assets.

(C) Application for benefits. Application for the benefits of this paragraph shall be made in such manner and at such time as the regulations prescribed under subparagraph (D) may require; except that the time so prescribed shall not be later than the time (including extensions) for filing the return for the first taxable year which ends on or after the day which is 12 months after the first day of the short period. Such application, in case the return was filed without regard to this paragraph, shall be considered a claim for credit or refund with respect to the amount by which the tax is reduced under this paragraph.

(D) Regulations. The Secretary shall prescribe such regulations as he deems necessary for the application of this paragraph.

(3) Modified taxable income defined. For purposes of this subsection the term "modified taxable income" means, with respect to any period, the gross income for such period minus the deductions allowed by this chapter for such period (but, in the case of a short period, only the adjusted amount of the deductions for personal exemptions).

(c) Adjustment in deduction for personal exemption.
In the case of a taxpayer other than a corporation, if a return is made for a short period by reason of subsection (a)(1) and if the tax is not computed under subsection (b)(2), then the exemptions allowed as a deduction under section 151 (and any deduction in lieu thereof) shall be reduced to amounts which bear the same ratio to the full exemptions as the number of months in the short period bears to 12.

(d) Adjustment in computing minimum tax and tax preferences.
If a return is made for a short period by reason of subsection (a)—

(1) the alternative minimum taxable income for the short period shall be placed on an annual basis by multiplying such amount by 12 and dividing the result by the number of months in the short period, and

(2) the amount computed under paragraph (1) of section 55(a) shall bear the same relation to the tax computed on the annual basis as the number of months in the short period bears to 12.

(e) Cross references.
For inapplicability of subsection (b) in computing—
(1) Accumulated earnings tax, see section 536.
(2) Personal holding company tax, see section 546.
(3) The taxable income of a regulated investment company, see section 852(b)(2)(E).
(4) The taxable income of a real estate investment trust, see section 857(b)(2)(C).

For returns for a period of less than 12 months in the case of a debtor's election to terminate a taxable year, see section 1398(d)(2)(E).

In 2004, P.L. 108-357, Sec. 413(c)(6), deleted para. (e)(3) and redesignated paras. (e)(4) and (e)(5) as (e)(3) and (e)(4), effective for tax. yrs. of foreign corporations begin. after 12/31/2004, and for tax. yrs. of United States shareholders with or within which such tax. yrs. of foreign corporations end.
Prior to deletion, para. (e)(3) read as follows:
"(3) Undistributed foreign personal holding company income, see section 557."
In 1986, P.L. 99-514, Sec. 104(b)(7)(A), deleted ", and adding the zero bracket amount" after "the short period," in para. (b)(1) . . . Sec. 104(b)(7)(B), amended clause (b)(2)(A)(ii), effective for tax. yrs. begin. after 12/31/86.
Prior to amendment, clause (b)(2)(A)(ii) read as follows:
"(ii) the tax computed on the sum of the modified taxable income for the short period plus the zero bracket amount."
—P.L. 99-514, Sec. 701(e)(3), amended subsec. (d), effective for tax. yrs. begin. after 12/31/86. For special rules, see Sec. 701(f)(2), (3) and (5) of this Act reproduced in note following Code Sec. 56.
Prior to amendment, subsec. (d) read as follows:
"(d) Adjustment in computing minimum tax for tax preferences.
"If a return is made for a short period by reason of subsection (a), then—
"(1) in the case of a taxpayer other than a corporation, the alternative minimum taxable income for the short period shall be placed on an annual basis by multiplying that amount by 12 and dividing the result by the number of months in the short period, and the amount computed under paragraph (1) of section 55(a) shall be the same part of the tax computed on the annual basis as the number of months in the short period is of 12 months; and

Tax accounting — Code Sec. 444(e)

"(2) the $10,000 amount specified in section 56 (relating to minimum tax for tax preferences), modified as provided by section 58, shall be reduced to the amount which bears the same ratio to such specified amount as the number of days in the short period bears to 365."

In 1983, P.L. 97-448, Sec. 304(a), substituted "section 1398(d)(2)(E)" for "section 1398(d)(3)(E)", in para. (e)(5), effective for any bankruptcy case begin. after 3/25/81 [more than 90 days after date of enactment (12/24/80)].

In 1980, P.L. 96-589, Sec. 3(d), added the sentence at the end of subsec. (e), effective for any bankruptcy case begin. after 3/25/81 [more than 90 days after the date of enactment (12/24/80)]. Sec. 7(g) of this Act provides:

"(g) Definitions.

"For purposes of this section—

"(1) Bankruptcy case. The term 'bankruptcy case' means any case under title 11 of the United States Code (as recodified by P.L. 95-598).

"(2) Similar judicial proceeding. The term 'similar judicial proceeding' means a receivership, foreclosure, or similar proceeding in a Federal or State court (as modified by section 368(a)(3)(D) of the Internal Revenue Code of 1954)."

—P.L. 96-222, Sec. 104(a)(4)(H)(iii), deleted "in the case of a corporation" before "the $10,000 amount" in para. (d)(2), effective for tax. yrs. begin. after 12/31/78.

In 1978, P.L. 95-600, Sec. 421(e)(2), amended subsec. (d), effective for tax. yrs. begin. after 12/31/78.

Prior to amendment, subsec. (d) read as follows:

"(d) Adjustment in exclusion for computing minimum tax for tax preferences.

"If a return is made for a short period by reason of subsection (a), then the $10,000 amount specified in section 56 (relating to minimum tax for tax preferences), modified as provided by section 58, shall be reduced to the amount which bears the same ratio to such specified amount as the number of days in the short period bears to 365."

—P.L. 95-600, Sec. 703(o)(1)(A), substituted "modified taxable income" for "taxable income" in clause (b)(2)(A)(i)... Sec. 703(o)(1)(B), amended clause (b)(2)(A)(ii)... Sec. 703(o)(2), substituted "modified taxable income for such short period" for "gross income for such short period (minus the deductions allowed by this chapter for the short period, but only the adjusted amount of the deductions for personal exemptions)" in para. (b)(1)... Sec. 703(o)(2), added para. (b)(3), effective for tax. yrs. begin. after 12/31/76.

Prior to amendment, clause (b)(2)(A)(ii) read as follows:

"(ii) the tax computed on the taxable income for the short period without placing the taxable income on an annual basis."

In 1977, P.L. 95-30, Sec. 102(b)(6), amended para. (b)(1), effective for tax. yrs. begin. after 12/31/76.

Prior to amendment, para. (b)(1) read as follows:

"(1) General rule. If a return is made under paragraph (1) of subsection (a), the taxable income for the short period shall be placed on an annual basis by multiplying such income by 12 and dividing the result by the number of months in the short period. The tax shall be the same part of the tax computed on the annual basis as the number of months in the short period is of 12 months."

In 1976, P.L. 94-528, Sec. 2(a), amended the effective date for the amendment made by Sec. 1204(c)(2) of P.L. 94-455, see below, to be effective for action taken under Code Sec. 6851, 6861 or 6862 where notice and demand takes place after 2/28/77, rather than effective for action taken under Code Sec. 6851, 6861 or 6862 where notice and demand takes place after 12/31/76.

—P.L. 94-455, Sec. 301(c), substituted "$10,000" for "$30,000" in subsec. (d), effective for items of tax preference for tax. yrs. begin. after 12/31/75.

—P.L. 94-455, Sec. 1204(c)(2), deleted para. (a)(3), effective [as amended by Sec. 2(a) of P.L. 94-528, see above] for action taken under Code Sec. 6851, 6861 or 6862 where the notice and demand takes place after 2/28/77.

Prior to amendment, para. (a)(3) read as follows:

"(3) Termination of taxable year for jeopardy. When the Secretary or his delegate terminates the taxpayer's taxable year under section 6851 (relating to tax in jeopardy)."

—P.L. 94-455, Sec. 1607(b)(1)(C), substituted "857(b)(2)(C)" for "857(b)(2)(D)" in para. (e)(5), for tax. yrs. end. after 10/4/76.

—P.L. 94-455, Sec. 1906(b)(13)(A), substituted "Secretary" for "Secretary or his delegate" in para. (a)(1) and subpara. (b)(2)(D), effective for tax. yrs. begin. after 12/31/76.

In 1969, P.L. 91-172, Sec. 301(b)(6), redesignated subsec. (d) as subsec. (e) and added subsec. (d), effective for tax. yrs. end. after 12/31/69.

In 1960, P.L. 86-779, Sec. 10(i), added subsec. (d)(5), effective for tax. yrs. of real estate investment trusts begin. after 12/31/60.

Sec. 444. Election of taxable year other than required taxable year.

(a) General rule.

Except as otherwise provided in this section, a partnership, S corporation, or personal service corporation may elect to have a taxable year other than the required taxable year.

(b) Limitations on taxable years which may be elected.

(1) In general. Except as provided in paragraphs (2) and (3), an election may be made under subsection (a) only if the deferral period of the taxable year elected is not longer than 3 months.

(2) Changes in taxable year. Except as provided in paragraph (3), in the case of an entity changing a taxable year, an election may be made under subsection (a) only if the deferral period of the taxable year elected is not longer than the shorter of—

(A) 3 months, or

(B) the deferral period of the taxable year which is being changed.

(3) Special rule for entities retaining 1986 taxable years. In the case of an entity's 1st taxable year beginning after December 31, 1986, an entity may elect a taxable year under subsection (a) which is the same as the entity's last taxable year beginning in 1986.

(4) Deferral period. For purposes of this subsection, except as provided in regulations, the term "deferral period" means, with respect to any taxable year of the entity, the months between—

(A) the beginning of such year, and

(B) the close of the 1st required taxable year ending within such year.

(c) Effect of election.

If an entity makes an election under subsection (a), then—

(1) in the case of a partnership or S corporation, such entity shall make the payments required by section 7519, and

(2) in the case of a personal service corporation, such corporation shall be subject to the deduction limitations of section 280H.

(d) Elections.

(1) Person making election. An election under subsection (a) shall be made by the partnership, S corporation, or personal service corporation.

(2) Period of election.

(A) In general. Any election under subsection (a) shall remain in effect until the partnership, S corporation, or personal service corporation changes its taxable year or otherwise terminates such election. Any change to a required taxable year may be made without the consent of the Secretary.

(B) No further election. If an election is terminated under subparagraph (A) or paragraph (3)(A), the partnership, S corporation, or personal service corporation may not make another election under subsection (a).

(3) Tiered structures, etc.

(A) In general. Except as otherwise provided in this paragraph—

(i) no election may be under subsection (a) with respect to any entity which is part of a tiered structure, and

(ii) an election under subsection (a) with respect to any entity shall be terminated if such entity becomes part of a tiered structure.

(B) Exceptions for structures consisting of certain entities with same taxable year. Subparagraph (A) shall not apply to any tiered structure which consists only of partnerships or S corporations (or both) all of which have the same taxable year.

(e) Required taxable year.

For purposes of this section, the term "required taxable year" means the taxable year determined under section 706(b), 1378, or 441(i) without taking into account any taxable year which is allowable by reason of business purposes. Solely for purposes of the preceding sentence, sections 706(b), 1378, and 441(i) shall be treated as in effect for taxable years beginning before January 1, 1987.

(f) Personal service corporation.

For purposes of this section, the term "personal service corporation" has the meaning given to such term by section 441(i)(2).

(g) Regulations.

The Secretary shall prescribe such regulations as may be necessary to carry out the provisions of this section, including regulations to prevent the avoidance of subsection (b)(2)(B) or (d)(2)(B) through the change in form of an entity.

In **1988**, P.L. 100-647, Sec. 2004(e)(1)(A), substituted "as otherwise provided in this section" for "as provided in subsections (b) and (c)" in subsec. (a) ... Sec. 2004(e)(1)(B), amended para. (d)(3) ... Sec. 2004(e)(1)(C), substituted "under subparagraph (A) or paragraph (3)(A)" for "under subparagraph (A)" in subpara. (d)(2)(B) ... Sec. 2004(e)(2)(A), redesignated subsec. (f) and (g) and added new subsec. (f) ... Sec. 2004(e)(12), added "or otherwise terminates such election" before the period at the end of the first sentence of subpara. (d)(2)(A) ... Sec. 2004(e)(13), substituted "except as provided in regulations, the term" for "the term" in para. (b)(4), effective for tax. yrs. begin. after 12/31/86 and as provided in Sec. 10206(a)(1) of P.L. 100-203, see below.

Prior to amendment, para. (d)(3) read as follows:

"(3) Tiered structures, etc. No election may be made under subsection (a) with respect to an entity which is part of a tiered structure other than a tiered structure comprised of 1 or more partnerships or S corporations all of which have the same taxable year."

— P.L. 100-647, Sec. 2004(e)(11), amended Sec. 10206(d)(4) of P.L. 100-203 [reproduced below], special rules for the amendments made by Sec. 10206(a)(1) of P.L. 100-203, by adding the last sentence, see below.

In **1987**, P.L. 100-203, Sec. 10206(a)(1), added Code Sec. 444, effective for tax. yrs. begin. after 12/31/86. Sec. 10206(d)(3) and (4) [as amended by Sec. 2004(e)(11) of P.L. 100-647, see above] of this Act provides:

"(3) Elections.— Any election under section 444 of the Internal Revenue Code of 1986 (as added by subsection (a)) for an entity's 1st taxable year beginning after December 31, 1986, shall not be required to be made before the 90th day after the date of the enactment of this Act.

"(4) Special rule for existing entities electing S corporation status.— If a C corporation (within the meaning of section 1361(a)(2)) of the Internal Revenue Code of 1986) with a taxable year other than the calendar year—

"(A) made an election after September 18, 1986, and before January 1, 1988, under section 1362 of such Code to be treated as an S corporation, and

"(B) elected to have the calendar year as the taxable year of the S corporation, then section 444(b)(2)(B) of such Code shall be applied by taking into account the deferral period of the last taxable year of the C corporation rather than the deferral period of the taxable year being changed. The preceding sentence shall apply only in the case of an election under section 444 of such Code made for a taxable year beginning before 1989."

PART II.—METHODS OF ACCOUNTING

Subpart

A. Methods of accounting in general.

B. Taxable year for which items of gross income included.

C. Taxable year for which deductions taken.

D. Inventories.

SUBPART A.—METHODS OF ACCOUNTING IN GENERAL

Sec.

446. General rule for methods of accounting.

447. Method of accounting for corporations engaged in farming.

448. Limitation on use of cash method of accounting.

In **1986**, P.L. 99-514, Sec. 801(c), added item 448.

In **1976**, P.L. 94-455, Sec. 207(c)(1)(B), added the item for 447.

Sec. 446. General rule for methods of accounting.

(a) General rule.

Taxable income shall be computed under the method of accounting on the basis of which the taxpayer regularly computes his income in keeping his books.

(b) Exceptions.

If no method of accounting has been regularly used by the taxpayer, or if the method used does not clearly reflect income, the computation of taxable income shall be made under such method as, in the opinion of the Secretary, does clearly reflect income.

(c) Permissible methods.

Subject to the provisions of subsections (a) and (b), a taxpayer may compute taxable income under any of the following methods of accounting—

(1) the cash receipts and disbursements method;

(2) an accrual method;

(3) any other method permitted by this chapter; or

(4) any combination of the foregoing methods permitted under regulations prescribed by the Secretary.

(d) Taxpayer engaged in more than one business.

A taxpayer engaged in more than one trade or business may, in computing taxable income, use a different method of accounting for each trade or business.

(e) Requirement respecting change of accounting method.

Except as otherwise expressly provided in this chapter, a taxpayer who changes the method of accounting on the basis of which he regularly computes his income in keeping his books shall, before computing his taxable income under the new method, secure the consent of the Secretary.

(f) Failure to request change of method of accounting.

If the taxpayer does not file with the Secretary a request to change the method of accounting, the absence of the consent of the Secretary to a change in the method of accounting shall not be taken into account—

(1) to prevent the imposition of any penalty, or the addition of any amount to tax, under this title, or

(2) to diminish the amount of such penalty or addition to tax.

In **2001**, P.L. 107-16, Sec. 658, of this Act, reads as follows:

"SEC. 658. CLARIFICATION OF TREATMENT OF CONTRIBUTIONS TO MULTIEMPLOYER PLAN.

"(a) Not considered method of accounting. For purposes of section 446 of the Internal Revenue Code of 1986, a determination under section 404(a)(6) of such Code regarding the taxable year with respect to which a contribution to a multiemployer pension plan is deemed made shall not be treated as a method of accounting of the taxpayer. No deduction shall be allowed for any taxable year for any contribution to a multiemployer pension plan with respect to which a deduction was previously allowed.

"(b) Regulations. The Secretary of the Treasury shall promulgate such regulations as necessary to clarify that a taxpayer shall not be allowed an aggregate amount of deductions for contributions to a multiemployer pension plan which exceeds the amount of such contributions made or deemed made under section 404(a)(6) of the Internal Revenue Code of 1986 to such plan.

"(c) Effective date. Subsection (a), and any regulations promulgated under subsection (b), shall be effective for years ending after the date of the enactment of this Act."

In **1984**, P.L. 98-369, Sec. 161(a), added subsec. (f), for tax. yrs. begin. after 7/18/84.

In **1981**, P.L. 97-34, Sec. 203(c)(2), provides

"(2) Change in method of accounting. Sections 446 and 481 of the Internal Revenue Code of 1954 shall not apply to the change in the method of depreciation [i.e., as defined in Code Sec. 168(g)(6)] to comply with the provisions of this subsection [i.e., Sec. 203(c)(1)]."

In **1976**, P.L. 94-455, Sec. 1906(b)(13)(A), substituted "Secretary" for "Secretary or his delegate" each place it appeared in Code Sec. 446, effective for tax. yrs. begin. after 12/31/76.

In **1960**, P.L. 86-459, Sec. 1, through 5 provide as follows:

"Dealer Reserve Income Adjustment Act of 1960"

"SEC 1. SHORT TITLE.

"This Act may be cited as the 'Dealer Reserve Income Adjustment Act of 1960'.

"SEC. 2. PERSONS TO WHOM THIS ACT APPLIES.

"This Act shall apply to any person who, for his most recent taxable year ending on or before June 22, 1959—

"(1) computed, or was required to compute, taxable income under an accrual method of accounting,

"(2) treated any dealer reserve income, which should have been taken into account (under the accrual method of accounting) for such taxable year, and

"(3) before September 1, 1960, makes an election under section 3(a) or 4(a) of this Act.

"SEC. 3. ELECTION TO HAVE SECTION 481 APPLY.

"(a) General rule.

"If—

"(1) for the year of the change (determined under subsection (b)), the treatment of dealer reserve income by any person to whom this Act applies is changed to a method proper under the accrual method of accounting (whether or not such person initiated the change),

"(2) such person makes an election under this subsection, and

"(3) such person does not make the election provided by section 4(a),

then, for purposes of section 481 of the Internal Revenue Code of 1954, the change described in paragraph (1) shall be treated as a change in method of accounting not initiated by the taxpayer.

"*(b) Year of change, etc.*

"In applying section 481 of the Internal Revenue Code of 1954 for purposes of this section, the 'year of the change' in the case of any person is—

"(1) except as provided in paragraph (2), the first taxable year ending after June 22, 1959, or

"(2) the earliest taxable year (whether the Internal Revenue Code of 1954 or the Internal Revenue Code of 1939 applies to such year) for which—

"(A) on or before June 22, 1959—

"(i) the Secretary of the Treasury or his delegate issued a notice of deficiency, or a written notice of a proposed deficiency, with respect to dealer reserve income, or

"(ii) such person, filed with the Secretary or his delegate a claim for refund or credit with respect to dealer reserve income, and

"(B) the assessment of any deficiency or the refund or credit of any overpayment, whichever is applicable, was not, on June 21, 1959, prevented by the operation of any law or rule of law.

For purposes of this section, section 481 of such Code shall be treated as applying to any year of the change to which the Internal Revenue Code of 1939 applies.

"Sec. 4. Election to have section 481 not apply; payment in installments.

"*(a) General rule.*

"If a person to whom this Act applies makes an election under this subsection, then for purposes of chapter 1 of the Internal Revenue Code of 1954 (and the corresponding provisions of prior law) a change in the treatment of dealer reserve income to a method proper under the accrual method of accounting shall be treated as not a change in method of accounting in respect of which section 481 of the Internal Revenue Code of 1954 applies. Any election under this subsection shall apply to all taxable years ending on or before June 22, 1959 (whether the provisions of the Internal Revenue Code of 1954 or the corresponding provisions of prior law apply), for which the assessment of any deficiency, or for which refund or credit of any overpayment, whichever is applicable, was on June 21, 1959, prevented by the operation of any law or rule of law.

"*(b) Election to pay tax in installments.*

"(1) Eligibility.—If the net increase in tax (as defined in paragraph (2)) which results solely from the effect of the election provided by subsection (a) exceeds $2,500, then the taxpayer may elect (at the time the election is made under subsection (a)) to pay in two or more (but not to exceed 10) equal annual installments any portion of such net increase which (on the date of such election) is unpaid.

"(2) Net increase in tax defined.—For purposes of this section, the term 'net increase in tax' means the amount (if any) by which—

"(A) the sum of the increases in tax (including interest) for all taxable years to which the election applies and which is attributable to the election, exceeds

"(B) the sum of the decreases in tax (including interest) for all taxable years to which the election applies and which is attributable to the election.

For purposes of this paragraph, interest for the period before the date of the election shall be computed as provided in chapter 67 of the Internal Revenue Code of 1954 (or the corresponding provisions of prior revenue laws).

"*(c) Due date for installments.*

"If an election is made under subsection (b), the first installment shall be paid on or before the date prescribed by section 6151(a) of the Internal Revenue Code of 1954 for payment of the tax for the taxable year in which the election was made, and each succeeding installment shall be paid on or before the date which is one year after the date prescribed by this subsection for payment of the preceding installment.

"*(d) Effect of subsequent redetermination of tax.—*

"(1) Redetermination.—If—

"(A) the taxpayer makes an election under subsection (b), and

"(B) there is a redetermination of the taxpayer's tax for any taxable year to which the election provided by subsection (a) applies, then the net increase in tax (as defined in subsection (b)(2)) shall be redetermined.

"(2) Effect of increase.—If the redetermination described in paragraph (1)(B) results in an increase in the net increase in tax (as defined in subsection (b)(2)), the resulting increase shall be prorated to all the installments. The part of such resulting increase so prorated to any installment the date for payment of which has not arrived shall be collected at the same time as, and as a part of, such installment. The part of such resulting increase so prorated to any installment the date for payment of which has arrived shall be paid upon notice and demand from the Secretary of the Treasury or his delegate.

"(3) Effect of decrease.—For treatment of a decrease in the net increase in tax as the result of a redetermination described in paragraph (1)(B), see section 6403 of the Internal Revenue Code of 1954 (relating to overpayment of installment).

"*(e) Suspension of interest.*

"(1) In general.—If an election under subsection (a) applies and there is a net increase in tax (as defined in subsection (b)(2)), no interest shall be imposed on any underpayment (and no interest shall be paid on any overpayment) attributable to such election for the period beginning on the date of such election and ending on the date prescribed by section 6151(a) of the Internal Revenue Code of 1954 for payment of the taxable year in which the election was made.

"(2) No interest during installation period.— If an election under subsection (b) applies, no interest shall be imposed for the period on or after the date fixed for payment of the first installment unless payment of unpaid installments is accelerated under subsection (f) or (g).

"(3) Interest where payment is accelerated. If payment is accelerated under subsection (f) or (g), interest determined in accordance with the provisions of section 6601 of the Internal Revenue Code of 1954 on the entire unpaid tax shall be payable—

"(A) if payment is accelerated under subsection (f), from the date of notice and demand provided by such subsection to the date such tax is paid, or

"(B) if payment is accelerated under subsection (g), from the date fixed for paying the unpaid installment to the date such tax is paid.

"*(f) Termination of installment payment privilege.*

"The extension of time provided by this section for payment of tax shall cease to apply, and any unpaid installments shall be paid upon notice and demand from the Secretary of the Treasury or his delegate, if—

"(1) in the case of a taxpayer who is an individual, he dies or ceases to engage in a trade or business,

"(2) in the case of a taxpayer who is a partner, the entire interest of such partner is transferred or liquidated or the partnership terminates, or

"(3) in the case of a taxpayer which is a corporation, the taxpayer ceases to engage in a trade or business, unless the unpaid portion of the tax payable in installments is required to be taken into account by the acquiring corporation under section 5(d).

"*(g) Failure to pay installment.*

"If any installment under this section is not paid on or before the date fixed for its payment by this section (including any extension of time for payment of such installment), the unpaid installments shall be paid upon notice and demand from the Secretary of the Treasury or his delegate.

"*(h) Suspension of running of periods of limitation.*

"The running of the periods of limitation provided by section 6502 of the Internal Revenue Code of 1954 (or corresponding provision of prior law) for the collection of any amount of tax payable in installments under this section shall be suspended for the period of any extension of time for payment granted under this section.

"Sec. 5. Definitions; Special Rules.

"*(a) Dealer reserve income.*

"For purposes of this Act, the term 'dealer reserve income' means—

"(1) that part of the consideration derived by any person from the sale or other disposition of customers' sales contracts, notes, and other evidences of indebtedness (or derived from customers' finance charges connected with such sales or other dispositions) which is—

"(A) attributable to the sale by such person to such customers, in the ordinary course of his trade or business, of real property or tangible personal property, and

"(B) held in a reserve account, by the financial institution to which such person disposed of such evidences of indebtedness, for the purpose of securing obligations of such person or of such customers, or both; and

"(2) that part of the consideration—

"(A) derived by any person from a sale described in paragraph (1)(A) in respect of which part or all of the purchase price of the property sold is provided by a financial institution to or for the customer to whom such property is sold, or

"(B) derived by such person from finance charges connected with the financing of such sale,

which is held in a reserve account by such financial institution for the purpose of securing obligations of such person or of such customer, or both.

"*(b) Financial institution.*

"For purposes of this Act, the term 'financial institution' means any person regularly engaged in the business of acquiring evidences of indebtedness of the kind described in subsection (a)(1), or of financing sales of the kind described in subsection (a)(2), or both.

"*(c) Other terms; application of other laws.*

"Except where otherwise distinctly expressed or manifestly intended, terms used in this Act shall have the same meaning as when used in the Internal Revenue Code of 1954 and all provisions of law shall apply with respect to this Act as if this Act were a part of such Code.

"*(d) Acquiring corporation.*

"In the case of the acquisition of assets of a corporation by another corporation in a distribution or transfer described in section 381(a) of the Internal Revenue Code of 1954, the acquiring corporation shall, for purposes of this Act, be treated as if it were the distributor or transferor corporation.

"*(e) Statutes of limitations.*

"(1) Extension of period for assessment and refund or credit.—For purposes of applying sections 3 and 4 of this Act, if the assessment of any deficiency, or the refund or credit of any overpayment, for any taxable year was not prevented on June 21, 1959, by the operation of any law or rule of law, but would be so prevented prior to September 1, 1961, the period within which such assessment, or such refund or credit, may be made shall not expire prior to September 1, 1961. An election by a taxpayer under section 3 or 4 of this Act shall be considered as a consent to the application of the provisions of this subsection.

"(2) Years closed by closing agreement or compromise.—For purposes of this Act, if the assessment of any deficiency, or the refund or credit of any overpayment, for any taxable year is prevented on the date of an election under section 3 or 4 of this Act by the operation of the provisions of chapter 74 of the Internal Revenue Code of 1954 (relating to closing agreements and compromises) or by the corresponding provisions of the Internal Revenue Code of 1939, such assessment, or such refund or credit, shall be considered as having been prevented on June 21, 1959.

Code Sec. 446   Tax accounting

"(f) Regulations.
"The Secretary of the Treasury or his delegate shall prescribe such regulations as may be necessary to carry out the purposes of this Act, including regulations relating to—
"(1) the application of the provisions of this Act in the case of partnerships, and
"(2) the manner in which the elections provided by this Act are to be made."

Sec. 447. Method of accounting for corporations engaged in farming.

(a) General rule.

Except as otherwise provided by law, the taxable income from farming of—

(1) a corporation engaged in the trade or business of farming, or

(2) a partnership engaged in the trade or business of farming, if a corporation is a partner in such partnership,

shall be computed on an accrual method of accounting. This section shall not apply to the trade or business of operating a nursery or sod farm or to the raising or harvesting of trees (other than fruit and nut trees).

(b) Preproductive period expenses.

For rules requiring capitalization of certain preproductive period expenses, see section 263A.

(c) Exception for certain corporations.

For purposes of subsection (a), a corporation shall be treated as not being a corporation if it is—

(1) an S corporation, or

(2) a corporation the gross receipts of which meet the requirements of subsection (d).

(d) Gross receipts requirements.

(1) In general. A corporation meets the requirements of this subsection if, for each prior taxable year beginning after December 31, 1975, such corporation (and any predecessor corporation) did not have gross receipts exceeding $1,000,000. For purposes of the preceding sentence, all corporations which are members of the same controlled group of corporations (within the meaning of section 1563(a)) shall be treated as 1 corporation.

(2) Special rules for family corporations.

(A) In general. In the case of a family corporation, paragraph (1) shall be applied—

(i) by substituting "December 31, 1985," for "December 31, 1975,"; and

(ii) by substituting "$25,000,000" for "$1,000,000".

(B) Gross receipts test.

(i) Controlled groups. Notwithstanding the last sentence of paragraph (1), in the case of a family corporation—

(I) except as provided by the Secretary, only the applicable percentage of gross receipts of any other member of any controlled group of corporations of which such corporation is a member shall be taken into account, and

(II) under regulations, gross receipts of such corporation or of another member of such group shall not be taken into account by such corporation more than once.

(ii) Pass-thru entities. For purposes of paragraph (1), if a family corporation holds directly or indirectly any interest in a partnership, estate, trust or other pass-thru entity, such corporation shall take into account its proportionate share of the gross receipts of such entity.

(iii) Applicable percentage. For purposes of clause (i), the term "applicable percentage" means the percentage equal to a fraction—

(I) the numerator of which is the fair market value of the stock of another corporation held directly or indirectly as of the close of the taxable year by the family corporation, and

(II) the denominator of which is the fair market value of all stock of such corporation as of such time.

For purposes of this clause, the term "stock" does not include stock described in section 1563(c)(1).

(C) Family corporation. For purposes of this section, the term "family corporation" means—

(i) any corporation if at least 50 percent of the total combined voting power of all classes of stock entitled to vote, and at least 50 percent of all other classes of stock of the corporation, are owned by members of the same family, and

(ii) any corporation described in subsection (h).

(e) Members of the same family.

For purposes of subsection (d)—

(1) the members of the same family are an individual, such individual's brothers and sisters, the brothers and sisters of such individual's parents and grandparents, the ancestors and lineal descendants of any of the foregoing, a spouse of any of the foregoing, and the estate of any of the foregoing,

(2) stock owned, directly or indirectly, by or for a partnership or trust shall be treated as owned proportionately by its partners or beneficiaries, and

(3) if 50 percent or more in value of the stock in a corporation (hereinafter in this paragraph referred to as "first corporation") is owned, directly or through paragraph (2), by or for members of the same family, such members shall be considered as owning each class of stock in a second corporation (or a wholly owned subsidiary of such second corporation) owned, directly or indirectly, by or for the first corporation, in that proportion which the value of the stock in the first corporation which such members so own bears to the value of all the stock in the first corporation.

For purposes of paragraph (1), individuals related by the half blood or by legal adoption shall be treated as if they were related by the whole blood.

(f) Coordination with section 481.

In the case of any taxpayer required by this section to change its method of accounting for any taxable year—

(1) such change shall be treated as having been made with the consent of the Secretary,

(2) for purposes of section 481(a)(2), such change shall be treated as a change not initiated by the taxpayer, and

(3) under regulations prescribed by the Secretary, the net amount of adjustments required by section 481(a) to be taken into account by the taxpayer in computing taxable income shall be taken into account in each of the 10 taxable years (or the remaining taxable years where there is a stated future life of less than 10 taxable years) beginning with the year of change.

(g) Certain annual accrual accounting methods.

(1) In general. Notwithstanding subsection (a) or section 263A, if—

(A) for its 10 taxable years ending with its first taxable year beginning after December 31, 1975, a corporation or qualified partnership used an annual accrual method of accounting with respect to its trade or business of farming,

(B) such corporation or qualified partnership raises crops which are harvested not less than 12 months after planting, and

(C) such corporation or qualified partnership has used such method of accounting for all taxable years intervening between its first taxable year beginning after December 31, 1975, and the taxable year,

such corporation or qualified partnership may continue to employ such method of accounting for the taxable year with respect to its qualified farming trade or business.

(2) Annual accrual method of accounting defined. For purposes of paragraph (1), the term "annual accrual method of accounting" means a method under which revenues, costs, and expenses are computed on an accrual method of accounting and the preproductive period expenses incurred during the taxable year are charged to harvested crops or deducted in determining the taxable income for such years.

(3) Certain nonrecognition transfers. For purposes of this subsection, if—

(A) a corporation acquired substantially all the assets of a qualified farming trade or business from another corporation in a transaction in which no gain or loss was recognized to the transferor or transferee corporation, or

(B) a qualified partnership acquired substantially all the assets of a qualified farming trade or business from one of its partners in a transaction to which section 721 applies,

the transferee corporation or qualified partnership shall be deemed to have computed its taxable income on an annual accrual method of accounting during the period for which the transferor corporation or partnership computed its taxable income from such trade or business on an annual accrual method.

(4) Qualified partnership defined. For purposes of this subsection—

(A) Qualified partnership. The term "qualified partnership" means a partnership which is engaged in a qualified farming trade or business and each of the partners of which is a corporation other than—

(i) an S corporation, or

(ii) a personal holding company (within the meaning of section 542(a)).

(B) Qualified farming trade or business.

(i) In general. The term "qualified farming trade or business" means the trade or business of farming—

(I) sugar cane,

(II) any plant with a preproductive period (as defined in section 263A(e)(3)) of 2 years or less, and

(III) any other plant (other than any citrus or almond tree) if an election by the corporation under this subparagraph is in effect.

In the case of a partnership and for purposes of paragraph (3)(A), subclauses (II) and (III) shall not apply.

(ii) Effect of election. For purposes of paragraphs (1) and (2) of section 263A(e), any election under this subparagraph shall be treated as if it were an election under subsection (d)(3) of section 263A.

(iii) Election. Unless the Secretary otherwise consents, an election under this subparagraph may be made only for the corporation's 1st taxable year which begins after December 31, 1986, and during which the corporation engages in a farming business. Any such election, once made, may be revoked only with the consent of the Secretary.

(h) Exception for certain closely held corporations.

(1) In general. A corporation is described in this subsection if, on October 4, 1976, and at all times thereafter—

(A) members of 2 families (within the meaning of subsection (e)(1)) have owned (directly or through the application of subsection (e)) at least 65 percent of the total combined voting power of all classes of stock of such corporation entitled to vote, and at least 65 percent of the total number of shares of all other classes of stock of such corporation; or

(B)(i) members of 3 families (within the meaning of subsection (e)(1)) have owned (directly or through the application of subsection (e)) at least 50 percent of the total combined voting power of all classes of stock of such corporation entitled to vote, and at least 50 percent of the total number of shares of all other classes of stock of such corporation; and

(ii) substantially all of the stock of such corporation which is not so owned (directly or through the application of subsection (e)) by members of such 3 families is owned directly—

(I) by employees of the corporation or members of their families (within the meaning of section 267(c)(4)), or

(II) by a trust for the benefit of the employees of such corporation which is described in section 401(a) and which is exempt from taxation under section 501(a).

(2) Stock held by employees, etc. For purposes of this subsection, stock which—

(A) is owned directly by employes [sic employees] of the corporation or members of their families (within the meaning of section 267(c)(4)) or by a trust described in paragraph (1)(B)(ii)(II), and

(B) was acquired on or after October 4, 1976, from the corporation or from a member of a family which, on October 4, 1976, was described in subparagraph (A) or (B)(i) of paragraph (1),

shall be treated as owned by a member of a family which, on October 4, 1976, was described in subparagraph (A) or (B)(i) of paragraph (1).

(3) Corporation must be engaged in farming. This subsection shall apply only in the case of a corporation which was, on October 4, 1976, and at all times thereafter, engaged in the trade or business of farming.

(i) Suspense account for family corporations.

(1) In general. If any family corporation is required by this section to change its method of accounting for any taxable year (hereinafter in this subsection referred to as the "year of the change"), notwithstanding subsection (f), such corporation shall establish a suspense account under this subsection in lieu of taking into account adjustments under section 481(a) with respect to amounts included in the suspense account.

(2) Initial opening balance. The initial opening balance of the account described in paragraph (1) shall be the lesser of—

(A) the net adjustments which would have been required to be taken into account under section 481 but for this subsection, or

(B) the amount of such net adjustments determined as of the beginning of the taxable year preceding the year of change.

If the amount referred to in subparagraph (A) exceeds the amount referred to in subparagraph (B), notwithstanding paragraph (1), such excess shall be included in gross income in the year of the change.

(3) Inclusion where corporation ceases to be a family corporation.

Code Sec. 447(i)(3)(A)   Tax accounting

(A) In general. If the corporation ceases to be a family corporation during any taxable year, the amount in the suspense account (after taking into account prior reductions) shall be included in gross income for such taxable year.

(B) Special rule for certain transfers. For purposes of subparagraph (A), any transfer in a corporation after December 15, 1987, shall be treated as a transfer to a person whose ownership could not qualify such corporation as a family corporation unless it is a transfer—

(i) to a member of the family of the transferor, or

(ii) in the case of a corporation described in subsection (h), to a member of a family which on December 15, 1987, held stock in such corporation which qualified the corporation under subsection (h).

(4) Subchapter C transactions. The application of this subsection with respect to a taxpayer which is a party to any transaction with respect to which there is nonrecognition of gain or loss to any party by reason of subchapter C shall be determined under regulations prescribed by the Secretary.

(5) Termination.

(A) In general. No suspense account may be established under this subsection by any corporation required by this section to change its method of accounting for any taxable year ending after June 8, 1997.

(B) Phaseout of existing suspense accounts.

(i) In general. Each suspense account under this subsection shall be reduced (but not below zero) for each taxable year beginning after June 8, 1997, by an amount equal to the lesser of—

(I) the applicable portion of such account, or

(II) 50 percent of the taxable income of the corporation for the taxable year, or, if the corporation has no taxable income for such year, the amount of any net operating loss (as defined in section 172(c)) for such taxable year.

For purposes of the preceding sentence, the amount of taxable income and net operating loss shall be determined without regard to this paragraph.

(ii) Coordination with other reductions. The amount of the applicable portion for any taxable year shall be reduced (but not below zero) by the amount of any reduction required for such taxable year under any other provision of this subsection.

(iv) [sic (iii)] Inclusion in income. Any reduction in a suspense account under this paragraph shall be included in gross income for the taxable year of the reduction.

(C) Applicable portion. For purposes of subparagraph (B), the term "applicable portion" means, for any taxable year, the amount which would ratably reduce the amount in the account (after taking into account prior reductions) to zero over the period consisting of such taxable year and the remaining taxable years in such first 20 taxable years.

(D) Amounts after 20th year. Any amount in the account as of the close of the 20th year referred to in subparagraph (C) shall be treated as the applicable portion for each succeeding year thereafter to the extent not reduced under this paragraph for any prior taxable year after such 20th year.

In 1997, P.L. 105-34, Sec. 1081(a), deleted paras. (i)(3) and (4), redesignated paras. (i)(5) and (6) as paras. (i)(3) and (4), and added new para. (i)(5), effective for tax. yrs. end. after 6/8/97.

Prior to deletion, paras. (i)(3) and (4) read as follows:

"(3) Reduction in account if farming business contracts. If—

"(A) the gross receipts of the corporation from the trade or business of farming for the year of the change or any subsequent taxable year, is less than

"(B) such gross receipts for the taxpayer's last taxable year beginning before the year of the change (or for the most recent taxable year for which a reduction in the suspense account was made under this paragraph),

the amount in the suspense account (after taking into account prior reductions) shall be reduced by the percentage by which the amount described in subparagraph (A) is less than the amount described in subparagraph (B).

"(4) Income inclusion. Any reduction in the suspense account under paragraph (3) shall be included in gross income for the taxable year of the reduction."

In 1990, P.L. 101-508, Sec. 11702(b)(1), amended subpara. (g)(4)(B)....Sec. 11702(b)(2), substituted "trade or business of farming" for "qualified farming trade or business" in subpara. (g)(1)(A), effective for costs incurred after 12/31/86, in tax. yrs. end. after 12/31/86. For special rules, see Sec. 803(d)(2)-(7) of P.L. 99-514 reproduced in note following Code Sec. 263A.

Prior to amendment, subpara. (g)(4)(B) read as follows:

"(B) Qualified farming trade or business. The term 'qualified farming trade or business' means the trade or business of farming sugar cane."

In 1988, P.L. 100-647, Sec. 1008(b)(5)(A), deleted "of" before "expenses" in subsec. (b)...Sec. 1008(b)(5)(B), deleted "of" before "expenses" in the heading of subsec. (b)...Sec. 1008(b)(6), substituted "qualified farming trade or business" for "trade or business of farming" each place it appeared subsec. (g), effective for costs incurred after 12/31/86, in tax. yrs. end. after 12/31/86. For special rules, see Sec. 803(d)(2)-(7) of P.L. 99-514 reproduced in note following Code Sec. 263A.

In 1987, P.L. 100-203, Sec. 10205(a), deleted subsecs. (c) and (e), redesignated subsec. (d) as (e) and added new subsecs. (c) and (d)...Sec. 10205(b), added new subsec. (i)...Sec. 10205(c)(1), substituted "subsection (d)" for "subsection (c)(2)" in subsec. (e) (as redesignated by Sec. 10205(a))...Sec. 10205(c)(2)(A), substituted "A corporation is described in this subsection" for "This section shall not apply to any corporation" in para. (h)(1)...Sec. 10205(c)(2)(B), substituted "subsection (e)" for "subsection (d)" each place it appeared in para. (h)(1)...Sec. 10205(c)(2)(C), substituted "subsection (e)(1)" for "subsection (d)(1)" each place it appeared in para. (h)(1), effective for tax. yrs. begin. after 12/31/87.

Prior to amendment, subsec. (c) read as follows:

"(c) Exception for small business and family corporations

For purposes of subsection (a), a corporation shall be treated as not being a corporation if it is—

"(1) an S corporation,

"(2) a corporation of which at least 50 percent of the total combined voting power of all classes of stock entitled to vote, and at least 50 percent of the total number of shares of all other classes of stock of the corporation, are owned by members of the same family, or

"(3) a corporation the gross receipts of which meet the requirements of subsection (e)"

Prior to amendment, subsec. (e) read as follows:

"(e) Corporations having gross receipts of $1,000,000 or less

A corporation meets the requirements of this subsection if, for each prior taxable year beginning after December 31, 1975, such corporation (and any predecessor corporation) did not have gross receipts exceeding $1,000,000. For purposes of the preceding sentence, all corporations which are members of a controlled group of corporations (within the meaning of section 1563(a)) shall be treated as one corporation."

In 1986, P.L. 99-514, Sec. 803(b)(7)(A), amended subsec. (b)....Sec. 803(b)(7)(B), deleted "and with the capitalization of preproductive period of expenses described in subsection (b)", after "on an accrual method of accounting" in subsec. (a)....Sec. 803(b)(7)(C), substituted "Notwithstanding subsection (a) or section 263A, if" for "If", in para. (g)(1), effective for costs incurred after 12/31/86, in tax. yrs. end. after 12/31/86. For special rules see Sec. 803(d)(2)-(7) reproduced in note following Code Sec. 263A.

Prior to amendment, subsec. (b) read as follows:

"(b) Preproductive period expenses

"(1) In general. For purposes of this section, the term 'preproductive period expenses' means any amount which is attributable to crops, animals, or any other property having a crop or yield during the preproductive period of such property.

"(2) Exceptions. Paragraph (1) shall not apply—

"(A) to taxes and interest, and

"(B) to any amount incurred on account of fire, storm, flood, or other casualty or on account of disease or drought.

"(3) Preproductive period defined. For purposes of this subsection, the term 'preproductive period' means—

"(A) in the case of property having a useful life of more than 1 year which will have more than 1 crop or yield, the period before the disposition of the first such marketable crop or yield, or

"(B) in the case of any other property, the period before such property is disposed of.

For purposes of this section, the use by the taxpayer in the trade or business of farming of any supply produced in such trade or business shall be treated as a disposition."

In 1982, P.L. 97-354, Sec. 5(a)(28), amended para. (c)(1)...Sec. 5(a)(29), amended clause (g)(4)(A)(i), effective for tax. yrs. begin. after 12/31/82.

Prior to amendment, para. (c)(1) read as follows:

"(1) an electing small business corporation (within the meaning of section 1371(b)),"

Prior to amendment, clause (g)(4)(A)(i) read as follows:

Tax accounting

"(i) an electing small business corporation (within the meaning of section 1371(b)), or"
—P.L. 97-248, Sec. 230(a)(1), added "or qualified partnership" after "corporation" each place it appeared in para. (g)(1) . . . Sec. 230(a)(2), amended para. (g)(3) . . . Sec. 230(a)(3), added para. (g)(4), effective for tax. yrs. begin. after 12/31/81.

Prior to amendment, para. (g)(3) read as follows:

"(3) Certain reorganizations. For purposes of this subsection, if a corporation acquired substantially all the assets of a farming trade or business from another corporation in a transaction in which no gain or loss was recognized to the transferor or transferee corporation, the transferee corporation shall be deemed to have computed its taxable income on an annual accrual method of accounting during the period for which the transferor corporation computed its taxable income from such trade or business on an annual accrual method."

In 1978, P.L. 95-600, Sec. 351(a), added subsec. (h), effective for tax. yrs. begin. after '77.

—P.L. 95-600, Sec. 353(a), substituted "nursery or sod farm" for "nursery" in subsec. (a), effective for tax. yrs. begin. after 12/31/76.

—P.L. 95-600, Sec. 701(l)(1), deleted "(except as otherwise provided in such regulations)" after "taxable income shall", and added "(or the remaining taxable years where there is a stated future life of less than 10 taxable years)" after "10 taxable years" in para. (f)(3), effective for tax. yrs. begin. after 1976. Sec. 701(l)(2) of the Act provides:

"(2) Automatic 10-year adjustment for farming syndicates changing to accrual accounting. If—

"(A) a farming syndicate (within the meaning of section 464(c) of the Internal Revenue Code of 1954) was in existence on December 31, 1975, and

"(B) such syndicate elects an accrual method of accounting (including the capitalization of preproductive period expenses described in section 447(b) of such Code) for a taxable year beginning before January 1, 1979,

then such election shall be treated as having been made with the consent of the Secretary of the Treasury or his delegate and, under regulations prescribed by the Secretary of the Treasury or his delegate, the net amount of the adjustments required by section 481(a) of such Code to be taken into account by the taxpayer in computing taxable income shall be taken into account in each of the 10 taxable years (or the remaining taxable years where there is a stated future life of less than 10 taxable years) beginning with the year of change."

—P.L. 95-600, Sec. 703(d), substituted "preproductive period expenses" for "preproductive expenses" in subsec. (a) and para. (g)(2), effective 10/4/76.

In 1977, P.L. 95-30, Sec. 404, amended Sec. 207(c)(2) of P.L. 94-455, which was the effective date for the amendment made by Sec. 207(c)(1)(A) of P.L. 94-455, see below. Sec. 207(c)(2) of P.L. 94-455, now reads as follows:

"(2) Effective dates.—

"(A) In general.—Except as provided in subparagraph (B), the amendments made by paragraph (1) shall apply to taxable years beginning after December 31, 1976.

"(B) Special rule for certain corporations.—In the case of a corporation engaged in the trade or business of farming and with respect to which—

"(i) members of two families (within the meaning of paragraph (1) of section 447(d) of the Internal Revenue Code of 1954, as added by paragraph (1)) owned, on October 4, 1976 (directly or through the application of such section 447(d)), at least 65 percent of the total combined voting power of all classes of stock of such corporation entitled to vote, and at least 65 percent of the total number of shares of all other classes of stock of such corporation; or

"(ii) members of three families (within the meaning of paragraph (1) of such section 447(d)) owned, on October 4, 1976 (directly or through the application of such section 447(d)), at least 50 percent of the total combined voting power of all classes of stock of such corporation entitled to vote, and at least 50 percent of the total number of shares of all other classes of stock of such corporation; and substantially all of the stock of such corporation which was not so owned (directly or through the application of such section 447(d)), by members of such three families was owned, on October 4, 1976, directly—

"(I) by employees of the corporation or members of the families (within the meaning of section 267(c)(4) of such Code) of such employees, or

"(II) by a trust for the benefit of the employees of such corporation which is described in section 401(a) of such Code and which is exempt from taxation under section 501(a) of such Code.

the amendments made by paragraph (1) shall apply to taxable years beginning after December 31, 1977."

In 1976, P.L. 94-455, Sec. 207(c)(1)(A), added Code Sec. 447, effective for tax. yrs. begin. after '76. Sec. 207(c)(3) provides as follows:

"(3) Election to change from static value method to accrual method of accounting.—

"(A) In general.—If—

"(i) a corporation has computed its taxable income on an annual accrual method of accounting together with a static value method of accounting for deferred costs of growing crops for the 10 taxable years ending with its first taxable year beginning after December 31, 1975,

"(ii) such corporation raises crops which are harvested not less than 12 months after planting, and

"(iii) such corporation elects, within one year after the date of the enactment of this Act and in such manner as the Secretary of the Treasury or his delegate prescribes, to change to the annual accrual method of accounting (within the meaning of section 447(g)(2) of the Internal Revenue Code of 1954) for taxable years beginning after December 31, 1976,

such change shall be treated as having been made with the consent of the Secretary of the Treasury, and, under regulations prescribed by the Secretary of the Treasury or his delegate, the net amount of the adjustments required by section 481(a) of the Internal Revenue Code of 1954 to be taken into account by the taxpayer in computing taxable income shall (except as otherwise provided in such regulations) be taken into account in each of the 10 taxable years beginning with the year of change.

"(B) Coordination with section 447 of the code.—A corporation which elects under subparagraph (A) to change to the annual accrual method of accounting shall, for purposes of section 447(g) of the Internal Revenue Code of 1954, be deemed to be a corporation which has computed its taxable income on an annual accrual method of accounting for its 10 taxable years ending with its first taxable year beginning after December 31, 1975.

"(C) Certain corporate reorganizations.—For purposes of this paragraph, if a corporation acquired substantially all the assets of a farming trade or business from another corporation in a transaction in which no gain or loss was recognized to the transferor or transferee corporation, the transferee corporation shall be deemed to have computed its taxable income on an annual accrual method of accounting together with a static value method of accounting for deferred costs of growing crops during the period for which the transferor corporation computed its taxable income from such trade or business on such accrual and static value method."

Sec. 448. Limitation on use of cash method of accounting.

(a) General rule.

Except as otherwise provided in this section, in the case of a—

(1) C corporation,

(2) partnership which has a C corporation as a partner, or

(3) tax shelter,

taxable income shall not be computed under the cash receipts and disbursements method of accounting.

(b) Exceptions.

(1) **Farming business.** Paragraphs (1) and (2) of subsection (a) shall not apply to any farming business.

(2) **Qualified personal service corporations.** Paragraphs (1) and (2) of subsection (a) shall not apply to a qualified personal service corporation, and such a corporation shall be treated as an individual for purposes of determining whether paragraph (2) of subsection (a) applies to any partnership.

(3) **Entities with gross receipts of not more than $5,000,000.** Paragraphs (1) and (2) of subsection (a) shall not apply to any corporation or partnership for any taxable year if, for all prior taxable years beginning after December 31, 1985, such entity (or any predecessor) met the $5,000,000 gross receipts test of subsection (c).

(c) $5,000,000 gross receipts test.

For purposes of this section—

(1) **In general.** A corporation or partnership meets the $5,000,000 gross receipts test of this subsection for any prior taxable year if the average annual gross receipts of such entity for the 3-taxable-year period ending with such prior taxable year does not exceed $5,000,000.

(2) **Aggregation rules.** All persons treated as a single employer under subsection (a) or (b) of section 52 or subsection (m) or (o) of section 414 shall be treated as one person for purposes of paragraph (1).

(3) **Special rules.** For purposes of this subsection—

(A) Not in existence for entire 3-year period. If the entity was not in existence for the entire 3-year period referred to in paragraph (1), such paragraph shall be applied on the basis of the period during which such entity (or trade or business) was in existence.

(B) Short taxable years. Gross receipts for any taxable year of less than 12 months shall be annualized by multiplying the gross receipts for the short period by 12 and dividing the result by the number of months in the short period.

(C) Gross receipts. Gross receipts for any taxable year shall be reduced by returns and allowances made during such year.

(D) Treatment of predecessors. Any reference in this subsection to an entity shall include a reference to any predecessor of such entity.

(d) Definitions and special rules. For purposes of this section—

(1) Farming business.

(A) In general. The term "farming business" means the trade or business of farming (within the meaning of section 263A(e)(4)).

(B) Timber and ornamental trees. The term "farming business" includes the raising, harvesting, or growing of trees to which section 263A(c)(5) applies.

(2) Qualified personal service corporation. The term "qualified personal service corporation" means any corporation—

(A) substantially all of the activities of which involve the performance of services in the fields of health, law, engineering, architecture, accounting, actuarial science, performing arts, or consulting, and

(B) substantially all of the stock of which (by value) is held directly (or indirectly through 1 or more partnerships, S corporations, or qualified personal service corporations not described in paragraph (2) or (3) of subsection (a)) by —

(i) employees performing services for such corporation in connection with the activities involving a field referred to in subparagraph (A),

(ii) retired employees who had performed such services for such corporation,

(iii) the estate of any individual described in clause (i) or (ii), or

(iv) any other person who acquired such stock by reason of the death of an individual described in clause (i) or (ii) (but only for the 2-year period beginning on the date of the death of such individual).

To the extent provided in regulations which shall be prescribed by the Secretary, indirect holdings through a trust shall be taken into account under subparagraph (B).

(3) Tax shelter defined. The term "tax shelter" has the meaning given such term by section 461(i)(3) (determined after application of paragraph (4) thereof). An S corporation shall not be treated as a tax shelter for purposes of this section merely by reason of being required to file a notice of exemption from registration with a State agency described in section 461(i)(3)(A), but only if there is a requirement applicable to all corporations offering securities for sale in the State that to be exempt from such registration the corporation must file such a notice.

(4) Special rules for application of paragraph (2). For purposes of paragraph (2)—

(A) community property laws shall be disregarded,

(B) stock held by a plan described in section 401(a) which is exempt from tax under section 501(a) shall be treated as held by an employee described in paragraph (2)(B)(i), and

(C) at the election of the common parent of an affiliated group (within the meaning of section 1504(a)), all members of such group may be treated as 1 taxpayer for purposes of paragraph (2)(B) if 90 percent or more of the activities of such group involve the performance of services in the same field described in paragraph (2)(A).

(5) Special rule for certain services.

(A) In general. In the case of any person using an accrual method of accounting with respect to amounts to be received for the performance of services by such person, such person shall not be required to accrue any portion of such amounts which (on the basis of such person's experience) will not be collected if—

(i) such services are in fields referred to in paragraph (2)(A), or

(ii) such person meets the gross receipts test of subsection (c) for all prior taxable years.

(B) Exception. This paragraph shall not apply to any amount if interest is required to be paid on such amount or there is any penalty for failure to timely pay such amount.

(C) Regulations. The Secretary shall prescribe regulations to permit taxpayers to determine amounts referred to in subparagraph (A) using computations or formulas which, based on experience, accurately reflect the amount of income that will not be collected by such person. A taxpayer may adopt, or request consent of the Secretary to change to, a computation or formula that clearly reflects the taxpayer's experience. A request under the preceding sentence shall be approved if such computation or formula clearly reflects the taxpayer's experience.

(6) Treatment of certain trusts subject to tax on unrelated business income. For purposes of this section, a trust subject to tax under section 511(b) shall be treated as a C corporation with respect to its activities constituting an unrelated trade or business.

(7) Coordination with section 481. In the case of any taxpayer required by this section to change its method of accounting for any taxable year—

(A) such change shall be treated as initiated by the taxpayer,

(B) such change shall be treated as made with the consent of the Secretary, and

(C) the period for taking into account the adjustments under section 481 by reason of such change—

(i) except as provided in clause (ii), shall not exceed 4 years, and

(ii) in the case of a hospital, shall be 10 years.

(8) Use of related parties, etc. The Secretary shall prescribe such regulations as may be necessary to prevent the use of related parties, pass-thru entities, or intermediaries to avoid the application of this section.

In 2002, P.L. 107-147, Sec. 403(a), amended para. (d)(5), effective for tax. yrs. end. after 3/9/2002. Sec. 403(b)(2) of this Act, relating to change in method of accounting, provides:

"(2) Change in method of accounting. In the case of any taxpayer required by the amendments made by this section to change its method of accounting for its first taxable year ending after the date of the enactment of this Act—

"(A) such change shall be treated as initiated by the taxpayer,

"(B) such change shall be treated as made with the consent of the Secretary of the Treasury, and

"(C) the net amount of the adjustments required to be taken into account by the taxpayer under section 481 of the Internal Revenue Code of 1986 shall be taken into account over a period of 4 years (or if less, the number of taxable years that the taxpayer used the method permitted under section 448(d)(5) of such Code as in effect before the date of the enactment of this Act) beginning with such first taxable year."

Prior to amendment, para. (d)(5) read as follows:

"(5) Special rule for services. In the case of any person using an accrual method of accounting with respect to amounts to be received for the performance of services by such person, such person shall not be required to accrue any portion of such amounts which (on the basis of experience) will not be collected. This paragraph shall not apply to any amount if interest is required to be paid on such amount or there is any penalty for failure to timely pay such amount."

In 1988, P.L. 100-647, Sec. 1008(a)(1)(A), substituted "(or indirectly through 1 or more partnerships, S corporations, or qualified personal service corporations not described in paragraph (2) or (3) of subsection (a))" for "or indirectly" in subpara. (d)(2)(B) . . . Sec. 1008(a)(1)(B), added para. (d)(8) . . . Sec. 1008(a)(2), substituted "such group" for "all such members" in subpara. (d)(4)(C) . . . Sec. 1008(a)(7), added the sentence at the end of para. (d)(3) . . . Sec. 1008(a)(8), substituted "90 percent or more of" for "substantially all of" in subpara. (d)(4)(C)

Tax accounting   Code Sec. 451(e)(2)

... Sec. 1008(a)(9), added subpara. (c)(3)(D), effective for tax. yrs. begin. after 12/31/86, except as provided in Secs. 801(d)(2)-(5) of P.L. 99-514 [as amended by Secs. 1008(a)(5) and (6) of P.L. 100-647] reproduced below.

—P.L. 100-647, Sec. 1008(a)(5), amended Sec. 801(d)(4)(C) [reproduced below] of P.L. 99-514, part of the special rules for Code Sec. 448, by substituting "a method of accounting for long-term contracts" for "the completed contract method"

—P.L. 100-647, Sec. 1008(a)(6), added Sec. 801(d)(5) [reproduced below] of P.L. 99-514 part of the special rules for Code Sec. 448, see below.

—P.L. 100-647, Sec. 6032(a), added the sentence at the end of para. (d)(2), effective for tax. yrs. begin. 12/31/86

In **1986**, P.L. 99-514, Sec. 801(a), added Code Sec. 448, effective for taxable years begin. after 12/31/86, except as provided in Sec. 801(d)(2)-(5) of this Act [as amended by Secs. 1008(a)(5) and (6) of P.L. 100-647, see above.] which reads as follows:

"(2) Election to retain cash method for certain transactions.— A taxpayer may elect not to have the amendments made by this section apply to any loan or lease, or any transaction with a related party (within the meaning of section 267(b) of the Internal Revenue Code of 1954, as in effect before the enactment of this Act), entered into on or before September 25, 1985. Any election under the preceding sentence may be made separately with respect to each transaction.

"(3) Certain contracts.— The amendments made by this section shall not apply to—

"(A) contracts for the acquisition or transfer of real property, and

"(B) contracts for services related to the acquisition or development of real property,

but only if such contracts were entered into before September 25, 1985, and the sole element of the contract which has not been performed as of September 25, 1985, is payment for such property or services.

"(4) Treatment of affiliated group providing engineering services.— Each member of an affiliated group of corporations (within the meaning of section 1504(a) of the Internal Revenue Code of 1986) shall be allowed to use the cash receipts and disbursements method of accounting for any trade or business of providing engineering services with respect to taxable years ending after December 31, 1986, if the common parent of such group—

"(A) was incorporated in the State of Delaware in 1970,

"(B) was the successor to a corporation that was incorporated in the State of Illinois in 1949, and

"(C) used a method of accounting for long-term contracts of accounting for a substantial part of its income from the performance of engineering services.

"(5) Special rule for paragraphs (2) and (3). If any loan, lease, contract, or evidence of any transaction to which paragraph (2) or (3) applies is transferred after June 10, 1987, to a person other than a related party (within the meaning of paragraph (2)), paragraph (2) or (3) shall cease to apply on and after the date of such transfer."

SUBPART B.— TAXABLE YEAR FOR WHICH ITEMS OF GROSS INCOME INCLUDED

Sec.
451. General rule for taxable year of inclusion.
452. Repealed.
453. Installment method.
453A. Special rules for nondealers.
453B. Gain or loss on disposition of installment obligations.
453C. Repealed.
454. Obligations issued at discount.
455. Prepaid subscription income.
456. Prepaid dues income of certain membership organizations.
457. Deferred compensation plans of State and local governments and tax-exempt organizations.
457A. Nonqualified deferred compensation from certain tax indifferent parties.
458. Magazines, paperbacks, and records returned after the close of the taxable year.
460. Special rules for long-term contracts.

In **1988**, P.L. 100-647, Sec. 5076(b)(2), amended item 453A.
Prior to Amendment, item 453A read as follows:
"453A. Special rules for nondealers of real property."
In **1987**, P.L. 100-203, Sec. 10202(a)(2), repealed the item for 453C.
Prior to repeal, item 453C read as follows:
"453C. Certain indebtedness treated as payments on installment obligations."
—P.L. 100-203, Sec. 10202(c)(2), amended item 453A.
Prior to amendment, item 453A read as follows:
"453A. Installment method for dealers in personal property."
In **1986**, P.L. 99-514, Sec. 804(c), added item 460 ... Sec. 811(b), added item 453C ... Sec. 1107(b), amended item 457.

Prior to amendment item 457 read:
"457. Deferred compensation plans with respect to service for state and local governments."
In **1980**, P.L. 96-471, Sec. 2(d), added items 453A and 453B.
In **1978**, P.L. 95-600, Sec. 131(b), added item 457.
—P.L. 95-600, Sec. 372(b), added item 458.
In **1961,** added item 456.
In **1958,** added item 455.
In **1955,** deleted item 452.
Prior to deletion, item 452 read as follows:
"452. Prepaid income."

Sec. 451. General rule for taxable year of inclusion.
(a) General rule.

The amount of any item of gross income shall be included in the gross income for the taxable year in which received by the taxpayer, unless, under the method of accounting used in computing taxable income, such amount is to be properly accounted for as of a different period.

(b) Special rule in case of death.

In the case of the death of a taxpayer whose taxable income is computed under an accrual method of accounting, any amount accrued only by reason of the death of the taxpayer shall not be included in computing taxable income for the period in which falls the date of the taxpayer's death.

(c) Special rule for employee tips.

For purposes of subsection (a), tips included in a written statement furnished an employer by an employee pursuant to section 6053(a) shall be deemed to be received at the time the written statement including such tips is furnished to the employer.

(d) Special rule for crop insurance proceeds or disaster payments.

In the case of insurance proceeds received as a result of destruction or damage to crops, a taxpayer reporting on the cash receipts and disbursements method of accounting may elect to include such proceeds in income for the taxable year following the taxable year of destruction or damage, if he establishes that, under his practice, income from such crops would have been reported in a following taxable year. For purposes of the preceding sentence, payments received under the Agricultural Act of 1949, as amended, or title II of the Disaster Assistance Act of 1988, as a result of (1) destruction or damage to crops caused by drought, flood, or any other natural disaster, or (2) the inability to plant crops because of such a natural disaster shall be treated as insurance proceeds received as a result of destruction or damage to crops. An election under this subsection for any taxable year shall be made at such time and in such manner as the Secretary prescribes.

(e) Special rule for proceeds from livestock sold on account of drought, flood, or other weather-related conditions.

(1) In general. In the case of income derived from the sale or exchange of livestock in excess of the number the taxpayer would sell if he followed his usual business practices, a taxpayer reporting on the cash receipts and disbursements method of accounting may elect to include such income for the taxable year following the taxable year in which such sale or exchange occurs if he establishes that, under his usual business practices, the sale or exchange would not have occurred in the taxable year in which it occurred if it were not for drought, flood, or other weather-related conditions, and that such conditions had resulted in the area being designated as eligible for assistance by the Federal Government.

(2) Limitation. Paragraph (1) shall apply only to a taxpayer whose principal trade or business is farming (within the meaning of section 6420(c)(3)).

2,121

(3) Special election rules. If section 1033(e)(2) applies to a sale or exchange of livestock described in paragraph (1), the election under paragraph (1) shall be deemed valid if made during the replacement period described in such section.

(f) Special rule for utility services.

(1) In general. In the case of a taxpayer the taxable income of which is computed under an accrual method of accounting, any income attributable to the sale or furnishing of utility services to customers shall be included in gross income not later than the taxable year in which such services are provided to such customers.

(2) Definition and special rule. For purposes of this subsection—

(A) Utility services. The term "utility services" includes—

(i) the providing of electrical energy, water, or sewage disposal,

(ii) the furnishing of gas or steam through a local distribution system,

(iii) telephone or other communication services, and

(iv) the transporting of gas or steam by pipeline.

(B) Year in which services provided. The taxable year in which services are treated as provided to customers shall not, in any manner, be determined by reference to—

(i) the period in which the customers' meters are read, or

(ii) the period in which the taxpayer bills (or may bill) the customers for such service.

(g) Treatment of interest on frozen deposits in certain financial institutions.

(1) In general. In the case of interest credited during any calendar year on a frozen deposit in a qualified financial institution, the amount of such interest includible in the gross income of a qualified individual shall not exceed the sum of—

(A) the net amount withdrawn by such individual from such deposit during such calendar year, and

(B) the amount of such deposit which is withdrawable as of the close of the taxable year (determined without regard to any penalty for premature withdrawals of a time deposit).

(2) Interest tested each year. Any interest not included in gross income by reason of paragraph (1) shall be treated as credited in the next calendar year.

(3) Deferral of interest deduction. No deduction shall be allowed to any qualified financial institution for interest not includible in gross income under paragraph (1) until such interest is includible in gross income.

(4) Frozen deposit. For purposes of this subsection, the term "frozen deposit" means any deposit if, as of the close of the calendar year, any portion of such deposit may not be withdrawn because of—

(A) the bankruptcy or insolvency of the qualified financial institution (or threat thereof), or

(B) any requirement imposed by the State in which such institution is located by reason of the bankruptcy or insolvency (or threat thereof) of 1 or more financial institutions in the State.

(5) Other definitions. For purposes of this subsection, the terms "qualified individual", "qualified financial institution", and "deposit" have the same respective meanings as when used in section 165(l).

(h) Special rule for cash options for receipt of qualified prizes.

(1) In general. For purposes of this title, in the case of an individual on the cash receipts and disbursements method of accounting, a qualified prize option shall be disregarded in determining the taxable year for which any portion of the qualified prize is properly includible in gross income of the taxpayer.

(2) Qualified prize option; qualified prize. For purposes of this subsection—

(A) In general. The term "qualified prize option" means an option which—

(i) entitles an individual to receive a single cash payment in lieu of receiving a qualified prize (or remaining portion thereof), and

(ii) is exercisable not later than 60 days after such individual becomes entitled to the qualified prize.

(B) Qualified prize. The term "qualified prize" means any prize or award which—

(i) is awarded as a part of a contest, lottery, jackpot, game, or other similar arrangement,

(ii) does not relate to any past services performed by the recipient and does not require the recipient to perform any substantial future service, and

(iii) is payable over a period of at least 10 years.

(3) Partnership, etc. The Secretary shall provide for the application of this subsection in the case of a partnership or other pass-through entity consisting entirely of individuals described in paragraph (1).

(i) Special rule for sales or dispositions to implement Federal Energy Regulatory Commission or State electric restructuring policy.

(1) In general. In the case of any qualifying electric transmission transaction for which the taxpayer elects the application of this section, qualified gain from such transaction shall be recognized—

(A) in the taxable year which includes the date of such transaction to the extent the amount realized from such transaction exceeds—

(i) the cost of exempt utility property which is purchased by the taxpayer during the 4-year period beginning on such date, reduced (but not below zero) by

(ii) any portion of such cost previously taken into account under this subsection, and

(B) ratably over the 8-taxable year period beginning with the taxable year which includes the date of such transaction, in the case of any such gain not recognized under subparagraph (A).

(2) Qualified gain. For purposes of this subsection, the term "qualified gain" means, with respect to any qualifying electric transmission transaction in any taxable year—

(A) any ordinary income derived from such transaction which would be required to be recognized under section 1245 or 1250 for such taxable year (determined without regard to this subsection), and

(B) any income derived from such transaction in excess of the amount described in subparagraph (A) which is required to be included in gross income for such taxable year (determined without regard to this subsection).

(3) Qualifying electric transmission transaction. For purposes of this subsection, the term "qualifying electric transmission transaction" means any sale or other disposition before January 1, 2008 (before January 1, 2012, in the case of a qualified electric utility), of—

(A) property used in the trade or business of providing electric transmission services, or
(B) any stock or partnership interest in a corporation or partnership, as the case may be, whose principal trade or business consists of providing electric transmission services,

but only if such sale or disposition is to an independent transmission company.

(4) Independent transmission company. For purposes of this subsection, the term "independent transmission company" means—
(A) an independent transmission provider approved by the Federal Energy Regulatory Commission,
(B) a person—
(i) who the Federal Energy Regulatory Commission determines in its authorization of the transaction under section 203 of the Federal Power Act (16 U.S.C. 824b) or by declaratory order is not a market participant within the meaning of such Commission's rules applicable to independent transmission providers, and
(ii) whose transmission facilities to which the election under this subsection applies are under the operational control of a Federal Energy Regulatory Commission-approved independent transmission provider before the close of the period specified in such authorization, but not later than the date which is 4 years after the close of the taxable year in which the transaction occurs, or
(C) in the case of facilities subject to the jurisdiction of the Public Utility Commission of Texas—
(i) a person which is approved by that Commission as consistent with Texas State law regarding an independent transmission provider, or
(ii) a political subdivision or affiliate thereof whose transmission facilities are under the operational control of a person described in clause (i).

(5) Exempt utility property. For purposes of this subsection—
(A) In general. The term "exempt utility property" means property used in the trade or business of—
(i) generating, transmitting, distributing, or selling electricity, or
(ii) producing, transmitting, distributing, or selling natural gas.
(B) Nonrecognition of gain by reason of acquisition of stock. Acquisition of control of a corporation shall be taken into account under this subsection with respect to a qualifying electric transmission transaction only if the principal trade or business of such corporation is a trade or business referred to in subparagraph (A).
(C) Exception for property located outside the United States. The term "exempt utility property" shall not include any property which is located outside the United States.

(6) Qualified electric utility. For purposes of this subsection, the term "qualified electric utility" means a person that, as of the date of the qualifying electric transmission transaction, is vertically integrated, in that it is both—
(A) a transmitting utility (as defined in section 3(23) of the Federal Power Act (16 U.S.C. 796(23))) with respect to the transmission facilities to which the election under this subsection applies, and
(B) an electric utility (as defined in section 3(22) of the Federal Power Act (16 U.S.C. 796(22))).

(7) Special rule for consolidated groups. In the case of a corporation which is a member of an affiliated group filing a consolidated return, any exempt utility property purchased by another member of such group shall be treated as purchased by such corporation for purposes of applying paragraph (1)(A).

(8) Time for assessment of deficiencies. If the taxpayer has made the election under paragraph (1) and any gain is recognized by such taxpayer as provided in paragraph (1)(B), then—
(A) the statutory period for the assessment of any deficiency, for any taxable year in which any part of the gain on the transaction is realized, attributable to such gain shall not expire prior to the expiration of 3 years from the date the Secretary is notified by the taxpayer (in such manner as the Secretary may by regulations prescribe) of the purchase of exempt utility property or of an intention not to purchase such property, and
(B) such deficiency may be assessed before the expiration of such 3-year period notwithstanding any law or rule of law which would otherwise prevent such assessment.

(9) Purchase. For purposes of this subsection, the taxpayer shall be considered to have purchased any property if the unadjusted basis of such property is its cost within the meaning of section 1012.

(10) Election. An election under paragraph (1) shall be made at such time and in such manner as the Secretary may require and, once made, shall be irrevocable.

(11) Nonapplication of installment sales treatment. Section 453 shall not apply to any qualifying electric transmission transaction with respect to which an election to apply this subsection is made.

In 2010, P.L. 111-312, Sec. 705(a), substituted "January 1, 2012" for "January 1, 2010" in para. (i)(3), effective for dispositions after 12/31/2009.

In 2008, P.L. 110-343, Sec. 109(a)(1)DivB, added "(before January 1, 2010, in the case of a qualified electric utility)" after "January 1, 2008" in para. (i)(3) . . . Sec. 109(a)(2)DivB, redesignated paras. (i)(6)-(10) as (7)-(11) and added para. (i)(6), effective for transactions after 12/31/2007.

—P.L. 110-343, Sec. 109(b)DivB, substituted "the date which is 4 years after the close of the taxable year in which the transaction occurs" for "December 31, 2007" in clause (i)(4)(B)(ii), effective [as if included in section 909 of the American Jobs Creation Act of 2004] for transactions occurring after 10/22/2004, in tax. yrs. end. after 10/22/2004.

—P.L. 110-343, Sec. 109(c)DivB, added subpara. (i)(5)(C), effective for transactions after 10/3/2008.

In 2005, P.L. 109-58, Sec. 1305(a), substituted "2008" for "2007" in para. (i)(3), effective for transactions occurring after 8/8/2005.

—P.L. 109-58, Sec. 1305(b), substituted "December 31, 2007" for "the close of the period applicable under subsection (a)(2)(B) as extended under paragraph (2)" in clause (i)(4)(B)(ii), effective for transactions occurring after 10/22/2004, in tax. yrs. end. after 10/22/2004 as if included in Sec. 909 of P.L. 108-357, the American Jobs Creation Act of 2004.

In 2004, P.L. 108-357, Sec. 311(c), added para. (e)(3), effective for any tax. yr. with respect to which the due date (without regard to extensions) for the return is after 12/31/2002.

—P.L. 108-357, Sec. 909(a), added subsec. (i), effective for transactions occurring after 10/22/2004, in tax. yrs. end. after 10/22/2004.

In 1998, P.L. 105-277, Sec. 5301(a), added subsec. (h), effective as provided by Sec. 5301(b), of this Act, which reads as follows:
"(b) Effective date.
"(1) In general. The amendment made by this section shall apply to any prize to which a person first becomes entitled after the date of enactment of this Act.
"(2) Transition rule. The amendment made by this section shall apply to any prize to which a person first becomes entitled on or before the date of enactment of this Act, except that in determining whether an option is a qualified prize option as defined in section 451(h)(2)(A) of the Internal Revenue Code of 1986 (as added by such amendment)—
"(A) clause (ii) of such section 451(h)(2)(A) shall not apply, and
"(B) such option shall be treated as a qualified prize option if it is exercisable only during all or part of the 18-month period beginning on July 1, 1999."

In 1997, P.L. 105-34, Sec. 913(a)(1), substituted "drought, flood, or other weather-related conditions, and that such conditions" for "drought conditions, and that these drought conditions" in para. (e)(1) . . . Sec. 913(a)(2), added ", flood, or other weather-related conditions" after "drought" in the heading of subsec. (e), effective for sales and exchanges after 12/31/96.

In 1991, P.L. 102-190, Sec. 662(b), of this Act provides:

"(b) Tax Treatment—Notwithstanding the Internal Revenue Code of 1986 and any other provision of law, any voluntary separation incentive paid to a member of the Armed Forces under section 1175 of title 10, United States Code (as added by subsection (a)), shall be includable in gross income for federal tax purposes only for the taxable year in which such incentive is paid to the participant or beneficiary of the member."

In 1988, P.L. 100-647, Sec. 1008(h), amended Sec. 821(b) of P.L. 99-514 [reproduced below], special rules for amendments made by Sec. 821(a) of P.L. 99-514, by adding the last sentence to para. (b)(3), see below.

—P.L. 100-647, Sec. 1009(d)(3), redesignated subsec. (f) [sic (g)] [as added by Sec. 905(b) of P.L. 99-514] as subsec. (g), effective for tax. yrs. begin. after 12/31/82, except as provided in Sec. 905(c)(2) of P.L. 99-514 [reproduced below].

—P.L. 100-647, Sec. 1009(d)(4), provides the following special rule:

"(4) if on the date of the enactment of this Act (or at any time before the date 1 year after such date of enactment) credit or refund of any overpayment of tax attributable to amendments made by section 905 of the Reform Act or by this subsection (or the assessment of any underpayment of tax so attributable) is barred by any law or rule of law—

"(A) credit or refund of any such overpayment may nevertheless be made if claim therefore is filed before the date 1 year after such date of enactment, and

"(B) assessment of any such underpayment may nevertheless be made if made before the date 1 year after such date of enactment."

—P.L. 100-647, Sec. 6030(a), deleted "(other than livestock described in section 1231(b)(3))" after "exchange of livestock" in para. (e)(1), effective for sales or exchanges occurring after 12/31/87.

—P.L. 100-647, Sec. 6033(a), added "or title II of the Disaster Assistance Act of 1988," after "the Agricultural Act of 1949, as amended," in subsec. (d), effective for payments received before, on, or after 11/10/88.

In 1986, P.L. 99-514, Sec. 821(a), added subsec. (f), effective for tax. yrs. begin. after 12/31/86. Sec. 821(b)(2) and (3) of this Act provides:

"(2) Change in method of accounting. If a taxpayer is required by the amendments made by this section to change its method of accounting for any taxable year—

"(A) such change shall be treated as initiated by the taxpayer,

"(B) such change shall be treated as having been made with the consent of the Secretary, and

"(C) the adjustments under section 481 of the Internal Revenue Code of 1954 by reason of such change shall be taken into account ratably over a period no longer than the first 4 taxable years beginning after December 31, 1986.

"(3) Special rule for certain cycle billing. If a taxpayer for any taxable year beginning before August 16, 1986, for purposes of chapter 1 of the Internal Revenue Code of 1986 took into account income from services described in section 451(f) of such Code (as added by subsection (a)) on the basis of the period in which the customers' meters were read, then such treatment for such year shall be deemed to be proper."

The preceding sentence shall also apply to any taxable year beginning after August 16, 1986, and before January 1, 1987, if the taxpayer treated such income in the same manner for the taxable year preceding such taxable year.

—P.L. 99-514, Sec. 905(b), added subsec. (f) [sic (g)], effective for tax. yrs. begin. after 12/31/82. Sec. 905(c)(2) of this Act provides [see Sec. 1009(d)(4) of P.L. 100-647, above]:

"(2) Special rules for subsection (b).

"(A) The amendment made by subsection (b) [Sec. 905(b)] shall apply to taxable years beginning after December 31, 1982, and before January 1, 1987, only if the qualified individual elects to have such amendment apply for all such taxable years.

"(B) In the case of interest attributable to the period beginning January 1, 1983, and ending December 31, 1987, the interest deduction of financial institutions shall be determined without regard to paragraph (3) of section 451(f) of the Internal Revenue Code of 1986 (as added by subsection (b))."

In 1984, P.L. 98-369, Sec. 712(m), added para. (c)(4) to Sec. 229 of P.L. 97-248, reproduced below.

In 1982, P.L. 97-248, Sec. 229, provided the following modifications of regulations on the completed contract method of accounting:

"SEC. 229. MODIFICATION OF REGULATIONS ON THE COMPLETED CONTRACT METHOD OF ACCOUNTING.

"(a) In general. The Secretary of the Treasury shall modify the income tax regulations relating to accounting for long-term contracts to—

"(1) clarify the time at which a contract is to be considered completed,

"(2) clarify when—

"(A) one agreement will be treated as more than one contract, and

"(B) two or more agreements will be treated as one contract, and

"(3) properly allocate all costs which directly benefit, or are incurred by reason of, the extended period long-term contract activities of the taxpayer.

"(b) Extended period long-term contracts defined. For purposes of this section—

"(1) In general.—The term 'extended period long-term contract' means any long-term contract which the taxpayer estimates (at the time such contract is entered into) will not be completed within the 2-year period beginning on the contract commencement date of such contract.

"(2) Certain construction contracts.—

"(A) In general.—The term 'extended period long-term contract' does not include any construction contract entered into by a taxpayer—

"(i) who estimates (at the time such contract is entered into) that such contract will be completed within the 3-year period beginning on the contract commencement date of such contract, or

"(ii) whose average annual gross receipts over the 3 taxable years preceding the taxable year in which such contract is entered into do not exceed $25,000,000.

"(B) Determination of taxpayer's gross receipts.—For purposes of subparagraph (A), the gross receipts of—

"(i) all trades or businesses (whether or not incorporated) which are under common control with the taxpayer (within the meaning of section 52(b)), and

"(ii) all members of any controlled group of corporations of which the taxpayer is a member,

for the 3 taxable years of such persons preceding the taxable year in which the contract described in subparagraph (A) is entered into shall be included in the gross receipts of the taxpayer for the period described in subparagraph (A). The Secretary shall prescribe regulations which provide attribution rules that take into account, in addition to the persons and entities described in the preceding sentence, taxpayers who engage in construction contracts through partnerships, joint ventures, and corporations.

"(C) Controlled group of corporations.—the term 'controlled group of corporations' has the meaning given to such term by section 1563(a), except that—

(i) 'more than 50 percent' shall be substituted for 'at least 80 percent' each place it appears in section 1563(a)(1), and

(ii) the determination shall be made without regard to subsections (a)(4) and (e)(3)(C) of section 1563.

"(3) Construction contract.—The term 'construction contract' means any contract for the building, construction, reconstruction, or rehabilitation of, or the installation of any integral component to, improvements to real property.

"(4) Contract commencement date.—The term 'contract commencement date' means, with respect to any contract, the first date on which any costs (other than costs such as bidding expenses or expenses incurred in connection with negotiating the contract) allocable to such contract are incurred.

"(c) Effective Dates; Special Rules.

"(1) In general.—The modifications to regulations which are required to be made under paragraphs (1) and (2) of subsection (a) shall apply with respect to taxable years ending after December 31, 1982.

"(2) Cost allocation.—

"(A) In general.—Any modification to Income Tax Regulation 1.451-3 made under subsection (a)(3) which requires additional costs to be allocated to a contract shall apply only to the applicable percentage of such additional costs incurred in taxable years beginning after December 31, 1982, with respect to contracts entered into after such date.

"(B) Applicable percentage.—for purposes of subparagraph (A), the applicable percentage shall be determined in accordance with the following table:

"If the taxable year begins in calendar year:	The applicable percentage is:
1983	33⅓
1984	66⅔
1985 or thereafter	100."

"(3) Special rules.—

"(A) Time of completion.—Any contract of a taxpayer which would (but for this paragraph) be treated as having been completed prior to the first taxable year of such taxpayer ending after December 31, 1982, solely by reason of any modification to regulations made under subsection (a)(1), shall be treated as having been completed on the first day of such taxable year.

"(B) Aggregation and severance.—Any contract of a taxpayer which would (but for this paragraph) be treated as having been completed prior to the first taxable year of such taxpayer ending after December 31, 1982—

"(i) solely by reason of any modification to regulations made under subsection (a)(2), or

"(ii) solely by reason of any modifications to regulations made under both paragraphs (1) and (2) of subsection (a),

shall be treated as having been completed on the first day after December 31, 1982, on which any contract which was severed from such contract (by reason of the modifications made by subsection (a)(2)) is completed (determined after the application of any modifications to regulations made under subsection (a)(1)).

"(4) Underpayments of estimated tax for 1982. To the extent provided in regulations, no addition to tax shall be made under section 6654 or 6655 of the Internal Revenue Code of 1954 for the taxpayer's first taxable year ending after December 31, 1982, by reason of a long-term contract, but only with respect to installments required to be paid before April 13, 1983."

In 1978, P.L. 95-600, Sec. 132, provided the following rules regarding certain private deferred compensation plans.

"SEC. 132. CERTAIN PRIVATE DEFERRED COMPENSATION PLANS.

"(a) General rule. The taxable year of inclusion in gross income of any amount covered by a private deferred compensation plan shall be determined in accordance with the principles set forth in regulations, rulings, and judicial decisions relating to deferred compensation which were in effect on February 1, 1978.

"(b) Private deferred compensation plan defined.—

"(1) In general. For purposes of this section, the term 'private deferred compensation plan' means a plan, agreement, or arrangement—

"(A) where the person for whom the service is performed is not a State (within the meaning of paragraph (1) of section 457(d) of the Internal Revenue Code of 1954) and not an organization which is exempt from tax under section 501 of such Code, and

(B) under which the payment or otherwise making available of compensation is deferred.

"(2) Certain plans excluded. Paragraph (1) shall not apply to—
"(A) a plan described in section 401(a) of the Internal Revenue Code of 1954 which includes a trust exempt from tax under section 501(a) of such Code,
"(B) an annuity plan or contract described in section 403 of such Code,
"(C) a qualified bond purchase plan described in section 405(a) of such Code,
"(D) that portion of any plan which consists of a transfer of property described in section 83 (determined without regard to subsection (e) thereof) of such Code, and
"(E) that portion of any plan which consists of a trust to which section 402(b) of such Code applies.
"(c) Effective date. This section shall apply to taxable years ending on or after February 1, 1978."

In 1976, P.L. 94-455, Sec. 1906(b)(13)(A), substituted "Secretary" for "Secretary or his delegate" in subsec. (d), effective for tax. yrs. begin. after 12/31/76.
— P.L. 94-455, Sec. 2102, amended subsec. (d), effective for payments received after 12/31/73, in tax. yrs. end. after 12/31/73.
Prior to amendment, subsec. (d) read as follows:
"(d) Special rule for crop insurance proceeds.
"In the case of insurance proceeds received as a result of destruction or damage to crops, a taxpayer reporting on the cash receipts and disbursements method of accounting may elect to include such proceeds in income for the taxable year following the taxable year of destruction or damage, if he establishes that, under his practice, income from such crops would have been reported in a following taxable year. An election under this subsection for any taxable year shall be made at such time and in such manner as the Secretary prescribes."
— P.L. 94-455, Sec. 2141(a), added subsec. (e), effective for tax. yrs. begin. after 12/31/75.

In 1969, P.L. 91-172, Sec. 215(a), added subsec. (d), effective for tax. yrs. end. after 12/30/69.

In 1965, P.L. 89-97, Sec. 313, added subsec. (c), effective for tips received after 1965.

Sec. 452. Repealed.

In 1955, P.L. 74, Sec. 1(a), repealed Code Sec. 452 which related to prepaid income, effective for all '54 Code years.
Prior to repeal, Code Sec. 452 read as follows:
"SEC. 452. PREPAID INCOME.
"(a) Prepaid income to be earned over short or indefinite period.
"(1) Short period. — In the case of any prepaid income to which this section applies, if the liability described in subsection (e)(2) is (at the time the income is received) to end before the first day of the sixth taxable year after the taxable year in which such income is received, then such income shall be included in gross income for the taxable year in which received, and for each of the 5 succeeding taxable years, to the extent proper under the method of accounting used under section 446 in computing taxable income for such year. If the liability does not in fact end before the first day of such sixth taxable year, such income shall be included in gross income for the taxable years specified in the preceding sentence except that with the consent of the Secretary or his delegate it shall be included in gross income in such proportions, and for such taxable years, as are specified in such consent.
"(2) Indefinite period. — In the case of any prepaid income to which this section applies, if the liability described in subsection (e)(2) is (at the time the income is received) of indefinite duration, then such income shall be included in gross income for the taxable year in which received and for each of the 5 succeeding taxable years, consistently with the principles prescribed in paragraph (1) and subsection (b), under regulations prescribed by the Secretary or his delegate. With the consent of the Secretary or his delegate the prepaid income shall be included in gross income in such proportions, and for such taxable years, as are specified in such consent.
"(b) Prepaid income to be earned over long period.
"In the case of any prepaid income to which this section applies, if the liability described in subsection (e)(2) is (at the time the income is received) to end after the close of the fifth taxable year after the taxable year in which such income is received, then—
"(1) one-sixth of the prepaid income shall be included in gross income for the taxable year in which received, and one-sixth shall be included in gross income for each of the 5 succeeding taxable years; except that
"(2) with the consent of the Secretary or his delegate, the prepaid income shall be included in gross income in such proportions, and for such taxable years, as are specified in such consent.
"(c) Where taxpayer's liability ceases.
"In the case of any prepaid income to which this section applies—
"(1) If the liability described in subsection (e)(2) ends, then so much of such income as was not includible in gross income under subsections (a) and (b) for preceding taxable years shall be included in gross income for the taxable year in which the liability ends.
"(2) If the taxpayer dies or ceases to exist, then so much of such income as was not includible in gross income under subsections (a) and (b) for preceding taxable years shall be included in gross income for the taxable year in which such death, or such cessation of existence, occurs.
"(d) Prepaid income to which this section applies.
"(1) Election of benefits. — This section shall apply to prepaid income if and only if the taxpayer makes an election under this section with respect to the trade or business in connection with which such income is received. The election shall be made in such manner as the Secretary or his delegate may by regulations prescribe. No election may be made with respect to a trade or business if in computing taxable income the cash receipts and disbursements method of accounting is used with respect to such trade or business.
"(2) Scope of election. — An election made under this section shall apply to all prepaid income received in connection with the trade or business with respect to which the taxpayer has made the election; except that the taxpayer may, to the extent permitted under regulations prescribed by the Secretary or his delegate, include in gross income for the taxable year of receipt the entire amount of any prepaid income if the liability from which it arose is to end within 12 months after the date of receipt. An election made under this section shall not apply to any prepaid income received before the first taxable year for which the election is made.
"(3) When election may be made.
"(A) Without consent. — A taxpayer may, without the consent of the Secretary or his delegate, make an election under this section for his first taxable year (i) which begins after December 31, 1953, and ends after the date on which this title is enacted, and (ii) in which he receives prepaid income in the trade or business. Such an election shall be made not later than the time prescribed by this subtitle for filing the return for such year (including extensions thereof).
"(B) With consent. — A taxpayer may, with the consent of the Secretary or his delegate, make an election under this section at any time.
"(e) Definitions.
"For purposes of this section—
"(1) Prepaid income. — The term 'prepaid income' means any amount (includible in gross income) which is received in connection with, and is directly attributable to, a liability which extends beyond the close of the taxable year in which such amount is received. Such term does not include any income treated as gain from the sale or other disposition of a capital asset.
"(2) Liability to render services, etc. — The term 'liability' means a liability to render services, furnish goods or other property, or allow the use of property.
"(3) Receipt of prepaid income. — Prepaid income shall be treated as received during the taxable year for which it is includible in gross income under section 451 (without regard to this section)."
— P.L. 74, Sec. 4, provided:
"SEC. 4. SAVING PROVISIONS.
"(a) Filing of statement.
"If—
"(1) the amount of any tax required to be paid for any taxable year ending on or before the date of the enactment of this Act is increased by reason of the enactment of this Act [repealing Code Secs. 452 and 462], and
"(2) the last date prescribed for payment of such tax (or any installment thereof) is before December 15, 1955,
then the taxpayer shall, on or before December 15, 1955, file a statement which shows the increase in the amount of such tax required to be paid by reason of the enactment of this Act.
"(b) Form and effect of statement.
"(1) Form of statement, etc. — The statement required by subsection (a) shall be filed at the place fixed for filing the return. Such statement shall be in such form, and shall include such information necessary or appropriate to show the increase in the amount of the tax required to be paid for the taxable year by reason of the enactment of this Act, as the Secretary of the Treasury or his delegate shall by regulations prescribe.
"(2) Treatment as amount shown on return. — The amount shown on a statement filed under subsection (a) as the increase in the amount of the tax required to be paid for the taxable year by reason of the enactment of this Act shall, for all purposes of the internal revenue laws, be treated as tax shown on the return. Notwithstanding the preceding sentence, that portion of the amount of increase in tax for any taxable year which is attributable to a decrease (by reason of the enactment of this Act) in the net operating loss for a succeeding taxable year shall not be treated as tax shown on the return.
"(3) Waiver of interest in case of payment on or before December 15, 1955. — If the taxpayer, on or before December 15, 1955, files the statement referred to in subsection (a) and pays in full that portion of the amount shown thereon for which the last date prescribed for payment is before December 15, 1955, then for purposes of computing interest (other than interest on overpayments) such portion shall be treated as having been paid on the last date prescribed for payment. This paragraph shall not apply if the amount shown on the statement as the increase in the amount of the tax required to be paid for the taxable year by reason of the enactment of this Act is greater than the actual increase unless the taxpayer establishes, to the satisfaction of the Secretary of the Treasury or his delegate, that his computation of the greater amount was based upon a reasonable interpretation and application of sections 452 and 462 of the Internal Revenue Code of 1954, as those sections existed before the enactment of this Act.
"(c) Special rules.
"(1) Interest for period before enactment. — Interest shall not be imposed on the amount of any increase in tax resulting from the enactment of this Act for any period before the day after the date of the enactment of this Act.
"(2) Estimated tax. — Any addition to the tax under section 294(d) of the Internal Revenue Code of 1939 shall be computed as if this Act had not been enacted. In the case of any installment for which the last date prescribed for payment is before December 15, 1955, any addition to the tax under section 6654 of the Internal Revenue Code of 1954 shall be computed as if this Act had not been enacted.
"(3) Treatment of certain payments which taxpayer is required to make. — If—
"(A) the taxpayer is required to make a payment (or an additional payment) to another person by reason of the enactment of this Act, and
"(B) the Internal Revenue Code of 1954 prescribes a period, which expires after the close of the taxable year, within which the taxpayer must make such payment (or additional payment) if the amount thereof is to be taken into account (as a deduction or otherwise) in computing taxable income for such taxable year,

then, subject to such regulations as the Secretary of the Treasury or his delegate may prescribe, if such payment (or additional payment) is made on or before December 15, 1955, it shall be treated as having been made within the period prescribed by such Code.

"(4) Treatment of certain dividends.— Subject to such regulations as the Secretary of the Treasury or his delegate may prescribe, for purposes of section 561(a)(1) of the Internal Revenue Code of 1954, dividends paid after the 15th day of the third month following the close of the taxable year and on or before December 15, 1955, may be treated as having been paid on the last day of the taxable year, but only to the extent (A) that such dividends are attributable to an increase in taxable income for the taxable year resulting from the enactment of this Act, and (B) elected by the taxpayer.

"(5) Determination of date prescribed.— For purposes of this section, the determination of the last date prescribed for payment or for filing a return shall be made without regard to any extension of time therefor and without regard to any provision of this section.

"(6) Regulations.— For requirement that the Secretary of the Treasury or his delegate shall prescribe all rules and regulations as may be necessary by reason of the enactment of this Act, see section 7805(a) of the Internal Revenue Code of 1954."

Sec. 453. Installment method.
(a) General rule.

Except as otherwise provided in this section, income from an installment sale shall be taken into account for purposes of this title under the installment method.

(b) Installment sale defined.

For purposes of this section—

(1) In general. The term "installment sale" means a disposition of property where at least 1 payment is to be received after the close of the taxable year in which the disposition occurs.

(2) Exceptions. The term "installment sale" does not include—

(A) Dealer dispositions. Any dealer disposition (as defined in subsection (l)).

(B) Inventories of personal property. A disposition of personal property of a kind which is required to be included in the inventory of the taxpayer if on hand at the close of the taxable year.

(c) Installment method defined.

For purposes of this section, the term "installment method" means a method under which the income recognized for any taxable year from a disposition is that proportion of the payments received in that year which the gross profit (realized or to be realized when payment is completed) bears to the total contract price.

(d) Election out.

(1) In general. Subsection (a) shall not apply to any disposition if the taxpayer elects to have subsection (a) not apply to such disposition.

(2) Time and manner for making election. Except as otherwise provided by regulations, an election under paragraph (1) with respect to a disposition may be made only on or before the due date prescribed by law (including extensions) for filing the taxpayer's return of the tax imposed by this chapter for the taxable year in which the disposition occurs. Such an election shall be made in the manner prescribed by regulations.

(3) Election revocable only with consent. An election under paragraph (1) with respect to any disposition may be revoked only with the consent of the Secretary.

(e) Second dispositions by related persons.

(1) In general. If—

(A) any person disposes of property to a related person (hereinafter in this subsection referred to as the "first disposition"), and

(B) before the person making the first disposition receives all payments with respect to such disposition, the related person disposes of the property (hereinafter in this subsection referred to as the "second disposition"),

then, for purposes of this section, the amount realized with respect to such second disposition shall be treated as received at the time of the second disposition by the person making the first disposition.

(2) 2-year cutoff for property other than marketable securities.

(A) In general. Except in the case of marketable securities, paragraph (1) shall apply only if the date of the second disposition is not more than 2 years after the date of the first disposition.

(B) Substantial diminishing of risk of ownership. The running of the 2-year period set forth in subparagraph (A) shall be suspended with respect to any property for any period during which the related person's risk of loss with respect to the property is substantially diminished by—

(i) the holding of a put with respect to such property (or similar property),

(ii) the holding by another person of a right to acquire the property, or

(iii) a short sale or any other transaction.

(3) Limitation on amount treated as received. The amount treated for any taxable year as received by the person making the first disposition by reason of paragraph (1) shall not exceed the excess of—

(A) the lesser of—

(i) the total amount realized with respect to any second disposition of the property occurring before the close of the taxable year, or

(ii) the total contract price for the first disposition, over

(B) the sum of—

(i) the aggregate amount of payments received with respect to the first disposition before the close of such year, plus

(ii) the aggregate amount treated as received with respect to the first disposition for prior taxable years by reason of this subsection.

(4) Fair market value where disposition is not sale or exchange. For purposes of this subsection, if the second disposition is not a sale or exchange, an amount equal to the fair market value of the property disposed of shall be substituted for the amount realized.

(5) Later payments treated as receipt of tax paid amounts. If paragraph (1) applies for any taxable year, payments received in subsequent taxable years by the person making the first disposition shall not be treated as the receipt of payments with respect to the first disposition to the extent that the aggregate of such payments does not exceed the amount treated as received by reason of paragraph (1).

(6) Exception for certain dispositions. For purposes of this subsection—

(A) Reacquisitions of stock by issuing corporation not treated as first dispositions. Any sale or exchange of stock to the issuing corporation shall not be treated as a first disposition.

(B) Involuntary conversions not treated as second dispositions. A compulsory or involuntary conversion (within the meaning of section 1033) and any transfer thereafter shall not be treated as a second disposition if the first disposition occurred before the threat or imminence of the conversion.

(C) Dispositions after death. Any transfer after the earlier of—

Tax accounting Code Sec. 453(h)(1)(B)(ii)

(i) the death of the person making the first disposition, or

(ii) the death of the person acquiring the property in the first disposition,

and any transfer thereafter shall not be treated as a second disposition.

(7) Exception where tax avoidance not a principal purpose. This subsection shall not apply to a second disposition (and any transfer thereafter) if it is established to the satisfaction of the Secretary that neither the first disposition nor the second disposition had as one of its principal purposes the avoidance of Federal income tax.

(8) Extension of statute of limitations. The period for assessing a deficiency with respect to a first disposition (to the extent such deficiency is attributable to the application of this subsection) shall not expire before the day which is 2 years after the date on which the person making the first disposition furnishes (in such manner as the Secretary may by regulations prescribe) a notice that there was a second disposition of the property to which this subsection may have applied. Such deficiency may be assessed notwithstanding the provisions of any law or rule of law which would otherwise prevent such assessment.

(f) Definitions and special rules.

For purposes of this section—

(1) Related person. Except for purposes of subsections (g) and (h), the term "related person" means—

(A) a person whose stock would be attributed under section 318(a) (other than paragraph (4) thereof) to the person first disposing of the property, or

(B) a person who bears a relationship described in section 267(b) to the person first disposing of the property.

(2) Marketable securities. The term "marketable securities" means any security for which, as of the date of the disposition, there was a market on an established securities market or otherwise.

(3) Payment. Except as provided in paragraph (4), the term "payment" does not include the receipt of evidences of indebtedness of the person acquiring the property (whether or not payment of such indebtedness is guaranteed by another person).

(4) Purchaser evidences of indebtedness payable on demand or readily tradable. Receipt of a bond or other evidence of indebtedness which—

(A) is payable on demand, or

(B) is readily tradable,

shall be treated as receipt of payment.

(5) Readily tradable defined. For purposes of paragraph (4), the term "readily tradable" means a bond or other evidence of indebtedness which is issued—

(A) with interest coupons attached or in registered form (other than one in registered form which the taxpayer establishes will not be readily tradable in an established securities market), or

(B) in any other form designed to render such bond or other evidence of indebtedness readily tradable in an established securities market.

(6) Like-kind exchanges. In the case of any exchange described in section 1031(b)—

(A) the total contract price shall be reduced to take into account the amount of any property permitted to be received in such exchange without recognition of gain,

(B) the gross profit from such exchange shall be reduced to take into account any amount not recognized by reason of section 1031(b), and

(C) the term "payment", when used in any provision of this section other than subsection (b)(1), shall not include any property permitted to be received in such exchange without recognition of gain.

Similar rules shall apply in the case of an exchange which is described in section 356(a) and is not treated as a dividend.

(7) Depreciable property. The term "depreciable property" means property of a character which (in the hands of the transferee) is subject to the allowance for depreciation provided in section 167.

(8) Payments to be received defined. The term "payments to be received" includes—

(A) the aggregate amount of all payments which are not contingent as to amount, and

(B) the fair market value of any payments which are contingent as to amount.

(g) Sale of depreciable property to controlled entity.

(1) In general. In the case of an installment sale of depreciable property between related persons—

(A) subsection (a) shall not apply,

(B) for purposes of this title—

(i) except as provided in clause (ii), all payments to be received shall be treated as received in the year of the disposition, and

(ii) in the case of any payments which are contingent as to the amount but with respect to which the fair market value may not be reasonably ascertained, the basis shall be recovered ratably, and

(C) the purchaser may not increase the basis of any property acquired in such sale by any amount before the time such amount is includible in the gross income of the seller.

(2) Exception where tax avoidance not a principal purpose. Paragraph (1) shall not apply if it is established to the satisfaction of the Secretary that the disposition did not have as one of its principal purposes the avoidance of Federal income tax.

(3) Related persons. For purposes of this subsection, the term "related persons" has the meaning given to such term by section 1239(b), except that such term shall include 2 or more partnerships having a relationship to each other described in section 707(b)(1)(B).

(h) Use of installment method by shareholders in certain liquidations.

(1) Receipt of obligations not treated as receipt of payment.

(A) In general. If, in a liquidation to which section 331 applies, the shareholder receives (in exchange for the shareholder's stock) an installment obligation acquired in respect of a sale or exchange by the corporation during the 12-month period beginning on the date a plan of complete liquidation is adopted and the liquidation is completed during such 12-month period, then, for purposes of this section, the receipt of payments under such obligation (but not the receipt of such obligation) by the shareholder shall be treated as the receipt of payment for the stock.

(B) Obligations attributable to sale of inventory must result from bulk sale. Subparagraph (A) shall not apply to an installment obligation acquired in respect of a sale or exchange of—

(i) stock in trade of the corporation,

(ii) other property of a kind which would properly be included in the inventory of the corporation if on hand at the close of the taxable year, and

(iii) property held by the corporation primarily for sale to customers in the ordinary course of its trade or business,

unless such sale or exchange is to 1 person in 1 transaction and involves substantially all of such property attributable to a trade or business of the corporation.

(C) Special rule where obligor and shareholder are related persons. If the obligor of any installment obligation and the shareholder are married to each other or are related persons (within the meaning of section 1239(b)), to the extent such installment obligation is attributable to the disposition by the corporation of depreciable property—

(i) subparagraph (A) shall not apply to such obligation, and

(ii) for purposes of this title, all payments to be received by the shareholder shall be deemed received in the year the shareholder receives the obligation.

(D) Coordination with subsection (e)(1)(A). For purposes of subsection (e)(1)(A), disposition of property by the corporation shall be treated also as disposition of such property by the shareholder.

(E) Sales by liquidating subsidiaries. For purposes of subparagraph (A), in the case of a controlling corporate shareholder (within the meaning of section 368(c)) of a selling corporation, an obligation acquired in respect of a sale or exchange by the selling corporation shall be treated as so acquired by such controlling corporate shareholder. The preceding sentence shall be applied successively to each controlling corporate shareholder above such controlling corporate shareholder.

(2) Distributions received in more than 1 taxable year of shareholder. If—

(A) paragraph (1) applies with respect to any installment obligation received by a shareholder from a corporation, and

(B) by reason of the liquidation such shareholder receives property in more than 1 taxable year,

then, on completion of the liquidation, basis previously allocated to property so received shall be reallocated for all such taxable years so that the shareholder's basis in the stock of the corporation is properly allocated among all property received by such shareholder in such liquidation.

(i) Recognition of recapture income in year of disposition.

(1) In general. In the case of any installment sale of property to which subsection (a) applies—

(A) notwithstanding subsection (a), any recapture income shall be recognized in the year of the disposition, and

(B) any gain in excess of the recapture income shall be taken into account under the installment method.

(2) Recapture income. For purposes of paragraph (1), the term "recapture income" means, with respect to any installment sale, the aggregate amount which would be treated as ordinary income under section 1245 or 1250 (or so much of section 751 as relates to section 1245 or 1250) for the taxable year of the disposition if all payments to be received were received in the taxable year of disposition.

(j) Regulations.

(1) In general. The Secretary shall prescribe such regulations as may be necessary or appropriate to carry out the provisions of this section.

(2) Selling price not readily ascertainable. The regulations prescribed under paragraph (1) shall include regulations providing for ratable basis recovery in transactions where the gross profit or the total contract price (or both) cannot be readily ascertained.

(k) Current inclusion in case of revolving credit plans, etc.

In the case of—

(1) any disposition of personal property under a revolving credit plan, or

(2) any installment obligation arising out of a sale of—

(A) stock or securities which are traded on an established securities market, or

(B) to the extent provided in regulations, property (other than stock or securities) of a kind regularly traded on an established market,

subsection (a) shall not apply, and, for purposes of this title, all payments to be received shall be treated as received in the year of disposition. The Secretary may provide for the application of this subsection in whole or in part for transactions in which the rules of this subsection otherwise would be avoided through the use of related parties, pass-thru entities, or intermediaries.

(l) Dealer dispositions.

For purposes of subsection (b)(2)(A)—

(1) In general. The term "dealer disposition" means any of the following dispositions:

(A) Personal property. Any disposition of personal property by a person who regularly sells or otherwise disposes of personal property of the same type on the installment plan.

(B) Real property. Any disposition of real property which is held by the taxpayer for sale to customers in the ordinary course of the taxpayer's trade or business.

(2) Exceptions. The term "dealer disposition" does not include—

(A) Farm property. The disposition on the installment plan of any property used or produced in the trade or business of farming (within the meaning of section 2032A(e)(4) or (5)).

(B) Timeshares and residential lots.

(i) In general. Any dispositions described in clause (ii) on the installment plan if the taxpayer elects to have paragraph (3) apply to any installment obligations which arise from such dispositions. An election under this paragraph shall not apply with respect to an installment obligation which is guaranteed by any person other than an individual.

(ii) Dispositions to which subparagraph applies. A disposition is described in this clause if it is a disposition in the ordinary course of the taxpayer's trade or business to an individual of—

(I) a timeshare right to use or a timeshare ownership interest in residential real property for not more than 6 weeks per year, or a right to use specified campgrounds for recreational purposes, or

(II) any residential lot, but only if the taxpayer (or any related person) is not to make any improvements with respect to such lot.

For purposes of subclause (I), a timeshare right to use (or timeshare ownership interest in) property held by the spouse, children, grandchildren, or parents of an individual shall be treated as held by such individual.

(C) Carrying charges or interest. Any carrying charges or interest with respect to a disposition described in subparagraph (A) or (B) which are added on the books of account of the seller to the established cash selling price of the property shall be included in the total contract price of the property and, if such charges or inter-

Tax accounting   Code Sec. 453

est are not so included, any payments received shall be treated as applying first against such carrying charges or interest.

(3) Payment of interest on timeshares and residential lots.

(A) In general. In the case of any installment obligation to which paragraph (2)(B) applies, the tax imposed by this chapter for any taxable year for which payment is received on such obligation shall be increased by the amount of interest determined in the manner provided under subparagraph (B).

(B) Computation of interest.

(i) In general. The amount of interest referred to in subparagraph (A) for any taxable year shall be determined —

(I) on the amount of the tax for such taxable year which is attributable to the payments received during such taxable year on installment obligations to which this subsection applies,

(II) for the period beginning on the date of sale, and ending on the date such payment is received, and

(III) by using the applicable Federal rate under section 1274 (without regard to subsection (d)(2) thereof) in effect at the time of the sale compounded semiannually.

(ii) Interest not taken into account. For purposes of clause (i), the portion of any tax attributable to the receipt of any payment shall be determined without regard to any interest imposed under subparagraph (A).

(iii) Taxable year of sale. No interest shall be determined for any payment received in the taxable year of the disposition from which the installment obligation arises.

(C) Treatment as interest. Any amount payable under this paragraph shall be taken into account in computing the amount of any deduction allowable to the taxpayer for interest paid or accrued during such taxable year.

In 2004, P.L. 108-357, Sec. 897(a), deleted "is issued by a corporation or a government or political subdivision thereof and" before "is readily tradable" in subpara. (f)(4)(B), effective for sales occurring on or after 10/22/2004.

In 2000, P.L. 106-573, Sec. 2(b), amended subsec. (a) and substituted "(a)" for "(a)(1)" each place it appeared in para. (d)(1), (i)(1) and subsec. (k), effective with respect to sales and other dispositions occurring on or after 12/17/99.

Prior to amendment, subsec. (a) read as follows:

"(a) Use of installment method.

"(1) In general. Except as otherwise provided in this section, income from an installment sale shall be taken into account for purposes of this title under the installment method.

"(2) Accrual method taxpayer. The installment method shall not apply to income from an installment sale if such income would be reported under an accrual method of accounting without regard to this section. The preceding sentence shall not apply to a disposition described in subparagraph (A) or (B) of subsection (l)(2)."

In 1999, P.L. 106-170, Sec. 536(a)(1), amended subsec. (a) . . . Sec. 536(a)(2), substituted "(a)(1)" for "(a)" each place it appeared in paras. (d)(1) and (i)(1) and subsec. (k), effective for sales or other dispositions occurring on or after 12/17/99.

Prior to amendment, subsec. (a) read as follows:

"(a) General rule. Except as otherwise provided in this section, income from an installment sale shall be taken into account for purposes of this title under the installment method."

In 1988, P.L. 100-647, Sec. 1006(e)(7)(A), substituted "to 1 person in 1 transaction" for "to one person" in subpara. (h)(1)(B) . . . Sec. 1006(e)(7)(B), substituted "section 368(c)" for "section 368(c)(1)" in subpara. (h)(1)(E), effective as provided in Sec. 633(a)(1) of P.L. 99-514 [reproduced below].

—P.L. 100-647, Sec. 1006(i)(1), amended subparas. (g)(1)(A) and (B) and added subpara. (g)(1)(C) . . . Sec. 1006(i)(2)(A), added para. (g)(3) . . . Sec. 1006(i)(2)(B), deleted "(within the meaning of section 1239(b))" after "related persons" in para. (g)(1), effective for sales after 10/22/86 in tax. yrs. end. after 10/22/86, except as provided in Sec. 642(c)(2) of P.L. 99-514 [reproduced below].

Prior to amendment, subparas. (g)(1)(A) and (B) read as follows:

"(A) subsection (a) shall not apply, and

"(B) for purposes of this title —

"(i) except as provided in clause (ii), all payments to be received shall be treated as received in the year of the disposition, and

"(ii) in the case of any payments which are contingent as to amount but with respect to which the fair market value may not be reasonably ascertained —

"(I) the basis shall be recovered ratably, and

"(II) the purchaser may not increase the basis of any property acquired in such sale by any amount before such time as the seller includes such amount in income."

—P.L. 100-647, Sec. 1006(i)(3), amended Sec. 642(c)(2) of P.L. 99-514 [reproduced below], transitional rule for amendments made by Sec. 642(a) of P.L. 99-514, by substituting "Transitional" for "Traditional" in the heading, see below.

—P.L. 100-647, Sec. 1008(g)(1), redesignated subsec. (j) (as added by Sec. 812(a) of P.L. 99-514) as subsec. (k), effective for tax. yrs. begin. after 12/31/86, except as provided in Sec. 812(c)(2)-(6) of P.L. 99-514, reproduced below.

—P.L. 100-647, Sec. 1008(g)(4), amended Sec. 812(c) of P.L. 99-514, part of the effective date for changes made by Sec. 812(a) of P.L. 99-514, by redesignating Sec. 812(c)(2) of P.L. 99-514 as Sec. 812(c)(3) and adding new Sec. 812(c)(2) of P.L. 99-514, reproduced below . . . Sec. 1008(g)(5), amended Sec. 812(c)(3)(B) and (C) (as redesignated) and added Sec. 812(c)(3)(D) of P.L. 99-514, reproduced below . . . Sec. 1008(g)(6), added Sec. 812(c)(4), (5) and (6) of P.L. 99-514, reproduced below.

Prior to amendment, Sec. 812(c)(3)(B) and (C) of P.L. 99-514 (as redesignated) read as follows:

"(B) such change shall be treated as having been made with the consent of the Secretary, and

"(C) the period for taking into account adjustments under section 481 of such Code by reason of such change shall not exceed 4 years."

—P.L. 100-647, Sec. 1018(u)(25), substituted "subsections (g)" for "subsection (g)" in para. (f)(1) . . . Sec. 1018(u)(26), substituted "payments to be" for "payment to be" in para. (f)(8), effective for sales made after 10/22/86, in tax. yrs. end. after 10/22/86, except as provided in Sec. 642(c)(2) of 99-514, reproduced below.

—P.L. 100-647, Sec. 2004(d)(1), substituted "disposes of personal property of the same type" for "disposes of personal property" in subpara. (l)(1)(A) . . . Sec. 2004(d)(5), deleted "and section 453A" following "subsection (a)" in subsec. (k), effective for dispositions in tax. yrs. begin. after 12/31/87, except as provided in Sec. 10202(e)(2), (3), and (5) of P.L. 99-514, reproduced below.

—P.L. 100-647, Sec. 2004(d)(3), added Sec. 10202(e)(3)(C) of P.L. 100-203 [reproduced below], part of the effective date for changes made by Sec. 10202(b)(1) of P.L. 100-203, see below . . . Sec. 2004(d)(4), added Sec. 10202(e)(2)(C) of P.L. 100-203, reproduced below . . . Sec. 2004(d)(6), amended Sec. 10202(e)(2)(A) of P.L. 100-203 [reproduced below] by substituting "section 453(l)(1) of the Internal Revenue Code of 1986 as added by this section" for "section 453A of the Internal Revenue Code of 1986, see below.

In 1987, P.L. 100-203, Sec. 10202(b)(1), amended subpara. (b)(2)(A) . . . Sec. 10202(b)(2), added subsec. (l), effective for dispositions in tax. yrs. begin. after 12/31/87, except as provided in Sec. 10202(e)(2), (3) and (5) of this Act [as amended by Sec. 2004(d)(3) of P.L. 100-647, (4) and (6), see above] which reads as follows:

"(2) Special rules for dealers.

"(A) In general. In the case of dealer dispositions (within the meaning of section 453(l)(1) of the Internal Revenue Code of 1986 as added by this section), the amendments made by subsections (a) [of Sec. 10202 of P.L. 100-203, repeal of Code Sec. 453C] and (b) [of Sec. 10202 of P.L. 100-203, addition of Code Sec. 453(l)] shall apply to installment obligations arising from dispositions after December 31, 1987.

"(B) Special rules for obligations arising from dealer dispositions after February 28, 1986, and before January 1, 1988.

"(i) In general. In the case of an applicable installment obligation arising from a disposition described in subclause (I) or (II) of section 453C(e)(1)(A)(i) of the Internal Revenue Code of 1986 (as in effect before the amendments made by this section) before January 1, 1988, the amendments made by subsections (a) [of Sec. 10202 of P.L. 100-203, repeal of Code Sec. 453C] and (b) [of Sec. 10202 of P.L. 100-203, addition of Code Sec. 453(l)] shall apply to taxable years beginning after December 31, 1987.

"(ii) Change in method of accounting. In the case of any taxpayer who is required by clause (i) to change its method of accounting for any taxable year with respect to obligations described in clause (i) —

"(I) such change shall be treated as initiated by the taxpayer,

"(II) such change shall be treated as made with the consent of the Secretary of the Treasury or his delegate, and

"(III) the net amount of adjustments required by section 481 of the Internal Revenue Code of 1986 shall be taken into account over a period not longer than 4 taxable years.

"(C) Certain rules made applicable. — For purposes of this paragraph, rules similar to the rules of paragraphs (4) and (5) of section 812(c) of the Tax Reform Act of 1986 [P.L. 99-514] (as added by the Technical and Miscellaneous Revenue Act of 1988 [P.L. 100-647]) shall apply.

"(3) Special rule for nondealers.

"(A) Election. A taxpayer may elect, at such time and in such manner as the Secretary of the Treasury or his delegate may prescribe, to have the amendments made by subsections (a) [of Sec. 10202 of P.L. 100-203, repeal of Code Sec. 453C] and (c) [of Sec. 10202 of P.L. 100-203, amendment of Code Sec. 453A] apply to taxable years ending after December 31, 1986, with respect to dispositions and pledges occurring after August 16, 1986.

"(B) Pledging rules. Except as provided in subparagraph (A) —

2,129

"(i) In general.—Section 453A(d) of the Internal Revenue Code of 1986 shall apply to any installment obligation which is pledged to secure any secured indebtedness (within the meaning of section 453A(d)(4) of such Code) after December 17, 1987, in taxable years ending after such date.

"(ii) Coordination with section 453C. For purposes of section 453C of such Code (as in effect before its repeal), the face amount of any obligation to which section 453A(d) of such Code applies shall be reduced by the amount treated as payments on such obligation under section 453A(d) of such Code and the amount of any indebtedness secured by it shall not be taken into account.

"(C) Certain dispositions deemed made on 1st day of taxable year.—If the taxpayer makes an election under subparagraph (A), in the case of the taxpayer's 1st taxable year ending after December 31, 1986—

"(i) dispositions after August 16, 1986, and before the 1st day of such taxable year shall be treated as made on such 1st day, and

"(ii) subsections (b)(2)(B) and (c)(4) of section 453A of such Code shall be applied separately with respect to such dispositions by substituting for '$5,000,000' the amount which bears the same ratio to $5,000,000 as the number of days after August 16, 1986, and before such 1st day bears to 365."

* * *

"(5) Coordination with Tax Reform Act of 1986. The amendments made by this section [Sec. 10202 of P.L. 100-203] shall not apply to any installment obligation or to any taxpayer during any period to the extent the amendments made by section 811 of the Tax Reform Act of 1986 do not apply to such obligation or during such period."

Prior to amendment, subpara. (b)(2)(A) read as follows:

"(A) Dealer disposition of personal property. A disposition of personal property on the installment plan by a person who regularly sells or otherwise disposes of personal property on the installment plan."

In 1986, P.L. 99-514, Sec. 631(e)(8)(A), amended subparas. (h)(1)(A) and (B) . . . Sec. 631(e)(8)(B), amended subpara. (h)(1)(E) . . . Sec. 631(e)(8)(C), substituted "certain" for "section 337" in the heading of subsec. (h), effective as provided in Sec. 633(a)(1) this Act, which read as follows:

"(a) General rule.

"Except as otherwise provided in this section [Sec. 633], the amendments made by this subtitle shall apply to—

"(1) any distribution in complete liquidation, and any sale or exchange, made by a corporation after July 31, 1986, unless such corporation is completely liquidated before January 1, 1987,"

Sec. 633(d) [sic (e)] of this Act provides:

"(d) [sic (e)] Complete liquidation defined.

"For purposes of this section, a corporation shall be treated as completely liquidated if all of the assets of such corporation are distributed in complete liquidation, less assets retained to meet claims."

Prior to amendment, subparas. (h)(1)(A) and (B) read as follows:

"(A) In general. If, in connection with a liquidation to which section 337 applies, in a transaction to which section 331 applies the shareholder receives (in exchange for the shareholder's stock) an installment obligation acquired in respect of a sale or exchange by the corporation during the 12-month period set forth in section 337(a), then, for purposes of this section, the receipt of payments under such obligation (but not the receipt of such obligation) by the shareholder shall be treated as the receipt of payment for the stock.

"(B) Obligations attributable to sale of inventory must result from bulk sale. Subparagraph (A) shall not apply to an installment obligation described in section 337(b)(1)(B) unless such obligation is also described in section 337(b)(2)(B)."

Prior to amendment, subpara. (h)(1)(E) read as follows:

"(E) Sales by liquidating subsidiary. For purposes of subparagraph (A), in any case to which section 337(c)(3) applies, an obligation acquired in respect of a sale or exchange by the selling corporation shall be treated as so acquired by the corporation distributing the obligation to the shareholder."

—P.L. 99-514, Sec. 642(a)(1)(D), substituted "controlled" for "80-percent owned" in the heading of subsec. (g) . . . Sec. 642(a)(3), amended para. (f)(1) . . . Sec. 642(b)(1), added para. (f)(8) . . . Sec. 642(b)(2), amended para. (g)(1), effective for sales after 10/22/86, in tax. yrs. end. after 10/22/86, except as provided in Sec. 642(c)(2) of this Act [as amended by Sec. 1006(i)(3) of P.L. 100-647, see above], which reads as follows:

"(2) Transitional rule for binding contracts.— The amendments made by this section shall not apply to sales made after August 14, 1986, which are made pursuant to a binding contract in effect on August 14, 1986, and at all times thereafter."

Prior to amendment, para. (f)(1) read as follows:

"(1) Related person. Except for purposes of subsections (g) and (h), the term 'related person' means a person whose stock would be attributed under section 318(a) (other than paragraph (4) thereof) to the person first disposing of the property."

Prior to amendment, para. (g)(1) read as follows:

"(1) In general. In the case of an installment sale of depreciable property between related persons within the meaning of section 1239(b), subsection (a) shall not apply, and, for purposes of this title, all payments to be received shall be deemed received in the year of the disposition."

—P.L. 99-514, Sec. 812(a), added subsec. (j) [redesignated subsec. (k) by Sec. 1008(g)(1) of P.L. 100-647, see above] effective for tax. yrs. begin. after 12/31/86, except as provided in Sec. 812(c)(2)-(6) [as amended by Sec. 1008(g)(4) of P.L. 100-647(6), see above] of this Act which reads as follows:

"(2) Sales of stock, etc.— Section 453(k)(2) of the Internal Revenue Code of 1986, as added by subsection (a) [Sec. 812(a)], shall apply to sales after December 31, 1986, in taxable years ending after such date.

"(3) Change in method of accounting.— In the case of any taxpayer who made sales under a revolving credit plan and was on the installment method under section 453 or 453A of the Internal Revenue Code of 1986 for such taxpayer's last taxable year beginning before January 1, 1987, the amendments made by this section shall be treated as a change in method of accounting for its 1st taxable year beginning after December 31, 1986, and—

"(A) such change shall be treated as initiated by the taxpayer,

"(B) such change shall be treated as having been made with the consent of the Secretary,

"(C) the period for taking into account adjustments under section 481 of such Code by reason of such change shall be equal to 4 years, and

"(D) except as provided in paragraph (4), the amount taken into account in each of such 4 years shall be the applicable percentage (determined in accordance with the following table) of the net adjustment:

"In the case of the:	The applicable percentage is:
1st taxable year	15
2nd taxable year	25
3rd taxable year	30
4th taxable year	30

If the taxpayer's last taxable year beginning before January 1, 1987, was the taxpayer's 1st taxable year in which sales were made under a revolving credit plan, all adjustments under section 481 of such Code shall be taken into account in the taxpayer's 1st taxable year beginning after December 31, 1986."

"(4) Acceleration of adjustments where contraction in amount of installment obligations.—

"(A) In general.— If the percentage determined under subparagraph (B) for any taxable year in the adjustment period exceeds the percentage which would otherwise apply under paragraph (3)(D) for such taxable year (determined after the application of this paragraph for prior taxable years in the adjustment period)—

"(i) the percentage determined under subparagraph (B) shall be substituted for the applicable percentage which would otherwise apply under paragraph (3)(D), and

"(ii) any increase in the applicable percentage by reason of clause (i) shall be applied to reduce the applicable percentage determined under paragraph (3)(D) for subsequent taxable years in the adjustment period (beginning with the 1st of such subsequent taxable years).

"(B) Determination of percentage.— For purposes of subparagraph (A), the percentage determined under this subparagraph for any taxable year in the adjustment period is the excess (if any) of—

"(i) the percentage determined by dividing the aggregate contraction in revolving installment obligations by the aggregate face amount of such obligations outstanding as of the close of the taxpayer's last taxable year beginning before January 1, 1987, over

"(ii) the sum of the applicable percentages under paragraph (3)(D) (as modified by this paragraph) for prior taxable years in the adjustment period.

"(C) Aggregate contraction in revolving installment obligations.— For purposes of subparagraph (B), the aggregate contraction in revolving installment obligations is the amount by which—

"(i) the aggregate face amount of the revolving installment obligations outstanding as of the close of the taxpayer's last taxable year beginning before January 1, 1987, exceeds

"(ii) the aggregate face amount of the revolving installment obligations outstanding as of the close of the taxable year involved.

"(D) Revolving installment obligations.— For purposes of this paragraph, the term 'revolving installment obligations' means installment obligations arising under a revolving credit plan.

"(E) Treatment of certain obligations disposed of on or before October 26, 1987.— For purposes of subparagraphs (B)(i) and (C)(i), in determining the aggregate face amount of revolving installment obligations outstanding as of the close of the taxpayer's last taxable year beginning before January 1, 1987, there shall not be taken into account any obligation—

"(i) which was disposed of to an unrelated person on or before October 26, 1987, or

"(ii) was disposed of to an unrelated person on or after such date pursuant to a binding written contract in effect on October 26, 1987, and at all times thereafter before such disposition.

For purposes of the preceding sentence, the term 'unrelated person' means any person who is not a related person (as defined in section 453(g) of the Internal Revenue Code of 1986).

"(5) Limitation on losses from sales of obligations under revolving credit plans.— If 1 or more obligations arising under a revolving credit plan and taken into account under paragraph (3) are disposed of during the adjustment period, then, notwithstanding any other provisions of law—

"(A) no losses from such dispositions shall be recognized, and

"(B) the aggregate amount of the adjustment for taxable years in the adjustment period (in reverse order of time) shall be reduced by the amount of such losses.

"(6) Adjustment period.— For purposes of paragraphs (4) and (5), the adjustment period is the 4-year period under paragraph (3)."

—P.L. 99-514, Sec. 1809(c), substituted "section 1245 or 1250 (or so much of section 751 as relates to section 1245 or 1250)" for "section 1245 or 1250" after "1250" in para (i)(2), effective for dispositions made after 6/6/84, except as provided by Secs. 112(b)(2) and (3) of P.L. 98-369, reproduced below.

In 1984, P.L. 98-369, Sec. 112(a), amended subsec. (i), effective for dispositions made after 6/6/84. Sec. 112(b)(2) and (3) of the Act provides:

"(2) Exception. The amendments made by this section (Sec. 112 of P.L. 98-369) shall not apply with respect to any disposition conducted pursuant to a contract which was binding on March 22, 1984, and at all times thereafter.

"(3) Special rule for certain dispositions before October 1, 1984. The amendments made by this section (Sec. 112 of P.L. 98-369) shall not apply to any disposition before October 1, 1984, of all or substantially all of the personal property of a cable television business pursuant to a written offer delivered by the seller on June 20, 1984, but only if the last payment under the installment contract is due no later than October 1, 1989."

Prior to amendment, subsec. (i) read as follows:

"(i) Application with section 179.

"(1) In general. In the case of an installment sale of section 179 property, subsection (a) shall not apply, and for purposes of this title, all payments to be received shall be deemed received in the year of disposition.

"(2) Limitation. Paragraph (1) shall apply only to the extent of the amount allowed as a deduction under section 179 with respect to the section 179 property."

—P.L. 98-369, Sec. 421(b)(6)(B), substituted "the obligor of any installment obligation and the shareholder are married to each other or are related persons" for "the obligor of any installment obligation and the shareholder are related persons" in subpara. (h)(1)(C) . . . Sec. 421(b)(6)(C), deleted "spouse or" after "property to" in the heading of subsec. (g), effective for transfers after 7/18/84, in tax. yrs. end. after 7/18/84. Sec. 421(d)(2) through (4) of the Act provides:

"(2) Election to have amendments apply to transfers after 1983. If both spouses or former spouses make an election under this paragraph, the amendments made by this section (Sec. 421 of P.L. 98-369) shall apply to all transfers made by such spouses (or former spouses) after December 31, 1983.

"(3) Exception for transfers pursuant to existing decrees. Except in the case of an election under paragraph (2), the amendments made by this section (Sec. 421 of P.L. 98-369) shall not apply to transfers under any instrument in effect on or before the date of the enactment of this Act unless both spouses (or former spouses) elect to have such amendments apply to transfers under such instrument.

"(4) Election. Any election under paragraph (2) or (3) shall be made in such manner, at such time, and subject to such conditions, as the Secretary of the Treasury or his delegate may by regulations prescribe."

In 1983, P.L. 97-448, Sec. 303, added ", when used in any provision of this section other than subsection (b)(1)," after "the term 'payment'" in subpara. (f)(6)(C), effective for dispositions made after 10/19/80, in tax. yrs. end. after 10/19/80.

In 1981, P.L. 97-34, Sec. 202(c), redesignated subsec. (i) as subsec. (j) and added new subsec. (i), effective for property placed in service after 12/31/80, in tax. yrs. end. after 12/31/80.

In 1980, P.L. 96-471, Sec. 2(a), amended Code Sec. 453, effective for dispositions made after 10/19/80 in tax. yrs. end. after 10/19/80 [date of enactment] except for subsec. (e) which is effective for first dispositions made after 5/14/80 and paras. (h)(1) and (2) which is effective for distributions of installment obligations after 3/31/80. Sec. 6(a)(7) of P.L. 96-471 provides:

"(7) Special rule for application of former section 453 to certain dispositions. In the case of any disposition made on or before the date of the enactment of this Act [10/19/80] in any taxable year ending after such date [10/19/80], the provisions of section 453(b) of the Internal Revenue Code of 1954, as in effect before such date [10/19/80], shall be applied with respect to such disposition without regard to—

"(A) paragraph (2) of such section 453(b), and

"(B) any requirement that more than 1 payment be received."

Prior to amendment, Code Sec. 453 read as follows:

"Sec. 453. Installment method.

"(a) Dealers in personal property.

"(1) In general. Under regulations prescribed by the Secretary, a person who regularly sells or otherwise disposes of personal property on the installment plan may return as income therefrom in any taxable year that proportion of the installment payments actually received in that year which the gross profit, realized or to be realized when payment is completed, bears to the total contract price.

"(2) Total contract price. For purposes of paragraph (1), the total contract price of all sales of personal property on the installment plan includes the amount of carrying charges or interest which is determined with respect to such sales and is added on the books of account of the seller to the established cash selling price of such property. This paragraph shall not apply with respect to sales of personal property under a revolving credit type plan or with respect to sales or other dispositions of property the income from which is, under subsection (b), returned on the basis and in the manner prescribed in paragraph (1).

"(b) Sales of realty and casual sales of personalty.

"(1) General rule. Income from—

"(A) a sale or other disposition of real property, or

"(B) a casual sale or other casual disposition of personal property (other than property of a kind which would properly be included in the inventory of the taxpayer if on hand at the close of the taxable year) for a price exceeding $1,000, may (under regulations prescribed by the Secretary) be returned on the basis and in the manner prescribed in subsection (a).

"(2) Limitation. Paragraph (1) shall apply only if in the taxable year of the sale or other disposition—

"(A) there are no payments, or

"(B) the payments (exclusive of evidences of indebtedness of the purchaser) do not exceed 30 percent of the selling price.

"(3) Purchaser evidences of indebtedness payable on demand or readily tradable. In applying this subsection, a bond or other evidence of indebtedness which is payable on demand, or which is issued by a corporation or a government or political subdivision thereof (A) with interest coupons attached or in registered form (other than one in registered form which the taxpayer establishes will not be readily tradable in an established securities market), or (B) in any other form designed to render such bond or other evidence of indebtedness readily tradable in an established securities market, shall not be treated as an evidence of indebtedness of the purchaser.

"(c) Change from accrual to installment basis.

"(1) General rule. If a taxpayer entitled to the benefits of subsection (a) elects for any taxable year to report his taxable income on the installment basis, then in computing his taxable income for such year (referred to in this subsection as year of change) or for any subsequent year—

"(A) installment payments actually received during any such year on account of sales or other dispositions of property made in any taxable year before the year of change shall not be excluded; but

"(B) the tax imposed by this chapter for any taxable year (referred to in this subsection as 'adjustment year') beginning after December 31, 1953, shall be reduced by the adjustment computed under paragraph (2).

"(2) Adjustment in tax for amounts previously taxed. In determining the adjustment referred to in paragraph (1)(B), first determine, for each taxable year before the year of change, the amount which equals the lesser of—

"(A) the portion of the tax for such prior taxable year which is attributable to the gross profit which was included in gross income for such prior taxable year, and which by reason of paragraph (1)(A) is includible in gross income for the taxable year, or

"(B) the portion of the tax for the adjustment year which is attributable to the gross profit described in subparagraph (A).

The adjustment referred to in paragraph (1)(B) for the adjustment year is the sum of the amounts determined under the preceding sentence.

"(3) Rule for applying paragraph (2). For purposes of paragraph (2), the portion of the tax for a prior taxable year, or for the adjustment year, which is attributable to the gross profit described in such paragraph is that amount which bears the same ratio to the tax imposed by this chapter other than by sections 55 and 56, for such taxable year (computed without regard to paragraph (2)) as the gross profit described in such paragraph bears to the gross income for such taxable year.

"(4) Revocation of election. An election under paragraph (1) to report taxable income on the installment basis may be revoked by filing a notice of revocation, in such manner as the Secretary prescribes by regulations, at any time before the expiration of 3 years following the date of the filing of the tax return for the year of change. If such notice of revocation is timely filed—

"(A) the provisions of paragraph (1) and subsection (a) shall not apply to the year of change or for any subsequent year;

"(B) the statutory period for the assessment of any deficiency for any taxable year ending before the filing of such notice, which is attributable to the revocation of the election to use the installment basis, shall not expire before the expiration of 2 years from the date of the filing of such notice, and such deficiency may be assessed before the expiration of such 2-year period notwithstanding the provisions of any law or rule of law which would otherwise prevent such assessment; and

"(C) if refund or credit of any overpayment, resulting from the revocation of the election to use the installment basis, for any taxable year ending before the date of the filing of the notice of revocation is prevented on the date of such filing, or within one year from such date, by the operation of any law or rule of law (other than section 7121 or 7122), refund or credit of such overpayment may nevertheless be made or allowed if claim therefor is filed within one year from such date. No interest shall be allowed on the refund or credit of such overpayment for any period prior to the date of the filing of the notice of revocation.

"(5) Election after revocation. If the taxpayer revokes under paragraph (4) an election under paragraph (1) to report taxable income on the installment basis, no election under paragraph (1) may be made, except with the consent of the Secretary, for any subsequent taxable year before the fifth taxable year following the year of change with respect to which such revocation is made.

"(d) Gain or loss on disposition of installment obligations.

"(1) General rule. If an installment obligation is satisfied at other than its face value or distributed, transmitted, sold, or otherwise disposed of, gain or loss shall result to the extent of the difference between the basis of the obligation and—

"(A) the amount realized, in the case of satisfaction at other than face value or a sale or exchange, or

"(B) the fair market value of the obligation at the time of distribution, transmission, or disposition, in the case of the distribution, transmission, or disposition otherwise than by sale or exchange.

Any gain or loss so resulting shall be considered as resulting from the sale or exchange of the property in respect of which the installment obligation was received.

"(2) Basis of obligation. The basis of an installment obligation shall be the excess of the face value of the obligation over an amount equal to the income which would be returnable were the obligation satisfied in full.

"(3) Special rule for transmission at death. Except as provided in section 691 (relating to recipients of income in respect of decedents), this subsection shall not apply to the transmission of installment obligations at death.

"(4) Effect of distribution in certain liquidations.

"(A) Liquidations to which section 332 applies. If—

"(i) an installment obligation is distributed in a liquidation to which section 332 (relating to complete liquidations of subsidiaries) applies, and

"(ii) the basis of such obligation in the hands of the distributee is determined under section 334(b)(1),

then no gain or loss with respect to the distribution of such obligation shall be recognized by the distributing corporation.

"(B) Liquidations to which section 337 applies. If—

"(i) an installment obligation is distributed by a corporation in the course of a liquidation, and

"(ii) under section 337 (relating to gain or loss on sales or exchanges in connection with certain liquidations) no gain or loss would have been recognized to the corporation if the corporation had sold or exchanged such installment obligation on the day of such distribution,

then no gain or loss shall be recognized to such corporation by reason of such distribution. The preceding sentence shall not apply to the extent that under paragraph (1) gain to the distributing corporation would be considered as gain to which section 341(f), 617(d)(1), 1245(a), 1250(a), 1251(c), 1252(a), or 1254(a) applies.

"(5) Life insurance companies. In the case of a disposition of an installment obligation by any person other than a life insurance company (as defined in section 801(a)) to such an insurance company or to a partnership of such such an insurance company is a partner, no provision of this subtitle providing for the nonrecognition of gain shall apply with respect to any gain resulting under paragraph (1). If a corporation which is a life insurance company for the taxable year was (for the preceding taxable year) a corporation which was not a life insurance company, such corporation shall, for purposes of this paragraph and paragraph (1), be treated as having transferred to a life insurance company, on the last day of the preceding taxable year, all installment obligations which it held on such last day. A partnership of which a life insurance company becomes a partner shall, for purposes of this paragraph and paragraph (1), be treated as having transferred to a life insurance company, on the last day of the preceding taxable year of such partnership, all installment obligations which it holds at the time such insurance company becomes a partner.

"(e) Carrying charges not included in total contract price.

"If the carrying charges or interest with respect to sales of personal property, the income from which is returned under subsection (a)(1), is not included in the total contract price, payments received with respect to such sales shall be treated as applying first against such carrying charges or interest. This subsection shall not apply with respect to sales or other dispositions of property the income from which is, under subsection (b), returned on the basis and in the manner prescribed in subsection (a)(1)."

—P.L. 96-471, Sec. 2(c)(4), repealed Sec. 403(b)(2)(B) of P.L. 96-223 which added the last sentence of subpara. (d)(4)(B) [see below], effective for distributions and dispositions pursuant to plans of liquidation adopted after 12/31/81.
Prior to repeal, the last sentence of subpara. (d)(4)(B) read as follows:

"In the case of any installment obligation which would have met the requirements of clauses (i) and (ii) of the first sentence of this subparagraph but for section 337(f), gain shall be recognized to such corporation by reason of such distribution only to the extent gain would have been recognized under section 337(f) if such corporation had sold, or exchanged such installment obligation on the day of such distribution."

—P.L. 96-223, Sec. 403(b)(2)(B), [repealed by Sec. 2(c)(4) of P.L. 96-471, see above], added the last sentence of subpara. (d)(4)(B), effective for distributions and dispositions pursuant to plans of liquidation adopted after 12/31/81.

—P.L. 96-222, Sec. 104(a)(4)(H)(iv), substituted "sections 55 and 56" for "section 56" in para. (c)(3), effective 10/4/76.

In 1978, P.L. 95-600, Sec. 703(j)(3), deleted "(or by the corresponding provisions of prior revenue laws)" following "by this chapter" in the first sentence of para. (c)(3) and deleted the last sentence of para. (c)(3), effective 10/4/76.
Prior to amendment, the last sentence of para. (c)(3) read as follows:

"For purposes of the preceding sentence, the provisions of chapter 1 (other than of subchapter D, relating to excess profits tax, and of subchapter E, relating to self-employment income) of the Internal Revenue Code of 1939 shall be treated as the corresponding provisions of the Internal Revenue Code of 1954."

In 1976, P.L. 94-455, Sec. 205(c)(1)(E), substituted "1252(a), or 1254(a)" for "or 1252(a)" in subpara. (d)(4)(B), effective for tax. yrs. end. after 12/31/75.

—P.L. 94-455, Sec. 1901(a)(66)(A), substituted "corresponding provisions of the Internal Revenue Code of 1954" for "corresponding provisions of the Internal Revenue Code of 1939" in para. (c)(3) ... Sec. 1901(a)(66)(B), substituted "617(d)(1)" for "section 617(d)(1)" in subpara. (d)(4)(B), effective for tax. yrs. begin. after 12/31/76.

—P.L. 94-455, Sec. 1906(b)(13)(A), substituted "Secretary" for "Secretary or his delegate" each place it appeared in Code Sec. 453, effective for tax. yrs. begin. after 12/31/76.

—P.L. 94-455, Sec. 1951(b)(7)(A), amended para. (b)(2), effective for tax. yrs. begin. after 12/31/76, except as provided in Sec. 1951(b)(7)(B) of the Act, which reads as follows:

"(B) Savings provision.

Notwithstanding subparagraph (A), in the case of installment payments received during taxable years beginning after December 31, 1976, on account of a sale or other disposition made during a taxable year beginning before January 1, 1954, subsection (b)(1) of section 453 (relating to sales of realty and casual sales of personalty) shall apply only if the income was (by reason of section 44(b) of the Internal Revenue Code of 1939) returnable on the basis and in the manner prescribed in section 44(a) of such Code."
Prior to amendment, para. (b)(2) read as follows:

"(2) Limitation. Paragraph (1) shall apply—

"(A) In the case of a sale or other disposition during a taxable year beginning after December 31, 1953 (whether or not such taxable year ends after the date of enactment of this title), only if in the taxable year of the sale or other disposition—

"(i) there are no payments, or

"(ii) the payments (exclusive of evidences of indebtedness of the purchaser) do not exceed 30 percent of the selling price.

"(B) In the case of a sale or other disposition during a taxable year beginning before January 1, 1954, only if the income was (by reason of section 44(b) of the Internal Revenue Code of 1939) returnable on the basis and in the manner prescribed in section 44(a) of such code."

In 1969, P.L. 91-172, Sec. 211(b)(5), substituted "1250(a), 1251(c), or 1252(a)" for "or 1250(a)" in subsec. (d)(4)(B), effective for tax. yrs. begin. after 12/31/69.

—P.L. 91-172, Sec. 301(b)(7), added ", other than by section 56," after "prior revenue laws)" in para. (c)(3), effective for tax. yrs. end. after 12/31/69.

—P.L. 91-172, Sec. 412(a), added new para. (b)(3), effective for sales or other dispositions occurring after 5/27/69, which are not made pursuant to a binding written contract entered into on or before such date.

—P.L. 91-172, Sec. 916, added paras. (c)(4) and (5), effective for an election made for any year of change (as defined in Sec. 453(c)(1)) ending on or after 12/30/69, and for any such year of change which ended before 12/30/69 if the 3-year statutory period for assessment of any deficiency for such year has not expired on 12/30/69.

In 1966, P.L. 89-809, Sec. 202(c), amended subpara. (d)(4)(A), effective with respect to distributions made after 11/13/66.
Prior to amendment, subpara. (d)(4)(A) read as follows:

"(i) an installment obligation is distributed by one corporation to another corporation in the course of liquidation, and

"(ii) under section 332 (relating to complete liquidations of subsidiaries) no gain or loss with respect to the receipt of such obligation is recognized in the case of the recipient corporation,

then no gain or loss with respect to the distribution of such obligation shall be recognized in the case of the distributing corporation. If the basis of the property of the liquidating corporation in the hands of the distributee is determined under section 334(b)(2) then the preceding sentence shall not apply to the extent that under paragraph (1) gain to the distributing corporation would be considered as gain to which section 341(f) or section 617(d)(1), 1245(a) or 1250(a) applies."

—P.L. 89-570, Sec. [1](b)(5), substituted "section 617(d)(1), 1245(a)," for "section 1245(a)" in subpara. (d)(4)(A) and (B), effective for tax. yrs. end. after 9/12/66, but only for expenditures paid or incurred after 9/12/66.

In 1964, P.L. 88-539, Sec. 3(a), amended subsec. (a), effective for sales made in tax. yrs. begin. on or after 1/1/60.
Prior to amendment, subsec. (a) read as follows:

"(a) Dealers in personal property. Under regulations prescribed by the Secretary or his delegate, a person who regularly sells or otherwise disposes of personal property on the installment plan may return as income therefrom in any taxable year that proportion of the installment payments actually received in that year which the gross profit, realized or to be realized when payment is completed, bears to the total contract price."

—P.L. 88-539, Sec. 3(b), amended subsec. (e), effective for sales made during tax. yrs. begin. after 12/31/63.
Prior to amendment, subsec. (e) read as follows:

"(e) Revolving credit type plans. For purposes of subsection (a), the term 'installment plan' includes a revolving credit type plan which provides that the purchaser of personal property at retail may pay for such property in a series of periodic payments of an agreed portion of the amounts due the seller under the plan, except that such term does not include any such plan with respect to a purchaser who uses his account primarily as an ordinary charge account."

—P.L. 88-484, Sec. [1](b)(2), added "section 341(f) or" before "section 1245(a)" in subpara. (d)(4)(A) and (B), effective for transactions after 8/22/64 in tax. yrs. end. after that date.

—P.L. 88-272, Sec. 231(b)(5), added "or 1250(a)" in subparas. (d)(4)(A) and (B), effective for dispositions after 12/31/63, in tax. yrs. end. after 12/31/63.

—P.L. 88-272, Sec. 222(a), added subsec. (e), effective for sales made in tax. yrs. begin. after 12/31/63.

In 1962, P.L. 87-834, Sec. 13(f)(5)(A), added the last sentence to subpara. (d)(4)(A) ... Sec. 13(f)(5)(B), added the last sentence to subpara. (d)(4)(B), effective for tax. yrs. begin. after 12/31/62.

In 1958, P.L. 85-866, Sec. 27, added para. (d)(5), effective for tax. yrs. end. after 12/31/57, but only as to transfers or other dispositions of installment obligations occurring after 12/31/57.

Sec. 453A. Special rules for nondealers.

(a) General rule.

In the case of an installment obligation to which this section applies—

(1) interest shall be paid on the deferred tax liability with respect to such obligation in the manner provided under subsection (c), and

(2) the pledging rules under subsection (d) shall apply.

(b) Installment obligations to which section applies.

(1) In general. This section shall apply to any obligation which arises from the disposition of any property under the installment method, but only if the sales price of such property exceeds $150,000.

(2) Special rule for interest payments. For purposes of subsection (a)(1), this section shall apply to an obligation described in paragraph (1) arising during a taxable year only if—

Tax accounting — Code Sec. 453A

(A) such obligation is outstanding as of the close of such taxable year, and

(B) the face amount of all such obligations held by the taxpayer which arose during, and are outstanding as of the close of, such taxable year exceeds $5,000,000.

Except as provided in regulations, all persons treated as a single employer under subsection (a) or (b) of section 52 shall be treated as one person for purposes of this paragraph and subsection (c)(4).

(3) Exception for personal use and farm property. An installment obligation shall not be treated as described in paragraph (1) if it arises from the disposition—

(A) by an individual of personal use property (within the meaning of section 1275(b)(3)), or

(B) of any property used or produced in the trade or business of farming (within the meaning of section 2032A(e)(4) or (5)).

(4) Special rule for timeshares and residential lots. An installment obligation shall not be treated as described in paragraph (1) if it arises from a disposition described in section 453(1)(2)(B), but the provisions of section 453(1)(3) (relating to interest payments on timeshares and residential lots) shall apply to such obligation.

(5) Sales price. For purposes of paragraph (1), all sales or exchanges which are part of the same transaction (or a series of related transactions) shall be treated as 1 sale or exchange.

(c) Interest on deferred tax liability.

(1) In general. If an obligation to which this section applies is outstanding as of the close of any taxable year, the tax imposed by this chapter for such taxable year shall be increased by the amount of interest determined in the manner provided under paragraph (2).

(2) Computation of interest. For purposes of paragraph (1), the interest for any taxable year shall be an amount equal to the product of—

(A) the applicable percentage of the deferred tax liability with respect to such obligation, multiplied by

(B) the underpayment rate in effect under section 6621(a)(2) for the month with or within which the taxable year ends.

(3) Deferred tax liability. For purposes of this section, the term "deferred tax liability" means, with respect to any taxable year, the product of—

(A) the amount of gain with respect to an obligation which has not been recognized as of the close of such taxable year, multiplied by

(B) the maximum rate of tax in effect under section 1 or 11, whichever is appropriate, for such taxable year.

For purposes of applying the preceding sentence with respect to so much of the gain which, when recognized, will be treated as long-term capital gain, the maximum rate on net capital gain under section 1(h) or 1201 (whichever is appropriate) shall be taken into account.

(4) Applicable percentage. For purposes of this subsection, the term "applicable percentage" means, with respect to obligations arising in any taxable year, the percentage determined by dividing—

(A) the portion of the aggregate face amount of such obligations outstanding as of the close of such taxable year in excess of $5,000,000, by

(B) the aggregate face amount of such obligations outstanding as of the close of such taxable year.

(5) Treatment as interest. Any amount payable under this subsection shall be taken into account in computing the amount of any deduction allowable to the taxpayer for interest paid or accrued during the taxable year.

(6) Regulations. The Secretary shall prescribe such regulations as may be necessary to carry out the provisions of this subsection including regulations providing for the application of this subsection in the case of contingent payments, short taxable years, and pass-thru entities.

(d) Pledges, etc., of installment obligations.

(1) In general. For purposes of section 453, if any indebtedness (hereinafter in this subsection referred to as "secured indebtedness") is secured by an installment obligation to which this section applies, the net proceeds of the secured indebtedness shall be treated as a payment received on such installment obligation as of the later of—

(A) the time the indebtedness becomes secured indebtedness, or

(B) the time the proceeds of such indebtedness are received by the taxpayer.

(2) Limitation based on total contract price. The amount treated as received under paragraph (1) by reason of any secured indebtedness shall not exceed the excess (if any) of—

(A) the total contract price, over

(B) any portion of the total contract price received under the contract before the later of the times referred to in subparagraph (A) or (B) of paragraph (1) (including amounts previously treated as received under paragraph (1) but not including amounts not taken into account by reason of paragraph (3)).

(3) Later payments treated as receipt of tax paid amounts. If any amount is treated as received under paragraph (1) with respect to any installment obligation, subsequent payments received on such obligation shall not be taken into account for purposes of section 453 to the extent that the aggregate of such subsequent payments does not exceed the aggregate amount treated as received under paragraph (1).

(4) Secured indebtedness. For purposes of this subsection indebtedness is secured by an installment obligation to the extent that payment of principal or interest on such indebtedness is directly secured (under the terms of the indebtedness or any underlying arrangements) by any interest in such installment obligation. A payment shall be treated as directly secured by an interest in an installment obligation to the extent an arrangement allows the taxpayer to satisfy all or a portion of the indebtedness with the installment obligation.

(e) Regulations.

The Secretary shall prescribe such regulations as may be necessary to carry out the purposes of this section, including regulations—

(1) disallowing the use of the installment method in whole or in part for transactions in which the rules of this section otherwise would be avoided through the use of related persons, pass-thru entities, or intermediaries, and

(2) providing that the sale of an interest in a partnership or other pass-thru entity will be treated as a sale of the proportionate share of the assets of the partnership or other entity.

In 1999, P.L. 106-170, Sec. 536(b), added a sentence at the end of para. (d)(4), effective for sales or other dispositions occurring on or after 12/17/99.

In 1993, P.L. 103-66, Sec. 13201(b)(4), added the last sentence of para. (c)(3), effective for tax. yrs. begin. after 12/31/92.

In 1989, P.L. 101-239, Sec. 7812(c)(2), substituted "(5)." for "(5)." in para. (b)(3), effective for dispositions in tax. yrs. begin. after 12/31/87 except as provided in Sec. 10202(e)(2), (3) and (5) of P.L. 100-203, reproduced in note of following Code Sec. 453.

—P.L. 101-239, Sec. 7815(g), amended para. (b)(3), effective for sales after 12/31/88, except as provided in Sec. 5076(c)(2) of P.L. 100-647, reproduced below.

Code Sec. 453A   Tax accounting

Prior to amendment, para. (b)(3) read as follows:

"(3) Exception for farm property. An installment obligation shall not be treated as described in paragraph (1) if it arises from the disposition of any property used or produced in the trade or business of farming (within the meaning of section 2032A(e)(4) or (5))."

—P.L. 101-239, Sec. 7821(a)(1), substituted "all such obligations held by the taxpayer" for "all obligations of the taxpayer described in paragraph (1)" in subpara. (b)(2)(B) . . . Sec. 7821(a)(2), substituted "before the later of the times referred to in subparagraph (A) or (B) of paragraph (1)" for "before such secured indebtedness was incurred" in subpara. (d)(2)(B) . . . Sec. 7821(a)(3), added "the time" before "the proceeds" in subpara. (d)(1)(B) . . . Sec. 7821(a)(4)(B), redesignated para. (c)(5) as (c)(6) and added new para. (c)(5), effective for dispositions in tax. yrs. begin. after 12/31/87, except as provided in Sec. 10202(e)(2), (3) and (5) of P.L. 100-203, reproduced in note following Code Sec. 453.

In **1988**, P.L. 100-647, Sec. 1008(g)(2), substituted "453(k)" for "453(j)" in subsec. (c), effective 10/22/86.

—P.L. 100-647, Sec. 2004(d)(2), added subsec. (e) . . . Sec. 2004(d)(7), added "and subsection (c)(4)" after "for purposes of this paragraph" in para. (b)(2) . . . Sec. 2004(d)(8), amended para. (b)(3), effective for dispositions in tax. yrs. begin. after 12/31/87, except as provided in Sec. 10202(e)(2), (3) and (5) of P.L. 100-203, reproduced in note following Code Sec. 453.

Prior to amendment, para. (b)(3) read as follows:

"(3) Exception for personal use and farm property. An installment obligation shall not be treated as described in paragraph (1) if it arises from the disposition—

"(A) by an individual of personal use property (within the meaning of section 1275(b)(3)), or

"(B) of any property used or produced in the trade or business of farming (within the meaning of section 2032A(e)(4) or (5))."

—P.L. 100-647, Sec. 5076(a), amended para. (b)(1) . . . Sec. 5076(b)(1), deleted "of real property" after "nondealers" from the heading of Code Sec. 453A, effective for sales after 12/31/88, except as provided in Sec. 5076(c)(2) of this Act which reads as follows:

"(2) Binding contract, etc.—The amendments made by this section shall not apply to any sale on or before December 31, 1990, if—

"(A) such sale is pursuant to a written binding contract in effect on October 21, 1988, and at all times thereafter before such sale,

"(B) such sale is pursuant to a letter of intent in effect on October 21, 1988, or

"(C) there is a board of directors or shareholder approval for such sale on or before October 21, 1988."

Prior to amendment, para. (b)(1) read as follows:

"(1) In general. This section shall apply to any obligation which arises from the disposition of real property under the installment method which is property used in the taxpayer's trade or business or property held for the production of rental income, but only if the sales price of such property exceeds $150,000."

—P.L. 100-647, Sec. 6031, provides the following:

"SEC. 6031. CERTAIN REPLEDGES PERMITTED.

"(a) General rule.— Section 453A(d) of the 1986 Code (relating to pledges, etc., of installment obligations) shall not apply to any pledge after December 17, 1987, of an installment obligation to secure any indebtedness if such indebtedness is incurred to refinance indebtedness which was outstanding on December 17, 1987, and which was secured on such date and all times thereafter before such refinancing by a pledge of such installment obligation.

"(b) Limitation.— Subsection (a) shall not apply to the extent that the principal amount of the indebtedness resulting from the refinancing exceeds the principal amount of the refinanced indebtedness immediately before the refinancing.

"(c) Certain refinancings permitted.— For purposes of subsection (a), if—

"(1) a refinancing is attributable to the calling of indebtedness by the creditor, and

"(2) such refinancing is not with the creditor under the refinanced indebtedness or a person related to such creditor,

such refinancing shall, to the extent the refinanced indebtedness qualifies under subsections (a) and (b), be treated as a continuation of such refinanced indebtedness."

In **1987**, P.L. 100-203, Sec. 10202(c), [sic 10202(c)(1)], amended Code Sec. 453A, effective for dispositions in tax. yrs. begin. after 12/31/87, except as provided in Sec. 10202(e)(2), (3), and (5) of this Act, reproduced in note following Code Sec. 453.

Prior to amendment by Sec. 10202(c) of this Act, Code Sec. 453A [as amended by Sec. 1008(g)(2) of P.L. 100-647, see above] read as follows:

"SEC. 453A. INSTALLMENT METHOD FOR DEALERS IN PERSONAL PROPERTY.

"(a) General rule.

"(1) In general. Under regulations prescribed by the Secretary, a person who regularly sells or otherwise disposes of personal property on the installment plan may return as income therefrom in any taxable year that proportion of the installment payments actually received in that year which the gross profit, realized or to be realized when payment is completed, bears to the total contract price.

"(2) Total contract price. For purposes of paragraph (1), the total contract price of all sales of personal property on the installment plan includes the amount of carrying charges or interest which is determined with respect to such sales and is added on the books of account of the seller to the established cash selling price of such property.

"(b) Carrying charges not included in total contract price.

"If the carrying charges or interest with respect to sales of personal property, the income from which is returned under subsection (a)(1), is not included in the total contract price, payments received with respect to such sales shall be treated as applying first against such carrying charges or interest.

"(c) Cross reference.

"For disallowance of use of installment method for certain obligations, see section 453(k)."

In **1986**, P.L. 99-514, Sec. 812(b)(1), deleted "This paragraph shall not apply with respect to sales of personal property under a revolving credit type plan." from the end of para. (a)(2) . . . Sec. 812(b)(2), added subsec. (c), effective 10/22/86. See Sec. 812(c)(2) of this Act reproduced in note following Code Sec. 453.

In **1980**, P.L. 96-471, Sec. 2(a), added Code Sec. 453A, effective for tax. yrs. end. after 10/19/80. For tax. yrs. end. before 10/20/80, see former Code Sec. 453 in note following Code Sec. 453.

Sec. 453B. Gain or loss on disposition of installment obligations.

(a) General rule.

If an installment obligation is satisfied at other than its face value or distributed, transmitted, sold, or otherwise disposed of, gain or loss shall result to the extent of the difference between the basis of the obligation and—

(1) the amount realized, in the case of satisfaction at other than face value or a sale or exchange, or

(2) the fair market value of the obligation at the time of distribution, transmission, or disposition, in the case of the distribution, transmission, or disposition otherwise than by sale or exchange.

Any gain or loss so resulting shall be considered as resulting from the sale or exchange of the property in respect of which the installment obligation was received.

(b) Basis of obligation.

The basis of an installment obligation shall be the excess of the face value of the obligation over an amount equal to the income which would be returnable were the obligation satisfied in full.

(c) Special rule for transmission at death.

Except as provided in section 691 (relating to recipients of income in respect of decedents), this section shall not apply to the transmission of installment obligations at death.

(d) Exception for distributions to which section 337(a) applies.

Subsection (a) shall not apply to any distribution to which section 337(a) applies.

(e) Life insurance companies.

(1) In general. In the case of a disposition of an installment obligation by any person other than a life insurance company (as defined in section 816(a)) to such an insurance company or to a partnership of which such an insurance company is a partner, no provision of this subtitle providing for the nonrecognition of gain shall apply with respect to any gain resulting under subsection (a). If a corporation which is a life insurance company for the taxable year was (for the preceding taxable year) a corporation which was not a life insurance company, such corporation shall, for purposes of this subsection and subsection (a), be treated as having transferred to a life insurance company, on the last day of the preceding taxable year, all installment obligations which it held on such last day. A partnership of which a life insurance company becomes a partner shall, for purposes of this subsection and subsection (a), be treated as having transferred to a life insurance company, on the last day of the preceding taxable year of such partnership, all installment obligations which it holds at the time such life insurance company becomes a partner.

(2) Special rule where life insurance company elects to treat income as not related to insurance business. Paragraph (1) shall not apply to any transfer or deemed transfer of an installment obligation if the life insurance company elects (at such time and in such manner as the Secretary may by regulations prescribe) to determine its life insurance company taxable income—

Tax accounting
Code Sec. 453C

(A) by returning the income on such installment obligation under the installment method prescribed in section 453, and

(B) as if such income were an item attributable to a noninsurance business (as defined in section 806(b)(3)).

(f) Obligation becomes unenforceable.

For purposes of this section, if any installment obligation is canceled or otherwise becomes unenforceable—

(1) the obligation shall be treated as if it were disposed of in a transaction other than a sale or exchange, and

(2) if the obligor and obligee are related persons (within the meaning of section 453(f)(1)), the fair market value of the obligation shall be treated as not less than its face amount.

(g) Transfers between spouses or incident to divorce.

In the case of any transfer described in subsection (a) of section 1041 (other than a transfer in trust)—

(1) subsection (a) of this section shall not apply, and

(2) the same tax treatment with respect to the transferred installment obligation shall apply to the transferee as would have applied to the transferor.

(h) Certain liquidating distributions by S corporations.

If—

(1) an installment obligation is distributed by an S corporation in a complete liquidation, and

(2) receipt of the obligation is not treated as payment for the stock by reason of section 453(h)(1),

then, except for purposes of any tax imposed by subchapter S, no gain or loss with respect to the distribution of the obligation shall be recognized by the distributing corporation. Under regulations prescribed by the Secretary, the character of the gain or loss to the shareholder shall be determined in accordance with the principles of section 1366(b).

In 1990, P.L. 101-508, Sec. 11702(a)(2), amended subsec. (d), effective as provided in Sec. 633(a)(1) of P.L. 99-514, reproduced below.
Prior to amendment, subsec. (d) read as follows:
"(d) Effect of distribution in liquidations to which section 332 applies.
If—
"(1) an installment obligation is distributed in a liquidation to which section 332 (relating to complete liquidations of subsidiaries) applies, and
"(2) the basis of such obligation in the hands of the distributee is determined under section 334(b)(1),
then no gain or loss with respect to the distribution of such obligation shall be recognized by the distributing corporation."
In 1988, P.L. 100-647, Sec. 1006(e)(22), added subsec. (h), effective as provided in Sec. 633(a)(1) of P.L. 99-514, reproduced below.
In 1986, P.L. 99-514, Sec. 631(e)(9), amended subsec. (d), effective as provided in Sec. 633(a)(1) of this Act, which read as follows:
"(a) General rule.—
"Except as otherwise provided in this section [Sec. 633], the amendments made by [Subtitle D] shall apply to—
"(1) any distribution in complete liquidation, and any sale or exchange, made by a corporation after July 31, 1986, unless such corporation is completely liquidated before January 1, 1987,"
Sec. 633(d) [sic (e)] of this Act provides:
"(d) [sic (e)] Complete liquidation defined.—
"For purposes of this section, a corporation shall be treated as completely liquidated if all of the assets of such corporation are distributed in complete liquidation, less assets retained to meet claims."
Prior to amendment, subsec. (d) read as follows:
"(d) Effect of distribution in certain liquidations.
"(1) Liquidations to which section 332 applies. If—
"(A) an installment obligation is distributed in a liquidation to which section 332 (relating to complete liquidations of subsidiaries) applies, and
"(B) the basis of such obligation in the hands of the distributee is determined under section 334(b)(1).
then no gain or loss with respect to the distribution of such obligation shall be recognized by the distributing corporation.
"(2) Liquidations to which section 337 applies. If—
"(A) an installment obligation is distributed by a corporation in the course of a liquidation, and
"(B) under section 337 (relating to gain or loss on sales or exchanges in connection with certain liquidations) no gain or loss would have been recognized to the corporation if the corporation had sold or exchanged such installment obligation on the day of such distribution,

then no gain or loss shall be recognized to such corporation by reason of such distribution. The preceding sentence shall not apply to the extent that under subsection (a) gain to the distributing corporation would be considered as gain to which section 341(f), 617(d)(1), 1245(a), 1250(a), 1252(a), 1254(a), or 1276(a) applies. In the case of any installment obligation which would have met the requirements of subparagraphs (A) and (B) of the first sentence of this paragraph but for section 337(f), gain shall be recognized to such corporation by reason of such distribution only to the extent gain would have been recognized under section 337(f) if such corporation had sold or exchanged such installment obligation on the date of such distribution."
—P.L. 99-514, Sec. 1011(b)(1), substituted "806(b)(3)" for "806(c)(3)" in subpara. (e)(2)(B), effective for tax. yrs. begin. after 12/31/86.
—P.L. 99-514, Sec. 1842(c), substituted "section 1041 (other than a transfer in trust)" for "section 1041" in subsec. (g), effective for transfers after 7/18/84 in tax. yrs. end. after 7/18/84.
In 1984, P.L. 98-369, Sec. 43(c)(2), substituted "1254(a), or 1276(a)" for "or 1254(a)" in para. (d)(2), effective for tax. yrs. end. after 7/18/84.
—P.L. 98-369, Sec. 211(b)(6)(A), substituted "section 816(a)" for "section 801(a)" in para. (e)(1) . . . Sec. 211(b)(6)(B), amended para. (e)(2), effective for tax. yrs. begin. after 12/31/83. Sec. 217(b) of this Act provides:
"(b) Treatment of elections under section 453B(e)(2).—If an election is made under section 453B(e)(2) before January 1, 1984, with respect to any installment obligation, any income from such obligation shall be treated as attributable to a noninsurance business (as defined in section 806(c)(3) of the Internal Revenue Code of 1954)."
Prior to amendment, para. (e)(2) read as follows:
"(2) Special rule where life insurance company elects to treat income as investment income. Paragraph (1) shall not apply to any transfer or deemed transfer of an installment obligation if the life insurance company elects (at such time and in such manner as the Secretary may by regulations prescribe) to determine its life insurance company taxable income—
"(A) by returning the income on such installment obligation under the installment method prescribed in section 453, and
"(B) if such income would not otherwise be returnable as an item referred to in section 804(b) or as long-term capital gain, as if the income on such obligations were income specified in section 804(b)."
—P.L. 98-369, Sec. 421(b)(3), added subsec. (g), effective for transfers after 7/18/84 in tax. yrs. end. after 7/18/84.
—P.L. 98-369, Sec. 492(b)(3), deleted "1251(c)," after "1250(a)," in para. (d)(2), effective for tax. yrs. begin. after 12/31/83.
In 1983, P.L. 97-448, Sec. 302, substituted "to the extent that under subsection (a)" for "to the extent under paragraph (1)" in para. (d)(2), effective for dispositions made after 10/19/80, in tax. yrs. end. after 10/19/80.
In 1980, P.L. 96-471, Sec. 2(a), added Code Sec. 453B, effective for dispositions made after 10/19/80 in tax. yrs. end. after 10/19/80 [date of enactment] except for subsec. (f) which is effective for installment obligations becoming unenforceable after 10/19/80. For dispositions made before 10/20/80, see former Code Sec. 453 in note following Code Sec. 453.

Sec. 453C. Repealed.

In 1998, P.L. 105-206, Sec. 6010(q), added "more than 1 year" before "after the date" in Sec. 1088(b)(2)(C) of P.L. 105-34, see below.
In 1997, P.L. 105-34, Sec. 1088(a), repealed Sec. 811(c)(2) of P.L. 99-514, [see below] effective for tax. yrs. begin. after 8/5/97, except as provided in Sec. 1088(b)(2) of this Act [as amended by Sec. 6010(q) of 105-206, see above], which reads as follows:
"(2) Coordination with section 481. In the case of any taxpayer required by this section to change its method of accounting for any taxable year—
"(A) such changes shall be treated as initiated by the taxpayer,
"(B) such changes shall be treated as made with the consent of the Secretary of the Treasury, and
"(C) the net amount of the adjustments required to be taken into account under section 481(a) of the Internal Revenue Code of 1986 shall be taken into account ratably over the 4 taxable year period beginning with the first taxable year beginning more than 1 year after the date of the enactment of this Act."
Prior to repeal, Sec. 811(c)(2) of P.L. 99-514 read as follows:
"(2) Exception for certain sales of property by a manufacturer to a dealer.—
"(A) In general.—The amendments made by this section shall not apply to any installment obligation arising from the disposition of tangible personal property by a manufacturer (or any affiliate) to a dealer if—
"(i) the dealer is obligated to pay on such obligation only when the dealer resells (or rents) the property,
"(ii) the manufacturer has the right to repurchase the property at a fixed (or ascertainable) price after no later than the 9-month period beginning with the date of the sale, and
"(iii) such disposition is in a taxable year with respect to which the requirements of subparagraph (B) are met.
"(B) Receivables must be at least 50 percent of total sales.—
"(i) In general.—The requirements of this subparagraph are met with respect to any taxable year if for such taxable year and the preceding taxable year the aggregate face amount of installment obligations described in subparagraph (A) is at least 50 percent of the total sales to dealers giving rise to such obligations.
"(ii) Taxpayer must fail for 2 consecutive years.— A taxpayer shall be treated as failing to meet the requirements of clause (i) only if the taxpayer fails to meet the 50-percent test for both the taxable year and the preceding taxable year.

"(C) Transition rule. — An obligation issued before the date of the enactment of this Act shall be treated as described in subparagraph (A) if, within 60 days after such date, the taxpayer modifies the terms of such obligation to conform to the requirements of subparagraph (A).

"(D) Application with other obligations. — In applying section 453C of the Internal Revenue Code of 1986 to any installment obligations to which the amendments made by this section apply, obligations described in subparagraph (A) shall not be treated as applicable installment obligations (within the meaning of section 453C(e)(1) of such Code).

"(E) Other requirements. — This paragraph shall apply only if the taxpayer meets the requirements of subparagraphs (A) and (B) for its first taxable year beginning after the date of the enactment of this Act."

In 1988, P.L. 100-647, Sec. 1008(f)(1)(A), substituted "as of the close of" for "at any time during" in para. (b)(4) . . . Sec. 1008(f)(1)(B), substituted "as of the close of such taxable year (determined by not taking into account any indebtedness described in paragraph (3)(B) in lieu" for "as of the close of such taxable year in lieu" in para. (b)(4) . . . Sec. 1008(f)(2), amended so much of para. (d)(2) that precedes subpara. (d)(2)(A) . . . Sec. 1008(f)(3), added the last sentence of subpara. (e)(1)(A) . . . Sec. 1008(f)(4), substituted "Except as provided in regulations, for" for "For" in para. (e)(2) . . . Sec. 1008(f)(5), deleted "or (3)" after "(d)(2)" in subpara. (e)(4)(B), effective for tax. yrs. end. after 12/31/86, for dispositions made after 2/28/86, except as provided in Sec. 811(c)(2)-(9) of P.L. 99-514, reproduced below. Sec. 1008(f)(9) of this Act provides:

"(9) For purposes of applying the amendments made by this subsection and the amendments made by section 10202 of the Revenue Act of 1987, the provisions of this subsection shall be treated as having been enacted immediately before the enactment of the Revenue Act of 1987."

Prior to amendment, so much of para. (d)(2) that preceded subpara. (d)(2)(A) read as follows:

"(2) Excess allocable installment indebtedness. If, after application of paragraph (1), the allocable installment indebtedness for any taxable year exceeds the amount which may be allocated to applicable installment obligations arising in (and outstanding as of the close of) such taxable year, such excess shall—"

—P.L. 100-647, Sec. 1008(f)(6), amended Sec. 811(c)(4) P.L. 99-514 [reproduced below], part of the effective date for amendments made by Sec. 811(a) of P.L. 99-514, by deleting the second Sec. 811(c)(4)(D) and (E) of P.L. 99-514, see below . . . Sec. 1008(f)(7), substituted "October 23, 1984" for "October 23, 1985" each place it appeared in Sec. 811(c)(5) P.L. 99-514 [reproduced below] . . . Sec. 1008(f)(8), added Sec. 811(c)(9) of P.L. 99-514, reproduced below.

Prior to deletion the second Sec. 811(c)(4)(D) and (E) read as follows:

"(D) the portion of the net adjustment taken into account in the 1st taxable year of the taxpayer ending after December 31, 1986, shall not exceed 15 percent of such adjustment, and

"(E) the remaining portion of such adjustment shall be taken into account ratably in the 2nd, 3rd, and 4th years ending after December 31, 1986."

In 1987, P.L. 100-203, Sec. 10202(a)(1), repealed Code Sec. 453C, effective for dispositions in tax. yrs. begin. after 12/31/87, except as provided in Sec. 10202(e)(2), (3) and (5) of this Act, reproduced in note following Code Sec. 453. Prior to repeal, Code Sec. 453C [as amended by Sec. 1008(f)(1) of P.L. 100-647-(5), see above] read as follows:

"SEC. 453C. CERTAIN INDEBTEDNESS TREATED AS PAYMENT ON INSTALLMENT OBLIGATIONS.

"(a) General rule.

"For purposes of sections 453 and 453A, if a taxpayer has allocable installment indebtedness for any taxable year, such indebtedness—

"(1) shall be allocated on a pro rata basis to any applicable installment obligation of the taxpayer which—

"(A) arises in such taxable year, and

"(B) is outstanding as of the close of such taxable year, and

"(2) shall be treated as a payment received on such obligation as of the close of such taxable year.

"(b) Allocable installment indebtedness.

"For purposes of this section—

"(1) In general. The term 'allocable installment indebtedness' means, with respect to any taxable year, the excess (if any) of—

"(A) the installment percentage of the taxpayer's average quarterly indebtedness for such taxable year, over

"(B) the aggregate amount treated as allocable installment indebtedness with respect to applicable installment obligations which—

"(i) are outstanding as of the close of such taxable year, but

"(ii) did not arise during such taxable year.

"(2) Installment percentage. The term 'installment percentage' means the percentage (not in excess of 100 percent) determined by dividing—

"(A) the face amount of all applicable installment obligations of the taxpayer outstanding as of the close of the taxable year, by

"(B) the sum of—

"(i) the aggregate adjusted bases of all assets not described in clause (ii) held as of the close of the taxable year, and

"(ii) the face amount of all installment obligations outstanding as of such time.

For purposes of subparagraph (B)(i), a taxpayer may elect to compute the aggregate adjusted bases of all assets using the deduction for depreciation which is used in computing earnings and profits under section 312(k).

"(3) Special rules for personal use property. For purposes of this subsection—

"(A) for purposes of paragraph (2)(B), there shall not be taken into account any personal use property (within the meaning of section 1275(b)(3)) held by an individual or any installment obligation arising from the sale of such property, and

"(B) for purposes of computing the taxpayer's average quarterly indebtedness under paragraph (1)(A), there shall not be taken into account any indebtedness with respect to which substantially all of the property securing such indebtedness is property described in subparagraph (A).

"(4) Special rule for casual sales. If the taxpayer has no applicable installment obligations described in subclause (I) or (II) of subsection (e)(1)(A)(i) outstanding as of the close of the taxable year, then the taxpayer's allocable installment indebtedness for such taxable year shall be computed by using the taxpayer's indebtedness as of the close of such taxable year (determined by not taking into account any indebtedness described in paragraph (3)(B)) in lieu of the taxpayer's average quarterly indebtedness.

"(c) Treatment of subsequent payments.

"(1) Payments treated as receipt of tax paid amounts. If any amount is treated as received under subsection (a) (after application of subsection (d)(2)) with respect to any applicable installment obligation, subsequent payments received on such obligation shall not be taken into account for purposes of sections 453 and 453A to the extent that the aggregate amount of such subsequent payments does not exceed the aggregate amount treated as received on such obligation under subsection (a).

"(2) Reduction of allocable installment indebtedness. For purposes of applying subsection (b)(1)(B) for the taxable year in which any payment to which paragraph (1) of this subsection applies was received (and for any subsequent taxable year), the allocable installment indebtedness with respect to the applicable installment obligation shall be reduced (but not below zero) by the amount of such payment not taken into account by reason of paragraph (1).

"(d) Limitation based on total contract price.

"(1) In general. The amount treated as received under subsection (a) (after application of paragraph (2)) with respect to any applicable installment obligation for any taxable year shall not exceed the excess (if any) of—

"(A) the total contract price, over

"(B) any portion of the total contract price received under the contract before the close of such taxable year—

"(i) including amounts so treated under subsection (a) for all preceding taxable years (after application of paragraph (2)), but

"(ii) not including amounts not taken into account by reason of subsection (c).

"(2) Excess allocable installment indebtedness. If the allocable installment indebtedness for any taxable year exceeds the amount which may be allocated under paragraph (1) to applicable installment obligations arising in (and outstanding as of the close of) such taxable year, such excess shall—".

"(A) subject to the limitations of paragraph (1), be allocated to applicable installment obligations outstanding as of the close of such taxable year which arose in preceding taxable years, beginning with applicable installment obligations arising in the earliest preceding taxable year, and

"(B) be treated as a payment under subsection (a)(2).

"(e) Definitions and special rules.

"For purposes of this section—

"(1) Applicable installment obligation.

"(A) In general. The term 'applicable installment obligation' means any obligation—

"(i) which arises from the disposition—

"(I) after February 28, 1986, of personal property under the installment method by a person who regularly sells or otherwise disposes of personal property of the same type on the installment plan,

"(II) after February 28, 1986, of real property under the installment method which is held by the taxpayer for sale to customers in the ordinary course of the taxpayer's trade or business, or

"(III) after August 16, 1986, of real property under the installment method which is property used in the taxpayer's trade or business or property held for the production of rental income, but only if the sales price of such property exceeds $150,000 (determined after application of the rule under the last sentence of section 1274(c)(3)(A)(ii)), and

"(ii) which is held by the seller or a member of the same affiliated group (within the meaning of section 1504(a), but without regard to section 1504(b)) as the seller.

"Such term also includes any obligation held by any person if the basis of such obligation in the hands of such person is determined (in whole or in part) by reference to the basis of such obligation in the hands of another person and such obligation was an applicable installment obligation in the hands of such other person."

"(B) Exception for personal use and farm property. The term 'applicable installment obligation' shall not include any obligation which arises from the disposition—

"(i) by an individual of personal use property (within the meaning of section 1275(b)(3)), or

"(ii) of any property used or produced in the trade or business of farming (within the meaning of section 2032A(e)(4) or (5)).

"(2) Aggregation rules. Except as provided in regulations, for purposes of this section, all persons treated as a single employer under section 52 shall be treated as 1 taxpayer. The Secretary shall prescribe regulations for the treatment under this section of transactions between such persons.

"(3) Aggregation of obligations. The Secretary may by regulations provide that all (or any portion of) applicable installment obligations of a taxpayer may be treated as 1 obligation.

"(4) Exception for sales of timeshares and residential lots.

"(A) In general. If a taxpayer elects the application of this paragraph, this section shall not apply to any installment obligation which—

"(i) arises from a sale in the ordinary course of the taxpayer's trade or business to an individual of—

"(I) a timeshare right to use or a timeshare ownership interest in residential real property for not more than 6 weeks, or a right to use specified campgrounds for recreational purposes, or

"(II) any residential lot but only if the taxpayer (or any related person) is not to make any improvements with respect to such lot, and

"(ii) which is not guaranteed by any person other than an individual.

For purposes of clause (i)(I), a timeshare right to use (or timeshare ownership interest in) property held by the spouse, children, grandchildren, or parents of an individual shall be treated as held by such individual.

"(B) Interest on deferred tax. If subparagraph (A) applies to any installment obligation, interest shall be paid on the portion of any tax for any taxable year (determined without regard to any deduction allowable for such interest) which is attributable to the receipt of payments on such obligation in such year (other than payments received in the taxable year of the sale). Such interest shall be computed for the period from the date of the sale to the date on which the payment is received using the applicable Federal rate under section 1274 (without regard to subsection (d)(2) thereof) in effect at the time of the sale, compounded semiannually.

"(C) Time for payment. Any interest payable under this paragraph with respect to a payment shall be treated as an addition to tax for the taxable year in which the payment is received, except that the amount of such interest shall be taken into account in computing the amount of any deduction allowable to the taxpayer for interest paid or accrued during such taxable year.

"(5) Regulations. The Secretary shall prescribe regulations as may be necessary to carry out the purposes of this section, including regulations—

"(A) disallowing the use of the installment method in whole or in part for transactions in which the rules of this section otherwise would be avoided through the use of related parties, pass-through entities, or intermediaries,

"(B) providing for the proper treatment of reserves (including consistent treatment with assets held in the reserves), and

"(C) providing that subsection (b)(4) shall not apply where necessary to prevent the avoidance of the application of this section."

In 1986, P.L. 99-514, Sec. 811(a), added Code Sec. 453C, effective for tax. yrs. ending after 12/31/86, for dispositions after 2/28/86. Sec. 811(c)(2)-(9) [as amended by Sec. 1071(a) of 105-34, and Secs. 1008(f)(6)-(8) of P.L. 100-647, see above] of this Act provides:

"(2) [Repealed]

"(3) Exception for certain obligations.— In applying the amendments made by this section to any installment obligation of a corporation incorporated on January 13, 1928, the following indebtedness shall not be taken into account in determining the allocable installment indebtedness of such corporation under section 453C of the Internal Revenue Code of 1986 (as added by this section):

"(A) 12⅝ percent subordinated debentures with a total face amount of $175,000,000 issued pursuant to a trust indenture dated as of September 1, 1985.

"(B) A revolving credit term loan in the maximum amount of $130,000,000 made pursuant to a revolving credit and security agreement dated as of September 6, 1985, payable in various stages with final payment due on August 31, 1992. This paragraph shall also apply to indebtedness which replaces indebtedness described in this paragraph if such indebtedness does not exceed the amount and maturity of the indebtedness it replaces.

"(4) Special rule for residential condominium project.— For purposes of applying the amendments made by this section, the term applicable installment obligation (within the meaning of section 453C(e)(1) of the Internal Revenue Code of 1986) shall not include any obligation arising in connection with sales from a residential condominium project—

"(A) for which a contract to purchase land for the project was entered into at least 5 years before the date of the enactment of this Act,

"(B) with respect to which land for the project was purchased before September 26, 1985,

"(C) with respect to which building permits for the project were obtained, and construction commenced, before September 26, 1985,

"(D) in conjunction with which not less than 80 units of low-income housing are deeded to a tax-exempt organization designated by a local government, and

"(E) with respect to which at least $1,000,000 of expenses were incurred before September 26, 1985.

"(5) Special rule for qualified buyout.— The amendments made by this section shall apply for taxable years ending after December 31, 1991, to a corporation if—

"(A) such corporation was incorporated on May 25, 1984, for the purpose of acquiring all of the stock of another corporation,

"(B) such acquisition took place on October 23, 1984,

"(C) in connection with such acquisition, the corporation incurred indebtedness of approximately $151,000,000, and

"(D) substantially all of the stock of the corporation is owned directly or indirectly by employees of the corporation the stock of which was acquired on October 23, 1984.

"(6) Special rule for sales of real property by dealers.— In the case of installment obligations arising from the sale of real property in the ordinary course of the trade or business of the taxpayer, any gain attributable to allocable installment indebtedness allocated to any such installment obligations which arise (or are deemed to arise)—

"(A) in the 1st taxable year of the taxpayer ending after December 31, 1986, shall be taken into account ratably over the 3 taxable years beginning with such 1st taxable year, and

"(B) in the 2nd taxable year of the taxpayer ending after December 31, 1986, shall be taken into account ratably over the 2 taxable years beginning with such 2nd taxable year.

"(7) Special rule for sales of personal property by dealers.— In the case of installment obligations arising from the sale of personal property in the ordinary course of the trade or business of the taxpayer, solely for purposes of determining the time for payment of tax and interest payable with respect to such tax—

"(A) any increase in tax imposed by chapter 1 of the Internal Revenue Code of 1986 for the 1st taxable year of the taxpayer ending after December 31, 1986, by reason of the amendments made by this section shall be treated as imposed ratably over the 3 taxable years beginning with such 1st taxable year, and

"(B) any increase in tax imposed by such chapter 1 for the 2nd taxable year of the taxpayer ending after December 31, 1986 (determined without regard to subparagraph (A)), by reason of the amendments made by this section shall be treated as imposed ratably over the 2 taxable years beginning with such 2nd taxable year.

"(8) Treatment of certain installment obligations.— Notwithstanding the amendments made by subtitle B of title III, gain with respect to installment payments received pursuant to notes issued in accordance with a note agreement dated as of August 29, 1980, where—

"(A) such note agreement was executed pursuant to an agreement of purchase and sale dated April 25, 1980,

"(B) more than ½ of the installment payments of the aggregate principal of such notes have been received by August 29, 1986, and

"(C) the last installment payment of the principal of such notes is due August 29, 1989,

shall be taxed at a rate of 28 percent."

"(9) Special rules. For purposes of section 453C of the 1986 Code (as added by subsection (a))—

"(A) Revolving credit plans, etc. The term 'applicable installment obligation' shall not include any obligation arising out of any disposition or sale described in paragraph (1) or (2) of section 453(k) of such Code (as added by section 812(a)).

"(B) Certain dispositions deemed made on first day of taxable year. In the case of a taxpayer's 1st taxable year ending after December 31, 1986, dispositions after February 28, 1986, and before the 1st day of such taxable year shall be treated as made on such 1st day."

Sec. 454. Obligations issued at discount.

(a) Non-interest-bearing obligations issued at a discount.

If, in the case of a taxpayer owning any non-interest-bearing obligation issued at a discount and redeemable for fixed amounts increasing at stated intervals or owning an obligation described in paragraph (2) of subsection (c), the increase in the redemption price of such obligation occurring in the taxable year does not (under the method of accounting used in computing his taxable income) constitute income to him in such year, such taxpayer may, at his election made in his return for any taxable year, treat such increase as income received in such taxable year. If any such election is made with respect to any such obligation, it shall apply also to all such obligations owned by the taxpayer at the beginning of the first taxable year to which it applies and to all such obligations thereafter acquired by him and shall be binding for all subsequent taxable years, unless on application by the taxpayer the Secretary permits him, subject to such conditions as the Secretary deems necessary, to change to a different method. In the case of any such obligations owned by the taxpayer at the beginning of the first taxable year to which his election applies, the increase in the redemption price of such obligations occurring between the date of acquisition (or, in the case of an obligation described in paragraph (2) of subsection (c), the date of acquisition of the series E bond involved) and the first day of such taxable year shall also be treated as income received in such taxable year.

(b) Short-term obligations issued on discount basis.

In the case of any obligation—

(1) of the United States; or

(2) of a State or a possession of the United States, or any political subdivision of any of the foregoing, or of the District of Columbia,

which is issued on a discount basis and payable without interest at a fixed maturity date not exceeding 1 year from the date of issue, the amount of discount at which such obligation is originally sold shall not be considered to accrue until the date on which such obligation is paid at maturity, sold, or otherwise disposed of.

Code Sec. 454(c) — Tax accounting

(c) Matured United States savings bonds.
In the case of a taxpayer who—
(1) holds a series E United States savings bond at the date of maturity, and
(2) pursuant to regulations prescribed under chapter 31 of title 31 (A) retains his investment in such series E bond in an obligation of the United States, other than a current income obligation, or (B) exchanges such series E bond for another nontransferable obligation of the United States in an exchange upon which gain or loss is not recognized because of section 1037 (or so much of section 1031 as relates to section 1037),
the increase in redemption value (to the extent not previously includible in gross income) in excess of the amount paid for such series E bond shall be includible in gross income in the taxable year in which the obligation is finally redeemed or in the taxable year of final maturity, whichever is earlier. This subsection shall not apply to a corporation, and shall not apply in the case of any taxable year for which the taxpayer's taxable income is computed under an accrual method of accounting or for which an election made by the taxpayer under subsection (a) applies.

In 1983, P.L. 97-452, Sec. 2(c)(2), substituted "chapter 31 of title 31" for "the Second Liberty Bond Act" in para. (c)(2).
In 1976, P.L. 94-455, Sec. 1901(c)(2), deleted ", a Territory," after "of a State" in para. (b)(2), effective for tax. yrs. begin. after 12/31/76.
—P.L. 94-455, Sec. 1906(b)(13)(A), substituted "Secretary" for "Secretary or his delegate" each place it appeared in subsec. (a), effective 2/1/77.
In 1959, P.L. 86-346, Sec. 102, amended para. (c)(2), effective 9/22/59.
Prior to amendment, para. (c)(2) read as follows:
"(2) pursuant to regulations prescribed under the Second Liberty Bond Act retains his investment in the maturity value of such series E bond in an obligation, other than a current income obligation, which matures not more than 10 years from the date of maturity of such series E bond,
the increase in redemption value (to the extent not previously includible in gross income) in excess of the amount paid for such series E bond shall be includible in gross income in the taxable year in which the obligation is finally redeemed or in the taxable year of final maturity, whichever is earlier."

Sec. 455. Prepaid subscription income.

(a) Year in which included.
Prepaid subscription income to which this section applies shall be included in gross income for the taxable years during which the liability described in subsection (d)(2) exists.

(b) Where taxpayer's liability ceases.
In the case of any prepaid subscription income to which this section applies—
(1) If the liability described in subsection (d)(2) ends, then so much of such income as was not includible in gross income under subsection (a) for preceding taxable years shall be included in gross income for the taxable year in which the liability ends.
(2) If the taxpayer dies or ceases to exist, then so much of such income as was not includible in gross income under subsection (a) for preceding taxable years shall be included in gross income for the taxable year in which such death, or such cessation of existence, occurs.

(c) Prepaid subscription income to which this section applies.
(1) **Election of benefits.** This section shall apply to prepaid subscription income if and only if the taxpayer makes an election under this section with respect to the trade or business in connection with which such income is received. The election shall be made in such manner as the Secretary may by regulations prescribe. No election may be made with respect to a trade or business if in computing taxable income the cash receipts and disbursements method of accounting is used with respect to such trade or business.

(2) **Scope of election.** An election made under this section shall apply to all prepaid subscription income received in connection with the trade or business with respect to which the taxpayer has made the election; except that the taxpayer may, to the extent permitted under regulations prescribed by the Secretary, include in gross income for the taxable year of receipt the entire amount of any prepaid subscription income if the liability from which it arose is to end within 12 months after the date of receipt. An election made under this section shall not apply to any prepaid subscription income received before the first taxable year for which the election is made.

(3) **When election may be made.**
(A) With consent. A taxpayer may, with the consent of the Secretary, make an election under this section at any time.
(B) Without consent. A taxpayer may, without the consent of the Secretary, make an election under this section for his first taxable year in which he receives prepaid subscription income in the trade or business. Such election shall be made not later than the time prescribed by law for filing the return for the taxable year (including extensions thereof) with respect to which such election is made.

(4) **Period to which election applies.** An election under this section shall be effective for the taxable year with respect to which it is first made and for all subsequent taxable years, unless the taxpayer secures the consent of the Secretary to the revocation of such election. For purposes of this title, the computation of taxable income under an election made under this section shall be treated as a method of accounting.

(d) Definitions.
For purposes of this section—
(1) **Prepaid subscription income.** The term "prepaid subscription income" means any amount (includible in gross income) which is received in connection with, and is directly attributable to, a liability which extends beyond the close of the taxable year in which such amount is received, and which is income from a subscription to a newspaper, magazine, or other periodical.
(2) **Liability.** The term "liability" means a liability to furnish or deliver a newspaper, magazine, or other periodical.
(3) **Receipt of prepaid subscription income.** Prepaid subscription income shall be treated as received during the taxable year for which it is includible in gross income under section 451 (without regard to this section).

(e) Deferral of income under established accounting procedures.
Notwithstanding the provisions of this section, any taxpayer who has, for taxable years prior to the first taxable year to which this section applies, reported his income under an established and consistent method or practice of accounting for prepaid subscription income (to which this section would apply if an election were made) may continue to report his income for taxable years to which this title applies in accordance with such method or practice.

In 1976, P.L. 94-455, Sec. 1901(a)(67), substituted "for his first taxable year in which he receives prepaid subscription income in the trade or business" for "for his first taxable year (i) which begins after December 31, 1957, and (ii) in which he receives prepaid subscription income in the trade or business" in subpara. (c)(3)(B), effective for tax. yrs. begin. after 12/31/76.
—P.L. 94-455, Sec. 1906(b)(13)(A), substituted "Secretary" for "Secretary or his delegate" each place it appeared in Code Sec. 455, effective for tax. yrs. begin. after 12/31/76.
In 1958, P.L. 85-866, Sec. 28, added Code Sec. 455, effective for tax. yrs. begin. after 12/31/57.

Sec. 456. Prepaid dues income of certain membership organizations.

(a) Year in which included.

Prepaid dues income to which this section applies shall be included in gross income for the taxable years during which the liability described in subsection (e)(2) exists.

(b) Where taxpayer's liability ceases.

In the case of any prepaid dues income to which this section applies—

(1) If the liability described in subsection (e)(2) ends, then so much of such income as was not includible in gross income under subsection (a) for preceding taxable years shall be included in gross income for the taxable year in which the liability ends.

(2) If the taxpayer ceases to exist, then so much of such income as was not includible in gross income under subsection (a) for preceding taxable years shall be included in gross income for the taxable year in which such cessation of existence occurs.

(c) Prepaid dues income to which this section applies.

(1) **Election of benefits.** This section shall apply to prepaid dues income if and only if the taxpayer makes an election under this section with respect to the trade or business in connection with which such income is received. The election shall be made in such manner as the Secretary may by regulations prescribe. No election may be made with respect to a trade or business if in computing taxable income the cash receipts and disbursements method of accounting is used with respect to such trade or business.

(2) **Scope of election.** An election made under this section shall apply to all prepaid dues income received in connection with the trade or business with respect to which the taxpayer has made the election; except that the taxpayer may, to the extent permitted under regulations prescribed by the Secretary, include in gross income for the taxable year of receipt the entire amount of any prepaid dues income if the liability from which it arose is to end within 12 months after the date of receipt. Except as provided in subsection (d), an election made under this section shall not apply to any prepaid dues income received before the first taxable year for which the election is made.

(3) **When election may be made.**

(A) With consent. A taxpayer may, with the consent of the Secretary, make an election under this section at any time.

(B) Without consent. A taxpayer may, without the consent of the Secretary, make an election under this section for its first taxable year in which it receives prepaid dues income in the trade or business. Such election shall be made not later than the time prescribed by law for filing the return for the taxable year (including extensions thereof) with respect to which such election is made.

(4) **Period to which election applies.** An election under this section shall be effective for the taxable year with respect to which it is first made and for all subsequent taxable years, unless the taxpayer secures the consent of the Secretary to the revocation of such election. For purposes of this title, the computation of taxable income under an election made under this section shall be treated as a method of accounting.

(d) Transitional rule.

(1) **Amount includible in gross income for election years.** If a taxpayer makes an election under this section with respect to prepaid dues income, such taxpayer shall include in gross income, for each taxable year to which such election applies, not only that portion of prepaid dues income received in such year otherwise includible in gross income for such year under this section, but shall also include in gross income for such year an additional amount equal to the amount of prepaid dues income received in the 3 taxable years preceding the first taxable year to which such election applies which would have been included in gross income in the taxable year had the election been effective 3 years earlier.

(2) **Deductions of amounts included in income more than once.** A taxpayer who makes an election with respect to prepaid dues income, and who includes in gross income for any taxable year to which the election applies an additional amount computed under paragraph (1), shall be permitted to deduct, for such taxable year and for each of the 4 succeeding taxable years, an amount equal to one-fifth of such additional amount, but only to the extent that such additional amount was also included in the taxpayer's gross income during any of the 3 taxable years preceding the first taxable year to which such election applies.

(e) Definitions.

For purposes of this section—

(1) **Prepaid dues income.** The term "prepaid dues income" means any amount (includible in gross income) which is received by a membership organization in connection with, and is directly attributable to, a liability to render services or make available membership privileges over a period of time which extends beyond the close of the taxable year in which such amount is received.

(2) **Liability.** The term "liability" means a liability to render services or make available membership privileges over a period of time which does not exceed 36 months, which liability shall be deemed to exist ratably over the period of time that such services are required to be rendered, or that such membership privileges are required to be made available.

(3) **Membership organization.** The term "membership organization" means a corporation, association, federation, or other organization—

(A) organized without capital stock of any kind, and

(B) no part of the net earnings of which is distributable to any member.

(4) **Receipt of prepaid dues income.** Prepaid dues income shall be treated as received during the taxable year for which it is includible in gross income under section 451 (without regard to this section).

In **1976**, P.L. 94-455, Sec. 1901(a)(68), substituted "for its first taxable year" for "for its first taxable year (i) which begins after December 31, 1960, and (ii)" in subpara. (c)(3)(B), effective for tax. yrs. begin. after 12/31/76.
—P.L. 94-455, Sec. 1906(b)(13)(A), substituted "Secretary" for "Secretary or his delegate" each place it appeared in Code Sec. 456, effective for tax. yrs. begin. after 12/31/76.
In **1961**, P.L. 87-109, Sec. 1(a), added Code Sec. 456, effective for tax. yrs. begin. after 1960.

Sec. 457. Deferred compensation plans of state and local governments and tax-exempt organizations.

(a) Year of inclusion in gross income.

(1) **In general.** Any amount of compensation deferred under an eligible deferred compensation plan, and any income attributable to the amounts so deferred, shall be includible in gross income only for the taxable year in which such compensation or other income—

(A) is paid to the participant or other beneficiary, in the case of a plan of an eligible employer described in subsection (e)(1)(A), and

(B) is paid or otherwise made available to the participant or other beneficiary, in the case of a plan of an eligible employer described in subsection (e)(1)(B).

(2) Special rule for rollover amounts. To the extent provided in section 72(t)(9), section 72(t) shall apply to any amount includible in gross income under this subsection.

(3) Special rule for health and long-term care insurance. In the case of a plan of an eligible employer described in subsection (e)(1)(A), to the extent provided in section 402(l), paragraph (1) shall not apply to amounts otherwise includible in gross income under this subsection.

(b) Eligible deferred compensation plan defined.

For purposes of this section, the term "eligible deferred compensation plan" means a plan established and maintained by an eligible employer—

(1) in which only individuals who perform service for the employer may be participants,

(2) which provides that (except as provided in paragraph (3)) the maximum amount which may be deferred under the plan for the taxable year (other than rollover amounts) shall not exceed the lesser of—

(A) the applicable dollar amount, or

(B) 100 percent of the participant's includible compensation,

(3) which may provide that, for 1 or more of the participant's last 3 taxable years ending before he attains normal retirement age under the plan, the ceiling set forth in paragraph (2) shall be the lesser of—

(A) twice the dollar amount in effect under subsection (b)(2)(A), or

(B) the sum of—

(i) the plan ceiling established for purposes of paragraph (2) for the taxable year (determined without regard to this paragraph), plus

(ii) so much of the plan ceiling established for purposes of paragraph (2) for taxable years before the taxable year as has not previously been used under paragraph (2) or this paragraph,

(4) which provides that compensation will be deferred for any calendar month only if an agreement providing for such deferral has been entered into before the beginning of such month,

(5) which meets the distribution requirements of subsection (d), and

(6) except as provided in subsection (g) which provides that—

(A) all amounts of compensation deferred under the plan,

(B) all property and rights purchased with such amounts, and

(C) all income attributable to such amounts, property, or rights,

shall remain (until made available to the participant or other beneficiary) solely the property and rights of the employer (without being restricted to the provision of benefits under the plan), subject only to the claims of the employer's general creditors.

A plan which is established and maintained by an employer which is described in subsection (e)(1)(A) and which is administered in a manner which is inconsistent with the requirements of any of the preceding paragraphs shall be treated as not meeting the requirements of such paragraph as of the 1st plan year beginning more than 180 days after the date of notification by the Secretary of the inconsistency unless the employer corrects the inconsistency before the 1st day of such plan year.

(c) Limitation.

The maximum amount of the compensation of any one individual which may be deferred under subsection (a) during any taxable year shall not exceed the amount in effect under subsection (b)(2)(A) (as modified by any adjustment provided under subsection (b)(3)).

(d) Distribution requirements.

(1) In general. For purposes of subsection (b)(5), a plan meets the distribution requirements of this subsection if—

(A) under the plan amounts will not be made available to participants or beneficiaries earlier than—

(i) the calendar year in which the participant attains age 70½,

(ii) when the participant has a severance from employment with the employer, or

(iii) when the participant is faced with an unforeseeable emergency (determined in the manner prescribed by the Secretary in regulations),

(B) the plan meets the minimum distribution requirements of paragraph (2), and

(C) in the case of a plan maintained by an employer described in subsection (e)(1)(A), the plan meets requirements similar to the requirements of section 401(a)(31).

Any amount transferred in a direct trustee-to-trustee transfer in accordance with section 401(a)(31) shall not be includible in gross income for the taxable year of transfer.

(2) Minimum distribution requirements. A plan meets the minimum distribution requirements of this paragraph if such plan meets the requirements of section 401(a)(9).

(3) Special rule for government plan. An eligible deferred compensation plan of an employer described in subsection (e)(1)(A) shall not be treated as failing to meet the requirements of this subsection solely by reason of making a distribution described in subsection (e)(9)(A).

(e) Other definitions and special rules.

For purposes of this section—

(1) Eligible employer. The term "eligible employer" means—

(A) a State, political subdivision of a State, and any agency or instrumentality of a State or political subdivision of a State, and

(B) any other organization (other than a governmental unit) exempt from tax under this subtitle.

(2) Performance of service. The performance of service includes performance of service as an independent contractor and the person (or governmental unit) for whom such services are performed shall be treated as the employer.

(3) Participant. The term "participant" means an individual who is eligible to defer compensation under the plan.

(4) Beneficiary. The term "beneficiary" means a beneficiary of the participant, his estate, or any other person whose interest in the plan is derived from the participant.

(5) Includible compensation. The term "includible compensation" has the meaning given to the term "participant's compensation" by section 415(c)(3).

(6) Compensation taken into account at present value. Compensation shall be taken into account at its present value.

(7) Community property laws. The amount of includible compensation shall be determined without regard to any community property laws.

(8) Income attributable. Gains from the disposition of property shall be treated as income attributable to such property.

(9) Benefits of tax exempt organization plans not treated as made available by reason of certain elections, etc. In the case of an eligible deferred compensation plan of an employer described in subsection (e)(1)(B)—

(A) Total amount payable is dollar limit or less. The total amount payable to a participant under the plan shall not be treated as made available merely because the participant may elect to receive such amount (or the plan may distribute such amount without the participant's consent) if—

(i) the portion of such amount which is not attributable to rollover contributions (as defined in section 411(a)(11)(D)) does not exceed the dollar limit under section 411(a)(11)(A), and

(ii) such amount may be distributed only if—

(I) no amount has been deferred under the plan with respect to such participant during the 2-year period ending on the date of the distribution, and

(II) there has been no prior distribution under the plan to such participant to which this subparagraph applied.

A plan shall not be treated as failing to meet the distribution requirements of subsection (d) by reason of a distribution to which this subparagraph applies.

(B) Election to defer commencement of distributions. The total amount payable to a participant under the plan shall not be treated as made available merely because the participant may elect to defer commencement of distributions under the plan if—

(i) such election is made after amounts may be available under the plan in accordance with subsection (d)(1)(A) and before commencement of such distributions, and

(ii) the participant may make only 1 such election.

(10) Transfers between plans. A participant shall not be required to include in gross income any portion of the entire amount payable to such participant solely by reason of the transfer of such portion from 1 eligible deferred compensation plan to another eligible deferred compensation plan.

(11) Certain plans excluded.

(A) In general. The following plans shall be treated as not providing for the deferral of compensation:

(i) Any bona fide vacation leave, sick leave, compensatory time, severance pay, disability pay, or death benefit plan.

(ii) Any plan paying solely length of service awards to bona fide volunteers (or their beneficiaries) on account of qualified services performed by such volunteers.

(B) Special rules applicable to length of service award plans.

(i) Bona fide volunteer. An individual shall be treated as a bona fide volunteer for purposes of subparagraph (A)(ii) if the only compensation received by such individual for performing qualified services is in the form of—

(I) reimbursement for (or a reasonable allowance for) reasonable expenses incurred in the performance of such services, or

(II) reasonable benefits (including length of service awards), and nominal fees for such services, customarily paid by eligible employers in connection with the performance of such services by volunteers.

(ii) Limitation on accruals. A plan shall not be treated as described in subparagraph (A)(ii) if the aggregate amount of length of service awards accruing with respect to any year of service for any bona fide volunteer exceeds $3,000.

(C) Qualified services. For purposes of this paragraph, the term "qualified services" means fire fighting and prevention services, emergency medical services, and ambulance services.

(D) Certain voluntary early retirement incentive plans.

(i) In general. If an applicable voluntary early retirement incentive plan—

(I) makes payments or supplements as an early retirement benefit, a retirement-type subsidy, or a benefit described in the last sentence of section 411(a)(9), and

(II) such payments or supplements are made in coordination with a defined benefit plan which is described in section 401(a) and includes a trust exempt from tax under section 501(a) and which is maintained by an eligible employer described in paragraph (1)(A) or by an education association described in clause (ii)(II),

such applicable plan shall be treated for purposes of subparagraph (A)(i) as a bona fide severance pay plan with respect to such payments or supplements to the extent such payments or supplements could otherwise have been provided under such defined benefit plan (determined as if section 411 applied to such defined benefit plan).

(ii) Applicable voluntary early retirement incentive plan. For purposes of this subparagraph, the term "applicable voluntary early retirement incentive plan" means a voluntary early retirement incentive plan maintained by—

(I) a local educational agency (as defined in section 9101 of the Elementary and Secondary Education Act of 1965 (20 U.S.C. 7801)), or

(II) an education association which principally represents employees of 1 or more agencies described in subclause (I) and which is described in section 501(c)(5) or (6) and exempt from tax under section 501(a).

(12) Exception for nonelective deferred compensation of nonemployees.

(A) In general. This section shall not apply to nonelective deferred compensation attributable to services not performed as an employee.

(B) Nonelective deferred compensation. For purposes of subparagraph (A), deferred compensation shall be treated as nonelective only if all individuals (other than those who have not satisfied any applicable initial service requirement) with the same relationship to the payor are covered under the same plan with no individual variations or options under the plan.

(13) Special rule for churches. The term "eligible employer" shall not include a church (as defined in section 3121(w)(3)(A)) or qualified church-controlled organization (as defined in section 3121(w)(3)(B)).

(14) Treatment of qualified governmental excess benefit arrangements. Subsections (b)(2) and (c)(1) shall not apply to any qualified governmental excess benefit arrangement (as defined in section 415(m)(3)), and benefits provided under such an arrangement shall not be taken into account in determining whether any other plan is an eligible deferred compensation plan.

(15) Applicable dollar amount.

(A) In general. The applicable dollar amount shall be the amount determined in accordance with the following table:

For taxable years beginning in calendar year:	The applicable dollar amount:
2002	$11,000
2003	$12,000
2004	$13,000
2005	$14,000
2006 or thereafter	$15,000

(B) Cost-of-living adjustments. In the case of taxable years beginning after December 31, 2006, the Secretary shall adjust the $15,000 amount under subparagraph (A) at the same time and in the same manner as under section 415(d), except that the base period shall be the calendar quarter beginning July 1, 2005, and any increase under this paragraph which is not a multiple of $500 shall be rounded to the next lowest multiple of $500.

(16) Rollover amounts.

(A) General rule. In the case of an eligible deferred compensation plan established and maintained by an employer described in subsection (e)(1)(A), if—

(i) any portion of the balance to the credit of an employee in such plan is paid to such employee in an eligible rollover distribution (within the meaning of section 402(c)(4)),

(ii) the employee transfers any portion of the property such employee receives in such distribution to an eligible retirement plan described in section 402(c)(8)(B), and

(iii) in the case of a distribution of property other than money, the amount so transferred consists of the property distributed,

then such distribution (to the extent so transferred) shall not be includible in gross income for the taxable year in which paid.

(B) Certain rules made applicable. The rules of paragraphs (2) through (7), (9), and (11) of section 402(c) and section 402(f) shall apply for purposes of subparagraph (A).

(C) Reporting. Rollovers under this paragraph shall be reported to the Secretary in the same manner as rollovers from qualified retirement plans (as defined in section 4974(c)).

(17) Trustee-to-trustee transfers to purchase permissive service credit. No amount shall be includible in gross income by reason of a direct trustee-to-trustee transfer to a defined benefit governmental plan (as defined in section 414(d)) if such transfer is—

(A) for the purchase of permissive service credit (as defined in section 415(n)(3)(A)) under such plan, or

(B) a repayment to which section 415 does not apply by reason of subsection (k)(3) thereof.

(18) Coordination with catch-up contributions for individuals age 50 or older. In the case of an individual who is an eligible participant (as defined by section 414(v)) and who is a participant in an eligible deferred compensation plan of an employer described in paragraph (1)(A), subsections (b)(3) and (c) shall be applied by substituting for the amount otherwise determined under the applicable subsection the greater of—

(A) the sum of—

(i) the plan ceiling established for purposes of subsection (b)(2) (without regard to subsection (b)(3)), plus

(ii) the applicable dollar amount for the taxable year determined under section 414(v)(2)(B)(i), or

(B) the amount determined under the applicable subsection (without regard to this paragraph).

(f) Tax treatment of participants where plan or arrangement of employer is not eligible.

(1) In general. In the case of a plan of an eligible employer providing for a deferral of compensation, if such plan is not an eligible deferred compensation plan, then—

(A) the compensation shall be included in the gross income of the participant or beneficiary for the 1st taxable year in which there is no substantial risk of forfeiture of the rights to such compensation, and

(B) the tax treatment of any amount made available under the plan to a participant or beneficiary shall be determined under section 72 (relating to annuities, etc.).

(2) Exceptions. Paragraph (1) shall not apply to—

(A) a plan described in section 401(a) which includes a trust exempt from tax under section 501(a),

(B) an annuity plan or contract described in section 403,

(C) that portion of any plan which consists of a transfer of property described in section 83,

(D) that portion of any plan which consists of a trust to which section 402(b) applies,

(E) a qualified governmental excess benefit arrangement described in section 415(m), and

(F) that portion of any applicable employment retention plan described in paragraph (4) with respect to any participant.

(3) Definitions. For purposes of this subsection—

(A) Plan includes arrangements, etc. The term "plan" includes any agreement or arrangement.

(B) Substantial risk of forfeiture. The rights of a person to compensation are subject to a substantial risk of forfeiture if such person's rights to such compensation are conditioned upon the future performance of substantial services by any individual.

(4) Employment retention plans. For purposes of paragraph (2)(F)—

(A) In general. The portion of an applicable employment retention plan described in this paragraph with respect to any participant is that portion of the plan which provides benefits payable to the participant not in excess of twice the applicable dollar limit determined under subsection (e)(15).

(B) Other rules.

(i) Limitation. Paragraph (2)(F) shall only apply to the portion of the plan described in subparagraph (A) for years preceding the year in which such portion is paid or otherwise made available to the participant.

(ii) Treatment. A plan shall not be treated for purposes of this title as providing for the deferral of compensation for any year with respect to the portion of the plan described in subparagraph (A).

(C) Applicable employment retention plan. The term "applicable employment retention plan" means an employment retention plan maintained by—

(i) a local educational agency (as defined in section 9101 of the Elementary and Secondary Education Act of 1965 (20 U.S.C. 7801), or

(ii) an education association which principally represents employees of 1 or more agencies described in

Tax accounting   Code Sec. 457

clause (i) and which is described in section 501(c)(5) or (6) and exempt from taxation under section 501(a).

(D) Employment retention plan. The term "employment retention plan" means a plan to pay, upon termination of employment, compensation to an employee of a local educational agency or education association described in subparagraph (C) for purposes of—

(i) retaining the services of the employee, or

(ii) rewarding such employee for the employee's service with 1 or more such agencies or associations.

(g) Governmental plans must maintain set-asides for exclusive benefit of participants.

(1) In general. A plan maintained by an eligible employer described in subsection (e)(1)(A) shall not be treated as an eligible deferred compensation plan unless all assets and income of the plan described in subsection (b)(6) are held in trust for the exclusive benefit of participants and their beneficiaries.

(2) Taxability of trusts and participants. For purposes of this title—

(A) a trust described in paragraph (1) shall be treated as an organization exempt from taxation under section 501(a), and

(B) notwithstanding any other provision of this title, amounts in the trust shall be includible in the gross income of participants and beneficiaries only to the extent, and at the time, provided in this section.

(3) Custodial accounts and contracts. For purposes of this subsection, custodial accounts and contracts described in section 401(f) shall be treated as trusts under rules similar to the rules under section 401(f).

(4) Death benefits under USERRA-qualified active military service. A plan described in paragraph (1) shall not be treated as an eligible deferred compensation plan unless such plan meets the requirements of section 401(a)(37).

In 2010, P.L. 111-312, Sec. 101(a)(1), substituted "December 31, 2012" for "December 31, 2010" both places it appeared in Sec. 901 of P.L. 107-16 [see below], effective as if included in the enactment of P.L. 107-16, EGTRRA, 6/7/2001.

In 2008, P.L. 110-245, Sec. 104(c)(3), added para. (g)(4), effective for deaths and disabilities occurring on or after 1/1/2007. Sec. 104(d)(2) of this Act provides:

"(2) Provisions relating to plan amendments.

"(A) In general. If this subparagraph applies to any plan or contract amendment, such plan or contract shall be treated as being operated in accordance with the terms of the plan during the period described in subparagraph (B)(iii).

"(B) Amendments to which subparagraph (a) applies.

"(i) In general. Subparagraph (A) shall apply to any amendment to any plan or annuity contract which is made—

"(I) pursuant to the amendments made by subsection (a) or pursuant to any regulation issued by the Secretary of the Treasury under subsection (a), and

"(II) on or before the last day of the first plan year beginning on or after January 1, 2010.

"In the case of a governmental plan (as defined in section 414(d) of the Internal Revenue Code of 1986), this clause shall be applied by substituting '2012' for '2010' in subclause (II).

"(ii) Conditions. This paragraph shall not apply to any amendment unless—

"(I) the plan or contract is operated as if such plan or contract amendment were in effect for the period described in clause (iii), and

"(II) such plan or contract amendment applies retroactively for such period.

"(iii) Period described. The period described in this clause is the period—

"(I) beginning on the effective date specified by the plan, and

"(II) ending on the date described in clause (i)(II) (or, if earlier, the date the plan or contract amendment is adopted)."

In 2006, P.L. 109-280, Sec. 811, of this Act [relating to Sec. 901 of P.L. 107-16, see below], provides:

"SEC. 811. PENSIONS AND INDIVIDUAL RETIREMENT ARRANGEMENT PROVISIONS OF ECONOMIC GROWTH AND TAX RELIEF RECONCILIATION ACT OF 2001 MADE PERMANENT.

"Title IX of the Economic Growth and Tax Relief Reconciliation Act of 2001 shall not apply to the provisions of, and amendments made by, subtitles A through F of title VI of such Act (relating to pension and individual retirement arrangement provisions)."

—P.L. 109-280, Sec. 825, of this Act, reads as follows:

"SEC. 825. ELIGIBILITY FOR PARTICIPATION IN RETIREMENT PLANS. An individual shall not be precluded from participating in an eligible deferred compensation plan by reason of having received a distribution under section 457(e)(9) of the Internal Revenue Code of 1986, as in effect prior to the enactment of the Small Business Job Protection Act of 1996."

—P.L. 109-280, Sec. 826, of this Act, reads as follows:

"SEC. 826. MODIFICATIONS OF RULES GOVERNING HARDSHIPS AND UNFORESEEN FINANCIAL EMERGENCIES. Within 180 days after the date of the enactment of this Act, the Secretary of the Treasury shall modify the rules for determining whether a participant has had a hardship for purposes of section 401(k)(2)(B)(i)(IV) of the Internal Revenue Code of 1986 to provide that if an event (including the occurrence of a medical expense) would constitute a hardship under the plan if it occurred with respect to the participant's spouse or dependent (as defined in section 152 of such Code), such event shall, to the extent permitted under a plan, constitute a hardship if it occurs with respect to a person who is a beneficiary under the plan with respect to the participant. The Secretary of the Treasury shall issue similar rules for purposes of determining whether a participant has had—

"(1) a hardship for purposes of section 403(b)(11)(B) of such Code; or

"(2) an unforeseen financial emergency for purposes of sections 409A(a)(2)(A)(vi), 409A(a)(2)(B)(ii), and 457(d)(1)(A)(iii) of such Code."

—P.L. 109-280, Sec. 829(a)(4), substituted ", (9), and (11)" for "and (9)" in subpara. (e)(16)(B), effective for distributions after 12/31/2006.

—P.L. 109-280, Sec. 845(b)(3), added para. (a)(3), effective for distributions in tax. yrs. begin. after 12/31/2006.

—P.L. 109-280, Sec. 1104(a)(1), added subpara. (e)(14)(D) ... Sec. 1104(b)(1), deleted "and" at the end of subpara. (f)(2)(D), substituted ", and" for the period at the end of subpara. (f)(2)(E), and added subpara. (f)(2)(F) ... Sec. 1104(b)(2), added para. (f)(4), effective for tax. yrs. end. after 8/17/2006, Sec. 1104(d)(4) of this Act, which reads as follows:

"(4) Construction. Nothing in the amendments made by this section shall alter or affect the construction of the Internal Revenue Code of 1986, the Employee Retirement Income Security Act of 1974, or the Age Discrimination in Employment Act of 1967 as applied to any plan, arrangement, or conduct to which such amendments do not apply."

In 2005, P.L. 109-135, Sec. 201(b)(4)(A), Repealed Sec. 101 of P.L. 109-73. Prior to repeal, Sec. 101 of P.L. 109-73 read as follows:

"SEC. 101. TAX-FAVORED WITHDRAWALS FROM RETIREMENT PLANS FOR RELIEF RELATING TO HURRICANE KATRINA.

"(a) In general. Section 72(t) of the Internal Revenue Code of 1986 shall not apply to any qualified Hurricane Katrina distribution.

"(b) Aggregate dollar limitation.

"(1) In general. For purposes of this section, the aggregate amount of distributions received by an individual which may be treated as qualified Hurricane Katrina distributions for any taxable year shall not exceed the excess (if any) of—

"(A) $100,000, over

"(B) the aggregate amounts treated as qualified Hurricane Katrina distributions received by such individual for all prior taxable years.

"(2) Treatment of plan distributions. If a distribution to an individual would (without regard to paragraph (1)) be a qualified Hurricane Katrina distribution, a plan shall not be treated as violating any requirement of the Internal Revenue Code of 1986 merely because the plan treats such distribution as a qualified Hurricane Katrina distribution, unless the aggregate amount of such distributions from all plans maintained by the employer (and any member of any controlled group which includes the employer) to such individual exceeds $100,000.

"(3) Controlled group. For purposes of paragraph (2), the term 'controlled group' means any group treated as a single employer under subsection (b), (c), (m), or (o) of section 414 of such Code.

"(c) Amount distributed may be repaid.

"(1) In general. Any individual who receives a qualified Hurricane Katrina distribution may, at any time during the 3-year period beginning on the day after the date on which such distribution was received, make one or more contributions in an aggregate amount not to exceed the amount of such distribution to an eligible retirement plan of which such individual is a beneficiary and to which a rollover contribution of such distribution could be made under section 402(c), 403(a)(4), 403(b)(8), 408(d)(3), or 457(e)(16) of such Code, as the case may be.

"(2) Treatment of repayments of distributions from eligible retirement plans other than IRAs. For purposes of such Code, if a contribution is made pursuant to paragraph (1) with respect to a qualified Hurricane Katrina distribution from an eligible retirement plan other than an individual retirement plan, then the taxpayer shall, to the extent of the amount of the contribution, be treated as having received the qualified Hurricane Katrina distribution in an eligible rollover distribution (as defined in section 402(c)(4) of such Code) and as having transferred the amount to the eligible retirement plan in a direct trustee to trustee transfer within 60 days of the distribution.

"(3) Treatment of repayments for distributions from IRAs. For purposes of such Code, if a contribution is made pursuant to paragraph (1) with respect to a qualified Hurricane Katrina distribution from an individual retirement plan (as defined by section 7701(a)(37) of such Code), then, to the extent of the amount of the contribution, the qualified Hurricane Katrina distribution shall be treated as a distribution described in section 408(d)(3) of such Code and as having been transferred to the eligible retirement plan in a direct trustee to trustee transfer within 60 days of the distribution.

"(d) Definitions. For purposes of this section—

"(1) Qualified Hurricane Katrina distribution. Except as provided in subsection (b), the term 'qualified Hurricane Katrina distribution' means any distribution from an eligible retirement plan made on or after August 25, 2005, and before January 1, 2007, to an individual whose principal place of abode on August 28,

2005, is located in the Hurricane Katrina disaster area and who has sustained an economic loss by reason of Hurricane Katrina.

"(2) Eligible retirement plan. The term 'eligible retirement plan' shall have the meaning given such term by section 402(c)(8)(B) of such Code.

"(e) Income inclusion spread over 3 year period for qualified Hurricane Katrina distributions.

"(1) In general. In the case of any qualified Hurricane Katrina distribution, unless the taxpayer elects not to have this subsection apply for any taxable year, any amount required to be included in gross income for such taxable year shall be so included ratably over the 3-taxable year period beginning with such taxable year.

"(2) Special rule. For purposes of paragraph (1), rules similar to the rules of subparagraph (E) of section 408A(d)(3) of such Code shall apply.

"(f) Special rules.

"(1) Exemption of distributions from trustee to trustee transfer and withholding rules. For purposes of sections 401(a)(31), 402(f), and 3405 of such Code, qualified Hurricane Katrina distributions shall not be treated as eligible rollover distributions.

"(2) Qualified Hurricane Katrina distributions treated as meeting plan distribution requirements. For purposes of such Code, a qualified Hurricane Katrina distribution shall be treated as meeting the requirements of sections 401(k)(2)(B)(i), 403(b)(7)(A)(ii), 403(b)(11), and 457(d)(1)(A) of such Code."

In 2002, P.L. 107-358, Sec. 2, added subsec. (c) in Sec. 901 of P.L. 107-16 [see below], effective 12/17/2002.

—P.L. 107-147, Sec. 411(o)(9), added para. (e)(18), effective for contributions in tax. yrs. begin. after 12/31/2001.

—P.L. 107-147, Sec. 411(p)(5), amended para. (e)(5), effective for yrs. begin. after 12/31/2001.

Prior to amendment, para. (e)(5) read as follows:

"(5) Includible compensation. The term 'includible compensation' means compensation for service performed for the employer which (taking into account the provisions of this section and other provisions of this chapter) is currently includible in gross income."

In 2001, P.L. 107-16, Sec. 611(d)(3)(B), substituted "402(g)(7)(A)(iii)" for "402(g)(8)(A)(iii)" in para. (c)(2) . . . Sec. 611(e)(1)(A), substituted "the applicable dollar amount" for "$7,500" in subpara. (b)(2)(A) and para. (c)(1) . . . Sec. 611(e)(1)(B), substituted "twice the dollar amount in effect under subsection (b)(2)(A)" for "$15,000" in subpara. (b)(3)(A) . . . Sec. 611(e)(2), amended para. (e)(15), effective for yrs. begin. after 12/31/2001.

Prior to amendment, para. (e)(15) read as follows:

"(15) Cost-of-living adjustment of maximum deferral amount. The Secretary shall adjust the $7,500 amount specified in subsections (b)(2) and (c)(1) at the same time and in the same manner as under section 415(d), except that the base period shall be the calendar quarter ending September 30, 1994, and any increase under this paragraph which is not a multiple of $500 shall be rounded to the next lowest multiple of $500."

—P.L. 107-16, Sec. 615(a), amended subsec. (c) [as amended by Sec. 611(d)(3)(B) and (e)(1)(A) of this Act, see above], effective for yrs. begin. after 12/31/2001.

Prior to amendment, subsec. (c) read as follows:

"(c) Individuals who are participants in more than 1 plan.

"(1) In general. The maximum of the compensation of any one individual which may be deferred under subsection (a) during any taxable year shall not exceed the applicable dollar amount (as modified by any adjustment provided under subsection (b)(3)).

"(2) Coordination with certain other deferrals. In applying paragraph (1) of this subsection—

"(A) any amount excluded from gross income under section 403(b) for the taxable year, and

"(B) any amount—

"(i) excluded from gross income under section 402(e)(3) or section 402(h)(1)(B) or (k) for the taxable year, or

"(ii) with respect to which a deduction is allowable by reason of a contribution to an organization described in section 501(c)(18) for the taxable year,

shall be treated as an amount deferred under subsection (a). In applying section 402(g)(7)(A)(ii) or 403(b)(2)(A)(ii), an amount deferred under subsection (a) for any year of service shall be taken into account as if described in section 402(g)(3)(C) or 403(b)(2)(A)(ii), respectively. Subparagraph (B) shall not apply in the case of a participant in a rural cooperative plan (as defined in section 401(k)(7))."

—P.L. 107-16, Sec. 632(c)(1), substituted "100 percent" for "33 ⅓ percent" in subpara. (b)(2)(B), effective for yrs. begin. after 12/31/2001.

—P.L. 107-16, Sec. 634, of this Act, reads as follows:

"SEC. 634. MODIFICATION TO MINIMUM DISTRIBUTION RULES. The Secretary of the Treasury shall modify the life expectancy tables under the regulations relating to minimum distribution requirements under sections 401(a)(9), 408(a)(6) and (b)(3), 403(b)(10), and 457(d)(2) of the Internal Revenue Code to reflect current life expectancy."

—P.L. 107-16, Sec. 641(a)(1)(A), added para. (e)(16) . . . Sec. 641(a)(1)(B), added "(other than rollover amounts)" after "taxable year" in para. (b)(2) . . . Sec. 641(a)(1)(C), deleted "and" at the end of subpara. (d)(1)(A), substituted ", and" for the period at the end of subpara. (d)(1)(B), and added subpara. (d)(1)(C), effective for distributions after 12/31/2001. Sec. 641(f)(2) and (3) of this Act, provides:

"(2) Reasonable notice. No penalty shall be imposed on a plan for the failure to provide the information required by the amendment made by subsection (c) with respect to any distribution made before the date that is 90 days after the date on which the Secretary of the Treasury issues a safe harbor rollover notice after the

date of the enactment of this Act, if the administrator of such plan makes a reasonable attempt to comply with such requirement.

"(3) Special rule. Notwithstanding any other provision of law, subsections (h)(3) and (h)(5) of section 1122 of the Tax Reform Act of 1986 shall not apply to any distribution from an eligible retirement plan (as defined in clause (iii) or (iv) of section 402(c)(8)(B) of the Internal Revenue Code of 1986) on behalf of an individual if there was a rollover to such plan on behalf of such individual which is permitted solely by reason of any amendment made by this section."

—P.L. 107-16, Sec. 646(a)(3), substituted "has a severance from employment" for "is separated from service" in clause (d)(1)(A)(ii), effective for distributions after 12/31/2001.

—P.L. 107-16, Sec. 647(b), added para. (e)(17), effective for trustee-to-trustee transfers after 12/31/2001.

—P.L. 107-16, Sec. 648(b), substituted "the portion of such amount which is not attributable to rollover contributions (as defined in section 411(a)(11)(D))" for "such amount" in clause (e)(9)(A)(i), effective for distributions after 12/31/2001.

—P.L. 107-16, Sec. 649(a), amended para. (d)(2) . . . Sec. 649(b)(1), amended subsec. (a) . . . Sec. 649(b)(2)(A), substituted "(9) Benefits of tax exempt organization plans not treated as made available by reason of certain elections, etc. In the case of an eligible deferred compensation plan of an employer described in subsection (e)(1)(B)—" for "(9) Benefits not treated as made available by reason of certain elections, etc." in para. (e)(9) . . . Sec. 649(b)(2)(B), added para. (d)(3), effective for distributions after 12/31/2001.

Prior to amendment, para. (d)(2) read as follows:

"(2) Minimum distribution requirements. A plan meets the minimum distribution requirements of this paragraph if such plan meets the requirements of subparagraphs (A), (B), and (C):

"(A) Application of section 401(a)(9). A plan meets the requirements of this subparagraph if the plan meets the requirements of section 401(a)(9).

"(B) Additional distribution requirements. A plan meets the requirements of this subparagraph if—

"(i) in the case of a distribution beginning before the death of the participant, such distribution will be made in a form under which—

"(I) the amounts payable with respect to the participant will be paid at times specified by the Secretary which are not later than the time determined under section 401(a)(9)(G) (relating to incidental death benefits), and

"(II) any amount not distributed to the participant during his life will be distributed after the death of the participant at least as rapidly as under the method of distributions being used under subclause (I) as of the date of his death, or

"(ii) in the case of a distribution which does not begin before the death of the participant, the entire amount payable with respect to the participant will be paid during a period not to exceed 15 years (or the life expectancy of the surviving spouse if such spouse is the beneficiary).

"(C) Nonincreasing benefits. A plan meets the requirements of this subparagraph if any distribution payable over a period of more than 1 year can only be made in substantially nonincreasing amounts (paid not less frequently than annually)."

Prior to amendment, subsec. (a) read as follows:

"(a) Year of inclusion in gross income. In the case of a participant in an eligible deferred compensation plan, any amount of compensation deferred under the plan, and any income attributable to the amounts so deferred, shall be includible in gross income only for the taxable year in which such compensation or other income is paid or otherwise made available to the participant or other beneficiary."

—P.L. 107-16, Sec. 901, of this Act [as amended by Sec. 2 of P.L. 107-358, and Sec. 101(a)(1) of P.L. 111-312, and as related to Sec. 811 of P.L. 109-280, see above], reads as follows:

"SEC. 901. SUNSET OF PROVISIONS OF ACT.

"(a) In general. All provisions of, and amendments made by, this Act shall not apply—

"(1) to taxable, plan, or limitation years beginning after December 31, 2012, or

"(2) in the case of title V, to estates of decedents dying, gifts made, or generation skipping transfers, after December 31, 2012.

"(b) Application of certain laws. The Internal Revenue Code of 1986 and the Employee Retirement Income Security Act of 1974 shall be applied and administered to years, estates, gifts, and transfers described in subsection (a) as if the provisions and amendments described in subsection (a) had never been enacted.

"(c) Exception. Subsection (a) shall not apply to section 803 (relating to no federal income tax on restitution received by victims of the Nazi regime or their heirs or estates)."

In 1997, P.L. 105-34, Sec. 1071(a)(2)(A), substituted "the dollar limit under section 411(a)(11)(A)" for "$3,500" in clause (e)(9)(A)(i) . . . Sec. 1071(a)(2)(B), substituted "dollar limit" for "$3,500" in the heading of subpara. (e)(9)(A), effective for plan yrs. begin. after 8/5/97.

In 1996, P.L. 104-188, Sec. 1421(b)(3)(C), substituted "section 402(h)(1)(B) or (k)" for "section 402(h)(1)(B)" in clause (c)(2)(B)(i), effective for tax. yrs. begin. after 12/31/96.

—P.L. 104-188, Sec. 1444(b)(2), added para. (e)(14) . . . Sec. 1444(b)(3), deleted "and" at the end of subpara. (f)(2)(C), substituted ", and" for the period at the end of subpara. (f)(2)(D), and added subpara. (f)(2)(E), effective for yrs. begin. after 12/31/94. Sec. 1444(e)(2) of this Act provides:

"(2) Treatment for years beginning before January 1, 1995. Nothing in the amendments made by this section shall be construed to imply that a governmental plan (as defined in section 414(d) of the Internal Revenue Code of 1986) fails to satisfy the requirements of section 415 of such Code for any taxable year beginning before January 1, 1995."

—P.L. 104-188, Sec. 1447(a), amended para. (e)(9) . . . Sec. 1447(b), added para. (e)(15), effective for tax. yrs. begin. after 12/31/96.

Prior to amendment, para. (e)(9) read as follows:

"(9) Benefits not treated as made available by reason of certain elections. If—

"(A) the total amount payable to a participant under the plan does not exceed $3,500, and

"(B) no additional amounts may be deferred under the plan with respect to the participant,

the amount payable to the participant under the plan shall not be treated as made available merely because such participant may elect to receive a lump sum payable after separation from service and within 60 days of the election."

—P.L. 104-188, Sec. 1448(a), added subsec. (g)... Sec. 1448(b), added "except as provided in subsection (g)" before "which provides that" in para. (b)(6), effective for assets and income described in Code Sec. 457(b)(6) held by a plan on or after date of enactment. Sec. 1448(c)(2) of this Act provides:

"(2) Transition rule. In the case of a plan in existence on the date of the enactment of this Act, a trust need not be established by reason of the amendments made by this section before January 1, 1999.

—P.L. 104-188, Sec. 1458(a), amended para. (e)(11), effective for accruals of length of service awards after 12/31/96.

Prior to amendment, para. (e)(11) read as follows:

"(11) Certain plans excepted. Any bona fide vacation leave, sick leave, compensatory time, severance pay, disability pay, or death benefit plan shall be treated as a plan not providing for the deferral of compensation."

In 1992, P.L. 102-318, Sec. 521(b)(26), substituted "section 402(e)(3)" for "section 402(a)(8)" in clause (c)(2)(B)(i), effective for distributions after 12/31/92. For special rule, see Sec. 521(e)(2) of this Act which reads as follows:

"(2) Special rule for partial distributions. For purposes of section 402(a)(5)(D)(i)(II) of the Internal Revenue Code of 1986 (as in effect before the amendments made by this section), a distribution before January 1, 1993, which is made before or at the same time as a series of periodic payments shall not be treated as one of such series if it is not substantially equal in amount to other payments in such series."

In 1989, P.L. 101-239, Sec. 7811(g)(4), substituted ", and" for the period at the end clause (d)(1)(A)(iii)... Sec. 7811(g)(5), added "and" at end of subclause (d)(2)(B)(i)(I), effective for tax. yrs. begin. after 12/31/88, except as provided by Sec. 1107(c)(2)-(c)(5) of P.L. 99-514, see below.

—P.L. 101-239, Sec. 7816(j), amended para. (e)(13), effective for tax. yrs. begin. after 12/31/87, except as provided in Secs. 6064(d)(2)-(4) of P.L. 100-647, see below.

Prior to amendment, para. (e)(13) read as follows:

"(13) Exception for church plans. The term 'eligible deferred compensation plan' shall not include a plan maintained by a church for church employees. For purposes of this paragraph, the term 'church' has the meaning given such term by section 3121(w)(3)(A), including a qualified church-controlled organization (as defined in section 3121(w)(3)(B)."

In 1988, P.L. 100-647, Sec. 1011(e)(1), deleted "and paragraphs (2) and (3) of subsection (b)" after "of this subsection" in para. (c)(2)... Sec. 1011(e)(2), amended subpara. (d)(1)(A)... Sec. 1011(e)(10), amended subclause (d)(2)(B)(i)(I), effective for tax. yrs. begin. after 12/31/88, except as provided by Sec. 1107(c)(2)-(c)(5) of P.L. 99-514, see below.

Prior to amendment, subpara. (d)(1)(A) read as follows:

"(A) the plan provides that amounts payable under the plan will be made available to participants or other beneficiaries not earlier than when the participant is separated from service with the employer or is faced with an unforeseeable emergency (determined in the manner prescribed by the Secretary by regulation), and"

Prior to amendment, subclause (d)(2)(B)(i)(I) read as follows:

"(I) at least 2/3 of the total amount payable with respect to the participant will be paid during the life expectancy of such participant (determined as of the commencement of the distribution), and"

—P.L. 100-647, Sec. 1011(e)(6)(A), deleted "eligible" each place it appeared in Sec. 1107(c)(3) of P.L. 99-514... Sec. 1011(e)(6)(B), added the sentence at the end of Sec. 1107(c)(3)(B) of P.L. 99-514 [reproduced below]... Sec. 1011(c)(7)(A), deleted "to employees on August 1, 1986, of" in Sec. 1107(c)(5) of P.L. 99-514... Sec. 1011(c)(7)(B), substituted "to employees on August 16, 1986," for "a deferred compensation plan" in Sec. 1107(c)(5)(A) of P.L. 99-514 ... Sec. 1011(c)(7)(C), added "maintaining a deferred compensation plan" after "Alabama" in Sec. 1107(c)(5)(A) of P.L. 99-514... Sec. 1011(c)(7)(D), substituted "to individuals eligible to participate on August 16, 1986, in a deferred compensation plan" for "a deferred compensation plan" in Sec. 1107(c)(5)(B) of P.L. Amendments above apply to the effective date for amendments made by Sec. 1107(a) of P.L. 99-514, see below.

—P.L. 100-647, Sec. 1011(e)(9), added "after separation from service and" before "within 60 days" in para. (e)(9), effective for yrs. begin. after 12/31/88.

—P.L. 100-647, Sec. 6064(a)(1), added para. (e)(11)... Sec. 6064(a)(2), added para. (d)(10) [before amendment by Sec. 1107(a) of P.L. 99-514,... Sec. 6064(b)(1), added para. (e)(12)... Sec. 6064(b)(2), added para. (d)(11) [before amendment by Sec. 1107(a) of P.L. 99-514, see below]... Sec. 6064(c), added para. (e)(13), effective for tax. yrs. begin. after 12/31/87, except as provided in Secs. 6064(d)(2)-(4) of this Act which read as follows:

"(2) Exception for plans collectively bargained plans.—

"(A) In general.— Section 457 of the 1986 Code (as in effect before and after the amendments made by section 1107 of the Reform Act) shall not apply to nonelective deferred compensation provided under a plan in existence on December 31, 1987, and maintained pursuant to a collective bargaining agreement.

"(B) Nonelective plan.— For purposes of this paragraph, a nonelective plan is a plan which covers a broad group of employees and under which the covered employees earn nonelective deferred compensation under a definite, fixed and uniform benefit formula.

"(C) Termination.— This paragraph shall cease to apply to a plan as of the elective date of the first material modification of the plan agreed to after December 31, 1987.

"(3) Treatment of certain nonelective deferred compensation.— Section 457 of the 1986 Code shall not apply to amounts deferred under a nonelective deferred compensation plan maintained by an eligible employer described in section 457(e)(1)(A) of the 1986 Code (as in effect after the Reform Act)—

"(A) if such amounts were deferred from periods before July 14, 1988, or

"(B) if—

"(i) such amounts are deferred from periods on or after such date pursuant to an agreement which—

"(I) was in writing on such date, and

"(II) on such date provides for a deferral for each taxable year covered by the agreement of a fixed amount or of an amount determined pursuant to a fixed formula, and

"(ii) the individual with respect to whom the deferral is made was covered under such agreement on such date.

Subparagraph (B) shall not apply to any taxable year ending after the date on which any modification of the amount or formula described in subparagraph (B)(i)(II) agreed to in writing before January 1, 1989, is effective. The preceding sentence shall not apply to a modification agreed to in writing before January 1, 1989, which does not increase any benefit of a participant. Amounts described in the first sentence of this paragraph shall be taken into account for purposes of applying section 457 of the 1986 Code to other amounts deferred under any eligible deferred compensation plan.

"(4) Study.— The Secretary of the Treasury or his delegate shall conduct a study on the tax treatment of deferred compensation paid by State and local governments and tax-exempt organizations (including deferred compensation paid to independent contractors). Not later than January 1, 1990, the Secretary shall submit to the Committee on Ways and Means of the House of Representatives and the Committee on Finance of the Senate a report on the study conducted under this paragraph together with such recommendations as he may deem advisable."

—P.L. 100-647, Sec. 6071(c), substituted "rural cooperative plan" for "rural electric cooperative plan" in para. (c)(2), effective for tax. yrs. begin. after 11/10/88.

In 1986, P.L. 99-514, Sec. 1107(a), amended Code Sec. 457, effective for tax. yrs. begin. after 12/31/88, except as provided by Sec. 1107(c)(2)-(c)(5) of this Act [as amended by Sec. 1011(e)(6) of P.L. 100-647 and (7), see above], which reads as follows:

"(2) Transfers and cash-outs. Paragraphs (9) and (10) of section 457(e) of the Internal Revenue Code of 1986 (as amended by this section) shall apply to taxable years beginning after December 31, 1986.

"(3) Application to tax-exempt organizations.

"(A) In general. Except as provided in subparagraph (B), the application of section 457 of the Internal Revenue Code of 1986 by reason of the amendments made by this section to deferred compensation plans established and maintained by organizations exempt from tax shall apply to taxable years beginning after December 31, 1986.

"(B) Existing deferrals and arrangements. Section 457 of such Code shall not apply to amounts deferred under a plan described in subparagraph (A) which—

"(i) were deferred from taxable years beginning before January 1, 1987, or

"(ii) are deferred from taxable years beginning after December 31, 1986, pursuant to an agreement which—

"(I) was in writing on August 16, 1986,

"(II) on such date provides for a deferral for each taxable year covered by the agreement of a fixed amount or of an amount determined pursuant to a fixed formula.

Clause (ii) shall not apply to any taxable year ending after the date on which any modification to the amount or formula described in subclause (II) is effective. Amounts described in the first sentence shall be taken into account for applying section 457 to other amounts deferred under any deferred compensation plan. This subparagraph shall only apply to individuals who were covered under the plan and agreement on August 16, 1986.

"(4) Deferred compensation plans for state judges. The amendments made by this section shall not apply to any qualified State judicial plan (as defined in section 131(c)(3)(B) of the Revenue Act of 1978 as amended by section 252 of the Tax Equity and Fiscal Responsibility Act of 1982).

"(5) Special rule for certain deferred compensation plans. The amendments made by this section shall not apply

"(A) to employees on August 16, 1986, of a nonprofit corporation organized under the laws of the State of Alabama maintaining a deferred compensation plan with respect to which the Internal Revenue Service issued a ruling dated March 17, 1976, that the plan would not affect the tax-exempt status of the corporation, or

"(B) to individuals eligible to participate on August 16, 1986, in a deferred compensation plan with respect to which a letter dated November 6, 1975, submitted the original plan to the Internal Revenue Service, an amendment was submitted on November 19, 1975, and the Internal Revenue Service responded with a letter dated December 24, 1975,

but only with respect to deferrals under such plan."

Prior to amendment, Code Sec. 457 read as follows:

"SEC. 457. DEFERRED COMPENSATION PLANS WITH RESPECT TO SERVICE FOR STATE AND LOCAL GOVERNMENTS.

"(a) Year of inclusion in gross income.

"In the case of a participant in an eligible State deferred compensation plan, any amount of compensation deferred under the plan, and any income attributable to the amounts so deferred, shall be includible in gross income only for the taxa-

Code Sec. 457

ble year in which such compensation or other income is paid or otherwise made available to the participant or other beneficiary.

"(b) Eligible state deferred compensation plan defined.

"For purposes of this section, the term 'eligible State deferred compensation plan' means a plan established and maintained by a State—

"(1) in which only individuals who perform service for the State may be participants,

"(2) which provides that (except as provided in paragraph (3)) the maximum that may be deferred under the plan for the taxable year shall not exceed the lesser of—

"(A) $7,500, or

"(B) 33⅓ percent of the participant's includible compensation,

"(3) which may provide that, for 1 or more of the participant's last 3 taxable years ending before he attains normal retirement age under the plan, the ceiling set forth in paragraph (2) shall be the lesser of—

"(A) $15,000, or

"(B) the sum of—

"(i) the plan ceiling established for purposes of paragraph (2) for the taxable year (determined without regard to this paragraph), plus

"(ii) so much of the plan ceiling established for purposes of paragraph (2) for taxable years before the taxable year as has not theretofore been used under paragraph (2) or this paragraph,

"(4) which provides that compensation will be deferred for any calendar month only if an agreement providing for such deferral has been entered into before the beginning of such month,

"(5) which does not provide that amounts payable under the plan will be made available to participants or other beneficiaries earlier than when the participant is separated from service with the State or is faced with an unforeseeable emergency (determined in the manner prescribed by the Secretary by regulation), and

"(6) which provides that—

"(A) all amounts of compensation deferred under the plan,

"(B) all property and rights purchased with such amounts, and

"(C) all income attributable to such amounts, property, or rights,

shall remain (until made available to the participant or other beneficiary) solely the property and rights of the State (without being restricted to the provision of benefits under the plan) subject only to the claims of the State's general creditors. A plan which is administered in a manner which is inconsistent with the requirements of any of the preceding paragraphs shall be treated as not meeting the requirements of such paragraph as of the first plan year beginning more than 180 days after the date of notification by the Secretary of the inconsistency unless the State corrects the inconsistency before the first day of such plan year.

"(c) Individuals who are participants in more than one plan.

"(1) In general. The maximum amount of the compensation of any one individual which may be deferred under subsection (a) during any taxable year shall not exceed $7,500 (as modified by any adjustment provided under subsection (b)(3)).

"(2) Coordination with section 403(b). In applying paragraph (1) of this subsection and paragraphs (2) and (3) of subsection (b), an amount excluded during a taxable year under section 403(b) shall be treated as an amount deferred under subsection (a). In applying clause (ii) of section 403(b)(2)(A), an amount deferred under subsection (a) for any year of service shall be taken into account as if described in such clause.

"(d) Other definitions and special rules.

"For purposes of this section—

"(1) State. The term 'State' means a State, a political subdivision of a State, and an agency or instrumentality of a State or political subdivision of a State.

"(2) Performance of service. The performance of service includes performance of service as an independent contractor.

"(3) Participant. The term 'participant' means an individual who is eligible to defer compensation under the plan.

"(4) Beneficiary. The term 'beneficiary' means a beneficiary of the participant, his estate, or any other person whose interest in the plan is derived from the participant.

"(5) Includible compensation. The term 'includible compensation' means compensation for service performed for the State which (taking into account the provisions of this section and section 403(b)) is currently includible in gross income.

"(6) Compensation taken into account at present value. Compensation shall be taken into account at its present value.

"(7) Community property laws. The amount of includible compensation shall be determined without regard to any community property laws.

"(8) Income attributable. Gains from the disposition of property shall be treated as income attributable to such property.

"(9) Section to apply to rural electric cooperatives.

"(A) In general. This section shall apply with respect to any participant in a plan of a rural electric cooperative in the same manner and to the same extent as if such plan were a plan of a State.

"(B) Rural Electric Cooperative Defined. For purposes of subparagraph (A), the term 'rural electric cooperative means

"(i) any organization which is exempt from tax under section 501(a) and which is engaged primarily in providing electric service on a mutual or cooperative basis, and

"(ii) any organization described in paragraph (4) or (6) of section 501(c) which is exempt from tax under section 501(a) and at least 80 percent of the members of which are organizations described in clause (i).

"(10) Certain plans excepted. Any bona fide vacation leave, sick leave, compensatory time, severance pay, disability pay, or death benefit plan shall be treated as a plan not providing for the deferral of compensation.

"(11) Exception for nonelective deferred compensation of nonemployees.

Tax accounting

"(A) In general. This section shall not apply to nonelective deferred compensation attributable to services not performed as an employee.

"(B) Nonelective deferred compensation. For purposes of subparagraph (a), deferred compensation shall be treated as nonelective only if all individuals (other than those who have not satisfied any applicable initial service requirement) with the same relationship to the payor are covered under the same plan with no individual variations or options under the plan.

"(e) Tax treatment of participants where plan or arrangement of state is not eligible.

"(1) In general. In the case of a plan of a State providing for a deferral of compensation, if such plan is not an eligible State deferred compensation plan, then—

"(A) the compensation shall be included in the gross income of the participant or beneficiary for the first taxable year in which there is no substantial risk of forfeiture of the rights to such compensation, and

"(B) the tax treatment of any amount made available under the plan to a participant or beneficiary shall be determined under section 72 (relating to annuities, etc.).

"(2) Exceptions. Paragraph (1) shall not apply to—

"(A) is a plan described in section 401(a) which includes a trust exempt from tax under section 501(a),

"(B) an annuity plan or contract described in section 403,

"(C) that portion of any plan which consists of a transfer of property described in section 83, and

"(D) that portion of any plan which consists of a trust to which section 402(b) applies.

"(3) Definitions. For purposes of this subsection—

"(A) Plan includes arrangements, etc. The term 'plan' includes any agreement or arrangement.

"(B) Substantial risk of forfeiture. The rights of a person to compensation are subject to a substantial risk of forfeiture if such person's rights to such compensation are conditioned upon the future performance of substantial services by any individual."

In 1984, P.L. 98-369, Sec. 491(d)(33), deleted subpara. (e)(2)(C) and redesignated subparas. (e)(2)(D) and (E) as subparas. (e)(2)(C) and (D), effective for obligations issued after 12/31/83.

Prior to deletion, subpara. (e)(2)(C) read as follows:

"(C) a qualified bond purchase plan described in section 405(a),"

In 1982, P.L. 97-248, Sec. 252, added para. (c)(3) to Sec. 131 of P.L. 95-600, reproduced below.

In 1980, P.L. 96-222, Sec. 101(a)(4), amended subpara. (d)(9)(B), effective for tax. yrs. begin. after 12/31/78. Secs. 131(c)(2) and (3) of P.L. 95-600 [as amended by Sec. 252 of P.L. 97-248, see above] provides transitional rules, reproduced below.

Prior to amendment, subpara. (d)(9)(B) read as follows:

"(B) Rural electric cooperative defined. For purposes of subparagraph (A), the term 'rural electric cooperative' means—

"(i) any organization described in section 501(c)(12) which is exempt from tax under section 501(a) and which is engaged primarily in providing electric service, and

"(ii) any organization described in section 501(c)(6) which is exempt from tax under section 501(a) and all the members of which are organizations described in clause (i)."

In 1978, P.L. 95-600, Sec. 131(a), added Code Sec. 457, effective for tax. yrs. begin. after 12/31/78. Secs. 131(c)(2) and (3) of this Act [as amended by Sec. 252 of P.L. 97-248, see above] provides transitional rules as follows:

"(2) Transitional rules.

"(A) In general. In the case of any taxable year beginning after December 31, 1978, and before January 1, 1982—

"(i) any amount of compensation deferred under a plan of a State providing for a deferral of compensation (other than a plan described in section 457(e)(2) of the Internal Revenue Code of 1954), and any income attributable to the amounts so deferred, shall be includible in gross income only for the taxable year in which such compensation or other income is paid or otherwise made available to the participant or other beneficiary, but

"(ii) the maximum amount of the compensation of any one individual which may be excluded from gross income by reason of clause (i) and by reason of section 457(a) of such Code during any such taxable year shall not exceed the lesser of—

"(I) $7,500, or

"(II) 33⅓ percent of the participant's includible compensation.

"(B) Application of catch-up provisions in certain cases. If, in the case of any participant for any taxable year, all of the plans are eligible State deferred compensation plans, then clause (ii) of subparagraph (A) of this paragraph shall be applied with the modification provided by paragraph (3) of section 457(b) of such Code.

"(C) Applications of certain coordination provisions.— In applying clause (ii) of subparagraph (A) of this paragraph and section 403(b)(2)(A)(ii) of such Code, rules similar to the rules of section 457(c)(2) of such Code shall apply.

"(D) Meaning of terms. Except as otherwise provided in this paragraph, terms used in this paragraph shall have the same meaning as when used in section 457 of such Code.

"(3) Deferred compensation plans for state judges.—

"(A) In general.— The amendments made by this section shall not apply to any qualified State judicial plan.

"(B) Qualified state judicial plan.— For purposes of subparagraph (A), the term 'qualified State judicial plan' means any retirement plan of a State for the exclusive benefit of judges or their beneficiaries if—

"(i) such plan has been continuously in existence since December 31, 1978,
"(ii) under such plan, all judges eligible to benefit under the plan—
"(I) are required to participate, and
"(II) are required to contribute the same fixed percentage of their basic or regular rate of compensation as judge,
"(iii) under such plan, no judge has an option as to contributions or benefits the exercise of which would affect the amount of includible compensation,
"(iv) the retirement payments of a judge under the plan are a percentage of the compensation of judges of that State holding similar positions, and
"(v) the plan during any year does not pay benefits with respect to any participant which exceed the limitations of section 415(b) of the Internal Revenue Code of 1954."

Sec. 457A. Nonqualified deferred compensation from certain tax indifferent parties.

(a) In general.
Any compensation which is deferred under a nonqualified deferred compensation plan of a nonqualified entity shall be includible in gross income when there is no substantial risk of forfeiture of the rights to such compensation.

(b) Nonqualified entity.
For purposes of this section, the term "nonqualified entity" means—
(1) any foreign corporation unless substantially all of its income is—
(A) effectively connected with the conduct of a trade or business in the United States, or
(B) subject to a comprehensive foreign income tax, and
(2) any partnership unless substantially all of its income is allocated to persons other than—
(A) foreign persons with respect to whom such income is not subject to a comprehensive foreign income tax, and
(B) organizations which are exempt from tax under this title.

(c) Determinability of amounts of compensation.
(1) In general. If the amount of any compensation is not determinable at the time that such compensation is otherwise includible in gross income under subsection (a)—
(A) such amount shall be so includible in gross income when determinable, and
(B) the tax imposed under this chapter for the taxable year in which such compensation is includible in gross income shall be increased by the sum of—
(i) the amount of interest determined under paragraph (2), and
(ii) an amount equal to 20 percent of the amount of such compensation.
(2) Interest. For purposes of paragraph (1)(B)(i), the interest determined under this paragraph for any taxable year is the amount of interest at the underpayment rate under section 6621 plus 1 percentage point on the underpayments that would have occurred had the deferred compensation been includible in gross income for the taxable year in which first deferred or, if later, the first taxable year in which such deferred compensation is not subject to a substantial risk of forfeiture.

(d) Other definitions and special rules.
For purposes of this section—
(1) **Substantial risk of forfeiture.**
(A) In general. The rights of a person to compensation shall be treated as subject to a substantial risk of forfeiture only if such person's rights to such compensation are conditioned upon the future performance of substantial services by any individual.
(B) Exception for compensation based on gain recognized on an investment asset.
(i) In general. To the extent provided in regulations prescribed by the Secretary, if compensation is determined solely by reference to the amount of gain recognized on the disposition of an investment asset, such compensation shall be treated as subject to a substantial risk of forfeiture until the date of such disposition.
(ii) Investment asset. For purposes of clause (i), the term "investment asset" means any single asset (other than an investment fund or similar entity)—
(I) acquired directly by an investment fund or similar entity,
(II) with respect to which such entity does not (nor does any person related to such entity) participate in the active management of such asset (or if such asset is an interest in an entity, in the active management of the activities of such entity), and
(III) substantially all of any gain on the disposition of which (other than such deferred compensation) is allocated to investors in such entity.
(iii) Coordination with special rule. Paragraph (3)(B) shall not apply to any compensation to which clause (i) applies.
(2) **Comprehensive foreign income tax.** The term "comprehensive foreign income tax" means, with respect to any foreign person, the income tax of a foreign country if—
(A) such person is eligible for the benefits of a comprehensive income tax treaty between such foreign country and the United States, or
(B) such person demonstrates to the satisfaction of the Secretary that such foreign country has a comprehensive income tax.
(3) **Nonqualified deferred compensation plan.**
(A) In general. The term "nonqualified deferred compensation plan" has the meaning given such term under section 409A(d), except that such term shall include any plan that provides a right to compensation based on the appreciation in value of a specified number of equity units of the service recipient.
(B) Exception. Compensation shall not be treated as deferred for purposes of this section if the service provider receives payment of such compensation not later than 12 months after the end of the taxable year of the service recipient during which the right to the payment of such compensation is no longer subject to a substantial risk of forfeiture.
(4) **Exception for certain compensation with respect to effectively connected income.** In the case a foreign corporation with income which is taxable under section 882, this section shall not apply to compensation which, had such compensation been paid in cash on the date that such compensation ceased to be subject to a substantial risk of forfeiture, would have been deductible by such foreign corporation against such income.
(5) **Application of rules.** Rules similar to the rules of paragraphs (5) and (6) of section 409A(d) shall apply.

(e) Regulations.
The Secretary shall prescribe such regulations as may be necessary or appropriate to carry out the purposes of this section, including regulations disregarding a substantial risk of forfeiture in cases where necessary to carry out the purposes of this section.

In 2008, P.L. 110-343, Sec. 801(a)DivC, added Code Sec. 457A, effective for amounts deferred which are attributable to services performed after 12/31/2008. Sec. 801(d)(2) through (d)(5) of this Act, provides:
"(2) Application to existing deferrals. In the case of any amount deferred to which the amendments made by this section do not apply solely by reason of the fact that the amount is attributable to services performed before January 1, 2009, to

the extent such amount is not includible in gross income in a taxable year beginning before 2018, such amounts shall be includible in gross income in the later of—

"(A) the last taxable year beginning before 2018, or

"(B) the taxable year in which there is no substantial risk of forfeiture of the rights to such compensation (determined in the same manner as determined for purposes of section 457A of the Internal Revenue Code of 1986, as added by this section).

"(3) Accelerated payments. No later than 120 days after the date of the enactment of this Act, the Secretary shall issue guidance providing a limited period of time during which a nonqualified deferred compensation arrangement attributable to services performed on or before December 31, 2008, may, without violating the requirements of section 409A(a) of the Internal Revenue Code of 1986, be amended to conform the date of distribution to the date the amounts are required to be included in income.

"(4) Certain back-to-back arrangements. If the taxpayer is also a service recipient and maintains one or more nonqualified deferred compensation arrangements for its service providers under which any amount is attributable to services performed on or before December 31, 2008, the guidance issued under paragraph (4) shall permit such arrangements to be amended to conform the dates of distribution under such arrangement to the date amounts are required to be included in the income of such taxpayer under this subsection.

"(5) Accelerated payment not treated as material modification. Any amendment to a nonqualified deferred compensation arrangement made pursuant to paragraph (4) or (5) shall not be treated as a material modification of the arrangement for purposes of section 409A of the Internal Revenue Code of 1986."

Sec. 458. Magazines, paperbacks, and records returned after the close of the taxable year.
(a) Exclusion from gross income.
A taxpayer who is on an accrual method of accounting may elect not to include in the gross income for the taxable year the income attributable to the qualified sale of any magazine, paperback, or record which is returned to the taxpayer before the close of the merchandise return period.
(b) Definitions and special rules.
For purposes of this section—
(1) **Magazine.** The term "magazine" includes any other periodical.
(2) **Paperback.** The term "paperback" means any book which has a flexible outer cover and the pages of which are affixed directly to such outer cover. Such term does not include a magazine.
(3) **Record.** The term "record" means a disc, tape, or similar object on which musical, spoken, or other sounds are recorded.
(4) **Separate application with respect to magazines, paperbacks, and records.** If a taxpayer makes qualified sales of more than one category of merchandise in connection with the same trade or business, this section shall be applied as if the qualified sales of each such category were made in connection with a separate trade or business. For purposes of the preceding sentence, magazines, paperbacks, and records shall each be treated as a separate category of merchandise.
(5) **Qualified sale.** A sale of a magazine, paperback, or record is a qualified sale if—
(A) at the time of sale, the taxpayer has a legal obligation to adjust the sales price of such magazine, paperback, or record if it is not resold, and
(B) the sales price of such magazine, paperback, or record is adjusted by the taxpayer because of a failure to resell it.
(6) **Amount excluded.** The amount excluded under this section with respect to any qualified sale shall be the lesser of—
(A) the amount covered by the legal obligation described in paragraph (5)(A), or
(B) the amount of the adjustment agreed to by the taxpayer before the close of the merchandise return period.

(7) **Merchandise return period.**
(A) Except as provided in subparagraph (B), the term "merchandise return period" means, with respect to any taxable year—
(i) in the case of magazines, the period of 2 months and 15 days first occurring after the close of taxable year, or
(ii) in the case of paperbacks and records, the period of 4 months and 15 days first occurring after the close of the taxable year.
(B) The taxpayer may select a shorter period than the applicable period set forth in subparagraph (A).
(C) Any change in the merchandise return period shall be treated as a change in the method of accounting.
(8) **Certain evidence may be substituted for physical return of merchandise.** Under regulations prescribed by the Secretary, the taxpayer may substitute, for the physical return of magazines, paperbacks, or records required by subsection (a), certification or other evidence that the magazine, paperback, or record has not been resold and will not be resold if such evidence—
(A) is in the possession of the taxpayer at the close of the merchandise return period, and
(B) is satisfactory to the Secretary.
(9) **Repurchased by the taxpayer not treated as resale.** A repurchase by the taxpayer shall be treated as an adjustment of the sales price rather than as a resale.
(c) Qualified sales to which section applies.
(1) **Election of benefits.** This section shall apply to qualified sales of magazines, paperbacks, or records, as the case may be, if and only if the taxpayer makes an election under this section with respect to the trade or business in connection with which such sales are made. An election under this section may be made without the consent of the Secretary. The election shall be made in such manner as the Secretary may by regulations prescribed and shall be made for any taxable year not later than the time prescribed by law for filing the return for such taxable year (including extensions thereof).
(2) **Scope of election.** An election made under this section shall apply to all qualified sales of magazines, paperbacks, or records, as the case may be, made in connection with the trade or business with respect to which the taxpayer has made the election.
(3) **Period to which election applies.** An election under this section shall be effective for the taxable year for which it is made and for all subsequent taxable years, unless the taxpayer secures the consent of the Secretary to the revocation of such election.
(4) **Treatment as method of accounting.** Except to the extent inconsistent with the provisions of this section, for purposes of this subtitle, the computation of taxable income under an election made under this section shall be treated as a method of accounting.
(d) 5-year spread of transitional adjustments for magazines.
In applying section 481(c) with respect to any election under this section which applies to magazines, the period for taking into account any decrease in taxable income resulting from the application of section 481(a)(2) shall be the taxable year for which the election is made and the 4 succeeding taxable years.
(e) Suspense account for paperbacks and records.
(1) **In general.** In the case of any election under this section which applies to paperbacks or records, in lieu of applying section 481, the taxpayer shall establish a suspense

account for the trade or business for the taxable year for which the election is made.

(2) Initial opening balance. The opening balance of the account described in paragraph (1) for the first taxable year to which the election applies shall be the largest dollar amount of returned merchandise which would have been taken into account under this section for any of the 3 immediately preceding taxable years if this section had applied to such preceding 3 taxable years. This paragraph and paragraph (3) shall be applied by taking into account only amounts attributable to the trade or business for which such account is established.

(3) Adjustments in suspense account. At the close of each taxable year the suspense account shall be—

(A) reduced the excess (if any) of—

(i) the opening balance of the suspense account for the taxable year, over

(ii) the amount excluded from gross income for the taxable year under subsection (a), or

(B) increased (but not in excess of the initial opening balance) by the excess (if any) of—

(i) the amount excluded from gross income for the taxable year under subsection (a), over

(ii) the opening balance of the account for the taxable year.

(4) Gross income adjustments.

(A) Reductions excluded from gross income. In the case of any reduction under paragraph (3)(A) in the account for the taxable year, an amount equal to such reduction shall be excluded from gross income for such taxable year.

(B) Increases added to gross income. In the case of any increase under paragraph (3)(B) in the account for the taxable year, an amount equal to such increase shall be included in gross income for such taxable year.

If the initial opening balance exceeds the dollar amount of returned merchandise which would have been taken into account under subsection (a) for the taxable year preceding the first taxable year for which the election is effective if this section had applied to such preceding taxable year, then an amount equal to the amount of such excess shall be included in gross income for such first taxable year.

(5) Subchapter C transactions. The application of this subsection with respect to a taxpayer which is a party to any transaction with respect to which there is nonrecognition of gain or loss to any party to the transaction by reason of subchapter C shall be determined under regulations prescribed by the Secretary.

In 1978, P.L. 95-600, Sec. 372(a), added Code Sec. 458, effective for tax. yrs. begin. after 9/30/79.

Sec. 460. Special rules for long-term contracts.
(a) Requirement that percentage of completion method be used.

In the case of any long-term contract, the taxable income from such contract shall be determined under the percentage of completion method (as modified by subsection (b)).

(b) Percentage of completion method.

(1) Requirements of percentage of completion method. Except as provided in paragraph (3), in the case of any long-term contract with respect to which the percentage of completion method is used—

(A) the percentage of completion shall be determined by comparing costs allocated to the contract under subsection (c) and incurred before the close of the taxable year with the estimated total contract costs, and

(B) upon completion of the contract (or, with respect to any amount properly taken into account after completion of the contract, when such amount is so properly taken into account), the taxpayer shall pay (or shall be entitled to receive) interest computed under the look-back method of paragraph (2).

In the case of any long-term contract with respect to which the percentage of completion method is used, except for purposes of applying the look-back method of paragraph (2), any income under the contract (to the extent not previously includible in gross income) shall be included in gross income for the taxable year following the taxable year in which the contract was completed. For purposes of subtitle F (other than sections 6654 and 6655), any interest required to be paid by the taxpayer under subparagraph (B) shall be treated as an increase in the tax imposed by this chapter for the taxable year in which the contract is completed (or, in the case of interest payable with respect to any amount properly taken into account after completion of the contract, for the taxable year in which the amount is so properly taken into account).

(2) Look-back method. The interest computed under the look-back method of this paragraph shall be determined by—

(A) first allocating income under the contract among taxable years before the year in which the contract is completed on the basis of the actual contract price and costs instead of the estimated contract price and costs,

(B) second, determining (solely for purposes of computing such interest) the overpayment or underpayment of tax for each taxable year referred to in subparagraph (A) which would result solely from the application of subparagraph (A), and

(C) then using the adjusted overpayment rate (as defined in paragraph (7)), compounded daily, on the overpayment or underpayment determined under subparagraph (B).

For purposes of the preceding sentence, any amount properly taken into account after completion of the contract shall be taken into account by discounting (using the Federal mid-term rate determined under section 1274(d) as of the time such amount was properly taken into account) such amount to its value as of the completion of the contract. The taxpayer may elect with respect to any contract to have the preceding sentence not apply to such contract.

(3) Special rules.

(A) Simplified method of cost allocation. In the case of any long-term contract, the Secretary may prescribe a simplified procedure for allocation of costs to such contract in lieu of the method of allocation under subsection (c).

(B) Look-back method not to apply to certain contracts. Paragraph (1)(B) shall not apply to any contract—

(i) the gross price of which (as of the completion of the contract) does not exceed the lesser of—

(I) $1,000,000, or

(II) 1 percent of the average annual gross receipts of the taxpayer for the 3 taxable years preceding the taxable year in which the contract was completed, and

(ii) which is completed within 2 years of the contract commencement date.

For purposes of this subparagraph, rules similar to the rules of subsections (e)(2) and (f)(3) shall apply.

(4) Simplified look-back method for pass-thru entities.
(A) In general. In the case of a pass-thru entity—
(i) the look-back method of paragraph (2) shall be applied at the entity level,
(ii) in determining overpayments and underpayments for purposes of applying paragraph (2)(B)—
(I) any increase in the income under the contract for any taxable year by reason of the allocation under paragraph (2)(A) shall be treated as giving rise to an underpayment determined by applying the highest rate for such year to such increase, and
(II) any decrease in such income for any taxable year by reason of such allocation shall be treated as giving rise to an overpayment determined by applying the highest rate for such year to such decrease, and
(iii) any interest required to be paid by the taxpayer under paragraph (2) shall be paid by such entity (and any interest entitled to be received by the taxpayer under paragraph (2) shall be paid to such entity).
(B) Exceptions.
(i) Closely held pass-thru entities. This paragraph shall not apply to any closely held pass-thru entity.
(ii) Foreign contracts. This paragraph shall not apply to any contract unless substantially all of the income from such contract is from sources in the United States.
(C) Other definitions. For purposes of this paragraph—
(i) Highest rate. The term "highest rate" means—
(I) the highest rate of tax specified in section 11, or
(II) if at all times during the year involved more than 50 percent of the interests in the entity are held by individuals directly or through 1 or more other pass-thru entities, the highest rate of tax specified in section 1.
(ii) Pass-thru entity. The term "pass-thru entity" means any—
(I) partnership,
(II) S corporation, or
(III) trust.
(iii) Closely held pass-thru entity. The term "closely held pass-thru entity" means any pass-thru entity if, at any time during any taxable year for which there is income under the contract, 50 percent or more (by value) of the beneficial interests in such entity are held (directly or indirectly) by or for 5 or fewer persons. For purposes of the preceding sentence, rules similar to the constructive ownership rules of section 1563(e) shall apply.

(5) Election to use 10-percent method.
(A) General rule. In the case of any long-term contract with respect to which an election under this paragraph is in effect, the 10-percent method shall apply in determining the taxable income from such contract.
(B) 10-percent method. For purposes of this paragraph—
(i) In general. The 10-percent method is the percentage of completion method, modified so that any item which would otherwise be taken into account in computing taxable income with respect to a contract for any taxable year before the 10-percent year is taken into account in the 10-percent year.
(ii) 10-percent year. The term "10-percent year" means the 1st taxable year as of the close of which at least 10 percent of the estimated total contract costs have been incurred.
(C) Election. An election under this paragraph shall apply to all long-term contracts of the taxpayer which are entered into during the taxable year in which the election is made or any subsequent taxable year.
(D) Coordination with other provisions.
(i) Simplified method of cost allocation. This paragraph shall not apply to any taxpayer which uses a simplified procedure for allocation of costs under paragraph (3)(A).
(ii) Look-back method. The 10-percent method shall be taken into account for purposes of applying the look-back method of paragraph (2) to any taxpayer making an election under this paragraph.

(6) Election to have look-back method not apply in de minimis cases.
(A) Amounts taken into account after completion of contract. Paragraph (1)(B) shall not apply with respect to any taxable year (beginning after the taxable year in which the contract is completed) if—
(i) the cumulative taxable income (or loss) under the contract as of the close of such taxable year, is within
(ii) 10 percent of the cumulative look-back taxable income (or loss) under the contract as of the close of the most recent taxable year to which paragraph (1)(B) applied (or would have applied but for subparagraph (B)).
(B) De minimis discrepancies. Paragraph (1)(B) shall not apply in any case to which it would otherwise apply if—
(i) the cumulative taxable income (or loss) under the contract as of the close of each prior contract year, is within
(ii) 10 percent of the cumulative look-back income (or loss) under the contract as of the close of such prior contract year.
(C) Definitions. For purposes of this paragraph—
(i) Contract year. The term "contract year" means any taxable year for which income is taken into account under the contract.
(ii) Look-back income or loss. The look-back income (or loss) is the amount which would be the taxable income (or loss) under the contract if the allocation method set forth in paragraph (2)(A) were used in determining taxable income.
(iii) Discounting not applicable. The amounts taken into account after the completion of the contract shall be determined without regard to any discounting under the 2nd sentence of paragraph (2).
(D) Contracts to which paragraph applies. This paragraph shall only apply if the taxpayer makes an election under this subparagraph. Unless revoked with the consent of the Secretary, such an election shall apply to all long-term contracts completed during the taxable year for which election is made or during any subsequent taxable year.

(7) Adjusted overpayment rate.
(A) In general. The adjusted overpayment rate for any interest accrual period is the overpayment rate in effect under section 6621 for the calendar quarter in which such interest accrual period begins.
(B) Interest accrual period. For purposes of subparagraph (A), the term "interest accrual period" means the period—

(i) beginning on the day after the return due date for any taxable year of the taxpayer, and

(ii) ending on the return due date for the following taxable year.

For purposes of the preceding sentence, the term "return due date" means the date prescribed for filing the return of the tax imposed by this chapter (determined without regard to extensions).

(c) Allocation of costs to contract.

(1) Direct and certain indirect costs. In the case of a long-term contract, all costs (including research and experimental costs) which directly benefit, or are incurred by reason of, the long-term contract activities of the taxpayer shall be allocated to such contract in the same manner as costs are allocated to extended period long-term contracts under section 451 and the regulations thereunder.

(2) Costs identified under cost-plus and certain federal contracts. In the case of a cost-plus long-term contract or a Federal long-term contract, any cost not allocated to such contract under paragraph (1) shall be allocated to such contract if such cost is identified by the taxpayer (or a related person), pursuant to the contract or Federal, State, or local law or regulation, as being attributable to such contract.

(3) Allocation of production period interest to contract.

(A) In general. Except as provided in subparagraphs (B) and (C), in the case of a long-term contract, interest costs shall be allocated to the contract in the same manner as interest costs are allocated to property produced by the taxpayer under section 263A(f).

(B) Production period. In applying section 263A(f) for purposes of subparagraph (A), the production period shall be the period—

(i) beginning on the later of—

(I) the contract commencement date, or

(II) in the case of a taxpayer who uses an accrual method with respect to long-term contracts, the date by which at least 5 percent of the total estimated costs (including design and planning costs) under the contract have been incurred, and

(ii) ending on the contract completion date.

(C) Application of de minimis rule. In applying section 263A(f) for purposes of subparagraph (A), paragraph (1)(B)(iii) of such section shall be applied on a contract-by-contract basis; except that, in the case of a taxpayer described in subparagraph (B)(i)(II) of this paragraph, paragraph (1)(B)(iii) of section 263A(f) shall be applied on a property-by-property basis.

(4) Certain costs not included. This subsection shall not apply to any—

(A) independent research and development expenses,

(B) expenses for unsuccessful bids and proposals, and

(C) marketing, selling, and advertising expenses.

(5) Independent research and development expenses. For purposes of paragraph (4), the term "independent research and development expenses" means any expenses incurred in the performance of research or development, except that such term shall not include—

(A) any expenses which are directly attributable to a long-term contract in existence when such expenses are incurred, or

(B) any expenses under an agreement to perform research or development.

(6) Special rule for allocation of bonus depreciation with respect to certain property.

(A) In general. Solely for purposes of determining the percentage of completion under subsection (b)(1)(A), the cost of qualified property shall be taken into account as a cost allocated to the contract as if subsection (k) of section 168 had not been enacted.

(B) Qualified property. For purposes of this paragraph, the term "qualified property" means property described in section 168(k)(2) which—

(i) has a recovery period of 7 years or less, and

(ii) is placed in service after December 31, 2009, and before January 1, 2011 (January 1, 2012, in the case of property described in section 168(k)(2)(B)).

(d) Federal long-term contract.

For purposes of this section—

(1) In general. The term "Federal long-term contract" means any long-term contract—

(A) to which the United States (or any agency or instrumentality thereof) is a party, or

(B) which is a subcontract under a contract described in subparagraph (A).

(2) Special rules for certain taxable entities. For purposes of paragraph (1), the rules of section 168(h)(2)(D) (relating to certain taxable entities not treated as instrumentalities) shall apply.

(e) Exception for certain construction contracts.

(1) In general. Subsections (a), (b), and (c)(1) and (2) shall not apply to—

(A) any home construction contract, or

(B) any other construction contract entered into by a taxpayer—

(i) who estimates (at the time such contract is entered into) that such contract will be completed within the 2-year period beginning on the contract commencement date of such contract, and

(ii) whose average annual gross receipts for the 3 taxable years preceding the taxable year in which such contract is entered into do not exceed $10,000,000.

In the case of a home construction contract with respect to which the requirements of clauses (i) and (ii) of subparagraph (B) are not met, section 263A shall apply notwithstanding subsection (c)(4) thereof.

(2) Determination of taxpayer's gross receipts. For purposes of paragraph (1), the gross receipts of—

(A) all trades or businesses (whether or not incorporated) which are under common control with the taxpayer (within the meaning of section 52(b)),

(B) all members of any controlled group of corporations of which the taxpayer is a member, and

(C) any predecessor of the taxpayer or a person described in subparagraph (A) or (B),

for the 3 taxable years of such persons preceding the taxable year in which the contract described in paragraph (1) is entered into shall be included in the gross receipts of the taxpayer for the period described in paragraph (1)(B). The Secretary shall prescribe regulations which provide attribution rules that take into account, in addition to the persons and entities described in the preceding sentence, taxpayers who engage in construction contracts through partnerships, joint ventures, and corporations.

(3) Controlled group of corporations. For purposes of this subsection, the term "controlled group of corporations" has the meaning given to such term by section 1563(a), except that—

(A) "more than 50 percent" shall be substituted for "at least 80 percent" each place it appears in section 1563(a)(1), and

(B) the determination shall be made without regard to subsections (a)(4) and (e)(3)(C) of section 1563.

(4) Construction contract. For purposes of this subsection, the term "construction contract" means any contract for the building, construction, reconstruction, or rehabilitation of, or the installation of any integral component to, or improvements of, real property.

(5) Special rule for residential construction contracts which are not home construction contracts. In the case of any residential construction contract which is not a home construction contract, subsection (a) (as in effect on the day before the date of the enactment [12/19/89] of the Revenue Reconciliation Act of 1989] shall apply except that such subsection shall be applied—

(A) by substituting "70 percent" for "90 percent" each place it appears, and

(B) by substituting "30 percent" for "10 percent".

(6) Definitions relating to residential construction contracts. For purposes of this subsection—

(A) Home construction contract. The term "home construction contract" means any construction contract if 80 percent or more of the estimated total contract costs (as of the close of the taxable year in which the contract was entered into) are reasonably expected to be attributable to activities referred to in paragraph (4) with respect to—

(i) dwelling units (as defined in section 168(e)(2)(A)(ii)) contained in buildings containing 4 or fewer dwelling units (as so defined), and

(ii) improvements to real property directly related to such dwelling units and located on the site of such dwelling units.

For purposes of clause (i), each townhouse or rowhouse shall be treated as a separate building.

(B) Residential construction contract. The term "residential construction contract" means any contract which would be described in subparagraph (A) if clause (i) of such subparagraph reads as follows:

"(i) dwelling units (as defined in section 168(e)(2)(A)(ii)), and".

(f) Long-term contract.

For purposes of this section—

(1) In general. The term "long-term contract" means any contract for the manufacture, building, installation, or construction of property if such contract is not completed within the taxable year in which such contract is entered into.

(2) Special rule for manufacturing contracts. A contract for the manufacture of property shall not be treated as a long-term contract unless such contract involves the manufacture of—

(A) any unique item of a type which is not normally included in the finished goods inventory of the taxpayer, or

(B) any item which normally requires more than 12 calendar months to complete (without regard to the period of the contract).

(3) Aggregation, etc. For purposes of this subsection, under regulations prescribed by the Secretary—

(A) 2 or more contracts which are interdependent (by reason of pricing or otherwise) may be treated as 1 contract, and

(B) a contract which is properly treated as an aggregation of separate contracts may be so treated.

(g) Contract commencement date.

For purposes of this section, the term "contract commencement date" means, with respect to any contract, the first date on which any costs (other than bidding expenses or expenses incurred in connection with negotiating the contract) allocable to such contract are incurred.

(h) Regulations.

The Secretary shall prescribe such regulations as may be necessary or appropriate to carry out the purposes of this section, including regulations to prevent the use of related parties, pass-thru entities, intermediaries, options, or other similar arrangements to avoid the application of this section.

In 2010, P.L. 111-240, Sec. 2023(a), added para. (c)(6), effective for property placed in service after 12/31/2009.

In 2005, P.L. 109-135, Sec. 403(s)(1), substituted "construction commencement date" for "contract commencement date" in Sec. 708(a) of P.L. 108-357 [see below]... Sec. 403(s)(2), redesignated Sec. 708(d) of P.L. 108-357 [see below] as Sec. 708(e) and added Sec. 708(d) [see below].

In 2004, P.L. 108-357, Sec. 708, of this Act [as amended by Sec. 403(s)(1) and (2) of P.L. 109-135, see above], provides:

"SEC. 708. METHOD OF ACCOUNTING FOR NAVAL SHIPBUILDERS.

"(a) In general. In the case of a qualified naval ship contract, the taxable income of such contract during the 5-taxable year period beginning with the taxable year in which the construction commencement date occurs shall be determined under a method identical to the method used in the case of a qualified ship contract (as defined in section 10203(b)(2)(B) of the Revenue Act of 1987).

"(b) Recapture of tax benefit. In the case of a qualified naval ship contract to which subsection (a) applies, the taxpayer's tax imposed by chapter 1 of the Internal Revenue Code of 1986 for the first taxable year following the 5-taxable year period described in subsection (a) shall be increased by the excess (if any) of—

"(1) the amount of tax which would have been imposed during such period if this section had not been enacted, over

"(2) the amount of tax so imposed during such period.

"(c) Qualified naval ship contract. For purposes of this section:

"(1) In general. The term 'qualified naval ship contract' means any contract or portion thereof that is for the construction in the United States of 1 ship or submarine for the Federal Government if the taxpayer reasonably expects the acceptance date will occur no later than 9 years after the construction commencement date.

"(2) Acceptance date. The term 'acceptance date' means the date 1 year after the date on which the Federal Government issues a letter of acceptance or other similar document for the ship or submarine.

"(3) Construction commencement date. The term 'construction commencement date' means the date on which the physical fabrication of any section or component of the ship or submrine begins in the taxpayer's shipyard.

"(d) Certain adjustments not to apply. Section 481 of the Internal Revenue Code of 1986 shall not apply with respect to any change in the method of accounting which is required by this section.

"(e) Effective date. This section shall apply to contracts for ships or submarines with respect to which the construction commencement date occurs after the date of the enactment of this Act."

In 1997, P.L. 105-34, Sec. 1211(a), added para. (b)(6), effective for contracts completed in tax. yrs. end. after 8/5/97.

—P.L. 105-34, Sec. 1211(b)(1), substituted "the adjusted overpayment rate (as defined in paragraph (7))" for "the overpayment rate established by section 6621" in subpara. (b)(2)(C)... Sec. 1211(b)(2), added para. (b)(7), effective for purposes of section 167(g) for property placed in service after 9/13/95.

In 1996, P.L. 104-188, Sec. 1702(h)(15), substituted "section 168(e)(2)(A)(ii)" for "section 167(k)" in subpara. (e)(6)(B), effective for property placed in service after 11/5/90, except as provided in Sec. 11812(c)(2) of P.L. 101-508, reproduced in note following Code Sec. 42.

—P.L. 104-188, Sec. 1704(t)(28), substituted "the look-back method of paragraph (2)" for "the look-back method of paragraph (3)" in para. (b)(1), effective 8/20/96.

In 1990, P.L. 101-508, Sec. 11812(b)(8), substituted "section 168(e)(2)(A)(ii)" for "section 167(k)" in clause (e)(6)(A)(i), effective for property placed in service after 11/5/90, except as provided in Sec. 11812(c)(2) of this Act, reproduced in note following Code Sec. 42.

In 1989, P.L. 101-239, Sec. 7621(a), amended subsec. (a)... Sec. 7621(b), added new para. (b)(5) [as amended by Sec. 7621(c)(1) of this Act]... Sec. 7621(c)(1), deleted para. (b)(1) and redesignated paras. (b)(2) through (b)(5) as paras. (b)(1) through (b)(4)... Sec. 7621(c)(2), substituted "paragraph (3)" for "paragraph (4)" and substituted "paragraph (2)" for "paragraph (3)" in para. (b)(1) [as redesignated]... Sec. 7621(c)(3), substituted "Paragraph (1)(B)" for "Paragraph (2)(B) and subsection (a)(2)" in para. (b)(3) [as redesignated]... Sec. 7621(c)(4)(A), substituted "paragraph (2)" for "paragraph (3)" each place it appeared in subpara. (b)(4)(A) [as redesignated]... Sec. 7621(c)(4)(B), substituted "paragraph (2)(B)" for "paragraph (3)(B)" in subpara. (b)(4)(A) [as redesignated]... Sec. 7621(c)(4)(C), substituted "paragraph (2)(A)" for "paragraph (3)(A)" in subpara. (b)(4)(A) [as redesignated]... Sec. 7621(c)(5), amended para. (e)(5), effective for contracts entered into on or after 7/11/89, except as provided in Sec. 7621(d)(2) and (3) of this Act which reads as follows.

"(2) Binding bids.— The amendments made by this section [Sec. 7621] shall not apply to any contract resulting from the acceptance of a bid made before July 11, 1989. The preceding sentence shall apply only if the bid could not have been revoked or altered at any time on or after July 11, 1989.

"(3) Special rule for certain ship contracts.— The amendments made by this section shall not apply in the case of a qualified ship contract (as defined in section 10203(b)(2)(B) of the Revenue Act of 1987 [P.L. 100-203])."

Prior to amendment, subsec. (a) [as amended by Sec. 7811(e)(1) of this Act, see above] read as follows:

"(a) Percentage of completion-capitalized cost method.

"(1) In general. In the case of any long-term contract—

"(A) 90 percent of the items with respect to such contract shall be taken into account under the percentage of completion method (as modified by subsection (b)), and

"(B) 10 percent of the items with respect to such contract shall be taken into account under the taxpayer's normal method of accounting.

"(2) 90 percent look-back method to apply. Upon completion of any long-term contract (or, with respect to any amount properly taken into account after completion of the contract, when such amount is so properly taken into account), the taxpayer shall pay (or shall be entitled to receive) interest determined by applying the look-back method of subsection (b)(3) to 90 percent of the items with respect to the contract."

Prior to deletion, para. (b)(1) read as follows:

"(1) Subsection (a) not to apply where percentage of completion method used. Subsection (a) shall not apply to any long-term contract with respect to which amounts includible in gross income are determined under the percentage of completion method."

Prior to amendment para. (e)(5) read as follows:

"(5) Special rule for residential construction contracts which are not home construction contracts. In the case of any residential construction contract which is not a home construction contract, subsection (a) shall be applied

"(A) by substituting '70 percent' for '90 percent' each place it appears, and

"(B) by substituting '30 percent' for '10 percent'".

—P.L. 101-239, Sec. 7811(e)(1), added "(or, with respect to any amount properly taken into account after completion of the contract, when such amount is so properly taken into account)" after "any long-term contract" in para. (a)(2) [before amended by Sec. 7621(a), see above] ... Sec. 7811(e)(2)(A), substituted "any amount properly taken into account" for "any amount received or accrued" in subpara. (b)(2)(B) [before redesignation by Sec. 7621(c)(1), see above] ... Sec. 7811(e)(2)(B), substituted "is so properly taken into account" for "is so received or accrued" in subpara. (b)(2)(B) [before redesignation by Sec. 7621(c)(1), see above] ... Sec. 7811(e)(3)(A), substituted "any amount properly taken into account" for "any amount received or accrued" in para. (b)(3) [before redesignation by Sec. 7621(c)(1), see above] ... Sec. 7811(e)(3)(B), substituted "such amount was properly taken into account" for "such amount was received or accrued" in para. (b)(3) [before redesignation by Sec. 7621(c)(10), see above] ... Sec. 7811(e)(4), added the second sentence to para. (b)(2) [before redesignation by Sec. 7621(c)(1), see above] ... Sec. 7811(e)(5), deleted "and" at the end of subpara. (e)(2)(A), added "and" at the end of subpara. (e)(2)(B), and added subpara. (e)(2)(C) ... Sec. 7811(e)(6), added the last sentence to para. (b)(2) [before redesignation by Sec. 7621(c)(1), see above], effective for contracts entered into after 2/28/86, and as provided in Sec. 804(d)(2) of P.L. 99-514, reproduced below.

—P.L. 101-239, Sec. 7815(e)(1)(A), substituted "activities referred to in paragraph (4) with respect to" for "the building, construction, reconstruction, or rehabilitation of" in subpara. (e)(6)(A) ... Sec. 7815(e)(1)(B), amended clause (e)(6)(A)(i), effective for contracts entered into on or after 6/21/88, except as provided by Sec. 5041(e)(1)(B) and (C) of Sec. 100-647, reproduced below.

Prior to amendment, clause (e)(6)(A)(i) read as follows:

"(i) dwelling units contained in buildings containing 4 or fewer dwelling units, and"

—P.L. 101-239, Sec. 7815(e)(3), amended Sec. 5041(e)(1)(C) of P.L. 100-647 [reproduced below], part of the effective date for changes made by Sec. 5041(a), and (b) of P.L. 100-647, by substituting "subsections (a) and (b)" for "subsections (a), (b), and (c)", see below.

In **1988**, P.L. 100-647, Sec. 1008(c)(1)(A), substituted "paragraph" for "subparagraph" in para. (b)(3) ... Sec. 1008(c)(1)(B), substituted "subparagraph (A)" for "paragraph (1)" each place it appeared in subpara. (b)(3)(B) ... Sec. 1008(c)(1)(C), substituted "subparagraph (B)" for "paragraph (1)" in subpara. (b)(3)(C) ... Sec. 1008(c)(2)(A), added para. (b)(4) ... Sec. 1008(c)(2)(B), substituted "Except as provided in paragraph (4), in" for "In" at the beginning of para. (b)(2) ... Sec. 1008(c)(4)(A), added the last two sentences to para. (b)(3) ... Sec. 1008(c)(4)(B), added "(or, with respect to any amount received or accrued after completion of the contract, when such amount is so received or accrued)" after "contract" in subpara. (b)(2)(B), effective for any contract entered into after 2/28/86 and as provided in Sec. 804(d)(2) of P.L. 99-514, [as amended by Sec. 1008(c)(3) of this Act, see below] reproduced below.

—P.L. 100-647, Sec. 1008(c)(3), amended Sec. 804(d)(2) of P.L. 99-514, by substituting "section 460(c)(5)" for "section 263A(c)(5)", see below.

—P.L. 100-647, Sec. 5041(a)(1), substituted "90 percent" for "70 percent" each place it appeared in subsec. (a) ... Sec. 5041(a)(2), substituted "10 percent" for "30 percent" in subpara. (a)(1)(B) ... Sec. 5041(b)(1), amended para. (e)(1) ... Sec. 5041(b)(2), added para. (e)(5) ... Sec. 5041(b)(3), added para. (e)(6) ... Sec. 5041(c), added subsec. (h), effective for contracts entered into after 6/21/88, except as provided by Sec. 5041(e)(1)(C) of this Act, [as amended by Sec. 7815(e)(3) of P.L. 101-239, see above], which reads as follows:

"(B) Binding bids. The amendments made by subsections (a), (b), and (c) shall not apply to any contract resulting from the acceptance of a bid made before June 21, 1988. The preceding sentence shall apply only if the bid could not have been revoked or altered at any time on or after June 21, 1988.

"(C) Special rule for certain ship contracts. The amendments made by subsections (a) and (b) shall not apply in the case of a qualified ship contract (as defined in section 10203(b)(2)(B) of the Revenue Act of 1987)."

Prior to amendment, para. (e)(1) read as follows:

"(1) In general. Subsections (a), (b), and (c)(1) and (2) shall not apply to any construction contract entered into by a taxpayer—

"(A) who estimates (at the time such contract is entered into) that such contract will be completed within the 2-year period beginning on the contract commencement date of such contract, and

"(B) whose average annual gross receipts for the 3 taxable years preceding the taxable year in which such contract is entered into do not exceed $10,000,000."

—P.L. 100-647, Sec. 5041(d), added para. (b)(5), effective for any contract entered into after 2/28/86 and as provided in Sec. 804(d)(2) of P.L. 99-514 [as amended by this Act, reproduced below]; except that such amendment shall not apply to any contract completed in a taxable year ending before 11/10/88, if the due date (determined with regard to extensions) for the return for such year is before 11/10/88.

In **1987**, P.L. 100-203, Sec. 10203(a)(1), substituted "70 percent" for "40 percent" each place it appeared in subsec. (a) ... Sec. 10203(a)(2), substituted "30 percent" for "60 percent" in para. (a)(2), effective for contracts entered into after 10/13/87, except as provided in Sec. 10203(b)(2) which reads as follows:

"Special rule for certain ship contracts.

"(A) In general.— The amendments made by this section shall not apply in the case of a qualified ship contract.

"(B) Qualified ship contract. For purposes of subparagraph (A), the term 'qualified ship contract' means any contract for the construction in the United States of not more than 5 ships if—

"(i) such ships will not be constructed (directly or indirectly) for the Federal Government, and

"(ii) the taxpayer reasonably expects to complete such contract within 5 years of the contract commencement date (as defined in section 460(g) of the Internal Revenue Code of 1986)."

For Amortization of past service pension costs, see Sec. 10204 of this Act reproduced in note following Code Sec. 263A.

In **1986**, P.L. 99-514, Sec. 804(a), added Code Sec. 460, effective for any contract entered into after 2/28/86, and as provided by Sec. 804(d)(2) [as amended by Sec. 1008(c)(3) of P.L. 100-647, see above] which reads as follows:

"(2) Clarification of treatment of independent research and development expenses.

"(A) In general.— For periods before, on, or after the date of enactment of this Act—

"(i) any independent research and development expenses taken into account in determining the total contract price shall not be severable from the contract, and

"(ii) any independent research and development expenses shall not be treated as amounts chargeable to capital account.

"(B) Independent research and development expenses.— For purposes of subparagraph (A), the term 'independent research and development expenses' has the meaning given to such term by section 460(c)(5) of the Internal Revenue Code of 1986, as added by this section."

Sec. 804(b) of this Act provides:

"(b) Change in regulations.

"The Secretary of the Treasury or his delegate shall modify the income tax regulations relating to accounting for long-term contracts to carry out the provisions of section 460 of the Internal Revenue Code of 1986 (as added by subsection (a))."

SUBPART C.—TAXABLE YEAR FOR WHICH DEDUCTIONS TAKEN

Sec.

461. General rule for taxable year of deduction.

462. Repealed.

463. Repealed.

464. Limitations on deductions for certain farming expenses.

465. Deductions limited to amount at risk.

467. Certain payments for the use of property or services.

468. Special rules for mining and solid waste reclamation and closing costs.

468A. Special rules for nuclear decommissioning costs.

468B. Special rules for designated settlement funds.

469. Passive activity losses and credits limited.

470. Limitation on deductions allocable to property used by governments or other tax-exempt entities.

In **2004**, P.L. 108-357, Sec. 848(b), added item 470.
In **1987**, P.L. 100-203, Sec. 10201(b)(7), repealed item 463.
Prior to repeal, item 463 read as follows:
"463. Accrual of vacation pay."

In **1986,** P.L. 99-514, Sec. 404(b)(2), substituted "for certain farming expenses" for "in case of farming syndicates", in item 464.
—P.L. 99-514, Sec. 501(b), added item 469.
—P.L. 99-514, Sec. 823(b)(2), deleted item 466.
Prior to deletion, item 466 read as follows:
"466. Qualified discount coupons redeemed after close of taxable year."
—P.L. 99-514, Sec. 1807(a)(7)(B), added item 468B.
—P.L. 99-514, Sec. 1599A(71), added "the" before "use" in item 467.
In **1984,** P.L. 98-369, Sec. 91(b)(2), added item 468 . . . Sec. 91(c)(2), added item 468A . . . Sec. 92(b), added item 467.
In **1978,** P.L. 95-600, Sec. 201(c)(2), amended item 465.
Prior to amendment, item 465 read as follows:
"465. Deductions limited to amount at risk in case of certain activities."
—P.L. 95-600, Sec. 373(b), added item 466.
In **1976,** P.L. 94-455, Sec. 204(b), added item 465.
—P.L. 94-455, Sec. 207(a)(2), added item 464.
In **1975,** P.L. 93-625, Sec. 4(b), added item 463.
In **1955,** struck out item 462, which dealt with reserves for estimated expenses.

Sec. 461. General rule for taxable year of deduction.
(a) General rule.
The amount of any deduction or credit allowed by this subtitle shall be taken for the taxable year which is the proper taxable year under the method of accounting used in computing taxable income.
(b) Special rule in case of death.
In the case of the death of a taxpayer whose taxable income is computed under an accrual method of accounting, any amount accrued as a deduction or credit only by reason of the death of the taxpayer shall not be allowed in computing taxable income for the period in which falls the date of the taxpayer's death.
(c) Accrual of real property taxes.
(1) In general. If the taxable income is computed under an accrual method of accounting, then, at the election of the taxpayer, any real property tax which is related to a definite period of time shall be accrued ratably over that period.
(2) When election may be made.
(A) Without consent. A taxpayer may, without the consent of the Secretary, make an election under this subsection for his first taxable year in which he incurs real property taxes. Such an election shall be made not later than the time prescribed by law for filing the return for such year (including extensions thereof).
(B) With consent. A taxpayer may, with the consent of the Secretary, make an election under this subsection at any time.
(d) Limitation on acceleration of accrual of taxes.
(1) General rule. In the case of a taxpayer whose taxable income is computed under an accrual method of accounting, to the extent that the time for accruing taxes is earlier than it would be but for any action of any taxing jurisdiction taken after December 31, 1960, then, under regulations prescribed by the Secretary, such taxes shall be treated as accruing at the time they would have accrued but for such action by such taxing jurisdiction.
(2) Limitation. Under regulations prescribed by the Secretary, paragraph (1) shall be inapplicable to any item of tax to the extent that its application would (but for this paragraph) prevent all persons (including successors in interest) from ever taking such item into account.
(e) Dividends or interest paid on certain deposits or withdrawable accounts.
Except as provided in regulations prescribed by the Secretary, amounts paid to, or credited to the accounts of, depositors or holders of accounts as dividends or interest on their deposits or withdrawable accounts (if such amounts paid or credited are withdrawable on demand subject only to customary notice to withdraw) by a mutual savings bank not having capital stock represented by shares, a domestic building and loan association, or a cooperative bank shall not be allowed as a deduction for the taxable year to the extent such amounts are paid or credited for periods representing more than 12 months. Any such amount not allowed as a deduction as the result of the application of the preceding sentence shall be allowed as a deduction for such other taxable year as the Secretary determines to be consistent with the preceding sentence.
(f) Contested liabilities.
If—
(1) the taxpayer contests an asserted liability,
(2) the taxpayer transfers money or other property to provide for the satisfaction of the asserted liability,
(3) the contest with respect to the asserted liability exists after the time of the transfer, and
(4) but for the fact that the asserted liability is contested, a deduction would be allowed for the taxable year of the transfer (or for an earlier taxable year) determined after application of subsection (h),
then the deduction shall be allowed for the taxable year of the transfer. This subsection shall not apply in respect of the deduction for income, war profits, and excess profits taxes imposed by the authority of any foreign country or possession of the United States.
(g) Prepaid interest.
(1) In general. If the taxable income of the taxpayer is computed under the cash receipts and disbursements method of accounting, interest paid by the taxpayer which, under regulations prescribed by the Secretary, is properly allocable to any period—
(A) with respect to which the interest represents a charge for the use or forbearance of money, and
(B) which is after the close of the taxable year in which paid,
shall be charged to capital account and shall be treated as paid in the period to which so allocable.
(2) Exception. This subsection shall not apply to points paid in respect of any indebtedness incurred in connection with the purchase or improvement of, and secured by, the principal residence of the taxpayer to the extent that, under regulations prescribed by the Secretary, such payment of points is an established business practice in the area in which such indebtedness is incurred, and the amount of such payment does not exceed the amount generally charged in such area.
(h) Certain liabilities not incurred before economic performance.
(1) In general. For purposes of this title, in determining whether an amount has been incurred with respect to any item during any taxable year, the all events test shall not be treated as met any earlier than when economic performance with respect to such item occurs.
(2) Time when economic performance occurs. Except as provided in regulations prescribed by the Secretary, the time when economic performance occurs shall be determined under the following principles:
(A) Services and property provided to the taxpayer. If the liability of the taxpayer arises out of—
(i) the providing of services to the taxpayer by another person, economic performance occurs as such person provides such services,
(ii) the providing of property to the taxpayer by another person, economic performance occurs as the person provides such property, or

(iii) the use of property by the taxpayer, economic performance occurs as the taxpayer uses such property.

(B) Services and property provided by the taxpayer. If the liability of the taxpayer requires the taxpayer to provide property or services, economic performance occurs as the taxpayer provides such property or services.

(C) Workers compensation and tort liabilities of the taxpayer. If the liability of the taxpayer requires a payment to another person and—

(i) arises under any workers compensation act, or

(ii) arises out of any tort,

economic performance occurs as the payments to such person are made. Subparagraphs (A) and (B) shall not apply to any liability described in the preceding sentence.

(D) Other items. In the case of any other liability of the taxpayer, economic performance occurs at the time determined under regulations prescribed by the Secretary.

(3) Exception for certain recurring items.

(A) In general. Notwithstanding paragraph (1) an item shall be treated as incurred during any taxable year if—

(i) the all events test with respect to such item is met during such taxable year (determined without regard to paragraph (1)),

(ii) economic performance with respect to such item occurs within the shorter of—

(I) a reasonable period after the close of such taxable year, or

(II) 8½ months after the close of such taxable year,

(iii) such item is recurring in nature and the taxpayer consistently treats items of such kind as incurred in the taxable year in which the requirements of clause (i) are met, and

(iv) either—

(I) such item is not a material item, or

(II) the accrual of such item in the taxable year in which the requirements of clause (i) are met results in a more proper match against income than accruing such item in the taxable year in which economic performance occurs.

(B) Financial statements considered under subparagraph (A)(iv). In making a determination under subparagraph (A)(iv), the treatment of such item on financial statements shall be taken into account.

(C) Paragraph not to apply to workers compensation and tort liabilities. This paragraph shall not apply to any item described in subparagraph (C) of paragraph (2).

(4) All events test. For purposes of this subsection, the all events test is met with respect to any item if all events have occurred which determine the fact of liability and the amount of such liability can be determined with reasonable accuracy.

(5) Subsection not to apply to certain items. This subsection shall not apply to any item for which a deduction is allowable under a provision of this title which specifically provides for a deduction for a reserve for estimated expenses.

(i) Special rules for tax shelters.

(1) Recurring item exception not to apply. In the case of a tax shelter, economic performance shall be determined without regard to paragraph (3) of subsection (h).

(2) Special rule for spudding of oil or gas wells.

(A) In general. In the case of a tax shelter, economic performance with respect to amounts paid during the taxable year for drilling an oil or gas well shall be treated as having occurred within a taxable year if drilling of the well commences before the close of the 90th day after the close of the taxable year.

(B) Deduction limited to cash basis.

(i) Tax shelter partnerships. In the case of a tax shelter which is a partnership, in applying section 704(d) to a deduction or loss for any taxable year attributable to an item which is deductible by reason of subparagraph (A), the term "cash basis" shall be substituted for the term "adjusted basis".

(ii) Other tax shelters. Under regulations prescribed by the Secretary, in the case of a tax shelter other than a partnership, the aggregate amount of the deductions allowable by reason of subparagraph (A) for any taxable year shall be limited in a manner similar to the limitation under clause (i).

(C) Cash basis defined. For purposes of subparagraph (B), a partner's cash basis in a partnership shall be equal to the adjusted basis of such partner's interest in the partnership, determined without regard to—

(i) any liability of the partnership, and

(ii) any amount borrowed by the partner with respect to such partnership which—

(I) was arranged by the partnership or by any person who participated in the organization, sale, or management of the partnership (or any person related to such person within the meaning of section 465(b)(3)(C)), or

(II) was secured by any asset of the partnership.

(3) Tax shelter defined. For purposes of this subsection, the term "tax shelter" means—

(A) any enterprise (other than a C corporation) if at any time interests in such enterprise have been offered for sale in any offering required to be registered with any Federal or State agency having the authority to regulate the offering of securities for sale,

(B) any syndicate (within the meaning of section 1256(e)(3)(B)), or

(C) any tax shelter (as defined in section 6662(d)(2)(C)(ii)).

(4) Special rules for farming. In the case of the trade or business of farming (as defined in section 464(e)), in determining whether an entity is a tax shelter, the definition of farming syndicate in section 464(c) shall be substituted for subparagraphs (A) and (B) of paragraph (3).

(5) Economic performance. For purposes of this subsection, the term "economic performance" has the meaning given such term by subsection (h).

(j) Limitation on excess farm losses of certain taxpayers.

(1) Limitation. If a taxpayer other than a C corporation receives any applicable subsidy for any taxable year, any excess farm loss of the taxpayer for the taxable year shall not be allowed.

(2) Disallowed loss carried to next taxable year. Any loss which is disallowed under paragraph (1) shall be treated as a deduction of the taxpayer attributable to farming businesses in the next taxable year.

(3) Applicable subsidy. For purposes of this subsection, the term "applicable subsidy" means—

(A) any direct or counter-cyclical payment under title I of the Food, Conservation, and Energy Act of 2008, or any payment elected to be received in lieu of any such payment, or

(B) any Commodity Credit Corporation loan.

(4) Excess farm loss. For purposes of this subsection—
(A) In general. The term "excess farm loss" means the excess of—
(i) the aggregate deductions of the taxpayer for the taxable year which are attributable to farming businesses of such taxpayer (determined without regard to whether or not such deductions are disallowed for such taxable year under paragraph (1)), over
(ii) the sum of—
(I) the aggregate gross income or gain of such taxpayer for the taxable year which is attributable to such farming businesses, plus
(II) the threshold amount for the taxable year.
(B) Threshold amount.
(i) In general. The term "threshold amount" means, with respect to any taxable year, the greater of—
(I) $300,000 ($150,000 in the case of married individuals filing separately), or
(II) the excess (if any) of the aggregate amounts described in subparagraph (A)(ii)(I) for the 5-consecutive taxable year period preceding the taxable year over the aggregate amounts described in subparagraph (A)(i) for such period.
(ii) Special rules for determining aggregate amounts. For purposes of clause (i)(II)—
(I) notwithstanding the disregard in subparagraph (A)(i) of any disallowance under paragraph (1), in the case of any loss which is carried forward under paragraph (2) from any taxable year, such loss (or any portion thereof) shall be taken into account for the first taxable year in which a deduction for such loss (or portion) is not disallowed by reason of this subsection, and
(II) the Secretary shall prescribe rules for the computation of the aggregate amounts described in such clause in cases where the filing status of the taxpayer is not the same for the taxable year and each of the taxable years in the period described in such clause.
(C) Farming business.
(i) In general. The term "farming business" has the meaning given such term in section 263A(e)(4).
(ii) Certain trades and businesses included. If, without regard to this clause, a taxpayer is engaged in a farming business with respect to any agricultural or horticultural commodity—
(I) the term "farming business" shall include any trade or business of the taxpayer of the processing of such commodity (without regard to whether the processing is incidental to the growing, raising, or harvesting of such commodity), and
(II) if the taxpayer is a member of a cooperative to which subchapter T applies, any trade or business of the cooperative described in subclause (I) shall be treated as the trade or business of the taxpayer.
(D) Certain losses disregarded. For purposes of subparagraph (A)(i), there shall not be taken into account any deduction for any loss arising by reason of fire, storm, or other casualty, or by reason of disease or drought, involving any farming business.
(5) Application of subsection in case of partnerships and S corporations. In the case of a partnership or S corporation—
(A) this subsection shall be applied at the partner or shareholder level, and
(B) each partner's or shareholder's proportionate share of the items of income, gain, or deduction of the partnership or S corporation for any taxable year from farming businesses attributable to the partnership or S corporation, and of any applicable subsidies received by the partnership or S corporation during the taxable year, shall be taken into account by the partner or shareholder in applying this subsection to the taxable year of such partner or shareholder with or within which the taxable year of the partnership or S corporation ends.
The Secretary may provide rules for the application of this paragraph to any other pass-thru entity to the extent necessary to carry out the provisions of this subsection.
(6) Additional reporting. The Secretary may prescribe such additional reporting requirements as the Secretary determines appropriate to carry out the purposes of this subsection.
(7) Coordination with section 469. This subsection shall be applied before the application of section 469.

In 2008, P.L. 110-246, Sec. 4, Repeals the duplicative enactment and provides effective date provisions of the Act entitled "An Act to provide for the continuation of agricultural programs through fiscal year 2012, and for other purposes" Sec. 4, P.L. 110-246 reads as follows:
"Sec. 4. Repeal of duplicative enactment.
"(a) In General- The Act entitled 'An Act to provide for the continuation of agricultural programs through fiscal year 2012, and for other purposes' (H.R. 2419 of the 110th Congress), and the amendments made by that Act, are repealed, effective on the date of enactment of that Act.
"(b) Effective Date- Except as otherwise provided in this Act, this Act and the amendments made by this Act shall take effect on the earlier of--
"(1) the date of enactment of this Act; or
"(2) the date of the enactment of the Act entitled 'An Act to provide for the continuation of agricultural programs through fiscal year 2012, and for other purposes' (H.R. 2419 of the 110th Congress)."
—P.L. 110-246, Sec. 15351(a), added subsec. (j), effective for tax. yrs. begin. after 12/31/2009. [Ed. Note: May 22, 2008 was the date of enactment for H.R. 2419 (PL 110-234), which was repealed by (2008 Farm Act § 4(a)) (PL 110-246, 6/18/2008), in connection with the reenactment of the farm bill to correct a technical deficiency in its original passage.]
In 2005, P.L. 109-135, Sec. 412(aa), substituted "section 6662(d)(2)(C)(ii)" for "section 6662(d)(2)(C)(iii)" in subpara. (i)(3)(C), effective 12/21/2005.
In 1996, P.L. 104-188, Sec. 1704(t)(24), amended Sec. 7721(c)(10) of P.L. 101-239, see below, by substituting "section 6661(b)(2)(C)(ii)" for "section 6662(b)(2)(C)(ii)" in the material stricken... Sec. 1704(t)(78), substituted "section 6662(d)(2)(C)(iii)" for "section 6662(d)(2)(C)(ii)" in subpara. (i)(3)(C), effective 8/20/96.
In 1990, P.L. 101-508, Sec. 11704(a)(5), amended subpara. (i)(3)(C), effective 11/5/90.
Prior to amendment subpara. (i)(3)(C) read as follows:
"(C) any tax shelter (within the meaning of section 6662(d)(2)(C)(ii))."
In 1989, P.L. 101-239, Sec. 7721(c)(10), [as amended by Sec. 1704(t)(24) of P.L. 104-188, see above] substituted "section 6662(d)(2)(C)(ii)" for "section 6661(b)(2)(C)(ii)" in subpara. (i)(3)(C), effective for returns the due date for which (determined without regard to extensions) is after 12/31/89.
In 1988, P.L. 100-647, Sec. 1008(a)(3), amended para. (i)(2), effective for tax. yrs. begin. after 12/31/86.
Prior to amendment, para. (i)(2) read as follows:
"(2) Special rule for spudding of oil or gas wells. In the case of a tax shelter, economic performance with respect to the act of drilling an oil or gas well shall be treated as having occurred within a taxable year if drilling of the well commences before the close of the 90th day after the close of the taxable year."
—P.L. 100-647, Sec. 1018(u)(5), amended Sec. 823(b)(1) of 99-514, see below.
Prior to amendment, Sec. 823(b)(1) of P.L. 99-514 read as follows:
"(1) Paragraph (5) of section 461(h) is amended by striking out subparagraph (C) and by redesignating subparagraph (D) as subparagraph (C)."
In 1987, P.L. 100-203, Sec. 10201(b)(5), amended para. (h)(5), effective for tax. yrs. begin. after 12/31/87.
Prior to amendment, para. (h)(5) read as follows:
"(5) Subsection not to apply to certain cases to which other provisions of this title specifically apply. This subsection shall not apply to any item to which any of the following provisions apply:
"(A) Section 463 (relating to vacation pay).
"(B) Any other provisions of this title which specifically provides for a deduction for a reserve for estimated expenses."
In 1986, P.L. 99-514, Sec. 801(b)(1), amended the heading of subsec. (i) and paras. (i)(1) and (i)(2)... Sec. 801(b)(2), amended para. (i)(4) [as amended by Sec. 1807(a)(2) of this Act, see below]... Sec. 805(c)(5), deleted subpara. (h)(5)(A) and redesignated subparas. (h)(5)(B), (C) and (D) as subparas. (h)(5)(A), (B) and (C)... Sec. 823(b)(1), [as amended by Sec. 1018(u)(5) of P.L. 100-647, see

Tax accounting   Code Sec. 461

above] deleted subpara. (h)(5)(B) (as redesignated by Sec. 805(c)(5) of this Act) and redesignated para. (h)(5)(C) (as redesignated by Sec. 805(c)(5) of this Act) as subpara. (h)(5)(B), effective for tax. yrs. begin. after 12/31/86.

For special rules and exceptions, see Secs. 801(d)(2)-(4) of P.L. 99-514, reproduced in Note following Code Sec. 448.

Prior to amendment, the heading of subsec. (i) and paras. (i)(1) and (i)(2) [as amended by Sec. 1807(a)(1) of this Act] read as follows:

"(i) Tax shelters may not deduct items earlier than when economic performance occurs.

"(1) In general. In the case of a tax shelter computing taxable income under the cash receipts and disbursements method of accounting, such tax shelter shall not be allowed a deduction under this chapter with respect to any item any earlier than the time when such item would be treated as incurred under subsection (h) (determined without regard to paragraph (3) thereof).

"(2) Exception (to extent of cash basis) when economic performance occurs on or before the 90th day after the close of the taxable year.

"(A) In general. Paragraph (1) shall not apply to any item if economic performance with respect to such item occurs before the close of the 90th day the close of the taxable year.

"(B) Deduction limited to cash basis.

"(i) Tax shelter partnerships. In the case of a tax shelter which is a partnership, in applying section 704(d) to a deduction or loss for any taxable year attributable to an item which is deductible by reason of subparagraph (A), the term 'cash basis' shall be substituted for the term 'adjusted basis'.

"(ii) Other tax shelters. Under regulations prescribed by the Secretary, in the case of a tax shelter other than a partnership, the aggregate amount of the deductions allowable by reason of subparagraph (A) for any taxable year shall be limited in a manner similar to the limitation under clause (i).

"(C) Cash basis defined. For purposes of subparagraph (B), a partner's cash basis in a partnership shall be equal to the adjusted basis of such partner's interest in the partnership, determined without regard to—

"(i) any liability of the partnership, and

"(ii) any amount borrowed by the partner with respect to such partnership which—

"(I) was arranged by the partnership or by any person who participated in the organization, sale, or management of the partnership (or any person related to such person within the meaning of section 168(e)(4)), or

"(II) was secured by any assets of the partnership.

"(D) Special cash basis rule for spudding of oil or gas wells. Solely for purposes of applying subparagraph (A), economic performance with respect to the act of drilling of an oil or gas well shall be treated as occurring when the drilling of the well is commenced."

Prior to amendment, para. (i)(4) [as amended by Sec. 1807(a)(2) of the Act] read as follows:

"(4) Special rules for farming. In the case of the trade or business of farming (as defined in section 464(e))—

"(A) any tax shelter described in paragraph (3)(C) shall be treated as a farming syndicate for purposes of section 464; except that this subparagraph shall not apply for purposes of determining the income of an individual meeting the requirements of section 464(c)(2),

"(B) section 464 shall be applied before this subsection, and

"(C) in determining whether an entity is a tax shelter, the definition of farming syndicate in section 464(c) shall be substituted for subparagraphs (A) and (B) of paragraph (3)."

Prior to deletion, subpara. (h)(5)(A) read as follows:

"(A) Subsection (c) or (f) of section 166 (relating to reserves for bad debts)."

Prior to deletion, subpara. (h)(5)(C) [before redesignation] read as follows:

"(C) Section 466 (relating to discount coupons)."

—P.L. 99-514, Sec. 1807(a)(1)(A), substituted "before the close of the 90th day after the close of the taxable year" for "within 90 days after the close of the taxable year" in subpara. (i)(2)(A) [before amendment by Sec. 801(b)(1) of this Act] . . . Sec. 1807(a)(1)(B), substituted "on or before the 90th day" for "within 90 days" in the heading of para. (i)(2) [before amendment by Sec. 801(b)(1) of this Act] . . . Sec. 1807(a)(2), amended subpara. (i)(4)(A) [before amendment by Sec. 801(b)(2) of this Act], effective as provided in Sec. 91(g), (h) and (i) of P.L. 98-369, reproduced below.

Prior to amendment, subpara. (i)(4)(A) read as follows:

"(A) section 464 shall be applied to any tax shelter described in paragraph (3)(C),"

—P.L. 99-514, Sec. 1807(a)(6), amended Sec. 91(g)(2)(A) of P.L. 98-369 [reproduced below], the effective date of changes made by Sec. 91 of P.L. 98-369, by substituting "incurred on or before" for "incurred before", by substituting "incurred after" for "incurred on or after" and by adding the last sentence [see below].

—P.L. 99-514, Sec. 1807(a)(8), provides:

"(8) Transitional rule for certain amounts.— For purposes of section 461(h) of the Internal Revenue Code of 1954, economic performance shall be treated as occurring on the date of a payment to an insurance company if—

"(A) such payment was made before November 23, 1985, for indemnification against a tort liability relating to personal injury or death caused by inhalation or ingestion of dust from asbestos-containing insulation products,

"(B) such insurance company is unrelated to taxpayer,

"(C) such payment is not refundable, and

"(D) the taxpayer is not engaged in the mining of asbestos nor is any member of any affiliated group which includes the taxpayer so engaged."

In 1984, P.L. 98-369, Sec. 91(a), added subsecs. (h) and (i) . . . Sec. 91(e), added "determined after application of subsection (h)" after "taxable year" in para.

(f)(4), effective as provided in Secs. 91(g), [as amended by Sec. 1807(a)(6) of P.L. 99-514, see above] (h) and (i) of the Act which read as follows:

"(g) Effective dates.

"(1) In general. — Except as provided in this subsection and subsections (h) and (i), the amendments made by this section shall apply to amounts with respect to which a deduction would be allowable under chapter 1 of the Internal Revenue Code of 1954 (determined without regard to such amendments) after—

"(A) in the case of amounts to which section 461(h) of such Code (as added by such amendments) applies, the date of the enactment of this Act, and

"(B) in the case of amounts to which section 461(i) of such Code (as so added) applies, after March 31, 1984.

"(2) Taxpayer may elect earlier application. —

"(A) In general. — In the case of amounts described in paragraph (1)(A), a taxpayer may elect to have the amendments made by this section apply to amounts which—

"(i) are incurred on or before the date of the enactment of this Act (determined without regard to such amendments), and

"(ii) are incurred after the date of the enactment of this Act (determined with regard to such amendments).

"The Secretary of the Treasury or his delegate may by regulations provide that (in lieu of an election under the preceding sentence) a taxpayer may (subject to such conditions as such regulations may provide) elect to have subsection (h) of section 461 of such Code apply to the taxpayer's entire taxable year in which occurs July 19, 1984.

"(B) Election treated as change in the method of accounting. — For purposes of section 481 of the Internal Revenue Code of 1954, if an election is made under subparagraph (A) with respect to any amount, the application of the amendments made by this section shall be treated as a change in method of accounting —

"(i) initiated by the taxpayer,

"(ii) made with the consent of the Secretary of the Treasury, and

"(iii) with respect to which section 481 of such Code shall be applied by substituting a 3-year adjustment period for a 10-year adjustment period.

"(3) Section 461(h) to apply in certain cases. — Notwithstanding paragraph (1), section 461(h) of the Internal Revenue Code of 1954 (as added by this subsection) shall be treated as being in effect to the extent necessary to carry out any amendments made by this section which take effect before section 461(h).

"(h) Exception for certain existing activities and contracts. If—

"(1) Existing accounting practices. — If, on March 1, 1984, any taxpayer was regularly computing his deduction for mining reclamation activities under a current cost method of accounting (as determined by the Secretary of the Treasury or his delegate), the liability for reclamation activities—

"(A) for land disturbed before the date of the enactment of this Act, or

"(B) to which paragraph (2) applies,

shall be treated as having been incurred when the land was disturbed.

"(2) Fixed price supply contract. —

"(A) In general. — In the case of any fixed price supply contract entered into before March 1, 1984, the amendments made by subsection (b) shall not apply to any minerals extracted from such property which are sold pursuant to such contract.

"(B) No extension or renegotiation. — Subparagraph (A) shall not apply —

"(i) to any extension of any contract beyond the period such contract was in effect on March 1, 1984, or

"(ii) to any renegotiation of, or other change in, the terms and conditions of such contract in effect on March 1, 1984.

"(i) Transitional rule for accrued vacation pay.

"(1) In general. — In the case of any taxpayer —

"(A) with respect to whom a deduction was allowable (other than under section 463 of the Internal Revenue Code of 1954) for vested accrued vacation pay for the last taxable year ending before the date of the enactment of this Act, and

"(B) who elects the application of section 463 of such Code for the first taxable year ending after the date of the enactment of this Act,

then, for purposes of section 463(b) of such Code, the opening balance of the taxpayer with respect to any vested accrued vacation pay shall be determined under section 463(b)(1) of such Code.

"(2) Vested accrued vacation pay. — For purposes of this subsection, the term 'vested accrued vacation pay' means any amount allowable under section 162(a) of such Code with respect to vacation pay of employees of the taxpayer (determined without regard to section 463 of such Code)."

In 1976, P.L. 94-455, Sec. 208(a), added subsec. (g), effective for amounts paid after 12/31/75, in tax. yrs. end. after 12/31/75, except as provided in Sec. 208(b)(2) of the Act, which reads as follows:

"(2) Certain amounts paid before 1977. — The amendment made by subsection (a) shall not apply to amounts paid before January 1, 1977, pursuant to a binding contract or written loan commitment which existed on September 16, 1975 (and at all times thereafter), and which required prepayment of such amounts by the taxpayer."

—P.L. 94-455, Sec. 1901(a)(69), deleted para. (c)(2), redesignated para. (c)(3) as (c)(2) and substituted "his first taxable year in which he" for "his first taxable year which begins after December 31, 1953, and ends after the date of enactment of this title in which the taxpayer" in para. (c)(2) (as redesignated), effective for tax. yrs. begin. after 12/31/76.

Prior to amendment, para. (c)(2) read as follows:

"(2) Special rules. Paragraph (1) shall not apply to any real property tax, to the extent that such tax was allowable as a deduction under the Internal Revenue Code of 1939 for a taxable year which began before January 1, 1954. In the case of any real property tax which would, but for this subsection, be allowable as a deduction for the first taxable year of the taxpayer which begins after December

2,157

Code Sec. 461 — Tax accounting

31, 1953, then, to the extent that such tax is related to any period before the first day of such first taxable year, the tax shall be allowable as a deduction for such first taxable year."

—P.L. 94-455, Sec. 1906(b)(13)(A), substituted "Secretary" for "Secretary or his delegate" each place it appeared in Code Sec. 461, effective for tax. yrs. begin. after 12/31/76.

In 1964, P.L. 88-272, Sec. 223(a)(1), added subsec. (f), effective for tax. yrs. begin. after 12/31/53 and end. after 8/16/54, except as provided in Sec. 223(c) and (d) which read as follows:

"(c) Election as to transfers in taxable years beginning before Jan. 1, 1964.

"(1) The amendments made by subsection (a) [adding subsec. (f)] shall not apply to any transfer of money or other property described in subsection (a) made in a taxable year beginning before January 1, 1964, if the taxpayer elects, in the manner provided by regulations prescribed by the Secretary of the Treasury or his delegate, to have this paragraph apply. Such an election—

"(A) must be made within one year after the date of the enactment of this Act [2/26/64],

"(B) may not be revoked after the expiration of such one-year period, and

"(C) shall apply to all transfers described in the first sentence of this paragraph (other than transfers described in paragraph (2)).

In the case of any transfer to which this paragraph applies, the deduction shall be allowed only for the taxable year in which the contest with respect to such transfer is settled.

"(2) Paragraph (1) shall not apply to any transfer if the assessment of any deficiency which, without regard to the application of the election in respect of such transfer is, on the date of the election under paragraph (1), prevented by the operation of any law or rule of law.

"(3) If the taxpayer makes an election under paragraph (1), and if, on the date of such election, the assessment of any deficiency which results from the application of the election in respect of any transfer is not prevented by the operation of any law or rule of law, the period within which assessment of such deficiency may be made shall not expire earlier than 2 years after the date of the enactment of this Act."

"(d) Certain other transfers in taxable years beginning before Jan. 1, 1964.

"The amendments made by subsection (a) [to this section, and section 43, Internal Revenue Code of 1939] shall not apply to any transfer of money or other property described in subsection (a) made in a taxable year beginning before January 1, 1964, if—

"(1) no deduction has been allowed in respect of such transfer for any taxable year before the taxable year in which the contest with respect to such transfer is settled, and

"(2) refund or credit of any overpayment which would result from the application of such amendments to such transfer is prevented by the operation of any law or rule of law. In the case of any transfer to which this subsection applies, the deduction shall be allowed for the taxable year in which the contest with respect to such transfer is settled."

In 1962, P.L. 87-876, added subsec. (e), effective for tax. yrs. end. after 1962.

In 1960, P.L. 86-781, added subsec. (d), effective for tax. yrs. end. after 1960.

Sec. 462. Repealed.

In 1955, P.L. 74, Sec. 1(b), repealed Code Sec. 462, effective for estimated expenses for all '54 Code years. For saving provisions see note to repealed Code Sec. 452.

Prior to repeal, Code Sec. 462 read as follows:

"SEC. 462. RESERVES FOR ESTIMATED EXPENSES, ETC.

"(a) General rule.

"In computing taxable income for the taxable year, there shall be taken into account (in the discretion of the Secretary or his delegate) a reasonable addition to each reserve for estimated expenses to which this section applies.

"(b) Adjustments where reserve becomes excessive.

"If it is determined that the amount of any reserve for estimated expenses to which this section applies is (as of the close of the taxable year) excessive, then (under regulations prescribed by the Secretary or his delegate) such excess shall be taken into account in computing taxable income for the taxable year.

"(c) Estimated expenses to which this section applies.

"(1) Election of benefits.—This section shall apply to estimated expenses if and only if the taxpayer makes an election under this section with respect to the trade or business to which such expenses are attributable. The election shall be made in such manner as the Secretary or his delegate may by regulations prescribe. No election may be made with respect to a trade or business if in computing taxable income the cash receipts and disbursements method of accounting is used with respect to such trade or business.

"(2) Scope of election.—An election made under this section shall apply to all estimated expenses attributable to the trade or business.

"(3) When election may be made.—

"(A) Without consent.—A taxpayer may, without the consent of the Secretary or his delegate, make an election under this section for his first taxable year (i) which begins after December 31, 1953, and ends after the date on which this title is enacted, and (ii) for which there are estimated expenses attributable to the trade or business. Such an election shall be made not later than the time prescribed by law for filing the return for such year (including extensions thereof).

"(B) With consent.—A taxpayer may, with the consent of the Secretary or his delegate, make an election under this section at any time.

"(d) Estimated expense defined.

"(1) General rule.—For purposes of this section, the term 'estimated expense' means a deduction allowable by this subtitle—

"(A) part or all of which would (but for this section) be required to be taken into account for a subsequent taxable year;

"(B) which is attributable to the income of the taxable year or prior taxable years for which an election under this section is in effect; and

"(C) which the Secretary or his delegate is satisfied can be estimated with reasonable accuracy.

"(2) Exceptions.—The term 'estimated expense' does not include—

"(A) any deduction attributable to income taken into account in computing taxable income for taxable years preceding the first taxable year for which the election is made;

"(B) any deduction attributable to prepaid income to which section 452 applies by reason of an election made under such section by the taxpayer; or

"(C) any deduction allowable under section 166 (relating to bad debts).

"(e) Special rule for deductions attributable to period before election.

"Any deduction attributable to income taken into account in computing taxable income for taxable years preceding the first taxable year for which the election is made shall be allowable in the same manner and to the same extent as if this section had not been enacted."

Sec. 463. Repealed.

In 1987, P.L. 100-203, Sec. 10201(a), repealed Code Sec. 463, effective for tax. yrs. begin after 12/31/87.

Sec. 10201(c)(2) of the Act provides:

"(2) Change in method of accounting. In the case of any taxpayer who elected to have section 463 of the Internal Revenue Code of 1986 apply for such taxpayer's last taxable year beginning before January 1, 1988, and who is required to change his method of accounting by reason of the amendments made by this section—

"(A) such change shall be treated as initiated by the taxpayer,

"(B) such change shall be treated as having been made with the consent of the Secretary, and

"(C) the net amount of adjustments required by section 481 of such Code to be taken into account by the taxpayer—

"(i) shall be reduced by the balance in the suspense account under section 463(c) of such Code as of the close of such last taxable year, and

"(ii) shall be taken into account over the 4-taxable year period beginning with the taxable year following such last taxable year as follows:

In the case of the:	The percentage taken into account is:
1st year	25
2nd year	5
3rd year	35
4th year	35

Notwithstanding subparagraph (C)(ii), if the period the adjustments are required to be taken into account under section 481 of such Code is less than 4 years, such adjustments shall be taken into account ratably over such shorter period."

Prior to repeal Code Sec. 463 read as follows:

"SEC. 463. ACCRUAL OF VACATION PAY.

"(a) Allowance of deduction.

"At the election of a taxpayer whose taxable income is computed under an accrual method of accounting, if the conditions of section 162(a) are otherwise satisfied, the deduction allowable under section 162(a) with respect to vacation pay shall be an amount equal to the sum of—

"(1) a reasonable addition to an account representing the taxpayer's liability for vacation pay earned by employees before the close of the taxable year and paid during the taxable year or within 8½ months following the close of the taxable year; plus

"(2) the amount (if any) of the reduction at the close of the taxable year in the suspense account provided in subsection (c)(2).

Such liability for vacation pay earned before the close of the taxable year shall include amounts which, because of contingencies, would not (but for this section) be deductible under section 162(a) as an accrued expense. All payments with respect to vacation pay shall be charged to such account.

"(b) Opening balance.

"The opening balance of the account described in subsection (a)(1) for its first taxable year shall, under regulations prescribed by the Secretary, be—

"(1) in the case of a taxpayer who maintained a predecessor account for vacation pay under section 97 of the Technical Amendments Act of 1958, as amended, for his last taxable year ending before January 1, 1973, and who makes an election under this section for his first taxable year ending after December 31, 1972, the larger of—

"(A) the balance in such predecessor account at the close of such last taxable year, or

"(B) the amount determined as if the taxpayer had maintained an account described in subsection (a)(1) for such last taxable year, or

"(2) in the case of any taxpayer not described in paragraph (1), an amount equal to the largest closing balance the taxpayer would have had for any of the taxpayer's 3 taxable years immediately preceding such first taxable year if the taxpayer had maintained such account throughout such 3 immediately preceding taxable years.

"(c) Suspense account for deferred deduction.

"(1) Initial suspense account. The amount of the suspense account at the beginning of the first taxable year for which the taxpayer maintains under this section an account (described in subsection (a)(1)) shall be the amount of the opening balance described in subsection (b) minus the amount, if any, allowed as deductions for prior taxable years for vacation pay accrued but not paid at the close of the taxable year preceding such first taxable year.

"(2) Adjustments in suspense account. At the close of each taxable year the suspense account shall be—

"(A) reduced by the excess, if any, of the amount in the suspense account at the beginning of the taxable year over the amount in the account described in subsection (a)(1) at the close of the taxable year (after making the additions and charges for such taxable year provided in subsection (a)), or

"(B) increased (but not to an amount greater than the initial balance of the suspense account) by the excess, if any of the amount in the account described in subsection (a)(1) at the close of the taxable year (after making the additions and charges for such taxable year provided in subsection (a)) over the amount in the suspense account at the beginning of the taxable year.

"(3) Section 381 acquisitions. The application of this subsection to any acquisition to which section 381(a) applies shall be determined under regulations prescribed by the Secretary.

"(d) Election.

"An election under this section shall be made at such time and in such manner as the Secretary may by regulations prescribe.

"(e) Changes in accounting method.

"(1) Establishment of account not considered change. The establishment of an account described in subsection (a)(1) shall not be considered a change in method of accounting for purposes of section 446(e) (relating to requirement respecting change of accounting method), and no adjustment shall be required under section 481 by reason of the establishment of such account.

"(2) Certain taxpayers treated as having initiated change. If the taxpayer treated vacation pay under section 97 of the Technical Amendments Act of 1958, as amended, for his last taxable year ending before January 1, 1973, and if such taxpayer fails to make an election under this section for his first taxable year ending after December 31, 1972, then, for purposes of section 481, such taxpayer shall be treated as having initiated a change in method of accounting with respect to vacation pay for his first taxable year ending after December 31, 1972."

In **1986**, P.L. 99-514, Sec. 1165(a), substituted "and paid during the taxable year or within 8½ months following the close of the taxable year" for "and expected to be paid during the taxable year or within 12 months following the close of the taxable year" in para. (a)(1), effective for tax. yrs. begin. after 12/31/86.

— P.L. 99-514, Sec. 1851(b)(1)(A), and (b)(1)(B) provide:

"(1) Transitional rule for certain taxpayers with fully vested vacation pay plans.—

"(A) In general.— In the case of any taxpayer—

"(i) who maintained a fully vested vacation pay plan where payments are expected to be paid (or are in fact paid) within 1 year after the accrual of the vacation pay, and

"(ii) who makes an election under section 463 of the Internal Revenue Code of 1954 for such taxpayer's 1st taxable year ending after the date of the enactment of the Tax Reform Act of 1984,

in lieu of establishing a suspense account under such section 463, such election shall be treated as a change in the taxpayer's method of accounting and the adjustments required as a result of such change shall be taken into account under section 481 of such Code.

"(B) Extension of time for making election.— In the case of any taxpayer who meets the requirements of subparagraph (A)(i), the time for making an election under section 463 of such Code for such taxpayer's 1st taxable year ending after the date of the enactment of the Tax Reform Act of 1984 shall not expire before the date 6 months after the date of the enactment of this Act."

In **1984**, P.L. 98-369, Sec. 561(a), substituted "and expected to be paid during" for "and payable during" in para. (a)(1), effective for tax. yrs. begin. after 3/31/84.

In **1976**, P.L. 94-455, Sec. 1906(b)(13)(A), substituted "Secretary" for "Secretary or his delegate" each place it appeared in Code Sec. 468, effective for tax yrs. begin. after 12/31/76.

In **1975**, P.L. 93-625, Sec. 4(a), added Code Sec. 463, effective for tax. yrs. begin. after 12/31/73 with the following exception: If the taxpayer maintained an account for vacation pay under section 97 of the Technical Amendments Act of 1958, as amended, for his last tax. yr. ending before 1/1/73, this section is effective with respect to tax. yrs. ending after 12/31/72.

Sec. 464. Limitations on deductions for certain farming.

(a) General rule.

In the case of any farming syndicate (as defined in subsection (c)), a deduction (otherwise allowable under this chapter) for amounts paid for feed, seed, fertilizer, or other similar farm supplies shall only be allowed for the taxable year in which such feed, seed, fertilizer, or other supplies are actually used or consumed, or, if later, for the taxable year for which allowable as a deduction (determined without regard to this section).

(b) Certain poultry expenses.

In the case of any farming syndicate (as defined in subsection (c))—

(1) the cost of poultry (including egg-laying hens and baby chicks) purchased for use in a trade or business (or both for use in a trade or business and for sale) shall be capitalized and deducted ratably over the lesser of 12 months or their useful life in the trade or business, and

(2) the cost of poultry purchased for sale shall be deducted for the taxable year in which the poultry is sold or otherwise disposed of.

(c) Farming syndicate defined.

(1) **In general.** For purposes of this section, the term "farming syndicate" means—

(A) a partnership or any other enterprise other than a corporation which is not an S corporation engaged in the trade or business of farming, if at any time interests in such partnership or enterprise have been offered for sale in any offering required to be registered with any Federal or State agency having authority to regulate the offering of securities for sale, or

(B) a partnership or any other enterprise other than a corporation which is not an S corporation engaged in the trade or business of farming, if more than 35 percent of the losses during any period are allocable to limited partners or limited entrepreneurs.

(2) **Holdings attributable to active management.** For purposes of paragraph (1)(B), the following shall be treated as an interest which is not held by a limited partner or a limited entrepreneur:

(A) in the case of any individual who has actively participated (for a period of not less than 5 years) in the management of any trade or business of farming, any interest in a partnership or other enterprise which is attributable to such active participation,

(B) in the case of any individual whose principal residence is on a farm, any partnership or other enterprise engaged in the trade or business of farming such farm,

(C) in the case of any individual who is actively participating in the management of any trade or business of farming or who is an individual who is described in subparagraph (A) or (B), any participation in the further processing of livestock which was raised in such trade or business (or in the trade or business referred to in subparagraph (A) or (B)),

(D) in the case of an individual whose principal business activity involves active participation in the management of a trade or business of farming, any interest in any other trade or business of farming, and

(E) any interest held by a member of the family (or a spouse of any such member) of a grandparent of an individual described in subparagraph (A), (B), (C), or (D) if the interest in the partnership or the enterprise is attributable to the active participation of the individual described in subparagraph (A), (B), (C), or (D).

For purposes of subparagraph (A), where one farm is substituted for or added to another farm, both farms shall be treated as one farm. For purposes of subparagraph (E), the term "family" has the meaning given to such term by section 267(c)(4).

(d) Exception.

Subsection (a) shall not apply to any amount paid for supplies which are on hand at the close of the taxable year on account of fire, storm, or other casualty, or on account of disease or drought.

(e) Definitions.
For purposes of this section—

(1) Farming. The term "farming" means the cultivation of land or the raising or harvesting of any agricultural or horticultural commodity including the raising, shearing, feeding, caring for, training, and management of animals. For purposes of the preceding sentence, trees (other than trees bearing fruit or nuts) shall not be treated as an agricultural or horticultural commodity.

(2) Limited entrepreneur. The term "limited entrepreneur" means a person who—

(A) has an interest in an enterprise other than as a limited partner, and

(B) does not actively participate in the management of such enterprise.

(f) Subsections (a) and (b) to apply to certain persons prepaying 50 percent or more of certain farming expenses.

(1) In general. In the case of a taxpayer to whom this subsection applies, subsections (a) and (b) shall apply to the excess prepaid farm supplies of such taxpayer in the same manner as if such taxpayer were a farming syndicate.

(2) Taxpayer to whom subsection applies. This subsection applies to any taxpayer for any taxable year if such taxpayer—

(A) does not use an accrual method of accounting,

(B) has excess prepaid farm supplies for the taxable year, and

(C) is not a qualified farm-related taxpayer.

(3) Qualified farm-related taxpayer.

(A) In general. For purposes of this subsection, the term "qualified farm-related taxpayer" means any farm-related taxpayer if—

(i)(I) the aggregate prepaid farm supplies for the 3 taxable years preceding the taxable year are less than 50 percent of,

(II) the aggregate deductible farming expenses (other than prepaid farm supplies) for such 3 taxable years, or

(ii) the taxpayer has excess prepaid farm supplies for the taxable year by reason of any change in business operation directly attributable to extraordinary circumstances.

(B) Farm-related taxpayer. For purposes of this paragraph, the term "farm-related taxpayer" means any taxpayer—

(i) whose principal residence (within the meaning of section 121) is on a farm,

(ii) who has a principal occupation of farming, or

(iii) who is a member of the family (within the meaning of subsection (c)(2)(E)) of a taxpayer described in clause (i) or (ii).

(4) Definitions. For purposes of this subsection—

(A) Excess prepaid farm supplies. The term "excess prepaid farm supplies" means the prepaid farm supplies for the taxable year to the extent the amount of such supplies exceeds 50 percent of the deductible farming expenses for the taxable year (other than prepaid farm supplies).

(B) Prepaid farm supplies. The term "prepaid farm supplies" means any amounts which are described in subsection (a) or (b) and would be allowable for a subsequent taxable year under the rules of subsections (a) and (b).

(C) Deductible farming expenses. The term "deductible farming expenses" means any amount allowable as a deduction under this chapter (including any amount allowable as a deduction for depreciation or amortization) which is properly allocable to the trade or business of farming.

(g) Termination.

Except as provided in subsection (f), subsections (a) and (b) shall not apply to any taxable year beginning after December 31, 1986.

In 1998, P.L. 105-206, Sec. 6005(e)(3), added "on or" before "before" each place it appears in Sec. 312(d)(2) [sic (e)(2)] of P.L. 105-34, see below.

In 1997, P.L. 105-34, Sec. 312(d)(1), substituted "section 121" for "section 1034" in clause (f)(3)(B)(i), effective for sales and exchanges after 5/6/97, except as provided in Secs. 312(d)(2)-(4) [sic (e)(2)-(4)] of this Act [as amended by Sec. 6005(e)(3) of 105-206, see above], which read as follows:

"(2) Sales on or before date of enactment. — At the election of the taxpayer, the amendments made by this section shall not apply to any sale or exchange on or before the date of the enactment of this Act.

"(3) Certain sales within 2 years after date of enactment. Section 121 of the Internal Revenue Code of 1986 (as amended by this section) shall be applied without regard to subsection (c)(2)(B) thereof in the case of any sale or exchange of property during the 2-year period beginning on the date of the enactment of this Act if the taxpayer held such property on the date of the enactment of this Act and fails to meet the ownership and use requirements of subsection (a) thereof with respect to such property.

"(4) Binding contracts. — At the election of the taxpayer, the amendments made by this section shall not apply to a sale or exchange after the date of the enactment of this Act, if—

"(A) such sale or exchange is pursuant to a contract which was binding on such date, or

"(B) without regard to such amendments, gain would not be recognized under section 1034 of the Internal Revenue Code of 1986 (as in effect on the day before the date of the enactment of this Act) on such sale or exchange by reason of a new residence acquired on or before such date or with respect to the acquisition of which by the taxpayer a binding contract was in effect on such date.

This paragraph shall not apply to any sale or exchange by an individual if the treatment provided by section 877(a)(1) of the Internal Revenue Code of 1986 applies to such individual."

In 1988, P.L. 100-647, Sec. 1008(a)(4), added subsec. (g), effective for amounts paid or incurred after 3/1/86 in tax. yrs. begin. after 3/1/86.

In 1986, P.L. 99-514, Sec. 404(a), added subsec. (f) . . . Sec. 404(b)(1), substituted "for certain farming" for "in case of farming syndicates", in the heading of Code Sec. 464, effective for amounts paid or incurred after 3/1/86 in tax yrs. begin. after 3/1/86.

—P.L. 99-514, Sec. 803(b)(8), amended subsec. (d), effective for costs incurred after 12/31/86 in tax yrs. end. after 12/31/86.

Prior to amendment, subsec. (d) read as follows:

"(d) Exceptions.

"Subsection (a) shall not apply to—

"(1) any amount paid for supplies which are on hand at the close of the taxable year on account of fire, storm, flood, or other casualty or on account of disease or drought, or

"(2) any amount required to be charged to capital account under section 278."

In 1982, P.L. 97-354, Sec. 5(a)(30), substituted "an S corporation" for "an electing small business corporation (as defined in section 1371(b))" each place it appeared in para. (c)(1), effective for tax. yrs. begin. after 12/31/82.

In 1978, P.L. 95-600, Sec. 701(1)(3), substituted "(or a spouse of any such member)" for "(within the meaning of section 267(c)(4))" in subpara. (c)(2)(E) and added the sentence at the end of para. (c)(2), effective as if included in the amendments made by Sec. 207(a)(1) of P.L. 94-455, see below.

In 1976, P.L. 94-455, Sec. 207(a)(1), added Code Sec. 464, effective for tax. yrs. begin. after 12/31/75, except in the case of a farming syndicate in existence on 12/31/75, and for which there was no change of membership throughout its taxable year beginning in '76, Code Sec. 464 is effective for tax. yrs. begin. after 12/31/76.

Sec. 465. Deductions limited to amount at risk.
(a) Limitation to amount at risk.

(1) In general. In the case of—

(A) an individual, and

(B) a C corporation with respect to which the stock ownership requirement of paragraph (2) of section 542(a) is met,

engaged in an activity to which this section applies, any loss from such activity for the taxable year shall be allowed only to the extent of the aggregate amount with respect to which the taxpayer is at risk (within the meaning of subsection (b)) for such activity at the close of the taxable year.

(2) Deduction in succeeding year. Any loss from an activity to which this section applies not allowed under this section for the taxable year shall be treated as a deduction allocable to such activity in the first succeeding taxable year.

(3) Special rules for applying paragraph (1)(B). For purposes of paragraph (1)(B)—

(A) section 544(a)(2) shall be applied as if such section did not contain the phrase "or by or for his partner"; and

(B) sections 544(a)(4)(A) and 544(b)(1) shall be applied by substituting "the corporation meet the stock ownership requirements of section 542(a)(2)" for "the corporation a personal holding company".

(b) Amounts considered at risk.

(1) In general. For purposes of this section, a taxpayer shall be considered at risk for an activity with respect to amounts including—

(A) the amount of money and the adjusted basis of other property contributed by the taxpayer to the activity, and

(B) amounts borrowed with respect to such activity (as determined under paragraph (2)).

(2) Borrowed amounts. For purposes of this section, a taxpayer shall be considered at risk with respect to amounts borrowed for use in an activity to the extent that he—

(A) is personally liable for the repayment of such amounts, or

(B) has pledged property, other than property used in such activity, as security for such borrowed amount (to the extent of the net fair market value of the taxpayer's interest in such property).

No property shall be taken into account as security if such property is directly or indirectly financed by indebtedness which is secured by property described in paragraph (1).

(3) Certain borrowed amounts excluded.

(A) In general. Except to the extent provided in regulations, for purposes of paragraph (1)(B), amounts borrowed shall not be considered to be at risk with respect to an activity if such amounts are borrowed from any person who has an interest in such activity or from a related person to a person (other than the taxpayer) having such an interest.

(B) Exceptions.

(i) Interest as creditor. Subparagraph (A) shall not apply to an interest as a creditor in the activity.

(ii) Interest as shareholder with respect to amounts borrowed by corporation. In the case of amounts borrowed by a corporation from a shareholder, subparagraph (A) shall not apply to an interest as a shareholder.

(C) Related person. For purposes of this subsection, a person (hereinafter in this paragraph referred to as the "related person") is related to any person if—

(i) the related person bears a relationship to such person specified in section 267(b) or section 707(b)(1), or

(ii) the related person and such person are engaged in trades or business under common control (within the meaning of subsections (a) and (b) of section 52).

For purposes of clause (i), in applying section 267(b) or 707(b)(1), "10 percent" shall be substituted for "50 percent".

(4) Exception. Notwithstanding any other provision of this section, a taxpayer shall not be considered at risk with respect to amounts protected against loss through nonrecourse financing, guarantees, stop loss agreements, or other similar arrangements.

(5) Amounts at risk in subsequent years. If in any taxable year the taxpayer has a loss from an activity to which subsection (a) applies, the amount with respect to which a taxpayer is considered to be at risk (within the meaning of subsection (b)) in subsequent taxable years with respect to that activity shall be reduced by that portion of the loss which (after the application of subsection (a)) is allowable as a deduction.

(6) Qualified nonrecourse financing treated as amount at risk. For purposes of this section—

(A) In general. Notwithstanding any other provision of this subsection, in the case of an activity of holding real property, a taxpayer shall be considered at risk with respect to the taxpayer's share of any qualified nonrecourse financing which is secured by real property used in such activity.

(B) Qualified nonrecourse financing. For purposes of this paragraph, the term "qualified nonrecourse financing" means any financing—

(i) which is borrowed by the taxpayer with respect to the activity of holding real property,

(ii) which is borrowed by the taxpayer from a qualified person or represents a loan from any Federal, State, or local government or instrumentality thereof, or is guaranteed by any Federal, State, or local government,

(iii) except to the extent provided in regulations, with respect to which no person is personally liable for repayment, and

(iv) which is not convertible debt.

(C) Special rule for partnerships. In the case of a partnership, a partner's share of any qualified nonrecourse financing of such partnership shall be determined on the basis of the partner's share of liabilities of such partnership incurred in connection with such financing (within the meaning of section 752).

(D) Qualified person defined. For purposes of this paragraph—

(i) In general. The term "qualified person" has the meaning given such term by section 49(a)(1)(D)(iv).

(ii) Certain commercially reasonable financing from related persons. For purposes of clause (i), section 49(a)(1)(D)(iv) shall be applied without regard to subclause (I) thereof (relating to financing from related persons) if the financing from the related person is commercially reasonable and on substantially the same terms as loans involving unrelated persons.

(E) Activity of holding real property. For purposes of this paragraph—

(i) Incidental personal property and services. The activity of holding real property includes the holding of personal property and the providing of services which are incidental to making real property available as living accommodations.

(ii) Mineral property. The activity of holding real property shall not include the holding of mineral property.

(c) Activities to which section applies.

(1) Types of activities. This section applies to any taxpayer engaged in the activity of—

(A) holding, producing, or distributing motion picture films or video tapes,

(B) farming (as defined in section 464(e)),
(C) leasing any section 1245 property (as defined in section 1245(a)(3)),
(D) exploring for, or exploiting, oil and gas resources, or
(E) exploring for, or exploiting, geothermal deposits (as defined in section 613(e)(2)).

as a trade or business or for the production of income.

(2) Separate activities. For purposes of this section—

(A) In general. Except as provided in subparagraph (B), a taxpayer's activity with respect to each—
(i) film or video tape,
(ii) section 1245 property which is leased or held for leasing,
(iii) farm,
(iv) oil and gas property (as defined under section 614), or
(v) geothermal property (as defined under section 614),

shall be treated as a separate activity.

(B) Aggregation rules.
(i) Special rule for leases of section 1245 property by partnerships or S corporations. In the case of any partnership or S corporation, all activities with respect to section 1245 properties which—
(I) are leased or held for lease, and
(II) are placed in service in any taxable year of the partnership or S corporation,
shall be treated as a single activity.
(ii) Other aggregation rules. Rules similar to the rules of subparagraphs (B) and (C) of paragraph (3) shall apply for purposes of this paragraph.

(3) Extension to other activities.

(A) In general. In the case of taxable years beginning after December 31, 1978, this section also applies to each activity—
(i) engaged in by the taxpayer in carrying on a trade or business or for the production of income, and
(ii) which is not described in paragraph (1).

(B) Aggregation of activities where taxpayer actively participates in management of trade or business. Except as provided in subparagraph (C), for purposes of this section, activities described in subparagraph (A) which constitute a trade or business shall be treated as one activity if—
(i) the taxpayer actively participates in the management of such trade or business, or
(ii) such trade or business is carried on by a partnership or an S corporation and 65 percent or more of the losses for the taxable year is allocable to persons who actively participate in the management of the trade or business.

(C) Aggregation or separation of activities under regulations. The Secretary shall prescribe regulations under which activities described in subparagraph (A) shall be aggregated or treated as separate activities.

(D) Application of subsection (b)(3). In the case of an activity described in subparagraph (A), subsection (b)(3) shall apply only to the extent provided in regulations prescribed by the Secretary.

(4) Exclusion for certain equipment leasing by closely-held corporations.

(A) In general. In the case of a corporation described in subsection (a)(1)(B) actively engaged in equipment leasing—

(i) the activity of equipment leasing shall be treated as a separate activity, and
(ii) subsection (a) shall not apply to losses from such activity.

(B) 50-percent gross receipts test. For purposes of subparagraph (A), a corporation shall not be considered to be actively engaged in equipment leasing unless 50 percent or more of the gross receipts of the corporation for the taxable year is attributable, under regulations prescribed by the Secretary, to equipment leasing.

(C) Component members of controlled group treated as a single corporation. For purposes of subparagraph (A), the component members of a controlled group of corporations shall be treated as a single corporation.

(5) Waiver of controlled group rule where there is substantial leasing activity.

(A) In general. In the case of the component members of a qualified leasing group, paragraph (4) shall be applied—
(i) by substituting "80 percent" for "50 percent" in subparagraph (B) thereof, and
(ii) as if paragraph (4) did not include subparagraph (C) thereof.

(B) Qualified leasing group. For purposes of this paragraph, the term "qualified leasing group" means a controlled group of corporations which, for the taxable year and each of the 2 immediately preceding taxable years, satisfied each of the following 3 requirements:
(i) At least 3 employees. During the entire year, the group had at least 3 full-time employees substantially all of the services of whom were services directly related to the equipment leasing activity of the qualified leasing members.
(ii) At least 5 separate leasing transactions. During the year, the qualified leasing members in the aggregate entered into at least 5 separate equipment leasing transactions.
(iii) At least $1,000,000 equipment leasing receipts. During the year, the qualified leasing members in the aggregate had at least $1,000,000 in gross receipts from equipment leasing.

The term "qualified leasing group" does not include any controlled group of corporations to which, without regard to this paragraph, paragraph (4) applies.

(C) Qualified leasing member. For purposes of this paragraph, a corporation shall be treated as a qualified leasing member for the taxable year only if for each of the taxable years referred to in subparagraph (B)—
(i) it is a component member of the controlled group of corporations, and
(ii) it meets the requirements of paragraph (4)(B) (as modified by subparagraph (A)(i) of this paragraph).

(6) Definitions relating to paragraphs (4) and (5). For purposes of paragraphs (4) and (5)—

(A) Equipment leasing. The term "equipment leasing" means—
(i) the leasing of equipment which is section 1245 property, and
(ii) the purchasing, servicing, and selling of such equipment.

(B) Leasing of master sound recordings, etc., excluded. The term "equipment leasing" does not include the leasing of master sound recordings, and other similar contractual arrangements with respect to tangible or intangible assets associated with literary, artistic, or musical properties.

(C) Controlled group of corporations; component member. The terms "controlled group of corporations" and "component member" have the same meanings as when used in section 1563. The determination of the taxable years taken into account with respect to any controlled group of corporations shall be made in a manner consistent with the manner set forth in section 1563.

(7) Exclusion of active businesses of qualified C corporations.

(A) In general. In the case of a taxpayer which is a qualified C corporation—

(i) each qualifying business carried on by such taxpayer shall be treated as a separate activity, and

(ii) subsection (a) shall not apply to losses from such business.

(B) Qualified C corporation. For purposes of subparagraph (A), the term "qualified C corporation" means any corporation described in subparagraph (B) of subsection (a)(1) which is not—

(i) a personal holding company (as defined in section 542(a)), or

(ii) a personal service corporation (as defined in section 269A(b) but determined by substituting "5 percent" for "10 percent" in section 269A(b)(2)).

(C) Qualifying business. For purposes of this paragraph, the term "qualifying business" means any active business if—

(i) during the entire 12-month period ending on the last day of the taxable year, such corporation had at least 1 full-time employee substantially all the services of whom were in the active management of such business,

(ii) during the entire 12-month period ending on the last day of the taxable year, such corporation had at least 3 full-time, nonowner employees substantially all of the services of whom were services directly related to such business,

(iii) the amount of the deductions attributable to such business which are allowable to the taxpayer solely by reason of sections 162 and 404 for the taxable year exceeds 15 percent of the gross income from such business for such year, and

(iv) such business is not an excluded business.

(D) Special rules for application of subparagraph (C).

(i) Partnerships in which taxpayer is a qualified corporate partner. In the case of an active business of a partnership, if—

(I) the taxpayer is a qualified corporate partner in the partnership, and

(II) during the entire 12-month period ending on the last day of the partnership's taxable year, there was at least 1 full-time employee of the partnership (or of a qualified corporate partner) substantially all the services of whom were in the active management of such business,

then the taxpayer's proportionate share (determined on the basis of its profits interest) of the activities of the partnership in such business shall be treated as activities of the taxpayer (and clause (i) of subparagraph (C) shall not apply in determining whether such business is a qualifying business of the taxpayer).

(ii) Qualified corporate partner. For purposes of clause (i), the term "qualified corporate partner" means any corporation if—

(I) such corporation is a general partner in the partnership,

(II) such corporation has an interest of 10 percent or more in the profits and losses of the partnership, and

(III) such corporation has contributed property to the partnership in an amount not less than the lesser of $500,000 or 10 percent of the net worth of the corporation.

For purposes of subclause (III), any contribution of property other than money shall be taken into account at its fair market value.

(iii) Deduction for owner employee compensation not taken into account. For purposes of clause (iii) of subparagraph (C), there shall not be taken into account any deduction in respect of compensation for personal services rendered by any employee (other than a non-owner employee) of the taxpayer or any member of such employee's family (within the meaning of section 318(a)(1)).

(iv) Special rule for banks. For purposes of clause (iii) of subparagraph (C), in the case of a bank (as defined in section 581) or a financial institution to which section 591 applies—

(I) gross income shall be determined without regard to the exclusion of interest from gross income under section 103, and

(II) in addition to the deductions described in such clause, there shall also be taken into account the amount of the deductions which are allowable for amounts paid or credited to the accounts of depositors or holders of accounts as dividends or interest on their deposits or withdrawable accounts under section 163 or 591.

(v) Special rule for life insurance companies.

(I) In general. Clause (iii) of subparagraph (C) shall not apply to any insurance business of a qualified life insurance company.

(II) Insurance business. For purposes of subclause (I), the term "insurance business" means any business which is not a noninsurance business (within the meaning of section 806(b)(3)).

(III) Qualified life insurance company. For purposes of subclause (I), the term "qualified life insurance company" means any company which would be a life insurance company as defined in section 816 if unearned premiums were not taken into account under subsections (a)(2) and (c)(2) of section 816.

(E) Definitions. For purposes of this paragraph—

(i) Non-owner employee. The term "non-owner employee" means any employee who does not own, at any time during the taxable year, more than 5 percent in value of the outstanding stock of the taxpayer. For purposes of the preceding sentence, section 318 shall apply, except that "5 percent" shall be substituted for "50 percent" in section 318(a)(2)(C).

(ii) Excluded business. The term "excluded business" means—

(I) equipment leasing (as defined in paragraph (6)), and

(II) any business involving the use, exploitation, sale, lease, or other disposition of master sound recordings, motion picture films, video tapes, or tangible or intangible assets associated with literary, artistic, musical, or similar properties.

(iii) Special rules relating to communications industry, etc.

(I) Business not excluded where taxpayer not completely at risk. A business involving the use, exploitation, sale, lease, or other disposition of property described in subclause (II) of clause (ii) shall not constitute an excluded business by reason of such subclause if the taxpayer is at risk with respect to all amounts paid or incurred (or chargeable to capital account) in such business.

(II) Certain licensed businesses not excluded. For purposes of subclause (II) of clause (ii), the provision of radio, television, cable television, or similar services pursuant to a license or franchise granted by the Federal Communications Commission or any other Federal, State, or local authority shall not constitute an excluded business by reason of such subclause.

(F) Affiliated group treated as 1 taxpayer. For purposes of this paragraph—

(i) In general. Except as provided in subparagraph (G), the component members of an affiliated group of corporations shall be treated as a single taxpayer.

(ii) Affiliated group of corporations. The term "affiliated group of corporations" means an affiliated group (as defined in section 1504(a)) which files or is required to file consolidated income tax returns.

(iii) Component member. The term "component member" means an includible corporation (as defined in section 1504) which is a member of the affiliated group.

(G) Loss of 1 member of affiliated group may not offset income of personal holding company or personal service corporation. Nothing in this paragraph shall permit any loss of a member of an affiliated group to be used as an offset against the income of any other member of such group which is a personal holding company (as defined in section 542(a)) or a personal service corporation (as defined in section 269A(b) but determined by substituting "5 percent" for "10 percent" in section 269A(b)(2)).

(d) Definition of loss.

For purposes of this section, the term "loss" means the excess of the deductions allowable under this chapter for the taxable year (determined without regard to the first sentence of subsection (a)) and allocable to an activity to which this section applies over the income received or accrued by the taxpayer during the taxable year from such activity (determined without regard to subsection (e)(1)(A)).

(e) Recapture of losses where amount at risk is less than zero.

(1) In general. If zero exceeds the amount for which the taxpayer is at risk in any activity at the close of any taxable year—

(A) the taxpayer shall include in his gross income for such taxable year (as income from such activity) an amount equal to such excess, and

(B) an amount equal to the amount so included in gross income shall be treated as a deduction allocable to such activity for the first succeeding taxable year.

(2) Limitation. The excess referred to in paragraph (1) shall not exceed—

(A) the aggregate amount of the reductions required by subsection (b)(5) with respect to the activity by reason of losses for all prior taxable years beginning after December 31, 1978, reduced by

(B) the amounts previously included in gross income with respect to such activity under this subsection.

In **2004,** P.L. 108-357, Sec. 413(c)(7), added "or" at the end of clause (c)(7)(B)(i), deleted clause (c)(7)(B)(ii), and redesignated clause (c)(7)(B)(iii) as clause (c)(7)(B)(ii), effective for tax. yrs. of foreign corporations begin. after 12/31/2004, and for tax. yrs. of United States shareholders with or within which such tax. yrs. of foreign corporations end.
Prior to deletion, clause (c)(7)(B)(ii) read as follows:
"(ii) a foreign personal holding company (as defined in section 552(a)), or"
In **1990,** P.L. 101-508, Sec. 11813(b)(15), substituted "49(a)(1)(D)(iv)" for "46(c)(8)(D)(iv)" each placed it appeared in subpara. (b)(6)(D), effective for property placed in service after 12/31/90, except as provided by Sec. 11813(c)(2) of this Act reproduced in note following Code Sec. 46.
— P.L. 101-508, Sec. 11815(b)(3), substituted "section 613(e)(2)" for "section 613(e)(3)" in subpara. (c)(1)(E), effective 11/5/90 except as provided in Sec. 11821 of this Act, reproduced in note following Code Sec. 613.
In **1988,** P.L. 100-647, Sec. 1002(c)(3), provided as follows:
"(3) Notwithstanding section 203 of the Reform Act, the amendments made by section 201 of the Reform Act shall apply to any real property which was acquired before January 1, 1987, and was converted on or after such date from personal use to a use for which depreciation is allowable."
In **1986,** P.L. 99-514, Sec. 201(d)(7)(A), amended subpara. (b)(3)(C), effective for property placed in service after 12/31/86, in tax. yrs. ending after 12/31/86, [see Sec. 1002(c)(3) of P.L. 100-647, reproduced above]. For transitional rules, see Sec. 203(b)-(e) of this Act reproduced in note following Code Sec. 168. Sec. 203(a)(1)(B) of this Act provides:
"(B) Election to have amendments made by section 201 apply.—A taxpayer may elect (at such time and in such manner as the Secretary of the Treasury or his delegate may prescribe) to have the amendments made by section 201 apply to any property placed in service after July 31, 1986, and before January 1, 1987."
Prior to amendment, subpara. (b)(3)(C) read as follows:
"(C) Related person defined. For purposes of subparagraph (A), the term 'related person' has the meaning given such term by section 168(e)(4)."
— P.L. 99-514, Sec. 503(a), deleted subpara (c)(3)(D) and redesignated subpara. (c)(3)(E) as subpara. (c)(3)(D) . . . Sec. 503(b), added para. (b)(6), effective for losses incurred after 12/31/86, for property placed in service by the taxpayer after 12/31/86, except as provided in Sec. 503(c)(2) and (3) of this Act, which read as follows:
"(2) Special rule for losses of s corporation, partnership, or pass-thru entity.—In the case of an interest in an S corporation, a partnership, or other pass-thru entity acquired after December 31, 1986, the amendments made by this section shall apply to losses after December 31, 1986, which are attributable to property placed in service by the S corporation, partnership, or pass-thru entity on, before, or after January 1, 1986.
"(3) Special rule for athletic stadium.—The amendments made by this section shall not apply to any losses incurred by a taxpayer with respect to the holding of a multi-use athletic stadium in Pittsburgh, Pennsylvania, which the taxpayer acquired in a sale for which a letter of understanding was entered into before April 16, 1986."
Prior to deletion, subpara. (c)(3)(D) read as follows:
"(D) Exclusion for real property. In the case of activities described in subparagraph (A), the holding of real property (other than mineral property) shall be treated as a separate activity, and subsection (a) shall not apply to losses from such activity. For purposes of the preceding sentence, personal property and services which are incidental to making real property available as living accommodations shall be treated as part of the activity of holding such real property."
— P.L. 99-514, Sec. 1011(b)(1), substituted "806(b)(3)" for "806(c)(3)" in clause (c)(7)(D)(v), effective for tax. yrs. begin. after 12/31/86.
In **1984,** P.L. 98-369, Sec. 432(a), added para. (c)(7) . . . Sec. 432(b), amended para. (c)(2) . . . Sec. 432(c), amended para. (b)(3), effective for tax. yrs. begin. after 12/31/83, except that any loss from an activity described in section 465(c)(7)(A) of the Internal Revenue Code of 1954 (as amended by this Sec. 432 of P.L. 98-369) which (but for the amendments made by this section) would have been treated as a deduction for the taxpayer's first taxable year beginning after December 31, 1983, under section 465(a)(2) of such Code shall be allowed as a deduction for such first taxable year notwithstanding such amendments."
Prior to amendment, para. (c)(2) read as follows:
"(2) Separate activities. For purposes of this section, a taxpayer's activity with respect to each—
"(A) film or video tape,
"(B) section 1245 property which is leased or held for leasing,
"(C) farm,
"(D) oil and gas property (as defined under section 614), or
"(E) geothermal property (as determined under section 614)
shall be treated as a separate activity. A partner's interest in a partnership or a shareholder's interest in an S corporation shall be treated as a single activity to the extent that the partnership or the S corporation is engaged in activities described in any subparagraph of this paragraph."
Prior to amendment, para. (b)(3) read as follows:
"(3) Certain borrowed amounts excluded. For purposes of paragraph (1)(B), amounts borrowed shall not be considered to be at risk with respect to an activity if such amounts are borrowed from any person who—
"(A) has an interest (other than an interest as a creditor) in such activity, or
"(B) has a relationship to the taxpayer specified within any one of the paragraphs of section 267(b)."
— P.L. 98-369, Sec. 721(x)(2), substituted "a C corporation" for "a corporation" in subpara. (a)(1)(B), effective for tax. yrs. begin. after 12/31/82.

In **1982**, P.L. 97-354, Sec. 5(a)(31)(A), added "and" to the end of subpara. (a)(1)(A), deleted subpara. (a)(1)(B), and redesignated subpara. (a)(1)(C) as subpara. (a)(1)(B)... Sec. 5(a)(31)(B), substituted "paragraph (1)(B)" for "paragraph (1)(C)" in para. (a)(3) and substituted "paragraph (1)(B)" for "paragraph (1)(C)" in the heading of para. (a)(3)... Sec. 5(a)(31)(C), substituted "an S corporation" for "an electing small business corporation" the first place it appeared in the last sentence of para. (c)(2) and substituted "the S corporation" for "an electing small business corporation" the second place it appeared in the last sentence of para. (c)(2)... Sec. 5(a)(31)(D), substituted "an S corporation" for "electing small business corporation (as defined in section 1371(b))" in clause (c)(3)(B)(ii)... Sec. 5(a)(31)(E), substituted "subsection (a)(1)(B)" for "subsection (a)(1)(C)" in subpara. (c)(4)(A), effective for tax. yrs. begin. after 12/31/82.

Prior to deletion, subpara. (a)(1)(B) read as follows:

"(B) an electing small business corporation (as defined in section 1371(b)), and"

In **1980**, P.L. 96-222, Sec. 102(a)(1)(A)(i), deleted "(determined by reference to the rules contained in section 318 rather than under section 544)" in subpara. (a)(1)(C)... Sec. 102(a)(1)(A)(ii), added new para. (a)(3), effective for tax. yrs. begin. after 12/31/78. For transitional rule, see Sec. 204(b) of P.L. 95-600, reproduced below.

—P.L. 96-222, Sec. 102(a)(1)(B), added "(determined without regard to subsection (e)(1)(A))" before the period at the end of subsec. (d), effective for tax. yrs. begin. after 12/31/78.

—P.L. 96-222, Sec. 102(a)(1)(C), added "by reason of losses" before "with respect to the activity" in subpara. (e)(2)(A), effective for tax. yrs. begin. after 12/31/78.

—P.L. 96-222, Sec. 102(a)(1)(D)(i), added paras. (c)(4), (c)(5) and (c)(6), effective for tax. yrs. begin. after 12/31/78.

—P.L. 96-222, Sec. 102(a)(1)(D)(ii), amended subpara. (c)(3)(D), effective for tax. yrs. begin. after 12/31/78.

Prior to amendment, subpara. (c)(3)(D) read as follows:

"(D) Exclusions.—

"(i) Real property. In the case of activities described in subparagraph (A), the holding of real property (other than mineral property) shall be treated as a separate activity, and subsection (a) shall not apply to losses from such activity. For purposes of the preceding sentence, personal property and services which are incidental to making real property available as living accommodations shall be treated as part of the activity of holding such real property.

"(ii) Equipment leasing by closely-held corporations.

"(I) In the case of a corporation described in subsection (a)(1)(C) actively engaged in leasing equipment which is section 1245 property, the activity of leasing such equipment shall be treated, for purposes of subsection (a), as a separate activity and subsection (a) shall not apply to losses from such activity.

"(II) A corporation described in subsection (a)(1)(C) shall not be considered to be actively engaged in leasing such equipment unless 50 percent or more of the gross receipts of the corporation for the taxable year are attributable, under regulations prescribed by the Secretary, to leasing and selling such equipment.

"(III) For purposes of this paragraph, the leasing of master sound recordings, and other similar contractual arrangements with respect to tangible or intangible assets associated with literary, artistic, or musical properties shall not be treated as leasing equipment which is section 1245 property.

"(IV) In the case of a controlled group of corporations (within the meaning of section 1563(a)), this paragraph shall be applied by treating the controlled group as a single corporation."

—P.L. 96-222, Sec. 102(a)(1)(D)(iii), substituted "to which subsection (a) applies" for "to which this section applies" in para. (b)(5), effective for tax yrs. begin. after 12/31/78.

—P.L. 96-222, Sec. 102(a)(1)(E), substituted "this subtitle" for "this section" in Sec. 204(b)(2)(A) of P.L. 95-600 [reproduced below].

In **1978**, P.L. 95-618, Sec. 402(d)(1), deleted "or" at the end of subpara. (c)(1)(C), added ", or" at the end of subpara. (c)(1)(D), added new subpara. (c)(1)(E), effective for wells commenced on or after 10/1/78, in tax. yrs. end. on or after 10/1/78.

—P.L. 95-618, Sec. 402(d)(2), deleted "or" at the end of subpara. (c)(2)(C), added "or" at the end of subpara. (c)(2)(D), added new subpara. (c)(2)(E), effective for wells commenced on or after 10/1/78, in tax. yrs. end. on or after 10/1/78.

—P.L. 95-600, Sec. 201(a), added para. (c)(3)... Sec. 201(c)(1), amended the heading of Code Sec. 465... Sec. 202, amended subsec. (a)... Sec. 203, added subsec. (e), effective for tax. yrs. begin. after 12/31/78. Sec. 204(b) of the Act provides:

"(b) Transitional rules.—

"(1) Recapture provisions.—If the amount for which the taxpayer is at risk in any activity as of the close of the taxpayer's last taxable year beginning before January 1, 1979, is less than zero, section 465(e)(1) of the Internal Revenue Code of 1954 (as added by section 203 of this Act) shall be applied with respect to such activity of the taxpayer by substituting such negative amount for zero.

"(2) Special transitional rules for leasing activities.—

"(A) Rule for leases.—In the case of any activity described in section 465(c)(1)(C) of such Code in which a corporation described in section 465(a)(1)(C) of such Code is engaged, the amendments made by this subtitle shall not apply with respect to—

"(i) leases entered into before November 1, 1978, and

"(ii) leases where the property was ordered by the lessor or lessee before November 1, 1978.

"(B) Holding of interests for purposes of subparagraph (A).—Subparagraph (A) shall apply only to taxpayers who held their interests in the property on October 31, 1978."

Prior to amendment, the heading of Code Sec. 465 read as follows:

"SEC. 465. DEDUCTIONS LIMITED TO AMOUNT AT RISK IN CASE OF CERTAIN ACTIVITIES."

Prior to amendment, subsec. (a) read as follows:

"(a) General rule.

"In the case of a taxpayer (other than a corporation which is neither an electing small business corporation (as defined in section 1371(b)) nor a personal holding company (as defined in section 542)) engaged in an activity to which this section applies, any loss from such activity for the taxable year shall be allowed only to the extent of the aggregate amount with respect to which the taxpayer is at risk (within the meaning of subsection (b)) for such activity at the close of the taxable year. Any loss from such activity not allowed under this section for the taxable year shall be treated as a deduction allocable to such activity in the first succeeding taxable year."

—P.L. 95-600, Sec. 701(k)(1), substituted "section 465(c)(1)(C)" for "section 465(c)(1)(B)" in Sec. 204(c)(3) of P.L. 94-455 (reproduced below)... Sec. 701(k)(2), substituted "(determined without regard to the first sentence of subsection (a))" for "(determined without regard to this section)" in subsec. (d), effective 10/4/76.

In **1976**, P.L. 94-455, Sec. 204(a), added Code Sec. 465. Sec. 204(c) of the Act provided as follows:

"(c) Effective Dates.—

"(1) In general.—Except as provided in paragraph (2) and (3), the amendments made by this section shall apply to losses attributable to amounts paid or incurred in taxable years beginning after December 31, 1975. For purposes of this subsection, any amount allowed or allowable for depreciation or amortization for any period shall be treated as an amount paid or incurred in such period.

"(2) Special transitional rules for movies and video tapes.—

"(A) In general.—In the case of any activity described in section 465(c)(1)(A) of the Internal Revenue Code of 1954, the amendments made by this section shall not apply to—

"(i) deductions for depreciation or amortization with respect to property the principal production of which began before September 11, 1975, and for the purchase of which there was on September 11, 1975, and at all times thereafter a binding contract, and

"(ii) deductions attributable to producing or distributing property the principal production of which began before September 11, 1975.

"(B) Exception for certain agreements where principal photography began before 1976.—In the case of any activity described in section 465(c)(1)(A) of the Internal Revenue Code of 1954, the amendments made by this section shall not apply to deductions attributable to the producing of a film the principal photography of which began on or before December 31, 1975, if—

"(i) on September 10, 1975, there was an agreement with the director or a principal motion picture star, or on or before September 10, 1975, there had been expended (or committed to the production) an amount not less than the lower of $100,000 or 10 percent of the estimated costs of producing the film, and

"(ii) the production takes place in the United States. Subparagraph (A) shall apply only to taxpayers who held their interest on September 10, 1975. Subparagraph (B) shall apply only to taxpayers who held their interests on December 31, 1975.

"(3) Special transitional rules for leasing activities.—

"(A) Rule for leases other than operating leases.—In the case of any activity described in section 465(c)(1)(B) of the Internal Revenue Code of 1954, the amendments made by this section shall not apply with respect to—

"(i) leases entered into before January 1, 1976, and

"(ii) leases where the property was ordered by the lessor or lessee before January 1, 1976.

"(B) Holding of interests for purposes of subparagraph (A).—Subparagraph (A) shall apply only to taxpayers who held their interests in the property on December 31, 1975.

"(C) Special rule for operating leases.—In the case of a lease described in section 46(e)(3)(B) of the Internal Revenue Code of 1954—

"(i) subparagraph (A) shall be applied by substituting 'May 1, 1976' for 'January 1, 1976' each place it appears therein, and

"(ii) subparagraph (B) shall be applied by substituting 'April 30, 1976' for 'December 31, 1975'."

Sec. 466. Repealed.

In **1986**, P.L. 99-514, Sec. 823(a), repealed Code Sec. 466, effective for tax. yrs. begin. after 12/31/86. Sec. 823(c)(2) of this Act provides:

"(2) Change in method of accounting. In the case of any taxpayer who elected to have section 466 of the Internal Revenue Code of 1954 apply for such taxpayer's last taxable year beginning before January 1, 1987, and is required to change its method of accounting by reason of the amendments made by this section for any taxable year—

"(A) such change shall be treated as initiated by the taxpayer,

"(B) such change shall be treated as having been made with the consent of the Secretary, and

"(C) the net amount of adjustments required by section 481 of the Internal Revenue Code of 1986 to be taken into account by the taxpayer shall—

"(i) be reduced by the balance in the suspense account under section 466(e) of such Code as of the close of such last taxable year, and

"(ii) be taken into account over a period not longer than 4 years."

Prior to repeal, Code Sec. 466 read as follows:

"SEC. 466. QUALIFIED DISCOUNT COUPONS REDEEMED AFTER CLOSE OF TAXABLE YEAR.

Code Sec. 466

"(a) Allowance of deduction.

"At the election of a taxpayer whose taxable income is computed under an accrual method of accounting, the deduction allowable under this chapter for the redemption costs of qualified discount coupons shall be an amount equal to the sum of—

"(1) such costs incurred by the taxpayer with respect to coupons—

"(A) which were outstanding at the close of the taxable year, and

"(B) which were received by the taxpayer before the close of the redemption period for the taxable year, plus

"(2) such costs (other than costs properly taken into account under paragraph (1) for a prior taxable year) incurred by the taxpayer during the taxable year.

"(b) Qualified discount coupons.

"For purposes of this section—

"(1) In general. The term 'qualified discount coupon' means a discount coupon which—

"(A) was issued by the taxpayer,

"(B) is redeemable by the taxpayer, and

"(C) allows a discount on the purchase price of merchandise or other tangible personal property.

"(2) Method of issuance not taken into account. The determination of whether or not a discount coupon is a qualified discount coupon shall be made without regard to whether the coupon was issued through a newspaper, magazine, or other publication, by mail, on the pack or in the pack of merchandise, or otherwise.

"(3) Discount on item cannot exceed $5. A coupon shall not be a qualified discount coupon if—

"(A) the face amount of such coupon is more than $5, or

"(B) such coupon may be used with other coupons to bring about a price discount of more than $5 with respect to any item.

"(4) There must be redemption chain. A coupon shall not be a qualified discount coupon if the issuer directly redeems such coupon from the person using the coupon to receive a price discount. For purposes of the preceding sentence, corporations which are members of the same controlled group of corporations (within the meaning of section 1563(a) as the issuer shall be treated as the issuer.

"(5) Redeemable by taxpayer. A coupon is redeemable by the taxpayer if the terms of the coupon require the taxpayer to redeem the coupon when presented for redemption in accordance with its terms.

"(c) Redemption costs; redemption period. For purposes of this section—

"(1) Redemption costs. The term 'redemption cost' means, with respect to any coupon—

"(A) the lesser of—

"(i) the amount of the discount provided by the terms of the coupon, or

"(ii) the amount incurred by the taxpayer for paying such discount, plus

"(B) the amount incurred by the taxpayer for a payment to the retailer (or other person redeeming the coupon from the person receiving the price discount), but only if the amount so payable is stated on the coupon.

"(2) Redemption period.

"(A) In general. Except as provided in subparagraph (B), the redemption period for any taxable year is the 6-month period immediately following the close of the taxable year.

"(B) Taxpayer may select shorter period. The taxpayer may select a redemption period which is shorter than 6 months.

"(C) Change in redemption period. Any change in the redemption period shall be treated as a change in the method of accounting.

"(d) Qualified discount coupons to which section applies.

"(1) Election of benefits. This section shall apply to qualified discount coupons if and only if the taxpayer makes an election under this section with respect to the trade or business in connection with which such coupons are issued. An election under this section may be made without the consent of the Secretary. The election shall be made in such manner as the Secretary may by regulations prescribe and shall be made for any taxable year not later than the time prescribed by law for filing the return for such taxable year (including extensions thereof).

"(2) Scope of election. An election made under this section shall apply to all qualified discount coupons issued in connection with the trade or business with respect to which the taxpayer has made the election.

"(3) Period to which election applies. An election under this section shall apply to the taxable year for which it is made and for all subsequent taxable years, unless the taxpayer secures the consent of the Secretary to the revocation of such election.

"(4) Treatment as method of accounting. Except to the extent inconsistent with the provisions of this section, for purposes of this subtitle, the computation of taxable income under an election made under this section shall be treated as a method of accounting.

"(e) Suspense account.

"(1) In general. In the case of any election under this section which (but for this subsection) would result in a net decrease in taxable income under section 481(a)(2), in lieu of applying section 481, the taxpayer shall establish a suspense account for the trade or business for the taxable year for which the election is made.

"(2) Initial opening balance. Initial opening balance of the account described in paragraph (1) for the first taxable year to which the election applies shall be the amount by which—

"(A) the largest dollar amount which would have been taken into account under subsection (a)(1) for any of the 3 immediately preceding taxable years if this section had applied to such 3 preceding taxable years, exceeds

"(B) the sum of the increases in income (and the decreases in deductions) which (but for this subsection) would result under section 481(a)(2) for such first taxable year.

This subsection shall be applied by taking into account only amounts attributable to the trade or business for which such account is established.

"(3) Adjustments in suspense account. At the close of each taxable year, the suspense account shall be—

"(A) reduced by the excess (if any) of—

"(i) the opening balance of the suspense account for the taxable year, over

"(ii) the amount deducted for the taxable year under subsection (a)(1), or

"(B) increased (but not in excess of the initial opening balance) by the excess (if any) of—

"(i) the amount deducted for the taxable year under subsection (a)(1), over

"(ii) the opening balance of the suspense account for the taxable year.

"(4) Income adjustments.

"Reductions allowed as deduction. In the case of any reduction under paragraph (3)

"(A) in the account for the taxable year, an amount equal to such reduction shall be allowed as a deduction for such taxable year.

"(B) Increases added to gross income. In the case of any increase under paragraph (3)(B) in the account for the taxable year, an amount equal to such increase shall be included in gross income for such taxable year.

If the amount described in paragraph (2)(A) exceeds the dollar amount which would have been taken into account under subsection (a)(1) for the taxable year preceding the first taxable year for which the election is effective if this section had applied to such preceding taxable year, then an amount equal to the amount of such excess shall be included in gross income for such first taxable year.

"(5) Subchapter C transactions. The application of this subsection with respect to a taxpayer which is a party to any transaction with respect to which there is nonrecognition of gain or loss to any party to the transaction by reason of subchapter C shall be determined under regulations prescribed by the Secretary.

"(f) 10-year spread of any net increase in taxable income under section 481(a)(2).

"In the case of any election under this section which results in a net increase in taxable income under section 481(a)(2), under regulations prescribed by the Secretary, such net increase shall (except as otherwise provided in such regulations) be taken into account by the taxpayer in computing taxable income in each of the 10 taxable years beginning with the year for which the election is made."

In 1980, P.L. 96-222, Sec. 103(a)(16), substituted "first taxable year" for "first taxable years" in subpara. (e)(2)(B), effective for tax. yrs. end. after 12/31/78.

In 1978, P.L. 95-600, Sec. 373(a), added Code Sec. 466, effective for tax. yrs. end. after 12/31/78. Sec. 373(c)(2) of the Act provides:

"(2) Application to certain prior taxable years.—

"(A) In General.—If—

"(i) the taxpayer makes an election under section 466 of the Internal Revenue Code of 1954 for his first taxable year ending after December 31, 1978, and

"(ii) for a continuous period of 1 or more taxable years each of which ends on or before December 31, 1978, the taxpayer used the method of accounting with respect to any type of discount coupons which was reasonably similar to the method of accounting provided by section 1.451-4 of the Income Tax Regulations,

then the taxpayer may make an election under this paragraph to have the method of accounting which he used for such continuous period treated as a valid method of accounting with respect to each such type of discount coupons for such period for purposes of the Internal Revenue Code of 1954. A taxpayer may make an election under this paragraph with respect to only one such continuous period.

"(B) Certain amounts to which method of accounting applies. An accounting method which the taxpayer used for the period described in subparagraph (A) may include—

"(i) costs of the type permitted by section 1.451-4 of the Income Tax Regulations to be included in the estimated average cost of redeeming coupons, plus

"(ii) any amount designated or referred to on the coupon payable by the taxpayer to the person who allowed the discount on a sale by such person to the user of the coupon.

"(C) Suspense account not required in certain cases. A taxpayer whose election under this paragraph applies to all types of discount coupons which he issued during the continuous period referred to in subparagraph (A)(ii) shall not be required to establish a suspense account under section 466(e) of the Internal Revenue Code of 1954.

"(D) Rules relating to election under this subsection. An election under this paragraph may be made only before the expiration of the period for making an election under section 466 of the Internal Revenue Code of 1954 for the taxpayer's first taxable year ending after December 31, 1978. An election under this paragraph shall be made in such manner and form as the Secretary of the Treasury or his delegate may by regulations prescribe. For purposes of the Internal Revenue Code of 1954, such an election shall be treated as a method of accounting, except that the approval of the Secretary of the Treasury or his delegate to the making of the election may not be required."

Sec. 467. Certain payments for the use of property or services.

(a) Accrual method on present value basis.

In the case of the lessor or lessee under any section 467 rental agreement, there shall be taken into account for purposes of this title for any taxable year the sum of—

(1) the amount of the rent which accrues during such taxable year as determined under subsection (b), and

(2) interest for the year on the amounts which were taken into account under this subsection for prior taxable years and which are unpaid.

(b) Accrual of rental payments.

(1) Allocation follows agreement. Except as provided in paragraph (2), the determination of the amount of the rent under any section 467 rental agreement which accrues during any taxable year shall be made—

(A) by allocating rents in accordance with the agreement, and

(B) by taking into account any rent to be paid after the close of the period in an amount determined under regulations which shall be based on present value concepts.

(2) Constant rental accrual in case of certain tax avoidance transactions, etc. In the case of any section 467 rental agreement to which this paragraph applies, the portion of the rent which accrues during any taxable year shall be that portion of the constant rental amount with respect to such agreement which is allocable to such taxable year.

(3) Agreements to which paragraph (2) applies. Paragraph (2) applies to any rental payment agreement if—

(A) such agreement is a disqualified leaseback or long-term agreement, or

(B) such agreement does not provide for the allocation referred to in paragraph (1)(A).

(4) Disqualified leaseback or long-term agreement. For purposes of this subsection, the term "disqualified leaseback or long-term agreement" means any section 467 rental agreement if—

(A) such agreement is part of a leaseback transaction or such agreement is for a term in excess of 75 percent of the statutory recovery period for the property, and

(B) a principal purpose for providing increasing rents under the agreement is the avoidance of tax imposed by this subtitle.

(5) Exceptions to disqualification in certain cases. The Secretary shall prescribe regulations setting forth circumstances under which agreements will not be treated as disqualified leaseback or long-term agreements, including circumstances relating to—

(A) changes in amounts paid determined by reference to price indices,

(B) rents based on a fixed percentage of lessee receipts or similar amounts,

(C) reasonable rent holidays, or

(D) changes in amounts paid to unrelated 3rd parties.

(c) Recapture of prior understated inclusions under leaseback or long-term agreements.

(1) In general. If—

(A) the lessor under any section 467 rental agreement disposes of any property subject to such agreement during the term of such agreement, and

(B) such agreement is a leaseback or long-term agreement to which paragraph (2) of subsection (b) did not apply,

the recapture amount shall be treated as ordinary income. Such gain shall be recognized notwithstanding any other provision of this subtitle.

(2) Recapture amount. For purposes of paragraph (1), the term "recapture amount" means the lesser of—

(A) the prior understated inclusions, or

(B) the excess of the amount realized (or in the case of a disposition other than a sale, exchange, or involuntary conversion, the fair market value of the property) over the adjusted basis of such property.

The amount determined under subparagraph (B) shall be reduced by the amount of any gain treated as ordinary income on the disposition under any other provision of this subtitle.

(3) Prior understated inclusions. For purposes of this subsection, the term "prior understated inclusion" means the excess (if any) of—

(A) the amount which would have been taken into account by the lessor under subsection (a) for periods before the disposition if subsection (b)(2) had applied to the agreement, over

(B) the amount taken into account under subsection (a) by the lessor for periods before the disposition.

(4) Leaseback or long-term agreement. For purposes of this subsection, the term "leaseback or long-term agreement" means any agreement described in subsection (b)(4)(A).

(5) Special rules. Under regulations prescribed by the Secretary—

(A) exceptions similar to the exceptions applicable under section 1245 or 1250 (whichever is appropriate) shall apply for purposes of this subsection,

(B) any transferee in a disposition excepted by reason of subparagraph (A) who has a transferred basis in the property shall be treated in the same manner as the transferor, and

---

• *Caution:* Code Sec. 467(c)(5)(C), following, was amended by Sec. 302(e)(4)(B)(ii), P.L. 108-27. These provisions generally sunset for tax years beginning after 12/31/2012. For specific sunset provisions see Sec. 303, P.L. 108-27 reproduced in history notes for this Code Sec.

(C) for purposes of sections 170(e) and 751(c), amounts treated as ordinary income under this section shall be treated in the same manner as amounts treated as ordinary income under section 1245 or 1250.

(d) Section 467 rental agreements.

(1) In general. Except as otherwise provided in this subsection, the term "section 467 rental agreements" means any rental agreement for the use of tangible property under which—

(A) there is at least one amount allocable to the use of property during a calendar year which is to be paid after the close of the calendar year following the calendar year in which such use occurs, or

(B) there are increases in the amount to be paid as rent under the agreement.

(2) Section not to apply to agreements involving payments of $250,000 or less. This section shall not apply to any amount to be paid for the use of property if the sum of the following amounts does not exceed $250,000—

(A) the aggregate amount of payments received as consideration for such use of property, and

(B) the aggregate value of any other consideration to be received for such use of property.

For purposes of the preceding sentence, rules similar to the rules of clauses (ii) and (iii) of section 1274(c)(4)(C) shall apply.

Code Sec. 467(e) — Tax accounting

(e) Definitions.
For purposes of this section—
(1) Constant rental amount. The term "constant rental amount" means, with respect to any section 467 rental agreement, the amount which, if paid as of the close of each lease period under the agreement, would result in an aggregate present value equal to the present value of the aggregate payments required under the agreement.
(2) Leaseback transaction. A transaction is a leaseback transaction if it involves a leaseback to any person who had an interest in such property at any time within 2 years before such leaseback (or to a related person).
(3) Statutory recovery period.
(A) In general.

In the case of:	The statutory recovery period is:
3-year property	3 years
5-year property	5 years
7-year property	7 years
10-year property	10 years
15-year and 20-year property	15 years
Residential rental property and nonresidential real property	19 years
Any railroad grading or tunnel bore	50 years

(B) Special rule for property not depreciable under section 168. In the case of property to which section 168 does not apply, subparagraph (A) shall be applied as if section 168 applies to such property.
(4) Discount and interest rate. For purposes of computing present value and interest under subsection (a)(2), the rate used shall be equal to 110 percent of the applicable Federal rate determined under section 1274(d) (compounded semiannually) which is in effect at the time the agreement is entered into with respect to debt instruments having a maturity equal to the term of the agreement.
(5) Related person. The term "related person" has the meaning given to such term by section 465(b)(3)(C).
(6) Certain options of lessee to renew not taken into account. Except as provided in regulations prescribed by the Secretary, there shall not be taken into account in computing the term of any agreement for purposes of this section any extension which is solely at the option of the lessee.
(f) Comparable rules where agreement for decreasing payments.
Under regulations prescribed by the Secretary, rules comparable to the rules of this section shall also apply in the case of any agreement where the amount paid under the agreement for the use of property decreases during the term of the agreement.
(g) Comparable rules for services.
Under regulations prescribed by the Secretary, rules comparable to the rules of subsection (a)(2) shall also apply in the case of payments for services which meet requirements comparable to the requirements of subsection (d). The preceding sentence shall not apply to any amount to which section 404 or 404A (or any other provision specified in regulations) applies.
(h) Regulations.
The Secretary shall prescribe such regulations as may be appropriate to carry out the purposes of this section, including regulations providing for the application of this section in the case of contingent payments.

In 2010, P.L. 111-312, Sec. 102(a), substituted "December 31, 2012" for "December 31, 2010" in Sec. 303, P.L. 108-27 [see below], effective as if included in the enactment of P.L. 108-27, 5/28/2003.
In 2006, P.L. 109-222, Sec. 102, substituted "December 31, 2010" for "December 31, 2008" in Sec. 303 of P.L. 108-27 [see below], effective 5/17/2006.
In 2004, P.L. 108-311, Sec. 402(a)(6), of this Act [which amended Sec. 302(f)(2) of P.L. 108-27, see below], provides:
"(2) Pass-thru entities. In the case of a pass-thru entity described in subparagraph (A), (B), (C), (D), (E), or (F) of section 1(h)(10) of the Internal Revenue Code of 1986, as amended by this Act, the amendments made by this section shall apply to taxable years ending after December 31, 2002; except that dividends received by such an entity on or before such date shall not be treated as qualified dividend income (as defined in section 1(h)(11)(B) of such Code, as added by this Act)."
In 2003, P.L. 108-27, Sec. 302(e)(4)(B)(ii), deleted ", 341(e)(12)," after "sections 170(e)" in subpara. (c)(5)(C), effective for tax. yrs. begin. after 12/31/2002. Sec. 302(f)(2), of this Act [prior to amendment by Sec. 402(a)(6) of P.L. 108-311 see above] provides:
"(2) Regulated investment companies and real estate investment trusts. In the case of a regulated investment company or a real estate investment trust, the amendments made by this section shall apply to taxable years ending after December 31, 2002; except that dividends received by such a company or trust on or before such date shall not be treated as qualified dividend income (as defined in section 1(h)(11)(B) of the Internal Revenue Code of 1986, as added by this Act)."
—P.L. 108-27, Sec. 303, of this Act [as amended by Sec. 102, P.L. 109-222, and Sec. 102(a), 111-312, see above], reads as follows:
"Sec. 303. Sunset of title. All provisions of, and amendments made by, this title [Secs. 301 and 302] shall not apply to taxable years beginning after December 31, 2012, and the Internal Revenue Code of 1986 shall be applied and administered to such years as if such provisions and amendments had never been enacted."
In 1988, P.L. 100-647, Sec. 1002(c)(3), provides:
"(3) Notwithstanding section 203 of the Reform Act, the amendments made by section 201 of the Reform Act shall apply to any real property which was acquired before January 1, 1987, and was converted on or after such date from personal use to a use for which depreciation is allowable."
—P.L. 100-647, Sec. 1002(i)(2)(H), added the last line to the table in subpara. (e)(3)(A), effective for that portion of the basis of any property which is attributable to expenditures paid or incurred after 12/31/86, except as provided in Sec. 242(c)(2) of P.L. 99-514, reproduced in note following Code Sec. 185.
—P.L. 100-647, Sec. 1005(c)(10), corrected Sec. 511(d)(2)(A) of P.L. 99-514 to delete "163(d)," instead of "section 163(d)," in subpara. (c)(5)(C), see below.
In 1986, P.L. 99-514, Sec. 201(d)(8)(A), amended para. (e)(3)... Sec. 201(d)(8)(B), substituted "465(b)(3)(C)" for "168(d)(4)(D)" ["168(e)(4)(D)", see Sec. 1807(b)(2)(D) of this Act, below] in para. (e)(5), effective for property placed in service after 12/31/86, in tax. years ending after 12/31/86. For transitional rules, see Sec. 203(b)-(e) of this Act reproduced in note following Code Sec. 168. Sec. 203(a)(1)(B) of this Act provides:
"(B) Election to have amendments made by section 201 apply.—A taxpayer may elect (at such time and in such manner as the Secretary of the Treasury or his delegate may prescribe) to have the amendments made by section 201 apply to any property placed in service after July 31, 1986, and before January 1, 1987."
Prior to amendment, para. (e)(3) read as follows:
"(3) Statutory recovery period.
"(A) In general.

"In the case of property which is:	The statutory recovery period is:
3-year property	3 years
5-year property	5 years
10-year property	10 years
Low-income housing	15 years
15-year public utility property	15 years
18-year real property	18 years

"(B) Special rule for property which is not recovery property. In the case of any property which is not recovery property, subparagraph (A) shall be applied as if such property were recovery property."
—P.L. 99-514, Sec. 511(d)(2)(A), [sic 511(c)(2)(A)], deleted "section 163(d)," [sic "163(d),"] before "170(e)," in subpara. (c)(5)(C), effective for tax. yrs. begin. after 12/31/86.
—P.L. 99-514, Sec. 631(e)(10), deleted "341(e)(12)," "453B(d)(2)," before "and 751(c)" in subpara. (c)(5)(C), effective as provided in Sec. 633(a)(1) of this Act:
"(a) General rule.
"Except as otherwise provided in this section [Sec. 633], the amendments made by this subtitle shall apply to—
"(1) any distribution in complete liquidation, and any sale or exchange, made by a corporation after July 31, 1986, unless such corporation is completely liquidated before January 1, 1987."
Sec. 633(d) [sic (e)] of this Act provides:
"(d) [sic (e)] Complete liquidation defined.
"For purposes of this section, a corporation shall be treated as completely liquidated if all of the assets of such corporation are distributed in complete liquidation, less assets retained to meet claims."
—P.L. 99-514, Sec. 1807(b)(1), added the sentence at the end of subsec. (g)... Sec. 1807(b)(2)(A), substituted "statutory recovery period" for "statutory recover period" in subpara. (b)(4)(A)... Sec. 1807(b)(2)(B), substituted "subsection

"(b)(4)(A)" for "subsection (b)(3)(A)" in para. (c)(4) . . . Sec. 1807(b)(2)(C), substituted "section 1274(c)(4)(C)" for "section 1274(c)(2)(C)" in the last sentence of para. (d)(2) . . . Sec. 1807(b)(2)(D), substituted "section 168(e)(4)(D)" for "section 168(d)(4)(D)" in para. (e)(5) [amended by Sec. 201(d)(8)(B) of this Act, above], effective for agreements entered into after 6/8/84, except as provided in Sec. 92(c)(2) of P.L. 98-369 and (c)(3), reproduced below.

—P.L. 99-514, Sec. 1879(f)(1)(A), substituted "19-year real property" for "18-year real property" in subpara. (e)(3)(A) . . . Sec. 1879(f)(1)(B), substituted "19 years" for "18 years" in subpara. (e)(3)(A), effective for property placed in service after 5/8/85, except as provided in Sec. 105(b)(2) of P.L. 99-121 reproduced in note following Code Sec. 168.

In 1984, P.L. 98-369, Sec. 92(a), added Code Sec. 467, effective for agreements entered into after 6/8/84 except as provided in Sec. 92(c)(2) and (c)(3) which reads as follows:

"(2) Exceptions.—The amendments made by this section [Sec. 92] shall not apply—

"(A) to any agreement entered into pursuant to a written agreement which was binding on June 8, 1984, and at all times thereafter,

"(B) subject to the provisions of paragraph (3), to any agreement to lease property if—

"(i) there was in effect a firm plan, evidenced by a board of directors' resolution, memorandum of agreement, or letter of intent on March 15, 1984, to enter into such an agreement, and

"(ii) construction of the property was commenced (but such property was not placed in service) on or before March 15, 1984, or

"(C) to any agreement to lease property if—

"(i) the lessee of such property adopted a firm plan to lease the property, evidenced by a resolution of the Finance Committee of the Board of Directors of such lessee, on February 10, 1984,

"(ii) the sum of the present values of the rents payable by the lessee under the lease at the inception thereof equals at least $91,223,034, assuming for purposes of this clause—

"(I) the annual discount rate is 12.6 percent,

"(II) the initial payment of rent occurs 12 months after the commencement of the lease, and

"(III) subsequent payments of rents occur on the anniversary date of the initial payment, and

"(iii) during—

"(I) the first 5 years of the lease, at least 9 percent of the rents payable by the lessee under the agreement are paid, and

"(II) the second 5 years of the lease, at least 16.25 percent of the rents payable by the lessee under the agreement are paid.

Paragraph (3)(B)(ii)(II) shall apply for purposes of clauses (ii) and (iii) of subparagraph (C), as if, as of the beginning of the last stage, the separate agreements were treated as 1 single agreement relating to all property covered by the agreements, including any property placed in service before the property to which the agreement for the last stage relates. If the lessor under the agreement described in subparagraph (C) leases the property from another person, this exception shall also apply to any agreement between the lessor and such person which is integrally related to, and entered into at the same time as, such agreement, and which calls for comparable payments of rent over the primary term of the agreement.

"(3) Schedule of deemed rental payments.—

"(A) In general.—In any case to which paragraph (2)(B) applies, for purposes of the Internal Revenue Code of 1954, the lessor shall be treated as having received or accrued (and the lessee shall be treated as having paid or incurred) rents equal to the greater of—

"(i) the amount of rents actually paid under the agreement during the taxable year, or

"(ii) the amount of rents determined in accordance with the schedule under subparagraph (B) for such taxable year.

"(B) Schedule.—

"(i) In general.—The schedule under this subparagraph is as follows:

Portion of lease term	Cumulative percentage of total rent deemed paid:
1st ⅕	10
2nd ⅕	25
3rd ⅕	45
4th ⅕	70
Last ⅕	100.

"(ii) Operating rules.—For purposes of this schedule—

"(I) the rent allocable to each taxable year within any portion of a lease term described in such schedule shall be a level pro rata amount properly allocable to such taxable year, and

"(II) any agreement relating to property which is to be placed in service in 2 or more stages shall be treated as 2 or more separate agreements.

"(C) Paragraph not to apply.—This paragraph shall not apply to any agreement if the sum of the present values of all payments under the agreement is greater than the sum of the present value of all the payments deemed to be paid or received under the schedule under subparagraph (B). For purposes of computing any present value under this subparagraph, the annual discount rate shall be equal to 12 percent, compounded semiannually."

Sec. 468. Special rules for mining and solid waste reclamation and closing costs.

(a) Establishment of reserves for reclamation and closing costs.

(1) Allowance of deduction. If a taxpayer elects the application of this section with respect to any mining or solid waste disposal property, the amount of any deduction for qualified reclamation or closing costs for any taxable year to which such election applies shall be equal to the current reclamation or closing costs allocable to—

(A) in the case of qualified reclamation costs, the portion of the reserve property which was disturbed during such taxable year, and

(B) in the case of qualified closing costs, the production from the reserve property during such taxable year.

(2) Opening balance and adjustments to reserve.

(A) Opening balance. The opening balance of any reserve for its first taxable year shall be zero.

(B) Increase for interest. A reserve shall be increased each taxable year by an amount equal to the amount of interest which would have been earned during such taxable year on the opening balance of such reserve for such taxable year if such interest were computed—

(i) at the Federal short-term rate or rates (determined under section 1274) in effect, and

(ii) by compounding semiannually.

(C) Reserve to be charged for amounts paid. Any amount paid by the taxpayer during any taxable year for qualified reclamation or closing costs allocable to portions of the reserve property for which the election under paragraph (1) was in effect shall be charged to the appropriate reserve as of the close of the taxable year.

(D) Reserve increased by amount deducted. A reserve shall be increased each taxable year by the amount allowable as a deduction under paragraph (1) for such taxable year which is allocable to such reserve.

(3) Allowance of deduction for excess amounts paid. There shall be allowed as a deduction for any taxable year the excess of—

(A) the amounts described in paragraph (2)(C) paid during such taxable year, over

(B) the closing balance of the reserve for such taxable year (determined without regard to paragraph (2)(C)).

(4) Limitation on balance as of the close of any taxable year.

(A) Reclamation reserves. In the case of any reserve for qualified reclamation costs, there shall be included in gross income for any taxable year an amount equal to the excess of—

(i) the closing balance of the reserve for such taxable year, over

(ii) the current reclamation costs of the taxpayer for all portions of the reserve property disturbed during any taxable year to which the election under paragraph (1) applies.

(B) Closing costs reserves. In the case of any reserve for qualified closing costs, there shall be included in gross income for any taxable year an amount equal to the excess of—

(i) the closing balance of the reserve for such taxable year, over

(ii) the current closing cost of the taxpayer with respect to the reserve property, determined as if all production with respect to the reserve property for any taxable year to which the election under paragraph (1) applies had occurred in such taxable year.

(C) Order of application. This paragraph shall be applied after all adjustments to the reserve have been made for the taxable year.

(5) Income inclusions on completion or disposition. Proper inclusion in income shall be made upon—

(A) the revocation of an election under paragraph (1), or

(B) completion of the closing, or disposition of any portion, of a reserve property.

(b) Allocation for property where election not in effect for all taxable years.

If the election under subsection (a)(1) is not in effect for 1 or more taxable years in which the reserved property is disturbed (or production occurs), items with respect to the reserve property shall be allocated to the reserve, in such manner as the Secretary may prescribe by regulations.

(c) Revocation of election; Separate reserves.

(1) Revocation of election.

(A) In general. The taxpayer may revoke an election under subsection (a)(1) with respect to any property. Such revocation, once made, shall be irrevocable.

(B) Time and manner of revocation. Any revocation under subparagraph (A) shall be made at such time and in such manner as the Secretary may prescribe.

(2) Separate reserves required. If a taxpayer makes an election under subsection (a)(1), the taxpayer shall establish with respect to the property for which the election was made—

(A) a separate reserve for qualified reclamation costs, and

(B) a separate reserve for qualified closing costs.

(d) Definitions and special rules relating to reclamation and closing costs.

For purposes of this section—

(1) Current reclamation and closing costs.

(A) Current reclamation costs. The term "current reclamation costs" means the amount which the taxpayer would be required to pay for qualified reclamation costs if the reclamation activities were performed currently.

(B) Current closing costs.

(i) In general. The term "current closing costs" means the amount which the taxpayer would be required to pay for qualified closing costs if the closing activities were performed currently.

(ii) Costs computed on unit-of-production or capacity method. Estimated closing costs shall—

(I) in the case of the closing of any mine site, be computed on the unit-of-production method of accounting, and

(II) in the case of the closing of any solid waste disposal site, be computed on the unit-of-capacity method.

(2) Qualified reclamation or closing costs. The term "qualified reclamation or closing costs" means any of the following expenses:

(A) Mining reclamation and closing costs. Any expenses incurred for any land reclamation or closing activity which is conducted in accordance with a reclamation plan (including an amendment or modification thereof)—

(i) which—

(I) is submitted pursuant to the provisions of section 511 or 528 of the Surface Mining Control and Reclamation Act of 1977 (as in effect on January 1, 1984), and

(II) is part of a surface mining and reclamation permit granted under the provisions of title V of such Act (as so in effect), or

(ii) which is submitted pursuant to any other Federal or State law which imposes surface mining reclamation and permit requirements substantially similar to the requirements imposed by title V of such Act (as so in effect).

(B) Solid waste disposal and closing costs.

(i) In general. Any expenses incurred for any land reclamation or closing activity in connection with any solid waste disposal site which is conducted in accordance with any permit issued pursuant to—

(I) any provision of the Solid Waste Disposal Act (as in effect on January 1, 1984) requiring such activity, or

(II) any other Federal, State, or local law which imposes requirements substantially similar to the requirements imposed by the Solid Waste Disposal Act (as so in effect).

(ii) Exception for certain hazardous waste sites. Clause (i) shall not apply to that portion of any property which is disturbed after the property is listed in the national contingency plan established under section 105 of the Comprehensive Environmental Response, Compensation, and Liability Act of 1980.

(3) Property. The term "property" has the meaning given such term by section 614.

(4) Reserve property. The term "reserve property" means any property with respect to which a reserve is established under subsection (a)(1).

In 1990, P.L. 101-508, Sec. 11802(c), amended subpara. (a)(2)(B), effective 11/5/90, except as provided in Sec. 11821(b) of this Act, reproduced in note following Code Sec. 422.

Prior to amendment, subpara. (a)(2)(B) read as follows:

"(B) increase for interest.

"(i) In general. A reserve shall be increased each taxable year by an amount equal to the amount of interest which would be earned during such taxable year on the opening balance of such reserve for such taxable year if such interest were computed—

"(I) at the Federal short-term rate or rates (determined under section 1274) in effect, and

"(II) by compounding semiannually.

"(ii) Phase-in of interest rate. In the case of taxable years ending before 1987, the rate determined under clause (i)(I) shall be equal to the following percentage of such rate (determined without regard to this clause):

In the case of taxable years ending in:	The percentage is:
1984 or 1985	70
1986	85."

In 1986, P.L. 99-514, Sec. 1807(a)(3)(A), added subpara. (a)(2)(D) . . . Sec. 1807(a)(3)(B), added Sec. 91(g)(4) to P.L. 98-367, the effective date for changes made by Sec. 91(b)(1), see below . . . Sec. 1807(a)(3)(C), substituted "this section" for "this subsection" in para. (a)(1), effective 7/18/84 for tax. yrs. ending after 7/18/84, except as provided in Sec. (h) and (i) of P.L. 98-369, reproduced in note following Code Sec. 461.

—P.L. 99-514, Sec. 1899A(14), substituted "Comprehensive Environmental Response, Compensation, and Liability Act of 1980" for "Comprehensive Environmental, Compensation, and Liability Act of 1980" in clause (d)(2)(B)(ii), effective 10/22/86.

In 1984, P.L. 98-369, Sec. 91(b)(1), added Code Sec. 468, effective 7/18/84 for tax. yrs. ending after 7/18/84, [as amended by Sec. 1807(a)(3)(B) of P.L. 99-574, see above] except as provided in Sec. 91 (h) and (i) of this Act, reproduced in note following Code Sec. 461.

Sec. 468A. Special rules for nuclear decommissioning costs.

(a) In general.

If the taxpayer elects the application of this section, there shall be allowed as a deduction for any taxable year the amount of payments made by the taxpayer to a Nuclear

Tax accounting

Decommissioning Reserve Fund (hereinafter referred to as the "Fund") during such taxable year.

(b) Limitation on amounts paid into Fund.

The amount which a taxpayer may pay into the Fund for any taxable year shall not exceed the ruling amount applicable to such taxable year.

(c) Income and deductions of the taxpayer.

(1) Inclusion of amounts distributed. There shall be includible in the gross income of the taxpayer for any taxable year—

(A) any amount distributed from the Fund during such taxable year, other than any amount distributed to pay costs described in subsection (e)(4)(B), and

(B) except to the extent provided in regulations, amounts properly includible in gross income in the case of any deemed distribution under subsection (e)(6), any termination under subsection (e)(7), or the disposition of any interest in the nuclear powerplant.

(2) Deduction when economic performance occurs. In addition to any deduction under subsection (a), there shall be allowable as a deduction for any taxable year the amount of the nuclear decommissioning costs with respect to which economic performance (within the meaning of section 461(h)(2)) occurs during such taxable year.

(d) Ruling amount.

For purposes of this section—

(1) Request required. No deduction shall be allowed for any payment to the Fund unless the taxpayer requests, and receives, from the Secretary a schedule of ruling amounts. For purposes of the preceding sentence, the taxpayer shall request a schedule of ruling amounts upon each renewal of the operating license of the nuclear powerplant.

(2) Ruling amount. The term "ruling amount" means, with respect to any taxable year, the amount which the Secretary determines under paragraph (1) to be necessary to—

(A) fund the total nuclear decommissioning costs with respect to such power plant over the estimated useful life of such power plant, and

(B) prevent any excessive funding of such costs or the funding of such costs at a rate more rapid than level funding, taking into account such discount rates as the Secretary deems appropriate.

(3) Review of amount. The Secretary shall at least once during the useful life of the nuclear powerplant (or, more frequently, upon the request of the taxpayer) review, and revise if necessary, the schedule of ruling amounts determined under paragraph (1).

(e) Nuclear Decommissioning Reserve Fund.

(1) In general. Each taxpayer who elects the application of this section shall establish a Nuclear Decommissioning Reserve Fund with respect to each nuclear powerplant to which such election applies.

(2) Taxation of Fund.

(A) In general. There is hereby imposed on the gross income of the Fund for any taxable year a tax at the rate of 20 percent, except that—

(i) there shall not be included in the gross income of the Fund any payment to the Fund with respect to which a deduction is allowable under subsection (a), and

(ii) there shall be allowed as a deduction to the Fund any amount paid by the Fund which is described in paragraph (4)(B) (other than an amount paid to the taxpayer) and which would be deductible under this chapter for purposes of determining the taxable income of a corporation.

(B) Tax in lieu of other taxation. The tax imposed by subparagraph (A) shall be in lieu of any other taxation under this subtitle of the income from assets in the Fund.

(C) Fund treated as corporation. For purposes of subtitle F—

(i) the Fund shall be treated as if it were a corporation, and

(ii) any tax imposed by this paragraph shall be treated as a tax imposed by section 11.

(3) Contributions to Fund. Except as provided in subsection (f), the Fund shall not accept any payments (or other amounts) other than payments with respect to which a deduction is allowable under subsection (a).

(4) Use of Fund. The Fund shall be used exclusively for—

(A) satisfying, in whole or in part, any liability of any person contributing to the Fund for the decommissioning of a nuclear powerplant (or unit thereof),

(B) to pay administrative costs (including taxes) and other incidental expenses of the Fund (including legal, accounting, actuarial, and trustee expenses) in connection with the operation of the Fund, and

(C) to the extent that a portion of the Fund is not currently needed for purposes described in subparagraph (A) or (B), making investments.

(5) Prohibitions against self-dealing. Under regulations prescribed by the Secretary, for purposes of section 4951 (and so much of this title as relates to such section), the Fund shall be treated in the same manner as a trust described in section 501(c)(21).

(6) Disqualification of Fund. In any case in which the Fund violates any provision of this section or section 4951, the Secretary may disqualify such Fund from the application of this section. In any case to which this paragraph applies, the Fund shall be treated as having distributed all of its funds on the date such determination takes effect.

(7) Termination upon completion. Upon substantial completion of the nuclear decommissioning of the nuclear powerplant with respect to which a Fund relates, the taxpayer shall terminate such Fund.

(f) Transfers into qualified funds.

(1) In general. Notwithstanding subsection (b), any taxpayer maintaining a Fund to which this section applies with respect to a nuclear power plant may transfer into such Fund not more than an amount equal to the present value of the portion of the total nuclear decommissioning costs with respect to such nuclear power plant previously excluded for such nuclear power plant under subsection (d)(2)(A) as in effect immediately before the date of the enactment of this subsection.

(2) Deduction for amounts transferred.

(A) In general. Except as provided in subparagraph (C), the deduction allowed by subsection (a) for any transfer permitted by this subsection shall be allowed ratably over the remaining estimated useful life (within the meaning of subsection (d)(2)(A)) of the nuclear power plant beginning with the taxable year during which the transfer is made.

(B) Denial of deduction for previously deducted amounts. No deduction shall be allowed for any transfer under this subsection of an amount for which a deduction was previously allowed to the taxpayer (or a predecessor) or a corresponding amount was not included in gross income of the taxpayer (or a predecessor). For purposes of the preceding sentence, a ratable portion of each transfer shall be treated as being from previously deducted or excluded amounts to the extent thereof.

(C) Transfers of qualified funds. If—

(i) any transfer permitted by this subsection is made to any Fund to which this section applies, and

(ii) such Fund is transferred thereafter,

any deduction under this subsection for taxable years ending after the date that such Fund is transferred shall be allowed to the transferor for the taxable year which includes such date.

(D) Special rules.

(i) Gain or loss not recognized on transfers to Fund. No gain or loss shall be recognized on any transfer described in paragraph (1).

(ii) Transfers of appreciated property to Fund. If appreciated property is transferred in a transfer described in paragraph (1), the amount of the deduction shall not exceed the adjusted basis of such property.

(3) New ruling amount required. Paragraph (1) shall not apply to any transfer unless the taxpayer requests from the Secretary a new schedule of ruling amounts in connection with such transfer.

(4) No basis in qualified funds. Notwithstanding any other provision of law, the taxpayer's basis in any Fund to which this section applies shall not be increased by reason of any transfer permitted by this subsection.

(g) Nuclear powerplant.

For purposes of this section, the term "nuclear powerplant" includes any unit thereof.

(h) Time when payments deemed made.

For purposes of this section, a taxpayer shall be deemed to have made a payment to the Fund on the last day of a taxable year if such payment is made on account of such taxable year and is made within 2½ months after the close of such taxable year.

In 2005, P.L. 109-58, Sec. 1310(a), amended subsec. (b)...Sec. 1310(b)(1), redesignated subsecs. (f) and (g) as subsecs. (g) and (h), and added subsec. (f)...Sec. 1310(b)(2), amended subpara. (d)(2)(A)...Sec. 1310(c), added "For purposes of the preceding sentence, the taxpayer shall request a schedule of ruling amounts upon each renewal of the operating license of the nuclear powerplant." at the end of para. (d)(1)...Sec. 1310(d), substituted "Except as provided in subsection (f), the Fund" for "The Fund" in para. (e)(3)...Sec. 1310(e)(1), substituted "rate of 20 percent" for "rate set forth in subparagraph (B)" in subpara. (e)(2)(A)...Sec. 1310(e)(2), deleted subpara. (e)(2)(B)...Sec. 1310(e)(3), redesignated subparas. (e)(2)(C) and (D) as subparas. (e)(2)(B) and (C), effective for tax. yrs. begin. after 12/31/2005.

Prior to amendment, subsec. (b) read as follows:

"(b) Limitation on amounts paid into Fund. The amount which a taxpayer may pay into the Fund for any taxable year shall not exceed the lesser of—

"(1) the amount of nuclear decommissioning costs allocable to the Fund which is included in the taxpayer's cost of service for ratemaking purposes for such taxable year, or

"(2) the ruling amount applicable to such taxable year."

Prior to amendment, subpara. (d)(2)(A) read as follows:

"(A) fund that portion of the nuclear decommissioning costs of the taxpayer with respect to the nuclear powerplant which bears the same ratio to the total nuclear decommissioning costs with respect to such nuclear powerplant as the period for which the Fund is in effect bears to the estimated useful life of such nuclear powerplant, and"

Prior to deletion, subpara. (e)(2)(B) read as follows:

"(B) Rate of tax. For purposes of subparagraph (A), the rate set forth in this subparagraph is—

"(i) 22 percent in the case of taxable years beginning in calendar year 1994 or 1995, and

"(ii) 20 percent in the case of taxable year beginning after December 31, 1995."

In 1996, P.L. 104-188, Sec. 1704(j)(6), amended Sec. 1917(b)(1) of P.L. 102-486 by substituting "at a rate" for "at the rate" in the material proposed to be stricken, see below.

In 1992, P.L. 102-486, Sec. 1917(a), deleted "described in section 501(c)(21)(B)(ii)" after "investments" in subpara. (e)(4)(C), effective for tax. yrs. begin. after 12/31/92.

—P.L. 102-486, Sec. 1917(b)(1), [amended by Sec. 1704(j)(6) of P.L. 104-188, see above] substituted "at the rate set forth in subparagraph (B)" for "at a rate equal to the highest rate of tax specified in section 11(b)", in subpara. (e)(2)(A)...Sec. 1917(b)(2), redesignated subparas. (e)(2)(B) and (C) as subparas.

(e)(2)(C) and (D) and added new subpara. (e)(2)(B), effective as provided in Sec. 1917(c)(2) of this Act, which reads as follows:

"(2) Subsection (b). The amendments made by subsection (b) shall apply to taxable years beginning after December 31, 1993. Section 15 of the Internal Revenue Code of 1986 shall not apply to any change in rate resulting from the amendment made by subsection (b)."

In 1986, P.L. 99-514, Sec. 1807(a)(4)(A)(i), added subsec. (g) effective 7/18/84 in tax. yrs. end. after 7/18/84. Sec. 1807(a)(4)(A)(ii) of this Act provides the following transitional rule:

"(ii) Transitional rule.—To the extent provided in regulations prescribed by the Secretary of the Treasury or his delegate, subsection (g) of section 468A of the Internal Revenue Code of 1954 (as added by clause (i)) shall be applied with respect to any payment on account of a taxable year beginning before January 1, 1987, as if it did not contain the requirements that the payment be made within 2½ months after the close of the taxable year. Such regulations may provide that, to the extent such payment to the Fund is made more than 2½ months after the close of the taxable year, any adjustment to the tax attributable to such payment shall not affect the amount of interest payable with respect to periods before the payment is made. Such regulations may provide appropriate adjustments to the deduction allowed under such section 468A for any such taxable year to take into account the fact that the payment to the Fund is made more than 2½ months after the close of the taxable year."

—P.L. 99-514, Sec. 1807(a)(4)(B), substituted "subsection (e)(4)(B)," for "subsection (e)(2)(B)," in subpara. (c)(1)(A)...Sec. 1807(a)(4)(C), amended para. (e)(2)...Sec. 1807(a)(4)(D), deleted "and" from the end of subpara. (e)(4)(A), substituted ", and" for the period at the end of subpara. (e)(4)(B), and added subpara. (e)(4)(C)...Sec. 1807(a)(4)(E)(i), substituted "this section" for "this subsection" in subsec. (a)...Sec. 1807(a)(4)(E)(ii), substituted "this section" for "this subsection" in subsec. (d)...Sec. 1807(a)(4)(E)(iii), substituted "reserve fund" for "trust fund" in the heading of subsec. (e)...Sec. 1807(a)(4)(E)(iv)(I), substituted "this section" for "this subsection" in para. (e)(1)...Sec. 1807(a)(4)(E)(iv)(II), substituted "Reserve Fund" for "Trust Fund" in para. (e)(1)...Sec. 1807(a)(4)(E)(v)(I), substituted "this section" for "this subsection" each place it appeared in para. (e)(6)...Sec. 1807(a)(4)(E)(v)(II), substituted "this paragraph" for "this subparagraph" in para. (e)(6)...Sec. 1807(a)(4)(E)(vi), substituted "For purposes of this section, the term" for "The term" in subsec. (f), effective 7/18/84 for tax. yrs. end. after 7/18/84. For exceptions and transitional rules, see Sec. 91(h) and (i) of P.L. 98-369 reproduced in note following Code Sec. 461.

Prior to amendment, para. (e)(2) read as follows:

"(2) Taxation of fund. There is imposed on the gross income of the Fund for any taxable year a tax at a rate equal to the maximum rate in effect under section 11(b), except that—

"(A) there shall not be included in the gross income of the Fund any payment to the Fund with respect to which a deduction is allowable under subsection (a), and

"(B) there shall be allowed as a deduction any amount paid by the Fund described in paragraph (4)(B) (other than to the taxpayer)."

—P.L. 99-514, Sec. 1807(a)(4), added Sec. 91(g)(5) to P.L. 98-369, the effective date for changes made by Sec. 91(c)(1), see below.

In 1984, P.L. 98-369, Sec. 91(c)(1), added Code Sec. 468A, effective 7/18/84 for tax. yrs. end. after 7/18/84 (as amended by Sec. 1807(a)(4) of P.L. 99-514, see above]. For exceptions and transitional rules, see Secs. 91(h) and (i) of P.L. 98-369 reproduced in note following Code Sec. 461.

Sec. 468B. Special rules for designated settlement funds.

(a) In general.

For purposes of section 461(h), economic performance shall be deemed to occur as qualified payments are made by the taxpayer to a designated settlement fund.

(b) Taxation of designated settlement fund.

(1) In general. There is imposed on the gross income of any designated settlement fund for any taxable year a tax at a rate equal to the maximum rate in effect for such taxable year under section 1(e).

(2) Certain expenses allowed. For purposes of paragraph (1), gross income for any taxable year shall be reduced by the amount of any administrative costs (including State and local taxes) and other incidental expenses of the designated settlement fund (including legal, accounting, and actuarial expenses)—

(A) which are incurred in connection with the operation of the fund, and

(B) which would be deductible under this chapter for purposes of determining the taxable income of a corporation.

No other deduction shall be allowed to the fund.

(3) Transfers to the fund. In the case of any qualified payment made to the fund—

(A) the amount of such payment shall not be treated as income of the designated settlement fund,

(B) the basis of the fund in any property which constitutes a qualified payment shall be equal to the fair market value of such property at the time of payment, and

(C) the fund shall be treated as the owner of the property in the fund (and any earnings thereon).

(4) Tax in lieu of other taxation. The tax imposed by paragraph (1) shall be in lieu of any other taxation under this subtitle of income from assets in the designated settlement fund.

(5) Coordination with subtitle F. For purposes of subtitle F—

(A) a designated settlement fund shall be treated as a corporation, and

(B) any tax imposed by this subsection shall be treated as a tax imposed by section 11.

(c) Deductions not allowed for transfer of insurance amounts.

No deduction shall be allowable for any qualified payment by the taxpayer of any amounts received from the settlement of any insurance claim to the extent such amounts are excluded from the gross income of the taxpayer.

(d) Definitions.

For purposes of this section—

(1) Qualified payment. The term "qualified payment" means any money or property which is transferred to any designated settlement fund pursuant to a court order, other than—

(A) any amount which may be transferred from the fund to the taxpayer (or any related person), or

(B) the transfer of any stock or indebtedness of the taxpayer (or any related person).

(2) Designated settlement fund. The term "designated settlement fund" means any fund—

(A) which is established pursuant to a court order and which extinguishes completely the taxpayer's tort liability with respect to claims described in subparagraph (D),

(B) with respect to which no amounts may be transferred other than in the form of qualified payments,

(C) which is administered by persons a majority of whom are independent of the taxpayer,

(D) which is established for the principal purpose of resolving and satisfying present and future claims against the taxpayer (or any related person or formerly related person) arising out of personal injury, death, or property damage,

(E) under the terms of which the taxpayer (or any related person) may not hold any beneficial interest in the income or corpus of the fund, and

(F) with respect to which an election is made under this section by the taxpayer.

An election under this section shall be made at such time and in such manner as the Secretary shall by regulation prescribe. Such an election, once made, may be revoked only with the consent of the Secretary.

(3) Related person. The term "related person" means a person related to the taxpayer within the meaning of section 267(b).

(e) Nonapplicability of section.

This section (other than subsection (g)) shall not apply with respect to any liability of the taxpayer arising under any workers' compensation Act or any contested liability of the taxpayer within the meaning of section 461(f).

(f) Other funds.

Except as provided in regulations, any payment in respect of a liability described in subsection (d)(2)(D) (and not described in subsection (e)) to a trust fund or escrow fund which is not a designated settlement fund shall not be treated as constituting economic performance.

(g) Clarification of taxation of certain funds.

(1) In general. Except as provided in paragraph (2), nothing in any provision of law shall be construed as providing that an escrow account, settlement fund, or similar fund is not subject to current income tax. The Secretary shall prescribe regulations providing for the taxation of any such account or fund whether as a grantor trust or otherwise.

(2) Exemption from tax for certain settlement funds. An escrow account, settlement fund, or similar fund shall be treated as beneficially owned by the United States and shall be exempt from taxation under this subtitle if—

(A) it is established pursuant to a consent decree entered by a judge of a United States District Court,

(B) it is created for the receipt of settlement payments as directed by a government entity for the sole purpose of resolving or satisfying one or more claims asserting liability under the Comprehensive Environmental Response, Compensation, and Liability Act of 1980,

(C) the authority and control over the expenditure of funds therein (including the expenditure of contributions thereto and any net earnings thereon) is with such government entity, and

(D) upon termination, any remaining funds will be disbursed to such government entity for use in accordance with applicable law.

For purposes of this paragraph, the term "government entity" means the United States, any State or political subdivision thereof, the District of Columbia, any possession of the United States, and any agency or instrumentality of any of the foregoing.

In 2006, P.L. 109-432, Sec. 409(a), deleted para. (g)(3), effective or accounts and funds established after 5/17/2006.
Prior to deletion, para. (g)(3) read as follows:
"(3) Termination.
"Paragraph (2) shall not apply to accounts and funds established after December 31, 2010."
—P.L. 109-222, Sec. 201(a), amended subsec. (g), effective for accounts and funds established after 5/17/2006.
Prior to amendment, subsec. (g) read as follows:
"(g) Clarification of taxation of certain funds. Nothing in any provision of law shall be construed as providing that an escrow account, settlement fund, or similar fund is not subject to current income tax. The Secretary shall prescribe regulations providing for the taxation of any such account or fund whether as a grantor trust or otherwise."

In 1990, P.L. 101-508, Sec. 11702(e)(1), substituted "This section (other than subsection (g))" for "This section" in subsec. (e), effective as provided in Sec. 91(g), (h), and (i) of P.L. 98-369 reproduced in note following Code Sec. 461. For special rules see Secs. 1807(a)(7)(C) and (D) of P.L. 99-514 reproduced below.

In 1988, P.L. 100-647, Sec. 1018(f)(1), substituted "the taxpayer (or any related person)" for "the taxpayer" in subparas. (d)(1)(A) and (d)(2)(E) . . . Sec. 1018(f)(2), amended subpara. (d)(2)(A) . . . Sec. 1018(f)(4)(A), substituted "a corporation." for "the corporation." in subpara. (b)(2)(B) . . . Sec. 1018(f)(4)(B), substituted "No other" for "no other" in para. (b)(2) . . . Sec. 1018(f)(5)(A), added subsec. (g), effective as provided in Secs. 91(g), (h), and (i) of P.L. 98-369, reproduced in the note following Code Sec. 461 and Sec. 1807(a)(7)(C) of P.L. 99-514, reproduced below.
Prior to amendment, subpara. (d)(2)(A) read as follows:
"(A) which is established pursuant to a court order,".
—P.L. 100-647, Sec. 1018(f)(3), amended Sec. 1807(a)(7)(C)(i) of P.L. 99-514 [reproduced below] part of the effective date for changes made by Sec. 1807(a)(7)(A) of P.L. 99-514 . . . Sec. 1018(f)(5)(B), repealed Sec. 1807(a)(7)(D) of P.L. 99-514, clarification of amendments made by Sec. 1807(a)(7)(A) of P.L. 99-514, see below.
Prior to amendment, Sec. 1807(a)(7)(C)(i) of P.L. 99-514 read as follows:
"(i) any portion of such fund which meets the requirements of subparagraphs (A), (C), (D), and (F) of section 468B(d)(2) of the Internal Revenue Code of 1954

(as added by this paragraph) shall be treated as a designated settlement fund for purposes of section 468B of such Code,".

Prior to repeal, Sec. 1807(a)(7)(D) of P.L. 99-514 read as follows:

"(D) Clarification of law with respect to certain funds.—

"(i) In general.—Nothing in any provision of law shall be construed as providing that an escrow account, settlement fund, or similar fund is not subject to current income tax. If contributions to such an account or fund are not deductible, then the account or fund shall be taxed as a grantor trust.

"(ii) Effective date.—The provisions of clause (i) shall apply to accounts or funds established after August 16, 1986."

In 1986, P.L. 99-514, Sec. 1807(a)(7)(A), added Code Sec. 468B, effective as provided in Secs. 91(g), (h), and (i) of P.L. 98-369, reproduced in note following Code Sec. 461. Sec. 1807(a)(7)(C) [as amended by Sec. 1018(f)(3) of P.L. 100-647, see above] of this Act and Sec. 1807(a)(7)(D) of this Act [repealed by Sec. 1018(f)(5)(B) of P.L. 100-647, see above] provides:

"(C) Special rule for taxpayer in bankruptcy reorganization. In the case of any settlement fund which is established for claimants against a corporation which filed a petition for reorganization under chapter 11 of title 11, United States Code, on August 26, 1982, and which filed with a United States district court a first amended and restated plan of reorganization before March 1, 1986—

"(i) any portion of such fund which is established pursuant to a court order and with qualified payments, which meets the requirements of subparagraphs (C) and (D) of section 468B(d)(2) of the Internal Revenue Code of 1954 (as added by this paragraph), and with respect to which an election is made under subparagraph (F) thereof, shall be treated as a designated successor settlement fund for purposes of section 468B of such Code,

"(ii) such corporation (or any successor thereof) shall be liable for the tax imposed by section 468B of such Code on such portion of the fund (and the fund shall not be liable for such tax), such tax shall be deductible by the corporation, and the rate of tax under section 468B of such Code for any taxable year shall be equal to 15 percent, and

"(iii) any transaction by any portion of the fund not described in clause (i) shall be treated as a transaction made by the corporation."

Sec. 469. Passive activity losses and credits limited.

(a) Disallowance.

(1) In general. If for any taxable year the taxpayer is described in paragraph (2), neither—

(A) the passive activity loss, nor

(B) the passive activity credit,

for the taxable year shall be allowed.

(2) Persons described. The following are described in this paragraph:

(A) any individual, estate, or trust,

(B) any closely held C corporation, and

(C) any personal service corporation.

(b) Disallowed loss or credit carried to next year.

Except as otherwise provided in this section, any loss or credit from an activity which is disallowed under subsection (a) shall be treated as a deduction or credit allocable to such activity in the next taxable year.

(c) Passive activity defined.

For purposes of this section—

(1) In general. The term "passive activity" means any activity—

(A) which involves the conduct of any trade or business, and

(B) in which the taxpayer does not materially participate.

(2) Passive activity includes any rental activity. Except as provided in paragraph (7), the term "passive activity" includes any rental activity.

(3) Working interests in oil and gas property.

(A) In general. The term "passive activity" shall not include any working interest in any oil or gas property which the taxpayer holds directly or through an entity which does not limit the liability of the taxpayer with respect to such interest.

(B) Income in subsequent years. If any taxpayer has any loss for any taxable year from a working interest in any oil or gas property which is treated as a loss which is not from a passive activity, then any net income from such property (or any property the basis of which is determined in whole or in part by reference to the basis of such property) for any succeeding taxable year shall be treated as income of the taxpayer which is not from a passive activity. If the preceding sentence applies to the net income from any property for any taxable year, any credits allowable under Subpart B (other than section 27(a)) or D of part IV of subchapter A for such taxable year which are attributable to such property shall be treated as credits not from a passive activity to the extent the amount of such credits does not exceed the regular tax liability of the taxpayer for the taxable year which is allocable to such net income.

(4) Material participation not required for paragraphs (2) and (3). Paragraphs (2) and (3) shall be applied without regard to whether or not the taxpayer materially participates in the activity.

(5) Trade or business includes research and experimentation activity. For purposes of paragraph (1)(A), the term "trade or business" includes any activity involving research or experimentation (within the meaning of section 174).

(6) Activity in connection with trade or business or production of income. To the extent provided in regulations, for purposes of paragraph (1)(A), the term "trade or business" includes—

(A) any activity in connection with a trade or business, or

(B) any activity with respect to which expenses are allowable as a deduction under section 212.

(7) Special rules for taxpayers in real property business.

(A) In general. If this paragraph applies to any taxpayer for a taxable year—

(i) paragraph (2) shall not apply to any rental real estate activity of such taxpayer for such taxable year, and

(ii) this section shall be applied as if each interest of the taxpayer in rental real estate were a separate activity.

Notwithstanding clause (ii), a taxpayer may elect to treat all interests in rental real estate as one activity. Nothing in the preceding provisions of this subparagraph shall be construed as affecting the determination of whether the taxpayer materially participates with respect to any interest in a limited partnership as a limited partner.

(B) Taxpayers to whom paragraph applies. This paragraph shall apply to a taxpayer for a taxable year if—

(i) more than one-half of the personal services performed in trades or businesses by the taxpayer during such taxable year are performed in real property trades or businesses in which the taxpayer materially participates, and

(ii) such taxpayer performs more than 750 hours of services during the taxable year in real property trades or businesses in which the taxpayer materially participates.

In the case of a joint return, the requirements of the preceding sentence are satisfied if and only if either spouse separately satisfies such requirements. For purposes of the preceding sentence, activities in which a spouse materially participates shall be determined under subsection (h).

(C) Real property trade or business. For purposes of this paragraph, the term "real property trade or business" means any real property development, redevelopment, construction, reconstruction, acquisition, conversion, rental, operation, management, leasing, or brokerage trade or business.

(D) Special rules for subparagraph (B).

(i) Closely held C Corporations. In the case of a closely held C corporation, the requirements of subparagraph (B) shall be treated as met for any taxable year if more than 50 percent of the gross receipts of such corporation for such taxable year are derived from real property trades or businesses in which the corporation materially participates.

(ii) Personal services as an employee. For purposes of subparagraph (B), personal services performed as an employee shall not be treated as performed in real property trades or businesses. The preceding sentence shall not apply if such employee is a 5-percent owner (as defined in section 416(i)(1)(B)) in the employer.

(d) Passive activity loss and credit defined.

For purposes of this section—

(1) Passive activity loss. The term "passive activity loss" means the amount (if any) by which—

(A) the aggregate losses from all passive activities for the taxable year, exceed

(B) the aggregate income from all passive activities for such year.

(2) Passive activity credit. The term "passive activity credit" means the amount (if any) by which—

(A) the sum of the credits from all passive activities allowable for the taxable year under—

(i) subpart D of part IV of subchapter A, or

(ii) subpart B (other than section 27(a)) of such part IV, exceeds

(B) the regular tax liability of the taxpayer for the taxable year allocable to all passive activities.

(e) Special rules for determining income or loss from a passive activity.

For purposes of this section—

(1) Certain income not treated as income from passive activity. In determining the income or loss from any activity—

(A) In general. There shall not be taken into account—

(i) any—

(I) gross income from interest, dividends, annuities, or royalties not derived in the ordinary course of a trade or business,

(II) expenses (other than interest) which are clearly and directly allocable to such gross income, and

(III) interest expense properly allocable to such gross income, and

(ii) gain or loss not derived in the ordinary course of a trade or business which is attributable to the disposition of property—

(I) producing income of a type described in clause (i), or

(II) held for investment.

For purposes of clause (ii), any interest in a passive activity shall not be treated as property held for investment.

(B) Return on working capital. For purposes of subparagraph (A), any income, gain, or loss which is attributable to an investment of working capital shall be treated as not derived in the ordinary course of a trade or business.

(2) Passive losses of certain closely held corporations may offset active income.

(A) In general. If a closely held C corporation (other than a personal service corporation) has net active income for any taxable year, the passive activity loss of such taxpayer for such taxable year (determined without regard to this paragraph)—

(i) shall be allowable as a deduction against net active income, and

(ii) shall not be taken into account under subsection (a) to the extent so allowable as a deduction.

A similar rule shall apply in the case of any passive activity credit of the taxpayer.

(B) Net active income. For purposes of this paragraph, the term "net active income" means the taxable income of the taxpayer for the taxable year determined without regard to—

(i) any income or loss from a passive activity, and

(ii) any item of gross income, expense, gain, or loss described in paragraph (1)(A).

(3) Compensation for personal services. Earned income (within the meaning of section 911(d)(2)(A)) shall not be taken into account in computing the income or loss from a passive activity for any taxable year.

(4) Dividends reduced by dividends received deduction. For purposes of paragraphs (1) and (2), income from dividends shall be reduced by the amount of any dividends received deduction under section 243, 244, or 245.

(f) Treatment of former passive activities.

For purposes of this section—

(1) In general. If an activity is a former passive activity for any taxable year—

(A) any unused deduction allocable to such activity under subsection (b) shall be offset against the income from such activity for the taxable year,

(B) any unused credit allocable to such activity under subsection (b) shall be offset against the regular tax liability (computed after the application of paragraph (1)) allocable to such activity for the taxable year, and

(C) any such deduction or credit remaining after the application of subparagraphs (A) and (B) shall continue to be treated as arising from a passive activity.

(2) Change in status of closely held C corporation or personal service corporation. If a taxpayer ceases for any taxable year to be a closely held C corporation or personal service corporation, this section shall continue to apply to losses and credits to which this section applied for any preceding taxable year in the same manner as if such taxpayer continued to be a closely held C corporation or personal service corporation, whichever is applicable.

(3) Former passive activity. The term "former passive activity" means any activity which, with respect to the taxpayer—

(A) is not a passive activity for the taxable year, but

(B) was a passive activity for any prior taxable year.

(g) Dispositions of entire interest in passive activity.

If during the taxable year a taxpayer disposes of his entire interest in any passive activity (or former passive activity), the following rules shall apply:

(1) Fully taxable transaction.

(A) In general. If all gain or loss realized on such disposition is recognized, the excess of—

(i) any loss from such activity for such taxable year (determined after the application of subsection (b)), over

(ii) any net income or gain for such taxable year from all other passive activities (determined after the application of subsection (b)),

shall be treated as a loss which is not from a passive activity.

(B) Subparagraph (A) not to apply to disposition involving related party. If the taxpayer and the person acquiring the interest bear a relationship to each other described in section 267(b) or section 707(b)(1), then subparagraph (A) shall not apply to any loss of the taxpayer until the taxable year in which such interest is acquired (in a transaction described in subparagraph (A)) by another person who does not bear such a relationship to the taxpayer.

(C) Income from prior years. To the extent provided in regulations, income or gain from the activity for preceding taxable years shall be taken into account under subparagraph (A)(ii) for the taxable year to the extent necessary to prevent the avoidance of this section.

(2) Disposition by death. If an interest in the activity is transferred by reason of the death of the taxpayer—

(A) paragraph (1)(A) shall apply to losses described in paragraph (1)(A) to the extent such losses are greater than the excess (if any) of—

(i) the basis of such property in the hands of the transferee, over

(ii) the adjusted basis of such property immediately before the death of the taxpayer, and

(B) any losses to the extent of the excess described in subparagraph (A) shall not be allowed as a deduction for any taxable year.

(3) Installment sale of entire interest. In the case of an installment sale of an entire interest in an activity to which section 453 applies, paragraph (1) shall apply to the portion of such losses for each taxable year which bears the same ratio to all such losses as the gain recognized on such sale during such taxable year bears to the gross profit from such sale (realized or to be realized when payment is completed).

(h) Material participation defined.

For purposes of this section—

(1) In general. A taxpayer shall be treated as materially participating in an activity only if the taxpayer is involved in the operations of the activity on a basis which is—

(A) regular,

(B) continuous, and

(C) substantial.

(2) Interests in limited partnerships. Except as provided in regulations, no interest in a limited partnership as a limited partner shall be treated as an interest with respect to which a taxpayer materially participates.

(3) Treatment of certain retired individuals and surviving spouses. A taxpayer shall be treated as materially participating in any farming activity for a taxable year if paragraph (4) or (5) of section 2032A(b) would cause the requirements of section 2032A(b)(1)(C)(ii) to be met with respect to real property used in such activity if such taxpayer had died during the taxable year.

(4) Certain closely held C corporations and personal service corporations. A closely held C corporation or personal service corporation shall be treated as materially participating in an activity only if—

(A) 1 or more shareholders holding stock representing more than 50 percent (by value) of the outstanding stock of such corporation materially participate in such activity, or

(B) in the case of a closely held C corporation (other than a personal service corporation), the requirements of section 465(c)(7)(C) (without regard to clause (iv)) are met with respect to such activity.

(5) Participation by spouse. In determining whether a taxpayer materially participates, the participation of the spouse of the taxpayer shall be taken into account.

(i) $25,000 offset for rental real estate activities.

(1) In general. In the case of any natural person, subsection (a) shall not apply to that portion of the passive activity loss or the deduction equivalent (within the meaning of subsection (j)(5)) of the passive activity credit for any taxable year which is attributable to all rental real estate activities with respect to which such individual actively participated in such taxable year (and if any portion of such loss or credit arose in another taxable year, in such other taxable year).

(2) Dollar limitation. The aggregate amount to which paragraph (1) applies for any taxable year shall not exceed $25,000.

(3) Phase-out of exemption.

(A) In general. In the case of any taxpayer, the $25,000 amount under paragraph (2) shall be reduced (but not below zero) by 50 percent of the amount by which the adjusted gross income of the taxpayer for the taxable year exceeds $100,000.

(B) Special phase-out of rehabilitation credit. In the case of any portion of the passive activity credit for any taxable year which is attributable to the rehabilitation credit determined under section 47, subparagraph (A) shall be applied by substituting "$200,000" for "$100,000".

(C) Exception for commercial revitalization deduction. Subparagraph (A) shall not apply to any portion of the passive activity loss for any taxable year which is attributable to the commercial revitalization deduction under section 1400I.

(D) Exception for low-income housing credit. Subparagraph (A) shall not apply to any portion of the passive activity credit for any taxable year which is attributable to any credit determined under section 42.

(E) Ordering rules to reflect exceptions and separate phase-outs. If subparagraph (B), (C), or (D) applies for a taxable year, paragraph (1) shall be applied—

(i) first to the portion of the passive activity loss to which subparagraph (C) does not apply,

(ii) second to the portion of such loss to which subparagraph (C) applies,

(iii) third to the portion of the passive activity credit to which subparagraph (B) or (D) does not apply,

(iv) fourth to the portion of such credit to which subparagraph (B) applies, and

(v) then to the portion of such credit to which subparagraph (D) applies.

> • **Caution:** Code Sec. 469(i)(3)(F), following, was amended by P.L. 107-16, EGTRRA. These provisions generally sunset for tax years beginning after 12/31/2012. For specific sunset provisions, see Sec. 901, P.L. 107-16 (as amended) reproduced in history notes for this Code Sec.

(F) Adjusted gross income. For purposes of this paragraph, adjusted gross income shall be determined without regard to—

(i) any amount includible in gross income under section 86,

(ii) the amounts excludable from gross income under sections 135 and 137,
(iii) the amounts allowable as a deduction under sections 199, 219, 221, and 222, and
(iv) any passive activity loss or any loss allowable by reason of subsection (c)(7).

(4) Special rule for estates.
(A) In general. In the case of taxable years of an estate ending less than 2 years after the date of the death of the decedent, this subsection shall apply to all rental real estate activities with respect to which such decedent actively participated before his death.
(B) Reduction for surviving spouse's exemption. For purposes of subparagraph (A), the $25,000 amount under paragraph (2) shall be reduced by the amount of the exemption under paragraph (1) (without regard to paragraph (3)) allowable to the surviving spouse of the decedent for the taxable year ending with or within the taxable year of the estate.

(5) Married individuals filing separately.
(A) In general. Except as provided in subparagraph (B), in the case of any married individual filing a separate return, this subsection shall be applied by substituting—
(i) "$12,500" for "$25,000" each place it appears,
(ii) "$50,000" for "$100,000" in paragraph (3)(A), and
(iii) "$100,000" for "$200,000" in paragraph (3)(B).
(B) Taxpayers not living apart. This subsection shall not apply to a taxpayer who—
(i) is a married individual filing a separate return for any taxable year, and
(ii) does not live apart from his spouse at all times during such taxable year.

(6) Active participation.
(A) In general. An individual shall not be treated as actively participating with respect to any interest in any rental real estate activity for any period if, at any time during such period, such interest (including any interest of the spouse of the individual) is less than 10 percent (by value) of all interests in such activity.
(B) No participation requirement for low-income housing, rehabilitation credit, or commercial revitalization deduction. Paragraphs (1) and (4)(A) shall be applied without regard to the active participation requirement in the case of—
(i) any credit determined under section 42 for any taxable year,
(ii) any rehabilitation credit determined under section 47, or
(iii) any deduction under section 1400I (relating to commercial revitalization deduction).
(C) Interest as a limited partner. Except as provided in regulations, no interest as a limited partner in a limited partnership shall be treated as an interest with respect to which the taxpayer actively participates.
(D) Participation by spouse. In determining whether a taxpayer actively participates, the participation of the spouse of the taxpayer shall be taken into account.

(j) Other definitions and special rules.
For purposes of this section—
(1) Closely held C corporation. The term "closely held C corporation" means any C corporation described in section 465(a)(1)(B).
(2) Personal service corporation. The term "personal service corporation" has the meaning given such term by section 269A(b)(1), except that section 269A(b)(2) shall be applied—
(A) by substituting "any" for "more than 10 percent", and
(B) by substituting "any" for "50 percent or more in value" in section 318(a)(2)(C).
A corporation shall not be treated as a personal service corporation unless more than 10 percent of the stock (by value) in such corporation is held by employee-owners (within the meaning of section 269A(b)(2), as modified by the preceding sentence).
(3) Regular tax liability. The term "regular tax liability" has the meaning given such term by section 26(b).
(4) Allocation of passive activity loss and credit. The passive activity loss and the passive activity credit (and the $25,000 amount under subsection (i)) shall be allocated to activities, and within activities, on a pro rata basis in such manner as the Secretary may prescribe.
(5) Deduction equivalent. The deduction equivalent of credits from a passive activity for any taxable year is the amount which (if allowed as a deduction) would reduce the regular tax liability for such taxable year by an amount equal to such credits.
(6) Special rule for gifts. In the case of a disposition of any interest in a passive activity by gift—
(A) the basis of such interest immediately before the transfer shall be increased by the amount of any passive activity losses allocable to such interest with respect to which a deduction has not been allowed by reason of subsection (a), and
(B) such losses shall not be allowable as a deduction for any taxable year.
(7) Qualified residence interest. The passive activity loss of a taxpayer shall be computed without regard to qualified residence interest (within the meaning of section 163(h)(3)).
(8) Rental activity. The term "rental activity" means any activity where payments are principally for the use of tangible property.
(9) Election to increase basis of property by amount of disallowed credit. For purposes of determining gain or loss from a disposition of any property to which subsection (g)(1) applies, the transferor may elect to increase the basis of such property immediately before the transfer by an amount equal to the portion of any unused credit allowable under this chapter which reduced the basis of such property for the taxable year in which such credit arose. If the taxpayer elects the application of this paragraph, such portion of the passive activity credit of such taxpayer shall not be allowed for any taxable year.
(10) Coordination with section 280A. If a passive activity involves the use of a dwelling unit to which section 280A(c)(5) applies for any taxable year, any income, deduction, gain, or loss allocable to such use shall not be taken into account for purposes of this section for such taxable year.
(11) Aggregation of members of affiliated groups. Except as provided in regulations, all members of an affiliated group which files a consolidated return shall be treated as 1 corporation.
(12) Special rule for distributions by estates or trusts. If any interest in a passive activity is distributed by an estate or trust—
(A) the basis of such interest immediately before such distribution shall be increased by the amount of any passive activity losses allocable to such interest, and

(B) such losses shall not be allowable as a deduction for any taxable year.

(k) Separate application of section in case of publicly traded partnerships.

(1) In general. This section shall be applied separately with respect to items attributable to each publicly traded partnership (and subsection (i) shall not apply with respect to items attributable to any such partnership). The preceding sentence shall not apply to any credit determined under section 42, or any rehabilitation credit determined under section 47, attributable to a publicly traded partnership to the extent the amount of any such credits exceeds the regular tax liability attributable to income from such partnership.

(2) Publicly traded partnership. For purposes of this section, the term "publicly traded partnership" means any partnership if—

(A) interests in such partnership are traded on an established securities market, or

(B) interests in such partnership are readily tradable on a secondary market (or the substantial equivalent thereof).

(3) Coordination with subsection (g). For purposes of subsection (g), a taxpayer shall not be treated as having disposed of his entire interest in an activity of a publicly traded partnership until he disposes of his entire interest in such partnership.

(4) Application to regulated investment companies. For purposes of this section, a regulated investment company (as defined in section 851) holding an interest in a qualified publicly traded partnership (as defined in section 851(h)) shall be treated as a taxpayer described in subsection (a)(2) with respect to items attributable to such interest.

(l) Regulations.

The Secretary shall prescribe such regulations as may be necessary or appropriate to carry out provisions of this section, including regulations—

(1) which specify what constitutes an activity, material participation, or active participation for purposes of this section,

(2) which provide that certain items of gross income will not be taken into account in determining income or loss from any activity (and the treatment of expenses allocable to such income),

(3) requiring net income or gain from a limited partnership or other passive activity to be treated as not from a passive activity,

(4) which provide for the determination of the allocation of interest expense for purposes of this section, and

(5) which deal with changes in marital status and changes between joint returns and separate returns.

(m) Phase-in of disallowance of losses and credits for interest held before date of enactment.

(1) In general. In the case of any passive activity loss or passive activity credit for any taxable year beginning in calendar years 1987 through 1990, subsection (a) shall not apply to the applicable percentage of that portion of such loss (or such credit) which is attributable to pre-enactment interests.

(2) Applicable percentage. For purposes of this subsection, the applicable percentage shall be determined in accordance with the following table:

In the case of taxable years beginning in:	The applicable percentage is:
1987	65
1988	40
1989	20
1990	10

(3) Portion of loss or credit attributable to pre-enactment interests. For purposes of this subsection—

(A) In general. The portion of the passive activity loss (or passive activity credit) for any taxable year which is attributable to pre-enactment interests is the lesser of—

(i) the amount of the passive activity loss (or passive activity credit) which is disallowed for the taxable year under subsection (a) (without regard to this subsection), or

(ii) the amount of the passive activity loss (or passive activity credit) which would be disallowed for the taxable year (without regard to this subsection and without regard to any amount allocable to an activity for the taxable year under subsection (b)) taking into account only pre-enactment interests.

(B) Pre-enactment interest.

(i) In general. The term "pre-enactment interest" means any interest in a passive activity held by a taxpayer on the date of the enactment [10/22/86] of the Tax Reform Act of 1986, and at all times thereafter.

(ii) Binding contract exception. For purposes of clause (i), any interest acquired after such date of enactment pursuant to a written binding contract in effect on such date, and at all times thereafter, shall be treated as held on such date.

(iii) Interest in activities. The term "pre-enactment interest" shall not include an interest in a passive activity unless such activity was being conducted on such date of enactment. The preceding sentence shall not apply to an activity commencing after such date if—

(I) the property used in such activity is acquired pursuant to a written binding contract in effect on August 16, 1986, and at all times thereafter, or

(II) construction of property used in such activity began on or before August 16, 1986.

In 2010, P.L. 111-312, Sec. 101(a)(1), substituted "December 31, 2012" for "December 31, 2010" both places it appeared in Sec. 901, P.L. 107-16 [see below], effective as if included in the enactment of P.L. 107-16, EGTRRA, 6/7/2001.

In 2005, P.L. 109-135, Sec. 403(a)(19), amended Sec. 102(e) of P.L. 108-357 [see below].

Prior to amendment, Sec. 102(e) of P.L. 108-357 [see below] read as follows:

"*(e) Effective date.* The amendments made by this section shall apply to taxable years beginning after December 31, 2004."

In 2004, P.L. 108-357, Sec. 102(d)(5), added "199," before "219" in clause (i)(3)(F)(iii), effective as provided by Sec. 102(e) of this Act [as amended by Sec. 403(a)(19) of P.L. 109-135, see above], which reads as follows:

"*(e) Effective date.*

"(1) The amendments made by this section shall apply to taxable years beginning after December 31, 2004.

"(2) Application to pass-thru entities, etc. In determining the deduction under section 199 of the Internal Revenue Code of 1986 (as added by this section), items arising from a taxable year of a partnership, S corporation, estate, or trust beginning before January 1, 2005, shall not be taken into account for purposes of subsection (d)(1) of such section."

—P.L. 108-357, Sec. 331(g), added para. (k)(4), effective for tax. yrs. begin. after 10/22/2004.

In 2002, P.L. 107-358, Sec. 2, added subsec. (c) in Sec. 901 of P.L. 107-16 [see below], effective 12/17/2002.

—P.L. 107-147, Sec. 412(a), deleted clauses (i)(3)(E)(ii)-(iv) and added new clauses (i)(3)(E)(ii)-(iv), effective as if included in Sec. 101 of the Community Renewal Tax Relief Act of 2000, P.L. 106-554, enacted 12/21/2000.

Prior to deletion, clauses (i)(3)(E)(ii)-(iv) read as follows:

"(ii) second to the portion of the passive activity credit to which subparagraph (B) or (D) does not apply,

"(iii) third to the portion of such credit to which subparagraph (B) applies,

"(iv) fourth to the portion of such loss to which subparagraph (C) applies, and"

Tax accounting Code Sec. 469

In 2001, P.L. 107-16, Sec. 431(c)(3), substituted ", 221, and 222" for "and 221" in subpara. (i)(3)(F), effective for payments made in tax. yrs. begin. after 12/31/2001.

—P.L. 107-16, Sec. 901, of this Act [as amended by Sec. 2, P.L. 107-358, and Sec. 101(a)(1), P.L. 111-312, see above], reads as follows:

"SEC. 901. SUNSET OF PROVISIONS OF ACT.

"(a) In general. All provisions of, and amendments made by, this Act shall not apply—

"(1) to taxable, plan, or limitation years beginning after December 31, 2012, or

"(2) in the case of title V, to estates of decedents dying, gifts made, or generation skipping transfers, after December 31, 2012.

"(b) Application of certain laws. The Internal Revenue Code of 1986 and the Employee Retirement Income Security Act of 1974 shall be applied and administered to years, estates, gifts, and transfers described in subsection (a) as if the provisions and amendments described in subsection (a) had never been enacted.

"(c) Exception. Subsection (a) shall not apply to section 803 (relating to no federal income tax on restitution received by victims of the Nazi regime or their heirs or estates)."

In 2000, P.L. 106-554, Sec. 1(a)(7), [which enacted into law Sec. 101(b)(1) of P.L. 106-554] redesignated subpara. (i)(3)(C), (D) and (E) as (i)(3)(D), (E) and (F), and added subpara. (i)(3)(C)... Sec. 1(a)(7), [which enacted into law Sec. 101(b)(2) of P.L. 106-554] amended subpara. (i)(3)(E) [as redesignated by Sec. 101(b)(1) of this Act, see above]... Sec. 1(a)(7), [which enacted into law Sec. 101(b)(3)(A) of P.L. 106-554] deleted "or" at the end of clause (i)(6)(B)(i), substituted ", or" for the period at the end of clause (i)(6)(B)(ii), and added clause (i)(6)(B)(iii)... Sec. 1(a)(7), [which enacted into law Sec. 101(b)(3)(B) of P.L. 106-554] substituted ", rehabilitation credit, or commercial revitalization deduction" for "or rehabilitation credit" in the heading of subpara. (i)(6)(B), effective 12/21/2000.

Prior to amendment subpara. (i)(3)(E) read as follows:

"(E) Ordering rules to reflect exception and separate phase-out. If subparagraph (B) or (C) applies for any taxable year, paragraph (1) shall be applied—

"(i) first to the passive activity loss,

"(ii) second to the portion of the passive activity credit to which subparagraph (B) or (C) does not apply,

"(iii) third to the portion of such credit to which subparagraph (B) applies, and

"(iv) then to the portion of such credit to which subparagraph (C) applies."

In 1998, P.L. 105-277, Sec. 4003(a)(2)(D), amended clause (i)(3)(E)(iii), effective as provided in Sec. 202(e) of P.L. 105-34, which reads as follows:

"(e) Effective date. The amendments made by this section shall apply to any qualified education loan (as defined in section 221(e)(1) of the Internal Revenue Code of 1986, as added by this section) incurred on, before, or after the date of the enactment of this Act, but only with respect to—

"(1) any loan interest payment due and paid after December 31, 1997, and

"(2) the portion of the 60-month period referred to in section 221(d) of the Internal Revenue Code of 1986 (as added by this section) after December 31, 1997."

Prior to amendment, clause (i)(3)(E)(iii) read as follows:

"(iii) any amount allowable as a deduction under section 219, and"

In 1996, P.L. 104-188, Sec. 1704(d)(1), added the sentence at the end of subpara. (c)(3)(B), effective for tax. yrs. begin. after 12/31/86.

—P.L. 104-188, Sec. 1704(e)(1), amended subpara. (g)(1)(A), effective for tax. yrs. begin. after 12/31/86.

Prior to amendment, subpara. (g)(1)(A) read as follows:

"(A) In general. If all gain or loss realized on such disposition is recognized, the excess of—

"(i) the sum of—

"(I) any loss from such activity for such taxable year (determined after application of subsection (b)), plus

"(II) any loss realized on such disposition, over

"(ii) net income or gain for such taxable year from all passive activities (determined without regard to losses described in clause (i)),

shall be treated as a loss which is not from a passive activity."

—P.L. 104-188, Sec. 1807(c)(4), amended clause (i)(3)(E)(ii), effective for tax. yrs. begin. after 12/31/96.

Prior to amendment, clause (i)(3)(E)(ii) read as follows:

"(ii) the amount excludable from gross income under section 135,"

In 1993, P.L. 103-66, Sec. 13143(a), added para. (c)(7)... Sec. 13143(b)(1), substituted "Except as provided in paragraph (7), the" for "The" in para. (c)(2)... Sec. 13143(b)(2), added "or any loss allowable by reason of subsection (c)(7)" after "loss" in clause (i)(3)(E)(iv), effective for tax. yrs. begin. after 12/31/93.

In 1990, P.L. 101-508, Sec. 11704(a)(6), substituted "pre-enactment" for "pre-nactment" in subpara. (m)(3)(A), effective 11/5/90.

—P.L. 101-508, Sec. 11813(b)(16)(A), substituted "rehabilitation credit determined under section 47" for "rehabilitation investment credit (within the meaning of section 48(o))" in subpara. (i)(3)(B) and clause (i)(6)(B)(ii)... Sec. 11813(b)(16)(B), substituted "rehabilitation credit determined under section 47" for "rehabilitation investment credit (within the meaning of section 48(o))" in para. (k)(1), effective for property placed in service after 12/31/90 except as provided in Sec. 11813(c)(2) of this Act, reproduced in note following Code Sec. 46.

In 1989, P.L. 101-239, Sec. 7109(a), redesignated subpara. (i)(3)(D) as (i)(3)(E), amended subparas. (i)(3)(B) and (i)(3)(C) and added subpara. (i)(3)(D), effective for property placed in service after 12/31/89, in tax. yrs. end. after 12/31/89 except as provided in Sec. 7109(b)(2) of this Act which reads as follows:

"(2) Special rule where interest held in pass-thru entity.—In the case of a taxpayer who holds an indirect interest in property described in paragraph (1), the amendments made by this section [Sec. 7109] shall apply only if such interest is acquired after December 31, 1989."

Prior to amendment, subparas. (i)(3)(B) and (i)(3)(C) read as follows:

"(B) Special phase-out of low-income housing and rehabilitation credits. In the case of any portion of the passive activity credit for any taxable year which is attributable to any credit to which paragraph (6)(B) applies, subparagraph (A) shall be applied by substituting '$200,000' for '$100,000'.

"(C) Ordering rule to reflect separate phase-outs. If subparagraph (B) applies for any taxable year, paragraph (1) shall be applied—

"(i) first to the passive activity loss,

"(ii) second to the portion of the passive activity credit to which subparagraph (B) does not apply, and

"(iii) then to the portion of such credit to which subparagraph (B) applies."

In 1988, P.L. 100-647, Sec. 1005(a)(1), added "not derived in the ordinary course of a trade or business which is" after "gain or loss" in clause (e)(1)(A)(ii)... Sec. 1005(a)(2)(A), amended subpara. (g)(1)(A)... Sec. 1005(a)(2)(B), amended subpara. (g)(1)(C)... Sec. 1005(a)(3)(A), substituted "paragraph (1)(A)" for "paragraph (1)" in subpara. (g)(2)(A)... Sec. 1005(a)(3)(B), substituted "losses described in paragraph (1)(A)" for "such losses" the first place it appeared in subpara. (g)(2)(A)... Sec. 1005(a)(4)(A), substituted "(realized or to be realized" for "realized (or to be realized)" in para. (g)(3)... Sec. 1005(a)(4)(B), added a closing parenthesis after "completed" in para. (g)(3)... Sec. 1005(a)(5), added "only" before "if" in para. (h)(4)... Sec. 1005(a)(6), substituted "in such taxable year (and if any portion of such loss or credit arose in another taxable year, in such other taxable year)" for "in the taxable year in which such portion of such loss or credit arose" in para. (i)(1)... Sec. 1005(a)(7), substituted "Except as provided in regulations, no" for "No" in subpara. (i)(6)(C)... Sec. 1005(a)(8), added "with respect to which a deduction has not been allowed by reason of subsection (a)" before ", and" in subpara. (j)(6)(A)... Sec. 1005(a)(9), added paras. (j)(10) and (j)(11)... Sec. 1005(a)(11), added para. (j)(12)... Sec. 1005(a)(12), amended all the material that preceded subpara. (m)(3)(B) in subsec. (m), effective for tax. yrs. begin. after 12/31/86. Secs. 501(c)(2) through (4) of P.L. 99-514 [as amended by Sec. 4003(b)(2) of this Act, see below] provides special rules, reproduced below. Sec. 502 of P.L. 99-514 [as amended by Secs. 1005(b)(1), (2) and (3) of P.L. 100-647, and Sec. 8073(a) of P.L. 99-509, see below] provides transitional rules, reproduced below.

Prior to amendment, subpara. (g)(1)(A) read as follows:

"(A) In general. If all gain or loss realized on such disposition is recognized, any loss from such activity which has not previously been allowed as a deduction (and in the case of a passive activity for the taxable year, any loss realized on such disposition) shall not be treated as a passive activity loss and shall be allowable as a deduction against income in the following order:

"(i) Income or gain from the passive activity for the taxable year (including any gain recognized on the disposition).

"(ii) Net income or gain for the taxable year from all passive activities.

"(iii) Any other income or gain."

Prior to amendment, subpara. (g)(1)(C) read as follows:

"(C) Coordination with section 1211. In the case of any loss realized on the disposition of an interest in a passive activity, section 1211 shall be applied before subparagraph (A) is applied."

Prior to amendment, all the material that preceded subpara. (m)(3)(B) of subsec. (m), read as follows:

"(m) Phase-in of disallowance of losses and credits for interests held before date of enactment.

"(1) In general. In the case of any passive activity loss or credit for any taxable year beginning in calendar years 1987 through 1990 which—

"(A) is attributable to a pre-enactment interest, but

"(B) is not attributable to a carryforward to such taxable year of any loss or credit which was disallowed under this section for a preceding taxable year,

there shall be disallowed under subsection (a) only the applicable percentage of the amount which (but for this subsection) would have been disallowed under subsection (a) for such taxable year.

"(2) Applicable percentage. For purposes of this subsection, the applicable percentage shall be determined in accordance with the following table:

In the case of taxable years beginning in:	The applicable percentage is:
1987	35
1988	60
1989	80
1990	90

"(3) Portion of loss or credit attributable to pre-enactment interests. For purposes of this subsection—

"(A) In general. The portion of the passive activity loss for any taxable year which is attributable to pre-enactment interests shall be equal to the lesser of—

"(i) the passive activity loss for such taxable year, or

"(ii) the passive activity loss for such taxable year determined by taking into account only pre-enactment interests. For purposes of this subparagraph, the deduction equivalent (within the meaning of subsection (j)(5)) of a passive activity credit shall be taken into account."

—P.L. 100-647, Sec. 1005(a)(10), added Sec. 501(c)(4) to P.L. 99-514

—P.L. 100-647, Sec. 1005(b)(1), amended Sec. 502(d)(1)(A) of P.L. 99-514... Sec. 1005(b)(2), added Sec. 502(d)(3) to P.L. 99-514... Sec. 1105(b)(3), redesignated Sec. 502(d) of P.L. 99-514 as Sec. 502(e) of P.L. 99-514, see below.

Prior to amendment, Sec. 502(d)(1)(A) of P.L. 99-514 read as follows:

"(A) if

Code Sec. 469 — Tax accounting

"(i) in the case of a project placed in service before August 16, 1986, such person held an interest in such project on August 16, 1986, and the taxpayer made his initial investment after December 31, 1983, or

"(ii) in the case of a project not described in subparagraph (A), such investor held an interest in such project on December 31, 1986, and"

—P.L. 100-647, Sec. 2004(g), added para. (k)(3), effective for tax. yrs. begin. after 12/31/86. Secs. 501(c)(2) through (4) of P.L. 99-514 [as amended by Sec. 4003(b)(2) of this Act, see below] provides special rules, reproduced below. Sec. 502 of P.L. 99-514 [as amended by Secs. 1005(b)(1), (2) and (3) of P.L. 100-647, see above, and Sec. 8073(a) of P.L. 99-509, see below] provides transitional rules, reproduced below.

—P.L. 100-647, Sec. 4003(b)(2), repealed Sec. 501(c)(3) of P.L. 99-514, part of the special rules for changes made by Sec. 501(a) of P.L. 99-514.

Prior to repeal, Sec. 501(c)(3) of P.L. 99-514 read as follows:

"(3) Special rule for low-income housing.—

"(A) In general.— Except as provided in subparagraph (B), section 469(i)(6)(B)(i) of the Internal Revenue Code of 1986 (as added by this section) shall not apply to any property placed in service after December 31, 1989.

"(B) Exception where at least 10 percent of costs incurred.— In the case of property placed in service after December 31, 1989, and before January 1, 1991, section 469(i)(6)(B)(i) of such Code shall apply to such property if at least 10 percent of the costs of such property were incurred before January 1, 1989."

—P.L. 100-647, Sec. 6009(c)(3), redesignated clauses (i)(3)(D)(ii) and (iii) as clauses (i)(3)(D)(iii) and (iv), and added new clause (i)(3)(D)(ii), effective for tax. yrs. begin. after 12/31/89.

In 1987, P.L. 100-203, Sec. 10212(a), redesignated subsecs. (k) and (l) as subsecs. (l) and (m), and added new subsec. (k), effective for tax. yrs. begin. after 12/31/86. Secs. 501(c)(2) through (4) of P.L. 99-514 [as amended by Sec. 4003(b)(2) of P.L. 100-647, see above] provides special rules, reproduced below.

In 1986, P.L. 99-514, Sec. 501(a), added Code Sec. 469, effective for tax. yrs. begin. after 12/31/86. Secs. 501(c)(2) through (4) of P.L. 99-514 [as amended by Sec. 4403(b)(2) of P.L. 100-647, see above] provides special rules as follows:

"(2) Special rule for carryovers.— The amendments made by this section shall not apply to any loss, deduction, or credit carried to a taxable year beginning after December 31, 1986, from a taxable year beginning before January 1, 1987.

"(3) Repealed [by Sec. 4003(b)(2) of P.L. 100-647, see above]

"(4) Income from sales of passive activities in taxable years beginning before January 1, 1987.— If—

"(A) gain is recognized in a taxable year beginning after December 31, 1986, from a sale or exchange of an interest in an activity in a taxable year beginning before January 1, 1987, and

"(B) such gain would have been treated as gain from a passive activity had section 469 of the Internal Revenue Code of 1986 (as added by this section) been in effect for the taxable year in which the sale or exchange occurred and for all succeeding taxable years,

then such gain shall be treated as gain from a passive activity for purposes of such section."

—P.L. 99-514, Sec. 502, [as amended by Secs. 1005(b)(1), (2) and (3) of P.L. 100-647, see above, and Sec. 8073(a) of P.L. 99-509, see below] provides transitional rules as follows:

"Sec. 502. Transitional rule for low-income housing.

"(a) General rule.

"Any loss sustained by a qualified investor with respect to an interest in a qualified low-income housing project for any taxable year in the relief period shall not be treated as a loss from a passive activity for purposes of section 469 of the Internal Revenue Code of 1986.

"(b) Relief period.

"For purposes of subsection (a), the term 'relief period' means the period beginning with the taxable year in which the investor made his initial investment in the qualified low-income housing project and ending with whichever of the following is the earliest—

"(1) the 6th taxable year after the taxable year in which the investor made his initial investment,

"(2) the 1st taxable year after the taxable year in which the investor is obligated to make his last investment, or

"(3) the taxable year preceding the 1st taxable year for which such project ceased to be a qualified low-income housing project.

"(c) Qualified low-income housing project.

"For purposes of this section, the term 'qualified low-income housing project' means any project if—

"(1) such project meets the requirements of clause (i), (ii), (iii), or (iv) of section 1250(a)(1)(B) as of the date placed in service and for each taxable year thereafter which begins after 1986 and for which a passive loss may be allowable with respect to such project,

"(2) the operator certifies to the Secretary of the Treasury or his delegate that such project met the requirements of paragraph (1) on the date of the enactment of this Act (or, if later, when placed in service) and annually thereafter,

"(3) such project is constructed or acquired pursuant to a binding written contract entered into on or before August 16, 1986, and

"(4) such project is placed in service before January 1, 1989.

"(d) Qualified investor.

"For purposes of this section—

"(1) In general.— The term 'qualified investor' means any natural person who holds (directly or through 1 or more entities) an interest in a qualified low-income housing project—

"(A) if—

"(i) in the case of a project placed in service on or before August 16, 1986, such person held an interest in such project on August 16, 1986, and such person made his initial investment after December 31, 1983, or

"(ii) in the case of a project placed in service after August 16, 1986, such person made his initial investment after December 31, 1983, and such person held an interest in such project on December 31, 1986, and"

"(B) if such investor is required to make payments after December 31, 1986, of 50 percent or more of the total original obligated investment for such interest.

For purposes of subparagraph (A), a person shall be treated as holding an interest on August 16, 1986, or December 31, 1986, if on such date such person had a binding contract to acquire such interest.

"(2) Treatment of estates.— The estate of a decedent shall succeed to the treatment under this section of the decedent but only with respect to the 1st 2 taxable years of such estate ending after the date of the decedent's death.

"(3) Special rule for certain partnerships.— In the case of any property which is held by a partnership—

"(A) which placed such property in service on or after December 31, 1985, and before August 17, 1986, and continuously held such property through the close of the taxable year for which the determination is being made, and

"(B) which was not treated as a new partnership or as terminated at any time on or after the date on which such property was placed in service and through the close of the taxable year for which the determination is being made, paragraph (1)(A)(i) shall be applied by substituting 'December 31, 1988' for 'August 16, 1986' the 2nd place it appears.

"(4) Special rule for certain rural housing.— In the case of any interest in a qualified low-income housing project which—

"(A) is assisted under section 515 of the Housing Act of 1949 (relating to the Farmers' Home Administration Program), and

"(B) is located in a town with a population of less than 10,000 and which is not part of a metropolitan statistical area,

paragraph (1)(B) shall be applied by substituting '35 percent' for '50 percent' and subsection (b)(1) shall be applied by substituting '5th taxable year' for '6th taxable year'. The preceding sentence shall not apply to any interest unless, on December 31, 1986, at least one-half of the number of payments required with respect to such interest remain to be paid.

"(e) Special rules.

"(1) Where more than 1 building in project.— If there is more than 1 building in any project, the determination of when such project is placed in service shall be based on when the 1st building in such project is placed in service.

"(2) Only cash and other property taken into account.— In determining the amount any person invests in (or is obligated to invest in) any interest, only cash and other property shall be taken into account.

"(3) Coordination with credit.— No low-income housing credit shall be determined under section 42 of the Internal Revenue Code of 1986 with respect to any project with respect to which any person has been allowed any benefit under this section."

—P.L. 99-509, Sec. 8073(a), added Sec. 502(d)(4) to P.L. 99-514, reproduced above.

Sec. 470. Limitation on deductions allocable to property used by governments or other tax-exempt entities.

(a) Limitation on losses.

Except as otherwise provided in this section, a tax-exempt use loss for any taxable year shall not be allowed.

(b) Disallowed loss carried to next year.

Any tax-exempt use loss with respect to any tax-exempt use property which is disallowed under subsection (a) for any taxable year shall be treated as a deduction with respect to such property in the next taxable year.

(c) Definitions.

For purposes of this section—

(1) Tax-exempt use loss. The term "tax-exempt use loss" means, with respect to any taxable year, the amount (if any) by which—

(A) the sum of—

(i) the aggregate deductions (other than interest) directly allocable to a tax-exempt use property, plus

(ii) the aggregate deductions for interest properly allocable to such property, exceed

(B) the aggregate income from such property.

(2) Tax-exempt use property.

(A) In general. The term "tax-exempt use property" has the meaning given to such term by section 168(h), except that such section shall be applied—

(i) without regard to paragraphs (1)(C) and (3) thereof, and

(ii) as if section 197 intangible property (as defined in section 197), and property described in paragraph

(1)(B) or (2) of section 167(f), were tangible property.

(B) Exception for partnerships. Such term shall not include any property which would (but for this subparagraph) be tax-exempt use property solely by reason of section 168(h)(6).

(C) Cross reference. For treatment of partnerships as leases to which section 168(h) applies, see section 7701(e).

(d) Exception for certain leases.

This section shall not apply to any lease of property which meets the requirements of all of the following paragraphs:

(1) Availability of funds.

(A) In general. A lease of property meets the requirements of this paragraph if (at all times during the lease term) not more than an allowable amount of funds are—

(i) subject to any arrangement referred to in subparagraph (B), or

(ii) set aside or expected to be set aside,

to or for the benefit of the lessor or any lender, or to or for the benefit of the lessee to satisfy the lessee's obligations or options under the lease. For purposes of clause (ii), funds shall be treated as set aside or expected to be set aside only if a reasonable person would conclude, based on the facts and circumstances, that such funds are set aside or expected to be set aside.

(B) Arrangements. The arrangements referred to in this subparagraph include a defeasance arrangement, a loan by the lessee to the lessor or any lender, a deposit arrangement, a letter of credit collateralized with cash or cash equivalents, a payment undertaking agreement, prepaid rent (within the meaning of the regulations under section 467), a sinking fund arrangement, a guaranteed investment contract, financial guaranty insurance, and any similar arrangement (whether or not such arrangement provides credit support).

(C) Allowable amount.

(i) In general. Except as otherwise provided in this subparagraph, the term "allowable amount" means an amount equal to 20 percent of the lessor's adjusted basis in the property at the time the lease is entered into.

(ii) Higher amount permitted in certain cases. To the extent provided in regulations, a higher percentage shall be permitted under clause (i) where necessary because of the credit-worthiness of the lessee. In no event may such regulations permit a percentage of more than 50 percent.

(iii) Option to purchase. If under the lease the lessee has the option to purchase the property for a fixed price or for other than the fair market value of the property (determined at the time of exercise), the allowable amount at the time such option may be exercised may not exceed 50 percent of the price at which such option may be exercised.

(iv) No allowable amount for certain arrangements. The allowable amount shall be zero with respect to any arrangement which involves—

(I) a loan from the lessee to the lessor or a lender,

(II) any deposit received, letter of credit issued, or payment undertaking agreement entered into by a lender otherwise involved in the transaction, or

(III) in the case of a transaction which involves a lender, any credit support made available to the lessor in which any such lender does not have a claim that is senior to the lessor.

For purposes of subclause (I), the term "loan" shall not include any amount treated as a loan under section 467 with respect to a section 467 rental agreement.

(2) Lessor must make substantial equity investment.

(A) In general. A lease of property meets the requirements of this paragraph if—

(i) the lessor—

(I) has at the time the lease is entered into an unconditional at-risk equity investment (as determined by the Secretary) in the property of at least 20 percent of the lessor's adjusted basis in the property as of that time, and

(II) maintains such investment throughout the term of the lease, and

(ii) the fair market value of the property at the end of the lease term is reasonably expected to be equal to at least 20 percent of such basis.

(B) Risk of loss. For purposes of clause (ii), the fair market value at the end of the lease term shall be reduced to the extent that a person other than the lessor bears a risk of loss in the value of the property.

(C) Paragraph not to apply to short-term leases. This paragraph shall not apply to any lease with a lease term of 5 years or less.

(3) Lessee may not bear more than minimal risk of loss.

(A) In general. A lease of property meets the requirements of this paragraph if there is no arrangement under which the lessee bears—

(i) any portion of the loss that would occur if the fair market value of the leased property were 25 percent less than its reasonably expected fair market value at the time the lease is terminated, or

(ii) more than 50 percent of the loss that would occur if the fair market value of the leased property at the time the lease is terminated were zero.

(B) Exception. The Secretary may by regulations provide that the requirements of this paragraph are not met where the lessee bears more than a minimal risk of loss.

(C) Paragraph not to apply to short-term leases. This paragraph shall not apply to any lease with a lease term of 5 years or less.

(4) Property with more than 7-year class life. In the case of a lease—

(A) of property with a class life (as defined in section 168(i)(1)) of more than 7 years, other than fixed-wing aircraft and vessels, and

(B) under which the lessee has the option to purchase the property,

the lease meets the requirements of this paragraph only if the purchase price under the option equals the fair market value of the property (determined at the time of exercise).

(e) Special rules.

(1) Treatment of former tax-exempt use property.

(A) In general. In the case of any former tax-exempt use property—

(i) any deduction allowable under subsection (b) with respect to such property for any taxable year shall be allowed only to the extent of any net income (without regard to such deduction) from such property for such taxable year, and

(ii) any portion of such unused deduction remaining after application of clause (i) shall be treated as a deduction allowable under subsection (b) with respect to such property in the next taxable year.

(B) Former tax-exempt use property. For purposes of this subsection, the term "former tax-exempt use property" means any property which—
(i) is not tax-exempt use property for the taxable year, but
(ii) was tax-exempt use property for any prior taxable year.

(2) Disposition of entire interest in property. If during the taxable year a taxpayer disposes of the taxpayer's entire interest in tax-exempt use property (or former tax-exempt use property), rules similar to the rules of section 469(g) shall apply for purposes of this section.

(3) Coordination with section 469. This section shall be applied before the application of section 469.

(4) Coordination with sections 1031 and 1033.
(A) In general. Sections 1031(a) and 1033(a) shall not apply if—
(i) the exchanged or converted property is tax-exempt use property subject to a lease which was entered into before March 13, 2004, and which would not have met the requirements of subsection (d) had such requirements been in effect when the lease was entered into, or
(ii) the replacement property is tax-exempt use property subject to a lease which does not meet the requirements of subsection (d).
(B) Adjusted basis. In the case of property acquired by the lessor in a transaction to which section 1031 or 1033 applies, the adjusted basis of such property for purposes of this section shall be equal to the lesser of—
(i) the fair market value of the property as of the beginning of the lease term, or
(ii) the amount which would be the lessor's adjusted basis if such sections did not apply to such transaction.

(f) Other definitions.
For purposes of this section—
(1) Related parties. The terms "lessor", "lessee", and "lender" each include any related party (within the meaning of section 197(f)(9)(C)(i)).
(2) Lease term. The term "lease term" has the meaning given to such term by section 168(i)(3).
(3) Lender. The term "lender" means, with respect to any lease, a person that makes a loan to the lessor which is secured (or economically similar to being secured) by the lease or the leased property.
(4) Loan. The term "loan" includes any similar arrangement.

(g) Regulations.
The Secretary shall prescribe such regulations as may be necessary or appropriate to carry out the purposes of this section, including regulations which—
(1) allow in appropriate cases the aggregation of property subject to the same lease, and
(2) provide for the determination of the allocation of interest expense for purposes of this section.

In 2007, P.L. 110-172, Sec. 7(c)(1), amended para. (c)(2) . . . Sec. 7(c)(2), substituted "(at all times during the lease term)" for "(at any time during the lease term)" in subpara. (d)(1)(A), effective as if included in the provisions of Sec. 849 of P.L. 108-357 [see below]

Prior to amendment, para. (c)(2) read as follows:
"(2) Tax-exempt use property. The term 'tax-exempt use property' has the meaning given to such term by section 168(h), except that such section shall be applied—
"(A) without regard to paragraphs (1)(C) and (3) thereof, and
"(B) as if property described in—
"(i) section 167(f)(1)(B),
"(ii) section 167(f)(2), and
"(iii) section 197 intangible,
were tangible property.
"Such term shall not include property which would (but for this sentence) be tax-exempt use property solely by reason of section 168(h)(6) if any credit is allowable under section 42 or 47 with respect to such property."

In 2005, P.L. 109-135, Sec. 403(ff), added ", and in the case of property treated as tax-exempt use property other than by reason of a lease, to property acquired after March 12, 2004" before the period at the end of Sec. 849(a) of P.L. 108-357 [see below]. Sec. 849(a) of P.L. 108-357 provides the effective date for the amendment made by Sec. 848(a) of such Act.

In 2004, P.L. 108-357, Sec. 848(a), added Code Sec. 470, effective as provided in Sec. 849(a) [as amended by Sec. 403(ff) of P.L. 109-135, see above] Sec. 849(a) and (b) of this Act, reads as follows:
"(a) In general. Except as provided in this section, the amendments made by this part shall apply to leases entered into after March 12, 2004, and in the case of property treated as tax-exempt use property other than by reason of a lease, to property acquired after March 12, 2004.
"(b) Exception.
"(1) In general. The amendments made by this part shall not apply to qualified transportation property.
"(2) Qualified transportation property. For purposes of paragraph (1), the term 'qualified transportation property' means domestic property subject to a lease with respect to which a formal application—
"(A) was submitted for approval to the Federal Transit Administration (an agency of the Department of Transportation) after June 30, 2003, and before March 13, 2004,
"(B) is approved by the Federal Transit Administration before January 1, 2006, and
"(C) includes a description of such property and the value of such property.
"(3) Exchanges and conversion of tax-exempt use property. Section 470(e)(4) of the Internal Revenue Code of 1986, as added by section 848, shall apply to property exchanged or converted after the date of the enactment of this Act.
"(4) Intangibles and Indian tribal governments. The amendments made subsections (b)(2), (b)(3), and (e) of section 847, and the treatment of property described in clauses (ii) and (iii) of section 470(c)(2)(B) of the Internal Revenue Code of 1986 (as added by section 848) as tangible property, shall apply to leases entered into after October 3, 2004."

SUBPART D.—INVENTORIES
Sec.
471. General rule for inventories.
472. Last-in, first-out inventories.
473. Qualified liquidations of LIFO inventories.
474. Simplified dollar-value LIFO method for certain small businesses.
475. Mark to market accounting method for dealers in securities.

In 1993, P.L. 103-66, Sec. 13223(b)(2), added item 475.
In 1986, P.L. 99-514, Sec. 802(b), amended item 474.
Prior to amendment, item 474 read as follows:
"474. Election by certain small businesses to use one inventory pool."
In 1981, P.L. 97-34, Sec. 237(b), added item 474.
In 1980, P.L. 96-223, Sec. 403(a)(2), added item 473.

Sec. 471. General rule for inventories.
(a) General rule.
Whenever in the opinion of the Secretary the use of inventories is necessary in order clearly to determine the income of any taxpayer, inventories shall be taken by such taxpayer on such basis as the Secretary may prescribe as conforming as nearly as may be to the best accounting practice in the trade or business and as most clearly reflecting the income.

(b) Estimates of inventory shrinkage permitted.
A method of determining inventories shall not be treated as failing to clearly reflect income solely because it utilizes estimates of inventory shrinkage that are confirmed by a physical count only after the last day of the taxable year if—
(1) the taxpayer normally does a physical count of inventories at each location on a regular and consistent basis, and

Tax accounting   Code Sec. 472(g)(1)

(2) the taxpayer makes proper adjustments to such inventories and to its estimating methods to the extent such estimates are greater than or less than the actual shrinkage.

(c) Cross reference.

For rules relating to capitalization of direct and indirect costs of property, see section 263A.

In 1997, P.L. 105-34, Sec. 961(a), redesignated subsec. (b) as subsec. (c) and added new subsec. (b), effective for tax. yrs. end. after 8/5/97. Sec. 951(b)(2) of this Act provides:

"(2) Coordination with section 481. In the case of any taxpayer permitted by this section to change its method of accounting to a permissible method for any taxable year—

"(A) such changes shall be treated as initiated by the taxpayer,

"(B) such changes shall be treated as made with the consent of the Secretary of the Treasury, and

"(C) the period for taking into account the adjustments under section 481 by reason of such change shall be 4 years."

In 1988, P.L. 100-647, Sec. 6252(a)(2), repealed Sec. 238 of P.L. 97-34.

Prior to repeal, Sec. 238 of P.L. 97-34 read as follows:

"SEC. 238. STUDY OF ACCOUNTING METHODS FOR INVENTORY.

"(a) Study.

"The Secretary of the Treasury shall conduct a full and complete study of methods of tax accounting for inventory with a view toward the development of simplified methods. Such study shall include (but shall not be limited to) an examination of the last-in first-out method and the cash receipts and disbursements method.

"(b) Report.

"Not later than December 31, 1982, the Secretary of the Treasury shall submit to the Committee on Ways and Means of the House of Representative and to the Committee on Finance of the Senate a report on the study conducted under subsection (a), together with such recommendations as he deems appropriate."

In 1986, P.L. 99-514, Sec. 803(b)(4)(A), substituted "(a) General rule— whenever" for "Whenever" in Code Sec. 471 . . . Sec. 803(b)(4)(B), added subsec. (b), effective for costs incurred after 12/31/86 in tax. yrs. end. after 12/31/86.

In 1981, P.L. 97-34, Sec. 238, providing for a study of accounting methods for inventory was repealed by Sec. 6252(a)(2) of P.L. 100-647, see above.

In 1978, P.L. 95-600, Sec. 352, provided the following rules on accounting for growing crops:

"SEC. 352. ACCOUNTING FOR GROWING CROPS.

"(a) Application of section.

"This section shall apply to a taxpayer who—

"(1) is a farmer, nurseryman, or florist,

"(2) is on an accrual method of accounting, and

"(3) is not required by section 447 of the Internal Revenue Code of 1954 to capitalize reproductive period expenses.

"(b) Taxpayer may not be required to inventory growing crops.

"A taxpayer to whom this section applies may not be required to inventory growing crops for any taxable year beginning after December 31, 1977.

"(c) Taxpayer may elect to change to cash method.

"A taxpayer to whom this section applies may, for any taxable year beginning after December 31, 1977 and before January 1, 1981, change to the cash receipts and disbursements method of accounting with respect to any trade or business in which the principal activity is growing crops.

"(d) Section 481 of code to apply.

"Any change in the way in which a taxpayer accounts for the costs of growing crops resulting from the application of subsection (b) or (c)—

"(1) shall not require the consent of the Secretary of the Treasury or his delegate, and

"(2) shall be treated, for purposes of section 481 of the Revenue Code of 1954, as a change in the method of accounting initiated by the taxpayer.

"(e) Growing crops.

"For purposes of this section, the term 'growing crops' does not include trees grown for lumber, pulp, or other nonlife purposes."

In 1976, P.L. 94-455, Sec. 1906(b)(13)(A), substituted "Secretary" for "Secretary or his delegate" each place it appeared in Code Sec. 471, effective for tax. yrs. begin. after 12/31/76.

—P.L. 94-455, Sec. 2119, covers the application of Code Sec. 471 to publishers' prepublication expenditures. See note to Code Sec. 174.

Sec. 472. Last-in, first-out inventories.

(a) Authorization.

A taxpayer may use the method provided in subsection (b) (whether or not such method has been prescribed under section 471) in inventorying goods specified in an application to use such method filed at such time and in such manner as the Secretary may prescribe. The change to, and the use of, such method shall be in accordance with such regulations as the Secretary may prescribe as necessary in order that the use of such method may clearly reflect income.

(b) Method applicable.

In inventorying goods specified in the application described in subsection (a), the taxpayer shall:

(1) Treat those remaining on hand at the close of the taxable year as being: First, those included in the opening inventory of the taxable year (in the order of acquisition) to the extent thereof; and second, those acquired in the taxable year;

(2) Inventory them at cost; and

(3) Treat those included in the opening inventory of the taxable year in which such method is first used as having been acquired at the same time and determine their cost by the average cost method.

(c) Condition.

Subsection (a) shall apply only if the taxpayer establishes to the satisfaction of the Secretary that the taxpayer has used no procedure other than that specified in paragraphs (1) and (3) of subsection (b) in inventorying such goods to ascertain the income, profit, or loss of the first taxable year for which the method described in subsection (b) is to be used, for the purpose of a report or statement covering such taxable year—

(1) to shareholders, partners, or other proprietors, or to beneficiaries, or

(2) for credit purposes.

(d) 3-year averaging for increases in inventory value.

The beginning inventory for the first taxable year for which the method described in subsection (b) is used shall be valued at cost. Any change in the inventory amount resulting from the application of the preceding sentence shall be taken into account ratably in each of the 3 taxable years beginning with the first taxable year for which the method described in subsection (b) is first used.

(e) Subsequent inventories.

If a taxpayer, having complied with subsection (a), uses the method described in subsection (b) for any taxable year, then such method shall be used in all subsequent taxable years unless—

(1) with the approval of the Secretary a change to a different method is authorized; or,

(2) the Secretary determines that the taxpayer has used for any such subsequent taxable year some procedure other than that specified in paragraph (1) of subsection (b) in inventorying the goods specified in the application to ascertain the income, profit, or loss of such subsequent taxable year for the purpose of a report or statement covering such taxable year (A) to shareholders, partners, or other proprietors, or beneficiaries, or (B) for credit purposes; and requires a change to a method different from that prescribed in subsection (b) beginning with such subsequent taxable year or any taxable year thereafter.

If paragraph (1) or (2) of this subsection applies, the change to, and the use of, the different method shall be in accordance with such regulations as the Secretary may prescribe as necessary in order that the use of such method may clearly reflect income.

(f) Use of government price indexes in pricing inventory.

The Secretary shall prescribe regulations permitting the use of suitable published governmental indexes in such manner and circumstances as determined by the Secretary for purposes of the method described in subsection (b).

(g) Conformity rules applied on controlled group basis.

(1) In general. Except as otherwise provided in regulations, all members of the same group of financially related corporations shall be treated as 1 taxpayer for purposes of subsections (c) and (e)(2).

2,183

(2) Group of financially related corporations. For purposes of paragraph (1), the term "group of financially related corporations" means—

(A) any affiliated group as defined in section 1504 determined by substituting "50 percent" for "80 percent" each place it appears in section 1504(a) and without regard to section 1504(b), and

(B) any other group of corporations which consolidate or combine for purposes of financial statements.

In 1984, P.L. 98-369, Sec. 95(a), added subsec. (g), effective for tax. yrs. begin. after 7/18/84.

In 1981, P.L. 97-34, Sec. 235, added subsec. (f), effective 8/13/81.

—P.L. 97-34, Sec. 236(a), amended subsec. (d), effective for tax. yrs. begin. after 12/31/81.

Prior to amendment subsec. (d) read as follows:

"*(d) Preceding closing inventory.*

"In determining income for the taxable year preceding the taxable year for which the method described in subsection (b) is first used, the closing inventory of such preceding year of the goods specified in the application referred to in subsection (a) shall be at cost."

In 1976, P.L. 94-455, Sec. 1901(b)(36)(A), repealed subsec. (f), effective for tax. yrs. begin. after 12/31/76.

Prior to amendment, subsec. (f) read as follows:

"*(f) Cross reference.*

"For provisions relating to involuntary liquidation and replacement of LIFO inventories, see section 1321."

—P.L. 94-455, Sec. 1906(b)(13)(A), substituted "Secretary" for "Secretary or his delegate" each place it appeared in Code Sec. 472, effective for tax. yrs. begin. after 12/31/76.

Sec. 473. Qualified liquidations of LIFO inventories.

(a) General rule.

If, for any liquidation year

(1) there is a qualified liquidation of goods which the taxpayer inventories under the LIFO method, and

(2) the taxpayer elects to have the provisions of this section apply with respect to such liquidation,

then the gross income of the taxpayer for such taxable year shall be adjusted as provided in subsection (b).

(b) Adjustment for replacements.

If the liquidated goods are replaced (in whole or in part) during any replacement year and such replacement is reflected in the closing inventory for such year, then the gross income for the liquidation year shall be

(1) decreased by an amount equal to the excess of

(A) the aggregate replacement cost of the liquidated goods so replaced during such year, over

(B) the aggregate cost of such goods reflected in the opening inventory of the liquidation year, or

(2) increased by an amount equal to the excess of

(A) the aggregate cost reflected in such opening inventory of the liquidated goods so replaced during such year, over

(B) such aggregate replacement cost.

(c) Qualified liquidation defined.

For purposes of this section—

(1) **In general.** The term "qualified liquidation" means—

(A) a decrease in the closing inventory of the liquidation year from the opening inventory of such year, but only if

(B) the taxpayer establishes to the satisfaction of the Secretary that such decrease is directly and primarily attributable to a qualified inventory interruption.

(2) **Qualified inventory interruption defined.**

(A) In general. The term "qualified inventory interruption" means a regulation, request, or interruption described in subparagraph (B) but only to the extent provided in the notice published pursuant to subparagraph (B).

(B) Determination by Secretary. Whenever the Secretary, after consultation with the appropriate Federal officers, determines

(i) that—

(I) any Department of Energy regulation or request with respect to energy supplies, or

(II) any embargo, international boycott, or other major foreign trade interruption,

has made difficult or impossible the replacement during the liquidation year of any class of goods for any class of taxpayers, and

(ii) that the application of this section to that class of goods and taxpayers is necessary to carry out the purposes of this section,

he shall publish a notice of such determinations in the Federal Register, together with the period to be affected by such notice.

(d) Other definitions and special rules.

For purposes of this section—

(1) **Liquidation year.** The term "liquidation year" means the taxable year in which occurs the qualified liquidation to which this section applies.

(2) **Replacement year.** The term "replacement year" means any taxable year in the replacement period; except that such term shall not include any taxable year after the taxable year in which replacement of the liquidated goods is completed.

(3) **Replacement period.** The term "replacement period" means the shorter of—

(A) the period of the 3 taxable years following the liquidation year, or

(B) the period specified by the Secretary in a notice published in the Federal Register with respect to that qualified inventory interruption.

Any period specified by the Secretary under subparagraph (B) may be modified by the Secretary in a subsequent notice published in the Federal Register.

(4) **LIFO method.** The term "LIFO method" means the method of inventorying goods described in section 472.

(5) **Election.**

(A) In general. An election under subsection (a) shall be made subject to such conditions, and in such manner and form and at such time, as the Secretary may prescribe by regulation.

(B) Irrevocable election. An election under this section shall be irrevocable and shall be binding for the liquidation year and for all determinations for prior and subsequent taxable years insofar as such determinations are affected by the adjustments under this section.

(e) Replacement; inventory basis.

For purposes of this chapter—

(1) **Replacements.** If the closing inventory of the taxpayer for any replacement year reflects an increase over the opening inventory of such goods for such year, the goods reflecting such increase shall be considered, in the order of their acquisition, as having been acquired in replacement of the goods most recently liquidated (whether or not in a qualified liquidation) and not previously replaced.

(2) **Amount at which replacement goods taken into account.** In the case of any qualified liquidation, any goods considered under paragraph (1) as having been acquired in replacement of the goods liquidated in such liquidation shall be taken into purchases and included in the closing inventory of the taxpayer for the replacement year at the inventory cost basis of the goods replaced.

(f) Special rules for application of adjustments.
  (1) Period of limitations. If—
    (A) an adjustment is required under this section for any taxable year by reason of the replacement of liquidated goods during any replacement year, and
    (B) the assessment of a deficiency, or the allowance of a credit or refund of an overpayment of tax attributable to such adjustment, for any taxable year, is otherwise prevented by the operation of any law or rule of law (other than section 7122, relating to compromises),
  then such deficiency may be assessed, or credit or refund allowed, within the period prescribed for assessing a deficiency or allowing a credit or refund for the replacement year if a notice for deficiency is mailed, or claim for refund is filed, within such period.
  (2) Interest. Solely for purposes of determining interest on any overpayment or underpayment attributable to an adjustment made under this section, such overpayment or underpayment shall be treated as an overpayment or underpayment (as the case may be) for the replacement year.
(g) Coordination with section 472.
  The Secretary shall prescribe such regulations as may be necessary to coordinate the provisions of this section with the provisions of section 472.

In 1980, P.L. 96-223, Sec. 403(a)(1), added Code Sec. 473, effective for qualified liquidations (within the meaning of Code Sec. 473(c) of the Internal Revenue Code of 1954) in tax. yrs. end. after 10/31/79.

Sec. 474. Simplified dollar-value LIFO method for certain small businesses.
(a) General rule.
  An eligible small business may elect to use the simplified dollar-value method of pricing inventories for purposes of the LIFO method.
(b) Simplified dollar-value method of pricing inventories.
  For purposes of this section—
  (1) In general. The simplified dollar-value method of pricing inventories is a dollar-value method of pricing inventories under which—
    (A) the taxpayer maintains a separate inventory pool for items in each major category in the applicable Government price index, and
    (B) the adjustment for each such separate pool is based on the change from the preceding taxable year in the component of such index for the major category.
  (2) Applicable government price index. The term "applicable Government price index" means—
    (A) except as provided in subparagraph (B), the Producer Price Index published by the Bureau of Labor Statistics, or
    (B) in the case of a retailer using the retail method, the Consumer Price Index published by the Bureau of Labor Statistics.
  (3) Major category. The term "major category" means—
    (A) in the case of the Producer Price Index, any of the 2-digit standard industrial classifications in the Producer Prices Data Report, or
    (B) in the case of the Consumer Price Index, any of the general expenditure categories in the Consumer Price Index Detailed Report.
(c) Eligible small business.
  For purposes of this section, a taxpayer is an eligible small business for any taxable year if the average annual gross receipts of the taxpayer for the 3 preceding taxable years do not exceed $5,000,000. For purposes of the preceding sentence, rules similar to the rules of section 448(c)(3) shall apply.
(d) Special rules.
  For purposes of this section—
  (1) Controlled groups.
    (A) In general. In the case of a taxpayer which is a member of a controlled group, all persons which are component members of such group shall be treated as 1 taxpayer for purposes of determining the gross receipts of the taxpayer.
    (B) Controlled group defined. For purposes of subparagraph (A), persons shall be treated as being component members of a controlled group if such persons would be treated as a single employer under section 52.
  (2) Election.
    (A) In general. The election under this section may be made without the consent of the Secretary.
    (B) Period to which election applies. The election under this section shall apply—
      (i) to the taxable year for which it is made, and
      (ii) to all subsequent taxable years for which the taxpayer is an eligible small business,
    unless the taxpayer secures the consent of the Secretary to the revocation of such election.
  (3) LIFO method. The term "LIFO method" means the method provided by section 472(b).
  (4) Transitional rules.
    (A) In general. In the case of a year of change under this section—
      (i) the inventory pools shall—
        (I) in the case of the 1st taxable year to which such an election applies, be established in accordance with the major categories in the applicable Government price index, or
        (II) in the case of the 1st taxable year after such election ceases to apply, be established in the manner provided by regulations under section 472;
      (ii) the aggregate dollar amount of the taxpayer's inventory as of the beginning of the year of change shall be the same as the aggregate dollar value as of the close of the taxable year preceding the year of change, and
      (iii) the year of change shall be treated as a new base year in accordance with procedures provided by regulations under section 472.
    (B) Year of change. For purposes of this paragraph, the year of change under this section is—
      (i) the 1st taxable year to which an election under this section applies, or
      (ii) in the case of a cessation of such an election, the 1st taxable year after such election ceases to apply.

In 1986, P.L. 99-514, Sec. 802(a), amended Code Sec. 474, effective for tax. yrs. begin. after 12/31/86. Sec. 802(c) of this Act provides the following:
"(2) Treatment of taxpayers who made elections under existing section 474.— The amendments made by this section shall not apply to any taxpayer who made an election under section 474 of the Internal Revenue Code of 1954 (as in effect on the day before the date of the enactment of this Act) for any period during which such election is in effect. Notwithstanding any provision of such section 474 (as so in effect), an election under such section may be revoked without the consent of the Secretary."
Prior to amendment, Code Sec. 474 read as follows:
"SEC. 474. ELECTION BY CERTAIN SMALL BUSINESSES TO USE ONE INVENTORY POOL.
"(a) In general.
"A taxpayer which is an eligible small business and which uses the dollar-value method of pricing inventories under the method provided by section 472(b) may elect to use one inventory pool for any trade or business of such taxpayer.
"(b) Eligible small business defined.
"For purposes of this section, a taxpayer is an eligible small business for any taxable year if the average annual gross receipts of the taxpayer do not exceed $2,000,000 for the 3-taxable-year period ending with the taxable year.

"(c) Special rules. For purposes of this section—
"(1) Controlled groups.
"(A) In general. In the case of a taxpayer which is a member of a controlled group, all persons which are component members of such group at any time during the calendar year shall be treated as one taxpayer for such year for purposes of determining the gross receipts of the taxpayer.
"(B) Controlled group defined. For purposes of subparagraph (A), persons shall be treated as being members of a controlled group if such persons would be treated as a single employer under the regulations prescribed under section 52(b).
"(2) Election.
"(A) In general. The election under this section may be made without the consent of the Secretary and shall be made at such time and in such manner as the Secretary may by regulations prescribe.
"(B) Period to which election applies. The election under this section shall apply—
"(i) to the taxable year for which it is made, and
"(ii) to all subsequent taxable years for which the taxpayer is an eligible small business,
unless the taxpayer secures the consent of the Secretary to the revocation of such election.
"(3) Transitional rules. In the case of a taxpayer who changes the number of inventory pools maintained by him in a taxable year by reason of an election (or cessation thereof) under this section—
"(A) the inventory pools combined or separated shall be combined or separated in the manner provided by regulations under section 472;
"(B) the aggregate dollar value of the taxpayer's inventory as of the beginning of the first taxable year—
"(i) for which an election under this section is in effect, or
"(ii) after such election ceases to apply, shall be the same as the aggregate dollar value as of the close of the taxable year preceding the taxable year described in clause (i) or (ii) (as the case may be), and
"(C) the first taxable year for which an election under this section is in effect or after such election ceases to apply (as the case may be) shall be treated as a new base year in accordance with procedures provided by regulations under section 472."

In 1981, P.L. 97-34, Sec. 237(a), added Code Sec. 474, effective for tax. yrs. begin. after 12/31/81.

Sec. 475. Mark to market accounting method for dealers in securities.

(a) General rule.
Notwithstanding any other provision of this subpart, the following rules shall apply to securities held by a dealer in securities:

(1) Any security which is inventory in the hands of the dealer shall be included in inventory at its fair market value.

(2) In the case of any security which is not inventory in the hands of the dealer and which is held at the close of any taxable year—

(A) the dealer shall recognize gain or loss as if such security were sold for its fair market value on the last business day of such taxable year, and

(B) any gain or loss shall be taken into account for such taxable year.

Proper adjustment shall be made in the amount of any gain or loss subsequently realized for gain or loss taken into account under the preceding sentence. The Secretary may provide by regulations for the application of this paragraph at times other than the times provided in this paragraph.

(b) Exceptions.

(1) In general. Subsection (a) shall not apply to—
(A) any security held for investment,
(B) (i) any security described in subsection (c)(2)(C) which is acquired (including originated) by the taxpayer in the ordinary course of a trade or business of the taxpayer and which is not held for sale, and (ii) any obligation to acquire a security described in clause (i) if such obligation is entered into in the ordinary course of such trade or business and is not held for sale, and
(C) any security which is a hedge with respect to—
(i) a security to which subsection (a) does not apply, or
(ii) a position, right to income, or a liability which is not a security in the hands of the taxpayer.

To the extent provided in regulations, subparagraph (C) shall not apply to any security held by a person in its capacity as a dealer in securities.

(2) Identification required. A security shall not be treated as described in subparagraph (A), (B), or (C) of paragraph (1), as the case may be, unless such security is clearly identified in the dealer's records as being described in such subparagraph before the close of the day on which it was acquired, originated, or entered into (or such other time as the Secretary may by regulations prescribe).

(3) Securities subsequently not exempt. If a security ceases to be described in paragraph (1) at any time after it was identified as such under paragraph (2), subsection (a) shall apply to any changes in value of the security occurring after the cessation.

(4) Special rule for property held for investment. To the extent provided in regulations, subparagraph (A) of paragraph (1) shall not apply to any security described in subparagraph (D) or (E) of subsection (c)(2) which is held by a dealer in such securities.

(c) Definitions.
For purposes of this section—

(1) Dealer in securities defined. The term "dealer in securities" means a taxpayer who—
(A) regularly purchases securities from or sells securities to customers in the ordinary course of a trade or business; or
(B) regularly offers to enter into, assume, offset, assign or otherwise terminate positions in securities with customers in the ordinary course of a trade or business.

(2) Security defined. The term "security" means any—
(A) share of stock in a corporation;
(B) partnership or beneficial ownership interest in a widely held or publicly traded partnership or trust;
(C) note, bond, debenture, or other evidence of indebtedness;
(D) interest rate, currency, or equity notional principal contract;
(E) evidence of an interest in, or a derivative financial instrument in, any security described in subparagraph (A), (B), (C), or (D), or any currency, including any option, forward contract, short position, and any similar financial instrument in such a security or currency; and
(F) position which—
(i) is not a security described in subparagraph (A), (B), (C), (D), or (E),
(ii) is a hedge with respect to such a security, and
(iii) is clearly identified in the dealer's records as being described in this subparagraph before the close of the day on which it was acquired or entered into (or such other time as the Secretary may by regulations prescribe).

Subparagraph (E) shall not include any contract to which section 1256(a) applies.

(3) Hedge. The term "hedge" means any position which manages the dealer's risk of interest rate or price changes or currency fluctuations, including any position which is reasonably expected to become a hedge within 60 days after the acquisition of the position.

(4) Special rules for certain receivables.
(A) In general. Paragraph (2)(C) shall not include any nonfinancial customer paper.

(B) **Nonfinancial customer paper.** For purposes of subparagraph (A), the term "nonfinancial customer paper" means any receivable which—

(i) is a note, bond, debenture, or other evidence of indebtedness;

(ii) arises out of the sale of nonfinancial goods or services by a person the principal activity of which is the selling or providing of nonfinancial goods or services; and

(iii) is held by such person (or a person who bears a relationship to such person described in section 267(b) or 707(b)) at all times since issue.

(d) Special rules.

For purposes of this section—

(1) Coordination with certain rules. The rules of sections 263(g), 263A, and 1256(a) shall not apply to securities to which subsection (a) applies, and section 1091 shall not apply (and section 1092 shall apply) to any loss recognized under subsection (a).

(2) Improper identification. If a taxpayer—

(A) identifies any security under subsection (b)(2) as being described in subsection (b)(1) and such security is not so described, or

(B) fails under subsection (c)(2)(F)(iii) to identify any position which is described in subsection (c)(2)(F) (without regard to clause (iii) thereof) at the time such identification is required,

the provisions of subsection (a) shall apply to such security or position, except that any loss under this section prior to the disposition of the security or position shall be recognized only to the extent of gain previously recognized under this section (and not previously taken into account under this paragraph) with respect to such security or position.

(3) Character of gain or loss.

(A) In general. Except as provided in subparagraph (B) or section 1236(b)—

(i) In general. Any gain or loss with respect to a security under subsection (a)(2) shall be treated as ordinary income or loss.

(ii) Special rule for dispositions. If—

(I) gain or loss is recognized with respect to a security before the close of the taxable year, and

(II) subsection (a)(2) would have applied if the security were held as of the close of the taxable year,

such gain or loss shall be treated as ordinary income or loss.

(B) Exception. Subparagraph (A) shall not apply to any gain or loss which is allocable to a period during which—

(i) the security is described in subsection (b)(1)(C) (without regard to subsection (b)(2)),

(ii) the security is held by a person other than in connection with its activities as a dealer in securities, or

(iii) the security is improperly identified (within the meaning of subparagraph (A) or (B) of paragraph (2)).

(e) Election of mark to market for dealers in commodities.

(1) In general. In the case of a dealer in commodities who elects the application of this subsection, this section shall apply to commodities held by such dealer in the same manner as this section applies to securities held by a dealer in securities.

(2) Commodity. For purposes of this subsection and subsection (f), the term "commodity" means—

(A) any commodity which is actively traded (within the meaning of section 1092(d)(1));

(B) any notional principal contract with respect to any commodity described in subparagraph (A);

(C) any evidence of an interest in, or a derivative instrument in, any commodity described in subparagraph (A) or (B), including any option, forward contract, futures contract, short position, and any similar instrument in such a commodity; and

(D) any position which—

(i) is not a commodity described in subparagraph (A), (B), or (C),

(ii) is a hedge with respect to such a commodity, and

(iii) is clearly identified in the taxpayer's records as being described in this subparagraph before the close of the day on which it was acquired or entered into (or such other time as the Secretary may by regulations prescribe).

(3) Election. An election under this subsection may be made without the consent of the Secretary. Such an election, once made, shall apply to the taxable year for which made and all subsequent taxable years unless revoked with the consent of the Secretary.

(f) Election of mark to market for traders in securities or commodities.

(1) Traders in securities.

(A) In general. In the case of a person who is engaged in a trade or business as a trader in securities and who elects to have this paragraph apply to such trade or business—

(i) such person shall recognize gain or loss on any security held in connection with such trade or business at the close of any taxable year as if such security were sold for its fair market value on the last business day of such taxable year, and

(ii) any gain or loss shall be taken into account for such taxable year.

Proper adjustment shall be made in the amount of any gain or loss subsequently realized for gain or loss taken into account under the preceding sentence. The Secretary may provide by regulations for the application of this subparagraph at times other than the times provided in this subparagraph.

(B) Exception. Subparagraph (A) shall not apply to any security—

(i) which is established to the satisfaction of the Secretary as having no connection to the activities of such person as a trader, and

(ii) which is clearly identified in such person's records as being described in clause (i) before the close of the day on which it was acquired, originated, or entered into (or such other time as the Secretary may by regulations prescribe).

If a security ceases to be described in clause (i) at any time after it was identified as such under clause (ii), subparagraph (A) shall apply to any changes in value of the security occurring after the cessation.

(C) Coordination with section 1259. Any security to which subparagraph (A) applies and which was acquired in the normal course of the taxpayer's activities as a trader in securities shall not be taken into account in applying section 1259 to any position to which subparagraph (A) does not apply.

(D) Other rules to apply. Rules similar to the rules of subsections (b)(4) and (d) shall apply to securities held by a person in any trade or business with respect to which an election under this paragraph is in effect. Subsection (d)(3) shall not apply under the preceding sentence for purposes of applying sections 1402 and 7704.

(2) Traders in commodities. In the case of a person who is engaged in a trade or business as a trader in commodities and who elects to have this paragraph apply to such trade or business, paragraph (1) shall apply to commodities held by such trader in connection with such trade or business in the same manner as paragraph (1) applies to securities held by a trader in securities.

(3) Election. The elections under paragraphs (1) and (2) may be made separately for each trade or business and without the consent of the Secretary. Such an election, once made, shall apply to the taxable year for which made and all subsequent taxable years unless revoked with the consent of the Secretary.

(g) Regulatory authority.

The Secretary shall prescribe such regulations as may be necessary or appropriate to carry out the purposes of this section, including rules—

(1) to prevent the use of year-end transfers, related parties, or other arrangements to avoid the provisions of this section,

(2) to provide for the application of this section to any security which is a hedge which cannot be identified with a specific security, position, right to income, or liability, and

(3) to prevent the use by taxpayers of subsection (c)(4) to avoid the application of this section to a receivable that is inventory in the hands of the taxpayer (or a person who bears a relationship to the taxpayer described in section 267(b) or 707(b)).

In **2002**, P.L. 107-147, Sec. 417(10), substituted "section" for "sections" in para. (g)(3), effective 3/9/2002.

In **2000**, P.L. 106-554, Sec. 1(a)(7), [which enacted into law Sec. 319(4) of P.L. 106-554] substituted "267(b) or" for "267(b) of" in para. (g)(3), effective 12/21/2000.

In **1999**, P.L. 106-170, Sec. 532(b)(1), substituted "manages" for "reduces" in para. (c)(3), effective for any instrument held, acquired, or entered into, any transaction entered into, and supplies held or acquired on or after 12/17/99.

In **1998**, P.L. 105-206, Sec. 6010(a)(3), added a sentence at the end of subpara. (f)(1)(D), effective for any constructive sale after 6/8/97, except as provided by Secs. 1001(d)(2)-(4), of P.L. 105-34, reproduced below.

—P.L. 105-206, Sec. 6010(a)(4), substituted "before the close of the 30th day after" for "within the 30-day period beginning on" in Sec. 1001(d)(3)(C) of P.L. 105-34 [see below].

—P.L. 105-206, Sec. 7003(a), added para. (c)(4) . . . Sec. 7003(b), deleted "and" at the end of para. (g)(1), substituted ", and" for the period at the end of para. (g)(2), and added para. (g)(3), effective for tax. yrs. end. after 7/22/98. Sec. 7003(c)(2) of this Act provides:

"(2) Change in method of accounting. In the case of any taxpayer required by the amendments made by this section to change its method of accounting for its first taxable year ending after the date of the enactment of this Act—

"(A) such change shall be treated as initiated by the taxpayer;

"(B) such change shall be treated as made with the consent of the Secretary of the Treasury; and

"(C) the net amount of the adjustments required to be taken into account by the taxpayer under section 481 of the Internal Revenue Code of 1986 shall be taken into account ratably over the 4-taxable year period beginning with such first taxable year."

In **1997**, P.L. 105-34, Sec. 1001(b), redesignated subsec. (e) as (g) and added subsecs. (e) and (f), effective for any constructive sale after 6/8/97, except as provided by Secs. 1001(d)(2)-(4) [as amended by Sec. 6010(a)(4) of 105-206, see above], which read as follows:

"(2) Exception for sales of positions, etc. held before June 9, 1997. If—

"(A) before June 9, 1997, the taxpayer entered into any transaction which is a constructive sale of any appreciated financial position, and

"(B) before the close of the 30-day period beginning on the date of the enactment of this Act [8/5/97], or before such later date as may be specified by the Secretary of the Treasury, such transaction and position are clearly identified in the taxpayer's records as offsetting,

such transaction and position shall not be taken into account in determining whether any other constructive sale after June 8, 1997, has occurred. The preceding sentence shall cease to apply as of the date such transaction is closed or the taxpayer ceases to hold such position.

"(3) Special rule. In the case of a decedent dying after June 8, 1997, if—

"(A) there was a constructive sale on or before such date of any appreciated financial position,

"(B) the transaction resulting in such constructive sale of such position remains open (with respect to the decedent or any related person)—

"(i) for not less than 2 years after the date of such transaction (whether such period is before or after June 8, 1997), and

"(ii) at any time during the 3-year period ending on the date of the decedent's death, and

"(C) such transaction is not closed before the close of the 30th day after the date of the enactment [8/5/97] of this Act,

then, for purposes of such Code, such position (and the transaction resulting in such constructive sale) shall be treated as property constituting rights to receive an item of income in respect of a decedent under section 691 of such Code. Section 1014(c) of such Code shall not apply to so much of such position's or property's value (as included in the decedent's estate for purposes of chapter 11 of such Code) as exceeds its fair market value as of the date such transaction is closed.

"(4) Election of mark to market by securities traders and traders and dealers in commodities.

"(A) In general. The amendments made by subsection (b) shall apply to taxable years ending after the date of the enactment of this Act.

"(B) 4-year spread of adjustments. In the case of a taxpayer who elects under subsection (e) or (f) of section 475 of the Internal Revenue Code of 1986 (as added by this section) to change its method of accounting for the taxable year which includes the date of the enactment of this Act—

"(i) any identification required under such subsection with respect to securities and commodities held on the date of the enactment of this Act shall be treated as timely made if made on or before the 30th day after such date of enactment, and

"(ii) the net amount of the adjustments required to be taken into account by the taxpayer under section 481 of such Code shall be taken into account ratably over the 4-taxable year period beginning with such first taxable year."

In **1993**, P.L. 103-66, Sec. 13223(a), added Code Sec. 475, effective for tax. yrs. end. on or after 12/31/93. For special rules, see Sec. 13223(c)(2) and (c)(3) of this Act, which reads as follows:

"(2) Change in method of accounting. In the case of any taxpayer required by this section to change its method of accounting for any taxable year—

"(A) such change shall be treated as initiated by the taxpayer,

"(B) such change shall be treated as made with the consent of the Secretary, and

"(C) except as provided in paragraph (3), the net amount of the adjustments required to be taken into account by the taxpayer under section 481 of the Internal Revenue Code of 1986 shall be taken into account ratably over the 5-taxable year period beginning with the first taxable year ending on or after December 31, 1993.

"(3) Special rule for floor specialists and market makers.

"(A) In general. If—

"(i) a taxpayer (or any predecessor) used the last-in first-out (LIFO) method of accounting with respect to any qualified securities for the 5-taxable year period ending with its last taxable year ending before December 31, 1993, and

"(ii) any portion of the net amount described in paragraph (2)(C) is attributable to the use of such method of accounting,

then paragraph (2)(C) shall be applied by taking such portion into account ratably over the 15-taxable year period beginning with the first taxable year ending on or after December 31, 1993.

"(B) Qualified security. For purposes of this paragraph, the term 'qualified security' means any security acquired—

"(i) by a floor specialist (as defined in section 1236(d)(2) of the Internal Revenue Code of 1986) in connection with the specialist's duties as a specialist on an exchange, but only if the security is one in which the specialist is registered with the exchange, or

"(ii) by a taxpayer who is a market maker in connection with the taxpayer's duties as a market maker, but only if—

"(I) the security is included on the National Association of Security Dealers Automated Quotation System,

"(II) the taxpayer is registered as a market maker in such security with the National Association of Security Dealers, and

"(III) as of the last day of the taxable year preceding the taxpayer's first taxable year ending on or after December 31, 1993, the taxpayer (or any predecessor) has been actively and regularly engaged as a market maker in such security for the 2-year period ending on such date (or, if shorter, the period beginning 61 days after the security was listed in such quotation system and ending on such date)."

PART III.—ADJUSTMENTS

Sec.

481. Adjustments required by changes in method of accounting.

482. Allocation of income and deductions among taxpayers.

483. Interest on certain deferred payments.

In **1964**, added item 483.

In **1960**, added Dealer Reserve Income Adjustment. See Note to Code Sec. 451.

Sec. 481. Adjustments required by changes in method of accounting.

(a) General rule.

In computing the taxpayer's taxable income for any taxable year (referred to in this section as the "year of the change")—

(1) if such computation is under a method of accounting different from the method under which the taxpayer's taxable income for the preceding taxable year was computed, then

(2) there shall be taken into account those adjustments which are determined to be necessary solely by reason of the change in order to prevent amounts from being duplicated or omitted, except there shall not be taken into account any adjustment in respect of any taxable year to which this section does not apply unless the adjustment is attributable to a change in the method of accounting initiated by the taxpayer.

(b) Limitation on tax where adjustments are substantial.

(1) **Three year allocation.** If—

(A) the method of accounting from which the change is made was used by the taxpayer in computing his taxable income for the 2 taxable years preceding the year of the change, and

(B) the increase in taxable income for the year of the change which results solely by reason of the adjustments required by subsection (a)(2) exceeds $3,000,

then the tax under this chapter attributable to such increase in taxable income shall not be greater than the aggregate increase in the taxes under this chapter (or under the corresponding provisions of prior revenue laws) which would result if one-third of such increase in taxable income were included in taxable income for the year of the change and one-third of such increase were included for each of the 2 preceding taxable years.

(2) **Allocation under new method of accounting.** If—

(A) the increase in taxable income for the year of the change which results solely by reason of the adjustments required by subsection (a)(2) exceeds $3,000, and

(B) the taxpayer establishes his taxable income (under the new method of accounting) for one or more taxable years consecutively preceding the taxable year of the change for which the taxpayer in computing taxable income used the method of accounting from which the change is made,

then the tax under this chapter attributable to such increase in taxable income shall not be greater than the net increase in the taxes under this chapter (or under the corresponding provisions of prior revenue laws) which would result if the adjustments required by subsection (a)(2) were allocated to the taxable year or years specified in subparagraph (B) to which they are properly allocable under the new method of accounting and the balance of the adjustments required by subsection (a)(2) was allocated to the taxable year of the change.

(3) **Special rules for computations under paragraphs (1) and (2).** For purposes of this subsection—

(A) There shall be taken into account the increase or decrease in tax for any taxable year preceding the year of the change to which no adjustment is allocated under paragraph (1) or (2) but which is affected by a net operating loss (as defined in section 172) or by a capital loss carryback or carryover (as defined in section 1212), determined with reference to taxable years with respect to which adjustments under paragraph (1) or (2) are allocated.

(B) The increase or decrease in the tax for any taxable year for which an assessment of any deficiency, or a credit or refund of any overpayment, is prevented by any law or rule of law, shall be determined by reference to the tax previously determined (within the meaning of section 1314(a)) for such year.

(C) In applying section 7807(b)(1), the provisions of chapter 1 (other than subchapter E, relating to self-employment income) and chapter 2 of the Internal Revenue Code of 1939 shall be treated as the corresponding provisions of the Internal Revenue Code of 1939.

(c) Adjustments under regulations.

In the case of any change described in subsection (a), the taxpayer may, in such manner and subject to such conditions as the Secretary may by regulations prescribe, take the adjustments required by subsection (a)(2) into account in computing the tax imposed by this chapter for the taxable year or years permitted under such regulations.

In 1981, P.L. 97-34, Sec. 203(c)(2), provides:

"(2) Change in method of accounting. Sections 446 and 481 of the Internal Revenue Code of 1954 shall not apply to the change in the method of depreciation [i.e., as defined in Code Sec. 168(g)(6)] to comply with the provisions of this subsection [i.e., Sec. 203(c)(1)]."

In 1980, P.L. 96-471, Sec. 2(b)(3), repealed subsec. (d), effective for dispositions made after 10/19/80 in tax yrs. end. after 10/19/80.

Prior to repeal, subsec. (d) read as follows:

"(d) *Exception for change to installment basis.*

"This section shall not apply to a change to which section 453 (relating to change to installment method) applies."

In 1976, P.L. 94-455, Sec. 1901(a)(70)(A), deleted paras. (b)(4), (5) and (6)... Sec. 1901(a)(70)(B), deleted ", other than the amount of such adjustments to which paragraph (4) or (5) applies,", after "subsection (a)(2)", each place it appeared in paras. (b)(1) and (2), effective for tax. yrs. begin. after 12/31/76.

Prior to amendment, paras. (b)(4), (5) and (6) read as follows:

"(4) *Special rule for pre-1954 adjustments generally.* Except as provided in paragraphs (5) and (6)—

"(A) *Amount of adjustments to which paragraph applies.* The net amount of the adjustments required by subsection (a), to the extent that such amount does not exceed the net amount of adjustments which would have been required if the change in method of accounting had been made in the first taxable year beginning after December 31, 1953, and ending after August 16, 1954, shall be taken into account by the taxpayer in computing taxable income in the manner provided in subparagraph (B), but only if such net amount of such adjustment would increase the taxable income of such taxpayer by more than $3,000.

"(B) *Years in which amounts are to be taken into account.* One-tenth of the net amount of the adjustments described in subparagraph (A) shall (except as provided in subparagraph (C)) be taken into account in each of the 10 taxable years beginning with the year of the change. The amount to be taken into account for each taxable year in the 10-year period shall be taken into account whether or not for such year the assessment of tax is prevented by operation of any law or rule of law. If the year of the change was a taxable year ending before January 1, 1958, and if the taxpayer so elects (at such time and in such manner as the Secretary or his delegate shall by regulations prescribe), the 10-year period shall begin with the first taxable year which begins after December 31, 1957. If the taxpayer elects under the preceding sentence to begin the 10-year period with the first taxable year which begins after December 31, 1957, the 10-year period shall be reduced by the number of years, beginning with the year of the change, in respect of which assessment of tax is prevented by operation of any law or rule of law on the date of the enactment of the Technical Amendments Act of 1958.

"(C) *Limitation on years in which adjustments can be taken into account.* The net amount of any adjustments described in subparagraph (A), to the extent not taken into account in prior taxable years under subparagraph (B)—

"(i) in the case of a taxpayer who is an individual, shall be taken into account in the taxable year in which he dies or ceases to engage in a trade or business,

"(ii) in the case of a taxpayer who is a partner, his distributive share of such net amount shall be taken into account in the taxable year in which the partnership terminates, or in which the entire interest of such partner is transferred or liquidated, or

"(iii) in the case of a taxpayer who is a corporation, shall be taken into account in the taxable year in which such corporation ceases to engage in a trade or business unless such net amount of such adjustment is required to be taken into account by the acquiring corporation under section 381(c)(21).

"(D) *Termination of application of paragraph.* The provisions of this paragraph shall not apply with respect to changes in methods of accounting made in taxable years beginning after December 31, 1963.

"(5) *Special rule for pre-1954 adjustments in case of certain decedents.* A change from the cash receipts and disbursements method to the accrual method in any case involving the use of inventories, made on or after August 16, 1954, and before January 1, 1958, for a taxable year to which this section applies, by the executor or administrator of a decedent's estate in the first return filed by such executor or administrator on behalf of the decedent, shall be given effect in determining taxable income (other than for the purpose of computing a net operating loss carryback to any prior taxable year of the decedent), and, if the net amount of any adjustments required by subsection (a) in respect of taxable years to which this section does not apply would increase the taxable income of the decedent by more than $3,000, then the tax attributable to such net adjustments shall not exceed and amount equal to the tax that would have been payable on the cash receipts and disbursements method for the years for which the executor or administrator filed returns on behalf of the decedent, computed for each such year as though a ratable portion of the taxable income for such year had been received in each of 10 taxable years beginning and ending on the same dates as the taxable year for which the tax is being computed.

"(6) Application of paragraph (4). Paragraph (4) shall not apply with respect to any taxpayer, if the taxpayer elects to take the net amount of the adjustments described in paragraph (4)(A) into account in the manner provided by paragraph (1) or (2). An election to take the net amount of such adjustments into account in the manner provided by paragraph (1) or (2) may be made only if the taxpayer consents in writing to the assessment, within such period as may be agreed on with the Secretary or his delegate, of any deficiency for the year of the change, to the extent attributable to taking the net amount of the adjustments described in paragraph (4)(A) into account in the manner provided by paragraph (1) or (2), even though at the time of filing such consent the assessment of such deficiency would otherwise be prevented by the operation of any law or rule of law. An election under this paragraph shall be made at such time and in such manner as the Secretary or his delegate shall by regulations prescribe."

—P.L. 94-455, Sec. 1906(b)(13)(A), substituted "Secretary" for "Secretary or his delegate" in subsec. (c), effective for tax. yrs. begin. after 12/31/76.

In **1969**, P.L. 91-172, Sec. 512(f)(4), substituted "loss carryback or carryover" for "loss carryover." effective for net capital losses sustained in tax. yrs. begin. after 12/31/69.

In **1960**, P.L. 86-459, authorized any person who computed taxable income under the accrual method of accounting for his most recent taxable year ending on or before June 22, 1959, and who treated dealer reserve income for such taxable year as accruable for a subsequent taxable year, to elect before Sept. 1, 1960, to have section 481 of this title apply to the treatment for income tax purposes of dealer reserve income.

In **1958**, P.L. 85-866, Sec. 29(a)(1), amended para. (a)(2) . . . Sec. 29(a)(2), added paras. (b)(4), (5) and (6) . . . Sec. 29(b)(1), added ", other than the amount of such adjustments to which paragraph (4) or (5) applies," after "subsection (a)(2)" each place it appeared in subsec. (b) . . . Sec. 29(b)(2), substituted "the aggregate increase in the taxes" for "the aggregate of the taxes" in para. (b)(1) . . . Sec. 29(b)(3), substituted "which would result if one-third of such increase in taxable income" for "which would result if one-third of such increase" in para. (b)(1) . . . Sec. 29(b)(4), added "(or under the corresponding provisions of prior revenue laws)" after "the net increase in the taxes under this chapter" in para. (b)(2) . . . Sec. 29(b)(5), substituted "paragraph (1) or (2)" for "paragraph (2)" each place it appeared in subpara. (b)(3)(A), effective for any change in method of accounting where the year of change (within the meaning of Code Sec. 481) is a tax. yr. begin. after 12/31/53, and end. after 8/16/54, except as provided in Sec. 29(d)(2) of this Act, which reads as follows:

"[d](2) Exception for certain agreements.—The amendments made . . . [to subsecs. (a)(2) and (b)(4)–(6)] . . . shall not apply if before the date of the enactment of this Act [9/2/58]—

"(A) the taxpayer applied for a change in the method of accounting in the manner provided by regulations prescribed by the Secretary of the Treasury or his delegate, and

"(B) the taxpayer and the Secretary of the Treasury or his delegate agreed to the terms and conditions for making the change."

—P.L. 85-866, Sec. 29(e), of this Act also provides:

"(e) Election To Return to Former Method of Accounting.

"(1) Election.— Any taxpayer who for any taxable year beginning after December 31, 1953, and ending after August 16, 1954, and before the date of enactment of this Act [9/2/58], computed his taxable income under a method of accounting different from the method under which his taxable income for the preceding taxable year was computed, may elect to recompute his taxable income, beginning with the taxable year for which taxable income was computed under such different method of accounting, under the method of accounting under which taxable income was computed for such preceding taxable year. An election under this paragraph shall be made within 6 months after the date of the enactment of this Act, and shall be made in such manner as the Secretary of the Treasury or his delegate may provide. This paragraph shall not apply to any taxpayer—

"(A) to whom subsection (d)(2) [the exception for certain agreements above] applies, or

"(B) who was required, before the date of the enactment of this Act, by the Secretary of the Treasury or his delegate to change his method of accounting.

"(2) Statute of limitations.— If assessment of any deficiency for any taxable year resulting from an election under paragraph (1) is prevented on the date on which such election is made, or at any time within one year after such date, by the operation of any law or rule of law, such assessment may, nevertheless, be made if made within one year after such date. An election by a taxpayer under paragraph (1) shall be considered as a consent to the assessment pursuant to this paragraph of any such deficiency. If refund or credit of any overpayment of income tax resulting from an election under paragraph (1) is prevented on the date on which such election is made, or at any time within one year after such date, by the operation of any law or rule of law, refund or credit of such overpayment may, nevertheless, be made or allowed if claim therefor is filed within one year after such date."

Prior to amendment, para. (a)(2) read as follows:

"(2) there shall be taken into account those adjustments which are determined to be necessary solely by reason of the change in order to prevent amounts from being duplicated or omitted, except there shall not be taken into account any adjustment in respect of any taxable year to which this section does not apply."

Sec. 482. Allocation of income and deductions among taxpayers.

In any case of two or more organizations, trades, or businesses (whether or not incorporated, whether or not organized in the United States, and whether or not affiliated) owned or controlled directly or indirectly by the same interests, the Secretary may distribute, apportion, or allocate gross income, deductions, credits, or allowances between or among such organizations, trades, or businesses, if he determines that such distribution, apportionment, or allocation is necessary in order to prevent evasion of taxes or clearly to reflect the income of any of such organizations, trades, or businesses. In the case of any transfer (or license) of intangible property (within the meaning of section 936(h)(3)(B)), the income with respect to such transfer or license shall be commensurate with the income attributable to the intangible.

In **2006**, P.L. 109-280, Sec. 1205(b)(2), of this Act, reads as follows:

"(2) Report to Congress. Not later than January 1, 2009, the Secretary of the Treasury shall submit to the Committee on Finance of the Senate and the Committee on Ways and Means of the House of Representatives a report on the effectiveness of the Internal Revenue Service in administering the amendments made by subsection (a) and on the extent to which payments by controlled entities (within the meaning of section 512(b)(13) of the Internal Revenue Code of 1986) to controlling organizations (within the meaning of section 512(b)(13) of such Code) meet the requirements under section 482 of such Code. Such report shall include the results of any audit of any controlling organization or controlled entity and recommendations relating to the tax treatment of payments from controlled entities to controlling organizations."

In **1988**, P.L. 100-647, Sec. 1012(n)(1), amended Sec. 1231(g)(2)(A) of P.L. 99-514, part of the effective for changes made by Sec. 1231(e)(1) of P.L. 99-514, by adding the last sentence, see below.

In **1986**, P.L. 99-514, Sec. 1231(e)(1), added the last sentence to Code Sec. 482, effective for tax. yrs. begin. after 12/31/86, except as provided in Sec. 1231(g)(2)(A) [as amended by Sec. 1012(n)(1) of P.L. 100-647, see above] which reads:

"(2) Special rule for transfer of intangibles.

"(A) In general.— The amendments made by subsection (e) shall apply to taxable years beginning after December 31, 1986, but only with respect to transfers after November 16, 1985, or licenses granted after such date (or before such date with respect to property not in existence or owned by the taxpayer on such date). In the case of any transfer (or license) which is not to a foreign person, the preceding sentence shall be applied by substituting 'August 16, 1986' for 'November 16, 1985'."

In **1984**, P.L. 98-369, Sec. 44(b)(2), provides:

"(2) Revision of section 482 regulations.—Not later than 180 days after the date of the enactment of this Act, the Secretary of the Treasury or his delegate shall modify the safe harbor interest rates applicable under the regulations prescribed under section 482 of the Internal Revenue Code of 1954 so that such rates are consistent with the rates applicable under section 483 of such Code by reason of the amendments made by section 41."

In **1976**, P.L. 94-455, Sec. 1906(b)(13)(A), substituted "Secretary" for "Secretary or his delegate" in Code Sec. 482, effective for tax. yrs. begin. after 12/31/76.

Sec. 483. Interest on certain deferred payments.
(a) Amount constituting interest.

For purposes of this title, in the case of any payment—

(1) under any contract for the sale or exchange of any property, and

(2) to which this section applies,

there shall be treated as interest that portion of the total unstated interest under such contract which, as determined in a manner consistent with the method of computing interest under section 1272(a), is properly allocable to such payment.
(b) Total unstated interest.

For purposes of this section, the term "total unstated interest" means, with respect to a contract for the sale or exchange of property, an amount equal to the excess of—

(1) the sum of the payments to which this section applies which are due under the contract, over

(2) the sum of the present values of such payments and the present values of any interest payments due under the contract.

For purposes of the preceding sentence, the present value of a payment shall be determined under the rules of section 1274(b)(2) using a discount rate equal to the applicable Federal rate determined under section 1274(d).

(c) Payments to which subsection (a) applies.

(1) In general. Except as provided in subsection (d), this section shall apply to any payment on account of the sale or exchange of property which constitutes part or all of the sales price and which is due more than 6 months after the date of such sale or exchange under a contract—

(A) under which some or all of the payments are due more than 1 year after the date of such sale or exchange, and

(B) under which there is total unstated interest.

(2) Treatment of other debt instruments. For purposes of this section, a debt instrument of the purchaser which is given in consideration for the sale or exchange of property shall not be treated as a payment, and any payment due under such debt instrument shall be treated as due under the contract for the sale or exchange.

(3) Debt instrument defined. For purposes of this subsection, the term "debt instrument" has the meaning given such term by section 1275(a)(1).

(d) Exceptions and limitations.

(1) Coordination with original issue discount rules. This section shall not apply to any debt instrument for which an issue price is determined under section 1273(b) (other than paragraph (4) thereof) or section 1274.

(2) Sales prices of $3,000 or less. This section shall not apply to any payment on account of the sale or exchange of property if it can be determined at the time of such sale or exchange that the sales price cannot exceed $3,000.

(3) Carrying charges. In the case of the purchaser, the tax treatment of amounts paid on account of the sale or exchange of property shall be made without regard to this section if any such amounts are treated under section 163(b) as if they included interest.

(4) Certain sales of patents. In the case of any transfer described in section 1235(a) (relating to sale or exchange of patents), this section shall not apply to any amount contingent on the productivity, use, or disposition of the property transferred.

(e) Maximum rate of interest on certain transfers of land between related parties.

(1) In general. In the case of any qualified sale, the discount rate used in determining the total unstated interest rate under subsection (b) shall not exceed 6 percent, compounded semiannually.

(2) Qualified sale. For purposes of this subsection, the term "qualified sale" means any sale or exchange of land by an individual to a member of such individual's family (within the meaning of section 267(c)(4)).

(3) $500,000 limitation. Paragraph (1) shall not apply to any qualified sale between individuals made during any calendar year to the extent that the sales price for such sale (when added to the aggregate sales price for prior qualified sales between such individuals during the calendar year) exceeds $500,000.

(4) Nonresident alien individuals. Paragraph (1) shall not apply to any sale or exchange if any party to such sale or exchange is a nonresident alien individual.

(f) Regulations.

The Secretary shall prescribe such regulations as may be necessary or appropriate to carry out the purposes of this section including regulations providing for the application of this section in the case of —

(1) any contract for the sale or exchange of property under which the liability for, or the amount or due date of, a payment cannot be determined at the time of the sale or exchange, or

(2) any change in the liability for, or the amount or due date of, any payment (including interest) under a contract for the sale or exchange of property.

(g) Cross references.

(1) For treatment of assumptions, see section 1274(c)(4).

(2) For special rules for certain transactions where stated principal amount does not exceed $2,800,000, see section 1274A.

(3) For special rules in case of the borrower under certain loans for personal use, see section 1275(b).

In 1986, P.L. 99-514, Sec. 1803(a)(9), provides:

"(9) Treatment of transfers of land between related parties. In the case of any sale or exchange before July 1, 1985, to which section 483(f) of the Internal Revenue Code of 1954 (as in effect on the day before the date of the enactment of P.L. 99-121) applies, such section shall be treated as providing that the discount rate to be used for purposes of section 483(c)(1) of such Code shall be 6 percent, compounded semiannually."

—P.L. 99-514, Sec. 1803(a)(14)(B), substituted "any debt instrument for which an issue price is determined under section 1273(b) (other than paragraph (4) thereof) or section 1274" for "any debt instrument to which section 1272 applies" in para (d)(1), effective for sales or exchanges after 12/31/84, but (as provided in Sec. 44(b)(1)(B) of P.L. 98-369, see below) this amendment "shall not apply to any sale or exchange pursuant to a written contract which was binding on March 1, 1984, and at all times thereafter before the sale or exchange."

—P.L. 99-514, Sec. 1803(b)(2), amended Sec. 44(b)(3)(A) of P.L. 98-369 (reproduced below) by deleting "and before January 1, 1985," after "March 1, 1984," in subclause (b)(3)(A)(i)(I), after "June 8, 1984," in subclause (b)(3)(A)(i)(II), and after "March 1, 1984," in clause (b)(3)(A)(ii) . . . Sec. 1803(b)(3), amended subpara. (b)(3)(B) of P.L. 98-369, reproduced below.

Prior to amendment, subpara. (b)(3)(B) of P.L. 98-369 read as follows:

"(B) Exception for binding contracts. Subparagraph (A) shall not apply to any sale or exchange pursuant to a written contract which was binding on March 1, 1984, and at all times thereafter before the sale or exchange."

In 1985, P.L. 99-121, Sec. 101(a)(2)(A), deleted "120 percent of" after "rate equal to" in the last sentence of subsec. (b) . . . Sec. 101(a)(2)(B), amended subpara. (c)(1)(B) . . . Sec. 102(c)(1), deleted subsec. (e) and redesignated subsecs. (f), [see Sec. 1803(a)(9) of P.L. 99-514 above for treatment of subsec. (f) before redesignation] (g) and (h) as subsecs. (e), (f), and (g) . . . Sec. 102(c)(2), substituted "6 percent" for "7 percent" in para. (e)(1) (as redesignated) . . . Sec. 102(c)(3), amended subsec. (g) (as redesignated), effective for sales and exchanges after 6/30/85, in tax. yrs. end. after 6/30/85. The amendment made by Sec. 2 of P.L. 98-612 [adding Sec. 44(b)(4)-(7) of P.L. 98-369, reproduced in note following Code Sec. 1274] shall not apply to sales and exchanges after 6/30/85, in tax. yrs. end. after 6/30/85.

Prior to amendment, subpara. (c)(1)(B) read as follows:

"(B) under which, using a discount rate equal to 110 percent of the applicable Federal rate determined under section 1274(d), there is total unstated interest."

Prior to deletion, subsec. (e) read as follows:

"(e) Interest rates in case of sales of principal residences or farm lands.

"(1) In general. In the case of any debt instrument arising from a sale or exchange to which the subsection applies, subsections (b) and (c)(1)(B) shall be applied by using, in lieu of the discount rates determined under such subsections, discount rates determined under subsections (b) and (c)(1), respectively, of this section as it was in effect before the amendments made by the Tax Reform Act of 1984.

"(2) Sales or exchanges to which subsection applies. This subsection shall apply—

"(A) to any sale or exchange by an individual of his principal residence (within the meaning of section 1034), and

"(B) to any sale or exchange by a person of land used by such person as a farm (within the meaning of section 6420(c)(2)).

"(3) Limitation. Paragraph (1) shall apply to any sale or exchange by an individual of his principal residence (within the meaning of section 1034), only to the extent the purchase price of such residence does not exceed $250,000. For purposes of the preceding sentence, the purchase price of a residence shall be determined without regard to this section."

Prior to amendment, subsec. (g) read as follows:

"(g) Cross reference. For special rules in the case of the borrower under certain loans for personal use, see section 1275(b)."

—P.L. 99-121, Sec. 104, provides:

"SEC. 104. SPECIAL RULE FOR CERTAIN WORKOUTS.

"(a) General rule. Sections 483 and 1274 of the Internal Revenue Code of 1954 shall not apply to the issuance or modification of any written indebtedness if—

"(1) such issuance or modification is in connection with a workout of a specified MLC loan which (as of May 31, 1985) was substantially in arrears, and

"(2) the aggregate principal amount of indebtedness resulting from such workout does not exceed the sum (as of the time of the workout) of the outstanding principal amount of the specified MLC loan and any arrearages on such loan.
"(b) Specified MLC loan. For purposes of subsection (a), the term specified MLC loan means any loan which, in a submission dated June 17, 1985, on behalf of the New York State Mortgage Loan Enforcement and Administration Corporation, had one of the following loan numbers: 001, 005, 007, 012, 025, 038, 041, 042, 043, 049, 053, 064, 068, 090, 141, 180, or 188."

In 1984, P.L. 98-612, Sec. 2, amended Sec. 44(b) of P.L. 98-369 by adding paras. (b)(4)–(7), reproduced in note following Code Sec. 1274.

—P.L. 98-369, Sec. 41(b), amended Code Sec. 483, effective for sales or exchanges after 12/31/84, but (as provided in Sec. 44(b)(1)(B) of the Act) this amendment "shall not apply to any sale or exchange pursuant to a written contract which was binding on March 1, 1984, and at all times thereafter before the sale or exchange."

—P.L. 98-369, Sec. 44(b)(3), [as amended by P.L. 99-514 Secs. 1803(b)(2) and (b)(3)] provides:

"(3) Clarification of interest accrual; fair market value rule in case of potentially abusive situations.

"(A) In general.

"(i) Clarification of interest accrual. In the case of any sale or exchange—

"(I) after March 1, 1984, nothing in section 483 of the Internal Revenue Code of 1954 shall permit any interest to be deductible before the period to which such interest is properly allocable, or

"(II) after June 8, 1984, notwithstanding section 483 of the Internal Revenue Code of 1954 or any other provision of law, no interest shall be deductible before the period to which such interest is properly allocable.

"(ii) Fair market rule. In the case of any sale or exchange after March 1, 1984, such section 483 shall be treated as including provisions similar to the provisions of section 1274(b)(3) of such Code (as added by section 41).

"(B) Exception for binding contracts.

"(i) Subparagraph (A)(i)(I) shall not apply to any sale or exchange pursuant to a written contract which was binding on March 1, 1984, and at all times thereafter before the sale or exchange.

"(ii) Subparagraph (A)(i)(II) shall not apply to any sale or exchange pursuant to a written contract which was binding on June 8, 1984, and at all times thereafter before the sale or exchange.

"(C) Interest accrual rule not to apply where substantially equal annual payments. Clause (i) of subparagraph (A) shall not apply to any debt instrument with substantially equal annual payments."

For special rules and exceptions see Sec. 44(b)(4)-(7) of this Act reproduced in note following Code Sec. 1274.

—P.L. 98-369, Sec. 44(j), provides:

"(j) Clarification that prior effective date rules not affected.—Nothing in the amendment made by section 41(a) shall affect the application of any effective date provision (including any transitional rule) for any provision which was a predecessor to any provision contained in part V of subchapter P of chapter 1 of the Internal Revenue Code of 1954 (as added by section 41)."

Prior to amendment, Code Sec. 483 read as follows:

"SEC. 483. INTEREST ON CERTAIN DEFERRED PAYMENTS.

"(a) Amount constituting interest.

"For purposes of this title, in the case of any contract for the sale or exchange of property there shall be treated as interest that part of a payment to which this section applies which bears the same ratio to the amount of such payment as the total unstated interest under such contract bears to the total of the payments to which this section applies which are due under such contract.

"(b) Total unstated interest.

"For purposes of this section, the term 'total unstated interest' means, with respect to a contract for the sale or exchange of property, an amount equal to the excess of—

"(1) the sum of the payments to which this section applies which are due under the contract, over

"(2) the sum of the present values of such payments and the present values of any interest payments due under the contract.

For purposes of paragraph (2), the present value of a payment shall be determined, as of the date of the sale or exchange, by discounting such payment at the rate, and in the manner, provided in regulations prescribed by the Secretary. Such regulations shall provide for discounting on the basis of 6-month brackets and shall provide that the present value of any interest payment due not more than 6 months after the date of sale or exchange is an amount equal to 100 percent of such payment.

"(c) Payments to which section applies.

"(1) In general. Except as provided in subsection (f), this section shall apply to any payment on account of the sale or exchange of property which constitutes part or all of the sales price and which is due more than 6 months after the date of such sale or exchange under a contract—

"(A) under which some or all of the payments are due more than one year after the date of such sale or exchange and

"(B) under which, using a rate provided by regulations prescribed by the Secretary for purposes of this subparagraph, there is total unstated interest.

Any rate prescribed for determining whether there is total unstated interest for purposes of subparagraph (B) shall be at least one percentage point lower than the rate prescribed for purposes of subsection (b)(2).

"(2) Treatment of evidence of indebtedness. For purposes of this section, an evidence of indebtedness of the purchaser given in consideration for the sale or exchange of property shall not be considered a payment, and any payment due under such evidence of indebtedness shall be treated as due under the contract for the sale or exchange.

"(d) Payments that are indefinite as to time, liability, or amount.

"In the case of a contract for the sale or exchange of property under which the liability for, or the amount or due date of, any portion of a payment cannot be determined at the time of the sale or exchange, this section shall be separately applied to such portion as if it (and any amount of interest attributable to such portion) were the only payments due under the contract; and such determinations of liability, amount, and due date shall be made at the time payment of such portion is made.

"(e) Change in terms of contract.

If the liability for, or the amount or due date of, any payment (including interest) under a contract for the sale or exchange of property is changed, the 'total unstated interest' under the contract shall be recomputed and allocated (with adjustment for prior interest (including unstated interest) payments) under regulations prescribed by the Secretary.

"(f) Exceptions and limitations.

"(1) Sales price of $3,000 or less. This section shall not apply to any payment on account of the sale or exchange of property if it can be determined at the time of such sale or exchange that the sales price cannot exceed $3,000.

"(2) Carrying charges. In the case of the purchaser, the tax treatment of amounts paid on account of the sale or exchange of property shall be made without regard to this section if any such amounts are treated under section 163(b) as if they included interest.

"(3) Treatment of seller. In the case of the seller, the tax treatment of any amounts received on account of the sale or exchange of property shall be made without regard to this section if all of the gain, if any, on such sale or exchange would be considered as ordinary income.

"(4) Sales or exchanges of patents. This section shall not apply to any payments made pursuant to a transfer described in section 1235(a) (relating to sale or exchange of patents).

"(5) Annuities. This section shall not apply to any amount the liability for which depends in whole or in part on the life expectancy of one or more individuals and which constitutes an amount received as an annuity to which section 72 applies.

"(g) Maximum rate of interest on certain transfers of land between related parties.

"(1) In general. In the case of any qualified sale, the maximum interest rate used in determining the total unstated interest rate under the regulations under subsection (b) shall not exceed 7 percent, compounded semiannually.

"(2) Qualified sale. For purposes of this subsection, the term 'qualified sale' means any sale or exchange of land by an individual to a member of such individual's family (within the meaning of section 267(c)(4)).

"(3) $500,000 limitation. Paragraph (1) shall not apply to any qualified sale between individuals made during any calendar year to the extent that the sales price for such sale (when added to the aggregate sales price for prior qualified sales between such individuals during the calendar year) exceeds $500,000.

"(4) Nonresident alien individuals. Paragraph (1) shall not apply to any sale or exchange if any party to such sale or exchange is a nonresident alien individual."

In 1983, P.L. 97-448, Sec. 101(g), substituted "Paragraph (1)" for "This section" in para. (g)(4), effective for payments made after 6/30/81 pursuant to sales or exchanges made after 6/30/81.

In 1981, P.L. 97-34, Sec. 126(a), added subsec. (g), effective for payments made after 6/30/81, pursuant to sales or exchanges made after 6/30/81.

In 1976, P.L. 94-455, Sec. 1901(b)(3)(B), substituted "all of the gain, if any, on such" for "no part of any gain on such", and substituted "ordinary income" for "gain from the sale or exchange of a capital asset or property described in section 1231" in para. (f)(3), effective for tax. yrs. begin. after 12/31/76.

—P.L. 94-455, Sec. 1906(b)(13)(A), substituted "Secretary" for "Secretary or his delegate" each place it appeared in Code Sec. 483, effective for tax. yrs. begin. after 12/31/76.

In 1964, P.L. 88-272, Sec. 224, added Code Sec. 483, effective for payments made after 12/31/63, on account of sales or exchanges of property after 6/30/63, other than a sale or exchange pursuant to written contract, including an irrevocable written option, entered into before 7/1/63.

Subchapter F.—Exempt Organizations

Part
I. General rule.
II. Private foundations.
III. Taxation of business income of certain exempt organizations.
IV. Farmers' cooperatives.
V. Shipowners' protection and indemnity associations.
VI. Political organizations.
VII. Certain homeowners associations.
VIII. Higher education savings entities.

In 1997, P.L. 105-34, Sec. 211(e)(1)(B), amended item for Part VIII Prior to amendment, the item for Part VIII read as follows:
"Qualified state tuition programs."

In **1976,** P.L. 94-455, Sec. 2101(d), added Part VII.
In **1975,** P.L. 93-625, Sec. 10(d), added Part VI.
In **1969,** P.L. 91-172, Sec. 101(j)(58), redesignated former parts II, III, and IV as parts III, IV, and V respectively and added new part II.

PART I.—GENERAL RULE
Sec.
501. Exemption from tax on corporations, certain trusts, etc.
502. Feeder organizations.
503. Requirements for exemption.
504. Status after organization ceases to qualify for exemption under section 501(c)(3) because of substantial lobbying or because of political activities.
505. Additional requirements for organizations described in paragraph (9), (17), or (20) of section 501(c).

In **1987,** P.L. 100-203, Sec. 10711(b)(2)(B), amended item 504.
Prior to amendment, item 504 read as follows:
"504. Status after organization ceases to qualify for exemption under section 501(c)(3) because of substantial lobbying."
In **1984,** P.L. 98-369, Sec. 513(b), added the item for Code Sec. 505.
In **1976,** P.L. 94-455, Sec. 1307(d)(3)(B), added the item for Code Sec. 504.
In **1969,** P.L. 91-172, Sec. 101(j)(61), repealed item 504 relating to denial of exemption.

Sec. 501. Exemption from tax on corporations, certain trusts, etc.
(a) Exemption from taxation.

An organization described in subsection (c) or (d) or section 401(a) shall be exempt from taxation under this subtitle unless such exemption is denied under section 502 or 503.

(b) Tax on unrelated business income and certain other activities.

An organization exempt from taxation under subsection (a) shall be subject to tax to the extent provided in parts II, III, and VI of this subchapter, but (notwithstanding parts II, III, and VI of this subchapter) shall be considered an organization exempt from income taxes for the purpose of any law which refers to organizations exempt from income taxes.

(c) List of exempt organizations.

The following organizations are referred to in subsection (a):

(1) Any corporation organized under Act of Congress which is an instrumentality of the United States but only if such corporation—
   (A) is exempt from Federal income taxes—
      (i) under such Act as amended and supplemented before July 18, 1984, or
      (ii) under this title without regard to any provision of law which is not contained in this title and which is not contained in a revenue Act, or
   (B) is described in subsection (l).

(2) Corporations organized for the exclusive purpose of holding title to property, collecting income therefrom, and turning over the entire amount thereof, less expenses, to an organization which itself is exempt under this section. Rules similar to the rules of subparagraph (G) of paragraph (25) shall apply for purposes of this paragraph.

(3) Corporations, and any community chest, fund, or foundation, organized and operated exclusively for religious, charitable, scientific, testing for public safety, literary, or educational purposes, or to foster national or international amateur sports competition (but only if no part of its activities involve the provision of athletic facilities or equipment), or for the prevention of cruelty to children or animals, no part of the net earnings of which inures to the benefit of any private shareholder or individual, no substantial part of the activities of which is carrying on propaganda, or otherwise attempting, to influence legislation (except as otherwise provided in subsection (h)), and which does not participate in, or intervene in (including the publishing or distributing of statements), any political campaign on behalf of (or in opposition to) any candidate for public office.

(4)(A) Civic leagues or organizations not organized for profit but operated exclusively for the promotion of social welfare, or local associations of employees, the membership of which is limited to the employees of a designated person or persons in a particular municipality, and the net earnings of which are devoted exclusively to charitable, educational, or recreational purposes.
(B) Subparagraph (A) shall not apply to an entity unless no part of the net earnings of such entity inures to the benefit of any private shareholder or individual.

(5) Labor, agricultural, or horticultural organizations.

(6) Business leagues, chambers of commerce, real-estate boards, boards of trade, or professional football leagues (whether or not administering a pension fund for football players), not organized for profit and no part of the net earnings of which inures to the benefit of any private shareholder or individual.

(7) Clubs organized for pleasure, recreation, and other nonprofitable purposes, substantially all of the activities of which are for such purposes and no part of the net earnings of which inures to the benefit of any private shareholder.

(8) Fraternal beneficiary societies, orders, or associations—
   (A) operating under the lodge system or for the exclusive benefit of the members of a fraternity itself operating under the lodge system, and
   (B) providing for the payment of life, sick, accident, or other benefits to the members of such society, order, or association or their dependents.

(9) Voluntary employees' beneficiary associations providing for the payment of life, sick, accident, or other benefits to the members of such association or their dependents or designated beneficiaries, if no part of the net earnings of such association inures (other than through such payments) to the benefit of any private shareholder or individual. For purposes of providing for the payment of sick and accident benefits to members of such an association and their dependents, the term "dependent" shall include any individual who is a child (as defined in section 152(f)(1)) of a member who as of the end of the caendar year has not attained age 27.

(10) Domestic fraternal societies, orders, or associations, operating under the lodge system—
   (A) the net earnings of which are devoted exclusively to religious, charitable, scientific, literary, educational, and fraternal purposes, and
   (B) which do not provide for the payment of life, sick, accident, or other benefits.

(11) Teachers' retirement fund associations of a purely local character, if—
   (A) no part of their net earnings inures (other than through payment of retirement benefits) to the benefit of any private shareholder or individual, and
   (B) the income consists solely of amounts received from public taxation, amounts received from assessments on the teaching salaries of members, and income in respect of investments.

(12)(A) Benevolent life insurance associations of a purely local character, mutual ditch or irrigation companies, mutual or cooperative telephone companies, or like or-

2,193

ganizations; but only if 85 percent or more of the income consists of amounts collected from members for the sole purpose of meeting losses and expenses.

(B) In the case of a mutual or cooperative telephone company, subparagraph (A) shall be applied without taking into account any income received or accrued—

(i) from a nonmember telephone company for the performance of communication services which involve members of the mutual or cooperative telephone company,

(ii) from qualified pole rentals,

(iii) from the sale of display listings in a directory furnished to the members of the mutual or cooperative telephone company, or

(iv) from the prepayment of a loan under section 306A, 306B, or 311 of the Rural Electrification Act of 1936 (as in effect on January 1, 1987).

(C) In the case of a mutual or cooperative electric company, subparagraph (A) shall be applied without taking into account any income received or accrued—

(i) from qualified pole rentals, or

(ii) from any provision or sale of electric energy transmission services or ancillary services if such services are provided on a nondiscriminatory open access basis under an open access transmission tariff approved or accepted by FERC or under an independent transmission provider agreement approved or accepted by FERC (other than income received or accrued directly or indirectly from a member),

(iii) from the provision or sale of electric energy distribution services or ancillary services if such services are provided on a nondiscriminatory open access basis to distribute electric energy not owned by the mutual or electric cooperative company—

(I) to end-users who are served by distribution facilities not owned by such company or any of its members (other than income received or accrued directly or indirectly from a member), or

(II) generated by a generation facility not owned or leased by such company or any of its members and which is directly connected to distribution facilities owned by such company or any of its members (other than income received or accrued directly or indirectly from a member),

(iv) from any nuclear decommissioning transaction, or

(v) from any asset exchange or conversion transaction.

(D) For purposes of this paragraph, the term "qualified pole rental" means any rental of a pole (or other structure used to support wires) if such pole (or other structure)—

(i) is used by the telephone or electric company to support one or more wires which are used by such company in providing telephone or electric services to its members, and

(ii) is used pursuant to the rental to support one or more wires (in addition to the wires described in clause (i)) for use in connection with the transmission by wire of electricity or of telephone or other communications.

For purposes of the preceding sentence, the term "rental" includes any sale of the right to use the pole (or other structure).

(E) For purposes of subparagraph (C)(ii), the term "FERC" means the Federal Energy Regulatory Commission and references to such term shall be treated as including the Public Utility Commission of Texas with respect to any ERCOT utility (as defined in section 212(k)(2)(B) of the Federal Power Act (16 U.S.C. 824k(k)(2)(B))).

(F) For purposes of subparagraph (C)(iv), the term "nuclear decommissioning transaction" means—

(i) any transfer into a trust, fund, or instrument established to pay any nuclear decommissioning costs if the transfer is in connection with the transfer of the mutual or cooperative electric company's interest in a nuclear power plant or nuclear power plant unit,

(ii) any distribution from any trust, fund, or instrument established to pay any nuclear decommissioning costs, or

(iii) any earnings from any trust, fund, or instrument established to pay any nuclear decommissioning costs.

(G) For purposes of subparagraph (C)(v), the term "asset exchange or conversion transaction" means any voluntary exchange or involuntary conversion of any property related to generating, transmitting, distributing, or selling electric energy by a mutual or cooperative electric company, the gain from which qualifies for deferred recognition under section 1031 or 1033, but only if the replacement property acquired by such company pursuant to such section constitutes property which is used, or to be used, for—

(i) generating, transmitting, distributing, or selling electric energy, or

(ii) producing, transmitting, distributing, or selling natural gas.

(H)(i) In the case of a mutual or cooperative electric company described in this paragraph or an organization described in section 1381(a)(2)(C), income received or accrued from a load loss transaction shall be treated as an amount collected from members for the sole purpose of meeting losses and expenses.

(ii) For purposes of clause (i), the term "load loss transaction" means any wholesale or retail sale of electric energy (other than to members) to the extent that the aggregate sales during the recovery period do not exceed the load loss mitigation sales limit for such period.

(iii) For purposes of clause (ii), the load loss mitigation sales limit for the recovery period is the sum of the annual load losses for each year of such period.

(iv) For purposes of clause (iii), a mutual or cooperative electric company's annual load loss for each year of the recovery period is the amount (if any) by which—

(I) the megawatt hours of electric energy sold during such year to members of such electric company are less than

(II) the megawatt hours of electric energy sold during the base year to such members.

(v) For purposes of clause (iv)(II), the term "base year" means—

(I) the calendar year preceding the start-up year, or

(II) at the election of the mutual or cooperative electric company, the second or third calendar years preceding the start-up year.

(vi) For purposes of this subparagraph, the recovery period is the 7-year period beginning with the start-up year.

(vii) For purposes of this subparagraph, the start-up year is the first year that the mutual or cooperative electric company offers nondiscriminatory open access or the calendar year which includes the date of the enactment of this subparagraph, if later, at the election of such company.

(viii) A company shall not fail to be treated as a mutual or cooperative electric company for purposes of this paragraph or as a corporation operating on a cooperative basis for purposes of section 1381(a)(2)(C) by reason of the treatment under clause (i).

(ix) For purposes of subparagraph (A), in the case of a mutual or cooperative electric company, income received, or accrued, indirectly from a member shall be treated as an amount collected from members for the sole purpose of meeting losses and expenses.

(13) Cemetery companies owned and operated exclusively for the benefit of their members or which are not operated for profit; and any corporation chartered solely for the purpose of the disposal of bodies by burial or cremation which is not permitted by its charter to engage in any business not necessarily incident to that purpose and no part of the net earnings of which inures to the benefit of any private shareholder or individual.

(14)(A) Credit unions without capital stock organized and operated for mutual purposes and without profit.

(B) Corporations or associations without capital stock organized before September 1, 1957, and operated for mutual purposes and without profit for the purpose of providing reserve funds for, and insurance of shares or deposits in—

(i) domestic building and loan associations,

(ii) cooperative banks without capital stock organized and operated for mutual purposes and without profit,

(iii) mutual savings banks not having capital stock represented by shares, or

(iv) mutual savings banks described in section 591(b)[.]

(C) Corporations or associations organized before September 1, 1957, and operated for mutual purposes and without profit for the purpose of providing reserve funds for associations or banks described in clause (i), (ii), or (iii) of subparagraph (B); but only if 85 percent or more of the income is attributable to providing such reserve funds and to investments. This subparagraph shall not apply to any corporation or association entitled to exemption under subparagraph (B).

(15)(A) Insurance companies (as defined in section 816(a)) other than life (including interinsurers and reciprocal underwriters) if—

(i)(I) the gross receipts for the taxable year do not exceed $600,000, and

(II) more than 50 percent of such gross receipts consist of premiums, or

(ii) in the case of a mutual insurance company—

(I) the gross receipts of which for the taxable year do not exceed $150,000, and

(II) more than 35 percent of such gross receipts consist of premiums.

Clause (ii) shall not apply to a company if any employee of the company, or a member of the employee's family (as defined in section 2032A(e)(2)), is an employee of another company exempt from taxation by reason of this paragraph (or would be so exempt but for this sentence).

(B) For purposes of subparagraph (A), in determining whether any company or association is described in subparagraph (A), such company or association shall be treated as receiving during the taxable year amounts described in subparagraph (A) which are received during such year by all other companies or associations which are members of the same controlled group as the insurance company or association for which the determination is being made.

(C) For purposes of subparagraph (B), the term "controlled group" has the meaning given such term by section 831(b)(2)(B)(ii), except that in applying section 831(b)(2)(B)(ii) for purposes of this subparagraph, subparagraphs (B) and (C) of section 1563(b)(2) shall be disregarded.

(16) Corporations organized by an association subject to part IV of this subchapter or members thereof, for the purpose of financing the ordinary crop operations of such members or other producers, and operated in conjunction with such association. Exemption shall not be denied any such corporation because it has capital stock, if the dividend rate of such stock is fixed at not to exceed the legal rate of interest in the State of incorporation or 8 percent per annum, whichever is greater, on the value of the consideration for which the stock was issued, and if substantially all such stock (other than nonvoting preferred stock, the owners of which are not entitled or permitted to participate, directly or indirectly, in the profits of the corporation, on dissolution or otherwise, beyond the fixed dividends) is owned by such association, or members thereof; nor shall exemption be denied any such corporation because there is accumulated and maintained by it a reserve required by State law or a reasonable reserve for any necessary purpose.

(17)(A) A trust or trusts forming part of a plan providing for the payment of supplemental unemployment compensation benefits, if—

(i) under the plan, it is impossible, at any time prior to the satisfaction of all liabilities with respect to employees under the plan, for any part of the corpus or income to be (within the taxable year or thereafter) used for, or diverted to, any purpose other than the providing of supplemental unemployment compensation benefits,

(ii) such benefits are payable to employees under a classification which is set forth in the plan and which is found by the Secretary not to be discriminatory in favor of employees who are highly compensated employees (within the meaning of section 414(q)), and

(iii) such benefits do not discriminate in favor of employees who are highly compensated employees (within the meaning of section 414(q)). A plan shall not be considered discriminatory within the meaning of this clause merely because the benefits received under the plan bear a uniform relationship to the total compensation, or the basic or regular rate of compensation, of the employees covered by the plan.

(B) In determining whether a plan meets the requirements of subparagraph (A), any benefits provided under any other plan shall not be taken into consideration, except that a plan shall not be considered discriminatory—

(i) merely because the benefits under the plan which are first determined in a nondiscriminatory manner within the meaning of subparagraph (A) are then reduced by any sick, accident, or unemployment compensation benefits received under State or Federal law (or reduced by a portion of such benefits if determined in a nondiscriminatory manner), or

(ii) merely because the plan provides only for employees who are not eligible to receive sick, accident, or unemployment compensation benefits under State or Federal law the same benefits (or a portion of such benefits if determined in a nondiscriminatory manner) which such employees would receive under such laws if such employees were eligible for such benefits, or

(iii) merely because the plan provides only for employees who are not eligible under another plan (which meets the requirements of subparagraph (A)) of supplemental unemployment compensation benefits provided wholly by the employer the same benefits (or a portion of such benefits if determined in a nondiscriminatory manner) which such employees would receive under such other plan if such employees were eligible under such other plan, but only if the employees eligible under both plans would make a classification which would be nondiscriminatory within the meaning of subparagraph (A).

(C) A plan shall be considered to meet the requirements of subparagraph (A) during the whole of any year of the plan if on one day in each quarter it satisfies such requirements.

(D) The term "supplemental unemployment compensation benefits" means only—

(i) benefits which are paid to an employee because of his involuntary separation from the employment of the employer (whether or not such separation is temporary) resulting directly from a reduction in force, the discontinuance of a plant or operation, or other similar conditions, and

(ii) sick and accident benefits subordinate to the benefits described in clause (i).

(E) Exemption shall not be denied under subsection (a) to any organization entitled to such exemption as an association described in paragraph (9) of this subsection merely because such organization provides for the payment of supplemental unemployment benefits (as defined in subparagraph (D)(i)).

(18) A trust or trusts created before June 25, 1959, forming part of a plan providing for the payment of benefits under a pension plan funded only by contributions of employees, if—

(A) under the plan, it is impossible, at any time prior to the satisfaction of all liabilities with respect to employees under the plan, for any part of the corpus or income to be (within the taxable year or thereafter) used for, or diverted to, any purpose other than the providing of benefits under the plan,

(B) such benefits are payable to employees under a classification which is set forth in the plan and which is found by the Secretary not to be discriminatory in favor of employees who are highly compensated employees (within the meaning of section 414(q)),

(C) such benefits do not discriminate in favor of employees who are highly compensated employees (within the meaning of section 414(q)). A plan shall not be considered discriminatory within the meaning of this subparagraph merely because the benefits received under the plan bear a uniform relationship to the total compensation, or the basic or regular rate of compensation, of the employees covered by the plan, and

(D) in the case of a plan under which an employee may designate certain contributions as deductible—

(i) such contributions do not exceed the amount with respect to which a deduction is allowable under section 219(b)(3),

(ii) requirements similar to the requirements of section 401(k)(3)(A)(ii) are met with respect to such elective contributions,

> • **Caution:** Code Sec. 501(c)(18)(D)(iii), following, was amended by Sec. 611(d)(3)(C), P.L. 107-16, the Economic Growth and Tax Relief Reconciliation Act of 2001 (EGTRRA). These provisions generally sunset for tax years beginning after 12/31/2012. For specific sunset provisions see Sec. 901, P.L. 107-16 (as amended) reproduced in history notes for this Code Sec.

(iii) such contributions are treated as elective deferrals for purposes of section 402(g), and

(iv) the requirements of section 401(a)(30) are met.

For purposes of subparagraph (D)(ii), rules similar to the rules of section 401(k)(8) shall apply. For purposes of section 4979, any excess contribution under clause (ii) shall be treated as an excess contribution under a cash or deferred arrangement.

(19) A post or organization of past or present members of the Armed Forces of the United States, or an auxiliary unit or society of, or a trust or foundation for, any such post or organization—

(A) organized in the United States or any of its possessions,

(B) at least 75 percent of the members of which are past or present members of the Armed Forces of the United States and substantially all of the other members of which are individuals who are cadets or are spouses, widows, widowers, ancestors, or lineal descendants of past or present members of the Armed Forces of the United States or of cadets, and

(C) no part of the net earnings of which inures to the benefit of any private shareholder or individual.

(20) an organization or trust created or organized in the United States, the exclusive function of which is to form part of a qualified group legal services plan or plans, within the meaning of section 120. An organization or trust which receives contributions because of section 120(c)(5)(C) shall not be prevented from qualifying as an organization described in this paragraph merely because it provides legal services or indemnification against the cost of legal services unassociated with a qualified group legal services plan.

(21)(A) A trust or trusts established in writing, created or organized in the United States, and contributed to by any person (except an insurance company) if—

(i) the purpose of such trust or trusts is exclusively—

(I) to satisfy, in whole or in part, the liability of such person for, or with respect to, claims for compensation for disability or death due to pneumoconiosis under Black Lung Acts,

(II) to pay premiums for insurance exclusively covering such liability,

(III) to pay administrative and other incidental expenses of such trust in connection with the operation of the trust and the processing of claims against such person under Black Lung Acts, and

(IV) to pay accident or health benefits for retired miners and their spouses and dependents (including administrative and other incidental expenses of such trust in connection therewith) or premiums for insurance exclusively covering such benefits; and

(ii) no part of the assets of the trust may be used for, or diverted to, any purpose other than—

(I) the purposes described in clause (i),

(II) investment (but only to the extent that the trustee determines that a portion of the assets is not currently needed for the purposes described in clause (i)) in qualified investments, or

(III) payment into the Black Lung Disability Trust Fund established under section 9501, or into the general fund of the United States Treasury (other than in satisfaction of any tax or other civil or criminal liability of the person who established or contributed to the trust).

(B) No deduction shall be allowed under this chapter for any payment described in subparagraph (A)(i)(IV) from such trust.

(C) Payments described in subparagraph (A)(i)(IV) may be made from such trust during a taxable year only to the extent that the aggregate amount of such payments during such taxable year does not exceed the excess (if any), as of the close of the preceding taxable year, of—

(i) the fair market value of the assets of the trust, over

(ii) 110 percent of the present value of the liability described in subparagraph (A)(i)(I) of such person.

The determinations under the preceding sentence shall be made by an independent actuary using actuarial methods and assumptions (not inconsistent with the regulations prescribed under section 192(c)(1)(A)) each of which is reasonable and which are reasonable in the aggregate.

(D) For purposes of this paragraph:

(i) The term "Black Lung Acts" means part C of title IV of the Federal Mine Safety and Health Act of 1977, and any State law providing compensation for disability or death due to that pneumoconiosis.

(ii) The term "qualified investments" means—

(I) public debt securities of the United States,

(II) obligations of a State or local government which are not in default as to principal or interest, and

(III) time or demand deposits in a bank (as defined in section 581) or an insured credit union (within the meaning of section 101(7) of the Federal Credit Union Act, 12 U.S.C. 1752(7)) located in the United States.

(iii) The term "miner" has the same meaning as such term has when used in section 402(d) of the Black Lung Benefits Act (30 U.S.C. 902(d)).

(iv) The term "incidental expenses" includes legal, accounting, actuarial, and trustee expenses.

(22) A trust created or organized in the United States and established in writing by the plan sponsors of multiemployer plans if—

(A) the purpose of such trust is exclusively—

(i) to pay any amount described in section 4223(c) or (h) of the Employee Retirement Income Security Act of 1974, and

(ii) to pay reasonable and necessary administrative expenses in connection with the establishment and operation of the trust and the processing of claims against the trust,

(B) no part of the assets of the trust may be used for, or diverted to, any purpose other than—

(i) the purposes described in subparagraph (A), or

(ii) the investment in securities, obligations, or time or demand deposits described in clause (ii) of paragraph (21)(D),

(C) such trust meets the requirements of paragraphs (2), (3), and (4) of section 4223(b), section 4223(h), or, if applicable, section 4223(c) of the Employee Retirement Income Security Act of 1974, and

(D) the trust instrument provides that, on dissolution of the trust, assets of the trust may not be paid other than to plans which have participated in the plan or, in the case of a trust established under section 4223(h) of such Act, to plans with respect to which employers have participated in the fund.

(23) Any association organized before 1880 more than 75 percent of the members of which are present or past members of the Armed Forces and a principal purpose of which is to provide insurance and other benefits to veterans or their dependents.

(24) A trust described in section 4049 of the Employee Retirement Income Security Act of 1974 (as in effect on the date of the enactment of the Single-Employer Pension Plan Amendments Act of 1986).

(25)(A) Any corporation or trust which—

(i) has no more than 35 shareholders or beneficiaries,

(ii) has only 1 class of stock or beneficial interest, and

(iii) is organized for the exclusive purposes of—

(I) acquiring real property and holding title to, and collecting income from, such property, and

(II) remitting the entire amount of income from such property (less expenses) to 1 or more organizations described in subparagraph (C) which are shareholders of such corporation or beneficiaries of such trust.

For purposes of clause (iii), the term "real property" shall not include any interest as a tenant in common (or similar interest) and shall not include any indirect interest.

(B) A corporation or trust shall be described in subparagraph (A) without regard to whether the corporation or trust is organized by 1 or more organizations described in subparagraph (C).

(C) An organization is described in this subparagraph if such organization is—

(i) a qualified pension, profit sharing, or stock bonus plan that meets the requirements of section 401(a),

(ii) a governmental plan (within the meaning of section 414(d)),

(iii) the United States, any State or political subdivision thereof, or any agency or instrumentality of any of the foregoing, or

(iv) any organization described in paragraph (3).

(D) A corporation or trust shall in no event be treated as described in subparagraph (A) unless such corporation or trust permits its shareholders or beneficiaries—

(i) to dismiss the corporation's or trust's investment adviser, following reasonable notice, upon a vote of the shareholders or beneficiaries holding a majority of interest in the corporation or trust, and

(ii) to terminate their interest in the corporation or trust by either, or both, of the following alternatives, as determined by the corporation or trust:

(I) by selling or exchanging their stock in the corporation or interest in the trust (subject to any Federal or State securities law) to any organization described in subparagraph (C) so long as the sale or exchange does not increase the number of shareholders or beneficiaries in such corporation or trust above 35, or

(II) by having their stock or interest redeemed by the corporation or trust after the shareholder or beneficiary has provided 90 days notice to such corporation or trust.

(E)(i) For purposes of this title—

(I) a corporation which is a qualified subsidiary shall not be treated as a separate corporation, and

(II) all assets, liabilities, and items of income, deduction, and credit of a qualified subsidiary shall be treated as assets, liabilities, and such items (as the case may be) of the corporation or trust described in subparagraph (A).

(ii) For purposes of this subparagraph, the term "qualified subsidiary" means any corporation if, at all times during the period such corporation was in existence, 100 percent of the stock of such corporation is held by the corporation or trust described in subparagraph (A).

(iii) For purposes of this subtitle, if any corporation which was a qualified subsidiary ceases to meet the requirements of clause (ii), such corporation shall be treated as a new corporation acquiring all of its assets (and assuming all of its liabilities) immediately before such cessation from the corporation or trust described in subparagraph (A) in exchange for its stock.

(F) For purposes of subparagraph (A), the term "real property" includes any personal property which is leased under, or in connection with, a lease of real property, but only if the rent attributable to such personal property (determined under the rules of section 856(d)(1)) for the taxable year does not exceed 15 percent of the total rent for the taxable year attributable to both the real and personal property leased under, or in connection with, such lease.

(G)(i) An organization shall not be treated as failing to be described in this paragraph merely by reason of the receipt of any otherwise disqualifying income which is incidentally derived from the holding of real property.

(ii) Clause (i) shall not apply if the amount of gross income described in such clause exceeds 10 percent of the organization's gross income for the taxable year unless the organization establishes to the satisfaction of the Secretary that the receipt of gross income described in clause (i) in excess of such limitation was inadvertent and reasonable steps are being taken to correct the circumstances giving rise to such income.

(26) Any membership organization if—

(A) such organization is established by a State exclusively to provide coverage for medical care (as defined in section 213(d)) on a not-for-profit basis to individuals described in subparagraph (B) through—

(i) insurance issued by the organization, or

(ii) a health maintenance organization under an arrangement with the organization,

(B) the only individuals receiving such coverage through the organization are individuals—

(i) who are residents of such State, and

(ii) who, by reason of the existence or history of a medical condition—

(I) are unable to acquire medical care coverage for such condition through insurance or from a health maintenance organization, or

(II) are able to acquire such coverage only at a rate which is substantially in excess of the rate for such coverage through the membership organization,

(C) the composition of the membership in such organization is specified by such State, and

(D) no part of the net earnings of the organization inures to the benefit of any private shareholder or individual.

A spouse and any qualifying child (as defined in section 24(c)) of an individual described in subparagraph (B) (without regard to this sentence) shall be treated as described in subparagraph (B).

(27)(A) Any membership organization if—

(i) such organization is established before June 1, 1996, by a State exclusively to reimburse its members for losses arising under workmen's compensation acts,

(ii) such State requires that the membership of such organization consist of—

(I) all persons who issue insurance covering workmen's compensation losses in such State, and

(II) all persons and governmental entities who self-insure against such losses, and

(iii) such organization operates as a non-profit organization by—

(I) returning surplus income to its members or workmen's compensation policyholders on a periodic basis, and

(II) reducing initial premiums in anticipation of investment income.

(B) Any organization (including a mutual insurance company) if—

(i) such organization is created by State law and is organized and operated under State law exclusively to—

(I) provide workmen's compensation insurance which is required by State law or with respect to which State law provides significant disincentives if such insurance is not purchased by an employer, and

(II) provide related coverage which is incidental to workmen's compensation insurance,

(ii) such organization must provide workmen's compensation insurance to any employer in the State (for employees in the State or temporarily assigned out-of-State) which seeks such insurance and meets other reasonable requirements relating thereto,

(iii) (I) the State makes a financial commitment with respect to such organization either by extending the full faith and credit of the State to the initial debt of such organization or by providing the initial operating capital of such organization, and (II) in the case of periods after the date of enactment of this subparagraph, the assets of such organization revert to the State upon dissolution or State law does not permit the dissolution of such organization, and

(iv) the majority of the board of directors or oversight body of such organization are appointed by the chief executive officer or other executive branch official of the State, by the State legislature, or by both.

Exempt organizations   Code Sec. 501(h)(2)(B)

(28) The National Railroad Retirement Investment Trust established under section 15(j) of the Railroad Retirement Act of 1974.

(29) **Co-op health insurance issuers.**

(A) In general. A qualified nonprofit health insurance issuer (within the meaning of section 1322 of the Patient Protection and Affordable Care Act) which has received a loan or grant under the CO-OP program under such section, but only with respect to periods for which the issuer is in compliance with the requirements of such section and any agreement with respect to the loan or grant.

(B) Conditions for exemption. Subparagraph (A) shall apply to an organization only if—

(i) the organization has given notice to the Secretary, in such manner as the Secretary may by regulations prescribe, that it is applying for recognition of its status under this paragraph,

(ii) except as provided in section 1322(c)(4) of the Patient Protection and Affordable Care Act, no part of the net earnings of which inures to the benefit of any private shareholder or individual,

(iii) no substantial part of the activities of which is carrying on propaganda, or otherwise attempting, to influence legislation, and

(iv) the organization does not participate in, or intervene in (including the publishing or distributing of statements), any political campaign on behalf of (or in opposition to) any candidate for public office.

(d) **Religious and apostolic organizations.**

The following organizations are referred to in subsection (a): Religious or apostolic associations or corporations, if such associations or corporations have a common treasury or community treasury, even if such associations or corporations engage in business for the common benefit of the members, but only if the members thereof include (at the time of filing their returns) in their gross income their entire pro rata shares, whether distributed or not, of the taxable income of the association or corporation for such year. Any amount so included in the gross income of a member shall be treated as a dividend received.

(e) **Cooperative hospital service organizations.**

For purposes of this title, an organization shall be treated as an organization organized and operated exclusively for charitable purposes, if—

(1) such organization is organized and operated solely—

(A) to perform, on a centralized basis, one or more of the following services which, if performed on its own behalf by a hospital which is an organization described in subsection (c)(3) and exempt from taxation under subsection (a), would constitute activities in exercising or performing the purpose or function constituting the basis for its exemption: data processing, purchasing (including the purchasing of insurance on a group basis), warehousing, billing and collection (including the purchase of patron accounts receivable on a recourse basis), food, clinical, industrial engineering, laboratory, printing, communications, record center, and personnel (including selection, testing, training, and education of personnel) services; and

(B) to perform such services solely for two or more hospitals each of which is—

(i) an organization described in subsection (c)(3) which is exempt from taxation under subsection (a),

(ii) a constituent part of an organization described in subsection (c)(3) which is exempt from taxation under subsection (a) and which, if organized and operated as a separate entity, would constitute an organization described in subsection (c)(3), or

(iii) owned and operated by the United States, a State, the District of Columbia, or a possession of the United States, or a political subdivision or an agency or instrumentality of any of the foregoing;

(2) such organization is organized and operated on a cooperative basis and allocates or pays, within 8 ½ months after the close of its taxable year, all net earnings to patrons on the basis of services performed for them; and

(3) if such organization has capital stock, all of such stock outstanding is owned by its patrons.

For purposes of this title, any organization which, by reason of the preceding sentence, is an organization described in subsection (c)(3) and exempt from taxation under subsection (a), shall be treated as a hospital and as an organization referred to in section 170(b)(1)(A)(iii).

(f) **Cooperative service organizations of operating educational organizations.**

For purposes of this title, if an organization is—

(1) organized and operated solely to hold, commingle, and collectively invest and reinvest (including arranging for and supervising the performance by independent contractors of investment services related thereto) in stocks and securities, the moneys contributed thereto by each of the members of such organization, and to collect income therefrom and turn over the entire amount thereof, less expenses, to such members,

(2) organized and controlled by one or more such members, and

(3) comprised solely of members that are organizations described in clause (ii) or (iv) of section 170(b)(1)(A)—

(A) which are exempt from taxation under subsection (a), or

(B) the income of which is excluded from taxation under section 115(a),

then such organization shall be treated as an organization organized and operated exclusively for charitable purposes.

(g) **Definition of agricultural.**

For purposes of subsection (c)(5), the term "agricultural" includes the art or science of cultivating land, harvesting crops or aquatic resources, or raising livestock.

(h) **Expenditures by public charities to influence legislation.**

(1) General rule. In the case of an organization to which this subsection applies, exemption from taxation under subsection (a) shall be denied because a substantial part of the activities of such organization consists of carrying on propaganda, or otherwise attempting, to influence legislation, but only if such organization normally—

(A) makes lobbying expenditures in excess of the lobbying ceiling amount for such organization for each taxable year, or

(B) makes grass roots expenditures in excess of the grass roots ceiling amount for such organization for each taxable year.

(2) Definitions. For purposes of this subsection—

(A) Lobbying expenditures. The term "lobbying expenditures" means expenditures for the purpose of influencing legislation (as defined in section 4911(d)).

(B) Lobbying ceiling amount. The lobbying ceiling amount for any organization for any taxable year is 150 percent of the lobbying nontaxable amount for such organization for such taxable year, determined under section 4911.

(C) **Grass roots expenditures.** The term "grass roots expenditures" means expenditures for the purpose of influencing legislation (as defined in section 4911(d) without regard to paragraph (1)(B) thereof).
(D) **Grass roots ceiling amount.** The grass roots ceiling amount for any organization for any taxable year is 150 percent of the grass roots nontaxable amount for such organization for such taxable year, determined under section 4911.
(3) **Organizations to which this subsection applies.** This subsection shall apply to any organization which has elected (in such manner and at such time as the Secretary may prescribe) to have the provisions of this subsection apply to such organization and which, for the taxable year which includes the date the election is made, is described in subsection (c)(3) and—
(A) is described in paragraph (4), and
(B) is not a disqualified organization under paragraph (5).
(4) **Organizations permitted to elect to have this subsection apply.** An organization is described in this paragraph if it is described in—
(A) section 170(b)(1)(A)(ii) (relating to educational institutions),
(B) section 170(b)(1)(A)(iii) (relating to hospitals and medical research organizations),
(C) section 170(b)(1)(A)(iv) (relating to organizations supporting government schools),
(D) section 170(b)(1)(A)(vi) (relating to organizations publicly supported by charitable contributions),
(E) section 509(a)(2) (relating to organizations publicly supported by admissions, sales, etc.), or
(F) section 509(a)(3) (relating to organizations supporting certain types of public charities) except that for purposes of this subparagraph, section 509(a)(3) shall be applied without regard to the last sentence of section 509(a).
(5) **Disqualified organizations.** For purposes of paragraph (3) an organization is a disqualified organization if it is—
(A) described in section 170(b)(1)(A)(i) (relating to churches),
(B) an integrated auxiliary of a church or of a convention or association of churches, or
(C) a member of an affiliated group of organizations (within the meaning of section 4911(f)(2)) if one or more members of such group is described in subparagraph (A) or (B).
(6) **Years for which election is effective.** An election by an organization under this subsection shall be effective for all taxable years of such organization which—
(A) end after the date the election is made, and
(B) begin before the date the election is revoked by such organization (under regulations prescribed by the Secretary).
(7) **No effect on certain organizations.** With respect to any organization for a taxable year for which—
(A) such organization is a disqualified organization (within the meaning of paragraph (5)), or
(B) an election under this subsection is not in effect for such organization,
nothing in this subsection or in section 4911 shall be construed to affect the interpretation of the phrase, "no substantial part of the activities of which is carrying on propaganda, or otherwise attempting, to influence legislation," under subsection (c)(3).

(8) **Affiliated organizations.** For rules regarding affiliated organizations, see section 4911(f).
(i) **Prohibition of discrimination by certain social clubs.**
Notwithstanding subsection (a), an organization which is described in subsection (c)(7) shall not be exempt from taxation under subsection (a) for any taxable year if, at any time during such taxable year, the charter, bylaws, or other governing instrument, of such organization or any written policy statement of such organization contains a provision which provides for discrimination against any person on the basis of race, color, or religion. The preceding sentence to the extent it relates to discrimination on the basis of religion shall not apply to—
(1) an auxiliary of a fraternal beneficiary society if such society—
(A) is described in subsection (c)(8) and exempt from tax under subsection (a), and
(B) limits its membership to the members of a particular religion, or
(2) a club which in good faith limits its membership to the members of a particular religion in order to further the teachings or principles of that religion, and not to exclude individuals of a particular race or color.
(j) **Special rules for certain amateur sports organizations.**
(1) **In general.** In the case of a qualified amateur sports organization—
(A) the requirement of subsection (c)(3) that no part of its activities involve the provision of athletic facilities or equipment shall not apply, and
(B) such organization shall not fail to meet the requirements of subsection (c)(3) merely because its membership is local or regional in nature.
(2) **Qualified amateur sports organization defined.** For purposes of this subsection, the term "qualified amateur sports organization" means any organization organized and operated exclusively to foster national or international amateur sports competition if such organization is also organized and operated primarily to conduct national or international competition in sports or to support and develop amateur athletes for national or international competition in sports.
(k) **Treatment of certain organizations providing child care.**
For purposes of subsection (c)(3) of this section and sections 170(c)(2), 2055(a)(2), and 2522(a)(2), the term "educational purposes" includes the providing of care of children away from their homes if—
(1) substantially all of the care provided by the organization is for purposes of enabling individuals to be gainfully employed, and
(2) the services provided by the organization are available to the general public.
(l) **Government corporations exempt under subsection (c)(1).**
For purposes of subsection (c)(1), the following organizations are described in this subsection:
(1) The Central Liquidity Facility established under title III of the Federal Credit Union Act (12 U.S.C. 1795 et seq.).
(2) The Resolution Trust Corporation established under section 21A of the Federal Home Loan Bank Act.
(3) The Resolution Funding Corporation established under section 21B of the Federal Home Loan Bank Act.
(4) The Patient-Centered Outcomes Research Institute established under section 1181(b) of the Social Security Act.

Exempt organizations   Code Sec. 501(o)

(m) **Certain organizations providing commercial-type insurance not exempt from tax.**

(1) **Denial of tax exemption where providing commercial-type insurance is substantial part of activities.** An organization described in paragraph (3) or (4) of subsection (c) shall be exempt from tax under subsection (a) only if no substantial part of its activities consists of providing commercial-type insurance.

(2) **Other organizations taxed as insurance companies on insurance business.** In the case of an organization described in paragraph (3) or (4) of subsection (c) which is exempt from tax under subsection (a) after the application of paragraph (1) of this subsection—

(A) the activity of providing commercial-type insurance shall be treated as an unrelated trade or business (as defined in section 513), and

(B) in lieu of the tax imposed by section 511 with respect to such activity, such organization shall be treated as an insurance company for purposes of applying subchapter L with respect to such activity.

(3) **Commercial-type insurance.** For purposes of this subsection, the term "commercial-type insurance" shall not include—

(A) insurance provided at substantially below cost to a class of charitable recipients,

(B) incidental health insurance provided by a health maintenance organization of a kind customarily provided by such organizations,

(C) property or casualty insurance provided (directly or through an organization described in section 414(e)(3)(B)(ii)) by a church or convention or association of churches for such church or convention or association of churches,

(D) providing retirement or welfare benefits (or both) by a church or a convention or association of churches (directly or through an organization described in section 414(e)(3)(A) or 414(e)(3)(B)(ii)) for the employees (including employees described in section 414(e)(3)(B)) of such church or convention or association of churches or the beneficiaries of such employees, and

(E) charitable gift annuities.

(4) **Insurance includes annuities.** For purposes of this subsection, the issuance of annuity contracts shall be treated as providing insurance.

(5) **Charitable gift annuity.** For purposes of paragraph (3)(E), the term "charitable gift annuity" means an annuity if—

(A) a portion of the amount paid in connection with the issuance of the annuity is allowable as a deduction under section 170 or 2055, and

(B) the annuity is described in section 514(c)(5) (determined as if any amount paid in cash in connection with such issuance were property).

(n) **Charitable risk pools.**

(1) **In general.** For purposes of this title—

(A) a qualified charitable risk pool shall be treated as an organization organized and operated exclusively for charitable purposes, and

(B) subsection (m) shall not apply to a qualified charitable risk pool.

(2) **Qualified charitable risk pool.** For purposes of this subsection, the term "qualified charitable risk pool" means any organization—

(A) which is organized and operated solely to pool insurable risks of its members (other than risks related to medical malpractice) and to provide information to its members with respect to loss control and risk management,

(B) which is comprised solely of members that are organizations described in subsection (c)(3) and exempt from tax under subsection (a), and

(C) which meets the organizational requirements of paragraph (3).

(3) **Organizational requirements.** An organization (hereinafter in this subsection referred to as the "risk pool") meets the organizational requirements of this paragraph if—

(A) such risk pool is organized as a non-profit organization under State law provisions authorizing risk pooling arrangements for charitable organizations,

(B) such risk pool is exempt from any income tax imposed by the State (or will be so exempt after such pool qualifies as an organization exempt from tax under this title),

(C) such risk pool has obtained at least $1,000,000 in startup capital from nonmember charitable organizations,

(D) such risk pool is controlled by a board of directors elected by its members, and

(E) the organizational documents of such risk pool require that—

(i) each member of such pool shall at all times be an organization described in subsection (c)(3) and exempt from tax under subsection (a),

(ii) any member which receives a final determination that it no longer qualifies as an organization described in subsection (c)(3) shall immediately notify the pool of such determination and the effective date of such determination, and

(iii) each policy of insurance issued by the risk pool shall provide that such policy will not cover the insured with respect to events occurring after the date such final determination was issued to the insured.

An organization shall not cease to qualify as a qualified charitable risk pool solely by reason of the failure of any of its members to continue to be an organization described in subsection (c)(3) if, within a reasonable period of time after such pool is notified as required under subparagraph (E)(ii), such pool takes such action as may be reasonably necessary to remove such member from such pool.

(4) **Other definitions.** For purposes of this subsection—

(A) Startup capital. The term "startup capital" means any capital contributed to, and any program-related investments (within the meaning of section 4944(c)) made in, the risk pool before such pool commences operations.

(B) Nonmember charitable organization. The term "nonmember charitable organization" means any organization which is described in subsection (c)(3) and exempt from tax under subsection (a) and which is not a member of the risk pool and does not benefit (directly or indirectly) from the insurance coverage provided by the pool to its members.

(o) **Treatment of hospitals participating in provider-sponsored organizations.**

An organization shall not fail to be treated as organized and operated exclusively for a charitable purpose for purposes of subsection (c)(3) solely because a hospital which is owned and operated by such organization participates in a provider-sponsored organization (as defined in section 1855(d) of the Social Security Act), whether or not the provider-sponsored organization is exempt from tax. For purposes of subsection (c)(3), any person with a material financial interest in such a provider-sponsored organization shall be treated as a private shareholder or individual with respect to the hospital.

(p) Suspension of tax-exempt status of terrorist organizations.

(1) **In general.** The exemption from tax under subsection (a) with respect to any organization described in paragraph (2), and the eligibility of any organization described in paragraph (2) to apply for recognition of exemption under subsection (a), shall be suspended during the period described in paragraph (3).

(2) **Terrorist organizations.** An organization is described in this paragraph if such organization is designated or otherwise individually identified—

(A) under section 212(a)(3)(B)(vi)(II) or 219 of the Immigration and Nationality Act as a terrorist organization or foreign terrorist organization,

(B) in or pursuant to an Executive order which is related to terrorism and issued under the authority of the International Emergency Economic Powers Act or section 5 of the United Nations Participation Act of 1945 for the purpose of imposing on such organization an economic or other sanction, or

(C) in or pursuant to an Executive order issued under the authority of any Federal law if—

(i) the organization is designated or otherwise individually identified in or pursuant to such Executive order as supporting or engaging in terrorist activity (as defined in section 212(a)(3)(B) of the Immigration and Nationality Act) or supporting terrorism (as defined in section 140(d)(2) of the Foreign Relations Authorization Act, Fiscal Years 1988 and 1989); and

(ii) such Executive order refers to this subsection.

(3) **Period of suspension.** With respect to any organization described in paragraph (2), the period of suspension—

(A) begins on the later of—

(i) the date of the first publication of a designation or identification described in paragraph (2) with respect to such organization, or

(ii) the date of the enactment of this subsection, and

(B) ends on the first date that all designations and identifications described in paragraph (2) with respect to such organization are rescinded pursuant to the law or Executive order under which such designation or identification was made.

(4) **Denial of deduction.** No deduction shall be allowed under any provision of this title, including sections 170, 545(b)(2), 556(b)(2), 642(c), 2055, 2106(a)(2), and 2522, with respect to any contribution to an organization described in paragraph (2) during the period described in paragraph (3).

(5) **Denial of administrative or judicial challenge of suspension or denial of deduction.** Notwithstanding section 7428 or any other provision of law, no organization or other person may challenge a suspension under paragraph (1), a designation or identification described in paragraph (2), the period of suspension described in paragraph (3), or a denial of a deduction under paragraph (4) in any administrative or judicial proceeding relating to the Federal tax liability of such organization or other person.

(6) **Erroneous designation.**

(A) In general. If—

(i) the tax exemption of any organization described in paragraph (2) is suspended under paragraph (1),

(ii) each designation and identification described in paragraph (2) which has been made with respect to such organization is determined to be erroneous pursuant to the law or Executive order under which such designation or identification was made, and

(iii) the erroneous designations and identifications result in an overpayment of income tax for any taxable year by such organization,

credit or refund (with interest) with respect to such overpayment shall be made.

(B) Waiver of limitations. If the credit or refund of any overpayment of tax described in subparagraph (A)(iii) is prevented at any time by the operation of any law or rule of law (including res judicata), such credit or refund may nevertheless be allowed or made if the claim therefor is filed before the close of the 1-year period beginning on the date of the last determination described in subparagraph (A)(ii).

(7) **Notice of suspensions.** If the tax exemption of any organization is suspended under this subsection, the Internal Revenue Service shall update the listings of tax-exempt organizations and shall publish appropriate notice to taxpayers of such suspension and of the fact that contributions to such organization are not deductible during the period of such suspension.

(q) Special rules for credit counseling organizations.

(1) **In general.** An organization with respect to which the provision of credit counseling services is a substantial purpose shall not be exempt from tax under subsection (a) unless such organization is described in paragraph (3) or (4) of subsection (c) and such organization is organized and operated in accordance with the following requirements:

(A) The organization—

(i) provides credit counseling services tailored to the specific needs and circumstances of consumers,

(ii) makes no loans to debtors (other than loans with no fees or interest) and does not negotiate the making of loans on behalf of debtors,

(iii) provides services for the purpose of improving a consumer's credit record, credit history, or credit rating only to the extent that such services are incidental to providing credit counseling services, and

(iv) does not charge any separately stated fee for services for the purpose of improving any consumer's credit record, credit history, or credit rating.

(B) The organization does not refuse to provide credit counseling services to a consumer due to the inability of the consumer to pay, the ineligibility of the consumer for debt management plan enrollment, or the unwillingness of the consumer to enroll in a debt management plan.

(C) The organization establishes and implements a fee policy which—

(i) requires that any fees charged to a consumer for services are reasonable,

(ii) allows for the waiver of fees if the consumer is unable to pay, and

(iii) except to the extent allowed by State law, prohibits charging any fee based in whole or in part on a percentage of the consumer's debt, the consumer's payments to be made pursuant to a debt management plan, or the projected or actual savings to the consumer resulting from enrolling in a debt management plan.

(D) At all times the organization has a board of directors or other governing body—

(i) which is controlled by persons who represent the broad interests of the public, such as public officials acting in their capacities as such, persons having special knowledge or expertise in credit or financial education, and community leaders,

(ii) not more than 20 percent of the voting power of which is vested in persons who are employed by the organization or who will benefit financially, directly or indirectly, from the organization's activities (other than through the receipt of reasonable directors' fees or the repayment of consumer debt to creditors other than the credit counseling organization or its affiliates), and

(iii) not more than 49 percent of the voting power of which is vested in persons who are employed by the organization or who will benefit financially, directly or indirectly, from the organization's activities (other than through the receipt of reasonable directors' fees).

(E) The organization does not own more than 35 percent of—

(i) the total combined voting power of any corporation (other than a corporation which is an organization described in subsection (c)(3) and exempt from tax under subsection (a)) which is in the trade or business of lending money, repairing credit, or providing debt management plan services, payment processing, or similar services,

(ii) the profits interest of any partnership (other than a partnership which is an organization described in subsection (c)(3) and exempt from tax under subsection (a)) which is in the trade or business of lending money, repairing credit, or providing debt management plan services, payment processing, or similar services, and

(iii) the beneficial interest of any trust or estate (other than a trust which is an organization described in subsection (c)(3) and exempt from tax under subsection (a)) which is in the trade or business of lending money, repairing credit, or providing debt management plan services, payment processing, or similar services.

(F) The organization receives no amount for providing referrals to others for debt management plan services, and pays no amount to others for obtaining referrals of consumers.

(2) Additional requirements for organizations described in subsection (c)(3).

(A) In general. In addition to the requirements under paragraph (1), an organization with respect to which the provision of credit counseling services is a substantial purpose and which is described in paragraph (3) of subsection (c) shall not be exempt from tax under subsection (a) unless such organization is organized and operated in accordance with the following requirements:

(i) The organization does not solicit contributions from consumers during the initial counseling process or while the consumer is receiving services from the organization.

(ii) The aggregate revenues of the organization which are from payments of creditors of consumers of the organization and which are attributable to debt management plan services do not exceed the applicable percentage of the total revenues of the organization.

(B) Applicable percentage.

(i) In general. For purposes of subparagraph (A)(ii), the applicable percentage is 50 percent.

(ii) Transition rule. Notwithstanding clause (i), in the case of an organization with respect to which the provision of credit counseling services is a substantial purpose and which is described in paragraph (3) of subsection (c) and exempt from tax under subsection (a) on the date of the enactment of this subsection, the applicable percentage is—

(I) 80 percent for the first taxable year of such organization beginning after the date which is 1 year after the date of the enactment of this subsection, and

(II) 70 percent for the second such taxable year beginning after such date, and

(III) 60 percent for the third such taxable year beginning after such date.

(3) Additional requirement for organizations described in subsection (c)(4). In addition to the requirements under paragraph (1), an organization with respect to which the provision of credit counseling services is a substantial purpose and which is described in paragraph (4) of subsection (c) shall not be exempt from tax under subsection (a) unless such organization notifies the Secretary, in such manner as the Secretary may by regulations prescribe, that it is applying for recognition as a credit counseling organization.

(4) Credit counseling services; debt management plan services. For purposes of this subsection—

(A) Credit counseling services. The term "credit counseling services" means—

(i) the providing of educational information to the general public on budgeting, personal finance, financial literacy, saving and spending practices, and the sound use of consumer credit,

(ii) the assisting of individuals and families with financial problems by providing them with counseling, or

(iii) a combination of the activities described in clauses (i) and (ii).

(B) Debt management plan services. The term "debt management plan services" means services related to the repayment, consolidation, or restructuring of a consumer's debt, and includes the negotiation with creditors of lower interest rates, the waiver or reduction of fees, and the marketing and processing of debt management plans.

(r) Additional requirements for certain hospitals.

(1) In general. A hospital organization to which this subsection applies shall not be treated as described in subsection (c)(3) unless the organization—

(A) meets the community health needs assessment requirements described in paragraph (3),

(B) meets the financial assistance policy requirements described in paragraph (4),

(C) meets the requirements on charges described in paragraph (5), and

(D) meets the billing and collection requirement described in paragraph (6).

(2) Hospital organizations to which subsection applies.

(A) In general. This subsection shall apply to—

(i) an organization which operates a facility which is required by a State to be licensed, registered, or similarly recognized as a hospital, and

(ii) any other organization which the Secretary determines has the provision of hospital care as its principal function or purpose constituting the basis for its exemption under subsection (c)(3) (determined without regard to this subsection).

(B) Organizations with more than 1 hospital facility. If a hospital organization operates more than 1 hospital facility—

(i) the organization shall meet the requirements of this subsection separately with respect to each such facility, and

(ii) the organization shall not be treated as described in subsection (c)(3) with respect to any such facility for which such requirements are not separately met.

> • *Caution:* The requirements of Sec. 501(r)(3), following, is effective for tax. yrs. begin. after 3/23/2012.

(3) Community health needs assessments.

(A) In general. An organization meets the requirements of this paragraph with respect to any taxable year only if the organization—

(i) has conducted a community health needs assessment which meets the requirements of subparagraph (B) in such taxable year or in either of the 2 taxable years immediately preceding such taxable year, and

(ii) has adopted an implementation strategy to meet the community health needs identified through such assessment.

(B) Community health needs assessment. A community health needs assessment meets the requirements of this paragraph if such community health needs assessment—

(i) takes into account input from persons who represent the broad interests of the community served by the hospital facility, including those with special knowledge of or expertise in public health, and

(ii) is made widely available to the public.

(4) Financial assistance policy. An organization meets the requirements of this paragraph if the organization establishes the following policies:

(A) Financial assistance policy. A written financial assistance policy which includes—

(i) eligibility criteria for financial assistance, and whether such assistance includes free or discounted care,

(ii) the basis for calculating amounts charged to patients,

(iii) the method for applying for financial assistance,

(iv) in the case of an organization which does not have a separate billing and collections policy, the actions the organization may take in the event of nonpayment, including collections action and reporting to credit agencies, and

(v) measures to widely publicize the policy within the community to be served by the organization.

(B) Policy relating to emergency medical care. A written policy requiring the organization to provide, without discrimination, care for emergency medical conditions (within the meaning of section 1867 of the Social Security Act (42 U.S.C. 1395dd)) to individuals regardless of their eligibility under the financial assistance policy described in subparagraph (A).

(5) Limitation on charges. An organization meets the requirements of this paragraph if the organization—

(A) limits amounts charged for emergency or other medically necessary care provided to individuals eligible for assistance under the financial assistance policy described in paragraph (4)(A) to not more than the amounts generally billed to individuals who have insurance covering such care, and

(B) prohibits the use of gross charges.

(6) Billing and collection requirements. An organization meets the requirement of this paragraph only if the organization does not engage in extraordinary collection actions before the organization has made reasonable efforts to determine whether the individual is eligible for assistance under the financial assistance policy described in paragraph (4)(A).

(7) Regulatory authority. The Secretary shall issue such regulations and guidance as may be necessary to carry out the provisions of this subsection, including guidance relating to what constitutes reasonable efforts to determine the eligibility of a patient under a financial assistance policy for purposes of paragraph (6).

(s) Cross reference.

For nonexemption of Communist-controlled organizations, see section 11(b) of the Internal Security Act of 1950 (64 Stat 997; 50 U.S.C. 790(b)).

In 2010, P.L. 111-312, Sec. 101(a)(1), substituted "December 31, 2012" for "December 31, 2010" both places it appeared in Sec. 901 of P.L. 107-16 [see below], effective as if included in the enactment of P.L. 107-16, EGTRRA, 6/7/2001.

—P.L. 111-152, Sec. 1004(d)(4), added "For purposes of providing for the payment of sick and accident benefits to members of such an association and their dependents, the term 'dependent' shall include any individual who is a child (as defined in section 152(f)(1) of a member who as of the end of the calendar year has not attained age 27." at the end of para. (c)(9), effective 3/30/2010.

—P.L. 111-148, Sec. 1322(h)(1), added para. (c)(29), effective 3/23/2010.

—P.L. 111-148, Sec. 6301(f), added para. (l)(4), effective 3/23/2010.

—P.L. 111-148, Sec. 9007(a), redesignated subsec. (r) as subsec. (s) and added subsec. (r), effective for tax. yrs. begin. after 3/23/2010, except as provided in Sec 9007(f)(2) of this Act, which reads as follows:

"(2) Community health needs assessment. The requirements of section 501(r)(3) of the Internal Revenue Code of 1986, as added by subsection (a) [Sec. 9007(a) of this Act, see above], shall apply to taxable years beginning after the date which is 2 years after the date of the enactment of this Act [3/23/2012]."

—P.L. 111-148, Sec. 9007(c), of this Act, reads as follows:

"(c) Mandatory review of tax exemption for hospitals. The Secretary of the Treasury or the Secretary's delegate shall review at least once every 3 years the community benefit activities of each hospital organization to which section 501(r) of the Internal Revenue Code of 1986 (as added by this section) applies."

—P.L. 111-148, Sec. 10903(a), substituted "the amounts generally billed" for "the lowest amounts charged" in subpara. (r)(5)(A) [as added by Sec. 9007 of this Act, see above], effective for tax. yrs. begin. after 3/23/2010.

In 2007, P.L. 110-141, Sec. 1, of this Act, reads as follows:

"Sec. 1. Exclusion from income for payments from the Hokie Spirit Memorial Fund. For purposes of the Internal Revenue Code of 1986, gross income shall not include any amount received from the Virginia Polytechnic Institute & State University, out of amounts transferred from the Hokie Spirit Memorial Fund established by the Virginia Tech Foundation, an organization organized and operated as described in section 501(c)(3) of the Internal Revenue Code of 1986, if such amount is paid on account of the tragic event on April 16, 2007, at such university."

In 2006, P.L. 109-280, Sec. 811, of this Act [relating to Sec. 901 of P.L. 107-16, see below], provides:

"SEC. 811. PENSIONS AND INDIVIDUAL RETIREMENT ARRANGEMENT PROVISIONS OF ECONOMIC GROWTH AND TAX RELIEF RECONCILIATION ACT OF 2001 MADE PERMANENT.

"Title IX of the Economic Growth and Tax Relief Reconciliation Act of 2001 shall not apply to the provisions of, and amendments made by, subtitles A through F of title VI of such Act (relating to pension and individual retirement arrangement provisions)."

—P.L. 109-280, Sec. 862(a), amended as much of subpara. (c)(21)(C) as precedes the last sentence, effective for tax. yrs. begin. after 12/31/2006.

Prior to amendment, as much of subpara. (c)(21)(C), as preceded the last sentence, read as follows: "(C) Payments described in subparagraph (A)(i)(IV) may be made from such trust during a taxable year only to the extent that the aggregate amount of such payments during such taxable year does not exceed the lesser of—

"(i) the excess (if any) (as of the close of the preceding taxable year) of—

"(I) the fair market value of the assets of the trust, over

"(II) 110 percent of the present value of the liability described in of such person, or

"(ii) the excess (if any) of—

"(I) the sum of a similar excess determined as of the close of the last taxable year ending before the date of the enactment of this subparagraph plus earnings thereon as of the close of the taxable year preceding the taxable year involved, over

"(II) the aggregate payments described in subparagraph (A)(i)(IV) made from the trust during all taxable years beginning after the date of the enactment of this subparagraph.

—P.L. 109-280, Sec. 1220(a), redesignated subsec. (q) as subsec. (r) and added a new subsec. (q), effective for tax. yrs. begin. after 8/17/2006, except as provided in Sec. 1220(c)(2) of this Act, which reads as follows:

"(2) Transition rule for existing organizations. In the case of any organization described in paragraph (3) or (4) section 501(c) of the Internal Revenue Code of 1986 and with respect to which the provision of credit counseling services is a substantial purpose on the date of the enactment of this Act, the amendments made by this section shall apply to taxable years beginning after the date which is 1 year after the date of the enactment of this Act."

—P.L. 109-280, Sec. 1226, of this Act provides:

"Sec. 1226. Study on donor advised funds and supporting organizations.

"(a) Study. The Secretary of the Treasury shall undertake a study on the organization and operation of donor advised funds (as defined in section 4966(d)(2) of the Internal Revenue Code of 1986, as added by this Act) and of organizations described in section 509(a)(3) of such Code. The study shall specifically consider—

"(1) whether the deductions allowed for the income, gift, or estate taxes for charitable contributions to sponsoring organizations (as defined in section 4966(d)(1) of such Code, as added by this Act) if donor advised funds or to organizations described in section 509(a)(3) of such Code are appropriate in consideration of—

"(A) the use of contributed assets (including the type, extent, and timing of such use), or

"(B) the use of the assets of such organizations for the benefit of the person making the charitable contribution (or a person related to such person),

"(2) whether donor advised funds should be required to distribute for charitable purposes a specified amount (whether based on the income or assets of the fund) in order to ensure that the sponsoring organization with respect to such donor advised fund is operating consistent with the purposes or functions constituting the basis for its exemption under section 501, or its status as an organization described in section 509(a), of such Code,

"(3) whether the retention by donors to organizations described in paragraph (1) of rights or privileges with respect to amounts transferred to such organizations (including advisory rights or privileges with respect to the making of grants or the investment of assets) is consistent with the treatment of such transfers as completed gifts that qualify for a deduction for income, gift, or estate taxes, and

"(4) whether the issues raised by paragraphs (1), (2), and (3) are also issues with respect to other forms of charities or charitable donations.

"(b) Report. Not later than 1 year after the date of the enactment of this Act, the Secretary of the Treasury shall submit to the Committee on Finance of the Senate and the Committee on Ways and Means of the House of Representatives a report on the study conducted under subsection (a) and make such recommendations as the Secretary of the Treasury considers appropriate."

Prior to amendment, subpara. (c)(21)(C) read as follows:

"(C) Payments described in subparagraph (A)(i)(IV) may be made from such trust during a taxable year only to the extent that the aggregate amount of such payments during such taxable year does not exceed the lesser of—

"(i) the excess (if any) (as of the close of the preceding taxable year) of—

"(I) the fair market value of the assets of the trust, over

"(II) 110 percent of the present value of the liability described in of such person, or

"(ii) the excess (if any) of—

"(I) the sum of a similar excess determined as of the close of the last taxable year ending before the date of the enactment of this subparagraph plus earnings thereon as of the close of the taxable year preceding the taxable year involved, over

"(II) the aggregate payments described in subparagraph (A)(i)(IV) made from the trust during all taxable years beginning after the date of the enactment of this subparagraph.

"The determinations under the preceding sentence shall be made by an independent actuary using actuarial methods and assumptions (not inconsistent with the regulations prescribed under section 192(c)(1)(A)) each of which is reasonable and which are reasonable in the aggregate."

In **2005**, P.L. 109-135, Sec. 412(bb)(1), substituted "subparagraph (C)(iv)" for "subparagraph (C)(iii)" in subpara. (c)(12)(F) . . . Sec. 412(bb)(2), substituted "subparagraph (C)(v)" for "subparagraph (C)(iv)" in subpara. (c)(12)(G) . . . Sec. 412(cc), substituted "clause (ii) of paragraph (21)(D)" for "clause (ii) of paragraph (21)(B)" in clause (c)(22)(B)(ii), effective 12/21/2005.

—P.L. 109-58, Sec. 1304(a), deleted "Clauses (ii) through (v) shall not apply to taxable years beginning after December 31, 2006." at the end of subpara. (c)(12)(C) . . . Sec. 1304(b), deleted clause (c)(12)(H)(x), effective 8/8/2005.

Prior to deletion, clause (c)(12)(H)(x) read as follows:

"(x) This subparagraph shall not apply to taxable years beginning after December 31, 2006."

In **2004**, P.L. 108-357, Sec. 319(a)(1), deleted clause (c)(12)(C)(ii) and added clauses (c)(12)(C)(ii)-(v) . . . Sec. 319(a)(2), added subparas. (c)(12)(E)-(G) . . . Sec. 319(b), added subpara. (c)(12)(H), effective for tax. yrs. begin. after 10/22/2004.

Prior to deletion, clause (c)(12)(C)(ii) read as follows:

"(ii) from the prepayment of a loan under section 306A, 306B, or 311 of the Rural Electrification Act of 1936 (as in effect on January 1, 1987)."

—P.L. 108-218, Sec. 206(a), amended subpara. (c)(15)(A) . . . Sec. 206(b), added ", except that in applying section 831(b)(2)(B)(ii) for purposes of this subparagraph, subparagraphs (B) and (C) of section 1563(b)(2) shall be disregarded"

before the period at the end of subpara. (c)(15)(C), effective for tax. yrs. begin. after 12/31/2003. Sec. 206(e)(2) of this Act, provides:

"(2) Transition rule for companies in receivership or liquidation. In the case of a company or association which—

"(A) for the taxable year which includes April 1, 2004, meets the requirements of section 501(c)(15)(A) of the Internal Revenue Code of 1986, as in effect for the last taxable year beginning before January 1, 2004, and

"(B) on April 1, 2004, is in a receivership, liquidation, or similar proceeding under the supervision of a State court,

"the amendments made by this section shall apply to taxable years beginning after the earlier of the date such proceeding ends or December 31, 2007."

Prior to amendment, subpara. (c)(15)(A) read as follows:

"(A) Insurance companies or associations other than life (including interinsurers and reciprocal underwriters) if the net written premiums (or, if greater, direct written premiums) for the taxable year do not exceed $350,000."

In **2003**, P.L. 108-121, Sec. 105(a), substituted ", widowers, ancestors, or lineal descendants" for "or widowers" in subpara. (c)(19)(B), effective for tax. yrs. begin. after 11/11/2003.

—P.L. 108-121, Sec. 108(a), redesignated subsec. (p) as subsec. (q) and added new subsec. (p), effective for designations made before, on, or after 11/11/2003.

In **2002**, P.L. 107-358, Sec. 2, added subsec. (c) in Sec. 901 of P.L. 107-16 [see below], effective 12/17/2002.

—P.L. 107-134, Sec. 104, of this Act, reads as follows:

"Sec. 104. Payments by charitable organizations treated as exempt payments.

"(a) In general. For purposes of the Internal Revenue Code of 1986—

"(1) payments made by an organization described in section 501(c)(3) of such Code by reason of the death, injury, wounding, or illness of an individual incurred as the result of the terrorist attacks against the United States on September 11, 2001, or an attack involving anthrax occurring on or after September 11, 2001, and before January 1, 2002, shall be treated as related to the purpose or function constituting the basis for such organization's exemption under section 501 of such Code if such payments are made in good faith using a reasonable and objective formula which is consistently applied, and

"(2) in the case of a private foundation (as defined in section 509 of such Code), any payment described in paragraph (1) shall not be treated as made to a disqualified person for purposes of section 4941 of such Code.

"(b) Effective date. This section shall apply to payments made on or after September 11, 2001."

In **2001**, P.L. 107-90, Sec. 202, added para. (c)(28), effective 12/21/2001.

—P.L. 107-16, Sec. 611(d)(3)(C), deleted "(other than paragraph (4) thereof)" after "section 402(g)" in clause (c)(18)(D)(iii), effective for yrs. begin. after 12/31/2001.

—P.L. 107-16, Sec. 901, of this Act [as amended by Sec. 2 of P.L. 107-358, and Sec. 101(a)(1) of P.L. 111-312, and as related to Sec. 811 of P.L. 109-280, see above], reads as follows:

"Sec. 901. Sunset of provisions of Act.

"(a) In general. All provisions of, and amendments made by, this Act shall not apply—

"(1) to taxable, plan, or limitation years beginning after December 31, 2012, or

"(2) in the case of title V, to estates of decedents dying, gifts made, or generation skipping transfers, after December 31, 2012.

"(b) Application of certain laws. The Internal Revenue Code of 1986 and the Employee Retirement Income Security Act of 1974 shall be applied and administered to years, estates, gifts, and transfers described in subsection (a) as if the provisions and amendments described in subsection (a) had never been enacted.

"(c) Exception. Subsection (a) shall not apply to section 803 (relating to no federal income tax on restitution received by victims of the Nazi regime or their heirs or estates)."

In **1998**, P.L. 105-206, Sec. 6023(6), substituted "subparagraph (E)(ii)" for "subparagraph (C)(ii)" in para. (n)(3) . . . Sec. 6023(7), substituted "secton 1855(d)" for "section 1853(e)" in subsec. (o), effective 7/22/98.

In **1997**, P.L. 105-33, Sec. 4041(a), redesignated subsec. (o) as subsec. (p) and added new subsec. (o), effective 8/5/97.

—P.L. 105-34, Sec. 101(c), added the sentence at the end of para. (c)(26), effective for tax. yrs. begin. after 12/31/97.

—P.L. 105-34, Sec. 963(a), added new subpara. (c)(27)(B) . . . Sec. 963(b), added "(A)" at the beginning of para. (c)(27), redesignated subparas. (c)(27)(A)-(C) as subparas. (c)(27)(A)(i)-(iii), redesignated clauses (c)(27)(B)(i) and (ii) as subclauses (c)(27)(A)(ii)(I) and (II), and redesignated clauses (c)(27)(C)(i) and (ii) as subclauses (c)(27)(A)(iii)(I) and (II), effective for tax. yrs. begin. after 12/31/97.

—P.L. 105-34, Sec. 974(a), added "(including the purchase of patron accounts receivable on a recourse basis)" after "billing and collection" in subpara. (e)(1)(A), effective for tax. yrs. begin. after 12/31/96.

In **1996**, P.L. 104-191, Sec. 1114(a), redesignated subsec. (n) as subsec. (o) and added a new subsec. (n), effective for tax. yrs. begin. after 8/21/96.

—P.L. 104-191, Sec. 341(a), added para. (c)(26), effective for tax. yrs. begin. after 12/31/96.

—P.L. 104-191, Sec. 342(a), added para. (c)(27), effective for tax. yrs. end. after 8/21/96.

—P.L. 104-188, Sec. 1704(j)(5), substituted "section 101(7)" for "section 101(6)" and substituted "1752(7)" for "1752(6)" in subclause (c)(21)(D)(ii)(III), effective 8/20/96.

—P.L. 104-168, Sec. 1311(b)(1), amended para. (c)(4) by redesignating para. (c)(4) as subpara. (c)(4)(A) and by adding subpara. (c)(4)(B), effective for inurement occurring on or after 9/14/95. Sec. 1311(d)(3)(B) of this Act provides:

"Binding contracts. The amendment made by subsection (b) shall not apply to any inurement occurring before January 1, 1997, pursuant to a written contract which was binding on September 13, 1995, and at all times thereafter before such inurement occurred.

—P.L. 104-168, Sec. 1311(b)(2), of this Act, reads as follows:

"(2) Special rule for certain cooperatives. In the case of an organization operating on a cooperative basis which, before the date of the enactment of this Act, was determined by the Secretary of the Treasury or his delegate, to be described in section 501(c)(4) of the Internal Revenue Code of 1986 and exempt from tax under section 501(a) of such Code,

the allocation or return of net margins or capital to the members of such organization in accordance with its incorporating statute and bylaws shall not be treated for purposes of such Code the inurement of the net earnings of such organization to the benefit of any private shareholder or individual. The preceding sentence shall apply only if such statute and bylaws are substantially as such statute and bylaws were in existence on the date of the enactment of this Act."

In **1993**, P.L. 103-66, Sec. 13146(a), added subpara. (c)(25)(G) . . . Sec. 13146(b), added "Rules similar to the rules of subparagraph (G) of paragraph (25) shall apply for purposes of this paragraph." to the end of para. (c)(2), effective for tax. yrs. begin. on or after 1/1/94.

In **1992**, P.L. 102-486, Sec. 1940(a), amended para. (c)(21), effective for tax. yrs. begin. after 12/31/91.

Prior to amendment, para. (c)(21) read as follows:

"(21) A trust or trusts established in writing, created or organized in the United States, and contributed to by any person (except an insurance company) if—

"(A) the purpose of such trust or trusts is exclusively—

"(i) to satisfy, in whole or in part, the liability of such person for, or with respect to, claims for compensation for disability or death due to pneumoconiosis under Black Lung Acts;

"(ii) to pay premiums for insurance exclusively covering such liability; and

"(iii) to pay administrative and other incidental expenses of such trust (including legal, accounting, actuarial, and trustee expenses) in connection with the operation of the trust and the processing of claims against such person under Black Lung Acts; and

"(B) no part of the assets of the trust may be used for, or diverted to, any purpose other than—

"(i) the purposes described in subparagraph (A), or

"(ii) investment (but only to the extent that the trustee determines that a portion of the assets is not currently needed for the purposes described in subparagraph (A)) in—

"(I) public debt securities of the United States,

"(II) obligations of a State or local government which are not in default as to principal or interest, or

"(III) time or demand deposits in a bank (as defined in section 581) or an insured credit union (within the meaning of section 101(6) of the Federal Credit Union Act, 12 U.S.C. 1752(6) located in the United States, or

"(iii) payment into the Black Lung Disability Trust Fund established under section 9501, or into the general fund of the United States Treasury (other than in satisfaction of any tax or other civil or criminal liability of the person who established or contributed to the trust).

For purposes of this paragraph the term 'Black Lung Acts' means part C of title IV of the Federal Mine Safety and Health Act of 1977, and any State law providing compensation for disability or death due to pneumoconiosis."

In **1989**, P.L. 101-73, Sec. 1402(a), amended subsec. (l), effective 8/9/89.

Prior to amendment, subsec. (l) read as follows:

"(l) Government corporations exempt under subsection (c)(1).

"The organization described in this subsection is the Central Liquidity Facility established under title III of the Federal Credit Union Act (12 U.S.C. 1795 et seq.)."

In **1988**, P.L. 100-647, Sec. 1010(b)(4)(A), deleted "and" at the end of subpara. (m)(3)(C), substituted ", and" for the period at the end of subpara. (m)(3)(D), and added subpara. (m)(3)(E) . . . Sec. 1010(b)(4)(B), added para. (m)(5), effective for tax. yrs. begin. after 12/31/86.

—P.L. 100-647, Sec. 1011(c)(7)(D), deleted "and" at the end of clause (c)(18)(D)(ii), substituted ", and" for the period at the end of clause (c)(18)(D)(iii), and added clause (c)(18)(D)(iv), effective for plan yrs. begin. after 12/31/87, except as provided in Sec. 1011(c)(7)(E)(ii) of this Act which reads:

"(ii) In the case of a plan described in section 1105(c)(2) of the Reform Act, the amendments made by this paragraph shall not apply to contributions made pursuant to an agreement described in such section for plan years beginning before the earlier of—

"(I) the later of January 1, 1988, or the date on which the last of such agreements terminates (determined without regard to any extension thereof after February 28, 1986), or

"(II) January 1, 1989."

—P.L. 100-647, Sec. 1013(i), provides:

"(i) Application to 501(c)(3) bonds.—In accordance with section 1302 of the Reform Act, each amendment and other provision of this Act which applies to private activity bonds shall, unless otherwise expressly provided, apply to qualified 501(c)(3) bonds."

—P.L. 100-647, Sec. 1016(a)(1)(A), added the last sentence to subpara. (c)(25)(A), effective or with respect to property acquired by the organization after 6/10/87, except that such amendment shall not apply to any property acquired after 6/10/87, pursuant to a binding written contract in effect on 6/10/87, and at all times thereafter before such acquisition.

—P.L. 100-647, Sec. 1016(a)(2), amended the part of subpara. (c)(25)(D) that precedes clause (c)(25)(D)(i) . . . Sec. 1016(a)(3)(A), added subpara. (c)(25)(E) . . .

Sec. 1016(a)(3)(B), added "or" at the end of clause (a)(3)(B)(iii), substituted a period for ", or" at the end of clause (a)(3)(B)(iv) and deleted clause (a)(3)(B)(v) . . . Sec. 1016(a)(4), added subpara. (c)(25)(F), effective for tax. yrs. begin. after 12/31/86.

Prior to amendment, the part of subpara. (c)(25)(D) that precedes clause (c)(25)(D)(i) read as follows:

"(D) A corporation or trust described in this paragraph must permit its shareholders or beneficiaries—"

Prior to deletion, clause (a)(3)(B)(v) read as follows:

"(v) any organization described in this paragraph"

—P.L. 100-647, Sec. 1018(u)(14), substituted "Any association" for "any association" in para. (c)(23), effective 9/3/82.

—P.L. 100-647, Sec. 1018(u)(15), substituted "Any corporation organized" for "any corporation organized" in para. (c)(1), effective 10/1/79.

—P.L. 100-647, Sec. 2003(a)(1), deleted "or" at the end of clause (c)(12)(B)(ii), substituted ", or" for the period at the end of clause (c)(12)(B)(iii) and added clause (c)(12)(B)(iv) . . . Sec. 2003(a)(2), amended subpara. (c)(12)(C), effective for tax. yrs. end. after 10/21/86.

Prior to amendment, subpara. (c)(12)(C) read as follows:

"(C) In the case of a mutual or cooperative electric company, subparagraph (A) shall be applied without taking into account any income received or accrued from qualified pole rentals."

—P.L. 100-647, Sec. 6202(a), added "(including the purchasing of insurance on a group basis)" after "purchasing" in subpara. (e)(1)(A), effective for purchases before, on, or after 11/10/88.

—P.L. 100-647, Sec. 6203, provides:

"SEC. 6203. CANCELLATION OF CERTAIN DEBTS ORIGINATED BY OR GUARANTEED BY THE UNITED STATES NOT TAKEN INTO ACCOUNT IN DETERMINING TAX EXEMPT STATUS OF CERTAIN ORGANIZATIONS.

"Subparagraph (A) of section 501(c)(12) of the 1986 Code shall be applied without taking into account any income attributable to the cancellation of any loan originally made or guaranteed by the United States (or any agency or instrumentality thereof) if such cancellation occurs after 1986 and before 1990."

In **1987**, P.L. 100-203, Sec. 10711(a)(2), substituted "on behalf of (or in opposition to) any candidate" for "on behalf of any candidate" in para. (c)(3), effective for activities after 12/22/87.

In **1986**, P.L. 99-514, Sec. 1012(a), redesignated subsec. (m) as subsec. (n) and added new subsec. (m), effective for tax. yrs. begin. after 12/31/86. Sec. 1012(c)(2) of this Act provides:

"(2) Study of fraternal beneficiary associations.—The Secretary of the Treasury or his delegate shall conduct a study of organizations described in section 501(c)(8) of the Internal Revenue Code of 1986 and which received gross annual insurance premiums in excess of $25,000,000 for the taxable years of such organizations which ended during 1984. Not later than January 1, 1988, the Secretary of the Treasury shall submit to the Committee on Ways and Means of the House of Representatives, the Committee on Finance of the Senate, and the Joint Committee on Taxation the results of such study, together with such recommendations as he determines to be appropriate. The Secretary of the Treasury shall have authority to require the furnishing of such information as may be necessary to carry out the purposes of this paragraph."

—P.L. 99-514, Sec. 1024(b), amended para. (c)(15), effective for tax. yrs. begin. after 12/31/86.

Prior to amendment, para. (c)(15) read as follows:

"(15) Mutual insurance companies or associations other than life or marine (including interinsurers and reciprocal underwriters) if the gross amount received during the taxable year from the items described in section 822(b) (other than paragraph (1)(D) thereof) and premiums (including deposits and assessments) does not exceed $150,000."

—P.L. 99-514, Sec. 1109(a), deleted "and" from the end of subpara. (c)(18)(B), substituted ", and" for the period at the end of subpara. (c)(18)(C) and added subpara. (c)(18)(D), effective for tax. yrs. begin. after 12/31/86.

—P.L. 99-514, Sec. 1114(b)(14), substituted "highly compensated employees (within the meaning of section 414(q))" for "officers, shareholders, persons whose principal duties consists of supervising the work of other employees, or highly compensated employees" in clause (c)(17)[A] (ii), clause (c)(17)[A](iii), subpara. (c)(18)(B) and subpara. (c)(18)(C), effective for yrs. begin. after 12/31/86.

—P.L. 99-514, Sec. 1302, [as amended by Sec. 1013(i) of P.L. 100-647, see above] provides:

"SEC. 1302. TREATMENT OF SECTION 501(C)(3) BONDS.

"Nothing in the treatment of section 501(c)(3) bonds as private activity bonds under the amendments made by this title shall be construed as indicating how section 501(c)(3) bonds will be treated in future legislation, and any change in future legislation applicable to private activity bonds shall apply to section 501(c)(3) bonds only if expressly provided in such legislation."

—P.L. 99-514, Sec. 1603, added para. (c)(25), effective for tax. yrs. begin. after 12/31/86.

—P.L. 99-514, Sec. 1879(k)(1)(A), deleted "or" at the end of clause (c)(14)(B)(ii) . . . Sec. 1879(k)(1)(B), substituted "or" for the period at the end of clause (c)(14)(B)(iii) . . . Sec. 1879(k)(1)(C), added clause (C)(14)(B)(iv), effective for tax. yrs. end. after 8/13/81.

—P.L. 99-514, Sec. 1899A(15), substituted "July, 18, 1984" for "the date of enactment of the Tax Reform Act of 1984" in clause (c)(1)(A)(i), effective 10/22/86.

In **1986**, P.L. 99-272, Sec. 11012(b), added para. (c)(24), effective 1/1/86.

In **1984**, P.L. 98-369, Sec. 1032(a), redesignated subsec. (k) as subsec. (l), and added new subsec. (k), effective for tax. yrs. begin. after 7/18/84.

Exempt organizations

Code Sec. 501

—P.L. 98-369, Sec. 1079, amended subpara. (c)(1)(A) (as added by Sec. 2813(b)(2)).

Prior to amendment, para. (c)(1)(A) read as follows:

"(A) is exempt from Federal income taxes under such Act, as amended and supplemented, or"

—P.L. 98-369, Sec. 2813(b)(l), redesignated subsec. (l) (as redesignated by Sec. 1032(a)) as subsec. (m) and added new subsec. (l)... Sec. 2813(b)(2), amended para. (c)(1), effective 10/1/79.

Prior to amendment, para. (c)(1) read as follows:

"(1) Corporations organized under Act of Congress, if such corporations are instrumentalities of the United States and if, under such Act, as amended and supplemented, such corporations are exempt from Federal income taxes."

In 1983, P.L. 97-448, Sec. 306(b)(5), substituted "75 percent" for "25 percent" in para. (c)(23), effective 9/3/82.

In 1982, P.L. 97-248, Sec. 286(a), redesignated subsec. (j) as subsec. (k) and added new subsec. (j), effective 10/5/76.

—P.L. 97-248, Sec. 354(a)(1), substituted "past or present members of the Armed Forces of the United States" for "war veterans" the first time it appeared in para. (c)(19)... Sec. 354(a)(2), amended subpara. (c)(19)(B)... Sec. 354(b), added para. (c)(23), effective 9/3/82.

Prior to amendment, subpara. (c)(19)(B) read as follows:

"(B) at least 75 percent of the members of which are war veterans and substantially all of the other members of which are individuals who are veterans (but not war veterans), or are cadets, or are spouses, widows, or widowers of war veterans or such individuals, and"

In 1981, P.L. 97-119, Sec. 103(c)(1), substituted "established under section 9501" for "established under section 3 of the Black Lung Benefits Revenue Act of 1977" in clause (c)(21)(B)(iii), effective 1/1/82.

—P.L. 97-34, Sec. 802(b), amended Sec. 2134(e)(1) of P.L. 94-455, the effective date for changes made by Sec. 2134(b), from tax. yrs. begin. after '76 and end. before '82 to tax. yrs. begin. after '76 [see below].

In 1980, P.L. 96-605, Sec. 106(a)(1), substituted "(12)(A)" for "(12)" in para. (c)(12)... Sec. 106(a)(2), deleted the second sentence of para. (c)(12)... Sec. 106(a)(3), added subparas. (c)(12)(B), (C)(12)(C), and (c)(12)(D), effective for tax. yrs. to which the Internal Revenue Code of 1954 applies.

—P.L. 96-601, Sec. 3(a), added the last sentence to subsec. (i), effective for tax. yrs. begin. after 10/20/76.

—P.L. 96-364, Sec. 209(a), added new para. (c)(22), effective for tax. yrs. ending after 9/26/80.

—P.L. 96-222, Sec. 108(b)(2)(B), substituted "Federal Mine Safety and Health Act of 1977" for "Federal Coal Mine Health and Safety Act of 1969" in para. (c)(21), effective in and for tax. yrs. begin. after '77, see Sec. 5 of P.L. 95-227 reproduced in note following Code Sec. 192.

In 1979, P.L. 96-74, Sec. 103, provides the following:

"Sec. 103. None of the funds made available pursuant to the provisions of this Act [Treasury Department Appropriations Act, 1980] shall be used to formulate or carry out any rule, policy, procedure, guideline, regulation, standard, or measure which would cause the loss of tax-exempt status to private, religious, or church-operated schools under section 501(c)(3) of the Internal Revenue Code of 1954 unless in effect prior to August 22, 1978."

—P.L. 96-74, Sec. 615, provides the following:

"SEC. 615. None of the funds available under this Act [Treasury, Postal Service, and General Government Appropriations Act, 1980] may be used to carry out proposed revenue procedure 4830-01-M of the Internal Revenue Service entitled 'Proposed Revenue Procedure on Private Tax-Exempt Schools' (44 F.R. 9451 through 9455, February 13, 1979, F.R. Document 79-4801), and proposed revenue procedure 4830-01 of the Internal Revenue Service entitled 'Proposed Revenue Procedure on Private Tax-Exempt Schools' (43 F.R. 37296 through 37298, August 22, 1978, F.R. Document 78-23515), or parts thereof."

In 1978, P.L. 95-600, Sec. 703(b)(2), substituted "this paragraph" for "section 501(c)(20)" in para. (c)(20), effective 10/4/76.

—P.L. 95-600, Sec. 703(g)(2)(A), amended the changes made by Sec. 2(a) of P.L. 94-568 by substituting "subsection (i) as subsection (j) by and by inserting after subsection (h)" for "subsection (h) as subsection (i) and by inserting after subsection (g)"... Sec. 703(g)(2)(B), redesignated subsec. (g) [sic (i)] (as added by Sec. 2(a) of P.L. 94-568) as subsec. (i), effective for tax. yrs. begin. after 10/20/76. See below.

—P.L. 95-345, Sec. 1(a), added a new sentence to the end of para. (c)(12), effective for tax. yrs. begin. after 12/31/74.

—P.L. 95-227, Sec. 4(a), added para. (c)(21), effective for contributions, acts, and expenditures made after '77, in and for tax. yrs. begin. after '77. See Sec. 5 of this Act, reproduced in note following Code Sec. 192.

In 1976, P.L. 94-568, Sec. 1(a), amended para. (c)(7), effective for tax. yrs. begin. after 10/20/76.

Prior to amendment, para. (c)(7) read as follows:

"(7) Clubs organized and operated exclusively for pleasure, recreation, and other nonprofitable purposes, no part of the net earnings of which inures to the benefit of any private shareholder."

—P.L. 94-568, Sec. 2(a), redesignated subsec. (h) as subsec. (i) [sic] and added new subsec. (g) [sic], for tax. yrs. begin. after 10/20/76. See above

—P.L. 94-455, Sec. 1307(a)(1), redesignated subsec. (h) as subsec. (i) (as previously amended by this Act), and added new subsec. (h), effective for tax. yrs. begin. after 12/31/76.

—P.L. 94-455, Sec. 1307(d)(1)(A), substituted "no substantial part of the activities of which is carrying on propaganda or otherwise attempting to influence legislation (except as otherwise provided in subsection (h))," for "no substantial part of the activities of which is carrying on propaganda or otherwise attempting to influence legislation," in para. (c)(3), effective for tax. yrs. begin. after 12/31/76.

—P.L. 94-455, Sec. 1312(a), added "clinical," following "food," in subpara. (e)(1)(A), effective for tax. yrs. end. after 12/31/76.

—P.L. 94-455, Sec. 1313(a), added "or to foster national or international amateur sports competition (but only if no part of its activities involve the provision of athletic facilities or equipment)," following "or educational purposes" in para. (c)(3), effective 10/5/76. Sec. 1313(c) of the Act provided the following:

"(c) An organization which (without regard to the amendments made by this section) is an organization described in section 170(c)(2)(B), 501(c)(3), 2055(a)(2), or 2522(a)(2) of the Internal Revenue Code of 1954 shall not be treated as an organization not so described as a result of the amendments made by this section."

—P.L. 94-455, Sec. 1906(b)(13)(A), substituted "Secretary" for "Secretary or his delegate" each time it appears in subsec. (c), effective for tax. yrs. begin. after 12/31/76.

—P.L. 94-455, Sec. 2113(a), redesignated subsec. (g) as subsec. (h), and added new subsec. (g), effective for tax. yrs. end. after 12/31/75.

—P.L. 94-455, Sec. 2134(b), added para. (c)(20), effective for tax. yrs. begin. after 12/31/76 and end. before 1/1/82.

In 1975, P.L. 93-625, Sec. 10(c), substituted "parts II, III, and VI" for "parts II and III" each place it appeared in subsec. (b), effective for tax. yrs. begin. after 12/31/74.

In 1974, P.L. 93-406, Sec. 1022(i), provided as follows:

"(i) Certain Puerto Rican Pension, etc., plans to be exempt from tax under section 501(a).

"(1) General rule. Effective for taxable years beginning after December 31, 1973, for purposes of section 501(a) of the Internal Revenue Code of 1954 (relating to exemption from tax), any trust forming part of a pension, profit-sharing, or stock bonus plan all of the participants of which are residents of the Commonwealth of Puerto Rico shall be treated as an organization described in section 401(a) of such Code if such trust—

"(A) forms part of a pension, profit-sharing, or stock bonus plan, and

"(B) is exempt from income tax under the laws of the Commonwealth of Puerto Rico.

"(2) Election to have provisions of, and amendments made by, title ii of this act apply.

"(A) If the administrator of a pension, profit-sharing, or stock bonus plan which is created or organized in Puerto Rico elects, at such time and in such manner as the Secretary of the Treasury may require, to have the provisions of this paragraph apply, for plan years beginning after the date of election any trust forming a part of such plan shall be treated as a trust created or organized in the United States for purposes of section 401(a) of the Internal Revenue Code of 1954.

"(B) An election under subparagraph (A), once made, is irrevocable.

"(C) This paragraph applies to plan years beginning after the date of enactment of this Act.

"(D) The source of any distributions made under a plan which makes an election under this paragraph to participants and beneficiaries residing outside of the United States shall be determined, for purposes of subchapter N of chapter 1 of the Internal Revenue Code of 1954, by the Secretary of the Treasury in accordance with regulations prescribed by him. For purposes of this subparagraph the United States means the United States as defined in section 7701(a)(9) of the Internal Revenue Code of 1954."

In 1974, P.L. 93-310, Sec. 3(a), redesignated subsec. (f) as subsec. (g), and added subsec. (f), effective for tax. yrs. end. after 12/31/73.

In 1972, P.L. 92-418, Sec. 1(a), added para. (c)(19), effective for tax. yrs. begin. after 12/31/69.

In 1970, P.L. 91-618, Sec. 1, amended para. (c)(13), effective for tax. yrs. end. after 12/31/70.

Prior to amendment, para. (c)(13) read as follows:

"(13) Cemetery companies owned and operated exclusively for the benefit of their members or which are not operated for profit; and any corporation chartered solely for burial purposes as a cemetery corporation and not permitted by its charter to engage in any business not necessarily incident to that purpose, no part of the net earnings of which inures to the benefit of any private shareholder or individual."

In 1969, P.L. 91-172, Sec. 101(j)(3), substituted "502 or 503" for "502, 503, or 504" in subsec. (a), effective for tax. yrs. begin. after 12/31/69... Sec. 101(j)(4), amended subsec. (b)... Sec. 101(j)(5), substituted "part IV" for "part III" in para. (c)(16)... Sec. 101(j)(6), substituted "section 170(b)(1)(A)(iii)." for "section 503(b)(5)." in the last sentence of subsec. (e), effective 1/1/70.

Prior to amendment, subsec. (b) read as follows:

"(b) Tax on unrelated business income. An organization exempt from taxation under subsection (a) shall be subject to tax to the extent provided in part II of this subchapter (relating to tax on unrelated income), but, notwithstanding part II, shall be considered an organization exempt from income taxes for the purpose of any law which refers to organizations exempt from income taxes."

—P.L. 91-172, Sec. 121(b)(5)(A), amended paras. (c)(9) and (c)(10),... Sec. 121(b)(6)(A), added para. (c)(18), effective for tax. yrs. begin. after 12/31/69.

Prior to amendment paras. (c)(9) and (c)(10) read as follows:

"(9) Voluntary employees' beneficiary associations providing for the payment of life, sick, accident, or other benefits to the members of such association or their dependents, if—

"(A) no part of their net earnings inures (other than through such payments) to the benefit of any private shareholder or individual, and

2,207

"(B) 85 percent or more of the income consists of amounts collected from members and amounts contributed to the association by the employer of the members for the sole purpose of making such payments and meeting expenses.

"(10) Voluntary employees' beneficiary associations providing for the payment of life, sick, accident, or other benefits to the members of such association or their dependents or their designated beneficiaries, if—

"(A) admission to membership in such association is limited to individuals who are officers or employees of the United States Government, and

"(B) no part of the net earnings of such association inures (other than through such payments) to the benefit of any private shareholder or individual."

In **1968**, P.L. 90-364, Sec. 109(a), redesignated subsec. (e) as subsec. (f), and added subsec. (e), effective for tax. yrs. end. after 6/28/68.

In **1966**, P.L. 89-800, Sec. 6(a), substituted "boards of trade, or professional football leagues (whether or not administering a pension fund for football players)" for "or boards of trade" in para. (c)(6), effective for tax. yrs. end. after 11/8/66.

—P.L. 89-352, Sec. 1, amended para. (c)(14), effective for tax. yrs. end. after 2/2/66.

Prior to amendment, para. (c)(14) read as follows:

"(14) Credit unions without capital stock organized and operated for mutual purposes and without profit; and corporations or associations without capital stock organized before September 1, 1957, and operated for mutual purposes and without profit for the purpose of providing reserve funds for, and insurance of, shares or deposits in—

"(A) domestic buildings and loan associations,

"(B) cooperative banks without capital stock organized and operated for mutual purposes and without profit, or

"(C) mutual savings banks not having capital stock represented by shares."

In **1965**, P.L. 89-44, Sec. 811, provided as follows:

"Sec. 811. Exchanges for sale of poultry.

"(a) Exemption From tax.

"A corporation, association, or organization organized and operated exclusively for the purpose of providing an exchange for the sale of poultry for the poultry growers of a particular locality shall be treated for purposes of the Internal Revenue Code of 1954 as an organization described in section 501(c) (relating to list of exempt organizations) of such Code, if—

"(1) such corporation, association, or organization has no capital stock and is not organized for profit,

"(2) no member of the governing body of such corporation, association, or organization receives any compensation from such corporation, association, or organization,

"(3) the net earnings of such corporation, association, or organization (except for reasonable additions to reserves for the operation of such exchange) are devoted exclusively to disseminating information as to the best methods of poultry culture and to other agricultural purposes, and

"(4) at all times on and after June 10, 1965, and before the close of its last taxable year beginning before January 1, 1966, all of the net assets of such corporation, association, or organization must, on liquidation for any reason, be transferred to an educational organization which is exempt from tax under section 501(a) of such Code or which is an agency or instrumentality of, or is owned or operated by, a State.

"(b) Application of subsection (a).

"Subsection (a) shall apply to taxable years beginning after December 31, 1953, and ending after August 16, 1954, which begin before January 1, 1966."

In **1962**, P.L. 87-834, Sec. 8(d), substituted "$150,000" for "$75,000" in para. (c)(15), effective for tax. yrs. begin. after 12/31/62.

In **1960**, P.L. 86-667, Sec. 1, added para. (c)(17), effective for tax. yrs. begin. after 12/31/59.

—P.L. 86-428, Sec. 1, substituted "1957" for "1951" in para. (c)(14), effective for tax. yrs. begin. after 12/31/59.

In **1956**, P.L. 429, Sec. 5(2), substituted "the items described in section 822(b) (other than paragraph (1)(D) thereof)" for "interest, dividends, rents," in para. (c)(15), effective for tax. yrs. begin. after 12/31/54.

Sec. 502. Feeder organizations.
(a) General rule.

An organization operated for the primary purpose of carrying on a trade or business for profit shall not be exempt from taxation under section 501 on the ground that all of its profits are payable to one or more organizations exempt from taxation under section 501.

(b) Special rule.

For purposes of this section, the term "trade or business" shall not include—

(1) the deriving of rents which would be excluded under section 512(b)(3), if section 512 applied to the organization,

(2) any trade or business in which substantially all the work in carrying on such trade or business is performed for the organization without compensation, or

(3) any trade or business which is the selling of merchandise, substantially all of which has been received by the organization as gifts or contributions.

In **1969**, P.L. 91-172, Sec. 121(b)(7), amended Code Sec. 502, effective for tax. yrs. begin. after 12/31/69.

Prior to amendment, Code Sec. 502 read as follows:

"Sec. 502. Feeder organizations.

"An organization operated for the primary purpose of carrying on a trade or business for profit shall not be exempt under section 501 on the ground that all of its profits are payable to one or more organizations exempt under section 501 from taxation. For purposes of this section, the term 'trade or business' shall not include the rental by an organization of its real property (including personal property leased with the real property)."

Sec. 503. Requirements for exemption.
(a) Denial of exemption to organizations engaged in prohibited transactions.

(1) General rule.

(A) An organization described in section 501(c)(17) shall not be exempt from taxation under section 501(a) if it has engaged in a prohibited transaction after December 31, 1959.

(B) An organization described in section 401(a) which is referred to in section 4975(g)(2) or (3) shall not be exempt from taxation under section 501(a) if it has engaged in a prohibited transaction after March 1, 1954.

(C) An organization described in section 501(c)(18) shall not be exempt from taxation under section 501(a) if it has engaged in a prohibited transaction after December 31, 1969.

(2) Taxable years affected. An organization described in section 501(c)(17) or (18) or paragraph [sic (a)] (1)(B) shall be denied exemption from taxation under section 501(a) by reason of paragraph (1) only for taxable years after the taxable year during which it is notified by the Secretary that it has engaged in a prohibited transaction, unless such organization entered into such prohibited transaction with the purpose of diverting corpus or income of the organization from its exempt purposes, and such transaction involved a substantial part of the corpus or income of such organization.

(b) Prohibited transactions.

For purposes of this section, the term "prohibited transaction" means any transaction in which an organization subject to the provisions of this section—

(1) lends any part of its income or corpus, without the receipt of adequate security and a reasonable rate of interest, to;

(2) pays any compensation, in excess of a reasonable allowance for salaries or other compensation for personal services actually rendered, to;

(3) makes any part of its services available on a preferential basis to;

(4) makes any substantial purchase of securities or any other property, for more than adequate consideration in money or money's worth, from;

(5) sells any substantial part of its securities or other property, for less than an adequate consideration in money or money's worth, to; or

(6) engages in any other transaction which results in a substantial diversion of its income or corpus to;

the creator of such organization (if a trust); a person who has made a substantial contribution to such organization; a member of the family (as defined in section 267(c)(4)) of an individual who is the creator of such trust or who has made a substantial contribution to such organization; or a corporation controlled by such creator or person through the ownership, directly or indirectly, of 50 percent or more of the total combined voting power of all classes of stock entitled to vote or 50 percent or more of the total value of shares of all classes of stock of the corporation.

(c) Future status of organizations denied exemption.

Any organization described in section 501(c)(17) or (18) or subsection (a)(1)(B) which is denied exemption under section 501(a) by reason of subsection (a) of this section, with respect to any taxable year following the taxable year in which notice of denial of exemption was received, may, under regulations prescribed by the Secretary, file claim for exemption, and if the Secretary, pursuant to such regulations, is satisfied that such organization will not knowingly again engage in a prohibited transaction, such organization shall be exempt with respect to taxable years after the year in which such claim is filed.

(d) Repealed.

(e) Special rules.

For purposes of subsection (b)(1), a bond, debenture, note, or certificate or other evidence of indebtedness (hereinafter in this subsection referred to as "obligation") shall not be treated as a loan made without the receipt of adequate security if—

(1) such obligation is acquired—

(A) on the market, either (i) at the price of the obligation prevailing on a national securities exchange which is registered with the Securities and Exchange Commission, or (ii) if the obligation is not traded on such a national securities exchange, at a price not less favorable to the trust than the offering price for the obligation as established by current bid and asked prices quoted by persons independent of the issuer;

(B) from an underwriter, at a price (i) not in excess of the public offering price for the obligation as set forth in a prospectus or offering circular filed with the Securities and Exchange Commission, and (ii) at which a substantial portion of the same issue is acquired by persons independent of the issuer; or

(C) directly from the issuer, at a price not less favorable to the trust than the price paid currently for a substantial portion of the same issue by persons independent of the issuer;

(2) immediately following acquisition of such obligation—

(A) not more than 25 percent of the aggregate amount of obligations issued in such issue and outstanding at the time of acquisition is held by the trust, and

(B) at least 50 percent of the aggregate amount referred to in subparagraph (A) is held by persons independent of the issuer; and

(3) immediately following acquisition of the obligation, not more than 25 percent of the assets of the trust is invested in obligations of persons described in subsection (b).

(f) Loans with respect to which employers are prohibited from pledging certain assets.

Subsection (b)(1) shall not apply to a loan made by a trust described in section 401(a) to the employer (or to a renewal of such a loan or, if the loan is repayable upon demand, to a continuation of such a loan) if the loan bears a reasonable rate of interest, and if (in the case of a making or renewal)—

(1) the employer is prohibited (at the time of such making or renewal) by any law of the United States or regulation thereunder from directly or indirectly pledging, as security for such a loan, a particular class or classes of his assets the value of which (at such time) represents more than one-half of the value of all his assets;

(2) the making or renewal, as the case may be, is approved in writing as an investment which is consistent with the exempt purposes of the trust by a trustee who is independent of the employer, and no other such trustee had previously refused to give such written approval; and

(3) immediately following the making or renewal, as the case may be, the aggregate amount loaned by the trust to the employer, without the receipt of adequate security, does not exceed 25 percent of the value of all the assets of the trust.

For purposes of paragraph (2), the term "trustee" means, with respect to any trust for which there is more than one trustee who is independent of the employer, a majority of such independent trustees. For purposes of paragraph (3), the determination as to whether any amount loaned by the trust to the employer is loaned without the receipt of adequate security shall be made without regard to subsection (e).

In 1990, P.L. 101-508, Sec. 11801(a)(22), deleted subsec. (d), effective 11/5/90, except as provided in Sec. 11821(b) of this Act, which reads as follows:
"(b) Savings provision.—If—
"(1) any provision amended or repealed by this part applied to—
"(A) any transaction occurring before the date of the enactment of this Act [11/5/90],
"(B) any property acquired before such date of enactment [11/5/90], or
"(C) any item of income, loss, deduction, or credit taken into account before such date of enactment [11/5/90], and
"(2) the treatment of such transaction, property, or item under such provision would (without regard to the amendments made by this part) affect liability for tax for periods ending after such date of enactment [11/5/90],
nothing in the amendments made by this part shall be construed to affect the treatment of such transaction, property, or item for purposes of determining liability for tax for periods ending after such date of enactment [11/5/90]."
Prior to deletion, subsec. (d) read as follows:
"(d) Special rule for loans. For purposes of the application of subsection (b)(1), in the case of a loan by a trust described in section 401(a), the following rules shall apply with respect to a loan made before March 1, 1954, which would constitute a prohibited transaction if made on or after March 1, 1954:
"(1) If any part of the loan is repayable prior to December 31, 1955, the renewal of such part of the loan for a period not extending beyond December 31, 1955, on the same terms, shall not be considered a prohibited transaction.
"(2) If the loan is repayable on demand, the continuation of the loan without the receipt of adequate security and a reasonable rate of interest beyond December 31, 1955, shall be considered a prohibited transaction."

In 1976, P.L. 94-455, Sec. 1906(b)(13)(A), substituted "Secretary" for "Secretary or his delegate" in subsec. (a), and each place it appeared in subsec. (c), effective for tax. yrs. begin. after 12/31/76.

In 1974, P.L. 93-406, Sec. 2003(b)(1), deleted "or 18" in subpara. (a)(1)(A)... Sec. 2003(b)(2), added "which is referred to in section 4975(g)(2) or (3)" after "described in section 401(a)" in subpara. (a)(1)(B)... Sec. 2003(b)(3), substituted "or paragraph (1)(B)" for "or section 401 [sic (a)]" in para. (a)(2)... Sec. 2003(b)(4), substituted "or subsection (a)(1)(B)" for "or section 401 [sic (a)]" in subsec. (c)... Sec. 2003(b)(5), deleted subsec. (g), effective 1/1/75.
Prior to deletion, subsec. (g) read as follows:
"(g) Trusts benefiting certain owner-employees.
"(1) Prohibited transactions.—In the case of a trust described in section 401(a) which is part of a plan providing contributions or benefits for employees some or all of whom are owner-employees (as defined in section 401(c)(3)) who control (within the meaning of section 401(d)(9)(B)) the trade or business with respect to which the plan is established, the term 'prohibited transaction' also means any transaction in which such trust, directly or indirectly—
"(A) lends any part of the corpus or income of the trust to;
"(B) pays any compensation for personal services rendered to the trust to;
"(C) makes any part of its services available on a preferential basis to; or
"(D) acquires for the trust any property from, or sells any property to;
any person described in subsection (b) or to any such owner-employee, a member of the family (as defined in section 267(c)(4)) of any such owner-employee, or a corporation controlled by any such owner-employee through the ownership, directly or indirectly, of 50 percent or more of the total combined voting power of all classes of stock entitled to vote or 50 percent or more of the total value of shares of all classes of stock of the corporation.
"(2) Special rule for loans.—For purposes of the application of paragraph (1)(A), the following rules shall apply with respect to a loan made before the date of the enactment of this subsection which would be a prohibited transaction if made in a taxable year beginning after December 31, 1962:
"(A) If any part of the loan is repayable prior to December 31, 1965, the renewal of such part of the loan for a period not extending beyond December 31, 1965, on the same terms, shall not be considered a prohibited transaction.
"(B) If the loan is repayable on demand, the continuation of the loan beyond December 31, 1965, shall be considered a prohibited transaction."

In 1969, P.L. 91-172, Sec. 101(j)(7), amended para. (a)(1)... Sec. 101(j)(8), substituted "Section 501(c)(17)" for "Section 501(c)(3) or (17)" in para. (a)(2)... Sec. 101(j)(9), substituted "501(c)(17)" for "501(c)(3) or (17)" in subsec. (c)... Sec. 101(j)(10), substituted "subsection (b)(1)," for "subsection (c)(1)," in subsec. (g)... Sec. 101(j)(11)(A), substituted "special rules.—" for "special rules relating to lending by section 401(a) and section 501(c)(17) trusts to certain persons.—" in the heading of subsec. (h)... Sec. 101(j)(11)(B), substituted "subsection (b)(1)" for "subsection (c)(1)" in subsec. (h)... Sec. 101(j)(11)(C), deleted "acquired by a trust described in section 401(a) or section 501(c)(17)"... Sec. 101(j)(11)(D), substituted "subsection (b)" for "subsection (c)" in para. (h)(3)... Sec. 101(j)(12)(A), substituted "Subsection (b)(1)" for "Subsection (c)(1)" in subsec. (1)... Sec. 101(j)(12)(B), substituted "subsection (e)" for "subsection (h)" in subsec. (i)... Sec. 101(j)(13), substituted "subsection (b)" for "subsection (c)" in para. (j)(1)... Sec. 101(j)(14), deleted subsecs. (b), (e), and (f) and redesignated subsecs. (c), (d), (g), (h), (i), and (j) as subsecs. (b), (c), (d), (e), (f), and (g), effective 1/1/70.

Prior to amendment, para. (a)(1) read as follows:

"(1) General rule.

"(A) An organization described in section 501(c)(3) which is subject to the provisions of this section shall not be exempt from taxation under section 501(a) if it has engaged in a prohibited transaction after July 1, 1950.

"(B) An organization described in section 501(c)(17) which is subject to the provisions of this section shall not be exempt from taxation under section 501(a) if it has engaged in a prohibited transaction after December 31, 1959.

"(C) An organization described in section 401(a) which is subject to the provisions of this section shall not be exempt from taxation under section 501(a) if it has engaged in a prohibited transaction after March 1, 1954."

Prior to deletion subsec. (b) read as follows:

"(b) Organizations to which section applies.

"This section shall apply to any organization described in section 501(c)(3) or (17) or section 401(a) except—

"(a) a religious organization (other than a trust);

"(2) an educational organization which normally maintains a regular faculty and curriculum and normally has a regularly enrolled body of pupils or students in attendance at the place where its educational activities are regularly carried on;

"(3) an organization which normally receives a substantial part of its support (exclusive of income received in the exercise or performance by such organization of its charitable, educational, or other purpose or function constituting the basis for its exemption under section 501(a)) from the United States or any State or political subdivision thereof or from direct or indirect contributions from the general public;

"(4) an organization which is operated, supervised, controlled, or principally supported by a religious organization (other than a trust) which is itself not subject to the provisions of this section; and

"(5) an organization the principal purposes or functions of which are the providing of medical or hospital care or medical education or medical research or agricultural research.

Prior to deletion, subsec. (e) read as follows:

"(e) Disallowance of certain charitable, etc., deductions.

"No gift or bequest for religious, charitable, scientific, literary, or educational purposes (including the encouragement of art and the prevention of cruelty to children or animals), otherwise allowable as a deduction under section 170, 642(c), 545(b)(2), 2055, 2106(a)(2), or 2522, shall be allowed as a deduction if made to an organization described in section 501(c)(3) which, in the taxable year or the organization in which the gift or bequest is made, is not exempt under section 501(a) by reason of this section. With respect to any taxable year of the organization for which the organization is not exempt pursuant to subsection (a) by reason of having engaged in a prohibited transaction with the purpose of diverting the corpus or income of such organization from its exempt purposes and such transaction involved a substantial part of such corpus or income, and which taxable year is the same, or prior to, the taxable year of the organization in which such transaction occurred, such deduction shall be disallowed the donor only if such donor or (if such donor is an individual) any member of his family (as defined in section 267(c)(4)) was a party to such prohibited transaction.

Prior to deletion, subsec. (f) read as follows:

"(f) Definition.

"For purposes of this section, the term 'gift or bequest' means any gift, contribution, bequest, devise, legacy, or transfer."

—P.L. 91-172, Sec. 121(b)(6)(B)(i), added subpara. (a)(1)(C)... Sec. 121(b)(6)(B)(ii), substituted "(c)(17) or (18)" for "(c)(17)" each place it appeared in Code Sec. 503, effective for tax. yrs. begin. after 12/31/69.

In 1962, P.L. 87-792, Sec. 6, added subsec. (j), effective for tax. yrs. begin. after 12/31/62.

In 1960, P.L. 86-667, Sec. 2(a)(1), amended para. (a)(1)... Sec. 2(a)(2), substituted "section 501(c)(3) or (17)" for "section 501(c)(3)" in para. (a)(2)... Sec. 2(b), substituted "section 501(c)(3) or (17)" for "section 501(c)(3)" in subsec. (b)... Sec. 2(c), substituted "section 501(c)(3) or (17)" for "section 501(c)(3)" in subsec. (d)... Sec. 2(d)(1), substituted "section 401(a) and section 501(c)(17)" for "section 401(a)" in the heading of subsec. (h)... Sec. 2(d)(2), substituted "section 401(a) or section 501(c)(17)" for "section 401(a)" in subsec. (h), effective for tax. yrs. begin. after 12/31/59 and for loans made, renewed or continued after 12/31/59.

Prior to amendment, para. (a)(1) read as follows:

"(1) General rule.—An organization described in section 501(c)(3) which is subject to the provisions of this section shall not be exempt from taxation under section 501(a) if it has engaged in a prohibited transaction after July 1, 1950; and an organization described in section 401(a) which is subject to the provisions of

this section shall not be exempt from taxation under section 501(a) if it has engaged in a prohibited transaction after March 1, 1954."

In 1958, P.L. 85-866, Sec. 30(a), added subsec. (h), effective for tax. yrs. end. after 3/15/56, except as provided in Sec. 30(c)(2) of this Act, reproduced below.

—P.L. 85-866, Sec. 30(b), added subsec. (i), effective for tax. yrs. end. after 9/2/58, but only for periods after 9/2/58, except as provided in Sec. 30(c)(2) of this Act, which reads as follows:

"(2) Exceptions. Nothing in subsection (a) shall be construed to make any transaction a prohibited transaction which, under announcements of the Internal Revenue Service made with respect to section 503 (c)(1) of the Internal Revenue Code of 1954 before the date of the enactment of this Act, [9/2/58] would not constitute a prohibited transaction. In the case of any bond, debenture, note, or certificate or other evidence of indebtedness acquired before the date of the enactment of this Act by a trust described in section 401 (a) of such Code which is held on such date, paragraphs (2) and (3) of section 503 (h) of such Code shall be treated as satisfied if such requirements would have been satisfied if such obligation had been acquired on such date of enactment."

Sec. 504. Status after organization ceases to qualify for exemption under section 501(c)(3) because of substantial lobbying or because of political activities.

(a) General rule.

An organization which—

(1) was exempt (or was determined by the Secretary to be exempt) from taxation under section 501(a) by reason of being an organization described in section 501(c)(3), and

(2) is not an organization described in section 501(c)(3)—

(A) by reason of carrying on propaganda, or otherwise attempting, to influence legislation, or

(B) by reason of participating in, or intervening in, any political campaign on behalf of (or in opposition to) any candidate for public office,

shall not at any time thereafter be treated as an organization described in section 501(c)(4).

(b) Regulations to prevent avoidance.

The Secretary shall prescribe such regulations as may be necessary or appropriate to prevent the avoidance of subsection (a), including regulations relating to a direct or indirect transfer of all or part of the assets of an organization to an organization controlled (directly or indirectly) by the same person or persons who control the transferor organization.

(c) Churches, etc.

Subsection (a) shall not apply to any organization which is a disqualified organization within the meaning of section 501(h)(5) (relating to churches, etc.) for the taxable year immediately preceding the first taxable year for which such organization is described in paragraph (2) of subsection (a).

In 1987, P.L. 100-203, Sec. 10711(b)(1), amended para. (a)(2)... Sec. 10711(b)(2)(A), substituted "substantial lobbying or because of political activities" for "substantial lobbying" in heading of Sec. 504, effective for activities after 12/22/87.

Prior to amendment para. (a)(2) read as follows:

"(2) is not an organization described in section 501(c)(3) by reason of carrying on propaganda, or otherwise attempting, to influence legislation,"

In 1976, P.L. 94-455, Sec. 1307(a)(2), added Code Sec. 504, effective for tax. yrs. begin. after '76. Sec. 1307(a)(3) of this Act provided the following rules of interpretation:

"(3) Rules of interpretation.—It is the intent of Congress that enactment of this section is not to be regarded in any way as an approval or disapproval of the decision of the Court of Appeals for the Tenth Circuit in Christian Echoes National Ministry, Inc. versus United States, 470 F.2d 849 (1972), or of the reasoning in any of the opinions leading to that decision."

In 1969, P.L. 91-172, Sec. 101(j)(15), repealed Code Sec. 504, for tax. yrs. begin. after 12/31/69.

Prior to repeal Code Sec. 504 read as follows:

"Sec. 504. Denial of exemption.

"(a) General rule.

"In the case of any organization described in section 501(c)(3) to which section 503 is applicable, exemption under section 501 shall be denied for the taxable year if the amounts accumulated out of income during the taxable year or any prior taxable year and not actually paid out by the end of the taxable year—

"(1) are unreasonable in amount or duration in order to carry out the charitable, educational, or other purpose or function constituting the basis for exemption under section 501(a) of an organization described in section 501(c)(3); or

"(2) are used to a substantial degree for purposes or functions other than those constituting the basis for exemption under section 501(a) of an organization described in section 501(c)(3); or

Exempt organizations   Code Sec. 505

"(3) are invested in such a manner as to jeopardize the carrying out of the charitable, educational, or other purpose or function constituting the basis for exemption under section 501(a) of an organization described in section 501(c)(3).

Paragraph (1) shall not apply to income attributable to property of a decedent dying before January 1, 1951, which is transferred under his will to a trust created by such will. In the case of a trust created by the will of a decedent dying on or after January 1, 1951, if income is required to be accumulated pursuant to the mandatory terms of the will creating the trust, paragraph (1) shall apply only to income accumulated during a taxable year of the trust beginning more than 21 years after the date of death of the last life in being designated in the trust instrument. Paragraph (1) shall not apply to income attributable to property transferred to a trust before January 1, 1951, by the creator of such trust, if such trust was irrevocable on such date and if such income is required to be accumulated pursuant to the mandatory terms (as in effect on such date and at all times thereafter) of the instrument creating such trust.

"(b) Cross references.

"For limitation on charitable contributions in case of unreasonable accumulations by certain trusts, see section 681(c)(2).''

In 1968, P.L. 90-630, Sec. 6(a), added the last sentence in subsec. (a) for tax. yrs. begin. after '53, and end. after Aug. 16, '54.

Sec. 505. Additional requirements for organizations described in paragraph (9), (17), or (20) of section 501(c).

(a) Certain requirements must be met in the case of organizations described in paragraph (9) or (20) of section 501(c).

(1) Voluntary Employees' Beneficiary Associations, etc. An organization described in paragraph (9) or (20) of subsection (c) of section 501 which is part of a plan shall not be exempt from tax under section 501(a) unless such plan meets the requirements of subsection (b) of this section.

(2) Exception for collective bargaining agreements. Paragraph (1) shall not apply to any organization which is part of a plan maintained pursuant to an agreement between employee representatives and 1 or more employers if the Secretary finds that such agreement is a collective bargaining agreement and that such plan was the subject of good faith bargaining between such employee representatives and such employer or employers.

(b) Nondiscrimination requirements.

(1) In general. Except as otherwise provided in this subsection, a plan meets the requirements of this subsection only if—

(A) each class of benefits under the plan is provided under a classification of employees which is set forth in the plan and which is found by the Secretary not to be discriminatory in favor of employees who are highly compensated individuals, and

(B) in the case of each class of benefits, such benefits do not discriminate in favor of employees who are highly compensated individuals.

A life insurance, disability, severance pay, or supplemental unemployment compensation benefit shall not be considered to fail to meet the requirements of subparagraph (B) merely because the benefits available bear a uniform relationship to the total compensation, or the basic or regular rate of compensation, of employees covered by the plan.

(2) Exclusion of certain employees. For purposes of paragraph (1), there may be excluded from consideration—

(A) employees who have not completed 3 years of service,

(B) employees who have not attained age 21,

(C) seasonal employees or less than half-time employees,

(D) employees not included in the plan who are included in a unit of employees covered by an agreement between employee representatives and 1 or more employers which the Secretary finds to be a collective bargaining agreement if the class of benefits involved was the subject of good faith bargaining between such employee representatives and such employer or employers, and

(E) employees who are nonresident aliens and who receive no earned income (within the meaning of section 911(d)(2)) from the employer which constitutes income from sources within the United States (within the meaning of section 861(a)(3)).

(3) Application of subsection where other nondiscrimination rules provided. In the case of any benefit for which a provision of this chapter other than this subsection provides nondiscrimination rules, paragraph (1) shall not apply but the requirements of this subsection shall be met only if the nondiscrimination rules so provided are satisfied with respect to such benefit.

(4) Aggregation rules. At the election of the employer, 2 or more plans of such employer may be treated as 1 plan for purposes of this subsection.

(5) Highly compensated individual. For purposes of this subsection, the determination as to whether an individual is a highly compensated individual shall be made under rules similar to the rules for determining whether an individual is a highly compensated employee (within the meaning of section 414(q)).

(6) Compensation. For purposes of this subsection, the term "compensation" has the meaning given such term by section 414(s).

> • **Caution:** Code Sec. 505(b)(7), following, was amended by Sec. 611(c)(1), P.L. 107-16, the Economic Growth and Tax Relief Reconciliation Act of 2001 (EGTRRA). These provisions generally sunset for tax years beginning after 12/31/2012. For specific sunset provisions see Sec. 901, P.L. 107-16 (as amended) reproduced in history notes for this Code Sec.

(7) Compensation limit. A plan shall not be treated as meeting the requirements of this subsection unless under the plan the annual compensation of each employee taken into account for any year does not exceed $200,000. The Secretary shall adjust the $200,000 amount at the same time, and by the same amount, as any adjustment under section 401(a)(17)(B). This paragraph shall not apply in determining whether the requirements of section 79(d) are met.

(c) Requirement that organization notify secretary that it is applying for tax-exempt status.

(1) In general. An organization shall not be treated as an organization described in paragraph (9), (17), or (20) of section 501(c)—

(A) unless it has given notice to the Secretary, in such manner as the Secretary may by regulations prescribe, that it is applying for recognition of such status, or

(B) for any period before the giving of such notice, if such notice is given after the time prescribed by the Secretary by regulations for giving notice under this subsection.

(2) Special rule for existing organizations. In the case of any organization in existence on July 18, 1984, the time for giving notice under paragraph (1) shall not expire before the date 1 year after such date of the enactment.

In 2010, P.L. 111-312, Sec. 101(a)(1), substituted "December 31, 2012" for "December 31, 2010" both places it appeared in Sec. 901 of P.L. 107-16 [see below], effective as if included in the enactment of P.L. 107-16, EGTRRA, 6/7/2001.

Code Sec. 505 — Exempt organizations

In 2006, P.L. 109-280, Sec. 811, of this Act [relating to Sec. 901 of P.L. 107-16, see below], provides:

"SEC. 811. PENSIONS AND INDIVIDUAL RETIREMENT ARRANGEMENT PROVISIONS OF ECONOMIC GROWTH AND TAX RELIEF RECONCILIATION ACT OF 2001 MADE PERMANENT.

"Title IX of the Economic Growth and Tax Relief Reconciliation Act of 2001 shall not apply to the provisions of, and amendments made by, subtitles A through F of title VI of such Act (relating to pension and individual retirement arrangement provisions)."

In 2002, P.L. 107-358, Sec. 2, added subsec. (c) in Sec. 901 of P.L. 107-16 [see below], effective 12/17/2002.

In 2001, P.L. 107-16, Sec. 611(c)(1), substituted "$200,000" for "$150,000" each place it appeared in para. (b)(7), effective for yrs. begin. after 12/31/2001.

—P.L. 107-16, Sec. 901, of this Act [as amended by Sec. 2 of P.L. 107-358, and Sec. 101(a)(1) of P.L. 111-312, and as related to Sec. 811 of P.L. 109-280, see above], reads as follows:

"SEC. 901. SUNSET OF PROVISIONS OF ACT.

"(a) In general. All provisions of, and amendments made by, this Act shall not apply—

"(1) to taxable, plan, or limitation years beginning after December 31, 2012, or

"(2) in the case of title V, to estates of decedents dying, gifts made, or generation skipping transfers, after December 31, 2012.

"(b) Application of certain laws. The Internal Revenue Code of 1986 and the Employee Retirement Income Security Act of 1974 shall be applied and administered to years, estates, gifts, and transfers described in subsection (a) as if the provisions and amendments described in subsection (a) had never been enacted.

"(c) Exception. Subsection (a) shall not apply to section 803 (relating to no federal income tax on restitution received by victims of the Nazi regime or their heirs or estates)."

In 1993, P.L. 103-66, Sec. 13212(c)(1)(A), substituted "$150,000" for "$200,000" in the first sentence of para. (b)(7) . . . Sec. 13212(c)(1)(B), amended the second sentence of para. (b)(7) . . . Sec. 13212(c)(2), deleted "$200,000" before "compensation" in the heading of para. (b)(7), effective for benefits accruing in plan yrs. begin. after 12/31/93, except as provided by Sec. 13212(d)(2) and (3) of this Act, which reads as follows:

"(2) Collectively bargained plans.— In the case of a plan maintained pursuant to 1 or more collective bargaining agreements between employee representatives and 1 or more employers ratified before the date of the enactment of this Act, the amendments made by this section shall not apply to contributions or benefits pursuant to such agreements for plan years beginning before the earlier of—

"(A) the latest of—

"(i) January 1, 1994

"(ii) the date on which the last of such collective bargaining agreements terminates (without regard to any extension, amendment, or modification of such agreements on or after such date of enactment [8/10/93]), or

"(iii) in the case of a plan maintained pursuant to collective bargaining under the Railway Labor Act, the date of execution of an extension or replacement of the last of such collective bargaining agreements in effect on such date of enactment, or

"(B) January 1, 1997.

"(3) Transition rule for state and local plans.—

"(A) In general.— In the case of an eligible participant in a governmental plan (within the meaning of section 414(d) of the Internal Revenue Code of 1986), the dollar limitation under section 401(a)(17) of such Code shall not apply to the extent the amount of compensation which is allowed to be taken into account under the plan would be reduced below the amount which was allowed to be taken into account under the plan as in effect on July 1, 1993.

"(B) Eligible participant.— For purposes of subparagraph (A), an eligible participant is an individual who first became a participant in the plan during a plan year beginning before the 1st plan year beginning after the earlier of—

"(i) the plan year in which the plan is amended to reflect the amendments made by this section, or

"(ii) December 31, 1995.

"(C) Plan must be amended to incorporate limits.— This paragraph shall not apply to any eligible participant of a plan unless the plan is amended so that the plan incorporates by reference the dollar limitation under section 401(a)(17) of the Internal Revenue Code of 1986, effective with respect to noneligible participants for plan years beginning after December 31, 1995 (or earlier if the plan amendment so provides)."

Prior to amendment, the second sentence of para. (b)(7) read as follows:

"The Secretary shall adjust the $200,000 amount at the same time and in the same manner as under section 415(d)."

In 1989, P.L. 101-140, Sec. 203(a)(1), repealed as if not enacted Sec. 1151(g)(6) of P.L. 99-514, which amended para. (b)(2).

—P.L. 101-140, Sec. 203(a)(2), repealed as if not enacted Sec. 1011B(a)(27)(C) of P.L. 100-647, which amended para. (a)(1).

—P.L. 101-140, Sec. 203(a)(2), repealed as if not enacted Sec. 1011B(a)(31)(B) of P.L. 100-647, which amended para. (b)(2).

—P.L. 101-140, Sec. 204(c), added the last sentence of para. (b)(7), effective as provided in Sec. 1151(k)(l) of P.L. 99-514, reproduced in note following Code Sec. 414.

—P.L. 101-136, Sec. 528, provided that "no monies appropriated by this Act [for the fiscal year ending September 30, '90] may be used to implement or enforce section 1151 of the Tax Reform Act of '86 [P.L. 99-514] or the amendments made by such section." [See below]

In 1988, P.L. 100-647, Sec. 1011B(a)(25), amended Sec. 1151(k)(1) of P.L. 99-514 [reproduced in the note following Code Sec. 414], part of the effective date for changes made by Sec. 1151(e)(2)(B), (g)(6), and (j)(3) of P.L. 99-514, by adding the last sentence, see below.

—P.L. 100-647, Sec. 1011B(a)(32), added para. (b)(7), effective as provided in Sec. 1151(k)(1) of P.L. 99-514 reproduced in note following Code Sec. 414.

In 1986, P.L. 99-514, Sec. 1114(b)(16), amended para. (b)(5), effective for yrs. begin. after 12/31/87.

Prior to amendment, para. (b)(5) read as follows:

"(5) Highly compensated individual. For purposes of this subsection, the term 'highly compensated individual' has the meaning given such term by section 105(h)(5). For purposes of the preceding sentence, section 105(h)(5) shall be applied by substituting '10 percent' for '25 percent'."

—P.L. 99-514, Sec. 1151(e)(2)(B), amended para. (b)(4) . . . Sec. 1151(j)(3), added para. (b)(6), effective as provided in Sec. 1151(k)(l) of this Act reproduced in note following Code Sec. 414.

Prior to amendment, para. (b)(4) read as follows:

"(4) Aggregation rules. For purposes of this subsection—

"(A) Aggregation of plans. At the election of the employer, 2 or more plans of such employer may be treated as 1 plan.

"(B) Treatment of related employers. Rules similar to the rules of subsections (b), (c), (m), and (n) of section 414 shall apply. For purposes of the preceding sentence, section 414(n) shall be applied without regard to paragraph (5)."

—P.L. 99-514, Sec. 1851(c)(1), deleted "of an employer" after "part of a plan" in para. (a)(1) . . . Sec. 1851(c)(2), substituted "as otherwise provided in this subsection" for "as provided in paragraph (2)" in para. (b)(1) . . . Sec. 1851(c)(3), substituted "highly compensated individuals" for "highly compensated employees" in subpara. (b)(1)(B) . . . Sec. 1851(c)(4), amended para. (a)(2), effective for yrs. begin. after 12/31/84, except as provided in Sec. 513(c)(2) of P.L. 98-369, reproduced below.

Prior to amendment, para. (a)(2) read as follows:

"(2) Exception for collective bargaining agreements. Paragraph (1) shall not apply to any organization which is part of a plan maintained pursuant to 1 or more collective bargaining agreements between 1 or more employee organizations and 1 or more employers."

—P.L. 99-514, Sec. 1899A(16), substituted "July 18, 1984" for "the date of the enactment of the Tax Reform Act of 1984" in para. (c)(2), effective 10/22/86.

In 1984, P.L. 98-369, Sec. 513(a), added Code Sec. 505, effective for yrs. begin. after 12/31/84. Sec. 513(c)(2) of the Act provides:

"(2) Treatment of certain benefits in pay status as of January 1, 1985.— For purposes of determining whether a plan meets the requirements of section 505(b) of the Internal Revenue Code of 1954 (as added by subsection (a)), there may (at the election of the employer) be excluded from consideration all disability or severance payments payable to individuals who are in pay status as of January 1, 1985. The preceding sentence shall not apply to any payment to the extent such payment is increased by any plan amendment adopted after June 22, 1984."

PART II.— PRIVATE FOUNDATIONS

Sec.
507. Termination of private foundation status.
508. Special rules with respect to section 501(c)(3) organizations.
509. Private foundation defined.

In 1969, P.L. 91-172, Sec. 101(a), added new Part II.

Sec. 507. Termination of private foundation status.

(a) General rule.

Except as provided in subsection (b), the status of any organization as a private foundation shall be terminated only if—

(1) such organization notifies the Secretary (at such time and in such manner as the Secretary may by regulations prescribe) of its intent to accomplish such termination, or

(2) (A) with respect to such organization, there have been either willful repeated acts (or failures to act), or a willful and flagrant act (or failure to act), giving rise to liability for tax under chapter 42, and

(B) the Secretary notifies such organization that, by reason of subparagraph (A), such organization is liable for the tax imposed by subsection (c),

and either such organization pays the tax imposed by subsection (c) (or any portion not abated under subsection (g)) or the entire amount of such tax is abated under subsection (g).

(b) Special rules.

(1) Transfer to, or operation as, public charity. The status as a private foundation of any organization, with respect to which there have not been either willful repeated acts (or failures to act) or a willful and flagrant act (or failure to act) giving rise to liability for tax under chapter 42, shall be terminated if—

(A) such organization distributes all of its net assets to one or more organizations described in section 170(b)(1)(A) (other than in clauses (vii) and (viii)) each of which has been in existence and so described for a continuous period of at least 60 calendar months immediately preceding such distribution, or

(B)(i) such organization meets the requirements of paragraph (1), (2), or (3) of section 509(a) by the end of the 12-month period beginning with its first taxable year which begins after December 31, 1969, or for a continuous period of 60 calendar months beginning with the first day of any taxable year which begins after December 31, 1969,

(ii) such organization notifies the Secretary (in such manner as the Secretary may by regulations prescribe) before the commencement of such 12-month or 60-month period (or before the 90th day after the day on which regulations first prescribed under this subsection become final) that it is terminating its private foundation status, and

(iii) such organization establishes to the satisfaction of the Secretary (in such manner as the Secretary may by regulations prescribe) immediately after the expiration of such 12-month or 60-month period that such organization has complied with clause (i).

If an organization gives notice under subparagraph (B)(ii) of the commencement of a 60-month period and such organization fails to meet the requirements of paragraph (1), (2), or (3) of section 509(a) for the entire 60-month period, this part and chapter 42 shall not apply to such organization for any taxable year within such 60-month period for which it does meet such requirements.

(2) Transferee foundations. For purposes of this part, in the case of a transfer of assets of any private foundation to another private foundation pursuant to any liquidation, merger, redemption, recapitalization, or other adjustment, organization, or reorganization, the transferee foundation shall not be treated as a newly created organization.

(c) Imposition of tax.

There is hereby imposed on each organization which is referred to in subsection (a) a tax equal to the lower of—

(1) the amount which the private foundation substantiates by adequate records or other corroborating evidence as the aggregate tax benefit resulting from the section 501(c)(3) status of such foundation, or

(2) the value of the net assets of such foundation.

(d) Aggregate tax benefit.

(1) In general. For purposes of subsection (c), the aggregate tax benefit resulting from the section 501(c)(3) status of any private foundation is the sum of—

(A) the aggregate increases in tax under chapters 1, 11, and 12 (or the corresponding provisions of prior law) which would have been imposed with respect to all substantial contributors to the foundation if deductions for all contributions made by such contributors to the foundation after February 28, 1913, had been disallowed, and

(B) the aggregate increases in tax under chapter 1 (or the corresponding provisions of prior law) which would have been imposed with respect to the income of the private foundation for taxable years beginning after December 31, 1912, if (i) it had not been exempt from tax under section 501(a) (or the corresponding provisions of prior law), and (ii) in the case of a trust, deductions under section 642(c) (or the corresponding provisions of prior law) had been limited to 20 percent of the taxable income of the trust (computed without the benefit of section 642(c) but with the benefit of section 170(b)(1)(A)), and

(C) interest on the increases in tax determined under subparagraphs (A) and (B) from the first date on which each such increase would have been due and payable to the date on which the organization ceases to be a private foundation.

(2) Substantial contributor.

(A) Definition. For purposes of paragraph (1), the term "substantial contributor" means any person who contributed or bequeathed an aggregate amount of more than $5,000 to the private foundation, if such amount is more than 2 percent of the total contributions and bequests received by the foundation before the close of the taxable year of the foundation in which the contribution or bequest is received by the foundation from such person. In the case of a trust, the term "substantial contributor" also means the creator of the trust.

(B) Special rules. For purposes of subparagraph (A)—

(i) each contribution or bequest shall be valued at fair market value on the date it was received,

(ii) in the case of a foundation which is in existence on October 9, 1969, all contributions and bequests received on or before such date shall be treated (except for purposes of clause (i)) as if received on such date,

(iii) an individual shall be treated as making all contributions and bequests made by his spouse, and

(iv) any person who is a substantial contributor on any date shall remain a substantial contributor for all subsequent periods.

(C) Person ceases to be substantial contributor in certain cases.

(i) In general. A person shall cease to be treated as a substantial contributor with respect to any private foundation as of the close of any taxable year of such foundation if—

(I) during the 10-year period ending at the close of such taxable year such person (and all related persons) have not made any contribution to such private foundation,

(II) at no time during such 10-year period was such person (or any related person) a foundation manager of such private foundation, and

(III) the aggregate contributions made by such person (and related persons) are determined by the Secretary to be insignificant when compared to the aggregate amount of contributions to such foundation by one other person.

For purposes of subclause (III), appreciation on contributions while held by the foundation shall be taken into account.

(ii) Related person. For purposes of clause (i), the term "related person" means, with respect to any person, any other person who would be a disqualified person (within the meaning of section 4946) by reason of his relationship to such person. In the case of a contributor which is a corporation, the term also includes any officer or director of such corporation.

(3) Regulations. For purposes of this section, the determination as to whether and to what extent there would have been any increase in tax shall be made in accordance with regulations prescribed by the Secretary.

(e) Value of assets.

For purposes of subsection (c), the value of the net assets shall be determined at whichever time such value is higher: (1) the first day on which action is taken by the organization which culminates in its ceasing to be a private foundation, or (2) the date on which it ceases to be a private foundation.

(f) Liability in case of transfers of assets from private foundation.

For purposes of determining liability for the tax imposed by subsection (c) in the case of assets transferred by the private foundation, such tax shall be deemed to have been imposed on the first day on which action is taken by the organization which culminates in its ceasing to be a private foundation.

(g) Abatement of taxes.

The Secretary may abate the unpaid portion of the assessment of any tax imposed by subsection (c), or any liability in respect thereof, if—

(1) the private foundation distributes all of its net assets to one or more organizations described in section 170(b)(1)(A) (other than in clauses (vii) and (viii)) each of which has been in existence and so described for a continuous period of at least 60 calendar months, or

(2) following the notification prescribed in section 6104(c) to the appropriate State officer, such State officer within one year notifies the Secretary, in such manner as the Secretary may by regulations prescribe, that corrective action has been initiated pursuant to State law to insure that the assets of such private foundation are preserved for such charitable or other purposes specified in section 501(c)(3) as may be ordered or approved by a court of competent jurisdiction, and upon completion of the corrective action, the Secretary receives certification from the appropriate State officer that such action has resulted in such preservation of assets.

In **1984,** P.L. 98-369, Sec. 313(a), added subpara. (d)(2)(C), effective for tax. yrs. begin. after 12/31/84.

In **1977,** P.L. 95-170, Sec. 3, of this Act provides as follows:

"Sec. 3 In determining whether a person is a substantial contributor within the meaning of section 507(d)(2) of the Internal Revenue Code of 1954 for purposes of applying section 4941 of such Code (relating to taxes on self-dealing), contributions made before October 9, 1969, which—

"(1) were made on account of or in lieu of payments required under a lease in effect before such date, and

"(2) were coincident with or by reason of the reduction in the required payments under such lease,

shall not be taken into account. For purposes of applying section 507(d)(2)(B)(iv) of such Code, the preceding sentence shall be treated as having taken effect on January 1, 1970."

In **1976,** P.L. 94-455, Sec. 1906(b)(13)(A), substituted "Secretary" for "Secretary or his delegate" each place it appeared in Code Sec. 507, effective for tax. yrs. begin. after 12/31/76.

In **1969,** P.L. 91-172, Sec. 101(a), added Code Sec. 507, effective 1/1/70.

Sec. 508. Special rules with respect to section 501(c)(3) organizations.

(a) New organizations must notify Secretary that they are applying for recognition of section 501(c)(3) status.

Except as provided in subsection (c), an organization organized after October 9, 1969, shall not be treated as an organization described in section 501(c)(3)—

(1) unless it has given notice to the Secretary, in such manner as the Secretary may by regulations prescribe, that it is applying for recognition of such status, or

(2) for any period before the giving of such notice, if such notice is given after the time prescribed by the Secretary by regulations for giving notice under this subsection.

(b) Presumption that organizations are private foundations.

Except as provided in subsection (c), any organization (including an organization in existence on October 9, 1969) which is described in section 501(c)(3) and which does not notify the Secretary, at such time and in such manner as the Secretary may by regulations prescribe, that it is not a private foundation shall be presumed to be a private foundation.

(c) Exceptions.

(1) **Mandatory exceptions.** Subsections (a) and (b) shall not apply to—

(A) churches, their integrated auxiliaries, and conventions or associations of churches, or

(B) any organization which is not a private foundation (as defined in section 509(a)) and the gross receipts of which in each taxable year are normally not more than $5,000.

(2) **Exceptions by regulations.** The Secretary may by regulations exempt (to the extent and subject to such conditions as may be prescribed in such regulations) from the provisions of subsection (a) or (b) or both—

(A) educational organizations described in section 170(b)(1)(A)(ii), and

(B) any other class of organizations with respect to which the Secretary determines that full compliance with the provisions of subsections (a) and (b) is not necessary to the efficient administration of the provisions of this title relating to private foundations.

(d) Disallowance of certain charitable, etc., deductions.

(1) **Gift or bequest to organizations subject to section 507(c) tax.** No gift or bequest made to an organization upon which the tax provided by section 507(c) has been imposed shall be allowed as a deduction under section 170, 545(b)(2), 642(c), 2055, 2106(a)(2), or 2522, if such gift or bequest is made—

(A) by any person after notification is made under section 507(a), or

(B) by a substantial contributor (as defined in section 507(d)(2)) in his taxable year which includes the first day on which action is taken by such organization which culminates in the imposition of tax under section 507(c) and any subsequent taxable year.

(2) **Gift or bequest to taxable private foundation, section 4947 trust, etc.** No gift or bequest made to an organization shall be allowed as a deduction under section 170, 545(b)(2), 642(c), 2055, 2106(a)(2), or 2522, if such gift or bequest is made—

(A) to a private foundation or a trust described in section 4947 in a taxable year for which it fails to meet the requirements of subsection (e) (determined without regard to subsection (e)(2)), or

(B) to any organization in a period for which it is not treated as an organization described in section 501(c)(3) by reason of subsection (a).

(3) **Exception.** Paragraph (1) shall not apply if the entire amount of the unpaid portion of the tax imposed by section 507(c) is abated by the Secretary under section 507(g).

(e) Governing instruments.

(1) **General rule.** A private foundation shall not be exempt from taxation under section 501(a) unless its governing instrument includes provisions the effects of which are—

(A) to require its income for each taxable year to be distributed at such time and in such manner as not to subject the foundation to tax under section 4942, and

(B) to prohibit the foundation from engaging in any act of self-dealing (as defined in section 4941(d)), from retaining any excess business holdings (as defined in section 4943(c)), from making any investments in such manner as to subject the foundation to tax under section 4944, and from making any taxable expenditures (as defined in section 4945(d)).

(2) **Special rules for existing private foundations.** In the case of any organization organized before January 1, 1970, paragraph (1) shall not apply—

(A) to any period after December 31, 1971, during the pendency of any judicial proceeding begun before January 1, 1972, by the private foundation which is necessary to reform, or to excuse such foundation from compliance with, its governing instrument or any other instrument in order to meet the requirements of paragraph (1), and

(B) to any period after the termination of any judicial proceeding described in subparagraph (A) during which its governing instrument or any other instrument does not permit it to meet the requirements of paragraph (1).

(f) Additional provisions relating to sponsoring organizations.

A sponsoring organization (as defined in section 4966(d)(1)) shall give notice to the Secretary (in such manner as the Secretary may provide) whether such organization maintains or intends to maintain donor advised funds (as defined in section 4966(d)(2)) and the manner in which such organization plans to operate such funds.

In 2006, P.L. 109-280, Sec. 1235(b)(1), added subsec. (f), effective for organizations applying for tax-exempt status after 8/17/2006.

In 2004, P.L. 108-357, Sec. 413(c)(30), deleted "556(b)(2)" each place it appeared in subsec. (d), effective for tax. yrs. of foreign corporations begin. after 12/31/2004, and for tax. yrs. of United States shareholders with or within which such tax. yrs. of foreign corporations end.

In 1976, P.L. 94-455, Sec. 1901(a)(71)(A), deleted the last sentence of subsecs. (a) and (b) . . . Sec. 1901(a)(71)(B), substituted "(e)(2)" for "(e)(2)(B) and (C)" in subpara. (d)(2)(A) . . . Sec. 1901(a)(71)(C), deleted subpara. (e)(2)(A), and redesignated subparas. (e)(2)(B) and (e)(2)(C) as (e)(2)(A) and (e)(2)(B), and substituted "(A)" for "(B)" in subpara. (e)(2)(B), as redesignated, effective for tax. yrs. begin. after 12/31/76.

Prior to deletion, the last sentence of subsec. (a) read as follows:
"For purposes of paragraph (2), the time prescribed for giving notice under this subsection shall not expire before the 90th day after the day on which regulations first prescribed under this subsection become final."

Prior to deletion, the last sentence of subsec. (b) read as follows:
"The time prescribed for giving notice under this subsection shall not expire before the 90th day after the day on which regulations first prescribed under this subsection become final."

Prior to deletion, subpara. (e)(2)(A) read as follows:
"(A) to any taxable year beginning before January 1, 1972."

—P.L. 94-455, Sec. 1901(b)(8)(E), amended subpara. (c)(2)(A), effective for tax. yrs. begin. after 12/31/76.

Prior to amendment, subpara. (c)(2)(A) read as follows:
"(A) educational organizations which normally maintain a regular faculty and curriculum and normally have a regularly enrolled body of pupils or students in attendance at the place where their educational activities are regularly carried on; and"

—P.L. 94-455, Sec. 1906(b)(13)(A), substituted "Secretary" for "Secretary or his delegate" each place it appeared in Code Sec. 508, effective for tax. yrs. begin. after 12/31/76.

In 1969, P.L. 91-172, Sec. 101(a), added Code Sec. 508; subsecs. (a), (b), and (c), effective on 10/9/69; subsecs. (d) and (e), effective 1/1/70; Sec. 101(l)(6) provides that: subsec. (e) shall not apply to require inclusion in governing instruments of any provisions inconsistent with this subsec.

Sec. 509. Private foundation defined.

(a) General rule.

For purposes of this title, the term "private foundation" means a domestic or foreign organization described in section 501(c)(3) other than—

(1) an organization described in section 170(b)(1)(A) (other than in clauses (vii) and (viii));

(2) an organization which—

(A) normally receives more than one-third of its support in each taxable year from any combination of—

(i) gifts, grants, contributions, or membership fees, and

(ii) gross receipts from admissions, sales of merchandise, performance of services, or furnishing of facilities, in an activity which is not an unrelated trade or business (within the meaning of section 513), not including such receipts from any person, or from any bureau or similar agency of a governmental unit (as described in section 170(c)(1)), in any taxable year to the extent such receipts exceed the greater of $5,000 or 1 percent of the organization's support in such taxable year,

from persons other than disqualified persons (as defined in section 4946) with respect to the organization, from governmental units described in section 170(c)(1), or from organizations described in section 170(b)(1)(A) (other than in clauses (vii) and (viii)), and

(B) normally receives not more than one-third of its support in each taxable year from the sum of—

(i) gross investment income (as defined in subsection (e)) and

(ii) the excess (if any) of the amount of the unrelated business taxable income (as defined in section 512) over the amount of the tax imposed by section 511;

(3) an organization which—

(A) is organized, and at all times thereafter is operated, exclusively for the benefit of, to perform the functions of, or to carry out the purposes of one or more specified organizations described in paragraph (1) or (2),

(B) is—

(i) operated, supervised, or controlled by one or more organizations described in paragraph (1) or (2),

(ii) supervised or controlled in connection with one or more such organizations, or

(iii) operated in connection with one or more such organizations, and

(C) is not controlled directly or indirectly by one or more disqualified persons (as defined in section 4946) other than foundation managers and other than one or more organizations described in paragraph (1) or (2); and

(4) an organization which is organized and operated exclusively for testing for public safety.

For purposes of paragraph (3), an organization described in paragraph (2) shall be deemed to include an organization described in section 501(c)(4), (5), or (6) which would be described in paragraph (2) if it were an organization described in section 501(c)(3).

(b) Continuation of private foundation status.

For purposes of this title, if an organization is a private foundation (within the meaning of subsection (a)) on October 9, 1969, or becomes a private foundation on any subsequent date, such organization shall be treated as a private foundation for all periods after October 9, 1969, or after such subsequent date, unless its status as such is terminated under section 507.

(c) Status of organization after termination of private foundation status.

For purposes of this part, an organization the status of which as a private foundation is terminated under section 507 shall (except as provided in section 507(b)(2)) be treated as an organization created on the day after the date of such termination.

(d) Definition of support.

For purposes of this part and chapter 42, the term "support" includes (but is not limited to)—

(1) gifts, grants, contributions, or membership fees,

(2) gross receipts from admissions, sales of merchandise, performance of services, or furnishing of facilities in any activity which is not an unrelated trade or business (within the meaning of section 513),

(3) net income from unrelated business activities, whether or not such activities are carried on regularly as a trade or business,

(4) gross investment income (as defined in subsection (e)),

(5) tax revenues levied for the benefit of an organization and either paid to or expended on behalf of such organization, and

(6) the value of services or facilities (exclusive of services or facilities generally furnished to the public without charge) furnished by a governmental unit referred to in section 170(c)(1) to an organization without charge.

Such term does not include any gain from the sale or other disposition of property which would be considered as gain from the sale or exchange of a capital asset, or the value of exemption from any Federal, State, or local tax or any similar benefit.

(e) Definition of gross investment income.

For purposes of subsection (d), the term "gross investment income" means the gross amount of income from interest, dividends, payments with respect to securities loans (as defined in section 512(a)(5)), rents, and royalties, but not including any such income to the extent included in computing the tax imposed by section 511. Such term shall also include income from sources similar to those in the preceding sentence.

(f) Requirements for supporting organizations.

(1) Type III supporting organizations. For purposes of subsection (a)(3)(B)(iii), an organization shall not be considered to be operated in connection with any organization described in paragraph (1) or (2) of subsection (a) unless such organization meets the following requirements:

(A) Responsiveness. For each taxable year beginning after the date of the enactment of this subsection, the organization provides to each supported organization such information as the Secretary may require to ensure that such organization is responsive to the needs or demands of the supported organization.

(B) Foreign supported organizations.

(i) In general. The organization is not operated in connection with any supported organization that is not organized in the United States.

(ii) Transition rule for existing organizations. If the organization is operated in connection with an organization that is not organized in the United States on the date of the enactment of this subsection, clause (i) shall not apply until the first day of the third taxable year of the organization beginning after the date of the enactment of this subsection.

(2) Organizations controlled by donors.

(A) In general. For purposes of subsection (a)(3)(B), an organization shall not be considered to be—

(i) operated, supervised, or controlled by any organization described in paragraph (1) or (2) of subsection (a), or

(ii) operated in connection with any organization described in paragraph (1) or (2) of subsection (a),

if such organization accepts any gift or contribution from any person described in subparagraph (B).

(B) Person described. A person is described in this subparagraph if, with respect to a supported organization of an organization described in subparagraph (A), such person is—

(i) a person (other than an organization described in paragraph (1), (2) or (4) of section 509(a)) who directly or indirectly controls, either alone or together with persons described in clauses (ii) and (iii), the governing body of such supported organization,

(ii) a member of the family (determined under section 4958(f)(4)) of an individual described in clause (i), or

(iii) a 35-percent controlled entity (as defined in section 4958(f)(3) by substituting "persons described in clause (i) or (ii) of section 509(f)(2)(B)" for "persons described in subparagraph (A) or (B) of paragraph (1)" in subparagraph (A)(i) thereof).

(3) Supported organization. For purposes of this subsection, the term "supported organization" means, with respect to an organization described in subsection (a)(3), an organization described in paragraph (1) or (2) of subsection (a)—

(A) for whose benefit the organization described in subsection (a)(3) is organized and operated, or

(B) with respect to which the organization performs the functions of, or carries out the purposes of.

In 2006, P.L. 109-280, Sec. 811, of this Act [relating to Sec. 901 of P.L. 107-16, see below], provides:

"SEC. 811. PENSIONS AND INDIVIDUAL RETIREMENT ARRANGEMENT PROVISIONS OF ECONOMIC GROWTH AND TAX RELIEF RECONCILIATION ACT OF 2001 MADE PERMANENT.

"Title IX of the Economic Growth and Tax Relief Reconciliation Act of 2001 shall not apply to the provisions of, and amendments made by, subtitles A through F of title VI of such Act (relating to pension and individual retirement arrangement provisions)."

—P.L. 109-280, Sec. 1221(a)(2), added "Such term shall also include income from sources similar to those in the preceding sentence." at the end of subsec. (e), effective for tax. yrs. begin. after 8/17/2006.

—P.L. 109-280, Sec. 1226, of this Act, provides:

"SEC. 1226. STUDY ON DONOR ADVISED FUNDS AND SUPPORTING ORGANIZATIONS.

"(a) Study. The Secretary of the Treasury shall undertake a study on the organization and operation of donor advised funds (as defined in section 4966(d)(2) of the Internal Revenue Code of 1986, as added by this Act) and of organizations described in section 509(a)(3) of such Code. The study shall specifically consider—

"(1) whether the deductions allowed for the income, gift, or estate taxes for charitable contributions to sponsoring organizations (as defined in section 4966(d)(1) of such Code, as added by this Act) of donor advised funds or to organizations described in section 509(a)(3) of such Code are appropriate in consideration of—

"(A) the use of contributed assets (including the type, extent, and timing of such use), or

"(B) the use of the assets of such organizations for the benefit of the person making the charitable contribution (or a person related to such person),

"(2) whether donor advised funds should be required to distribute for charitable purposes a specified amount (whether based on the income or assets of the fund) in order to ensure that the sponsoring organization with respect to such donor advised fund is operating consistent with the purposes or functions constituting the basis for its exemption under section 501, or its status as an organization described in section 509(a), of such Code,

"(3) whether the retention by donors to organizations described in paragraph (1) of rights or privileges with respect to amounts transferred to such organizations (including advisory rights or privileges with respect to the making of grants or the investment of assets) is consistent with the treatment of such transfers as completed gifts that qualify for a deduction for income, gift, or estate taxes, and

"(4) whether the issues raised by paragraphs (1), (2), and (3) are also issues with respect to other forms of charities or charitable donations.

"(b) Report. Not later than 1 year after the date of the enactment of this Act, the Secretary of the Treasury shall submit to the Committee on Finance of the Senate and the Committee on Ways and Means of the House of Representatives a report on the study conducted under subsection (a) and make such recommendations as the Secretary of the Treasury considers appropriate."

—P.L. 109-280, Sec. 1241(a), amended subpara, (a)(3)(B)... Sec. 1241(b), added subsec. (f), effective 8/17/2006. Sec. 1241(e)(2) of this Act provides:

"(2) CHARITABLE TRUSTS WHICH ARE TYPE III SUPPORTING ORGANIZATIONS. Subsection (c) shall take effect—

"(A) in the case of trusts operated in connection with an organization described in paragraph (1) or (2) of section 509(a) of the Internal Revenue Code of 1986 on

Exempt organizations   Code Sec. 511

the date of the enactment of this Act, on the date that is one year after the date of the enactment of this Act, and

"(B) in the case of any other trust, on the date of the enactment of this Act."

—P.L. 109-280, Sec. 1241(c), and (d) of this Act provides:

"(c) Charitable trusts which are type iii supporting organizations. For purposes of section 509(a)(3)(B)(iii) of the Internal Revenue Code of 1986, an organization which is a trust shall not be considered to be operated in connection with any organization described in paragraph (1) or (2) of section 509(a) of such Code solely because—

"(1) it is a charitable trust under State law,

"(2) the supported organization (as defined in section 509(f)(3) of such Code) is a beneficiary of such trust, and

"(3) the supported organization (as so defined) has the power to enforce the trust and compel an accounting."

—P.L. 109-280, Sec. 1241(d), of this Act provides:

"(d) Payout requirements for type III supporting organizations.

"(1) In general. The Secretary of the Treasury shall promulgate new regulations under section 509 of the Internal Revenue Code of 1986 on payments required by type III supporting organizations which are not functionally integrated type III supporting organizations. Such regulations shall require such organizations to make distributions of a percentage of either income or assets to supported organizations (as defined in section 509(f)(3) of such Code) in order to ensure that a significant amount is paid to such organizations.

"(2) Type III supporting organization; functionally integrated type iii supporting organization. For purposes of paragraph (1), the terms 'type III supporting organization' and 'functionally integrated type III supporting organization' have the meanings given such terms under subparagraphs (A) and (B) of section 4943(f)(5) of the Internal Revenue Code of 1986 (as added by this Act), respectively."

Prior to amendment, subpara. (a)(3)(B) read as follows:

"(B) is operated, supervised, or controlled by or in connection with one or more organizations described in paragraph (1) or, and"

In **1978**, P.L. 95-345, Sec. 2(a)(1), added "payments with respect to securities loans (as defined in section 512(a)(5))," after "dividends," in subsec. (e), effective for amounts received after 12/31/76 as payments with respect to securities loans (as defined in Code Sec. 512(a)(5)).

In **1975**, P.L. 94-81, Sec. 3(a), amended subpara. (a)(2)(B), effective for unrelated business taxable income derived from trades and businesses which are acquired by the organization after 6/30/75.

Prior to amendment, subpara. (a)(2)(B) read as follows:

"(B) normally receives not more than one-third of its support in each taxable year from gross investment income (as defined in subsection (e));"

In **1969**, P.L. 91-172, Sec. 101(a), added Code Sec. 509, effective 1/1/70. Sec. 101(l)(7) of this Act provides:

"(7) Section 509(a).— In the case of any trust created under the terms of a will or a codicil to a will executed on or before March 30, 1924, by which the testator bequeathed all of the outstanding common stock of a corporation in trust, the income of which trust is to be used principally for the benefit of those from time to time employed by the corporation and their families, the trustees of which trust are elected or selected from among the employees of such corporation, and which trust does not own directly any stock in any other corporation, if the trust makes an irrevocable election under this paragraph within one year after the date of the enactment of this Act, such trust shall be treated as not being a private foundation for purposes of the Internal Revenue Code of 1954 but shall be treated for purposes of such Code as if it were not exempt from tax under section 501(a) for any taxable year beginning after the date of the enactment of this Act and before the date (if any) on which such trust has complied with the requirements of section 507 for termination of the status of an organization as a private foundation."

PART III.— TAXATION OF BUSINESS INCOME OF CERTAIN EXEMPT ORGANIZATIONS

Sec.

511. Imposition of tax on unrelated business income of charitable, etc., organizations.

512. Unrelated business taxable income.

513. Unrelated trade or business.

514. Unrelated debt-financed income.

515. Taxes of foreign countries and possessions of the United States.

In **1969**, P.L. 91-172, Sec. 101(a), redesignated Part II as Part III.

—P.L. 91-172, Sec. 121(d)(3)(C), amended item 514 which previously read "Business leases."

Sec. 511. Imposition of tax on unrelated business income of charitable, etc., organizations.

(a) Charitable, etc., organizations taxable at corporation rates.

(1) Imposition of tax. There is hereby imposed for each taxable year on the unrelated business taxable income (as defined in section 512) of every organization described in paragraph (2) a tax computed as provided in section 11. In making such computation for purposes of this section, the term "taxable income" as used in section 11 shall be read as "unrelated business taxable income".

(2) Organizations subject to tax.

(A) Organizations described in sections 401(a) and 501(c). The tax imposed by paragraph (1) shall apply in the case of any organization (other than a trust described in subsection (b) or an organization described in section 501(c)(1)) which is exempt, except as provided in this part or part II (relating to private foundations), from taxation under this subtitle by reason of section 501(a).

(B) State colleges and universities. The tax imposed by paragraph (1) shall apply in the case of any college or university which is an agency or instrumentality of any government or any political subdivision thereof, or which is owned or operated by a government or any political subdivision thereof, or by any agency or instrumentality of one or more governments or political subdivisions. Such tax shall also apply in the case of any corporation wholly owned by one or more such colleges or universities.

(b) Tax on charitable, etc., trusts.

(1) Imposition of tax. There is hereby imposed for each taxable year on the unrelated business taxable income of every trust described in paragraph (2) a tax computed as provided in section 1(e). In making such computation for purposes of this section, the term "taxable income" as used in section 1 shall be read as "unrelated business taxable income" as defined in section 512.

(2) Charitable, etc., trusts subject to tax. The tax imposed by paragraph (1) shall apply in the case of any trust which is exempt, except as provided in this part or part II (relating to private foundations), from taxation under this subtitle by reason of section 501(a) and which, if it were not for such exemption, would be subject to subchapter J (sec. 641 and following, relating to estates, trusts, beneficiaries, and decedents).

(c) Special rule for section 501(c)(2) corporations.

If a corporation described in section 501(c)(2)—

(1) pays any amount of its net income for a taxable year to an organization exempt from taxation under section 501(a) (or which would pay such an amount but for the fact that the expenses of collecting its income exceed its income), and

(2) such corporation and such organization file a consolidated return for the taxable year,

such corporation shall be treated, for purposes of the tax imposed by subsection (a), as being organized and operated for the same purposes as such organization, in addition to the purposes described in section 501(c)(2).

In **1988**, P.L. 100-647, Sec. 1007(g)(6), repealed subsec. (d), effective for tax. yrs. begin after 12/31/86.

Prior to deletion, subsec. (d) read as follows:

"(d) Tax preferences.

"(1) Organizations taxable at corporate rates. If an organization is subject to tax on unrelated business taxable income pursuant to subsection (a), the tax imposed by section 56 shall apply to such organizations with respect to items of tax preference which enter into the computation of unrelated business taxable income in the same manner as section 56 applies to corporations.

"(2) Organizations taxable as trusts. If an organization is subject to tax on unrelated business taxable income pursuant to subsection (b), the taxes imposed by section 55 shall apply to such organization with respect to items of tax preference which enter into the computation of unrelated business taxable income."

In **1983**, P.L. 97-448, Sec. 306(a)(1)(A)(i), redesignated the second Sec. 201(c) of P.L. 97-248 as Sec. 201(d) of P.L. 97-248, see below.

In **1982**, P.L. 97-248, Sec. 201(d)(5), deleted "and section 56 (as the case may be)" after "section 55" in para. (d)(2), effective for tax. yrs. begin. after 12/31/82.

In 1978, P.L. 95-600, Sec. 301(b)(5)(A), substituted "a tax" for "a normal tax and a surtax" in para. (a)(1)... Sec. 301(b)(5)(B), substituted "tax" for "taxes" each place it appeared in para. (a)(2), effective for tax. yrs. begin. after 12/31/78.
—P.L. 95-600, Sec. 421(e)(3), amended subsec. (d), effective for tax. yrs. begin. after 12/31/78.
Prior to amendment, subsec. (d) read as follows:
"(d) Tax preferences.
"The tax imposed by section 56 shall apply to an organization subject to tax under this section with respect to items of tax preference which enter into the computation of unrelated business taxable income."
In 1977, P.L. 95-30, Sec. 101(d)(6), substituted "section 1(e)" for "section 1(d)" in para. (b)(1), effective for tax. yrs. begin. after 12/31/76.
In 1969, P.L. 91-172, Sec. 121(a)(1), amended subpara. (a)(2)(A)... Sec. 121(a)(2), amend para. (b)(2)... Sec. 121(a)(3), amended subsec. (c), effective for tax. yrs. begin. after 12/31/69.
Prior to amendment subsec. (a)(2)(A) read as follows:
"(A) Organizations described in section 501(c)(2), (3), (5), (6), (14)(B) or (C), and (17), and section 401(a). The taxes imposed by paragraph (1) shall apply in the case of any organization (other than a church, a convention or association of churches, or a trust described in subsec. (b)) which is exempt, except as provided in this part, from taxation under this subtitle by reason of section 401(a) or of paragraph (3), (5), (6), 14(B) or (C), or (17), of section 501(c). Such taxes shall also apply in the case of a corporation described in section 501(c)(2) if the income is payable to an organization which itself is subject to the taxes imposed by paragraph (1) or to a church or to a convention or association of churches."
Prior to amendment subsec. (b)(2) read as follows:
"(2) Charitable, etc., trusts subject to tax. The tax imposed by paragraph (1) shall apply in the case of any trust which is exempt, except as provided in this part, from taxation under this subtitle by reason of section 501(c)(3) or (17) or section 401(a) and which, if it were not for such exemption, would be subject to subchapter J (sec. 641 and following, relating to estates, trusts, beneficiaries, and decedents)."
Prior to amendment subsec. (c) read as follows:
"(c) Effective date.
"The tax imposed by this section shall apply, in the case of a trust described in section 401(a), only for taxable years beginning after June 30, 1954."
—P.L. 91-172, Sec. 301(b)(8), added subsec. (d), effective for tax. yrs. end. after 12/31/69.
—P.L. 91-172, Sec. 803(d)(2), substituted "section 1(d)" for "section 1" in the first sentence of subsec. (b)(1), effective for tax. yrs. begin. after 12/31/70.
In 1966, P.L. 89-352, Sec. 2, added "(14)(B) or (C)," after "(6)" in the heading and text of subpara. (a)(2)(A), effective for tax. yrs. begin. after 2/2/66.
In 1960, P.L. 86-667, Sec. 3, included organizations described in section 501(c)(17) within subsec. (a)(2)(A); added a reference to section 501(c)(17) in subsec. (b), effective for tax. yrs. begin. after 12/31/59.

Sec. 512. Unrelated business taxable income.
(a) Definition.

For purposes of this title—

(1) General rule. Except as otherwise provided in this subsection, the term "unrelated business taxable income" means the gross income derived by any organization from any unrelated trade or business (as defined in section 513) regularly carried on by it, less the deductions allowed by this chapter which are directly connected with the carrying on of such trade or business, both computed with the modifications provided in subsection (b).

(2) Special rule for foreign organizations. In the case of an organization described in section 511 which is a foreign organization, the unrelated business taxable income shall be—

(A) its unrelated business taxable income which is derived from sources within the United States and which is not effectively connected with the conduct of a trade or business within the United States, plus

(B) its unrelated business taxable income which is effectively connected with the conduct of a trade or business within the United States.

(3) Special rules applicable to organizations described in paragraph (7), (9), (17), or (20) of section 501(c).

(A) General rule. In the case of an organization described in paragraph (7), (9), (17), or (20) of section 501(c), the term "unrelated business taxable income" means the gross income (excluding any exempt function income), less the deductions allowed by this chapter which are directly connected with the production of the gross income (excluding exempt function income), both computed with the modifications provided in paragraphs (6), (10), (11), and (12) of subsection (b). For purposes of the preceding sentence, the deductions provided by sections 243, 244, and 245 (relating to dividends received by corporations) shall be treated as not directly connected with the production of gross income.

(B) Exempt function income. For purposes of subparagraph (A), the term "exempt function income" means the gross income from dues, fees, charges, or similar amounts paid by members of the organization as consideration for providing such members or their dependents or guests goods, facilities, or services in furtherance of the purposes constituting the basis for the exemption of the organization to which such income is paid. Such term also means all income (other than an amount equal to the gross income derived from any unrelated trade or business regularly carried on by such organization computed as if the organization were subject to paragraph (1)), which is set aside—

(i) for a purpose specified in section 170(c)(4), or

(ii) in the case of an organization described in paragraph (9), (17), or (20) of section 501(c), to provide for the payment of life, sick, accident, or other benefits,

including reasonable costs of administration directly connected with a purpose described in clause (i) or (ii). If during the taxable year, an amount which is attributable to income so set aside is used for a purpose other than that described in clause (i) or (ii), such amount shall be included, under subparagraph (A), in unrelated business taxable income for the taxable year.

(C) Applicability to certain corporations described in section 501(c)(2). In the case of a corporation described in section 501(c)(2), the income of which is payable to an organization described in paragraph (7), (9), (17), or (20) of section 501(c), subparagraph (A) shall apply as if such corporation were the organization to which the income is payable. For purposes of the preceding sentence, such corporation shall be treated as having exempt function income for a taxable year only if it files a consolidated return with such organization for such year.

(D) Nonrecognition of gain. If property used directly in the performance of the exempt function of an organization described in paragraph (7), (9), (17), or (20) of section 501(c) is sold by such organization, and within a period beginning 1 year before the date of such sale, and ending 3 years after such date, other property is purchased and used by such organization directly in the performance of its exempt function, gain (if any) from such sale shall be recognized only to the extent that such organization's sales price of the old property exceeds the organization's cost of purchasing the other property. For purposes of this subparagraph, the destruction in whole or in part, theft, seizure, requisition, or condemnation of property, shall be treated as the sale of such property, and rules similar to the rules provided by subsections (b), (c), (e), and (j) of section 1034 (as in effect on the day before the date of the enactment [8/5/97] of the Taxpayer Relief Act of 1997) shall apply.

(E) Limitation on amount of setaside in the case of organizations described in paragraph (9), (17), or (20) of section 501(c).

(i) In general. In the case of any organization described in paragraph (9), (17), or (20) of section 501(c), a set-aside for any purpose specified in clause

(ii) of subparagraph (B) may be taken into account under subparagraph (B) only to the extent that such set-aside does not result in an amount of assets set aside for such purpose in excess of the account limit determined under section 419A (without regard to subsection (f)(6) thereof) for the taxable year (not taking into account any reserve described in section 419A(c)(2)(A) for post-retirement medical benefits).

(ii) Treatment of existing reserves for post-retirement medical or life insurance benefits.

(I) Clause (i) shall not apply to any income attributable to an existing reserve for post-retirement medical or life insurance benefits.

(II) For purposes of subclause (I), the term "reserve for post-retirement medical or life insurance benefits" means the greater of the amount of assets set aside for purposes of post-retirement medical or life insurance benefits to be provided to covered employees as of the close of the last plan year ending before the date of the enactment [7/18/84] of the Tax Reform Act of 1984 or on July 18, 1984.

(III) All payments during plan years ending on or after the date of the enactment [7/18/84] of the Tax Reform Act of 1984 of post-retirement medical benefits or life insurance benefits shall be charged against the reserve referred to in subclause (II). Except to the extent provided in regulations prescribed by the Secretary, all plans of an employer shall be treated as 1 plan for purposes of the preceding sentence.

(iii) Treatment of tax exempt organizations. This subparagraph shall not apply to any organization if substantially all of the contributions to such organization are made by employers who were exempt from tax under this chapter throughout the 5-taxable year period ending with the taxable year in which the contributions are made.

(4) Special rule applicable to organizations described in section 501(c)(19). In the case of an organization described in section 501(c)(19), the term "unrelated business taxable income" does not include any amount attributable to payments for life, sick, accident, or health insurance with respect to members of such organizations or their dependents which is set aside for the purpose of providing for the payment of insurance benefits or for a purpose specified in section 170(c)(4). If an amount set aside under the preceding sentence is used during the taxable year for a purpose other than a purpose described in the preceding sentence, such amount shall be included, under paragraph (1), in unrelated business taxable income for the taxable year.

(5) Definition of payments with respect to securities loans.

(A) The term "payments with respect to securities loans" includes all amounts received in respect of a security (as defined in section 1236(c)) transferred by the owner to another person in a transaction to which section 1058 applies (whether or not title to the security remains in the name of the lender) including—

(i) amounts in respect of dividends, interest, or other distributions,

(ii) fees computed by reference to the period beginning with the transfer of securities by the owner and ending with the transfer of identical securities back to the transferor by the transferee and the fair market value of the security during such period,

(iii) income from collateral security for such loan, and

(iv) income from the investment of collateral security.

(B) Subparagraph (A) shall apply only with respect to securities transferred pursuant to an agreement between the transferor and the transferee which provides for—

(i) reasonable procedures to implement the obligation of the transferee to furnish to the transferor, for each business day during such period, collateral with a fair market value not less than the fair market value of the security at the close of business on the preceding business day,

(ii) termination of the loan by the transferor upon notice of not more than 5 business days, and

(iii) return to the transferor of securities identical to the transferred securities upon termination of the loan.

(b) Modifications.

The modifications referred to in subsection (a) are the following:

(1) There shall be excluded all dividends, interest, payments with respect to securities loans (as defined in subsection (a)(5)), amounts received or accrued as consideration for entering into agreements to make loans, and annuities, and all deductions directly connected with such income.

(2) There shall be excluded all royalties (including overriding royalties) whether measured by production or by gross or taxable income from the property, and all deductions directly connected with such income.

(3) In the case of rents—

(A) Except as provided in subparagraph (B), there shall be excluded—

(i) all rents from real property (including property described in section 1245(a)(3)(C)), and

(ii) all rents from personal property (including for purposes of this paragraph as personal property any property described in section 1245(a)(3)(B)) leased with such real property, if the rents attributable to such personal property are an incidental amount of the total rents received or accrued under the lease, determined at the time the personal property is placed in service.

(B) Subparagraph (A) shall not apply—

(i) if more than 50 percent of the total rent received or accrued under the lease is attributable to personal property described in subparagraph (A)(ii), or

(ii) if the determination of the amount of such rent depends in whole or in part on the income or profits derived by any person from the property leased (other than an amount based on a fixed percentage or percentages of receipts or sales).

(C) There shall be excluded all deductions directly connected with rents excluded under subparagraph (A).

(4) Notwithstanding paragraph (1), (2), (3), or (5), in the case of debt-financed property (as defined in section 514) there shall be included, as an item of gross income derived from an unrelated trade or business, the amount ascertained under section 514(a)(1), and there shall be allowed, as a deduction, the amount ascertained under section 514(a)(2).

(5) There shall be excluded all gains or losses from the sale, exchange, or other disposition of property other than—

(A) stock in trade or other property of a kind which would properly be includible in inventory if on hand at the close of the taxable year, or

(B) property held primarily for sale to customers in the ordinary course of the trade or business.

There shall also be excluded all gains or losses recognized, in connection with the organization's investment activities, from the lapse or termination of options to buy or sell securities (as defined in section 1236(c)) or real property and all gains or losses from the forfeiture of good-faith deposits (that are consistent with established business practice) for the purchase, sale, or lease of real property in connection with the organization's investment activities. This paragraph shall not apply with respect to the cutting of timber which is considered, on the application of section 631, as a sale or exchange of such timber.

(6) The net operating loss deduction provided in section 172 shall be allowed, except that—

(A) the net operating loss for any taxable year, the amount of the net operating loss carryback or carryover to any taxable year, and the net operating loss deduction for any taxable year shall be determined under section 172 without taking into account any amount of income or deduction which is excluded under this part in computing the unrelated business taxable income; and

(B) the terms "preceding taxable year" and "preceding taxable years" as used in section 172 shall not include any taxable year for which the organization was not subject to the provisions of this part.

(7) There shall be excluded all income derived from research for (A) the United States, or any of its agencies or instrumentalities, or (B) any State or political subdivision thereof; and there shall be excluded all deductions directly connected with such income.

(8) In the case of a college, university, or hospital, there shall be excluded all income derived from research performed for any person, and all deductions directly connected with such income.

(9) In the case of an organization operated primarily for purposes of carrying on fundamental research the results of which are freely available to the general public, there shall be excluded all income derived from research performed for any person, and all deductions directly connected with such income.

(10) In the case of any organization described in section 511(a), the deduction allowed by section 170 (relating to charitable etc. contributions and gifts) shall be allowed (whether or not directly connected with the carrying on of the trade or business), but shall not exceed 10 percent of the unrelated business taxable income computed without the benefit of this paragraph.

(11) In the case of any trust described in section 511(b), the deduction allowed by section 170 (relating to charitable etc. contributions and gifts) shall be allowed (whether or not directly connected with the carrying on of the trade or business), and for such purpose a distribution made by the trust to a beneficiary described in section 170 shall be considered as a gift or contribution. The deduction allowed by this paragraph shall be allowed with the limitations prescribed in section 170(b)(1)(A) and (B) determined with reference to the unrelated business taxable income computed without the benefit of this paragraph (in lieu of with reference to adjusted gross income).

(12) Except for purposes of computing the net operating loss under section 172 and paragraph (6), there shall be allowed a specific deduction of $1,000. In the case of a diocese, province of a religious order, or a convention or association of churches, there shall also be allowed, with respect to each parish, individual church, district, or other local unit, a specific deduction equal to the lower of—

(A) $1,000, or

(B) the gross income derived from any unrelated trade or business regularly carried on by such local unit.

(13) Special rules for certain amounts received from controlled entities.

(A) In general. If an organization (in this paragraph referred to as the "controlling organization") receives or accrues (directly or indirectly) a specified payment from another entity which it controls (in this paragraph referred to as the "controlled entity"), notwithstanding paragraphs (1), (2), and (3), the controlling organization shall include such payment as an item of gross income derived from an unrelated trade or business to the extent such payment reduces the net unrelated income of the controlled entity (or increases any net unrelated loss of the controlled entity). There shall be allowed all deductions of the controlling organization directly connected with amounts treated as derived from an unrelated trade or business under the preceding sentence.

(B) Net unrelated income or loss. For purposes of this paragraph—

(i) Net unrelated income. The term "net unrelated income" means—

(I) in the case of a controlled entity which is not exempt from tax under section 501(a), the portion of such entity's taxable income which would be unrelated business taxable income if such entity were exempt from tax under section 501(a) and had the same exempt purposes as the controlling organization, or

(II) in the case of a controlled entity which is exempt from tax under section 501(a), the amount of the unrelated business taxable income of the controlled entity.

(ii) Net unrelated loss. the term "net unrelated loss" means the net operating loss adjusted under rules similar to the rules of clause (i).

(C) Specified payment. For purposes of this paragraph, the term "specified payment" means any interest, annuity, royalty, or rent.

(D) Definition of control. For purposes of this paragraph—

(i) Control. The term "control" means—

(I) in the case of a corporation, ownership (by vote or value) of more than 50 percent of the stock in such corporation,

(II) in the case of a partnership, ownership of more than 50 percent of the profits interests or capital interests in such partnership, or

(III) in any other case, ownership of more than 50 percent of the beneficial interests in the entity.

(ii) Constructive ownership. Section 318 (relating to constructive ownership of stock) shall apply for purposes of determining ownership of stock in a corporation. Similar principles shall apply for purposes of determining ownership of interests in any other entity.

(E) Paragraph to apply only to certain excess payments.

(i) In general. Subparagraph (A) shall apply only to the portion of a qualifying specified payment received or accrued by the controlling organization that exceeds the amount which would have been paid or accrued if such payment met the requirements prescribed under section 482.

(ii) Addition to tax for valuation misstatements. The tax imposed by this chapter on the controlling organization shall be increased by an amount equal to 20 percent of the larger of—

(I) such excess determined without regard to any amendment or supplement to a return of tax, or

(II) such excess determined with regard to all such amendments and supplements.

(iii) Qualifying specified payment. The term "qualifying specified payment" means a specified payment which is made pursuant to—

(I) a binding written contract in effect on the date of the enactment of this subparagraph, or

(II) a contract which is a renewal, under substantially similar terms, of a contract described in subclause (I).

(iv) Termination. This subparagraph shall not apply to payments received or accrued after December 31, 2011.

(F) Related persons. The Secretary shall prescribe such rules as may be necessary or appropriate to prevent avoidance of the purposes of this paragraph through the use of related persons.

(14) Repealed.

(15) Except as provided in paragraph (4), in the case of a trade or business—

(A) which consists of providing services under license issued by a Federal regulatory agency,

(B) which is carried on by a religious order or by an educational organization described in section 170(b)(1)(A)(ii) maintained by such religious order, and which was so carried on before May 27, 1959, and

(C) less than 10 percent of the net income of which for each taxable year is used for activities which are not related to the purpose constituting the basis for the religious order's exemption,

there shall be excluded all gross income derived from such trade or business and all deductions directly connected with the carrying on of such trade or business, so long as it is established to the satisfaction of the Secretary that the rates or other charges for such services are competitive with rates or other charges charged for similar services by persons not exempt from taxation.

(16)(A) Notwithstanding paragraph (5)(B), there shall be excluded all gains or losses from the sale, exchange, or other disposition of any real property described in subparagraph (B) if—

(i) such property was acquired by the organization from—

(I) a financial institution described in section 581 or 591(a) which is in conservatorship or receivership, or

(II) the conservator or receiver of such an institution (or any government agency or corporation succeeding to the rights or interests of the conservator or receiver),

(ii) such property is designated by the organization within the 9-month period beginning on the date of its acquisition as property held for sale, except that not more than one-half (by value determined as of such date) of property acquired in a single transaction may be so designated,

(iii) such sale, exchange, or disposition occurs before the later of—

(I) the date which is 30 months after the date of the acquisition of such property, or

(II) the date specified by the Secretary in order to assure an orderly disposition of property held by persons described in subparagraph (A), and

(iv) while such property was held by the organization, the aggregate expenditures on improvements and development activities included in the basis of the property are (or were) not in excess of 20 percent of the net selling price of such property.

(B) Property is described in this subparagraph if it is real property which—

(i) was held by the financial institution at the time it entered into conservatorship or receivership, or

(ii) was foreclosure property (as defined in section 514(c)(9)(H)(v)) which secured indebtedness held by the financial institution at such time.

For purposes of this subparagraph, real property includes an interest in a mortgage.

(17) Treatment of certain amounts derived from foreign corporations.

(A) In general. Notwithstanding paragraph (1), any amount included in gross income under section 951(a)(1)(A) shall be included as an item of gross income derived from an unrelated trade or business to the extent the amount so included is attributable to insurance income (as defined in section 953) which, if derived directly by the organization, would be treated as gross income from an unrelated trade or business. There shall be allowed all deductions directly connected with amounts included in gross income under the preceding sentence.

(B) Exception.

(i) In general. Subparagraph (A) shall not apply to income attributable to a policy of insurance or reinsurance with respect to which the person (directly or indirectly) insured is—

(I) such organization,

(II) an affiliate of such organization which is exempt from tax under section 501(a), or

(III) a director or officer of, or an individual who (directly or indirectly) performs services for, such organization or affiliate but only if the insurance covers primarily risks associated with the performance of services in connection with such organization or affiliate.

(ii) Affiliate. For purposes of this subparagraph—

(I) In general. The determination as to whether an entity is an affiliate of an organization shall be made under rules similar to the rules of section 168(h)(4)(B).

(II) Special rule. Two or more organizations (and any affiliates of such organizations) shall be treated as affiliates if such organizations are colleges or universities described in section 170(b)(1)(A)(ii) or organizations described in section 170(b)(1)(A)(iii) and participate in an insurance arrangement that provides for any profits from such arrangement to be returned to the policyholders in their capacity as such.

(C) Regulations. The Secretary shall prescribe such regulations as may be necessary or appropriate to carry out the purposes of this paragraph, including regulations for the application of this paragraph in the case of income paid through 1 or more entities or between 2 or more chains of entities.

(18) Treatment of mutual or cooperative electric companies. In the case of a mutual or cooperative electric company described in section 501(c)(12), there shall be excluded income which is treated as member income under subparagraph (H) thereof.

(19) Treatment of gain or loss on sale or exchange of certain brownfield sites.

(A) In general. Notwithstanding paragraph (5)(B), there shall be excluded any gain or loss from the qualified sale, exchange, or other disposition of any qualifying brownfield property by an eligible taxpayer.

(B) Eligible taxpayer. For purposes of this paragraph—

(i) In general. The term "eligible taxpayer" means, with respect to a property, any organization exempt from tax under section 501(a) which—

(I) acquires from an unrelated person a qualifying brownfield property, and

(II) pays or incurs eligible remediation expenditures with respect to such property in an amount which exceeds the greater of $550,000 or 12 percent of the fair market value of the property at the time such property was acquired by the eligible taxpayer, determined as if there was not a presence of a hazardous substance, pollutant, or contaminant on the property which is complicating the expansion, redevelopment, or reuse of the property.

(ii) Exception. Such term shall not include any organization which is—

(I) potentially liable under section 107 of the Comprehensive Environmental Response, Compensation, and Liability Act of 1980 with respect to the qualifying brownfield property,

(II) affiliated with any other person which is so potentially liable through any direct or indirect familial relationship or any contractual, corporate, or financial relationship (other than a contractual, corporate, or financial relationship which is created by the instruments by which title to any qualifying brownfield property is conveyed or financed or by a contract of sale of goods or services), or

(III) the result of a reorganization of a business entity which was so potentially liable.

(C) Qualifying brownfield property. For purposes of this paragraph—

(i) In general. The term "qualifying brownfield property" means any real property which is certified, before the taxpayer incurs any eligible remediation expenditures (other than to obtain a Phase I environmental site assessment), by an appropriate State agency (within the meaning of section 198(c)(4)) in the State in which such property is located as a brownfield site within the meaning of section 101(39) of the Comprehensive Environmental Response, Compensation, and Liability Act of 1980 (as in effect on the date of the enactment of this paragraph).

(ii) Request for certification. Any request by an eligible taxpayer for a certification described in clause (i) shall include a sworn statement by the eligible taxpayer and supporting documentation of the presence of a hazardous substance, pollutant, or contaminant on the property which is complicating the expansion, redevelopment, or reuse of the property given the property's reasonably anticipated future land uses or capacity for uses of the property (including a Phase I environmental site assessment and, if applicable, evidence of the property's presence on a local, State, or Federal list of brownfields or contaminated property) and other environmental assessments prepared or obtained by the taxpayer.

(D) Qualified sale, exchange, or other disposition. For purposes of this paragraph—

(i) In general. A sale, exchange, or other disposition of property shall be considered as qualified if—

(I) such property is transferred by the eligible taxpayer to an unrelated person, and

(II) within 1 year of such transfer the eligible taxpayer has received a certification from the Environmental Protection Agency or an appropriate State agency (within the meaning of section 198(c)(4)) in the State in which such property is located that, as a result of the eligible taxpayer's remediation actions, such property would not be treated as a qualifying brownfield property in the hands of the transferee.

For purposes of subclause (II), before issuing such certification, the Environmental Protection Agency or appropriate State agency shall respond to comments received pursuant to clause (ii)(V) in the same form and manner as required under section 117(b) of the Comprehensive Environmental Response, Compensation, and Liability Act of 1980 (as in effect on the date of the enactment of this paragraph).

(ii) Request for certification. Any request by an eligible taxpayer for a certification described in clause (i) shall be made not later than the date of the transfer and shall include a sworn statement by the eligible taxpayer certifying the following:

(I) Remedial actions which comply with all applicable or relevant and appropriate requirements (consistent with section 121(d) of the Comprehensive Environmental Response, Compensation, and Liability Act of 1980) have been substantially completed, such that there are no hazardous substances, pollutants, or contaminants which complicate the expansion, redevelopment, or reuse of the property given the property's reasonably anticipated future land uses or capacity for uses of the property.

(II) The reasonably anticipated future land uses or capacity for uses of the property are more economically productive or environmentally beneficial than the uses of the property in existence on the date of the certification described in subparagraph (C)(i). For purposes of the preceding sentence, use of property as a landfill or other hazardous waste facility shall not be considered more economically productive or environmentally beneficial.

(III) A remediation plan has been implemented to bring the property into compliance with all applicable local, State, and Federal environmental laws, regulations, and standards and to ensure that the remediation protects human health and the environment.

(IV) The remediation plan described in subclause (III), including any physical improvements required to remediate the property, is either complete or substantially complete, and, if substantially complete, sufficient monitoring, funding, institutional controls, and financial assurances have been put in place to ensure the complete remediation of the property in accordance with the remediation plan as soon as is reasonably practicable after the sale, exchange, or other disposition of such property.

(V) Public notice and the opportunity for comment on the request for certification was completed before the date of such request. Such notice and opportunity for comment shall be in the same form and manner as required for public participation required under section 117(a) of the Comprehensive Environmental Response, Compensation, and Liability Act of 1980 (as in effect on the date of the enactment of this paragraph). For purposes of this subclause, public notice shall include, at a minimum, publication in a major local newspaper of general circulation.

(iii) Attachment to tax returns. A copy of each of the requests for certification described in clause (ii) of subparagraph (C) and this subparagraph shall be included in the tax return of the eligible taxpayer (and, where applicable, of the qualifying partnership) for the taxable year during which the transfer occurs.

(iv) Substantial completion. For purposes of this subparagraph, a remedial action is substantially complete when any necessary physical construction is complete, all immediate threats have been eliminated, and all long-term threats are under control.

(E) Eligible remediation expenditures. For purposes of this paragraph—

(i) In general. The term "eligible remediation expenditures" means, with respect to any qualifying brownfield property, any amount paid or incurred by the eligible taxpayer to an unrelated third person to obtain a Phase I environmental site assessment of the property, and any amount so paid or incurred after the date of the certification described in subparagraph (C)(i) for goods and services necessary to obtain a certification described in subparagraph (D)(i) with respect to such property, including expenditures—

(I) to manage, remove, control, contain, abate, or otherwise remediate a hazardous substance, pollutant, or contaminant on the property,

(II) to obtain a Phase II environmental site assessment of the property, including any expenditure to monitor, sample, study, assess, or otherwise evaluate the release, threat of release, or presence of a hazardous substance, pollutant, or contaminant on the property,

(III) to obtain environmental regulatory certifications and approvals required to manage the remediation and monitoring of the hazardous substance, pollutant, or contaminant on the property, and

(IV) regardless of whether it is necessary to obtain a certification described in subparagraph (D)(i)(II), to obtain remediation cost-cap or stop-loss coverage, re-opener or regulatory action coverage, or similar coverage under environmental insurance policies, or financial guarantees required to manage such remediation and monitoring.

(ii) Exceptions. Such term shall not include—

(I) any portion of the purchase price paid or incurred by the eligible taxpayer to acquire the qualifying brownfield property,

(II) environmental insurance costs paid or incurred to obtain legal defense coverage, owner/operator liability coverage, lender liability coverage, professional liability coverage, or similar types of coverage,

(III) any amount paid or incurred to the extent such amount is reimbursed, funded, or otherwise subsidized by grants provided by the United States, a State, or a political subdivision of a State for use in connection with the property, proceeds of an issue of State or local government obligations used to provide financing for the property the interest of which is exempt from tax under section 103, or subsidized financing provided (directly or indirectly) under a Federal, State, or local program provided in connection with the property, or

(IV) any expenditure paid or incurred before the date of the enactment of this paragraph.

For purposes of subclause (III), the Secretary may issue guidance regarding the treatment of government-provided funds for purposes of determining eligible remediation expenditures.

(F) Determination of gain or loss. For purposes of this paragraph, the determination of gain or loss shall not include an amount treated as gain which is ordinary income with respect to section 1245 or section 1250 property, including amounts deducted as section 198 expenses which are subject to the recapture rules of section 198(e), if the taxpayer had deducted such amounts in the computation of its unrelated business taxable income.

(G) Special rules for partnerships.

(i) In general. In the case of an eligible taxpayer which is a partner of a qualifying partnership which acquires, remediates, and sells, exchanges, or otherwise disposes of a qualifying brownfield property, this paragraph shall apply to the eligible taxpayer's distributive share of the qualifying partnership's gain or loss from the sale, exchange, or other disposition of such property.

(ii) Qualifying partnership. The term "qualifying partnership" means a partnership which—

(I) has a partnership agreement which satisfies the requirements of section 514(c)(9)(B)(vi) at all times beginning on the date of the first certification received by the partnership under subparagraph (C)(i),

(II) satisfies the requirements of subparagraphs (B)(i), (C), (D), and (E), if "qualified partnership" is substituted for "eligible taxpayer" each place it appears therein (except subparagraph (D)(iii)), and

(III) is not an organization which would be prevented from constituting an eligible taxpayer by reason of subparagraph (B)(ii).

(iii) Requirement that tax-exempt partner be a partner since first certification. This paragraph shall apply with respect to any eligible taxpayer which is a partner of a partnership which acquires, remediates, and sells, exchanges, or otherwise disposes of a qualifying brownfield property only if such eligible taxpayer was a partner of the qualifying partnership at all times beginning on the date of the first certification received by the partnership under subparagraph (C)(i) and ending on the date of the sale, exchange, or other disposition of the property by the partnership.

(iv) Regulations. The Secretary shall prescribe such regulations as are necessary to prevent abuse of the requirements of this subparagraph, including abuse through—

(I) the use of special allocations of gains or losses, or

(II) changes in ownership of partnership interests held by eligible taxpayers.

(H) Special rules for multiple properties.

(i) In general. An eligible taxpayer or a qualifying partnership of which the eligible taxpayer is a partner may make a 1-time election to apply this paragraph to more than 1 qualifying brownfield property by averaging the eligible remediation expenditures for all such properties acquired during the election period. If the eligible taxpayer or qualifying partnership makes such an election, the election shall apply to all qualified sales, exchanges, or other dispositions of qualifying brownfield properties the acquisition and transfer of which occur during the period for which the election remains in effect.

(ii) Election. An election under clause (i) shall be made with the eligible taxpayer's or qualifying partnership's timely filed tax return (including extensions) for the first taxable year for which the taxpayer or qualifying partnership intends to have the election apply. An election under clause (i) is effective for the period—

(I) beginning on the date which is the first day of the taxable year of the return in which the election is included or a later day in such taxable year selected by the eligible taxpayer or qualifying partnership, and

(II) ending on the date which is the earliest of a date of revocation selected by the eligible taxpayer or qualifying partnership, the date which is 8 years after the date described in subclause (I), or, in the case of an election by a qualifying partnership of which the eligible taxpayer is a partner, the date of the termination of the qualifying partnership.

(iii) Revocation. An eligible taxpayer or qualifying partnership may revoke an election under clause (i)(II) by filing a statement of revocation with a timely filed tax return (including extensions). A revocation is effective as of the first day of the taxable year of the return in which the revocation is included or a later day in such taxable year selected by the eligible taxpayer or qualifying partnership. Once an eligible taxpayer or qualifying partnership revokes the election, the eligible taxpayer or qualifying partnership is ineligible to make another election under clause (i) with respect to any qualifying brownfield property subject to the revoked election.

(I) Recapture. If an eligible taxpayer excludes gain or loss from a sale, exchange, or other disposition of property to which an election under subparagraph (H) applies, and such property fails to satisfy the requirements of this paragraph, the unrelated business taxable income of the eligible taxpayer for the taxable year in which such failure occurs shall be determined by including any previously excluded gain or loss from such sale, exchange, or other disposition allocable to such taxpayer, and interest shall be determined at the overpayment rate established under section 6621 on any resulting tax for the period beginning with the due date of the return for the taxable year during which such sale, exchange, or other disposition occurred, and ending on the date of payment of the tax.

(J) Related persons. For purposes of this paragraph, a person shall be treated as related to another person if—

(i) such person bears a relationship to such other person described in section 267(b) (determined without regard to paragraph (9) thereof), or section 707(b)(1), determined by substituting "25 percent" for "50 percent" each place it appears therein, and

(ii) in the case such other person is a nonprofit organization, if such person controls directly or indirectly more than 25 percent of the governing body of such organization.

(K) Termination. Except for purposes of determining the average eligible remediation expenditures for properties acquired during the election period under subparagraph (H), this paragraph shall not apply to any property acquired by the eligible taxpayer or qualifying partnership after December 31, 2009.

(c) Special rules for partnerships.

(1) In general. If a trade or business regularly carried on by a partnership of which an organization is a member is an unrelated trade or business with respect to such organization, such organization in computing its unrelated business taxable income shall, subject to the exceptions, additions, and limitations contained in subsection (b), include its share (whether or not distributed) of the gross income of the partnership from such unrelated trade or business and its share of the partnership deductions directly connected with such gross income.

(2) Special rule where partnership year is different from organization's year. If the taxable year of the organization is different from that of the partnership, the amounts to be included or deducted in computing the unrelated business taxable income under paragraph (1) shall be based upon the income and deductions of the partnership for any taxable year of the partnership ending within or with the taxable year of the organization.

(d) Treatment of dues of agricultural or horticultural organizations.

(1) In general. If—

(A) an agricultural or horticultural organization described in section 501(c)(5) requires annual dues to be paid in order to be a member of such organization, and

(B) the amount of such required annual dues does not exceed $100,

in no event shall any portion of such dues be treated as derived by such organization from an unrelated trade or business by reason of any benefits or privileges to which members of such organization are entitled.

(2) Indexation of $100 amount. In the case of any taxable year beginning in a calendar year after 1995, the $100 amount in paragraph (1) shall be increased by an amount equal to—

(A) $100, multiplied by

(B) the cost-of-living adjustment determined under section 1(f)(3) for the calendar year in which the taxable year begins, by substituting "calendar year 1994" for "calendar year 1992" in subparagraph (B) thereof.

(3) Dues. For purposes of this subsection, the term "dues" means any payment (whether or not designated as dues) which is required to be made in order to be recognized by the organization as a member of the organization.

(e) Special rules applicable to S corporations.

(1) In general. If an organization described in section 1361(c)(2)(A)(vi) or 1361(c)(6) holds stock in an S corporation—

(A) such interest shall be treated as an interest in an unrelated trade or business; and

(B) notwithstanding any other provision of this part—

(i) all items of income, loss, or deduction taken into account under section 1366(a), and

(ii) any gain or loss on the disposition of the stock in the S corporation

shall be taken into account in computing the unrelated business taxable income of such organization.

(2) Basis reduction. Except as provided in regulations, for purposes of paragraph (1), the basis of any stock acquired by purchase (as defined in section 1361(e)(1)(C))

Exempt organizations Code Sec. 512

shall be reduced by the amount of any dividends received by the organization with respect to the stock.

(3) Exception for ESOPs. This subsection shall not apply to employer securities (within the meaning of section 409(l)) held by an employee stock ownership plan described in section 4975(e)(7).

In 2010, P.L. 111-312, Sec. 747(a), substituted "December 31, 2011" for "December 31, 2009" in clause (b)(13)(E)(iv), effective for payments received or accrued after 12/31/2009.

In 2008, P.L. 110-343, Sec. 306(a)DivC, substituted "December 31, 2009" for "December 31, 2007" in clause (b)(13)(E)(iv), effective for payments received or accrued after 12/31/2007.

In 2006, P.L. 109-280, Sec. 1205(a), redesignated subpara. (b)(13)(E) as subpara. (b)(13)(F) and added subpara. (b)(13)(E), effective for payments received or accrued after 12/31/2005.

In 2005, P.L. 109-135, Sec. 412(dd), substituted "subsection (a)(5)" for "section 512(a)(5)" in para. (b)(1) . . . Sec. 412(ee)(1), redesignated para. (b)(18) [as added by Sec. 702(a) of P.L. 108-357, see below] as para. (b)(19) . . . Sec. 412(ee)(2), redesignated the text of para. (b)(18) [as added by Sec. 702(a) of P.L. 108-357, see below] as the text for redesignated para. (b)(19), effective 12/21/2005.

In 2004, P.L. 108-357, Sec. 233(d), added "1361(c)(2)(A)(vi) or" before "1361(c)(6)" in para. (e)(1), effective 10/22/2004.

— P.L. 108-357, Sec. 319(c), added para. (b)(18), effective for tax. yrs. begin. after 10/22/2004.

— P.L. 108-357, Sec. 702(a), added para. (b)(18) [sic (19)], effective for any gain or loss on the sale, exchange, or other disposition of any property acquired by the taxpayer after 12/31/2004.

— P.L. 108-357, Sec. 702(c), of this Act, reads as follows:

"(c) *Savings clause*. Nothing in the amendments made by this section shall affect any duty, liability, or other requirement imposed under any other Federal or State law. Notwithstanding section 128(h) of the Comprehensive Environmental Response, Compensation, and Liability Act of 1980, a certification provided by the Environmental Protection Agency or an appropriate State agency (within the meaning of section 198(c)(4) of the Internal Revenue Code of 1986) shall not affect the liability of any person under section 107(a) of such Act."

In 1998, P.L. 105-206, Sec. 6005(e)(3), added "on or" before "before" each place it appeared in the text and heading of Sec. 312(d)(2) [sic (e)(2)] of P.L. 105-34 [see below].

— P.L. 105-206, Sec. 6010(j)(1), added "or accrues" after "receives" in subpara. (b)(13)(A) . . . Sec. 6010(j)(2), deleted "(as defined in section 513A(a)(5)(A))" after "exempt purposes" in subclause (b)(13)(B)(i)(I), effective for tax. yrs. begin. after 8/5/97, except as provided in Sec. 1041(b)(2) of P.L. 105-34 [reproduced below].

— P.L. 105-206, Sec. 6010(j)(3), amended Sec. 1041(b)(2) of P.L. 105-34 [reproduced below].

Prior to amendment, Sec. 1041(b)(2) of P.L. 105-34, read as follows:

"(2) Binding contracts. The amendments made by this section shall not apply to any payment made during the first 2 taxable years beginning on or after the date of the enactment of this Act if such payment is made pursuant to a written binding contract in effect on June 8, 1997, and at all times thereafter before such payment."

— P.L. 105-206, Sec. 6023(8), substituted "rule" for "Rule" in the heading of subclause (b)(17)(B)(ii)(II), effective 7/22/98.

In 1997, P.L. 105-34, Sec. 312(d)(5), added "(as in effect on the day before the date of the enactment of the Taxpayer Relief Act of 1997)" after "1034" in subpara. (a)(3)(D), effective for sales and exchanges after 5/6/97, except as provided in Secs. 312(d)(2)-(4) [sic (e)(2)-(4)] of this Act [as amended by Sec. 6005(e)(3) of P.L. 105-206, see above], which reads as follows:

"(2) Sales on or before date of enactment. At the election of the taxpayer, the amendments made by this section shall not apply to any sale or exchange on or before the date of the enactment of this Act.

"(3) Certain sales within 2 years after date of enactment. Section 121 of the Internal Revenue Code of 1986 (as amended by this section) shall be applied without regard to subsection (c)(2)(B) thereof in the case of any sale or exchange of property during the 2-year period beginning on the date of the enactment of this Act if the taxpayer held such property on the date of the enactment of this Act and fails to meet the ownership and use requirements of subsection (a) thereof with respect to such property.

"(4) Binding contracts. At the election of the taxpayer, the amendments made by this section shall not apply to a sale or exchange after the date of the enactment of this Act, if—

"(A) such sale or exchange is pursuant to a contract which was binding on such date, or

"(B) without regard to such amendments, gain would not be recognized under section 1034 of the Internal Revenue Code of 1986 (as in effect on the day before the date of the enactment of this Act) on such sale or exchange by reason of a new residence acquired on or before such date or with respect to the acquisition of which by the taxpayer a binding contract was in effect on such date.

This paragraph shall not apply to any sale or exchange by an individual if the treatment provided by section 877(a)(1) of the Internal Revenue Code of 1986 applies to such individual."

— P.L. 105-34, Sec. 1041(a), amended para. (b)(13), effective for tax. yrs. begin. after 8/5/97, except as provided in Sec. 1041(b)(2) of this Act [as amended by Sec. 6010(j)(3) of P.L. 105-206, see above], which reads as follows:

"(2) Binding contracts. The amendments made by this section shall not apply to any amount received or accrued during the first 2 taxable years beginning on or after the date of the enactment of this Act if such amount is received or accrued pursuant to a written binding contract in effect on June 8, 1997, and at all times thereafter before such amount is received or accrued. The preceding sentence shall not apply to any amount which would (but for the exercise of an option to accelerate payment of such amount) be received or accrued after such 2 taxable years."

Prior to amendment, para. (b)(13) read as follows:

"(13) Notwithstanding paragraphs (1), (2), or (3), amounts of interest, annuities, royalties, and rents derived from any organization (in this paragraph called the 'controlled organization') of which the organization deriving such amounts (in this paragraph called the 'controlling organization') has control (as defined in section 368(c)) shall be included as an item of gross income (whether or not the activity from which such amounts are derived represents a trade or business or is regularly carried on) in an amount which bears the same ratio as—

"(A)(i) in the case of a controlled organization which is not exempt from taxation under section 501(a), the excess of the amount of taxable income of the controlled organization over the amount of such organization's taxable income which if derived directly by the controlling organization would not be unrelated business taxable income, or

"(ii) in the case of a controlled organization which is exempt from taxation under section 501(a), the amount of unrelated business taxable income of the controlled organization, bears to

"(B) the taxable income of the controlled organization (determined in the case of a controlled organization to which subparagraph (A)(ii) applies as if it were not an organization exempt from taxation under section 501(a)), but not less than the amount determined in clause (i) or (ii), as the case may be, of subparagraph (A), both amounts computed without regard to amounts paid directly or indirectly to the controlling organization. There shall be allowed all deductions directly connected with amounts included in gross income under the preceding sentence."

— P.L. 105-34, Sec. 1523(a), added para. (e)(3), effective for tax. yrs. begin. after 12/31/97.

— P.L. 105-34, Sec. 1601(c)(4)(A), substituted "as defined in section 1361(e)(1)(C)" for "within the meaning of section 1012" in para. (e)(2) . . . Sec. 1601(c)(4)(D), substituted "section 1361(e)(6)" for "section 1361(c)(7)" in para. (e)(1), effective for tax. yrs. begin. after 12/31/97.

In 1996, P.L. 104-188, Sec. 1115(a), added subsec. (d), effective for tax. yrs. begin. after 12/31/86. Secs. 1115(b)(2) and (3) of this Act read as follows:

"(2) Transitional rule. If—

"(A) for purposes of applying part III of subchapter F of chapter 1 of the Internal Revenue Code of 1986 to any taxable year beginning before January 1, 1987, an agricultural or horticultural organization did not treat any portion of membership dues received by it as income derived in an unrelated trade or business, and

"(B) such organization had a reasonable basis for not treating such dues as income derived in an unrelated trade or business,

then, for purposes of applying such part III to any such taxable year, in no event shall any portion of such dues be treated as derived in an unrelated trade or business.

"(3) Reasonable basis. For purposes of paragraph (2), an organization shall be treated as having a reasonable basis for not treating membership dues as income derived in an unrelated trade or business if the taxpayer's treatment of such dues was in reasonable reliance on any of the following:

"(A) Judicial precedent, published rulings, technical advice with respect to the organization, or a letter ruling to the organization.

"(B) A past Internal Revenue Service audit of the organization in which there was no assessment attributable to the reclassification of membership dues for purposes of the tax on unrelated business income.

"(C) Long-standing recognized practice of agricultural or horticultural organizations."

— P.L. 104-188, Sec. 1316(c), added subsec. (e), effective for tax. yrs. begin. after 12/31/97.

— P.L. 104-188, Sec. 1603(a), added para. (b)(17), effective for amounts included in gross income for any tax. yrs. begin. after 12/31/95.

In 1993, P.L. 103-66, Sec. 13145(a)(1), deleted para. (c)(2) . . . Sec. 13145(a)(2), redesignated para. (c)(3) as para. (c)(2) . . . Sec. 13145(a)(3), substituted "paragraph (1)" for "paragraph (1) or (2)" in para. (c)(2) [as redesignated], effective for partnership yrs. begin. on or after 1/1/94.

Prior to deletion, para. (c)(2) read as follows:

"(2) Special rule for publicly traded partnerships. Notwithstanding any other provision of this section—

"(A) any organization's share (whether or not distributed) of the gross income of a publicly traded partnership (as defined in section 469(k)(2)) shall be treated as gross income derived from an unrelated trade or business, and

"(B) such organization's share of the partnership deductions shall be allowed in computing unrelated business taxable income."

— P.L. 103-66, Sec. 13147(a), added para. (b)(16), effective for property acquired on or after 1/1/94.

— P.L. 103-66, Sec. 13148(a), added "amounts received or accrued as consideration for entering into agreements to make loans," before "and annuities" in para. (b)(1) . . . Sec. 13148(b)(1), substituted "all gains or losses recognized, in connection with the organization's investment activities, from" for "all gains on" in the second sentence of para. (b)(5) . . . Sec. 13148(b)(2), deleted ", written by the organization in connection with its investment activities," after "termination of options" in the second sentence of para. (b)(5) . . . Sec. 13148(b)(3), added "or real property and all gains or losses from the forfeiture of good-faith deposits (that are consistent with established business practice) for the purchase, sale, or lease of real property in connection with the organization's investment activities" before

2,225

the period at the end of the second sentence of para. (b)(5), effective for amounts received on or after 1/1/94.

In **1990**, P.L. 101-508, Sec. 11801(a)(23), deleted para. (b)(14), effective 11/5/90 except as provided in Sec. 11821(b) of this Act, which reads as follows:

"(b) Savings provision. If—

"(1) any provision amended or repealed by this part applied to—

"(A) any transaction occurring before the date of the enactment of this Act [11/5/90],

"(B) any property acquired before such date of enactment [11/5/90], or

"(C) any item of income, loss, deduction, or credit taken into account before such date of enactment [11/5/90], and

"(2) the treatment of such transaction, property, or item under such provision would (without regard to the amendments made by this part) affect liability for tax for periods ending after such date of enactment [11/5/90],

nothing in the amendments made by this part shall be construed to affect the treatment of such transaction, property, or item for purposes of determining liability for tax for periods ending after such date of enactment [11/5/90]."

Prior to deletion, para. (b)(14) read as follows:

"(14) Except as provided in paragraph (4), in the case of a church, or convention or association of churches, for taxable years beginning before January 1, 1976, there shall be excluded all gross income derived from a trade or business and all deductions directly connected with the carrying on of such trade or business if such trade or business was carried on by such organization or its predecessor before May 27, 1969."

In **1988**, P.L. 100-647, Sec. 1018(t)(2)(B), substituted "subclause (I)" for "subclause (II)" in subclause (a)(3)(E)(ii)(II) and substituted a period for the comma at the end of subclause (a)(3)(E)(ii)(II), effective for contributions paid or accrued after 12/31/85, in tax. yrs. end. after 12/31/85.

In **1987**, P.L. 100-203, Sec. 10213(a), amended subsec. (c), effective for partnership interests acquired after 12/17/87.

Prior to amendment, subsec. (c) read as follows:

"(c) Special rules applicable to partnerships.

"If a trade or business regularly carried on by a partnership of which an organization is a member is an unrelated trade or business with respect to such organization, such organization in computing its unrelated business taxable income shall, subject to the exceptions, additions, and limitations contained in subsection (b), include its share (whether or not distributed) of the gross income of the partnership from such unrelated trade or business and its share of the partnership deductions directly connected with such gross income. If the taxable year of the organization is different from that of the partnership, the amounts to be so included or deducted in computing the unrelated business taxable income shall be based upon the income and deductions of the partnership for any taxable year of the partnership ending within or with the taxable year of the organization."

In **1986**, P.L. 99-514, Sec. 1851(a)(10)(A), substituted "determined under section 419A (without regard to subsection (f)(6) thereof)" for "determined under section 419A(c)" in clause (a)(3)(E)(i) . . . Sec. 1851(a)(10)(B), deleted clause (a)(3)(E)(ii) and redesignated clauses (a)(3)(E)(iii) and (iv) as clauses (a)(3)(E)(ii) and (iii), respectively . . . Sec. 1851(a)(10)(C)(i), substituted "an existing reserve" for "a existing reserve" in subclause (a)(3)(E)(ii)(I) [as redesignated, see above] . . . Sec. 1851(a)(10)(C)(ii), amended subclause (a)(3)(E)(ii)(II) [as redesignated, see above] . . . Sec. 1851(a)(10)(D), substituted "subparagraph shall not" for "paragraph shall not" in clause (a)(3)(E)(iii) [as redesignated, see above], effective for contributions paid or accrued after 12/31/85, in tax. yrs. end. after 12/31/85, except as provided in Sec. 511(e)(2)-(5) of P.L. 98-369, reproduced in note following Code Sec. 419, and as provided in Sec. 511(e)(6) of P.L. 98-369 [as added by Sec. 1851(a)(12) of this Act, see below] reproduced below.

Prior to deletion, clause (a)(3)(E)(ii) read as follows:

"(ii) No set aside for facilities. No set aside for assets used in the provision of benefits described in clause (ii) of subparagraph (B) shall be taken into account."

Prior to amendment, subclause (a)(3)(E)(ii)(II) read as follows:

"(II) For purposes of subclause (I), the term 'existing reserve [f]or post-retirement medical or life insurance benefit' means the amount of assets set aside as of the close of the last plan year ending before the date of the enactment of the Tax Reform Act of 1984 for purposes of post-retirement medical benefits or life insurance benefits to be provided to covered employees."

—P.L. 99-514, Sec. 1851(a)(12), added Sec. 511(e)(6) to P.L. 98-369, the effective date for changes made by Sec. 511(b) of P.L. 98-369, see above and below.

In **1984**, P.L. 98-369, Sec. 511(b)(1)(A), substituted "paragraph (7), (9), (17), or (20) of section 501(c)" for "section 501(c)(7) or (9)" each place it appeared (including the paragraph heading) in para. (a)(3) . . . Sec. 511(b)(1)(B), substituted "paragraph (9), (17), or (20) of section 501(c)" for "section 501(c)(9)" in clause (a)(3)(B)(ii) . . . Sec. 511(b)(2), added subpara. (a)(3)(E), effective as provided in Sec. 511(e)(6) of this Act [as added by Sec. 1851(a)(12) of P.L. 99-514, see above], which reads as follows:

"(6) Amendments related to tax on unrelated business income.—The amendments made by subsection (b) [Sec. 511(b)] shall apply with respect to taxable years ending after December 31, 1985. For purposes of section 15 of the Internal Revenue Code of 1954, such amendments shall be treated as a change in the rate of a tax imposed by chapter 1 of such Code."

In **1983**, P.L. 97-448, Sec. 102(m)(3), substituted "10 percent" for "5 percent" in para. (b)(10), effective for tax. yrs. begin. after 12/31/81.

In **1978**, P.L. 95-345, Sec. 2(a)(2), added "payments with respect to securities loans (as defined in section 512(a)(5))," after "interest" in para. (b)(1) . . . Sec. 2(b), added para. (a)(5), effective for amounts received after 12/31/76, as payments with respect to securities loans as defined in Code Sec. 512(a)(5)) and for transfers of securities under agreements described in Code Sec. 1058 occurring after 12/31/76.

In **1976**, P.L. 94-568, Sec. 1(b), added the sentence to the end of subpara. (a)(3)(A), effective for tax. yrs. begin. after 10/20/76.

—P.L. 94-455, Sec. 1901(b)(8)(F), substituted "educational organization described in section 170(b)(1)(A)(ii)" for "educational institution (as defined in section 151(c)(4))" in subpara. (b)(15)(B) [as redesignated by Sec. 1951(b)(8)(A) of this Act, see below] . . . Sec. 1906(b)(13)(A), substituted "Secretary" for "Secretary or his delegate" in para. (b)(15) [as redesignated by Sec. 1951(b)(8)(A) of this Act, see below], effective for tax. yrs. begin. after 12/31/76.

—P.L. 94-455, Sec. 1951(b)(8)(A), deleted paras. (b)(13) and (14), and redesignated paras. (b)(15), (16) and (17) as (b)(13), (14) and (15), effective for tax. yrs. begin. after 12/31/76. Sec. 1951(b)(8)(B) of the Act provided the following savings provision:

"(B) Savings provision.—Notwithstanding subparagraph (A), income received in a taxable year beginning after December 31, 1975, shall be excluded from gross income in determining unrelated business taxable income, if such income would have been excluded by paragraph (13) or (14) of section 512(b) if received in a taxable year beginning before such date. Any deductions directly connected with income excluded under the preceding sentence in determining unrelated business taxable income shall also be excluded for such purpose."

Prior to deletion, paras. (b)(13) and (14) read as follows:

"(13) in the case of a trust—

"(A) created by virtue of the provisions of the will of an individual who died after August 16, 1954, and before January 1, 1957,

"(B) which, by virtue of the provisions of such will, is a limited partner in a partnership created under the laws of a State (i) providing for the creation of limited partnerships, and (ii) under which a limited partner has no right to take part in the control of the business without becoming liable as a general partner,

"(C) which, at no time before or during a taxable year of the partnership ending within or with the taxable year of the trust, was (or was liable as) a general partner in such partnership, and

"(D) which is required to distribute all of its income (within the meaning of section 643(b)) currently exclusively for religious, charitable, scientific, literary, or educational purposes, and which is required to distribute all of the corpus exclusively for such purposes,

there shall be excluded its share (determined under subsection (c) without regard to this paragraph and paragraph (11)) of gross income of the partnership as such limited partner and of the partnership deductions directly connected with such income, but, if such share of gross income exceeds such share of deductions, only to the extent that the partnership makes distributions during its taxable year which are attributable to such gross income. For purposes of the preceding sentence (i) any distribution made after the close of a partnership taxable year and on or before the 15th day of the fourth calendar month after the close of such taxable year shall be treated as made on the last day of such taxable year, and (ii) distributions shall be treated as attributable first to gross income other than gross income described in the preceding sentence, and shall be properly adjusted (under regulations prescribed by the Secretary or his delegate) to the extent necessary to reflect capital contributions to the partnership made by the trust, income of the partnership exempt from tax under this title, and other items.

"(14) In the case of an organization which is described in section 501(c)(5), there shall be excluded all income used to establish, maintain, or operate a retirement home, hospital, or other similar facility for the exclusive use and benefit of the aged and infirm members of such an organization, which is derived from agricultural pursuits conducted on a ground contiguous to the retirement home, hospital, or similar facility and further provided that such income does not provide more than 75 percent of the cost of maintaining and operating the retirement home, hospital, or similar facility; and there shall be excluded all deductions directly connected with such income."

—P.L. 94-396, Sec. 1(a), added the second sentence to para. (b)(5), effective for gain from options which lapse or terminate on or after 1/1/76, in tax. yrs. end. on or after 1/1/76.

In **1972**, P.L. 92-418, Sec. 1(b), added para. (a)(4), effective for tax. yrs. begin. after 12/31/69.

In **1969**, P.L. 91-172, Sec. 121(b)(1), amended subsec. (a), . . . Sec. 121(b)(2)(A), amended paras. (b)(3) and (4) . . . Sec. 121(b)(2)(B), amended para. (b)(12) . . . Sec. 121(b)(2)(C), added paras. (b)(15), (16) and (17) . . . Sec. 121(b)(2)(D), amended so much of subsec. (b) as precedes para. (b)(1), effective for tax. yrs. begin. after 12/31/69.

Prior to amendment, subsec. (a) read as follows:

"(a) Definition.

The term 'unrelated business taxable income' means the gross income derived by any organization from any unrelated trade or business (as defined in section 513) regularly carried on by it, less the deductions allowed by this chapter which are directly connected with the carrying on of such trade or business, both computed with the exceptions, additions, and limitations provided in subsection (b). In the case of an organization described in section 511 which is a foreign organization, the unrelated business taxable income shall be its unrelated business taxable income which is effectively connected with the conduct of a trade or business within the United States."

Prior to amendment, paras. (b)(3) and (4) read as follows:

"(3) There shall be excluded all rents from real property (including personal property leased with the real property), and all deductions directly connected with such rents.

"(4) Notwithstanding paragraph (3), in the case of a business lease (as defined in section 514) there shall be included, as an item of gross income derived from an unrelated trade or business, the amount ascertained under section 514(a)(1), and there shall be allowed, as a deduction, the amount ascertained under section 514(a)(2)."

Prior to amendment, para. (b)(12) read as follows:

"(12) There shall be allowed a specific deduction of $1,000."
Prior to amendment, so much of subsec. (b) as precedes para. (b)(1) read as follows:
"(b) Exceptions, additions, and limitations
"The exceptions, additions, and limitations applicable in determining unrelated business taxable income are the following"
In 1966, P.L. 89-809, Sec. 104(g), amended the sentence at the end of subsec. (a), effective for tax. yrs. begin. after 12/31/66.
Prior to amendment, the sentence at the end of subsec. (a) read as follows:
"In the case of an organization described in section 511 which is a foreign organization, the unrelated business taxable income shall be its unrelated business taxable income derived from sources within the United States determined under subchapter N (Sec. 861 and following, relating to tax based on income from sources within or without the United States)."
In 1964, P.L. 88-380, added para. (b)(14), effective for tax. yrs. begin. after 12/31/63.
In 1958, P.L. 85-367, added para. (b)(13), effective for tax. yrs. of trusts begin. after 12/31/55.

Sec. 513. Unrelated trade or business.

(a) General rule.

The term "unrelated trade or business" means, in the case of any organization subject to the tax imposed by section 511, any trade or business the conduct of which is not substantially related (aside from the need of such organization for income or funds or the use it makes of the profits derived) to the exercise or performance by such organization of its charitable, educational, or other purpose or function constituting the basis for its exemption under section 501 (or, in the case of an organization described in section 511(a)(2)(B), to the exercise or performance of any purpose or function described in section 501(c)(3)), except that such term does not include any trade or business—

(1) in which substantially all the work in carrying on such trade or business is performed for the organization without compensation; or

(2) which is carried on, in the case of an organization described in section 501(c)(3) or in the case of a college or university described in section 511(a)(2)(B), by the organization primarily for the convenience of its members, students, patients, officers, or employees, or, in the case of a local association of employees described in section 501(c)(4) organized before May 27, 1969, which is the selling by the organization of items of work-related clothes and equipment and items normally sold through vending machines, through food dispensing facilities, or by snack bars, for the convenience of its members at their usual places of employment; or

(3) which is the selling of merchandise, substantially all of which has been received by the organization as gifts or contributions.

(b) Special rule for trusts.

The term "unrelated trade or business" means, in the case of—

(1) a trust computing its unrelated business taxable income under section 512 for purposes of section 681; or

(2) a trust described in section 401(a), or section 501(c)(17), which is exempt from tax under section 501(a);

any trade or business regularly carried on by such trust or by a partnership of which it is a member.

(c) Advertising, etc., activities.

For purposes of this section, the term "trade or business" includes any activity which is carried on for the production of income from the sale of goods or the performance of services. For purposes of the preceding sentence, an activity does not lose identity as a trade or business merely because it is carried on within a larger aggregate of similar activities or within a larger complex of other endeavors which may, or may not, be related to the exempt purposes of the organization. Where an activity carried on for profit constitutes an unrelated trade or business, no part of such trade or business shall be excluded from such classification merely because it does not result in profit.

(d) Certain activities of trade shows, state fairs, etc.

(1) General rule. The term "unrelated trade or business" does not include qualified public entertainment activities of an organization described in paragraph (2)(C), or qualified convention and trade show activities of an organization described in paragraph (3)(C).

(2) Qualified public entertainment activities. For purposes of this subsection—

(A) Public entertainment activity. The term "public entertainment activity" means any entertainment or recreational activity of a kind traditionally conducted at fairs or expositions promoting agricultural and educational purposes, including, but not limited to, any activity one of the purposes of which is to attract the public to fairs or expositions or to promote the breeding of animals or the development of products or equipment.

(B) Qualified public entertainment activity. The term "qualified public entertainment activity" means a public entertainment activity which is conducted by a qualifying organization described in subparagraph (C) in—

(i) conjunction with an international, national, State, regional, or local fair or exposition,

(ii) accordance with the provisions of State law which permit the activity to be operated or conducted solely by such an organization, or by an agency, instrumentality, or political subdivision of such State, or

(iii) accordance with the provisions of State law which permit such an organization to be granted a license to conduct not more than 20 days of such activity on payment to the State of a lower percentage of the revenue from such licensed activity than the State requires from organizations not described in section 501(c)(3), (4), or (5).

(C) Qualifying organization. For purposes of this paragraph, the term "qualifying organization" means an organization which is described in section 501(c)(3), (4), or (5) which regularly conducts, as one of its substantial exempt purposes, an agricultural and educational fair or exposition.

(3) Qualified convention and trade show activities.

(A) Convention and trade show activity. The term "convention and trade show activity" means any activity of a kind traditionally conducted at conventions, annual meetings, or trade shows, including, but not limited to, any activity one of the purposes of which is to attract persons in an industry generally (without regard to membership in the sponsoring organization) as well as members of the public to the show for the purpose of displaying industry products or to stimulate interest in, and demand for, industry products or services, or to educate persons engaged in the industry in the development of new products and services or new rules and regulations affecting the industry.

(B) Qualified convention and trade show activity. The term "qualified convention and trade show activity" means a convention and trade show activity carried out by a qualifying organization described in subparagraph (C) in conjunction with an international, national, State, regional, or local convention, annual meeting, or show conducted by an organization described in subparagraph (C) if one of the purposes of such organization in sponsoring the activity is the promotion and stimulation of interest in, and demand for, the products and services of that industry in general or to educate persons in attendance regarding new developments or products and services related to the exempt activities of the organization, and the show is designed to achieve such purpose through the character of the exhibits and the extent of the industry products displayed.

(C) **Qualifying organization.** For purposes of this paragraph, the term "qualifying organization" means an organization described in section 501(c)(3), (4), (5), or (6) which regularly conducts as one of its substantial exempt purposes a show which stimulates interest in, and demand for, the products of a particular industry or segment of such industry or which educates persons in attendance regarding new developments or products and services related to the exempt activities of the organization.

(4) Such activities not to affect exempt status. An organization described in section 501(c)(3), (4), or (5) shall not be considered as not entitled to the exemption allowed under section 501(a) solely because of qualified public entertainment activities conducted by it.

(e) Certain hospital services.

In the case of a hospital described in section 170(b)(1)(A)(iii), the term "unrelated trade or business" does not include the furnishing of one or more of the services described in section 501(e)(1)(A) to one or more hospitals described in section 170(b)(1)(A)(iii) if—

(1) such services are furnished solely to such hospitals which have facilities to serve not more than 100 inpatients;

(2) such services, if performed on its own behalf by the recipient hospital, would constitute activities in exercising or performing the purpose or function constituting the basis for its exemption; and

(3) such services are provided at a fee or cost which does not exceed the actual cost of providing such services, such cost including straight line depreciation and a reasonable amount for return on capital goods used to provide such services.

(f) Certain bingo games.

(1) In general. The term "unrelated trade or business" does not include any trade or business which consists of conducting bingo games.

(2) Bingo game defined. For purposes of paragraph (1), the term "bingo game" means any game of bingo—

(A) of a type in which usually—
  (i) the wagers are placed,
  (ii) the winners are determined, and
  (iii) the distribution of prizes or other property is made,
in the presence of all persons placing wagers in such game,
(B) the conducting of which is not an activity ordinarily carried out on a commercial basis, and
(C) the conducting of which does not violate any State or local law.

(g) Certain pole rentals.

In the case of a mutual or cooperative telephone or electric company, the term "unrelated trade or business" does not include engaging in qualified pole rentals (as defined in section 501(c)(12)(D)).

(h) Certain distributions of low cost articles without obligation to purchase and exchanges and rentals of member lists.

(1) In general. In the case of an organization which is described in section 501 and contributions to which are deductible under paragraph (2) or (3) of section 170(c), the term "unrelated trade or business" does not include—

(A) activities relating to the distribution of low cost articles if the distribution of such articles is incidental to the solicitation of charitable contributions, or

(B) any trade or business which consists of—
  (i) exchanging with another such organization names and addresses of donors to (or members of) such organization, or
  (ii) renting such names and addresses to another such organization.

(2) Low cost article defined. For purposes of this subsection—

(A) **In general.** The term "low cost article" means any article which has a cost not in excess of $5 to the organization which distributes such item (or on whose behalf such item is distributed).

(B) **Aggregation rule.** If more than 1 item is distributed by or on behalf of an organization to a single distributee in any calendar year, the aggregate of the items so distributed in such calendar year to such distributee shall be treated as 1 article for purposes of subparagraph (A).

(C) **Indexation of $5 amount.** In the case of any taxable year beginning in a calendar year after 1987, the $5 amount in subparagraph (A) shall be increased by an amount equal to—
  (i) $5, multiplied by
  (ii) the cost-of-living adjustment determined under section 1(f)(3) for the calendar year in which the taxable year begins, by substituting "calendar year 1987" for "calendar year 1992" in subparagraph (B) thereof.

(3) Distribution which is incidental to the solicitation of charitable contributions described. For purposes of this subsection, any distribution of low cost articles by an organization shall be treated as a distribution incidental to the solicitation of charitable contributions only if—

(A) such distribution is not made at the request of the distributee,
(B) such distribution is made without the express consent of the distributee, and
(C) the articles so distributed are accompanied by—
  (i) a request for a charitable contribution (as defined in section 170(c)) by the distributee to such organization, and
  (ii) a statement that the distributee may retain the low cost article regardless of whether such distributee makes a charitable contribution to such organization.

(i) Treatment of certain sponsorship payments.

(1) In general. The term "unrelated trade or business" does not include the activity of soliciting and receiving qualified sponsorship payments.

(2) Qualified sponsorship payments. For purposes of this subsection—

(A) **In general.** The term "qualified sponsorship payment" means any payment made by any person engaged in a trade or business with respect to which there is no arrangement or expectation that such person will receive any substantial return benefit other than the use or acknowledgement of the name or logo (or product lines) of such person's trade or business in connection with the activities of the organization that receives such payment. Such a use or acknowledgement does not include advertising such person's products or services (including messages containing qualitative or comparative language, price information, or other indications of savings or value, an endorsement, or an inducement to purchase, sell, or use such products or services).

(B) Limitations.

(i) Contingent payments. The term "qualified sponsorship payment" does not include any payment if the amount of such payment is contingent upon the level of attendance at one or more events, broadcast ratings, or other factors indicating the degree of public exposure to one or more events.

(ii) Safe harbor does not apply to periodicals and qualified convention and trade show activities. The term "qualified sponsorship payment" does not include—

(I) any payment which entities the payor to the use or acknowledgement of the name or logo (or product lines) of the payor's trade or business in regularly scheduled and printed material published by or on behalf of the payee organization that is not related to and primarily distributed in connection with a specific event conducted by the payee organization, or

(II) any payment made in connection with any qualified convention or trade show activity (as defined in subsection (d)(3)(B)).

(3) Allocation of portions of single payment. For purposes of this subsection, to the extent that a portion of a payment would (if made as a separate payment) be a qualified sponsorship payment, such portion of such payment and the other portion of such payment shall be treated as separate payments.

(j) Debt management plan services.

The term "unrelated trade or business" includes the provision of debt management plan services (as defined in section 501(q)(4)(B)) by any organization other than an organization which meets the requirements of section 501(q).

In 2006, P.L. 109-280, Sec. 1220(b), added subsec. (j), effective for tax. yrs. begin. after 8/17/2006, except as provided in Sec. 1220(c)(2), of this Act, which reads as follows:

"(2) Transition rule for existing organizations. In the case of any organization described in paragraph (3) or (4) section 501(c) of the Internal Revenue Code of 1986 and with respect to which the provision of credit counseling services is a substantial purpose on the date of the enactment of this Act, the amendments made by this section shall apply to taxable years beginning after the date which is 1 year after the date of the enactment of this Act."

In 1997, P.L. 105-34, Sec. 965(a), added subsec. (i), effective for payments solicited or received after 12/31/97.

In 1993, P.L. 103-66, Sec. 13201(b)(3)(H), substituted "1992" for "1989" in clause (h)(2)(C)(ii), effective for tax. yrs. begin. after 12/31/92.

In 1990, P.L. 101-508, Sec. 11101(d)(1)(G), added "by substituting 'calendar year 1987' for 'calendar year 1989' in subparagraph (B) thereof" before the period at the end of subpara. (h)(2)(C), effective for tax. yrs. begin. after 12/31/90.

In 1988, P.L. 100-647, Sec. 6201, provides:

"SEC. 6201. CERTAIN GAMES OF CHANCE NOT TREATED AS UNRELATED TRADE OR BUSINESS.

"Section 1834 of the Reform Act is amended by adding at the end thereof the following new sentence: 'The amendment made by this section shall apply to games of chance conducted after October 22, 1986, in taxable years ending after such date'."

In 1986, P.L. 99-514, Sec. 1601(a), added subsec. (h), effective for distributions of low cost articles and exchanges and rentals of member lists after 10/22/86.

— P.L. 99-514, Sec. 1602(a), added "or to educate persons in attendance regarding new developments or products and services related to the exempt activities of the organization" after "industry in general" in subpara. (d)(3)(B)... Sec. 1602(b)(1), substituted "501(c)(3), (4), (5), or (6)" for "501(c)(5) or (6)" in subpara. (d)(3)(C)... Sec. 1602(b)(2), added "or which educates persons in attendance regarding new developments or products and services related to the exempt activities of the organization" before the period at the end of subpara. (d)(3)(C), effective for activities in tax. yrs. begin. after 10/22/86.

— P.L. 99-514, Sec. 1834, amended Sec. 311(a)(3)(A) of P.L. 98-369 [reproduced below], the general rule for the application of Code Sec. 513 to businesses consisting of conducting games of chance, by substituting "a State law (originally enacted on April 22, 1977)" for "a State law" [see Sec. 6201 of P.L. 100-647, reproduced above].

In 1984, P.L. 98-369, Sec. 311(a), [as amended by Sec. 1834 of P.L. 99-514, see above] provides the following general rule, effective for games of chance conducted after 6/30/81, in tax. yrs. end. after 6/30/81, [see Sec. 6201 of P.L. 100-647, reproduced above]:

"(a) General rule. — For purposes of section 513 of the Internal Revenue Code of 1954 (defining unrelated trade or business), the term 'unrelated trade or business' does not include any trade or business which consists of conducting any game of chance if—

"(1) such game of chance is conducted by a nonprofit organization,

"(2) the conducting of such game by such organization does not violate any State or local law, and

"(3) as of October 5, 1983—

"(A) there was a State law (originally enacted on April 22, 1977) in effect which permitted the conducting of such game of chance by such nonprofit organization, but

"(B) the conducting of such game of chance by organizations which were not nonprofit organizations would have violated such law."

In 1980, P.L. 96-605, Sec. 106(b), added subsec. (g), effective for tax. yrs. begin. after 12/31/69.

In 1978, P.L. 95-502, Sec. 301(a), added subsec. (f), effective for tax. yrs. begin. after 12/31/69.

In 1976, P.L. 94-455, Sec. 1305, added subsec. (d), effective for qualified public entertainment activities in tax. yrs. begin. after 12/31/62, and to qualified convention and trade show activities in tax. yrs. begin. after 10/4/76.

— P.L. 94-455, Sec. 1311, added subsec. (e), effective for tax. yrs. to which the Internal Revenue Code of 1954 applies.

In 1969, P.L. 91-172, Sec. 121(b)(4), substituted "employees, or, in the case of a local association of employees described in section 501(c)(4) organized before May 27, 1969, which is the selling by the organization of items of work-related clothes and equipment and items normally sold through vending machines, through food dispensing facilities, or by snack bars, for the convenience of its members at their usual places of employment; or" for "employees; or" in subsec. (a)(2)... Sec. 121(c), amended subsec. (c), effective for tax. yrs. begin. after 12/31/69.

Prior to amendment, subsec. (c) read as follows:

"(c) Special rule for certain publishing businesses.

"If a publishing business carried on by an organization during a taxable year beginning before January 1, 1953, is, without regard to this subsection, an unrelated trade or business, but before the beginning of the third succeeding taxable year the business is carried on by it (or by a successor who acquired such business in a liquidation which would have constituted a tax-free exchange under section 112(b)(6) of the Internal Revenue Code of 1939) in such manner that the conduct thereof is substantially related to the exercise or performance by such organization (or such successor) or its educational or other purpose or function described in section 501(c)(3), such publishing business shall not be considered, for the taxable year, as an unrelated trade or business."

In 1960, P.L. 86-667, Sec. 4, substituted "section 401(a), or 501(c)(17)" for "section 401(a)" in para. (b)(2), effective for tax. yrs. begin. after 12/31/59.

Sec. 514. Unrelated debt-financed income.

(a) Unrelated debt-financed income and deductions.

In computing under section 512 the unrelated business taxable income for any taxable year—

(1) Percentage of income taken into account. There shall be included with respect to each debt-financed property as an item of gross income derived from an unrelated trade or business an amount which is the same percentage (but not in excess of 100 percent) of the total gross income derived during the taxable year from or on account of such property as (A) the average acquisition indebtedness (as defined in subsection (c)(7)) for the taxable year with respect to the property is of (B) the average amount (determined under regulations prescribed by the Secretary) of the adjusted basis of such property during the period it is held by the organization during such taxable year.

(2) Percentage of deductions taken into account. There shall be allowed as a deduction with respect to each debt-financed property an amount determined by applying (except as provided in the last sentence of this paragraph) the percentage derived under paragraph (1) to the sum determined under paragraph (3). The percentage derived under this paragraph shall not be applied with respect to the deduction of any capital loss resulting from the carryback or carryover of net capital losses under section 1212.

(3) Deductions allowable. The sum referred to in paragraph (2) is the sum of the deductions under this chapter which are directly connected with the debt-financed property or the income therefrom, except that if the debt-financed property is of a character which is subject to the allowance for depreciation provided in section 167, the allowance shall be computed only by use of the straight-line method.

(b) Definition of debt-financed property.

(1) In general. For purposes of this section, the term "debt-financed property" means any property which is held to produce income and with respect to which there is an acquisition indebtedness (as defined in subsection (c)) at any time during the taxable year (or, if the property was disposed of during the taxable year, with respect to which there was an acquisition indebtedness at any time during the 12-month period ending with the date of such disposition), except that such term does not include—

(A)(i) any property substantially all the use of which is substantially related (aside from the need of the organization for income or funds) to the exercise or performance by such organization of its charitable, educational, or other purpose or function constituting the basis for its exemption under section 501 (or, in the case of an organization described in section 511(a)(2)(B), to the exercise or performance of any purpose or function designated in section 501(c)(3)), or

(ii) any property to which clause (i) does not apply, to the extent that its use is so substantially related;

(B) except in the case of income excluded under section 512(b)(5), any property to the extent that the income from such property is taken into account in computing the gross income of any unrelated trade or business;

(C) any property to the extent that the income from such property is excluded by reason of the provisions of paragraph (7), (8), or (9) of section 512(b) in computing the gross income of any unrelated trade or business;

(D) any property to the extent that it is used in any trade or business described in paragraph (1), (2), or (3) of section 513(a); or

(E) any property the gain or loss from the sale, exchange, or other disposition of which would be excluded by reason of the provisions of section 512(b)(19) in computing the gross income of any unrelated trade or business.

For purposes of subparagraph (A), substantially all the use of a property shall be considered to be substantially related to the exercise or performance by an organization of its charitable, educational, or other purpose or function constituting the basis for its exemption under section 501 if such property is real property subject to a lease to a medical clinic entered into primarily for purposes which are substantially related (aside from the need of such organization for income or funds or the use it makes of the rents derived) to the exercise or performance by such organization of its charitable, educational, or other purpose or function constituting the basis for its exemption under section 501.

(2) Special rule for related uses. For purposes of applying paragraphs (1)(A), (C), and (D), the use of any property by an exempt organization which is related to an organization shall be treated as use by such organization.

(3) Special rules when land is acquired for exempt use within 10 years.

(A) Neighborhood land. If an organization acquires real property for the principal purpose of using the land (commencing within 10 years of the time of acquisition) in the manner described in paragraph (1)(A) and at the time of acquisition the property is in the neighborhood of other property owned by the organization which is used in such manner, the real property acquired for such future use shall not be treated as debt-financed property so long as the organization does not abandon its intent to so use the land within the 10-year period. The preceding sentence shall not apply for any period after the expiration of the 10-year period, and shall apply after the first 5 years of the 10-year period only if the organization establishes to the satisfaction of the Secretary that it is reasonably certain that the land will be used in the described manner before the expiration of the 10-year period.

(B) Other cases. If the first sentence of subparagraph (A) is inapplicable only because—

(i) the acquired land is not in the neighborhood referred to in subparagraph (A), or

(ii) the organization (for the period after the first 5 years of the 10-year period) is unable to establish to the satisfaction of the Secretary that it is reasonably certain that the land will be used in the manner described in paragraph (1)(A) before the expiration of the 10-year period,

but the land is converted to such use by the organization within the 10-year period, the real property (subject to the provisions of subparagraph (D)) shall not be treated as debt-financed property for any period before such conversion. For purposes of this subparagraph, land shall not be treated as used in the manner described in paragraph (1)(A) by reason of the use made of any structure which was on the land when acquired by the organization.

(C) Limitations. Subparagraphs (A) and (B)—

(i) shall apply with respect to any structure on the land when acquired by the organization, or to the land occupied by the structure, only if (and so long as) the intended future use of the land in the manner described in paragraph (1)(A) requires that the structure be demolished or removed in order to use the land in such manner;

(ii) shall not apply to structures erected on the land after the acquisition of the land; and

(iii) shall not apply to property subject to a lease which is a business lease (as defined in this section immediately before the enactment of the Tax Reform Act of 1976).

(D) Refund of taxes when subparagraph (B) applies. If an organization for any taxable year has not used land in the manner to satisfy the actual use condition of subparagraph (B) before the time prescribed by law (including extensions thereof) for filing the return for such taxable year, the tax for such year shall be computed without regard to the application of subparagraph (B), but if and when such use condition is satisfied, the provisions of subparagraph (B) shall then be applied to such taxable year. If the actual use condition of subparagraph (B) is satisfied for any taxable year after such time for filing the return, and if credit or refund of any overpayment for the taxable year resulting from the satisfaction of such use condition is prevented at the close of the taxable year in which the use condition is satisfied, by the operation of any law or rule of law (other than chapter 74, relating to closing agreements and compromises), credit or refund of such overpayment may nevertheless be allowed or made if claim therefor is filed before the expiration of 1 year after the close of the taxable year in which the use condition is satisfied.

(E) Special rule for churches. In applying this paragraph to a church or convention or association of churches, in lieu of the 10-year period referred to in subparagraphs (A) and (B) a 15-year period shall be applied, and subparagraphs (A) and (B)(ii) shall apply whether or not the acquired land meets the neighborhood test.

(c) Acquisition indebtedness.

(1) General rule. For purposes of this section, the term "acquisition indebtedness" means, with respect to any debt-financed property, the unpaid amount of—

(A) the indebtedness incurred by the organization in acquiring or improving such property;

(B) the indebtedness incurred before the acquisition or improvement of such property if such indebtedness would not have been incurred but for such acquisition or improvement; and

(C) the indebtedness incurred after the acquisition or improvement of such property if such indebtedness would not have been incurred but for such acquisition or improvement and the incurrence of such indebtedness was reasonably foreseeable at the time of such acquisition or improvement.

(2) Property acquired subject to mortgage, etc. For purposes of this subsection—

(A) General rule. Where property (no matter how acquired) is acquired subject to a mortgage or other similar lien, the amount of the indebtedness secured by such mortgage or lien shall be considered as an indebtedness of the organization incurred in acquiring such property even though the organization did not assume or agree to pay such indebtedness.

(B) Exceptions. Where property subject to a mortgage is acquired by an organization by bequest or devise, the indebtedness secured by the mortgage shall not be treated as acquisition indebtedness during a period of 10 years following the date of the acquisition. If an organization acquires property by gift subject to a mortgage which was placed on the property more than 5 years before the gift, which property was held by the donor more than 5 years before the gift, the indebtedness secured by such mortgage shall not be treated as acquisition indebtedness during a period of 10 years following the date of such gift. This subparagraph shall not apply if the organization, in order to acquire the equity in the property by bequest, devise, or gift, assumes and agrees to pay the indebtedness secured by the mortgage, or if the organization makes any payment for the equity in the property owned by the decedent or the donor.

(C) Liens for taxes or assessments. Where State law provides that—

(i) a lien for taxes, or

(ii) a lien for assessments,

made by a State or a political subdivision thereof attaches to property prior to the time when such taxes or assessments become due and payable, then such lien shall be treated as similar to a mortgage (within the meaning of subparagraph (A)) but only after such taxes or assessments become due and payable and the organization has had an opportunity to pay such taxes or assessments in accordance with State law.

(3) Extension of obligations. For purposes of this section, an extension, renewal, or refinancing of an obligation evidencing a pre-existing indebtedness shall not be treated as the creation of a new indebtedness.

(4) Indebtedness incurred in performing exempt purpose. For purposes of this section, the term "acquisition indebtedness" does not include indebtedness the incurrence of which is inherent in the performance or exercise of the purpose or function constituting the basis of the organization's exemption, such as the indebtedness incurred by a credit union described in section 501(c)(14) in accepting deposits from its members.

(5) Annuities. For purposes of this section, the term "acquisition indebtedness" does not include an obligation to pay an annuity which—

(A) is the sole consideration (other than a mortgage to which paragraph (2)(B) applies) issued in exchange for property if, at the time of the exchange, the value of the annuity is less than 90 percent of the value of the property received in the exchange,

(B) is payable over the life of one individual in being at the time the annuity is issued, or over the lives of two individuals in being at such time, and

(C) is payable under a contract which—

(i) does not guarantee a minimum amount of payments or specify a maximum amount of payments, and

(ii) does not provide for any adjustment of the amount of the annuity payments by reference to the income received from the transferred property or any other property.

(6) Certain federal financing.

(A) In general. For purposes of this section, the term "acquisition indebtedness" does not include—

(i) an obligation, to the extent that it is insured by the Federal Housing Administration, to finance the purchase, rehabilitation, or construction of housing for low and moderate income persons, or

(ii) indebtedness incurred by a small business investment company licensed after the date of the enactment of the American Jobs Creation Act of 2004 under the Small Business Investment Act of 1958 if such indebtedness is evidenced by a debenture—

(I) issued by such company under section 303(a) of such Act, and

(II) held or guaranteed by the Small Business Administration.

(B) Limitation. Subparagraph (A)(ii) shall not apply with respect to any small business investment company during any period that—

(i) any organization which is exempt from tax under this title (other than a governmental unit) owns more than 25 percent of the capital or profits interest in such company, or

(ii) organizations which are exempt from tax under this title (including governmental units other than any agency or instrumentality of the United States) own, in the aggregate, 50 percent or more of the capital or profits interest in such company.

(7) Average acquisition indebtedness. For purposes of this section, the term "average acquisition indebtedness" for any taxable year with respect to a debt-financed property means the average amount, determined under regulations prescribed by the Secretary, of the acquisition indebtedness during the period the property is held by the organization during the taxable year, except that for the purpose of computing the percentage of any gain or loss to be taken into account on a sale or other disposition of debt-financed property, such term means the highest amount of the acquisition indebtedness with respect to such property during the 12-month period ending with the date of the sale or other disposition.

(8) Securities subject to loans. For purposes of this section—

(A) payments with respect to securities loans (as defined in section 512(a)(5)) shall be deemed to be derived from the securities loaned and not from collateral security or the investment of collateral security from such loans,

(B) any deductions which are directly connected with collateral security for such loan, or with the investment of collateral security, shall be deemed to be deductions which are directly connected with the securities loaned, and

(C) an obligation to return collateral security shall not be treated as acquisition indebtedness (as defined in paragraph (1)).

(9) Real property acquired by a qualified organization.
(A) In general. Except as provided in subparagraph (B), the term "acquisition indebtedness" does not, for purposes of this section, include indebtedness incurred by a qualified organization in acquiring or improving any real property. For purposes of this paragraph, an interest in a mortgage shall in no event be treated as real property.

(B) Exceptions. The provisions of subparagraph (A) shall not apply in any case in which—

(i) the price for the acquisition or improvement is not a fixed amount determined as of the date of the acquisition or the completion of the improvement;

(ii) the amount of any indebtedness or any other amount payable with respect to such indebtedness, or the time for making any payment of any such amount, is dependent, in whole or in part, upon any revenue, income, or profits derived from such real property;

(iii) the real property is at any time after the acquisition leased by the qualified organization to the person selling such property to such organization or to any person who bears a relationship described in section 267(b) or 707(b) to such person;

(iv) the real property is acquired by a qualified trust from, or is at any time after the acquisition leased by such trust to, any person who—

(I) bears a relationship which is described in subparagraph (C), (E), or (G) of section 4975(e)(2) to any plan with respect to which such trust was formed, or

(II) bears a relationship which is described in subparagraph (F) or (H) of section 4975(e)(2) to any person described in subclause (I);

(v) any person described in clause (iii) or (iv) provides the qualified organization with financing in connection with the acquisition or improvement; or

(vi) the real property is held by a partnership unless the partnership meets the requirements of clauses (i) through (v) and unless—

(I) all of the partners of the partnership are qualified organizations,

(II) each allocation to a partner of the partnership which is a qualified organization is a qualified allocation (within the meaning of section 168(h)(6)), or

(III) such partnership meets the requirements of subparagraph (E).

For purposes of subclause (I) of clause (vi), an organization shall not be treated as a qualified organization if any income of such organization is unrelated business taxable income.

(C) Qualified organization. For purposes of this paragraph, the term "qualified organization" means—

(i) an organization described in section 170(b)(1)(A)(ii) and its affiliated support organizations described in section 509(a)(3);

(ii) any trust which constitutes a qualified trust under section 401;

(iii) an organization described in section 501(c)(25); or

(iv) a retirement income account described in section 403(b)(9).

(D) Other pass-thru entities; tiered entities. Rules similar to the rules of subparagraph (B)(vi) shall also apply in the case of any pass-thru entity other than a partnership and in the case of tiered partnerships and other entities.

(E) Certain allocations permitted.

(i) In general. A partnership meets the requirements of this subparagraph if—

(I) the allocation of items to any partner which is a qualified organization cannot result in such partner having a share of the overall partnership income for any taxable year greater than such partner's share of the overall partnership loss for the taxable year for which such partner's loss share will be the smallest, and

(II) each allocation with respect to the partnership has substantial economic effect within the meaning of section 704(b)(2).

For purposes of this clause, items allocated under section 704(c) shall not be taken into account.

(ii) Special rules.

(I) Chargebacks. Except as provided in regulations, a partnership may without violating the requirements of this subparagraph provide for chargebacks with respect to disproportionate losses previously allocated to qualified organizations and disproportionate income previously allocated to other partners. Any chargeback referred to in the preceding sentence shall not be at a ratio in excess of the ratio under which the loss or income (as the case may be) was allocated.

(II) Preferred rates of return, etc. To the extent provided in regulations, a partnership may without violating the requirements of this subparagraph provide for reasonable preferred returns or reasonable guaranteed payments.

(iii) Regulations. The Secretary shall prescribe such regulations as may be necessary to carry out the purposes of this subparagraph, including regulations which may provide for exclusion or segregation of items.

(F) Special rules for organizations described in section 501(c)(25).

(i) In general. In computing under section 512 the unrelated business taxable income of a disqualified holder of an interest in an organization described in section 501(c)(25), there shall be taken into account—

(I) as gross income derived from an unrelated trade or business, such holder's pro rata share of the items of income described in clause (ii)(I) of such organization, and

(II) as deductions allowable in computing unrelated business taxable income, such holder's pro rata share of the items of deduction described in clause (ii)(II) of such organization.

Such amounts shall be taken into account for the taxable year of the holder in which (or with which) the taxable year of such organization ends.

(ii) Description of amounts. For purposes of clause (i)—

(I) gross income is described in this clause to the extent such income would (but for this paragraph) be treated under subsection (a) as derived from an unrelated trade or business, and

(II) any deduction is described in this clause to the extent it would (but for this paragraph) be allowable under subsection (a)(2) in computing unrelated business taxable income.

(iii) Disqualified holder. For purposes of this subparagraph, the term "disqualified holder" means any shareholder (or beneficiary) which is not described in clause (i) or (ii) of subparagraph (C).

(G) Special rules for purposes of the exceptions. Except as otherwise provided by regulations—

(i) Small leases disregarded. For purposes of clauses (iii) and (iv) of subparagraph (B), a lease to a person described in such clause (iii) or (iv) shall be disregarded if no more than 25 percent of the leasable floor space in a building (or complex of buildings) is covered by the lease and if the lease is on commercially reasonable terms.

(ii) Commercially reasonable financing. Clause (v) of subparagraph (B) shall not apply if the financing is on commercially reasonable terms.

(H) Qualifying sales by financial institutions.

(i) In general. In the case of a qualifying sale by a financial institution, except as provided in regulations, clauses (i) and (ii) of subparagraph (B) shall not apply with respect to financing provided by such institution for such sale.

(ii) Qualifying sale. For purposes of this clause, there is a qualifying sale by a financial institution if—

(I) a qualified organization acquires property described in clause (iii) from a financial institution and any gain recognized by the financial institution with respect to the property is ordinary income,

(II) the stated principal amount of the financing provided by the financial institution does not exceed the amount of the outstanding indebtedness (including accrued but unpaid interest) of the financial institution with respect to the property described in clause (iii) immediately before the acquisition referred to in clause (iii) or (v), whichever is applicable, and

(III) the present value (determined as of the time of the sale and by using the applicable Federal rate determined under section 1274(d)) of the maximum amount payable pursuant to the financing that is determined by reference to the revenue, income, or profits derived from the property cannot exceed 30 percent of the total purchase price of the property (including the contingent payments).

(iii) Property to which subparagraph applies. Property is described in this clause if such property is foreclosure property, or is real property which—

(I) was acquired by the qualified organization from a financial institution which is in conservatorship or receivership, or from the conservator or receiver of such an institution, and

(II) was held by the financial institution at the time it entered into conservatorship or receivership.

(iv) Financial institution. For purposes of this subparagraph, the term "financial institution" means—

(I) any financial institution described in section 581 or 591(a),

(II) any other corporation which is a direct or indirect subsidiary of an institution referred to in subclause (I) but only if, by virtue of being affiliated with such institution, such other corporation is subject to supervision and examination by a Federal or State agency which regulates institutions referred to in subclause (I), and

(III) any person acting as a conservator or receiver of an entity referred to in subclause (I) or (II) (or any government agency or corporation succeeding to the rights or interest of such person).

(v) Foreclosure property. For purposes of this subparagraph, the term "foreclosure property" means any real property acquired by the financial institution as the result of having bid on such property at foreclosure, or by operation of an agreement or process of law, after there was a default (or a default was imminent) on indebtedness which such property secured.

(d) Basis of debt-financed property acquired in corporate liquidation.

For purposes of this subtitle, if the property was acquired in a complete or partial liquidation of a corporation in exchange for its stock, the basis of the property shall be the same as it would be in the hands of the transferor corporation, increased by the amount of gain recognized to the transferor corporation upon such distribution and by the amount of any gain to the organization which was included, on account of such distribution, in unrelated business taxable income under subsection (a).

(e) Allocation rules.

Where debt-financed property is held for purposes described in subsection (b)(1)(A), (B), (C), or (D) as well as for other purposes, proper allocation shall be made with respect to basis, indebtedness, and income and deductions. The allocations required by this section shall be made in accordance with regulations prescribed by the Secretary to the extent proper to carry out the purposes of this section.

(f) Personal property leased with real property.

For purposes of this section, the term "real property" includes personal property of the lessor leased by it to a lessee of its real estate if the lease of such personal property is made under, or in connection with, the lease of such real estate.

(g) Regulations.

The Secretary shall prescribe such regulations as may be necessary or appropriate to carry out the purposes of this section, including regulations to prevent the circumvention of any provision of this section through the use of segregated asset accounts.

In **2006**, P.L. 109-280, Sec. 866(a), deleted "or" at the end of clause (c)(9)(C)(ii), substituted "; or" for the period at the end of clause (c)(9)(C)(iii), and added clause (c)(9)(C)(iv), effective for tax. yrs. begin. on or after 8/17/2006.

In **2005**, P.L. 109-135, Sec. 412(ee)(2), substituted "section 512(b)(19)" for "section 512(b)(18)" in subpara. (b)(1)(E), effective 12/21/2005.

In **2004**, P.L. 108-357, Sec. 247(a), amended para. (c)(6), effective for indebtedness incurred after 10/22/2004 by a small business investment company licensed after 10/22/2004.

Prior to amendment, para. (c)(6) read as follows:

"(6) Certain federal financing. For purposes of this section, the term 'acquisition indebtedness' does not include an obligation, to the extent that it is insured by the Federal Housing Administration, to finance the purchase, rehabilitation, or construction of housing for low and moderate income persons."

—P.L. 108-357, Sec. 702(b), deleted "or" at the end of subpara. (b)(1)(C), substituted "; or" for the period at the end of subpara. (b)(1)(D) and added subpara. (b)(1)(E), effective for any gain or loss on the sale, exchange, or other disposition of any property acquired by the taxpayer after 12/31/2004.

—P.L. 108-357, Sec. 702(c), of this Act, reads as follows:

"(c) Savings clause. Nothing in the amendments made by this section shall affect any duty, liability, or other requirement imposed under any other Federal or State law. Notwithstanding section 128(b) of the Comprehensive Environmental Response, Compensation, and Liability Act of 1980, a certification provided by the Environmental Protection Agency or an appropriate State agency (within the meaning of section 198(c)(4) of the Internal Revenue Code of 1986) shall not affect the liability of any person under section 107(a) of such Act."

In 1993, P.L. 103-66, Sec. 13144(a), added subparas. (c)(9)(G) and (H) . . . Sec. 13144(b)(1), added "For purposes of this paragraph, an interest in a mortgage shall in no event be treated as real property." at the end of subpara. (c)(9)(A) . . . Sec. 13144(b)(2), deleted the last sentence of subpara. (c)(9)(B), effective for acquisitions on or after 1/1/94. Sec. 13144(c)(2) of this Act provides:

"(2) Small leases. The provisions of section 514(c)(9)(G)(i) of the Internal Revenue Code of 1986 shall, in addition to any leases to which the provisions apply by reason of paragraph (1), apply to leases entered into on or after January 1, 1994."

Prior to deletion, the last sentence of subpara. (c)(9)(B) read as follows:

"For purposes of this paragraph, an interest in a mortgage shall in no event be treated as real property."

In 1989, P.L. 101-239, Sec. 7811(1), redesignated subpara. (c)(9)(E) [sic (F)] [as added by Sec. 1016(a)(5)(A) of P.L. 100-647, see below] as subpara. (c)(9)(F), effective as provided in Sec. 1016(a)(5)(B) of P.L. 100-647, see below.

In 1988, P.L. 100-647, Sec. 1002(c)(3), of this Act provides:

"(3) Notwithstanding section 203 of the Reform Act, the amendments made by section 201 of the Reform Act shall apply to any real property which was acquired before January 1, 1987, and was converted on or after such date from personal use to a use for which depreciation is allowable."

—P.L. 100-647, Sec. 1016(a)(5)(A), added subpara. (c)(9)(E) [sic (F)], effective as provided in Sec. 1016(a)(5)(B) of this Act which reads as follows:

"(B) The amendment made by subparagraph (A) shall apply with respect to interests in the organization acquired after June 10, 1987, except that such amendment shall not apply to any such interest acquired after June 10, 1987, pursuant to a binding written contract in effect on June 10, 1987, and at all times thereafter before such acquisition."

—P.L. 100-647, Sec. 1016(a)(6), substituted "this paragraph" for "clause (vi)" in subpara. (c)(9)(B), effective for tax. yrs. begin. after 12/31/86.

—P.L. 100-647, Sec. 1018(u)(13)(A), substituted "second to the last sentence of section 514(c)(9)(B) (as amended by paragraph (3))" for "last sentence of section 514(c)(9)(B) (relating to exceptions)" in Sec. 1878(e)(1) of P.L. 99-514, see below . . . Sec. 1018(u)(13)(B), substituted", and the last sentence of such section, are amended" for "is amended" in Sec. 1878(e)(3) of P.L. 99-514, see below.

—P.L. 100-647, Sec. 2004(h)(1), added clause (c)(9)(E)(iii) . . . Sec. 2004(h)(2), deleted subclause (c)(9)(E)(i)(I) and redesignated subclauses (c)(9)(E)(i)(II) and (III) as subclauses (c)(9)(E)(i)(I) and (II), effective as provided in Secs. 10214(c)(1) and (2) of P.L. 100-203, see below.

Prior to deletion, subclause (c)(9)(E)(i)(I) read as follows:

"(I) the allocation of items to any partner other than a qualified organization cannot result in such partner having a share of the overall partnership loss for any taxable year greater than such partner's share of the overall partnership income for the taxable year for which such partner's income share will be the smallest,"

In 1987, P.L. 100-203, Sec. 10214(a), amended clause (c)(9)(B)(vi) . . . Sec. 10214(b), added subpara. (c)(9)(E), effective as provided in Secs. 10214(c)(1) and (2) which read as follows:

"(1) property acquired by the partnership after October 13, 1987, and

"(2) partnership interests acquired after October 13, 1987,

except that such amendments shall not apply in the case of any property (or partnership interest) acquired pursuant to a written binding contract in effect on October 13, 1987, and at all times thereafter before such property (or interest) is acquired."

Prior to amendment, clause (c)(9)(B)(vi) read as follows:

"(vi) the real property is held by a partnership (which does not fail to meet the requirements of clauses (i) through (v)), and—

"(I) any partner of the partnership is not a qualified organization, and

"(II) the principal purpose of any allocation to any partner of the partnership which is a qualified organization which is not a qualified allocation (within the meaning of section 168(h)(6)) is the avoidance of income tax."

In 1986, P.L. 99-514, Sec. 201(d)(9), substituted "section 168(h)(6)" for "section 168(j)(9)" in subclause (c)(9)(B)(vi)(II) [as amended by Sec. 1878(e)(3) of this Act, see below], effective for property placed in service after 12/31/86, in tax. yrs. end. after 12/31/86 [see Sec. 1002(c)(3) of P.L. 100-647, above]. For other rules, see Sec. 203(b)-(e) of this Act, reproduced in note following Code Sec. 168.

—P.L. 99-514, Sec. 1603(b)(1), deleted "or" at the end of clause (c)(9)(C)(i) . . . Sec. 1603(b)(2), substituted"; or" for the period at the end of clause (c)(9)(C)(ii) . . . Sec. 1603(b)(3), added clause (c)(9)(C)(iii), effective for tax. yrs. begin. after 12/31/86.

—P.L. 99-514, Sec. 1607, provides transitional rule as follows:

"SEC. 1607. TRANSITION RULE FOR ACQUISITION INDEBTEDNESS WITH RESPECT TO CERTAIN LAND.

"For purposes of applying section 514(c) of the Internal Revenue Code of 1986, with respect to a disposition during calendar year 1986 or calendar year 1987 of land acquired during calendar year 1984, the term 'acquisition indebtedness' does not include indebtedness incurred in connection with bonds issued after January 1, 1984, and before July 19, 1984, on behalf of an organization which is a community college and which is described in section 511(a)(2)(B) of such Code."

—P.L. 99-514, Sec. 1878(e)(1), [as amended by Sec. 1018(u)(13)(A) of P.L. 100-647, see above], substituted "is unrelated business taxable income" for "would be unrelated business taxable income (determined without regard to this paragraph)" in the second to last sentence of subpara. (c)(9)(B) [as amended by Sec. 1878(e)(3) of this Act, see below] . . . Sec. 1878(e)(2), substituted "section 509(a)(3)" for "section 509(a)" in clause (c)(9)(C)(i) . . . Sec. 1878(e)(3), [as amended by Sec. 1018(u)(13)(B) of P.L. 100-647, see above], amended clause (c)(9)(B)(vi) and the sentence at the end of subpara. (c)(9)(B), effective for indebtedness incurred after 7/18/84, except as provided by Sec. 1034(c)(2) and (3) of P.L. 98-369, reproduced below.

Prior to amendment, clause (c)(9)(B)(vi) read as follows:

"(vi) the real property is held by a partnership unless the partnership meets the requirements of clauses (i) through (v) and unless—

"(I) all of the partners of the partnership are qualified organizations, or

"(II) each allocation to a partner of the partnership which is a qualified organization is a qualified allocation (within the meaning of section 168(j)(9))."

Prior to amendment, the sentence at the end of subpara. (c)(9)(B) read as follows:

"For purposes of clause (vi)(I), an organization shall not be treated as a qualified organization if any income of such organization would be unrelated business taxable income (determined without regard to this paragraph)."

In 1984, P.L. 98-369, Sec. 174(b)(5)(B), substituted "section 267(b) or 707(b)" for "section 267(b)" in clause (c)(9)(B)(iii), effective for transactions after 12/31/83, in tax. yrs. end. after 12/31/83.

—P.L. 98-369, Sec. 1034(a), amended para. (c)(9) . . . Sec. 1034(b), added subsec. (g), effective for indebtedness incurred after 7/18/84. Sec. 1034(c)(2) and (3) of this Act provides exceptions as follows:

"(2) Exception for indebtedness on certain property acquired before January 1, 1985.—

"(A) The amendment made by subsection (a) shall not apply to any indebtedness incurred before January 1, 1985, by a partnership described in subparagraph (B) if such indebtedness is incurred with respect to property acquired (directly or indirectly) by such partnership before such date.

"(B) A partnership is described in this subparagraph if—

"(i) before October 21, 1983, the partnership was organized, a request for exemption with respect to such partnership was filed with the Department of Labor, and a private placement memorandum stating the maximum number of units in the partnership that would be offered had been circulated,

"(ii) the interest in the property to be acquired, directly or indirectly (including through acquiring an interest in another partnership) by such partnership was described in such private placement memorandum, and

"(iii) the marketing of partnership interests in such partnership is completed not later than 2 years after the later of the date of enactment of this Act or the date of publication in the Federal Register of such exemption by the Department of Labor and the aggregate number of units in such partnership sold does not exceed the amount described in clause (i).

"(3) Exception for indebtedness on certain property acquired before January 1, 1986.—

"(A) The amendment made by subsection (a) shall not apply to any indebtedness incurred before January 1, 1986, by a partnership described in subparagraph (B) if such indebtedness is incurred with respect to property acquired (directly or indirectly) by such partnership before such date.

"(B) A partnership is described in this paragraph if—

"(i) before March 6, 1984, the partnership was organized and publicly announced, the maximum amount of interest which would be sold in such partnership, and

"(ii) the marketing of partnership interests in such partnership is completed not later than the 90th day after the date of the enactment of this Act and the aggregate amount of interests in such partnership sold does not exceed the maximum amount described in clause (i).

For purposes of clause (i), the maximum amount taken into account shall be the greatest of the amounts shown in the registration statement, prospectus, or partnership agreement.

"(C) Binding contracts.—For purposes of this paragraph, property shall be deemed to have been acquired before January 1, 1986, if such property is acquired pursuant to a written contract which, on January 1, 1986, and at all times thereafter, required the acquisition of such property and such property is placed in service not later than 6 months after the date such contract was entered into."

Prior to amendment, para. (c)(9) read as follows:

"(9) Real property acquired by qualified trust. For purposes of this section—

"(A) In general. Except as provided in subparagraph (B), the term 'acquisition indebtedness' does not include indebtedness incurred by a qualified trust in acquiring or improving any real property.

"(B) Exceptions. The provisions of subparagraph (A) shall not apply in any case in which—

"(i) the acquisition price is not a fixed amount determined as of the date of acquisition;

"(ii) the amount of any indebtedness or any other amount payable with respect to such indebtedness, or the time for making any payment of any such amount, is dependent, in whole or in part, upon any revenue, income, or profits derived from such real property;

"(iii) the real property is at any time after the acquisition leased by the qualified trust to the person selling such property to such trust or to any person who bears a relationship described in section 267(b) or 707(b) to such person;

"(iv) the real property is acquired from, or is at any time after the acquisition leased by the qualified trust to, any person who—

"(I) bears a relationship which is described in section 4975(e)(2)(C), (E), or (G) to any plan with respect to which such trust was formed, or

"(II) bears a relationship which is described in section 4975(e)(2)(F) or (H) to any person described in subclause (I); or

"(v) any person described in clause (iii) or (iv) provides the qualified trust with nonrecourse financing in connection with such transaction and such debt—

"(I) is subordinate to any other indebtedness on such property, or

"(II) bears interest at a rate which is significantly less than the rate available from any person not described in clause (iii) or (iv) at the time such indebtedness is incurred.

"(C) Qualified trust. For purposes of this paragraph, the term 'qualified trust' means any trust which constitutes a qualified trust under section 401."

In 1980, P.L. 96-608, Sec. 6, provides:

"SEC. 6. TREATMENT OF CERTAIN INDEBTEDNESS INCURRED BEFORE 1965 FOR PURPOSES OF SECTION 514.

"(a) General rule.

"For purposes of applying section 514 of the Internal Revenue Code of 1954 with respect to any sale of real property during 1976, indebtedness incurred before January 1, 1965, by an organization to finance the construction of a building on such property shall not be treated as acquisition indebtedness if the parcel of real property on which such building was constructed—

"(1) was acquired by such organization before January 1, 1952, and

"(2) is contiguous to another parcel of real property which—

"(A) was acquired by such organization before January 1, 1952, and

"(B) was used by such organization, on January 1, 1952, and at all times thereafter before the date of the enactment of this Act, in a manner which meets the requirements of section 514(b)(1)(A) of such Code (relating to property used in carrying out exempt purpose).

"(b) Effective date.

"The provisions of subsection (a) shall apply to sales during calendar year 1976."

—P.L. 96-605, Sec. 110(a), added para. (c)(9), effective for tax. yrs. begin. after 12/31/80. Sec. 110(b) of this Act provides as follows:

"(b) No Precedent.

"The amendment [Code Sec. 514(c)(9)] made by subsection (a) shall not be considered a precedent with respect to extending such amendment (or similar rules) to any other person."

In 1978, P.L. 95-345, Sec. 2(c), added para. (c)(8), effective as provided in Sec. 2(e) of this Act, which reads as follows:

"(e) Effective date.

"The amendments made by this section apply with respect to—

"(1) amounts received after December 31, 1976, as payments with respect to securities loans (as defined in section 512(a)(5) of the Internal Revenue Code of 1954), and

"(2) transfers of securities, under agreements described in section 1058 of such Code, occurring after such date."

In 1976, P.L. 94-455, Sec. 1308(a), added subpara. (c)(2)(C), effective for tax. yrs. end. after 12/31/69.

—P.L. 94-455, Sec. 1901(a)(72)(A), substituted a period for ", except that in the case of any taxable year beginning before January 1, 1972, any indebtedness incurred before June 28, 1966, shall not be taken into account. In the case of an organization (other than a church or convention or association of churches) such indebtedness incurred before June 28, 1966, shall be taken into account if such indebtedness constitutes business lease indebtedness (as defined in subsection (g))." in subpara. (c)(1)(C) ... Sec. 1901(a)(72)(B), deleted subsecs. (f) and (g), and redesignated subsec. (h) as subsec. (f) ... Sec. 1901(a)(72)(C), amended clause (b)(3)(C)(iii) ... Sec. 1901(a)(72)(D), substituted "includes" for "and the term 'premises' include" in subsec. (f) [as redesignated by Sec. 1901(a)(72)(B) of this Act, see above], effective for tax. yrs. begin. after 12/31/76.

Prior to deletion, subsecs. (f) and (g) read as follows:

"(f) Definition of business lease.

"(1) General rule. For purposes of this section, the term 'business lease' means a lease for a term of more than 5 years of real property by an organization (or by a partnership of which it is a member), if at the close of the lessor's taxable year there is a business lease indebtedness (as defined in subsection (g)) with respect to such property.

"(2) Special rules for applying paragraph (1).

"For purposes of paragraph (1)—

"(A) In computing the term of a lease which contains an option for renewal or extension, the term of such lease shall be considered as including any period for which such option may be exercised; and the term of any lease made pursuant to an exercise of such option shall include the period during which the prior lease was in effect. If real property is acquired subject to a lease, the term of such lease shall be considered to begin on the date of such acquisition.

"(B) If the property has been occupied by the same lessee for a total period of more than 5 years commencing not earlier than the date of acquisition of the property by the organization or trust (whether such occupancy is under one or more leases, renewals, extensions, or continuations thereof), the occupancy of such lessee shall be considered to be under a lease for a term of more than 5 years within the meaning of paragraph (1). However, subsection (a) shall apply in the case of a tenancy described in this subparagraph (and not within subparagraph (A)) only with respect to the sixth and succeeding years of occupancy by the same lessee. For purposes of this subparagraph, the term 'same lessee' shall include any lessee of the property whose relationship with a lessee of the same property is such that losses in respect of sales or exchanges of property between the 2 lessees would be disallowed under section 267(a).

"(3) Exceptions.

"(A) No lease shall be considered a business lease if—

"(i) such lease is entered into primarily for purposes which are substantially related (aside from the need of such organization for income or funds or the use it makes of the rents derived) to the exercise or performance by such organization of its charitable, educational, or other purpose or function constituting the basis for its exemption under section 501, or

"(ii) the lease is of premises in a building primarily designed for occupancy, and occupied, by the organization.

"(B) If a lease for more than 5 years to a tenant is for only a portion of the real property, and space in the real property is rented during the taxable year under a lease for not more than 5 years to any other tenant of the organization, leases of the real property for more than 5 years shall be considered as business leases during the taxable year only if—

"(i) the rents derived from the real property during the taxable year under leases for more than 5 years (not including, as a lease for more than 5 years, an occupancy which is considered as such a lease by reason of paragraph (2)(B)) represent 50 percent or more of the total rents derived during the taxable year from the real property; or the area of the premises occupied under leases for more than 5 years (not including, as a lease for more than 5 years, an occupancy which is considered as such a lease by reason of paragraph (2)(B)) represents, at any time during the taxable year, 50 percent or more of the total area of the real property rented at such time; or

"(ii) the rent derived from the real property during the taxable year from any tenant under a lease for more than 5 years (including as a lease for more than 5 years an occupancy which is considered as such a lease by reason of paragraph (2)(B)), or from a group of tenants (under such leases) who are either members of an affiliated group (as defined in section 1504) or partners, represents more than 10 percent of the total rents derived during the taxable year from such property; or the area of the premises occupied by any one such tenant, or by any such group of tenants, represents at any time during the taxable year more than 10 percent of the total area of the real property rented at such time.

In the application of clause (i), if during the last half of the term of a lease a new lease is made to take effect after the expiration of such lease, the unexpired portion of such lease on the date the second lease is made shall not be treated as a part of the term of the second lease.

"(g) Business lease indebtedness.

"(1) General rule. The term 'business lease indebtedness' means, with respect to any real property leased for a term of more than 5 years, the unpaid amount of—

"(A) the indebtedness incurred by the lessor in acquiring or improving such property;

"(B) the indebtedness incurred before the acquisition or improvement of such property if such indebtedness would not have been incurred but for such acquisition or improvement; and

"(C) the indebtedness incurred after the acquisition or improvement of such property if such indebtedness would not have been incurred but for such acquisition or improvement and the incurrence of such indebtedness was reasonably foreseeable at the time of such acquisition or improvement.

"(2) Property acquired subject to mortgage, etc. Where real property is acquired subject to a mortgage or other similar lien, the amount of the indebtedness secured by such mortgage or lien shall be considered (whether the acquisition was by gift, devise, or purchase) as an indebtedness of the lessor incurred in acquiring such property even though the lessor did not assume or agree to pay such indebtedness, except that where real property was acquired by gift, bequest, or devise before July 1, 1950, subject to a mortgage or other similar lien, the amount of such mortgage or other similar lien shall not be considered as an indebtedness of the lessor incurred in acquiring such property.

"(3) Certain property acquired by gift, etc. Where real property was acquired by gift, bequest, or devise before July 1, 1950, subject to a lease requiring improvements in such property on the happening of stated contingencies, indebtedness incurred in improving such property in accordance with the terms of such lease shall not be considered as an indebtedness for purposes of this subsection.

"(4) Certain corporations described in section 501(c)(2). In the case of a corporation described in section 501(c)(2), all of the stock of which was acquired before July 1, 1950, by an organization described in paragraph (3), (5), or (6) of section 501(c) (and more than one-third of such stock was acquired by such organization by gift or bequest), any indebtedness incurred by such corporation before July 1, 1950, and any indebtedness incurred by such corporation on or after such date in improving real property in accordance with the terms of a lease entered into before such date, shall not be considered as an indebtedness with respect to such corporation or such organization for purposes of this subsection.

"(5) Certain trusts described in section 401(a). In the case of a trust described in section 401(a), or in the case of a corporation described in section 501(c)(2) all of the stock of which was acquired prior to March 1, 1954, by a trust described in section 401(a), any indebtedness incurred by such trust or such corporation before March 1, 1954, in connection with real property which is leased before March 1, 1954, and any indebtedness incurred by such trust or such corporation on or after such date necessary to carry out the terms of such lease, shall not be considered as an indebtedness with respect to such trust or such corporation for purposes of this subsection.

"(6) Business lease on portion of property. In determining the amount of the business lease indebtedness where only a portion of the real property is subject to a business lease, proper allocation to the premises covered by such lease shall be made of the indebtedness incurred by the lessor with respect to the real property.

"(7) Special rule applicable to trusts described in section 401(a). In the application of paragraph (1), if a trust described in section 401(a) forming part of a stock bonus, pension, or profit-sharing plan of an employer lends any money to another trust described in section 401(a) forming part of a stock bonus, pension, or profit-sharing plan of the same employer, such loan shall not be treated as an indebtedness of the borrowing trust, except to the extent that the loaning trust—

"(A) incurs any indebtedness in order to make such loan;

"(B) incurred indebtedness before the making of such loan which would not have been incurred but for the making of such loan; or

"(C) incurred indebtedness after the making of such loan which would not have been incurred but for the making of such loan and which was reasonably foreseeable at the time of making such loan.

"(8) Trusts described in section 501(c)(17).

"(A) In the case of a trust described in section 501(c)(17), or in the case of a corporation described in section 501(c)(2), all of the stock of which was acquired before January 1, 1960, by a trust described in section 501(c)(17), any indebtedness incurred by such trust or such corporation before January 1, 1960, in connection with real property which is leased before January 1, 1960, and any indebtedness incurred by such trust or such corporation on or after such date necessary to carry out the terms of such lease, shall not be considered as an indebtedness with respect to such trust or such corporation for purposes of this subsection.

"(B) In the application of paragraph (1), if a trust described in section 501(c)(17) forming part of a supplemental unemployment compensation benefit plan lends any money to another trust described in section 501(c)(17) forming part of the same plan, such loan shall not be treated as an indebtedness of the borrowing trust, except to the extent that the loaning trust—

"(i) incurs any indebtedness in order to make such loan,

"(ii) incurred indebtedness before the making of such loan which would not have been incurred but for the making of such loan, or

"(iii) incurred indebtedness after the making of such loan which would not have been incurred but for the making of such loan and which was reasonably foreseeable at the time of making such loan."

Prior to amendment, clause (b)(3)(C)(iii) read as follows:

"(iii) shall not apply to property subject to a lease which is a business lease (defined in subsection (f))."

—P.L. 94-455, Sec. 1906(b)(13)(A), substituted "Secretary" for "Secretary or his delegate" each place it appeared in Code Sec. 514, effective for tax. yrs. begin. after 12/31/76.

In 1975, P.L. 93-625, Sec. 7(b)(2), deleted the sentence at the end of subpara. (b)(3)(D), effective 7/1/75 and apply to amounts outstanding on 7/1/75 or arising thereafter.

Prior to deletion, the sentence at the end of subpara. (b)(3)(D) read as follows: "Interest on any overpayment for a taxable year resulting from the application of subparagraph (B) after the actual use condition is satisfied shall be allowed and paid at the rate of 4 percent per annum in lieu of 6 percent per annum."

In 1969, P.L. 91-172, Sec. 121(d)(1), amended so much of Code Sec. 514 as precedes subsec. (b) [adding new subsecs. (a), (b), (c), (d) and (e)]... Sec. 121(d)(3)(A), redesignated existing subsecs. (b), (c) and (d) as subsecs. (f), (g) and (h)... Sec. 121(d)(3)(B), substituted "subsection (g)" for "subsection (c)" in para. (f)(1) [as redesignated by Sec. 121(d)(3)(A) of this Act, see above], effective for tax. yrs. begin. after 12/31/69. Sec. 121(g) of this Act provides a special rule as follows:

"(g) Effective dates.

"The amendments made by this section (other than by subsections (b)(3) and (e)) shall apply to taxable years beginning after December 31, 1969. The amendments made by subsection (b)(3) shall apply to taxable years beginning after December 31, 1970. The amendments made by subsection (e) shall apply with respect to transfers of property after December 31, 1969. Where an organization makes a bargain purchase of property before October 9, 1969, which is subject to a mortgage which was placed on the property more than 5 years before the purchase, and the organization paid the seller a total amount no greater than the amount of the seller's cost (including attorneys' fees) directly related to the transfer of such property to the organization (but in any event no more than 10 percent of the value of the seller's equity in the property), the indebtedness securing by such mortgage shall not be treated, notwithstanding the amendments made by subsection (d)(1), as acquisition indebtedness for purposes of section 514(c)(1) of the Internal Revenue Code of 1954 during a period of 10 years following the date of the transaction."

Prior to amendment, so much of Code Sec. 514 as precedes subsec. (b) read as follows:

"SEC. 514. BUSINESS LEASES.

"(a) Business lease rents and deductions.

"In computing under section 512 the unrelated business taxable income for any taxable year—

"(1) Percentage of rents taken into account. There shall be included with respect to each business lease, as an item of gross income derived from an unrelated trade or business, an amount which is the same percentage (but not in excess of 100 percent) of the total rents derived during the taxable year under such lease as (A) the business lease indebtedness, at the close of the taxable year, with respect to the premises covered by such lease is of (B) the adjusted basis, at the close of the taxable year, of such premises.

"(2) Percentage of deductions taken into account. There shall be allowed with respect to each business lease, as a deduction to be taken into account in computing unrelated business taxable income, an amount determined by applying the percentage derived under paragraph (1) to the sum determined under paragraph (3).

"(3) Deductions allowable. The sum referred to in paragraph (2) is the sum of the following deductions allowable under this chapter:

"(A) Taxes and other expenses paid or accrued during the taxable year on or with respect to the real property subject to the business lease.

"(B) Interest paid or accrued during the taxable year on the business lease indebtedness.

"(C) A reasonable allowance for exhaustion, wear and tear (including a reasonable allowance for obsolescence) of the real property subject to such lease.

Where only a portion of the real property is subject to the business lease, there shall be taken into account under subparagraphs (A), (B), and (C) only those amounts which are properly allocable to the premises covered by such lease."

In 1960, P.L. 86-667, Sec. 5, added para. (c)(8), effective for tax. yrs. begin. after 12/31/59.

Sec. 515. Taxes of foreign countries and possessions of the United States.

The amount of taxes imposed by foreign countries and possessions of the United States shall be allowed as a credit against the tax of an organization subject to the tax imposed by section 511 to the extent provided in section 901; and in the case of the tax imposed by section 511, the term "taxable income" as used in section 901 shall be read as "unrelated business taxable income."

PART IV.—FARMERS' COOPERATIVES

Sec.

521. Exemption of farmers' cooperatives from tax.

522. Repealed.

In 1969, P.L. 91-172, Sec. 101(a), redesignated Part III as Part IV.

In 1962, P.L. 87-834, Sec. 17, struck out item 522 which dealt with tax on farmers' cooperatives.

Sec. 521. Exemption of farmers' cooperatives from tax.

(a) Exemption from tax.

A farmers' cooperative organization described in subsection (b)(1) shall be exempt from taxation under this subtitle except as otherwise provided in part I of subchapter T (sec. 1381 and following). Notwithstanding part I of subchapter T (sec. 1381 and following), such an organization shall be considered an organization exempt from income taxes for purposes of any law which refers to organizations exempt from income taxes.

(b) Applicable rules.

(1) Exempt farmers' cooperatives. The farmers' cooperatives exempt from taxation to the extent provided in subsection (a) are farmers', fruit growers', or like associations organized and operated on a cooperative basis (A) for the purpose of marketing the products of members or other producers, and turning back to them the proceeds of sales, less the necessary marketing expenses, on the basis of either the quantity or the value of the products furnished by them, or (B) for the purpose of purchasing supplies and equipment for the use of members or other persons, and turning over such supplies and equipment to them at actual cost, plus necessary expenses.

(2) Organizations having capital stock. Exemption shall not be denied any such association because it has capital stock, if the dividend rate of such stock is fixed at not to exceed the legal rate of interest in the State of incorporation or 8 percent per annum, whichever is greater, on the value of the consideration for which the stock was issued, and if substantially all such stock (other than nonvoting preferred stock, the owners of which are not entitled or permitted to participate, directly or indirectly, in the profits of the association, upon dissolution or otherwise, beyond the fixed dividends) is owned by producers who market their products or purchase their supplies and equipment through the association.

(3) Organizations maintaining reserve. Exemption shall not be denied any such association because there is accumulated and maintained by it a reserve required by State law or a reasonable reserve for any necessary purpose.

(4) Transactions with nonmembers. Exemption shall not be denied any such association which markets the products of nonmembers in an amount the value of which does not exceed the value of the products marketed for members, or which purchases supplies and equipment for nonmembers in an amount the value of which does not exceed the value of the supplies and equipment purchased for members, provided the value of the purchases made for persons who are neither members nor producers does not exceed 15 percent of the value of all its purchases.

(5) Business for the United States. Business done for the United States or any of its agencies shall be disregarded in determining the right to exemption under this section.

(6) Netting of losses. Exemption shall not be denied any such association because such association computes its net earnings for purposes of determining any amount available for distribution to patrons in the manner described in paragraph (1) of section 1388(j).

(7) Cross reference. For treatment of value-added processing involving animals, see section 1388(k).

In 2004, P.L. 108-357, Sec. 316(b), added para. (b)(7), effective for tax. yrs. begin. after 10/22/2004.

In 1986, P.L. 99-272, Sec. 13210(b), added para. (b)(6), effective for tax. yrs. begin. after 12/31/62. For special rules, see Sec. 13210(c)(2) and (3) of this Act reproduced in note following Code Sec. 1388.

In 1962, P.L. 87-834, Sec. 17(b)(1), substituted "part I of subchapter T (sec. 1381 and following)" for "section 522" each place it appeared in subsec. (a), effective for tax. yrs. begin. after 12/31/62.

Sec. 522. Repealed.

In 1962, P.L. 87-834, Sec. 17, repealed Code Sec. 522, effective as provided in Sec. 17(c)(3) of this act, which reads:

"(3) Application of existing law. In the case of any money, written notice of allocation, or other property paid by any organization described in section 1381(a)—

"(A) before the first day of the first taxable year of such organization beginning after December 31, 1962, or

"(B) on or after such first day with respect to patronage occurring before such first day,

the tax treatment of such money, written notice of allocation, or other property (including the tax treatment of gain or loss on the redemption, sale, or other disposition of such written notice of allocation) by any person shall be made under the Code of 1954 without regard to subchapter T of chapter 1 of such Code [§§ 1381 thru 1388]."

Prior to repeal, Code Sec. 522, read as follows:

"SEC. 522. TAX ON FARMERS' COOPERATIVES.

"(a) Imposition of tax.

"An organization exempt from taxation under section 521 shall be subject to the taxes imposed by section 11 or section 1201.

"(b) Computation of taxable income.

"(1) General rule.— In computing the taxable income of such an organization there shall be allowed as deductions from gross income (in addition to other deductions allowable under this chapter)—

"(A) amounts paid as dividends during the taxable year on its capital stock, and

"(B) amounts allocated during the taxable year to patrons with respect to its income not derived from patronage (whether or not such income was derived during such taxable year) whether paid in cash, merchandise, capital stock, revolving fund certificates, retain certificates, certificates of indebtedness, letters of advice, or in some other manner that discloses to each patron the dollar amount allocated to him. Allocations made after the close of the taxable year and on or before the 15th day of the 9th month following the close of such year shall be considered as made on the last day of such taxable year to the extent the allocations are attributable to income derived before the close of such year.

"(2) Patronage dividends, etc.—Patronage dividends, refunds, and rebates to patrons with respect to their patronage in the same or preceding years (whether paid in cash, merchandise, capital stock, revolving fund certificates, retain certificates, certificates of indebtedness, letters of advice, or in some other manner that discloses to each patron the dollar amount of such dividend, refund, or rebate) shall be taken into account in computing taxable income in the same manner as in the case of a cooperative organization not exempt under section 521. Such dividends, refunds, and rebates made after the close of the taxable year and on or before the 15th day of the 9th month following the close of such year shall be considered as made on the last day of such taxable year to the extent the dividends, refunds, or rebates, are attributable to patronage occurring before the close of such year."

PART V.—SHIPOWNERS' PROTECTION AND INDEMNITY ASSOCIATIONS

Sec.
526. Shipowners' protection and indemnity associations.

In 1969, P.L. 91-172, Sec. 101(a), redesignated Part IV as Part V.

Sec. 526. Shipowners' protection and indemnity associations.

There shall not be included in gross income the receipts of shipowners' mutual protection and indemnity associations not organized for profit, and no part of the net earnings of which inures to the benefit of any private shareholder; but such corporations shall be subject as other persons to the tax on their taxable income from interest, dividends, and rents.

PART VI.—POLITICAL ORGANIZATIONS

Sec.
527. Political Organizations.

Sec. 527. Political organizations.

(a) General rule.

A political organization shall be subject to taxation under this subtitle only to the extent provided in this section. A political organization shall be considered an organization exempt from income taxes for the purpose of any law which refers to organizations exempt from income taxes.

(b) Tax imposed.

(1) In general. A tax is hereby imposed for each taxable year on the political organization taxable income of every political organization. Such tax shall be computed by multiplying the political organization taxable income by the highest rate of tax specified in section 11(b).

(2) Alternative tax in case of capital gains. If for any taxable year any political organization has a net capital gain, then, in lieu of the tax imposed by paragraph (1), there is hereby imposed a tax (if such a tax is less than the tax imposed by paragraph (1)) which shall consist of the sum of—

(A) a partial tax, computed as provided by paragraph (1), on the political organization taxable income determined by reducing such income by the amount of such gain, and

(B) an amount determined as provided in section 1201(a) on such gain.

(c) Political organization taxable income defined.

(1) Taxable income defined. For purposes of this section, the political organization taxable income of any organization for any taxable year is an amount equal to the excess (if any) of—

(A) the gross income for the taxable year (excluding any exempt function income), over

(B) the deductions allowed by this chapter which are directly connected with the production of the gross income (excluding exempt function income), computed with the modifications provided in paragraph (2).

(2) Modifications. For purposes of this subsection—

(A) there shall be allowed a specific deduction of $100,

(B) no net operating loss deduction shall be allowed under section 172, and

(C) no deduction shall be allowed under part VIII of subchapter B (relating to special deductions for corporations).

(3) Exempt function income. For purposes of this subsection, the term "exempt function income" means any amount received as—

(A) a contribution of money or other property,

(B) membership dues, a membership fee or assessment from a member of the political organization,

(C) proceeds from a political fundraising or entertainment event, or proceeds from the sale of political campaign materials, which are not received in the ordinary course of any trade or business, or

(D) proceeds from the conducting of any bingo game (as defined in section 513(f)(2)), to the extent such amount is segregated for use only for the exempt function of the political organization.

(d) Certain uses not treated as income to candidate.
For purposes of this title, if any political organization—
(1) contributes any amount to or for the use of any political organization which is treated as exempt from tax under subsection (a) of this section,
(2) contributes any amount to or for the use of any organization described in paragraph (1) or (2) of section 509(a) which is exempt from tax under section 501(a), or
(3) deposits any amount in the general fund of the Treasury or in the general fund of any State or local government,

such amount shall be treated as an amount not diverted for the personal use of the candidate or any other person. No deduction shall be allowed under this title for the contribution or deposit of any amount described in the preceding sentence.

(e) Other definitions.
For purposes of this section—
(1) Political organization. The term "political organization" means a party, committee, association, fund, or other organization (whether or not incorporated) organized and operated primarily for the purpose of directly or indirectly accepting contributions or making expenditures, or both, for an exempt function.
(2) Exempt function. The term "exempt function" means the function of influencing or attempting to influence the selection, nomination, election, or appointment of any individual to any Federal, State, or local public office or office in a political organization, or the election of Presidential or Vice-Presidential electors, whether or not such individual or electors are selected, nominated, elected, or appointed. Such term includes the making of expenditures relating to an office described in the preceding sentence which, if incurred by the individual, would be allowable as a deduction under section 162(a).
(3) Contributions. The term "contributions" has the meaning given to such term by section 271(b)(2).
(4) Expenditures. The term "expenditures" has the meaning given to such term by section 271(b)(3).
(5) Qualified State or local political organization.
  (A) In general. The term "qualified State or local political organization" means a political organization—
    (i) all the exempt functions of which are solely for the purposes of influencing or attempting to influence the selection, nomination, election, or appointment of any individual to any State or local public office or office in a State or local political organization,
    (ii) which is subject to State law that requires the organization to report (and it so reports)—
      (I) information regarding each separate expenditure from and contribution to such organization, and
      (II) information regarding the person who makes such contribution or receives such expenditure,
    which would otherwise be required to be reported under this section, and
    (iii) with respect to which the reports referred to in clause (ii) are (I) made public by the agency with which such reports are filed, and (II) made publicly available for inspection by the organization in the manner described in section 6104(d).
  (B) Certain State law differences disregarded. An organization shall not be treated as failing to meet the requirements of subparagraph (A)(ii) solely by reason of 1 or more of the following:

    (i) The minimum amount of any expenditure or contribution required to be reported under State law is not more than $300 greater than the minimum amount required to be reported under subsection (j).
    (ii) The State law does not require the organization to identify 1 or more of the following:
      (I) The employer of any person who makes contributions to the organization.
      (II) The occupation of any person who makes contributions to the organization.
      (III) The employer of any person who receives expenditures from the organization.
      (IV) The occupation of any person who receives expenditures from the organization.
      (V) The purpose of any expenditure of the organization.
      (VI) The date any contribution was made to the organization.
      (VII) The date of any expenditure of the organization.
  (C) De minimis errors. An organization shall not fail to be treated as a qualified State or local political organization solely because such organization makes de minimis errors in complying with the State reporting requirements and the public inspection requirements described in subparagraph (A) as long as the organization corrects such errors within a reasonable period after the organization becomes aware of such errors.
  (D) Participation of Federal candidate or office holder. The term "qualified State or local political organization" shall not include any organization otherwise described in subparagraph (A) if a candidate for nomination or election to Federal elective public office or an individual who holds such office—
    (i) controls or materially participates in the direction of the organization,
    (ii) solicits contributions to the organization (unless the Secretary determines that such solicitations resulted in de minimis contributions and were made without the prior knowledge and consent, whether explicit or implicit, of the organization or its officers, directors, agents, or employees), or
    (iii) directs, in whole or in part, disbursements by the organization.

(f) Exempt organization which is not political organization must include certain amounts in gross income.
(1) In general. If an organization described in section 501(c) which is exempt from tax under section 501(a) expends any amount during the taxable year directly (or through another organization) for an exempt function (within the meaning of subsection (e)(2)), then, notwithstanding any other provision of law, there shall be included in the gross income of such organization for the taxable year, and shall be subject to tax under subsection (b) as if it constituted political organization taxable income, an amount equal to the lesser of—
  (A) the net investment income of such organization for the taxable year, or
  (B) the aggregate amount so expended during the taxable year for such an exempt function.
(2) Net investment income. For purposes of this subsection, the term "net investment income" means the excess of—
  (A) the gross amount of income from interest, dividends, rents, and royalties, plus the excess (if any) of gains from the sale or exchange of assets over the losses from the sale or exchange of assets, over

(B) the deductions allowed by this chapter which are directly connected with the production of the income referred to in subparagraph (A).

For purposes of the preceding sentence, there shall not be taken into account items taken into account for purposes of the tax imposed by section 511 (relating to tax on unrelated business income).

> • **Caution:** Code Sec. 527(f)(3), following, contains a reference to 18 USC 610, which was repealed by Sec. 201(a) of P.L. 94-293 (5/11/76). No conforming amendment was made to Code Sec. 527(f)(3).

(3) Certain separate segregated funds. For purposes of this subsection and subsection (e)(1), a separate segregated fund (within the meaning of section 610 of title 18 or of any similar State statute, or within the meaning of any State statute which permits the segregation of dues moneys for exempt functions (within the meaning of subsection (e)(2))) which is maintained by an organization described in section 501(c) which is exempt from tax under section 501(a) shall be treated as a separate organization.

(g) Treatment of newsletter funds.
(1) In general. For purposes of this section, a fund established and maintained by an individual who holds, has been elected to, or is a candidate (within the meaning of paragraph (3)) for nomination or election to, any Federal, State, or local elective public office for use by such individual exclusively for the preparation and circulation of such individual's newsletter shall, except as provided in paragraph (2), be treated as if such fund constituted a political organization.

(2) Additional modifications. In the case of any fund described in paragraph (1)—
(A) the exempt function shall be only the preparation and circulation of the newsletter, and
(B) the specific deduction provided by subsection (c)(2)(A) shall not be allowed.

(3) Candidate. For purposes of paragraph (1), the term "candidate" means, with respect to any Federal, State, or local elective public office, an individual who—
(A) publicly announces that he is a candidate for nomination or election to such office, and
(B) meets the qualifications prescribed by law to hold such office.

(h) Special rule for principal campaign committees.
(1) In general. In the case of a political organization which is a principal campaign committee, paragraph (1) of subsection (b) shall be applied by substituting "the appropriate rates" for "the highest rate".

(2) Principal campaign committee defined.
(A) In general. For purposes of this subsection, the term "principal campaign committee" means the political committee designated by a candidate for Congress as his principal campaign committee for purposes of—
(i) section 302(e) of the Federal Election Campaign Act of 1971 (2 U.S.C. 432(e)), and
(ii) this subsection.
(B) Designation. A candidate may have only 1 designation in effect under subparagraph (A)(ii) at any time and such designation—
(i) shall be made at such time and in such manner as the Secretary may prescribe by regulations, and
(ii) once made, may be revoked only with the consent of the Secretary.

Nothing in this subsection shall be construed to require any designation where there is only one political committee with respect to a candidate.

(i) Organizations must notify Secretary that they are section 527 organizations.
(1) In general. Except as provided in paragraph (5), an organization shall not be treated as an organization described in this section—
(A) unless it has given notice to the Secretary electronically that it is to be so treated, or
(B) if the notice is given after the time required under paragraph (2), the organization shall not be so treated for any period before such notice is given or, in the case of any material change in the information required under paragraph (3), for the period beginning on the date on which the material change occurs and ending on the date on which such notice is given.

(2) Time to give notice. The notice required under paragraph (1) shall be transmitted not later than 24 hours after the date on which the organization is established or, in the case of any material change in the information required under paragraph (3), not later than 30 days after such material change.

(3) Contents of notice. The notice required under paragraph (1) shall include information regarding—
(A) the name and address of the organization (including any business address, if different) and its electronic mailing address,
(B) the purpose of the organization,
(C) the names and addresses of its officers, highly compensated employees, contact person, custodian of records, and members of its Board of Directors,
(D) the name and address of, and relationship to, any related entities (within the meaning of section 168(h)(4)),
(E) whether the organization intends to claim an exemption from the requirements of subsection (j) or section 6033, and
(F) such other information as the Secretary may require to carry out the internal revenue laws.

(4) Effect of failure. In the case of an organization failing to meet the requirements of paragraph (1) for any period, the taxable income of such organization shall be computed by taking into account any exempt function income (and any deductions directly connected with the production of such income) or, in the case of a failure relating to a material change, by taking into account such income and deductions only during the period beginning on the date on which the material change occurs and ending on the date on which notice is given under this subsection. For purposes of the preceding sentence, the term "exempt function income" means any amount described in a subparagraph of subsection (c)(3), whether or not segregated for use for an exempt function.

(5) Exceptions. This subsection shall not apply to any organization—
(A) to which this section applies solely by reason of subsection (f)(1),
(B) which reasonably anticipates that it will not have gross receipts of $25,000 or more for any taxable year, or
(C) which is a political committee of a State or local candidate or which is a State or local committee of a political party.

(6) Coordination with other requirements. This subsection shall not apply to any person required (without regard to this subsection) to report under the Federal Election Campaign Act of 1971 (2 U.S.C. 431 et seq.) as a political committee.

(j) Required disclosure of expenditures and contributions.
(1) Penalty for failure. In the case of—
  (A) a failure to make the required disclosures under paragraph (2) at the time and in the manner prescribed therefor, or
  (B) a failure to include any of the information required to be shown by such disclosures or to show the correct information,
there shall be paid by the organization an amount equal to the rate of tax specified in subsection (b)(1) multiplied by the amount to which the failure relates. For purposes of subtitle F, the amount imposed by this paragraph shall be assessed and collected in the same manner as penalties imposed by section 6652(c).
(2) Required disclosure. A political organization which accepts a contribution, or makes an expenditure, for an exempt function during any calendar year shall file with the Secretary either—
  (A)(i) in the case of a calendar year in which a regularly scheduled election is held—
    (I) quarterly reports, beginning with the first quarter of the calendar year in which a contribution is accepted or expenditure is made, which shall be filed not later than the fifteenth day after the last day of each calendar quarter, except that the report for the quarter ending on December 31 of such calendar year shall be filed not later than January 31 of the following calendar year,
    (II) a pre-election report, which shall be filed not later than the twelfth day before (or posted by registered or certified mail not later than the fifteenth day before) any election with respect to which the organization makes a contribution or expenditure, and which shall be complete as of the twentieth day before the election, and
    (III) a post-general election report, which shall be filed not later than the thirtieth day after the general election and which shall be complete as of the twentieth day after such general election, and
  (ii) in the case of any other calendar year, a report covering the period beginning January 1 and ending June 30, which shall be filed no later than July 31 and a report covering the period beginning July 1 and ending December 31, which shall be filed no later than January 31 of the following calendar year, or
  (B) monthly reports for the calendar year, beginning with the first month of the calendar year in which a contribution is accepted or expenditure is made, which shall be filed not later than the twentieth day after the last day of the month and shall be complete as if the last day of the month, except that, in lieu of filing the reports otherwise due in November and December of any year in which a regularly scheduled general election is held, a pre-general election report shall be filed in accordance with subparagraph (A)(i)(II), a post-general election report shall be filed in accordance with subparagraph (A)(i)(III), and a year end report shall be filed not later than January 31 of the following calendar year.
(3) Contents of report. A report required under paragraph (2) shall contain the following information:
  (A) The amount, date, and purpose of each expenditure made to a person if the aggregate amount of expenditures to such person during the calendar year equals or exceeds $500 and the name and address of the person (in the case of an individual, including the occupation and name of employer of such individual).
  (B) The name and address (in the case of an individual, including the occupation and name of employer of such individual) of all contributors which contributed an aggregate amount of $200 or more to the organization during the calendar year and the amount and date of the contribution.
Any expenditure or contribution disclosed in a previous reporting period is not required to be included in the current reporting period.
(4) Contracts to spend or contribute. For purposes of this subsection, a person shall be treated as having made an expenditure or contribution if the person has contracted or is otherwise obligated to make the expenditure or contribution.
(5) Coordination with other requirements. This subsection shall not apply—
  (A) to any person required (without regard to this subsection) to report under the Federal Election Campaign Act of 1971 (2 U.S.C. 431 et seq.) as a political committee,
  (B) to any State or local committee of a political party or political committee of a State or local candidate,
  (C) to any organization which is a qualified State or local political organization,
  (D) to any organization which reasonably anticipates that it will not have gross receipts of $25,000 or more for any taxable year,
  (E) to any organization to which this section applies solely by reason of subsection (f)(1), or
  (F) with respect to any expenditure which is an independent expenditure (as defined in section 301 of such Act).
(6) Election. For purposes of this subsection, the term "election" means—
  (A) a general, special, primary, or runoff election for a Federal office,
  (B) a convention or caucus of a political party which has authority to nominate a candidate for Federal office,
  (C) a primary election held for the selection of delegates to a national nominating convention of a political party, or
  (D) a primary election held for the expression of a preference for the nomination of individuals for election to the office of President.
(7) Electronic filing. Any report required under paragraph (2) with respect to any calendar year shall be filed in electronic form if the organization has, or has reason to expect to have, contributions exceeding $50,000 or expenditures exceeding $50,000 in such calendar year.
(k) Public availability of notices and reports.
(1) In general. The Secretary shall make any notice described in subsection (i)(1) or report described in subsection (j)(7) available for public inspection on the Internet not later than 48 hours after such notice or report has been filed (in addition to such public availability as may be made under section 6104(d)(7)).
(2) Access. The Secretary shall make the entire database of notices and reports which are made available to the public under paragraph (1) searchable by the following items (to the extent the items are required to be included in the notices and reports):

Exempt organizations — Code Sec. 528(c)(1)(A)

(A) Names, States, zip codes, custodians of records, directors, and general purposes of the organizations.
(B) Entities related to the organizations.
(C) Contributors to the organizations.
(D) Employers of such contributors.
(E) Recipients of expenditures by the organizations.
(F) Ranges of contributions and expenditures.
(G) Time periods of the notices and reports.

Such database shall be downloadable.

(l) Authority to waive.
The Secretary may waive all or any portion of the—
(1) tax assessed on an organization by reason of the failure of the organization to comply with the requirements of subsection (i), or
(2) amount imposed under subsection (j) for a failure to comply with the requirements thereof,
on a showing that such failure was due to reasonable cause and not due to willful neglect.

In **2002**, P.L. 107-276, Sec. 1(a), deleted "or" at the end of subpara. (i)(5)(A), substituted ", or" for the period at the end of subpara. (i)(5)(B), and added subpara. (i)(5)(C), effective 7/1/2000, except as provided in Sec. 1(d)(2) of P.L. 106-230 [see below].
—P.L. 107-276, Sec. 2(a), redesignated subparas. (j)(5)(C)-(E) as (j)(5)(D)-(F), and added subpara. (j)(5)(C) . . . Sec. 2(b), added para. (e)(5), effective as provided in Sec. 2(d) of P.L. 106-230 [see below].
—P.L. 107-276, Sec. 4, of this Act, provides:
"Sec. 4. Notification of interaction of reporting requirements.
"(a) In general. The Secretary of the Treasury, in consultation with the Federal Election Commission, shall publicize—
"(1) the effect of the amendments made by this Act, and
"(2) the interaction of requirements to file a notification or report under section 527 of the Internal Revenue Code of 1986 and reports under the Federal Election Campaign Act of 1971.
"(b) Information. Information provided under subsection (a) shall be included in any appropriate form, instruction, notice, or other guidance issued to the public by the Secretary of the Treasury or the Federal Election Commission regarding reporting requirements of political organizations (as defined in section 527 of the Internal Revenue Code of 1986) or reporting requirements under the Federal Election Campaign Act of 1971."
—P.L. 107-276, Sec. 5(a), added subsec. (k) [prior to redesignation by Sec. 6(e)(3) of this Act, see below], effective for any tax assessed or amount imposed after 6/30/2000.
—P.L. 107-276, Sec. 6(a), added a sentence at the end of para. (i)(4) . . . Sec. 6(b), added a sentence at the end of para. (j)(1), effective for failures occurring on or after 11/2/2002.
—P.L. 107-276, Sec. 6(c), substituted "electronically" for ", electronically and in writing," in subpara. (i)(1)(A), effective 7/1/2000, except as provided in Sec. 1(d)(2) of P.L. 106-230 [see below].
—P.L. 107-276, Sec. 6(e)(1)(A), added ", date, and purpose" after "The amount" in subpara. (j)(3)(A) . . . Sec. 6(e)(1)(B), added "and date" after "the amount" in subpara. (j)(3)(B), effective for reports and notices required to be filed more than 30 days after 11/2/2002.
—P.L. 107-276, Sec. 6(e)(2), added para. (j)(7) . . . Sec. 6(e)(3), redesignated subsec. (k) [as added by Sec. 5(a) of this Act, see above] as (l) and added subsec. (k), effective for reports required to be filed on or after 6/30/2003.
—P.L. 107-276, Sec. 6(f), deleted "and" at the end of subpara. (i)(3)(D), redesignated subpara. (i)(3)(E) as (F), and added subpara. (i)(3)(E), effective for reports and notices required to be filed more than 30 days after 11/2/2002.
—P.L. 107-276, Sec. 6(g)(1), added "or, in the case of any material change in the information required under paragraph (3), for the period beginning on the date on which the material change occurs and ending on the date on which such notice is given" after "given" in subpara. (i)(1)(B) . . . Sec. 6(g)(2), added "or, in the case of any material change in the information required under paragraph (3), not later than 30 days after such material change" after "established" in para. (i)(2) . . . Sec. 6(g)(3), added "or, in the case of a failure relating to a material change, by taking into account such income and deductions only during the period beginning on the date on which the material change occurs and ending on the date on which notice is given under this subsection" before the period at the end of para. (i)(4), effective for material changes on or after 11/2/2002. Sec. 6(h)(6)(B) of this Act, provides:
"(B) Transition rule. In the case of a material change occurring during the 30-day period beginning on the date of the enactment of this Act [11/2/2002], a notice under section 527(i) of the Internal Revenue Code of 1986 (as amended by this Act) shall not be required to be filed under such section before the later of—
"(i) 30 days after the date of such material change, or
"(ii) 45 days after the date of the enactment of this Act [11/2/2002]."
In **2000**, P.L. 106-230, Sec. 1(a), added subsec. (i), effective 7/1/2000, except as provided in Sec. 1(d)(2) of this Act, which reads as follows:
"(2) Organizations already in existence. In the case of an organization established before the date of the enactment of this section, the time to file the notice under section 527(i)(2) of the Internal Revenue Code of 1986, as added by this section, shall be 30 days after the date of the enactment of this section."
—P.L. 106-230, Sec. 2(a), added subsec. (j), effective as provided in Sec. 2(d) of this Act, which reads as follows:
"(d) Effective date. The amendment made by subsection (a) shall apply to expenditures made and contributions received after 7/1/2000, except that such amendment shall not apply to expenditures made, or contributions received, after 7/1/2000 pursuant to a contract entered into on or before 7/1/2000."
In **1988**, P.L. 100-647, Sec. 1001(b)(3)(B), added the sentence at the end of para. (e)(2), effective for tax. yrs. begin. after 12/31/86.
In **1986**, P.L. 99-514, Sec. 112(b)(1)(A), substituted "paragraph (3)" for "section 24(c)(2)" in para. (g)(1) . . . Sec. 112(b)(1)(B), added para. (g)(3), effective for tax. yrs. begin. after 12/31/86.
In **1984**, P.L. 98-369, Sec. 474(r)(16), substituted "section 24(c)(2)" for "section 41(c)(2)" in para. (g)(1), effective for tax. yrs. begin. after 12/31/83, and for carrybacks for tax. yrs. begin. after 12/31/83.
—P.L. 98-369, Sec. 722(c), added the sentence at the end of subpara. (h)(2)(B), effective for tax. yrs. begin. after 12/31/81.
In **1981**, P.L. 97-34, Sec. 128(a), added subsec. (h), effective for tax. yrs. begin. after 12/31/81.
In **1978**, P.L. 95-600, Sec. 301(b)(6), amended para. (b)(1), effective for tax. yrs. begin. after 12/31/78.
Prior to amendment, para. (b)(1) read as follows:
"(1) In general. A tax is hereby imposed for each taxable year on the political organization taxable income of every political organization. Such tax shall consist of a normal tax and surtax computed as provided in section 11 as though the political organization were a corporation and as though the political organization taxable income were the taxable income referred to in section 11. For purposes of this subsection, the surtax exemption provided by section 11(d) shall not be allowed."
—P.L. 95-502, Sec. 302(a), deleted "or" at the end of subpara (c)(3)(B), added "or" at the end of subpara. (c)(3)(C), and added new subpara. (c)(3)(D). Sec. 302(b) provides as follows:
"(b)(1) The amendment made by subsection (a) shall apply to taxable years beginning after December 31, 1974, except that notwithstanding any other provision of law to the contrary, no amounts held at the date of enactment of this bill by an organization described in section 527(e)(1) of the Internal Revenue Code of 1954 in escrow, in separate accounts for the payment of Federal taxes, or in any other fund which are proceeds described in section 527(c)(3)(D) of such Code may be used, directly or indirectly, to make a contribution or expenditure (as defined in section 301(e) and (f) of the Federal Election Campaign Act of 1971; 2 U.S.C. 431(f) in connection with any election held before January 1, 1979.
"(2) Such amounts as described in (1) above shall not be considered as security or collateral for any loan by any State or national bank or any other person or organization."
In **1976**, P.L. 94-455, Sec. 1901(b)(33)(C), substituted "net capital gain" for "net section 1201 gain" in para. (b)(2), effective for tax. yrs. begin. after 12/31/76.
In **1975**, P.L. 93-625, Sec. 10(a), added Code Sec. 527, effective for tax. yrs. begin. after 12/31/74.

PART VII.—CERTAIN HOMEOWNERS ASSOCIATIONS

Sec.
528. Certain homeowners associations.

Sec. 528. Certain homeowners associations.
(a) General rule.
A homeowners association (as defined in subsection (c)) shall be subject to taxation under this subtitle only to the extent provided in this section. A homeowners association shall be considered an organization exempt from income taxes for the purpose of any law which refers to organizations exempt from income taxes.
(b) Tax imposed.
A tax is hereby imposed for each taxable year on the homeowners association taxable income of every homeowners association. Such tax shall be equal to 30 percent of the homeowners association taxable income (32 percent of such income in the case of a timeshare association).
(c) Homeowners association defined.
For purposes of this section—
(1) Homeowners association. The term "homeowners association" means an organization which is a condominium management association, a residential real estate management association, or a timeshare association if—
(A) such organization is organized and operated to provide for the acquisition, construction, management, maintenance, and care of association property,

(B) 60 percent or more of the gross income of such organization for the taxable year consists solely of amounts received as membership dues, fees, or assessments from—
  (i) owners of residential units in the case of a condominium management association,
  (ii) owners of residences or residential lots in the case of a residential real estate management association, or
  (iii) owners of timeshare rights to use, or timeshare ownership interests in, association property in the case of a timeshare association,
(C) 90 percent or more of the expenditures of the organization for the taxable year are expenditures for the acquisition, construction, management, maintenance, and care of association property and, in the case of a timeshare association, for activities provided to or on behalf of members of the association,
(D) no part of the net earnings of such organization inures (other than by acquiring, constructing, or providing management, maintenance, and care of association property, and other than by a rebate of excess membership dues, fees, or assessments) to the benefit of any private shareholder or individual, and
(E) such organization elects (at such time and in such manner as the Secretary by regulations prescribes) to have this section apply for the taxable year.

(2) Condominium management association. The term "condominium management association" means any organization meeting the requirement of subparagraph (A) of paragraph (1) with respect to a condominium project substantially all of the units of which are used by individuals for residences.

(3) Residential real estate management association. The term "residential real estate management association" means any organization meeting the requirements of subparagraph (A) of paragraph (1) with respect to a subdivision, development, or similar area substantially all the lots or buildings of which may only be used by individuals for residences.

(4) Timeshare association. The term "timeshare association" means any organization (other than a condominium management association) meeting the requirement of subparagraph (A) of paragraph (1) if any member thereof holds a timeshare right to use, or a timeshare ownership interest in, real property constituting association property.

(5) Association property. The term "association property" means—
  (A) property held by the organization,
  (B) property commonly held by the members of the organization,
  (C) property within the organization privately held by the members of the organization, and
  (D) property owned by a governmental unit and used for the benefit of residents of such unit.
In the case of a timeshare association, such term includes property in which the timeshare association, or members of the association, have rights arising out of recorded easements, covenants, or other recorded instruments to use property related to the timeshare project.

(d) Homeowners association taxable income defined.
(1) Taxable income defined. For purposes of this section, the homeowners association taxable income of any organization for any taxable year is an amount equal to the excess (if any) of—
  (A) the gross income for the taxable year (excluding any exempt function income), over
  (B) the deductions allowed by this chapter which are directly connected with the production of the gross income (excluding exempt function income), computed with the modifications provided in paragraph (2).

(2) Modifications. For purposes of this subsection—
  (A) there shall be allowed a specific deduction of $100,
  (B) no net operating loss deduction shall be allowed under section 172, and
  (C) no deduction shall be allowed under part VIII of subchapter B (relating to special deductions for corporations).

(3) Exempt function income. For purposes of this subsection, the term "exempt function income" means any amount received as membership dues, fees, or assessments from—
  (A) owners of condominium housing units in the case of a condominium management association,
  (B) owners of real property in the case of a residential real estate management association, or
  (C) owners of timeshare rights to use, or timeshare ownership interests in, real property in the case of a timeshare association.

In **1997**, P.L. 105-34, Sec. 966(a)(1)(A), substituted ", a residential real estate management association, or a timeshare association" for "or a residential real estate management association" in para. (c)(1) . . . Sec. 966(a)(1)(B), deleted "or" at the end of clause (c)(1)(B)(i), substituted ", or" for the period at the end of clause (c)(1)(B)(ii) and added clause (c)(1)(B)(iii) . . . Sec. 966(a)(1)(C), added "and, in the case of a timeshare association, for activities provided to or on behalf of members of the association" before the comma at the end of subpara. (c)(1)(C) . . . Sec. 966(a)(2), redesignated para. (c)(4) as para. (c)(5), and added new para. (c)(4) . . . Sec. 966(b), deleted "or" at the end of subpara. (d)(3)(A), substituted ", or" for the period at the end of subpara. (d)(3)(B), and added subpara. (d)(3)(C) . . . Sec. 966(c), added sentence at end of para. (c)(5) . . . Sec. 966(d), added "(32 percent of such income in the case of a timeshare association)" before the period at the end of subsec. (b), effective for tax. yrs. begin. after 12/31/96.

In **1980**, P.L. 96-605, Sec. 105(a), amended subsec. (b), effective for tax. yrs. begin. after 12/31/80.
Prior to amendment, subsec. (b) read as follows:
"*(b) Tax imposed.*
"(1) In general. A tax is hereby imposed for each taxable year on the homeowners association taxable income of every homeowners association. Such tax shall be computed by multiplying the homeowners association taxable income by the highest rate of tax specified in section 11(b).
"(2) Alternative tax in case of capital gains. If for any taxable year any homeowners association has a net capital gain, then in lieu of the tax imposed by paragraph (1), there is hereby imposed a tax (if such tax is less than the tax imposed by paragraph (1)) which shall consist of the sum of—
"(A) a partial tax, computed as provided by paragraph (1), on the homeowners association taxable income determined by reducing such income by the amount of such gain, and
"(B) an amount determined as provided in section 1201(a) on such gain."

In **1978**, P.L. 95-600, Sec. 301(b)(7), amended para. (b)(1), effective for tax. yrs. begin. after 12/31/78.
Prior to amendment, para. (b)(1) read as follows:
"(1) In general. A tax is hereby imposed for each taxable year on the homeowners association taxable income of every homeowners association. Such tax shall consist of a normal tax and surtax computed as provided in section 11 as though the homeowners association were a corporation and as though the homeowners association taxable income were the taxable income referred to in section 11. For purposes of this subsection, the surtax exemption provided by section 11(d) shall not be allowed."
— P.L. 95-600, Sec. 403(c)(2), amended subpara. (b)(2)(B), effective 11/6/78.
Prior to amendment, subpara. (b)(2)(B) read as follows:
"(B) a tax of 30 percent of such gain."
— P.L. 95-600, Sec. 701(n)(1), substituted "by individuals for residences" for "as residences" in para. (c)(2), effective for tax. yrs. begin. after 12/31/73.

In **1976**, P.L. 94-455, Sec. 2101(a), added Code Sec. 528, effective for tax. yrs. begin. after 12/31/73.

PART VIII.—HIGHER EDUCATION SAVINGS ENTITIES

Sec.
529. Qualified tuition programs.
530. Coverdell education savings accounts.

In **2001**, P.L. 107-22, Sec. 1(a)(6), amended item 530.
Prior to amendment, item 530 read as follows:

Exempt organizations Code Sec. 529(c)(3)(B)(iii)

"530. Education individual retirement accounts."
—P.L. 107-16, Sec. 402(a)(4)(E), amended item 529.
Prior to amendment, item 529 read as follows:
"529. Qualified State tuition programs."
In 1997, P.L. 105-34, Sec. 211(e)(1)(A), amended the heading of Part VIII... Sec. 213(e)(3), added item 530
Prior to amendment, the heading of Part VIII read as follows:
"QUALIFIED STATE TUITION PROGRAMS."
In 1996, P.L. 104-188, Sec. 1806(a), added part VIII.

> • *Caution:* Code Sec. 529, following, was amended by P.L. 107-16, the Economic Growth and Tax Relief Reconciliation Act of 2001 (EGTRRA). These provisions generally sunset for tax years beginning after 12/31/2012. For specific sunset provisions see Sec. 901, P.L. 107-16 (as amended) reproduced in history notes for this Code Sec.

Sec. 529. Qualified tuition programs.
(a) General rule.
A qualified tuition program shall be exempt from taxation under this subtitle. Notwithstanding the preceding sentence, such program shall be subject to the taxes imposed by section 511 (relating to imposition of tax on unrelated business income of charitable organizations).
(b) Qualified tuition program.
For purposes of this section—
(1) In general. The term "qualified tuition program" means a program established and maintained by a State or agency or instrumentality thereof or by 1 or more eligible educational institutions—
  (A) under which a person—
    (i) may purchase tuition credits or certificates on behalf of a designated beneficiary which entitle the beneficiary to the waiver or payment of qualified higher education expenses of the beneficiary, or
    (ii) in the case of a program established and maintained by a State or agency or instrumentality thereof, may make contributions to an account which is established for the purpose of meeting the qualified higher education expenses of the designated beneficiary of the account, and
  (B) which meets the other requirements of this subsection.
Except to the extent provided in regulations, a program established and maintained by 1 or more eligible educational institutions shall not be treated as a qualified tuition program unless such program provides that amounts are held in a qualified trust and such program has received a ruling or determination that such program meets the applicable requirements for a qualified tuition program. For purposes of the preceding sentence, the term "qualified trust" means a trust which is created or organized in the United States for the exclusive benefit of designated beneficiaries and with respect to which the requirements of paragraphs (2) and (5) of section 408(a) are met.
(2) Cash contributions. A program shall not be treated as a qualified tuition program unless it provides that purchases or contributions may only be made in cash.
(3) Separate accounting. A program shall not be treated as a qualified tuition program unless it provides separate accounting for each designated beneficiary.
(4) No investment direction. A program shall not be treated as a qualified tuition program unless it provides that any contributor to, or designated beneficiary under, such program may not directly or indirectly direct the investment of any contributions to the program (or any earnings thereon).
(5) No pledging of interest as security. A program shall not be treated as a qualified tuition program if it allows any interest in the program or any portion thereof to be used as security for a loan.
(6) Prohibition on excess contributions. A program shall not be treated as a qualified tuition program unless it provides adequate safeguards to prevent contributions on behalf of a designated beneficiary in excess of those necessary to provide for the qualified higher education expenses of the beneficiary.
(c) Tax treatment of designated beneficiaries and contributors.
(1) In general. Except as otherwise provided in this subsection, no amount shall be includible in gross income of—
  (A) a designated beneficiary under a qualified tuition program, or
  (B) a contributor to such program on behalf of a designated beneficiary,
with respect to any distribution or earnings under such program.
(2) Gift tax treatment of contributions. For purposes of chapters 12 and 13—
  (A) In general. Any contribution to a qualified tuition program on behalf of any designated beneficiary—
    (i) shall be treated as a completed gift to such beneficiary which is not a future interest in property, and
    (ii) shall not be treated as a qualified transfer under section 2503(e).
  (B) Treatment of excess contributions. If the aggregate amount of contributions described in subparagraph (A) during the calendar year by a donor exceeds the limitation for such year under section 2503(b), such aggregate amount shall, at the election of the donor, be taken into account for purposes of such section ratably over the 5-year period beginning with such calendar year.
(3) Distributions.
  (A) In general. Any distribution under a qualified tuition program shall be includible in the gross income of the distributee in the manner as provided under section 72 to the extent not excluded from gross income under any other provision of this chapter.
  (B) Distributions for qualified higher education expenses. For purposes of this paragraph—
    (i) In-kind distributions. No amount shall be includible in gross income under subparagraph (A) by reason of a distribution which consists of providing a benefit to the distributee which, if paid for by the distributee, would constitute payment of a qualified higher education expense.
    (ii) Cash distributions. In the case of distributions not described in clause (i), if—
      (I) such distributions do not exceed the qualified higher education expenses (reduced by expenses described in clause (i)), no amount shall be includible in gross income, and
      (II) in any other case, the amount otherwise includible in gross income shall be reduced by an amount which bears the same ratio to such amount as such expenses bear to such distributions.
    (iii) Exception for institutional programs. In the case of any taxable year beginning before January 1, 2004, clauses (i) and (ii) shall not apply with respect to any distribution during such taxable year under a

qualified tuition program established and maintained by 1 or more eligible educational institutions.

(iv) Treatment as distributions. Any benefit furnished to a designated beneficiary under a qualified tuition program shall be treated as a distribution to the beneficiary for purposes of this paragraph.

(v) Coordination with hope and lifetime learning credits. The total amount of qualified higher education expenses with respect to an individual for the taxable year shall be reduced—

(I) as provided in section 25A(g)(2), and

(II) by the amount of such expenses which were taken into account in determining the credit allowed to the taxpayer or any other person under section 25A.

(vi) Coordination with Coverdell education savings accounts. If, with respect to an individual for any taxable year—

(I) the aggregate distributions to which clauses (i) and (ii) and section 530(d)(2)(A) apply, exceed

(II) the total amount of qualified higher education expenses otherwise taken into account under clauses (i) and (ii) (after the application of clause (v)) for such year,

the taxpayer shall allocate such expenses among such distributions for purposes of determining the amount of the exclusion under clauses (i) and (ii) and section 530(d)(2)(A).

(C) Change in beneficiaries or programs.

(i) Rollovers. Subparagraph (A) shall not apply to that portion of any distribution which, within 60 days of such distribution, is transferred—

(I) to another qualified tuition program for the benefit of the designated beneficiary, or

(II) to the credit of another designated beneficiary under a qualified tuition program who is a member of the family of the designated beneficiary with respect to which the distribution was made.

(ii) Change in designated beneficiaries. Any change in the designated beneficiary of an interest in a qualified tuition program shall not be treated as a distribution for purposes of subparagraph (A) if the new beneficiary is a member of the family of the old beneficiary.

(iii) Limitation on certain rollovers. Clause (i)(I) shall not apply to any transfer if such transfer occurs within 12 months from the date of a previous transfer to any qualified tuition program for the benefit of the designated beneficiary.

(D) Operating rules. For purposes of applying section 72—

(i) to the extent provided by the Secretary, all qualified tuition programs of which an individual is a designated beneficiary shall be treated as one program,

(ii) except to the extent provided by the Secretary, all distributions during a taxable year shall be treated as one distribution, and

(iii) except to the extent provided by the Secretary, the value of the contract, income on the contract, and investment in the contract shall be computed as of the close of the calendar year in which the taxable year begins.

(4) Estate tax treatment.

(A) In general. No amount shall be includible in the gross estate of any individual for purposes of chapter 11 by reason of an interest in a qualified tuition program.

(B) Amounts includible in estate of designated beneficiary in certain cases. Subparagraph (A) shall not apply to amounts distributed on account of the death of a beneficiary.

(C) Amounts includible in estate of donor making excess contributions. In the case of a donor who makes the election described in paragraph (2)(B) and who dies before the close of the 5-year period referred to in such paragraph, notwithstanding subparagraph (A), the gross estate of the donor shall include the portion of such contributions properly allocable to periods after the date of death of the donor.

(5) Other gift tax rules. For purposes of chapters 12 and 13—

(A) Treatment of distributions. Except as provided in subparagraph (B), in no event shall a distribution from a qualified tuition program be treated as a taxable gift.

(B) Treatment of designation of new beneficiary. The taxes imposed by chapters 12 and 13 shall apply to a transfer by reason of a change in the designated beneficiary under the program (or a rollover to the account of a new beneficiary) unless the new beneficiary is—

(i) assigned to the same generation as (or a higher generation than) the old beneficiary (determined in accordance with section 2651), and

(ii) a member of the family of the old beneficiary.

(6) Additional tax. The tax imposed by section 530(d)(4) shall apply to any payment or distribution from a qualified tuition program in the same manner as such tax applies to a payment or distribution from an [a] Coverdell education savings account. This paragraph shall not apply to any payment or distribution in any taxable year beginning before January 1, 2004, which is includible in gross income but used for qualified higher education expenses of the designated beneficiary.

(d) Reports.

Each officer or employee having control of the qualified tuition program or their designee shall make such reports regarding such program to the Secretary and to designated beneficiaries with respect to contributions, distributions, and such other matters as the Secretary may require. The reports required by this subsection shall be filed at such time and in such manner and furnished to such individuals at such time and in such manner as may be required by the Secretary.

(e) Other definitions and special rules.

For purposes of this section—

(1) Designated beneficiary. The term "designated beneficiary" means—

(A) the individual designated at the commencement of participation in the qualified tuition program as the beneficiary of amounts paid (or to be paid) to the program,

(B) in the case of a change in beneficiaries described in subsection (c)(3)(C), the individual who is the new beneficiary, and

(C) in the case of an interest in a qualified tuition program purchased by a State or local government (or agency or instrumentality thereof) or an organization described in section 501(c)(3) and exempt from taxation under section 501(a) as part of a scholarship program operated by such government or organization, the individual receiving such interest as a scholarship.

(2) Member of family. The term "member of the family" means, with respect to any designated beneficiary—

(A) the spouse of such beneficiary;

(B) an individual who bears a relationship to such beneficiary which is described in subparagraphs (A) through (G) of section 152(d)(2);

(C) the spouse of any individual described in subparagraph (B); and

(D) any first cousin of such beneficiary.

(3) Qualified higher education expenses.

(A) In general. The term "qualified higher education expenses" means—

(i) tuition, fees, books, supplies, and equipment required for the enrollment or attendance of a designated beneficiary at an eligible educational institution;

(ii) expenses for special needs services in the case of a special needs beneficiary which are incurred in connection with such enrollment or attendance

(iii) expenses paid or incurred in 2009 or 2010 for the purchase of any computer technology or equipment (as defined in section 170(e)(6)(F)(i)) or Internet access and related services, if such technology, equipment, or services are to be used by the beneficiary and the beneficiary's family during any of the years the beneficiary is enrolled at an eligible educational institution.

Clause (iii) shall not include expenses for computer software designed for sports, games, or hobbies unless the software is predominantly educational in nature.

(B) Room and board included for students who are at least half-time.

(i) In general. In the case of an individual who is an eligible student (as defined in section 25A(b)(3)) for any academic period, such term shall also include reasonable costs for such period (as determined under the qualified tuition program) incurred by the designated beneficiary for room and board while attending such institution. For purposes of subsection (b)(6), a designated beneficiary shall be treated as meeting the requirements of this clause.

(ii) Limitation. The amount treated as qualified higher education expenses by reason of clause (i) shall not exceed—

(I) the allowance (applicable to the student) for room and board included in the cost of attendance (as defined in section 472 of the Higher Education Act of 1965 (20 U.S.C. 1087ll), as in effect on the date of the enactment [6/7/2001] of the Economic Growth and Tax Relief Reconciliation Act of 2001) as determined by the eligible educational institution for such period, or

(II) if greater, the actual invoice amount the student residing in housing owned or operated by the eligible educational institution is charged by such institution for room and board costs for such period.

(4) Application of section 514. An interest in a qualified tuition program shall not be treated as debt for purposes of section 514.

(5) Eligible educational institution. The term "eligible educational institution" means an institution—

(A) which is described in section 481 of the Higher Education Act of 1965 (20 U.S.C. 1088), as in effect on the date of the enactment [6/7/2001] of this paragraph, and

(B) which is eligible to participate in a program under title IV of such Act.

(f) Regulations.

Notwithstanding any other provision of this section, the Secretary shall prescribe such regulations as may be necessary or appropriate to carry out the purposes of this section and to prevent abuse of such purposes, including regulations under chapters 11, 12, and 13 of this title.

In 2010, P.L. 111-312, Sec. 101(a)(1), substituted "December 31, 2012" for "December 31, 2010" both places it appeared in Sec. 901 of P.L. 107-16 [see below], effective as if included in the enactment of P.L. 107-16, EGTRRA, 6/7/2001.

In 2009, P.L. 111-5, Sec. 1005(a), deleted "and" at the end of subpara. (e)(3)(A)(i), deleted the period at the end of subpara. (e)(3)(A)(ii), and added clause (e)(3)(A)(iii), effective for expenses paid or incurred after 12/31/2008.

In 2006, P.L. 109-280, Sec. 1304(a), of this Act [relating to Sec. 901 of P.L. 107-16, see below], provides:

"Sec. 1304. Qualified tuition programs.

"(a) Permanent extension of modifications. Section 901 of the Economic Growth and Tax Relief Reconciliation Act of 2001 (relating to sunset provisions) shall not apply to section 402 of such Act (relating to modifications to qualified tuition programs)."

—P.L. 109-280, Sec. 1304(b), added subsec. (f), enacted 8/17/2006.

In 2005, P.L. 109-135, Sec. 412(ee)(3), substituted 'Coverdell education savings account' for 'education individual retirement account' in para. (c)(6), effective 12/21/2005.

In 2004, P.L. 108-311, Sec. 207(21), substituted 'subparagraphs (A) through (G) of section 152(d)(2)' for 'paragraphs (1) through (8) of section 152(a)' in subpara. (e)(2)(B), effective for tax. yrs. begin. after 12/31/2004.

—P.L. 108-311, Sec. 406(a), amended subpara. (c)(5)(B), effective for transfers (including designations of new beneficiaries) made after 8/5/97 (as provided in Sec. 211(f)(5)(A) of P.L. 105-34). For special rules, see Sec. 211(f)(6) of P.L. 105-34, reproduced below.

Prior to amendment, subpara. (c)(5)(B) read as follows:

"(B) Treatment of designation of new beneficiary. The taxes imposed by chapters 12 and 13 shall apply to a transfer by reason of a change in the designated beneficiary under the program (or a rollover to the account of a new beneficiary) only if the new beneficiary is a generation below the generation of the old beneficiary (determined in accordance with section 2651)."

In 2002, P.L. 107-358, Sec. 2, added subsec. (c) in Sec. 901 of P.L. 107-16 [see below], effective 12/17/2002.

—P.L. 107-147, Sec. 417(11), substituted "subsection (b)(6)" for "subsection (b)(7)" in clause (e)(3)(B)(i), effective 3/9/2002.

In 2001, P.L. 107-22, Sec. 1(b)(3)(C), substituted "Coverdell education savings" for "education individual retirement" in the heading of clause (c)(3)(B)(vi), effective 7/26/2001.

—P.L. 107-16, Sec. 402(a)(1)(A), added "or by 1 or more eligible educational institutions" after "instrumentality thereof" in para. (b)(1) . . . Sec. 402(a)(1)(B), added a flush sentence at the end of para. (b)(1) . . . Sec. 402(a)(2), added "in the case of a program established and maintained by a State or agency or instrumentality thereof," before "may make" in clause (b)(1)(A)(ii) . . . Sec. 402(a)(3)(A), deleted para. (b)(3) and redesignated paras. (b)(4)-(7) as (b)(3)-(6) . . . Sec. 402(a)(3)(B), added para. (c)(6) . . . Sec. 402(a)(4)(A), substituted "qualified tuition" for "qualified State tuition" each place it appeared in Code Sec. 529 . . . Sec. 402(a)(4)(C), substituted "qualified tuition" for "qualified State tuition" in the heading of subsec. (b) . . . Sec. 402(a)(4)(D), deleted "State" after "Qualified" in the heading of Code Sec. 529 . . . Sec. 402(b)(1), amended subpara. (c)(3)(B) . . . Sec. 402(c)(1), amended clause (c)(3)(C)(i) . . . Sec. 402(c)(2), added clause (c)(3)(C)(iii) . . . Sec. 402(c)(3), added "or programs" after "beneficiaries" in the heading of subpara. (c)(3)(C) . . . Sec. 402(d), deleted "and" at the end of subpara. (e)(2)(B), substituted "; and" for the period at the end of subpara. (e)(2)(C), and added subpara. (e)(2)(D) . . . Sec. 402(e), amended clause (e)(3)(B)(ii) . . . Sec. 402(f), amended subpara. (e)(3)(A) . . . Sec. 402(g)(1), added "except to the extent provided by the Secretary," before "all distributions" in clause (c)(3)(D)(ii) . . . Sec. 402(g)(2), added "except to the extent provided by the Secretary," before "the value" in clause (c)(3)(D)(iii), effective for tax. yrs. begin. after 12/31/2001.

Prior to deletion, para. (b)(3) read as follows:

"(3) Refunds. A program shall not be treated as a qualified State tuition program unless it imposes a more than de minimis penalty on any refund of earnings from the account which are not—

"(A) used for qualified higher education expenses of the designated beneficiary,

"(B) made on account of the death or disability of the designated beneficiary, or

"(C) made on account of a scholarship (or allowance or payment described in section 135(d)(1)(B) or (C)) received by the designated beneficiary to the extent the amount of the refund does not exceed the amount of the scholarship, allowance, or payment."

Prior to amendment, subpara. (c)(3)(B) read as follows:

"(B) In-kind distributions. Any benefit furnished to a designated beneficiary under a qualified State tuition program shall be treated as a distribution to the beneficiary."

Prior to amendment, clause (c)(3)(C)(i) read as follows:

"(i) Rollovers. Subparagraph (A) shall not apply to that portion of any distribution which, within 60 days of such distribution, is transferred to the credit of another designated beneficiary under a qualified State tuition program who is a member of the family of the designated beneficiary with respect to which the distribution was made."

Prior to amendment, clause (e)(3)(B)(ii) read as follows:

"(ii) Limitation. The amount treated as qualified higher education expenses by reason of the preceding sentence shall not exceed the minimum amount (applicable to the student) included for room and board for such period in the cost of attendance (as defined in section 472 of the Higher Education Act of 1965, 20

U.S.C. 1087ll, as in effect on the date of the enactment of this paragraph) for the eligible educational institution for such period."

Prior to amendment, subpara. (e)(3)(A) read as follows:

"(A) In general. The term 'qualified higher education expenses' means tuition, fees, books, supplies, and equipment required for the enrollment or attendance of a designated beneficiary at an eligible educational institution."

Prior to amendment, clause (e)(3)(B)(ii) read as follows:

"(ii) Limitation. The amount treated as qualified higher education expenses by reason of the preceding sentence shall not exceed the minimum amount (applicable to the student) included for room and board for such period in the cost of attendance (as defined in section 472 of the Higher Education Act of 1965, 20 U.S.C. 1087ll, as in effect on the date of the enactment of this paragraph) for the eligible educational institution for such period."

—P.L. 107-16, Sec. 901, of this Act [as amended by Sec. 2 of P.L. 107-358, and Sec. 101(a)(1) of P.L. 111-312, see above], reads as follows:

"SEC. 901. SUNSET OF PROVISIONS OF ACT.

"(a) In general. All provisions of, and amendments made by, this Act shall not apply—

"(1) to taxable, plan, or limitation years beginning after December 31, 2012, or

"(2) in the case of title V, to estates of decedents dying, gifts made, or generation skipping transfers, after December 31, 2012.

"(b) Application of certain laws. The Internal Revenue Code of 1986 and the Employee Retirement Income Security Act of 1974 shall be applied and administered to years, estates, gifts, and transfers described in subsection (a) as if the provisions and amendments described in subsection (a) had never been enacted.

"(c) Exception. Subsection (a) shall not apply to section 803 (relating to no federal income tax on restitution received by victims of the Nazi regime or their heirs or estates)."

In 2000, P.L. 106-554, Sec. 1(a)(7), [which enacted into law Sec. 319(5) of P.L. 106-554 deleted "under guaranteed plans" after "for students" in subpara. (e)(3)(B), effective 12/21/2000.

In 1998, P.L. 105-206, Sec. 6004(c)(2), substituted "section 72" for "section 72(b)" in subpara. (c)(3)(A) . . . Sec. 6004(c)(3), amended para. (e)(2), effective 1/1/98. For transition rule, see Sec. 211(f)(6) of P.L. 105-34 [reproduced below].

Prior to amendment, para. (e)(2) read as follows:

"(2) Member of family. The term 'member of the family' means—

"(A) an individual who bears a relationship to another individual which is a relationship described in paragraphs (1) through (8) of section 152(a), and

"(B) the spouse of any individual described in subparagraph (A)."

In 1997, P.L. 105-34, Sec. 211(a), amended para. (e)(3), effective for tax. yrs. end. after 8/20/96. Sec. 211(f)(6) of this Act provides:

"(6) Transition rule for pre-August 20, 1996 contracts. In the case of any contract issued prior to August 20, 1996, section 529(c)(3)(C) of the Internal Revenue Code of 1986 shall be applied for taxable years ending after August 20, 1996, without regard to the requirement that a distribution be transferred to a member of the family or the requirement that a change in beneficiaries may be made only to a member of the family."

Prior to amendment, para. (e)(3) read as follows:

"(3) Qualified higher education expenses. The term 'qualified higher education expenses' means tuition, fees, books, supplies, and equipment required for the enrollment or attendance of a designated beneficiary at an eligible educational institution (as defined in section 135(c)(3))."

—P.L. 105-34, Sec. 211(b)(1), amended para. (e)(2), effective 1/1/98. For special rules see Sec. 211(f)(6) of this Act, reproduced above.

Prior to amendment, para. (e)(2) read as follows:

"(2) Member of family. The term 'member of the family' has the same meaning given such term as section 2032A(e)(2)."

—P.L. 105-34, Sec. 211(b)(2), added para. (e)(5), effective for distributions after 12/31/97, for expenses paid after 12/31/97 (in tax. yrs. end. after 12/31/97), for education furnished in academic periods begin. after 12/31/97. For special rules see Sec. 211(f)(6) of this Act, reproduced above.

—P.L. 105-34, Sec. 211(b)(3)(A)(i), amended para. (c)(2) . . . Sec. 211(b)(3)(A)(ii), amended para. (c)(5), effective for transfers (including designations of new beneficiaries) made after 8/5/97. For special rules see Sec. 211(f)(6) of this Act, reproduced above.

Prior to amendment, para. (c)(2) read as follows:

"(2) Contributions. In no event shall a contribution to a qualified State tuition program on behalf of a designated beneficiary be treated as a taxable gift for purposes of chapter 12."

Prior to amendment, para. (c)(5) read as follows:

"(5) Special rule for applying section 2503(e). For purposes of section 2503(e), the waiver (or payment to an educational institution) of qualified higher education expenses of a designated beneficiary under a qualified State tuition program shall be treated as a qualified transfer."

—P.L. 105-34, Sec. 211(b)(3)(B), amended para. (c)(4), effective for estates of decedents dying after 6/8/97. For special rules see Sec. 211(f)(6) of this Act, reproduced above.

Prior to amendment, para. (c)(4) read as follows:

"(4) Estate tax inclusion. The value of any interest in any qualified State tuition program which is attributable to contributions made by an individual to such program on behalf of any designated beneficiary shall be includible in the gross estate of the contributor for purposes of chapter 11."

—P.L. 105-34, Sec. 211(d), substituted "section 72(b)" for "section 72" in subpara. (b)(5) . . . Sec. 211(d), substituted "section 72(b)" for "section 72" in subpara. (c)(3)(A) . . . Sec. 211(e)(2)(A), amended subsec. (d), effective 1/1/98. For special rules, see Sec. 211(f)(6) of this Act, reproduced above.

Prior to amendment, subsec. (d) read as follows:

"(d) Reporting requirements.

"(1) In general. If there is a distribution to any individual with respect to an interest in a qualified State tuition program during any calendar year, each officer or employee having control of the qualified State tuition program or their designee shall make such reports as the Secretary may require regarding such distribution to the Secretary and to the designated beneficiary or the individual to whom the distribution was made. Any such report shall include such information as the Secretary may prescribe.

"(2) Timing of reports. Any report required by this subsection—

"(A) shall be filed at such time and in such matter as the Secretary prescribes, and

"(B) shall be furnished to individuals not later than January 31 of the calendar year following the calendar year to which such report relates."

—P.L. 105-34, Sec. 1601(h)(1)(A), substituted "subsection (c)(3)(C)" for "subsection (c)(2)(C)" in subpara. (e)(1)(B) . . . Sec. 1601(h)(1)(B), added "(or agency or instrumentality thereof)" after "local government" in subpara. (e)(1)(C), effective for tax. yrs. end. after 8/20/96. For Sec. 1806(c)(2) of P.L. 104-188 [as amended by Sec. 1601(h)(1)(C) of this Act, see above], see below

—P.L. 105-34, Sec. 1601(h)(1)(C), substituted "then such program (as in effect on August 20, 1996) shall be treated as a qualified State tuition program with respect to contributions (and earnings allocable thereto) pursuant to contracts entered into under such program before the first date on which such program meets such requirements (determined without regard to this paragraph) and the provisions of such program (as so in effect) shall apply in lieu of section 529(b) of the Internal Revenue Code of 1986 with respect to such contributions and earnings." for "the amendments made by this section shall apply to contributions (and earnings allocable thereto) made before the date such program meets the requirements of such amendments without regard to whether any requirements of such amendments are met with respect to such contributions and earnings." in Sec. 1806(c)(2) of P.L. 104-188, [see below]

In 1996, P.L. 104-188, Sec. 1806(a), added Code Sec. 529, effective for tax. yrs. end. after 8/20/96. Sec. 1806(c)(2), of this Act [as amended by Sec. 1601(h)(1)(C) of P.L. 105-34, see above], provides:

"(2) Transition rule. If—

"(A) a State or agency or instrumentality thereof maintains, on the date of the enactment of this Act, a program under which persons may purchase tuition credits or certificates on behalf of, or make contributions for education expenses of, a designated beneficiary, and

"(B) such program meets the requirements of a qualified State tuition program before the later of—

"(i) the date which is 1 year after such date of enactment, or

"(ii) the first day of the first calendar quarter after the close of the first regular session of the State legislature that begins after such date of enactment,

then such program (as in effect on August 20, 1996) shall be treated as a qualified State tuition program with respect to contributions (and earnings allocable thereto) pursuant to contracts entered under such program before the first date on which such program meets such requirements (determined without regard to this paragraph) and the provisions of such program (as so in effect) shall apply in lieu of section 529(b) of the Internal Revenue Code of 1986 with respect to such contributions and earnings.

For purposes of subparagraph (B)(ii), if a State has a 2-year legislative session, each year of such session shall be deemed to be a separate regular session of the State legislature."

Sec. 530. Coverdell education savings accounts.

(a) General rule.

A Coverdell education savings account shall be exempt from taxation under this subtitle. Notwithstanding the preceding sentence, the Coverdell education savings account shall be subject to the taxes imposed by section 511 (relating to imposition of tax on unrelated business income of charitable organizations).

• *Caution:* Code Sec. 530(b), following, was amended by P.L. 107-16, the Economic Growth and Tax Relief Reconciliation Act of 2001 (EGTRRA). These provisions generally sunset for tax years beginning after 12/31/2012. For specific sunset provisions, see Sec. 901, P.L. 107-16 (as amended) reproduced in history notes for this Code Sec.

(b) Definitions and special rules.

For purposes of this section—

(1) Coverdell education savings account. The term "Coverdell education savings account" means a trust created or organized in the United States exclusively for the purpose of paying the qualified education expenses of an individual who is the designated beneficiary of the trust (and designated as a Coverdell education savings account at the time created or organized), but only if the written governing instrument creating the trust meets the following requirements:

(A) No contribution will be accepted—
(i) unless it is in cash,
(ii) after the date on which such beneficiary attains age 18, or
(iii) except in the case of rollover contributions, if such contribution would result in aggregate contributions for the taxable year exceeding $2,000.

(B) The trustee is a bank (as defined in section 408(n)) or another person who demonstrates to the satisfaction of the Secretary that the manner in which that person will administer the trust will be consistent with the requirements of this section or who has so demonstrated with respect to any individual retirement plan.

(C) No part of the trust assets will be invested in life insurance contracts.

(D) The assets of the trust shall not be commingled with other property except in a common trust fund or common investment fund.

(E) Except as provided in subsection (d)(7), any balance to the credit of the designated beneficiary on the date on which the beneficiary attains age 30 shall be distributed within 30 days after such date to the beneficiary or, if the beneficiary dies before attaining age 30, shall be distributed within 30 days after the date of death of such beneficiary.

The age limitations in subparagraphs (A)(ii) and (E), and paragraphs (5) and (6) of subsection (d), shall not apply to any designated beneficiary with special needs (as determined under regulations prescribed by the Secretary).

(2) Qualified education expenses.
(A) In general. The term "qualified education expenses" means—
(i) qualified higher education expenses (as defined in section 529(e)(3)), and
(ii) qualified elementary and secondary education expenses (as defined in paragraph (3)).

(B) Qualified tuition programs. Such term shall include any contribution to a qualified tuition program (as defined in section 529(b)) on behalf of the designated beneficiary (as defined in section 529(e)(1)); but there shall be no increase in the investment in the contract for purposes of applying section 72 by reason of any portion of such contribution which is not includible in gross income by reason of subsection (d)(2).

(3) Qualified elementary and secondary education expenses.
(A) In general. The term "qualified elementary and secondary education expenses" means—
(i) expenses for tuition, fees, academic tutoring, special needs services in the case of a special needs beneficiary, books, supplies, and other equipment which are incurred in connection with the enrollment or attendance of the designated beneficiary of the trust as an elementary or secondary school student at a public, private, or religious school,
(ii) expenses for room and board, uniforms, transportation, and supplementary items and services (including extended day programs) which are required or provided by a public, private, or religious school in connection with such enrollment or attendance, and
(iii) expenses for the purchase of any computer technology or equipment (as defined in section 170(e)(6)(F)(i)) or Internet access and related services, if such technology, equipment, or services are to be used by the beneficiary and the beneficiary's family during any of the years the beneficiary is in school.

Clause (iii) shall not include expenses for computer software designed for sports, games, or hobbies unless the software is predominantly educational in nature.

(B) School. The term "school" means any school which provides elementary education or secondary education (kindergarten through grade 12), as determined under State law.

(4) Time when contributions deemed made. An individual shall be deemed to have made a contribution to a Coverdell education savings account on the last day of the preceding taxable year if the contribution is made on account of such taxable year and is made not later than the time prescribed by law for filing the return for such taxable year (not including extensions thereof).

(c) Reduction in permitted contributions based on adjusted gross income.

> • *Caution:* Code Sec. 530(c)(1), following, was amended by P.L. 107-16, the Economic Growth and Tax Relief Reconciliation Act of 2001 (EGTRRA). These provisions generally sunset for tax years beginning after 12/31/2012. For specific sunset provisions, see Sec. 901, P.L. 107-16 (as amended) reproduced in history notes for this Code Sec.

(1) In general. In the case of a contributor who is an individual, the maximum amount the contributor could otherwise make to an account under this section shall be reduced by an amount which bears the same ratio to such maximum amount as—
(A) the excess of—
(i) the contributor's modified adjusted gross income for such taxable year, over
(ii) $95,000 ($190,000 in the case of a joint return), bears to
(B) $15,000 ($30,000 in the case of a joint return).

(2) Modified adjusted gross income. For purposes of paragraph (1), the term "modified adjusted gross income" means the adjusted gross income of the taxpayer for the taxable year increased by any amount excluded from gross income under section 911, 931, or 933.

(d) Tax treatment of distributions.
(1) In general. Any distribution shall be includible in the gross income of the distributee in the manner as provided in section 72.

> • *Caution:* Code Sec. 530(d)(2), following, was amended by P.L. 107-16, the Economic Growth and Tax Relief Reconciliation Act of 2001 (EGTRRA) and P.L. 108-311. These provisions generally sunset for tax years beginning after 12/31/2012. For specific sunset provisions, see Sec. 901, P.L. 107-16 (as amended) reproduced in history notes for this Code Sec.

(2) Distributions for qualified education expenses.
(A) In general. No amount shall be includible in gross income under paragraph (1) if the qualified education expenses of the designated beneficiary during the taxa-

ble year are not less than the aggregate distributions during the taxable year.

(B) Distributions in excess of expenses. If such aggregate distributions exceed such expenses during the taxable year, the amount otherwise includible in gross income under paragraph (1) shall be reduced by the amount which bears the same ratio to the amount which would be includible in gross income under paragraph (1) (without regard to this subparagraph) as the qualified education expenses bear to such aggregate distributions.

(C) Coordination with hope and lifetime learning credits and qualified tuition programs. For purposes of subparagraph (A)—

(i) Credit coordination. The total amount of qualified education expenses with respect to an individual for the taxable year shall be reduced—

(I) as provided in section 25A(g)(2), and

(II) by the amount of such expenses which were taken into account in determining the credit allowed to the taxpayer or any other person under section 25A.

(ii) Coordination with qualified tuition programs. If, with respect to an individual for any taxable year—

(I) the aggregate distributions during such year to which subparagraph (A) and section 529(c)(3)(B) apply, exceed

(II) the total amount of qualified education expenses (after the application of clause (i)) for such year,

the taxpayer shall allocate such expenses among such distributions for purposes of determining the amount of the exclusion under subparagraph (A) and section 529(c)(3)(B).

(D) Disallowance of excluded amounts as deduction, credit, or exclusion. No deduction, credit, or exclusion shall be allowed to the taxpayer under any other section of this chapter for any qualified education expenses to the extent taken into account in determining the amount of the exclusion under this paragraph.

(3) Special rules for applying estate and gift taxes with respect to account. Rules similar to the rules of paragraphs (2), (4), and (5) of section 529(c) shall apply for purposes of this section.

(4) Additional tax for distributions not used for educational expenses.

(A) In general. The tax imposed by this chapter for any taxable year on any taxpayer who receives a payment or distribution from a Coverdell education savings account which is includible in gross income shall be increased by 10 percent of the amount which is so includible.

(B) Exceptions. Subparagraph (A) shall not apply if the payment or distribution is—

(i) made to a beneficiary (or to the estate of the designated beneficiary) on or after the death of the designated beneficiary,

(ii) attributable to the designated beneficiary's being disabled (within the meaning of section 72(m)(7)),

(iii) made on account of a scholarship, allowance, or payment described in section 25A(g)(2) received by the designated beneficiary to the extent the amount of the payment or distribution does not exceed the amount of the scholarship, allowance, or payment,

(iv) made on account of the attendance of the designated beneficiary at the United States Military Academy, the United States Naval Academy, the United States Air Force Academy, the United States Coast Guard Academy, or the United States Merchant Marine Academy, to the extent that the amount of the payment or distribution does not exceed the costs of advanced education (as defined by section 2005(e)(3) of title 10, United States Code, as in effect on the date of the enactment of this section) attributable to such attendance, or

(v) an amount which is includible in gross income solely by application of paragraph (2)(C)(i)(II) for the taxable year.

> • *Caution:* Code Sec. 530(d)(4)(C), following, was amended by P.L. 107-16, the Economic Growth and Tax Relief Reconciliation Act of 2001 (EGTRRA). These provisions generally sunset for tax years beginning after 12/31/2012. For specific sunset provisions, see Sec. 901, P.L. 107-16 (as amended) reproduced in history notes for this Code Sec.

(C) Contributions returned before certain date. Subparagraph (A) shall not apply to the distribution of any contribution made during a taxable year on behalf of the designated beneficiary if—

(i) such distribution is made before the first day of the sixth month of the taxable year following the taxable year, and

(ii) such distribution is accompanied by the amount of net income attributable to such excess contribution.

Any net income described in clause (ii) shall be included in gross income for the taxable year in which such excess contribution was made.

(5) Rollover contributions. Paragraph (1) shall not apply to any amount paid or distributed from a Coverdell education savings account to the extent that the amount received is paid, not later than the 60th day after the date of such payment or distribution, into another Coverdell education savings account for the benefit of the same beneficiary or a member of the family (within the meaning of section 529(e)(2)) of such beneficiary who has not attained age 30 as of such date. The preceding sentence shall not apply to any payment or distribution if it applied to any prior payment or distribution during the 12-month period ending on the date of the payment or distribution.

(6) Change in beneficiary. Any change in the beneficiary of a Coverdell education savings account shall not be treated as a distribution for purposes of paragraph (1) if the new beneficiary is a member of the family (as so defined) of the old beneficiary and has not attained age 30 as of the date of such change.

(7) Special rules for death and divorce. Rules similar to the rules of paragraphs (7) and (8) of section 220(f) shall apply. In applying the preceding sentence, members of the family (as so defined) of the designated beneficiary shall be treated in the same manner as the spouse under such paragraph (8).

(8) Deemed distribution on required distribution date. In any case in which a distribution is required under subsection (b)(1)(E), any balance to the credit of a designated beneficiary as of the close of the 30-day period referred to in such subsection for making such distribution shall be deemed distributed at the close of such period.

Exempt organizations   **Code Sec. 530**

(9) Military death gratuity.

(A) In general. For purposes of this section, the term "rollover contribution" includes a contribution to a Coverdell education savings account made before the end of the 1-year period beginning on the date on which the contributor receives an amount under section 1477 of title 10, United States Code, or section 1967 of title 38 of such Code, with respect to a person, to the extent that such contribution does not exceed—

(i) the sum of the amounts received during such period by such contributor under such sections with respect to such person, reduced by

(ii) the amounts so received which were contributed to a Roth IRA under section 408A(e)(2) or to another Coverdell education savings account.

(B) Annual limit on number of rollovers not to apply. The last sentence of paragraph (5) shall not apply with respect to amounts treated as a rollover by the subparagraph (A).

(C) Application of section 72. For purposes of applying section 72 in the case of a distribution which is includible in gross income under paragraph (1), the amount treated as a rollover by reason of subparagraph (A) shall be treated as investment in the contract.

(e) Tax treatment of accounts.

Rules similar to the rules of paragraphs (2) and (4) of section 408(e) shall apply to any Coverdell education savings account.

(f) Community property laws.

This section shall be applied without regard to any community property laws.

(g) Custodial accounts.

For purposes of this section, a custodial account shall be treated as a trust if the assets of such account are held by a bank (as defined in section 408(n)) or another person who demonstrates, to the satisfaction of the Secretary, that the manner in which he will administer the account will be consistent with the requirements of this section, and if the custodial account would, except for the fact that it is not a trust, constitute an account described in subsection (b)(1). For purposes of this title, in the case of a custodial account treated as a trust by reason of the preceding sentence, the custodian of such account shall be treated as the trustee thereof.

(h) Reports.

The trustee of a Coverdell education savings account shall make such reports regarding such account to the Secretary and to the beneficiary of the account with respect to contributions, distributions, and such other matters as the Secretary may require. The reports required by this subsection shall be filed at such time and in such manner and furnished to such individuals at such time and in such manner as may be required.

In 2010, P.L. 111-312, Sec. 101(a)(1), substituted "December 31, 2012" for "December 31, 2010" both places it appeared in Sec. 901, P.L. 107-16 [see below], effective as if included in the enactment of P.L. 107-16, EGTRRA, 6/7/2001.

In 2008, P.L. 110-245, Sec. 109(c), added para. (d)(9), effective for deaths from injuries occurring on or after 6/17/2008. ... Sec. 109(d)(2), and (3) of this Act provides:

"(2) Application of amendments to deaths from injuries occurring on or after october 7, 2001, and before enactment. The amendments made by this section shall apply to any contribution made pursuant to section 408A(e)(2) or 530(d)(5) of the Internal Revenue Code of 1986, as amended by this Act, with respect to amounts received under section 1477 of title 10, United States Code, or under section 1967 of title 38 of such Code, for deaths from injuries occurring on or after October 7, 2001, and before the date of the enactment of this Act if such contribution is made not later than 1 year after the date of the enactment of this Act.

"(3) Pension protection act changes. Section 408A(e)(1) of the Internal Revenue Code of 1986 (as in effect after the amendments made by subsection (b)) shall apply to taxable years beginning after December 31, 2007."

In 2006, P.L. 109-280, Sec. 1304(a), of this Act [relating to Sec. 901 of P.L. 107-16, see below], provides:

"Sec. 1304. Qualified tuition programs.

"(a) Permanent Extension of Modifications. Section 901 of the Economic Growth and Tax Relief Reconciliation Act of 2001 (relating to sunset provisions) shall not apply to section 402 of such Act (relating to modifications to qualified tuition programs)."

In 2005, P.L. 109-135, Sec. 412(ff)(1), deleted para. (b)(3) and redesignated paras. (b)(4) and (5) as paras. (b)(3) and (4) ... Sec. 412(ff)(2), substituted "paragraph (3)" for "paragraph (4)" in clause (b)(2)(A)(ii), effective 12/21/2005.

Prior to deletion, para. (b)(3) read as follows:

"(3) Eligible educational institution. The term 'eligible educational institution' has the meaning given such term by section 529(e)(5)."

In 2004, P.L. 108-311, Sec. 404(a), deleted "higher" after "qualified" in clause (d)(2)(C)(i), effective for tax. yrs. begin. after 12/31/2001 as if included in Sec. 401 of the Economic Growth and Tax Relief Reconciliation Act of 2001, P.L. 107-16.

—P.L. 108-311, Sec. 406(b), substituted "designated beneficiary" for "account holder" in clause (d)(4)(B)(iii), effective for tax. yrs. begin. after 12/31/97 as if included in Sec. 213 of the Taxpayer Relief Act of 1997, P.L. 105-34.

In 2003, P.L. 108-121, Sec. 107(a), deleted "or" at the end of clause (d)(4)(B)(iii), redesignated clause (d)(4)(B)(iv) as clause (d)(4)(B)(v), and added new clause (d)(4)(B)(iv), effective for tax. yrs. begin. after 12/31/2002.

In 2002, P.L. 107-358, Sec. 2, added subsec. (c) in Sec. 901 of P.L. 107-16 [see below], effective 12/17/2002.

—P.L. 107-147, Sec. 411(f), substituted "by application of paragraph (2)(C)(i)(II)" for "because the taxpayer elected under paragraph (2)(C) to waive the application of paragraph (2)" in clause (d)(4)(B)(iv), effective for tax. yrs. begin. after 12/31/2001.

In 2001, P.L. 107-22, Sec. 1(a)(1), substituted "a Coverdell education savings account" for "an education individual retirement account" each place it appeared in Code Sec. 530 ... Sec. 1(a)(2)(A), substituted "A Coverdell education savings account" for "An education individual retirement account" in subsec. (a) ... Sec. 1(a)(2)(B), substituted "the Coverdell education savings account" for "the education individual retirement account" in subsec. (a) ... Sec. 1(a)(3)(A), substituted "Coverdell education savings account" for "education individual retirement account" in para. (b)(1) ... Sec. 1(a)(3)(B), substituted "Coverdell education savings account" for "Education individual retirement account" in the heading of para. (b)(1) ... Sec. 1(a)(4), substituted "Coverdell education savings account" for "education individual retirement account" in para. (d)(5) and subsec. (e) ... Sec. 1(a)(5), substituted "Sec. 530. Coverdell education savings accounts." for "Sec. 530. Education individual retirement accounts." in the heading of Code Sec. 530, effective 7/26/2001.

—P.L. 107-16, Sec. 401(a)(1), substituted "$2,000" for "$500" in clause (b)(1)(A)(iii) ... Sec. 401(b)(1), substituted "$190,000" for "$150,000" in clause (c)(1)(A)(ii) ... Sec. 401(b)(2), substituted "$30,000" for "$10,000" in subpara. (c)(1)(B) ... Sec. 401(c)(1), amended para. (b)(2) ... Sec. 401(c)(2), added para. (b)(4) ... Sec. 401(c)(3)(A), deleted "higher" after "qualified" each place it appeared in paras. (b)(1) and (d)(2) ... Sec. 401(c)(3)(B), deleted "higher" after "qualified" in the heading of para. (b)(2) ... Sec. 401(d), added a flush sentence at the end of para. (b)(1) ... Sec. 401(e), substituted "In the case of a contributor who is an individual, the maximum amount the contributor" for "The maximum amount which a contributor" in para. (c)(1) ... Sec. 401(f)(1), added para. (b)(5) ... Sec. 401(f)(2)(A), amended clause (d)(4)(C)(i) ... Sec. 401(f)(2)(B), substituted "certain date" for "due date of return" in the heading of subpara. (d)(4)(C) ... Sec. 401(g)(1), amended subpara. (d)(2)(C) [Editor's Note: The word "higher" should probably be deleted in subpara. (d)(2)(C) consistent with the amendment made by Sec. 401(c)(3)(A) of this Act, see above.] ... Sec. 401(g)(2)(C)(i), substituted ", credit, or exclusion" for "or credit" in subpara. (d)(2)(D) ... Sec. 401(g)(2)(C)(ii), substituted "deduction, credit, or exclusion" for "credit or deduction" in the heading of subpara. (d)(2)(D), effective for tax. yrs. begin. after 12/31/2001.

Prior to amendment para. (b)(2) read as follows:

"(2) Qualified higher education expenses.

"(A) In general. The term 'qualified higher education expenses' has the meaning given such term by section 529(e)(3), reduced as provided in section 25A(g)(2).

"(B) Qualified State tuition programs. Such term shall include amounts paid or incurred to purchase tuition credits or certificates, or to make contributions to an account, under a qualified State tuition program (as defined in section 529(b)) for the benefit of the beneficiary of the account."

Prior to amendment, clause (d)(4)(C)(i) read as follows:

"(i) such distribution is made on or before the day prescribed by law (including extensions of time) for filing the beneficiary's return of tax for the taxable year or, if the beneficiary is not required to file such a return, the 15th day of the 4th month of the taxable year following the taxable year; and"

Prior to amendment, subpara. (d)(2)(C) read as follows:

"(C) Election to waive exclusion. A taxpayer may elect to waive the application of this paragraph for any taxable year."

—P.L. 107-16, Sec. 402(a)(4)(A), substituted "qualified tuition" for "qualified State tuition" in subpara. (b)(2)(B) ... Sec. 402(a)(4)(C), substituted "Qualified tuition" for "Qualified State tuition" in the heading of subpara. (b)(2)(B), effective for tax. yrs. begin. after 12/31/2001.

—P.L. 107-16, Sec. 901, of this Act [as amended by Sec. 2, P.L. 107-358 and Sec. 101(a)(1), P.L. 111-312, and as related to Sec. 1304(a) of P.L. 109-280, see above], reads as follows:

"Sec. 901. Sunset of provisions of Act.

"(a) In general. All provisions of, and amendments made by, this Act shall not apply—
"(1) to taxable, plan, or limitation years beginning after December 31, 2012, or
"(2) in the case of title V, to estates of decedents dying, gifts made, or generation skipping transfers, after December 31, 2012.
"(b) Application of certain laws. The Internal Revenue Code of 1986 and the Employee Retirement Income Security Act of 1974 shall be applied and administered to years, estates, gifts, and transfers described in subsection (a) as if the provisions and amendments described in subsection (a) had never been enacted.
"(c) Exception. Subsection (a) shall not apply to section 803 (relating to no federal income tax on restitution received by victims of the Nazi regime or their heirs or estates)."

In 2000, P.L. 106-554, Sec. 1(a)(7), [which enacted into law Sec. 319(6) of P.L. 106-554] substituted ", or" for "; or" at the end of clause (d)(4)(B)(iii), effective 12/21/2000.

In 1998, P.L. 105-206, Sec. 6004(d)(1), added "an individual who is" before "the designated beneficiary" in the matter preceding subpara. (b)(1)(A) . . . Sec. 6004(d)(2)(A), amended subpara. (b)(1)(E) . . . Sec. 6004(d)(2)(B), added a sentence at the end of para. (d)(7) . . . Sec. 6004(d)(2)(C), added para. (d)(8) . . . Sec. 6004(d)(3)(A), substituted "section 72" for "section 72(b)" in para. (d)(1) . . . Sec. 6004(d)(5), added subpara. (d)(2)(D) . . . Sec. 6004(d)(6), deleted "or" at the end of clause (d)(4)(B)(ii), substituted "; or" for the period at the end of clause (d)(4)(B)(iii) and added clause (d)(4)(B)(iv) . . . Sec. 6004(d)(7), amended the matter in subpara. (d)(4)(C) preceding clause (d)(4)(C)(ii) . . . Sec. 6004(d)(8)(A), amended the first sentence of para. (d)(5) . . . Sec. 6004(d)(8)(B), added "and has not attained age 30 as of the date of such change" before the period at the end of para. (d)(6), effective for tax. yrs. begin. after 12/31/97.
Prior to amendment, subpara. (b)(1)(E) read as follows:
"(E) Upon the death of the designated beneficiary, any balance to the credit of the beneficiary shall be distributed within 30 days after the date of death to the estate of such beneficiary."
Prior to amendment, the matter in subpara. (d)(4)(C) preceding clause (d)(4)(C)(ii) read as follows:
"(C) Excess contributions returned before due date of return. Subparagraph (A) shall not apply to the distribution of any contribution made during a taxable year on behalf of a designated beneficiary to the extent that such contribution exceeds $500 if—
"(i) such distribution is received on or before the day prescribed by law (including extensions of time) for filing such contributor's return for such taxable year, and"
Prior to amendment, the first sentence of para. (d)(5) read as follows:
"Paragraph (1) shall not apply to any amount paid or distributed from an education individual retirement account to the extent that the amount received is paid into another education individual retirement account for the benefit of the same beneficiary or a member of the family (within the meaning of section 529(e)(2)) of such beneficiary not later than the 60th day after the date of such payment or distribution."

In 1997, P.L. 105-34, Sec. 213(a), added Code Sec. 530, effective for tax. yrs. begin. after 12/31/97.

Subchapter G.—Corporations Used to Avoid Income Tax on Shareholders

Part
    I. Corporations improperly accumulating surplus.
    II. Personal holding companies.
   III. [Repealed] Foreign personal holding companies.
   IV. Deduction for dividends paid.

PART I.—CORPORATIONS IMPROPERLY ACCUMULATING SURPLUS

Sec.
531. Imposition of accumulated earnings tax.
532. Corporations subject to accumulated earnings tax.
533. Evidence of purpose to avoid income tax.
534. Burden of proof.
535. Accumulated taxable income.
536. Income not placed on annual basis.
537. Reasonable needs of the business.

> • **Caution:** Code Sec. 531, following, was amended by P.L. 108-27 and P.L. 107-16. These provisions generally sunset for tax years beginning after 12/31/2012. For specific sunset provisions, see Sec. 303, P.L. 108-27, as amended by Sec. 102(a), P.L. 111-312 and Sec. 901, P.L. 107-16, as amended by Sec. 101(a)(1), P.L. 111-312, reproduced in history notes for this Code Sec.

Sec. 531. Imposition of accumulated earnings tax.

In addition to other taxes imposed by this chapter, there is hereby imposed for each taxable year on the accumulated taxable income (as defined in section 535) of each corporation described in section 532, an accumulated earnings tax equal to 15 percent of the accumulated taxable income.

In 2010, P.L. 111-312, Sec. 101(a)(1), substituted "December 31, 2012" for "December 31, 2010" both places it appeared in Sec. 901 of P.L. 107-16 [see below], effective as if included in the enactment of P.L. 107-16, EGTRRA, 6/7/2001.
—P.L. 111-312, Sec. 102(a), substituted "December 31, 2012" for "December 31, 2010" in Sec. 303 of P.L. 108-27 [see below], effective as if included in the enactment of the Jobs and Growth Tax Relief Reconciliation Act, P.L. 108-27, 5/28/2003.

In 2006, P.L. 109-222, Sec. 102, substituted "December 31, 2010" for "December 31, 2008" in Sec. 303 of P.L. 108-27 [see below], effective 5/17/2006.

In 2004, P.L. 108-311, Sec. 402(a)(6), of this Act [which amended Sec. 302(f)(2) of P.L. 108-27, see below], provides:
"(2) Pass-thru entities. In the case of a pass-thru entity described in subparagraph (A), (B), (C), (D), (E), or (F) of section 1(h)(10) of the Internal Revenue Code of 1986, as amended by this Act, the amendments made by this section shall apply to taxable years ending after December 31, 2002; except that dividends received by such an entity on or before such date shall not be treated as qualified dividend income (as defined in section 1(h)(11)(B) of such Code, as added by this Act)."

In 2003, P.L. 108-27, Sec. 302(e)(5), substituted "equal to 15 percent of the accumulated taxable income." for "equal to the product of the highest rate of tax under section 1(c) and the accumulated taxable income." in Code Sec. 531, effective for tax. yrs. begin. after 12/31/2002. Sec. 302(f)(2), of this Act [prior to amendment by Sec. 402(a)(6) of P.L. 108-311 see above] provides:
"(2) Regulated investment companies and real estate investment trusts. In the case of a regulated investment company or a real estate investment trust, the amendments made by this section shall apply to taxable years ending after December 31, 2002; except that dividends received by such a company or trust on or before such date shall not be treated as qualified dividend income (as defined in section 1(h)(11)(B) of the Internal Revenue Code of 1986, as added by this Act)."
—P.L. 108-27, Sec. 303, of this Act [as amended by Sec. 102, P.L. 109-222, and Sec. 102(a), P.L. 111-312, see above], reads as follows:
"Sec. 303. Sunset of title. All provisions of, and amendments made by, this title [Secs. 301 and 302] shall not apply to taxable years beginning after December 31, 2012, and the Internal Revenue Code of 1986 shall be applied and administered to such years as if such provisions and amendments had never been enacted."

In 2002, P.L. 107-358, Sec. 2, added subsec. (c) in Sec. 901 of P.L. 107-16 [see below], effective 12/17/2002.

In 2001, P.L. 107-16, Sec. 101(c)(4), substituted "equal to the product of the highest rate of tax under section 1(c) and the accumulated taxable income." for "equal to 39.6 percent of the accumulated taxable income." in Code Sec. 531, effective for tax. yrs. begin. after 12/31/2000.
—P.L. 107-16, Sec. 901, of this Act [as amended by Sec. 2, P.L. 107-358, and Sec. 101(a)(1), P.L. 111-312, see above], reads as follows:
"Sec. 901. Sunset of provisions of Act.
"(a) In general. All provisions of, and amendments made by, this Act shall not apply—
"(1) to taxable, plan, or limitation years beginning after December 31, 2012, or
"(2) in the case of title V, to estates of decedents dying, gifts made, or generation skipping transfers, after December 31, 2012.
"(b) Application of certain laws. The Internal Revenue Code of 1986 and the Employee Retirement Income Security Act of 1974 shall be applied and administered to years, estates, gifts, and transfers described in subsection (a) as if the provisions and amendments described in subsection (a) had never been enacted.
"(c) Exception. Subsection (a) shall not apply to section 803 (relating to no federal income tax on restitution received by victims of the Nazi regime or their heirs or estates)."

In 1993, P.L. 103-66, Sec. 13201(b)(1), substituted "36 percent" for "28 percent" in Code Sec. 531, effective for tax. yrs. begin. after 12/31/92.
—P.L. 103-66, Sec. 13202(b), substituted "39.6 percent" for "36 percent" in Code Sec. 531, effective for tax. yrs. begin. after 12/31/92.

In 1988, P.L. 100-647, Sec. 1001(a)(2)(A), amended Code Sec. 531, effective for tax. yrs. begin. after 12/31/87.
Prior to amendment, Code Sec. 531 read as follows:
"SEC. 531. IMPOSITION OF ACCUMULATED EARNINGS TAX.
In addition to other taxes imposed by this chapter, there is hereby imposed for each taxable year on the accumulated taxable income (as defined in section 535) of every corporation described in section 532, an accumulated earnings tax equal to the sum of —
"(1) 27½ percent of the accumulated taxable income not in excess of $100,000, plus
"(2) 38½ percent of the accumulated taxable income in excess of $100,000."

Accumulated earnings tax   Code Sec. 535(b)(1)

Sec. 532. Corporations subject to accumulated earnings tax.
(a) General rule.

The accumulated earnings tax imposed by section 531 shall apply to every corporation (other than those described in subsection (b)) formed or availed of for the purpose of avoiding the income tax with respect to its shareholders or the shareholders of any other corporation, by permitting earnings and profits to accumulate instead of being divided or distributed.

(b) Exceptions.

The accumulated earnings tax imposed by section 531 shall not apply to—

(1) a personal holding company (as defined in section 542),

(2) a corporation exempt from tax under subchapter F (section 501 and following), or

(3) a passive foreign investment company (as defined in section 1297).

(c) Application determined without regard to number of shareholders.

The application of this part to a corporation shall be determined without regard to the number of shareholders of such corporation.

In 2005, P.L. 109-135, Sec. 403(n)(1), deleted para. (b)(2) and redesignated paras. (b)(3) and (b)(4) as paras. (b)(2) and (b)(3), effective for tax. yrs. of foreign corporations begin. after 12/31/2004, and for tax. yrs. of United States shareholders with or within which such tax. yrs. of foreign corporations end, as if included in Sec. 413 of the American Jobs Creation Act of 2004, P.L. 108-357.

Prior to deletion, para. (b)(2) read as follows:

"(2) a foreign personal holding company (as defined in section 552),"

In 1997, P.L. 105-34, Sec. 1122(d)(1), substituted "section 1297" for "section 1296" in para. (b)(4), effective for tax. yrs. of United States persons begin. after 12/31/97, and tax. yrs. of foreign corporations end. with or within such tax. yrs. of United States persons.

In 1986, P.L. 99-514, Sec. 1235(f)(1), deleted "or" at the end of para. (b)(2), substituted ", or" for the period at the end of para. (b)(3), and added para. (b)(4), effective for tax. yrs. of foreign corporations begin. after 12/31/86.

In 1984, P.L. 98-369, Sec. 58(a), added subsec. (c), effective for tax. yrs. begin. after 7/18/84.

Sec. 533. Evidence of purpose to avoid income tax.
(a) Unreasonable accumulation determinative of purpose.

For purposes of section 532, the fact that the earnings and profits of a corporation are permitted to accumulate beyond the reasonable needs of the business shall be determinative of the purpose to avoid the income tax with respect to shareholders, unless the corporation by the preponderance of the evidence shall prove to the contrary.

(b) Holding or investment company.

The fact that any corporation is a mere holding or investment company shall be prima facie evidence of the purpose to avoid the income tax with respect to shareholders.

Sec. 534. Burden of proof.
(a) General rule.

In any proceeding before the Tax Court involving a notice of deficiency based in whole or in part on the allegation that all or any part of the earnings and profits have been permitted to accumulate beyond the reasonable needs of the business, the burden of proof with respect to such allegation shall—

(1) if notification has not been sent in accordance with subsection (b), be on the Secretary, or

(2) if the taxpayer has submitted the statement described in subsection (c), be on the Secretary with respect to the grounds set forth in such statement in accordance with the provisions of such subsection.

(b) Notification by Secretary.

Before mailing the notice of deficiency referred to in subsection (a), the Secretary may send by certified mail or registered mail a notification informing the taxpayer that the proposed notice of deficiency includes an amount with respect to the accumulated earnings tax imposed by section 531.

(c) Statement by taxpayer.

Within such time (but not less than 30 days) after the mailing of the notification described in subsection (b) as the Secretary may prescribe by regulations, the taxpayer may submit a statement of the grounds (together with facts sufficient to show the basis thereof) on which the taxpayer relies to establish that all or any part of the earnings and profits have not been permitted to accumulate beyond the reasonable needs of the business.

(d) Jeopardy assessment.

If pursuant to section 6861(a) a jeopardy assessment is made before the mailing of the notice of deficiency referred to in subsection (a), for purposes of this section such notice of deficiency shall, to the extent that it informs the taxpayer that such deficiency includes the accumulated earnings tax imposed by section 531, constitute the notification described in subsection (b), and in that event the statement described in subsection (c) may be included in the taxpayer's petition to the Tax Court.

In 1976, P.L. 94-455, Sec. 1901(a)(73)(A), deleted the last sentence of subsec. (b) . . . Sec. 1901(a)(73)(B), deleted subsec. (e), effective for tax. yrs. begin. after 12/31/76.

Prior to amendment, the last sentence of subsec. (b) read as follows:

"In the case of a notice of deficiency to which subsection (e)(2) applies and which is mailed on or before the 30th day after the date of the enactment of this sentence [8/11/55], the notification referred to in the preceding sentence may be mailed at any time on or before such 30th day."

Prior to deletion, subsec. (e) read as follows:

"(e) Application of section.

"(1) Notwithstanding any other provision of law, this section shall apply with respect to taxable years to which this subchapter applies and (except as provided in paragraph (2)) to taxable years to which the corresponding provisions of prior revenue laws apply.

"(2) In the case of a notice of deficiency for a taxable year to which this subchapter does not apply, this section shall apply only in the case of proceedings tried on the merits after the date of the enactment of this paragraph [8/11/55]."

—P.L. 94-455, Sec. 1906(b)(13)(A), substituted "Secretary" for "Secretary or his delegate" each place it appeared in Code Sec. 534, effective for tax. yrs. begin. after 12/31/76.

In 1958, P.L. 85-866, Sec. 89(b), substituted "certified mail or registered mail" for "registered mail" in subsec. (b), effective if mailing occurred after 9/2/58.

In 1955, ch. 805, Secs. 4, 5, added second sentence of subsec. (b), and added in subsec. (e) the permission, in certain instances, to apply this section to cases involving taxable years to which prior revenue laws apply.

Sec. 535. Accumulated taxable income.
(a) Definition.

For purposes of this subtitle, the term "accumulated taxable income" means the taxable income, adjusted in the manner provided in subsection (b), minus the sum of the dividends paid deduction (as defined in section 561) and the accumulated earnings credit (as defined in subsection (c)).

(b) Adjustments to taxable income.

For purposes of subsection (a), taxable income shall be adjusted as follows:

(1) Taxes. There shall be allowed as a deduction Federal income and excess profits taxes and income, war profits, and excess profits taxes of foreign countries and possessions of the United States (to the extent not allowable as a deduction under section 275(a)(4)), accrued during the taxable year or deemed to be paid by a domestic corporation under section 902(a) or 960(a)(1) for the taxable year, but not including the accumulated earnings tax imposed by section 531, the personal holding company tax imposed

2,251

by section 541, or the taxes imposed by corresponding sections of a prior income tax law.

(2) Charitable contributions. The deduction for charitable contributions provided under section 170 shall be allowed without regard to section 170(b)(2).

(3) Special deductions disallowed. The special deductions for corporations provided in part VIII (except section 248) of subchapter B (section 241 and following, relating to the deduction for dividends received by corporations, etc.) shall not be allowed.

(4) Net operating loss. The net operating loss deduction provided in section 172 shall not be allowed.

(5) Capital losses.

(A) In general. Except as provided in subparagraph (B), there shall be allowed as a deduction an amount equal to the net capital loss for the taxable year (determined without regard to paragraph (7)(A)).

(B) Recapture of previous deductions for capital gains. The aggregate amount allowable as a deduction under subparagraph (A) for any taxable year shall be reduced by the lesser of—

(i) the nonrecaptured capital gains deductions, or

(ii) the amount of the accumulated earnings and profits of the corporation as of the close of the preceding taxable year.

(C) Nonrecaptured capital gains deductions. For purposes of subparagraph (B), the term "nonrecaptured capital gains deductions" means the excess of—

(i) the aggregate amount allowable as a deduction under paragraph (6) for preceding taxable years beginning after July 18, 1984, over

(ii) the aggregate of the reductions under subparagraph (B) for preceding taxable years.

(6) Net capital gains.

(A) In general. There shall be allowed as a deduction—

(i) the net capital gain for the taxable year (determined with the application of paragraph (7)), reduced by

(ii) the taxes attributable to such net capital gain.

(B) Attributable taxes. For purposes of subparagraph (A), the taxes attributable to the net capital gain shall be an amount equal to the difference between—

(i) the taxes imposed by this subtitle (except the tax imposed by this part) for the taxable year, and

(ii) such taxes computed for such year without including in taxable income the net capital gain for the taxable year (determined without the application of paragraph (7)).

(7) Capital loss carryovers.

(A) Unlimited carryforward. The net capital loss for any taxable year shall be treated as a short-term capital loss in the next taxable year.

(B) Section 1212 inapplicable. No allowance shall be made for the capital loss carryback or carryforward provided in section 1212.

(8) Special rules for mere holding or investment companies. In the case of a mere holding or investment company—

(A) Capital loss deduction, etc., not allowed. Paragraphs (5) and (7)(A) shall not apply.

(B) Deduction for certain offsets. There shall be allowed as a deduction the net short-term capital gain for the taxable year to the extent such gain does not exceed the amount of any capital loss carryover to such taxable year under section 1212 (determined without regard to paragraph (7)(B)).

(C) Earnings and profits. For purposes of subchapter C, the accumulated earnings and profits at any time shall not be less than they would be if this subsection had applied to the computation of earnings and profits for all taxable years beginning after July 18, 1984.

(9) Special rule for capital gains and losses of foreign corporations. In the case of a foreign corporation, paragraph (6) shall only be applied by taking into account only gains and losses which are effectively connected with the conduct of a trade or business within the United States and are not exempt from tax under treaty.

(10) Controlled foreign corporations. There shall be allowed as a deduction the amount of the corporation's income for the taxable year which is included in the gross income of a United States shareholder under section 951(a). In the case of any corporation the accumulated taxable income of which would (but for this sentence) be determined without allowance of any deductions, the deduction under this paragraph shall be allowed and shall be appropriately adjusted to take into account any deductions which reduced such inclusion.

(c) Accumulated earnings credit.

(1) General rule. For purposes of subsection (a), in the case of a corporation other than a mere holding or investment company the accumulated earnings credit is (A) an amount equal to such part of the earnings and profits for the taxable year as are retained for the reasonable needs of the business, minus (B) the deduction allowed by subsection (b)(6). For purposes of this paragraph, the amount of the earnings and profits for the taxable year which are retained is the amount by which the earnings and profits for the taxable year exceed the dividends paid deduction (as defined in section 561) for such year.

(2) Minimum credit.

(A) In general. The credit allowable under paragraph (1) shall in no case be less than the amount by which $250,000 exceeds the accumulated earnings and profits of the corporation at the close of the preceding taxable year.

(B) Certain service corporations. In the case of a corporation the principal function of which is the performance of services in the field of health, law, engineering, architecture, accounting, actuarial science, performing arts, or consulting, subparagraph (A) shall be applied by substituting "$150,000" for "$250,000".

(3) Holding and investment companies. In the case of a corporation which is a mere holding or investment company, the accumulated earnings credit is the amount (if any) by which $250,000 exceeds the accumulated earnings and profits of the corporation at the close of the preceding taxable year.

(4) Accumulated earnings and profits. For purposes of paragraphs (2) and (3), the accumulated earnings and profits at the close of the preceding taxable year shall be reduced by the dividends which under section 563(a) (relating to dividends paid after the close of the taxable year) are considered as paid during such taxable year.

(5) Cross reference. For denial of credit provided in paragraph (2) or (3) where multiple corporations are formed to avoid tax, see section 1551, and for limitation on such credit in the case of certain controlled corporations, see section 1561.

(d) Income distributed to United States-owned foreign corporation retains United States connection.

(1) In general. For purposes of this part, if 10 percent or more of the earnings and profits of any foreign corporation for any taxable year—

Accumulated earnings tax — Code Sec. 537(a)(3)

(A) is derived from sources within the United States, or
(B) is effectively connected with the conduct of a trade or business within the United States,

any distribution out of such earnings and profits (and any interest payment) received (directly or through 1 or more other entities) by a United States-owned foreign corporation shall be treated as derived by such corporation from sources within the United States.

(2) United States-owned foreign corporation. The term "United States-owned foreign corporation" has the meaning given to such term by section 904(h)(6).

In 2005, P.L. 109-135, Sec. 403(n)(2), added para. (b)(10), effective for tax. yrs. of foreign corporations begin. after 12/31/2004, and for tax. yrs. of United States shareholders in which or within which such tax. yrs. of foreign corporations end as if included in Sec. 413 of the American Jobs Creation Act of 2004, P.L. 108-357.

In 2004, P.L. 108-357, Sec. 402(b)(1), substituted "section 904(h)(6)" for "section 904(g)(6)" in para. (d)(2), effective for losses for tax. yrs. begin. after 12/31/2006.

In 1990, P.L. 101-508, Sec. 11801(c)(18), substituted "section 1561" for "sections 1561 and 1564" in para. (c)(5), effective 11/5/90, except as provided in Sec. 11821(b) of this Act, reproduced in note following Code Sec. 1564.

In 1988, P.L. 100-647, Sec. 1012(k), amended Sec. 1225(c) of P.L. 99-514, the effective date for changes made by Sec. 1225 of P.L. 99-514, by substituting "January 1, 1986" for "March 1, 1986", see below.

In 1986, P.L. 99-514, Sec. 1225(a), added para. (b)(9), effective for gains and losses realized on or after 1/1/86 [as amended by Sec. 1012(k) of P.L. 100-647].

—P.L. 99-514, Sec. 1899A(17), substituted "July 18, 1984" for "the date of the enactment of the Tax Reform Act of 1984" in clause (b)(5)(C)(i) and subpara. (b)(8)(C), effective 10/22/86.

In 1984, P.L. 98-369, Sec. 58(b), amended paras. (b)(5), (6), and (7) and added new para. (b)(8), effective for tax. yrs. begin. after 7/18/84.

Prior to amendment, paras. (b)(5), (6), and (7) read as follows:

"(5) Capital losses. There shall be allowed as deductions losses from sales or exchanges of capital assets during the taxable year which are disallowed as deductions under section 1211(a).

"(6) Net capital gains. There shall be allowed as a deduction the net capital gain for the taxable year (determined without regard to the capital loss carryback or carryover provided in section 1212) minus the taxes imposed by this subtitle attributable to such net capital gain. The taxes attributable to such net capital gain shall be an amount equal to the difference between—

"(A) the taxes imposed by this subtitle (except the tax imposed by this part) for such year, and

"(B) such taxes computed for such year without including in taxable income the net capital gain for the taxable year (determined with regard to the capital loss carryback and carryover provided in section 1212).

"(7) Capital loss carryover. No allowance shall be made for the capital loss carryback or carryover provided in section 1212."

—P.L. 98-369, Sec. 125(a), added subsec. (d), effective for distributions and interest payments received by a United States-owned foreign corporation (within the meaning of Code Sec. 535(d)) on or after 5/23/83, in tax. yrs. end. on or after 5/23/83. Sec. 125(b)(2) of this Act provides:

"(2) Corporations in existence on May 23, 1983.—In the case of a United States-owned foreign corporation (as so defined) in existence on May 23, 1983, the amendment made by subsection (a) shall apply to taxable years beginning after December 31, 1984."

In 1981, P.L. 97-34, Sec. 232(a), amended para. (c)(2) ... Sec. 232(b)(1), substituted "$250,000" for "$150,000" in para. (c)(3), effective for tax. yrs. begin. after 12/31/81.

Prior to amendment, para. (c)(2) read as follows:

"(2) Minimum credit. The credit allowable under paragraph (1) shall in no case be less than the amount by which $150,000 exceeds the accumulated earnings and profits of the corporation at the close of the preceding taxable year."

In 1976, P.L. 94-455, Sec. 1033(b)(3), substituted "section 902(a) or 960(a)(1)" for "section 902(a)(1) or 960(a)(1)(C)" in para. (b)(1). Sec. 1033(c), of the Act provided the following effective dates for amendments made by Sec. 1033 of the Act:

"(c) Effective dates. The amendments made by this section shall apply —

"(1) in respect of any distribution received by a domestic corporation after December 31, 1977, and

"(2) in respect of any distribution received by a domestic corporation before January 1, 1978, in a taxable year of such corporation beginning after December 31, 1975, but only to the extent that such distribution is made out of the accumulated profits of a foreign corporation for a taxable year (of such foreign corporation) beginning after December 31, 1975.

For purposes of paragraph (2), a distribution made by a foreign corporation out of its profits which are attributable to a distribution received from a foreign corporation to which section 902(b) of the Internal Revenue Code of 1954 applies shall be treated as made out of the accumulated profits of a foreign corporation for a taxable year beginning before January 1, 1976, to the extent that such distribution was paid out of the accumulated profits of such foreign corporation for a taxable year beginning before January 1, 1976."

—P.L. 94-455, Sec. 1901(a)(74), deleted "(other than the excess profits tax imposed by subchapter E of chapter 2 of the Internal Revenue Code of 1939 for taxable years beginning after December 31, 1940)" after "Federal income and excess profits taxes" in para. (b)(1), effective for tax. yrs. begin. after 12/31/76.

—P.L. 94-455, Sec. 1901(b)(20)(A), deleted para. (b)(8), effective for tax. yrs. begin. after 12/31/76.

Prior to amendment, para. (b)(8) read as follows:

"(8) Bank affiliates. There shall be allowed the deduction described in section 601 (relating to bank affiliates)."

—P.L. 94-455, Sec. 1901(b)(32)(C), deleted paras. (b)(9) and (b)(10), effective for tax. yrs. begin. after 12/31/76.

Prior to amendment, paras. (b)(9) and (10) read as follows:

"(9) Distributions of divested stock. There shall be allowed as a deduction the amount of any dividend distribution received of divested stock (as defined in subsection (e) of section 1111), minus the taxes imposed by this subtitle attributable to such receipt, but only if the stock with respect to which the distribution is made was owned by the distributee on September 6, 1961, or was owned by the distributee for at least 2 years prior to the date on which the antitrust order (as defined in subsection (d) of section 1111) was entered.

"(10) Special adjustment on disposition of antitrust stock received as a dividend. If—

"(A) a corporation received antitrust stock (as defined in section 301(f)) in a distribution to which section 301 applied,

"(B) the amount of the distribution determined under section 301(f)(2) exceeded the basis of the stock determined under section 301(f)(3), and

"(C) paragraph (9) did not apply in respect of such distribution,

then proper adjustment shall be made, under regulations prescribed by the Secretary or his delegate, if such stock (or other property the basis of which is determined by reference to the basis of such stock) is sold or exchanged."

—P.L. 94-455, Sec. 1901(b)(33)(D), substituted "Net" for "Long-term" in the heading of para. (b)(6), substituted "the net capital gain for the taxable year" for "the excess of the net long-term capital gain for the taxable year over the net short-term capital loss for such year" each place it appeared in para. (b)(6), and substituted "such net capital gain" for "such excess" each place it appeared in para. (b)(6), effective for tax. yrs. begin. after 12/31/76.

In 1975, P.L. 94-12, Sec. 304(a), substituted "$150,000" for "$100,000" in paras. (c)(2) and (c)(3), effective for tax. yrs. begin. after 12/31/74.

In 1969, P.L. 91-172, Sec. 401(b)(2)(C), substituted "section 1551, and for limitation on such credit in the case of certain controlled corporations, see sections 1561 and 1564" for "section 1551" in subsec. (c)(5), effective for tax. yrs. begin. after 12/31/69.

—P.L. 91-172, Sec. 512(f)(5), substituted "capital loss carryback or carryover" for "capital loss carryover" in the first sentence of para. (b)(6), substituted "capital loss carryback and carryover" for "capital loss carryover" in subpara. (b)(6)(B), and added "carryback or" after "capital loss" in para. (b)(7), effective for net capital losses sustained in tax. yrs. begin. after 12/31/69.

In 1964, P.L. 88-272, Sec. 207(b)(4), substituted "section 275(a)(4)" for "section 164(b)(6)" in para. (b)(1), effective for tax. yrs. begin. after '63.

In 1962, P.L. 87-834, Sec. 9(d)(2), substituted "accrued during the taxable year or deemed to be paid by a domestic corporation under section 902(a)(1) or 960(a)(1)(C) for the taxable year" for "accrued during the taxable year" in para. (b)(1), effective for any distribution received by a domestic corporation after '64, and in respect of any distribution received by a domestic corporation before '65, in a taxable year of such corporation beginning after '62, but only to the extent that such distribution is made out of the accumulated profits of a foreign corporation for a taxable year (of such foreign corporation) beginning after '62.

—P.L. 87-403, Sec. 3(b), added paras. (b)(9), (10), effective for distributions after 2/2/62.

In 1958, P.L. 85-866, Sec. 31, deleted "the limitation in" after "without regard to" in para. (b)(2) ... and substituted "in taxable income the excess of the net long-term capital gain for the taxable year over the net short-term capital loss for such year (determined without regard to the capital loss carryover provided in section 1212)" for "such excess in taxable income" in subpara. (b)(6)(B), effective for tax. yrs. begin. after 12/31/53, and end. after 8/16/54.

—P.L. 85-866, Sec. 205(a), substituted "$100,000" for "$60,000" in paras. (c)(2) and (3), effective for tax. yrs. begin. after 12/31/57.

Sec. 536. Income not placed on annual basis.

Section 443(b) (relating to computation of tax on change of annual accounting period) shall not apply in the computation of the accumulated earnings tax imposed by section 531.

Sec. 537. Reasonable needs of the business.

(a) General rule.

For purposes of this part, the term "reasonable needs of the business" includes—

(1) the reasonably anticipated needs of the business,

(2) the section 303 redemption needs of the business, and

(3) the excess business holdings redemption needs of the business.

Code Sec. 537(b) — Accumulated earnings tax

(b) Special rules.
For purposes of subsection (a)—

(1) Section 303 redemption needs. The term "section 303 redemption needs" means, with respect to the taxable year of the corporation in which a shareholder of the corporation died or any taxable year thereafter, the amount needed (or reasonably anticipated to be needed) to make a redemption of stock included in the gross estate of the decedent (but not in excess of the maximum amount of stock to which section 303(a) may apply).

(2) Excess business holdings redemption needs. The term "excess business holdings redemption needs" means the amount needed (or reasonably anticipated to be needed) to redeem from a private foundation stock which—

(A) such foundation held on May 26, 1969 (or which was received by such foundation pursuant to a will or irrevocable trust to which section 4943(c)(5) applies), and

(B) constituted excess business holdings on May 26, 1969, or would have constituted excess business holdings as of such date if there were taken into account (i) stock received pursuant to a will or trust described in subparagraph (A), and (ii) the reduction in the total outstanding stock of the corporation which would have resulted solely from the redemption of stock held by the private foundation.

(3) Obligations incurred to make redemptions. In applying paragraphs (1) and (2), the discharge of any obligation incurred to make a redemption described in such paragraphs shall be treated as the making of such redemption.

(4) Product liability loss reserves. The accumulation of reasonable amounts for the payment of reasonably anticipated product liability losses (as defined in section 172(f)), as determined under regulations prescribed by the Secretary, shall be treated as accumulated for the reasonably anticipated needs of the business.

(5) No inference as to prior taxable years. The application of this part to any taxable year before the first taxable year specified in paragraph (1) shall be made without regard to the fact that distributions in redemption coming within the terms of such paragraphs were subsequently made.

In 1996, P.L. 104-188, Sec. 1704(t)(33), substituted "section 172(f)" for "section 172(i)" in para. (b)(4), effective 8/20/96.

In 1978, P.L. 95-600, Sec. 371(c), redesignated para. (b)(4) as para. (b)(5) and added new para. (b)(4), effective for tax. yrs. begin. after 9/30/79.

In 1976, P.L. 94-455, Sec. 1901(a)(75)(A), deleted ", with respect to taxable years of the corporation ending after May 26, 1969," after "'excess business holdings redemption needs' means" in para. (b)(2)... Sec. 1901(a)(75)(B), deleted "or (2)" after "paragraph (1)" in para. (b)(4), effective for tax. yrs. begin. after 12/31/76.

In 1969, P.L. 91-172, Sec. 906(a), amended Code Sec. 537, effective for tax imposed under Code Sec. 531, with respect to tax. yrs. end. after 5/26/69.
Prior to amendment, Code Sec. 537 read as follows:
"Sec. 537. Reasonable Needs Of The Business.
"For purposes of this part, the term 'reasonable needs of the business' includes the reasonably anticipated needs of the business."

PART II.—PERSONAL HOLDING COMPANIES

Sec.
541. Imposition of personal holding company tax.
542. Definition of personal holding company.
543. Personal holding company income.
544. Rules for determining stock ownership.
545. Undistributed personal holding company income.
546. Income not placed on annual basis.
547. Deduction for deficiency dividends.

• **Caution:** Code Sec. 541, following, was amended by P.L. 108-27 and P.L. 107-16, EGTRRA. These provisions generally sunset for tax years beginning after 12/31/2012. For specific sunset provisions, see Sec. 303, P.L. 108-27, as amended by Sec. 102(a), P.L. 111-312, and Sec. 901, P.L. 107-16, as amended by Sec. 101(a)(1), P.L. 111-312, reproduced in history notes for this Code Sec.

Sec. 541. Imposition of personal holding company tax.

In addition to other taxes imposed by this chapter, there is hereby imposed for each taxable year on the undistributed personal holding company income (as defined in section 545) of every personal holding company (as defined in section 542) a personal holding company tax equal to 15 percent of the undistributed personal holding company income.

In 2010, P.L. 111-312, Sec. 101(a)(1), substituted "December 31, 2012" for "December 31, 2010" both places it appeared in Sec. 901 of P.L. 107-16 [see below], effective as if included in the enactment of P.L. 107-16, EGTRRA, 6/7/2001.
—P.L. 111-312, Sec. 102(a), substituted "December 31, 2012" for "December 31, 2010" in Sec. 303 of P.L. 108-27 [see below], effective as if included in the enactment of the Jobs and Growth Tax Relief Reconciliation Act of 2003, 5/28/2003.

In 2006, P.L. 109-222, Sec. 102, substituted "December 31, 2010" for "December 31, 2008" in Sec. 303 of P.L. 108-27 [see below], effective 5/17/2006.

In 2004, P.L. 108-311, Sec. 402(a)(6), of this Act [which amended Sec. 302(f)(2) of P.L. 108-27, see below], provides:
"(2) Pass-thru entities. In the case of a pass-thru entity described in subparagraph (A), (B), (C), (D), (E), or (F) of section 1(h)(10) of the Internal Revenue Code of 1986, as amended by this Act, the amendments made by this section shall apply to taxable years ending after December 31, 2002; except that dividends received by such an entity on or before such date shall not be treated as qualified dividend income (as defined in section 1(h)(11)(B) of such Code, as added by this Act)."

In 2003, P.L. 108-27, Sec. 302(e)(6), substituted "equal to 15 percent of the undistributed personal holding company income." for "equal to the product of the highest rate of tax under section 1(c) and the undistributed personal holding company income." in Code Sec. 541, effective for tax. yrs. begin. after 12/31/2002. Sec. 302(f)(2), of this Act [prior to amendment by Sec. 402(a)(6) of P.L. 108-311, see above] provides:
"(2) Regulated investment companies and real estate investment trusts. In the case of a regulated investment company or a real estate investment trust, the amendments made by this section shall apply to taxable years beginning after December 31, 2002; except that dividends received by such a company or trust on or before such date shall not be treated as qualified dividend income (as defined in section 1(h)(11)(B) of the Internal Revenue Code of 1986, as added by this Act)."
—P.L. 108-27, Sec. 303, of this Act [as amended by Sec. 102, P.L. 109-222, and Sec. 102(a), P.L. 111-312, see above], reads as follows:
"Sec. 303. Sunset of title. All provisions of, and amendments made by, this title [Secs. 301 and 302] shall not apply to taxable years beginning after December 31, 2012, and the Internal Revenue Code of 1986 shall be applied and administered to such years as if such provisions and amendments had never been enacted."

In 2002, P.L. 107-358, Sec. 2, added subsec. (c) in Sec. 901 of P.L. 107-16 [see below], effective 12/17/2002.

In 2001, P.L. 107-16, Sec. 101(c)(5), substituted "equal to the product of the highest rate of tax under section 1(c) and the undistributed personal holding company income." for "equal to 39.6 percent of the undistributed personal holding company income." in Code Sec. 541, effective for tax. yrs. begin. after 12/31/2000.
—P.L. 107-16, Sec. 901, of this Act [as amended by Sec. 2, P.L. 107-358, and Sec. 101(a)(1), P.L. 111-312, see above], reads as follows:
"Sec. 901. Sunset of provisions of Act.
"(a) In general. All provisions of, and amendments made by, this Act shall not apply—
"(1) to taxable, plan, or limitation years beginning after December 31, 2012, or
"(2) in the case of title V, to estates of decedents dying, gifts made, or generation skipping transfers, after December 31, 2012.
"(b) Application of certain laws. The Internal Revenue Code of 1986 and the Employee Retirement Income Security Act of 1974 shall be applied and administered to years, estates, gifts, and transfers described in subsection (a) as if the provisions and amendments described in subsection (a) had never been enacted.
"(c) Exception. Subsection (a) shall not apply to section 803 (relating to no federal income tax on restitution received by victims of the Nazi regime or their heirs or estates)."

Personal holding companies   Code Sec. 542(c)(7)

In 1993, P.L. 103-66, Sec. 13201(b)(2), substituted "36 percent" for "28 percent" in Code Sec. 541, effective for tax. yrs. begin. after 12/31/92.
—P.L. 103-66, Sec. 13202(b), substituted "39.6 percent" for "36 percent" in Code Sec. 541, effective for tax. yrs. begin. after 12/31/92.
In 1990, P.L. 101-508, Sec. 11802(f)(1), deleted "(38.5 percent in the case of taxable years beginning in 1987)" after "28 percent" in Code Sec. 541, effective 11/5/90 except as provided in Sec. 11821(b) of this Act, reproduced in note following Code Sec. 545.
In 1986, P.L. 99-514, Sec. 104(b)(8), substituted "28 percent (38.5 percent in the case of taxable years beginning in 1987" for "50 percent" in Code Sec. 541, effective for tax. yrs. begin. after 12/31/86.
In 1981, P.L. 97-34, Sec. 101(d)(2), substituted "50 percent" for "70 percent" in Code Sec. 541, effective for tax. yrs. begin. after 12/31/81.
In 1964, P.L. 88-272, Sec. 225(a), substituted "tax equal to 70 percent of the undistributed personal holding company income." for "tax equal to the sum of—
   (1) 75 percent of the undistributed personal company income not in excess of $2,000, plus
   (2) 85 percent of the undistributed personal holding company income in excess of $2,000.' in Code Sec. 541, effective for tax. yrs. begin. after 12/31/63.

Sec. 542. Definition of personal holding company.
(a) General rule.

For purposes of this subtitle, the term "personal holding company" means any corporation (other than a corporation described in subsection (c)) if—

   (1) Adjusted ordinary gross income requirement. At least 60 percent of its adjusted ordinary gross income (as defined in section 543(b)(2)) for the taxable year is personal holding company income (as defined in section 543(a)), and

   (2) Stock ownership requirement. At any time during the last half of the taxable year more than 50 percent in value of its outstanding stock is owned, directly or indirectly, by or for not more than 5 individuals. For purposes of this paragraph, an organization described in section 401(a), 501(c)(17), or 509(a) or a portion of a trust permanently set aside or to be used exclusively for the purposes described in section 642(c) or a corresponding provision of a prior income tax law shall be considered an individual.

(b) Corporations filing consolidated returns.

   (1) General rule. In the case of an affiliated group of corporations filing or required to file a consolidated return under section 1501 for any taxable year, the adjusted ordinary gross income requirement of subsection (a)(1) of this section shall, except as provided in paragraphs (2) and (3), be applied for such year with respect to the consolidated adjusted ordinary gross income and the consolidated personal holding company income of the affiliated group. No member of such an affiliated group shall be considered to meet such adjusted ordinary gross income requirement unless the affiliated group meets such requirement.

   (2) Ineligible affiliated group. Paragraph (1) shall not apply to an affiliated group of corporations if—

      (A) any member of the affiliated group of corporations (including the common parent corporation) derived 10 percent or more of its adjusted ordinary gross income for the taxable year from sources outside the affiliated group, and

      (B) 80 percent or more of the amount described in subparagraph (A) consists of personal holding company income (as defined in section 543).

   For purposes of this paragraph, section 543 shall be applied as if the amount described in subparagraph (A) were the adjusted ordinary gross income of the corporation.

   (3) Excluded corporations. Paragraph (1) shall not apply to an affiliated group of corporations if any member of the affiliated group (including the common parent corporation) is a corporation excluded from the definition of personal holding company under subsection (c).

   (4) Certain dividend income received by a common parent. In applying paragraph (2)(A) and (B), personal holding company income and adjusted ordinary gross income shall not include dividends received by a common parent corporation from another corporation if—

      (A) the common parent corporation owns, directly or indirectly, more than 50 percent of the outstanding voting stock of such other corporation, and

      (B) such other corporation is not a personal holding company for the taxable year in which the dividends are paid.

   (5) Certain dividend income received from a nonincludible life insurance company. In the case of an affiliated group of corporations filing or required to file a consolidated return under section 1501 for any taxable year, there shall be excluded from consolidated personal holding company income and consolidated adjusted ordinary gross income for purposes of this part dividends received by a member of the affiliated group from a life insurance company taxable under section 801 that is not a member of the affiliated group solely by reason of the application of paragraph (2) of subsection (b) of section 1504.

(c) Exceptions.

The term "personal holding company" as defined in subsection (a) does not include—

   (1) a corporation exempt from tax under subchapter F (sec. 501 and following);

   (2) a bank as defined in section 581, or a domestic building and loan association within the meaning of section 7701(a)(19);

   (3) a life insurance company;

   (4) a surety company;

   (5) a foreign corporation,

   (6) a lending or finance company if—

      (A) 60 percent or more of its ordinary gross income (as defined in section 543(b)(1)) is derived directly from the active and regular conduct of a lending or finance business;

      (B) the personal holding company income for the taxable year (computed without regard to income described in subsection (d)(3) and income derived directly from the active and regular conduct of a lending or finance business, and computed by including as personal holding company income the entire amount of the gross income from rents, royalties, produced film rents, and compensation for use of corporate property by shareholders) is not more than 20 percent of the ordinary gross income;

      (C) the sum of the deductions which are directly allocable to the active and regular conduct of its lending or finance business equals or exceeds the sum of—

         (i) 15 percent of so much of the ordinary gross income derived therefrom as does not exceed $500,000, plus

         (ii) 5 percent of so much of the ordinary gross income derived therefrom as exceeds $500,000; and

      (D) the loans to a person who is a shareholder in such company during the taxable year by or for whom 10 percent or more in value of its outstanding stock is owned directly or indirectly (including, in the case of an individual, stock owned by members of his family as defined in section 544(a)(2)), outstanding at any time during such year do not exceed $5,000 in principal amount;

   (7) a small business investment company which is licensed by the Small Business Administration and operating under the Small Business Investment Act of 1958 (15

U.S.C. 661 and following) and which is actively engaged in the business of providing funds to small business concerns under that Act. This paragraph shall not apply if any shareholder of the small business investment company owns at any time during the taxable year directly or indirectly (including, in the case of an individual, ownership by the members of his family as defined in section 544(a)(2)) a 5 per centum or more proprietary interest in a small business concern to which funds are provided by the investment company or 5 per centum or more in value of the outstanding stock of such concern; and

(8) a corporation which is subject to the jurisdiction of the court in a title 11 or similar case (within the meaning of section 368(a)(3)(A)) unless a major purpose of instituting or continuing such case is the avoidance of the tax imposed by section 541.

(d) **Special rules for applying subsection (c)(6).**

(1) **Lending or finance business defined.**

(A) In general. Except as provided in subparagraph (B), for purposes of subsection (c)(6), the term "lending or finance business" means a business of—

(i) making loans,

(ii) purchasing or discounting accounts receivable, notes, or installment obligations,

(iii) rendering services or making facilities available in connection with activities described in clauses (i) and (ii) carried on by the corporation rendering services or making facilities available, or

(iv) rendering services or making facilities available to another corporation which is engaged in the lending or finance business (within the meaning of this paragraph), if such services or facilities are related to the lending or finance business (within such meaning) of such other corporation and such other corporation and the corporation rendering services or making facilities available are members of the same affiliated group (as defined in section 1504).

(B) Exceptions. For purposes of subparagraph (A), the term "lending or finance business" does not include the business of—

(i) making loans, or purchasing or discounting accounts receivable, notes, or installment obligations, if (at the time of the loan, purchase, or discount) the remaining maturity exceeds 144 months; unless—

(I) the loans, notes, or installment obligations are evidenced or secured by contracts of conditional sale, chattel mortgages, or chattel lease agreements arising out of the sale of goods or services in the course of the borrower's or transferor's trade or business, or

(II) the loans, notes, or installment obligations are made or acquired by the taxpayer and meet the requirements of subparagraph (C), or

(ii) making loans evidenced by, or purchasing, certificates of indebtedness issued in a series, under a trust indenture, and in registered form or with interest coupons attached.

For purposes of clause (i), the remaining maturity shall be treated as including any period for which there may be a renewal or extension under the terms of an option exercisable by the borrower.

(C) Indefinite maturity credit transactions. For purposes of subparagraph (B)(i), a loan, note, or installment obligation meets the requirements of this subparagraph if it is made under an agreement—

(i) under which the creditor agrees to make loans or advances (not in excess of an agreed upon maximum amount) from time to time to or for the account of the debtor upon request, and

(ii) under which the debtor may repay the loan or advance in full or in installments.

(2) **Business deductions.** For purposes of subsection (c)(6)(C), the deductions which may be taken into account shall include only—

(A) deductions which are allowable only by reason of section 162 or section 404, except there shall not be included any such deduction in respect of compensation for personal services rendered by shareholders (including members of the shareholder's family as described in section 544(a)(2)), and

(B) deductions allowable under section 167, and deductions allowable under section 164 for real property taxes, but in either case only to the extent that the property with respect to which such deductions are allowable is used directly in the active and regular conduct of the lending or finance business.

(3) **Income received from certain affiliated corporations.** For purposes of subsection (c)(6)(B), in the case of a lending or finance company which meets the requirements of subsection (c)(6)(A), there shall not be treated as personal holding company income the lawful income received from a corporation which meets the requirements of subsection (c)(6) and which is a member of the same affiliated group (as defined in section 1504) of which such company is a member.

In **2004**, P.L. 108-357, Sec. 413(b)(1)(A), amended para. (c)(5)... Sec. 413(b)(1)(B), deleted paras. (c)(7) and (c)(10), and redesignated paras. (c)(8)-(9) as paras. (c)(7)-(8)... Sec. 413(b)(1)(C), added "and" at the end of para. (c)(7) [as redesignated by Sec. 413(b)(1)(B) of this Act, see above]... Sec. 413(b)(1)(D), substituted a period for "; and" at the end of para. (c)(8) [as redesignated by Sec. 413(b)(1)(B) of this Act, see above], effective for tax. yrs. of foreign corporations begin. after 12/31/2004, and for tax. yrs. of United States shareholders with or within which such tax. yrs. of foreign corporations end.
Prior to amendment, para. (c)(5) read as follows:
"(5) a foreign personal holding company as defined in section 552;"
Prior to deletion, para. (c)(7) read as follows:
"(7) a foreign corporation (other than a corporation which has income to which section 543(a)(7) applies for the taxable year), if all of its stock outstanding during the last half of the taxable year is owned by nonresident alien individuals, whether directly or indirectly through foreign estates, foreign trusts, foreign partnerships, or other foreign corporations;"
Prior to deletion, para. (c)(10) read as follows:
"(10) a passive foreign investment company (as defined in section 1297)."
In **1997**, P.L. 105-34, Sec. 1122(d)(1), substituted "section 1297" for "section 1296" in para. (c)(10), effective for tax. yrs. of United States persons begin. after 12/31/97, and tax. yrs. of foreign corporations end. with or within such tax. yrs. of United States persons.
In **1988**, P.L. 100-647, Sec. 6280(a)-(d), provide:
"SEC. 6280. TREATMENT OF CERTAIN BANK HOLDING COMPANIES.
"(a) General rule.
"For purposes of subtitle A of the 1986 Code, the term 'personal holding company income' shall not include any dividend received by a qualified bank holding company from a 25-percent owned bank during any taxable year ending in 1989 or 1990.
"(b) $3,000,000 limitation.
"The aggregate amount excluded from the personal holding company income of any qualified bank holding company under subsection (a) for the taxable year shall not exceed $3,000,000.
"(c) Qualified bank holding company.
"For purposes of this section, the term 'qualified bank holding company' means any bank holding company (as defined in section 2(a) of the Bank Holding Company Act of 1956) if 80 percent or more (by value) of the assets of such company at all times during the taxable year consist of stock in 1 or more 25-percent owned banks.
"(d) 25-percent owned bank.
"For purposes of this section, the term '25-percent owned bank' means any bank (as defined in section 581 of the 1986 Code) if at least 25 percent of the stock of such bank (by vote and value) is owned by the bank holding company."
In **1986**, P.L. 99-514, Sec. 1235(f)(2), deleted "and" at the end of para. (c)(8), substituted "; and" for the period at the end of para. (c)(9), and added para. (c)(10), effective for tax. yrs. of foreign corporations begin. after 12/31/86.
In **1984**, P.L. 98-369, Sec. 211(b)(7), substituted "section 801" for "section 802" in para. (b)(5), effective for tax. yrs. begin. after 12/31/83.

In 1982, P.L. 97-248, Sec. 293(a), deleted "but not $1,000,000" after "$500,000" in clause (c)(6)(C)(ii), effective for tax. yrs. begin. after 12/31/81.

—P.L. 97-248, Sec. 293(b), amended clause (d)(1)(B)(i) . . . Sec. 293(c), added subpara. (d)(1)(C), effective for tax. yrs. begin. after 12/31/80.

Prior to amendment, clause (d)(1)(B)(i) read as follows:

"(i) making loans, or purchasing or discounting accounts receivable, notes, or installment obligations, if (at the time of the loan, purchase, or discount) the remaining maturity exceeds 60 months, unless the loans, notes, or installment obligations are evidenced or secured by contracts of conditional sale, chattel mortgages, or chattel lease agreements arising out of the sale of goods or services in the course of the borrower's or transferor's trade or business, or"

In 1980, P.L. 96-589, Sec. 5(a), substituted "; and" for the period at the end of para. (c)(8) and added para. (c)(9). Sec. 7(d)(1) of this Act makes this amendment effective for any bankruptcy case or similar judicial proceeding begun after 12/31/80. Secs. 7(f) and (g) of this Act provide:

"(f) Election to substitute September 30, 1979, for December 31, 1980.

"(1) In general. The debtor (or debtors) in a bankruptcy case or similar judicial proceeding may (with the approval of the court) elect to apply [subsection 7(d) of this Act] by substituting 'September 30, 1979' for 'December 31, 1980' each place it appears in such subsections.

"(2) Effect of election. Any election made under paragraph (1) with respect to any proceeding shall apply to all parties to the proceeding.

"(3) Revocation only with consent. Any election under this subsection may be revoked only with the consent of the Secretary of the Treasury or his delegate.

"(4) Time and manner of election. Any election under this subsection shall be made at such time, and in such manner, as the Secretary of the Treasury or his delegate may by regulations prescribe.

"(g) Definitions.

"For purposes of this section—

"(1) Bankruptcy case. The term 'bankruptcy case' means any case under title 11 of the United States Code (as recodified by P.L. 95-598).

"(2) Similar judicial proceeding. The term 'similar judicial proceeding' means a receivership, foreclosure, or similar proceeding in a Federal or State court (as modified by section 368(a)(3)(D) of the Internal Revenue Code of 1954)."

In 1978, P.L. 95-600, Sec. 701(o)(1), provides the following with respect to the definition of a personal holding company, effective for tax. yrs. begin. after 12/31/76.

"(1) In general. The last sentence of section 542(a)(2) of the Internal Revenue Code of 1954 (relating to stock ownership requirement) shall not apply in the case of an organization or trust organized or created before July 1, 1950, if at all times on or after July 1, 1950, and before the close of the taxable year such organization or trust has owned all of the common stock and at least 80 percent of the total number of shares of all other classes of stock of the corporation."

In 1976, P.L. 94-455, Sec. 1901(a)(76)(A), deleted the last sentence in para. (a)(2) . . . Sec. 1901(a)(76)(B), deleted "other than an affiliated group of railroad corporations the common parent of which would be eligible to file a consolidated return under section 141 of the Internal Revenue Code of 1939 prior to its amendment by the Internal Revenue Act of 1942," after "an affiliate group of corporations," in para. (b)(2) . . . Sec. 1901(a)(76)(C), deleted "without regard to subparagraphs (D) and (E) thereof" after "section 7701(a)(19)" in para. (c)(2) . . . Sec. 1901(a)(76)(D), added "(15 U.S.C. 661 and following)" after "Small Business Investment Act of 1958" in para. (c)(8), effective for tax. yrs. begin. after 12/31/76.

Prior to amendment, the last sentence of para. (a)(2) read as follows:

"The preceding sentence shall not apply in the case of an organization or trust organized or created before July 1, 1950, if at all times on or after July 1, 1950, and before the close of the taxable year such organization or trust has owned all of the common stock and at least 80 percent of the total number of shares of all other classes of stock of the corporation."

In 1974, P.L. 93-480, Sec. 3(a), added para. (b)(5), effective for tax. yrs. begin. after 12/31/73.

In 1969, P.L. 91-172, Sec. 101(j)(16), amended para. (a)(2), effective for tax. yrs. begin. after 12/31/69.

Prior to amendment, para. (a)(2) read as follows:

"(2) Stock ownership requirements. At any time during the last half of the taxable year more than 50 percent in value of its outstanding stock is owned, directly or indirectly, by or for not more than 5 individuals. For purposes of this paragraph, an organization described in section 503(b) or a portion of a trust permanently set aside or to be used exclusively for the purposes described in section 642(c) or a corresponding provision of a prior income tax law shall be considered an individual. The preceding sentence shall not apply in the case of an organization or trust organized or created before July 1, 1950, if at all times on or after July 1, 1950, and before the close of the taxable year such organization or trust has owned all of the common stock and at least 80 percent of the total number of shares of all other classes of stock of the corporation, but only if such organization or trust is not denied exemption under section 504 or an unlimited charitable deduction is not denied under section 681(c) and, for this purpose—

"(A) all income of the corporation which is available for distribution as dividends to its shareholders at the close of any taxable year shall be deemed to have been distributed at the close of such year whether or not any portion of such income was in fact distributed; and

"(B) section 504(a)(1) and section 681(c)(1) shall also not apply to income attributable to property of a decedent dying before January 1, 1951, which was transferred during his lifetime to a trust or property that was transferred under his will to such trust."

In 1966, P.L. 89-809, Sec. 104, amended para. (c)(7), effective for tax. yrs. begin. after 12/31/66.

Prior to amendment, para. (c)(7) read as follows:

"(7) a foreign corporation if—

"(A) its gross income from sources within the United States for the period specified in section 861(a)(2)(B) is less than 50 percent of its total gross income from all sources, and

"(B) all of its stock outstanding during the last half of the taxable year is owned by nonresident alien individuals, whether directly or indirectly through other foreign corporations;"

In 1964, P.L. 88-272, Sec. 225(b), amended para. (a)(1) . . . Sec. 225(k)(1), substituted "adjusted ordinary gross income" for "gross income" each place it appeared in subsec. (b) . . . Sec. 225(c)(2), deleted paras. (c)(6), (7), (8) and (9), redesignated paras. (c)(10) and (11) as paras. (c)(7) and (8), and added new para. (c)(6) . . . Sec. 225(c)(3), added subsec. (d), effective for tax. yrs. begin. after 12/31/63.

Prior to amendment, para. (a)(1) read as follows:

"(1) Gross income requirement. At least 80 percent of its gross income for the taxable year is personal holding company income as defined in section 543, and"

Prior to deletion, paras. (c)(6), (7), (8) and (9) read as follows:

"(6) a licensed personal finance company under State supervision, 80 percent or more of the gross income of which is lawful interest received from loans made to individuals in accordance with the provisions of applicable State law if at least 60 percent of such gross income is lawful interest—

"(A) received from individuals each of whose indebtedness to such company did not at any time during the taxable year exceed in principal amount the limit prescribed for small loans by such law (or, if there is no such limit, $500), and

"(B) not payable in advance or compounded and computed only on unpaid balances, and if the loans to a person, who is a shareholder in such company during the taxable year by or for whom 10 percent or more in value of its outstanding stock is owned directly or indirectly (including, in the case of an individual, stock owned by the members of his family as defined in section 544(a)(2)), outstanding at any time during such year do not exceed $5,000 in principal amount;

"(7) a lending company, not otherwise excepted by this subsection, authorized to engage in and actively and regularly engaged in the small loan business (consumer finance business) under one or more State statutes providing for the direct regulations of such business, 80 percent or more of the gross income of which consists of either or both of the following—

"(A) lawful interest, discount, or other authorized charges received from loans made to individuals in accordance with the provisions of applicable State law, and

"(B) lawful income received from domestic subsidiary corporations (of which stock possessing at least 80 percent of the voting power of all classes of stock and of which at least 80 percent of each class of the nonvoting stock is owned directly by such lending company), which are themselves excepted under this paragraph or paragraph (6), (8), or (9) of this subsection,

if at least 60 percent of the gross income is lawful interest, discount, or other authorized charges received from loans made in accordance with the provisions of such small loan (consumer finance) laws to individuals, each of whose indebtedness to such company did not at any time during the taxable year exceed in principal amount the limit prescribed for small loans by such law (or, if there is no such limit, $1,500), and if the deductions allowed to such company under section 162 (relating to trade or business expenses), other than for compensation for personal services rendered by shareholders (including members of the shareholder's family as described in section 544(a)(2)), constitute 15 percent or more of its gross income, and the loans to a person, who is a shareholder in such company during the taxable year by or for whom 10 percent or more in value of its outstanding stock is owned directly or indirectly (including, in the case of an individual, stock owned by the members of his family as defined in section 544(a)(2)), outstanding at any time during such year do not exceed $5,000 in principal amount;

"(8) a loan or investment corporation, a substantial part of the business of which consists of receiving funds not subject to check and evidenced by installment or fully paid certificates of indebtedness or investment, and making loans and discounts, and the loans to a person who is a shareholder in such corporation during such taxable year by or for whom 10 percent or more in value of its outstanding stock is owned directly or indirectly (including, in the case of an individual, stock owned by the members of his family as defined in section 544(a)(2)) outstanding at any time during such year do not exceed $5,000 in principal amount;

"(9) a finance company, actively and regularly engaged in the business of purchasing or discounting accounts or notes receivable or installment obligations, or making loans secured by any of the foregoing or by tangible personal property, at least 80 percent of the gross income of which is derived from such business in accordance with the provisions of applicable State law or does not constitute personal holding company income as defined in section 543, if 60 percent of the gross income is derived from one or more of the following classes of transactions—

"(A) purchasing or discounting accounts or notes receivable, or installment obligations evidenced or secured by contracts of conditional sale, chattel mortgages, or chattel lease agreements, arising out of the sale of goods or services in the course of the transferor's trade or business;

"(B) making loans, maturing in not more than 36 months, to, and for the business purposes of, persons engaged in trade or business, secured by—

"(i) accounts or notes receivable, or installment obligations, described in subparagraph (A);

"(ii) warehouse receipts, bills of lading, trust receipts, chattel mortgages, bailments, or factor's liens, covering or evidencing the borrower's inventories;

"(iii) a chattel mortgage on property used in the borrower's trade or business; except loans to any single borrower which for more than 90 days in the taxable year of the company exceed 15 percent of the average funds employed by the company during such taxable year;

"(C) making loans, in accordance with the provisions of applicable State law, secured by chattel mortgages on tangible personal property, the original amount of each of which is not less than the limit referred to in, or prescribed by, paragraph (6)(A), and the aggregate principal amount of which owing by any one borrower to the company at any time during the taxable year of the company does not exceed $5,000; and

"(D) if 30 percent or more of the gross income of the company is derived from one or more of the classes of transactions described in subparagraphs (A), (B), and (C), purchasing, discounting, or lending upon the security of, installment obligations of individuals where the transferor or borrower acquired such obligations either in transactions of the classes described in subparagraphs (A) and (C) or as a result of loans made by such transferor or borrower in accordance with the provisions of subparagraphs (A) and (B) of paragraph (6) or of subparagraphs (A) and (B) of paragraph (7) of this subsection, if the funds so supplied at all times bear an agreed ratio to the unpaid balance of the assigned installment obligations, and documents evidencing such obligations are held by the company;

provided that the deductions allowable under section 162 (relating to trade or business expenses), other than compensation for personal services rendered by shareholders (including members of the shareholder's family as described in section 544(a)(2)), constitute 15 percent or more of the gross income, and that loans to a person who is a shareholder in such company during such taxable year by or for whom 10 percent or more in value of its outstanding stock is owned directly or indirectly (including, in the case of an individual, stock owned by members of his family as defined in section 544(a)(2)) outstanding at any time during such year do not exceed $5,000 in principal amount; "

—P.L. 88-272, Sec. 225(c)(1), amended para. (c)(2), effective for tax. yrs. begin. after 10/16/62.

Prior to amendment, para. (c)(2) read as follows:

"(2) a bank as defined in section 581;"

In 1962, P.L. 87-768, amended para. (c)(7), effective for tax. yrs. begin. after 12/31/61.

Prior to amendment, para. (c)(7) read as follows:

"(7) a lending company, not otherwise excepted by this subsection, authorized to engage in the small loan business under one or more State statutes providing for the direct regulation of such business, 80 percent or more of the gross income of which is lawful interest, discount or other authorized charges—

"(A) received from loans maturing in not more than 36 months made to individuals in accordance with the provisions of applicable State law, and

"(B) which do not, in the case of any individual loan, exceed in the aggregate an amount equal to simple interest at the rate of 3 percent per month not payable in advance and computed only on unpaid balances, if at least 60 percent of the gross income is lawful interest, discount or other authorized charges received from individuals each of whose indebtedness to such company did not at any time during the taxable year exceed in principal amount the limit prescribed for small loans by such law (or, if there is no such limit, $500), and if the deductions allowed to such company under section 162 (relating to trade or business expenses), other than for compensation for personal services rendered by shareholders (including members of the shareholder's family as described in section 544(a)(2)) constitute 15 percent or more of its gross income, and the loans to a person, who is a shareholder in such company during the taxable year by or for whom 10 percent or more in value of its outstanding stock is owned directly or indirectly (including, in the case of an individual, stock owned by the members of his family as defined in section 544(a)(2)), outstanding at any time during such year do not exceed $5,000 in principal amount;"

In 1959, P.L. 86-376, Sec. 3(a), added para. (c)(11), effective for tax. yrs. begin. after '58.

In 1955, ch. 871, Sec. 3, added the sentence at the end of para. (a)(2), effective for tax. yrs. begin. after 12/31/54.

Sec. 543. Personal holding company income.

(a) General rule.

For purposes of this subtitle, the term "personal holding company income" means the portion of the adjusted ordinary gross income which consists of—

(1) **Dividends, etc.** Dividends, interest, royalties (other than mineral, oil, or gas royalties or copyright royalties), and annuities. This paragraph shall not apply to—

(A) interest constituting rent (as defined in subsection (b)(3)),

(B) interest on amounts set aside in a reserve fund under chapter 533 or 535 of title 46, United States Code,

(C) active business computer software royalties (within the meaning of subsection (d)), and

(D) interest received by a broker or dealer (within the meaning of section 3(a)(4) or (5) of the Securities and Exchange Act of 1934) in connection with—

(i) any securities or money market instruments held as property described in section 1221(a)(1),

(ii) margin accounts, or

(iii) any financing for a customer secured by securities or money market instruments.

(2) **Rents.** The adjusted income from rents; except that such adjusted income shall not be included if—

(A) such adjusted income constitutes 50 percent or more of the adjusted ordinary gross income, and

(B) the sum of—

(i) the dividends paid during the taxable year (determined under section 562),

(ii) the dividends considered as paid on the last day of the taxable year under section 563(d) (as limited by the second sentence of section 563(b)), and

(iii) the consent dividends for the taxable year (determined under section 565),

equals or exceeds the amount, if any, by which the personal holding company income for the taxable year (computed without regard to this paragraph and paragraph (6), and computed by including as personal holding company income copyright royalties and the adjusted income from rents, mineral, oil, and gas royalties) exceeds 10 percent of the ordinary gross income.

(3) **Mineral, oil, and gas royalties.** The adjusted income from mineral, oil, and gas royalties; except that such adjusted income shall not be included if—

(A) such adjusted income constitutes 50 percent or more of the adjusted ordinary gross income,

(B) the personal holding company income for the taxable year (computed without regard to this paragraph, and computed by including as personal holding company income copyright royalties and the adjusted income from rents) is not more than 10 percent of the ordinary gross income, and

(C) the sum of the deductions which are allowable under section 162 (relating to trade or business expenses) other than—

(i) deductions for compensation for personal services rendered by the shareholders, and

(ii) deductions which are specifically allowable under sections other than section 162,

equals or exceeds 15 percent of the adjusted ordinary gross income.

(4) **Copyright royalties.** Copyright royalties; except that copyright royalties shall not be included if—

(A) such royalties (exclusive of royalties received for the use of, or right to use, copyrights or interests in copyrights on works created in whole, or in part, by any shareholder) constitute 50 percent or more of the ordinary gross income,

(B) the personal holding company income for the taxable year computed—

(i) without regard to copyright royalties, other than royalties received for the use of, or right to use, copyrights or interests in copyrights in works created in whole, or in part, by any shareholder owning more than 10 percent of the total outstanding capital stock of the corporation,

(ii) without regard to dividends from any corporation in which the taxpayer owns at least 50 percent of all classes of stock entitled to vote and at least 50 percent of the total value of all classes of stock and which corporation meets the requirements of this subparagraph and subparagraphs (A) and (C), and

(iii) by including as personal holding company income the adjusted income from rents and the adjusted income from mineral, oil, and gas royalties,

Personal holding companies — Code Sec. 543(b)(2)(B)(iv)

is not more than 10 percent of the ordinary gross income, and

(C) the sum of the deductions which are properly allocable to such royalties and which are allowable under section 162, other than—

(i) deductions for compensation for personal services rendered by the shareholders,

(ii) deductions for royalties paid or accrued, and

(iii) deductions which are specifically allowable under sections other than section 162,

equals or exceeds 25 percent of the amount by which the ordinary gross income exceeds the sum of the royalties paid or accrued and the amounts allowable as deductions under section 167 (relating to depreciation) with respect to copyright royalties.

For purposes of this subsection, the term "copyright royalties" means compensation, however designated, for the use of, or the right to use, copyrights in works protected by copyright issued under title 17 of the United States Code and to which copyright protection is also extended by the laws of any country other than the United States of America by virtue of any international treaty, convention, or agreement, or interests in any such copyrighted works, and includes payments from any person for performing rights in any such copyrighted work and payments (other than produced film rents as defined in paragraph (5)(B)) received for the use of, or right to use, films. For purposes of this paragraph, the term "shareholder" shall include any person who owns stock within the meaning of section 544. This paragraph shall not apply to active business computer software royalties.

(5) Produced film rents.

(A) Produced film rents; except that such rents shall not be included if such rents constitute 50 percent or more of the ordinary gross income.

(B) For purposes of this section, the term "produced film rents" means payments received with respect to an interest in a film for the use of, or right to use, such film, but only to the extent that such interest was acquired before substantial completion of production of such film. In the case of a producer who actively participates in the production of the film, such term includes an interest in the proceeds or profits from the film, but only to the extent such interest is attributable to such active participation.

(6) Use of corporate property by shareholder.

(A) Amounts received as compensation (however designated and from whomever received) for the use of, or the right to use, tangible property of the corporation in any case where, at any time during the taxable year, 25 percent or more in value of the outstanding stock of the corporation is owned, directly or indirectly, by or for an individual entitled to the use of the property (whether such right is obtained directly from the corporation or by means of a sublease or other arrangement).

(B) Subparagraph (A) shall apply only to a corporation which has personal holding company income in excess of 10 percent of its ordinary gross income.

(C) For purposes of the limitation in subparagraph (B), personal holding company income shall be computed—

(i) without regard to subparagraph (A) or paragraph (2),

(ii) by excluding amounts received as compensation for the use of (or right to use) intangible property (other than mineral, oil, or gas royalties or copyright royalties) if a substantial part of the tangible property used in connection with such intangible property is owned by the corporation and all such tangible and intangible property is used in the active conduct of a trade or business by an individual or individuals described in subparagraph (A), and

(iii) by including copyright royalties and adjusted income from mineral, oil, and gas royalties.

(7) Personal service contracts.

(A) Amounts received under a contract under which the corporation is to furnish personal services; if some person other than the corporation has the right to designate (by name or by description) the individual who is to perform the services, or if the individual who is to perform the services is designated (by name or by description) in the contract; and

(B) amounts received from the sale or other disposition of such a contract.

This paragraph shall apply with respect to amounts received for services under a particular contract only if at some time during the taxable year 25 percent or more in value of the outstanding stock of the corporation is owned, directly or indirectly, by or for the individual who has performed, is to perform, or may be designated (by name or by description) as the one to perform, such services.

(8) Estates and trusts. Amounts includible in computing the taxable income of the corporation under part I of subchapter J (sec. 641 and following, relating to estates, trusts, and beneficiaries).

(b) Definitions.

For purposes of this part—

(1) Ordinary gross income. The term "ordinary gross income" means the gross income determined by excluding—

(A) all gains from the sale or other disposition of capital assets, and

(B) all gains (other than those referred to in subparagraph (A)) from the sale or other disposition of property described in section 1231(b).

(2) Adjusted ordinary gross income. The term "adjusted ordinary gross income" means the ordinary gross income adjusted as follows:

(A) Rents. From the gross income from rents (as defined in the second sentence of paragraph (3) of this subsection) subtract the amount allowable as deductions for—

(i) exhaustion, wear and tear, obsolescence, and amortization of property other than tangible personal property which is not customarily retained by any one lessee for more than three years,

(ii) property taxes,

(iii) interest, and

(iv) rent,

to the extent allocable, under regulations prescribed by the Secretary, to such gross income from rents. The amount subtracted under this subparagraph shall not exceed such gross income from rents.

(B) Mineral royalties, etc. From the gross income from mineral, oil, and gas royalties described in paragraph (4), and from the gross income from working interests in an oil or gas well, subtract the amount allowable as deductions for—

(i) exhaustion, wear and tear, obsolescence, amortization, and depletion,

(ii) property and severance taxes,

(iii) interest, and

(iv) rent,

to the extent allocable, under regulations prescribed by the Secretary, to such gross income from royalties or such gross income from working interests in oil or gas wells. The amount subtracted under this subparagraph with respect to royalties shall not exceed the gross income from such royalties, and the amount subtracted under this subparagraph with respect to working interests shall not exceed the gross income from such working interests.

(C) Interest. There shall be excluded—

(i) interest received on a direct obligation of the United States held for sale to customers in the ordinary course of trade or business by a regular dealer who is making a primary market in such obligations, and

(ii) interest on a condemnation award, a judgment, and a tax refund.

(D) Certain excluded rents. From the gross income consisting of compensation described in subparagraph (D) of paragraph (3) subtract the amount allowable as deductions for the items described in clauses (i), (ii), (iii), and (iv) of subparagraph (A) to the extent allocable, under regulations prescribed by the Secretary, to such gross income. The amount subtracted under this subparagraph shall not exceed such gross income.

(3) Adjusted income from rents. The term "adjusted income from rents" means the gross income from rents, reduced by the amount subtracted under paragraph (2)(A) of this subsection. For purposes of the preceding sentence, the term "rents" means compensation, however designated, for the use of, or right to use, property, and the interest on debts owed to the corporation, to the extent such debts represent the price for which real property held primarily for sale to customers in the ordinary course of its trade or business was sold or exchanged by the corporation; but such term does not include—

(A) amounts constituting personal holding company income under subsection (a)(6),

(B) copyright royalties (as defined in subsection (a)(4)),

(C) produced film rents (as defined in subsection (a)(5)(B)),

(D) compensation, however designated, for the use of, or the right to use, any tangible personal property manufactured or produced by the taxpayer, if during the taxable year the taxpayer is engaged in substantial manufacturing or production of tangible personal property of the same type, or

(E) active business computer software royalties (as defined in subsection (d)).

(4) Adjusted income from mineral, oil, and gas royalties. The term "adjusted income from mineral, oil, and gas royalties" means the gross income from mineral, oil, and gas royalties (including production payments and overriding royalties), reduced by the amount subtracted under paragraph (2)(B) of this subsection in respect of such royalties.

(c) Gross income of insurance companies other than life insurance companies.

In the case of an insurance company other than a life insurance company, the term "gross income" as used in this part means the gross income, as defined in section 832(b)(1), increased by the amount of losses incurred, as defined in section 832(b)(5), and the amount of expenses incurred, as defined in section 832(b)(6), and decreased by the amount deductible under section 832(c)(7) (relating to tax-free interest).

(d) Active business computer software royalties.

(1) In general. For purposes of this section, the term "active business computer software royalties" means any royalties—

(A) received by any corporation during the taxable year in connection with the licensing of computer software, and

(B) with respect to which the requirements of paragraphs (2), (3), (4), and (5) are met.

(2) Royalties must be received by corporation actively engaged in computer software business. The requirements of this paragraph are met if the royalties described in paragraph (1)—

(A) are received by a corporation engaged in the active conduct of the trade or business of developing, manufacturing, or producing computer software, and

(B) are attributable to computer software which—

(i) is developed, manufactured, or produced by such corporation (or its predecessor) in connection with the trade or business described in subparagraph (A), or

(ii) is directly related to such trade or business.

(3) Royalties must constitute at least 50 percent of income. The requirements of this paragraph are met if the royalties described in paragraph (1) constitute at least 50 percent of the ordinary gross income of the corporation for the taxable year.

(4) Deductions under sections 162 and 174 relating to royalties must equal or exceed 25 percent of ordinary gross income.

(A) In general. The requirements of this paragraph are met if—

(i) the sum of the deductions allowable to the corporation under sections 162, 174, and 195 for the taxable year which are properly allocable to the trade or business described in paragraph (2) equals or exceeds 25 percent of the ordinary gross income of such corporation for such taxable year, or

(ii) the average of such deductions for the 5-taxable year period ending with such taxable year equals or exceeds 25 percent of the average ordinary gross income of such corporation for such period.

If a corporation has not been in existence during the 5-taxable year period described in clause (ii), then the period of existence of such corporation shall be substituted for such 5-taxable year period.

(B) Deductions allowable under section 162. For purposes of subparagraph (A), a deduction shall not be treated as allowable under section 162 if it is specifically allowable under another section.

(C) Limitation on allowable deductions. For purposes of subparagraph (A), no deduction shall be taken into account with respect to compensation for personal services rendered by the 5 individual shareholders holding the largest percentage (by value) of the outstanding stock of the corporation. For purposes of the preceding sentence—

(i) individuals holding less than 5 percent (by value) of the stock of such corporation shall not be taken into account, and

(ii) stock deemed to be owned by a shareholder solely by attribution from a partner under section 544(a)(2) shall be disregarded.

(5) Dividends must equal or exceed excess of personal holding company income over 10 percent of ordinary gross income.

Personal holding companies
Code Sec. 543

(A) In general. The requirements of this paragraph are met if the sum of—

(i) the dividends paid during the taxable year (determined under section 562),

(ii) the dividends considered as paid on the last day of the taxable year under section 563(d) (as limited by the second sentence of section 563(b)), and

(iii) the consent dividends for the taxable year (determined under section 565),

equals or exceeds the amount, if any, by which the personal holding company income for the taxable year exceeds 10 percent of the ordinary gross income of such corporation for such taxable year.

(B) Computation of personal holding company income. For purposes of this paragraph, personal holding company income shall be computed—

(i) without regard to amounts described in subsection (a)(1)(C),

(ii) without regard to interest income during any taxable year—

(I) which is in the 5-taxable year period beginning with the later of the 1st taxable year of the corporation or the 1st taxable year in which the corporation conducted the trade or business described in paragraph (2)(A), and

(II) during which the corporation meets the requirements of paragraphs (2), (3), and (4), and

(iii) by including adjusted income from rents and adjusted income from mineral, oil, and gas royalties (within the meaning of paragraphs (2) and (3) of subsection (a)).

(6) Special rules for affiliated group members.

(A) In general. In any case in which—

(i) the taxpayer receives royalties in connection with the licensing of computer software, and

(ii) another corporation which is a member of the same affiliated group as the taxpayer meets the requirements of paragraphs (2), (3), (4), and (5) with respect to such computer software,

the taxpayer shall be treated as having met such requirements.

(B) Affiliated group. For purposes of this paragraph, the term "affiliated group" has the meaning given such term by section 1504(a).

In 2006, P.L. 109-304, Sec. 17(e)(3), substituted "chapter 533 or 535 of title 46, United States Code" for "section 511 or 607 of the Merchant Marine Act, 1936 (46 U.S.C. App. 1161 or 1177)" in subpara. (a)(1)(B), enacted 10/6/2006.

In 2004, P.L. 108-357, Sec. 413(c)(8), added "and" at the end of subpara. (b)(1)(A), substituted a period for ", and" at the end of subpara. (b)(1)(B), and deleted subpara. (b)(1)(C), effective for tax. yrs. of foreign corporations begin. after 12/31/2004, and for tax. yrs. of United States shareholders with or within which such tax. yrs. of foreign corporations end.

Prior to deletion, subpara. (b)(1)(C) read as follows:

"(C) in the case of a foreign corporation all of the outstanding stock of which during the last half of the taxable year is owned by nonresident alien individuals (whether directly or indirectly through foreign estates, foreign trusts, foreign partnerships, or other foreign corporations), all items of income which would, but for this subparagraph, constitute personal holding company income under any paragraph of subsection (a) other than paragraph (7) thereof:[(.)]"

In 1999, P.L. 106-170, Sec. 532(c)(2)(E), substituted "section 1221(a)(1)" for "section 1221(1)" in clause (a)(1)(D)(i), effective for any instrument held, acquired, or entered into, any transaction entered into, and supplies held or acquired on or after 12/17/99.

In 1998, P.L. 105-206, Sec. 6023(9), substituted "section 563(d)" for "section 563(c)" in clause (d)(5)(A)(ii), effective 7/22/98.

In 1996, P.L. 104-188, Sec. 1704(t)(6), substituted "section 563(d)" for "section 563(c)" in clause (a)(2)(B)(ii), effective 8/20/96.

In 1988, P.L. 100-647, Sec. 1010(f)(5)(A), substituted "insurance companies" for "or mutual" in the heading of subsec. (c)... Sec. 1010(f)(5)(B), substituted "a life insurance company" for "life or mutual" in subsec. (c), effective for tax. yrs. begin. after 12/31/86. For transitional rules, see Sec. 1024(d) of P.L. 99-514 reproduced in Code Sec. 832.

—P.L. 100-647, Sec. 6279(a), deleted "and" at the end of subpara. (a)(1)(B), substituted ", and" for the period at the end of subpara. (a)(1)(C), and added subpara. (a)(1)(D), effective for interest received after 11/10/88, in tax. yrs. ending after 11/10/88.

In 1986, P.L. 99-514, Sec. 645(a)(1)(A)-(C), deleted "and" at the end of subpara. (a)(1)(A), substituted ", and" for the period at the end of subpara. (a)(1)(B), and added subpara. (a)(1)(C)... Sec. 645(a)(2), added subsec. (d)... Sec. 645(a)(4)(A), added the sentence at the end of para. (a)(4)... Sec. 645(a)(4)(B)(i)-(iii), deleted "or" at the end of subpara. (b)(3)(C), substituted ", or" for the period at the end of subpara. (b)(3)(D), and added subpara. (b)(3)(E), effective for royalties received before, on, or after 12/31/86.

—P.L. 99-514, Sec. 645(b)-(d), provides the following special rules:

"(b) Special rules for broker-dealers. In the case of a broker-dealer which is part of an affiliated group which files a consolidated Federal income tax return, the common parent of which was incorporated in Nevada on January 27, 1972, the personal holding company income (within the meaning of section 543 of the Internal Revenue Code of 1986) of such broker-dealer, shall not include any interest received after the date of the enactment of this Act with respect to—

"(1) any securities or money market instruments held as inventory,

"(2) margin accounts, or

"(3) any financing for a customer secured by securities or money market instruments.

"(c) Special rule for royalties received by qualified taxpayer.

"(1) In general. Any qualified royalty received or accrued in taxable years beginning after December 31, 1981, by a qualified taxpayer shall be treated in the same manner as a royalty with respect to software is treated under the amendments made by this section.

"(2) Qualified taxpayer. For purposes of this subsection, a qualified taxpayer is any taxpayer incorporated on September 7, 1978, which is engaged in the trade or business of manufacturing dolls and accessories.

"(3) Qualified royalty. For purposes of this subsection, the term 'qualified royalty' means any royalty arising from an agreement entered into in 1982 which permits the licensee to manufacture and sell dolls and accessories.

"(d) Special rule for treatment of active business computer royalties for S corporation purposes. In the case of a taxpayer which was incorporated on May 3, 1977, in California which elected to be taxed as an S corporation for its taxable year ending on December 31, 1985, any active business computer royalties (within the meaning of section 543(d) of the Internal Revenue Code of 1986 as added by this Act) which are received by the taxpayer in taxable years beginning after December 31, 1984, shall not be treated as passive investment income (within the meaning of section 1362(d)(3)(D)) for purposes of subchapter S of chapter 1 of such Code."

—P.L. 99-514, Sec. 1899A(18), substituted "46 U.S.C. App." for "46 U.S.C." in subpara. (a)(1)(B), effective 10/22/86.

In 1984, P.L. 98-369, Sec. 712(i)(3), deleted subpara. (a)(1)(C), added "and" at the end of subpara. (a)(1)(A), and substituted a period for ", and" at the end of subpara. (a)(1)(B), effective for distributions after 8/31/82. For exceptions and special rules, see Sec. 222(f)(2)-(4) of P.L. 97-248 reproduced in note following Code Sec. 302.

Prior to deletion, subpara. (a)(1)(C) read as follows:

"(C) dividends to which section 302(b)(4) would apply if the corporation were an individual."

In 1982, P.L. 97-248, Sec. 222(e)(6)(A), deleted "and" at end of subpara. (a)(1)(A)... Sec. 222(e)(6)(B), substituted ", and" for the period at the end of subpara. (a)(1)(B) and added subpara. (a)(1)(C), effective for distributions after 8/31/82. For exceptions and special rules, see Sec. 222(f)(2)-(4) of this Act reproduced in note following Code Sec. 302.

In 1976, P.L. 94-553, Sec. 105(d), deleted "(other than by reason of section 2 or 6 thereof)" after "copyright issued under title 17 of the United States Code" in para. (a)(4), effective 10/19/76.

—P.L. 94-455, Sec. 211(a), added the last sentence in subpara. (a)(5)(B), effective for tax. yrs. end. on or after 12/31/75.

—P.L. 94-455, Sec. 1901(b)(32)(D), added "and" at the end of subpara. (a)(1)(A), deleted subparas. (a)(1)(B) and (C) and added new subpara. (a)(1)(B), effective for tax. yrs. begin. after 12/31/76.

Prior to amendment, subparas (a)(1)(B) and (C) read as follows:

"(B) interest on amounts set aside in a reserve fund under section 511 or 607 of the Merchant Marine Act, 1936, and

"(C) a dividend distribution of divested stock (as defined in subsection (e) of section 1111), but only if the stock with respect to which the distribution is made was owned by the distributee on September 6, 1961, or was owned by the distributee for at least 2 years before the date on which the antitrust order (as defined in subsection (d) of section 1111) was entered."

—P.L. 94-455, Sec. 1906(b)(13)(A), substituted "Secretary" for "Secretary or his delegate" each place it appeared in para. (b)(2), effective for tax. yrs. begin. after 12/31/76.

—P.L. 94-455, Sec. 2106(a), amended para. (a)(6), effective for tax. yrs. begin. after 12/31/76.

Prior to amendment, para. (a)(6) read as follows:

"(6) Use of corporation property by shareholder. Amounts received as compensation (however designated and from whomsoever received) for the use of, or right to use, property of the corporation in any case where, at any time during the taxable year, 25 percent or more in value of the outstanding stock of the corporation is owned, directly or indirectly, by or for an individual entitled to the use of the property; whether such right is obtained directly from the corporation or by means of a sublease or other arrangement. This paragraph shall apply only to a corporation which has personal holding company income for the taxable year (computed without regard to this paragraph and paragraph (2), and computed by including as personal holding company income copyright royalties and the adjusted income from mineral, oil, and gas royalties) in excess of 10 percent of its ordinary gross income."

In 1966, P.L. 89-809, Sec. 206(b)(1), deleted the last sentence of para. (a)(2), effective for tax. yrs. begin. after 11/13/66. Such amendments shall also apply, at the election of the taxpayer (made at such time and in such manner as the Secretary or his delegate may prescribe), to taxable years beginning or before such date and ending after Dec. 31, '65.

Prior to deletion, the last sentence of para. (a)(2) read as follows:

"For purposes of applying this paragraph, royalties received for the use of, or for the privilege of using, a patent, invention, model, or design (whether or not patented), secret formula or process, or any other similar property right shall be treated as rent, if such property right is also used by the corporation receiving such royalties in the manufacture or production of tangible personal property held for lease to customers, and if the amount (computed without regard to this sentence) constituting rent from such leases to customers meets the requirements of subparagraph (A).

—P.L. 89-809, Sec. 104(h)(2), deleted "and" at the end of subpara. (b)(1)(A), substituted ", and" for the period at the end of subpara. (b)(1)(B), and added subsec. (b)(1)(C), effective for tax. yrs. begin. after 12/31/66.

—P.L. 89-809, Sec. 206(b)(2), added subsec. (b)(1)(D) . . . Sec. 206(a), expanded subsec. (b)(3) into subparas. (A)—(C) and added (D), for tax. yrs. begin. after 11/13/66. Such amendments shall also apply, at the election of the taxpayer (made at such time and in such manner as the Secretary or his delegate may prescribe), to taxable years beginning on or before such date and ending after Dec. 31, '65.

In 1964, P.L. 88-484, Sec. 3, added last sentence to para. (a)(2), effective for tax. yrs. begin. after 12/31/63.

—P.L. 88-272, Sec. 225(d), amended subsecs. (a) and (b) . . . Sec. 225(k)(2), deleted subsec. (d), effective for tax. yrs. begin. after 12/31/69.

Prior to amendment, subsecs. (a) and (b) read as follows:

"SEC. 543. PERSONAL HOLDING COMPANY INCOME.

"(a) General rule.—

"For purposes of this subtitle, the term 'personal holding company income' means the portion of the gross income which consists of:

"(1) Dividends, etc.—Dividends, interest, royalties (other than mineral, oil, or gas royalties or copyright royalties), and annuities. This paragraph shall not apply to interest constituting rent as defined in paragraph (7) or to interest on amounts set aside in a reserve fund under section 511 or 607 of the Merchant Marine Act, 1936. This paragraph shall not apply to a dividend distribution of divested stock (as defined in subsection (e) of section 1111) but only if the stock with respect to which the distribution is made was owned by the distributee on September 6, 1961, or was owned by the distributee for at least 2 years prior to the date on which the antitrust order (as defined in subsection (d) of section 1111) was entered.

"(2) Stock and securities transactions.—Except in the case of regular dealers in stock or securities, gains from the sale or exchange of stock or securities.

"(3) Commodities transactions.—Gains from futures transactions in any commodity on or subject to the rules of a board of trade or commodity exchange. This paragraph shall not apply to gains by a producer, processor, merchant, or handler of the commodity which arise out of bona fide hedging transactions reasonably necessary to the conduct of its business in the manner in which such business is customarily and usually conducted by others.

"(4) Estates and trusts.—Amounts includible in computing the taxable income of the corporation under part I of subchapter J (Sec. 641 and following, relating to estates, trusts, and beneficiaries; and gains from the sale or other disposition of any interest in an estate or trust.

"(5) Personal service contracts.—

"(A) Amounts received under a contract under which the corporation is to furnish personal services; if some person other than the corporation has the right to designate (by name or by description) the individual who is to perform the services, or if the individual who is to perform the services is designated (by name or by description) in the contract; and

"(B) amounts received from the sale or other disposition of such a contract. This paragraph shall apply with respect to amounts received for services under a particular contract only if at some time during the taxable year 25 percent or more in value of the outstanding stock of the corporation is owned, directly or indirectly, by or for the individual who has performed, is to perform, or may be designated (by name or by description) as the one to perform, such services.

"(6) Use of corporation property by shareholder.—Amounts received as compensation (however designated and from whomsoever received) for the use of, or right to use, property of the corporation in any case where, at any time during the taxable year, 25 percent or more in value of the outstanding stock of the corporation is owned, directly or indirectly, by or for an individual entitled to the use of the property; whether such right is obtained directly from the corporation or by means of a sublease or other arrangement. This paragraph shall apply only to a corporation which has personal holding company income for the taxable year, computed without regard to this paragraph and paragraph (7), in excess of 10 percent of its gross income. For purposes of the preceding sentence, copyright royalties constitute personal holding company income.

"(7) Rents.—Rents, unless constituting 50 percent or more of the gross income. For purposes of this paragraph, the term 'rents' means compensation, however designated, for the use of, or right to use, property, and the interest on debts owed to the corporation, to the extent such debts represent the price for which real property held primarily for sale to customers in the ordinary course of its trade or business was sold or exchanged by the corporation; but does not include amounts constituting personal holding company income under paragraph (6).

"(8) Mineral, oil, or gas royalties.—Mineral, oil, or gas royalties, unless—

"(A) such royalties constitute 50 percent or more of the gross income, and

"(B) the deductions allowable under section 162 (relating to trade or business expenses) other than compensation for personal services rendered by the shareholders, constitute 15 percent or more of the gross income.

"(9) Copyright royalties.—Copyright royalties, unless—

"(A) such royalties (exclusive of royalties received for the use of, or right to use, copyrights or interests in copyrights on works created in whole, or in part, by any shareholder) constitute 50 percent or more of the gross income,

"(B) the personal holding company income for the taxable year not taking into account—

"(i) copyright royalties, other than royalties received for the use of, or right to use, copyrights or interests in copyrights in works created in whole, or in part, by any shareholder owning more than 10 percent of the total outstanding capital stock of the corporation, and

"(ii) dividends from any corporation in which the taxpayer owns at least 50 percent of all classes of stock entitled to vote and at least 50 percent of the total value of all classes of stock and which corporation meets the requirements of this subparagraph and subparagraphs (A) and (C)

is 10 percent or less of the gross income, and

"(C) the deductions allowable under section 162 (other than deductions for compensation for personal services rendered by the shareholders and other than deductions for royalties to shareholders) constitute 50 percent or more of the gross income.

For purposes of this subsection, the term 'copyright royalties' means compensation, however designated, for the use of, or the right to use, copyrights in works protected by copyright issued under title 17 of the United States Code (other than by reason of section 2 or 6 thereof), and to which copyright protection is also extended by the laws of any country other than the United States of America by virtue of any international treaty, convention or agreement, or interests in any such copyrighted works, and includes payments from any person for performing rights in any such copyrighted work. For purposes of this paragraph the term 'shareholder' shall include any person who owns stock within the meaning of section 544. This paragraph shall not apply to compensation which is rent within the meaning of paragraph (7), determined without regard to the requirement that rents constitute 50 percent or more of the gross income.

"(b) Limitation on gross income in certain transactions.

"For purposes of this part—

"(1) gross income and personal holding company income determined with respect to transactions described in section 543(a)(2) (relating to gains from stock and security transactions) shall include only the excess of gains over losses from such transactions, and

"(2) gross income and personal holding company income determined with respect to transactions described in section 543(a)(3) (relating to gains from commodity transactions) shall include only the excess of gains over losses from such transactions."

Prior to deletion, subsec. (d) read as follows:

"(d) Special adjustment on disposition of antitrust stock received as a dividend.

"If—

"(1) a corporation received antitrust stock (as defined in section 301(f)) in a distribution to which section 301 applied,

"(2) the amount of the distribution determined under section 301(f)(2) exceeded the basis of the stock determined under section 301(f)(3), and

"(3) such distribution was includible in personal holding company income under subsection (a)(1), then proper adjustment shall be made, under regulations prescribed by the Secretary or his delegate, to the amount includible in personal holding company income under subsection (a)(2) with respect to such stock (or other property the basis of which is determined by reference to the basis of such stock)."

In 1962, P.L. 87-403, Sec. 3(c), added to sentence at the end of para. (a)(1) and added subsec. (d), effective for distributions after 2/2/62.

In 1960, P.L. 86-435, Sec. 1(a), added para. (a)(9) . . . Sec. 1(b)(1), substituted "(other than mineral, oil, or gas royalties or copyright royalties)" for "(other then mineral, oil, or gas royalties)" in para. (a)(1) . . . Sec. 1(b)(2), added the sentence at the end of para. (a)(6), effective for tax. yrs. begin. after 12/31/59.

Sec. 544. Rules for determining stock ownership.
(a) Constructive ownership.

For purposes of determining whether a corporation is a personal holding company, insofar as such determination is based on stock ownership under section 542(a)(2), section 543(a)(7), section 543(a)(6), or section 543(a)(4)—

(1) Stock not owned by individual. Stock owned, directly or indirectly, by or for a corporation, partnership, estate, or trust shall be considered as being owned proportionately by its shareholders, partners, or beneficiaries.

(2) Family and partnership ownership. An individual shall be considered as owning the stock owned, directly or indirectly, by or for his family or by or for his partner. For purposes of this paragraph, the family of an individual includes only his brothers and sisters (whether by the whole or half blood), spouse, ancestors, and lineal descendants.

(3) Options. If any person has an option to acquire stock, such stock shall be considered as owned by such person. For purposes of this paragraph, an option to acquire such an option, and each one of a series of such options, shall be considered as an option to acquire such stock.

(4) Application of family-partnership and option rules. Paragraphs (2) and (3) shall be applied—

(A) for purposes of the stock ownership requirement provided in section 542(a)(2), if, but only if, the effect is to make the corporation a personal holding company;

(B) for purposes of section 543(a)(7) (relating to personal service contracts), of section 543(a)(6) (relating to use of property by shareholders), or of section 543(a)(4) (relating to copyright royalties), if, but only if, the effect is to make the amounts therein referred to includible under such paragraph as personal holding company income.

(5) Constructive ownership as actual ownership. Stock constructively owned by a person by reason of the application of paragraph (1) or (3), shall, for purposes of applying paragraph (1) or (2), be treated as actually owned by such person; but stock constructively owned by an individual by reason of the application of paragraph (2) shall not be treated as owned by him for purposes of again applying such paragraph in order to make another the constructive owner of such stock.

(6) Option rule in lieu of family and partnership rule. If stock may be considered as owned by an individual under either paragraph (2) or (3) it shall be considered as owned by him under paragraph (3).

(b) Convertible securities.

Outstanding securities convertible into stock (whether or not convertible during the taxable year) shall be considered as outstanding stock—

(1) for purposes of the stock ownership requirement provided in section 542(a)(2), but only if the effect of the inclusion of all such securities is to make the corporation a personal holding company;

(2) for purposes of section 543(a)(7) (relating to personal service contracts), but only if the effect of the inclusion of all such securities is to make the amounts therein referred to includible under such paragraph as personal holding company income;

(3) for purposes of section 543(a)(6) (relating to the use of property by shareholders), but only if the effect of the inclusion of all such securities is to make the amounts therein referred to includible under such paragraph as personal holding company income; and

(4) for purposes of section 543(a)(4) (relating to copyright royalties), but only if the effect of the inclusion of all such securities is to make the amounts therein referred to includible under such paragraph as personal holding company income.

The requirement in paragraphs (1), (2), (3), and (4) that all convertible securities must be included if any are to be included shall be subject to the exception that, where some of the outstanding securities are convertible only after a later date than in the case of others, the class having the earlier conversion date may be included although the others are not included, but no convertible securities shall be included unless all outstanding securities having a prior conversion date are also included.

In **1964**, P.L. 88-272, Sec. 255(k)(3), substituted "section 543(a)(7)" for "section 543(a)(5)", and "section 543(a)(4)" for "section 543(a)(9)", each place they appeared in Code Sec. 544, effective for tax. yrs. begin. after 12/31/63.

In **1959**, P.L. 86-435, Sec. 1(c)(1), substituted "For purposes of determining whether a corporation is a personal holding company, insofar as such determination is based on stock ownership under section 542(a)(2), section 543(a)(5), section 543(a)(6), or section 543(a)(9)" for "For purposes of determining whether a corporation is a personal holding company, insofar as such determination is based on stock ownership under section 542(a)(2), section 543(a)(5), or section 543(a)(6)" in subsec (a)... Sec. 1(c)(2), amended subpara. (a)(4)(B)... Sec. 1(d)(1), deleted "and" at the end of para. (b)(2)... Sec. 1(d)(2), substituted ";" and" for the period at the end of para. (b)(3)... Sec. 1(d)(3), added para. (b)(4)... Sec. 1(d)(4), substituted "paragraphs (1), (2), (3), and (4)" for "paragraphs (1), (2), and (3)" in the last sentence of subsec. (b), effective for tax. yrs. begin. after 12/31/59.

Sec. 545. Undistributed personal holding company income.

(a) Definition.

For purposes of this part, the term "undistributed personal holding company income" means the taxable income of a personal holding company adjusted in the manner provided in subsections (b), (c), and (d), minus the dividends paid deduction as defined in section 561. In the case of a personal holding company which is a foreign corporation, not more than 10 percent in value of the outstanding stock of which is owned (within the meaning of section 958(a)) during the last half of the taxable year by United States persons, the term "undistributed personal holding company income" means the amount determined by multiplying the undistributed personal holding company income (determined without regard to this sentence) by the percentage in value of its outstanding stock which is the greatest percentage in value of its outstanding stock so owned by United States persons on any one day during such period.

(b) Adjustments to taxable income.

For the purposes of subsection (a), the taxable income shall be adjusted as follows:

(1) Taxes. There shall be allowed as a deduction Federal income and excess profits taxes and income, war profits and excess profits taxes of foreign countries and possessions of the United States (to the extent not allowable as a deduction under section 275(a)(4)), accrued during the taxable year or deemed to be paid by a domestic corporation under section 902(a) or 960(a)(1) for the taxable year, but not including the accumulated earnings tax imposed by section 531, the personal holding company tax imposed by section 541, or the taxes imposed by corresponding sections of a prior income tax law.

(2) Charitable contributions. The deduction for charitable contributions provided under section 170 shall be allowed, but in computing such deduction the limitations in section 170(b)(1)(A), (B), (D), and (E) shall apply, and section 170(b)(2) and (d)(1) shall not apply. For purposes of this paragraph, the term "contribution base" when used in section 170(b)(1) means the taxable income computed with the adjustments (other than the 10-percent limitation) provided in section 170(b)(2) and (d)(1) and without deduction of the amount disallowed under paragraph (6) of this subsection.

(3) Special deductions disallowed. The special deductions for corporations provided in part VIII (except section 248) of subchapter B (section 241 and following, relating to the deduction for dividends received by corporations, etc.) shall not be allowed.

(4) Net operating loss. The net operating loss deduction provided in section 172 shall not be allowed, but there shall be allowed as a deduction the amount of the net operating loss (as defined in section 172(c)) for the preceding taxable year computed without the deductions provided in part VIII (except section 248) of subchapter B.

(5) Net capital gains. There shall be allowed as a deduction the net capital gain for the taxable year, minus the taxes imposed by this subtitle attributable to such net cap-

Code Sec. 545(b)(5)   Personal holding companies

ital gain. The taxes attributable to such net capital gain shall be an amount equal to the difference between—

(A) the taxes imposed by this subtitle (except the tax imposed by this part) for such year, and

(B) such taxes computed for such year without including such net capital gain in taxable income.

(6) Expenses and depreciation applicable to property of the taxpayer. The aggregate of the deductions allowed under section 162 (relating to trade or business expenses) and section 167 (relating to depreciation), which are allocable to the operation and maintenance of property owned or operated by the corporation, shall be allowed only in an amount equal to the rent or other compensation received for the use of, or the right to use, the property, unless it is established (under regulations prescribed by the Secretary) to the satisfaction of the Secretary—

(A) that the rent or other compensation received was the highest obtainable, or, if none was received, that none was obtainable;

(B) that the property was held in the course of a business carried on bona fide for profit; and

(C) either that there was reasonable expectation that the operation of the property would result in a profit, or that the property was necessary to the conduct of the business.

(7) Special rule for capital gains and losses of foreign corporations. In the case of a foreign corporation, paragraph (5) shall be applied by taking into account only gains and losses which are effectively connected with the conduct of a trade or business within the United States and are not exempt from tax under treaty.

(c) Certain foreign corporations.

In the case of a foreign corporation all of the outstanding stock of which during the last half of the taxable year is owned by nonresident alien individuals (whether directly or indirectly through foreign estates, foreign trusts, foreign partnerships, or other foreign corporations), the taxable income for purposes of subsection (a) shall be the income which constitutes personal holding company income under section 543(a)(7), reduced by the deductions attributable to such income, and adjusted, with respect to such income, in the manner provided in subsection (b).

In 2006, P.L. 109-280, Sec. 1206(b)(2), substituted "(D), and (E)" for "and (D)" in para. (b)(2), effective for contributions in tax. yrs. begin. after 12/31/2005.

In 1990, P.L. 101-508, Sec. 11801(a)(24), deleted subsec. (c)... Sec. 11801(c)(10)(B), redesignated subsec. (d) as subsec. (c), effective 11/5/90 except as provided in Sec. 11821(b) of this Act, which reads as follows:

"(b) Savings provision.

"If —

"(1) any provision amended or repealed by this part applied to—

"(A) any transaction occurring before the date of the enactment of this Act [11/5/90],

"(B) any property acquired before such date of enactment [11/5/90], or

"(C) any item of income, loss, deduction, or credit taken into account before such date of enactment [11/5/90], and

"(2) the treatment of such transaction, property, or item under such provision would (without regard to the amendments made by this part) affect liability for tax periods ending after such date of enactment [11/5/90],

nothing in the amendments made by this part shall be construed to affect the treatment of such transaction, property, or item for purposes of determining liability for tax for periods ending after such date of enactment [11/5/90]."

Prior to deletion, subsec. (c) read as follows:

"(c) Special adjustment to taxable income.

"(1) In general. Except as otherwise provided in this subsection, for purposes of subsection (a) there shall be allowed as a deduction amounts used, or amounts irrevocably set aside (to the extent reasonable with reference to the size and terms of the indebtedness), to pay or retire qualified indebtedness.

"(2) Corporations to which applicable. This subsection shall apply only with respect to a corporation—

"(A) which for at least one of the two most recent taxable years ending before February 26, 1964 was not a personal holding company under section 542, but would have been a personal holding company under section 542 for such taxable year if the law applicable for the first taxable year beginning after December 31, 1963, had been applicable to such taxable year, or

"(B) to the extent that it succeeds to the deduction referred to in paragraph (1) by reason of section 381(c)(15).

"(3) Qualified indebtedness.

"(A) In general. Except as otherwise provided in this paragraph, for purposes of this subsection the term 'qualified indebtedness' means—

"(i) the outstanding indebtedness incurred by the taxpayer after December 31, 1933, and before January 1, 1964, and

"(ii) the outstanding indebtedness incurred after December 31, 1963, for the purpose of making a payment or set-aside referred to in paragraph (1) in the same taxable year, but, in the case of such a payment or set-aside which is made on or after the first day of the first taxable year beginning after December 31, 1963, only to the extent the deduction otherwise allowed in paragraph (1) with respect to such payment or set-aside is treated as nondeductible by reason of the election provided in paragraph (4).

"(B) Exception. For purposes of subparagraph (A), qualified indebtedness does not include any amounts which were, at any time after December 31, 1963, and before the payment or set-aside, owed to a person who at such time owned (or was considered as owning within the meaning of section 318(a)) more than 10 percent in value of the taxpayer's outstanding stock.

"(C) Reduction for amounts irrevocably set aside. For purposes of subparagraph (A), the qualified indebtedness with respect to a contract shall be reduced by amounts irrevocably set aside before the taxable year to pay or retire such indebtedness; and no deduction shall be allowed under paragraph (1) for payments out of amounts so set aside.

"(4) Election not to deduct. A taxpayer may elect, under regulations prescribed by the Secretary, to treat as non-deductible an amount otherwise deductible under paragraph (1); but only if the taxpayer files such election on or before the 15th day of the third month following the close of the taxable year with respect to which such election applies, designating therein the amounts which are to be treated as nondeductible and specifying the indebtedness (referred to in paragraph (3)(A)(ii)) incurred for the purpose of making the payment or set-aside.

"(5) Limitations. The deduction otherwise allowed by this subsection for the taxable year shall be reduced by the sum of—

"(A) the amount, if any, by which—

"(i) the deductions allowed for the taxable year and all preceding taxable years beginning after December 31, 1963, for exhaustion, wear and tear, obsolescence, amortization, or depletion (other than such deductions which are disallowed in computing undistributed personal holding company income under subsection (b)(6)), exceed

"(ii) any reduction, by reason of this subparagraph, of the deductions otherwise allowed by this subsection for such preceding taxable years, and

"(B) the amount, if any, by which—

"(i) the deductions allowed under subsection (b)(5) in computing undistributed personal holding company income for the taxable year and all preceding taxable years beginning after December 31, 1963, exceed

"(ii) any reduction, by reason of this subparagraph, of the deductions otherwise allowed by this subsection for such preceding taxable years.

"(6) Pro-rata reduction in certain cases. For purposes of paragraph (3)(A), if property (of a character which is subject to an allowance for exhaustion, wear and tear, obsolescence, amortization or depletion) is disposed of after December 31, 1963, the total amounts of qualified indebtedness of the taxpayer shall be reduced pro-rata in the taxable year of such disposition by the amount, if any, by which—

"(A) the adjusted basis of such property at the time of such disposition, exceeds

"(B) the amount of qualified indebtedness which ceased to be qualified indebtedness with respect to the taxpayer by reason of the assumption of the indebtedness by the transferee."

In 1988, P.L. 100-647, Sec. 1012(k), amended Sec. 1225(c) of P.L. 99-514, the effective date for changes made by Sec. 1225 of P.L. 99-514, by substituting "January 1, 1986" for "March 1, 1986", see below.

In 1986, P.L. 99-514, Sec. 1225(b), added para. (b)(7), effective for gains and losses realized on or after 1/1/86 [as amended by Sec. 1012(k) of P.L. 100-647, see above].

In 1983, P.L. 97-448, Sec. 102(m)(2), substituted "10-percent" for "5-percent" in para. (b)(2), effective for tax. yrs. begin. after 12/31/81.

In 1976, P.L. 94-455, Sec. 1033(b)(4), substituted "section 902(a) or 960(a)(1)" for "section 902(a)(1) or 960(a)(1)(C)" in para. (b)(1). For the effective dates for Sec. 1033 of the Act, see the note for Code Sec. 535.

—P.L. 94-455, Sec. 1901(a)(77)(A)(i), deleted "(other than the excess profits tax imposed by subchapter E of chapter 2 of the Internal Revenue Code of 1939 for taxable years beginning after December 31, 1940)"... Sec. 1901(a)(77)(A)(ii), deleted the last two sentences in para. (b)(1)... Sec. 1901(a)(77)(B), deleted para. (b)(7)... Sec. 1901(a)(77)(C), substituted "February 26, 1964" for "the date of the enactment of this subsection" following "taxable years ending before" in subpara. (c)(2)(A), effective for tax. yrs. begin. after 12/31/76.

Prior to deletion, para. (b)(7) read as follows:

"(7) Payment of indebtedness incurred prior to January 1, 1934. There shall be allowed as a deduction amounts used or irrevocably set aside to pay or to retire indebtedness of any kind incurred before January 1, 1934, if such amounts are reasonable with reference to the size and terms of such indebtedness."

—P.L. 94-455, Sec. 1901(b)(20)(B)(i), deleted para. (b)(6) and redesignated para. (b)(8) as para. (b)(6)... Sec. 1901(b)(20)(B)(ii), substituted "paragraph (6)" for "paragraph (8)" in para. (b)(2)... Sec. 1901(b)(20)(B)(iii), substituted "subsection (b)(6)" for "subsection (b)(8)" in para. (c)(5), effective for tax. yrs. begin. after 12/31/76.

Prior to deletion, para. (b)(6) read as follows:

"(6) Bank affiliates. There shall be allowed the deduction described in section 601 (relating to bank affiliates)."

—P.L. 94-455, Sec. 1901(b)(32)(E), deleted paras. (b)(10) and (b)(11), effective for tax. yrs. begin. after 12/31/76.

Prior to deletion, paras. (b)(10) and (b)(11) read as follows:

"(10) Distributions of divested stock. There shall be allowed as a deduction the amount of any income attributable to the receipt of a distribution of divested stock (as defined in subsection (e) of section 1111), minus the taxes imposed by this subtitle attributable to such receipt, but only if the stock with respect to which the distribution is made was owned by the distributee on September 6, 1961, or was owned by the distributee for at least 2 years prior to the date on which the antitrust order (as defined in subsection (d) of section 1111) was entered.

"(11) Special adjustment on disposition of antitrust stock received as a dividend. If—

"(A) a corporation received antitrust stock (as defined in section 301(f)) in a distribution to which section 301 applied,

"(B) the amount of the distribution determined under section 301(f)(2) exceeded the basis of the stock determined under section 301(f)(3), and

"(C) paragraph (10) did not apply in respect of such distribution,

then proper adjustment shall be made, under regulations prescribed by the Secretary or his delegate, if such stock (or other property the basis of which is determined by reference to the basis of such stock) is sold or exchanged."

—P.L. 94-455, Sec. 1901(b)(33)(D), substituted "Net" for "Long-term" in the heading ... substituted "the net capital gain for the taxable year" for "the excess of the net long-term capital gain for the taxable year over the net short-term capital loss for such year" following "There shall be allowed as a deduction" ... substituted "such net capital gain" for "such excess" each time it appears in para. (b)(5), effective for tax. yrs. begin. after 12/31/76.

—P.L. 94-455, Sec. 1906(b)(13)(A), substituted "Secretary" for "Secretary or his delegate" each time it appears in para. (b)(6), as previously redesignated by the Act and para. (c)(2), effective for tax. yrs. begin. after 12/31/76.

—P.L. 94-455, Sec. 1951(b)(9)(A), deleted para. (b)(9), effective for tax. yrs. begin. after 12/31/76.

Prior to deletion, para. (b)(9) read as follows:

"(9) Amount of a lien in favor of the United States. There shall be allowed as a deduction the amount, not to exceed the taxable income of the taxpayer, of any lien in favor of the United States (notice of which has been filed as provided in section 6323(f) to which the taxpayer is subject at the close of the taxable year. The sum of the amounts deducted under this paragraph with respect to any lien shall, for the purposes of this section, be added to the taxable income of the taxpayer for the taxable year in which such lien is satisfied or released. Where an amount is added to the taxable income of a corporation by reason of the preceding sentence of this paragraph, the shareholders of the corporations may, pursuant to regulations prescribed by the Secretary or his delegate, elect to compute the income tax with respect to such dividends as are attributable to such amount as though they were received ratably over the period the lien was in effect."

Sec. 1951(b)(9)(B) provided the following savings provision:

"(B) Savings provision.—Not withstanding subparagraph (A), if any amount was deducted under paragraph (9) of section 545(b) in a taxable year beginning before January 1, 1977, on account of a lien which is satisfied or released in a taxable year beginning on or after such date, the amount so deducted shall be included in income, for purposes of section 545, as provided in the second sentence of such paragraph. Shareholders of any corporation which has amounts included in its income by reason of the preceding sentence may elect to compute the income tax on dividends attributable to amounts so included as provided in the third sentence of such paragraph."

In 1969, P.L. 91-172, Sec. 201(a)(2)(B)(i), substituted "section 170(b)(1)(A), (B), and (D)" for "section 170(b)(1)(A) and (B)" in the first sentence of para. (b)(2) ... Sec. 201(a)(2)(B)(ii), substituted "section 170(b)(2) and (d)(1)" for "section 170(b)(a) and (5)" in the first sentence of para. (b)(2) ... Sec. 201(a)(2)(B)(iii), substituted "contribution base'" for "adjusted gross income'" in the second sentence of para. (b)(2) ... Sec. 201(a)(2)(B)(iv), substituted "section 170(b)(2) and (d)(1)" for "the first sentence of section 170(b)(2) and (5)" in the second sentence of para. (b)(2), effective for tax. yrs. begin. after 12/31/69.

In 1966, P.L. 89-809, Sec. 104(h)(3)(A), amended subsec. (a) ... Sec. 104(h)(3)(B), added subsec. (d), effective for tax. yrs. begin. after 12/31/66.

Prior to amendment, subsec. (a) read as follows:

"(a) Definition.

"For purposes of this part, the term 'undistributed personal holding company income' means the taxable income of a personal holding company adjusted in the manner provided in subsections (b) and (c), minus the dividends paid deduction as defined in section 561."

—P.L. 89-719, Sec. 101(b)(2), substituted "section 6323(f)" for "section 6323(a)(1), (2), or (3)" in para. (d)(9), effective after 11/2/66, except as provided in Sec 114(b) at note following Code Sec. 6323

In 1964, P.L. 88-272, Sec. 225(i)(1), substituted "subsections (b) and (c)" for "subsection (b)" in subsec. (a) ... Sec. 225(i)(2), added subsec. (c) ... Sec. 207(b)(5), substituted "section 275(a)(4)" for "section 164(b)(6)" in the first sentence of para. (b)(1) ... Sec. 209(c)(2), substituted "section 170(b)(2) and (5)" for "section 170(b)(2)" in para. (b)(2), effective for tax. yrs. begin. after 12/31/63.

In 1962, P.L. 87-834, Sec. 9(d)(2), substituted "accrued during the taxable year or deemed to be paid by a domestic corporation under section 902(a)(1) or 960(a)(C) for the taxable year" for "accrued during the taxable year," in the first sentence of para. (b)(1), effective for distribution received by a domestic corporation after 12/31/64, and in respect of any distribution received by a domestic corporation before 1/1/65, in a taxable year of such corporation beginning after 12/31/62, but only to the extent that such distribution is made out of the accumulated profits of a foreign corporation for a taxable year (of such foreign corporation) beginning after 12/31/62.

—P.L. 87-403, Sec. 3(d), added paras. (b)(10), and (b)(11), effective for distributions made after 2/2/62.

In 1958, P.L. 85-866, Sec. 32(a), amended para. (b)(2), effective 1/1/54.

Prior to amendment, para. (b)(2) read as follows:

"(2) Charitable contributions.—The deduction for charitable contributions provided under section 170 shall be allowed but with the limitations in section 170(b)(1)(A) and (B) (in lieu of the limitation in section 170(b)(2)). For purposes of this paragraph, the term 'adjusted gross income' when used in section 170(b)(1) means the taxable income computed with the adjustments provided in section 170(b)(2) and without the deduction of the amount disallowed under paragraph (8) of this subsection."

—P.L. 85-866, Sec. 32(b), added "computed without the deductions provided in Part VIII (except section 248) of subchapter B" before the period at the end of para. (b)(4), effective for tax. yrs. begin. after 12/31/57.

Sec. 546. Income not placed on annual basis.

Section 443(b) (relating to computation of tax on change of annual accounting period) shall not apply in the computation of the personal holding company tax imposed by section 541.

Sec. 547. Deduction for deficiency dividends.

(a) General rule.

If a determination (as defined in subsection (c)) with respect to a taxpayer establishes liability for personal holding company tax imposed by section 541 (or by a corresponding provision of a prior income tax law) for any taxable year, a deduction shall be allowed to the taxpayer for the amount of deficiency dividends (as defined in subsection (d)) for the purpose of determining the personal holding company tax for such year, but not for the purpose of determining interest, additional amounts, or assessable penalties computed with respect to such personal holding company tax.

(b) Rules for application of section.

(1) Allowance of deduction. The deficiency dividend deduction shall be allowed as of the date the claim for the deficiency dividend deduction is filed.

(2) Credit or refund. If the allowance of a deficiency dividend deduction results in an overpayment of personal holding company tax for any taxable year, credit or refund with respect to such overpayment shall be made as if on the date of the determination 2 years remained before the expiration of the period of limitation on the filing of claim for refund for the taxable year to which the overpayment relates. No interest shall be allowed on a credit or refund arising from the application of this section.

(c) Determination.

For purposes of this section, the term "determination" means—

(1) a decision by the Tax Court or a judgment, decree, or other order by any court of competent jurisdiction, which has become final;

(2) a closing agreement made under section 7121; or

(3) under regulations prescribed by the Secretary, an agreement signed by the Secretary and by, or on behalf of, the taxpayer relating to the liability of such taxpayer for personal holding company tax.

(d) Deficiency dividends.

(1) Definition. For purposes of this section, the term "deficiency dividends" means the amount of the dividends paid by the corporation on or after the date of the determination and before filing claim under subsection (e), which would have been includible in the computation of the deduction for dividends paid under section 561 for the taxable year with respect to which the liability for personal holding company tax exists, if distributed during such taxable year. No dividends shall be considered as deficiency dividends for purposes of subsection (a) unless distributed within 90 days after the determination.

(2) Effect on dividends paid deduction.

(A) For taxable year in which paid. Deficiency dividends paid in any taxable year (to the extent of the portion thereof taken into account under subsection (a) in determining personal holding company tax) shall not be included in the amount of dividends paid for such year for purposes of computing the dividends paid deduction for such year and succeeding years.

(B) For prior taxable year. Deficiency dividends paid in any taxable year (to the extent of the portion thereof taken into account under subsection (a) in determining personal holding company tax) shall not be allowed for purposes of section 563(b) in the computation of the dividends paid deduction for the taxable year preceding the taxable year in which paid.

(e) Claim required.

No deficiency dividend deduction shall be allowed under subsection (a) unless (under regulations prescribed by the Secretary) claim therefor is filed within 120 days after the determination.

(f) Suspension of statute of limitations and stay of collection.

(1) Suspension of running of statute. If the corporation files a claim, as provided in subsection (e), the running of the statute of limitations provided in section 6501 on the making of assessments, and the bringing of distraint or a proceeding in court for collection, in respect of the deficiency and all interest, additional amounts, or assessable penalties, shall be suspended for a period of 2 years after the date of the determination.

(2) Stay of collection. In the case of any deficiency with respect to the tax imposed by section 541 established by a determination under this section—

(A) the collection of the deficiency and all interest, additional amounts, and assessable penalties shall, except in cases of jeopardy, be stayed until the expiration of 120 days after the date of the determination, and

(B) if claim for deficiency dividend deduction is filed under subsection (e), the collection of such part of the deficiency as is not reduced by the deduction for deficiency dividends provided in subsection (a) shall be stayed until the date the claim is disallowed (in whole or in part), and if disallowed in part collection shall be made only with respect to the part disallowed.

No distraint or proceeding in court shall be begun for the collection of an amount the collection of which is stayed under subparagraph (A) or (B) during the period for which the collection of such amount is stayed.

(g) Deduction denied in case of fraud, etc.

No deficiency dividend deduction shall be allowed under subsection (a) if the determination contains a finding that any part of the deficiency is due to fraud with intent to evade tax, or to wilful failure to file an income tax return within the time prescribed by law or prescribed by the Secretary in pursuance of law.

In 1976, P.L. 94-455, Sec. 1901(a)(78), deleted subsec. (h), effective for tax. yrs. begin. after 12/31/76.
Prior to deletion, subsec. (h) read as follows:
"(h) Effective date.
"Subsections (a) through (f) inclusive, shall apply only with respect to determinations made more than 90 days after the date of enactment of this title. In the taxable year with respect to which the deficiency is asserted before January 1, 1954, the term 'deficiency dividend' includes only amounts which would have been includible in the computation under the Internal Revenue Code of 1939 of the basic surtax credit for such taxable year. Subsection (g) shall apply only if the taxable year with respect to which the deficiency is asserted begins after December 31, 1953."

—P.L. 94-455, Sec. 1906(b)(13)(A), substituted "Secretary" for "Secretary or his delegate" each place it appeared in para. (c)(3) and subsecs. (e) and (g), effective for tax. yrs. begin. after 12/31/76.

PART III.—REPEALED [FOREIGN PERSONAL HOLDING COMPANIES]

Sec.
551. Repealed [Foreign personal holding company income taxed to United States shareholders.]
552. Repealed [Definition of foreign personal holding company.]
553. Repealed [Foreign personal holding company income.]
554. Repealed [Stock ownership.]
555. Repealed [Gross income of foreign personal holding companies.]
556. Repealed [Undistributed foreign personal holding company income.]
557. Repealed [Income not placed on annual basis.]
558. Repealed [Returns of officers, directors, and shareholders of foreign personal holding companies.]

In 2004, P.L. 108-357, Sec. 413(c)(31), deleted part III of subchapter G of chapter 1, effective for tax. yrs. of foreign corporations begin. after 12/31/2004, and for tax. yrs. of United States shareholders with or within which such tax. yrs. of foreign corporations end.
In 1958, added item 558.

Sec. 551. Repealed.

In 2004, P.L. 108-357, Sec. 413(a)(1), repealed Code Sec. 551, effective for tax. yrs. of foreign corporations begin. after 12/31/2004, and for tax. yrs. of United States shareholders with or within which such tax. yrs. of foreign corporations end.

Prior to repeal, Code Sec. 551 read as follows:
"SEC. 551. FOREIGN PERSONAL HOLDING COMPANY INCOME TAXED TO UNITED STATES SHAREHOLDERS.

"(a) General rule. The undistributed foreign personal holding company income of a foreign personal holding company shall be included in the gross income of the citizens or residents of the United States, domestic corporations, domestic partnerships, and estates or trusts (other than foreign estates or trusts), who are shareholders in such foreign personal holding company (hereinafter called 'United States shareholders') in the manner and to the extent set forth in this part.

"(b) Amount included in gross income. Each United States shareholder, who was a shareholder on the day in the taxable year of the company which was the last day on which a United States group (as defined in section 552(a)(2)) existed with respect to the company, shall include in his gross income, as a dividend, for the taxable year in which or with which the taxable year of the company ends, the amount he would have received as a dividend (determined as if any distribution in liquidation actually made in such taxable year had not been made) if on such last day there had been distributed by the company, and received by the shareholders, an amount which bears the same ratio to the undistributed foreign personal holding company income of the company for the taxable year as the portion of such taxable year up to and including such last day bears to the entire taxable year.

"(c) Information in return. Every United States shareholder who is required under subsection (b) to include in his gross income any amount with respect to the undistributed foreign personal holding company income of a foreign personal holding company and who, on the last day on which a United States group existed with respect to the company, owned 5 percent or more in value of the outstanding stock of such company, shall set forth in his return in complete detail the gross income, deductions and credits, taxable income, foreign personal holding company income, and undistributed foreign personal holding company income of such company.

"(d) Effect on capital account of foreign personal holding company. An amount which bears the same ratio to the undistributed foreign personal holding company income of the foreign personal holding company for its taxable year as the portion of such taxable year up to and including the last day on which a United States group existed with respect to the company bears to the entire taxable year, shall, for the purpose of determining the effect of distributions in subsequent taxable years by the corporation, be considered as paid-in surplus or as a contribution to capital, and the accumulated earnings and profits as of the close of the taxable year shall be correspondingly reduced, if such amount or any portion thereof is required to be included as a dividend, directly or indirectly, in the gross income of United States shareholders.

"(e) Basis of stock in hands of shareholders. The amount required to be included in the gross income of a United States shareholder under subsection (b) shall, for the purpose of adjusting the basis of his stock with respect to which the distribution would have been made (if it had been made), be treated as having been reinvested by the shareholder as a contribution to the capital of the corporation; but only to the extent to which such amount is included in his gross income in his return, increased or decreased by any adjustment of such amount in the last

Foreign personal holding companies Code Sec. 552

determination of the shareholder's tax liability, made before the expiration of 6 years after the date prescribed by law for filing the return.

"(f) Stock held through foreign entity. For purposes of this section, stock of a foreign personal holding company owned (directly or through the application of this subsection) by—

"(1) a foreign partnership or an estate or trust which is a foreign estate or trust, or

"(2) a foreign corporation which is not a foreign personal holding company,

"shall be considered as being owned proportionately by its partners, beneficiaries, or shareholders. In any case to which the preceding sentence applies, the Secretary may by regulations provide that rules similar to the rules of section 1298(b)(5) shall apply, and provide for such other adjustments in the application of this subchapter as may be necessary to carry out the purposes of this subsection.

"(g) Coordination with passive foreign investment company provisions. If, but for this subsection, an amount would be included in the gross income of any person under subsection (a) and under section 1293 (relating to current taxation of income from certain passive foreign investment companies), such amount shall be included in the gross income of such person only under subsection (a).

"(h) Cross references.

"(1) For basis of stock or securities in a foreign personal holding company acquired from a decedent, see section 1014(b)(5).

"(2) For period of limitation on assessment and collection without assessment, in case of failure to include in gross income the amount properly includible therein under subsection (b), see section 6501."

In 1997, P.L. 105-34, Sec. 1122(d)(2), substituted "section 1298(b)(5)" for "section 1297(b)(5)" in subsec. (f), effective for tax. yrs. of United States persons begin. after 12/31/97, and tax. yrs. of foreign corporations end. with or within such tax. yrs. of United States persons.

In 1988, P.L. 100-647, Sec. 1012(bb)(1)(A)(i), amended para. (f)(1) . . . Sec. 1012(bb)(1)(A)(ii), amended the last sentence of subsec. (f) . . . Sec. 1012(bb)(1)(B), substituted "(other than foreign estates or trusts)" for "(other than estates or trusts the gross income of which under this subtitle includes only income from sources within the United States)" in subsec. (a), effective for tax. yrs. of foreign corporations begin. after 12/31/86.

Prior to amendment, para. (f)(1) read as follows:

"(1) a partnership, estate, or trust which is not a United States shareholder or an estate or trust which is a foreign estate or trust, or"

Prior to amendment, the last sentence of subsec. (f) read as follows:

"In any case to which the preceding sentence applies, the Secretary may by regulations provide for such adjustments in the application of this part as may be necessary to carry out the purposes of the preceding sentence."

In 1986, P.L. 99-514, Sec. 1235(e), redesignated subsec. (g) as subsec. (h) and added new subsec. (g), effective for tax. yrs. of foreign corporations begin. after 12/31/86.

—P.L. 99-514, Sec. 1810(h)(2), substituted "United States shareholder or an estate or trust which is a foreign estate or trust" for "United States shareholder" in para. (f)(1), effective for tax. yrs. of foreign corporations begin. after 12/31/83, except as provided in Sec. 1012(d)(1)(B) of P.L. 98-369, reproduced below.

In 1984, P.L. 98-369, Sec. 132(b), redesignated subsec. (f) as subsec. (g) and added new subsec. (f), effective for tax. yrs. of foreign corporations begin. after 12/31/83, except as provided in Sec. 132(d)(1)(B) of the Act, which reads as follows:

"(B) 1-year extension for certain trusts created before June 30, 1953.—

"(i) In general.— The amendment made by subsection (b) [Sec. 132(b) of P.L. 98-369] shall apply to taxable years of a foreign corporation beginning after December 31, 1984, with respect to stock of such corporation which is held (directly or indirectly, within the meaning of section 554 of the Internal Revenue Code of 1954) by a trust created before June 30, 1953, if—

"(I) none of the beneficiaries of such trust was a citizen or resident of the United States at the time of its creation or within 5 years thereafter, and

"(II) such trust does not, after July 1, 1983, acquire (directly or indirectly) stock of any foreign personal holding company other than a company described in clause (ii).

"(ii) Description of company.— A company is described in this clause if—

"(I) substantially all of the assets of such company are stock or assets previously held by such trust, or

"(II) such company ceases to be a foreign personal holding company before January 1, 1985."

In 1976, P.L. 94-455, Sec. 1901(a)(79), substituted "taxable income, foreign personal holding company income," for "taxable income, foreign personal holding company," in subsec. (c) [as redesignated by Sec. 1901(b)(1)(F)(i) of this Act, see below], effective for tax. yrs. begin. after 12/31/76.

—P.L. 94-455, Sec. 1901(b)(1)(F)(i), deleted subsec. (c), and redesignated subsecs. (d), (e), (f) and (g) as subsecs. (c), (d), (e) and (f), respectively, effective for tax. yrs. begin. after 12/31/76.

Prior to deletion, subsec. (c) read as follows:

"(c) Deduction for obligations of United States and its instrumentalities.

"Each United States shareholder shall take into account in determining his income tax his proportionate share of partially tax-exempt interest on obligations described in section 35 or 242 which is included in the gross income of the company otherwise than by the application of the provisions of section 555(b) (relating to the inclusion in the gross income of a foreign personal holding company of its distributive share of the undistributed foreign personal holding company income of another foreign personal holding company in which it is a shareholder). If the foreign personal holding company elects under section 171 to amortize the premiums on such obligations, for purposes of the preceding sentence each United States shareholder's proportionate share of such interest received by the foreign personal holding company shall be his proportionate share of such interest (determined without regard to this sentence) reduced by so much of the deduction under section 171 as is attributable to such share."

—P.L. 94-455, Sec. 1901(b)(12)(A), deleted para. (f)(3) [as redesignated by Sec. 1901(b)(1)(F) of this Act, see above], effective for tax. yrs. begin. after 12/31/76.

Prior to deletion, para. (f)(3) read as follows:

"(3) For treatment of gain on liquidation of certain foreign personal holding companies, see section 342."

In 1964, P.L. 88-272, Sec. 225(f)(4), substituted "received as a dividend (determined as if any distribution in liquidation actually made in such taxable year had not been made)" for "received as a dividend" in subsec. (b), effective for distributions made in any tax. yr. of distributing corporation begin. after 12/31/63.

Sec. 552. Repealed.

In 2004, P.L. 108-357, Sec. 413(a)(1), repealed Code Sec. 552, effective for tax. yrs. of foreign corporations begin. after 12/31/2004, and for tax. yrs. of United States shareholders with or within which such tax. yrs. of foreign corporations end.

Prior to repeal, Code Sec. 552 read as follows:

"SEC. 552. DEFINITION OF FOREIGN PERSONAL HOLDING COMPANY.

"(a) General rule. For purposes of this subtitle, the term 'foreign personal holding company' means any foreign corporation if—

"(1) Gross income requirement. At least 60 percent of its gross income (as defined in section 555(a)) for the taxable year is foreign personal holding company income as defined in section 553; but if the corporation is a foreign personal holding company with respect to any taxable year ending after August 26, 1937, then, for each subsequent taxable year, the minimum percentage shall be 50 percent in lieu of 60 percent, until a taxable year during the whole of which the stock ownership required by paragraph (2) does not exist, or until the expiration of three consecutive taxable years in each of which less than 50 percent of the gross income is foreign personal holding company income. For purposes of this paragraph, there shall be included in the gross income the amount includible therein as a dividend by reason of the application of section 555(c)(2); and

"(2) Stock ownership requirement. At any time during the taxable year more than 50 percent of—

"(A) the total combined voting power of all classes of stock of such corporation entitled to vote, or

"(B) the total value of the stock of such corporation,

"is owned (directly or indirectly) by or for not more than 5 individuals who are citizens or residents of the United States (hereinafter in this part referred to as the 'United States group').

"(b) Exceptions. The term 'foreign personal holding company' does not include—

"(1) a corporation exempt from tax under subchapter F (sec. 501 and following); and

"(2) a corporation organized and doing business under the banking and credit laws of a foreign country if it is established (annually or at other periodic intervals) to the satisfaction of the Secretary that such corporation is not formed or availed of for the purpose of evading or avoiding United States income taxes which would otherwise be imposed upon its shareholders. If the Secretary is satisfied that such corporation is not so formed or availed of, he shall issue to such corporation annually or at other periodic intervals a certification that the corporation is not a foreign personal holding company.

"Each United States shareholder of a foreign corporation which would, except for the provisions of paragraph (2), be a foreign personal holding company, shall attach to and file with his income tax return for the taxable year a copy of the certification by the Secretary made pursuant to paragraph (2). Such copy shall be filed with the taxpayer's return for the taxable year if he has been a shareholder of such corporation for any part of such year.

"(c) Look-thru for certain dividends and interest.

"(1) In general. For purposes of this part, any related person dividend or interest shall be treated as foreign personal holding company income only to the extent such dividend or interest is attributable (determined under rules similar to the rules of subparagraphs (C) and (D) of section 904(d)(3)) to income of the related person which would be foreign personal holding company income.

"(2) Related person dividend or interest. For purposes of paragraph (1), the term 'related person dividend or interest' means any dividend or interest which—

"(A) is described in subparagraph (A) of section 954(c)(3), and

"(B) is received from a related person which is not a foreign personal holding company (determined without regard to this subsection).

"For purposes of the preceding sentence, the term 'related person' has the meaning given such term by section 954(d)(3) (determined by substituting 'foreign personal holding company' for 'controlled foreign corporation' each place it appears)."

In 1988, P.L. 100-647, Sec. 1012(bb)(1)(C), amended subsec. (c) effective for tax. yrs. of foreign corporations begin. after 12/31/86.

Prior to amendment, subsec. (c) read as follows:

"(c) Certain dividends and interest not taken into account.

"For purposes of subsection (a)(1) and section 553(a)(1), gross income and foreign personal holding company income shall not include any dividends and interest which—

"(1) are described in subparagraph (A) of section 954(c)(4), and

"(2) are received from a related person which is not a foreign personal holding company (determined without regard to this subsection).

2,267

Code Sec. 552 — Foreign personal holding companies

For purposes of the preceding sentence, the term 'related person' has the meaning given such term by section 954(d)(3) (determined by substituting 'foreign personal holding company' for 'controlled foreign corporation' each place it appears)."

In 1986, P.L. 99-514, Sec. 1222(b), amended para. (a)(2), effective for tax. yrs. of foreign corporations begin. after 12/31/86; except that for purposes of applying Code Secs. 951(a)(1)(B) and 956, the effective date is 8/16/86. Sec. 1222(c)(2)-(3) of this Act provides:

"(2) Transitional rule. — In the case of any corporation treated as a controlled foreign corporation by reason of the amendments made by this section, property acquired before August 16, 1986, shall not be taken into account under section 956(b) of the Internal Revenue Code of 1986.

"(3) Special rule for beneficiary of trust. — In the case of an individual —

"(A) who is a beneficiary of a trust which was established on December 7, 1979, under the laws of a foreign jurisdiction, and

"(B) who was not a citizen or resident of the United States on the date the trust was established,

amounts which are included in the gross income of such beneficiary under section 951(a) of the Internal Revenue Code of 1986 with respect to stock held by the trust (and treated as distributed to the trust) shall be treated as the first amounts which are distributed by the trust to such beneficiary and as amounts to which section 959(a) of such Code applies."

Prior to amendment, para. (a)(2) read as follows:

"(2) Stock ownership requirement. At any time during the taxable year more than 50 percent in value of its outstanding stock is owned, directly or indirectly, by or for not more than five individuals who are citizens or residents of the United States, hereinafter called 'United States group'."

— P.L. 99-514, Sec. 1810(h)(1), added the last sentence to para. (c)(2), effective for tax. yrs. of foreign corporation begin. after 3/15/84.

In 1984, P.L. 98-369, Sec. 132(c)(2), added subsec. (c), effective for tax. yrs. of foreign corporations begin. after 3/15/84.

In 1976, P.L. 94-455, Sec. 1906(b)(13)(A), substituted "Secretary" for "Secretary or his delegate" each place it appeared in subsec. (c), effective for tax. yrs. begin. after 12/31/76.

Sec. 553. Repealed.

In 2004, P.L. 108-357, Sec. 413(a)(1), repealed Code Sec. 553, effective for tax. yrs. of foreign corporations begin. after 12/31/2004, and for tax. yrs. of United States shareholders with or within which such tax. yrs. of foreign corporations end.

Prior to repeal, Code Sec. 553 read as follows:

"SEC. 553. FOREIGN PERSONAL HOLDING COMPANY INCOME.

"(a) Foreign personal holding company income. For purposes of this subtitle, the term 'foreign personal holding company income' means that portion of the gross income, determined for purposes of section 552, which consists of:

"(1) Dividends, etc. Dividends, interest, royalties, and annuities. This paragraph shall not apply to active business computer software royalties (as defined in section 543(d)).

"(2) Stock and securities transactions. Except in the case of regular dealers in stock or securities, gains from the sale or exchange of stock or securities.

"(3) Commodities transactions. Gains from futures transactions in any commodity on or subject to the rules of a board of trade or commodity exchange. This paragraph shall not apply to gains by a producer, processor, merchant, or handler of the commodity which arise out of bona fide hedging transactions reasonably necessary to the conduct of its business in the manner in which such business is customarily and usually conducted by others.

"(4) Estates and trusts. Amounts includible in computing the taxable income of the corporation under part I of subchapter J (sec. 641 and following, relating to estates, trusts, and beneficiaries); and gains from the sale or other disposition of any interest in an estate or trust.

"(5) Personal service contracts.

"(A) Amounts received under a contract under which the corporation is to furnish personal services; if some person other than the corporation has the right to designate (by name or by description) the individual who is to perform the services, or if the individual who is to perform the services is designated (by name or by description) in the contract; and

"(B) amounts received from the sale or other disposition of such a contract.

"This paragraph shall apply with respect to amounts received for services under a particular contract only if at some time during the taxable year 25 percent or more in value of the outstanding stock of the corporation is owned, directly or indirectly, by or for the individual who has performed, is to perform, or may be designated (by name or by description) as the one to perform, such services.

"(6) Use of corporation property by shareholder. Amounts received as compensation (however designated and from whomsoever received) for the use of, or right to use, property of the corporation in any case where, at any time during the taxable year, 25 percent or more in value of the outstanding stock of the corporation is owned, directly or indirectly, by or for an individual entitled to the use of the property; whether such right is obtained directly from the corporation or by means of a sublease or other arrangement. This paragraph shall apply only to a corporation which has foreign personal holding company income for the taxable year, computed without regard to this paragraph and paragraph (7), in excess of 10 percent of its gross income.

"(7) Rents. Rents, unless constituting 50 percent or more of the gross income. For purposes of this paragraph, the term 'rents' means compensation, however designated, for the use of, or right to use, property; but does not include amounts constituting foreign personal holding company income under paragraph (6).

"(b) Limitation on gross income in certain transactions. For purposes of this part —

"(1) gross income and foreign personal holding company income determined with respect to transactions described in subsection (a)(2) (relating to gains from stock and security transactions) shall include only the excess of gains over losses from such transactions, and

"(2) gross income and foreign personal holding company income determined with respect to transactions described in subsection (a)(3) (relating to gains from commodity transactions) shall include only the excess of gains over losses from such transactions."

In 1986, P.L. 99-514, Sec. 645(a)(3), added the sentence at the end of para. (a)(1), effective for royalties received before, on, and after effective 12/31/86.

In 1976, P.L. 94-455, Sec. 1901(b)(32)(F), amended para. (a)(1), effective for tax. yrs. begin. after 12/31/76.

Prior to amendment, para. (a)(1) read as followed:

"(1) Dividends, etc. Dividends, interest, royalties, and annuities. This paragraph shall not apply to a dividend distribution of divested stock (as defined in subsection (e) of section 1111) but only if the stock with respect to which the distribution is made was owned by the distributee on September 6, 1961, or was owned by the distributee for at least 2 years before the date on which the antitrust order (as defined in subsection (d) of section 1111) was entered."

In 1964, P.L. 88-272, Sec. 225(e), amended Code Sec. 553, effective for tax. yrs. begin. after 12/31/63.

Prior to amendment, Code Sec. 553 read as follows:

"SEC. 553. FOREIGN PERSONAL HOLDING COMPANY INCOME.

"For purposes of this subtitle, the term 'foreign personal holding company income' means the portion of the gross income, determined for purposes of section 552, which consists of personal holding company income, as defined in section 543, except that all interest, whether or not treated as rent, and all royalties, whether or not mineral, oil, or gas royalties or copyright royalties, shall constitute 'foreign personal holding company income'."

In 1960, P.L. 86-435, Sec. 1(e), substituted "all royalties, whether or not mineral, oil, or gas royalties or copyright royalties" for "all royalties, whether or not mineral, oil, or gas royalties" in Code Sec. 553, effective only for tax. yrs. begin. after 12/31/59.

Sec. 554. Repealed.

In 2004, P.L. 108-357, Sec. 413(a)(1), repealed Code Sec. 554, effective for tax. yrs. of foreign corporations begin. after 12/31/2004, and for tax. yrs. of United States shareholders with or within which such tax. yrs. of foreign corporations end.

Prior to repeal, Code Sec. 554 read as follows:

"SEC. 554. STOCK OWNERSHIP.

"(a) Constructive ownership. For purposes of determining whether a corporation is a foreign personal holding company, insofar as such determination is based on stock ownership under section 552(a)(2), section 553(a)(5), or section 553(a)(6) —

"(1) Stock not owned by individual. Stock owned, directly or indirectly, by or for a corporation, partnership, estate, or trust shall be considered as being owned proportionately by its shareholders, partners, or beneficiaries.

"(2) Family and partnership ownership. An individual shall be considered as owning the stock owned, directly or indirectly, by or for his family or by or for his partner. For purposes of this paragraph, the family of an individual includes only his brothers and sisters (whether by the whole or half blood), spouse, ancestors, and lineal descendants.

"(3) Options. If any person has an option to acquire stock, such stock shall be considered as owned by such person. For purposes of this paragraph, an option to acquire such an option, and each one of a series of such options, shall be considered as an option to acquire such stock.

"(4) Application of family-partnership and option rules. Paragraphs (2) and (3) shall be applied —

"(A) for purposes of the stock ownership requirement provided in section 552(a)(2), if, but only if, the effect is to make the corporation a foreign personal holding company;

"(B) for purposes of section 553(a)(5) (relating to personal service contracts) or of section 553(a)(6) (relating to the use of property by shareholders), if, but only if, the effect is to make the amounts therein referred to includible under such paragraph as foreign personal holding company income.

"(5) Constructive ownership as actual ownership. Stock constructively owned by a person by reason of the application of paragraph (1) or (3) shall, for purposes of applying paragraph (1) or (2), be treated as actually owned by such person; but stock constructively owned by an individual by reason of the application of paragraph (2) shall not be treated as owned by him for purposes of again applying such paragraph in order to make another the constructive owner of such stock.

"(6) Option rule in lieu of family and partnership rule. If stock may be considered as owned by an individual under either paragraph (2) or (3) it shall be considered as owned by him under paragraph (3).

"(b) Convertible securities. Outstanding securities convertible into stock (whether or not convertible during the taxable year) shall be considered as outstanding stock —

"(1) for purposes of the stock ownership requirement provided in section 552(a)(2), but only if the effect of the inclusion of all such securities is to make the corporation a foreign personal holding company;

"(2) for purposes of section 553(a)(5) (relating to personal service contracts), but only if the effect of the inclusion of all such securities is to make the amounts therein referred to includible under such paragraph as foreign personal holding company income; and

"(3) for purposes of section 553(a)(6) (relating to the use of property by shareholders), but only if the effect of the inclusion of all such securities is to make the amounts therein referred to includible under such paragraph as foreign personal holding company income.

"The requirement in paragraphs (1), (2), and (3) that all convertible securities must be included if any are to be included shall be subject to the exception that, where some of the outstanding securities are convertible only after a later date than in the case of others, the class having the earlier conversion date may be included although the others are not included, but no convertible securities shall be included unless all outstanding securities having a prior conversion date are also included.

"(c) Special rules for application of subsection (a)(2). For purposes of the stock ownership requirement provided in section 552(a)(2)—

"(1) stock owned by a nonresident alien individual (other than a foreign trust or foreign estate) shall not be considered by reason of so much of subsection (a)(2) as relates to attribution through family membership as owned by a citizen or by a resident alien individual who is not the spouse of the nonresident individual and who does not otherwise own stock in such corporation (determined after the application of subsection (a), other than attribution through family membership), and

"(2) stock of a corporation owned by any foreign person shall not be considered by reason of so much of subsection (a)(2) as relates to attribution through partners as owned by a citizen or resident of the United States who does not otherwise own stock in such corporation (determined after application of subsection (a) and paragraph (1), other than attribution through partners)."

In 1984, P.L. 98-369, Sec. 132(a), added subsec. (c), effective for tax. yrs. of foreign corporations begin. after 12/31/83.

In 1964, P.L. 88-272, Sec. 225(e), amended Code Sec. 554, effective for tax. yrs. begin. after 12/31/63.

Prior to amendment, Code Sec. 554 read as follows:

"SEC. 554. STOCK OWNERSHIP.

"For purposes of determining whether a foreign corporation is a foreign personal holding company, insofar as such determination is based on stock ownership, the rules provided in section 54 shall be applicable as if any reference in such section to a personal holding company was a reference to a foreign personal holding company and as if any reference in such section to a provision of part II (relating to personal holding companies) was a reference to the corresponding provision of this part."

Sec. 555. Repealed.

In 2004, P.L. 108-357, Sec. 413(a)(1), repealed Code Sec. 555, effective for tax. yrs. of foreign corporations begin. after 12/31/2004, and for tax. yrs. of United States shareholders with or within which such tax. yrs. of foreign corporations end.

Prior to repeal, Code Sec. 555 read as follows:

"SEC. 555. GROSS INCOME OF FOREIGN PERSONAL HOLDING COMPANIES.

"(a) General rule. For purposes of this part, the term 'gross income' means, with respect to a foreign corporation, gross income computed (without regard to the provisions of subchapter N (sec. 861 and following)) as if the foreign corporation were a domestic corporation which is a personal holding company.

"(b) Additions to gross income. In the case of a foreign personal holding company (whether or not a United States group, as defined in section 552(a)(2), existed with respect to such company on the last day of its taxable year) which was a shareholder in another foreign personal holding company on the day in the taxable year of the second company which was the last day on which a United States group existed with respect to the second company, there shall be included, as a dividend, in the gross income of the first company, for the taxable year in which or with which the taxable year of the second company ends, the amount the first company would have received as a dividend if on such last day there had been distributed by the second company, and received by the shareholders, an amount which bears the same ratio to the undistributed foreign personal holding company income of the second company for its taxable year as the portion of such taxable year up to and including such last day bears to the entire taxable year.

"(c) Application of subsection (b). The rule provided in subsection (b)—

"(1) shall be applied in the case of a foreign personal holding company for the purpose of determining its undistributed foreign personal holding company income which, or a part of which, is to be included in the gross income of its shareholders, whether United States shareholders or other foreign personal holding companies;

"(2) shall be applied in the case of every foreign corporation with respect to which a United States group exists on some day of its taxable year, for the purpose of determining whether such corporation meets the gross income requirements of section 552(a)(1)."

Sec. 556. Repealed.

In 2004, P.L. 108-357, Sec. 413(a)(1), repealed Code Sec. 556, effective for tax. yrs. of foreign corporations begin. after 12/31/2004, and for tax. yrs. of United States shareholders with or within which such tax. yrs. of foreign corporations end.

Prior to repeal, Code Sec. 556 read as follows:

"SEC. 556. UNDISTRIBUTED FOREIGN PERSONAL HOLDING COMPANY INCOME.

"(a) Definition. For purposes of this part, the term 'undistributed foreign personal holding company income' means the taxable income of a foreign personal holding company adjusted in the manner provided in subsection (b), minus the dividends paid deduction (as defined in section 561).

"(b) Adjustments to taxable income. For the purposes of subsection (a), the taxable income shall be adjusted as follows:

"(1) Taxes. There shall be allowed as a deduction Federal income and excess profits taxes and income, war profits, and excess-profits taxes of foreign countries and possessions of the United States (to the extent not allowable as a deduction under section 275(a)(4)), accrued during the taxable year, but not including the accumulated earnings tax imposed by section 531, the personal holding company tax imposed by section 541 , or the taxes imposed by corresponding sections of a prior income tax law.

"(2) Charitable contributions. The deduction for charitable contributions provided under section 170 shall be allowed, but in computing such deduction the limitations in section 170(b)(1)(A), (B), and (D) shall apply, and section 170(b)(2) and (d)(1) shall not apply. For purposes of this paragraph, the term 'contribution base' when used in section 170(b)(1) means the taxable income computed with the adjustments (other than the 10-percent limitation) provided in section 170(b)(2) and (d)(1) and without the deduction of the amounts disallowed under paragraphs (5) and (6) of this subsection or the inclusion in gross income of the amounts includible therein as dividends by reason of the application of the provisions of section 555(b) (relating to the inclusion in gross income of a foreign personal holding company of its distributive share of the undistributed foreign personal holding company income of another company in which it is a shareholder).

"(3) Special deductions disallowed. The special deductions for corporations provided in part VIII (except section 248) of subchapter B (section 241 and following, relating to the deduction for dividends received by corporations, etc.) shall not be allowed.

"(4) Net operating loss. The net operating loss deduction provided in section 172 shall not be allowed, but there shall be allowed as a deduction the amount of the net operating loss (as defined in section 172(c)) for the preceding taxable year computed without the deductions provided in part VIII (except section 248) of subchapter B.

"(5) Expenses and depreciation applicable to property of the taxpayer. The aggregate of the deductions allowed under section 162 (relating to trade or business expenses) and section 167 (relating to depreciation) which are allocable to the operation and maintenance of property owned or operated by the company, shall be allowed only in an amount equal to the rent or other compensation received for the use of, or the right to use, the property, unless it is established (under regulations prescribed by the Secretary) to the satisfaction of the Secretary—

"(A) that the rent or other compensation received was the highest obtainable, or, if none was received, that none was obtainable;

"(B) that the property was held in the course of a business carried on bona fide for profit; and

"(C) either that there was reasonable expectation that the operation of the property would result in a profit, or that the property was necessary to the conduct of the business.

"(6) Taxes and contributions to pension trusts. The deductions provided in section 164(e) (relating to taxes of a shareholder paid by the corporation) and in section 404 (relating to pension, etc., trusts) shall not be allowed."

In 1990, P.L. 101-508, Sec. 11802(d)(1), deleted the last two sentences of para. (b)(1), effective 11/5/90, except as provided in Sec. 11821(b) of this Act reproduced at note following Code Sec. 545.

—P.L. 101-508, Sec. 11802(d)(2), provides:

"(2) The amendment made by paragraph (1) [Sec. 11802(d)(1) of this Act] shall not apply to any corporation with respect to which an election under the second sentence of section 556(b)(1) of the Internal Revenue Code of 1986 (as in effect before the amendment made by paragraph (1)) is in effect unless such corporation elects to have such amendment apply and agrees to such adjustments as the Secretary of the Treasury or his delegate may require."

Prior to deletion, the last two sentences of para. (b)(1) read as follows:

"A taxpayer which, for each taxable year in which it was subject to the provisions of supplement P of the Internal Revenue Code of 1939, deducted Federal income and excess profits taxes when paid for the purpose of computing undistributed supplement P net income under such code, shall deduct taxes under this paragraph when paid, unless the corporation elects, under regulations prescribed by the Secretary, after the date of enactment of this title to deduct the taxes described in this paragraph when accrued. Such election shall be irrevocable and shall apply to the taxable year for which the election is made and to all subsequent taxable years."

In 1983, P.L. 97-448, Sec. 102(m)(2), substituted "10-percent" for "5-percent" in para. (b)(2), effective for tax. yrs. begin. after 12/31/81.

In 1976, P.L. 94-455, Sec. 1901(a)(80), deleted "(other than the excess profits tax imposed by subchapter E of chapter 2 of the Internal Revenue Code of 1939 for taxable year beginning after December 1, 1940)", after "Federal income and excess profits taxes", in para. (b)(1), effective for tax. yrs. begin. after 12/31/76.

—P.L. 94-455, Sec. 1901(b)(32)(G), deleted paras. (b)(7) and (b)(8), effective for tax. yrs. begin. after 12/31/76.

Prior to amendment, paras. (b)(7) and (b)(8) read as follows:

"(7) Distributions of divested stock. There shall be allowed as a deduction the amount of any income attributable to the receipt of a distribution of divested stock (as defined in subsection (e) of section 1111), minus the taxes imposed by this subtitle attributable to such receipt, but only if the stock with respect to which the distribution is made was owned by the distributee on September 6, 1961, or was owned by the distributee for at least 2 years prior to the date on which the antitrust order (as defined in subsection (d) of section 1111) was entered.

"(8) Special adjustment on disposition of antitrust stock received as a dividend. If—

"(A) a corporation received antitrust stock (as defined in section 301(f)) in a distribution to which section 301 applied.

"(B) the amount of the distribution determined under section 301(f)(2) exceeded the basis of the stock determined under section 301(f)(3), and

"(C) paragraph (7) did not apply in respect of such distribution, then proper adjustment shall be made, under regulations prescribed by the Secretary or his delegate, if such stock (or other property the basis of which is determined by reference to the basis of such stock) is sold or exchanged."

—P.L. 94-455, Sec. 1906(b)(13)(A), substituted "Secretary" for "Secretary or his delegate" each place it appeared in paras. (b)(1) and (b)(5), effective for tax. yrs. begin. after 12/31/76.

In **1969**, P.L. 91-172, Sec. 201(a)(2)(B)(i), substituted "section 170(b)(1)(A), (B), and (D)" for "section 170(b)(1)(A) and (B)" in the first sentence of para. (b)(2) ... Sec. 201(a)(2)(B)(ii), substituted "section 170(b)(2) and (d)(1)" for "section 170(b)(2) and (5)" in the first sentence of para. (b)(2) ... Sec. 201(a)(2)(B)(iii), substituted "'contribution base'" for "'adjusted gross income'" in the second sentence of para. (b)(2) ... Sec. 201(a)(2)(B)(iv), substituted "section 170(b)(2) and (d)(1)" for "the first sentence of section 170(b)(2) and (5)" in the second sentences of subsec. (b)(2), effective for tax. yrs. begin. after 12/31/69.

In **1964**, P.L. 88-272, Sec. 207(b)(6), substituted "section 275(a)(4)" for "section 164(b)(6)" in the first sentence of para. (b)(1), effective for tax. yrs. begin. after 12/31/63.

—P.L. 88-272, Sec. 209(c)(2), substituted "section 170(b)(2) and (5)" for "section 170(b)(2)" in para. (b)(2), effective for contributions which are paid in tax. yrs. begin. after 12/31/63.

In **1962**, P.L. 87-403, Sec. 3(e), added paras. (c)(7) and (8), effective for distributions made after 2/2/62.

In **1958**, P.L. 85-866, Sec. 33(a)(1), amended the first sentence of para. (b)(2) ... Sec. 33(a)(2), substituted "the taxable income computed with the adjustments (other than the 5-percent limitation) provided in the first sentence of section 170(b)(2)" for "the taxable income computed with the adjustments provided in section 170(b)(2)" in the second sentence of para. (b)(2), effective for tax. yrs. begin. after 12/31/53, and end. after 8/16/54.

Prior to amendment, the first sentence of para. (b)(2) read as follows:

"The deduction for charitable contributions provided under section 170 shall be allowed, but with the limitation in section 170(b)(1)(A) and (B) (in lieu of the limitation in section 170(b)(2))."

—P.L. 85-866, Sec. 33(b)(1), substituted "section 248" for "sections 242 and 248" in para. (b)(3), effective for tax. yrs. end. after 12/31/57.

—P.L. 85-866, Sec. 33(c)(1), added "computed without the deductions provided in part VIII (except section 248) of subchapter B" before the period at the end of para. (b)(4), effective for adjustments under Code Sec. 556(b)(4), for tax. yrs. end. after 12/31/57.

Sec. 557. Repealed.

In **2004**, P.L. 108-357, Sec. 413(a)(1), repealed Code Sec. 557, effective for tax. yrs. of foreign corporations begin. after 12/31/2004, and for tax. yrs. of United States shareholders with or within which such tax. yrs. of foreign corporations end.

Prior to repeal, Code Sec. 557 read as follows:

"SEC. 557. INCOME NOT PLACED ON ANNUAL BASIS.

"Section 443(b) (relating to computation of tax on change of annual accounting period) shall not apply in the computation of the undistributed foreign personal holding company income under section 556."

Sec. 558. Repealed.

In **2004**, P.L. 108-357, Sec. 413(a)(1), repealed Code Sec. 558, effective for tax. yrs. of foreign corporations begin. after 12/31/2004, and for tax. yrs. of United States shareholders with or within which such tax. yrs. of foreign corporations end.

Prior to repeal, Code Sec. 558 read as follows:

"SEC. 558. RETURNS OF OFFICERS, DIRECTORS, AND SHAREHOLDERS OF FOREIGN PERSONAL HOLDING COMPANIES.

"For provisions relating to returns of officers, directors, and shareholders of foreign personal holding companies, see section 6035."

In **1958**, P.L. 85-866, Sec. 33(d)(1), added Code Sec. 558, effective for tax. yrs. begin. after 12/31/53, and end. after 8/16/54.

PART IV.—DEDUCTION FOR DIVIDENDS PAID

Sec.
561. Definition of deduction for dividends paid.
562. Rules applicable in determining dividends eligible for dividends paid deduction.
563. Rules relating to dividends paid after close of taxable year.
564. Dividend carryover.
565. Consent dividends.

Sec. 561. Definition of deduction for dividends paid.

(a) General rule.

The deduction for dividends paid shall be the sum of—

(1) the dividends paid during the taxable year,

(2) the consent dividends for the taxable year (determined under section 565), and

(3) in the case of a personal holding company, the dividend carryover described in section 564.

(b) Special rules applicable.

In determining the deduction for dividends paid, the rules provided in section 562 (relating to rules applicable in determining dividends eligible for dividends paid deduction) and section 563 (relating to dividends paid after the close of the taxable year) shall be applicable.

In **1976**, P.L. 94-455, Sec. 1901(b)(32)(H), amended subsec. (b), effective for tax. yrs. begin. after 12/31/76.

Prior to amendment, subsec. (b) read as follows:

"(b) Special rules applicable.

"(1) In determining the deduction for dividends paid, the rules provided in section 562 (relating to rules applicable in determining dividends eligible for dividends paid deduction) and section 563 (relating to dividends paid after the close of the taxable year) shall be applicable.

"(2) If a corporation received antitrust stock (as defined in section 301(f)) in a distribution to which section 301 applied and such corporation distributes such stock (or other property the basis of which is determined by reference to the basis of such stock) to its shareholders, proper adjustment shall be made, under regulations prescribed by the Secretary or his delegate, to the amount of the deduction provided for in subsection (a)."

In **1962**, P.L. 87-403, Sec. 3(f), amended subsec. (b), effective for distributions made after 2/2/62.

Prior to amendment, subsec. (b) read as follows:

"(b) Special rules applicable. In determining the deduction for dividends paid, the rules provided in section 562 (relating to rules applicable in determining dividends eligible for dividends paid deduction) and section 563 (relating to dividends paid after the close of the taxable year) shall be applicable."

Sec. 562. Rules applicable in determining dividends eligible for dividends paid deduction.

(a) General rule.

For purposes of this part, the term "dividend" shall, except as otherwise provided in this section, include only dividends described in section 316 (relating to definition of dividends for purposes of corporate distributions).

(b) Distributions in liquidation.

(1) Except in the case of a personal holding company described in section 542—

(A) in the case of amounts distributed in liquidation, the part of such distribution which is properly chargeable to earnings and profits accumulated after February 28, 1913, shall be treated as a dividend for purposes of computing the dividends paid deduction, and

(B) in the case of a complete liquidation occurring within 24 months after the adoption of a plan of liquidation, any distribution within such period pursuant to such plan shall, to the extent of the earnings and profits (computed without regard to capital losses) of the corporation for the taxable year in which such distribution is made, be treated as a dividend for purposes of computing the dividends paid deduction.

For purposes of subparagraph (A), a liquidation includes a redemption of stock to which section 302 applies. Except to the extent provided in regulations, the preceding sentence shall not apply in the case of any mere holding or investment company which is not a regulated investment company.

(2) In the case of a complete liquidation of a personal holding company, occurring within 24 months after the adoption of a plan of liquidation, the amount of any distribution within such period pursuant to such plan shall be treated as a dividend for purposes of computing the dividends paid deduction, to the extent that such amount is

Deduction for dividends paid — Code Sec. 563

distributed to corporate distributees and represents such corporate distributees' allocable share of the undistributed personal holding company income for the taxable year of such distribution computed without regard to this paragraph and without regard to subparagraph (B) of section 316(b)(2).

(c) Preferential dividends.

Except in the case of a publicly offered regulated investment company (as defined in section 67(c)(2)(B)), the amount of any distribution shall not be considered as a dividend for purposes of computing the dividends paid deduction, unless such distribution is pro rata, with no preference to any share of stock as compared with other shares of the same class, and with no preference to one class of stock as compared with another class except to the extent that the former is entitled (without reference to waivers of their rights by shareholders) to such preference. In the case of a distribution by a regulated investment company (other than a publicly offered regulated investment company (as so defined)) to a shareholder who made an initial investment of at least $10,000,000 in such company, such distribution shall not be treated as not being pro rata or as being preferential solely by reason of an increase in the distribution by reason of reductions in administrative expenses of the company.

(d) Distributions by a member of an affiliated group.

In the case where a corporation which is a member of an affiliated group of corporations filing or required to file a consolidated return for a taxable year is required to file a separate personal holding company schedule for such taxable year, a distribution by such corporation to another member of the affiliated group shall be considered as a dividend for purposes of computing the dividends paid deduction if such distribution would constitute a dividend under the other provisions of this section to a recipient which is not a member of an affiliated group.

(e) Special rules for real estate investment trusts.

In the case of a real estate investment trust, in determining the amount of dividends under section 316 for purposes of computing the dividends paid deduction, the earnings and profits of such trust for any taxable year beginning after December 31, 1980, shall be increased by the total amount of gain (if any) on the sale or exchange of real property by such trust during such taxable year.

---

taxable year in which such distribution is made, be treated as a dividend for purposes of computing the dividends paid deduction."

Sec. 563. Rules relating to dividends paid after close of taxable year.

(a) Accumulated earnings tax.

In the determination of the dividends paid deduction for purposes of the accumulated earnings tax imposed by section 531, a dividend paid after the close of any taxable year and on or before the 15th day of the third month following the close of such taxable year shall be considered as paid during such taxable year.

(b) Personal holding company tax.

In the determination of the dividends paid deduction for purposes of the personal holding company tax imposed by section 541, a dividend paid after the close of any taxable year and on or before the 15th day of the third month following the close of such taxable year shall, to the extent the taxpayer elects in its return for the taxable year, be considered as paid during such taxable year. The amount allowed as a dividend by reason of the application of this subsection with respect to any taxable year shall not exceed either—

(1) The undistributed personal holding company income of the corporation for the taxable year, computed without regard to this subsection, or

(2) 20 percent of the sum of the dividends paid during the taxable year, computed without regard to this subsection.

(c) Dividends considered as paid on last day of taxable year.

For the purpose of applying section 562(a), with respect to distributions under subsection (a) or (b) of this section, a distribution made after the close of a taxable year and on or before the 15th day of the third month following the close of the taxable year shall be considered as made on the last day of such taxable year.

In 2010, P.L. 111-325, Sec. 307(a), substituted "Except in the case of a publicly offered regulated investment company (as defined in section 67(c)(2)(B)), the amount" for "The amount" in the first sentence of subsec. (c)...Sec. 307(b), added "(other than a publicly offered regulated investment company (as so defined))" after "regulated investment company" in the second sentence of subsec. (c), effective for distributions in tax. yrs. begin. after 12/22/2010.

In 2004, P.L. 108-357, Sec. 413(c)(9), deleted "or a foreign personal holding company described in section 552" after "section 542" in para. (b)(1), effective for tax. yrs. of foreign corporations begin. after 12/31/2004, and for tax. yrs. of United States shareholders with or within which such tax. yrs. of foreign corporations end.

In 1986, P.L. 99-514, Sec. 657(a), added the sentence at the end of subsec. (c), effective for distributions made after 10/22/86.

—P.L. 99-514, Sec. 1804(d)(1), added the last sentence to para. (b)(1), effective for distributions after 9/27/85.

In 1983, P.L. 97-448, Sec. 102(c)(2), added subsec. (e), effective for property placed in service after 12/31/80 in tax yrs. end. after 12/31/80.

In 1982, P.L. 97-248, Sec. 222(e)(7), added the last sentence to para. (b)(1), effective for distributions after 8/31/82. For exceptions and special rules see Sec. 222(f)(2)–(4) of this Act reproduced in note following Code Sec. 302.

In 1964, P.L. 88-272, Sec. 225(f)(3), amended subsec. (b), effective for distributions made in any tax. year of the distributing corporation begin. after 12/31/63. Prior to amendment, subsec. (b) read as follows:

"(b) Distributions in liquidation. In the case of amounts distributed in liquidation, the part of such distribution which is properly chargeable to earnings and profits accumulated after February 28, 1913, shall be treated as a dividend for purposes of computing the dividends paid deduction. In the case of a complete liquidation occurring within 24 months after the adoption of a plan of liquidation, any distribution within such period pursuant to such plan shall, to the extent of the earnings and profits (computed without regard to capital losses) of the corporation for the

In 2004, P.L. 108-357, Sec. 413(c)(10)(A), deleted subsec. (c)...Sec. 413(c)(10)(B), redesignated subsec. (d) as subsec. (c)...Sec. 413(c)(10)(C), substituted "subsection (a) or (b)" for "subsection (a), (b), or (c)" in subsec. (c) [as redesignated by Sec. 413(c)(10)(B) of this Act, see above], effective for tax. yrs. of foreign corporations begin. after 12/31/2004, and for tax. yrs. of United States shareholders with or within which such tax. yrs. of foreign corporations end. Prior to deletion, subsec. (c) read as follows:

"(c) Foreign personal holding company tax.

"(1) In general. In the determination of the dividends paid deduction for purposes of part III, a dividend paid after the close of any taxable year and on or before the 15th day of the 3rd month following the close of such taxable year shall, to the extent the company designates such dividend as being taken into account under this subsection, be considered as paid during such taxable year. The amount allowed as a deduction by reason of the application of this subsection with respect to any taxable year shall not exceed the undistributed foreign personal holding company income of the corporation for the taxable year computed without regard to this subsection.

"(2) Special rules. In the case of any distribution referred to in paragraph (1)—

"(A) paragraph (1) shall apply only if such distribution is to the person who was the shareholder of record (as of the last day of the taxable year of the foreign personal holding company) with respect to the stock for which such distribution is made,

"(B) the determination of the person required to include such distribution in gross income shall be made under the principles of section 551(f), and

"(C) any person required to include such distribution in gross or distributable net income shall include such distribution in income for such person's taxable year in which the taxable year of the foreign personal holding company ends."

In 1989, P.L. 101-239, Sec. 7401(b)(1), redesignated subsec. (c) as subsec. (d) and added new subsec. (c)...Sec. 7401(b)(2), substituted "subsection (a), (b), or (c)" for "subsection (a) or (b)" in subsec. (d) [as amended by Sec. 7401(b)(1) of this Act], effective for tax. yrs. of foreign corporations begin. after 7/10/89, except as provided in Sec. 7401(d)(2) of this Act which reads as follows:

"(2) Special rules.— If any foreign corporation is required by the amendments made by this section to change its taxable year for its first taxable year beginning after July 10, 1989—

"(A) such change shall be treated as initiated by the taxpayer,

"(B) such change shall be treated as having been made with the consent of the Secretary of the Treasury or his delegate, and

"(C) if, by reason of such change, any United States person is required to include in gross income for 1 taxable year amounts attributable to 2 taxable years of such foreign corporation, the amount which would otherwise be required to be included in gross income for such 1 taxable year by reason of the short taxable year of the foreign corporation resulting from such change shall be included in gross income ratably over the 4-taxable-year period beginning with such 1 taxable year."

In 1969, P.L. 91-172, Sec. 914(a), substituted "20 percent" for "10 percent" in para. (b)(2), effective for tax. yrs. begin. after 12/31/69.

Sec. 564. Dividend carryover.
(a) General rule.

For purposes of computing the dividends paid deduction under section 561, in the case of a personal holding company the dividend carryover for any taxable year shall be the dividend carryover to such taxable year, computed as provided in subsection (b), from the two preceding taxable years.

(b) Computation of dividend carryover.

The dividend carryover to the taxable year shall be determined as follows:

(1) For each of the 2 preceding taxable years there shall be determined the taxable income computed with the adjustments provided in section 545 (whether or not the taxpayer was a personal holding company for either of such preceding taxable years), and there shall also be determined for each such year the deduction for dividends paid during such year as provided in section 561 (but determined without regard to the dividend carryover to such year).

(2) There shall be determined for each such taxable year whether there is an excess of such taxable income over such deduction for dividends paid or an excess of such deduction for dividends paid over such taxable income, and the amount of each such excess.

(3) If there is an excess of such deductions for dividends paid over such taxable income for the first preceding taxable year, such excess shall be allowed as a dividend carryover to the taxable year.

(4) If there is an excess of such deduction for dividends paid over such taxable income for the second preceding taxable year, such excess shall be reduced by the amount determined in paragraph (5), and the remainder of such excess shall be allowed as a dividend carryover to the taxable year.

(5) The amount of the reduction specified in paragraph (4) shall be the amount of the excess of the taxable income, if any, for the first preceding taxable year over such deduction for dividends paid, if any, for the first preceding taxable year.

In 1976, P.L. 94-455, Sec. 1901(a)(81), deleted subsec. (c), effective for tax. yrs. begin. after 12/31/76.
Prior to deletion, subsec. (c) read as follows:
"(c) Determination of dividend carryover from taxable years to which this subtitle does not apply. In a case where the first or second preceding taxable year began before the taxpayer's first taxable year under this subtitle, the amount of the dividend carryover to taxable years to which this subtitle applies shall be determined under the provisions of the Internal Revenue Code of 1939."

Sec. 565. Consent dividends.
(a) General rule.

If any person owns consent stock (as defined in subsection (f)(1)) in a corporation on the last day of the taxable year of such corporation, and such person agrees, in a consent filed with the return of such corporation in accordance with regulations prescribed by the Secretary, to treat as a dividend the amount specified in such consent, the amount so specified shall, except as provided in subsection (b), constitute a consent dividend for purposes of section 561 (relating to the deduction for dividends paid).

(b) Limitations.

A consent dividend shall not include—

(1) an amount specified in a consent which, if distributed in money, would constitute, or be part of, a distribution which would be disqualified for purposes of the dividends paid deduction under section 562(c) (relating to preferential dividends), or

(2) an amount specified in a consent which would not constitute a dividend (as defined in section 316) if the total amounts specified in consents filed by the corporation had been distributed in money to shareholders on the last day of the taxable year of such corporation.

(c) Effect of consent.

The amount of a consent dividend shall be considered, for purposes of this title—

(1) as distributed in money by the corporation to the shareholder on the last day of the taxable year of the corporation, and

(2) as contributed to the capital of the corporation by the shareholder on such day.

(d) Consent dividends and other distributions.

If a distribution by a corporation consists in part of consent dividends and in part of money or other property, the entire amount specified in the consents and the amount of such money or other property shall be considered together for purposes of applying this title.

(e) Nonresident aliens and foreign corporations.

In the case of a consent dividend which, if paid in money would be subject to the provisions of section 1441 (relating to withholding of tax on nonresident aliens) or section 1442 (relating to withholding of tax on foreign corporations), this section shall not apply unless the consent is accompanied by money, or such other medium of payment as the Secretary may by regulations authorize, in an amount equal to the amount that would be required to be deducted and withheld under sections 1441 or 1442 if the consent dividend had been, on the last day of the taxable year of the corporation, paid to the shareholder in money as a dividend. The amount accompanying the consent shall be credited against the tax imposed by this subtitle on the shareholder.

(f) Definitions.

(1) **Consent stock.** Consent stock, for purposes of this section, means the class or classes of stock entitled, after the payment of preferred dividends, to a share in the distribution (other than in complete or partial liquidation) within the taxable year of all the remaining earnings and profits, which share constitutes the same proportion of such distribution regardless of the amount of such distribution.

(2) **Preferred dividends.** Preferred dividends, for purposes of this section, means a distribution (other than in complete or partial liquidation), limited in amount, which must be made on any class of stock before a further distribution (other than in complete or partial liquidation) of earnings and profits may be made within the taxable year.

In 1976, P.L. 94-455, Sec. 1906(b)(13)(A), substituted "Secretary" for "Secretary or his delegate" in subsecs. (a) and (e), for tax. yrs. begin. after '76.

Subchapter H.—Banking Institutions
Part
    I. Rules of general application to banking institutions.
   II. Mutual savings banks, etc.

In 1976, P.L. 94-455, Sec. 1907(b)(20)(C), deleted the item for Part III.
Prior to deletion the item for Part III read as follows:

Banking institutions Code Sec. 582

"III. Bank affiliates."

PART I.—RULES OF GENERAL APPLICATION TO BANKING INSTITUTIONS

Sec.
581. Definition of bank.
582. Bad debts, losses, and gains with respect to securities held by financial institutions.
583. Repealed.
584. Common trust funds.
585. Reserves for losses on loans of banks.

In 1986, P.L. 99-514, Sec. 901(d)(4)(H), deleted item 586.
Prior to deletion, item 586 read as follows:
"586. Reserves for losses on loans of small business investment companies, etc."
In 1976, P.L. 94-455, Sec. 1901(b)(18), repealed Code Sec. 583, for tax. yrs. begin. after '76.
In 1969, P.L. 91-172, Sec. 431(c), substituted "Bad debts, losses, and gains with respect to securities held by financial institutions." for "Bad debt and loss deduction with respect to securities held by banks." in item 582 . . . . added items 585 and 586.

Sec. 581. Definition of bank.

For purposes of sections 582 and 584, the term "bank" means a bank or trust company incorporated and doing business under the laws of the United States (including laws relating to the District of Columbia) or of any State, a substantial part of the business of which consists of receiving deposits and making loans and discounts, or of exercising fiduciary powers similar to those permitted to national banks under authority of the Comptroller of the Currency, and which is subject by law to supervision and examination by State, or Federal authority having supervision over banking institutions. Such term also means a domestic building and loan association.

In 1976, P.L. 94-455, Sec. 1901(c)(5), substituted "or of any State" for "of any State, or of any Territory", and deleted "Territorial," after "examination by State," in Code Sec. 581, effective for tax. yrs. begin. after 12/31/76.
In 1962, P.L. 87-722, Sec. 5, substituted "authority of the Comptroller of the Currency" for "section 11(k) of the Federal Reserve Act (38 Stat. 262; 12 U.S.C. 248(k))", effective 9/28/62.

Sec. 582. Bad debts, losses, and gains with respect to securities held by financial institutions.

(a) Securities.

Notwithstanding sections 165(g)(1) and 166(e), subsections (a) and (b) of section 166 (relating to allowance of deduction for bad debts) shall apply in the case of a bank to a debt which is evidenced by a security as defined in section 165(g)(2)(C).

(b) Worthless stock in affiliated bank.

For purposes of section 165(g)(1), where the taxpayer is a bank and owns directly at least 80 percent of each class of stock of another bank, stock in such other bank shall not be treated as a capital asset.

(c) Bond, etc., losses and gains of financial institutions.

(1) General rule. For purposes of this subtitle, in the case of a financial institution referred to in paragraph (2), the sale or exchange of a bond, debenture, note, or certificate or other evidence of indebtedness shall not be considered a sale or exchange of a capital asset. For purposes of the preceding sentence, any regular or residual interest in a REMIC shall be treated as an evidence of indebtedness.

(2) Financial institutions to which paragraph (1) applies.

(A) In general. For purposes of paragraph (1), the financial institutions referred to in this paragraph are—
(i) any bank (and any corporation which would be a bank except for the fact it is a foreign corporation),
(ii) any financial institution referred to in section 591,
(iii) any small business investment company operating under the Small Business Investment Act of 1958, and
(iv) any business development corporation.
(B) Business development corporation. For purposes of subparagraph (A), the term "business development corporation" means a corporation which was created by or pursuant to an act of a State legislature for purposes of promoting, maintaining, and assisting the economy and industry within such State on a regional or statewide basis by making loans to be used in trades and businesses which would generally not be made by banks within such region or State in the ordinary course of their business (except on the basis of a partial participation), and which is operated primarily for such purposes.
(C) Limitations on foreign banks. In the case of a foreign corporation referred to in subparagraph (A)(i), paragraph (1) shall only apply to gains and losses which are effectively connected with the conduct of a banking business in the United States.

In 2008, P.L. 110-343, Sec. 301DivA, of this Act provides:
"Sec. 301. Gain or loss from sale or exchange of certain preferred stock.
"(a) In general. For purposes of the Internal Revenue Code of 1986, gain or loss from the sale or exchange of any applicable preferred stock by any applicable financial institution shall be treated as ordinary income or loss.
"(b) Applicable preferred stock. For purposes of this section, the term "applicable preferred stock" means any stock—
"(1) which is preferred stock in—
"(A) the Federal National Mortgage Association, established pursuant to the Federal National Mortgage Association Charter Act (12 U.S.C. 1716 et seq.), or
"(B) the Federal Home Loan Mortgage Corporation, established pursuant to the Federal Home Loan Mortgage Corporation Act (12 U.S.C. 1451 et seq.), and
"(2) which—
"(A) was held by the applicable financial institution on September 6, 2008, or
"(B) was sold or exchanged by the applicable financial institution on or after January 1, 2008, and before September 7, 2008.
"(c) Applicable financial institution. For purposes of this section:
"(1) In general. Except as provided in paragraph (2), the term "applicable financial institution" means—
"(A) a financial institution referred to in section 582(c)(2) of the Internal Revenue Code of 1986, or
"(B) a depository institution holding company (as defined in section 3(w)(1) of the Federal Deposit Insurance Act (12 U.S.C. 1813(w)(1))).
"(2) Special rules for certain sales. In the case of—
"(A) a sale or exchange described in subsection (b)(2)(B), an entity shall be treated as an applicable financial institution only if it was an entity described in subparagraph (A) or (B) of paragraph (1) at the time of the sale or exchange, and
"(B) a sale or exchange after September 6, 2008, of preferred stock described in subsection (b)(2)(A), an entity shall be treated as an applicable financial institution only if it was an entity described in subparagraph (A) or (B) of paragraph (1) at all times during the period beginning on September 6, 2008, and ending on the date of the sale or exchange of the preferred stock.
"(d) Special rule for certain property not held on September 6, 2008. The Secretary of the Treasury or the Secretary's delegate may extend the application of this section to all or a portion of the gain or loss from a sale or exchange in any case where—
"(1) an applicable financial institution sells or exchanges applicable preferred stock after September 6, 2008, which the applicable financial institution did not hold on such date, but the basis of which in the hands of the applicable financial institution at the time of the sale or exchange is the same as the basis in the hands of the person which held such stock on such date, or
"(2) the applicable financial institution is a partner in a partnership which—
"(A) held such stock on September 6, 2008, and later sold or exchanged such stock, or
"(B) sold or exchanged such stock during the period described in subsection (b)(2)(B).
"(e) Regulatory authority. The Secretary of the Treasury or the Secretary's delegate may prescribe such guidance, rules, or regulations as are necessary to carry out the purposes of this section.
"(f) Effective date. This section shall apply to sales or exchanges occurring after December 31, 2007, in taxable years ending after such date.
In 2004, P.L. 108-357, Sec. 835(b)(3), deleted ', and any regular interest in a FASIT,' after 'REMIC' in para. (c)(1), effective 1/1/2005, except as provided in Sec. 835(c)(2) of this Act, which reads as follows:
"(2) Exception for existing FASITs. Paragraph (1) shall not apply to any FASIT in existence on the date of the enactment of this Act to the extent that regular in-

2,273

terests issued by the FASIT before such date continue to remain outstanding in accordance with the original terms of issuance."

In 1996, P.L. 104-188, Sec. 1621(b)(4), added ", and any regular interest in a FASIT," after "REMIC" in para. (c)(1), effective 9/1/97.

In 1990, P.L. 101-508, Sec. 11801(a)(25), deleted paras. (c)(2), (c)(3) and (c)(4) . . . Sec. 11801(c)(11)(A), substituted "paragraph (2)" for "paragraph (5)" in para. (c)(1) . . . Sec. 11801(c)(11)(B), redesignated para. (c)(5) as para. (c)(2), effective 11/5/90, except as provided in Sec. 11821(b) of this Act, which reads as follows:
"(b) Savings provision.
"If—
"(1) any provision amended or repealed by this part applied to—
"(A) any transaction occurring before the date of the enactment of this Act [11/5/90],
"(B) any property acquired before such date of enactment [11/5/90], or
"(C) any item of income, loss, deduction, or credit taken into account before such date of enactment [11/5/90], and
"(2) the treatment of such transaction, property, or item under such provision would (without regard to the amendments made by this part) affect liability for tax for periods ending after such date of enactment [11/5/90],
nothing in the amendments made by this part shall be construed to affect the treatment of such transaction, property, or item for purposes of determining liability for tax for periods ending after such date of enactment [11/5/90]."

Prior to deletion, paras. (c)(2), (c)(3) and (c)(4) read as follows:
"(2) Transitional rule for banks. In the case of a bank, if the net long-term capital gains of the taxable year from sales or exchanges of qualifying securities exceed the net short-term capital losses of the taxable year from such sales or exchanges, such excess shall be considered as gain from the sale of a capital asset held for more than 1 year to the extent it does not exceed the net gain on sales and exchanges described in paragraph (1).
"(3) Special rules. For purposes of this subsection—
"(A) The term 'qualifying security' means a bond, debenture, note, or certificate or other evidence of indebtedness held by a bank on July 11, 1969.
"(B) The amount treated as capital gain or loss from the sale or exchange of a qualifying security shall be determined by multiplying the amount of capital gain or loss from the sale or exchange of such security (determined without regard to this subsection) by a fraction, the numerator of which is the number of days before July 12, 1969, that such security was held by the bank, and the denominator of which is the number of days the security was held by the bank.
"(4) Transitional rule for banks. In the case of a corporation which would be a bank except for the fact that it is a foreign corporation, the net gain, if any, for the taxable year on sales and exchanges described in paragraph (1) shall be considered as gain from the sale or exchange of a capital asset to the extent such net gain does not exceed the portion of any capital loss carryover to such taxable year which is attributable to capital losses on sales or exchanges described in paragraph (1) for a taxable year beginning before July 12, 1969. For purposes of the preceding sentence, the portion of a net capital loss for a taxable year which is attributable to capital losses on sales or exchanges described in paragraph (1) is the amount of the net capital loss on such sales or exchanges for such taxable year (but not in excess of the net capital loss for such taxable year)."

In 1988, P.L. 100-647, Sec. 1006(w)(3), amended Sec. 675(a) of P.L. 99-514, the effective date for changes made by Sec. 671(a), by substituting "the amendments made by this subtitle shall take effect on January 1, 1987" for "the amendments made by this part shall apply to taxable years beginning after December 31, 1986", see below.

—P.L. 100-647, Sec. 1008(d)(3), substituted "subsections (a) and (b) of section 166" for "subsections (a), (b), and (c) of section 166", effective for tax. yrs. begin. after 12/31/86, except as provided by Sec. 805(d)(2) of P.L. 99-514, reproduced in note following Code Sec. 166.

In 1986, P.L. 99-514, Sec. 671(b)(4), added the sentence at the end of para. (c)(1), effective on 1/1/87 [as amended by Sec. 1006(w)(1) of P.L. 100-647, see above].

—P.L. 99-514, Sec. 901(d)(3)(A), substituted "a financial institution referred to in paragraph (5)" for "a financial institution to which section 585, 586, or 593 applies" in para. (c)(1) . . . Sec. 901(d)(3)(B), added para. (c)(5), effective for tax. yrs. begin. after 12/31/86.

In 1984, P.L. 98-369, Sec. 1001(b)(6), substituted "6 months" for "1 year" in para. (c)(2), effective for property acquired after 6/22/84, and before 1/1/88.

In 1976, P.L. 94-455, Sec. 1044(a), added para. (c)(4), effective for tax. yrs. begin. after 7/11/69. Sec. 1044(b)(2) of this Act provides:
"(2) If the refund or credit of any overpayment attributable to the application of the amendment made by subsection (a) to any taxable year is otherwise prevented by the operation of any law or rule of law (other than section 7122 of the Internal Revenue Code of 1954, relating to compromises) on the day which is one year after the date of the enactment of this Act, such credit or refund shall be nevertheless allowed or made if claim therefor is filed on or before such day."

—P.L. 94-455, Sec. 1402(b)(1)(G), substituted "9 months" for "6 months" in para. (c)(2), effective for tax. yrs. begin. in '77.

—P.L. 94-455, Sec. 1402(b)(2), substituted "1 year" for "9 months" in para. (c)(2), effective for tax. yrs. begin. after '77. Sec. 1402(c) of this Act provided a transitional rule for certain installment obligations (see note at Code Sec. 1222).

In 1969, P.L. 91-172, Sec. 433(a), amended subsec. (c), effective for tax. yrs. begin. after 7/11/69. Sec. 433(d)(2) provides as follows:
"(2) Election for small business investment companies and business development corporations. Notwithstanding paragraph (1), in the case of a financial institution described in section 586(a) of the Internal Revenue Code of 1954, the amendments made by this section shall not apply for its taxable years beginning

after 7/11/69, and before 7/11/74, unless the taxpayer so elects at such time and in such manner as shall be prescribed by the Secretary of the Treasury or his delegate. Such election shall be irrevocable and shall apply to all such taxable years."
Prior to amendment, subsec. (c) read as follows:
"(c) Bond, etc., losses of banks.
"For purposes of this subtitle, in the case of a bank, if the losses of the taxable year from sales or exchanges of bonds, debentures, notes, or certificates, or other evidences of indebtedness, issued by any corporation (including one issued by a government or political subdivision thereof), exceed the gains of the taxable year from such sales or exchanges, no such sale or exchange shall be considered a sale or exchange of a capital asset."

In 1958, P.L. 85-866, Sec. 34, deleted "with interest coupons or in registered form," before "exceed the gains" in subsec. (c), effective for tax. yrs. begin. after 12/31/53, and end. after 8/16/54.

Sec. 583. Repealed.

In 1976, P.L. 94-455, Sec. 1901(a)(82), repealed Code Sec. 583, for tax. yrs. begin. after '76.
Prior to repeal Code Sec. 583 read as follows:
"Sec. 583. Deductions of dividends paid on certain preferred stock.
"In computing the taxable income of any national banking association, or of any bank or trust company organized under the laws of any State, Territory, possession of the United States, or the Canal Zone, or of any other banking corporation engaged in the business of industrial banking and under the supervision of a State banking department or of the Comptroller of the Currency, or of any incorporated domestic insurance company, there shall be allowed as a deduction from gross income, in addition to deductions otherwise provided for in this subtitle, any dividend (not including any distribution in liquidation) paid, within the taxable year, to the United States or to any instrumentality thereof exempt from Federal income taxes, on the preferred stock of the corporation owned by the United States or such instrumentality. The amount allowable as a deduction under this section shall reduce the deduction for dividends paid otherwise computed under section 561."

Sec. 584. Common trust funds.
(a) Definitions.

For purposes of this subtitle, the term "common trust fund" means a fund maintained by a bank—

(1) exclusively for the collective investment and reinvestment of moneys contributed thereto by the bank in its capacity—

(A) as a trustee, executor, administrator, or guardian, or

(B) as a custodian of accounts—

(i) which the Secretary determines are established pursuant to a State law which is substantially similar to the Uniform Gifts to Minors Act as published by the American Law Institute, and

(ii) with respect to which the bank establishes, to the satisfaction of the Secretary, that it has duties and responsibilities similar to duties and responsibilities of a trustee or guardian; and

(2) in conformity with the rules and regulations, prevailing from time to time, of the Board of Governors of the Federal Reserve System or the Comptroller of the Currency pertaining to the collective investment of trust funds by national banks.

For purposes of this subsection, two or more banks which are members of the same affiliated group (within the meaning of section 1504) shall be treated as one bank for the period of affiliation with respect to any fund of which any of the member banks is trustee or two or more of the member banks are co-trustees.

(b) Taxation of common trust funds.

A common trust fund shall not be subject to taxation under this chapter and for purposes of this chapter shall not be considered a corporation.

> • **Caution:** Code Sec. 584(c), following, was amended by Sec. 302(e)(7), P.L. 108-27. These provisions generally sunset for tax years beginning after 12/31/2012. For specific sunset provisions see Sec. 303, P.L. 108-27, as

amended by Sec. 102(a), P.L. 111-312, reproduced in history notes for this Code Sec.

(c) Income of participants in fund.

Each participant in the common trust fund in computing its taxable income shall include, whether or not distributed and whether or not distributable—

(1) as part of its gains and losses from sales or exchanges of capital assets held for not more than 1 year, its proportionate share of the gains and losses of the common trust fund from sales or exchanges of capital assets held for not more than 1 year,

(2) as part of its gains and losses from sales or exchanges of capital assets held for more than 1 year, its proportionate share of the gains and losses of the common trust fund from sales or exchanges of capital assets held for more than 1 year, and

(3) its proportionate share of the ordinary taxable income or the ordinary net loss of the common trust fund, computed as provided in subsection (d).

The proportionate share of each participant in the amount of dividends received by the common trust fund and to which section 1(h)(11) applies shall be considered for purposes of such paragraph as having been received by such participant.

(d) Computation of common trust fund income.

The taxable income of a common trust fund shall be computed in the same manner and on the same basis as in the case of an individual, except that—

(1) there shall be segregated the gains and losses from sales or exchanges of capital assets;

(2) after excluding all items of gain and loss from sales or exchanges of capital assets, there shall be computed—

(A) an ordinary taxable income which shall consist of the excess of the gross income over deductions; or

(B) an ordinary net loss which shall consist of the excess of the deductions over the gross income; and

(3) the deduction provided by section 170 (relating to charitable, etc., contributions and gifts) shall not be allowed.

(e) Admission and withdrawal.

No gain or loss shall be realized by the common trust fund by the admission or withdrawal of a participant. The admission of a participant shall be treated with respect to the participant as the purchase of, or an exchange for, the participating interest. The withdrawal of any participating interest by a participant shall be treated as a sale or exchange of such interest by the participant.

(f) Different taxable years of common trust fund and participant.

If the taxable year of the common trust fund is different from that of a participant, the inclusions with respect to the taxable income of the common trust fund, in computing the taxable income of the participant for its taxable year, shall be based upon the taxable income of the common trust fund for any taxable year of the common trust fund ending within or with the taxable year of the participant.

(g) Net operating loss deduction.

The benefit of the deduction for net operating losses provided by section 172 shall not be allowed to a common trust fund, but shall be allowed to the participants in the common trust fund under regulations prescribed by the Secretary.

(h) Nonrecognition treatment for certain transfers to regulated investment companies.

(1) In general. If—

(A) a common trust fund transfers substantially all of its assets to one or more regulated investment companies in exchange solely for stock in the company or companies to which such assets are so transferred, and

(B) such stock is distributed by such common trust fund to participants in such common trust fund in exchange solely for their interests in such common trust fund,

no gain or loss shall be recognized by such common trust fund by reason of such transfer or distribution, and no gain or loss shall be recognized by any participant in such common trust fund by reason of such exchange.

(2) Basis rules.

(A) Regulated investment company. The basis of any asset received by a regulated investment company in a transfer referred to in paragraph (1)(A) shall be the same as it would be in the hands of the common trust fund.

(B) Participants. The basis of the stock which is received in an exchange referred to in paragraph (1)(B) shall be the same as that of the property exchanged. If stock in more than one regulated investment company is received in such exchange, the basis determined under the preceding sentence shall be allocated among the stock in each such company on the basis of respective fair market values.

(3) Treatment of assumptions of liability.

(A) In general. In determining whether the transfer referred to in paragraph (1)(A) is in exchange solely for stock in one or more regulated investment companies, the assumption by any such company of a liability of the common trust fund shall be disregarded.

(B) Special rule where assumed liabilities exceed basis.

(i) In general. If, in any transfer referred to in paragraph (1)(A), the assumed liabilities exceed the aggregate adjusted bases (in the hands of the common trust fund) of the assets transferred to the regulated investment company or companies—

(I) notwithstanding paragraph (1), gain shall be recognized to the common trust fund on such transfer in an amount equal to such excess,

(II) the basis of the assets received by the regulated investment company or companies in such transfer shall be increased by the amount so recognized, and

(III) any adjustment to the basis of a participant's interest in the common trust fund as a result of the gain so recognized shall be treated as occurring immediately before the exchange referred to in paragraph (1)(B).

If the transfer referred to in paragraph (1)(A) is to two or more regulated investment companies, the basis increase under subclause (II) shall be allocated among such companies on the basis of the respective fair market values of the assets received by each of such companies.

(ii) Assumed liabilities. For purposes of clause (i), the term "assumed liabilities" means any liability of the common trust fund assumed by any regulated investment company in connection with the transfer referred to in paragraph (1)(A).

(C) Assumption. For purposes of this paragraph, in determining the amount of any liability assumed, the rules of section 357(d) shall apply.

(4) Common trust fund must meet diversification rules. This subsection shall not apply to any common trust fund which would not meet the requirements of section 368(a)(2)(F)(ii) if it were a corporation. For purposes of the preceding sentence, Government securities shall not be treated as securities of an issuer in applying the 25-percent

Code Sec. 584(h)(4)   **Banking institutions**

and 50-percent test and such securities shall not be excluded for purposes of determining total assets under clause (iv) of section 368(a)(2)(F).

(i) Taxable year of common trust fund.

For purposes of this subtitle, the taxable year of any common trust fund shall be the calendar year.

In 2010, P.L. 111-312, Sec. 102(a), substituted "December 31, 2012" for "December 31, 2010" in Sec. 303, P.L. 108-27 [see below], effective as if included in the enactment of P.L. 108-27, 5/28/2003.

In 2006, P.L. 109-222, Sec. 102, substituted "December 31, 2010" for "December 31, 2008" in Sec. 303 of P.L. 108-27 [see below], effective 5/17/2006.

In 2004, P.L. 108-311, Sec. 402(a)(6), of this Act [which amended Sec. 302(f)(2) of P.L. 108-27, see below], provides:

"(2) Pass-thru entities. In the case of a pass-thru entity described in subparagraph (A), (B), (C), (D), (E), or (F) of section 1(h)(10) of the Internal Revenue Code of 1986, as amended by this Act, the amendments made by this section shall apply to taxable years ending after December 31, 2002; except that dividends received by such an entity on or before such date shall not be treated as qualified dividend income (as defined in section 1(h)(11)(B) of such Code, as added by this Act)."

In 2003, P.L. 108-27, Sec. 302(e)(3), added a flush sentence at the end of subsec. (c), effective for tax. yrs. begin. after 12/31/2002. Sec. 302(f)(2), of this Act [prior to amendment by Sec. 402(a)(6) of P.L. 108-311 see above] provides:

"(2) Regulated investment companies and real estate investment trusts. In the case of a regulated investment company or a real estate investment trust, the amendments made by this section shall apply to taxable years ending after December 31, 2002; except that dividends received by such a company or trust on or before such date shall not be treated as qualified dividend income (as defined in section 1(h)(11)(B) of the Internal Revenue Code of 1986, as added by this Act)."

—P.L. 108-27, Sec. 303, of this Act [as amended by Sec. 102, P.L. 109-222, and Sec. 102(a), P.L. 111-312, see above], reads as follows:

"Sec. 303. SUNSET OF TITLE. All provisions of, and amendments made by, this title [Secs. 301 and 302] shall not apply to taxable years beginning after December 31, 2012, and the Internal Revenue Code of 1986 shall be applied and administered to such years as if such provisions and amendments had never been enacted."

In 1999, P.L. 106-36, Sec. 3001(c)(1)(A), deleted ", and the fact that any property transferred by the common trust fund is subject to a liability," after "the common trust fund" in subpara. (h)(3)(A) . . . Sec. 3001(c)(1)(B), amended clause (h)(3)(B)(ii) and added subpara. (h)(3)(C), effective for transfers after 10/18/98.

Prior to amendment, clause (h)(3)(B)(ii) read as follows:

"(ii) Assumed liabilities. For purposes of clause (i), the term 'assumed liabilities' means the aggregate of—

"(I) any liability of the common trust fund assumed by any regulated investment company in connection with the transfer referred to in paragraph (1)(A), and

"(II) any liability to which property so transferred is subject."

In 1996, P.L. 104-188, Sec. 1805(a), redesignated subsec. (h) as subsec. (i) and added a new subsec. (h), effective for transfers after 12/31/95.

In 1988, P.L. 100-647, Sec. 1008(e)(5)(A), added subsec. (h), effective as provided in Sec. 1008(e)(5)(B) of this Act which reads as follows:

"(B) The amendment made by subparagraph (A) [Sec. 1008(e)(5)(A)] shall take effect as if included in the amendments made by section 806 of the Reform Act [P.L. 99-514], except that section 806(e)(1) [reproduced in notes following Code Sec. 706] shall be applied by substituting 'December 31, 1987' for 'December 31, 1986'. For purposes of section 806(e)(2) [reproduced in notes following Code Sec. 706] of the Reform Act—

"(i) a participant in a common trust fund shall be treated in the same manner as a partner, and

"(ii) subparagraph (C) thereof shall be applied by substituting 'December 31, 1987' for 'December 31, 1986' and as if it did not contain the election to include all income in the short taxable year."

In 1986, P.L. 99-514, Sec. 612(b)(2)(A), amended subsec. (c), effective for tax. yrs. begin. after 12/31/86. Sec. 612(b)(2)(B) of this Act provides:

"(B) If the amendments made by section 1001 of the Tax Reform Act of 1984 cease to apply, effective with respect to property to which such amendments do not apply, subsection (c) of section 584 is amended by striking out '6 months' each place it appears and inserting in lieu thereof '1 year'."

Prior to amendment, subsec. (c) read as follows:

"(c) Income of participants in fund.

"(1) Inclusions in taxable income. Each participant in the common trust fund in computing its taxable income shall include, whether or not distributed and whether or not distributable—

"(A) as part of its gains and losses from sales or exchanges of capital assets held for not more than 6 months, its proportionate share of the gains and losses of the common trust fund from sales or exchanges of capital assets held for not more than 6 months;

"(B) as part of its gains and losses from sales or exchanges of capital assets held for more than 6 months, its proportionate share of the gains and losses of the common trust fund from sales or exchanges of capital assets held for more than 6 months;

"(C) its proportionate share of the ordinary taxable income of the ordinary net loss of the common trust fund, computed as provided in subsection (d).

"(2) Dividends or interest received. The proportionate share of each participant in the amount of dividends or interest received by the common trust fund to which section 116 or 128 applies shall be considered for purposes of such section as having been received by such participant."

In 1984, P.L. 98-369, Sec. 1001(b)(7), substituted "6 months" for "1 year" each place it appeared in subparas. (c)(1)(A) and (B), effective for property acquired after 6/22/84, and before 1/1/88.

In 1983, P.L. 97-448, Sec. 103(a)(2), amended para. (c)(2), effective for tax. yrs. end. after 9/30/81.

Prior to amendment, para. (c)(2) read as follows:

"(2) Dividends or interest received. The proportionate share of each participant in the amount of dividends or interest received by the common trust fund and to which section 116 applies shall be considered for purposes of such section as having been received by such participant."

In 1981, P.L. 97-34, Sec. 301(b)(3), added "or 128" after "116" in para. (c)(2) (as in effect for tax. yrs. begin. in '81), effective for tax. yrs. end. after 9/30/81.

—P.L. 97-34, Sec. 301(b)(6)(A), added "or interest" after "dividends" in the text and heading of para. (c)(2) (as in effect for tax. yrs. begin. after 12/31/81), effective for tax. yrs. begin. after 12/31/81.

—P.L. 97-34, Sec. 302(b)(1), amended the effective date for changes made by Sec. 404(b)(3) of P.L. 96-223 from tax. yrs. begin. after 12/31/80 and before 1/1/83 to tax. yrs. begin. after 12/31/80 and before 1/1/82 [see below].

In 1980, P.L. 96-223, Sec. 404(b)(3), added "or interest" after "dividends" in the heading and text of para. (c)(2), effective [as amended by Sec. 302(b)(1) of P.L. 97-34, see above] for tax. yrs. begin. after 12/31/80, and before 1/1/82.

In 1977, P.L. 95-30, Sec. 101(d)(7), added "and" at the end of para. (d)(2), substituted a period for "; and" at the end of para. (d)(3), and deleted para. (d)(4), effective for tax. yrs. begin. after 12/31/76.

Prior to deletion, para. (d)(4) read as follows:

"(4) the standard deduction provided in section 141 shall not be allowed."

In 1976, P.L. 94-455, Sec. 1402(b)(1)(H), substituted "9 months" for "6 months" in subparas. (c)(1)(A) and (c)(1)(B), effective for tax. yrs. begin. in 1977.

—P.L. 94-455, Sec. 1402(b)(2), substituted "1 year" for "9 months" in subparas. (c)(1)(A) and (c)(1)(B), effective for tax. yrs. begin. after 12/31/77.

—P.L. 94-455, Sec. 1402(c), of the Act provides a transitional rule for certain installment obligations (see note at Code Sec. 1222).

—P.L. 94-455, Sec. 1901(b)(1)(G), amended para. (c)(2), effective for tax. yrs. begin. after 12/31/76.

Prior to amendment, para. (c)(2) read as follows:

"(2) Dividends and partially tax exempt interest. The proportionate share of each participant in the amount of dividends to which section 116 applies, and in the amount of partially tax exempt interest on obligations described in section 35 or section 242, received by the common trust fund shall be considered for purposes of such sections as having been received by such participant. If the common trust fund elects under section 171 (relating to amortizable bond premium) to amortize the premium on such obligations, for purposes of the preceding sentence the proportionate share of the participant of such interest received by the common trust fund shall be his proportionate share of such interest (determined without regard to this sentence) reduced by so much of the deduction under section 171 as is attributable to such share."

—P.L. 94-455, Sec. 1906(b)(13)(A), substituted "Secretary" for "Secretary or his delegate" in subsec. (g), effective for tax. yrs. begin. after 12/31/76.

—P.L. 94-455, Sec. 2131(d), added a sentence after "withdrawal of a participant" in subsec. (e), effective on 4/8/76, in tax. yrs. end. on or after 4/8/76.

—P.L. 94-455, Sec. 2138(a), amended para. (a)(1), effective 10/4/76.

Prior to amendment, para. (a)(1) read as follows:

"(1) exclusively for the collective investment and reinvestment of moneys contributed thereto by the bank in its capacity as a trustee, executor, administrator, or guardian; and"

—P.L. 94-414, Sec. 1, added the sentence at the end of subsec. (a), effective for tax. yrs. begin. after 12/31/75.

In 1964, P.L. 88-272, Sec. 201(d)(5), deleted "section 34 or" before "section 116 applies" in subsec. (c)(2), effective for dividends received after 12/31/64 in tax. yrs. end. after 12/31/64.

In 1962, P.L. 87-722, Sec. 4, added "or the Comptroller of the Currency" after "the Board of Governors of the Federal Reserve System." in para. (a)(2).

Sec. 585. Reserves for losses on loans of banks.

(a) Reserve for bad debts.

(1) In general. Except as provided in subsection (c), a bank shall be allowed a deduction for a reasonable addition to a reserve for bad debts. Such deduction shall be in lieu of any deduction under section 166(a).

(2) Bank. For purposes of this section—

(A) In general. The term "bank" means any bank (as defined in section 581).

(B) Banking business of United States branch of foreign corporation. The term "bank" also includes any corporation to which subparagraph (A) would apply except for the fact that it is a foreign corporation. In the case of any such foreign corporation, this section shall apply only with respect to loans outstanding the interest on

Banking institutions   Code Sec. 585(c)(4)

which is effectively connected with the conduct of a banking business within the United States.

(b) Addition to reserves for bad debts.

(1) General rule. For purposes of subsection (a), the reasonable addition to the reserve for bad debts of any financial institution to which this section applies shall be an amount determined by the taxpayer which shall not exceed the addition to the reserve for losses on loans determined under the experience method as provided in paragraph (2).

(2) Experience method. The amount determined under this paragraph for a taxable year shall be the amount necessary to increase the balance of the reserve for losses on loans (at the close of the taxable year) to the greater of—

(A) the amount which bears the same ratio to loans outstanding at the close of the taxable year as (i) the total bad debts sustained during the taxable year and the 5 preceding taxable years (or, with the approval of the Secretary, a shorter period), adjusted for recoveries of bad debts during such period, bears to (ii) the sum of the loans outstanding at the close of such 6 or fewer taxable years, or

(B) the lower of—

(i) the balance of the reserve at the close of the base year, or

(ii) if the amount of loans outstanding at the close of the taxable year is less than the amount of loans outstanding at the close of the base year, the amount which bears the same ratio to loans outstanding at the close of the taxable year as the balance of the reserve at the close of the base year bears to the amount of loans outstanding at the close of the base year.

For purposes of this paragraph, the base year shall be the last taxable year before the most recent adoption of the experience method, except that for taxable years beginning after 1987 the base year shall be the last taxable year beginning before 1988.

(3) Regulations; definition of loan. The Secretary shall define the term loan and prescribe such regulations as may be necessary to carry out the purposes of this section.

(c) Section not to apply to large banks.

(1) In general. In the case of a large bank, this section shall not apply (and no deduction shall be allowed under any other provision of this subtitle for any addition to a reserve for bad debts).

(2) Large banks. For purposes of this subsection, a bank is a large bank if, for the taxable year (or for any preceding taxable year beginning after December 31, 1986)—

(A) the average adjusted bases of all assets of such bank exceeded $500,000,000, or

(B) such bank was a member of a parent-subsidiary controlled group and the average adjusted bases of all assets of such group exceeded $500,000,000.

(3) 4-year spread of adjustments.

(A) In general. Except as provided in paragraph (4), in the case of any bank which for its last taxable year before the disqualification year maintained a reserve for bad debts—

(i) the provisions of this subsection shall be treated as a change in the method of accounting of such bank for the disqualification year,

(ii) such change shall be treated as having been made with the consent of the Secretary, and

(iii) the net amount of adjustments required by section 481(a) to be taken into account by the taxpayer shall be taken into account in each of the 4 taxable years beginning with the disqualification year with—

(I) the amount taken into account for the 1st of such taxable years being the greater of 10 percent of such net amount or such higher percentage of such net amount as the taxpayer may elect, and

(II) the amount taken into account in each of the 3 succeeding taxable years being equal to the applicable fraction (determined in accordance with the following table for the taxable year involved) of the portion of such net amount not taken into account under subclause (I).

If the case of the—	The applicable fraction is—
1st succeeding year	2/9
2nd succeeding year	1/3
3rd succeeding year	4/9

(B) Suspension of recapture for taxable year for which bank is financially troubled.

(i) In general. In the case of a bank which is a financially troubled bank for any taxable year—

(I) no adjustment shall be taken into account under subparagraph (A) for such taxable year, and

(II) such taxable year shall be disregarded in determining whether any other taxable year is a taxable year for which an adjustment is required to be taken into account under subparagraph (A) or the amount of such adjustment.

(ii) Exception for elective recapture for 1st year. Clause (i) shall not apply to the 1st taxable year referred to in subparagraph (A)(iii)(I) if the taxpayer elects a higher percentage in accordance with such subparagraph.

(iii) Financially troubled bank. For purposes of clause (i), the term "financially troubled bank" means any bank if, for the taxable year, the nonperforming loan percentage of such bank exceeds 75 percent.

(iv) Nonperforming loan percentage. For purposes of clause (iii), the term "nonperforming loan percentage" means the percentage determined by dividing—

(I) the sum of the outstanding balances of nonperforming loans of the bank as of the close of each quarter of the taxable year, by

(II) the sum of the amounts of equity of the bank as of the close of each such quarter.

In the case of a bank which is a member of a parent-subsidiary controlled group for the taxable year, the preceding sentence shall be applied with respect to such group.

(v) Other definitions. For purposes of this subparagraph—

(I) Nonperforming loans. The term "nonperforming loan" means any loan which is considered to be nonperforming by the primary Federal regulatory agency with respect to the bank.

(II) Equity. The term "equity" means the equity of the bank as determined for Federal regulatory purposes.

(C) Coordination with estimated tax payments. For purposes of applying section 6655(e)(2)(A)(i) with respect to any installment, the determination under subparagraph (B) of whether an adjustment is required to be taken into account under subparagraph (A) shall be made as of the last day prescribed for payment of such installment.

(4) Elective cut-off method. If a bank makes an election under this paragraph for the disqualification year—

2,277

Code Sec. 585(c)(4)(A) — Banking institutions

(A) the provisions of this subsection shall not be treated as a change in the method of accounting of the taxpayer for purposes of section 481,

(B) the taxpayer shall continue to maintain its reserve for loans held by the bank as of the 1st day of the disqualification year and charge against such reserve any losses resulting from loans held by the bank as of such 1st day, and

(C) no deduction shall be allowed under this section (or any other provision of this subtitle) for any addition to such reserve for the disqualification year or any subsequent taxable year.

If the amount of the reserve referred to in subparagraph (B) as of the close of any taxable year exceeds the outstanding balance (as of such time) of the loans referred to in subparagraph (B), such excess shall be included in gross income for such taxable year.

(5) Definitions. For purposes of this subsection—

(A) Parent-subsidiary controlled group. The term "parent-subsidiary controlled group" means any controlled group of corporations described in section 1563(a)(1). In determining the average adjusted bases of assets held by such a group, interests held by one member of such group in another member of such group shall be disregarded.

(B) Disqualification year. The term "disqualification year" means, with respect to any bank, the 1st taxable year beginning after December 31, 1986, for which such bank was a large bank if such bank maintained a reserve for bad debts for the preceding taxable year.

(C) Election made by each member. In the case of a parent-subsidiary controlled group, any election under this section shall be made separately by each member of such group.

In **1996**, P.L. 104-188, Sec. 1616(b)(6), deleted "other than an organization to which section 593 applies" from subpara. (a)(2)(A), effective for tax. yrs. begin. after 12/31/95.

In **1993**, P.L. 103-66, Sec. 13224, of this Act, relating to clarification of treatment of certain FSLIC financial assistance, is reproduced in note following Code Sec. 165.

In **1990**, P.L. 101-508, Sec. 11801(a)(26), deleted para. (b)(2) . . . Sec. 11801(c)(12)(C), substituted "shall not exceed the addition to the reserve for losses on loans determined under the experience method as provided in paragraph (2)." for "shall not exceed the greater of—

"(A) for taxable years beginning before 1988 the addition to the reserve for losses on loans determined under the percentage method as provided in paragraph (2), or

"(B) the addition to the reserve for losses on loans determined under the experience method as provided in paragraph (3)." in para. (b)(1) . . . Sec. 11801(c)(12)(D), redesignated paras. (b)(3) and (b)(4) as paras. (b)(2) and (b)(3) . . . Sec. 11801(c)(12)(E), amended para. (b)(3) (as redesignated by Sec. 11801(c)(12)(D)), effective 11/5/90, except as provided in Sec. 11821(b) of this Act which reads as follows:

"(b) Savings provision. If—

"(1) any provision amended or repealed by this part applied to—

"(A) any transaction occurring before the date of the enactment of this Act [11/5/90],

"(B) any property acquired before such date of enactment [11/5/90], or

"(C) any item of income, loss, deduction, or credit taken into account before such date of enactment [11/5/90], and

"(2) the treatment of such transaction, property, or item under such provision would (without regard to the amendments made by this part) affect liability for tax for periods ending after such date of enactment [11/5/90],

nothing in the amendments made by this part shall be construed to affect the treatment of such transaction, property, or item for purposes of determining liability for tax for periods ending after such date of enactment [11/5/90]."

Prior to deletion, para. (b)(2) read as follows:

"(2) Percentage method. The amount determined under this paragraph for a taxable year shall be the amount necessary to increase the balance of the reserve for losses on loans (at the close of the taxable year) to the allowable percentage of eligible loans outstanding at such time, except that—

"(A) If the reserve for losses on loans at the close of the base year is less than the allowable percentage of eligible loans outstanding at such time, the amount determined under this paragraph with respect to the difference shall not exceed one-fifth of such difference.

"(B) If the reserve for losses on loans at the close of the base year is not less than the allowable percentage of eligible loans outstanding at such time, the amount determined under this paragraph shall be the amount necessary to increase the balance of the reserve at the close of the taxable year to (i) the allowable percentage of eligible loans outstanding at such time, or (ii) the balance of the reserve at the close of the base year, whichever is greater, but if the amount of eligible loans outstanding at the close of the taxable year is less than the amount of such loans outstanding at the close of the base year, the amount determined under clause (ii) shall be the amount necessary to increase the balance of the reserve at the close of the taxable year to the amount which bears the same ratio to eligible loans outstanding at the close of the taxable year as the balance of the reserve at the close of the base year bears to the amount of eligible loans outstanding at the close of the base year.

For purposes of this paragraph, the term 'allowable percentage' means 1.8 percent for taxable years beginning before 1976; 1.2 percent for taxable years beginning after 1975 but before 1982; 1.0 percent for taxable years beginning in 1982; and 0.6 percent for taxable years beginning after 1982. The amount determined under this paragraph shall not exceed 0.6 percent of eligible loans outstanding at the close of the taxable year or an amount sufficient to increase the reserve for losses on loans to 0.6 percent of eligible loans outstanding at the close of the taxable year, whichever is greater. For purposes of this paragraph, the term 'base year' means: for taxable years beginning before 1976, the last taxable year beginning on or before July 11, 1969, for taxable years beginning after 1975 but before 1983, the last taxable year beginning before 1976, and for taxable years beginning after 1982, the last taxable year beginning before 1983; except that for purposes of subparagraph (A) such term means the last taxable year before the most recent adoption of the percentage method, if later."

Prior to amendment, para. (b)(3) (as redesignated) read as follows:

"(3) Regulations; definition of eligible loan, etc. The Secretary shall define the terms 'loan' and 'eligible loan' and prescribe such regulations as may be necessary to carry out the purposes of this section; except that the term 'eligible loan' shall not include—

"(A) a loan to a bank (as defined in section 581),

"(B) a loan to a domestic branch of a foreign corporation to which subsection (a)(2) applies,

"(C) a loan secured by a deposit (i) in the lending bank, or (ii) in an institution described in subparagraph (A) or (B) if the lending bank has control over withdrawal of such deposit,

"(D) a loan to or guaranteed by the United States, a possession or instrumentality thereof, or a State or a political subdivision thereof,

"(E) a loan evidenced by a security as defined in section 165(g)(2)(C),

"(F) a loan of Federal funds, and

"(G) commercial paper, including short-term promissory notes which may be purchased on the open market."

In **1988**, P.L. 100-647, Sec. 1009(a)(2)(A), added subpara. (c)(5)(C) . . . Sec. 1009(a)(2)(B), substituted "or such higher percentage of such net amount as the taxpayer may elect" for "or such greater amount as the taxpayer may designate" in clause (c)(3)(A)(iii)(I) . . . Sec. 1009(a)(2)(C), substituted "elects a higher percentage" for "designates an amount" in clause (c)(3)(B)(ii) . . . Sec. 1009(a)(3), added the sentence at the end of para. (c)(4), effective for tax. yrs. begin. after 12/31/86.

In **1987**, P.L. 100-203, Sec. 10301(b)(2), substituted "section 6655(e)(2)(A)(i)" for "section 6655(d)(3)" in subpara. (c)(3)(C), effective for tax. yrs. begin. after 12/31/87.

In **1986**, P.L. 99-514, Sec. 901(a)(1), amended subsec. (a) . . . Sec. 901(a)(2), added subsec. (c) . . . Sec. 901(d)(1), substituted "subsection (a)" for "section 166(c)" in para. (b)(1), effective for tax. yrs. begin. after 12/31/86.

Prior to amendment, subsec. (a) read as follows:

"(a) Institutions to which section applies.

This section shall apply to the following financial institutions:

"(1) any bank (as defined in section 581) other than an organization to which section 593 applies, and

"(2) any corporation to which paragraph (1) would apply except for the fact that it is a foreign corporation, and in the case of any such foreign corporation this section shall apply only with respect to loans outstanding the interest on which is effectively connected with the conduct of a banking business within the United States."

In **1981**, P.L. 97-34, Sec. 267(a)(1), substituted "but before 1982; 1.0 percent for taxable years beginning in 1982; and 0.6 percent for taxable years beginning after 1982" for "but before 1982, and 0.6 percent for taxable years beginning after 1981", in the first sentence of subpara. (b)(2)(B) . . . Sec. 267(a)(2), substituted "but before 1983, the last taxable year beginning before 1976, and for taxable years beginning after 1982, the last taxable year beginning before 1983" for "but before 1982, the last taxable year beginning before 1976, and for taxable years beginning after 1981, the last taxable year beginning before 1982" in the last sentence of para. (b)(2), effective for tax. yrs. begin. after 1981.

In **1976**, P.L. 94-455, Sec. 1906(b)(13)(A), substituted "Secretary" for "Secretary or his delegate" in subpara. (b)(3)(A) and para. (b)(4), effective 2/1/77.

In **1969**, P.L. 91-172, Sec. 431(a), added Code Sec. 585, effective for tax. yrs. begin. after 7/11/69.

Sec. 586. Repealed.

In **1986**, P.L. 99-514, Sec. 901(c), repealed Code Sec. 586, effective for tax. yrs. begin. after 12/31/86.

Prior to repeal, Code Sec. 586 read as follows:

"SEC. 586. RESERVES FOR LOSSES ON LOANS OF SMALL BUSINESS INVESTMENT COMPANIES, ETC.

"(a) *Institutions to which section applies.*

"This section shall apply to the following financial institutions:

"(1) any small business investment company operating under the Small Business Investment Act of 1958, and

"(2) any business development corporation.

For purposes of this section, the term 'business development corporation' means a corporation which was created by or pursuant to an act of a State legislature for purposes of promoting, maintaining, and assisting the economy and industry within such State on a regional or statewide basis by making loans to be used in trades and businesses which would generally not be made by banks (as defined in section 581) within such region or State in the ordinary course of their business (except on the basis of a partial participation), and which is operated primarily for such purposes.

"(b) *Addition to reserves for bad debts.*

"(1) General rule. For purposes of section 166(c), except as provided in paragraph (2) the reasonable addition to the reserve for bad debts of any financial institution to which this section applies shall be an amount determined by the taxpayer which shall not exceed the amount necessary to increase the balance of the reserve for bad debts (at the close of the taxable year) to the greater of—

"(A) the amount which bears the same ratio to loans outstanding at the close of the taxable year as (i) the total bad debts sustained during the taxable year and the 5 preceding taxable years (or, with the approval of the Secretary, a shorter period), adjusted for recoveries of bad debts during such period, bears to (ii) the sum of the loans outstanding at the close of such 6 or fewer taxable years, or

"(B) the lower of—

"(i) the balance of the reserve at the close of the base year, or

"(ii) if the amount of loans outstanding at the close of the taxable year is less than the amount of loans outstanding at the close of the base year, the amount which bears the same ratio to loans outstanding at the close of the taxable year as the balance of the reserve at the close of the base year bears to the amount of loans outstanding at the close of the base year.

For purposes of this subparagraph, the term 'base year' means the last taxable year beginning on or before July 11, 1969.

"(2) New financial institutions. In the case of any taxable year beginning not more than 10 years after the day before the first day on which a financial institution (or any predecessor) was authorized to do business as a financial institution described in subsection (a), the reasonable addition to the reserve for bad debts of such financial institution shall not exceed the larger of the amount determined under paragraph (1) or the amount necessary to increase the balance of the reserve for bad debts at the close of the taxable year to the amount which bears the same ratio (as determined by the Secretary) to loans outstanding at the close of the taxable year as (i) the total bad debts sustained by all institutions described in the applicable paragraph of subsection (a) during the 6 preceding taxable years (adjusted for recoveries of bad debts during such period), bears to (ii) the sum of the loans by all such institutions outstanding at the close of such taxable years."

In 1976, P.L. 94-455, Sec. 1906(b)(13)(A), substituted "Secretary" for "Secretary or his delegate" each place it appeared in subsec. (b), effective for tax. yrs. begin. after 12/31/76.

In 1969, P.L. 91-172, Sec. 431(a), added Code Sec. 586, effective for tax. yrs. begin. after 7/11/69.

PART II.—MUTUAL SAVINGS BANKS, ETC.

Sec.

591. Deduction for dividends paid on deposits.
592. Repealed.
593. Reserves for losses on loans.
594. Alternative tax for mutual savings banks conducting life insurance business.
595. Repealed [Foreclosure on property securing loans.]
596. Repealed. [Limitation on dividends received deduction.]
597. Treatment of transactions in which Federal financial assistance provided.

In 1996, P.L. 104-188, Sec. 1616(b)(16), deleted items 595 and 596.

Prior to deletion, item 595 read as follows:
"Sec. 595. Foreclosure on property securing loans."
Prior to deletion, item 596 read as follows:
"Sec. 596. Limitation on dividends received deduction."

In 1989, amended item 597.

In 1988, P.L. 100-647, Sec. 4012(b)(2)(D)(ii), added "or FDIC" after "FSLIC" in item 597, as deleted by Sec. 904(b)(2) of P.L. 99-514.

In 1986, P.L. 99-514, Sec. 904(b)(2), deleted item 597.

Prior to deletion, item 597 [as amended by Sec. 4012(b)(2)(D) of P.L. 100-647(ii), see above] read as follows:
"597. FSLIC or FDIC financial assistance."

In 1981, P.L. 97-34, Sec. 244(b), added item 597.

In 1976, P.L. 94-455, Sec. 1901(b)(19), repealed Code Sec. 592, for tax. yrs. begin. after '76.

Prior to repeal, the item for Code Sec. 592 read as follows:
"592. Deduction for repayment of certain loans."

In 1969, P.L. 91-172, Sec. 434(b), added item 596.

In 1962, substituted "Reserves for losses on loans" for "Additions to reserve for bad debts" in item 593, and added item 595.

Sec. 591. Deduction for dividends paid on deposits.

(a) In general.

In the case of mutual savings banks, cooperative banks, domestic building and loan associations, and other savings institutions chartered and supervised as savings and loan or similar associations under Federal or State law, there shall be allowed as deductions in computing taxable income amounts paid to, or credited to the accounts of, depositors or holders of accounts as dividends or interest on their deposits or withdrawable accounts, if such amounts paid or credited are withdrawable on demand subject only to customary notice of intention to withdraw.

(b) Mutual savings bank to include certain banks with capital stock.

For purposes of this part, the term "mutual savings bank" includes any bank—

(1) which has capital stock represented by shares, and
(2) which is subject to, and operates under, Federal or State laws relating to mutual savings bank.

In 1981, P.L. 97-34, Sec. 245(a)(1), added "(a) In general." before "In" in Code Sec. 591 . . . Sec. 245(a)(2), added subsec. (b), effective for tax. yrs. end. after 8/13/81.

In 1962, P.L. 87-834, Sec. 6(f)(1), substituted "domestic building and loan associations, and other savings institutions chartered and supervised as savings and loan or similar associations under Federal or State law" for "and domestic building and loan associations" in Code Sec. 591 . . . Sec. 6(f)(2), added "or interest" after "dividends" in Code Sec. 591, effective 10/17/62.

Sec. 592. Repealed.

In 1976, P.L. 94-455, Sec. 1901(a)(83), repealed Code Sec. 592, effective for tax. yrs. begin. after '76.

Prior to repeal Code Sec. 592 read as follows:
"Sec. 592. Deduction for repayment of certain loans.

"In the case of a mutual savings bank not having capital stock represented by shares, a domestic building and loan association, or a cooperative bank without capital stock organized and operated for mutual purposes and without profit, there shall be allowed as deductions in computing taxable income amounts paid by the taxpayer during the taxable year in repayment of loans made before September 1, 1951, by (1) the United States or any agency or instrumentality thereof which is wholly owned by the United States, or (2) any mutual fund established under the authority of the laws of any State."

Sec. 593. Reserves for losses on loans.

(a) Reserve for bad debts.

(1) In general. Except as provided in paragraph (2), in the case of—

(A) any domestic building and loan association,
(B) any mutual savings bank, or
(C) any cooperative bank without capital stock organized and operated for mutual purposes and without profit,

there shall be allowed a deduction for a reasonable addition to a reserve for bad debts. Such deduction shall be in lieu of any deduction under section 166(a).

(2) Organization must meet 60-percent asset test of section 7701(a)(19). This section shall apply to an association or bank referred to in paragraph (1) only if it meets the requirements of section 7701(a)(19)(C).

(b) Addition to reserves for bad debts.

(1) In general. For purposes of subsection (a), the reasonable addition for the taxable year to the reserve for bad debts of any taxpayer described in subsection (a) shall be an amount equal to the sum of—

(A) the amount determined to be a reasonable addition to the reserve for losses on nonqualifying loans, com-

2,279

puted in the same manner as is provided with respect to additions to the reserves for losses on loans of banks under section 585(b)(2), plus

(B) the amount determined by the taxpayer to be a reasonable addition to the reserve for losses on qualifying real property loans, but such amount shall not exceed the amount determined under paragraph (2) or (3), whichever is the larger but the amount determined under this subparagraph shall in no case be greater than the larger of—

(i) the amount determined under paragraph (3), or

(ii) the amount which, when added to the amount determined under subparagraph (A), equals the amount by which 12 percent of the total deposits or withdrawable accounts of depositors of the taxpayer at the close of such year exceeds the sum of its surplus, undivided profits, and reserves at the beginning of such year (taking into account any portion thereof attributable to the period before the first taxable year beginning after December 31, 1951).

(2) Percentage of taxable income method.

(A) In general. Subject to subparagraphs (B) and (C), the amount determined under this paragraph for the taxable year shall be an amount equal to 8 percent of the taxable income for such year.

(B) Reduction for amounts referred to in paragraph (1)(A). The amount determined under subparagraph (A) shall be reduced (but not below 0) by the amount determined under paragraph (1)(A).

(C) Overall limitation on paragraph. The amount determined under this paragraph shall not exceed the amount necessary to increase the balance at the close of the taxable year of the reserve for losses on qualifying real property loans to 6 percent of such loans outstanding at such time.

(D) Computation of taxable income. For purposes of this paragraph, taxable income shall be computed—

(i) by excluding from gross income any amount included therein by reason of subsection (e),

(ii) without regard to any deduction allowable for any addition to the reserve for bad debts,

(iii) by excluding from gross income an amount equal to the net gain for the taxable year arising from the sale or exchange of stock of a corporation or of obligations the interest on which is excludable from gross income under section 103,

(iv) by excluding from gross income dividends with respect to which a deduction is allowable by part VIII of subchapter B, reduced by an amount equal to 8 percent of the dividends received deduction (determined without regard to section 596) for the taxable year, and

(v) if there is a capital gain rate differential (as defined in section 904(b)(3)(D)) for the taxable year, by excluding from gross income the rate differential portion (within the meaning of section 904(b)(3)(E)) of the lesser of—

(I) the net long-term capital gain for the taxable year, or

(II) the net long-term capital gain for the taxable year from the sale or exchange of property other than property described in clause (iii).

(3) Experience method. The amount determined under this paragraph for the taxable year shall be computed in the same manner as is provided with respect to additions to the reserves for losses on loans of banks under section 585(b)(2).

(c) Treatment of reserves for bad debts.

(1) Establishment of reserves. Each taxpayer described in subsection (a) which uses the reserve method of accounting for bad debts shall establish and maintain a reserve for losses on qualifying real property loans, a reserve for losses on nonqualifying loans, and a supplemental reserve for losses on loans. For purposes of this title, such reserves shall be treated as reserves for bad debts, but no deduction shall be allowed for any addition to the supplemental reserve for losses on loans.

(2) Certain pre-1963 reserves. Notwithstanding the second sentence of paragraph (1), any amount allocated pursuant to paragraph (5) (as in effect immediately before the enactment of the Tax Reform Act of 1976) during a taxable year beginning before January 1, 1977, to the reserve for losses on qualifying real property loans out of the surplus, undivided profits, and bad debt reserves (determined as of December 31, 1962) attributable to the period before the first taxable year beginning after December 31, 1951, shall not be treated as a reserve for bad debts for any purpose other than determining the amount referred to in subsection (b)(1)(B), and for such purpose such amount shall be treated as remaining in such reserve.

(3) Charging of bad debts to reserves. Any debt becoming worthless or partially worthless in respect of a qualifying real property loan shall be charged to the reserve for losses on such loans, and any debt becoming worthless or partially worthless in respect of a nonqualifying loan shall be charged to the reserve for losses on nonqualifying loans; except that any such debt may, at the election of the taxpayer, be charged in whole or in part to the supplemental reserve for losses on loans.

(d) Loans defined.

For purposes of this section—

(1) Qualifying real property loans. The term "qualifying real property loan" means any loan secured by an interest in improved real property or secured by an interest in real property which is to be improved out of the proceeds of the loan, but such term does not include—

(A) any loan evidenced by a security (as defined in section 165(g)(2)(C));

(B) any loan, whether or not evidenced by a security (as defined in section 165(g)(2)(C)), the primary obligor on which is—

(i) a government or political subdivision or instrumentality thereof;

(ii) a bank (as defined in section 581); or

(iii) another member of the same affiliated group;

(C) any loan, to the extent secured by a deposit in or share of the taxpayer; or

(D) any loan which, within a 60-day period beginning in one taxable year of the creditor and ending in its next taxable year, is made or acquired and then repaid or disposed of, unless the transactions by which such loan was made or acquired and then repaid or disposed of are established to be for bona fide business purposes.

For purposes of subparagraph (B)(iii), the term "affiliated group" has the meaning assigned to such term by section 1504(a); except that (i) the phrase "more than 50 percent" shall be substituted for the phrase "at least 80 percent" each place it appears in section 1504(a), and (ii) all corporations shall be treated as includible corporations (without any exclusion under section 1504(b)).

(2) Nonqualifying loans. The term "nonqualifying loan" means any loan which is not a qualifying real property loan.

(3) Loan. The term "loan" means debt, as the term "debt" is used in section 166.

(4) Treatment of interests in REMIC's. A regular or residual interest in a REMIC shall be treated as a qualifying real property loan; except that, if less than 95 percent of the assets of such REMIC are qualifying real property loans (determined as if the taxpayer held the assets of the REMIC), such interest shall be so treated only in the proportion which the assets of such REMIC consist of such loans. For purposes of determining whether any interest in a REMIC qualifies under the preceding sentence, any interest in another REMIC held by such REMIC shall be treated as a qualifying real property loan under principles similar to the principles of the preceding sentence, except that if such REMIC's are part of a tiered structure, they shall be treated as 1 REMIC for purposes of this paragraph.

(e) Distributions to shareholders.

(1) In general. For purposes of this chapter, any distribution of property (as defined in section 317(a)) by a taxpayer having a balance described in subsection (g)(2)(A)(ii) to a shareholder with respect to its stock, if such distribution is not allowable as a deduction under section 591, shall be treated as made—

(A) first out of its earnings and profits accumulated in taxable years beginning after December 31, 1951, (and, in the case of an S corporation, the accumulated adjustments account, as defined in section 1368(e)(1)) to the extent thereof,

(B) then out of the balance taken into account under subsection (g)(2)(A)(ii) (properly adjusted for amounts charged against such reserves for taxable years beginning after December 31, 1987),

(C) then out of the supplemental reserve for losses on loans, to the extent thereof,

(D) then out of such other accounts as may be proper.

This paragraph shall apply in the case of any distribution in redemption of stock or in partial or complete liquidation of a taxpayer having a balance described in subsection (g)(2)(A)(ii), except that any such distribution shall be treated as made first out of the amount referred to in subparagraph (B), second out of the amount referred to in subparagraph (C), third out of the amount referred to in subparagraph (A), and then out of such other accounts as may be proper. This paragraph shall not apply to any transaction to which section 381 applies, or to any distribution to the Federal Savings and Loan Insurance Corporation (or any successor thereof) or the Federal Deposit Insurance Corporation in redemption of an interest in a taxpayer having a balance described in subsection (g)(2)(A)(ii), if such interest was originally received by any such entity in exchange for assistance provided under a provision of law referred to in section 597(c). This paragraph shall not apply to any distribution of all of the stock of a bank (as defined in section 581) to another corporation if, immediately after the distribution, such bank and such other corporation are members of the same affiliated group (as defined in section 1504) and the provisions of section 5(e) of the Federal Deposit Insurance Act (as in effect on December 31, 1995) or similar provisions are in effect.

(2) Amounts charged to reserve accounts and included in gross income. If any distribution is treated under paragraph (1) as having been made out of the reserves described in subparagraphs (B) and (C) of such paragraph, the amount charged against such reserve shall be the amount which, when reduced by the amount of tax imposed under this chapter and attributable to the inclusion of such amount in gross income, is equal to the amount of such distribution; and the amount so charged against such reserve shall be included in gross income of the taxpayer.

(3) Special rules.

(A) For purposes of paragraph (1)(B), additions to the reserve for losses on qualifying real property loans for the taxable year in which the distribution occurs shall be taken into account.

(B) For purposes of computing under this section the amount of a reasonable addition to the reserve for losses on qualifying real property loans for any taxable year, any amount charged during any year to such reserve pursuant to the provisions of paragraph (2) shall not be taken into account.

(f) Termination of reserve method.

Subsections (a), (b), (c), and (d) shall not apply to any taxable year beginning after December 31, 1995.

(g) 6-Year spread of adjustments.

(1) In general. In the case of any taxpayer who is required by reason of subsection (f) to change its method of computing reserves for bad debts—

(A) such change shall be treated as a change in a method of accounting,

(B) such change shall be treated as initiated by the taxpayer and as having been made with the consent of the Secretary, and

(C) the net amount of the adjustments required to be taken into account by the taxpayer under section 481(a)—

(i) shall be determined by taking into account only applicable excess reserves, and

(ii) as so determined, shall be taken into account ratably over the 6-taxable year period beginning with the first taxable year beginning after December 31, 1995.

(2) Applicable excess reserves.

(A) In general. For purposes of paragraph (1), the term "applicable excess reserves" means the excess (if any) of—

(i) the balance of the reserves described in subsection (c)(1) (other than the supplemental reserve) as of the close of the taxpayer's last taxable year beginning before January 1, 1996, over

(ii) the lesser of—

(I) the balance of such reserves as of the close of the taxpayer's last taxable year beginning before January 1, 1988, or

(II) the balance of the reserves described in subclause (I), reduced in the same manner as under section 585(b)(2)(B)(ii) on the basis of the taxable years described in clause (i) and this clause.

(B) Special rule for thrifts which become small banks. In the case of a bank (as defined in section 581) which was not a large bank (as defined in section 585(c)(2)) for its first taxable year beginning after December 31, 1995—

(i) the balance taken into account under subparagraph (A)(ii) shall not be less than the amount which would be the balance of such reserves as of the close of its last taxable year beginning before such date if the additions to such reserves for all taxable years had been determined under section 585(b)(2)(A), and

(ii) the opening balance of the reserve for bad debts as of the beginning of such first taxable year shall be the balance taken into account under subparagraph (A)(ii) (determined after the application of clause (i) of this subparagraph).

The preceding sentence shall not apply for purposes of paragraphs (5) and (6) or subsection (e)(1).

(3) Recapture of pre-1988 reserves where taxpayer ceases to be bank. If, during any taxable year beginning after December 31, 1995, a taxpayer to which paragraph (1) applied is not a bank (as defined in section 581), paragraph (1) shall apply to the reserves described in paragraph (2)(A)(ii) and the supplemental reserve; except that such reserves shall be taken into account ratably over the 6-taxable year period beginning with such taxable year.

(4) Suspension of recapture if residential loan requirement met.

(A) In general. In the case of a bank which meets the residential loan requirement of subparagraph (B) for the first taxable year beginning after December 31, 1995, or for the following taxable year—

(i) no adjustment shall be taken into account under paragraph (1) for such taxable year, and

(ii) such taxable year shall be disregarded in determining—

(I) whether any other taxable year is a taxable year for which an adjustment is required to be taken into account under paragraph (1), and

(II) the amount of such adjustment.

(B) Residential loan requirement. A taxpayer meets the residential loan requirement of this subparagraph for any taxable year if the principal amount of the residential loans made by the taxpayer during such year is not less than the base amount for such year.

(C) Residential loan. For purposes of this paragraph, the term "residential loan" means any loan described in clause (v) of section 7701(a)(19)(C) but only if such loan is incurred in acquiring, constructing, or improving the property described in such clause.

(D) Base amount. For purposes of subparagraph (B), the base amount is the average of the principal amounts of the residential loans made by the taxpayer during the 6 most recent taxable years beginning on or before December 31, 1995. At the election of the taxpayer who made such loans during each of such 6 taxable years, the preceding sentence shall be applied without regard to the taxable year in which such principal amount was the highest and the taxable year in such principal amount was the lowest. Such an election may be made only for the first taxable year beginning after such date, and, if made for such taxable year, shall apply to the succeeding taxable year unless revoked with the consent of the Secretary.

(E) Controlled groups. In the case of a taxpayer which is a member of any controlled group of corporations described in section 1563(a)(1), subparagraph (B) shall be applied with respect to such group.

(5) Continued application of fresh start under section 585 transitional rules. In the case of a taxpayer to which paragraph (1) applied and which was not a large bank (as defined in section 585(c)(2)) for its first taxable year beginning after December 31, 1995:

(A) In general. For purposes of determining the net amount of adjustments referred to in section 585(c)(3)(A)(iii), there shall be taken into account only the excess (if any) of the reserve for bad debts as of the close of the last taxable year before the disqualification year over the balance taken into account by such taxpayer under paragraph (2)(A)(ii) of this subsection.

(B) Treatment under elective cut-off method. For purposes of applying section 585(c)(4)—

(i) the balance of the reserve taken into account under subparagraph (B) thereof shall be reduced by the balance taken into account by such taxpayer under paragraph (2)(A)(ii) of this subsection, and

(ii) no amount shall be includible in gross income by reason of such reduction.

(6) Suspended reserve included as section 381(c) items. The balance taken into account by a taxpayer under paragraph (2)(A)(ii) of this subsection and the supplemental reserve shall be treated as items described in section 381(c).

(7) Conversions to credit unions. In the case of a taxpayer to which paragraph (1) applied which becomes a credit union described in section 501(c) and exempt from taxation under section 501(a)—

(A) any amount required to be included in the gross income of the credit union by reason of this subsection shall be treated as derived from an unrelated trade or business (as defined in section 513), and

(B) for purposes of paragraph (3), the credit union shall not be treated as if it were a bank.

(8) Regulations. The Secretary shall prescribe such regulations as may be necessary to carry out this subsection and subsection (e), including regulations providing for the application of such subsections in the case of acquisitions, mergers, spinoffs, and other reorganizations.

In 1997, P.L. 105-34, Sec. 1601(f)(5)(A), added "(and, in the case of an S corporation, the accumulated adjustments account, as defined in section 1368(e)(1))" after "1951," in subpara. (e)(1)(A), effective for tax. yrs. begin. after 12/31/95.

In 1996, P.L. 104-188, Sec. 1616(a), added subsecs. (f) and (g)... Sec. 1616(b)(7)(A), substituted "by a taxpayer having a balance described in subsection (g)(2)(A)(ii)" for "by a domestic building and loan association or an institution that is treated as a mutual savings bank under section 591(b)" in para. (e)(1), effective for tax. yrs. begin. after 12/31/95.

—P.L. 104-188, Sec. 1616(b)(7)(B), amended subpara. (e)(1)(B), effective for tax. yrs. begin. after 12/31/95, except as provided in Sec. 1616(c)(2) of this Act, which reads as follows:

"(2) Subsection (b)(7)(B). The amendments made by subsection (b)(7)(B) shall not apply to any distribution with respect to preferred stock if—

"(A) such stock is outstanding at all times after October 31, 1995, and before the distribution, and

"(B) such distribution is made before the date which is 1 year after the date of the enactment of this Act (or, in the case of stock which may be redeemed, if later, the date which is 30 days after the earliest date that such stock may be redeemed).

Prior to amendment, subpara. (e)(1)(B) read as follows:

"(B) then out of the reserve for losses on qualifying real property loans, to the extent additions to such reserve exceed the additions which would have been allowed under subsection (b)(3),"

—P.L. 104-188, Sec. 1616(b)(7)(C), substituted "a taxpayer having a balance described in subsection (g)(2)(A)(ii)" for "the association or an institution that is treated as a mutual savings bank under section 591(b)" in the second sentence of para. (e)(1)... Sec. 1616(b)(7)(D), substituted "a taxpayer having a balance described in subsection (g)(2)(A)(ii)" for "an association" in the third sentence of para. (e)(1)... Sec. 1616(b)(7)(E), added the sentence at the end of para. (e)(1), effective for tax. yrs. begin. after 12/31/95.

—P.L. 104-188, Sec. 1704(t)(51), amended Sec. 11801(c)(12)(F) of P.L. 101-508 by substituting "and (3)" for "and (E)", see below.

In 1993, P.L. 103-66, Sec. 13224, of this Act, relating to clarification of treatment of certain FSLIC financial assistance, is reproduced in note following Code Sec. 165.

In 1990, P.L. 101-508, Sec. 11801(c)(12)(F), [as amended by Sec. 1704(t)(51) of P.L. 104-188, see above] substituted "section 585(b)(2)" for "section 585(b)(3)" in subpara. (b)(1)(A) and (3), effective 11/5/90 except as provided in Sec. 11821(b) of this Act, reproduced in note following Code Sec. 585.

In 1989, P.L. 101-73, Sec. 1401(b)(3), amended the last sentence of para. (e)(1), effective 8/9/89.

Prior to amendment, the last sentence of para. (e)(1) read as follows:

"This paragraph shall not apply to any transaction to which section 381 (relating to carryovers in certain corporate acquisitions) applies, or to any distribution to the Federal Savings and Loan Insurance Corporation in redemption of an interest

Banking institutions — Code Sec. 593

in an association, if such interest was originally received by the Federal Savings and Loan Insurance Corporation in exchange for financial assistance pursuant to section 406(f) of the National Housing Act (12 U.S.C. Sec. 1729(f))."

In 1988, P.L. 100-647, Sec. 1003(c), deleted "and" at the end of clause (b)(2)(D)(iii), substituted ", and" for the period in clause (b)(2)(D)(iv) and added clause (b)(2)(D)(v), effective for tax. yrs. begin. after 12/31/86.

—P.L. 100-647, Sec. 1006(t)(25)(B), added the sentence at the end of para. (d)(4), effective on 1/1/87.

—P.L. 100-647, Sec. 1006(w)(1), amended Sec. 675(a) of P.L. 99-514, the effective date for changes made by Sec. 671(b)(2), by substituting "the amendments made by this subtitle shall take effect on January 1, 1987" for "the amendments made by this part shall apply to taxable years beginning after December 31, 1986" see below.

In 1986, P.L. 99-514, Sec. 311(b)(2), added "and" at the end of clause (b)(2)(E)(iii), deleted clause (b)(2)(E)(iv) and redesignated clause (v) as clause (iv), effective for tax. yrs. begin. after 12/31/86.

Prior to deletion, clause (b)(2)(E)(iv) read as follows:

"(iv) by excluding from gross income an amount equal to the lesser of $^{18}/_{46}$ of the net long-term capital gain for the taxable year of $^{18}/_{46}$ of the net long-term capital gain for the taxable year from the sale or exchange of property other than property described in clause (iii), and"

—P.L. 99-514, Sec. 671(b)(2), added para. (d)(4), effective on 1/1/87 [as amended by Sec. 1006(w)(1) of P.L. 100-647, see above].

—P.L. 99-514, Sec. 901(b)(1), amended subsec. (a)...Sec. 901(b)(2), deleted subparas. (b)(2)(A)-(C), added new subparas. (b)(2)(A) and (B) and redesignated subparas. (b)(2)(D) and (E) as (b)(2)(C)(D)...Sec. 901(b)(3), deleted paras. (b)(3) and (b)(5) and redesignated para. (b)(4) as (b)(3)...Sec. 901(d)(2)(A), substituted "subsection (a)" for "section 166(c)" in para. (b)(1)...Sec. 901(d)(2)(B), substituted "paragraph (2) or (3), whichever is the larger," for "paragraph (2), (3), or (4), whichever amount is the largest" in subpara. (b)(1)(B) and substituted "paragraph (3)" for "paragraph (4)" in clause (b)(1)(B)(i)...Sec. 901(d)(2)(B), [(C)], substituted "8 percent" for "the applicable percentage (determined under subparagraphs (A) and (B))" in subpara. (b)(2)(D) [as redesignated]...Sec. 901(d)(2)(C), [(D)], substituted "subsection (b)(3)" for "subsection (b)(4)" in subpara. (e)(1)(B), effective for tax. yrs. begin. after 12/31/86.

Prior to amendment, subsec. (a) read as follows:

"(a) Organizations to which section applies.

"This section shall apply to any mutual savings bank, domestic building and loan association, or cooperative bank without capital stock organized and operated for mutual purposes and without profit."

Prior to amendment, subparas. (b)(2)(A)-(C), read as follows:

"(A) In general. Subject to subparagraphs (B), (C), and (D), the amount determined under this paragraph for the taxable year shall be an amount equal to the applicable percentage of the taxable income for such year (determined under the following table):

"For a taxable year beginning in—	The applicable percentage under this paragraph shall be—
1976	43 percent.
1977	42 percent.
1978	41 percent.
1979 or thereafter	40 percent.

"(B) Reduction of applicable percentage in certain cases. If, for the taxable year, the percentage of the assets of a taxpayer described in subsection (a), which are assets described in section 7701(a)(19)(C), is less than—

"(i) 82 percent of the total assets in the case of a taxpayer other than a mutual savings bank which is not described in section 591(b), the applicable percentage for such year provided by subparagraph (A) shall be reduced by ¾ of 1 percentage point for each 1 percentage point of such difference, or

"(ii) 72 percent of the total assets in the case of a mutual savings bank which is not described in section 591(b), the applicable percentage for such year provided by subparagraph (A) shall be reduced by 1½ percentage points for each 1 percentage point of such difference.

If, for the taxable year, the percentage of the assets of such taxpayer which are assets described in section 7701(a)(19)(C) is less than 60 percent (50 percent for a taxable year beginning before 1973 in the case of a mutual savings bank which is not described in section 591(b)), this paragraph shall not apply.

"(C) Reduction for amounts referred to in paragraph (1)(A). The amount determined under subparagraph (A) shall be reduced by that portion of the amount referred to in paragraph (1)(A) for the taxable year (not in excess of 100 percent) which bears the same ratio to such amount as (i) 18 percent (28 percent in the case of mutual savings banks which is not described in section 591(b)) bears to (ii) the percentage of the assets of the taxpayer for such year which are not assets described in section 7701(a)(19)(C)."

Prior to deletion, paras. (b)(3) and (b)(5) read as follows:

"(3) Percentage method. The amount determined under this paragraph to be a reasonable addition to the reserve for losses on qualifying real property loans shall be computed in the same manner as is provided with respect to additions to the reserves for losses on loans of banks under section 585(b)(2), reduced by the amount referred to in paragraph (1)(A) for the taxable year.

"(5) Determination of reserve for percentage method. For purposes of paragraph (3), the amount deemed to be the balance of the reserve for losses on loans at the beginning of the taxable year shall be the total of the balances at such time of the reserve for losses on nonqualifying loans, the reserve for losses on qualifying real property loans, and the supplemental reserve for losses on loans."

In 1981, P.L. 97-34, Sec. 243, substituted "applies, or to any distribution to the Federal Savings and Loan Insurance Corporation in redemption of an interest in an association, if such interest was originally received by the Federal Savings and Loan Insurance Corporation in exchange for financial assistance pursuant to section 406(f) of the National Housing Act (12 U.S.C. Sec. 1729(f))." for "applies." in para. (e)(1), effective for any distribution made on or after 1/1/81.

—P.L. 97-34, Sec. 245(b)(1), added "which is not described in section 591(b)" after "mutual savings bank" each time it appears in subpara. (b)(2)(B)...Sec. 245(b)(2), added "which are not described in section 591(b)" after "mutual savings banks" in subpara. (b)(2)(C)...Sec. 245(c)(1), deleted "not having capital stock represented by shares" after "mutual savings bank" in subsec. (a)...Sec. 245(c)(2), added "or an institution that is treated as a mutual savings bank under section 591(b)" after "association" each time it appears in para. (e)(1), effective for tax. yrs. end. after 8/13/81.

In 1980, P.L. 96-222, Sec. 104(a)(3)(C), substituted "$^{18}/_{46}$" for "$^{3}/_{5}$" each time it appeared in clause (b)(2)(E)(iv), effective for tax. yrs. begin. after 12/31/76.

In 1976, P.L. 94-455, Sec. 1901(a)(84)(A), amended subpara. (b)(2)(A), effective for tax. yrs. begin. after 12/31/76.

Prior to amendment, subpara. (b)(2)(A) read as follows:

"(A) In general. Subject to subparagraphs (B), (C), and (D), the amount determined under this paragraph for the taxable year shall be an amount equal to the applicable percentage of the taxable income for such year (determined under the following table):

For a taxable year beginning in—	The applicable percentage under this paragraph shall be—
1969	60 percent.
1970	57 percent.
1971	54 percent.
1972	51 percent.
1973	49 percent.
1974	47 percent.
1975	45 percent.
1976	43 percent.
1977	42 percent.
1978	41 percent.
1979 or thereafter	40 percent."

—P.L. 94-455, Sec. 1901(a)(84)(B), deleted paras. (c)(2), (c)(3), (c)(4), and (c)(5), redesignated para. (c)(6) as (c)(3) and added new para. (c)(2) following para. (c)(1), effective for tax. yrs. begin. after 12/31/76.

Prior to amendment paras. (c)(2), (c)(3), (c)(4) and (c)(5) read as follows:

"(2) Allocation of pre-1963 reserves. For purposes of this section, the pre-1963 reserves, shall, as of the close of December 31, 1962, be allocated to, and constitute the opening balance of—

"(A) the reserve for losses on nonqualifying loans,

"(B) the reserve for losses on qualifying real property loans, and

"(C) the supplemental reserve for losses on loans.

"(3) Method of allocation. The allocation provided by paragraph (2) shall be made—

"(A) first, to the reserve described in paragraph (2)(A), to the extent such reserve is not increased above the amount which would be a reasonable addition under section 166(c) for a period in which the nonqualifying loans increased from zero to the amount thereof outstanding at the close of December 31, 1962;

"(B) second, to the reserve described in paragraph (2)(B), to the extent such reserve is not increased above the amount which would be determined under paragraph (3)(A) or (4) of subsection (b) (whichever such amount is the larger) for a period in which the qualifying real property loans increased from zero to the amount thereof outstanding at the close of December 31, 1962; and

"(C) then to the supplemental reserve for losses on loans.

"(4) Pre-1963 reserves defined. For purposes of this subsection, the term 'pre-1963 reserves' means the net amount, determined as of the close of December 31, 1962 (after applying subsection (d)(1)), accumulated in the reserve for bad debts pursuant to section 166(c) (or the corresponding provisions of prior revenue laws) for taxable years beginning after December 31, 1951.

"(5) Certain pre-1952 surplus. If after the application of paragraph (3), the opening balance of the reserve described in paragraph (2)(B) is less than the amount described in paragraph (3)(B), then, for purposes of this subsection, the term 'pre-1963 reserves' includes so much of the surplus, undivided profits, and bad debt reserves (determined as of December 31, 1952) attributable to the period before the first taxable year beginning after December 31, 1951, as does not exceed the amount by which such opening balance is less than the amount described in paragraph (3)(B). For purposes of the preceding sentence, the surplus, undivided profits, and bad debt reserves attributable to the period before the first taxable year beginning after December 31, 1951, shall be reduced by the amount thereof which is attributable to interest which would have been excludable from gross income under section 22(b)(4) of the Internal Revenue Code of 1939 (relating to interest on governmental obligations) or the corresponding provisions of prior laws. Notwithstanding the second sentence of paragraph (1), any amount which, by reason of the application of the first sentence of this paragraph, is allocated to the reserve described in paragraph (2)(B) shall not be treated as a reserve for bad debts for any purpose other than determining the amount referred to in subsection (b)(1)(B), and for such purpose such amount shall be treated as remaining in such reserve."

—P.L. 94-455, Sec. 1901(a)(84)(C), deleted subsec. (d) and redesignated subsecs. (e) and (f) as (d) and (e) respectively, effective for tax. yrs. begin. after 12/31/76.

Prior to amendment, subsec. (d) read as follows:

"(d) Taxable years beginning in 1962 and ending in 1963.

"In the case of a taxable year beginning before January 1, 1963, and ending after December 31, 1962, of a taxpayer described in subsection (a) which uses the reserve method of accounting for bad debts, the taxable income shall be the sum of—

"(1) that portion of the taxable income allocable to the part of the taxable year occurring before January 1, 1963, reduced by the amount of the deduction for an addition to a reserve for bad debts which would be allowable under section 166(c) (without regard to the amendments made by section 6 of the Revenue Act of 1962) if such part year constituted a taxable year, plus

"(2) that portion of the taxable income allocable to the part of the taxable year occurring after December 31, 1962, reduced by the amount of the deduction for an addition to a reserve for bad debts which would be allowed under section 166(c) (taking into account the amendments made by section 6 of the Revenue Act of 1962) if such part year constituted a taxable year.

For purposes of the preceding sentence, the taxable income shall be determined without regard to any deduction under section 166(c), and the portion thereof allocable to each part year shall be determined on the basis of the ratio which the number of days in such part year bears to the number of days in the entire taxable year."

—P.L. 94-455, Sec. 1901(a)(84)(D), substituted "subsection (e)" for "subsection (f)" in clause (b)(2)(E)(i), effective for tax. yrs. begin. after 12/31/76.

In **1969**, P.L. 91-172, Sec. 432(a), amended subsec. (b), . . . Sec. 432(b), added the sentence of the end of para. (f)(1), effective for tax. yrs. begin. after 7/11/69. Prior to amendment, subsec. (b) read as follows:

"(b) Addition to reserves for bad debts.

"(1) In general. For purposes of section 166(c), the reasonable addition to the taxable year to the reserve for bad debts of any taxpayer described in subsection (a) shall be an amount equal to the sum of—

"(A) the amount determined under section 166(c) to be a reasonable addition to the reserve for losses on nonqualifying loans, plus

"(B) the amount determined by the taxpayer to be a reasonable addition to the reserve for losses on qualifying real property loans, but such amount shall not exceed the amount determined under paragraph (2), (3), or (4), whichever amount is the largest, but the amount determined under this subparagraph shall in no case be greater than the larger of—

"(i) the amount determined under paragraph (4), or

"(ii) the amount which, when added to the amount determined under subparagraph (A), equals the amount by which 12 percent of the total deposits or withdrawable accounts of depositors of the taxpayer at the close of such year exceeds the sum of its surplus, undivided profits, and reserves at the beginning of such year (taking into account any portion thereof attributable to the period before the first taxable year beginning after December 31, 1951).

"(2) Percentage of taxable income method. The amount determined under this paragraph for the taxable year shall be the excess of—

"(A) an amount equal to 60 percent of the taxable income for such year, over

"(B) the amount referred to in paragraph (1)(A) for such year,

but the amount determined under this paragraph shall not exceed the amount necessary to increase the balance (as of the close of the taxable year) of the reserve for losses on qualifying real property loans to 6 percent of such loans outstanding at such time. For purposes of this paragraph, taxable income shall be computed (i) by excluding from gross income any amount included therein by reason of subsection (f), and (ii) without regard to any deduction allowable for any addition to the reserve for bad debts.

"(3) Percentage of real property loans method. The amount determined under this paragraph for the taxable year shall be an amount equal to the amount necessary to increase the balance (as of the close of the taxable year) of the reserve for losses on amount equal to—

"(A) 3 percent of such loans outstanding at such time, plus

"(B) in the case of a taxpayer which is a new company and which does not have capital stock with respect to which distributions of property (as defined in section 317(a)) are not allowable as a deduction under section 591, an amount equal to—

"(i) 2 percent of so much of the amount of such loans outstanding at such time as does not exceed $4,000,000 reduced (but not below zero) by

"(ii) the amount, if any, of the balance (as of the close of such taxable year) of the taxpayer's supplemental reserve for losses on loans.

"For purposes of subparagraph (B), a taxpayer is a new company for any taxable year only if such taxable year begins not more than 10 years after the first day on which it (or any predecessor) was authorized to do business as an organization described in subsection (a).

"(4) Experience method. The amount determined under this paragraph for the taxable year shall be an amount equal to the amount determined under section 166(c) (without regard to this subsection) to be a reasonable addition to the reserve for losses on qualifying real property loans.

"(5) Limitation in case of certain domestic building and loan associations. If the percentage of the assets of a domestic building and loan association which are not assets described in section 7701(a)(19)(D)(ii) exceeds 36 percent for the taxable year (as determined for purposes of section 7701(a)(19) for such year), the amount determined under paragraph (2), and the amount determined under paragraph (3), shall in each case be the amount (determined without regard to this paragraph but with regard to the limits contained in paragraphs (2), (3), and (1)(B)) reduced by the amount determined under the following table:

"If the percentage exceeds—	but does not exceed—	the reduction shall be the following proportion of the amount so determined without regard to this paragraph—
36 percent	37 percent	½
37 percent	38 percent	⅙
38 percent	39 percent	¼
39 percent	40 percent	⅓
40 percent	41 percent	5/12

In **1962**, P.L. 87-834, amended Code Sec. 593 to read as above, effective for tax. yrs. end. after '62, except that section 593(f) shall apply to distributions after 12/31/62, in tax. yrs. end. after 12/31/62.

Prior to amendment, Code Sec. 593 read as follows:

"SEC. 593. ADDITIONS TO RESERVE FOR BAD DEBTS.

"In the case of a mutual savings bank not having capital stock represented by shares, a domestic building and loan association, and a cooperative bank without capital stock organized and operated for mutual purposes and without profit, the reasonable addition to a reserve for bad debts under section 166(c) shall be determined with due regard to the amount of the taxpayer's surplus or bad debt reserves existing at the close of December 31, 1951.

"In the case of a taxpayer described in the preceding sentence, the reasonable addition to a reserve for bad debts for any taxable year shall in no case be less than the amount determined by the taxpayer as the reasonable addition for such year; except that the amount determined by the taxpayer under this sentence shall not be greater than the lesser of—

"(1) the amount of its taxable income for the taxable year, computed without regard to this section, or

"(2) the amount by which 12 percent of the total deposits or withdrawable accounts of its depositors at the close of such year exceeds the sum of its surplus, undivided profits, and reserves at the beginning of the taxable year."

Sec. 594. Alternative tax for mutual savings banks conducting life insurance business.

(a) Alternative tax.

In the case of a mutual savings bank not having capital stock represented by shares, authorized under State law to engage in the business of issuing life insurance contracts, and which conducts a life insurance business in a separate department the accounts of which are maintained separately from the other accounts of the mutual savings bank, there shall be imposed in lieu of the taxes imposed by section 11 or section 1201(a), a tax consisting of the sum of the partial taxes determined under paragraphs (1) and (2):

(1) A partial tax computed on the taxable income determined without regard to any items of gross income or deductions properly allocable to the business of the life insurance department, at the rates and in the manner as if this section had not been enacted; and

(2) a partial tax computed on the income of the life insurance department determined without regard to any items of gross income or deductions not properly allocable to such department, at the rates and in the manner provided in subchapter L (sec. 801 and following) with respect to life insurance companies.

(b) Limitations of section.

Subsection (a) shall apply only if the life insurance department would, if it were treated as a separate corporation, qualify as a life insurance company under section 816.

In **1984**, P.L. 98-369, Sec. 211(b)(8), substituted "section 816" for "section 801" in subsec. (b), effective for tax. yrs. begin. after 12/31/83.

In **1956**, ch. 83, Sec. 5(3), substituted "the income" for "the taxable income (as defined in section 803)" in para. (a)(2), effective for tax. yrs. begin. after '54.

Sec. 595. Repealed.

In **1996**, P.L. 104-188, Sec. 1616(b)(8), repealed Code Sec. 595, effective for property acquired in tax. yrs. begin. after 12/31/95.

Prior to repeal, Code Sec. 595 read as follows:

"Code Sec. 595. Foreclosure on property securing loans.

"(a) Nonrecognition of gain or loss as a result of foreclosure. In the case of a creditor which is an organization described in section 593(a), no gain or loss shall be recognized, and no debt shall be considered as becoming worthless or partially worthless, as the result of such organization having bid in at foreclosure, or having otherwise reduced to ownership or possession by agreement or process of law, any property which was security for the payment of any indebtedness.

"(b) Character of property. For purposes of sections 166 and 1221, any property acquired in a transaction with respect to which gain or loss to an organization was not recognized by reason of subsection (a) shall be considered as property having the same characteristics as the indebtedness for which such property was security. Any amount realized by such organization with respect to such property shall be treated for purposes of this chapter as a payment on account of such indebtedness, and any loss with respect thereto shall be treated as a bad debt to which the provisions of section 166 (relating to allowance of a deduction for bad debts) apply.

Banking institutions

Code Sec. 597

"(c) Basis. The basis of any property to which subsection (a) applies shall be the basis of the indebtedness for which such property was security (determined as of the date of the acquisition of such property), properly increased for costs of acquisition.

"(d) Regulatory authority. The Secretary shall prescribe such regulations as he may deem necessary to carry out the purposes of this section."

In 1976, P.L. 94-455, Sec. 1906(b)(13)(A), substituted "Secretary" for "Secretary or his delegate" in subsec. (d), effective for tax. yrs. begin. after 12/31/76.

In 1962, P.L. 87-834, Sec. 6(b), added Code Sec. 595, effective for transactions described in Code Sec. 595(a) occurring after 12/31/62, in tax. yrs. end after 12/31/62.

Sec. 596. Repealed.

In 1996, P.L. 104-188, Sec. 1616(b)(9), repealed Code Sec. 596, effective for tax. yrs. begin. after 12/31/95.

Prior to repeal, Code Sec. 596 read as follows:

"Sec. 596 Limitation on dividends received deduction.

"In the case of an organization to which section 593 applies and which computes additions to the reserve for losses on loans for the taxable year under section 593(b)(2), the total amount allowed under sections 243, 244, and 245 (determined without regard to this section) for the taxable year as a deduction with respect to dividends received shall be reduced by an amount equal to 8 percent of such total amount."

In 1986, P.L. 99-514, Sec. 901(d)(4)(D), substituted "an amount equal to 8 percent of such total amount." for "an amount equal to the applicable percentage for such year (determined under subparagraphs (A) and (B) of section 593(b)(2)) of such total amount." in Code Sec. 596, effective for tax. yrs. begin. after 12/31/86.

In 1969, P.L. 91-172, Sec. 434(a), added Code Sec. 596, effective for tax. yrs. begin. after 7/11/69.

Sec. 597. Treatment of transactions in which federal financial assistance provided.

(a) General rule

The treatment for purposes of this chapter of any transaction in which Federal financial assistance is provided with respect to a bank or domestic building and loan association shall be determined under regulations prescribed by the Secretary.

(b) Principles used in prescribing regulations.

(1) Treatment of taxable asset acquisitions. In the case of any acquisition of assets to which section 381(a) does not apply, the regulations prescribed under subsection (a) shall—

(A) provide that Federal financial assistance shall be properly taken into account by the institution from which the assets were acquired, and

(B) provide the proper method of allocating basis among the assets so acquired (including rights to receive Federal financial assistance).

(2) Other transactions. In the case of any transaction not described in paragraph (1), the regulations prescribed under subsection (a) shall provide for the proper treatment of Federal financial assistance and appropriate adjustments to basis or other tax attributes in connection with such assistance.

(3) Denial of double benefit. No regulations prescribed under this section shall permit the utilization of any deduction (or other tax benefit) if such amount was in effect reimbursed by nontaxable Federal financial assistance.

(c) Federal financial assistance.

For purposes of this section, the term "Federal financial assistance" means—

(1) any money or other property provided with respect to a domestic building and loan association by the Federal Savings and Loan Insurance Corporation or the Resolution Trust Corporation pursuant to section 406(f) of the National Housing Act or section 21A of the Federal Home Loan Bank Act (or under any other similar provision of law), and

(2) any money or other property provided with respect to a bank or domestic building and loan association by the Federal Deposit Insurance Corporation pursuant to section 11(f) or 13(c) of the Federal Deposit Insurance Act (or under any other similar provision of law),

regardless of whether any note or other instrument is issued in exchange therefor.

(d) Domestic building and loan association.

For purposes of this section, the term "domestic building and loan association" has the meaning given such term by section 7701(a)(19) without regard to subparagraph (C) thereof.

In 1990, P.L. 101-508, Sec. 11704(a)(7), substituted "For purposes of" for "The purposes of" in subsec. (c), effective 11/5/90.

In 1989, P.L. 101-239, Sec. 7841(e)(1), substituted "in connection with such assistance" for "to reflect such treatment" in para. (b)(2), effective as provided in Secs. 1401(c)(3) and (c)(7) of P.L. 101-73, reproduced below.

—P.L. 101-73, Sec. 1401(a)(3)(A), amended Code Sec. 597, effective as provided in Sec. 1401(c)(3) and (c)(7) of this Act:

"(3) Subsection (a)(3). [Sec. 1401(a)(3)]

"(A) In general.— The amendments made by subsection (a)(3) [Sec. 1401(a)(3)] shall apply to any amount received or accrued by the financial institution on or after May 10, 1989, except that such amendments shall not apply to transfers on or after such date pursuant to an acquisition to which the amendment made by subsection (a)(1) does not apply.

"(B) Interim rule.— In the case of any payment pursuant to a transaction on or after May 10, 1989, and before the date on which the Secretary of the Treasury (or his delegate) takes action in exercise of his regulatory authority under section 597 of the Internal Revenue Code of 1986 (as amended by subsection (a)(3)), [Sec. 1401(a)(3)] the taxpayer may rely on the legislative history for the amendments made by subsection (a)(3) [Sec. 1401(a)(3)] in determining the proper treatment of such payment."

* * *

"(7) Clarification of prior law.— Any reference to the Federal Savings and Loan Insurance Corporation in section 597 of the Internal Revenue Code of 1986 (as in effect on the day before the date of the enactment of this Act) shall be treated as including a reference to the Resolution Trust Corporation and the FSLIC Resolution Fund."

Prior to amendment, Code Sec. 597 read as follows:

"SEC. 597. FSLIC OR FDIC FINANCIAL ASSISTANCE.

"(a) Exclusion from gross income.

"Gross income of a domestic building and loan association does not include any amount of money or other property received from the Federal Savings and Loan Insurance Corporation pursuant to section 406(f) of the National Housing Act (12 U.S.C. sec. 1729(f)), regardless of whether any note or other instrument is issued in exchange therefor. Gross income of bank does not include any amount of money or other property received from the Federal Deposit Insurance Corporation pursuant to sections 13(c), 15(c)(1), and 15(c)(2) of the Federal Deposit Insurance Act (12 U.S.C. 1821(f) and 1823(c)(1) and (c)(2)), regardless of whether any note or other instrument is issued in exchange therefor.

"(b) No reduction in basis of assets.

"No reduction in the basis of assets of a domestic building and loan association or bank shall be made on account of money or other property received under the circumstances referred to in subsection (a).

"(c) Reduction of tax attributes by 50 percent of amounts excludable under subsection (a).

"(1) In general. 50 percent of any amount excludable under subsection (a) for any taxable year shall be applied to reduce the tax attributes of the taxpayer as provided in paragraph (2).

"(2) Tax attributes reduced; order of reduction. The reduction referred to in paragraph (1) shall be made in the following tax attributes in the following order.—

"(A) Nol. Any pre-assistance net operating loss for the taxable year.

"(B) Interest. The amount of any interest with respect to which a deduction is allowable for the taxable year.

"(C) Built-in portfolio losses. Recognized build-in portfolio losses for the taxable year.

"(3) Pre-assistance net operating loss. For purposes of paragraph (2)(A)—

"(A) In general. The pre-assistance net operating loss shall be determined in the same manner as a pre-change loss under section 382(d), except that—

"(i) the applicable financial institution shall be treated as the old loss corporation, and

"(ii) the determination date shall be substituted for the change date.

"(B) Ordering rule. The reduction under paragraph (2)(A) shall be made in the carryovers in the order in which carryovers are taken into account under this chapter for the taxable year.

"(4) Recognized built-in portfolio losses. For purposes of paragraph (2)(C) recognized built-in portfolio losses shall be determined in the same manner as recognized built-in losses under section 382(h), except that—

"(A) the only assets taken into account shall be—

"(i) the loan portfolio,

"(ii) marketable securities (within the meaning of section 453(f)(2)), and

"(iii) property described in section 595(a),

"(B) the rules of clauses (i) and (ii) of paragraph (3)(A) shall apply,

"(C) there shall be no limit on the number of years in the recognition period, and

"(D) section 382(h) shall be applied without regard to paragraph (3)(B) thereof.

Code Sec. 597 — Banking institutions

"(5) Definitions and special rules. For purposes of this subsection—

"(A) Applicable financial institution. The term 'applicable financial institution' means the domestic building and loan association or bank the financial condition of which was determined by the Federal Savings and Loan Insurance Corporation or the Federal Deposit Insurance Corporation to require the financial assistance described in subsection (a).

"(B) Determination date. The term 'determination date' means the date of the determination under subparagraph (A). Except as provided by the Secretary, any subsequent revision or modification of such determination shall be treated as made on the original determination date.

"(C) Taxable asset acquisitions.

"(i) In general. In the case of any acquisition of the assets of any applicable financial institution to which section 381 does not apply—

"(I) paragraph (1) shall not apply to any amounts excludable under subsection (a) which are payments made at the time of the acquisition to the person acquiring such assets, and

"(II) rights to receive future payments excludable under subsection (a) in connection with the acquisition shall be treated as provided in clause (ii).

"(ii) Treatment of future payments.

"(I) In general. Rights to receive future payments described in clause (i)(II) shall be treated as assets to which basis is allocated.

"(II) Recovery of basis. Any basis allocated under subclause (I) shall be recovered in such manner as the Secretary may provide, but in no event shall the amount recovered for any taxable year beginning before the taxable year in which the rights expire exceed the aggregate payments received with respect to such rights for all taxable years reduced by the amount of basis recovered with respect to such rights in preceding taxable years.

"(III) Application of paragraph (1). Paragraph (1) shall apply to payments described in subclause (I) in a taxable year only to the extent such payments exceed the amount of basis recovered in such taxable year.

"(D) Treatment of repayments. If a taxpayer repays an amount to which paragraph (1) applied in a preceding taxable year, there shall be allowed as a deduction for the taxable year of repayment an amount equal to the reduction in tax attributes under paragraph (1) attributable to the amount repaid.

"(E) Carryovers. If 50 percent of the amount excludable under subsection (a) for any taxable year exceeds the amount of the tax attributes described in paragraph (2) for such taxable year, then, for purposes of this subsection, the amount excludable under subsection (a) for the succeeding taxable year shall be increased by an amount equal to twice the amount of such excess.

"(F) Regulations. The Secretary shall prescribe such regulations as may be necessary to carry out the provisions of this subsection.

"(d) Domestic building and loan association.

"For purposes of this section, the term 'domestic building and loan association' has the meaning given such term by section 7701(a)(19) without regard to subparagraph (C) thereof."

—P.L. 101-73, Sec. 1401(a)(3)(B), repealed Sec. 904(c)(2)(B) of P.L. 99-514, part of the effective date for amendments made by Sec. 904(b)(1) of P.L. 99-514, effective as provided in Sec. 1401(c)(3) of this Act reproduced above.

Prior to repeal Sec. 904(c)(2)(B) of P.L. 99-514 [as amended by Sec. 4012(c)(2) of P.L. 100-647, see below] read as follows:

"(B) Clarification of treatment of amounts excluded under section 597.—Section 265 of the Internal Revenue Code of 1986 (as amended by this title [Title IX]) shall not deny any deduction by reason of such deduction being allocable to amounts excluded from gross income under section 597 of the Internal Revenue Code of 1954 (as in effect on the day before the date of the enactment of this Act [10/22/86])."

—P.L. 101-73, Sec. 1401(b)(1), repealed as if not enacted Sec. 904 of P.L. 99-514 (except Sec. 904(c)(2)(B) of P.L. 99-514, see above] of P.L. 99-514, see Sec. 1401(a)(3)(B) of P.L. 101-73, above], effective 10/22/86, see below.

—P.L. 101-73, Sec. 1401(b)(2), amended the last sentence of Sec. 4012(c)(3) [reproduced below] of P.L. 100-647, part of the effective date for amendments made by Sec. 4012(c)(1) of P.L. 100-647, effective 11/10/88.

Prior to amendment the last sentence of Sec. 4012(c)(3) of P.L. 100-647 read as follows:

"In the case of a taxpayer to which the amendments made by subsection (b)(1) apply, subparagraphs (A) and (B) shall be applied by substituting 'the date of the enactment of this Act' for 'December 31, 1988'."

In 1988, P.L. 100-647, Sec. 4012(a)(2), amended Sec. 904(c)(2)(A) [repealed as if not enacted by Sec. 1401(b)(1) of P.L. 101-73, see above] of P.L. 99-514 part of the effective date for changes made by Sec. 904(b)(1) of Sec. 99-514 [repealed as if not enacted by Sec. 1401(b)(1) of P.L. 101-73, see above]

—P.L. 100-647, Sec. 4012(b)(2)(A), added the sentence at the end of subsec. (a) . . . Sec. 4012(b)(2)(B), added subsec. (d) . . . Sec. 4012(b)(2)(C), added "or bank" after "association" in subsec. (b) . . . Sec. 4012(b)(2)(D)(i), added "or FDIC" after "FSLIC" in the heading of Code Sec. 597 effective as provided in Sec. 4012(b)(2)(E) of this Act:

"(E) The amendments made by this paragraph shall apply to any transfer—

"(i) after the date of the enactment of this Act, and before January 1, 1990, unless such transfer is pursuant to an acquisition occurring on or before such date of enactment, or

"(ii) after December 31, 1989, if such transfer is pursuant to an acquisition occurring after such date of enactment and before January 1, 1990."

—P.L. 100-467, Sec. 4012(c)(1), added subsec. (c), effective as provided in Sec. 4012(c)(3) [as amended by Sec. 1401(b)(2) of P.L. 101-73, see above] of this Act:

"(3) Effective date.—The amendments made by this subsection shall apply to any transfer—

"(A) after December 31, 1988, and before January 1, 1990, unless such transfer is pursuant to an acquisition occurring before January 1, 1989, and

"(B) after December 31, 1989, if such transfer is pursuant to an acquisition occurring after December 31, 1988, and before January 1, 1990.

In the case of any bank or any institution treated as a domestic building and loan association for purposes of section 597 of the 1986 Code by reason of the amendment made by subsection (b)(2)(B) [Sec. 4012], the amendments made by this subsection shall also apply to any transfer before January 1, 1989, to which the amendments made by subsection (b)(2) [Sec. 4012] apply."

—P.L. 100-647, Sec. 4012(c)(2), amended Sec. 904(c)(2)(B) of P.L. 99-514, [repealed by Sec. 1401(a)(3)(B) of P.L. 101-73, see above] part of the effective date of Code Sec. 597, by substituting "265" for "265(a)(1)".

In 1986, P.L. 99-514, Sec. 904(b)(1), repealed Code Sec. 597 effective as provided in Sec. 904(c)(2)(A) [repealed as if not enacted by Sec. 1401(b)(1) of P.L. 101-73, see above]

—P.L. 99-514, Sec. 904(c)(2)(B), dealing with Clarification of treatment of amounts excluded under Code Sec. 597 [as amended by Sec. 4012(c)(2) of P.L. 100-647, see above] is repealed by Sec. 1401(a)(3)(B) of P.L. 101-73, see above.

In 1981, P.L. 97-34, Sec. 244(a), added Code Sec. 597, effective for any payment made on or after 1/1/81.

PART III. Repealed

Sec.
601. Repealed.

In 1976, P.L. 94-455, Sec. 1901(a)(85), repealed Part III of subchapter H of chapter 1, effective for tax. yrs. begin. after '76.
Prior to repeal Part III read as follows:
"Part III. BANK AFFILIATES
Sec.
601. Special deduction for bank affiliates.
"SEC. 601. SPECIAL DEDUCTION FOR BANK AFFILIATES.
"In the case of a holding company affiliate (as defined in section 2 of the Banking Act of 1933; 12 U.S.C. 221a(c)), there shall be allowed as a deduction, for purposes of section 535(b)(8) (relating to the computation of accumulated taxable income) and section 545(b)(6) (relating to the computation of undistributed personal holding company income), the amount of the earnings and profits which the Board of Governors of the Federal Reserve System certifies to the Secretary or to his delegate has been devoted by such affiliate during the taxable year to the acquisition of readily marketable assets other than bank stock in compliance with section 5144 of the Revised Statutes (12 U.S.C. 61). The amount of the deduction under this section for any taxable year shall not exceed the taxable income for such year computed without regard to the special deductions for corporations provided in part VIII (except section 248) of subchapter B (section 241 and following, relating to the deduction for dividends received by corporations, etc.). The aggregate of the deductions allowable under this section and the credits allowable under the corresponding provision of any prior income tax law for all taxable years shall not exceed the amount required to be devoted under such section 5144 to such purposes."

Sec. 601. Repealed.

In 1976, P.L. 94-455, Sec. 1901(a)(85), repealed Code Sec. 601, effective for tax. yrs. begin. after 12/31/76.
Prior to repeal, Code Sec. 601 read as follows:
"Sec. 601. Special deduction for bank affiliates.
"In the case of a holding company affiliate (as defined in section 2 of the Banking Act of 1933; (12 U.S.C. 221a(c)), there shall be allowed as a deduction, for purposes of section 535(b)(8) (relating to the computation of accumulated taxable income) and section 545(b)(6) (relating to the computation of undistributed personal holding company income), the amount of the earnings and profits which the Board of Governors of the Federal Reserve System certifies to the Secretary or to his delegate has been devoted by such affiliate during the taxable year to the acquisition of readily marketable assets other than bank stock in compliance with section 5144 of the Revised Statutes (12 U.S.C. 61). The amount of the deduction under this section for any taxable year shall not exceed the taxable income for such year computed without regard to the special deductions for corporations provided in part VIII (except section 248) of subchapter B (section 241 and following, relating to the deduction for dividends received by corporations, etc.). The aggregate of the deductions allowable under this section and the credits allowable under the corresponding provision of any prior income tax law for all taxable years shall not exceed the amount required to be devoted under such section 5144 to such purposes."

Subchapter I.— Natural Resources

Part
   I. Deductions.
   II. Repealed.
   III. Sales and exchanges.
   IV. Mineral production payments.

Natural resources

V. Continental shelf areas.

In 1990, P.L. 101-508, Sec. 11801(b)(7), deleted the item for Part II. Prior to deletion, the item for Part II read as follows:
"II. Exclusions from gross income."
In 1969, P.L. 91-172, Sec. 503(b), added part IV.
—P.L. 91-172, Sec. 505(c), added part V.

PART I.—DEDUCTIONS

Sec.
611. Allowance of deduction for depletion.
612. Basis for cost depletion.
613. Percentage depletion.
[613A. Limitations on percentage depletion in case of oil and gas wells.]
614. Definition of property.
615. Repealed. [Pre-1970 exploration expenditures.]
616. Development expenditures.
617. Deduction and recapture of certain mining exploration expenditures.

In 1976, P.L. 94-455, Sec. 1901(b)(21)(H), repealed item 615. Prior to repeal, item 615 read as follows:
"Pre-1970 exploration expenditures."
In 1975, P.L. 94-12, Sec. 501(a), added Code Sec. 613A. The Act did not add item 613A to the list of Code Secs. for Part I above, but Congress presumably intended to do so.
In 1969, P.L. 91-172, Sec. 504(c), added "Pre-1970" to item 615 and substituted "Deduction and recapture of certain mining exploration expenditures." for "Additional exploration expenditures in the case of domestic mining." in item 617.
In 1966, P.L. 89-570, Sec. [1](d), added item 617.

Sec. 611. Allowance of deduction for depletion.
(a) General rule.

In the case of mines, oil and gas wells, other natural deposits, and timber, there shall be allowed as a deduction in computing taxable income a reasonable allowance for depletion and for depreciation of improvements, according to the peculiar conditions in each case; such reasonable allowance in all cases to be made under regulations prescribed by the Secretary. For purposes of this part, the term "mines" includes deposits of waste or residue, the extraction of ores or minerals from which is treated as mining under section 613(c). In any case in which it is ascertained as a result of operations or of development work that the recoverable units are greater or less than the prior estimate thereof, then such prior estimate (but not the basis for depletion) shall be revised and the allowance under this section for subsequent taxable years shall be based on such revised estimate.

(b) Special rules.
(1) **Leases.** In the case of a lease, the deduction under this section shall be equitably apportioned between the lessor and lessee.
(2) **Life tenant and remainderman.** In the case of property held by one person for life with remainder to another person, the deduction under this section shall be computed as if the life tenant were the absolute owner of the property and shall be allowed to the life tenant.
(3) **Property held in trust.** In the case of property held in trust, the deduction under this section shall be apportioned between the income beneficiaries and the trustee in accordance with the pertinent provisions of the instrument creating the trust, or, in the absence of such provisions, on the basis of the trust income allocable to each.
(4) **Property held by estate.** In the case of an estate, the deduction under this section shall be apportioned between the estate and the heirs, legatees, and devisees on the basis of the income of the estate allocable to each.

(c) Cross reference.
For other rules applicable to depreciation of improvements, see section 167.

In 1976, P.L. 94-455, Sec. 1906(b)(13)(A), substituted "Secretary" for "Secretary or his delegate" in Code Sec. 611, effective for tax. yrs. begin. after 12/31/76.
In 1958, P.L. 85-866, Sec. 35, substituted "devisees" for "devises" in para. (d)(4), effective for tax. yrs. begin after 12/31/53, and end. after 8/16/54.

Sec. 612. Basis for cost depletion.
Except as otherwise provided in this subchapter, the basis on which depletion is to be allowed in respect of any property shall be the adjusted basis provided in section 1011 for the purpose of determining the gain upon the sale or other disposition of such property.

Sec. 613. Percentage depletion.
(a) General rule.

In the case of the mines, wells, and other natural deposits listed in subsection (b), the allowance for depletion under section 611 shall be the percentage, specified in subsection (b), of the gross income from the property excluding from such gross income an amount equal to any rents or royalties paid or incurred by the taxpayer in respect of the property. Such allowance shall not exceed 50 percent (100 percent in the case of oil and gas properties) of the taxpayer's taxable income from the property (computed without allowances for depletion and without the deduction under section 199). For purposes of the preceding sentence, the allowable deductions taken into account with respect to expenses of mining in computing the taxable income from the property shall be decreased by an amount equal to so much of any gain which (1) is treated under section 1245 (relating to gain from disposition of certain depreciable property) as ordinary income, and (2) is properly allocable to the property. In no case shall the allowance for depletion under section 611 be less than it would be if computed without reference to this section.

(b) Percentage depletion rates.
The mines, wells, and other natural deposits, and the percentages, referred to in subsection (a) are as follows:
(1) **22 percent.**
  (A) sulphur and uranium; and
  (B) if from deposits in the United States—anorthosite, clay, laterite, and nephelite syenite (to the extent that alumina and aluminum compounds are extracted therefrom), asbestos, bauxite, celestite, chromite, corundum, fluorspar, graphite, ilmenite, kyanite, mica, olivine, quartz crystals (radio grade), rutile, block steatite talc, and zircon, and ores of the following metals: antimony, beryllium, bismuth, cadmium, cobalt, columbium, lead, lithium, manganese, mercury, molybdenum, nickel, platinum and platinum group metals, tantalum, thorium, tin, titanium, tungsten, vanadium, and zinc.
(2) **15 percent.** If from deposits in the United States—
  (A) gold, silver, copper, and iron ore, and
  (B) oil shale (except shale described in paragraph (5)).
(3) **14 percent.**
  (A) metal mines (if paragraph (1)(B) or (2)(A) does not apply), rock asphalt, and vermiculite; and
  (B) if paragraph (1)(B), (5), or (6)(B) does not apply, ball clay, bentonite, china clay, sagger clay, and clay used or sold for use for purposes dependent on its refractory properties.
(4) **10 percent.** Asbestos (if paragraph (1)(B) does not apply), brucite, coal, lignite, perlite, sodium chloride, and wollastonite.
(5) **7½ percent.** Clay and shale used or sold for use in the manufacture of sewer pipe or brick, and clay, shale, and

slate used or sold for use as sintered or burned lightweight aggregates.

(6) 5 percent.
  (A) gravel, peat, pumice, sand, scoria, shale (except shale described in paragraph (2)(B) or (5)), and stone (except stone described in paragraph (7));
  (B) clay used, or sold for use, in the manufacture of drainage and roofing tile, flower pots, and kindred products; and
  (C) if from brine wells—bromine, calcium chloride, and magnesium chloride.

(7) 14 percent. All other minerals, including, but not limited to, aplite, barite, borax, calcium carbonates, diatomaceous earth, dolomite, feldspar, fullers earth, garnet, gilsonite, granite, limestone, magnesite, magnesium carbonates, marble, mollusk shells (including clam shells and oyster shells), phosphate rock, potash, quartzite, slate, soapstone, stone (used or sold for use by the mine owner or operator as dimension stone or ornamental stone), thenardite, tripoli, trona, and (if paragraph (1)(B) does not apply) bauxite, flake graphite, fluorspar, lepidolite, mica, spodumene, and talc (including pyrophyllite), except that, unless sold on bid in direct competition with a bona fide bid to sell a mineral listed in paragraph (3), the percentage shall be 5 percent for any such other mineral (other than slate to which paragraph (5) applies) when used, or sold for use, by the mine owner or operator as rip rap, ballast, road material, rubble, concrete aggregates, or for similar purposes. For purposes of this paragraph, the term "all other minerals" does not include—
  (A) soil, sod, dirt, turf, water, or mosses;
  (B) minerals from sea water, the air, or similar inexhaustible sources; or
  (C) oil and gas wells.

For the purposes of this subsection, minerals (other than sodium chloride) extracted from brines pumped from a saline perennial lake within the United States shall not be considered minerals from an inexhaustible source.

(c) Definition of gross income from property.

For purposes of this section—

(1) Gross income from the property. The term "gross income from the property" means, in the case of a property other than an oil or gas well and other than a geothermal deposit, the gross income from mining.

(2) Mining. The term "mining" includes not merely the extraction of the ores or minerals from the ground but also the treatment processes considered as mining described in paragraph (4) (and the treatment processes necessary or incidental thereto), and so much of the transportation of ores or minerals (whether or not by common carrier) from the point of extraction from the ground to the plants or mills in which such treatment processes are applied thereto as is not in excess of 50 miles unless the Secretary finds that the physical and other requirements are such that the ore or mineral must be transported a greater distance to such plants or mills.

(3) Extraction of the ores or minerals from the ground. The term "extraction of the ores or minerals from the ground" includes the extraction by mine owners or operators of ores or minerals from the waste or residue of prior mining. The preceding sentence shall not apply to any such extraction of the mineral or ore by a purchaser of such waste or residue or of the rights to extract ores or minerals therefrom.

(4) Treatment processes considered as mining. The following treatment processes where applied by the mine owner or operator shall be considered as mining to the extent they are applied to the ore or mineral in respect of which he is entitled to a deduction for depletion under section 611:
  (A) In the case of coal—cleaning, breaking, sizing, dust allaying, treating to prevent freezing, and loading for shipment;
  (B) in the case of sulfur recovered by the Frasch process—cleaning, pumping to vats, cooling, breaking, and loading for shipment;
  (C) in the case of iron ore, bauxite, ball and sagger clay, rock asphalt, and ores or minerals which are customarily sold in the form of a crude mineral product—sorting, concentrating, sintering, and substantially equivalent processes to bring to shipping grade and form, and loading for shipment;
  (D) in the case of lead, zinc, copper, gold, silver, uranium, or fluorspar ores, potash, and ores or minerals which are not customarily sold in the form of the crude mineral product—crushing, grinding, and beneficiation by concentration (gravity, flotation, amalgamation, electrostatic, or magnetic), cyanidation, leaching, crystallization, precipitation (but not including electrolytic deposition, roasting, thermal or electric smelting, or refining), or by substantially equivalent processes or combination of processes used in the separation or extraction of the product or products from the ore or the mineral or minerals from other material from the mine or other natural deposit;
  (E) the pulverization of talc, the burning of magnesite, the sintering and nodulizing of phosphate rock, the decarbonation of trona, and the furnacing of quicksilver ores;
  (F) in the case of calcium carbonates and other minerals when used in making cement—all processes (other than preheating of the kiln feed) applied prior to the introduction of the kiln feed into the kiln, but not including any subsequent process;
  (G) in the case of clay to which paragraph (5) or (6)(B) of subsection (b) applies—crushing, grinding, and separating the mineral from waste, but not including any subsequent process;
  (H) in the case of oil shale—extraction from the ground, crushing, loading into the retort, and retorting (including in situ retorting), but not hydrogenation, refining, or any other process subsequent to retorting; and
  (I) any other treatment process provided for by regulations prescribed by the Secretary which, with respect to the particular ore or mineral, is not inconsistent with the preceding provisions of this paragraph.

(5) Treatment processes not considered as mining. Unless such processes are otherwise provided for in paragraph (4) (or are necessary or incidental to processes so provided for), the following treatment processes shall not be considered as "mining": electrolytic deposition, roasting, calcining, thermal or electric smelting, refining, polishing, fine pulverization, blending with other materials, treatment effecting a chemical change, thermal action, and molding or shaping.

(d) Denial of percentage depletion in case of oil and gas wells.

Except as provided in section 613A, in the case of any oil or gas well, the allowance for depletion shall be computed without reference to this section.

(e) Percentage depletion for geothermal deposits.

(1) In general. In the case of geothermal deposits located in the United States or in a possession of the United States, for purposes of subsection (a)—

Natural resources   **Code Sec. 613**

(A) such deposits shall be treated as listed in subsection (b), and

(B) 15 percent shall be deemed to be the percentage specified in subsection (b).

(2) Geothermal deposit defined. For purposes of paragraph (1), the term "geothermal deposit" means a geothermal reservoir consisting of natural heat which is stored in rocks or in an aqueous liquid or vapor (whether or not under pressure). Such a deposit shall in no case be treated as a gas well for purposes of this section or section 613A, and this section shall not apply to a geothermal deposit which is located outside the United States or its possessions.

(3) Percentage depletion not to include lease bonuses, etc. In the case of any geothermal deposit, the term "gross income from the property" shall, for purposes of this section, not include any amount described in section 613A(d)(5).

In 2005, P.L. 109-135, Sec. 403(a)(19), amended Sec. 102(e) of P.L. 108-357 [see below].
Prior to amendment, Sec. 102(e) of P.L. 108-357 [see below] read as follows:
"*(e) Effective date.* The amendments made by this section shall apply to taxable years beginning after December 31, 2004."
—P.L. 109-135, Sec. 412(gg), added "(including in situ retorting)" after "and retorting" in subpara. (c)(4)(H), effective 12/21/2005.
In 2004, P.L. 108-357, Sec. 102(d)(6), added "and without the deduction under section 199" after "without allowance for depletion" in subsec. (a), effective as provided by Sec. 102(e) of this Act [as amended by Sec. 403(a)(19) of P.L. 109-135, see above], which reads as follows:
"*(e) Effective date.*
"(1) The amendments made by this section shall apply to taxable years beginning after December 31, 2004.
"(2) Application to pass-thru entities, etc. In determining the deduction under section 199 of the Internal Revenue Code of 1986 (as added by this section), items arising from a taxable year of a partnership, S corporation, estate, or trust beginning before January 1, 2005, shall not be taken into account for purposes of subsection (d)(1) of such section."
In 1996, P.L. 104-188, Sec. 1704(t)(34), substituted a period for the comma at the end of subpara. (e)(1)(B), effective 8/20/96.
In 1990, P.L. 101-508, Sec. 11522(a), added "(100 percent in the case of oil and gas properties)" after "50 percent" in the second sentence of subsec. (a), effective for tax. yrs. begin. after 12/31/90.
—P.L. 101-508, Sec. 11815(b)(1), deleted para. (e)(2) and redesignated paras. (e)(3) and (e)(4) as paras. (e)(2) and (e)(3) . . . Sec. 11815(b)(2), amended subpara. (e)(1)(B), effective 11/5/90 except as provided in Sec. 11821(b) of this Act, which reads as follows:
"(b) Savings provision. If—
"(1) any provision amended or repealed by this part applied to—
"(A) any transaction occurring before the date of the enactment of this Act [11/5/90],
"(B) any property acquired before such date of enactment [11/5/90], or
"(C) any item of income, loss, deduction, or credit taken into account before such date of enactment [11/5/90], and
"(2) the treatment of such transaction, property, or item under such provision would (without regard to the amendments made by this part) affect liability for tax for periods ending after such date of enactment [11/5/90],
nothing in the amendment by this part shall be construed to affect the treatment of such transaction, property, or item for purposes of determining liability for tax for periods ending after such date of enactment [11/5/90]."
Prior to deletion, para. (e)(2) read as follows:
"(2) Applicable percentage. For purposes of paragraph (1)—

In the case of taxable years beginning in calendar year—	The applicable percentage is—
1978, 1979, or 1980	22
1981	20
1982	18
1983	16
1984 and thereafter	15".

Prior to amendment, subpara. (e)(1)(B) read as follows:
"(B) the applicable percentage (determined under the table contained in paragraph (2) shall be deemed to be the percentage specified in subsection (b)."
In 1986, P.L. 99-514, Sec. 412(a)(2), added para. (d)(4), effective for amounts received or accrued after 8/16/86, in tax. yrs. end. after 8/16/86.
In 1978, P.L. 95-618, Sec. 403(a)(1), added subsec. (e) . . . Sec. 403(a)(2)(A), added "and other than a geothermal deposit" after "oil or gas well" in para. (c)(1), effective 10/1/78 for tax. yrs. end. on or after 10/1/78.
In 1976, P.L. 94-455, Sec. 1901(b)(3)(K), substituted "ordinary income" for "gain from the sale or exchange of property which is neither a capital asset nor property described in section 1231" in subsec. (a), effective for tax. yrs. begin. after 12/31/76.
—P.L. 94-455, Sec. 1906(b)(13)(A), substituted "Secretary" for "Secretary or his delegate" in paras. (c)(2) and (c)(5), for tax. yrs. begin. after '76.
In 1975, P.L. 94-12, Sec. 501(b)(2), deleted subpara. (b)(1)(A) and redesignated subparas. (b)(1)(B) and (b)(1)(C) as (b)(1)(A) and (b)(1)(B), substituted "(1)(B)" for "(1)(C)" each place it appeared in paras. (b)(3), (b)(4), and (b)(7), deleted "or" at the end of subpara. (b)(7)(A), substituted "; or" for the period at the end of subpara. (b)(7)(B), and added new subpara. (b)(7)(C), effective 1/1/75 for tax. yrs. end. after 12/31/74.
Prior to deletion, subpara. (b)(1)(A) read as follows:
"(A) oil and gas wells;"
—P.L. 94-12, Sec. 501(b)(1), amended subsec. (d), effective 1/1/75 for tax. yrs. end. after 12/31/74.
Prior to amendment, subsec. (d) read as follows:
"(d) Application of percentage depletion rates to certain taxable years ending in 1954.
"(1) General rule. At the election of the taxpayer in respect of any property (within the meaning of the Internal Revenue Code of 1939), the percentage specified in subsection (b) in the case of any mine, well, or other natural deposit listed in such subsection shall apply to a taxable year ending after December 31, 1953, to which the Internal Revenue Code of 1939 applies.
"(2) Method of computation. The allowance for depletion, in respect of any property for which an election is made under paragraph (1) for any taxable year, shall be an amount equal to the sum of—
"(A) that portion of a tentative allowance, computed under the Internal Revenue Code of 1939 without regard to paragraph (1) of this subsection, which the number of days in such taxable year before January 1, 1954, bears to the total number of days in such taxable year; plus
"(B) that portion of a tentative allowance, computed under the Internal Revenue Code of 1939 (as modified solely by the application of paragraph (1) of this subsection), which the number of days in such taxable year after December 31, 1953, bears to the total number of days in such taxable year."
In 1974, P.L. 93-499, Sec. 2(a), added "the decarbonation of trona," after "phosphate rock," in subpara. (c)(4)(E), effective with respect to tax. yrs. begin. after 12/31/70.
In 1969, P.L. 91-172, Sec. 501(a), amended subsec. (b), effective for tax. yrs. begin. after 10/9/69.
Prior to amendment, subsec. (b) read as follows:
"(b) Percentage depletion rates.
The mines, wells, and other natural deposits, and the percentages, referred to in subsection (a) are as follows:
"(1) 27½ percent— oil and gas wells.
"(2) 23 percent—
"(A) sulfur and uranium; and
"(B) if from deposits in the United States— anorthosite clay, laterite, and nepheline syenite (to the extent that alumina and aluminum compounds are extracted therefrom), asbestos, bauxite, celestite, chromite corundum, fluorspar, graphite, ilmenite, kyanite, mica, olivine, quartz crystals (radio grade), rutile, block steatite talc, and zircon, and ores of the following metals; antimony, beryllium, bismuth, cadmium, cobalt, columbium, lead, lithium, manganese, mercury, nickel, platinum and platinum group metals, tantalum, thorium, tin, titanium, tungsten, vanadium, and zinc.
"(3) 15 percent—
"(A) metal mines (if paragraph (2)(B) does not apply), rock asphalt, and vermiculite; and
"(B) If neither paragraph (2)(B), (5), or 6(B) applies, ball clay, bentonite, china clay, sagger clay, and clay used or sold for use for purposes dependent on its refractory properties.
"(4) 10 percent— asbestos (if paragraph (2)(B) does not apply), brucite, coal, lignite, perlite, sodium chloride, and wollastonite.
"(5) 7½ percent— clay and shale used or sold for use in the manufacture of sewer pipe or brick, and clay, shale, and slate used or sold for use as sintered or burned lightweight aggregates.
"(6) 5 percent—
"(A) gravel, peat, pumice, sand, scoria, shale (except shale described in paragraph (5)), and stone (except stone described in paragraph (7));
"(B) clay used, or sold for use, in the manufacture of drainage and roofing tile, flower pots, and kindred products; and
"(C) if from brine wells— bromine, calcium chloride, and magnesium chloride.
"(7) 15 percent— all other minerals (including, but not limited to, aplite, barite, borax, calcium carbonates, diatomaceous earth, dolomite, feldspar, fullers earth, garnet, gilsonite, granite, limestone, magnesite, magnesium carbonates, marble, mollusk shells (including clam shells and oyster shells), phosphate rock, potash, quartzite, slate, soapstone, stone (used or sold for use by the mine owner or operator as dimension stone or ornamental stone), thenardite, tripoli, trona, and (if paragraph (2)(B) does not apply) bauxite, flake graphite, fluorspar, lepidolite, mica, spodumene, and talc, including pyrophyllite), except that, unless sold on bid in direct competition with a bona fide bid to sell a mineral listed in paragraph (3), the percentage shall be 5 percent for any such other mineral (other than slate to which paragraph (5) applies) when used, or sold for use, by the mine owner or operator as rip rap, ballast, road material, rubble, concrete aggregates, or other purposes. For purposes of this paragraph, the term 'all other minerals' does not include—
"(A) soil, sod, dirt, turf, water, or mosses; or
"(B) minerals from sea water, the air, or similar inexhaustible sources."Sec. 502 of P.L. 91-172 struck out "and" from the end of subpara. (c)(4)(G), redesignated

Code Sec. 613

subpara. (c)(4)(H) as subpara. (I) and added new subpara. (H), for tax. yrs. begin. after 12/30/69.

In 1966, P.L. 89-809, Sec. 207, thru 209(a) amended subsec. (b) . . . Sec. 209(b), substituted "paragraph (5) or (6)(B)" for "paragraph (5)(B)" in subpara. (c)(4)(G), effective for tax yrs. begin. after 11/13/66.

Prior to amendment, subsec. (b) read as follows:

"(b) Percentage depletion rates.

The mines, wells, and other natural deposits, and the percentages, referred to in subsection (a) are as follows:

"(1) 27½ percent — oil and gas wells.

"(2) 23 percent —

"(A) sulfur and uranium; and

"(B) if from deposits in the United States — anorthosite (to the extent that a alumina and aluminum compounds, are extracted therefrom), asbestos, bauxite, celestite, chromite, corundum, fluorspar, graphite, ilmenite, kyanite, mica, olivine, quartz crystals, (radio grade), rutile, block steatite talc, and zircon, and ores of the following metals: antimony, beryllium, bismuth, cadmium, cobalt, columbium, lead, lithium, manganese, mercury, nickel, platinum and platinum group metals, tantalum, thorium, tin, titanium, tungsten, vanadium, and zinc.

"(3) 15 percent —

"(A) metal mines (if paragraph (2)(B) does not apply), rock asphalt, and vermiculite; and

"(B) if paragraph (5)(B) does not apply, ball clay, bentonite, china clay, sagger clay, and clay used or sold for use for purposes dependent on its refractory properties.

"(4) 10 percent — asbestos (if paragraph (2)(B) does not apply), brucite, coal, lignite, perlite, sodium chloride, and wollastonite.

"(5) 5 percent —

"(A) gravel, mollusk shells (including clam shells and oyster shells), peat, pumice, sand, scoria, shale, and stone, except stone described in paragraph (6); and

"(B) clay used, or sold for use, in the manufacture of building or paving brick, drainage and roofing tile, sewer pipe, flower pots, and kindred products; and

"(C) if from brine wells — bromine, calcium chloride, and magnesium chloride.

"(6) 15 percent — all other minerals (including, but not limited to, aplite, barite, borax, calcium carbonates, diatomaceous earth, dolomite, feldspar, fullers earth, garnet, gilsonite, granite, limestone, magnesite, magnesium, carbonates, marble, phosphate rock, potash, quartzite, slate, soapstone, stone (used or sold for use by the mine owner or operator as dimension stone or ornamental stone), thenardite, tripoli, trona, and (if paragraph (2)(B) does not apply) bauxite, flake graphite, fluorspar, lepidolite, mica, spodumene, and talc, including pyrophyllite), except that, unless sold on bid in direct competition with a bona fide bid to sell a mineral listed in paragraph (3), the percentage shall be 5 percent for any such other mineral when used, or sold for use, by the mine owner or operator as rip rap, ballast, road material, rubble, concrete aggregates, or for similar purposes. For purposes of this paragraph, the term 'all other minerals' does not include—

"(A) soil, sod, dirt, turf, water, or mosses; or

"(B) minerals from sea water, the air, or similar inexhaustible sources."

In 1964, P.L. 88-571, added "beryllium" after "antimony" in subpara. (b)(2)(B), and deleted "beryl" following "bauxite" in subpara. (b)(2)(B) and para. (b)(6), effective for tax. yrs. begin. after 12/31/63.

In 1962, P.L. 87-834, Sec. 13(e), added the third sentence in subsec. (a), effective for tax. yrs. begin. after 12/31/62.

In 1961, P.L. 87-312, Sec. 1, provided:

"(a) Election for past years.

In the case of brick and tile clay, fire clay, or shale used by the mineowner or operator in the manufacture of building or paving brick, drainage and roofing tile, sewer pipe, flower pots, and kindred products (without regard to the applicable rate of percentage depletion), if an election is made under subsection (c), for the purpose of applying section 613(c) of the Internal Revenue Code of 1954 (and corresponding provision of the Internal Revenue Code of 1939) for each of the taxable years with respect to which the election is effective —

"(1) gross income from the property shall be 50 per centum of the amount for which the manufactured products are sold during the taxable year except that with respect to such manufactured products, gross income from the property shall not exceed an amount equal to $12.50 multiplied by the number of short tons used in the manufactured products sold during the taxable year, and

"(2) for purposes of computing the 50 per centum limitation under section 613(a) of the Internal Revenue Code of 1954 (or the corresponding provision of the Internal Revenue Code of 1939), the taxable income from the property (computed without allowance for depletion) shall be 50 per centum of the taxable income from the manufactured products sold during the taxable year (computed without allowance for depletion).

"(b) Years to which applicable.

An election made under subsection (c) to have the provisions of this section apply shall be effective for all taxable years beginning before January 1, 1961, in respect of which—

"(1) the assessment of a deficiency,

"(2) the refund or credit of an overpayment, or

"(3) the commencement of a suit for recovery of a refund under section 7405 of the Internal Revenue Code of 1954,

is not prevented on the date of the enactment of this Act [9/26/61] by the operation of any law or rule of law. Such election shall also be effective for any taxable year beginning before January 1, 1961, in respect of which an assessment of a deficiency has been made but not collected on or before the date of the enactment of this Act.

"(c) Time and manner of election.

Natural resources

An election to have the provisions of this section apply shall be made by the taxpayer on or before the sixtieth day after the date of publication in the Federal Register of final regulations issued under authority of subsection (f), and shall be made in such form and manner as the Secretary of the Treasury or his delegate shall prescribe by regulations. Such election, if made, may not be revoked.

"(d) Statutes of limitation.

Notwithstanding any other law, the period within which an assessment of a deficiency attributable to the election under subsection (c) may be made with respect to any taxable year for which such election is effective, and the period within which a claim for refund or credit of an overpayment attributable to the election under such subsection may be made with respect to any such taxable year, shall not expire prior to one year after the last day for making an election under subsection (c). An election by a taxpayer under subsection (c) shall be considered as a consent to the application of the provisions of this subsection.

"(e) Terms; applicability of other laws.

Except where otherwise distinctly expressed or manifestly intended, terms used in this section shall have the same meaning as when used in the Internal Revenue Code of 1954 (or corresponding provisions of the Internal Revenue Code of 1939) and all provisions of law shall apply with respect to this section as if this section were a part of such Code (or corresponding provisions of the Internal Revenue Code of 1939).

"(f) Regulations.

The Secretary of the Treasury or his delegate shall prescribe such regulations as may be necessary to carry out the provisions of this section."

—P.L. 87-321, Sec. 2, provided that:

"(a) Election for past years.

If an election is made under subsection (c), in the case of quartzite and clay used by the mine owner or operator in the production of refractory products, for the purpose of applying section 613(c) of the Internal Revenue Code of 1954 (and corresponding provisions of the Internal Revenue Code of 1939) for each of the taxable years with respect to which the election is effective—

"(1) the term 'ordinary treatment processes' shall include crushing, grinding, and separating the mineral from waste, but shall not include any subsequent process; and

"(2) the gross income from mining for each short ton of such quartzite or clay used in the production of all refractory products sold during the taxable year shall be equal to 87½ percent of the lesser of—

"(A) the average lowest published or advertised price, or

"(B) the average lowest actual selling price, at which, during the taxable year, the mine owner or operator offered to sell, or sold, such quartzite or clay (in the form and condition of such products after the application of only the processes described in paragraph (1) and before transportation from the plant in which such processes were applied.)

For purposes of this paragraph, exceptional, unusual, or nominal sales or selling prices shall be disregarded. If the mine owner or operator makes no sales of, or makes only exceptional, unusual, or nominal sales of, such quartzite or clay after application of only the processes described in paragraph (1), then in lieu of the price provided for in subparagraph (A) or (B) there shall be used the average lowest recognized selling price for the taxable year for such quartzite or clay in the marketing area of the mine owner or operator published in a trade journal or other industry publication.

"(b) Years to which applicable.

An election made under subsection (c) to have the provisions of this section apply shall be effective on and after January 1, 1951, for all taxable years beginning before January 1, 1961, in respect of which—

"(1) the assessment of a deficiency,

"(2) the refund or credit of an overpayment, or

"(3) the commencement of a suit for recovery of a refund under section 7405 of the Internal Revenue Code of 1954,

is not prevented on the date of the enactment of this Act [9/26/61] by the operation of any law or rule of law. Such election shall also be effective on and after January 1, 1951, for any taxable year beginning before January 1, 1961, in respect of which an assessment of a deficiency has been made but not collected on or before the date of the enactment of this Act.

"(c) Time and manner of election.

An election to have the provisions of this section apply shall be made by the taxpayer on or before the 60th day after the date of publication in the Federal Register of final regulations issued under authority of subsection (f), and shall be made in such form and manner as the Secretary of the Treasury or his delegate shall prescribe by regulations. Such election, if made, may not be revoked.

"(d) Statutes of limitations.

Notwithstanding any other law, the period within which an assessment of a deficiency attributable to the election under subsection (c) may be made with respect to any taxable year for which such election is effective, and the period within which a claim for refund or credit of an overpayment attributable to the election under such subsection may be made with respect to any such taxable year, shall not expire prior to one year after the last day for making an election under subsection (c). An election by a taxpayer under subsection (c) shall be considered as a consent to the application of the provisions of this subsection.

"(e) Terms; applicability of other laws.

Except where otherwise distinctly expressed or manifestly intended, terms used in this section shall have the same meaning as when used in the Internal Revenue Code of 1954 (or corresponding provisions of the Internal Revenue Code of 1939) and all provisions of law shall apply with respect to this section as if this section were a part of such Code (or corresponding provisions of the Internal Revenue Code of 1939).

"(f) Regulations.

Natural resources

The Secretary of the Treasury or his delegate shall prescribe such regulations as may be necessary to carry out the provisions of this section.

In 1960, P.L. 86-564, Sec. 302, limited the 15% allowance in subsec. (b)(3) for ball clay, bentonite, china clay, and sagger clay to cases where paragraph (5)(B) does not apply, and authorized a 15% allowance, if paragraph (5)(B) does not apply, for clay used or sold for use for purposes dependent on its refractory properties ... substituted provisions in subsec. (b)(5) authorizing a 5% allowance for clay used, or sold for use, in the manufacture of building or paving brick, drainage and roofing tile, sewer pipe, flower pots, and kindred products for provisions which authorized a 5% allowance for brick and tile clay ... eliminated provisions in subsec. (b)(6) which authorized a 15% allowance for refractory and fire clay. (See subsec. (b)(3)) ... substituted in subsec. (c)(2) "the treatment processes considered as mining described in paragraph (4) (and the treatment processes necessary or incidental thereto)" for "the ordinary treatment processes normally applied by mine owners or operators in order to obtain the commercially marketable mineral product or products", and "such treatment processes" for "the ordinary treatment processes". ... substituted in subsec. (c)(4) "The following treatment processes were applied by the mine owner or operator shall be considered as mining to the extent they are applied to the ore or mineral in respect of which he is entitled to a deduction for depletion under section 611" for "The term 'ordinary treatment processes' includes the following" in the opening provisions, included cleaning in clause (B), substituted "ores or minerals which" for "minerals which", and included substantially equivalent processes in clause (C), included uranium and minerals which are not customarily sold in the form of the crude mineral product and substituted "from the ore or the mineral or minerals from other material from the mine or other natural deposit" for "from the ore, including the furnacing of quicksilver ores" in cl. (D), included the furnacing of quicksilver ores in cl. (E), and added cls. (F–H) ... added subsec. (c)(5), for tax. yrs. begin. after '60, except that Sec. 302(c)(2) of the P. L. provided:

"(2) Calcium carbonates, etc.—

"(A) Election for past years.—In the case of calcium carbonates or other minerals when used in making cement, if an election is made by the taxpayer under subparagraph (C)—

"(i) the amendments made by subsection (b) shall apply to taxable years with respect to which such election is effective and

"(ii) provisions having the same effect as the amendments made by subsection (b) shall be deemed to be included in the Internal Revenue Code of 1939 and shall apply to taxable years with respect to which such election is effective in lieu of the corresponding provisions of such Code.

"(B) Years to which applicable.—An election made under subparagraph (C) to have the provisions of this paragraph apply shall be effective for all taxable years beginning after January 1, 1961, in respect of which—

"(i) the assessment of a deficiency,

"(ii) the refund or credit of an overpayment, or

"(iii) the commencement of a suit for recovery of a refund under section 7405 of the Internal Revenue Code of 1954, is not prevented on the date of the enactment of this paragraph [9/14/60] by the operation of any law or rule of law. Such election shall also be effective for any taxable year beginning before January 1, 1961, in respect of which an assessment of a deficiency has been made but not collected on or before the date of the enactment of this paragraph.

"(C) Time and manner of election.—An election to have the provisions of this paragraph apply shall be made by the taxpayer on or before the 60th day after the date of publication in the Federal Register of final regulations issued under authority of subparagraph (F), and shall be made in such form and manner as the Secretary of the Treasury or his delegate shall prescribe by regulations. Such election, if made, may not be revoked.

"(D) Statutes of limitation.—Notwithstanding any other law, the period within which an assessment of a deficiency attributable to the application of the amendments made by subsection (b) may be made with respect to any taxable year to which such amendments apply under an election made under subparagraph (C), and the period within which a claim for refund or credit of an overpayment attributable to the application of such amendments may be made with respect to any such taxable year, shall not expire prior to one year after the last day for making an election under subparagraph (C). An election by a taxpayer under subparagraph (C) shall be considered as a consent to the application of the provisions of this subparagraph.

"(E) Terms; applicability of other laws.— Except where otherwise distinctly expressed or manifestly intended, terms used in this paragraph shall have the same meaning as when used in the Internal Revenue Code of 1954 (or corresponding provisions of the Internal Revenue Code of 1939) and all provisions of law shall apply with respect to this paragraph as if this paragraph were a part of such Code (or corresponding provisions of the Internal Revenue Code of 1939).

"(F) Regulations.—The Secretary of the Treasury or his delegate shall prescribe such regulations as may be necessary to carry out the provisions of this paragraph."

In 1958, P.L. 85-866, Sec. 36, added subsec. (d), for '54 Code years. But Sec. 36(b) of the P. L. provided that:

"If refund or credit of any overpayment resulting from the application of the amendment made by subsection (a) of this section is prevented on the date of the enactment of this Act [9/2/58], or within 6 months from such date, by the operation of any law or rule of law (other than section 3760 of the Internal Revenue Code of 1939 or section 7121 of the Internal Revenue Code of 1954, relating to closing agreements, and other than section 3761 of the Internal Revenue Code of 1939 or section 7122 of the Internal Revenue Code of 1954, relating to compromises), refund or credit of such overpayment may, nevertheless, be made or allowed if claim therefor is filed within 6 months from such date. No interest shall be paid on any overpayment resulting from the application of the amendment made by subsection (a) of this section."

Sec. 613A. Limitations on percentage depletion in case of oil and gas wells.

(a) General rule.

Except as otherwise provided in this section, the allowance for depletion under section 611 with respect to any oil or gas well shall be computed without regard to section 613.

(b) Exemption for certain domestic gas wells.

(1) In general. The allowance for depletion under section 611 shall be computed in accordance with section 613 with respect to—

(A) regulated natural gas, and

(B) natural gas sold under a fixed contract,

and 22 percent shall be deemed to be specified in subsection (b) of section 613 for purposes of subsection (a) of that section.

(2) Natural gas from geopressured brine. The allowance for depletion under section 611 shall be computed in accordance with section 613 with respect to any qualified natural gas from geopressured brine, and 10 percent shall be deemed to be specified in subsection (b) of section 613 for purposes of subsection (a) of such section.

(3) Definitions. For purposes of this subsection—

(A) Natural gas sold under a fixed contract. The term "natural gas sold under a fixed contract" means domestic natural gas sold by the producer under a contract, in effect on February 1, 1975, and at all times thereafter before such sale, under which the price for such gas cannot be adjusted to reflect to any extent the increase in liabilities of the seller for tax under this chapter by reason of the repeal of percentage depletion for gas. Price increases after February 1, 1975, shall be presumed to take increases in tax liabilities into account unless the taxpayer demonstrates to the contrary by clear and convincing evidence.

(B) Regulated natural gas. The term "regulated natural gas" means domestic natural gas produced and sold by the producer, before July 1, 1976, subject to the jurisdiction of the Federal Power Commission, the price for which has not been adjusted to reflect to any extent the increase in liability of the seller for tax under this chapter by reason of the repeal of percentage depletion for gas. Price increases after February 1, 1975, shall be presumed to take increases in tax liabilities into account unless the taxpayer demonstrates the contrary by clear and convincing evidence.

(C) Qualified natural gas from geopressured brine. The term "qualified natural gas from geopressured brine" means any natural gas—

(i) which is determined in accordance with section 503 of the Natural Gas Policy Act of 1978 to be produced from geopressured brine, and

(ii) which is produced from any well the drilling of which began after September 30, 1978, and before January 1, 1984.

(c) Exemption for independent producers and royalty owners.

(1) In general. Except as provided in subsection (d), the allowance for depletion under section 611 shall be computed in accordance with section 613 with respect to—

(A) so much of the taxpayer's average daily production of domestic crude oil as does not exceed the taxpayer's depletable oil quantity; and

(B) so much of the taxpayer's average daily production of domestic natural gas as does not exceed the taxpayer's depletable natural gas quantity;

and 15 percent shall be deemed to be specified in subsection (b) of section 613 for purposes of subsection (a) of that section.

(2) Average daily production. For purposes of paragraph (1)—

(A) the taxpayer's average daily production of domestic crude oil or natural gas for any taxable year, shall be determined by dividing his aggregate production of domestic crude oil or natural gas, as the case may be, during the taxable year by the number of days in such taxable year, and

(B) in the case of a taxpayer holding a partial interest in the production from any property (including an interest held in a partnership) such taxpayer's production shall be considered to be that amount of such production determined by multiplying the total production of such property by the taxpayer's percentage participation in the revenues from such property.

(3) Depletable oil quantity.

(A) In general. For purposes of paragraph (1), the taxpayer's depletable oil quantity shall be equal to—

(i) the tentative quantity determined under subparagraph (B), reduced (but not below zero) by

(ii) except in the case of a taxpayer making an election under paragraph (6)(B), the taxpayer's average daily marginal production for the taxable year.

(B) Tentative quantity. For purposes of subparagraph (A), the tentative quantity is 1,000 barrels.

(4) Daily depletable natural gas quantity. For purposes of paragraph (1), the depletable natural gas quantity of any taxpayer for any taxable year shall be equal to 6,000 cubic feet multiplied by the number of barrels of the taxpayer's depletable oil quantity to which the taxpayer elects to have this paragraph apply. The taxpayer's depletable oil quantity for any taxable year shall be reduced by the number of barrels with respect to which an election under this paragraph applies. Such election shall be made at such time and in such manner as the Secretary shall by regulations prescribe.

(5) Repealed.

(6) Oil and natural gas produced from marginal properties.

(A) In general. Except as provided in subsection (d) and subparagraph (B), the allowance for depletion under section 611 shall be computed in accordance with section 613 with respect to—

(i) so much of the taxpayer's average daily marginal production of domestic crude oil as does not exceed the taxpayer's depletable oil quantity (determined without regard to paragraph (3)(A)(ii)), and

(ii) so much of the taxpayer's average daily marginal production of domestic natural gas as does not exceed the taxpayer's depletable natural gas quantity (determined without regard to paragraph (3)(A)(ii)),

and the applicable percentage shall be deemed to be specified in subsection (b) of section 613 for purposes of subsection (a) of that section.

(B) Election to have paragraph apply to pro rata portion of marginal production. If the taxpayer elects to have this subparagraph apply for any taxable year, the rules of subparagraph (A) shall apply to the average daily marginal production of domestic crude oil or domestic natural gas of the taxpayer to which paragraph (1) would have applied without regard to this paragraph.

(C) Applicable percentage. For purposes of subparagraph (A), the term "applicable percentage" means the percentage (not greater than 25 percent) equal to the sum of—

(i) 15 percent, plus

(ii) 1 percentage point for each whole dollar by which $20 exceeds the reference price for crude oil for the calendar year preceding the calendar year in which the taxable year begins.

For purposes of this paragraph, the term "reference price" means, with respect to any calendar year, the reference price determined for such calendar year under section 45K(d)(2)(C).

(D) Marginal production. The term "marginal production" means domestic crude oil or domestic natural gas which is produced during any taxable year from a property which—

(i) is a stripper well property for the calendar year in which the taxable year begins, or

(ii) is a property substantially all of the production of which during such calendar year is heavy oil.

(E) Stripper well property. For purposes of this paragraph, the term "stripper well property" means, with respect to any calendar year, any property with respect to which the amount determined by dividing—

(i) the average daily production of domestic crude oil and domestic natural gas from producing wells on such property for such calendar year, by

(ii) the number of such wells,

is 15 barrel equivalents or less.

(F) Heavy Oil. For purposes of this paragraph, the term "heavy oil" means domestic crude oil produced from any property if such crude oil had a weighted average gravity of 20 degrees API or less (corrected to 60 degrees Fahrenheit).

(G) Average daily marginal production. For purposes of this subsection—

(i) the taxpayer's average daily marginal production of domestic crude oil or natural gas for any taxable year shall be determined by dividing the taxpayer's aggregate marginal production of domestic crude oil or natural gas, as the case may be, during the taxable year by the number of days in such taxable year, and

(ii) in the case of a taxpayer holding a partial interest in the production from any property (including any interest held in any partnership), such taxpayer's production shall be considered to be that amount of such production determined by multiplying the total production of such property by the taxpayer's percentage participation in the revenues from such property.

(H) Temporary suspension of taxable income limit with respect to marginal production. The second sentence of subsection (a) of section 613 shall not apply to so much of the allowance for depletion as is determined under subparagraph (A) for any taxable year—

(i) beginning after December 31, 1997, and before January 1, 2008, or

(ii) beginning after December 31, 2008, and before January 1, 2012.

(7) Special rules.

(A) Production of crude oil in excess of depletable oil quantity. If the taxpayer's average daily production of domestic crude oil exceeds his depletable oil quantity, the allowance under paragraph (1)(A) with respect to oil produced during the taxable year from each property in the United States shall be that amount which bears the same ratio to the amount of depletion which would have been allowable under section 613(a) for all of the taxpayer's oil produced from such property during the taxable year (computed as if section 613 applied to all of such production at the rate specified in paragraph (1) or (6), as the case may be) as his depletable oil quantity bears to the aggregate number of barrels representing the average daily production of domestic crude oil of the taxpayer for such year.

(B) Production of natural gas in excess of depletable natural gas quantity. If the taxpayer's average daily production of domestic natural gas exceeds his depletable natural gas quantity, the allowance under paragraph (1)(B) with respect to natural gas produced during the taxable year from each property in the United States shall be that amount which bears the same ratio to the amount of depletion which would have been allowable under section 613(a) for all of the taxpayers natural gas produced from such property during the taxable year (computed as if section 613 applied to all of such production at the rate specified in paragraph (1) or (6), as the case may be) as the amount of his depletable natural gas quantity in cubic feet bears to the aggregate number of cubic feet representing the average daily production of domestic natural gas of the taxpayer for such year.

(C) Taxable income from the property. If both oil and gas are produced from the property during the taxable year, for purposes of subparagraphs (A) and (B) the taxable income from the property, in applying the taxable income limitation in section 613(a), shall be allocated between the oil production and the gas production in proportion to the gross income during the taxable year from each.

(D) Partnerships. In the case of a partnership, the depletion allowance shall be computed separately by the partners and not by the partnership. The partnership shall allocate to each partner his proportionate share of the adjusted basis of each partnership oil or gas property. The allocation is to be made as of the later of the date of acquisition of the oil or gas property by the partnership, or January 1, 1975. A partner's proportionate share of the adjusted basis of partnership property shall be determined in accordance with his interest in partnership capital or income and, in the case of property contributed to the partnership by a partner, section 704(c) (relating to contributed property) shall apply in determining such share. Each partner shall separately keep records of his share of the adjusted basis in each oil and gas property of the partnership, adjust such share of the adjusted basis for any depletion taken on such property, and use such adjusted basis each year in the computation of his cost depletion or in the computation of his gain or loss on the disposition of such property by the partnership. For purposes of section 732 (relating to basis of distributed property other than money), the partnership's adjusted basis in mineral property shall be an amount equal to the sum of the partners' adjusted basis in such property as determined under this paragraph.

(8) Businesses under common control; members of the same family.
(A) Component members of controlled group treated as one taxpayer. For purposes of this subsection, persons who are members of the same controlled group of corporations shall be treated as one taxpayer.
(B) Aggregation of business entities under common control. If 50 percent or more of the beneficial interest in two or more corporations, trusts, or estates is owned by the same or related persons (taking into account only persons who own at least 5 percent of such beneficial interest), the tentative quantity determined under paragraph (3)(B) shall be allocated among all such entities in proportion to the respective production of domestic crude oil during the period in question by such entities.
(C) Allocation among members of the same family. In the case of individuals who are members of the same family, the tentative quantity determined under paragraph (3)(B) shall be allocated among such individuals in proportion to the respective production of domestic crude oil during the period in question by such individuals.
(D) Definition and special rules. For purposes of this paragraph—
(i) the term "controlled group of corporations" has the meaning given to such term by section 1563(a), except that section 1563(b)(2) shall not apply and except that "more than 50 percent" shall be substituted for "at least 80 percent" each place it appears in section 1563(a),
(ii) a person is a related person to another person if such persons are members of the same controlled group of corporations or if the relationship between such persons would result in a disallowance of losses under section 267 or 707(b), except that for this purpose the family of an individual includes only his spouse and minor children,
(iii) the family of an individual includes only his spouse and minor children, and
(iv) each 6,000 cubic feet of domestic natural gas shall be treated as 1 barrel of domestic crude oil.

(9) Special rule for fiscal year taxpayers. In applying this subsection to a taxable year which is not a calendar year, each portion of such taxable year which occurs during a single calendar year shall be treated as if it were a short taxable year.

(10) Certain production not taken into account. In applying this subsection, there shall not be taken into account the production of natural gas with respect to which subsection (b) applies.

(11) Subchapter S corporations.
(A) Computation of depletion allowance at shareholder level. In the case of an S corporation, the allowance for depletion with respect to any oil or gas property shall be computed separately by each shareholder.
(B) Allocation of basis. The S corporation shall allocate to each shareholder his pro rata share of the adjusted basis of the S corporation in each oil or gas property held by the S corporation. The allocation shall be made as of the later of the date of acquisition of the property by the S corporation, or the first day of the first taxable year of the S corporation to which the Subchapter S Revision Act of 1982 applies. Each shareholder shall separately keep records of his share of the adjusted basis in each oil and gas property of the S corporation, adjust such share of the adjusted basis for any depletion taken on such property, and use such adjusted basis each year in the computation of his cost depletion or in the computation of his gain or loss on the disposition of such property by the S corporation. In the case of any distribution of oil or gas property to its shareholders by the S corporation, the corporation's adjusted basis in the property shall be an amount equal to the sum of the shareholders' adjusted bases in such property, as determined under this subparagraph.

Code Sec. 613A(d) — Natural resources

(d) Limitations on application of subsection (c).

(1) Limitation based on taxable income. The deduction for the taxable year attributable to the application of subsection (c) shall not exceed 65 percent of the taxpayer's taxable income for the year computed without regard to—

(A) any depletion on production from an oil or gas property which is subject to the provisions of subsection (c),

(B) any deduction allowable under section 199,

(C) any net operating loss carryback to the taxable year under section 172,

(D) any capital loss carryback to the taxable year under section 1212, and

(E) in the case of a trust, any distributions to its beneficiary, except in the case of any trust where any beneficiary of such trust is a member of the family (as defined in section 267(c)(4)) of a settlor who created inter vivos and testamentary trusts for members of the family and such settlor died within the last six days of the fifth month in 1970, and the law in the jurisdiction in which such trust was created requires all or a portion of the gross or net proceeds of any royalty or other interest in oil, gas, or other mineral representing any percentage depletion allowance to be allocated to the principal of the trust.

If an amount is disallowed as a deduction for the taxable year by reason of application of the preceding sentence, the disallowed amount shall be treated as an amount allowable as a deduction under subsection (c) for the following taxable year, subject to the application of the preceding sentence to such taxable year. For purposes of basis adjustments and determining whether cost depletion exceeds percentage depletion with respect to the production from a property, any amount disallowed as a deduction on the application of this paragraph shall be allocated to the respective properties from which the oil or gas was produced in proportion to the percentage depletion otherwise allowable to such properties under subsection (c).

(2) Retailers excluded. Subsection (c) shall not apply in the case of any taxpayer who directly, or through a related person, sells oil or natural gas (excluding bulk sales of such items to commercial or industrial users), or any product derived from oil or natural gas (excluding bulk sales of aviation fuels to the Department of Defense)—

(A) through any retail outlet operated by the taxpayer or a related person, or

(B) to any person—

(i) obligated under an agreement or contract with the taxpayer or a related person to use a trademark, trade name, or service mark or name owned by such taxpayer or a related person, in marketing or distributing oil or natural gas or any product derived from oil or natural gas, or

(ii) given authority, pursuant to an agreement or contract with the taxpayer or a related person, to occupy any retail outlet owned, leased, or in any way controlled by the taxpayer or a related person.

Notwithstanding the preceding sentence this paragraph shall not apply in any case where the combined gross receipts from the sale of such oil, natural gas, or any product derived therefrom, for the taxable year of all retail outlets taken into account for purposes of this paragraph do not exceed $5,000,000. For purposes of this paragraph, sales of oil, natural gas, or any product derived from oil or natural gas shall not include sales made of such items outside the United States, if no domestic production of the taxpayer or a related person is exported during the taxable year or the immediately preceding taxable year.

(3) Related person. For purposes of this subsection, a person is a related person with respect to the taxpayer if a significant ownership interest in either the taxpayer or such person is held by the other, or if a third person has a significant ownership interest in both the taxpayer and such person. For purposes of the preceding sentence, the term "significant ownership interest" means—

(A) with respect to any corporation, 5 percent or more in value of the outstanding stock of such corporation,

(B) with respect to a partnership, 5 percent or more interest in the profits or capital of such partnership, and

(C) with respect to an estate or trust, 5 percent or more of the beneficial interests in such estate or trust.

For purposes of determining a significant ownership interest, an interest owned by or for a corporation, partnership, trust, or estate shall be considered as owned directly both by itself and proportionately by its shareholders, partners, or beneficiaries, as the case may be.

(4) Certain refiners excluded. If the taxpayer or one or more related persons engages in the refining of crude oil, subsection (c) shall not apply to the taxpayer for a taxable year if the average daily refinery runs of the taxpayer and such persons for the taxable year exceed 75,000 barrels. For purposes of this paragraph, the average daily refinery runs for any taxable year shall be determined by dividing the aggregate refinery runs for the taxable year by the number of days in the taxable year.

(5) Percentage depletion not allowed for lease bonuses, etc. In the case of any oil or gas property to which subsection (c) applies, for purposes of section 613, the term "gross income from the property" shall not include any lease bonus, advance royalty, or other amount payable without regard to production from property.

(e) Definitions. For purposes of this section—

(1) Crude oil. The term "crude oil" includes a natural gas liquid recovered from a gas well in lease separators or field facilities.

(2) Natural gas. The term "natural gas" means any product (other than crude oil) of an oil or gas well if a deduction for depletion is allowable under section 611 with respect to such product.

(3) Domestic. The term "domestic" refers to production from an oil or gas well located in the United States or in a possession of the United States.

(4) Barrel. The term "barrel" means 42 United States gallons.

In **2010**, P.L. 111-312, Sec. 706(a), substituted "January 1, 2012" for "January 1, 2010" in clause (c)(6)(H)(ii), effective for tax. yrs. begin. after 12/31/2009.

In **2008**, P.L. 110-343, Sec. 210DivB, amended subpara. (c)(6)(H), enacted 10/3/2008.

Prior to amendment, subpara. (c)(6)(H) read as follows:

"(H) Temporary suspension of taxable income limit with respect to marginal production. The second sentence of subsection (a) of section 613 shall not apply to so much of the allowance for depletion as is determined under subparagraph (A) for any taxable year beginning after December 31, 1997, and before January 1, 2008."

In **2006**, P.L. 109-432, Sec. 118(a), substituted "2008" for "2006" in subpara. (c)(6)(H) effective for tax. yrs. begin. after 12/31/2005.

In **2005**, P.L. 109-135, Sec. 403(a)(18), redesignated subparas. (d)(1)(B)-(D) as subparas. (d)(1)(C)-(E) and added subpara. (d)(1)(B), effective as provided by Sec. 102 of the American Jobs Creation Act of 2004, P.L. 108-357 [as amended by Sec. 403(a)(19) of P.L. 109-135], which reads as follows:

"(e) Effective date.

"(1) The amendments made by this section shall apply to taxable years beginning after December 31, 2004.

"(2) Application to pass-thru entities, etc. In determining the deduction under section 199 of the Internal Revenue Code of 1986 (as added by this section), items arising from a taxable year of a partnership, S corporation, estate, or trust

Natural resources Code Sec. 613A

beginning before January 1, 2005, shall not be taken into account for purposes of subsection (d)(1) of such section."

— P.L. 109-58, Sec. 1322(a)(3)(B), substituted "section 45K(d)(2)(C)" for "section 29(d)(2)(C)" in subpara. (c)(6)(C), effective for credits determined under the Internal Revenue Code of 1986 for tax. yrs. end. after 12/31/2005.

— P.L. 109-58, Sec. 1328(a), amended para. (d)(4), effective for tax. yrs. end. after 8/8/2005.

Prior to amendment, para. (d)(4) read as follows:

"(4) Certain refiners excluded. If the taxpayer or a related person engages in the refining of crude oil, subsection (c) shall not apply to such taxpayer if on any day during the taxable year the refinery runs of the taxpayer and such person exceed 50,000 barrels."

In 2004, P.L. 108-311, Sec. 314(a), substituted "January 1, 2006" for "January 1, 2004" in subpara. (c)(6)(H), effective for tax. yrs. begin. after 12/31/2003.

In 2002, P.L. 107-147, Sec. 607(a), substituted "2004" for "2002" in subpara. (c)(6)(H), effective for tax. yrs. begin. after 12/31/2001.

In 1999, P.L. 106-170, Sec. 504(a), substituted "January 1, 2002" for "January 1, 2000" in subpara. (c)(6)(H), effective for tax. yrs. begin. after 12/31/99.

In 1997, P.L. 105-34, Sec. 972(a), added subpara. (c)(6)(H), effective for tax. yrs. begin. after 12/31/97.

In 1996, P.L. 104-188, Sec. 1702(e)(2), deleted "the table contained in" after "determined under" in clause (c)(2)(A)(i), effective for tax. yrs. begin. after 12/31/90.

In 1990, P.L. 101-508, Sec. 11521(a), deleted paras. (c)(9) [as amended by Sec 11815(a)(2)(B) of this Act, see below] and (c)(10), and redesignated paras. (c)(11)-(c)(13) as paras. (c)(9)-(c)(11) . . . Sec. 11521(b), deleted subparas. (c)(11)(C) and (c)(11)(D) [as redesignated], effective for transfers after 10/11/90. Prior to deletion, paras. (c)(9) and (c)(10) read as follows:

"(9) Transfer of oil or gas property.

"(A) In the case of a transfer (including the subleasing of a lease) after December 31, 1974 of an interest (including an interest in a partnership or trust) in any proven oil or gas property, this subsection shall not apply to the transferee (or sublessee) with respect to production of crude oil or natural gas attributable to such interest, and such production shall not be taken into account for any computation by the transferee (or sublessee) under this subsection. A property shall be treated as a proven oil or gas property if at the time of the transfer the principal value of the property has been demonstrated by prospecting or exploration or discovery work.

"(B) Subparagraph (A) shall not apply in the case of—

"(i) a transfer of property at death, or

"(ii) the transfer in an exchange to which section 351 applies if following the exchange of the tentative quantity determined under paragraph (3)(B) is allocated under paragraph (8) between the transferor or transferee,

"(iii) a change of beneficiaries of a trust by reason of the death, birth, or adoption of any vested beneficiary if the transferee was a beneficiary of such trust or is a lineal descendent of the settlor or any other vested beneficiary of such trust, except in the case of any trust where any beneficiary of such trust is a member of the family (as defined in section 267(c)(4)) of a settlor who created inter vivos and testamentary trusts for members of the family and such settlor died within the last six days of the fifth month in 1970, and the law in the jurisdiction in which such trust was created requires all or a portion of the gross or net proceeds of any royalty or other interest in oil, gas, or other mineral representing any percentage depletion allowance to be allocated to the principal of the trust,

"(iv) a transfer of property between corporations which are members of the same controlled group of corporations (as defined in paragraph (8)(D)(ii)), or

"(v) a transfer of property between business entities which are under common control (within the meaning of paragraph (8)(B)) or between related persons in the same family (within the meaning of paragraph (8)(C)), or

"(vi) A transfer of property between a trust and related persons in the same family (within the meaning of paragraph (8)(C) to the extent that the beneficiaries of that trust are and continue to be related persons in the family that transferred the property, and to the extent that the tentative oil quantity is allocated among the members of the family (within the meaning of paragraph (8)(C)).

Clause (iv) or (v) shall apply only so long as the tentative oil quantity determined under paragraph (3)(B) is allocated under paragraph (8) between the transferor and transferee.

"(10) Transfers by individuals to corporations.

"(A) In general. Paragraph (9)(A) shall not apply to a transfer by an individual of qualified property to a qualified transferee corporation solely in exchange for stock in such corporation,

"(B) 1,000-barrel limit for corporation. A tentative quantity shall be determined for the qualified transferee corporation under this subsection.

"(C) Transferor's tentative quantity reduced.

"(i) In general. The tentative quantity for the transferor (and his family) for any period shall be reduced by the transferor's pro rata share of the corporation's depletable quantity for such period.

"(ii) Pro rata share. For purposes of clause (i), a transferor's pro rata share for any period shall be—

"(I) in the case of production from property to which subparagraph (A) applies, that portion of the corporation's depletable quantity which is allocable to production from such property, and

"(II) in the case of production from all other property, that portion of the corporation's depletable quantity which is allocable to the production from such property, multiplied by a fraction the numerator of which is the fair market value of the transferor's stock in the corporation, and the denominator of which is the fair market value of all stock in the corporation.

"(iii) Depletable quantity. For purposes of this paragraph, a corporation's depletable quantity for any period in the lessor of—

"(I) such corporation's tentative quantity for such period (determined under paragraphs (3) and (8)), or

"(II) such corporation's average daily production for such period.

"(D) Qualified transferee corporation defined. For purposes of this paragraph, the term 'qualified transferee corporation' means a corporation all of the outstanding stock of which has been issued to individuals solely in exchange for qualified property held by such individuals.

"(E) Qualified property defined. For purposes of this paragraph, the term 'qualified property' means oil or gas property with respect to which—

"(i) there has been no prior transfer to which paragraph (9)(A) applied, and

"(ii) the transferor has made an election to have this paragraph apply.

The term also includes cash (not to exceed $1,000 in the aggregate) which one or more individuals transfer to the corporation and, in the case of any property, also includes necessary production equipment for such property which is in place when the property is transferred.

"(F) Transferor must retain stock during lifetime. If at any time during his lifetime any transferor disposes of stock in the corporation (other than to a member of his family), then the depletable quantity of the corporation (determined without regard to this subparagraph) shall be reduced (for all periods on or after the date of the disposition) by an amount which bears the same ratio to such quantity as the fair market value of the stock so disposed of bears to the aggregate fair market value of all stock of the corporation on such date of disposition.

"(G) Special rules relating to family of transferor.

"(i) In general. For purposes of this paragraph—

"(I) the issuance of stock to a member of the family of the transferor shall be treated as issuance of stock to the transferor, and

"(II) during the lifetime of the transferor, stock transferred to a member of the family of the transferor shall be treated as held by the transferor.

If stock described in the preceding sentence ceases to be held by a member of the family of the transferor, the transferor shall be treated as having disposed of such stock at the time of such cessation.

"(ii) Family defined. For purposes of this paragraph, the members of the family of an individual include only his spouse and his minor children.

"(H) Property subject to liabilities. For purposes of this paragraph, section 357 shall be applied as if—

"(i) references to section 351 include references to subparagraph (A) of this paragraph, and

"(ii) the reference in subsection (a)(1) of section 357 to the nonrecognition of gain includes a reference to the nonapplication of paragraph (9)(A) of this subsection.

"(I) Election. A transferor may make an election under this paragraph only in such manner as the Secretary may by regulations prescribe and only on or before the due date (including extensions) for filing the return of the corporation of the taxes imposed by this chapter for the corporation's first taxable year ending after the date of the transfer (or, if later, after the date of the enactment of this paragraph).

"(J) Regulations. The Secretary shall prescribe such regulations as may be necessary to carry out the purposes of this paragraph."

Prior to deletion, subparas. (c)(11)(C) and (c)(11)(D) [as redesignated] read as follows:

"(C) Coordination with transfer rule of paragraph (9). For purposes of paragraph (9)—

"(i) an S corporation shall be treated as a partnership, and the shareholders of the S corporation shall be treated as partners, and

"(ii) an election by a C corporation to become an S corporation shall be treated as a transfer of all its properties effective on the day on which such election first takes effect.

"(D) Coordination with transfer rule or paragraph (10). For purposes of paragraphs (9) and (10), if an S corporation becomes a C corporation, each shareholder shall be treated as having transferred to such corporation his pro rata share of all the assets of the S corporation."

— P.L. 101-508, Sec. 11522(b)(1), substituted "taxable income" for "50 percent" in subpara. (c)(7)(C) . . . Sec. 11523(a), amended para. (c)(6) . . . Sec. 11523(b)(1), substituted "(ii) except in the case of the taxpayer making an election under paragraph (6)(B), the taxpayer's average daily marginal production for the taxable year." for "(ii) the taxpayer's average daily secondary or tertiary production for the taxable year." in subpara. (c)(3)(A) . . . Sec. 11523(b)(2), deleted "Clause (ii) shall not apply after December 31, 1983.", the last sentence in subpara. (c)(3)(A), effective for tax. yrs. begin. after 12/31/90.

Prior to amendment, para. (c)(6) read as follows:

"(6) Oil and natural gas resulting from secondary or tertiary processes.

"(A) In general. Except as provided in subsection (d), the allowance for depletion under section 611 shall be computed in accordance with section 613 with respect to—

"(i) so much of the taxpayer's average daily secondary or tertiary production of domestic crude oil as does not exceed the taxpayer's depletable oil quantity (determined without regard to paragraph (3)(A)(ii)); and

"(ii) so much of the taxpayer's average daily secondary or tertiary production of domestic natural gas as does not exceed the taxpayer's depletable natural gas quantity (determined without regard to paragraph (3)(A)(ii));

and 22 percent shall be deemed to be specified in subsection (b) of section 613 for purposes of subsection (a) of that section.

"(B) Average daily secondary or tertiary production. For purposes of this subsection—

2,295

"(i) the taxpayer's average daily secondary or tertiary production of domestic crude oil or natural gas for any taxable year shall be determined by dividing his aggregate production of domestic crude oil or natural gas as the case may be, resulting from secondary or tertiary processes during the taxable year by the number of days in such taxable year, and

"(ii) in the case of a taxpayer holding a partial interest in the production from any property (including any interest held in any partnership) such taxpayer's production shall be considered to be that amount of such production determined by multiplying the total production of such property by the taxpayer's percentage participation in the revenues from such property.

"(C) Termination. This paragraph shall not apply after December 31, 1983."

—P.L. 101-508, Sec. 11815(a)(1)(A), substituted "15 percent" for "the applicable percentage (determined in accordance with the table contained in paragraph (5))" in para. (c)(1) . . . Sec. 11815(a)(1)(B), amended subpara. (c)(3)(B) . . . Sec. 11815(a)(1)(C), deleted para. (c)(5) and subpara. (c)(7)(E) . . . Sec. 11815(a)(2)(A), substituted "specified in paragraph (1)" for "specified in paragraph (5)" in subparas. (c)(7)(A) and (c)(7)(B) . . . Sec. 11815(a)(2)(B), substituted "determined under paragraph (3)(B)" for "determined under the table contained in paragraph (3)(B)" in subparas. (c)(8)(B) and (c)(8)(C) and para. (c)(9) as deleted by Sec. 11521(a), see above, effective 11/15/90, except as provided in Sec. 11821(b) of this Act reproduced in note following Code Sec. 613.

Prior to amendment, subpara. (c)(3)(B) read as follows:

"(B) Phase-out table. For purposes of subparagraph (A)—

In the case of production during the calendar year:	The tentative quantity in barrels is:
1975	2,000
1976	1,800
1977	1,600
1978	1,400
1979	1,200
1980 and thereafter	1,000"

Prior to deletion, para. (c)(5) read as follows:

"(5) Applicable percentage. For purposes of paragraph (1)—

In the case of production during the calendar year:	The applicable percentage is:
1975	22
1976	22
1977	22
1978	22
1979	22
1980	22
1981	20
1982	18
1983	16
1984 and thereafter	15"

Prior to deletion, subpara. (c)(7)(E) read as follows:

"(E) Secondary or tertiary production. If the taxpayer has production from secondary or tertiary recovery processes during the taxable year, this paragraph (under regulations prescribed by the Secretary) shall be applied separately with respect to such production. This subparagraph shall not apply after December 31, 1983."

In **1986**, P.L. 99-514, Sec. 104(b)(9), deleted "(reduced in the case of an individual by the zero bracket amount)" after "taxable income" in para. (d)(1), effective for tax. yrs. begin. after 12/31/86.

—P.L. 99-514, Sec. 412(a)(1), added para. (d)(5), effective for amounts received or accrued after 8/16/86, in tax. yrs. end. after 8/16/86.

In **1984**, P.L. 98-369, Sec. 25(b)(1), deleted "In applying this paragraph, there shall not be taken into account any production of crude oil or natural gas resulting from secondary or tertiary processes (as defined in regulations prescribed by the Secretary)." in para. (c)(2) . . . Sec. 25(b)(2), added the last sentence of subpara. (c)(3)(A) . . . Sec. 25(b)(3), added the last sentence of subpara. (c)(7)(E) . . . Sec. 25(b)(4), substituted "this subsection" for "paragraph (1)" in subpara. (c)(9)(A), effective 1/1/84.

—P.L. 98-369, Sec. 71(b), amended subpara. (c)(7)(D), effective for property contributed to the partnership after 3/31/84, in tax. yrs. end. after 3/31/84.

Prior to amendment, subpara. (c)(7)(D) read as follows:

"(D) Partnerships. In the case of a partnership, the depletion allowance shall be computed separately by the partners and not by the partnership. The partnership shall allocate to each partner his proportionate share of the adjusted basis of each partnership oil or gas property. The allocation is to be made as of the later of the date of acquisition of the oil or gas property by the partnership, or January 1, 1975. A partner's proportionate share of the adjusted basis of partnership property shall be determined in accordance with his interest in partnership capital or income and, in the case of an agreement described in section 704(c)(2) (relating to effect of a partnership agreement on contributed property), such share shall be determined by taking such agreement into account. Each partner shall separately keep records of his share of the adjusted basis in each oil and gas property of the partnership, adjust such share of the adjusted basis for any depletion taken on such property, and use such adjusted basis each year in the computation of his cost depletion or in the computation of his gain or loss on the disposition of such property by the partnership. For purposes of section 732 (relating to basis of distributed property other than money), the partnership's adjusted basis in mineral property shall be amount equal to the sum of the partners' adjusted basis in such property as determined under this paragraph."

In **1983**, P.L. 97-448, Sec. 202(d)(1), added "and, in the case of any property, also includes necessary production equipment for such property which is in place when the property is transferred" before the period at the end of subpara. (c)(10)(E), effective as provided in Sec. 203(b)(3)(A) of this Act which reads as follows:

"(A) The amendment made by section 202(d)(1) [P.L. 97-448] shall apply to transfers in taxable years ending after December 31, 1974, but only for purposes of applying section 613A of the Internal Revenue Code of 1954 to periods after December 31, 1979."

—P.L. 97-448, Sec. 202(d)(2), added "(excluding bulk sales of aviation fuels to the Department of Defense)" after "any product derived from oil or natural gas" the first place it appeared in para. (d)(2), effective for bulk sales after 9/18/82.

In **1982**, P.L. 97-354, Sec. 3(a), added para. (c)(13), effective for tax. yrs. begin. after 12/31/82.

In **1980**, P.L. 96-603, Sec. 3(a), redesignated paras. (c)(10) and (11) as paras. (c)(11) and (12) and added new para. (c)(10), effective for transfers in tax. yrs. ending after 12/31/74, but only for purposes of applying Code Sec. 613A to periods after 12/31/79.

In **1978**, P.L. 95-618, Sec. 403(a)(2)(B), inserted "and" at the end of subpara. (b)(1)(A), deleted "and" at the end of subpara. (b)(1)(B), and deleted subpara. (b)(1)(C), effective 10/1/78 for tax. yrs. end. on or after 10/1/78.

Prior to deletion, subpara. (b)(1)(C) read as follows:

"(C) any geothermal deposit in the United States or in a possession of the United States which is determined to be a gas well,"

—P.L. 95-618, Sec. 403(b), redesignated para. (b)(2) as para. (b)(3) . . . added new para. (b)(2) . . . added subpara. (b)(3)(C) as redesignated by this Act, effective 10/1/78 for tax. yrs. end. on or after 10/1/78. Sec. 403(d) of the Act provides:

"(d) Coordination with other provision. Any allowance for depletion allowed by reason of the amendments made by subsection (b) shall not be treated as a credit, exemption, deduction, or comparable adjustment applicable to the computation of any Federal tax which is specifically allowable with respect to any high-cost natural gas (or category thereof) for purposes of section 107(d) of the Natural Gas Policy Act of 1978."

In **1977**, P.L. 95-30, Sec. 102(b)(7), added "(reduced in the case of an individual by the zero bracket amount)" after "the taxpayer's taxable income" in para. (d)(1), effective for tax. yrs. begin. after 12/31/76.

In **1976**, P.L. 94-455, Sec. 1901(a)(86)(A), deleted "within the meaning of section 613(b)(1)(A)" after "determined to be a gas well" in subpara. (b)(1)(C), effective for tax. yrs. begin. after '76.

—P.L. 94-455, Sec. 1901(a)(86)(B), substituted "determined without" for "determined with" in clause "(c)(6)(i)" [sic] for tax. yrs. begin. after '76

—P.L. 94-455, Sec. 1906(b)(13)(A), substituted "Secretary" for "Secretary or his delegate" each place it appeared in Code Sec 613A, effective for tax. yrs. begin. after 12/31/76.

—P.L. 94-455, Sec. 2115(a), added "(excluding bulk sales of such items to commercial or industrial users)" after "natural gas" the first time it appeared, and added the last paragraph of para. (d)(2) . . . Sec. 2115(b)(1), deleted "or" at the end of clause (c)(9)(B)(i), substituted ", or" for the period at the end of clause (c)(9)(B)(ii), and added new clause (c)(9)(B)(iii) . . . Sec. 2115(b)(2)(A), amended subpara. (d)(1)(A) . . . Sec. 2115(b)(2)(B), deleted "and" at the end of subpara. (d)(1)(B) . . . Sec. 2115(b)(2)(C), substituted ", and" for the period at the end of subpara. (d)(1)(C) . . . Sec. 2115(b)(2)(D), added subpara. (d)(1)(D), effective 1/1/75, and applicable to tax. yrs. end after 12/31/74.

Prior to amendment, subpara. (d)(1)(A) read as follows:

"(A) depletion with respect to production of oil and gas subject to the provisions of subsection (e),"

—P.L. 94-455, Sec. 2115(c)(1), amended subpara. (c)(7)(D), for tax. yrs. end. after 12/31/74.

Prior to amendment, subpara. (c)(7)(D) read as follows:

"(D) Partnerships. In the case of a partnership, the depletion allowance in the case of oil and gas wells to which this subsection applies shall be computed separately by the partners and not by the partnership."

—P.L. 94-455, Sec. 2115(d), added the last paragraph in para. (d)(3), effective 1/1/75, and applicable to tax. yrs. end after 12/31/74.

—P.L. 94-455, Sec. 2115(e), substituted a comma for ", or" at the end of clause (c)(9)(B)(ii), substituted a period for the comma at the end of clause (c)(9)(B)(iii), as previously amended by the Act, added clauses (c)(9)(B)(iv), (v) and (vi), effective for tax. yrs. end. after 12/31/74.

In **1975**, P.L. 94-12, Sec. 501(a), added Code Sec. 613A, effective 1/1/75 for tax. yrs. end. after 12/31/74. The reference to section "613(b)(1)(A)" in para. (b)(1) presumably is to that provision as it existed prior to the amendment made by P.L. 94-12, Sec. 501(b)(2), which struck out that provision and redesignated subpara. (b)(1)(B) as (b)(1)(A).

Sec. 614. Definition of property.
(a) General rule.

For the purpose of computing the depletion allowance in the case of mines, wells, and other natural deposits, the term "property" means each separate interest owned by the taxpayer in each mineral deposit in each separate tract or parcel of land.

(b) Special rules as to operating mineral interests in oil and gas wells or geothermal deposits.

In the case of oil and gas wells or geothermal deposits—

(1) In general. Except as otherwise provided in this subsection—
  (A) all of the taxpayer's operating mineral interests in a separate tract or parcel of land shall be combined and treated as one property, and
  (B) the taxpayer may not combine an operating mineral interest in one tract or parcel of land with an operating mineral interest in another tract or parcel of land.
(2) Election to treat operating mineral interests as separate properties. If the taxpayer has more than one operating mineral interest in a single tract or parcel of land, he may elect to treat one or more of such operating mineral interests as separate properties. The taxpayer may not have more than one combination of operating mineral interests in a single tract or parcel of land. If the taxpayer makes the election provided in this paragraph with respect to any interest in a tract or parcel of land, each operating mineral interest which is discovered or acquired by the taxpayer in such tract or parcel of land after the taxable year for which the election is made shall be treated—
  (A) if there is no combination of interests in such tract or parcel, as a separate property unless the taxpayer elects to combine it with another interest, or
  (B) if there is a combination of interests in such tract or parcel, as part of such combination unless the taxpayer elects to treat it as a separate property.
(3) Certain unitization or pooling arrangements.
  (A) In general. Under regulations prescribed by the Secretary, if one or more of the taxpayer's operating mineral interests participate, under a voluntary or compulsory unitization or pooling agreement, in a single cooperative or unit plan of operation, then for the period of such participation—
    (i) they shall be treated for all purposes of this subtitle as one property, and
    (ii) the application of paragraphs (1), (2), and (4) in respect of such interests shall be suspended.
  (B) Limitation. Subparagraph (A) shall apply to a voluntary agreement only if all the operating mineral interests covered by such agreement—
    (i) are in the same deposit, or are in 2 or more deposits the joint development or production of which is logical from the standpoint of geology, convenience, economy, or conservation, and
    (ii) are in tracts or parcels of land which are contiguous or in close proximity.
  (C) Special rule in the case of arrangements entered into in taxable years beginning before January 1, 1964. If—
    (i) two or more of the taxpayer's operating mineral interests participate under a voluntary or compulsory unitization or pooling agreement entered into in any taxable year beginning before January 1, 1964, in a single cooperative or unit plan of operation,
    (ii) the taxpayer, for the last taxable year beginning before January 1, 1964, treated such interests as two or more separate properties, and
    (iii) it is determined that such treatment was proper under the law applicable to such taxable year,
  such taxpayer may continue to treat such interests in a consistent manner for the period of such participation.
(4) Manner, time, and scope of election.
  (A) Manner and time. Any election provided in paragraph (2) shall be made for each operating mineral interest, in the manner prescribed by the Secretary by regulations, not later than the time prescribed by law for filing the return (including extensions thereof) for whichever of the following taxable years is the later: The first taxable year beginning after December 31, 1963, or the first taxable year in which any expenditure for development or operation in respect of such operating mineral interest is made by the taxpayer after the acquisition of such interest.
  (B) Scope. Any election under paragraph (2) shall be for all purposes of this subtitle and shall be binding on the taxpayer for all subsequent taxable years.
(5) Treatment of certain properties. If, on the day preceding the first day of the first taxable year beginning after December 31, 1963, the taxpayer has any operating mineral interests which he treats under subsection (d) of this section (as in effect before the amendments made by the Revenue Act of 1964), such treatment shall be continued and shall be deemed to have been adopted pursuant to paragraphs (1) and (2) of this subsection (as amended by such Act).
(c) Special rules as to operating mineral interests in mines.
  (1) Election to aggregate separate interests. Except in the case of oil and gas wells and geothermal deposits, if a taxpayer owns two or more separate operating mineral interests which constitute part or all of an operating unit, he may elect (for all purposes of this subtitle)—
    (A) to form an aggregation of, and to treat as one property, all such interests owned by him which comprise any one mine or any two or more mines; and
    (B) to treat as a separate property each such interest which is not included within an aggregation referred to in subparagraph (A).
  For purposes of this paragraph, separate operating mineral interests which constitute part or all of an operating unit may be aggregated whether or not they are included in a single tract or parcel of land and whether or not they are included in contiguous tracts or parcels. For purpcses of this paragraph, a taxpayer may elect to form more than one aggregation of operating mineral interests within any one operating unit; but no aggregation may include any operating mineral interest which is a part of a mine without including all of the operating mineral interests which are a part of such mine in the first taxable year for which the election to aggregate is effective, and any operating mineral interest which thereafter becomes a part of such mine shall be included in such aggregation.
  (2) Election to treat a single interest as more than one property. Except in the case of oil and gas wells and geothermal deposits, if a single tract or parcel of land contains a mineral deposit which is being extracted, or will be extracted, by means of two or more mines for which expenditures for development or operation have been made by the taxpayer, then the taxpayer may elect to allocate to such mines, under regulations prescribed by the Secretary, all of the tract or parcel of land and of the mineral deposit contained therein, and to treat as a separate property that portion of the tract or parcel of land and of the mineral deposit so allocated to each mine. A separate property formed pursuant to an election under this paragraph shall be treated as a separate property for all purposes of this subtitle (including this paragraph). A separate property so formed may, under regulations prescribed by the Secretary, be included as a part of an aggregation in accordance with paragraphs (1) and (3). The election provided by this paragraph may not be made with respect to any property which is a part of an aggregation formed by the taxpayer under paragraph (1) except with the consent of the Secretary.

(3) Manner and scope of election. The elections provided by paragraphs (1) and (2) shall be made, in accordance with regulations prescribed by the Secretary, not later than the time prescribed for filing the return (including extensions thereof) for the first taxable year—

(A) in which, in the case of an election under paragraph (1), any expenditure for development or operation in respect of the separate operating mineral interest is made by the taxpayer after the acquisition of such interest, or

(B) in which, in the case of an election under paragraph (2), expenditures for development or operation of more than one mine in respect of a property are made by the taxpayer after the acquisition of the property.

An election made under paragraph (1) or (2) for a taxable year shall be binding upon the taxpayer for such year and all subsequent taxable years, except that the Secretary may consent to a different treatment of any interest with respect to which an election has been made.

(d) Operating mineral interests defined.

For purposes of this section, the term "operating mineral interest" includes only an interest in respect of which the costs of production of the mineral are required to be taken into account by the taxpayer for purposes of computing the taxable income limitation provided for in section 613, or would be so required if the mine, well, or other natural deposit were in the production stage.

(e) Special rule as to nonoperating mineral interests.

(1) Aggregation of separate interests. If a taxpayer owns two or more separate nonoperating mineral interests in a single tract or parcel of land or in two or more adjacent tracts or parcels of land, the Secretary shall, on showing by the taxpayer that a principal purpose is not the avoidance of tax, permit the taxpayer to treat (for all purposes of this subtitle) all such mineral interests in each separate kind of mineral deposit as one property. If such permission is granted for any taxable year, the taxpayer shall treat such interests as one property for all subsequent taxable years unless the Secretary consents to a different treatment.

(2) Nonoperating mineral interests defined. For purposes of this subsection, the term "nonoperating mineral interests" includes only interests which are not operating mineral interests.

In 1990, P.L. 101-508, Sec. 11522(b)(2), substituted "taxable income" for "50 percent" in subsec. (d), effective for tax. yrs. begin. after 12/31/90.

In 1978, P.L. 95-618, Sec. 402(a)(2)(C), added "or geothermal deposits" following "gas wells" in the heading of subsec. (b) and in so much of the text as precedes para. (b)(1) . . . Sec. 403(a)(2)(D), substituted "oil and gas wells and geothermal deposits" for "oil and gas wells" each place it appeared in subsec. (c), effective 10/1/78 for tax. yrs. end. on or after 10/1/78.

In 1976, P.L. 94-455, Sec. 1901(a)(87)(A), deleted para. (c)(4), effective for elections to form aggregations of operating mineral interests made under section 614(c)(1) for tax. yrs. begin. after 12/31/76.

Prior to amendment, para. (c)(4) read as follows:

"(4) Special rule as to deductions under section 615(a) prior to aggregation.

"(A) In general. If an aggregation of operating mineral interests formed under paragraph (1) includes any interest or interests in respect of which exploration expenditures, paid or incurred after the acquisition of such interest or interests, were deducted by the taxpayer under section 615(a) for any taxable year all or any portion of which precedes the date on which such aggregation becomes effective, or the date on which such interest or interests become a part of such aggregation (as the case may be), then the tax imposed by this chapter for such taxable year shall be recomputed as provided in subparagraph (B). In the case of any taxable year beginning before January 1, 1958, this subparagraph shall apply to exploration expenditures deducted in respect of any interest or interests for such taxable year, only if such interest or interests constitute part or all of any operating unit with respect to which the taxpayer makes an election pursuant to paragraph (3)(B) which is applicable with respect to such taxable year.

"(B) Recomputation of tax. A recomputation of the tax imposed by this chapter shall be made for each taxable year described in subparagraph (A) for which exploration expenditures were deducted as though, for each such year, an election had been made to aggregate the separate operating mineral interest or interests with respect to which such exploration expenditures were deducted with those operating mineral interests included in the aggregation formed under paragraph (1) in respect of which any expenditure for exploration, development, or operation had been made by the taxpayer before or during the taxable year to which such election would apply. A recomputation of the tax imposed by this chapter (or by the corresponding provisions of the Internal Revenue Code of 1939) shall also be made for taxable years affected by the recomputation described in the preceding sentence. If the tax so recomputed for any taxable year or years, by reason of the application of this paragraph, exceeds the tax liability previously determined for such year or years, such excess shall be taken into account in the first taxable year to which the election to aggregate under paragraph (1) applies and succeeding taxable years as provided in subparagraph (C).

"(C) Increase in tax. The tax imposed by this chapter for the first taxable year to which the election to aggregate under paragraph (1) applies, and for each succeeding taxable year until the full amount of the excess described in subparagraph (B) has been taken into account, shall be increased by an amount equal to the quotient obtained by dividing such excess by the total number of taxable years described in subparagraph (A) in respect of which—

"(i) exploration expenditures were deducted by the taxpayer under section 615(a), and

"(ii) the recomputation of tax described in the first sentence of subparagraph (B) results in an increase in tax or a reduction of a net operating loss.

If the taxpayer dies or ceases to exist, then so much of the excess described in subparagraph (B) as was not taken into account under the preceding sentence for taxable years preceding such death, or such cessation of existence, shall be taken into account for the taxable year in which such death, or such cessation of existence, occurs.

"(D) Basis adjustment. If the tax liability of a taxpayer is increased by reason of the application of this paragraph, proper adjustments shall be made with respect to the basis of the aggregated property owned by such taxpayer, in accordance with regulations prescribed by the Secretary or his delegate, as though the tax liability of the taxpayer for the prior taxable year or years had been determined in accordance with the recomputation of tax described in subparagraph (B)."

—P.L. 94-455, Sec. 1901(a)(87)(B), substituted "A separate property so formed may, under regulations prescribed by the Secretary, be included as part of an aggregation in accordance with paragraphs (1) and (3)." for "A separate property so formed may, under regulations prescribed by the Secretary or his delegate, be included as part of an aggregation in accordance with paragraphs (1) and (3), but the provisions of paragraph (4) shall not apply with respect to such separate property." in the third sentence of para. (c)(2), effective for tax. yrs. begin. after 12/31/76.

—P.L. 94-455, Sec. 1901(a)(87)(C), amended para. (c)(3), effective for tax. yrs. begin. after 12/31/76.

Prior to amendment, para. (c)(3) read as follows:

"(3) Manner and scope of election.

"(A) In general. Except as provided in subparagraph (D), the election provided by paragraph (1) shall be made for each operating mineral interest, in accordance with regulations prescribed by the Secretary or his delegate, not later than the time prescribed by law for filing the return (including extensions thereof) for whichever of the following taxable years is the later: The first taxable year beginning after December 31, 1957, or the first taxable year in which any expenditure for development or operation in respect of the separate operating mineral interest is made by the taxpayer after the acquisition of such interest. Except as provided in subparagraph (D), the election provided by paragraph (2) shall be made for any property, in accordance with regulations prescribed by the Secretary or his delegate, not later than the time prescribed by law for filing the return (including extensions thereof) for whichever of the following taxable years is the later: The first taxable year beginning after December 31, 1957, or the first taxable year in which expenditures for development or operation of more than one mine in respect of the property are made by the taxpayer after the acquisition of the property. No election may be made pursuant to this subparagraph for any operating mineral interest which constitutes part of all of an operating unit if the taxpayer makes an election pursuant to subparagraph (B) with respect to any operating mineral interest which constitutes part or all of such operating unit.

"(B) Taxable years beginning before January 1, 1958. The election provided by paragraph (1) may, at the election of the taxpayer, be made for each operating mineral interest, in accordance with regulations prescribed by the Secretary or his delegate, within the time provided in subparagraph (D), for whichever of the following taxable years is the later (not including any taxable year in respect of which an assessment of deficiency is prevented on the date of the enactment of the Technical Amendments Act of 1958 by the operation of any law or rule of law): The first taxable year of the taxpayer which begins after December 31, 1953, and ends after August 16, 1954, or the first taxable year in which any expenditure for development or operation in respect of the separate operating mineral interest is made by the taxpayer after the acquisition of such interest. The election provided by paragraph (2) may, at the election of the taxpayer, be made for any property, in accordance with regulations prescribed by the Secretary or his delegate, within the time prescribed in subparagraph (D), for whichever of the following taxable years is the later (not including any taxable year in respect of which an assessment of deficiency is prevented on the date of the enactment of the Technical Amendments Act of 1958 by the operation of any law or rule of law): The first taxable year beginning after December 31, 1953, and ending after August 16, 1954, or the first taxable year in which expenditures for development or operation of more than one mine in respect of the property are made by the taxpayer after the acquisition of the property.

"(C) Effect. An election made under paragraph (1) or (2) shall be binding upon the taxpayer for all subsequent taxable years, except that the Secretary or his delegate may consent to a different treatment of any interest with respect to which an election has been made.

"(D) Election after final regulations. Notwithstanding any other provision of this paragraph the time for making an election under paragraph (1) or (2) shall not expire prior to the first day of the first month which begins more than 90 days after the date of publication in the Federal Register of final regulations issued under the authority of this subsection.

"(E) Statute of limitations. If the taxpayer makes an election pursuant to subparagraph (B) and if assessment of any deficiency for any taxable year resulting from such election is prevented on the first day of the first month which begins more than 90 days after the date of publication in the Federal Register of final regulations issued under authority of this subsection, or at any time within one year after such day, by the operation of any law or rule of law, such assessment may, nevertheless, be made if made within one year after such day. An election by a taxpayer pursuant to subparagraph (B) shall be considered as a consent to the assessment pursuant to this subparagraph of any such deficiency. If refund or credit of any overpayment of income tax resulting from an election made pursuant to subparagraph (B) is prevented on such day, or at any time within one year after such day, by the operation of any law or rule of law, refund or credit of such overpayment may, nevertheless, be made or allowed if claim therefor is filed within one year after such day. This subparagraph shall not apply to any taxable year in respect of which an assessment of a deficiency, or a refund or credit of an overpayment, as the case may be, is prevented by the operation of any law or rule of law on the date of the enactment of the Technical Amendments Act of 1958."

— P.L. 94-455, Sec. 1906(b)(13)(A), substituted "Secretary" for "Secretary or his delegate" each time it appears in subsecs. (b), (c), and (e), effective for tax. yrs. begin. after 12/31/76.

In 1964, P.L. 88-272, Sec. 226(a), amended subsec. (b) ... Sec. 226(b)(1), amended the heading of subsec. (c) ... Sec. 226(b)(2), deleted para. (c)(5) ... Sec. 226(b)(3), amended subsec. (d) ... Sec. 226(b)(4), deleted "within the meaning of subsection (b)(3)" in para. (e)(2), effective for tax. yrs. begin. after 12/31/63.

Prior to amendment subsec. (b) read as follows:

"(b) Special rule as to operating mineral interests.

"(1) Election to aggregate separate interests. — If a taxpayer owns two or more separate operating mineral interests which constitute part or all of an operating unit, he may elect (for all purposes of this subtitle)—

"(A) to form one aggregation of, and to treat as one property, any two or more of such interests; and

"(B) to treat as a separate property each such interest which he does not elect to include within the aggregation referred to in subparagraph (A). For purposes of the preceding sentence, separate operating mineral interests which constitute part or all of an operating unit may be aggregated whether or not they are included in a single tract or parcel of land and whether or not they are included in contiguous tracts or parcels. A taxpayer may not elect to form more than one aggregation of operating mineral interests within any one operating unit.

"(2) Manner and scope of election. — The election provided by paragraph (1) shall be made, for each operating mineral interest in accordance with regulations prescribed by the Secretary or his delegate, not later than the time prescribed by law for filing the return (including extensions thereof) for whichever of the following taxable years is the later: The first taxable year beginning after December 31, 1953, or the first taxable year in which any expenditure for exploration, development, or operation in respect of the separate operating mineral interest is made by the taxpayer after the acquisition of such interest. Such an election shall be binding upon the taxpayer for all subsequent taxable years, except that the Secretary or his delegate may consent to a different treatment of the interest with respect to which the election has been made.

"(3) Operating mineral interests defined. — For purposes of this subsection, the term 'operating mineral interest' includes only an interest in respect of which the costs of production of the mineral are required to be taken into account by the taxpayer for purposes of computing the 50 percent limitation provided for in section 613, or would be so required if the mine, well, or other natural deposit were in the production stage.

"(4) Termination with respect to mines. — Except in the case of oil and gas wells —

"(A) an election made under the provisions of this subsection shall not apply with respect to any taxable year beginning after December 31, 1957, and

"(B) if a taxpayer makes an election under the provisions of subsection (c)(3)(B) for any operating mineral interest which constitutes part or all of an operating unit, an election made under the provisions of this subsection shall not apply with respect to any operating mineral interest which constitutes part or all of such operating unit for any taxable year for which the election under subsection (c)(3)(B) is effective."

Prior to amendment, heading of subsec. (c) read as follows:

"1958 Special rules as to operating mineral interest in mines."

Prior to amendment, para. (c)(5) read as follows:

"(5) Operating mineral interests defined. — For purposes of this subsection, the term 'operating mineral interest' has the meaning as assigned to it by subsection (b)(3)."

Prior to amendment, subsec. (d) read as follows:

"(d) 1939 code treatment with respect to operating mineral interests in case of oil and gas wells. In the case of oil and gas wells, any taxpayer may treat any property (determined as if the Internal Revenue Code of 1939 continued to apply) as if subsections (a) and (b) had not been enacted. If any such treatment would constitute an aggregation under subsection (b), such treatment shall be taken into account in applying subsection (b) to other property of the taxpayer."

— P.L. 88-272, Sec. 226(c), provided that

"For purposes of the Internal Revenue Code of 1954—

"(1) Fair market value rule. — Except as provided in paragraph (2), if a taxpayer has a section 614(b) aggregation, then the adjusted basis (as of the first day of the first taxable year beginning after December 31, 1963) of each property included in such aggregation shall be determined by multiplying the adjusted basis of the aggregation by a fraction—

"(A) the numerator of which is the fair market value of such property, and

"(B) the denominator of which is the fair market value of such aggregation.

For purposes of this paragraph, the adjusted basis and the fair market value of the aggregation, and the fair market value of each property included therein, shall be determined as of the day preceding the first day of the first taxable year which begins after December 31, 1963.

"(2) Allocation of adjustments, etc. — If the taxpayer makes an election under this paragraph with respect to any section 614(b) aggregation, then the adjusted basis (as of the first day of the first taxable year beginning December 31, 1963) of each property included in such aggregation shall be the adjusted basis of such property at the time it was first included in the aggregation by the taxpayer, adjusted for that portion of those adjustments to the basis of the aggregation which are reasonably attributable to such property. If, under the preceding sentence, the total of the adjusted bases of the interests included in the aggregation exceeds the adjusted basis of the aggregation (as of the day preceding the first day of the first taxable year which begins after December 31, 1963), the adjusted bases of the properties which include such interests shall be adjusted, under regulations prescribed by the Secretary of the Treasury or his delegate, so that the total of the adjusted basis of such interests equals the adjusted basis of the aggregation. An election under this paragraph shall be made at such time and in such manner as the Secretary of the Treasury or his delegate shall by regulations prescribe.

"(3) Definitions. — For purposes of this subsection—

"(A) Section 614(b) aggregation. —

"The term 'section 614(b) aggregation' means any aggregation to which section 614(b)(1)(A) of the Internal Revenue Code of 1954 (as in effect before the amendments made by subsection (a) of this section) applied for the day preceding the first day of the first taxable year beginning after December 31, 1963.

"(B) Property.

"The term 'property' has the same meaning as is applicable, under section 614 of the Internal Revenue Code of 1954, to the taxpayer for the first taxable year beginning after December 31, 1963."

In 1958, P.L. 85-866, Sec. 37(a), added para. (b)(4) ... Sec. 37(c), added subsec. (d), effective for tax. yrs. begin. after 12/31/53, and end. after 8/16/54.

— P.L. 85-866, Sec. 37(b), redesignated subsec. (c) as (e) and added subsec. (d), effective for tax. yrs. begin. after 12/31/57, except that such amendments shall, at the election of the taxpayer made in conformity with such amendments, apply to tax. yrs. begin. after 12/31/53, and end. after 8/16/54.

— P.L. 85-866, Sec. 37(d), amended the first sentence of para. (e)(1), effective for tax. yrs. begin. after 12/31/57, except that with respect to any taxpayer such amendment shall, at the election of the taxpayer, apply to tax. yrs. begin. after 12/31/53, and end. after 8/16/54.

Prior to amendment, first sentence of para. (e)(1) read as follows:

"If a taxpayer owns two or more separate nonoperating mineral interests in a single tract or parcel of land, or in two or more contiguous tracts or parcels of land, the Secretary or his delegate may, on showing of undue hardship, permit the taxpayer to treat (for all purposes of this subtitle) all such mineral interests as one property."

Sec. 615. Repealed.

In 1976, P.L. 94-455, Sec. 1901(a)(88), repealed Code Sec. 615, for tax. yrs. begin. after '76.

Prior to amendment, Code Sec. 615 read as follows:

"SEC. 615. PRE-1970 EXPLORATION EXPENDITURES.

"(a) In general.

"In the case of expenditures paid or incurred during the taxable year for the purpose of ascertaining the existence, location, extent, or quality of any deposit of ore or other mineral, and paid or incurred before the beginning of the development stage of the mine or deposit, there shall be allowed as a deduction in computing taxable income so much of such expenditures as does not exceed $100,000. This section shall apply only with respect to the amount of such expenditures which, but for this section, would not be allowable as a deduction for the taxable year. This section shall not apply to expenditures for the acquisition or improvement of property of a character which is subject to the allowance for depreciation provided in section 167, but allowances for depreciation shall be considered, for purposes of this section, as expenditures paid or incurred. In no case shall this section apply with respect to amounts paid or incurred for the purpose of ascertaining the existence, location, extent, or quality of any deposit of oil or gas.

"(b) Election of taxpayer.

"If the taxpayer elects, in accordance with regulations prescribed by the Secretary or his delegate, to treat as deferred expenses any portion of the amount deductible for the taxable year under subsection (a), such portion shall not be deductible in the manner provided in subsection (a) but shall be deductible on a ratable basis as the units of produced ores or minerals discovered or explored by reason of such expenditures are sold. An election made under this subsection for any taxable year shall be binding for such year.

"(c) Limitation.

"(1) In general. This section shall not apply to any amount paid or incurred to the extent that it would, when added to the amounts which have been deducted under subsection (a) and the amounts which have been treated as deferred expenses under subsection (b), or the corresponding provisions of prior law, exceed $400,000.

"(2) Amounts taken into account. For purposes of paragraph (1), there shall be taken into account amounts deducted and amounts treated as deferred expenses by—

"(A) the taxpayer, and

"(B) any individual or corporation who has transferred to the taxpayer any mineral property.

"(3) Application of paragraph (2)(B). Paragraph (2)(B) shall apply with respect to all amounts deducted and all amounts treated as deferred expenses which were paid or incurred before the latest such transfer from the individual or corporation to the taxpayer. Paragraph (2)(B) shall apply only if—

"(A) the taxpayer acquired any mineral property from the individual or corporation under circumstances which make paragraph (7), (8), (11), (15), (17), (20), or (22) of section 113(a) of the Internal Revenue Code of 1939 apply to such transfer;

"(B) the taxpayer would be entitled under section 381(c)(10) to deduct expenses deferred under this section had the distributor or transferor corporation elected to defer such expenses; or

"(C) the taxpayer acquired any mineral property from the individual or corporation under circumstances which make sections 334(b), 362(a) and (b), 372(a), 373(b)(1), 1051, or 1082 apply to such transfer.

"(d) Adjusted basis of mine or deposit.

"The amount of expenditures which are treated under subsection (b) as deferred expenses shall be taken into account in computing the adjusted basis of the mine or deposit, but such amounts, and the adjustments to basis provided in section 1016(a)(10) shall be disregarded in determining the adjusted basis of the property for the purpose of computing a deduction for depletion under section 611.

"(e) Election to have section apply.

"This section (other than subsections (f) and (g)) shall apply only if the taxpayer so elects in such manner as the Secretary or his delegate may by regulations prescribe. Such election shall be made before the expiration of 3 years after the time prescribed by law (determined without any extension thereof) for filing the return for the first taxable year ending after the date of the enactment of this subsection in which expenditures described in subsection (a) are paid or incurred after such date. Such election may not be revoked after the expiration of such 3 years.

"(f) Section 615 and section 617 elections to be mutually exclusive.

"A taxpayer who has made an election under subsection (e) (which he has not revoked) may not make an election under section 617(a). A taxpayer who has made an election under section 617(a) (which he has not revoked) may not make an election under subsection (e) of this section.

"(g) Effect of transfer of mineral property.

"(1) Transfer before election. If—

"(A) any person transfers any mineral property to another person in a transaction as a result of which the basis of such property in the hands of the transferee is determined by reference to the basis in the hands of the transferor, and

"(B) the transferor has not, at the time of the transfer, made an election under either subsection (a) of section 617 or subsection (e) of this section,

then no election by the transferor under either such subsection shall apply with respect to expenditures which are made by the transferor after the date of the enactment of this subsection and before the date of the transfer and which are properly chargeable to such property.

For purposes of the preceding sentence, a transferor of mineral property who made an election under subsection (a) of section 617 or subsection (e) of this section before the transfer but who revokes such election after the transfer shall be treated with respect to such property as not having made an election under either such subsection.

"(2) Effect of election by transferee under section 617. If—

"(A) the taxpayer receives mineral property in a transaction described in paragraph (1)(A),

"(B) an election made by the transferor under subsection (e) applies with respect to expenditures which are made by him after the date of the enactment of this subsection and before the date of the transfer and which are properly chargeable to such property, and

"(C) the taxpayer has made or makes an election under section 617(a),

then in applying section 617 with respect to the transferee, the amounts allowed as deductions under this section to the transferor, which (but for the transferor's election) would be reflected in the adjusted basis of such property in the hands of the transferee, shall be treated as expenditures allowed as deductions under section 617(a) to the transferor. Notwithstanding subsections (b) and (d) of this section (and section 381(c)(10)), any deferred expenses described in subsection (b) which are not allowed as deductions to the transferor for a period before the transfer may not be deducted by the transferee and in his hands shall be charged to capital account.

"(h) Termination.

"The provisions of this section shall not apply with respect to expenditures paid or incurred after December 31, 1969."

In **1969**, P.L. 91-172, Sec. 504(a), added "Pre-1970" to heading of Code Sec. and added subsec. (h), for exploration expenditures paid or incurred after 12/31/69.

In **1966**, P.L. 89-570, Sec. 2(a), added subsecs. (e), (f), and (g) for tax. yrs. ending after Sept. 12, '66, but only for expenditures paid or incurred after Sept. 12, '66.

In **1960**, P.L. 86-594, Sec. 1, amended subsec. (c) for tax. yrs. begin. after 7/6/60. Before amendment subsec. (c) read as follows:

"(c) Limitation.

"This section shall not apply to any amount paid or incurred in any taxable year if in any 4 preceding years a deduction or election under this section, or the corresponding provision of prior laws, has been allowed to, or exercised by—

"(1) the taxpayer, or

"(2) the individual or corporation who has transferred to the taxpayer any mineral property.

Paragraph (2) shall apply only if (A) the taxpayer was required to take into account under section 23(ff)(3) of the Internal Revenue Code of 1939 the deduction allowed to or election exercised by such individual or corporation; (B) the taxpayer would be entitled under section 381(c)(10) to deduct expenses deferred under this section had the distributor or transferor corporation elected to defer such expenses; or (C) the taxpayer acquired any mineral property under circumstances which make section 334(b), 362(a), and (b), 372(a), 373(b)(1), 723, 732, 1051, or 1082 apply to such transfer."

Sec. 616. Development expenditures.

(a) In general.

Except as provided in subsections (b) and (d), there shall be allowed as a deduction in computing taxable income all expenditures paid or incurred during the taxable year for the development of a mine or other natural deposit (other than an oil or gas well) if paid or incurred after the existence of ores or minerals in commercially marketable quantities has been disclosed. This section shall not apply to expenditures for the acquisition or improvement of property of a character which is subject to the allowance for depreciation provided in section 167, but allowances for depreciation shall be considered, for purposes of this section, as expenditures.

(b) Election of taxpayer.

At the election of the taxpayer, made in accordance with regulations prescribed by the Secretary, expenditures described in subsection (a) paid or incurred during the taxable year shall be treated as deferred expenses and shall be deductible on a ratable basis as the units of produced ores or minerals benefited by such expenditures are sold. In the case of such expenditures paid or incurred during the development stage of the mine or deposit, the election shall apply only with respect to the excess of such expenditures during the taxable year over the net receipts during the taxable year from the ores or minerals produced from such mine or deposit. The election under this subsection, if made, must be for the total amount of such expenditures, or the total amount of such excess, as the case may be, with respect to the mine or deposit, and shall be binding for such taxable year.

(c) Adjusted basis of mine or deposit.

The amount of expenditures which are treated under subsection (b) as deferred expenses shall be taken into account in computing the adjusted basis of the mine or deposit, except that such amount, and the adjustments to basis provided in section 1016(a)(9), shall be disregarded in determining the adjusted basis of the property for the purpose of computing a deduction for depletion under section 611.

(d) Special rules for foreign development.

In the case of any expenditures paid or incurred with respect to the development of a mine or other natural deposit (other than an oil, gas, or geothermal well) located outside of the United States—

(1) subsections (a) and (b) shall not apply, and

(2) such expenditures shall—

(A) at the election of the taxpayer, be included in adjusted basis for purposes of computing the amount of any deduction allowable under section 611 (without regard to section 613), or

(B) if subparagraph (A) does not apply, be allowed as a deduction ratably over the 10-taxable year period beginning with the taxable year in which such expenditures were paid or incurred.

(e) Cross reference.

For election of 10-year amortization of expenditures allowable as a deduction under subsection (a), see section 59(e).

In **1988**, P.L. 100-647, Sec. 1007(g)(7), substituted "section 59(e)" for "section 58(i)" in subsec. (e), effective for costs paid or incurred after 12/31/86, in tax. yrs. end. after 12/31/86.

In 1986, P.L. 99-514, Sec. 411(b)(2)(A), redesignated subsec. (d) as subsec. (e) and added new subsec. (d) . . . Sec. 411(b)(2)(C)(i), substituted "subsections (b) and (d)" for "subsection (b)" in subsec. (a), effective for costs paid or incurred after 12/31/86, in tax. yrs. end. after 12/31/86. Sec. 411(c)(2) of this Act provides a transitional rule as follows:

"(2) Transition rule.—The amendments made by this section shall not apply with respect to intangible drilling and development costs incurred by United States companies pursuant to a minority interest in a license for Netherlands or United Kingdom North Sea development if such interest was acquired on or before December 31, 1985."

In 1983, P.L. 97-448, Sec. 306(a)(1)(A)(i), redesignated the second Sec. 201(c) of P.L. 97-248 as Sec. 201(d) of P.L. 97-248, see below.

In 1982, P.L. 97-248, Sec. 201(d)(9)(C), [as redesignated by Sec. 306(a)(1)(A)(i) of P.L. 97-448, see above] added subsec. (d), effective for tax. yrs. begin. after 12/31/82.

In 1976, P.L. 94-455, Sec. 1906(b)(13)(A), substituted "Secretary" for "Secretary or his delegate" in subsec. (b), effective for tax. yrs. begin. after 12/31/76.

Sec. 617. Deduction and recapture of certain mining exploration expenditures.

(a) Allowance of deduction.

(1) **General rule.** At the election of the taxpayer, expenditures paid or incurred during the taxable year for the purpose of ascertaining the existence, location, extent, or quality of any deposit of ore or other mineral, and paid or incurred before the beginning of the development stage of the mine, shall be allowed as a deduction in computing taxable income. This subsection shall apply only with respect to the amount of such expenditures which, but for this subsection, would not be allowable as a deduction for the taxable year. This subsection shall not apply to expenditures for the acquisition or improvement of property of a character which is subject to the allowance for depreciation provided in section 167, but allowances for depreciation shall be considered, for purposes of this subsection, as expenditures paid or incurred. In no case shall this subsection apply with respect to amounts paid or incurred for the purpose of ascertaining the existence, location, extent, or quality of any deposit of oil or gas or of any mineral with respect to which a deduction for percentage depletion is not allowable under section 613.

(2) **Elections.**

(A) Method. Any election under this subsection shall be made in such manner as the Secretary may by regulations prescribe.

(B) Time and scope. The election provided by paragraph (1) for the taxable year may be made at any time before the expiration of the period prescribed for making a claim for credit or refund of the tax imposed by this chapter for the taxable year. Such an election for the taxable year shall apply to all expenditures described in paragraph (1) paid or incurred by the taxpayer during the taxable year or during any subsequent taxable year. Such an election may not be revoked unless the Secretary consents to such revocation.

(C) Deficiencies. The statutory period for the assessment of any deficiency for any taxable year, to the extent such deficiency is attributable to an election or revocation of an election under this subsection, shall not expire before the last day of the 2-year period beginning on the day after the date on which such election or revocation of election is made; and such deficiency may be assessed at any time before the expiration of such 2-year period, notwithstanding any law or rule of law which would otherwise prevent such assessment.

(b) Recapture on reaching producing stage.

(1) **Recapture.** If, in any taxable year, any mine with respect to which expenditures were deducted pursuant to subsection (a) reaches the producing stage, then—

(A) If the taxpayer so elects with respect to all such mines reaching the producing stage during the taxable year, he shall include in gross income for the taxable year an amount equal to the adjusted exploration expenditures with respect to such mines, and the amount so included in income shall be treated for purposes of this subtitle as expenditures which (i) are paid or incurred on the respective dates on which the mines reach the producing stage, and (ii) are properly chargeable to capital account.

(B) If subparagraph (A) does not apply with respect to any such mine, then the deduction for depletion under section 611 with respect to the property shall be disallowed until the amount of depletion which would be allowable but for this subparagraph equals the amount of the adjusted exploration expenditures with respect to such mine.

(2) **Elections.**

(A) Method. Any election under this subsection shall be made in such manner as the Secretary may by regulations prescribe.

(B) Time and scope. The election provided by paragraph (1) for any taxable year may be made or changed not later than the time prescribed by law for filing the return (including extensions thereof) for such taxable year.

(c) Recapture in case of bonus or royalty.

If an election has been made under subsection (a) with respect to expenditures relating to a mining property and the taxpayer receives or accrues a bonus or a royalty with respect to such property, then the deduction for depletion under section 611 with respect to the bonus or royalty shall be disallowed until the amount of depletion which would be allowable but for this subsection equals the amount of the adjusted exploration expenditures with respect to the property to which the bonus or royalty relates.

(d) Gain from dispositions of certain mining property.

(1) **General rule.** Except as otherwise provided in this subsection, if mining property is disposed of the lower of—

(A) the adjusted exploration expenditures with respect to such property, or

(B) the excess of—

(i) the amount realized (in the case of a sale, exchange, or involuntary conversion), or the fair market value (in the case of any other disposition), over

(ii) the adjusted basis of such property,

shall be treated as ordinary income. Such gain shall be recognized notwithstanding any other provision of this subtitle.

(2) **Disposition of portion of property.** For purposes of paragraph (1)—

(A) In the case of the disposition of a portion of a mining property (other than an undivided interest), the entire amount of the adjusted exploration expenditures with respect to such property shall be treated as attributable to such portion to the extent of the amount of the gain to which paragraph (1) applies.

(B) In the case of the disposition of an undivided interest in a mining property (or a portion thereof), a proportionate part of the adjusted exploration expenditures with respect to such property shall be treated as attributable to such undivided interest to the extent of the amount of the gain to which paragraph (1) applies.

This paragraph shall not apply to any expenditure to the extent the taxpayer establishes to the satisfaction of the Secretary that such expenditure relates neither to the portion (or interest therein) disposed of nor to any mine, in the property held by the taxpayer before the disposition, which has reached the producing stage.

(3) Exceptions and limitations. Paragraphs (1), (2), and (3) of section 1245(b) (relating to exceptions and limitations with respect to gain from disposition of certain depreciable property) shall apply in respect of this subsection in the same manner and with the same effect as if references in section 1245(b) to section 1245 or any provision thereof were references to this subsection or the corresponding provisions of this subsection and as if references to section 1245 property were references to mining property.

(4) Application of subsection. This subsection shall apply notwithstanding any other provision of this subtitle.

(5) Coordination with section 1254. This subsection shall not apply to any disposition to which section 1254 applies.

(e) Basis of property.

(1) Basis. The basis of any property shall not be reduced by the amount of any depletion which would be allowable but for the application of this section.

(2) Adjustments. The Secretary shall prescribe such regulations as he may deem necessary to provide for adjustments to the basis of property to reflect gain recognized under subsection (d)(1).

(f) Definitions.

For purposes of this section—

(1) Adjusted exploration expenditures. The term "adjusted exploration expenditures" means, with respect to any property or mine—

(A) the amount of the expenditures allowed for the taxable year and all preceding taxable years as deductions under subsection (a) to the taxpayer or any other person which are properly chargeable to such property or mine and which (but for the election under subsection (a)) would be reflected in the adjusted basis of such property or mine, reduced by

(B) for the taxable year and for each preceding taxable year, the amount (if any) by which (i) the amount which would have been allowable for percentage depletion under section 613 but for the deduction of such expenditures, exceeds (ii) the amount allowable for depletion under section 611,

properly adjusted for any amounts included in gross income under subsection (b) or (c) and for any amounts of gain to which subsection (d) applied.

(2) Mining property. The term "mining property" means any property (within the meaning of section 614 after the application of subsections (c) and (e) thereof) with respect to which any expenditures allowed as a deduction under subsection (a)(1) are properly chargeable.

(3) Disposal of coal or domestic iron ore with a retained economic interest. A transaction which constitutes a disposal of coal or iron ore under section 631(c) shall be treated as a disposition. In such a case, the excess referred to in subsection (d)(1)(B) shall be treated as equal to the gain (if any) referred to in section 631(c).

(g) Special rules relating to partnership property.

(1) Property distributed to partner. In the case of any property or mine received by the taxpayer in a distribution with respect to part or all of his interest in a partnership, the adjusted exploration expenditures with respect to such property or mine include the adjusted exploration expenditures (not otherwise included under subsection (f)(1)) with respect to such property or mine immediately prior to such distribution, but the adjusted exploration expenditures with respect to any such property or mine shall be reduced by the amount of gain to which section 751(b) applied realized by the partnership (as constituted after the distribution) on the distribution of such property or mine.

(2) Property retained by partnership. In the case of any property or mine held by a partnership after a distribution to a partner to which section 751(b) applied, the adjusted exploration expenditures with respect to such property or mine shall, under regulations prescribed by the Secretary, be reduced by the amount of gain to which section 751(b) applied realized by such partner with respect to such distribution on account of such property or mine.

(h) Special rules for foreign exploration.

In the case of any expenditures paid or incurred before the development stage for the purpose of ascertaining the existence, location, extent, or quality of any deposit of ore or other mineral (other than an oil, gas, or geothermal well) located outside the United States—

(1) subsection (a) shall not apply, and

(2) such expenditures shall—

(A) at the election of the taxpayer, be included in adjusted basis for purposes of computing the amount of any deduction allowable under section 611 (without regard to section 613), or

(B) if subparagraph (A) does not apply, be allowed as a deduction ratably over the 10-taxable year period beginning with the taxable year in which such expenditures were paid or incurred.

(i) Cross reference.

For election of 10-year amortization of expenditures allowable as a deduction under this section, see section 59(e).

In 1990, P.L. 101-508, Sec. 11801(a)(27), deleted subsec. (i)... Sec. 11801(c)(13), redesignated subsec. (j) as subsec. (i), effective 11/5/90 except as provided in Sec. 11821(b) of this Act, which reads as follows:
"(b) Savings provision. If—
"(1) any provision amended or repealed by this part applied to—
"(A) any transaction occurring before the date of the enactment of this Act [11/5/90],
"(B) any property acquired before such date of enactment [11/5/90], or
"(C) any item of income, loss, deduction, or credit taken into account before such date of enactment [11/5/90], and
"(2) the treatment of such transaction, property, or item under such provision would (without regard to the amendments made by this part) affect liability for tax periods ending after such date of enactment [11/5/90],
nothing in the amendments made by this part shall be construed to affect the treatment of such transaction, property, or item for purposes of determining liability for tax for periods ending after such date of enactment [11/5/90]."
Prior to deletion, subsec. (i) read as follows:
"(i) Certain pre-1970 exploration expenditures. If—
"(1) the taxpayer receives mineral property in a transaction as a result of which the basis of such property in the hands of the transferee is determined by reference to the basis in the hands of the transferor,
"(2) an election made by the transferor under subsection (e) of section 615(e) (as in effect before the enactment of the Tax Reform Act of 1976) applied with respect to expenditures which were made by him and which were properly chargeable to such property, and
"(3) the taxpayer has made or makes an election under subsection (a),
then in the application of this section with respect to the transferee, the amounts allowed as deductions under such section 615 to the transferor, which (but for the transferor's election) would be reflected in the adjusted basis of such property in the hands of the transferee, shall be treated as expenditures allowed as deductions under subsection (a) to the transferor."
In 1988, P.L. 100-647, Sec. 1007(g)(7), substituted "section 59(e)" for "section 58(i)" in subsec. (j), effective for costs paid or incurred after 12/31/86, in tax. years end. after 12/31/86.
In 1986, P.L. 99-514, Sec. 411(b)(2)(B), amended subsec. (h), effective for costs paid or incurred after 12/31/86, in tax. yrs. end. after 12/31/86. Sec. 411(c)(2) of this Act provides a transitional rule as follows:
"(2) Transition rule.—The amendments made by this section shall not apply with respect to intangible drilling and development costs incurred by United States companies pursuant to a minority interest in a license for Netherlands or United Kingdom North Sea development if such interest was acquired on or before December 31, 1985."
Prior to amendment, subsec. (h) read as follow:
"(h) Limitations.
"(1) In general. Subsection (a) shall apply to any amount paid or incurred after December 31, 1969, with respect to any deposit of ore or other mineral located

Natural resources Code Sec. 631(a)

outside the United States, only to the extent that such amount, when added to the amounts which are or have been deducted under subsection (a) and subsection (a) of section 615 as in effect before the enactment of the Tax Reform Act of 1976, or the corresponding provisions of prior law, does not exceed $400,000.

"(2) Amounts taken into account. For purposes of paragraph (1), there shall be taken into account amounts deducted and amounts treated as deferred expenses by—
"(A) the taxpayer, and
"(B) any individual or corporation who has transferred to the taxpayer any mineral property.
"(3) Application of paragraph (2)(B). Paragraph (2)(B) shall apply with respect to all amounts deducted before the latest such transfer from the individual or corporation to the taxpayer. Paragraph (2)(B) shall apply only if—
"(A) the taxpayer acquired any mineral property from the individual or corporation under circumstances which make paragraph (7), (8), (11), (15), (17), (20), or (22) of section 113(a) of the Internal Revenue Code of 1939 apply to such transfer; or
"(B) the taxpayer acquired any mineral property from the individual or corporation under circumstances which make section 334(b), 338, 362(a) and (b), 372(a), 374(b)(1), 1051, or 1082 apply to such transfer."
—P.L. 99-514, Sec. 413(b), added para. (d)(5), effective for any disposition of property which is placed in service by the taxpayer after 12/31/86. Sec. 413(c)(2) of this Act provides an exception as follows:
"(2) Exception for binding contracts. The amendments made by this section shall not apply to any disposition of property placed in service after December 31, 1986, if such property was acquired pursuant to a written contract which was entered into before September 26, 1985, and which was binding at all times thereafter."
In 1983, P.L. 97-448, Sec. 306(a)(1)(A)(i), redesignated the second Sec. 201(c) of P.L. 97-448 as Sec. 201(d) of P.L. 97-448, see below.
In 1982, P.L. 97-448, Sec. 201(d)(9)(D), [as amended by Sec. 306(a)(1)(A)(i) of P.L. 97-448, see above] added subsec. (j), effective for tax. yrs. begin. after 12/31/82.
—P.L. 97-248, Sec. 224(c)(8), added "338," after "334(b)" in subpara. (h)(3)(B). For effective date see Sec. 224(d) of this Act reproduced in note following Code Sec. 338.
In 1976, P.L. 94-455, Sec. 1901(a)(89), substituted "may not be revoked unless" for "may not be revoked after the last day of the third month following the month in which the final regulations issued under the authority of this subsection are published in the Federal Register, unless" in subpara. (a)(2)(B) . . . Sec. 1901(b)(3)(K), substituted "ordinary income" for "gain from the sale or exchange of property which is neither a capital asset nor property described in section 1231" in para. (d)(1) . . . Sec. 1901(b)(21)(C), substituted "and subsection (a) of section 615 (as in effect before the enactment of the Tax Reform Act of 1976)" for "and section 615(a) and the amounts which are or have been treated as deferred expenses under section 615(b)" in para. (h)(1) . . . Sec. 1901(b)(21)(D), amended para. (h)(3) . . . Sec. 1901(b)(21)(E), added subsec. (i) . . . Sec. 1906(b)(13)(A), substituted "Secretary" for "Secretary or his delegate" each place it appeared in subsecs. (a), (b), (d), (e) and (g), effective for tax. yrs. begin. after 12/31/76.
Prior to amendment, para. (h)(3) read as follows:
"(3) Application of paragraph (2)(B). Paragraph (2)(B) shall apply with respect to all amounts deducted and all amounts treated as deferred expenses which were paid or incurred before from the individual or corporation to the taxpayer. Paragraph (2)(B) shall apply only if—
"(A) the taxpayer acquired any mineral property from the individual or corporation under circumstances which make paragraph (7), (8), (11), (15), (17), (20), or (22) of section 113(a) of the Internal Revenue Code of 1939 apply to such transfer;
"(B) the taxpayer would be entitled under section 381(c)(10) to deduct expenses deferred under section 615(b) had the distributor or transferor corporation elected to defer such expenses; or
"(C) the taxpayer acquired any mineral property from the individual or corporation under circumstances which make section 334(b), 362(a) and (b), 372(a), 373(b)(1), 1051, or 1082 apply to such transfer."
In 1969, P.L. 91-172, Sec. 504(b)(1), amended the heading of Code Sec. 617 . . . Sec. 504(b)(2), deleted "in the United States or on the Outer Continental Shelf (within the meaning of section 2 of the Outer Continental Shelf Lands Act, as amended and supplemented; 43 U.S.C. 1331)" after "deposit of ore or other mineral" in para. (a)(1) . . . Sec. 504(b)(3), amended subsec. (h), effective for exploration expenditures paid or incurred after 12/31/69. Sec. 504(d)(2) of this Act provides as follows:
"(2) Presumption of election under section 617. For purposes of section 617 of the Internal Revenue Code of 1954, an election under section 615(e) of such Code, which is effective with respect to exploration expenditures paid or incurred before January 1, 1970, shall be treated as an election under section 617(a) of such Code with respect to exploration expenditures paid or incurred after December 31, 1969. The preceding sentence shall not apply to any taxpayer who notifies the Secretary of the Treasury or his delegate (at such time and in such manner as the Secretary or his delegate prescribes by regulations) that he does not desire his election under section 615(e) to be so treated."
Prior to amendment, the heading of Code Sec. 617 read as follows:
"SEC. 617. ADDITIONAL EXPLORATION EXPENDITURES IN THE CASE OF DOMESTIC MINING."
Prior to amendment, subsec. (h) read as follows:
"(h) Cross reference. For additional rules applicable for purposes of this section, see subsections (f) and (g) of section 615."

In 1966, P.L. 89-570, Sec. [1], added Code Sec. 617, effective for tax. yrs. end. after 9/12/66, but only for expenditures paid or incurred after 9/12/66.

PART II.— EXCLUSIONS FROM GROSS INCOME [REPEALED]
Sec.
621. Repealed [Payments to encourage exploration, development, and mining for defense purposes].

In 1990, P.L. 101-508, Sec. 11801(a)(28), repealed Part II of Subchapter I of Chapter 1.

Sec. 621. Repealed.

In 1990, P.L. 101-508, Sec. 11801(a)(28), repealed Code Sec. 621, effective 11/5/90, except as provided in Sec. 11821(b) of this Act which reads as follows:
"(b) Savings provision. If—
"(1) any provision amended or repealed by this part applied to—
"(A) any transaction occurring before the date of the enactment of this Act [11/5/90],
"(B) any property acquired before such date of enactment [11/5/90], or
"(C) any item of income, loss, deduction, or credit taken into account before such date of enactment [11/5/90], and
"(2) the treatment of such transaction, property, or item under such provision would (without regard to the amendments made by this part) affect liability for tax for periods ending after such date of enactment [11/5/90],
nothing in the amendments made by this part shall be construed to affect the treatment of such transaction, property, or item for purposes of determining liability for tax for periods ending after such date of enactment [11/5/90]."
Prior to repeal, Code Sec. 621 read as follows:
"SEC. 621. PAYMENTS TO ENCOURAGE EXPLORATION, DEVELOPMENT, AND MINING FOR DEFENSE PURPOSES.
There shall not be included in gross income any amount paid to a taxpayer by the United States (or any agency or instrumentality thereof), whether by grant or loan, and whether or not repayable, for the encouragement of exploration, development, or mining of critical and strategic minerals or metals pursuant to or in connection with any undertaking approved by the United States (or any of its agencies or instrumentalities) and for which an accounting is made or required to be made to an appropriate governmental agency, or any forgiveness or discharge of any part of such amount. Any expenditures (other than expenditures made after the repayment of such grant or loan) attributable to such grant or loan shall not be deductible by the taxpayer as an expense nor increase the basis of the taxpayer's property either for determining gain or loss on sale, exchange, or other disposition or for computing depletion or depreciation, but on the repayment of any portion of any such grant or loan which has been expended in accordance with the terms thereof such deductions and such increase in basis shall to the extent of such repayment be allowed as if made at the time of such repayment."

PART III.— SALES AND EXCHANGES
Sec.
631. Gain or loss in the case of timber, coal, or domestic iron ore.
632. Repealed.

In 1976, P.L. 94-455, Sec. 1901(b)(22)(A), repealed the item for Code Sec. 632.
Prior to amendment, the item for Code Sec. 632 read as follows:
"SEC. 632. SALE OF OIL OR GAS PROPERTIES."
In 1964, inserted reference to domestic iron ore in item 631.

Sec. 631. Gain or loss in the case of timber, coal, or domestic iron ore.
(a) Election to consider cutting as sale or exchange.

If the taxpayer so elects on his return for a taxable year, the cutting of timber (for sale or for use in the taxpayer's trade or business) during such year by the taxpayer who owns, or has a contract right to cut, such timber (providing he has owned such timber or has held such contract right for a period of more than 1 year) shall be considered as a sale or exchange of such timber cut during such year. If such election has been made, gain or loss to the taxpayer shall be recognized in an amount equal to the difference between the fair market value of such timber, and the adjusted basis for depletion of such timber in the hands of the taxpayer. Such fair market value shall be the fair market value as of the first day of the taxable year in which such timber is cut, and shall thereafter be considered as the cost of such cut timber to the taxpayer for all purposes for which such cost is a necessary factor. If a taxpayer makes an election under this subsection, such election shall apply with respect to all timber which is owned by the taxpayer or which the taxpayer has a contract right to cut and shall be binding on the taxpayer for the taxable year for which the election is made and for all subsequent years, unless the Secretary, on showing of undue hardship, permits the taxpayer to revoke his election; such revocation, however, shall preclude any further elections under this subsection except with the consent of the Secretary. For purposes of this subsection and subsection (b), the term "timber" includes evergreen trees which are more than 6 years old at the time severed from the roots and are sold for ornamental purposes.

(b) Disposal of timber.

In the case of the disposal of timber held for more than 1 year before such disposal, by the owner thereof under any form or type of contract by virtue of which such owner either retains an economic interest in such timber or makes an outright sale of such timber, the difference between the amount realized from the disposal of such timber and the adjusted depletion basis thereof, shall be considered as though it were a gain or loss, as the case may be, on the sale of such timber. In determining the gross income, the adjusted gross income, or the taxable income of the lessee, the deductions allowable with respect to rents and royalties shall be determined without regard to the provisions of this subsection. In the case of disposal of timber with a retained economic interest, the date of disposal of such timber shall be deemed to be the date such timber is cut, but if payment is made to the owner under the contract before such timber is cut the owner may elect to treat the date of such payment as the date of disposal of such timber. For purposes of this subsection, the term "owner" means any person who owns an interest in such timber, including a sublessor and a holder of a contract to cut timber.

(c) Disposal of coal or domestic iron ore with a retained economic interest.

In the case of the disposal of coal (including lignite), or iron ore mined in the United States, held for more than 1 year before such disposal, by the owner thereof under any form of contract by virtue of which such owner retains an economic interest in such coal or iron ore, the difference between the amount realized from the disposal of such coal or iron ore and the adjusted depletion basis thereof plus the deductions disallowed for the taxable year under section 272 shall be considered as though it were a gain or loss, as the case may be, on the sale of such coal or iron ore. If for the taxable year of such gain or loss the maximum rate of tax imposed by this chapter on any net capital gain is less than such maximum rate for ordinary income, such owner shall not be entitled to the allowance for percentage depletion provided in section 613 with respect to such coal or iron ore. This subsection shall not apply to income realized by any owner as a co-adventurer, partner, or principal in the mining of such coal or iron ore, and the word "owner" means any person who owns an economic interest in coal or iron ore in place, including a sublessor. The date of disposal of such coal or iron ore shall be deemed to be the date such coal or iron ore is mined. In determining the gross income, the adjusted gross income, or the taxable income of the lessee, the deductions allowable with respect to rents and royalties shall be determined without regard to the provisions of this subsection. This subsection shall have no application, for purposes of applying subchapter G, relating to corporations used to avoid income tax on shareholders (including the determinations of the amount of the deductions under section 535(b)(6) or section 545(b)(5)). This subsection shall not apply to any disposal of iron ore or coal—

(1) to a person whose relationship to the person disposing of such iron ore or coal would result in the disallowance of losses under section 267 or 707(b), or

(2) to a person owned or controlled directly or indirectly by the same interests which own or control the person disposing of such iron ore or coal.

In 2005, P.L. 109-135, Sec. 403(a)(19), amended Sec. 102(e) of P.L. 108-357 to read as follows:
"(e) Effective date.
"(1) In general. The amendments made by this section shall apply to taxable years beginning after December 31, 2004.
"(2) Application to pass-thru entities, etc. In determining the deduction under section 199 of the Internal Revenue Code of 1986 (as added by this section), items arising from a taxable year of a partnership, S corporation, estate, or trust beginning before January 1, 2005, shall not be taken into account for purposes of subsection (d)(1) of such section."
Prior to amendment, Sec. 102(e) of P.L. 108-357 read as follows:
"(e) Effective date. The amendments made by this section shall apply to taxable years beginning after December 31, 2004."

In 2004, P.L. 108-357, Sec. 102(c), of this Act, provides:
"(c) Special rule relating to election to treat cutting of timber as a sale or exchange. Any election under section 631(a) of the Internal Revenue Code of 1986 made for a taxable year ending on or before the date of the enactment of this Act may be revoked by the taxpayer for any taxable year ending after such date. For purposes of determining whether such taxpayer may make a further election under such section, such election (and any revocation under this section) shall not be taken into account."
—P.L. 108-357, Sec. 315(a), substituted "either retains an economic interest in such timber or makes an outright sale of such timber" for "retains an economic interest in such timber" in the first sentence of subsec. (b) . . . Sec. 315(b)(1), substituted "In the case of disposal of timber with a retained economic interest, the date of disposal" for "The date of disposal" in the third sentence of subsec. (b) . . . Sec. 315(b)(2), deleted "with a retained economic interest" after "timber" in the heading of subsec. (b), effective for sales after 12/31/2004.

In 1986, P.L. 99-514, Sec. 311(b)(3), substituted "If for the taxable year of such gain or loss the maximum rate of tax imposed by this chapter or any net capital gain is less than such maximum rate for ordinary income, such owner" for "Such owner" in the second sentence of subsec. (c), effective for tax. yrs. begin. after 12/31/86. For transitional rules, see Sec. 311(d) of this Act reproduced in note following Code Sec. 1201.

In 1984, P.L. 98-369, Sec. 178(a), added "or coal" after "iron ore" each place it appeared in the sentence at the end of subsec. (c), effective for dispositions after 9/30/85. Sec. 178(b)(2) of this Act provides a special rule as follows:
"(2) Special rule for fixed contracts.—
"(A) In general.— The amendment made by subsection (a) shall not apply to any disposition of an interest in coal by a person to a related person if such coal is subsequently sold before January 1, 1990, by either such person—
"(i) to a person who is not a related person with respect to either such person, and
"(ii) pursuant to a qualified fixed contract.
"(B) Allocation where more than 1 contract.— If, for any taxable year, there is a disposition described in a subparagraph (A) which is not specifically allocable to a qualified fixed contract or to a contract which is not a qualified fixed contract, such disposition shall be treated as first allocable to the qualified fixed contract.
"(C) Qualified fixed contract defined.— The term 'qualified fixed contract' means any contract for the sale of coal which—
"(i) was entered into before June 12, 1984,
"(ii) is binding at all times thereafter, and
"(iii) cannot be adjusted to reflect to any extent the increase in liabilities of the person disposing of the coal for tax under chapter 1 of the Internal Revenue Code of 1954 by reason of the amendment made by subsection (a).
"(D) Related person.— For purposes of this paragraph, the term 'related person' means a person who bears a relationship to another person described in the last sentence of section 631(c)."
—P.L. 98-369, Sec. 1001(c)(1), substituted "on the first day of such year and for a period of more than 6 months before such cutting" for "for a period of more than 1 year" in subsec. (a) . . . Sec. 1001(c)(2), substituted "6 months" for "1 year" in subsecs. (b) and (c), effective for property acquired after 6/22/84, and before 1/1/88.

In 1976, P.L. 94-455, Sec. 1402(b)(1)(I), substituted "9 months" for "6 months" each place it appeared in Code Sec. 631, effective for tax. yrs. begin. in 1977.
—P.L. 94-455, Sec. 1402(b)(2), substituted "1 year" for "9 months" each place it appeared in Code Sec. 631, effective for tax. yrs. begin. after 12/31/77.
—P.L. 94-455, Sec. 1402(b)(3), deleted "before the beginning of such year" in subsec. (a) . . . Sec. 1906(b)(13)(A), substituted "Secretary" for "Secretary or his delegate" each place it appeared in Code Sec. 631, effective for tax. yrs. begin. after 12/31/76.

In 1964, P.L. 88-272, Sec. 227(a)(1)(A), amended the heading of subsec. (c) . . . Sec. 227(a)(1)(B), added "or iron ore mined in the United States," after "coal (including lignite)," in subsec. (c) . . . Sec. 227(a)(1)(C), added "or iron ore" after

Natural resources Part I

"coal" each place it appeared in subsec. (c)... Sec. 227(a)(1)(D), added "This subsection shall not apply to any disposal of iron ore—" to the end of subsec. (c) and added paras. (c)(1) and (2)... Sec. 227(b)(1), amended the heading of Code Sec. 631, effective for amounts received or accrued in tax. yrs. begin. after 12/31/63, attributable to iron ore mined in such tax. yrs.
Prior to amendment, the heading of subsec. (c) read as follows:
"(c) Disposal of coal with a retained economic interest"
Prior to amendment, the heading of Code Sec. 631 read as follows:
"SEC. 631. GAIN OR LOSS IN THE CASE OF TIMBER OR COAL."

Sec. 632. Repealed.

In **1976**, P.L. 94-455, Sec. 1901(a)(90), repealed Code Sec. 632, for tax. yrs. begin. after '76.
Prior to amendment, Code Sec. 632 read as follows:
"SEC. 632. SALE OF OIL OR GAS PROPERTIES.
"In the case of a bona fide sale of any oil or gas property, or any interest therein, where the principal value of the property has been demonstrated by prospecting or exploration or discovery work done by the taxpayer, the portion of the tax imposed by section 1 attributable to such sale shall not exceed 33 percent of the selling price of such property or interest."
In **1969**, P.L. 91-172, Sec. 803(d)(4), substituted "tax" for "surtax" and substituted "33 percent", for tax. yrs. begin. after 12/31/70.

PART IV.—MINERAL PRODUCTION PAYMENTS

Sec.
636. Income tax treatment of mineral production payments.

Sec. 636. Income tax treatment of mineral production payments.

(a) Carved-out production payment.

A production payment carved out of mineral property shall be treated, for purposes of this subtitle, as if it were a mortgage loan on the property, and shall not qualify as an economic interest in the mineral property. In the case of a production payment carved out for exploration or development of a mineral property, the preceding sentence shall apply only if and to the extent gross income from the property (for purposes of section 613) would be realized, in the absence of the application of such sentence, by the person creating the production payment.

(b) Retained production payment on sale of mineral property.

A production payment retained on the sale of a mineral property shall be treated, for purposes of this subtitle, as if it were a purchase money mortgage loan and shall not qualify as an economic interest in the mineral property.

(c) Retained production payment on lease of mineral property.

A production payment retained in a mineral property by the lessor in a leasing transaction shall be treated, for purposes of this subtitle, insofar as the lessee (or his successors in interest) is concerned, as if it were a bonus granted by the lessee to the lessor payable in installments. The treatment of the production payment in the hands of the lessor shall be determined without regard to the provisions of this subsection.

(d) Definition.

As used in this section, the term "mineral property" has the meaning assigned to the term "property" in section 614(a).

(e) Regulations.

The Secretary shall prescribe such regulations as may be necessary to carry out the purposes of this section.

In **1976**, P.L. 94-455, Sec. 1906(b)(13)(A), substituted "Secretary" for "Secretary or his delegate" in subsec. (e), effective for tax. yrs. begin. after 12/31/76.
In **1969**, P.L. 91-172, Sec. 503(a), added Code Sec. 636 as part of Part IV of subchapter I of chapter 1, effective as provided in Sec. 503(c) of this Act which reads as follows:
"(c)(1) GENERAL RULE.—The amendments made by this section shall apply with respect to mineral production payments created on or after August 7, 1969, other than mineral production payments created before January 1, 1971, pursuant to a binding contract entered into before August 7, 1969.

"(2) ELECTION.—At the election of the taxpayer (made at such time and in such manner as the Secretary of the Treasury or his delegate prescribes by regulations), the amendments made by this section shall apply with respect to all mineral production payments which the taxpayer carved out of mineral properties after the beginning of his last taxable year ending before August 7, 1969. No interest shall be allowed on any refund or credit of any overpayment resulting from such election for any taxable year ending before August 7, 1969.

"(3) SPECIAL RULE.—With respect to a taxpayer who does not elect the treatment provided in paragraph (2) and who carves out one or more mineral production payments on or after August 7, 1969, during the taxable year which includes such date, the amendments made by this section shall apply to such production payments only to the extent the aggregate amount of such production payments exceeds the lesser of—

"(A) the excess of—

"(i) the aggregate amount of production payments carved out and sold by the taxpayer during the 12-month period immediately preceding his taxable year which includes August 7, 1969, over

"(ii) the aggregate amount of production payments carved out before August 7, 1969, by the taxpayer during his taxable year which includes such date, or

"(B) the amount necessary to increase the amount of the taxpayer's gross income, within the meaning of chapter 1 of subtitle A of the Internal Revenue Code of 1954, for the taxable year which includes August 7, 1969, to an amount equal to the amount of deductions (other than any deduction under section 172 of such Code) allowable for such year under such chapter.

"The preceding sentence shall not apply for purposes of determining the amount of any deduction allowable under section 611 or the amount of foreign tax credit allowable under section 904 of such Code."

PART V.—CONTINENTAL SHELF AREAS

Sec.
638. Continental shelf areas.

Sec. 638. Continental shelf areas.

For purposes of applying the provisions of this chapter (including sections 861(a)(3) and 862(a)(3) in the case of the performance of personal services) with respect to mines, oil and gas wells, and other natural deposits—

(1) the term "United States" when used in a geographical sense includes the seabed and subsoil of those submarine areas which are adjacent to the territorial waters of the United States and over which the United States has exclusive rights, in accordance with international law, with respect to the exploration and exploitation of natural resources; and

(2) the terms "foreign country" and "possession of the United States" when used in a geographical sense include the seabed and subsoil of those submarine areas which are adjacent to the territorial waters of the foreign country or such possession and over which the foreign country (or the United States in case of such possession) has exclusive rights, in accordance with international law, with respect to the exploration and exploitation of natural resources, but this paragraph shall apply in the case of a foreign country only if it exercises, directly or indirectly, taxing jurisdiction with respect to such exploration or exploitation.

No foreign country shall, by reason of the application of this section, be treated as a country contiguous to the United States.

In **1969**, P.L. 91-172, Sec. 505(a), added Code Sec. 638.

Subchapter J.—Estates, Trusts, Beneficiaries, and Decedents

Part
I. Estates, trusts, and beneficiaries.
II. Income in respect of decedents.

PART I.—ESTATES, TRUSTS, AND BENEFICIARIES

Subpart
A. General rules for taxation of estates and trusts.
B. Trusts which distribute current income only.
C. Estates and trusts which may accumulate income or which distribute corpus.

2,305

D. Treatment of excess distributions by trusts.
E. Grantors and others treated as substantial owners.
F. Miscellaneous.

SUBPART A.—GENERAL RULES FOR TAXATION OF ESTATES AND TRUSTS

Sec.
641. Imposition of tax.
642. Special rules for credits and deductions.
643. Definitions applicable to subparts A, B, C, and D.
644. Taxable year of trusts.
645. Certain revocable trusts treated as part of estate.
646. Tax treatment of electing Alaska Native Settlement Trusts.

In 2001, P.L. 107-16, Sec. 671(c)(1), added item 646.
In 1998, P.L. 105-206, Sec. 6013(a)(2), redesignated item 646 as item 645.
In 1997, P.L. 105-34, Sec. 507(b)(3), deleted item 644 and redesignated item 645 as item 645 ... Sec. 1305(c), added item 646.
Prior to deletion, item 644 read as follows:
"644. Special rule for gain on property transferred to trust at less than fair market value".
In 1986, P.L. 99-514, Sec. 1403(b), added item 645.
In 1976, P.L. 94-455, Sec. 701(g)(2), added item 644.

Sec. 641. Imposition of tax.
(a) Application of tax.
The tax imposed by section 1(e) shall apply to the taxable income of estates or of any kind of property held in trust, including—

(1) income accumulated in trust for the benefit of unborn or unascertained persons or persons with contingent interests, and income accumulated or held for future distribution under the terms of the will or trust;

(2) income which is to be distributed currently by the fiduciary to the beneficiaries, and income collected by a guardian of an infant which is to be held or distributed as the court may direct;

(3) income received by estates of deceased persons during the period of administration or settlement of the estate; and

(4) income which, in the discretion of the fiduciary, may be either distributed to the beneficiaries or accumulated.

(b) Computation and payment.
The taxable income of an estate or trust shall be computed in the same manner as in the case of an individual, except as otherwise provided in this part. The tax shall be computed on such taxable income and shall be paid by the fiduciary. For purposes of this subsection, a foreign trust or foreign estate shall be treated as a nonresident alien individual who is not present in the United States at any time.

(c) Special rules for taxation of electing small business trusts.

(1) **In general.** For purposes of this chapter—

(A) the portion of any electing small business trust which consists of stock in 1 or more S corporations shall be treated as a separate trust, and

(B) the amount of the tax imposed by this chapter on such separate trust shall be determined with the modifications of paragraph (2).

(2) **Modifications.** For purposes of paragraph (1), the modifications of this paragraph are the following:

(A) Except as provided in section 1(h), the amount of the tax imposed by section 1(e) shall be determined by using the highest rate of tax set forth in section 1(e).

(B) The exemption amount under section 55(d) shall be zero.

(C) The only items of income, loss, deduction, or credit to be taken into account are the following:

(i) The items required to be taken into account under section 1366.

(ii) Any gain or loss from the disposition of stock in an S corporation.

(iii) To the extent provided in regulations, State or local income taxes or administrative expenses to the extent allocable to items described in clauses (i) and (ii).

(iv) Any interest expense paid or accrued on indebtedness incurred to acquire stock in an S corporation.

No deduction or credit shall be allowed for any amount not described in this paragraph, and no item described in this paragraph shall be apportioned to any beneficiary.

(D) No amount shall be allowed under paragraph (1) or (2) of section 1211(b).

(3) **Treatment of remainder of trust and distributions.** For purposes of determining—

(A) the amount of the tax imposed by this chapter on the portion of any electing small business trust not treated as a separate trust under paragraph (1), and

(B) the distributable net income of the entire trust,

the items referred to in paragraph (2)(C) shall be excluded. Except as provided in the preceding sentence, this subsection shall not affect the taxation of any distribution from the trust.

(4) **Treatment of unused deductions where termination of separate trust.** If a portion of an electing small business trust ceases to be treated as a separate trust under paragraph (1), any carryover or excess deduction of the separate trust which is referred to in section 642(h) shall be taken into account by the entire trust.

(5) **Electing small business trust.** For purposes of this subsection, the term "electing small business trust" has the meaning given such term by section 1361(e)(1).

In 2007, P.L. 110-28, Sec. 8236(a), added clause (c)(2)(C)(iv), effective for tax. yrs. begin. after 12/31/2006.
In 1998, P.L. 105-206, Sec. 6007(f)(2), deleted subsec. (c) and redesignated subsec. (d) as (c), effective for sales or exchanges after 8/5/97.
Prior to deletion, subsec. (c) read as follows:
"(c) Exclusion of includible gain from taxable income.
"(1) General rule. For purposes of this part, the taxable income of a trust does not include the amount of any includible gain as defined in section 644(b) reduced by any deductions properly allocable thereto.
"(2) Cross reference. For the taxation of any includible gain, see section 644."
In 1997, P.L. 105-34, Sec. 1601(i)(3)(B), added the sentence at the end of subsec. (b), effective 8/20/96.
In 1996, P.L. 104-188, Sec. 1302(d), added subsec. (d), effective for tax. yrs. begin. after 12/31/96.
In 1977, P.L. 95-30, Sec. 101(d)(8), substituted "section 1(e)" for "section 1(d)" in subsec. (a), effective for tax. yrs. begin. after 12/31/76.
In 1976, P.L. 94-455, Sec. 701(e)(2), added subsec. (c), effective for transfers in trust made after 5/21/76.
In 1969, P.L. 91-172, Sec. 803(d)(3), substituted "The tax imposed by section 1(d)" for "The taxes imposed by this chapter on individuals" in subsec. (a), effective for tax. yrs. begin. after 12/31/70.

Sec. 642. Special rules for credits and deductions.
(a) Foreign tax credit allowed.
An estate or trust shall be allowed the credit against tax for taxes imposed by foreign countries and possessions of the United States, to the extent allowed by section 901, only in respect of so much of the taxes described in such section as is not properly allocable under such section to the beneficiaries.

(b) Deduction for personal exemption.

(1) **Estates.** An estate shall be allowed a deduction of $600.

(2) Trusts.
(A) In general. Except as otherwise provided in this paragraph, a trust shall be allowed a deduction of $100.
(B) Trusts distributing income currently. A trust which, under its governing instrument, is required to distribute all of its income currently shall be allowed a deduction of $300.
(C) Disability trusts.
(i) In general. A qualified disability trust shall be allowed a deduction equal to the exemption amount under section 151(d), determined—
(I) by treating such trust as an individual described in section 151(d)(3)(C)(iii), and
(II) by applying section 67(e) (without the reference to section 642(b)) for purposes of determining the adjusted gross income of the trust.
(ii) Qualified disability trust. For purposes of clause (i), the term "qualified disability trust" means any trust if—
(I) such trust is a disability trust described in subsection (c)(2)(B)(iv) of section 1917 of the Social Security Act (42 U.S.C. 1396p), and
(II) all of the beneficiaries of the trust as of the close of the taxable year are determined by the Commissioner of Social Security to have been disabled (within the meaning of section 1614(a)(3) of the Social Security Act, 42 U.S.C. 1382c(a)(3)) for some portion of such year.

A trust shall not fail to meet the requirements of subclause (II) merely because the corpus of the trust may revert to a person who is not so disabled after the trust ceases to have any beneficiary who is so disabled.
(3) Deductions in lieu of personal exemption. The deductions allowed by this subsection shall be in lieu of the deductions allowed under section 151 (relating to deduction for personal exemption).

(c) Deduction for amounts paid or permanently set aside for a charitable purpose.
(1) General rule. In the case of an estate or trust (other than a trust meeting the specifications of subpart B), there shall be allowed as a deduction in computing its taxable income (in lieu of the deduction allowed by section 170(a), relating to deduction for charitable, etc., contributions and gifts) any amount of the gross income, without limitation, which pursuant to the terms of the governing instrument is, during the taxable year, paid for a purpose specified in section 170(c) (determined without regard to section 170(c)(2)(A)). If a charitable contribution is paid after the close of such taxable year and on or before the last day of the year following the close of such taxable year, then the trustee or administrator may elect to treat such contribution as paid during such taxable year. The election shall be made at such time and in such manner as the Secretary prescribes by regulations.
(2) Amounts permanently set aside. In the case of an estate, and in the case of a trust (other than a trust meeting the specifications of subpart B) required by the terms of its governing instrument to set aside amounts which was—
(A) created on or before October 9, 1969, if—
(i) an irrevocable remainder interest is transferred to or for the use of an organization described in section 170(c), or
(ii) the grantor is at all times after October 9, 1969, under a mental disability to change the terms of the trust; or

(B) established by a will executed on or before October 9, 1969, if—
(i) the testator dies before October 9, 1972, without having republished the will after October 9, 1969, by codicil or otherwise,
(ii) the testator at no time after October 9, 1969, had the right to change the portions of the will which pertain to the trust, or
(iii) the will is not republished by codicil or otherwise before October 9, 1972, and the testator is on such date and at all times thereafter under a mental disability to republish the will by codicil or otherwise,

there shall also be allowed as a deduction in computing its taxable income any amount of the gross income, without limitation, which pursuant to the terms of the governing instrument is, during the taxable year, permanently set aside for a purpose specified in section 170(c), or is to be used exclusively for religious, charitable, scientific, literary, or educational purposes, or for the prevention of cruelty to children or animals, or for the establishment, acquisition, maintenance, or operation of a public cemetery not operated for profit. In the case of a trust, the preceding sentence shall apply only to gross income earned with respect to amounts transferred to the trust before October 9, 1969, or transferred under a will to which subparagraph (B) applies.
(3) Pooled income funds. In the case of a pooled income fund (as defined in paragraph (5)), there shall also be allowed as a deduction in computing its taxable income any amount of the gross income attributable to gain from the sale of a capital asset held for more than 1 year, without limitation, which pursuant to the terms of the governing instrument is, during the taxable year, permanently set aside for a purpose specified in section 170(c).
(4) Adjustments. To the extent that the amount otherwise allowable as a deduction under this subsection consists of gain described in section 1202(a), proper adjustment shall be made for any exclusion allowable to the estate or trust under section 1202. In the case of a trust, the deduction allowed by this subsection shall be subject to section 681 (relating to unrelated business income).
(5) Definition of pooled income fund. For purposes of paragraph (3), a pooled income fund is a trust—
(A) to which each donor transfers property, contributing an irrevocable remainder interest in such property to or for the use of an organization described in section 170(b)(1)(A) (other than in clauses (vii) or (viii)), and retaining an income interest for the life of one or more beneficiaries (living at the time of such transfer),
(B) in which the property transferred by each donor is commingled with property transferred by other donors who have made or make similar transfers,
(C) which cannot have investments in securities which are exempt from the taxes imposed by this subtitle,
(D) which includes only amounts received from transfers which meet the requirements of this paragraph,
(E) which is maintained by the organization to which the remainder interest is contributed and of which no donor or beneficiary of an income interest is a trustee, and
(F) from which each beneficiary of an income interest receives income, for each year for which he is entitled to receive the income interest referred to in subparagraph (A), determined by the rate of return earned by the trust for such year.

For purposes of determining the amount of any charitable contribution allowable by reason of a transfer of property to a pooled fund, the value of the income interest shall be determined on the basis of the highest rate of return earned by the fund for any of the 3 taxable years immediately preceding the taxable year of the fund in which the transfer is made. In the case of funds in existence less than 3 taxable years preceding the taxable year of the fund in which a transfer is made, the rate of return shall be deemed to be 6 percent per annum, except that the Secretary may prescribe a different rate of return.

(6) Taxable private foundations. In the case of a private foundation which is not exempt from taxation under section 501(a) for the taxable year, the provisions of this subsection shall not apply and the provisions of section 170 shall apply.

(d) Net operating loss deduction.

The benefit of the deduction for net operating losses provided by section 172 shall be allowed to estates and trusts under regulations prescribed by the Secretary.

(e) Deduction for depreciation and depletion.

An estate or trust shall be allowed the deduction for depreciation and depletion only to the extent not allowable to beneficiaries under sections 167(d) and 611(b).

(f) Amortization deductions.

The benefit of the deductions for amortization provided by sections 169 and 197 shall be allowed to estates and trusts in the same manner as in the case of an individual. The allowable deduction shall be apportioned between the income beneficiaries and the fiduciary under regulations prescribed by the Secretary.

(g) Disallowance of double deductions.

Amounts allowable under section 2053 or 2054 as a deduction in computing the taxable estate of a decedent shall not be allowed as a deduction (or as an offset against the sales price of property in determining gain or loss) in computing the taxable income of the estate or of any other person, unless there is filed, within the time and in the manner and form prescribed by the Secretary, a statement that the amounts have not been allowed as deductions under section 2053 or 2054 and a waiver of the right to have such amounts allowed at any time as deductions under section 2053 or 2054. Rules similar to the rules of the preceding sentence shall apply to amounts which may be taken into account under section 2621(a)(2) or 2622(b). This subsection shall not apply with respect to deductions allowed under part II (relating to income in respect of decedents).

(h) Unused loss carryovers and excess deductions on termination available to beneficiaries.

If on the termination of an estate or trust, the estate or trust has—

(1) a net operating loss carryover under section 172 or a capital loss carryover under section 1212, or

(2) for the last taxable year of the estate or trust deductions (other than the deductions allowed under subsections (b) or (c)) in excess of gross income for such year,

then such carryover or such excess shall be allowed as a deduction, in accordance with regulations prescribed by the Secretary to the beneficiaries succeeding to the property of the estate or trust.

(i) Certain distributions by cemetery perpetual care funds.

In the case of a cemetery perpetual care fund which—

(1) was created pursuant to local law by a taxable cemetery corporation for the care and maintenance of cemetery property, and

(2) is treated for the taxable year as a trust for purposes of this subchapter,

any amount distributed by such fund for the care and maintenance of gravesites which have been purchased from the cemetery corporation before the beginning of the taxable year of the trust and with respect to which there is an obligation to furnish care and maintenance shall be considered to be a distribution solely for purposes of sections 651 and 661, but only to the extent that the aggregate amount so distributed during the taxable year does not exceed $5 multiplied by the aggregate number of such gravesites.

In **2002**, P.L. 107-134, Sec. 116(a), amended subsec. (b), effective for tax. yrs. end. on or after 9/11/2001.
Prior to amendment, subsec. (b) read as follows:
"(b) Deduction for personal exemption. An estate shall be allowed a deduction of $600. A trust which, under its governing instrument, is required to distribute all of its income currently shall be allowed a deduction of $300. All other trusts shall be allowed a deduction of $100. The deductions allowed by this subsection shall be in lieu of the deductions allowed under section 151 (relating to deduction for personal exemption)."
In **1996**, P.L. 104-188, Sec. 1703(l), amended Sec. 13261(g)(2)(A)(iii) of P.L. 103-66 by substituting "by the taxpayer or a related person" for "by the taxpayer", see below.
—P.L. 104-188, Sec. 1704(t)(8), substituted "under section 2621(a)(2)" for "under 2621(a)(2)" in subsec. (g), effective 8/20/96.
In **1993**, P.L. 103-66, Sec. 13113(d)(2), amended para. (c)(4), effective for stock issued after 8/10/93.
Prior to amendment, para. (c)(4) read as follows:
"(4) Coordination with section 681.
In the case of a trust, the deduction allowed by this subsection shall be subject to section 681 (relating to unrelated business income)."
—P.L. 103-66, Sec. 13261(f)(2), substituted "sections 169 and 197" for "section 169" in subsec. (f), effective for property acquired after 8/10/93, except as provided in Sec. 13261(g)(2) [as amended by Sec. 1703(l) of P.L. 104-188, see above] and (3) which reads as follows:
"(2) Election to have amendments apply to property acquired after July 25, 1991.
"(A) In general. If an election under this paragraph applies to the taxpayer—
"(i) the amendments made by this section shall apply to property acquired by the taxpayer after July 25, 1991,
"(ii) subsection (c)(1)(A) of section 197 of the Internal Revenue Code of 1986 (as added by this section) and so much of subsection (f)(9)(A) of such section 197 as precedes clause (i) thereof) shall be applied with respect to the taxpayer or a related person by treating July 25, 1991, as the date of the enactment of such section, and
"(iii) in applying subsection (f)(9) of such section, with respect to any property acquired by the taxpayer or a related person on or before the date of the enactment of this Act, only holding or use on July 25, 1991, shall be taken into account.
"(B) Election. An election under this paragraph shall be made at such time and in such manner as the Secretary of the Treasury or his delegate may prescribe. Such an election by any taxpayer, once made—
"(i) may be revoked only with the consent of the Secretary, and
"(ii) shall apply to the taxpayer making such election and any other taxpayer under common control with the taxpayer (within the meaning of subparagraphs (A) and (B) of section 41(f)(1) of such Code) at any time after August 2, 1993, and on or before the date on which such election is made.
"(3) Elective binding contract exception.
"(A) In general. The amendments made by this section shall not apply to any acquisition of property by the taxpayer if—
"(i) such acquisition is pursuant to a written binding contract in effect on the date of the enactment of this Act and at all times thereafter before such acquisition,
"(ii) an election under paragraph (2) does not apply to the taxpayer, and
"(iii) the taxpayer makes an election under this paragraph with respect to such contract.
"(B) Election. An election under this paragraph shall be made at such time and in such manner as the Secretary of the Treasury or his delegate shall prescribe. Such an election, once made—
"(i) may be revoked only with the consent of the Secretary, and
"(ii) shall apply to all property acquired pursuant to the contract with respect to which such election was made."
In **1990**, P.L. 101-508, Sec. 11801(c)(6)(B), substituted "section 169" for "sections 169, 184, 187, and 188" in subsec. (f), effective 11/5/90 except as provided in Sec. 11821(b) of this Act, reproduced in note following Code Sec. 184.
—P.L. 101-508, Sec. 11812(b)(9), substituted "167(d)" for "167(h)" in subsec. (e), effective for property placed in service after 11/5/90 except as provided in Sec. 11812(c)(2) of this Act reproduced in note following Code Sec. 42.
In **1989**, P.L. 101-239, Sec. 7811(j)(3), added the second sentence to subsec. (g), effective for any generation-skipping transfer (within the meaning of '86 Code Sec. 2611) made after 10/22/86, except as provided in Sec. 1433(b)-(d) of P.L. 99-514, reproduced in the note following Code Sec. 2601.

Estates, trusts, beneficiaries — Code Sec. 643(a)(1)

In **1986**, P.L. 99-514, Sec. 112(b)(2), amended subsec. (a)... Sec. 301(b)(6)(A), deleted the first sentence of para. (c)(4)... Sec. 301(b)(6)(B), substituted "Coordination with section 681" for "Adjustments" in heading of para. (c)(4)... Sec. 612(b)(3), deleted subsec. (j), effective for tax. yrs. begin. after 12/31/86.

Prior to amendment, subsec. (a) read as follows:

"(a) Credits against tax.

"(1) Foreign taxes. An estate or trust shall be allowed the credit against tax for taxes imposed by foreign countries and possessions of the United States, to the extent allowed by section 901, only in respect of so much of the taxes described in such section as is not properly allocable under such section to the beneficiaries.

"(2) Political contributions. An estate or trust shall not be allowed the credit against tax for political contributions provided by section 24."

Prior to deletion, the first sentence of para. (c)(4) read as follows: "To the extent that the amount otherwise allowable as a deduction under this subsection consists of gain from the sale or exchange of capital assets held for more than 6 months, [1 year for property acquired before 6/23/84 and after 12/31/87] proper adjustment shall be made for any deduction allowable to the estate or trust under section 1202 (relating to deduction for excess of capital gains over capital losses)."

Prior to deletion, subsec. (j) read as follows:

"(j) Cross reference.

"For special rule for determining the time of receipt of dividends by a beneficiary under section 652 or 662, see section 116(c)(3)."

In **1984**, P.L. 98-369, Sec. 474(r)(17), substituted "section 24" for "section 41" in para. (a)(2), effective for tax. yrs. begin. after 12/31/83, and for carrybacks from such yrs.

—P.L. 98-369, Sec. 1001(b)(8), substituted "6 months" for "1 year" each place it appeared in paras. (c)(3) and (4), effective for property acquired after 6/22/84, and before 1/1/88.

In **1983**, P.L. 97-448, Sec. 102(f)(1), amended Sec. 212(e)(2)(B) of P.L. 97-34, part of the effective date for changes made by Sec. 212(d)(2)(D) of P.L. 97-34, see below.

Prior to amendment, Sec. 212(e)(2)(B) of P.L. 97-34 read as follows:

"(B) such building meets the requirements of paragraph (1) of section 48(g) of the Internal Revenue Code of 1954 (as in effect on the day before the date of enactment of this Act) but does not meet the requirements of such paragraph (1) (as amended by this Act)."

In **1981**, P.L. 97-34, Sec. 212(d)(2)(D), substituted "and 188" for "188, and 191" in subsec. (f), for expenditures incurred after 12/21/81 in tax. yrs. end. after 12/31/81. Sec. 212(e)(2) of this Act [as amended by Sec. 102(f)(1) of P.L. 97-448, see above] provides:

"(2) Transitional rule. The amendments made by this section shall not apply with respect to any rehabilitation of a building if—

"(A) the physical work on such rehabilitation began before January 1, 1982, and

"(B) such building does not meet the requirements of paragraph (1) of section 48(g) of the Internal Revenue Code of 1954 (as amended by this Act)."

In **1980**, P.L. 96-541, Sec. 2(e)(1), deleted Sec. 2124(a)(4) of P.L. 94-455, the effective date for changes made by Sec. 2124(a)(3)(B) of P.L. 94-455, see below.

Prior to amendment, Sec. 2124(a)(4) of P.L. 94-455 read as follows:

"(4) Effective date. The amendments made by this subsection shall apply with respect to additions to capital account made after June 14, 1976 and before June 15, 1981."

In **1978**, P.L. 95-600, Sec. 113(a)(2)(B), deleted subsec. (i) and redesignated subsec. (j) and (k) as subsec. (i) and (j), for contributions the payment of which is made after 12/31/78, in tax. yrs. begin. on or after 12/31/78.

Prior to amendment, subsec. (i) read as follows:

"(i) Political contributions.

"An estate or trust shall not be allowed the deduction for contributions to candidates for public office provided by section 218."

In **1977**, P.L. 95-30, Sec. 101(d)(9), amended subsec. (k), effective for tax. yrs. begin. after 12/31/76.

Prior to amendment, subsec. (k) read as follows:

"(k) Cross references.

"(1) For disallowance of standard deduction in case of estates and trusts, see section 142(b)(4).

"(2) For special rule for determining the time of receipt of dividends by a beneficiary under section 652 or 662, see section 116(c)(3)."

In **1976**, P.L. 94-528, Sec. 1(a), redesignated subsec. (j) as subsec. (k) and added new subsec. (j), effective 10/1/77 and for amounts distributed during tax. yrs. end. after 12/31/63.

—P.L. 94-455, Sec. 1402(b)(1)(J), substituted "9 months" for "6 months" in paras. (c)(3) and (c)(4), effective for tax. yrs. begin. in '77.

—P.L. 94-455, Sec. 1402(b)(2), substituted "1 year" for "9 months" in para. (c)(3) and (c)(4), effective for tax. yrs. begin. after '77.

—P.L. 94-455, Sec. 1402(c), provided a transitional rule for certain installment obligations (see note at Code Sec. 1222).

—P.L. 94-455, Sec. 1901(b)(1)(H)(i), deleted para. (a)(1) and redesignated paras. (a)(2) and (a)(3) as (a)(1) and (2), respectively, effective for tax. yrs. begin. after 12/31/76.

Prior to amendment, para. (a)(1) read as follows:

"(1) Partially tax-exempt interest. An estate or trust shall be allowed the credit against tax for partially tax-exempt interest provided by section 35 only in respect of so much of such interest as is not properly allocable to any beneficiary under section 652 or 662. If the estate or trust elects under section 171 to treat as amortizable the premium on bonds with respect to the interest on which the credit is allowable under section 35, such credit (whether allowable to the estate or trust or to the beneficiary) shall be reduced under section 171(a)(3)."

—P.L. 94-455, Sec. 1906(b)(13)(A), substituted "Secretary" for "Secretary or his delegate" each place it appeared in Code Sec. 642, effective for tax. yrs. begin. after 12/31/76.

—P.L. 94-455, Sec. 1951(c)(2)(B), deleted "168," following "provided by sections" in subsec. (f), effective for tax. yrs. begin. after 12/31/76.

—P.L. 94-455, Sec. 2009(d), added "(or as an offset against the sales price of property in determining gain or loss)" following "shall not be allowed as a deduction" in subsec. (g), effective for tax. yrs. end. after 10/4/76.

—P.L. 94-455, Sec. 2124(a)(3)(B), substituted "188, and 191" for "and 188" in subsec. (f). For amendments made to Sec. 2124(a)(4), the effective date, see Sec. 2(e)(1) of P.L. 96-541 above.

In **1971**, P.L. 92-178, Sec. 303(c)(4), substituted "187, and 188" for "and 187" in subsec (f) effective for tax. yrs. end. after 12/31/71.

—P.L. 92-178, Sec. 701(b), added para. (a)(3),... Sec. 702(b), redesignated subsec. (i) as subsec. (j) and added new subsec. (i), effective for tax. yrs. end. after 12/31/71, but only with respect to political contributions, payment of which is made after 12/31/71.

In **1969**, P.L. 91-172, Sec. 201(b), amended subsec. (c). Sec. 201(g)(2) provides as follows:

"(2) The amendments made by subsection (b) shall apply with respect to amounts paid, permanently set aside, or to be used for a charitable purpose in taxable years beginning after December 31, 1969, except that section 642(c)(5) of the Internal Revenue Code of 1954 (as added by subsection (b)) shall apply to transfers in trust made after July 31, 1969."

Prior to amendment, subsec. (c) read as follows:

"(c) Deduction for amounts paid or permanently set aside for a charitable purpose.

"In the case of an estate or trust (other than a trust meeting the specifications of subpart B) there shall be allowed as a deduction in computing its taxable income (in lieu of the deductions allowed by section 170(a), relating to deduction for charitable, etc., contributions and gifts) any amount of the gross income, without limitation, which pursuant to the terms of the governing instrument is, during the taxable year, paid or permanently set aside for a purpose specified in section 170(c), or is to be used exclusively for religious, charitable, scientific, literary, or educational purposes, or for the prevention of cruelty to children or animals, or for the establishment, acquisition, maintenance or operation of a public cemetery not operated for profit. For this purpose, to the extent that such amount consists of gain from the sale or exchange of capital assets held for more than 6 months, proper adjustment of the deduction otherwise allowable under this subsection shall be made for any deduction allowable to the estate or trust under section 1202 (relating to deduction for excess of capital gains over capital losses). In the case of a trust, the deduction allowed by this subsection shall be subject to section 681 (relating to unrelated business income and prohibited transactions)."

—P.L. 91-172, Sec. 704(b)(2), amended the heading and first sentence of subsec. (f), effective for tax. yrs. end. after 12/31/68.

Prior to amendment, the heading and first sentence of subsec. (f) read as follows:

"(f) Amortization of emergency or grain storage facilities.

"The benefit of the deductions for amortization of emergency and grain storage facilities provided by sections 168 and 169 shall be allowed to estates and trusts in the same manner as in the case of an individual."

In **1966**, P.L. 89-621, Sec. 2, added "or of any other person" in subsec. (g), effective for tax. yrs. end. after 10/4/66 but only for amounts paid or incurred and losses sustained after that date.

In **1964**, P.L. 88-272, Sec. 201(d)(6)(A), deleted para. (a)(3)... Sec. 201(d)(6)(B), amended subsec. (i), effective for dividends received after 12/31/64, in tax. yrs. end. after 12/31/64.

Prior to deletion, para. (a)(3) read as follows:

"(3) Dividends received by individuals.—An estate or trust shall be allowed the credit against tax for dividends received provided by section 34 only in respect of so much of such dividends as is not properly allocable to any beneficiary under section 652 or 662. For purposes of determining the time of receipt of dividends under section 34 and section 116, the amount of dividends properly allocable to a beneficiary under section 652 or 662 shall be deemed to have been received by the beneficiary ratably on the same dates that the dividends were received by the estate or trust."

Prior to amendment, subsec. (i) read as follows:

"(i) Cross references.

For disallowance of standard deduction in case of estates and trusts, see section 142(b)(4)."

In **1962**, P.L. 87-834, Sec. 13(c)(2), substituted "167(h)" for a "167(g)" in subsec. (e), effective for tax. yrs. begin. after 12/31/61, and end. after 10/16/62.

Sec. 643. Definitions applicable to subparts A, B, C, and D.

(a) Distributable net income.

For purposes of this part, the term "distributable net income" means, with respect to any taxable year, the taxable income of the estate or trust computed with the following modifications—

(1) Deduction for distributions. No deduction shall be taken under sections 651 and 661 (relating to additional deductions).

(2) Deduction for personal exemption. No deduction shall be taken under section 642(b) (relating to deduction for personal exemptions).

(3) Capital gains and losses. Gains from the sale or exchange of capital assets shall be excluded to the extent that such gains are allocated to corpus and are not (A) paid, credited, or required to be distributed to any beneficiary during the taxable year, or (B) paid, permanently set aside, or to be used for the purposes specified in section 642(c). Losses from the sale or exchange of capital assets shall be excluded, except to the extent such losses are taken into account in determining the amount of gains from the sale or exchange of capital assets which are paid, credited, or required to be distributed to any beneficiary during the taxable year. The exclusion under section 1202 shall not be taken into account.

(4) Extraordinary dividends and taxable stock dividends. For purposes only of subpart B (relating to trusts which distribute current income only), there shall be excluded those items of gross income constituting extraordinary dividends or taxable stock dividends which the fiduciary, acting in good faith, does not pay or credit to any beneficiary by reason of his determination that such dividends are allocable to corpus under the terms of the governing instrument and applicable local law.

(5) Tax-exempt interest. There shall be included any tax-exempt interest to which section 103 applies, reduced by any amounts which would be deductible in respect of disbursements allocable to such interest but for the provisions of section 265 (relating to disallowance of certain deductions).

(6) Income of foreign trust. In the case of a foreign trust—

(A) There shall be included the amounts of gross income from sources without the United States, reduced by any amounts which would be deductible in respect of disbursements allocable to such income but for the provisions of section 265(a)(1) (relating to disallowance of certain deductions).

(B) Gross income from sources within the United States shall be determined without regard to section 894 (relating to income exempt under treaty).

(C) Paragraph (3) shall not apply to a foreign trust. In the case of such a trust, there shall be included gains from the sale or exchange of capital assets, reduced by losses from such sales or exchanges to the extent such losses do not exceed gains from such sales or exchanges.

(7) Abusive transactions. The Secretary shall prescribe such regulations as may be necessary or appropriate to carry out the purposes of this part, including regulations to prevent avoidance of such purposes.

If the estate or trust is allowed a deduction under section 642(c), the amount of the modifications specified in paragraphs (5) and (6) shall be reduced to the extent that the amount of income which is paid, permanently set aside, or to be used for the purposes specified in section 642(c) is deemed to consist of items specified in those paragraphs. For this purpose, such amount shall (in the absence of specific provisions in the governing instrument) be deemed to consist of the same proportion of each class of items of income of the estate or trust as the total of each class bears to the total of all classes.

(b) Income.

For purposes of this subpart and subparts B, C, and D, the term "income", when not preceded by the words "taxable", "distributable net", "undistributed net", or "gross", means the amount of income of the estate or trust for the taxable year determined under the terms of the governing instrument and applicable local law. Items of gross income constituting extraordinary dividends or taxable stock dividends which the fiduciary, acting in good faith, determines to be allocable to corpus under the terms of the governing instrument and applicable local law shall not be considered income.

(c) Beneficiary.

For purposes of this part, the term "beneficiary" includes heir, legatee, devisee.

(d) Coordination with back-up withholding.

Except to the extent otherwise provided in regulations, this subchapter shall be applied with respect to payments subject to withholding under section 3406—

(1) by allocating between the estate or trust and its beneficiaries any credit allowable under section 31(c) (on the basis of their respective shares of any such payment taken into account under this subchapter),

(2) by treating each beneficiary to whom such credit is allocated as if an amount equal to such credit has been paid to him by the estate or trust, and

(3) by allowing the estate or trust a deduction in an amount equal to the credit so allocated to beneficiaries.

(e) Treatment of property distributed in kind.

(1) Basis of beneficiary. The basis of any property received by a beneficiary in a distribution from an estate or trust shall be—

(A) the adjusted basis of such property in the hands of the estate or trust immediately before the distribution, adjusted for

(B) any gain or loss recognized to the estate or trust on the distribution.

(2) Amount of distribution. In the case of any distribution of property (other than cash), the amount taken into account under sections 661(a)(2) and 662(a)(2) shall be the lesser of—

(A) the basis of such property in the hands of the beneficiary (as determined under paragraph (1)), or

(B) the fair market value of such property.

(3) Election to recognize gain.

(A) In general. In the case of any distribution of property (other than cash) to which an election under this paragraph applies—

(i) paragraph (2) shall not apply,

(ii) gain or loss shall be recognized by the estate or trust in the same manner as if such property had been sold to the distributee at its fair market value, and

(iii) the amount taken into account under sections 661(a)(2) and 662(a)(2) shall be the fair market value of such property.

(B) Election. Any election under this paragraph shall apply to all distributions made by the estate or trust during a taxable year and shall be made on the return of such estate or trust for such taxable year.

Any such election, once made, may be revoked only with the consent of the Secretary.

(4) Exception for distributions described in section 663(a). This subsection shall not apply to any distribution described in section 663(a).

(f) Treatment of multiple trusts.

For purposes of this subchapter, under regulations prescribed by the Secretary, 2 or more trusts shall be treated as 1 trust if—

(1) such trusts have substantially the same grantor or grantors and substantially the same primary beneficiary or beneficiaries, and

Estates, trusts, beneficiaries — Code Sec. 643

(2) a principal purpose of such trusts is the avoidance of the tax imposed by this chapter.

For purposes of the preceding sentence, a husband and wife shall be treated as 1 person.

(g) Certain payments of estimated tax treated as paid by beneficiary.

(1) **In general.** In the case of a trust—

(A) the trustee may elect to treat any portion of a payment of estimated tax made by such trust for any taxable year of the trust as a payment made by a beneficiary of such trust,

(B) any amount so treated shall be treated as paid or credited to the beneficiary on the last day of such taxable year, and

(C) for purposes of subtitle F, the amount so treated—

(i) shall not be treated as a payment of estimated tax made by the trust, but

(ii) shall be treated as a payment of estimated tax made by such beneficiary on January 15 following the taxable year.

(2) **Time for making election.** An election under paragraph (1) shall be made on or before the 65th day after the close of the taxable year of the trust and in such manner as the Secretary may prescribe.

(3) **Extension to last year of estate.** In the case of a taxable year reasonably expected to be the last taxable year of an estate—

(A) any reference in this subsection to a trust shall be treated as including a reference to an estate, and

(B) the fiduciary of the estate shall be treated as the trustee.

(h) Distributions by certain foreign trusts through nominees.

For purposes of this part, any amount paid to a United States person which is derived directly or indirectly from a foreign trust of which the payor is not the grantor shall be deemed in the year of payment to have been directly paid by the foreign trust to such United States person.

(i) Loans from foreign trusts.

For purposes of subparts B, C, and D—

(1) **General rules.** Except as provided in regulations, if a foreign trust makes a loan of cash or marketable securities (or permits the use of any other trust property) directly or indirectly to or by—

(A) any grantor or beneficiary of such trust who is a United States person, or

(B) any United States person not described in subparagraph (A) who is related to such grantor or beneficiary, the amount of such loan (or the fair market value of the use of such property) shall be treated as a distribution by such trust to such grantor or beneficiary (as the case may be).

(2) **Definitions and special rules.** For purposes of this subsection—

(A) Cash. The term "cash" includes foreign currencies and cash equivalents.

(B) Related person.

(i) In general. A person is related to another person if the relationship between such persons would result in a disallowance of losses under section 267 or 707(b). In applying section 267 for purposes of the preceding sentence, section 267(c)(4) shall be applied as if the family of an individual includes the spouses of the members of the family.

(ii) Allocation. If any person described in paragraph (1)(B) is related to more than one person, the grantor or beneficiary to whom the treatment under this subsection applies shall be determined under regulations prescribed by the Secretary.

(C) Exclusion of tax-exempts. The term "United States person" does not include any entity exempt from tax under this chapter.

(D) Trust not treated as simple trust. Any trust which is treated under this subsection as making a distribution shall be treated as not described in section 651.

(E) Exception for compensated use of property. In the case of the use of any trust property other than a loan of cash or marketable securities, paragraph (1) shall not apply to the extent that the trust is paid the fair market value of such use within a reasonable period of time of such use.

(3) **Subsequent transactions.** If any loan (or use of property) is taken into account under paragraph (1), any subsequent transaction between the trust and the original borrower regarding the principal of the loan (by way of complete or partial repayment, satisfaction, cancellation, discharge, or otherwise) or the return of such property shall be disregarded for purposes of this title.

In 2010, P.L. 111-147, Sec. 533(a)(1), substituted "(or permits the use of any other trust property) directly or indirectly to or by" for "directly or indirectly to" in para. (i)(1) . . . Sec. 533(a)(2), added "(or the fair market value of the use of such property)" after "the amount of such loan" in para. (i)(1) . . . Sec. 533(b), added subpara. (i)(2)(E) . . . Sec. 533(d)(1), added "(or use of property)" after "If any loan" in para. (i)(3) . . . Sec. 533(d)(2), added "or the return of such property" before "shall be disregarded" in para (i)(3) . . . Sec. 533(d)(3), deleted "regarding loan principal" after "Subsequent transactions" in the heading of para. (i)(3), effective for loans made, and uses of property, after 3/18/2010.

In 1996, P.L. 104-188, Sec. 1904(c)(1), added subsec. (h), effective 8/20/96, except as provided in Secs. 1904(d)(2) and (e) of this Act, which read as follows:

"(2) Exception for certain trusts. The amendments made by this section shall not apply to any trust—

"(A) which is treated as owned by the grantor under section 676 or 677 (other than subsection (a)(3) thereof) of the Internal Revenue Code of 1986, and

"(B) which is in existence on September 19, 1995.

The preceding sentence shall not apply to the portion of any such trust attributable to any transfer to such trust after September 19, 1995.

"(e) Transitional rule. If—

"(1) by reason of the amendments made by this section, any person other than a United States person ceases to be treated as the owner of a portion of a domestic trust, and

"(2) before January 1, 1997, such trust becomes a foreign trust, or the assets of such trust are transferred to a foreign trust,

no tax shall be imposed by section 1491 of the Internal Revenue Code of 1986 by reason of such trust becoming a foreign trust or the assets of such trust being transferred to a foreign trust."

—P.L. 104-188, Sec. 1906(b), added para. (a)(7), effective 8/20/96.

—P.L. 104-188, Sec. 1906(c)(1), added subsec. (i), effective for loans of cash or marketable securities made after 9/19/95.

In 1993, P.L. 103-66, Sec. 13113(d)(3), added the sentence at the end of para. (a)(3), effective for stock issued after 8/10/93.

In 1989, P.L. 101-239, Sec. 7811(b)(1), amended subpara. (a)(6)(C) . . . Sec. 7811(b)(2), deleted subpara. (a)(6)(D), effective for tax. yrs. begin. after 12/31/86. Prior to amendment, subpara. (a)(6)(C) read as follows:

"(C) Paragraph (3) shall not apply to a foreign trust. In the case of such a trust, (i) there shall be included gains from the sale or exchange of capital assets, reduced by losses from such sales or exchanges to the extent such losses do not exceed gains from such sales or exchanges, and (ii) the deduction under section 1202 (relating to deduction for excess of capital gains over capital losses) shall not be taken into account."

Prior to deletion, subpara. (a)(6)(D) read as follows:

"(D) Effective for distributions made in taxable years beginning after December 31, 1975, the undistributed net income of each foreign trust for each taxable year beginning on or before December 31, 1975, shall be redetermined by taking into account the deduction allowed by section 1202."

—P.L. 101-239, Sec. 7811(f)(1), substituted "section 265(a)(1)" for "section 265(1)" in subpara. (a)(6)(A), effective for tax. yrs. end. after 12/31/86, except as provided in Secs. 902(f)(2)-(4) of P.L. 99-514, reproduced in notes following Code Sec. 265.

In 1988, P.L. 100-647, Sec. 1014(d)(3)(A), deleted the last sentence of para. (g)(1) . . . Sec. 1014(d)(3)(B), amended para. (g)(2) . . . Sec. 1014(d)(4), added para. (g)(3), effective for tax. yrs. begin. after 12/31/86.

Prior to deletion, the last sentence of para. (g)(1) read as follows:

"The preceding sentence shall apply only to the extent the payments of estimated tax made by the trust for the taxable year exceed the tax imposed by this chapter shown on its return for the taxable year."

Code Sec. 643 — Estates, trusts, beneficiaries

Prior to amendment, para. (g)(2) read as follows:

"(2) Time for making election. An election under paragraph (1) may be made—

"(A) only on the trust's return of the tax imposed by this chapter for the taxable year, and

"(B) only if such return is filed on or before the 65th day after the close of the taxable year."

—P.L. 100-647, Sec. 1018(e)(1)-(3), provide:

"(e) Provision Related to Section 1806 of the Reform Act. If—

"(1) on a return for the 1st taxable year of the trusts involved beginning after March 1 1984, 2 or more trusts were treated as a single trust for purposes of the tax imposed by chapter 1 of the Internal Revenue Code of 1954,

"(2) such trusts would have been required to be so treated but for the amendment made by section 1806(b) of the Reform Act, and

"(3) such trusts did not accumulate any income during such taxable year and did not make any accumulation distributions during such taxable year,

then, notwithstanding the amendment made by section 1806(b) of the Reform Act, such trusts shall be treated as one trust for purposes of such taxable year."

In 1986, P.L. 99-514, Sec. 301(b)(7), deleted the last sentence in para. (a)(3)... Sec. 612(b)(4), deleted para. (a)(7)... Sec. 1404(b), added subsec. (g), effective for tax. yrs. begin. after 12/31/86.

Prior to deletion, the last sentence of para. (a)(3) read as follows:

"The deduction under section 1202 (relating to deduction for excess of capital gains over capital losses) shall not be taken into account."

Prior to deletion, para. (a)(7) read as follows:

"(7) Dividends or interest. There shall be included the amount of any dividends or interest excluded from gross income pursuant to section 116 (relating to partial exclusion of dividends) or section 128 (relating to certain interest)."

—P.L. 99-514, Sec. 1806(a), amended subpara. (e)(3)(B) [as redesignated by Sec. 1806(c)(1) of this Act, following], effective for distributions after 6/1/84, in tax. yrs. end. after 6/1/84, except as provided in Sec. 81(b)(2), reproduced below. [see Secs. 1018(e)(1)-(3) of P.L. 100-647, reproduced above]

Prior to amendment subpara. (e)(3)(B) read as follows:

"(B) Election. Any election under this paragraph shall be made by the estate or trust on its return for the taxable year for which the distribution was made."

—P.L. 99-514, Sec. 1806(b), amended Sec. 82(b) of P.L. 98-369, the effective date of changes made by Sec. 82(a) of P.L. 98-369, by adding the clause following the semicolon, [see below].

—P.L. 99-514, Sec. 1806(c)(1), redesignated subsec. (d) (relating to treatment of property distributed in kind) [as added by Sec. 82(b) of P.L. 98-369] as subsec. (e)... Sec. 1806(c)(2), redesignated subsec. (e) [as added by Sec. 82(a) of P.L. 98-369] as subsec. (f), effective for tax. yrs. begin. after 3/1/84; except that, in the case of a trust which is attributable to contributions to corpus after 3/1/84 [as added by Sec. 1806(b) of P.L. 99-514, see above].

In 1984, P.L. 98-369, Sec. 81(a), added subsec. (d), effective for distributions after 6/1/84, in tax. yrs. end. after 6/1/84. Sec. 81(b)(2) of the Act provides:

"(2) Time for making election. In the case of any distribution before the date of the enactment of this Act—

"(A) the time for making an election under section 643(d)(3) of the Internal Revenue Code of 1954 (as added by this section) shall not expire before January 1, 1985, and

"(B) the requirement that such election be made on the return of the estate or trust shall not apply."

—P.L. 98-369, Sec. 82(a), added subsec. (e), effective for tax. yrs. begin. after 3/1/84; except that, in the case of a trust which was irrevocable on March 1, 1984, such amendment shall so apply only to that portion of the trust which is attributable to contributions to corpus after March 1, 1984 [as added by Sec. 1806(b) of P.L. 99-514, see above.].

—P.L. 98-369, Sec. 722(h)(3), added subsec. (d), effective with respect to payments made after 12/31/83.

In 1983, P.L. 97-448, Sec. 103(a)(3), amended para. (a)(7), effective for tax. yrs. end. after 9/30/81.

Prior to amendment, para. (a)(7) read as follows:

"(7) Dividends or interest. There shall be included the amount of any dividends or interest excluded from gross income pursuant to section 116 (relating to partial exclusion of dividends or interest received)."

In 1981, P.L. 97-34, Sec. 301(b)(4), added "or section 128 (relating to interest on certain savings certificates)" after "received)" in para. (a)(7) (as in effect for tax. yrs. begin. in '81), effective for tax. yrs. end. after 9/30/81.

—P.L. 97-34, Sec. 301(b)(6)(B), added "or interest" after "dividends" in the text and heading of para. (a)(7) (as in effect for tax. yrs. begin. after 12/31/81), effective for tax. yrs. begin. after 12/31/81.

—P.L. 97-34, Sec. 302(b)(1), amended the effective date for changes made by Sec. 404(b)(4) of P.L. 96-223 to be effective for tax. yrs. begin. after 12/31/80 and before 1/1/82 rather than effective for tax. yrs. begin. after 12/31/80 and before 1/1/83, see below.

In 1980, P.L. 96-223, Sec. 404(b)(4), added "or interest" after "dividends" each time it appeared in the caption or text of para. (a)(7), effective [as amended by Sec. 302(b)(1) of P.L. 97-34, see above] for tax. yrs. begin. after 12/31/80 and before 1/1/82.

In 1976, P.L. 94-455, Sec. 1013(c)(1), substituted "foreign trust" for "foreign trust created by a United States person" in subpara. (a)(6)(C), effective for tax. yrs. begin. after 12/31/75.

—P.L. 94-455, Sec. 1013(c)(2), added subpara. (a)(6)(D), effective for tax. yrs. begin. after 12/31/75.

—P.L. 94-455, Sec. 1013(e)(2), deleted subsec. (d), effective for tax. yrs. end. after 12/31/75, but only in the case of foreign trusts created after 5/21/74, and transfers of property to foreign trusts after 5/21/74.

Prior to amendment, subsec. (d) read as follows:

"(d) Foreign trust created by United States persons. For purposes of this part, the term 'foreign trust created by a United States person' means that portion of a foreign trust (as defined in section 7701(a)(31)) attributable to money or property transferred directly or indirectly by a United States person (as defined in section 7701(a)(30)), or under the will of a decedent who at the date of his death was a United States citizen or resident."

In 1962, P.L. 87-834, Sec. 7, substituted "Income of foreign trust" for "Foreign income" in the heading of para. (a)(6), designated existing material as subpara. (a)(6)(A), added subparas. (a)(16)(B) and (C), and added subsec. (d), effective for distributions made after 12/31/62.

Sec. 644. Taxable year of trusts.

(a) In general.

For purposes of this subtitle, the taxable year of any trust shall be the calendar year.

(b) Exception for trusts exempt from tax and charitable trusts.

Subsection (a) shall not apply to a trust exempt from taxation under section 501(a) or to a trust described in section 4947(a)(1).

In 1997, P.L. 105-34, Sec. 507(b)(1), redesignated Code Sec. 645 as Code Sec. 644, effective for sales and exchanges after 8/5/97.

In 1988, P.L. 100-647, Sec. 1014(c)(1)-(4), provide:

"(c) Amendments related to section 1403 of the Reform Act.

"(1) If a beneficiary of a trust to which section 664 of the 1986 Code applies elects (at such time and in such manner as the Secretary of the Treasury or his delegate may prescribe) to have this paragraph apply, such beneficiary shall be entitled to the benefits of section 1403(c)(2) of the Reform Act with respect to amounts included in gross income under section 664(b) of the 1986 Code in the same manner as if such amounts were included in gross income under section 652(a) of the 1986 Code.

"(2) Any trust beneficiary may elect (at such time and in such manner as the Secretary of the Treasury or his delegate may prescribe) to waive the benefits of section 1403(c)(2) of the Reform Act.

"(3)(A) For purposes of determining the gross income of any pass-thru entity, such pass-thru entity shall not be allowed the benefits of section 806(e)(2)(C) (other than with respect to income from a common trust fund) or 1403(c)(2) of the Reform Act if such pass-thru entity is required to change its taxable year by reason of the amendments made by section 806 or 1403 of the Reform Act.

"(B) For purposes of subparagraph (A), the term 'pass-thru entity' means any trust, partnership, S corporation, or common trust fund.

"(4) If any trust required to change its taxable year by the amendments made by section 1403 of the Reform Act, such change shall be treated as initiated by such trust and approved by the Secretary of the Treasury or his delegate."

In 1986, P.L. 99-514, Sec. 1403(a), added Code Sec. 645, effective for tax. yrs. begin. after 12/31/86. Sec. 1403(c)(2) of this Act provides the following transitional rule [see Secs. 1014(c)(1)-(4) of P.L. 100-647, reproduced above]:

"(2) Transition rule. With respect to any trust beneficiary who is required to include in gross income amounts under sections 652(a) or 662(a) of the Internal Revenue Code of 1986 in the 1st taxable year of the beneficiary beginning after December 31, 1986, by reason of any short taxable year of the trust required by the amendments made by this section, such income shall be ratably included in the income of the trust beneficiary over the 4-taxable year period beginning with such taxable year."

Sec. 644. Repealed

In 1997, P.L. 105-34, Sec. 507(b)(1), repealed Code Sec. 644, effective for sales and exchanges after 8/5/97.

Prior to repeal, Code Sec. 644 read as follows:

"Sec. 644 Special rule for gain on property transferred to trust at less than fair market value.

"(a) Imposition of tax.

"(1) In general. If—

"(A) a trust (or another trust to which the property is distributed) sells or exchanges property at a gain not more than 2 years after the date of the initial transfer of the property in trust by the transferor, and

"(B) the fair market value of such property at the time of the initial transfer in trust by the transferor exceeds the adjusted basis of such property immediately after such transfer,

there is hereby imposed a tax determined in accordance with paragraph (2) on the includible gain recognized on such sale or exchange.

"(2) Amount of tax. The amount of the tax imposed by paragraph (1) on any includible gain recognized on the sale or exchange of any property shall be equal to the sum of—

"(A) the excess of—

"(i) the tax which would have been imposed under this chapter for the taxable year of the transferor in which the sale or exchange of such property occurs had the amount of the includible gain recognized on such sale or exchange, reduced by any deductions properly allocable to such gain, been included in the gross income of the transferor for such taxable year, over

"(ii) the tax actually imposed under this chapter for such taxable year on the transferor, plus

"(B) if such sale or exchange occurs in a taxable year of the transferor which begins after the beginning of the taxable year of the trust in which such sale or exchange occurs, an amount equal to the amount determined under subparagraph (A) multiplied by the underpayment rate established under section 6621.

The determination of tax under clause (i) of subparagraph (A) shall be made by not taking into account any carryback, and by not taking into account any loss or deduction to the extent that such loss or deduction may be carried by the transferor to any other taxable year.

"(3) Taxable year for which tax imposed. The tax imposed by paragraph (1) shall be imposed for the taxable year of the trust which begins with or within the taxable year of the transferor in which the sale or exchange occurs.

"(4) Tax to be in addition to other taxes. The tax imposed by this subsection for any taxable year of the trust shall be in addition to any other tax imposed by this chapter for such taxable year.

"(b) Definition of includible gain. For purposes of this section, the term 'includible gain' means the lesser of—

"(1) the gain recognized by the trust on the sale or exchange of any property, or

"(2) the excess of the fair market value of such property at the time of the initial transfer in trust by the transferor over the adjusted basis of such property immediately after such transfer.

"(c) Character of includible gain. For purposes of subsection (a)—

"(1) the character of the includible gain shall be determined as if the property had actually been sold or exchanged by the transferor, and any activities of the trust with respect to the sale or exchange of the property shall be deemed to be activities of the transferor, and

"(2) the portion of the includible gain subject to the provisions of section 1245 and section 1250 shall be determined in accordance with regulations prescribed by the Secretary.

"(d) Special rules.

"(1) Short sales. If the trust sells the property referred to in subsection (a) in a short sale within the 2-year period referred to in such subsection, such 2-year period shall be extended to the date of the closing of such short sale.

"(2) Substituted basis property. For purposes of this section, in the case of any property held by the trust which has a basis determined in whole or in part by reference to the basis of any other property which was transferred to the trust—

"(A) the initial transfer of such property in trust by the transferor shall be treated as having occurred on the date of the initial transfer in trust of such other property,

"(B) subsections (a)(1)(B) and (b)(2) shall be applied by taking into account the fair market value and the adjusted basis of such other property, and

"(C) the amount determined under subsection (b)(2) with respect to such other property shall be allocated (under regulations prescribed by the Secretary) among such other property and all properties held by the trust which have a basis determined in whole or in part by reference to the basis of such other property.

"(e) Exceptions. Subsection (a) shall not apply to property—

"(1) acquired by the trust from a decedent or which passed to a trust from a decedent (within the meaning of section 1014); or

"(2) acquired by a pooled income fund (as defined in section 642(c)(5)); or

"(3) acquired by a charitable remainder annuity trust (as defined in section 664(d)(1)) or a charitable remainder unitrust (as defined in sections 664(d)(2) and (3)), or

"(4) if the sale or exchange of the property occurred after the death of the transferor.

"(f) Special rule for installment sales. If the trust reports income under section 453 on any sale or exchange to which subsection (a) applies, under regulations prescribed by the Secretary—

"(1) subsection (a) (other than the 2-year requirement of paragraph (1)(A) thereof) shall be applied as if each installment were a separate sale or exchange of property to which such subsection applies, and

"(2) the term 'includible gain' shall not include any portion of an installment received by the trust after the death of the transferor."

In 1986, P.L. 99-514, Sec. 1511(c)(5), substituted "the underpayment rate established under section 6621" for "the annual rate established under section 6621" in subpara. (a)(2)(B), effective for determining interest for periods after 12/31/86.

In 1980, P.L. 96-471, Sec. 2(b)(4), substituted "reports income under section 453" for "elects to report income under section 453" in subsec. (f), effective for dispositions made after 10/19/80 in tax. yrs. ending after 10/19/80.

In 1978, P.L. 95-600, Sec. 701(p)(1)(A), substituted "gain recognized" for "gain realized" each place it appeared in paras. (a)(1), (a)(2) and (b)(1) ... Sec. 701(p)(1)(B), amended subsec. (d) ... Sec. 701(p)(2), added the sentence at the end of para. (a)(2) ... Sec. 701(p)(3), substituted "subsection (a) (other than the 2-year requirement of paragraph (1)(A) thereof)" for "subsection (a)" in para. (f)(1), effective for transfers in trust made after 5/21/78.

Prior to amendment, subsec. (d) read as follows:

"(d) Special rule for short sales.

"If the trust sells the property referred to in subsection (a) in a short sale within the 2-year period referred to in such subsection, such 2-year period shall be extended to the date of the closing of such short sale."

—P.L. 95-600, Sec. 701(p)(4), repealed Sec. 1402(b)(1)(K) of P.L. 94-455, effective 10/4/76. See below.

In 1976, P.L. 94-455, Sec. 701(e)(1), added Code Sec. 644, effective for transfers in trust made after 5/21/76.

—P.L. 94-455, Sec. 1402(b)(1)(K), substituted "9 months" for "6 months" each place it appeared in Code Sec. 644 ... Sec. 1402(b)(2), substituted "1 year" "9 months" each place it appeared in Code Sec. 644 [as amended by Sec. 1402(b)(1)(I) of this Act, see above] [unworkable amendments, "6 months" does not appear in Code Sec. 644, these amendments repealed by Sec. 701(p)(4) of P.L. 95-600, see above], effective for tax. yrs. begin. in 1977.

Sec. 645. Certain revocable trusts treated as part of estate.

(a) General rule.

For purposes of this subtitle, if both the executor (if any) of an estate and the trustee of a qualified revocable trust elect the treatment provided in this section, such trust shall be treated and taxed as part of such estate (and not as a separate trust) for all taxable years of the estate ending after the date of the decedent's death and before the applicable date.

(b) Definitions.

For purposes of subsection (a)—

(1) Qualified revocable trust. The term "qualified revocable trust" means any trust (or portion thereof) which was treated under section 676 as owned by the decedent of the estate referred to in subsection (a) by reason of a power in the grantor (determined without regard to section 672(e)).

(2) Applicable date. The term "applicable date" means—

(A) if no return of tax imposed by chapter 11 is required to be filed, the date which is 2 years after the date of the decedent's death, and

(B) if such a return is required to be filed, the date which is 6 months after the date of the final determination of the liability for tax imposed by chapter 11.

(c) Election.

The election under subsection (a) shall be made not later than the time prescribed for filing the return of tax imposed by this chapter for the first taxable year of the estate (determined with regard to extensions) and, once made, shall be irrevocable.

In 1998, P.L. 105-206, Sec. 6013(a)(1), redesignated Code Sec. 646 as Code Sec. 645, effective for estates of decedents dying after 8/5/97.

In 1997, P.L. 105-34, Sec. 1305(a), added Code Sec. 646, effective for estates of decedents dying after 8/5/97.

• **Caution:** Code Sec. 646, following, was added by P.L. 107-16, the Economic Growth and Tax Relief Reconciliation Act of 2001 (EGTRRA). These provisions generally sunset for tax years beginning after 12/31/2012. For specific sunset provisions, see Sec. 901, P.L. 107-16 (as amended) reproduced in history notes for this Code Sec.

Sec. 646. Tax treatment of electing Alaska Native Settlement Trusts.

(a) In general.

If an election under this section is in effect with respect to any Settlement Trust, the provisions of this section shall apply in determining the income tax treatment of the Settlement Trust and its beneficiaries with respect to the Settlement Trust.

(b) Taxation of income of trust.

Except as provided in subsection (f)(1)(B)(ii)—

(1) In general. There is hereby imposed on the taxable income of an electing Settlement Trust, other than its net capital gain, a tax at the lowest rate specified in section 1(c).

(2) Capital gain. In the case of an electing Settlement Trust with a net capital gain for the taxable year, a tax is hereby imposed on such gain at the rate of tax which would apply to such gain if the taxpayer were subject to a tax on its other taxable income at only the lowest rate specified in section 1(c).

Any such tax shall be in lieu of the income tax otherwise imposed by this chapter on such income or gain.

(c) One-time election.

  (1) In general. A Settlement Trust may elect to have the provisions of this section apply to the trust and its beneficiaries.

  (2) Time and method of election. An election under paragraph (1) shall be made by the trustee of such trust—

   (A) on or before the due date (including extensions) for filing the Settlement Trust's return of tax for the first taxable year of such trust ending after the date of the enactment of this section, and

   (B) by attaching to such return of tax a statement specifically providing for such election.

  (3) Period election in effect. Except as provided in subsection (f), an election under this subsection—

   (A) shall apply to the first taxable year described in paragraph (2)(A) and all subsequent taxable years, and

   (B) may not be revoked once it is made.

(d) Contributions to trust.

  (1) Beneficiaries of electing trust not taxed on contributions. In the case of an electing Settlement Trust, no amount shall be includible in the gross income of a beneficiary of such trust by reason of a contribution to such trust.

  (2) Earnings and profits. The earnings and profits of the sponsoring Native Corporation shall not be reduced on account of any contribution to such Settlement Trust.

(e) Tax treatment of distributions to beneficiaries.

Amounts distributed by an electing Settlement Trust during any taxable year shall be considered as having the following characteristics in the hands of the recipient beneficiary:

  (1) First, as amounts excludable from gross income for the taxable year to the extent of the taxable income of such trust for such taxable year (decreased by any income tax paid by the trust with respect to the income) plus any amount excluded from gross income of the trust under section 103.

  (2) Second, as amounts excludable from gross income to the extent of the amount described in paragraph (1) for all taxable years for which an election is in effect under subsection (c) with respect to the trust, and not previously taken into account under paragraph (1).

  (3) Third, as amounts distributed by the sponsoring Native Corporation with respect to its stock (within the meaning of section 301(a)) during such taxable year and taxable to the recipient beneficiary as amounts described in section 301(c)(1), to the extent of current or accumulated earnings and profits of the sponsoring Native Corporation as of the close of such taxable year after proper adjustment is made for all distributions made by the sponsoring Native Corporation during such taxable year.

  (4) Fourth, as amounts distributed by the trust in excess of the distributable net income of such trust for such taxable year.

Amounts distributed to which paragraph (3) applies shall not be treated as a corporate distribution subject to section 311(b), and for purposes of determining the amount of a distribution for purposes of paragraph (3) and the basis to the recipients, section 643(e) and not section 301(b) or (d) shall apply.

(f) Special rules where transfer restrictions modified.

  (1) Transfer of beneficial interests. If, at any time, a beneficial interest in an electing Settlement Trust may be disposed of to a person in a manner which would not be permitted by section 7(h) of the Alaska Native Claims Settlement Act (43 U.S.C. 1606(h)) if such interest were Settlement Common Stock—

   (A) no election may be made under subsection (c) with respect to such trust, and

   (B) if such an election is in effect as of such time—

    (i) such election shall cease to apply as of the first day of the taxable year in which such disposition is first permitted,

    (ii) the provisions of this section shall not apply to such trust for such taxable year and all taxable years thereafter, and

    (iii) the distributable net income of such trust shall be increased by the current or accumulated earnings and profits of the sponsoring Native Corporation as of the close of such taxable year after proper adjustment is made for all distributions made by the sponsoring Native Corporation during such taxable year.

In no event shall the increase under clause (iii) exceed the fair market value of the trust's assets as of the date the beneficial interest of the trust first becomes so disposable. The earnings and profits of the sponsoring Native Corporation shall be adjusted as of the last day of such taxable year by the amount of earnings and profits so included in the distributable net income of the trust.

  (2) Stock in corporation. If—

   (A) stock in the sponsoring Native Corporation may be disposed of to a person in a manner which would not be permitted by section 7(h) of the Alaska Native Claims Settlement Act (43 U.S.C. 1606(h)) if such stock were Settlement Common Stock, and

   (B) at any time after such disposition of stock is first permitted, such corporation transfers assets to a Settlement Trust,

paragraph (1)(B) shall be applied to such trust on and after the date of the transfer in the same manner as if the trust permitted dispositions of beneficial interests in the trust in a manner not permitted by such section 7(h).

  (3) Certain distributions. For purposes of this section, the surrender of an interest in a Native Corporation or an electing Settlement Trust in order to accomplish the whole or partial redemption of the interest of a shareholder or beneficiary in such corporation or trust, or to accomplish the whole or partial liquidation of such corporation or trust, shall be deemed to be a transfer permitted by section 7(h) of the Alaska Native Claims Settlement Act.

(g) Taxable income.

For purposes of this title, the taxable income of an electing Settlement Trust shall be determined under section 641(b) without regard to any deduction under section 651 or 661.

(h) Definitions.

For purposes of this section—

  (1) Electing Settlement Trust. The term "electing Settlement Trust" means a Settlement Trust which has made the election, effective for a taxable year, described in subsection (c).

  (2) Native Corporation. The term "Native Corporation" has the meaning given such term by section 3(m) of the Alaska Native Claims Settlement Act (43 U.S.C. 1602(m)).

Estates, trusts, beneficiaries   **Code Sec. 661(a)**

(3) **Settlement Common Stock.** The term "Settlement Common Stock" has the meaning given such term by section 3(p) of the Alaska Native Claims Settlement Act (43 U.S.C. 1602(p)).

(4) **Settlement Trust.** The term "Settlement Trust" means a trust that constitutes a settlement trust under section 3(t) of the Alaska Native Claims Settlement Act (43 U.S.C. 1602(t)).

(5) **Sponsoring Native Corporation.** The term "sponsoring Native Corporation" means the Native Corporation which transfers assets to an electing Settlement Trust.

(i) **Special loss disallowance rule.**

Any loss that would otherwise be recognized by a shareholder upon a disposition of a share of stock of a sponsoring Native Corporation shall be reduced (but not below zero) by the per share loss adjustment factor. The per share loss adjustment factor shall be the aggregate of all contributions to all electing Settlement Trusts sponsored by such Native Corporation made on or after the first day each trust is treated as an electing Settlement Trust expressed on a per share basis and determined as of the day of each such contribution.

(j) **Cross reference.**

For information required with respect to electing Settlement Trusts and sponsoring Native Corporations, see section 6039H.

In 2010, P.L. 111-312, Sec. 101(a)(1), substituted "December 31, 2012" for "December 31, 2010" both places it appeared in Sec. 901, P.L. 107-16 [see below], effective as if included in the enactment of P.L. 107-16, EGTRRA, 6/7/2001.

In 2002, P.L. 107-358, Sec. 2, added subsec. (c) in Sec. 901 of P.L. 107-16 [see below], effective 12/17/2002.

In 2001, P.L. 107-16, Sec. 671(a), added Code Sec. 646, effective for tax. yrs. ending after 6/7/2001 and for contributions made to electing Settlement Trusts for such year or any subsequent year.

—P.L. 107-16, Sec. 901, of this Act [as amended by Sec. 2, P.L. 107-358, and Sec. 101(a)(1), P.L. 111-312, see above], reads as follows:

"Sec. 901. Sunset of provisions of Act.

"(a) In general. All provisions of, and amendments made by, this Act shall not apply—

"(1) to taxable, plan, or limitation years beginning after December 31, 2012, or

"(2) in the case of title V, to estates of decedents dying, gifts made, or generation skipping transfers, after December 31, 2012.

"(b) Application of certain laws. The Internal Revenue Code of 1986 and the Employee Retirement Income Security Act of 1974 shall be applied and administered to years, estates, gifts, and transfers described in subsection (a) as if the provisions and amendments described in subsection (a) had never been enacted.

"(c) Exception. Subsection (a) shall not apply to section 803 (relating to no federal income tax on restitution received by victims of the Nazi regime or their heirs or estates)."

Subpart B.—Trusts Which Distribute Current Income Only

Sec.
651. Deduction for trusts distributing current income only.
652. Inclusion of amounts in gross income of beneficiaries of trusts distributing current income only.

Sec. 651. Deduction for trusts distributing current income only.

(a) **Deduction.**

In the case of any trust the terms of which—

(1) provide that all of its income is required to be distributed currently, and

(2) do not provide that any amounts are to be paid, permanently set aside, or used for the purposes specified in section 642(c) (relating to deduction for charitable, etc., purposes),

there shall be allowed as a deduction in computing the taxable income of the trust the amount of the income for the taxable year which is required to be distributed currently. This section shall not apply in any taxable year in which the trust distributes amounts other than amounts of income described in paragraph (1).

(b) **Limitation on deduction.**

If the amount of income required to be distributed currently exceeds the distributable net income of the trust for the taxable year, the deduction shall be limited to the amount of the distributable net income. For this purpose, the computation of distributable net income shall not include items of income which are not included in the gross income of the trust and the deductions allocable thereto.

Sec. 652. Inclusion of amounts in gross income of beneficiaries of trusts distributing current income only.

(a) **Inclusion.**

Subject to subsection (b), the amount of income for the taxable year required to be distributed currently by a trust described in section 651 shall be included in the gross income of the beneficiaries to whom the income is required to be distributed, whether distributed or not. If such amount exceeds the distributable net income, there shall be included in the gross income of each beneficiary an amount which bears the same ratio to distributable net income as the amount of income required to be distributed to such beneficiary bears to the amount of income required to be distributed to all beneficiaries.

(b) **Character of amounts.**

The amounts specified in subsection (a) shall have the same character in the hands of the beneficiary as in the hands of the trust. For this purpose, the amounts shall be treated as consisting of the same proportion of each class of items entering into the computation of distributable net income of the trust as the total of each class bears to the total distributable net income of the trust, unless the terms of the trust specifically allocate different classes of income to different beneficiaries. In the application of the preceding sentence, the items of deduction entering into the computation of distributable net income shall be allocated among the items of distributable net income in accordance with regulations prescribed by the Secretary.

(c) **Different taxable years.**

If the taxable year of a beneficiary is different from that of the trust, the amount which the beneficiary is required to include in gross income in accordance with the provisions of this section shall be based upon the amount of income of the trust for any taxable year or years of the trust ending within or with his taxable year.

In 1976, P.L. 94-455, Sec. 1906(b)(13)(A), substituted "Secretary" for "Secretary or his delegate" in subsec. (b), effective 2/1/77.

Subpart C.—Estates and Trusts Which May Accumulate Income or Which Distribute Corpus

Sec.
661. Deduction for estates and trusts accumulating income or distributing corpus.
662. Inclusion of amounts in gross income of beneficiaries of estates and trusts accumulating income or distributing corpus.
663. Special rules applicable to sections 661 and 662.
664. Charitable remainder trusts.

In 1969, P.L. 91-172, Sec. 201(e)(2), added item 664.

Sec. 661. Deduction for estates and trusts accumulating income or distributing corpus.

(a) **Deduction.**

In any taxable year there shall be allowed as a deduction in computing the taxable income of an estate or trust (other than a trust to which subpart B applies), the sum of—

(1) any amount of income for such taxable year required to be distributed currently (including any amount required to be distributed which may be paid out of income or corpus to the extent such amount is paid out of income for such taxable year); and

(2) any other amounts properly paid or credited or required to be distributed for such taxable year;

but such deduction shall not exceed the distributable net income of the estate or trust.

(b) Character of amounts distributed.

The amount determined under subsection (a) shall be treated as consisting of the same proportion of each class of items entering into the computation of distributable net income of the estate or trust as the total of each class bears to the total distributable net income of the estate or trust in the absence of the allocation of different classes of income under the specific terms of the governing instrument. In the application of the preceding sentence, the items of deduction entering into the computation of distributable net income (including the deduction allowed under section 642(c)) shall be allocated among the items of distributable net income in accordance with regulations prescribed by the Secretary.

(c) Limitation on deduction.

No deduction shall be allowed under subsection (a) in respect of any portion of the amount allowed as a deduction under that subsection (without regard to this subsection) which is treated under subsection (b) as consisting of any item of distributable net income which is not included in the gross income of the estate or trust.

In 1976, P.L. 94-455, Sec. 1906(b)(13)(A), substituted "Secretary" for "Secretary or his delegate" in subsec. (b), effective 2/1/77.

Sec. 662. Inclusion of amounts in gross income of beneficiaries of estates and trusts accumulating income or distributing corpus.

(a) Inclusion.

Subject to subsection (b), there shall be included in the gross income of a beneficiary to whom an amount specified in section 661(a) is paid, credited, or required to be distributed (by an estate or trust described in section 661), the sum of the following amounts:

(1) **Amounts required to be distributed currently.** The amount of income for the taxable year required to be distributed currently to such beneficiary, whether distributed or not. If the amount of income required to be distributed currently to all beneficiaries exceeds the distributable net income (computed without the deduction allowed by section 642(c), relating to deduction for charitable, etc., purposes) of the estate or trust, then, in lieu of the amount provided in the preceding sentence, there shall be included in the gross income of the beneficiary an amount which bears the same ratio to distributable net income (as so computed) as the amount of income required to be distributed currently to such beneficiary bears to the amount required to be distributed currently to all beneficiaries. For purposes of this section, the phrase "the amount of income for the taxable year required to be distributed currently" includes any amount required to be paid out of income or corpus to the extent such amount is paid out of income for such taxable year.

(2) **Other amounts distributed.** All other amounts properly paid, credited, or required to be distributed to such beneficiary for the taxable year. If the sum of—

(A) the amount of income for the taxable year required to be distributed currently to all beneficiaries, and

(B) all other amounts properly paid, credited, or required to be distributed to all beneficiaries

exceeds the distributable net income of the estate or trust, then, in lieu of the amount provided in the preceding sentence, there shall be included in the gross income of the beneficiary an amount which bears the same ratio to distributable net income (reduced by the amounts specified in (A)) as the other amounts properly paid, credited or required to be distributed to the beneficiary bear to the other amounts properly paid, credited, or required to be distributed to all beneficiaries.

(b) Character of amounts.

The amounts determined under subsection (a) shall have the same character in the hands of the beneficiary as in the hands of the estate or trust. For this purpose, the amounts shall be treated as consisting of the same proportion of each class of items entering into the computation of distributable net income as the total of each class bears to the total distributable net income of the estate or trust unless the terms of the governing instrument specifically allocate different classes of income to different beneficiaries. In the application of the preceding sentence, the items of deduction entering into the computation of distributable net income (including the deduction allowed under section 642(c)) shall be allocated among the items of distributable net income in accordance with regulations prescribed by the Secretary. In the application of this subsection to the amount determined under paragraph (1) of subsection (a), distributable net income shall be computed without regard to any portion of the deduction under section 642(c) which is not attributable to income of the taxable year.

(c) Different taxable years.

If the taxable year of a beneficiary is different from that of the estate or trust, the amount to be included in the gross income of the beneficiary shall be based on the distributable net income of the estate or trust and the amounts properly paid, credited, or required to be distributed to the beneficiary during any taxable year or years of the estate or trust ending within or with his taxable year.

In 1976, P.L. 94-455, Sec. 1906(b)(13)(A), substituted "Secretary" for "Secretary or his delegate" in subsec. (b), effective 2/1/77.

Sec. 663. Special rules applicable to sections 661 and 662.

(a) Exclusions.

There shall not be included as amounts falling within section 661(a) or 662(a)—

(1) **Gifts, bequests, etc.** Any amount which, under the terms of the governing instrument, is properly paid or credited as a gift or bequest of a specific sum of money or of specific property and which is paid or credited all at once or in not more than 3 installments. For this purpose an amount which can be paid or credited only from the income of the estate or trust shall not be considered as a gift or bequest of a specific sum of money.

(2) **Charitable, etc., distributions.** Any amount paid or permanently set aside or otherwise qualifying for the deduction provided in section 642(c) (computed without regard to sections 508(d), 681, and 4948(c)(4)).

(3) **Denial of double deduction.** Any amount paid, credited, or distributed in the taxable year, if section 651 or section 661 applied to such amount for a preceding taxable year of an estate or trust because credited or required to be distributed in such preceding taxable year.

(b) Distributions in first sixty-five days of taxable year.

(1) **General rule.** If within the first 65 days of any taxable year of an estate or a trust, an amount is properly paid or credited, such amount shall be considered paid or credited on the last day of the preceding taxable year.

(2) Limitation. Paragraph (1) shall apply with respect to any taxable year of an estate or a trust only if the executor of such estate or the fiduciary of such trust (as the case may be) elects, in such manner and at such time as the Secretary prescribes by regulations, to have paragraph (1) apply for such taxable year.

(c) Separate shares treated as separate estates or trusts.

For the sole purpose of determining the amount of distributable net income in the application of sections 661 and 662, in the case of a single trust having more than one beneficiary, substantially separate and independent shares of different beneficiaries in the trust shall be treated as separate trusts. Rules similar to the rules of the preceding provisions of this subsection shall apply to treat substantially separate and independent shares of different beneficiaries in an estate having more than 1 beneficiary as separate estates. The existence of such substantially separate and independent shares and the manner of treatment as separate trusts or estates, including the application of subpart D, shall be determined in accordance with regulations prescribed by the Secretary.

In 1997, P.L. 105-34, Sec. 1306(a), added "an estate or" before "a trust" each place it appeared in subsec. (b) . . . Sec. 1306(b), substituted "the executor of such estate or the fiduciary of such trust (as the case may be)" for "the fiduciary of such trust" in para. (b)(2), effective for tax. yrs. begin. after 8/5/97.

—P.L. 105-34, Sec. 1307(a)(1), added a sentence after "shall be treated as separate trusts." in subsec. (c) . . . Sec. 1307(a)(2), added "or estates" after "trusts" at the end of subsec. (c) . . . Sec. 1307(b), added "estates or" before "trusts" in the heading of subsec. (c), effective for estates of decedents dying after 8/5/97

In 1976, P.L. 94-455, Sec. 1906(b)(13)(A), substituted "Secretary" for "Secretary or his delegate" in subsecs. (b) and (c), effective for tax. yrs. begin. after 12/31/76.

In 1969, P.L. 91-172, Sec. 101(j)(17), substituted "sections 508(d), 681, and 4948(c)(4)" for "section 681" in para. (a)(2), effective 1/1/70.

—P.L. 91-172, Sec. 331(b), amended para. (b)(2), effective for tax. yrs. begin. after 12/31/68.

Prior to amendment, para. (b)(2) read as follows:

"(2) Limitations. This subsection shall apply only to a trust—

"(A) which was in existence prior to January 1, 1954.

"(B) which, under the terms of its governing instrument, may not distribute in any taxable year amounts in excess of the income of the preceding taxable year, and

"(C) on behalf of which the fiduciary elects to have this subsection apply.

The election authorized by subparagraph (C) shall be made for the first taxable year to which this part is applicable in accordance with such regulations as the Secretary or his delegate shall prescribe and shall be made not later than the time prescribed by law for filing the return for such year (including extensions thereof). If such election is made with respect to a taxable year, this subsection shall apply to all amounts property paid or credited within the first 65 days of all subsequent taxable years of such trust."

Sec. 664. Charitable remainder trusts.

(a) General rule.

Notwithstanding any other provision of this subchapter, the provisions of this section shall, in accordance with regulations prescribed by the Secretary, apply in the case of a charitable remainder annuity trust and a charitable remainder unitrust.

(b) Character of distributions.

Amounts distributed by a charitable remainder annuity trust or by a charitable remainder unitrust shall be considered as having the following characteristics in the hands of a beneficiary to whom is paid the annuity described in subsection (d)(1)(A) or the payment described in subsection (d)(2)(A):

(1) First, as amounts of income (other than gains, and amounts treated as gains, from the sale or other disposition of capital assets) includible in gross income to the extent of such income of the trust for the year and such undistributed income of the trust for prior years;

(2) Second, as a capital gain to the extent of the capital gain of the trust for the year and the undistributed capital gain of the trust for prior years;

(3) Third, as other income to the extent of such income of the trust for the year and such undistributed income of the trust for prior years; and

(4) Fourth, as a distribution of trust corpus.

For purposes of this section, the trust shall determine the amount of its undistributed capital gain on a cumulative net basis.

(c) Taxation of trusts.

(1) Income tax. A charitable remainder annuity trust and a charitable remainder unitrust shall, for any taxable year, not be subject to any tax imposed by this subtitle.

(2) Excise tax.

(A) In general. In the case of a charitable remainder annuity trust or a charitable remainder unitrust which has unrelated business taxable income (within the meaning of section 512, determined as if part III of subchapter F applied to such trust) for a taxable year, there is hereby imposed on such trust or unitrust an excise tax equal to the amount of such unrelated business taxable income.

(B) Certain rules to apply. The tax imposed by subparagraph (A) shall be treated as imposed by chapter 42 for purposes of this title other than subchapter E of chapter 42.

(C) Tax court proceedings. For purposes of this paragraph, the references in section 6212(c)(1) to section 4940 shall be deemed to include references to this paragraph.

(d) Definitions.

(1) Charitable remainder annuity trust. For purposes of this section, a charitable remainder annuity trust is a trust—

(A) from which a sum certain (which is not less than 5 percent nor more than 50 percent of the initial net fair market value of all property placed in trust) is to be paid, not less often than annually, to one or more persons (at least one of which is not an organization described in section 170(c) and, in the case of individuals, only to an individual who is living at the time of the creation of the trust) for a term of years (not in excess of 20 years) or for the life or lives of such individual or individuals,

(B) from which no amount other than the payments described in subparagraph (A) and other than qualified gratuitous transfers described in subparagraph (C) may be paid to or for the use of any person other than an organization described in section 170(c),

(C) following the termination of the payments described in subparagraph (A), the remainder interest in the trust is to be transferred to, or for the use of, an organization described in section 170(c) or is to be retained by the trust for such a use or, to the extent the remainder interest is in qualified employer securities (as defined in subsection (g)(4)), all or part of such securities are to be transferred to an employee stock ownership plan (as defined in section 4975(e)(7)) in a qualified gratuitous transfer (as defined by subsection (g)), and

(D) the value (determined under section 7520) of such remainder interest is at least 10 percent of the initial net fair market value of all property placed in the trust.

(2) Charitable remainder unitrust. For purposes of this section, a charitable remainder unitrust is a trust—

(A) from which a fixed percentage (which is not less than 5 percent nor more than 50 percent) of the net fair market value of its assets, valued annually, is to be paid, not less often than annually, to one or more persons (at least one of which is not an organization described in section 170(c) and, in the case of individuals, only to an individual who is living at the time of the creation of the trust) for a term of years (not in excess of 20 years) or for the life or lives of such individual or individuals,

(B) from which no amount other than the payments described in subparagraph (A) and other than qualified gratuitous transfers described in subparagraph (C) may be paid to or for the use of any person other than an organization described in section 170(c),

(C) following the termination of the payments described in subparagraph (A), the remainder interest in the trust is to be transferred to, or for the use of, an organization described in section 170(c) or is to be retained by the trust for such a use or, to the extent the remainder interest is in qualified employer securities (as defined in subsection (g)(4)), all or part of such securities are to be transferred to an employee stock ownership plan (as defined in section 4975(e)(7)) in a qualified gratuitous transfer (as defined by subsection (g)), and

(D) with respect to each contribution of property to the trust, the value (determined under section 7520) of such remainder interest in such property is at least 10 percent of the net fair market value of such property as of the date such property is contributed to the trust.

(3) **Exception.** Notwithstanding the provisions of paragraphs (2)(A) and (B), the trust instrument may provide that the trustee shall pay the income beneficiary for any year—

(A) the amount of the trust income, if such amount is less than the amount required to be distributed under paragraph (2)(A), and

(B) any amount of the trust income which is in excess of the amount required to be distributed under paragraph (2)(A), to the extent that (by reason of subparagraph (A)) the aggregate of the amounts paid in prior years was less than the aggregate of such required amounts.

(4) **Severance of certain additional contributions.** If—

(A) any contribution is made to a trust which before the contribution is a charitable remainder unitrust, and

(B) such contribution would (but for this paragraph) result in such trust ceasing to be a charitable unitrust by reason of paragraph (2)(D),

such contribution shall be treated as a transfer to a separate trust under regulations prescribed by the Secretary.

(e) **Valuation for purposes of charitable contribution.**

For purposes of determining the amount of any charitable contribution, the remainder interest of a charitable remainder annuity trust or charitable remainder unitrust shall be computed on the basis that an amount equal to 5 percent of the net fair market value of its assets (or a greater amount, if required under the terms of the trust instrument) is to be distributed each year.

(f) **Certain contingencies permitted.**

(1) **General rule.** If a trust would, but for a qualified contingency, meet the requirements of paragraph (1)(A) or (2)(A) of subsection (d), such trust shall be treated as meeting such requirements.

(2) **Value determined without regard to qualified contingency.** For purposes of determining the amount of any charitable contribution (or the actuarial value of any interest), a qualified contingency shall not be taken into account.

(3) **Qualified contingency.** For purposes of this subsection, the term "qualified contingency" means any provision of a trust which provides that, upon the happening of a contingency, the payments described in paragraph (1)(A) or (2)(A) of subsection (d) (as the case may be) will terminate not later than such payments would otherwise terminate under the trust.

• *Caution:* Code Sec. 664(g), following, was amended by P.L. 107-16, the Economic Growth and Tax Relief Reconciliation Act of 2001 (EGTRRA). These provisions generally sunset for tax years beginning after 12/31/2012. For specific sunset provisions see Sec. 901, P.L. 107-16 (as amended) reproduced in history notes for this Code Sec.

(g) **Qualified gratuitous transfer of qualified employer securities.**

(1) **In general.** For purposes of this section, the term "qualified gratuitous transfer" means a transfer of qualified employer securities to an employee stock ownership plan (as defined in section 4975(e)(7)) but only to the extent that—

(A) the securities transferred previously passed from a decedent dying before January 1, 1999, to a trust described in paragraph (1) or (2) of subsection (d),

(B) no deduction under section 404 is allowable with respect to such transfer,

(C) such plan contains the provisions required by paragraph (3),

(D) such plan treats such securities as being attributable to employer contributions but without regard to the limitations otherwise applicable to such contributions under section 404, and

(E) the employer whose employees are covered by the plan described in this paragraph files with the Secretary a verified written statement consenting to the application of sections 4978 and 4979A with respect to such employer.

(2) **Exception.** The term "qualified gratuitous transfer" shall not include a transfer of qualified employer securities to an employee stock ownership plan unless—

(A) such plan was in existence on August 1, 1996,

(B) at the time of the transfer, the decedent and members of the decedent's family (within the meaning of section 2032A(e)(2)) own (directly or through the application of section 318(a)) no more than 10 percent of the value of the stock of the corporation referred to in paragraph (4), and

(C) immediately after the transfer, such plan owns (after the application of section 318(a)(4)) at least 60 percent of the value of the outstanding stock of the corporation.

(3) **Plan requirements.** A plan contains the provisions required by this paragraph if such plan provides that—

(A) the qualified employer securities so transferred are allocated to plan participants in a manner consistent with section 401(a)(4),

(B) plan participants are entitled to direct the plan as to the manner in which such securities which are entitled to vote and are allocated to the account of such participant are to be voted,

(C) an independent trustee votes the securities so transferred which are not allocated to plan participants,

(D) each participant who is entitled to a distribution from the plan has the rights described in subparagraphs (A) and (B) of section 409(h)(1),

(E) such securities are held in a suspense account under the plan to be allocated each year, up to the applicable limitation under paragraph (7) (determined on the basis of fair market value of securities when allocated to participants), after first allocating all other annual additions for the limitation year, up to the limitations under sections 415(c) and (e), and

(F) on termination of the plan, all securities so transferred which are not allocated to plan participants as of such termination are to be transferred to, or for the use of, an organization described in section 170(c).

For purposes of the preceding sentence, the term "independent trustee" means any trustee who is not a member of the family (within the meaning of section 2032A(e)(2)) of the decedent or a 5-percent shareholder. A plan shall not fail to be treated as meeting the requirements of section 401(a) by reason of meeting the requirements of this subsection.

(4) Qualified employer securities. For purposes of this section, the term "qualified employer securities" means employer securities (as defined in section 409(l)) which are issued by a domestic corporation—

(A) which has no outstanding stock which is readily tradable on an established securities market, and

(B) which has only 1 class of stock.

(5) Treatment of securities allocated by employee stock ownership plan to persons related to decedent or 5-percent shareholders.—

(A) In general. If any portion of the assets of the plan attributable to securities acquired by the plan in a qualified gratuitous transfer are allocated to the account of—

(i) any person who is related to the decedent (within the meaning of section 267(b)) or a member of the decedent's family (within the meaning of section 2032A(e)(2)), or

(ii) any person who, at the time of such allocation or at any time during the 1-year period ending on the date of the acquisition of qualified employer securities by the plan, is a 5-percent shareholder of the employer maintaining the plan,

the plan shall be treated as having distributed (at the time of such allocation) to such person or shareholder the amount so allocated.

(B) 5-percent shareholder. For purposes of subparagraph (A), the term "5-percent shareholder" means any person who owns (directly or through the application of section 318(a)) more than 5 percent of the outstanding stock of the corporation which issued such qualified employer securities or of any corporation which is a member of the same controlled group of corporations (within the meaning of section 409(l)(4)) as such corporation. For purposes of the preceding sentence, section 318(a) shall be applied without regard to the exception in paragraph (2)(B)(i) thereof.

(C) Cross reference. For excise tax on allocations described in subparagraph (A), see section 4979A.

(6) Tax on failure to transfer unallocated securities to charity on termination of plan. If the requirements of paragraph (3)(F) are not met with respect to any securities, there is hereby imposed a tax on the employer maintaining the plan in an amount equal to the sum of—

(A) the amount of the increase in the tax which would be imposed by chapter 11 if such securities were not transferred as described in paragraph (1), and

(B) interest on such amount at the underpayment rate under section 6621 (and compounded daily) from the due date for filing the return of the tax imposed by chapter 11.

(7) Applicable limitation.

(A) In general. For purposes of paragraph (3)(E), the applicable limitation under this paragraph with respect to a participant is an amount equal to the lesser of—

(i) $30,000, or

(ii) 25 percent of the participant's compensation (as defined in section 415(c)(3)).

(B) Cost-of-living adjustment. The Secretary shall adjust annually the $30,000 amount under subparagraph (A)(i) at the same time and in the same manner as under section 415(d), except that the base period shall be the calendar quarter beginning October 1, 1993, and any increase under this subparagraph which is not a multiple of $5,000 shall be rounded to the next lowest multiple of $5,000.

In 2010, P.L. 111-312, Sec. 101(a)(1), substituted "December 31, 2012" for "December 31, 2010" both places it appeared in Sec. 901 of P.L. 107-16 [see below], effective as if included in the enactment of P.L. 107-16, EGTRRA, 6/7/2001.

In 2006, P.L. 109-432, Sec. 424(a), amended subsec. (c), effective for tax. yrs. begin. after 12/31/2006.

Prior to amendment, subsec. (c) read as follows:

"(c) Exemption from income taxes.

"A charitable remainder annuity trust and a charitable remainder unitrust shall, for any taxable year, not be subject to any tax imposed by this subtitle, unless such trust, for such year, has unrelated business taxable income (within the meaning of section 512, determined as if part III of subchapter F applied to such trust)."

—P.L. 109-280, Sec. 811, of this Act [relating to Sec. 901 of P.L. 107-16, see below], provides:

"SEC. 811. PENSIONS AND INDIVIDUAL RETIREMENT ARRANGEMENT PROVISIONS OF ECONOMIC GROWTH AND TAX RELIEF RECONCILIATION ACT OF 2001 MADE PERMANENT.

"Title IX of the Economic Growth and Tax Relief Reconciliation Act of 2001 shall not apply to the provisions of, and amendments made by, subtitles A through F of title VI of such Act (relating to pension and individual retirement arrangement provisions)."

—P.L. 109-280, Sec. 868(a), added "(determined on the basis of fair market value of securities when allocated to participants)" after "paragraph (7)" in subpara. (g)(3)(E), effective 8/17/2006.

In 2002, P.L. 107-358, Sec. 2, added subsec. (c) in Sec. 901 of P.L. 107-16 [see below], effective 12/17/2002.

In 2001, P.L. 107-16, Sec. 632(a)(3)(H)(i), substituted "applicable limitation under paragraph (7)" for "limitations under section 415(c)" in subpara. (g)(3)(E) ... Sec. 632(a)(3)(H)(ii), added para. (g)(7), effective for yrs. begin. after 12/31/2001.

—P.L. 107-16, Sec. 901, of this Act [as amended by Sec. 2 of P.L. 107-358, and Sec. 101(a)(1) of P.L. 111-312, and as related to Sec. 811 of P.L. 109-280, see above], reads as follows:

"SEC. 901. SUNSET OF PROVISIONS OF ACT.

"(a) In general. All provisions of, and amendments made by, this Act shall not apply—

"(1) to taxable, plan, or limitation years beginning after December 31, 2012, or

"(2) in the case of title V, to estates of decedents dying, gifts made, or generation skipping transfers, after December 31, 2012.

"(b) Application of certain laws. The Internal Revenue Code of 1986 and the Employee Retirement Income Security Act of 1974 shall be applied and administered to years, estates, gifts, and transfers described in subsection (a) as if the provisions and amendments described in subsection (a) had never been enacted.

"(c) Exception. Subsection (a) shall not apply to section 803 (relating to no federal income tax on restitution received by victims of the Nazi regime or their heirs or estates)."

In 2000, P.L. 106-554, Sec. 1(a)(7), [which enacted into law Sec. 312(b) of P.L. 106-554] added "(7)(A)(i)(II)," after "(5)(A)(ii)(I)," in Sec. 4003(b) of P.L. 105-277, see below.

—P.L. 106-554, Sec. 1(a)(7), [which enacted into law Sec. 319(7) of P.L. 106-554] deleted the period after "subsection (g))" in paras. (d)(1)(C) and (d)(2)(C); this amendment cannot be made to this Code Sec. as it currently exists, effective 12/21/2000.

In 1998, P.L. 105-277, Sec. 4003(b), of this Act, reads as follows:

"(b) Provision related to section 311 of 1997 Act. In the case of any capital gain distribution made after 1997 by a trust to which section 664 of the 1986 Code applies with respect to amounts properly taken into account by such trust during 1997, paragraphs (5)(A)(i)(I), (5)(A)(ii)(I), (7)(A)(i)(II), and (13)(A) of section 1(h) of the 1986 Code (as in effect for taxable years ending on December 31, 1997) shall not apply."

—P.L. 105-206, Sec. 6010(r), added ", and" at the end of subparas. (d)(1)(C) and (d)(2)(C), effective for transfers in trust after 7/28/97. For special rules, see Sec. 1089(b)(6)(B) of P.L. 105-34 [reproduced below].

In 1997, P.L. 105-34, Sec. 1089(a)(1), added "nor more than 50 percent" after "not less than 5 percent" in subparas. (d)(1)(A) and (d)(2)(A), effective for transfers in trust after 6/18/97.

—P.L. 105-34, Sec. 1089(b)(1), deleted "and" at the end of subpara. (d)(1)(B), deleted the period at the end of subpara. (d)(1)(C), and added subpara. (d)(1)(D) ... Sec. 1089(b)(2), deleted "and" at the end of subpara. (d)(2)(B), deleted the period at the end of subpara. (d)(2)(C), and added subpara. (d)(2)(D) ... Sec. 1089(b)(4), added para. (d)(4), effective for transfers in trust after 7/28/97. Sec. 1089(b)(6)(B) of this Act provides:

"(B) Special rule for certain decedents. The amendments made by this subsection shall not apply to transfers in trust under the terms of a will (or other testamentary instrument) executed on or before July 28, 1997, if the decedent —

"(i) dies before January 1, 1999, without having republished the will (or amended such instrument) by codicil or otherwise, or

"(ii) on July 28, 1997, under a mental disability to change the disposition of his property and did not regain his competence to dispose of such property before the date of his death."

—P.L. 105-34, Sec. 1530(a), substituted "or, to the extent the remainder interest is in qualified employer securities (as defined in subsection (g)(4)), all or part of such securities are to be transferred to an employee stock ownership plan (as defined in section 4975(e)(7)) in a qualified gratuitous transfer (as defined by subsection (g))." for the period at the end of subpara. (d)(1)(C) [prior to amendment by Sec. 1089(1) of this Act, see above] and (d)(2)(C) [prior to amendment by Sec. 1089(1) of this Act, see above] ... Sec. 1530(b), added subsec. (g) ... Sec. 1530(c)(5), added "and other than qualified gratuitous transfers described in subparagraph (C)" after "subparagraph (A)" in subparas. (d)(1)(B) and (d)(2)(B), effective for transfers made by trusts to, or for the use of, an employee stock ownership plan after 8/5/97.

In **1984**, P.L. 98-369, Sec. 1022(d), added subsec. (f), effective for transfers after 12/31/78. Sec. 1022(e)(3) of this Act, provides:

"(3) Statute of limitations.

"(A) In general.—If on the date of the enactment of this Act [7/18/84] (or at any time before the date 1 year after such date of enactment), credit or refund of any overpayment of tax attributable to the amendments made by this section is barred by any law or rule of law, such credit or refund of such overpayment may nevertheless be made if claim therefor is filed before the date 1 year after the date of the enactment of this Act.

"(B) No interest where statute closed on date of enactment. In any case where the making of the credit or refund of the overpayment described in subparagraph (A) is barred on the date of the enactment of this Act [7/18/84], no interest shall be allowed with respect to such overpayment (or any related adjustment) for the period before the date 180 days after the date on which the Secretary of the Treasury (or his delegate) is notified that the reformation has occurred."

In **1976**, P.L. 94-455, Sec. 1906(b)(13)(A), substituted "Secretary" for "Secretary or his delegate" in subsec. (a), effective for tax. yrs. begin. after 12/31/76.

In **1969**, P.L. 91-172, Sec. 201(e)(1), added Code Sec. 664, effective for transfers in trust made after 7/31/69.

SUBPART D.—TREATMENT OF EXCESS DISTRIBUTIONS BY TRUSTS

Sec.
665. Definitions applicable to subpart D.
666. Accumulation distribution allocated to preceding years.
667. Treatment of amounts deemed distributed by trust in preceding years.
668. Interest charge on accumulation distributions from foreign sources.
669. Repealed.

In **1976**, P.L. 94-455, Sec. 701(g)(1), deleted the items for Code Secs. 667, 668, and 669 ... added "Sec. 667. Treatment of amounts deemed distributed by trust in preceding years."

—P.L. 94-455, Sec. 1014(c), added the item for Code Sec. 668.

In **1969**, P.L. 91-172, Sec. 331(a), amended Subpart D.

Prior to amendment Subpart D read as follows:

"SUBPART D.—TREATMENT OF EXCESS DISTRIBUTIONS BY TRUSTS
"Sec.
"665. Definitions applicable to subpart D.
"666. Accumulation distribution allocated to 5 preceding years.
"667. Denial of refund to trusts.
"668. Treatment of amounts deemed distributed in preceding years.
"669. Special rules applicable to certain foreign trusts."

In **1962**, added item 669.

Sec. 665. Definitions applicable to subpart D.
(a) Undistributed net income.

For purposes of this subpart, the term "undistributed net income" for any taxable year means the amount by which the distributable net income of the trust for such taxable year exceeds the sum of—

(1) the amounts for such taxable year specified in paragraphs (1) and (2) of section 661(a), and

(2) the amount of taxes imposed on the trust attributable to such distributable net income.

(b) Accumulation distribution.

For purposes of this subpart, except as provided in subsection (c), the term "accumulation distribution" means, for any taxable year of the trust, the amount by which—

(1) the amounts specified in paragraph (2) of section 661(a) for such taxable year, exceed

(2) distributable net income for such year reduced (but not below zero) by the amounts specified in paragraph (1) of section 661(a).

For purposes of section 667 (other than subsection (c) thereof, relating to multiple trusts), the amounts specified in paragraph (2) of section 661(a) shall not include amounts properly paid, credited, or required to be distributed to a beneficiary from a trust (other than a foreign trust) as income accumulated before the birth of such beneficiary or before such beneficiary attains the age of 21. If the amounts properly paid, credited, or required to be distributed by the trust for the taxable year do not exceed the income of the trust for such year, there shall be no accumulation distribution for such year.

(c) Exception for accumulation distributions from certain domestic trusts.

For purposes of this subpart—

(1) In general. In the case of a qualified trust, any distribution in any taxable year beginning after the date of the enactment of this subsection shall be computed without regard to any undistributed net income.

(2) Qualified trust. For purposes of this subsection, the term "qualified trust" means any trust other than—

(A) a foreign trust (or, except as provided in regulations, a domestic trust which at any time was a foreign trust), or

(B) a trust created before March 1, 1984, unless it is established that the trust would not be aggregated with other trusts under section 643(f) if such section applied to such trust.

(d) Taxes imposed on the trust.

For purposes of this subpart—

(1) In general. The term "taxes imposed on the trust" means the amount of the taxes which are imposed for any taxable year of the trust under this chapter (without regard to this subpart or part IV of subchapter A) and which, under regulations prescribed by the Secretary, are properly allocable to the undistributed portions of distributable net income and gains in excess of losses from sales or exchanges of capital assets. The amount determined in the preceding sentence shall be reduced by any amount of such taxes deemed distributed under section 666(b) and (c) to any beneficiary.

(2) Foreign trusts. In the case of any foreign trust, the term "taxes imposed on the trust" includes the amount, reduced as provided in the last sentence of paragraph (1), of any income, war profits, and excess profits taxes imposed by any foreign country or possession of the United States on such foreign trust which, as determined under paragraph (1), are so properly allocable. Under rules or regulations prescribed by the Secretary, in the case of any foreign trust of which the settlor or another person would be treated as owner of any portion of the trust under subpart E but for section 672(f), the term "taxes imposed on the trust" includes the allocable amount of any income, war profits, and excess profits taxes imposed by any foreign country or possession of the United States on the settlor or such other person in respect of trust income.

Estates, trusts, beneficiaries Code Sec. 665

(e) Preceding taxable year.

For purposes of this subpart—

(1) In the case of a foreign trust created by a United States person, the term "preceding taxable year" does not include any taxable year of the trust to which this part does not apply.

(2) In the case of a preceding taxable year with respect to which a trust qualified, without regard to this subpart, under the provisions of subpart B, for purposes of the application of this subpart to such trust for such taxable year, such trust shall, in accordance with regulations prescribed by the Secretary, be treated as a trust to which subpart C applies.

In 1997, P.L. 105-34, Sec. 507(a)(1), added subsec. (c) ... Sec. 507(a)(2), added "except as provided in subsection (c)," after "subpart," in subsec. (b), effective for tax. yrs. begin. after 8/5/97.

—P.L. 105-34, Sec. 1604(g)(2), deleted "or 669(d) and (e)" after "666(b) and (c)" in para. (d)(1), effective 8/5/97.

In 1996, P.L. 104-188, Sec. 1904(b)(1), added the sentence to the end of para. (d)(2) ... Sec. 1904(c)(2), deleted subsec. (c), effective 8/20/96, except as provided in Secs. 1904(d)(2) and (e), which provide:

"(2) Exception for certain trusts. The amendments made by this section shall not apply to any trust—

"(A) which is treated as owned by the grantor under section 676 or 677 (other than subsection (a)(3) thereof) of the Internal Revenue Code of 1986, and

"(B) which is in existence on September 19, 1995.

The preceding sentence shall not apply to the portion of any such trust attributable to any transfer to such trust after September 19, 1995.

"(c) Transitional rule. If—

'(1) by reason of the amendments made by this section, any person other than a United States person ceases to be treated as the owner of a portion of a domestic trust, and

"(2) before January 1, 1997, such trust becomes a foreign trust, or the assets of such trust are transferred to a foreign trust,

no tax shall be imposed by section 1491 of the Internal Revenue Code of 1986 by reason of such trust becoming a foreign trust or the assets of such trust being transferred to a foreign trust."

Prior to deletion, subsec. (c) read as follows:

"(c) Special rule applicable to distributions by certain foreign trusts.

For purposes of this subpart, any amount paid to a United States person which is from a payor who is not a United States person and which is derived directly or indirectly from a foreign trust created by a United States person shall be deemed in the year of payment to have been directly paid by the foreign trust."

In 1990, P.L. 101-508, Sec. 11802(f)(2), amended subsec. (e), effective 11/5/90 except as provided in Sec. 11821(b) of this Act, reproduced in note following Code Sec. 613.

Prior to amendment, subsec. (e) read as follows:

"(e) Preceding taxable year.

"For purposes of this subpart—

"(1) in the case of a trust (other than a foreign trust created by a United States person), the term 'preceding taxable year' does not include any taxable year of the trust—

"(A) which precedes by more than 5 years the taxable year of the trust in which an accumulation distribution is made, if it is made in a taxable year beginning before January 1, 1974, or

"(B) which begins before January 1, 1969, in the case of an accumulation distribution made during a taxable year beginning after December 31, 1973, and

"(2) in the case of a foreign trust created by a United States person, such term does not include any taxable year of the trust to which this part does not apply.

In the case of a preceding taxable year with respect to which a trust qualifies (without regard to this subpart) under the provisions of subpart B, for purposes of the application of this subpart to such trust for such taxable year, such trust shall, in accordance with regulations prescribed by the Secretary, be treated as a trust to which subpart C applies."

In 1986, P.L. 99-514, Sec. 1847(b)(16), substituted "part IV" for "subpart A of part IV" in para. (d)(1), effective for distributions made in tax. yrs. begin. after 12/31/75.

In 1978, P.L. 95-600, Sec. 701(q)(1)(A), amended subsec. (d), effective for distributions made in tax. yrs. begin. after 12/31/75.

Prior to amendment, subsec. (d) read as follows:

"(d) Taxes imposed on the trust.

"For purposes of this subpart, the term 'taxes imposed on the trust' means the amount of the taxes which are imposed for any taxable year of the trust under this chapter (without regard to this subpart) and which, under regulations prescribed by the Secretary are properly allocable to the undistributed portions of distributable net income and gains in excess of losses from sales or exchanges of capital assets. The amount determined in the preceding sentence shall be reduced by any amount of such taxes deemed distributed under section 666(b) and (c) or 669(d) and (e) to any beneficiary.

In 1976, P.L. 94-455, Sec. 701(b), added the sentence at the end of subsec. (b) ... Sec. 701(c), added the sentence at the end of subsec. (b) [as amended by Sec. 701(b) of this Act, see above] ... Sec. 701(d)(2)(A), deleted subpara. (e)(1)(C) ... Sec. 701(d)(2)(B), added "or" to the end of subpara. (e)(1)(A) ... Sec. 701(d)(2)(C), substituted "; and" for "; or" at the end of subpara. (e)(1)(B) ... Sec. 701(d)(3), deleted subsecs. (f) and (g), effective for distributions made in tax. yrs. begin. after 12/31/75.

Prior to deletion, subpara. (e)(1)(C) read as follows:

"(C) which begins before January 1, 1969, in the case of capital gain distribution made during a taxable year beginning after December 31, 1968; and"

Prior to deletion, subsecs. (f) and (g) read as follows:

"(f) Undistributed capital gain.

"For purposes of this subpart, the term 'undistributed capital gain' means for any taxable year of the trust beginning after December 31, 1968, the amount by which

"(1) gains in excess of losses from the sale or exchange of capital assets, to the extent that such gains are allocated to corpus and are not

"(A) paid, credited, or required to be distributed to any beneficiary during such taxable year, or

"(B) paid, permanently set aside, or used for the purposes specified in section 642(c), exceed

"(2) the amount of taxes imposed on the trust attributable to such gains.

For purposes of paragraph (1), the deduction under section 1202 (relating to deduction for excess of capital gains over capital losses) shall not be taken into account

"(g) Capital gain distribution.

"For purposes of this subpart, the term 'capital gain distribution' for any taxable year of the trust means to the extent of undistributed capital gain, that portion of

"(1) the excess of the amounts specified in paragraph (2) of section 661(a) for such taxable year over distributable net income for such year reduced (but not below zero) by the amounts specified in paragraph (1) of section 661(a), over

"(2) the undistributed net income of the trust for all preceding taxable years."

—P.L. 94-455, Sec. 1906(b)(13)(A), substituted "Secretary" for "Secretary or his delegate" in subsec. (d) and para. (e)(2), effective for tax. yrs. begin. after 12/31/76.

In 1971, P.L. 92-178, Sec. 306(a), deleted "for such taxable year" after "undistributed capital gain" in subsec. (g), effective for tax. yrs. begin. after 12/31/68.

In 1969, P.L. 91-172, Sec. 331(a), amended Code Sec..665, for tax. yrs. begin. after 12/31/68. Sec. 331(d)(2)(A) of this Act provides an exception as follows:

"(A) Amounts paid, credited, or required to be distributed by a trust (other than a foreign trust created by a United States person) on or before the last day of a taxable year of the trust beginning before January 1, 1974, shall not be deemed to be accumulation distributions to the extent that such amounts were accumulated by a trust in taxable years of such trust beginning before January 1, 1969, and would have been excepted from the definition of an accumulation distribution by reason of paragraphs (1), (2), (3), or (4) of section 665(b) of the Internal Revenue Code of 1954, as in effect on December 31, 1968, if they had been distributed on the last day of the last taxable year of the trust beginning before January 1, 1969."

Prior to amendment, Code Sec. 665 read as follows:

"SEC. 665. DEFINITIONS APPLICABLE TO SUBPART D.

"(a) Undistributed net income.

"For purposes of this subpart, the term 'undistributed net income' for any taxable year means the amount by which distributable net income of the trust for such taxable year exceeds the sum of—

"(1) the amounts for such taxable year specified in paragraphs (1) and (2) of section 661(a); and

"(2) the amount of taxes imposed on the trust.

"(b) Accumulation distributions of trusts other than certain foreign trusts.

"For purposes of this subpart, in the case of a trust (other than a foreign trust created by a United States person), the term 'accumulation distribution' for any taxable year of the trust means the amount (if in excess of $2,000) by which the amounts specified in paragraph (2) of section 661(a) for such taxable year exceed distributable net income reduced by the amounts specified in paragraph (1) of section 661(a). For purposes of this subsection, the amount specified in paragraph (2) of section 661(a) shall be determined without regard to section 666 and shall not include—

"(1) amounts paid, credited, or required to be distributed to a beneficiary as income accumulated before the birth of such beneficiary or before such beneficiary attains the age of 21;

"(2) amounts properly paid or credited to a beneficiary to meet the emergency needs of such beneficiary;

"(3) amounts properly paid or credited to a beneficiary upon such beneficiary's attaining a specified age or ages if—

"(A) the total number of such distributions cannot exceed 4 with respect to such beneficiary,

"(B) the period between each such distribution to such beneficiary is 4 years or more, and

"(C) as of January 1, 1954, such distributions are required by the specific terms of the governing instrument; and

"(4) amounts properly paid or credited to a beneficiary as a final distribution of the trust if such final distribution is made more than 9 years after the date of the last transfer to such trust.

"(c) Accumulation distribution of certain foreign trusts.

"For purposes of this subpart, in the case of a foreign trust created by a United States person, the term 'accumulation distribution' for any taxable year of the trust means the amount by which the amounts specified in paragraph (2) of section 661(a) for such taxable year exceed distributable net income, reduced by the amounts specified in paragraph (1) of section 661(a). For purposes of this subsection, the amount specified in paragraph (2) of section 661(a) shall be determined without regard to section 666. Any amount paid to a United States person which is from a payor who is not a United States person and which is derived directly or indirectly from a foreign trust created by a United States person shall be deemed in the year of payment to have been directly paid by the foreign trust.

"(d) Taxes imposed on the trust.

"For purposes of this subpart, the term 'taxes imposed on the trust' means the amount of the taxes which are imposed for any taxable year on the trust under this chapter (without regard to this subpart) and which, under regulations prescribed by the Secretary or his delegate, are properly allocable to the undistributed portion of the distributable net income. The amount determined in the preceding sentence shall be reduced by any amount of such taxes allowed, under sections 667 and 668, as a credit to any beneficiary on account of any accumulation distribution determined for any taxable year.

"(e) Preceding taxable year.

"For purposes of this subpart, the term 'preceding taxable year' does not include any taxable year of the trust to which this part does not apply. In the case of a preceding taxable year with respect to which a trust qualifies (without regard to this subpart) under the provisions of subpart B, for purposes of the application of this subpart to such trust for such taxable year, such trust shall, in accordance with regulations prescribed by the Secretary or his delegate, he treated as a trust to which subpart C applies."

In 1962, P.L. 87-834, Sec. 7(b)(1), amended the heading of subsec. (b) and substituted "For purposes of this subpart, in the case of a trust (other than a foreign trust created by a United States person)." for "For purposes of this subpart," immediately following the heading of subsec. (b) [as amended by this Sec., see above] ... Sec. 7(b)(2), redesignated subsecs. (c) and (d) as subsecs. (d) and (e) and added new subsec. (c), effective for distributions made after 12/31/62.

Prior to amendment, the heading of subsec. (b) read as follows:

"(b) Accumulation distribution."

Sec. 666. Accumulation distribution allocated to preceding years.

(a) Amount allocated.

In the case of a trust which is subject to subpart C, the amount of the accumulation distribution of such trust for a taxable year shall be deemed to be an amount within the meaning of paragraph (2) of section 661(a) distributed on the last day of each of the preceding taxable years, commencing with the earliest of such years, to the extent that such amount exceeds the total of any undistributed net income for all earlier preceding taxable years. The amount deemed to be distributed in any such preceding taxable year under the preceding sentence shall not exceed the undistributed net income for such preceding taxable year. For purposes of this subsection, undistributed net income for each of such preceding taxable years shall be computed without regard to such accumulation distribution and without regard to any accumulation distribution determined for any succeeding taxable year.

(b) Total taxes deemed distributed.

If any portion of an accumulation distribution for any taxable year is deemed under subsection (a) to be an amount within the meaning of paragraph (2) of section 661(a) distributed on the last day of any preceding taxable year, and such portion of such distribution is not less than the undistributed net income for such preceding taxable year, the trust shall be deemed to have distributed on the last day of such preceding taxable year an additional amount within the meaning of paragraph (2) of section 661(a). Such additional amount shall be equal to the taxes (other than the tax imposed by section 55) imposed on the trust for such preceding taxable year attributable to the undistributed net income. For purposes of this subsection, the undistributed net income and the taxes imposed on the trust for such preceding taxable year attributable to such undistributed net income shall be computed without regard to such accumulation distribution and without regard to any accumulation distribution determined for any succeeding taxable year.

(c) Pro rata portion of taxes deemed distributed.

If any portion of an accumulation distribution for any taxable year is deemed under subsection (a) to be an amount within the meaning of paragraph (2) of section 661(a) distributed on the last day of any preceding taxable year and such portion of the accumulation distribution is less than the undistributed net income for such preceding taxable year, the trust shall be deemed to have distributed on the last day of such preceding taxable year an additional amount within the meaning of paragraph (2) of section 661(a). Such additional amount shall be equal to the taxes (other than the tax imposed by section 55) imposed on the trust for such taxable year attributable to the undistributed net income multiplied by the ratio of the portion of the accumulation distribution to the undistributed net income of the trust for such year. For purposes of this subsection, the undistributed net income and the taxes imposed on the trust for such preceding taxable year attributable to such undistributed net income shall be computed without regard to the accumulation distribution and without regard to any accumulation distribution determined for any succeeding taxable year.

(d) Rule when information is not available.

If adequate records are not available to determine the proper application of this subpart to an amount distributed by a trust, such amount shall be deemed to be an accumulation distribution consisting of undistributed net income earned during the earliest preceding taxable year of the trust in which it can be established that the trust was in existence.

(e) Denial of refund to trusts and beneficiaries.

No refund or credit shall be allowed to a trust or a beneficiary of such trust for any preceding taxable year by reason of a distribution deemed to have been made by such trust in such year under this section.

In 1980, P.L. 96-222, Sec. 104(a)(4)(H)(vi), added "(other than the tax imposed by section 55)" after "equal to the taxes" in subsec. (c), effective for tax. yrs. begin. after 12/31/78.

In 1978, P.L. 95-600, Sec. 421(d), substituted "taxes (other than the tax imposed by section 55)" for "taxes" in the second sentence of subsec. (b), effective for tax. yrs. begin. after 12/31/78.

In 1976, P.L. 94-455, Sec. 701(a)(2), added subsec. (e), effective for distributions made in tax. yrs. begin. after 12/31/75.

In 1969, P.L. 91-172, Sec. 331(a), amended Code Sec. 666, effective for tax. yrs. begin. after 12/31/68. Sec. 331(d)(2)(B) of this Act provides an exception as follows:

"(B) For taxable years of a trust beginning before January 1, 1970, the first sentence of section 666(a) of the Internal Revenue Code of 1954 (as amended by this section) shall not apply, and the amount of the accumulation distribution of the trust for such taxable years shall be deemed to be an amount within the meaning of paragraph (2) of section 661(a) distributed on the last day of each of the preceding taxable years to the extent that such amount exceeds the total of any undistributed net income for any taxable years intervening between the taxable year with respect to which the accumulation distribution is determined and such preceding taxable year."

Prior to amendment, Code Sec. 666 read as follows:

"Sec. 666. Accumulation Distribution Allocated to 5 Preceding Years.

"(a) Amount allocated.

"In the case of a trust (other than a foreign trust created by a United States person) which for a taxable year beginning after December 31, 1953, is subject to subpart C, the amount of the accumulation distribution of such trust for such taxable year shall be deemed to be an amount within the meaning of paragraph (2) of section 661(a) distributed on the last day of each of the 5 preceding taxable years to the extent that such amount exceeds the total of any undistributed net incomes for any taxable years intervening between the taxable year with respect to which the accumulation distribution is determined and such preceding taxable year. The amount deemed to be distributed in any such preceding taxable year under the preceding sentence shall not exceed the undistributed net income of such preceding taxable year. For purposes of this subsection, undistributed net income for each of such 5 preceding taxable years shall be computed without regard to such accumulation distribution and without regard to any accumulation distribution determined for any succeeding taxable year. In the case of a foreign trust created by a United States person, this subsection shall apply to the preceding taxable years of the trust without regard to any provision of the preceding sentences which would (but for this sentence) limit its application to the 5 preceding taxable years.

"(b) Total taxes deemed distributed.

"If any portion of an accumulation distribution for any taxable year is deemed under subsection (a) to be an amount within the meaning of paragraph (2) of section 661(a) distributed on the last day of any preceding taxable year, and such portion of such accumulation distribution is not less than the undistributed net income for such preceding taxable year, the trust shall be deemed to have distributed on the last day of such preceding taxable year an additional amount within the meaning of paragraph (2) of section 661(a). Such additional amount shall be equal to the taxes imposed on the trust for such preceding taxable year. For purposes of this subsection, the undistributed net income and the taxes imposed on the trust for such preceding taxable year shall be computed without regard to such accumulation distribution and without regard to any accumulation distribution determined for any succeeding taxable year.

"(c) Pro rata portion of taxes deemed distributed.

"If any portion of an accumulation distribution for any taxable year is deemed under subsection (a) to be an amount within the meaning of paragraph (2) of section 661(a) distributed on the last day of any preceding taxable year and such portion of the accumulation distribution is less than the undistributed net income for such preceding taxable year, the trust shall be deemed to have distributed on the last day of such preceding taxable year an additional amount within the meaning of paragraph (2) of section 661(a). Such additional amount shall be equal to the taxes imposed on the trust for such taxable year multiplied by the ratio of the portion of the accumulation distribution to the undistributed net income of the trust for such year. For purposes of this subsection, the undistributed net income and the taxes imposed on the trust for such preceding taxable year shall be computed without regard to the accumulation distribution and without regard to any accumulation distribution determined for any succeeding taxable year."

In 1962, P.L. 87-834, Sec. 7(c)(1), substituted "(a) Amount allocated.—In the case of a trust (other than a foreign trust created by a United States person)" for "(a) Amount allocated.—In the case of a trust" in subsec. (a) . . . Sec. 7(c)(2), added the sentence at the end of subsec. (a), effective for distributions made after 12/31/62.

Sec. 667. Treatment of amounts deemed distributed by trust in preceding years.

(a) General rule.

The total of the amounts which are treated under section 666 as having been distributed by a trust in a preceding taxable year shall be included in the income of a beneficiary of the trust when paid, credited, or required to be distributed to the extent that such total would have been included in the income of such beneficiary under section 662(a)(2) (and, with respect to any tax-exempt interest to which section 103 applies, under section 662(b)) if such total had been paid to such beneficiary on the last day of such preceding taxable year. The tax imposed by this subtitle on a beneficiary for a taxable year in which any such amount is included in his income shall be determined only as provided in this section and shall consist of the sum of—

(1) a partial tax computed on the taxable income reduced by an amount equal to the total of such amounts, at the rate and in the manner as if this section had not been enacted,

(2) a partial tax determined as provided in subsection (b) of this section, and

(3) in the case of a foreign trust, the interest charge determined as provided in section 668.

(b) Tax on distribution.

(1) In general. The partial tax imposed by subsection (a)(2) shall be determined—

(A) by determining the number of preceding taxable years of the trust on the last day of which an amount is deemed under section 666(a) to have been distributed,

(B) by taking from the 5 taxable years immediately preceding the year of the accumulation distribution the 1 taxable year for which the beneficiary's taxable income was the highest and the 1 taxable year for which his taxable income was the lowest,

(C) by adding to the beneficiary's taxable income for each of the 3 taxable years remaining after the application of subparagraph (B) an amount determined by dividing the amount deemed distributed under section 666 and required to be included in income under subsection (a) by the number of preceding taxable years determined under subparagraph (A), and

(D) by determining the average increase in tax for the 3 taxable years referred to in subparagraph (C) resulting from the application of such subparagraph.

The partial tax imposed by subsection (a)(2) shall be the excess (if any) of the average increase in tax determined under subparagraph (D), multiplied by the number of preceding taxable years determined under subparagraph (A), over the amount of taxes (other than the amount of taxes described in section 665(d)(2)) deemed distributed to the beneficiary under sections 666(b) and (c).

(2) Treatment of loss years. For purposes of paragraph (1), the taxable income of the beneficiary for any taxable year shall be deemed to be not less than zero.

(3) Certain preceding taxable years not taken into account. For purposes of paragraph (1), if the amount of the undistributed net income deemed distributed in any preceding taxable year of the trust is less than 25 percent of the amount of the accumulation distribution divided by the number of preceding taxable years to which the accumulation distribution is allocated under section 666(a), the number of preceding taxable years of the trust with respect to which an amount is deemed distributed to a beneficiary under section 666(a) shall be determined without regard to such year.

(4) Effect of other accumulation distributions. In computing the partial tax under paragraph (1) for any beneficiary, the income of such beneficiary for each of his prior taxable years shall include amounts previously deemed distributed to such beneficiary in such year under section 666 as a result of prior accumulation distributions (whether from the same or another trust).

(5) Multiple distributions in the same taxable year. In the case of accumulation distributions made from more than one trust which are includible in the income of a beneficiary in the same taxable year, the distributions shall be deemed to have been made consecutively in whichever order the beneficiary shall determine.

(6) Adjustment in partial tax for estate and generation-skipping transfer taxes attributable to partial tax.

(A) In general. The partial tax shall be reduced by an amount which is equal to the pre-death portion of the partial tax multiplied by a fraction—

(i) the numerator of which is that portion of the tax imposed by chapter 11 or 13, as the case may be, which is attributable (on a proportionate basis) to amounts included in the accumulation distribution, and

(ii) the denominator of which is the amount of the accumulation distribution which is subject to the tax imposed by chapter 11 or 13, as the case may be.

(B) Partial tax determined without regard to this paragraph. For purposes of this paragraph, the term "partial tax" means the partial tax imposed by subsection (a)(2) determined under this subsection without regard to this paragraph.

(C) Pre-death portion. For purposes of this paragraph, the pre-death portion of the partial tax shall be an amount which bears the same ratio to the partial tax as the portion of the accumulation distribution which is attributable to the period before the date of the death of the decedent or the date of the generation-skipping transfer bears to the total accumulation distribution.

(c) Special rule for multiple trusts.

(1) In general. If, in the same prior taxable year of the beneficiary in which any part of the accumulation distribution from a trust (hereinafter in this paragraph referred to as "third trust") is deemed under section 666(a) to have been distributed to such beneficiary, some part of prior distributions by each of 2 or more other trusts is deemed under section 666(a) to have been distributed to such beneficiary, then subsections (b) and (c) of section 666 shall not apply with respect to such part of the accumulation distribution from such third trust.

(2) **Accumulation distributions from trust not taken into account unless they equal or exceed $1,000.** For purposes of paragraph (1), an accumulation distribution from a trust to a beneficiary shall be taken into account only if such distribution, when added to any prior accumulation distributions from such trust which are deemed under section 666(a) to have been distributed to such beneficiary for the same prior taxable year of the beneficiary, equals or exceeds $1,000.

(d) **Special rules for foreign trust.**

(1) **Foreign tax deemed paid by beneficiary.**

(A) **In general.** In determining the increase in tax under subsection (b)(1)(D) for any computation year, the taxes described in section 665(d)(2) which are deemed distributed under section 666(b) or (c) and added under subsection (b)(1)(C) to the taxable income of the beneficiary for any computation year shall, except as provided in subparagraphs (B) and (C), be treated as a credit against the increase in tax for such computation year under subsection (b)(1)(D).

(B) **Deduction in lieu of credit.** If the beneficiary did not choose the benefits of subpart A of part III of subchapter N with respect to the computation year, the beneficiary may in lieu of treating the amounts described in subparagraph (A) (without regard to subparagraph (C)) as a credit may treat such amounts as a deduction in computing the beneficiary's taxable income under subsection (b)(1)(C) for the computation year.

(C) **Limitation on credit; retention of character.**

(i) **Limitation on credit.** For purposes of determining under subparagraph (A) the amount treated as a credit for any computation year, the limitations under subpart A of part III of subchapter N shall be applied separately with respect to amounts added under subsection (b)(1)(C) to the taxable income of the beneficiary for such computation year. For purposes of computing the increase in tax under subsection (b)(1)(D) for any computation year for which the beneficiary did not choose the benefits of subpart A of part III of subchapter N, the beneficiary shall be treated as having chosen such benefits for such computation year.

(ii) **Retention of character.** The items of income, deduction, and credit of the Trust shall retain their character (subject to the application of section 904(f)(5)) to the extent necessary to apply this paragraph.

(D) **Computation year.** For purposes of this paragraph, the term "computation year" means any of the three taxable years remaining after application of subsection (b)(1)(B).

(e) **Retention of character of amounts distributed from accumulation trust to nonresident aliens and foreign corporations.**

In the case of a distribution from a trust to a nonresident alien individual or a foreign corporation, the first sentence of subsection (a) shall be applied as if the reference to the determination of character under section 662(b) applied to all amounts instead of just to tax-exempt interest.

In 1986, P.L. 99-514, Sec. 104(b)(10), amended para. (b)(2), effective for tax. yrs. begin. after 12/31/86.
Prior to amendment, para. (b)(2) read as follows:
"(2) Treatment of loss years. For purposes of paragraph (1), the taxable income of the beneficiary for any taxable year shall be deemed to be not less than—
"(A) in the case of a beneficiary who is an individual, the zero bracket amount for such year, or
"(B) in the case of a beneficiary who is a corporation, zero."
In 1978, P.L. 95-600, Sec. 701(q)(1)(B), added subsec. (d) ... Sec. 701(q)(1)(C), added "(other than the amount of taxes described in section 665(d)(2))" after "taxes" in the last sentence of para. (b)(1), for distributions made in tax. yrs. begin. after 12/31/75.
—P.L. 95-600, Sec. 701(r)(1), added subsec. (e), effective for distributions made in tax. yrs. begin. after 12/31/75.
—P.L. 95-600, Sec. 702(o)(1), added para. (b)(6), effective for Chapter 11 [Estate Tax] taxes to estates of decedents dying after 12/31/79 and effective for Chapter 13 [Tax on Certain Generation-Skipping Transfers] taxes to any generation-skipping transfer (within the meaning of Code Sec. 2611(a)) made after 6/11/76.
In 1977, P.L. 95-30, Sec. 102(b)(8), amended para. (b)(2), effective for tax. yrs. begin. after 12/31/76.
Prior to amendment, para. (b)(2) read as follows:
"(2) Treatment of loss years. For purposes of paragraph (1), the taxable income of the beneficiary for any taxable year shall be deemed not to be less than zero."
In 1976, P.L. 94-455, Sec. 701(a)(1), amended Code Sec. 667, for tax. yrs. begin. after 12/31/75.
Prior to amendment, Code Sec. 667, read as follows:
"SEC. 667. DENIAL OF REFUND TO TRUSTS; AUTHORIZATION OF CREDIT TO BENEFICIARIES.
"(a) *Denial of refund to trusts.*
"No refund or credit shall be allowed to a trust for any preceding taxable year by reason of a distribution deemed to have been made by such trust in such year under section 666 or 669.
"(b) *Authorization of credit to beneficiary.*
"There shall be allowed as a credit (without interest) against the tax imposed by this subtitle on the beneficiary an amount equal to the amount of the taxes deemed distributed to such beneficiary by the trust under sections 666(b) and (c) and 669(d) and (e) during preceding taxable years of the trust on the last day of which the beneficiary was in being, reduced by the amount of the taxes deemed distributed to such beneficiary for such preceding taxable years to the extent that such taxes are taken into account under sections 668(b)(1) and 669(b) in determining the amount of the tax imposed by section 668."
—P.L. 94-455, Sec. 1014(a), deleted ", and" at the end of para. (a)(1) substituted "; and" for the period at the end of para. (a)(2), and added para. (a)(3), as previously amended by the Act, effective for tax. yrs. begin. after 12/31/76.
In 1969, P.L. 91-172, Sec. 331(a), amended Code Sec. 667, effective for tax. yrs. begin. after 12/31/68.
Prior to amendment Code Sec. 667 read as follows:
"SEC. 667. DENIAL OF REFUND TO TRUSTS.
"The amount of taxes imposed on the trust under this chapter, which would not have been payable by the trust for any preceding taxable year had the trust in fact made distributions at the times and in the amounts deemed under section 666, shall not be refunded or credited to the trust, but shall be allowed as a credit under section 668(b) against the tax of the beneficiaries who are treated as having received the distributions. For purposes of the preceding sentence, the amount of taxes which may not be refunded or credited to the trust shall be an amount equal to the excess of (1) the taxes imposed on the trust for any preceding taxable year (computed without regard to the accumulation distribution for the taxable year) over (2) the amount of taxes for such preceding taxable year imposed on the undistributed portion of distributable net income of the trust for such preceding taxable year after the application of this subpart on account of the accumulation distribution determined for such taxable year."

Sec. 668. Interest charge on accumulation distributions from foreign trusts.

(a) **General rule.**

For purposes of the tax determined under section 667(a)—

(1) **Interest determined using underpayment rates.** The interest charge determined under this section with respect to any distribution is the amount of interest which would be determined on the partial tax computed under section 667(b) for the period described in paragraph (2) using the rates and the method under section 6621 applicable to underpayments of tax.

(2) **Period.** For purposes of paragraph (1), the period described in this paragraph is the period which begins on the date which is the applicable number of years before the date of the distribution and which ends on the date of the distribution.

(3) **Applicable number of years.** For purposes of paragraph (2)—

(A) **In general.** The applicable number of years with respect to a distribution is the number determined by dividing—

(i) the sum of the products described in subparagraph (B) with respect to each undistributed income year, by

(ii) the aggregate undistributed net income.

The quotient determined under the preceding sentence shall be rounded under procedures prescribed by the Secretary.

(B) Product described. For purposes of subparagraph (A), the product described in this subparagraph with respect to any undistributed income year is the product of—

(i) the undistributed net income for such year, and

(ii) the sum of the number of taxable years between such year and the taxable year of the distribution (counting in each case the undistributed income year but not counting the taxable year of the distribution).

(4) Undistributed income year. For purposes of this subsection, the term "undistributed income year" means any prior taxable year of the trust for which there is undistributed net income, other than a taxable year during all of which the beneficiary receiving the distribution was not a citizen or resident of the United States.

(5) Determination of undistributed net income. Notwithstanding section 666, for purposes of this subsection, an accumulation distribution from the trust shall be treated as reducing proportionately the undistributed net income for undistributed income years.

(6) Periods before 1996. Interest for the portion of the period described in paragraph (2) which occurs before January 1, 1996, shall be determined—

(A) by using an interest rate of 6 percent, and

(B) without compounding until January 1, 1996.

(b) Limitation.

The total amount of the interest charge shall not, when added to the total partial tax computed under section 667(b), exceed the amount of the accumulation distribution (other than the amount of tax deemed distributed by section 666(b) or (c)) in respect of which such partial tax was determined.

(c) Interest charge not deductible.

The interest charge determined under this section shall not be allowed as a deduction for purposes of any tax imposed by this title.

In 1996, P.L. 104-188, Sec. 1906(a), amended subsec. (a), effective for distributions after 8/20/96.
Prior to amendment, subsec. (a) read as follows:
"(a) General rule.
For purposes of the tax determined under section 667(a), the interest charge is an amount equal to 6 percent of the partial tax computed under section 667(b) multiplied by a fraction—
"(1) the numerator of which is the sum of the number of taxable years between each taxable year to which the distribution is allocated under section 666(a) and the taxable year of the distribution (counting in each case the taxable year to which the distribution is allocated but not counting the taxable year of the distribution), and
"(2) the denominator of which is the number of taxable years to which the distribution is allocated under section 666(a)."
In 1990, P.L. 101-508, Sec. 11802(f)(3), amended subsec. (c), effective 11/5/90 except as provided in Sec. 11821(b) of this Act reproduced at note following Code Sec. 545.
Prior to amendment, subsec. (c) read as follows:
"(c) Special rules.
"(1) Interest charge not deductible. The interest charge determined under this section shall not be allowed as a deduction for purposes of any tax imposed by this title.
"(2) Transitional rule. For purposes of this section, undistributed net income existing in a trust as of January 1, 1977, shall be treated as allocated under section 666(a) to the first taxable year beginning after December 31, 1976."
In 1976, P.L. 94-455, Sec. 701(a)(3), repealed Code Sec. 668, effective for distributions made in tax. yrs. begin. after 12/31/75.
Prior to repeal, Code Sec. 668 read as follows:
"SEC. 668. TREATMENT OF AMOUNTS DEEMED DISTRIBUTED IN PRECEDING YEARS.
"(a) General rule.
The total of the amounts which are treated under sections 666 and 669 as having been distributed by the trust in a preceding taxable year shall be included in the income of a beneficiary of the trust when paid, credited, or required to be distributed to the extent that such total would have been included in the income of such beneficiary under section 662(a)(2) and (b) if such total had been paid to such beneficiary on the last day of such preceding taxable year. The tax imposed by this subtitle on a beneficiary for a taxable year in which any such amount is included in his income shall be determined only as provided in this section and shall consist of the sum of—
"(1) a partial tax computed on the taxable income reduced by an amount equal to the total of such amounts, at the rate and in the manner as if this section had not been enacted,
"(2) a partial tax determined as provided in subsection (b) of this section, and
"(3) in the case of a beneficiary of a trust which is not required to distribute all of its income currently, a partial tax determined as provided in section 669.
For purposes of this subpart, a trust shall not be considered to be a trust which is not required to distribute all of its income currently for any taxable year prior to the first taxable year in which income is accumulated.
"(b) Tax on distribution.
"(1) Alternative methods. Except as provided in paragraph (2), the partial tax imposed by subsection (a)(2) shall be the lesser of—
"(A) the aggregate of the taxes attributable to the amounts deemed distributed under section 666 had they been included in the gross income of the beneficiary on the last day of each respective preceding taxable year, or
"(B) the tax determined by multiplying, by the number of preceding taxable years of the trust, on the last day of which an amount is deemed under section 666(a) to have been distributed, the average of the increase in tax attributable to recomputing the beneficiary's gross income for each of the beneficiary's 3 taxable years immediately preceding the year of the accumulation distribution by adding to the income of each of such years an amount determined by dividing the amount deemed distributed under section 666 and required to be included in income under subsection (a) by such number of preceding taxable years of the trust, less an amount equal to the amount of taxes deemed distributed to the beneficiary under sections 666(b) and (c).
"(2) Special rules.
"(A) If a beneficiary was not in existence on the last day of a preceding taxable year of the trust with respect to which a distribution is deemed made under section 666(a), the partial tax under either paragraph (1)(A) or (1)(B) shall be computed as if the beneficiary were in existence on the last day of such year on the basis that the beneficiary had no gross income (other than amounts deemed distributed to him under sections 666 and 669 by the same or other trusts) and no deductions for such year.
"(B) The partial tax shall not be computed under the provisions of subparagraph (B) of paragraph (1) if, in the same prior taxable year of the beneficiary in which any part of the accumulation distribution is deemed under section 666(a) to have been distributed to such beneficiary, some part of prior accumulation distributions by each of two or more other trusts is deemed under section 666(a) to have been distributed to such beneficiary.
"(C) If the partial tax is computed under paragraph (1)(B), and the amount of the undistributed net income deemed distributed in any preceding taxable year of the trust is less than 25 per cent of the amount of the accumulation distribution divided by the number of preceding taxable years to which the accumulation distribution is allocated under section 666(a), the number of preceding taxable years of the trust with respect to which an amount is deemed distributed to a beneficiary under section 666(a) shall be determined without regard to such year.
"(3) Effect of other accumulation distributions and capital gain distributions. In computing the partial tax under paragraph (1) for any beneficiary, the income of such beneficiary for each of his prior taxable years—
"(A) shall include amounts previously deemed distributed to such beneficiary in such year under section 666 or 669 as a result of prior accumulation distributions or capital gain distributions (whether from the same or another trust), and
"(B) shall not include amounts deemed distributed to such beneficiary in such year under section 669 as a result of a capital gain distribution from the same trust in the current year.
"(4) Multiple distributions in the same taxable year. In the case of accumulation distributions made from more than one trust which are includible in the income of a beneficiary in the same taxable year, the distributions shall be deemed to have been made consecutively in whichever order the beneficiary shall determine.
"(5) Information requirements with respect to beneficiary.
"(A) Except as provided in subparagraph (B), the partial tax shall not be computed under the provisions of paragraph (1)(A) unless the beneficiary supplies such information with respect to his income, for each taxable year with which or in which ends a taxable year of the trust on the last day of which an amount is deemed distributed under section 666(a), as the Secretary or his delegate prescribes by regulations.
"(B) If by reason of paragraph (2)(B) the provisions of paragraph (1)(B) do not apply, the determination of the amount of the beneficiary's income for a taxable year for which the beneficiary has not supplied the information required under subparagraph (A) shall be made by the Secretary or his delegate on the basis of information available to him."
—P.L. 94-455, Sec. 1014(b), added new Code Sec. 668, effective for tax. yrs. begin. after 12/31/76.
In 1969, P.L. 91-172, Sec. 331(a), amended Code Sec. 668, effective for tax. yrs. begin. after 12/31/68.
Prior to amendment, Code Sec. 668 read as follows:
"SEC. 668. TREATMENT OF AMOUNTS DEEMED DISTRIBUTED IN PRECEDING YEARS.
"(a) Amounts treated as received in prior taxable years.
The total of the amounts which are treated under section 666 as having been distributed by the trust in a preceding taxable year shall be included in the income of a beneficiary or beneficiaries of the trust when paid, credited, or required to be distributed to the extent that such total would have been included in the income of such beneficiary or beneficiaries under section 662(a)(2) and (b) if such total had been paid to such beneficiary or beneficiaries on the last day of such preceding taxable year. The portion of such total included under the preceding sentence in

the income of any beneficiary shall be based upon the same ratio as determined under the second sentence of section 662(a)(2) for the taxable year in respect of which the accumulation distribution is determined, except that proper adjustment of such ratio shall be made, in accordance with regulations prescribed by the Secretary or his delegate, for amounts which fall within paragraphs (1) through (4) of section 665 (b). The tax of the beneficiaries attributable to the amounts treated as having been received on the last day of such preceding taxable year of the trust shall not be greater than the aggregate of the taxes attributable to those amounts had they been included in the gross income of the beneficiaries on such day in accordance with section 662(a)(2) and (b). Except as provided in section 669, in the case of a foreign trust created by a United States person the preceding sentence shall not apply to any beneficiary who is a United States person.

"(b) Credit for taxes paid by trust.

The tax imposed on beneficiaries under this chapter shall be credited with a pro rata portion of the taxes imposed on the trust under this chapter for such preceding taxable year which would not have been payable by the trust for such preceding taxable year had the trust in fact made distributions to such beneficiaries at the times and in the amounts specified in section 666."

In 1962, P.L. 87-834, Sec. 7(d), added the sentence at the end of subsec. (a), effective for distributions made after 12/31/62.

Sec. 669. Repealed.

In 1976, P.L. 94-455, Sec. 701(d)(1), repealed Code Sec. 669, effective for tax. yrs. begin. after 12/31/75.

Prior to amendment, Code Sec. 669 read as follows:

"SEC. 669. TREATMENT OF CAPITAL GAIN DEEMED DISTRIBUTED IN PRECEDING YEARS.

"(a) Amount allocated.

"In the case of a trust which is not required to distribute all of its income currently, the amount of a capital gain distribution of such trust for a taxable year shall be deemed to be an amount properly paid, credited, or required to be distributed on the last day of each of the preceding taxable years, commencing with the earliest of such years, to the extent that such amount exceeds the total of any undistributed capital gain for all earlier preceding taxable years. The amount deemed to be distributed in any such preceding taxable year under the preceding sentence shall not exceed the undistributed capital gain for such preceding taxable year. For purposes of this subsection, undistributed capital gain for each of such preceding taxable years shall be computed without regard to such capital gain distribution and without regard to any capital gain distribution determined for any succeeding taxable year.

"(b) Tax on distribution.

"The partial tax imposed by section 668(a)(3) shall be the lesser of—

"(1) the aggregate of the taxes attributable to the amounts deemed distributed under this section, had such amounts been included in the gross income of the beneficiary on the last day of each respective preceding taxable year, or

"(2) the tax determined by multiplying by the number of preceding taxable years of the trust, on the last day of which net gains from the sale or exchange of capital assets are deemed under subsection (a) to have been distributed, the average of the increase in tax attributable to recomputing the beneficiary's gross income for each of the beneficiary's 3 taxable years immediately preceding the year of the capital gain distribution by adding to the income of each of such years an amount determined by dividing the total of the amounts deemed distributed under this section and required to be included in income under section 668(a) by such number of preceding taxable years of the trust,

less an amount equal to the amount of taxes deemed distributed to the beneficiary under subsections (d) and (e) which are attributable to the capital gain distribution.

"(c) Effect of other distributions; special rules, etc.

"In computing the partial tax under subsection (b) for any beneficiary, the income of such beneficiary for each of his prior taxable years—

"(1) shall include amounts previously deemed distributed to such beneficiary in such year under section 666 or 669 as a result of prior accumulation distributions or capital gain distributions (whether from the same or another trust), and

"(2) shall include amounts deemed distributed to such beneficiary in such year under section 666 as a result of an accumulation distribution from the same trust in the current year.

Under regulations prescribed by the Secretary or his delegate, rules similar to the rules provided by paragraphs (2), (4), and (5) of section 668(b) shall be applied for purposes of this section.

"(d) Total taxes deemed distributed.

"If any portion of a capital gain distribution for any taxable year is deemed under subsection (a) to be an amount properly paid, credited or required to be distributed on the last day of any preceding taxable year, and such portion of such capital gain distribution is not less than the undistributed capital gain for such preceding taxable year, the trust shall be deemed to have properly distributed on the last day of such preceding taxable year an additional amount. Such additional amount shall be equal to the taxes imposed on the trust for such preceding taxable year attributable to such undistributed capital gain. For purposes of this subsection, the undistributed capital gain and the taxes imposed on the trust for such preceding taxable year attributable to such gain shall be computed without regard to such capital gain distribution and without regard to any capital gain distribution for any succeeding taxable year.

"(e) Pro rata portion of taxes deemed distributed.

"If any portion of a capital gain distribution for any taxable year is deemed under subsection (a) to be an amount properly paid, credited, or required to be distributed on the last day of any preceding taxable year and such portion of the capital gain distribution is less than the undistributed capital gain for such preceding taxable year, the trust shall be deemed to have properly distributed on the last day of such preceding taxable year an additional amount. Such additional amount shall be equal to the taxes imposed on the trust for such taxable year attributable to such undistributed capital gain multiplied by the ratio of the portion of the capital gain distribution to be undistributed capital gain of the trust for such year. For purposes of this subsection, the undistributed capital gain and the taxes imposed on the trust for such preceding taxable year attributable to such gain shall be computed without regard to the capital gain distribution and without regard to the capital gain distribution determined for any succeeding taxable year.

"(f) Character of capital gain.

"For purposes of this section, the character of the capital gain of a trust for any taxable year with respect to a beneficiary shall be the same as it was with respect to the trust."

In 1969, P.L. 91-172, Sec. 331(a), amended Code Sec. 669, effective for tax. yrs. begin. after 12/31/68, except that Sec. 331(d)(2)(c) provides that in the case of a trust which was in existence on December 31, 1969, section 669 of the Internal Revenue Code of 1954, as amended by this section, shall not apply to capital gain distributions made to a beneficiary before January 1, 1973. If the beneficiary receives capital gain distributions from more than one such trust before January 1, 1973, the preceding sentence shall apply to capital gain distributions from only one of such trusts, such one to be designated by the taxpayer in accordance with regulations prescribed by the Secretary or his delegate. For purposes of the preceding sentence, capital gain distributions received from a trust-qualifying under section 2056(b)(5) of the Internal Revenue Code of 1954 by a surviving spouse (who is the beneficiary of only one such trust) shall be disregarded. (Sec. 331(d)(2)(C), '69 Tax Reform Act, as amended by Sec. 306(b) of P.L. 92-178)

Prior to amendment Code Sec. 669 read as follows:

SEC. 669. SPECIAL RULES APPLICABLE TO CERTAIN FOREIGN TRUSTS.

"(a) Limitation on tax.

"(1) General rule. At the election of a beneficiary who is a United States person (as defined in section 7701(a)(30)) and who satisfies the requirements of subsection (b), the tax attributable to the amounts treated under section 668(a) as having been received by him from a foreign trust created by a United States person on the last day of a preceding taxable year of the trust shall not be greater than—

"(A) the tax determined under the next to the last sentence of section 668(a), or

"(B) the tax determined by multiplying by the number of preceding taxable years of the trust, on the last day of each of which an amount is deemed under section 666(a) to have been distributed, the average of the increase in tax attributable to recomputing the beneficiary's gross income for the taxable year and each of his 2 taxable years immediately preceding the year of the accumulation distribution by adding to the income of each of such year an amount determined by dividing the amount required to be included in income under section 688(a) by such number of preceding taxable years of the trust. The recomputation for the taxable year shall be made without regard to the inclusion in income required by section 668(a) of any amount other than pursuant to this paragraph.

"(2) Exceptions.

"(A) When an accumulation distribution is deemed under section 666(a) to have been distributed on the last day of less than 3 taxable years of the trust, the taxable years of the beneficiary for which a recomputation is made under subsection (a)(1)(B) shall equal the number of years to which section 666(a) applies, commencing with the most recent taxable year of the beneficiary.

"(B) If a beneficiary was not alive on the last day of each preceding taxable year of the trust with respect to which a distribution is deemed made under section 666(a), paragraph (1)(A) of this subsection shall not apply. In applying paragraph (1)(B) of this subsection, no recomputation shall be made for a beneficiary for a taxable year for which he was not alive; if he has no preceding taxable year, the recomputation shall be made on the basis of his taxable year without regard to the inclusion in income required by section 668(a) of any amount other than pursuant to paragraph (1)(B).

"(3) Effect of prior election. In computing the limitation on tax under paragraph (1) of this subsection for any beneficiary—

"(A) Subsequent election under paragraph (1)(A). If an election has been made under paragraph (1)(B) of this subsection, for purposes of a subsequent election under paragraph (1)(A) the income of any year with respect to which an amount is deemed distributed to a beneficiary under section 666(a) shall include amounts previously deemed distributed to such beneficiary for such year as a result of an accumulation distribution with respect to which an election under paragraph (1)(B) was made.

"(B) Subsequent election under paragraph (1)(B). If with respect to an accumulation distribution an election has been made under either paragraph (1)(A) or paragraph (1)(B) of this subsection, or the next to the last sentence of section 668(a) has applied, for purposes of a subsequent election under paragraph (1)(B) the number of preceding taxable years of the trust with respect to which an amount is deemed distributed to a beneficiary under section 666(a) shall be determined without regard to any such year with respect to which an amount was previously deemed distributed to such beneficiary.

"(b) Information requirement.

"The election of a beneficiary to apply the limitations on tax provided in subsection (a) of this section shall not be effective unless the beneficiary at the time of making the election supplies such information with respect to the operation and accounts of the trust, for each taxable year on the last day of which an amount is deemed distributed under section 666(a), as the Secretary or his delegate may by regulations prescribe."

In 1962, P.L. 87-834, Sec. 7, added Code Sec. 669, effective for distributions made after '62.

SUBPART E.—GRANTORS AND OTHERS TREATED AS SUBSTANTIAL OWNERS

Sec.
671. Trust income, deductions, and credits attributable to grantors and others as substantial owners.
672. Definitions and rules.
673. Reversionary interests.
674. Power to control beneficial enjoyment.
675. Administrative powers.
676. Power to revoke.
677. Income for benefit of grantor.
678. Person other than grantor treated as substantial owner.
679. Foreign trusts having one or more United States beneficiaries.

In 1976, P.L. 94-455, Sec. 1013(e)(1), added the item for Code Sec. 679.

Sec. 671. Trust income, deductions, and credits attributable to grantors and others as substantial owners.

Where it is specified in this subpart that the grantor or another person shall be treated as the owner of any portion of a trust, there shall then be included in computing the taxable income and credits of the grantor or the other person those items of income, deductions, and credits against tax of the trust which are attributable to that portion of the trust to the extent that such items would be taken into account under this chapter in computing taxable income or credits against the tax of an individual. Any remaining portion of the trust shall be subject to subparts A through D. No items of a trust shall be included in computing the taxable income and credits of the grantor or of any other person solely on the grounds of his dominion and control over the trust under section 61 (relating to definition of gross income) or any other provision of this title, except as specified in this subpart.

Sec. 672. Definitions and rules.
(a) Adverse party.

For purposes of this subpart, the term "adverse party" means any person having a substantial beneficial interest in the trust which would be adversely affected by the exercise or nonexercise of the power which he possesses respecting the trust. A person having a general power of appointment over the trust property shall be deemed to have a beneficial interest in the trust.

(b) Nonadverse party.

For purposes of this subpart, the term "nonadverse party" means any person who is not an adverse party.

(c) Related or subordinate party.

For purposes of this subpart, the term "related or subordinate party" means any nonadverse party who is—

(1) the grantor's spouse if living with the grantor;
(2) any one of the following: The grantor's father, mother, issue, brother or sister; an employee of the grantor; a corporation or any employee of a corporation in which the stock holdings of the grantor and the trust are significant from the viewpoint of voting control; a subordinate employee of a corporation in which the grantor is an executive.

For purposes of subsection (f) and sections 674 and 675, a related or subordinate party shall be presumed to be subservient to the grantor in respect of the exercise or nonexercise of the powers conferred on him unless such party is shown not to be subservient by a preponderance of the evidence.

(d) Rule where power is subject to condition precedent.

A person shall be considered to have a power described in this subpart even though the exercise of the power is subject to a precedent giving of notice or takes effect only on the expiration of a certain period after the exercise of the power.

(e) Grantor treated as holding any power or interest of grantor's spouse.

(1) In general. For purposes of this subpart, a grantor shall be treated as holding any power or interest held by—

(A) any individual who was the spouse of the grantor at the time of the creation of such power or interest, or
(B) any individual who became the spouse of the grantor after the creation of such power or interest, but only with respect to periods after such individual became the spouse of the grantor.

(2) Marital status. For purposes of paragraph (1)(A), an individual legally separated from his spouse under a decree of divorce or of separate maintenance shall not be considered as married.

(f) Subpart not to result in foreign ownership.

(1) In general. Notwithstanding any other provision of this subpart, this subpart shall apply only to the extent such application results in an amount (if any) being currently taken into account (directly or through 1 or more entities) under this chapter in computing the income of a citizen or resident of the United States or a domestic corporation.

(2) Exceptions.

(A) Certain revocable and irrevocable trusts. Paragraph (1) shall not apply to any portion of a trust if—

(i) the power to revest absolutely in the grantor title to the trust property to which such portion is attributable is exercisable solely by the grantor without the approval or consent of any other person or with the consent of a related or subordinate party who is subservient to the grantor, or
(ii) the only amounts distributable from such portion (whether income or corpus) during the lifetime of the grantor are amounts distributable to the grantor or the spouse of the grantor.

(B) Compensatory trusts. Except as provided in regulations, paragraph (1) shall not apply to any portion of a trust distributions from which are taxable as compensation for services rendered.

(3) Special rules. Except as otherwise provided in regulations prescribed by the Secretary—

(A) a controlled foreign corporation (as defined in section 957) shall be treated as a domestic corporation for purposes of paragraph (1), and
(B) paragraph (1) shall not apply for purposes of applying section 1297.

(4) Recharacterization of purported gifts. In the case of any transfer directly or indirectly from a partnership or foreign corporation which the transferee treats as a gift or bequest, the Secretary may recharacterize such transfer in such circumstances as the Secretary determines to be appropriate to prevent the avoidance of the purposes of this subsection.

(5) Special rule where grantor is foreign person. If—

(A) but for this subsection, a foreign person would be treated as the owner of any portion of a trust, and
(B) such trust has a beneficiary who is a United States person,

such beneficiary shall be treated as the grantor of such portion to the extent such beneficiary has made (directly or indirectly) transfers of property (other than in a sale for full and adequate consideration) to such foreign person. For purposes of the preceding sentence, any gift shall not be taken into account to the extent such gift would be excluded from taxable gifts under section 2503(b).

(6) Regulations. The Secretary shall prescribe such regulations as may be necessary or appropriate to carry out the purposes of this subsection, including regulations providing that paragraph (1) shall not apply in appropriate cases.

In **1998,** P.L. 105-206, Sec. 6011(c)(1), substituted "section 1297" for "section 1296" in subpara. (f)(3)(B), effective for tax. yrs. of U.S. persons begin. after 12/31/97 and tax. yrs. of foreign corporations end. with or within such tax. yrs. of U.S. persons.

In **1996,** P.L. 104-188, Sec. 1904(a)(1), amended subsec. (f) . . . Sec. 1904(a)(2), added "subsection (f) and" before "sections 674" in subsec. (c), effective 8/20/96, except as provided in Secs. 1904(d)(2) and (e) of this Act, which read as follows:

"(2) Exception for certain trusts. The amendments made by this section shall not apply to any trust—

"(A) which is treated as owned by the grantor under section 676 or 677 (other than subsection (a)(3) thereof) of the Internal Revenue Code of 1986, and

"(B) which is in existence on September 19, 1995.

The preceding sentence shall not apply to the portion of any such trust attributable to any transfer to such trust after September 19, 1995.

"(e) Transitional rule. If—

"(1) by reason of the amendments made by this section, any person other than a United States person ceases to be treated as the owner of a portion of a domestic trust, and

"(2) before January 1, 1997, such trust becomes a foreign trust, or the assets of such trust are transferred to a foreign trust,

no tax shall be imposed by section 1491 of the Internal Revenue Code of 1986 by reason of such trust becoming a foreign trust or the assets of such trust being transferred to a foreign trust."

Prior to amendment, subsec. (f) read as follows:

"(f) Special rule where grantor is foreign person.

"(1) In general. If—

"(A) but for this subsection, a foreign person would be treated as the owner of any portion of a trust, and

"(B) such trust has a beneficiary who is a United States person,

such beneficiary shall be treated as the grantor of such portion to the extent such beneficiary has made transfers of property by gift (directly or indirectly) to such foreign person. For purposes of the preceding sentence, any gift shall not be taken into account to the extent such gift would be excluded from taxable gifts under section 2503(b).

"(2) Regulations. The Secretary shall prescribe such regulations as may be necessary to carry out the purposes of this subsection."

In **1990,** P.L. 101-508, Sec. 11343(a), added subsec. (f), effective as provided in Sec. 11343(b) of this Act, which reads as follows:

"(b) Effective date.

"The amendments made by this section shall apply to—

"(1) any trust created after the date of the enactment of this Act [11/5/90], and

"(2) any portion of a trust created on or before such date which is attributable to amounts contributed to the trust after such date."

In **1988,** P.L. 100-647, Sec. 1014(a)(1), amended subsec. (e), effective for transfers in trust made after 3/1/86.

Prior to amendment, subsec. (e) read as follows:

"(e) Grantor treated as holding any power or interests of grantor's spouse.

"For purposes of this subpart, if a grantor's spouse is living with the grantor at the time of the creation of any power or interest held by such spouse, the grantor shall be treated as holding such power or interest."

In **1986,** P.L. 99-514, Sec. 1401(a), added subsec. (e), effective for transfers in trust made after 3/1/86.

Sec. 673. Reversionary interests.
(a) General rule.

The grantor shall be treated as the owner of any portion of a trust in which he has a reversionary interest in either the corpus or the income therefrom, if, as of the inception of that portion of the trust, the value of such interest exceeds 5 percent of the value of such portion.

(b) Reversionary interest taking effect at death of minor lineal descendant beneficiary.

In the case of any beneficiary who—

(1) is a lineal descendant of the grantor, and

(2) holds all of the present interests in any portion of a trust,

the grantor shall not be treated under subsection (a) as the owner of such portion solely by reason of a reversionary interest in such portion which takes effect upon the death of such beneficiary before such beneficiary attains age 21.

(c) Special rule for determining value of reversionary interest.

For purposes of subsection (a), the value of the grantor's reversionary interest shall be determined by assuming the maximum exercise of discretion in favor of the grantor.

(d) Postponement of date specified for reacquisition.

Any postponement of the date specified for the reacquisition of possession or enjoyment of the reversionary interest shall be treated as a new transfer in trust commencing with the date on which the postponement is effective and terminating with the date prescribed by the postponement. However, income for any period shall not be included in the income of the grantor by reason of the preceding sentence if such income would not be so includible in the absence of such postponement.

In **1988,** P.L. 100-647, Sec. 1014(b), added subsecs. (c) and (d), effective for transfers in trust made after 3/1/86, except as provided in as Sec. 1402(c)(2) of P.L. 99-514, reproduced below.

In **1986,** P.L. 99-514, Sec. 1402(a), amended Code Sec. 673, effective for transfers in trust made after 3/1/86, except as provided in Sec. 1402(c)(2) of this Act which read as follows:

"(2) Transfers pursuant to property settlement agreement.—The amendments made by this section [Sec. 1402] shall not apply to any transfer in trust made after March 1, 1986, pursuant to a binding property settlement agreement entered into on or before March 1, 1986, which required the taxpayer to establish a grantor trust and for the transfer of a specified sum of money or property to the trust by the taxpayer. This paragraph shall apply only to the extent of the amount required to be transferred under the agreement described in the preceding sentence."

Prior to amendment, Code Sec. 673 read as follows:

"SEC. 673. REVERSIONARY INTERESTS.

"(a) General rule.

"The grantor shall be treated as the owner of any portion of a trust in which he has a reversionary interest in either the corpus or the income therefrom if, as of the inception of that portion of the trust, the interest will or may reasonably be expected to take effect in possession or enjoyment within 10 years commencing with the date of the transfer of that portion of the trust.

"(c) Reversionary interest taking effect at death of income beneficiary.

"The grantor shall not be treated under subsection (a) as the owner of any portion of a trust where his reversionary interest in such portion is not to take effect in possession or enjoyment until the death of the person or persons to whom the income therefrom is payable.

"(d) Postponement of date specified for reacquisition.

"Any postponement of the date specified for the reacquisition of possession or enjoyment of the reversionary interest shall be treated as a new transfer in trust commencing with the date on which the postponement is effected and terminating with the date prescribed by the postponement. However, income for any period shall not be included in the income of the grantor by reason of the preceding sentence if such income would not be so includible in the absence of such postponement."

In **1969,** P.L. 91-172, Sec. 201(c), deleted subsec. (b), effective for transfers in trust made after 4/22/69.

Prior to deletion, subsec. (b) read as follows:

"(b) Exception where income is payable to charitable beneficiaries. Subsection (a) shall not apply to the extent that the income of a portion of a trust in which the grantor has a reversionary interest is, under the terms of the trust, irrevocably payable for a period of at least 2 years (commencing with the date of the transfer) to a designated beneficiary, which beneficiary is of a type described in section 170(b)(1)(A)(i), (ii), or (iii)."

Sec. 674. Power to control beneficial enjoyment.
(a) General rule.

The grantor shall be treated as the owner of any portion of a trust in respect of which the beneficial enjoyment of the corpus or the income therefrom is subject to a power of disposition, exercisable by the grantor or a nonadverse party, or both, without the approval or consent of any adverse party.

(b) Exceptions for certain powers.

Subsection (a) shall not apply to the following powers regardless of by whom held:

(1) Power to apply income to support of a dependent. A power described in section 677(b) to the extent that the grantor would not be subject to tax under that section.

(2) Power affecting beneficial enjoyment only after occurrence of event. A power, the exercise of which can only affect the beneficial enjoyment of the income for a period commencing after the occurrence of an event such that a grantor would not be treated as the owner under section 673 if the power were a reversionary interest; but the grantor may be treated as the owner after the occurrence of the event unless the power is relinquished.

(3) Power exercisable only by will. A power exercisable only by will, other than a power in the grantor to appoint by will the income of the trust where the income is accumulated for such disposition by the grantor or may be so accumulated in the discretion of the grantor or a nonadverse party, or both, without the approval or consent of any adverse party.

(4) Power to allocate among charitable beneficiaries. A power to determine the beneficial enjoyment of the corpus or the income therefrom if the corpus or income is irrevocably payable for a purpose specified in section 170(c) (relating to definition of charitable contributions) or to an employee stock ownership plan (as defined in section 4975(e)(7)) in a qualified gratuitous transfer (as defined in section 664(g)(1)).

(5) Power to distribute corpus. A power to distribute corpus either—

(A) to or for a beneficiary or beneficiaries or to or for a class of beneficiaries (whether or not income beneficiaries) provided that the power is limited by a reasonably definite standard which is set forth in the trust instrument; or

(B) to or for any current income beneficiary, provided that the distribution of corpus must be chargeable against the proportionate share of corpus held in trust for the payment of income to the beneficiary as if the corpus constituted a separate trust.

A power does not fall within the powers described in this paragraph if any person has a power to add to the beneficiary or beneficiaries or to a class of beneficiaries designated to receive the income or corpus, except where such action is to provide for after-born or after-adopted children.

(6) Power to withhold income temporarily. A power to distribute or apply income to or for any current income beneficiary or to accumulate the income for him, provided that any accumulated income must ultimately be payable—

(A) to the beneficiary from whom distribution or application is withheld, to his estate, or to his appointees (or persons named as alternate takers in default of appointment) provided that such beneficiary possesses a power of appointment which does not exclude from the class of possible appointees any person other than the beneficiary, his estate, his creditors, or the creditors of his estate, or

(B) on termination of the trust, or in conjunction with a distribution of corpus which is augmented by such accumulated income, to the current income beneficiaries in shares which have been irrevocably specified in the trust instrument.

Accumulated income shall be considered so payable although it is provided that if any beneficiary does not survive a date of distribution which could reasonably have been expected to occur within the beneficiary's lifetime, the share of the deceased beneficiary is to be paid to his appointees or to one or more designated alternate takers (other than the grantor or the grantor's estate) whose shares have not been irrevocably specified. A power does not fall within the powers described in this paragraph if any person has a power to add to the beneficiary or beneficiaries or to a class of beneficiaries designated to receive the income or corpus except where such action is to provide for after-born or after-adopted children.

(7) Power to withhold income during disability of a beneficiary. A power exercisable only during—

(A) the existence of a legal disability of any current income beneficiary, or

(B) the period during which any income beneficiary shall be under the age of 21 years,

to distribute or apply income to or for such beneficiary or to accumulate and add the income to corpus. A power does not fall within the powers described in this paragraph if any person has a power to add to the beneficiary or beneficiaries or to a class of beneficiaries designated to receive the income or corpus, except where such action is to provide for after-born or after-adopted children.

(8) Power to allocate between corpus and income. A power to allocate receipts and disbursements as between corpus and income, even though expressed in broad language.

(c) Exception for certain powers of independent trustees.

Subsection (a) shall not apply to a power solely exercisable (without the approval or consent of any other person) by a trustee or trustees, none of whom is the grantor, and no more than half of whom are related or subordinate parties who are subservient to the wishes of the grantor—

(1) to distribute, apportion, or accumulate income to or for a beneficiary or beneficiaries, or to, for, or within a class of beneficiaries; or

(2) to pay out corpus to or for a beneficiary or beneficiaries or to or for a class of beneficiaries (whether or not income beneficiaries).

A power does not fall within the powers described in this subsection if any person has a power to add to the beneficiary or beneficiaries or to a class of beneficiaries designated to receive the income or corpus, except where such action is to provide for after-born or after-adopted children. For periods during which an individual is the spouse of the grantor (within the meaning of section 672(e)(2)), any reference in this subsection to the grantor shall be treated as including a reference to such individual.

(d) Power to allocate income if limited by a standard.

Subsection (a) shall not apply to a power solely exercisable (without the approval or consent of any other person) by a trustee or trustees, none of whom is the grantor or spouse living with the grantor, to distribute, apportion, or accumulate income to or for a beneficiary or beneficiaries, or to, for, or within a class of beneficiaries, whether or not the conditions of paragraph (6) or (7) of subsection (b) are satisfied, if such power is limited by a reasonably definite external standard which is set forth in the trust instrument. A power does not fall within the powers described in this subsection if any person has a power to add to the beneficiary or beneficiaries or to a class of beneficiaries designated to receive the income or corpus except where such action is to provide for after-born or after-adopted children.

In 1997, P.L. 105-34, Sec. 1530(c)(6), added "or to an employee stock ownership plan (as defined in section 4975(e)(7)) in a qualified gratuitous transfer (as defined in section 664(g)(1))" before the period at the end of para. (b)(4), effective for transfers made by trusts to, or for the use of, an employee stock ownership plan after 8/5/97.

In 1988, P.L. 100-647, Sec. 1014(a)(3), added the sentence at the end of subsec. (c), effective for transfers in trust made after 3/1/86.

In 1986, P.L. 99-514, Sec. 1402(b)(1)(A), substituted "the occurrence of an event" for "the expiration of a period" in para. (b)(2) . . . Sec. 1402(b)(1)(B), substituted "the occurrence of the event" for "the expiration of the period" in para. (b)(2) . . . Sec. 1402(b)(1)(C), substituted "occurrence of event" for "expiration of 10-year period" in the heading of para. (b)(2), effective for transfers in trust made after 3/1/86, except as provided in Sec. 1402(c)(2) of this Act which read as follows:

"(2) Transfers pursuant to property settlement agreement.—The amendments made by this section [Sec. 1402] shall not apply to any transfer in trust made after March 1, 1986, pursuant to a binding property settlement agreement entered into on or before March 1, 1986, which required the taxpayer to establish a grantor trust and for the transfer of a specified sum of money or property to the trust by the taxpayer. This paragraph shall apply only to the extent of the amount required to be transferred under the agreement described in the preceding sentence."

Sec. 675. Administrative powers.

The grantor shall be treated as the owner of any portion of a trust in respect of which—

(1) Power to deal for less than adequate and full consideration. A power exercisable by the grantor or a nonadverse party, or both, without the approval or consent of any adverse party enables the grantor or any person to purchase, exchange, or otherwise deal with or dispose of the corpus or the income therefrom for less than an adequate consideration in money or money's worth.

(2) Power to borrow without adequate interest or security. A power exercisable by the grantor or a nonadverse party, or both, enables the grantor to borrow the corpus or income, directly or indirectly, without adequate interest or without adequate security except where a trustee (other than the grantor) is authorized under a general lending power to make loans to any person without regard to interest or security.

(3) Borrowing of the trust funds. The grantor has directly or indirectly borrowed the corpus or income and has not completely repaid the loan, including any interest, before the beginning of the taxable year. The preceding sentence shall not apply to a loan which provides for adequate interest and adequate security, if such loan is made by a trustee other than the grantor and other than a related or subordinate trustee subservient to the grantor. For periods during which an individual is the spouse of the grantor (within the meaning of section 672(e)(2)), any reference in this paragraph to the grantor shall be treated as including a reference to such individual.

(4) General powers of administration. A power of administration is exercisable in a nonfiduciary capacity by any person without the approval or consent of any person in a fiduciary capacity. For purposes of this paragraph, the term "power of administration" means any one or more of the following powers: (A) a power to vote or direct the voting of stock or other securities of a corporation in which the holdings of the grantor and the trust are significant from the viewpoint of voting control; (B) a power to control the investment of the trust funds either by directing investments or reinvestments, or by vetoing proposed investments or reinvestments, to the extent that the trust funds consist of stocks or securities of corporations in which the holdings of the grantor and the trust are significant from the viewpoint of voting control; or (C) a power to reacquire the trust corpus by substituting other property of an equivalent value.

In **1988**, P.L. 100-647, Sec. 1014(a)(2), added the last sentence in para. (3), effective for transfers in trust made after 3/1/86.

Sec. 676. Power to revoke.
(a) General rule.

The grantor shall be treated as the owner of any portion of a trust, whether or not he is treated as such owner under any other provision of this part, where at any time the power to revest in the grantor title to such portion is exercisable by the grantor or a nonadverse party, or both.

(b) Power affecting beneficial enjoyment only after occurrence of event.

Subsection (a) shall not apply to a power the exercise of which can only affect the beneficial enjoyment of the income for a period commencing after the occurrence of an event such that a grantor would not be treated as the owner under section 673 if the power were a reversionary interest. But the grantor may be treated as the owner after the occurrence of such event unless the power is relinquished.

In **1986**, P.L. 99-514, Sec. 1402(b)(2)(A), substituted "the occurrence of an event" for "the expiration of a period" in subsec. (b) . . . Sec. 1402(b)(2)(B), substituted "the occurrence of such event" for "the expiration of such period" in subsec. (b) . . . Sec. 1402(b)(2)(C), substituted, "occurrence of event" for "expiration of 10-year period" in the heading of subsec. (b), effective for transfers in trust made after 3/1/86, except as provided in Sec. 1402(c)(2) of this Act which read as follows:

"(2) Transfers pursuant to property settlement agreement.—The amendments made by this section [Sec. 1402] shall not apply to any transfer in trust made after March 1, 1986, pursuant to a binding property settlement agreement entered into on or before March 1, 1986, which required the taxpayer to establish a grantor trust and for the transfer of a specified sum of money or property to the trust by the taxpayer. This paragraph shall apply only to the extent of the amount required to be transferred under the agreement described in the preceding sentence."

Sec. 677. Income for benefit of grantor.
(a) General rule.

The grantor shall be treated as the owner of any portion of a trust, whether or not he is treated as such owner under section 674, whose income without the approval or consent of any adverse party is, or, in the discretion of the grantor or a nonadverse party, or both, may be—

(1) distributed to the grantor or the grantor's spouse;

(2) held or accumulated for future distribution to the grantor or the grantor's spouse; or

(3) applied to the payment of premiums on policies of insurance on the life of the grantor or the grantor's spouse (except policies of insurance irrevocably payable for a purpose specified in section 170(c) (relating to definition of charitable contributions)).

This subsection shall not apply to a power the exercise of which can only affect the beneficial enjoyment of the income for a period commencing after the occurrence of an event such that the grantor would not be treated as the owner under section 673 if the power were a reversionary interest; but the grantor may be treated as the owner after the occurrence of the event unless the power is relinquished.

(b) Obligations of support.

Income of a trust shall not be considered taxable to the grantor under subsection (a) or any other provision of this chapter merely because such income in the discretion of another person, the trustee, or the grantor acting as trustee or co-trustee, may be applied or distributed for the support or maintenance of a beneficiary (other than the grantor's spouse) whom the grantor is legally obligated to support or maintain, except to the extent that such income is so applied or distributed. In cases where the amounts so applied or distributed are paid out of corpus or out of other than income for the taxable year, such amounts shall be considered to be an amount paid or credited within the meaning of paragraph (2) of section 661(a) and shall be taxed to the grantor under section 662.

In **1986**, P.L. 99-514, Sec. 1402(b)(3)(A), substituted, "the occurrence of an event" for "the expiration of a period" in subsec. (a) . . . Sec. 1402(b)(3)(B), substituted, "the occurrence of the event" for "the expiration of the period" in subsec. (a), effective for transfers in trust made after 3/1/86, except as provided in Sec. 1402(c)(2) of this Act which read as follows:

"(2) Transfers pursuant to property settlement agreement.—The amendments made by this section [Sec. 1402] shall not apply to any transfer in trust made after March 1, 1986, pursuant to a binding property settlement agreement entered into on or before March 1, 1986, which required the taxpayer to establish a grantor trust and for the transfer of a specified sum of money or property to the trust by the taxpayer. This paragraph shall apply only to the extent of the amount required to be transferred under the agreement described in the preceding sentence.

In 1969, P.L. 91-172, Sec. 332(a)(1), substituted "the grantor or the grantor's spouse" for "the grantor" in subsecs. (a)(1), (2) and (3)... Sec. 332(a)(2), substituted "beneficiary" for "beneficiary (other than the grantor's spouse)" in subsec. (b), effective for property transferred in trust after 10/9/69.

Sec. 678. Person other than grantor treated as substantial owner.

(a) General rule.

A person other than the grantor shall be treated as the owner of any portion of a trust with respect to which:

(1) such person has a power exercisable solely by himself to vest the corpus or the income therefrom in himself, or

(2) such person has previously partially released or otherwise modified such a power and after the release or modification retains such control as would, within the principles of sections 671 to 677, inclusive, subject a grantor of a trust to treatment as the owner thereof.

(b) Exception where grantor is taxable.

Subsection (a) shall not apply with respect to a power over income, as originally granted or thereafter modified, if the grantor of the trust or a transferor (to whom section 679 applies) is otherwise treated as the owner under the provisions of this subpart other than this section.

(c) Obligations of support.

Subsection (a) shall not apply to a power which enables such person, in the capacity of trustee or co-trustee, merely to apply the income of the trust to the support or maintenance of a person whom the holder of the power is obligated to support or maintain except to the extent that such income is so applied. In cases where the amounts so applied or distributed are paid out of corpus or out of other than income of the taxable year, such amounts shall be considered to be an amount paid or credited within the meaning of paragraph (2) of section 661(a) and shall be taxed to the holder of the power under section 662.

(d) Effect of renunciation or disclaimer.

Subsection (a) shall not apply with respect to a power which has been renounced or disclaimed within a reasonable time after the holder of the power first became aware of its existence.

(e) Cross reference.

For provision under which beneficiary of trust is treated as owner of the portion of the trust which consists of stock in an S corporation, see section 1361(d).

In 2000, P.L. 106-554, Sec. 1(a)(7), [which enacted into law Sec. 319(8)(A) of P.L. 106-554] substituted "an S corporation" for "an electing small business corporation" in subsec. (e), effective 12/21/2000.

In 1983, P.L. 97-448, Sec. 102(i)(2), added subsec. (e), effective for tax. yrs. begin. after 12/31/81.

In 1976, P.L. 94-455, Sec. 1013(b), substituted "if the grantor of the trust or a transferor (to whom section 679 applies) is otherwise treated as the owner under the provisions of this subpart other than this section." for "if the grantor of the trust is otherwise treated as the owner under sections 671 to 677, inclusive." in subsec. (b), effective for tax. yrs. end. after 12/31/75. Sec. 1013(f) provided as follows:

"(1) In general.—The amendments made by this section (other than subsection (c)) shall apply to taxable years ending after December 31, 1975, but only in the case of—

"(A) foreign trusts created after May 21, 1974, and

"(B) transfers of property to foreign trusts after May 21, 1974."

Sec. 679. Foreign trusts having one or more United States beneficiaries.

(a) Transferor treated as owner.

(1) In general. A United States person who directly or indirectly transfers property to a foreign trust (other than a trust described in section 6048(a)(3)(B)(ii)) shall be treated as the owner for his taxable year of the portion of such trust attributable to such property if for such year there is a United States beneficiary of any portion of such trust.

(2) Exceptions. Paragraph (1) shall not apply—

(A) Transfers by reason of death. To any transfer by reason of the death of the transferor.

(B) Transfers at fair market value. To any transfer of property to a trust in exchange for consideration of at least the fair market value of the transferred property. For purposes of the preceding sentence, consideration other than cash shall be taken into account at its fair market value.

(3) Certain obligations not taken into account under fair market value exception.

(A) In general. In determining whether paragraph (2)(B) applies to any transfer by a person described in clause (ii) or (iii) of subparagraph (C), there shall not be taken into account—

(i) except as provided in regulations, any obligation of a person described in subparagraph (C), and

(ii) to the extent provided in regulations, any obligation which is guaranteed by a person described in subparagraph (C).

(B) Treatment of principal payments on obligation. Principal payments by the trust on any obligation referred to in subparagraph (A) shall be taken into account on and after the date of the payment in determining the portion of the trust attributable to the property transferred.

(C) Persons described. The persons described in this subparagraph are—

(i) the trust,

(ii) any grantor, owner, or beneficiary of the trust, and

(iii) any person who is related (within the meaning of section 643(i)(2)(B)) to any grantor, owner, or beneficiary of the trust.

(4) Special rules applicable to foreign grantor who later becomes a United States person.

(A) In general. If a nonresident alien individual has a residency starting date within 5 years after directly or indirectly transferring property to a foreign trust, this section and section 6048 shall be applied as if such individual transferred to such trust on the residency starting date an amount equal to the portion of such trust attributable to the property transferred by such individual to such trust in such transfer.

(B) Treatment of undistributed income. For purposes of this section, undistributed net income for periods before such individual's residency starting date shall be taken into account in determining the portion of the trust which is attributable to property transferred by such individual to such trust but shall not otherwise be taken into account.

(C) Residency starting date. For purposes of this paragraph, an individual's residency starting date is the residency starting date determined under section 7701(b)(2)(A).

(5) Outbound trust migrations. If—

(A) an individual who is a citizen or resident of the United States transferred property to a trust which was not a foreign trust, and

(B) such trust becomes a foreign trust while such individual is alive,

then this section and section 6048 shall be applied as if such individual transferred to such trust on the date such trust becomes a foreign trust an amount equal to the portion of such trust attributable to the property previously transferred by such individual to such trust. A rule similar to the rule of paragraph (4)(B) shall apply for purposes of this paragraph.

(b) Trusts acquiring United States beneficiaries.
If—
(1) subsection (a) applies to a trust for the transferor's taxable year, and
(2) subsection (a) would have applied to the trust for his immediately preceding taxable year but for the fact that for such preceding taxable year there was no United States beneficiary for any portion of the trust,

then, for purposes of this subtitle, the transferor shall be treated as having income for the taxable year (in addition to his other income for such year) equal to the undistributed net income (at the close of such immediately preceding taxable year) attributable to the portion of the trust referred to in subsection (a).

(c) Trusts treated as having a United States beneficiary.
(1) **In general.** For purposes of this section, a trust shall be treated as having a United States beneficiary for the taxable year unless—
   (A) under the terms of the trust, no part of the income or corpus of the trust may be paid or accumulated during the taxable year to or for the benefit of a United States person, and
   (B) if the trust were terminated at any time during the taxable year, no part of the income or corpus of such trust could be paid to or for the benefit of a United States person.

For purposes of subparagraph (A), an amount shall be treated as accumulated for the benefit of a United States person even if the United States person's interest in the trust is contingent on a future event.

(2) **Attribution of ownership.** For purposes of paragraph (1), an amount shall be treated as paid or accumulated to or for the benefit of a United States person if such amount is paid to or accumulated for a foreign corporation, foreign partnership, or foreign trust or estate, and—
   (A) in the case of a foreign corporation, such corporation is a controlled foreign corporation (as defined in section 957(a)),
   (B) in the case of a foreign partnership, a United States person is a partner of such partnership, or
   (C) in the case of a foreign trust or estate, such trust or estate has a United States beneficiary (within the meaning of paragraph (1)).

(3) **Certain United States beneficiaries disregarded.** A beneficiary shall not be treated as a United States person in applying this section with respect to any transfer of property to foreign trust if such beneficiary first became a United States person more than 5 years after the date of such transfer.

(4) **Special rule in case of discretion to identify beneficiaries.** For purposes of paragraph (1)(A), if any person has the discretion (by authority given in the trust agreement, by power of appointment, or otherwise) of making a distribution from the trust to, or for the benefit of, any person, such trust shall be treated as having a beneficiary who is a United States person unless—
   (A) the terms of the trust specifically identify the class of persons to whom such distributions may be made, and
   (B) none of those persons are United States persons during the taxable year.

(5) **Certain agreements and understandings treated as terms of the trust.** For purposes of paragraph (1)(A), if any United States person who directly or indirectly transfers property to the trust is directly or indirectly involved in any agreement or understanding (whether written, oral, or otherwise) that may result in the income or corpus of the trust being paid or accumulated to or for the benefit of a United States person, such agreement or understanding shall be treated as a term of the trust.

(6) **Uncompensated use of trust property treated as a payment.** For purposes of this subsection, a loan of cash or marketable securities (or the use of any other trust property) directly or indirectly to or by any United States person (whether or not a beneficiary under the terms of the trust) shall be treated as paid or accumulated for the benefit of a United States person. The preceding sentence shall not apply to the extent that the United States person repays the loan at a market rate of interest (or pays the fair market value of the use of such property) within a reasonable period of time.

(d) Presumption that foreign trust has United States beneficiary.
If a United States person directly or indirectly transfers property to a foreign trust (other than a trust described in section 6048(a)(3)(B)(ii)), the Secretary may treat such trust as having a United States beneficiary for purposes of applying this section to such transfer unless such person—
(1) submits such information to the Secretary as the Secretary may require with respect to such transfer, and
(2) demonstrates to the satisfaction of the Secretary that such trust satisfies the requirements of subparagraphs (A) and (B) of subsection (c)(1).

(e) Regulations.
The Secretary shall prescribe such regulations as may be necessary or appropriate to carry out the purposes of this section.

In 2010, P.L. 111-147, Sec. 531(a), added matter at the end of para. (c)(1) . . . Sec. 531(b), added para. (c)(4) . . . Sec. 531(c), added para. (c)(5), enacted 3/18/2010.
—P.L. 111-147, Sec. 532(a), redesignated subsec. (d) as (e) and added new subsec. (d), effective for transfers of property after 3/18/2010.
—P.L. 111-147, Sec. 533(c), added para. (c)(6), effective for loans made, and uses of property, after 3/18/2010.
In 1998, P.L. 105-206, Sec. 6018(g), amended Sec. 1903(b) of P.L. 104-188 by substituting "OR" for "or" in the material to be deleted [see below].
In 1997, P.L. 105-34, Sec. 1601(i)(2), added ", owner," after "grantor" in clauses (a)(3)(C)(ii) and (iii), effective for transfers of property after 2/6/95.
In 1996, P.L. 104-188, Sec. 1903(a)(1), amended subpara. (a)(2)(B) . . . Sec. 1903(a)(2), added para. (a)(3) . . . Sec. 1903(b), substituted "section 6048(a)(3)(B)(ii)" for "section 404(a)(4) or [sic section] 404A" in para. (a)(1) . . . Sec. 1903(c), added paras. (a)(4) and (5) . . . Sec. 1903(d), added para. (c)(3) . . . Sec. 1903(e), amended subpara. (c)(2)(A) . . . Sec. 1903(f), added subsec. (d), effective for transfers of property after 2/6/95.
Prior to amendment, subpara. (a)(2)(B) read as follows:
"(B) Transfers where gain is recognized to transferor. To any sale or exchange of the property at its fair market value in a transaction in which all of the gain to the transferor is realized at the time of the transfer and is recognized either at such time or is returned as provided in section 453."
Prior to amendment, subpara. (c)(2)(A) read as follows:
"(A) in the case of a foreign corporation, more than 50 percent of the total combined voting power of all classes of stock entitled to vote of such corporation is owned (within the meaning of section 958(a)) or is considered to be owned (within the meaning of section 958(b)) by United States shareholders (as defined in section 951(b))."
In 1980, P.L. 96-603, Sec. 2(b), added "[o]r section 404A" after "section 404(a)(4)" in para. (a)(1), effective for employer contributions or accruals for tax. yrs. begin. after 12/31/79. For special election, see Sec. 2(e) of this Act reproduced in note following Code Sec 404A.
In 1976, P.L. 94-455, Sec. 1013(a), added Code Sec. 679, effective for tax yrs. end. after 12/31/75. For special rules, see Sec. 1013(f) of this Act, reproduced in note following Code Sec. 678.

SUBPART F.—MISCELLANEOUS
681. Limitation on charitable deduction.
682. Income of an estate or trust in case of divorce, etc.

Estates, trusts, beneficiaries   **Code Sec. 682(a)**

683. Use of trust as an exchange fund.
684. Recognition of gain on certain transfers to certain foreign trusts and estates [before 1/1/2010].
684. Recognition of gain on certain transfers to certain foreign trusts and estates and nonresident aliens [after 12/31/2009].
685. Treatment of funeral trusts.

In **2001**, P.L. 107-16, Sec. 542(e)(1)(D), added "and nonresident aliens" after "estates" in item 684.

In **1997**, P.L. 105-34, Sec. 1131(c)(6) sic [(d)], added item 684 . . . Sec. 1309(b), added item 685.

Sec. 681. Limitation on charitable deduction.
(a) Trade or business income.

In computing the deduction allowable under section 642(c) to a trust, no amount otherwise allowable under section 642(c) as a deduction shall be allowed as a deduction with respect to income of the taxable year which is allocable to its unrelated business income for such year. For purposes of the preceding sentence, the term "unrelated business income" means an amount equal to the amount which, if such trust were exempt from tax under section 501(a) by reason of section 501(c)(3), would be computed as its unrelated business taxable income under section 512 (relating to income derived from certain business activities and from certain property acquired with borrowed funds).

(b) Cross reference.

For disallowance of certain charitable, etc., deductions otherwise allowable under section 642(c), see sections 508(d) and 4948(c)(4).

In **1969**, P.L. 91-172, Sec. 101(j)(18), deleted subsecs. (b) and (c) . . . Sec. 101(j)(19), redesignated subsec. (d) as subsec. (b) and substituted "sections 508(d) and 4948(c)(4)" for "section 503(e)" in subsec. (b) [as redesignated by this Sec., see above], effective 1/1/70.

Prior to deletion, subsecs. (b) and (c) read as follows:

"(b) *Operations of trusts.*

"(1) Limitation on charitable, etc., deduction. The amount otherwise allowable under section 642(c) as a deduction shall not exceed 20 percent of the taxable income of the trust (computed without the benefit of section 642(c) but with the benefit of section 170(b)(1)(A)) if the trust has engaged in a prohibited transaction, as defined in paragraph (2).

"(2) Prohibited transactions. For purposes of this subsection, the term 'prohibited transaction' means any transaction after July 1, 1950, in which any trust while holding income or corpus which has been permanently set aside or is to be used exclusively for charitable or other purposes described in section 642(c)—

"(A) lends any part of such income or corpus, without receipt of adequate security and a reasonable rate of interest, to;

"(B) pays any compensation from such income or corpus, in excess of a reasonable allowance for salaries or other compensation for personal services actually rendered, to;

"(C) makes any part of its services available on a preferential basis to;

"(D) uses such income or corpus to make any substantial purchase of securities or any other property, for more than an adequate consideration in money or money's worth, from;

"(E) sells any substantial part of the securities or other property comprising such income or corpus, for less than an adequate consideration in money or money's worth, to; or

"(F) engages in any other transaction which results in a substantial diversion of such income or corpus to;

the creator of such trust; any person who has made a substantial contribution to such trust; a member of a family (as defined in section 267(c)(4)) of an individual who is the creator of the trust or who has made a substantial contribution to the trust; or a corporation controlled by any such creator or person through the ownership, directly or indirectly, of 50 percent or more of the total combined voting power of all classes of stock entitled to vote or 50 percent or more of the total value of shares of all classes of stock of the corporation.

"(3) Taxable years affected. The amount otherwise allowable under section 642(c) as a deduction shall be limited as provided in paragraph (1) only for taxable years after the taxable year during which the trust is notified by the Secretary that it has engaged in such transaction, unless such trust entered into such prohibited transaction with the purpose of diverting such corpus or income from the purposes described in section 642(c), and such transaction involved a substantial part of such corpus or income.

"(4) Future charitable, etc., deductions of trusts denied deduction under paragraph (3). If the deduction of any trust under section 642(c) has been limited as provided in this subsection, such trust, with respect to any taxable year following the taxable year in which notice is received of limitation of deduction under section 642(c), may, under regulations prescribed by the Secretary or his delegate, file claim for the allowance of the unlimited deduction under section 642(c), and if the Secretary, pursuant to such regulations, is satisfied that such trust will not knowingly again engage in a prohibited transaction, the limitation provided in paragraph (1) shall not apply with respect to taxable years after the year in which such claim is filed.

"(5) Disallowance of certain charitable, etc., deductions. No gift or bequest for religious, charitable, scientific, literary, or educational purposes (including the encouragement of art and the prevention of cruelty to children or animals), otherwise allowable as a deduction under section 170, 545(b)(2), 642(c), 2055, 2106(a)(2), or 2522, shall be allowed as a deduction if made in trust and, in the taxable year of the trust in which the gift or bequest is made, the deduction allowed the trust under section 642(c) is limited by paragraph (1). With respect to any taxable year of a trust in which such deduction has been so limited by reason of entering into a prohibited transaction with the purpose of diverting such corpus or income from the purposes described in section 642(c), and such transaction involved in a substantial part of such income or corpus, and which taxable year is the same, or before the taxable year of the trust in which such prohibited transaction occurred, such deduction shall be disallowed the donor only if such donor or (if such donor is an individual) any member of his family (as defined in section 267(c)(4)) was a party to such prohibited transaction.

"(6) Definition. For purposes of this subsection, the term 'gift or bequest' means any gift, contribution, bequest, devise, or legacy, or any transfer without adequate consideration.

"(c) *Accumulated income.*

"If the amounts permanently set aside, or to be used exclusively for the charitable and other purposes described in section 642(c) during the taxable year or any prior taxable year and not actually paid out by the end of the taxable year—

"(1) are unreasonable in amount or duration in order to carry out such purposes of the trust;

"(2) are used to a substantial degree for purposes other than those prescribed in section 642(c); or

"(3) are invested in such a manner as to jeopardize the interests of the religious, charitable, scientific, etc., beneficiaries,

the amount otherwise allowable under section 642(c) as a deduction shall be limited to the amount actually paid out during the taxable year and shall not exceed 20 percent of the taxable income of the trust (computed without the benefit of section 642(c) but with the benefit of section 170(b)(1)(A)). Paragraph (1) shall not apply to income attributable to property of a decedent dying before January 1, 1951, which is transferred under his will to a trust created by such will. In the case of a trust created by the will of a decedent dying on or after January 1, 1951, if income is required to be accumulated pursuant to the mandatory terms of the will creating the trust, paragraph (1) shall apply only to income accumulated during a taxable year of the trust beginning more than 21 years after the date of death of the last life in being designated in the trust instrument. Paragraph (1) shall not apply to income attributable to property transferred to a trust before January 1, 1951, by the creator of such trust, if such trust was irrevocable on such date and if such income is required to be accumulated pursuant to the mandatory terms (as in effect on such date and at all times thereafter) of the instrument creating such trust."

—P.L. 91-172, Sec. 121(d)(2)(B), substituted "certain property acquired with borrowed funds" for "certain leases" in the second sentence of subsec. (a), effective for tax. yrs. begin. after 12/31/69.

In **1968**, P.L. 90-630, Sec. 6(b), added the third sentence in subsec. (c), effective for tax. yrs. begin. after 12/31/53 and end. after 8/16/54.

Sec. 682. Income of an estate or trust in case of divorce, etc.
(a) Inclusion in gross income of wife.

There shall be included in the gross income of a wife who is divorced or legally separated under a decree of divorce or of separate maintenance (or who is separated from her husband under a written separation agreement) the amount of the income of any trust which such wife is entitled to receive and which, except for this section, would be includible in the gross income of her husband, and such amount shall not, despite any other provision of this subtitle, be includible in the gross income of such husband. This subsection shall not apply to that part of any such income of the trust which the terms of the decree, written separation agreement, or trust instrument fix, in terms of an amount of money or a portion of such income, as a sum which is payable for the support of minor children of such husband. In case such income is less than the amount specified in the decree, agreement, or instrument, for the purpose of applying the preceding sentence, such income, to the extent of such sum payable for such support, shall be considered a payment for such support.

2,333

(b) Wife considered a beneficiary.

For purposes of computing the taxable income of the estate or trust and the taxable income of a wife to whom subsection (a) applies, such wife shall be considered as the beneficiary specified in this part.

(c) Cross reference.

For definitions of "husband" and "wife," as used in this section, see section 7701(a)(17).

In **1984**, P.L. 98-369, Sec. 422(d)(2)(A), deleted "or section 71" after "subsection (a)" in subsec. (b) . . . Sec. 422(d)(2)(B), deleted the last sentence of subsec. (b), effective for divorce or separation instruments (as defined in Code Sec. 71(b)(2), as amended), executed after 12/31/84. Sec. 422(e)(2) of this Act also provides:

"(2) Modifications of instruments executed before January 1, 1985—The amendments made by this section shall also apply to any divorce or separation instrument (as so defined) executed before January 1, 1985, but modified on or after such date if the modification expressly provides that the amendments made by this section shall apply to such modification."

Prior to deletion, the last sentence in subsec. (b) read as follows:

"A periodic payment under section 71 to any portion of which this part applies shall be included in the gross income of the beneficiary in the taxable year in which under this part such portion is required to be included."

Sec. 683. Use of trust as an exchange fund.
(a) General rule.

Except as provided in subsection (b), if property is transferred to a trust in exchange for an interest in other trust property and if the trust would be an investment company (within the meaning of section 351) if it were a corporation, then gain shall be recognized to the transferor.

(b) Exception for pooled income funds.

Subsection (a) shall not apply to any transfer to a pooled income fund (within the meaning of section 642(c)(5)).

In **1976**, P.L. 94-455, Sec. 2131(e)(1), amended Code Sec. 683, effective 4/8/76, in tax. yrs. ending on or after 4/8/76.

Prior to amendment, Code Sec. 683 read as follows:

"SEC. 683. APPLICABILITY OF PROVISIONS.

"(a) General rule.

"This part shall apply only to taxable years beginning after December 31, 1953, and ending after the date of the enactment of this title.

"(b) Exceptions.

"In the case of any beneficiary of an estate or trust—

"(1) this part shall not apply to any amount paid, credited, or to be distributed by the estate or trust in any taxable year of such estate or trust to which this part does not apply, and

"(2) the Internal Revenue Code of 1939 shall apply for purposes of determining the amount includible in the gross income of the beneficiary.

To the extent that any amount paid, credited, or to be distributed by an estate or trust in the first taxable year of such estate or trust to which this part applies would be treated, if the Internal Revenue Code of 1939 were applicable, as paid, credited, or to be distributed on the last day of the preceding taxable year, such amount shall not be taken into account for purposes of this part but shall be taken into account as provided in the Internal Revenue Code of 1939."

• **Caution:** Sec. 301(a), P.L. 111-312, (reproduced in the history notes following this Code Sec.) provides that the amendments made by Sec. 542(e)(1)(A)-(C), P.L. 107-16, EGTRRA, will apply as if never enacted. Code Sec. 684, following, reflects the removal of these amendments, effective for estates of decedents dying, and transfers made, after 12/31/2009.

Sec. 684. Recognition of gain on certain transfers to certain foreign trusts and estates.
(a) In general.

Except as provided in regulations, in the case of any transfer of property by a United States person to a foreign estate or trust or to a nonresident alien, for purposes of this subtitle, such transfer shall be treated as a sale or exchange for an amount equal to the fair market value of the property transferred, and the transferor shall recognize as gain the excess of—

(1) the fair market value of the property so transferred, over

(2) the adjusted basis (for purposes of determining gain) of such property in the hands of the transferor.

(b) Exceptions.

(1) **Transfers to certain trusts.** Subsection (a) shall not apply to a transfer to a trust by a United States person to the extent that any United States person is treated as the owner of such trust under section 671.

(2) **Lifetime transfers to nonresident aliens.** Subsection (a) shall not apply to a lifetime transfer to a nonresident alien.

(c) Treatment of trusts which become foreign trusts.

If a trust which is not a foreign trust becomes a foreign trust, such trust shall be treated for purposes of this section as having transferred, immediately before becoming a foreign trust, all of its assets to a foreign trust.

• **Caution:** Code Sec. 684, following reflects amendments made by Sec. 542(e)(1)(A)-(C), P.L. 107-16, EGTRRA. As provided in Sec. 301(a), P.L. 111-312, these amendments will apply as if never enacted, effective for estates of decedents dying, and transfers made, after 12/31/2009.

Sec. 684. Recognition of gain on certain transfers to certain foreign trusts and estates and nonresident aliens.
(a) In general.

Except as provided in regulations, in the case of any transfer of property by a United States person to a foreign estate or trust, for purposes of this subtitle, such transfer shall be treated as a sale or exchange for an amount equal to the fair market value of the property transferred, and the transferor shall recognize as gain the excess of—

(1) the fair market value of the property so transferred, over

(2) the adjusted basis (for purposes of determining gain) of such property in the hands of the transferor.

(b) Exception.

Subsection (a) shall not apply to a transfer to a trust by a United States person to the extent that any person is treated as the owner of such trust under section 671.

(c) Treatment of trusts which become foreign trusts.

If a trust which is not a foreign trust becomes a foreign trust, such trust shall be treated for purposes of this section as having transferred, immediately before becoming a foreign trust, all of its assets to a foreign trust.

In **2010**, P.L. 111-312, Sec. 101(a)(1), substituted "December 31, 2012" for "December 31, 2010" both places it appeared in Sec. 901, P.L. 107-16 [see below], effective as if included in the enactment of P.L. 107-16, EGTRRA, 6/7/2001.

—P.L. 111-312, Sec. 301(a), provides that Code Sec. 684, as amended by Sec. 542(e)(1)(A)-(C) [see below] will read as if such provisions had never been enacted, effective for estates of decedents dying, and transfers made, after 12/31/2009.

Sec. 301(a), P.L. 111-312, 12/17/2010, provides:

"(a) In general. Each provision of law amended by subtitle A or E of title V of the Economic Growth and Tax Relief Reconciliation Act of 2001 is amended to read as such provision would read if such subtitle had never been enacted."

Prior to the enactment of Sec. 301(a), P.L. 111-312, Code Sec. 684 read as follows:

"Sec. 684. Recognition of gain on certain transfers to certain foreign trusts and estates and nonresident aliens.

"(a) In general. Except as provided in regulations, in the case of any transfer of property by a United States person to a foreign estate or trust or to a nonresident alien, for purposes of this subtitle, such transfer shall be treated as a sale or ex-

change for an amount equal to the fair market value of the property transferred, and the transferor shall recognize as gain the excess of—
"(1) the fair market value of the property so transferred, over
"(2) the adjusted basis (for purposes of determining gain) of such property in the hands of the transferor.
"(b) Exceptions.
"(1) Transfers to certain trusts. Subsection (a) shall not apply to a transfer to a trust by a United States person to the extent that any United States person is treated as the owner of such trust under section 671.
"(2) Lifetime transfers to nonresident aliens. Subsection (a) shall not apply to a lifetime transfer to a nonresident alien.
"(c) Treatment of trusts which become foreign trusts. If a trust which is not a foreign trust becomes a foreign trust, such trust shall be treated for purposes of this section as having transferred, immediately before becoming a foreign trust, all of its assets to a foreign trust."
—P.L. 111-312, Sec. 301(c), of this Act, provides
"(c) Special election with respect to estates of decedents dying in 2010. Notwithstanding subsection (a), in the case of an estate of a decedent dying after December 31, 2009, and before January 1, 2011, the executor (within the meaning of section 2203 of the Internal Revenue Code of 1986) may elect to apply such Code as though the amendments made by subsection (a) do not apply with respect to chapter 11 of such Code and with respect to property acquired or passing from such decedent (within the meaning of section 1014(b) of such Code). Such election shall be made at such time and in such manner as the Secretary of the Treasury or the Secretary's delegate shall provide. Such an election once made shall be revocable only with the consent of the Secretary of the Treasury or the Secretary's delegate. For purposes of section 2652(a)(1) of such Code, the determination of whether any property is subject to the tax imposed by such chapter 11 shall be made without regard to any election made under this subsection."
—P.L. 111-312, Sec. 301(d), of this Act, provides
" (d) Extension of time for performing certain acts.
" (1) Estate tax. In the case of the estate of a decedent dying after December 31, 2009, and before the date of the enactment of this Act, the due date for—
" (A) filing any return under section 6018 of the Internal Revenue Code of 1986 (including any election required to be made on such a return) as such section is in effect after the date of the enactment of this Act without regard to any election under subsection (c),
" (B) making any payment of tax under chapter 11 of such Code, and
" (C) making any disclaimer described in section 2518(b) of such Code of an interest in property passing by reason of the death of such decedent, shall not be earlier than the date which is 9 months after the date of the enactment of this Act.
" (2) Generation-skipping tax. In the case of any generation-skipping transfer made after December 31, 2009, and before the date of the enactment of this Act, the due date for filing any return under section 2662 of the Internal Revenue Code of 1986 (including any election required to be made on such a return) shall not be earlier than the date which is 9 months after the date of the enactment of this Act."
In 2002, P.L. 107-358, Sec. 2, added subsec. (c) in Sec. 901 of P.L. 107-16 [see below], effective 12/17/2002.
In 2001, P.L. 107-16, Sec. 542(e)(1)(A), added "or to a nonresident alien" after "or trust" in subsec. (a)... Sec. 542(e)(1)(B), amended subsec. (b)... Sec. 542(e)(1)(C), added "and nonresident aliens" after "estates" in the heading of Code Sec. 684, effective for transfers after 12/31/2009. Sec. 301(a), P.L. 111-312 (reproduced above) provides that these amendments shall be treated as never enacted.
Prior to amendment, subsec. (b) read as follows:
"(b) Exception. Subsection (a) shall not apply to a transfer to a trust by a United States person to the extent that any person is treated as the owner of such trust under section 671."
—P.L. 107-16, Sec. 901, of this Act [as amended by Sec. 2, P.L. 107-358 and Sec. 101(a)(1), P.L. 111-312, see above], reads as follows:
"Sec. 901. Sunset of provisions of Act.
"(a) In general. All provisions of, and amendments made by, this Act shall not apply—
"(1) to taxable, plan, or limitation years beginning after December 31, 2012, or
"(2) in the case of title V, to estates of decedents dying, gifts made, or generation skipping transfers, after December 31, 2012.
"(b) Application of certain laws. The Internal Revenue Code of 1986 and the Employee Retirement Income Security Act of 1974 shall be applied and administered to years, estates, gifts, and transfers described in subsection (a) as if the provisions and amendments described in subsection (a) had never been enacted.
"(c) Exception. Subsection (a) shall not apply to section 803 (relating to no federal income tax on restitution received by victims of the Nazi regime or their heirs or estates)."
In 1997, P.L. 105-34, Sec. 1131(b), added Code Sec. 684, effective 8/5/97.

Sec. 685. Treatment of funeral trusts.
(a) In general.
In the case of a qualified funeral trust—
(1) subparts B, C, D, and E shall not apply, and
(2) no deduction shall be allowed by section 642(b).
(b) Qualified funeral trust.
For purposes of this subsection, the term "qualified funeral trust" means any trust (other than a foreign trust) if—

(1) the trust arises as a result of a contract with a person engaged in the trade or business of providing funeral or burial services or property necessary to provide such services,
(2) the sole purpose of the trust is to hold, invest, and reinvest funds in the trust and to use such funds solely to make payments for such services or property for the benefit of the beneficiaries of the trust,
(3) the only beneficiaries of such trust are individuals with respect to whom such services or property are to be provided at their death under contracts described in paragraph (1),
(4) the only contributions to the trust are contributions by or for the benefit of such beneficiaries,
(5) the trustee elects the application of this subsection, and
(6) the trust would (but for the election described in paragraph (5)) be treated as owned under subpart E by the purchasers of the contracts described in paragraph (1).
A trust shall not fail to be treated as meeting the requirement of paragraph (6) by reason of the death of an individual but only during the 60-day period beginning on the date of such death.
(c) Application of rate schedule.
Section 1(e) shall be applied to each qualified funeral trust by treating each beneficiary's interest in each such trust as a separate trust.
(d) Treatment of amounts refunded to purchaser on cancellation.
No gain or loss shall be recognized to a purchaser of a contract described in subsection (b)(1) by reason of any payment from such trust to such purchaser by reason of cancellation of such contract. If any payment referred to in the preceding sentence consists of property other than money, the basis of such property in the hands of such purchaser shall be the same as the trust's basis in such property immediately before the payment.
(e) Simplified reporting.
The Secretary may prescribe rules for simplified reporting of all trusts having a single trustee and of trusts terminated during the year.

In 2008, P.L. 110-317, Sec. 9(a), deleted subsec. (c)... Sec. 9(b), redesignated subsecs. (d), (e), and (f) as subsecs. (c), (d), and (e) respectively, effective for tax. yrs. begin. after 8/29/2008.
Prior to deletion, subsec (c) read as follows:
"(c) Dollar limitation on contributions.
"(1) In general. The term 'qualified funeral trust' shall not include any trust which accepts aggregate contributions by or for the benefit of an individual in excess of $7,000.
"(2) Related trusts. For purposes of paragraph (1), all trusts having trustees which are related persons shall be treated as 1 trust. For purposes of the preceding sentence, persons are related if—
"(A) the relationship between such persons is described in section 267 or 707(b),
"(B) such persons are treated as a single employer under subsection (a) or (b) of section 52, or
"(C) the Secretary determines that treating such persons as related is necessary to prevent avoidance of the purposes of this section.
"(3) Inflation adjustment. In the case of any contract referred to in subsection (b)(1) which is entered into during any calendar year after 1998, the dollar amount referred to paragraph (1) shall be increased by an amount equal to—
"(A) such dollar amount, multiplied by
"(B) the cost-of-living adjustment determined under section 1(f)(3) for such calendar year, by substituting 'calendar year 1997' for 'calendar year 1992' in subparagraph (B) thereof.
"If any dollar amount after being increased under the preceding sentence is not a multiple of $100, such dollar amount shall be rounded to the nearest multiple of $100."
In 1998, P.L. 105-206, Sec. 6013(b)(1), added a flush sentence at the end of subsec. (b)... Sec. 6013(b)(2), added "and of trusts terminated during the year" before the period at the end of subsec. (f), effective for tax. yrs. end. after 8/5/97.
In 1997, P.L. 105-34, Sec. 1309(a), added Code Sec. 685, effective for tax. yrs. end. after 8/5/97.

Part II — Income in Respect of Decedents

Sec.
691. Recipients of income in respect of decedents.
692. Income taxes of members of Armed Forces, astronauts, and victims of certain terrorist attacks on death.

In 2003, P.L. 108-121, Sec. 110(a)(3)(B), amended item 692.
Prior to amendment, item 692 read as follows:
"Sec. 692. Income taxes of members of Armed Forces and victims of certain terrorist attacks on death."
In 2002, P.L. 107-134, Sec. 101(c)(2), amended item 692.
Prior to amendment, item 692 read as follows:
"Sec. 692. Income taxes of members of Armed Forces on death."

Sec. 691. Recipients of income in respect of decedents.

(a) Inclusion in gross income.

(1) General rule. The amount of all items of gross income in respect of a decedent which are not properly includible in respect of the taxable period in which falls the date of his death or a prior period (including the amount of all items of gross income in respect of a prior decedent, if the right to receive such amount was acquired by reason of the death of the prior decedent or by bequest, devise, or inheritance from the prior decedent) shall be included in the gross income, for the taxable year when received, of:

(A) the estate of the decedent, if the right to receive the amount is acquired by the decedent's estate from the decedent;

(B) the person who, by reason of the death of the decedent, acquires the right to receive the amount, if the right to receive the amount is not acquired by the decedent's estate from the decedent; or

(C) the person who acquires from the decedent the right to receive the amount by bequest, devise, or inheritance, if the amount is received after a distribution by the decedent's estate of such right.

(2) Income in case of sale, etc. If a right, described in paragraph (1), to receive an amount is transferred by the estate of the decedent or a person who received such right by reason of the death of the decedent or by bequest, devise, or inheritance from the decedent, there shall be included in the gross income of the estate or such person, as the case may be, for the taxable period in which the transfer occurs, the fair market value of such right at the time of such transfer plus the amount by which any consideration for the transfer exceeds such fair market value. For purposes of this paragraph, the term "transfer" includes sale, exchange, or other disposition, or the satisfaction of an installment obligation at other than face value, but does not include transmission at death to the estate of the decedent or a transfer to a person pursuant to the right of such person to receive such amount by reason of the death of the decedent or by bequest, devise, or inheritance from the decedent.

(3) Character of income determined by reference to decedent. The right, described in paragraph (1), to receive an amount shall be treated, in the hands of the estate of the decedent or any person who acquired such right by reason of the death of the decedent, or by bequest, devise, or inheritance from the decedent, as if it had been acquired by the estate or such person in the transaction in which the right to receive the income was originally derived and the amount includible in gross income under paragraph (1) or (2) shall be considered in the hands of the estate or such person to have the character which it would have had in the hands of the decedent if the decedent had lived and received such amount.

(4) Installment obligations acquired from decedent. In the case of an installment obligation reportable by the decedent on the installment method under section 453, if such obligation is acquired by the decedent's estate from the decedent or by any person by reason of the death of the decedent or by bequest, devise, or inheritance from the decedent—

(A) an amount equal to the excess of the face amount of such obligation over the basis of the obligation in the hands of the decedent (determined under section 453B) shall, for the purpose of paragraph (1), be considered as an item of gross income in respect of the decedent; and

(B) such obligation shall, for purposes of paragraphs (2) and (3), be considered a right to receive an item of gross income in respect of the decedent, but the amount includible in gross income under paragraph (2) shall be reduced by an amount equal to the basis of the obligation in the hands of the decedent (determined under section 453B).

(5) Other rules relating to installment obligations.

(A) In general. In the case of an installment obligation reportable by the decedent on the installment method under section 453, for purposes of paragraph (2)—

(i) the second sentence of paragraph (2) shall be applied by inserting "(other than the obligor)" after "or a transfer to a person",

(ii) any cancellation of such an obligation shall be treated as a transfer, and

(iii) any cancellation of such an obligation occurring at the death of the decedent shall be treated as a transfer by the estate of the decedent (or, if held by a person other than the decedent before the death of the decedent, by such person).

(B) Face amount treated as fair market value in certain cases. In any case to which the first sentence of paragraph (2) applies by reason of subparagraph (A), if the decedent and the obligor were related persons (within the meaning of section 453(f)(1)), the fair market value of the installment obligation shall be treated as not less than its face amount.

(C) Cancellation includes becoming unenforceable. For purposes of subparagraph (A), an installment obligation which becomes unenforceable shall be treated as if it were canceled.

(b) Allowance of deductions and credit. The amount of any deduction specified in section 162, 163, 164, 212, or 611 (relating to deductions for expenses, interest, taxes, and depletion) or credit specified in section 27 (relating to foreign tax credit), in respect of a decedent which is not properly allowable to the decedent in respect of the taxable period in which falls the date of his death, or a prior period, shall be allowed:

(1) Expenses, interest, and taxes. In the case of a deduction specified in section 162, 163, 164, or 212 and a credit specified in section 27, in the taxable year when paid—

(A) to the estate of the decedent; except that

(B) if the estate of the decedent is not liable to discharge the obligation to which the deduction or credit relates, to the person who, by reason of the death of the decedent or by bequest, devise, or inheritance acquires, subject to such obligation, from the decedent an interest in property of the decedent.

(2) Depletion. In the case of the deduction specified in section 611, to the person described in subsection (a)(1)(A), (B), or (C) who, in the manner described therein, receives the income to which the deduction relates, in the taxable year when such income is received.

(c) Deduction for estate tax.
(1) Allowance of deduction.
(A) General rule. A person who includes an amount in gross income under subsection (a) shall be allowed, for the same taxable year, as a deduction an amount which bears the same ratio to the estate tax attributable to the net value for estate tax purposes of all the items described in subsection (a)(1) as the value for estate tax purposes of the items of gross income or portions thereof in respect of which such person included the amount in gross income (or the amount included in gross income, whichever is lower) bears to the value for estate tax purposes of all the items described in subsection (a)(1).

(B) Estates and trusts. In the case of an estate or trust, the amount allowed as a deduction under subparagraph (A) shall be computed by excluding from the gross income of the estate or trust the portion (if any) of the items described in subsection (a)(1) which is properly paid, credited, or to be distributed to the beneficiaries during the taxable year.

(2) Method of computing deduction. For purposes of paragraph (1)—

(A) The term "estate tax" means the tax imposed on the estate of the decedent or any prior decedent under section 2001 or 2101, reduced by the credits against such tax.

(B) The net value for estate tax purposes of all the items described in subsection (a)(1) shall be the excess of the value for estate tax purposes of all the items described in subsection (a)(1) over the deductions from the gross estate in respect of claims which represent the deductions and credit described in subsection (b). Such net value shall be determined with respect to the provisions of section 421(c)(2), relating to the deduction for estate tax with respect to stock options to which part II of subchapter D applies.

(C) The estate tax attributable to such net value shall be an amount equal to the excess of the estate tax over the estate tax computed without including in the gross estate such net value.

(3) Special rule for generation-skipping transfers. In the case of any tax imposed by chapter 13 on a taxable termination or a direct skip occurring as a result of the death of the transferor, there shall be allowed a deduction (under principles similar to the principles of this subsection) for the portion of such tax attributable to items of gross income of the trust which were not properly includible in the gross income of the trust for periods before the date of such termination.

• *Caution:* Code Sec. 691(c)(4), following, was amended by Sec. 402(a)(4), P.L. 108-311. These provisions generally sunset for tax years beginning after 12/31/2012. For specific sunset provisions see Sec. 303, P.L. 108-27, as amended by Sec. 102(a), P.L. 111-312, reproduced in history notes for this Code Sec.

(4) Coordination with capital gain provisions. For purposes of sections 1(h), 1201, 1202, and 1211, the amount taken into account with respect to any item described in subsection (a)(1) shall be reduced (but not below zero) by the amount of the deduction allowable under paragraph (1) of this subsection with respect to such item.

(d) Amounts received by surviving annuitant under joint and survivor annuity contract.
(1) Deduction for estate tax. For purposes of computing the deduction under subsection (c)(1)(A), amounts received by a surviving annuitant—

(A) as an annuity under a joint and survivor annuity contract where the decedent annuitant died after December 31, 1953, and after the annuity starting date (as defined in section 72(c)(4)), and

(B) during the surviving annuitant's life expectancy period,

shall, to the extent included in gross income under section 72, be considered as amounts included in gross income under subsection (a).

(2) Net value for estate tax purposes. In determining the net value for estate tax purposes under subsection (c)(2)(B) for purposes of this subsection, the value for estate tax purposes of the items described in paragraph (1) of this subsection shall be computed—

(A) by determining the excess of the value of the annuity at the date of the death of the deceased annuitant over the total amount excludable from the gross income of the surviving annuitant under section 72 during the surviving annuitant's life expectancy period, and

(B) by multiplying the figure so obtained by the ratio which the value of the annuity for estate tax purposes bears to the value of the annuity at the date of the death of the deceased.

(3) Definitions. For purposes of this subsection—

(A) The term "life expectancy period" means the period beginning with the first day of the first period for which an amount is received by the surviving annuitant under the contract and ending with the close of the taxable year with or in which falls the termination of the life expectancy of the surviving annuitant. For purposes of this subparagraph, the life expectancy of the surviving annuitant shall be determined, as of the date of the death of the deceased annuitant, with reference to actuarial tables prescribed by the Secretary.

(B) The surviving annuitant's expected return under the contract shall be computed, as of the death of the deceased annuitant, with reference to actuarial tables prescribed by the Secretary.

(e) Cross reference.

For application of this section to income in respect of a deceased partner, see section 753.

In 2010, P.L. 111-312, Sec. 102(a), substituted "December 31, 2010" for "December 31, 2008" in Sec. 303 of P.L. 108-27 [see below], effective as if included in the enactment of the Jobs and Growth Tax Relief Act of 2003, P.L. 108-27, 5/28/2003.

In 2006, P.L. 109-222, Sec. 102, substituted "December 31, 2010" for "December 31, 2008" in Sec. 303 of P.L. 108-27 [see below], effective 5/17/2006.

In 2004, P.L. 108-311, Sec. 402(a)(4), deleted "of any gain" after "the amount" in para. (c)(4), effective for tax. yrs. begin. after 12/31/2002 as if included in Sec. 302 of the Jobs and Growth Tax Relief Reconciliation Act of 2003, P.L. 108-27. For sunset provision, see Sec. 303 of P.L. 108-27, reproduced below. Sec. 302(f)(2) of P.L. 108-27 (as amended by Sec. 402(a)(6) of P.L. 108-311), provides:

"(2) Pass-thru entities. In the case of a pass-thru entity described in subparagraph (A), (B), (C), (D), (E), or (F) of section 1(h)(10) of the Internal Revenue Code of 1986, as amended by this Act, the amendments made by this section shall apply to taxable years ending after December 31, 2002; except that dividends received by such an entity on or before such date shall not be treated as qualified dividend income (as defined in section 1(h)(11)(B) of such Code, as added by this Act)."

Sec. 302(f)(2) of P.L. 108-27, prior to amendment by Sec. 402(a)(6) of P.L. 108-311, read as follows:

"(2) Regulated investment companies and real estate investment trusts. In the case of a regulated investment company or a real estate investment trust, the amendments made by this section shall apply to taxable years ending after December 31, 2002; except that dividends received by such a company or trust on or

Code Sec. 691 — Decedents

before such date shall not be treated as qualified dividend income (as defined in section 1(h)(11)(B) of the Internal Revenue Code of 1986, as added by this Act)."
— P.L. 108-27, Sec. 303, of P.L. 108-27 [as amended by Sec. 102, P.L. 109-222 and Sec. 102(a), 12/17/2010, see above] reads as follows:

"Sec. 303. Sunset of title. All provisions of, and amendments made by, this title [Secs. 301 and 302] shall not apply to taxable years beginning after December 31, 2012, and the Internal Revenue Code of 1986 shall be applied and administered to such years as if such provisions and amendments had never been enacted."

In 1997, P.L. 105-34, Sec. 1073(b)(1), deleted subpara. (c)(1)(C), effective for estates of decedents dying after 12/31/96.
Prior to deletion, subpara. (c)(1)(C) read as follows:

"(C) Excess retirement accumulation tax. For purposes of this subsection, no deduction shall be allowed for the portion of the estate tax attributable to the increase in such tax under section 4980A(d)."

In 1996, P.L. 104-188, Sec. 1401(b)(9), deleted para. (c)(5), effective for tax. yrs. begin. after 12/31/99, except as provided in Sec. 1401(c)(2), of this Act, which reads as follows:

"(2) Retention of certain transition rules. The amendments made by this section shall not apply to any distribution for which the taxpayer is eligible to elect the benefits of section 1122(h)(3) or (5) of the Tax Reform Act of 1986. Notwithstanding the preceding sentence, individuals who elect such benefits after December 31, 1999, shall not be eligible for 5-year averaging under section 402(d) of the Internal Revenue Code of 1986 (as in effect immediately before such amendments)."

Prior to deletion, para. (c)(5) read as follows:

"(5) Coordination with section 402(d). For purposes of section 402(d) (other than paragraph (1)(C) thereof), the total taxable amount of any lump sum distribution shall be reduced by the amount of the deduction allowable under paragraph (1) of this subsection which is attributable to the total taxable amount (determined without regard to this paragraph)."

— P.L. 104-188, Sec. 1704(t)(73), amended Sec. 521(b)(27) of P.L. 102-318 by substituting "Section 691(c)(5)" for "Section 691(c)", see below.

In 1993, P.L. 103-66, Sec. 13113(d)(4), substituted "1201, 1202, and 1211" for "1201, and 1211" in para. (c)(4), effective for stock issued after 8/10/93.

In 1992, P.L. 102-318, Sec. 521(b)(27), [as amended by Sec. 1704(t)(73) of P.L. 104-188, see above] substituted "402(d)" for "402(e)" in the heading and text of para. (c)(5), effective for distributions after 12/31/92. For special rule, see Sec. 521(e)(2) of this Act which reads as follows:

"(2) Special rule for partial distributions. For purposes of section 402(a)(5)(D)(i)(II) of the Internal Revenue Code of 1986 (as in effect before the amendments made by this section), a distribution before January 1, 1993, which is made before or at the same time as a series of periodic payments shall not be treated as one of such series if it is not substantially equal in amount to other payments in such series."

In 1990, P.L. 101-508, Sec. 11101(d)(4), substituted "1(h)" for "1(j)" in para. (c)(4), effective for tax. yrs. begin. after 12/31/90.

In 1989, P.L. 101-239, Sec. 7841(d)(3), substituted "paragraph (1)(C)" for "paragraph (1)(D)" in para. (c)(5), effective 12/19/89.

In 1988, P.L. 100-647, Sec. 1011A(g)(10), added subpara. (c)(1)(C), effective for distributions made after 12/31/86, except as provided in Secs. 1133(c)(2) and (c)(3) of P.L. 99-514, reproduced in note following Code Sec. 4980A.

In 1987, P.L. 100-203, Sec. 10202(c)(3), deleted "or 453A" each place it appeared in paras. (a)(4) and (a)(5), effective for dispositions in tax. yrs. begin. after 12/31/87.

In 1986, P.L. 99-514, Sec. 301(b)(8)(A), substituted "1(j), 1201, and 1211" for "1201, 1202, and 1211, and for purposes of section 57(a)(9)" in para. (c)(4) . . . Sec. 301(b)(8)(B), substituted "capital gain provisions" for "capital gain deduction, etc." in the heading of para. (c)(4), effective for tax. yrs. begin. after 12/31/86.

— P.L. 99-514, Sec. 1432(a)(3), amended para. (c)(3), effective for any generation-skipping transfers made after 10/22/86. For special rules see Sec. 1433(b)-(d) reproduced in note following Code Sec. 2601.
Prior to amendment, para. (c)(3) read as follows:

"(3) Special rule for generation-skipping transfers. For purposes of this section —

"(A) the tax imposed by section 2601 or any State inheritance tax described in section 2602(c)(5)(B) on any generation-skipping transfer shall be treated as a tax imposed by section 2001 on the estate of the deemed transferor (as defined in section 2612(a));

"(B) any property transferred in such a transfer shall be treated as if it were included in the gross estate of the deemed transferor at the value of such property taken into account for purposes of the tax imposed by section 2601; and

"(C) under regulations prescribed by the secretary, any item of gross income subject to the tax imposed under section 2601 shall be treated as income described in subsection (a) if such item is not properly includible in the gross income of the trust on or before the date of the generation-skipping transfer (within the meaning of section 2611(a)) and if such transfer occurs at or after the death of the deemed transferor (as so defined)."

In 1984, P.L. 98-369, Sec. 474(r)(18), substituted "section 27" for "section 33" each place it appeared in subsec. (b), effective for tax. yrs. begin. after 12/31/83, and for carrybacks from tax. yrs. begin. after 12/31/83.

In 1981, P.L. 97-34, Sec. 403(a)(2)(C), substituted "section 2602(c)(5)(B)" for "section 2602(c)(5)(C)" in subpara. (c)(3)(A), effective for the estates of decedents dying after 12/31/81.

— P.L. 97-34, Sec. 428, amended Sec. 2006(c)(2)(B) of P.L. 94-455 (as amended by Sec. 702(n)(1) of P.L. 95-600) by substituting "January 1, 1983" for "January 1, 1982" [see below].

In 1980, P.L. 96-471, Sec. 2(b)(5), substituted "reportable by the decedent on the installment method under section 453 or 453A" for "received by a decedent on the sale or other disposition of property, the income from which was properly reportable by the decedent on the installment basis under section 453", in para. (a)(4) and substituted "section 453B" for "453(d)" each time it appeared in para. (a)(4), effective for dispositions made after 10/19/80 in tax. yrs. end. after 10/19/80.

— P.L. 96-471, Sec. 3, added para. (a)(5), effective for decedents dying after 10/19/80.

— P.L. 96-223, Sec. 401(a), repealed Sec. 2005(a)(4) of P.L. 94-455 and the amendments made by Sec. 2005(a)(4), effective for decedents dying after '76 [see below]. Sec. 401(b) of P.L. 96-223 provides as follows:
"(b) Revival of prior law.

"Except to the extent necessary to carry out subsection (d), the Internal Revenue Code of 1954 shall be applied and administered as if the provisions repealed by subsection (a), and the amendments made by those provisions, had not been enacted."

— P.L. 96-222, Sec. 101(a)(8)(A), added para. (c)(5), presumably intended by Congress to be effective for the estates of decedents dying after 4/1/80 [Sec. 101(b)(1)(D)] although technically effective as if included in the provision of the Revenue Act of 1978 to which para. (c)(5) relates [Sec. 101(b)(2)].

In 1978, P.L. 95-600, Sec. 515(6), extended the effective date for amendments made by Sec. 2005(a)(4) of P.L. 94-455 to apply to estates of decedents dying after '79.
Prior to amendment the effective date applied to decedents dying after '76. [inoperative]

— P.L. 95-600, Sec. 702(b)(1), added para. (c)(4), effective for decedent's dying after 11/6/78.

— P.L. 95-600, Sec. 702(n)(1), substituted "June 11, 1976" for "April 30, 1976" each place it appeared in Sec. 2006(c) of P.L. 94-455 [see below].

In 1976, P.L. 94-455, Sec. 1901(a)(91), deleted "This subparagraph shall apply to the same taxable years, and to the same extent as is provided in section 683." at the end of subpara. (c)(1)(B), effective for tax. yrs. begin. after 12/31/76.

— P.L. 94-455, Sec. 1906(b)(13)(A), substituted "Secretary" for "Secretary or his delegate" each place it appeared in Code Sec. 691, effective for tax. yrs. begin. after 12/31/76.

— P.L. 94-455, Sec. 1951(b)(10)(A), deleted subsec. (e) . . . redesignated subsec. (f) as subsec. (e), effective for tax. yrs. begin. 12/31/76. Sec. 1951(b)(10)(B) of the Act provided as follows:

"(B) Savings provision. Notwithstanding subparagraph (A), any election made under section 691(e) to have subsection (a)(4) of such section apply in the case of an installment obligation shall continue to be effective with respect to taxable years beginning after December 31, 1976. Section 691(c) shall not apply in respect of any amount included in gross income by reason of the preceding sentence. The liability under bond filed under section 44(d) of the Internal Revenue Code of 1939 (or corresponding provisions of prior law) in respect of which such an election applies is hereby released with respect to taxable years to which such election applies."

Prior to deletion, subsec. (e) read as follows:
"(e) Installment obligations transmitted at death when prior law applied to transmission.

"(1) In general. Effective with respect to the first taxable year to which the election referred to in paragraph (2) applies and to each taxable year thereafter, subsection (a)(4) shall apply in the case of installment obligations in respect of which section 44(d) of the Internal Revenue Code of 1939 (or the corresponding provisions of prior law) did not apply by reason of the filing of the bond referred to in such section or provisions. Subsection (c) of this section shall not apply in respect of any amount included in gross income by reason of this paragraph.

"(2) Election. Installment obligations referred to in paragraph (1) may, at the election of the taxpayer holding such obligations, be treated as obligations in respect of which subsection (a)(4) applies. An election under this subsection for any taxable year shall be made not later than the time prescribed by law (including extensions thereof) for filing the return for such taxable year. The election shall be made in such manner as the Secretary or his delegate may by regulations prescribe.

"(3) Release of bond. The liability under any bond filed under section 44(d) of the Internal Revenue Code of 1939 (or the corresponding provisions of prior law) in respect of which an election under this subsection applies is hereby released with respect to taxable years to which such election applies."

— P.L. 94-455, Sec. 2005(a)(4)(A), amended subpara. (c)(2)(A), effective [see Sec. 515(6) of P.L. 95-600, above] for estates of decedents dying after '76, but was repealed by Sec. 401(a) of P.L. 96-223 [see above]. Subpara. (c)(2)(A) as amended by Sec. 2005(a)(4)(A) read as follows:

"(A) The term 'estate tax' means Federal and State estate taxes within the meaning of section 1023(f)(3))."

— P.L. 94-455, Sec. 2005(a)(4)(B), amended subpara. (c)(2)(C), effective [see Sec. 515(6) of P.L. 95-600, above] for estates of decedents dying after '76, but was repealed by Sec. 401(a) of P.L. 96-223 [see above]. Subpara. (c)(2)(C) as amended by Sec. 2005(a)(4)(B) read as follows:

"(C) The estate tax attributable to such net value shall be an amount which bears the same ratio to the estate tax as such net value bears to the value of the gross estate."

— P.L. 94-455, Sec. 2006(b)(3), added para. (c)(3), effective for generation-skipping transfers made after 6/11/76. Sec. 2006(c)(2) [as amended by Sec. 702(n)(1) of P.L. 95-600, see above] of this Act, made the following exceptions for generation-skipping transfers:

"(2) Exceptions. — The amendments made by this section shall not apply to any generation-skipping transfer —

"(A) under a trust which was irrevocable on June 11, 1976, but only to the extent that the transfer is not made out of corpus added to the trust after June 11, 1976, or

"(B) in the case of a decedent dying before January 1, 1983, pursuant to a will (or revocable trust) which was in existence on June 11, 1976, and was not amended at any time after that date in any respect which will result in the creation of, or increasing the amount of, any generation-skipping transfer.

For purposes of subparagraph (B), if the decedent on June 11, 1976, was under a mental disability to change the disposition of his property, the period set forth in such subparagraph shall not expire before the date which is 2 years after the date on which he first regains his competence to dispose of such property."

In 1964, P.L. 88-272, Sec. 221(c)(2), substituted "421(c)(2), relating to the deduction for estate tax with respect to stock options to which part II of subchapter D applies" for "421(d)(6)(B), relating to the deduction for estate tax with respect to restricted stock options" in subsec. (c)(2)(B), effective for tax. yrs. end. after 12/31/63.

—P.L. 88-570, Sec. 1, added subsec. (e) and redesignated subsec. (e) as (f).

Sec. 692. Income taxes of members of Armed Forces, astronauts, and victims of certain terrorist attacks on death.

(a) General rule.

In the case of any individual who dies while in active service as a member of the Armed Forces of the United States, if such death occurred while serving in a combat zone (as determined under section 112) or as a result of wounds, disease, or injury incurred while so serving—

(1) any tax imposed by this subtitle shall not apply with respect to the taxable year in which falls the date of his death, or with respect to any prior taxable year ending on or after the first day he so served in a combat zone after June 24, 1950; and

(2) any tax under this subtitle and under the corresponding provisions of prior revenue laws for taxable years preceding those specified in paragraph (1) which is unpaid at the date of his death (including interest, additions to the tax, and additional amounts) shall not be assessed, and if assessed the assessment shall be abated, and if collected shall be credited or refunded as an overpayment.

(b) Individuals in missing status.

For purposes of this section, in the case of an individual who was in a missing status within the meaning of section 6013(f)(3)(A), the date of his death shall be treated as being not earlier than the date on which a determination of his death is made under section 556 of title 37 of the United States Code. Except in the case of the combat zone designated for purposes of the Vietnam conflict, the preceding sentence shall not cause subsection (a)(1) to apply for any taxable year beginning more than 2 years after the date designated under section 112 as the date of termination of combatant activities in a combat zone.

(c) Certain military or civilian employees of the United States dying as a result of injuries.

(1) In general. In the case of any individual who dies while a military or civilian employee of the United States, if such death occurs as a result of wounds or injury which was incurred while the individual was a military or civilian employee of the United States and which was incurred in a terroristic or military action, any tax imposed by this subtitle shall not apply—

(A) with respect to the taxable year in which falls the date of his death, and

(B) with respect to any prior taxable year in the period beginning with the last taxable year ending before the taxable year in which the wounds or injury were incurred.

(2) Terroristic or military action. For purposes of paragraph (1), the term "terroristic or military action" means—

(A) any terroristic activity which a preponderance of the evidence indicates was directed against the United States or any of its allies, and

(B) any military action involving the Armed Forces of the United States and resulting from violence or aggression against the United States or any of its allies (or threat thereof).

For purposes of the preceding sentence, the term "military action" does not include training exercises.

(3) Treatment of multinational forces. For purposes of paragraph (2), any multinational force in which the United States is participating shall be treated as an ally of the United States.

(d) Individuals dying as a result of certain attacks.

(1) In general. In the case of a specified terrorist victim, any tax imposed by this chapter shall not apply—

(A) with respect to the taxable year in which falls the date of death, and

(B) with respect to any prior taxable year in the period beginning with the last taxable year ending before the taxable year in which the wounds, injury, or illness referred to in paragraph (3) were incurred.

(2) $10,000 minimum benefit. If, but for this paragraph, the amount of tax not imposed by paragraph (1) with respect to a specified terrorist victim is less than $10,000, then such victim shall be treated as having made a payment against the tax imposed by this chapter for such victim's last taxable year in an amount equal to the excess of $10,000 over the amount of tax not so imposed.

(3) Taxation of certain benefits. Subject to such rules as the Secretary may prescribe, paragraph (1) shall not apply to the amount of any tax imposed by this chapter which would be computed by only taking into account the items of income, gain, or other amounts attributable to—

(A) deferred compensation which would have been payable after death if the individual had died other than as a specified terrorist victim, or

(B) amounts payable in the taxable year which would not have been payable in such taxable year but for an action taken after September 11, 2001.

(4) Specified terrorist victim. For purposes of this subsection, the term "specified terrorist victim" means any decedent—

(A) who dies as a result of wounds or injury incurred as a result of the terrorist attacks against the United States on April 19, 1995, or September 11, 2001, or

(B) who dies as a result of illness incurred as a result of an attack involving anthrax occurring on or after September 11, 2001, and before January 1, 2002.

Such term shall not include any individual identified by the Attorney General to have been a participant or conspirator in any such attack or a representative of such an individual.

(5) Relief with respect to astronauts. The provisions of this subsection shall apply to any astronaut whose death occurs in the line of duty, except that paragraph (3)(B) shall be applied by using the date of the death of the astronaut rather than September 11, 2001.

In 2003, P.L. 108-121, Sec. 110(a)(1), added para. (d)(5) . . . Sec. 110(a)(3)(A), added ", astronauts," after "Forces" in the heading of Code Sec. 692, effective for any astronaut whose death occurs after 12/31/2002.

In 2002, P.L. 107-134, Sec. 101(a), added subsec. (d) . . . Sec. 101(c)(1), amended the heading of Code Sec. 692, effective for tax. yrs. end. before, on, or after 9/11/2001. Sec. 101(d)(2) of this Act, provides:

"(2) Waiver of limitations. If refund or credit of any overpayment of tax resulting from the amendments made by this section is prevented at any time before the close of the 1-year period beginning on the date of the enactment of this Act by the operation of any law or rule of law (including res judicata), such refund or

credit may nevertheless be made or allowed if claim therefor is filed before the close of such period."
Prior to amendment, the heading of Code Sec. 692 read as follows:
"SEC. 692. INCOME TAXES OF MEMBERS OF ARMED FORCES ON DEATH."
—P.L. 107-134, Sec. 113(b)(1), deleted "outside the United States" after "was incurred" in para. (c)(1) . . . Sec. 113(b)(2), deleted "sustained overseas" after "of injuries" in the heading of subsec. (c), effective for tax. yrs. end. on or after 9/11/2001.

In **1996**, P.L. 104-117, Sec. 1(a)(3) and (b), of this Act, regarding treatment of certain individuals performing services in certain hazardous duty areas, effective 11/21/95, provides:

"(a) General rule. For purposes of the following provisions of the Internal Revenue Code of 1986, a qualified hazardous duty area shall be treated in the same manner as if it were a combat zone (as determined under section 112 of such Code):

* * *

"(3) Section 692 (relating to income taxes of members of Armed Forces on death).

* * *

"(b) Qualified hazardous duty area. For purposes of this section, the term 'qualified hazardous duty area' means Bosnia and Herzegovina, Croatia, or Macedonia, if as of the date of the enactment [3/20/96] of this section any member of the Armed Forces of the United States is entitled to special pay under section 310 of title 37, United States Code (relating to special pay; duty subject to hostile fire or imminent danger) for services performed in such country. Such term includes any such country only during the period such entitlement is in effect. Solely for purposes of applying section 7508 of the Internal Revenue Code of 1986, in the case of an individual who is performing services as part of Operation Joint Endeavor outside the United States while deployed away from such individual's permanent duty station, the term 'qualified hazardous duty area' includes, during the period for which such entitlement is in effect, any area in which such services are performed."

In **1986**, P.L. 99-514, Sec. 1708(a)(2), amended the last sentence of subsec. (b), effective for tax. yrs. begin. after 12/31/82.
Prior to amendment, the last sentence of subsec. (b) read as follows:
"The preceding sentence shall not cause subsection (a)(1) to apply for any taxable year beginning—
"(1) after December 31, 1982, in the case of service in the combat zone designated for purposes of the Vietnam conflict, or
"(2) more than 2 years after the date designated under section 112 as the date of termination of combatant activities in that zone, in the case of any combat zone other than that referred to in paragraph (1)."

In **1984**, P.L. 98-369, Sec. 722(g)(1), amended Sec. 1(b) of P.L. 98-259, the effective date for changes made by Sec. 1(a) of P.L. 98-259, by substituting "November 17, 1978" for "December 31, 1979", see below.
—P.L. 98-369, Sec. 722(g)(2), substituted "as a result of wounds or injury which was incurred while the individual was a military or civilian employee of the United States and which was incurred" for "as a result of wounds or injury incurred" in para. (c)(1) . . . Sec. 722(g)(3), amended subpara. (c)(2)(A), effective for all tax. yrs. (whether begin. before, on, or after 4/10/84) for individuals dying after 11/17/78, as a result of wounds or injuries incurred after 11/17/78. Sec. 722(g)(4) and (g)(5)(B) of this Act provide:
"(4) Treatment of director general of multinational force. For purposes of section 692(c) of the Internal Revenue Code of 1954, the Director General of the Multinational Force and Observers in the Sinai who died on February 15, 1984, shall be treated as if he were a civilian employee of the United States while he served as such Director General."

* * *

"(B) Statute of limitations waived. Notwithstanding section 6511 of the Internal Revenue Code of 1954, the time for filing a claim for credit or refund of any overpayment of tax resulting from the amendments made by this subsection shall not expire before the date 1 year after the date of the enactment of this Act."
Prior to amendment, subpara. (c)(2)(A) read as follows:
"(A) any terrorist activity directed against the United States or any of its allies, and"
—P.L. 98-259, Sec. 1(a), added subsec. (c), effective for all tax. yrs. (whether begin. before, on, or after 4/10/84) for individuals dying after 11/17/78, as a result of wounds or injuries incurred after 11/17/78. Sec. 1(b)(2) of this Act provides:
"(2) Statute of limitations waived. Notwithstanding section 6511 of the Internal Revenue Code of 1954, the time for filing a claim for credit or refund of any overpayment of tax resulting from the amendment made by subsection (a) shall not expire before the date 1 year after the date of the enactment of this Act."

In **1983**, P.L. 97-448, Sec. 307(b), substituted "December 31, 1982" for "January 2, 1978" in para. (b)(1), effective 1/12/83.

In **1976**, P.L. 94-569, Sec. 3(c), amended the second sentence of subsec. (b), effective 10/20/76.
Prior to amendment, the second sentence of subsec. (b) read as follows:
"The preceding sentence shall not cause subsection (a)(1) to apply for any taxable year beginning more than 2 years after—
"(1) the date of the enactment of this subsection, in the case of service in the combat zone designated for purposes of the Vietnam conflict, or
"(2) the date designated under section 112 as the date of termination of combatant activities in that zone, in the case of any combat zone other than that referred to in paragraph (1)."
—P.L. 94-455, Sec. 1901(a)(92), amended the heading of Code Sec. 692.
Prior to amendment, the heading of Code Sec. 692 read as follows:

"Sec. 692. Income taxes on members of Armed Forces on death."
In **1975**, P.L. 93-597, Sec. 4(a), substituted "(a) General rule.—In the case of any individual who dies" for "In the case of any individual who dies during an induction period (as defined in section 112(c)(5))", and added new subsec. (b), effective for tax. yrs. end. on or after 2/28/61.
—P.L. 93-597, Sec. 4(c), of this Act provides:
"(c) Refunds and credits resulting from section 692 of Code. If the refund or credit of any overpayment for any taxable year ending on or after February 28, 1961, resulting from the application of section 692 of the Internal Revenue Code of 1954 (as amended by subsection (a) of this section) is prevented at any time before the expiration of one year after the date of the enactment of this Act by the operation of any law or rule of law, but would not have been so prevented if claim for refund or credit therefor were made on the due date for the return for the taxable year of his death (or any later year), refund or credit of such overpayment may, nevertheless, be made or allowed if claim therefor is filed before the expiration of such one-year period."

Subchapter K.—Partners and Partnerships

Part

I. Determination of tax liability.
II. Contributions, distributions, and transfers.
III. Definitions.
IV. Special rules for electing large partnerships.

In **1997**, P.L. 105-34, Sec. 1221(b), added item for Part IV.
In **1976**, P.L. 99-455, Sec. 1901(b)(23), deleted the item for Part IV.

PART I.—DETERMINATION OF TAX LIABILITY

Sec.
701. Partners, not partnership, subject to tax.
702. Income and credits of partner.
703. Partnership computations.
704. Partner's distributive share.
705. Determination of basis of partner's interest.
706. Taxable years of partner and partnership.
707. Transactions between partner and partnership.
708. Continuation of partnership.
709. Treatment of organization and syndication fees.

In **1976**, P.L. 94-455, Sec. 213(b)(2), added the item for 709.

Sec. 701. Partners, not partnership, subject to tax.

A partnership as such shall not be subject to the income tax imposed by this chapter. Persons carrying on business as partners shall be liable for income tax only in their separate or individual capacities.

Sec. 702. Income and credits of partner.

(a) General rule.

In determining his income tax, each partner shall take into account separately his distributive share of the partnership's—

(1) gains and losses from sales or exchanges of capital assets held for not more than 1 year,

(2) gains and losses from sales or exchanges of capital assets held for more than 1 year,

(3) gains and losses from sales or exchanges of property described in section 1231 (relating to certain property used in a trade or business and involuntary conversions),

(4) charitable contributions (as defined in section 170(c)),

• *Caution:* Code Sec. 702(a)(5), following, was amended by Sec. 302(e)(8), P.L. 108-27. These provisions generally sunset for tax years beginning after 12/31/2012. For specific sunset provisions see Sec. 303, P.L. 108-27 reproduced in history notes for this Code Sec.

(5) dividends with respect to which section 1(h)(11) or part VIII of subchapter B applies,

(6) taxes, described in section 901, paid or accrued to foreign countries and to possessions of the United States,

(7) other items of income, gain, loss, deduction, or credit, to the extent provided by regulations prescribed by the Secretary, and

(8) taxable income or loss, exclusive of items requiring separate computation under other paragraphs of this subsection.

(b) Character of items constituting distributive share.

The character of any item of income, gain, loss, deduction, or credit included in a partner's distributive share under paragraphs (1) through (7) of subsection (a) shall be determined as if such item were realized directly from the source from which realized by the partnership, or incurred in the same manner as incurred by the partnership.

(c) Gross income of a partner.

In any case where it is necessary to determine the gross income of a partner for purposes of this title, such amount shall include his distributive share of the gross income of the partnership.

(d) Cross reference.

For rules relating to procedures for determining the tax treatment of partnership items see subchapter C of chapter 63 (section 6221 and following).

In 2010, P.L. 111-312, Sec. 102(a), substituted "December 31, 2012" for "December 31, 2010" in Sec. 303, P.L. 108-27 [see below], effective as if included in the enactment of P.L. 108-27, 5/28/2003.

In 2006, P.L. 109-222, Sec. 102, substituted "December 31, 2010" for "December 31, 2008" in Sec. 303 of P.L. 108-27 [see below], effective 5/17/2006.

In 2004, P.L. 108-311, Sec. 402(a)(6), of this Act [which amended Sec. 302(f)(2) of P.L. 108-27, see below], provides:

"(2) Pass-thru entities. In the case of a pass-thru entity described in subparagraph (A), (B), (C), (D), (E), or (F) of section 1(h)(10) of the Internal Revenue Code of 1986, as amended by this Act, the amendments made by this section shall apply to taxable years ending after December 31, 2002; except that dividends received by such an entity on or before such date shall not be treated as qualified dividend income (as defined in section 1(h)(11)(B) of such Code, as added by this Act)."

In 2003, P.L. 108-27, Sec. 302(e)(8), amended para. (a)(5), effective for tax. yrs. begin. after 12/31/2002. Sec. 302(f)(2), of this Act [prior to amendment by Sec. 402(a)(6) of P.L. 108-311 see above] provides:

"(2) Regulated investment companies and real estate investment trusts. In the case of a regulated investment company or a real estate investment trust, the amendments made by this section shall apply to taxable years ending after December 31, 2002; except that dividends received by such a company or trust on or before such date shall not be treated as qualified dividend income (as defined in section 1(h)(11)(B) of the Internal Revenue Code of 1986, as added by this Act)."
Prior to amendment, para. (a)(5) read as follows:

"(5) dividends with respect to which there is a deduction under part VIII of subchapter B,"

—P.L. 108-27, Sec. 303, of this Act [as amended by Sec. 102 of P.L. 109-222, and Sec. 102(a), P.L. 111-312, see above], reads as follows:

"SEC. 303. SUNSET OF TITLE. All provisions of, and amendments made by, this title [Secs. 301 and 302] shall not apply to taxable years beginning after December 31, 2012, and the Internal Revenue Code of 1986 shall be applied and administered to such years as if such provisions and amendments had never been enacted."

In 1986, P.L. 99-514, Sec. 612(b)(5), amended para. (a)(5), effective for tax. yrs. begin. after 12/31/86.
Prior to amendment, para. (a)(5) read as follows:

"(5) dividends or interest with respect to which there is an exclusion under section 116 or 128, or a deduction under part VIII of subchapter B,"

In 1984, P.L. 98-369, Sec. 1001(b)(9), substituted "6 months" for "1 year" each place it appeared in paras. (a)(1) and (2), effective for property acquired after 6/22/84 and before 1/1/88.

In 1983, P.L. 97-448, Sec. 103(a)(4), amended para. (a)(5), effective for tax. yrs. end. after 9/30/81.
Prior to amendment, para. (a)(5) read as follows:

"(5) dividends or interest with respect to which there is provided an exclusion under section 116 or a deduction under part VIII of subchapter B,"

In 1982, P.L. 97-248, Sec. 402(c)(1), added subsec. (d), effective for partnership tax. yrs. begin. after 9/3/82. Sec. 407(a)(3) of this Act provides:

"(3) The amendments made by sections 402, 403, and 404 [of this Act] apply to any partnership taxable year (or in the case of section 6232 of such Code, to any period) ending after the date of the enactment of this Act [9/3/82] if the partnership, each partner, and each indirect partner requests such application and the Secretary of the Treasury or his delegate consents to such application."

In 1981, P.L. 97-34, Sec. 301(b)(5), added "or 128" after "116" in para. (a)(5) (as in effect for tax. yrs. begin. in 1981), effective for tax. yrs. end. after 9/30/81.

—P.L. 97-34, Sec. 301(b)(6)(C), added "or interest" after "dividends" in para. (a)(5) (as in effect for tax. yrs. begin. after 12/31/81), effective for tax. yrs. begin. after 12/31/81.

—P.L. 97-34, Sec. 302(b)(1), amended the effective date for changes made by Sec. 404(b)(5) of P.L. 96-223 from tax. yrs. begin. after 12/31/80 and before 1/1/83 to tax. yrs. begin. after 12/31/80 and before 1/1/82 [see below].

In 1980, P.L. 96-223, Sec. 404(b)(5), added "or interest" after "dividends" in para. (a)(5), effective [as amended by Sec. 302(b)(1) of P.L. 97-34, see above] for tax. yrs. begin. after 12/31/80 and before 1/1/82.

In 1976, P.L. 94-455, Sec. 1402(b)(1)(L), substituted "9 months" for "6 months" in paras. (a)(1) and (a)(2), effective for tax. yrs. begin. in 1977.

—P.L. 94-455, Sec. 1402(b)(2), of the Act substituted "1 year" for "9 months" in paras. (a)(1) and (a)(2), for tax. yrs. begin. after 12/31/77.

—P.L. 94-455, Sec. 1402(c), of this Act provided a transitional rule for certain installment obligations (see note at Code Sec. 1222).

—P.L. 94-455, Sec. 1901(b)(1)(I)(i), deleted para. (a)(7), and redesignated paras. (a)(8) and (a)(9) as paras. (a)(7) and (a)(8), effective for tax. yrs. begin. after 1976.

Prior to amendment para. (a)(7) read as follows:

"(7) partially tax-exempt interest on obligations of the United States or on obligations of instrumentalities of the United States as described in section 35 or section 242 (but, if the partnership elects to amortize the premiums on bonds as provided in section 171, the amount received on such obligations shall be reduced by the reduction provided under section 171(a)(3))."

—P.L. 94-455, Sec. 1901(b)(1)(I)(ii), substituted "paragraphs (1) and (7)" for "paragraphs (1) and (8)" in subsec. (b), effective for tax. yrs. begin. after 1976.

—P.L. 94-455, Sec. 1906(b)(13)(A), substituted "Secretary" for "Secretary, or his delegate" in para. (a)(7), (as designated by Sec. 1901(b)(1)(I)(i) of this Act), effective for tax. yrs. begin. after 12/31/76.

In 1964, P.L. 88-272, Sec. 201(d)(7), deleted "a credit under section 34," preceding "an exclusion" in para. (a)(5), effective for dividends received after 12/31/64 in tax. yrs. end. after 12/31/64.

Sec. 703. Partnership computations.
(a) Income and deductions.

The taxable income of a partnership shall be computed in the same manner as in the case of an individual except that—

(1) the items described in section 702(a) shall be separately stated, and

(2) the following deductions shall not be allowed to the partnership:

(A) the deductions for personal exemptions provided in section 151,

(B) the deduction for taxes provided in section 164(a) with respect to taxes, described in section 901, paid or accrued to foreign countries and to possessions of the United States,

(C) the deduction for charitable contributions provided in section 170,

(D) the net operating loss deduction provided in section 172,

(E) the additional itemized deductions for individuals provided in part VII of subchapter B (sec. 211 and following), and

(F) the deduction for depletion under section 611 with respect to oil and gas wells.

(b) Elections of the partnership.

Any election affecting the computation of taxable income derived from a partnership shall be made by the partnership, except that any election under—

(1) subsection (b)(5) or (c)(3) of section 108 (relating to income from discharge of indebtedness),

(2) section 617 (relating to deduction and recapture of certain mining exploration expenditures), or

(3) section 901 (relating to taxes of foreign countries and possessions of the United States),

shall be made by each partner separately.

In 1993, P.L. 103-66, Sec. 13150(c)(9), substituted "subsection (b)(5) or (c)(3)" for "subsection (b)(5)" in para. (b)(1), effective for discharges after 12/31/92, in tax. yrs. end. after 12/31/92.

In 1988, P.L. 100-647, Sec. 1008(i), deleted "or (d)(4)" after "(b)(5)" in para. (b)(1), effective for discharges after 12/31/86.

In 1986, P.L. 99-514, Sec. 511(d)(2)(B), [sic (c)(2)(B)], deleted para. (b)(3) and redesignated paras. (b)(4) and (b)(5) as (b)(3) and (b)(4) . . . Sec. 701(e)(4)(E), deleted para. (b)(1) and redesignated paras. (b)(2), (b)(3) and (b)(4) as (b)(1), (b)(2) and (b)(3), effective for tax. yrs. begin. after 12/31/86.

Prior to deletion, para. (b)(3) read as follows:

"(3) section 163(d) (relating to limitation of interest on investment indebtedness),"

Prior to deletion, para. (b)(1) read as follows:

"(1) section 57(c) (defining net lease),"

In 1980, P.L. 96-589, Sec. 2(e)(1), amended subsec. (b), effective for any transaction which occurs after 12/31/80, other than a transaction which occurs in a proceeding in a bankruptcy case or similar judicial proceeding (or in a proceeding under the Bankruptcy Act) commencing on or before 12/31/80. Sec. 7(g) of this Act provides definitions of the above as follows:

"(g) Definitions.

"For purposes of this section—

"(1) Bankruptcy case. The term 'bankruptcy case' means any case under title 11 of the United States Code (as recodified by P.L. 95-598).

"(2) Similar judicial proceeding. The term 'similar judicial proceeding' means a receivership, foreclosure, or similar proceeding in a Federal or State court (as modified by section 368(a)(3)(D) of the Internal Revenue Code of 1954)."

Prior to amendment, subsec. (b) read as follows:

"(b) Elections of the partnership.

"Any election affecting the computation of taxable income derived from a partnership shall be made by the partnership, except that the election under section 901, relating to taxes of foreign countries and possessions of the United States, and any election under section 617 (relating to deduction and recapture of certain mining exploration expenditures) under section 57(c) (relating to definition of net lease) or under section 163(d) (relating to limitation on interest on investment indebtedness) shall be made by each partner separately."

In 1977, P.L. 95-30, Sec. 101(d)(10), deleted subpara. (a)(2)(A) and redesignated subparas. (a)(2)(B) through (a)(2)(G) as subparas. (a)(2)(A) through (a)(2)(F), effective for tax. yrs. begin. after 12/31/76.

Prior to deletion, subpara. (a)(2)(A) read as follows:

"(A) the standard deduction provided in section 141,"

In 1976, P.L. 94-455, Sec. 1901(b)(21)(F), deleted "under section 615 (relating to pre-1970 exploration expenditures)," after "and any election" in subsec. (b), effective for tax. yrs. begin. after 12/31/76.

—P.L. 94-455, Sec. 2115(c)(2), substituted "wells" for "production subject to the provisions of section 613A(c)" in subpara. (a)(2)(G), effective 1/1/75, for tax. yrs. end. after 12/31/74.

In 1975, P.L. 94-12, Sec. 501(b)(3), deleted "and" at the end of subpara. (a)(2)(E), substituted ", and" for the period at the end of subpara. (a)(2)(F), and added new subpara. (a)(2)(G), effective 1/1/75 for tax. yrs. end. after 12/31/74.

In 1971, P.L. 92-178, Sec. 304(c)(1), substituted a comma for "or" after "(relating to pre-1970 exploration expenditures)" in subsec. (b) . . . Sec. 304(c)(2), added "under section 57(c) (relating to definition of net lease), or under section 163(d) (relating to limitation on interest on investment indebtedness)" after "(relating to deduction and recapture of certain mining exploration expenditures)" in subsec. (b).

In 1969, P.L. 91-172, Sec. 504(c)(3), substituted "(relating to pre-1970 exploration expenditures) or under section 617 (relating to deduction and recapture of certain mining exploration expenditures)" for "(relating to exploration expenditures) or under section 617 (relating to additional exploration expenditures in the case of domestic mining)" in subsec. (b), effective for exploration expenditures paid or incurred after 12/31/69.

In 1966, P.L. 89-570, Sec. 2(b), added "and any election under section 615 (relating to exploration expenditures) or under section 617 (relating to additional exploration expenditures in the case of domestic mining)," after "United States," in subsec. (b), effective for tax. yrs. end. after 9/12/66, but only for expenditures paid or incurred after 9/12/66.

Sec. 704. Partner's distributive share.

(a) Effect of partnership agreement.

A partner's distributive share of income, gain, loss, deduction, or credit shall, except as otherwise provided in this chapter, be determined by the partnership agreement.

(b) Determination of distributive share.

A partner's distributive share of income, gain, loss, deduction, or credit (or item thereof) shall be determined in accordance with the partner's interest in the partnership (determined by taking into account all facts and circumstances), if—

(1) the partnership agreement does not provide as to the partner's distributive share of income, gain, loss, deduction, or credit (or item thereof), or

(2) the allocation to a partner under the agreement of income, gain, loss, deduction, or credit (or item thereof) does not have substantial economic effect.

(c) Contributed property.

(1) In general. Under regulations prescribed by the Secretary—

(A) income, gain, loss, and deduction with respect to property contributed to the partnership by a partner shall be shared among the partners so as to take account of the variation between the basis of the property to the partnership and its fair market value at the time of contribution,

(B) if any property so contributed is distributed (directly or indirectly) by the partnership (other than to the contributing partner) within 7 years of being contributed—

(i) the contributing partner shall be treated as recognizing gain or loss (as the case may be) from the sale of such property in an amount equal to the gain or loss which would have been allocated to such partner under subparagraph (A) by reason of the variation described in subparagraph (A) if the property had been sold at its fair market value at the time of the distribution,

(ii) the character of such gain or loss shall be determined by reference to the character of the gain or loss which would have resulted if such property had been sold by the partnership to the distributee, and

(iii) appropriate adjustments shall be made to the adjusted basis of the contributing partner's interest in the partnership and to the adjusted basis of the property distributed to reflect any gain or loss recognized under this subparagraph, and

(C) if any property so contributed has a built-in loss—

(i) such built-in loss shall be taken into account only in determining the amount of items allocated to the contributing partner, and

(ii) except as provided in regulations, in determining the amount of items allocated to other partners, the basis of the contributed property in the hands of the partnership shall be treated as being equal to its fair market value at the time of contribution.

For purposes of subparagraph (C), the term "built-in loss" means the excess of the adjusted basis of the property (determined without regard to subparagraph (C)(ii)) over its fair market value at the time of contribution.

(2) Special rule for distributions where gain or loss would not be recognized outside partnerships. Under regulations prescribed by the Secretary, if—

(A) property contributed by a partner (hereinafter referred to as the "contributing partner") is distributed by the partnership to another partner, and

(B) other property of a like kind (within the meaning of section 1031) is distributed by the partnership to the contributing partner not later than the earlier of—

(i) the 180th day after the date of the distribution described in subparagraph (A), or

(ii) the due date (determined with regard to extensions) for the contributing partner's return of the tax imposed by this chapter for the taxable year in which the distribution described in subparagraph (A) occurs, then to the extent of the value of the property described in subparagraph (B), paragraph (1)(B) shall be applied as if the contributing partner had contributed to the partnership the property described in subparagraph (B).

(3) Other rules. Under regulations prescribed by the Secretary, rules similar to the rules of paragraph (1) shall apply to contributions by a partner (using the cash receipts and disbursements method of accounting) of accounts payable and other accrued but unpaid items. Any reference in paragraph (1) or (2) to the contributing partner shall be treated as including a reference to any successor of such partner.

(d) Limitation on allowance of losses.

A partner's distributive share of partnership loss (including capital loss) shall be allowed only to the extent of the adjusted basis of such partner's interest in the partnership at the end of the partnership year in which such loss occurred. Any excess of such loss over such basis shall be allowed as a deduction at the end of the partnership year in which such excess is repaid to the partnership.

(e) Family partnerships.

(1) Recognition of interest created by purchase or gift. A person shall be recognized as a partner for purposes of this subtitle if he owns a capital interest in a partnership in which capital is a material income-producing factor, whether or not such interest was derived by purchase or gift from any other person.

(2) Distributive share of donee includible in gross income. In the case of any partnership interest created by gift, the distributive share of the donee under the partnership agreement shall be includible in his gross income, except to the extent that such share is determined without allowance of reasonable compensation for services rendered to the partnership by the donor, and except to the extent that the portion of such share attributable to donated capital is proportionately greater than the share of the donor attributable to the donor's capital. The distributive share of a partner in the earnings of the partnership shall not be diminished because of absence due to military service.

(3) Purchase of interest by member of family. For purposes of this section, an interest purchased by one member of a family from another shall be considered to be created by gift from the seller, and the fair market value of the purchased interest shall be considered to be donated capital. The "family" of any individual shall include only his spouse, ancestors, and lineal descendants, and any trusts for the primary benefit of such persons.

(f) Cross reference.

For rules in the case of the sale, exchange, liquidation, or reduction of a partner's interest, see section 706(c)(2).

In 2004, P.L. 108-357, Sec. 833(a), deleted "and" at the end of subpara. (c)(1)(A), substituted ", and" for the period at the end of subpara. (c)(1)(B), and added subpara. (c)(1)(C), effective for contributions made after 10/22/2004.
In 1997, P.L. 105-34, Sec. 1063(a), substituted "7 years" for "5 years" in subpara. (c)(1)(B), effective for property contributed to a partnership after 6/8/97. Sec. 1063(b)(2) of this Act reads as follows:

"(2) Binding contracts. The amendments made by subsection (a) shall not apply to any property contributed pursuant to a written binding contract in effect on June 8, 1997, and at all times thereafter before such contribution if such contract provides for the contribution of a fixed amount of property."
In 1992, P.L. 102-486, Sec. 1937(b)(1), substituted "is distributed (directly or indirectly)" for "is distributed" in subpara. (c)(1)(B), effective for distributions on or after 6/25/92.
In 1989, P.L. 101-239, Sec. 7642(a), amended subsec. (c), effective for property contributed to a partnership after 10/3/89 in tax. yrs. end. after 10/3/89.
Prior to amendment, subsec. (c) read as follows:
"(c) Contributed property.
"Under regulations prescribed by the Secretary, income, gain, loss, and deduction with respect to property contributed to the partnership by a partner shall be shared among partners so as to take account of the variation between the basis of the property to the partnership and its fair market value at the time of contribution. Under regulations prescribed by the Secretary, rules similar to the rules of the preceding sentence shall apply to contributions by a partner (using the cash receipts and disbursements method of accounting) of accounts payable and other accrued but unpaid items."
In 1984, P.L. 98-369, Sec. 71(a), amended subsec. (c), effective for property contributed to the partnership after 3/31/84, in tax. yrs. end. after 3/31/84.
Prior to amendment, subsec. (c) read as follows:
"(c) Contributed property.
"(1) General rule. In determining a partner's distributive share of items described in section 702(a), depreciation, depletion, or gain or loss with respect to property contributed to the partnership by a partner shall, except to the extent otherwise provided in paragraph (2) or (3), be allocated among the partners in the same manner as if such property had been purchased by the partnership.
"(2) Effect of partnership agreement. If the partnership agreement so provides, depreciation, depletion, or gain or loss with respect to property contributed to the partnership by a partner shall, under regulations prescribed by the Secretary, be shared among the partners so as to take account of the variation between the basis of the property to the partnership and its fair market value at the time of contribution.
"(3) Undivided interests. If the partnership agreement does not provide otherwise, depreciation, depletion, or gain or loss with respect to undivided interests in property contributed to a partnership shall be determined as though such undivided interests had not been contributed to the partnership. This paragraph shall apply only if all the partners had undivided interests in such property prior to contribution and their interests in the capital and profits of the partnership correspond with such undivided interests."
In 1978, P.L. 95-600, Sec. 201(b)(1), deleted the last two sentences of subsec. (d), effective for tax. yrs. begin. after 12/31/78. Sec. 201(b)(2) of this Act provides:

"(2) Transitional rule. In the case of a loss which was not allowed for any taxable year by reason of the last 2 sentences of section 704(d) of the Internal Revenue Code of 1954 (as in effect before the date of the enactment of this Act), such loss shall be treated as a deduction (subject to section 465(a) of such Code) for the first taxable year beginning after December 31, 1978. Section 465(a) of such Code (as amended by this section) shall not apply with respect to partnership liabilities to which the last 2 sentences of section 704(d) of such Code (as in effect on the day before the date of enactment of this Act) did not apply because of the provisions of section 213(f)(2) of the Tax Reform Act of 1976."
Prior to deletion, the last two sentences of subsec. (d) read as follows:
"For purposes of this subsection, the adjusted basis of any partner's interest in the partnership shall not include any portion of any partnership liability with respect to which the partner has no personal liability. The preceding sentence shall not apply with respect to any activity to the extent that section 465 (relating to limiting deductions to amounts at risk in case of certain activities) applies, nor shall it apply to any partnership the principal activity of which is investing in real property (other than mineral property)."
In 1976, P.L. 94-455, Sec. 213(c)(2), substituted "except as otherwise provided in the chapter" for "except as otherwise provided in this section" in subsec. (a), effective for partnership tax. yrs. begin. after 12/31/75.
—P.L. 94-455, Sec. 213(c)(3)(A), added subsec. (f), effective for partnership tax. yrs. begin. after 12/31/75.
—P.L. 94-455, Sec. 213(d), amended subsec. (b), effective for partnership tax. yrs. begin. after 12/31/75.
Prior to amendment, subsec. (b) read as follows:
"(b) Distributive share determined by income or loss ratio.
"A partner's distributive share of any item of income, gain, loss, deduction, or credit shall be determined in accordance with his distributive share of taxable income or loss of the partnership, as described in section 702(a)(9), for the taxable year, if—
"(1) the partnership agreement does not provide as to the partner's distributive share of such item, or
"(2) the principal purpose of any provision in the partnership agreement with respect to the partner's distributive share of such item is the avoidance or evasion of any tax imposed by this subtitle."
—P.L. 94-445, Sec. 213(e), added the last two sentences to subsec. (d), effective for liabilities incurred after 12/31/76.
—P.L. 94-455, Sec. 1906(b)(13)(A), substituted "Secretary" for "Secretary or his delegate" in para. (c)(2), effective for tax. yrs. begin. after 12/31/76.

Sec. 705. Determination of basis of partner's interest.
(a) General rule.

The adjusted basis of a partner's interest in a partnership shall, except as provided in subsection (b), be the basis of such interest determined under section 722 (relating to contributions to a partnership) or section 742 (relating to transfers of partnership interests)—

(1) increased by the sum of his distributive share for the taxable year and prior taxable years of—

(A) taxable income of the partnership as determined under section 703(a),

(B) income of the partnership exempt from tax under this title, and

(C) the excess of the deductions for depletion over the basis of the property subject to depletion;

(2) decreased (but not below zero) by distributions by the partnership as provided in section 733 and by the sum of his distributive share for the taxable year and prior taxable years of—

(A) losses of the partnership, and

(B) expenditures of the partnership not deductible in computing its taxable income and not properly chargeable to capital account; and

(3) decreased (but not below zero) by the amount of the partner's deduction for depletion for any partnership oil and gas property to the extent such deduction does not exceed the proportionate share of the adjusted basis of such property allocated to such partner under section 613A(c)(7)(D).

(b) Alternative rule.

The Secretary shall prescribe by regulations the circumstances under which the adjusted basis of a partner's interest in a partnership may be determined by reference to his proportionate share of the adjusted basis of partnership property upon a termination of the partnership.

In **1984**, P.L. 98-369, Sec. 722(e)(1), amended para. (a)(3), effective 1/1/75. Prior to amendment, para. (a)(3) read as follows:

"(3) decreased (but not below zero), by the amount of the partner's deduction for depletion under section 611 with respect to oil and gas wells."

In **1976**, P.L. 94-455, Sec. 1906(b)(13)(A), substituted "Secretary" for "Secretary or his delegate" in subsec. (b), for tax. yrs. begin. after 12/31/76.

—P.L. 94-455, Sec. 2115(c)(3)(A), deleted "and" at the end of subpara. (a)(1)(C)
. . . Sec. 2115(c)(3)(B), substituted "; and" for the period at the end of para. (a)(2)
. . . Sec. 2115(c)(3)(C), added para. (a)(3), effective 1/1/75, and for tax. yrs. end. after 12/31/74.

Sec. 706. Taxable years of partner and partnership.

(a) Year in which partnership income is includible.

In computing the taxable income of a partner for a taxable year, the inclusions required by section 702 and section 707(c) with respect to a partnership shall be based on the income, gain, loss, deduction, or credit of the partnership for any taxable year of the partnership ending within or with the taxable year of the partner.

(b) Taxable year.

(1) **Partnership's taxable year.**

(A) Partnership treated as taxpayer. The taxable year of a partnership shall be determined as though the partnership were a taxpayer.

(B) Taxable year determined by reference to partners. Except as provided in subparagraph (C), a partnership shall not have a taxable year other than—

(i) the majority interest taxable year (as defined in paragraph (4)),

(ii) if there is no taxable year described in clause (i), the taxable year of all the principal partners of the partnership, or

(iii) if there is no taxable year described in clause (i) or (ii), the calendar year unless the Secretary by regulations prescribes another period.

(C) Business purpose. A partnership may have a taxable year not described in subparagraph (B) if it establishes, to the satisfaction of the Secretary, a business purpose therefor. For purposes of this subparagraph, any deferral of income to partners shall not be treated as a business purpose.

(2) **Partner's taxable year.** A partner may not change to a taxable year other than that of a partnership in which he is a principal partner unless he establishes, to the satisfaction of the Secretary, a business purpose therefor.

(3) **Principal partner.** For the purpose of this subsection, a principal partner is a partner having an interest of 5 percent or more in partnership profits or capital.

(4) **Majority interest taxable year; limitation on required changes.**

(A) Majority interest taxable year defined. For purposes of paragraph (1)(B)(i)—

(i) In general. The term "majority interest taxable year" means the taxable year (if any) which, on each testing day, constituted the taxable year of 1 or more partners having (on such day) an aggregate interest in partnership profits and capital of more than 50 percent.

(ii) Testing days. The testing days shall be—

(I) the 1st day of the partnership taxable year (determined without regard to clause (i)), or

(II) the days during such representative period as the Secretary may prescribe.

(B) Further change not required for 3 years. Except as provided in regulations necessary to prevent the avoidance of this section, if, by reason of paragraph (1)(B)(i), the taxable year of a partnership is changed, such partnership shall not be required to change to another taxable year for either of the 2 taxable years following the year of change.

(5) **Application with other sections.** Except as provided in regulations, for purposes of determining the taxable year to which a partnership is required to change by reason of this subsection, changes in taxable years of other persons required by this subsection, section 441(i), section 584(h), section 644, or section 1378(a) shall be taken into account.

(c) Closing of partnership year.

(1) **General rule.** Except in the case of a termination of a partnership and except as provided in paragraph (2) of this subsection, the taxable year of a partnership shall not close as the result of the death of a partner, the entry of a new partner, the liquidation of a partner's interest in the partnership, or the sale or exchange of a partner's interest in the partnership.

(2) **Treatment of dispositions.**

(A) Disposition of entire interest. The taxable year of a partnership shall close with respect to a partner whose entire interest in the partnership terminates (whether by reason of death, liquidation, or otherwise).

(B) Disposition of less than entire interest. The taxable year of a partnership shall not close (other than at the end of a partnership's taxable year as determined under subsection (b)(1)) with respect to a partner who sells or exchanges less than his entire interest in the partnership or with respect to a partner whose interest is reduced (whether by entry of a new partner, partial liquidation of a partner's interest, gift, or otherwise).

(d) Determination of distributive share when partner's interest changes.

(1) **In general.** Except as provided in paragraphs (2) and (3), if during any taxable year of the partnership there is a change in any partner's interest in the partnership, each partner's distributive share of any item of income, gain, loss, deduction, or credit of the partnership for such taxable year shall be determined by the use of any method prescribed by the Secretary by regulations which takes into account the varying interests of the partners in the partnership during such taxable year.

(2) **Certain cash basis items prorated over period to which attributable.**

(A) In general. If during any taxable year of the partnership there is a change in any partner's interest in the partnership, then (except to the extent provided in regulations) each partner's distributive share of any allocable cash basis item shall be determined—

(i) by assigning the appropriate portion of such item to each day in the period to which it is attributable, and

(ii) by allocating the portion assigned to any such day among the partners in proportion to their interests in the partnership at the close of such day.

(B) Allocable cash basis item. For purposes of this paragraph, the term "allocable cash basis item" means any of the following items with respect to which the partnership uses the cash receipts and disbursements method of accounting:

(i) Interest.
(ii) Taxes.
(iii) Payments for services or for the use of property.
(iv) Any other item of a kind specified in regulations prescribed by the Secretary as being an item with respect to which the application of this paragraph is appropriate to avoid significant misstatements of the income of the partners.

(C) Items attributable to periods not within taxable year. If any portion of any allocable cash basis item is attributable to—

(i) any period before the beginning of the taxable year, such portion shall be assigned under subparagraph (A)(i) to the first day of the taxable year, or
(ii) any period after the close of the taxable year, such portion shall be assigned under subparagraph (A)(i) to the last day of the taxable year.

(D) Treatment of deductible items attributable to prior periods. If any portion of a deductible cash basis item is assigned under subparagraph (C)(i) to the first day of any taxable year—

(i) such portion shall be allocated among persons who are partners in the partnership during the period to which such portion is attributable in accordance with their varying interests in the partnership during such period, and
(ii) any amount allocated under clause (i) to a person who is not a partner in the partnership on such first day shall be capitalized by the partnership and treated in the manner provided for in section 755.

(3) Items attributable to interest in lower tier partnership prorated over entire taxable year. If—

(A) during any taxable year of the partnership there is a change in any partner's interest in the partnership (hereinafter in this paragraph referred to as the "upper tier partnership"), and

(B) such partnership is a partner in another partnership (hereinafter in this paragraph referred to as the "lower tier partnership"),

then (except to the extent provided in regulations) each partner's distributive share of any item of the upper tier partnership attributable to the lower tier partnership shall be determined by assigning the appropriate portion (determined by applying principles similar to the principles of subparagraphs (C) and (D) of paragraph (2)) of each such item to the appropriate days during which the upper tier partnership is a partner in the lower tier partnership and by allocating the portion assigned to any such day among the partners in proportion to their interests in the upper tier partnership at the close of such day.

(4) Taxable year determined without regard to subsection (c)(2)(A). For purposes of this subsection, the taxable year of a partnership shall be determined without regard to subsection (c)(2)(A).

In 1997, P.L. 105-34, Sec. 507(b)(2), substituted "section 644" for "section 645" in para. (b)(5), effective for sales or exchanges after 8/5/97.

—P.L. 105-34, Sec. 1246(a), amended subpara. (c)(2)(A) . . . Sec. 1246(b), amended the heading of para. (c)(2), effective for partnership tax. yrs. begin. after 12/31/97.

Prior to amendment, the heading of para. (c)(2) read as follows:
"(2) Partner who retires or sells interest in partnership."
Prior to amendment subpara. (c)(2)(A) read as follows:
"(A) Disposition of entire interest. The taxable year of a partnership shall close—
"(i) with respect to a partner who sells or exchanges his entire interest in a partnership, and
"(ii) with respect to a partner whose interest is liquidated, except that the taxable year of a partnership with respect to a partner who dies shall not close prior to the end of the partnership's taxable year."

In 1988, P.L. 100-647, Sec. 1008(e)(1)(A), amended clause (b)(1)(B)(i) . . . Sec. 1008(e)(1)(B), amended para. (b)(4) . . . Sec. 1008(e)(2), substituted "unless the Secretary by regulations prescribes another period" for "or such other period as the Secretary may prescribe in regulation" in clause (b)(1)(B)(iii) . . . Sec. 1008(e)(3), added para. (b)(5), effective as provided in Sec. 806(e) of P.L. 99-514, reproduced below.

Prior to amendment, clause (b)(1)(B)(i) read as follows:
"(i) the taxable year of 1 or more of its partners who have an aggregate interest in partnership profits and capital of greater than 50 percent,"
Prior to amendment, para. (b)(4) read as follows:
"(4) Application of majority interest rule. Clause (i) of paragraph (1)(B) shall not apply to any taxable year of a partnership unless the period which constitutes the taxable year of 1 or more of its partners who have an aggregate interest in partnership profits and capital of greater than 50 percent has been the same for—
"(A) the 3-taxable year period of such partner or partners ending on or before the beginning of such taxable year of the partnership, or
"(B) if the partnership has not been in existence during all of such 3-taxable year period, the taxable years of such partner or partners ending with or within the period of existence.
This paragraph shall apply without regard to whether the same partners or interest are taken into account in determining the 50 percent interest during any period"

—P.L. 100-647, Sec. 1008(e)(7)(A), amended Sec. 806(e)(2)(C) of P.L. 99-514 [reproduced below], part of the effective date for changes made by Sec. 806(a)(1)-(3) of P.L. 99-514, by deleting "(including such short taxable year)" after "first 4 taxable years", see below . . . Sec. 1008(e)(7)(B), substituted "the partners's or shareholder's taxable year with or within which the partnership's or S corporation's short taxable year ends" for "short taxable year" the second place it appeared in Sec. 806(e)(2)(C) of P.L. 99-514 [reproduced below] . . . Sec. 1008(e)(8)(A), substituted "the taxpayer's first taxable year beginning after December 31, 1986" for "any taxable year" in Sec. 806(e)(2) of P.L. 99-514 [reproduced below] . . . Sec. 1008(e)(8)(B), substituted "partnership, S corporation, or personal service corporation" for "taxpayer" each place it appeared in Sec. 806(e)(2) of P.L. 99-514 [reproduced below] . . . Sec. 1008(e)(10), added Sec. 806(c)(3) of P.L. 99-514 [reproduced below]. Sec. 1008(e)(9) of this Act provides:

"(9) Nothing in section 806 of the Reform Act or in any legislative history relating thereto shall be construed as requiring the Secretary of the Treasury or his delegate to permit an automatic change of a taxable year."

—P.L. 100-647, Sec. 1014(c)(3), provides:
"(c) Amendments related to section 1403 of the Reform Act.
"(3)(A) For purposes of determining the gross income of any pass-thru entity, such pass-thru entity shall not be allowed the benefits of section 806(e)(2)(C) (other than with respect to income from a common trust fund) or 1403(c)(2) of the Reform Act if such pass-thru entity is required to change its taxable year by reason of the amendments made by section 806 or 1403 of the Reform Act.
"(B) For purposes of subparagraph (A), the term 'pass-thru entity' means any trust, partnership, S corporation, or common trust fund."

In 1986, P.L. 99-514, Sec. 806(a)(1), amended para. (b)(1) . . . Sec. 806(a)(2), added para. (b)(4) . . . Sec. 806(a)(3), deleted "Adoption of" in the heading of subsec. (b), effective as provided in Sec. 806(e) of this Act [as amended by Sec. 1008(e)(7) of P.L. 100-647-(10), see above] which reads as follows:
"(1) In general.— The amendments made by this section shall apply to taxable years beginning after December 31, 1986.
"(2) Change in accounting period. In the case of any partnership, S corporation, or personal service corporation required by the amendments made by this section to change its accounting period for the taxpayer's first taxable year beginning after December 31, 1986—
"(A) such change shall be treated as initiated by the partnership, S corporation, or personal service corporation,
"(B) such change shall be treated as having been made with the consent of the Secretary, and
"(C) with respect to any partner or shareholder of an S corporation which is required to include the items from more than 1 taxable year of the partnership or S corporation in any 1 taxable year, income in excess of expenses of such partnership or corporation for the short taxable year required by such amendments shall be taken into account ratably in each of the first 4 taxable years beginning after December 31, 1986, unless such partner or shareholder elects to include all such income in the partner's or shareholder's taxable year with or within which the partnership's or S corporation's short taxable year ends.
Subparagraph (C) shall apply to a shareholder of an S corporation only if such corporation was an S corporation for a taxable year beginning in 1986.
"(3) Basis, etc. rules.—
"(A) Basis rule.— The adjusted basis of any partner's interest in a partnership or shareholder's stock in an S corporation shall be determined as if all of the income to be taken into account ratably in the 4 taxable years referred to in paragraph (2)(C) were included in gross income for the 1st of such taxable years.

"(B) Treatment of dispositions.—If any interest in a partnership or stock in an S corporation is disposed of before the last taxable year in the spread period, all amounts which would be included in the gross income of the partner or shareholder for subsequent taxable years in the spread period under paragraph (2)(C) and attributable to the interest or stock disposed of shall be included in gross income for the taxable year in which the disposition occurs. For purposes of the preceding sentence, the term 'spread period' means the period consisting of the 4 taxable years referred to in paragraph (2)(C)."

Prior to amendment, para. (b)(1) read as follows:

"(1) Partnership's taxable year. The taxable year of a partnership shall be determined as though the partnership were a taxpayer. A partnership may not change to, or adopt, a taxable year other than that of all its principal partners unless it establishes, to the satisfaction of the Secretary, a business purpose therefor."

—P.L. 99-514, Sec. 1805(a)(1)(A), substituted "such item" for "each such item" in clause (d)(2)(A)(i)...Sec. 1805(a)(1)(B), deleted "which are described in paragraph (1) and" following "of the following items" in subpara. (d)(2)(B)...Sec. 1805(a)(2), substituted "the first day of the taxable year" for "the first day of such taxable year" in clause (d)(2)(C)(i), effective as provided in Secs. 72(c)(1) and (2) of P.L. 98-369, reproduced below.

In **1984**, P.L. 98-369, Sec. 72(a), added subsec. (d)...Sec. 72(b)(1), deleted the last sentence in subpara. (c)(2)(A)...Sec. 72(b)(2), deleted ", but such partner's distributive share of items described in section 702(a) shall be determined by taking into account his varying interests in the partnership during the taxable year" after "or otherwise)" in subpara. (c)(2)(B), effective as provided in Secs. 72(c)(1) and (2), which read as follows:

"(c) Effective date.—The amendments made by this section shall apply

"(1) in the case of items described in section 706(d)(2) of the Internal Revenue Code of 1954 (as added by Sec. 72(a) of P.L. 98-369), to amounts attributable to periods after March 31, 1984, and

"(2) in the case of items described in section 706(d)(3) of such Code (as added by Sec. 72(a) of P.L. 98-369), to amounts paid or accrued by the other partnership after March 31, 1984.

Prior to deletion, the last sentence in subpara. (c)(2)(A) read as follows:

"Such partner's distributive share of items described in section 702(a) for such year shall be determined, under regulations prescribed by the Secretary, for the period ending with such sale, exchange, or liquidation."

In **1976**, P.L. 94-455, Sec. 213(c)(1), substituted "or with respect to a partner whose interest is reduced (whether by entry of a new partner, partial liquidation of a partner's interest, gift, or otherwise)" for "or with respect to a partner whose interest is reduced" in subpara. (c)(2)(B), effective for partnership tax. yrs. begin. after 12/31/75.

—P.L. 94-455, Sec. 1906(b)(13)(A), substituted "Secretary" for "Secretary or his delegate" in paras. (b)(1) and (b)(2) and subsec. (c), for tax. yrs. begin. after 12/31/79.

Sec. 707. Transactions between partner and partnership.

(a) Partner not acting in capacity as partner.

(1) In general. If a partner engages in a transaction with a partnership other than in his capacity as a member of such partnership, the transaction shall, except as otherwise provided in this section, be considered as occurring between the partnership and one who is not a partner.

(2) Treatment of payments to partners for property or services. Under regulations prescribed by the Secretary—

(A) Treatment of certain services and transfers of property. If—

(i) a partner performs services for a partnership or transfers property to a partnership,

(ii) there is a related direct or indirect allocation and distribution to such partner, and

(iii) the performance of such services (or such transfer) and the allocation and distribution, when viewed together, are properly characterized as a transaction occurring between the partnership and a partner acting other than in his capacity as a member of the partnership,

such allocation and distribution shall be treated as a transaction described in paragraph (1).

(B) Treatment of certain property transfers. If—

(i) there is a direct or indirect transfer of money or other property by a partner to a partnership,

(ii) there is a related direct or indirect transfer of money or other property by the partnership to such partner (or another partner), and

(iii) the transfers described in clauses (i) and (ii), when viewed together, are properly characterized as a sale or exchange of property,

such transfers shall be treated either as a transaction described in paragraph (1) or as a transaction between 2 or more partners acting other than in their capacity as members of the partnership.

(b) Certain sales or exchanges of property with respect to controlled partnerships.

(1) Losses disallowed. No deduction shall be allowed in respect of losses from sales or exchanges of property (other than an interest in the partnership), directly or indirectly, between—

(A) a partnership and a person owning, directly or indirectly, more than 50 percent of the capital interest, or the profits interest, in such partnership, or

(B) two partnerships in which the same persons own, directly or indirectly, more than 50 percent of the capital interests or profits interests.

In the case of a subsequent sale or exchange by a transferee described in this paragraph, section 267(d) shall be applicable as if the loss were disallowed under section 267(a)(1). For purposes of section 267(a)(2), partnerships described in subparagraph (B) of this paragraph shall be treated as persons specified in section 267(b).

(2) Gains treated as ordinary income. In the case of a sale or exchange, directly or indirectly, of property, which in the hands of the transferee, is property other than a capital asset as defined in section 1221—

(A) between a partnership and a person owning, directly or indirectly, more than 50 percent of the capital interest, or profits interest, in such partnership, or

(B) between two partnerships in which the same persons own, directly or indirectly, more than 50 percent of the capital interest or profits interests,

any gain recognized shall be considered as ordinary income.

(3) Ownership of a capital or profits interest. For purposes of paragraphs (1) and (2) of this subsection, the ownership of a capital or profits interest in a partnership shall be determined in accordance with the rules for constructive ownership of stock provided in section 267(c) other than paragraph (3) of such section.

(c) Guaranteed payments.

To the extent determined without regard to the income of the partnership, payments to a partner for services or the use of capital shall be considered as made to one who is not a member of the partnership, but only for the purposes of section 61(a) (relating to gross income) and, subject to section 263, for purposes of section 162(a) (relating to trade or business expenses).

In **1988**, P.L. 100-647, Sec. 1006(i), amended Sec. 642(c)(2) [reproduced below] of P.L. 99-514, part of the transitional rules for changes made by Sec. 642(a) of P.L. 99-514, by substituting "Transitional" for "Traditional" in the heading, see below.

In **1986**, P.L. 99-514, Sec. 642(a)(2), substituted "50 percent" for "80 percent" in subparas. (b)(2)(A) and (b)(2)(B), effective for sales after 10/22/86, in tax. yrs. end. after 10/22/86. Sec. 642(c)(2) [as amended by Sec. 1006(i)(3) of P.L. 100-647, see above] of this Act provides:

"(2) Transitional Rule for Binding Contracts. The amendments made by this section [Sec. 642] shall not apply to sales made after August 14, 1986, which are made pursuant to a binding contract in effect on August 14, 1986, and at all times thereafter."

—P.L. 99-514, Sec. 1805(b), substituted "sale or exchange of property" for "sale of property" in clause (a)(2)(B)(ii), effective as provided in Secs. 73(b)(1)-(3) of P.L. 98-369, reproduced below.

—P.L. 99-514, Sec. 1812(c)(3)(A), substituted "a person" for "a partner" in subparas. (b)(1)(A) and (b)(2)(A), effective for sales or exchanges after 9/27/85.

—P.L. 99-514, Sec. 1812(c)(3)(B), added the last sentence to para. (b)(1), effective as provided in Sec. 174(c) of P.L. 98-369, reproduced in the note following Code Sec. 267.

In 1984, P.L. 98-369, Sec. 73(a), amended subsec. (a), effective as provided in Secs. 73(b)(1)–(3) of this Act, which read as follows:

"*(b) Effective date.—*

"(1) In general.—The amendment made by subsection (a) [Sec. 73(a) of P.L. 98-369] shall apply—

"(A) in the case of arrangements described in section 707(a)(2)(A) of the Internal Revenue Code of 1954 (as amended by subsection (a)), to services performed or property transferred after February 29, 1984, and

"(B) in the case of transfers described in section 707(a)(2)(B) of such Code (as so amended), to property transferred after March 31, 1984.

"(2) Binding contract exception.—The amendment made by subsection (a) shall not apply to a transfer of property described in section 707(a)(2)(B)(i) if such transfer is pursuant to a binding contract in effect on March 31, 1984, and at all times thereafter before the transfer.

"(3) Exception for certain transfers.—The amendment made by subsection (a) shall not apply to a transfer of property described in section 707(a)(2)(B)(i) that is made before December 31, 1984, if—

"(A) such transfer was proposed in a written private offering memorandum circulated before February 28, 1984;

"(B) the out-of-pocket costs incurred with respect to such offering exceeded $250,000 as of February 28, 1984;

"(C) the encumbrances placed on such property in anticipation of such transfer all constitute obligations for which neither the partnership nor any partner is liable; and

"(D) the transferor of such property is the sole general partner of the partnership."

Prior to amendment, subsec. (a) read as follows:

"*(a) Partner not acting in capacity as partner.*—

"If a partner engages in a transaction with a partnership other than in his capacity as a member of such partnership, the transaction shall, except as otherwise provided in this section, be considered as occurring between the partnership and one who is not a partner."

In 1976, P.L. 94-455, Sec. 213(b)(3), substituted "and, subject to section 263, for purposes of section 162(a)" for "and section 162(a)" in subsec. (c), effective for partnership tax. yrs. begin. after 12/31/75.

—P.L. 94-455, Sec. 1901(b)(3)(C), substituted "as ordinary income" for "as gain from the sale or exchange of property other than a capital asset" in para. (b)(2), effective for tax. yrs. begin. after 12/31/76.

Sec. 708. Continuation of partnership.
(a) General rule.

For purposes of this subchapter, an existing partnership shall be considered as continuing if it is not terminated.

(b) Termination.

(1) General rule. For purposes of subsection (a), a partnership shall be considered as terminated only if—

(A) no part of any business, financial operation, or venture of the partnership continues to be carried on by any of its partners in a partnership, or

(B) within a 12-month period there is a sale or exchange of 50 percent or more of the total interest in partnership capital and profits.

(2) Special rules.

(A) Merger or consolidation. In the case of the merger or consolidation of two or more partnerships, the resulting partnership shall, for purposes of this section, be considered the continuation of any merging or consolidating partnership whose members own an interest of more than 50 percent in the capital and profits of the resulting partnership.

(B) Division of a partnership. In the case of a division of a partnership into two or more partnerships, the resulting partnerships (other than any resulting partnership the members of which had an interest of 50 percent or less in the capital and profits of the prior partnership) shall, for purposes of this section, be considered a continuation of the prior partnership.

Sec. 709. Treatment of organization and syndication fees.
(a) General rule.

Except as provided in subsection (b), no deduction shall be allowed under this chapter to the partnership or to any partner for any amounts paid or incurred to organize a partnership or to promote the sale of (or to sell) an interest in such partnership.

(b) Deduction of organization fees.

(1) Allowance of deduction. If a partnership elects the application of this subsection (in accordance with regulations prescribed by the Secretary) with respect to any organizational expenses—

(A) the partnership shall be allowed a deduction for the taxable year in which the partnership begins business in an amount equal to the lesser of—

(i) the amount of organizational expenses with respect to the partnership, or

(ii) $5,000, reduced (but not below zero) by the amount by which such organizational expenses exceed $50,000, and

(B) the remainder of such organizational expenses shall be allowed as a deduction ratably over the 180-month period beginning with the month in which the partnership begins business.

(2) Dispositions before close of amortization period. In any case in which a partnership is liquidated before the end of the period to which paragraph (1)(B) applies, any deferred expenses attributable to the partnership which were not allowed as a deduction by reason of this section may be deducted to the extent allowable under section 165.

(3) Organizational expenses defined. The organizational expenses to which paragraph (1) applies, are expenditures which—

(A) are incident to the creation of the partnership;

(B) are chargeable to capital account; and

(C) are of a character which, if expended incident to the creation of a partnership having an ascertainable life, would be amortized over such life.

In 2005, P.L. 109-135, Sec. 403(ll), substituted "partnership" for "taxpayer" each place it appeared in para. (b)(1), effective for amounts paid or incurred after 10/22/2004 as if included in Sec. 902 of the American Jobs Creation Act of 2004, P.L. 108-357.

In 2004, P.L. 108-357, Sec. 902(c)(1), amended para. (b)(1), redesignated para. (b)(2) as (b)(3), and added para. (b)(2) . . . Sec. 902(c)(2), substituted "Deduction" for "Amortization" in the heading of subsec. (b), effective for amounts paid or incurred after 10/22/2004.

Prior to amendment, para. (b)(1) read as follows:

"(1) Deduction. Amounts paid or incurred to organize a partnership may, at the election of the partnership (made in accordance with regulations prescribed by the Secretary), be treated as deferred expenses. Such deferred expenses shall be allowed as a deduction ratably over such period of not less than 60 months as may be selected by the partnership (beginning with the month in which the partnership begins business), or if the partnership is liquidated before the end of such 60-month period, such deferred expenses (to the extent not deducted under this section) may be deducted to the extent provided in section 165."

In 1976, P.L. 94-455, Sec. 213(b)(1), added Code Sec. 709. Subsec. (a) is effective for partnership tax. yrs. begin. after 12/31/75, and subsec. (b) is effective for amounts paid or incurred in tax. yrs. begin. after 12/31/76.

PART II.—CONTRIBUTIONS, DISTRIBUTIONS, AND TRANSFERS

Subpart

A. Contributions to a partnership.
B. Distributions by a partnership.
C. Transfers of interests in a partnership.
D. Provisions common to other subparts.

SUBPART A.—CONTRIBUTIONS TO A PARTNERSHIP

Sec.

721. Nonrecognition of gain or loss on contribution.
722. Basis of contributing partner's interest.
723. Basis of property contributed to partnership.

724. Character of gain or loss on contributed unrealized receivables, inventory items, and capital loss property.

In **1984**, P.L. 98-369, Sec. 74(c), added the item for Code Sec. 724.

Sec. 721. Nonrecognition of gain or loss on contribution.
(a) General rule.
No gain or loss shall be recognized to a partnership or to any of its partners in the case of a contribution of property to the partnership in exchange for an interest in the partnership.
(b) Special rule.
Subsection (a) shall not apply to gain realized on a transfer of property to a partnership which would be treated as an investment company (within the meaning of section 351) if the partnership were incorporated.
(c) Regulations relating to certain transfers to partnerships.
The Secretary may provide by regulations that subsection (a) shall not apply to gain realized on the transfer of property to a partnership if such gain, when recognized, will be includible in the gross income of a person other than a United States person.
(d) Transfers of intangibles.
For regulatory authority to treat intangibles transferred to a partnership as sold, see section 367(d)(3).

In **1997**, P.L. 105-34, Sec. 1131(b)(3), [sic (c)(3)], added subsec. (c)... Sec. 1131(b)(5)(B), [sic (c)(5)(B)], added subsec. (d), effective 8/5/97.
In **1976**, P.L. 94-455, Sec. 2131(b), amended Code Sec. 721, effective for transfers made after 2/17/76, in tax. yrs. end. after 2/17/76, except as provided in Secs. 2131(f)(4) and (f)(5) of this Act which reads as follows:
"(4) The amendments made by subsections (b) and (c) shall not apply to transfers to a partnership made on or before the 90th day after the date of the enactment of this Act if—
"(A) either—
"(i) a ruling request with respect to such transfers was filed with the Internal Revenue Service before March 27, 1976, or
"(ii) a registration statement with respect to such transfers was filed with the Securities and Exchange Commission before March 27, 1976,
"(B) the securities transferred were deposited on or before the 60th day after the date of the enactment of this Act, and
"(C) either—
"(i) the aggregate value (determined as of the close of the 60th day referred to in subparagraph (B), or, if earlier, the close of the deposit period) of the securities so transferred does not exceed $100,000,000, or
"(ii) the securities transferred were all on deposit on February 29, 1976, pursuant to a registration statement referred to in subparagraph (A)(ii).
"(5) If no registration statement was required to be filed with the Securities and Exchange Commission with respect to the transfer of securities to any partnership, then paragraph (4) shall be applied to such transfers—
"(A) as if paragraph (4) did not contain subparagraph (A)(ii) thereof, and
"(B) by substituting '$25,000,000' for '$100,000,000' in subparagraph (C)(i) thereof."
Prior to amendment, Code Sec. 721 read as follows:
"SEC. 721. NONRECOGNITION OF GAIN OR LOSS ON CONTRIBUTION.
"No gain or loss shall be recognized to a partnership or to any of its partners in the case of a contribution of property to the partnership in exchange for an interest in the partnership."

Sec. 722. Basis of contributing partner's interest.
The basis of an interest in a partnership acquired by a contribution of property, including money, to the partnership shall be the amount of such money and the adjusted basis of such property to the contributing partner at the time of the contribution increased by the amount (if any) of gain recognized under section 721(b) to the contributing partner at such time.

In **1984**, P.L. 98-369, Sec. 722(f)(1), added "under section 721(b)" after "gain recognized" in Code Sec. 722, effective for transfers made after 2/17/76, in tax. yrs. end. after 2/17/76, except as provided in Sec. 2131(f)(4) and (5) of P.L. 94-455, reproduced in note following Code Sec. 721.
In **1976**, P.L. 94-455, Sec. 2131(c), substituted "contribution increased by the amount (if any) of gain recognized to the contributing partner at such time" for "contribution.", in Code Sec. 722, effective for transfers made after 2/17/76, in tax. yrs. end. after 2/17/76, except as provided in Sec. 2131(f)(4) and (5) of this Act, reproduced in note following Code Sec. 721.

Sec. 723. Basis of property contributed to partnership.
The basis of property contributed to a partnership by a partner shall be the adjusted basis of such property to the contributing partner at the time of the contribution increased by the amount (if any) of gain recognized under section 721(b) to the contributing partner at such time.

In **1984**, P.L. 98-369, Sec. 722(f)(1), added "under section 721(b)" after "gain recognized" in Code Sec. 723, effective for transfers made after 2/17/76, in tax. yrs. end. after 2/17/76, except as provided in Sec. 2131(f)(4) and (5) of P.L. 94-455, reproduced in note following Code Sec. 721.
In **1976**, P.L. 94-455, Sec. 2131(c), substituted "contribution increased by the amount (if any) of gain recognized to the contributing partner at such time" for "contribution." in Code Sec. 723, effective for transfers made after 2/17/76, in tax. yrs. end. after 2/17/76, except as provided in Sec. 2131(f)(4) and (5) of this Act, reproduced in note following Code Sec. 721.

Sec. 724. Character of gain or loss on contributed unrealized receivables, inventory items, and capital loss property.
(a) Contributions of unrealized receivables.
In the case of any property which—
(1) was contributed to the partnership by a partner, and
(2) was an unrealized receivable in the hands of such partner immediately before such contribution,
any gain or loss recognized by the partnership on the disposition of such property shall be treated as ordinary income or ordinary loss, as the case may be.
(b) Contributions of inventory items.
In the case of any property which—
(1) was contributed to the partnership by a partner, and
(2) was an inventory item in the hands of such partner immediately before such contribution,
any gain or loss recognized by the partnership on the disposition of such property during the 5-year period beginning on the date of such contribution shall be treated as ordinary income or ordinary loss, as the case may be.
(c) Contributions of capital loss property.
In the case of any property which—
(1) was contributed by a partner to the partnership, and
(2) was a capital asset in the hands of such partner immediately before such contribution,
any loss recognized by the partnership on the disposition of such property during the 5-year period beginning on the date of such contribution shall be treated as a loss from the sale of a capital asset to the extent that, immediately before such contribution, the adjusted basis of such property in the hands of the partner exceeded the fair market value of such property.
(d) Definitions.
For purposes of this section—
(1) Unrealized receivable. The term "unrealized receivable" has the meaning given such term by section 751(c) (determined by treating any reference to the partnership as referring to the partner).
(2) Inventory item. The term "inventory item" has the meaning given such term by section 751(d) (determined by treating any reference to the partnership as referring to the partner and by applying section 1231 without regard to any holding period therein provided).
(3) Substituted basis property.
(A) In general. If any property described in subsection (a), (b), or (c) is disposed of in a nonrecognition transaction, the tax treatment which applies to such property under such subsection shall also apply to any substituted basis property resulting from such transaction. A

similar rule shall also apply in the case of a series of non-recognition transactions.

(B) Exception for stock in C corporation. Subparagraph (A) shall not apply to any stock in a C corporation received in an exchange described in section 351.

In 1997, P.L. 105-34, Sec. 1062(b)(3), substituted "section 751(d)" for "section 751(d)(2)" in para. (d)(2), effective for sales, exchanges, and distributions after 8/5/97. Sec. 1062(c)(2) of this Act reads as follows:

"(2) Binding contracts. The amendments made by this section shall apply to sales, exchanges, and distributions after date of enactment."

In 1996, P.L. 104-188, Sec. 1704(t)(63), substituted "Subparagraph" for "Subparagraph" in subpara. (d)(3)(B), effective 8/20/96.

In 1984, P.L. 98-369, Sec. 741(a), added Code Sec. 724, effective for property contributed to a partnership after 3/31/84, in tax. yrs. end. after 3/31/84.

SUBPART B.—DISTRIBUTIONS BY A PARTNERSHIP

Sec.
731. Extent of recognition of gain or loss on distribution.
732. Basis of distributed property other than money.
733. Basis of distributee partner's interest.
734. Adjustment to basis of undistributed partnership property where section 754 election or substantial basis reduction.
735. Character of gain or loss on disposition of distributed property.
736. Payments to a retiring partner or a deceased partner's successor in interest.
737. Recognition of precontribution gain in case of certain distributions to contributing partner.

In 2004, P.L. 108-357, Sec. 833(c)(5)(B), amended item 734.
Prior to amendment, item 734 read as follows:
"734. Optional adjustment to basis of undistributed partnership property."
In 1992, P.L. 102-486, Sec. 1937(b)(3), added item 737.

Sec. 731. Extent of recognition of gain or loss on distribution.

(a) Partners.

In the case of a distribution by a partnership to a partner—

(1) gain shall not be recognized to such partner, except to the extent that any money distributed exceeds the adjusted basis of such partner's interest in the partnership immediately before the distribution, and

(2) loss shall not be recognized to such partner, except that upon a distribution in liquidation of a partner's interest in a partnership where no property other than that described in subparagraph (A) or (B) is distributed to such partner, loss shall be recognized to the extent of the excess of the adjusted basis of such partner's interest in the partnership over the sum of—

(A) any money distributed, and

(B) the basis to the distributee, as determined under section 732, of any unrealized receivables (as defined in section 751(c)) and inventory (as defined in section 751(d)).

Any gain or loss recognized under this subsection shall be considered as gain or loss from the sale or exchange of the partnership interest of the distributee partner.

(b) Partnerships.

No gain or loss shall be recognized to a partnership on a distribution to a partner of property, including money.

(c) Treatment of marketable securities.

(1) In general. For purposes of subsection (a)(1) and section 737—

(A) the term "money" includes marketable securities, and

(B) such securities shall be taken into account at their fair market value as of the date of the distribution.

(2) Marketable securities. For purposes of this subsection:

(A) In general. The term "marketable securities" means financial instruments and foreign currencies which are, as of the date of the distribution, actively traded (within the meaning of section 1092(d)(1)).

(B) Other property. Such term includes—

(i) any interest in—

(I) a common trust fund, or

(II) a regulated investment company which is offering for sale or has outstanding any redeemable security (as defined in section 2(a)(32) of the Investment Company Act of 1940) of which it is the issuer,

(ii) any financial instrument which, pursuant to its terms or any other arrangement, is readily convertible into, or exchangeable for, money or marketable securities,

(iii) any financial instrument the value of which is determined substantially by reference to marketable securities,

(iv) except to the extent provided in regulations prescribed by the Secretary, any interest in a precious metal which, as of the date of the distribution, is actively traded (within the meaning of section 1092(d)(1)) unless such metal was produced, used, or held in the active conduct of a trade or business by the partnership,

(v) except as otherwise provided in regulations prescribed by the Secretary, interests in any entity if substantially all of the assets of such entity consist (directly or indirectly) of marketable securities, money, or both, and

(vi) to the extent provided in regulations prescribed by the Secretary, any interest in an entity not described in clause (v) but only to the extent of the value of such interest which is attributable to marketable securities, money, or both.

(C) Financial instrument. The term "financial instrument" includes stocks and other equity interests, evidences of indebtedness, options, forward or futures contracts, notional principal contracts, and derivatives.

(3) Exceptions.

(A) In general. Paragraph (1) shall not apply to the distribution from a partnership of a marketable security to a partner if—

(i) the security was contributed to the partnership by such partner, except to the extent that the value of the distributed security is attributable to marketable securities or money contributed (directly or indirectly) to the entity to which the distributed security relates,

(ii) to the extent provided in regulations prescribed by the Secretary, the property was not a marketable security when acquired by such partnership, or

(iii) such partnership is an investment partnership and such partner is an eligible partner thereof.

(B) Limitation on gain recognized. In the case of a distribution of marketable securities to a partner, the amount taken into account under paragraph (1) shall be reduced (but not below zero) by the excess (if any) of—

(i) such partner's distributive share of the net gain which would be recognized if all of the marketable securities of the same class and issuer as the distrib-

2,349

uted securities held by the partnership were sold (immediately before the transaction to which the distribution relates) by the partnership for fair market value, over

(ii) such partner's distributive share of the net gain which is attributable to the marketable securities of the same class and issuer as the distributed securities held by the partnership immediately after the transaction, determined by using the same fair market value as used under clause (i).

Under regulations prescribed by the Secretary, all marketable securities held by the partnership may be treated as marketable securities of the same class and issuer as the distributed securities.

(C) Definitions relating to investment partnerships. For purposes of subparagraph (A)(iii):

(i) Investment partnership. The term "investment partnership" means any partnership which has never been engaged in a trade or business and substantially all of the assets (by value) of which have always consisted of—

(I) money,

(II) stock in a corporation,

(III) notes, bonds, debentures, or other evidences of indebtedness,

(IV) interest rate, currency, or equity notional principal contracts,

(V) foreign currencies,

(VI) interests in or derivative financial instruments (including options, forward or futures contracts, short positions, and similar financial instruments) in any asset described in any other subclause of this clause or in any commodity traded on or subject to the rules of a board of trade or commodity exchange,

(VII) other assets specified in regulations prescribed by the Secretary, or

(VIII) any combination of the foregoing.

(ii) Exception for certain activities. A partnership shall not be treated as engaged in a trade or business by reason of—

(I) any activity undertaken as an investor, trader, or dealer in any asset described in clause (i), or

(II) any other activity specified in regulations prescribed by the Secretary.

(iii) Eligible partner.

(I) In general. The term "eligible partner" means any partner who, before the date of the distribution, did not contribute to the partnership any property other than assets described in clause (i).

(II) Exception for certain nonrecognition transactions. The term "eligible partner" shall not include the transferor or transferee in a nonrecognition transaction involving a transfer of any portion of an interest in a partnership with respect to which the transferor was not an eligible partner.

(iv) Look-thru of partnership tiers. Except as otherwise provided in regulations prescribed by the Secretary—

(I) a partnership shall be treated as engaged in any trade or business engaged in by, and as holding (instead of a partnership interest) a proportionate share of the assets of, any other partnership in which the partnership holds a partnership interest, and

(II) a partner who contributes to a partnership an interest in another partnership shall be treated as contributing a proportionate share of the assets of the other partnership.

If the preceding sentence does not apply under such regulations with respect to any interest held by a partnership in another partnership, the interest in such other partnership shall be treated as if it were specified in a subclause of clause (i).

(4) **Basis of securities distributed.**

(A) In general. The basis of marketable securities with respect to which gain is recognized by reason of this subsection shall be—

(i) their basis determined under section 732, increased by

(ii) the amount of such gain.

(B) Allocation of basis increase. Any increase in basis attributable to the gain described in subparagraph (A)(ii) shall be allocated to marketable securities in proportion to their respective amounts of unrealized appreciation before such increase.

(5) **Subsection disregarded in determining basis of partner's interest in partnership and of basis of partnership property.** Sections 733 and 734 shall be applied as if no gain were recognized, and no adjustment were made to the basis of property, under this subsection.

(6) **Character of gain recognized.** In the case of a distribution of a marketable security which is an unrealized receivable (as defined in section 751(c)) or an inventory item (as defined in section 751(d)), any gain recognized under this subsection shall be treated as ordinary income to the extent of any increase in the basis of such security attributable to the gain described in paragraph (4)(A)(ii).

(7) **Regulations.** The Secretary shall prescribe such regulations as may be necessary or appropriate to carry out the purposes of this subsection, including regulations to prevent the avoidance of such purposes.

(d) **Exceptions.**

This section shall not apply to the extent otherwise provided by section 736 (relating to payments to a retiring partner or a deceased partner's successor in interest), section 751 (relating to unrealized receivables and inventory items), and section 737 (relating to recognition of precontribution gain in case of certain distributions).

In 1997, P.L. 105-34, Sec. 1062(b)(3), substituted "section 751(d)" for "section 751(d)(2)" in subpara. (a)(2)(B) and para. (c)(6), effective for sales, exchanges, and distributions after 8/5/97. Sec. 1062(c)(2) of this Act reads as follows:

"(2) Binding contracts. The amendments made by this section shall apply to sales, exchanges, and distributions after date of enactment."

In 1994, P.L. 103-465, Sec. 741(a), redesignated subsec. (c) as subsec. (d) and added new subsec. (c), effective for distributions after 12/8/94, except as provided in Sec. 741(c)(2)-(5) of this Act, which reads as follows:

"(2) Certain distributions before January 1, 1995.—The amendments made by this section shall not apply to any marketable security distributed before January 1, 1995, by the partnership which held such security on July 27, 1994.

"(3) Distributions in liquidation of partner's interest.—The amendments made by this section shall not apply to the distribution of a marketable security in liquidation of a partner's interest in a partnership if—

"(A) such liquidation is pursuant to a written contract which was binding on July 15, 1994, and at all times thereafter before the distribution, and

"(B) such contract provides for the purchase of such interest not later than a date certain for—

"(i) a fixed value of marketable securities that are specified in the contract, or

"(ii) other property.

"The preceding sentence shall not apply if the partner has the right to elect that such distribution be made other than in marketable securities.

"(4) Distributions in complete liquidation of publicity traded partnerships.—

"(A) In general.—The amendments made by this section shall not apply to the distribution of a marketable security in a qualified partnership liquidation if—

"(i) the marketable securities were received by the partnership in a nonrecognition transaction in exchange for substantially all of the assets of the partnership, "(ii) the marketable securities are distributed by the partnership within 90 days after their receipt by the partnership, and

"(iii) the partnership is liquidated before the beginning of the 1st taxable year of the partnership beginning after December 31, 1997.

"(B) Qualified partnership liquidation.— For purposes of subparagraph (A), the term 'qualified partnership liquidation' means —

"(i) a complete liquidation of a publicly traded partnership (as defined in section 7704(b) of the Internal Revenue Code of 1986) which is an existing partnership (as defined in section 10211(c)(2) of the Revenue Act of 1987), and

"(ii) a complete liquidation of a partnership which is related to a partnership described in clause (i) if such liquidation is related to a complete liquidation of the partnership described in clause (i).

"(5) Marketable securities.— For purposes of this subsection, the term 'marketable securities' has the meaning given such term by section 731(c) of the Internal Revenue Code of 1986, as added by this section."

In 1992, P.L. 102-486, Sec. 1937(b)(2)(A), substituted ", section 751" for "and section 751" in subsec. (c)... Sec. 1937(b)(2)(B), added ", and section 737 (relating to recognition of precontribution gain in case of certain distributions)" at the end of subsec. (c), effective for distributions on or after 6/25/92.

Sec. 732. Basis of distributed property other than money.

(a) Distributions other than in liquidation of a partner's interest.

(1) **General rule.** The basis of property (other than money) distributed by a partnership to a partner other than in liquidation of the partner's interest shall, except as provided in paragraph (2), be its adjusted basis to the partnership immediately before such distribution.

(2) **Limitation.** The basis to the distributee partner of property to which paragraph (1) is applicable shall not exceed the adjusted basis of such partner's interest in the partnership reduced by any money distributed in the same transaction.

(b) Distributions in liquidation.

The basis of property (other than money) distributed by a partnership to a partner in liquidation of the partner's interest shall be an amount equal to the adjusted basis of such partner's interest in the partnership reduced by any money distributed in the same transaction.

(c) Allocation of basis.

(1) **In general.** The basis of distributed properties to which subsection (a)(2) or (b) is applicable shall be allocated—

(A)(i) first to any unrealized receivables (as defined in section 751(c)) and inventory items (as defined in section 751(d)) in an amount equal to the adjusted basis of each such property to the partnership, and

(ii) if the basis to be allocated is less than the sum of the adjusted bases of such properties to the partnership, then, to the extent any decrease is required in order to have the adjusted bases of such properties equal the basis to be allocated, in the manner provided in paragraph (3), and

(B) to the extent of any basis remaining after the allocation under subparagraph (A), to other distributed properties—

(i) first by assigning to each such other property such other property's adjusted basis to the partnership, and

(ii) then, to the extent any increase or decrease in basis is required in order to have the adjusted bases of such other distributed properties equal such remaining basis, in the manner provided in paragraph (2) or (3), whichever is appropriate.

(2) **Method of allocating increase.** Any increase required under paragraph (1)(B) shall be allocated among the properties—

(A) first to properties with unrealized appreciation in proportion to their respective amounts of unrealized appreciation before such increase (but only to the extent of each property's unrealized appreciation), and

(B) then, to the extent such increase is not allocated under subparagraph (A), in proportion to their respective fair market values.

(3) **Method of allocating decrease.** Any decrease required under paragraph (1)(A) or (1)(B) shall be allocated—

(A) first to properties with unrealized depreciation in proportion to their respective amounts of unrealized depreciation before such decrease (but only to the extent of each property's unrealized depreciation), and

(B) then, to the extent such decrease is not allocated under subparagraph (A), in proportion to their respective adjusted bases (as adjusted under subparagraph (A)).

(d) Special partnership basis to transferee.

For purposes of subsections (a), (b), and (c), a partner who acquired all or a part of his interest by a transfer with respect to which the election provided in section 754 is not in effect, and to whom a distribution of property (other than money) is made with respect to the transferred interest within 2 years after such transfer, may elect, under regulations prescribed by the Secretary, to treat as the adjusted partnership basis of such property the adjusted basis such property would have if the adjustment provided in section 743(b) were in effect with respect to the partnership property. The Secretary may by regulations require the application of this subsection in the case of a distribution to a transferee partner, whether or not made within 2 years after the transfer, if at the time of the transfer the fair market value of the partnership property (other than money) exceeded 110 percent of its adjusted basis to the partnership.

(e) Exception.

This section shall not apply to the extent that a distribution is treated as a sale or exchange of property under section 751(b) (relating to unrealized receivables and inventory items).

(f) Corresponding adjustment to basis of assets of a distributed corporation controlled by a corporate partner.

(1) **In general.** If—

(A) a corporation (hereafter in this subsection referred to as the "corporate partner") receives a distribution from a partnership of stock in another corporation (hereafter in this subsection referred to as the "distributed corporation"),

(B) the corporate partner has control of the distributed corporation immediately after the distribution or at any time thereafter, and

(C) the partnership's adjusted basis in such stock immediately before the distribution exceeded the corporate partner's adjusted basis in such stock immediately after the distribution,

then an amount equal to such excess shall be applied to reduce (in accordance with subsection (c)) the basis of property held by the distributed corporation at such time (or, if the corporate partner does not control the distributed corporation at such time, at the time the corporate partner first has such control).

(2) **Exception for certain distributions before control acquired.** Paragraph (1) shall not apply to any distribution of stock in the distributed corporation if—

(A) the corporate partner does not have control of such corporation immediately after such distribution, and

(B) the corporate partner establishes to the satisfaction of the Secretary that such distribution was not part of a plan or arrangement to acquire control of the distributed corporation.

(3) Limitations on basis reduction.
 (A) In general. The amount of the reduction under paragraph (1) shall not exceed the amount by which the sum of the aggregate adjusted bases of the property and the amount of money of the distributed corporation exceeds the corporate partner's adjusted basis in the stock of the distributed corporation.
 (B) Reduction not to exceed adjusted basis of property. No reduction under paragraph (1) in the basis of any property shall exceed the adjusted basis of such property (determined without regard to such reduction).
(4) Gain recognition where reduction limited. If the amount of any reduction under paragraph (1) (determined after the application of paragraph (3)(A)) exceeds the aggregate adjusted bases of the property of the distributed corporation—
 (A) such excess shall be recognized by the corporate partner as long-term capital gain, and
 (B) the corporate partner's adjusted basis in the stock of the distributed corporation shall be increased by such excess.
(5) Control. For purposes of this subsection, the term "control" means ownership of stock meeting the requirements of section 1504(a)(2).
(6) Indirect distributions. For purposes of paragraph (1), if a corporation acquires (other than in a distribution from a partnership) stock the basis of which is determined (by reason of being distributed from a partnership) in whole or in part by reference to subsection (a)(2) or (b), the corporation shall be treated as receiving a distribution of such stock from a partnership.
(7) Special rule for stock in controlled corporation. If the property held by a distributed corporation is stock in a corporation which the distributed corporation controls, this subsection shall be applied to reduce the basis of the property of such controlled corporation. This subsection shall be reapplied to any property of any controlled corporation which is stock in a corporation which it controls.
(8) Regulations. The Secretary shall prescribe such regulations as may be necessary to carry out the purposes of this subsection, including regulations to avoid double counting and to prevent the abuse of such purposes.

In 1999, P.L. 106-170, Sec. 538(a), added subsec. (f), effective for distributions made after 7/14/99, except as provided in Sec. 538(b)(2) of this Act, which reads as follows:

"(2) Partnerships in existence on July 14, 1999. In the case of a corporation which is a partner in a partnership as of July 14, 1999, the amendment made by this section shall apply to any distribution made (or treated as made) to such partner from such partnership after June 30, 2001, except that this paragraph shall not apply to any distribution after the date of the enactment of this Act unless the partner makes an election to have this paragraph apply to such distribution on the partner's return of Federal income tax for the taxable year in which such distribution occurs."

In 1997, P.L. 105-34, Sec. 1061(a), amended subsec. (c), effective for distributions after 8/5/97.

Prior to amendment, subsec. (c) read as follows:
"(c) Allocation of basis.
 "The basis of distributed properties to which subsection (a)(2) or subsection (b) is applicable shall be allocated—
  "(1) first to any unrealized receivables (as defined in section 751(c)) and inventory items (as defined in section 751(d)(2)) in an amount equal to the adjusted basis of each such property to the partnership (or if the basis to be allocated is less than the sum of the adjusted bases of such properties to the partnership, in proportion to such bases), and
  "(2) to the extent of any remaining basis, to any other distributed properties in proportion to their adjusted bases to the partnership."

—P.L. 105-34, Sec. 1062(b)(3), substituted "751(d)" for "751(d)(2)" in subpara. (c)(1)(A) [as amended by Sec. 1064(a) above], effective for sales, exchanges, and distributions after 8/5/97. For exceptions, see Sec. 1062(c)(2) of this Act, which provides:

"(2) Binding contracts. The amendments made by this section shall not apply to any sale or exchange pursuant to a written binding contract in effect on June 8, 1997, and at all times thereafter before such sale or exchange."

In 1976, P.L. 94-455, Sec. 1906(b)(13)(A), substituted "Secretary" for "Secretary or his delegate" each place it appeared in Code Sec. 732, effective for tax. yrs. begin. after 12/31/76.

Sec. 733. Basis of distributee partner's interest.
 In the case of a distribution by a partnership to a partner other than in liquidation of a partner's interest, the adjusted basis to such partner of his interest in the partnership shall be reduced (but not below zero) by—
 (1) the amount of any money distributed to such partner, and
 (2) the amount of the basis to such partner of distributed property other than money, as determined under section 732.

Sec. 734. Adjustment to basis of undistributed partnership property where section 754 election or substantial basis reduction.

(a) General rule.
 The basis of partnership property shall not be adjusted as the result of a distribution of property to a partner unless the election, provided in section 754 (relating to optional adjustment to basis of partnership property), is in effect with respect to such partnership or unless there is a substantial basis reduction with respect to such distribution.

(b) Method of adjustment.
 In the case of a distribution of property to a partner by a partnership with respect to which the election provided in section 754 is in effect or with respect to which there is a substantial basis reduction, the partnership shall—
 (1) increase the adjusted basis of partnership property by—
  (A) the amount of any gain recognized to the distributee partner with respect to such distribution under section 731(a)(1), and
  (B) in the case of distributed property to which section 732(a)(2) or (b) applies, the excess of the adjusted basis of the distributed property to the partnership immediately before the distribution (as adjusted by section 732(d)) over the basis of the distributed property to the distributee, as determined under section 732, or
 (2) decrease the adjusted basis of partnership property by—
  (A) the amount of any loss recognized to the distributee partner with respect to such distribution under section 731(a)(2), and
  (B) in the case of distributed property to which section 732(b) applies, the excess of the basis of the distributed property to the distributee, as determined under section 732, over the adjusted basis of the distributed property to the partnership immediately before such distribution (as adjusted by section 732(d)).

Paragraph (1)(B) shall not apply to any distributed property which is an interest in another partnership with respect to which the election provided in section 754 is not in effect.

(c) Allocation of basis.
 The allocation of basis among partnership properties where subsection (b) is applicable shall be made in accordance with the rules provided in section 755.

(d) Substantial basis reduction.
 (1) In general. For purposes of this section, there is a substantial basis reduction with respect to a distribution if the sum of the amounts described in subparagraphs (A) and (B) of subsection (b) exceeds $250,000.
 (2) Regulations. For regulations to carry out this subsection, see section 743(d)(2).

(e) Exception for securitization partnerships.
 For purposes of this section, a securitization partnership (as defined in section 743(f)) shall not be treated as having a

substantial basis reduction with respect to any distribution of property to a partner.

In 2005, P.L. 109-135, Sec. 403(bb)(1), added "with respect to such distribution" before the period at the end of subsec. (a) . . . Sec. 403(bb)(2), amended so much of subsec. (b) as precedes para. (b)(1), effective for distributions after 10/22/2004 as if included in Sec. 833 of the American Jobs Creation Act of 2004, P.L. 108-357.

Prior to amendment, so much of subsec. (b) as precedes para. (b)(1) read as follows:

"(b) Method of adjustment. In the case of a distribution of property to a partner, a partnership, with respect to which the election provided in section 754 is in effect or unless there is a substantial basis reduction, shall—"

In 2004, P.L. 108-357, Sec. 833(c)(1), added "or unless there is a substantial basis reduction" before the period in subsec. (a) . . . Sec. 833(c)(2), added "or unless there is a substantial basis reduction" after "section 754 is in effect" in subsec. (b) . . . Sec. 833(c)(3), added subsec. (d) . . . Sec. 833(c)(4), added subsec. (e) . . . Sec. 833(c)(5)(A), amended the heading of Code Sec. 734, effective for distributions after 10/22/2004.

Prior to amendment, the heading of Code Sec. 734 read as follows:

"SEC. 734. OPTIONAL ADJUSTMENT TO BASIS OF UNDISTRIBUTED PARTNERSHIP PROPERTY."

In 1984, P.L. 98-369, Sec. 78(a), added the sentence at the end of subsec. (b), effective for distributions after 3/1/84, in tax. yrs. end. after 3/1/84.

Sec. 735. Character of gain or loss on disposition of distributed property.

(a) Sale or exchange of certain distributed property.

(1) Unrealized receivables. Gain or loss on the disposition by a distributee partner of unrealized receivables (as defined in section 751(c)) distributed by a partnership, shall be considered as ordinary income or as ordinary loss, as the case may be.

(2) Inventory items. Gain or loss on the sale or exchange by a distributee partner of inventory items (as defined in section 751(d)) distributed by a partnership shall, if sold or exchanged within 5 years from the date of the distribution, be considered as ordinary income or as ordinary loss, as the case may be.

(b) Holding period for distributed property.

In determining the period for which a partner has held property received in a distribution from a partnership (other than for purposes of subsection (a)(2)), there shall be included the holding period of the partnership, as determined under section 1223, with respect to such property.

(c) Special rules.

(1) Waiver of holding periods contained in section 1231. For purposes of this section, section 751(d) (defining inventory item) shall be applied without regard to any holding period in section 1231(b).

(2) Substituted basis property.

(A) In general. If any property described in subsection (a) is disposed of in a nonrecognition transaction, the tax treatment which applies to such property under such subsection shall also apply to any substituted basis property resulting from such transaction. A similar rule shall also apply in the case of a series of nonrecognition transactions.

(B) Exception for stock in C corporation. Subparagraph (A) shall not apply to any stock in a C corporation received in an exchange described in section 351.

In 1997, P.L. 105-34, Sec. 1062(b)(3), substituted "section 751(d)" for "section 751(d)(2)" in paras. (a)(2) and (c)(1), effective for sales, exchanges, and distributions after 8/5/97. Sec. 1062(c)(2) of this Act reads as follows:

"(2) Binding contracts. The amendments made by this section shall not apply to any asle or exchange pursuant to a written binding contract in effect on June 8, 1997, and at all times thereafter before such sale or exchange."

In 1984, P.L. 98-369, Sec. 74(b), added subsec. (c), effective for property distributed after 3/1/84, in tax. yrs. end. after 3/1/84.

In 1976, P.L. 94-455, Sec. 1901(b)(3)(D), substituted "as ordinary income or as ordinary loss, as the case may be" for "gain or loss from the sale or exchange of property other than a capital asset" in paras. (a)(1) and (a)(2), effective for tax. yrs. begin. after 12/31/75.

Sec. 736. Payments to a retiring partner or a deceased partner's successor in interest.

(a) Payments considered as distributive share or guaranteed payment.

Payments made in liquidation of the interest of a retiring partner or a deceased partner shall, except as provided in subsection (b), be considered—

(1) as a distributive share to the recipient of partnership income if the amount thereof is determined with regard to the income of the partnership, or

(2) as a guaranteed payment described in section 707(c) if the amount thereof is determined without regard to the income of the partnership.

(b) Payments for interest in partnership.

(1) General rule. Payments made in liquidation of the interest of a retiring partner or a deceased partner shall, to the extent such payments (other than payments described in paragraph (2)) are determined, under regulations prescribed by the Secretary, to be made in exchange for the interest of such partner in partnership property, be considered as a distribution by the partnership and not as a distributive share or guaranteed payment under subsection (a).

(2) Special rules. For purposes of this subsection, payments in exchange for an interest in partnership property shall not include amounts paid for—

(A) unrealized receivables of the partnership (as defined in section 751(c)), or

(B) good will of the partnership, except to the extent that the partnership agreement provides for a payment with respect to good will.

(3) Limitation on application of paragraph (2). Paragraph (2) shall apply only if—

(A) capital is not a material income-producing factor for the partnership, and

(B) the retiring or deceased partner was a general partner in the partnership.

In 1993, P.L. 103-66, Sec. 13262(a), added para. (b)(3) . . . Sec. 13262(b)(2)(B), deleted subsec. (c), effective for partners retiring or dying on or after 1/5/93, except as provided in Sec. 13262(c)(2) of this Act which reads as follows:

"(2) Binding contract exception. The amendments made by this section shall not apply to any partner retiring on or after January 5, 1993, if a written contract to purchase such partner's interest in the partnership was binding on January 4, 1993, and at all times thereafter before such purchase."

Prior to deletion, subsec. (c) read as follows:

"(c) Cross reference.

For limitation on the tax attributable to certain gain connected with section 1248 stock, see section 751(e)."

In 1978, P.L. 95-600, Sec. 701(u)(13)(B), added subsec. (c), effective for transfers begin. after 10/9/75, and for sales, exchanges and distributions taking place after 10/9/75.

In 1976, P.L. 94-455, Sec. 1906(b)(13)(A), substituted "Secretary" for "Secretary or his delegate" in para. (b)(1), effective for tax. yrs. begin. after 12/31/76.

Sec. 737. Recognition of precontribution gain in case of certain distributions to contributing partner.

(a) General rule.

In the case of any distribution by a partnership to a partner, such partner shall be treated as recognizing gain in an amount equal to the lesser of—

(1) the excess (if any) of (A) the fair market value of property (other than money) received in the distribution over (B) the adjusted basis of such partner's interest in the partnership immediately before the distribution reduced (but not below zero) by the amount of money received in the distribution, or

(2) the net precontribution gain of the partner.

Gain recognized under the preceding sentence shall be in addition to any gain recognized under section 731. The character of such gain shall be determined by reference to the proportionate character of the net precontribution gain.

(b) Net precontribution gain.

For purposes of this section, the term "net precontribution gain" means the net gain (if any) which would have been recognized by the distributee partner under section 704(c)(1)(B) if all property which—

(1) had been contributed to the partnership by the distributee partner within 7 years of the distribution, and

(2) is held by such partnership immediately before the distribution,

had been distributed by such partnership to another partner.

(c) Basis rules.

(1) Partner's interest. The adjusted basis of a partner's interest in a partnership shall be increased by the amount of any gain recognized by such partner under subsection (a). For purposes of determining the basis of the distributed property (other than money), such increase shall be treated as occurring immediately before the distribution.

(2) Partnership's basis in contributed property. Appropriate adjustments shall be made to the adjusted basis of the partnership in the contributed property referred to in subsection (b) to reflect gain recognized under subsection (a).

(d) Exceptions.

(1) Distributions of previously contributed property. If any portion of the property distributed consists of property which had been contributed by a distributee partner to the partnership, such property shall not be taken into account under subsection (a)(1) and shall not be taken into account in determining the amount of the net precontribution gain. If the property distributed consists of an interest in an entity, the preceding sentence shall not apply to the extent that the value of such interest is attributable to property contributed to such entity after such interest had been contributed to the partnership.

(2) Coordination with section 751. This section shall not apply to the extent section 751(b) applies to such distribution.

(e) Marketable securities treated as money.

For treatment of marketable securities as money for purposes of this section, see section 731(c).

In 1997, P.L. 105-34, Sec. 1063(a), substituted "7 years" for "5 years" in para. (b)(1), effective for property contributed to a partnership after 6/8/97. Sec. 1063(b)(2) of this Act provides:

"(2) Binding contracts. The amendment made by subsection (a) shall not apply to any property contributed pursuant to a written binding contract in effect on June 8, 1997, and at all times thereafter before such contribution if such contract provides for the contribution of a fixed amount of property."

In 1994, P.L. 103-465, Sec. 741(b)(1), amended the last sentence in para. (c)(1) ... Sec. 741(b)(2), added subsec. (e), effective for distributions after 12/8/94, except as provided in Sec. 741(c)(2)-(5) of this Act, which reads as follows:

"(2) Certain distributions before January 1, 1995. The amendments made by this section shall not apply to any marketable security distributed before January 1, 1995, by the partnership which held such security on July 27, 1994.

"(3) Distributions in liquidation of partner's interest. The amendments made by this section shall not apply to the distribution of a marketable security in liquidation of a partner's interest in a partnership if—

"(A) such liquidation is pursuant to a written contract which was binding on July 15, 1994, and at all times thereafter before the distribution, and

"(B) such contract provides for the purchase of such interest not later than a date certain for—

"(i) a fixed value of marketable securities that are specified in the contract, or

"(ii) other property.

"The preceding sentence shall not apply if the partner has the right to elect that such distribution be made other than in marketable securities.

"(4) Distributions in complete liquidation of publicly traded partnerships.

"(A) In general. The amendments made by this section shall not apply to the distribution of a marketable security in a qualified partnership liquidation if—

"(i) the marketable securities were received by the partnership in a nonrecognition transaction in exchange for substantially all of the assets of the partnership,

"(ii) the marketable securities are distributed by the partnership within 90 days after their receipt by the partnership, and

"(iii) the partnership is liquidated before the beginning of the 1st taxable year of the partnership beginning after December 31, 1997.

"(B) Qualified partnership liquidation. For purposes of subparagraph (A), the term 'qualified partnership liquidation' means—

"(i) a complete liquidation of a publicly traded partnership (as defined in section 7704(b) of the Internal Revenue Code of 1986) which is an existing partnership (as defined in section 10211(c)(2) of the Revenue Act of 1987), and

"(ii) a complete liquidation of a partnership which is related to a partnership described in clause (i) if such liquidation is related to a complete liquidation of the partnership described in clause (i).

"(5) Marketable securities. For purposes of this subsection, the term 'marketable securities' has the meaning given such term by section 731(c) of the Internal Revenue Code of 1986, as added by this section."

Prior to amendment, the last sentence of para. (c)(1) read as follows:

"Except for purposes of determining the amount recognized under subsection (a), such increase shall be treated as occurring immediately before this distribution."

In 1992, P.L. 102-486, Sec. 1937(a), added Code Sec. 737, effective for distributions on or after 6/25/92.

SUBPART C.—TRANSFERS OF INTEREST IN A PARTNERSHIP

Sec.

741. Recognition and character of gain or loss on sale or exchange.

742. Basis of transferee partner's interest.

743. Special rules where section 754 election or substantial built-in loss.

In 2004, P.L. 108-357, Sec. 833(b)(6)(B), amended item 743.
Prior to amendment, item 743 read as follows:
"743. Optional adjustment to basis of partnership property."

Sec. 741. Recognition and character of gain or loss on sale or exchange.

In the case of a sale or exchange of an interest in a partnership, gain or loss shall be recognized to the transferor partner. Such gain or loss shall be considered as gain or loss from the sale or exchange of a capital asset, except as otherwise provided in section 751 (relating to unrealized receivables and inventory items).

In 2002, P.L. 107-147, Sec. 417(12), deleted "which have appreciated substantially in value" after "inventory items" in Code Sec. 741, effective 3/9/2002.

Sec. 742. Basis of transferee partner's interest.

The basis of an interest in a partnership acquired other than by contribution shall be determined under part II of subchapter O (sec. 1011 and following).

Sec. 743. Special rules where section 754 election or substantial built-in loss.

(a) General rule.

The basis of partnership property shall not be adjusted as the result of a transfer of an interest in a partnership by sale or exchange or on the death of a partner unless the election provided by section 754 (relating to optional adjustment to basis of partnership property) is in effect with respect to such partnership or unless the partnership has a substantial built-in loss immediately after such transfer.

(b) Adjustment to basis of partnership property.

In the case of a transfer of an interest in a partnership by sale or exchange or upon the death of a partner, a partnership with respect to which the election provided in section 754 is in effect or which has a substantial built-in loss immediately after such transfer shall—

(1) increase the adjusted basis of the partnership property by the excess of the basis to the transferee partner of his interest in the partnership over his proportionate share of the adjusted basis of the partnership property, or

(2) decrease the adjusted basis of the partnership property by the excess of the transferee partner's proportionate share of the adjusted basis of the partnership property over the basis of his interest in the partnership.

Under regulations prescribed by the Secretary, such increase or decrease shall constitute an adjustment to the basis of partnership property with respect to the transferee partner only. A partner's proportionate share of the adjusted basis of partnership property shall be determined in accordance with his interest in partnership capital and, in the case of property contributed to the partnership by a partner, section 704(c) (relating to contributed property) shall apply in determining such share. In the case of an adjustment under this subsection to the basis of partnership property subject to depletion, any depletion allowable shall be determined separately for the transferee partner with respect to his interest in such property.

(c) Allocation of basis.
The allocation of basis among partnership properties where subsection (b) is applicable shall be made in accordance with the rules provided in section 755.

(d) Substantial built-in loss.
   (1) In general. For purposes of this section, a partnership has a substantial built-in loss with respect to a transfer of an interest in a partnership if the partnership's adjusted basis in the partnership property exceeds by more than $250,000 the fair market value of such property.
   (2) Regulations. The Secretary shall prescribe such regulations as may be appropriate to carry out the purposes of paragraph (1) and section 734(d), including regulations aggregating related partnerships and disregarding property acquired by the partnership in an attempt to avoid such purposes.

(e) Alternative rules for electing investment partnerships.
   (1) No adjustment of partnership basis. For purposes of this section, an electing investment partnership shall not be treated as having a substantial built-in loss with respect to any transfer occurring while the election under paragraph (6)(A) is in effect.
   (2) Loss deferral for transferee partner. In the case of a transfer of an interest in an electing investment partnership, the transferee partner's distributive share of losses (without regard to gains) from the sale or exchange of partnership property shall not be allowed except to the extent that it is established that such losses exceed the loss (if any) recognized by the transferor (or any prior transferor to the extent not fully offset by a prior disallowance under this paragraph) on the transfer of the partnership interest.
   (3) No reduction in partnership basis. Losses disallowed under paragraph (2) shall not decrease the transferee partner's basis in the partnership interest.
   (4) Effect of termination of partnership. This subsection shall be applied without regard to any termination of a partnership under section 708(b)(1)(B).
   (5) Certain basis reductions treated as losses. In the case of a transferee partner whose basis in property distributed by the partnership is reduced under section 732(a)(2), the amount of the loss recognized by the transferor on the transfer of the partnership interest which is taken into account under paragraph (2) shall be reduced by the amount of such basis reduction.
   (6) Electing investment partnership. For purposes of this subsection, the term "electing investment partnership" means any partnership if—
      (A) the partnership makes an election to have this subsection apply,
      (B) the partnership would be an investment company under section 3(a)(1)(A) of the Investment Company Act of 1940 but for an exemption under paragraph (1) or (7) of section 3(c) of such Act,
      (C) such partnership has never been engaged in a trade or business,
      (D) substantially all of the assets of such partnership are held for investment,
      (E) at least 95 percent of the assets contributed to such partnership consist of money,
      (F) no assets contributed to such partnership had an adjusted basis in excess of fair market value at the time of contribution,
      (G) all partnership interests of such partnership are issued by such partnership pursuant to a private offering before the date which is 24 months after the date of the first capital contribution to such partnership,
      (H) the partnership agreement of such partnership has substantive restrictions on each partner's ability to cause a redemption of the partner's interest, and
      (I) the partnership agreement of such partnership provides for a term that is not in excess of 15 years.
   The election described in subparagraph (A), once made, shall be irrevocable except with the consent of the Secretary.
   (7) Regulations. The Secretary shall prescribe such regulations as may be appropriate to carry out the purposes of this subsection, including regulations for applying this subsection to tiered partnerships.

(f) Exception for securitization partnerships.
   (1) No adjustment of partnership basis. For purposes of this section, a securitization partnership shall not be treated as having a substantial built-in loss with respect to any transfer.
   (2) Securitization partnership. For purposes of paragraph (1), the term "securitization partnership" means any partnership the sole business activity of which is to issue securities which provide for a fixed principal (or similar) amount and which are primarily serviced by the cash flows of a discrete pool (either fixed or revolving) of receivables or other financial assets that by their terms convert into cash in a finite period, but only if the sponsor of the pool reasonably believes that the receivables and other financial assets comprising the pool are not acquired so as to be disposed of.

In 2004, P.L. 108-357, Sec. 833(b)(1), added "or unless the partnership has a substantial built-in loss immediately after such transfer" after "such partnership" at the end of subsec. (a). . . Sec. 833(b)(2), added "or which has a substantial built-in loss immediately after such transfer" after "section 754 is in effect" in subsec. (b) . . . Sec. 833(b)(3), added subsec. (d) . . . Sec. 833(b)(4)(A), added subsec. (e) . . . Sec. 833(b)(5), added subsec. (f) . . . Sec. 833(b)(6)(A), amended the heading of Code Sec. 743, effective for transfers after 10/22/2004, except as provided by Sec. 833(d)(2)(B) of this Act, which reads as follows:

"(B) Transition rule. In the case of an electing investment partnership which is in existence on June 4, 2004, section 743(e)(6)(H) of the Internal Revenue Code of 1986, as added by this section, shall not apply to such partnership and section 743(e)(6)(I) of such Code, as so added, shall be applied by substituting '20 years' for '15 years'."

Prior to amendment, the heading of Code Sec. 743 read as follows:
"SEC. 743. OPTIONAL ADJUSTMENT TO BASIS OF PARTNERSHIP PROPERTY."

In 1984, P.L. 98-369, Sec. 71(b), substituted "property contributed to the partnership by a partner, section 704(c) (relating to contributed property) shall apply in determining such share" for "an agreement described in section 704(c)(2) (relating to effect of partnership agreement on contributed property), such share shall be determined by taking such agreement into account" in subsec. (b), effective for property contributed to the partnership after 3/31/84, in tax. yrs. end. after 3/31/84.

In 1976, P.L. 94-455, Sec. 1906(b)(13)(A), substituted "Secretary" for "Secretary or his delegate" in subsec. (b), effective for tax. yrs. begin. after 12/31/76.

SUBPART D.—PROVISIONS COMMON TO OTHER SUBPARTS

Sec.
751. Unrealized receivables and inventory items.
752. Treatment of certain liabilities.
753. Partner receiving income in respect of decedent.

754. Manner of electing optional adjustment to basis of partnership property.
755. Rules for allocation of basis.

Sec. 751. Unrealized receivables and inventory items.

(a) Sale or exchange of interest in partnership.

The amount of any money, or the fair market value of any property, received by a transferor partner in exchange for all or a part of his interest in the partnership attributable to—

(1) unrealized receivables of the partnership, or

(2) inventory items of the partnership,

shall be considered as an amount realized from the sale or exchange of property other than a capital asset.

(b) Certain distributions treated as sales or exchanges.

(1) *General rule.* To the extent a partner receives in a distribution—

(A) partnership property which is—
(i) unrealized receivables, or
(ii) inventory items which have appreciated substantially in value,

in exchange for all or a part of his interest in other partnership property (including money), or

(B) partnership property (including money) other than property described in subparagraph (A)(i) or (ii) in exchange for all or a part of his interest in partnership property described in subparagraph (A)(i) or (ii),

such transactions shall, under regulations prescribed by the Secretary, be considered as a sale or exchange of such property between the distributee and the partnership (as constituted after the distribution).

(2) *Exceptions.* Paragraph (1) shall not apply to—

(A) a distribution of property which the distributee contributed to the partnership, or

(B) payments, described in section 736(a), to a retiring partner or successor in interest of a deceased partner.

(3) *Substantial appreciation.* For purposes of paragraph (1)—

(A) In general. Inventory items of the partnership shall be considered to have appreciated substantially in value if their fair market value exceeds 120 percent of the adjusted basis to the partnership of such property.

(B) Certain property excluded. For purposes of subparagraph (A), there shall be excluded any inventory property if a principal purpose for acquiring such property was to avoid the provisions of this subsection relating to inventory items.

(c) Unrealized receivables.

For purposes of this subchapter, the term "unrealized receivables" includes, to the extent not previously includible in income under the method of accounting used by the partnership, any rights (contractual or otherwise) to payment for—

(1) goods delivered, or to be delivered, to the extent the proceeds therefrom would be treated as amounts received from the sale or exchange of property other than a capital asset, or

(2) services rendered, or to be rendered.

For purposes of this section and, sections 731, 732, and 741 (but not for purposes of section 736), such term also includes mining property (as defined in section 617(f)(2)), stock in a DISC (as described in section 992(a)), section 1245 property (as defined in section 1245(a)(3)), stock in certain foreign corporations (as described in section 1248), section 1250 property (as defined in section 1250(c)), farm land (as defined in section 1252(a)), franchises, trademarks, or trade names (referred to in section 1253(a)), and an oil, gas, or geothermal property (described in section 1254) but only to the extent of the amount which would be treated as gain to which section 617(d)(1), 995(c), 1245(a), 1248(a), 1250(a), 1252(a), 1253(a) or 1254(a) would apply if (at the time of the transaction described in this section or section 731, 732, or 741, as the case may be) such property had been sold by the partnership at its fair market value. For purposes of this section and, sections 731, 732, and 741 (but not for purposes of section 736), such term also includes any market discount bond (as defined in section 1278) and any short-term obligation (as defined in section 1283) but only to the extent of the amount which would be treated as ordinary income if (at the time of the transaction described in this section or section 731, 732, or 741, as the case may be) such property had been sold by the partnership.

(d) Inventory items.

For purposes of this subchapter, the term "inventory items" means—

(1) property of the partnership of the kind described in section 1221(a)(1),

(2) any other property of the partnership which, on sale or exchange by the partnership, would be considered property other than a capital asset and other than property described in section 1231, and

(3) any other property held by the partnership which, if held by the selling or distributee partner, would be considered property of the type described in paragraph (1) or (2).

(e) Limitation on tax attributable to deemed sales of section 1248 stock.

For purposes of applying this section and sections 731 and 741 to any amount resulting from the reference to section 1248(a) in the second sentence of subsection (c), in the case of an individual, the tax attributable to such amount shall be limited in the manner provided by subsection (b) of section 1248 (relating to gain from certain sales or exchanges of stock in certain foreign corporation).

(f) Special rules in the case of tiered partnerships, etc.

In determining whether property of a partnership is—

(1) an unrealized receivable, or

(2) an inventory item,

such partnership shall be treated as owning its proportionate share of the property of any other partnership in which it is a partner. Under regulations, rules similar to the rules of the preceding sentence shall also apply in the case of interests in trusts.

In 2004, P.L. 108-357, Sec. 413(c)(11), added "and" at the end of para. (d)(2), deleted para. (d)(3), redesignated para. (d)(4) as (d)(3), and substituted "paragraph (1) or (2)" for "paragraph (1), (2), or (3)" in para. (d)(3) [as redesignated], effective for tax. yrs. of foreign corporations begin. after 12/31/2004, and for tax. yrs. of U.S. shareholders with or within which such tax. yrs. of foreign corporations end.

Prior to deletion, para. (d)(3) read as follows:

"(3) any other property of the partnership which, if sold or exchanged by the partnership, would result in a gain taxable under subsection (a) of section 1246 (relating to gain on foreign investment company stock), and"

In 1999, P.L. 106-170, Sec. 532(c)(2)(F), substituted "section 1221(a)(1)" for "section 1221(1)" in para. (d)(1), effective for any instrument held, acquired, or entered into, any transaction entered into, and supplies held or acquired on or after 12/17/99.

In 1998, P.L. 105-206, Sec. 6010(m), substituted "731, 732," for "731" each place it appeared in subsec. (c), effective for distributions after 8/5/97.

In 1997, P.L. 105-34, Sec. 1062(a), amended para. (a)(2) . . . Sec. 1062(b)(1)(A), amended subparas. (b)(1)(A) and (b)(1)(B) . . . Sec. 1062(b)(1)(B), added para. (b)(3) . . . Sec. 1062(b)(2), amended subsec. (d), effective for sales, exchanges, and distributions after 8/5/97. Sec. 1062(c)(2) of this Act provides:

"(2) Binding contracts. The amendments made by this section shall not apply to any sale or exchange pursuant to a written binding contract in effect on June 8, 1997, and at all thereafter before such sale or exchange."

Prior to amendment, para. (a)(2) read as follows:

"(2) inventory items of the partnership which have appreciated substantially in value,"

Prior to amendment, subparas. (b)(1)(A) and (b)(1)(B) read as follows:

Partners and partnerships
Code Sec. 752

"(A) partnership property described in subsection (a)(1) or (2) in exchange for all or a part of his interest in other partnership property (including money), or

"(B) partnership property (including money) other than property described in subsection (a)(1) or (2) in exchange for all or a part of his interest in partnership property described in subsection (a)(1) or (2),"

Prior to amendment, subsec. (d) read as follows:

"(d) Inventory items which have appreciated substantially in value.

"(1) Substantial appreciation.

"(A) In general. Inventory items of the partnership shall be considered to have appreciated substantially in value if their fair market value exceeds 120 percent of the adjusted basis to the partnership of such property.

"(B) Certain property excluded. For purposes of subparagraph (A), there shall be excluded any inventory property if a principal purpose for acquiring such property was to avoid the provisions of this section relating to inventory items.

"(2) Inventory items. For purposes of this subchapter the term 'inventory items' means —

"(A) property of the partnership of the kind described in section 1221(1),

"(B) any other property of the partnership which, on sale or exchange by the partnership, would be considered property other than a capital asset and other than property described in section 1231,

"(C) any other property of the partnership which, if sold or exchanged by the partnership, would result in a gain taxable under subsection (a) of section 1246 (relating to gain on foreign investment company stock), and

"(D) any other property held by the partnership which, if held by the selling or distributee partner, would be considered property of the type described in subparagraph (A), (B), or (C)."

In 1993, P.L. 103-66, Sec. 13206(e)(1), amended para. (d)(1), effective for sales, exchanges, and distributions after 4/30/93.

Prior to amendment, para. (d)(1) read as follows:

"(1) Substantial appreciation. Inventory items of the partnership shall be considered to have appreciated substantially in value if their fair market value exceeds —

"(A) 120 percent of the adjusted basis to the partnership of such property, and

"(B) 10 percent of the fair market value of all partnership property, other than money."

—P.L. 103-66, Sec. 13262(b)(1)(A), substituted ", sections 731 and 741 (but not for purposes of section 736)" for "sections 731, 736, and 741" each place it appeared in subsec. (c). . . . Sec. 13262(b)(1)(B), substituted "section 731 or 741" for "section 731, 736, or 741" each place it appeared in subsec. (c). . . . Sec. 13262(b)(2)(A), substituted "sections 731 and 741" for "sections 731, 736, and 741" in subsec. (e), effective in the case of partners retiring or dying on or after 1/5/93, except as provided in Sec. 13262(c)(2) of this Act, which reads as follows:

"(2) Binding contract exception. The amendments made by this section shall not apply to any partner retiring on or after January 5, 1993, if a written contract to purchase such partner's interest in the partnership was binding on January 4, 1993, and at all times thereafter before such purchase."

In 1988, P.L. 100-647, Sec. 1002(c)(3), of this Act provides:

"(3) Notwithstanding section 203 of the Reform Act, [P.L. 99-514] the amendments made by section 201 of the Reform Act [P.L. 99-514] shall apply to any real property which was acquired before January 1, 1987, and was converted on or after such date from personal use to a use for which depreciation is allowable.".

In 1986, P.L. 99-514, Sec. 201(d)(10), deleted "section 1245 recovery property (as defined in section 1245(a)(5))," following "(as defined in section 1245(a)(3))," in subsec. (c), effective for property placed in service after 12/31/86, [see Sec. 1002(c)(3) of P.L. 100-647, reproduced above] in tax. yrs. end. after 12/31/86. For transitional rules, see Sec. 203(b)-(e) of this Act, reproduced in note following Code Sec. 168. Sec. 203(a)(1)(B) of this Act provides:

"(B) Election to have amendments made by section 201 apply. — A taxpayer may elect (at such time and in such manner as the Secretary of the Treasury or his delegate may prescribe) to have the amendments made by section 201 apply to any property placed in service after July 31, 1986, and before January 1, 1987."

—P.L. 99-514, Sec. 1899A(19), substituted "section 617(f)(2)," for "section 617(f)(2), stock," effective 10/22/86.

In 1984, P.L. 98-369, Sec. 43(c)(3), added the last sentence of subsec. (c), effective for tax. yrs. end. after 7/18/84.

—P.L. 98-369, Sec. 76(a), added subsec. (f), effective for distributions sales, and exchanges made after 3/31/84, in tax. yrs. end. after 3/31/84.

—P.L. 98-369, Sec. 492(b)(4), deleted "farm recapture property (as defined in section 1251(e)(1)," after "as defined in section 1250(c)," and deleted "1251(c)" after "1250(a)" in subsec. (c), effective for tax. yrs. begin. after 12/31/83.

In 1983, P.L. 97-448, Sec. 102(a)(6), added "section 1245 recovery property (as defined in section 1245(a)(5))," after "section 1245(a)(3)," in the second sentence of subsec. (c), effective for property placed in service after 12/31/80 in tax. yrs. end. after 12/31/80.

In 1978, P.L. 95-618, Sec. 402(c)(5), substituted "oil, gas, or geothermal property" for "oil and gas property" in subsec. (c), effective with respect to wells commenced on or after 10/1/78, in tax. yrs. end. on or after 10/1/78.

—P.L. 95-600, Sec. 701(u)(13)(A), added subsec. (e), effective for transfers begin. after 10/9/75, and for sales, exchanges and distributions taking place after 10/9/75.

In 1976, P.L. 94-455, Sec. 205(b), substituted "farm land (as defined in section 1252(a))," and an oil or gas property (described in section 1254)" for "and farm land (as defined in section 1252(a))" and substituted "1252(a), or 1254(a)" for "or 1252(a)" in subsec. (c), effective for tax. yrs. end. after 12/31/75.

—P.L. 94-455, Sec. 1042(c)(2), substituted "(as defined in section 1245(a)(3)), stock in certain foreign corporations (as described in section 1248)," for "(as defined in section 1245(a)(3))" and substituted "1245(a), 1248(a)," for "1245(a)," in subsec. (c), effective for transfers begin. after 10/9/75, and to sales, exchanges, and distributions taking place after 10/9/75.

—P.L. 94-455, Sec. 1101(d)(2), substituted "(as defined in section 617(f)(2), stock in a DISC (as described in section 992(a))," for "(as defined in section 617(f)(2))," and substituted "617(d)(1), 995(c), 1245(a)," for "617(d)(1), 1245(a)" in subsec. (c), effective for sales, exchanges, or other dispositions after 12/31/75, in tax. yrs. end. after 12/31/75.

—P.L. 94-455, Sec. 1901(a)(93), substituted "1245(a), 1250(a)," for "1254(a), or 1250(a)," [sic ; presumably meaning "1245(a), or 1250(a),"] in subsec. (c), effective for tax. yrs. begin. after '76.

—P.L. 94-455, Sec. 1906(b)(13)(A), substituted "Secretary" for "Secretary or his delegate" in para. (b)(1), effective for tax. yrs. begin. after 12/31/76.

—P.L. 94-455, Sec. 2110(a)(1), substituted "farm land (as defined in section 1252(a)), franchises, trademarks, or trade names (referred to in section 1253(a))," for "farm land (as defined in section 1252(a))," in subsec. (c); (as previously amended by this Act) . . . Sec. 2110(a)(2), substituted "1252(a), 1253(a)" for "1252(a)" in subsec. (c), (as previously amended by this Act), effective for transactions described in sections 731, 736, 741 or 751 which occur after 12/31/76, in tax. yrs. end. after 12/31/76.

In 1969, P.L. 91-172, Sec. 211(b)(6), substituted "section 1250 property (as defined in section 1250(c)), farm recapture property (as defined in section 1251(e)(1)), and farm land (as defined in section 1252(a))" for "and section 1250 property (as defined in section 1250(c))", and substituted "1250(a), 1251(c), or 1252(a)" for "1250(a)" in subsec. (c), effective for tax. yrs. begin. after 12/31/69.

In 1966, P.L. 89-570, Sec. [1](c)(1), substituted "mining property (as defined in section 617(f)(2)), section 1245 property (as defined in section 1245(a)(3))," for "section 1245 property (as defined in section 1245(a)(3))" in the last sentence of subsec. (c). . . Sec. [1](c)(2), substituted "section 617(d)(1), 1245(a)," for "section 1245(a)" in the last sentence of subsec. (c), effective for tax. yrs. end. after 9/12/66, but only for expenditures paid or incurred after 9/12/66.

In 1964, P.L. 88-272, Sec. 231(b)(6), substituted "(as defined in section 1245(a)(3)) and section 1250 property (as defined in section 1250(c))" for "(as defined in section 1245(a)(3))" in subsec. (c), and substituted "to which section 1245(a) or 1250(a)" for "to which section 1245(a)" in subsec. (c), effective for dispositions after 12/31/63, in tax. yrs. end. after 12/31/63.

In 1962, P.L. 87-834, Sec. 13(f)(1), added last sentence in subsec. (c) . . . Sec. 14(b)(2), deleted "and" at the end of subpara. (d)(2)(B), amended subpara. (d)(2)(C), and added subpara. (d)(2)(D), effective for tax. yrs. begin. after 12/31/62.

Prior to amendment, subpara. (d)(2)(C) read as follows:

"(C) any other property held by the partnership which, if held by the selling or distributee partner, would be considered property of the type described in subparagraph (A) or (B)."

Sec. 752. Treatment of certain liabilities.
(a) Increase in partner's liabilities.

Any increase in a partner's share of the liabilities of a partnership, or any increase in a partner's individual liabilities by reason of the assumption by such partner of partnership liabilities, shall be considered as a contribution of money by such partner to the partnership.

(b) Decrease in partner's liabilities.

Any decrease in a partner's share of the liabilities of a partnership, or any decrease in a partner's individual liabilities by reason of the assumption by the partnership of such individual liabilities, shall be considered as a distribution of money to the partner by the partnership.

(c) Liability to which property is subject.

For purposes of this section, a liability to which property is subject shall, to the extent of the fair market value of such property, be considered as a liability of the owner of the property.

(d) Sale or exchange of an interest.

In the case of a sale or exchange of an interest in a partnership, liabilities shall be treated in the same manner as liabilities in connection with the sale or exchange of property not associated with partnerships.

In 1984, P.L. 98-369, Sec. 79(a), and (b), provided:

"(a) General rule. — Section 752 of the Internal Revenue Code of 1954 (and the regulations prescribed thereunder) shall be applied without regard to the result reached in the case of Raphan vs the United States, 3 Cl. Ct. 457 (1983).

"(b) Regulations. — In amending the regulations prescribed under section 752 of such Code to reflect subsection (a), the Secretary of the Treasury or his delegate shall prescribe regulations relating to liabilities, including the treatment of guarantees, assumptions, indemnity agreements, and similar arrangements."

Sec. 753. Partner receiving income in respect of decedent.

The amount includible in the gross income of a successor in interest of a deceased partner under section 736(a) shall be considered income in respect of a decedent under section 691.

Sec. 754. Manner of electing optional adjustment to basis of partnership property.

If a partnership files an election, in accordance with regulations prescribed by the Secretary, the basis of partnership property shall be adjusted, in the case of a distribution of property, in the manner provided in section 734 and, in the case of a transfer of a partnership interest, in the manner provided in section 743. Such an election shall apply with respect to all distributions of property by the partnership and to all transfers of interests in the partnership during the taxable year with respect to which such election was filed and all subsequent taxable years. Such election may be revoked by the partnership, subject to such limitations as may be provided by regulations prescribed by the Secretary.

In **1976**, P.L. 94-455, Sec. 1906(b)(13)(A), substituted "Secretary" for "Secretary or his delegate" each place it appeared in Code Sec. 754, effective for tax. yrs. begin. after 12/31/76.

Sec. 755. Rules for allocation of basis.
(a) General rule.

Any increase or decrease in the adjusted basis of partnership property under section 734(b) (relating to the optional adjustment to the basis of undistributed partnership property) or section 743(b) (relating to the optional adjustment to the basis of partnership property in the case of a transfer of an interest in a partnership) shall, except as provided in subsection (b), be allocated—

(1) in a manner which has the effect of reducing the difference between the fair market value and the adjusted basis of partnership properties, or

(2) in any other manner permitted by regulations prescribed by the Secretary.

(b) Special rule.

In applying the allocation rules provided in subsection (a), increases or decreases in the adjusted basis of partnership property arising from a distribution of, or a transfer of an interest attributable to, property consisting of—

(1) capital assets and property described in section 1231(b), or

(2) any other property of the partnership,

shall be allocated to partnership property of a like character except that the basis of any such partnership property shall not be reduced below zero. If, in the case of a distribution, the adjustment to basis of property described in paragraph (1) or (2) is prevented by the absence of such property or by insufficient adjusted basis for such property, such adjustment shall be applied to subsequently acquired property of a like character in accordance with regulations prescribed by the Secretary.

(c) No allocation of basis decrease to stock of corporate partner.

In making an allocation under subsection (a) of any decrease in the adjusted basis of partnership property under section 734(b)—

(1) no allocation may be made to stock in a corporation (or any person related (within the meaning of sections 267(b) and 707(b)(1)) to such corporation) which is a partner in the partnership, and

(2) any amount not allocable to stock by reason of paragraph (1) shall be allocated under subsection (a) to other partnership property.

Gain shall be recognized to the partnership to the extent that the amount required to be allocated under paragraph (2) to other partnership property exceeds the aggregate adjusted basis of such other property immediately before the allocation required by paragraph (2).

In **2004**, P.L. 108-357, Sec. 834(a), added subsec. (c), effective for distributions after 10/22/2004.
In **1976**, P.L. 94-455, Sec. 1906(b)(13)(A), substituted "Secretary" for "Secretary or his delegate" in para. (a)(2) and subsec. (b), effective for tax. yrs. begin. after 12/31/76.

PART III.—DEFINITIONS

Sec.
761. Terms defined.

Sec. 761. Terms defined.
(a) Partnership.

For purposes of this subtitle, the term "partnership" includes a syndicate, group, pool, joint venture, or other unincorporated organization through or by means of which any business, financial operation, or venture is carried on, and which is not, within the meaning of this title, a corporation or a trust or estate. Under regulations the Secretary may, at the election of all the members of an unincorporated organization, exclude such organization from the application of all or part of this subchapter, if it is availed of—

(1) for investment purposes only and not for the active conduct of a business,

(2) for the joint production, extraction, or use of property, but not for the purpose of selling services or property produced or extracted, or

(3) by dealers in securities for a short period for the purpose of underwriting, selling, or distributing a particular issue of securities,

if the income of the members of the organization may be adequately determined without the computation of partnership taxable income.

(b) Partner.

For purposes of this subtitle, the term "partner" means a member of a partnership.

(c) Partnership agreement.

For purposes of this subchapter, a partnership agreement includes any modifications of the partnership agreement made prior to, or at, the time prescribed by law for the filing of the partnership return for the taxable year (not including extensions) which are agreed to by all the partners, or which are adopted in such other manner as may be provided by the partnership agreement.

(d) Liquidation of a partner's interest.

For purposes of this subchapter, the term "liquidation of a partner's interest" means the termination of a partner's entire interest in a partnership by means of a distribution, or a series of distributions, to the partner by the partnership.

(e) Distributions of partnership interests treated as exchanges.

Except as otherwise provided in regulations, for purposes of—

(1) section 708 (relating to continuation of partnership),

(2) section 743 (relating to optional adjustment to basis of partnership property), and

(3) any other provision of this subchapter specified in regulations prescribed by the Secretary,

any distribution of an interest in a partnership (not otherwise treated as an exchange) shall be treated as an exchange.

(f) Qualified joint venture.
  (1) In general. In the case of a qualified joint venture conducted by a husband and wife who file a joint return for the taxable year, for purposes of this title—
    (A) such joint venture shall not be treated as a partnership,
    (B) all items of income, gain, loss, deduction, and credit shall be divided between the spouses in accordance with their respective interests in the venture, and
    (C) each spouse shall take into account such spouse's respective share of such items as if they were attributable to a trade or business conducted by such spouse as a sole proprietor.
  (2) Qualified joint venture. For purposes of paragraph (1), the term "qualified joint venture" means any joint venture involving the conduct of a trade or business if—
    (A) the only members of such joint venture are a husband and wife,
    (B) both spouses materially participate (within the meaning of section 469(h) without regard to paragraph (5) thereof) in such trade or business, and
    (C) both spouses elect the application of this subsection.
(g) Cross reference.
  For rules in the case of the sale, exchange, liquidation, or reduction of a partner's interest, see sections 704(b) and 706(c)(2).

In **2007**, P.L. 110-28, Sec. 8215(a), redesignated subsec. (f) as subsec. (g) and added new subsec. (f), effective for tax. yrs. begin. after 12/31/2006.
In **1986**, P.L. 99-514, Sec. 1805(c)(2)(A), substituted "Except as otherwise provided in regulations, for purposes of" for "For purposes of" in subsec. (e) . . . Sec. 1805(c)(2)(B), substituted "any distribution of an interest in a partnership (not otherwise treated as an exchange)" for "any distribution (not otherwise treated as an exchange)" in subsec. (e) . . . Sec. 1805(c)(2)(C), substituted "Distributions of partnership interests" for "Distributions" in the heading of subsec. (e), effective for distributions, sales and exchanges made after 3/31/84, in tax. yrs. end. after 3/31/84.
In **1984**, P.L. 98-369, Sec. 75(b), redesignated subsec. (e) as subsec. (f) and added new subsec. (e), effective for distributions, sales, and exchanges made after 3/31/84, in tax. yrs. end. after 3/31/84.
In **1980**, P.L. 96-222, Sec. 102(a)(2)(C), deleted "or" at the end of para. (a)(1), added "or" at the end of para. (a)(2), and added para. (a)(3), effective for tax. yrs. begin. after 12/31/78.
In **1976**, P.L. 94-455, Sec. 213(c)(3)(B), added subsec. (e), effective for tax. yrs. begin. after 12/31/75.
—P.L. 94-455, Sec. 1906(b)(13)(A), substituted "Secretary" for "Secretary or his delegate" in subsec. (a), effective for tax. yrs. begin. after 12/31/76.

PART IV.—SPECIAL RULES FOR ELECTING LARGE PARTNERSHIPS
Sec.
771. Application of subchapter to electing large partnerships.
772. Simplified flow-through.
773. Computations at partnership level.
774. Other modifications.
775. Electing large partnership defined.
776. Special rules for partnerships holding oil and gas properties.
777. Regulations.

In **1997**, P.L. 105-34, Sec. 1221(a), added Part IV to Subchapter K.

Sec. 771. Application of subchapter to electing large partnerships.
  The preceding provisions of this subchapter to the extent inconsistent with the provisions of this part shall not apply to an electing large partnership and its partners.

In **1997**, P.L. 105-34, Sec. 1221(a), added Code Sec. 771, effective for partnership tax. yrs. begin. after 12/31/97.

Sec. 772. Simplified flow-through.
(a) General rule.
  In determining the income tax of a partner of an electing large partnership, such partner shall take into account separately such partner's distributive share of the partnership's—
  (1) taxable income or loss from passive loss limitation activities,
  (2) taxable income or loss from other activities,
  (3) net capital gain (or net capital loss)—
    (A) to the extent allocable to passive loss limitation activities, and
    (B) to the extent allocable to other activities,
  (4) tax-exempt interest,
  (5) applicable net AMT adjustment separately computed for—
    (A) passive loss limitation activities, and
    (B) other activities,
  (6) general credits,
  (7) low-income housing credit determined under section 42,
  (8) rehabilitation credit determined under section 47,
  (9) foreign income taxes, and
  (10) other items to the extent that the Secretary determines that the separate treatment of such items is appropriate.
(b) Separate computations.
  In determining the amounts required under subsection (a) to be separately taken into account by any partner, this section and section 773 shall be applied separately with respect to such partner by taking into account such partner's distributive share of the items of income, gain, loss, deduction, or credit of the partnership.
(c) Treatment at partner level.
  (1) In general. Except as provided in this subsection, rules similar to the rules of section 702(b) shall apply to any partner's distributive share of the amounts referred to in subsection (a).
  (2) Income or loss from passive loss limitation activities. For purposes of this chapter, any partner's distributive share of any income or loss described in subsection (a)(1) shall be treated as an item of income or loss (as the case may be) from the conduct of a trade or business which is a single passive activity (as defined in section 469). A similar rule shall apply to a partner's distributive share of amounts referred to in paragraphs (3)(A) and (5)(A) of subsection (a).
  (3) Income or loss from other activities.
    (A) In general. For purposes of this chapter, any partner's distributive share of any income or loss described in subsection (a)(2) shall be treated as an item of income or expense (as the case may be) with respect to property held for investment.
    (B) Deductions for loss not subject to section 67. The deduction under section 212 for any loss described in subparagraph (A) shall not be treated as a miscellaneous itemized deduction for purposes of section 67.
  (4) Treatment of net capital gain or loss. For purposes of this chapter, any partner's distributive share of any gain or loss described in subsection (a)(3) shall be treated as a long-term capital gain or loss, as the case may be.
  (5) Minimum tax treatment. In determining the alternative minimum taxable income of any partner, such partner's distributive share of any applicable net AMT adjustment shall be taken into account in lieu of making the

separate adjustments provided in sections 56, 57, and 58 with respect to the items of the partnership. Except as provided in regulations, the applicable net AMT adjustment shall be treated, for purposes of section 53, as an adjustment or item of tax preference not specified in section 53(d)(1)(B)(ii).

(6) General credits. A partner's distributive share of the amount referred to in paragraph (6) of subsection (a) shall be taken into account as a current year business credit.

(d) Operating rules.

For purposes of this section—

(1) Passive loss limitation activity. The term "passive loss limitation activity" means—

(A) any activity which involves the conduct of a trade or business, and

(B) any rental activity.

For purposes of the preceding sentence, the term "trade or business" includes any activity treated as a trade or business under paragraph (5) or (6) of section 469(c).

(2) Tax-exempt interest. The term "tax-exempt interest" means interest excludable from gross income under section 103.

(3) Applicable net AMT adjustment.

(A) In general. The applicable net AMT adjustment is—

(i) with respect to taxpayers other than corporations, the net adjustment determined by using the adjustments applicable to individuals, and

(ii) with respect to corporations, the net adjustment determined by using the adjustments applicable to corporations.

(B) Net adjustment. The term "net adjustment" means the net adjustment in the items attributable to passive loss activities or other activities (as the case may be) which would result if such items were determined with the adjustments of sections 56, 57, and 58.

(4) Treatment of certain separately stated items.

(A) Exclusion for certain purposes. In determining the amounts referred to in paragraphs (1) and (2) of subsection (a), any net capital gain or net capital loss (as the case may be), and any item referred to in subsection (a)(11), shall be excluded.

(B) Allocation rules. The net capital gain shall be treated—

(i) as allocable to passive loss limitation activities to the extent the net capital gain does not exceed the net capital gain determined by only taking into account gains and losses from sales and exchanges of property used in connection with such activities, and

(ii) as allocable to other activities to the extent such gain exceeds the amount allocated under clause (i).

A similar rule shall apply for purposes of allocating any net capital loss.

(C) Net capital loss. The term "net capital loss" means the excess of the losses from sales or exchanges of capital assets over the gains from sales or exchange of capital assets.

(5) General credits. The term "general credits" means any credit other than the low-income housing credit, the rehabilitation credit, and the foreign tax credit.

(6) Foreign income taxes. The term "foreign income taxes" means taxes described in section 901 which are paid or accrued to foreign countries and to possessions of the United States.

(e) Special rule for unrelated business tax.

In the case of a partner which is an organization subject to tax under section 511, such partner's distributive share of any items shall be taken into account separately to the extent necessary to comply with the provisions of section 512(c)(1).

(f) Special rules for applying passive loss limitations.

If any person holds an interest in an electing large partnership other than as a limited partner—

(1) paragraph (2) of subsection (c) shall not apply to such partner, and

(2) such partner's distributive share of the partnership items allocable to passive loss limitation activities shall be taken into account separately to the extent necessary to comply with the provisions of section 469.

The preceding sentence shall not apply to any items allocable to an interest held as a limited partner.

In 2005, P.L. 109-58, Sec. 1322(a)(3)(I), added "and" at the end of para. (a)(9), deleted para. (a)(10), and redesignated para. (a)(11) as (10) . . . Sec. 1322(a)(3)(J), substituted "and the foreign tax credit" for "the foreign tax credit, and the credit allowable under section 29" in para. (d)(5), effective for credits determined under the Internal Revenue Code of 1986 for tax. yrs. end. after 12/31/2005.
Prior to deletion, para. (a)(10) read as follows:
"(10) the credit allowable under section 29, and"
In 1997, P.L. 105-34, Sec. 1221(a), added Code Sec. 772, effective for partnership tax. yrs. begin. after 12/31/97.

Sec. 773. Computations at partnership level.

(a) General rule.

(1) Taxable income. The taxable income of an electing large partnership shall be computed in the same manner as in the case of an individual except that—

(A) the items described in section 772(a) shall be separately stated, and

(B) the modifications of subsection (b) shall apply.

(2) Elections. All elections affecting the computation of the taxable income of an electing large partnership or the computation of any credit of an electing large partnership shall be made by the partnership; except that the election under section 901, and any election under section 108, shall be made by each partner separately.

(3) Limitations, etc.

(A) In general. Except as provided in subparagraph (B), all limitations and other provisions affecting the computation of the taxable income of an electing large partnership or the computation of any credit of an electing large partnership shall be applied at the partnership level (and not at the partner level).

(B) Certain limitations applied at partner level. The following provisions shall be applied at the partner level (and not at the partnership level):

(i) Section 68 (relating to overall limitation on itemized deductions).

(ii) Sections 49 and 465 (relating to at risk limitations).

(iii) Section 469 (relating to limitation on passive activity losses and credits).

(iv) Any other provision specified in regulations.

(4) Coordination with other provisions. Paragraphs (2) and (3) shall apply notwithstanding any other provision of this chapter other than this part.

(b) Modifications to determination of taxable income.

In determining the taxable income of an electing large partnership—

(1) Certain deductions not allowed. The following deductions shall not be allowed:

(A) The deduction for personal exemptions provided in section 151.

Partners and partnerships   Code Sec. 775(b)(2)(C)

(B) The net operating loss deduction provided in section 172.

(C) The additional itemized deductions for individuals provided in part VII of subchapter B (other than section 212 thereof).

(2) Charitable deductions. In determining the amount allowable under section 170, the limitation of section 170(b)(2) shall apply.

(3) Coordination with section 67. In lieu of applying section 67, 70 percent of the amount of the miscellaneous itemized deductions shall be disallowed.

(c) Special rules for income from discharge of indebtedness.

If an electing large partnership has income from the discharge of any indebtedness—

(1) such income shall be excluded in determining the amounts referred to in section 772(a), and

(2) in determining the income tax of any partner of such partnership—

  (A) such income shall be treated as an item required to be separately taken into account under section 772(a), and

  (B) the provisions of section 108 shall be applied without regard to this part.

In 1997, P.L. 105-34, Sec. 1221(a), added Code Sec. 773, effective for partnership tax. yrs. begin. after 12/31/97.

Sec. 774. Other modifications.
(a) Treatment of certain optional adjustments, etc.

In the case of an electing large partnership—

(1) computations under section 773 shall be made without regard to any adjustment under section 743(b) or 108(b), but

(2) a partner's distributive share of any amount referred to in section 772(a) shall be appropriately adjusted to take into account any adjustment under section 743(b) or 108(b) with respect to such partner.

(b) Credit recapture determined at partnership level.

(1) **In general.** In the case of an electing large partnership—

  (A) any credit recapture shall be taken into account by the partnership, and

  (B) the amount of such recapture shall be determined as if the credit with respect to which the recapture is made had been fully utilized to reduce tax.

(2) **Method of taking recapture into account.** An electing large partnership shall take into account a credit recapture by reducing the amount of the appropriate current year credit to the extent thereof, and if such recapture exceeds the amount of such current year credit, the partnership shall be liable to pay such excess.

(3) **Dispositions not to trigger recapture.** No credit recapture shall be required by reason of any transfer of an interest in an electing large partnership.

(4) **Credit recapture.** For purposes of this subsection, the term "credit recapture" means any increase in tax under section 42(j) or 50(a).

(c) Partnership not terminated by reason of change in ownership.

Subparagraph (B) of section 708(b)(1) shall not apply to an electing large partnership.

(d) Partnership entitled to certain credits.

The following shall be allowed to an electing large partnership and shall not be taken into account by the partners of such partnership:

(1) The credit provided by section 34.

(2) Any credit or refund under section 852(b)(3)(D) or 857(b)(3)(D).

(e) Treatment of REMIC residuals.

For purposes of applying section 860E(e)(6) to any electing large partnership—

(1) all interests in such partnership shall be treated as held by disqualified organizations,

(2) in lieu of applying subparagraph (C) of section 860E(e)(6), the amount subject to tax under section 860E(e)(6) shall be excluded from the gross income of such partnership, and

(3) subparagraph (D) of section 860E(e)(6) shall not apply.

(f) Special rules for applying certain installment sale rules.

In the case of an electing large partnership—

(1) the provisions of sections 453(l)(3) and 453A shall be applied at the partnership level, and

(2) in determining the amount of interest payable under such sections, such partnership shall be treated as subject to tax under this chapter at the highest rate of tax in effect under section 1 or 11.

In 1998, P.L. 105-206, Sec. 6012(c), added "or 857(b)(3)(D)" before the period at the end of para. (d)(2), effective for partnership tax. yrs. begin. after 12/31/97.
In 1997, P.L. 105-34, Sec. 1221(a), added Code Sec. 774, effective for partnership tax. yrs. begin. after 12/31/97.

Sec. 775. Electing large partnership defined.
(a) General rule.

For purposes of this part—

(1) **In general.** The term "electing large partnership" means, with respect to any partnership taxable year, any partnership if—

  (A) the number of persons who were partners in such partnership in the preceding partnership taxable year equaled or exceeded 100, and

  (B) such partnership elects the application of this part.

To the extent provided in regulations, a partnership shall cease to be treated as an electing large partnership for any partnership taxable year if in such taxable year fewer than 100 persons were partners in such partnership.

(2) **Election.** The election under this subsection shall apply to the taxable year for which made and all subsequent taxable years unless revoked with the consent of the Secretary.

(b) Special rules for certain service partnerships.

(1) **Certain partners not counted.** For purposes of this section, the term "partner" does not include any individual performing substantial services in connection with the activities of the partnership and holding an interest in such partnership, or an individual who formerly performed substantial services in connection with such activities and who held an interest in such partnership at the time the individual performed such services.

(2) **Exclusion.** For purposes of this part, an election under subsection (a) shall not be effective with respect to any partnership if substantially all the partners of such partnership—

  (A) are individuals performing substantial services in connection with the activities of such partnership or are personal service corporations (as defined in section 269A(b)) the owner-employees (as defined in section 269A(b)) of which perform such substantial services,

  (B) are retired partners who had performed such substantial services, or

  (C) are spouses of partners who are performing (or had previously performed) such substantial services.

2,361

(3) Special rule for lower tier partnerships. For purposes of this subsection, the activities of a partnership shall include the activities of any other partnership in which the partnership owns directly an interest in the capital and profits of at least 80 percent.

(c) Exclusion of commodity pools.

For purposes of this part, an election under subsection (a) shall not be effective with respect to any partnership the principal activity of which is the buying and selling of commodities (not described in section 1221(a)(1)), or options, futures, or forwards with respect to such commodities.

(d) Secretary may rely on treatment on return.

If, on the partnership return of any partnership, such partnership is treated as an electing large partnership, such treatment shall be binding on such partnership and all partners of such partnership but not on the Secretary.

In **1999**, P.L. 106-170, Sec. 532(c)(2)(G), substituted "section 1221(a)(1)" for "section 1221(1)" in subsec. (c), effective for any instrument held, acquired, or entered into, any transaction entered into, and supplies held or acquired on or after 12/17/99.

In **1997**, P.L. 105-34, Sec. 1221(a), added Code Sec. 775, effective for partnership tax. yrs. begin. after 12/31/97.

Sec. 776. Special rules for partnerships holding oil and gas properties.

(a) Computation of percentage depletion.

In the case of an electing large partnership, except as provided in subsection (b)—

(1) the allowance for depletion under section 611 with respect to any partnership oil or gas property shall be computed at the partnership level without regard to any provision of section 613A requiring such allowance to be computed separately by each partner,

(2) such allowance shall be determined without regard to the provisions of section 613A(c) limiting the amount of production for which percentage depletion is allowable and without regard to paragraph (1) of section 613A(d), and

(3) paragraph (3) of section 705(a) shall not apply.

(b) Treatment of certain partners.

(1) In general. In the case of a disqualified person, the treatment under this chapter of such person's distributive share of any item of income, gain, loss, deduction, or credit attributable to any partnership oil or gas property shall be determined without regard to this part. Such person's distributive share of any such items shall be excluded for purposes of making determinations under sections 772 and 773.

(2) Disqualified person. For purposes of paragraph (1), the term "disqualified person" means, with respect to any partnership taxable year—

(A) any person referred to in paragraph (2) or (4) of section 613A(d) for such person's taxable year in which such partnership taxable year ends, and

(B) any other person if such person's average daily production of domestic crude oil and natural gas for such person's taxable year in which such partnership taxable year ends exceeds 500 barrels.

(3) Average daily production. For purposes of paragraph (2), a person's average daily production of domestic crude oil and natural gas for any taxable year shall be computed as provided in section 613A(c)(2)—

(A) by taking into account all production of domestic crude oil and natural gas (including such person's proportionate share of any production of a partnership),

(B) by treating 6,000 cubic feet of natural gas as a barrel of crude oil, and

(C) by treating as 1 person all persons treated as 1 taxpayer under section 613A(c)(8) or among whom allocations are required under such section.

In **1997**, P.L. 105-34, Sec. 1221(a), added Code Sec. 776, effective for partnership tax. yrs. begin. after 12/31/97.

Sec. 777. Regulations.

The Secretary shall prescribe such regulations as may be appropriate to carry out the purposes of this part.

In **1997**, P.L. 105-34, Sec. 1221(a), added Code Sec. 777, effective for partnership tax. yrs. begin. after 12/31/97.

PART IV. REPEALED

In **1976**, P.L. 94-455, Sec. 1901(a)(94), repealed Part IV of subchapter K, for tax. yrs. begin. after '76.
Prior to amendment Part IV read as follows:
"PART IV.—EFFECTIVE DATE FOR SUBCHAPTER
"Sec.
771. Effective date.
"SEC. 771. EFFECTIVE DATE.
"(a) General rule.
"(1) Taxable years beginning after December 31, 1954. Except as provided in subsection (b), this subchapter shall apply with respect to—
"(A) any partnership taxable year beginning after December 31, 1954, and
"(B) any part of a partner's taxable year falling within such partnership taxable year.
"(2) Application of prior provisions. Except as provided in subsection (b), sections 113(a)(13), 181 to 191 (inclusive), and 3797(a)(2) of the Internal Revenue Code of 1939 shall apply with respect to—
"(A) any partnership taxable year beginning before January 1, 1955, and
"(B) any part of a partner's taxable year falling within such partnership taxable year.
"(b) Special rules.
"(1) Adoption of taxable year. Section 706(b) (relating to the adoption of a taxable year by a partnership or partner) shall apply to—
"(A) any partnership which adopts, or changes to, a taxable year beginning after April 1, 1954, and
"(B) any partner who changes to a taxable year beginning after April 1, 1954. For the purpose of applying this paragraph, section 708 (relating to the continuation of a partnership) shall be effective for taxable years beginning after April 1, 1954.
"(2) Property distributed by a partnership. Section 735(a) (relating to the character of gain or loss on the disposition of property distributed by a partnership) shall apply only to property distributed by a partnership after March 9, 1954.
"(3) Unrealized receivables and inventory items. Section 751 (relating to unrealized receivables and inventory items) shall apply with respect to gain or loss to a seller, distributee, or partnership in the case of a sale, exchange, or distribution occurring after March 9, 1954. For the purpose of applying this paragraph in the case of a taxable year beginning before January 1, 1955, the other sections of this subchapter shall be applicable to the extent provided by regulations prescribed by the Secretary or his delegate.
"(4) Partner receiving income in respect of decedent. Section 753 (relating to income in respect of a decedent) shall apply only in the case of payments made with respect to decedents dying after December 31, 1954.
"(c) Optional treatment of certain distributions.
"In the case of a partnership taxable year beginning after December 31, 1953, and before January 1, 1955, a partnership may elect, under regulations prescribed by the Secretary or his delegate, with respect to distributions made during such year to any partner, other than in liquidation of the partner's interest, to apply the rules in sections 731, 732(a), (c), and (e), 733, 735, and 751(b), (c), and (d) (and, to the extent applicable, the rules provided in sections 705, 752, and 761(d)). If a partnership so elects, such rules shall be effective for the partnership and all members of such partnership with respect to such distributions."

Subchapter L.—Insurance Companies

Part
  I. Life insurance companies.
 II. Other insurance companies.
III. Provisions of general application.

In **1988**, P.L. 100-647, Sec. 1018(u)(32), deleted the items for Parts II-IV, and added the items for Parts II and III.
Prior to amendment, Parts II-IV read as follows:
"II. Mutual insurance companies (other than life and certain marine insurance companies and other than fire or flood insurance companies which operate on basis of perpetual policies or premium deposits).

"III. Other insurance companies.
"IV. Provisions of general application."
In 1984, P.L. 98-369, Sec. 211(a), amended Part I of Subchapter L.

In 1962, substituted "and certain marine and other than fire or flood insurance companies which operate on basis of perpetual policies or premium deposits" for "or marine or fire insurance compaines issuing perpetual policies" in the heading of Part II.

In 1959, P.L. 86-69, Sec. 2(a), amended Part I of Subchapter L.

In 1956, P.L. 429, Sec. 2, amended Part I of Subchapter L.

PART I.—LIFE INSURANCE COMPANIES
Subpart
A. Tax imposed.
B. Life insurance gross income.
C. Life insurance deductions.
D. Accounting, allocation, and foreign provisions.
E. Definitions and special rules.

In 1984, P.L. 98-369, Sec. 211(a), amended Part I of Subchapter L. Prior to amendment, Part I read as follows:

"PART I.—LIFE INSURANCE COMPANIES
 "Subpart
 "A. Definition; tax imposed.
 "B. Investment income.
 "C. Gain and loss from operations.
 "D. Distributions to shareholders.
 "E. Miscellaneous provisions."

"SUBPART A.— DEFINITION; TAX IMPOSED
 "Sec.
 "801. Definition of life insurance company.
 "802. Tax imposed."

"SEC. 801. DEFINITION OF LIFE INSURANCE COMPANY.
"(a) Life insurance company defined.

"For purposes of this subtitle, the term 'life insurance company' means an insurance company which is engaged in the business of issuing life insurance and annuity contracts (either separately or combined with heal and accident insurance), or noncancellable contracts of health and accident insurance, if—

"(1) its life insurance reserves (as defined in subsection (b)), plus

"(2) unearned premiums and unpaid losses (whether or not ascertained) on noncancellable life, health, or accident policies not included in life insurance reserves, comprise more than 50 percent of its total reserves (as defined in subsection (c)).

"(b) Life insurance reserves defined.

"(1) In general. For purposes of this part, the term 'life insurance reserves' means amounts—

"(A) which are computed or estimated on the basis of recognized mortality of morbidity tables and assumed rates of interest, and

"(B) which are set aside to mature or liquidate, either by payment or reinsurance, future unaccrued claims arising from life insurance, annuity, and noncancellable health and accident insurance contracts (including life insurance or annuity contracts combined with noncancellable health and accident insurance) involving, at the time with respect to which the reserve is computed, life, health, or accident contingencies.

"(2) Reserves must be required by law. Except—

"(A) in the case of policies covering life, health, and accident insurance combined in one policy issued on the weekly premium payment plan, continuing for life and not subject to cancellation, and

"(B) as provided in paragraph (3),

in addition to the requirements set forth in paragraph (1), life insurance reserves must be required by law.

"(3) Assessment companies. In the case of an assessment life insurance company or association, the term 'life insurance reserves' includes—

"(A) sums actually deposited by such company or association with State officers pursuant to law as guaranty or reserve funds, and

"(B) any funds maintained, under the charter or articles of incorporation or association (or bylaws approved by a State insurance commissioner) of such company or association, exclusively for the payment of claims arising under certificates of membership or policies issued on the assessment plan and not subject to any other use.

For purposes of this part, the rate of interest assumed in calculating the reserves described in subparagraphs (A) and (B) shall be 3 percent.

"(4) Deficiency reserves excluded. The term 'life insurance reserves' does not include deficiency reserves. For purposes of this subsection and subsection (c), the deficiency reserve for any contract is that portion of the reserve for such contract equal to the amount (if any) by which—

"(A) the present value of the future net premiums required for such contracts, exceeds

"(B) the present value of the future actual premiums and consideration charged for such contract.

"(5) Amount of reserves. For purposes of this subsection, subsection (a), and subsection (c), the amount of any reserve (or portion thereof) for any taxable year shall be the mean of such reserve (or portion thereof) at the beginning and end of the taxable year.

"(c) Total reserves defined.

"For purposes of subsection (a), the term 'total reserves' means—

"(1) life insurance reserves,

"(2) unearned premiums, and unpaid losses (whether or not ascertained), not included in life insurance reserves, and

"(3) all other insurance reserves required by law.

The term 'total reserves' does not include deficiency reserves (within the meaning of subsection (b)(4)).

"(d) Adjustments in reserves for policy loans.

"For purposes only of determining under subsection (a) whether or not an insurance company is a life insurance company, the life insurance reserves, and the total reserves, shall each be reduced by an amount equal to the mean of the aggregates, at the beginning and end of the taxable year, of the policy loans outstanding with respect to contracts for which life insurance reserves are maintained.

"(e) Guaranteed renewable contracts.

"For purposes of this part, guaranteed renewable life, health, and accident insurance shall be treated in the same manner as noncancellable life, health, and accident insurance.

"(f) Burial and funeral benefit insurance companies.

"A burial or funeral benefit insurance company engaged directly in the manufacture of funeral supplies of the performance of funeral services shall not be taxable under this part but shall be taxable under section 821 or section 831.

"(g) Contracts with reserves based on segregated asset accounts.

"(1) Definitions.

"(A) Annuity contracts include variable annuity contracts. For purposes of this part, an 'annuity contract' includes a contract which provides for the payment of a variable annuity computed on the basis of recognized mortality tables and the investment experience of the company issuing the contract.

"(B) Contracts with reserves based on a segregated asset account. For purposes of this part, a 'contract with reserves based on a segregated asset account' is a contract—

"(i) which provides for the allocation of all or part of the amounts received under the contract to an account which, pursuant to State law or regulation, is segregated from the general asset accounts of the company,

"(ii) which is described in any paragraph of section 805(d) (other than a life, health or accident, property, casualty, or liability insurance contract) or which provides for the payment of annuities, and

"(iii) under which the amounts paid in, or the amount paid out, reflect the investment return and the market value of the segregated asset account.

If a contract ceases to reflect current investment return and current market value, such contract shall not be considered as meeting the requirements of clause (iii) after such cessation.

"(2) Life insurance reserves. For purposes of subsection (b)(1)(A) of this section, the reflection of the investment return and the market value of the segregated asset account shall be considered an assumed rate of interest.

"(3) Separate accounting. For purposes of this part, a life insurance company which issues contracts with reserves based on segregated asset accounts shall separately account for the various income, exclusion, deduction, asset, reserve, and other liability items properly attributable to such segregated asset accounts. For such items as are not accounted for directly, separate accounting shall be made—

"(A) in accordance with the method regularly employed by such company, if such method is reasonable, and

"(B) in all other cases, in accordance with regulations prescribed by the Secretary.

"(4) Investment yield.

"(A) In general. For purposes of this part, the policy and other contract liability requirements, and the life insurance company's share of investment yield, shall be separately computed—

"(i) with respect to the items separately accounted for in accordance with paragraph (3), and

"(ii) excluding the items taken into account under clause (i).

"(B) Capital gains and losses. If, without regard to subparagraph (A), the net short-term capital gain exceeds the net long-term capital loss, such excess shall be allocated between clauses (i) and (ii) of subparagraph (A) in proportion to the respective contributions to such excess of the items taken into account under each such clause.

"(5) Policy and other contract liability requirements. For purposes of this part—

"(A) with respect to life insurance reserves based on segregated asset accounts, the adjusted reserves rate and the current earnings rate for purposes of section 805(b), and the rate of interest assumed by the taxpayer for purposes of sections 805(c) and 809(a)(2), shall be a rate equal to the current earnings rate determined under section 805(b)(2) with respect to the items separately accounted for in accordance with paragraph (3) reduced by the percentage obtained by dividing—

"(i) any amount retained with respect to such reserves by the life insurance company from gross investment income (as defined in section 804(b)) on segregated assets, to the extent such retained amount exceeds the deductions allowable under section 804(c) which are attributable to such reserves, by

"(ii) the means of such reserves; and

"(B) with respect to reserves based on segregated asset accounts other than life insurance reserves, an amount equal to the product of—

"(i) the rate of interest assumed as defined in subparagraph (A), and

"(ii) the means of such reserves,

shall be included as interest paid within the meaning of section 805(e)(1).

2,363

"(6) Increases and decreases in reserves. For purposes of subsections (a) and (b) of section 810, the sum of the items described in section 810(c) taken into account as of the close of the taxable year shall, under regulations prescribed by the Secretary, be adjusted—

"(A) by subtracting therefrom an amount equal to the sum of the amounts added from time to time (for the taxable year) to the reserves separately accounted for in accordance with paragraph (3) by reason of appreciation in value of assets (whether or not the assets have been disposed of), and

"(B) by adding thereto an amount equal to the sum of the amounts subtracted from time to time (for the taxable year) from such reserves by reason of depreciation in value of assets (whether or not the assets have been disposed of).

The deduction allowable for items described in paragraphs (1) and (7) of section 809(d) with respect to segregated asset accounts shall be reduced to the extent that the amount of such items is increased for the taxable year by appreciation (or increased to the extent that the amount of such items is decreased for the taxable year by depreciation) not reflected in adjustments under the preceding sentence.

"(7) Basis of assets held for qualified pension plan contracts. In the case of contracts described in any paragraph of section 805(d), the basis of each asset in a segregated asset account shall (in addition to all other adjustments to basis) be—

"(A) increased by the amount of any appreciation in value, and

"(B) decreased by the amount of any depreciation in value,

to the extent that such appreciation and depreciation are from time to time reflected in the increases and decreases in reserves or other items in paragraph (6) with respect to such contracts.

"(8) Additional separate computations. Under regulations prescribed by the Secretary, such additional separate computations shall be made, with respect to the items separately accounted for in accordance with paragraph (3), as may be necessary to carry out the purposes of this subsection and this part."

In 1978, P.L. 95-600, Sec. 703(j)(4), substituted "any paragraph of section 805(d)" for "subparagraph (A), (B), (C), (D), or (E) of section 805(d)(1)" in clause (g)(1)(B)(ii) and para. (g)(7), effective 10/4/76.

In 1976, P.L. 94-455, Sec. 1505(a), amended clause (g)(1)(B)(ii) and substituted "out" for "as annuities" in clause (g)(1)(B)(iii), for distributions and payments made after 12/31/75.

Prior to amendment, clause (g)(1)(B)(ii) read as follows:

"(ii) which provides for the payment of annuities, and"

—P.L. 95-455, Sec. 1901(c)(6), deleted "or Territorial" in subpara. (b)(3)(A), effective for tax. yrs. begin. after 12/31/76.

—P.L. 95-455, Sec. 1906(b)(13)(A), substituted "Secretary" for "Secretary or his delegate" each time it appeared in subsec. (g), effective for tax. yrs. begin. after 12/31/76.

In 1974, P.L. 93-406, Sec. 2002(g)(11), substituted "(D), or (E)" for "or (D)" in para. (g)(7), effective 1/1/75.

In 1969, P.L. 91-172, Sec. 121(b)(5)(B), added "and" at the end of subpara. (b)(2)(A), deleted subpara. (b)(2)(B) and redesignated subpara. (b)(2)(C) as (b)(2)(B), effective for tax. yrs. begin. after 12/31/69.

Prior to deletion, subpara. (b)(2)(B) read as follows:

"(B) in the case of policies issued by an organization which meets the requirements of section 501(c)(9) other than the requirement of subparagraph (B) thereof, and"

In 1962, P.L. 87-858, Sec. 3(a), amended subsec. (g), effective for tax. yrs. begin. after 12/31/61.

Prior to amendment, subsec. (g) read as follows:

"(g) Variable annuities.

"(1) In general. For purposes of this part, an annuity contract includes a contract which provides for the payment of a variable annuity computed on the basis of recognized mortality tables and the investment experience of the company issuing the contract.

"(2) Adjusted reserves rate; assumed rate. For purposes of this part—

"(A) the adjusted reserves rate for any taxable year with respect to annuity contracts described in paragraph (1), and

"(B) the rate of interest assumed by the taxpayer for any taxable year in calculating the reserve on any such contract,

shall be a rate equal to the current earnings rate determined under paragraph (3).

"(3) Current earnings rate. For purposes of this part, the current earnings rate for any taxable year with respect to annuity contracts described in paragraph (1) is the current earnings rate determined under section 805(b)(2) with respect to such contracts, reduced by the percentage obtained by dividing—

"(A) the amount of the actuarial margin charge on all annuity contracts described in paragraph (1) issued by the taxpayer, by

"(B) the mean of the reserves for such contracts.

"(4) Increases and decreases in reserves. For purposes of subsections (a) and (b) of section 810, the sum of the items described in section 801(c) taken into account as of the close of the taxable year shall, under regulations prescribed by the Secretary or his delegate, be adjusted—

"(A) by subtracting therefrom an amount equal to the sum of the amounts added from time to time (for the taxable year) to the reserves for annuity contracts described in paragraph (1) by reason of appreciation in value of assets (whether or not the assets have been disposed of), and

"(B) by adding thereto an amount equal to the sum of the amounts subtracted from time to time (for the taxable year) from such reserves by reason of depreciation in value of assets (whether or not the assets have been disposed of).

"(5) Companies issuing variable annuities and other contracts. In the case of a life insurance company which issues both annuity contracts described in paragraph (1) and other contracts, under regulations prescribed by the Secretary or his delegate—

"(A) the policy and other contract liability requirements shall be considered to be the sum of—

"(i) the policy and other contract liability requirements computed by reference to the items which relate to annuity contracts described in paragraph (1), and

"(ii) the policy and other contract liability requirements computed by excluding the items taken into account under clause (i); and

"(B) such additional separate computations, with respect to such annuity contracts and such other contracts, shall be made as may be necessary to carry out the purposes of this subsection and this part.

"(6) Termination. Paragraphs (1), (2), (3), (4), and (5) shall not apply with respect to any taxable year beginning after December 31, 1962."

"Sec. 802. Tax imposed.

"(a) Tax imposed.

"(1) In general. A tax is hereby imposed for each taxable year on the life insurance company taxable income of every life insurance company. Such tax shall consist of a tax computed as provided in section 11 as though the life insurance company taxable income were the taxable income referred to in section 11.

"(2) Alternative tax in case of capital gains. If for any taxable year any life insurance company has a net capital gain, then, in lieu of the tax imposed by paragraph (1), there is hereby imposed a tax (if such tax is less than the tax imposed by such paragraph) which shall consist of the sum of—

"(A) a partial tax, computed as provided by paragraph (1), on the life insurance company taxable income determined by reducing the taxable investment income, and the gain from operations, by the amount of such net capital gain, and

"(B) an amount determined as provided in section 1201(a) on such net capital gain.

"(b) Life insurance company taxable income defined.

"For purposes of this part, the term 'life insurance company taxable income' means the sum of—

"(1) the taxable investment income (as defined in section 804) or, if smaller, the gain from operations (as defined in section 809),

"(2) if the gain from operations exceeds the taxable investment income, an amount equal to 50 percent of such excess, plus

"(3) the amount subtracted from the policyholders surplus account for the taxable year, as determined under section 815."

In 1978, P.L. 95-600, Sec. 301(b)(8), substituted "a tax" for "a normal tax and surtax" in para. (a)(1), effective for tax. yrs. begin. after 12/31/78.

In 1976, P.L. 94-455, Sec. 1901(a)(95), deleted "beginning after December 31, 1957," in para. (a)(1), deleted "beginning after December 31, 1961," in para. (a)(2), deleted para. (a)(3), effective for tax. yrs. begin. after 12/31/76.

Prior to deletion, para. (a)(3) read as follows:

"(3) Special rule for 1959 and 1960. If any amount is subtracted from the policyholders surplus account under section 815(c)(3) for a taxable year beginning in 1959 or 1960 on account of a distribution in 1959 or 1960 (not including any distribution treated under section 815(d)(2)(B) as made in 1959 or 1960), the tax imposed for such taxable year on the life insurance company taxable income shall be the amount determined under paragraph (1) reduced by the following percentage of the amount by which the tax imposed by paragraph (1) is (without regard to this paragraph) increased, on account of the amount so subtracted, by reason of section 802(b)(3)—

"(A) in the case of a taxable year beginning in 1959, 66⅔ percent; and

"(B) in the case of a taxable year beginning in 1960, 33⅓ percent.

The preceding sentence shall not apply with respect to any payment treated as a distribution under section 815(d)(3)."

—P.L. 94-455, Sec. 1901(b)(33)(E), substituted "any life insurance company has a net capital gain" for "the net long-term capital gain of any life insurance company exceeds the net short-term capital loss" in para. (a)(2) and substituted "such net capital gain" for "such excess" in subparas. (a)(2)(A) and (a)(2)(B), effective for tax. yrs. begin. after 12/31/76.

In 1969, P.L. 91-172, Sec. 511(c)(1), substituted "determined as provided in section 1201(a) on" for "equal to 25 percent of" in subpara. (a)(2)(B), effective for tax. yrs. begin. after 12/31/69.

In 1964, P.L. 88-272, Sec. 235(c)(1), amended para. (a)(1), effective for tax. yrs. end. after 12/31/63.

Prior to amendment, para. (a)(1) read as follows:

"(1) In general. A tax is hereby imposed for each taxable year beginning after December 31, 1957, on the life insurance company taxable income of every life insurance company. Such tax shall consist of—

"(A) a normal tax on such income computed at the rate provided by section 11(b), and

"(B) a surtax, on so much of such income as exceeds $25,000, computed at the rate provided by section 11(c)."

In 1962, P.L. 87-858, Sec. 3(b), amended para. (a)(2), effective for tax. yrs. begin. after 12/31/61.

Prior to amendment, para. (a)(2) read as follows:

"(2) Tax in case of capital gains. If for any taxable year beginning after December 31, 1958, the net long-term capital gain of any life insurance company exceeds the net short-term capital loss, there is hereby imposed a tax equal to 25 percent of such excess."

"Subpart B. Investment income

"Sec.

"804. Taxable investment income.

"805. Policy and other contract liability requirements.

Partners and partnerships   Part I

"806. Certain changes in reserves and assets."

"SEC. 804. TAXABLE INVESTMENT INCOME.
"(a) In general.
"(1) Exclusion of policyholders' share of investment yield. The policyholders' share of each and every item of investment yield (including tax-exempt interest, and dividends received) of any life insurance company shall not be included in taxable investment income. For purposes of the preceding sentence, the policyholders' share of any item shall be that percentage obtained by dividing the policy and other contract liability requirements by the investment yield; except that if the policy and other contract liability requirements exceed the investment yield, then the policyholders' share of any item shall be 100 percent.
"(2) Taxable investment income defined. For purposes of this part, the taxable investment income for any taxable year shall be an amount (not less than zero) equal to the amount (if any) of the net capital gain plus the sum of the life insurance company's share of each and every item of investment yield (including tax-exempt interest, and dividends received), reduced by—
"(A) the sum of—
"(i) the life insurance company's share of interest which under section 103 is excluded from gross income, and
"(ii) the deductions for dividends received provided by sections 243, 244, and 245 (as modified by paragraph (4)) computed with respect to the life insurance company's share of the dividends received; and
"(B) the small business deduction provided by paragraph (3).
For purposes of the preceding sentence, the life insurance company's share of any item shall be that percentage which, when added to the percentage obtained under the second sentence of paragraph (1), equals 100 percent.
"(3) Small business deduction. For purposes of this part, the small business deduction is an amount equal to 10 percent of the investment yield for the taxable year. The deduction under this paragraph shall not exceed $25,000.
"(4) Application of section 246(b). In applying section 246(b) (relating to limitation on aggregate amount of deductions for dividends received) for purposes of this subsection, the limit on the aggregate amount of the deductions allowed by sections 243(a)(1), 244(a), and 245 shall be 85 percent of the taxable investment income computed without regard to the deductions allowed by such sections.
"(b) Gross investment income.
"For purposes of this part, the term 'gross investment income' means the sum of the following:
"(1) Interest, etc. The gross amount of income from—
"(A) interest, dividends, rents, and royalties,
"(B) the entering into of any lease, mortgage, or other instrument or agreement from which the life insurance company derives interest, rents, or royalties, and
"(C) the alteration or termination of any instrument or agreement described in subparagraph (B).
"(2) Short-term capital gain. The amount (if any) by which the net short-term capital gain exceeds the net long-term capital loss.
"(3) Trade or business income. The gross income from any trade or business (other than an insurance business) carried on by the life insurance company, or by a partnership of which the life insurance company is a partner. In computing gross income under this paragraph, there shall be excluded any item described in paragraph (1).
Except as provided in paragraph (2), in computing gross investment income under this subsection, there shall be excluded any gain from the sale or exchange of a capital asset, and any gain considered as gain from the sale or exchange of a capital asset.
"(c) Investment yield defined.
"For purposes of this part, the term 'investment yield' means the gross investment income less the following deductions—
"(1) Investment expenses. Investment expenses for the taxable year. If any general expenses are in part assigned to or included in the investment expenses, the total deduction under this paragraph shall not exceed the sum of—
"(A) one-fourth of one percent of the mean of the assets (as defined in section 805(b)(4)) held at the beginning and end of the taxable year,
"(B) the amount of the mortgage service fees for the taxable year, plus
"(C) whichever of the following is the greater:
"(i) one-fourth of the amount by which the investment yield (computed without any deduction for investment expenses allowed by this paragraph) exceeds 3¾ percent of the mean of the assets (as defined in section 805(b)(4)) held at the beginning and end of the taxable year, reduced by the amount described in subparagraph (B), or
"(ii) one-fourth of one percent of the mean of the value of mortgages held at the beginning and end of the taxable year for which there are no mortgage service fees for the taxable year.
"(2) Real estate expenses. The amount of taxes (as provided in section 164), and other expenses, for the taxable year exclusively on or with respect to the real estate owned by the company. No deduction shall be allowed under this paragraph for any amount paid out for new buildings, or for permanent improvements or betterments made to increase the value of any property.
"(3) Depreciation. The deduction allowed by section 167. The deduction under this paragraph and paragraph (2) on account of any real estate owned and occupied for insurance purposes in whole or in part by a life insurance company shall be limited to an amount which bears the same ratio to such deduction (computed without regard to this sentence) as the rental value of the space not so occupied bears to the rental value of the entire property.
"(4) Depletion. The deduction allowed by section 611 (relating to depletion).
"(5) Trade or business deductions. The deductions allowed by this subtitle (without regard to this part) which are attributable to any trade or business (other than an insurance business) carried on by the life insurance company, or by a partnership of which the life insurance company is a partner; except that in computing the deduction under this paragraph—
"(A) There shall be excluded losses—
"(i) from (or considered as from) sales or exchanges of capital assets,
"(ii) from sales or exchanges of property used in the trade or business (as defined in section 1231(b)), and
"(iii) from the compulsory or involuntary conversion (as a result of destruction, in whole or in part, theft or seizure, or an exercise of the power of requisition or condemnation or the threat or imminence thereof) of property used in the trade or business (as so defined).
"(B) Any item, to the extent attributable to the carrying on of the insurance business, shall not be taken into account.
"(C) The deduction for net operating losses provided in section 172, and the special deductions for corporations provided in part VIII of subchapter B, shall not be allowed.
"(d) Cross reference.
"For reduction of the $25,000 amount provided in subsection (a)(4) in the case of certain controlled corporations, see sections 1561 and 1564."

In 1976, P.L. 94-455, Sec. 1901(a)(96), deleted para. (a)(6) and substituted "The" for "In the case of a taxable year beginning after December 31, 1958, the" in para. (b)(2), effective for tax. yrs. begin. after 12/31/76. . . . Sec. 1901(b)(1)(J)(i), deleted para. (a)(3), redesignated paras. (a)(4) and (5) as paras. (a)(3) and (4), effective for tax. yrs. begin. after 12/31/76. . . . Sec. 1901(b)(1)(J)(iii), substituted "paragraph (4)" for "paragraph (5)" and "paragraph (3)" for "paragraph (4)" in para. (a)(2), effective for tax .yrs. begin. after 12/31/76. . . . Sec. 1901(b)(1)(K), deleted clause (a)(2)(A)(ii), added "and" at the end of clause (a)(2)(A)(i) and redesignated clause (a)(2)(A)(iii) as clause (a)(2)(A)(ii), effective for tax. yrs. begin. after 12/31/76. . . . Sec. 1901(b)(1)(M), deleted ", partially tax-exempt interest," in paras. (a)(1) and (2), effective for tax. yrs. begin. after 12/31/76. . . . Sec. 1901(b)(33)(F), substituted "of the net capital gain" for "by which the net long-term capital gain exceeds the net short-term capital loss" in para. (a)(2), effective for tax .yrs. begin. after 12/31/76.
Prior to deletion, para. (a)(6) read as follows:
"(6) Exception. If it is established in any case that the application of the definition of taxable investment income contained in paragraph (2) results in the imposition of tax on—
"(A) any interest which under section 103 is excluded from gross income,
"(B) any amount of interest which under section 242 (as modified by paragraph (3)) is allowable as a deduction, or
"(C) any amount of dividends received which under sections 243, 244, and 245 (as modified by paragraph (5)) is allowable as a deduction,
adjustment shall be made to the extent necessary to prevent such imposition."
Prior to deletion, para. (a)(3) read as follows:
"(3) Partially tax-exempt interest. For purposes of this part, the deduction allowed by section 242 shall be an amount which bears the same ratio to the amount determined under such section without regard to this paragraph as (A) the normal tax rate for the taxable year prescribed by section 11, bears to (B) the sum of the normal tax rate and the surtax rate for the taxable year prescribed by section 11."
Prior to deletion, clause (a)(2)(A)(ii) read as follows:
"(ii) the deduction for partially tax-exempt interest provided by section 242 (as modified by paragraph (3)) computed with respect to the life insurance company's share of such interest, and"
In 1969, P.L. 91-172, Sec. 401(b)(2)(D), added subsec. (d), effective for tax .yrs. begin. after 12/31/69.
In 1964, P.L. 88-272, Sec. 214(b)(3), substituted "243(a)(1), 244(a)" for "243(a), 244" in para. (a)(5), effective for tax. yrs. end. after 12/31/63.
In 1962, P.L. 87-858, Sec. 3(b)(2), substituted "equal to the amount (if any) by which the long-term capital gain exceeds the net short-term capital loss plus the sum" for "equal to the sum" in para. (a)(2), effective for tax. yrs. begin. after 12/31/61.

"SEC. 805. POLICY AND OTHER CONTRACT LIABILITY REQUIREMENTS.
"(a) In general.
"For purposes of this part, the term 'policy and other contract liability requirements' means, for any taxable year, the sum of—
"(1) the adjusted life insurance reserves, multiplied by the adjusted reserves rate,
"(2) the mean of the pension plan reserves at the beginning and end of the taxable year, multiplied by the current earnings rate, and
"(3) the interest paid.
"(b) Adjusted reserves rate and earnings rates.
"(1) Adjusted reserves rate. For purposes of this part, the adjusted reserves rate for any taxable year is the average earnings rate or, if lower, the current earnings rate.
"(2) Current earnings rate. For purposes of this part, the current earnings rate for any taxable year is the amount determined by dividing—
"(A) the taxpayer's investment yield for such taxable year, by
"(B) the mean of the taxpayer's assets at the beginning and end of the taxable year.
"(3) Average earnings rate.
"(A) In general. For purposes of this part, the average earnings rate for any taxable year is the average of the current earnings rates for such taxable year and for each of the 4 taxable years immediately preceding such taxable year (excluding

2,365

Part I

Partners and partnerships

any of such 4 taxable years for which the taxpayer was not an insurance company.

"(B) Special rule. For purposes of subparagraph (A), the current earnings rate for any taxable year of any company which, for such year, is an insurance company (but not a life insurance company) shall be determined as if this part applied to such company for such year.

"(4) Assets. For purposes of this part, the term 'assets' means all assets of the company (including nonadmitted assets), other than real and personal property (excluding money) used by it in carrying on an insurance trade or business. For purposes of this paragraph, the amount attributable to—

"(A) real property and stock shall be the fair market value thereof, and

"(B) any other asset shall be the adjusted basis of such asset for purposes of determining gain on sale or other disposition.

"(c) Adjusted life insurance reserves.

"(1) Adjusted life insurance reserves defined. For purposes of this part, the term 'adjusted life insurance reserves' means—

"(A) the mean of the life insurance reserves (as defined in section 801(b)), other than pension plan reserves or reserves on any qualified contract, at the beginning and end of the taxable year, multiplied by

"(B) 0.9 raised to the power of n where n is the number (positive or negative) determined by subtracting—

"(i) 100 times the average rate of interest assumed by the taxpayer in calculating such reserves, from

"(ii) 100 times the adjusted reserves rate.

"(2) Average interest rate assumed. For purposes of this part, the average rate of interest assumed in calculating reserves shall be computed—

"(A) by multiplying each assumed rate of interest by the means of the amounts of such reserves computed at that rate at the beginning and end of the taxable year, and

"(B) by dividing (i) the sum of the products ascertained under subparagraph (A), by (ii) the mean of the total of such reserves at the beginning and end of the taxable year.

"(d) Pension plan reserves.

"For purposes of this part, the term 'pension plan reserves' means that portion of the life insurance reserves which is allocable to contracts—

"(1) purchased under contracts entered into with trusts which (as of the time the contracts were entered into) were deemed to be (A) trusts described in section 401(a) and exempt from tax under section 501(a), or (B) trusts exempt from tax under section 165 of the Internal Revenue Code of 1939 or the corresponding provisions of prior revenue laws;

"(2) purchased under contracts entered into under plans which (as of the time the contracts were entered into) were deemed to be plans described in section 403(a), or plans meeting the requirements of paragraphs (3), (4), (5), and (6) of section 165(a) of the Internal Revenue Code of 1939;

"(3) provided for employees of the life insurance company under a plan which, for the taxable year, meets the requirements of paragraphs (3), (4), (5), (6), (7), (8), (11), (12), (13), (14), (15), (16), (19), (20), and (22) of section 401(a);

"(4) purchased to provide retirement annuities for its employees by an organization which (as of the time the contracts were purchased) was an organization described in section 501(c)(3) which was exempt from tax under section 501(a) or was an organization described under section 101(6) of the Internal Revenue Code of 1939 or the corresponding provisions of prior revenue laws, or purchased to provide retirement annuities for employees described in section 403(b)(1)(A)(ii) by an employer which is a State, a political subdivision of a State, or an agency or instrumentality of any one or more of the foregoing;

"(5) purchased under contracts entered into with trusts which (at the time the contracts were entered into) were individual retirement accounts described in section 408(a) or under contracts entered into with individual retirement annuities described in section 408(b); or

"(6) purchased by—

"(A) a governmental plan (within the meaning of section 414(d)), or

"(B) the Government of the United States, the government of any State or political subdivision thereof, or by any agency or instrumentality of the foregoing, for use in satisfying an obligation of such government, political subdivision, or agency or instrumentality to provide a benefit under a plan described in subparagraph (A).

"(e) Interest paid.

"For purposes of this part, the interest paid for any taxable year is the sum of—

"(1) Interest on indebtedness. All interest for the taxable year on indebtedness, except on indebtedness incurred or continued to purchase or carry obligations the interest on which is wholly exempt from taxation under this chapter.

"(2) Amounts in the nature of interest. All amounts in the nature of interest, whether or not guaranteed, for the taxable year on insurance or annuity contracts (including contracts supplementary thereto) which do not involve, at the time of accrual, life, health, or accident contingencies.

"(3) Discount on prepaid premiums. All amounts accrued for the taxable year for discounts in the nature of interest, whether or not guaranteed, on premiums or other consideration paid in advance on insurance or annuity contracts.

"(4) Interest on certain special contingency reserves. Interest for the taxable year on special contingency reserves under contracts of group term life insurance or group health and accident insurance which are established and maintained for the provision of insurance on retired lives, for premium stabilization, or for a combination thereof.

"(5) Qualified guaranteed interest. Qualified guaranteed interest (within the meaning of subsection (f)).

For purposes of this subpart, the interest paid for any taxable year shall not include any interest paid or accrued after December 31, 1981, by a ceding company (or its affiliates) to any person in connection with a reinsurance agreement (other than interest on account of delay in making periodic settlements of income and expense items under the terms of the agreement).

"(f) Qualified guaranteed interest and qualified contracts.

"For purposes of this section—

"(1) In general. The term 'qualified guaranteed interest' means any amount in the nature of interest for the taxable year on qualified contracts, but only if such amount is determined pursuant to—

"(A) a stated rate of interest which is guaranteed—

"(i) before the beginning of the period for which the interest accrues, and

"(ii) for a period of not less than 12 months (or for a period ending not earlier than the close of the taxable year in which the contract was issued), or

"(B) a rate or rates of interest which—

"(i) meet the requirements of clause (i) of subparagraph (A), and

"(ii) is determined under a formula or other method the terms of which—

"(I) during the period referred to in subparagraph (A)(ii) may not be changed by the taxpayer, and

"(II) are independent of the experience of the taxpayer.

"(2) Qualified contract. The term 'qualified contract' means any annuity contract (other than any contract described in subsection (d)) which—

"(A) involves (at the time the qualified interest is credited under the contract) life contingencies,

"(B) provides no right under State law for the policyholder to participate in the divisible surplus of the taxpayer, and

"(C) provides that the taxpayer may from time to time credit amounts in the nature of interest in excess of amounts computed on the basis of any rate or rates guaranteed in the contract at the time it was entered into.

"(3) Special rule for participating contracts.

"(A) In general. In the case of an annuity contract which is not a qualified contract solely because it fails to satisfy the requirements of subparagraph (B) of paragraph (2), such contract shall be treated as a qualified contract and the amount taken into account as qualified guaranteed interest with respect to such contract shall be equal to the sum of—

"(i) the amount of interest which would be assumed in calculating reserves with respect to such contract under section 810(c) if such interest were not taken into account under subsection (e), plus

"(ii) 92.5 percent of the excess of—

"(I) the amount of qualified guaranteed interest (determined without regard to this paragraph and as if such contract were a qualified contract), over

"(II) the amount determined under clause (i).

"(B) Interest not otherwise taken into account. No deduction shall be allowed under any other provision of this part for the 7.5 percent of the excess described in subparagraph (A)(ii) which is not treated as qualified guaranteed interest.

"(g) Special limitation for group pension contracts.

"The amount determined under paragraphs (2) and (3) of subsection (a) for policy and other contract liability requirements for group pension contracts shall not exceed the amount actually credited to the policyholders whether such crediting is through premium rate computations, reserve increases, excess interest, experience rate credits, policyholder dividends or otherwise. The Secretary shall prescribe such regulations as may be necessary to carry out the purposes of this subsection."

In 1982, P.L. 97-248, Sec. 257(a), added the last sentence of subsec. (e), effective 9/3/82. Sec. 257(b) of this Act provides:

"(b) Special transitional rule where at least 20 percent of the liabilities reinsured are paid in cash, etc. The amendment made by subsection (a) shall not apply with respect to any interest paid or incurred by a ceding company to a person who is a member of the same affiliated group (within the meaning of section 1504 of the Internal Revenue Code of 1954) on indebtedness evidenced by a note—

"(1) which was entered into after December 31, 1981, with respect to a reinsurance contract under the terms of which an amount not less than 20 percent of the amounts reinsured was paid in cash to the reinsurer on the effective date of such contract,

"(2) at least 40 percent of the principal of which had been paid by the ceding company in cash as of July 1, 1982, and

"(3) the remaining balance of which is paid in cash before January 1, 1983."

—P.L. 97-248, Sec. 260(b), added subsec. (g), effective for tax. yrs. begin. after 12/31/81 and before 1/1/84. Sec. 260(c) of this Act provides:

"(c) Prohibition against changing the qualification status of life insurance companies. For any taxable year ending before January 1, 1984, a taxpayer shall not be treated as other than a life insurance company (as defined in section 801(a) of such Code) because of the effect of amounts held under contracts which would be described in section 805(d) of the Internal Revenue Code of 1954, except for the fact that such contracts do not contain permanent annuity purchase rate guarantees."

—P.L. 97-248, Sec. 261, amended subpara. (c)(1)(B), effective for tax. yrs. begin. after 12/31/81 and before 1/1/82.

Prior to amendment, subpara. (c)(1)(B) read as follows:

"(B) that percentage which equals 100 percent—

"(i) increased by that percentage which is 10 times the average rate of interest assumed by the taxpayer in calculating such reserves, and

"(ii) reduced by that percentage which is 10 times the adjusted reserves rate."

—P.L. 97-248, Sec. 264(a), added para. (e)(5) . . . Sec. 264(b), added subsec. (f) . . . Sec. 264(c)(1), added "or reserves on any qualified contract" after "pension plan reserves" in subpara. (c)(1)(A), effective for tax. yrs. begin. after 12/31/81. Sec. 264(d)(2) of this Act provides:

"(2) Guarantees for less than 12 months.

"(A) Moneys held before August 14, 1982. The requirements of subparagraph (A)(ii) or (B)(ii)(I) of section 805(f)(1) of the Internal Revenue Code of 1954 (as added by subsection (b)) shall not apply to any moneys held under any contract on August 13, 1982 (and any interest on such moneys after such date).

"(B) Contracts entered into after August 13, 1982, and before January 1, 1983. A contract entered into after August 13, 1982, and before January 1, 1983, shall be treated as meeting the requirements of subparagraph (A)(ii) or (B)(ii)(I) of such Code if it meets such requirements on the first contract anniversary date."

In 1980, P.L. 96-222, Sec. 101(a)(7)(B), corrected Sec. 141(g) of P.L. 95-600 [see below].

Prior to correction, Sec. 141(g) of P.L. 95-600 read as follows:

"(g) Effective dates.

"(1) In general. The amendments made by this section (other than by subsection (f)(3)) shall apply with respect to qualified investment for taxable years beginning after December 31, 1978. The amendment made by subsection (f)(7) shall apply to years beginning after December 31, 1978.

"(2) Retroactive application of amendment made by subsection (d). In determining the regular tax deduction under section 6 of the Internal Revenue Code of 1954 for any taxable year beginning before January 1, 1979, the amount of the credit allowable under section 38 shall be determined without regard to section 46(a)(2)(B) of such Code (as in effect before the enactment of the Energy Tax Act of 1978)."

In 1978, P.L. 95-600, Sec. 141(f)(9), substituted "(20), and (22)" for "and (20)" in subsec. (d), effective for qualified investments for tax. yrs. begin. after 12/31/78. Sec. 141(g)(1) and (2) of this Act reads as follows:

"(1) In general. Except as otherwise provided in this subsection and subsection (h), the amendments made by this section shall apply with respect to qualified investment for taxable years beginning after December 31, 1978.

"(2) Election to have amendments apply during 1978. At the election of the taxpayer, paragraph (1) shall be applied by substituting 'December 31, 1977' for 'December 31, 1978'; except that in the case of a plan in existence before December 31, 1978, any such election shall not affect the required allocation of employer securities attributable to qualified investment for taxable years beginning before January 1, 1979. An election under the preceding sentence shall be made at such time and in such manner as the Secretary of the Treasury or his delegate shall prescribe. Such an election, once made, shall be irrevocable."

—P.L. 95-600, Sec. 155, deleted "or" at the end of para. (d)(4), substituted "; or" for the period at the end of para. (d)(5), and added para. (d)(6), effective for tax. yrs. begin. after 12/31/78.

In 1976, P.L. 94-455, Sec. 1901(a)(97)(A), amended subpara. (b)(3)(B) . . . Sec. 1901(a)(97)(B), deleted "(determined without regard to fair market value on December 31, 1958)" in subpara. (b)(4)(B) . . . Sec. 1901(a)(97)(C), amended subsec. (d), effective for tax. yrs. begin. after 12/31/76.

Prior to amendment, subpara. (b)(3)(B) read as follows:

"(B) Special rules. For purposes of subparagraph (A)—

"(i) the current earnings rate for any taxable year beginning before January 1, 1958, shall be determined as if this part (as in effect for 1958) and section 381(c)(22) applied to such taxable year, and

"(ii) the current earnings rate for any taxable year of any company which, for such year, is an insurance company (but not a life insurance company) shall be determined as if this part applied to such company for such year."

Prior to amendment, subsec. (d) read as follows:

"(d) Pension plan reserves.

"(1) Pension plan reserves defined. For purposes of this part, the term 'pension plan reserves' means that portion of the life insurance reserves which is allocable to contracts—

"(A) purchased under contracts entered into with trusts which (as of the time the contracts were entered into) were deemed to be (i) trusts described in section 401(a) and exempt from tax under section 501(a), or (ii) trusts exempt from tax under section 165 of the Internal Revenue Code of 1939 or the corresponding provisions of prior revenue laws;

"(B) purchased under contracts entered into under plans which (as of the time the contracts were entered into) were deemed to be plans described in section 403(a), or plans meeting the requirements of section 165(a) (3), (4), (5), and (6) of the Internal Revenue Code of 1939;

"(C) provided for employees of the life insurance company under a plan which, for the taxable year, meets the requirements of section 401(a) (3), (4), (5), (6), (7), (8), (11), (12), (13), (14), (15), (16), (19) and (20);

"(D) purchased to provide retirement annuities for its employees by an organization which (as of the time the contracts were purchased) was an organization described in section 501(c)(3) which was exempt from tax under section 501(a) or was an organization exempt from tax under section 101(6) of the Internal Revenue Code of 1939 or the corresponding provisions of prior revenue laws, or purchased to provide retirement annuities for employees described in section 403(b)(1)(A)(ii) by an employer which is a State, a political subdivision of a State, or an agency or instrumentality of any one or more of the foregoing; or

"(E) purchased under contracts entered into with trusts which (at the time the contracts were entered into) were individual retirement accounts described in section 408(a) or under contracts entered into with individual retirement annuities described in section 408(b).

"(2) Special transitional rule. For purposes of this part, the amount taken into account as pension plan reserves shall be—

"(A) in the case of a taxable year beginning after December 31, 1957, and before January 1, 1959, zero;

"(B) in the case of a taxable year beginning after December 31, 1958, and before January 1, 1960, 33⅓ percent of the amount thereof (determined without regard to this paragraph);

"(C) in the case of a taxable year beginning after December 31, 1959, and before January 1, 1961, 66⅔ percent of the amount thereof (determined without regard to this paragraph); and

"(D) in the case of a taxable year beginning after December 31, 1960, 100 percent of the amount thereof."

—P.L. 94-267, Sec. [1](c)(4), substituted "(19), and (20)" for "and (19)" in subpara. (d)(1)(C), effective for payments made to an employee on or after 7/4/74.

In 1974, P.L. 93-406, Sec. 1016(a)(6), substituted "(8), (11), (12), (13), (14), and (15)" for "and (8)" in subpara. (d)(1)(C), effective 9/2/74 or other date as specified in Sec. 1017 of this Act (reproduced following Code Sec. 401).

—P.L. 93-406, Sec. 2002(g)(9), deleted "or" at the end of subpara. (d)(1)(C), substituted "foregoing; or" for "foregoing," in subpara. (d)(1)(D) and added subpara. (d)(1)(E), effective 1/1/75.

—P.L. 93-406, Sec. 2004(c)(3), substituted "(15), (16), and (19)" for "and (15)" in subpara. (d)(1)(C), as amended by Sec. 1016 of this Act, effective for yrs. begin. after 12/31/75.

In 1969, P.L. 91-172, Sec. 907(a)(1), amended para. (e)(4), effective for tax. yrs. begin. after 12/31/57.

Prior to amendment, para. (e)(4) read as follows:

"(4) Interest on certain special contingency reserves. Interest for the taxable year on special contingency reserves established pursuant to section 8(d) of the Federal Employees' Group Life Insurance Act of 1954 (5 USC § 2097(d))."

In 1964, P.L. 88-571, Sec. 5, added ", or purchased to provide retirement annuities for employees described in section 403(b)(1)(A)(ii) by an employer which is a State, a political subdivision of a State, or an agency or instrumentality of any one or more of the foregoing," in subpara. (d)(1)(D), effective for tax. yrs. begin. after 12/31/63.

In 1962, P.L. 87-792, Sec. 7(g)(1), substituted "described in section 403(a), or plans meeting" for "meeting the requirements of section 401(a)(3), (4), (5), and (6) or" in subpara. (d)(1)(B) . . . Sec. 7(g)(2), substituted "(6), (7), and (8)" for "and (6)" in subpara. (d)(1)(C), effective for tax. yrs. begin. after 12/31/62.

"Sec. 806. Certain changes in reserves and assets.

"(a) Adjustments to means for certain transfers of liabilities.

"For purposes of this part, if, during the taxable year, there is a change in life insurance reserves attributable to the transfer between the taxpayer and another person of liabilities under contracts taken into account in computing such reserves, then, under regulations prescribed by the Secretary, the means of such reserves, and the mean of the assets, shall be appropriately adjusted, on a daily basis, to reflect the amounts involved in such transfer. This subsection shall not apply to reinsurance ceded to the taxpayer or to another person.

"(b) Change of basis in computing reserves.

"If the basis for determining the amount of any item referred to in section 810(c) as of the close of the taxable year differs from the basis for such determination as of the beginning of the taxable year, then for purposes of this subpart the amount of such item—

"(1) as of the close of the taxable year shall be computed on the old basis, and

"(2) as of the beginning of the next taxable year shall be computed on the new basis."

In 1976, P.L. 94-455, Sec. 1906(b)(13)(A), substituted "Secretary" for "Secretary or his delegate" in subsec. (a) for tax. yrs. begin. after 12/31/76.

"Subpart C. Gain and loss from operations.

"Sec.

"809. In general.

"810. Rules for certain reserves.

"811. Dividends to policyholders.

"812. Operations loss deduction.

"Sec. 809. In general.

"(a) Exclusion of share of investment yield set aside for policyholders.

"(1) Amount. The share of each and every item of investment yield (including tax-exempt interest, and dividends received) of any life insurance company set aside for policyholders shall not be included in gain or loss from operations. For purposes of the preceding sentence, the share of any item set aside for policyholders shall be that percentage obtained by dividing the required interest by the investment yield; except that if the required interest exceeds the investment yield, then the share of any item set aside for policyholders shall be 100 percent.

"(2) Required interest. For purposes of this part, the required interest for any taxable year is the sum of the amount of qualified guaranteed interest (within the meaning of section 805(f)(1)) and the products obtained by multiplying—

"(A) each rate of interest required, or assumed by the taxpayer, in calculating the reserves described in section 810(c), by

"(B) the means of the amount of such reserves computed at that rate at the beginning and end of the taxable year.

For purposes of subparagraphs (A) and (B), reserves on qualified contracts (within the meaning of section 805(f)(2)) shall not be taken into account.

"(b) Gain and loss from operations

"(1) Gain from operations defined. For purposes of this part, the term 'gain from operations' means the amount by which the sum of the following exceeds the deductions provided by subsection (d):

"(A) the life insurance company's share of each and every item of investment yield (including tax-exempt interest, and dividends received);

"(B) the amount (if any) of the net capital gain; and

"(C) the sum of the items referred to in subsection (c).

"(2) Loss from operations defined. For purposes of this part, the term 'loss from operations' means the amount by which the sum of the deductions provided by subsection (d) exceeds the sum of—

"(A) the life insurance company's share of each and every item of investment yield (including tax-exempt interest, and dividends received);

"(B) the amount (if any) of the net capital gain; and

"(C) the sum of the items referred to in subsection (c).

"(3) Life insurance company's share. For purposes of this subpart, the life insurance company's share of any item shall be that percentage which, when added to the percentage obtained under the second sentence of subsection (a)(1), equals 100 percent.

"(c) Gross amount.

"For purposes of subsections (b)(1) and (2), the following items shall be taken into account:

"(1) Premiums. The gross amount of premiums and other consideration, including—

"(A) advance premiums,

"(B) deposits,

"(C) fees,

"(D) assessments,

"(E) consideration in respect of assuming liabilities under contracts not issued by the taxpayer, and

"(F) the amount of dividends to policyholders reimbursed to the taxpayer by a reinsurer in respect of reinsured policies,

on insurance and annuity contracts (including contracts supplementary thereto); less return premiums, and premiums and other consideration arising out of reinsurance ceded. Except in the case of amounts of premiums or other consideration returned to another life insurance company in respect of reinsurance ceded, amounts returned where the amount is not fixed in the contract but depends on the experience of the company or the discretion of the management shall not be included in return premiums.

"(2) Decreases in certain reserves. Each net decrease in reserves which is required by section 810 or 811(b)(2) to be taken into account for purposes of this paragraph.

"(3) Other amounts. All amounts, not included in computing investment yield and not includible under paragraph (1) or (2), which under this subtitle are includible in gross income.

Except as included in computing investment yield, there shall be excluded any gain from the sale or exchange of a capital asset, and any gain considered as gain from the sale or exchange of a capital asset.

"(d) Deductions.

"For purposes of subsections (b)(1) and (2), there shall be allowed the following deductions:

"(1) Death benefits, etc. All claims and benefits accrued, and all losses incurred (whether or not ascertained), during the taxable year on insurance and annuity contracts (including contracts supplementary thereto).

"(2) Increases in certain reserves. The net increase in reserves which is required by section 810 to be taken into account for purposes of this paragraph.

"(3) Dividends to policyholders. The deduction for dividends to policyholders (determined under section 811(b)), other than the deduction provided under paragraph (12).

"(4) Operations loss deduction. The operations loss deduction (determined under section 812).

"(5) Certain nonparticipating contracts. An amount equal to 10 percent of the increase for the taxable year in the reserves for nonparticipating contracts or (if greater) an amount equal to 3 percent of the premiums for the taxable year (excluding that portion of the premiums which is allocable to annuity features) attributable to nonparticipating contracts (other than group contracts) which are issued or renewed for periods of 5 years or more. For purposes of this paragraph, the term 'reserves for nonparticipating contracts' means such part of the life insurance reserves (excluding that portion of the reserves which is allocable to annuity features) as relates to nonparticipating contracts (other than group contracts). For purposes of this paragraph and paragraph (6), the term 'premiums' means the net amount of the premiums and other consideration taken into account under subsection (c)(1). For purposes of this paragraph, the period for which any contract is issued or renewed includes the period for which such contract is guaranteed renewable.

"(6) Certain accident and health insurance and group life insurance. An amount equal to 2 percent of the premiums for the taxable year attributable to accident and health insurance contracts (other than those to which paragraph (5) applies) and group life insurance contracts. The deduction under this paragraph for the taxable year and all preceding taxable years shall not exceed an amount equal to 50 percent of the premiums for the taxable year attributable to such contracts.

"(7) Assumption by another person of liabilities under insurance, etc., contracts. The consideration (other than consideration arising out of reinsurance ceded) in respect of the assumption by another person of liabilities under insurance and annuity contracts (including contracts supplementary thereto).

"(8) Tax-exempt interest, dividends, etc.

"(A) Life insurance company's share. Each of the following items:

"(i) the life insurance company's share of interest which under section 103 is excluded from gross income, and

"(ii) the deductions for dividends received provided by sections 243, 244, and 245 (as modified by subparagraph (B)) computed with respect to the life insurance company's share of the dividends received.

"(B) Application of section 246(b). In applying section 246(b) (relating to limitation on aggregate amount of deductions for dividends received) for purposes of subparagraph (A)(ii), the limit on the aggregate amount of the deductions allowed by sections 243(a)(1), 244(a), and 245 shall be 85 percent of the gain from operations computed without regard to—

"(i) the deductions provided by paragraphs (3), (5), and (6) of this subsection,

"(ii) the operations loss deduction provided by section 812, and

"(iii) the deductions allowed by sections 243(a)(1), 244(a), and 245,

but such limit shall not apply for any taxable year for which there is a loss from operations.

"(9) Investment expenses, etc. Investment expenses to the extent not allowed as a deduction under section 804(c)(1) in computing investment yield, and the amount (if any) by which the sum of the deductions allowable under section 804(c) exceeds the gross investment income.

"(10) Small business deduction. A small business deduction in an amount equal to the amount determined under section 804(a)(2).

"(11) Other deductions. Subject to the modifications provided by subsection (e), all other deductions allowed under this subtitle for purposes of computing taxable income to the extent not allowed as deductions in computing investment yield.

"(12) Dividends reimbursed. The deduction for the amount of dividends to policyholders reimbursed by the taxpayer to another insurance company in respect of policies the taxpayer has reinsured (determined under section 811(c)).

Except as provided in paragraph (3), no amount shall be allowed as a deduction under this subsection in respect of dividends to policyholders.

"(e) Modifications.

"The modifications referred to in subsection (d)(11) are as follows:

"(1) Interest. In applying section 163 (relating to deduction for interest), no deduction shall be allowed for qualified guaranteed interest (within the meaning of section 805(f)(1)) or interest in respect of items described in section 810(c).

"(2) Bad debts. Section 166(c) (relating to reserve for bad debts) shall not apply.

"(3) Charitable, etc., contributions and gifts. In applying section 170—

"(A) the limit on the total deductions under such section provided by section 170(b)(2) shall be 10 percent of the gain from operations computed without regard to—

"(i) the deduction provided by section 170,

"(ii) the deductions provided by paragraphs (3), (5), (6), and (8) of subsection (d), and

"(iii) any operations loss carryback to the taxable year under section 812; and

"(B) under regulations prescribed by the Secretary, a rule similar to the rule contained in section 170(d)(2)(B) shall be applied.

"(4) Amortizable bond premium. Section 171 shall not apply.

"(5) Net operating loss deduction. Except as provided by section 844, the deduction for net operating losses provided in section 172 shall not be allowed.

"(6) Dividends received. The deductions for dividends received provided by sections 243, 244, and 245 shall not be allowed.

"(f) Limitation on certain deductions.

"(1) In general. The amount of the deductions under paragraphs (3), (5), and (6) of subsection (d) shall not exceed $250,000 plus the amount (if any) by which—

"(A) the gain from operations for the taxable year, computed without regard to such deductions, exceeds

"(B) the taxable investment income for the taxable year.

"(2) Application of limitation. The limitation provided by paragraph (1) shall apply first to the amount of the deduction under subsection (d)(3), then to the amount of the deduction under subsection (d)(6), and finally to the amount of the deduction under subsection (d)(5)."

In 1984, P.L. 98-369, Sec. 217(g), provides:

"(g) Treatment of reinsurance agreements required by NAIC.

"Effective for taxable years beginning after December 31, 1981, and before January 1, 1984, subsections (c)(1)(F) and (d)(12) of section 809 of the Internal Revenue Code of 1954 (as in effect on 7/17/84) shall not apply to dividends to policyholders reimbursed to the taxpayer by a reinsurer in respect of accident and health policies reinsured under a reinsurance agreement entered into before June 30, 1955, pursuant to the direction of the National Association of Insurance Commissioners and approved by the State insurance commissioner of the taxpayer's State of domicile. For purposes of subchapter L of chapter 1 of such Code (as in effect on the date before 7/18/84) any such dividends shall be treated as dividends of the reinsurer and not the taxpayer."

In 1983, P.L. 97-448, Sec. 102(m)(1), substituted "10 percent" for "5 percent" in para. (e)(3), effective for tax. yrs. begin. after 12/31/81.

In 1982, P.L. 97-248, Sec. 255(b)(2), amended the first sentence of para. (c)(1) ... Sec. 255(b)(3), added ", other than the deduction provided under paragraph (12)" before the period at the end of para. (d)(3) ... Sec. 255(b)(4), added para. (d)(12), effective for tax. yrs. begin. after 12/31/81. Sec. 255(c)(2) of this Act provides:

"(2) Rules applicable to taxable years beginning before January 1, 1982.

"(A) In general. In the case of any taxable year beginning before January 1, 1982—

"(i) any determination as to whether any contract met the requirements of subsection (b) of section 820 of the Internal Revenue Code of 1954 (as in effect before its repeal by this section) shall be made solely by reference to the terms of the contract, and

2,368

Partners and partnerships — Part I

"(ii) the treatment of such contract under subsection (c) of such section 820 shall be made in accordance with the regulations under such section which were in effect on December 31, 1981.

"(B) Paragraph not to apply if fraud involved. The provisions of subparagraph (A) shall not apply with respect to any deficiency which the Secretary of the Treasury or his delegate establishes was due to fraud with intent to evade tax."

Prior to amendment, the first sentence of para. (c)(1) read as follows:

"The gross amount of premiums and other consideration (including advance premiums, deposits, fees, assessments, and consideration in respect of assuming liabilities under contracts not issued by the taxpayer) on insurance and annuity contracts (including contracts supplementary thereto); less return premiums, and premiums and other consideration arising out of reinsurance ceded."

—P.L. 97-248, Sec. 259(a), amended subsec. (f), effective for tax. yrs. begin. after 12/31/81 and before 1/1/84. Secs. 263(b)(1) and (3) of this Act provide as follows:

"(b) Special rules for certain transactions in taxable years beginning before January 1, 1982.

"(1) Certain interest and premiums.

"(A) In general. In the case of any taxable year beginning before January 1, 1982, if a taxpayer, on his return of tax for such taxable year, treated—

"(i) any amount described in subparagraph (B) as an amount which was not a dividend to policyholders (within the meaning of section 811 of the Internal Revenue Code of 1954), or

"(ii) any amount described in subparagraph (C) as not described in section 809(c)(1),

then such amounts shall be so treated for purposes of the Internal Revenue Code of 1954.

"(B) Certain interest. An amount is described in this subparagraph if such amount is in the nature of interest accrued for the taxable year on an insurance or annuity contract pursuant to—

"(i) an interest rate guaranteed or fixed before the period of payment of such amount begins, or

"(ii) any other method (fixed before such period begins) the terms of which during the period are beyond the control and are independent of the experience of the company, whether or not the interest rate or other method was guaranteed or fixed for any specified period of time.

"(C) Amounts not treated as premiums. An amount is described in this subparagraph if such amount represents the difference between—

"(i) the amount of premiums received or mortality charges made under rates fixed in advance of the premium or mortality charge due date, and

"(ii) the maximum premium or mortality charge which could be charged under the terms of the insurance or annuity contract.

"(D) No inference. The provisions of this paragraph shall constitute no inference with respect to the treatment of any item in taxable years beginning after December 31, 1981.

"* * *

"(3) Taxable years where period of limitation has run. This subsection shall not apply to any taxable year with respect to which the statute of limitations for filing a claim for credit or refund has expired under any provision of law or by operation of law."

Prior to amendment, subsec. (f) read as follows:

"(f) Limitation on certain deductions.

"(1) In general. The amount of the deductions under paragraphs (3), (5), and (6) of subsection (d) shall not exceed $250,000 plus the amount (if any) by which—

"(A) the gain from operations for the taxable year, computed without regard to such deductions, exceeds

"(B) the taxable investment income for the taxable year.

"(2) Application of limitation. The limitation provided by paragraph (1) shall apply first to the amount of the deduction under subsection (d)(3), then to the amount of the deduction under subsection (d)(6), and finally to the amount of the deduction under subsection (d)(5)."

Subsec. (f), effective for tax. yrs. begin. after 12/31/81 and before 1/1/84, read as follows:

"(f) Limitation on certain deductions.

"(1) In general. The amount of the deductions under paragraphs (3), (5), and (6) of subsection (d) shall not exceed the greater of—

"(A) $1,000,000, plus the amount (if any) by which—

"(i) the gain from operations for the taxable year (computed without regard to such deductions) exceeds

"(ii) the taxable investment income for the taxable year, or

"(B) if the taxpayer elects for any taxable year, the amount determined under paragraph (2).

"(2) Alternative limitation. The amount determined under this paragraph for any taxable year shall be equal to the sum of—

"(A) that portion of the deduction under subsection (d)(3) which is allocable to any contract described in section 805(d), and

"(B) an amount equal to the sum of—

"(i) so much of the base amount as does not exceed $1,000,000, plus

"(ii) in the case of—

"(I) a mutual life insurance company, 77.5 percent of the base amount, or

"(II) a stock life insurance company, 85 percent of the base amount.

"(3) Reduction in $1,000,000 amount for large insurers. If the sum of the deductions under paragraphs (3), (5), and (6) of subsection (d) exceeds $4,000,000, then each of the $1,000,000 amounts in paragraphs (1) and (2) shall be reduced (but not below zero) by the amount which bears the same ratio to $1,000,000 as—

"(A) the amount of such excess bears to,

"(B) $4,000,000.

"(4) Base amount. For purposes of paragraph (2)(B), the term 'base amount' means the excess of—

"(A) the amount of the deductions under paragraphs (3) and (5) of subsection (d) for the taxable year, over

"(B) the amount determined under paragraph (2)(A) for such taxable year.

"(5) Application of limitation. The limitation provided by paragraph (1) shall apply first to the amount of the deduction under subsection (d)(3), then to the amount of the deduction under subsection (d)(5), and finally to the amount of the deduction under subsection (d)(6)."

—P.L. 97-248, Sec. 264(c)(2), added "the amount of qualified guaranteed interest (within the meaning of section 805(f)(1))" after "the sum of" in para. (a)(2), and added "For purposes of subparagraphs (A) and (B), reserves on qualified contracts (within the meaning of section 805(f)(2)) shall not be taken into account." at the end of para. (a)(2)... Sec. 264(c)(3), added "qualified guaranteed interest (within the meaning of section 805(f)(1)) or" after "allowed for" in para. (e)(1), effective for tax. yrs. begin. after 12/31/81. Sec. 264(d)(2) of this Act provides:

"(2) Guarantees for less than 12 months.

"(A) Moneys held before August 14, 1982. The requirements of subparagraph (A)(ii) or (B)(ii)(I) of section 805(f)(1) of the Internal Revenue Code of 1954 (as added by subsection (b)) shall not apply to any moneys held under any contract on August 13, 1982 (and any interest on such moneys after such date).

"(B) Contracts entered into after August 13, 1982, and before January 1, 1983. A contract entered into after August 13, 1982, and before January 1, 1983, shall be treated as meeting the requirements of subparagraph (A)(ii) or (B)(ii)(I) of such Code if it meets such requirements on the first contract anniversary date."

In 1976, P.L. 94-455, Sec. 1508, added a sentence to the end of para. (d)(5), effective for tax. yrs. begin. after 12/31/57.

—P.L. 94-455, Sec. 1901(a)(98)(A), deleted para. (b)(4)... Sec. 1901(a)(98)(B)(i), deleted para. (d)(11) and redesignated para. (d)(12) as (d)(11)... Sec. 1901(a)(98)(B)(ii), substituted "subsection (d)(11)" for "subsection (d)(12)" in subsec. (e)... Sec. 1901(a)(98)(C), deleted subsec. (g), effective for tax. yrs. begin. after 12/31/76.

Prior to deletion, para. (b)(4) read as follows:

"(4) Exception. If it is established in any case that the application of the definition of gain from operations contained in paragraph (1) results in the imposition of tax on—

"(A) any interest which under section 103 is excluded from gross income,

"(B) any amount of interest which under section 242 (as modified by section 804(a)(3)) is allowable as a deduction, or

"(C) any amount of dividends received which under sections 243, 244, and 245 (as modified by subsection (d)(8)(B)) is allowable as a deduction,

adjustment shall be made to the extent necessary to prevent such imposition."

Prior to deletion, para. (d)(11) read as follows:

"(11) Certain mutualization distributions. The amount of distributions to shareholders made in 1958, 1959, 1960, 1961, and 1962 in acquisition of stock pursuant to a plan of mutualization adopted before January 1, 1958."

Prior to deletion, subsec. (g) read as follows:

"(g) Limitations on deduction for certain mutualization distributions.

"(1) Deduction not to reduce taxable investment income. The amount of the deduction under subsection (d)(11) shall not exceed the amount (if any) by which—

"(A) the gain from operations for the taxable year, computed without regard to such deduction (but after the application of subsection (f)), exceeds

"(B) the taxable investment income for the taxable year.

"(2) Deduction not to reduce tax below 1957 law. The deduction under subsection (d)(11) for the taxable year shall be allowed only to the extent that such deduction (after the application of all other deductions provided by subsection (d)) does not reduce the amount of the tax imposed by section 802(a)(1) for such taxable year below the amount of tax which would have been imposed by section 802(a) as in effect for 1957, if this part, as in effect for 1957, applied for such taxable year.

"(3) Application of section 815. That portion of any distribution with respect to which a deduction is allowed under subsection (d)(11) shall not be treated as a distribution to shareholders for purposes of section 815; except that in the case of any distribution made in 1959, 1960, 1961, or 1962, such portion shall be treated as a distribution with respect to which a reduction is required under section 815(e)(2)(B)."

—P.L. 94-455, Sec. 1901(b)(1)(J)(iv), substituted "section 804(a)(3)" for "section 804(a)(4)" in para. (d)(10)... Sec. 1901(b)(1)(L)(i), deleted clause (d)(8)(A)(ii), added "and" at the end of clause (d)(8)(A)(i), and redesignated clause (d)(8)(A)(iii) as clause (d)(8)(A)(ii)... Sec. 1901(b)(1)(L)(ii), substituted "subparagraph (A)(ii)" for "subparagraph (A)(iii)" in subpara. (d)(8)(B)... Sec. 1901(b)(1)(M), deleted "partially tax-exempt interest," in para. (a)(1), subparas. (b)(1)(A), and (b)(2)(A)... Sec. 1901(b)(1)(N), deleted para. (e)(6) and redesignated para. (e)(7) as para. (e)(6)... Sec. 1901(b)(33)(G), substituted "of the net capital gain" for "by which the net long-term capital gain exceeds the net short-term capital loss" in subparas. (b)(1)(B) and (b)(2)(B), effective for tax. yrs. begin. after 12/31/76.

Prior to deletion, clause (d)(8)(A)(ii) read as follows:

"(ii) the deduction for partially tax-exempt interest provided by section 242 (as modified by section 804(a)(3)) computed with respect to the life insurance company's share of such interest," and

Prior to deletion, para. (e)(6) read as follows:

"(6) Partially tax-exempt interest. The deduction for partially tax-exempt interest provided by section 242 shall not be allowed."

—P.L. 94-455, Sec. 1906(b)(13)(A), substituted "Secretary" for "Secretary or his delegate" in subpara. (e)(3)(B), effective for tax. yrs. begin. after 12/31/76.

2,369

In 1969, P.L. 91-172, Sec. 201(a)(2)(C), deleted "the first sentence of" in subpara. (e)(3)(A) and substituted "170(d)(2)(B)" for "section 170(b)(3)" in subpara. (e)(3)(B), effective for tax. yrs. begin. after 12/31/69.
—P.L. 91-172, Sec. 907(c)(2)(B), substituted "Except as provided by section 844, the" for "The" in para. (e)(5), effective for losses incurred in tax. yrs. begin. after 12/31/62, but shall not affect any tax liability for any tax. yrs. begin. before 1/1/67.
In 1964, P.L. 88-272, Sec. 214(b)(4), substituted "243(a)(1), 244(a)" for "243(a), 244" wherever appearing in subsec. (d)(8)(B), effective for dividends received in tax. yrs. end. after 12/31/63.
—P.L. 88-272, Sec. 228(a)(1), added the year 1962 in para. (d)(11) . . . Sec. 228(a)(2), added the year 1962 in para. (g)(3), effective for tax. yrs. begin. after 12/31/61.
In 1962, P.L. 87-858, Sec. 3(b)(3), deleted "and" at the end of subparas. (b)(1)(A) and (b)(2)(A), added subparas. (b)(1)(B) and (b)(2)(B) and redesignated former subparas. (b)(1)(B) and (b)(2)(B) as (b)(1)(C) and (b)(2)(C), respectively . . . Sec. 3(c), amended para. (f)(2), effective for tax. yrs. begin. after 12/31/61.
Prior to amendment, para. (f)(2) read as follows:
  "(2) Application of limitation. The limitation provided by paragraph (1) shall apply first to the amount of the deduction under subsection (d)(6), then to the amount of the deduction under subsection (d)(5), and finally to the amount of the deduction under subsection (d)(3)."
—P.L. 87-790, Sec. 3(a)(1), substituted "accident and health insurance contracts (other than those to which paragraph (5) applies) and group life insurance contracts" for "group life insurance contracts and group accident and health insurance contracts" in para. (d)(6) . . . Sec. 3(a)(2), amended the heading of para. (d)(6), effective for tax. yrs. begin. after 12/31/62.
Prior to amendment, the heading of para. (d)(6) read as follows:
  "(6) Group life, accident, and health insurance."
In 1961, P.L. 87-59, Sec. 2(a), substituted "in 1958, 1959, 1960, and 1961" for "in 1958 and 1959" in para. (d)(11) . . . Sec. 2(b), substituted '"in 1959, 1960, or 1961" for "in 1959" in para. (g)(3), effective for tax. yrs. begin. after 12/31/59.

"SEC. 810. RULES FOR CERTAIN RESERVES.
"(a) Adjustment for decrease.
  "If the sum of the items described in subsection (c) as of the beginning of the taxable year exceeds the sum of such items as of the close of the taxable year (reduced by the amount of investment yield not included in gain or loss from operations for the taxable year by reason of section 809(a)(1)), the excess shall be taken into account as a net decrease referred to in section 809(c)(2).
"(b) Adjustment for increase.
  "If the sum of the items described in subsection (c) as of the close of the taxable year (reduced by the amount of investment yield not included in gain or loss from operations for the taxable year by reason of section 809(a)(1)) exceeds the sum of such items as of the beginning of the taxable year, the excess shall be taken into account as a net increase referred to in section 809(d)(2).
"(c) Items taken into account.
  "The items referred to in subsections (a) and (b) are as follows:
  "(1) The life insurance reserves (as defined in section 801(b)).
  "(2) The unearned premiums and unpaid losses included in total reserves under section 801(c)(2).
  "(3) The amounts (discounted at the rates of interest assumed by the company) necessary to satisfy the obligations under insurance or annuity contracts (including contracts supplementary thereto), but only if such obligations do not involve (at the time with respect to which the computation is made under this paragraph) life, health, or accident contingencies.
  "(4) Dividend accumulations, and other amounts, held at interest in connection with insurance or annuity contracts (including contracts supplementary thereto).
  "(5) Premiums received in advance, and liabilities for premium deposit funds.
  "(6) Special contingency reserves under contracts of group term life insurance or group health and accident insurance which are established and maintained for the provision of insurance on retired lives, for premium stabilization, or for a combination thereof.
In applying this subsection, the same item shall be counted only once.
"(d) Adjustment for change in computing reserves.
  "(1) In general. If the basis for determining any item referred to in subsection (c) as of the close of any taxable year differs from the basis for such determination as of the close of the preceding taxable year, then so much of the difference between—
  "(A) the amount of the item at the close of the taxable year, computed on the new basis, and
  "(B) the amount of the item at the close of the taxable year, computed on the old basis, as is attributable to contracts issued before the taxable year shall be taken into account for purposes of this subpart as follows:
  "(i) if the amount determined under subparagraph (A) exceeds the amount determined under subparagraph (B), 1/10 of such excess shall be taken into account, for each of the succeeding 10 taxable years, as a net increase to which section 809(d)(2) applies; or
  "(ii) if the amount determined under subparagraph (B) exceeds the amount determined under subparagraph (A), 1/10 of such excess shall be taken into account for each of the 10 succeeding taxable years, as a net decrease to which section 809(c)(2) applies.
  "(2) Termination as life insurance company. Except as provided in section 381(c)(22) (relating to carryovers in certain corporate readjustments), if for any taxable year the taxpayer is not a life insurance company, the balance of any adjustments under this paragraph shall be taken into account for the preceding taxable year.

"(3) Effect of preliminary term election. An election under section 818(c) shall not be treated as a change in the basis for determining an item referred to in subsection (c) to which this subsection applies. If an election under section 818(c) applies for the taxable year, the amounts of the items referred to in subparagraphs (A) and (B) of paragraph (1) shall be determined without regard to such election. If such an election would apply in respect of such item for the taxable year but for the new basis, the amount of the item referred to in subparagraph (B) shall be determined on the basis which would have been applicable under section 818(c) if the election applied in respect of the item for the taxable year."

In 1969, P.L. 91-172, Sec. 121(b)(5)(B), deleted subsec. (e), effective for tax. yrs. begin. after 12/31/69.
Prior to deletion, subsec. (e) read as follows:
"(e) Certain decreases in reserves of voluntary employees' beneficiary associations.
  "(1) Decreases due to voluntary lapses of policies issued before January 1, 1958. For purposes of subsections (a) and (b), in the case of a life insurance company which meets the requirements of section 501(c)(9) other than the requirement of subparagraph (B) thereof, there shall be taken into account only 11½ percent of any decrease in the life insurance reserve on any policy issued before January 1, 1958, which is attributable solely to the voluntary lapse of such policy on or after January 1, 1958. In applying the preceding sentence, the decrease in the reserve for any policy shall be determined by reference to the amount of such reserve as of the beginning of the taxable year, reduced by any amount allowable as a deduction under section 809(d)(1) in respect of such policy by reason of such lapse. This paragraph shall apply for any taxable year only if the taxpayer has made an election under paragraph (3) which is effective for such taxable year.
  "(2) Disallowance of carryovers from pre-1958 losses from operations. In the case of a life insurance company to which paragraph (1) applies for the taxable year, section 812(b)(1) shall not apply with respect to any loss from operations for any taxable year beginning before January 1, 1958.
  "(3) Election. Paragraph (1) shall apply to any taxpayer for any taxable year only if the taxpayer elects, not later than the time prescribed by law (including extensions thereof) for filing the return for such taxable year, to have such paragraph apply. Such election shall be made in such manner as the Secretary or his delegate shall prescribe by regulations. Such election shall be effective for the taxable year for which made and for all succeeding taxable years, and shall not be revoked except with the consent of the Secretary or his delegate."
—P.L. 91-172, Sec. 907(a)(2), added para. (c)(6), effective for tax. yrs. begin. after 12/31/57.

"SEC. 811. DIVIDENDS TO POLICYHOLDERS.
"(a) Dividends to policyholders defined.
  "For purposes of this part, the term 'dividends to policyholders' means dividends and similar distributions to policyholders in their capacity as such. Such term does not include interest paid (as defined in section 805(e)).
"(b) Amount of deduction.
  "(1) In general. Except as limited by section 809(f), the deduction for dividends to policyholders for any taxable year shall be an amount equal to the dividends to policyholders paid during the taxable year—
  "(A) increased by the excess of (i) the amounts held at the end of the taxable year as reserves for dividends to policyholders (as defined in subsection (a)) payable during the year following the taxable year, over (ii) such amounts held at the end of the preceding taxable year, or
  "(B) decreased by the excess of (i) such amounts held at the end of the preceding taxable year, over (ii) such amounts held at the end of the taxable year.
For purposes of subparagraphs (A) and (B), there shall be included as amounts held at the end of any taxable year amounts set aside, before the 16th day of the third month of the year following such taxable year (or, in the case of a mutual savings bank subject to the tax imposed by section 594, before the 16th day of the fourth month of the year following such taxable year), for payment during the year following such taxable year.
  "(2) Certain amounts to be treated as net decreases. If the amount determined under paragraph (1)(B) exceeds the dividends to policyholders paid during the taxable year, the amount of such excess shall be a net decrease referred to in section 809(c)(2).
"(c) Special rule for dividends to policyholders under reinsurance contracts.
  "If, under the terms of a reinsurance contract, a life insurance company (hereinafter referred to as 'the reinsurer') is obligated to reimburse another life insurance company (hereinafter referred to as 'the reinsured') for dividends to policyholders on the policies reinsured, the amount of the deduction for dividends reimbursed shall, for purposes of section 809(d)(12), be equal to the amount of dividends to policyholders—
  "(1) which were paid by the reinsured, and
  "(2) with respect to which the reinsurer reimbursed the reinsured under the terms of such contract.
The amount determined under the preceding sentence shall be properly adjusted to reflect the adjustments under subsection (b)(1)."

In 1984, P.L. 98-369, Sec. 714(a), substituted "reinsurance contract" for "conventional coinsurance contract" in subsec. (c), effective for tax. yrs. begin. after 12/31/81.
In 1982, P.L. 97-248, Sec. 255(b)(1), added subsec. (c), effective for tax. yrs. begin. after 12/31/81.
—P.L. 97-248, Sec. 263(b), provides:
  "(b) Special rules for certain transactions in taxable years beginning before January 1, 1982.

Partners and partnerships — Part I

"(1) Certain interest and premiums

"(A) In general. In the case of any taxable year beginning before January 1, 1982, if a taxpayer, on his return of tax for such taxable year, treated—

"(i) any amount described in subparagraph (B) as an amount which was not a dividend to policyholders (within the meaning of section 811 of the Internal Revenue Code of 1954), or

"(ii) any amount described in subparagraph (C) as not described in section 809(c)(1),

then such amounts shall be so treated for purposes of the Internal Revenue Code of 1954.

"(B) Certain interest. An amount is described in this subparagraph if such amount is in the nature of interest accrued for the taxable year on an insurance or annuity contract pursuant to—

"(i) an interest rate guaranteed or fixed before the period of payment of such amount begins, or

"(ii) any other method (fixed before such period begins) the terms of which during the period are beyond the control and are independent of the experience of the company, whether or not the interest rate or other method was guaranteed or fixed for any specified period of time.

"(C) Not treated as premiums. An amount is described in this subparagraph if such amount represents the difference between—

"(i) the amount of premiums received or mortality charges made under rates fixed in advance of the premium or mortality charge due date, and

"(ii) the maximum premium or mortality charge which could be charged under the terms of the insurance or annuity contract.

"(D) No inference. The provisions of this paragraph shall constitute no inference with respect to the treatment of any item in taxable years beginning after December 31, 1981.

"(2) Consolidated returns. The provisions of section 818(f) of such Code, as amended by section 262, shall apply to any taxable year beginning before January 1, 1982, if the taxpayer filed a consolidated return before July 1, 1982 for such taxable year under section 1501 of such Code which, on such date (determined without regard to any amended return filed after June 30, 1982), was consistent with the provisions of section 818(f) of such Code, as so amended. In the case of a taxable year beginning in 1981, the preceding sentence shall be applied by substituting 'September 16' for 'July 1' and 'September 15' for 'June 30'.

"(3) Taxable years where period of limitation has run. This subsection shall not apply to any taxable year with respect to which the statute of limitations for filing a claim for credit or refund has expired under any provision of law or by operation of law.".

"SEC. 812. OPERATIONS LOSS DEDUCTION.

"(a) Deduction allowed.

"There shall be allowed as a deduction for the taxable year an amount equal to the aggregate of—

"(1) the operations loss carryovers to such year, plus

"(2) the operations loss carrybacks to such year.

For purposes of this part, the term 'operations loss deduction' means the deduction allowed by this subsection.

"(b) Operations loss carrybacks and carryovers.

"(1) Years to which loss may be carried. The loss from operations for any taxable year (hereinafter in this section referred to as the 'loss year') shall be—

"(A) an operations loss carryback to each of the 3 taxable years preceding the loss year,

"(B) an operations loss carryover to each of the 5 taxable years following the loss year, and

"(C) subject to subsection (e), if the life insurance company is a new company for the loss year, an operations loss carryover to each of the 3 taxable years following the 5 taxable years described in subparagraph (B).

In the case of an operations loss for any taxable year ending after December 31, 1975, this paragraph shall be applied by substituting '15 taxable years' for '5 taxable years'.

"(2) Amount of carrybacks and carryovers. The entire amount of the loss from operations for any loss year shall be carried to the earliest of the taxable years to which (by reason of paragraph (1)) such loss may be carried. The portion of such loss which shall be carried to each of the other taxable years shall be the excess (if any) of the amount of such loss over the sum of the offsets (as defined in subsection (d)) for each of the prior taxable years to which such loss may be carried.

"(3) Election for operations loss carrybacks. In the case of a loss from operations for any taxable year ending after December 31, 1975, the taxpayer may elect to relinquish the entire carryback period for such loss. Such election shall be made by the due date (including extensions of time) for filing the return for the taxable year of the loss from operations for which the election is to be in effect, and once made for any taxable year, such election shall be irrevocable for that taxable year.

"(c) Computation of loss from operations.

"In computing the loss from operations for purposes of this section—

"(1) The operations loss deduction shall not be allowed.

"(2) The deductions allowed by sections 243 (relating to dividends received by corporations), 244 (relating to dividends received on certain preferred stock of public utilities), and 245 (relating to dividends received from certain foreign corporations) shall be computed without regard to section 246(b) as modified by section 809(d)(8)(B).

"(d) Offset defined.

"(1) In general. For purposes of subsection (b)(2), the term 'offset' means, with respect to any taxable year, an amount equal to that increase in the operations loss deduction for the taxable year which reduces the life insurance company taxable income (computed without regard to section 802(b)(3)) for such year to zero.

"(2) Operations loss deduction. For purposes of paragraph (1), the operations loss deduction for any taxable year shall be computed without regard to the loss from operations for the loss year or for any taxable year thereafter.

"(e) New company defined.

"For purposes of this part, a life insurance company is a new company for any taxable year only if such taxable year begins not more than 5 years after the first day on which it (or any predecessor, if section 381(c)(22) applies or would have applied if in effect) was authorized to do business as an insurance company.

"(f) Application of subtitle A and subtitle F.

"Except as provided in section 809(e), subtitle A and subtitle F shall apply in respect of operations loss carrybacks, operations loss carryovers, and the operations loss deduction under this part in the same manner and to the same extent as such subtitles apply in respect of net operating loss carrybacks, net operating loss carryovers, and the net operating loss deduction."

In **1983**, P.L. 97-448, Sec. 102(d)(2), added para. (c)(3) to Sec. 209 of P.L. 97-34, the effective date for amendments made by Sec. 207(b) of P.L. 97-34, see below.

In **1981**, P.L. 97-34, Sec. 207(b), substituted "15" for "7" in para. (b)(1), effective for net operating losses in tax. yrs. end. after 12/31/75. Sec. 209(c)(3) of this Act [as added by Sec. 102(d)(2) of P.L. 97-448, see above] provides:

"(3) Carryover must have been alive in 1981. The amendments made by subsections (a), (b), and (c) of section 207 shall not apply to any amount which, under the law in effect on the day before the date of the enactment of this Act, could not be carried to a taxable year ending in 1981."

In **1976**, P.L. 94-455, Sec. 806(d)(1)(A), added a sentence at the end of para. (b)(1), as previously amended by this Act, see below, effective for tax. yrs. end. after 12/31/75.

—P.L. 94-455, Sec. 806(d)91)(B), added para. (b)(3), effective for tax. yrs. end. after 12/31/75.

—P.L. 94-455, Sec. 1901(a)(99), amended para. (b)(1), effective for tax. yrs. begin. after 12/31/76.

Prior to amendment, para. (b)(1) read as follows:

"(1) Years to which loss may be carried.

"(A) In general. The loss from operations for any taxable year (hereinafter in this section referred to as the 'loss year') beginning after December 31, 1954, shall be—

"(i) an operations loss carryback to each of the 3 taxable years preceding the loss year,

"(ii) an operations loss carryover to each of the 5 taxable years following the loss year, and

"(iii) subject to subsection (e), if the life insurance company is a new company for the loss year, an operations loss carryover to each of the 3 taxable years following the 5 taxable years described in clause (ii).

"(B) Special transitional rules for carrybacks. A loss from operations for any taxable year beginning before January 1, 1958, shall not be an operations loss carryback to any taxable year beginning before January 1, 1955. A loss from operations for any taxable year beginning after December 31, 1957, shall not be an operations loss carryback to any taxable year beginning before January 1, 1958.

"(C) Application for years prior to 1958. For purposes of this section, this part (as in effect for 1958) and section 381(c)(22) shall be treated as applying to all taxable years beginning after December 31, 1954, and before January 1, 1958."

In **1964**, P.L. 88-571, Sec. 1(a), amended subsec. (e), effective as provided in Sec. 1(b) of this Act, which reads as follows:

"(b) The amendment made by subsection (a) shall apply to a loss from operations for taxable years beginning after December 31, 1955; except that, in the case of a nonqualified corporation as defined in section 812(e)(2)(B) of the Internal Revenue Code of 1954 as in effect before such amendment—

"(1) a loss from operations for a taxable year beginning in 1956 shall not be an operating loss carryover to the years 1962 and 1963, and there shall be no reduction in the portion of such loss from operations which may be carried to 1964 by reason of an offset with respect to the year 1962 or 1963, and

"(2) a loss from operations for a taxable year beginning in 1957 shall not be an operating loss carryover to the year 1963, and there shall be no reduction in the portion of such loss from operations which may be carried to 1964 and 1965 by reason of an offset with respect to the year 1963."

Prior to amendment, subsec. (e) read as follows:

"(e) Rules relating to new companies.

"(1) New company defined. For purposes of this part, a life insurance company is a new company for any taxable year only if such taxable year begins not more than 5 years after the first day on which it (or any predecessor, if section 381(c)(22) applies or would have applied if in effect) was authorized to do business as an insurance company.

"(2) Limitations on 8-year carryover.

"(A) In general. For purposes of subsection (b)(1)(A)(iii), a life insurance company shall not be treated as a new company for any loss year if at any time during such year it was a nonqualified corporation. If, at any time during any taxable year after the loss year, the life insurance company is a nonqualified corporation, subsection (b)(1)(A)(iii) shall cease to apply with respect to such loss for such taxable year and all subsequent taxable years.

"(B) Nonqualified corporation defined. For purposes of subparagraph (A), the term 'nonqualified corporation' means any corporation connected through stock ownership with any other corporation (except a corporation taxable under part II or part III of this subchapter), if either of such corporations possesses at least 50 percent of the voting power of all classes of stock of the other such corporation.

2,371

For purposes of subparagraph (A), a corporation shall be treated as becoming a nonqualified corporation at any time at which it becomes a party to a reorganization (other than a reorganization which is not described in any subparagraph of section 368(a)(1) other than subparagraphs (E) and (F) thereof)."

In 1962, P.L. 87-858, Sec. 3(d)(1), added "(except a corporation taxable under part II or part III of this subchapter)" after "with any other corporation" in subpara. (e)(2)(B), effective for tax. yrs. begin. after 12/31/54.

"SUBPART D.—DISTRIBUTIONS TO SHAREHOLDERS.
"Sec.
"815. Distributions to shareholders.

"SEC. 815. DISTRIBUTIONS TO SHAREHOLDERS.
"(a) General rule.
"For purposes of this section and section 802(b)(3), any distribution to shareholders after December 31, 1958, shall be treated as made—
"(1) first out of the shareholders surplus account, to the extent thereof,
"(2) then out of the policyholders surplus account, to the extent thereof, and
"(3) finally out of other accounts.
"(b) Shareholders surplus account.
"(1) In general. Each stock life insurance company shall, for purposes of this part, establish and maintain a shareholders surplus account. The amount in such account on January 1, 1958, shall be zero.
"(2) Additions to account. The amount added to the shareholders surplus account for any taxable year beginning after December 31, 1957, shall be the amount by which—
"(A) the sum of—
"(i) the life insurance company taxable income (computed without regard to section 802(b)(3)),
"(ii) in the case of a taxable year beginning after December 31, 1958, the amount (if any) by which the net long-term capital gain exceeds the net short-term capital loss, reduced (in the case of a taxable year beginning after December 31, 1961) of the net capital gain,
"(iii) the deduction for dividends received provided by sections 243, 244, and 245 (as modified by section 809(d)(8)(B)), and the amount of interest excluded from gross income under section 103, and
"(iv) the small business deduction provided by section 809(d)(10), exceeds
"(B) the taxes imposed for the taxable year by section 802(a), determined without regard to section 802(b)(3).
"(3) Subtractions from account.
"(A) In general. There shall be subtracted from the shareholders surplus account for any taxable year the amount which is treated under this section as distributed out of such account.
"(B) Distributions in 1958. There shall be subtracted from the shareholders surplus account (to the extent thereof) for any taxable year beginning in 1958 the amount of distributions to shareholders made during 1958.
"(c) Policyholders surplus account.
"(1) In general. Each stock life insurance company shall, for purposes of this part, establish and maintain a policyholders surplus account. The amount in such account on January 1, 1959, shall be zero.
"(2) Additions to account. The amount added to the policyholders surplus account for any taxable year beginning after December 31, 1958, shall be the sum of—
"(A) an amount equal to 50 percent of the amount by which the gain from operations exceeds the taxable investment income,
"(B) the deduction for certain nonparticipating contracts provided by section 809(d)(%) (as limited by section 809(f), and
"(C) the deduction for accident and health insurance and group life insurance contracts provided by section 809(d)(6) (as limited by section 809(f)).
"(3) Subtractions from account. There shall be subtracted from the policyholders surplus account for any taxable year an amount equal to the sum of—
"(A) the amount which (without regard to subparagraph (B)) is treated under this section as distributed out of the policyholders surplus account, and
"(B) the amount by which the tax imposed for the taxable year by section 802() is increased by reason of section 802(b)(3).
"(d) Special rules.
"(1) Election to transfer amounts from policyholders surplus account to shareholders surplus account.
"(A) In general. A taxpayer may elect for any taxable year for which it is a life insurance company to subtract from its policyholders surplus account any amount in such account as of the close of such taxable year. The amount so subtracted, less the amount of the tax imposed with respect to such amount by reason of section 802(b)(3), shall be added to the shareholders surplus account as of the beginning of the succeeding taxable year.
"(B) Manner and effect of election. The election provided by subparagraph (A) shall be made (in such manner and in such form as the Secretary may by regulations prescribe) after the close of the taxable year and not later than the time prescribed by law for filing the return (including extensions thereof) for the taxable year. Such an election, once made, shall not be revoked.
"(2) Termination as life insurance company.
"(A) Effect of termination. Except as provided in section 381(c)(22) (relating to carryovers in certain corporate readjustments), of—
"(i) for any taxable year the taxpayer is not an insurance company, or
"(ii) for any two successive taxable years the taxpayer is not a life insurance company,

then the amount taken into account under section 802(b)(3) for the last preceding taxable year for which it was a life insurance company shall be increased (after the application of subparagraph (B)) by the amount remaining in its policyholders surplus account at the close of such last preceding taxable year.
"(B) Effect of certain distributions. If for any taxable year the taxpayer is an insurance company but not a life insurance company, then any distribution to shareholders during such taxable year shall be treated as made on the last day of the last preceding taxable year for which the taxpayer was a life insurance company.
"(3) Treatment of certain indebtedness. If—
"(A) the taxpayer makes any payment in discharge of its indebtedness, and
"(B) such indebtedness is attributable to a distribution by the taxpayer to its shareholders after February 9, 1959.
then the amount of such payment shall, for purposes of this section and section 802(b)(3), be treated as a distribution in cash to shareholders, but only to the extent that the distribution referred to in subparagraph (B) was treated as made out of accounts other than the shareholders and policyholders surplus accounts.
"(4) Limitation on amount in policyholders surplus account. There shall be treated as a subtraction from the policyholders surplus account for a taxable year for which the taxpayer is a life insurance company the amount by which the policyholders surplus account (computed at the end of the taxable year without regard to this paragraph) exceeds whichever of the following is the greatest—
"(A) 15 percent of life insurance reserves at the end of the taxable year,
"(B) 25 percent of the amount by which the life insurance reserves at the end of the taxable year exceed the life insurance reserves at the end of 1958, and
"(C) 50 percent of the net amount of the premiums and other consideration taken into account for the taxable year under section 809(c)(1).
The amount so treated as subtracted, less the amount of the tax imposed with respect to such amount by reason of section 802(b)(3), shall be added to the shareholders surplus account as of the beginning of the succeeding taxable year.
"(5) Reduction of policyholders surplus account for certain unused deductions. If—
"(A) an amount added to the policyholders surplus account for any taxable year increased (or created) a loss from operations for such year, and
"(B) any portion of the increase (or amount created) in the loss from operations referred to in subparagraph (A) did not reduce the life insurance company taxable income for any taxable year to which such loss was carried,
the policyholders surplus account for the taxable year referred to in subparagraph (A) shall be reduced by the amount described in subparagraph (B).
"(6) Restoration of amounts distributed out of policyholders surplus account. Notwithstanding any other provision of this subchapter, no amount shall be subtracted from a taxpayer's policyholders surplus account with respect to a distribution made during the last month of the taxable year which, without regard to this paragraph, would be treated in whole or in part as a distribution out of the policyholders surplus account, to the extent that amounts so distributed are returned to the taxpayer no later than the time prescribed by law (including extensions thereof) for filing the taxpayer's return for the taxable year in which the distribution was made. For purposes of this paragraph, amounts returned to a taxpayer with respect to a distribution shall be first applied to the return of amounts which, without regard to this paragraph, would have been treated as distributed out of the policyholders surplus account. This paragraph shall not apply if, at the time such distribution was made, the taxpayer intended to avail itself of the provisions of this paragraph by having its shareholders return all or a part of such distribution. Nothing in this paragraph shall affect the tax treatment of the receipt of the distribution by any shareholder, and the basis to a shareholder of his stock in the taxpayer shall not be increased by reason of amounts returned under this paragraph to the extent that a dividends received deduction or exclusion was allowable in respect of the distribution of such amount under any provision of this title.
"(e) Special rule for certain mutualizations.
"(1) In general. For purposes of this section and section 802(b)(3), any distribution to shareholders after December 31, 1958, in acquisition of stock pursuant to a plan of mutualization shall be treated—
"(A) first, as made out of paid-in capital and paid-in surplus, to the extent thereof,
"(B) thereafter, as made in two allocable parts—
"(i) one part of which is made out of the other accounts referred to in subsection (a)(3), and
"(ii) the remainder of which is a distribution to which subsection (a) applies.
"(2) Special rules.
"(A) Allocation ratio. The part referred to in paragraph (1)(B)(i) is the amount which means the same ratio to the amount to which paragraph (1)(B) applies as—
"(i) the excess (determined as of December 31, 1958, and adjusted to the beginning of the year of the distribution as provided in subparagraph (B)) of the assets over the total liabilities, bears to
"(ii) the sum (determined as of the beginning of the year of the distribution) of the excess described in clause (i), the amount in the shareholders surplus account, plus the amount in the policyholders surplus account.
"(B) Adjustment for certain distributions. The excess described in subparagraph (A)(i) shall be reduced by the aggregate of the prior distributions which have been treated under subsection (a)(3) as made out of accounts other than the shareholders surplus account and the policyholders surplus account.
"(f) Distribution defined.
"For purposes of this section, the term 'distribution' includes any distribution in redemption of stock or in partial or complete liquidation of the corporation, but does not include—
"(1) any distribution made by the corporation in its stock or in rights to acquire its stock;
"(2) except for purposes of subsection (a)(3) and subsection (e)(2)(B), any distribution in redemption of stock issued before 1958, which at all times on and af-

2,372

ter the date of issuance and on and before the date of redemption is limited as to dividends and is callable, at the option of the issuer, at a price not in excess of 105 percent of the sum of the issue price and the amount of any contribution to surplus made by the original purchaser at the time of his purchase.

"(3) any distribution after December 31, 1963, of the stock of a controlled corporation to which section 355 applies, is such controlled corporation is an insurance company subject to the tax imposed by section 831 and if—

"(A) control was acquired prior to January 1, 1958, or

"(B) control has been acquired after December 31, 1957—

"(i) in a transaction qualifying as a reorganization under section 368(a)(1)(B), if the distributing corporation has at all times since December 31, 1957, owned stock representing not less than 50 percent of the total combined voting power of all classes of stock entitled to vote, and not less than 50 percent of the value of all classes of stock, of the controlled corporation, or

"(ii) solely in exchange for stock of the distributing corporation which stock is immediately exchanged by the controlled corporation in a transaction qualifying as a reorganization under section 368(a)(1)(A) or (C), if the controlled corporation has at all times since its organization been wholly owned by the distributing corporation and the distributing corporation has at all times since December 31, 1957, owned stock representing not less than 50 percent of the total combined voting power of all classes of stock entitled to vote, and not less than 50 percent of the value of all classes of stock, of the corporation the assets of which have been transferred to the controlled corporation in the section 368(a)(1)(A) or (C) reorganization;

"(4) any distribution after December 31, 1966, of the stock of a controlled corporation to which section 355 applies, if such distribution is made to a corporation which immediately after the distribution is in control (within the meaning of section 268(c)) of both the distributing corporation and such controlled corporation and if such controlled corporation is a life insurance company of which the distributing corporation has been in control at all times since December 31, 1957; or

"(5) any distribution after December 31, 1968 of the stock of a controlled corporation to which section 355 applies, if such distribution is made to a corporation which immediately after the distribution is the owner of all the stock of such controlled corporation and if, immediately before the distribution, the distributing corporation had been the owner of all of the stock in all classes of such controlled corporation at all times since December 31, 1957.

Paragraphs (3), (4), and (5) shall not apply to that portion of the distribution of stock of the controlled corporation equal to the increase in the aggregate adjusted basis of such stock after December 31, 1957, except to the extent such increase results from an acquisition of stock in the controlled corporation in a transaction described in paragraph (3)(B). If any part of the increase in the aggregate adjusted basis of stock of the controlled corporation after December 31, 1957, results from the transfer (other than as part of a transaction described in paragraph (3)(B)) by the distributing corporation to the controlled corporation of property which has a fair market value in excess of its adjusted basis at the time of the transfer, paragraphs (3), (4), and (5) also shall not apply to that portion of the distribution equal to such excess.

"(g) Certain distributions related to former subsidiaries.

"If subsection (f)(5) applied to the distribution by a life insurance company of the stock of a corporation which was a controlled corporation—

"(1) any distribution by such corporation to its shareholders (after the date of the distribution of its stock by the life insurance company), and

"(2) any disposition of the stock of such corporation by the distributee corporation,

shall, for purposes of this section, be treated as a distribution to its shareholders by such life insurance company, until the amounts so treated equal the amount of the distribution of such stock which by reason of subsection (f)(5) was not included as a distribution for purposes of this section.

In 1976, P.L. 94-331, Sec. 1(a), added para. (d)(6), effective for tax. yrs. end. after 12/31/57.

—P.L. 94-445, Sec. 1901(b)(1)(O), amended clause (b)(1)(A)(iii) . . . Sec. 1901(b)(24), deleted '(determined without regard to section 802(a)(3))' in subpara. (c)(3)(B) . . . Sec. 1901(b)(33)(H), substituted 'of the net capital gain' for 'by which the net long-term capital gain exceeds the net short-term capital loss' in clause (b)(2)(A)(ii), effective for tax. yrs. begin. after 12/31/76.

Prior to amendment, clause (b)(1)(A)(iii) read as follows:

"(iii) the deduction for partially tax-exempt interest provided by section 242 (as modified by section 804(a)(3)), the deductions for dividends received provided by sections 243, 244, and 245 (as modified by section 809(d)(8)(B)), and the amount of interest excluded from gross income under section 103, and"

—P.L. 94-455, Sec. 1906(b)(13)(A), substituted "Secretary" for "Secretary or his delegate" in para. (d)(1), effective for tax. yrs. begin. after 12/31/76.

In 1969, P.L. 91-172, Sec. 907(b)(1)(A), deleted "or" at the end of para. (f)(3) . . . Sec. 907(b)(1)(B), substituted "; or" for the period at the end of para. (f)(4) . . . Sec. 907(b)(1)(C), added para. (f)(5) . . . Sec. 907(b)(1)(D), substituted "Paragraphs (3), (4), and (5) shall not apply" for "Neither paragraph (3) nor paragraph (4) shall apply" in the next to last sentence in subsec. (f) . . . Sec. 907(b)(1)(E), substituted "paragraphs (3) , (4), and (5)" for "paragraphs (3) and (4)" in subsec. (f), effective for tax. yrs. begin. after 12/31/57.

—P.L. 91-172, Sec. 907(b)(2), added subsec. (g), effective for tax. yrs. begin. after 12/31/68.

In 1967, P.L. 90-225, Sec. 4(a)(1), deleted "or" at the end of para. (f)(3) . . . Sec. 4(a)(2), substituted "; or" for the period at the end of para. (f)(3) . . . Sec. 4(a)(3), added para. (f)(4) . . . Sec. 4(b)(1)(A), substituted "Neither paragraph (3) nor paragraph (4) shall" for "Paragraph (3) shall not" in the next to last sentence in sub-

sec. (f) . . . Sec. 4(b)(1)(B), substituted "subparagraph (3)(B)" for " subparagraph (B) of such paragraph" in subsec. (f) . . . Sec. 4(b)(2), substituted "paragraphs (3) and (4) also" for "paragraph (3) also" in the last sentence of subsec. (f), effective for tax. yrs. begin. after 12/31/66.

In 1964, P.L. 88-571, Sec. 2, added "reduced (in the case of a taxable year beginning after December 31, 1961) by the amount referred to in clause (i)" in clause (b)92)(A)(ii), effective 9/2/64.

—P.L. 88-571, Sec. 3(a), added para. (d)(5), effective for amounts added to policyholders surplus accounts (within the meaning of Code Sec. 815(c)), for tax. yrs. begin. after 12/31/58.

—P.L. 88-571, Sec. 4(a)(1), deleted the second and third sentences of subsec. (a) . . . Sec. 4(a)(2), added subsec. (f), effective for tax. yrs. begin. after 12/31/63.

Prior to deletion, the second and third sentence of subsec. (a) read as follows:

"For purposes of this section, the term 'distribution' includes any distribution in redemption of stock or in partial or complete liquidation of the corporation, but does not include any distribution made by the corporation in its stock or in rights to acquire its stock, and does not (except for purposes of paragraph (3) and subsection (e)(2)(B)) include any distribution in redemption of stock issued before 1958 which at all times on and after the date of issuance and on and before the date of redemption is limited as to dividends and is callable, at the option of the issuer, at a price not in excess of 105 percent of the sum of the issue price and the amount of any contribution to surplus made by the original purchaser at the time of his purchase. Further, for purposes of this section, the term 'distribution' does not include any distribution before January 1, 1964, of the stock of a controlled corporation to which section 355 applies, if such controlled corporation is an insurance company subject to the tax imposed by section 831 and control has been acquired prior to January 1, 1963, in a transaction qualifying as a reorganization under section 368(a)(1)(B)."

In 1962, P.L. 87-585, Sec. 3(b)(4), substituted "802(a)" for "802(a)(1)" in subpara. (c)(3)(B) . . . Sec. 3(e), added the third sentence in subsec. (a), effective for tax. yrs. begin. after 12/31/61.

—P.L. 87-790, Sec. 2(b), substituted "accident and health insurance and group life insurance contracts" for "group life and group accident and health insurance contracts" in subpara. (c)(2)(C), effective for tax. yrs. begin. after 12/31/62.

"Subpart E.—Miscellaneous Provisions

"Sec.

"817. Rules relating to certain gains and losses.

"818. Accounting provisions.

"819. Foreign life insurance companies.

"819A. Contiguous country branches of domestic life insurance companies.

"820. Repealed."

In 1982, P.L. 97-248, Sec. 255(b)(5), deleted item 820.

Prior to deletion, item 820 read as follows:

"820. Optional treatment of policies reinsured under modified coinsurance contracts."

In 1976, P.L. 94-455, Sec. 1043(b), added item 819A.

"Sec. 817. Rules relating to certain gains and losses.

"(a) Treatment of capital gains and losses, etc.

"In the case of a life insurance company—

"(1) in applying section 1231(a), the term 'property used in the trade or business' shall be treated as including only—

"(A) property used in carrying on an insurance business, of a character which is subject to the allowance for depreciation provided in section 167, held for more than 1 year, and real property used in carrying on an insurance business, held for more than 6 months, which is not described in section 1231(b)(1)(A), (b), or (C), and

"(B) property described in section 1231(b)(2), and

"(2) in applying section 1221(2), he reference to property used in trade or business shall be treated as including only property used in carrying on an insurance business.

"(b) Gain on property held on December 31, 1958, and certain substituted property acquired after 1958.

"(1) Property held on December 31, 1958. In the case of property held by the taxpayer on December 31, 1958, if—

"(A) the fair market value of such property on such date exceeds the adjusted basis for determining gain as of such date, and

"(B) the taxpayer has been a life insurance company at all times on and after December 31, 1958,

the gain on the sale or other disposition of such property shall be treated as an amount (not less than zero) equal to the amount by which the gain (teremined without regard to this subsection) exceeds the difference between the fair market value on December 31, 1958, and the adjusted basis for determining gain as of such date.

"(2) Certain property acquired after December 31, 1958. In the case of property acquired after December 31, 1958, and having a substituted basis (within the meaning of section 1016(b))—

"(A) for purposes of paragraph (1), such property shall be deemed held continuously by the taxpayer since the beginning of the holding period thereof, determined with reference to section 1223,

"(B) the fair market value and adjusted basis referred to in paragraph (1) shall be that of that property for which the holding period taken into account includes December 31, 1958,

2,373

"(C) paragraph (1) shall apply only if the property or properties the holding periods of which are taken into account were held only by life insurance companies after December 31, 1958, during the holding periods so taken into account,

"(D) the difference between the fair market value and adjusted basis referred to in paragraph (1) shall be reduced (not less than zero) by the excess of (i) the gain that would have been recognized but for this subsection on all prior sales or dispositions after December 31, 1958, of properties referred to in subparagraph (C), over (ii) the gain that was recognized on such sales or other dispositions, and

"(E) the basis of such property shall be determined as if the gain which would have been recognized but for this subsection were recognized gain.

"(3) Property defined. For purposes of paragraphs (1) and (2), the term 'property' does not include insurance and annuity contracts (and contracts supplementary thereto) and property described in paragraph (1) of section 1221."

In 1976, P.L. 94-455, Sec. 1351(b)(11)(A), repealed subsec. (d), effective 1/2/77, except as provided in Sec. 1351(b)(11)(B) of this Act, which reads as follows:

"(B) Savings provision. Notwithstanding subparagraph (A), if any gain in a taxable year beginning after December 31, 1976, from any sale or other disposition of property prior to January 1, 1959, would be excluded or not taken into account for purposes of part I of subchapter L of chapter 1 if subsection (d) of section 817 of such Code were still in effect for such taxable year, such gain shall be excluded for purposes of such part."

Prior to repeal, subsec. (d) read as follows:

"(d) Gain on transactions occurring prior to January 1, 1959.

"For purposes of this part, there shall be excluded any gain from the sale or exchange or a capital asset, and any gain considered as gain from the sale or exchange of a capital asset, resulting from sales or other dispositions of property prior to January 1, 1959. Any gain after December 31, 1958, resulting from the sale or other disposition of property prior to January 1, 1959, which, but for this sentence, would be taken into account under section 1231, shall not be taken into account under section 1231 for purposes of this part."

—P.L. 94-455, Sec. 1402(b)(1)(M), substituted "9 months" for "6 months" in subpara. (a)(1)(A), effective for tax. yrs. begin. in 12/31/77.

—P.L. 94-455, Sec. 1402(b)(2), substituted "1 year" for "9 months" in subpara. (a)(1)(A), effective for tax. yrs. begin. after 12/31/77. Sec. 1402(c) of this Act, reproduced as a note after Code Sec. 1222, provided a transitional rule for certain installment obligations.

—P.L. 94-455, Sec. 1901(a)(100), deleted subsecs. (c) and (e), effective for tax. yrs. begin. after 12/31/76.

Prior to deletion, subsec. (c) read as follows:

"(c) Limitation on capital loss carryovers.

"A net capital loss for any taxable year beginning before January 1, 1959, shall not be taken into account."

Prior to deletion, subsec. (e) read as follows:

"(e) Certain reinsurance transactions in 1958.

"For purposes of this part, the reinsurance in a single transaction, or in a series of related transactions, occurring in 1958, by a life insurance company of all or its insurance contracts by a particular type, through the asuaption by another company or companies of all liabilities under such contracts, shall be treated as a sale of a capital asset."

"SEC. 818. ACCOUNTING PROVISIONS.

"(a) Method of accounting.

"All computations entering into the determination of the taxes imposed by this part shall be made—

"(1) under an accrual method of accounting, or

"(2) to the extent permitted under regulations prescribed by the Secretary, under a combination of an accrual method or accounting with any other method permitted by this chapter (other than the cash receipts and disbursements method).

Except as provided in the preceding sentence, all such computations shall be made in a manner consistent with the manner required for purposes of the annual statement approved by the National Association of Insurance Commissioners.

"(b) Amortization of premium and accrual of discount.

"(1) In general. The appropriate items of income, deductions, and adjustments under this part shall be adjusted to reflect the appropriate amortization of premium and the appropriate accrual of discount attributable to the taxable year on bonds, notes, debentures, or other evidences of indebtedness held by a life insurance company. Such amortization and accrual shall be determined—

"(A) in accordance with the method regularly employed by such company, if such method is reasonable, and

"(B) in all other cases, in accordance with regulations prescribed by the secretary.

"(2) Special rules.

"(A) Amortization of bond premium. In the case of any bond (as defined in section 171(d)) acquired after December 31, 1957, the amount of bond premium, and the amortizable bond premium for the taxable year, shall be determined under section 171(b) as if the election set forth in section 171(c) had been made.

"(B) Convertible evidences of indebtedness. In no case shall the amount of premium on a convertible evidence of indebtedness include any amount attributable to the conversion features of the evidence of indebtedness.

"(3) Exception. For taxable years beginning after December 31, 1962, no accrual of discount shall be required under paragraph (1) on any bond (as defined in section 171(d)), except in the case of discount which is—

"(A) interest to which section 103 applies, or

"(B) original issued discount (as defined in section 1232(b)).

For purposes of section 805(b)(3)(A), the current earnings rate for any taxable year beginning before January 1, 1963, shall be determined as if the preceding sentence applied to such taxable year.

"(c) Life insurance reserves computed on preliminary term basis.

"For purposes of this part (other than section 801), at the election of the taxpayer the amount taken into account as life insurance reserves with respect to contracts for which such reserves are computed on a preliminary term basis may be determined on either of the following bases:

"(1) Exact revaluation. As if the reserves for all such contracts had been comptued on a net level premium basis (using the same mortality assumptions and interest rates for both the preliminary term basis and the net level premium basis).

"(2) Approximate revaluation. The amount computed without regard to this subsection—

"(A) increased by $19 per $1,000 of insurance in force (other than term insurance) under such contracts, less 1.9 percent of reserves under such contacts, and

"(A) increased by $5 per $1,000 of term insurance in force under such contracts which at the time of issuance cover a period of more than 15 years, less 0.5 percent of reserves under such contracts.

If the taxpayer makes an election under either paragraph (1) or (2) for any taxable year, the basis adopted shall be adhered to in making the computations under this part (other than section 801) for the taxable year and all subsequent taxable years unless a change in the basis of computing such reserve is approved by the Secretary, except that if, pursuant to an election made for a taxable year beginning in 1958, or in effect for a taxable year beginning in 1981, the basis adopted is the basis provided in paragraph (2), the taxpayer may adopt the basis provided by paragraph (1) for its first taxable year beginning after 1958 or 1981, which ever is applicable.

"(d) Short taxable years.

"If any return of a corporation made under this part is for a period of less than the entire calendar year (referred to in this subsection as 'short period'), then section 443 shall not apply in respect of such period, but—

"(1) the taxable investment income and the gain or loss from operations shall be determined, under regulations prescribed by the Secretary, on an annual basis by a ratable daily projection of the appropriate figures for the short period,

"(2) that portion of the life insurance company taxable income described in paragraphs (1) and (2) of section 802(b) shall be determined on an annual basis by treating the amounts ascertained under paragraph 981) as the taxable investment income and the gain or loss from operations for the taxable year, and

"(3) that portion of the life insurance company taxable income described in paragraphs (1) and (2) of section 802(b) for the short period shall be the amount which bears the same ratio to the amount ascertained under paragraph (2) as the number of days in the short period bears to the number of days in the entire calendar year.

"(e) Denial of double deductions.

"Nothing in this part shall permit the same item to be deducted more than once under subpart B and once under subpart C.

"(f) Special rules for consolidated return computations.

"For purposes of this part, in the case of life insurance company filing or required to file a consolidated return under section 1501 for a taxable year, the following rules shall apply:

"(1) Policyholders' share of investment yield. The computation of the policyholders' share of investment yield under subparts B and C (including all determinations and computations incident thereto) shall be made as if such company were not filing a consolidated return.

"(2) Life insurance company taxable income.

"(A) In general. The amount of the consolidated life insurance company taxable income under paragraphs (1) and (2) of section 802(b) shall be determined by taking into account the life insurance company taxable income (including any case where deductions exceed income) of each life insurance company which is a member of the group (as computed separately under such paragraphs).

"(B) Certain amounts computed separately. For purposes of subparagraph (A), the determination of a life insurance company's taxable investment income and gain or loss from operations (after applying the limitation provided by section 809(f)) shall be made without regard to the taxable investment income or gain or loss from operations of any other such company.

"(3) Consolidated net capital gain. If there is a consolidated net capital gain, then the partial tax referred to in section 902(a)(2)(A) shall be computed on—

"(A) the consolidated life insurance company taxable income, reduced (ut not below the sum of the amounts determined under section 802(b)(3)) by

"(B) the amount of such consolidated net capital gain.

"(g) Allocation in case of reinsurance agreement involving tax avoidance or evation.

"In the case of 2 or more related persons (within the meaning of section 1239(b)) who are parties to a reinsurance agreement, the Secretary may—

"(1) allocate between or among such persons income (whether investment income, premium, or otherwise), deductions, assets, reserves, credits, and other items related to such agreement, or

"(2) recharacterize any such items,

if he determines that such allocation or recharacterization is necessary to reflect the proper source and character of the taxable income (or any item described in paragraph (1) relating to such taxable income) of each such person.

"(h) Method for computing reserves on contract where interest is guaranteed beyond end of taxable year.

"For purposes of this part (other than section 801), interest payable under any contract which is computed at a rate which—

"(1) is in excess of the lowest rates which are assumed under such contract for any period in calculating the reserves under section 810(C) for the contract under which such interest is payable, and

"(2) is guaranteed beyond the end of the taxable year on which the reserves are being computed,
shall be taken into account in computing the reserves with respect to such contract as if such interest were guaranteed only up to the end of the taxable year."

In 1982, P.L. 97-248, Sec. 258(a), added subsec. (g), effective for agreements entered into after 9/3/82.
—P.L. 97-248, Sec. 260(a), added subsec. (h), effective for reserves computed for tax. yrs. begin. after 12/31/81 and before 1/1/84 with respect to guarantees made after 7/1/82 and before 1/1/84. Sec. 263(a)(3)(B) of this Act provides:
"(B) Special rule relating to reserves. If, for any taxable year beginning before January 1, 1982—
"(i) the taxpayer increased reserves pursuant to section 810(c)(4) of the Internal Revenue Code of 1954 to reflect interest guaranteed beyond the end of such taxable year, and
"(ii) the Federal income tax liability of such taxpayer for all taxable years would be the same if such liability was computed with or without regard to such reserves,
then such reserves shall, as of the beginning of the first taxable year of the taxpayer beginning after December 31, 1981, be recomputed as if section 818(h) of such Code (as added by this Act) applied to such reserves. If this subparagraph applies to any taxpayer, subparagraph (A) shall be applied with respect to such taxpayer by striking out 'after July 1, 1982, and'."
—P.L. 97-248, Sec. 262, amended subsec. (f), effective for tax. yrs. begin. after 12/31/81. Secs. 263(b)(2) and (3) of this Act provide:
"(2) Consolidated returns. The provisions of section 818(f) of such Code, as amended by section 262, shall apply to any taxable year beginning before January 1, 1982, if the taxpayer filed a consolidated return before July, 1982 for such taxable year under section 1501 of such Code, which, on such date (determined without regard to any amended return files after June 30, 1982), was consistent with the provisions of section 818(f) of such Code, as so amended. In the case of a taxable year beginning in 1981, the preceding sentence shall be applied by substituting 'September 16' for 'July 1' and 'September 15' for 'June 30'.
"(3) Taxable years where period of limitation has run. This subsection shall not apply to any taxable year with respect to which the statue of limitations for filing a claim for credit or refund has expired under any provision o law or by operation of law."
Prior to amendment, subsec. (f) read as follows:
"(f) Computation on colidilated returns of policyholders' share of investment yield.
"For purposes of this part, in the case of a life insurance company filing or required to file a consolidated return under section 1051 for a taxable year, under the computations of the policyholder's share of investment yield under subparts B and C (including all determinations and computations incident thereto) shall be made as if such company were not filing a consolidated return."
—P.L. 87-248, Sec. 267(a)(1)(A), substituted "$21" for "$19" in subpara. (c)(2)(A) . . . Sec. 267(a)(1)(B), substituted "1.9 percent" for "21. percent" in subpara. (c)(2)(A) . . . Sec. 267(a)(2)(A), and (B) added "or in effect for a taxable year beginning in 1982" after 1958" the first time it appeared in the last sentence of subsec. (C), and added 'or 1981, whichever is applicable" after the second time '1958" appeared in the last sentence of subsec. (c), effective for tax. yrs. begin. after 2/31/81, but only with respect to reserves established under contracts entered into after 3/31/82.

In 1976, P.L. 94-455, Sec. 1901(a)(101), deleted subsec. (e), redesignated subsecs. (f) and (g) as subsecs. (e) and (f), effective for tax. yrs. begin. after 12/31/76.
Prior to deletion, subsec. (e) read as follows:
"(e) Transitional rule for changes in method of accounting.
"(1) In general. If the method of accounting required to be used in computing the taxpayer's taxes under this part for the taxable year 1958 is different from the method used in computing its taxes under this part for 1957, then there shall be ascertained the net amount of those adjustments which are determined (as of the close of 1957) to be necessary solely by reason of the change to the method required by subsection (a) in order to prevent amounts from being duplicated or omitted. The amount o the taxpayer's tax for 1957 shall be recomputed (under the law applicable to 1957, modified as provided in paragraph (4)) taking into account an amount equal to 1/10 of the net amount of the adjustments determined under the preceding sentence. The amount of increase or decrease (as the case may be) referred to in paragraph (2) or (3) shall be the amount of the increase or decrease ascertained under the preceding sentence, multiplied by 10.
"(2) Treatment of decrease. For purposes of subtitle F, if the recomputation under paragraph (1) results in a decrease, the amount there of shall be a decrease in the tax imposed for 1957; except that for purposes of computing the period of limitation on the making of refunds or the allowance of credits with respect to such overpayment, the amount of such decrease shall be treated as an overpayment of tax for 1959. No interest shall be paid, for any period before March 15, 1960, on any overpayment of tax imposed for 1957 which is attributable to such decrease.
"(3) Treatment of increase.
"(A) In general. For purposes of subtitle F (other than sections 6016 and 6655), if the recomputation under paragraph (1) results in an increase, the amount there of shall be treated as a tax imposed by this subsection for 1959. Such tax shall be payable in 10 equal annual installments, beginning with March 15, 1960.
"(B) Special rules. For purposes of subparagraph (A)—
"(i) No interest shall be paid on any installment described in subparagraph (A) for any period before the time prescribed in such subparagraph for the payment of such installment.

"(ii) Section 6152(c) (relating to proration of deficiencies to installments) shall apply.
"(iii) In applying section 6502(a)(1) (relating to collection after assessment), the assessment of any installment described in subparagraph (A) shall be treated as made at the time prescribed by such subparagraph for the payment of such installment.
"(iv) Except as provided in section 381(c)(22), if for any taxable year the taxpayer is not a life insurance company, the time for payment of any remaining installments described in subparagraph (A) shall be the date (determined without regard to any extension of time) for filing the return for such taxable year.
"(4) Modifications of 1957 tax computation. In recomputing the taxpayer's tax for 1957 for purposes of paragraph (1)—
"(A) section 804(b) (as in effect in 1957) shall not apply with respect to any amount required to be taken into account by such paragraph, and
"(B) the amount of the deduction allowed by section 805 (as in effect in 1957) shall not be reduced by reason of any amount required to be taken into account by such paragraph."
—P.L. 94-455, Sec. 1906(b)(13)(A), substituted 'Secretary" for "Secretary or his delegate" in subsecs. (a), (B), (c), and (d), effective for tax. yrs. begin. after 12/31/76.

In 1971, P.L. 91-688, Sec. 1(a), added subsec. (g), effective for tax. yrs. begin. after 12/31/57.

In 1964, P.L. 88-272, Sec. 228(b)(1), added para. (b)(3), effective for tax. yrs. begin. after 12/31/57.

"SEC. 819. FOREIGN LIFE INSURANCE COMPANIES.
"(a) Adjustment where surplus held in Unites States is less than specified minimum.
"(1) In general. In the case of any foreign company taxable under this part, if the minimum figure determined under paragraph (2) exceeds the surplus held in the United Sates, then—
"(A) the amount of the policy and other contract liability requirements (determined under section 805 without regard to this subsection), and
"(B) the amount of the required interest (determined under section 809(a)(2) without regard to this subsection),
shall each be reduced by an amount determined by multiplying such excess by the current earnings rate (as defined in section 805(b)(2)).
"(2) Definitions. For purposes of paragraph (1)—
"(A) The minimum figure is the amount determined by multiplying the taxpayer's total insurance liabilities on United States business by a percentage for the taxable year to be determined and proclaimed by the Secretary
"(i) in the case of a taxable year beginning before January 1, 1959, 9 percent, and
"(ii) in the case of a taxable year beginning after December 31, 1958, a percentage for such year to be determined and proclaimed by the Secretary.
The percentage determined and proclaimed by the Secretary under the preceding sentence shall be based on such data with respect to domestic life insurance companies for the preceding taxable year as the Secretary considers representative. Such percentage shall be computed on the basis of a ratio the numerator of which is the excess of the assets over the total insurance liabilities, and the denominator of which is the total insurance liabilities.
"(B) The surplus held in the United States is the excess of the assets held in the United States over the total insurance liabilities on United States business.
For purposes of this paragraph and subsection (b), the term 'total insurance liabilities' means the sum of the total reserves (as defined in section 801(c)) plus (to the extent not included in total reserves) the items referred to in paragraphs (3), (4), and (5) of section 810(c).
"(3) Reduction of section 881 tax. In the case of any foreign corporation taxable under this part, there shall be determined—
"(A) the amount which would be subject of tax under section 881 if the amount taxable under such section were determined without regard to sections 103 and 894, and
"(B) the amount of the reduction provided by paragraph (1).
The tax under section 881 (determined without regard to this paragraph) shall be reduced *but not below zero) by an amount which is the same proportion of such tax as the amount referred to in subparagraph)B) is of the amount referred to in subparagraph (A); but such reduction in tax shall not exceed the increase in tax under this part by reason of the reduction provided by paragraph (1).
"(b) Distributions to shareholders.
"(1) In general. In applying section 802(b)(3) and 815 with respect to a foreign corporation, the amount of the distributions to shareholders shall be determined by multiplying the total amount of the distributions to shareholders (within the meaning of section 815) of the foreign corporation by whichever of the following percentages is selected by the taxpayer for the taxable year:
"(A) the percentage which the minimum figure for the taxable year (determined under subsection (a)(2)(A)) is of the excess of the assets of the company over the total insurance liabilities; or
"(B) the percentage which the total insurance liabilities on United Stated business for the taxable year is of the company's total insurance liabilities.
"(2) Distributions pursuant to certain mutualizations. In applying section 815(e) with respect to a foreign corporation—
"(A) the paid-in capital and paid-in surplus referred to in section 815(e)(1)(A) of a foreign corporation is the portion of such capital and surplus determined by multiplying such capital and surplus by the percentage selected for the taxable year under paragraph (1); and
"(B) the excess referred to in section 815(e)(2)(A)(i) (without the adjustment provided by section 815(e)(2)(B)) is whichever of the following is the greater:

"(i) the minimum figure for 1958 determined under subsection (a)92(A) computed by using a percentage of 9 percent in lieu of the percentage determined and proclaimed by the Secretary, or

"(ii) the surplus described in subsection (a)(2)(B) (determined as of December 31, 1958).

"(c) Cross reference.

"3For taxation of foreign corporations carrying on life insurance business within the United States, see section 842."

In **1976**, P.L. 94-455, Sec. 1901(a)(102)(A), amended the first sentence of subpara. (a)(2)(A) . . . Sec. 1901(a)(102)(B), substituted "under the preceding sentence" for "under clause (ii)" in the second sentence of subpara. (a)(2)(A) . . . Sec. 1901(a)(102)(C), amended clause (b)(2)(B)(i), effective for tax. yrs. begin. after 12/31/76.

Prior to amendment, the first sentence of subpara. (a)(2)(A) read as follows:

"The minimum figure is the amount determined by multiplying the taxpayer's total insurance liabilities on the Unites States business by—"

Prior to amendment, clause (b)(2)(B)(i) read as follows:

"(i) the minimum figure for 1958 determined under subsection (a)(2)(A), or"

—P.L. 94-455, Sec. 1906(a)(13)(A), substituted "Secretary" for "Secretary or his delegate" each time it appeared in para. (a)(2), effective for tax. yrs. begin. after 12/31/76.

In **1966**, P.L. 98-809, Sec. 104, amended Code Sec. 819, effective for tax. yrs. begin. after 12/31/66.

Prior to amendment, Code Sec. 819 read as follows:

"SEC. 819. FOREIGN LIFE INSURANCE COMPANIES.

"(a) Carrying on United States insurance business.

"A foreign life insurance company carrying on a life insurance business within the United States, if with respect to its United States business it would qualify as a life insurance company under section 801, shall be taxable on the Unites States business of such company in the same manner as a domestic life insurance company.

"(b) Adjustment where surplus held in Unites States is less than specified minimum.

"(1) In general. In the case of any foreign company taxable under this part, if the minimum figure determined under paragraph (2) exceeds the surplus held in the United Sates, then—

"(A) the amount of the policy and other contract liability requirements (determined under section 805 without regard to this subsection), and

"(B) the amount of the required interest (determined under section 809(a)(2) without regard to this subsection),

shall each be reduced by an amount determined by multiplying such excess by the current earnings rate (as defined in section 805(b)(2)).

"(2) Definitions. For purposes of paragraph (1)—

"(A) The minimum figure is the amount determined by multiplying the taxpayer's total insurance liabilities on United States business by a percentage for the taxable year to be determined and proclaimed by the Secretary

"(i) in the case of a taxable year beginning before January 1, 1959, 9 percent, and

"(ii) in the case of a taxable year beginning after December 31, 1958, a percentage for such year to be determined and proclaimed by the Secretary.

The percentage determined and proclaimed by the Secretary under the preceding sentence shall be based on such data with respect to domestic life insurance companies for the preceding taxable year as the Secretary considers representative. Such percentage shall be computed on the basis of a ratio the numerator of which is the excess of the assets over the total insurance liabilities, and the denominator of which is the total insurance liabilities.

"(B) The surplus held in the United States is the excess of the assets held in the United States over the total insurance liabilities on United States business.

For purposes of this paragraph and subsection (b), the term 'total insurance liabilities' means the sum of the total reserves (as defined in section 801(c)) plus (to the extent not included in total reserves) the items referred to in paragraphs (3), (4), and (5) of section 810(c).

"(c) Distributions to shareholders.

"(1) In general. In applying section 802(b)(3) and 815 with respect to a foreign corporation, the amount of the distributions to shareholders shall be determined by multiplying the total amount of the distributions to shareholders (within the meaning of section 815) of the foreign corporation by whichever of the following percentages is selected by the taxpayer for the taxable year:

"(A) the percentage which the minimum figure for the taxable year (determined under subsection (a)(2)(A)) is of the excess of the assets of the company over the total insurance liabilities; or

"(B) the percentage which the total insurance liabilities on United Stated business for the taxable year is of the company's total insurance liabilities.

"(2) Distributions pursuant to certain mutualizations. In applying section 815(e) with respect to a foreign corporation—

"(A) the paid-in capital and paid-in surplus referred to in section 815(e)(1)(A) of a foreign corporation is the portion of such capital and surplus determined by multiplying such capital and surplus by the percentage selected for the taxable year under paragraph (1); and

"(B) the excess referred to in section 815(e)(2)(A)(i) (without the adjustment provided by section 815(e)(2)(B)) is whichever of the following is the greater:

"(i) the minimum figure for 1958 determined under subsection (a)92(A) computed by using a percentage of 9 percent in lieu of the percentage determined and proclaimed by the Secretary, or

"(ii) the surplus described in subsection (a)(2)(B) (determined as of December 31, 1958).

"(d) No United States insurance business.

"Foreign life insurance companies not carrying on an insurance business within the United States shall not be taxable under this section but shall be taxable as other foreign corporations."

"SEC. 819A. CONTIGUOUS COUNTRY RANCHES OF DOMESTIC LIFE INSURANCE COMPANIES.

"(a) Exclusion of items.

"In the case of a domestic mutual insurance company which—

"(1) is a life insurance company,

"(2) has a contiguous country life insurance branch, and

"(3) makes the election provided by subsection (g) with respect to such branch, there shall be excluded from each and every item involved in the determination of life insurance company taxable income the items separately accounted for in accordance with subsection (c).

"(b) Contiguous country life insurance branch.

"For purposes of this section, the term 'contiguous country life insurance branch' means a branch which—

"(1) issues insurance contracts insuring risks in connection with the lives or health of residents of a country which is contiguous to the United States,

"(2) has its principal place of business in such contiguous country, and

"(3) would constitute a mutual life insurance company if such branch were a separate domestic insurance company.

For purposes of this section, the term ' insurance contract' means any life, health, accident, or annuity contract or reinsurance contract or any contract relating thereto.

"(c) Separate accounting required.

"Any taxpayer which makes the election provided by subsection (g) shall establish and maintain a separate account for the various income, exclusion, deduction, asset, reserve, liability, and surplus items properly attributable to the contracts described in subsection (b). Such separate accounting shall be made—

"(1) in accordance with the method regularly employed by such company, if such method clearly reflects income derived from, and the other items attributable to, the contracts described in subsection (b), and

"(2) in all other cases, in accordance with regulations prescribed by the Secretary.

"(d) Recognition of gain on assets in branch account.

"If the aggregate fair market value of all the invested assets and tangible property which are separately accounted for by the domestic life insurance company in the branch account established pursuant to subsection (c) exceeds the aggregate adjusted basis of such assets for purposes of determining gain, then the domestic life insurance company shall be treated as having sold all such assets on the first day of the first taxable year for which the election is in effect at their fair market value on such first day. Notwithstanding any other provision of this chapter, the net gain shall be recognized to the domestic life insurance company on the deemed sale described in the preceding sentence.

"(e) Transactions between contiguous country branch and domestic life insurance company.

"(1) Reimbursement for home office services, etc. Any payment, transfer, reimbursement, credit, or allowance which is made from a separate account established pursuant to subsection (c) to one or more other accounts of a domestic life insurance company as reimbursement for costs incurred for or with respect to the insurance (or reinsurance) of risks accounted for in such separate account shall be taken into account by the domestic life insurance company in the same manner as if such payment, transfer, reimbursement, credit, or allowance had been received from a separate person.

"(2) Repatriation of income.

"(A) In general. Except as provided in subparagraph (B), any amount directly or indirectly transferred or credited from a branch account established pursuant to subsection (c) to one or more other accounts of such company shall, unless such transfer or credit is a reimbursement to which paragraph (1) applies, be added to the life insurance company taxable income of the domestic life insurance company (as computed without regard to this paragraph).

"(B) Limitation. The addition provided by subparagraph (A) for the taxable year with respect to any contiguous country life insurance branch shall not exceed the amount by which—

"(i) the aggregate decrease in the life insurance company taxable income of the domestic life insurance company for the taxable year and for all prior taxable years resulting solely from the application of subsection (a) of this section with respect to such branch, exceeds

"(ii) the amount of additions to life insurance company taxable income pursuant to subparagraph (A) with respect to such contiguous country branch for all prior taxable years.

"(f) Other rules.

"(1) Treatment of foreign taxes.

"(A) In general. No income, war profits, or excess profits taxes paid or accrued to any foreign country or possession of the United States which is attributable to cinoem excluded under subsection (a) shall be taken into account for purposes of subpart A of Part III of subchapter N (relating to foreign tax credit) or allowable as a deduction.

"(B) Treatment of repatriated amounts. For purposes of sections 78 and 902, where any amount is added to the life insurance company taxable income of the domestic life insurance company by reason of subsection (e)92), the contiguous country life insurance branch shall be treated as a foreign corporation. Any amount so added shall be treated as a dividend paid by a foreign corporation, and the taxes paid to any foreign country or possession of the United States with respect to such amount shall be deemed to have been paid by such branch.

Partners and partnerships — Part I

"(2) United States source income allocable to cintiguous country branch. For purposes of sections 881, 882, and 1442, each contiguous country life insurance branch shall be treated as a foreign corporation. Such section shall be applied to each such branch in the same manner as if such sections contained the provisions of any treaty to which the United States and the contiguous country are parties, to the same extent such provisions would apply if such branch were incorporated in such contiguous country.

"(g) Election

"A taxpayer may make the election provided by this subsection with respect to any contiguous country for any taxable year beginning after December 31,1 975. An election made under this subsection for any taxable year shall remain in effect for all subsequent taxable years, except that it may be revoked with the consent of the Secretary. The election provided by this subsection shall be made not later than the time prescribed by law for filing the return for the taxable year (including extensions thereof) with respect to which such election is made, and such election and any approved revocation thereof shall be made in the manner provided by the Secretary.

"(h) Special rule for domestic stock life insurance companies.

"At the election of a domestic stock life insurance company which has a contiguous country life insurance branch described in subsection (b) (without regard to the mutual requirement in subsection (b)(3)), the assets of such branch may be transferred to a foreign corporation organized under the laws of the contiguous country without the application of section 267 or 1491. Subsection (a) shall apply to the stock of such foreign corporation as if such domestic company were a mutual company and as if the stock were an item described in subsection (c). Subsection (e)(2) shall apply to amounts transferred or credited to such domestic company as if such domestic company and such foreign corporation constituted one domestic mutual life insurance company. The insurance contracts which may be transferred pursuant to this subsection shall include only those which are similar to the types of insurance contracts issued by a mutual life insurance company. Notwithstanding the first sentence of this subsection, if the aggregate fair market value of the invested assets and tangible property which are separately accounted for by the domestic life insurance company in the branch account exceeds the aggregate adjusted basis of such assets for purposes of determining gain, the domestic life insurance company shall be deemed to have sold all such assets on the first day of the taxable year for which the election under this subsection applies and the net gain shall be recognized to the domestic life insurance company on the deemed sale, but not in excess of the proportion of such net gain which equals the proportion which the aggregate fair market value of such assets which are transferred pursuant to this subsection is of the aggregate fair market value of all such assets.

In 1976, P.L. 94-455, Sec. 1043(a), added Code. Sec. 819A, effective for tax. yrs. begin. after 12/31/75.

"Sec. 820. Repealed.

In 1982, P.L. 97-248, Sec. 255(a), repealed Code Sec. 820, effective for tax. yrs. begin. after 12/31/81. Sec. 255(c)(2) of this Act provides:

"(2) Rules applicable to taxable years beginning before January 1, 1982.

"(A) In general. In the case of any taxable year beginning before January 1, 1982—

"(i) any determination as to whether any contract met the requirements of subsection (B) of section 820 of the Internal Revenue Code of 1954 (as in effect before its repeal by this section) shall be made solely by reference to the terms of the contract, and

"(ii) the treatment of such contract under subsection (c) of such section 820 shall be made in accordance with the regulations under such section which were in effect on December 31, 1981.

"(B) Paragraph not to apply if fraud involved. The provisions of subparagraph (A) shall not apply with respect to any deficiency which the Secretary of the Treasury or his delegate establishes was due to fraud with intent to evade tax."
— P.L. 97-248, Sec. 256, provides:

"Sec. 256. Special accounting rules relating to repeal of section 820.

"(a) In general.

"For purposes of subchapter L of chapter 1 of the Internal Revenue Code of 1954, the provisions of this section shall apply to any contract—

"(1) which was in effect on December 31, 1981, and

"(2) to which section 820(a)(1) of such Code (as in effect before its repeal by section 255(a)) applied.

"(b) Treatment of reserves and assets.

"Except as provided in subsections (c) and (d), the reserves on the contract described in subsection (a) and the assets in relation to such reserves shall—

"(1) as of the beginning of taxable year 1982, be treated as the reserves and assets of the reinsurer (and not the reinsured), and

"(2) as of the end of taxable year 1982, bet treated as the reserves and assets of the reinsured (and not the reinsurer).

"(c) Allocation of certain section 820(c) items.

"Any amount described in paragraphs (1), (2), (4), and (5) of section 820(C) of such Code (as so in effect) with respect to any contract described in subsection (a) shall, beginning with taxable year 1982, be taken into account by the reinsured and the reinsurer in the same manner as such amounts would be taken into account under a modified coinsurance contract to which section 820(a)(1) of such Code (As so in effect) does not apply.

"(d) Amounts treated as returned under the contract.

"(1) In general. For taxable year 1982—

"(A) in the case of the reinsurer, there shall be allowed as a deduction for ordinary and necessary business expenses under section 809(d)(11) of such Code an amount equal to the termination amount (and such amount shall not otherwise be taken into account in determining gain or loss from operations under section 809 of such Code), and

"(B) in the case of the reinsured, the gross amount under section 809(c)(3) of such Code shall be increased by the termination amount.

"(2) Adjustment for reserves of reinsured. For purposes of subsections (a) and (b) of section 810 of such Code, the amount taken into account as of the close of taxable year 1982 by the reinsured shall be reduced for such taxable year (but not for purposes of determining such amount at the beginning of the next succeeding taxable year) by the excess (if any) of—

"(A) the reserves on the contract as of January 1, 1982, (determined under the reinsured's method of computing reserves for tax purposes), over

"(B) the termination amount.

This paragraph shall not apply to any portion of any policies with respect to which the taxpayer is both the reinsured and the reinsurer under contracts to which this section applies.

"(3) Termination amount. For purposes of this subsection, the term 'termination amount' means the amount under the contract which the reinsurer would have returned to the reinsured upon termination of the contract if the contract had been terminated as of January 1, 1982.

"(4) Certain amounts not taken into account under section 809(d)(5). Any amount treated as the reserves of the reinsured by reason of subsection (b)92) shall not be taken into account under section 809(d)(5) of the Internal Revenue Code of 1954.

"(e) 3-Year installment payment of taxes owned by reinsurer resulting from repeal of section 820.

"(1) In general. That portion of any tax imposed under chapter 1 of such Code (reduced by the sum of the credits allowable under subpart A of part IV of such chapter) on a reinsurer for taxable year 1982 which is attributable to the excess (if any) of—

"(A) any decrease in reserves for such taxable year by reason of subsection (b), over

"(B) the amount allowable as a deduction for such taxable year by reason of subsection (d)(1)(A),
may, at the election of the reinsurer, be paid in 3 equal annual installments.

"(2) Time for payments.

"(A) In general. The 3 installments under paragraph (1) shall be paid on March 15 of 1983, 1984, and 1985.

"(B) First installment may be made in 2 payments. The reinsurer may elect to pay one-half of the installment due March 15, 1983, on June 1, 1983.

"(3) Acceleration of payments. If—

"(A) an election is made under paragraph (1), and

"(B) before the tax attributable to such excess is paid in full any installment under this section is not paid on or before the date fixed by this section for its payment,
then the extension of time for payment of tax provided in this subsection shall cease to apply, and any portion of the tax payable in installments shall be paid on notice and demand from the Secretary of the Treasury or his delegate.

"(4) Proration of deficiency to installments. If an election is made under paragraph (1) and a deficiency attributable to the excess has been assessed, the deficiency shall be prorated to such installments. The part of the deficiency so prorated to any installment the date for payment of which has not arrived shall be collected at the same time as, and as part of, such installment. The part of the deficiency so prorated to any installment the date for payment of which has arrived shall be paid on notice and demand from the Secretary of the Treasury or his delegate. This paragraph shall not apply if the deficiency is due to negligence, to intentional disregard of rules or regulations, or to fraud with intent to evade tax.

"(5) Bond may be required. If an election is made under this section, section 165 of the Internal Revenue Code or 1954 shall apply as though the Secretary of the Treasury or his delegate were extending the time for payment of the tax.

"(6) Extension of period of limitations. The running of any period of limitations for the collection of the tax with respect to which an election is made under paragraph (1) shall be suspended for the period during which there are any unpaid installments of such tax.

"(7) Interest on installments. Rules similar to the rules of section 6601(b)(2) of such Code (without regard to the last sentence thereof) shall apply with respect to any tax for which an election is made under paragraph (1).

"(f) Special rule allowing reinsured to revoke an election under section 820.

"(1) In general. In any case in which—

"(A) a taxpayer is the reinsured under any contract—

"(i) which took effect in 1980 or 1981, and

"(ii) with respect to which an election under section 820 of the Internal Revenue Code of 1954 was made.

"(B) the taxpayer has a loss from operations or its gain from operations (determined with regard to any deduction under paragraph (3), (5), and (6) of section 809(d) of such Code) for the taxable year in which such contract took effect does not exceed the taxpayer's taxable investment income for such taxable year.

"(C) such contract was not a contract with a person who, during the taxable year in which such contract took effect, was a member of the same affiliated group (determined under section 1504 of such Code without regard to subsection (b)) of which the taxpayer is a member, and

"(D) the taxpayer makes an election under this subsection within 6 months after the date of the enactment of this Act,
then the provisions of paragraph (2) shall apply.

2,377

"(2) Rules which apply if this subsection applies. In any case described in paragraph (1)—
"(A) the taxpayer shall, for all taxable years, be treated as not having made an election under section 820 of such Code with respect to the contract described in paragraph (1), but
"(B) all other parties to the contract shall be treated as having made such election with respect to such contract for all taxable years.
"(g) Taxable year 1982.
"For purposes of this section, the term 'taxable year 1982' means, with resect to any taxpayer, the first taxable year of the taxpayer beginning after December 31, 1981.
"(h) Regulations.
"The secretary of the Treasury or his delegate shall prescribe such regulations as may be necessary or appropriate to carry out the purposes of this section."
Prior to repeal, Code Sec. 820 read as follows:
"SEC. 820. OPTIONAL TREATMENT OF POLICIES REINSURED UNDER MODIFIED COINSURANCE CONTRACTS.
"(a) In general.
"(1) Treatment as reinsured under conventional coinsurance contract. Under regulations prescribed by the Secretary or his delegate, an insurance or annuity policy reinsured under a modified coinsurance contract (as defined in subsection (b)) shall be treated, for purposes of this part (other than for purposes of section 801), as if such policy were reinsured under a conventional coinsurance contract.
"(2) Consent of reinsured and reinsurer. Paragraph (1) shall apply to an insurance or annuity policy reinsured under a modified coinsurance contract only if the reinsured and reinsurer consent, in such manner as the Secretary shall prescribe by regulations—
"(A) to the application of paragraph (1) to all insurance and annuity policies reinsured under such modified coinsurance contract, and
"(B) to the application of the rules provided by subsection (c) and the rules prescribed under such subsection.
Such consent, once given, may not be rescinded except with the approval of the Secretary.
"(b) Definition of modified coinsurance contract.
"For purposes of this section, the term 'modified coinsurance contract' means an indemnity reinsurance contract under the terms of which—
"(1) a life insurance company (hereinafter referred to as 'the reinsurer') agrees to indemnify another life insurance company (hereinafter referred to as 'the reinsured') against a risk assumed by the reinsured under the insurance or annuity policy reinsured,
"(2) the reinsured retains ownership of the assets in relation to the revers on the policy reinsured,
"(3) all or part of the gross investment income denied from such assets is paid by the reinsured to the reinsurer as a part of the consideration for the reinsurance of such policy, and
"(4) the reinsurer is obligated for expenses incurred, and for Federal income taxes imposed, in respect to such gross investment income.
"(c) Special rules.
"Under regulations prescribed by the Secretary, in applying subsection (a)(1) with respect to any insurance or annuity policy the following rules shall (to the extent not improper under the terms of the modified coinsurance contract under which such policy is reinsured) be applied in respect of the amount of such policy reinsured:
"(1) Premiums and gross investment income. The premiums (to the extent allocable to the participation of the reinsurer therein) received for the policy reinsured shall be treated as received by the reinsurer and not by the reinsured. The gross investment income (to the extent allocable to the participation of the reinsurer therein) derived from the assets in relation to the reserve on the policy reinsured shall be treated as gross investment income of the reinsurer and not of the reinsured. The gross investment income so treated shall be considered as derived proportionately from each of the various sources of gross investment income of the reinsured.
"(2) Capital gains and losses. The gains and losses from sales and exchanges of capital assets, and gains and losses considered as gains and losses from sales and exchanges of capital assets, of the reinsured shall (to the extent of the participation therein by the reinsurer under the terms of the modified coinsurance contract) be treated as gains and losses from sales and exchanges of capital assets of the reinsurer and not of the reinsured.
"(3) Reserves and assets. The reserve on the policy reinsured shall be treated as a part of the reserves of the reinsurer and not of the reinsured, and the assets in relation to such reserve shall be treated as owned by the reinsurer and not by the reinsured.
"(4) Expenses. The expenses (to the extent reimbursable by the reinsurer) incurred with respect to the assets referred to in paragraph (3) shall be treated as insured by the reinsurer and not by the reinsured.
"(5) Dividends to policyholders. The dividends to policyholders paid in respect of the policy reinsured shall be treated as paid by the reinsurer and not by the reinsured. For purposes of the preceding sentence, the amount of dividends to policyholders treated as paid by the reinsurer shall be the amount paid, in respect of the policy reinsured, by the reinsurer to the reinsured as reimbursement for dividends to policyholders paid by the reinsured. This paragraph shall apply also in respect of an insurance or annuity policy reinsured under a conventional coinsurance contract.
"(6) Rules prescribed by the Secretary. Such other rule as may be prescribed by the Secretary.
In applying the rules provided in paragraphs (1), (2), (3), (4), and (5), and the rules prescribed under paragraph (6), an item shall be taken into account as income only once under subpart B and only once under subpart C by both the reinsured and the reinsurer, and an item shall be allowed as a deduction only once under subpart B and only once under subpart C to both the reinsured and the reinsurer."
In 1976, P.L. 94-455, Sec. 1901(a)(103)(A), deleted para. (c)(6) and redesignated para. (c)(7) as para. (c)(6) . . . Sec. 1901(a)(103)(B), substituted "and (5) and the rules prescribed by paragraph (6)" for "(5), and (6) and the rules prescribed by paragraph (7)", effective for tax. yrs. begin. after 12/31/76.
Prior to deletion, para. (c)(6) read as follows:
"(6) Reimbursement for 1957 Federal income tax. Any amount paid in 1958 or any subsequent year by the reinsurer to the reinsured as reimbursement for Federal income taxes imposed for a taxable year beginning in 1957 or any preceding taxable year shall not be taken into account by the reinsured as an item under section 809(c) or by the reinsurer as a deduction under section 809(d)."
— P.L. 94-455, Sec. 1906(b)(13)(A), substituted "Secretary" for "Secretary or his delegate" in para. (a)(2) and subsec. (c), effective for tax. yrs. begin. after 12/31/76.

In 1959, P.L. 86-69, Sec. 2(a), amended Part I of Subchapter L, effective for all tax yrs. begin. after 12/31/54. Sec. 7 of this Act provided:
"Sec. 7 In the case of any taxpayer subject to tax under section 802 or 807 of the Internal Revenue Code of 1954 (as such sections where in effect before the enactment of this Act), no addition to the tax shall be made under section 6655 of such Code (relating to failure by corporation to pay estimated tax) with respect to estimated tax for a taxable year beginning in 1955. In the case of any taxpayer subject to tax under section 821 of such Code (imposing tax on certain mutual insurance companies), any addition to the tax under section 6655 of such Code with respect to estimated tax for a taxable year beginning in 1955 shall in no case be larger than such addition would have been if this Act had not been enacted."
Prior to amendment, Part I read as follows:
"PART I.— LIFE INSURANCE COMPANIES
"Subpart
"A. 1955 formula.
"B. 1942 formula.
"C. Miscellaneous provisions.
"SUBPART A.— 1955 FORMULA
"Sec.
"801. Definition of life insurance company.
"802. Tax imposed.
"803. Income and deductions.
"804. Reserve and other policy liability deduction.
"805. Special interest deduction.
In 1958, P.L. 85-345, Sec. 2(b), amended item 802.
Prior to amendment, item 802 read as follows:
"802. Tax imposed for 1955 and 1956."
In 1956, P.L. 784, Sec. 2(a), added "and 1956" after "1955" in item 802.

"SEC. 801. DEFINITION OF LIFE INSURANCE COMPANY.
"(a) Life insurance company defined.
"For purposes of this subtitle, the term 'life insurance company' means an insurance company which is engaged in the business of issuing life insurance and annuity contracts (either separately or combined with health and accident insurance), or noncancellable contracts of health and accident insurance, if—
"(1) its life insurance reserves (as defined in subsection (b)), plus
"(2) unearned premiums and unpaid losses on noncancellable life, health, or accident policies not included in life insurance reserves, comprise more than 50 percent of its total reserves (as defined in subsection (c)).
"(b) Life insurance reserves defined.
"(1) In general. For purposes of this part, the term 'life insurance reserves' means amounts—
"(A) which are computed or estimated on the basis of recognized mortality or morbidity tables and assumed rates of interest, and
"(B) which are set aside to mature or liquidate, either by payment or reinsurance, future unaccrued claims arising from life insurance, annuity, and noncancellable health and accident insurance contracts (including life insurance or annuity contracts combined with noncancellable health and accident insurance) involving, at the time with respect to which the reserve is computed, life, health, or accident contingencies.
"(2) Reserves must be required by law. Except—
"(A) in the case of policies covering life, health, and accident insurance combined in one policy issued on the weekly premium payment plan, continuing for life and not subject to cancellation, and
"(B) as provided in paragraph (3),
in addition to the requirements set forth in paragraph (1), life insurance reserves must be required by law.
"(3) Assessment companies. In the case of an assessment life insurance company or association, the term 'life insurance reserves' includes—
"(A) sums actually deposited by such company or association with State or Territorial officers pursuant to law as guaranty or reserve funds, and
"(B) any funds maintained, under the charter or articles of incorporation or association (or bylaws approved by a State insurance commissioner) of such company or association, exclusively for the payment of claims arising under certificates of membership or policies issued on the assessment plan and not subject to any other use.
"(4) Amount of reserve. For purposes of this subsection, subsection (a), and subsection (c), the amount of any reserve (or portion thereof) for any taxable year

shall be the mean of such reserve (or portion thereof) at the beginning and end of the taxable year.

"(c) Total reserves defined.

"For purposes of subsection (a), the term 'total reserves' means

"(1) life insurance reserves,

"(2) unearned premiums and unpaid losses not included in life insurance reserves, and

"(3) all other insurance reserves required by law.

"(d) Adjustments in reserves for policy loans.

"For purposes only of determining under subsection (a) whether or not an insurance company is a life insurance company, the life insurance reserves, and the total reserves, shall each be reduced by an amount equal to the mean of the aggregates, at the beginning and end of the taxable year, of the policy loans outstanding with respect to contracts for which life insurance reserves are maintained.

"(e) Burial and funeral benefit insurance companies.

"A burial or funeral benefit insurance company engaged directly in the manufacture of burial supplies or the performance of funeral services shall not be taxable under this part but shall be taxable under section 821 or section 831."

"SEC. 802. TAX IMPOSED.

"(a) Tax imposed.

"A tax is hereby imposed for each taxable year beginning after December 31, 1954 and before January 1, 1958 on the income of every life insurance company. Except as provided in subsection (c), such tax shall consist of a normal tax (computed under section 11(b)) and a surtax (computed under section 11(c)) on the sum of—

"(1) the life insurance taxable income (as defined in subsection (b)), plus

"(2) the nonlife insurance taxable income (as defined in subsection (f)).

"(b) Life insurance taxable income defined.

"For purposes of this subpart, the term 'life insurance taxable income' means the net investment income (as defined in section 803(c)), minus the sum of—

"(1) the net investment income allocable to non-life insurance reserves (determined under section 804(d)),

"(2) the reserve and other policy liability deduction (determined under section 804), and

"(3) the special interest deduction, in any, allowed by section 805.

"(c) Alternative tax in the case of companies having non-life insurance reserves.

"(1) In general. In the case of a life insurance company which has non-life insurance reserves, the tax imposed by subsection (a) of this section for any taxable year beginning after December 31, 1954 and before January 1, 1958 shall be the tax computed under such subsection (or under section 1201(a) if applicable) or the tax computed under paragraph (2) of this subsection, whichever is the greater.

"(2) Alternative 1 percent tax on non-life insurance business. The tax referred to in paragraph (1) is a tax equal to the sum of the following:

"(A) A partial tax consisting of a normal tax (computed under section 11(b)) and a surtax (computed under section 11(c)) on the life insurance taxable income.

"(B) A partial tax consisting of—

"(i) 1 percent of the amount which bears the same ratio to the gross investment income (reduced by the deduction for wholly-exempt interest allowed by section 803(c)(1)) as the non-life insurance reserves bear to the qualified reserves (determined under section 804(c)), plus

"(ii) 1 percent of the excess of the amount by which the net premiums on contracts meeting the requirements of section 804(d)(2)(A) exceed the dividends to policyholders on such contracts. For purposes of this clause, net premiums, and dividends to policyholders, shall be computed in the manner provided in section 823.

"(d) Deductions for partially tax-exempt interest.

"(1) Computations under subsection (a). For purposes of computing the normal tax under subsection (a), there shall be allowed as a deduction an amount which bears the same ratio to the amount of the deduction provided by section 242 for partially tax-exempt interest as (A) the sum of the life insurance taxable income and the net investment income allocable to non-life insurance reserves bears to (B) the net investment income.

"(2) Computations under subsection (c)(2)(A). In computing the normal tax for purposes of subsection (c)(2)(A), there shall be allowed as a deduction an amount which bears the same ratio to the amount of the deduction provided by section 242 for partially tax-exempt interest as (A) the life insurance taxable income bears to (B) the net investment income.

"(e) Alternative tax on capital gains.

"In the case of a life insurance company which has non-life insurance reserves, the term 'excess' used in section 1201(a) (relating to alternative tax on capital gains of corporations) means, for purposes of section 1201(a), an amount which bears the same ratio to the excess described in such section as the non-life insurance reserves (determined under section 804(d)) bear to the qualified reserves (determined under section 804(c)). For purposes of any such computation, a net capital loss for any taxable year beginning before January 1, 1955, shall not be taken into account.

"(f) Non-life insurance taxable income defined.

"For purposes of this subpart, the term 'non-life insurance taxable income' means the net investment income allocable to non-life insurance reserves (determined under section 804(d))—

"(1) increased by an amount which bears the same ratio to the net capital gain as the non-life insurance reserves bear to the qualified reserves; and

"(2) decreased by an amount which bears the same ratio to the total of the deductions provided in sections 243, 244, and 245 as the non-life insurance reserves bear to the qualified reserves.

In computing a net capital gain for purposes of paragraph (1) of this subsection, a net capital loss for any taxable year beginning before January 1, 1955, shall not be taken into account."

In **1958**, P.L. 85-345, Sec. 1, substituted "beginning after December 31, 1954, and before January 1, 1958," for "beginning in 1955 or in 1956" in subsecs. (a) and (c) . . . Sec. 2(a), amended the heading of Sec. 802.

Prior to amendment, the heading of Sec. 802 read as follows:

"Sec. 802. Tax imposed for 1955 and 1956."

In **1956**, P.L. 784, Sec. 1, added "or in 1956" after "in 1955" in subsecs. (a) and (c) . . . Sec. (2)(b), added "and 1956" after "1955" in the name of Sec. 802, effective for tax. yrs. beginning after 12/31/55.

"SEC. 803. INCOME AND DEDUCTIONS.

"(a) Application of section.

"The definitions and rules contained in this section shall apply only in the case of life insurance companies.

"(b) Gross investment income.

"For purposes of this part, the term 'gross investment income' means the sum of the following:

"(1) The gross amount of income received or accrued from—

"(A) interest, dividends, rents, and royalties,

"(B) the entering into of any lease, mortgage, or other instrument or agreement from which the life insurance company derives interests, rents, or royalties, and

"(C) the alteration or termination of any instrument or agreement described in subparagraph (B).

"(2) The gross income from any trade or business (other than an insurance business) carried on by the life insurance company, or by a partnership of which the life insurance company is a partner. In computing gross income under this paragraph, there shall be excluded any item described in paragraph (1).

In computing gross investment income under this subsection, there shall be excluded any gain from the sale or exchange of a capital asset, and any gain considered as gain from the sale or exchange of a capital asset.

"(c) Net investment income defined.

"The term 'net investment income' means the gross investment income less the following deductions:

"(1) Tax-free interest. The amount of interest received or accrued during the taxable year which under section 103 is excluded from gross income.

"(2) Investment expenses.

"(A) Investment expenses paid or accrued during the taxable year.

"(B) If any general expenses are in part assigned to or included in the investment expenses, the total deduction under this paragraph shall not exceed—

"(i) One-fourth of 1 percent of the mean of the book value of the invested assets held at the beginning and end of the taxable year, plus

"(ii) one-fourth of the amount by which the net investment income (computed without any deduction for investment expenses allowed by this paragraph, or for tax-free interest allowed by paragraph (1)) exceeds 3¾ percent of the book value of the mean of the invested assets held at the beginning and end of the taxable year.

"(3) Real estate expenses. Taxes (as provided in section 164), and other expenses, paid or accrued during the taxable year exclusively on or with respect to the real estate owned by the company. No deduction shall be allowed under this paragraph for any amount paid out for new buildings, or for permanent improvements or betterments made to increase the value of any property.

"(4) Depreciation. The depreciation deduction allowed by section 167.

"(5) Depletion. The deduction allowed by section 611 (relating to depletion).

"(6) Trade or business deductions. The deductions allowed by this subtitle (without regard to this part) which are attributable to any trade or business (other than an insurance business) carried on by the life insurance company, or by a partnership of which the life insurance company is a partner; except that for purposes of this paragraph—

"(A) There shall be excluded losses from—

"(i) sales or exchanges of capital assets,

"(ii) sales or exchanges of property used in the trade or business (as defined in section 1231(b)), and

"(iii) the compulsory or involuntary conversion (as a result of destruction, in whole or in part, theft or seizure, or an exercise of the power of requisition or condemnation or the threat or imminence thereof) of property used in the trade or business (as so defined).

"(B) Any item, to the extent attributable to the carrying on of the insurance business, shall not be taken into account.

"(C) The deduction for net operating losses provided in section 172, and the special deductions for corporations provided in part VIII of subchapter B, shall not be allowed.

"(d) Rental value of real estate.

"The deduction under subsection (c)(3) and (4) on account of any real estate owned and occupied in whole or in part by a life insurance company shall be limited to an amount which bears the same ratio to such deduction (computed without regard to this subsection) as the rental value of the space not so occupied bears to the rental value of the entire property.

"(e) Amortization of premium and accrual of discount.

"The gross investment income, the deduction for wholly-exempt interest allowed by subsection (c)(1), and the deduction allowed by section 242 (relating to partially tax-exempt interest) shall each be decreased to reflect the appropriate amortization of premium and increased to reflect the appropriate accrual of discount attributable to the taxable year on bonds, notes, debentures, or other evidences of indebtedness held by a life insurance company. Such amortization and accrual shall be determined—

"(1) in accordance with the method regularly employed by such company, if such method is reasonable, and

"(2) in all other cases, in accordance with regulations prescribed by the Secretary or his delegate."

"SEC. 804. RESERVE AND OTHER POLICY LIABILITY DEDUCTION.

"(a) General rule.

"Except as provided in subsection (b), for purposes of this subpart the term 'reserve and other policy liability deduction' means the sum of the amounts determined by applying the following percentages to the excess of the net investment income over the net investment income allocable to non-life insurance reserves (determined under subsection (d))—

"(1) 87.5 percent of so much of such excess as does not exceed $1,000,000; and

"(2) 85 percent of so much of such excess as exceeds $1,000,000.

"(b) Maximum deduction.

"(1) In general. The reserve and other policy liability deduction shall in no case exceed that amount which is equal to the sum of the following:

"(A) the amount equal to 2 times the amount determined under paragraph (1) of section 805(c) (relating to required interest on life insurance reserves);

"(B) the amount determined under paragraph (2) of section 805(c) (relating to required interest on reserves for deferred dividends);

"(C) the amount of the interest paid (as defined in section 805(d));

"(D) the dividends to policyholders paid or declared (other than dividends on contracts meeting the requirements of subsection (d)(2)(A)); and

"(E) in the case of a mutual assessment life insurance company or association, the amount equal to 2 times whichever of the following is the lesser: (i) the amount of the net investment income on life insurance reserves described in subparagraph (A) or (B) of section 801(b)(3), or (ii) 3 percent of the life insurance reserves so described,

reduced by the amount of the adjustment for policy loans provided in paragraph (2) of this subsection. For purposes of subparagraph (B) of the preceding sentence, the term 'paid or declared' shall be construed according to the method of accounting regularly employed in keeping the books of the insurance company.

"(2) Reduction for certain policy loans. The adjustment described in paragraph (1) of this subsection shall be an amount equal to—

"(A) the mean of the aggregates, at the beginning and end of the taxable year, of the outstanding policy loans with respect to contracts for which life insurance reserves are maintained, multiplied by

"(B) the average rate of interest applicable to life insurance reserves.

For purposes of subparagraph (B) of the preceding sentence, the term 'average rate of interest applicable to life insurance reserves' means the ratio obtained by dividing the sum obtained under paragraph (1) of section 805(c) by the sum obtained under paragraph (1)(B) of section 805(c).

"(3) Dividends received deduction where maximum limit applies.

"(A) If paragraph (1) of this subsection reduces the reserve and other policy liability deduction allowed by this section or section 812 for the taxable year, then in computing life insurance taxable income under section 802(b), and in computing life insurance company taxable income under section 811(b), there shall be allowed an additional deduction in an amount determined under subparagraph (B).

"(B) The amount of the additional deduction referred to in subparagraph (A) shall be the amount which bears the same ratio to the total of the deductions provided in sections 243, 244, and 245 as the net investment income reduced by the sum of—

"(i) the net investment income allocable to non-life insurance reserves (or, for purposes of section 811(b), the amount of the adjustment for certain reserves provided in section 813), and

"(ii) 100/85 of the maximum limitation determined under paragraphs (1) and (2) of this subsection,

bears to the net investment income.

"(c) Qualified reserves defined.

"For purposes of this subpart, the term 'qualified reserves' means the sum of the following:

"(1) The life insurance reserves (as defined in section 801(b)), plus 7 percent of that portion of such reserves as are computed on a preliminary term basis.

"(2) The non-life insurance reserves (as defined in subsection (d)(2)).

"(3) The amounts (discounted at the rates of interest assumed by the company) necessary to satisfy the obligations under insurance and annuity contracts (including contracts supplementary thereto), but only if (A) such obligations when satisfied will reflect an increment in the nature of interest, and (B) such obligations do not involve (at the time with respect to which the computation is made under this paragraph) life, health, or accident contingencies.

"(4) The amounts held at the end of the taxable year as reserves for dividends to policy holders, the payment of which dividends is deferred for a period which expires not earlier than 5 years from the date of the policy contract. This paragraph does not apply to dividends payable during the year following the taxable year.

"(5) Dividend accumulations, and other amounts, held at interest in connection with insurance or annuity contracts (including contracts supplementary thereto).

"(6) Premiums received in advance, and liabilities for premium deposit funds. In applying this subsection the same item shall be counted only once. For purposes of this section (other than paragraph (4) of this subsection), the amount of any reserve (or portion thereof) for any taxable year shall be the mean of such reserve (or portion thereof) at the beginning and end of the taxable year.

"(d) Net investment income allocable to non-life insurance reserves.

"(1) Allocation ratio. For purposes of this subpart, the net investment income allocable to non-life insurance reserves is that amount which bears the same ratio to the net investment income as such reserves bear to the qualified reserves.

"(2) Non-life insurance reserves defined. For purposes of this subpart the term 'non-life insurance reserves' means the sum of the unearned premiums and the unpaid losses (whether or not ascertained)—

"(A) on contracts other than life insurance, annuity, and noncancellable health and accident insurance contracts (including life insurance or annuity contracts combined with noncancellable health and accident insurance), and

"(B) which are not included in life insurance reserves (as defined in section 801(b)).

For purposes of this paragraph, such unearned premiums shall not be considered to be less than 25 percent of the net premiums written during the taxable year on such other contracts.

"(3) Adjustments with respect to certain non-life insurance contracts. For the purposes of this subpart, if—

"(A) any computation under this subpart is made by reference to a contract meeting the requirements of paragraph (2)(A) of this subsection, and

"(B) part of the reserves for such contract are life insurance reserves, then, under regulations prescribed by the Secretary or his delegate, proper adjustment shall be made in the amount taken into account with respect to such contract for purposes of such computation."

"SEC. 805. SPECIAL INTEREST DEDUCTION.

"(a) Special interest deduction.

"For purposes of the tax imposed by section 802 (and the tax imposed by section 811), there shall be allowed a special interest deduction determined as follows:

"(1) Divide the amount of the adjusted net investment income (as defined in subsection (b)) by the amount of the required interest (as defined in subsection (c)).

"(2) If the quotient obtained in paragraph (1) is 1.05 or more, the special interest deduction shall be zero.

"(3) If the quotient obtained in paragraph (1) is 1.00 or less, the special interest deduction shall be an amount equal to 50 percent of the amount by which—

"(A) the net investment income (reduced by the net investment income allocable to non-life insurance reserves), exceeds

"(B) the reserve and other policy liability deduction for the taxable year.

"(4) If the quotient obtained in paragraph (1) is more than 1.00 but less than 1.05, the special interest deduction shall be the amount obtained by multiplying—

"(A) the amount by which (i) the net investment income (reduced by the net investment income allocable to non-life insurance reserves) exceeds (ii) the reserve and other policy liability deduction for the taxable year, by

"(B) 10 times the difference between the figure 1.05 and the quotient obtained in paragraph (1).

"(b) Adjusted net investment income.

"For purposes of subsection (a)(1), the term 'adjusted net investment income' means—

"(1) the net investment income (computed without the deduction for wholly-exempt interest allowed by section 803(C)(1)), minus

"(2) 50 percent of the net investment income allocable to non-life insurance reserves.

"(c) Required interest.

"For purposes of subsection (a)(1), the term 'required interest' means the total of—

"(1) the sum of the amounts obtained by multiplying—

"(A) each rate of interest assumed in computing the taxpayer's life insurance reserves, by

"(B) the means of the amounts of the taxpayer's life insurance reserves computed at such rate at the beginning and end of the taxable year, plus 7 percent of the portion of such reserves at such rates as are computed on a preliminary term basis;

"(2) the sum of the amounts obtained by multiplying—

"(A) each rate of interest assumed in computing the taxpayer's reserves for deferred dividends described in section 804(c)(4), by

"(B) the means of the amounts of such reserves computed at such rate at the end of the taxable year; and

"(3) interest paid.

"(d) Interest paid.

"For purposes of subsection (c)(3), the term '*In re*interest paid' means—

"(1) all interest paid or accrued within the taxable year on indebtedness except on indebtedness incurred or continued to purchase or carry obligations (other than obligations of the United States issued after September 24, 1917, and originally subscribed for by the taxpayer) the interest on which is wholly exempt from taxation under this chapter; and

"(2) all amounts in the nature of interest, whether or not guaranteed, paid or accrued within the taxable year on insurance or annuity contracts (or contracts arising out of insurance or annuity contracts) which do not involve, at the time of payment or accrual, life, health, or accident contingencies."

"SUBPART B.— 1942 FORMULA

"Sec.

"811. Tax imposed.

"812. Reserve and other policy liability deduction.

"813. Adjustment for certain reserves.

Partners and partnerships — Part I

"SEC. 811. TAX IMPOSED.
"(a) Tax imposed.
"A tax is hereby imposed, on the life insurance company taxable income of every life insurance company, for each taxable year beginning after December 31, 1957. Such tax shall consist of—
"(1) a normal tax on such income computed under section 11(b), and
"(2) a surtax on such income computed under section 11(c).
"(b) Life insurance company taxable income defined.
"For purposes of this subpart, the term 'life insurance company taxable income' means the net investment income (as defined in section 803(c))—
"(1) minus the reserve and other policy liability deduction allowed by section 812,
"(2) minus the special interest deduction, if any, allowed by section 805, and
"(3) plus the amount of the adjustment for certain reserves provided in section 813.
For purposes of the normal tax, life insurance company taxable income shall be reduced by the deduction provided in section 242 for partially tax-exempt interest.
"(c) Rule for computation of special interest deduction.
"In computing the special interest deduction under section 805 in the case of any taxable year with respect to which a tax is imposed under this section—
"(1) in lieu of the reduction of the net investment income provided in paragraphs (3)(A) and (4)(A) of section 805(a), the net investment income shall be reduced by the amount of the adjustment for certain reserves provided in section 813, and
"(2) in lieu of subtracting the amount provided in paragraph (2) of section 805(b), subtract 50 percent of the amount of the adjustment for certain reserves provided in section 813."

In 1958, P.L. 85-345, Sec. 2(c), substituted "December 31, 1957" for "December 31, 1956" in subsec. (a).
In 1956, P.L. 784, Sec. 2(c), substituted "December 1956" for "December 1955" in subsec. (a), effective for tax. yrs. begin. after 12/31/55.

"SEC. 812. RESERVE AND OTHER POLICY LIABILITY DEDUCTION.
"(a) General Rule.
"For purposes of this subpart, the term 'reserve and other policy liability deduction' means an amount computed by multiplying the net investment income by a figure, to be determined and proclaimed by the Secretary or his delegate for each taxable year with respect to which a tax is imposed by section 811. This figure shall be based on such data with respect to life insurance companies for the preceding taxable year as the Secretary or his delegate considers representative and shall be computed in accordance with the following formula: The ratio which a numerator comprised of the aggregate of the sums of—
"(1) 2 percent of the reserves for deferred dividends,
"(2) interest paid, and
"(3) the product of—
"(A) the mean of the adjusted reserves at the beginning and end of the taxable year, and
"(B) the reserve earnings rate,
bears to a denominator comprised of the aggregate of the excess of net investment incomes (computed without the deduction for wholly-exempt interest allowed by section 803(c)(1)) over the adjustment for certain reserves provided in section 813.
"(b) Definitions.
"For purposes of subsection (a)—
"(1) Reserves for deferred dividends. The term 'reserves for deferred dividends' has the same meaning as when used in section 804(c)(4).
"(2) Interest paid. The term 'interest paid' has the meaning given to such term by section 805(d).
"(3) Adjusted reserves. The term 'adjusted reserves' means the life insurance reserves (as defined in section 801(b)), plus 7 percent of that portion of such reserves as are computed on a preliminary term basis.
"(4) Reserve earnings rate. The term 'reserve earnings rate' means a rate computed by adding 2.1125 percent (65 percent of 3¼ percent) to 35 percent of the average rate of interest assumed in computing life insurance reserves. Such average rate shall be calculated by multiplying each assumed rate of interest by the means of the amounts of the adjusted reserves computed at that rate at the beginning and end of the taxable year and dividing the sum of the products by the mean of the total adjusted reserves at the beginning and end of the taxable year.
"(c) Maximum deduction.
"The reserve and other policy liability deduction allowed by subsection (a) of this section shall in no case exceed an amount equal to the amount which would be determined under subsection (b) of section 804 if such subsection applied with respect to the taxable year."

"SEC. 813. ADJUSTMENT FOR CERTAIN RESERVES.
"In the case of a life insurance company writing contracts other than life insurance, annuity, and noncancellable health and accident insurance contracts (including life insurance or annuity contracts combined with noncancellable health and accident insurance), the term 'adjustment for certain reserves' means, for purposes of this subpart, an amount equal to 3¼ percent of the unearned premiums and unpaid losses on such other contracts which are not included in life insurance reserves (as defined in section 801(b)). For purposes of this section, such unearned premiums shall not be considered to be less than 25 percent of the net premiums written during the taxable year on such other contracts."

"SUBPART C.— MISCELLANEOUS PROVISIONS
"Sec.
"816. Foreign life insurance companies.
"817. Denial of double deductions.
"818. Certain new insurance companies.

"SEC. 816. FOREIGN LIFE INSURANCE COMPANIES.
"(a) Carrying on United States insurance business.
"A foreign life insurance company carrying on a life insurance business within the United States, if with respect to its United States business it would qualify as a life insurance company under section 801, shall be taxable in the same manner as a domestic life insurance company; except that the determinations necessary for purposes of this subtitle shall be made on the basis of the income, disbursements, assets, and liabilities reported in the annual statement for the taxable year of the United States business of such company on the form approved for life insurance companies by the National Association of Insurance Commissioners.
"(b) No United States insurance business.
"Foreign life insurance companies not carrying on an insurance business within the United States shall not be taxable under this part but shall be taxable as other foreign corporations."

"SEC. 817. DENIAL OF DOUBLE DEDUCTIONS.
"Nothing in this part shall permit the same item to be deducted more than once."

"SEC. 818. CERTAIN NEW INSURANCE COMPANIES.
"(a) General rule.
"If the taxable year begins not more than 9 years after the first day on which the taxpayer was authorized to do business as an insurance company, then—
"(1) for purposes of subpart A, the life insurance taxable income shall not exceed (A) the amount of the net gain from operations after dividends to policy holders, reduced by (B)(i) the net investment income allocable to non-life insurance reserves and (ii) the special reduction for dividends received provided by subsection (c); or
"(2) for purposes of subpart B, the life insurance company taxable income shall not exceed (A) the amount of the net gain from operations after dividends to policyholders, reduced by (B) the special reduction for dividends received provided by subsection (c).
For purposes of this subsection, the net gain from operations after dividends to policyholders shall be computed in the manner required for purposes of the annual statement approved by the National Convention of Insurance Commissioners, except that no reduction shall be made for any Federal income tax.
"(b) Limitation.
"This section shall not reduce the tax for any taxable year below the amount which (but for this section) would be imposed by section 802 or section 811, as the case may be, computed without the applicable limitation on the reserve and other policy liability deduction contained in section 804(b) or section 812(c).
"(c) Special rule for dividends received.
"The reduction referred to in paragraph (1)(B)(ii) and in paragraph (2)(B) of subsection (a) shall be an amount computed under section 804(b)(3), except that, for purposes of such computation, the maximum limitation referred to in section 804(b)(3)(B)(ii) shall be—
"(1) in the case of a taxable year with respect to which tax is imposed by 802, the amount by which (A) the net investment income (reduced by the net investment income allocable to non-life insurance reserves), exceeds (B) the life insurance taxable income (computed without regard to the reduction provided by this subsection); or
"(2) in the case of a taxable year with respect to which tax is imposed by section 811, the amount by which (A) the sum of the net investment income and the amount of the adjustment for certain reserves provided in section 813, exceeds (B) the life insurance company taxable income (computed without regard to the reduction provided by this subsection)."

In 1956, P.L. 429, Sec. 2, amended Part I of Subchapter L.
Prior to amendment, Part I read as follows:
"PART I.— LIFE INSURANCE COMPANIES
"Sec.
"801. Definition of life insurance company
"802. Imposition of tax
"803. Other definitions and rules.
"804. Reserve and other policy liability deduction.
"805. 1954 life insurance company taxable income.
"806. Adjustment for certain reserves.
"807. Foreign life insurance companies."

"SEC. 801. DEFINITION OF LIFE INSURANCE COMPANY.
"For purposes of this subtitle, the term 'life insurance company' means an insurance company which is engaged in the business of issuing life insurance and annuity contracts (either separately or combined with health and accident insurance), or noncancellable contracts of health and accident insurance, if its life insurance reserves (as defined in section 803(b)), plus unearned premiums and unpaid losses on noncancellable life, health, or accident policies not included in life insurance reserves, comprise more than 50 percent of its total reserves. For purposes of this section, the term 'total reserves' means life insurance reserves, unearned premiums and unpaid losses not included in life insurance reserves, and all other insurance reserves required by law. A burial or funeral benefit insurance

2,381

Part I
Partners and partnerships

company engaged directly in the manufacture of funeral supplies or the performance of funeral services shall not be taxable under section 802 but shall be taxable under section 821 or section 831."

"SEC. 802. IMPOSITION OF TAX.
"(a) In general.

"Except as otherwise provided in subsection (b), there shall be imposed for each taxable year on the life insurance company taxable income of every life insurance company a tax consisting of a normal tax and a surtax computed as provided in section 11. For purposes of such tax, the term 'life insurance company taxable income' means the taxable income (as defined in section 803(g)) minus the reserve and other policy liability deduction provided in section 804 and plus the amount of the adjustment for certain reserves provided in section 806. For purposes of the surtax, such taxable income shall be computed without regard to the deduction provided in section 242 for partially tax-exempt interest.

"(b) Taxable years beginning in 1954.

"In lieu of the tax imposed by subsection (a) there shall be imposed, for taxable years beginning in 1954, on the 1954 life insurance company taxable income (as defined in section 805) of every life insurance company a tax equal to the sum of the following:

"(1) 3¾ percent of the amount thereof not in excess of $200,00, plus
"(2) 6½ percent of the amount thereof in excess of $200,000."

"SEC. 803. OTHER DEFINITIONS AND RULES.
"(a) Application of section; gross income.

"(1) Application. The definitions and rules contained in this section shall apply only in the case of life insurance companies.

"(2) Gross income. The term 'gross income' means the gross amount of income received or accrued during the taxable year from interest, dividends, and rents.

"(b) Life insurance reserves.

"The term 'life insurance reserves' means amounts which are computed or estimated on the basis of recognized mortality or morbidity tables and assumed rates of interest, and which are set aside to mature or liquidate, either by payment or reinsurance, future unaccrued claims arising from life insurance, annuity, and noncancellable health and accident insurance contracts (including life insurance or annuity contracts combined with noncancellable health and accident insurance) involving, at the time with respect to which the reserve is computed, life, health, or accident contingencies. Such life insurance reserves, except in the case of policies covering life, health, and accident insurance combined in one policy issued on the weekly premium payment plan, continuing for life and not subject to cancellation and except as hereinafter provided in the case of assessment life insurance, must also be required by law. In the case of an assessment life insurance company or association, the term 'life insurance reserves' includes sums actually deposited by such company or association with State or Territorial officers pursuant to law as guaranty or reserve funds, and any funds maintained, under the charter or articles of incorporation or association (or bylaws approved by a State insurance commissioner) of such company or association, exclusively for the payment of claims arising under certificates of membership or policies issued on the assessment plan and not subject to any other use.

"(c) Adjusted reserves.

"The term 'adjusted reserves' means life insurance reserves plus 7 percent of that portion of such reserves as are computed on a preliminary term basis.

"(d) Reserve earnings rate.

"The term 'reserve earnings rate' means a rate computed by adding 2.1125 percent (65 percent of 3¼ percent) to 35 percent of the average rate of interest assumed in computing life insurance reserves. Such average rate shall be calculated by multiplying each assumed rate of interest by the means of the amounts of the adjusted reserves computed at that rate at the beginning and end of the taxable year and dividing the sum of the products by the mean of the total adjusted reserves at the beginning and end of the taxable year.

"(e) Reserve for deferred dividends.

"The term 'reserve for deferred dividends' means sums held at the end of the taxable year as a reserve for dividends (other than dividends payable during the year following the taxable year) the payment of which is deferred for a period of not less than 5 years from the date of the policy contract.

"(f) Interest paid.

"The term 'interest paid' means—

"(1) All interest paid or accrued within the taxable year on indebtedness, except on indebtedness incurred or continued to purchase or carry obligations (other than obligations of the United States issued after September 24, 1917, and originally subscribed for by the taxpayer) the interest upon which is wholly exempt from taxation under this chapter, and

"(2) All amounts in the nature of interest, whether or not guaranteed, paid or accrued within the taxable year on insurance or annuity contracts (or contracts arising out of insurance or annuity contracts) which do not involve, at the time of payment or accrual, life, health, or accident contingencies.

"(g) Taxable income.

"The term 'taxable income' means the gross income less the following deductions:

"(1) Tax-free interest. The amount of interest received or accrued during the taxable year which under section 103 is excluded from gross income.

"(2) Investment expenses. Investment expenses paid or incurred during the table year. If any general expenses are in part assigned to or included in the investment expenses, the total deduction under this paragraph shall not exceed one-fourth of 1 percent of the mean of the book value of the invested assets held at the beginning and end of the taxable year plus one-fourth of the amount by which taxable income (computed without any deduction for investment expenses allowed by this paragraph, for tax-free interest allowed by paragraph (1), or for partially tax-exempt interest and dividends received allowed by paragraph (5)) exceeds 3¾ percent of the book value of the mean of the invested assets held at the beginning and end of the taxable year.

"(3) Real estate expenses. Taxes and other expenses paid or accrued during the taxable year exclusively on or with respect to the real estate owned by the company, not including taxes assessed against local benefits of a kind tending to increase the value of the property assessed, and not including any amount paid out for new buildings, or for permanent improvements or betterments made to increase the value of any property. The deduction allowed by this paragraph shall be allowed in the case of taxes imposed on a shareholder of a company on his interest as shareholder, which are paid or accrued by the company without reimbursement from the shareholder, but in such cases no deduction shall be allowed the shareholder for the amount of such taxes.

"(4) Depreciation. The depreciation deduction allowed by section 167.
"(5) Special deductions. The special deductions allowed by part VIII of subchapter B (except section 248).

"(h) Rental value of real estate.

"The deduction under subsection (g)(3) and (4) on account of any real estate owned and occupied in whole or in part by a life insurance company shall be limited to an amount which bears the same ratio to such deduction (computed without regard to this subsection) as the rental value of the space not so occupied bears to the rental value of the entire property.

"(i) Amortization of premium and accrual of discount.

"The gross income, the deduction provided in subsection (g)(1), and the deduction allowed by section 242 (relating to partially tax-exempt interest) shall each be decreased to reflect the appropriate amortization of premium and increased to reflect the appropriate accrual of discount attributable to the taxable year on bonds, notes, debentures, or other evidences of indebtedness held by a life insurance company. Such amortization and accrual shall be determined—

"(1) in accordance with the method regularly employed by such company, if such method is reasonable, and

"(2) in all other cases, in accordance with regulations prescribed by the Secretary or his delegate.

"(j) Double deductions.

"Nothing in this part shall permit the same item to be deducted more than once."

"SEC. 804. RESERVE AND OTHER POLICY LIABILITY DEDUCTION.
"(a) In general.

"For purposes of this subpart, the term 'reserve and other policy liability deduction' means an amount computed by multiplying the taxable income by a figure, to be determined and proclaimed by the Secretary or his delegate for each taxable year. This figure shall be based on such data with respect to life insurance companies for the preceding taxable year as the Secretary or his delegate considers representative and shall be computed in accordance with the following formula: The ratio which a numerator comprised of the aggregate of the sums of—

"(1) 2 percent of the reserves for deferred dividends,
"(2) interest paid, and
"(3) the product of—
"(A) the mean of the adjusted reserves at the beginning and end of the taxable year and
"(B) the reserve earnings rate,

bears to a denominator comprised of the aggregate of the excess of taxable incomes (computed without any deduction for tax-free interest, partially tax-exempt interest, or dividends received) over the adjustment for certain reserves provided in section 806.

"(b) Surtax computation.

"In determining the life insurance company taxable income for purposes of the surtax, the taxable income to be multiplied by the figure determined and proclaimed under subsection (a) shall be computed without regard to the deduction provided in section 242 for partially tax-exempt interest."

"SEC. 805. 1954 LIFE INSURANCE COMPANY TAXABLE INCOME.
"(a) Definition.

"For purposes of section 802(b), the term '1954 life insurance company taxable income' means the taxable income (as defined in section 803(g)), plus 8 times the amount of the adjustment for certain reserves provided in section 806, and minus the reserve interest credit, if any, provided in subsection (b) of this section.

"(b) Reserve interest credit. For purposes of subsection (a), the reserve interest credit shall be an amount determined as follows:

"(1) Divide the amount of the adjusted taxable income (as defined in subsection (c)) by the amount of the required interest (as defined in subsection (d)).

"(2) If the quotient obtained in paragraph (1) os 1.05 or more, the reserve interest credit shall be zero.

"(3) If the quotient obtained in paragraph (1) is 1.00 or less, the reserve interest credit shall be an amount equal to 50 percent of the taxable income.

"(4) If the quotient obtained in paragraph (1) is more than 1.00 but less than 1.05, the reserve interest credit shall be the amount obtained by multiplying the taxable income by 10 times the difference between the figures 1.05 and such quotient.

"(c) Adjusted taxable income.

"For purposes of subsection (b)(1), the term 'adjusted taxable income' means the taxable income (computed without the deductions provided in section 803(g)(1) or (5)) minus 50 percent of the amount of the adjustment for certain reserves provided in section 806.

"(d) Required interest.

2,382

Insurance companies — Subpart C

"For purposes of subsection (b)(1), the term 'required interest' means the total of—
"(1) the sum of the amounts obtained by multiplying—
"(A) each rate of interest assumed in computing the taxpayer's life insurance reserves by
"(B) the means of the amounts of the taxpayer's adjusted reserves computed at that rate at the beginning and end of the taxable year.
"(2) 2 percent of the reserve for deferred dividends, and
"(3) interest paid."

"Sec. 806. Adjustment for certain reserves.
"In the case of a life insurance company writing contracts other than life insurance or annuity contracts (either separately or combined with noncancellable health and accident insurance), the term 'adjusted for certain reserves' means an amount equal to 3¼ percent of the unearned premiums and unpaid losses on such other contracts which are not included in life insurance reserves (as defined in section 803(b)). For purposes of this section, such unearned premiums shall not be considered to be less than 25 percent of the net premiums written during the taxable year on such other contracts."

"Sec. 807. Foreign life insurance companies.
"(a) Carrying on United States insurance business.
"A foreign life insurance company carrying on a life insurance business within the United States, if with respect to its United States business it would qualify as a life insurance company under section 801, shall be taxable in the same manner as a domestic life insurance company; except that the determinations necessary for purposes of this subtitle shall be made on the basis of the income, disbursements, assets, and liabilities reported in the annual statement for the taxable year of the United States business of such company on the form approved for life insurance companies by the National Association of Insurance Commissioners.
"(b) No United States insurance business.
"Foreign life insurance companies not carrying on an insurance business within the United States shall not be taxable under this section but shall be taxable as other foreign corporations."

Subpart A.—Tax Imposed

Sec.
801. Tax imposed.
Sec. 801. Tax imposed.
(a) Tax imposed.
  (1) In general. A tax is hereby imposed for each taxable year on the life insurance company taxable income of every life insurance company. Such tax shall consist of a tax computed as provided in section 11 as though the life insurance company taxable income were the taxable income referred to in section 11.
  (2) Alternative tax in case of capital gains.
    (A) In general. If a life insurance company has a net capital gain for the taxable year, then (in lieu of the tax imposed by paragraph (1)), there is hereby imposed a tax (if such tax is less than the tax imposed by paragraph (1)).
    (B) Amount of tax. The amount of the tax imposed by this paragraph shall be the sum of—
      (i) a partial tax, computed as provided by paragraph (1), on the life insurance company taxable income reduced by the amount of the net capital gain, and
      (ii) an amount determined as provided in section 1201(a) on such net capital gain.
    (C) Net capital gain not taken into account in determining small life insurance company deduction. For purposes of subparagraph (B)(i), the amount allowable as a deduction under paragraph (2) of section 804 shall be determined by reducing the tentative LICTI by the amount of the net capital gain (determined without regard to items attributable to noninsurance businesses).
(b) Life insurance company taxable income.
  For purposes of this part, the term "life insurance company taxable income" means—
    (1) life insurance gross income, reduced by
    (2) life insurance deductions.

(c) Taxation of distributions from pre-1984 policyholders surplus account.
  For provision taxing distributions to shareholders from pre-1984 policyholders surplus account, see section 815.

In **1986**, P.L. 99-514, Sec. 1011(b)(3)(A), substituted "the amount allowable as a deduction under paragraph (2)" for "the amounts allowable as deductions under paragraphs (2) and (3)" in subpara. (a)(2)(C) . . . Sec. 1011(b)(3)(B), deleted "special life insurance company deduction and" before "small life insurance company" in the heading of subpara. (a)(2)(C), effective for tax. yrs. begin. after 12/31/86. For provisions on waiver of interest on certain underpayments of tax, see Sec. 1829 of this Act reproduced in note following Code Sec. 6601.
In **1984**, P.L. 98-369, Sec. 211(a), added Code Sec. 801 as part of the amendments to part I of Subchapter L, effective for tax. yrs. begin. after 12/31/83. For transitional rules, see Secs. 216(b)(3)(B), (C) and Sec. 216(b)(4) of this Act reproduced in note following Code Sec. 807.

Subpart B.—Life Insurance Gross Income

Sec.
803. Life insurance gross income.
Sec. 803. Life insurance gross income.
(a) In general.
  For purposes of this part, the term "life insurance gross income" means the sum of the following amounts:
    (1) Premiums.
      (A) The gross amount of premiums and other consideration on insurance and annuity contracts, less
      (B) return premiums, and premiums and other consideration arising out of indemnity reinsurance.
    (2) Decreases in certain reserves. Each net decrease in reserves which is required by section 807(a) to be taken into account under this paragraph.
    (3) Other amounts. All amounts not includible under paragraph (1) or (2) which under this subtitle are includible in gross income.
(b) Special rules for premiums.
  (1) Certain items included. For purposes of subsection (a)(1)(A), the term "gross amount of premiums and other consideration" includes—
    (A) advance premiums,
    (B) deposits,
    (C) fees,
    (D) assessments,
    (E) consideration in respect of assuming liabilities under contracts not issued by the taxpayer, and
    (F) the amount of policyholder dividends reimbursable to the taxpayer by a reinsurer in respect of reinsured policies,
  on insurance and annuity contracts.
  (2) Policyholder dividends excluded from return premiums. For purposes of subsection (a)(1)(B)—
    (A) In general. Except as provided in subparagraph (B), the term "return premiums" does not include any policyholder dividends.
    (B) Exception for indemnity reinsurance. Subparagraph (A) shall not apply to amounts of premiums or other consideration returned to another life insurance company in respect of indemnity reinsurance.

In **1984**, P.L. 98-369, Sec. 211(a), added Code Sec. 803 as part of the amendments to part I of Subchapter L, effective for tax. yrs. begin. after 12/31/83.

Subpart C.—Life Insurance Deductions

Sec.
804. Life insurance deductions.
805. General deductions.
806. Small life insurance company deduction.
807. Rules for certain reserves.

2,383

Subpart C   **Insurance companies**

808. Policyholder dividends deduction.
809. [Repealed] Reduction in certain deductions of mutual life insurance companies.
810. Operations loss deduction.

In 2004, P.L. 108-218, Sec. 205(b)(7), repealed the item for Code Sec. 809, effective for tax. yrs. begin. after 12/31/2004.
Prior to repeal, the item for Code Sec. 809 read as follows:
"Sec. 809. Reduction in certain deductions of mutual life insurance companies."
In 1986, P.L. 99-514, Sec. 1011(b)(11)(B), amended item 806.
Prior to amendment, item 806 read as follows:
"806. Special deductions."

Sec. 804. Life insurance deductions.

For purposes of this part, the term "life insurance deductions" means—

(1) the general deductions provided in section 805, and

(2) the small life insurance company deduction (if any) determined under section 806(a).

In 1986, P.L. 99-514, Sec. 1011(b)(2), added "and" at the end of para. (1), deleted paras. (2) and (3), and added new para. (2), effective for tax. yrs. begin. after 12/31/86.
Prior to deletion, paras. (2) and (3) read as follows:
"(2) the special life insurance company deduction determined under section 806(a), and
"(3) the small life insurance company deduction (if any) determined under section 806(b)."
In 1984, P.L. 98-369, Sec. 211(a), added Code Sec. 804 as part of the amendments to part I of subchapter L of chapter 1, effective for tax. yrs. begin. after 12/31/83.

Sec. 805. General deductions.
(a) General rule.

For purposes of this part, there shall be allowed the following deductions:

(1) Death benefits, etc. All claims and benefits accrued, and all losses incurred (whether or not ascertained), during the taxable year on insurance and annuity contracts.

(2) Increases in certain reserves. The net increase in reserves which is required by section 807(b) to be taken into account under this paragraph.

(3) Policyholder dividends. The deduction for policyholder dividends (determined under section 808(c)).

(4) Dividends received by company.

(A) In general. The deductions provided by sections 243, 244, and 245 (as modified by subparagraph (B))—

(i) for 100 percent dividends received, and

(ii) for the life insurance company's share of the dividends (other than 100 percent dividends) received.

(B) Application of section 246(b). In applying section 246(b) (relating to limitation on aggregate amount of deductions for dividends received) for purposes of subparagraph (A), the limit on the aggregate amount of the deductions allowed by sections 243(a)(1), 244(a), and 245 shall be the percentage determined under section 246(b)(3) of the life insurance company taxable income (and such limitation shall be applied as provided in section 246(b)(3)), computed without regard to—

(i) the small life insurance company deduction,

(ii) the operations loss deduction provided by section 810,

(iii) the deductions allowed by sections 243(a)(1), 244(a), and 245, and

(iv) any capital loss carryback to the taxable year under section 1212(a)(1),

but such limit shall not apply for any taxable year for which there is a loss from operations.

(C) 100 percent dividend. For purposes of subparagraph (A)—

(i) In general. Except as provided in clause (ii), the term "100 percent dividend" means any dividend if the percentage used for purposes of determining the deduction allowable under section 243, 244, or 245(b) is 100 percent.

(ii) Treatment of dividends from noninsurance companies. The term "100 percent dividend" does not include any distribution by a corporation which is not an insurance company to the extent such distribution is out of tax-exempt interest, or out of the increase for the taxable year in policy cash values (within the meaning of subparagraph (F)) of life insurance policies and annuity and endowment contracts to which section 264(f) applies, or out of dividends which are not 100 percent dividends (determined with the application of this clause as if it applies to distributions by all corporations including insurance companies).

(D) Special rules for certain dividends from insurance companies.

(i) In general. In the case of any 100 percent dividend paid to any life insurance company out of the earnings and profits for any taxable year beginning after December 31, 1983, of another life insurance company if—

(I) the paying company's share determined under section 812 for such taxable year, exceeds

(II) the receiving company's share determined under section 812 for its taxable year in which the dividend is received or accrued,

the deduction allowed under section 243, 244, or 245(b) (as the case may be) shall be reduced as provided in clause (ii).

(ii) Amount of reduction. The reduction under this clause for a dividend is an amount equal to—

(I) the portion of such dividend attributable to prorated amounts, multiplied by

(II) the percentage obtained by subtracting the share described in subclause (II) of clause (i) from the share described in subclause (I) of such clause.

(iii) Prorated amounts. For purposes of this subparagraph, the term "prorated amounts" means tax-exempt interest, the increase for the taxable year in policy cash values (within the meaning of subparagraph (F)) of life insurance policies and annuity and endowment contracts to which section 264(f) applies, and dividends other than 100 percent dividends.

(iv) Portion of dividend attributable to prorated amounts. For purposes of this subparagraph, in determining the portion of any dividend attributable to prorated amounts—

(I) any dividend by the paying corporation shall be treated as paid first out of earnings and profits for taxable years beginning after December 31, 1983, attributable to prorated amounts (to the extent thereof), and

(II) by determining the portion of earnings and profits so attributable without any reduction for the tax imposed by this chapter.

(v) Subparagraph to apply to dividends from other insurance companies. Rules similar to the rules of this subsection shall apply in the case of 100 percent dividends paid by an insurance company which is not a life insurance company.

(E) Certain dividends received by foreign corporations. Subparagraph (A)(i) (and not subparagraph (A)(ii)) shall apply to any dividend received by a foreign corporation from a domestic corporation which would be a 100 per-

Insurance companies   Code Sec. 805

cent dividend if section 1504(b)(3) did not apply for purposes of applying section 243(b)(2).

(F) Increase in policy cash values. For purposes of subparagraphs (C) and (D)—

(i) In general. The increase in the policy cash value for any taxable year with respect to policy or contract is the amount of the increase in the adjusted cash value during such taxable year determined without regard to—

(I) gross premiums paid during such taxable year, and

(II) distributions (other than amounts includible in the policyholder's gross income) during such taxable year to which section 72(e) applies.

(ii) Adjusted cash value. For purposes of clause (i), the term "adjusted cash value" means the cash surrender value of the policy or contract increased by the sum of—

(I) commissions payable with respect to such policy or contract for the taxable year, and

(II) asset management fees, surrender charges, mortality and expense charges, and any other fees or charges specified in regulations prescribed by the Secretary which are imposed (or which would be imposed were the policy or contract canceled) with respect to such policy or contract for the taxable year.

(5) Operations loss deduction. The operations loss deduction (determined under section 810).

(6) Assumption by another person of liabilities under insurance, etc., contracts. The consideration (other than consideration arising out of indemnity reinsurance) in respect of the assumption by another person of liabilities under insurance and annuity contracts.

(7) Reimbursable dividends. The amount of policyholder dividends which—

(A) are paid or accrued by another insurance company in respect of policies the taxpayer has reinsured, and

(B) are reimbursable by the taxpayer under the terms of the reinsurance contract.

(8) Other deductions. Subject to the modifications provided by subsection (b), all other deductions allowed under this subtitle for purposes of computing taxable income.

Except as provided in paragraph (3), no amount shall be allowed as a deduction under this part in respect of policyholder dividends.

(b) Modifications.

The modifications referred to in subsection (a)(8) are as follows:

(1) Interest. In applying section 163 (relating to deduction for interest), no deduction shall be allowed for interest in respect of items described in section 807(c).

(2) Charitable, etc., contributions and gifts. In applying section 170—

(A) the limit on the total deductions under such section provided by section 170(b)(2) shall be 10 percent of the life insurance company taxable income computed without regard to—

(i) the deduction provided by section 170,

(ii) the deductions provided by paragraphs (3) and (4) of subsection (a),

(iii) the small life insurance company deduction,

(iv) any operations loss carryback to the taxable year under section 810, and

(v) any capital loss carryback to the taxable year under section 1212(a)(1), and

(B) under regulations prescribed by the Secretary, a rule similar to the rule contained in section 170(d)(2)(B) (relating to special rule for net operating loss carryovers) shall be applied.

(3) Amortizable bond premium.

(A) In general. Section 171 shall not apply.

(B) Cross reference.

For rules relating to amortizable bond premium, see section 811(b).

(4) Net operating loss deduction. Except as provided by section 844, the deduction for net operating losses provided in section 172 shall not be allowed.

(5) Dividends received deduction. Except as provided in subsection (a)(4), the deductions for dividends received provided by sections 243, 244, and 245 shall not be allowed.

In 1998, P.L. 105-206, Sec. 6010(o)(3)(B), substituted "except that, in the case of a master contract (within the meaning of section 264(f)(4)(E) of the Internal Revenue Code of 1986), the addition of covered lives shall be treated as a new contract only with respect to such additional covered lives." for "but the addition of covered lives shall be treated as a new contract only with respect to such additional covered lives. For purposes of this subsection, an increase in the death benefit under a policy or contract issued in connection with a lapse described in section 501(d)(2) of the Health Insurance Portability and Accountability Act of 1996 shall not be treated as a new contract." in Sec. 1084(d)[sic (f)] of P.L. 105-34 [reproduced below].

In 1997, P.L. 105-34, Sec. 1084(b)(1)(A) [sic (d)(1)(A)], added ", or out of the increase for the taxable year in policy cash values (within the meaning of subparagraph (F)) of life insurance policies and annuity and endowment contracts to which section 264(f) applies" after "tax-exempt interest" in clause (a)(4)(C)(ii) . . . Sec. 1084(b)(1)(B) [sic (d)(1)(B)], substituted ", the increase for the taxable year in policy cash values (within the meaning of subparagraph (F)) of life insurance policies and annuity and endowment contracts to which section 264(f) applies, and" for "and" in clause (a)(4)(D)(iii) . . . Sec. 1084(b)(1)(C) [sic (d)(1)(C)], added subpara. (a)(4)(F), effective as provided in Sec. 1084(d)[sic (f)] of this Act [as amended by Sec. 6010(o)(3)(B), 105-206, see above], which reads:

"(d) Effective date.— The amendments made by this section shall apply to contracts issued after June 8, 1997, in taxable years ending after such date. For purposes of the preceding sentence, any material increase in the death benefit or other material change in the contract shall be treated as a new contract except that, in the case of a master contract (within the meaning of section 264(f)(4)(E) of the Internal Revenue Code of 1986), the addition of covered lives shall be treated as a new contract only with respect to such additional covered lives."

In 1996, P.L. 104-188, Sec. 1702(h)(3), substituted "243(b)(2)" for "243(b)(5)" in subpara. (a)(4)(E), effective for tax. yrs. begin. after 12/31/90, except as provided in Sec. 11814(c)(2) of P.L. 101-508, reproduced in note following Code Sec. 243.

In 1988, P.L. 100-647, Sec. 2004(i)(1), changed the effective date for amendments made by Sec. 10221(c)(2) of P.L. 100-203, from Sec. 10221(e)(1) of P.L. 100-203 to Sec. 10221(e)(2) of P.L. 100-203. The change made by Sec. 10221(c)(2) of P.L. 100-203, is now effective in tax. yrs. begin. after 12/31/87. Prior to the amendment made by 2004(i)(1) of this Act, the change made by Sec. 10221(c)(2) of P.L. 100-203, was effective for dividends received or accrued after 12/31/87 in tax. yrs. end. after 12/31/87.

In 1987, P.L. 100-203, Sec. 10221(c)(2), substituted "shall be the percentage determined under section 246(b)(3) of the life insurance company taxable income (and such limitation shall be applied as provided in section 246(b)(3))" for "shall be 80 percent of the life insurance company taxable income" in subpara. (a)(4)(B), effective for tax. yrs. begin. after 12/31/87 [as amended by Sec. 2004(i)(1) of P.L. 100-647].

In 1986, P.L. 99-514, Sec. 611(a)(5), substituted "80 percent" for "85 percent" in subpara. (a)(4)(B), effective for dividends received or accrued after 12/31/86 in tax. yrs. ending after 12/31/86.

—P.L. 99-514, Sec. 805(c)(6), deleted para. (b)(2), and redesignated paras. (b)(3)-(6) as paras. (b)(2)-(5), effective for tax. yrs. begin. after 12/31/86. For special rules, see Sec. 805(d)(2) reproduced in note following Code Sec. 166.
Prior to deletion, para. (b)(2) read as follows:

"(2) Bad debts. Section 166(c) (relating to reserve for bad debts) shall not apply."

—P.L. 99-514, Sec. 1011(b)(4), deleted "the special life insurance company deduction and" before "the small life insurance" in clauses (a)(4)(B)(i), (b)(3)(A)(iii), effective for tax. yrs. begin. after 12/31/86.

—P.L. 99-514, Sec. 1821(p), redesignated subpara. (a)(4)(D) as (a)(4)(E), deleted subpara. (a)(4)(C), and added new subparas. (a)(4)(C), and (a)(4)(D), effective for tax. yrs. begin. after 12/31/83.
Prior to deletion, subpara. (a)(4)(C) read as follows:

"(C) 100 percent dividend. For purposes of subparagraph (A), the term '100 percent dividend' means any dividend if the percentage used for purposes of determining the deduction allowable under section 243 or 244 is 100 percent. Such term does not include any dividend to the extent it is a distribution out of tax-exempt interest or out of dividends which are not 100 percent dividends (determined with the application of this sentence)."

In 1984, P.L. 98-369, Sec. 211(a), added Code Sec. 805 as part of the amendments to part I of Subchapter L, effective for tax. yrs. begin. after 12/31/83.

Sec. 806. Small life insurance company deduction.
(a) Small life insurance company deduction.

(1) In general. For purposes of section 804, the small life insurance company deduction for any taxable year is 60 percent of so much of the tentative LICTI for such taxable year as does not exceed $3,000,000.

(2) Phaseout between $3,000,000 and $15,000,000. The amount of the small life insurance company deduction determined under paragraph (1) for any taxable year shall be reduced (but not below zero) by 15 percent of so much of the tentative LICTI for such taxable year as exceeds $3,000,000.

(3) Small life insurance company deduction not allowable to company with assets of $500,000,000 or more.

(A) In general. The small life insurance company deduction shall not be allowed for any taxable year to any life insurance company which, at the close of such taxable year, has assets equal to or greater than $500,000,000.

(B) Assets. For purposes of this paragraph, the term "assets" means all assets of the company.

(C) Valuation of assets. For purposes of this paragraph, the amount attributable to—

(i) real property and stock shall be the fair market value thereof, and

(ii) any other asset shall be the adjusted basis of such asset for purposes of determining gain on sale or other disposition.

(D) Special rule for interests in partnerships and trusts. For purposes of this paragraph—

(i) an interest in a partnership or trust shall not be treated as an asset of the company, but

(ii) the company shall be treated as actually owning its proportionate share of the assets held by the partnership or trust (as the case may be).

(b) Tentative LICTI.
For purposes of this part—

(1) In general. The term "tentative LICTI" means life insurance company taxable income determined without regard to the small life insurance company deduction.

(2) Exclusion of items attributable to noninsurance businesses. The amount of the tentative LICTI for any taxable year shall be determined without regard to all items attributable to noninsurance businesses.

(3) Noninsurance business.

(A) In general. The term "noninsurance business" means any activity which is not an insurance business.

(B) Certain activities treated as insurance businesses. For purposes of subparagraph (A), any activity which is not an insurance business shall be treated as an insurance business if—

(i) it is of a type traditionally carried on by life insurance companies for investment purposes, but only if the carrying on of such activity (other than in the case of real estate) does not constitute the active conduct of a trade or business, or

(ii) it involves the performance of administrative services in connection with plans providing life insurance, pension, or accident and health benefits.

(C) Limitation on amount of loss from noninsurance business which may offset income from insurance business. In computing the life insurance company taxable income of any life insurance company, any loss from a noninsurance business shall be limited under the principles of section 1503(c).

(c) Special rule for controlled groups.

(1) Small life insurance company deduction determined on controlled group basis. For purposes of subsection (a)—

(A) all life insurance companies which are members of the same controlled group shall be treated as 1 life insurance company, and

(B) any small life insurance company deduction determined with respect to such group shall be allocated among the life insurance companies which are members of such group in proportion to their respective tentative LICTI's.

(2) Nonlife insurance members included for asset test. For purposes of subsection (a)(3), all members of the same controlled group (whether or not life insurance companies) shall be treated as 1 company.

(3) Controlled group. For purposes of this subsection, the term "controlled group" means any controlled group of corporations (as defined in section 1563(a)); except that subsections (a)(4) and (b)(2)(D) of section 1563 shall not apply.

(4) Adjustments to prevent excess detriment or benefit. Under regulations prescribed by the Secretary, proper adjustments shall be made in the application of this subsection to prevent any excess detriment or benefit (whether from year-to-year or otherwise) arising from the application of this subsection.

In 1986, P.L. 99-514, Sec. 1011(a), deleted subsec. (a), and redesignated subsecs. (b), (c), and (d), as subsecs. (a), (b), and (c) . . . Sec. 1011(b)(5), substituted "without regard to the small life insurance company deduction." for "without regard to—

"(A) the special life insurance company deduction, and

"(B) the small life insurance company deduction.' in para. (b)(1) [as redesignated] . . . Sec. 1011(b)(6)(A), substituted 'subsection (a)' for 'subsections (a) and (b)' in para. (c)(1) [as redesignated] . . . Sec. 1101(b)(6)(B), deleted 'any special life insurance company deduction and' before 'any small life' in subpara. (c)(1)(B) [as redesignated] . . . Sec. 1101(b)(6)(C), substituted 'Small' for 'Special life insurance company deduction and small' in the heading of para. (c)(1) [as redesignated] . . . Sec. 1101(b)(7), substituted 'subsection (a)(3)' for 'subsection (b)(3)' in para. (c)(2) [as redesignated] . . . Sec. 1101(b)(8), deleted para. (c)(4) [as redesignated] and redesignated para. (c)(5) as (c)(4) . . . Sec. 1011(b)(11)(A), substituted 'Small life insurance company deduction' for 'Special deductions' in the heading of Code Sec. 806 . . . Sec. 1011(c)(2), amended Sec. 217(k) of P.L. 98-369 [reproduced below], special rules for the changes made by Sec. 211(a) of P.L. 98-369, by substituting 'the small life insurance company deduction under section 806(a)' for 'the special deductions under section 806' and by adding the last sentence, see below, effective for tax. yrs. begin. after 12/31/86. Prior to deletion, subsec. (a) read as follows:

"*(a) Special life insurance company deduction.* For purposes of section 804, the special life insurance company deduction for any taxable year is 20 percent of the excess of the tentative LICTI for such taxable year over the small life insurance company deduction (if any)."

Prior to deletion, para. (c)(4) read as follows:

"(4) Election with respect to loss from operations of member of group.

"(A) In general. Any life insurance company which is a member of a controlled group may elect to have its loss from operations for any taxable year not taken into account for purposes of determining the amount of the special life insurance company deduction for the life insurance companies which are members of such group and which do not file a consolidated return with such life insurance company for the taxable year.

"(B) Limitation on amount of loss which may offset nonlife income. In the case of that portion of any loss from operations for any taxable year of a life insurance company which (but for subparagraph (A)) would have reduced tentative LICTI of other life insurance companies for such taxable year—

"(i) only 80 percent of such portion may be used to offset nonlife income, and

"(ii) to the extent such portion is used to offset nonlife income, the loss shall be treated as used at a rate of $1 for each 80 cents of income so offset.

For purposes of the preceding sentence, any such portion shall be used before the remaining portion of the loss from the same year and shall be treated as first being offset against income which is not nonlife income.

"(C) Nonlife income.

"(i) In general. The term 'nonlife income' means the portion of the life insurance company's taxable income for which the special life insurance company de-

Insurance companies   Code Sec. 807(c)(3)

duction was not allowable and any income of a corporation not subject to tax under this part.

"(ii) Special rule for taxable years beginning before January 1, 1984. In the case of a taxable year beginning before January 1, 1984, all life insurance company taxable income shall be treated as nonlife income."

In 1984, P.L. 98-369, Sec. 211(a), added Code Sec. 806 as part of the amendments to part I of Subchapter L, effective for tax. yrs. begin. after 12/31/83. For transitional rules, see Sec. 216(b)(3)(D) of this Act reproduced in note following Code Sec. 807.

—P.L. 98-369, Sec. 217(c), provides:

"(c) Determination of tentative LICTI where corporation made certain acquisitions in 1980, 1981, 1982, and 1983.— If —

"(1) a corporation domiciled or having its principal place of business in Alabama, Arkansas, Oklahoma, or Texas acquired the assets of 1 or more insurance companies after 1979 and before April 1, 1983, and

"(2) the bases of such assets in the hands of the corporation were determined under section 334(b)(2) of the Internal Revenue Code of 1954 or such corporation made an election under section 338 of such Code with respect to such assets,

then the tentative LICTI of the corporation holding such assets for taxable years beginning after December 31, 1983, shall, for purposes of determining the amount of the special deductions under section 806 of such Code, be increased by the deduction allowable under chapter 1 of such Code for the amortization of the cost of insurance contracts acquired in such asset acquisition (and any portion of any operations loss deduction attributable to such amortization)."

—P.L. 98-369, Sec. 217(h), provides:

"(h) Determination of assets of controlled group for purposes of small life insurance company deduction for 1984.—

"(1) In general.— For purposes of applying paragraph (2) of section 806(d) of the Internal Revenue Code of 1954 (relating to nonlife insurance members included for asset test) for the first taxable year beginning after December 31, 1983, the members of the controlled group referred to in such paragraph shall be treated as including only those members of such group which are described in paragraph (2) of this subsection if—

"(A) an election under section 1504(c)(2) of such Code is not in effect for the controlled group for such taxable year,

"(B) during such taxable year, the controlled group does not include a member which is taxable under part I of subchapter L of chapter 1 of such Code and which became a member of such group after September 27, 1983, and

"(C) the sum of the contributions to capital received by members of the controlled group which are taxable under such part I during such taxable year from the members of the controlled group which are not taxable under such part does not exceed the aggregate dividends paid during such taxable year by the members of such group which are taxable under such part I.

"(2) Members of group taken into account.— For purposes of paragraph (1), the members of the controlled group which are described in this paragraph are—

"(A) any financial institution to which section 585 or 593 of such Code applies,

"(B) any lending or finance business (as defined by section 542(d)),

"(C) any insurance company subject to tax imposed by subchapter L of chapter 1 of such Code, and

"(D) any securities broker."

—P.L. 98-369, Sec. 217(k), [as amended by Sec. 1011(c)(2) of P.L. 99-514, see above], (l), and (m) provide:

"(k) Special rule for certain debt-financed acquisition of stock.— If —

"(1) a life insurance company owns the stock of another corporation through a partnership of which it is a partner,

"(2) the stock of the corporation was acquired on January 14, 1981, and

"(3) such stock was acquired by debt financing,

then, for purposes of determining the small life insurance company deduction under section 806(a) of the Internal Revenue Code of 1954 (as amended by this subtitle), the amount of tentative LICTI of such life insurance company shall be computed without taking into account any income, gain, loss, or deduction attributable to the ownership of such stock. For purposes of determining taxable income, the amount of any income, gain, loss, or deduction attributable to the ownership of such stock shall be an amount equal to 46 times the amount of such income, gain, loss, or deduction, divided by 36.8.

"(l) Treatment of losses from certain guaranteed interest contracts.—

"(1) In general.— For purposes of determining the amount of the special deductions under section 806 of the Internal Revenue Code of 1954 (as amended by this subtitle), for any taxable year beginning before January 1, 1988, the amount of tentative LICTI of any qualified life insurance company shall be computed without taking into account any income, gain, loss, or deduction attributable to a qualified GIC.

"(2) Qualified life insurance company.— For purposes of this subsection, the term 'qualified life insurance company' means any life insurance company if—

"(A) the accrual of discount less amortization of premium for bonds and short-term investments (as shown in the first footnote to Exhibit 3 of its 1983 annual statement for life insurance companies approved by the National Association of Insurance Commissioners (but excluding separate accounts) filed in its State of domicile) exceeds $72,000,000 but does not exceed $73,000,000, and

"(B) such life insurance company makes an election under this subsection on its return for its first taxable year beginning after December 31, 1983.

"(3) Qualified GIC.— The term 'qualified GIC' means any group contract—

"(A) which is issued before January 1, 1984,

"(B) which specifies the contract maturity or renewal date,

"(C) under which funds deposited by the contract holder plus interest guaranteed at the inception of the contract for the term of the contract and net of any specified expenses are paid as directed by the contract holder, and

"(D) which is a pension plan contract (as defined in section 818(a) of the Internal Revenue Code of 1954).

"(4) Scope of election.— An election under this subsection shall apply to all qualified GIC's of a qualified life insurance company. Any such election, once made, shall be irrevocable.

"(5) Income on underlying assets taken into account.— In determining the amount of any income attributable to a qualified GIC, income on any asset attributable to such contract (as determined in the manner provided by the Secretary of the Treasury or his delegate) shall be taken into account.

"(6) Limitation on tax benefit.— The amount of any reduction in tax for any taxable year by reason of this subsection for any qualified life insurance company (or controlled group within the meaning of section 806(d)(3) of the Internal Revenue Code of 1954) shall not exceed the applicable amount set forth in the following table:

In the case of taxable years beginning in:	The reduction may not exceed:
1984	$4,500,000
1985	$4,500,000
1986	$3,000,000
1987	$2,000,000

"(m) Special rule for certain interests in oil and gas properties.—

"(1) In general.— For purposes of section 806 of the Internal Revenue Code of 1954, the ownership by a qualified life insurance company of any undivided interest in operating mineral interests with respect to any oil or gas properties held on December 31, 1983, shall be treated as an insurance business.

"(2) Qualified life insurance company.— For purposes of paragraph (1), the term 'qualified life insurance company' means a mutual life insurance company which—

"(A) was originally incorporated in March of 1857, and

"(B) has a cost to such company (as of December 31, 1983) in the operating mineral interests described in paragraph (1) in excess of $250,000,000."

Sec. 807. Rules for certain reserves.

(a) Decrease treated as gross income.

If for any taxable year—

(1) the opening balance for the items described in subsection (c), exceeds

(2) (A) the closing balance for such items, reduced by

(B) the amount of the policyholders' share of tax-exempt interest and the amount of the policyholder's share of the increase for the taxable year in policy cash values (within the meaning of section 805(a)(4)(F)) of life insurance policies and annuity and endowment contracts to which section 264(f) applies,

such excess shall be included in gross income under section 803(a)(2).

(b) Increase treated as deduction.

If for any taxable year—

(1)(A) the closing balance for the items described in subsection (c), reduced by

(B) the amount of the policyholders' share of tax-exempt interest and the amount of the policyholder's share of the increase for the taxable year in policy cash values (within the meaning of section 805(a)(4)(F)) of life insurance policies and annuity and endowment contracts to which section 264(f) applies, exceeds

(2) the opening balance for such items,

such excess shall be taken into account as a deduction under section 805(a)(2).

(c) Items taken into account.

The items referred to in subsections (a) and (b) are as follows:

(1) The life insurance reserves (as defined in section 816(b)).

(2) The unearned premiums and unpaid losses included in total reserves under section 816(c)(2).

(3) The amounts (discounted at the appropriate rate of interest) necessary to satisfy the obligations under insurance and annuity contracts, but only if such obligations do not involve (at the time with respect to which the computation is made under this paragraph) life, accident, or health contingencies.

(4) Dividend accumulations, and other amounts, held at interest in connection with insurance and annuity contracts.

(5) Premiums received in advance, and liabilities for premium deposit funds.

(6) Reasonable special contingency reserves under contracts of group term life insurance or group accident and health insurance which are established and maintained for the provision of insurance on retired lives, for premium stabilization, or for a combination thereof.

For purposes of paragraph (3), the appropriate rate of interest for any obligation is whichever of the following rates is the highest as of the time such obligation first did not involve life, accident, or health contingencies: the applicable Federal interest rate under subsection (d)(2)(B)(i), the prevailing State assumed interest rate under subsection (d)(2)(B)(ii), or the rate of interest assumed by the company in determining the guaranteed benefit. In no case shall the amount determined under paragraph (3) for any contract be less than the net surrender value of such contract. For purposes of paragraph (2) and section 805(a)(1), the amount of the unpaid losses (other than losses on life insurance contracts) shall be the amount of the discounted unpaid losses as defined in section 846.

(d) Method of computing reserves for purposes of determining income.

  (1) In general. For purposes of this part (other than section 816), the amount of the life insurance reserves for any contract shall be the greater of—

    (A) the net surrender value of such contract, or

    (B) the reserve determined under paragraph (2).

In no event shall the reserve determined under the preceding sentence for any contract as of any time exceed the amount which would be taken into account with respect to such contract as of such time in determining statutory reserves (as defined in paragraph (6)).

  (2) Amount of reserve. The amount of the reserve determined under this paragraph with respect to any contract shall be determined by using—

    (A) the tax reserve method applicable to such contract,

    (B) the greater of—

      (i) the applicable Federal interest rate, or

      (ii) the prevailing State assumed interest rate, and

    (C) the prevailing commissioners' standard tables for mortality and morbidity adjusted as appropriate to reflect the risks (such as substandard risks) incurred under the contract which are not otherwise taken into account.

  (3) Tax reserve method. For purposes of this subsection—

    (A) In general. The term "tax reserve method" means—

      (i) Life insurance contracts. The CRVM in the case of a contract covered by the CRVM.

      (ii) Annuity contracts. The CARVM in the case of a contract covered by the CARVM.

      (iii) Noncancellable accident and health insurance contracts. In the case of any noncancellable accident and health insurance contract (other than a qualified long-term care insurance contract, as defined in section 7702B(b)), a 2-year full preliminary term method.

      (iv) Other contracts. In the case of any contract not described in clause (i), (ii), or (iii)—

        (I) the reserve method prescribed by the National Association of Insurance Commissioners which covers such contract (as of the date of issuance), or

        (II) if no reserve method has been prescribed by the National Association of Insurance Commissioners which covers such contract, a reserve method which is consistent with the reserve method required under clause (i), (ii), or (iii) or under subclause (I) of this clause as of the date of the issuance of such contract (whichever is most appropriate).

    (B) Definition of CRVM and CARVM. For purposes of this paragraph—

      (i) CRVM. The term "CRVM" means the Commissioners' Reserve Valuation Method prescribed by the National Association of Insurance Commissioners which is in effect on the date of the issuance of the contract.

      (ii) CARVM. The term "CARVM" means the Commissioners' Annuities Reserve Valuation Method prescribed by the National Association of Insurance Commissioners which is in effect on the date of the issuance of the contract.

    (C) No additional reserve deduction allowed for deficiency reserves. Nothing in any reserve method described under this paragraph shall permit any increase in the reserve because the net premium (computed on the basis of assumptions required under this subsection) exceeds the actual premiums or other consideration charged for the benefit.

  (4) Applicable Federal interest rate; prevailing State assumed interest rate. For purposes of this subsection—

    (A) Applicable Federal interest rate.

      (i) In general. Except as provided in clause (ii), the term "applicable Federal interest rate" means the annual rate determined by the Secretary under section 846(c)(2) for the calendar year in which the contract was issued.

      (ii) Election to recompute Federal interest rate every 5 years.

        (I) In general. In computing the amount of the reserve with respect to any contract to which an election under this clause applies for periods during any recomputation period, the applicable Federal interest rate shall be the annual rate determined by the Secretary under section 846(c)(2) for the 1st year of such period. No change in the applicable Federal interest rate shall be made under the preceding sentence unless such change would equal or exceed ½ of 1 percentage point.

        (II) Recomputation period. For purposes of subclause (I), the term "recomputation period" means, with respect to any contract, the 5 calendar year period beginning with the 5th calendar year beginning after the calendar year in which the contract was issued (and each subsequent 5 calendar year period).

        (III) Election. An election under this clause shall apply to all contracts issued during the calendar year for which the election was made or during any subsequent calendar year unless such election is revoked with the consent of the Secretary.

        (IV) Spread not available. Subsection (f) shall not apply to any adjustment required under this clause.

    (B) Prevailing State assumed interest rate.

      (i) In general. The term "prevailing State assumed interest rate" means, with respect to any contract, the highest assumed interest rate permitted to be used in computing life insurance reserves for insurance contracts or annuity contracts (as the case may be) under

Insurance companies   Code Sec. 807(e)(4)(B)

the insurance laws of at least 26 States. For purposes of the preceding sentence, the effect of nonforfeiture laws of a State on interest rates for reserves shall not be taken into account.

(ii) When rate determined. The prevailing State assumed interest rate with respect to any contract shall be determined as of the beginning of the calendar year in which the contract was issued.

(5) Prevailing commissioners' standard tables. For purposes of this subsection—

(A) In general. The term "prevailing commissioners' standard tables" means, with respect to any contract, the most recent commissioners' standard tables prescribed by the National Association of Insurance Commissioners which are permitted to be used in computing reserves for that type of contract under the insurance laws of at least 26 States when the contract was issued.

(B) Insurer may use old tables for 3 years when tables change. If the prevailing commissioners' standard tables as of the beginning of any calendar year (hereinafter in this subparagraph referred to as the "year of change") is different from the prevailing commissioners' standard tables as of the beginning of the preceding calendar year, the issuer may use the prevailing commissioners' standard tables as of the beginning of the preceding calendar year with respect to any contract issued after the change and before the close of the 3-year period beginning on the first day of the year of change.

(C) Special rule for contracts for which there are no commissioners' standard tables. If there are no commissioners' standard tables applicable to any contract when it is issued, the mortality and morbidity tables used for purposes of paragraph (2)(C) shall be determined under regulations prescribed by the Secretary. When the Secretary by regulation changes the table applicable to a type of contract, the new table shall be treated (for purposes of subparagraph (B) and for purposes of determining the issue dates of contracts for which it shall be used) as if it were a new prevailing commissioner's standard table adopted by the twenty-sixth State as of a date (no earlier than the date the regulation is issued) specified by the Secretary.

(D) Special rule for contracts issued before 1948. If—

(i) a contract was issued before 1948, and

(ii) there were no commissioners' standard tables applicable to such contract when it was issued,

the mortality and morbidity tables used in computing statutory reserves for such contracts shall be used for purposes of paragraph (2)(C).

(E) Special rule where more than 1 table or option applicable. If, with respect to any category of risks, there are 2 or more tables (or options under 1 or more tables) which meet the requirements of subparagraph (A) (or, where applicable, subparagraph (B) or (C)), the table (and option thereunder) which generally yields the lowest reserves shall be used for purposes of paragraph (2)(C).

(6) Statutory reserves. The term "statutory reserves" means the aggregate amount set forth in the annual statement with respect to items described in section 807(c). Such term shall not include any reserve attributable to a deferred and uncollected premium if the establishment of such reserve is not permitted under section 811(c).

(e) Special rules for computing reserves.

(1) Net surrender value. For purposes of this section—

(A) In general. The net surrender value of any contract shall be determined—

(i) with regard to any penalty or charge which would be imposed on surrender, but

(ii) without regard to any market value adjustment on surrender.

(B) Special rule for pension plan contracts. In the case of a pension plan contract, the balance in the policyholder's fund shall be treated as the net surrender value of such contract. For purposes of the preceding sentence, such balance shall be determined with regard to any penalty or forfeiture which would be imposed on surrender but without regard to any market value adjustment.

(2) Issuance date in case of group contracts. For purposes of this section, in the case of a group contract, the date on which such contract is issued shall be the date as of which the master plan is issued (or, with respect to a benefit guaranteed to a participant after such date, the date as of which such benefit is guaranteed).

(3) Supplemental benefits.

(A) Qualified supplemental benefits treated separately. For purposes of this part, the amount of the life insurance reserve for any qualified supplemental benefit—

(i) shall be computed separately as though such benefit were under a separate contract, and

(ii) shall, except to the extent otherwise provided in regulations, be the reserve taken into account for purposes of the annual statement approved by the National Association of Insurance Commissioners.

(B) Supplemental benefits which are not qualified supplemental benefits. In the case of any supplemental benefit described in subparagraph (D) which is not a qualified supplemental benefit, the amount of the reserve determined under paragraph (2) of subsection (d) shall, except to the extent otherwise provided in regulations, be the reserve taken into account for purposes of the annual statement approved by the National Association of Insurance Commissioners.

(C) Qualified supplemental benefit. For purposes of this paragraph, the term "qualified supplemental benefit" means any supplemental benefit described in subparagraph (D) if—

(i) there is a separately identified premium or charge for such benefit, and

(ii) any net surrender value under the contract attributable to any other benefit is not available to fund such benefit.

(D) Supplemental benefits. For purposes of this paragraph, the supplemental benefits described in this subparagraph are any—

(i) guaranteed insurability,

(ii) accidental death or disability benefit,

(iii) convertibility,

(iv) disability waiver benefit, or

(v) other benefit prescribed by regulations,

which is supplemental to a contract for which there is a reserve described in subsection (c).

(4) Certain contracts issued by foreign branches of domestic life insurance companies.

(A) In general. In the case of any qualified foreign contract, the amount of the reserve shall be not less than the minimum reserve required by the laws, regulations, or administrative guidance of the regulatory authority of the foreign country referred to in subparagraph (B) (but not to exceed the net level reserves for such contract).

(B) Qualified foreign contract. For purposes of subparagraph (A), the term "qualified foreign contract" means any contract issued by a foreign life insurance branch (which has its principal place of business in a foreign country) of a domestic life insurance company if—

(i) such contract is issued on the life or health of a resident of such country,

(ii) such domestic life insurance company was required by such foreign country (as of the time it began operations in such country) to operate in such country through a branch, and

(iii) such foreign country is not contiguous to the United States.

(5) Treatment of substandard risks.

(A) Separate computation. Except to the extent provided in regulations, the amount of the life insurance reserve for any qualified substandard risk shall be computed separately under subsection (d)(1) from any other reserve under the contract.

(B) Qualified substandard risk. For purposes of subparagraph (A), the term "qualified substandard risk" means any substandard risk if—

(i) the insurance company maintains a separate reserve for such risk,

(ii) there is a separately identified premium or charge for such risk,

(iii) the amount of the net surrender value under the contract is not increased or decreased by reason of such risk, and

(iv) the net surrender value under the contract is not regularly used to pay premium charges for such risk.

(C) Limitation on amount of life insurance reserve. The amount of the life insurance reserve determined for any qualified substandard risk shall in no event exceed the sum of the separately identified premiums charged for such risk plus interest less mortality charges for such risk.

(D) Limitation on amount of contracts to which paragraph applies. The aggregate amount of insurance in force under contracts to which this paragraph applies shall not exceed 10 percent of the insurance in force (other than term insurance) under life insurance contracts of the company.

(6) Special rules for contracts issued before January 1, 1989, under existing plans of insurance, with term insurance or annuity benefits. For purposes of this part—

(A) In general. In the case of a life insurance contract issued before January 1, 1989, under an existing plan of insurance, the life insurance reserve for any benefit to which this paragraph applies shall be computed separately under subsection (d)(1) from any other reserve under the contract.

(B) Benefits to which this paragraph applies. This paragraph applies to any term insurance or annuity benefit with respect to which the requirements of clauses (i) and (ii) of paragraph (3)(C) are met.

(C) Existing plan of insurance. For purposes of this paragraph, the term "existing plan of insurance" means, with respect to any contract, any plan of insurance which was filed by the company using such contract in one or more States before January 1, 1984, and is on file in the appropriate State for such contract.

(7) Special rules for treatment of certain nonlife reserves.

(A) In general. The amount taken into account for purposes of subsections (a) and (b) as—

(i) the opening balance of the items referred to in subparagraph (C), and

(ii) the closing balance of such items,

shall be 80 percent of the amount which (without regard to this subparagraph) would have been taken into account as such opening or closing balance, as the case may be.

(B) Transitional rule.

(i) In general. In the case of any taxable year beginning on or after September 30, 1990, and before September 30, 1996, there shall be included in the gross income of any life insurance company an amount equal to 3 ⅓ percent of such company's closing balance of the items referred to in subparagraph (C) for its most recent taxable year beginning before September 30, 1990.

(ii) Termination as life insurance company. Except as provided in section 381(c)(22), if, for any taxable year beginning on or before September 30, 1996, the taxpayer ceases to be a life insurance company, the aggregate inclusions which would have been made under clause (i) for such taxable year and subsequent taxable years but for such cessation shall be taken into account for the taxable year preceding such cessation year.

(C) Description of items. For purposes of this paragraph, the items referred to in this subparagraph are the items described in subsection (c) which consist of unearned premiums and premiums received in advance under insurance contracts not described in section 816(b)(1)(B).

(f) Adjustment for change in computing reserves.

(1) 10-year spread.

(A) In general. For purposes of this part, if the basis for determining any item referred to in subsection (c) as of the close of any taxable year differs from the basis for such determination as of the close of the preceding taxable year, then so much of the difference between—

(i) the amount of the item at the close of the taxable year, computed on the new basis, and

(ii) the amount of the item at the close of the taxable year, computed on the old basis,

as is attributable to contracts issued before the taxable year shall be taken into account under the method provided in subparagraph (B).

(B) Method. The method provided in this subparagraph is as follows:

(i) if the amount determined under subparagraph (A)(i) exceeds the amount determined under subparagraph (A)(ii), ¹⁄₁₀ of such excess shall be taken into account, for each of the succeeding 10 taxable years, as a deduction under section 805(a)(2); or

(ii) if the amount determined under subparagraph (A)(ii) exceeds the amount determined under subparagraph (A)(i), ¹⁄₁₀ of such excess shall be included in gross income, for each of the 10 succeeding taxable years, under section 803(a)(2).

(2) Termination as life insurance company. Except as provided in section 381(c)(22) (relating to carryovers in certain corporate readjustments), if for any taxable year the taxpayer is not a life insurance company, the balance of any adjustments under this subsection shall be taken into account for the preceding taxable year.

In 2004, P.L. 108-218, Sec. 205(b)(1), deleted "the sum of (i)" and "plus (ii) any excess described in section 809(a)(2) for the taxable year," in subparas. (a)(2)(B) and (b)(1)(B) . . . Sec. 205(b)(2)(A), substituted "paragraph (6)" for "section 809(b)(4)(B)" in para. (d)(1) . . . Sec. 205(b)(2)(B), added para. (d)(6), effective for tax. yrs. begin. after 12/31/2004.

In 1998, P.L. 105-206, Sec. 6010(o)(3)(B), substituted "except that, in the case of a master contract (within the meaning of section 264(f)(4)(E) of the Internal Revenue Code of 1986), the addition of covered lives shall be treated as a new contract only with respect to such additional covered lives." for "but the addition of covered lives shall be treated as a new contract only with respect to such additional covered lives. For purposes of this subsection, an increase in the death benefit under a policy or contract issued in connection with a lapse described in section 501(d)(2) of the Health Insurance Portability and Accountability Act of 1996 shall not be treated as a new contract." in Sec. 1084(d)[sic (f)] of P.L. 105-34 [reproduced below].

In 1997, P.L. 105-34, Sec. 1084(b)(2)(A) [sic (d)(2)(A)], substituted "interest and the amount of the policyholder's share of the increase for the taxable year in policy cash values (within the meaning of section 805(a)(4)(F)) of life insurance policies and annuity and endowment contracts to which section 264(f) applies," for "interest," in subpara. (a)(2)(B) . . . Sec. 1084(b)(2)(B) [sic (d)(2)(B)], substituted "interest and the amount of the policyholder's share of the increase for the taxable year in policy cash values (within the meaning of section 805(a)(4)(F)) of life insurance policies and annuity and endowment contracts to which section 264(f) applies," for "interest," in subpara. (b)(1)(B), effective as provided in Sec. 1084(d)[sic (f)] of this Act [as amended by Sec. 6010(o)(3)(B), 105-206, see above], which reads:

"(d) Effective date. — The amendments made by this section shall apply to contracts issued after June 8, 1997, in taxable years ending after such date. For purposes of the preceding sentence, any material increase in the death benefit or other material change in the contract shall be treated as a new contract except that, in the case of a master contract (within the meaning of section 264(f)(4)(E) of the Internal Revenue Code of 1986), the addition of covered lives shall be treated as a new contract only with respect to such additional covered lives."

In 1996, P.L. 104-188, Sec. 1704(t)(61), substituted "Commissioners'" for "Commissoners'" in clause (d)(3)(B)(ii), effective 8/20/96.

— P.L. 104-191, Sec. 321(b), added "(other than a qualified long-term care insurance contract, as defined in section 7702B(b))" after "insurance contract" in clause (d)(3)(A)(iii), effective for contracts issued after 12/31/97. For other provisions, see Sec. 321(d)(2) – (5) of this Act, which reads as follows:

"(2) Continuation of existing policies. In the case of any contract issued before January 1, 1997, which met the long-term care insurance requirements of the State in which the contract was used at the time the contract was issued —

"(A) such contract shall be treated for purposes of the Internal Revenue Code of 1986 as a qualified long-term care insurance contract (as defined in section 7702B(b) of such Code), and

"(B) services provided under, or reimbursed by, such contract shall be treated for such purposes as qualified long-term care services (as defined in section 7702B(c) of such Code).

In the case of an individual who is covered on December 31, 1996, under a State long-term care plan (as defined in section 7702B(f)(2) of such Code), the terms of such plan on such date shall be treated for purposes of the preceding sentence as a contract issued on such date which met the long-term care insurance requirements of such State.

"(3) Exchanges of existing policies. If, after the date of enactment of this Act and before January 1, 1998, a contract providing for long-term care insurance coverage is exchanged solely for a qualified long-term care insurance contract (as defined in section 7702B(b) of such Code), no gain or loss shall be recognized on the exchange. If, in addition to a qualified long-term care insurance contract, money or other property is received in the exchange, then any gain shall be recognized to the extent of the sum of the money and the fair market value of the other property received. For purposes of this paragraph, the cancellation of a contract providing for long-term care insurance coverage and reinvestment of the cancellation proceeds in a qualified long-term care insurance contract within 60 days thereafter shall be treated as an exchange.

"(4) Issuance of certain riders permitted. For purposes of applying sections 101(f), 7702, and 7702A of the Internal Revenue Code of 1986 to any contract —

"(A) the issuance of a rider which is treated as a qualified long-term care insurance contract under section 7702B, and

"(B) the addition of any provision required to conform any other long-term care rider to be so treated,

shall not be treated as a modification or material change of such contract.

"(5) Application of per diem limitation to existing contracts. The amount of per diem payments made under a contract issued on or before July 31, 1996, with respect to an insured which are excludable from gross income by reason of section 7702B of the Internal Revenue Code of 1986 (as added by this section) shall not be reduced under subsection (d)(2)(B) thereof by reason of reimbursements received under a contract issued on or before such date. The preceding sentence shall cease to apply as of the date (after July 31, 1996) such contract is exchanged or there is any contract modification which results in an increase in the amount of such per diem payments or the amount of such reimbursements."

In 1990, P.L. 101-508, Sec. 11302(a), added para. (e)(7), effective for tax. yrs. begin. on or after 9/30/90.

In 1988, P.L. 100-647, Sec. 1018(i), amended Sec. 216(b)(4)(C)(i) of P.L. 98-369 by substituting "subclause (I)" for "clause (i)", see below.

In 1987, P.L. 100-203, Sec. 10241(a), amended subpara. (d)(2)(B) . . . Sec. 10241(b)(1), amended para. (d)(4) . . . Sec. 10241(b)(2)(A), substituted "whichever of the following rates is the highest as of the time such obligation first did not involve life, accident, or health contingencies: the applicable Federal interest rate under subsection (d)(2)(B)(i), the prevailing State assumed interest rate under subsection (d)(2)(B)(ii), or the rate of interest assumed by the company in determining the guaranteed benefit." for "the higher of the prevailing State assumed interest rate as of the time such obligation first did not involve life, accident, or health contingencies or the rate of interest assumed by the company (as of such time) in determining the guaranteed benefit." in the third to the last sentence of subsec. (c), effective for contracts issued in tax. yrs. begin. after 12/31/87.

Prior to amendment, subpara. (d)(2)(B) read as follows:

"(B) the prevailing State assumed interest rate, and".

Prior to amendment, para. (d)(4) read as follows:

"(4) Prevailing state assumed interest rate. For purposes of this subsection

"(A) In general. The term 'prevailing State assumed interest rate' means, with respect to any contract, the highest assumed interest rate permitted to be used in computing life insurance reserves for insurance contracts or annuity contracts (as the case may be) under the insurance laws of at least 26 States. For purposes of the preceding sentence, the effect of the nonforfeiture laws of a State on interest rates for reserves shall not be taken into account.

"(B) When rate determined. Except as provided in subparagraph (C), the prevailing State assumed rate with respect to any contract shall be determined as of the beginning of the calendar year in which the contract was issued.

"(C) Election for nonannuity contracts. In the case of a contract other than an annuity contract, the issuer may elect (at such time and in such manner as the Secretary shall by regulations prescribe) to determine the prevailing State assumed rate as of the beginning of the calendar year preceding the calendar year in which the contract was issued.

"(D) Rate for noncancellable accident and health insurance contracts. If there is no prevailing State assumed interest rate applicable under subparagraph (A) to any noncancellable accident and health insurance contract when it is issued, the prevailing State assumed interest rate for such contract shall be the prevailing State assumed interest rate which would be determined under subparagraph (A) for a whole life insurance contract issued on the date on which the noncancellable accident and health insurance contract is issued."

In 1986, P.L. 99-514, Sec. 1023(b), added the last sentence to subsec. (c), effective for tax. yrs. begin. after 12/31/86.

— P.L. 99-514, Sec. 1821(a), added the next-to-last sentence to subsec. (c) . . . Sec. 1821(s), added the last sentence to subpara. (d)(5)(C), effective for tax. yrs. begin. after 12/31/83.

— P.L. 99-514, Sec. 1822(a), amended Sec. 216(b)(3)(C) of P.L. 98-369 by substituting "would have been required to be taken into account" for "was required to have been taken into account" . . . Sec. 1822(b), amended Sec. 216(b)(4)(B) of P.L. 98-369 by substituting "Paragraph (3) and subparagraph (A)" for "Subparagraph (A)" . . . Sec. 1822(c)(1), amended Sec. 216(c)(2)(A)(ii) of P.L. 98-369 by substituting "$3,000,000 (determined with regard to this subparagraph)" for "$3,000,000" . . . Sec. 1822(c)(2), amended Sec. 216(c)(2)(A) of P.L. 98-369 by substituting "be equal to the greater of the statutory reserve for such contract (adjusted as provided in subparagraph (B)) or the net surrender value of such contract (as defined in section 807(e)(1) of the Internal Revenue Code of 1954)." for "be equal to the statutory reserve for such contract, adjusted as provided in subparagraph (B)" . . . Sec. 1822(c)(3)(A), amended Sec. 216(c)(2)(B) of P.L. 98-369 by substituting "opening and closing statutory reserves" for "statutory reserves" . . . Sec. 1822(c)(3)(B), amended Sec. 216(c)(2)(B) of P.L. 98-369 by substituting "under the principles of section 805(c)(1) of such Code" for "under section 805(c)(1) of such Code" . . . Sec. 1822(d), amended Sec. 216(b)(3)(A) of P.L. 98-369 by adding the last sentence . . . Sec. 1822(e), amended Sec. 216(b)(1) of P.L. 98-369 by adding the last two sentences . . . Sec. 1822(f), added Sec. 216(b)(4)(C) of P.L. 98-369.

— P.L. 99-514, Sec. 1823, amended Sec. 217(n) of P.L. 98-369, reproduced below.

Prior to amendment, Sec. 217(n) of P.L. 98-369 read as follows:

"(n) Special rule for companies using net level reserve method for noncancellable accident and health insurance contracts. A company shall be treated as meeting the requirement of section 807(d)(3)(A)(iii) of the Internal Revenue Code of 1954, as amended by this Act, with respect to any noncancellable accident and health insurance contract for any taxable year if such company —

"(1) uses the net level reserve method to compute its tax reserves under section 807 of such Code on such contracts for such taxable year,

"(2) was using the net level reserve method to compute its statutory reserves on such contracts as of December 31, 1982, and

"(3) has continuously used such method for computing such reserves on such contracts after December 31, 1982, and through such taxable year."

In 1984, P.L. 98-369, Sec. 211(a), added Code Sec. 807 as part of the amendments to part I of Subchapter L, effective for tax. yrs. begin. after 12/31/83.

— P.L. 98-369, Sec. 216, transitional rules for changes made by Sec. 211 of this Act [as amended by Sec. 1822 of P.L. 99-514, and Sec. 1018(i) of P.L. 100-647, see above] provides:

"SEC. 216. RESERVES COMPUTED ON NEW BASIS; FRESH START.

"(a) Recomputation of reserves.

"(1) In general. As of the beginning of the first taxable year beginning after December 31, 1983, for purposes of subchapter L of the Internal Revenue Code of 1954 (other than section 816 thereof), the reserve for any contract shall be recomputed as if the amendments made by this subtitle had applied to such contract when it was issued.

"(2) Premiums earned. For the first taxable year beginning after December 31, 1983, in determining 'premiums earned on insurance contracts during the taxable year' as provided in section 832(b)(4) of the Internal Revenue Code of 1954, life insurance reserves which are included in unearned premiums on outstanding business at the end of the preceding taxable year shall be determined as provided in section 807 of the Internal Revenue Code of 1954, as amended by this subtitle, as though section 807 was applicable to such reserves in such preceding taxable year.

"(3) Issuance date for group contracts. For purposes of this subsection, the issuance date of any group contract shall be determined under section 807(e)(2) of the Internal Revenue Code of 1954 (as added by this subtitle), except that if such issuance date cannot be determined, the issuance date shall be determined on the basis prescribed by the Secretary of the Treasury or his delegate for purposes of this subsection.

"(b) Fresh start.

"(1) In general. Except as provided in paragraph (2), in the case of any insurance company, any change in the method of accounting (and any change in the method of computing reserves) between such company's first taxable year beginning after December 31, 1983, and the preceding taxable year which is required solely by the amendments made by this subtitle shall be treated as not being a change in the method of accounting (or change in the method of computing reserves) for purposes of the Internal Revenue Code of 1954. The preceding sentence shall apply for purposes of computing the earnings and profits of any insurance company for its 1st taxable year beginning in 1984. The preceding sentence shall be applied by substituting '1985' for '1984' in the case of an insurance company which is a member of a controlled group (as defined in section 806(d)(3)), the common parent of which is

"(A) a company having its principal place of business in Alabama and incorporated in Delaware on November 29, 1979, or

"(B) a company having its principal place of business in Houston, Texas, and incorporated in Delaware on June 9, 1947.

"(2) Treatment of adjustments from years before 1984.

"(A) Adjustments attributable to decreases in reserves. No adjustment under section 810(d) of the Internal Revenue Code of 1954 (as in effect on the day before the date of the enactment of this Act) attributable to any decrease in reserves as a result of a change in a taxable year beginning before 1984 shall be taken into account in any taxable year beginning after 1983.

"(B) Adjustments attributable to increases in reserves.

"(i) In general. Any adjustment under section 810(d) of the Internal Revenue Code of 1954 (as so in effect) attributable to an increase in reserves as a result of a change in a taxable year beginning before 1984 shall be taken into account in taxable years beginning after 1983 to the extent that—

"(I) the amount of the adjustments which would be taken into account under such section in taxable years beginning after 1983 without regard to this subparagraph, exceeds

"(II) the amount of any fresh start adjustment attributable to contracts for which there was such an increase in reserves as a result of such change.

"(ii) Fresh start adjustment. For purposes of clause (i), the fresh start adjustment with respect to any contract is the excess (if any) of—

"(I) the reserve attributable to such contract as of the close of the taxpayer's last taxable year beginning before January 1, 1984, over

"(II) the reserve for such contract as of the beginning of the taxpayer's first taxable year beginning after 1983 as recomputed under subsection (a) of this section.

"(C) Related income inclusions not taken into account to the extent deduction disallowed under subparagraph (b). No premium shall be included in income to the extent such premium is directly related to an increase in a reserve for which a deduction is disallowed by subparagraph (B).

"(3) Reinsurance transactions, and reserve strengthening, after September 27, 1983.

"(A) In general. Paragraph (1) shall not apply (and section 807(f) of the Internal Revenue Code of 1954 as amended by this subtitle shall apply)—

"(i) to any reserve transferred pursuant to—

"(I) a reinsurance agreement entered into after September 27, 1983, and before January 1, 1984, or

"(II) a modification of a reinsurance agreement made after September 27, 1983, and before January 1, 1984, and

"(ii) to any reserve strengthening reported for Federal income tax purposes after September 27, 1983, for a taxable year ending before January 1, 1984.

Clause (ii) shall not apply to the computation of reserves on any contract issued if such computation employs the reserve practice used for purposes of the most recent annual statement filed before September 27, 1983, for the type of contract with respect to which such reserves are set up. For purposes of this subparagraph, if the reinsurer's taxable year is not a calendar year, the first day of the reinsurer's first taxable year beginning after December 31, 1983, shall be substituted for 'January 1, 1984' each place it appears.

"(B) Treatment of reserve attributable to section 818(c) election. In the case of any reserve described in subparagraph (A), for purposes of section 807(f) of the Internal Revenue Code of 1954, any change in the treatment of any contract to which an election under section 818(c) of such Code (as in effect on the date before the date of the enactment of this Act) applied shall be treated as a change in the basis for determining the amount of any reserve.

"(C) 10-year spread inapplicable where no 10-year spread under prior law. In the case of any item to which section 807(f) of such Code applies by reason of subparagraph (A) or (B), such item shall be taken into account for the first taxable year beginning after December 31, 1983 (in lieu of over the 10-year period otherwise provided in such section) unless the item would have been required to be taken into account over a period of 10 taxable years under section 810(d) of such Code (as in effect on the day before the date of the enactment of this Act).

"(D) Disallowance of special life insurance company deduction and small life insurance company deduction. Any amount included in income under section 807(f) of such Code by reason of subparagraph (A) or (B) (and any income attributable to expenses transferred in connection with the transfer of reserves described in subparagraph (A)) shall not be taken into account for purposes of determining the amount of special life insurance company deduction and the small life insurance company deduction.

"(E) Disallowance of deductions under section 809(d). No deduction shall be allowed under paragraph (5) or (6) of section 809(d) of such Code (as in effect before the amendments made by this subtitle) with respect to any amount described in either such paragraph which is transferred in connection with the transfer of reserves described in subparagraph (A).

"(4) Elections under section 818(c) after September 27, 1983, not to take effect

"(A) In general. Except as provided in subparagraph (B), any election after September 27, 1983, under section 818(c) of the Internal Revenue Code of 1954 (as in effect on the day before the date of the enactment of this Act) shall not take effect.

"(B) Exception for certain contracts issued under plan of insurance first filed after March 1, 1982, and before September 28, 1983. Paragraph (3) and subparagraph (A) shall not apply to any election under such section 818(c) if more than 95 percent of the reserves computed in accordance with such election are attributable to risks under life insurance contracts issued by the taxpayer under a plan of insurance first filed after March 1, 1982, and before September 28, 1983.

"(C) Section 818(c) elections made by certain acquired companies

"(i) In general. If the case of any corporation—

"(I) which made an election under such section 818(c) before September 28, 1983, and

"(II) which was acquired in a qualified stock purchase (as defined in section 338(c) of the Internal Revenue Code of 1954) before December 31, 1983,

the fact that such corporation is treated as a new corporation under section 338 of such Code shall not result in the election described in subclause (I) not applying to such new corporation.

"(ii) Time for making section 818(c) or 338 election. In the case of any corporation described in clause (i), the time for making an election under section 818(c) of such Code (with respect to the first taxable year of the corporation beginning in 1983 and ending after September 28, 1983), or making an election under section 338 of such Code with respect to the qualified stock purchase described in clause (i)(II), shall not expire before the close of the 60th day after the date of the enactment of the Tax Reform Act of 1986.

"(iii) Statute of limitations. In the case of any such election under section 818(c) or 338 of such Code which would not have been timely made but for clause (ii), the period for assessing any deficiency attributable to such election (or for filing claim for credit or refund of any overpayment attributable to such election) shall not expire before the date 2 years after the date of the enactment of this Act.

"(5) Recapture of reinsurance after December 31, 1983. If (A) insurance or annuity contracts in force on December 31, 1983, are subject to a conventional coinsurance agreement entered into after December 31, 1981, and before January 1, 1984, and (B) such contracts are recaptured by the reinsured in any taxable year beginning after December 31, 1983, then—

"(i) if the amount of the reserves with respect to the recaptured contracts, computed at the date of recapture, that the reinsurer would have taken into account under section 810(c) of the Internal Revenue Code of 1954 (as in effect on the day before the date of the enactment of this Act) exceeds the amount of the reserves with respect to the recaptured contracts, computed at the date of recapture, taken into account by the reinsurer under section 807(c) of the Internal Revenue Code of 1954 (as amended by this subtitle), such excess (but not greater than the amount of such excess if computed on January 1, 1984) shall be taken into account by the reinsurer under the method described in section 807(f)(1)(B)(ii) of the Internal Revenue Code of 1954 (as amended by this subtitle) commencing with the taxable year of recapture, and

"(ii) the amount, if any, taken into account by the reinsurer under clause (i) for purposes of part I of subchapter L of chapter 1 of the Internal Revenue Code of 1954 shall be taken into account by the reinsured under the method described in section 807(f)(1)(B)(i) of the Internal Revenue Code of 1954 (as amended by this subtitle) commencing with the taxable year of recapture.

"The excess described in clause (i) shall be reduced by any portion of such excess to which section 807(f) of the Internal Revenue Code of 1954 applies by reason of paragraph (3) of this subsection. For purposes of this paragraph, the term 'reinsurer' refers to the taxpayer that held reserves with respect to the recaptured contracts as of the end of the taxable year preceding the first taxable year beginning after December 31, 1983, and the term 'reinsured' refers to the taxpayer to which such reserves are ultimately transferred upon termination.

"(c) Election not to have reserves recomputed

"(1) In general. If a qualified life insurance company makes an election under this paragraph—

"(A) subsection (a) shall not apply to such company, and

"(B) as of the beginning of the first taxable year beginning after December 31, 1983, and thereafter, the reserve for any contract issued before the first day of such taxable year by such company shall be the statutory reserve for such contract (within the meaning of section 809(b)(4)(B)(i) of the Internal Revenue Code of 1954).

"(2) Election with respect to contracts issued after 1983 and before 1989.

"(A) In general. If—

"(i) a qualified life insurance company makes an election under paragraph (1), and

"(ii) the tentative LICTI (within the meaning of section 806(c) of such Code) of such company for its first taxable year beginning after December 31, 1983, does not exceed $3,000,000 (determined with regard to this paragraph)

such company may elect under this paragraph to have the reserve for any contract issued on or after the first day of such first taxable year and before January 1, 1989, be equal to the greater of the statutory reserve for such contract (adjusted as provided in subparagraph (B)) or the net surrender value of such contract (as defined in section 807(e)(1) of the Internal Revenue Code of 1954).

"(B) Adjustment to reserves. If this paragraph applies to any contract the opening and closing statutory reserves for such contract shall be adjusted as provided under the principles of section 805(c)(1) of such Code (as in effect for taxable

Insurance companies
Code Sec. 808(f)(6)

years beginning in 1982 and 1983), except that section 805(c)(1)(B)(ii) of such Code (as so in effect) shall be applied by substituting—

"(i) the prevailing State assumed interest rate (within the meaning of section 807(c)(4) of such Code), for

"(ii) the adjusted reserves rate.

"(3) Qualified life insurance company. For purposes of this subsection, the term 'qualified life insurance company' means any life insurance company which, as of December 31, 1983, had assets of less than $100,000,000 (determined in the same manner as under section 806(b)(3) of such Code).

"(4) Special rules for controlled groups. For purposes of applying the dollar limitations of paragraphs (2) and (3), rules similar to the rules of section 806(d) of such Code shall apply.

"(5) Elections. Any election under paragraph (1) or (2)—

"(A) shall be made at such time and in such manner as the Secretary of the Treasury may prescribe, and

"(B) once made, shall be irrevocable."

—P.L. 98-369, Sec. 217(f), provides:

"(f) Treatment of certain assessment life insurance companies.

"(1) Mortality and morbidity tables.—In the case of a contract issued by an assessment life insurance company, the mortality and morbidity tables used in computing statutory reserves for such contract shall be used for purposes of paragraph (2)(C) of section 807(d) of the Internal Revenue Code of 1954 (as amended by this subtitle) if such tables were—

"(A) in use since 1965, and

"(B) developed on the basis of the experience of assessment life insurance companies in the State in which such assessment life insurance company is domiciled.

"(2) Treatment of certain mutual assessment life insurance companies.—In the case of any contract issued by a mutual assessment life insurance company which—

"(A) has been in existence since 1965, and

"(B) operates under chapter 13 or 14 of the Texas Insurance Code, for purposes of part I of subchapter L of chapter 1 of the Internal Revenue Code of 1954, the amount of the life insurance reserves for such contract shall be equal to the amount taken into account with respect to such contract in determining statutory reserves.

"(3) Statutory reserves.—For purposes of this subsection, the term 'statutory reserves' has the meaning given to such term by section 809(b)(4)(B) of such Code."

—P.L. 98-369, Sec. 217(n), [as amended by Sec. 1823 of P.L. 99-514, see above], provides the following special rule:

"(n) Special rule for companies using net level reserve method for noncancellable accident and health insurance contracts. A company shall be treated as meeting the requirements of section 807(d)(3)(A)(iii) of the Internal Revenue Code of 1954, as amended by this Act, with respect to any directly-written noncancellable accident and health insurance contract (whether under existing or new plans of insurance) for any taxable year if—

"(1) such company—

"(A) was using the net level reserve method to compute at least 99 percent of its statutory reserves on such contracts as of December 31, 1982, and

"(B) received more than half its total direct premiums in 1982 from directly-written noncancellable accident and health insurance,

"(2) after December 31, 1983, and through such taxable year, such company has continuously used the net level reserve method for computing at least 99 percent of its tax and statutory reserves on such contracts, and

"(3) for any such contract for which the company does not use the net level reserve method, such company uses the same method for computing tax reserves as such company uses for computing its statutory reserves."

Sec. 808. Policyholder dividends deduction.
(a) Policyholder dividend defined.

For purposes of this part, the term "policyholder dividend" means any dividend or similar distribution to policyholders in their capacity as such.

(b) Certain amounts included.

For purposes of this part, the term "policyholder dividend" includes—

(1) any amount paid or credited (including as an increase in benefits) where the amount is not fixed in the contract but depends on the experience of the company or the discretion of the management,

(2) excess interest,

(3) premium adjustments, and

(4) experience-rated refunds.

(c) Amount of deduction.

The deduction for policyholder dividends for any taxable year shall be an amount equal to the policyholder dividends paid or accrued during the taxable year.

(d) Definitions.

For purposes of this section—

(1) Excess interest. The term "excess interest" means any amount in the nature of interest—

(A) paid or credited to a policyholder in his capacity as such, and

(B) in excess of interest determined at the prevailing State assumed rate for such contract.

(2) Premium adjustment. The term "premium adjustment" means any reduction in the premium under an insurance or annuity contract which (but for the reduction) would have been required to be paid under the contract.

(3) Experience-rated refund. The term "experience-rated refund" means any refund or credit based on the experience of the contract or group involved.

(e) Treatment of policyholder dividends.

For purposes of this part, any policyholder dividend which—

(1) increases the cash surrender value of the contract or other benefits payable under the contract, or

(2) reduces the premium otherwise required to be paid,

shall be treated as paid to the policyholder and returned by the policyholder to the company as a premium.

(f) Coordination of 1984 fresh-start adjustment with acceleration of policyholder dividends deduction through change in business practice.

(1) In general. The amount determined under paragraph (1) of subsection (c) for the year of change shall (before any reduction under paragraph (2) of subsection (c)) be reduced by so much of the accelerated policyholder dividends deduction for such year as does not exceed the 1984 fresh-start adjustment for policyholder dividends (to the extent such adjustment was not previously taken into account under this subsection).

(2) Year of change. For purposes of this subsection, the term "year of change" means the taxable year in which the change in business practices which results in the accelerated policyholder dividends deduction takes effect.

(3) Accelerated policyholder dividends deduction defined. For purposes of this subsection, the term "accelerated policyholder dividends deduction" means the amount which (but for this subsection) would be determined for the taxable year under paragraph (1) of subsection (c) but which would have been determined (under such paragraph) for a later taxable year under the business practices of the taxpayer as in effect at the close of the preceding taxable year.

(4) 1984 fresh-start adjustment for policyholder dividends. For purposes of this subsection, the term "1984 fresh-start adjustment for policyholder dividends" means the amounts held as of December 31, 1983, by the taxpayer as reserves for dividends to policyholders under section 811(b) (as in effect on the day before the date of the enactment [7/18/84] of the Tax Reform Act of 1984) other than for dividends which accrued before January 1, 1984. Such amounts shall be properly reduced to reflect the amount of previously nondeductible policyholder dividends (as determined under section 809(f) as in effect on the day before the date of the enactment [7/18/84] of the Tax Reform Act of 1984).

(5) Separate application with respect to lines of business. This subsection shall be applied separately with respect to each line of business of the taxpayer.

(6) Subsection not to apply to mere change in dividend amount. This subsection shall not apply to a mere change in the amount of policyholder dividends.

(7) Subsection not to apply to policies issued after December 31, 1983.

(A) In general. This subsection shall not apply to any policyholder dividend paid or accrued with respect to a policy issued after December 31, 1983.

(B) Exchanges of substantially similar policies. For purposes of subparagraph (A), any policy issued after December 31, 1983, in exchange for a substantially similar policy issued on or before such date shall be treated as issued before January 1, 1984. A similar rule shall apply in the case of a series of exchanges.

(8) Subsection to apply to policies provided under employee benefit plans. This subsection shall not apply to any policyholder dividend paid or accrued with respect to a group policy issued in connection with a plan to provide welfare benefits to employees (within the meaning of section 419(e)(2)).

In 2004, P.L. 108-218, Sec. 205(b)(3), amended subsec. (c), effective for tax. yrs. begin. after 12/31/2004.

Prior to amendment, subsec. (c) read as follows:

"(c) Amount of deduction.

"(1) In general. Except as limited by paragraph (2), the deduction for policyholder dividends for any taxable year shall be an amount equal to the policyholder dividends paid or accrued during the taxable year.

"(2) Reduction in case of mutual companies. In the case of a mutual life insurance company, the deduction for policyholder dividends for any taxable year shall be reduced by the amount determined under section 809."

In 1986, P.L. 99-514, Sec. 1821(b), amended subpara. (d)(1)(B) . . . Sec. 1821(c), added subsec. (f), effective for tax. yrs. begin. after 12/31/83.

Prior to amendment, subpara. (d)(1)(B) read as follows:

"(B) determined at a rate in excess of the prevailing State assumed interest rate for such contract."

In 1984, P.L. 98-369, Sec. 211(a), added Code Sec. 808 as part of the amendments to part I of Subchapter L, effective for tax. yrs. begin. after 12/31/83.

Sec. 809. Repealed.

In 2004, P.L. 108-218, Sec. 205(a), repealed Code Sec. 809, effective for tax. yrs. begin. after 12/31/2004.

Prior to repeal, Code Sec. 809 read as follows:

"Sec. 809. Reduction in certain deductions of mutual life insurance companies.

"(a) General rule.

"(1) Policyholder dividends. In the case of any mutual life insurance company, the amount of the deduction allowed under section 808 shall be reduced (but not below zero) by the differential earnings amount.

"(2) Reduction in reserve deduction in certain cases. In the case of any mutual life insurance company, if the differential earnings amount exceeds the amount allowable as a deduction under section 808 for the taxable year (determined without regard to this section), such excess shall be taken into account under subsections (a) and (b) of section 807.

"(3) Differential earnings amount. For purposes of this section, the term 'differential earnings amount' means, with respect to any taxable year, an amount equal to the product of—

"(A) the life insurance company's average equity base for the taxable year, multiplied by

"(B) the differential earnings rate for such taxable year.

"(b) Average equity base. For purposes of this section—

"(1) In general. The term 'average equity base' means, with respect to any taxable year, the average of—

"(A) the equity base determined as of the close of the taxable year, and

"(B) the equity base determined as of the close of the preceding taxable year.

"(2) Equity base. The term 'equity base' means an amount determined in the manner prescribed by regulations equal to—

"(A) the surplus and capital,

"(B) adjusted as provided in paragraphs (3), (4), (5), and (6) of this subsection.

"No item shall be taken into account more than once in determining equity base.

"(3) Increase for nonadmitted financial assets.

"(A) In general. The amount of the surplus and capital shall be increased by the amount of the nonadmitted financial assets.

"(B) Nonadmitted financial assets. For purposes of subparagraph (A), the term 'nonadmitted financial asset' means any nonadmitted asset of the company which is—

"(i) a bond,

"(ii) stock,

"(iii) real estate,

"(iv) a mortgage loan on real estate, or

"(v) any other invested asset.

"(4) Increase where statutory reserves exceed tax reserves.

"(A) In general. If—

"(i) the aggregate amount of statutory reserves, exceeds

"(ii) the aggregate amount of tax reserves,

"the amount of the surplus and capital shall be increased by the amount of such excess.

"(B) Definitions. For purposes of this paragraph—

"(i) Statutory reserves. The term 'statutory reserves' means the aggregate amount set forth in the annual statement with respect to items described in section 807(c). Such term shall not include any reserve attributable to a deferred and uncollected premium if the establishment of such reserve is not permitted under section 811(c).

"(ii) Tax reserves. The term 'tax reserves' means the aggregate of the items described in section 807(c) as determined for purposes of section 807.

"(5) Increase by amount of certain other reserves. The amount of the surplus and capital shall be increased by the sum of—

"(A) the amount of any mandatory securities valuation reserve,

"(B) the amount of any deficiency reserve, and

"(C) the amount of any voluntary reserve or similar liability not described in subparagraph (A) or (B).

"(6) Adjustment for next year's policyholder dividends. The amount of the surplus and capital shall be increased by 50 percent of the amount of any provision for policyholder dividends (or other similar liability) payable in the following taxable year.

"(c) Differential earnings rate.

"(1) In general. For purposes of this section, the differential earnings rate for any taxable year is the excess of—

"(A) the imputed earnings rate for the taxable year, over

"(B) the average mutual earnings rate for the second calendar year preceding the calendar year in which the taxable year begins.

"(2) Transitional rule. The differential earnings rate—

"(A) for any taxable year beginning in 1984, or

"(B) for purposes of computing the amount of underpayment under section 6655 (including the application of section 6655(d)(3)) for any taxable year beginning in 1985,

"shall be equal to 7.8 percent.

"(3) Coordination with estimated tax payments. For purposes of applying section 6655 with respect to any installment of estimated tax, the amount of tax shall be determined by using the lesser of—

"(A) the differential earnings rate of the second tax year preceding the taxable year for which the installment is made, or

"(B) the differential earnings rate for the taxable year for which the installment is made.

"(d) Imputed earnings rate.

"(1) In general. For purposes of this section, the imputed earnings rate for any taxable year is—

"(A) 16.5 percent in the case of taxable years beginning in 1984, and

"(B) in the case of taxable years beginning after 1984, an amount which bears the same ratio to 16.5 percent as the current stock earnings rate for the taxable year bears to the base period stock earnings rate.

"(2) Current stock earnings rate. For purposes of this subsection, the term 'current stock earnings rate' means, with respect to any taxable year, the average of the stock earnings rates determined under paragraph (4) for the 3 calendar years preceding the calendar year in which the taxable year begins.

"(3) Base period stock earnings rate. For purposes of this subsection, the base period stock earnings rate is the average of the stock earnings rates determined under paragraph (4) for calendar years 1981, 1982, and 1983.

"(4) Stock earnings rate.

"(A) In general. For purposes of this subsection, the stock earnings rate for any calendar year is the numerical average of the earnings rates of the 50 largest stock companies.

"(B) Earnings rate. For purposes of subparagraph (A), the earnings rate of any stock company is the percentage (determined by the Secretary) which—

"(i) the statement gain or loss from operations for the calendar year of such company, is of

"(ii) such company's average equity base for such year.

"(C) 50 largest stock companies. For purposes of this paragraph, the term '50 largest stock companies' means a group (as determined by the Secretary) of stock life insurance companies which consists of the 50 largest domestic stock life insurance companies which are subject to tax under this part. The Secretary—

"(i) shall, for purposes of determining the base period stock earnings rate, exclude from the group determined under the preceding sentence any company which had a negative equity base at any time during 1981, 1982, or 1983,

"(ii) shall exclude from such group for any calendar year any company which has a negative equity base, and

"(iii) may by regulations exclude any other company which otherwise would have been included in such group if the inclusion of the excluded company or companies would, by reason of the small equity base of such company, seriously distort the stock earnings rate.

"The aggregate number of companies excluded by the Secretary under clause (iii) shall not exceed the excess of 2 over the number of companies excluded under clause (ii).

"(D) Treatment of affiliated groups. For purposes of this paragraph, all stock life insurance companies which are members of the same affiliated group shall be treated as one stock life insurance company.

"(e) Average mutual earnings rate. For purposes of this section, the average mutual earnings rate for any calendar year is the percentage (determined by the Secretary) which—

"(1) the aggregate statement gain or loss from operations for such year of domestic mutual life insurance companies, is of

"(2) their aggregate average equity bases for such year.

"(f) Recomputation in subsequent year.

"(1) Inclusion in income where recomputed amount greater. In the case of any mutual life insurance company, if—

"(A) the recomputed differential earnings amount for any taxable year, exceeds

"(B) the differential earnings amount determined under this section for such taxable year,

"such excess shall be included in life insurance gross income for the succeeding taxable year.

"(2) Deduction where recomputed amount smaller. In the case of any mutual life insurance company, if—

"(A) the differential earnings amount determined under this section for any taxable year, exceeds

"(B) the recomputed differential earnings amount for such taxable year,

"such excess shall be allowed as a life insurance deduction for the succeeding taxable year.

"(3) Recomputed differential earnings amount. For purposes of this subsection, the term 'recomputed differential earnings amount' means, with respect to any taxable year, the amount which would be the differential earnings amount for such taxable year if the average mutual earnings rate taken into account under subsection (c)(1)(B) were the average mutual earnings rate for the calendar year in which the taxable year begins.

"(4) Special rule where company ceases to be mutual life insurance company. Except as provided in section 381(c)(22), if—

"(A) a life insurance company is a mutual life insurance company for any taxable year, but

"(B) such life insurance company is not a mutual life insurance company for the succeeding taxable year,

"any adjustment under paragraph (1) or (2) by reason of the recomputed differential earnings amount for the first of such taxable years shall be taken into account for the first of such taxable years.

"(5) Subsection not to apply for purposes of estimated tax. Section 6655 shall be applied to any taxable year without regard to any adjustments under this subsection for such year.

"(g) Definitions and special rules. For purposes of this section—

"(1) Statement gain or loss from operations. The term 'statement gain or loss from operations' means the net gain or loss from operations required to be set forth in the annual statement, determined without regard to Federal income taxes, and—

"(A) determined by substituting for the amount shown for policyholder dividends the amount of deduction for policyholder dividends determined under section 808 (without regard to section 808(c)(2)),

"(B) determined on the basis of the tax reserves rather than statutory reserves, and

"(C) properly adjusted for realized capital gains and losses and other relevant items.

"(2) Other terms. Except as otherwise provided in this section, the terms used in this section shall have the same respective meanings as when used in the annual statement.

"(3) Determinations based on amount set forth in annual statement. Except as otherwise provided in this section or in regulations, all determinations under this section shall be made on the basis of the amounts required to be set forth on the annual statement.

"(4) Annual statement. The term 'annual statement' means the annual statement for life insurance companies approved by the National Association of Insurance Commissioners.

"(5) Reduction in equity base for portion of equity allocable to life insurance business in noncontiguous Western Hemisphere countries. The equity base of any mutual life insurance company shall be reduced by an amount equal to the portion of the equity base attributable to the life insurance business multiplied by a fraction—

"(A) the numerator of which is the portion of the tax reserves which is allocable to life insurance contracts issued on the life of residents of countries in the Western Hemisphere which are not contiguous to the United States, and

"(B) the denominator of which is the amount of the tax reserves allocable to life insurance contracts.

"The preceding sentence shall not apply unless the fraction determined under the preceding sentence exceeds ½₀.

"(6) Special rule for certain contracts issued before January 1, 1985. In determining the amount of tax reserves of a subsidiary of a mutual insurance company for purposes of subsection (b)(4), section 811(d) shall not apply with respect to any life insurance contract issued before January 1, 1985, under a plan of life insurance in existence on July 1, 1983.

"(h) Treatment of stock companies owned by mutual life insurance companies.

"(1) Treatment as mutual life insurance companies for purposes of determining stock earnings rates and mutual earnings rates. Solely for purposes of subsections (d) and (e), a stock life insurance company shall be treated as a mutual life insurance company if stock possessing—

"(A) at least 80 percent of the total combined voting power of all classes of stock of such stock life insurance company entitled to vote, or

"(B) at least 80 percent of the total value of shares of all classes of stock of such stock life insurance company,

"is owned at any time during the calendar year directly (or through the application of section 318) by one or more mutual life insurance companies.

"(2) Treatment of affiliated group which includes mutual parent and stock subsidiary. In the case of an affiliated group of corporations which includes a common parent which is a mutual life insurance company and one or more stock life insurance companies, for purposes of determining the average equity base of such common parent (and the statement gain or loss from operations)—

"(A) stock in such stock life insurance companies held by such common parent (and dividends on such stock) shall not be taken into account, and

"(B) such common parent and such stock life insurance companies shall be treated as though they were one mutual life insurance company.

"(3) Adjustment where stock company not member of affiliated group. In the case of any stock life insurance company which is described in paragraph (1) but is not a member of an affiliated group described in paragraph (2), under regulations, proper adjustments shall be made in the average equity bases (and statement gains or losses from operations) of mutual life insurance companies owning stock in such company as may be necessary or appropriate to carry out the purposes of this section.

"(i) Transitional rule for certain high surplus mutual life insurance companies.

"(1) In general. For purposes of subsection (a)(3), the average equity base of a high surplus mutual life insurance company for any taxable year shall not include the applicable percentage of the excess equity base of such company for such taxable year.

"(2) Definitions. For purposes of this subsection—

"(A) Excess equity base. The term 'excess equity base' means the excess of—

"(i) the average equity base of the company for the taxable year, over

"(ii) the amount which would be its average equity base if its equity percentage equaled the following percentage:

For taxable years beginning in:	The percentage is:
1984	14.5
1985 or 1986	14
1987 or 1988	13.5

"In no case shall the excess equity base for any taxable year be greater than the excess equity base for the company's first taxable year beginning in 1984.

"(B) Applicable percentage. The term 'applicable percentage' means the percentage determined in accordance with the following table:

For taxable years beginning in:	The applicable percentage is:
1984	100
1985	80
1986	60
1987	40
1988	20
1989 or thereafter	0.

"(C) High surplus mutual life insurance company. The term 'high surplus mutual life insurance company' means any mutual life insurance company if, for the taxable year beginning in 1984, its equity percentage exceeded 14.5 percent.

"(D) Equity percentage. The term 'equity percentage' means, with respect to any mutual life insurance company, the percentage which—

"(i) the average equity base of such company (determined under this section without regard to this subsection) for a taxable year bears to

"(ii) the average of—

"(I) the assets of such company as of the close of the preceding taxable year, and

"(II) the assets of such company as of the close of the taxable year.

"For purposes of the preceding sentence, the assets of a company shall include all assets taken into account under this section in determining its equity base (after applying the principles of subsection (h)).

"(j) Differential earnings rate treated as zero for certain years. Notwithstanding subsection (c) or (f), the differential earnings rate shall be treated as zero for purposes of computing both the differential earnings amount and the recomputed differential earnings amount for a mutual life insurance company's taxable years beginning in 2001, 2002, or 2003."

In 2002, P.L. 107-147, Sec. 611(a), added subsec. (j), effective for tax. yrs. begin. after 12/31/2000.

In 1988, P.L. 100-647, Sec. 1018(u)(47), substituted "The Secretary" for "the Secretary" in subpara. (d)(4)(C), effective for tax. yrs. begin. after 12/31/83.

In 1986, P.L. 99-514, Sec. 1821(d), added the sentence at the end of para. (b)(2) ... Sec. 1821(e)(1), amended the last sentence of subpara. (d)(4)(C) ... Sec. 1821(e)(2)(A), substituted "largest domestic stock life insurance companies" for "largest stock life insurance companies" in subpara. (d)(4)(C) ... Sec. 1821(e)(2)(B), substituted "domestic mutual life insurance companies" for "mutual life insurance companies" in para. (e)(1) ... Sec. 1821(f), amended as much of para. (g)(1) as preceded subpara. (g)(1)(B) ... Sec. 1821(g), added para. (c)(3) ... Sec. 1821(h), added para. (f)(5) ... Sec. 1821(r), substituted "subsection (c)(1)(B)" for "subsection (c)(2)" in para. (f)(3), effective for tax. yrs. begin. after 12/31/83. Sec. 1821(q) of this Act provides:

"(q) *Special rule for application of high surplus mutual rules*

"In the case of any mutual life insurance company—

"(1) which was incorporated on February 23, 1888, and

"(2) which acquired a stock subsidiary during 1982,

the amount of such company's excess equity base for purposes of section 809(i) of such Code shall, notwithstanding the last sentence of section 809(i)(2)(D), equal $175,000,000."

Prior to amendment, the last sentence of subpara. (d)(4)(C) read as follows:

"The Secretary may by regulations provide for exclusion from the group determined under the preceding sentence of any stock life insurance company if (i) the equity of such company is not great enough for such company to be 1 of the 50 largest stock life insurance companies if the determination were made on the basis of equity, and (ii) by reason of the small equity base of such company, it has an earnings rate which would seriously distort the stock earnings rate."

Prior to amendment, so much of para. (g)(1) as preceded subpara. (g)(1)(B) read as follows:

"(1) Statement gain or loss from operations. The term 'statement gain or loss from operations' means the net gain or loss from operations required to be set forth in the annual statement—

"(A) determined with regard to policyholder dividends (as defined in section 808) but without regard to Federal income taxes,"

In 1984, P.L. 98-369, Sec. 211(a), added Code Sec. 809 as part of the amendments to part I of Subchapter L, effective for tax. yrs. begin. after 12/31/83. For transitional rules, see Sec. 216(b)(3)(E) of this Act, reproduced in note following Code Sec. 807.

—P.L. 98-369, Sec. 217(j), provides:

"(j) Reduction in equity base for mutual successor of fraternal benefit society.— In the case of any mutual life insurance company which—

"(1) is the successor to a fraternal benefit society, and

"(2) which assumed the surplus of such fraternal benefit society in 1950 or in March of 1961, for purposes of section 809 of the Internal Revenue Code of 1954 (as amended by this subtitle), the equity base of such mutual life insurance company shall be reduced by the amount of the surplus so assumed plus earnings thereon, (i) for taxable years before 1984, at a 7 percent interest rate, and (ii) for taxable years 1984 and following, at the average mutual earnings rate for such year."

—P.L. 98-369, Sec. 219, provides:

"SEC. 219. CLARIFICATION OF AUTHORITY TO REQUIRE CERTAIN INFORMATION.

"Nothing in any provision of law shall be construed to prevent the Secretary of the Treasury or his delegate from requiring (from time to time) life insurance companies to provide such data with respect to taxable years beginning before January 1, 1984, as may be necessary to carry out the provisions of section 809 of such Code (as added by this title)."

In 1984, P.L. 98-369, Sec. 211(a), amended Code Sec. 809 as part of the amendments to Part I of Subchapter L, effective for tax. yrs. begin. after 12/31/83. For transitional rules, see Secs. 216(b)(3)(B), (C) and Sec. 216(b)(4) of this Act reproduced in note following Code Sec. 807.

Prior to amendment, Code Sec. 809 read as follows:

"SEC. 809. IN GENERAL.

"(a) Exclusion of share of investment yield set aside for policyholders.

"(1) Amount. The share of each and every item of investment yield (including tax-exempt interest, and dividends received) of any life insurance company set aside for policyholders shall not be included in gain or loss from operations. For purposes of the preceding sentence, the share of any item set aside for policyholders shall be that percentage obtained by dividing the required interest by the investment yield; except that if the required interest exceeds the investment yield, then the share of any item set aside for policyholders shall be 100 percent.

"(2) Required interest. For purposes of this part, the required interest for any taxable year is the sum of the amount of qualified guaranteed interest (within the meaning of section 805(f)(1)) and the products obtained by multiplying—

"(A) each rate of interest required, or assumed by the taxpayer, in calculating the reserves described in section 810(c), by

"(B) the means of the amount of such reserves computed at that rate at the beginning and end of the taxable year.

For purposes of subparagraphs (A) and (B), reserves on qualified contracts (within the meaning of section 805(f)(2)) shall not be taken into account.

"(b) Gain and loss from operations

"(1) Gain from operations defined. For purposes of this part, the term 'gain from operations' means the amount by which the sum of the following exceeds the deductions provided by subsection (d):

"(A) the life insurance company's share of each and every item of investment yield (including tax-exempt interest, and dividends received);

"(B) the amount (if any) of the net capital gain; and

"(C) the sum of the items referred to in subsection (c).

"(2) Loss from operations defined. For purposes of this part, the term 'loss from operations' means the amount by which the sum of the deductions provided by subsection (d) exceeds the sum of—

"(A) the life insurance company's share of each and every item of investment yield (including tax-exempt interest, and dividends received);

"(B) the amount (if any) of the net capital gain; and

"(C) the sum of the items referred to in subsection (c).

"(3) Life insurance company's share. For purposes of this subpart, the life insurance company's share of any item shall be that percentage which, when added to the percentage obtained under the second sentence of subsection (a)(1), equals 100 percent.

"(c) Gross amount.

"For purposes of subsections (b)(1) and (2), the following items shall be taken into account:

"(1) Premiums. The gross amount of premiums and other consideration, including—

"(A) advance premiums,

"(B) deposits,

"(C) fees,

"(D) assessments,

"(E) consideration in respect of assuming liabilities under contracts not issued by the taxpayer, and

"(F) the amount of dividends to policyholders reimbursed to the taxpayer by a reinsurer in respect of reinsured policies,

on insurance and annuity contracts (including contracts supplementary thereto); less return premiums, and premiums and other consideration arising out of reinsurance ceded. Except in the case of amounts of premiums or other consideration returned to another life insurance company in respect of reinsurance ceded, amounts returned where the amount is not fixed in the contract but depends on the experience of the company or the discretion of the management shall not be included in return premiums.

"(2) Decreases in certain reserves. Each net decrease in reserves which is required by section 810 or 811(b)(2) to be taken into account for purposes of this paragraph.

"(3) Other amounts. All amounts, not included in computing investment yield and not includible under paragraph (1) or (2), which under this subtitle are includible in gross income.

Except as included in computing investment yield, there shall be excluded any gain from the sale or exchange of a capital asset, and any gain considered as gain from the sale or exchange of a capital asset.

"(d) Deductions.

"For purposes of subsections (b)(1) and (2), there shall be allowed the following deductions:

"(1) Death benefits, etc. All claims and benefits accrued, and all losses incurred (whether or not ascertained), during the taxable year on insurance and annuity contracts (including contracts supplementary thereto).

"(2) Increases in certain reserves. The net increase in reserves which is required by section 810 to be taken into account for purposes of this paragraph.

"(3) Dividends to policyholders. The deduction for dividends to policyholders (determined under section 811(b)), other than the deduction provided under paragraph (12).

"(4) Operations loss deduction. The operations loss deduction (determined under section 812).

"(5) Certain nonparticipating contracts. An amount equal to 10 percent of the increase for the taxable year in the reserves for nonparticipating contracts or (if greater) an amount equal to 3 percent of the premiums for the taxable year (excluding that portion of the premiums which is allocable to annuity features) attributable to nonparticipating contracts (other than group contracts) which are issued or renewed for periods of 5 years or more. For purposes of this paragraph, the term 'reserves for nonparticipating contracts' means such part of the life insurance reserves (excluding that portion of the reserves which is allocable to annuity features) as relates to nonparticipating contracts (other than group contracts). For purposes of this paragraph and paragraph (6), the term 'premiums' means the net amount of the premiums and other consideration taken into account under subsection (c)(1). For purposes of this paragraph, the period for which any contract is issued or renewed includes the period for which such contract is guaranteed renewable.

"(6) Certain accident and health insurance and group life insurance. An amount equal to 2 percent of the premiums for the taxable year attributable to accident and health insurance contracts (other than those to which paragraph (5) applies) and group life insurance contracts. The deduction under this paragraph for the taxable year and all preceding taxable years shall not exceed an amount equal to 50 percent of the premiums for the taxable year attributable to such contracts.

"(7) Assumption by another person of liabilities under insurance, etc., contracts. The consideration (other than consideration arising out of reinsurance ceded) in respect of the assumption by another person of liabilities under insurance and annuity contracts (including contracts supplementary thereto).

"(8) Tax-exempt interest, dividends, etc.

"(A) Life insurance company's share. Each of the following items:

"(i) the life insurance company's share of interest which under section 103 is excluded from gross income, and

"(ii) the deductions for dividends received provided by sections 243, 244, and 245 (as modified by subparagraph (B)) computed with respect to the life insurance company's share of the dividends received.

"(B) Application of section 246(b). In applying section 246(b) (relating to limitation on aggregate amount of deductions for dividends received) for purposes of subparagraph (A)(ii), the limit on the aggregate amount of the deductions allowed by sections 243(a)(1), 244(a), and 245 shall be 85 percent of the gain from operations computed without regard to—

"(i) the deductions provided by paragraphs (3), (5), and (6) of this subsection,

"(ii) the operations loss deduction provided by section 812, and

"(iii) the deductions allowed by sections 243(a)(1), 244(a), and 245,

but such limit shall not apply for any taxable year for which there is a loss from operations.

"(9) Investment expenses, etc. Investment expenses to the extent not allowed as a deduction under section 804(c)(1) in computing investment yield, and the amount (if any) by which the sum of the deductions allowable under section 804(c) exceeds the gross investment income.

"(10) Small business deduction. A small business deduction in an amount equal to the amount determined under section 804(a)(2).

Insurance companies — Code Sec. 809

"(11) Other deductions. Subject to the modifications provided by subsection (e), all other deductions allowed under this subtitle for purposes of computing taxable income to the extent not allowed as deductions in computing investment yield.

"(12) Dividends reimbursed. The deduction for the amount of dividends to policyholders reimbursed by the taxpayer to another insurance company in respect of policies the taxpayer has reinsured (determined under section 811(c)).

Except as provided in paragraph (3), no amount shall be allowed as a deduction under this subsection in respect of dividends to policyholders.

"(e) Modifications.

"The modifications referred to in subsection (d)(11) are as follows:

"(1) Interest. In applying section 163 (relating to deduction for interest), no deduction shall be allowed for qualified guaranteed interest (within the meaning of section 805(f)(1)) or interest in respect of items described in section 810(c).

"(2) Bad debts. Section 166(c) (relating to reserve for bad debts) shall not apply.

"(3) Charitable, etc., contributions and gifts. In applying section 170—

"(A) the limit on the total deductions under such section provided by section 170(b)(2) shall be 10 percent of the gain from operations computed without regard to—

"(i) the deduction provided by section 170,

"(ii) the deductions provided by paragraphs (3), (5), (6), and (8) of subsection (d), and

"(iii) any operations loss carryback to the taxable year under section 812; and

"(B) under regulations prescribed by the Secretary, a rule similar to the rule contained in section 170(d)(2)(B) shall be applied.

"(4) Amortizable bond premium. Section 171 shall not apply.

"(5) Net operating loss deduction. Except as provided by section 844, the deduction for net operating losses provided in section 172 shall not be allowed.

"(6) Dividends received. The deductions for dividends received provided by sections 243, 244, and 245 shall not be allowed.

"(f) Limitation on certain deductions.

"(1) In general. The amount of the deductions under paragraphs (3), (5), and (6) of subsection (d) shall not exceed $250,000 plus the amount (if any) by which—

"(A) the gain from operations for the taxable year, computed without regard to such deductions, exceeds

"(B) the taxable investment income for the taxable year.

"(2) Application of limitation. The limitation provided by paragraph (1) shall apply first to the amount of the deduction under subsection (d)(3), then to the amount of the deduction under subsection (d)(6), and finally to the amount of the deduction under subsection (d)(5)."

In 1984, P.L. 98-369, Sec. 217(g), provides:

"(g) Treatment of reinsurance agreements required by NAIC.

"Effective for taxable years beginning after December 31, 1981, and before January 1, 1984, subsections (c)(1)(F) and (d)(12) of section 809 of the Internal Revenue Code of 1954 (as in effect on 7/17/84) shall not apply to dividends to policyholders reimbursed to the taxpayer by a reinsurer in respect of accident and health policies reinsured under a reinsurance agreement entered into before June 30, 1955, pursuant to the direction of the National Association of Insurance Commissioners and approved by the State insurance commissioner of the taxpayer's State of domicile. For purposes of subchapter L of chapter 1 of such Code (as in effect on the date before 7/18/84) any such dividends shall be treated as dividends of the reinsurer and not the taxpayer."

In 1983, P.L. 97-448, Sec. 102(m)(1), substituted "10 percent" for "5 percent" in para. (e)(3), effective for tax. yrs. begin. after 12/31/81.

In 1982, P.L. 97-248, Sec. 255(b)(2), amended the first sentence of para. (c)(1) . . . Sec. 255(b)(3), added ", other than the deduction provided under paragraph (12)" before the period at the end of para. (d)(3) . . . Sec. 255(b)(4), added para. (d)(12), effective for tax. yrs. begin. after 12/31/81. Sec. 255(c)(2) of this Act provides:

"(2) Rules applicable to taxable years beginning before January 1, 1982.

"(A) In general. In the case of any taxable year beginning before January 1, 1982—

"(i) any determination as to whether any contract met the requirements of subsection (b) of section 820 of the Internal Revenue Code of 1954 (as in effect before its repeal by this section) shall be made solely by reference to the terms of the contract, and

"(ii) the treatment of such contract under subsection (c) of such section 820 shall be made in accordance with the regulations under such section which were in effect on December 31, 1981.

"(B) Paragraph not to apply if fraud involved. The provisions of subparagraph (A) shall not apply with respect to any deficiency which the Secretary of the Treasury or his delegate establishes was due to fraud with intent to evade tax."

Prior to amendment, the first sentence of para. (c)(1) read as follows:

"The gross amount of premiums and other consideration (including advance premiums, deposits, fees, assessments, and consideration in respect of assuming liabilities under contracts not issued by the taxpayer) on insurance and annuity contracts (including contracts supplementary thereto); less return premiums, and premiums and other consideration arising out of reinsurance ceded."

—P.L. 97-248, Sec. 259(a), amended subsec. (f), effective for tax. yrs. begin. after 12/31/81 and before 1/1/84. Secs. 263(b)(1) and (3) of this Act provide as follows:

"(b) Special rules for certain transactions in taxable years beginning before January 1, 1982.

"(1) Certain interest and premiums.

"(A) In general. In the case of any taxable year beginning before January 1, 1982, if a taxpayer, on his return of tax for such taxable year, treated—

"(i) any amount described in subparagraph (B) as an amount which was not a dividend to policyholders (within the meaning of section 811 of the Internal Revenue Code of 1954), or

"(ii) any amount described in subparagraph (C) as not described in section 809(c)(1),

then such amounts shall be so treated for purposes of the Internal Revenue Code of 1954.

"(B) Certain interest. An amount is described in this subparagraph if such amount is in the nature of interest accrued for the taxable year on an insurance or annuity contract pursuant to—

"(i) an interest rate guaranteed or fixed before the period of payment of such amount begins, or

"(ii) any other method (fixed before such period begins) the terms of which during the period are beyond the control and are independent of the experience of the company, whether or not the interest rate or other method was guaranteed or fixed for any specified period of time.

"(C) Amounts not treated as premiums. An amount is described in this subparagraph if such amount represents the difference between—

"(i) the amount of premiums received or mortality charges made under rates fixed in advance of the premium or mortality charge due date, and

"(ii) the maximum premium or mortality charge which could be charged under the terms of the insurance or annuity contract.

"(D) No inference. The provisions of this paragraph shall constitute no inference with respect to the treatment of any item in taxable years beginning after December 31, 1981.

* * *

"(3) Taxable years where period of limitation has run. This subsection shall not apply to any taxable year with respect to which the statute of limitations for filing a claim for credit or refund has expired under any provision of law or by operation of law."

Prior to amendment, subsec. (f) read as follows:

"(f) Limitation on certain deductions.

"(1) In general. The amount of the deductions under paragraphs (3), (5), and (6) of subsection (d) shall not exceed $250,000 plus the amount (if any) by which—

"(A) the gain from operations for the taxable year, computed without regard to such deductions, exceeds

"(B) the taxable investment income for the taxable year.

"(2) Application of limitation. The limitation provided by paragraph (1) shall apply first to the amount of the deduction under subsection (d)(3), then to the amount of the deduction under subsection (d)(6), and finally to the amount of the deduction under subsection (d)(5)."

Subsec. (f), effective for tax. yrs. begin. after 12/31/81 and before 1/1/84, read as follows:

"(f) Limitation on certain deductions.

"(1) In general. The amount of the deductions under paragraphs (3), (5), and (6) of subsection (d) shall not exceed the greater of—

"(A) $1,000,000, plus the amount (if any) by which—

"(i) the gain from operations for the taxable year (computed without regard to such deductions), exceeds

"(ii) the taxable investment income for the taxable year, or

"(B) if the taxpayer elects for any taxable year, the amount determined under paragraph (2).

"(2) Alternative limitation. The amount determined under this paragraph for any taxable year shall be equal to the sum of—

"(A) that portion of the deduction under subsection (d)(3) which is allocable to any contract described in section 805(d), and

"(B) an amount equal to the sum of—

"(i) so much of the base amount as does not exceed $1,000,000, plus

"(ii) in the case of—

"(I) a mutual life insurance company, 77.5 percent of the base amount, or

"(II) a stock life insurance company, 85 percent of the base amount.

"(3) Reduction in $1,000,000 amount for large insurers. If the sum of the deductions under paragraphs (3), (5), and (6) of subsection (d) exceeds $4,000,000, then each of the $1,000,000 amounts in paragraphs (1) and (2) shall be reduced (but not below zero) by the amount which bears the same ratio to $1,000,000 as—

"(A) the amount of such excess bears to,

"(B) $4,000,000.

"(4) Base amount. For purposes of paragraph (2)(B), the term 'base amount' means the excess of—

"(A) the amount of the deductions under paragraphs (3) and (5) of subsection (d) for the taxable year, over

"(B) the amount determined under paragraph (2)(A) for such taxable year.

"(5) Application of limitation. The limitation provided by paragraph (1) shall apply first to the amount of the deduction under subsection (d)(3), then to the amount of the deduction under subsection (d)(5), and finally to the amount of the deduction under subsection (d)(6)."

—P.L. 97-248, Sec. 264(c)(2), added "the amount of qualified guaranteed interest (within the meaning of section 805(f)(1)) and" after "the sum of" in para. (a)(2), and added "For purposes of subparagraphs (A) and (B), reserves on qualified contracts (within the meaning of section 805(f)(2)) shall not be taken into account." at the end of para. (a)(2). . . . Sec. 264(c)(3), added "qualified guaranteed interest (within the meaning of section 805(f)(1)) or" after "allowed for" in para. (e)(1), effective for tax. yrs. begin. after 12/31/81. Sec. 264(d)(2) of this Act provides:

"(2) Guarantees for less than 12 months.

"(A) Moneys held before August 14, 1982. The requirements of subparagraph (A)(ii) or (B)(ii)(I) of section 805(f)(1) of the Internal Revenue Code of 1954 (as

2,397

added by subsection (b)) shall not apply to any moneys held under any contract on August 13, 1982 (and any interest on such moneys after such date).

"(B) Contracts entered into after August 13, 1982, and before January 1, 1983. A contract entered into after August 13, 1982, and before January 1, 1983, shall be treated as meeting the requirements of subparagraph (A)(ii) or (B)(ii)(I) of such Code if it meets such requirements on the first contract anniversary date."

In 1976, P.L. 94-455, Sec. 1508, added a sentence to the end of para. (d)(5), effective for tax. yrs. begin. after 12/31/57.

—P.L. 94-455, Sec. 1901(a)(98)(A), deleted para. (b)(4) ... Sec. 1901(a)(98)(B)(i), deleted para. (d)(11) and redesignated para. (d)(12) as (d)(11) ... Sec. 1901(a)(98)(B)(ii), substituted "subsection (d)(11)" for "subsection (d)(12)" in subsec. (e) ... Sec. 1901(a)(98)(C), deleted subsec. (g), effective for tax. yrs. begin. after 12/31/76.

Prior to deletion, para. (b)(4) read as follows:

"(4) Exception. If it is established in any case that the application of the definition of gain from operations contained in paragraph (1) results in the imposition of tax on—

"(A) any interest which under section 103 is excluded from gross income,

"(B) any amount of interest which under section 242 (as modified by section 804(a)(3)) is allowable as a deduction, or

"(C) any amount of dividends received which under sections 243, 244, and 245 (as modified by subsection (d)(8)(B)) is allowable as a deduction,

adjustment shall be made to the extent necessary to prevent such imposition."

Prior to deletion, para. (d)(11) read as follows:

"(11) Certain mutualization distributions. The amount of distributions to shareholders made in 1958, 1959, 1960, 1961, and 1962 in acquisition of stock pursuant to a plan of mutualization adopted before January 1, 1958."

Prior to deletion, subsec. (g) read as follows:

"(g) Limitations on deduction for certain mutualization distributions.

"(1) Deduction not to reduce taxable investment income. The amount of the deduction under subsection (d)(11) shall not exceed the amount (if any) by which—

"(A) the gain from operations for the taxable year, computed without regard to such deduction (but after the application of subsection (f)), exceeds

"(B) the taxable investment income for the taxable year.

"(2) Deduction not to reduce tax below 1957 law. The deduction under subsection (d)(11) for the taxable year shall be allowed only to the extent that such deduction (after the application of all other deductions provided by subsection (d)) does not reduce the amount of the tax imposed by section 802(a)(1) for such taxable year below the amount of tax which would have been imposed by section 802(a) as in effect for 1957, if this part, as in effect for 1957, applied for such taxable year.

"(3) Application of section 815. That portion of any distribution with respect to which a deduction is allowed under subsection (d)(11) shall not be treated as a distribution to shareholders for purposes of section 815; except that in the case of any distribution made in 1959, 1960, 1961, or 1962, such portion shall be treated as a distribution with respect to which a reduction is required under section 815(e)(2)(B)."

—P.L. 94-455, Sec. 1901(b)(1)(J)(iv), substituted "section 804(a)(3)" for "section 804(a)(4)" in para. (d)(10) ... Sec. 1901(b)(1)(L)(i), deleted clause (d)(8)(A)(ii), added "and" at the end of clause (d)(8)(A)(i), and redesignated clause (d)(8)(A)(iii) as clause (d)(8)(A)(ii) ... Sec. 1901(b)(1)(L)(ii), substituted "subparagraph (A)(ii)" for "subparagraph (A)(iii)" in subpara. (d)(8)(B) ... Sec. 1901(b)(1)(M), deleted "partially tax-exempt interest," in para. (a)(1), subparas. (b)(1)(A), and (b)(2)(A) ... Sec. 1901(b)(1)(N), deleted para. (e)(6) and redesignated para. (e)(7) as para. (e)(6) ... Sec. 1901(b)(33)(G), substituted "of the net capital gain" for "by which the net long-term capital gain exceeds the net short-term capital loss" in subparas. (b)(1)(B) and (b)(2)(B), effective for tax. yrs. begin. after 12/31/76.

Prior to deletion, clause (d)(8)(A)(ii) read as follows:

"(ii) the deduction for partially tax-exempt interest provided by section 242 (as modified by section 804(a)(3)) computed with respect to the life insurance company's share of such interest, and"

Prior to deletion, para. (e)(6) read as follows:

"(6) Partially tax-exempt interest. The deduction for partially tax-exempt interest provided by section 242 shall not be allowed."

—P.L. 94-455, Sec. 1906(b)(13)(A), substituted "Secretary" for "Secretary or his delegate" in subpara. (e)(3)(B), effective for tax. yrs. begin. after 12/31/76.

In 1969, P.L. 91-172, Sec. 201(a)(2)(C), deleted "the first sentence of" in subpara. (e)(3)(A) and substituted "170(d)(2)(B)" for "section 170(b)(3)" in subpara. (e)(3)(B), effective for tax. yrs. begin. after 12/31/69.

—P.L. 91-172, Sec. 907(c)(2)(B), substituted "Except as provided by section 844, the" for "The" in para. (e)(5), effective for losses incurred in tax. yrs. begin. after 12/31/62, but shall not affect any tax liability for any tax. yrs. begin. before 1/1/67.

In 1964, P.L. 88-272, Sec. 214(b)(4), substituted "243(a)(1), 244(a)" for "243(a), 244" wherever appearing in subsec. (d)(8)(B), effective for dividends received in tax. yrs. end. after 12/31/63.

—P.L. 88-272, Sec. 228(a)(1), added the year 1962 in para. (d)(11) ... Sec. 228(a)(2), added the year 1962 in para. (g)(3), effective for tax. yrs. begin. after 12/31/61.

In 1962, P.L. 87-858, Sec. 3(b)(3), deleted "and" at the end of subparas. (b)(1)(A) and (b)(2)(A), added subparas. (b)(1)(B) and (b)(2)(B) and redesignated former subparas. (b)(1)(B) and (b)(2)(B) as (b)(1)(C) and (b)(2)(C), respectively ... Sec. 3(c), amended para. (f)(2), effective for tax. yrs. begin. after 12/31/61.

Prior to amendment, para. (f)(2) read as follows:

"(2) Application of limitation. The limitation provided by paragraph (1) shall apply first to the amount of the deduction under subsection (d)(6), then to the amount of the deduction under subsection (d)(5), and finally to the amount of the deduction under subsection (d)(3)."

—P.L. 87-790, Sec. 3(a)(1), substituted "accident and health insurance contracts (other than those to which paragraph (5) applies) and group life insurance contracts" for "group life insurance contracts and group accident and health insurance contracts" in para. (d)(6) ... Sec. 3(a)(2), amended the heading of para. (d)(6), effective for tax. yrs. begin. after 12/31/62.

Prior to amendment, the heading of para. (d)(6) read as follows:

"(6) Group life, accident, and health insurance."

In 1961, P.L. 87-59, Sec. 2(a), substituted "in 1958, 1959, 1960, and 1961" for "in 1958 and 1959" in para. (d)(11) ... Sec. 2(b), substituted "in 1959, 1960, or 1961" for "in 1959" in para. (g)(3), effective for tax. yrs. begin. after 12/31/59.

Sec. 810. Operations loss deduction.
(a) Deduction allowed.

There shall be allowed as a deduction for the taxable year an amount equal to the aggregate of—

(1) the operations loss carryovers to such year, plus

(2) the operations loss carrybacks to such year.

For purposes of this part, the term "operations loss deduction" means the deduction allowed by this subsection.

(b) Operations loss carrybacks and carryovers.

(1) **Years to which loss may be carried.** The loss from operations for any taxable year (hereinafter in this section referred to as the "loss year") shall be—

(A) an operations loss carryback to each of the 3 taxable years preceding the loss year,

(B) an operations loss carryover to each of the 15 taxable years following the loss year, and

(C) if the life insurance company is a new company for the loss year, an operations loss carryover to each of the 3 taxable years following the 15 taxable years described in subparagraph (B).

(2) **Amount of carrybacks and carryovers.** The entire amount of the loss from operations for any loss year shall be carried to the earliest of the taxable years to which (by reason of paragraph (1)) such loss may be carried. The portion of such loss which shall be carried to each of the other taxable years shall be the excess (if any) of the amount of such loss over the sum of the offsets (as defined in subsection (d)) for each of the prior taxable years to which such loss may be carried.

(3) **Election for operations loss carrybacks.** In the case of a loss from operations for any taxable year, the taxpayer may elect to relinquish the entire carryback period for such loss. Such election shall be made by the due date (including extensions of time) for filing the return for the taxable year of the loss from operations for which the election is to be in effect, and, once made for any taxable year, such election shall be irrevocable for that taxable year.

(4) **Carryback for 2008 or 2009 losses.**

(A) In general. In the case of an applicable loss from operations with respect to which the taxpayer has elected the application of this paragraph, paragraph (1)(A) shall be applied by substituting any whole number elected by the taxpayer which is more than 3 and less than 6 for "3".

(B) Applicable loss from operations. For purposes of this paragraph, the term "applicable loss from operations" means the taxpayer's loss from operations for a taxable year ending after December 31, 2007, and beginning before January 1, 2010.

(C) Election.

(i) In general. Any election under this paragraph may be made only with respect to 1 taxable year.

(ii) Procedure. Any election under this paragraph shall be made in such manner as may be prescribed by the Secretary, and shall be made by the due date (including extension of time) for filing the return for

Insurance companies   Code Sec. 811(b)(1)

the taxpayer's last taxable year beginning in 2009. Any such election, once made, shall be irrevocable.

(D) Limitation on amount of loss carryback to 5th preceding taxable year.

(i) In general. The amount of any loss from operations which may be carried back to the 5th taxable year preceding the taxable year of such loss under subparagraph (A) shall not exceed 50 percent of the taxpayer's taxable income (computed without regard to the loss from operations for the loss year or any taxable year thereafter) for such preceding taxable year.

(ii) Carrybacks and carryovers to other taxable years. Appropriate adjustments in the application of the second sentence of paragraph (2) shall be made to take into account the limitation of clause (i).

(c) Computation of loss from operations.

For purposes of this section—

(1) In general. The term "loss from operations" means the excess of the life insurance deductions for any taxable year over the life insurance gross income for such taxable year.

(2) Modifications. For purposes of paragraph (1)—

(A) the operations loss deduction shall not be allowed, and

(B) the deductions allowed by sections 243 (relating to dividends received by corporations), 244 (relating to dividends received on certain preferred stock of public utilities), and 245 (relating to dividends received from certain foreign corporations) shall be computed without regard to section 246(b) as modified by section 805(a)(4).

(d) Offset defined.

(1) In general. For purposes of subsection (b)(2), the term "offset" means, with respect to any taxable year, an amount equal to that increase in the operations loss deduction for the taxable year which reduces the life insurance company taxable income (computed without regard to paragraphs (2) and (3) of section 804) for such year to zero.

(2) Operations loss deduction. For purposes of paragraph (1), the operations loss deduction for any taxable year shall be computed without regard to the loss from operations for the loss year or for any taxable year thereafter.

(e) New company defined.

For purposes of this part, a life insurance company is a new company for any taxable year only if such taxable year begins not more than 5 years after the first day on which it (or any predecessor, if section 381(c)(22) applies) was authorized to do business as an insurance company.

(f) Application of subtitles A and F in respect of operation losses.

Except as provided in section 805(b)(5), subtitles A and F shall apply in respect of operation loss carrybacks, operation loss carryovers, and the operations loss deduction under this part, in the same manner and to the same extent as such subtitles apply in respect of net operating loss carrybacks, net operating loss carryovers, and the net operating loss deduction.

(g) Transitional rule.

For purposes of this section and section 812 (as in effect before the enactment of the Life Insurance Tax Act of 1984), this section shall be treated as a continuation of such section 812.

In 2009, P.L. 111-92, Sec. 13(c), added para. (b)(4), effective effective for net operating losses arising in tax. yrs. end. after 12/31/2007

—P.L. 111-92, Sec. 13(d), of this Act, provides:

"(d) Anti-abuse rules. The Secretary of Treasury or the Secretary's designee shall prescribe such rules as are necessary to prevent the abuse of the purposes of the amendments made by this section, including anti-stuffing rules, anti-churning rules (including rules relating to sale-leasebacks), and rules similar to the rules under section 1091 of the Internal Revenue Code of 1986 relating to losses from wash sales."

—P.L. 111-92, Sec. 13(f), of this Act, provides:

"(f) Exception for tarp recipients. The amenfments made by this section shall not apply to—

"(1) any taxpayer if—

"(A) the Federal Government acquired before the date of the enactment of this Act an equity interest in the taxpayer pursuant to the Emergency Economic Stabilization Act of 2008,

"(B) the Federal Government acquired before such date of enactment any warrant (or other right) to acquire any equity interest with respect to the taxpayer pursuant to the Emergency Economic Stabilization Act of 2008, or

"(C) such taxpayer receives after such date of enactment funds from the Federal Government in exchange for an interest described in subparagraph (A) or (B) pursuant to a program established under title I of division A of the Emergency Economic Stabilization Act of 2008 (unless such taxpayer is a financial institution (as defined in section 3 of such Act) and the funds are received pursuant to a program established by the Secretary of the Treasury for the stated purpose of increasing the availability of credit to small businesses using funding made available under such Act), or

"(2) the Federal National Mortgage Association and the Federal Home Loan Mortgage Corporation, and

"(3) any taxpayer which at any time in 2008 or 2009 was or is a member of the same affiliated group (as defined in section 1504 of the Internal Revenue Code of 1986, determined without regard to subsection (b) thereof) as a taxpayer described in paragraph (1) or (2)."

In 1984, P.L. 98-369, Sec. 211(a), added Code Sec. 810 as part of the amendments to part I of Subchapter L, effective for tax. yrs. begin. after 12/31/83.

SUBPART D.—ACCOUNTING, ALLOCATION, AND FOREIGN PROVISIONS

Sec.

811. Accounting provisions.

812. Definition of company's share and policyholders' share.

813. Repealed.

814. Contiguous country branches of domestic life insurance companies.

815. Distributions to shareholders from pre-1984 policyholders surplus account.

In 1987, P.L. 100-203, Sec. 10242(c)(4), repealed item 813.
Prior to repeal, item 813 read as follows:
"813. Foreign life insurance companies."

Sec. 811. Accounting provisions.

(a) Method of accounting.

All computations entering into the determination of the taxes imposed by this part shall be made—

(1) under an accrual method of accounting, or

(2) to the extent permitted under regulations prescribed by the Secretary, under a combination of an accrual method of accounting with any other method permitted by this chapter (other than the cash receipts and disbursements method).

To the extent not inconsistent with the preceding sentence or any other provision of this part, all such computations shall be made in a manner consistent with the manner required for purposes of the annual statement approved by the National Association of Insurance Commissioners.

(b) Amortization of premium and accrual of discount.

(1) In general. The appropriate items of income, deductions, and adjustments under this part shall be adjusted to reflect the appropriate amortization of premium and the appropriate accrual of discount attributable to the taxable year on bonds, notes, debentures, or other evidences of indebtedness held by a life insurance company. Such amortization and accrual shall be determined—

(A) in accordance with the method regularly employed by such company, if such method is reasonable, and

(B) in all other cases, in accordance with regulations prescribed by the Secretary.

(2) Special rules.

(A) Amortization of bond premium. In the case of any bond (as defined in section 171(d)), the amount of bond premium, and the amortizable bond premium for the taxable year, shall be determined under section 171(b) as if the election set forth in section 171(c) had been made.

(B) Convertible evidence of indebtedness. In no case shall the amount of premium on a convertible evidence of indebtedness include any amount attributable to the conversion features of the evidence of indebtedness.

(3) Exception. No accrual of discount shall be required under paragraph (1) on any bond (as defined in section 171(d)), except in the case of discount which is—

(A) interest to which section 103 applies, or

(B) original issue discount (as defined in section 1273).

(c) No double counting.

Nothing in this part shall permit—

(1) a reserve to be established for any item unless the gross amount of premiums and other consideration attributable to such item are required to be included in life insurance gross income,

(2) the same item to be counted more than once for reserve purposes, or

(3) any item to be deducted (either directly or as an increase in reserves) more than once.

(d) Method of computing reserves on contract where interest is guaranteed beyond end of taxable year.

For purposes of this part (other than section 816), amounts in the nature of interest to be paid or credited under any contract for any period which is computed at a rate which—

(1) exceeds the greater of the prevailing State assumed interest rate or applicable Federal interest rate in effect under section 807 for the contract for such period, and

(2) is guaranteed beyond the end of the taxable year on which the reserves are being computed,

shall be taken into account in computing the reserves with respect to such contract as if such interest were guaranteed only up to the end of the taxable year.

(e) Short taxable years.

If any return of a corporation made under this part is for a period of less than the entire calendar year (referred to in this subsection as "short period"), then section 443 shall not apply in respect to such period, but life insurance company taxable income shall be determined, under regulations prescribed by the Secretary, on an annual basis by a ratable daily projection of the appropriate figures for the short period.

In **1988**, P.L. 100-647, Sec. 2004(p)(1), substituted "the greater of the prevailing State assumed interest rate or applicable Federal interest rate in effect under section 807 for the contract" for "the prevailing State assumed interest rate for the contract" in para. (d)(1), effective for contracts issued in tax. yrs. begin. after 12/31/87.

In **1984**, P.L. 98-369, Sec. 42(a)(8), substituted "section 1273" for "section 1232(b)" in para. (b)(3) [as added by Sec. 211(a) of this Act, see below], effective for tax. yrs. end. after 7/18/84.

—P.L. 98-369, Sec. 211(a), added Code Sec. 811 as part of the amendments to part I of Subchapter L, effective for tax. yrs. begin. after 12/31/83. For transitional rules, see Secs. 216(b)(3)(B), (C) and Sec. 216(b)(4) of this Act reproduced in note following Code Sec. 807.

Prior to this amendment, Code Sec. 811 read as follows:

"Sec. 811. Dividends to policyholders.

"(a) Dividends to policyholders defined. For purposes of this part, the term 'dividends to policyholders' means dividends and similar distributions to policyholders in their capacity as such. Such term does not include interest paid (as defined in section 805(e)).

"(b) Amount of deduction.

"(1) In general. Except as limited by section 809(f), the deduction for dividends to policyholders for any taxable year shall be an amount equal to the dividends to policyholders paid during the taxable year—

"(A) increased by the excess of (i) the amounts held at the end of the taxable year as reserves for dividends to policyholders (as defined in subsection (a)) payable during the year following the taxable year, over (ii) such amounts held at the end of the preceding taxable year, or

"(B) decreased by the excess of (i) such amounts held at the end of the preceding taxable year, over (ii) such amounts held at the end of the taxable year.

For purposes of subparagraphs (A) and (B), there shall be included as amounts held at the end of any taxable year amounts set aside, before the 16th day of the third month of the year following such taxable year (or, in the case of a mutual savings bank subject to the tax imposed by section 594, before the 16th day of the fourth month of the year following such taxable year), for payment during the year following such taxable year.

"(2) Certain amounts to be treated as net decreases. If the amount determined under paragraph (1)(B) exceeds the dividends to policyholders paid during the taxable year, the amount of such excess shall be a net decrease referred to in section 809(c)(2).

"(c) Special rule for dividends to policyholders under reinsurance contracts. If, under the terms of a reinsurance contract, a life insurance company (hereinafter referred to as 'the reinsurer') is obligated to reimburse another life insurance company (hereinafter referred to as 'the reinsured') for dividends to policyholders on the policies reinsured, the amount of the deduction for dividends reimbursed shall, for purposes of section 809(d)(12), be equal to the amount of dividends to policyholders—

"(1) which were paid by the reinsured, and

"(2) with respect to which the reinsurer reimbursed the reinsured under the terms of such contract.

The amount determined under the preceding sentence shall be properly adjusted to reflect the adjustments under subsection (b)(1)."

In **1982**, P.L. 97-248, Sec. 255(b)(1), added subsec. (c), effective for tax. yrs. begin. after 12/31/81.

Sec. 812. Definition of company's share and policyholders' share.

(a) General rule.

(1) Company's share. For purposes of section 805(a)(4), the term "company's share" means, with respect to any taxable year, the percentage obtained by dividing—

(A) the company's share of the net investment income for the taxable year, by

(B) the net investment income for the taxable year.

(2) Policyholders' share. For purposes of section 807, the term "policyholders' share" means, with respect to any taxable year, the excess of 100 percent over the percentage determined under paragraph (1).

(b) Company's share of net investment income.

(1) In general. For purposes of this section, the company's share of net investment income is the excess (if any) of—

(A) the net investment income for the taxable year, over

(B) the sum of—

(i) the policy interest, for the taxable year, plus

(ii) the gross investment income's proportionate share of policyholder dividends for the taxable year.

(2) Policy interest. For purposes of this subsection, the term "policy interest" means—

(A) required interest (at the greater of the prevailing State assumed rate or the applicable Federal interest rate) on reserves under section 807(c) (other than paragraph (2) thereof),

(B) the deductible portion of excess interest,

(C) the deductible portion of any amount (whether or not a policyholder dividend), and not taken into account under subparagraph (A) or (B), credited to—

(i) a policyholder's fund under a pension plan contract for employees (other than retired employees), or

(ii) a deferred annuity contract before the annuity starting date, and

(D) interest on amounts left on deposit with the company.

In any case where neither the prevailing State assumed interest rate nor the applicable Federal interest rate is used,

Insurance companies   Code Sec. 812

another appropriate rate shall be used for purposes of subparagraph (A).

(3) Gross investment income's proportionate share of policyholder dividends. For purposes of paragraph (1), the gross investment income's proportionate share of policyholder dividends is—

(A) the deduction for policyholders' dividends determined under section 808 for the taxable year, but not including—

(i) the deductible portion of excess interest,

(ii) the deductible portion of policyholder dividends on contracts referred to in clauses (i) and (ii) of paragraph (2)(C), and

(iii) the deductible portion of the premium and mortality charge adjustments with respect to contracts paying excess interest for such year,

multiplied by

(B) the fraction—

(i) the numerator of which is gross investment income for the taxable year (reduced by the policy interest for such year), and

(ii) the denominator of which is life insurance gross income reduced by the excess (if any) of the closing balance for the items described in section 807(c) over the opening balance for such items for the taxable year.

For purposes of subparagraph (B)(ii), life insurance gross income shall be determined by including tax-exempt interest and by applying section 807(a)(2)(B) as if it did not contain clause (i) thereof.

(c) Net investment income.

For purposes of this section, the term "net investment income" means—

(1) except as provided in paragraph (2), 90 percent of gross investment income; or

(2) in the case of gross investment income attributable to assets held in segregated asset accounts under variable contracts, 95 percent of gross investment income.

(d) Gross investment income.

For purposes of this section, the term "gross investment income" means the sum of the following:

(1) Interest, etc. The gross amount of income from—

(A) interest (including tax-exempt interest), dividends, rents, and royalties,

(B) the entering into of any lease, mortgage, or other instrument or agreement from which the life insurance company derives interest, rents, or royalties,

(C) the alteration or termination of any instrument or agreement described in subparagraph (B), and

(D) the increase for any taxable year in the policy cash values (within the meaning of section 805(a)(4)(F)) of life insurance policies and annuity and endowment contracts to which section 264(f) applies.

(2) Short-term capital gain. The amount (if any) by which the net short-term capital gain exceeds the net long-term capital loss.

(3) Trade or business income. The gross income from any trade or business (other than an insurance business) carried on by the life insurance company, or by a partnership of which the life insurance company is a partner. In computing gross income under this paragraph, there shall be excluded any item described in paragraph (1).

Except as provided in paragraph (2), in computing gross investment income under this subsection, there shall be excluded any gain from the sale or exchange of a capital asset, and any gain considered as gain from the sale or exchange of a capital asset.

(e) Dividends from certain subsidiaries not included in gross investment income.

(1) In general. For purposes of this section, the term "gross investment income" shall not include any dividend received by the life insurance company which is a 100 percent dividend.

(2) 100 percent dividend defined.

(A) In general. Except as provided in subparagraphs (B) and (C), the term "100 percent dividend" means any dividend if the percentage used for purposes of determining the deduction allowable under section 243, 244, or 245(b) is 100 percent.

(B) Certain dividends out of tax-exempt interest, etc. The term "100 percent dividend" does not include any distribution by a corporation to the extent such distribution is out of tax-exempt interest or out of dividends which are not 100 percent dividends (determined with the application of this subparagraph).

(C) Certain dividends received by foreign corporations. The term "100 percent dividends" does not include any dividend described in section 805(a)(4)(E) (relating to certain dividends in the case of foreign corporations).

(f) No double counting.

Under regulations, proper adjustments shall be made in the application of this section to prevent an item from being counted more than once.

In **2004**, P.L. 108-218, Sec. 205(b)(4), substituted "section 808" for "sections 808 and 809" in subpara. (b)(3)(A), effective for tax. yrs. begin. after 12/31/2004.

In **1998**, P.L. 105-206, Sec. 6010(o)(3)(B), substituted "except that, in the case of a master contract (within the meaning of section 264(f)(4)(E) of the Internal Revenue Code of 1986), the addition of covered lives shall be treated as a new contract only with respect to such additional covered lives." for "but the addition of covered lives shall be treated as a new contract only with respect to such additional covered lives. For purposes of this subsection, an increase in the death benefit under a policy or contract issued in connection with a lapse described in section 501(d)(2) of the Health Insurance Portability and Accountability Act of 1996 shall not be treated as a new contract." in Sec. 1084(d)[sic (f)] of P.L. 105-34 [reproduced below].

In **1997**, P.L. 105-34, Sec. 1084(b)(5) [sic (d)(5)], deleted "and" at the end of subpara. (d)(1)(B), substituted ", and" for the period at the end of subpara. (d)(1)(C) and added subpara. (d)(1)(D), effective as provided in Sec. 1084(d)[sic (f)] of this Act [as amended by Sec. 6010(o)(3)(B), 105-206, see above], which reads:

"(d) Effective date.— The amendments made by this section shall apply to contracts issued after June 8, 1997, in taxable years ending after such date. For purposes of the preceding sentence, any material increase in the death benefit or other material change in the contract shall be treated as a new contract except that, in the case of a master contract (within the meaning of section 264(f)(4)(E) of the Internal Revenue Code of 1986), the addition of covered lives shall be treated as a new contract only with respect to such additional covered lives."

In **1996**, P.L. 104-188, Sec. 1602(b)(2), deleted subsec. (g), effective for loans made after 8/20/96. For notes regarding refinancings and exceptions, see Secs. 1602(c)(2) and (3) of this Act, which read as follows::

"(2) Refinancings. The amendments made by this section shall not apply to loans made after the date of the enactment of this Act to refinance securities acquisition loans (determined without regard to section 133(b)(1)(B) of the Internal Revenue Code of 1986, as in effect on the day before the date of the enactment of this Act) made on or before such date or to refinance loans described in this paragraph if—

"(A) the refinancing loans meet the requirements of section 133 of such Code (as so in effect),

"(B) immediately after the refinancing the principal amount of the loan resulting from the refinancing does not exceed the principal amount of the refinanced loan (immediately before the refinancing), and

"(C) the term of such refinancing loan does not extend beyond the last day of the term of the original securities acquisition loan.

For purposes of this paragraph, the term 'securities acquisition loan' includes a loan from a corporation to an employee stock ownership plan described in section 133(b)(3) of such Code (as so in effect).

"(3) Exception. Any loan made pursuant to a binding written contract in effect before June 10, 1996, and at all times thereafter before such loan is made, shall be treated for purposes of paragraphs (1) and (2) as a loan made on or before the date of the enactment of this Act."

Prior to deletion, subsec. (g) read as follows:

"(g) Treatment of interest partially tax-exempt under section 133. For purposes of this section and subsections (a) and (b) of section 807, the terms 'gross investment income' and 'tax-exempt interest' shall not include any interest received with respect to a securities acquisition loan (as defined in section 133(b)). Such interest shall not be included in life insurance gross income for purposes of subsection (b)(3)."

In **1988**, P.L. 100-647, Sec. 1018(h)(1), amended subsec. (e), effective for contracts issued in tax. yrs. begin. after 12/31/83.

Prior to amendment, subsec. (e) read as follows:

"(e) Dividends from certain subsidiaries not included in gross investment income.

"For purposes of this section, the term 'gross investment income' shall not include any dividend received by the life insurance company which is a 100-percent dividend (as defined in section 805(a)(4)(C)). Such term also shall not include any dividend described in section 805(a)(4)(D) (relating to certain dividends in the case of foreign corporations)."

— P.L. 100-647, Sec. 2004(p)(2), amended the last sentence of para. (b)(2), effective for tax. yrs. begin. after 12/31/87.

Prior to amendment the last sentence of para. (b)(2) read as follows:

"In any case where the prevailing State assumed rate is not used, another appropriate rate shall be treated as the prevailing State assumed rate for purposes of subparagraph (A)."

In **1987**, P.L. 100-203, Sec. 10241(b)(2)(B)(i), substituted "at the greater of the prevailing State assumed rate or the applicable Federal interest rate" for "at the prevailing State assumed rate or, where such rate is not used, another appropriate rate" in para. (b)(2)... Sec. 10241(b)(2)(B)(ii), added the sentence at the end of para. (b)(2), effective for contracts included in taxable yrs. begin. after 12/31/87.

In **1986**, P.L. 99-514, Sec. 1821(i)(1)(A), substituted "the prevailing State assumed rate or, where such rate is not used, another appropriate rate" for "the prevailing State assumed rate" in para. (b)(2)... Sec. 1821(i)(1)(B), deleted "and" from the end of subpara. (b)(2)(B)... Sec. 1821(i)(1)(C), substituted ", and" for the period at the end of subpara. (b)(2)(C)... Sec. 1821(i)(1)(D), added subpara. (b)(2)(D)... Sec. 1812(i)(2)(A), deleted "(including tax exempt interest)" after "gross income" in clause (b)(3)(B)(ii)... Sec. 1821(i)(2)(B), added the last sentence to subpara. (b)(3)(B)... Sec. 1821(i)(3), amended subsec. (c)... Sec. 1821(i)(4), added subsec. (g), effective for tax. yrs. begin. after 12/31/83.

Prior to amendment, subsec. (c) read as follows:

"(c) Net investment income.

"For purposes of this section, the term 'net investment income' means 90 percent of gross investment income."

In **1984**, P.L. 98-369, Sec. 211(a), added Code Sec. 812 as part of the amendments to part I of Subchapter L, effective for tax. yrs. begin. after 12/31/83. For transitional rules, see Secs. 216(b)(3)(B), (C) and Sec. 216(b)(4) of this Act reproduced in note following Code Sec. 807.

Sec. 813. Repealed.

In **1988**, P.L. 100-647, Sec. 1010(a)(1), deleted "the special life insurance company deduction and" before "the small life insurance company" in para. (a)(1), effective for tax. yrs. begin. after 12/31/86.

In **1987**, P.L. 100-203, Sec. 10242(c)(1), repealed Code Sec. 813, effective for tax. yrs. begin. after 12/31/87.

Prior to repeal, Code Sec. 813 read as follows:

"SEC. 813. FOREIGN LIFE INSURANCE COMPANIES.

"(a) Adjustment where surplus held in the United States is less than specified minimum.

"(1) In general. In the case of any foreign company taxable under this part, if—

"(A) the required surplus determined under paragraph (2), exceeds

"(B) the surplus held in the United States.

then its income effectively connected with the conduct of an insurance business within the United States shall be increased by an amount determined by multiplying such excess by such company's current investment yield. The preceding sentence shall be applied before computing the amount of the small life insurance company deduction, and any increase under the preceding sentence shall be treated as gross investment income.

"(2) Required surplus For purposes of this subsection —

"(A) In general. The term 'required surplus' means the amount determined by multiplying the taxpayer's total insurance liabilities on United States business by a percentage for the taxable year determined and proclaimed by the Secretary under subparagraph (B).

"(B) Determination of percentage. The percentage determined and proclaimed by the Secretary under this subparagraph shall be based on such data with respect to domestic life insurance companies for the preceding taxable year as the Secretary considers representative. Such percentage shall be computed on the basis of a ratio the numerator of which is the excess of the assets over the total insurance liabilities, and the denominator of which is the total insurance liabilities.

"(3) Current investment yield. For purposes of this subsection—

"(A) In general. The term 'current investment yield' means the percent obtained by dividing—

"(i) the net investment income on assets held in the United States, by

"(ii) the mean of the assets held in the United States during the taxable year.

"(B) Determinations based on amount set forth in the annual statement. Except as otherwise provided in regulations, determinations under subparagraph (A) shall be made on the basis of the amounts required to be set forth on the annual statement approved by the National Association of Insurance Commissioners.

"(4) Other definitions. For purposes of this subsection —

"(A) Surplus held in the United States. The surplus held in the United States is the excess of the assets (determined under section 806(a)(3)(C)) held in the United States over the total insurance liabilities on United States business.

"(B) Total insurance liabilities. For purposes of this subsection, the term 'total insurance liabilities' means the sum of the total reserves (as defined in section 816(c)) plus (to the extent not included in total reserves) the items referred to in paragraphs (3), (4), (5), and (6) of section 807(c).

"(5) Reduction of section 881 taxes. In the case of any foreign company taxable under this part, there shall be determined —

"(A) the amount which would be subject to taxes under section 881 if the amount taxable under such section were determined without regard to sections 103 and 894, and

"(B) the amount of the increase provided by paragraph (1).

The tax under section 881 (determined without regard to this paragraph) shall be reduced (but not below zero) by an amount which is the same proportion of such tax as the amount referred to in subparagraph (B) is of the amount referred to in subparagraph (A); but such reduction in taxes shall not exceed the increase in taxes under this part by reason of the increase provided by paragraph (1).

"(b) Adjustment to limitation on deduction for policyholder dividends in the case of foreign mutual life insurance companies.

"For purposes of section 809, the equity base of any foreign mutual life insurance company as of the close of any taxable year shall be increased by the amount of any excess determined under paragraph (1) of subsection (a) with respect to such taxable year.

"(c) Cross reference.

"For taxation of foreign corporations carrying on life insurance business within the United States, see section 842."

In **1986**, P.L. 99-514, Sec. 1011(b)(9), substituted "section 806(a)(3)(C)" for "section 806(b)(3)(C) in subpara. (a)(4)(A), effective for tax. yrs. begin. after 12/31/86.

— P.L. 99-514, Sec. 1821(j), added the last sentence to para. (a)(1), effective for tax. yrs. begin. after 12/31/83.

In **1984**, P.L. 98-369, Sec. 211(a), added Code Sec. 813 as part of the amendments to part I of Subchapter L, effective for tax. yrs. begin. after 12/31/83.

In **1959**, P.L. 86-69, Sec. 2(a), amended Code Sec. 813 as part of the amendments to Part I of Subchapter L, effective for tax. yrs. begin. after 12/31/54.

Prior to amendment, Code Sec. 813 read as follows:

"SEC. 813. ADJUSTMENT FOR CERTAIN RESERVES.

"In the case of a life insurance company writing contracts other than life insurance, annuity, and noncancellable health and accident insurance contracts (including life insurance or annuity contracts combined with noncancellable health and accident insurance), the term 'adjustment for certain reserves' means, for purposes of this subpart, an amount equal to 3¼ percent of the unearned premiums and unpaid losses on such other contracts which are not included in life insurance reserves (as defined in section 801(b)). For purposes of this section, such unearned premiums shall not be considered to be less than 25 percent of the net premiums written during the taxable year on such other contracts."

Sec. 814. Contiguous country branches of domestic life insurance companies.

(a) Exclusion of items.

In the case of a domestic mutual insurance company which—

(1) is a life insurance company,

(2) has a contiguous country life insurance branch, and

(3) makes the election provided by subsection (g) with respect to such branch,

there shall be excluded from each item involved in the determination of life insurance company taxable income the items separately accounted for in accordance with subsection (c).

(b) Contiguous country life insurance branch.

For purposes of this section, the term contiguous country life insurance branch means a branch which—

(1) issues insurance contracts insuring risks in connection with the lives or health of residents of a country which is contiguous to the United States,

(2) has its principal place of business in such contiguous country, and

(3) would constitute a mutual life insurance company if such branch were a separate domestic insurance company.

For purposes of this section, the term "insurance contract" means any life, health, accident, or annuity contract or reinsurance contract or any contract relating thereto.

(c) Separate accounting required.

Any taxpayer which makes the election provided by subsection (g) shall establish and maintain a separate account

Insurance companies

Code Sec. 814(h)

for the various income, exclusion, deduction, asset, reserve, liability, and surplus items properly attributable to the contracts described in subsection (b). Such separate accounting shall be made—

(1) in accordance with the method regularly employed by such company, if such method clearly reflects income derived from, and the other items attributable to, the contracts described in subsection (b), and

(2) in all other cases, in accordance with regulations prescribed by the Secretary.

(d) Recognition of gain on assets in branch account.

If the aggregate fair market value of all the invested assets and tangible property which are separately accounted for by the domestic life insurance company in the branch account established pursuant to subsection (c) exceeds the aggregate adjusted basis of such assets for purposes of determining gain, then the domestic life insurance company shall be treated as having sold all such assets on the first day of the first taxable year for which the election is in effect at their fair market value on such first day. Notwithstanding any other provision of this chapter, the net gain shall be recognized to the domestic life insurance company on the deemed sale described in the preceding sentence.

(e) Transactions between contiguous country branch and domestic life insurance company.

(1) Reimbursement for home office services, etc. Any payment, transfer, reimbursement, credit, or allowance which is made from a separate account established pursuant to subsection (c) to one or more other accounts of a domestic life insurance company as reimbursement for costs incurred for or with respect to the insurance (or reinsurance) of risks accounted for in such separate account shall be taken into account by the domestic life insurance company in the same manner as if such payment, transfer, reimbursement, credit, or allowance had been received from a separate person.

(2) Repatriation of income.

(A) In general. Except as provided in subparagraph (B), any amount directly or indirectly transferred or credited from a branch account established pursuant to subsection (c) to one or more other accounts of such company shall, unless such transfer or credit is a reimbursement to which paragraph (1) applies, be added to the income of the domestic life insurance company.

(B) Limitation. The addition provided by subparagraph (A) for the taxable year with respect to any contiguous country life insurance branch shall not exceed the amount by which—

(i) the aggregate decrease in the tentative LICTI of the domestic life insurance company for the taxable year and for all prior taxable years resulting solely from the application of subsection (a) of this section with respect to such branch, exceeds

(ii) the amount of additions to tentative LICTI pursuant to subparagraph (A) with respect to such contiguous country branch for all prior taxable years.

(C) Transitional rule. For purposes of this paragraph, in the case of a prior taxable year beginning before January 1, 1984, the term "tentative LICTI" means life insurance company taxable income determined under this part (as in effect for such year) without regard to this paragraph.

(f) Other rules.

(1) Treatment of foreign taxes.

(A) In general. No income, war profits, or excess profits taxes paid or accrued to any foreign country or possession of the United States which is attributable to income excluded under subsection (a) shall be taken into account for purposes of subpart A of part III of subchapter N (relating to foreign tax credit) or allowable as a deduction.

(B) Treatment of repatriated amounts. For purposes of sections 78 and 902, where any amount is added to the life insurance company taxable income of the domestic life insurance company by reason of subsection (e)(2), the contiguous country life insurance branch shall be treated as a foreign corporation. Any amount so added shall be treated as a dividend paid by a foreign corporation, and the taxes paid to any foreign country or possession of the United States with respect to such amount shall be deemed to have been paid by such branch.

(2) United States source income allocable to contiguous country branch. For purposes of sections 881, 882, and 1442, each contiguous country life insurance branch shall be treated as a foreign corporation. Such sections shall be applied to each such branch in the same manner as if such sections contained the provisions of any treaty to which the United States and the contiguous country are parties, to the same extent such provisions would apply if such branch were incorporated in such contiguous country.

(g) Election.

A taxpayer may make the election provided by this subsection with respect to any contiguous country for any taxable year. An election made under this subsection for any taxable year shall remain in effect for all subsequent taxable years, except that it may be revoked with the consent of the Secretary. The election provided by this subsection shall be made not later than the time prescribed by law for filing the return for the taxable year (including extensions thereof) with respect to which such election is made, and such election and any approved revocation thereof shall be made in the manner provided by the Secretary.

(h) Special rule for domestic stock life insurance companies.

At the election of a domestic stock life insurance company which has a contiguous country life insurance branch described in subsection (b) (without regard to the mutual requirement in subsection (b)(3)), the assets of such branch may be transferred to a foreign corporation organized under the laws of the contiguous country without the application of section 367. Subsection (a) shall apply to the stock of such foreign corporation as if such domestic company were a mutual company and as if the stock were an item described in subsection (c). Subsection (e)(2) shall apply to amounts transferred or credited to such domestic company as if such domestic company and such foreign corporation constituted one domestic mutual life insurance company. The insurance contracts which may be transferred pursuant to this subsection shall include only those which are similar to the types of insurance contracts issued by a mutual life insurance company. Notwithstanding the first sentence of this subsection, if the aggregate fair market value of the invested assets and tangible property which are separately accounted for by the domestic life insurance company in the branch account exceeds the aggregate adjusted basis of such assets for purposes of determining gain, the domestic life insurance company shall be deemed to have sold all such assets on the first day of the taxable year for which the election under this subsection applies and the net gain shall be recognized to the domestic life insurance company on the deemed sale, but not in excess of the proportion of such net gain which equals the proportion which the aggregate fair market value of such as-

Code Sec. 814(h)

sets which are transferred pursuant to this subsection is of the aggregate fair market value of all such assets.

In 1997, P.L. 105-34, Sec. 1131(c)(1), [sic (d)(1)], deleted "or 1491" after "section 367" in subsec. (h), effective 8/5/97.
In 1984, P.L. 98-369, Sec. 211(a), added Code Sec. 814 as part of the amendments to part I of Subchapter L, effective for tax. yrs. begin. after 12/31/83.
—P.L. 98-369, Sec. 217(a), provides:
"(a) New section 814 treated as continuation of section 819A. For purposes of section 814 of the Internal Revenue Code of 1954 (relating to contiguous country branches of domestic life insurance companies)—

"(1) any election under section 819A of such Code (as in effect on the day before the date of the enactment of this Act) shall be treated as an election under such section 814, and

"(2) any reference to a provision of such section 814 shall be treated as including a reference to the corresponding provision of such section 819A."

Sec. 815. Distributions to shareholders from pre-1984 policyholders surplus account.

(a) General rule.

In the case of a stock life insurance company which has an existing policyholders surplus account, the tax imposed by section 801 for any taxable year shall be the amount which would be imposed by such section for such year on the sum of—

(1) life insurance company taxable income for such year (but not less than zero), plus

(2) the amount of direct and indirect distributions during such year to shareholders from such account.

For purposes of the preceding sentence, the term "indirect distribution" shall not include any bona fide loan with arms-length terms and conditions.

(b) Ordering rule.

For purposes of this section, any distribution to shareholders shall be treated as made—

(1) first out of the shareholders surplus account, to the extent thereof,

(2) then out of the policyholders surplus account, to the extent thereof, and

(3) finally, out of other accounts.

(c) Shareholders surplus account.

(1) **In general.** Each stock life insurance company which has an existing policyholders surplus account shall continue its shareholders surplus account for purposes of this part.

(2) **Additions to account.** The amount added to the shareholders surplus account for any taxable year beginning after December 31, 1983, shall be the excess of—

(A) the sum of—

(i) the life insurance company's taxable income (but not below zero),

(ii) the small life insurance company deduction provided by section 806, and

(iii) the deductions for dividends received provided by sections 243, 244, and 245 (as modified by section 805(a)(4)) and the amount of interest excluded from gross income under section 103, over

(B) the taxes imposed for the taxable year by section 801 (determined without regard to this section).

If for any taxable year a tax is imposed by section 55, under regulations proper adjustments shall be made for such year and all subsequent taxable years in the amounts taken into account under subparagraphs (A) and (B) of this paragraph and subparagraph (B) of subsection (d)(3).

(3) **Subtractions from account.** There shall be subtracted from the shareholders surplus account for any taxable year the amount which is treated under this section as distributed out of such account.

(d) Policyholders surplus account.

(1) **In general.** Each stock life insurance company which has an existing policyholders surplus account shall continue such account.

(2) **No additions to account.** No amount shall be added to the policyholders surplus account for any taxable year beginning after December 31, 1983.

(3) **Subtractions from account.** There shall be subtracted from the policyholders surplus account for any taxable year an amount equal to the sum of—

(A) the amount which (without regard to subparagraph (B)) is treated under this section as distributed out of the policyholders surplus account, and

(B) the amount by which the tax imposed for the taxable year by section 801 is increased by reason of this section.

(e) Existing policyholders surplus account.

For purposes of this section, the term "existing policyholders surplus account" means any policyholders surplus account which has a balance as of the close of December 31, 1983.

(f) Other rules applicable to policyholders surplus account continued.

Except to the extent inconsistent with the provisions of this part, the provisions of subsections (d), (e), (f), and (g) of section 815 (and of sections 819(b), 6501(c)(6), 6501(k), 6511(d)(6), 6601(d)(3), and 6611(f)(4)) as in effect before the enactment of the Tax Reform Act of 1984 are hereby made applicable in respect of any policyholders surplus account for which there was a balance as of December 31, 1983.

(g) Special rules applicable during 2005 and 2006.

In the case of any taxable year of a stock life insurance company beginning after December 31, 2004, and before January 1, 2007—

(1) the amount under subsection (a)(2) for such taxable year shall be treated as zero, and

(2) notwithstanding subsection (b), in determining any subtractions from an account under subsections (c)(3) and (d)(3), any distribution to shareholders during such taxable year shall be treated as made first out of the policyholders surplus account, then out of the shareholders surplus account, and finally out of other accounts.

In 2004, P.L. 108-357, Sec. 705(a), added subsec. (g), effective for tax. yrs. begin. after 12/31/2004.
In 1988, P.L. 100-647, Sec. 1010(j)(1), added the sentence at the end of para. (c)(2), effective for tax. yrs. begin. after 12/31/86.
In 1986, P.L. 99-514, Sec. 1011(b)(10), substituted "small life insurance company deduction" for "special deductions" in clause (c)(2)(A)(ii), effective for tax. yrs. begin. after 12/31/86.
—P.L. 99-514, Sec. 1013, provides as follows:
"Sec. 1013. Operations loss deduction of insolvent companies may offset distributions from policyholders surplus account.
"(a) In general.—
"If—
"(1) on November 15, 1985, a life insurance company was insolvent,
"(2) pursuant to the order of any court of competent jurisdiction in a title 11 or similar case (as defined in section 368(a)(3) of the Internal Revenue Code of 1954), such company is liquidated, and
"(3) as a result of such liquidation, the tax imposed by section 801 of such Code for any taxable year (hereinafter in this subsection referred to as the 'liquidation year') would (but for this subsection) be increased under section 815(a) of such Code,
then the amount described in section 815(a)(2) of such Code shall be reduced by the loss from operations (if any) for the liquidation year, and by the unused operations loss carryovers (if any) to the liquidation year (determined after the application of section 810 of such Code for such year). No carryover of any loss from operations of such company arising during the liquidation year (or any prior taxable year) shall be allowable for any taxable year succeeding the liquidation year.
"(b) Definitions.—
"For purposes of subsection (a)—

Insurance companies   Code Sec. 816

"(1) Insolvent.— The term insolvent means the excess of liabilities over the fair market value of assets.
"(2) Loss from operations.— The term loss from operations has the meaning given such term by section 810(c) of such Code.
"(c) Effective date.—
"This section shall apply to liquidations on or after November 15, 1985, in taxable years ending after such date."
—P.L. 99-514, Sec. 1821(k)(1), substituted "sections 819(b), 6501(c)(6)" for "section 6501(c)(6)" in subsec. (f) . . . Sec. 1821(k)(2), added the sentence at the end of subsec. (a), effective for tax. yrs. begin. after 12/31/83. Sec. 1821(k)(3) of this Act provides as follows:
"(3) In the case of any loan made before March 1, 1986 (other than a loan which is renegotiated, extended, renewed, or revised after February 28, 1986), which does not meet the requirements of the last sentence of section 815(a) of the Internal Revenue Code of 1954 (as added by paragraph (2)), the amount of the indirect distribution for purposes of such section 815(a) shall be the foregone interest on the loan (determined by using the lowest rate which would have met the arms-length requirements of such sentence for such a loan)."
In 1984, P.L. 98-369, Sec. 211(a), added Code Sec. 815 as part of the amendments to part I of Subchapter L, effective for tax. yrs. begin. after 12/31/83.

SUBPART E.— DEFINITIONS AND SPECIAL RULES
Sec.
816. Life insurance company defined.
817. Treatment of variable contracts.
817A. Special rules for modified guaranteed contracts.
818. Other definitions and special rules.

In 1996, P.L. 104-188, Sec. 1612(b), added item 817A.
In 1984, P.L. 98-369, Sec. 211(a), amended Part I of Subchapter L.

Sec. 816. Life insurance company defined.
(a) Life insurance company defined.

For purposes of this subtitle, the term "life insurance company" means an insurance company which is engaged in the business of issuing life insurance and annuity contracts (either separately or combined with accident and health insurance), or noncancellable contracts of health and accident insurance, if—

(1) its life insurance reserves (as defined in subsection (b)), plus

(2) unearned premiums, and unpaid losses (whether or not ascertained), on noncancellable life, accident, or health policies not included in life insurance reserves,

comprise more than 50 percent of its total reserves (as defined in subsection (c)). For purposes of the preceding sentence, the term "insurance company" means any company more than half of the business of which during the taxable year is the issuing of insurance or annuity contracts or the reinsuring of risks underwritten by insurance companies.

(b) Life insurance reserves defined.

(1) **In general.** For purposes of this part, the term "life insurance reserves" means amounts—

(A) which are computed or estimated on the basis of recognized mortality or morbidity tables and assumed rates of interest, and

(B) which are set aside to mature or liquidate, either by payment or reinsurance, future unaccrued claims arising from life insurance, annuity, and noncancellable accident and health insurance contracts (including life insurance or annuity contracts combined with noncancellable accident and health insurance) involving, at the time with respect to which the reserve is computed, life, accident, or health contingencies.

(2) **Reserves must be required by law.** Except—

(A) in the case of policies covering life, accident, and health insurance combined in one policy issued on the weekly premium payment plan, continuing for life and not subject to cancellation, and

(B) as provided in paragraph (3),

in addition to the requirements set forth in paragraph (1), life insurance reserves must be required by law.

(3) **Assessment companies.** In the case of an assessment life insurance company or association, the term "life insurance reserves" includes—

(A) sums actually deposited by such company or association with State officers pursuant to law as guaranty or reserve funds, and

(B) any funds maintained, under the charter or articles of incorporation or association (or bylaws approved by a State insurance commissioner) of such company or association, exclusively for the payment of claims arising under certificates of membership or policies issued on the assessment plan and not subject to any other use.

(4) **Amount of reserves.** For purposes of this subsection, subsection (a), and subsection (c), the amount of any reserve (or portion thereof) for any taxable year shall be the mean of such reserve (or portion thereof) at the beginning and end of the taxable year.

(c) Total reserves defined.

For purposes of subsection (a), the term "total reserves" means—

(1) life insurance reserves,

(2) unearned premiums, and unpaid losses (whether or not ascertained), not included in life insurance reserves, and

(3) all other insurance reserves required by law.

(d) Adjustments in reserves for policy loans.

For purposes only of determining under subsection (a) whether or not an insurance company is a life insurance company, the life insurance reserves, and the total reserves, shall each be reduced by an amount equal to the mean of the aggregates, at the beginning and end of the taxable year, of the policy loans outstanding with respect to contracts for which life insurance reserves are maintained.

(e) Guaranteed renewable contracts.

For purposes of this part, guaranteed renewable life, accident, and health insurance shall be treated in the same manner as noncancellable life, accident, and health insurance.

(f) Amounts not involving life, accident, or health contingencies.

For purposes only of determining under subsection (a) whether or not an insurance company is a life insurance company, amounts set aside and held at interest to satisfy obligations under contracts which do not contain permanent guarantees with respect to life, accident, or health contingencies shall not be included in reserves described in paragraph (1) or (3) of subsection (c).

(g) Burial and funeral benefit insurance companies.

A burial or funeral benefit insurance company engaged directly in the manufacture of funeral supplies or the performance of funeral services shall not be taxable under this part but shall be taxable under section 831.

(h) Treatment of deficiency reserves.

For purposes of this section and section 842(b)(2)(B)(i), the terms "life insurance reserves" and "total reserves" shall not include deficiency reserves.

In 1988, P.L. 100-647, Sec. 1010(f)(6), deleted "section 821 or" after "taxable under" in subsec. (g), effective for tax. yrs. begin. after 12/31/86.
—P.L. 100-647, Sec. 1010(h)(1), amended Sec. 217(i)(2) of P.L. 98-369 [reproduced below], effective for tax. yrs. begin. after 12/31/86 and before 1/1/92. Sec. 1010(h)(3) of this Act provides:
"(3) Revenue loss limited.— The decrease in the amount of Federal revenue by reason of the amendment made by this subsection shall not exceed $300,000 per taxable year."
Prior to amendment Sec. 217(i)(2) of P.L. 98-369 read as follows:
"(2) Effect of election on subsidiaries of electing parent.—
"(A) Treated as mutual life insurance company.— Any stock life insurance company which is a member of an affiliated group which has a common parent which made an election under paragraph (1), for purposes of part 1 of subchapter

L, of the Internal Revenue Code of 1954, such stock life insurance company shall be treated as though it were a mutual life insurance company.

"(B) Income of electing parent taken into account in determining small life insurance company deduction of any subsidiary.— For purposes of determining the amount of the small life insurance company deduction of any controlled group which includes a mutual company which made an election under paragraph (1), the taxable income of such electing company shall be taken into account under section 806(b)(2) of the Internal Revenue Code of 1954 (relating to phase-out of small life insurance company deduction)."

— P.L. 100-647, Sec. 2004(q)(1), substituted "section 842(b)(2)(B)(i)" for "section 842(c)(1)(A)" in subsec. (h), effective for tax. yrs. begin. after 12/31/87.

In **1987**, P.L. 100-203, Sec. 10242(c)(2), substituted "842(c)(1)(A)" for "813(a)(4)(B)" in subsec. (h), effective for tax. yrs. begin. after 12/31/87.

In **1986**, P.L. 99-514, Sec. 1821(1), added subsec. (h), effective for tax. yrs. begin. after 12/31/83.

In **1984**, P.L. 98-369, Sec. 211(a), added Code Sec. 816 as part of the amendments to part I of Subchapter L, effective for tax. yrs. begin. after 12/31/83.

— P.L. 98-369, Sec. 217(e), provides:

"(e) *Treatment of certain companies operating both as stock and mutual company.* — If, during the 10-year period ending on December 31, 1983, a company has, as authorized by the law of the State in which the company is domiciled, been operating as a mutual life insurance company with shareholders, such company shall be treated as a stock life insurance company."

— P.L. 98-369, Sec. 217(i), [as amended by Sec. 1010(h)(1) of P.L. 100-647, see above], provides:

"(i) *Special election to treat individual noncancellable accident and health contracts as cancellable.*—

"(1) In general.— A mutual life insurance company may elect to treat all individual noncancellable (or guaranteed renewable) accident and health insurance contracts as though they were cancellable for purposes of section 816 of subchapter L of chapter 1 of the Internal Revenue Code of 1954.

"(2) Effect of election on subsidiaries of electing parent.— For purposes of determining the amount of the small life insurance company deduction of any controlled group which includes a mutual company which made an election under paragraph (1), the taxable income of such electing company shall be taken into account under section 806(b)(2) of the Internal Revenue Code of 1954 (relating to phaseout of small life insurance company deduction).

"(3) Election.— An election under paragraph (1) shall apply to the company's first taxable year beginning after December 31, 1983, and all taxable years thereafter.

"(4) Time and manner.— An election under paragraph (1) shall be made—

"(A) on the return of the taxpayer for its first taxable year beginning after December 31, 1983, and

"(B) in such manner as the Secretary of the Treasury or his delegate may prescribe."

Sec. 817. Treatment of variable contracts.
(a) Increases and decreases in reserves.

For purposes of subsections (a) and (b) of section 807, the sum of the items described in section 807(c) taken into account as of the close of the taxable year with respect to any variable contract shall, under regulations prescribed by the Secretary, be adjusted—

(1) by subtracting therefrom an amount equal to the sum of the amounts added from time to time (for the taxable year) to the reserves separately accounted for in accordance with subsection (c) by reason of appreciation in value of assets (whether or not the assets have been disposed of), and

(2) by adding thereto an amount equal to the sum of the amounts subtracted from time to time (for the taxable year) from such reserves by reason of depreciation in value of assets (whether or not the assets have been disposed of).

The deduction allowable for items described in paragraphs (1) and (6) of section 805(a) with respect to variable contracts shall be reduced to the extent that the amount of such items is increased for the taxable year by appreciation (or increased to the extent that the amount of such items is decreased for the taxable year by depreciation) not reflected in adjustments under the preceding sentence.

(b) Adjustment to basis of assets held in segregated asset account.

In the case of variable contracts, the basis of each asset in a segregated asset account shall (in addition to all other adjustments to basis) be—

(1) increased by the amount of any appreciation in value, and

(2) decreased by the amount of any depreciation in value, to the extent such appreciation and depreciation are from time to time reflected in the increases and decreases in reserves or other items referred to in subsection (a) with respect to such contracts.

(c) Separate accounting.

For purposes of this part, a life insurance company which issues variable contracts shall separately account for the various income, exclusion, deduction, asset, reserve, and other liability items properly attributable to such variable contracts. For such items as are not accounted for directly, separate accounting shall be made—

(1) in accordance with the method regularly employed by such company, if such method is reasonable, and

(2) in all other cases, in accordance with regulations prescribed by the Secretary.

(d) Variable contract defined.

For purposes of this part, the term "variable contract" means a contract—

(1) which provides for the allocation of all or part of the amounts received under the contract to an account which, pursuant to State law or regulation, is segregated from the general asset accounts of the company,

(2) which—

(A) provides for the payment of annuities,

(B) is a life insurance contract, or

(C) provides for funding of insurance on retired lives as described in section 807(c)(6), and

(3) under which—

(A) in the case of an annuity contract, the amounts paid in, or the amount paid out, reflect the investment return and the market value of the segregated asset account,

(B) in the case of a life insurance contract, the amount of the death benefit (or the period of coverage) is adjusted on the basis of the investment return and the market value of the segregated asset account , or

(C) in the case of funds held under a contract described in paragraph (2)(C), the amounts paid in, or the amounts paid out, reflect the investment return and the market value of the segregated asset account.

If a contract ceases to reflect current investment return and current market value, such contract shall not be considered as meeting the requirements of paragraph (3) after such cessation. Paragraph (3) shall be applied without regard to whether there is a guarantee, and obligations under such guarantee which exceed obligations under the contract without regard to such guarantee shall be accounted for as part of the company's general account.

(e) Pension plan contracts treated as paying annuity.

A pension plan contract which is not a life, accident, or health, property, casualty, or liability insurance contract shall be treated as a contract which provides for the payments of annuities for purposes of subsection (d).

(f) Other special rules.

(1) Life insurance reserves. For purposes of subsection (b)(1)(A) of section 816, the reflection of the investment return and the market value of the segregated asset account shall be considered an assumed rate of interest.

(2) Additional separate computations. Under regulations prescribed by the Secretary, such additional separate computations shall be made, with respect to the items separately accounted for in accordance with subsection (c), as may be necessary to carry out the purposes of this section and this part.

Insurance companies　　　　　　　　　　　　　　　　　　　　　　　　　　　　　　　　　Code Sec. 817A(c)

(g) Variable annuity contracts treated as annuity contracts.

For purposes of this part, the term "annuity contract" includes a contract which provides for the payment of a variable annuity computed on the basis of—

(1) recognized mortality tables, and

(2)(A) the investment experience of a segregated asset account, or

(B) the company-wide investment experience of the company.

Paragraph (2)(B) shall not apply to any company which issues contracts which are not variable contracts.

(h) Treatment of certain nondiversified contracts.

(1) In general. For purposes of subchapter L, section 72 (relating to annuities), and section 7702(a) (relating to definition of life insurance contract), a variable contract (other than a pension plan contract) which is otherwise described in this section and which is based on a segregated asset account shall not be treated as an annuity, endowment, or life insurance contract for any period (and any subsequent period) for which the investments made by such account are not, in accordance with regulations prescribed by the Secretary, adequately diversified.

(2) Safe harbor for diversification. A segregated asset account shall be treated as meeting the requirements of paragraph (1) for any quarter of a taxable year if as of the close of such quarter—

(A) it meets the requirements of section 851(b)(3), and

(B) no more than 55 percent of the value of the total assets of the account are assets described in section 851(b)(3)(A)(i).

(3) Special rule for investments in United States obligations. To the extent that any segregated asset account with respect to a variable life insurance contract is invested in securities issued by the United States Treasury, the investments made by such account shall be treated as adequately diversified for purposes of paragraph (1).

(4) Look-through in certain cases. For purposes of this subsection, if all of the beneficial interests in a regulated investment company or in a trust are held by 1 or more—

(A) insurance companies (or affiliated companies) in their general account or in segregated asset accounts, or

(B) fund managers (or affiliated companies) in connection with the creation or management of the regulated investment company or trust,

the diversification requirements of paragraph (1) shall be applied by taking into account the assets held by such regulated investment company or trust.

(5) Independent investment advisors permitted. Nothing in this subsection shall be construed as prohibiting the use of independent investment advisors.

(6) Government securities funds. In determining whether a segregated asset account is adequately diversified for purposes of paragraph (1), each United States Government agency or instrumentality shall be treated as a separate issuer.

In 2004, P.L. 108-218, Sec. 205(b)(5), deleted "(other than section 809)" after "For purposes of this part" in the first sentence of subsec. (c), effective for tax. yrs. begin. after 12/31/2004.

In 1997, P.L. 105-34, Sec. 1271(b)(8)(A), substituted "851(b)(3)" for "851(b)(4)," in subpara. (h)(2)(A) . . . Sec. 1271(b)(8)(B), substituted "851(b)(3)(A)(i)" for "851(b)(4)(A)(i)" in subpara. (h)(2)(B), effective for tax. yrs. begin. after 8/5/97.

In 1996, P.L. 104-188, Sec. 1611(a)(1), deleted "or" at the end of subpara. (d)(2)(A), substituted "or" for "and" at the end of subpara. (d)(2)(B) and added subpara. (d)(2)(C). . . . Sec. 1611(a)(2), deleted "or" at the end of subpara.

(d)(3)(A), substituted "or" for the period at the end of subpara. (d)(3)(B) and added subpara. (d)(3)(C), effective for tax. yrs. begin. after 12/31/95.

In 1988, P.L. 100-647, Sec. 1010(i)(1)-(3), amended the effective date for applying '86 Code Sec. 817(h), see below.

—P.L. 100-647, Sec. 6080(a), added para. (h)(6), effective for tax. yrs. begin. after 12/31/87.

In 1986, P.L. 99-514, Sec. 1821(m)(1), amended paras. (h)(3) and (h)(4), and added para. (h)(5) . . . Sec. 1821(m)(2), deleted the last sentence from para. (h)(1), effective for tax. yrs begin. after 12/31/83. Secs. 1010(i)(1)-(3) of P.L. 100-647, provide:

"(i) Delay in effective date for diversification requirements with respect to accounts for certain immediate annuities. Section 817(h) of the 1986 Code shall not apply until January 1, 1989 with respect to a variable contract (as defined in section 817(d) of the 1986 Code) if—

"(1) such contract provides for the payment of an immediate annuity (as defined in section 72(u)(4) of the 1986 Code),

"(2) such contract was outstanding on September 12, 1986, and

"(3) the segregated asset account on which such contract is based was, on September 12, 1986, wholly invested in deposits insured by the Federal Deposit Insurance Corporation or the Federal Savings and Loan Insurance Corporation."

Prior to amendment, paras. (h)(3) and (4) read as follows:

"(3) Special rule for variable life insurance contracts investing in United States obligations. In the case of a segregated asset account with respect to variable life insurance contracts, paragraph (1) shall not apply in the case of securities issued by the United States Treasury which are owned by a regulated investment company or by a trust all the beneficial interests in which are held by 1 or more segregated asset accounts of the company issuing the contract.

"(4) Independent investment advisors permitted. Nothing in this subsection shall be construed as prohibiting the use of independent investment advisors."

Prior to deletion, the last sentence of para. (h)(1) read as follows:

"For purposes of this paragraph and paragraph (2), beneficial interests in a regulated investment company or in a trust shall not be treated as 1 investment if all of the beneficial interests in such company or trust are held by 1 or more segregated asset accounts of 1 or more insurance companies."

—P.L. 99-514, Sec. 1821(t)(1), added the sentence at the end of subsec (d), effective for contracts issued after 12/31/86 and for contracts issued before 1/1/87, if such contract was treated as a variable contract on the taxpayer's return.

In 1984, P.L. 98-369, Sec. 211(a), added Code Sec. 817 as part of the amendments to part I of Subchapter L, effective for tax. yrs. begin. after 12/31/83.

Sec. 817A. Special rules for modified guaranteed contracts.

(a) Computation of reserves.

In the case of a modified guaranteed contract, clause (ii) of section 807(e)(1)(A) shall not apply.

(b) Segregated assets under modified guaranteed contracts marked to market.

(1) In general. In the case of any life insurance company, for purposes of this subtitle—

(A) Any gain or loss with respect to a segregated asset shall be treated as ordinary income or loss, as the case may be.

(B) If any segregated asset is held by such company as of the close of any taxable year—

(i) such company shall recognize gain or loss as if such asset were sold for its fair market value on the last business day of such taxable year, and

(ii) any such gain or loss shall be taken into account for such taxable year.

Proper adjustment shall be made in the amount of any gain or loss subsequently realized for gain or loss taken into account under the preceding sentence. The Secretary may provide by regulations for the application of this subparagraph at times other than the times provided in this subparagraph.

(2) Segregated asset. For purposes of paragraph (1), the term "segregated asset" means any asset held as part of a segregated account referred to in subsection (d)(1) under a modified guaranteed contract.

(c) Special rule in computing life insurance reserves.

For purposes of applying section 816(b)(1)(A) to any modified guaranteed contract, an assumed rate of interest shall include a rate of interest determined, from time to time, with reference to a market rate of interest.

(d) Modified guaranteed contract defined.

For purposes of this section, the term "modified guaranteed contract" means a contract not described in section 817—

(1) all or part of the amounts received under which are allocated to an account which, pursuant to State law or regulation, is segregated from the general asset accounts of the company and is valued from time to time with reference to market values,

(2) which—

(A) provides for the payment of annuities,

(B) is a life insurance contract, or

(C) is a pension plan contract which is not a life, accident, or health, property, casualty, or liability contract,

(3) for which reserves are valued at market for annual statement purposes, and

(4) which provides for a net surrender value or a policyholder's fund (as defined in section 807(e)(1)).

If only a portion of a contract is not described in section 817, such portion shall be treated for purposes of this section as a separate contract.

(e) Regulations.

The Secretary may prescribe regulations—

(1) to provide for the treatment of market value adjustments under sections 72, 7702, 7702A, and 807(e)(1)(B),

(2) to determine the interest rates applicable under sections 807(c)(3), 807(d)(2)(B), and 812 with respect to a modified guaranteed contract annually, in a manner appropriate for modified guaranteed contracts and, to the extent appropriate for such a contract, to modify or waive the applicability of section 811(d),

(3) to provide rules to limit ordinary gain or loss treatment to assets constituting reserves for modified guaranteed contracts (and not other assets) of the company,

(4) to provide appropriate treatment of transfers of assets to and from the segregated account, and

(5) as may be necessary or appropriate to carry out the purposes of this section.

In **1996**, P.L. 104-188, Sec. 1612(a), added Code Sec. 817A, effective for tax. yrs. begin. after 12/31/95. Secs. 1612(c)(2) and (3) of this Act provide:

"(2) Treatment of net adjustments. Except as provided in paragraph (3), in the case of any taxpayer required by the amendments made by this section to change its calculation of reserves to take into account market value adjustments and to mark segregated assets to market for any taxable year—

"(A) such changes shall be treated as a change in method of accounting initiated by the taxpayer,

"(B) such changes shall be treated as made with the consent of the Secretary, and

"(C) the adjustments required by reason of section 481 of the Internal Revenue Code of 1986, shall be taken into account as ordinary income by the taxpayer for the taxpayer's first taxable year beginning after December 31, 1995.

"(3) Limitation on loss recognition and on deduction for reserve increases.

"(A) Limitation on loss recognition.

"(i) In general. The aggregate loss recognized by reason of the application of section 481 of the Internal Revenue Code of 1986 with respect to section 817A(b) of such Code (as added by this section) for the first taxable year of the taxpayer beginning after December 31, 1995, shall not exceed the amount included in the taxpayer's gross income for such year by reason of the excess (if any) of—

"(I) the amount of life insurance reserves as of the close of the prior taxable year, over

"(II) the amount of such reserves as of the beginning of such first taxable year, to the extent such excess is attributable to subsection (a) of such section 817A. Notwithstanding the preceding sentence, the adjusted basis of each segregated asset shall be determined as if all such losses were recognized.

"(ii) Disallowed loss allowed over period. The amount of the loss which is not allowed under clause (i) shall be allowed ratably over the period of 7 taxable years beginning with the taxpayer's first taxable year beginning after December 31, 1995.

"(B) Limitation on deduction for increase in reserves.

"(i) In general. The deduction allowed for the first taxable year of the taxpayer beginning after December 31, 1995, by reason of the application of section 481 of such Code with respect to section 817A(a) of such Code (as added by this section) shall not exceed the aggregate built-in gain recognized by reason of the application of such section 481 with respect to section 817A(b) of such Code (as added by this section) for such first taxable year.

"(ii) Disallowed deduction allowed over period. The amount of the deduction which is disallowed under clause (i) shall be allowed ratably over the period of 7 taxable years beginning with the taxpayer's first taxable year beginning after December 31, 1995.

"(iii) Built-in gain. For purposes of this subparagraph, the built-in gain on an asset is the amount equal to the excess of—

"(I) the fair market value of the asset as of the beginning of the first taxable year of the taxpayer beginning after December 31, 1995, over

"(II) the adjusted basis of such asset as of such time."

Sec. 818. Other definitions and special rules.
(a) Pension plan contracts.

For purposes of this part, the term "pension plan contract" means any contract—

(1) entered into with trusts which (as of the time the contracts were entered into) were deemed to be trusts described in section 401(a) and exempt from tax under section 501(a) (or trusts exempt from tax under section 165 of the Internal Revenue Code of 1939 or the corresponding provisions of prior revenue laws);

(2) entered into under plans which (as of the time the contracts were entered into) were deemed to be plans described in section 403(a), or plans meeting the requirements of paragraphs (3), (4), (5), and (6) of section 165(a) of the Internal Revenue Code of 1939;

(3) provided for employees of the life insurance company under a plan which, for the taxable year, meets the requirements of paragraphs (3), (4), (5), (6), (7), (8), (11), (12), (13), (14), (15), (16), (17), (19), (20), (22), (26), and (27) of section 401(a);

(4) purchased to provide retirement annuities for its employees by an organization which (as of the time the contracts were purchased) was an organization described in section 501(c)(3) which was exempt from tax under section 501(a) (or was an organization exempt from tax under section 101(6) of the Internal Revenue Code of 1939 or the corresponding provisions of prior revenue laws), or purchased to provide retirement annuities for employees described in section 403(b)(1)(A)(ii) by an employer which is a State, a political subdivision of a State, or an agency or instrumentality of any one or more of the foregoing;

(5) entered into with trusts which (at the time the contracts were entered into) were individual retirement accounts described in section 408(a) or under contracts entered into with individual retirement annuities described in section 408(b); or

(6) purchased by—

(A) a governmental plan (within the meaning of section 414(d)) or an eligible deferred compensation plan (within the meaning of section 457(b)), or

(B) the Government of the United States, the government of any State or political subdivision thereof, or by any agency or instrumentality of the foregoing, or any organization (other than a governmental unit) exempt from tax under this subtitle, for use in satisfying an obligation of such government, political subdivision, agency or instrumentality, or organization to provide a benefit under a plan described in subparagraph (A).

(b) Treatment of capital gains and losses, etc.

In the case of a life insurance company,—

(1) in applying section 1231(a), the term "property used in the trade or business" shall be treated as including only—

(A) property used in carrying on an insurance business, of a character which is subject to the allowance for depreciation provided in section 167, held for more than 1 year, and real property used in carrying on an insurance

Insurance companies   Code Sec. 818

business, held for more than 1 year, which is not described in section 1231(b)(1)(A), (B), or (C), and

(B) property described in section 1231(b)(2), and

(2) in applying section 1221(a)(2), the reference to property used in trade or business shall be treated as including only property used in carrying on an insurance business.

(c) Gain on property held on December 31, 1958 and certain substituted property acquired after 1958.

(1) Property held on December 31, 1958. In the case of property held by the taxpayer on December 31, 1958, if—

(A) the fair market value of such property on such date exceeds the adjusted basis for determining gain as of such date, and

(B) the taxpayer has been a life insurance company at all times on and after December 31, 1958,

the gain on the sale or other disposition of such property shall be treated as an amount (not less than zero) equal to the amount by which the gain (determined without regard to this subsection) exceeds the difference between the fair market value on December 31, 1958, and the adjusted basis for determining gain as of such date.

(2) Certain property acquired after December 31, 1958. In the case of property acquired after December 31, 1958, and having a substituted basis (within the meaning of section 1016(b))—

(A) for purposes of paragraph (1), such property shall be deemed held continuously by the taxpayer since the beginning of the holding period thereof, determined with reference to section 1223,

(B) the fair market value and adjusted basis referred to in paragraph (1) shall be that of that property for which the holding period taken into account includes December 31, 1958,

(C) paragraph (1) shall apply only if the property or properties the holding periods of which are taken into account were held only by life insurance companies after December 31, 1958, during the holding periods so taken into account,

(D) the difference between the fair market value and adjusted basis referred to in paragraph (1) shall be reduced (to not less than zero) by the excess of (i) the gain that would have been recognized but for this subsection on all prior sales or dispositions after December 31, 1958, of properties referred to in subparagraph (C), over (ii) the gain which was recognized on such sales or other dispositions, and

(E) the basis of such property shall be determined as if the gain which would have been recognized but for this subsection were recognized gain.

(3) Property defined. For purposes of paragraphs (1) and (2), the term "property" does not include insurance and annuity contracts and property described in paragraph (1) of section 1221(a).

(d) Insurance or annuity contract includes contracts supplementary thereto.

For purposes of this part, the term "insurance or annuity contract" includes any contract supplementary thereto.

(e) Special rules for consolidated returns.

(1) Items of companies other than life insurance companies. If an election under section 1504(c)(2) is in effect with respect to an affiliated group for the taxable year, all items of the members of such group which are not life insurance companies shall not be taken into account in determining the amount of the tentative LICTI of members of such group which are life insurance companies.

(2) Dividends within group. In the case of a life insurance company filing or required to file a consolidated return under section 1501 with respect to any affiliated group for any taxable year, any determination under this part with respect to any dividend paid by one member of such group to another member of such group shall be made as if such group was not filing a consolidated return.

(f) Allocation of certain items for purposes of foreign tax credit, etc.

(1) In general. Under regulations, in applying sections 861, 862, and 863 to a life insurance company, the deduction for policyholder dividends (determined under section 808(c)), reserve adjustments under subsections (a) and (b) of section 807, and death benefits and other amounts described in section 805(a)(1) shall be treated as items which cannot definitely be allocated to an item or class of gross income.

(2) Election of alternative allocation.

(A) In general. On or before September 15, 1985, any life insurance company may elect to treat items described in paragraph (1) as properly apportioned or allocated among items of gross income to the extent (and in the manner) prescribed in regulations.

(B) Election irrevocable. Any election under subparagraph (A), once made, may be revoked only with the consent of the Secretary.

(3) Items described in section 807(c) treated as not interest for source rules, etc. For purposes of part I of subchapter N, items described in any paragraph of section 807(c) shall be treated as amounts which are not interest.

(g) Qualified accelerated death benefit riders treated as life insurance.

For purposes of this part—

(1) In general. Any reference to a life insurance contract shall be treated as including a reference to a qualified accelerated death benefit rider on such contract.

(2) Qualified accelerated death benefit riders. For purposes of this subsection, the term "qualified accelerated death benefit rider" means any rider on a life insurance contract if the only payments under the rider are payments meeting the requirements of section 101(g).

(3) Exception for long-term care riders. Paragraph (1) shall not apply to any rider which is treated as a long-term care insurance contract under section 7702B.

In 1999, P.L. 106-170, Sec. 532(c)(1)(D), substituted "section 1221(a)" for "section 1221" in para. (c)(3) . . . Sec. 532(c)(3), substituted "section 1221(a)(2)" for "section 1221(2)" in para. (b)(2), effective for any instrument held, acquired, or entered into, any transaction entered into, and supplies held or acquired on or after 12/17/99.

In 1996, P.L. 104-191, Sec. 332(a), added subsec. (g), effective 1/1/97. Sec. 332(b)(2), of this Act, provides:

"(2) Issuance of rider not treated as material change. For purposes of applying sections 101(f), 7702, and 7702A of the Internal Revenue Code of 1986 to any contract—

"(A) the issuance of a qualified accelerated death benefit rider (as defined in section 818(g) of such Code (as added by this Act), and

"(B) the addition of any provision required to conform an accelerated death benefit rider to the requirements of such section 818(g),

shall not be treated as a modification or material change of such contract."

In 1988, P.L. 100-647, Sec. 1010(k), added para. (f)(3) effective for tax. yrs. begin. after 12/31/86.

—P.L. 100-647, Sec. 1011(e)(5)(A), deleted "State" after "eligible" in subpara. (a)(6)(A), added "or any organization (other than a governmental unit) exempt from tax under this subtitle," after "foregoing" in subpara. (a)(6)(B), deleted "or" before "agency" in subpara. (a)(6)(B), added "organization" after "instrumentality" the second place it appeared in subpara. (a)(6)(B), effective for contracts issued after 12/31/86.

In 1986, P.L. 99-514, Sec. 1106(d)(3)(C), added "(17)," after "(16)" in para. (a)(3), effective for benefits accruing in years begin. after 12/31/88, except as provided in Sec. 1106(i)(5)(B) of this Act which provides:

"(B) Collective bargaining agreements. In the case of a plan described in paragraph (2), the amendments made by subsection (d) shall apply to benefits accruing in years beginning on or after the earlier of—

Code Sec. 818

"(i) the later of—
"(I) the date determined under paragraph (2)(A), or
"(II) January 1, 1989, or
"(ii) January 1, 1991."
— P.L. 99-514, Sec. 1112(d)(4), substituted "(22), and (26)" for "and (22)" in para. (a)(3), effective for plan years begin. after 12/31/88.
— P.L. 99-514, Sec. 1136(b), substituted "(26) and (27)" for "and (26)" in para. (a)(3), effective 10/22/86.
— P.L. 99-514, Sec. 1821(n), amended para. (a)(6)(A) . . . Sec. 1821(o), amended subsec. (e), effective for tax. yrs. begin. after 12/31/83.
Prior to amendment, subpara. (a)(6)(A) read as follows:
"(A) a governmental plan (within the meaning of section 414(d)), or"
Prior to amendment, subsec. (e) read as follows:
"(e) *Special rule for consolidated returns.* If an election under section 1504(c)(2) is in effect with respect to an affiliated group for the taxable year, all items of the members of such group which are not life insurance companies shall not be taken into account in determining the amount of the tentative LICTI of members of such group which are life insurance companies."
In 1984, P.L. 98-369, Sec. 211(a), added Code Sec. 818 as part of the amendments to part I of Subchapter L, effective for tax. yrs. begin. after 12/31/83.
— P.L. 98-369, Sec. 1001(b)(10), substituted "6 months" for "1 year" each place it appeared in subpara. (b)(1)(A), effective for property acquired after 6/22/84, and before 1/1/88.

PART II. Repealed [MUTUAL INSURANCE COMPANIES (OTHER THAN LIFE AND CERTAIN MARINE INSURANCE COMPANIES AND OTHER THAN FIRE OR FLOOD INSURANCE COMPANIES WHICH OPERATE ON BASIS OF PERPETUAL POLICIES OR PREMIUM DEPOSITS)]

Sec.
821. Repealed. [Tax on mutual insurance companies to which part II applies.]
822. [Determination of taxable investment income]
823. Repealed. [Determination of statutory underwriting income or loss.]
824. Repealed. [Adjustments to provide protection against losses.]
825. Repealed. [Unused loss deduction.]
826. [Election by reciprocal]

In 1986, P.L. 99-514, Sec. 1024(a)(1), Repealed Part II, effective for tax. yrs. begin. after 12/31/86. . . . Sec. 1024(a)(3), redesignated Code Sec. 822 as Code Sec. 834, and redesignated Code Sec. 826 as Code Sec. 835.
Prior to repeal, Part II read as follows:
"Part II. Mutual insurance companies (other than life and certain marine insurance companies and other than fire or flood insurance companies which operate on basis of perpetual policies or premium deposits)
"Sec.
"821. Tax on mutual insurance companies to which part II applies.
"822. Determination of taxable investment income
"823. Determination of statutory underwriting income or loss.
"824. Adjustments to provide protection against losses.
"825. Unused loss deduction.
"826. Election by reciprocal"
In 1962, P.L. 87-834, Sec. 8, amended the table for Part II and added items 824–826.
Prior to amendment, Part II read as follows:
"Part II. Mutual insurance companies (other than life or marine or fire insurance companies issuing perpetual policies)
"Sec.
"821. Tax on mutual insurance companies (other than life or marine or fire insurance companies issuing perpetual policies)
"822. Determination of mutual insurance company taxable income
"823. Other definitions"

Sec. 821. Repealed.

In 1986, P.L. 99-514, Sec. 1024(a)(1), repealed Code Sec. 821, effective for tax. yrs. begin after 12/31/86.
Prior to repeal, Code Sec. 821 read as follows:
"SEC. 821. TAX ON MUTUAL INSURANCE COMPANIES TO WHICH PART II APPLIES.
"(a) Imposition of tax.
"(1) In general. A tax is hereby imposed for each taxable year on the mutual insurance company taxable income of every mutual insurance company (other than a life insurance company and other than a fire, flood, or marine insurance company subject to the tax imposed by section 831). Such tax shall be computed by multiplying the mutual insurance company taxable income by the rates provided in section 11(b).

"(2) Cap on tax where income is less than $12,000. The tax imposed by paragraph (1) on so much of the mutual insurance company taxable income as does not exceed $12,000 shall not exceed 32 percent (30 percent for taxable years beginning after December 31, 1982) of the amount by which such income exceeds $6,000.
"(b) Mutual insurance company taxable income defined.
"For purposes of this part, the term 'mutual insurance company taxable income' means, with respect to any taxable year, the amount by which—
"(1) the sum of—
"(A) the taxable investment income (as defined in section 822(a)(1)),
"(B) the statutory underwriting income (as defined in section 823(a)(1)), and
"(C) the amounts required by section 824(d) to be subtracted from the protection against loss account, exceeds
"(2) the sum of—
"(A) the investment loss (as defined in section 822(a)(2)),
"(B) the statutory underwriting loss (as defined in section 823(a)(2)), and
"(C) the unused loss deduction provided by section 825(a).
"(c) Alternative tax for certain small companies.
"(1) Imposition of tax.
"(A) In general. There is hereby imposed for each taxable year on the income of every mutual insurance company to which this subsection applies a tax (which shall be in lieu of the tax imposed by subsection (a)). Such tax shall be computed by multiplying the taxable investment income by the rates provided in section 11(b).
"(B) Cap where income is less than $6,000. The tax imposed by subparagraph (A) on so much of the taxable investment income as does not exceed $6,000 shall not exceed 32 percent (30 percent for taxable years beginning after December 31, 1982) of the amount by which such income exceeds $3,000.
"(2) Gross amount received over $150,000 but less than $250,000. If the gross amount received during the taxable year from the items described in section 822(b) (other than paragraph (1)(D) thereof) and premiums (including deposits and assessments) is over $150,000 but less than $250,000, the tax imposed by paragraph (1) shall be reduced to an amount which bears the same proportion to the amount of the tax determined under paragraph (1) as the excess over $150,000 of such gross amount received bears to $100,000.
"(3) Companies to which subsection applies.
"(A) In general. Except as provided in subparagraph (B), this subsection shall apply to every mutual insurance company (other than a life insurance company and other than a fire, flood, or marine insurance company subject to the tax imposed by section 831) which received during the taxable year from the items described in section 822(b) (other than paragraph (1)(D) thereof) and premiums (including deposits and assessments) a gross amount in excess of $150,000 but not in excess of $500,000.
"(B) Exceptions. This subsection shall not apply to a mutual insurance company for the taxable year if—
"(i) there is in effect an election by such company made under subsection (d) to be taxable under subsection (a); or
"(ii) there is any amount in the protection against loss account at the beginning of the taxable year.
"(d) Election to include statutory underwriting income or loss.
"(1) In general. Any mutual insurance company which is subject to the tax imposed by subsection (c) may elect, in such manner and at such time as the Secretary may by regulations prescribe, to be subject to the tax imposed by subsection (a).
"(2) Effect of election. If an election is made under paragraph (1), the electing company shall be subject to the tax imposed by subsection (a) and shall not be subject to the tax imposed by subsection (c) for the first taxable year for which such election is made and for all taxable years thereafter unless the Secretary consents to a revocation of such election.
"(e) Tax applicable to member of group filing consolidated return.
"Notwithstanding any other provision of this section, if a mutual insurance company to which this section applies joins in the filing of a consolidated return (or is required to so file), the applicable tax shall consist of a normal tax and a surtax computed as provided in section 11 as though the mutual insurance company taxable income of such company were the taxable income referred to in section 11.
"(f) Cross references.
"(1) For exemption from tax of certain mutual insurance companies, see section 501(c)(15).
"(2) For alternative tax in case of capital gains, see section 1201(a).
"(3) For taxation of foreign corporations carrying on an insurance business within the United States, see section 842."
— P.L. 99-514, Sec. 1879(q)(1)-(4), provides as follows:
"(q) Treatment of certain self-insured workers' compensation funds.
"(1) Moratorium on collection activities. During the period beginning on the date of the enactment of this Act [10/22/86] and ending on August 16, 1987, the Secretary of the Treasury or his delegate—
"(A) shall suspend any pending audit of any self-insured workers' compensation fund where the audit involves the issue of whether such fund is a mutual insurance company,
"(B) shall not initiate any audit of any such fund involving such issue, and
"(C) shall take no steps to collect from such fund any underpayment, interest, or penalty involving such issue.
"(2) Suspension of running of interest. No interest shall be payable under chapter 67 of the Internal Revenue Code of 1986 on any underpayment by a self-insured workers' compensation fund involving such issue for the period beginning on August 16, 1986, and ending on August 16, 1987.

Insurance companies Code Sec. 821

"(3) Additional time to file tax court proceeding. If the period during which a petition involving such issue could have been filed with the Tax Court by any self-insured workers' compensation fund had not expired before August 16, 1986, such period shall not expire before August 16, 1987.

"(4) Self-insured workers' compensation fund. For purposes of this subsection, the term 'self-insured workers' compensation fund' means any self-insured workers' compensation fund established pursuant to applicable State law regulating self-insured workers' compensation funds."

In 1981, P.L. 97-34, Sec. 231(b)(1), amended para. (a)(2)... Sec. 231(b)(2), amended subpara. (c)(1)(B), effective as provided in Sec. 231(b)(3) of this Act which reads as follows:

"(3) The amendments made by paragraphs (1) and (2) [Sec. 231(b)] shall apply to taxable years beginning after December 31, 1978; except that for purposes of applying sections 821(a)(2) and 821(c)(1)(B) of the Internal Revenue Code of 1954 (as amended by this subsection) to taxable years beginning before January 1, 1982, the percentage referred to in such section shall be deemed to be 34 percent."

Prior to amendment, para. (a)(2) read as follows:

"(2) Cap on tax where income is less than $12,000. The tax imposed by paragraph (1) shall not exceed 34 percent of the amount by which the mutual insurance company taxable income exceeds $6,000."

Prior to amendment, subpara. (c)(1)(B) read as follows:

"(B) Cap where income is less than $6,000. The tax imposed by subparagraph (A) shall not exceed 34 percent of the amount by which the taxable investment income exceeds $3,000."

In 1978, P.L. 95-600, Sec. 301(b)(9)(A), amended subsec. (a)... Sec. 301(b)(9)(B), amended para. (c)(1), effective for tax. yrs. begin. after 12/31/78.

Prior to amendment, subsec. (a) read as follows:

"(a) Imposition of tax.

"A tax is hereby imposed for each taxable year on the mutual insurance company taxable income of every mutual insurance company (other than a life insurance company and other than a fire, flood, or marine insurance company subject to the tax imposed by section 831). Such tax shall consist of—

"(1) Normal tax. A normal tax equal to—

"(A) in the case of a taxable year ending after December 31, 1978, 22 percent of the mutual insurance company taxable income, or 44 percent of the amount by which such taxable income exceeds $6,000, whichever is lesser, or

"(B) in the case of a taxable year ending after December 31, 1974, and before January 1, 1979—

"(i) 20 percent of so much of the mutual insurance company taxable income as does not exceed $25,000, plus

"(ii) 22 percent of so much of the mutual insurance company taxable income as exceeds $25,000,

or 44 percent of the amount by which such taxable income exceeds $6,000, whichever is lesser, plus.

"(2) Surtax. A surtax on the mutual insurance company taxable income computed as provided in section 11(c) as though the mutual insurance company taxable income were the taxable income referred to in section 11(c)."

Prior to amendment, para. (c)(1) read as follows:

"(c) Alternative tax for certain small companies.

"(1) Imposition of tax. There is hereby imposed for each taxable year on the income of each mutual insurance company to which this subsection applies a tax (which shall be in lieu of the tax imposed by subsection (a)) computed as follows:

"(A) Normal tax. A normal tax equal to—

"(i) in the case of a taxable year ending after December 31, 1978, 22 percent of the taxable investment income, or 44 percent of the amount by which such taxable income exceeds $3,000, whichever is lesser, or

"(ii) in the case of a taxable year ending after December 31, 1974, and before January 1, 1979, 20 percent of so much of the taxable investment income as does not exceed $25,000, plus 22 percent of so much of the taxable investment income as exceeds $25,000, or 44 percent of the amount by which such taxable income exceeds $3,000, whichever is lesser, plus.

"(B) Surtax. A surtax on the taxable investment income computed as provided in section 11(c) as though the taxable investment income were the taxable income referred to in section 11(c)."

In 1977, P.L. 95-30, Sec. 201(3) and (4), substituted "December 31, 1978" for "December 31, 1977" and "January 1, 1979" for "January 1, 1978" in para. (a)(1) and subpara. (c)(1)(A), effective 5/23/77.

In 1976, P.L. 94-455, Sec. 901(b)(1), amended para. (a)(1), effective for tax. yrs. end. after 12/31/74.

Prior to amendment, para. (a)(1) read as follows:

"(1) Normal tax. A normal tax of 22 percent of the mutual insurance company taxable income, or 44 percent of the amount by which such taxable income exceeds $6,000, whichever is the lesser; plus"

— P.L. 94-455, Sec. 901(b)(2), amended subpara. (c)(1)(A), effective for tax. yrs. end. after 12/31/74.

Prior to amendment, subpara. (c)(1)(A) read as follows:

"(A) Normal tax. A normal tax of 22 percent of the taxable investment income, or 44 percent of the amount by which such taxable income exceeds $3,000, whichever is the lesser; plus"

— P.L. 94-455, Sec. 1507(b)(1), redesignated subsec. (e) as (f) and added new subsec. (e), effective for distributions and payments made after 12/31/75, in tax. yrs. begin. after 12/31/75.

— P.L. 94-455, Sec. 1901(a)(104), deleted "beginning after December 31, 1963," after "taxable year" in the first sentence of subsec. (a), substituted "There is" for "In the case of taxable years beginning after December 31, 1963, there is" in

para. (c)(1), deleted subsec. (e) and redesignated subsec. (f) as subsec. (e), effective for tax. yrs. begin. after 12/31/76.

Prior to repeal, subsec. (e) read as follows:

"(e) Special transitional underwriting loss.

"(1) Companies to which subsection applies. This subsection shall apply to every mutual insurance company which has been subject to the tax imposed by this section (as in effect before the enactment of this subsection) for the 5 taxable years immediately preceding January 1, 1962, and has incurred an underwriting loss for each of such 5 taxable years.

"(2) Reduction of statutory underwriting income. For purposes of this part, the statutory underwriting income of a company described in paragraph (1) for the taxable year shall be the statutory underwriting income for the taxable year (determined without regard to this subsection) reduced by the amount by which—

"(A) the sum of the underwriting losses of such company for the 5 taxable years immediately preceding January 1, 1962, exceeds

"(B) the total amount by which the company's statutory underwriting income was reduced by reason of this subsection for prior taxable years.

"(3) Underwriting loss defined. For purposes of this subsection, the term 'underwriting loss' means statutory underwriting loss, computed without any deduction under section 824(a) and without any deduction under section 832(c)(11).

"(4) Years to which subsection applies. This subsection shall apply with respect to any taxable year beginning after December 31, 1962, and before January 1, 1968, for which the taxpayer is subject to the tax imposed by subsection (a)."

— P.L. 94-455, Sec. 1906(b)(13)(A), substituted "Secretary" for "Secretary or his delegate" each place it appeared in subsec. (d), effective for tax. yrs. begin. after 12/31/76.

In 1966, P.L. 89-809, Sec. 104, deleted subsec. (e), redesignated subsecs. (f) and (g) as subsecs. (e) and (f) and added para. (f)(3), effective for tax. yrs. begin. after 12/31/66.

Prior to deletion, subsec. (e) read as follows:

"(e) No United States insurance business.

"Foreign mutual insurance companies (other than a life insurance company and other than a fire, flood, or marine insurance company subject to the tax imposed by section 831) not carrying on an insurance business within the United States shall not be subject to this part but shall be taxable as other foreign corporations."

In 1964, P.L. 88-272, Sec. 123(a)(1), amended subsec. (a)... Sec. 123(a)(2), amended para. (c)(1), effective for tax. yrs. begin. after 12/31/63.

Prior to amendment, subsec. (a) read as follows:

"(a) Imposition of tax.

"A tax is hereby imposed for each taxable year beginning after December 31, 1962, on the mutual insurance company taxable income of every mutual insurance company (other than a life insurance company and other than a fire, flood, or marine insurance company subject to the tax imposed by section 831). Such tax shall consist of—

"(1) Normal tax.

"(A) Taxable years beginning before July 1, 1964. In the case of taxable years beginning before July 1, 1964, a normal tax of 30 percent of the mutual insurance company taxable income, or 60 percent of the amount by which such taxable income exceeds $6,000, whichever is the lesser;

"(B) Taxable years beginning after June 30, 1964. In the case of taxable years beginning after June 30, 1964, a normal tax of 25 percent of the mutual insurance company taxable income, or 50 percent of the amount by which such taxable income exceeds $6,000, whichever is the lesser; plus

"(2) Surtax. A surtax of 22 percent of the mutual insurance company taxable income (computed without regard to the deduction provided in section 242 for partially tax-exempt interest) in excess of $25,000."

Prior to amendment, para. (c)(1) read as follows:

"(c) Alternative tax for certain small companies.

"(1) Imposition of tax. In the case of taxable years beginning after December 31, 1962, there is hereby imposed for each taxable year on the income of each mutual insurance company to which this subsection applies a tax (which shall be in lieu of the tax imposed by subsection (a)) computed as follows:

"(A) Normal tax.

"(i) Taxable years beginning before July 1, 1964. In the case of taxable years beginning before July 1, 1964, a normal tax of 30 percent of the taxable investment income, or 60 percent of the amount by which such taxable income exceeds $3,000, whichever is the lesser;

"(ii) Taxable years beginning after June 30, 1964. In the case of taxable years beginning after June 30, 1964, a normal tax of 25 percent of the taxable investment income, or 50 percent of the amount by which such taxable income exceeds $3,000, whichever is the lesser; plus

"(B) Surtax. A surtax of 22 percent of the taxable investment income (computed without regard to the deduction provided in section 242 for partially tax-exempt interest) in excess of $25,000."

In 1963, P.L. 88-52, Sec. 2(1), substituted "July 1, 1964" for "July 1, 1963" in the heading of subpara. (a)(1)(A)... Sec. 2(2), substituted "July 1, 1964" for "July 1, 1963" in subpara. (a)(1)(A)... Sec. 2(3), substituted "June 30, 1964" for "June 30, 1963" in the heading of clauses (c)(1)(A)(i) and (ii)... Sec. 2(4), substituted "June 30, 1964" for "June 30, 1963" in clause (c)(1)(A), effective 6/29/63.

In 1962, P.L. 87-834, Sec. 8, amended Code Sec. 821, effective for tax. yrs. begin. after 12/31/62.

Prior to amendment, Code Sec. 821 read as follows:

"SEC. 821. TAX ON MUTUAL INSURANCE COMPANIES (OTHER THAN LIFE OR MARINE OR FIRE INSURANCE COMPANIES ISSUING PERPETUAL POLICIES).

"(a) Imposition of tax on mutual companies other than interinsurers.

2,411

Code Sec. 821 — Insurance companies

"There shall be imposed for each taxable year on the income of every mutual insurance company (other than a life or a marine insurance company or a fire insurance company subject to the tax imposed by section 831 and other than an interinsurer or reciprocal underwriter) a tax computed under paragraph (1) or paragraph (2), whichever is the greater:

"(1) If the mutual insurance company taxable income (computed without regard to the deduction provided in section 242 for partially tax-exempt interest) is over $3,000, a tax computed as follows:

"(A) Normal tax.

"(i) Taxable years beginning before July 1, 1963. In the case of taxable years beginning before July 1, 1963, a normal tax of 30 percent of the mutual insurance company taxable income, or 60 percent of the amount by which such taxable income exceeds $3,000, whichever is the lesser;

"(ii) Taxable years beginning after June 30, 1963. In the case of taxable years beginning after June 30, 1963, a normal tax of 25 percent of the mutual insurance company taxable income, or 50 percent of the amount by which such taxable income exceeds $3,000, whichever is the lesser; plus

"(B) Surtax. A surtax of 22 percent of the mutual insurance company taxable income (computed without regard to the deduction provided in section 242 for partially tax-exempt interest) in excess of $25,000.

"(2) If for the taxable year the gross amount of income from the items described in section 822(b) (other than paragraph (1)(D) thereof) and net premiums, minus dividends to policyholders, minus the interest which under section 103 is excluded from gross income, exceeds $75,000, a tax equal to 1 percent of the amount so computed, or 2 percent of the excess of the amount so computed over $75,000, whichever is the lesser.

"(b) Imposition of tax on interinsurers.

"In the case of every mutual insurance company which is an interinsurer or reciprocal underwriter (other than a life or a marine insurance company or a fire insurance company (subject to the tax imposed by section 831), if the mutual insurance company taxable income (computed as provided in subsection (a)(1)) is over $50,000, there shall be imposed for each taxable year on the mutual insurance company taxable income a tax computed as follows:

"(1) Normal tax.

"(A) Taxable years beginning before July 1, 1963. In the case of taxable years beginning before July 1, 1963, a normal tax of 30 percent of the mutual insurance company taxable income, or 60 percent of the amount by which such taxable income exceeds $50,000, whichever is the lesser;

"(B) Taxable years beginning after June 30, 1963. In the case of a taxable year beginning after June 30, 1963, a normal tax of 25 percent of the mutual insurance company taxable income, or 50 percent of the amount by which such taxable income exceeds $50,000, whichever is the lesser; plus

"(2) Surtax. A surtax of 22 percent of the mutual insurance company taxable income (computed as provided in subsection (a)(1)) in excess of $25,000, or 33 percent of the amount by which such taxable income exceeds $50,000, whichever is the lesser.

"(c) Gross amount received, over $75,000 but less than $125,000.

"If the gross amount received during the taxable year from the items described in section 822(b) (other than paragraph (1)(D) thereof) and premiums (including deposits and assessments) is over $75,000 but less than $125,000, the tax imposed by subsection (a) or subsection (b), whichever applies, shall be reduced to an amount which bears the same proportion to the amount of the tax determined under such subsection as the excess over $75,000 of such gross amount received bears to $50,000.

"(d) No United States insurance business.

"Foreign mutual insurance companies (other than a life or marine insurance company or a fire insurance company subject to the tax imposed by section 831) not carrying on an insurance business within the United States shall not be subject to this part but shall be taxable as other foreign corporations.

"(e) Alternative tax on capital gains.

"For alternative tax in case of capital gains, see section 1201(a)."

—P.L. 87-508, Sec. 2(1), substituted "July 1, 1963" for "July 1, 1962" in the heading of clauses (a)(1)(A)(i) and (ii)... Sec. 2(2), substituted "July 1, 1963" for "July 1, 1962" in subpara. (a)(1)(A)... Sec. 2(3), substituted "June 30, 1963" for "June 30, 1962" in the heading of subparas. (b)(1)(A) and (B)... Sec. 2(4), substituted "June 30, 1963" for "June 30, 1962" in para. (b)(1), effective 6/28/62.

In 1961, P.L. 87-72, Sec. 2(1), substituted "July 1, 1962" for "July 1, 1961" in the heading of clauses (a)(1)(A)(i) and (ii)... Sec. 2(2), substituted "July 1, 1962" for "July 1, 1961" in subpara. (a)(1)(A)... Sec. 2(3), substituted "June 30, 1962" for "June 30, 1961" in the heading of subparas. (b)(1)(A) and (B)... Sec. 2(4), substituted "June 30, 1962" for "June 30, 1961" in para. (b)(1), effective 6/30/61.

In 1960, P.L. 86-564, Sec. 2(1), substituted "July 1, 1961" for "July 1, 1960" in the heading of clauses. (a)(1)(A)(i) and (ii)... Sec. 2(2), substituted "July 1, 1961" for "July 1, 1960" in subpara. (a)(1)(A)... Sec. 2(3), substituted "June 30, 1961" for "June 30, 1960" in the heading of subparas. (b)(1)(A) and (B)... Sec. 2(4), substituted "June 30, 1961" for "June 30, 1960" in para. (b)(1), effective 6/30/60.

In 1959, P.L. 86-75, Sec. 2(1), substituted "July 1, 1960" for "July 1, 1959" in the heading of clauses (a)(1)(A)(i) and (ii)... Sec. 2(2), substituted "July 1, 1960" for "July 1, 1959" in subpara. (a)(1)(A)... Sec. 2(3), substituted "June 30, 1960" for "June 30, 1959" in the heading of subparas. (b)(1)(A) and (B)... Sec. 2(4), substituted "June 30, 1960" for "June 30, 1959" in para. (b)(1), effective 6/30/59.

In 1958, P.L. 85-475, Sec. 2(1), substituted "July 1, 1959" for "July 1, 1958" in the heading of clauses (a)(1)(A)(i) and (ii)... Sec. 2(2), substituted "July 1, 1959" for "July 1, 1958" in subpara. (a)(1)(A)... Sec. 2(3), substituted "June 30, 1959" for "June 30, 1958" in the heading of subparas. (b)(1)(A) and (B)... Sec. 2(4), substituted "June 30, 1959" for "June 30, 1958" in para. (b)(1), effective 6/30/58.

In 1957, P.L. 85-12, Sec. 2(1), substituted "July 1, 1958" for "April 1, 1957" in the heading of clauses (a)(1)(A)(i) and (ii)... Sec. 2(2), substituted "July 1, 1958" for "April 1, 1957" in subpara. (a)(1)(A)... Sec. 2(3), substituted "June 30, 1958" for "March 31, 1957" in the heading of subparas. (b)(1)(A) and (B)... Sec. 2(4), substituted "June 30, 1958" for "March 31, 1957" in para. (b)(1), effective 3/29/57.

In 1956, P.L. 458, Sec. 2(1), substituted "April 1, 1957" for "April 1, 1956" in the heading of clauses (a)(1)(A)(i) and (ii)... Sec. 2(2), substituted "April 1, 1957" for "April 1, 1956" in subpara. (a)(1)(A)... Sec. 2(3), substituted "March 31, 1957" for "March 31, 1956" in the heading of subparas. (b)(1)(A) and (B)... Sec. 2(4), substituted "March 31, 1957" for "March 31, 1956" in para. (b)(1), effective 3/29/56.

—P.L. 429, Sec. 3(a)(1), substituted "the items described in section 822(b) (other than paragraph (1)(D) thereof)" for "interest, dividends, rents," in para. (a)(2)... Sec. 3(a)(2), substituted "the items described in section 822(b) (other than paragraph (1)(D) thereof)" for "interest, dividends, rents," in subsec. (c), effective for tax. yrs. begin. after 12/31/54.

In 1955, P.L. 18, Sec. 2(1), substituted "April 1, 1956" for "April 1, 1955" in the heading of clauses (a)(1)(A)(i) and (ii)... Sec. 2(2), substituted "April 1, 1956" for "April 1, 1955" in subpara. (a)(1)(A)... Sec. 2(3), substituted "March 31, 1956" for "March 31, 1955" in the heading of subparas. (b)(1)(A) and (B)... Sec. 2(4), substituted "March 31, 1956" for "March 31, 1955" in para. (b)(1), effective 3/30/55.

Sec. 823. Repealed.

In 1986, P.L. 99-514, Sec. 1024(a)(1), repealed Code Sec. 823, effective for tax. yrs. begin. after 12/31/86.

Prior to repeal, Code Sec. 823 read as follows:

"SEC. 823. DETERMINATION OF STATUTORY UNDERWRITING INCOME OR LOSS.

"(a) In general.

"For purposes of this part—

"(1) The term 'statutory underwriting income' means the amount by which—

"(A) the gross income which would be taken into account in computing taxable income under section 832 if the taxpayer were subject to the tax imposed by section 831, reduced by the gross investment income, exceeds

"(B) the sum of (i) the deductions which would be taken into account in computing taxable income if the taxpayer were subject to the tax imposed by section 831, reduced by the deductions provided in section 822(c), plus (ii) the deductions provided in subsection (c) and section 824(a).

"(2) The term 'statutory underwriting loss' means the excess of the amount referred to in paragraph (1)(B) over the amount referred to in paragraph (1)(A).

"(b) Modifications.

"In applying subsection (a)—

"(1) Net operating loss deduction. Except as provided by section 844, the deduction for net operating losses provided in section 172 shall not be allowed.

"(2) Interinsurers. In the case of a mutual insurance company which is an interinsurer or reciprocal underwriter—

"(A) there shall be allowed as a deduction the increase for the taxable year in savings credited to subscriber accounts, or

"(B) there shall be included as an item of gross income the decrease for the taxable year in savings credited to subscriber accounts.

For purposes of the preceding sentence, the term 'savings credited to subscriber accounts' means such portion of the surplus as is credited to the individual accounts of subscribers before the 16th day of the third month following the close of the taxable year, but only if the company would be obligated to pay such amount promptly to such subscriber if he terminated his contract at the close of the company's taxable year. For purposes of determining his taxable income, the subscriber shall treat any such savings credited to his account as a dividend paid or declared.

"(c) Special deduction for small company having gross amount of less than $1,100,000.

"(1) In general. If the gross amount received during the taxable year by a taxpayer subject to the tax imposed by section 821(a) from the items described in section 822(b) (other than paragraph (1)(D) thereof) and premiums (including deposits and assessments) does not equal or exceed $1,100,000, then in determining the statutory underwriting income or loss for the taxable year there shall be allowed an additional deduction of $6,000; except that if such gross amount exceeds $500,000, such additional deduction shall be equal to 1 percent of the amount by which $1,100,000 exceeds such gross amount.

"(2) Limitation. The amount of the deduction allowed under paragraph (1) shall not exceed the statutory underwriting income for the taxable year, computed without regard to any deduction under this subsection or section 824(a)."

In 1969, P.L. 91-172, Sec. 907(c)(2)(B), substituted "Except as provided by section 844, the" for "The" in para. (b)(1), effective for losses incurred in tax. yrs. begin. after 12/31/62, but shall not affect any tax liability for any tax. yr. begin. before 1/1/67.

In 1962, P.L. 87-834, Sec. 8, added Code Sec. 823, effective for tax. yrs. begin. after 12/31/62. A prior Code Sec. 823 was redesignated Code Sec. 822(f).

Insurance companies

Sec. 824. Repealed.

In 1988, P.L. 100-647, Sec. 1010(f)(8), amended Sec. 1041(d)(1) of P.L. 99-514 [reproduced below], transitional rules for amendments made by Sec. 1024(a)(1) of P.L. 99-514, by adding the last sentence, see below.

In 1986, P.L. 99-514, Sec. 1024(a)(1), repealed Code Sec. 824, effective for tax. yrs. begin. after 12/31/86. Sec. 1024(d)(1) [as amended by Sec. 1010(f)(8) of P.L. 100-647, see above] of this Act provides as follows:

"(d) Transitional rules.—

"(1) Treatment of amounts in protection against loss account.—In the case of any insurance company which had a protection against loss account for its last taxable year beginning before January 1, 1987, there shall be included in the gross income of such company for any taxable year beginning after December 31, 1986, the amount which would have been included in gross income for such taxable year under section 824 of the Internal Revenue Code of 1954 (as in effect on the day before the date of the enactment of this Act). For purposes of the preceding sentence, no addition to such account shall be made for any taxable year beginning after December 31, 1986. In the case of a company taxable under section 831(b) of the Internal Revenue Code of 1986 (as amended by subsection (a)), any amount included in gross income under this paragraph shall be treated as gross investment income."

Prior to repeal, Code Sec. 824 read as follows:

"SEC. 824. ADJUSTMENTS TO PROVIDE PROTECTION AGAINST LOSSES.

"(a) Allowance of deduction.

"(1) In general. In determining the statutory underwriting income or loss for any taxable year there shall be allowed as a deduction the sum of—

"(A) an amount equal to 1 percent of the losses incurred during the taxable year (as determined under section 832(b)(5)), plus

"(B) an amount equal to 25 percent of the underwriting gain for the taxable year, plus

"(C) if the concentrated windstorm, etc., premium percentage for the taxable year exceeds 40 percent, an amount determined by applying so much of such percentage as exceeds 40 percent to the underwriting gain for the taxable year.

For purposes of this paragraph, the term 'underwriting gain' means statutory underwriting income, computed without any deduction under this subsection.

"(2) Special rule for companies having concentrated windstorm, etc., risks. For purposes of paragraph (1)(C), the term 'concentrated windstorm, etc., premium percentage' means, with respect to any taxable year, the percentage obtained by dividing—

"(A) the amount of the premiums earned on insurance contracts during the taxable year (as defined in section 832(b)(4)), to the extent attributable to insuring against losses arising, either in any one State or within 200 miles of any fixed point selected by the taxpayer, from windstorm, hail, flood, earthquake, or similar hazards, by

"(B) the amount of the premiums earned on insurance contracts during the taxable year (as so defined).

"(b) Protection against loss account.

"Each insurance company subject to the tax imposed by section 821(a) for any taxable year shall, for purposes of this part, establish and maintain a protection against loss account.

"(c) Additions to account.

"There shall be added to the protection against loss account for each taxable year an amount equal to the amount allowable as a deduction for the taxable year under subsection (a)(1).

"(d) Subtractions.

"(1) Annual subtractions. After applying subsection (c), there shall be subtracted for the taxable year from the protection against loss account—

"(A) first, an amount equal to the excess (if any) of the deduction allowed under subsection (a) for the taxable year over the underwriting gain (within the meaning of subsection (a)(1)) for the taxable year,

"(B) then, the amount (if any) by which—

"(i) the sum of the investment loss for such year and the statutory underwriting loss (reduced by the amount referred to in subparagraph (A)) for such year, exceeds

"(ii) the sum of the statutory underwriting income for such taxable year and the taxable investment income for such taxable year,

"(C) next (in the order in which the losses occurred), amounts equal to the unused loss carryovers to such year,

"(D) next, any amount remaining which was added to the account for the fifth preceding taxable year, minus one-half of the amount remaining in the account for such taxable year which was added by reason of subsection (a)(1)(B), and

"(E) finally, the amount by which the total amount in the account exceeds whichever of the following is the greater:

"(i) 10 percent of premiums earned on insurance contracts during the taxable year (as defined in section 832(b)(4)) less dividends to policyholders (as defined in section 832(c)(11)), or

"(ii) the total amount in the account at the close of the preceding taxable year.

"(2) Rules for ceiling on protection against loss account. For purposes of paragraph (1)(E), the total amount in the account shall be determined—

"(A) after the application of this section without regard to paragraph (1)(E), and

"(B) without taking into consideration amounts remaining in the account which were added, with respect to all taxable years, by reason of subsection (a)(1)(B).

"(3) Priorities. The amounts required to be subtracted from the protection against loss account—

"(A) under subparagraphs (A), (B), and (C) of paragraph (1) shall be subtracted—

"(i) first (on a first-in, first-out basis) from amounts in the account with respect to the five preceding taxable years and the taxable year, and

"(ii) then from amounts in the account with respect to earlier years,

"(B) under subparagraph (E) of paragraph (1) shall be subtracted only from amounts in the account with respect to the taxable year, and

"(C) under paragraphs (A), (B), (C), and (E) of paragraph (1) shall, if the amount to be subtracted from the total amounts in the account with respect to any taxable year is less than such total, be subtracted from each of the amounts (referred to in subsection (a)(1)) in the account with respect to such year in the proportion which each bears to such total.

"(4) Termination of taxability under section 821. If the taxpayer is not subject to tax under section 821 for any taxable year, the entire amount in the account at the close of the preceding taxable year shall be subtracted from the account in such preceding taxable year.

"(5) Election to subtract amount from account.

"(A) A taxpayer may elect for any taxable year for which it is subject to tax under section 821(a) to subtract from its protection against loss account any amount which, but for the application of this subparagraph, would be in such account as of the close of such taxable year.

"(B) The election provided by subparagraph (A) for any taxable year shall be made (in such manner and in such form as the Secretary may by regulations prescribe) after the close of such taxable year and not later than the time prescribed by law for filing the return (including extensions thereof) for the taxable year following such taxable year. Such an election, once made, may not be revoked."

In 1976, P.L. 94-455, Sec. 1906(b)(13)(A), substituted "Secretary" for "Secretary or his delegate" in subpara. (d)(5)(B), effective for tax. yrs. begin. after 12/31/76.

In 1962, P.L. 87-834, Sec. 8, added Code Sec. 824, effective for tax. yrs. begin. after 12/31/62.

Sec. 825. Repealed.

In 1986, P.L. 99-514, Sec. 1024(a)(1), repealed Code Sec. 825, effective for tax. yrs. begin after 12/31/86. For transitional rule, see Sec. 1024(d)(2) of this Act reproduced in note following Code Sec. 832.

Prior to repeal, Code Sec. 825 read as follows:

"SEC. 825. UNUSED LOSS DEDUCTION.

"(a) Amount of deduction.

"For purposes of this Part, the unused loss deduction for the taxable year shall be an amount equal to the unused loss carryovers or carrybacks to the taxable year.

"(b) Unused loss defined.

"For purposes of this part, the term 'unused loss' means, with respect to any taxable year, the amount (if any) by which—

"(1) the sum of the statutory underwriting loss and the investment loss, exceeds

"(2) the sum of—

"(A) the taxable investment income,

"(B) the statutory underwriting income, and

"(C) the amounts required by section 824(d) to be subtracted from the protection against loss account.

"(c) Loss year defined.

"For purposes of this part, the term 'loss year' means, with respect to any company subject to the tax imposed by section 821(a), any taxable year in which the unused loss (as defined in subsection (b)) of such taxpayer is more than zero.

"(d) Years to which carried.

"(1) In general. The unused loss for any taxable year shall be—

"(A) an unused loss carryback to each of the 3 taxable years preceding the loss year, and

"(B) an unused loss carryover to each of the 5 taxable years following the loss year.

In the case of an unused loss for a taxable year ending after December 31, 1975, such unused loss shall be an unused loss carryover to each of the 15 taxable years following the loss year.

"(2) Election for unused loss carrybacks. In the case of an unused loss for any taxable year ending after December 31, 1975, the taxpayer may elect to relinquish the entire carryback period for such loss. Such election shall be made by the due date (including extensions of time) for filing the return for the taxable year of the unused loss for which the election is to be in effect, and once made for any taxable year, such election shall be irrevocable for that taxable year.

"(e) Amount of carrybacks and carryovers.

"The entire amount of the unused loss for any loss year shall be carried to the earliest of the taxable years to which such loss may be carried. The portion of such loss which shall be carried to each of the other taxable years shall be the excess (if any) of the amount of such loss over the sum of the offsets (as defined in subsection (f)) for each of the prior taxable years to which such loss may be carried.

"(f) Offset defined.

"For purposes of subsection (e), the term 'offset' means with respect to any taxable year (hereinafter referred to as the 'offset year'—

"(1) in the case of an unused loss carryback from the loss year to the offset year, the mutual insurance company taxable income for the offset year; or

"(2) in the case of an unused loss carryover from the loss year to the offset year, an amount equal to the sum of—

"(A) the amount required to be subtracted from the protection against loss account under section 824(d)(1)(C) for the offset year, plus

"(B) the mutual insurance company taxable income for the offset year.

Code Sec. 825

For purposes of paragraphs (1) and (2)(B), the mutual insurance company taxable income for the offset year shall be determined without regard to any unused loss carryback or carryover from the loss year or any taxable year thereafter.

"(g) Limitations.

"For purposes of this part, an unused loss shall not be carried—

"(1) except as provided by Section 844, to or from any taxable year for which the insurance company is not subject to the tax imposed by section 821(a), nor

"(2) except as provided by section 844, to any taxable year if, between the loss year and such taxable year, there is an intervening taxable year for which the insurance company was not subject to the tax imposed by section 821(a)."

In 1983, P.L. 97-448, Sec. 102(d)(2), added para. (c)(3) to Sec. 209 of P.L. 97-34, the effective date for amendments made by Sec. 207(b) of P.L. 97-34, see below.

In 1981, P.L. 97-34, Sec. 207(b), substituted "15" for "7" in para. (d)(1), effective for net operating losses in tax. yrs. end. after 12/31/75. Sec. 209(c)(3) of this Act provides:

"(3) Carryover must have been alive in 1981.— The amendments made by subsections (a), (b), and (c) of section 207 shall not apply to any amount which, under the law in effect on the day before the date of the enactment of this Act, could not be carried to a taxable year ending in 1981."

In 1976, P.L. 94-455, Sec. 806(d)(2), amended subsec. (d), effective for losses incurred in tax. yrs. end. after 12/31/75.

Prior to amendment, subsec. (d) read as follows:

"(d) Years to which carried.

"The unused loss for any loss year shall be—

"(1) an unused loss carryback to each of the 3 taxable years preceding the loss year, and

"(2) an unused loss carryover to each of the 5 taxable years following the loss year."

—P.L. 94-455, Sec. 1901(a)(106), deleted para. (g)(1), redesignated paras. (g)(2) and (g)(3) as para. (g)(1) and (g)(2), effective for tax. yrs. begin. after 12/31/76. Prior to amendment, para. (g)(1) read as follows:

"(1) to or from any taxable year beginning before January 1, 1963,"

In 1969, P.L. 91-172, Sec. 907(c)(2), added "except as provided by section 844," to the beginning of paras. (g)(2) and (3), effective for losses incurred in tax. yrs. begin. after 12/31/62, but shall not affect any tax liability for any tax. yr. begin. before 1/1/67.

In 1962, P.L. 87-834, Sec. 8, added Code Sec. 825, effective for tax. yrs. begin. after 12/31/62.

PART II.—OTHER INSURANCE COMPANIES

Sec.
831. Tax on insurance companies other than life insurance companies.
832. Insurance company taxable income.
833. Treatment of Blue Cross and Blue Shield organizations, etc.
834. Determination of taxable investment income.
835. Election by reciprocal.

In 1988, P.L. 100-647, Sec. 1010(f)(7), amended the item 831.
Prior to amendment, item 831 read as follows:
"831. Tax on insurance companies (other than life or mutual), mutual marine insurance companies, and certain mutual fire or flood insurance companies."

In 1986, P.L. 99-514, Sec. 1024(a)(2), redesignated Part III as Part II . . . Sec. 1012(b)(2), added item 833 . . . Sec. 1024(c)(18), added items 834 and 835.

In 1962, substituted "and certain mutual fire or flood insurance companies" for "and mutual fire insurance companies issuing perpetual policies" in item 831.

Sec. 831. Tax on insurance companies other than life insurance companies.

(a) General rule.

Taxes computed as provided in section 11 shall be imposed for each taxable year on the taxable income of every insurance company other than a life insurance company.

(b) Alternative tax for certain small companies.

(1) **In general.** In lieu of the tax otherwise applicable under subsection (a), there is hereby imposed for each taxable year on the income of every insurance company to which this subsection applies a tax computed by multiplying the taxable investment income of such company for such taxable year by the rates provided in section 11(b).

(2) **Companies to which this subsection applies.**

(A) **In general.** This subsection shall apply to every insurance company other than life (including interinsurers and reciprocal underwriters) if—

(i) the net written premiums (or, if greater, direct written premiums) for the taxable year do not exceed $1,200,000, and

(ii) such company elects the application of this subsection for such taxable year.

The election under clause (ii) shall apply to the taxable year for which made and for all subsequent taxable years for which the requirements of clause (i) are met. Such an election, once made, may be revoked only with the consent of the Secretary.

(B) **Controlled group rules.**

(i) **In general.** For purposes of subparagraph (A), in determining whether any company is described in clause (i) of subparagraph (A), such company shall be treated as receiving during the taxable year amounts described in such clause (i) which are received during such year by all other companies which are members of the same controlled group as the insurance company for which the determination is being made.

(ii) **Controlled group.** For purposes of clause (i), the term "controlled group" means any controlled group of corporations (as defined in section 1563(a)); except that—

(I) "more than 50 percent" shall be substituted for "at least 80 percent" each place it appears in section 1563(a), and

(II) subsections (a)(4) and (b)(2)(D) of section 1563 shall not apply.

(3) **Limitation on use of net operating losses.** For purposes of this part, except as provided in section 844, a net operating loss (as defined in section 172) shall not be carried—

(A) to or from any taxable year for which the insurance company is not subject to the tax imposed by subsection (a), or

(B) to any taxable year if, between the taxable year from which such loss is being carried and such taxable year, there is an intervening taxable year for which the insurance company was not subject to the tax imposed by subsection (a).

(c) Insurance company defined.

For purposes of this section, the term "insurance company" has the meaning given to such term by section 816(a).

(d) Cross references.

(1) For alternative tax in case of capital gains, see section 1201(a).

(2) For taxation of foreign corporations carrying on an insurance business within the United States, see section 842.

(3) For exemption from tax for certain insurance companies other than life, see section 501(c)(15).

In 2004, P.L. 108-218, Sec. 206(c), redesignated subsec. (c) as subsec. (d) and added subsec. (c) . . . Sec. 206(d), deleted "exceed $350,000 but" after "for the taxable year" in clause (b)(2)(A)(i), effective for tax. yrs. begin. after 12/31/2003. Sec. 206(e)(2) of this Act, provides:

"(2) Transition rule for companies in receivership or liquidation. In the case of a company or association which—

"(A) for the taxable year which includes April 1, 2004, meets the requirements of section 501(c)(15)(A) of the Internal Revenue Code of 1986, as in effect for the last taxable year beginning before January 1, 2004, and

"(B) on April 1, 2004, is in a receivership, liquidation, or similar proceeding under the supervision of a State court,

the amendments made by this section shall apply to taxable years beginning after the earlier of the date such proceeding ends or December 31, 2007."

In 1989, P.L. 101-239, Sec. 7816(m), provides:

"(m) *Provision related to section 6076 of the 1988 Act.[reproduced below]*

"If, for the 1st taxable year beginning on or after January 1, 1987, a qualified group self-insurers fund changes its treatment of policyholder dividends to take into account such dividends no earlier than the date that the State regulatory authority determines the amount of the policyholder dividend that may be paid, then such change shall be treated as a change in a method of accounting and no adjustment under section 481(a) of the Internal Revenue Code of 1986 shall be made with respect to such change in method of accounting."

In 1988, P.L. 100-647, Sec. 1010(f)(1), added the sentence at the end of subpara (b)(2)(A) . . . Sec. 1010(f)(9), added para. (b)(3), effective for tax. yrs. begin. after 12/31/86

—P.L. 100-647, Sec. 1010(g)(1), amended Sec. 1031(a)(1) of P.L. 99-514 [reproduced below] by adding "(whether made in a lump sum or a series of substantially equal payments over a period of not more than 6 years)" after "any initial payment" . . . Sec. 1010(g)(2), and (3) amended Sec. 1031(a)(2) of P.L. 99-514 [reproduced below] by substituting "initial payment referred to in paragraph (1)" for "initial payment" each place it appeared, and by substituting "the Internal Revenue Code of 1986" for "this title" each place it appeared, see below

—P.L. 100-647, Sec. 6076, [see Sec. 7816(m) of P.L. 101-239, above] provides:

"SEC. 6076. TREATMENT OF CERTAIN WORKERS' COMPENSATION FUNDS.

"(a) Treatment for Taxable Years Beginning Before 1987.

"In the case of any taxable year beginning before January 1, 1987, a deficiency shall not be assessed against (and if assessed, shall not be collected from) any qualified group self-insurers' fund to the extent such deficiency is attributable to the timing of policyholder dividend deductions.

"(b) Qualified group self-insurers' fund.

For purposes of this section, the term 'qualified group self-insurers' fund' means any group of 2 or more employers which has been in existence for not less than 2 years, and who enter into agreements to pool their liabilities under the State workers' disability compensation laws for the purpose of qualifying as a self-insurer under such laws, if—

"(1) the group has received a certificate of approval from, and is subject to regulation by, the State board or agency that is responsible for administering the State workers' disability compensation laws,

"(2) each employer who is a member of the group, by written agreement, is jointly and severally bound to assume and discharge, by payment, any lawful judgment or award entered by a court of competent jurisdiction or by the State agency responsible for administering the State workers' disability compensation laws against a member of the group,

"(3) the group is prohibited by State law or regulation from using the monies collected for a purpose other than to pay, or to reserve against, claims under the State workers' disability compensation laws and expenses,

"(4) the group is prohibited by State law or regulation from taking projected investment income into account in determining members' premiums,

"(5) the group is required by State law or regulation to submit to the State board or agency that is responsible for administering the State workers' disability compensation laws an audited financial statement,

"(6) the group's investments are limited by State law or regulation to bonds, notes, or other evidences of indebtedness issued, assumed or guaranteed by the United States of America, or by an agency or instrumentality thereof, certificates of deposit in a federally insured bank, shares or savings deposits in a federally insured savings and loan association or credit union, and certificates of deposit issued by a commercial bank duly chartered under State law, and other investments which are approved by the State board or agency that is responsible for administering the State workers' disability compensation laws, and

"(7) the group exclusively covers workers' compensation liability, is not a commercial insurance carrier or company licensed by the State board, agency, or commissioner responsible for regulating and licensing insurance carriers and companies; and is not subject to filing under the regulatory statements of the National Association of Insurance Commissioners."

In 1986, P.L. 99-514, Sec. 1024(a)(4), amended Code Sec. 831, effective for tax. yrs. begin. after 12/31/86.

Prior to amendment, Code Sec. 831 read as follows:

"SEC. 831. TAX ON INSURANCE COMPANIES (OTHER THAN LIFE OR MUTUAL), MUTUAL MARINE INSURANCE COMPANIES, AND CERTAIN MUTUAL FIRE OR FLOOD INSURANCE COMPANIES.

"(a) Imposition of tax.

"Taxes computed as provided in section 11 shall be imposed for each taxable year on the taxable income of—

"(1) every insurance company (other than a life or mutual insurance company),

"(2) every mutual marine insurance company, and

"(3) every mutual fire or flood insurance company—

"(A) exclusively issuing perpetual policies, or

"(B) whose principal business is the issuance of policies for which the premium deposits are the same, regardless of the length of the term for which the policies are written, if the unabsorbed portion of such premium deposits not required for losses, expenses, or establishment of reserves is returned or credited to the policyholder on cancellation or expiration of the policy.

"(b) Election for multiple line company to be taxed on total income.

"(1) In general. Any mutual insurance company engaged in writing marine, fire, and casualty insurance which for any 5-year period beginning after December 31, 1941, and ending before January 1, 1962, was subject to the tax imposed by section 831 (or the tax imposed by corresponding provisions of prior law) may elect, in such manner and at such time as the Secretary may by regulations prescribe, to be subject to the tax imposed by section 831, whether or not marine insurance is its predominant source of premium income.

"(2) Effect of election. If an election is made under paragraph (1), the electing company shall (in lieu of being subject to the tax imposed by section 821) be subject to the tax imposed by this section for taxable years beginning after December 31, 1961.Such election shall not be revoked except with the consent of the Secretary.

"(c) Cross references.

"(1) For alternative tax in case of capital gains, see section 1201(a).

"(2) For taxation of foreign corporations carrying on an insurance business within the United States, see section 842."

—P.L. 99-514, Sec. 1031, [as amended by P.L. 100-647, Secs, 1010(g)(1)-(3)] provides as follows:

"SEC. 1031. PHYSICIANS AND SURGEONS' MUTUAL PROTECTION AND INTERINDEMNITY ARRANGEMENTS OR ASSOCIATIONS.

"(a) Certain physicians' and surgeons' mutual protection and interindemnity arrangements or associations.—

"(1) Treatment of arrangements or associations.—

"(A) Capital contributions.—There shall not be included in the gross income of any eligible physicians' and surgeons' mutual protection and interindemnity arrangement or association any initial payment (whether made in a lump sum or a series of substantially equal payments over a period of not more than 6 years) made during any taxable year to such arrangement or association by a member joining such arrangement or association which—

"(i) does not release such member from obligations to pay current or future dues, assessments, or premiums; and

"(ii) is a condition precedent to receiving benefits of membership

Such initial payment shall be included in the gross income of such arrangement or association for such taxable year if it is reasonable to expect that such payment will be deductible pursuant to paragraph (2) by any member of such arrangement or association.

"(B) Return of contributions.—

"(i) In general.—The repayment to any member of any amount of any payment excluded under subparagraph (A) shall not be treated as policyholder dividend, and is not deductible by the arrangement or association.

"(ii) Source of returns.—Except in the case of the termination of a member's interest in the arrangement or association, any amount distributed to any member shall be treated as paid out of surplus in excess of amounts excluded under subparagraph (A).

"(2) Deduction for members of eligible arrangements or associations—

"(A) Payment as trade or business expenses.—To the extent not otherwise allowable under the Internal Revenue Code of 1986 any member of any eligible arrangement or association may treat any initial payment referred to in paragraph (1) made during a taxable year to such arrangement or association as an ordinary and necessary expense incurred in connection with a trade or business for purposes of the deduction allowable under section 162, to the extent such payment does not exceed the amount which would be payable to an independent insurance company for similar annual insurance coverage (as determined by the Secretary), and further reduced by any annual dues, assessments, or premiums paid during such taxable year. Such deduction shall not be allowable as to any initial payment referred to in paragraph (1) made to an eligible arrangement or association by any person who is a member of any other eligible arrangement or association on or after the effective date of the Tax Reform Act of 1986. Any excess amount not allowed as a deduction for the taxable year in which such payment was made pursuant to the limitation contained in the 1st sentence of this subparagraph shall, subject to such limitation, be allowable as a deduction in any of the 5 succeeding taxable years, in order of time, to the extent not previously allowed as a deduction under this sentence.

"(B) Refunds of initial payment referred to in paragraph (1).—Any amount attributable to any initial payment referred to in paragraph (1) to such arrangement or association described in paragraph (1) which is later refunded for any reason shall be included in the gross income of the recipient in the taxable year received, to the extent a deduction for such payment was allowed. Any amount refunded in excess of such payment shall be included in gross income except to the extent otherwise excluded from income by the Internal Revenue Code of 1986.

"(3) Eligible arrangements or associations.— The terms 'eligible physicians' and surgeons' mutual protection and interindemnity arrangement or association' and 'eligible arrangement or association' mean and are limited to any mutual protection and interindemnity arrangement or association that provides only medical malpractice liability protection for its members or medical malpractice liability protection in conjunction with protection against other liability claims incurred in the course of, or related to, the professional practice of a physician or surgeon and which—

"(A) was operative and was providing such protection, or had received a permit for the offer and sale of memberships, under the laws of any State before January 1, 1984, to no disqualification if excess contributions distributed) shall apply for purposes of the preceding sentence.

"(B) is not subject to regulation by any State insurance department,

"(C) has a right to make unlimited assessments against all members to cover current claims and losses, and

"(D) is not a member of, nor subject to protection by, any insurance guaranty plan or association of any State.

"(b) Effective date.—

"The provisions of subsection (a) shall apply to payments made to and receipts of physicians' and surgeons' mutual protection and interindemnity arrangements or associations, and refunds of payments by such arrangements or associations, after the date of the enactment of this Act, in taxable years ending after such date."

In 1976, P.L. 94-455, Sec. 1901(a)(107), substituted "on the taxable income" for "or the taxable income" in subsec. (a), effective for tax. yrs. begin. after 12/31/76.

—P.L. 94-455, Sec. 1906(b)(13)(A), substituted "Secretary" for "Secretary or his delegate" each time it appears in subsec. (b), for tax. yrs. begin. after '76.

In 1966, P.L. 89-809, Sec. 104, deleted subsec. (b), redesignated subsecs. (c) and (d) as subsecs. (b) and (c), and added para. (c)(2), effective for tax. yrs. begin. after 12/31/66.

Code Sec. 831   Insurance companies

Prior to deletion, former subsec. (b) read as follows:

"(b) *No United States insurance business.*

"Foreign insurance companies (other than a life or mutual insurance company), foreign mutual marine insurance companies, and foreign mutual fire insurance companies described in subsection (a), not carrying on an insurance business within the United States, shall not be subject to this part but shall be taxable as other foreign corporations."

In 1962, P.L. 87-834, Sec. 8, substituted "and certain mutual fire or flood insurance companies" for "and mutual fire insurance companies issuing perpetual policies" in the section catchline, amended subsec. (a), redesignated subsec. (c) as (d), and added new subsec. (c), effective for tax. yrs. begin. after '62.

Prior to amendment, subsec. (a) read as follows:

"(a) *Imposition of tax.*

"Taxes computed as provided in section 11 shall be imposed for each taxable year or the taxable income of—

"(1) every insurance company (other than a life or mutual insurance company),

"(2) every mutual marine insurance company, and

"(3) every mutual fire or flood insurance company—

"(A) exclusively issuing perpetual policies, or

"(B) whose principal business is the issuance of policies for which the premium deposits are the same, regardless of the length of the term for which the policies are written, if the unabsorbed portion of such premium deposits not required for losses, expenses, or establishment of reserves is returned or credited to the policyholder on cancellation or expiration of the policy."

Sec. 832. Insurance company taxable income.

(a) Definition of taxable income.

In the case of an insurance company subject to the tax imposed by section 831, the term "taxable income" means the gross income as defined in subsection (b)(1) less the deductions allowed by subsection (c).

(b) Definitions.

In the case of an insurance company subject to the tax imposed by section 831—

(1) Gross income. The term "gross income" means the sum of—

(A) the combined gross amount earned during the taxable year, from investment income and from underwriting income as provided in this subsection, computed on the basis of the underwriting and investment exhibit of the annual statement approved by the National Association of Insurance Commissioners,

(B) gain during the taxable year from the sale or other disposition of property,

(C) all other items constituting gross income under subchapter B, except that, in the case of a mutual fire insurance company exclusively issuing perpetual policies, the amount of single deposit premiums paid to such company shall not be included in gross income,

(D) in the case of a mutual fire or flood insurance company whose principal business is the issuance of policies—

(i) for which the premium deposits are the same (regardless of the length of the term for which the policies are written), and

(ii) under which the unabsorbed portion of such premium deposits not required for losses, expenses, or establishment of reserves is returned or credited to the policyholder on cancellation or expiration of the policy,

an amount equal to 2 percent of the premiums earned on insurance contracts during the taxable year with respect to such policies after deduction of premium deposits returned or credited during the same taxable year, and

(E) in the case of a company which writes mortgage guaranty insurance, the amount required by subsection (e)(5) to be subtracted from the mortgage guaranty account.

(2) Investment income. The term "investment income" means the gross amount of income earned during the taxable year from interest, dividends, and rents, computed as follows: To all interest, dividends, and rents received during the taxable year, add interest, dividends, and rents due and accrued at the end of the taxable year, and deduct all interest, dividends, and rents due and accrued at the end of the preceding taxable year.

(3) Underwriting income. The term "underwriting income" means the premiums earned on insurance contracts during the taxable year less losses incurred and expenses incurred.

(4) Premiums earned. The term "premiums earned on insurance contracts during the taxable year" means an amount computed as follows:

(A) From the amount of gross premiums written on insurance contracts during the taxable year, deduct return premiums and premiums paid for reinsurance.

(B) To the result so obtained, add 80 percent of the unearned premiums on outstanding business at the end of the preceding taxable year and deduct 80 percent of the unearned premiums on outstanding business at the end of the taxable year.

(C) To the result so obtained, in the case of a taxable year beginning after December 31, 1986, and before January 1, 1993, add an amount equal to 3 $\frac{1}{3}$ percent of unearned premiums on outstanding business at the end of the most recent taxable year beginning before January 1, 1987.

For purposes of this subsection, unearned premiums shall include life insurance reserves, as defined in section 816(b) but determined as provided in section 807. For purposes of this subsection, unearned premiums of mutual fire or flood insurance companies described in paragraph (1)(D) means (with respect to the policies described in paragraph (1)(D)) the amount of unabsorbed premium deposits which the company would be obligated to return to its policyholders at the close of the taxable year if all of its policies were terminated at such time; and the determination of such amount shall be based on the schedule of unabsorbed premium deposit returns for each such company then in effect. Premiums paid by the subscriber of a mutual flood insurance company described in paragraph (1)(D) or issuing exclusively perpetual policies shall be treated, for purposes of computing the taxable income of such subscriber, in the same manner as premiums paid by a policyholder to a mutual fire insurance company described in subparagraph (C) or (D) of paragraph (1).

(5) Losses incurred.

(A) In general. The term "losses incurred" means losses incurred during the taxable year on insurance contracts computed as follows:

(i) To losses paid during the taxable year, deduct salvage and reinsurance recovered during the taxable year.

(ii) To the result so obtained, add all unpaid losses on life insurance contracts plus all discounted unpaid losses (as defined in section 846) outstanding at the end of the taxable year and deduct all unpaid losses on life insurance contracts plus all discounted unpaid losses outstanding at the end of the preceding taxable year.

(iii) To the results so obtained, add estimated salvage and reinsurance recoverable as of the end of the preceding taxable year and deduct estimated salvage and reinsurance recoverable as of the end of the taxable year.

The amount of estimated salvage recoverable shall be determined on a discounted basis in accordance with procedures established by the Secretary.

(B) Reduction of deduction. The amount which would (but for this subparagraph) be taken into account under subparagraph (A) shall be reduced by an amount equal to 15 percent of the sum of—

(i) tax-exempt interest received or accrued during such taxable year,

(ii) the aggregate amount of deductions provided by sections 243, 244, and 245 for—

(I) dividends (other than 100 percent dividends) received during the taxable year, and

(II) 100 percent dividends received during the taxable year to the extent attributable (directly or indirectly) to prorated amounts, and

(iii) the increase for the taxable year in policy cash values (within the meaning of section 805(a)(4)(F)) of life insurance policies and annuity and endowment contracts to which section 264(f) applies.

In the case of a 100 percent dividend paid by an insurance company, the portion attributable to prorated amounts shall be determined under subparagraph (E)(ii).

(C) Exception for investments made before August 8, 1986.

(i) In general. Except as provided in clause (ii), subparagraph (B) shall not apply to any dividend or interest received or accrued on any stock or obligation acquired before August 8, 1986.

(ii) Special rule for 100 percent dividends. For purposes of clause (i), the portion of any 100 percent dividend which is attributable to prorated amounts shall be treated as received with respect to stock acquired on the later of—

(I) the date the payor acquired the stock or obligation to which the prorated amounts are attributable, or

(II) the 1st day on which the payor and payee were members of the same affiliated group (as defined in section 243(b)(2)).

(D) Definitions. For purposes of this paragraph—

(i) Prorated amounts. The term "prorated amounts" means tax-exempt interest and dividends with respect to which a deduction is allowable under section 243, 244, or 245 (other than 100 percent dividends).

(ii) 100 percent dividend.

(I) In general. The term "100 percent dividend" means any dividend if the percentage used for purposes of determining the deduction allowable under section 243, 244, or 245(b) is 100 percent.

(II) Certain dividends received by foreign corporations. A dividend received by a foreign corporation from a domestic corporation which would be a 100 percent dividend if section 1504(b)(3) did not apply for purposes of applying section 243(b)(2) shall be treated as a 100 percent dividend.

(E) Special rules for dividends subject to proration at subsidiary level.

(i) In general. In the case of any 100 percent dividend paid to an insurance company to which this part applies by any insurance company, the amount of the decrease in the deductions of the payee company by reason of the portion of such dividend attributable to prorated amounts shall be reduced (but not below zero) by the amount of the decrease in the deductions (or increase in income) of the payor company attributable to the application of this section or section 805(a)(4)(A) to such amounts.

(ii) Portion of dividend attributable to prorated amounts. For purposes of this subparagraph, in determining the portion of any dividend attributable to prorated amounts—

(I) any dividend by the paying corporation shall be treated as paid first out of earnings and profits attributable to prorated amounts (to the extent thereof), and

(II) by determining the portion of earnings and profits so attributable without any reduction for the tax imposed by this chapter.

(6) Expenses incurred. The term "expenses incurred" means all expenses shown on the annual statement approved by the National Association of Insurance Commissioners, and shall be computed as follows: To all expenses paid during the taxable year, add expenses unpaid at the end of the taxable year and deduct expenses unpaid at the end of the preceding taxable year. For purposes of this subchapter, the term "expenses unpaid" shall not include any unpaid loss adjustment expenses shown on the annual statement, but such unpaid loss adjustment expenses shall be included in unpaid losses. For the purpose of computing the taxable income subject to the tax imposed by section 831, there shall be deducted from expenses incurred (as defined in this paragraph) all expenses incurred which are not allowed as deductions by subsection (c).

(7) Special rules for applying paragraph (4).

(A) Reduction not to apply to life insurance reserves. Subparagraph (B) of paragraph (4) shall be applied with respect to insurance contracts described in section 816(b)(1)(B) by substituting "100 percent" for "80 percent" each place it appears in such subparagraph (B), and subparagraph (C) of paragraph (4) shall be applied by not taking such contracts into account.

(B) Special treatment of premiums attributable to insuring certain securities. In the case of premiums attributable to insurance against default in the payment of principal or interest on securities described in section 165(g)(2)(C) with maturities of more than 5 years—

(i) subparagraph (B) of paragraph (4) shall be applied by substituting "90 percent" for "80 percent" each place it appears, and

(ii) subparagraph (C) of paragraph (4) shall be applied by substituting "1 ⅔ percent" for "3 ⅓ percent".

(C) Termination as insurance company taxable under section 831(a). Except as provided in section 381(c)(22) (relating to carryovers in certain corporate readjustments), if, for any taxable year beginning before January 1, 1993, the taxpayer ceases to be an insurance company taxable under section 831(a), the aggregate adjustments which would be made under paragraph (4)(C) for such taxable year and subsequent taxable years but for such cessation shall be made for the taxable year preceding such cessation year.

(D) Treatment of companies which become taxable under section 831(a).

(i) Exception to phase-in for companies which were not taxable, etc., before 1987. Subparagraph (C) of paragraph (4) shall not apply to any insurance company which, for each taxable year beginning before January 1, 1987, was not subject to the tax imposed by section 821(a) or 831(a) (as in effect on the day before the date of the enactment [10/22/86] of the Tax Reform Act of 1986) by reason of being—

(I) subject to tax under section 821(c) (as so in effect), or

(II) described in section 501(c) (as so in effect) and exempt from tax under section 501(a).

2,417

(ii) Phase-in beginning at later date for companies not 1st taxable under section 831(a) in 1987. In the case of an insurance company—
  (I) which was not subject to the tax imposed by section 831(a) for its 1st taxable year beginning after December 31, 1986, by reason of being subject to tax under section 831(b), or described in section 501(c) and exempt from tax under section 501(a), and
  (II) which, for any taxable year beginning before January 1, 1987, was subject to the tax imposed by section 821(a) or 831(a) (as in effect on the day before the date of the enactment of the Tax Reform Act of 1986),
subparagraph (C) of paragraph (4) shall apply beginning with the 1st taxable year beginning after December 31, 1986, for which such company is subject to the tax imposed by section 831(a) and shall be applied by substituting the last day of the preceding taxable year for "December 31, 1986" and the 1st day of the 7th succeeding taxable year for "January 1, 1993".

(E) Treatment of certain reciprocal insurers. In the case of a reciprocal (within the meaning of section 835(a)) which reports (as required by State law) on its annual statement reserves on unearned premiums net of premium acquisition expenses—
  (i) subparagraph (B) of paragraph (4) shall be applied by treating unearned premiums as including an amount equal to such expenses, and
  (ii) appropriate adjustments shall be made under subparagraph (c) of paragraph (4) to reflect the amount by which—
    (I) such reserves at the close of the most recent taxable year beginning before January 1, 1987, are greater or less than,
    (II) 80 percent of the sum of the amount under subclause (I) plus such premium acquisition expenses,[.]

(8) Special rules for applying paragraph (4) to title insurance premiums.
(A) In general. In the case of premiums attributable to title insurance—
  (i) subparagraph (B) of paragraph (4) shall be applied by substituting "the discounted unearned premiums" for "80 percent of the unearned premiums" each place it appears, and
  (ii) subparagraph (C) of paragraph (4) shall not apply.
(B) Method of discounting. For purposes of subparagraph (A), the amount of the discounted unearned premiums as of the end of any taxable year shall be the present value of such premiums (as of such time and separately with respect to premiums received in each calendar year) determined by using—
  (i) the amount of the undiscounted unearned premiums at such time,
  (ii) the applicable interest rate, and
  (iii) the applicable statutory premium recognition pattern.
(C) Determination of applicable factors. In determining the amount of the discounted unearned premiums as of the end of any taxable year—
  (i) Undiscounted unearned premiums. The term "undiscounted unearned premiums" means the unearned premiums shown in the yearly statement filed by the taxpayer for the year ending with or within such taxable year.

(ii) Applicable interest rate. The term "applicable interest rate" means the annual rate determined under 846(c)(2) for the calendar year in which the premiums are received.
(iii) Applicable statutory premium recognition pattern. The term "applicable statutory premium recognition pattern" means the statutory premium recognition pattern—
  (I) which is in effect for the calendar year in which the premiums are received, and
  (II) which is based on the statutory premium recognition pattern which applies to premiums received by the taxpayer in such calendar year.
For purposes of the preceding sentence, premiums received during any calendar year shall be treated as received in the middle of such year.

(c) Deductions allowed.
In computing the taxable income of an insurance company subject to the tax imposed by section 831, there shall be allowed as deductions:
(1) all ordinary and necessary expenses incurred, as provided in section 162 (relating to trade or business expenses);
(2) all interest, as provided in section 163;
(3) taxes, as provided in section 164;
(4) losses incurred, as defined in subsection (b)(5) of this section;
(5) capital losses to the extent provided in subchapter P (sec. 1201 and following, relating to capital gains and losses) plus losses from capital assets sold or exchanged in order to obtain funds to meet abnormal insurance losses and to provide for the payment of dividends and similar distributions to policyholders. Capital assets shall be considered as sold or exchanged in order to obtain funds to meet abnormal insurance losses and to provide for the payment of dividends and similar distributions to policyholders to the extent that the gross receipts from their sale or exchange are not greater than the excess, if any, for the taxable year of the sum of dividends and similar distributions paid to policyholders in their capacity as such, losses paid, and expenses paid over the sum of the items described in section 834(b) (other than paragraph (1)(D) thereof) and net premiums received. In the application of section 1212 for purposes of this section, the net capital loss for the taxable year shall be the amount by which losses for such year from sales or exchanges of capital assets exceeds the sum of the gains from such sales or exchanges and whichever of the following amounts is the lesser:
  (A) the taxable income (computed without regard to gains or losses from sales or exchanges of capital assets); or
  (B) losses from the sale or exchange of capital assets sold or exchanged to obtain funds to meet abnormal insurance losses and to provide for the payment of dividends and similar distributions to policyholders;
(6) debts in the nature of agency balances and bills receivable which become worthless within the taxable year;
(7) the amount of interest earned during the taxable year which under section 103 is excluded from gross income;
(8) the depreciation deduction allowed by section 167 and the deduction allowed by section 611 (relating to depletion);
(9) charitable, etc., contributions, as provided in section 170;
(10) deductions (other than those specified in this subsection) as provided in part VI of subchapter B (sec. 161 and

following, relating to itemized deductions for individuals and corporations) and in part I of subchapter D (sec. 401 and following, relating to pension, profit-sharing, stock bonus plans, etc.);

(11) dividends and similar distributions paid or declared to policyholders in their capacity as such, except in the case of a mutual fire insurance company described in subsection (b)(1)(C). For purposes of the preceding sentence, the term "dividends and similar distributions" includes amounts returned or credited to policyholders on cancellation or expiration of policies described in subsection (b)(1)(D). For purposes of this paragraph, the term "paid or declared" shall be construed according to the method of accounting regularly employed in keeping the books of the insurance company;

(12) the special deductions allowed by part VIII of subchapter B (sec. 241 and following, relating to dividends received); and

(13) in the case of a company which writes mortgage guaranty insurance, the deduction allowed by subsection (e).

(d) Double deductions.

Nothing in this section shall permit the same item to be deducted more than once.

(e) Special deduction and income account.

In the case of taxable years beginning after December 31, 1966, of a company which writes mortgage guaranty insurance—

(1) **Additional deduction.** There shall be allowed as a deduction for the taxable year, if bonds are purchased as required by paragraph (2), the sum of—

(A) an amount representing the amount required by State law or regulation to be set aside in a reserve for mortgage guaranty insurance losses resulting from adverse economic cycles; and

(B) an amount representing the aggregate of amounts so set aside in such reserve for the 8 preceding taxable years to the extent such amounts were not deducted under this paragraph in such preceding taxable years,

except that the deduction allowable for the taxable year under this paragraph shall not exceed the taxable income for the taxable year computed without regard to this paragraph or to any carryback of a net operating loss. For purposes of this paragraph, the amount required by State law or regulation to be so set aside in any taxable year shall not exceed 50 percent of premiums earned on insurance contracts (as defined in subsection (b)(4)) with respect to mortgage guaranty insurance for such year. For purposes of this subsection, all amounts shall be taken into account on a first-in-time basis. The computation and deduction under this section of losses incurred (including losses resulting from adverse economic cycles) shall not be affected by the provisions of this subsection. For purposes of this subsection, the terms "preceding taxable years" and "preceding taxable year" shall not include taxable years which began before January 1, 1967.

(2) **Purchase of bonds.** The deduction under paragraph (1) shall be allowed only to the extent that tax and loss bonds are purchased in an amount equal to the tax benefit attributable to such deduction, as determined under regulations prescribed by the Secretary, on or before the date that any taxes (determined without regard to this subsection) due for the taxable year for which the deduction is allowed are due to be paid. If a deduction would be allowed but for the fact that tax and loss bonds were not timely purchased, such deduction shall be allowed to the extent such purchases are made within a reasonable time, as determined by the Secretary, if all interest and penalties, computed as if this sentence did not apply, are paid.

(3) **Mortgage guaranty account.** Each company which writes mortgage guaranty insurance shall, for purposes of this part, establish and maintain a mortgage guaranty account.

(4) **Additions to account.** There shall be added to the mortgage guaranty account for each taxable year an amount equal to the amount allowed as a deduction for the taxable year under paragraph (1).

(5) **Subtractions from account and inclusion in gross income.** After applying paragraph (4), there shall be subtracted for the taxable year from the mortgage guaranty account and included in gross income—

(A) the amount (if any) remaining which was added to the account for the tenth preceding taxable year,

(B) the excess (if any) of the aggregate amount in the mortgage guaranty account over the aggregate amount in the reserve referred to in paragraph (1)(A). For purposes of determining such excess, the aggregate amount in the mortgage guaranty account shall be determined after applying subparagraph (A), and the aggregate amount in the reserve referred to in paragraph (1)(A) shall be determined by disregarding any amounts remaining in such reserve added for taxable years beginning before January 1, 1967,

(C) an amount (if any) equal to the net operating loss for the taxable year computed without regard to this subparagraph, and

(D) any amount improperly subtracted from the account under subparagraph (A), (B), or (C) to the extent that tax and loss bonds were redeemed with respect to such amount.

If a company liquidates or otherwise terminates its mortgage guaranty insurance business and does not transfer or distribute such business in an acquisition of assets referred to in section 381(a), the entire amount remaining in such account shall be subtracted. Except in the case where a company transfers or distributes its mortgage guaranty insurance in an acquisition of assets referred to in section 381(a), if the company is not subject to the tax imposed by section 831 for any taxable year, the entire amount in the account at the close of the preceding taxable year shall be subtracted from the account in such preceding taxable year.

(6) **Lease guaranty insurance; Insurance of state and local obligations.** In the case of any taxable year beginning after December 31, 1970, the provisions of this subsection shall also apply in all respects to a company which writes lease guaranty insurance or insurance on obligations the interest on which is excludable from gross income under section 103. In applying this subsection to such a company, any reference to mortgage guaranty insurance contained in this section shall be deemed to be a reference also to lease guaranty insurance and to insurance on obligations the interest on which is excludable from gross income under section 103; and in the case of insurance on obligations the interest on which is excludable from gross income under section 103, the references in paragraph (1) to "losses resulting from adverse economic cycles" include losses from declining revenues related to such obligations (as well as losses resulting from adverse economic cycles), and the time specified in subparagraph (A) of paragraph (5) shall be the twentieth preceding taxable year.

Code Sec. 832(f) — Insurance companies

(f) Interinsurers.

In the case of a mutual insurance company which is an interinsurer or reciprocal underwriter—

(1) there shall be allowed as a deduction the increase for the taxable year in savings credited to subscriber accounts, or

(2) there shall be included as an item of gross income the decrease for the taxable year in savings credited to subscriber accounts.

For purposes of the preceding sentence, the term "savings credited to subscriber accounts" means such portion of the surplus as is credited to the individual accounts of subscribers before the 16th day of the 3rd month following the close of the taxable year, but only if the company would be obligated to pay such amount promptly to such subscriber if he terminated his contract at the close of the company's taxable year. For purposes of determining his taxable income, the subscriber shall treat any such savings credited to his account as a dividend paid or declared.

(g) Dividends within group.

In the case of an insurance company subject to tax under section 831(a) filing or required to file a consolidated return under section 1501 with respect to any affiliated group for any taxable year, any determination under this part with respect to any dividend paid by one member of such group to another member of such group shall be made as if such group were not filing a consolidated return.

In 1998, P.L. 105-206, Sec. 6010(o)(3)(B), substituted "except that, in the case of a master contract (within the meaning of section 264(f)(4)(E) of the Internal Revenue Code of 1986), the addition of covered lives shall be treated as a new contract only with respect to such additional covered lives." for "but the addition of covered lives shall be treated as a new contract only with respect to such additional covered lives. For purposes of this subsection, an increase in the death benefit under a policy or contract issued in connection with a lapse described in section 501(c)(2) of the Health Insurance Portability and Accountability Act of 1996 shall not be treated as a new contract." In Sec. 1084(d)[sic (f)] of P.L. 105-34 [reproduced below].

In 1997, P.L. 105-34, Sec. 1084(b)(4) [sic (d)(4)], deleted "and" at the end of clause (b)(5)(B)(i), substituted ", and" for the period at the end of clause (b)(5)(B)(ii), and added clause (b)(5)(B)(iii), effective as provided in Sec. 1084(d)[sic (f)] of this Act [as amended by Sec. 6010(o)(3)(B), 105-206, see above], which reads:

"(d) Effective date.—The amendments made by this section shall apply to contracts issued after June 8, 1997, in taxable years ending after such date. For purposes of the preceding sentence, any material increase in the death benefit or other material change in the contract shall be treated as a new contract except that, in the case of a master contract (within the meaning of section 264(f)(4)(E) of the Internal Revenue Code of 1986), the addition of covered lives shall be treated as a new contract only with respect to such additional covered lives."

In 1996, P.L. 104-188, Sec. 1702(c)(4), of this Act provides:

"(4) The earnings and profits of any insurance company to which section 11305(c)(3) of the Revenue Reconciliation Act of 1990 applies shall be determined without regard to any deduction allowed under such section; except that, for purposes of applying sections 56 and 902, and subpart F of part III of subchapter N of chapter 1 of the Internal Revenue Code of 1986, such deduction shall be taken into account."

— P.L. 104-188, Sec. 1702(h)(3), substituted "243(b)(2)" for "243(b)(5)" in subclause (b)(5)(C)(ii)(II) and (b)(5)(D)(ii)(II), effective for tax. yrs. begin. after 12/31/90.

— P.L. 104-188, Sec. 1704(t)(45), substituted "paragraph" for "subparagraph" in Sec. 11303(b) of P.L. 101-508, see below], effective 8/20/96.

In 1990, P.L. 101-508, Sec. 11303(a), substituted "section 807." for "section 807, pertaining to the life, burial, or funeral insurance, or annuity business of an insurance company subject to the tax imposed by section 831 and not qualifying as a life insurance company under section 816." in para. (b)(4) . . . Sec. 11303(b)(1), substituted "insurance contracts described in section 816(b)(1)(B)" for "amounts included in unearned premiums under the 2nd sentence of such paragraph" in subpara. (b)(7)(A) [as amended by Sec. 1704(t)(45) of P.L. 104-188, see above] . . . Sec. 11303(b)(2), substituted "such contracts into account" for "such amounts into account", effective for tax. yrs. begin. on or after 9/30/90 except as provided in Sec. 11303(c)(2) and (3) of this Act, which reads as follows:

"(2) Amendments treated as change in method of accounting. In the case of any taxpayer who is required by reason of the amendments made by this section to change his method of computing reserves—

"(A) such change shall be treated as a change in a method of accounting,

"(B) such change shall be treated as initiated by the taxpayer,

"(C) such change shall be treated as having been made with the consent of the Secretary, and

"(D) the net adjustments which are required by section 481 of the Internal Revenue Code of 1986 to be taken into account by the taxpayer shall be taken into account over a period not to exceed 4 taxable years beginning with the taxpayer's first taxable year beginning on or after September 30, 1990.

"(3) Coordination with section 832(b)(4)(C). The amendments made by this section shall not affect the application of section 832(b)(4)(C) of the Internal Revenue Code of 1986."

— P.L. 101-508, Sec. 11305(a), amended subpara. (b)(5)(A), effective for tax. yrs. begin. after 12/31/89 except as provided in Sec. 11305(c)(2)-(5) of this Act, which reads as follows:

"(2) Amendments treated as change in method of accounting.

"(A) In general. In the case of any taxpayer who is required by reason of the amendments made by this section to change his method of computing losses incurred.—

"(i) such change shall be treated as a change in a method of accounting,

"(ii) such change shall be treated as initiated by the taxpayer, and

"(iii) such change shall be treated as having been made with the consent of the Secretary.

"(B) Adjustments. In applying section 481 of the Internal Revenue Code of 1986 with respect to the change referred to in subparagraph (A)—

"(i) only 13 percent of the net amount of adjustments (otherwise required by such section 481 to be taken into account by the taxpayer) shall be taken into account, and

"(ii) the portion of such net adjustments which is required to be taken into account by the taxpayer (after the application of clause (i)) shall be taken into account over a period not to exceed 4 taxable years beginning with the taxpayer's 1st taxable year beginning after December 31, 1989.

"(3) Treatment of companies which took into account salvage recoverable. In the case of any insurance company which took into account salvage recoverable in determining losses incurred for its last taxable year beginning before January 1, 1990, 87 percent of the discounted amount of estimated salvage recoverable as of the close of such last taxable year shall be allowed as a deduction ratably over its 1st 4 taxable years beginning after December 31, 1989.

"(4) Special rule for overestimates. If for any taxable year beginning after December 31, 1989— 87 percent of such excess (adjusted for discounting used in determining the amount of salvage recoverable as of the close of the last taxable year of the taxpayer beginning before January 1, 1990) shall be included in gross income for such taxable year.

"(5) Effect on earnings and profits. The earnings and profits of any insurance company for its 1st taxable year beginning after December 31, 1989, shall be increased by the amount of the section 481 adjustment which would have been required but for paragraph (2). For purposes of applying sections 56, 902, 952(c)(1), and 960 of the Internal Revenue Code of 1986, earnings and profits of a corporation shall be determined by applying the principles of paragraph (2)(B)."

Prior to amendment, subpara. (b)(5)(A) read as follows:

"(A) In general. The term 'losses incurred' means losses incurred during the taxable year on insurance contracts, computed as follows:

"(i) To losses paid during the taxable year, add salvage and reinsurance recoverable outstanding at the end of the preceding taxable year and deduct salvage and reinsurance recoverable outstanding at the end of the taxable year.

"(ii) To the result so obtained, add all unpaid losses on life insurance contracts plus all discounted unpaid losses (as defined in section 846) outstanding at the end of the taxable year and deduct unpaid losses on life insurance contracts plus all discounted unpaid losses outstanding at the end of the preceding taxable year."

In 1988, P.L. 100-647, Sec. 1010(c)(1)(A), substituted "section 831(a)" for "this part" in subpara. (b)(7)(C) . . . Sec. 1010(c)(1)(B), substituted "insurance company taxable under section 831(a)" for "nonlife insurance company" in the heading of subpara. (b)(7)(C) . . . Sec. 1010(c)(2), added subparas. (b)(7)(D) and (E) . . . Sec. 1010(c)(3), deleted "and" at the end of subpara. (e)(5)(A) and substituted a comma for the period at the end of subpara. (e)(5)(B), effective for tax. yrs. begin. after 12/31/86.

— P.L. 100-647, Sec. 1010(d)(1), added subsec. (g) . . . Sec. 1010(d)(2), added "(directly or indirectly)" after "attributable" in subclause (b)(5)(B)(ii)(II), effective for tax. yrs. begin. after 12/31/86. Sec. 1010(d)(3) of this Act provides:

"(3) For purposes of section 832(b)(5)(C)(i) of the 1986 Code, any stock or obligation acquired on or after August 8, 1986, by an insurance company subject to the tax imposed by section 831 of the 1986 Code (hereinafter in this paragraph referred to as the 'acquiring company') from another insurance company so subject (hereinafter in this paragraph referred to as the 'transferor company') shall be treated as acquired on the date on which such stock or obligation was acquired by the transferor company if—

"(A) the transferor company acquired such stock or obligation before August 8, 1986, and

"(B) at all times after the date on which such stock or obligation was acquired by the transferor company and before the date of the acquisition by the acquiring company, the transferor company and the acquiring company were members of the same affiliated group filing a consolidated return.

For purposes of the preceding sentence, the date on which the stock or obligation was acquired by the transferor company shall be determined with regard to any prior application of the preceding sentence. For purposes of this paragraph, if the acquiring corporation or transferor corporation was a party to a reorganization described in section 368(a)(1)(F) of the 1986 Code, any reference to such corporation shall include a reference to any predecessor thereof involved in such reorganization."

— P.L. 100-647, Sec. 1010(e)(3), amended Sec. 1023(e) of P.L. 99-514, transitional rules for amendments made by Sec. 1023 of P.L. 99-514, by adding Sec. 1023(e)(4), reproduced below.

Insurance companies Code Sec. 832

—P.L. 100-647, Sec. 1010(f)(8), amended Sec. 1024(d)(1) of P.L. 99-514 [reproduced below], transitional rules for changes made by Sec. 1024(c)(1) of P.L. 99-514, by adding the last sentence, see below.

In 1986, P.L. 99-514, Sec. 1021(a), amended para. (b)(4)(B) and added para. (b)(4)(C)... Sec. 1021(b), added paras. (b)(7) and (b)(8), effective for tax. yrs. begin. after 12/31/86. Sec. 1021(c)(2) of this Act provides:

"(2) Special transitional rule for title insurance companies. For the 1st taxable year beginning after December 31, 1986, in the case of premiums attributable to title insurance —

"(A) In general. The unearned premiums at the end of the preceding taxable year as defined in paragraph (4) of section 832(b) shall be determined as if the amendments made by this section had applied to such unearned premiums in the preceding taxable year and by using the interest rate and premium recognition pattern applicable to years ending in calendar year 1987.

"(B) Fresh start. Except as provided in subparagraph (C), any difference between —

"(i) the amount determined to be unearned premiums for the year preceding the first taxable year of a title insurance company beginning after December 31, 1986, determined without regard to subparagraph (A), and

"(ii) such amount determined with regard to subparagraph (A),

shall not be taken into account for purposes of the Internal Revenue Code of 1986.

"(C) Effect on earnings and profits. The earnings and profits of any insurance company for its 1st taxable year beginning after December 31, 1986, shall be increased by the amount of the difference determined under subparagraph (A) with respect to such company."

Prior to amendment, subpara. (b)(4)(B) read as follows:

"(B) To the result so obtained, add unearned premiums on outstanding business at the end of the preceding taxable year and deduct unearned premiums on outstanding business at the end of the taxable year."

—P.L. 99-514, Sec. 1022(a), amended para. (b)(5), effective for tax. yrs. begin. after 12/31/86.

Prior to amendment, para. (b)(5) read as follows:

"(5) Losses incurred. The term 'losses incurred' means losses incurred during the taxable year on insurance contracts, computed as follows:

"(A) To losses paid during the taxable year, add salvage and reinsurance recoverable outstanding at the end of the preceding taxable year and deduct salvage and reinsurance recoverable outstanding at the end of the taxable year.

"(B) To the result so obtained, add all unpaid losses outstanding at the end of the taxable year and deduct unpaid losses outstanding at the end of the preceding taxable year."

—P.L. 99-514, Sec. 1023(a)(1), amended clause (b)(5)(A)(ii) (as amended by Sec. 1022 of this Act)... Sec. 1023(a)(2), added the second sentence to para. (b)(6), effective for tax. yrs. begin. after 12/31/86. Secs. 1023(e)(2)-(4) [as amended by Sec. 1010(e)(3) of P.L. 100-647, above] of this Act provide:

"(2) Transitional rule. — For the first taxable year beginning after December 31, 1986—

"(A) the unpaid losses and the expenses unpaid (as defined in paragraphs (5)(B) and (6) of section 832(b) of the Internal Revenue Code of 1986) at the end of the preceding taxable year, and

"(B) the unpaid losses as defined in sections 807(c)(2) and 805(a)(1) of such Code at the end of the preceding taxable year,

shall be determined as if the amendments made by this section had applied to such unpaid losses and expenses unpaid in the preceding taxable year and by using the interest rate and loss payment patterns applicable to accident years ending with calendar year 1987. For subsequent taxable years, such amendments shall be applied with respect to such unpaid losses and expenses unpaid by using the interest rate and loss payment patterns applicable to accident years ending with calendar year 1987.

"(3) Fresh start. —

"(A) In general. — Except as otherwise provided in this paragraph, any difference between—

"(i) the amount determined to be the unpaid losses and expenses unpaid for the year preceding the 1st taxable year of an insurance company beginning after December 31, 1986, determined without regard to paragraph (2), and

"(ii) such amount determined with regard to paragraph (2),

shall not be taken into account for purposes of the Internal Revenue Code of 1986.

"(B) Reserve strengthening in years after 1985. — Subparagraph (A) shall not apply to any reserve strengthening in a taxable year beginning in 1986, and such strengthening shall be treated as occurring in the taxpayer's 1st taxable year beginning after December 31, 1986.

"(C) Effect on earnings and profits. — The earnings and profits of any insurance company for its 1st taxable year beginning after December 31, 1986, shall be increased by the amount of the difference determined under subparagraph (A) with respect to such company."

"(4) Application of fresh start to companies which become subject to section 831(a) tax in later taxable year. If —

"(A) an insurance company was not subject to tax under section 831(a) of the Internal Revenue Code of 1986 for its 1st taxable year beginning after December 31, 1986, by reason of being —

"(i) subject to tax under section 831(b) of such Code, or

"(ii) described in section 501(c) of such Code and exempt from tax under section 501(a) of such Code, and

"(B) such company becomes subject to tax under such section 831(a) for any later taxable year,

paragraph (2) and subparagraphs (A) and (C) of paragraph (3) shall be applied by treating such later taxable year as its 1st taxable year beginning after December 31, 1986, and by treating the calendar year in which such later taxable year begins as 1987; and paragraph (3)(B) shall not apply."

Prior to amendment, clause (b)(5)(A)(ii) [as amended by Sec. 1022 of this Act] read as follows:

"(ii) To the result so obtained, add all unpaid losses outstanding at the end of the taxable year and deduct unpaid losses outstanding at the end of the preceding taxable year."

—P.L. 99-514, Sec. 1024(c)(1), substituted "a mutual fire insurance company exclusively issuing perpetual policies" for "a mutual fire insurance company described in section 831(a)(3)(A)" in subpara. (b)(1)(C)... Sec. 1024(c)(2), amended subpara. (b)(1)(D)... Sec. 1024(c)(3)(A), substituted "paragraph (1)(d)" for "section 831(a)(3)(B)" each time it appeared in para. (b)(4)... Sec. 1024(c)(3)(B), amended the last sentence of para. (b)(4)... Sec. 1024(c)(4), substituted "section 834(b)" for "section 822(b)" in para. (c)(5)... Sec. 1024(c)(5)(A), substituted "subsection (b)(1)(C)" for "section 831(a)(3)(A)" in para. (c)(11)... Sec. 1024(c)(5)(B), substituted "subsection (b)(1)(D)" for "section 831(a)(3)(B)" in para. (c)(11)... Sec. 1024(c)(6), added subsec. (f), effective for tax. yrs. begin. after 12/31/86. Sec. 1024(d) of this Act, [as amended by Sec. 1010(f)(8) of P.L. 100-647, above] provides:

"(d) Transitional rules.

"(1) Treatment of amounts in protection against loss account. — In the case of any insurance company which had a protection against loss account for its last taxable year beginning before January 1, 1987, there shall be included in the gross income of such company for any taxable year beginning after December 31, 1986, the amount which would have been included in gross income for such taxable year under section 824 of the Internal Revenue Code of 1954 (as in effect on the day before the date of the enactment of this Act). For purposes of the preceding sentence, no addition to such account shall be made for any taxable year beginning after December 31, 1986. In the case of a company taxable under section 831(b) of the Internal Revenue Code of 1986 (as amended by subsection (a)), any amount included in gross income under this paragraph shall be treated as gross investment income.

"(2) Transitional rule for unused loss carryover under section 825. Any unused loss carryover under section 825 of the Internal Revenue Code of 1954 (as in effect on the day before the date of the enactment of this Act) which —

"(A) is from a taxable year beginning before January 1, 1987, and

"(B) could have been carried under such section to a taxable year beginning after December 31, 1986, but for the repeal made by subsection (a)(1),

shall be included in the net operating loss deduction under section 832(c)(10) of such Code without regard to the limitations of section 844(b) of such Code."

Prior to amendment, subpara. (b)(1)(D) read as follows:

"(D) in the case of a mutual fire or flood insurance company described in section 831(a)(3)(B), an amount equal to 2 percent of the premiums earned on insurance contracts during the taxable year with respect to policies described in section 831(a)(3)(B) after deduction of premium deposits returned or credited during the same taxable year, and,"

Prior to amendment, the last sentence of para. (b)(4) read as follows:

"Premiums paid by the subscriber of a mutual flood insurance company referred to in paragraph (3) of section 831(a) shall be treated, for purposes of computing the taxable income of such subscriber, in the same manner as premiums paid by a policyholder to a mutual fire insurance company referred to in such paragraph (3)."

In 1984, P.L. 98-369, Sec. 211(b)(9), substituted "section 816(b) but determined as provided in section 807" for "section 801(b)" and substituted "section 816" for "section 801" in para. (b)(4), effective for tax. yrs. begin. after 12/31/83.

In 1982, P.L. 97-248, Sec. 234(b)(2)(A), deleted ", as if no election to make installment payments under section 6152 is made" after "due to be paid" in para. (e)(2), effective for tax. yrs. begin. after 12/31/82.

In 1976, P.L. 94-455, Sec. 1901(a)(108), substituted "Association" for "Convention" in paras. (b)(1) and (b)(6)... Sec. 1901(b)(1)(T), deleted "or to the deductions provided in section 242 for partially tax-exempt interest" after "capital assets" in subpara. (c)(5)(A)... Sec. 1901(b)(1)(U), deleted "partially tax-exempt interest and to" after "relating to" in para. (c)(12)... Sec. 1906(b)(13)(A), substituted "Secretary" for "Secretary or his delegate" in para. (e)(2), effective for tax. yrs. begin. after 12/31/76.

In 1974, P.L. 93-483, Sec. 5, added para. (6) to subsec. (e), effective with respect to tax. yrs. beginning after 12/31/70.

In 1968, P.L. 90-240, Sec. 5(a), deleted "and" at the end of subpara. (b)(1)(C), substituted ", and" for the period at the end of subpara. (b)(1)(D), and added subpara. (b)(1)(E)... Sec. 5(b), deleted the period at the end of para. (c)(11), substituted "; and" for the period at the end or para. (c)(12), and added para. (c)(13) ... Sec. 5(c), add new subsec. (e), effective for tax. yrs. begin. after 12/31/66, except that so much of new para. (e)(2) as provides for payment of interest and penalties for failure to make a timely purchase of tax and loss bonds shall not apply with respect to any period during which such bonds are not available for purchase.

—P.L. 90-240, Sec. (5)(g), also provides as follows:

"In the case of taxable years beginning before 1967, a company shall treat additions to a reserve, required by State law or regulations for mortgage guaranty insurance losses resulting from adverse economic cycles, as unearned premiums for purposes of section 832(b)(4) of the Internal Revenue Code of 1954, but the amount so treated as unearned premiums in a taxable year shall not exceed 50 percent of premiums earned on insurance contracts (as defined in section 832(b)(4) of such Code), determined without regard to amounts added to the reserve, with respect to amounts added to the reserve, with respect to mortgage guaranty insurance for such year. The amount of unearned premiums at the close of 1966 shall be determined without regard to the preceding sentence for the purpose of applying 832(b)(4) of such Code to 1967. Additions to such a reserve shall not be treated as unearned premiums for any taxable year beginning after 1966.

"If a mortgage guaranty insurance company made additions to a reserve which were so treated as unearned premiums described in paragraph (1), such company, in taxable years beginning after 1966, shall include in gross income (in addition to the items specified in section 832(b)(1) of such Code) the sum of the following amounts until there is included in gross income an amount equal to the aggregate additions to the reserve described in paragraph (1) for taxable years beginning before 1967:

"(A) an amount (if any) equal to the excess of losses incurred (as defined in section 832(b)(5) of such Code) for the taxable year over 35 percent of premiums earned on insurance contracts during the taxable year (as defined in section 832(b)(4) of such Code), determined without regard to amounts added to the reserve referred to in paragraph (1), with respect to mortgage guaranty insurance,

"(B) the amount (if any) remaining which was added to the reserve for the tenth preceding taxable year, and

"(C) the excess (if any) of—

"(i) the aggregate of amounts so treated as unearned premiums for all taxable years beginning before 1967 less the total of the amounts included in gross income under this paragraph for prior taxable years and the amounts included in gross income under subparagraphs (A) and (B) for the taxable year, over

"(ii) the aggregate of the additions made for taxable years beginning before 1967 which remain in the reserve at the close of the taxable year.

"Amounts shall be taken into account on a first-in-time basis. For purposes of section 832(e) of such Code and this paragraph, if part of the reserve is reduced under State law or regulations, such reduction shall first apply to the extent of amounts added to the reserve for taxable years beginning before 1967, and only then to amounts added thereafter.

"The provisions of this subsection shall apply to taxable years beginning after December 31, 1956."

In 1966, P.L. 89-809, Sec. 104(i)(7), deleted subsec. (d) and redesignated subsec. (e) as subsec. (d) effective for tax. yrs. begin. 12/31/66.

Prior to deletion, subsec. (d) read as follows:
"(d) Taxable income of foreign insurance companies other than life or mutual and foreign mutual marine.

"In the case of a foreign insurance company (other than a life or mutual insurance company), a foreign mutual marine insurance company, and a foreign mutual fire insurance company described in section 831(a), the taxable income shall be the taxable income from sources within the United States. In the case of a company to which the preceding sentence applies, the deductions allowed in this section shall be allowed to the extent provided in subpart B of part II of subchapter N (sec 881 and following) in the case of a foreign corporation engaged in trade or business within the United States."

In 1964, P.L. 88-272, Sec. 228(c), added "and in Part I of subchapter D (Sec. 401 and following, relating to pension, profit-sharing, stock bonus plans, etc.)" to para. (c)(10), effective for tax. yrs. begin. after 12/31/53, and end, after 8/16/54.

In 1962, P.L. 87-834, Sec. 8(e)(2), added the last two sentences to para. (b)(4) ... Sec. 8(e)(3), substituted "section 831(a)(3)(A)" for "section 831(a)" in subpara. (b)(1)(C) ... Sec. 8(e)(4), amended para. (c)(11) ... Sec. 8(e)(5), deleted "and" at the end of subpara. (b)(1)(B), substituted ", and" for the period at the end of subpara. (b)(1)(C), and added new subpara. (b)(1)(D), effective for tax. yrs. begin. after 12/31/62.

Prior to amendment, para. (c)(11) read as follows:
"(11) dividends and similar distributions paid or declared to policyholders in their capacity as such, except in the case of a mutual fire insurance company described in section 831(a). For purposes of the preceding sentence, the term 'paid or declared' shall be construed according to the method of accounting regularly employed in keeping the books of the insurance company; and"

In 1956, P.L. 84-429, Sec. 3(b)(1), substituted "section 801(b)" for "section 806" in subpara. [sic (b)(4)] ... Sec. 3(b)(2), substituted "the items described in section 822(b) (other than paragraph (1)(D) thereof) and net premiums received. In the application of section 1212" for "interest, dividends, rents, and net premiums received. In the application of section 1211" ... Sec. 3(b)(3), added "and the deduction allowed by section 611 (relating to depletion)" after "section 167" in para. (c)(8) effective for tax. yrs. begin. after 12/31/54.

Sec. 833. Treatment of Blue Cross and Blue Shield organizations, etc.

(a) General rule. In the case of any organization to which this section applies—

(1) Treated as stock company. Such organization shall be taxable under this part in the same manner as if it were a stock insurance company.

(2) Special deduction allowed. The deduction determined under subsection (b) for any taxable year shall be allowed.

(3) Reductions in unearned premium reserves not to apply. Subparagraph (B) of paragraph (4) of section 832(b) shall be applied by substituting "100 percent" for "80 percent", and subparagraph (C) of such paragraph (4) shall not apply.

(b) Amount of deduction.

(1) In general. Except as provided in paragraph (2), the deduction determined under this subsection for any taxable year is the excess (if any) of—

(A) 25 percent of the sum of—

(i) the claims incurred during the taxable year and liabilities incurred during the taxable year under cost-plus contracts, and

(ii) the expenses incurred during the taxable year in connection with the administration, adjustment, or settlement of claims or in connection with the administration of cost-plus contracts, over

(B) the adjusted surplus as of the beginning of the taxable year.

(2) Limitation. The deduction determined under paragraph (1) for any taxable year shall not exceed taxable income for such taxable year (determined without regard to such deduction).

(3) Adjusted surplus. For purposes of this subsection—

(A) In general. The adjusted surplus as of the beginning of any taxable year is an amount equal to the adjusted surplus as of the beginning of the preceding taxable year—

(i) increased by the amount of any adjusted taxable income for such preceding taxable year, or

(ii) decreased by the amount of any adjusted net operating loss for such preceding taxable year.

(B) Special rule. The adjusted surplus as of the beginning of the organization's 1st taxable year beginning after December 31, 1986, shall be its surplus as of such time. For purposes of the preceding sentence and subsection (c)(3)(C), the term "surplus" means the excess of the total assets over total liabilities as shown on the annual statement.

(C) Adjusted taxable income. The term "adjusted taxable income" means taxable income determined—

(i) without regard to the deduction determined under this subsection,

(ii) without regard to any carryforward or carryback to such taxable year, and

(iii) by increasing gross income by an amount equal to the net exempt income for the taxable year.

(D) Adjusted net operating loss. The term "adjusted net operating loss" means the net operating loss for any taxable year determined with the adjustments set forth in subparagraph (C).

(E) Net exempt income. The term "net exempt income" means—

(i) any tax-exempt interest received or accrued during the taxable year, reduced by any amount (not otherwise deductible) which would have been allowable as a deduction for the taxable year if such interest were not tax-exempt, and

(ii) the aggregate amount allowed as a deduction for the taxable year under sections 243, 244, and 245.

The amount determined under clause (ii) shall be reduced by the amount of any decrease in deductions allowable for the taxable year by reason of section 832(b)(5)(B) to the extent such decrease is attributable to deductions under sections 243, 244, and 245.

(4) Only health-related items taken into account. Any determination under this subsection shall be made by only taking into account items attributable to the health-related business of the taxpayer.

Insurance companies Code Sec. 833

(c) Organizations to which section applies.
 (1) In general. This section shall apply to—
  (A) any existing Blue Cross or Blue Shield organization, and
  (B) any other organization meeting the requirements of paragraph (3).
 (2) Existing Blue Cross or Blue Shield organization. The term "existing Blue Cross or Blue Shield organization" means any Blue Cross or Blue Shield organization if—
  (A) such organization was in existence on August 16, 1986,
  (B) such organization is determined to be exempt from tax for its last taxable year beginning before January 1, 1987, and
  (C) no material change has occurred in the operations of such organization or in its structure after August 16, 1986, and before the close of the taxable year.
 To the extent permitted by the Secretary, any successor to an organization meeting the requirements of the preceding sentence, and any organization resulting from the merger or consolidation of organizations each of which met such requirements, shall be treated as an existing Blue Cross or Blue Shield organization.
 (3) Other organizations.
  (A) In general. An organization meets the requirements of this paragraph for any taxable year if—
   (i) substantially all the activities of such organization involve the providing of health insurance,
   (ii) at least 10 percent of the health insurance provided by such organization is provided to individuals and small groups (not taking into account any medicare supplemental coverage),
   (iii) such organization provides continuous full-year open enrollment (including conversions) for individuals and small groups,
   (iv) such organization's policies covering individuals provide full coverage of pre-existing conditions of high-risk individuals without a price differential (with a reasonable waiting period), and coverage is provided without regard to age, income, or employment status of individuals under age 65,
   (v) at least 35 percent of its premiums are determined on a community rated basis, and
   (vi) no part of its net earnings inures to the benefit of any private shareholder or individual.
  (B) Small group defined. For purposes of subparagraph (A), the term "small group" means the lesser of—
   (i) 15 individuals, or
   (ii) the number of individuals required for a small group under applicable State law.
  (C) Special rule for determining adjusted surplus. For purposes of subsection (b), the adjusted surplus of any organization meeting the requirements of this paragraph as of the beginning of the 1st taxable year for which it meets such requirements shall be its surplus as of such time.
 (4) Treatment as existing Blue Cross or Blue Shield organization.
  (A) In general. Paragraph (2) shall be applied to an organization described in subparagraph (B) as if it were a Blue Cross or Blue Shield organization.
  (B) Applicable organization. An organization is described in this subparagraph if it—
   (i) is organized under, and governed by, State laws which are specifically and exclusively applicable to not-for-profit health insurance or health service type organizations, and
   (ii) is not a Blue Cross or Blue Shield organization or health maintenance organization.
 (5) Nonapplication of section in case of low medical loss ratio. Notwithstanding the preceding paragraphs, this section shall not apply to any organization unless such organization's percentage of total premium revenue expended on reimbursement for clinical services provided to enrollees under its policies during such taxable year (as reported under section 2718 of the Public Health Service Act) is not less than 85 percent.

In 2010, P.L. 111-148, Sec. 9016(a), added para. (c)(5), effective for tax. yrs. begin. after 12/31/2009.
In 1998, P.L. 105-277, Sec. 4003(g), of this Act, reads as follows:
"(g) Provision related to section 1042 of 1997 Act. Rules similar to the rules of section 1.1502-75(d)(5) of the Treasury Regulations shall apply with respect to any organization described in section 1042(b) of the 1997 Act."
In 1997, P.L. 105-34, Sec. 1042, of this Act, reads as follows:
"SEC. 1042. TERMINATION OF CERTAIN EXCEPTIONS FROM RULES RELATING TO EXEMPT ORGANIZATIONS WHICH PROVIDE COMMERCIAL-TYPE INSURANCE.
"(a) In general. Subparagraphs (A) and (B) of section 1012(c)(4) of the Tax Reform Act of 1986 shall not apply to any taxable year beginning after December 31, 1997.
"(b) Special rules. In the case of an organization to which section 501(m) of the Internal Revenue Code of 1986 applies solely by reason of the amendment made by subsection (a)—
"(1) no adjustment shall be made under section 481 (or any other provision) of such Code on account of a change in its method of accounting for its first taxable year beginning after December 31, 1997, and
"(2) for purposes of determining gain or loss, the adjusted basis of any asset held on the 1st day of such taxable year shall be treated as equal to its fair market value as of such day.
"(c) Reserve weakening after June 8, 1997. Any reserve weakening after June 8, 1997, by an organization described in subsection (b) shall be treated as occurring in such organization's 1st taxable year beginning after December 31, 1997.
"(d) Regulations. The Secretary of the Treasury or his delegate may prescribe rules for providing proper adjustments for organizations described in subsection (b) with respect to short taxable years which begin during 1998 by reason of section 843 of the Internal Revenue Code of 1986."
—P.L. 105-34, Sec. 1604(d)(2)(A)(i), added "and liabilities incurred during the taxable year under cost-plus contracts" before the comma at the end of clause (b)(1)(A)(i) . . . Sec. 1604(d)(2)(A)(ii), added "or in connection with the administration of cost-plus contracts" before the comma at the end of clause (b)(1)(A)(ii), effective for tax. yrs. begin. after 12/31/86.
In 1996, P.L. 104-191, Sec. 351(a), added para. (c)(4), effective for tax. yrs. end. after 12/31/96.
In 1988, P.L. 100-647, Sec. 1010(b)(1), amended Sec. 1012(c)(4)(C)(iv) of P.L. 99-514 [reproduced below] . . . Sec. 1010(b)(2), substituted "Plan" for "Association" in Sec. 1012(c)(4)(C)(ii) of P.L. 99-514, [reproduced below].
Prior to amendment, Sec. 1012(c)(4)(C)(iv) of P.L. 99-514, read as follows:
"(iv) dental benefit coverage provided by Delta Dental Plans Association through contracts with independent professional service provided as long as the provision of such coverage is the principal activity of such Association."
—P.L. 100-647, Sec. 1010(b)(3), of this Act provides:
"(3) The Secretary of the Treasury or his delegate may prescribe rules providing proper adjustments for taxpayers which become subject to subchapter L of chapter 1 of the 1986 Code by reason of the amendments made by section 1012 of the Reform Act with respect to short taxable years which begin during 1987 by reason of section 843 of such Code."
In 1986, P.L. 99-514, Sec. 1012(b)(1), added Code Sec. 833, for tax. yrs. begin. after 12/31/86. Secs. 1012(c)(2)-(c)(4) [as amended by P.L. 100-647, Secs 1010(b)(1) and (2), for additional rules, see Sec. 1042 of P.L. 105-34, see above, for additional rules see Sec. 1042 of P.L. 105-34] of this Act provide:
"(2) Study of fraternal beneficiary associations.—The Secretary of the Treasury or his delegate shall conduct a study of organizations described in section 501(c)(8) of the Internal Revenue Code of 1986 and which received gross annual insurance premiums in excess of $25,000,000 for the taxable years of such organizations which ended during 1984. Not later than January 1, 1988, the Secretary of the Treasury shall submit to the Committee on Ways and Means of the House of Representatives, the Committee on Finance of the Senate, and the Joint Committee on Taxation the results of such study, together with such recommendations as he determines to be appropriate. The Secretary of the Treasury shall have authority to require the furnishing of such information as may be necessary to carry out the purposes of this paragraph.
"(3) Special rules for existing blue cross or blue shield organizations.—
"(A) In general.—In the case of any existing Blue Cross or Blue Shield organization (as defined in section 833(c)(2) of the Internal Revenue Code of 1986 as added by this section)—
"(i) no adjustment shall be made under section 481 (or any other provision) of such Code on account of a change in its method of accounting for its 1st taxable year beginning after December 31, 1986, and

2,423

"(ii) for purposes of determining gain or loss, the adjusted basis of any asset held on the 1st day of such taxable year shall be treated as equal to its fair market value as of such day.

"(B) Treatment of certain distributions.— For purposes of section 833(b)(3)(B), the surplus of any organization as of the beginning of its 1st taxable year beginning after December 31, 1986, shall be increased by the amount of any distribution (other than to policyholders) made by such organization after August 16, 1986, and before the beginning of such taxable year.

"(C) Reserve weakening after August 16, 1986.— Any reserve weakening after August 16, 1986, by an existing Blue Cross or Blue Shield organization shall be treated as occurring in such organization's 1st taxable year beginning after December 31, 1986.

"(4) Other special rules.—

"(A) The amendments made by this section shall not apply with respect to that portion of the business of Mutual of America which is attributable to pension business.

"(B) The amendments made by this section shall not apply to that portion of the business of the Teachers Insurance Annuity Association-College Retirement Equities Fund which is attributable to pension business.

"(C) The amendments made by this section shall not apply to—

"(i) the retirement fund of the YMCA,

"(ii) the Missouri Hospital Plan,

"(iii) administrative services performed by municipal leagues, or

"(iv) dental benefit coverage provided by Delta Dental Plans Association organization through contracts with independent professional service providers so long as the provision of such coverage is the principal activity of such organization.

"(D) For purposes of this paragraph, the term 'pension business' means the administration of any plan described in section 401(a) of the Internal Revenue Code of 1954 which includes a trust exempt from tax under section 501(a), any plan under which amounts are contributed by an individual's employer for an annuity contract described in section 403(b) of such Code, any individual retirement plan described in section 408 of such Code, and any eligible deferred compensation plan to which section 457(a) of such Code applies."

Sec. 834. Determination of taxable investment income.
(a) General rule.

For purposes of section 831(b), the term "taxable investment income" means the gross investment income, minus the deductions provided in subsection (c).

(b) Gross investment income.

For purposes of subsection (a), the term "gross investment income" means the sum of the following:

(1) The gross amount of income during the taxable year from—

(A) interest, dividends, rents, and royalties,

(B) the entering into of any lease, mortgage, or other instrument or agreement from which the insurance company derives interest, rents, or royalties,

(C) the alteration or termination of any instrument or agreement described in subparagraph (B), and

(D) gains from sales or exchanges of capital assets to the extent provided in subchapter P (sec. 1201 and following, relating to capital gains and losses).

(2) The gross income during the taxable year from any trade or business (other than an insurance business) carried on by the insurance company, or by a partnership of which the insurance company is a partner. In computing gross income under this paragraph, there shall be excluded any item described in paragraph (1).

(c) Deductions.

In computing taxable investment income, the following deductions shall be allowed:

(1) Tax-free interest. The amount of interest which under section 103 is excluded for the taxable year from gross income.

(2) Investment expenses. Investment expenses paid or accrued during the taxable year. If any general expenses are in part assigned to or included in the investment expenses, the total deduction under this paragraph shall not exceed one-fourth of 1 percent of the mean of the book value of the invested assets held at the beginning and end of the taxable year plus one-fourth of the amount by which taxable investment income (computed without any deduction for investment expenses allowed by this paragraph, for tax-free interest allowed by paragraph (1), or for dividends received allowed by paragraph (7)), exceeds 3¾ percent of the book value of the mean of the invested assets held at the beginning and end of the taxable year.

(3) Real estate expenses. Taxes (as provided in section 164), and other expenses, paid or accrued during the taxable year exclusively on or with respect to the real estate owned by the company. No deduction shall be allowed under this paragraph for any amount paid out for new buildings, or for permanent improvements or betterments made to increase the value of any property.

(4) Depreciation. The depreciation deduction allowed by section 167.

(5) Interest paid or accrued. All interest paid or accrued within the taxable year on indebtedness, except on indebtedness incurred or continued to purchase or carry obligations the interest on which is wholly exempt from taxation under this subtitle.

(6) Capital losses. Capital losses to the extent provided in subchapter P (sec. 1201 and following) plus losses from capital assets sold or exchanged in order to obtain funds to meet abnormal insurance losses and to provide for the payment of dividends and similar distributions to policyholders. Capital assets shall be considered as sold or exchanged in order to obtain funds to meet abnormal insurance losses and to provide for the payment of dividends and similar distributions to policyholders to the extent that the gross receipts from their sale or exchange are not greater than the excess, if any, for the taxable year of the sum of dividends and similar distributions paid to policyholders, losses paid, and expenses paid over the sum of the items described in subsection (b) (other than paragraph (1)(D) thereof) and net premiums received. In the application of section 1212 for purposes of this section, the net capital loss for the taxable year shall be the amount by which losses for such year from sales or exchanges of capital assets exceeds the sum of the gains from such sales or exchanges and whichever of the following amounts is the lesser:

(A) the taxable investment income (computed without regard to gains or losses from sales or exchanges of capital assets); or

(B) losses from the sale or exchange of capital assets sold or exchanged to obtain funds to meet abnormal insurance losses and to provide for the payment of dividends and similar distributions to policyholders.

(7) Special deductions. The special deductions allowed by part VIII (except section 248) of subchapter B (sec. 241 and following, relating to dividends received). In applying section 246(b) (relating to limitation on aggregate amount of deductions for dividends received) for purposes of this paragraph, the reference in such section to "taxable income" shall be treated as a reference to "taxable investment income".

(8) Trade or business deductions. The deductions allowed by this subtitle (without regard to this part) which are attributable to any trade or business (other than an insurance business) carried on by the insurance company, or by a partnership of which the insurance company is a partner; except that for purposes of this paragraph—

(A) any item, to the extent attributable to the carrying on of the insurance business, shall not be taken into account, and

(B) the deduction for net operating losses provided in section 172 shall not be allowed.

(9) Depletion. The deduction allowed by section 611 (relating to depletion).

Insurance companies Code Sec. 835(b)

(d) Other applicable rules.
(1) Rental value of real estate. The deduction under subsection (c)(3) or (4) on account of any real estate owned and occupied in whole or in part by a mutual insurance company subject to the tax imposed by section 831 shall be limited to an amount which bears the same ratio to such deduction (computed without regard to this paragraph) as the rental value of the space not so occupied bears to the rental value of the entire property.

(2) Amortization of premium and accrual of discount. The gross amount of income during the taxable year from interest and the deduction provided in subsection (c)(1) shall each be decreased to reflect the appropriate amortization of premium and increased to reflect the appropriate accrual of discount attributable to the taxable year on bonds, notes, debentures, or other evidences of indebtedness held by a mutual insurance company subject to the tax imposed by section 831. Such amortization and accrual shall be determined—

(A) in accordance with the method regularly employed by such company, if such method is reasonable, and

(B) in all other cases, in accordance with regulations prescribed by the Secretary.

No accrual of discount shall be required under this paragraph on any bond (as defined in section 171(d)) except in the case of discount which is original issue discount (as defined in section 1273).

(3) Double deductions. Nothing in this part shall permit the same item to be deducted more than once.

(e) Definitions.
For purposes of this part—

(1) Net premiums. The term "net premiums" means gross premiums (including deposits and assessments) written or received on insurance contracts during the taxable year less return premiums and premiums paid or incurred for reinsurance. Amounts returned where the amount is not fixed in the insurance contract but depends on the experience of the company or the discretion of the management shall not be included in return premiums but shall be treated as dividends to policyholders under paragraph (2).

(2) Dividends to policyholders. The term "dividends to policyholders" means dividends and similar distributions paid or declared to policyholders. For purposes of the preceding sentence, the term "paid or declared" shall be construed according to the method regularly employed in keeping the books of the insurance company.

In 1986, P.L. 99-514, Sec. 1024(a)(3), redesignated Code Sec. 822, as Code Sec. 834 . . . Sec. 1024(c)(7), amended subsec. (a) . . . Sec. 1024(c)(8)(A), substituted "section 831" for "section 821" each place it appeared in subsec. (d) . . . Sec. 1024(c)(8)(B), added "except in the case of discount which is original issue discount (as defined in section 1273)" before the period at the end of the sentence at the end of para. (d)(2), effective for tax. yrs. begin. after 12/31/86.
Prior to amendment, subsec. (a) read as follows:
"(a) Definitions.
"For purposes of this part—
"(1) The term 'taxable investment income' means the gross investment income, minus the deductions provided in subsection (c).
"(2) The term 'investment loss' means the amount by which the deductions provided in subsection (c) exceed the gross investment income."
In 1976, P.L. 94-455, Sec. 1901(a)(105)(A), deleted "(other than obligations of the United States issued after September 24, 1917, and originally subscribed for by the taxpayer)" after "obligations" in para. (c)(5) . . . Sec. 1901(a)(105)(B), substituted "No accrual" for "For taxable years beginning after December 31, 1962, no accrual" in the sentence at the end of para. (d)(2) . . . Sec. 1901(b)(1)(P), deleted "partially tax-exempt interest and" after "paragraph (1), or for" in para. (c)(2) . . . Sec. 1901(b)(1)(Q), deleted "or to the deduction provided in section 242 for partially tax-exempt interest" after "capital assets" in subpara. (c)(6)(A) . . . Sec. 1901(b)(1)(R), deleted "partially tax-exempt interest and to" before "relating to" in para. (c)(7) . . . Sec. 1901(b)(1)(S), substituted "and the deduction provided in subsection (c)(1)" for ", the deduction provided in subsection (c)(1), and the deduction allowed by section 242 (relating to partially tax-exempt interest)" in para. (d)(2) . . . Sec. 1906(b)(13)(A), substituted "Secretary" for "Secretary of his delegate" each place it appeared in Code Sec. 822, effective for tax. yrs. begin. after 12/31/76.
In 1966, P.L. 89-809, Sec. 104(i)(5), deleted subsec. (e), and redesignated subsec. (f) as subsec. (e), effective for tax. yrs. begin. after 12/31/66.
Prior to deletion, subsec. (e) read as follows:
"(e) Foreign mutual insurance companies other than life or marine. In the case of a foreign mutual insurance company (other than a life or marine insurance company or a fire insurance company subject to the tax imposed by section 831), the taxable investment income shall be the taxable income from sources within the United States (computed without regard to the deductions allowed by subsection (c)(7)), and the gross amount of income from the items described in subsection (b) (other than paragraph (1)(D) thereof) and net premiums shall be the amount of such income from sources within the United States. In the case of a company to which the preceding sentence applies, the deductions allowed in this section shall be allowed to the extent provided in subpart B of part II of subchapter N (sec. 881 and following) in the case of a foreign corporation engaged in trade or business within the United States."
In 1964, P.L. 88-272, Sec. 228(b)(2), added the sentence at the end of para. (d)(2), effective 2/26/54.
In 1962, P.L. 87-834, Sec. 8(b)(1), amended the heading of Code Sec. 822, and amended subsec. (a) . . . Sec. 8(b)(2), substituted "taxable investment income" for "mutual insurance company taxable income" each place it appeared in subsecs. (c) and (e) . . . Sec. 8(b)(3), added the sentence at the end of para. (c)(7) . . . Sec. 8(b)(4), redesignated Code Sec. 823 as subsec. (f), and deleted "Other" before "definitions" in the heading of subsec. (f) [as redesignated], effective for tax. yrs. begin. after 12/31/62.
Prior to amendment, the heading of Code Sec. 822 and subsec. (a) read as follows:
"SEC. 822. DETERMINATION OF MUTUAL INSURANCE COMPANY TAXABLE INCOME.
"(a) Definitions.—For purposes of section 821, the term 'mutual insurance company taxable income' means the gross investment income minus the deductions provided in subsection (c)."
In 1956, P.L. 429, Sec. 3(a)(3), amended subsec. (b) . . . Sec. 3(a)(4), amended para. (c)(3) . . . Sec. 3(a)(5), substituted "the sum of the items described in subsection (b) (other than paragraph (1)(D) thereof) and net premiums received. In the application of section 1212" for "the sum of interest, dividends, rents, and net premiums received. In the application of section 1211" in para. (c)(6) . . . Sec. 3(a)(6), added paras. (c)(8) and (9) . . . Sec. 3(a)(7), substituted "subsection (c)(3) or (4)" for "subsection (e)(3) or (4)" in para. (d)(1) . . . Sec. 3(a)(8), substituted "items described in subsection (b) (other than paragraph (1)(D) thereof)" for "interest, dividends, rents," in subsec. (e), effective only for tax. yrs. begin. after 12/31/54.
Prior to amendment, subsec. (b) read as follows:
"(b) Gross investment income.
"For purposes of subsection (a), the term 'gross investment income' means the gross amount of income during the taxable year from interest, dividends, rents, and gains from sales or exchanges of capital assets to the extent provided in subchapter P (sec. 1201 and following, relating to capital gains and losses)."
Prior to amendment, para. (c)(3) read as follows:
"(3) Real estate expenses.—Taxes and other expenses paid or accrued during the taxable year exclusively on or with respect to the real estate owned by the company, not including taxes assessed against local benefits of a kind tending to increase the value of the property assessed, and not including any amount paid out for new buildings, or for permanent improvements or betterments made to increase the value of any property. The deduction allowed by this paragraph shall be allowed in the case of taxes imposed on a shareholder of a company on his interest as shareholder, which are paid or accrued by the company without reimbursement from the shareholder, but in such cases no deduction shall be allowed the shareholder for the amount of such taxes."

Sec. 835. Election by reciprocal.
(a) In general.
Except as otherwise provided in this section, any mutual insurance company which is an interinsurer or reciprocal underwriter (hereinafter in this section referred to as a "reciprocal") subject to the taxes imposed by section 831(a) may, under regulations prescribed by the Secretary, elect to be subject to the limitation provided in subsection (b). Such election shall be effective for the taxable year for which made and for all succeeding taxable years, and shall not be revoked except with the consent of the Secretary.

(b) Limitation.
The deduction for amounts paid or incurred in the taxable year to the attorney-in-fact by a reciprocal making the election provided in subsection (a) shall be limited to, but in no case increased by, the deductions of the attorney-in-fact allocable, in accordance with regulations prescribed by the Secretary, to the income received by the attorney-in-fact from the reciprocal.

2,425

Code Sec. 835(c) — Insurance companies

(c) Exception.

An election may not be made by a reciprocal under subsection (a) unless the attorney-in-fact of such reciprocal—

(1) is subject to the tax imposed by section 11;

(2) consents in such manner as the Secretary shall prescribe by regulations to make available such information as may be required during the period in which the election provided in subsection (a) is in effect, under regulations prescribed by the Secretary;

(3) reports the income received from the reciprocal and the deductions allocable thereto under the same method of accounting under which the reciprocal reports deductions for amounts paid to the attorney-in-fact; and

(4) files its return on the calendar year basis.

(d) Credit.

Any reciprocal electing to be subject to the limitation provided in subsection (b) shall be credited with so much of the tax paid by the attorney-in-fact as is attributable, under regulations prescribed by the Secretary, to the income received by the attorney-in-fact from the reciprocal in such taxable year.

(e) Benefits of graduated rates denied.

Any increase in the taxable income of a reciprocal attributable to the limits provided in subsection (b) shall be taxed at the highest rate of tax specified in section 11(b).

(f) Adjustment for refund.

If for any taxable year an attorney-in-fact is allowed a credit or refund for taxes paid with respect to which credit or refund to the reciprocal resulted under subsection (d), the taxes of such reciprocal for such taxable year shall be properly adjusted under regulations prescribed by the Secretary.

(g) Taxes of attorney-in-fact unaffected.

Nothing in this section shall increase or decrease the taxes imposed by this chapter on the income of the attorney-in-fact.

In 1988, P.L. 100-647, Sec. 1010(f)(2), substituted "section 831(a)" for "section 821(a)" in subsec. (a) ... Sec. 1010(f)(3), substituted "subsection (d)" for "subsection (e)" in subsec. (f), effective for tax. yrs. begin. after 12/31/86.

In 1986, P.L. 99-514, Sec. 1024(a)(3), redesignated Code Sec. 826 as Code Sec. 835 ... Sec. 1024(c)(9)(A), deleted subsec. (d) and redesignated subsecs. (c), (f), (g) and (h) as subsecs. (d), (e), (f) and (g) ... Sec. 1024(c)(9)(B), amended subsec (e) (as redesignated by Sec. 1024(c)(9)(A)), effective for tax. yrs. begin. after 12/31/86.

Prior to deletion, subsec. (d) read as follows:

"(d) Special rule. In applying section 824(d)(1)(D), any amount which was added to the protection against loss account by reason of an election under this section shall be treated as having been added by reason of section 824(a)(1)(A)."

Prior to amendment, subsec. (e) (as redesignated by Sec. 1024(c)(9)(A)) read as follows:

"(e) Surtax exemption denied. Any increase in taxable income of a reciprocal attributable to the limitation provided in subsection (b) shall be taxed without regard to the surtax exemption provided in section 821(a)(2)."

In 1978, P.L. 95-600, Sec. 301(b)(10), amended para. (c)(1), effective for tax. yrs. begin. after 12/31/78.

Prior to amendment, para. (c)(1) read as follows:

"(1) is subject to the taxes imposed by section 11(b) and (c);"

In 1976, P.L. 94-455, Sec. 1906(b)(13)(A), substituted "Secretary" for "Secretary or his delegate" each place it appeared in Code Sec. 835, effective for tax. yrs. begin after 12/31/76.

In 1962, P.L. 87-834, Sec. 8, added Code Sec. 826, effective for tax. yrs. begin. after 12/31/62.

PART III.—PROVISIONS OF GENERAL APPLICATION

Sec.
841. Credit for foreign taxes.
842. Foreign companies carrying on insurance business.
843. Annual accounting period.
844. Special loss carryover rules.
845. Certain reinsurance agreements.
846. Discounted unpaid losses defined.
847. Special estimated tax payments.
848. Capitalization of certain policy acquisition expenses.

In 1990, P.L. 101-508, Sec. 11301(c), added item 848.
In 1989, P.L. 101-239, Sec. 7821(d)(1), substituted "companies" for "corporations" in item 842.
In 1988, P.L. 100-647, Sec. 6077(b), added item 847.
In 1986, P.L. 99-514, Sec. 1024(a)(2), redesignated Part IV as Part III ... Sec. 1023(d), added item 846.
In 1984, P.L. 98-369, Sec. 212(b), added item 845.
In 1969, P.L. 91-172, Sec. 907(c), added item 844.
In 1966, P.L. 89-809, Sec. 104, changed the title of item 842 from "Computation of gross income."
In 1956, added item 843.

Sec. 841. Credit for foreign taxes.

The taxes imposed by foreign countries or possessions of the United States shall be allowed as a credit against the tax of a domestic insurance company subject to the tax imposed by section 801 or 831, to the extent provided in the case of a domestic corporation in section 901 (relating to foreign tax credit). For purposes of the preceding sentence (and for purposes of applying section 906 with respect to a foreign corporation subject to tax under this subchapter), the term "taxable income" as used in section 904 means—

(1) in the case of the tax imposed by section 801, the life insurance company taxable income (as defined in section 801(b)), and

(2) in the case of the tax imposed by section 831, the taxable income (as defined in section 832(a)).

In 1986, P.L. 99-514, Sec. 1024(c)(10)(A)-(D), substituted "801 or 831" for "801, 821, or 831" in Code Sec. 841, added "and" at the end of para. (1), deleted para. (2) and redesignated para. (3) as para. (2), effective for tax. yrs. begin. after 12/31/86.

Prior to deletion, para. (2) read as follows:

"(2) in the case of the tax imposed by section 821(a), the mutual insurance company taxable income (as defined in section 821(b)); and in the case of the tax imposed by section 821(c), the taxable investment income (as defined in section 822(a))," and

In 1984, P.L. 98-369, Sec. 211(b)(10)(A), and (B), substituted "section 801" for "section 802" each place it appeared in Code Sec. 841 and substituted "section 801(b)" for "section 802(b)" in para. (1), effective for tax. yrs. begin. after 12/31/83.

In 1966, P.L. 89-809, Sec. 104(i)(8), added "(and for purposes of applying section 906 with respect to a foreign corporation subject to tax under this subchapter)" after "sentence" in the second sentence of Code Sec. 841, effective for tax. yrs. begin. after '66.

In 1962, P.L. 87-834, added para. (2) and redesignated para. (2) as para. (3), effective for tax. yrs. begin. after 12/31/62.

In 1959, P.L. 86-69, Sec. 3(b), deleted "811," after "802," in the first sentence, and substituted "section 802, the life insurance company taxable income (as defined in section 802(b))," and "section 802 or 811, the net investment income (as defined in section 803(c))" in para. (1), effective for tax. yrs. begin. after 12/31/57.

In 1956, P.L. 429, Sec. 5(8), added "811," after "802," in the first sentence, effective for tax. yrs. begin. after 12/31/54.

Sec. 842. Foreign companies carrying on insurance business.

(a) Taxation under this subchapter.

If a foreign company carrying on an insurance business within the United States would qualify under part I or II of this subchapter for the taxable year if (without regard to income not effectively connected with the conduct of any trade or business within the United States) it were a domestic corporation, such company shall be taxable under such part on its income effectively connected with its conduct of any trade or business within the United States. With respect to the remainder of its income which is from sources within the United States, such a foreign company shall be taxable as provided in section 881.

Insurance companies
Code Sec. 842

(b) Minimum effectively connected net investment income.

(1) In general. In the case of a foreign company taxable under part I or II of this subchapter for the taxable year, its net investment income for such year which is effectively connected with the conduct of an insurance business within the United States shall be not less than the product of—

(A) the required U.S. assets of such company, and

(B) the domestic investment yield applicable to such company for such year.

(2) Required U.S. assets.

(A) In general. For purposes of paragraph (1), the required U.S. assets of any foreign company for any taxable year is an amount equal to the product of—

(i) the mean of such foreign company's total insurance liabilities on United States business, and

(ii) the domestic asset/liability percentage applicable to such foreign company for such year.

(B) Total insurance liabilities. For purposes of this paragraph—

(i) Companies taxable under part I. In the case of a company taxable under part I, the term "total insurance liabilities" means the sum of the total reserves (as defined in section 816(c)) plus (to the extent not included in total reserves) the items referred to in paragraphs (3), (4), (5), and (6) of section 807(c).

(ii) Companies taxable under part II. In the case of a company taxable under part II, the term "total insurance liabilities" means the sum of unearned premiums and unpaid losses.

(C) Domestic asset/liability percentage. The domestic asset/liability percentage applicable for purposes of subparagraph (A)(ii) to any foreign company for any taxable year is a percentage determined by the Secretary on the basis of a ratio—

(i) the numerator of which is the mean of the assets of domestic insurance companies taxable under the same part of this subchapter as such foreign company, and

(ii) the denominator of which is the mean of the total insurance liabilities of the same companies.

(3) Domestic investment yield. The domestic investment yield applicable for purposes of paragraph (1)(B) to any foreign company for any taxable year is the percentage determined by the Secretary on the basis of a ratio—

(A) the numerator of which is the net investment income of domestic insurance companies taxable under the same part of this subchapter as such foreign company, and

(B) the denominator of which is the mean of the assets of the same companies.

(4) Election to use worldwide yield.

(A) In general. If the foreign company makes an election under this paragraph, such company's worldwide current investment yield shall be taken into account in lieu of the domestic investment yield for purposes of paragraph (1)(B).

(B) Worldwide current investment yield. For purposes of subparagraph (A), the term "worldwide current investment yield" means the percentage obtained by dividing—

(i) the net investment income of the company from all sources, by

(ii) the mean of all assets of the company (whether or not held in the United States).

(C) Election. An election under this paragraph shall apply to the taxable year for which made and all subsequent taxable years unless revoked with the consent of the Secretary.

(5) Net investment income. For purposes of this subsection, the term "net investment income" means—

(A) gross investment income (within the meaning of section 834(b)), reduced by

(B) expenses allocable to such income.

(c) Special rules for purposes of subsection (b).

(1) Coordination with small life insurance company deduction. In the case of a foreign company taxable under part I, subsection (b) shall be applied before computing the small life insurance company deduction.

(2) Reduction in section 881 taxes.

(A) In general. The tax under section 881 (determined without regard to this paragraph) shall be reduced (but not below zero) by an amount which bears the same ratio to such tax as—

(i) the amount of the increase in effectively connected income of the company resulting from subsection (b), bears to

(ii) the amount which would be subject to tax under section 881 if the amount taxable under such section were determined without regard to sections 103 and 894.

(B) Limitation on reduction. The reduction under subparagraph (A) shall not exceed the increase in taxes under part I or II (as the case may be) by reason of the increase in effectively connected income of the company resulting from subsection (b).

(3) Data used in determining domestic asset/liability percentages and domestic investment yields. Each domestic asset/liability percentage, and each domestic investment yield, for any taxable year shall be based on such representative data with respect to domestic insurance companies for the second preceding taxable year as the Secretary considers appropriate.

(d) Regulations.

The Secretary shall prescribe such regulations as may be necessary or appropriate to carry out the purposes of this section, including regulations—

(1) providing for the proper treatment of segregated asset accounts,

(2) providing for proper adjustments in succeeding taxable years where the company's actual net investment income for any taxable year which is effectively connected with the conduct of an insurance business within the United States exceeds the amount required under subsection (b)(1),

(3) providing for the proper treatment of investments in domestic subsidiaries, and

(4) which may provide that, in the case of companies taxable under part II of this subchapter, determinations under subsection (b) will be made separately for categories of such companies established in such regulations.

In **2004,** P.L. 108-218, Sec. 205(b)(6), deleted para. (c)(3) and redesignated para. (c)(4) as (c)(3), effective for tax. yrs. begin. after 12/31/2004.

Prior to deletion, para. (c)(3) read as follows:

"(3) Adjustment to limitation on deduction for policyholder dividends in the case of foreign mutual life insurance companies. For purposes of section 809, the equity base of any foreign mutual life insurance company as of the close of any taxable year shall be increased by the excess of—

"(A) the required U.S. assets of the company (determined under subsection (b)(2)), over

"(B) the mean of the assets held in the United States during the taxable year."

In **1989,** P.L. 101-239, Sec. 7821(d)(2), substituted "yields" for "yeilds" in the heading of para. (c)(4), effective for tax. yrs. begin. after 12/31/87.

In **1988,** P.L. 100-647, Sec. 2004(q)(2)(A), deleted "held for the production of such income" after "the same companies" in subpara. (b)(3)(B)... Sec. 2004(q)(2)(B), deleted "held for the production of investment income" after "United States" in subpara. (b)(4)(B)... Sec. 2004(q)(3), deleted "and" at the end of para. (d)(2), substituted "and" for the period at the end of para. (d)(3) and added para. (d)(4), effective for tax. yrs. begin. after 12/31/87.

In **1987,** P.L. 100-203, Sec. 10242(a), amended Code Sec. 842, effective for tax. yrs. begin. after 12/31/87.

Prior to amendment, Code Sec. 842 read as follows:

"SEC. 842. FOREIGN CORPORATIONS CARRYING ON INSURANCE BUSINESS.

"If a foreign corporation carrying on an insurance business within the United States would qualify under part I or II of this subchapter for the taxable year if (without regard to income not effectively connected with the conduct of any trade or business within the United States) it were a domestic corporation, such corporation shall be taxable under such part on its income effectively connected with its conduct of any trade or business within the United States. With respect to the remainder of its income, which is from sources within the United States, such a foreign corporation shall be taxable as provided in section 881."

In **1986,** P.L. 99-514, Sec. 1024(c)(11), substituted "part I or II" for "part I, II, or III" in Code Sec. 842, effective for tax. yrs. begin. after 12/31/86.

In **1966,** P.L. 89-809, Sec. 104, amended Code Sec. 842, effective for tax. yrs. begin. after 12/31/66.

Prior to amendment, Code Sec. 842 read as follows:

"SEC. 842. COMPUTATION OF GROSS INCOME.

"The gross income of insurance companies subject to the tax imposed by section 802 or 831 shall not be determined in the manner provided in part I of subchapter N (relating to determination of sources of income)."

In **1959,** P.L. 86-69, Sec. 3(f)(1), deleted ", 811" after "802" in Code Sec. 842, effective for tax. yrs. begin. after 12/31/57.

In **1956,** ch. 83, Sec. 5(5), substituted "802, 811, or 831" for "802 or 831" in Code Sec. 842, effective for tax. yrs. begin. after 12/31/54.

Sec. 843. Annual accounting period.

For purposes of this subtitle, the annual accounting period for each insurance company subject to a tax imposed by this subchapter shall be the calendar year.

Under regulations prescribed by the Secretary, an insurance company which joins in the filing of a consolidated return (or is required to so file) may adopt the taxable year of the common parent corporation even though such year is not a calendar year.

In **1976,** P.L. 94-455, Sec. 1507(b)(2), added a sentence at the end of Code Sec. 843, effective for tax. yrs. begin. after 12/31/80.

In **1956,** ch. 83, Sec. 4(a), added Code Sec. 843, effective for tax. yrs. begin. after 12/31/54.

Sec. 844. Special loss carryover rules.
(a) General rule.

If an insurance company—

(1) is subject to the tax imposed by part I or II of this subchapter for the taxable year, and

(2) was subject to the tax imposed by a different part of this subchapter for a prior taxable year,

then any operations loss carryover under section 810 (or the corresponding provisions of prior law) or net operating loss carryover under section 172 (as the case may be) arising in such prior taxable year shall be included in its operations loss deduction under section 810(a) or net operating loss deduction under section 832(c)(10), as the case may be.

(b) Limitation.

The amount included under section 810(a) or 832(c)(10) (as the case may be) by reason of the application of subsection (a) shall not exceed the amount that would have constituted the loss carryover under such section if for all relevant taxable years the company had been subject to the tax imposed by the part referred to in subsection (a)(1) rather than the part referred to in subsection (a)(2). For purposes of applying the preceding sentence, section 810(b)(1)(C) (relating to additional years to which losses may be carried by new life insurance companies) shall not apply.

(c) Regulations.

The Secretary shall prescribe such regulations as may be necessary to carry out the purposes of this section.

In **1989,** P.L. 101-239, Sec. 7841(d)(16), substituted "for a prior taxable year" for "for the taxable year" in para. (a)(2), effective 12/19/89.

In **1986,** P.L. 99-514, Sec. 1024(c)(12), amended subsecs. (a) and (b), effective for tax. yrs. begin. after 12/31/86.

Prior to amendment, subsecs. (a) and (b) read as follows:

"(a) General rule.

"If an insurance company—

"(1) is subject to the tax imposed by part I, II, or III of this subchapter for the taxable year, and

"(2) was subject to the tax imposed by a different part of this subchapter for a prior taxable year beginning after December 31, 1962,

then any operations loss carryover under section 810 (or the corresponding provisions of prior law), unused loss carryover under section 825, or net operating loss carryover under section 172, as the case may be, arising in such prior taxable year shall be included in its operations loss deduction under section 810(a), unused loss deduction under section 825(a), or net operating loss deduction under section 832(c)(10), as the case may be.

"(b) Limitation.

"The amount included under section 810(a), 825(a), or 832(c)(10), as the case may be, by reason of the application of subsection (a) shall not exceed the amount that would have constituted the loss carryover under such section if for all relevant taxable years such company had been subject to the tax imposed by the part referred to in subsection (a)(1) rather than the part referred to in subsection (a)(2). For purposes of applying the preceding sentence—

"(1) in the case of a mutual insurance company which becomes a stock insurance company, an amount equal to 25 percent of the deduction under section 832(c)(11) (relating to dividends to policyholders) shall not be allowed, and

"(2) section 810(b)(1)(C) (relating to additional years to which losses may be carried by new life insurance companies) shall not apply."

—P.L. 99-514, Sec. 1899A(20), substituted "prior law), unused loss" for "prior law) unused loss" in subsec. (a), effective 10/22/86.

In **1984,** P.L. 98-369, Sec. 211(b)(11)(A)(i), substituted "section 810 (or the corresponding provisions of prior law)," for "section 812" in subsec. (a)... Sec. 211(b)(11)(A)(ii), substituted "section 810(a)" for "section 812(a)" in subsec. (a)... Sec. 211(b)(11)(B)(i), substituted "section 810(a)" for "section 812(a)" in subsec. (b)... Sec. 211(b)(11)(B)(ii), substituted "section 810(b)(1)(C)" for "section 812(b)(1)(C)" in subsec. (b), effective for tax. yrs. begin. after 12/31/83.

In **1976,** P.L. 94-455, Sec. 1901(b)(25), substituted "section 812(b)(1)(C)" for "section 812(b)(1)(A)(iii)" in para. (b)(2), for tax. yrs. begin. after '76.

—P.L. 94-455, Sec. 1906(b)(13)(A), substituted "Secretary" effective for "Secretary or his delegate" in subsec. (c), for tax. yrs. begin. after 12/31/76.

In **1969,** P.L. 91-172, Sec. 907(c), added Code Sec. 844, effective for losses incurred in tax. yrs. begin. after 12/31/62, but shall not affect any tax liability for any tax. yr. begin. before 1/1/67.

Sec. 845. Certain reinsurance agreements.
(a) Allocation in case of reinsurance agreement involving tax avoidance or evasion.

In the case of 2 or more related persons (within the meaning of section 482) who are parties to a reinsurance agreement (or where one of the parties to a reinsurance agreement is, with respect to any contract covered by the agreement, in effect an agent of another party to such agreement or a conduit between related persons), the Secretary may—

(1) allocate between or among such persons income (whether investment income, premium, or otherwise), deductions, assets, reserves, credits, and other items related to such agreement,

(2) recharacterize any such items, or

(3) make any other adjustment,

if he determines that such allocation, recharacterization, or adjustment is necessary to reflect the proper amount, source, or character of the taxable income (or any item described in paragraph (1) relating to such taxable income) of each such person.

(b) Reinsurance contract having significant tax avoidance effect.

If the Secretary determines that any reinsurance contract has a significant tax avoidance effect on any party to such contract, the Secretary may make proper adjustments with respect to such party to eliminate such tax avoidance effect (including treating such contract with respect to such party as terminated on December 31 of each year and reinstated on January 1 of the next year).

Insurance companies   Code Sec. 846(d)(3)(C)(ii)

In 2004, P.L. 108-357, Sec. 803(a), substituted "amount, source, or character" for "source and character" in subsec. (a), effective for any risk reinsured after 10/22/2004.

In 1984, P.L. 98-369, Sec. 212(a), added new Code Sec. 845, subsec. (a) of which is effective for any risk reinsured on or after 9/27/83 and subsec. (b) of which is effective for risks reinsured after 12/31/84. Sec. 217(e) of the Act provides:

"(e) Treatment of certain companies operating both as stock and mutual company. If, during the 10-year period ending on December 31, 1983, a company has, as authorized by the law of the State in which the company is domiciled, been operating as a mutual life insurance company with shareholders, such company shall be treated as a stock life insurance company."

Sec. 846. Discounted unpaid losses defined.

(a) Discounted losses determined.

(1) Separately computed for each accident year. The amount of the discounted unpaid losses as of the end of any taxable year shall be the sum of the discounted unpaid losses (as of such time) separately computed under this section with respect to unpaid losses in each line of business attributable to each accident year.

(2) Method of discounting. The amount of the discounted unpaid losses as of the end of any taxable year attributable to any accident year shall be the present value of such losses (as of such time) determined by using—

(A) the amount of the undiscounted unpaid losses as of such time,

(B) the applicable interest rate, and

(C) the applicable loss payment pattern.

(3) Limitation on amount of discounted losses. In no event shall the amount of the discounted unpaid losses with respect to any line of business attributable to any accident year exceed the aggregate amount of unpaid losses with respect to such line of business for such accident year included on the annual statement filed by the taxpayer for the year ending with or within the taxable year.

(4) Determination of applicable factors. In determining the amount of the discounted unpaid losses attributable to any accident year—

(A) the applicable interest rate shall be the interest rate determined under subsection (c) for the calendar year with which such accident year ends, and

(B) the applicable loss payment pattern shall be the loss payment pattern determined under subsection (d) which is in effect for the calendar year with which such accident year ends.

(b) Determination of undiscounted unpaid losses.

For purposes of this section—

(1) In general. Except as otherwise provided in this subsection, the term "undiscounted unpaid losses" means the unpaid losses shown in the annual statement filed by the taxpayer for the year ending with or within the taxable year of the taxpayer.

(2) Adjustment if losses discounted on annual statement. If—

(A) the amount of unpaid losses shown in the annual statement is determined on a discounted basis, and

(B) the extent to which the losses were discounted can be determined on the basis of information disclosed on or with the annual statement,

the amount of the unpaid losses shall be determined without regard to any reduction attributable to such discounting.

(c) Rate of interest.

(1) In general. For purposes of this section, the rate of interest determined under this subsection shall be the annual rate determined by the Secretary under paragraph (2).

(2) Determination of annual rate.

(A) In general. The annual rate determined by the Secretary under this paragraph for any calendar year shall be a rate equal to the average of the applicable Federal mid-term rates (as defined in section 1274(d) but based on annual compounding) effective as of the beginning of each of the calendar months in the test period.

(B) Test period. For purposes of subparagraph (A), the test period is the most recent 60-calendar-month period ending before the beginning of the calendar year for which the determination is made; except that there shall be excluded from the test period any month beginning before August 1, 1986.

(d) Loss payment pattern.

(1) In general. For each determination year, the Secretary shall determine a loss payment pattern for each line of business by reference to the historical loss payment pattern applicable to such line of business. Any loss payment pattern determined by the Secretary shall apply to the accident year ending with the determination year and to each of the 4 succeeding accident years.

(2) Method of determination. Determinations under paragraph (1) for any determination year shall be made by the Secretary—

(A) by using the aggregate experience reported on the annual statements of insurance companies,

(B) on the basis of the most recent published aggregate data from such annual statements relating to loss payment patterns available on the 1st day of the determination year,

(C) as if all losses paid or treated as paid during any year are paid in the middle of such year, and

(D) in accordance with the computational rules prescribed in paragraph (3).

(3) Computational rules. For purposes of this subsection—

(A) In general. Except as otherwise provided in this paragraph, the loss payment pattern for any line of business shall be based on the assumption that all losses are paid—

(i) during the accident year and the 3 calendar years following the accident year, or

(ii) in the case of any line of business reported in the schedule or schedules of the annual statement relating to auto liability, other liability, medical malpractice, workers' compensation, and multiple peril lines, during the accident year and the 10 calendar years following the accident year.

(B) Treatment of certain losses. Except as otherwise provided in this paragraph—

(i) in the case of any line of business not described in subparagraph (A)(ii), losses paid after the 1st year following the accident year shall be treated as paid equally in the 2nd and 3rd year following the accident year, and

(ii) in the case of a line of business described in subparagraph (A)(ii), losses paid after the close of the period applicable under subparagraph (A)(ii) shall be treated as paid in the last year of such period.

(C) Special rule for certain long-tail lines. In the case of any long-tail line of business—

(i) the period taken into account under subparagraph (A)(ii) shall be extended (but not by more than 5 years) to the extent required under clause (ii), and

(ii) the amount of losses which would have been treated as paid in the 10th year after the accident year shall be treated as paid in such 10th year and each

2,429

subsequent year in an amount equal to the amount of the losses treated as paid in the 9th year after the accident year (or, if lesser, the portion of the unpaid losses not theretofore taken into account).

Notwithstanding clause (ii), to the extent such unpaid losses have not been treated as paid before the last year of the extension, they shall be treated as paid in such last year.

(D) **Long-tail line of business.** For purposes of subparagraph (C), the term "long-tail line of business" means any line of business described in subparagraph (A)(ii) if the amount of losses which (without regard to subparagraph (C)) would be treated as paid in the 10th year after the accident year exceeds the losses treated as paid in the 9th year after the accident year.

(E) **Special rule for international and reinsurance lines of business.** Except as otherwise provided by regulations, any determination made under subsection (a) with respect to unpaid losses relating to the international or reinsurance lines of business shall be made using, in lieu of the loss payment pattern applicable to the respective lines of business, a pattern determined by the Secretary under paragraphs (1) and (2) based on the combined losses for all lines of business described in subparagraph (A)(ii).

(F) **Adjustments if loss experience information available for longer periods.** The Secretary shall make appropriate adjustments in the application of this paragraph if annual statement data with respect to payment of losses is available for longer periods after the accident year than the periods assumed under the rules of this paragraph.

(G) **Special rule for 9th year if negative or zero.** If the amount of the losses treated as paid in the 9th year after the accident year is zero or a negative amount, subparagraphs (C)(ii) and (D) shall be applied by substituting the average of the losses treated as paid in the 7th, 8th, and 9th years after the accident year for the losses treated as paid in the 9th year after the accident year.

(4) **Determination year.** For purposes of this section, the term "determination year" means calendar year 1987 and each 5th calendar year thereafter.

(e) **Election to use company's historical payment pattern.**

(1) **In general.** The taxpayer may elect to apply subsection (a)(2)(C) with respect to all lines of business by using a loss payment pattern determined by reference to the taxpayer's loss payment pattern for the most recent calendar year for which an annual statement was filed before the beginning of the accident year. Any such determination shall be made with the application of the rules of paragraphs (2)(C) and (3) of subsection (d).

(2) **Election.**

(A) In general. An election under paragraph (1) shall be made separately with respect to each determination year under subsection (d).

(B) Period for which election in effect. Unless revoked with the consent of the Secretary, an election under paragraph (1) with respect to any determination year shall apply to accident years ending with the determination year and to each of the 4 succeeding accident years.

(C) Time for making election. An election under paragraph (1) with respect to any determination year shall be made on the taxpayer's return for the taxable year in which (or with which) the determination year ends.

(3) **No election for international or reinsurance business.** No election under this subsection shall apply to any international or reinsurance line of business.

(4) **Regulations.** The Secretary shall prescribe such regulations as may be necessary or appropriate to carry out the purposes of this subsection including—

(A) regulations providing that a taxpayer may not make an election under this subsection if such taxpayer does not have sufficient historical experience for the line of business to determine a loss payment pattern, and

(B) regulations to prevent the avoidance (through the use of separate corporations or otherwise) of the requirement of this subsection that an election under this subsection applies to all lines of business of the taxpayer.

(f) **Other definitions and special rules.**

For purposes of this section—

(1) **Accident year.** The term "accident year" means the calendar year in which the incident occurs which gives rise to the related unpaid loss.

(2) **Unpaid loss adjustment expenses.** The term "unpaid losses" includes any unpaid loss adjustment expenses shown on the annual statement.

(3) **Annual statement.** The term "annual statement" means the annual statement approved by the National Association of Insurance Commissioners which the taxpayer is required to file with insurance regulatory authorities of a State.

(4) **Line of business.** The term "line of business" means a category for the reporting of loss payment patterns determined on the basis of the annual statement for fire and casualty insurance companies for the calendar year ending with or within the taxable year, except that the multiple peril lines shall be treated as a single line of business.

(5) **Multiple peril lines.** The term "multiple peril lines" means the lines of business relating to farmowners multiple peril, homeowners multiple peril, commercial multiple peril, ocean marine, aircraft (all perils) and boiler and machinery.

(6) **Special rule for certain accident and health insurance lines of business.** Any determination under subsection (a) with respect to unpaid losses relating to accident and health insurance lines of businesses (other than credit disability insurance) shall be made—

(A) in the case of unpaid losses relating to disability income, by using the general rules prescribed under section 807(d) applicable to noncancellable accident and health insurance contracts and using a mortality or morbidity table reflecting the taxpayer's experience; except that—

(i) the prevailing State assumed interest rate shall be the rate in effect for the year in which the loss occurred rather than the year in which the contract was issued, and

(ii) the limitation of subsection (a)(3) shall apply in lieu of the limitation of the last sentence of section 807(d)(1), and

(B) in all other cases, by using an assumption (in lieu of a loss payment pattern) that unpaid losses are paid in the middle of the year following the accident year.

(g) **Regulations.**

The Secretary shall prescribe such regulations as may be necessary or appropriate to carry out the purposes of this section, including—

(1) regulations providing proper treatment of allocated reinsurance, and

(2) regulations providing appropriate adjustments in the application of this section to a taxpayer having a taxable year which is not the calendar year.

Insurance companies Code Sec. 847(6)(A)

In 1996, P.L. 104-188, Sec. 1702(c)(4), of this Act, regarding the earnings and profit of insurance companies, is reproduced in note following Code Sec. 832.

In 1990, P.L. 101-508, Sec. 11305(b), added "and" at the end of para. (g)(1), deleted para. (g)(2) and redesignated para. (g)(3) as (g)(2), effective for tax. yrs. begin. after 12/31/89. For special rules see Sec. 11305 (c)(2)-(5) of this Act, reproduced in note following Code Sec. 832.

Prior to deletion, para. (g)(2) read as follows:

"(2) regulations providing proper treatment of salvage and reinsurance recoverable attributable to unpaid losses, and"

In 1988, P.L. 100-647, Sec. 1010(e)(1), substituted "paid in the middle of the year" for "paid during the year" in subpara. (f)(6)(B) . . . Sec. 1010(e)(2), deleted "and" from the end of para. (g)(1), substituted ", and" for the period at the end of para. (g)(2) and added para. (g)(3), effective for tax. yrs. begin. after 12/31/86.

— P.L. 100-647, Sec. 1010(e)(3), amended Sec. 1023(e) of P.L. 99-514, the transitional rules for changes made by Sec. 1023(c) of P.L. 99-514, by adding Sec. 1023(e)(4) of P.L. 99-514, see below.

In 1986, P.L. 99-514, Sec. 1023(c), added Code Sec. 846, effective for tax. yrs. begin. after 12/31/86. Secs. 1023(e)(2)-(4) [as amended by Sec. 1010(e)(3) of P.L. 100-647, see above] of this Act provide:

"(2) Transitional rule — For the first taxable year beginning after December 31, 1986 —

"(A) the unpaid losses and the expenses unpaid (as defined in paragraphs (5)(B) and (6)) of section 832(b) of the Internal Revenue Code of 1986) at the end of the preceding taxable year, and

"(B) the unpaid losses as defined in sections 807(c)(2) and 805(a)(1) of such Code at the end of the preceding taxable year,

shall be determined as if the amendments made by this section had applied to such unpaid losses and expenses unpaid in the preceding taxable year and by using the interest rate and loss payment patterns applicable to accident years ending with calendar year 1987. For subsequent taxable years, such amendments shall be applied with respect to such unpaid losses and expenses unpaid by using the interest rate and loss payment patterns applicable to accident years ending with calendar year 1987.

"(3) Fresh start. —

"(A) In general. — Except as otherwise provided in this paragraph, any difference between —

"(i) the amount determined to be the unpaid losses and expenses unpaid for the year preceding the 1st taxable year of an insurance company beginning after December 31, 1986, determined without regard to paragraph (2), and

"(ii) such amount determined with regard to paragraph (2),

shall not be taken into account for purposes of the Internal Revenue Code of 1986.

"(B) Reserve strengthening in years after 1985. — Subparagraph (A) shall not apply to any reserve strengthening in a taxable year beginning in 1986, and such strengthening shall be treated as occurring in the taxpayer's 1st taxable year beginning after December 31, 1986.

"(C) Effect on earnings and profits. — The earnings and profits of any insurance company for its 1st taxable year beginning after December 31, 1986, shall be increased by the amount of the difference determined under subparagraph (A) with respect to such company."

"(4) Application of fresh start to companies which become subject to section 831(a) tax in later taxable year. If —

"(A) an insurance company was not subject to tax under section 831(a) of the Internal Revenue Code of 1986 for its 1st taxable year beginning after December 31, 1986, by reason of being —

"(i) subject to tax under section 831(b) of such Code, or

"(ii) described in section 501(c) of such Code and exempt from tax under section 501(a) of such Code, and

"(B) such company becomes subject to tax under such section 831(a) for any later taxable year,

paragraph (2) and subparagraphs (A) and (C) of paragraph (3) shall be applied by treating such later taxable year as its 1st taxable year beginning after December 21, 1986, and by treating the calendar year in which such later taxable year begins as 1987; and paragraph (3)(B) shall not apply."

Sec. 847. Special estimated tax payments.

In the case of taxable years beginning after December 31, 1987, of an insurance company required to discount unpaid losses (as defined in section 846) —

(1) Additional deduction. There shall be allowed as a deduction for the taxable year, if special estimated tax payments are made as required by paragraph (2), an amount not to exceed the excess of —

(A) the amount of the undiscounted, unpaid losses (as defined in section 846(b)) attributable to losses incurred in taxable years beginning after December 31, 1986, over

(B) the amount of the related discounted, unpaid losses determined under section 846,

to the extent such amount was not deducted under this paragraph in a preceding taxable year. Section 6655 shall be applied to any taxable year without regard to the deduction allowed under the preceding sentence.

(2) Special estimated tax payments. The deduction under paragraph (1) shall be allowed only to the extent that such deduction would result in a tax benefit for the taxable year for which such deduction is allowed or any carryback year and only to the extent that special estimated tax payments are made in an amount equal to the tax benefit attributable to such deduction on or before the due date (determined without regard to extensions) for filing the return for the taxable year for which the deduction is allowed. If a deduction would be allowed but for the fact that special estimated tax payments were not timely made, such deduction shall be allowed to the extent such payments are made within a reasonable time, as determined by the Secretary, if all interest and penalties, computed as if this sentence did not apply, are paid. If amounts are included in gross income under paragraph (5) or (6) for any taxable year and an additional tax is due for such year (or any other year) as a result of such inclusion, an amount of special estimated tax payments equal to such additional tax shall be applied against such additional tax. If, after any such payment is so applied, there is an adjustment reducing the amount of such additional tax, in lieu of any credit or refund for such reduction, a special estimated tax payment shall be treated as made in an amount equal to the amount otherwise allowable as a credit or refund. To the extent that a special estimated tax payment is not used to offset additional tax due for any of the first 15 taxable years beginning after the year for which the payment was made, such special estimated tax payment shall be treated as an estimated tax payment made under section 6655 for the 16th year after the year for which the payment was made.

(3) Special loss discount account. Each company which is allowed a deduction under paragraph (1) shall, for purposes of this part, establish and maintain a special loss discount account.

(4) Additions to special loss discount account. There shall be added to the special loss discount account for each taxable year an amount equal to the amount allowed as a deduction for the taxable year under paragraph (1).

(5) Subtractions from special loss discount account and inclusion in gross income. After applying paragraph (4), there shall be subtracted for the taxable year from the special loss discount account and included in gross income:

(A) The excess (if any) of the amount in the special loss discount account with respect to losses incurred in each taxable year over the amount of the excess referred to in paragraph (1) with respect to losses incurred in that year, and

(B) Any amount improperly subtracted from the special loss discount account under subparagraph (A) to the extent special estimated tax payments were used with respect to such amount.

To the extent that any amount added to the special loss discount account is not subtracted from such account before the 15th year after the year for which the amount was so added, such amount shall be subtracted from such account for such 15th year and included in gross income for such 15th year.

(6) Rules in the case of liquidation or termination of taxpayer's insurance business.

(A) In general. If a company liquidates or otherwise terminates its insurance business and does not transfer or distribute such business in an acquisition of assets referred to in section 381(a), the entire amount remaining in such special loss discount account shall be subtracted

2,431

and included in gross income. Except in the case where a company transfers or distributes its insurance business in an acquisition of assets referred to in section 381(a), if the company is not subject to the tax imposed by section 801 or section 831 for any taxable year, the entire amount in the account at the close of the preceding taxable year shall be subtracted from the account in such preceding taxable year and included in gross income.

(B) Elimination of balance of payments. In any case to which subparagraph (A) applies, any special estimated tax payment remaining after the credit attributable to the inclusion under subparagraph (A) shall be voided.

(7) Modification of the amount of special estimated tax payments in the event of subsequent marginal rate reduction or increase. In the event of a reduction in any tax rate provided under section 11 for any tax year after the enactment of this section, the Secretary shall prescribe regulations providing for a reduction in the amount of any special estimated tax payments made for years before the effective date of such section 11 rate reductions. Such reduction in the amount of such payments shall reduce the amount of such payments to the amount that they would have been if the special deduction permitted under paragraph (1) had occurred during a year that the lower marginal rate under section 11 applied. Similar rules shall be applied in the event of a marginal rate increase.

(8) Tax benefit determination. The tax benefit attributable to the deduction under paragraph (1) shall be determined under regulations prescribed by the Secretary, by taking into account tax benefits that would arise from the carryback of any net operating loss for the year, as well as current year tax benefits. Tax benefits for the current year and carryback years shall include those that would arise from the filing of a consolidated return with another insurance company required to determine discounted, unpaid losses under section 846 without regard to the limitations on consolidation contained in section 1503(c). The limitations on consolidation contained in section 1503(c) shall not apply to the deduction allowed under paragraph (1).

(9) Effect on earnings and profits. In determining the earnings and profits.—

(A) any special estimated tax payment made for any taxable year shall be treated as a payment of income tax imposed by this title for such taxable year, and

(B) any deduction or inclusion under this section shall not be taken into account.

Nothing in the preceding sentence shall be construed to affect the application of section 56(g) (relating to adjustments based on adjusted current earnings).

(10) Regulations. The Secretary shall prescribe such regulations as may be necessary or appropriate to carry out the purposes of this section, including regulations—

(A) providing for the separate application of this section with respect to each accident year,

(B) such adjustments in the application of this section as may be necessary to take into account the tax imposed by section 55, and

(C) providing for the application of this section in cases where the deduction allowed under paragraph (1) for any taxable year is less than the excess referred to in paragraph (1) for such year.

In 1989, P.L. 101-239, Sec. 7816(n)(1)(A), substituted "special estimated tax" for "separate estimated tax" in para. (1)... Sec. 7816(n)(1)(B), substituted "in taxable years beginning after December 31, 1986" for "after December 31, 1986" in subpara. (1)(A)... Sec. 7816(n)(2), amended the first sentence in para. (2)... Sec. 7816(n)(3), added the last sentence to para. (5)... Sec. 7816(n)(4), deleted "and" at the end of subpara. (9)(A), substituted ", and" for the period at the end

of subpara. (9)(B) and added subpara. (9)(C) [before redesignation by Sec. 7816(n)(5) of this Act, see below]... Sec. 7816(n)(5), redesignated para. (9) as para. (10) and added new para. (9)... Sec. 7816(n)(6), added the sentence at the end of para. (8), effective for tax. yrs. begin. after 12/31/87.

Prior to amendment, the first sentence in para. (2) read as follows: "The deduction under paragraph (1) shall be allowed only to the extent that special estimated tax payments are made in an amount equal to the tax benefit attributable to such deduction, on or before the date that any taxes (determined without regard to this section) for the taxable year for which the deduction is allowed are due to be paid."

In 1988, P.L. 100-647, Sec. 6077(a), added Code Sec. 847, effective for tax. yrs. begin. after 12/31/87.

Sec. 848. Capitalization of certain policy acquisition expenses.

(a) General rule.

In the case of an insurance company—

(1) specified policy acquisition expenses for any taxable year shall be capitalized, and

(2) such expenses shall be allowed as a deduction ratably over the 120-month period beginning with the first month in the second half of such taxable year.

(b) 5-Year amortization for first $5,000,000 of specified policy acquisition expenses.

(1) In general. Paragraph (2) of subsection (a) shall be applied with respect to so much of the specified policy acquisition expenses of an insurance company for any taxable year as does not exceed $5,000,000 by substituting "60-month" for "120-month".

(2) Phase-out. If the specified policy acquisition expenses of an insurance company exceed $10,000,000 for any taxable year, the $5,000,000 amount under paragraph (1) shall be reduced (but not below zero) by the amount of such excess.

(3) Special rule for members of controlled group. In the case of any controlled group—

(A) all insurance companies which are members of such group shall be treated as 1 company for purposes of this subsection, and

(B) the amount to which paragraph (1) applies shall be allocated among such companies in such manner as the Secretary may prescribe.

For purposes of the preceding sentence, the term "controlled group" means any controlled group of corporations as defined in section 1563(a); except that subsections (a)(4) and (b)(2)(D) of section 1563 shall not apply, and subsection (b)(2)(C) of section 1563 shall not apply to the extent it excludes a foreign corporation to which section 842 applies.

(4) Exception for acquisition expenses attributable to certain reinsurance contracts. Paragraph (1) shall not apply to any specified policy acquisition expenses for any taxable year which are attributable to premiums or other consideration under any reinsurance contract.

(c) Specified policy acquisition expenses.

For purposes of this section—

(1) In general. The term "specified policy acquisition expenses" means, with respect to any taxable year, so much of the general deductions for such taxable year as does not exceed the sum of—

(A) 1.75 percent of the net premiums for such taxable year on specified insurance contracts which are annuity contracts,

(B) 2.05 percent of the net premiums for such taxable year on specified insurance contracts which are group life insurance contracts, and

(C) 7.7 percent of the net premiums for such taxable year on specified insurance contracts not described in subparagraph (A) or (B).

(2) General deductions. The term "general deductions" means the deductions provided in part VI of subchapter B (Sec. 161 and following, relating to itemized deductions) and in part I of subchapter D (Sec. 401 and following, relating to pension, profit sharing, stock bonus plans, etc.).

(d) Net premiums.
For purposes of this section—
(1) In general. The term "net premiums" means, with respect to any category of specified insurance contracts set forth in subsection (c)(1), the excess (if any) of—
(A) the gross amount of premiums and other consideration on such contracts, over
(B) return premiums on such contracts and premiums and other consideration incurred for reinsurance of such contracts.
The rules of section 803(b) shall apply for purposes of the preceding sentence.
(2) Amounts determined on accrual basis. In the case of an insurance company subject to tax under part II of this subchapter, all computations entering into determinations of net premiums for any taxable year shall be made in the manner required under section 811(a) for life insurance companies.
(3) Treatment of certain policyholder dividends and similar amounts. Net premiums shall be determined without regard to section 808(e) and without regard to other similar amounts treated as paid to, and returned by, the policyholder.
(4) Special rules for reinsurance.
(A) Premiums and other consideration incurred for reinsurance shall be taken into account under paragraph (1)(B) only to the extent such premiums and other consideration are includible in the gross income of an insurance company taxable under this subchapter or are subject to tax under this chapter by reason of subpart F of part III of subchapter N.
(B) The Secretary shall prescribe such regulations as may be necessary to ensure that premiums and other consideration with respect to reinsurance are treated consistently by the ceding company and the reinsurer.

(e) Classification of contracts.
For purposes of this section—
(1) Specified insurance contract.
(A) In general. Except as otherwise provided in this paragraph, the term "specified insurance contract" means any life insurance, annuity, or noncancellable accident and health insurance contract (or any combination thereof).
(B) Exceptions. The term "specified insurance contract" shall not include—
(i) any pension plan contract (as defined in section 818(a)),
(ii) any flight insurance or similar contract,
(iii) any qualified foreign contract (as defined in section 807(e)(4) without regard to paragraph (5) of this subsection),
(iv) any contract which is an Archer MSA (as defined in section 220(d)), and
(v) any contract which is a health savings account (as defined in section 223(d)).
(2) Group life insurance contract. The term "group life insurance contract" means any life insurance contract—
(A) which covers a group of individuals defined by reference to employment relationship, membership in an organization, or similar factor,
(B) the premiums for which are determined on a group basis, and
(C) the proceeds of which are payable to (or for the benefit of) persons other than the employer of the insured, an organization to which the insured belongs, or other similar person.
(3) Treatment of annuity contracts combined with noncancellable accident and health insurance. Any annuity contract combined with noncancellable accident and health insurance shall be treated as a noncancellable accident and health insurance contract and not as an annuity contract.
(4) Treatment of guaranteed renewable contracts. The rules of section 816(e) shall apply for purposes of this section.
(5) Treatment of reinsurance contract. A contract which reinsures another contract shall be treated in the same manner as the reinsured contract.
(6) Treatment of certain qualified long-term care insurance contract arrangements. An annuity or life insurance contract which includes a qualified long-term care insurance contract as a part of or a rider on such annuity or life insurance contract shall be treated as a specified insurance contract not described in subparagraph (A) or (B) of subsection (c)(1).

(f) Special rule where negative net premiums.
(1) In general. If for any taxable year there is a negative capitalization amount with respect to any category of specified insurance contracts set forth in subsection (c)(1)—
(A) the amount otherwise required to be capitalized under this section for such taxable year with respect to any other category of specified insurance contracts shall be reduced (but not below zero) by such negative capitalization amount, and
(B) such negative capitalization amount (to the extent not taken into account under subparagraph (A))—
(i) shall reduce (but not below zero) the unamortized balance (as of the beginning of such taxable year) of the amounts previously capitalized under subsection (a) (beginning with the amount capitalized for the most recent taxable year), and
(ii) to the extent taken into account as such a reduction, shall be allowed as a deduction for such taxable year.
(2) Negative capitalization amount. For purposes of paragraph (1), the term "negative capitalization amount" means, with respect to any category of specified insurance contracts, the percentage (applicable under subsection (c)(1) to such category) of the amount (if any) by which—
(A) the amount determined under subparagraph (B) of subsection (d)(1) with respect to such category, exceeds
(B) the amount determined under subparagraph (A) of subsection (d)(1) with respect to such category.

(g) Treatment of certain ceding commissions.
Nothing in any provision of law (other than this section or section 197) shall require the capitalization of any ceding commission incurred on or after September 30, 1990, under any contract which reinsures a specified insurance contract.

(h) Secretarial authority to adjust capitalization amounts.
(1) In general. Except as provided in paragraph (2), the Secretary may provide that a type of insurance contract will be treated as a separate category for purposes of this section (and prescribe a percentage applicable to such category) if the Secretary determines that the deferral of acquisition expenses for such type of contract which would otherwise result under this section is substantially greater

than the deferral of acquisition expenses which would have resulted if actual acquisition expenses (including indirect expenses) and the actual useful life for such type of contract had been used.

(2) Adjustment to other contracts. If the Secretary exercises his authority with respect to any type of contract under paragraph (1), the Secretary shall adjust the percentage which would otherwise have applied under subsection (c)(1) to the category which includes such type of contract so that the exercise of such authority does not result in a decrease in the amount of revenue received under this chapter by reason of this section for any fiscal year.

(i) Treatment of qualified foreign contracts under adjusted current earnings preference.

For purposes of determining adjusted current earnings under section 56(g), acquisition expenses with respect to contracts described in clause (iii) of subsection (e)(1)(B) shall be capitalized and amortized in accordance with the treatment generally required under generally accepted accounting principles as if this subsection applied to such contracts for all taxable years.

(j) Transitional rule.

In the case of any taxable year which includes September 30, 1990, the amount taken into account as the net premiums (or negative capitalization amount) with respect to any category of specified insurance contracts shall be the amount which bears the same ratio to the amount which (but for this subsection) would be so taken into account as the number of days in such taxable year on or after September 30, 1990, bears to the total number of days in such taxable year.

In 2006, P.L. 109-280, Sec. 844(e), added para. (e)(6), effective for specified policy acquisition expenses determined for tax. yrs. begin. after 12/31/2009.
In 2003, P.L. 108-173, Sec. 1201(h), deleted "and" at the end of clause (e)(1)(B)(iii), substituted ", and" for the period at the end of clause (e)(1)(B)(iv), and added clause (e)(1)(B)(v), effective for tax. yrs. begin. after 12/31/2003.
In 2000, P.L. 106-554, Sec. 1(a)(7), [which enacted into law Sec. 202(a)(5) of P.L. 106-554] substituted "Archer MSA" for "medical savings account" in clause (e)(1)(B)(iv), effective 12/21/2000.
In 1996, P.L. 104-188, Sec. 1703(l), substituted "by the taxpayer or a related person" for "by the taxpayer" in Sec. 13261(g)(2)(A)(iii) of P.L. 103-66 [see below], effective for property acquired after 8/10/93, except as provided in Sec. 13261(g)(2) and (3) of P.L. 103-66]see below].
—P.L. 104-191, Sec. 301(h), deleted "and" at the end of clause (e)(1)(B)(ii), substituted ", and" for the period at the end of clause (e)(1)(B)(iii), and added clause (e)(1)(B)(iv), effective for tax. yrs. begin. after 12/31/96.
—P.L. 104-191, Sec. 501(d), of this Act, regarding spread of income inclusion on surrender of contracts, is reproduced in note following Code Sec. 264.
In 1993, P.L. 103-66, Sec. 13261(d), substituted "this section or section 197" for "this section" in subsec. (g), effective for property acquired after 8/10/93, except as provided in Sec. 13261(g)(2) and (3) of this Act [as amended by Sec. 1703(l) of P.L. 104-188, see above], which reads as follows:

"(2) Election to have amendments apply to property acquired after July 25, 1991.
"(A) In general. If an election under this paragraph applies to the taxpayer—
"(i) the amendments made by this section shall apply to property acquired by the taxpayer after July 25, 1991,
"(ii) subsection (c)(1)(A) of section 197 of the Internal Revenue Code of 1986 (as added by this section) (and so much of subsection (f)(9)(A) of such section 197 as precedes clause (i) thereof) shall be applied with respect to the taxpayer by treating July 25, 1991, as the date of the enactment of such section, and
"(iii) in applying subsection (f)(9) of such section, with respect to any property acquired by the taxpayer or a related person on or before the date of the enactment of this Act, only holding or use on July 25, 1991, shall be taken into account.
"(B) Election. An election under this paragraph shall be made at such time and in such manner as the Secretary of the Treasury or his delegate may prescribe. Such an election by any taxpayer, once made—
"(i) may be revoked only with the consent of the Secretary, and
"(ii) shall apply to the taxpayer making such election and any other taxpayer under common control with the taxpayer (within the meaning of subparagraphs (A) and (B) of section 41(f)(1) of such Code) at any time after August 2, 1993, and on or before the date on which such election is made.
"(3) Elective binding contract exception.
"(A) In general. The amendments made by this section shall not apply to any acquisition of property by the taxpayer if—

"(i) such acquisition is pursuant to a written binding contract in effect on the date of the enactment of this Act and at all times thereafter before such acquisition,
"(ii) an election under paragraph (2) does not apply to the taxpayer, and
"(iii) the taxpayer makes an election under this paragraph with respect to such contract.
"(B) Election. An election under this paragraph shall be made at such time and in such manner as the Secretary of the Treasury or his delegate shall prescribe. Such an election, once made—
"(i) may be revoked only with the consent of the Secretary, and
"(ii) shall apply to all property, acquired pursuant to the contract with respect to which such election was made."
In 1990, P.L. 101-508, Sec. 11301(a), added Code Sec. 848, effective as provided in Sec. 11301(d)(1) of this Act, which reads as follows:
"(1) In general.— The amendments made by subsections (a) and (c) shall apply to taxable years ending on or after September 30, 1990. Any capitalization required by reason of such amendments shall not be treated as a change in method of accounting for purposes of the Internal Revenue Code of 1986."

Subchapter M.— Regulated Investment Companies and Real Estate Investment Trusts

Part
I. Regulated investment companies.
II. Real estate investment trusts.
III. Provisions which apply to both regulated investment companies and real estate investment trusts.
IV. Real estate mortgage investment conduits.
V. Repealed [Financial asset securitization trusts.]

In 2004, P.L. 108-357, Sec. 835(b)(12), removed the item for Part V.
In 1996, P.L. 104-188, Sec. 1621(a), added the item for Part V.
In 1988, P.L. 100-647, Sec. 1018(u)(30), added the item for Part IV.
In 1978, P.L. 95-600, Sec. 362(d)(8), added Part III.

PART I.— REGULATED INVESTMENT COMPANIES

Sec.
851. Definition of regulated investment company.
852. Taxation of regulated investment companies and their shareholders.
853. Foreign tax credit allowed to shareholders.
853A. Credits from tax credit bonds allowed to shareholders.
854. Limitations applicable to dividends and taxable interest received from regulated investment company.
855. Dividends paid by regulated investment company after close of taxable year.

In 2009, P.L. 111-5, Sec. 1541(b)(3), added item 853A.
In 1988, P.L. 96-223, Sec. 404(b)(7), added "and taxable interest" after "dividends" to item 854.
In 1960, added "and Real Estate Investment Trusts" to the Subchapter M heading, and Part II designation.

Sec. 851. Definition of regulated investment company.
(a) General rule.

For purposes of this subtitle, the term "regulated investment company" means any domestic corporation—

(1) which, at all times during the taxable year—

(A) is registered under the Investment Company Act of 1940, as amended (15 U.S.C. 80a-1 to 80b-2) as a management company or unit investment trust, or

(B) has in effect an election under such Act to be treated as a business development company, or

(2) which is a common trust fund or similar fund excluded by section 3(c)(3) of such Act (15 U.S.C. 80a-3(c)) from the definition of "investment company" and is not included in the definition of "common trust fund" by section 584(a).

Regulated investment companies Code Sec. 851(d)(2)(A)

(b) Limitations.
A corporation shall not be considered a regulated investment company for any taxable year unless—
 (1) it files with its return for the taxable year an election to be a regulated investment company or has made such election for a previous taxable year;
 (2) at least 90 percent of its gross income is derived from—
  (A) dividends, interest, payments with respect to securities loans (as defined in section 512(a)(5)), and gains from the sale or other disposition of stock or securities (as defined in section 2(a)(36) of the Investment Company Act of 1940, as amended) or foreign currencies, or other income (including but not limited to gains from options, futures or forward contracts) derived with respect to its business of investing in such stock, securities, or currencies, and
  (B) net income derived from an interest in a qualified publicly traded partnership (as defined in subsection (h)); and
 (3) at the close of each quarter of the taxable year—
  (A) at least 50 percent of the value of its total assets is represented by—
   (i) cash and cash items (including receivables), Government securities and securities of other regulated investment companies, and
   (ii) other securities for purposes of this calculation limited, except and to the extent provided in subsection (e), in respect of any one issuer to an amount not greater in value than 5 percent of the value of the total assets of the taxpayer and to not more than 10 percent of the outstanding voting securities of such issuer, and
  (B) not more than 25 percent of the value of its total assets is invested in—
   (i) the securities (other than Government securities or the securities of other regulated investment companies) of any one issuer,
   (ii) the securities (other than the securities of other regulated investment companies) of two or more issuers which the taxpayer controls and which are determined, under regulations prescribed by the Secretary, to be engaged in the same or similar trades or businesses or related trades or businesses, or
   (iii) the securities of one or more qualified publicly traded partnerships (as defined in subsection (h)).
For purposes of paragraph (2), there shall be treated as dividends amounts included in gross income under section 951(a)(1)(A)(i) or 1293(a) for the taxable year to the extent that, under section 959(a)(1) or 1293(c) (as the case may be), there is a distribution out of the earnings and profits of the taxable year which are attributable to the amounts so included. For purposes of paragraph (2), the Secretary may by regulation exclude from qualifying income foreign currency gains which are not directly related to the company's principal business of investing in stock or securities (or options and futures with respect to stock or securities). For purposes of paragraph (2), amounts excludable from gross income under section 103(a) shall be treated as included in gross income. Income derived from a partnership (other than a qualified publicly traded partnership as defined in subsection (h)) or trust shall be treated as described in paragraph (2) only to the extent such income is attributable to items of income of the partnership or trust (as the case may be) which would be described in paragraph (2) if realized by the regulated investment company in the same manner as realized by the partnership or trust.

(c) Rules applicable to subsection (b)(3).
For purposes of subsection (b)(3) and this subsection—
 (1) In ascertaining the value of the taxpayer's investment in the securities of an issuer, for the purposes of subparagraph (B), there shall be included its proper proportion of the investment of any other corporation, a member of a controlled group, in the securities of such issuer, as determined under regulations prescribed by the Secretary.
 (2) The term "controls" means the ownership in a corporation of 20 percent or more of the total combined voting power of all classes of stock entitled to vote.
 (3) The term "controlled group" means one or more chains of corporations connected through stock ownership with the taxpayer if—
  (A) 20 percent or more of the total combined voting power of all classes of stock entitled to vote of each of the corporations (except the taxpayer) is owned directly by one or more of the other corporations, and
  (B) the taxpayer owns directly 20 percent or more of the total combined voting power of all classes of stock entitled to vote, of at least one of the other corporations.
 (4) The term "value" means, with respect to securities (other than those of majority-owned subsidiaries) for which market quotations are readily available, the market value of such securities; and with respect to other securities and assets, fair value as determined in good faith by the board of directors, except that in the case of securities of majority-owned subsidiaries which are investment companies such fair value shall not exceed market value or asset value, whichever is higher.
 (5) The term "outstanding voting securities of such issuer" shall include the equity securities of a qualified publicly traded partnership (as defined in subsection (h)).
 (6) All other terms shall have the same meaning as when used in the Investment Company Act of 1940, as amended.

(d) Determination of status.
 (1) In general. A corporation which meets the requirements of subsections (b)(3) and (c) at the close of any quarter shall not lose its status as a regulated investment company because of a discrepancy during a subsequent quarter between the value of its various investments and such requirements unless such discrepancy exists immediately after the acquisition of any security or other property and is wholly or partly the result of such acquisition. A corporation which does not meet such requirements at the close of any quarter by reason of a discrepancy existing immediately after the acquisition of any security or other property which is wholly or partly the result of such acquisition during such quarter shall not lose its status for such quarter as a regulated investment company if such discrepancy is eliminated within 30 days after the close of such quarter and in such cases it shall be considered to have met such requirements at the close of such quarter for purposes of applying the preceding sentence.
 (2) Special rules regarding failure to satisfy requirements. If paragraph (1) does not preserve a corporation's status as a regulated investment company for any particular quarter—
  (A) In general. A corporation that fails to meet the requirements of subsection (b)(3) (other than a failure described in subparagraph (B)(i)) for such quarter shall nevertheless be considered to have satisfied the requirements of such subsection for such quarter if—

(i) following the corporation's identification of the failure to satisfy the requirements of such subsection for such quarter, a description of each asset that causes the corporation to fail to satisfy the requirements of such subsection at the close of such quarter is set forth in a schedule for such quarter filed in the manner provided by the Secretary,

(ii) the failure to meet the requirements of such subsection for such quarter is due to reasonable cause and not due to willful neglect, and

(iii)

(I) the corporation disposes of the assets set forth on the schedule specified in clause (i) within 6 months after the last day of the quarter in which the corporation's identification of the failure to satisfy the requirements of such subsection occurred or such other time period prescribed by the Secretary and in the manner prescribed by the Secretary, or

(II) the requirements of such subsection are otherwise met within the time period specified in subclause (I).

(B) Rule for certain de minimis failures. A corporation that fails to meet the requirements of subsection (b)(3) for such quarter shall nevertheless be considered to have satisfied the requirements of such subsection for such quarter if—

(i) such failure is due to the ownership of assets the total value of which does not exceed the lesser of—

(I) 1 percent of the total value of the corporation's assets at the end of the quarter for which such measurement is done, or

(II) $10,000,000, and

(ii)

(I) the corporation, following the identification of such failure, disposes of assets in order to meet the requirements of such subsection within 6 months after the last day of the quarter in which the corporation's identification of the failure to satisfy the requirements of such subsection occurred or such other time period prescribed by the Secretary and in the manner prescribed by the Secretary, or

(II) the requirements of such subsection are otherwise met within the time period specified in subclause (I).

(C) Tax.

(i) Tax imposed. If subparagraph (A) applies to a corporation for any quarter, there is hereby imposed on such corporation a tax in an amount equal to the greater of—

(I) $50,000, or

(II) the amount determined (pursuant to regulations promulgated by the Secretary) by multiplying the net income generated by the assets described in the schedule specified in subparagraph (A)(i) for the period specified in clause (ii) by the highest rate of tax specified in section 11.

(ii) Period. For purposes of clause (i)(II), the period described in this clause is the period beginning on the first date that the failure to satisfy the requirements of subsection (b)(3) occurs as a result of the ownership of such assets and ending on the earlier of the date on which the corporation disposes of such assets or the end of the first quarter when there is no longer a failure to satisfy such subsection.

(iii) Administrative provisions. For purposes of subtitle F, a tax imposed by this subparagraph shall be treated as an excise tax with respect to which the deficiency procedures of such subtitle apply.

(e) **Investment companies furnishing capital to development corporations.**

(1) **General rule.** If the Securities and Exchange Commission determines, in accordance with regulations issued by it, and certifies to the Secretary not earlier than 60 days prior to the close of the taxable year of a management company or a business development company described in subsection (a)(1), that such investment company is principally engaged in the furnishing of capital to other corporations which are principally engaged in the development or exploitation of inventions, technological improvements, new processes, or products not previously generally available, such investment company may, in the computation of 50 percent of the value of its assets under subparagraph (A) of subsection (b)(3) for any quarter of such taxable year, include the value of any securities of an issuer, whether or not the investment company owns more than 10 percent of the outstanding voting securities of such issuer, the basis of which, when added to the basis of the investment company for securities of such issuer previously acquired, did not exceed 5 percent of the value of the total assets of the investment company at the time of the subsequent acquisition of securities. The preceding sentence shall not apply to the securities of an issuer if the investment company has continuously held any security of such issuer (or of any predecessor company of such issuer as determined under regulations prescribed by the Secretary) for 10 or more years preceding such quarter of such taxable year.

(2) **Limitation.** The provisions of this subsection shall not apply at the close of any quarter of a taxable year to an investment company if at the close of such quarter more than 25 percent of the value of its total assets is represented by securities of issuers with respect to each of which the investment company holds more than 10 percent of the outstanding voting securities of such issuer and in respect of each of which or any predecessor thereof the investment company has continuously held any security for 10 or more years preceding such quarter unless the value of its total assets so represented is reduced to 25 percent or less within 30 days after the close of such quarter.

(3) **Determination of status.** For purposes of this subsection, unless the Securities and Exchange Commission determines otherwise, a corporation shall be considered to be principally engaged in the development or exploitation of inventions, technological improvements, new processes, or products not previously generally available, for at least 10 years after the date of the first acquisition of any security in such corporation or any predecessor thereof by such investment company if at the date of such acquisition the corporation or its predecessor was principally so engaged, and an investment company shall be considered at any date to be furnishing capital to any company whose securities it holds if within 10 years prior to such date it has acquired any of such securities, or any securities surrendered in exchange therefor, from such other company or predecessor thereof. For purposes of the certification under this subsection, the Securities and Exchange Commission shall have authority to issue such rules, regulations and orders, and to conduct such investigations and hearings, either public or private, as it may deem appropriate.

Regulated investment companies — Code Sec. 851

(4) Definitions. The terms used in this subsection shall have the same meaning as in subsections (b)(3) and (c) of this section.

(f) Certain unit investment trusts.

For purposes of this title—

(1) A unit investment trust (as defined in the Investment Company Act of 1940)—

(A) which is registered under such Act and issues periodic payment plan certificates (as defined in such Act) in one or more series,

(B) substantially all of the assets of which, as to all such series, consist of (i) securities issued by a single management company (as defined in such Act) and securities acquired pursuant to subparagraph (C), or (ii) securities issued by a single other corporation, and

(C) which has no power to invest in any other securities except securities issued by a single other management company, when permitted by such Act or the rules and regulations of the Securities and Exchange Commission,

shall not be treated as a person.

(2) In the case of a unit investment trust described in paragraph (1)—

(A) each holder of an interest in such trust shall, to the extent of such interest, be treated as owning a proportionate share of the assets of such trust;

(B) the basis of the assets of such trust which are treated under subparagraph (A) as being owned by a holder of an interest in such trust shall be the same as the basis of his interest in such trust; and

(C) in determining the period for which the holder of an interest in such trust has held the assets of the trust which are treated under subparagraph (A) as being owned by him, there shall be included the period for which such holder has held his interest in such trust.

This subsection shall not apply in the case of a unit investment trust which is a segregated asset account under the insurance laws or regulations of a State.

(g) Special rule for series funds.

(1) In general. In the case of a regulated investment company (within the meaning of subsection (a)) having more than one fund, each fund of such regulated investment company shall be treated as a separate corporation for purposes of this title (except with respect to the definitional requirement of subsection (a)).

(2) Fund defined. For purposes of paragraph (1) the term "fund" means a segregated portfolio of assets, the beneficial interests in which are owned by the holders of a class or series of stock of the regulated investment company that is preferred over all other classes or series in respect of such portfolio of assets.

(h) Qualified publicly traded partnership.

For purposes of this section, the term "qualified publicly traded partnership" means a publicly traded partnership described in section 7704(b) other than a partnership which would satisfy the gross income requirements of section 7704(c)(2) if qualifying income included only income described in subsection (b)(2)(A).

(i) Failure to satisfy gross income test.

(1) Disclosure requirement. A corporation that fails to meet the requirement of paragraph (2) of subsection (b) for any taxable year shall nevertheless be considered to have satisfied the requirement of such paragraph for such taxable year if—

(A) following the corporation's identification of the failure to meet such requirement for such taxable year, a description of each item of its gross income described in such paragraph is set forth in a schedule for such taxable year filed in the manner provided by the Secretary, and

(B) the failure to meet such requirement is due to reasonable cause and not due to willful neglect.

(2) Imposition of tax on failures. If paragraph (1) applies to a regulated investment company for any taxable year, there is hereby imposed on such company a tax in an amount equal to the excess of—

(A) the gross income of such company which is not derived from sources referred to in subsection (b)(2), over

(B) $\frac{1}{9}$ of the gross income of such company which is derived from such sources.

In 2010, P.L. 111-325, Sec. 201(a)(1), substituted "(1) In general. A corporation which meets" for "A corporation which meets" in subsec. (d) . . . Sec. 201(a)(2), added para. (d)(2) . . . Sec. 201(b), added subsec. (i), effective for tax. yrs. with respect to which the due date (determined with regard to any extensions) of the return of tax for such tax. year is after the 12/22/2010.

In 2004, P.L. 108-357, Sec. 331(a), amended para. (b)(2) . . . Sec. 331(b), added "(other than a qualified publicly traded partnership as defined in subsection (h))" after "derived from a partnership" in subsec. (b) . . . Sec. 331(c), redesignated para. (c)(5) as para. (c)(6) and added new para. (c)(5) . . . Sec. 331(d), added subsec. (h), . . . Sec. 331(f), amended subpara. (b)(3)(B), effective for tax. yrs. begin. after 10/22/2004.

Prior to amendment, para. (b)(2) read as follows:

"(2) at least 90 percent of its gross income is derived from dividends, interest, payments with respect to securities loans (as defined in section 512(a)(5)), and gains from the sale or other disposition of stock or securities (as defined in section 2(a)(36) of the Investment Company Act of 1940, as amended) or foreign currencies, or other income (including but not limited to gains from options, futures, or forward contracts) derived with respect to its business of investing in such stock, securities, or currencies; and"

Prior to amendment, subpara. (b)(3)(B) read as follows:

"(B) not more than 25 percent of the value of its total assets is invested in the securities (other than Government securities or the securities of other regulated investment companies) of any one issuer, or of two or more issuers which the taxpayer controls and which are determined, under regulations prescribed by the Secretary, to be engaged in the same or similar trades or businesses or related trades or businesses."

In 1997, P.L. 105-34, Sec. 1271(a), deleted para. (b)(3), added "and" at the end of para. (b)(2), and redesignated para. (b)(4) as para. (b)(3) . . . Sec. 1271(b)(1)(A), substituted "paragraph (2)" for "paragraphs (2) and (3)" in para. (b)(3) [as redesignated by Sec. 1271(a) of this Act, see above] . . . Sec. 1271(b)(1)(B), deleted "In the case of the taxable year in which a regulated investment company is completely liquidated, there shall not be taken into account under paragraph (3) any gain from the sale, exchange, or distribution of any property after the adoption of the plan of complete liquidation." at the end of para. (b)(3) [as redesignated by Sec. 1271(a) of this Act, see above] . . . Sec. 1271(b)(2), substituted "subsection (b)(3)" for "subsection (b)(4)" each place it appeared in the text and heading of subsec. (c) . . . Sec. 1271(b)(3), substituted "subsections (b)(3)" for "subsections (b)(4)" in subsec. (d) . . . Sec. 1271(b)(4), substituted "subsection (b)(3)" for "subsection (b)(4)" in para. (e)(1) . . . Sec. 1271(b)(5), substituted "subsections (b)(3)" for "subsections (b)(4)" in para. (e)(4) . . . Sec. 1271(b)(6), deleted subsec. (g) and redesignated subsec. (h) as subsec. (g) . . . Sec. 1271(b)(7), deleted para. (g)(3) [as redesignated by Sec. 1271(b)(6) of this Act, see above], effective for tax. yrs. begin. after 8/5/97.

Prior to deletion para. (b)(3) read as follows:

"(3) less than 30 percent of its gross income is derived from the sale or disposition of any of the following which was held for less than 3 months:

"(A) stock or securities (as defined in section 2(a)(36) of the Investment Company Act of 1940, as amended),

"(B) options, futures, or forward contracts (other than options, futures, or forward contracts on foreign currencies), or

"(C) foreign currencies (or options, futures, or forward contracts on foreign currencies) but only if such currencies (or options, futures, or forward contracts) are not directly related to the company's principal business of investing in stock or securities (or options and futures with respect to stocks or securities), and"

Prior to deletion, subsec. (g) read as follows:

"(g) Treatment of certain hedging transactions.

"(1) In general. In the case of any designated hedge, for purposes of subsection (b)(3), increases (and decreases) during the period of the hedge in the value of positions which are part of such hedge shall be netted.

"(2) Designated hedge. For purposes of this subsection, there is a designated hedge where—

"(A) the taxpayer's risk of loss with respect to any position in property is reduced by reason of—

"(i) the taxpayer having an option to sell, being under a contractual obligation to sell, or having made (and not closed) a short sale of substantially identical property,

"(ii) the taxpayer being the grantor of an option to buy substantially identical property, or

"(iii) under regulations prescribed by the Secretary, the taxpayer holding 1 or more other positions, and

2,437

"(B) the positions which are part of the hedge are clearly identified by the taxpayer in the manner prescribed by regulations."

Prior to deletion, para. (g)(3) [as redesignated by Sec. 1271(b)(6) of this Act, see above] read as follows:

"(3) Special rule for abnormal redemptions.

"(A) In general. Any fund treated as a separate corporation under paragraph (1) shall not be disqualified under subsection (b)(3) for any taxable year by reason of sales resulting from abnormal redemptions on any day and occurring before the close of the 5th business day after such day if—

"(i) the sum of the percentages determined under subparagraph (B) for the abnormal redemptions on such day and for abnormal redemptions on prior days during such taxable year exceeds 30 percent; and

"(ii) the regulated investment company of which such fund is a part would meet the requirements of subsection (b)(3) for such taxable year if all the funds which are part of such company were treated as a single company.

"(B) Abnormal redemptions. For purposes of subparagraph (A), the term 'abnormal redemptions' means redemptions occurring on any day if the net redemptions on such day exceed 1 percent of the fund's net asset value.

"(C) Determination of net asset value. For purposes of this paragraph, net asset value for any day shall be determined as of the close of the preceding day.

"(D) Limitation. For purposes of subparagraph (A), any sale or other disposition of stock or securities held less than 3 months occurring during any day shall be deemed to result from abnormal redemptions until the cumulative proceeds from such sales or dispositions occurring during such day, plus the cumulative net positive cash flow of the fund for preceding business days (if any) following the day with abnormal redemptions, exceed the amount of net redemptions on the day with abnormal redemptions."

In 1988, P.L. 100-647, Sec. 1006(m)(1), amended para. (a)(1) . . . Sec. 1006(m)(2), substituted "a management company or a business development company described in subsection (a)(1)" for "a registered management company or registered business development company" in para. (e)(1), effective for tax. yrs. begin. after 12/31/86.

Prior to amendment, para. (a)(1) read as follows:

"(1) which, at all times during the taxable year, is registered under the Investment Company Act of 1940, as amended (15 USC 80a-1 to 80b-2) as a management company, business development company, or unit investment trust or"

—P.L. 100-647, Sec. 1006(n)(1), added the last sentence [the next to the last sentence, see Sec. 1006(n)(5) of this Act, below] of subsec. (b), effective for tax. yrs. begin. after 10/22/86.

—P.L. 100-647, Sec. 1006(n)(2)(A), amended para. (b)(3) . . . Sec. 1006(n)(2)(B), substituted "which are not directly related" for "which are not ancillary" in subsec. (b), effective for tax. yrs. begin. after 11/10/88.

Prior to amendment, para. (b)(3) read as follows:

"(3) less than 30 percent of its gross income is derived from the sale or other disposition of stock or securities held for less than 3 months; and"

—P.L. 100-647, Sec. 1006(n)(4), substituted "contractual obligation" for "contractual option" in clause (g)(2)(A)(i) . . . Sec. 1006(n)(5), added the last sentence of subsec. (b) . . . Sec. 1006(o)(1), redesignated subsec. (q) [as added by Sec. 654(a) of P.L. 99-514, below] as subsec. (h) . . . Sec. 1006(o)(2), added para. (h)(3), effective for tax. yrs. begin. after 10/22/86.

In 1986, P.L. 99-514, Sec. 652(a), substituted "as a management company, business development company, or unit investment trust" for "either as a management company or as a unit investment trust" in para. (a)(1) . . . Sec. 652(b), substituted "registered management company or registered business development company" for "registered management company" in para. (e)(1), effective for tax. yrs. begin. after 12/31/86.

—P.L. 99-514, Sec. 653(a), added subsec. (g) . . . Sec. 653(b), substituted "(as defined in section 2(a)(36) of the Investment Company Act of 1940, as amended) or foreign currencies, or other income (including but not limited to gains from options, futures, or forward contracts) derived with respect to its business of investing in such stock, securities, or currencies;" for the semicolon, in para. (b)(2) . . . Sec. 653(c), added the next to the last sentence in subsec. (b), effective for tax. yrs. begin. after 10/22/86.

—P.L. 99-514, Sec. 654(a), added subsec. (q) [sic (h)], effective for tax. yrs. begin. after 10/22/86. Sec. 654(b)(2) of this Act provides:

"(2) Treatment of certain existing series funds.—In the case of a regulated investment company which has more than one fund on the date of the enactment of this act [10/22/86], and has before such date been treated for Federal income tax purposes as a single corporation—

"(A) the amendment made by subsection (a) [Sec. 654(a)], and the resulting treatment of each fund as a separate corporation, shall not give rise to the realization or recognition of income or loss by such regulated investment company, its funds, or its shareholders, and

"(B) the tax attributes of such regulated investment company shall be appropriately allocated among its funds."

—P.L. 99-514, Sec. 1235(f)(3), substituted "section 951(a)(1)(A)(i) or 1293(a)" for "section 951(a)(1)(A)(i)" and substituted "section 959(a)(1) or 1293(c) (as the case may be)" for "section 959(a)(1)" in subsec. (b), effective for tax. yrs. of foreign corporations begin. after 12/31/86.

In 1984, P.L. 98-369, Sec. 1071(a)(1), deleted "(other than a personal holding company as defined in section 542)" after "domestic corporation" in subsec. (a), effective for tax. yrs. begin. after 12/31/82.

In 1983, P.L. 97-424, Sec. 547(b)(1), substituted "103(a)" for "103(a)(1)" in subsec. (b), effective 1/6/83.

In 1978, P.L. 95-600, Sec. 701(s)(1), added the last sentence of subsec. (b), effective for tax. yrs. begin. after 12/31/75.

—P.L. 95-345, Sec. 2(a)(3), added "payments with respect to securities loans (as defined in section 512(a)(5))," after "interest," in para. (b)(2), effective for amounts received after 12/31/76 as payments with respect to securities loans (as defined in Code Sec. 512(a)(5)) and for transfers of securities under agreements described in Code Sec. 1058, occurring after such date.

In 1976, P.L. 94-455, Sec. 1901(a)(109), deleted "54 Stat. 789;" before "15 U.S.C. 80a-1" in para. (a)(1), deleted "which began after December 31, 1941" after "taxable year" in para. (b)(1), effective for tax. yrs. begin. after 12/31/76.

—P.L. 94-455, Sec. 1906(b)(13)(A), substituted "Secretary" for "Secretary or his delegate" in paras. (a)(4)(B), (c)(1), and (e)(1), effective for tax. yrs. begin. after 12/31/76.

In 1975, P.L. 94-12, Sec. 602(a)(2), added the final sentence to subsec. (b), effective for tax. yrs. of foreign corporations begin. after 12/31/75, and for tax. yrs. of U.S. shareholders (within the meaning of Code Sec. 951(b)) within which or with which such tax. yrs. of such foreign corporations end.

In 1969, P.L. 91-172, Sec. 908, added subsec. (f), effective for tax. yrs. of unit investment trusts end. after 12/31/68, and to taxable years of holders of interests in such trusts ending with or within such taxable years of such trusts. The enactment of this section shall not be construed to result in the realization of gain or loss by any unit investment trust or by any holder of an interest in a unit investment trust.

In 1958, P.L. 85-866, Sec. 38, substituted "not earlier than 60 days" for "not less than 60 days" in para. (e)(1), and substituted "issuer" for "issues" in para. (e)(2), effective for tax. yrs. begin. after 12/31/53, and end after 8/16/54.

Sec. 852. Taxation of regulated investment companies and their shareholders.

(a) Requirements applicable to regulated investment companies.

The provisions of this part (other than subsection (c) of this section) shall not be applicable to a regulated investment company for a taxable year unless—

(1) the deduction for dividends paid during the taxable year (as defined in section 561, but without regard to capital gain dividends) equals or exceeds the sum of—

(A) 90 percent of its investment company taxable income for the taxable year determined without regard to subsection (b)(2)(D); and

(B) 90 percent of the excess of (i) its interest income excludable from gross income under section 103(a) over (ii) its deductions disallowed under sections 265, 171(a)(2), and

(2) either—

(A) the provisions of this part applied to the investment company for all taxable years ending on or after November 8, 1983, or

(B) as of the close of the taxable year, the investment company has no earnings and profits accumulated in any taxable year to which the provisions of this part (or the corresponding provisions of prior law) did not apply to it.

The Secretary may waive the requirements of paragraph (1) for any taxable year if the regulated investment company establishes to the satisfaction of the Secretary that it was unable to meet such requirements by reason of distributions previously made to meet the requirements of section 4982.

(b) Method of taxation of companies and shareholders.

(1) Imposition of tax on regulated investment companies. There is hereby imposed for each taxable year upon the investment company taxable income of every regulated investment company a tax computed as provided in section 11, as though the investment company taxable income were the taxable income referred to in section 11. In the case of a regulated investment company which is a personal holding company (as defined in section 542) or which fails to comply for the taxable year with regulations prescribed by the Secretary for the purpose of ascertaining the actual ownership of its stock, such tax shall be computed at the highest rate of tax specified in section 11(b).

(2) Investment company taxable income. The investment company taxable income shall be the taxable income of the regulated investment company adjusted as follows:

Regulated investment companies   Code Sec. 852(b)(3)(D)(iv)

(A) There shall be excluded the amount of the net capital gain, if any.
(B) The net operating loss deduction provided in section 172 shall not be allowed.
(C) The deductions for corporations provided in part VIII (except section 248) in subchapter B (section 241 and following, relating to the deduction for dividends received, etc.) shall not be allowed.
(D) The deduction for dividends paid (as defined in section 561) shall be allowed, but shall be computed without regard to capital gain dividends and exempt-interest dividends.
(E) The taxable income shall be computed without regard to section 443(b) (relating to computation of tax on change of annual accounting period).
(F) The taxable income shall be computed without regard to section 454(b) (relating to short-term obligations issued on a discount basis) if the company so elects in a manner prescribed by the Secretary.
(G) There shall be deducted an amount equal to the tax imposed by subsections (d)(2) and (i) of section 851 for the taxable year.

(3) Capital gains.

(A) Imposition of tax. There is hereby imposed for each taxable year in the case of every regulated investment company a tax, determined as provided in section 1201(a), on the excess, if any, of the net capital gain over the deduction for dividends paid (as defined in section 561) determined with reference to capital gain dividends only.
(B) Treatment of capital gain dividends by shareholders. A capital gain dividend shall be treated by the shareholders as a gain from the sale or exchange of a capital asset held for more than 1 year.
(C) Definition of capital gain dividend. For purposes of this part—
   (i) In general. Except as provided in clause (ii), a capital gain dividend is any dividend, or part thereof, which is reported by the company as a capital gain dividend in written statements furnished to its shareholders.
   (ii) Excess reported amounts. If the aggregate reported amount with respect to the company for any taxable year exceeds the net capital gain of the company for such taxable year, a capital gain dividend is the excess of—
      (I) the reported capital gain dividend amount, over
      (II) the excess reported amount which is allocable to such reported capital gain dividend amount.
   (iii) Allocation of excess reported amount.
      (I) In general. Except as provided in subclause (II), the excess reported amount (if any) which is allocable to the reported capital gain dividend amount is that portion of the excess reported amount which bears the same ratio to the excess reported amount as the reported capital gain dividend amount bears to the aggregate reported amount.
      (II) Special rule for noncalendar year taxpayers. In the case of any taxable year which does not begin and end in the same calendar year, if the post-December reported amount equals or exceeds the excess reported amount for such taxable year, subclause (I) shall be applied by substituting "post-December reported amount" for "aggregate reported amount" and no excess reported amount shall be allocated to any dividend paid on or before December 31 of such taxable year.

(iv) Definitions. For purposes of this subparagraph—
   (I) Reported capital gain dividend amount. The term "reported capital gain dividend amount" means the amount reported to its shareholders under clause (i) as a capital gain dividend.
   (II) Excess reported amount. The term "excess reported amount" means the excess of the aggregate reported amount over the net capital gain of the company for the taxable year.
   (III) Aggregate reported amount. The term "aggregate reported amount" means the aggregate amount of dividends reported by the company under clause (i) as capital gain dividends for the taxable year (including capital gain dividends paid after the close of the taxable year described in section 855).
   (IV) Post-December reported amount. The term "post-December reported amount" means the aggregate reported amount determined by taking into account only dividends paid after December 31 of the taxable year.
(v) Adjustment for determinations. If there is an increase in the excess described in subparagraph (A) for the taxable year which results from a determination (as defined in section 860(e)), the company may, subject to the limitations of this subparagraph, increase the amount of capital gain dividends reported under clause (i).
(vi) Special rule for losses late in the calendar year. For special rule for certain losses after October 31, see paragraph (8).
(D) Treatment by shareholders of undistributed capital gains.
   (i) Every shareholder of a regulated investment company at the close of the company's taxable year shall include, in computing his long-term capital gains in his return for his taxable year in which the last day of the company's taxable year falls, such amount as the company shall designate in respect of such shares in a written notice mailed to its shareholders at any time prior to the expiration of 60 days after close of its taxable year, but the amount so includible by any shareholder shall not exceed that part of the amount subjected to tax in subparagraph (A) which he would have received if all of such amount had been distributed as capital gain dividends by the company to the holders of such shares at the close of its taxable year.
   (ii) For purposes of this title, every such shareholder shall be deemed to have paid, for his taxable year under clause (i), the tax imposed by subparagraph (A) on the amounts required by this subparagraph to be included in respect of such shares in computing his long-term capital gains for that year; and such shareholder shall be allowed credit or refund, as the case may be, for the tax so deemed to have been paid by him.
   (iii) The adjusted basis of such shares in the hands of the shareholder shall be increased, with respect to the amounts required by this subparagraph to be included in computing his long-term capital gains, by the difference between the amount of such includible gains and the tax deemed paid by such shareholder in respect of such shares under clause (ii).
   (iv) In the event of such designation the tax imposed by subparagraph (A) shall be paid by the regulated investment company within 30 days after close of its taxable year.

(v) The earnings and profits of such regulated investment company, and the earnings and profits of any such shareholder which is a corporation, shall be appropriately adjusted in accordance with regulations prescribed by the Secretary.

(E) Certain distributions. In the case of a distribution to which section 897 does not apply by reason of the second sentence of section 897(h)(1), the amount of such distribution which would be included in computing long-term capital gains for the shareholder under subparagraph (B) or (D) (without regard to this subparagraph)—

(i) shall not be included in computing such shareholder's long-term capital gains, and

(ii) shall be included in such shareholder's gross income as a dividend from the regulated investment company.

(4) Loss on sale or exchange of stock held 6 months or less.

(A) Loss attributable to capital gain dividend. If—

(i) subparagraph (B) or (D) of paragraph (3) provides that any amount with respect to any share is to be treated as long-term capital gain, and

(ii) such share is held by the taxpayer for 6 months or less,

then any loss (to the extent not disallowed under subparagraph (B)) on the sale or exchange of such share shall, to the extent of the amount described in clause (i), be treated as a long-term capital loss.

(B) Loss attributable to exempt-interest dividend. If—

(i) a shareholder of a regulated investment company receives an exempt-interest dividend with respect to any share, and

(ii) such share is held by the taxpayer for 6 months or less,

then any loss on the sale or exchange of such share shall, to the extent of the amount of such exempt-interest dividend, be disallowed.

(C) Determination of holding periods. For purposes of this paragraph, in determining the period for which the taxpayer has held any share of stock—

(i) the rules of paragraphs (3) and (4) of section 246(c) shall apply, and

(ii) there shall not be taken into account any day which is more than 6 months after the date on which such share becomes ex-dividend.

(D) Losses incurred under a periodic liquidation plan. To the extent provided in regulations, subparagraphs (A) and (B) shall not apply to losses incurred on the sale or exchange of shares of stock in a regulated investment company pursuant to a plan which provides for the periodic liquidation of such shares.

(E) Exception to holding period requirement for certain regularly declared exempt-interest dividends.

(i) Daily dividend companies. Except as otherwise provided by regulations, subparagraph (B) shall not apply with respect to a regular dividend paid by a regulated investment company which declares exempt-interest dividends on a daily basis in an amount equal to at least 90 percent of its net tax-exempt interest and distributes such dividends on a monthly or more frequent basis.

(ii) Authority to shorten required holding period with respect to other companies. In the case of a regulated investment company (other than a company described in clause (i)) which regularly distributes at least 90 percent of its net tax-exempt interest, the Secretary may by regulations prescribe that subparagraph (B) (and subparagraph (C) to the extent it relates to subparagraph (B)) shall be applied on the basis of a holding period requirement shorter than 6 months; except that such shorter holding period requirement shall not be shorter than the greater of 31 days or the period between regular distributions of exempt-interest dividends.

(5) Exempt-interest dividends. If, at the close of each quarter of its taxable year, at least 50 percent of the value (as defined in section 851(c)(4)) of the total assets of the regulated investment company consists of obligations described in section 103(a), such company shall be qualified to pay exempt-interest dividends, as defined herein, to its shareholders.

(A) Definition of exempt-interest dividend.

(i) In general. Except as provided in clause (ii), an exempt-interest dividend is any dividend or part thereof (other than a capital gain dividend) paid by a regulated investment company and reported by the company as an exempt-interest dividend in written statements furnished to its shareholders.

(ii) Excess reported amounts. If the aggregate reported amount with respect to the company for any taxable year exceeds the exempt interest of the company for such taxable year, an exempt-interest dividend is the excess of—

(I) the reported exempt-interest dividend amount, over

(II) the excess reported amount which is allocable to such reported exempt-interest dividend amount.

(iii) Allocation of excess reported amount—

(I) In general. Except as provided in subclause (II), the excess reported amount (if any) which is allocable to the reported exempt-interest dividend amount is that portion of the excess reported amount which bears the same ratio to the excess reported amount as the reported exempt-interest dividend amount bears to the aggregate reported amount.

(II) Special rule for noncalendar year taxpayers. In the case of any taxable year which does not begin and end in the same calendar year, if the post-December reported amount equals or exceeds the excess reported amount for such taxable year, subclause (I) shall be applied by substituting "post-December reported amount" for "aggregate reported amount" and no excess reported amount shall be allocated to any dividend paid on or before December 31 of such taxable year.

(iv) Definitions. For purposes of this subparagraph—

(I) Reported exempt-interest dividend amount. The term "reported exempt-interest dividend amount" means the amount reported to its shareholders under clause (i) as an exempt-interest dividend.

(II) Excess reported amount. The term "excess reported amount" means the excess of the aggregate reported amount over the exempt interest of the company for the taxable year.

(III) Aggregate reported amount. The term "aggregate reported amount" means the aggregate amount of dividends reported by the company under clause (i) as exempt-interest dividends for the taxable year (including exempt-interest dividends paid after the close of the taxable year described in section 855).

Regulated investment companies   Code Sec. 852(c)(2)

(IV) Post-december reported amount. The term "post-December reported amount" means the aggregate reported amount determined by taking into account only dividends paid after December 31 of the taxable year.

(V) Exempt interest. The term "exempt interest" means, with respect to any regulated investment company, the excess of the amount of interest excludable from gross income under section 103(a) over the amounts disallowed as deductions under sections 265 and 171(a)(2).

(B) Treatment of exempt-interest dividends by shareholders. An exempt-interest dividend shall be treated by the shareholders for all purposes of this subtitle as an item of interest excludable from gross income under section 103(a). Such purposes include but are not limited to—

(i) the determination of gross income and taxable income,

(ii) the determination of distributable net income under subchapter J,

(iii) the allowance of, or calculation of the amount of, any credit or deduction, and

(iv) the determination of the basis in the hands of any shareholder of any share of stock of the company.

(6) Section 311(b) not to apply to certain distributions. Section 311(b) shall not apply to any distribution by a regulated investment company to which this part applies, if such distribution is in redemption of its stock upon the demand of the shareholder.

(7) Time certain dividends taken into account. For purposes of this title, any dividend declared by a regulated investment company in October, November, or December of any calendar year and payable to shareholders of record on a specified date in such a month shall be deemed—

(A) to have been received by each shareholder on December 31 of such calendar year, and

(B) to have been paid by such company on December 31 of such calendar year (or, if earlier, as provided in section 855).

The preceding sentence shall apply only if such dividend is actually paid by the company during January of the following calendar year.

(8) Elective deferral of certain late-year losses.

(A) In general. Except as otherwise provided by the Secretary, a regulated investment company may elect for any taxable year to treat any portion of any qualified late-year loss for such taxable year as arising on the first day of the following taxable year for purposes of this title.

(B) Qualified late-year loss. For purposes of this paragraph, the term "qualified late-year loss" means—

(i) any post-October capital loss, and

(ii) any late-year ordinary loss.

(C) Post-October Capital loss. For purposes of this paragraph, the term "post-October capital loss" means the greatest of—

(i) the net capital loss attributable to the portion of the taxable year after October 31,

(ii) the net long-term capital loss attributable to such portion of the taxable year, or

(iii) the net short-term capital loss attributable to such portion of the taxable year.

(D) Late-year ordinary loss. For purposes of this paragraph, the term "late-year ordinary loss" means the excess (if any) of—

(i) the sum of—

(I) the specified losses (as defined in section 4982(e)(5)(B)(ii)) attributable to the portion of the taxable year after October 31, plus

(II) the ordinary losses not described in subclause (I) attributable to the portion of the taxable year after December 31, over

(ii) the sum of—

(I) the specified gains (as defined in section 4982(e)(5)(B)(i)) attributable to the portion of the taxable year after October 31, plus

(II) the ordinary income not described in subclause (I) attributable to the portion of the taxable year after December 31.

(E) Special rule for companies determining required capital gain distributions on taxable year basis. In the case of a company to which an election under section 4982(e)(4) applies—

(i) if such company's taxable year ends with the month of November, the amount of qualified late-year losses (if any) shall be computed without regard to any income, gain, or loss described in subparagraphs (C), (D)(i)(I), and (D)(ii)(I), and

(ii) if such company's taxable year ends with the month of December, subparagraph (A) shall not apply.

(9) Dividends treated as received by company on ex-dividend date. For purposes of this title, if a regulated investment company is the holder of record of any share of stock on the record date for any dividend payable with respect to such stock, such dividend shall be included in gross income by such company as of the later of—

(A) the date such share became ex-dividend with respect to such dividend, or

(B) the date such company acquired such share.

(c) Earnings and profits.

(1) Treatment of nondeductible items.

(A) Net capital loss. If a regulated investment company has a net capital loss for any taxable year—

(i) such net capital loss shall not be taken into account for purposes of determining the company's earnings and profits, and

(ii) any capital loss arising on the first day of the next taxable year by reason of clause (ii) or (iii) of section 1212(a)(3)(A) shall be treated as so arising for purposes of determining earnings and profits.

(B) Other nondeductible items.

(i) In general. The earnings and profits of a regulated investment company for any taxable year (but not its accumulated earnings and profits) shall not be reduced by any amount which is not allowable as a deduction (other than by reason of section 265 or 171(a)(2)) in computing its taxable income for such taxable year.

(ii) Coordination with treatment of net capital losses. Clause (i) shall not apply to a net capital loss to which subparagraph (A) applies.

(2) Coordination with tax on undistributed income. For purposes of applying this chapter to distributions made by a regulated investment company with respect to any calendar year, the earnings and profits of such company shall be determined without regard to any net capital loss attributable to the portion of the taxable year after October 31 and without regard to any late-year ordinary loss (as defined in subsection (b)(8)(D)).The preceding sentence shall apply—

2,441

(A) only to the extent that the amount distributed by the company with respect to the calendar year does not exceed the required distribution for such calendar year (as determined under section 4982 by substituting "100 percent" for each percentage set forth in section 4982(b)(1)), and

(B) except as provided in regulations, only if an election under section 4982(e)(4) is not in effect with respect to such company.

(3) Distributions to meet requirements of subsection (a)(2)(B). Any distribution which is made in order to comply with the requirements of subsection (a)(2)(B)—

(A) shall be treated for purposes of this subsection and subsection (a)(2)(B) as made from earnings and profits which, but for the distribution, would result in a failure to meet such requirements (and allocated to such earnings on a first-in, first-out basis), and

(B) to the extent treated under subparagraph (A) as made from accumulated earnings and profits, shall not be treated as a distribution for purposes of subsection (b)(2)(D) and section 855.

(4) Regulated investment company. For purposes of this subsection, the term "regulated investment company" includes a domestic corporation which is a regulated investment company determined without regard to the requirements of subsection (a).

(d) Distributions in redemption of interests in unit investment trusts.

In the case of a unit investment trust—

(1) which is registered under the Investment Company Act of 1940 (15 U.S.C. 80a-1 and following) and issues periodic payment plan certificates (as defined in such Act), and

(2) substantially all of the assets of which consist of securities issued by a management company (as defined in such Act),

section 562(c) (relating to preferential dividends) shall not apply to a distribution by such trust to a holder of an interest in such trust in redemption of part or all of such interest, with respect to the capital gain net income of such trust attributable to such redemption.

(e) Procedures similar to deficiency dividend procedures made applicable.

(1) In general. If—

(A) there is a determination that the provisions of this part do not apply to an investment company for any taxable year (hereinafter in this subsection referred to as the "non-RIC year"), and

(B) such investment company meets the distribution requirements of paragraph (2) with respect to the non-RIC year,

for purposes of applying subsection (a)(2) to subsequent taxable years, the provisions of this part shall be treated as applying to such investment company for the non-RIC year. If the determination under subparagraph (A) is solely as a result of the failure to meet the requirements of subsection (a)(2), the preceding sentence shall also apply for purposes of applying subsection (a)(2) to the non-RIC year and the amount referred to in paragraph (2)(A)(i) shall be the portion of the accumulated earnings and profits which resulted in such failure.

(2) Distribution requirements.

(A) In general. The distribution requirements of this paragraph are met with respect to any non-RIC year if, within the 90-day period beginning on the date of the determination (or within such longer period as the Secretary may permit), the investment company makes 1 or more qualified designated distributions and the amount of such distributions is not less than the excess of—

(i) the portion of the accumulated earnings and profits of the investment company (as of the date of the determination) which are attributable to the non-RIC year, over

(ii) any interest payable under paragraph (3).

(B) Qualified designated distribution. For purposes of this paragraph, the term "qualified designated distribution" means any distribution made by the investment company if—

(i) section 301 applies to such distribution, and

(ii) such distribution is designated (at such time and in such manner as the Secretary shall by regulations prescribe) as being taken into account under this paragraph with respect to the non-RIC year.

(C) Effect on dividends paid deduction. Any qualified designated distribution shall not be included in the amount of dividends paid for purposes of computing the dividends paid deduction for any taxable year.

(3) Interest charge.

(A) In general. If paragraph (1) applies to any non-RIC year of an investment company, such investment company shall pay interest at the underpayment rate established under section 6621—

(i) on an amount equal to 50 percent of the amount referred to in paragraph (2)(A)(i),

(ii) for the period—

(I) which begins on the last day prescribed for payment of the tax imposed for the non-RIC year (determined without regard to extensions), and

(II) which ends on the date the determination is made.

(B) Coordination with subtitle F. Any interest payable under subparagraph (A) may be assessed and collected at any time during the period during which any tax imposed for the taxable year in which the determination is made may be assessed and collected.

(4) Provision not to apply in the case of fraud. The provisions of this subsection shall not apply if the determination contains a finding that the failure to meet any requirement of this part was due to fraud with intent to evade tax.

(5) Determination. For purposes of this subsection, the term "determination" has the meaning given to such term by section 860(e). Such term also includes a determination by the investment company filed with the Secretary that the provisions of this part do not apply to the investment company for a taxable year.

(f) Treatment of certain load charges.

(1) In general. If—

(A) the taxpayer incurs a load charge in acquiring stock in a regulated investment company and, by reason of incurring such charge or making such acquisition, the taxpayer acquires a reinvestment right,

(B) such stock is disposed of before the 91st day after the date on which such stock was acquired, and

(C) the taxpayer acquires, during the period beginning on the date of the disposition referred to in subparagraph (B) and ending on January 31 of the calendar year following the calendar year that includes the date of such disposition, stock in such regulated investment company or in another regulated investment company and the otherwise applicable load charge is reduced by reason of the reinvestment right,

Regulated investment companies   Code Sec. 852

the load charge referred to in subparagraph (A) (to the extent it does not exceed the reduction referred to in subparagraph (C)) shall not be taken into account for purposes of determining the amount of gain or loss on the disposition referred to in subparagraph (B). To the extent such charge is not taken into account in determining the amount of such gain or loss, such charge shall be treated as incurred in connection with the acquisition referred to in subparagraph (C) (including for purposes of reapplying this paragraph).

(2) Definitions and special rules. For purposes of this subsection—

(A) Load charge. The term "load charge" means any sales or similar charge incurred by a person in acquiring stock of a regulated investment company. Such term does not include any charge incurred by reason of the reinvestment of a dividend.

(B) Reinvestment right. The term "reinvestment right" means any right to acquire stock of 1 or more regulated investment companies without the payment of a load charge or with the payment of a reduced charge.

(C) Nonrecognition transactions. If the taxpayer acquires stock in a regulated investment company from another person in a transaction in which gain or loss is not recognized, the taxpayer shall succeed to the treatment of such other person under this subsection.

(g) Special rules for fund of funds.

(1) In general. In the case of a qualified fund of funds—

(A) such fund shall be qualified to pay exempt-interest dividends to its shareholders without regard to whether such fund satisfies the requirements of the first sentence of subsection (b)(5), and

(B) such fund may elect the application of section 853 (relating to foreign tax credit allowed to shareholders) without regard to the requirement of subsection (a)(1) thereof.

(2) Qualified fund of funds. For purposes of this subsection, the term "qualified fund of funds" means a regulated investment company if (at the close of each quarter of the taxable year) at least 50 percent of the value of its total assets is represented by interests in other regulated investment companies.

In 2010, P.L. 111-325, Sec. 201(c), added subpara. (b)(2)(G), effective for tax. yrs. with respect to which the due date (determined with regard to any extensions) of the return of tax for such tax. year is after 12/22/2010.

— P.L. 111-325, Sec. 301(a)(1), amended subpara. (b)(3)(C)

Prior to amendment, subpara. (b)(3)(C) read as follows:

"(C) Definition of capital gain dividend. For purposes of this part, a capital gain dividend is any dividend, or part thereof, which is designated by the company as a capital gain dividend in a written notice mailed to its shareholders not later than 60 days after the close of its taxable year; except that, if there is an increase in the excess described in subparagraph (A) of this paragraph for such year which results from a determination (as defined in section 860(e)), such designation may be made with respect to such increase at any time before the expiration of 120 days after the date of such determination. If the aggregate amount so designated with respect to a taxable year of the company (including capital gains dividends paid after the close of the taxable year described in section 855) is greater than the net capital gain of the taxable year, the portion of each distribution which shall be a capital gain dividend shall be only that proportion of the amount so designated which such net capital gain bears to the aggregate amount so designated. For purposes of this subparagraph, the amount of the net capital gain for a taxable year (to which an election under section 4982(e)(4) does not apply) shall be determined without regard to any net capital loss or net long-term capital loss attributable to transactions after October 31 of such year, and any such net capital loss or net long-term capital loss shall be treated as arising on the 1st day of the next taxable year. To the extent provided in regulations, the preceding sentence shall apply also for purposes of computing the taxable income of the regulated investment company." . . . Sec. 301(b), amended subpara. (b)(5)(A), effective for tax. yrs. begin. after 12/22/2010.

Prior to amendment, subpara. (b)(5)(A) read as follows:

"(A) Definition. An exempt-interest dividend means any dividend or part thereof (other than a capital gain dividend) paid by a regulated investment company and designated by it as an exempt-interest dividend in a written notice mailed to its shareholders not later than 60 days after the close of its taxable year. If the aggregate amount so designated with respect to a taxable year of the company (including exempt-interest dividends paid after the close of the taxable year as described in section 855) is greater than the excess of—

"(i) the amount of interest excludable from gross income under section 103(a), over

"(ii) the amounts disallowed as deductions under sections 265 and 171(a)(2),

"the portion of such distribution which shall constitute an exempt-interest dividend shall be only that proportion of the amount so designated as the amount of such excess for such taxable year bears to the amount so designated."

— P.L. 111-325, Sec. 302(a), amended para. (c)(1)

Prior to amendment, para. (c)(1) read as follows:

"(1) In general. The earnings and profits of a regulated investment company for any taxable year (but not its accumulated earnings and profits) shall not be reduced by any amount which is not allowable as a deduction in computing its taxable income for such taxable year. For purposes of this subsection, the term 'regulated investment company' includes a domestic corporation which is a regulated investment company determined without regard to the requirements of subsection (a)." . . . Sec. 302(b)(1), added para. (c)(4), effective for tax. yrs. begin. after 12/22/2010.

— P.L. 111-325, Sec. 303(a), added subsec. (g), effective for tax. yrs. begin. after 12/22/2010.

— P.L. 111-325, Sec. 308(a), amended para. (b)(8).

Prior to amendment, para. (b)(8) read as follows:

"(8) Special rule for treatment of certain foreign currency losses. To the extent provided in regulations, the taxable income of a regulated investment company (other than a company to which an election under section 4982(e)(4) applies) shall be computed without regard to any net foreign currency loss attributable to transactions after October 31 of such year, and any such net foreign currency loss shall be treated as arising on the 1st day of the following taxable year. . . . Sec. 308(b)(1), deleted para. (b)(10)

Prior to deletion, para. (b)(10) read as follows:

"(10) Special rule for certain losses on stock in passive foreign investment company.

"To the extent provided in regulations, the taxable income of a regulated investment company (other than a company to which an election under section 4982(e)(4) applies) shall be computed without regard to any net reduction in the value of any stock of a passive foreign investment company with respect to which an election under section 1296(k) is in effect occurring after October 31 of the taxable year, and any such reduction shall be treated as occurring on the first day of the following taxable year. " . . . Sec. 308(b)(2), substituted "For purposes of applying this chapter to distributions made by a regulated investment company with respect to any calendar year, the earnings and profits of such company shall be determined without regard to any net capital loss attributable to the portion of the taxable year after October 31 and without regard to any late-year ordinary loss (as defined in subsection (b)(8)(D))." for "For purposes of applying this chapter to distributions made by a regulated investment company with respect to any calendar year, the earnings and profits of such company shall be determined without regard to any net capital loss (or net foreign currency loss) attributable to transactions after October 31 of such year, without regard to any net reduction in the value of any stock of a passive foreign investment company with respect to which an election under section 1296(k) is in effect occurring after October 31 of such year, and with such other adjustments as the Secretary may by regulations prescribe." in para. (c)(2), effective for tax. yrs. begin. after 12/22/2010.

— P.L. 111-325, Sec. 309(a), substituted new subpara. (b)(4)(E)(i)-(ii) for "Authority to shorten required holding period." . . . Sec. 309(b), added "(other than a company described in clause (i))" after "regulated investment company" in clause (b)(4)(E)(ii) [as added above], effective for losses incurred on shares of stock for which the taxpayer's holding period begins after 12/22/2010.

— P.L. 111-325, Sec. 502(a), substituted "acquires, during the period beginning on the date of the disposition referred to in subparagraph (B) and ending on January 31 of the calendar year following the calendar year that includes the date of such disposition," for "subsequently acquires" in subpara. (f)(1)(C), effective for charges incurred in tax. yrs. begin. after 12/22/2010.

In 2007, P.L. 110-172, Sec. 11(a)(17)(A), amended subpara. (b)(4)(C), enacted 12/29/2007.

Prior to amendment, subpara. (b)(4)(C) read as follows:

"(C) Determination of holding periods. For purposes of this paragraph, the rules of paragraphs (3) and (4) of section 246(c) shall apply in determining the period for which the taxpayer has held any share of stock; except that "6 months" shall be substituted for each number of days specified in subparagraph (B) of section 246(c)(3)."

In 2006, P.L. 109-222, Sec. 505(c)(1), added subpara. (b)(3)(E), effective for tax. yrs. of qualified investment entities begin. after 12/31/2005, except that no amount shall be required to be withheld under Code Secs. 1441, 1442, or 1445 with respect to any distribution before 5/17/2006 if such amount was not otherwise required to be withheld under any such section as in effect before such amendments.

In 1999, P.L. 106-170, Sec. 566(a)(1), added para. (c)(3) . . . Sec. 566(c), added a sentence at the end of para. (e)(1), effective for distributions after 12/31/2000.

In 1997, P.L. 105-34, Sec. 1122(c)(2), added para. (b)(10) . . . Sec. 1122(c)(3), added ", without regard to any net reduction in the value of any stock of a passive foreign investment company with respect to which an election under section 1296(k) is in effect occurring after October 31 of such year," after "October 31 of such year" in para. (c)(2), effective for tax. yrs. of U.S. persons begin. after 12/31/97, and tax. yrs. of foreign corporations end. with or within such tax. yrs. of U.S. persons.

—P.L. 105-34, Sec. 1254(b)(2), substituted "by the difference between the amount of such includible gains and the tax deemed paid by such shareholder in respect of such shares under clause (ii)." for "by 65 percent of so much of such amounts as equals the amount subject to tax in accordance with section 1201(a)." in clause (b)(3)(D)(iii), effective for tax. yrs. begin. after 8/5/97.

In 1996, P.L. 104-188, Sec. 1602(b)(3), deleted subpara. (b)(5)(C), effective for loans made after 8/20/96. For notes regarding refinancings and exceptions, see Secs. 1602(c)(2) and (3) of this Act, which read as follows:

"(2) Refinancings. The amendments made by this section shall not apply to loans made after the date of the enactment of this Act to refinance securities acquisition loans (determined without regard to section 133(b)(1)(B) of the Internal Revenue Code of 1986, as in effect on the day before the date of the enactment of this Act) made on or before such date or to refinance loans described in this paragraph if—

"(A) the refinancing loans meet the requirements of section 133 of such Code (as so in effect),

"(B) immediately after the refinancing the principal amount of the loan resulting from the refinancing does not exceed the principal amount of the refinanced loan (immediately before the refinancing), and

"(C) the term of such refinancing loan does not extend beyond the last day of the term of the original securities acquisition loan.

For purposes of this paragraph, the term 'securities acquisition loan' includes a loan from a corporation to an employee stock ownership plan described in section 133(b)(3) of such Code (as so in effect).

"(3) Exception. Any loan made pursuant to a binding written contract in effect before June 10, 1996, and at all times thereafter before such loan is made, shall be treated for purposes of paragraphs (1) and (2) as a loan made on or before the date of the enactment of this Act."

Prior to deletion, subpara. (b)(5)(C) read as follows:

"(C) Interest on certain loans used to acquire employer securities. For purposes of this section—

"(i) 50 percent of the amount of any loan of the regulated investment company which qualifies as a securities acquisition loan (as defined in section 133) shall be treated as an obligation described in section 103(a), and

"(ii) 50 percent of the interest received on such loan shall be treated as interest excludable from gross income under section 103."

In 1993, P.L. 103-66, Sec. 13221(c)(1), substituted "65 percent" for "66 percent" in clause (b)(3)(D)(iii), effective for tax. yrs. begin. on or after 1/1/93.

In 1989, P.L. 101-239, Sec. 7204(b)(1), added subsec. (f), effective for charges incurred after 10/3/89 in tax. yrs. end. after 10/3/89.

—P.L. 101-239, Sec. 7204(c)(1), added para. (b)(9), effective for dividends in cases where the stock becomes ex-dividend after 12/19/89.

In 1988, P.L. 100-647, Sec. 1006(l)(1)(A), redesignated para. (b)(6) [as added by Sec. 651(b)(1)(A) of P.L. 99-514, see below] as para. (b)(7) . . . Sec. 1006(l)(3), amended para. (c)(2) . . . Sec. 1006(l)(4)(A), substituted "net capital loss or net long-term capital loss" for "net capital loss" each place it appeared in the third sentence of subpara. (b)(3)(C) . . . Sec. 1006(l)(4)(B), substituted "the taxable income of the regulated investment company" for "regulated investment company taxable income" in the sentence at the end of subpara. (b)(3)(C) . . . Sec. 1006(l)(7), added para. (b)(8) . . . Sec. 1006(l)(8), added the sentence at the end of subsec. (a) . . . Sec. 1006(l)(10), substituted "subsection (a)(2)" for "subsection (a)(3)" in para. (e)(1), effective for calendar yrs. begin. after 12/31/86.

Prior to amendment, para. (c)(2) read as follows:

"(2) Coordination with tax on undistributed income. A regulated investment company shall be treated as having sufficient earnings and profits to treat as a dividend any distribution (other than in a redemption to which section 302(a) applies) which is treated as a dividend by such company. The preceding sentence shall not apply to the extent that the amount distributed during any calendar year by the company exceeds the required distribution for such calendar year (as determined under section 4982)."

—P.L. 100-647, Sec. 1006(l)(9)(A), substituted "in October, November, or December" for "in December" in para. (b)(7) [as redesignated by Sec. 1006(l)(1)(A) of this Act, see above] . . . Sec. 1006(l)(9)(B), substituted "in such a month" for "in such month" in para. (b)(7) [as redesignated] . . . Sec. 1006(l)(9)(C), substituted "on December 31 of such calendar year" for "on such date" in subparas. (b)(7)(A) and (b)(7)(B) [as redesignated] . . . Sec. 1006(l)(9)(D), substituted "during January" for "before February 1", in para. (b)(7) [as redesignated], effective for dividends declared in 1988 and subsequent tax. years.

—P.L. 100-647, Sec. 1011B(h)(4), substituted "section" for "paragraph" in subpara. (b)(5)(C), effective for loans used to acquire employer securities after 10/22/86, including loans used to refinance loans used to acquire employer securities before 10/22/86 if such loans were used to acquire employer securities after 5/23/84.

—P.L. 100-647, Sec. 1018(p), substituted "subsection (a)(2)" for "subsection (a)(3)" [same amendment made by Sec. 1006(l)(10) of this Act, see above], in para. (e)(1) effective for tax yrs. begin. after 12/31/82.

In 1986, P.L. 99-514, Sec. 311(b)(1), substituted "66 percent" for "72 percent" in clause (b)(3)(D)(iii), effective for tax. yrs. begin. after 12/31/86.

—P.L. 99-514, Sec. 631(e)(11), added para. (b)(6), effective as provided in Sec. 633(a) of this Act, which reads as follows:

"(a) General rule. Except as otherwise provided in this section, the amendments made by this subtitle shall apply to—

"(1) any distribution in complete liquidation, and any sale or exchange, made by a corporation after July 31, 1986, unless such corporation is completely liquidated before January 1, 1987,

"(2) any transaction described in section 338 of the Internal Revenue Code of 1986 for which the acquisition date occurs after December 31, 1986, and

"(3) any distribution (not in complete liquidation) made after December 31, 1986."

—P.L. 99-514, Sec. 651(b)(1)(A), added para. (b)(6) [sic (b)(7), later redesignated as para. (b)(7) by Sec. 1006(l)(1)(A) of P.L. 100-647, see above] . . . Sec. 651(b)(2), amended subsec. (c) . . . Sec. 651(b)(3), added the two sentences at the end of subpara. (b)(3)(C), effective for calendar yrs. begin. after 12/31/86.

Prior to amendment, subsec. (c) read as follows:

"(c) Earnings and profits.

"The earnings and profits of a regulated investment company for any taxable year (but not its accumulated earnings and profits) shall not be reduced by any amount which is not allowable as a deduction in computing its taxable income for such taxable year. For purposes of this subsection, the term 'regulated investment company' includes a domestic corporation which is a regulated investment company determined without regard to the requirements of subsection (a)."

—P.L. 99-514, Sec. 655(a)(1), substituted "60 days" for "45 days" each place it appeared in para. (b)(3) . . . Sec. 655(a)(2), substituted "60 days" for "45 days" each place it appeared in subpara. (b)(5)(A), effective for tax. yrs. begin. after 10/22/86.

—P.L. 99-514, Sec. 1173(b)(1)(B), added subpara. (b)(5)(C), effective for loans used to acquire employer securities after 10/22/86, including loans used to refinance loans used to acquire employer securities before 10/22/86 if such loans were used to acquire employer securities after 5/23/84.

—P.L. 99-514, Sec. 1511(c)(6), substituted "the underpayment rate established under section 6621" for "the annual rate established under section 6621" in subpara. (e)(3)(A), effective for purposes of determining interest for periods after 12/31/86.

—P.L. 99-514, Sec. 1804(c)(1), substituted "for 6 months or less" for "for less than 31 days" in clause (b)(4)(B)(ii) . . . Sec. 1804(c)(2), amended subpara. (b)(4)(C) . . . Sec. 1804(c)(3), substituted "subparagraphs (A) and (B)" for "subparagraph (A)" in subpara. (b)(4)(D) . . . Sec. 1804(c)(4), added subpara. (b)(4)(E) . . . Sec. 1804(c)(5), substituted "6 months or less" for "less than 31 days" in the heading of para. (b)(4), effective for stock for which the taxpayer's holding period beings after 3/28/85.

Prior to amendment, subpara. (b)(4)(C) read as follows:

"(C) Determination of holding periods. For purposes of this paragraph, the rules of paragraphs (3) and (4) of section 246(c) shall apply in determining the period for which the taxpayer held any share of stock; except that for the number of days specified in subparagraph (B) of section 246(c)(3) there shall be substituted—

"(i) '6 months' for purposes of subparagraph (A), and

"(ii) '30 days' for purposes of subparagraph (B)."

—P.L. 99-514, Sec. 1878(j)(1), added "and" at the end of para. (a)(1), deleted para. (a)(2) and redesignated para. (a)(3) as para. (a)(2) . . . Sec. 1878(j)(2), substituted "In the case of a regulated investment company which is a personal holding company (as defined in section 542) or which fails to comply for the taxable year with regulations prescribed by the Secretary for the purpose of ascertaining the actual ownership of its stock, such tax shall be computed at the highest rate of tax specified in section 11(b)" for "In the case of a regulated investment company which is a personal holding company (as defined in section 542), that tax shall be computed at the highest rate of tax specified in section 11(b)" in para. (b)(1), effective for tax. yrs. begin. after 12/31/82.

Prior to deletion, para. (a)(2) read as follows:

"(2) the investment company complies for such year with regulations prescribed by the Secretary for the purpose of ascertaining the actual ownership of its outstanding stock, and"

In 1984, P.L. 98-369, Sec. 55(a)(1), amended subpara. (b)(4)(A) . . . Sec. 55(a)(2), amended subpara. (b)(4)(C) . . . Sec. 55(a)(3), added subpara. (b)(4)(D), effective for losses incurred for shares of stock and beneficial interest for which the taxpayer's holding period begins after 7/18/84.

Prior to amendment, subpara. (b)(4)(A) read as follows:

"(A) Loss attributable to capital gain dividend. If—

"(i) under subparagraph (B) or (D) of paragraph (3) a shareholder of a regulated investment company is required, with respect to any share, to treat any amount as a long-term capital gain, and

"(ii) such share is held by the taxpayer for less than 31 days,

then any loss (to the extent not disallowed under subparagraph (B)) on the sale or exchange of such share shall, to the extent of the amount described in clause (i), be treated as a long-term capital loss."

Prior to amendment, subpara. (b)(4)(C) read as follows:

"(C) Determination of holding periods. For purposes of this paragraph, the rules of section 246(c)(3) shall apply in determining whether any share of stock has been held for less than 31 days; except that '30 days' shall be substituted for the number of days specified in subparagraph (B) of section 246(C)(3)."

—P.L. 98-369, Sec. 1001(b)(11), substituted "6 months" for "1 year" in subpara. (b)(3)(B), effective for property acquired after 6/22/84, and before 1/1/88.

—P.L. 98-369, Sec. 1071(a)(2), added the sentence at the end of para. (b)(1) . . . Sec. 1071(a)(3), deleted "and" at the end of para. (a)(1), substituted ", and" for the period at the end of para. (a)(2), and added para. (a)(3) . . . Sec. 1071(a)(4), added subsec. (e), effective for tax. yrs. begin. after 12/31/82. Secs. 1071(a)(5)(B)–(D) of the Act provide special rules as follows:

"(B) Investment companies which were regulated investment companies for years ending before November 8, 1983.—In the case of any investment company to which the provisions of part I of subchapter M of chapter 1 of the Internal Revenue Code of 1954 applied for any taxable year ending before November 8, 1983, for purposes of section 852(a)(3)(B) of the Internal Revenue Code of 1954 (as amended by this subsection), no earnings and profits accumulated in any taxable year ending before January 1, 1984, shall be taken into account.

"(C) Investment companies beginning business in 1983.—In the case of an investment company which began business in 1983 (and was not a successor corpo-

Regulated investment companies   Code Sec. 853(a)(2)

ration), earnings and profits accumulated during its first taxable year shall not be taken into account for purposes of section 852(a)(3)(B) of such Code (as so amended).

"(D) Investment companies registering before November 8, 1983 — In the case of any investment company —

"(i) which, during the period after December 31, 1981, and before November 8, 1983 —

"(I) was engaged in the active conduct of a trade or business,

"(II) sold substantially all of its operating assets, and

"(III) registered under the Investment Company Act of 1940 as either a management company or a unit investment trust, and

"(ii) to which the provisions of part I of subchapter M of chapter 1 of the Internal Revenue Code of 1954 applied for its first taxable year beginning after November 8, 1983,

for purposes of section 852(a)(3)(A) of such Code (as amended by paragraph (3)), the provisions of part I of subchapter M of chapter 1 of such Code shall be treated as applying to such investment company for its first taxable year ending after November 8, 1983. For purposes of the preceding sentence, all members of an affiliated group (as defined in section 1504(a) of such Code) filing a consolidated return shall be treated as 1 taxpayer."

— P.L. 98-369, Sec. 1071(b)(1), added subpara. (b)(2)(F), effective for tax. yrs. begin. after 12/31/78.

In 1983, P.L. 97-424, Sec. 547(b)(2), substituted "103(a)" for "103(a)(1)" each place it appears in Code Sec. 852, effective 1/6/83.

In 1980, P.L. 96-222, Sec. 103(a)(11)(A), substituted "860(e)" for "860(d)" in Sec. 362(e) of P.L. 95-600 [the effective date for amendments made by Sec. 362(c) of P.L. 95-600, see below].

— P.L. 96-222, Sec. 104(a)(3)(B), substituted "72 percent" for "70 percent" in clause (b)(3)(D)(iii), effective as if the amendment was included in Sec. 403 of P.L. 95-600. Sec. 403(d) of P.L. 95-600 provides as follows:

"(d) Effective dates.

"(1) The amendments made by subsections (a) and (b) shall apply to taxable years ending after December 31, 1978.

"(2) The amendment made by paragraph (1) of subsection (c) shall apply to gifts made after December 31, 1978.

"(3) The amendments made by paragraphs (2), (3), and (4) of subsection (c) shall take effect on the date of the enactment of this Act."

In 1978, P.L. 95-600, Sec. 301(b)(11), amended para. (b)(1), effective for tax. yrs. begin. after 12/31/78.

Prior to amendment, para. (b)(1) read as follows:

"(1) Imposition of normal tax and surtax on regulated investment companies. There is hereby imposed for each taxable year upon the investment company taxable income of every regulated investment company a normal tax and surtax computed as provided in section 11, as though the investment company taxable income were the taxable income referred to in section 11."

— P.L. 95-600, Sec. 362(c), added "; except that, if there is an increase in the excess described in subparagraph (A) of this paragraph for such year which results from a determination (as defined in section 860(e)), such designation may be made with respect to such increase at any time before the expiration of 120 days after the date of such determination" before the period at the end of the first sentence of subpara. (b)(3)(C), effective [as amended by Sec. 103(a)(11)(A) of P.L. 96-222, see above] for determinations (as defined in Code Sec. 860(e)) after 11/6/78.

— P.L. 95-600, Sec. 701(s)(2), amended para. (b)(4), effective for tax. yrs. begin. after 12/31/75.

Prior to amendment, para. (b)(4) read as follows:

"(4) Loss on sale or exchange of stock held less than 31 days. If —

"(A) under subparagraph (B) or (D) of paragraph (3) a shareholder of a regulated investment company is required, with respect to any share, to treat any amount as a long-term capital gain, and

"(B) such share is held by the taxpayer for less than 31 days,

then any loss on the sale or exchange of such share shall, to the extent of the amount described in subparagraph (A) of this paragraph, be treated as loss from the sale or exchange of a capital asset held for more than 9 months [1 year for tax. yrs. begin. after '77]. For purposes of this paragraph, the rules of section 246(c)(3) shall apply in determining whether any share of stock has been held for less than 31 days; except that '30 days' shall be substituted for the number of days specified in subparagraph (B) of section 246(c)(3)."

In 1976, P.L. 94-455, Sec. 1402(b)(1)(N), substituted "9 months" for "6 months" in subpara. (b)(3)(B) and para. (b)(4), effective for tax. yrs. begin. in 1977.

— P.L. 94-455, Sec. 1402(b)(2), substituted "1 year" for "9 months" in subpara. (b)(3)(B) and para. (b)(4) [as amended by Sec. 1402(b)(1)(N) of this Act, see above], effective for tax. yrs. begin. after 1977. Sec. 1402(c) of this Act provides a transitional rule, reproduced in note following Code Sec. 1222.

— P.L. 94-455, Sec. 1901(a)(110)(A), deleted the third sentence in para. (b)(3), effective for tax. yrs. begin. after 12/31/76.

Prior to deletion, the third sentence in para. (b)(3) read as follows:

"For purposes of subparagraph (A)(ii), the deduction for dividends paid shall, in the case of a taxable year beginning before January 1, 1975, first be made from the amount subject to tax in accordance with section 1201(a)(1)(B), to the extent thereof and then from the amount subject to tax in accordance with section 1201(a)(1)(A)."

— P.L. 94-455, Sec. 1901(a)(110)(B)(i), substituted "by 70 percent of so much of such amounts as equals the amount subject to tax in accordance with section 1201(a)" for "by 75 percent of so much of such amounts as equals the amount subject to tax in accordance with section 1201(a)(1)(A) and by 70 percent (72 percent in the case of a taxable year beginning after December 31, 1969, and before

January 1, 1971) of so much of such amounts as equals the amount subject to tax in accordance with section 1201(a)(1)(B) or (2)" in clause (b)(3)(D)(iii), effective for tax. yrs. begin. after 12/31/76. Sec. 1901(a)(110)(B)(ii) of this Act provides a special rule as follows:

"(ii) The amendment made by clause (i) shall not be considered to affect the amount of any increase in the basis of stock under the provisions of section 852(b)(3)(D)(iii) of the Internal Revenue Code of 1954 which is based upon amounts subject to tax under section 1201 of such Code in taxable years beginning before January 1, 1975."

— P.L. 94-455, Sec. 1901(a)(110)(C), added "(15 U.S.C. 80a-1 and following)" after "Investment Company Act of 1940" in subsec. (d) . . . Sec. 1901(b)(1)(V), deleted the sentence at the end of para. (b)(1) . . . Sec. 1901(b)(6)(B), substituted "section 103(a)" for "section 103(a)(1)" in subpara. (a)(1)(B) [as added by Sec. 2137(a) of this Act, see below] . . . Sec. 1901(b)(33)(I), substituted "the amount of the net capital gain, if any" for "the excess, if any, of the net long-term capital gain over the net short-term capital loss" in subpara. (b)(2)(A) . . . Sec. 1901(b)(33)(J)(i), amended subpara. (b)(3)(A) . . . Sec. 1901(b)(33)(J)(ii), substituted "net capital gain" for "excess of the net long-term capital gain over the net short-term capital loss" each place it appeared in the second sentence of subpara. (b)(3)(C) . . . Sec. 1901(b)(33)(N), substituted "capital gain net income" for "net capital gain" in subsec. (d) . . . Sec. 1906(b)(13)(A), substituted "Secretary" for "Secretary or his delegate" each place it appeared in Code Sec. 852, effective for tax. yrs. begin. after 12/31/76.

Prior to deletion, the sentence at the end of para. (b)(1) read as follows:

"For purposes of computing the normal tax under section 11, the taxable income and the dividends paid deduction of such investment company for the taxable year (computed without regard to capital gains dividends) shall be reduced by the deduction provided by section 242 (relating to partially tax-exempt interest)."

Prior to amendment, subpara. (b)(3)(A) read as follows:

"(A) Imposition of tax. There is hereby imposed for each taxable year in the case of every regulated investment company a tax, determined as provided in section 1201(a), on the excess, if any, of the net long-term capital loss, and capital gain over the sum of —

"(i) the net short-term capital loss, and

"(ii) the deduction for dividends paid (as defined in section 561) determined with reference to capital gains dividends only."

— P.L. 94-455, Sec. 2137(a), amended para. (a)(1) . . . Sec. 2137(b), amended subpara. (b)(2)(D) . . . Sec. 2137(c), added para. (b)(5), effective for tax. yrs. begin. after 12/31/75.

Prior to amendment, para. (a)(1) read as follows:

"(1) the deduction for dividends paid during the taxable year (as defined in section 561, but without regard to capital gains dividends) equals or exceeds 90 percent of its investment company taxable income for the taxable year (determined without regard to subsection (b)(2)(D)), and"

Prior to amendment, subpara. (b)(2)(D) read as follows:

"(D) The deduction for dividends paid (as defined in section 561) shall be allowed, but shall be computed without regard to capital gains dividends."

In 1969, P.L. 91-172, Sec. 511(c)(2)(A), substituted ", determined as provided in section 1201(a), on" for "of 25 percent of" in subpara. (b)(3)(A) . . . Sec. 511(c)(2)(B), added the sentence at the end of subpara. (b)(3)(C) . . . Sec. 511(c)(2)(C), deleted "of 25 percent" in clause (b)(3)(D)(ii) . . . Sec. 511(c)(2)(D), amended clause (b)(3)(D)(iii), effective for tax. yrs. begin. after 12/31/69.

Prior to amendment, clause (b)(3)(D)(iii) read as follows:

"(iii) The adjusted basis of such shares in the hands of the shareholder shall be increased by 75 percent of the amounts required by this subparagraph to be included in computing his long-term capital gains."

In 1964, P.L. 88-272, Sec. 229(a)(1), substituted "45 days" for "30 days" each place it appeared in subpara. (b)(3)(C) . . . Sec. 229(a)(2), substituted "45 days" for "30 days" each place it appeared in clause (b)(3)(D)(i), effective for tax. yrs. of regulated investment companies end. on or after 2/26/64.

— P.L. 88-272, Sec. 229(b), added subsec. (d), effective for tax. yrs. of regulated investment companies end. after 12/31/63.

In 1960, P.L. 86-779, Sec. 10(b)(2), substituted "this part" for "this subchapter" in subsec. (a) . . . Sec. 10(b)(3), substituted "For purposes of this part, a capital gain dividend is" for "A capital gain dividend means" in subpara. (b)(3)(C), effective for tax. yrs. of real estate investment trusts begin. after 12/31/60.

In 1958, P.L. 85-866, Sec. 39(a), added para. (b)(4), effective for tax. yrs. end. after 12/31/57, but only for shares of stock acquired after 12/31/57.

— P.L. 85-866, Sec. 101(a), substituted "this subchapter (other than subsection (c) of this section)" for "this subchapter" in subsec. (a) . . . Sec. 101(b), added the sentence at the end of subsec. (c), effective for tax. yrs. of regulated investment companies begin. on or after 3/1/58.

In 1956, P.L. 700, Sec. 2(a), added subpara. (b)(3)(D), effective only for tax. yrs. of regulated investment companies begin. after 12/31/56.

Sec. 853.   Foreign tax credit allowed to shareholders.

(a) General rule.

A regulated investment company —

(1) more than 50 percent of the value (as defined in section 851(c)(4)) of whose total assets at the close of the taxable year consists of stock or securities in foreign corporations, and

(2) which meets the requirements of section 852(a) for the taxable year,

2,445

may, for such taxable year, elect the application of this section with respect to income, war profits, and excess profits taxes described in section 901(b)(1), which are paid by the investment company during such taxable year to foreign countries and possessions of the United States.

(b) Effect of election.

If the election provided in subsection (a) is effective for a taxable year—

(1) the regulated investment company—

(A) shall not, with respect to such taxable year, be allowed a deduction under section 164(a) or a credit under section 901 for taxes to which subsection (a) is applicable, and

(B) shall be allowed as an addition to the dividends paid deduction for such taxable year the amount of such taxes;

(2) each shareholder of such investment company shall—

(A) include in gross income and treat as paid by him his proportionate share of such taxes, and

(B) treat as gross income from sources within the respective foreign countries and possessions of the United States, for purposes of applying subpart A of part III of subchapter N, the sum of his proportionate share of such taxes and the portion of any dividend paid by such investment company which represents income derived from sources within foreign countries or possessions of the United States.

(c) Statements to shareholders.

The amounts to be treated by the shareholder, for purposes of subsection (b)(2), as his proportionate share of—

(1) taxes paid to any foreign country or possession of the United States, and

(2) gross income derived from sources within any foreign country or possession of the United States,

shall not exceed the amounts so reported by the company in a written statement furnished to such shareholder.

(d) Manner of making election.

The election provided in subsection (a) shall be made in such manner as the Secretary may prescribe by regulations.

(e) Treatment of certain taxes not allowed as a credit under section 901.

This section shall not apply to any tax with respect to which the regulated investment company is not allowed a credit under section 901 by reason of subsection (k) or (l) of such section.

(f) Cross references.

(1) For treatment by shareholders of taxes paid to foreign countries and possessions of the United States, see section 164(a) and section 901.

(2) For definition of foreign corporation, see section 7701(a)(5).

In **2010**, P.L. 111-325, Sec. 301(c)(1)(A), substituted "so reported by the company in a written statement furnished to such shareholder" for "so designated by the company in a written notice mailed to its shareholders not later than 60 days after the close of the taxable year" in subsec. (c)

—P.L. 111-325, Sec. 301(c)(1)(B), substituted "statements" for "notice" in the heading of subsec. (c)

—P.L. 111-325, Sec. 301(c)(2)(A), deleted "and the notice to shareholders required by subsection (c)" in subsec. (d)

—P.L. 111-325, Sec. 301(c)(2)(B), deleted "and notifying shareholders" in the heading of subsec. (d), effective for tax. yrs. begin. after 12/22/2010.

In **2005**, P.L. 109-135, Sec. 403(aa)(1), amended subsec. (e), effective for amounts paid or accrued more than 30 days after 10/22/2004 as if included in Sec. 832 of the American Jobs Creation Act of 2004, P.L. 108-357.

Prior to amendment, subsec. (e) read as follows:

"(e) Treatment of taxes not allowed as a credit under section 901(k). This section shall not apply to any tax with respect to which the regulated investment company is not allowed a credit under section 901 by reason of section 901(k)."

In **1998**, P.L. 105-206, Sec. 6010(k)(1), redesignated subsec. (e) as (f) and added subsec. (e) . . . Sec. 6010(k)(2), deleted the sentence at the end of subsec. (c), effective for dividends paid or accrued more than 30 days after 8/5/97.

Prior to deletion, the sentence at the end of subsec. (c) read as follows:

"Such notice shall also include the amount of such taxes which (without regard to the election under this section) would not be allowable as a credit under section 901(a) to the regulated investment company by reason of section 901(k)."

In **1997**, P.L. 105-34, Sec. 1053(b), added the sentence to the end of subsec. (c), effective for dividends paid or accrued more than 30 days after 8/5/97.

In **1986**, P.L. 99-514, Sec. 655(a)(3), substituted "60 days" for "45 days" in para. (c)(2), effective for tax. yrs. begin. after 10/22/86.

In **1976**, P.L. 94-455, Sec. 1906(b)(13)(A), substituted "Secretary" for "Secretary or his delegate" in subsec. (d), effective for tax. yrs. begin. after 12/31/76.

In **1964**, P.L. 88-272, Sec. 229(a), substituted "45 days" for "30 days" in subsec. (c), effective for tax. yrs. end. after 2/25/64.

Sec. 853A. Credits from tax credit bonds allowed to shareholders.

(a) General rule.

A regulated investment company—

(1) which holds (directly or indirectly) one or more tax credit bonds on one or more applicable dates during the taxable year, and

(2) which meets the requirements of section 852(a) for the taxable year,

may elect the application of this section with respect to credits allowable to the investment company during such taxable year with respect to such bonds.

(b) Effect of election.

If the election provided in subsection (a) is in effect for any taxable year—

(1) the regulated investment company shall not be allowed any credits to which subsection (a) applies for such taxable year,

(2) the regulated investment company shall—

(A) include in gross income (as interest) for such taxable year an amount equal to the amount that such investment company would have included in gross income with respect to such credits if this section did not apply, and

(B) increase the amount of the dividends paid deduction for such taxable year by the amount of such income, and

(3) each shareholder of such investment company shall—

(A) include in gross income an amount equal to such shareholder's proportionate share of the interest income attributable to such credits, and

(B) be allowed the shareholder's proportionate share of such credits against the tax imposed by this chapter.

(c) Statements to shareholders.

For purposes of subsection (b)(3), the shareholder's proportionate share of—

(1) credits described in subsection (a), and

(2) gross income in respect of such credits, shall not exceed the amounts so reported by the regulated investment company in a written statement furnished to such shareholder.

(d) Manner of making election.

The election provided in subsection (a) shall be made in such manner as the Secretary may prescribe.

(e) Definitions and special rules.

(1) **Definitions.** For purposes of this subsection—

(A) Tax credit bond. The term "tax credit bond" means—

(i) a qualified tax credit bond (as defined in section 54A(d)),

(ii) a build America bond (as defined in section 54AA(d)), and

(iii) any bond for which a credit is allowable under subpart H of part IV of subchapter A of this chapter.

(B) Applicable date. The term "applicable date" means—
(i) in the case of a qualified tax credit bond or a bond described in subparagraph (A)(iii), any credit allowance date (as defined in section 54A(e)(1)), and
(ii) in the case of a build America bond (as defined in section 54AA(d)), any interest payment date (as defined in section 54AA(e)).

(2) Stripped tax credit bonds. If the ownership of a tax credit bond is separated from the credit with respect to such bond, subsection (a) shall be applied by reference to the instruments evidencing the entitlement to the credit rather than the tax credit bond.

(f) Regulations, etc.
The Secretary shall prescribe such regulations or other guidance as may be necessary or appropriate to carry out the purposes of this section, including methods for determining a shareholder's proportionate share of credits.

In 2010, P.L. 111-325, Sec. 301(d)(1)(A), substituted "so reported by the regulated investment company in a written statement furnished to such shareholder" for "so designated by the regulated investment company in a written notice mailed to its shareholders not later than 60 days after the close of its taxable year" in subsec. (c)(2)... Sec. 301(d)(1)(B), substituted "Statements" for "Notice" in the heading of subsec. (c)... Sec. 301(d)(2)(A), deleted "and the notice to shareholders required by subsection (c)" after "The election provided in subsection (a)" in subsec. (d)... Sec. 301(d)(2)(B), deleted "and Notifying Shareholders" after "Manner of making election" in the heading of subsec. (d), effective for tax. yrs. begin. after 12/22/2010.
In 2009, P.L. 111-5, Sec. 1541(a), added Code Sec. 853A, effective for tax. yrs end. after 2/17/2009.

Sec. 854. Limitations applicable to dividends received from regulated investment company.

> • *Caution:* Code Sec. 854, following, was amended by Sec. 301(c), P.L. 108-27. These provisions generally sunset for tax years beginning after 12/31/2012. For specific sunset provisions see Sec. 303, P.L. 108-27 (as amended) reproduced in history notes for this Code Sec.

(a) Capital gain dividend.
For purposes of section 1(h)(11) (relating to maximum rate of tax on dividends) and section 243 (relating to deductions for dividends received by corporations), a capital gain dividend (as defined in section 852(b)(3)) received from a regulated investment company shall not be considered as a dividend.

(b) Other dividends.
(1) Amount treated as dividend.
(A) Deduction under section 243. In any case in which—
(i) a dividend is received from a regulated investment company (other than a dividend to which subsection (a) applies), and
(ii) such investment company meets the requirements of section 852(a) for the taxable year during which it paid such dividend,
then, in computing any deduction under section 243, there shall be taken into account only that portion of such dividend reported by the regulated investment company as eligible for such deduction in written statements furnished to its shareholders and such dividend shall be treated as received from a corporation which is not a 20-percent owned corporation.
(B) Maximum rate under section 1(h).
(i) In general. In any case in which—
(I) a dividend is received from a regulated investment company (other than a dividend to which subsection (a) applies),
(II) such investment company meets the requirements of section 852(a) for the taxable year during which it paid such dividend, and
(III) the qualified dividend income of such investment company for such taxable year is less than 95 percent of its gross income,
then, in computing qualified dividend income, there shall be taken into account only that portion of such dividend reported by the regulated investment company as qualified dividend income in written statements furnished to its shareholders.
(ii) Gross income. For purposes of clause (i), in the case of 1 or more sales or other dispositions of stock or securities, the term "gross income" includes only the excess of—
(I) the net short-term capital gain from such sales or dispositions, over
(II) the net long-term capital loss from such sales or dispositions.
(C) Limitations.
(i) Subparagraph (A). The aggregate amount which may be reported as dividends under subparagraph (A) shall not exceed the aggregate dividends received by the company for the taxable year.
(ii) Subparagraph (B). The aggregate amount which may be reported as qualified dividend income under subparagraph (B) shall not exceed the sum of—
(I) the qualified dividend income of the company for the taxable year, and
(II) the amount of any earnings and profits which were distributed by the company for such taxable year and accumulated in a taxable year with respect to which this part did not apply.

(2) Aggregate dividends. For purposes of this subsection—
(A) In general. In computing the amount of aggregate dividends received, there shall only be taken into account dividends received from domestic corporations.
(B) Dividends. For purposes of subparagraph (A), the term "dividend" shall not include any distribution from—
(i) a corporation which, for the taxable year of the corporation in which the distribution is made, or for the next preceding taxable year of the corporation, is a corporation exempt from tax under section 501 (relating to certain charitable, etc., organizations) or section 521 (relating to farmers' cooperative associations), or
(ii) a real estate investment trust which, for the taxable year of the trust in which the dividend is paid, qualifies under part II of subchapter M (section 856 and following).
(C) Limitations on dividends from regulated investment companies. In determining the amount of any dividend for purposes of this paragraph, a dividend received from a regulated investment company shall be subject to the limitations prescribed in this section.

(3) Special rule for computing deduction under section 243. For purposes of subparagraph (A) of paragraph (1), an amount shall be treated as a dividend for the purpose of paragraph (1) only if a deduction would have been allowable under section 243 to the regulated investment company determined—

(A) as if section 243 applied to dividends received by a regulated investment company,

(B) after the application of section 246 (but without regard to subsection (b) thereof), and

(C) after the application of section 246A.

(4) Qualified dividend income. For purposes of this subsection, the term "qualified dividend income" has the meaning given such term by section 1(h)(11)(B).

In 2010, P.L. 111-325, Sec. 301(e)(1)(A), substituted "reported by the regulated investment company as eligible for such deduction in written statements furnished to its shareholders" for "designated under this subparagraph by the regulated investment company" in subpara. (b)(1)(A)... Sec. 301(e)(1)(B), substituted "reported by the regulated investment company as qualified dividend income in written statements furnished to its shareholders" for "designated by the regulated investment company" in clause (b)(1)(B)(i)... Sec. 301(e)(1)(C), substituted "reported" for "designated" in clause (b)(1)(C)(ii)... Sec. 301(e)(1)(D), substituted "reported" for "designated" in clause (b)(1)(C)(ii)... Sec. 301(e)(2), repealed para. (b)(2) and redesignated paras. (b)(3)-(5) as (b)(2)-(4), effective for tax. yrs. begin. after 12/22/2010.

—P.L. 111-325, Sec. 301(i), of this Act provides:

"Application of JGTRRA sunset. Section 303 of the Jobs and Growth Tax Relief Reconciliation Act of 2003 shall apply to the amendments made by subparagraphs (B) and (D) of subsection (e)(1) to the same extent and in the same manner as section 303 of such Act applies to the amendments made by section 302 of such Act."

—P.L. 111-312, Sec. 102(a), substituted "December 31, 2012" for "December 31, 2010" in Sec. 303 of P.L. 108-27 [see below], effective as if included in the enactment of P.L. 108-27, 5/28/2003.

In 2006, P.L. 109-222, Sec. 102, substituted "December 31, 2010" for "December 31, 2008" in Sec. 303 of P.L. 108-27 [see below], effective 5/17/2006.

In 2004, P.L. 108-311, Sec. 402(a)(5)(A)(i), deleted clause (b)(1)(B)(iii) and (iv) ... Sec. 402(a)(5)(A)(ii), amended clause (b)(1)(B)(i) ... Sec. 402(a)(5)(B), amended subpara. (b)(1)(C) ... Sec. 402(a)(5)(C), substituted "as qualified dividend income for purposes of section 1(h)(11) and as dividends for purposes of" for "as a dividend for purposes of the maximum rate under section 1(h)(11) and" in para. (b)(2)... Sec. 402(a)(5)(D), amended para. (b)(5)... Sec. 402(a)(6), amended Sec. 302(f)(2) of P.L. 108-27, effective for tax. yrs. begin. after 12/31/2002 as if included in Sec. 302 of the Jobs and Growth Tax Relief Reconciliation Act of 2003, P.L. 108-27. For Sec. 302(f)(2) of P.L. 108-27 [as amended by Sec. 402(a)(6) of P.L. 108-311], see below.... Sec. 402(a)(5)(F), of this Act, provides:

"(F) With respect to any taxable year of a regulated investment company or real estate investment trust ending on or before November 30, 2003, the period for providing notice of the qualified dividend amount to shareholders under sections 854(b)(2) and 857(c)(2)(C) of the Internal Revenue Code of 1986, as amended by this section, shall not expire before the date on which the statement under section 6042(c) of such Code is required to be furnished with respect to the last calendar year beginning in such taxable year."

Prior to deletion, clause (b)(1)(B)(iii) and (iv) read as follows:

"(iii) Dividends from real estate investment trusts. For purposes of clause (i)—

"(I) paragraph (3)(B)(ii) shall not apply, and

"(II) in the case of a distribution from a trust described in such paragraph, the amount of such distribution which is a dividend shall be subject to the limitations under section 857(c).

"(iv) Dividends from qualified foreign corporations. For purposes of clause (i), dividends received from qualified foreign corporations (as defined in section 1(h)(11)) shall also be taken into account in computing aggregate dividends received."

Prior to amendment, clause (b)(1)(B)(i) read as follows:

"(i) In general. If the aggregate dividends received by a regulated investment company during any taxable year are less than 95 percent of its gross income, then, in computing the maximum rate under section 1(h)(11), rules similar to the rules of subparagraph (A) shall apply."

Prior to amendment, subpara. (b)(1)(C) read as follows:

"(C) Limitation. The aggregate amount which may be designated as dividends under subparagraph (A) or (B) shall not exceed the aggregate dividends received by the company for the taxable year."

Prior to amendment, para. (b)(5) read as follows:

"(5) Coordination with section 1(h)(11). For purposes of paragraph (1)(B), an amount shall be treated as a dividend only if the amount is qualified dividend income (within the meaning of section 1(h)(11)(B))."

Prior to amendment by Sec. 402(a)(6) of P.L. 108-311, Sec. 302(f)(2) of P.L. 108-27 reads as follows:

"(2) Regulated investment companies and real estate investment trusts. In the case of a regulated investment company or a real estate investment trust, the amendments made by this section shall apply to taxable years ending after December 31, 2002; except that dividends received by such a company or trust on or before such date shall not be treated as qualified dividend income (as defined in section 1(h)(11)(B) of the Internal Revenue Code of 1986, as added by this Act)."

Sec. 303 of P.L. 108-27 [as amended by Sec. 102 of P.L. 109-222, and Sec. 102(a), P.L. 111-312, see above], reads as follows:

"SEC. 303. SUNSET OF TITLE. All provisions of, and amendments made by, this title [Secs. 301 and 302] shall not apply to taxable years beginning after December 31, 2012, and the Internal Revenue Code of 1986 shall be applied and administered to such years as if such provisions and amendments had never been enacted."

In 2003, P.L. 108-27, Sec. 302(c)(1), added "section 1(h)(11) (relating to maximum rate of tax on dividends) and" after "For purposes of" in subsec. (a)... Sec. 302(c)(2), redesignated subpara. (b)(1)(B) as (C) and added subpara. (b)(1)(B)... Sec. 302(c)(3), substituted "subparagraph (A) or (B)" for "subparagraph (A)" in subpara. (b)(1)(C) [as redesignated by Sec. 302(c)(2) of this Act, see above]... Sec. 302(c)(4), added "the maximum rate under section 1(h)(11) and" after "for purposes of" in para. (b)(2)... Sec. 302(c)(5), added para. (b)(5), effective for tax. yrs. begin. after 12/31/2002. Sec. 302(f)(2), as amended by Sec. 402(a)(6) of P.L. 108-311, see above, of this Act, provides:

"(2) Pass-thru entities. In the case of a pass-thru entity described in subparagraph (A), (B), (C), (D), (E), or (F) of section 1(h)(10) of the Internal Revenue Code of 1986, as amended by this Act, the amendments made by this section shall apply to taxable years ending after December 31, 2002; except that dividends received by such an entity on or before such date shall not be treated as qualified dividend income (as defined in section 1(h)(11)(B) of such Code, as added by this Act)."

—P.L. 108-27, Sec. 303, of this Act [as amended by Sec. 102 of P.L. 109-222, and Sec. 102(a) of P.L. 111-312, see above], reads as follows:

"SEC. 303. SUNSET OF TITLE. All provisions of, and amendments made by, this title [Secs. 301 and 302] shall not apply to taxable years beginning after December 31, 2012, and the Internal Revenue Code of 1986 shall be applied and administered to such years as if such provisions and amendments had never been enacted."

In 1988, P.L. 100-647, Sec. 1006(b)(2), amended para. (b)(3), effective for tax. yrs. begin. after 12/31/86.

Prior to amendment, para. (b)(3) read as follows:

"(3) Definitions. For purposes of this subsection—

"(A) In the case of 1 or more sales or other dispositions of stock and securities, the term 'gross income' includes only the excess of—

"(i) the net short-term capital gain from such sales or dispositions, over

"(ii) the net long-term capital loss from such sales or dispositions.

"(B)"(i) The term 'aggregate dividends received' includes only dividends received from domestic corporations.

"(ii) For purposes of clause (i), the term 'dividend' shall not include any distribution from—

"(I) a corporation which, for the taxable year of the corporation in which the distribution is made, or for the next preceding taxable year of the corporation, is a corporation exempt from tax under section 501 (relating to certain charitable, etc., organizations) or section 521 (relating to farmers' cooperative associations), or

"(II) a real estate investment trust which, for the taxable year of the trust in which the dividend is paid, qualifies under part II of subchapter M (section 856 and following).

"(iii) In determining the amount of any dividend for purposes of this subparagraph, a dividend received from a regulated investment company shall be subject to the limitations prescribed in this section."

In 1987, P.L. 100-203, Sec. 10221(d)(3), added "and such dividend shall be treated as received from a corporation which is not a 20-percent owned corporation" after "investment company" in subpara. (b)(1)(A), effective for dividends received or accrued after 12/31/87, in tax. yrs. end. after 12/31/87.

In 1986, P.L. 99-514, Sec. 612(b)(6)(A), deleted "section 116 (relating to an exclusion for dividends received by individuals), and" after "For purposes of" in subsec. (a)... Sec. 612(b)(6)(B)(i)-(iv), deleted subpara. (b)(1)(B), redesignated subpara. (b)(1)(C) as (b)(1)(B), deleted "or (B)" after "subparagraph (A)" in subpara. (b)(1)(B) [as redesignated], deleted "the exclusion under section 116 and" after "for purposes of" in para. (b)(2), and amended subpara. (b)(3)(B), effective for tax. yrs. begin. after 12/31/86.

Prior to amendment, subpara. (b)(1)(B), read as follows:

"(B) Exclusion under section 116. If the aggregate dividends received by a regulated investment company during any taxable year are less than 95 percent of its gross income, then, in computing the exclusion under section 116, rules similar to the rules of subparagraph (A) shall apply."

Prior to amendment, subpara. (b)(3)(B) read as follows:

"(B) The term 'aggregate dividends received' includes only dividends received for domestic corporations other than dividends described in section 116(b) (relating to dividends excluded from gross income). In determining the amount of any dividend for purposes of this subparagraph, the rules provided in section 116(c) (relating to certain distributions) shall apply."

—P.L. 99-514, Sec. 655(a)(1), substituted "60 days" for "45 days" in para. (b)(2), effective for tax. yrs. begin. after 10/22/86.

In 1984, P.L. 98-369, Sec. 16(a), repealed as if not enacted Sec. 302(c) of P.L. 97-34 which amended subsec. (b) for tax. yrs. begin. after 12/31/84.

—P.L. 98-369, Sec. 52(a), amended para. (b)(1)... Sec. 52(b), added para. (b)(4) ... Sec. 52(c), amended subpara. (b)(3)(A), effective for tax. yrs. of regulated investment companies begin. after 7/18/84.

Prior to amendment, para. (b)(1) read as follows:

"(1) General rule. In the case of a dividend received from a regulated investment company (other than a dividend to which subsection (a) applies)—

"(A) if such investment company meets the requirements of section 852(a) for the taxable year during which it paid such dividends; and

"(B) the aggregate dividends received by such company during such taxable year are less than 75 percent of its gross income,

then, in computing the exclusion under section 116 and the deduction under section 243, there shall be taken into account only that portion of the dividend which bears the same ratio to the amount of such dividend as the aggregate dividends received by such company during such taxable year bear to its gross income for such taxable year."

Real estate investment trusts — Code Sec. 856(c)(1)

Prior to amendment, subpara. (b)(3)(A) read as follows:

"(A) The term 'gross income' does not include gain from the sale or other disposition of stock or securities."

In 1981, P.L. 97-34, Sec. 302(b)(1), amended the effective date for changes made by Sec. 404(b)(6) of P.L. 96-233 from tax. yrs. begin. after 12/31/80 and before 1/1/83 to tax. yrs. begin. after 12/31/80 and before 1/1/82 [see below].

In 1980, P.L. 96-223, Sec. 404(b)(6)(A), added "and taxable interest" after "dividends" in the caption of subsec. (b) . . . Sec. 404(b)(6)(B), substituted "Deduction under section 243" for "General rule" in the caption of para. (b)(1) . . . Sec. 404(b)(6)(C), deleted "the exclusion under section 116 and" in para. (b)(1) . . . Sec. 404(b)(6)(D), redesignated paras. (2) and (3) as (3) and (4) in subsec. (b) . . . Sec. 404(b)(6)(E), added new para. (2) to subsec. (b) . . . Sec. 404(b)(6)(F), substituted "116(b)(2)" for "116(b)" in subpara. (b)(4)(B) (as redesignated by Sec. 404(b)(6)(D) of this Act) . . . Sec. 404(b)(6)(G), substituted "section 116(c)(2)" for "section 116(c)" in subpara. (b)(4)(B) (as redesignated by Sec. 404(b)(6)(D) of this Act) . . . Sec. 404(b)(6)(H), added new subpara. (C) at the end of para. (b)(4) (as redesignated by Sec. 404(b)(6)(D) of this Act), effective [as amended by Sec. 302(b)(1) of P.L. 97-34, see above] for tax. yrs. begin. after 12/31/80, and before 1/1/82.

In 1965, P.L. 88-272, Sec. 201, deleted "section 34(a) (relating to credit for dividends received by individuals)," before "section 116" in subsec. (a) and deleted "the credit under section 34(a)," preceding "the exclusion" in subsec. (b)(1) and (2), effective for dividends received after 12/31/64 in tax. yrs. end. after 12/31/64 —P.L. 88-272, Sec. 229(a), substituted "45 days" for "30 days" in subsec. (b)(2), effective for tax. yrs. end. after 2/25/64.

Sec. 855. Dividends paid by regulated investment company after close of taxable year.

(a) General rule.

For purposes of this chapter, if a regulated investment company—

(1) declares a dividend before the later of—

(A) the 15th day of the 9th month following the close of the taxable year, or

(B) in the case of an extension of time for filing the company's return for the taxable year, the due date for filing such return taking into account such extension, and

(2) distributes the amount of such dividend to shareholders in the 12-month period following the close of such taxable year and not later than the date of the the first dividend payment of the same type of dividend made after such declaration,

the amount so declared and distributed shall, to the extent the company elects in such return in accordance with regulations prescribed by the Secretary, be considered as having been paid during such taxable year, except as provided in subsections (b) and (c). For purposes of paragraph (2), a dividend attributable to any short-term capital gain with respect to which a notice is required under the Investment Company Act of 1940 shall be treated as the same type of dividend as a capital gain dividend.

(b) Receipt by shareholder.

Except as provided in section 852(b)(7), amounts to which subsection (a) is applicable shall be treated as received by the shareholder in the taxable year in which the distribution is made.

(c) Foreign tax election.

If an investment company to which section 853 is applicable for the taxable year makes a distribution as provided in subsection (a) of this section, the shareholders shall consider the amounts described in section 853(b)(2) allocable to such distribution as paid or received, as the case may be, in the taxable year in which the distribution is made.

In 2010, P.L. 111-325, Sec. 301(g)(1), repealed subsec. (c) and redesignated subsec. (d) as subsec. (c) . . . Sec. 301(g)(2), substituted "and (c)" for ", (c) and (d)" in subsec. (a), effective for tax. yrs. begin. after 12/22/2010.

Prior to repeal, subsec. (c) read as follows:

"Notice to shareholders. In the case of amounts to which subsection (a) is applicable, any notice to shareholders required under this part with respect to such amounts shall be made not later than 60 days after the close of the taxable year in which the distribution is made."

—P.L. 111-325, Sec. 304(c), added "For purposes of paragraph (2), a dividend attributable to any short-term capital gain with respect to which a notice is required under the Investment Company Act of 1940 shall be treated as the same type of dividend as a capital gain dividend" at the end of subsec. (a) . . . Sec. 304(a), amended para. (a)(1) . . . Sec. 304(b), substituted "the first dividend payment of the same type of dividend" for "the first regular dividend payment" in para. (a)(2), effective for distributions in tax. yrs. begin. after 12/22/2010.

Prior to amendment, para. (a)(1) read as follows:

"(1) declares a dividend prior to the time prescribed by law for the filing of its return for a taxable year (including the period of any extension of time granted for filing such return), and"

In 1988, P.L. 100-647, Sec. 1006(1)(1)(B), substituted "section 852(b)(7)" for "section 852(b)(6)" in subsec. (b), effective for calendar yrs. begin. after 12/31/86.

In 1986, P.L. 99-514, Sec. 651(b)(1)(B), substituted "Except as provided in section 852(b)(6), amounts" for "Amounts" in subsec (b), effective for calendar yrs. begin. after 12/31/86.

—P.L. 99-514, Sec. 655(a)(5), substituted "60 days" for "45 days" in subsec. (c), effective for tax. yrs. begin. after 10/22/86.

In 1976, P.L. 94-455, Sec. 1906(b)(13)(A), substituted "Secretary" for "Secretary or his delegate" in subsec. (a), effective for tax. yrs. begin. after 12/31/76.

In 1964, P.L. 88-272, Sec. 229(a), substituted "45 days" for "30 days" in subsec. (c), effective for tax. yrs. end. after 2/25/64.

In 1960, P.L. 86-779, Sec. 10(b), substituted "this part" for "this subchapter" in subsec. (c).

PART II.—REAL ESTATE INVESTMENT TRUSTS

Sec.

856. Definition of real estate investment trust.

857. Taxation of real estate investment trusts and their beneficiaries.

858. Dividends paid by real estate investment trust after close of taxable year.

859. Adoption of annual accounting period.

In 1978, P.L. 95-600, Sec. 362(d)(6), deleted item 859 and redesignated item 860 as item 859.

Prior to deletion, item 859 read as follows:

"859. Deduction for deficiency dividends."

In 1976, P.L. 94-455, Sec. 1601(a)(2), added the item for Code Sec. 859.

—P.L. 94-455, Sec. 1604(i)(2), added the item for Code Sec. 860.

In 1960, added Part II.

Sec. 856. Definition of real estate investment trust.

(a) In general.

For purposes of this title, the term "real estate investment trust" means a corporation, trust, or association—

(1) which is managed by one or more trustees or directors;

(2) the beneficial ownership of which is evidenced by transferable shares, or by transferable certificates of beneficial interest;

(3) which (but for the provisions of this part) would be taxable as a domestic corporation;

(4) which is neither (A) a financial institution referred to in section 582(c)(2), nor (B) an insurance company to which subchapter L applies;

(5) the beneficial ownership of which is held by 100 or more persons;

(6) subject to the provisions of subsection (k), which is not closely held (as determined under subsection (h)); and

(7) which meets the requirements of subsection (c).

(b) Determination of status.

The conditions described in paragraphs (1) to (4), inclusive, of subsection (a) must be met during the entire taxable year, and the condition described in paragraph (5) must exist during at least 335 days of a taxable year of 12 months, or during a proportionate part of a taxable year of less than 12 months.

(c) Limitations.

A corporation, trust, or association shall not be considered a real estate investment trust for any taxable year unless—

(1) it files with its return for the taxable year an election to be a real estate investment trust or has made such election for a previous taxable year, and such election has not been terminated or revoked under subsection (g);

(2) at least 95 percent (90 percent for taxable years beginning before January 1, 1980) of its gross income (excluding gross income from prohibited transactions) is derived from—
  (A) dividends;
  (B) interest;
  (C) rents from real property;
  (D) gain from the sale or other disposition of stock, securities, and real property (including interests in real property and interests in mortgages on real property) which is not property described in section 1221(a)(1);
  (E) abatements and refunds of taxes on real property;
  (F) income and gain derived from foreclosure property (as defined in subsection (e));
  (G) amounts (other than amounts the determination of which depends in whole or in part on the income or profits of any person) received or accrued as consideration for entering into agreements (i) to make loans secured by mortgages on real property or on interests in real property or (ii) to purchase or lease real property (including interests in real property and interests in mortgages on real property);
  (H) gain from the sale or other disposition of a real estate asset which is not a prohibited transaction solely by reason of section 857(b)(6); and
  (I) mineral royalty income earned in the first taxable year beginning after the date of the enactment of this subparagraph from real property owned by a timber real estate investment trust and held, or once held, in connection with the trade or business of producing timber by such real estate investment trust;

(3) at least 75 percent of its gross income (excluding gross income from prohibited transactions) is derived from—
  (A) rents from real property;
  (B) interest on obligations secured by mortgages on real property or on interests in real property;
  (C) gain from the sale or other disposition of real property (including interests in real property and interests in mortgages on real property) which is not property described in section 1221(a)(1);
  (D) dividends or other distributions on, and gain (other than gain from prohibited transactions) from the sale or other disposition of, transferable shares (or transferable certificates of beneficial interest) in other real estate investment trusts which meet the requirements of this part;
  (E) abatements and refunds of taxes on real property;
  (F) income and gain derived from foreclosure property (as defined in subsection (e));
  (G) amounts (other than amounts the determination of which depends in whole or in part on the income or profits of any person) received or accrued as consideration for entering into agreements (i) to make loans secured by mortgages on real property or on interests in real property or (ii) to purchase or lease real property (including interests in real property and interests in mortgages on real property);
  (H) gain from the sale or other disposition of a real estate asset which is not a prohibited transaction solely by reason of section 857(b)(6); and
  (I) qualified temporary investment income; and

(4) at the close of each quarter of the taxable year—
  (A) at least 75 percent of the value of its total assets is represented by real estate assets, cash and cash items (including receivables), and Government securities; and
  (B)(i) not more than 25 percent of the value of its total assets is represented by securities (other than those includible under subparagraph (A)),
  (ii) not more than 25 percent of the value of its total assets is represented by securities of one or more taxable REIT subsidiaries,
  (iii) except with respect to a taxable REIT subsidiary and securities includible under subparagraph (A)—
    (I) not more than 5 percent of the value of its total assets is represented by securities of any one issuer,
    (II) the trust does not hold securities possessing more than 10 percent of the total voting power of the outstanding securities of any one issuer, and
    (III) the trust does not hold securities having a value of more than 10 percent of the total value of the outstanding securities of any one issuer.

A real estate investment trust which meets the requirements of this paragraph at the close of any quarter shall not lose its status as a real estate investment trust because of a discrepancy during a subsequent quarter between the value of its various investments and such requirements (including a discrepancy caused solely by the change in the foreign currency exchange rate used to value a foreign asset) unless such discrepancy exists immediately after the acquisition of any security or other property and is wholly or partly the result of such acquisition. A real estate investment trust which does not meet such requirements at the close of any quarter by reason of a discrepancy existing immediately after the acquisition of any security or other property which is wholly or partly the result of such acquisition during such quarter shall not lose its status for such quarter as a real estate investment trust if such discrepancy is eliminated within 30 days after the close of such quarter and in such cases it shall be considered to have met such requirements at the close of such quarter for purposes of applying the preceding sentence.

(5) For purposes of this part—
  (A) The term "value" means, with respect to securities for which market quotations are readily available, the market value of such securities; and with respect to other securities and assets, fair value as determined in good faith by the trustees, except that in the case of securities of real estate investment trusts such fair value shall not exceed market value or asset value, whichever is higher.
  (B) The term "real estate assets" means real property (including interests in real property and interests in mortgages on real property) and shares (or transferable certificates of beneficial interest) in other real estate investment trusts which meet the requirements of this part. Such term also includes any property (not otherwise a real estate asset) attributable to the temporary investment of new capital, but only if such property is stock or a debt instrument, and only for the 1-year period beginning on the date the real estate trust receives such capital.
  (C) The term "interests in real property" includes fee ownership and co-ownership of land or improvements thereon, leaseholds of land or improvements thereon, options to acquire land or improvements thereon, and options to acquire leaseholds of land or improvements thereon, but does not include mineral, oil, or gas royalty interests.
  (D) Qualified temporary investment income.
    (i) In general. The term "qualified temporary investment income" means any income which—

(I) is attributable to stock or a debt instrument (within the meaning of section 1275(a)(1)),
(II) is attributable to the temporary investment of new capital, and
(III) is received or accrued during the 1-year period beginning on the date on which the real estate investment trust receives such capital.
(ii) New capital. The term "new capital" means any amount received by the real estate investment trust—
(I) in exchange for stock (or certificates of beneficial interests) in such trust (other than amounts received pursuant to a dividend reinvestment plan), or
(II) in a public offering of debt obligations of such trust which have maturities of at least 5 years.
(E) A regular or residual interest in a REMIC shall be treated as a real estate asset, and any amount includible in gross income with respect to such an interest shall be treated as interest on an obligation secured by a mortgage on real property; except that, if less than 95 percent of the assets of such REMIC are real estate assets (determined as if the real estate investment trust held such assets), such real estate investment trust shall be treated as holding directly (and as receiving directly) its proportionate share of the assets and income of the REMIC. For purposes of determining whether any interest in a REMIC qualifies under the preceding sentence, any interest held by such REMIC in another REMIC shall be treated as a real estate asset under principles similar to the principles of the preceding sentence, except that, if such REMIC's are part of a tiered structure, they shall be treated as one REMIC for purposes of this subparagraph.
(F) All other terms shall have the same meaning as when used in the Investment Company Act of 1940, as amended (15 U.S.C. 80a-1 and following).
(G) Treatment of certain hedging instruments. Except to the extent as determined by the Secretary—
(i) any income of a real estate investment trust from a hedging transaction (as defined in clause (ii) or (iii) of section 1221(b)(2)(A)) which is clearly identified pursuant to section 1221(a)(7), including gain from the sale or disposition of such a transaction, shall not constitute gross income under paragraphs (2) and (3) to the extent that the transaction hedges any indebtedness incurred or to be incurred by the trust to acquire or carry real estate assets, and
(ii) any income of a real estate investment trust from a transaction entered into by the trust primarily to manage risk of currency fluctuations with respect to any item of income or gain described in paragraph (2) or (3) (or any property which generates such income or gain), including gain from the termination of such a transaction, shall not constitute gross income under paragraphs (2) and (3), but only if such transaction is clearly identified as such before the close of the day on which it was acquired, originated, or entered into (or such other time as the Secretary may prescribe).
(H) Treatment of timber gains.
(i) In general. Gain from the sale of real property described in paragraph (2)(D) and (3)(C) shall include gain which is—
(I) recognized by an election under section 631(a) from timber owned by the real estate investment trust, the cutting of which is provided by a taxable REIT subsidiary of the real estate investment trust;
(II) recognized under section 631(b); or
(III) income which would constitute gain under subclause (I) or (II) but for the failure to meet the 1-year holding period requirement.
(ii) Special rules.
(I) For purposes of this subtitle, cut timber, the gain from which is recognized by a real estate investment trust pursuant to an election under section 631(a) described in clause (i)(I) or so much of clause (i)(III) as relates to clause (i)(I), shall be deemed to be sold to the taxable REIT subsidiary of the real estate investment trust on the first day of the taxable year.
(II) For purposes of this subtitle, income described in this subparagraph shall not be treated as gain from the sale of property described in section 1221(a)(1).
(iii) Termination. This subparagraph shall not apply to dispositions after the termination date.
(I) Timber real estate investment trust. The term "timber real estate investment trust" means a real estate investment trust in which more than 50 percent in value of its total assets consists of real property held in connection with the trade or business of producing timber.
(J) Secretarial authority to exclude other items of income. To the extent necessary to carry out the purposes of this part, the Secretary is authorized to determine, solely for purposes of this part, whether any item of income or gain which—
(i) does not otherwise qualify under paragraph (2) or (3) may be considered as not constituting gross income for purposes of paragraphs (2) or (3), or
(ii) otherwise constitutes gross income not qualifying under paragraph (2) or (3) may be considered as gross income which qualifies under paragraph (2) or (3).
(K) Cash. If the real estate investment trust or its qualified business unit (as defined in section 989) uses any foreign currency as its functional currency (as defined in section 985(b)), the term "cash" includes such foreign currency but only to the extent such foreign currency—
(i) is held for use in the normal course of the activities of the trust or qualified business unit which give rise to items of income or gain described in paragraph (2) or (3) of subsection (c) or are directly related to acquiring or holding assets described in subsection (c)(4), and
(ii) is not held in connection with an activity described in subsection (n)(4).
(6) A corporation, trust, or association which fails to meet the requirements of paragraph (2) or (3), or of both such paragraphs, for any taxable year shall nevertheless be considered to have satisfied the requirements of such paragraphs for such taxable year if—
(A) following the corporation, trust, or association's identification of the failure to meet the requirements of paragraph (2) or (3), or of both such paragraphs, for any taxable year, a description of each item of its gross income described in such paragraphs is set forth in a schedule for such taxable year filed in accordance with regulations prescribed by the Secretary, and
(B) the failure to meet the requirements of paragraph (2) or (3), or of both such paragraphs, is due to reasonable cause and not due to willful neglect.
(7) **Rules of application for failure to satisfy paragraph (4).**

(A) In general. A corporation, trust, or association that fails to meet the requirements of paragraph (4) (other than a failure to meet the requirements of paragraph (4)(B)(iii) which is described in subparagraph (B)(i) of this paragraph) for a particular quarter shall nevertheless be considered to have satisfied the requirements of such paragraph for such quarter if—

(i) following the corporation, trust, or association's identification of the failure to satisfy the requirements of such paragraph for a particular quarter, a description of each asset that causes the corporation, trust, or association to fail to satisfy the requirements of such paragraph at the close of such quarter of any taxable year is set forth in a schedule for such quarter filed in accordance with regulations prescribed by the Secretary,

(ii) the failure to meet the requirements of such paragraph for a particular quarter is due to reasonable cause and not due to willful neglect, and

(iii)(I) the corporation, trust, or association disposes of the assets set forth on the schedule specified in clause (i) within 6 months after the last day of the quarter in which the corporation, trust or association's identification of the failure to satisfy the requirements of such paragraph occurred or such other time period prescribed by the Secretary and in the manner prescribed by the Secretary, or

(II) the requirements of such paragraph are otherwise met within the time period specified in subclause (I).

(B) Rule for certain de minimis failures. A corporation, trust, or association that fails to meet the requirements of paragraph (4)(B)(iii) for a particular quarter shall nevertheless be considered to have satisfied the requirements of such paragraph for such quarter if—

(i) such failure is due to the ownership of assets the total value of which does not exceed the lesser of—

(I) 1 percent of the total value of the trust's assets at the end of the quarter for which such measurement is done, and

(II) $10,000,000, and

(ii)(I) the corporation, trust, or association, following the identification of such failure, disposes of assets in order to meet the requirements of such paragraph within 6 months after the last day of the quarter in which the corporation, trust or association's identification of the failure to satisfy the requirements of such paragraph occurred or such other time period prescribed by the Secretary and in the manner prescribed by the Secretary, or

(II) the requirements of such paragraph are otherwise met within the time period specified in subclause (I).

(C) Tax.

(i) Tax imposed. If subparagraph (A) applies to a corporation, trust, or association for any taxable year, there is hereby imposed on such corporation, trust, or association a tax in an amount equal to the greater of—

(I) $50,000, or

(II) the amount determined (pursuant to regulations promulgated by the Secretary) by multiplying the net income generated by the assets described in the schedule specified in subparagraph (A)(i) for the period specified in clause (ii) by the highest rate of tax specified in section 11.

(ii) Period. For purposes of clause (i)(II), the period described in this clause is the period beginning on the first date that the failure to satisfy the requirements of such paragraph (4) occurs as a result of the ownership of such assets and ending on the earlier of the date on which the trust disposes of such assets or the end of the first quarter when there is no longer a failure to satisfy such paragraph (4).

(iii) Administrative provisions. For purposes of subtitle F, the taxes imposed by this subparagraph shall be treated as excise taxes with respect to which the deficiency procedures of such subtitle apply.

(8) Termination date. For purposes of this subsection, the term "termination date" means, with respect to any taxpayer, the last day of the taxpayer's first taxable year beginning after the date of the enactment of this paragraph and before the date that is 1 year after such date of enactment.

(d) Rents from real property defined.

(1) Amounts included. For purposes of paragraphs (2) and (3) of subsection (c), the term "rents from real property" includes (subject to paragraph (2))—

(A) rents from interests in real property,

(B) charges for services customarily furnished or rendered in connection with the rental of real property, whether or not such charges are separately stated, and

(C) rent attributable to personal property which is leased under, or in connection with, a lease of real property, but only if the rent attributable to such personal property for the taxable year does not exceed 15 percent of the total rent for the taxable year attributable to both the real and personal property leased under, or in connection with, such lease.

For purposes of subparagraph (C), with respect to each lease of real property, rent attributable to personal property for the taxable year is that amount which bears the same ratio to total rent for the taxable year as the average of the fair market values of the personal property at the beginning and at the end of the taxable year bears to the average of the aggregate fair market values of both the real property and the personal property at the beginning and at the end of such taxable year.

(2) Amounts excluded. For purposes of paragraphs (2) and (3) of subsection (c), the term "rents from real property" does not include—

(A) except as provided in paragraphs (4) and (6), any amount received or accrued, directly or indirectly, with respect to any real or personal property, if the determination of such amount depends in whole or in part on the income or profits derived by any person from such property (except that any amount so received or accrued shall not be excluded from the term "rents from real property" solely by reason of being based on a fixed percentage or percentages of receipts or sales);

(B) except as provided in paragraph (8), any amount received or accrued directly or indirectly from any person if the real estate investment trust owns, directly or indirectly—

(i) in the case of any person which is a corporation, stock of such person possessing 10 percent or more of the total combined voting power of all classes of stock entitled to vote, or 10 percent or more of the total value of shares of all classes of stock of such person; or

(ii) in the case of any person which is not a corporation, an interest of 10 percent or more in the assets or net profits of such person; and

(C) any impermissible tenant service income (as defined in paragraph (7)).

(3) Independent contractor defined. For purposes of this subsection and subsection (e), the term "independent contractor" means any person—

(A) who does not own, directly or indirectly, more than 35 percent of the shares, or certificates of beneficial interest, in the real estate investment trust; and

(B) if such person is a corporation, not more than 35 percent of the total combined voting power of whose stock (or 35 percent of the total shares of all classes of whose stock), or, if such person is not a corporation, not more than 35 percent of the interest in whose assets or net profits is owned, directly or indirectly, by one or more persons owning 35 percent or more of the shares or certificates of beneficial interest in the trust.

In the event that any class of stock of either the real estate investment trust or such person is regularly traded on an established securities market, only persons who own, directly or indirectly, more than 5 percent of such class of stock shall be taken into account as owning any of the stock of such class for purposes of applying the 35 percent limitation set forth in subparagraph (B) (but all of the outstanding stock of such class shall be considered outstanding in order to compute the denominator for purpose of determining the applicable percentage of ownership).

(4) Special rule for certain contingent rents. Where a real estate investment trust receives or accrues, with respect to real or personal property, any amount which would be excluded from the term "rents from real property" solely because the tenant of the real estate investment trust receives or accrues, directly or indirectly, from subtenants any amount the determination of which depends in whole or in part on the income or profits derived by any person from such property, only a proportionate part (determined pursuant to regulations prescribed by the Secretary) of the amount received or accrued by the real estate investment trust from that tenant will be excluded from the term "rents from real property".

(5) Constructive ownership of stock. For purposes of this subsection, the rules prescribed by section 318(a) for determining the ownership of stock shall apply in determining the ownership of stock, assets, or net profits of any person; except that—

(A) "10 percent" shall be substituted for "50 percent" in subparagraph (C) of paragraphs (2) and (3) of section 318(a), and

(B) section 318(a)(3)(A) shall be applied in the case of a partnership by taking into account only partners who own (directly or indirectly) 25 percent or more of the capital interest, or the profits interest, in the partnership.

(6) Special rule for certain property subleased by tenant of real estate investment trusts.

(A) In general. If—

(i) a real estate investment trust receives or accrues, with respect to real or personal property, amounts from a tenant which derives substantially all of its income with respect to such property from the subleasing of substantially all of such property, and

(ii) a portion of the amount such tenant receives or accrues, directly or indirectly, from subtenants consists of qualified rents,

then the amounts which the trust receives or accrues from the tenant shall not be excluded from the term "rents from real property" by reason of being based on the income or profits of such tenant to the extent the amounts so received or accrued are attributable to qualified rents received or accrued by such tenant.

(B) Qualified rents. For purposes of subparagraph (A), the term "qualified rents" means any amount which would be treated as rents from real property if received by the real estate investment trust.

(7) Impermissible tenant service income. For purposes of paragraph (2)(C)—

(A) In general. The term "impermissible tenant service income" means, with respect to any real or personal property, any amount received or accrued directly or indirectly by the real estate investment trust for—

(i) services furnished or rendered by the trust to the tenants of such property, or

(ii) managing or operating such property.

(B) Disqualification of all amounts where more than de minimis amount. If the amount described in subparagraph (A) with respect to a property for any taxable year exceeds 1 percent of all amounts received or accrued during such taxable year directly or indirectly by the real estate investment trust with respect to such property, the impermissible tenant service income of the trust with respect to the property shall include all such amounts.

(C) Exceptions. For purposes of subparagraph (A)—

(i) services furnished or rendered, or management or operation provided, through an independent contractor from whom the trust itself does not derive or receive any income or through a taxable REIT subsidiary of such trust shall not be treated as furnished, rendered, or provided by the trust, and

(ii) there shall not be taken into account any amount which would be excluded from unrelated business taxable income under section 512(b)(3) if received by an organization described in section 511(a)(2).

(D) Amount attributable to impermissible services. For purposes of subparagraph (A), the amount treated as received for any service (or management or operation) shall not be less than 150 percent of the direct cost of the trust in furnishing or rendering the service (or providing the management or operation).

(E) Coordination with limitations. For purposes of paragraphs (2) and (3) of subsection (c), amounts described in subparagraph (A) shall be included in the gross income of the corporation, trust, or association.

(8) Special rule for taxable REIT subsidiaries. For purposes of this subsection, amounts paid to a real estate investment trust by a taxable REIT subsidiary of such trust shall not be excluded from rents from real property by reason of paragraph (2)(B) if the requirements of either of the following subparagraphs are met:

(A) Limited rental exception.

(i) In general. The requirements of this subparagraph are met with respect to any property if at least 90 percent of the leased space of the property is rented to persons other than taxable REIT subsidiaries of such trust and other than persons described in paragraph (2)(B).

(ii) Rents must be substantially comparable. Clause (i) shall apply only to the extent that the amounts paid to the trust as rents from real property (as defined in paragraph (1) without regard to paragraph (2)(B)) from such property are substantially comparable to such rents paid by the other tenants of the trust's property for comparable space.

(iii) Times for testing rent comparability. The substantial comparability requirement of clause (ii) shall be treated as met with respect to a lease to a taxable REIT subsidiary of the trust if such requirement is met under the terms of the lease—

(I) at the time such lease is entered into,

(II) at the time of each extension of the lease, including a failure to exercise a right to terminate, and

(III) at the time of any modification of the lease between the trust and the taxable REIT subsidiary if the rent under such lease is effectively increased pursuant to such modification.

With respect to subclause (III), if the taxable REIT subsidiary of the trust is a controlled taxable REIT subsidiary of the trust, the term "rents from real property" shall not in any event include rent under such lease to the extent of the increase in such rent on account of such modification.

(iv) Controlled taxable REIT subsidiary. For purposes of clause (iii), the term "controlled taxable REIT subsidiary" means, with respect to any real estate investment trust, any taxable REIT subsidiary of such trust if such trust owns directly or indirectly—

(I) stock possessing more than 50 percent of the total voting power of the outstanding stock of such subsidiary, or

(II) stock having a value of more than 50 percent of the total value of the outstanding stock of such subsidiary.

(v) Continuing qualification based on third party actions. If the requirements of clause (i) are met at a time referred to in clause (iii), such requirements shall continue to be treated as met so long as there is no increase in the space leased to any taxable REIT subsidiary of such trust or to any person described in paragraph (2)(B).

(vi) Correction period. If there is an increase referred to in clause (v) during any calendar quarter with respect to any property, the requirements of clause (iii) shall be treated as met during the quarter and the succeeding quarter if such requirements are met at the close of such succeeding quarter.

(B) Exception for certain lodging facilities and health care property. The requirements of this subparagraph are met with respect to an interest in real property which is a qualified lodging facility (as defined in paragraph (9)(D)) or a qualified health care property (as defined in subsection (e)(6)(D)(i)) leased by the trust to a taxable REIT subsidiary of the trust if the property is operated on behalf of such subsidiary by a person who is an eligible independent contractor. For purposes of this section, a taxable REIT subsidiary is not considered to be operating or managing a qualified health care property or qualified lodging facility solely because it—

(i) directly or indirectly possesses a license, permit, or similar instrument enabling it to do so, or

(ii) employs individuals working at such facility or property located outside the United States, but only if an eligible independent contractor is responsible for the daily supervision and direction of such individuals on behalf of the taxable REIT subsidiary pursuant to a management agreement or similar service contract.

(9) Eligible independent contractor. For purposes of paragraph (8)(B)—

(A) In general. The term "eligible independent contractor" means, with respect to any qualified lodging facility or qualified health care property (as defined in subsection (e)(6)(D)(i)), any independent contractor if, at the time such contractor enters into a management agreement or other similar service contract with the taxable REIT subsidiary to operate such qualified lodging facility or qualified health care property, such contractor (or any related person) is actively engaged in the trade or business of operating qualified lodging facilities or qualified health care properties, respectively, for any person who is not a related person with respect to the real estate investment trust or the taxable REIT subsidiary.

(B) Special rules. Solely for purposes of this paragraph and paragraph (8)(B), a person shall not fail to be treated as an independent contractor with respect to any qualified lodging facility or qualified health care property (as so defined) by reason of the following:

(i) The taxable REIT subsidiary bears the expenses for the operation of such qualified lodging facility or qualified health care property pursuant to the management agreement or other similar service contract.

(ii) The taxable REIT subsidiary receives the revenues from the operation of such qualified lodging facility or qualified health care property, net of expenses for such operation and fees payable to the operator pursuant to such agreement or contract.

(iii) The real estate investment trust receives income from such person with respect to another property that is attributable to a lease of such other property to such person that was in effect as of the later of—

(I) January 1, 1999, or

(II) the earliest date that any taxable REIT subsidiary of such trust entered into a management agreement or other similar service contract with such person with respect to such qualified lodging facility or qualified health care property.

(C) Renewals, etc., of existing leases. For purposes of subparagraph (B)(iii)—

(i) a lease shall be treated as in effect on January 1, 1999, without regard to its renewal after such date, so long as such renewal is pursuant to the terms of such lease as in effect on whichever of the dates under subparagraph (B)(iii) is the latest, and

(ii) a lease of a property entered into after whichever of the dates under subparagraph (B)(iii) is the latest shall be treated as in effect on such date if—

(I) on such date, a lease of such property from the trust was in effect, and

(II) under the terms of the new lease, such trust receives a substantially similar or lesser benefit in comparison to the lease referred to in subclause (I).

(D) Qualified lodging facility. For purposes of this paragraph—

(i) In general. The term "qualified lodging facility" means any lodging facility unless wagering activities are conducted at or in connection with such facility by any person who is engaged in the business of accepting wagers and who is legally authorized to engage in such business at or in connection with such facility.

(ii) Lodging facility. The term "lodging facility" means a—

(I) hotel,

(II) motel, or

(III) other establishment more than one-half of the dwelling units in which are used on a transient basis.

(iii) Customary amenities and facilities. The term "lodging facility" includes customary amenities and facilities operated as part of, or associated with, the lodging facility so long as such amenities and facilities are customary for other properties of a comparable size and class owned by other owners unrelated to such real estate investment trust.

(E) Operate includes manage. References in this paragraph to operating a property shall be treated as including a reference to managing the property.

(F) Related person. Persons shall be treated as related to each other if such persons are treated as a single employer under subsection (a) or (b) of section 52.

(e) Special rules for foreclosure property.

(1) Foreclosure property defined. For purposes of this part, the term "foreclosure property" means any real property (including interests in real property), and any personal property incident to such real property, acquired by the real estate investment trust as the result of such trust having bid in such property at foreclosure, or having otherwise reduced such property to ownership or possession by agreement or process of law, after there was default (or default was imminent) on a lease of such property or on an indebtedness which such property secured. Such term does not include property acquired by the real estate investment trust as a result of indebtedness arising from the sale or other disposition of property of the trust described in section 1221(a)(1) which was not originally acquired as foreclosure property.

(2) Grace period. Except as provided in paragraph (3), property shall cease to be foreclosure property with respect to the real estate investment trust as of the close of the 3d taxable year following the taxable year in which the trust acquired such property.

(3) Extensions. If the real estate investment trust establishes to the satisfaction of the Secretary that an extension of the grace period is necessary for the orderly liquidation of the trust's interests in such property, the Secretary may grant one extension of the grace period for such property. Any such extension shall not extend the grace period beyond the close of the 3d taxable year following the last taxable year in the period under paragraph (2).

(4) Termination of grace period in certain cases. Any foreclosure property shall cease to be such on the first day (occurring on or after the day on which the real estate investment trust acquired the property) on which—

(A) a lease is entered into with respect to such property which, by its terms, will give rise to income which is not described in subsection (c)(3) (other than subparagraph (F) of such subsection), or any amount is received or accrued, directly or indirectly, pursuant to a lease entered into on or after such day which is not described in such subsection,

(B) any construction takes place on such property (other than completion of a building, or completion of any other improvement, where more than 10 percent of the construction of such building or other improvement was completed before default became imminent), or

(C) if such day is more than 90 days after the day on which such property was acquired by the real estate investment trust and the property is used in a trade or business which is conducted by the trust (other than through an independent contractor (within the meaning of section (d)(3)) from whom the trust itself does not derive or receive any income).

For purposes of subparagraph (C), property shall not be treated as used in a trade or business by reason of any activities of the real estate investment trust with respect to such property to the extent that such activities would not result in amounts received or accrued, directly or indirectly, with respect to such property being treated as other than rents from real property.

(5) Taxpayer must make election. Property shall be treated as foreclosure property for purposes of this part only if the real estate investment trust so elects (in the manner provided in regulations prescribed by the Secretary) on or before the due date (including any extensions of time) for filing its return of tax under this chapter for the taxable year in which such trust acquires such property. A real estate investment trust may revoke any such election for a taxable year by filing the revocation (in the manner provided by the Secretary) on or before the due date (including any extension of time) for filing its return of tax under this chapter for the taxable year. If a trust revokes an election for any property, no election may be made by the trust under this paragraph with respect to the property for any subsequent taxable year.

(6) Special rule for qualified health care properties. For purposes of this subsection—

(A) Acquisition at expiration of lease. The term "foreclosure property" shall include any qualified health care property acquired by a real estate investment trust as the result of the termination of a lease of such property (other than a termination by reason of a default, or the imminence of a default, on the lease).

(B) Grace period. In the case of a qualified health care property which is foreclosure property solely by reason of subparagraph (A), in lieu of applying paragraphs (2) and (3)—

(i) the qualified health care property shall cease to be foreclosure property as of the close of the second taxable year after the taxable year in which such trust acquired such property, and

(ii) if the real estate investment trust establishes to the satisfaction of the Secretary that an extension of the grace period in clause (i) is necessary to the orderly leasing or liquidation of the trust's interest in such qualified health care property, the Secretary may grant one or more extensions of the grace period for such qualified health care property.

Any such extension shall not extend the grace period beyond the close of the 6th year after the taxable year in which such trust acquired such qualified health care property.

(C) Income from independent contractors. For purposes of applying paragraph (4)(C) with respect to qualified health care property which is foreclosure property by reason of subparagraph (A) or paragraph (1), income derived or received by the trust from an independent contractor shall be disregarded to the extent such income is attributable to—

(i) any lease of property in effect on the date the real estate investment trust acquired the qualified health care property (without regard to its renewal after such date so long as such renewal is pursuant to the terms of such lease as in effect on such date), or

(ii) any lease of property entered into after such date if—

(I) on such date, a lease of such property from the trust was in effect, and

(II) under the terms of the new lease, such trust receives a substantially similar or lesser benefit in comparison to the lease referred to in subclause (I).

(D) Qualified health care property.

(i) **In general.** The term "qualified health care property" means any real property (including interests therein), and any personal property incident to such real property, which—
   (I) is a health care facility, or
   (II) is necessary or incidental to the use of a health care facility.
(ii) **Health care facility.** For purposes of clause (i), the term "health care facility" means a hospital, nursing facility, assisted living facility, congregate care facility, qualified continuing care facility (as defined in section 7872(g)(4)), or other licensed facility which extends medical or nursing or ancillary services to patients and which, immediately before the termination, expiration, default, or breach of the lease of or mortgage secured by such facility, was operated by a provider of such services which was eligible for participation in the medicare program under title XVIII of the Social Security Act with respect to such facility.

(f) Interest.
(1) **In general.** For purposes of paragraphs (2)(B) and (3)(B) of subsection (c), the term "interest" does not include any amount received or accrued, directly or indirectly, if the determination of such amount depends in whole or in part on the income or profits of any person except that—
   (A) any amount so received or accrued shall not be excluded from the term "interest" solely by reason of being based on a fixed percentage or percentages of receipts or sales, and
   (B) where a real estate investment trust receives any amount which would be excluded from the term "interest" solely because the debtor of the real estate investment trust receives or accrues any amount the determination of which depends in whole or in part on the income or profits of any person, only a proportionate part (determined pursuant to regulations prescribed by the Secretary) of the amount received or accrued by the real estate investment trust from the debtor will be excluded from the term "interest".
(2) **Special rule.** If—
   (A) a real estate investment trust receives or accrues with respect to an obligation secured by a mortgage on real property or an interest in real property amounts from a debtor which derives substantially all of its gross income with respect to such property (not taking into account any gain on any disposition) from the leasing of substantially all of its interests in such property to tenants, and
   (B) a portion of the amount which such debtor receives or accrues, directly or indirectly, from tenants consists of qualified rents (as defined in subsection (d)(6)(B)),
then the amounts which the trust receives or accrues from such debtor shall not be excluded from the term "interest" by reason of being based on the income or profits of such debtor to the extent the amounts so received are attributable to qualified rents received or accrued by such debtor.

(g) Termination of election.
(1) **Failure to qualify.** An election under subsection (c)(1) made by a corporation, trust, or association shall terminate if the corporation, trust, or association is not a real estate investment trust to which the provisions of this part apply for the taxable year with respect to which the election is made, or for any succeeding taxable year unless paragraph (5) applies. Such termination shall be effective for the taxable year for which the corporation, trust, or association is not a real estate investment trust to which the provisions of this part apply, and for all succeeding taxable years.
(2) **Revocation.** An election under subsection (c)(1) made by a corporation, trust, or association may be revoked by it for any taxable year after the first taxable year for which the election is effective. A revocation under this paragraph shall be effective for the taxable year in which made and for all succeeding taxable years. Such revocation must be made on or before the 90th day after the first day of the first taxable year for which the revocation is to be effective. Such revocation shall be made in such manner as the Secretary shall prescribe by regulations.
(3) **Election after termination or revocation.** Except as provided in paragraph (4), if a corporation, trust, or association has made an election under subsection (c)(1) and such election has been terminated or revoked under paragraph (1) or paragraph (2), such corporation, trust, or association (and any successor corporation, trust, or association) shall not be eligible to make an election under subsection (c)(1) for any taxable year prior to the fifth taxable year which begins after the first taxable year for which such termination or revocation is effective.
(4) **Exception.** If the election of a corporation, trust, or association has been terminated under paragraph (1), paragraph (3) shall not apply if—
   (A) the corporation, trust, or association does not willfully fail to file within the time prescribed by law an income tax return for the taxable year with respect to which the termination of the election under subsection (c)(1) occurs;
   (B) the inclusion of any incorrect information in the return referred to in subparagraph (A) is not due to fraud with intent to evade tax; and
   (C) the corporation, trust, or association establishes to the satisfaction of the Secretary that its failure to qualify as a real estate investment trust to which the provisions of this part apply is due to reasonable cause and not due to willful neglect.
(5) **Entities to which paragraph applies.** This paragraph applies to a corporation, trust, or association—
   (A) which is not a real estate investment trust to which the provisions of this part apply for the taxable year due to one or more failures to comply with one or more of the provisions of this part (other than paragraph (2), (3), or (4) of subsection (c)),
   (B) such failures are due to reasonable cause and not due to willful neglect, and
   (C) if such corporation, trust, or association pays (as prescribed by the Secretary in regulations and in the same manner as tax) a penalty of $50,000 for each failure to satisfy a provision of this part due to reasonable cause and not willful neglect.

(h) Closely held determinations.
(1) **Section 542(a)(2) applied.**
   (A) **In general.** For purposes of subsection (a)(6), a corporation, trust, or association is closely held if the stock ownership requirement of section 542(a)(2) is met.
   (B) **Waiver of partnership attribution, etc.** For purposes of subparagraph (A)—
      (i) paragraph (2) of section 544(a) shall be applied as if such paragraph did not contain the phrase "or by or for his partner", and
      (ii) sections 544(a)(4)(A) and 544(b)(1) shall be applied by substituting "the entity meet the stock ownership requirement of section 542(a)(2)" for "the corporation a personal holding company".

(2) Subsections (a)(5) and (6) not to apply to 1st year. Paragraphs (5) and (6) of subsection (a) shall not apply to the 1st taxable year for which an election is made under subsection (c)(1) by any corporation, trust, or association.

(3) Treatment of trusts described in section 401(a).

(A) Look-thru treatment.

(i) In general. Except as provided in clause (ii), in determining whether the stock ownership requirement of section 542(a)(2) is met for purposes of paragraph (1)(A), any stock held by a qualified trust shall be treated as held directly by its beneficiaries in proportion to their actuarial interests in such trust and shall not be treated as held by such trust.

(ii) Certain related trusts not eligible. Clause (i) shall not apply to any qualified trust if one or more disqualified persons (as defined in section 4975(e)(2), without regard to subparagraphs (B) and (I) thereof) with respect to such qualified trust hold in the aggregate 5 percent or more in value of the interests in the real estate investment trust and such real estate investment trust has accumulated earnings and profits attributable to any period for which it did not qualify as a real estate investment trust.

(B) Coordination with personal holding company rules. If any entity qualifies as a real estate investment trust for any taxable year by reason of subparagraph (A), such entity shall not be treated as a personal holding company for such taxable year for purposes of part II of subchapter G of this chapter.

(C) Treatment for purposes of unrelated business tax. If any qualified trust holds more than 10 percent (by value) of the interests in any pension-held REIT at any time during a taxable year, the trust shall be treated as having for such taxable year gross income from an unrelated trade or business in an amount which bears the same ratio to the aggregate dividends paid (or treated as paid) by the REIT to the trust for the taxable year of the REIT with or within which the taxable year of the trust ends (the "REIT year") as—

(i) the gross income (less direct expenses related thereto) of the REIT for the REIT year from unrelated trades or businesses (determined as if the REIT were a qualified trust), bears to

(ii) the gross income (less direct expenses related thereto) of the REIT for the REIT year.

This subparagraph shall apply only if the ratio determined under the preceding sentence is at least 5 percent.

(D) Pension-held REIT. The purposes of subparagraph (C)—

(i) In general. A real estate investment trust is a pension-held REIT if such trust would not have qualified as a real estate investment trust but for the provisions of this paragraph and if such trust is predominantly held by qualified trusts.

(ii) Predominantly held. For purposes of clause (i), a real estate investment trust is predominantly held by qualified trusts if—

(I) at least 1 qualified trust holds more than 25 percent (by value) of the interests in such real estate investment trust, or

(II) 1 or more qualified trusts (each of whom own more than 10 percent by value of the interests in such real estate investment trust) hold in the aggregate more than 50 percent (by value) of the interests in such real estate investment trust.

(E) Qualified trust. For purposes of this paragraph, the term "qualified trust" means any trust described in section 401(a) and exempt from tax under section 501(a).

(i) Treatment of certain wholly owned subsidiaries.

(1) In general. For purposes of this title—

(A) a corporation which is a qualified REIT subsidiary shall not be treated as a separate corporation, and

(B) all assets, liabilities, and items of income, deduction, and credit of a qualified REIT subsidiary shall be treated as assets, liabilities, and such items (as the case may be) of the real estate investment trust.

(2) Qualified REIT subsidiary. For purposes of this subsection, the term "qualified REIT subsidiary" means any corporation if 100 percent of the stock of such corporation is held by the real estate investment trust. Such term shall not include a taxable REIT subsidiary.

(3) Treatment of termination of qualified subsidiary status. For purposes of this subtitle, if any corporation which was a qualified REIT subsidiary ceases to meet the requirements of paragraph (2), such corporation shall be treated as a new corporation acquiring all of its assets (and assuming all of its liabilities) immediately before such cessation from the real estate investment trust in exchange for its stock.

(j) Treatment of shared appreciation mortgages.

(1) In general. Solely for purposes of subsection (c) of this section and section 857(b)(6), any income derived from a shared appreciation provision shall be treated as gain recognized on the sale of the secured property.

(2) Treatment of income. For purposes of applying subsection (c) of this section and section 857(b)(6) to any income described in paragraph (1)—

(A) the real estate investment trust shall be treated as holding the secured property for the period during which it held the shared appreciation provision (or, if shorter, for the period during which the secured property was held by the person holding such property), and

(B) the secured property shall be treated as property described in section 1221(a)(1) if it is so described in the hands of the person holding the secured property (or it would be so described if held by the real estate investment trust).

(3) Coordination with prohibited transactions safe harbor. For purposes of section 857(b)(6)(C)—

(A) the real estate investment trust shall be treated as having sold the secured property when it recognizes any income described in paragraph (1), and

(B) any expenditures made by any holder of the secured property shall be treated as made by the real estate investment trust.

(4) Coordination with 4-year holding period.

(A) In general. For purposes of section 857(b)(6)(C), if a real estate investment trust is treated as having sold secured property under paragraph (3)(A), the trust shall be treated as having held such property for at least 4 years if—

(i) the secured property is sold or otherwise disposed of pursuant to a case under title 11 of the United States Code,

(ii) the seller is under the jurisdiction of the court in such case, and

(iii) the disposition is required by the court or is pursuant to a plan approved by the court.

(B) Exception. Subparagraph (A) shall not apply if—

(i) the secured property was acquired by the seller with the intent to evict or foreclose, or

(ii) the trust knew or had reason to know that default on the obligation described in paragraph (5)(A) would occur.

(5) **Definitions.** For purposes of this subsection—

(A) Shared appreciation provision. The term "shared appreciation provision" means any provision—

(i) which is in connection with an obligation which is held by the real estate investment trust and is secured by an interest in real property, and

(ii) which entitles the real estate investment trust to receive a specified portion of any gain realized on the sale or exchange of such real property (or of any gain which would be realized if the property were sold on a specified date) or appreciation in value as of any specified date.

(B) Secured property. The term "secured property" means the real property referred to in subparagraph (A).

(k) Requirement that entity not be closely held treated as met in certain cases.

A corporation, trust, or association—

(1) which for a taxable year meets the requirements of section 857(f)(1), and

(2) which does not know, or exercising reasonable diligence would not have known, whether the entity failed to meet the requirement of subsection (a)(6),

shall be treated as having met the requirement of subsection (a)(6) for the taxable year.

(l) Taxable REIT subsidiary.

For purposes of this part—

(1) **In general.** The term "taxable REIT subsidiary" means, with respect to a real estate investment trust, a corporation (other than a real estate investment trust) if—

(A) such trust directly or indirectly owns stock in such corporation, and

(B) such trust and such corporation jointly elect that such corporation shall be treated as a taxable REIT subsidiary of such trust for purposes of this part.

Such an election, once made, shall be irrevocable unless both such trust and corporation consent to its revocation. Such election, and any revocation thereof, may be made without the consent of the Secretary.

(2) **35 percent ownership in another taxable REIT subsidiary.** The term "taxable REIT subsidiary" includes, with respect to any real estate investment trust, any corporation (other than a real estate investment trust) with respect to which a taxable REIT subsidiary of such trust owns directly or indirectly—

(A) securities possessing more than 35 percent of the total voting power of the outstanding securities of such corporation, or

(B) securities having a value of more than 35 percent of the total value of the outstanding securities of such corporation.

The preceding sentence shall not apply to a qualified REIT subsidiary (as defined in subsection (i)(2)). For purposes of subparagraph (B), securities described in subsection (m)(2)(A) shall not be taken into account.

(3) **Exceptions.** The term "taxable REIT subsidiary" shall not include—

(A) any corporation which directly or indirectly operates or manages a lodging facility or a health care facility, and

(B) any corporation which directly or indirectly provides to any other person (under a franchise, license, or otherwise) rights to any brand name under which any lodging facility or health care facility is operated.

Subparagraph (B) shall not apply to rights provided to an eligible independent contractor to operate or manage a lodging facility or a health care facility if such rights are held by such corporation as a franchisee, licensee, or in a similar capacity and such lodging facility or health care facility is either owned by such corporation or is leased to such corporation from the real estate investment trust.

(4) **Definitions.** For purposes of paragraph (3)—

(A) Lodging facility. The term "lodging facility" has the meaning given to such term by subsection (d)(9)(D)(ii).

(B) Health care facility. The term "health care facility" has the meaning given to such term by subsection (e)(6)(D)(ii).

(m) Safe harbor in applying subsection (c)(4).

(1) **In general.** In applying subclause (III) of subsection (c)(4)(B)(iii), except as otherwise determined by the Secretary in regulations, the following shall not be considered securities held by the trust:

(A) Straight debt securities of an issuer which meet the requirements of paragraph (2).

(B) Any loan to an individual or an estate.

(C) Any section 467 rental agreement (as defined in section 467(d)), other than with a person described in subsection (d)(2)(B).

(D) Any obligation to pay rents from real property (as defined in subsection (d)(1)).

(E) Any security issued by a State or any political subdivision thereof, the District of Columbia, a foreign government or any political subdivision thereof, or the Commonwealth of Puerto Rico, but only if the determination of any payment received or accrued under such security does not depend in whole or in part on the profits of any entity not described in this subparagraph or payments on any obligation issued by such an entity,

(F) Any security issued by a real estate investment trust.

(G) Any other arrangement as determined by the Secretary.

(2) **Special rules relating to straight debt securities.**

(A) In general. For purposes of paragraph (1)(A), securities meet the requirements of this paragraph if such securities are straight debt, as defined in section 1361(c)(5) (without regard to subparagraph (B)(iii) thereof).

(B) Special rules relating to certain contingencies. For purposes of subparagraph (A), any interest or principal shall not be treated as failing to satisfy section 1361(c)(5)(B)(i) solely by reason of the fact that—

(i) the time of payment of such interest or principal is subject to a contingency, but only if—

(I) any such contingency does not have the effect of changing the effective yield to maturity, as determined under section 1272, other than a change in the annual yield to maturity which does not exceed the greater of ¼ of 1 percent or 5 percent of the annual yield to maturity, or

(II) neither the aggregate issue price nor the aggregate face amount of the issuer's debt instruments held by the trust exceeds $1,000,000 and not more than 12 months of unaccrued interest can be required to be prepaid thereunder, or

(ii) the time or amount of payment is subject to a contingency upon a default or the exercise of a prepayment right by the issuer of the debt, but only if such contingency is consistent with customary commercial practice.

(C) Special rules relating to corporate or partnership issuers. In the case of an issuer which is a corporation or a partnership, securities that otherwise would be described in paragraph (1)(A) shall be considered not to be so described if the trust holding such securities and any of its controlled taxable REIT subsidiaries (as defined in subsection (d)(8)(A)(iv)) hold any securities of the issuer which—

(i) are not described in paragraph (1) (prior to the application of this subparagraph), and

(ii) have an aggregate value greater than 1 percent of the issuer's outstanding securities determined without regard to paragraph (3)(A)(i).

(3) Look-through rule for partnership securities.

(A) In general. For purposes of applying subclause (III) of subsection (c)(4)(B)(iii)—

(i) a trust's interest as a partner in a partnership (as defined in section 7701(a)(2)) shall not be considered a security, and

(ii) the trust shall be deemed to own its proportionate share of each of the assets of the partnership.

(B) Determination of trust's interest in partnership assets. For purposes of subparagraph (A), with respect to any taxable year beginning after the date of the enactment of this subparagraph—

(i) the trust's interest in the partnership assets shall be the trust's proportionate interest in any securities issued by the partnership (determined without regard to subparagraph (A)(i) and paragraph (4), but not including securities described in paragraph (1)), and

(ii) the value of any debt instrument shall be the adjusted issue price thereof, as defined in section 1272(a)(4).

(4) Certain partnership debt instruments not treated as a security. For purposes of applying subclause (III) of subsection (c)(4)(B)(iii)—

(A) any debt instrument issued by a partnership and not described in paragraph (1) shall not be considered a security to the extent of the trust's interest as a partner in the partnership, and

(B) any debt instrument issued by a partnership and not described in paragraph (1) shall not be considered a security if at least 75 percent of the partnership's gross income (excluding gross income from prohibited transactions) is derived from sources referred to in subsection (c)(3).

(5) Secretarial guidance. The Secretary is authorized to provide guidance (including through the issuance of a written determination, as defined in section 6110(b)) that an arrangement shall not be considered a security held by the trust for purposes of applying subclause (III) of subsection (c)(4)(B)(iii) notwithstanding that such arrangement otherwise could be considered a security under subparagraph (F) of subsection (c)(5).

(6) Transition rule.

(A) In general. Notwithstanding paragraph (2)(C), securities held by a trust shall not be considered securities held by the trust for purposes of subsection (c)(4)(B)(iii)(III) during any period beginning on or before October 22, 2004, if such securities—

(i) are held by such trust continuously during such period, and

(ii) would not be taken into account for purposes of such subsection by reason of paragraph (7)(C) of subsection (c) (as in effect on October 22, 2004) if the amendments made by section 243 of the American Jobs Creation Act of 2004 had never been enacted.

(B) Rule not to apply to securities held after maturity date. Subparagraph (A) shall not apply with respect to any security after the later of October 22, 2004, or the latest maturity date under the contract (as in effect on October 22, 2004) taking into account any renewal or extension permitted under the contract if such renewal or extension does not significantly modify any other terms of the contract.

(C) Successors. If the successor of a trust to which this paragraph applies acquires securities in a transaction to which section 381 applies, such trusts shall be treated as a single entity for purposes of determining the holding period of such securities under subparagraph (A).

(n) Rules regarding foreign currency transactions.

(1) In general. For purposes of this part—

(A) passive foreign exchange gain for any taxable year shall not constitute gross income for purposes of subsection (c)(2), and

(B) real estate foreign exchange gain for any taxable year shall not constitute gross income for purposes of subsection (c)(3).

(2) Real estate foreign exchange gain. For purposes of this subsection, the term "real estate foreign exchange gain" means—

(A) foreign currency gain (as defined in section 988(b)(1)) which is attributable to—

(i) any item of income or gain described in subsection (c)(3),

(ii) the acquisition or ownership of obligations secured by mortgages on real property or on interests in real property (other than foreign currency gain attributable to any item of income or gain described in clause (i)), or

(iii) becoming or being the obligor under obligations secured by mortgages on real property or on interests in real property (other than foreign currency gain attributable to any item of income or gain described in clause (i)),

(B) section 987 gain attributable to a qualified business unit (as defined by section 989) of the real estate investment trust, but only if such qualified business unit meets the requirements under—

(i) subsection (c)(3) for the taxable year, and

(ii) subsection (c)(4)(A) at the close of each quarter that the real estate investment trust has directly or indirectly held the qualified business unit, and

(C) any other foreign currency gain as determined by the Secretary.

(3) Passive foreign exchange gain. For purposes of this subsection, the term "passive foreign exchange gain" means—

(A) real estate foreign exchange gain,

(B) foreign currency gain (as defined in section 988(b)(1)) which is not described in subparagraph (A) and which is attributable to—

(i) any item of income or gain described in subsection (c)(2),

(ii) the acquisition or ownership of obligations (other than foreign currency gain attributable to any item of income or gain described in clause (i)), or

(iii) becoming or being the obligor under obligations (other than foreign currency gain attributable to any item of income or gain described in clause (i)), and

(C) any other foreign currency gain as determined by the Secretary.

(4) Exception for income from substantial and regular trading. Notwithstanding this subsection or any other provision of this part, any section 988 gain derived by a corporation, trust, or association from dealing, or engaging in substantial and regular trading, in securities (as defined in section 475(c)(2)) shall constitute gross income which does not qualify under paragraph (2) or (3) of subsection (c). This paragraph shall not apply to income which does not constitute gross income by reason of subsection (c)(5)(G).

In 2008, P.L. 110-289, Sec. 3031(a), added subsec. (n), effective for gains and items of income recognized after 7/30/2008.
—P.L. 110-289, Sec. 3031(b), amended subpara. (c)(5)(G), effective for transactions entered into after 7/30/2008.
Prior to amendment, subpara. (c)(5)(G) read as follows:
"(G) Treatment of certain hedging instruments. Except to the extent provided by regulations, any income of a real estate investment trust from a hedging transaction (as defined in clause (ii) or (iii) of section 1221(b)(2)(A)) which is clearly identified pursuant to section 1221(a)(7), including gain from the sale or disposition of such a transaction, shall not constitute gross income under paragraph (2) to the extent that the transaction hedges any indebtedness incurred or to be incurred by the trust to acquire or carry real estate assets."
—P.L. 110-289, Sec. 3031(c), added subpara. (c)(5)(J), effective for gains and items of income recognized after 7/30/2008.
—P.L. 110-289, Sec. 3032(a), added "(including a discrepancy caused solely by the change in the foreign currency exchange rate used to value a foreign asset)" after "such requirements" in subclause (c)(4)(B)(iii)(III) . . . Sec. 3032(b), added subpara. (c)(5)(K), effective tax. yrs. begin. after 7/30/2008.
—P.L. 110-289, Sec. 3041(1), substituted "25 percent" for "20 percent" in clause (c)(4)(B)(ii) . . . Sec. 3041(2), substituted "REIT subsidiaries," for "REIT subsidiaries (in the case of a quarter which closes on or before the termination date, 25 percent in the case of a timber real estate investment trust) and" in clause (c)(4)(B)(ii), effective for tax. yrs. begin. after 7/30/2008.
—P.L. 110-289, Sec. 3061(a), amended subpara. (d)(8)(B) . . . Sec. 3061(b), amended subparas. (d)(9)(A) and (B)
Prior to amendment, subpara. (d)(8)(B) read as follows:
"(B) Exception for certain lodging facilities. The requirements of this subparagraph are met with respect to an interest in real property which is a qualified lodging facility leased by the trust to a taxable REIT subsidiary of the trust if the property is operated on behalf of such subsidiary by a person who is an eligible independent contractor."
Prior to amendment, subparas. (d)(9)(A) and (B) read as follows:
"(A) In general. The term 'eligible independent contractor' means, with respect to any qualified lodging facility, any independent contractor if, at the time such contractor enters into a management agreement or other similar service contract with the taxable REIT subsidiary to operate the facility, such contractor (or any related person) is actively engaged in the trade or business of operating qualified lodging facilities for any person who is not a related person with respect to the real estate investment trust or the taxable REIT subsidiary."
"(B) Special rules. Solely for purposes of this paragraph and paragraph (8)(B), a person shall not fail to be treated as an independent contractor with respect to any qualified lodging facility by reason of any of the following:"
"(i) The taxable REIT subsidiary bears the expenses for the operation of the facility pursuant to the management agreement or other similar service contract."
"(ii) The taxable REIT subsidiary receives the revenues from the operation of such facility, net of expenses for such operation and fees payable to the operator pursuant to such agreement or contract."
"(iii) he real estate investment trust receives income from such person with respect to another property that is attributable to a lease of such other property to such person that was in effect as of the later of—
"(I) January 1, 1999, or"
"(II) the earliest date that any taxable REIT subsidiary of such trust entered into a management agreement or other similar service contract with such person with respect to such qualified lodging facility."
—P.L. 110-289, Sec. 3061(c)(1), added "or a health care facility" after "a lodging facility" in para. (l)(3) . . . Sec. 3061(c)(2), added "or a health care facility" after "such lodging facility" in para. (l)(3), effective to tax. yrs. begin. after 7/30/2008.
—P.L. 110-246, Sec. 4, Repeals the duplicative enactment and provides effective date provisions of the Act entitled "An Act to provide for the continuation of agricultural programs through fiscal year 2012, and for other purposes" Sec. 4, P.L. 110-246 reads as follows:
"Sec. 4. Repeal of duplicative enactment.
"(a) In General- The Act entitled 'An Act to provide for the continuation of agricultural programs through fiscal year 2012, and for other purposes' (H.R. 2419 of the 110th Congress), and the amendments made by that Act, are repealed, effective on the date of enactment of that Act.
"(b) Effective Date- Except as otherwise provided in this Act, this Act and the amendments made by this Act shall take effect on the earlier of--
"(1) the date of enactment of this Act; or

"(2) the date of the enactment of the Act entitled 'An Act to provide for the continuation of agricultural programs through fiscal year 2012, and for other purposes' (H.R. 2419 of the 110th Congress)."
—P.L. 110-246, Sec. 15313(a), deleted "and" at the end of subpara. (c)(2)(G), inserted "and" at the end of subpara. (c)(2)(H), and added subpara. (c)(2)(I)
—P.L. 110-246, Sec. 15314(a), added "(in the case of a quarter which closes on or before the termination date, 25 percent in the case of a timber real estate investment trust)" after "REIT subsidiaries" in clause (c)(4)(B)(ii), effective for tax. yrs. begin. after 5/22/2008.
—P.L. 110-246, Sec. 15312(a), added subpara. (c)(5)(H), effective for dispositions in tax. yrs. begin. after 5/22/2008.
—P.L. 110-246, Sec. 15313(b), added subpara. (c)(5)(I), effective for tax. yrs. begin. after 5/22/08.
—P.L. 110-246, Sec. 15312(b), added para. (c)(8), effective for dispositions in tax. yrs. begin. after 5/22/08. [Ed. Note: May 22, 2008 was the date of enactment for H.R. 2419 (PL 110-234), which was repealed by (2008 Farm Act § 4(a)) (PL 110-246, 6/18/2008), in connection with the reenactment of the farm bill to correct a technical deficiency in its original passage.]
In 2007, P.L. 110-172, Sec. 9(b), amended clause (d)(8)(D)(ii), effective (as if included in PL 106-170, Sec. 542) for tax. yrs. begin. after 12/30/2000.
Prior to amendment, clause (d)(9)(D)(ii) read as follows:
"(ii) Lodging facility. The term 'lodging facility' means a hotel, motel, or other establishment more than one-half of the dwelling units in which are used on a transient basis."
—P.L. 110-172, Sec. 11(a)(18), amended the last sentence of para. (l)(2), enacted 12/29/2007.
Prior to amendment, the last sentence of para. (l)(2) read as follows:
"The rule of section 856(c)(7) shall apply for purposes of subparagraph (B)."
In 2005, P.L. 109-135, Sec. 403(d)(1), amended para. (c)(7) . . . Sec. 403(d)(2), added para. (m)(6), effective as if included in Sec. 243 of P.L. 108-357, as provided by Sec. 243(g) of the American Jobs Creation Act of 2004, P.L. 108-357 (as amended by Sec. 403(d)(4) of this Act) which reads as follows:
"(g) Effective dates.
"(1) Subsections (a) and (b). The amendments made by subsections (a) and (b) shall apply to taxable years beginning after December 31, 2000.
"(2) Subsections (c) and (e). The amendments made by subsections (c) and (e) shall apply to taxable years beginning after the date of the enactment of this Act.
"(3) Subsection (d). The amendment made by subsection (d) shall apply to transactions entered into after December 31, 2004.
"(4) Subsection (f).
"(A) The amendment made by paragraph (1) of subsection (f) shall apply to failures with respect to which the requirements of subparagraph (A) or (B) of section 856(c)(7) of the Internal Revenue Code of 1986 (as added by such paragraph) are satisfied after the date of the enactment of this Act.
"(B) The amendment made by paragraph (2) of subsection (f) shall apply to failures with respect to which the requirements of paragraph (6) of section 856(c) of the Internal Revenue Code of 1986 (as amended by such paragraph) are satisfied after the date of the enactment of this Act.
"(C) The amendments made by paragraph (3) of subsection (f) shall apply to failures with respect to which the requirements of paragraph (5) of section 856(g) of the Internal Revenue Code of 1986 (as added by such paragraph) are satisfied after the date of the enactment of this Act.
"(D) The amendment made by paragraph (4) of subsection (f) shall apply to taxable years ending after the date of the enactment of this Act.
"(E) The amendments made by paragraph (5) of subsection (f) shall apply to statements filed after the date of the enactment of this Act."
Prior to amendment, para. (c)(7) read as follows:
"(7) Rules of application for failure to satisfy paragraph (4).
"(A) De minimis failure. A corporation, trust, or association that fails to meet the requirements of paragraph (4)(B)(iii) for a particular quarter shall nevertheless be considered to have satisfied the requirements of such paragraph for such quarter if—
"(i) such failure is due to the ownership of assets the total value of which does not exceed the lesser of—
"(I) 1 percent of the total value of the trust's assets at the end of the quarter for which such measurement is done, and
"(II) $10,000,000, and
"(ii)(I) the corporation, trust, or association, following the identification of such failure, disposes of assets in order to meet the requirements of such paragraph within 6 months after the last day of the quarter in which the corporation, trust or association's identification of the failure to satisfy the requirements of such paragraph occurred or such other time period prescribed by the Secretary and in the manner prescribed by the Secretary, or
"(II) the requirements of such paragraph are otherwise met within the time period specified in subclause (I).
"(B) Failures exceeding de minimis amount. A corporation, trust, or association that fails to meet the requirements of paragraph (4) for a particular quarter shall nevertheless be considered to have satisfied the requirements of such paragraph for such quarter if—
"(i) such failure involves the ownership of assets the total value of which exceeds the de minimis standard described in subparagraph (A)(i) at the end of the quarter for which such measurement is done,
"(ii) following the corporation, trust, or association's identification of the failure to satisfy the requirements of such paragraph for a particular quarter, a description of each asset that causes the corporation, trust, or association to fail to satisfy the requirements of such paragraph at the close of such quarter of any taxable year is

Real estate investment trusts Code Sec. 856

set forth in a schedule for such quarter filed in accordance with regulations prescribed by the Secretary,

"(iii) the failure to meet the requirements of such paragraph for a particular quarter is due to reasonable cause and not due to willful neglect,

"(iv) the corporation, trust, or association pays a tax computed under subparagraph (C), and

"(v)(I) the corporation, trust, or association disposes of the assets set forth on the schedule specified in clause (ii) within 6 months after the last day of the quarter in which the corporation, trust or association's identification of the failure to satisfy the requirements of such paragraph occurred or such other time period prescribed by the Secretary and in the manner prescribed by the Secretary, or

"(II) the requirements of such paragraph are otherwise met within the time period specified in subclause (I).

"(C) Tax. For purposes of subparagraph (B)(iv)—

"(i) Tax imposed. If a corporation, trust, or association elects the application of this subparagraph, there is hereby imposed a tax on the failure described in subparagraph (B) of such corporation, trust, or association. Such tax shall be paid by the corporation, trust, or association.

"(ii) Tax computed. The amount of the tax imposed by clause (i) shall be the greater of—

"(I) $50,000, or

"(II) the amount determined (pursuant to regulations promulgated by the Secretary) by multiplying the net income generated by the assets described in the schedule specified in subparagraph (B)(ii) for the period specified in clause (iii) by the highest rate of tax specified in section 11.

"(iii) Period. For purposes of clause (ii)(II), the period described in this clause is the period beginning on the first date that the failure to satisfy the requirements of such paragraph (4) occurs as a result of the ownership of such assets and ending on the earlier of the date on which the trust disposes of such assets or the end of the first quarter when there is no longer a failure to satisfy such paragraph (4).

"(iv) Administrative provisions. For purposes of subtitle F, the taxes imposed by this subparagraph shall be treated as excise taxes with respect to which the deficiency procedures of such subtitle apply."

—P.L. 109-135, Sec. 403(d)(4), amended Sec. 243(g) of P.L. 108-357

Prior to amendment, Sec. 243(g) of P.L. 108-357, read as follows:

"(g) Effective dates.

"(1) In general. Except as provided in paragraph (2), the amendments made by this section shall apply to taxable years beginning after December 31, 2000.

"(2) Subsections (c) through (f). The amendments made by subsections (c), (d), (e), and (f) shall apply to taxable years beginning after the date of the enactment of this Act."

—P.L. 109-135, Sec. 412(hh), substituted "paragraph (2), (3), or (4) of subsection (c)" for "subsection (c)(6) or (c)(7) of section 856" in subpara. (g)(5)(A), effective 12/21/2005.

In 2004, P.L. 108-357, Sec. 243(a)(1), deleted para. (c)(7) . . . Sec. 243(a)(2), added subsec. (m) . . . Sec. 243(b), amended subpara. (d)(8)(A), effective for tax. yrs. begin. after 12/31/2000 [as amended by Sec. 403(d)(4) of P.L. 109-135, see above].

Prior to deletion, para. (c)(7) read as follows:

"(7) Straight debt safe harbor in applying paragraph (4). Securities of an issuer which are straight debt (as defined in section 1361(c)(5) without regard to subparagraph (B)(iii) thereof) shall not be taken into account in applying paragraph (4)(B)(iii)(III) if—

"(A) the issuer is an individual, or

"(B) the only securities of such issuer which are held by the trust or a taxable REIT subsidiary of the trust are straight debt (as so defined), or

"(C) the issuer is a partnership and the trust holds at least a 20 percent profits interest in the partnership."

Prior to amendment, subpara. (d)(8)(A) read as follows:

"(A) Limited rental exception. The requirements of this subparagraph are met with respect to any property if at least 90 percent of the leased space of the property is rented to persons other than taxable REIT subsidiaries of such trust and other than persons described in section 856(d)(2)(B). The preceding sentence shall apply only to the extent that the amounts paid to the trust as rents from real property (as defined in paragraph (1) without regard to paragraph (2)(B)) from such property are substantially comparable to such rents made by the other tenants of the trust's property for comparable space."

—P.L. 108-357, Sec. 243(d), amended subpara. (c)(5)(G), effective for transactions entered into after 12/31/2004 [as amended by Sec. 403(d)(4) of P.L. 109-58, see above]

Prior to amendment, subpara. (c)(5)(G) read as follows:

"(G) Treatment of certain hedging instruments. Except to the extent provided by regulations, any—

"(i) payment to a real estate investment trust under an interest rate swap or cap agreement, option, futures contract, forward rate agreement, or any similar financial instrument, entered into by the trust in a transaction to reduce the interest rate risks with respect to any indebtedness incurred or to be incurred by the trust to acquire or carry real estate assets, and

"(ii) gain from the sale or other disposition of any such investment,

shall be treated as income qualifying under paragraph (2)."

—P.L. 108-357, Sec. 243(f)(1), added para. (c)(7) . . . Sec. 243(f)(2), deleted subparas. (c)(6)(A) and (B), redesignated subpara. (c)(6)(C) as (c)(6)(B) and added subpara. (c)(6)(A) . . . Sec. 243(f)(3)(A), added "unless paragraph (5) applies" after "succeeding taxable year" in para. (g)(1) . . . Sec. 243(f)(3)(B), added para. (g)(5), effective as provided in Sec. 243(g)(4) [as amended by Sec. 403(d)(4), P.L. 109-135, see above], which reads as follows:

"(4) Subsection (f).

"(A) The amendment made by paragraph (1) of subsection (f) shall apply to failures with respect to which the requirements of subparagraph (A) or (B) of section 856(c)(7) of the Internal Revenue Code of 1986 (as added by such paragraph) are satisfied after the date of the enactment of this Act.

"(B) The amendment made by paragraph (2) of subsection (f) shall apply to failures with respect to which the requirements of paragraph (6) of section 856(c) of the Internal Revenue Code of 1986 (as amended by such paragraph) are satisfied after the date of the enactment of this Act.

"(C) The amendments made by paragraph (3) of subsection (f) shall apply to failures with respect to which the requirements of paragraph (5) of section 856(g) of the Internal Revenue Code of 1986 (as added by such paragraph) are satisfied after the date of the enactment of this Act.

"(D) The amendment made by paragraph (4) of subsection (f) shall apply to taxable years ending after the date of the enactment of this Act.

"(E) The amendments made by paragraph (5) of subsection (f) shall apply to statements filed after the date of the enactment of this Act."

Prior to deletion, subparas. (c)(6)(A) and (B) read as follows:

"(A) the nature and amount of each item of its gross income described in such paragraphs is set forth in a schedule attached to its income tax return for such taxable year;

"(B) the inclusion of any incorrect information in the schedule referred to in subparagraph (A) is not due to fraud with intent to evade tax; and"

—P.L. 108-357, Sec. 835(b)(4), deleted "The principles of the preceding provisions of this subparagraph shall apply to regular interests in a FASIT." at the end of subpara. (c)(5)(E), effective 1/1/2005. Sec. 835(c)(2) of this Act reads as follows:

"(2) Exception for existing FASITs. Paragraph (1) shall not apply to any FASIT in existence on the date of the enactment of this Act to the extent that regular interests issued by the FASIT before such date continue to remain outstanding in accordance with the original terms of issuance."

In 2000, P.L. 106-554, Sec. 1(a)(7), [which enacted into law Sec. 319(9) of P.L. 106-554] substituted "paragraph (4)(B)(iii)(III)" for "paragraph (4)(B)(ii)(III)" in para. (c)(7) . . . Sec. 1(a)(7), [which enacted into law Sec. 319(10) of P.L. 106-554] substituted "subsection (d)(9)(D)(ii)" for "paragraph (9)(D)(ii)" in subpara. (l)(4)(A), effective 12/21/2000.

In 1999, P.L. 106-170, Sec. 532(c)(2)(H), substituted "section 1221(a)(1)" for "section 1221(1)" in subpara. (c)(2)(D) . . . Sec. 532(c)(2)(I), substituted "section 1221(a)(1)" for "section 1221(1)" in subpara. (c)(3)(C) . . . Sec. 532(c)(2)(J), substituted "section 1221(a)(1)" for "section 1221(1)" in para. (e)(1) . . . Sec. 532(c)(2)(K), substituted "section 1221(a)(1)" for "section 1221(1)" in subpara. (j)(2)(B), effective for any instrument held, acquired, or entered into, any transaction entered into, and supplies held or acquired on or after 12/17/99.

—P.L. 106-170, Sec. 541(a), amended subpara. (c)(4)(B) . . . Sec. 541(b), added para. (c)(7), effective for tax. yrs. begin. after 12/31/2000. For transitional rules see Sec. 546(b) of this Act, which reads as follows:

"(b) Transitional rules related to section 541.

"(1) Existing arrangements.

"(A) In general. Except as otherwise provided in this paragraph, the amendment made by section 541 shall not apply to a real estate investment trust with respect to—

"(i) securities of a corporation held directly or indirectly by such trust on July 12, 1999,

"(ii) securities of a corporation held by an entity on July 12, 1999, if such trust acquires control of such entity pursuant to a written binding contract in effect on such date and at all times thereafter before such acquisition,

"(iii) securities received by such trust (or a successor) in exchange for, or with respect to, securities described in clause (i) or (ii) in a transaction in which gain or loss is not recognized, and

"(iv) securities acquired directly or indirectly by such trust as part of a reorganization (as defined in section 368(a)(1) of the Internal Revenue Code of 1986) with respect to such trust if such securities are described in clause (i), (ii), or (iii) with respect to any other real estate investment trust.

"(B) New trade or business or substantial new assets. Subparagraph (A) shall cease to apply to securities of a corporation as of the first day after July 12, 1999, on which such corporation engages in a substantial new line of business, or acquires any substantial asset, other than—

"(i) pursuant to a binding contract in effect on such date and at all times thereafter before the acquisition of such asset,

"(ii) in a transaction in which gain or loss is not recognized by reason of section 1031 or 1033 of the Internal Revenue Code of 1986, or

"(iii) in a reorganization (as so defined) with another corporation the securities of which are described in paragraph (1)(A) of this subsection.

"(C) Limitation on transition rules. Subparagraph (A) shall cease to apply to securities of a corporation held, acquired, or received, directly or indirectly, by a real estate investment trust as of the first day after July 12, 1999, on which such trust acquires any additional securities of such corporation other than—

"(i) pursuant to a binding contract in effect on July 12, 1999, and at all times thereafter, or

"(ii) in a reorganization (as so defined) with another corporation the securities of which are described in paragraph (1)(A) of this subsection.

"(2) Tax-free conversion. If—

"(A) at the time of an election for a corporation to become a taxable REIT subsidiary, the amendment made by section 541 does not apply to such corporation by reason of paragraph (1), and

"(B) such election first takes effect before January 1, 2004,

such election shall be treated as a reorganization qualifying under section 368(a)(1)(A) of such Code."

2,461

Prior to amendment, subpara. (c)(4)(B) read as follows:

"(B) not more than 25 percent of the value of its total assets is represented by securities (other than those includible under subparagraph (A)) for purposes of this calculation limited in respect of any one issuer to an amount not greater in value than 5 percent of the value of the total assets of the trust and to not more than 10 percent of the outstanding voting securities of such issuer."

—P.L. 106-170, Sec. 542(a), added "or through a taxable REIT subsidiary of such trust" after "receive any income" in clause (d)(7)(C)(i) . . . Sec. 542(b)(1), added paras. (d)(8) and (9) . . . Sec. 542(b)(2), added "except as provided in paragraph (8)" at the beginning of subpara. (d)(2)(B), effective for tax. yrs. begin. after 12/31/2000.

—P.L. 106-170, Sec. 542(b)(3)(A)(i), substituted "fair market values" for "adjusted bases" each place it appeared in para. (d)(1), effective for tax. yrs. begin. after 12/31/2000.

—P.L. 106-170, Sec. 542(b)(3)(B)(i), substituted "value" for "number" in clause (d)(2)(B)(i), effective for amounts received or accrued in tax. yrs. begin. after 12/31/2000, except for amounts paid pursuant to leases in effect on 7/12/99, or pursuant to a binding contract in effect on 7/12/99 and at all times thereafter.

—P.L. 106-170, Sec. 543(a), added subsec. (l) . . . Sec. 543(b), added a sentence at the end of para. (i)(2), effective for tax. yrs. begin. after 12/31/2000.

—P.L. 106-170, Sec. 551(a), added para. (e)(6), effective for tax. yrs. begin. after 12/31/2000.

—P.L. 106-170, Sec. 561(a), added a flush sentence at the end of para. (d)(3), effective for tax. yrs. begin. after 12/31/2000.

In 1997, P.L. 105-34, Sec. 1251(b)(1), added subsec. (k) . . . Sec. 1251(b)(2), added "subject to the provisions of subsection (k)," before "which is not" in para. (a)(6) . . . Sec. 1252(a), deleted subpara. (d)(2)(C) and the last sentence of para. (d)(2) and added a new subpara. (d)(2)(C) . . . Sec. 1252(b), added para. (d)(7) . . . Sec. 1253, amended para. (d)(5) . . . Sec. 1255(a)(1), added "and" at the end of subpara. (c)(3)(I) . . . Sec. 1255(a)(2), deleted paras. (c)(4) and (c)(8) . . . Sec. 1255(a)(3), redesignated paras. (c)(5)-(7) as paras. (c)(4)-(6) . . . Sec. 1255(b)(1), deleted "and such agreement shall be treated as a security for purposes of paragraph (4)(A)" after "under paragraph (2)" in subpara. (c)(5)(G) [as redesignated by Sec. 1255(a)(3) of this Act, see above] . . . Sec. 1257(a)(1), substituted "as of the close of the 3d taxable year following the taxable year in which the trust acquired such property" for "on the date which is 2 years after the date the trust acquired such property" in para. (e)(2) . . . Sec. 1257(a)(2)(A), substituted "extension" for "or more extensions" in para. (e)(3) . . . Sec. 1257(a)(2)(B), substituted "Any such extension shall not extend the grace period beyond the close of the 3d taxable year following the last taxable year in the period under paragraph (2)." for "Any such extension shall not extend the grace period beyond the date which is 6 years after the date such trust acquired such property." in para. (e)(3) . . . Sec. 1257(b), substituted "A real estate investment trust may revoke any such election for a taxable year by filing the revocation (in the manner provided by the Secretary) on or before the due date (including any extension of time) for filing its return of tax under this chapter for the taxable year. If a trust revokes an election for any property, no election may be made by the trust under this paragraph with respect to the property for any subsequent taxable year." for "Any such election shall be irrevocable." in para. (e)(5) . . . Sec. 1257(c), added a flush sentence at the end of para. (e)(4) . . . Sec. 1258, amended subpara. (c)(5)(G) . . . Sec. 1261(a), redesignated para. (j)(4) as para. (j)(5) and added new para. (j)(4) . . . Sec. 1261(b), added "or appreciation in value as of any specified date" before the period at the end of clause (j)(5)(A)(ii) [as redesignated by Sec. 1261(a) of this Act, see above] . . . Sec. 1262, deleted "at all times during the period such corporation was in existence" after "real estate investment trust" in para. (i)(2), effective for tax. yrs. begin. after 8/5/97.

Prior to deletion, subpara. (d)(2)(C) and the last sentence of para. (d)(2) read as follows:

"(C) any amount received or accrued, directly or indirectly, with respect to any real or personal property if the real estate investment trust furnishes or renders services to the tenants of such property, or manages or operates such property, other than through an independent contractor from whom the trust itself does not derive or receive any income.

Subparagraph (C) shall not apply with respect to any amount if such amount would be excluded from unrelated business taxable income under section 512(b)(3) if received by an organization described in section 511(a)(2)."

Prior to amendment, para. (d)(5) read as follows:

"(5) Constructive ownership of stock.

"For purposes of this subsection, the rules prescribed by section 318(a) for determining the ownership of stock shall apply in determining the ownership of stock, assets, or net profits of any person; except that '10 percent' shall be substituted for '50 percent' in subparagraph (C) of section 318(a)(2) and 318(a)(3)."

Prior to deletion para. (c)(4) read as follows:

"(4) less than 30 percent of its gross income is derived from the sale or other disposition of—

"(A) stock or securities held for less than 1 year;

"(B) property in a transaction which is a prohibited transaction; and

"(C) real property (including interests in real property and interests in mortgages on real property) held for less than 4 years other than—

"(i) property compulsorily or involuntarily converted within the meaning of section 1033, and

"(ii) property which is foreclosure property within the definition of section 856(e); and"

Prior to deletion, para. (c)(8) read as follows:

"(8) Treatment of liquidating gains. In the case of the taxable year in which a real estate investment trust is completely liquidated, there shall not be taken into account under paragraph (4) any gain from the sale, exchange, or distribution of any property after the adoption of the plan of complete liquidation."

In 1996, P.L. 104-188, Sec. 1621(b)(5), added sentence at the end of subpara. (c)(6)(E), effective 9/1/97.

—P.L. 104-188, Sec. 1704(t)(35), substituted "section 582(c)(2)" for "section 582(c)(5)" in para (a)(4), effective 8/20/96.

In 1993, P.L. 103-66, Sec. 13149(a), added para. (h)(3), effective for tax. yrs. begin. after 12/31/93.

In 1988, P.L. 100-647, Sec. 1006(p)(1), substituted "debt instrument (within the meaning of section 1275(a)(1)" for "debt instrument" in subclause (c)(6)(D)(i)(I), effective for tax. yrs. begin. after 12/31/86.

—P.L. 100-647, Sec. 1006(p)(2), changed the effective date for changes made by Sec. 662(c) of P.L. 99-514 from "tax. yrs. begin. after 12/31/86" to "tax. yrs. begin. after 12/31/86, but only in the case of obligations acquired after 10/22/86" .

—P.L. 100-647, Sec. 1006(p)(3), added para. (c)(8), effective for tax. yrs. begin. after 12/31/86.

—P.L. 100-647, Sec. 1006(p)(4)(A), added subpara. (c)(6)(G), effective for tax. yrs. end. after 11/10/88.

—P.L. 100-647, Sec. 1006(p)(5), substituted "stock (or certificates of beneficial interests) in" for "stock in" in subclause (c)(6)(D)(ii)(I), effective for tax. yrs. begin. after 12/31/86.

—P.L. 100-647, Sec. 1006(q)(1), amended subpara. (d)(6)(A) . . . Sec. 1006(q)(2), amended subsec. (f), effective for tax. yrs. begin. after 12/31/86, except as provided in Sec. 669(c) of P.L. 99-514 [reproduced below].

Prior to amendment, subpara. (d)(6)(A) read as follows:

"(A) In general. If—

"(i) a real estate investment trust receives or accrues, with respect to real or personal property, amounts from a tenant which derives substantially all of its income with respect to such property from the subleasing of substantially all of such property, and

"(ii) such tenant receives or accrues, directly or indirectly, from subtenants only amounts which are qualified rents,

then the amounts that the trust receives or accrues from the tenant shall not be excluded from the term 'rents from real property' solely by reason of being based on the income or profits of such tenant."

Prior to amendment, subsec. (f) read as follows:

"(f) Interest.

"(1) In general. For purposes of paragraphs (2)(B) and (3)(B) of subsection (c), the term 'interest' does not include any amount received or accrued (directly or indirectly) if the determination of such amount depends (in whole or in part) on the income or profits of any person, except that—

"(A) any amount so received or accrued shall not be excluded from the term 'interest' solely by reason of being based on a fixed percentage or percentages of receipts or sales, and

"(B) any amount so received or accrued with respect to an obligation secured by a mortgage on real property or an interest in real property shall not be excluded from the term 'interest' solely by reason of being based on the income or profits of the debtor from such property, if—

"(i) the debtor derives substantially all of its gross income with respect to such property from the leasing of substantially all of its interests in such property to tenants, and

"(ii) the amounts received or accrued directly or indirectly by the debtor from such tenants are only qualified rents (as defined in subsection (d)(6)(B)).

"(2) Special rule. Where a real estate investment trust receives or accrues any amount which would be excluded from the term 'interest' solely because the debtor of the real estate investment trust receives or accrues any amount the determination of which depends (in whole or in part) on the income or profits of any person, only a proportionate part (determined under regulations prescribed by the Secretary) of the amount received or accrued by the real estate investment trust shall be excluded from the term 'interest'."

—P.L. 100-647, Sec. 1006(t)(11), redesignated subpara. (c)(6)(E)[sic (F)] as (F), deleted subpara. (c)(6)(D) [(E)] added by Sec. 671(b)(1) of P.L. 99-514, and added subpara. (c)(6)(E), effective for tax. yrs. begin. after 12/31/86.

Prior to deletion, subpara. (c)(6)(D) [(E)] , added by Sec. 671(b)(1) read as follows:

"(D) [(E)] A regular or residual interest in a REMIC shall be treated as an interest in real property, and any amount includible in gross income with respect to such an interest shall be treated as interest; except that, if less than 95 percent of the assets of such REMIC are interests in real property (determined as if the taxpayer held such assets), such interest shall be so treated only in the proportion which the assets of the REMIC consist of such interests."

In 1986, P.L. 99-514, Sec. 661(a)(1), amended para. (a)(6) . . . Sec. 661(a)(2), added subsec. (h) . . . Sec. 662(a), added subsec. (i) . . . Sec. 662(b)(1), deleted "and" at the end of subpara. (c)(3)(G), added "and" at the end of subpara. (c)(3)(H), and added subpara. (c)(3)(I) . . . Sec. 662(b)(2), added the last sentence to subpara. (c)(6)(B) . . . Sec. 662(b)(3), redesignated subpara. (c)(6)(D) as subpara. (c)(6)(E) and added new subpara. (c)(6)(D) effective for tax yrs. begin. after 12/31/86.

Prior to amendment, para. (a)(6) read as follows:

"(6) which would not be a personal holding company (as defined in section 542) if all of its adjusted ordinary gross income (as defined in section 543(b)(2)) constituted personal holding company income (as defined in section 543); and"

—P.L. 99-514, Sec. 662(c), added subsec. (j), effective [as provided in Sec. 1006(p)(2) of P.L. 100-647, see above] for tax. yrs. begin. after 12/31/86, but only in the case of obligations acquired after 10/22/86.

—P.L. 99-514, Sec. 663(a), added the last sentence to para. (d)(2) . . . Sec. 663(b)(1), added para. (d)(6), effective for tax. yrs. begin. after 12/31/86.

—P.L. 99-514, Sec. 663(b)(2), amended subsec. (f), effective for tax. yrs. begin. after 12/31/86, except as provided in Sec. 669(c) of this act which reads:

"(c) Retention of existing transitional rule.

"The amendment made by section 663(b)(2) shall not apply with respect to amounts received or accrued pursuant to loans made before May 28, 1976. For purposes of the preceding sentence, a loan is considered to be made before May 28, 1976, if such loan is made pursuant to a binding commitment entered into before May 28, 1976."

Prior to amendment, subsec. (f) read as follows:

"(f) Interest.

"For purposes of paragraphs (2)(B) and (3)(B) of subsection (c), the term interest does not include any amount received or accrued, directly or indirectly, if the determination of such amount depends in whole or in part on the income or profits of any person except that:

"(1) any amount so received or accrued shall not be excluded from the term interest solely by reason of being based on a fixed percentage or percentages of receipts or sales, and

"(2) where a real estate investment trust receives or accrues any amount which would be excluded from the term interest solely because the debtor of the real estate investment trust receives or accrues any amount the determination of which depends in whole or in part on the income or profits of any person, only a proportionate part (determined pursuant to regulations prescribed by the Secretary) of the amount received or accrued by the real estate investment trust from such debtor will be excluded from the term interest.

The provisions of this subsection shall apply only with respect to amounts received or accrued pursuant to loans made after May 27, 1976. For purposes of the preceding sentence, a loan is considered to be made before May 28, 1976, if such loan is made pursuant to a binding commitment entered into before May 28, 1976."

—P.L. 99-514, Sec. 663(b)(3), substituted "paragraphs (4) and (6)" for "paragraph (4)" in subpara. (d)(2)(A), effective for tax. yrs. begin. after 12/31/86.

—P.L. 99-514, Sec. 671(b)(1), added subpara. (c)(6)(D), effective for tax. yrs. begin after 12/31/86.

—P.L. 99-514, Sec. 901(d)(4)(E), substituted "referred to in section 582(c)(5)" for "to which section 585, 586, or 593 applies" in para. (a)(4), effective for tax. yrs. begin. after 12/31/86.

In 1984, P.L. 98-369, Sec. 1001(b)(12), substituted "6 months" for "1 year" each place it appeared in subpara. (c)(4)(A), effective for property acquired after 6/22/84 and before 1/1/88.

In 1978, P.L. 95-600, Sec. 363(a), deleted "and" at the end of subparas. (c)(2)(F) and (c)(3)(F), added "and" at the end of subparas. (c)(2)(G) and (c)(3)(G), added subparas. (c)(2)(H) and (c)(3)(H), amended subpara. (c)(4)(B), effective for tax. yrs. end. after 11/6/78.

Prior to amendment, subpara. (c)(4)(B) read as follows:

"(B) section 1221(1) property (other than foreclosure property); and"

—P.L. 95-600, Sec. 363(c), amended para. (e)(3), effective for extensions granted after 11/6/78, for periods beginning after 12/31/77.

Prior to amendment, para. (e)(3) read as follows:

"(3) Extensions. If the real estate investment trust establishes to the satisfaction of the Secretary that an extension of the grace period is necessary for the orderly liquidation of the trust's interest in such property, the Secretary may extend the grace period for such property. Any such extension shall be for a period of not more than 1 year, and not more than 2 extensions shall be granted with respect to any property."

—P.L. 95-600, Sec. 701(t)(2), added "(other than gain from prohibited transactions)" following "and gain" in subpara. (c)(3)(D), effective 10/4/76.

In 1976, P.L. 94-455, Sec. 1402(b)(1), substituted "9 months" for "6 months" in subpara. (c)(4)(A), as previously amended by the Act, for tax. yrs. begin. in '77.

—P.L. 94-455, Sec. 1402(b)(2), substituted "1 year" for "9 months" in para. (c)(4)(A) for tax. yrs. begin. after '77.

—P.L. 94-455, Sec. 1402(c), provided a transitional rule for certain installment obligations (see note at Code Sec. 1222).

—P.L. 94-455, Sec. 1602(a), added para. (c)(7), effective as provided in Sec. 1608(b) of this act which reads:

"(b) Trust not disqualified in certain cases where income tests not met.

The amendment made by section 1602 shall apply to taxable years of real estate investment trusts beginning after the date of the enactment of this Act. In addition, the amendments made by section 1602 shall apply to a taxable year of a real estate investment trust beginning before the date of the enactment of this Act if, as the result of a determination (as defined in section 859(c) of the Internal Revenue Code of 1954) with respect to such trust occurring after the date of the enactment of this Act, such trust for such taxable years does not meet the requirements of section 856(c)(2) or section 856(c)(3), or of both such sections, of such Code as in effect for such taxable year. In any case, the amendment made by section 1602(a) requiring a schedule to be attached to the income tax return of certain real estate investment trusts shall apply only to taxable years of such trusts beginning after the date of the enactment of this Act. If the amendments made by section 1602 apply to a taxable year ending on or before the date of enactment of this Act, the reference to paragraph (2)(B) in section 857(b)(5) of such Code, as amended, shall be considered to be a reference to paragraph (2)(C) of section 857(b) of such Code, as in effect immediately before the enactment of this Act."

—P.L. 94-455, Sec. 1603(a), deleted para. (a)(4), effective for tax. yrs. of real estate investment trusts begin. after 10/4/76.

Prior to amendment, para. (a)(4) read as follows:

"(4) which does not hold any property (other than foreclosure property, as defined in subsection (e)) primarily for sale to customers in the ordinary course of its trade or business."

Sec. 1608(d)(2) of the Act, provided as follows:

"(2) If, as a result of a determination (as defined in section 859(c) of the Internal Revenue Code of 1954), occurring after the date of enactment of this Act, with respect to the real estate investment trust, such trust does not meet the requirement of section 856(a)(4) of the Internal Revenue Code of 1954 (as in effect before the amendment of such section by this Act) for any taxable year beginning on or before the date of the enactment of this Act, such trust may elect, within 60 days after such determination in the manner provided in regulations prescribed by the Secretary of the Treasury or his delegate, to have the provisions of section 1603 (other than paragraphs (1), (2), (3), and (4) of section 1603(c)) apply with respect to such taxable year. Where the provisions of section 1603 apply to a real estate investment trust with respect to any taxable year beginning on or before the date of the enactment of this Act—

"(A) credit or refund of any overpayment of tax which results from the application of section 1603 to such taxable year shall be made as if on the date of the determination (as defined in section 859(c) of the Internal Revenue Code of 1954) 2 years remained before the expiration of the period of limitation prescribed by section 6511 of such Code on the filing of claim for refund for the taxable year to which the overpayment relates,

"(B) the running of the statute of limitations provided in section 6501 of such Code on the making of assessments, and the bringing of distraint or a proceeding in court for collection, in respect of any deficiency (as defined in section 6211 of such Code) established by such a determination, and all interest, additions to tax, additional amounts, or assessable penalties in respect thereof, shall be suspended for a period of 2 years after the date of such determination, and

"(C) the collection of any deficiency (as defined in section 6211 of such Code) established by such determination and all interest, additions to tax, additional amounts, and assessable penalties in respect thereof shall, except in cases of jeopardy, be stayed until the expiration of 60 days after the date of such determination.

No distraint or proceeding in court shall be begun for the collection of an amount the collection of which is stayed under subparagraph (C) during the period for which the collection of such amount is stayed."

—P.L. 94-455, Sec. 1603(c)(1), substituted "(3) at least 75 percent of its gross income (excluding gross income from prohibited transactions) is derived from—" for "(3) at least 75 percent of its gross income is derived from—" in para. (c)(3), effective for tax. yrs. of real estate investment trusts begin. after 10/4/76.

—P.L. 94-455, Sec. 1603(c)(2), added "which is not property described in section 1221(1)" before the semicolon, in subpara. (c)(2)(D), effective for tax. yrs. of real estate investment trusts begin. after 10/4/76.

—P.L. 94-455, Sec. 1603(c)(3), added "which is not property described in section 1221(1)" before the semicolon in subpara. (c)(3)(C), effective for tax. yrs. of real estate investment trusts begin. after 10/4/76.

—P.L. 94-455, Sec. 1603(c)(4), added the last sentence in para. (e)(1), effective for tax. yrs. of real estate investment trusts begin. after 10/4/76.

—P.L. 94-455, Sec. 1604(a), substituted "95 percent (90 percent for taxable years beginning before January 1, 1980) of its gross (excluding gross income from prohibited transactions)" for "90 percent of its gross income" in para. (c)(2), effective for tax. yrs. of real estate investment trusts begin. after 10/4/76.

—P.L. 94-455, Sec. 1604(b), amended subsec. (d), effective for tax. yrs. of real estate investment trusts begin. after 10/4/76.

Prior to amendment, subsec. (d) read as follows:

"(d) Rents from real property defined.

"For purposes of paragraphs (2) and (3) of subsection (c), the terms 'rents from real property' includes rents from interests in real property but does not include—

"(1) any amount received or accrued, directly or indirectly, with respect to any real property, if the determination of such amount depends in whole or in part on the income or profits derived by any person from such property (except that any amount so received or accrued shall not be excluded from the term 'rents from real property' solely by reason of being based on a fixed percentage or percentages of receipts or sales);

"(2) any amount received or accrued directly or indirectly from any person if the real estate investment trust owns, directly or indirectly—

"(A) in the case of any person which is a corporation, stock of such person possessing 10 percent or more of the total combined voting power of all classes of stock entitled to vote, or 10 percent or more of the total number of shares of all classes of stock of such person; or

"(B) in the case of any person which is not a corporation, an interest of 10 percent or more in the assets or net profits of such person; and

"(3) any amount received or accrued, directly or indirectly, with respect to any real property, if the real estate investment trust furnishes or renders services to the tenants of such property, or manages or operates such property, other than through an independent contractor from whom the trust itself does not derive or receive any income. For purposes of this paragraph, the term 'independent contractor' means—

"(A) a person who does not own, directly or indirectly, more than 35 percent of the shares, or certificates of beneficial interest, in the real estate investment trust, or

"(B) a person, if a corporation, not more than 35 percent of the total combined voting power of whose stock (or 35 percent of the total shares of all classes of whose stock), or, if not a corporation, not more than 35 percent of the interest in whose assets or net profits is owned, directly or indirectly, by one or more persons owning 35 percent or more of the shares or certificates of beneficial interest in the trust.

"For purposes of paragraphs (2) and (3), the rules prescribed by section 318(a) for determining the ownership of stock shall apply in determining the ownership of stock, assets, or net profits of any person; except that '10 percent' shall be substituted for '50 percent' in subparagraph (C) of sections 318(a)(2) and 318(a)(3)."

Code Sec. 856   Real estate investment trusts

—P.L. 94-455, Sec. 1604(c)(1), deleted "and" at the end of subparas. (c)(2)(E) and (c)(3)(E), added "and" at the end of subparas. (c)(2)(F) and (c)(3)(F), added subparas. (c)(2)(G) and (c)(3)(G), effective for tax. yrs. of real estate investment trusts begin. after 10/4/76. Sec. 1608(d)(3) of the Act, provided as follows:

"(3) Section 856(g)(3) of the Internal Revenue Code of 1954, as added by section 1604 of this Act, shall not apply with respect to a termination of an election, filed by a taxpayer under section 856(c)(1) of such Code on or before the date of the enactment of this Act, unless the provisions of part II of subchapter M of chapter 1 of subtitle A of such Code apply to such taxpayer for a taxable year ending after the date of the enactment of this Act for which such election is in effect."

—P.L. 94-455, Sec. 1604(d), amended para. (c)(4), effective for tax. yrs. of real estate investment trusts begin. after 10/4/76.

Prior to amendment, para. (c)(4) read as follows:

"(4) less than 30 percent of its gross income is derived from the sale or other disposition of—

"(A) stock or securities held for less than 6 months; and

"(B) real property (including interest in real property) not compulsorily or involuntarily converted within the meaning of section 1033, held for less than 4 years; and"

—P.L. 94-455, Sec. 1604(e), amended subpara. (c)(6)(C), effective for tax. yrs. of real estate investment trusts begin. after 10/4/76.

Prior to amendment, subpara. (c)(6)(C) read as follows:

"(C) The term 'interests in real property' includes fee ownership and co-ownership of land or improvements thereon and leaseholds of land or improvements thereon, but does not include mineral, oil, or gas royalty interests."

—P.L. 94-455, Sec. 1604(f)(1), amended subsec. (a), for tax. yrs. of real estate investment trusts begin. after 10/4/76.

Prior to amendment subsec. (a) read as follows:

"(a) In general.

"For purposes of this subtitle, the term 'real estate investment trust' means an unincorporated trust or an unincorporated association—

"(1) which is managed by one or more trustees;

"(2) the beneficial ownership of which is evidenced by transferable shares, or by transferable certificates of beneficial interest;

"(3) which (but for the provisions of this part) would be taxable as a domestic corporation;

"(4) which does not hold any property (other than foreclosure property, as defined in subsection (e)) primarily for sale to customers in the ordinary course of its trade or business;

"(5) the beneficial ownership of which is held by 100 or more persons;

"(6) which would not be a personal holding company (as defined in section 542) if all of its adjusted ordinary gross income (as defined in section 543(b)(2)) constituted personal holding company income (as defined in section 543); and

"(7) which meets the requirements of subsection (c)."

—P.L. 94-455, Sec. 1604(f)(2), added new para. (a)(4), effective for tax. yrs. of real estate investment trusts begin. after 10/4/76.

—P.L. 94-455, Sec. 1604(f)(3)(A), substituted "A corporation, trust, or association" for "A trust or association" in subsec. (c), effective for tax. yrs. of real estate investment trusts begin. after 10/4/76.

—P.L. 94-455, Sec. 1604(g), added subsec. (f), effective for tax. yrs. of real estate investment trusts begin. after 10/4/76.

—P.L. 94-455, Sec. 1604(k)(1), added subsec. (g), effective for tax. yrs. of real estate investment trusts begin. after 10/4/76.

—P.L. 94-455, Sec. 1604(k)(2)(A), substituted ", and such election has not been terminated or revoked under subsection (g);" for the semicolon at the end of para. (c)(1), effective for tax. yrs. of real estate investment trusts begin. after 10/4/76.

—P.L. 94-455, Sec. 1901(a)(111), deleted "which began December 31, 1960" in para. (c)(1), added "(15 U.S.C. 80a-1 and following)" after "Investment Company Act of 1940, as amended" in subpara. (c)(6)(D), effective for tax. yrs. begin. after 12/31/76.

—P.L. 94-455, Sec. 1906(b)(13)(A), substituted "Secretary" for "Secretary or his delegate" in paras. (e)(3) and (e)(5), effective for tax. yrs. begin. after 12/31/76.

In 1975, P.L. 93-625, Sec. 6(b), added "(other than foreclosure property, as defined in subsection (e))" after "property" in para. (a)(4) . . . Sec. 6(d)(1), deleted the "and" at the end of subpara. (D), added "and" at the end of subpara. (E), and added new subpara. (F) to both para. (c)(2) and para. (c)(3) . . . Sec. 6(a), added subsec. (e), effective for foreclosure property acquired after 12/31/73. Sec. 6(e) states that, notwithstanding Code Sec. 856(e)(5), any taxpayer required to make an election with respect to foreclosure property sooner than 90 days after the date of enactment of the Act (1/3/75) may make that election at any time before the 91st day after the date of enactment (4/4/75).

In 1964, P.L. 88-272, Sec. 225(k)(4), substituted "adjusted ordinary gross income (as defined in section 543(b)(2))" for "gross income" in para. (a)(6), effective for tax. yrs. begin. after 12/31/63.

—P.L. 88-554, Sec. 5(b)(4), substituted "sections 318(a)(2) and 318(a)(3)" for "section 318(a)(2)" in subsec. (d), effective 8/31/64.

In 1960, P.L. 86-779, Sec. 10(a), added Code Sec. 856, effective for tax. yrs. of real estate investment trusts begin. after '60.

Sec. 857. Taxation of real estate investment trusts and their beneficiaries.

(a) Requirements applicable to real estate investment trusts.

The provisions of this part (other than subsection (d) of this section and subsection (g) of section 856) shall not apply to a real estate investment trust for a taxable year unless—

(1) the deduction for dividends paid during the taxable year (as defined in section 561, but determined without regard to capital gains dividends) equals or exceeds—

(A) the sum of—

(i) 90 percent of the real estate investment trust taxable income for the taxable year (determined without regard to the deduction for dividends paid (as defined in section 561) and by excluding any net capital gain); and

(ii) 90 percent of the excess of the net income from foreclosure property over the tax imposed on such income by subsection (b)(4)(A); minus

(B) any excess noncash income (as determined under subsection (e)); and

(2) either—

(A) the provisions of this part apply to the real estate investment trust for all taxable years beginning after February 28, 1986, or

(B) as of the close of the taxable year, the real estate investment trust has no earnings and profits accumulated in any non-REIT year.

For purposes of the preceding sentence, the term "non-REIT year" means any taxable year to which the provisions of this part did not apply with respect to the entity.

The Secretary may waive the requirements of paragraph (1) for any taxable year if the real estate investment trust establishes to the satisfaction of the Secretary that it was unable to meet such requirements by reason of distributions previously made to meet the requirements of section 4981.

(b) Method of taxation of real estate investment trusts and holders of shares or certificates of beneficial interest.

(1) Imposition of tax on real estate investment trusts. There is hereby imposed for each taxable year on the real estate investment trust taxable income of every real estate investment trust a tax computed as provided in section 11, as though the real estate investment trust taxable income were the taxable income referred to in section 11.

(2) Real estate investment trust taxable income. For purposes of this part, the term "real estate investment trust taxable income" means the taxable income of the real estate investment trust, adjusted as follows:

(A) The deductions for corporations provided in part VIII (except section 248) of subchapter B (section 241 and following, relating to the deduction for dividends received, etc.) shall not be allowed.

(B) The deduction for dividends paid (as defined in section 561) shall be allowed, but shall be computed without regard to that portion of such deduction which is attributable to the amount excluded under subparagraph (D).

(C) The taxable income shall be computed without regard to section 443(b) (relating to computation of tax on change of annual accounting period).

(D) There shall be excluded an amount equal to the net income from foreclosure property.

(E) There shall be deducted an amount equal to the tax imposed by paragraphs (5) and (7) of this subsection,

section 856(c)(7)(C), and section 856(g)(5) for the taxable year.

(F) There shall be excluded an amount equal to any net income derived from prohibited transactions.

(3) Capital gains.

(A) Alternative tax in case of capital gains. If for any taxable year a real estate investment trust has a net capital gain, then, in lieu of the tax imposed by subsection (b)(1), there is hereby imposed a tax (if such tax is less than the tax imposed by such subsection) which shall consist of the sum of—

(i) a tax, computed as provided in subsection (b)(1), on the real estate investment trust taxable income (determined by excluding such net capital gain and by computing the deduction for dividends paid without regard to capital gain dividends), and

(ii) a tax determined at the rates provided in section 1201(a) on the excess of the net capital gain over the deduction for dividends paid (as defined in section 561) determined with reference to capital gains dividends only.

(B) Treatment of capital gain dividends by shareholders. A capital gain dividend shall be treated by the shareholders or holders of beneficial interests as a gain from the sale or exchange of a capital asset held for more than 1 year.

(C) Definition of capital gain dividend. For purposes of this part, a capital gain dividend is any dividend, or part thereof, which is designated by the real estate investment trust as a capital gain dividend in a written notice mailed to its shareholders or holders of beneficial interests at any time before the expiration of 30 days after the close of its taxable year (or mailed to its shareholders or holders of beneficial interests with its annual report for the taxable year); except that, if there is an increase in the excess described in subparagraph (A)(ii) of this paragraph for such year which results from a determination (as defined in section 860(e)), such designation may be made with respect to such increase at any time before the expiration of 120 days after the date of such determination. If the aggregate amount so designated with respect to a taxable year of the trust (including capital gain dividends paid after the close of the taxable year described in section 858) is greater than the net capital gain of the taxable year, the portion of each distribution which shall be a capital gain dividend shall be only that proportion of the amount so designated which such net capital gain bears to the aggregate amount so designated. For purposes of this subparagraph, the amount of the net capital gain for any taxable year which is not a calendar year shall be determined without regard to any net capital loss attributable to transactions after December 31 of such year, and any such net capital loss shall be treated as arising on the 1st day of the next taxable year. To the extent provided in regulations, the preceding sentence shall apply also for purposes of computing the taxable income of the real estate investment trust.

(D) Treatment by shareholders of undistributed capital gains.

(i) Every shareholder of a real estate investment trust at the close of the trust's taxable year shall include, in computing his long-term capital gains in his return for his taxable year in which the last day of the trust's taxable year falls, such amount as the trust shall designate in respect of such shares in a written notice mailed to its shareholders at any time prior to the expiration of 60 days after the close of its taxable year (or mailed to its shareholders or holders of beneficial interests with its annual report for the taxable year), but the amount so includible by any shareholder shall not exceed that part of the amount subjected to tax in subparagraph (A)(ii) which he would have received if all of such amount had been distributed as capital gain dividends by the trust to the holders of such shares at the close of its taxable year.

(ii) For purposes of this title, every such shareholder shall be deemed to have paid, for his taxable year under clause (i), the tax imposed by subparagraph (A)(ii) on the amounts required by this subparagraph to be included in respect of such shares in computing his long-term capital gains for that year; and such shareholders shall be allowed credit or refund as the case may be, for the tax so deemed to have been paid by him.

(iii) The adjusted basis of such shares in the hands of the holder shall be increased with respect to the amounts required by this subparagraph to be included in computing his long-term capital gains, by the difference between the amount of such includible gains and the tax deemed paid by such shareholder in respect of such shares under clause (ii).

(iv) In the event of such designation, the tax imposed by subparagraph (A)(ii) shall be paid by the real estate investment trust within 30 days after the close of its taxable year.

(v) The earnings and profits of such real estate investment trust, and the earnings and profits of any such shareholder which is a corporation, shall be appropriately adjusted in accordance with regulations prescribed by the Secretary.

(vi) As used in this subparagraph, the terms "shares" and "shareholders" shall include beneficial interests and holders of beneficial interests, respectively.

(E) Coordination with net operating loss provisions. For purposes of section 172, if a real estate investment trust pays capital gain dividends during any taxable year, the amount of the net capital gain for such taxable year (to the extent such gain does not exceed the amount of such capital gain dividends) shall be excluded in determining—

(i) the net operating loss for the taxable year, and

(ii) the amount of the net operating loss of any prior taxable year which may be carried through such taxable year under section 172(b)(2) to a succeeding taxable year.

(F) Certain distributions. In the case of a shareholder of a real estate investment trust to whom section 897 does not apply by reason of the second sentence of section 897(h)(1), the amount which would be included in computing long-term capital gains for such shareholder under subparagraph (B) or (D) (without regard to this subparagraph)—

(i) shall not be included in computing such shareholder's long-term capital gains, and

(ii) shall be included in such shareholder's gross income as a dividend from the real estate investment trust.

(4) Income from foreclosure property.

(A) Imposition of tax. A tax is hereby imposed for each taxable year on the net income from foreclosure property of every real estate investment trust. Such tax shall be computed by multiplying the net income from foreclosure property by the highest rate of tax specified in section 11(b).

(B) Net income from foreclosure property. For purposes of this part, the term "net income from foreclosure property" means the excess of—

(i) gain (including any foreign currency gain, as defined in section 988(b)(1)) from the sale or other disposition of foreclosure property described in section 1221(a)(1) and the gross income for the taxable year derived from foreclosure property (as defined in section 856(e)), but only to the extent such gross income is not described in (or, in the case of foreign currency gain, not attributable to gross income described in) section 856(c)(3) other than subparagraph (F) thereof, over

(ii) the deductions allowed by this chapter which are directly connected with the production of the income referred to in clause (i).

(5) **Imposition of tax in case of failure to meet certain requirements.** If section 856(c)(6) applies to a real estate investment trust for any taxable year, there is hereby imposed on such trust a tax in an amount equal to the greater of—

(A) the excess of —

(i) 95 percent of the gross income (excluding gross income from prohibited transactions) of the real estate investment trust, over

(ii) the amount of such gross income which is derived from sources referred to in section 856(c)(2); or

(B) the excess of—

(i) 75 percent of the gross income (excluding gross income from prohibited transactions) of the real estate investment trust, over

(ii) the amount of such gross income which is derived from sources referred to in section 856(c)(3),

multiplied by a fraction the numerator of which is the real estate investment trust taxable income for the taxable year (determined without regard to the deductions provided in paragraphs (2)(B) and (2)(E), without regard to any net operating loss deduction, and by excluding any net capital gain) and the denominator of which is the gross income for the taxable year (excluding gross income from prohibited transactions; gross income and gain from foreclosure property (as defined in section 856(e)), but only to the extent such gross income and gain is not described in subparagraph (A), (B), (C), (D), (E), or (G) of section 856(c)(3)); long-term capital gain; and short-term capital gain to the extent of any short-term capital loss).

(6) **Income from prohibited transactions.**

(A) Imposition of tax. There is hereby imposed for each taxable year of every real estate investment trust a tax equal to 100 percent of the net income derived from prohibited transactions.

(B) Definitions. For purposes of this part—

(i) the term "net income derived from prohibited transactions" means the excess of the gain (including any foreign currency gain, as defined in section 988(b)(1)) from prohibited transactions over the deductions (including any foreign currency loss, as defined in section 988(b)(2)) allowed by this chapter which are directly connected with prohibited transactions;

(ii) in determining the amount of the net income derived from prohibited transactions, there shall not be taken into account any item attributable to any prohibited transaction for which there was a loss; and

(iii) the term "prohibited transaction" means a sale or other disposition of property described in section 1221(a)(1) which is not foreclosure property.

(C) Certain sales not to constitute prohibited transactions. For purposes of this part, the term "prohibited transaction" does not include a sale of property which is real estate asset (as defined in section 856(c)(5)(B)) and which is described in section 1221(a)(1) if—

(i) the trust has held the property for not less than 2 years;

(ii) aggregate expenditures made by the trust, or any partner of the trust, during the 2 year period preceding the date of sale which are includible in the basis of the property do not exceed 30 percent of the net selling price of the property;

(iii) (I) during the taxable year the trust does not make more than 7 sales of property (other than sales of foreclosure property or sales to which section 1033 applies), or (II) the aggregate adjusted bases (as determined for purposes of computing earnings and profits) of property (other than sales of foreclosure property or sales to which section 1033 applies) sold during the taxable year does not exceed 10 percent of the aggregate bases (as so determined) of all of the assets of the trust as of the beginning of the taxable year, or (III) the fair market value of property (other than sales of foreclosure property or sales to which section 1033 applies) sold during the taxable year does not exceed 10 percent of the fair market value of all of the assets of the trust as of the beginning of the taxable year;

(iv) in the case of property, which consists of land or improvements, not acquired through foreclosure (or deed in lieu of foreclosure), or lease termination, the trust has held the property for not less than 2 years for production of rental income; and

(v) if the requirement of clause (iii)(I) is not satisfied, substantially all of the marketing and development expenditures with respect to the property were made through an independent contractor (as defined in section 856(d)(3)) from whom the trust itself does not derive or receive any income.

(D) Certain sales not to constitute prohibited transactions. For purposes of this part, the term "prohibited transaction" does not include a sale of property which is a real estate asset (as defined in section 856(c)(5)(B)) and which is described in section 1221(a)(1) if—

(i) the trust held the property for not less than 2 years in connection with the trade or business of producing timber,

(ii) the aggregate expenditures made by the trust, or a partner of the trust, during the 2 year period preceding the date of sale which—

(I) are includible in the basis of the property (other than timberland acquisition expenditures), and

(II) are directly related to operation of the property for the production of timber or for the preservation of the property for use as timberland,

do not exceed 30 percent of the net selling price of the property,

(iii) the aggregate expenditures made by the trust, or a partner of the trust, during the 2 year period preceding the date of sale which—

(I) are includible in the basis of the property (other than timberland acquisition expenditures), and

(II) are not directly related to operation of the property for the production of timber, or for the preservation of the property for use as timberland, do not exceed 5 percent of the net selling price of the property,

(iv)(I) during the taxable year the trust does not make more than 7 sales of property (other than sales of foreclosure property or sales to which section 1033 applies), or

(II) the aggregate adjusted bases (as determined for purposes of computing earnings and profits) of property (other than sales of foreclosure property or sales to which section 1033 applies) sold during the taxable year does not exceed 10 percent of the aggregate bases (as so determined) of all of the assets of the trust as of the beginning of the taxable year, or

(III) the fair market value of property (other than sales of foreclosure property or sales to which section 1033 applies) sold during the taxable year does not exceed 10 percent of the fair market value of all of the assets of the trust as of the beginning of the taxable year,

(v) in the case that the requirement of clause (iv)(I) is not satisfied, substantially all of the marketing expenditures with respect to the property were made through an independent contractor (as defined in section 856(d)(3)) from whom the trust itself does not derive or receive any income, or, in the case of a sale on or before the termination date, a taxable REIT subsidiary, and

(vi) the sales price of the property sold by the trust is not based in whole or in part on income or profits, including income or profits derived from the sale or operation of such property.

(E) Special rules. In applying subparagraphs (C) and (D) the following special rules apply:

(i) The holding period of property acquired through foreclosure (or deed in lieu of foreclosure), or termination of the lease, includes the period for which the trust held the loan which such property secured, or the lease of such property.

(ii) In the case of a property acquired through foreclosure (or deed in lieu of foreclosure), or termination of a lease, expenditures made by, or for the account of, the mortgagor or lessee after default became imminent will be regarded as made by the trust.

(iii) Expenditures (including expenditures regarded as made directly by the trust, or indirectly by any partner of the trust, under clause (ii)) will not be taken into account if they relate to foreclosure property and did not cause the property to lose its status as foreclosure property.

(iv) Expenditures will not be taken into account if they are made solely to comply with standards or requirements of any government or governmental authority having relevant jurisdiction, or if they are made to restore the property as a result of losses arising from fire, storm or other casualty.

(v) The term "expenditures" does not include advances on a loan made by the trust.

(vi) The sale of more than one property to one buyer as part of one transaction constitutes one sale.

(vii) The term "sale" does not include any transaction in which the net selling price is less than $10,000.

(F) Sales not meeting requirements. In determining whether or not any sale constitutes a "prohibited transaction" for purposes of subparagraph (A), the fact that such sale does not meet the requirements of subparagraph (C) or (D) shall not be taken into account; and such determination, in the case of a sale not meeting such requirements, shall be made as if subparagraphs (C), (D), and (E) had not been enacted.

(G) Sales of property that are not a prohibited transaction. In the case of a sale on or before the termination date, the sale of property which is not a prohibited transaction through the application of subparagraph (D) shall be considered property held for investment or for use in a trade or business and not property described in section 1221(a)(1) for all purposes of this subtitle. For purposes of the preceding sentence, the reference to subparagraph (D) shall be a reference to such subparagraph as in effect on the day before the enactment of the Housing Assistance Tax Act of 2008, as modified by subparagraph (G) as so in effect.

(H) Termination date. For purposes of this paragraph, the term "termination date" has the meaning given such term by section 856(c)(8).

(7) Income from redetermined rents, redetermined deductions, and excess interest.

(A) Imposition of tax. There is hereby imposed for each taxable year of the real estate investment trust a tax equal to 100 percent of redetermined rents, redetermined deductions, and excess interest.

(B) Redetermined rents.

(i) In general. The term "redetermined rents" means rents from real property (as defined in section 856(d)) to the extent the amount of the rents would (but for subparagraph (E)) be reduced on distribution, apportionment, or allocation under section 482 to clearly reflect income as a result of services furnished or rendered by a taxable REIT subsidiary of the real estate investment trust to a tenant of such trust.

(ii) Exception for de minimis amounts. Clause (i) shall not apply to amounts described in section 856(d)(7)(A) with respect to a property to the extent such amounts do not exceed the one percent threshold described in section 856(d)(7)(B) with respect to such property.

(iii) Exception for comparably priced services. Clause (i) shall not apply to any service rendered by a taxable REIT subsidiary of a real estate investment trust to a tenant of such trust if—

(I) such subsidiary renders a significant amount of similar services to persons other than such trust and tenants of such trust who are unrelated (within the meaning of section 856(d)(8)(F)) to such subsidiary, trust, and tenants, but

(II) only to the extent the charge for such service so rendered is substantially comparable to the charge for the similar services rendered to persons referred to in subclause (I).

(iv) Exception for certain separately charged services. Clause (i) shall not apply to any service rendered by a taxable REIT subsidiary of a real estate investment trust to a tenant of such trust if—

(I) the rents paid to the trust by tenants (leasing at least 25 percent of the net leasable space in the trust's property) who are not receiving such service from such subsidiary are substantially comparable to the rents paid by tenants leasing comparable space who are receiving such service from such subsidiary, and

(II) the charge for such service from such subsidiary is separately stated.

(v) Exception for certain services based on subsidiary's income from the services. Clause (i) shall not apply to any service rendered by a taxable REIT subsidiary of a real estate investment trust to a tenant of such trust if the gross income of such subsidiary from such service is not less than 150 percent of such subsidiary's direct cost in furnishing or rendering the service.

(vi) Exceptions granted by Secretary. The Secretary may waive the tax otherwise imposed by subparagraph (A) if the trust establishes to the satisfaction of the Secretary that rents charged to tenants were established on an arms' length basis even though a taxable REIT subsidiary of the trust provided services to such tenants.

(C) Redetermined deductions. The term "redetermined deductions" means deductions (other than redetermined rents) of a taxable REIT subsidiary of a real estate investment trust to the extent the amount of such deductions would (but for subparagraph (E)) be decreased on distribution, apportionment, or allocation under section 482 to clearly reflect income as between such subsidiary and such trust.

(D) Excess interest. The term "excess interest" means any deductions for interest payments by a taxable REIT subsidiary of a real estate investment trust to such trust to the extent that the interest payments are in excess of a rate that is commercially reasonable.

(E) Coordination with section 482. The imposition of tax under subparagraph (A) shall be in lieu of any distribution, apportionment, or allocation under section 482.

(F) Regulatory authority. The Secretary shall prescribe such regulations as may be necessary or appropriate to carry out the purposes of this paragraph. Until the Secretary prescribes such regulations, real estate investment trusts and their taxable REIT subsidiaries may base their allocations on any reasonable method.

(8) Loss on sale or exchange of stock held 6 months or less.

(A) In general. If—

(i) subparagraph (B) or (D) of paragraph (3) provides that any amount with respect to any share or beneficial interest is to be treated as a long-term capital gain, and

(ii) the taxpayer has held such share or interest for 6 months or less,

then any loss on the sale or exchange of such share or interest shall, to the extent of the amount described in clause (i), be treated as a long-term capital loss.

(B) Determination of holding periods. For purposes of this paragraph, in determining the period for which the taxpayer has held any share of stock or beneficial interest—

(i) the rules of paragraphs (3) and (4) of section 246(c) shall apply, and

(ii) there shall not be taken into account any day which is more than 6 months after the date on which such share or interest becomes ex-dividend.

(C) Exception for losses incurred under periodic liquidation plans. To the extent provided in regulations, subparagraph (A) shall not apply to any loss incurred on the sale or exchange of shares of stock of, or beneficial interest in, a real estate investment trust pursuant to a plan which provides for the periodic liquidation of such shares or interests.

(9) Time certain dividends taken into account. For purposes of this title, any dividend declared by a real estate investment trust in October, November, or December of any calendar year and payable to shareholders of record on a specified date in such a month shall be deemed—

(A) to have been received by each shareholder on December 31 of such calendar year, and

(B) to have been paid by such trust on December 31 of such calendar year (or, if earlier, as provided in section 858).

The preceding sentence shall apply only if such dividend is actually paid by the company during January of the following calendar year.

> • *Caution:* Code Sec. 857(c), following, was amended by Sec. 302(d), P.L. 108-27. These provisions generally sunset for tax years beginning after 12/31/2012. For specific sunset provisions see Sec. 303, P.L. 108-27, as amended by Sec. 102(a), P.L. 111-312, reproduced in history notes for this Code Sec.

(c) Restrictions applicable to dividends received from real estate investment trusts.

(1) Section 243. For purposes of section 243 (relating to deductions for dividends received by corporations), a dividend received from a real estate investment trust which meets the requirements of this part shall not be considered a dividend.

(2) Section (1)(h)(11).

(A) In general. In any case in which—

(i) a dividend is received from a real estate investment trust (other than a capital gain dividend), and

(ii) such dividend meets the requirements of section 856(a) for the taxable year during which it paid such dividend,

then, in computing qualified dividend income, there shall be taken into account only that portion of such dividend designated by the real estate investment trust.

(B) Limitation. The aggregate amount which may be designated as qualified dividend income under subparagraph (A) shall not exceed the sum of—

(i) the qualified dividend income of the trust for the taxable year,

(ii) the excess of—

(I) the sum of the real estate investment trust taxable income computed under section 857(b)(2) for the preceding taxable year and the income subject to tax by reason of the application of the regulations under section 337(d) for such preceding taxable year, over

(II) the sum of the taxes imposed on the trust for such preceding taxable year under section 857(b)(1) and by reason of the application of such regulations, and

(iii) the amount of any earnings and profits which were distributed by the trust for such taxable year and accumulated in a taxable year with respect to which this part did not apply.

(C) Notice to shareholders. The amount of any distribution by a real estate investment trust which may be taken into account as qualified dividend income shall not exceed the amount so designated by the trust in a

Real estate investment trusts — Code Sec. 857

written notice to its shareholders mailed not later than 60 days after the close of its taxable year.

(D) Qualified dividend income. For purposes of this paragraph, the term "qualified dividend income" has the meaning given such term by section 1(h)(11)(B).

(d) Earnings and profits.

(1) **In general.** The earnings and profits of a real estate investment trust for any taxable year (but not its accumulated earnings) shall not be reduced by any amount which is not allowable in computing its taxable income for such taxable year. For purposes of this subsection, the term "real estate investment trust" includes a domestic corporation, trust, or association which is a real estate investment trust determined without regard to the requirements of subsection (a).

(2) **Coordination with tax on undistributed income.** A real estate investment trust shall be treated as having sufficient earnings and profits to treat as a dividend any distribution (other than in a redemption to which section 302(a) applies) which is treated as a dividend by such trust. The preceding sentence shall not apply to the extent that the amount distributed during any calendar year by the trust exceeds the required distribution for such calendar year (as determined under section 4981).

(3) **Distributions to meet requirements of subsection (a)(2)(B).** Any distribution which is made in order to comply with the requirements of subsection (a)(2)(B)—

(A) shall be treated for purposes of this subsection and subsection (a)(2)(B) as made from earnings and profits which, but for the distribution, would result in a failure to meet such requirements (and allocated to such earnings on a first-in, first-out basis), and

(B) to the extent treated under subparagraph (A) as made from accumulated earnings and profits, shall not be treated as a distribution for purposes of subsection (b)(2)(B) and section 858.

(e) Excess noncash income.

(1) **In general.** For purposes of subsection (a)(1)(B), the term "excess noncash income" means the excess (if any) of—

(A) the amount determined under paragraph (2) for the taxable year, over

(B) 5 percent of the real estate investment trust taxable income for the taxable year determined without regard to the deduction for dividends paid (as defined in section 561) and by excluding any net capital gain.

(2) **Determination of amount.** The amount determined under this paragraph for the taxable year is the sum of—

(A) the amount (if any) by which—

(i) the amounts includible in gross income under section 467 (relating to certain payments for the use of property or services), exceed

(ii) the amounts which would have been includible in gross income without regard to such section,

(B) any income on the disposition of a real estate asset if—

(i) there is a determination (as defined in section 860(e)) that such income is not eligible for nonrecognition under section 1031, and

(ii) failure to meet the requirements of section 1031 was due to reasonable cause and not to willful neglect,

(C) the amount (if any) by which—

(i) the amounts includible in gross income with respect to instruments to which section 860E(a) or 1272 applies, exceed

(ii) the amount of money and the fair market value of other property received during the taxable year under such instruments, and

(D) amounts includible in income by reason of cancellation of indebtedness.

(f) Real estate investment trusts to ascertain ownership.

(1) **In general.** Each real estate investment trust shall each taxable year comply with regulations prescribed by the Secretary for the purposes of ascertaining the actual ownership of the outstanding shares, or certificates of beneficial interest, of such trust.

(2) **Failure to comply.**

(A) In general. If a real estate investment trust fails to comply with the requirements of paragraph (1) for a taxable year, such trust shall pay (on notice and demand by the Secretary and in the same manner as tax) a penalty of $25,000.

(B) Intentional disregard. If any failure under paragraph (1) is due to intentional disregard of the requirement under paragraph (1), the penalty under subparagraph (A) shall be $50,000.

(C) Failure to comply after notice. The Secretary may require a real estate investment trust to take such actions as the Secretary determines appropriate to ascertain actual ownership if the trust fails to meet the requirements of paragraph (1). If the trust fails to take such actions, the trust shall pay (on notice and demand by the Secretary and in the same manner as tax) an additional penalty equal to the penalty determined under subparagraph (A) or (B), whichever is applicable.

(D) Reasonable cause. No penalty shall be imposed under this paragraph with respect to any failure if it is shown that such failure is due to reasonable cause and not to willful neglect.

(g) Cross reference.

For provisions relating to excise tax based on certain real estate investment trust taxable income not distributed during the taxable year, see section 4981.

In 2010, P.L. 111-312, Sec. 102(a), substituted "December 31, 2012" for "December 31, 2010" in Sec. 303, P.L. 108-27 [see below], effective as if included in the enactment of P.L. 108-27, 5/28/2003.

In 2008, P.L. 110-289, Sec. 3033(a), amended clause (b)(4)(B)(i) . . . Sec. 3033(b), amended clause (b)(6)(B)(i), effective for gains recognized after 7/30/2008.

Prior to amendment, clause (b)(4)(B)(i) read as follows:

"(i) gain from the sale or other disposition of foreclosure property described in section 1221(a)(1) and the gross income for the taxable year derived from foreclosure property (as defined in section 856(e)), but only to the extent such gross income is not described in subparagraph (A), (B), (C), (D), (E), or (G) of section 856(c)(3), over"

Prior to amendment, clause (b)(6)(B)(i) read as follows:

"(i) the term 'net income derived from prohibited transactions' means the excess of the gain from prohibited transactions over the deductions allowed by this chapter which are directly connected with prohibited transactions;"

—P.L. 110-289, Sec. 3051(a)(1), substituted "2 years" for "4 years" in clause (b)(6)(C)(i), (b)(6)(C)(iv), and (b)(6)(D)(i) . . . Sec. 3051(a)(2), substituted "2 year period" for "4-year period" in (b)(6)(C)(ii), (b)(6)(D)(ii), and (b)(6)(D)(iii) . . . Sec. 3051(a)(3), substituted "real estate asset (as defined in section 856(c)(5)(B)) and which is described in section 1221(a)(1) if" for "real estate asset as defined in section 856(c)(5)(B) if—" in subparas. (b)(6)(C) and (b)(6)(D) . . . Sec. 3051(b)(1), deleted subpara. (b)(6)(G) and redesignated subparas. (b)(6)(H) and (I) as (b)(6)(G) and (H) . . . Sec. 3051(b)(2), added "For purposes of the preceding sentence, the reference to subparagraph (D) shall be a reference to such subparagraph as in effect on the day before the enactment of the Housing Assistance Tax Act of 2008, as modified by subparagraph (G) as so in effect." at the end to subpara. (b)(6)(G), as redesignated by Sec. 3051(b)(1) of this Act . . . Sec. 3052(1), substituted ', or (III) the fair market value of property (other than sales of foreclosure property or sales to which section 1033 applies) sold during the taxable year does not exceed 10 percent of the fair market value of all of the assets of the trust as of the beginning of the taxable year;' for ';' in clause (b)(6)(C)(iii) . . . Sec. 3052(2), added 'or' at the end of subclause (b)(6)(D)(iv)(II) and added a new subclause (b)(6)(D)(iv)(III), effective for sales made after 7/30/2008.

Prior to deletion, subpara (b)(6)(G) read as follows:

"(G) Special rules for sales to qualified organizations.

"(i) In general. In the case of the sale of a real estate asset (as defined in section 856(c)(5)(B)) to a qualified organization (as defined in section 170(h)(3)) exclusively for conservation purposes (within the meaning of section 170(h)(1)(C)), subparagraph (D) shall be applied—

"(I) by substituting '2 years' for '4 years' in clause (i), and
"(II) by substituting '2-year period' for '4-year period' in clauses (ii) and (iii).
"(ii) Termination. This subparagraph shall not apply to sales after the termination date."
—P.L. 110-246, Sec. 4, Repeals the duplicative enactment and provides effective date provisions of the Act entitled "An Act to provide for the continuation of agricultural programs through fiscal year 2012, and for other purposes" Sec. 4, P.L. 110-246 reads as follows:

"Sec. 4. Repeal of duplicative enactment.
"(a) In General- The Act entitled 'An Act to provide for the continuation of agricultural programs through fiscal year 2012, and for other purposes' (H.R. 2419 of the 110th Congress), and the amendments made by that Act, are repealed, effective on the date of enactment of that Act.
"(b) Effective Date- Except as otherwise provided in this Act, this Act and the amendments made by this Act shall take effect on the earlier of--
"(1) the date of enactment of this Act; or
"(2) the date of the enactment of the Act entitled 'An Act to provide for the continuation of agricultural programs through fiscal year 2012, and for other purposes' (H.R. 2419 of the 110th Congress)."
—P.L. 110-246, Sec. 15311(c), substituted "rates" for "rate" in clause (b)(3)(A)(ii), effective for tax. yrs. end. after 5/22/2008.
—P.L. 110-246, Sec. 15315(a), added subpara. (b)(6)(G) . . . Sec. 15315(b), added ", or, in the case of a sale on or before the termination date, a taxable REIT subsidiary" after "any income" in clause (b)(6)(D)(v) . . . Sec. 15315(c), added subpara. (b)(6)(H) . . . Sec. 15315(d), added subpara. (b)(6)(I), effective for dispositions in tax. yrs. begin. after 5/22/2008. [Ed. Note: May 22, 2008 was the date of enactment for H.R. 2419 (PL 110-234), which was repealed by (2008 Farm Act § 4(a)) (PL 110-246, 6/18/2008), in connection with the reenactment of the farm bill to correct a technical deficiency in its original passage.]

In **2007**, P.L. 110-172, Sec. 11(a)(17)(B), amended subpara. (b)(8)(B), enacted 12/29/2007.
Prior to amendment, subpara. (b)(8)(B) read as follows:
"(B) Determination of holding period. For purposes of this paragraph, the rules of paragraphs (3) and (4) of section 246(c) shall apply in determining the period for which the taxpayer has held any share of stock or beneficial interest; except that "6 months" shall be substituted for the number of days specified in subparagraph (B) of section 246(c)(3)."

In **2006**, P.L. 109-222, Sec. 102, substituted "December 31, 2010" for "December 31, 2008" in Sec. 303 of P.L. 108-27 [see below], effective 5/17/2006.

In **2005**, P.L. 109-135, Sec. 403(d)(3), substituted "section 856(c)(7)(C), and section 856(g)(5)" for "section 856(c)(7)(B)(iii), and section 856(g)(1). [sic]" in subpara. (b)(2)(E), effective as provided by Sec. 243(g)(4) of P.L. 108-357 [as amended by Sec. 403(d)(4) of this Act, see below].
—P.L. 109-135, Sec. 403(d)(4), amended Sec. 243(g) of P.L. 108-357 [see below].
Prior to amendment, Sec. 243(g) of P.L. 108-357 [see below] read as follows:
"(g) Effective dates.
"(1) In general. Except as provided in paragraph (2), the amendments made by this section shall apply to taxable years beginning after December 31, 2000.
"(2) Subsections (c) through (f). The amendments made by subsections (c), (d), (e), and (f) shall apply to taxable years beginning after the date of the enactment of this Act."
—P.L. 109-135, Sec. 403(p)(2), amended Sec. 418(c) of P.L. 108-357 [see below].
Prior to amendment, Sec. 418(c) of P.L. 108-357 [see below] read as follows:
"(c) Effective date. The amendments made by this section shall apply to taxable years beginning after the date of the enactment of this Act."
—P.L. 109-135, Sec. 412(ii)(1), substituted "subparagraphs (C) and (D)" for "subparagraph (C) or (D)" in subpara. (b)(6)(E) . . . Sec. 412(ii)(2)(A), substituted "subparagraph (C) or (D)" for "subparagraph (C) of this paragraph" in subpara. (b)(6)(F) . . . Sec. 412(ii)(2)(B), substituted "subparagraphs (C), (D), and (E)" for "subparagraphs (C) and (D)" in subpara. (b)(6)(F), effective 12/21/2005.

In **2004**, P.L. 108-357, Sec. 243(c), deleted clause (b)(7)(B)(ii) and redesignated clauses (b)(7)(B)(iii)-(vii) as (b)(7)(B)(ii)-(vi) . . . Sec. 243(e), substituted "95 percent" for "90 percent" in clause (b)(5)(A)(i) . . . Sec. 243(f)(4), substituted "(7) of this subsection, section 856(c)(7)(B)(iii), and section 856(g)(1)." for "(7)" in subpara. (b)(2)(E), effective as provided by Sec. 243(g) of this Act [as amended by Sec. 403(d)(4) of P.L. 109-135, see above], which reads as follows:
"(g) Effective dates.
"(1) Subsections (a) and (b). The amendments made by subsections (a) and (b) shall apply to taxable years beginning after December 31, 2000.
"(2) Subsections (c) and (e). The amendments made by subsections (c) and (e) shall apply to taxable years beginning after the date of the enactment of this Act.
"(3) Subsection (d). The amendment made by subsection (d) shall apply to transactions entered into after December 31, 2004.
"(4) Subsection (f).
"(A) The amendment made by paragraph (1) of subsection (f) shall apply to failures with respect to which the requirements of subparagraph (A) or (B) of section 856(c)(7) of the Internal Revenue Code of 1986 (as added by such paragraph) are satisfied after the date of the enactment of this Act.
"(B) The amendment made by paragraph (2) of subsection (f) shall apply to failures with respect to which the requirements of paragraph (6) of section 856(c) of the Internal Revenue Code of 1986 (as amended by such paragraph) are satisfied after the date of the enactment of this Act.
"(C) The amendments made by paragraph (3) of subsection (f) shall apply to failures with respect to which the requirements of paragraph (5) of section 856(g) of the Internal Revenue Code of 1986 (as added by such paragraph) are satisfied after the date of the enactment of this Act.
"(D) The amendment made by paragraph (4) of subsection (f) shall apply to taxable years ending after the date of the enactment of this Act.
"(E) The amendments made by paragraph (5) of subsection (f) shall apply to statements filed after the date of the enactment of this Act.'
Prior to deletion, clause (b)(7)(B)(ii) read as follows:
"(ii) Exception for certain amounts. Clause (i) shall not apply to amounts received directly or indirectly by a real estate investment trust—
"(I) for services furnished or rendered by a taxable REIT subsidiary that are described in paragraph (1)(B) of section 856(d), or
"(II) from a taxable REIT subsidiary that are described in paragraph (7)(C)(ii) of such section."
—P.L. 108-357, Sec. 321(a), redesignated subparas. (b)(6)(D) and (E) as (b)(6)(E) and (F) and added subpara. (b)(6)(D), effective for tax. yrs. begin. after 10/22/2004.
—P.L. 108-357, Sec. 418(b), added subpara. (b)(3)(F), effective as provided by Sec. 418(c) of this Act [as amended by Sec. 403(p)(2) of P.L. 109-135, see above], which reads as follows:
"(c) Effective date. The amendments made by this section shall apply to—
"(1) any distribution by a real estate investment trust which is treated as a deduction for a taxable year of such trust beginning after the date of the enactment of this Act, and
"(2) any distribution by a real estate investment trust made after such date which is treated as a deduction under section 860 for a taxable year of such trust beginning on or before such date."
—P.L. 108-311, Sec. 402(a)(5)(E), amended para. (c)(2) . . . Sec. 402(a)(6), amended Sec. 302(f)(2) of P.L. 108-27, effective for tax. yrs. begin. after 12/31/2002, except as provided in Sec. 302(f)(2) of P.L. 108-27 [as amended by Sec. 402(a)(6) of P.L. 108-311] which reads as follows:
"(2) Pass-thru entities. In the case of a pass-thru entity described in subparagraph (A), (B), (C), (D), (E), or (F) of section 1(h)(10) of the Internal Revenue Code of 1986, as amended by this Act, the amendments made by this section shall apply to taxable years ending after December 31, 2002; except that dividends received by such an entity on or before such date shall not be treated as qualified dividend income (as defined in section 1(h)(11)(B) of such Code, as added by this Act)."
Prior to amendment, para. (c)(2) read as follows:
"(2) Section 1(h)(11). For purposes of section 1(h)(11) (relating to maximum rate of tax on dividends)—
"(A) rules similar to the rules of subparagraphs (B) and (C) of section 854(b)(1) shall apply to dividends received from a real estate investment trust which meets the requirements of this part, and
"(B) for purposes of such rules, such a trust shall be treated as receiving qualified dividend income during any taxable year in an amount equal to the sum of—
"(i) the excess of the real estate investment trust taxable income computed under section 857(b)(2) for the preceding taxable year over the tax payable by the trust under section 857(b)(1) for such preceding taxable year, and
"(ii) the excess of the income subject to tax by reason of the application of the regulations under section 337(d) for the preceding taxable year over the tax payable by the trust on such income for such preceding taxable year."
Prior to amendment, Sec. 302(f)(2) of P.L. 108-27 read as follows:
"(2) Regulated investment companies and real estate investment trusts. In the case of a regulated investment company or a real estate investment trust, the amendments made by this section shall apply to taxable years ending after December 31, 2002; except that dividends received by such a company or trust on or before such date shall not be treated as qualified dividend income (as defined in section 1(h)(11)(B) of the Internal Revenue Code of 1986, as added by this Act)."
—P.L. 108-311, Sec. 402(a)(5)(F), of this Act, provides:
"(F) With respect to any taxable year of a regulated investment company or real estate investment trust ending on or before November 30, 2003, the period for providing notice of the qualified dividend amount to shareholders under sections 854(b)(2) and 857(c)(2)(C) of the Internal Revenue Code of 1986, as amended by this section, shall not expire before the date on which the statement under section 6042(c) of such Code is required to be furnished with respect to the last calendar year beginning in such taxable year."

In **2003**, P.L. 108-27, Sec. 302(d), amended subsec. (c), effective for tax. yrs. begin. after 12/31/2002, except as provided in Sec. 302(f)(2) of this Act [as amended by Sec. 402(a)(6) of P.L. 108-311, see above], which reads as follows:
"(2) Pass-thru entities. In the case of a pass-thru entity described in subparagraph (A), (B), (C), (D), (E), or (F) of section 1(h)(10) of the Internal Revenue Code of 1986, as amended by this Act, the amendments made by this section shall apply to taxable years ending after December 31, 2002; except that dividends received by such an entity on or before such date shall not be treated as qualified dividend income (as defined in section 1(h)(11)(B) of such Code, as added by this Act)."
Prior to amendment, subsec. (c) read as follows:
"(c) Restrictions applicable to dividends received from real estate investment trusts. For purposes of section 243 (relating to deductions for dividends received by corporations), a dividend received from a real estate investment trust which meets the requirements of this part shall not be considered as a dividend."
—P.L. 108-27, Sec. 303, of this Act [as amended by Sec. 102, P.L. 109-222, and Sec. 102(a), P.L. 111-312, see above], reads as follows:

"SEC. 303. SUNSET OF TITLE. All provisions of, and amendments made by, this title [Secs. 301 and 302] shall not apply to taxable years beginning after December 31, 2012, and the Internal Revenue Code of 1986 shall be applied and administered to such years as if such provisions and amendments had never been enacted."

In 2002, P.L. 107-147, Sec. 413(a)(1), substituted "to the extent the amount of the rents" for "the amount of which" in clause (b)(7)(B)(i) . . . Sec. 413(a)(2), substituted "to the extent the amount" for "if the amount" in subpara. (b)(7)(C), effective for tax. yrs. begin. after 12/31/2000.

—P.L. 107-147, Sec. 417(13), substituted "section 856(d)" for "subsection 856(d)" in clause (b)(7)(B)(i), effective 3/9/2002.

In 2000, P.L. 106-554, Sec. 1(a)(7), [which enacted into law Sec. 311(b) of P.L. 106-554] amended clause (b)(7)(B)(ii), effective for tax. yrs. begin. after 12/31/2000.

Prior to amendment, clause (b)(7)(B)(ii) read as follows:

"(ii) Exception for certain services. Clause (i) shall not apply to amounts received directly or indirectly by a real estate investment trust for services described in paragraph (1)(B) or (7)(C)(i) of section 856(d)."

In 1999, P.L. 106-170, Sec. 532(c)(2)(L), substituted "section 1221(a)(1)" for "section 1221(1)" in clause (b)(4)(B)(i) . . . Sec. 532(c)(2)(M), substituted "section 1221(a)(1)" for "section 1221(1)" in clause (b)(6)(B)(iii), effective for any instrument held, acquired, or entered into, any transaction entered into, and supplies held or acquired on or after 12/17/99.

—P.L. 106-170, Sec. 545(a), redesignated paras. (b)(7) and (8) as (b)(8) and (9), and added para. (b)(7) . . . Sec. 545(b), substituted "paragraphs (5) and (7)" for "paragraph (5)" in subpara. (b)(2)(E), effective for tax. yrs. begin. after 12/31/2000.

—P.L. 106-170, Sec. 556(a), substituted "90 percent" for "95 percent (90 percent for taxable years beginning before January 1, 1980)" in clauses (a)(1)(A)(i) and (ii) . . . Sec. 556(b), substituted "90 percent" for "95 percent (90 percent in the case of taxable years beginning before January 1, 1980)" in clause (b)(5)(A)(i), effective for tax. yrs. begin. after 12/31/2000.

—P.L. 106-170, Sec. 566(a)(2), amended subpara. (d)(3)(A) . . . Sec. 566(b), added "and section 858" at the end of subpara. (d)(3)(B), effective for distributions after 12/31/2000.

Prior to amendment, subpara. (d)(3)(A) read as follows:

"(A) shall be treated for purposes of this subsection and subsection (a)(2)(B) as made from the earliest earnings and profits accumulated in any taxable year to which the provisions of this part did not apply rather than the most recently accumulated earnings and profits, and"

In 1998, P.L. 105-206, Sec. 6012(g), substituted "earliest earnings and profits accumulated in any taxable year to which the provisions of this part did not apply" for "earliest accumulated earnings and profits (other than earnings and profits to which subsection (a)(2)(A) applies)" in subpara. (d)(3)(A), effective for tax. yrs. begin. after 8/5/97.

In 1997, P.L. 105-34, Sec. 1251(a)(1), deleted para. (a)(2) and redesignated para. (a)(3) as para. (a)(2) . . . Sec. 1251(a)(2), redesignated subsec. (f) as subsec. (g) and added new subsec. (f) . . . Sec. 1254(a), redesignated subpara. (b)(3)(D) as subpara. (b)(3)(E) and added new subpara. (b)(3)(D) . . . Sec. 1254(b)(1), substituted "subparagraph (B) or (D)" for "subparagraph (B)" in clause (b)(7)(A)(i) . . . Sec. 1255(b)(2), substituted "section 856(c)(6)" for "section 856(c)(7)" in para. (b)(5) . . . Sec. 1255(b)(3), substituted "section 856(c)(5)(B)" for "section 856(c)(6)(B)" in subpara. (b)(6)(C) . . . Sec. 1256, added para. (d)(3) . . . Sec. 1259(1), deleted subpara. (e)(2)(B) . . . Sec. 1259(2), substituted a comma for the period at the end of subpara. (e)(2)(C) . . . Sec. 1259(3), redesignated subpara. (e)(2)(C) as subpara. (e)(2)(B) . . . Sec. 1259(4), added subparas. (e)(2)(C) and (D) . . . Sec. 1260, substituted "(other than sales of foreclosure property or sales to which section 1033 applies)" for "(other than foreclosure property)" each place it appeared in clause (b)(6)(C)(iii), effective for tax. yrs. begin. after 8/5/97.

Prior to deletion, para. (a)(2) read as follows:

"(2) the real estate investment trust complies for such year with regulations prescribed by the Secretary for the purpose of ascertaining the actual ownership of the outstanding shares, or certificates of beneficial interest, of such trust, and"

Prior to deletion, subpara. (e)(2)(B) read as follows:

"(B) in the case of a real estate investment trust using the cash receipts and disbursements method of accounting, the amount (if any) by which—

"(i) the amounts includible in gross income with respect to instruments to which section 1274 (relating to certain debt instruments issued for property) applies, exceed

"(ii) the amount of money and the fair market value of other property received during the taxable year under such instruments; plus"

In 1990, P.L. 101-508, Sec. 11704(a)(37), added "net" before "capital loss" each place it appeared in Sec. 1018(u)(28) of P.L. 100-647, see below.

In 1988, P.L. 100-647, Sec. 1006(r), substituted "with respect to instruments" for "as original issue discount on instruments" in clause (e)(2)(B)(i) effective for tax. yrs. begin after 12/31/86

—P.L. 100-647, Sec. 1006(s)(2), substituted "the taxable income of the real estate investment trust" for "real estate investment trust taxable income" in the last sentence in subpara. (b)(3)(C) . . . Sec. 1006(s)(4), added a new sentence to the end of subsec. (a), effective for calendar yrs. begin. after 12/31/86.

—P.L. 100-647, Sec. 1006(s)(5)(A), substituted "in October, November, or December" for "in December" in para. (b)(8) . . . Sec. 1006(s)(5)(B), substituted "in such a month" for "in such month" in para. (b)(8) . . . Sec. 1006(s)(5)(C), substituted "on December 31 of such calendar year" for "on such date" in subparas. (b)(8)(A) and (b)(8)(B) . . . Sec. 1006(s)(5)(D), substituted "during January" for "before February 1" in para. (b)(8), effective for dividends declared in 1988 and subsequent calendar yrs.

—P.L. 100-647, Sec. 1018(u)(28), [as amended by Sec. 11704(a)(37) of P.L. 101-508, see above] substituted "such net capital loss shall" for "such net capital loss such" in the second to last sentence of subpara. (b)(3)(C), effective for tax. yrs. begin. after 12/31/86.

In 1986, P.L. 99-514, Sec. 612(b)(7), deleted "section 116 (relating to an exclusion for dividends received by individuals), and" after "For purposes of" from the first sentence of subsec. (c), effective for tax. yrs. begin. after 12/31/86.

—P.L. 99-514, Sec. 661(b), deleted "and" from the end of para. (a)(1), substituted ", and" for the period at the end of para. (a)(2), and added new para. (a)(3), effective for tax. yrs. begin. after 12/31/86.

—P.L. 99-514, Sec. 664(a), amended subpara. (a)(1)(B) . . . Sec. 664(b), redesignated subsec. (e) as subsec. (f) and added new subsec. (e), effective for tax. yrs. begin. after 12/31/86.

Prior to amendment, subpara. (a)(1)(B) read as follows:

"(B) the sum of—

"(i) the amount of any penalty imposed on the real estate investment trust by section 6697 which is paid by such trust during the taxable year; and

"(ii) the net loss derived from prohibited transactions,"

—P.L. 99-514, Sec. 665(a)(1), added subpara. (b)(3)(D) . . . Sec. 665(a)(2), deleted the last sentence of subpara. (b)(3)(C) . . . Sec. 665(b)(1), substituted "the close of its taxable year (or mailed to its shareholders or holders of beneficial interests with its annual report for the taxable year)" for "the close of its taxable year" in subpara. (b)(3)(C), effective for tax. yrs. begin. after 12/31/86.

Prior to deletion, the last sentence of subpara. (b)(3)(C) read as follows:

"For purposes of this subparagraph, the net capital gain shall be deemed not to exceed the real estate investment trust taxable income (determined without regard to the deduction for dividends paid (as defined in section 561) for the taxable year)."

—P.L. 99-514, Sec. 666(a)(1), amended clause (b)(6)(C)(iii) . . . Sec. 666(a)(2), substituted "30 percent" for "20 percent" in clause (b)(6)(C)(ii) . . . Sec. 666(a)(3), deleted "and" at the end of clause (b)(6)(C)(iii), substituted "; and" for the period at the end of clause (b)(6)(C)(iv), and added new clause (b)(6)(C)(v) . . . Sec. 666(b)(1), amended clause (b)(6)(B)(ii) . . . Sec. 666(b)(2), deleted "and there shall be included an amount equal to any net loss derived from prohibited transactions" before the period in subpara. (b)(2)(F), effective for tax. yrs. begin. after 12/31/86.

Prior to amendment, clause (b)(6)(C)(ii) read as follows:

"(ii) the term 'net loss derived from prohibited transactions' means the excess of the deductions allowed by this chapter which are directly connected with prohibited transactions over the gain from prohibited transactions; and"

Prior to amendment, clause (b)(6)(C)(iii) read as follows:

"(iii) during the taxable year the trust does not make more than 5 sales of property (other than foreclosure property); and"

Prior to amendment, clause (b)(6)(B)(ii) read as follows:

—P.L. 99-514, Sec. 668(b)(1)(A), added para. (b)(8) . . . Sec. 668(b)(2), amended subsec. (d) . . . Sec. 668(b)(3), added the last two sentences to subpara. (b)(3)(C), effective for calendar yrs. begin. after 12/31/86.

Prior to amendment, subsec. (d) read as follows:

"(d) Earnings and profits.

"The earnings and profits of a real estate investment trust for any taxable year (but not its accumulated earnings and profits) shall not be reduced by any amount which is not allowable as a deduction in computing its taxable income for such taxable year. For purposes of this subsection, the term 'real estate investment trust' includes a domestic corporation, trust, or association which is a real estate investment trust determined without regard to the requirements of subsection (a)."

In 1984, P.L. 98-369, Sec. 16(a), repealed as if not enacted Sec. 302(c) of P.L. 97-34 which amended subsec. (c) for tax. yrs. begin. after 12/31/84.

—P.L. 98-369, Sec. 55(b), amended para. (b)(7), effective for losses for shares of stock and beneficial interests with respect to which the taxpayer's holding period begins after 7/18/84.

Prior to amendment, para. (b)(7) read as follows:

"(7) Loss on sale or exchange of stock held less than 31 days. If—

"(A) Under subparagraph (B) of paragraph (3) a shareholder of, or a holder of a beneficial interest in, a real estate investment trust is required, with respect to any share or beneficial interest, to treat any amount as a long-term capital gain, and

"(B) such share or interest is held by the taxpayer for less than 31 days,

then any loss on the sale or exchange of such share or interest shall, to the extent of the amount described in subparagraph (A) of this paragraph, be treated as loss from the sale or exchange of a capital asset held for more than 6 months [1 year for property acquired before 6/23/84]. For purposes of this paragraph, the rules of section 246(c)(3) shall apply in determining whether any share of stock or beneficial interest has been held for less than 31 days; except that '30 days' shall be substituted for the number of days specified in subparagraph (B) of section 246(c)(3)."

—P.L. 98-369, Sec. 1001(b)(13), substituted "6 months" for "1 year" each place it appeared in subpara. (b)(3)(B) and para. (b)(7) (before amend. by Sec. 55(b) of this Act), effective for property acquired after 6/22/84 and before 1/1/88.

In 1981, P.L. 97-34, Sec. 302(b)(1), amended the effective date for changes made by Sec. 404(b)(8) of P.L. 96-233 from tax. yrs. begin. after 12/31/80 and before 1/1/83 to tax. yrs. begin. after 12/31/80 and before 1/1/82 [see below].

In 1980, P.L. 96-223, Sec. 404(b)(8), amended subsec. (c), effective [as amended by Sec. 302(b)(1) of P.L. 97-34, see above] for tax. yrs. begin. after 12/31/80 and before 1/1/82.

Prior to amendment, subsec. (c) read as follows:

"(c) Restrictions applicable to dividends received from real estate investment trusts.

For purposes of section 116 (relating to an exclusion for dividends received by individuals) and section 243 (relating to deductions for dividends received by corporations), a dividend received from a real estate investment trust which meets the requirements of this part shall not be considered as a dividend."

—P.L. 96-222, Sec. 103(a)(11)(A), amended Sec. 362(e) of P.L. 95-600, the effective date for changes made by Sec. 362 of P.L. 95-600, by substituting "860(e)" for "860(d)" [see below].

—P.L. 96-222, Sec. 103(a)(1), amended subpara. (b)(4)(A), effective for tax. yrs. begin. after '78.

Prior to amendment, subpara. (b)(4)(A) read as follows:

"(A) Imposition of tax. There is hereby imposed for each taxable year on the net income from foreclosure property of every real estate investment trust a tax determined by applying section 11 to such income as if such income constituted the taxable income of a corporation taxable under section 11. For purposes of the preceding sentence, the surtax exemption shall be zero."

In 1978, P.L. 95-600, Sec. 301(b)(12), amended para. (b)(1), effective for tax. yrs. begin. after 12/31/78.

Prior to amendment, para. (b)(1) read as follows:

"(1) Imposition of normal tax and surtax on real estate investment trusts. There is hereby imposed for each taxable year on the real estate investment trust taxable income of every real estate investment trust a normal tax and surtax computed as provided in section 11, as though the real estate investment trust taxable income were the taxable income referred to in section 11."

—P.L. 95-600, Sec. 362(d)(3), substituted "section 860(e)" for "section 859(c)" in subpara. (b)(3)(C), effective for determinations (as defined in Code Sec. 860(e)) after 11/6/78.

—P.L. 95-600, Sec. 363(b), added subparas. (b)(6)(C), (D) and (E), effective for tax. yrs. ending after 11/6/78.

—P.L. 95-600, Sec. 403(c)(3), substituted "a tax determined at the rate provided in section 1201(a) on" for "a tax of 30 percent of" in clause (b)(3)(A)(ii), effective 11/6/78.

In 1976, P.L. 94-455, Sec. 1402(b)(1)(P), substituted "9 months" for "6 months" in subpara. (b)(3)(B) and para. (b)(5), effective for tax. yrs. begin. in '77.

—P.L. 94-455, Sec. 1402(b)(2), of the Act substituted "1 year" for "9 months" in subpara. (b)(3)(B) and para. (b)(5), effective for tax. yrs. begin. after '77.

—P.L. 94-455, Sec. 1402(c), of the Act provided a transitional rule for certain installment obligations (see note at Code Sec. 1222).

—P.L. 94-455, Sec. 1601(c), added "; except that, if there is an increase in the excess described in subparagraph (A)(ii) of this paragraph for such year which results from a determination (as defined in section 859(c)), such designation may be made with respect to such increase at any time before the expiration of 120 days after the date of such determination" before the period at the end of the first sentence in subpara. (b)(3)(C), for determinations occurring after 10/4/76. Sec. 1608(a) of the Act provided as follows:

"(a) Deficiency dividend procedures.

The amendments made by section 1601 shall apply with respect to determinations (as defined in section 859(c) of the Internal Revenue Code of 1954) occurring after the date of the enactment of this Act. If the amendments made by section 1601 apply to a taxable year ending on or before the date of enactment of this Act—

"(1) the reference to section 857(b)(3)(A)(ii) in sections 857(b)(3)(C) and 859(b)(1)(B) of such Code, as amended, shall be considered to be a reference to section 857(b)(3)(A) of such Code, as in effect immediately before the enactment of this Act, and

"(2) the reference to section 857(b)(2)(B) in section 859(a) of such Code, as amended, shall be considered to be a reference to section 857(b)(2)(C) of such Code, as in effect immediately before the enactment of this Act."

—P.L. 94-455, Sec. 1602(b)(1), redesignated para. (b)(5) as (b)(7), and added new para. (b)(5), effective for tax. yrs. of real estate investment trusts begin. after 10/4/76. For trusts not disqualified in certain cases where income tests aren't met, see Sec. 1608(b) of this Act reproduced in note following Code Sec. 856.

—P.L. 94-455, Sec. 1602(b)(2), added new subpara. (b)(2)(E) following subpara. (b)(2)(D), as redesignated by Sec. 1606(a) of this Act, effective for tax. yrs. of real estate investment trusts begin. after 10/4/76. For trusts not disqualified in certain cases where income tests aren't met, see Sec. 1608(b) of this Act reproduced in note following Code Sec. 856.

—P.L. 94-455, Sec. 1603(b), added new para. (b)(6) following new para. (b)(5), as previously added by the Act, for tax. yrs. of real estate investment trusts begin. after 10/4/76.

—P.L. 94-455, Sec. 1603(c)(5), added new subpara. (b)(2)(F) following subpara. (b)(2)(E), as previously added by the Act, effective for tax. yrs. of real estate investment trusts begin. after 10/4/76.

—P.L. 94-455, Sec. 1604(c)(2), substituted "(D), (E), or (G)" for "(D), or (E)" in clause (b)(4)(B)(i), effective for tax. yrs. of real estate investment trusts begin. after 10/4/76.

—P.L. 94-455, Sec. 1604(f)(3)(B), substituted "a domestic corporation, trust," for "a domestic unincorporated trust" in subsec. (c), for tax. yrs. of real estate investment trusts begin. after 10/4/76.

—P.L. 94-455, Sec. 1604(j), amended para. (a)(1), effective for tax. yrs. of real estate investment trusts begin. after 10/4/76.

Prior to amendment, para. (a)(1) read as follows:

"(1) the deduction for dividends paid during the taxable year (as defined in section 561, but determined without regard to capital gains dividends) equals or exceeds the sum of—

"(A) 90 percent of the real estate investment trust taxable income for the taxable year (determined without regard to the deduction for dividends paid (as defined in section 561)); and

"(B) 90 percent of the excess of (i) the net income from foreclosure property over (ii) the tax imposed on such income by subsection (b)(4)(A), and"

—P.L. 94-455, Sec. 1604(k)(2)(B), substituted "(other than subsection (d) of this section and subsection (g) of section 856)" for "(other than subsection (d) of this section)" in subsec. (a), effective for tax. yrs. of real estate investment trusts begin. after 10/4/76.

—P.L. 94-455, Sec. 1605(b)(2), added subsec. (e), effective for tax. yrs. of real estate investment trusts begin. after 10/4/76.

—P.L. 94-455, Sec. 1606(a), deleted subpara. (b)(2)(E), and redesignated subpara. (b)(2)(F) as (b)(2)(D), effective for tax. yrs. end. after 10/4/76.

Prior to amendment, subpara. (b)(2)(E) read as follows:

"(E) The net operating loss deduction provided in section 172 shall not be allowed."

For alternative tax and net operating loss, see the note for Code Sec. 857(b)(2)(A).

—P.L. 94-455, Sec. 1606(d), substituted "subparagraph (D)" for "subparagraph (F)" in subpara. (b)(2)(B), effective for tax. yrs. end. after 10/4/76. For alternative tax and net operating loss, see Sec. 1608(c), reproduced below.

—P.L. 94-455, Sec. 1607(a), amended subpara. (b)(3)(A), effective for tax. yrs. end. after 10/4/76.

Prior to amendment, subpara. (b)(3)(A) read as follows:

"(A) Imposition of tax. There is hereby imposed for each taxable year in the case of every real estate investment trust a tax, determined as provided in section 1201(a) on the excess, if any, of the net long-term capital gain over the sum of—

"(i) the net short-term capital loss; and

"(ii) the deduction for dividends paid (as defined in section 561) determined with reference to capital gains dividends only."

For alternative and net operating loss, see the note at Code Sec. 857(b)(2)(A).

—P.L. 94-455, Sec. 1607(b)(1)(A), deleted subpara. (b)(2)(A) and redesignated subparas. (b)(2)(B), (C), (D) as subparas. (b)(2)(A), (B) and (C), respectively, effective for tax. yrs. end. after 10/4/76. Sec. 1608(c) of the Act provided as follows:

"(c) Alternative tax and net operating loss.

The amendments made by sections 1606 and 1607 shall apply to taxable years ending after the date of the enactment of this Act, except that in the case of a taxpayer which has a net operating loss (as defined in section 172(c) of the Internal Revenue Code of 1954) for any taxable year ending after the date of enactment of this Act for which the provisions of part II of subchapter M of chapter 1 of subtitle A of such Code apply to such taxpayer, such loss shall not be a net operating loss carryback under section 172 of such Code to any taxable year ending on or before the date of enactment of this Act."

Prior to amendment, subpara. (b)(2)(A) read as follows:

"(A) There shall be excluded the excess, if any, of the net long-term capital gain over the net short-term capital loss."

—P.L. 94-455, Sec. 1607(b)(2), deleted "shall be computed without regard to capital gains dividends and" following "(as defined in section 561) shall be allowed, but" in subpara. (b)(2)(B), as previously redesignated by the Act, for tax. yrs. end. after 10/4/76. For alternative tax and net operating loss, see Sec. 1608(c) of this Act, reproduced above.

—P.L. 94-455, Sec. 1607(b)(3), added a new last sentence, in subpara. (b)(3)(C), as previously amended by the Act, for tax. yrs. end. after 10/4/76. For alternative tax and net operating loss, see Sec. 1608(c) of this Act, reproduced above.

—P.L. 94-455, Sec. 1901(a)(112), deleted the last sentence of subpara. (b)(3)(C), effective for tax. yrs. begin. after 12/31/76.

Prior to amendment, subpara. (b)(3)(C) read as follows:

"(C) Definition of capital gain dividend. For purposes of this part, a capital gain dividend is any dividend, or part thereof, which is designated by the real estate investment trust as a capital gain dividend in a written notice mailed to its shareholders or holders of beneficial interests at any time before the expiration of 30 days after the close of its taxable year. If the aggregate amount so designated with respect to a taxable year of the trust (including capital gain dividends paid after the close of the taxable year described in section 858) is greater than the excess of the net long-term capital gain over the net short-term capital loss of the taxable year, the portion of each distribution which shall be a capital gain dividend shall be only that proportion of the amount so designated which such excess of the net long-term capital gain over the net short-term capital loss bears to the aggregate amount so designated. For purposes of subparagraph (A)(ii), in the case of a taxable year beginning before January 1, 1975, the deduction for dividends paid shall first be made from the amount subject to tax in accordance with section 1201(a)(1)(B), to the extent thereof, and then from the amount subject to tax in accordance with section 1201(a)(1)(A)."

—P.L. 94-455, Sec. 1901(b)(1)(V), deleted the last sentence in para. (b)(1), effective for tax. yrs. begin. after 12/31/76.

Prior to amendment, para. (b)(1) read as follows:

"(1) Imposition of normal tax and surtax on real estate investment trusts. There is hereby imposed for each taxable year on the real estate investment trust taxable income of every real estate investment trust a normal tax and surtax computed as provided in section 11, as though the real estate investment trust taxable income were the taxable income referred to in section 11. For purposes of computing the normal tax under section 11, the taxable income and the dividends paid deduction of such real estate investment trust for the taxable year (computed without regard to capital gains dividends) shall be reduced by the deduction provided by section 242 (relating to partially tax-exempt interest)."

—P.L. 94-455, Sec. 1901(b)(33)(K), substituted "net capital gain" for "excess of the net long-term capital gain over the net short-term capital loss" each time it appeared in subpara. (b)(3)(C), effective for tax. yrs. begin. after 12/31/76.

Real estate investment trusts Code Sec. 859

—94-455, Sec. 1906(b)(13)(A), substituted "Secretary" for "Secretary or his delegate" each place it appeared in Code Sec. 857, effective for tax. yrs. begin. after 12/31/76.

In 1975, P.L. 93-625, Sec. 6(d)(2), amended para. (a)(1).

Prior to amendment, para. (a)(1) read as follows:

"(1) the deduction for dividends paid during the taxable year (as defined in section 561, but without regard to capital gains dividends) equals or exceeds 90 percent of its real estate investment trust taxable income for the taxable year (determined without regard to subsection (b)(2)(c)), and" . . . Sec. 6(d)(3), added new subpara. (b)(2)(F) . . . Sec. 6(d)(4), added "and shall be computed without regard to that portion of such deduction which is attributable to the amount excluded under subparagraph (F)" before the period at the end of subpara. (b)(2)(C) . . . Sec. 6(c), redesignated para. (b)(4) as (b)(5) and added new para. (b)(4), effective with respect to foreclosure property acquired after 12/31/73. Sec. 6(e) states that, notwithstanding the provisions of Code Sec. 856(e)(5), any taxpayer required to make an election with respect to foreclosure property sooner than 90 days after the date of enactment of the Act (1/3/75) may make that election at any time before the 91st day after the date of enactment (4/4/75).

In 1969, P.L. 91-172, Sec. 511(c)(3), substituted ", determined as provided in section 1201(a), on" for "of 25 percent of" in subpara. (b)(3)(A) and added a new sentence to the end of subpara. (b)(3)(C), effective for tax. yrs. begin. after 12/31/69.

In 1964, P.L. 88-272, Sec. 201(d)(11), deleted "section 34(a) (relating to credit for dividends received by individuals)," preceding "section 116" in subsec. (c), effective for dividends received after '64 in tax. yrs. end. after '64.

In 1960, P.L. 86-779, Sec. 10(a), added Code Sec. 857, effective for tax. yrs. of real estate investment trusts begin. after 1960.

Sec. 858. Dividends paid by real estate investment trust after close of taxable year.
(a) General rule.

For purposes of this part, if a real estate investment trust—

(1) declares a dividend before the time prescribed by law for the filing of its return for a taxable year (including the period of any extension of time granted for filing such return), and

(2) distributes the amount of such dividend to shareholders or holders of beneficial interests in the 12-month period following the close of such taxable year and not later than the date of the first regular dividend payment made after such declaration,

the amount so declared and distributed shall, to the extent the trust elects in such return (and specifies in dollar amounts) in accordance with regulations prescribed by the Secretary, be considered as having been paid only during such taxable year, except as provided in subsections (b) and (c).

(b) Receipt by shareholder.

Except as provided in section 857(b)(8), amounts to which subsection (a) applies shall be treated as received by the shareholder or holder of a beneficial interest in the taxable year in which the distribution is made.

(c) Notice to shareholders.

In the case of amounts to which subsection (a) applies, any notice to shareholders or holders of beneficial interests required under this part with respect to such amounts shall be made not later than 30 days after the close of the taxable year in which the distribution is made (or mailed to its shareholders or holders of beneficial interests with its annual report for the taxable year).

In 1988, P.L. 100-647, Sec. 1018(u)(27), amended Sec. 668(b)(1)(B) making a correction to Code Sec. 858 instead of 856, see below

In 1986, P.L. 99-514, Sec. 665(b)(2), added "(or mailed to its shareholders or holders of beneficial interests with its annual report for the taxable year)" after "distribution is made" in subsec. (c), effective for tax. yrs. begin. after 12/31/86.

—P.L. 99-514, Sec. 668(b)(1)(B), [as amended by Sec. 1018(u)(27) of P.L. 100-647, see above] substituted "Except as provided in section 857(b)(8)" for "Amounts", in subsec. (b), effective for calendar yrs. begin. after 12/31/86.

In 1976, P.L. 94-455, Sec. 1604(h), added "(and specifies in dollar amounts)" after "to the extent the trust elects in such return" in subsec. (a), and substituted "paid only during such taxable year" for "paid during such taxable year" in subsec. (a), effective for tax. yrs. of real estate investment trusts begin. after 10/4/76.

—P.L. 94-455, Sec. 1906(b)(13)(A), substituted "Secretary" for "Secretary or his delegate" in para. (a)(2), effective for tax. yrs. begin. after 12/31/76.

In 1960, P.L. 86-779, Sec. 10(a), added Code Sec. 858, effective for tax. yrs. of real estate investment trusts begin. after 1960.

Sec. 859. Adoption of annual accounting period.
(a) General rule.

For purposes of this subtitle—

(1) a real estate investment trust shall not change to any accounting period other than the calendar year, and

(2) a corporation, trust, or association may not elect to be a real estate investment trust for any taxable year beginning after October 4, 1976, unless its accounting period is the calendar year.

Paragraph (2) shall not apply to a corporation, trust, or association which was considered to be a real estate investment trust for any taxable year beginning on or before October 4, 1976.

(b) Change of accounting period without approval.

Notwithstanding section 442, an entity which has not engaged in any active trade or business may change its accounting period to a calendar year without the approval of the Secretary if such change is in connection with an election under section 856(c).

In 1986, P.L. 99-514, Sec. 661(c)(1), added subsec. (b) . . . Sec. 661(c)(2), substituted "(a) General rule. For purposes" for "For purposes" following the heading of Code Sec. 859, effective for tax. yrs. begin. after 12/31/86.

In 1978, P.L. 95-600, Sec. 362(d)(6), redesignated Code Sec. 860 as Code Sec. 859, effective for determinations (as defined in Code Sec. 860(d)) after 11/6/78.

—P.L. 95-600, Sec. 701(t)(1), amended Code Sec. 859, as redesignated by Sec. 362(d)(6) of this Act, effective 10/4/76.

Prior to amendment, Code Sec. 859 read as follows:

"SEC. 859. ADOPTION OF ANNUAL ACCOUNTING PERIOD.

"For purposes of this subtitle, a real estate investment trust shall not change to or adopt any annual accounting period other than the calendar year."

In 1976, P.L. 94-455, Sec. 1604(i)(1), added Code Sec. 860, for tax. yrs. of real estate investment trusts begin. after 10/4/76.

Sec. 859. Repealed.

In 1978, P.L. 95-600, Sec. 362(d)(6), repealed Code Sec. 859, for determinations (as defined in Code Sec. 860(d)) after 11/6/78.

Prior to amendment, Code Sec. 859 read as follows:

"Sec. 859. Deduction for deficiency dividends.

"(a) General rule.

"If a determination (as defined in subsection (c)) with respect to a real estate investment trust results in any adjustment (as defined in subsection (b)(1)) for any taxable year, a deduction shall be allowed to such trust for the amount of deficiency dividends (as defined in subsection (d)) for purposes of determining the deduction for dividends paid (for purposes of section 857) for such year.

"(b) Rules for application of section.

"(1) Adjustment. For purposes of this section, the term 'adjustment' means—

"(A) any increase in the sum of—

"(i) the real estate investment trust taxable income of the real estate investment trust (determined without regard to the deduction for dividends paid (as defined in section 561) and by excluding any net capital gain), and

"(ii) the excess of the net income from foreclosure property (as defined in section 857(b)(4)(B)) over the tax on such income imposed by section 857(b)(4)(A),

"(B) any increase in the amount of the excess described in section 857(b)(3)(A)(ii) (relating to the excess of the net capital gain over the deduction for capital gains dividends paid), and

"(C) any decrease in the deduction for dividends paid (as defined in section 561) determined without regard to capital gains dividends.

"(2) Interest and additions to tax determined with respect to the amount of deficiency dividend deduction allowed. For purposes of determining interest, additions to tax, and additional amounts—

"(A) the tax imposed by this chapter (after taking into account the deduction allowed by subsection (a)) on the real estate investment trust for the taxable year with respect to which the determination is made shall be deemed to be increased by an amount equal to the deduction allowed by subsection (a) with respect to such taxable year,

"(B) the last date prescribed for payment of such increase in tax shall be deemed to have been the last date prescribed for the payment of tax (determined in the manner provided by section 6601(b)) for the taxable year with respect to which the determination was made, and

"(C) such increase in tax shall be deemed to be paid as of the date the claim for the deficiency dividend deduction is filed.

"(3) Credit or refund. If the allowance of a deficiency dividend deduction results in an overpayment of tax for any taxable year, credit or refund with respect to such overpayment shall be made as if on the date of the determination 2 years remained before the expiration of the period of limitations on the filing of claim for refund for the taxable year to which the overpayment relates.

"(c) Determination.

"For purposes of this section, the term 'determination' means—

"(1) a decision by the Tax Court, or a judgment, decree, or other order by any court of competent jurisdiction, which has become final;

"(2) a closing agreement made under section 7121; or

"(3) under regulations prescribed by the Secretary, an agreement signed by the Secretary and by, or on behalf of, the real estate investment trust relating to the liability of such trust for tax.

"(d) Deficiency dividends.

"(1) Definition. For purposes of this section, the term 'deficiency dividends' means a distribution of property made by the real estate investment trust on or after the date of the determination and before filing claim under subsection (e), which would have been includible in the computation of the deduction for dividends paid under section 561 for the taxable year with respect to which the liability for tax resulting from the determination exists, if distributed during such taxable year. No distribution of property shall be considered as deficiency dividends for purposes of subsection (a) unless distributed within 90 days after the determination, and unless a claim for a deficiency dividend deduction with respect to such distribution is filed pursuant to subsection (e).

"(2) Limitations.

"(A) Ordinary dividends. The amount of deficiency dividends (other than deficiency dividends qualifying as capital gain dividends) paid by a real estate investment trust for the taxable year with respect to which the liability for tax resulting from the determination exists shall not exceed the sum of—

"(i) the excess of the amount of increase referred to in subparagraph (A) of subsection (b)(1) over the amount of any increase in the deduction for dividends paid (computed without regard to capital gain dividends) for such taxable year which results from such determination, and

"(ii) the amount of decrease referred to in subparagraph (C) of subsection (b)(1).

"(B) Capital gain dividends. The amount of deficiency dividends qualifying as capital gain dividends paid by a real estate investment trust for the taxable year with respect to which the liability for tax resulting from the determination exists shall not exceed the amount by which (i) the increase referred to in subparagraph (B) of subsection (b)(1) exceeds (ii) the amount of any dividends paid during such taxable year which are designated as capital gain dividends after such determination.

"(3) Effect on dividends paid deduction.

"(A) For taxable year in which paid. Deficiency dividends paid in any taxable year shall not be included in the amount of dividends paid for such year for purposes of computing the dividends paid deduction for such year.

"(B) For prior taxable year. Deficiency dividends paid in any taxable year shall not be allowed for purposes of section 858(a) in the computation of the dividends paid deduction for the taxable year preceding the taxable year in which paid.

"(e) Claim required.

"No deficiency dividend deduction shall be allowed under subsection (a) unless (under regulations prescribed by the Secretary) claim therefor is filed within 120 days after the date of the determination.

"(f) Suspension of statute of limitations and stay of collection.

"(1) Suspension of running of statute. If the real estate investment trust files a claim as provided in subsection (e), the running of the statute of limitations provided in section 6501 on the making of assessments, and the bringing of distraint or a proceeding in court for collection, in respect of the deficiency established by a determination under this section, and all interest, additions to tax, additional amounts, or assessable penalties in respect thereof, shall be suspended for a period of 2 years after the date of the determination.

"(2) Stay of collection. In the case of any deficiency established by a determination under this section—

"(A) The collection of the deficiency, and all interest, additions to tax, additional amounts, and assessable penalties in respect thereof, shall, except in cases of jeopardy, be stayed until the expiration of 120 days after the date of the determination, and

"(B) if claim for a deficiency dividend deduction is filed under subsection (e), the collection of such part of the deficiency as is not reduced by the deduction for deficiency dividends provided in subsection (a) shall be stayed until the date the claim is disallowed (in whole or in part), and if disallowed in part collection shall be made only with respect to the part disallowed.

"No distraint or proceeding in court shall be begun for the collection of an amount the collection of which is stayed under subparagraph (A) or (B) during the period for which the collection of such amount is stayed.

"(g) Deduction denied in case of fraud.

"No deficiency dividend deduction shall be allowed under subsection (a) if the determination contains a finding that any part of any deficiency attributable to an adjustment with respect to the taxable year is due to fraud with intent to evade tax or to willful failure to file an income return within the time prescribed by law or prescribed by the Secretary in pursuance of law.

"(h) Penalty.

"For assessable penalty with respect to liability for tax of real estate investment trust which is allowed a deduction under subsection (a), see section 6697."

—P.L. 95-600, Sec. 701(t)(4), substituted "section 6601(b)" for "section 6601(c)" in subpara. (b)(2)(B), effective 10/4/76.

In 1976, P.L. 94-455, Sec. 1601(a)(1), added Code Sec. 859. Sec. 1608(a) of the Act provided the following effective date.

"(a) Deficiency dividend procedures.

"The amendments made by section 1601 shall apply with respect to determinations (as defined in section 859(c) of the Internal Revenue Code of 1954) occurring after the date of the enactment of this Act [10/4/76]. If the amendments made by section 1601 apply to a taxable year ending on or before the date of enactment of this Act:

"(1) the reference to section 857(b)(3)(A)(ii) in sections 857(b)(3)(C) and 859(b)(1)(B) of such Code, as amended, shall be considered to be a reference to section 857(b)(3)(A) of such Code, as in effect immediately before the enactment of this Act, and

"(2) the reference to section 857(b)(2)(B) in section 859(a) of such Code, as amended, shall be considered to be a reference to section 857(b)(2)(C) of such Code, as in effect immediately before the enactment of this Act."

PART III.—PROVISIONS WHICH APPLY TO BOTH REGULATED INVESTMENT COMPANIES AND REAL ESTATE INVESTMENT TRUSTS

Sec.
860. Deduction for deficiency dividends.

Sec. 860. Deduction for deficiency dividends.

(a) General rule.

If a determination with respect to any qualified investment entity results in any adjustment for any taxable year, a deduction shall be allowed to such entity for the amount of deficiency dividends for purposes of determining the deduction for dividends paid (for purposes of section 852 or 857, whichever applies) for such year.

(b) Qualified investment entity defined.

For purposes of this section, the term "qualified investment entity" means—

(1) a regulated investment company, and

(2) a real estate investment trust.

(c) Rules for application of section.

(1) Interest and additions to tax determined with respect to the amount of deficiency dividend deduction allowed. For purposes of determining interest, additions to tax, and additional amounts—

(A) the tax imposed by this chapter (after taking into account the deduction allowed by subsection (a)) on the qualified investment entity for the taxable year with respect to which the determination is made shall be deemed to be increased by an amount equal to the deduction allowed by subsection (a) with respect to such taxable year,

(B) the last date prescribed for payment of such increase in tax shall be deemed to have been the last date prescribed for the payment of tax (determined in the manner provided by section 6601(b)) for the taxable year with respect to which the determination is made, and

(C) such increase in tax shall be deemed to be paid as of the date the claim for the deficiency dividend deduction is filed.

(2) Credit or refund. If the allowance of a deficiency dividend deduction results in an overpayment of tax for any taxable year, credit or refund with respect to such overpayment shall be made as if on the date of the determination 2 years remained before the expiration of the period of limitations on the filing of claim for refund for the taxable year to which the overpayment relates.

(d) Adjustment.

For purposes of this section—

(1) Adjustment in the case of regulated investment company. In the case of any regulated investment company, the term "adjustment" means—

(A) any increase in the investment company taxable income of the regulated investment company (determined without regard to the deduction for dividends paid (as defined in section 561)),

(B) any increase in the amount of the excess described in section 852(b)(3)(A) (relating to the excess of the net

Real estate investment trusts Code Sec. 860(i)

capital gain over the deduction for capital gain dividends paid), and

(C) any decrease in the deduction for dividends paid (as defined in section 561) determined without regard to capital gains dividends.

(2) Adjustment in the case of real estate investment trust. In the case of any real estate investment trust, the term "adjustment" means—

(A) any increase in the sum of—

(i) the real estate investment trust taxable income of the real estate investment trust (determined without regard to the deduction for dividends paid (as defined in section 561) and by excluding any net capital gain), and

(ii) the excess of the net income from foreclosure property (as defined in section 857(b)(4)(B)) over the tax on such income imposed by section 857(b)(4)(A),

(B) any increase in the amount of the excess described in section 857(b)(3)(A)(ii) (relating to the excess of the net capital gain over the deduction for capital gains dividends paid), and

(C) any decrease in the deduction for dividends paid (as defined in section 561) determined without regard to capital gains dividends.

(e) Determination.

For purposes of this section, the term "determination" means—

(1) a decision by the Tax Court, or a judgment, decree, or other order by any court of competent jurisdiction, which has become final;

(2) a closing agreement made under section 7121;

(3) under regulations prescribed by the Secretary, an agreement signed by the Secretary and by, or on behalf of, the qualified investment entity relating to the liability of such entity for tax; or

(4) a statement by the taxpayer attached to its amendment or supplement to a return of tax for the relevant tax year.

(f) Deficiency dividends.

(1) Definition. For purposes of this section, the term "deficiency dividends" means a distribution of property made by the qualified investment entity on or after the date of the determination and before filing claim under subsection (g), which would have been includible in the computation of the deduction for dividends paid under section 561 for the taxable year with respect to which the liability for tax resulting from the determination exists if distributed during such taxable year. No distribution of property shall be considered as deficiency dividends for purposes of subsection (a) unless distributed within 90 days after the determination, and unless a claim for a deficiency dividend deduction with respect to such distribution is filed pursuant to subsection (g).

(2) Limitations.

(A) Ordinary dividends. The amount of deficiency dividends (other than deficiency dividends qualifying as capital gain dividends) paid by a qualified investment entity for the taxable year with respect to which the liability for tax resulting from the determination exists shall not exceed the sum of—

(i) the excess of the amount of increase referred to in subparagraph (A) of paragraph (1) or (2) of subsection (d) (whichever applies) over the amount of any increase in the deduction for dividends paid (computed without regard to capital gain dividends) for such taxable year which results from such determination, and

(ii) the amount of decreased [decrease] referred to in subparagraph (C) of paragraph (1) or (2) of subsection (d) (whichever applies).

(B) Capital gain dividends. The amount of deficiency dividends qualifying as capital gain dividends paid by a qualified investment entity for the taxable year with respect to which the liability for tax resulting from the determination exists shall not exceed the amount by which (i) the increase referred to in subparagraph (B) of paragraph (1) or (2) of subsection (d) (whichever applies), exceeds (ii) the amount of any dividends paid during such taxable year which are designated or reported (as the case may be) as capital gain dividends after such determination.

(3) Effect on dividends paid deduction.

(A) For taxable year in which paid. Deficiency dividends paid in any taxable year shall not be included in the amount of dividends paid for such year for purposes of computing the dividends paid deduction for such year.

(B) For prior taxable year. Deficiency dividends paid in any taxable year shall not be allowed for purposes of section 855(a) or 858(a) in the computation of the dividends paid deduction for the taxable year preceding the taxable year in which paid.

(g) Claim required.

No deficiency dividend deduction shall be allowed under subsection (a) unless (under regulations prescribed by the Secretary) claim therefore is filed within 120 days after the date of the determination.

(h) Suspension of statute of limitations and stay of collection.

(1) Suspension of running of statute. If the qualified investment entity files a claim as provided in subsection (g), the running of the statute of limitations provided in section 6501 on the making of assessments, and the bringing of distraint or a proceeding in court for collection, in respect of the deficiency established by a determination under this section, and all interest, additions to tax, additional amounts, or assessable penalties in respect thereof, shall be suspended for a period of 2 years after the date of the determination.

(2) Stay of collection. In the case of any deficiency established by a determination under this section—

(A) the collection of the deficiency, and all interest, additions to tax, additional amounts, and assessable penalties in respect thereof, shall, except in cases of jeopardy, be stayed until the expiration of 120 days after the date of the determination, and

(B) if claim for a deficiency dividend deduction is filed under subsection (g), the collection of such part of the deficiency as is not reduced by the deduction for deficiency dividends provided in subsection (a) shall be stayed until the date the claim is disallowed (in whole or in part), and if disallowed in part collection shall be made only with respect to the part disallowed.

No distraint or proceeding in court shall be begun for the collection of an amount the collection of which is stayed under subparagraph (A) or (B) during the period for which the collection of such amount is stayed.

(i) Deduction denied in case of fraud.

No deficiency dividend deduction shall be allowed under subsection (a) if the determination contains a finding that any part of any deficiency attributable to an adjustment with respect to the taxable year is due to fraud with intent to evade tax or to willful failure to file an income tax return

2,475

within the time prescribed by law or prescribed by the Secretary in pursuance of law.

(j)
Repealed.

In 2010, P.L. 111-325, Sec. 301(a)(2), added "or reported (as the case may be)" after "designated", in subpara. (f)(2)(B), effective for tax. yrs. begin. after 12/22/2010.
—P.L. 111-325, Sec. 501(b), repealed subsec. (j), effective for tax. yrs. begin. after 12/22/2010.
Prior to repeal, subsec. (j) read as follow:
"Penalty. For assessable penalty with respect to liability for tax of a regulated investment company which is allowed a deduction under subsection (a), see section 6697."

In 2005, P.L. 109-135, Sec. 403(d)(4), amended Sec. 243(g) of P.L. 108-357, [relating to the effective date of the amendment made by Sec. 243(f)(5), see below] to read as follows:
"(g) Effective dates.
"(1) Subsections (a) and (b). The amendments made by subsections (a) and (b) shall apply to taxable years beginning after December 31, 2000.
"(2) Subsections (c) and (e). The amendments made by subsections (c) and (e) shall apply to taxable years beginning after the date of the enactment of this Act.
"(3) Subsection (d). The amendment made by subsection (d) shall apply to transactions entered into after December 31, 2004.
"(4) Subsection (f).
"(A) The amendment made by paragraph (1) of subsection (f) shall apply to failures with respect to which the requirements of subparagraph (A) or (B) of section 856(c)(7) of the Internal Revenue Code of 1986 (as added by such paragraph) are satisfied after the date of the enactment of this Act.
"(B) The amendment made by paragraph (2) of subsection (f) shall apply to failures with respect to which the requirements of paragraph (6) of section 856(c) of the Internal Revenue Code of 1986 (as amended by such paragraph) are satisfied after the date of the enactment of this Act.
"(C) The amendments made by paragraph (3) of subsection (f) shall apply to failures with respect to which the requirements of paragraph (5) of section 856(g) of the Internal Revenue Code of 1986 (as added by such paragraph) are satisfied after the date of the enactment of this Act.
"(D) The amendment made by paragraph (4) of subsection (f) shall apply to taxable years ending after the date of the enactment of this Act.
"(E) The amendments made by paragraph (5) of subsection (f) shall apply to statements filed after the date of the enactment of this Act."

In 2004, P.L. 108-357, Sec. 243(f)(5), deleted "or" at the end of para. (e)(2), substituted "; or" for the period at the end of para. (e)(3), and added para. (e)(4), effective for statements filed after 10/22/2004 [as provided by Sec. 403(d)(4) of P.L. 109-135, see above].

In 1986, P.L. 99-514, Sec. 667(b)(1), substituted "regulated investment company" for "qualified investment entity" in subsec. (j), effective for tax. yrs. begin. after 12/31/86.

In 1980, P.L. 96-222, Sec. 103(a)(11)(A), amended Sec. 362(e) of P.L. 95-600, the effective date for changes made by Sec. 362 of P.L. 95-600, by substituting "860(e)" for "860(d)" [see below].
—P.L. 96-222, Sec. 103(a)(11)(B), substituted "Deficiency" for "Efficiency" in the heading of subsec. (f), for determinations (as defined in subsec. (e)) after 11/6/78.
—P.L. 96-222, Sec. 103(a)(11)(C), substituted "(computed without regard" for "computed without regard" in clause (f)(2)(A)(i), for determinations (as defined in subsec. (e)) after 11/6/78.

In 1978, P.L. 95-600, Sec. 362(a), added Code Sec. 860, for determinations (as defined in subsec. (e), as amended by Sec. 103(a)(11)(A) of P.L. 96-222, see above) after 11/6/78. For determinations before 11/7/78, see Code Sec. 859 (repealed).

PART IV.—REAL ESTATE MORTGAGE INVESTMENT CONDUITS

Sec.
860A. Taxation of REMIC's.
860B. Taxation of holders of regular interests.
860C. Taxation of residual interests.
860D. REMIC defined.
860E. Treatment of income in excess of daily accruals on residual interests.
860F. Other rules.
860G. Other definitions and special rules.

In 1986, P.L. 99-514, Sec. 671(a), added part IV to Subchapter M of chapter 1.

Sec. 860A. Taxation of REMIC's.
(a) General rule.
Except as otherwise provided in this part, a REMIC shall not be subject to taxation under this subtitle (and shall not be treated as a corporation, partnership, or trust for purposes of this subtitle).
(b) Income taxable to holders.
The income of any REMIC shall be taxable to the holders of interests in such REMIC as provided in this part.

In 1990, P.L. 101-508, Sec. 11832(5), repealed Sec. 675(d) of P.L. 99-514 as added by Sec. 1006(w)(2) of P.L. 100-647 [see below].
Prior to repeal, Sec. 675(d) of P.L. 99-514 read as follows:
"(d) Study.
"The Secretary of the Treasury or his delegate shall conduct a study of the operation of the amendments made by this part and their competitive impact on savings and loan institutions and similar financial institutions. Not later than January 1, 1990, the Secretary shall submit a report of such study to the Committee on Ways and Means of the House of Representatives and the Committee on Finance of the Senate (together with such recommendations as he may deem advisable)."

In 1988, P.L. 100-647, Sec. 1006(t)(20), substituted "this subtitle" for "this chapter" each place it appeared in subsec. (a), effective 1/1/87.
—P.L. 100-647, Sec. 1006(w)(1), amended Sec. 675(a) of P.L. 99-514, the effective date for changes made by Sec. 671(a) of P.L. 99-514, by substituting "the amendments made by this subtitle shall take effect on January 1, 1987" for "the amendments made by this part shall apply to taxable years beginning after December 31, 1986," see below . . . Sec. 1006(w)(2), added Sec. 675(d) of P.L. 99-514 [repealed by Sec. 11832(5) of P.L. 101-508, see above].

In 1986, P.L. 99-514, Sec. 671(a), added Code Sec. 860A as part of Part IV of subchapter M of chapter 1, effective on 1/1/87 [as amended by Sec. 1006(w)(1) of P.L. 100-647, see above]. Sec. 675(d) of this Act [as added by Sec. 1006(w)(2) of P.L. 100-647, see above] provides a study [repealed by Sec. 11832(5) of P.L. 101-508, see above].

Sec. 860B. Taxation of holders of regular interests.
(a) General rule.
In determining the tax under this chapter of any holder of a regular interest in a REMIC, such interest (if not otherwise a debt instrument) shall be treated as a debt instrument.
(b) Holders must use accrual method.
The amounts includible in gross income with respect to any regular interest in a REMIC shall be determined under the accrual method of accounting.
(c) Portion of gain treated as ordinary income.
Gain on the disposition of a regular interest shall be treated as ordinary income to the extent such gain does not exceed the excess (if any) of—
(1) the amount which would have been includible in the gross income of the taxpayer with respect to such interest if the yield on such interest were 110 percent of the applicable Federal rate (as defined in section 1274(d) without regard to paragraph (2) thereof) as of the beginning of the taxpayer's holding period, over
(2) the amount actually includible in gross income with respect to such interest by the taxpayer.
(d) Cross reference.
For special rules in determining inclusion of original issue discount on regular interests, see section 1272(a)(6).

In 1988, P.L. 100-647, Sec. 1006(w)(1), amended Sec. 675(a) of P.L. 99-514, the effective date for changes made by Sec. 671(a), by substituting "the amendments made by this subtitle shall take effect on January 1, 1987" for "the amendments made by this part shall apply to taxable years beginning after December 31, 1986," see below.

In 1986, P.L. 99-514, Sec. 671(a), added Code Sec. 860B, as part of Part IV of Subchapter M of chapter 1, effective on 1/1/87 [as amended by Sec. 1006(w)(1) of P.L. 100-647, see above].

Sec. 860C. Taxation of residual interests.
(a) Pass-thru of income or loss.
(1) **In general.** In determining the tax under this chapter of any holder of a residual interest in a REMIC, such holder shall take into account his daily portion of the taxable income or net loss of such REMIC for each day dur-

ing the taxable year on which such holder held such interest.

(2) Daily portion. The daily portion referred to in paragraph (1) shall be determined—

(A) by allocating to each day in any calendar quarter its ratable portion of the taxable income (or net loss) for such quarter, and

(B) by allocating the amount so allocated to any day among the holders (on such day) of residual interests in proportion to their respective holdings on such day.

(b) Determination of taxable income or net loss.

For purposes of this section—

(1) Taxable income. The taxable income of a REMIC shall be determined under an accrual method of accounting and, except as provided in regulations, in the same manner as in the case of an individual, except that—

(A) regular interests in such REMIC (if not otherwise debt instruments) shall be treated as indebtedness of such REMIC,

(B) market discount on any market discount bond shall be included in gross income for the taxable years to which it is attributable as determined under the rules of section 1276(b)(2) (and sections 1276(a) and 1277 shall not apply),

(C) there shall not be taken into account any item of income, gain, loss, or deduction allocable to a prohibited transaction,

(D) the deductions referred to in section 703(a)(2) (other than any deduction under section 212) shall not be allowed, and

(E) the amount of the net income from foreclosure property (if any) shall be reduced by the amount of the tax imposed by section 860G(c).

(2) Net loss. The net loss of any REMIC is the excess of—

(A) the deductions allowable in computing the taxable income of such REMIC, over

(B) its gross income.

Such amount shall be determined with the modifications set forth in paragraph (1).

(c) Distributions.

Any distribution by a REMIC—

(1) shall not be included in gross income to the extent it does not exceed the adjusted basis of the interest, and

(2) to the extent it exceeds the adjusted basis of the interest, shall be treated as gain from the sale or exchange of such interest.

(d) Basis rules.

(1) Increase in basis. The basis of any person's residual interest in a REMIC shall be increased by the amount of the taxable income of such REMIC taken into account under subsection (a) by such person with respect to such interest.

(2) Decreases in basis. The basis of any person's residual interest in a REMIC shall be decreased (but not below zero) by the sum of the following amounts:

(A) any distributions to such person with respect to such interest, and

(B) any net loss of such REMIC taken into account under subsection (a) by such person with respect to such interest.

(e) Special rules.

(1) Amounts treated as ordinary. Any amount taken into account under subsection (a) by any holder of a residual interest in a REMIC shall be treated as ordinary income or ordinary loss, as the case may be.

(2) Limitation on losses.

(A) In general. The amount of the net loss of any REMIC taken into account by a holder under subsection (a) with respect to any calendar quarter shall not exceed the adjusted basis of such holder's residual interest in such REMIC as of the close of such calendar quarter (determined without regard to the adjustment under subsection (d)(2)(B) for such calendar quarter).

(B) Indefinite carryforward. Any loss disallowed by reason of subparagraph (A) shall be treated as incurred by the REMIC in the succeeding calendar quarter with respect to such holder.

(3) Cross reference. For special treatment of income in excess of daily accruals, see section 860E.

In **1988**, P.L. 100-647, Sec. 1006(t)(1), amended para. (e)(1)...Sec. 1006(t)(8)(C), deleted "and" at the end of subpara. (b)(1)(C), substituted ", and" for the period at the end of subpara. (b)(1)(D), and added subpara. (b)(1)(E),...Sec. 1006(t)(21), substituted "and, except as provided in regulations, in the same manner" for "and in the same manner," in para. (b)(1), effective on 1/1/87.

Prior to amendment, subsec. (e)(1) read as follows:

"(1) Amounts treated as ordinary income. Any amount included in the gross income of any holder of a residual interest in a REMIC by reason of subsection (a) shall be treated as ordinary income."

—P.L. 100-647, Sec. 1006(w)(1), amended Sec. 675(a) of P.L. 99-514, changed the the effective date for amendments made by Sec. 671(a) of P.L. 99-514 from effective for tax yrs. begin after 12/31/86 to effective on 1/1/87.

In **1986**, P.L. 99-514, Sec. 671(a), added Code Sec. 860C, as part of Part IV of Subchapter M of chapter 1, effective 1/1/87 [as amended by Sec. 1006(w)(1) of P.L. 100-647, see above].

Sec. 860D. REMIC defined.

(a) General rule.

For purposes of this title, the terms "real estate mortgage investment conduit" and "REMIC" mean any entity—

(1) to which an election to be treated as a REMIC applies for the taxable year and all prior taxable years,

(2) all of the interests in which are regular interests or residual interests,

(3) which has 1 (and only 1) class of residual interests (and all distributions, if any, with respect to such interests are pro rata),

(4) as of the close of the 3rd month beginning after the startup day and at all times thereafter, substantially all of the assets of which consist of qualified mortgages and permitted investments,

(5) which has a taxable year which is a calendar year, and

(6) with respect to which there are reasonable arrangements designed to ensure that—

(A) residual interests in such entity are not held by disqualified organizations (as defined in section 860E(e)(5)), and

(B) information necessary for the application of section 860E(e) will be made available by the entity.

In the case of a qualified liquidation (as defined in section 860F(a)(4)(A)), paragraph (4) shall not apply during the liquidation period (as defined in section 860F(a)(4)(B)).

(b) Election.

(1) In general. An entity (otherwise meeting the requirements of subsection (a)) may elect to be treated as a REMIC for its 1st taxable year. Such an election shall be made on its return for such 1st taxable year. Except as provided in paragraph (2), such an election shall apply to the taxable year for which made and all subsequent taxable years.

(2) Termination.

(A) In general. If any entity ceases to be a REMIC at any time during the taxable year, such entity shall not be treated as a REMIC for such taxable year or any succeeding taxable year.

(B) **Inadvertent terminations.** If—

(i) an entity ceases to be a REMIC,

(ii) the Secretary determines that such cessation was inadvertent,

(iii) no later than a reasonable time after the discovery of the event resulting in such cessation, steps are taken so that such entity is once more a REMIC, and

(iv) such entity, and each person holding an interest in such entity at any time during the period specified pursuant to this subsection, agrees to make such adjustments (consistent with the treatment of such entity as a REMIC or a C corporation) as may be required by the Secretary with respect to such period,

then, notwithstanding such terminating event, such entity shall be treated as continuing to be a REMIC (or such cessation shall be disregarded for purposes of subparagraph (A)) whichever the Secretary determines to be appropriate.

In 1990, P.L. 101-508, Sec. 11704(a)(8), added a closing parenthesis before the period in the last sentence of subsec. (a), effective 11/5/90.

In 1988, P.L. 100-647, Sec. 1006(t)(2)(A)(i), substituted "3rd month beginning after" for "4th month ending after" in para. (a)(4), effective 1/1/87.

—P.L. 100-647, Sec. 1006(t)(2)(A)(ii), substituted "and at all times thereafter" for "and each quarter ending thereafter" in para. (a)(4), effective 1/1/87.

—P.L. 100-647, Sec. 1006(t)(16)(A), deleted "and" at the end of para. (a)(4), substituted ", and" for the period at the end of para. (a)(5) and added para. (a)(6), effective as provided in Sec. 1006(t)(16)(D)(i) of this Act which reads as follows:

"(D)(i) The amendments made by subparagraph (A) [1006(t)(16)(A)] shall apply in the case of any REMIC where the start-up day (as defined in section 860G(a)(9) of the 1986 Code, as in effect on the day before the date of the enactment of this Act) is after March 31, 1988; except that such amendments shall not apply in the case of a REMIC formed pursuant to a binding written contract in effect on such date."

—P.L. 100-647, Sec. 1006(t)(19), added the last sentence of subsec. (a), effective 1/1/87.

—P.L. 100-647, Sec. 1006(w)(1), amended Sec. 675(a) of P.L. 99-514, the effective date for changes made by Sec. 671(a) of P.L. 99-514, by substituting "the amendments made by this subtitle shall take effect on January 1, 1987" for "the amendments made by this part shall apply to taxable years beginning after December 31, 1986," see below.

In 1986, P.L. 99-514, Sec. 671(a), added Code Sec. 860D as part of Part IV of subchapter M of chapter 1 effective 1/1/87 [as amended by Sec. 1006(w)(1) of P.L. 100-647, see above].

Sec. 860E. Treatment of income in excess of daily accruals on residual interests.

(a) Excess inclusions may not be offset by net operating losses.

(1) In general. The taxable income of any holder of a residual interest in a REMIC for any taxable year shall in no event be less than the excess inclusion for such taxable year.

(2) Special rule for affiliated groups. All members of an affiliated group filing a consolidated return shall be treated as 1 taxpayer for purposes of this subsection.

(3) Coordination with section 172. Any excess inclusion for any taxable year shall not be taken into account—

(A) in determining under section 172 the amount of any net operating loss for such taxable year, and

(B) in determining taxable income for such taxable year for purposes of the 2nd sentence of section 172(b)(2).

(4) Coordination with minimum tax. For purposes of part IV of subchapter A of this chapter—

(A) the reference in section 55(b)(2) to taxable income shall be treated as a reference to taxable income determined without regard to this subsection,

(B) the alternative minimum taxable income of any holder of a residual interest in a REMIC for any taxable year shall in no event be less than the excess inclusion for such taxable year, and

(C) any excess inclusion shall be disregarded for purposes of computing the alternative tax net operating loss deduction.

(b) Organizations subject to unrelated business tax.

If the holder of any residual interest in a REMIC is an organization subject to the tax imposed by section 511, the excess inclusion of such holder for any taxable year shall be treated as unrelated business taxable income of such holder for purposes of section 511.

(c) Excess inclusion.

For purposes of this section—

(1) In general. The term "excess inclusion" means, with respect to any residual interest in a REMIC for any calendar quarter, the excess (if any) of—

(A) the amount taken into account with respect to such interest by the holder under section 860C(a), over

(B) the sum of the daily accruals with respect to such interest for days during such calendar quarter while held by such holder.

To the extent provided in regulations, if residual interests in a REMIC do not have significant value, the excess inclusions with respect to such interests shall be the amount determined under subparagraph (A) without regard to subparagraph (B).

(2) Determination of daily accruals.

(A) **In general.** For purposes of this subsection, the daily accrual with respect to any residual interest for any day in any calendar quarter shall be determined by allocating to each day in such quarter its ratable portion of the product of—

(i) the adjusted issue price of such interest at the beginning of such quarter, and

(ii) 120 percent of the long-term Federal rate (determined on the basis of compounding at the close of each calendar quarter and properly adjusted for the length of such quarter).

(B) **Adjusted issue price.** For purposes of this paragraph, the adjusted issue price of any residual interest at the beginning of any calendar quarter is the issue price of the residual interest (adjusted for contributions)—

(i) increased by the amount of daily accruals for prior quarters, and

(ii) decreased (but not below zero) by any distribution made with respect to such interest before the beginning of such quarter.

(C) **Federal long-term rate.** For purposes of this paragraph, the term "Federal long-term rate" means the Federal long-term rate which would have applied to the residual interest under section 1274(d) (determined without regard to paragraph (2) thereof) if it were a debt instrument.

(d) Treatment of residual interests held by real estate investment trusts.

If a residual interest in a REMIC is held by a real estate investment trust, under regulations prescribed by the Secretary—

(1) any excess of—

(A) the aggregate excess inclusions determined with respect to such interests, over

(B) the real estate investment trust taxable income (within the meaning of section 857(b)(2), excluding any net capital gain),

shall be allocated among the shareholders of such trust in proportion to the dividends received by such shareholders from such trust, and

Real estate mortgage investment conduits — Code Sec. 860E

(2) any amount allocated to a shareholder under paragraph (1) shall be treated as an excess inclusion with respect to a residual interest held by such shareholder.

Rules similar to the rules of the preceding sentence shall apply also in the case of regulated investment companies, common trust funds, and organizations to which part I of subchapter T applies.

(e) Tax on transfers of residual interests to certain organizations, etc.

(1) In general. A tax is hereby imposed on any transfer of a residual interest in a REMIC to a disqualified organization.

(2) Amount of tax. The amount of the tax imposed by paragraph (1) on any transfer of a residual interest shall be equal to the product of—

(A) the amount (determined under regulations) equal to the present value of the total anticipated excess inclusions with respect to such interest for periods after such transfer, multiplied by

(B) the highest rate of tax specified in section 11(b)(1).

(3) Liability. The tax imposed by paragraph (1) on any transfer shall be paid by the transferor; except that, where such transfer is through an agent for a disqualified organization, such tax shall be paid by such agent.

(4) Transferee furnishes affidavit. The person (otherwise liable for any tax imposed by paragraph (1)) shall be relieved of liability for the tax imposed by paragraph (1) with respect to any transfer if—

(A) the transferee furnishes to such person an affidavit that the transferee is not a disqualified organization, and

(B) as of the time of the transfer, such person does not have actual knowledge that such affidavit is false.

(5) Disqualified organization. For purposes of this section, the term "disqualified organization" means—

(A) the United States, any State or political subdivision thereof, any foreign government, any international organization, or any agency or instrumentality of any of the foregoing,

(B) any organization (other than a cooperative described in section 521) which is exempt from tax imposed by this chapter unless such organization is subject to the tax imposed by section 511, and

(C) any organization described in section 1381(a)(2)(C).

For purposes of subparagraph (A), the rules of section 168(h)(2)(D) (relating to treatment of certain taxable instrumentalities) shall apply; except that, in the case of the Federal Home Loan Mortgage Corporation, clause (ii) of such section shall not apply.

(6) Treatment of pass-thru entities.

(A) Imposition of tax. If, at any time during any taxable year of a pass-thru entity, a disqualified organization is the record holder of an interest in such entity, there is hereby imposed on such entity for such taxable year a tax equal to the product of—

(i) the amount of excess inclusions for such taxable year allocable to the interest held by such disqualified organization, multiplied by

(ii) the highest rate of tax specified in section 11(b)(1).

(B) Pass-thru entity. For purposes of this paragraph, the term "pass-thru entity" means—

(i) any regulated investment company, real estate investment trust, or common trust fund,

(ii) any partnership, trust, or estate, and

(iii) any organization to which part I of subchapter T applies.

Except as provided in regulations, a person holding an interest in a pass-thru entity as a nominee for another person shall, with respect to such interest, be treated as a pass-thru entity.

(C) Tax to be deductible. Any tax imposed by this paragraph with respect to any excess inclusion of any pass-thru entity for any taxable year shall, for purposes of this title (other than this subsection), be applied against (and operate to reduce) the amount included in gross income with respect to the residual interest involved.

(D) Exception where holder furnishes affidavit. No tax shall be imposed by subparagraph (A) with respect to any interest in a pass-thru entity for any period if—

(i) the record holder of such interest furnishes to such pass-thru entity an affidavit that such record holder is not a disqualified organization, and

(ii) during such period, the pass-thru entity does not have actual knowledge that such affidavit is false.

(7) Waiver. The Secretary may waive the tax imposed by paragraph (1) on any transfer if—

(A) within a reasonable time after discovery that the transfer was subject to tax under paragraph (1), steps are taken so that the interest is no longer held by the disqualified organization, and

(B) there is paid to the Secretary such amounts as the Secretary may require.

(8) Administrative provisions. For purposes of subtitle F, the taxes imposed by this subsection shall be treated as excise taxes with respect to which the deficiency procedures of such subtitle apply.

(f) Treatment of variable insurance contracts.

Except as provided in regulations, with respect to any variable contract (as defined in section 817), there shall be no adjustment in the reserve to the extent of any excess inclusion.

In 1996, P.L. 104-188, Sec. 1616(b)(10)(A), substituted "The" for "Except as provided in paragraph (2), the" in para. (a)(1) . . . Sec. 1616(b)(10)(B), repealed paras. (a)(2) and (a)(4) and redesignated paras. (a)(3), (a)(5), and (a)(6) [as added by Sec. 1704(h)(1) of this Act, see below] as paras. (a)(2)-(4) . . . Sec. 1616(b)(10)(C), substituted a period for ", except that paragraph (2) shall be applied separately with respect to each corporation which is a member of such group and to which section 593 applies." in para. (a)(2) [as redesignated by Sec. 1616(b)(10)(B), see above] . . . Sec. 1616(b)(10)(D), deleted "The preceding sentence shall not apply to any organization to which section 593 applies, except to the extent provided in regulations prescribed by the Secretary under paragraph (2)." at the end of para. (a)(4) [as added by Sec. 1704(h)(1) of this Act, see below, and redesignated by Sec. 1616(b)(10)(B), see above], effective for tax. yrs. begin. after 12/31/95. Sec. 1616(c)(4) of this Act provides:

"(4) Subsection (b)(10). The amendments made by subsection (b)(10) shall not apply to any residual interest held by a taxpayer if such interest has been held by such taxpayer at all times after October 31, 1995."

Prior to deletion, para. (a)(2) read as follows:

"(2) Exception for certain financial institutions. Paragraph (1) shall not apply to any organization to which section 593 applies. The Secretary may by regulations provide that the preceding sentence shall not apply where necessary or appropriate to prevent avoidance of tax imposed by this chapter."

Prior to deletion, para. (a)(4) read as follows:

"(4) Treatment of certain subsidiaries.

"(A) In general. For purposes of this subsection, a corporation to which section 593 applies and each qualified subsidiary of such corporation shall be treated as a single corporation to which section 593 applies.

"(B) Qualified subsidiary. For purposes of this subsection, the term 'qualified subsidiary' means any corporation—

"(i) all the stock of which, and substantially all the indebtedness of which, is held directly by the corporation to which section 593 applies, and

"(ii) which is organized and operated exclusively in connection with the organization and operation of 1 or more REMIC's."

—P.L. 104-188, Sec. 1704(h)(1), added para. (a)(6), effective 1/1/87, unless the taxpayer elects to apply this amendment only to tax. yrs. begin. after 8/20/96.

In 1988, P.L. 100-647, Sec. 1006(t)(13), substituted "issue price of the residual interest" for "issue price of residual interest" in subpara. (c)(2)(B), . . . Sec. 1006(t)(15), added paras. (a)(3) and (a)(4), effective on 1/1/87.

—P.L. 100-647, Sec. 1006(t)(16)(B), added subsec. (e), effective as provided in Secs. 1006(t)(16)(D)(ii)-(iv) of this Act, which read as follows:

2,479

"(ii) The amendments made by subparagraphs (B) and (C) (except to the extent they relate to paragraph (6) of section 860E(e) of the 1986 Code as added by such amendments) shall apply to transfers after March 31, 1988; except that such amendments shall not apply to any transfer pursuant to a binding written contract in effect on such date.

"(iii) Except as provided in clause (iv), the amendments made by subparagraph (B) and (C) (to the extent they relate to paragraph (6) of section 860E(e) of the 1986 Code as so added) shall apply to excess inclusions for periods after March 31, 1988 but only to the extent such inclusions are—

"(I) allocable to an interest in a pass-thru entity acquired after March 31, 1988, or

"(II) allocable to an interest in a pass-thru entity acquired on or before March 31, 1988, but attributable to a residual interest acquired by the pass-thru entity after March 31, 1988.

For purposes of the preceding sentence, any interest in a pass-thru entity (or residual interest) acquired after March 31, 1988, pursuant to a binding written contract in effect on such date shall be treated as acquired before such date.

"(iv) In the case of any real estate investment trust, regulated investment company, common trust fund, or publicly traded partnership, no tax shall be imposed under section 860E(e)(6) of the 1986 Code (as added by the amendment made by subparagraph (B)) for any taxable year beginning before January 1, 1989."

—P.L. 100-647, Sec. 1006(t)(17)(A), added "(adjusted for contributions)" after "the residual interest" the second place it appeared in subpara. (c)(2)(B) . . . Sec. 1006(f)(17)(B), substituted "decreased (but not below zero) by" for "decreased by" in clause (c)(2)(B)(ii) . . . Sec. 1006(t)(23), added the last sentence to subsec. (d) . . . Sec. 1006(t)(26), added subsec. (f) . . . Sec. 1006(t)(27), added para. (a)(5), effective on 1/1/87.

—P.L. 100-647, Sec. 1006(w)(1), amended Sec. 675(a) of P.L. 99-514, the effective date for changes made by Sec. 671(a) of P.L. 99-514, by substituting "the amendments made by this subtitle shall take effect on January 1, 1987" for "the amendments made by this part shall apply to taxable years beginning after December 31, 1986," see below.

In 1986, P.L. 99-514, Sec. 671(a), added Code Sec. 860E, as part of Part IV of Subchapter M of chapter 1, effective on 1/1/87 [as amended by Sec. 1006(w)(1) of P.L. 100-647, see above].

Sec. 860F. Other rules.

(a) 100 percent tax on prohibited transactions.

(1) Tax imposed. There is hereby imposed for each taxable year of a REMIC a tax equal to 100 percent of the net income derived from prohibited transactions.

(2) Prohibited transaction. For purposes of this part, the term "prohibited transaction" means—

(A) Disposition of qualified mortgage. The disposition of any qualified mortgage transferred to the REMIC other than a disposition pursuant to—

(i) the substitution of a qualified replacement mortgage for a qualified mortgage (or the repurchase in lieu of substitution of a defective obligation),

(ii) a disposition incident to the foreclosure, default, or imminent default of the mortgage,

(iii) the bankruptcy or insolvency of the REMIC, or

(iv) a qualified liquidation.

(B) Income from nonpermitted assets. The receipt of any income attributable to any asset which is neither a qualified mortgage nor a permitted investment.

(C) Compensation for services. The receipt by the REMIC of any amount representing a fee or other compensation for services.

(D) Gain from disposition of cash flow investments. Gain from the disposition of any cash flow investment other than pursuant to any qualified liquidation.

(3) Determination of net income. For purposes of paragraph (1), the term "net income derived from prohibited transactions" means the excess of the gross income from prohibited transactions over the deductions allowed by this chapter which are directly connected with such transactions; except that there shall not be taken into account any item attributable to any prohibited transaction for which there was a loss.

(4) Qualified liquidation. For purposes of this part—

(A) In general. The term "qualified liquidation" means a transaction in which—

(i) the REMIC adopts a plan of complete liquidation,

(ii) such REMIC sells all its assets (other than cash) within the liquidation period, and

(iii) all proceeds of the liquidation (plus the cash), less assets retained to meet claims, are credited or distributed to holders of regular or residual interests on or before the last day of the liquidation period.

(B) Liquidation period. The term "liquidation period" means the period—

(i) beginning on the date of the adoption of the plan of liquidation, and

(ii) ending at the close of the 90th day after such date.

(5) Exceptions. Notwithstanding subparagraphs (A) and (D) of paragraph (2), the term "prohibited transaction" shall not include any disposition—

(A) required to prevent default on a regular interest where the threatened default resulted from a default on 1 or more qualified mortgages, or

(B) to facilitate a clean-up call (as defined in regulations).

(b) Treatment of transfers to the REMIC.

(1) Treatment of transferor.

(A) Nonrecognition gain or loss. No gain or loss shall be recognized to the transferor on the transfer of any property to a REMIC in exchange for regular or residual interests in such REMIC.

(B) Adjusted bases of interests. The adjusted bases of the regular and residual interests received in a transfer described in subparagraph (A) shall be equal to the aggregate adjusted bases of the property transferred in such transfer. Such amount shall be allocated among such interests in proportion to their respective fair market values.

(C) Treatment of nonrecognized gain. If the issue price of any regular or residual interest exceeds its adjusted basis as determined under subparagraph (B), for periods during which such interest is held by the transferor (or by any other person whose basis is determined in whole or in part by reference to the basis of such interest in the hand of the transferor)—

(i) in the case of a regular interest, such excess shall be included in gross income (as determined under rules similar to rules of section 1276(b)), and

(ii) in the case of a residual interest, such excess shall be included in gross income ratably over the anticipated period during which the REMIC will be in existence.

(D) Treatment of nonrecognized loss. If the adjusted basis of any regular or residual interest received in a transfer described in subparagraph (A) exceeds its issue price, for periods during which such interest is held by the transferor (or by any other person whose basis is determined in whole or in part by reference to the basis of such interest in the hand of the transferor)—

(i) in the case of a regular interest, such excess shall be allowable as a deduction under rules similar to the rules of section 171, and

(ii) in the case of a residual interest, such excess shall be allowable as a deduction ratably over the anticipated period during which the REMIC will be in existence.

(2) Basis to REMIC. The basis of any property received by a REMIC in a transfer described in paragraph (1)(A) shall be its fair market value immediately after such transfer.

Real estate mortgage investment conduits

(c) Distributions of property.

If a REMIC makes a distribution of property with respect to any regular or residual interest—

(1) notwithstanding any other provision of this subtitle, gain shall be recognized to such REMIC on the distribution in the same manner as if it had sold such property to the distributee at its fair market value, and

(2) the basis of the distributee in such property shall be its fair market value.

(d) Coordination with wash sale rules.

For purposes of section 1091—

(1) any residual interest in a REMIC shall be treated as a security, and

(2) in applying such section to any loss claimed to have been sustained on the sale or other disposition of a residual interest in a REMIC—

(A) except as provided in regulations, any residual interest in any REMIC and any interest in a taxable mortgage pool (as defined in section 7701(i)) comparable to a residual interest in a REMIC shall be treated as substantially identical stock or securities, and

(B) subsections (a) and (e) of such section shall be applied by substituting "6 months" for "30 days" each place it appears.

(e) Treatment under subtitle F.

For purposes of subtitle F, a REMIC shall be treated as a partnership (and holders of residual interests in such REMIC shall be treated as partners). Any return required by reason of the preceding sentence shall include the amount of the daily accruals determined under section 860E(c). Such return shall be filed by the REMIC. The determination of who may sign such return shall be made without regard to the first sentence of this subsection.

In 1996, P.L. 104-188, Sec. 1704(t)(74), substituted "paragraph (2)" for "paragraph (1)" in para. (a)(5), effective 8/20/96.

In 1988, P.L. 100-647, Sec. 1006(t)(3)(A), amended clause (a)(2)(A)(i) . . . Sec. 1006(t)(3)(B)(i), deleted the last sentence of subpara. (a)(2)(A) . . . Sec. 1006(t)(3)(B)(ii), added para. (a)(5) . . . Sec. 1006(t)(3)(C), deleted "described in subsection (b)" before the period at the end of subpara. (a)(2)(D) . . . Sec. 1006(t)(4), substituted "the transfer of any property to a REMIC in exchange for regular or residual interests in such REMIC" for "the transfer of any property to a REMIC" in subpara. (b)(1)(A) . . . Sec. 1006(t)(14), substituted "the REMIC" for "the real estate mortgage pool" in clause (b)(1)(D)(ii), effective on 1/1/87. Prior to amendment clause (a)(2)(A)(i) read as follows:

"(i) the substitution of a qualified replacement mortgage for a qualified mortgage,"

Prior to deletion the last sentence of para. (a)(2)(A) read as follows:

"Notwithstanding the preceding sentence, the term 'prohibited transaction' shall not include any disposition required to prevent default on a regular interest where the threatened default resulted from a default on 1 or more qualified mortgages."

—P.L. 100-647, Sec. 1006(t)(18)(A), added the last two sentences of subsec. (e), effective as provided in Sec. 1006(t)(18)(B) of this Act, which reads as follows:

"(B) Unless the REMIC otherwise elects, the amendment made by subparagraph (A) [Sec. 1006(t)(18)(A)] shall not apply to any REMIC where the start-up day (as defined in section 860G(a)(9) of the 1986 Code as in effect on the day before the date of the enactment of this Act) is before the date of the enactment of this Act [11/10/88]."

—P.L. 100-647, Sec. 1006(t)(22)(B)-(E), substituted "REMIC" for "real estate mortgage pool" in clause (a)(2)(A)(iii), subpara. (a)(2)(C) and clauses (b)(1)(C)(ii) and (b)(1)(D)(ii) [same amendment by Sec. 1006(t)(14) of this Act, above], effective on 1/1/87.

—P.L. 100-647, Sec. 1006(w)(1), amended Sec. 675(a) of P.L. 99-514, the effective date for changes made by Sec. 671(a) of P.L. 99-514, by substituting "the amendments made by this subtitle shall take effect on January 1, 1987" for "the amendments made by this part shall apply to taxable years beginning after December 31, 1986," see below.

In 1986, P.L. 99-514, Sec. 671(a), added Code Sec. 860F as part of Part IV of subchapter M of chapter 1, effective on 1/1/87 [as amended by Sec. 1006(w)(1) of P.L. 100-647 see above].

Sec. 860G. Other definitions and special rules.

(a) Definitions.

For purposes of this part—

(1) Regular interest. The term "regular interest" means any interest in a REMIC which is issued on the startup day with fixed terms and which is designated as a regular interest if—

(A) such interest unconditionally entitles the holder to receive a specified principal amount (or other similar amount), and

(B) interest payments (or other similar amount), if any, with respect to such interest at or before maturity—

(i) are payable based on a fixed rate (or to the extent provided in regulations, at a variable rate), or

(ii) consist of a specified portion of the interest payments on qualified mortgages and such portion does not vary during the period such interest is outstanding.

The interest shall not fail to meet the requirements of subparagraph (A) merely because the timing (but not the amount) of the principal payments (or other similar amounts) may be contingent on the extent of prepayments on qualified mortgages and the amount of income from permitted investments. An interest shall not fail to qualify as a regular interest solely because the specified principal amount of the regular interest (or the amount of interest accrued on the regular interest) can be reduced as a result of the nonoccurrence of 1 or more contingent payments with respect to any reverse mortgage loan held by the REMIC if, on the startup day for the REMIC, the sponsor reasonably believes that all principal and interest due under the regular interest will be paid at or prior to the liquidation of the REMIC.

(2) Residual interest. The term "residual interest" means an interest in a REMIC which is issued on the startup day, which is not a regular interest, and which is designated as a residual interest.

(3) Qualified mortgage. The term "qualified mortgage" means—

(A) any obligation (including any participation or certificate of beneficial ownership therein) which is principally secured by an interest in real property and which—

(i) is transferred to the REMIC on the startup day in exchange for regular or residual interests in the REMIC,

(ii) is purchased by the REMIC within the 3-month period beginning on the startup day if, except as provided in regulations, such purchase is pursuant to a fixed-price contract in effect on the startup day, or

(iii) represents an increase in the principal amount under the original terms of an obligation described in clause (i) or (ii) if such increase—

(I) is attributable to an advance made to the obligor pursuant to the original terms of a reverse mortgage loan or other obligation,

(II) occurs after the startup day, and

(III) is purchased by the REMIC pursuant to a fixed price contract in effect on the startup day.

(B) any qualified replacement mortgage, and

(C) any regular interest in another REMIC transferred to the REMIC on the startup day in exchange for regular or residual interests in the REMIC.

For purposes of subparagraph (A), any obligation secured by stock held by a person as a tenant-stockholder (as defined in section 216) in a cooperative housing corporation (as so defined) shall be treated as secured by an interest in real property. For purposes of subparagraph (A), any obligation originated by the United States or any State (or any political subdivision, agency, or instrumentality of the United States or any State) shall be treated as principally secured by an interest in real property if more than 50 percent of such obligations which are transferred to, or purchased by, the REMIC are principally secured by an interest in real property (determined without regard to this sentence).

(4) Qualified replacement mortgage. The term "qualified replacement mortgage" means any obligation—

(A) which would be a qualified mortgage if transferred on the startup day in exchange for regular or residual interests in the REMIC, and

(B) which is received for—

(i) another obligation within the 3-month period beginning on the startup day, or

(ii) a defective obligation within the 2-year period beginning on the startup day.

(5) Permitted investments. The term "permitted investments" means any—

(A) cash flow investment,

(B) qualified reserve asset, or

(C) foreclosure property.

(6) Cash flow investment. The term "cash flow investment" means any investment of amounts received under qualified mortgages for a temporary period before distribution to holders of interests in the REMIC.

(7) Qualified reserve asset.

(A) In general. The term "qualified reserve asset" means any intangible property which is held for investment and as part of a qualified reserve fund.

(B) Qualified reserve fund. For purposes of subparagraph (A), the term "qualified reserve fund" means any reasonably required reserve to—

(i) provide for full payment of expenses of the REMIC or amounts due on regular interests in the event of defaults on qualified mortgages or lower than expected returns on cash flow investments, or

(ii) provide a source of funds for the purchase of obligations described in clause (ii) or (iii) of paragraph (3)(A).

The aggregate fair market value of the assets held in any such reserve shall not exceed 50 percent of the aggregate fair market value of all of the assets of the REMIC on the startup day, and the amount of any such reserve shall be promptly and appropriately reduced to the extent the amount held in such reserve is no longer reasonably required for purposes specified in clause (i) or (ii) of this subparagraph.

(C) Special rule. A reserve shall not be treated as a qualified reserve for any taxable year (and all subsequent taxable years) if more than 30 percent of the gross income from the assets in such fund for the taxable year is derived from the sale or other disposition of property held for less than 3 months. For purposes of the preceding sentence, gain on the disposition of a qualified reserve asset shall not be taken into account if the disposition giving rise to such gain is required to prevent default on a regular interest where the threatened default resulted from a default on 1 or more qualified mortgages.

(8) Foreclosure property. The term "foreclosure property" means property—

(A) which would be foreclosure property under section 856(e) (without regard to paragraph (5) thereof) if acquired by a real estate investment trust, and

(B) which is acquired in connection with the default or imminent default of a qualified mortgage held by the REMIC.

Solely for purposes of section 860D(a), the determination of whether any property is foreclosure property shall be made without regard to section 856(e)(4).

(9) Startup day. The term "startup day" means the day on which the REMIC issues all of its regular and residual interests. To the extent provided in regulations, all interests issued (and all transfers to the REMIC) during any period (not exceeding 10 days) permitted in such regulations shall be treated as occurring on the day during such period selected by the REMIC for purposes of this paragraph.

(10) Issue price. The issue price of any regular or residual interest in a REMIC shall be determined under section 1273(b) in the same manner as if such interest were a debt instrument; except that if the interest is issued for property, paragraph (3) of section 1273(b) shall apply whether or not the requirements of such paragraph are met.

(b) Treatment of nonresident aliens and foreign corporations.

If the holder of a residual interest in a REMIC is a nonresident alien individual or a foreign corporation, for purposes of sections 871(a), 881, 1441 and 1442—

(1) amounts includible in the gross income of such holder under this part shall be taken into account when paid or distributed (or when the interest is disposed of), and

(2) no exemption from the taxes imposed by such sections (and no reduction in the rates of such taxes) shall apply to any excess inclusion.

The Secretary may by regulations provide that such amounts shall be taken into account earlier than as provided in paragraph (1) where necessary or appropriate to prevent the avoidance of tax imposed by this chapter.

(c) Tax on income from foreclosure property.

(1) In general. A tax is hereby imposed for each taxable year on the net income from foreclosure property of each REMIC. Such tax shall be computed by multiplying the net income from foreclosure property by the highest rate of tax specified in section 11(b).

(2) Net income from foreclosure property. For purposes of this part, the term "net income from foreclosure property" means the amount which would be the REMIC's net income from foreclosure property under section 857(b)(4)(B) if the REMIC were a real estate investment trust.

(d) Tax on contributions after startup date.

(1) In general. Except as provided in paragraph (2), if any amount is contributed to a REMIC after the startup day, there is hereby imposed a tax for the taxable year of the REMIC in which the contribution is received equal to 100 percent of the amount of such contribution.

(2) Exceptions. Paragraph (1) shall not apply to any contribution which is made in cash and is described in any of the following subparagraphs:

(A) Any contribution to facilitate a clean-up call (as defined in regulations) or a qualified liquidation.

(B) Any payment in the nature of a guarantee.

(C) Any contribution during the 3-month period beginning on the startup day.

(D) Any contribution to a qualified reserve fund by any holder of a residual interest in the REMIC.

(E) Any other contribution permitted in regulations.

Real estate mortgage investment conduits — Part V

(e) Regulations.

The Secretary shall prescribe such regulations as may be necessary or appropriate to carry out the purposes of this part, including regulations—

(1) to prevent unreasonable accumulations of assets in a REMIC,

(2) permitting determinations of the fair market value of property transferred to a REMIC and issue price of interests in a REMIC to be made earlier than otherwise provided,

(3) requiring reporting to holders of residual interests of such information as frequently as is necessary or appropriate to permit such holders to compute their taxable income accurately,

(4) providing appropriate rules for treatment of transfers of qualified replacement mortgages to the REMIC where the transferor holds any interest in the REMIC, and

(5) providing that a mortgage will be treated as a qualified replacement mortgage only if it is part of a bona fide replacement (and not part of a swap of mortgages).

In 2005, P.L. 109-135, Sec. 403(cc)(1), substituted "a reverse mortgage loan or other obligation" for "the obligation" in subclause (a)(3)(A)(iii)(I)... Sec. 403(cc)(2), amended the flush para. following subclause. (a)(3)(C), effective 1/1/2005 [as if included in Sec. 835 of the American Jobs Creation Act of 2004, P.L. 108-357], except as provided in Sec. 835(c)(2) of such Act, which reads as follows:

"(2) Exception for existing FASITs. Paragraph (1) shall not apply to any FASIT in existence on the date of the enactment of this Act to the extent that regular interests issued by the FASIT before such date continue to remain outstanding in accordance with the original terms of issuance."

Prior to amendment, the flush para. following subpara. (a)(3)(C) read as follows:

"For purposes of subparagraph (A), any obligation secured by stock held by a person as a tenant-stockholder (as defined in section 216) in a cooperative housing corporation (as so defined) shall be treated as secured by an interest in real property, and any reverse mortgage loan (and each balance increase on such loan meeting the requirements of subparagraph (A)(iii)) shall be treated as an obligation secured by an interest in real property. For purposes of subparagraph (A), if more than 50 percent of the obligations transferred to, or purchased by, the REMIC are originated by the United States or any State (or any political subdivision, agency, or instrumentality of the United States or any State) and are principally secured by an interest in real property, then each obligation transferred to, or purchased by, the REMIC shall be treated as secured by an interest in real property."

In 2004, P.L. 108-357, Sec. 835(b)(5)(A), added "An interest shall not fail to qualify as a regular interest solely because the specified principal amount of the regular interest (or the amount of interest accrued on the regular interest) can be reduced as a result of the nonoccurrence of 1 or more contingent payments with respect to any reverse mortgage loan held by the REMIC if, on the startup day for the REMIC, the sponsor reasonably believes that all principal and interest due under the regular interest will be paid at or prior to the liquidation of the REMIC." at the end of para. (a)(1)... Sec. 835(b)(5)(B), added ", and any reverse mortgage loan (and each balance increase on such loan meeting the requirements of subparagraph (A)(iii)) shall be treated as an obligation secured by an interest in real property" before the period at the end of para. (a)(3)... Sec. 835(b)(6), added "and" at the end of subpara. (a)(3)(B), substituted a period for ", and" at the end of subpara. (a)(3)(C), and deleted subpara. (a)(3)(D)... Sec. 835(b)(7), added "For purposes of subparagraph (A), if more than 50 percent of the obligations transferred to, or purchased by, the REMIC are originated by the United States or any State (or any political subdivision, agency, or instrumentality of the United States or any State) and are principally secured by an interest in real property, then each obligation transferred to, or purchased by, the REMIC shall be treated as secured by an interest in real property." at the end of para. (a)(3)... Sec. 835(b)(8)(A), deleted "or" at the end of clause (a)(3)(A)(i), added "or" at the end of clause (a)(3)(A)(ii), and added clause (a)(3)(A)(iii)... Sec. 835(b)(8)(B), amended subpara. (a)(7)(B), effective 1/1/2005, except as provided in Sec. 835(c)(2) of this Act, which reads as follows:

"(2) Exception for existing fasits. Paragraph (1) shall not apply to any FASIT in existence on the date of the enactment of this Act to the extent that regular interests issued by the FASIT before such date continue to remain outstanding in accordance with the original terms of issuance."

Prior to deletion, subpara. (a)(3)(D) read as follows:

"(D) any regular interest in a FASIT which is transferred to, or purchased by, the REMIC as described in clauses (i) and (ii) of subparagraph (A) but only if 95 percent or more of the value of the assets of such FASIT is at all times attributable to obligations described in subparagraph (A) (without regard to such clauses)."

Prior to amendment, subpara. (a)(7)(B) read as follows:

"(B) Qualified reserve fund. For purposes of subparagraph (A), the term 'qualified reserve fund' means any reasonably required reserve to provide for full payment of expenses of the REMIC or amounts due on regular interests in the event of defaults on qualified mortgages or lower than expected returns on cash-flow investments. The amount of any such reserve shall be promptly and appropriately reduced as payments of qualified mortgages are received."

In 1996, P.L. 104-188, Sec. 1621(b)(6), deleted "and" at the end of subpara. (a)(3)(B), substituted ", and" for the period at the end of subpara. (a)(3)(C), and added subpara. (a)(3)(D), effective 9/1/97.

In 1990, P.L. 101-508, Sec. 11704(a)(9), deleted the comma after "secured" in subpara. (a)(3)(A), effective 11/5/90.

In 1989, P.L. 101-239, Sec. 7811(c)(9), substituted "subparagraph (A)" for "this subparagraph" in para. (a)(3), effective 1/1/87.

In 1988, P.L. 100-647, Sec. 1006(t)(5)(A), amended para. (a)(1)... Sec. 1006(t)(5)(B), amended para. (a)(2)... Sec. 1006(t)(5)(C), substituted "on the startup day in exchange for regular or residual interests in the REMIC" for "on or before the startup day" in clause (a)(3)(A)(i), added "if, except as provided in regulations, such purchase is pursuant to a fixed price contract in effect on the startup day" before the comma at the end of clause (a)(3)(A)(ii), and substituted "on the startup day in exchange for regular or residual interests in the REMIC" for "on or before the startup day" in subpara. (a)(3)(C)... Sec. 1006(t)(5)(D), amended subpara. (a)(4)(A)... Sec. 1006(t)(5)(E), amended para. (a)(9), effective as provided in Sec. 1006(t)(5)(F) of this Act, which reads as follows:

"(F) The amendments made by this paragraph shall not apply to any REMIC where the startup day (as defined in section 860G(a)(9) of the 1986 Code as in effect on the day before the date of the enactment of this Act [11/10/88]) is before July 1, 1987."

Prior to amendment, para. (a)(1) read as follows:

"(1) Regular interest. The term 'regular interest' means an interest in a REMIC the terms of which are fixed on the startup day, and which—

"(A) unconditionally entitles the holder to receive a specified principal amount (or other similar amount), and

"(B) provides that interest payments (or other similar amounts), if any, at or before maturity are payable based on a fixed rate (or to the extent provided in regulations, at a variable rate).

"An interest shall not fail to meet the requirements of subparagraph (A) merely because the timing (but not the amount) of the principal payments (or other similar amounts) may be contingent on the extent of prepayments on qualified mortgages and the amount of income from permitted investments."

Prior to amendment, para. (a)(2) read as follows:

"(2) Residual interest. The term 'residual interest' means an interest in a REMIC which is not a regular interest and is designated as a residual interest."

Prior to amendment, subpara. (a)(4)(A) read as follows:

"(A) which would be described in paragraph (3)(A) if it were transferred to the REMIC on or before the startup day, and"

Prior to amendment, para. (a)(9) read as follows:

"(9) Startup day. The term 'startup day' means any day selected by a REMIC which is on or before the 1st day on which interests in such REMIC are issued."

—P.L. 100-647, Sec. 1006(t)(6)(A), deleted "directly or indirectly" which followed "principally secured," in subpara. (a)(3)(A)... Sec. 1006(t)(6)(B), added the last sentence of para. (a)(3)... Sec. 1006(t)(7), added, for "or lower than expected returns on cash flow investments" before the period at the end of the first sentence in subpara. (a)(7)(B)... Sec. 1006(t)(8)(A), substituted "section 856(e) (without regard to paragraph (5) thereof)" for "section 856(e)" in subpara. (a)(8)(A) and amended the last sentence in para. (a)(8)... Sec. 1006(t)(8)(B), redesignated subsec. (c) as subsec. (d) and added new subsec. (c)... Sec. 1006(t)(10), deleted "and" at the end of para. (e)(2) (as redesignated by Sec. 1006(t)(9) of this Act), substituted a comma for the period at the end of para. (e)(3), and added paras. (e)(4) and (5), effective on 1/1/87.

Prior to amendment, the last sentence in para. (a)(8) read as follows:

"Property shall cease to be foreclosure property with respect to the REMIC on the date which is 1 year after the date such real estate mortgage pool acquired such property."

—P.L. 100-647, Sec. 1006(t)(9)(A), redesignated subsec. (d) (as redesignated by Sec. 1006(t)(8)(B) of this Act) as subsec. (e) and added new subsec. (d), effective as provided in Sec. 1006(t)(9)(B) of this Act, which reads as follows:

"(B) The amendment made by subparagraph (A) shall not apply to any REMIC where the startup day (as defined in section 860G(a)(9) of the 1986 Code as in effect on the day before the date of the enactment of this Act [11/10/88]) is before July 1, 1987."

—P.L. 100-647, Sec. 1006(w)(1), amended Sec. 675(a) of P.L. 99-514, the effective date for changes made by Sec. 671(a) of P.L. 99-514, by substituting "the amendments made by this subtitle shall take effect on January 1, 1987" for "the amendments made by this part shall apply to taxable years beginning after December 31, 1986," see below.

In 1986, P.L. 99-514, Sec. 671(a), added Code Sec. 860G as part of Part IV of subchapter M of Chapter 1, effective on 1/1/87 [as amended by Sec. 1006(w)(1) of P.L. 100-647, see above].

PART V. Repealed [FINANCIAL ASSET SECURITIZATION INVESTMENT TRUSTS]

Sec.

860H. Repealed [Taxation of a FASIT; other general rules.]

860I. Repealed [Gain recognition on contributions to a FASIT and in other cases.]

Part V — Real estate mortgage investment conduits

860J. Repealed [Non-FASIT losses not to offset certain FASIT inclusions.]

860K. Repealed [Treatment of transfers of high-yield interests to disqualified holders.]

860L. Repealed [Definitions and other special rules.]

In 2004, P.L. 108-357, Sec. 835(a), repealed Part V of subchapter M of chapter 1, effective 1/1/2005.

In 1996, P.L. 104-188, Sec. 1621(a), added Part V.

Sec. 860H. Repealed.

In 2004, P.L. 108-357, Sec. 835(a), repealed Code Sec. 860H, effective 1/1/2005, except as provided in Sec. 835(c)(2) of this Act, which reads as follows:
"(2) Exception for existing FASITs. Paragraph (1) shall not apply to any FASIT in existence on the date of the enactment of this Act to the extent that regular interests issued by the FASIT before such date continue to remain outstanding in accordance with the original terms of issuance."

Prior to repeal, Code Sec. 860H read as follows:

"SEC. 860H. TAXATION OF A FASIT; OTHER GENERAL RULES.

"(a) Taxation of FASIT. A FASIT as such shall not be subject to taxation under this subtitle (and shall not be treated as a trust, partnership, corporation, or taxable mortgage pool).

"(b) Taxation of holder of ownership interest. In determining the taxable income of the holder of the ownership interest in a FASIT—

"(1) all assets, liabilities, and items of income, gain, deduction, loss, and credit of a FASIT shall be treated as assets, liabilities, and such items (as the case may be) of such holder,

"(2) the constant yield method (including the rules of section 1272(a)(6)) shall be applied under an accrual method of accounting in determining all interest, acquisition discount, original issue discount, and market discount and all premium deductions or adjustments with respect to each debt instrument of the FASIT,

"(3) there shall not be taken into account any item of income, gain, or deduction allocable to a prohibited transaction, and

"(4) interest accrued by the FASIT which is exempt from tax imposed by this subtitle shall, when taken into account by such holder, be treated as ordinary income.

"(c) Treatment of regular interests. For purposes of this title—

"(1) a regular interest in a FASIT, if not otherwise a debt instrument, shall be treated as a debt instrument,

"(2) section 163(e)(5) shall not apply to such an interest, and

"(3) amounts includible in gross income with respect to such an interest shall be determined under an accrual method of accounting."

In 1996, P.L. 104-188, Sec. 1621(a), added Code Sec. 860H, effective 9/1/97.

—P.L. 104-188, Sec. 1621(e), of this Act, provides:

"(e) Treatment of existing securitization entities.

"(1) In general. In the case of the holder of the ownership interest in a pre-effective date FASIT—

"(A) gain shall not be recognized under section 860L(d)(2) of the Internal Revenue Code of 1986 on property deemed contributed to the FASIT, and

"(B) gain shall not be recognized under section 860I of such Code on property contributed to such FASIT,

until such property (or portion thereof) ceases to be properly allocable to a pre-FASIT interest.

"(2) Allocation of property to pre-FASIT interest. For purposes of paragraph (1), property shall be allocated to a pre-FASIT interest in such manner as the Secretary of the Treasury may prescribe, except that all property in a FASIT shall be treated as properly allocable to pre-FASIT interests if the fair market value of all such property does not exceed 107 percent of the aggregate principal amount of all outstanding pre-FASIT interests.

"(3) Definitions. For purposes of this subsection—

"(A) Pre-effective date FASIT. The term 'pre-effective date FASIT' means any FASIT if the entity (with respect to which the election under section 860L(a)(3) of such Code was made) is in existence on August 31, 1997.

"(B) Pre-FASIT interest. The term 'pre-FASIT interest' means any interest in the entity referred to in subparagraph (A) which was issued before the startup day (other than any interest held by the holder of the ownership interest in the FASIT)."

Sec. 860I. Repealed.

In 2004, P.L. 108-357, Sec. 835(a), repealed Code Sec. 860I, effective 1/1/2005, except as provided in Sec. 835(c)(2) of this Act, which reads as follows:
"(2) Exception for existing FASITs. Paragraph (1) shall not apply to any FASIT in existence on the date of the enactment of this Act to the extent that regular interests issued by the FASIT before such date continue to remain outstanding in accordance with the original terms of issuance."

Prior to repeal, Code Sec. 860I read as follows:

"SEC. 860I. GAIN RECOGNITION ON CONTRIBUTIONS TO A FASIT AND IN CERTAIN CASES.

"(a) Treatment of property acquired by FASIT.

"(1) Property acquired from holder of ownership interest or related person. If property is sold or contributed to a FASIT by the holder of the ownership interest in such FASIT (or by a related person) gain (if any) shall be recognized to such holder (or person) in an amount equal to the excess (if any) of such property's value under subsection (d) on the date of such sale or contribution over its adjusted basis on such date.

"(2) Property acquired other than from holder of ownership interest or related person. Property which is acquired by a FASIT other than in a transaction to which paragraph (1) applies shall be treated—

"(A) as having been acquired by the holder of the ownership interest in the FASIT for an amount equal to the FASIT's cost of acquiring such property, and

"(B) as having been sold by such holder to the FASIT at its value under subsection (d) on such date.

"(b) Gain recognition on property outside FASIT which supports regular interests. If property held by the holder of the ownership interest in a FASIT (or by any person related to such holder) supports any regular interest in such FASIT—

"(1) gain shall be recognized to such holder (or person) in the same manner as if such holder (or person) had sold such property at its value under subsection (d) on the earliest date such property supports such an interest, and

"(2) such property shall be treated as held by such FASIT for purposes of this part.

"(c) Deferral of gain recognition. The Secretary may prescribe regulations which—

"(1) provide that gain otherwise recognized under subsection (a) or (b) shall not be recognized before the earliest date on which such property supports any regular interest in such FASIT or any indebtedness of the holder of the ownership interest (or of any person related to such holder), and

"(2) provide such adjustments to the other provisions of this part to the extent appropriate in the context of the treatment provided under paragraph (1).

"(d) Valuation. For purposes of this section—

"(1) In general. The value of any property under this subsection shall be—

"(A) in the case of a debt instrument which is not traded on an established securities market, the sum of the present values of the reasonably expected payments under such instrument determined (in the manner provided by regulations prescribed by the Secretary)—

"(i) as of the date of the event resulting in the gain recognition under this section, and

"(ii) by using a discount rate equal to 120 percent of the applicable Federal rate (as defined in section 1274(d)), or such other discount rate specified in such regulations, compounded semiannually, and

"(B) in the case of any other property, its fair market value.

"(2) Special rule for revolving loan accounts. For purposes of paragraph (1)—

"(A) each extension of credit (other than the accrual of interest) on a revolving loan account shall be treated as a separate debt instrument, and

"(B) payments on such extensions of credit having substantially the same terms shall be applied to such extensions beginning with the earliest such extension.

"(e) Special rules.

"(1) Nonrecognition rules not to apply. Gain required to be recognized under his section shall be recognized notwithstanding any other provision of this subtitle.

"(2) Basis adjustments. The basis of any property on which gain is recognized under this section shall be increased by the amount of gain so recognized."

In 1996, P.L. 104-188, Sec. 1621(a), added Code Sec. 860I, effective 9/1/97.

—P.L. 104-188, Sec. 1621(e), regarding treatment of existing securitization entities, is reproduced in note following Code Sec. 0860H.

Sec. 860J. Repealed.

In 2004, P.L. 108-357, Sec. 835(a), repealed Code Sec. 860J, effective 1/1/2005, except as provided in Sec. 835(c)(2) of this Act, which reads as follows:
"(2) Exception for existing FASITs. Paragraph (1) shall not apply to any FASIT in existence on the date of the enactment of this Act to the extent that regular interests issued by the FASIT before such date continue to remain outstanding in accordance with the original terms of issuance."

Prior to repeal, Code Sec. 860J read as follows:

"SEC. 860J. NON-FASIT LOSSES NOT TO OFFSET CERTAIN FASIT INCLUSIONS.

"(a) In general. The taxable income of the holder of the ownership interest or any high-yield interest in a FASIT for any taxable year shall in no event be less than the sum of—

"(1) such holder's taxable income determined solely with respect to such interests (including gains and losses from sales and exchanges of such interests), and

"(2) the excess inclusion (if any) under section 860E(a)(1) for such taxable year.

"(b) Coordination with section 172. Any increase in the taxable income of any holder of the ownership interest or a high-yield interest in a FASIT for any taxable year by reason of subsection (a) shall be disregarded—

"(1) in determining under section 172 the amount of any net operating loss for such taxable year, and

"(2) in determining taxable income for such taxable year for purposes of the second sentence of section 172(b)(2).

"(c) Coordination with minimum tax. For purposes of part VI of subchapter A of this chapter—

"(1) the reference in section 55(b)(2) to taxable income shall be treated as a reference to taxable income determined without regard to this section,

"(2) the alternative minimum taxable income of any holder of the ownership interest or a high-yield interest in a FASIT for any taxable year shall in no event be less than such holder's taxable income determined solely with respect to such interests, and

Real estate mortgage investment conduits — Code Sec. 860L

"(3) any increase in taxable income under this section shall be disregarded for purposes of computing the alternative tax net operating loss deduction.

"(d) Affiliated groups. All members of an affiliated group filing a consolidated return shall be treated as one taxpayer for purposes of this section."

In 1996, P.L. 104-188, Sec. 1621(a), added Code Sec. 860J, effective 9/1/97.

—P.L. 104-188, Sec. 1621(e), regarding treatment of existing securitization entities, is reproduced in note following Code Sec. 0860H.

Sec. 860K. Repealed.

In 2004, P.L. 108-357, Sec. 835(a), repealed Code Sec. 860K, effective 1/1/2005, except as provided in Sec. 835(c)(2) of this Act, which reads as follows:

"(2) Exception for existing FASITs. Paragraph (1) shall not apply to any FASIT in existence on the date of the enactment of this Act to the extent that regular interests issued by the FASIT before such date continue to remain outstanding in accordance with the original terms of issuance."

Prior to repeal, Code Sec. 860K read as follows:

"SEC. 860K. TREATMENT OF TRANSFERS OF HIGH-YIELD INTERESTS TO DISQUALIFIED HOLDERS.

"(a) General rule. In the case of any high-yield interest which is held by a disqualified holder—

"(1) the gross income of such holder shall not include any income (other than gain) attributable to such interest, and

"(2) amounts not includible in the gross income of such holder by reason of paragraph (1) shall be included (at the time otherwise includible under paragraph (1)) in the gross income of the most recent holder of such interest which is not a disqualified holder.

"(b) Exceptions. Rules similar to the rules of paragraphs (4) and (7) of section 860E(e) shall apply to the tax imposed by reason of the inclusion in gross income under subsection (a).

"(c) Disqualified holder. For purposes of this section, the term 'disqualified holder' means any holder other than—

"(1) an eligible corporation (as defined in section 860L(a)(2)), or

"(2) a FASIT.

"(d) Treatment of interests held by securities dealers.

"(1) In general. Subsection (a) shall not apply to any high-yield interest held by a disqualified holder if such holder is a dealer in securities who acquired such interest exclusively for sale to customers in the ordinary course of business (and not for investment).

"(2) Change in dealer status.

"(A) In general. In the case of a dealer in securities which is not an eligible corporation (as defined in section 860L(a)(2)), if—

"(i) such dealer ceases to be a dealer in securities, or

"(ii) such dealer commences holding the high-yield interest for investment,

"there is hereby imposed (in addition to other taxes) an excise tax equal to the product of the highest rate of tax specified in section 11(b)(1) and the income of such dealer attributable to such interest for periods after the date of such cessation or commencement.

"(B) Holding for 31 days or less. For purposes of subparagraph (A)(ii), a dealer shall not be treated as holding an interest for investment before the thirty-second day after the date such dealer acquired such interest unless such interest is so held as part of a plan to avoid the purposes of this paragraph.

"(C) Administrative provisions. The deficiency procedures of subtitle F shall apply to the tax imposed by this paragraph.

"(e) Treatment of high-yield interests in pass-thru entities.

"(1) In general. If a pass-thru entity (as defined in section 860E(e)(6)) issues a debt or equity interest—

"(A) which is supported by any regular interest in a FASIT, and

"(B) which has an original yield to maturity which is greater than each of—

"(i) the sum determined under clauses (i) and (ii) of section 163(i)(1)(B) with respect to such debt or equity interest, and

"(ii) the yield to maturity to such entity on such regular interest (determined as of the date such entity acquired such interest),

"there is hereby imposed on the pass-thru entity a tax (in addition to other taxes) equal to the product of the highest rate of tax specified in section 11(b)(1) and the income of the holder of such debt or equity interest which is properly attributable to such regular interest. For purposes of the preceding sentence, the yield to maturity of any equity interest shall be determined under regulations prescribed by the Secretary.

"(2) Exception. Paragraph (1) shall not apply to arrangements not having as a principal purpose the avoidance of the purposes of this subsection."

In 1996, P.L. 104-188, Sec. 1621(a), added Code Sec. 860K, effective 9/1/97.

—P.L. 104-188, Sec. 1621(e), regarding treatment of existing securitization entities, is reproduced in note following Code Sec. 0860H.

Sec. 860L. Repealed.

In 2004, P.L. 108-357, Sec. 835(a), repealed Code Sec. 860L, effective 1/1/2005, except as provided in Sec. 835(c)(2) of this Act, which reads as follows:

"(2) Exception for existing FASITs. Paragraph (1) shall not apply to any FASIT in existence on the date of the enactment of this Act to the extent that regular interests issued by the FASIT before such date continue to remain outstanding in accordance with the original terms of issuance."

Prior to repeal, Code Sec. 860L read as follows:

"SEC. 860L. DEFINITIONS AND OTHER SPECIAL RULES.

"(a) FASIT.

"(1) In general. For purposes of this title, the terms 'financial asset securitization investment trust' and 'FASIT' mean any entity—

"(A) for which an election to be treated as a FASIT applies for the taxable year,

"(B) all of the interests in which are regular interests or the ownership interest,

"(C) which has only one ownership interest and such ownership interest is held directly by an eligible corporation,

"(D) as of the close of the third month beginning after the day of its formation and at all times thereafter, substantially all of the assets of which (including assets treated as held by the entity under section 860I(b)(2)) consist of permitted assets, and

"(E) which is not described in section 851(a).

"A rule similar to the rule of the last sentence of section 860D(a) shall apply for purposes of this paragraph.

"(2) Eligible corporation. For purposes of paragraph (1)(C), the term 'eligible corporation' means any domestic C corporation other than—

"(A) a corporation which is exempt from, or is not subject to, tax under this chapter,

"(B) an entity described in section 851(a) or 856(a),

"(C) a REMIC, and

"(D) an organization to which part I of subchapter T applies.

"(3) Election. An entity (otherwise meeting the requirements of paragraph (1)) may elect to be treated as a FASIT. Except as provided in paragraph (5), such an election shall apply to the taxable year for which made and all subsequent taxable years unless revoked with the consent of the Secretary.

"(4) Termination. If any entity ceases to be a FASIT at any time during the taxable year, such entity shall not be treated as a FASIT after the date of such ceasation.

"(5) Inadvertent terminations, etc. Rules similar to the rules of section 860D(b)(2)(B) shall apply to inadvertent failures to qualify or remain qualified as a FASIT.

"(6) Permitted assets not treated as interest in FASIT. Except as provided in regulations prescribed by the Secretary, any asset which is a permitted asset at the time acquired by a FASIT shall not be treated at any time as an interest in such FASIT.

"(b) Interests in FASIT. For purposes of this part—

"(1) Regular interest.

"(A) In general. The term 'regular interest' means any interest which is issued by a FASIT on or after the startup date with fixed terms and which is designated as a regular interest if—

"(i) such interest unconditionally entitles the holder to receive a specified principal amount (or other similar amount),

"(ii) interest payments (or other similar amounts), if any, with respect to such interest are determined based on a fixed rate, or, except as otherwise provided by the Secretary, at a variable rate permitted under section 860G(a)(1)(B)(i),

"(iii) such interest does not have a stated maturity (including options to renew) greater than 30 years (or such longer period as may be permitted by regulations),

"(iv) the issue price of such interest does not exceed 125 percent of its stated principal amount, and

"(v) the yield to maturity on such interest is less than the sum determined under section 163(i)(1)(B) with respect to such interest.

"An interest shall not fail to meet the requirements of clause (i) merely because the timing (but not the amount) of the principal payments (or other similar amounts) may be contingent on the extent that payments on debt instruments held by the FASIT are made in advance of anticipated payments and on the amount of income from permitted assets.

"(B) High-yield interests.

"(i) In general. The term 'regular interest' includes any high-yield interest.

"(ii) High-yield interest. The term 'high-yield interest' means any interest which would be described in subparagraph (A) but for—

"(I) failing to meet the requirements of one or more of clauses (i), (iv), or (v) thereof , or

"(II) failing to meet the requirement of clause (ii) thereof but only if interest payments (or other similar amounts), if any, with respect to such interest consist of a specified portion of the interest payments on permitted assets and such portion does not vary during the period such interest is outstanding.

"(2) Ownership interest. The term 'ownership interest' means the interest issued by a FASIT after the startup day which is designated as an ownership interest and which is not a regular interest.

"(c) Permitted assets. For purposes of this part—

"(1) In general. The term 'permitted asset' means—

"(A) cash or cash equivalents,

"(B) any debt instrument (as defined in section 1275(a)(1)) under which interest payments (or other similar amounts), if any, at or before maturity meet the requirements applicable under clause (i) or (ii) of section 860G(a)(1)(B).

"(C) foreclosure property,

"(D) any asset—

"(i) which is an interest rate or foreign currency notional principal contract, letter of credit, insurance, guarantee against payment defaults, or other similar instrument permitted by the Secretary, and

"(ii) which is reasonably required to guarantee or hedge against the FASIT's risks associated with being the obligor on interests issued by the FASIT,

"(E) contract rights to acquire debt instruments described in subparagraph (B) or assets described in subparagraph (D),

"(F) any regular interest in another FASIT, and

"(G) any regular interest in a REMIC.

"(2) Debt issued by holder of ownership interest not permitted asset. The term 'permitted asset' shall not include any debt instrument issued by the holder of the ownership interest in the FASIT or by any person related to such holder or any direct or indirect interest in such a debt instrument. The preceding sentence shall not apply to cash equivalents and to any other investment specified in regulations prescribed by the Secretary.

"(3) Foreclosure property.

"(A) In general. The term 'foreclosure property' means property—

"(i) which would be foreclosure property under section 856(e) (determined without regard to paragraph (5) thereof) if such property were real property acquired by a real estate investment trust, and

"(ii) which is acquired in connection with the default or imminent default of a debt instrument held by the FASIT unless the security interest in such property was created for the principal purpose of permitting the FASIT to invest in such property.

"Solely for purposes of subsection (a)(1), the determination of whether any property is foreclosure property shall be made without regard to section 856(e)(4).

"(B) Authority to reduce grace period. In the case of property other than real property and other than personal property incident to real property, the Secretary may by regulation reduce for purposes of subparagraph (A) the periods otherwise applicable under paragraphs (2) and (3) of section 856(e).

"(d) Startup day. For purposes of this part—

"(1) In general. The term 'startup day' means the date designated in the election under subsection (a)(3) as the startup day of the FASIT. Such day shall be the beginning of the first taxable year of the FASIT.

"(2) Treatment of property held on startup day. All property held (or treated as held under section 860I(b)(2)) by an entity as of the startup day shall be treated as contributed to such entity on such day by the holder of the ownership interest in such entity.

"(e) Tax on prohibited transactions.

"(1) In general. There is hereby imposed for each taxable year of a FASIT a tax equal to 100 percent of the net income derived from prohibited transactions. Such tax shall be paid by the holder of the ownership interest in the FASIT.

"(2) Prohibited transactions. For purposes of this part, the term 'prohibited transaction' means—

"(A) except as provided in paragraph (3), the receipt of any income derived from any asset that is not a permitted asset,

"(B) except as provided in paragraph (3), the disposition of any permitted asset other than foreclosure property,

"(C) the receipt of any income derived from any loan originated by the FASIT, and

"(D) the receipt of any income representing a fee or other compensation for services (other than any fee received as compensation for a waiver, amendment, or consent under permitted assets (other than foreclosure property) held by the FASIT).

"(3) Exception for income from certain dispositions.

"(A) In general. Paragraph (2)(B) shall not apply to a disposition which would not be a prohibited transaction (as defined in section 860F(a)(2)) by reason of—

"(i) clause (ii), (iii), or (iv) of section 860F(a)(2)(A), or

"(ii) section 860F(a)(5),

"if the FASIT were treated as a REMIC and permitted assets (other than cash or cash equivalents) were treated as qualified mortgages.

"(B) Substitution of debt instruments; reduction of over-collateralization. Paragraph (2)(B) shall not apply to—

"(i) the substitution of a debt instrument described in subsection (c)(1)(B) for another debt instrument which is a permitted asset, or

"(ii) the distribution of any debt instrument contributed by the holder of the ownership interest to such holder in order to reduce over-collateralization of the FASIT,

"but only if a principal purpose of acquiring the debt instrument which is disposed of was not the recognition of gain (or the reduction of a loss) as a result of an increase in the market value of the debt instrument after its acquisition by the FASIT.

"(C) Liquidation of class of regular interests. Paragraph (2)(B) shall not apply to the complete liquidation of any class of regular interests.

"(D) Income from dispositions of former hedge assets. Paragraph (2)(A) shall not apply to income derived from the disposition of—

"(i) an asset which was described in subsection (c)(1)(D) when first acquired by the FASIT but on the date of such disposition was no longer described in subsection (c)(1)(D)(ii), or

"(ii) a contract right to acquire an asset described in clause (i).

"(4) Net income. For purposes of this subsection, net income shall be determined in accordance with section 860F(a)(3).

"(f) Coordination with other provisions.

"(1) Wash sales rules. Rules similar to the rules of section 860F(d) shall apply to the ownership interest in a FASIT.

"(2) Section 475. Except as provided by the Secretary by regulations, if any security which is sold or contributed to a FASIT by the holder of the ownership interest in such FASIT was required to be marked-to-market under section 475 by such holder, section 475 shall continue to apply to such security; except that in applying section 475 while such security is held by the FASIT, the fair market value of such security for purposes of section 475 shall not be less than its value under section 860I(d).

"(g) Related person. For purposes of this part, a person (hereinafter in this subsection referred to as the 'related person') is related to any person if—

"(1) the related person bears a relationship to such person specified in section 267(b) or section 707(b)(1), or

"(2) the related person and such person are engaged in trades or businesses under common control (within the meaning of subsections (a) and (b) of section 52).

"For purposes of paragraph (1), in applying section 267(b) or 707(b)(1), '20 percent' shall be substituted for '50 percent'.

"(h) Regulations. The Secretary shall prescribe such regulations as may be necessary or appropriate to carry out the purposes of this part, including regulations to prevent the abuse of the purposes of this part through transactions which are not primarily related to securitization of debt instruments by a FASIT."

In **1997**, P.L. 105-34, Sec. 1601(f)(6)(A), substituted "on or after the startup date" for "after the startup date" in subpara. (b)(1)(A)... Sec. 1601(f)(6)(B), substituted "section 860I(b)(2)" for "section 860I(c)(2)" in para. (d)(2)... Sec. 1601(f)(6)(C), added "other than foreclosure property" after "any permitted asset" in subpara. (e)(2)(B)... Sec. 1601(f)(6)(D), substituted "if the FASIT were treated as a REMIC and permitted assets (other than cash or cash equivalents) were treated as qualified mortgages." for "if the FASIT were treated as a REMIC and debt instruments described in subsection (c)(1)(B) were treated as qualified mortgages." in subpara. (e)(3)(A)... Sec. 1601(c)(6)(E)(i), added subpara. (e)(3)(D)... Sec. 1601(c)(6)(E)(ii), added "except as provided in paragraph (3)," before "the receipt" in subpara. (e)(2)(A), effective 9/1/97. Sec. 1621(e) of P.L. 104-188, regarding treatment of existing securitization entities, is reproduced in note following Code Sec. 0860H.

In **1996**, P.L. 104-188, Sec. 1621(a), added Code Sec. 860L, effective 9/1/97.

—P.L. 104-188, Sec. 1621(e), regarding treatment of existing securitization entities, is reproduced in note following Code Sec. 0860H.

Subchapter N.—Tax Based on Income From Sources Within or Without the United States

Part

I. Determination of sources of income.

II. Nonresident aliens and foreign corporations.

III. Income from sources without the United States.

IV. Domestic International Sales Corporations.

V. International Boycott determinations.

In **1976**, P.L. 94-455, Sec. 1064(b), added the item for Part V.

PART I.—DETERMINATION OF SOURCES OF INCOME

Sec.

861. Income from sources within the United States.

862. Income from sources without the United States.

863. Special rules for determining source.

864. Definitions and special rules.

865. Source rules for personal property sales.

In **1988**, P.L. 100-647, Sec. 1012(e)(3)(B), amended item 863... Sec. 1018(u)(37), added item 865.

Prior to amendment, item 863 read as follows:

"863. Items not specified in section 861 or 862."

In **1986**, P.L. 99-514, Sec. 1215(b)(2), added "and special rules" after "Definitions" in item 864.

Sec. 861. Income from sources within the United States.
(a) Gross income from sources within United States.

The following items of gross income shall be treated as income from sources within the United States:

(1) Interest. Interest from the United States, or the District of Columbia, and interest on bonds, notes, or other interest-bearing obligations of noncorporate residents or domestic corporations not including—

(A) interest—

(i) on deposits with a foreign branch of a domestic corporation or a domestic partnership if such branch is engaged in the commercial banking business, and

(ii) on amounts satisfying the requirements of subparagraph (B) of section 871(i)(3) which are paid by a foreign branch of a domestic corporation or a domestic partnership, and

(B) in the case of a foreign partnership, which is predominantly engaged in the active conduct of a trade or business outside the United States, any interest not paid by a trade or business engaged in by the partnership in the United States and not allocable to income which is effectively connected (or treated as effectively connected) with the conduct of a trade or business in the United States.

(2) Dividends. The amount received as dividends—

(A) from a domestic corporation other than a corporation which has an election in effect under section 936, or

(B) from a foreign corporation unless less than 25 percent of the gross income from all sources of such foreign corporation for the 3-year period ending with the close of its taxable year preceding the declaration of such dividends (or for such part of such period as the corporation has been in existence) was effectively connected (or treated as effectively connected other than income described in section 884(d)(2)) with the conduct of a trade or business within the United States; but only in an amount which bears the same ratio to such dividends as the gross income of the corporation for such period which was effectively connected (or treated as effectively connected other than income described in section 884(d)(2)) with the conduct of a trade or business within the United States bears to its gross income from all sources; but dividends (other than dividends for which a deduction is allowable under section 245(b)) from a foreign corporation shall, for purposes of subpart A of part III (relating to foreign tax credit), be treated as income from sources without the United States to the extent (and only to the extent) exceeding the amount which is 100/70th of the amount of the deduction allowable under section 245 in respect of such dividends, or

(C) from a foreign corporation to the extent that such amount is required by section 243(e) (relating to certain dividends from foreign corporations) to be treated as dividends from a domestic corporation which is subject to taxation under this chapter, and to such extent subparagraph (B) shall not apply to such amount, or

(D) from a DISC or former DISC (as defined in section 992(a)) except to the extent attributable (as determined under regulations prescribed by the Secretary) to qualified export receipts described in section 993(a)(1) (other than interest and gains described in section 995(b)(1)).

In the case of any dividend from a 20-percent owned corporation (as defined in section 243(c)(2)), subparagraph (B) shall be applied by substituting "100/80th" for "100/70th".

• *Caution:* Code Sec. 861(a)(3), following, was amended by Sec. 621(a), P.L. 107-16, the Economic Growth and Tax Relief Reconciliation Act of 2001 (EGTRRA). These provisions generally sunset for tax years beginning after 12/31/2012. For specific sunset provisions see Sec. 901, P.L. 107-16 (as amended) reproduced in history notes for this Code Sec.

---

(3) Personal services. Compensation for labor or personal services performed in the United States; except that compensation for labor or services performed in the United States shall not be deemed to be income from sources within the United States if—

(A) the labor or services are performed by a nonresident alien individual temporarily present in the United States for a period or periods not exceeding a total of 90 days during the taxable year,

(B) such compensation does not exceed $3,000 in the aggregate, and

(C) the compensation is for labor or services performed as an employee of or under a contract with—

(i) a nonresident alien, foreign partnership, or foreign corporation, not engaged in trade or business within the United States, or

(ii) an individual who is a citizen or resident of the United States, a domestic partnership, or a domestic corporation, if such labor or services are performed for an office or place of business maintained in a foreign country or in a possession of the United States by such individual, partnership, or corporation.

In addition, compensation for labor or services performed in the United States shall not be deemed to be income from sources within the United States if the labor or services are performed by a nonresident alien individual in connection with the individual's temporary presence in the United States as a regular member of the crew of a foreign vessel engaged in transportation between the United States and a foreign country or a possession of the United States.

(4) Rentals and royalties. Rentals or royalties from property located in the United States or from any interest in such property, including rentals or royalties for the use of or for the privilege of using in the United States patents, copyrights, secret processes and formulas, good will, trade-marks, trade brands, franchises, and other like property.

(5) Disposition of United States real property interest. Gains, profits, and income from the disposition of a United States real property interest (as defined in section 897(c)).

(6) Sale or exchange of inventory property. Gains, profits, and income derived from the purchase of inventory property (within the meaning of section 865(i)(1)) without the United States (other than within a possession of the United States) and its sale or exchange within the United States.

(7) Amounts received as underwriting income (as defined in section 832(b)(3)) derived from the issuing (or reinsuring) of any insurance or annuity contract—

(A) in connection with property in, liability arising out of an activity in, or in connection with the lives or health of residents of, the United States, or

(B) in connection with risks not described in subparagraph (A) as a result of any arrangement whereby another corporation receives a substantially equal amount of premiums or other consideration in respect to issuing (or reinsuring) any insurance or annuity contract in connection with property in, liability arising out of activity in, or in connection with the lives or health of residents of, the United States.

(8) Social security benefits. Any social security benefit (as defined in section 86(d)).

(9) Guarantees. Amounts received, directly or indirectly, from—

(A) a noncorporate resident or domestic corporation for the provision of a guarantee of any indebtedness of such resident or corporation, or

(B) any foreign person for the provision of a guarantee of any indebtedness of such person, if such amount is connected with income which is effectively connected (or treated as effectively connected) with the conduct of a trade or business in the United States.

(b) Taxable income from sources within United States.

From the items of gross income specified in subsection (a) as being income from sources within the United States there shall be deducted the expenses, losses, and other deductions properly apportioned or allocated thereto and a ratable part of any expenses, losses, or other deductions which cannot definitely be allocated to some item or class of gross income. The remainder, if any, shall be included in full as taxable income from sources within the United States. In the case of an individual who does not itemize deductions, an amount equal to the standard deduction shall be considered a deduction which cannot definitely be allocated to some item or class of gross income.

(c) Special rule for application of subsection (a)(2)(B).

For purposes of subsection (a)(2)(B), if the foreign corporation has no gross income from any source for the 3-year period (or part thereof) specified, the requirements of such subsection shall be applied with respect to the taxable year of such corporation in which the payment of the dividend is made.

(d) Income from certain railroad rolling stock treated as income from sources within the United States.

(1) **General rule.** For purposes of subsection (a) and section 862(a), if—

(A) a taxpayer leases railroad rolling stock which is section 1245 property (as defined in section 1245(a)(3)) to a domestic common carrier by railroad or a corporation which is controlled, directly or indirectly, by one or more such common carriers, and

(B) the use under such lease is expected to be use[d] within the United States,

all amounts includible in gross income by the taxpayer with respect to such railroad rolling stock (including gain from sale or other disposition of such railroad rolling stock) shall be treated as income from sources within the United States. The requirements of subparagraph (B) of the preceding sentence shall be treated as satisfied if the only expected use outside the United States is use by a person (whether or not a United States person) in Canada or Mexico on a temporary basis which is not expected to exceed a total of 90 days in any taxable year.

(2) **Paragraph (1) not to apply where lessor is a member of controlled group which includes a railroad.** Paragraph (1) shall not apply to a lease between two members of the same controlled group of corporations (as defined in section 1563) if any member of such group is a domestic common carrier by railroad or a switching or terminal company all of whose stock is owned by one or more domestic common carriers by railroad.

(3) **Denial of foreign tax credit** No credit shall be allowed under section 901 for any payments to foreign countries with respect to any amount received by the taxpayer with respect to railroad rolling stock which is subject to paragraph (1).

(e) Cross reference.

For treatment of interest paid by the branch of a foreign corporation, see section 884(f).

In 2010, P.L. 111-312, Sec. 101(a)(1), substituted "December 31, 2012" for "December 31, 2010" both places it appeared in Sec. 901 of P.L. 107-16, [see below] effective as if included in the enactment of P.L. 107-16, EGTRRA, 6/7/2001.

—P.L. 111-240, Sec. 2122(a), added para. (a)(9), effective to guarantees issued after 9/27/2010. P.L. 111-226, Sec. 217(a), deleted subpara. (a)(1)(A) and redesignated subpara. (a)(1)(B)-(C) as subpara. (a)(1)(A)-(B)

Prior to deletion, subpara. (a)(1)(A) read as follows:

"(A) interest from a resident alien individual or domestic corporation, if such individual or corporation meets the 80-percent foreign business requirements of subsection (c)(1)," P.L. 111-226, Sec. 217(c)(1), deleted subsec. (c) and redesignated subsec. (d)-(f) as subsec. (c)-(e), effective for tax. yrs. begin. after 12/31/2010.

Prior to deletion, subsec. (c) read as follows:

"(c) Foreign business requirements.

"(1) Foreign business requirements.

"(A) In general. An individual or corporation meets the 80-percent foreign business requirements of this paragraph if it is shown to the satisfaction of the Secretary that at least 80 percent of the gross income from all sources of such individual or corporation for the testing period is active foreign business income.

"(B) Active foreign business income. For purposes of subparagraph (A), the term 'active foreign business income' means gross income which—

"(i) is derived from sources outside the United States (as determined under this subchapter) or, in the case of a corporation, is attributable to income so derived by a subsidiary of such corporation, and

"(ii) is attributable to the active conduct of a trade or business in a foreign country or possession of the United States by the individual or corporation (or by a subsidiary).

"For purposes of this subparagraph, the term 'subsidiary' means any corporation in which the corporation referred to in this subparagraph owns (directly or indirectly) stock meeting the requirements of section 1504(a)(2) (determined by substituting '50 percent' for '80 percent' each place it appears).

"(C) Testing period. For purposes of this subsection, the term 'testing period' means the 3-year period ending with the close of the taxable year of the individual or corporation preceding the payment (or such part of such period as may be applicable). If the individual or corporation has no gross income for such 3-year period (or part thereof), the testing period shall be the taxable year in which the payment is made.

"(2) Look-thru where related person receives interest.

"(A) In general. In the case of interest received by a related person from a resident alien individual or domestic corporation meeting the 80-percent foreign business requirements of paragraph (1), subsection (a)(1)(A) shall apply only to a percentage of such interest equal to the percentage which—

"(i) the gross income of such individual or corporation for the testing period from sources outside the United States (as determined under this subchapter), is of

"(ii) the total gross income of such individual or corporation for the testing period.

"(B) Related person. For purposes of this paragraph, the term 'related person' has the meaning given such term by section 954(d)(3), except that—

"(i) such section shall be applied by substituting 'the individual or corporation making the payment' for 'controlled foreign corporation' each place it appears, and

"(ii) such section shall be applied by substituting '10 percent or more' for 'more than 50 percent' each place it appears."

Sec. 217(d)(2) of this Act reads as follows:

"(2) Grandfather rule for outstanding debt obligations.

"(A) In general. The amendments made by this section shall not apply to payments of interest on obligations issued before the date of the enactment of this Act.

"(B) Exception for related party debt. Subparagraph (A) shall not apply to any interest which is payable to a related person (determined under rules similar to the rules of section 954(d)(3)).

"(C) Significant modifications treated as new issues. For purposes of subparagraph (A), a significant modification of the terms of any obligation (including any extension of the term of such obligation) shall be treated as a new issue."

In 2006, P.L. 109-280, Sec. 811, of this Act [relating to Sec. 901 of P.L. 107-16, see below], provides:

"SEC. 811. PENSIONS AND INDIVIDUAL RETIREMENT ARRANGEMENT PROVISIONS OF ECONOMIC GROWTH AND TAX RELIEF RECONCILIATION ACT OF 2001 MADE PERMANENT.

"Title IX of the Economic Growth and Tax Relief Reconciliation Act of 2001 shall not apply to the provisions of, and amendments made by, subtitles A through F of title VI of such Act (relating to pension and individual retirement arrangement provisions)."

In 2004, P.L. 108-357, Sec. 410(a), deleted "and" at the end of subpara. (a)(1)(A), substituted ", and" for the period at the end of subpara. (a)(1)(B), and added subpara. (a)(1)(C), effective for tax. yrs. begin. after 12/31/2003.

In 2002, P.L. 107-358, Sec. 2, added subsec. (c) in Sec. 901 of P.L. 107-16 [see below], effective 12/17/2002.

In 2001, P.L. 107-16, Sec. 621(a), deleted "except for purposes of sections 79 and 105 and subchapter D," after "In addition," in para. (a)(3), effective for remuneration for services performed in plan yrs. begin. after 12/31/2001.

—P.L. 107-16, Sec. 901, of this Act [as amended by Sec. 2 of P.L. 107-358, and Sec. 101(a)(1) of P.L. 111-312, see above], reads as follows:

"SEC. 901. SUNSET OF PROVISIONS OF ACT.

"(a) In general. All provisions of, and amendments made by, this Act shall not apply—

"(1) to taxable, plan, or limitation years beginning after December 31, 2012, or

"(2) in the case of title V, to estates of decedents dying, gifts made, or generation skipping transfers, after December 31, 2012.

"(b) Application of certain laws. The Internal Revenue Code of 1986 and the Employee Retirement Income Security Act of 1974 shall be applied and administered to years, estates, gifts, and transfers described in subsection (a) as if the provisions and amendments described in subsection (a) had never been enacted.

"(c) Exception. Subsection (a) shall not apply to section 803 (relating to no federal income tax on restitution received by victims of the Nazi regime or their heirs or estates)."

In 1997, P.L. 105-34, Sec. 1174(a)(1), added the sentence at the end of para. (a)(3), effective for remuneration for services performed in tax. yrs. begin. after 12/31/97.

In 1996, P.L. 104-188, Sec. 1702(h)(9), amended Sec. 11813(b)(17) of P.L. 101-508 to include the closing parenthesis with material deleted from subpara. (e)(1)(A) [see below].

In 1990, P.L. 101-508, Sec. 11801(a)(29), deleted subparas. (a)(1)(C) and (a)(1)(D) . . . Sec. 11801(c)(6)(C), substituted "all of whose stock is owned by one or more domestic common carriers by railroad" for "referred to in subparagraph (B) of section 184(d)(1)" in para. (e)(2) . . . Sec. 11801(c)(14), added "and" at the end of subpara. (a)(1)(A) and substituted a period for the comma at the end of subpara. (a)(1)(B), effective 11/5/90 except as provided in Sec. 11821(b) of this Act, which reads as follows:

"*(b) Savings provision.*

"If—

"(1) any provision amended or repealed by this part applied to—

"(A) any transaction occurring before the date of the enactment of this Act [11/5/90],

"(B) any property acquired before such date of enactment [11/5/90], or

"(C) any item of income, loss, deduction, or credit taken into account before such date of enactment [11/5/90], and

"(2) the treatment of such transaction, property, or item under such provision would (without regard to the amendments made by this part) affect liability for tax for periods ending after such date of enactment [11/5/90],

nothing in the amendments made by this part shall be construed to affect the treatment of such transaction, property, or item for purposes of determining liability for tax for periods ending after such date of enactment [11/5/90]."

Prior to deletion, subparas. (a)(1)(C) and (a)(1)(D) read as follows:

"(C) interest on a debt obligation which was part of an issue with respect to which an election has been made under subsection (c) of section 4192 (as in effect before July 1, 1974) and which, when issued (or treated as issued under subsection (c)(2) of such section), had a maturity not exceeding 15 years and, when issued, was purchased by one or more underwriters with a view to distribution through resale, but only with respect to interest attributable to periods after the date of such election, and

"(D) interest on a debt obligation which was part of an issue which—

"(i) was part of an issue outstanding on April 1, 1971,

"(ii) was guaranteed by a United States person,

"(iii) was treated under chapter 41 as a debt obligation of a foreign obligor,

"(iv) as of June 30, 1974, had a maturity of not more than 15 years, and

"(v) when issued, was purchased by one or more underwriters for the purpose of distribution through resale."

—P.L. 101-508, Sec. 11813(b)(17), substituted "which is section 1245 property (as defined in section 1245(a)(3))" for "which is section 38 property (or would be section 38 property but for section 48(a)(5))" [as amended by Sec. 1702(h)(9) of P.L. 104-188, see above] in subpara. (e)(1)(A), effective for property placed in service after 12/31/90 except as provided in Sec. 11813(c)(2) of this Act, reproduced in note following Code Sec. 46.

In 1989, P.L. 101-239, Sec. 7811(i)(2), substituted "865(i)(1)" for "865(h)(1)" in para. (a)(6), effective for tax. yrs. begin. after 12/31/86, except as provided in Secs. 1211(c)(2) and (d) of P.L. 99-514 reproduced in note following Code Sec. 865.

—P.L. 101-239, Sec. 7841(d)(9), substituted "section 862(a)" for "section 826(a)" in subsec. (e), effective 12/19/89.

In 1988, P.L. 100-647, Sec. 1006(b)(1)(B), provides:

"(b) Amendments related to sections 611 and 612 of the Reform Act.

"(1) In the case of dividends received or accrued during 1987—

* * *

"(B) subparagraph (B) of section 861(a)(2) of the 1986 Code shall be applied by substituting '¹⁰⁄₁₀₀ths' for the fraction specified therein."

—P.L. 100-647, Sec. 1012(g)(1)(A), amended Sec. 1214(d)(1) of P.L. 99-514 [reproduced below] the effective date for changes made by Sec. 1214(c)(1) of P.L. 99-514, by substituting "payments made in a taxable year of the payor beginning after December 31, 1986" for "payments after December 31, 1986", see below. Sec. 1012(g)(1)(B) of this Act provides:

"(B) A taxpayer may elect not to have the amendment made by subparagraph (A) apply and to have section 1214(d)(1) of the Reform Act apply as in effect before such amendment. Such election shall be made at such time and in such manner as the Secretary of the Treasury or his delegate may prescribe."

Prior to amendment Sec. 1214(d)(1) of P.L. 99-514 read as follows:

"(d) Effective dates.

"(1) In general. The amendments made by this section shall apply to payments after December 31, 1986."

—P.L. 100-647, Sec. 1012(g)(2), amended Sec. 1214(d)(2)(B) of P.L. 99-514 [reproduced below], part of the effective date for changes made by Sec. 1214 of P.L. 99-514, by substituting "section 904(a)(2)(H)" for "section 904(d)(2)(G)", see below.

—P.L. 100-647, Sec. 1012(g)(3)(A), substituted "subchapter) or, in the case of a corporation, is attributable to income so derived by a subsidiary of such corporation" for "subchapter)" in clause (c)(1)(B)(i) . . . Sec. 1012(g)(3)(B), deleted "or chain of subsidiaries of such corporation" in clause (c)(1)(B)(ii) . . . Sec. 1012(g)(3)(C), added the last sentence in clause (c)(1)(B)(ii), effective for payments made in a tax. year of the payor begin. after 12/31/86 (as provided in Secs. 1214(d)(2)-(4) of the 1986 Act as amended by P.L. 100-647, Secs. 1012(g)(1) and (2), see below.

—P.L. 100-647, Sec. 1012(i)(10), amended para. (a)(7) . . . Sec. 1012(i)(14)(B), amended clause (c)(2)(B)(ii), effective for tax. yrs. of foreign corporations begin. after 12/31/86, except as provided in Sec. 1221(g)(3) of P.L. 99-514 reproduced in note following Code Sec. 953.

Prior to amendment, para. (a)(7) read as follows:

"(7) Amounts received as underwriting income (as defined in section 832(b)(3)) derived from the insurance of United States risks (as defined in section 953(a))."

Prior to amendment, clause (c)(2)(B)(ii) read as follows:

"(ii) such section shall be applied by substituting '10 percent' for '50 percent' each place it appears."

—P.L. 100-647, Sec. 1012(q)(7), substituted "other than income described in section 884(d)(2)" for "other than under section 884(d)(2)" each place it appeared in subpara. (a)(2)(B) . . . Sec. 1012(q)(9), added subsec. (f) . . . Sec. 1012(q)(15), substituted "243(e)" for "section 243(d)" in subpara. (a)(2)(C), effective for tax. yrs. begin. after 12/31/86.

—P.L. 100-647, Sec. 1012(aa)(3)(A), (D), (F) and (4), provide:

"(3) Certain amendments not to apply to the extent inconsistent with treaties. The following amendments made by the Reform Act shall not apply to the extent the application of such amendments would be contrary to any treaty obligation of the United States in effect on the date of the enactment of the Reform Act:

"(A) The amendments made by section 1211 of the Reform Act to the extent—

"(i) such amendments apply in the case of an individual treated as a resident of a foreign country under a treaty obligation of the United States as so in effect, or

"(ii) such amendments relate to income of a nonresident from the sale or exchange of inventory property which would otherwise be sourced under section 865(e)(2) of the 1986 Code.

* * *

"(D) The amendments made by section 1214 of the Reform Act; except for purposes of determining the amount of the foreign tax credit.

* * *

"(F) The amendment made by section 1241(b)(2)(A) of the Reform Act (see below).

* * *

"(4) Treatment of technical corrections.—For purposes of paragraphs (2) and (3), any amendment made by this title shall be treated as if it had been included in the provision of the Reform Act to which such amendment relates."

—P.L. 100-647, Sec. 1018(u)(39), substituted "inventory property" for "personal property" in the heading of para. (a)(6), effective for tax. yrs. begin. after 12/31/86. For special rule for foreign persons, see Sec. 1211(c)(2) of this Act reproduced in note following Code Sec. 805.

—P.L. 100-647, Sec. 4009, provides:

"Sec 4009. Allocation of research and experimental expenditures.

"(a) General rule.

"For purposes of sections 861(b), 862(b), and 863(b) of the 1986 Code, qualified research and experimental expenditures shall be allocated and apportioned as follows:

"(1) any qualified research and experimental expenditures expended solely to meet legal requirements imposed by a political entity with respect to the improvement or marketing of specific products or processes for purposes not reasonably expected to generate gross income (beyond de minimis amounts) outside the jurisdiction of the political entity shall be allocated only to gross income from sources within such jurisdiction.

"(2) In the case of any qualified research and experimental expenditures (not allocated under paragraph (1) to the extent—

"(A) that such expenditures are attributable to activities conducted in the United States, 64 percent of such expenditures shall be allocated and apportioned to income from sources within the United States and deducted from such income in determining the amount of taxable income from sources within the United States, and

"(B) that such expenditures are attributable to activities conducted outside the United States, 64 percent of such expenditures shall be allocated and apportioned to income from sources outside the United States and deducted from such income in determining the amount of taxable income from sources outside the United States.

"(3) The remaining portion of qualified research and experimental expenditures (not allocated under paragraphs (1) and (2)) shall be apportioned, at the annual election of the taxpayer, on the basis of gross sales or gross income, except that, if the taxpayer elects to apportion on the basis of gross income, the amount apportioned to income from sources outside the United States shall be at least 30 percent of the amount which would be so apportioned on the basis of gross sales.

"(b) Qualified research and experimental expenditures. For purposes of this section, the term 'qualified research and experimental expenditures' means amounts which are research and experimental expenditures within the meaning of section 174 of the 1986 Code. For purposes of this subsection, rules similar to the rules of subsection (c) of section 174 of the 1986 Code shall apply.

"(c) Special rules for expenditures attributable to activities conducted in space, etc.

"(1) In general. Any qualified research and experimental expenditures described in paragraph (2)—

"(A) if incurred by a United States person, shall be allocated and apportioned under this section in the same manner as if they were attributable to activities conducted in the United States, and

"(B) if incurred by a person other than a United States person, shall be allocated and apportioned under this section in the same manner as if they were attributable to activities conducted outside the United States.

"(2) Description of expenditures. For purposes of paragraph (1) qualified research and experimental expenditures are described in this paragraph if such expenditures are attributable to activities conducted—

"(A) in space,

"(B) on or under water not within the jurisdiction (as recognized by the United States) of a foreign country, possession of the United States, or the United States, or

"(C) in Antarctica.
"(d) Affiliated group.
"(1) Except as provided in paragraph (2), the allocation and apportionment required by subsection (a) shall be determined as if all members of the affiliated group (as defined in subsection (e)(5) of section 864 of the 1986 Code) were a single corporation.
"(2) For purposes of the allocation and apportionment required by subsection (a)—
"(A) sales and gross income from products produced in whole or in part in a possession by an electing corporation (within the meaning of section 936(h)(5)(E) of the 1986 Code); and
"(B) dividends from an electing corporation, shall not be taken into account, except that this paragraph shall not apply to sales of (and gross income and dividends attributable to sales of) products with respect to which an election under section 936(h)(5)(F) of the 1986 Code is not in effect.
"(3) The qualified research and experimental expenditures taken into account for purposes of subsection (a) shall be adjusted to reflect the amount of such expenditures included in computing the cost-sharing amount (determined under section 936(h)(5)(C)(i)(I) of the 1986 Code).
"(4) The Secretary of the Treasury or his delegate may prescribe such regulations as may be necessary to carry out the purposes of this subsection, including regulations providing for the source of gross income and the allocation and apportionment of deductions to take into account the adjustments required by paragraph (3).
"(5) Paragraph (6) of section 864(e) of the 1986 Code shall not apply to qualified research and experimental expenditures.
"(e) Years to which section applies.
"(1) In general. Except as provided in this subsection, this section shall apply to the taxpayer's 1st taxable year beginning after August 1, 1987.
"(2) Reduction in amounts to which section applies. Notwithstanding paragraph (1), this section shall only apply to that portion of the qualified research and experimental expenditures for the taxable year referred to in paragraph (1) which bears the same ratio to the total amount of such expenditures as—
"(A) the lesser of 4 months or the number of months in the taxable year, bears to
"(B) the number of months in the taxable year."
In 1987, P.L. 100-203, Sec. 10221(d)(4)(A), substituted "100/70th" for "100/85th" in para. (a)(2)... Sec. 10221(d)(4)(B), added the last sentence to para. (a)(2), effective for dividends received or accrued after 12/31/87, in tax. yrs. end. after 12/31/87.
In 1986, P.L. 99-514, Sec. 104(b)(11), substituted "the standard deduction" for "the zero bracket amount" in subsec. (b), effective for tax. yrs. begin. after 12/31/86.
—P.L. 99-514, Sec. 1211(b)(1)(B), substituted "inventory property (within the meaning of section 865(h)(1))" for "personal property" in para. (a)(6), generally effective for tax. yrs. begin. after 12/31/86 [see Sec. 1012 of P.L. 100-647(aa)(3)(A), above]. For special rule for foreign persons, see Sec. 1211(c)(2) of this Act reproduced in note following Code Sec. 865.
—P.L. 99-514, Sec. 1212(d), deleted subsec. (e) and redesignated subsec. (f) as (e), effective for tax. yrs. begin. after 12/31/86, except as provided in Secs. 1212(f)(2) and (3) of this Act:
"(2) Special rule for certain leased property.— The amendments made by subsections (a) and (d) shall not apply to any income attributable to property held by the taxpayer on January 1, 1986, if such property was first leased by the taxpayer before January 1, 1986, in a lease to which section 863(c)(2)(B) or 861(e) of the Internal Revenue Code of 1954 (as in effect on the day before the date of the enactment of this Act) applied.
"(3) Special rule for certain ships leased by the United States Navy.—
"(A) In general.— In the case of any property described in subparagraph (B), paragraph (2) shall be applied by substituting '1987' for '1986' each place it appears.
"(B) Property to which paragraph applies.— Property described in this subparagraph consists of 4 ships which are to be leased by the United States Navy and which are the subject of Internal Revenue Service rulings bearing the following dates and which involved the following amount of financing, respectively:

"March 5, 1986 . . . . $ 176,844,000
February 5, 1986   64,567,000
April 22, 1986   64,598,000
May 22, 1986 . . . . 175,300,000 ."

Prior to deletion, subsec. (e) read as follows:
"(e) Income from certain leased aircraft, vessels, and spacecraft treated as income from sources within the United States.
"(1) In general. For purposes of subsection (a) and section 862(a), if—
"(A) a taxpayer owning a craft which is section 38 property (or would be section 38 property but for section 48(a)(5)) leases such craft to a United States person, other than a member of the same controlled group of corporations (as defined in section 1563) as the taxpayer, and
"(B) such craft is manufactured or constructed in the United States,
then all amounts includible in gross income by the taxpayer with respect to such craft for any taxable year ending after the commencement of such lease (whether during or after the period of such lease), including gain from sale, exchange, or other disposition of such craft, shall be treated as income from sources within the United States.
"(2) Certain transfers involving carryover basis. If the taxpayer transfers or distributes a craft to which paragraph (1) applied and the basis of such craft in the hands of the transferee or distributee is determined by reference to its basis in the hands of the transferor or distributor, paragraph (1) shall continue to apply to such craft in the hands of the transferee or distributee.
"(3) Craft defined. For purposes of this subsection, the term 'craft' means a vessel, aircraft, or spacecraft."
—P.L. 99-514, Sec. 1214(a)(1), amended subpara. (a)(1)(B)... Sec. 1214(a)(2), amended subsec. (c)... Sec. 1214(b), amended subpara. (a)(2)(A)... Sec. 1214(c)(5)(A), deleted subparas. (a)(1)(A) and (E), and redesignated subparas. (a)(1)(B), (C), (D), (F), (G), and (H) as subparas. (a)(1)(A), (B), (C), (D), (E), and (F),... Sec. 1214(c)(5)(B), substituted "subparagraph (B) of section 871(i)(3)" for "paragraph (2) of subsection (c)" in subpara. (a)(1)(D) [as redesignated]... Sec. 1214(c)(5)(C), amended subsec. (d), effective as provided in Secs. 1214(d)(1)-(4) of this Act [as amended by P.L. 100-647, Secs. 1012(g)(1) and (2), see above] (see Sec. 1012(aa)(3)(A) and (D) of P.L. 100-647, above) which reads as follows:
"(d) Effective dates.
"(1) In general. The amendments made by this section shall apply to payments made in a taxable year of the payor beginning after December 31, 1986.
"(2) Treatment of certain interest.
"(A) In general.— The amendments made by this section shall not apply to any interest paid or accrued on any obligation outstanding on December 31, 1985. The preceding sentence shall not apply to any interest paid pursuant to any extension or renewal of such an obligation agreed to after December 31, 1985.
"(B) Special rule for related payee.— If the payee of any interest to which subparagraph (A) applies is related (within the meaning of section 904(d)(2)(H) of the Internal Revenue Code of 1986) to the payor, such interest shall be treated for purposes of section 904 of such Code as if the payor were a controlled foreign corporation (within the meaning of section 957(a) of such Code).
"(3) Transitional rule.
"(A) Years before 1988.— In applying the amendments made by this section to any payment made by a corporation in a taxable year of such corporation beginning before January 1, 1988, the requirements of clause (ii) of section 861(c)(1)(B) of the Internal Revenue Code of 1986 (relating to active business requirements), as amended by this section, shall not apply to gross income of such corporation for taxable years beginning before January 1, 1987.
"(B) Years after 1987. In applying the amendments made by this section to any payment made by a corporation in a taxable year of such corporation beginning after December 31, 1987, the testing period for purposes of section 861(c) of such Code (as so amended) shall not include any taxable year beginning before January 1, 1987.
"(4) Certain dividends.
"(A) In general. The amendments made by this section shall not apply to any dividend paid before January 1, 1991, by a qualified corporation with respect to stock which was outstanding on May 31, 1985.
"(B) Qualified corporation. For purposes of subparagraph (A), the term 'qualified corporation' means any business systems corporation which—
"(i) was incorporated in Delaware in February, 1979,
"(ii) is headquartered in Garden City, New York, and
"(iii) the parent corporation of which is a resident of Sweden."
Sec. 1216 of this Act provides:
"1-Year modification in regulations providing for allocation of research and experimental expenditures.
"(a) General rule.
"For purposes of section 861(b), section 862(b), and section 863(b) of the Internal Revenue Code of 1954, notwithstanding section 864(e) of such Code—
"(1) 50 percent of all amounts allowable as a deduction for qualified research and experimental expenditures shall be apportioned to income from sources within the United States and deducted from such income in determining the amount of taxable income from sources within the United States, and
"(2) the remaining portion of such amounts shall be apportioned on the basis of gross sales or gross income.
The preceding sentence shall not apply to any expenditures described in section 1.861-8(e)(3)(i)(B) of the Income Tax Regulations.
"(b) Qualified research and experimental expenditures.
"For purposes of this section—
"(1) In general. The term 'qualified research and experimental expenditures' means amounts—
"(A) which are research and experimental expenditures within the meaning of section 174 of such Code, and
"(B) which are attributable to activities conducted in the United States.
"(2) Treatment of depreciation, etc.— Rules similar to the rules of section 174(c) of such Code shall apply.
"(c) Effective date.
"This section shall apply to taxable years beginning after August 1, 1986, and on or before August 1, 1987."
Prior to amendment, subpara. (a)(1)(B) read as follows:
"(B) interest received from a resident alien individual or a domestic corporation, when it is shown to the satisfaction of the Secretary that less than 20 percent of the gross income from all sources of such individual or such corporation has been derived from sources within the United States, as determined under the provisions of this part, for the 3-year period ending with the close of the taxable year of such individual or such corporation preceding the payment of such interest, or for such part of such period as may be applicable."
Prior to amendment, subsec. (c) read as follows:
"(c) Interest on deposits, etc.
"For purposes of subsection (a)(1)(A), the amounts described in this subsection are—
"(1) deposits with persons carrying on the banking business.

Source of income Code Sec. 861

"(2) deposits or withdrawable accounts with savings institutions chartered and supervised as savings and loan or similar associations under Federal or State law, but only to the extent that amounts paid or credited on such deposits or accounts are deductible under section 591 (determined without regard to section 265) in computing the taxable income of such institutions, and

"(3) amounts held by an insurance company under an agreement to pay interest thereon."

Prior to amendment, subpara. (a)(2)(A) read as follows:

"(A) from a domestic corporation other than a corporation which has an election in effect under section 936, and other than a corporation less than 20 percent of whose gross income is shown to the satisfaction of the Secretary to have been derived from sources within the United States, as determined under the provisions of this part, for the 3-year period ending with the close of the taxable year of such corporation preceding the declaration of such dividends (or for such part of such period as the corporation has been in existence), or"

Prior to deletion, subpara. (a)(1)(A) read as follows:

"(A) interest on amounts described in subsection (c) received by a nonresident alien individual or a foreign corporation, if such interest is not effectively connected with the conduct of a trade or business within the United States."

Prior to deletion, subpara. (a)(1)(E) read as follows:

"(E) income derived by a foreign central bank of issue from bankers acceptances."

Prior to amendment, subsec. (d) read as follows:

"(d) Special rules for application of paragraphs (1)(B), (1)(C), (1)(D), and (2)(B) of subsection (a).

"(1) New entities. For purposes of paragraphs (1)(B), (1)(C), (1)(D), and (2)(B) of subsection (a), if the resident alien individual, domestic corporation, or foreign corporation, as the case may be, has no gross income from any source for the 3-year period (or part thereof) specified, the 20 percent test or the 50 percent test, as the case may be, shall be applied with respect to the taxable year of the payor in which payment of the interest or dividends, as the case may be, is made.

"(2) Transition rule. For purposes of paragraphs (1)(C), (1)(D), and (2)(B) of subsection (a), the gross income of the foreign corporation for any period before the first taxable year beginning after December 31, 1966, which is effectively connected with the conduct of a trade or business within the United States is an amount equal to the gross income for such period from sources within the United States."

—P.L. 99-514, Sec. 1241(b)(1)(A), substituted "noncorporate residents or domestic corporations" for "residents, corporate and otherwise," in para. (a)(1) . . . Sec. 1241(b)(1)(B), deleted subparas. (a)(1)(B) and (C) [as redesignated by Sec. 1214, see above], and redesignated subparas. (a)(1)(D), (E), and (F) as subparas. (a)(1)(B), (C), and (D) . . . Sec. 1241(b)(2)(A), substituted "25 percent" for "50 percent" in subpara. (a)(2)(B) . . . Sec. 1241(b)(2)(B), substituted "effectively connected (or treated as effectively connected other than under section 884(d)(2))" for "effectively connected" each place appeared in subpara. (a)(2)(B), effective for tax. yrs. begin. after 12/31/86 (see Sec. 1012 of P.L. 100-647(aa)(3)(F), above).

Prior to deletion, subparas. (a)(1)(B) and (C) [as redesignated by Sec. 1214] read as follows

"(B) interest received from a foreign corporation (other than interest paid or credited by a domestic branch of a foreign corporation, if such branch is engaged in the commercial banking business), when it is shown to the satisfaction of the Secretary that less than 50 percent of the gross income from all sources of such foreign corporation for the 3-year period ending with the close of its taxable year preceding the payment of such interest (or for such part of such period as the corporation has been in existence) was effectively connected with the conduct of a trade or business within the United States,

"(C) in the case of interest received from a foreign corporation (other than interest paid or credited by a domestic branch of a foreign corporation, if such branch is engaged in the commercial banking business), 50 percent or more of the gross income of which from all sources for the 3-year period ending with the close of its taxable year preceding the payment of such interest (or for such part of such period as the corporation has been in existence) was effectively connected with the conduct of a trade or business within the United States, an amount of such interest which bears the same ratio to such interest as the gross income of such foreign corporation for such period which was not effectively connected with the conduct of a trade or business within the United States bears to its gross income from all sources."

—P.L. 99-272, Sec. 13211, amended Sec. 126(c) of P.L. 98-369 by substituting "1986" for "1985" and by substituting "4th" for "3rd" each place it appeared [see below].

In 1984, P.L. 98-369, Sec. 126, [as amended by Sec. 13211 of P.L. 99-272, see above] provides:

"SEC. 126. ALLOCATION UNDER SECTION 861 OF RESEARCH AND EXPERIMENTAL EXPENDITURES.

"(a) In general. For purposes of section 861(b), section 862(b), and section 863(b) of the Internal Revenue Code of 1954, all amounts allowable as a deduction for qualified research and experimental expenditures shall be allocated to income from sources within the United States and deducted from such income in determining the amount of taxable income from sources within the United States.

"(b) Qualified research and experimental expenditures. For purposes of this section—

"(1) In general.—The term 'qualified research and experimental expenditures' means amounts—

"(A) which are research and experimental expenditures within the meaning of section 174 of such Code, and

"(B) which are attributable to activities conducted in the United States.

"(2) Treatment of depreciation, etc.—Rules similar to the rules of subsection (c) of section 174 of such Code shall apply.

"(c) Effective dates.

"(1) In general. —This section shall apply to taxable years beginning after August 13, 1983, and on or before August 1, 1986.

"(2) Special rule.—If the taxpayer's 4th taxable year beginning after 8/13/81, is not described in paragraph (1), this section shall apply also to such 4th taxable year."

In 1983, P.L. 98-21, Sec. 121(d), added para. (a)(8), effective for benefits received after 12/31/83, in tax. yrs. end. after 12/31/83. Sec. 121(g)(2) of the Act provides as follows:

"(2) Treatment of certain lump-sum payments received after December 31, 1983.—The amendments made by this section shall not apply to any portion of a lump-sum payment of social security benefits (as defined in section 86(d) of the Internal Revenue Code of 1954) received after December 31, 1983, if the generally applicable payment date for such portion was before January 1, 1984."

In 1981, P.L. 97-34, Sec. 223, provides for suspension of regulations relating to allocation under Code Sec. 861 of research and experimental expenditures. [Sec. 223 of P.L. 97-34 reproduced in note following Code Sec. 174.]

In 1980, P.L. 96-605, Sec. 104(a), amended subsec. (e), effective for property first leased after 12/28/80.

Prior to amendment, subsec. (e) read as follows:

"(e) Election to treat income from certain aircraft and vessels as income from sources within the United States.

"(1) In general. For purposes of subsection (a) and section 862(a), if a taxpayer owning an aircraft or vessel which is section 38 property (or would be section 38 property but for section 48(a)(5)) leases such aircraft or vessel to a United States person, other than a member of the same controlled group of corporations (as defined in section 1563) as the taxpayer, and if such aircraft or vessel is manufactured or constructed in the United States, the taxpayer may elect, for any taxable year ending after the commencement of such lease, to treat all amounts includible in gross income with respect to such aircraft or vessel (whether during or after the period of any such lease), including gain from sale, exchange, or other disposition of such aircraft or vessel, as income from sources within the United States.

"(2) Effect of election. An election under paragraph (1) made with respect to any aircraft or vessel shall apply to the taxable year for which made and to all subsequent taxable years. Such election may not be revoked except with the consent of the Secretary.

"(3) Manner and time of election and revocation. An election under paragraph (1), and any revocation of such election, shall be made in such manner and at such time as the Secretary prescribes by regulations.

"(4) Certain transfers involving carryover basis. If the taxpayer transfers or distributes an aircraft or vessel which is subject to an election under paragraph (1) and the basis of such aircraft or vessel in the hands of the basis in the hands of the transferor or distributor, the transferee or distributee shall, for purposes of paragraph (1), be treated as having made an election with respect to such aircraft or vessel."

—P.L. 96-499, Sec. 1124, amended para. (a)(5), effective for dispositions after 6/18/80.

Prior to amendment, para. (a)(5) read as follows:

"(5) Sale or exchange of real property. Gains, profits, and income from the sale or exchange of real property located in the United States."

In 1978, P.L. 95-600, Sec. 370(a), added new subsec. (f), effective for all railroad rolling stock placed in service with respect to the taxpayer after 11/6/78. Sec. 370(b)(2) of this Act provides:

"(2) Election to extend section 861(f) to railroad rolling stock placed in service before date of enactment.

"(A) In general. At the election of the taxpayer, the amendment made by subsection (a) shall also apply, for taxable years beginning after the date of the enactment of this Act, to all railroad rolling stock placed in service with respect to the taxpayer on or before such date of enactment. Such an election may not be revoked except with the consent of the Secretary of the Treasury or his delegate.

"(B) Manner and time of election and revocation. An election under subparagraph (A), and any revocation of such an election, shall be made in such manner and at such time as the Secretary of the Treasury or his delegate may by regulations prescribe."

—P.L. 95-600, Sec. 540(a), amended subpara. (a)(1)(F), effective for tax. yrs. begin. after 11/6/78.

Prior to amendment, subpara. (a)(1)(F) read as follows:

"(F) interest on deposits with a foreign branch of a domestic corporation or a domestic partnership, if such branch is engaged in the commercial banking business,"

In 1977, P.L. 95-30, Sec. 102(b)(9), added the last sentence in subsec. (b), effective for tax. yrs. begin. after 12/31/76.

In 1976, P.L. 94-455, Sec. 1036(a), added para. (a)(7), effective for tax. yrs. begin. after 12/31/76.

—P.L. 94-455, Sec. 1041, deleted the last sentence of subsec. (c), effective 10/4/76.

Prior to deletion, the last sentence of subsec. (c) read as follows:

"Effective with respect to amounts paid or credited after December 31, 1976, subsection (a)(1)(A) and this subsection shall cease to apply."

—P.L. 94-455, Sec. 1051(h)(3), substituted "other than a corporation which has an election in effect under section 936," for "other than a corporation entitled to the benefits of section 931," following "(A) for a domestic corporation" in subpara. (a)(2)(A), effective for tax. yrs. begin. after '75, except that "qualified possession source investment income" as defined in section 936(d)(2) of the Internal Revenue Code of 1954 shall include income from any source outside the United

2,491

Code Sec. 861 — Source of income

States if the taxpayer establishes to the satisfaction of the Secretary of the Treasury or his delegate that the income from such sources was earned before 10/1/76.
—P.L. 94-455, Sec. 1901(b)(26)(A), substituted "sale or exchange" for "sale" each time it appeared in paras. (a)(5) and (a)(6), effective for tax. yrs. begin. after 12/31/76.
—P.L. 94-455, Sec. 1901(b)(26)(B), substituted "sale, exchange, or other disposition" for "sale or other disposition" following "(whether during or after the period of any such lease), including gain from" in para. (e)(1), effective for tax. yrs. begin. after 12/31/76.
—P.L. 94-455, Sec. 1901(c)(7), deleted "any Territory, any political subdivision of a Territory," following "Interest from the United States," in the first sentence of para. (a)(1), effective for tax. yrs. begin. after 12/31/76.
—P.L. 94-455, Sec. 1904(b)(10)(B)(i), substituted "subsection (c) of section 4912 (as in effect before July 1, 1974)" for "section 4912(c)" in subpara. (a)(1)(G) . . . Sec. 1904(a)(10)(B)(ii), substituted "subsection (c)(2) of such section" for "section 4912(c)(2)" in subpara. (a)(1)(G), effective 2/1/77.
—P.L. 94-455, Sec. 1906(b)(13)(A), substituted "Secretary" for "Secretary or his delegate" each place it appeared in subsecs. (a) and (e), effective for tax. yrs. begin. after 12/31/76.
In 1975, P.L. 93-625, Sec. 9(a)(1), struck out "and" at the end of subpara. (a)(1)(F) . . . Sec. 9(a)(2), substituted ", and" for the period at the end of subpara. (a)(1)(G), Sec. 9(a)(3) added new subpara. (a)(1)(H), effective for interest paid after 1/3/75.
—P.L. 93-625, Sec. 8, substituted "1976" for "1975" in the last sentence of subsec. (c), effective 1/3/75.
In 1971, P.L. 92-178, Sec. 503(1), substituted ", or" for the period at the end of subpara. (a)(2)(C) . . . Sec. 503(2), added subpara. (a)(2)(D), effective for tax. yrs. end. after 12/31/71, except that a corporation may not be a DISC for any tax. yr. begin. before 1/1/72.
—P.L. 92-178, Sec. 314(a), added subsec. (e), effective for tax. yrs. end. after 8/15/71, but only for leases entered into after 8/15/71.
—P.L. 92-9, Sec. 3(a)(2)(A), deleted "and" at the end of subpara. (a)(1)(E) . . . Sec. 3(a)(2)(B), substituted ", and" for the period at the end of subpara. (a)(1)(F) . . . Sec. 3(a)(2)(C), added subpara. (a)(1)(G), effective 4/1/71.
In 1969, P.L. 91-172, Sec. 435(a)(1), deleted "after December 31, 1972," in subparas. (a)(1)(C) and (a)(1)(D), effective for amounts paid or credited after 12/31/69
—P.L. 91-172, Sec. 435(a)(2), substituted "1975" for "1972" in subsec. (c).
In 1966, P.L. 89-809, Sec. 102(a)(1)(A), amended subpara. (a)(1)(A) . . . Sec. 102(a)(1)(B), added subsec. (c) . . . Sec. 102(a)(2), amended subparas. (a)(1)(B) and (a)(1)(C), and added subparas. (a)(1)(D), (a)(1)(E), and (a)(1)(F) . . . Sec. 102(a)(3), added after subsec. (c) (as added by this Act, see above) subsec. (d) . . . Sec. 102(c), amended clause (a)(3)(C)(ii), effective for tax. yrs. begin. after 12/31/66.
Prior to amendment, subpara. (a)(1)(A) read as follows:
"(A) interest on deposits with persons carrying on the banking business paid to persons not engaged in business within the United States."
Prior to amendment, subpara. (a)(1)(B) read as follows:
"(B) interest received from a resident alien individual, a resident foreign corporation, or a domestic corporation, when it is shown to the satisfaction of the Secretary or his delegate that less than 20 percent of the gross income of such resident payor or domestic corporation has been derived from sources within the United States, as determined under the provisions of this part, for the 3-year period ending with the close of the taxable year of such payor preceding the payment of such interest, or for such part of such period as may be applicable, and"
Prior to amendment, subpara. (a)(1)(C) read as follows:
"(C) income derived by a foreign central bank of issue from bankers' acceptances."
Prior to amendment, clause (a)(3)(C)(ii) read as follows:
"(ii) a domestic corporation, if such labor or services are performed for an office or place of business maintained in a foreign country or in a possession of the United States by such corporation."
Sec. 102(b) of P.L. 89-809, amended subpara. (a)(2)(B), effective for amounts received after 12/31/66.
Prior to amendment, subpara. (a)(2)(B) read as follows:
"(B) from a foreign corporation unless less than 50 percent of the gross income of such foreign corporation for the 3-year period ending with the close of its taxable year preceding the declaration of such dividends (or for such part of such period as the corporation has been in existence) was derived from sources within the United States as determined under the provisions of this part; but only in an amount which bears the same ratio to such dividends as the gross income of the corporation for such period derived from sources within the United States bears to its gross income from all sources; but dividends from a foreign corporation shall, for purposes of subpart A of part III (relating to foreign tax credit), be treated as income from sources without the United States to the extent exceeding the amount which is 100/85ths of the amount of the deduction allowable under section 245 in respect of such dividends, or"
In 1962, P.L. 87-834, Sec. 9(c), substituted "to the extent exceeding the amount which is 100/85ths of the amount of the deduction allowable under section 245 in respect of such dividends" for "to the extent exceeding the amount of the deduction allowable under section 245 in respect of such dividends" in subpara. (a)(2)(B), effective for any distribution received by a domestic corporation after 12/31/64, and for any distribution received by a domestic corporation before 1/1/65, in a tax. yr. of such corporation begin. after 12/31/62, but only to the extent that such distribution is made out of the accumulated profits of a foreign corporation for a tax. yr. (of such foreign corporation) begin. after 12/31/62.

In 1960, P.L. 86-779, Sec. 3(b), substituted ", or" for the period at the end of subpara. (a)(2)(B) and added subpara. (a)(2)(C), effective for dividends received after 12/31/59 in tax. yrs. end. after 12/31/59.

Sec. 862. Income from sources without the United States.

(a) Gross income from sources without United States.

The following items of gross income shall be treated as income from sources without the United States:

(1) interest other than that derived from sources within the United States as provided in section 861(a)(1);

(2) dividends other than those derived from sources within the United States as provided in section 861(a)(2);

(3) compensation for labor or personal services performed without the United States;

(4) rentals or royalties from property located without the United States or from any interest in such property, including rentals or royalties for the use of or for the privilege of using without the United States patents, copyrights, secret processes and formulas, good will, trademarks, trade brands, franchises, and other like properties;

(5) gains, profits, and income from the sale or exchange of real property located without the United States;

(6) gains, profits, and income derived from the purchase of inventory property (within the meaning of section 865(i)(1)) within the United States and its sale or exchange without the United States;

(7) underwriting income other than that derived from sources within the United States as provided in section 861(a)(7);

(8) gains, profits, and income from the disposition of a United States real property interest (as defined in section 897(c)) when the real property is located in the Virgin Islands; and

(9) amounts received, directly or indirectly, from a foreign person for the provision of a guarantee of indebtedness of such person other than amounts which are derived from sources within the United States as provided in section 861(a)(9).

(b) Taxable income from sources without United States.

From the items of gross income specified in subsection (a) there shall be deducted the expenses, losses, and other deductions properly apportioned or allocated thereto, and a ratable part of any expenses, losses, or other deductions which cannot definitely be allocated to some item or class of gross income. The remainder, if any, shall be treated in full as taxable income from sources without the United States. In the case of an individual who does not itemize deductions, an amount equal to the standard deduction shall be considered a deduction which cannot definitely be allocated to some item or class of gross income.

In 2010, P.L. 111-240, Sec. 2122(b), struck out "and" at the end of para. (a)(7), substituted "; and" for the period at the end of para. (a)(8) and added para. (b)(9), effective for guarantees issued after 9/27/2010.
In 1989, P.L. 101-239, Sec. 7811(i)(2), substituted "865(i)(1)" for "865(h)(1)" in para. (a)(6), effective for tax. yrs. begin. after 12/31/86.
In 1988, P.L. 100-647, Sec. 1012(e)(4), deleted subsec. (c), effective for tax yrs. begin. after 12/31/86.
Prior to deletion, subsec. (c) read as follows:
"(c) *Cross reference.* For source of amounts attributable to certain aircraft and vessels, see section 861(e)."
—P.L. 100-647, Sec. 1012(aa)(3)(A) and (4), provides:
"(3) Certain amendments not to apply to the extent inconsistent with treaties. The following amendments made by the Reform Act shall not apply to the extent the application of such amendments would be contrary to any treaty obligation of the United States in effect on the date of the enactment of the Reform Act:
"(A) The amendments made by section 1211 of the Reform Act to the extent—
"(i) such amendments apply in the case of an individual treated as a resident of a foreign country under a treaty obligation of the United States as so in effect, or

Source of income — Code Sec. 863(d)(1)

"(ii) such amendments relate to income of a non-resident from the sale or exchange of inventory property which would otherwise be sourced under section 865(e)(2) of the 1986 Code."

* * *

"(4) Treatment of technical corrections. For purposes of paragraphs (2) and (3), any amendment made by this title shall be treated as if it had been included in the provision of the Reform Act to which such amendment relates."

—P.L. 100-647, Sec. 4009, provides rules for the allocation of research and experimental expenditures. Sec. 4009 of this Act is reproduced in the note following Code Sec. 861.

—P.L. 100-647, Sec. 1012(aa)(3)(A), provides that amendments made by Sec. 1211 of P.L. 99-514 shall not apply to the extent that the application of such amendments would be contrary to any treaty obligation of the U.S. in effect on 10/22/86 to the extent as provided in Secs. 1012(aa)(3)(A)(i) and (ii) which read as follows:

"(i) such amendments apply in the case of an individual treated as a resident of a foreign country under a treaty obligation of the United States as so in effect, or

"(ii) such amendments relate to income of a non-resident from the sale or exchange of inventory property which would otherwise be sourced under section 865(e)(2) of the 1986 Code."

In 1986, P.L. 99-514, Sec. 104(b)(12), substituted "standard deduction" for "zero bracket amount" in subsec. (b), effective for tax. yrs. begin. after 12/31/86.

—P.L. 99-514, Sec. 1211(b)(1)(C), substituted "inventory property (within the meaning of section 865(h)(1))" for "personal property" in para. (a)(6), effective for tax. yrs. begin. after 12/31/86. For special rule, see Sec. 1211(c)(2) of this Act reproduced in note following Code Sec. 865. For provisions on modifications of regulations for research and experimental expenditures, see Sec. 1216 of this Act, reproduced in note following Code Sec. 861.

—P.L. 99-272, Sec. 13211, amended Sec. 126(c) of P.L. 98-369 by substituting "1986" for "1985" and by substituting "4th" for "3rd" each place it appeared [see below]

In 1984, P.L. 98-369, Sec. 126, [as amended by Sec. 13211 of P.L. 99-272, see above] provides:

"Sec. 126. Allocation under section 861 of research and experimental expenditures.

"(a) In general. For purposes of section 861(b), section 862(b), and section 863(b) of the Internal Revenue Code of 1954, all amounts allowable as a deduction for qualified research and experimental expenditures shall be allocated to income from sources within the United States and deducted from such income in determining the amount of taxable income from sources within the United States.

"(b) Qualified research and experimental expenditures. For purposes of this section—

"(1) In general. The term 'qualified research and experimental expenditures' means amounts—

"(A) which are research and experimental expenditures within the meaning of section 174 of such Code, and

"(B) which are attributable to activities conducted in the United States.

"(2) Treatment of depreciation, etc. Rules similar to the rules of subsection (c) of section 174 of such Code shall apply.

"(c) Effective dates.

"(1) In general. This section shall apply to taxable years beginning after August 13, 1983, and on or before August 1, 1986.

"(2) Special rule. If the taxpayer's 4th taxable year beginning after August 13, 1981, is not described in paragraph (1), this section shall apply also to such 4th taxable year."

In 1981, P.L. 97-34, Sec. 831(a)(2), deleted "and" at the end of para. (a)(5), substituted a semicolon for the period at the end of para. (a)(6), substituted "underwriting" for "Underwriting" in para. (a)(7), substituted "; and" for the period at the end of para. (a)(7), and added para. (a)(8), effective for dispositions after 6/18/80, in tax. yrs. ending after 6/18/80.

In 1977, P.L. 95-30, Sec. 102(b)(10), added the last sentence in subsec. (b), effective for tax. yrs. begin. after 12/31/76.

In 1976, P.L. 94-455, Sec. 1036(b), added para. (a)(7), effective for tax. yrs. begin. after 12/31/76.

—P.L. 94-455, Sec. 1901(b)(26)(C), substituted "sale or exchange" for "sale" in paras. (a)(5) and (6), effective for tax. yrs. begin. after 12/31/76.

In 1971, P.L. 92-178, Sec. 314(b), added subsec. (c).

Sec. 863. Special rules for determining source.

(a) Allocation under regulations.

Items of gross income, expenses, losses, and deductions, other than those specified in sections 861(a) and 862(a), shall be allocated or apportioned to sources within or without the United States, under regulations prescribed by the Secretary. Where items of gross income are separately allocated to sources within the United States, there shall be deducted (for the purpose of computing the taxable income therefrom) the expenses, losses, and other deductions properly apportioned or allocated thereto and a ratable part of other expenses, losses, or other deductions which cannot definitely be allocated to some item or class of gross income. The remainder, if any, shall be included in full as taxable income from sources within the United States.

(b) Income partly from within and partly from without the United States.

In the case of gross income derived from sources partly within and partly without the United States, the taxable income may first be computed by deducting the expenses, losses, or other deductions apportioned or allocated thereto and a ratable part of any expenses, losses, or other deductions which cannot be definitely allocated to some item or class of gross income; and the portion of such taxable income attributable to sources within the United States may be determined by processes or formulas of general apportionment prescribed by the Secretary. Gains, profits, and income—

(1) from services rendered partly within and partly without the United States,

(2) from the sale or exchange of inventory property (within the meaning of section 865(i)(1)) produced (in whole or in part) by the taxpayer within and sold or exchanged without the United States, or produced (in whole or in part) by the taxpayer without and sold or exchanged within the United States, or

(3) derived from the purchase of inventory property (within the meaning of section 865(i)(1)) within a possession of the United States and its sale or exchange within the United States,

shall be treated as derived partly from sources within and partly from sources without the United States.

(c) Source rule for certain transportation income.

(1) Transportation beginning and ending in the United States. All transportation income attributable to transportation which begins and ends in the United States shall be treated as derived from sources within the United States.

(2) Other transportation having United States connection.

(A) In general. 50 percent of all transportation income attributable to transportation which—

(i) is not described in paragraph (1), and

(ii) begins or ends in the United States,

shall be treated as from sources in the United States.

(B) Special rule for personal service income. Subparagraph (A) shall not apply to any transportation income which is income derived from personal services performed by the taxpayer, unless such income is attributable to transportation which—

(i) begins in the United States and ends in a possession of the United States, or

(ii) begins in a possession of the United States and ends in the United States.

In the case of transportation income derived from, or in connection with, a vessel, this subparagraph shall only apply if the taxpayer is a citizen or resident alien.

(3) Transportation income. For purposes of this subsection, the term "transportation income" means any income derived from, or in connection with—

(A) the use (or hiring or leasing for use) of a vessel or aircraft, or

(B) the performance of services directly related to the use of a vessel or aircraft.

For purposes of the preceding sentence, the term "vessel or aircraft" includes any container used in connection with a vessel or aircraft.

(d) Source rules for space and certain ocean activities.

(1) In general. Except as provided in regulations, any income derived from a space or ocean activity—

2,493

(A) if derived by a United States person, shall be sourced in the United States, and

(B) if derived by a person other than a United States person, shall be sourced outside the United States.

(2) Space or ocean activity. For purposes of paragraph (1)—

(A) In general. The term "space or ocean activity" means—

(i) any activity conducted in space, and

(ii) any activity conducted on or under water not within the jurisdiction (as recognized by the United States) of a foreign country, possession of the United States, or the United States.

Such term includes any activity conducted in Antarctica.

(B) Exception for certain activities. The term "space or ocean activity" shall not include—

(i) any activity giving rise to transportation income (as defined in section 863(c)),

(ii) any activity giving rise to international communications income (as defined in subsection (e)(2)), and

(iii) any activity with respect to mines, oil and gas wells, or other natural deposits to the extent within the United States or any foreign country or possession of the United States (as defined in section 638).

For purposes of applying section 638, the jurisdiction of any foreign country shall not include any jurisdiction not recognized by the United States.

(e) International communications income.

(1) Source rules.

(A) United States persons. In the case of any United States person, 50 percent of any international communications income shall be sourced in the United States and 50 percent of such income shall be sourced outside the United States.

(B) Foreign persons.

(i) In general. Except as provided in regulations or clause (ii), in the case of any person other than a United States person, any international communications income shall be sourced outside the United States.

(ii) Special rule for income attributable to office or fixed place of business in the United States. In the case of any person (other than a United States person) who maintains an office or other fixed place of business in the United States, any international communications income attributable to such office or other fixed place of business shall be sourced in the United States.

(2) Definition. For purposes of this section, the term "international communications income" includes all income derived from the transmission of communications or data from the United States to any foreign country (or possession of the United States) or from any foreign country (or possession of the United States) to the United States.

In 1997, P.L. 105-34, Sec. 1174(a)(2), added a sentence at the end of subpara. (c)(2)(B), effective for remuneration for services performed in tax. yrs. begin. after 12/31/97.

In 1989, P.L. 101-239, Sec. 7811(i)(2), substituted "865(i)(1)" for "865(h)(1)", in paras. (b)(2) and (b)(3), effective for tax. yrs. begin. after 12/31/86.

In 1988, P.L. 100-647, Sec. 1012(e)(3)(A), amended the heading of Code Sec. 863 effective for tax. yrs. begin. after 12/31/86.
Prior to amendment, the heading read as follows:
"Sec. 863. Items not specified in section 861 or 862."

—P.L. 100-647, Sec. 1012(f), substituted "foreign country (or possession of the United States)" for "foreign country" each place it appeared in para. (e)(2), effective for tax. yrs. begin. after 12/31/86.

—P.L. 100-647, Sec. 1012(aa)(3)(A), (B), and (aa)(4), provide:

"(3) Certain amendments not to apply to the extent inconsistent with treaties. The following amendments made by the Reform Act shall not apply to the extent the application of such amendments would be contrary to any treaty obligation of the United States in effect on the date of the enactment of the Reform Act:

"(A) The amendments made by section 1211 of the Reform Act to the extent—
"(i) such amendments apply in the case of an individual treated as a resident of a foreign country under a treaty obligation of the United States as so in effect, or
"(ii) such amendments relate to income of a nonresident from the sale or exchange of inventory property which would otherwise be sourced under section 865(e)(2) of the 1986 Code.

"(B) The amendments made by section 1212(a) of the Reform Act; except for purposes of determining the amount of the foreign tax credit."

—P.L. 100-647, Sec. 4009, provides rules for the allocation of research and experimental expenditures. Sec. 4009 of this Act is reproduced in the note following Code Sec. 861.

In 1986, P.L. 99-514, Sec. 1211(b)(1)(A), substituted "inventory property (within the meaning of section 865(h)(1))" for "personal property" in paras. (b)(2) and (3), effective for tax. yrs. begin. after 12/31/86. For special rule, see Sec. 1211(c)(2) of this Act [see Sec. 1012 of P.L. 100-647(aa)(3)(A), (B) and (aa)(4), above] reproduced in note following Code Sec. 865.

—P.L. 99-514, Sec. 1212(a), amended para. (c)(2) ... Sec. 1212(e), substituted "services" for "transportation or other services" in para. (b)(1), effective for tax. yrs. begin. after 12/31/86 except as provided in Secs. 1212(f)(2) and (3) of this Act, which reads as follows:

"(2) Special rule for certain leased property.— The amendments made by subsections (a) and (d) [Sec. 1212] shall not apply to any income attributable to property held by the taxpayer on January 1, 1986, if such property was first leased by the taxpayer before January 1, 1986, in a lease to which section 863(c)(2)(B) or 861(e) of the Internal Revenue Code of 1954 (as in effect on the day before the date of the enactment of this Act) applied.

"(3) Special rule for certain ships leased by the United States Navy.—
"(A) In general.— In the case of any property described in subparagraph (B), paragraph (2) shall be applied by substituting '1987' for '1986' each place it appears.

"(B) Property to which paragraph applies.— Property described in this subparagraph consists of 4 ships which are to be leased by the United States Navy and which are the subject of Internal Revenue Service rulings bearing the following dates and which involved the following amount of financing respectively:

"March 5, 1986 . . . . $ 176,844,000
February 5, 1986 64,567,000
April 22, 1986 64,598,000
May 22, 1986 . . . . 175,300,000."

Prior to amendment, para. (c)(2) read as follows:
"(2) Transportation between United States and any possession.
"(A) In general. 50 percent of all transportation income attributable to transportation which—
"(i) begins in the United States and ends in a possession of the United States, or
"(ii) begins in a possession of the United States and ends in the United States, shall be treated as derived from sources within the United States
"(B) Special rule for certain lessors of aircraft. If—
"(i) the taxpayer owns an aircraft which is section 38 property and leases such aircraft to a United States person (other than a member of the same controlled group of corporations (as defined in section 1563) as the taxpayer), and
"(ii) such United States person is a regularly scheduled air carrier,
subparagraph (A) shall be applied by substituting 100 percent for 50 percent."

—P.L. 99-514, Sec. 1213(a), added subsecs. (d) and (e), effective for tax. yrs. begin. after 12/31/86. For provisions on modifications of regulations for research and experimental expenditures, see Sec. 1216 of this Act, reproduced in note following Code Sec. 861.

—P.L. 99-272, Sec. 13211, amended Sec. 126(c) of P.L. 98-369 by substituting "1986" for "1985" and by substituting "4th" for "3rd" each place it appeared [see below].

In 1984, P.L. 98-369, Sec. 124(a), added subsec. (c), effective for transportation begin. after 7/18/84 in tax. yrs. end. after 7/18/84.

—P.L. 98-369, Sec. 126, [as amended by Sec. 13211 of P.L. 99-272, see above] provides:

"SEC. 126. ALLOCATION UNDER SECTION 861 OF RESEARCH AND EXPERIMENTAL EXPENDITURES.

"(a) In general.— For purposes of section 861(b), section 862(b), and section 863(b) of the Internal Revenue Code of 1954, all amounts allowable as a deduction for qualified research and experimental expenditures shall be allocated to income from sources within the United States and deducted from such income in determining the amount of taxable income from sources within the United States.

"(b) Qualified research and experimental expenditures. For purposes of this section—
"(1) In general. The term 'qualified research and experimental expenditures' means amounts—
"(A) which are research and experimental expenditures within the meaning of section 174 of such Code, and
"(B) which are attributable to activities conducted in the United States.
"(2) Treatment of depreciation, etc.— Rules similar to the rules of subsection (c) of section 174 of such Code shall apply.

"(c) Effective dates.—
(1) In general.— This section shall apply to taxable years beginning after August 13, 1983, and on or before August 1, 1986.

"(2) Special rule.— If the taxpayer's 4th taxable year beginning after August 13, 1981, is not described in paragraph (1), this section shall apply also to such 4th taxable year."

In 1976, P.L. 94-455, Sec. 1906(b)(13)(A), substituted "Secretary" for "Secretary or his delegate" in subsecs. (a) and (b) . . . Sec. 1901(b)(26)(C), substituted "sale or exchange" for "sale" in paras. (b)(2) and (b)(3) . . . Sec. 1901(b)(26)(D), substituted "sold or exchanged" for "sold" each place it appeared in para. (b)(2), effective for tax. yrs. begin. after 12/31/76.

Sec. 864. Definitions and special rules.

(a) Produced.

For purposes of this part, the term "produced" includes created, fabricated, manufactured, extracted, processed, cured, or aged.

(b) Trade or business within the United States.

For purposes of this part, part II, and chapter 3, the term "trade or business within the United States" includes the performance of personal services within the United States at any time within the taxable year, but does not include—

(1) **Performance of personal services for foreign employer.** The performance of personal services—

(A) for a nonresident alien individual, foreign partnership, or foreign corporation, not engaged in trade or business within the United States, or

(B) for an office or place of business maintained in a foreign country or in a possession of the United States by an individual who is a citizen or resident of the United States or by a domestic partnership or a domestic corporation,

by a nonresident alien individual temporarily present in the United States for a period or periods not exceeding a total of 90 days during the taxable year and whose compensation for such services does not exceed in the aggregate $3,000.

(2) **Trading in securities or commodities.**

(A) Stocks and securities.

(i) In general. Trading in stocks or securities through a resident broker, commission agent, custodian, or other independent agent.

(ii) Trading for taxpayer's own account. Trading in stocks or securities for the taxpayer's own account, whether by the taxpayer or his employees or through a resident broker, commission agent, custodian, or other agent, and whether or not any such employee or agent has discretionary authority to make decisions in effecting the transactions. This clause shall not apply in the case of a dealer in stocks or securities.

(B) Commodities.

(i) In general. Trading in commodities through a resident broker, commission agent, custodian, or other independent agent.

(ii) Trading for taxpayer's own account. Trading in commodities for the taxpayer's own account, whether by the taxpayer or his employees or through a resident broker, commission agent, custodian, or other agent, and whether or not any such employee or agent has discretionary authority to make decisions in effecting the transactions. This clause shall not apply in the case of a dealer in commodities.

(iii) Limitation. Clauses (i) and (ii) shall apply only if the commodities are of a kind customarily dealt in on an organized commodity exchange and if the transaction is of a kind customarily consummated at such place.

(C) Limitation. Subparagraphs (A)(i) and (B)(i) shall apply only if, at no time during the taxable year, the taxpayer has an office or other fixed place of business in the United States through which or by the direction of which the transactions in stocks or securities, or in commodities, as the case may be, are effected.

(c) Effectively connected income, etc.

(1) **General rule.** For purposes of this title—

(A) In the case of a nonresident alien individual or a foreign corporation engaged in trade or business within the United States during the taxable year, the rules set forth in paragraphs (2), (3), (4), (6), and (7) shall apply in determining the income, gain, or loss which shall be treated as effectively connected with the conduct of a trade or business within the United States.

(B) Except as provided in paragraph (6) or (7) or in section 871(d) or sections 882(d) and (e), in the case of a nonresident alien individual or a foreign corporation not engaged in trade or business within the United States during the taxable year, no income, gain, or loss shall be treated as effectively connected with the conduct of a trade or business within the United States.

(2) **Periodical, etc., income from sources within United States—factors.** In determining whether income from sources within the United States of the types described in section 871(a)(1), section 871(h), section 881(a), or section 881(c), or whether gain or loss from sources within the United States from the sale or exchange of capital assets, is effectively connected with the conduct of a trade or business within the United States, the factors taken into account shall include whether—

(A) the income, gain, or loss is derived from assets used in or held for use in the conduct of such trade or business, or

(B) the activities of such trade or business were a material factor in the realization of the income, gain, or loss.

In determining whether an asset is used in or held for use in the conduct of such trade or business or whether the activities of such trade or business were a material factor in realizing an item of income, gain, or loss, due regard shall be given to whether or not such asset or such income, gain, or loss was accounted for through such trade or business.

(3) **Other income from sources within United States.** All income, gain, or loss from sources within the United States (other than income, gain, or loss to which paragraph (2) applies) shall be treated as effectively connected with the conduct of a trade or business within the United States.

(4) **Income from sources without United States.**

(A) Except as provided in subparagraphs (B) and (C), no income, gain, or loss from sources without the United States shall be treated as effectively connected with the conduct of a trade or business within the United States.

(B) Income, gain, or loss from sources without the United States shall be treated as effectively connected with the conduct of a trade or business within the United States by a nonresident alien individual or a foreign corporation if such person has an office or other fixed place of business within the United States to which such income, gain, or loss is attributable and such income, gain, or loss—

(i) consists of rents or royalties for the use of or for the privilege of using intangible property described in section 862(a)(4) derived in the active conduct of such trade or business;

(ii) consists of dividends, interest, or amounts received for the provision of guarantees of indebtedness, and either is derived in the active conduct of a banking, financing, or similar business within the

United States or is received by a corporation the principal business of which is trading in stocks or securities for its own account; or

(iii) is derived from the sale or exchange (outside the United States) through such office or other fixed place of business of personal property described in section 1221(a)(1), except that this clause shall not apply if the property is sold or exchanged for use, consumption, or disposition outside the United States and an office or other fixed place of business of the taxpayer in a foreign country participated materially in such sale.

Any income or gain which is equivalent to any item of income or gain described in clause (i), (ii), or (iii) shall be treated in the same manner as such item for purposes of this subparagraph.

(C) In the case of a foreign corporation taxable under part I or part II of subchapter L, any income from sources without the United States which is attributable to its United States business shall be treated as effectively connected with the conduct of a trade or business within the United States.

(D) No income from sources without the United States shall be treated as effectively connected with the conduct of a trade or business within the United States if it either—

(i) consists of dividends, interest, or royalties paid by a foreign corporation in which the taxpayer owns (within the meaning of section 958(a)), or is considered as owning (by applying the ownership rules of section 958(b)), more than 50 percent of the total combined voting power of all classes of stock entitled to vote, or

(ii) is subpart F income within the meaning of section 952(a).

(5) Rules for application of paragraph (4)(B). For purposes of subparagraph (B) of paragraph (4)—

(A) in determining whether a nonresident alien individual or a foreign corporation has an office or other fixed place of business, an office or other fixed place of business of an agent shall be disregarded unless such agent (i) has the authority to negotiate and conclude contracts in the name of the nonresident alien individual or foreign corporation and regularly exercises that authority or has a stock of merchandise from which he regularly fills orders on behalf of such individual or foreign corporation, and (ii) is not a general commission agent, broker, or other agent of independent status acting in the ordinary course of his business,

(B) income, gain, or loss shall not be considered as attributable to an office or other fixed place of business within the United States unless such office or fixed place of business is a material factor in the production of such income, gain, or loss and such office or fixed place of business regularly carries on activities of the type from which such income, gain, or loss is derived, and

(C) the income, gain, or loss which shall be attributable to an office or other fixed place of business within the United States shall be the income, gain, or loss property allocable thereto, but, in the case of a sale or exchange described in clause (iii) of such subparagraph, the income which shall be treated as attributable to an office or other fixed place of business within the United States shall not exceed the income which would be derived from sources within the United States if the sale or exchange were made in the United States.

(6) Treatment of certain deferred payments, etc. For purposes of this title, in the case of any income or gain of a nonresident alien individual or a foreign corporation which—

(A) is taken into account for any taxable year, but

(B) is attributable to a sale or exchange of property or the performance of services (or any other transaction) in any other taxable year,

the determination of whether such income or gain is taxable under section 871(b) or 882 (as the case may be) shall be made as if such income or gain were taken into account in such other taxable year and without regard to the requirement that the taxpayer be engaged in a trade or business within the United States during the taxable year referred to in subparagraph (A).

(7) Treatment of certain property transactions. For purposes of this title, if—

(A) any property ceases to be used or held for use in connection with the conduct of a trade or business within the United States, and

(B) such property is disposed of within 10 years after such cessation,

the determination of whether any income or gain attributable to such disposition is taxable under section 871(b) or 882 (as the case may be) shall be made as if such sale or exchange occurred immediately before such cessation and without regard to the requirement that the taxpayer be engaged in a trade or business within the United States during the taxable year for which such income or gain is taken into account.

(d) Treatment of related person factoring income.

(1) In general. For purposes of the provisions set forth in paragraph (2), if any person acquires (directly or indirectly) a trade or service receivable from a related person, any income of such person from the trade or service receivable so acquired shall be treated as if it were interest on a loan to the obligor under the receivable.

(2) Provisions to which paragraph (1) applies. The provisions set forth in this paragraph are as follows:

(A) Section 904 (relating to limitation on foreign tax credit).

(B) Subpart F of part III of this subchapter (relating to controlled foreign corporations).

(3) Trade or service receivable. For purposes of this subsection, the term "trade or service receivable" means any account receivable or evidence of indebtedness arising out of—

(A) the disposition by a related person of property described in section 1221(a)(1), or

(B) the performance of services by a related person.

(4) Related person. For purposes of this subsection, the term "related person" means—

(A) any person who is a related person (within the meaning of section 267(b)), and

(B) any United States shareholder (as defined in section 951(b)) and any person who is a related person (within the meaning of section 267(b)) to such a shareholder.

(5) Certain provisions not to apply.

(A) Certain exceptions. The following provisions shall not apply to any amount treated as interest under paragraph (1) or (6):

(i) Subparagraphs (A)(iii)(II), (B)(ii), and (C)(iii)(II) of section 904(d)(2) (relating to exceptions for export financing interest).

Source of income   Code Sec. 864(e)(5)(A)(ii)

(ii) Subparagraph (A) of section 954(b)(3) (relating to exception where foreign base company income is less than 5 percent or $1,000,000).

(iii) Subparagraph (B) of section 954(c)(2) (relating to certain export financing).

(iv) Clause (i) of section 954(c)(3)(A) (relating to certain income received from related persons).

(B) Special rules for possessions. An amount treated as interest under paragraph (1) shall not be treated as income described in subparagraph (A) or (B) of section 936(a)(1) unless such amount is from sources within a possession of the United States (determined after the application of paragraph (1)).

(6) Special rule for certain income from loans of a controlled foreign corporation. Any income of a controlled foreign corporation (within the meaning of section 957(a)) from a loan to a person for the purpose of financing—

(A) the purchase of property described in section 1221(a)(1) of a related person, or

(B) the payment for the performance of services by a related person,

shall be treated as interest described in paragraph (1).

(7) Exception for certain related persons doing business in same foreign country. Paragraph (1) shall not apply to any trade or service receivable acquired by any person from a related person if—

(A) the person acquiring such receivable and such related person are created or organized under the laws of the same foreign country and such related person has a substantial part of its assets used in its trade or business located in such same foreign country, and

(B) such related person would not have derived any foreign base company income (as defined in section 954(a), determined without regard to section 954(b)(3)(A)), or any income effectively connected with the conduct of a trade or business within the United States, from such receivable if it had been collected by such related person.

(8) Regulations. The Secretary shall prescribe such regulations as may be necessary to prevent the avoidance of the provisions of this subsection or section 956(b)(3).

(e) Rules for allocating interest, etc.

For purposes of this subchapter—

(1) Treatment of affiliated groups. The taxable income of each member of an affiliated group shall be determined by allocating and apportioning interest expense of each member as if all members of such group were a single corporation.

(2) Gross income method may not be used for interest. All allocations and apportionments of interest expense shall be made on the basis of assets rather than gross income.

(3) Tax-exempt assets not taken into account. For purposes of allocating and apportioning any deductible expense, any tax-exempt asset (and any income from such an asset) shall not be taken into account. A similar rule shall apply in the case of the portion of any dividend (other than a qualifying dividend as defined in section 243(b)) equal to the deduction allowable under section 243 or 245(a) with respect to such dividend and in the case of a like portion of any stock the dividends on which would be so deductible and would not be qualifying dividends (as so defined).

(4) Basis of stock in nonaffiliated 10-percent owned corporations adjusted for earnings and profits changes.

(A) In general. For purposes of allocating and apportioning expenses on the basis of assets, the adjusted basis of any stock in a nonaffiliated 10-percent owned corporation shall be—

(i) increased by the amount of the earnings and profits of such corporation attributable to such stock and accumulated during the period the taxpayer held such stock, or

(ii) reduced (but not below zero) by any deficit in earnings and profits of such corporation attributable to such stock for such period.

(B) Nonaffiliated 10-percent owned corporation. For purposes of this paragraph, the term "nonaffiliated 10-percent owned corporation" means any corporation if—

(i) such corporation is not included in the taxpayer's affiliated group, and

(ii) members of such affiliated group own 10 percent or more of the total combined voting power of all classes of stock of such corporation entitled to vote.

(C) Earnings and profits of lower tier corporations taken into account.

(i) In general. If, by reason of holding stock in a nonaffiliated 10-percent owned corporation, the taxpayer is treated under clause (iii) as owning stock in another corporation with respect to which the stock ownership requirements of clause (ii) are met, the adjustment under subparagraph (A) shall include an adjustment for the amount of the earnings and profits (or deficit therein) of such other corporation which are attributable to the stock the taxpayer is so treated as owning and to the period during which the taxpayer is treated as owning such stock.

(ii) Stock ownership requirements. The stock ownership requirements of this clause are met with respect to any corporation if members of the taxpayer's affiliated group own (directly or through the application of clause (iii)) 10 percent or more of the total combined voting power of all classes of stock of such corporation entitled to vote.

(iii) Stock owned through entities. For purposes of this subparagraph, stock owned (directly or indirectly) by a corporation, partnership, or trust shall be treated as being owned proportionately by its shareholders, partners, or beneficiaries. Stock considered to be owned by a person by reason of the application of the preceding sentence, shall, for purposes of applying such sentence, be treated as actually owned by such person.

(D) Coordination with subpart F, etc. For purposes of this paragraph, proper adjustment shall be made to the earnings and profits of any corporation to take into account any earnings and profits included in gross income under section 951 or under any other provision of this title and reflected in the adjusted basis of the stock.

(5) Affiliated group. For purposes of this subsection—

(A) In general. Except as provided in subparagraph (B), the term "affiliated group" has the meaning given such term by section 1504 (determined without regard to paragraph (4) of section 1504(b)). Notwithstanding the preceding sentence, a foreign corporation shall be treated as a member of the affiliated group if—

(i) more than 50 percent of the gross income of such foreign corporation for the taxable year is effectively connected with the conduct of a trade or business within the United States, and

(ii) at least 80 percent of either the vote or value of all outstanding stock of such foreign corporation is owned directly or indirectly by members of the affiliated group (determined with regard to this sentence).

(B) Treatment of certain financial institutions. For purposes of subparagraph (A), any corporation described in subparagraph (C) shall be treated as an includible corporation for purposes of section 1504 only for purposes of applying such section separately to corporations so described. This subparagraph shall not apply for purposes of paragraph (6).

(C) Description. A corporation is described in this subparagraph if—

(i) such corporation is a financial institution described in section 581 or 591,

(ii) the business of such financial institution is predominantly with persons other than related persons (within the meaning of subsection (d)(4)) or their customers, and

(iii) such financial institution is required by State or Federal law to be operated separately from any other entity which is not such an institution.

(D) Treatment of bank holding companies. To the extent provided in regulations—

(i) a bank holding company (within the meaning of section 2(a) of the Bank Holding Company Act of 1956), and

(ii) any subsidiary of a financial institution described in section 581 or 591 or of any bank holding company if such subsidiary is predominantly engaged (directly or indirectly) in the active conduct of a banking, financing, or similar business,

shall be treated as a corporation described in subparagraph (C).

(6) Allocation and apportionment of other expenses. Expenses other than interest which are not directly allocable or apportioned to any specific income producing activity shall be allocated and apportioned as if all members of the affiliated group were a single corporation.

(7) Regulations. The Secretary shall prescribe such regulations as may be necessary or appropriate to carry out the purposes of this section, including regulations providing—

(A) for the resourcing of income of any member of an affiliated group or modifications to the consolidated return regulations to the extent such resourcing or modification is necessary to carry out the purposes of this section,

(B) for direct allocation of interest expense incurred to carry out an integrated financial transaction to any interest (or interest-type income) derived from such transaction and in other circumstances where such allocation would be appropriate to carry out the purposes of this subsection,

(C) for the apportionment of expenses allocated to foreign source income among the members of the affiliated group and various categories of income described in section 904(d)(1),

(D) for direct allocation of interest expense in the case of indebtedness resulting in a disallowance under section 246A,

(E) for appropriate adjustments in the application of paragraph (3) in the case of an insurance company,

(F) preventing assets or interest expense from being taken into account more than once, and

(G) that this subsection shall not apply for purposes of any provision of this subchapter to the extent the Secretary determines that the application of this subsection for such purposes would not be appropriate.

(f) Election to allocate interest, etc. on worldwide basis.

For purposes of this subchapter, at the election of the worldwide affiliated group—

(1) Allocation and apportionment of interest expense.

(A) In general. The taxable income of each domestic corporation which is a member of a worldwide affiliated group shall be determined by allocating and apportioning interest expense of each member as if all members of such group were a single corporation.

(B) Treatment of worldwide affiliated group. The taxable income of the domestic members of a worldwide affiliated group from sources outside the United States shall be determined by allocating and apportioning the interest expense of such domestic members to such income in an amount equal to the excess (if any) of—

(i) the total interest expense of the worldwide affiliated group multiplied by the ratio which the foreign assets of the worldwide affiliated group bears to all the assets of the worldwide affiliated group, over

(ii) the interest expense of all foreign corporations which are members of the worldwide affiliated group to the extent such interest expense of such foreign corporations would have been allocated and apportioned to foreign source income if this subsection were applied to a group consisting of all the foreign corporations in such worldwide affiliated group.

(C) Worldwide affiliated group. For purposes of this paragraph, the term "worldwide affiliated group" means a group consisting of—

(i) the includible members of an affiliated group (as defined in section 1504(a), determined without regard to paragraphs (2) and (4) of section 1504(b)), and

(ii) all controlled foreign corporations in which such members in the aggregate meet the ownership requirements of section 1504(a)(2) either directly or indirectly through applying paragraph (2) of section 958(a) or through applying rules similar to the rules of such paragraph to stock owned directly or indirectly by domestic partnerships, trusts, or estates.

(2) Allocation and apportionment of other expenses. Expenses other than interest which are not directly allocable or apportioned to any specific income producing activity shall be allocated and apportioned as if all members of the affiliated group were a single corporation. For purposes of the preceding sentence, the term "affiliated group" has the meaning given such term by section 1504 (determined without regard to paragraph (4) of section 1504(b)).

(3) Treatment of tax-exempt assets; basis of stock in nonaffiliated 10-percent owned corporations. The rules of paragraphs (3) and (4) of subsection (e) shall apply for purposes of this subsection, except that paragraph (4) shall be applied on a worldwide affiliated group basis.

(4) Treatment of certain financial institutions.

(A) In general. For purposes of paragraph (1), any corporation described in subparagraph (B) shall be treated as an includible corporation for purposes of section 1504 only for purposes of applying this subsection separately to corporations so described.

(B) Description. A corporation is described in this subparagraph if—

(i) such corporation is a financial institution described in section 581 or 591,

(ii) the business of such financial institution is predominantly with persons other than related persons (within the meaning of subsection (d)(4)) or their customers, and

(iii) such financial institution is required by State or Federal law to be operated separately from any other entity which is not such an institution.

(C) Treatment of bank and financial holding companies. To the extent provided in regulations—

(i) a bank holding company (within the meaning of section 2(a) of the Bank Holding Company Act of 1956 (12 U.S.C. 1841(a)),

(ii) a financial holding company (within the meaning of section 2(p) of the Bank Holding Company Act of 1956 (12 U.S.C. 1841(p)), and

(iii) any subsidiary of a financial institution described in section 581 or 591, or of any such bank or financial holding company, if such subsidiary is predominantly engaged (directly or indirectly) in the active conduct of a banking, financing, or similar business,

shall be treated as a corporation described in subparagraph (B).

(5) Election to expand financial institution group of worldwide group.

(A) In general. If a worldwide affiliated group elects the application of this subsection, all financial corporations which—

(i) are members of such worldwide affiliated group, but

(ii) are not corporations described in paragraph (4)(B),

shall be treated as described in paragraph (4)(B) for purposes of applying paragraph (4)(A). This subsection (other than this paragraph) shall apply to any such group in the same manner as this subsection (other than this paragraph) applies to the pre-election worldwide affiliated group of which such group is a part.

(B) Financial corporation. For purposes of this paragraph, the term "financial corporation" means any corporation if at least 80 percent of its gross income is income described in section 904(d)(2)(D)(ii) and the regulations thereunder which is derived from transactions with persons who are not related (within the meaning of section 267(b) or 707(b)(1)) to the corporation. For purposes of the preceding sentence, there shall be disregarded any item of income or gain from a transaction or series of transactions a principal purpose of which is the qualification of any corporation as a financial corporation.

(C) Anti-abuse rules. In the case of a corporation which is a member of an electing financial institution group, to the extent that such corporation—

(i) distributes dividends or makes other distributions with respect to its stock after the date of the enactment of this paragraph to any member of the pre-election worldwide affiliated group (other than to a member of the electing financial institution group) in excess of the greater of—

(I) its average annual dividend (expressed as a percentage of current earnings and profits) during the 5-taxable-year period ending with the taxable year preceding the taxable year, or

(II) 25 percent of its average annual earnings and profits for such 5-taxable-year period, or

(ii) deals with any person in any manner not clearly reflecting the income of the corporation (as determined under principles similar to the principles of section 482),

an amount of indebtedness of the electing financial institution group equal to the excess distribution or the understatement or overstatement of income, as the case may be, shall be recharacterized (for the taxable year and subsequent taxable years) for purposes of this paragraph as indebtedness of the worldwide affiliated group (excluding the electing financial institution group). If a corporation has not been in existence for 5 taxable years, this subparagraph shall be applied with respect to the period it was in existence.

(D) Election. An election under this paragraph with respect to any financial institution group may be made only by the common parent of the pre-election worldwide affiliated group and may be made only for the first taxable year beginning after December 31, 2020, in which such affiliated group includes 1 or more financial corporations. Such an election, once made, shall apply to all financial corporations which are members of the electing financial institution group for such taxable year and all subsequent years unless revoked with the consent of the Secretary.

(E) Definitions relating to groups. For purposes of this paragraph—

(i) Pre-election worldwide affiliated group. The term "pre-election worldwide affiliated group" means, with respect to a corporation, the worldwide affiliated group of which such corporation would (but for an election under this paragraph) be a member for purposes of applying paragraph (1).

(ii) Electing financial institution group. The term "electing financial institution group" means the group of corporations to which this subsection applies separately by reason of the application of paragraph (4)(A) and which includes financial corporations by reason of an election under subparagraph (A).

(F) Regulations. The Secretary shall prescribe such regulations as may be appropriate to carry out this subsection, including regulations—

(i) providing for the direct allocation of interest expense in other circumstances where such allocation would be appropriate to carry out the purposes of this subsection,

(ii) preventing assets or interest expense from being taken into account more than once, and

(iii) dealing with changes in members of any group (through acquisitions or otherwise) treated under this paragraph as an affiliated group for purposes of this subsection.

(6) Election. An election to have this subsection apply with respect to any worldwide affiliated group may be made only by the common parent of the domestic affiliated group referred to in paragraph (1)(C) and may be made only for the first taxable year beginning after December 31, 2020, in which a worldwide affiliated group exists which includes such affiliated group and at least 1 foreign corporation. Such an election, once made, shall apply to such common parent and all other corporations which are members of such worldwide affiliated group for such taxable year and all subsequent years unless revoked with the consent of the Secretary.

(7) Repealed.

(g) Allocation of research and experimental expenditures.

(1) In general. For purposes of sections 861(b), 862(b), and 863(b), qualified research and experimental expenditures shall be allocated and apportioned as follows:

(A) Any qualified research and experimental expenditures expended solely to meet legal requirements imposed by a political entity with respect to the improvement or marketing of specific products or processes for purposes not reasonably expected to generate gross income (beyond de minimis amounts) outside the jurisdiction of the political entity shall be allocated only to gross income from sources within such jurisdiction.

(B) In the case of any qualified research and experimental expenditures (not allocated under subparagraph (A)) to the extent—

(i) that such expenditures are attributable to activities conducted in the United States, 50 percent of such expenditures shall be allocated and apportioned to income from sources within the United States and deducted from such income in determining the amount of taxable income from sources within the United States, and

(ii) that such expenditures are attributable to activities conducted outside the United States, 50 percent of such expenditures shall be allocated and apportioned to income from sources outside the United States and deducted from such income in determining the amount of taxable income from sources outside the United States.

(C) The remaining portion of qualified research and experimental expenditures (not allocated under subparagraphs (A) and (B)) shall be apportioned, at the annual election of the taxpayer, on the basis of gross sales or gross income, except that, if the taxpayer elects to apportion on the basis of gross income, the amount apportioned to income from sources outside the United States shall at least be 30 percent of the amount which would be so apportioned on the basis of gross sales.

(2) Qualified research and experimental expenditures. For purposes of this section, the term "qualified research and experimental expenditures" means amounts which are research and experimental expenditures within the meaning of section 174. For purposes of this paragraph, rules similar to the rules of subsection (c) of section 174 shall apply. Any qualified research and experimental expenditures treated as deferred expenses under subsection (b) of section 174 shall be taken into account under this subsection for the taxable year for which such expenditures are allowed as a deduction under such subsection.

(3) Special rules for expenditures attributable to activities conducted in space, etc.

(A) In general. Any qualified research and experimental expenditures described in subparagraph (B)—

(i) if incurred by a United States person, shall be allocated and apportioned under this section in the same manner as if they were attributable to activities conducted in the United States, and

(ii) if incurred by a person other than a United States person, shall be allocated and apportioned under this section in the same manner as if they were attributable to activities conducted outside the United States.

(B) Description of expenditures. For purposes of subparagraph (A), qualified research and experimental expenditures are described in this subparagraph if such expenditures are attributable to activities conducted—

(i) in space,

(ii) on or under water not within the jurisdiction (as recognized by the United States) of a foreign country, possession of the United States, or the United States, or

(iii) in Antarctica.

(4) Affiliated group.

(A) Except as provided in subparagraph (B), the allocation and apportionment required by paragraph (1) shall be determined as if all members of the affiliated group (as defined in subsection (e)(5)) were a single corporation.

(B) For purposes of the allocation and apportionment required by paragraph (1)—

(i) sales and gross income from products produced in whole or in part in a possession by an electing corporation (within the meaning of section 936(h)(5)(E)), and

(ii) dividends from an electing corporation,

shall not be taken into account, except that this subparagraph shall not apply to sales of (and gross income and dividends attributable to sales of) products with respect to which an election under section 936(h)(5)(F) is not in effect.

(C) The qualified research and experimental expenditures taken into account for purposes of paragraph (1) shall be adjusted to reflect the amount of such expenditures included in computing the cost-sharing amount (determined under section 936(h)(5)(C)(i)(I)).

(D) The Secretary may prescribe such regulations as may be necessary to carry out the purposes of this paragraph, including regulations providing for the source of gross income and the allocation and apportionment of deductions to take into account the adjustments required by subparagraph (B) or (C).

(E) Paragraph (6) of subsection (e) shall not apply to qualified research and experimental expenditures.

(5) Regulations. The Secretary shall prescribe such regulations as may be appropriate to carry out the purposes of this subsection, including regulations relating to the determination of whether any expenses are attributable to activities conducted in the United States or outside the United States and regulations providing such adjustments to the provisions of this subsection as may be appropriate in the case of cost-sharing arrangements and contract research.

(6) Applicability. This subsection shall apply to the taxpayer's first taxable year (beginning on or before August 1, 1994) following the taxpayer's last taxable year to which Revenue Procedure 92-56 applies or would apply if the taxpayer elected the benefits of such Revenue Procedure.

In **2010**, P.L. 111-240, Sec. 2122(c), substituted "dividends, interest, or amounts received for the provision of guarantees of indebtedness" for "dividends or interest" in clause (c)(4)(B)(ii), effective for guarantees issued after 9/27/2010.

—P.L. 111-226, Sec. 216(a), added text at the end of subpara. (e)(5)(A), effective for tax. yrs. begin. after 8/10/2010.

—P.L. 111-147, Sec. 551(a), substituted "December 31, 2020" for 'December 31, 2017" in subpara. (f)(5)(D) and para. (f)(6), effective 3/18/2010.

In **2009**, P.L. 111-92, Sec. 15(a), substituted "December 31, 2017" for "December 31, 2010" in subpara. (f)(5)(D) and para. (f)(6) . . . Sec. 15(b), deleted para. (f)(7), effective for tax. yrs. begin. after 12/31/2010.

Prior to deletion, para. (f)(7) read as follows:

"(7) Transition. In the case of the first taxable year to which this subsection applies, the increase (if any) in the amount of the interest expense allocable to sources within the United States by reason of the application of this subsection shall be 30 percent of the amount of such increase determined without regard to this paragraph."

In **2008**, P.L. 110-289, Sec. 3093(a), substituted "December 31, 2010" for "December 31, 2008" in paras. (f)(5)(D) and (f)(6) . . . Sec. 3093(b), added para. (f)(7), effective for tax. yrs. begin. after 12/31/2008.

In **2006**, P.L. 109-222, Sec. 513(a), amended Sec. 5(c)(1) of P.L. 106-519 [see below] . . . Sec. 513(b), repealed Sec. 101(f) of P.L. 108-357 [see below], effective for tax. yrs. begin. after 5/17/2006.

Prior to amendment, Sec. 5(c)(1) of P.L. 106-519 read as follows:

"(1) In general. In the case of a FSC (as so defined) in existence on September 30, 2000, and at all times thereafter, the amendments made by this Act shall not apply to any transaction in the ordinary course of trade or business involving a FSC which occurs—

"(A) before January 1, 2002; or

"(B) after December 31, 2001, pursuant to a binding contract—

"(i) which is between the FSC (or any related person) and any person which is not a related person; and

"(ii) which is in effect on September 30, 2000, and at all times thereafter."

For purposes of this paragraph, a binding contract shall include a purchase option, renewal option, or replacement option which is included in such contract and which is enforceable against the seller or lessor."

Source of income   Code Sec. 864

Prior to repeal, Sec. 101(f) of P.L. 108-357 read as follows:

"(f) Binding contracts. The amendments made by this section shall not apply to any transaction in the ordinary course of a trade or business which occurs pursuant to a binding contract—

"(1) which is between the taxpayer and a person who is not a related person (as defined in section 943(b)(3) of such Code, as in effect on the day before the date of the enactment of this Act), and

"(2) which is in effect on September 17, 2003, and at all times thereafter.

"For purposes of this subsection, a binding contract shall include a purchase option, renewal option, or replacement option which is included in such contract and which is enforceable against the seller or lessor."

In 2005, P.L. 109-135, Sec. 403(l), added subsec. (d) to Sec. 403 of P.L. 108-357, which reads as follows:

"(d) Transition rule. If the taxpayer elects (at such time and in such form and manner as the Secretary of the Treasury may prescribe) to have the rules of this subsection apply—

"(1) the amendments made by this section shall not apply to taxable years beginning after December 31, 2002, and before January 1, 2005, and

"(2) in the case of taxable years beginning after December 31, 2004, clause (iv) of section 904(d)(4)(C) of the Internal Revenue Code of 1986 (as amended by this section) shall be applied by substituting 'January 1, 2005' for 'January 1, 2003' both places it appears."

In 2004, P.L. 108-357, Sec. 101(b)(6)(A), substituted "(3) Tax-exempt assets not taken into account. For purposes of" for "(3) Tax-exempt assets not taken into account. (A) In general. For purposes of" in para. (e)(3) . . . Sec. 101(b)(6)(B), deleted subpara. (e)(3)(B), effective for transactions after 12/31/2004. Sec. 101(d)-(f) [subsec. (f) was repealed by Sec. 513(b) of P.L. 109-222, see above] of this Act, reads as follows:

"(d) Transitional rule for 2005 and 2006.

"(1) In general. In the case of transactions during 2005 or 2006, the amount includible in gross income by reason of the amendments made by this section shall not exceed the applicable percentage of the amount which would have been so included but for this subsection.

"(2) Applicable percentage. For purposes of paragraph (1), the applicable percentage shall be as follows:

"(A) For 2005, the applicable percentage shall be 20 percent.

"(B) For 2006, the applicable percentage shall be 40 percent.

"(e) Revocation of election to be treated as domestic corporation. If, during the 1-year period beginning on the date of the enactment of this Act, a corporation for which an election is in effect under section 943(e) of the Internal Revenue Code of 1986 revokes such election, no gain or loss shall be recognized with respect to property treated as transferred under clause (ii) of section 943(e)(4)(B) of such Code to the extent such property—

"(1) was treated as transferred under clause (i) thereof, or

"(2) was acquired during a taxable year to which such election applies and before May 1, 2003, in the ordinary course of its trade or business.

The Secretary of the Treasury (or such Secretary's delegate) may prescribe such regulations as may be necessary to prevent the abuse of the purposes of this subsection.

"(f)" [Repealed by Sec. 513(b) of P.L. 109-222, see above]

—P.L. 108-357, Sec. 401(a), redesignated subsec. (f) as subsec. (g), and added subsec. (f), . . . Sec. 401(b)(1), added "and in other circumstances where such allocation would be appropriate to carry out the purposes of this subsection" before the comma at the end of subpara. (e)(7)(B) . . . Sec. 401(b)(2), deleted "and" at the end of subpara. (e)(7)(E), redesignated subpara. (e)(7)(F) as subpara. (e)(7)(G), and added subpara (e)(7)(F), effective for tax. yrs. begin. after 12/31/2008.

—P.L. 108-357, Sec. 403(b)(6), substituted "(C)(iii)(II)" for "(C)(iii)(III)" in clause (d)(5)(A)(i), effective for tax. yrs. begin. after 12/31/2002. For transition rule, see Sec. 403(l) of P.L. 109-135, reproduced above.

—P.L. 108-357, Sec. 413(c)(12), deleted subpara. (d)(2)(A) and redesignated subparas. (d)(2)(B)-(C) as subparas. (d)(2)(A)-(B), effective for tax. yrs. of foreign corporations begin. after 12/31/2004, and for tax. yrs. of United States shareholders with or within which such tax. yrs. of foreign corporations end.

Prior to deletion, subpara. (d)(2)(A) read as follows:

"(A) Part III of subchapter G of this chapter (relating to foreign personal holding companies)."

—P.L. 108-357, Sec. 894(a), added "Any income or gain which is equivalent to any item of income or gain described in clause (i), (ii), or (iii) shall be treated in the same manner as such item for purposes of this subparagraph" flush at the end of subpara. (c)(4)(B), effective for tax. yrs. begin. after 10/22/2004.

In 2000, P.L. 106-519, Sec. 4(3)(A), substituted "(A) In general. For purposes of" for "For purposes of" in para. (e)(3) . . . Sec. 4(3)(B), added subpara. (e)(3)(B), effective for transactions after 9/30/2000. Sec. 5(b)–(d) [para. (c)(1) as amended by Sec. 513(a) of P.L. 109-222, see above] of this Act, provides:

"(b) No new FSCs; termination of inactive FSCs—

"(1) No new FSCs. No corporation may elect after September 30, 2000, to be a FSC (as defined in section 922 of the Internal Revenue Code of 1986, as in effect before the amendments made by this Act).

"(2) Termination of inactive FSCs. If a FSC has no foreign trade income (as defined in section 923(b) of such Code, as so in effect) for any period of 5 consecutive taxable years beginning after December 31, 2001, such FSC shall cease to be treated as a FSC for purposes of such Code for any taxable year beginning after such period.

"(c) Transition period for existing Foreign Sales Corporations.

"(1) In general. In the case of a FSC (as so defined) in existence on September 30, 2000, and at all times thereafter, the amendments made by this Act shall not apply to any transaction in the ordinary course of trade or business involving a FSC which occurs before January 1, 2002.

"(2) Election to have amendments apply earlier. A taxpayer may elect to have the amendments made by this Act apply to any transaction by a FSC or any related person to which such amendments would apply but for the application of paragraph (1). Such election shall be effective for the taxable year for which made and all subsequent taxable years, and, once made, may be revoked only with the consent of the Secretary of the Treasury.

"(3) Exception for old earnings and profits of certain corporations.

"(A) In general. In the case of a foreign corporation to which this paragraph applies—

"(i) earnings and profits of such corporation accumulated in taxable years ending before October 1, 2000, shall not be included in the gross income of the persons holding stock in such corporation by reason of section 943(e)(4)(B)(i), and

"(ii) rules similar to the rules of clauses (ii), (iii), and (iv) of section 953(d)(4)(B) shall apply with respect to such earnings and profits.

The preceding sentence shall not apply to earnings and profits acquired in a transaction after September 30, 2000, to which section 381 applies unless the distributor or transferor corporation was immediately before the transaction a foreign corporation to which this paragraph applies.

"(B) Existing FSCs. This paragraph shall apply to any controlled foreign corporation (as defined in section 957) if—

"(i) such corporation is a FSC (as so defined) in existence on September 30, 2000,

"(ii) such corporation is eligible to make the election under section 943(e) by reason of being described in paragraph (2)(B) of such section, and

"(iii) such corporation makes such election not later than for its first taxable year beginning after December 31, 2001.

"(C) Other corporations. This paragraph shall apply to any controlled foreign corporation (as defined in section 957), and such corporation shall (notwithstanding any provision of section 943(e)) be treated as an applicable foreign corporation for purposes of section 943(e), if—

"(i) such corporation is in existence on September 30, 2000;

"(ii) as of such date, such corporation is wholly owned (directly or indirectly) by a domestic corporation (determined without regard to any election under section 943(e));

"(iii) for each of the 3 taxable years preceding the first taxable year to which the election under section 943(e) by such controlled foreign corporation applies—

"(I) all of the gross income of such corporation is subpart F income (as defined in section 952), including by reason of section 954(b)(3)(B); and

"(II) in the ordinary course of such corporation's trade or business, such corporation regularly sold (or paid commissions) to a FSC which on September 30, 2000, was a related person to such corporation;

"(iv) such corporation has never made an election under section 922(a)(2) (as in effect before the date of the enactment of this paragraph) to be treated as a FSC; and

"(v) such corporation makes the election under section 943(e) not later than for its first taxable year beginning after December 31, 2001.

The preceding sentence shall cease to apply as of the date that the domestic corporation referred to in clause (ii) ceases to wholly own (directly or indirectly) such controlled foreign corporation.

"(4) Related person. For purposes of this subsection, the term 'related person' has the meaning given to such term by section 943(b)(3).

"(5) Section references. Except as otherwise expressly provided, any reference in this subsection to a section or other provision shall be considered to be a reference to a section or other provision of the Internal Revenue Code of 1986, as amended by this Act.

"(d) Special rules relating to leasing transactions.

"(1) Sales income. If foreign trade income in connection with the lease or rental of property described in section 927(a)(1)(B) of such Code (as in effect before the amendments made by this Act) is treated as exempt foreign trade income for purposes of section 921(a) of such Code (as so in effect), such property shall be treated as property described in section 941(c)(1)(B) of such Code (as added by this Act) for purposes of applying section 941(c)(2) of such Code (as so added) to any subsequent transaction involving such property to which the amendments made by this Act apply.

"(2) Limitation on use of gross receipts method. If any person computed its foreign trade income from any transaction with respect to any property on the basis of a transfer price determined under the method described in section 925(a)(1) of such Code (as in effect before the amendments made by this Act), then the qualifying foreign trade income (as defined in section 941(a) of such Code, as in effect after such amendment) of such person (or any related person) with respect to any other transaction involving such property (and to which the amendments made by this Act apply) shall be zero."

In 1999, P.L. 106-170, Sec. 532(c)(2)(N), substituted "section 1221(a)(1)" for "section 1221(1)" in clause (c)(4)(B)(iii) . . . Sec. 532(c)(2)(O), substituted "section 1221(a)(1)" for "section 1221(1)" in subpara. (d)(3)(A) . . . Sec. 532(c)(2)(P), substituted "section 1221(a)(1)" for "section 1221(1)" in subpara. (d)(6)(A), effective for any instrument held, acquired, or entered into, any transaction entered into, and supplies held or acquired on or after 12/17/99.

In 1997, P.L. 105-34, Sec. 1162(a), substituted a period for ", or in the case of a corporation (other than a corporation which is, or but for section 542(c)(7), 542(c)(10), or 543(b)(1)(C) would be, a personal holding company) the principal business of which is trading in stocks or securities for its own account, if its principal office is in the United States." in clause (b)(2)(A)(ii), effective for tax. yrs. begin. after 12/31/97.

2,501

Code Sec. 864 — Source of income

In 1996, P.L. 104-191, Sec. 521(a), repealed Sec. 1215(c)(5) of P.L. 99-514 [see below], effective for tax. yrs. begin. after 12/31/95. For special rules, see Sec. 521(b)(2), of this Act, which reads as follows:

"(2) Special rule. In the case of the first taxable year beginning after December 31, 1995, the pre-effective date portion of the interest expense of the corporation referred to in such paragraph (5) of such section 1215(c) for such taxable year shall allocated and apportioned without regard to such amendment. For purposes of the preceding sentence, the pre-effective date portion is the amount which bears the same ratio to the interest expense for such taxable year as the number of days during such taxable year before the date of the enactment of this Act bears to 366."

Prior to repeal, Sec. 1215(c)(5) of P.L. 99-514 read as follows:

"(5) Special rule for financial corporation.— For purposes of section 864(e)(5) of the Internal Revenue Code of 1986 (as added by this section), a corporation shall be treated as described in subparagraph (C) of such section for any taxable year if—

"(A) such corporation is a Delaware corporation incorporated on August 20, 1959, and

"(B) such corporation was primarily engaged in the financing of dealer inventory or consumer purchases on May 29, 1985, and at all times thereafter before the close of the taxable year."

In 1993, P.L. 103-66, Sec. 13234(a), substituted "50 percent" for "64 percent" each place it appeared in subpara. (f)(1)(B) . . . Sec. 13234(b)(1), amended para. (f)(5) and added para. (f)(6) . . . Sec. 13234(b)(2), substituted "subparagraph (B) or (C)" for "subparagraph (C)" in subpara. (f)(4)(D), effective 8/10/93.

Prior to amendment, para. (f)(5) read as follows:

"(5) Years to which rule applies.

"(A) In general. This subsection shall apply to the taxpayer's first 3 taxable years beginning after August 1, 1989, and on or before August 1, 1992.

"(B) Reduction. Notwithstanding subparagraph (A), in the case of the taxpayer's first taxable year beginning after August 1, 1991, this subsection shall only apply to qualified research and experimental expenditures incurred during the first 6 months of such taxable year."

In 1991, P.L. 102-227, Sec. 101(a), amended para. (f)(5), effective for tax yrs. begin. after 8/1/89.

Prior to amendment, para. (f)(5) read as follows:

"(5) Years to which rule applies. This subsection shall apply to the taxpayer's first 2 taxable years beginning after August 1, 1989, and on or before August 1, 1991."

In 1990, P.L. 101-508, Sec. 11401(a), amended para. (f)(5), effective for tax. yrs. begin. after 8/1/89.

Prior to amendment para. (f)(5) read as follows:

"(5) Year to which rule applies.

"(A) In general. Except as provided in this paragraph, this subsection shall apply to the taxpayer's first taxable year beginning after August 1, 1989, and before August 2, 1990.

"(B) Reduction. Notwithstanding subparagraph (A), this subsection shall only apply to that portion of the qualified research and experimental expenditures for the taxable year referred to in subparagraph (A) which bears the same ratio to the total amount of such expenditures as—

"(i) the lesser of 9 months or the number of months in the taxable year, bears to

"(ii) the number of months in the taxable year."

In 1989, P.L. 101-239, Sec. 7111, added subsec. (f), effective 12/19/89.

In 1988, P.L. 100-647, Sec. 1012(a)(1)(B), substituted "(C)(iii)(III)" for "(C)(iii)" in clause (d)(5)(A)(i) . . . Sec. 1012(d)(7), deleted "or" at the end of clause (c)(4)(B)(i), substituted "; or" for the period at the end of clause (c)(4)(B)(ii) and added clause (c)(4)(B)(iii) . . . Sec. 1012(d)(10)(A) and (B), deleted "(including any gain or loss realized on the sale or exchange of such property)" after "section 862(a)(4)" in clause (c)(4)(B)(i) and deleted ", or gain or loss from the sale or exchange of stock or notes, bonds, or other evidences of indebtedness" after "dividends or interest" in clause (c)(4)(B)(ii), effective for tax. yrs. begin. after 12/31/86.

—P.L. 100-647, Sec. 1012(g)(5), deleted the last sentence of para. (c)(2), effective for payments after 12/31/86.

Prior to amendment, the last sentence in para. (c)(2) read as follows:

"In applying this paragraph and paragraph (4), interest referred to in section 861(a)(1)(A) shall be considered income from sources within the United States."

—P.L. 100-647, Sec. 1012(h)(1), amended para. (e)(4) . . . Sec. 1012(h)(2)(A), deleted "from sources outside the United States" after "affiliated group" in para. (e)(1) . . . Sec. 1012(h)(3), amended the last sentence in para. (e)(3) . . . Sec. 1012(h)(4)(A), added subpara. (e)(5)(D) . . . Sec. 1012(h)(4)(B), added the last sentence of subpara. (e)(5)(B) . . . Sec. 1012(h)(5), substituted "directly allocable or apportioned" for "directly allocable and apportioned" in para. (e)(6) . . . Sec. 1012(h)(6)(A), deleted "and" at the end of subpara. (e)(7)(B), deleted the period at the end of subpara. added subparas. (e)(7)(D), (E) and (F) . . . Sec. 1012(h)(6)(B), deleted "(except as provided in the regulations)" after "subchapter" in the material preceding para. (e)(1), effective for tax. yrs. begin. after 12/31/86, except as provided in Sec. 1215(c)(2)-(6) of P.L. 99-514, reproduced below.

Prior to amendment, para. (e)(4) read as follows:

"(4) Basis of stock in certain corporations adjusted for earnings and profits changes. For purposes of allocating and apportioning expenses on the basis of assets, the adjusted basis of any asset which is stock in a corporation which is not included in the affiliated group and in which members of the affiliated group own 10 percent or more of the total combined voting power of all classes of stock entitled to vote in such corporation shall be—

"(A) increased by the amount of the earnings and profits of such corporation attributable to such stock and accumulated during the period the taxpayer held such stock, or

"(B) reduced (but not below zero) by any deficit in earnings and profits of such corporation attributable to such stock for such period."

Prior to amendment, the last sentence in para. (e)(3) read as follows:

"A similar rule shall apply in the case of any dividend (other than a qualifying dividend as defined in section 243(b)) for which a deduction is allowable under section 243 or 245(a) and any stock the dividends on which would be so deductible and would not be qualifying dividends (as so defined)."

—P.L. 100-647, Sec. 1012(h)(7), amended Sec. 1215(c)(2) of P.L. 99-514 [reproduced below], transitional rules for amendments made by Sec. 1215(c) of P.L. 99-514, see below.

Prior to amendment Sec. 1215(c)(2) of P.L. 99-514 read as follows:

"(2) Transitional rules.—

"(A) General phase-in.—Except as provided in subparagraph (B), in the case of the 1st 3 taxable years of the taxpayer beginning after December 31, 1986, the amendments made by this section shall apply only to the applicable percentage (determined under the following table) of the interest expenses paid or accrued by the taxpayer during the taxable year with respect to an aggregate amount of indebtedness which does not exceed the aggregate amount of indebtedness outstanding on November 16, 1985:

"In the case of the:	The applicable percentage is:
1st taxable year	25
2nd taxable year	50
3rd taxable year	75.

"(B) Consolidation rule not to apply to certain interest.—

"(i) Interest attributable to increase in indebtedness from January 1, 1984, through May 28, 1985.—In the case of the first 5 taxable years of the taxpayer beginning after December 31, 1986, with respect to interest expenses attributable to the excess of—

"(I) the amount of the outstanding debt of the taxpayer on May 29, 1985, over

"(II) the amount of the outstanding debt of the taxpayer on December 31, 1983, paragraph (1) of section 864(e) of the Internal Revenue Code of 1986 (as added by this section) shall apply only to the applicable percentage (determined under the following table) of such interest expenses paid or accrued by the taxpayer during the taxable year:

"In the case of the:	The applicable percentage is:
1st taxable year	16⅔
2nd taxable year	33⅓
3rd taxable year	50
4th taxable year	66⅔
5th taxable year	83⅓.

"(ii) Interest attributable to increase in indebtedness from January 1, 1983, through December 31, 1983.—In the case of the first 4 taxable years of the taxpayer beginning after December 31, 1986, with respect to interest expenses attributable to the excess of—

"(I) the amount of the outstanding debt of the taxpayer on January 1, 1984, over

"(II) the amount of the outstanding debt of the taxpayer on December 31, 1982, paragraph (1) of section 864(e) of the Internal Revenue Code of 1986 (as added by this section) shall apply only to the applicable percentage (determined under the following table) of such interest expenses paid or accrued by the taxpayer during the taxable year:

"In the case of the:	The applicable percentage is:
1st taxable year	20
2nd taxable year	40
3rd taxable year	60
4th taxable year	80.

"(iii) Ordering rule.—For purposes of this subparagraph, indebtedness outstanding on November 16, 1985, shall be treated as attributable first to any excess described in clause (i), then to any excess described in clause (ii), and then to other indebtedness.

"(iv) Treatment of affiliated group.—For purposes of this subparagraph, all members of the same affiliated group of corporations (as defined in section 864(e)(5)(A) of the Internal Revenue Code of 1986, as added by this section) shall be treated as one taxpayer whether or not such members filed a consolidated return.

"(C) Special rule.—In the case of the first 9 taxable years beginning after December 31, 1986, the following applicable percentages shall be applied (in lieu of those set forth in subparagraph (A)) to interest expenses paid or accrued with respect to the amount of indebtedness described in subparagraph (D) or (E):

Source of income   **Code Sec. 864**

"In the case of the:	The applicable percentage is:
1st taxable year	10
2nd taxable year	20
3rd taxable year	30
4th taxable year	40
5th taxable year	50
6th taxable year	60
7th taxable year	70
8th taxable year	80
9th taxable year	90.

"(D) Indebtedness outstanding on May 29, 1985.— Indebtedness is described in this subparagraph if it is indebtedness (which was outstanding on May 29, 1985) of a corporation incorporated on June 13, 1917, which has its principal place of business in Bartlesville, Oklahoma.

"(E) Indebtedness outstanding on May 29, 1985.— Indebtedness is described in this subparagraph if it is indebtedness (which was outstanding on May 29, 1985) of a member of an affiliated group (as defined in section 1504(a)), the common parent of which was incorporated on August 26, 1926, and has its principal place of business in Harrison, New York."

—P.L. 100-647, Sec. 1012(p)(30), substituted "section 542(c)(7), 542(c)(10)," for "section 542(c)(7)" in clause (b)(2)(A)(ii), effective for tax. yrs. of foreign corporations begin. after 12/31/86.

—P.L. 100-647, Sec. 1012(r)(1), amended para. (c)(7) . . . Sec. 1012(r)(2), amended para. (c)(6), effective for tax. yrs. begin. after 12/31/86.

Prior to amendment, para. (c)(7) read as follows:

"(7) Treatment of certain property transactions. For purposes of this title, if any property ceases to be used or held for use in connection with the conduct of a trade or business within the United States, the determination of whether any income or gain attributable to a sale or exchange of such property occurring within 10 years after such cessation is effectively connected with the conduct of a trade or business within the United States shall be made as if such sale or exchange occurred immediately before such cessation."

Prior to amendment, para. (c)(6) read as follows:

"(6) Treatment of certain deferred payments, etc. For purposes of this title, any income or gain of a nonresident alien individual or a foreign corporation for any taxable year which is attributable to a sale or exchange of property or the performance of services (or any other transaction) in any other taxable year shall be treated as effectively connected with the conduct of a trade or business within the United States if it would have been so treated if such income or gain were taken into account in such other taxable year."

—P.L. 100-647, Sec. 1012(aa)(2)(A), (3)(A) and (H), and (4), provides:

"(2) Certain Amendments to Apply Notwithstanding Treaties. The following amendments made by the Reform Act [P.L. 99-514] shall apply notwithstanding any treaty obligation of the United States in effect on the date of the enactment of the Reform Act:

"(A) The amendments made by section 1201 of the Reform Act."

* * *

"(3) Certain Amendments not to apply to the Extent Inconsistent with Treaties. The following amendments made by the Reform Act shall not apply to the extent the application of such amendments would be contrary to any treaty obligation of the United States in effect on the date of the enactment of the Reform Act:

"(A) The amendments made by section 1211 of the Reform Act to the extent—

"(i) such amendments apply in the case of an individual treated as a resident of a foreign country under a treaty obligation of the United States as so in effect, or

"(ii) such amendments relate to income of a nonresident from the sale or exchange of inventory property which would otherwise be sourced under section 865(e)(2) of the 1986 Code."

* * *

"(H) The amendments made by section 1242 of the Reform Act to the extent they relate to paragraph (7) of section 864(c) of the 1986 Code."

* * *

"(4) Treatment of technical corrections. For purposes of paragraphs (2) and (3), any amendment made by this title shall be treated as if it had been included in the provision of the Reform Act to which such amendment relates."

—P.L. 100-647, Sec. 6128(a), amended Sec. 127(g)(3)(B) of P.L. 98-369 [special rules for changes made by Sec. 127(f) of P.L. 98-369, see below] by adding the material following "73-110", effective 11/10/88, see below.

In 1987, P.L. 100-203, Sec. 10242(b), added "or part II" after "part I" in subpara. (c)(4)(C), effective for tax. yrs. begin. after 12/31/87.

In 1986, P.L. 99-514, Sec. 1201(d)(4), amended clause (d)(5)(A)(i), effective for tax. yrs. begin. after 12/31/86 (see Sec. 1012 of P.L. 100-647(aa)(2)(A), above). For special rule, see Sec. 1201(e)(3) of this Act, reproduced in note following Code Sec. 904.

Prior to amendment, clause (d)(5)(A)(i) [as amended by Sec. 1810(c)(3) of this Act, see below] read as follows:

"(i) Subparagraphs (A), (B), (C), and (D) of section 904(d)(2) (relating to interest income to which separate limitation applies) and subparagraph (J) of section 904(d)(3) (relating to interest from members of same affiliated group)."

—P.L. 99-514, Sec. 1211(b)(2), added "or" to the end of clause (c)(4)(B)(i), substituted a period for "; or" at the end of clause (c)(4)(B)(ii), and deleted clause (c)(4)(B)(iii), effective for tax. yrs. begin. after 12/31/86 (see Sec. 1012 of P.L. 100-647(aa)(3)(A), above). For special rule, see Sec. 1211(c)(2) of this Act reproduced in note following Code Sec. 865.

Prior to deletion, clause (c)(4)(B)(iii) read as follows:

"(iii) is derived from the sale or exchange (without the United States) through such office or other fixed place of business of personal property described in section 1221(1), except that this clause shall not apply if the property is sold or exchanged for use, consumption, or disposition outside the United States and an office or other fixed place of business of the taxpayer outside the United States participated materially in such sale or exchange."

—P.L. 99-514, Sec. 1215(a), added subsec. (e) . . . Sec. 1215(b)(1), added "and special rules" after "Definitions" in the heading of Code Sec. 864, effective for tax. yrs. begin. after 12/31/86, except as provided Sec. 1215(c)(2)-(6) [as amended by Sec. 1012(h)(7) of P.L. 100-647 and Sec. 521(a) of P.L. 104-191, see above] of this Act which read:

"(2) Transitional rules.

"(A) General phase-in.

"(i) In general. In the case of the 1st 3 taxable years of the taxpayer beginning after December 31, 1986, the amendments made by this section shall not apply to interest expenses paid or accrued by the taxpayer during the taxable year with respect to an aggregate amount of indebtedness which does not exceed the general phase-in amount.

"(ii) General phase-in amount. Except as provided in clause (iii), the general phase-in amount for purposes of clause (i) is the applicable percentage (determined under the following table) of the aggregate amount of indebtedness of the taxpayer outstanding on November 16, 1985:

"In the case of the:	The applicable percentage is:
1st taxable year	75
2nd taxable year	50
3rd taxable year	25.

"(iii) Lower limit where taxpayer reduces indebtedness. For purposes of applying this subparagraph to interest expenses attributable to any month, the general phase-in amount shall in no event exceed the lowest amount of indebtedness of the taxpayer outstanding as of the close of any preceding month beginning after November 16, 1985. To the extent provided in regulations, the average amount of indebtedness outstanding during any month shall be used (in lieu of the amount outstanding as of the close of such month) for purposes of the preceding sentence.

"(B) Consolidation rule not to apply to certain interest.

"(i) In general. In the case of the 1st 5 taxable years of the taxpayer beginning after December 31, 1986—

"(I) subparagraph (A) shall not apply for purposes of paragraph (1) of section 864(e) of the Internal Revenue Code of 1986 (as added by this section), but

"(II) such paragraph (1) shall not apply to interest expenses paid or accrued by the taxpayer during the taxable year with respect to an aggregate amount of indebtedness which does not exceed the special phase-in amount.

"(ii) Special phase-in amount. The special phase-in amount for purposes of clause (i) is the sum of—

"(I) the general phase-in amount as determined for purposes of subparagraph (A),

"(II) the 5-year phase-in amount, and

"(III) the 4-year phase-in amount. For purposes of applying this subparagraph to interest expense attributable to any month, the special phase-in amount shall in no event exceed the limitation determined under subparagraph (A)(iii).

"(iii) 5-year phase-in amount. The 5-year phase-in amount is the lesser of—

"(I) the applicable percentage (determined under the following table for purposes of this subclause) of the 5-year debt amount, or

"(II) the applicable percentage (determined under the following table for purposes of this subclause) of the 5-year debt amount reduced by paydowns:

"In the case of the:	The applicable percentage for purposes of subclause (I) is:	The applicable percentage for purposes of subclause (II) is:
1st taxable year	8⅓	10
2nd taxable year	16⅔	25
3rd taxable year	25	50
4th taxable year	33⅓	100
5th taxable year	16⅔	100

"(iv) 4-year phase-in amount.— The 4-year phase-in amount is the lesser of—

"(I) the applicable percentage (determined under the following table for purposes of this subclause) of the 4-year debt amount, or

"(II) the applicable percentage (determined under the following table for purposes of this subclause) of the 4-year debt amount reduced by paydowns to the extent such paydowns exceed the 5-year debt amount:

"In the case of the:	The applicable percentage for purposes of subclause (I) is:	The applicable percentage for purposes of subclause (II) is:
1st taxable year	5	6¼
2nd taxable year	10	16⅔
3rd taxable year	15	37½
4th taxable year	20	100
5th taxable year	0	0

"(v) 5-year debt amount.— The term '5-year debt amount' means the excess (if any) of—

"(I) the amount of the outstanding indebtedness of the taxpayer on May 29, 1985, over

"(II) the amount of the outstanding indebtedness of the taxpayer as of the close of December 31, 1983.
The 5-year debt amount shall not exceed the aggregate amount of indebtedness of the taxpayer outstanding on November 16, 1985.

"(vi) 4-year debt amount. The term '4-year debt amount' means the excess (if any) of—

"(I) the amount referred to in clause (v)(II), over

"(II) the amount of the outstanding indebtedness of the taxpayer as of the close of December 31, 1982.
The 4-year debt amount shall not exceed the aggregate amount of indebtedness of the taxpayer outstanding on November 16, 1985, reduced by the 5-year debt amount.

"(vii) Paydowns. For purposes of applying this subparagraph to interest expenses attributable to any month, the term 'paydowns' means the excess (if any) of—

"(I) the aggregate amount of indebtedness of the taxpayer outstanding on November 16, 1985, over

"(II) the lowest amount of indebtedness of the taxpayer outstanding as of the close of any preceding month beginning after November 16, 1985 (or, to the extent provided in regulations under subparagraph (A)(iii), the average amount of indebtedness outstanding during any such month),

"(C) Coordination of subparagraphs (A) and (B).—In applying subparagraph (B), there shall first be taken into account indebtedness to which subparagraph (A) applies.

"(D) Special rules.

"(i) In the case of the 1st 9 taxable years of the taxpayer beginning after December 31, 1986, the amendments made by this section shall not apply to interest expenses paid or accrued by the taxpayer during the taxable year with respect to an aggregate amount of indebtedness which does not exceed the applicable percentage (determined under the following table) of the indebtedness described in clause (iii) or (iv):

"In the case of the:	The applicable percentage is:
1st taxable year	90
2nd taxable year	80
3rd taxable year	70
4th taxable year	60
5th taxable year	50
6th taxable year	40
7th taxable year	30
8th taxable year	20
9th taxable year	10

"(ii) The provisions of this subparagraph shall apply in lieu of the provisions of subparagraphs (A) and (B).

"(iii) indebtedness outstanding on May 29, 1985. Indebtedness is described in this clause if it is indebtedness (which was outstanding on May 29, 1985) of a corporation incorporated on June 13, 1917, which has its principal place of business in Bartlesville, Oklahoma.

"(iv) Indebtedness outstanding on May 25, 1985. Indebtedness is described in this clause if it is indebtedness (which was outstanding on May 29, 1985) of a member of an affiliated group (as defined in section 1504(a)), the common parent of which was incorporated on August 26, 1926, and has its principal place of business in Harrison, New York.

"(E) Treatment of affiliated group. For purposes of this paragraph, all members of the same affiliated group of corporations (as defined in section 864(e)(5)(A) of the Internal Revenue Code of 1986, as added by this section) shall be treated as 1 taxpayer whether or not such members filed a consolidated return."

"(F) Election to have paragraph not apply. A taxpayer may elect (at such time and in such manner as the Secretary of the Treasury or his delegate may prescribe) to have this paragraph not apply. In the case of members of the same affiliated group (as so defined), such an election may be made only if each member consents to such election.

"(3) Special rule.—

"(A) In general.—In the case of a qualified corporation, in lieu of applying paragraph (2), the amendments made by this section shall not apply to interest expenses allocable to any indebtedness to the extent such indebtedness does not exceed $500,000,000 if—

"(i) the indebtedness was incurred to develop or improve existing property that is owned by the taxpayer on November 16, 1985, and was acquired with the intent to develop or improve the property,

"(ii) the loan agreement with respect to the indebtedness provides that the funds are to be utilized for purposes of developing or improving the above property, and

"(iii) the debt to equity ratio of the companies that join in the filing of the consolidated return is less than 15 percent.

"(B) Qualified corporation.—For purposes of subparagraph (A), the term 'qualified corporation' means a corporation—

"(i) which was incorporated in Delaware on June 29, 1964,

"(ii) the principal subsidiary of which is a resident of Arkansas, and

"(iii) which is a member of an affiliated group the average daily United States production of oil of which is less than 50,000 barrels and the average daily United States refining of which is less than 150,000 barrels.

"(4) Special rules for subsidiary.—The amendments made by this section shall not apply to interest on up to the applicable dollar amount of indebtedness of a subsidiary incorporated on February 11, 1975, the indebtedness of which on May 6, 1986, included—

"(A) $100,000,000 face amount of 11¾ percent notes due in 1990,

"(B) $100,000,000 of 8¾ percent notes due in 1989,

"(C) 6¾ percent Japanese yen notes due in 1991, and

"(D) 5⅜ percent Swiss franc bonds due in 1994.
For purposes of this paragraph, the term 'applicable dollar amount' means $600,000,000 in the case of taxable years beginning in 1987 through 1991, $500,000,000 in the case of the taxable year beginning in 1992, $400,000,000 in the case of the taxable year beginning 1993, $300,000,000 in the case of the taxable year beginning in 1994, $200,000,000 in the case of the taxable year beginning in 1995, $100,000,000 in the case of the taxable year beginning in 1996, and zero in the case of taxable years beginning after 1996.

"(5) Repealed.

"(6) Special rules for allocating general and administrative expenses.—

"(A) In general.—In the case of an affiliated group of domestic corporations the common parent of which has its principal office in New Brunswick, New Jersey, and has a certificate of organization which was filed with the Secretary of the State of New Jersey on November 10, 1887, the amendments made by this section shall not apply to the phase-in percentage of general and administrative expenses paid or incurred in its 1st 3 taxable years beginning after December 31, 1986.

"(B) Phase-in percentage.—For purposes of subparagraph (A):

"In the case of taxable years beginning in:	The phase-in percentage is:
1987	75
1988	50
1989	25."

—P.L. 99-514, Sec. 1221(a)(2), amended clauses (d)(5)(A)(iii) and (iv), effective for tax. yrs. of foreign corporations begin. after 12/31/86. For special rules, see Sec. 1221(g)(3) of this Act reproduced in note following Code Sec. 954.
Prior to amendment, clauses (d)(5)(A)(iii) and (iv) read as follows:

"(iii) Subparagraph (B) of section 954(c)(3) (relating to certain income derived in active conduct of trade or business).

"(iv) Subparagraphs (A) and (B) of section 954(c)(4) (relating to exception for certain income received from related persons)."

—P.L. 99-514, Sec. 1223(b)(1), substituted "less than 5 percent or $1,000,000" for "less than 10 percent" in clause (d)(5)(A)(ii), effective for tax. yrs. begin. after 12/31/86.

—P.L. 99-514, Sec. 1242(a), added paras. (c)(6) and (7) (see Sec. 1012 of P.L. 100-647(aa)(3)(H), above) . . . Sec. 1242(b), substituted "(4), (6), and (7)" for "and (4)" in subpara. (c)(1)(A) and substituted "as provided in paragraph (6) or (7) or in" for "as provided in" in subpara. (c)(1)(B), effective for tax. yrs. begin. after 12/31/86.

—P.L. 99-514, Sec. 1275(c)(7), amended subpara. (d)(5)(B), effective for tax. yrs. begin. after 12/31/86. For special rules, see Sec. 1277(b) and (d)-(f), reproduced in note following Code Sec. 931.
Prior to amendment, subpara. (d)(5)(B) read as follows:

"(B) Special rules for possessions.

"(i) Puerto Rico and possessions tax credit. Any amount treated as interest under paragraph (1) shall not be treated as income described in subparagraph (A) or (B) of section 936(a)(1) unless such amount is from sources within a possession of the United States (determined after the application of paragraph (1)).

"(ii) Virgin Islands corporations.—Subsection (b) of section 934 shall not apply to any amount treated as interest under paragraph (1) unless such amount is from sources within the Virgin Islands (determined after the application of paragraph (1))."

—P.L. 99-514, Sec. 1810(c)(2), redesignated para. (d)(7) as (d)(8), and added new para. (d)(7) . . . Sec. 1810(c)(3), added "and subparagraph (J) of section 904(d)(3) (relating to interest from members of same affiliated group)" after "applies)" in clause (d)(5)(A)(i), effective for accounts receivable and evidences of indebtedness transferred after 3/1/84, in tax. yrs. end. after 3/1/84.

—P.L. 99-514, Sec. 1899A(21), added a comma and a space after "section 871(h)" in the matter preceding subpara. (c)(2)(A), effective 10/22/86.

In 1984, P.L. 98-369, Sec. 123(a), added subsec. (d), effective for accounts receivable and evidences of indebtedness transferred after 3/1/84, in tax. yrs. end. after 3/1/84. Sec. 123(c)(2) of the Act provides the following transitional rule:

"(2) Transitional rule.—The amendments made by this section shall not apply to accounts receivable and evidences of indebtedness acquired after March 1, 1984, and before March 1, 1994, by a Belgian corporation in existence on March 1, 1984, in any taxable year ending after such date, but only to the extent that the amount includible in gross income by reason of section 956 of the Internal Revenue Code of 1954 with respect to such corporation for all such taxable years is not reduced by reason of this paragraph by more than the lesser of—

"(A) $15,000,000 or

"(B) the amount of the Belgian corporation's adjusted basis on March 1, 1984, in stock of a foreign corporation formed to issue bonds outside the United States to the public."

—P.L. 98-369, Sec. 127(c), substituted "section 871(a)(1), section 871(h), section 881(a), or section 881(c)" for "section 871(a)(1) or section 881(a)" in para. (c)(2), effective for interest received after 7/18/84 for obligations issued after 7/18/84, in tax. yrs. end. after 7/18/84. Sec. 127(g)(3) [as amended by Sec. 6128(a) of P.L. 100-647, see above] of the Act provides the following special rule:

"(3) Special rule for certain United States affiliate obligations.—

"(A) In general.—For purposes of the Internal Revenue Code of 1954, payments of interest on a United States affiliate obligation to an applicable CFC in

Source of income   Code Sec. 865(e)(1)(A)

existence on or before June 22, 1984, shall be treated as payments to a resident of the country in which the applicable CFC is incorporated.

"(B) Exception.—Subparagraph (A) shall not apply to any applicable CFC which did not meet requirements which are based on the principles set forth in Revenue Rulings 69-501, 69-377, 70-645, and 73-110 as such principles are applied in Revenue Ruling 86-6, except that the maximum debt-to-equity ratio described in such Revenue Rulings shall be increased from 5-to-1 to 25-to-1.

"(C) Definitions. —

"(i) The term 'applicable CFC' has the meaning given such term by section 121(b)(2)(D) of this Act, except that such section shall be applied by substituting 'the date of interest payment' for 'March 31, 1984,' in clause (i) thereof.

"(ii) The term 'United States affiliate obligation' means an obligation described in section 121(b)(2)(F) of this Act which was issued before June 22, 1984."

In 1976, P.L. 94-455, Sec. 1901(a)(113)(A), amended subsec. (a), effective for tax. yrs. begin. after 12/31/76.

Prior to amendment, subsec. (a) read as follows:

"(a) Sale, etc.

"For purposes of this part, the word 'sale' includes 'exchange'; the word 'sold' includes 'exchange'; and the word 'produced' includes 'created,' 'fabricated,' 'manufactured,' 'extracted,' 'processed,' 'cured,' or 'aged.' "

—P.L. 94-455, Sec. 1901(a)(113)(B), substituted "sale or exchange" for "sale" each time it appeared in clauses (c)(4)(B)(i) and (iii) and in subpara. (c)(5)(C), effective for tax. yrs. begin. after 12/31/76.

—P.L. 94-455, Sec. 1901(a)(113)(C), substituted "sold or exchanged" for "sold" in clause (c)(4)(B)(iii), effective for tax. yrs. begin. after 12/31/76.

In 1966, P.L. 89-809, Sec. 102, designated existing language as subsec. (a), and added subsecs. (b) and (c) for tax. yrs. begin. after '66, except that in applying section 864(c)(4)(B)(iii) of the Internal Revenue Code of 1954 with respect to a binding contract entered into on or before February 24, 1966, activities in the United States on or before such date in negotiating or carrying out such contract shall not be taken into account.

Sec. 865. Source rules for personal property sales.
(a) General rule.

Except as otherwise provided in this section, income from the sale of personal property—

(1) by a United States resident shall be sourced in the United States, or

(2) by a nonresident shall be sourced outside the United States.

(b) Exception for inventory property.

In the case of income derived from the sale of inventory property—

(1) this section shall not apply, and

(2) such income shall be sourced under the rules of sections 861(a)(6), 862(a)(6), and 863.

Notwithstanding the preceding sentence, any income from the sale of any unprocessed timber which is a softwood and was cut from an area in the United States shall be sourced in the United States and the rules of sections 862(a)(6) and 863(b) shall not apply to any such income. For purposes of the preceding sentence, the term "unprocessed timber" means any log, cant, or similar form of timber.

(c) Exception for depreciable personal property.

(1) **In general.** Gain (not in excess of the depreciation adjustments) from the sale of depreciable personal property shall be allocated between sources in the United States and sources outside the United States—

(A) by treating the same proportion of such gain as sourced in the United States as the United States depreciation adjustments with respect to such property bear to the total depreciation adjustments, and

(B) by treating the remaining portion of such gain as sourced outside the United States.

(2) **Gain in excess of depreciation.** Gain (in excess of the depreciation adjustments) from the sale of depreciable personal property shall be sourced as if such property were inventory property.

(3) **United States depreciation adjustments.** For purposes of this subsection—

(A) **In general.** The term "United States depreciation adjustments" means the portion of the depreciation adjustments to the adjusted basis of the property which are attributable to the depreciation deductions allowable in computing taxable income from sources in the United States.

(B) **Special rule for certain property.** Except in the case of property of a kind described in section 168(g)(4), if, for any taxable year—

(i) such property is used predominantly in the United States, or

(ii) such property is used predominantly outside the United States,

all of the depreciation deductions allowable for such year shall be treated as having been allocated to income from sources in the United States (or, where clause (ii) applies, from sources outside the United States).

(4) **Other definitions.** For purposes of this subsection—

(A) **Depreciable personal property.** The term "depreciable personal property" means any personal property if the adjusted basis of such property includes depreciation adjustments.

(B) **Depreciation adjustments.** The term "depreciation adjustments" means adjustments reflected in the adjusted basis of any property on account of depreciation deductions (whether allowed with respect to such property or other property and whether allowed to the taxpayer or to any other person).

(C) **Depreciation deductions.** The term "depreciation deductions" means any deductions for depreciation or amortization or any other deduction allowable under any provision of this chapter which treats an otherwise capital expenditure as a deductible expense.

(d) Exception for intangibles.

(1) **In general.** In the case of any sale of an intangible—

(A) this section shall apply only to the extent the payments in consideration of such sale are not contingent on the productivity, use, or disposition of the intangible, and

(B) to the extent such payments are so contingent, the source of such payments shall be determined under this part in the same manner as if such payments were royalties.

(2) **Intangible.** For purposes of paragraph (1), the term "intangible" means any patent, copyright, secret process or formula, goodwill, trademark, trade brand, franchise, or other like property.

(3) **Special rule in the case of goodwill.** To the extent this section applies to the sale of goodwill, payments in consideration of such sale shall be treated as from sources in the country in which such goodwill was generated.

(4) **Coordination with subsection (c).**

(A) Gain not in excess of depreciation adjustments sourced under subsection (c). Notwithstanding paragraph (1), any gain from the sale of an intangible shall be sourced under subsection (c) to the extent such gain does not exceed the depreciation adjustments with respect to such intangible.

(B) **Subsection (c)(2) not to apply to intangibles.** Paragraph (2) of subsection (c) shall not apply to any gain from the sale of an intangible.

(e) Special rules for sales through offices or fixed places of business.

(1) **Sales by residents.**

(A) **In general.** In the case of income not sourced under subsection (b), (c), (d)(1)(B) or (3), or (f), if a United States resident maintains an office or other fixed place of business in a foreign country, income from sales of personal property attributable to such office or other fixed place of business shall be sourced outside the United States.

2,505

(B) **Tax must be imposed.** Subparagraph (A) shall not apply unless an income tax equal to at least 10 percent of the income from the sale is actually paid to a foreign country with respect to such income.

(2) **Sales by nonresidents.**

(A) **In general.** Notwithstanding any other provisions of this part, if a nonresident maintains an office or other fixed place of business in the United States, income from any sale of personal property (including inventory property) attributable to such office or other fixed place of business shall be sourced in the United States. The preceding sentence shall not apply for purposes of section 971 (defining export trade corporation).

(B) **Exception.** Subparagraph (A) shall not apply to any sale of inventory property which is sold for use, disposition, or consumption outside the United States if an office or other fixed place of business of the taxpayer in a foreign country materially participated in the sale.

(3) **Sales attributable to an office or other fixed place of business.** The principles of section 864(c)(5) shall apply in determining whether a taxpayer has an office or other fixed place of business and whether a sale is attributable to such an office or other fixed place of business.

(f) **Stock of affiliates.**

If—

(1) a United States resident sells stock in an affiliate which is a foreign corporation,

(2) such sale occurs in a foreign country in which such affiliate is engaged in the active conduct of a trade or business, and

(3) more than 50 percent of the gross income of such affiliate for the 3-year period ending with the close of such affiliate's taxable year immediately preceding the year in which the sale occurred was derived from the active conduct of a trade or business in such foreign country,

any gain from such sale shall be sourced outside the United States. For purposes of paragraphs (2) and (3), the United States resident may elect to treat an affiliate and all other corporations which are wholly owned (directly or indirectly) by the affiliate as one corporation.

(g) **United States resident; nonresident.**

For purposes of this section—

(1) **In general.** Except as otherwise provided in this subsection—

(A) United States resident. The term "United States resident" means—

(i) any individual who—

(I) is a United States citizen or a resident alien and does not have a tax home (as defined in section 911(d)(3)) in a foreign country, or

(II) is a nonresident alien and has a tax home (as so defined) in the United States, and

(ii) any corporation, trust, or estate which is a United States person (as defined in section 7701(a)(30)).

(B) Nonresident. The term "nonresident" means any person other than a United States resident.

(2) **Special rules for United States citizens and resident aliens.** For purposes of this section, a United States citizen or resident alien shall not be treated as a nonresident with respect to any sale of personal property unless an income tax equal to at least 10 percent of the gain derived from such sale is actually paid to a foreign country with respect to that gain.

(3) **Special rule for certain stock sales by residents of Puerto Rico.** Paragraph (2) shall not apply to the sale by an individual who was a bona fide resident of Puerto Rico during the entire taxable year of stock in a corporation if—

(A) such corporation is engaged in the active conduct of a trade or business in Puerto Rico, and

(B) more than 50 percent of its gross income for the 3-year period ending with the close of such corporation's taxable year immediately preceding the year in which such sale occurred was derived from the active conduct of a trade or business in Puerto Rico.

For purposes of the preceding sentence, the taxpayer may elect to treat a corporation and all other corporations which are wholly owned (directly or indirectly) by such corporation as one corporation.

(h) **Treatment of gains from sale of certain stock or intangibles and from certain liquidations.**

(1) **In general.** In the case of gain to which this subsection applies—

(A) such gain shall be sourced outside the United States, but

(B) subsections (a), (b), and (c) of section 904 and sections 902, 907, and 960 shall be applied separately with respect to such gain.

(2) **Gain to which subsection applies.** This subsection shall apply to—

(A) Gain from sale of certain stock or intangibles. Any gain—

(i) which is from the sale of stock in a foreign corporation or an intangible (as defined in subsection (d)(2)) and which would otherwise be sourced in the United States under this section,

(ii) which, under a treaty obligation of the United States (applied without regard to this section), would be sourced outside the United States, and

(iii) with respect to which the taxpayer chooses the benefits of this subsection.

(B) Gain from liquidation in possession. Any gain which is derived from the receipt of any distribution in liquidation of a corporation—

(i) which is organized in a possession of the United States, and

(ii) more than 50 percent of the gross income of which during the 3-taxable year period ending with the close of the taxable year immediately preceding the taxable year in which the distribution is received from the active conduct of a trade or business in such possession.

(i) **Other definitions.**

For purposes of this section—

(1) **Inventory property.** The term "inventory property" means personal property described in paragraph (1) of section 1221(a).

(2) **Sale includes exchange.** The term "sale" includes an exchange or any other disposition.

(3) **Treatment of possessions.** Any possession of the United States shall be treated as a foreign country.

(4) **Affiliate.** The term "affiliate" means a member of the same affiliated group (within the meaning of section 1504(a) without regard to section 1504(b)).

(5) **Treatment of partnerships.** In the case of a partnership, except as provided in regulations, this section shall be applied at the partner level.

(j) **Regulations.**

The Secretary shall prescribe such regulations as may be necessary or appropriate to carry out the purpose of this section, including regulations—

Foreign taxpayers

(1) relating to the treatment of losses from sales of personal property,

(2) applying the rules of this section to income derived from trading in futures contracts, forward contracts, options contracts, and other instruments, and

(3) providing that, subject to such conditions (which may include provisions comparable to section 877) as may be provided in such regulations, subsections (e)(1)(B) and (g)(2) shall not apply for purposes of sections 931, 933, and 936.

(k) Cross references.

(1) For provisions relating to the characterization as dividends for source purposes of gains from the sale of stock in certain foreign corporations, see section 1248.

(2) For sourcing of income from certain foreign currency transactions, see section 988.

In 1999, P.L. 106-170, Sec. 532(c)(1)(E), substituted "section 1221(a)" for "section 1221" in para. (i)(1), effective for any instrument held, acquired, or entered into, any transaction entered into, and supplies held or acquired on or after 12/17/99.

In 1996, P.L. 104-188, Sec. 1704(f)(4)(A), substituted "863" for "863(b)" in para. (b)(2), effective for tax. yrs. begin. after 12/31/86, [see Sec. 1012 of P.L. 100-647(aa)(3)(A), below] except as provided in Secs. 1211(c)(2) and (d) of this Act [reproduced below].

In 1993, P.L. 103-66, Sec. 13239(c), added the last sentences of subsec. (b) following para. (b)(2), effective for sales, exchanges, or other dispositions after 8/10/93.

In 1990, P.L. 101-508, Sec. 11813(b)(18), substituted "section 168(g)(4)" for "section 48(a)(2)(B)" in subpara. (c)(3)(B), effective for property placed in service after 12/31/90 except as provided in Sec. 11813(c)(2) of this Act, reproduced in note following Code Sec. 46.

In 1988, P.L. 100-647, Sec. 1012(d)(1), added para. (d)(4)... Sec. 1012(d)(2), substituted "(d)(1)(B) or (3), or (f)" for "(d), or (f)" in subpara. (e)(1)(A)... Sec. 1012(d)(3)(A), deleted "partnership" which followed "corporation," in clause (g)(1)(A)(ii)... Sec. 1012(d)(3)(B), added para. (h)(5)... Sec. 1012(d)(4), amended subsec. (f)... Sec. 1012(d)(6)(A), added para. (g)(3)... Sec. 1012(d)(6)(B), deleted "and" from para. (i)(1) [(j)(1) as redesignated by Sec. 1012(d)(8) of this Act] substituted "and" for the period at the end of para. (i)(2) [(j)(2) as redesignated by Sec. 1012(d)(8) of this Act] and added para. (i)(3) [(j)(3) as redesignated by Sec. 1012(d)(8) of this Act]... Sec. 1012(d)(8), redesignated subsecs. (h), (i) and (j) as subsecs. (i), (j) and (k) and added new subsec. (h)... Sec. 1012(d)(9), substituted "in a foreign country" for "outside the United States" in subpara. (e)(1)(A)... Sec. 1012(d)(11), amended clause (g)(1)(A)(i)... Sec. 1012(d)(12), added "franchise," after "trade brand," in para. (d)(2), effective for tax. yrs. begin after 12/31/86, except as provided in Secs. 1211(c)(2) and (d) of P.L. 99-514, reproduced below.

Prior to amendment, subsec. (f) read as follows:

"(f) Stock of affiliates.

"If —

"(1) A United States resident sells stock in an affiliate which is a foreign corporation,

"(2) such affiliate is engaged in the active conduct of a trade or business, and

"(3) such sale occurs in the foreign country in which the affiliate derived more than 50 percent of its gross income for the 3-year period ending with the close of the affiliate's taxable year immediately preceding the year during which such sale occurred,

any gain from such sale shall be sourced outside the United States."

Prior to amendment, clause (g)(1)(A)(i) read as follows:

"(i) any individual who has a tax home (as defined in section 911(d)(3)) in the United States, and"

—P.L. 100-647, Sec. 1012(d)(5), amended subpara. (e)(2)(B), effective for tax. yrs. begin after 12/31/87.

Prior to amendment, subpara. (e)(2)(B) read as follows:

"(B) Exceptions. Subparagraph (A) shall not apply to —

"(i) any sale of inventory property which is sold for use, disposition, or consumption outside the United States if an office or other fixed place of business of the taxpayer outside the United States materially participated in the sale, or

"(ii) any amount included in gross income under section 951(a)(1)(A)."

—P.L. 100-647, Sec. 1012(aa)(3)(A) and (4), provides:

"(3) Certain amendments not to apply to the extent inconsistent with treaties. The following amendments made by the Reform Act shall not apply to the extent the application of such amendments would be contrary to any treaty obligation of the United States in effect on the date of the enactment of the Reform Act:

"(A) The amendments made by section 1211 of the Reform Act to the extent —

"(i) such amendments apply in the case of an individual treated as a resident of a foreign country under a treaty obligation of the United States as so in effect, or

"(ii) such amendments relate to income of a nonresident from the sale or exchange of inventory property which would otherwise be sourced under section 865(e)(2) of the 1986 Code."

* * *

"(4) Treatment of technical corrections. For purposes of paragraphs (2) and (3), any amendment made by this title shall be treated as if it had been included in the provision of the Reform Act to which such amendment relates."

In 1986, P.L. 99-514, Sec. 1211(a), added Code Sec. 865, effective for tax. yrs. begin. after 12/31/86, [see Sec. 1012 of P.L. 100-647(aa)(3)(A), above] except as provided in Secs. 1211(c)(2) and (d) of this Act, which read:

"(2) Special rule for foreign persons. In the case of any foreign person other than any controlled foreign corporations (within the meaning of section 957(a) of the Internal Revenue Code of 1954), the amendments made by this section shall apply to transactions entered into after March 18, 1986.

"(d) Study. The Secretary of the Treasury or his delegate shall conduct a study of the source rules for sales of inventory property. Not later than September 30, 1987, the Secretary of the Treasury or his delegate shall submit to the Committee on Ways and Means of the House of Representatives and the Committee on Finance of the Senate a report of such study (together with such recommendations as he may deem advisable)."

PART II. — NONRESIDENT ALIENS AND FOREIGN CORPORATIONS

Subpart

A. Nonresident alien individuals.

B. Foreign corporations.

C. Tax on gross transportation income.

D. Miscellaneous provisions.

SUBPART A. — NONRESIDENT ALIEN INDIVIDUALS

Sec.

871. Tax on nonresident alien individuals.

872. Gross income.

873. Deductions.

874. Allowance of deductions and credits.

875. Partnerships; beneficiaries of estates and trusts.

876. Alien residents of Puerto Rico, Guam, American Samoa, or the Northern Mariana Islands.

877. Expatriation to avoid tax.

877A. Tax responsibilities of expatriation.

878. Foreign educational, charitable, and certain other exempt organizations.

879. Tax treatment of certain community income in the case of nonresident alien individuals.

In 2008, P.L. 110-245, Sec. 301(f), added item 877A.

In 1986, P.L. 99-514, Sec. 1272(d)(13), amended item 876.

Prior to amendment, item 876 read as follows:

"876. Alien residents of Puerto Rico."

In 1984, P.L. 98-369, Sec. 139(b)(2), amended the item for Code Sec. 879.

Prior to amendment the item for Code Sec. 879 read as follows:

"879. Tax treatment of certain community income in the case of a resident or citizen of the United States who is married to a nonresident alien individual."

In 1976, P.L. 94-455, Sec. 1012(b)(3)(A), added item 879.

In 1966, P.L. 89-809, Sec. 103, added to item 875 "; beneficiaries of estates or trusts", added item 877 and redesignated former item 877 as item 878.

Sec. 871. Tax on nonresident alien individuals.

(a) Income not connected with United States business — 30 percent tax.

(1) Income other than capital gains. Except as provided in subsection (h), there is hereby imposed for each taxable year a tax of 30 percent of the amount received from sources within the United States by a nonresident alien individual as —

(A) interest (other than original issue discount as defined in section 1273), dividends, rents, salaries, wages, premiums, annuities, compensations, remunerations, emoluments, and other fixed or determinable annual or periodical gains, profits, and income,

(B) gains described in section 631(b) or (c), and gains on transfers described in section 1235 made on or before October 4, 1966,

(C) in the case of —

(i) a sale or exchange of an original issue discount obligation, the amount of the original issue discount accruing while such obligation was held by the nonresident alien individual (to the extent such discount was not theretofore taken into account under clause (ii)), and

(ii) a payment on an original issue discount obligation, an amount equal to the original issue discount accruing while such obligation was held by the nonresident alien individual (except that such original issue discount shall be taken into account under this clause only to the extent such discount was not theretofore taken into account under this clause and only to the extent that the tax thereon does not exceed the payment less the tax imposed by subparagraph (A) thereon), and

(D) gains from the sale or exchange after October 4, 1966, of patents, copyrights, secret processes and formulas, good will, trademarks, trade brands, franchises, and other like property, or of any interest in any such property, to the extent such gains are from payments which are contingent on the productivity, use, or disposition of the property or interest sold or exchanged,

but only to the extent the amount so received is not effectively connected with the conduct of a trade or business within the United States.

(2) Capital gains of aliens present in the United States 183 days or more. In the case of a nonresident alien individual present in the United States for a period or periods aggregating 183 days or more during the taxable year, there is hereby imposed for such year a tax of 30 percent of the amount by which his gains, derived from sources within the United States, from the sale or exchange at any time during such year of capital assets exceed his losses, allocable to sources within the United States, from the sale or exchange at any time during such year of capital assets. For purposes of this paragraph, gains and losses shall be taken into account only if, and to the extent that, they would be recognized and taken into account if such gains and losses were effectively connected with the conduct of a trade or business within the United States, except that such gains and losses shall be determined without regard to section 1202 and such losses shall be determined without the benefits of the capital loss carryover provided in section 1212. Any gain or loss which is taken into account in determining the tax under paragraph (1) or subsection (b) shall not be taken into account in determining the tax under this paragraph. For purposes of the 183-day requirement of this paragraph, a nonresident alien individual not engaged in trade or business within the United States who has not established a taxable year for any prior period shall be treated as having a taxable year which is the calendar year.

(3) Taxation of social security benefits. For purposes of this section and section 1441—

(A) 85 percent of any social security benefit (as defined in section 86(d)) shall be included in gross income (notwithstanding section 207 of the Social Security Act), and

(B) section 86 shall not apply.

For treatment of certain citizens of possessions of the United States, see section 932(c).

(b) Income connected with United States business—graduated rate of tax.

(1) Imposition of tax. A nonresident alien individual engaged in trade or business within the United States during the taxable year shall be taxable as provided in section 1 or 55 on his taxable income which is effectively connected with the conduct of a trade or business within the United States.

(2) Determination of taxable income. In determining taxable income for purposes of paragraph (1), gross income includes only gross income which is effectively connected with the conduct of a trade or business within the United States.

(c) Participants in certain exchange or training programs.

For purposes of this section, a nonresident alien individual who (without regard to this subsection) is not engaged in trade or business within the United States and who is temporarily present in the United States as a nonimmigrant under subparagraph (F), (J), (M), or (Q) of section 101(a)(15) of the Immigration and Nationality Act, as amended (8 U.S.C. 1101(a)(15)(F), (J), (M), or (Q), shall be treated as a nonresident alien individual engaged in trade or business within the United States, and any income described in the second sentence of section 1441(b) which is received by such individual shall, to the extent derived from sources within the United States, be treated as effectively connected with the conduct of a trade or business within the United States.

(d) Election to treat real property income as income connected with United States business.

(1) In general. A nonresident alien individual who during the taxable year derives any income—

(A) from real property held for the production of income and located in the United States, or from any interest in such real property, including (i) gains from the sale or exchange of such real property or an interest therein, (ii) rents or royalties from mines, wells, or other natural deposits, and (iii) gains described in section 631(b) or (c), and

(B) which, but for this subsection, would not be treated as income which is effectively connected with the conduct of a trade or business within the United States,

may elect for such taxable year to treat all such income as income which is effectively connected with the conduct of a trade or business within the United States. In such case, such income shall be taxable as provided in subsection (b)(1) whether or not such individual is engaged in trade or business within the United States during the taxable year. An election under this paragraph for any taxable year shall remain in effect for all subsequent taxable years, except that it may be revoked with the consent of the Secretary with respect to any taxable year.

(2) Election after revocation. If an election has been made under paragraph (1) and such election has been revoked, a new election may not be made under such paragraph for any taxable year before the 5th taxable year which begins after the first taxable year for which such revocation is effective, unless the Secretary consents to such new election.

(3) Form and time of election and revocation. An election under paragraph (1), and any revocation of such an election, may be made only in such manner and at such time as the Secretary may by regulations prescribe.

(e) Repealed.

(f) Certain annuities received under qualified plans.

(1) In general. For purposes of this section, gross income does not include any amount received as an annuity under a qualified annuity plan described in section 403(a)(1), or from a qualified trust described in section 401(a) which is exempt from tax under section 501(a), if—

(A) all of the personal services by reason of which the annuity is payable were either—

Foreign taxpayers — Code Sec. 871(h)(3)(A)

(i) personal services performed outside the United States by an individual who, at the time of performance of such personal services, was a nonresident alien, or

(ii) personal services described in section 864(b)(1) performed within the United States by such individual, and

(B) at the time the first amount is paid as an annuity under the annuity plan or by the trust, 90 percent or more of the employees for whom contributions or benefits are provided under such annuity plan, or under the plan or plans of which the trust is a part, are citizens or residents of the United States.

(2) Exclusion. Income received during the taxable year which would be excluded from gross income under this subsection but for the requirement of paragraph (1)(B) shall not be included in gross income if—

(A) the recipient's country of residence grants a substantially equivalent exclusion to residents and citizens of the United States; or

(B) the recipient's country of residence is a beneficiary developing country under title V of the Trade Act of 1974 (19 U.S.C. 2461 et seq.).

(g) Special rules for original issue discount.

For purposes of this section and section 881—

(1) Original issue discount obligation.

(A) In general. Except as provided in subparagraph (B), the term "original issue discount obligation" means any bond or other evidence of indebtedness having original issue discount (within the meaning of section 1273).

(B) Exceptions. The term "original issue discount obligation" shall not include—

(i) Certain short-term obligations. Any obligation payable 183 days or less from the date of original issue (without regard to the period held by the taxpayer).

(ii) Tax-exempt obligations. Any obligation the interest on which is exempt from tax under section 103 or under any other provision of law without regard to the identity of the holder.

(2) Determination of portion of original issue discount accruing during any period. The determination of the amount of the original issue discount which accrues during any period shall be made under the rules of section 1272 (or the corresponding provisions of prior law) without regard to any exception for short-term obligations.

(3) Source of original issue discount. Except to the extent provided in regulations prescribed by the Secretary, the determination of whether any amount described in subsection (a)(1)(C) is from sources within the United States shall be made at the time of the payment (or sale or exchange) as if such payment (or sale or exchange) involved the payment of interest.

(4) Stripped bonds. The provisions of section 1286 (relating to the treatment of stripped bonds and stripped coupons as obligations with original issue discount) shall apply for purposes of this section.

(h) Repeal of tax on interest of nonresident alien individuals received from certain portfolio debt investments.

(1) In general. In the case of any portfolio interest received by a nonresident individual from sources within the United States, no tax shall be imposed under paragraph (1)(A) or (1)(C) of subsection (a).

• *Caution:* Code Sec. 871(h)(2), following, is effective for obligations issued before 3/19/2012. For Code Sec. 871(h)(2), effective for obligations issued after 3/18/2012, see below.

(2) Portfolio interest. For purposes of this subsection, the term "portfolio interest" means any interest (including original issue discount) which would be subject to tax under subsection (a) but for this subsection and which is described in any of the following subparagraphs:

(A) Certain obligations which are not registered. Interest which is paid on any obligation which—

(i) is not in registered form, and

(ii) is described in section 163(f)(2)(B).

(B) Certain registered obligations. Interest which is paid on an obligation—

(i) which is in registered form, and

(ii) with respect to which the United States person who would otherwise be required to deduct and withhold tax from such interest under section 1441(a) receives a statement (which meets the requirements of paragraph (5)) that the beneficial owner of the obligation is not a United States person.

• *Caution:* Code Sec. 871(h)(2), following, is effective for obligations issued after 3/18/2012. For Code Sec. 871(h)(2), effective for obligations issued before 3/19/2012, see above.

(2) Portfolio interest. For purposes of this subsection, the term "portfolio interest" means any interest (including original issue discount) which—

(A) would be subject to tax under subsection (a) but for this subsection, and

(B) is paid on an obligation—

(i) which is in registered form, and

(ii) with respect to which—

(I) the United States person who would otherwise be required to deduct and withhold tax from such interest under section 1441(a) receives a statement (which meets the requirements of paragraph (5)) that the beneficial owner of the obligation is not a United States person, or

(II) the Secretary has determined that such a statement is not required in order to carry out the purposes of this subsection.

(3) Portfolio interest not to include interest received by 10-percent shareholders. For purposes of this subsection—

• *Caution:* Code Sec. 871(h)(3)(A), following, is effective for obligations issued before 3/19/2012. For Code Sec. 871(h)(3)(A), effective for obligations issued after 3/18/2012, see below.

(A) In general. The term "portfolio interest" shall not include any interest described in subparagraph (A) or (B) of paragraph (2) which is received by a 10-percent shareholder.

Code Sec. 871(h)(3)(A) — **Foreign taxpayers**

> • *Caution:* Code Sec. 871(h)(3)(A), following, is effective for obligations issued after 3/18/2012. For Code Sec. 871(h)(3)(A), effective for obligations issued before 3/19/2012, see above.

(A) In general. The term "portfolio interest" shall not include any interest described in paragraph (2) which is received by a 10-percent shareholder.

(B) 10-Percent shareholder. The term "10-percent shareholder" means—

(i) in the case of an obligation issued by a corporation, any person who owns 10 percent or more of the total combined voting power of all classes of stock of such corporation entitled to vote, or

(ii) in the case of an obligation issued by a partnership, any person who owns 10 percent or more of the capital or profits interest in such partnership.

(C) Attribution rules. For purposes of determining ownership of stock under subparagraph (B)(i) the rules of section 318(a) shall apply, except that—

(i) section 318(a)(2)(C) shall be applied without regard to the 50-percent limitation therein,

(ii) section 318(a)(3)(C) shall be applied—

(I) without regard to the 50-percent limitation therein; and

(II) in any case where such section would not apply but for subclause (I), by considering a corporation as owning the stock (other than stock in such corporation) which is owned by or for any shareholder of such corporation in that proportion which the value of the stock which such shareholder owns in such corporation bears to the value of all stock in such corporation, and

(iii) any stock which a person is treated as owning after application of section 318(a)(4) shall not, for purposes of applying paragraphs (2) and (3) of section 318(a), be treated as actually owned by such person.

Under regulations prescribed by the Secretary, rules similar to the rules of the preceding sentence shall be applied in determining the ownership of the capital or profits interest in a partnership for purposes of subparagraph (B)(ii).

(4) Portfolio interest not to include certain contingent interest. For purposes of this subsection—

(A) In general. Except as otherwise provided in this paragraph, the term "portfolio interest" shall not include—

(i) any interest if the amount of such interest is determined by reference to—

(I) any receipts, sales or other cash flow of the debtor or a related person,

(II) any income or profits of the debtor or a related person,

(III) any change in value of any property of the debtor or a related person, or

(IV) any dividend, partnership distributions, or similar payments made by the debtor or a related person, or

(ii) any other type of contingent interest that is identified by the Secretary by regulation, where a denial of the portfolio interest exemption is necessary or appropriate to prevent avoidance of Federal income tax.

(B) Related person. The term "related person" means any person who is related to the debtor within the meaning of section 267(b) or 707(b)(1), or who is a party to any arrangement undertaken for a purpose of avoiding the application of this paragraph.

(C) Exceptions. Subparagraph (A)(i) shall not apply to—

(i) any amount of interest solely by reason of the fact that the timing of any interest or principal payment is subject to a contingency,

(ii) any amount of interest solely by reason of the fact that the interest is paid with respect to nonrecourse or limited recourse indebtedness,

(iii) any amount of interest all or substantially all of which is determined by reference to any other amount of interest not described in subparagraph (A) (or by reference to the principal amount of indebtedness on which such other interest is paid),

(iv) any amount of interest solely by reason of the fact that the debtor or a related person enters into a hedging transaction to manage the risk of interest rate or currency fluctuations with respect to such interest,

(v) any amount of interest determined by reference to—

(I) changes in the value of property (including stock) that is actively traded (within the meaning of section 1092(d)) other than property described in section 897(c)(1) or (g),

(II) the yield on property described in subclause (I), other than a debt instrument that pays interest described in subparagraph (A), or stock or other property that represents a beneficial interest in the debtor or a related person, or

(III) changes in any index of the value of property described in subclause (I) or of the yield on property described in subclause (II), and

(vi) any other type of interest identified by the Secretary by regulation.

(D) Exception for certain existing indebtedness. Subparagraph (A) shall not apply to any interest paid or accrued with respect to any indebtedness with a fixed term—

(i) which was issued on or before April 7, 1993, or

(ii) which was issued after such date pursuant to a written binding contract in effect on such date and at all times thereafter before such indebtedness was issued.

(5) Certain statements. A statement with respect to any obligation meets the requirements of this paragraph if such statement is made by—

(A) the beneficial owner of such obligation, or

(B) a securities clearing organization, a bank, or other financial institution that holds customers' securities in the ordinary course of its trade or business.

The preceding sentence shall not apply to any statement with respect to payment of interest on any obligation by any person if, at least one month before such payment, the Secretary has published a determination that any statement from such person (or any class including such person) does not meet the requirements of this paragraph.

(6) Secretary may provide subsection not to apply in cases of inadequate information exchange.

(A) In general. If the Secretary determines that the exchange of information between the United States and a foreign country is inadequate to prevent evasion of the United States income tax by United States persons, the Secretary may provide in writing (and publish a statement) that the provisions of this subsection shall not apply to payments of interest to any person within such foreign country (or payments addressed to, or for the

account of, persons within such foreign country) during the period—
(i) beginning on the date specified by the Secretary, and
(ii) ending on the date that the Secretary determines that the exchange of information between the United States and the foreign country is adequate to prevent the evasion of United States income tax by United States persons.
(B) Exception for certain obligations. Subparagraph (A) shall not apply to the payment of interest on any obligation which is issued on or before the date of the publication of the Secretary's determination under such subparagraph.
(7) Registered form. For purposes of this subsection, the term "registered form" has the same meaning given such term by section 163(f).
(i) Tax not to apply to certain interest and dividends.
(1) In general. No tax shall be imposed under paragraph (1)(A) or (1)(C) of subsection (a) on any amount described in paragraph (2).
(2) Amounts to which paragraph (1) applies. The amounts described in this paragraph are as follows:
(A) Interest on deposits, if such interest is not effectively connected with the conduct of a trade or business within the United States.
(B) The active foreign business percentage of—
(i) any dividend paid by an existing 80/20 company, and
(ii) any interest paid by an existing 80/20 company.
(C) Income derived by a foreign central bank of issue from bankers' acceptances.
(D) Dividends paid by a foreign corporation which are treated under section 861(a)(2)(B) as income from sources within the United States.
(3) Deposits. For purposes of paragraph (2), the term "deposits" means amounts which are—
(A) deposits with persons carrying on the banking business,
(B) deposits or withdrawable accounts with savings institutions chartered and supervised as savings and loan or similar associations under Federal or State law, but only to the extent that amounts paid or credited on such deposits or accounts are deductible under section 591 (determined without regard to sections 265 and 291) in computing the taxable income of such institutions, and
(C) amounts held by an insurance company under an agreement to pay interest thereon.
(j) Exemption for certain gambling winnings.
No tax shall be imposed under paragraph (1)(A) of subsection (a) on the proceeds from a wager placed in any of the following games: blackjack, baccarat, craps, roulette, or big-6 wheel. The preceding sentence shall not apply in any case where the Secretary determines by regulation that the collection of the tax is administratively feasible.
(k) Exemption for certain dividends of regulated investment companies.
(1) Interest-related dividends.
(A) In general. Except as provided in subparagraph (B), no tax shall be imposed under paragraph (1)(A) of subsection (a) on any interest-related dividend received from a regulated investment company which meets the requirements of section 852(a) for the taxable year with respect to which the dividend is paid.
(B) Exceptions. Subparagraph (A) shall not apply—

(i) to any interest-related dividend received from a regulated investment company by a person to the extent such dividend is attributable to interest (other than interest described in subparagraph (E)(i) or (iii)) received by such company on indebtedness issued by such person or by any corporation or partnership with respect to which such person is a 10-percent shareholder,
(ii) to any interest-related dividend with respect to stock of a regulated investment company unless the person who would otherwise be required to deduct and withhold tax from such dividend under chapter 3 receives a statement (which meets requirements similar to the requirements of subsection (h)(5)) that the beneficial owner of such stock is not a United States person, and
(iii) to any interest-related dividend paid to any person within a foreign country (or any interest-related dividend payment addressed to, or for the account of, persons within such foreign country) during any period described in subsection (h)(6) with respect to such country.
Clause (iii) shall not apply to any dividend with respect to any stock which was acquired on or before the date of the publication of the Secretary's determination under subsection (h)(6).
(C) Interest-related dividend. For purposes of this paragraph—
(i) In general. Except as provided in clause (ii), an interest related dividend is any dividend, or part thereof, which is reported by the company as an interest related dividend in written statements furnished to its shareholders.
(ii) Excess reported amounts. If the aggregate reported amount with respect to the company for any taxable year exceeds the qualified net interest income of the company for such taxable year, an interest related dividend is the excess of—
(I) the reported interest related dividend amount, over
(II) the excess reported amount which is allocable to such reported interest related dividend amount.
(iii) Allocation of excess reported amount.
(I) In general. Except as provided in subclause (II), the excess reported amount (if any) which is allocable to the reported interest related dividend amount is that portion of the excess reported amount which bears the same ratio to the excess reported amount as the reported interest related dividend amount bears to the aggregate reported amount.
(II) Special rule for noncalendar year taxpayers. In the case of any taxable year which does not begin and end in the same calendar year, if the post-December reported amount equals or exceeds the excess reported amount for such taxable year, subclause (I) shall be applied by substituting "post-December reported amount" for "aggregate reported amount" and no excess reported amount shall be allocated to any dividend paid on or before December 31 of such taxable year.
(iv) Definitions. For purposes of this subparagraph—
(I) Reported interest related dividend amount. The term "reported interest related dividend amount" means the amount reported to its shareholders under clause (i) as an interest related dividend.

(II) Excess reported amount. The term "excess reported amount" means the excess of the aggregate reported amount over the qualified net interest income of the company for the taxable year.

(III) Aggregate reported amount. The term "aggregate reported amount" means the aggregate amount of dividends reported by the company under clause (i) as interest related dividends for the taxable year (including interest related dividends paid after the close of the taxable year described in section 855).

(IV) Post-december reported amount. The term "post-December reported amount" means the aggregate reported amount determined by taking into account only dividends paid after December 31 of the taxable year.

(v) Termination. The term "interest related dividend" shall not include any dividend with respect to any taxable year of the company beginning after December 31, 2011.

(D) Qualified net interest income. For purposes of subparagraph (C), the term "qualified net interest income" means the qualified interest income of the regulated investment company reduced by the deductions properly allocable to such income.

(E) Qualified interest income. For purposes of subparagraph (D), the term "qualified interest income" means the sum of the following amounts derived by the regulated investment company from sources within the United States:

(i) Any amount includible in gross income as original issue discount (within the meaning of section 1273) on an obligation payable 183 days or less from the date of original issue (without regard to the period held by the company).

(ii) Any interest includible in gross income (including amounts recognized as ordinary income in respect of original issue discount or market discount or acquisition discount under part V of subchapter P and such other amounts as regulations may provide) on an obligation which is in registered form; except that this clause shall not apply to—

(l) any interest on an obligation issued by a corporation or partnership if the regulated investment company is a 10-percent shareholder in such corporation or partnership, and

(ll) any interest which is treated as not being portfolio interest under the rules of subsection (h)(4).

(iii) Any interest referred to in subsection (i)(2)(A) (without regard to the trade or business of the regulated investment company).

(iv) Any interest-related dividend includable in gross income with respect to stock of another regulated investment company.

(F) 10-percent shareholder. For purposes of this paragraph, the term "10-percent shareholder" has the meaning given such term by subsection (h)(3)(B).

(2) Short-term capital gain dividends.

(A) In general. Except as provided in subparagraph (B), no tax shall be imposed under paragraph (1)(A) of subsection (a) on any short-term capital gain dividend received from a regulated investment company which meets the requirements of section 852(a) for the taxable year with respect to which the dividend is paid.

(B) Exception for aliens taxable under subsection (a)(2). Subparagraph (A) shall not apply in the case of any nonresident alien individual subject to tax under subsection (a)(2).

(C) Short-term capital gain dividend. For purposes of this paragraph—

(i) In general. Except as provided in clause (ii), the term "short-term capital gain dividend" means any dividend, or part thereof, which is reported by the company as a short-term capital gain dividend in written statements furnished to its shareholders.

(ii) Excess reported amounts. If the aggregate reported amount with respect to the company for any taxable year exceeds the qualified short-term gain of the company for such taxable year, the term "short-term capital gain dividend" means the excess of—

(I) the reported short-term capital gain dividend amount, over

(II) the excess reported amount which is allocable to such reported short-term capital gain dividend amount.

(iii) Allocation of excess reported amount.

(I) In general. Except as provided in subclause (II), the excess reported amount (if any) which is allocable to the reported short-term capital gain dividend amount is that portion of the excess reported amount which bears the same ratio to the excess reported amount as the reported short-term capital gain dividend amount bears to the aggregate reported amount.

(II) Special rule for noncalendar year taxpayers. In the case of any taxable year which does not begin and end in the same calendar year, if the post-December reported amount equals or exceeds the excess reported amount for such taxable year, subclause (I) shall be applied by substituting "post-December reported amount" for "aggregate reported amount" and no excess reported amount shall be allocated to any dividend paid on or before December 31 of such taxable year.

(iv) Definitions. For purposes of this subparagraph—

(I) Reported short-term capital gain dividend amount. The term "reported short-term capital gain dividend amount" means the amount reported to its shareholders under clause (i) as a short-term capital gain dividend.

(II) Excess reported amount. The term "excess reported amount" means the excess of the aggregate reported amount over the qualified short-term gain of the company for the taxable year.

(III) Aggregate reported amount. The term "aggregate reported amount" means the aggregate amount of dividends reported by the company under clause (i) as short-term capital gain dividends for the taxable year (including short-term capital gain dividends paid after the close of the taxable year described in section 855).

(IV) Post-december reported amount. The term "post-December reported amount" means the aggregate reported amount determined by taking into account only dividends paid after December 31 of the taxable year.

(v) Termination. The term "short-term capital gain dividend" shall not include any dividend with respect to'". any taxable year of the company beginning after December 31, 2011.

(D) Qualified short-term gain. For purposes of subparagraph (C), the term "qualified short-term gain" means the excess of the net short-term capital gain of the regulated investment company for the taxable year over the net long-term capital loss (if any) of such company for such taxable year. For purposes of this subparagraph, the net short-term capital gain of the regulated investment company shall be computed by treating any short-term capital gain dividend includible in gross income with respect to stock of another regulated investment company as a short-term capital gain.

(E) Certain distributions. In the case of a distribution to which section 897 does not apply by reason of the second sentence of section 897(h)(1), the amount which would be treated as a short-term capital gain dividend to the shareholder (without regard to this subparagraph)—

(i) shall not be treated as a short-term capital gain dividend, and

(ii) shall be included in such shareholder's gross income as a dividend from the regulated investment company.

(l) Rules relating to existing 80/20 companies.
For purposes of this subsection and subsection (i)(2)(B)—

(1) Existing 80/20 company.

(A) In general. The term "existing 80/20 company" means any corporation if—

(i) such corporation met the 80-percent foreign business requirements of section 861(c)(1) (as in effect before the date of the enactment of this subsection) for such corporation's last taxable year beginning before January 1, 2011,

(ii) such corporation meets the 80-percent foreign business requirements of subparagraph (B) with respect to each taxable year after the taxable year referred to in clause (i), and

(iii) there has not been an addition of a substantial line of business with respect to such corporation after the date of the enactment of this subsection.

(B) Foreign business requirements.

(i) In general. Except as provided in clause (iv), a corporation meets the 80-percent foreign business requirements of this subparagraph if it is shown to the satisfaction of the Secretary that at least 80 percent of the gross income from all sources of such corporation for the testing period is active foreign business income.

(ii) Active foreign business income. For purposes of clause (i), the term "active foreign business income" means gross income which—

(I) is derived from sources outside the United States (as determined under this subchapter), and

(II) is attributable to the active conduct of a trade or business in a foreign country or possession of the United States.

(iii) Testing period. For purposes of this subsection, the term "testing period" means the 3-year period ending with the close of the taxable year of the corporation preceding the payment (or such part of such period as may be applicable). If the corporation has no gross income for such 3-year period (or part thereof), the testing period shall be the taxable year in which the payment is made.

(iv) Transition rule. In the case of a taxable year for which the testing period includes 1 or more taxable years beginning before January 1, 2011—

(I) a corporation meets the 80-percent foreign business requirements of this subparagraph if and only if the weighted average of—

(aa) the percentage of the corporation's gross income from all sources that is active foreign business income (as defined in subparagraph (B) of section 861(c)(1) (as in effect before the date of the enactment of this subsection)) for the portion of the testing period that includes taxable years beginning before January 1, 2011, and

(bb) the percentage of the corporation's gross income from all sources that is active foreign business income (as defined in clause (ii) of this subparagraph) for the portion of the testing period, if any, that includes taxable years beginning on or after January 1, 2011, is at least 80 percent, and

(II) the active foreign business percentage for such taxable year shall equal the weighted average percentage determined under subclause (I).

(2) Active foreign business percentage. Except as provided in paragraph (1)(B)(iv), the term "active foreign business percentage" means, with respect to any existing 80/20 company, the percentage which—

(A) the active foreign business income of such company for the testing period, is of

(B) the gross income of such company for the testing period from all sources.

(3) Aggregation rules. For purposes of applying paragraph (1) (other than subparagraphs (A)(i) and (B)(iv) thereof) and paragraph (2)—

(A) In general. The corporation referred to in paragraph (1)(A) and all of such corporation's subsidiaries shall be treated as one corporation.

(B) Subsidiaries. For purposes of subparagraph (A), the term "subsidiary" means any corporation in which the corporation referred to in subparagraph (A) owns (directly or indirectly) stock meeting the requirements of section 1504(a)(2) (determined by substituting "50 percent" for "80 percent" each place it appears and without regard to section 1504(b)(3)).

(4) Regulations. The Secretary may issue such regulations or other guidance as is necessary or appropriate to carry out the purposes of this section, including regulations or other guidance which provide for the proper application of the aggregation rules described in paragraph (3).

(m) Treatment of dividend equivalent payments.

(1) In general. For purposes of subsection (a), sections 881 and 4948(a), and chapters 3 and 4, a dividend equivalent shall be treated as a dividend from sources within the United States.

(2) Dividend equivalent. For purposes of this subsection, the term "dividend equivalent" means—

(A) any substitute dividend made pursuant to a securities lending or a sale-repurchase transaction that (directly or indirectly) is contingent upon, or determined by reference to, the payment of a dividend from sources within the United States,

(B) any payment made pursuant to a specified notional principal contract that (directly or indirectly) is contingent upon, or determined by reference to, the payment of a dividend from sources within the United States, and

(C) any other payment determined by the Secretary to be substantially similar to a payment described in subparagraph (A) or (B).

(3) Specified notional principal contract. For purposes of this subsection, the term "specified notional principal contract" means—

(A) any notional principal contract if—

(i) in connection with entering into such contract, any long party to the contract transfers the underlying security to any short party to the contract,

(ii) in connection with the termination of such contract, any short party to the contract transfers the underlying security to any long party to the contract,

(iii) the underlying security is not readily tradable on an established securities market,

(iv) in connection with entering into such contract, the underlying security is posted as collateral by any short party to the contract with any long party to the contract, or

(v) such contract is identified by the Secretary as a specified notional principal contract,

(B) in the case of payments made after the date which is 2 years after the date of the enactment of this subsection, any notional principal contract unless the Secretary determines that such contract is of a type which does not have the potential for tax avoidance.

(4) Definitions. For purposes of paragraph (3)(A)—

(A) Long party. The term "long party" means, with respect to any underlying security of any notional principal contract, any party to the contract which is entitled to receive any payment pursuant to such contract which is contingent upon, or determined by reference to, the payment of a dividend from sources within the United States with respect to such underlying security.

(B) Short party. The term "short party" means, with respect to any underlying security of any notional principal contract, any party to the contract which is not a long party with respect to such underlying security.

(C) Underlying security. The term "underlying security" means, with respect to any notional principal contract, the security with respect to which the dividend referred to in paragraph (2)(B) is paid. For purposes of this paragraph, any index or fixed basket of securities shall be treated as a single security.

(5) Payments determined on gross basis. For purposes of this subsection, the term "payment" includes any gross amount which is used in computing any net amount which is transferred to or from the taxpayer.

(6) Prevention of over-withholding. In the case of any chain of dividend equivalents one or more of which is subject to tax under subsection (a) or section 881, the Secretary may reduce such tax, but only to the extent that the taxpayer can establish that such tax has been paid with respect to another dividend equivalent in such chain, or is not otherwise due, or as the Secretary determines is appropriate to address the role of financial intermediaries in such chain. For purposes of this paragraph, a dividend shall be treated as a dividend equivalent.

(7) Coordination with chapters 3 and 4. For purposes of chapters 3 and 4, each person that is a party to any contract or other arrangement that provides for the payment of a dividend equivalent shall be treated as having control of such payment.

(n) Cross references.

(1) For tax treatment of certain amounts distributed by the United States to nonresident alien individuals, see section 402(e)(2).

(2) For taxation of nonresident alien individuals who are expatriate United States citizens, see section 877.

(3) For doubling of tax on citizens of certain foreign countries, see section 891.

(4) For adjustment of tax in case of nationals or residents of certain foreign countries, see section 896.

(5) For withholding of tax at source on nonresident alien individuals, see section 1441.

(6) For election to treat married nonresident alien individual as resident of United States in certain cases, see subsections (g) and (h) of section 6013.

(7) For special tax treatment of gain or loss from the disposition by a nonresident alien individual of a United States real property interest, see section 897.

In 2010, P.L. 111-312, Sec. 748(a), substituted "December 31, 2011" for "December 31, 2009" in subparas. (k)(1)(C) and (k)(2)(C), effective for tax. yrs. begin. after 12/31/2009.

—P.L. 111-325, Sec. 301(f)(1), amended the portion of subpara. (k)(1)(C) that precedes "any taxable year of the company beginning" . . . Sec. 301(f)(2), amended the portion of subpara. (k)(2)(C) that precedes "any taxable year of the company beginning", effective for tax. yrs. begin. after 12/22/2010.

Prior to amendment, the amended portion of subpara. (k)(1)(C) read as follows:

"(C) Interest-related dividend. For purposes of this paragraph, the term 'interest related dividend' means any dividend (or part thereof) which is designated by the regulated investment company as an interest-related dividend in a written notice mailed to its shareholders not later than 60 days after the close of its taxable year. If the aggregate amount so designated with respect to a taxable year of the company (including amounts so designated with respect to dividends paid after the close of the taxable year described in section 855) is greater than the qualified net interest income of the company for such taxable year, the portion of each distribution which shall be an interest-related dividend shall be only that portion of the amounts so designated which such qualified net interest income bears to the aggregate amount so designated. Such term shall not include any dividend with respect to"

Prior to amendment, the amended portion of subpara. (k)(2)(C) read as follows:

"(C) Short-term capital gain dividend. For purposes of this paragraph, the term 'short-term capital gain dividend' means any dividend (or part thereof) which is designated by the regulated investment company as a short-term capital gain dividend in a written notice mailed to its shareholders not later than 60 days after the close of its taxable year. If the aggregate amount so designated with respect to a taxable year of the company (including amounts so designated with respect to dividends paid after the close of the taxable year described in section 855) is greater than the qualified short-term gain of the company for such taxable year, the portion of each distribution which shall be a short-term capital gain dividend shall be only that portion of the amounts so designated which such qualified short-term gain bears to the aggregate amount so designated. Such term shall not include any dividend with respect to"

—P.L. 111-325, Sec. 302(b)(2), added "which meets the requirements of section 852(a) for the taxable year with respect to which the dividend is paid" before the period in subpara. (k)(1)(A) and (k)(2)(C), effective for tax. yrs. begin. after 12/22/2010.

—P.L. 111-325, Sec. 308(b)(3), substituted "For purposes of this subparagraph, the net short-term capital gain of the regulated investment company shall be computed by treating any short-term capital gain dividend includible in gross income with respect to stock of another regulated investment company as a short-term capital gain." for the last 2 sentences in subpara. (k)(2)(D), effective for tax. yrs. begin. after 12/22/2010.

Prior to deletion, the last two sentences of subpara. (k)(2)(D) read as follows:

"For purposes of this subparagraph—

"(i) the net short-term capital gain of the regulated investment company shall be computed by treating any short-term capital gain dividend includible in gross income with respect to stock of another regulated investment company as a short-term capital gain, and

"(ii) the excess of the net short-term capital gain for a taxable year over the net long-term capital loss for a taxable year (to which an election under section 4982(e)(4) does not apply) shall be determined without regard to any net capital loss or net short-term capital loss attributable to transactions after October 31 of such year, and any such net capital loss or net short-term capital loss shall be treated as arising on the 1st day of the next taxable year.

"To the extent provided in regulations, clause (ii) shall apply also for purposes of computing the taxable income of the regulated investment company. "

—P.L. 111-226, Sec. 217(b)(1), amended subpara. (i)(2)(B)

Prior to amendment, subpara. (i)(2)(B) read as follows:

"(B) A percentage of any dividend paid by a domestic corporation meeting the 80-percent foreign business requirements of section 861(c)(1) equal to the percentage determined for purposes of section 861(c)(2)(A)." . . . Sec. 217(b)(2), redesignated subsecs. (l)-(m) as subsecs. (m)-(n) and added subsec. (l), effective for tax. yrs. begin. after 12/31/2010. . . . Sec. 217(d)(2), of this Act, reads as follows:

"(2) Grandfather rule for outstanding debt obligations.

"(A) In general. The amendments made by this section shall not apply to payments of interest on obligations issued before the date of the enactment of this Act.

"(B) Exception for related party debt. Subparagraph (A) shall not apply to any interest which is payable to a related person (determined under rules similar to the rules of section 954(d)(3)).

"(C) Significant modifications treated as new issues. For purposes of subparagraph (A), a significant modification of the terms of any obligation (including any extension of the term of such obligation) shall be treated as a new issue."

—P.L. 111-147, Sec. 502(b)(1), amended para. (h)(2) . . . Sec. 502(b)(2)(A), deleted "subparagraph (A) or (B) of" in subpara. (h)(3)(A), effective for obligations issued after 3/18/2012.

—P.L. 111-147, Sec. 541(a), redesignated subsec. (l) as subsec. (m) and added subsec. (l), effective for payments made on or after 9/14/2010.

In 2008, P.L. 110-343, Sec. 206(a)DivC, substituted "December 31, 2009" for "December 31, 2007" in Subpara. (k)(1)(C)

—P.L. 110-343, Sec. 206(b)DivC, substituted "December 31, 2009" for "December 31, 2007" in Subpara. (k)(2)(C), effective for dividends with respect to tax. yrs. of regulated investment companies beginning after 12/31/2007.

In 2006, P.L. 109-222, Sec. 505(c)(2), added subpara. (k)(2)(E), effective for tax. yrs. of qualified investment entities begin. after 12/31/2005, except that no amount shall be required to be withheld under Code Secs. 1441, 1442, or 1445 with respect to any distribution before 5/17/2006 if such amount was not otherwise required to be withheld under any such section as in effect before such amendments.

In 2004, P.L. 108-357, Sec. 409(a), added subpara. (i)(2)(D), effective for payments made after 12/31/2004.

—P.L. 108-357, Sec. 411(a)(1), redesignated subsec. (k) as (l) and added subsec. (k), effective for dividends with respect to tax. yrs. of regulated investment companies begin. after 12/31/2004.

In 2000, P.L. 106-554, Sec. 1(a)(7), [which enacted into law Sec. 319(11) of P.L. 106-554] substituted "(19 U.S.C." for "19 U.S.C." in subpara. (f)(2)(B), effective 12/21/2000.

In 1999, P.L. 106-170, Sec. 532(b)(2), substituted "to manage" for "to reduce" in clause (h)(4)(C)(iv), effective for any instrument held, acquired, or entered into, any transaction entered into, and supplies held or acquired on or after 12/17/99.

In 1998, P.L. 105-206, Sec. 6023(10), substituted "[(]19 U.S.C. 2461 et seq.)" for "(19 U.S.C. 2462)" in subpara. (f)(2)(B), effective 7/22/98.

In 1996, P.L. 104-188, Sec. 1401(b)(10), substituted "section 1 or 55" for "section 1, 55, or 402(d)(1)" in para. (b)(1), effective for tax. yrs. begin. after 12/31/99. For transitional rules, see Sec. 1401(c)(2), of this Act, which reads as follows:

"(2) Retention of certain transition rules. The amendments made by this section shall not apply to any distribution for which the taxpayer is eligible to elect the benefits of section 1122(h)(3) or (5) of the Tax Reform Act of 1986. Notwithstanding the preceding sentence, individuals who elect such benefits after December 31, 1999, shall not be eligible for 5-year averaging under section 402(d) of the Internal Revenue Code of 1986 (as in effect immediately before such amendments)."

—P.L. 104-188, Sec. 1954(b)(1), substituted "under title V" for "within the meaning of section 502" in subpara. (f)(2)(B), effective 8/20/96.

In 1994, P.L. 103-465, Sec. 733(a), substituted "85 percent" for "one-half" in subpara. (a)(3)(A), effective for benefits paid after 12/31/94, in tax. yrs. end. after 12/31/94.

—P.L. 103-296, Sec. 320(a)(1)(A), substituted "(J), (M), or (Q)" for "(J), or (M)" in subsec. (c), effective with the calendar quarter following 8/15/94.

In 1993, P.L. 103-66, Sec. 13113(d)(5), added "such gains and losses shall be determined without regard to section 1202 and" after "except that" in the second sentence of para. (a)(2), effective for stock issued after 8/10/93.

—P.L. 103-66, Sec. 13237(a)(1), redesignated paras. (h)(4), (5), and (6) as paras. (h)(5), (6), and (7) and added new para. (h)(4) . . . Sec. 13237(c)(1), substituted "paragraph (5)" for "paragraph (4)" in clause (h)(2)(B)(ii), effective for interest received after 12/31/93.

In 1992, P.L. 102-318, Sec. 521(b)(28), deleted "402(a)(2), 403(a)(2), or" after "in section" in subpara. (a)(1)(B) . . . Sec. 521(b)(29), substituted "402(d)(1)" for "402(e)(1)" in para. (b)(1) . . . Sec. 521(b)(30), substituted "section 402(e)(2)" for "section 402(a)(4)" in para. (k)(1), effective for distributions after 12/31/92. For special rule, see Sec. 521(e)(2) of this Act which reads as follows:

"(2) Special rule for partial distributions. For purposes of section 402(a)(5)(D)(i)(II) of the Internal Revenue Code of 1986 (as in effect before the amendments made by this section), a distribution before January 1, 1993, which is made before or at the same time as a series of periodic payments shall not be treated as one of such series if it is not substantially equal in amount to other payments in such series."

In 1988, P.L. 100-647, Sec. 1001(d)(2)(B), substituted "the second sentence of section 1441(b)" for "section 1441(b)(1) or (2)" and substituted "(F), (J), or (M)" for "(F) or (J)" each place it appeared in subsec. (c), effective for tax. yrs. begin. after 12/31/86, but only in the case of scholarships and fellowships granted after 8/16/86.

—P.L. 100-647, Sec. 1012(g)(1)(A), amended Sec. 1214(d)(1) of P.L. 99-514, the effective date for amendments made by Sec. 1214(c)(1) of P.L. 99-514, by substituting "payments made in a taxable year of the payor beginning after December 31, 1986" for "payments after December 31, 1986", see below. Sec. 1012(g)(1)(B) of this Act provides:

"(B) A taxpayer may elect not to have the amendment made by subparagraph (A) apply and to have section 1214(d)(1) of the Reform Act apply as in effect before such amendment. Such election shall be made at such time and in such manner as the Secretary of the Treasury or his delegate may prescribe.

—P.L. 100-647, Sec. 1012(aa)(3)(A), (D) and (4), provides:

"(3) Certain amendments not to apply to the extent inconsistent with treaties.—The following amendments made by the Reform Act shall not apply to the extent the application of such amendments would be contrary to any treaty obligation of the United States in effect on the date of the enactment of the Reform Act:

"(A) The amendments made by section 1211 of the Reform Act to the extent—

"(i) such amendments apply in the case of an individual treated as a resident of a foreign country under a treaty obligation of the United States as so in effect, or

"(ii) such amendments relate to income of a non-resident from the sale or exchange of inventory property which would otherwise be sourced under section 865(e)(2) of the 1986 Code."

* * *

"(D) The amendments made by section 1214 of the Reform Act; except for purposes of determining the amount of the foreign tax credit."

* * *

"(4) Treatment of technical corrections. For purposes of paragraphs (2) and (3), any amendment made by this title shall be treated as if it had been included in the provision of the Reform Act to which such amendment relates."

—P.L. 100-647, Sec. 6134(a)(1), redesignated subsec. (j) as (k) and added subsec. (j), effective 11/10/88.

In 1986, P.L. 99-514, Sec. 301(b)(9), deleted "such gains and losses shall be determined without regard to section 1202 (relating to deduction for capital gains) and" after "within the United States, except that" in para. (a)(2), effective for tax. yrs. begin. after 12/31/86.

—P.L. 99-514, Sec. 1211(b)(4), deleted "or from payments which are treated as being so contingent under subsection (e)," before the period at the end of subpara. (a)(1)(D) . . . Sec. 1211(b)(5), deleted subsec. (e), effective for tax. yrs. begin. after 12/31/86, except as provided in Sec. 1211(c)(2) of this Act [see Sec. 1012 of P.L. 100-647(aa)(3)(A) and (4) above] which reads:

"(2) Special rule for foreign persons.—In the case of any foreign person other than any controlled foreign corporations (within the meaning of section 957(a) of the Internal Revenue Code of 1954), the amendments made by this section shall apply to transactions entered into after March 18, 1986."

Prior to deletion, subsec. (e) read as follows:

"(e) Gains from sale or exchange of certain intangible property. For purposes of subsection (a)(1)(D), and for purposes of sections 881(a)(4), 1441(b), and 1442(a)—

"(1) Payments treated as contingent on use, etc. If more than 50 percent of the gain for any taxable year from the sale or exchange of any patent, copyright, secret process or formula, good will, trademark, trade brand, franchise, or other like property, or of any interest in any such property, is from payments which are contingent on the productivity, use, or disposition of such property or interest, all of the gain for the taxable year from the sale or exchange of such property or interest shall be treated as being from payments which are contingent on the productivity, use, or disposition of such property or interest.

"(2) Source rule. In determining whether gains described in subsection (a)(1)(D) and section 881(a)(4) are received from sources within the United States, such gains shall be treated as rentals or royalties for the use of, or privilege of using, property or an interest in property."

—P.L. 99-514, Sec. 1214(c)(1), redesignated subsec. (i) as subsec. (j), and added subsec. (i), effective [as amended by Sec. 1012(g)(1)(A) of P.L. 100-647, see above] for payments made in a tax. yr. of the payor begin. after 12/31/86, except as provided in Sec. 1214(d)(2)-(4) of this Act reproduced in note following Code Sec. 861 [see Sec. 1012 of P.L. 100-647(aa)(3)(D), above].

—P.L. 99-514, Sec. 1810(d)(1)(A), substituted "which would be subject to tax under subsection (a) but for this subsection and which is described in" for "which is described in" in para. (h)(2) . . . Sec. 1810(d)(2), deleted "and" from the end of clause (h)(3)(C)(i), redesignated clause (h)(3)(C)(ii) as (iii) and added new clause (h)(3)(C)(ii) . . . Sec. 1810(d)(3)(A), substituted "subsection (h)" for "subsection (i)" in para. (a)(1) . . . Sec. 1810(d)(3)(B), substituted "receives" for "has received" in clause (h)(2)(B)(ii), effective for interest received after 7/18/84 for obligations issued after 7/18/84, in tax. yrs. end. after 7/18/84.

—P.L. 99-514, Sec. 1810(e)(2)(A), amended subpara. (a)(1)(C), effective for payments made on or after 9/16/84, for obligations issued after 3/31/72.

Prior to amendment, subpara. (a)(1)(C) read as follows:

"(C) in the case of—

"(i) a sale or exchange of an original issue discount obligation, the amount of any gain not in excess of the original issue discount accruing while such obligation was held by the nonresident alien individual (to the extent such discount was not theretofore taken into account under clause (ii)), and

"(ii) the payment of interest on an original issue discount obligation, an amount equal to the original issue discount accrued on such obligation since the last payment of interest thereon (except that such original issue discount shall be taken into account under this clause only to the extent that the tax thereon does not exceed the interest payment less the tax imposed by subparagraph (A) thereon), and"

—P.L. 99-272, Sec. 12103(b), added the last sentence to para. (a)(3), effective for benefits received after 12/31/83, in tax. yrs. end. after 12/31/83.

In 1984, P.L. 98-369, Sec. 42(a)(9), substituted "section 1273" for "section 1232(b)" in subpara. (a)(1)(A), effective for tax. yrs. end. after 7/18/84.

—P.L. 98-369, Sec. 127(a)(1), redesignated subsec. (h) (as redesignated by Sec. 128(a)(2) of this Act see below) as subsec. (i) and added new subsec. (h) . . . Sec. 127(a)(2), substituted "Except as provided in subsection (i), there" for "There" in para. (a)(1), effective for interest received after 7/18/84 for obligations issued after 7/18/84, in tax. yrs. end. after 7/18/84. Sec. 127(g)(3) of the Act provides a special rule, see note following Code Sec. 864.

—P.L. 98-369, Sec. 128(a)(1), amended subpara. (a)(1)(C) . . . Sec. 128(a)(2), redesignated subsec. (g) as subsec. (h) and added new subsec. (g), effective for payments made on or after 9/16/84 for obligations issued after 3/31/72.

Prior to amendment, subpara. (a)(1)(C) read as follows:

"(C) in the case of—

"(i) bonds or other evidences of indebtedness issued after September 28, 1965, and before April 1, 1972, amounts which under section 1232(a)(2)(B) are considered as ordinary income, and, in the case of corporate obligations issued after May 27, 1969, and before April 1, 1972, amounts which would be so considered but for the fact the obligations were issued after May 27, 1969, "(ii) bonds or other evidences of indebtedness issued after March 31, 1972, and payable more than 6 months from the date of original issue (without regard to the period held by the taxpayer), amounts which under section 1232(a)(2)(B) would be considered as ordinary income but for the fact such obligations were issued after May 27, 1969, and

"(iii) the payment of interest on an obligation described in clause (ii), an amount equal to the original issue discount (but not in excess of such interest less the tax imposed by subparagraph (A) thereon) accrued on such obligation since the last payment of interest thereon, and"

—P.L. 98-369, Sec. 412(b)(1), deleted para. (g)(6) (before redesignation by Secs. 127(a)(1) and 128(a)(1) of the Act) and redesignated paras. (g)(7) and (8) as paras. (g)(6) and (7), effective for tax. yrs. begin. after 12/31/84.

Prior to deletion, para. (g)(6) read as follows:

"(6) For the requirement of making a declaration of estimated tax by certain nonresident alien individuals, see section 6015(j)."

In 1983, P.L. 98-21, Sec. 121(c)(1), added para. (a)(3), effective as provided in Sec. 121(g) which reads as follows:

"(g) Effective dates.

"(1) In general.—Except as provided in paragraph (2), the amendments made by this section shall apply to benefits received after December 31, 1983, in taxable years ending after such date.

"(2) Treatment of certain lump-sum payments received after December 31, 1983.—The amendments made by this section shall not apply to any portion of a lump-sum payment of social security benefits (as defined in section 86(d) of he Internal Revenue Code of 1954) received after December 31, 1983, if the generally applicable payment date for such portion was before January 1, 1984."

—P.L. 98-21, Sec. 335(b)(2)(B), added "(notwithstanding section 207 of the Social Security Act)" after "income" in subpara. (a)(3)(A) [as added by Sec. 121(c)(1), above].

In 1981, P.L. 97-34, Sec. 725(c)(1), substituted "6015(j)" for "6015(i)" in para. (g)(6), effective for estimated tax for tax. yrs. begin. after 12/31/80.

In 1980, P.L. 96-605, Sec. 227(a), amended subsec. (f), effective for amounts received after 7/1/79.

Prior to amendment, subsec. (f) read as follows:

"(f) Certain annuities received under qualified plans.

"For purposes of this section, gross income does not include any amount received as an annuity under a qualified annuity plan described in section 403(a)(1), or from a qualified trust described in section 401(a) which is exempt from tax under section 501(a), if—

"(1) all of the personal services by reason of which such annuity is payable were either (A) personal services performed outside the United States by an individual who, at the time of performance of such personal services, was a nonresident alien, or (B) personal services described in section 864(b)(1) performed within the United States by such individual, and

"(2) at the time the first amount is paid as such annuity under such annuity plan, or by such trust, 90 percent or more of the employees for whom contributions or benefits are provided under such annuity plan, or under the plan or plans of which such trust is a part, are citizens or residents of the United States."

—P.L. 96-499, Sec. 1122(c)(1), added para. (g)(8), effective for dispositions after 6/18/80.

—P.L. 96-222, Sec. 104(a)(4)(H)(v), substituted "55" for "section 55" in para. (b)(1), effective for tax. yrs. begin. after 12/31/78.

In 1978, P.L. 95-600, Sec. 401(b)(3), substituted "section 1 or 402(e)(1)" for "section 1, 402(e)(1), or 1201(b)" in para. (b)(1), effective for tax. yrs. begin. after 12/31/78.

—P.L. 95-600, Sec. 421(e)(4), added ", section 55," after "section 1" in para. (b)(1), effective for tax. yrs. begin. after 12/31/78.

In 1976, P.L. 94-455, Sec. 1012(a)(2), added para. (g)(7), effective for tax. yrs. end. on or after 12/31/75.

—P.L. 94-455, Sec. 1901(b)(3)(I), substituted "ordinary income" for "gain from the sale or exchange of property which is not a capital asset", following "considered as" in clauses (a)(1)(C)(i) and (ii), effective for tax. yrs. begin. after 12/31/76.

—P.L. 94-455, Sec. 1906(b)(13)(A), substituted "Secretary" for "Secretary or his delegate" each place it appeared in Code Sec. 871, effective for tax. yrs. begin. after 12/31/76.

In 1974, P.L. 93-406, Sec. 2005(c)(8), added ", 402(e)(1)," after "section 1" in para. (b)(1), effective for distributions or payments made after 12/31/73 in tax. yrs. begin. after 12/31/73.

In 1971, P.L. 92-178, Sec. 313(a), added "(other than original issue discount as defined in section 1232(b))" after "interest" in subpara. (a)(1)(A) . . . Sec. 313(b), amended subpara. (a)(1)(C), effective for tax. yrs. begin. after 12/31/66.

Prior to amendment, subpara. (a)(1)(C) read as follows:

"(C) in the case of bonds or other evidences of indebtedness issued after September 28, 1965, amounts which under section 1232 are considered as gains from the sale or exchange of property which is not a capital asset, and"

In 1966, P.L. 89-809, Sec. 103, amended Code Sec. 871, effective for tax. yrs. begin. after 12/31/66.

Prior to amendment, Code Sec. 871 read as follows:

"SEC. 871. TAX ON NONRESIDENT ALIEN INDIVIDUALS.

"(a) No United States business—30 percent tax.

"(1) Imposition of tax.—Except as otherwise provided in subsection (b) there is hereby imposed for each taxable year, in lieu of the tax imposed by section 1, on the amount received, by every non-resident alien individual not engaged in trade or business within the United States, from sources within the United States, as interest (except interest on deposits with persons carrying on the banking business), dividends, rents, salaries, wages, premiums, annuities, compensations, remunerations, emoluments, or other fixed or determinable annual or periodical gains, profits, and income (including amounts described in sections 402(a)(2), section 403(a)(2), section 631(b) and (c), and section 1235, which are considered to be gains from the sale or exchange of capital assets, a tax of 30 percent of such amount.

"(2) Capital gains of aliens temporarily present in the United States.—In the case of a nonresident alien individual not engaged in trade or business in the United States, there is hereby imposed for each taxable year, in addition to the tax imposed by paragraph (1)—

"(A) if he is present in the United States for a period or periods aggregating less than 90 days during such taxable year—a tax of 30 percent of the amount by which his gains, derived from sources within the United States, from sales or exchanges of capital assets effected during his presence in the United States exceed his losses, allocable to sources within the United States, from such sales or exchanges effected during such presence; or

"(B) if he is present in the United States for a period or periods aggregating 90 days or more during such taxable year—a tax of 30 percent of the amount by which his gains, derived from sources within the United States, from sales or exchanges of capital assets effected at any time during such year exceed his losses, allocable to sources within the United States, from such sales or exchanges effected at any time during such year.

"For purposes of this paragraph, gains and losses shall be taken into account only if, and to the extent that, they would be recognized and taken into account if such individual were engaged in trade or business in the United States, except that such gains and losses shall be computed without regard to section 1202 (relating to deduction for capital gains) and such losses shall be determined without the benefits of the capital loss carryover provided in section 1212.

"(b) No United States business— regular tax.

"A nonresident alien individual not engaged in trade or business within the United States shall be taxable without regard to subsection (a) if during the taxable year the sum of the aggregate amount received from the sources specified in subsection (a)(1), plus the amount by which gains from sales or exchanges of capital assets exceed losses from such sales or exchanges (determined in accordance with subsection (a)(2)) is more than $19,000 in the case of a taxable year beginning in 1964 or more than $21,200 in the case of a taxable year beginning after 1964, except that—

"(1) the gross income shall include only income from the sources specified in subsection (a)(1) plus any gain (to the extent provided in subchapter P; sec. 1201 and following, relating to capital gains and losses) from a sale or exchange of a capital asset if such gain would be taken into account were the tax being determined under subsection (a)(2);

"(2) the deductions (other than the deduction for charitable contributions and gifts provided in section 873(c)) shall be allowed only if and to the extent that they are properly allocable to the gross income from the sources specified in subsection (a), except that any loss from the sale or exchange of a capital asset shall be allowed (to the extent provided in subchapter P without the benefit of the capital loss carryover provided in section 1212) if such loss would be taken into account were the tax being determined under subsection (a)(2).

"If (without regard to this sentence) the amount of the taxes imposed in the case of such an individual under section 1 or under section 1201(b), minus the credit under section 35, is an amount which is less than 30 percent of the sum of—

"(A) the aggregate amount received from the sources specified in subsection (a)(1), plus

"(B) the amount determined under subsection (a)(2), by which gains from sales or exchanges of capital assets exceed losses from such sales or exchanges,

then this subsection shall not apply and subsection (a) shall apply. For purposes of this subsection, the term 'aggregate amount received from the sources specified in subsection (a)(1)' shall be applied without any exclusion under section 116.

"(c) United States business.

"A nonresident alien individual engaged in trade or business within the United States shall be taxable without regard to subsection (a). For purposes of part I, this section, sections 881 and 882, and chapter 3, the terms 'engaged in trade or business within the United States' includes the performance of personal services within the United States at any time within the taxable year, but does not include the performance of personal services—

"(1) for a nonresident alien individual, foreign partnership, or foreign corporation, not engaged in trade or business within the United States, or

"(2) for an office or place of business maintained by a domestic corporation in a foreign country or in a possession of the United States,

by a nonresident alien individual temporarily present in the United States for a period or periods not exceeding a total of 90 days during the taxable year and whose compensation for such services does not exceed in the aggregate $3,000. Such term does not include the effecting, through a resident broker, commission agent, or custodian, of transactions in the United States in stocks or securities, or in commodities (if of a kind customarily dealt in on an organized commodity exchange, if the transaction is of the kind customarily consummated at such place, and if the alien, partnership, or corporation has no office or place of business in the United States at any time during the taxable year through which or by the direction of which such transactions in commodities are effected).

"(d) Participants in certain exchange or training programs.

"For purposes of this section, a nonresident alien individual who (without regard to this subsection is not engaged in trade or business within the United States and who is temporarily present in the United States as a nonimmigrant under subparagraph (F) or (I) of section 101 (a)(15) of the Immigration and Nationality Act, as amended, shall be treated as a nonresident alien individual engaged in trade or business within the United States.

"(e) Cross references.

"(1) For doubling of tax on citizens of certain foreign countries, see section 891.

"(2) For tax treatment of certain amounts distributed by the United States to nonresident alien individuals, see section 402(a)(4)."

In 1964, P.L. 88-272, Sec. 113(b)(1), substituted "is more than $19,000 in the case of a taxable year beginning in 1964 or more $21,200 in the case of a taxable year beginning after 1964, except that—" for "is more than $15,400, except that—" in subsec. (b)... Sec. 113(b)(2), amended the heading of subsec. (a)... Sec. 113(b)(3), amended the heading of subsec. (b), effective for tax. yrs. begin. after 12/31/63.

Prior to amendment, the heading of subsec. (a) read as follows:
"(a) No United States business and gross income of not more than $15,400."
Prior to amendment, the heading of subsec. (b) read as follows:
"(b) No United States business and gross income or more than $15,400."
—P.L. 88-272, Sec. 201(d)(12), substituted "the credit under section 35" for "the sum of the credits under sections 34 and 35" in subsec. (b), effective for dividends received after 12/31/64, in tax. yrs. end. after 12/31/64.

In 1961, P.L. 87-256, redesignated subsec. (d) as subsec. (e) and added new subsec. (d), effective for tax. yrs. begin. after '61.

In 1960, P.L. 86-437, Sec. 2(b), amended subsec. (d), effective for tax. yrs. begin. after 12/31/59.

Prior to amendment, subsec. (d) read as follows:
"(d) Doubling of tax. For doubling of tax on citizens of certain foreign countries, see section 891."

In 1958, P.L. 85-866, Sec. 40, added "section 403(a)(2)," after "section 402(a)(2)" in para. (a)(1), effective for tax. yrs. end. after 9/2/58.
—P.L. 85-866, Sec. 41, deleted para. (b)(3), effective for tax. yrs. begin. after 12/31/57.

Prior to deletion, para. (b)(3) read as follows:
"(3) the taxes imposed by this subtitle (under section 1, or under section 1201(b)) shall, in no case, be less than 30 percent of the sum of—
"(A) the aggregate amount received from the sources specified in subsection (a)(1), plus
"(B) the amount, determined under subsection (a)(2), by which gains from sales or exchanges of capital assets exceed losses from such sales or exchanges."

Sec. 872. Gross income.
(a) General rule.

In the case of a nonresident alien individual, except where the context clearly indicates otherwise, gross income includes only—

(1) gross income which is derived from sources within the United States and which is not effectively connected with the conduct of a trade or business within the United States, and

(2) gross income which is effectively connected with the conduct of a trade or business within the United States.

(b) Exclusions.

The following items shall not be included in gross income of a nonresident alien individual, and shall be exempt from taxation under this subtitle:

(1) Ships operated by certain nonresidents. Gross income derived by an individual resident of a foreign country from the international operation of a ship or ships if such foreign country grants an equivalent exemption to individual residents of the United States.

(2) Aircraft operated by certain nonresidents. Gross income derived by an individual resident of a foreign country from the international operation of aircraft if such foreign country grants an equivalent exemption to individual residents of the United States.

(3) Compensation of participants in certain exchange or training programs. Compensation paid by a foreign employer to a nonresident alien individual for the period he is temporarily present in the United States as a non-immigrant under subparagraph (F), (J), or (Q) of section 101(a)(15) of the Immigration and Nationality Act, as amended. For purposes of this paragraph, the term "foreign employer" means—

(A) a nonresident alien individual, foreign partnership, or foreign corporation, or

(B) an office or place of business maintained in a foreign country or in a possession of the United States by a domestic corporation, a domestic partnership, or an individual who is a citizen or resident of the United States.

(4) Certain bond income of residents of the Ryukyu Islands or the Trust Territory of the Pacific Islands. Income derived by a nonresident alien individual from a series E or series H United States savings bond, if such individual acquired such bond while a resident of the Ryukyu Islands or the Trust Territory of the Pacific Islands.

(5) Income derived from wagering transactions in certain parimutuel pools. Gross income derived by a nonresident alien individual from a legal wagering transaction initiated outside the United States in a parimutuel pool with respect to a live horse race or dog race in the United States.

(6) Certain rental income. Income to which paragraphs (1) and (2) apply shall include income which is derived from the rental on a full or bareboat basis of a ship or ships or aircraft, as the case may be.

(7) Application to different types of transportation. The Secretary may provide that this subsection be applied separately with respect to income from different types of transportation.

(8) Treatment of possessions. To the extent provided in regulations, a possession of the United States shall be treated as a foreign country for purposes of this subsection.

In 2004, P.L. 108-357, Sec. 419(a), redesignated paras. (b)(5), (6) and (7) as paras. (b)(6), (7) and (8), and added para. (b)(5), effective for wagers made after 10/22/2004.

In 1994, P.L. 103-296, Sec. 320(a)(2), substituted "(F), (J), or (Q)" for "(F) or (J)" in para. (b)(3), effective with the calendar quarter following 8/15/94.

In 1989, P.L. 101-239, Sec. 7811(i)(8)(C), added para. (b)(7), effective for tax. yrs. begin. after 12/31/86.

In 1988, P.L. 100-647, Sec. 1012(e)(2)(B), substituted "to individual residents of the United States" for "to citizens of the United States and to corporations organized in the United States" in paras. (b)(1) and (2)... Sec. 1012(e)(5), substituted "international operation" for "operation" in paras. (b)(1) and (2)... Sec. 1012(s)(2)(A), substituted "the case of a nonresident alien individual, except where the context clearly indicates otherwise" for "the case of a nonresident alien individual" in subsec. (a), effective for tax. yrs. begin. after 12/31/86.
—P.L. 100-647, Sec. 1012(aa)(3)(C) and (4), provides:

"(3) Certain amendments not to apply to the extent inconsistent with treaties. The following amendments made by the Reform Act shall not apply to the extent the application of such amendments would be contrary to any treaty obligation of the United States in effect on the date of the enactment of the Reform Act:

"(C) The amendments made by subsections (b) and (c) of section 1212 of the Reform Act."

* * *

"(4) Treatment of technical corrections. For purposes of paragraphs (2) and (3), any amendment made by this title shall be treated as if it had been included in the provision of the Reform Act to which such amendment relates."

In 1986, P.L. 99-514, Sec. 1212(c)(1), amended paras. (b)(1) and (b)(2)... Sec. 1212(c)(2), added paras. (b)(5) and (b)(6), effective for tax. yrs. begin. after 12/31/86 [see Sec. 1012 of P.L. 100-647(aa)(3)(C) and (4), above].

Prior to amendment, paras. (b)(1) and (b)(2) read as follows:

"(1) Ships under foreign flag. Earnings derived from the operation of a ship or ships documented under the laws of a foreign country which grants an equivalent exemption to citizens of the United States and to corporations organized in the United States.

"(2) Aircraft of foreign registry. Earnings derived from the operation of aircraft registered under the laws of a foreign country which grants an equivalent exemption to citizens of the United States and to corporations organized in the United States."

In 1966, P.L. 89-809, Sec. 103, amended subsec. (a), substituted "by a domestic partnership, or an individual who is a citizen or resident of the United States" for "by a domestic corporation" in subpara. (b)(3)(B), and added subsec. (b)(4), effective for tax. yrs. begin. after 12/31/66.

Prior to amendment, subsec. (a) read as follows:
"(a) General rule.
"In the case of a nonresident alien individual gross income includes only the gross income from sources within the United States."

In 1961, P.L. 87-256, Sec. 110(c), added para. (b)(3), effective for tax. yrs. begin. after 1961.

Sec. 873. Deductions.

(a) General rule.

In the case of a nonresident alien individual, the deductions shall be allowed only for purposes of section 871(b) and (except as provided by subsection (b)) only if and to the extent that they are connected with income which is effectively connected with the conduct of a trade or business within the United States; and the proper apportionment and allocation of the deductions for this purpose shall be determined as provided in regulations prescribed by the Secretary.

(b) Exceptions.

The following deductions shall be allowed whether or not they are connected with income which is effectively connected with the conduct of a trade or business within the United States:

(1) Losses. The deduction allowed by section 165 for casualty or theft losses described in paragraph (2) or (3) of section 165(c), but only if the loss is of property located within the United States.

(2) Charitable contributions. The deduction for charitable contributions and gifts allowed by section 170.

(3) Personal exemption. The deduction for personal exemptions allowed by section 151, except that only one exemption shall be allowed under section 151 unless the taxpayer is a resident of a contiguous country or is a national of the United States.

(c) Cross reference.

For rule that certain foreign taxes are not to be taken into account in determining deduction or credit, see section 906(b)(1).

In **1998**, P.L. 105-277, Sec. 4004(b)(3), amended para. (b)(1), effective for tax. yrs. begin. after 12/31/83.
Prior to amendment, para. (b)(1) read as follows:
"(1) Losses. The deduction for losses allowed by section 165(c)(3), but only if the loss is of property located within the United States."
In **1984**, P.L. 98-369, Sec. 711(c)(2)(A)(iv), substituted "for losses" for ", for losses of property not connected with the trade or business if arising from certain casualties or theft," in para. (b)(1), effective for tax. yrs. begin. after 12/31/83.
In **1977**, P.L. 95-30, Sec. 101(d)(11), amended subsec. (c), effective for tax. yrs. begin. after 12/31/76.
Prior to amendment, subsec. (c) read as follows:
"(c) Cross references.
"(1) For disallowance of standard deduction, see section 142(b)(1).
"(2) For rule that certain foreign taxes are not to be taken into account in determining deduction or credit, see section 906(b)(1)."
In **1976**, P.L. 94-455, Sec. 1906(b)(13)(A), substituted "Secretary" for "Secretary or his delegate" in subsec. (a), for tax. yrs. begin. after 12/31/76.
In **1972**, P.L. 92-580, Sec. 1(b), amended para. (b)(3), effective for tax. yrs. begin. after 12/31/71.
Prior to amendment subsec. (b)(3) read as follows:
"(3) Personal exemption. The deduction for personal exemptions allowed by section 151, except that in the case of a nonresident alien individual who is not a resident of a contiguous country only one exemption shall be allowed under Section 151."
In **1966**, P.L. 89-809, Sec. 103, amended Code Sec. 873, effective for tax. yrs. begin. after 12/31/66.
Prior to amendment, Code Sec. 873 read as follows:
"SEC. 873. DEDUCTIONS.
"(a) General rule.
"In the case of a nonresident alien individual the deductions shall be allowed only if and to the extent that they are connected with income from sources within the United States; and the proper apportionment and allocation of the deductions with respect to sources of income within and without the United States shall be determined as provided in part I, under regulations prescribed by the Secretary or his delegate.
"(b) Losses.
"(1) The deduction, for losses not connected with the trade or business if incurred in transactions entered into for profit, allowed by section 165(c)(2) (relating to losses) shall be allowed whether or not connected with income from sources within the United States, but only if the profit, if such transaction had resulted in a profit, would be taxable under this subtitle.
"(2) The deduction for losses of property not connected with the trade or business if arising from certain casualties or theft, allowed by section 165(c)(3), shall be allowed whether or not connected with income from sources within the United States, but only if the loss is of property within the United States.
"(c) Charitable contributions.

"The deduction for charitable contributions and gifts provided by section 170 shall be allowed whether or not connected with income from sources within the United States, but only as to contributions or gifts made to domestic corporations, or to community chests, funds, or foundations, created in the United States.
"(d) Personal exemption.
"In the case of a nonresident alien individual who is not a resident of a contiguous country, only one exemption under section 151 shall be allowed as a deduction.
"(e) Standard deduction.
"For disallowance of standard deduction, see section 142(b)(1)."

Sec. 874. Allowance of deductions and credits.

(a) Return prerequisite to allowance.

A nonresident alien individual shall receive the benefit of the deductions and credits allowed to him in this subtitle only by filing or causing to be filed with the Secretary a true and accurate return, in the manner prescribed in subtitle F (sec. 6001 and following, relating to procedure and administration), including therein all the information which the Secretary may deem necessary for the calculation of such deductions and credits. This subsection shall not be construed to deny the credits provided by sections 31 and 33 for tax withheld at source or the credit provided by section 34 for certain uses of gasoline and special fuels.

(b) Tax withheld at source.

The benefit of the deduction for exemptions under section 151 may, in the discretion of the Secretary, and under regulations prescribed by the Secretary, be received by a nonresident alien individual entitled thereto, by filing a claim therefor with the withholding agent.

(c) Foreign tax credit.

Except as provided in section 906, a nonresident alien individual shall not be allowed the credits against the tax for taxes of foreign countries and possessions of the United States allowed by section 901.

In **1984**, P.L. 98-369, Sec. 474(r)(19), substituted "33" for "32" and substituted "section 34" for "section 39" in subsec. (a), effective for tax. yrs. begin. after 12/31/83, and to carrybacks from tax. yrs. begin. after 12/31/83.
In **1983**, P.L. 97-424, Sec. 515(b)(6)(E), substituted "and special fuels" for ", special fuels, and lubricating oil" in subsec. (a), effective for articles sold after 1/6/83.
In **1976**, P.L. 94-455, Sec. 1906(b)(13)(A), substituted "Secretary" for "Secretary or his delegate" each place it appeared in subsecs. (a) and (b), effective for tax. yrs. begin. after 12/31/76.
In **1970**, P.L. 91-258, Sec. 207(d)(1), substituted "uses of gasoline, special fuels, and lubricating oil" for "uses of gasoline and lubricating oil" in subsec. (a), effective 7/1/70.
In **1966**, P.L. 89-809, Sec. 103, amended subsec. (a) . . . Sec. 106, substituted "(c) Foreign tax credit. Except as provided in section 906, a nonresident" for "(c) Foreign tax credit not allowed. A nonresident", effective for tax. yrs. begin. after 12/31/66.
Prior to amendment, subsec. (a) read as follows:
"(a) Return prerequisite to allowance.
"A nonresident alien individual shall receive the benefit of the deductions and credits allowed to him in this subtitle only by filing or causing to be filed a true and accurate return of his total income received from all sources in the United States, in the manner prescribed in subtitle F (sec. 6001 and following, relating to procedure and administration), including therein all the information which the Secretary or his delegate may deem necessary for the calculation of such deductions and credits. This subsection shall not be construed to deny the credits provided by sections 31 and 32 for tax withheld at the source or the credit provided by section 39 for certain uses of gasoline and lubricating oil."
In **1965**, P.L. 89-44, Sec. 809, added "or the credit provided by section 39 for certain uses of gasoline and lubricating oil", in subsec. (a), effective for tax. yrs. begin. after 6/30/65.

Sec. 875. Partnerships; beneficiaries of estates and trusts.

For purposes of this subtitle—

(1) a nonresident alien individual or foreign corporation shall be considered as being engaged in a trade or business within the United States if the partnership of which such individual or corporation is a member is so engaged, and

(2) a nonresident alien individual or foreign corporation which is a beneficiary of an estate or trust which is engaged in any trade or business within the United States shall be treated as being engaged in such trade or business within the United States.

In 1966, P.L. 89-809, Sec. 103, amended Code Sec. 875, effective for tax. yrs. begin. after 12/31/66.
Prior to amendment, Code Sec. 875 read as follows:
"SEC. 875. PARTNERSHIPS.
For purposes of this subtitle, a nonresident alien individual shall be considered as being engaged in a trade or business within the United States if the partnership of which he is a member is so engaged."

Sec. 876. Alien residents of Puerto Rico, Guam, American Samoa, or the Northern Mariana Islands.
(a) General rule.
This subpart shall not apply to any alien individual who is a bona fide resident of Puerto Rico, Guam, American Samoa, or the Northern Mariana Islands during the entire taxable year and such alien shall be subject to the tax imposed by section 1.
(b) Cross references.
For exclusion from gross income of income derived from sources within—
(1) Guam, American Samoa, and the Northern Mariana Islands, see section 931, and
(2) Puerto Rico, see section 933.

In 1986, P.L. 99-514, Sec. 1272(b), amended Code Sec. 876, effective for tax. yrs. begin. after 12/31/86. For special rules, see Sec. 1271 and Sec. 1277(b) of P.L. 99-514, reproduced in note following Code Sec. 931.
Prior to amendment, Code Sec. 876 read as follows:
"SEC. 876. ALIEN RESIDENTS OF PUERTO RICO.
"(a) No application to certain alien residents of Puerto Rico.
"This subpart shall not apply to an alien individual who is a bona fide resident of Puerto Rico during the entire taxable year, and such alien shall be subject to the tax imposed by section 1.
"(b) Cross reference.
"For exclusion from gross income of income derived from sources within Puerto Rico, see section 933."

Sec. 877. Expatriation to avoid tax.
(a) Treatment of expatriates.
(1) In general. Every nonresident alien individual to whom this section applies and who, within the 10-year period immediately preceding the close of the taxable year, lost United States citizenship shall be taxable for such taxable year in the manner provided in subsection (b) if the tax imposed pursuant to such subsection (after any reduction in such tax under the last sentence of such subsection) exceeds the tax which, without regard to this section, is imposed pursuant to section 871.
(2) Individuals subject to this section. This section shall apply to any individual if—
(A) the average annual net income tax (as defined in section 38(c)(1)) of such individual for the period of 5 taxable years ending before the date of the loss of United States citizenship is greater than $124,000,
(B) the net worth of the individual as of such date is $2,000,000 or more, or
(C) such individual fails to certify under penalty of perjury that he has met the requirements of this title for the 5 preceding taxable years or fails to submit such evidence of such compliance as the Secretary may require.
In the case of the loss of United States citizenship in any calendar year after 2004, such $124,000 amount shall be increased by an amount equal to such dollar amount multiplied by the cost-of-living adjustment determined under section 1(f)(3) for such calendar year by substituting "2003" for "1992" in subparagraph (B) thereof. Any increase under the preceding sentence shall be rounded to the nearest multiple of $1,000.

(b) Alternative tax.
A nonresident alien individual described in subsection (a) shall be taxable for the taxable year as provided in section 1 or 55, except that—
(1) the gross income shall include only the gross income described in section 872(a) (as modified by subsection (d) of this section), and
(2) the deductions shall be allowed if and to the extent that they are connected with the gross income included under this section, except that the capital loss carryover provided by section 1212(b) shall not be allowed; and the proper allocation and apportionment of the deductions for this purpose shall be determined as provided under regulations prescribed by the Secretary.

For purposes of paragraph (2), the deductions allowed by section 873(b) shall be allowed; and the deduction (for losses not connected with the trade or business if incurred in transactions entered into for profit) allowed by section 165(c)(2) shall be allowed, but only if the profit, if such transaction had resulted in a profit, would be included in gross income under this section. The tax imposed solely by reason of this section shall be reduced (but not below zero) by the amount of any income, war profits, and excess profits taxes (within the meaning of section 903) paid to any foreign country or possession of the United States on any income of the taxpayer on which tax is imposed solely by reason of this section.

(c) Exceptions.
(1) In general. Subparagraphs (A) and (B) of subsection (a)(2) shall not apply to an individual described in paragraph (2) or (3).
(2) Dual citizens.
(A) In general. An individual is described in this paragraph if—
(i) the individual became at birth a citizen of the United States and a citizen of another country, and continues to be a citizen of such other country, and
(ii) the individual has had no substantial contacts with the United States.
(B) Substantial contacts. An individual shall be treated as having no substantial contacts with the United States only if the individual—
(i) was never a resident of the United States (as defined in section 7701(b)),
(ii) has never held a United States passport, and
(iii) was not present in the United States for more than 30 days during any calendar year which is 1 of the 10 calendar years preceding the individual's loss of United States citizenship.
(3) Certain minors. An individual is described in this paragraph if—
(A) the individual became at birth a citizen of the United States,
(B) neither parent of such individual was a citizen of the United States at the time of such birth,
(C) the individual's loss of United States citizenship occurs before such individual attains age 18½, and
(D) the individual was not present in the United States for more than 30 days during any calendar year which is 1 of the 10 calendar years preceding the individual's loss of United States citizenship.

(d) Special rules for source, etc.
For purposes of subsection (b)—
(1) Source rules. The following items of gross income shall be treated as income from sources within the United States:
(A) Sale of property. Gains on the sale or exchange of property (other than stock or debt obligations) located in the United States.
(B) Stock or debt obligations. Gains on the sale or exchange of stock issued by a domestic corporation or debt obligations of United States persons or of the United States, a State or political subdivision thereof, or the District of Columbia.
(C) Income or gain derived from controlled foreign corporation. Any income or gain derived from stock in a foreign corporation, but only—
(i) if the individual losing United States citizenship owned (within the meaning of section 958(a)), or is considered as owning (by applying the ownership rules of section 958(b)), at any time during the 2-year period ending on the date of the loss of United States citizenship, more than 50 percent of—
(I) the total combined voting power of all classes of stock entitled to vote of such corporation, or
(II) the total value of the stock of such corporation, and
(ii) to the extent such income or gain does not exceed the earnings and profits attributable to such stock which were earned or accumulated before the loss of citizenship and during periods that the ownership requirements of clause (i) are met.
(2) Gain recognition on certain exchanges.
(A) In general. In the case of any exchange of property to which this paragraph applies, notwithstanding any other provision of this title, such property shall be treated as sold for its fair market value on the date of such exchange, and any gain shall be recognized for the taxable year which includes such date.
(B) Exchanges to which paragraph applies. This paragraph shall apply to any exchange during the 10-year period beginning on the date the individual loses United States citizenship if—
(i) gain would not (but for this paragraph) be recognized on such exchange in whole or in part for purposes of this subtitle,
(ii) income derived from such property was from sources within the United States (or, if no income was so derived, would have been from such sources), and
(iii) income derived from the property acquired in the exchange would be from sources outside the United States.
(C) Exception. Subparagraph (A) shall not apply if the individual enters into an agreement with the Secretary which specifies that any income or gain derived from the property acquired in the exchange (or any other property which has a basis determined in whole or part by reference to such property) during such 10-year period shall be treated as from sources within the United States. If the property transferred in the exchange is disposed of by the person acquiring such property, such agreement shall terminate and any gain which was not recognized by reason of such agreement shall be recognized as of the date of such disposition.
(D) Secretary may extend period. To the extent provided in regulations prescribed by the Secretary, subparagraph (B) shall be applied by substituting the 15-year period beginning 5 years before the loss of United States citizenship for the 10-year period referred to therein. In the case of any exchange occurring during such 5 years, any gain recognized under this subparagraph shall be recognized immediately after such loss of citizenship.
(E) Secretary may require recognition of gain in certain cases. To the extent provided in regulations prescribed by the Secretary—
(i) the removal of appreciated tangible personal property from the United States, and
(ii) any other occurrence which (without recognition of gain) results in a change in the source of the income or gain from property from sources within the United States to sources outside the United States,
shall be treated as an exchange to which this paragraph applies.
(3) Substantial diminishing of risks of ownership. For purposes of determining whether this section applies to any gain on the sale or exchange of any property, the running of the 10-year period described in subsection (a) and the period applicable under paragraph (2) shall be suspended for any period during which the individual's risk of loss with respect to the property is substantially diminished by—
(A) the holding of a put with respect to such property (or similar property),
(B) the holding by another person of a right to acquire the property, or
(C) a short sale or any other transaction.
(4) Treatment of property contributed to controlled foreign corporations.
(A) In general. If—
(i) an individual losing United States citizenship contributes property during the 10-year period beginning on the date the individual loses United States citizenship to any corporation which, at the time of the contribution, is described in subparagraph (B), and
(ii) income derived from such property immediately before such contribution was from sources within the United States (or, if no income was so derived, would have been from such sources),
any income or gain on such property (or any other property which has a basis determined in whole or part by reference to such property) received or accrued by the corporation shall be treated as received or accrued directly by such individual and not by such corporation. The preceding sentence shall not apply to the extent the property has been treated under subparagraph (C) as having been sold by such corporation.
(B) Corporation described. A corporation is described in this subparagraph with respect to an individual if, were such individual a United States citizen—
(i) such corporation would be a controlled foreign corporation (as defined in 957), and
(ii) such individual would be a United States shareholder (as defined in section 951(b)) with respect to such corporation.
(C) Disposition of stock in corporation. If stock in the corporation referred to in subparagraph (A) (or any other stock which has a basis determined in whole or part by reference to such stock) is disposed of during the 10-year period referred to in subsection (a) and while the property referred to in subparagraph (A) is held by such corporation, a pro rata share of such property (determined on the basis of the value of such

stock) shall be treated as sold by the corporation immediately before such disposition.

(D) Anti-abuse rules. The Secretary shall prescribe such regulations as may be necessary to prevent the avoidance of the purposes of this paragraph, including where—

(i) the property is sold to the corporation, and

(ii) the property taken into account under subparagraph (A) is sold by the corporation.

(E) Information reporting. The Secretary shall require such information reporting as is necessary to carry out the purposes of this paragraph.

(e) Comparable treatment of lawful permanent residents who cease to be taxed as residents.

(1) In general. Any long-term resident of the United States who ceases to be a lawful permanent resident of the United States (within the meaning of section 7701(b)(6)) shall be treated for purposes of this section and sections 2107, 2501, and 6039G in the same manner as if such resident were a citizen of the United States who lost United States citizenship on the date of such cessation or commencement.

(2) Long-term resident. For purposes of this subsection, the term "long-term resident" means any individual (other than a citizen of the United States) who is a lawful permanent resident of the United States in at least 8 taxable years during the period of 15 taxable years ending with the taxable year during which the event described in subparagraph (A) or (B) of paragraph (1) occurs. For purposes of the preceding sentence, an individual shall not be treated as a lawful permanent resident for any taxable year if such individual is treated as a resident of a foreign country for the taxable year under the provisions of a tax treaty between the United States and the foreign country and does not waive the benefits of such treaty applicable to residents of the foreign country.

(3) Special rules.

(A) Exceptions not to apply. Subsection (c) shall not apply to an individual who is treated as provided in paragraph (1).

(B) Step-up in basis. Solely for purposes of determining any tax imposed by reason of this subsection, property which was held by the long-term resident on the date the individual first became a resident of the United States shall be treated as having a basis on such date of not less than the fair market value of such property on such date. The preceding sentence shall not apply if the individual elects not to have such sentence apply. Such an election, once made, shall be irrevocable.

(4) Authority to exempt individuals. This subsection shall not apply to an individual who is described in a category of individuals prescribed by regulation by the Secretary.

(5) Regulations. The Secretary shall prescribe such regulations as may be appropriate to carry out this subsection, including regulations providing for the application of this subsection in cases where an alien individual becomes a resident of the United States during the 10-year period after being treated as provided in paragraph (1).

(f) Burden of proof.

If the Secretary establishes that it is reasonable to believe that an individual's loss of United States citizenship would, but for this section, result in a substantial reduction for the taxable year in the taxes on his probable income for such year, the burden of proving for such taxable year that such loss of citizenship did not have for one of its principal purposes the avoidance of taxes under this subtitle or subtitle B shall be on such individual.

(g) Physical presence.

(1) In general. This section shall not apply to any individual to whom this section would otherwise apply for any taxable year during the 10-year period referred to in subsection (a) in which such individual is physically present in the United States at any time on more than 30 days in the calendar year ending in such taxable year, and such individual shall be treated for purposes of this title as a citizen or resident of the United States, as the case may be, for such taxable year.

(2) Exception.

(A) In general. In the case of an individual described in any of the following subparagraphs of this paragraph, a day of physical presence in the United States shall be disregarded if the individual is performing services in the United States on such day for an employer. The preceding sentence shall not apply if—

(i) such employer is related (within the meaning of section 267 and 707) to such individual, or

(ii) such employer fails to meet such requirements as the Secretary may prescribe by regulations to prevent the avoidance of the purposes of this paragraph.

Not more than 30 days during any calendar year may be disregarded under this subparagraph.

(B) Individuals with ties to other countries. An individual is described in this subparagraph if—

(i) the individual becomes (not later than the close of a reasonable period after loss of United States citizenship or termination of residency) a citizen or resident of the country in which—

(I) such individual was born,

(II) if such individual is married, such individual's spouse was born, or

(III) either of such individual's parents were born, and

(ii) the individual becomes fully liable for income tax in such country.

(C) Minimal prior physical presence in the United States. An individual is described in this subparagraph if, for each year in the 10-year period ending on the date of loss of United States citizenship or termination of residency, the individual was physically present in the United States for 30 days or less. The rule of section 7701(b)(3)(D) shall apply for purposes of this subparagraph.

(h) Termination.

This section shall not apply to any individual whose expatriation date (as defined in section 877A(g)(3)) is on or after the date of the enactment of this subsection.

In 2008, P.L. 110-245, Sec. 301(c)(2)(A), amended para. (e)(1) . . . Sec. 301(d), added subsec. (h), effective for any individual whose expatriation date (as so defined) is on or after 6/17/2008.

Prior to amendment, para. (e)(1) read as follows:

"(1) In general. Any long-term resident of the United States who—

"(A) ceases to be a lawful permanent resident of the United States (within the meaning of section 7701(b)(6)), or

"(B) commences to be treated as a resident of a foreign country under the provisions of a tax treaty between the United States and the foreign country and who does not waive the benefits of such treaty applicable to residents of the foreign country,

"shall be treated for purposes of this section and sections 2107, 2501, and 6039G in the same manner as if such resident were a citizen of the United States who lost United States citizenship on the date of such cessation or commencement."

In 2005, P.L. 109-135, Sec. 403(v)(1), substituted "section 7701(b)(3)(D)" for "section 7701(b)(3)(D)(ii)" in subpara. (g)(2)(C), effective for individuals who expatriate after 6/3/2004 as if included in Sec. 804 of the American Jobs Creation Act of 2004, P.L. 108-357.

In 2004, P.L. 108-357, Sec. 804(a)(1), amended subsec. (a)... Sec. 804(a)(2), amended subsec. (c)... Sec. 804(c), added subsec. (g), effective for individuals who expatriate after 6/3/2004.

Prior to amendment, subsec. (a) read as follows:

"(a) Treatment of expatriates.

"(1) In general. Every nonresident alien individual who, within the 10-year period immediately preceding the close of the taxable year, lost United States citizenship, unless such loss did not have for one of its principal purposes the avoidance of taxes under this subtitle or subtitle B, shall be taxable for such taxable year in the manner provided in subsection (b) if the tax imposed pursuant to such subsection (after any reduction in such tax under the last sentence of such subsection) exceeds the tax which, without regard to this section, is imposed pursuant to section 871.

"(2) Certain individuals treated as having tax avoidance purpose. For purposes of paragraph (1), an individual shall be treated has having a principal purpose to avoid such taxes if—

"(A) the average annual net income tax (as defined in section 38(c)(1)) of such individual for the period of 5 taxable years ending before the date of the loss of United States citizenship is greater than $100,000, or

"(B) the net worth of the individual as of such date is $500,000 or more. In the case of the loss of United States citizenship in any calendar year after 1996, such $100,000 and $500,000 amounts shall be increased by an amount equal to such dollar amount multiplied by the cost-of-living adjustment determined under section 1(f)(3) for such calendar year by substituting '1994' for '1992' in subparagraph (B) thereof. Any increase under the preceding sentence shall be rounded to the nearest multiple of $1,000.".

Prior to amendment, subsec. (c) read as follows:

"(c) Tax avoidance not presumed in certain cases.

"(1) In general. Subsection (a)(2) shall not apply to an individual if—

"(A) such individual is described in a subparagraph of paragraph (2) of this subsection, and

"(B) within the 1-year period beginning on the date of the loss of United States citizenship, such individual submits a ruling request for the Secretary's determination as to whether such loss has for one of its principal purposes the avoidance of taxes under this subtitle or subtitle B.

"(2) Individuals described.

"(A) Dual citizenship, etc. An individual is described in this subparagraph if—

"(i) the individual became at birth a citizen of the United States and a citizen of another country and continues to be a citizen of such other country, or

"(ii) the individual becomes (not later than the close of a reasonable period after loss of United States citizenship) a citizen of the country in which—

"(I) such individual was born,

"(II) if such individual is married, such individual's spouse was born, or

"(III) either of such individual's parents were born.

"(B) Long-term foreign residents. An individual is described in this subparagraph if, for each year in the 10-year period ending on the date of loss of United States citizenship, the individual was present in the United States for 30 days or less. The rule of section 7701(b)(3)(D)(ii) shall apply for purposes of this subparagraph.

"(C) Renunciation upon reaching age of majority. An individual is described in this subparagraph if the individual's loss of United States citizenship occurs before such individual attains age 18½.

"(D) Individuals specified in regulations. An individual is described in this subparagraph if the individual is described in a category of individuals prescribed by regulation by the Secretary."

In 1997, P.L. 105-34, Sec. 1602(g)(1), substituted "the 10-year period beginning on the date the individual loses United States citizenship" for "the 10-year period described in subsection (a)" in subpara. (d)(2)(B) ... Sec. 1602(g)(2), added the sentence at the end of subpara. (d)(2)(D) ... Sec. 1602(g)(3), added "and the period applicable under paragraph (2)" after "subsection (a)" in para. (d)(3) ... Sec. 1602(g)(4)(A), added "during the 10-year period beginning on the date the individual loses United States citizenship" after "contributes property" in clause (d)(4)(A)(i) ... Sec. 1602(g)(4)(B), added "immediately before such contribution" after "from such property" in clause (d)(4)(A)(ii) ... Sec. 1602(g)(4)(C), deleted "during the 10-year period referred to in subsection (a)," before "any income or gain" in subpara. (d)(4)(A), effective as provided in Sec. 511(g) of P.L. 104-191, reproduced below.

—P.L. 105-34, Sec. 1602(h)(3), substituted "6039G" for "6039F" in para. (e)(1), effective as provided in Sec. 512(c) of P.L. 104-191, reproduced in note after Code Sec. 6039G.

In 1996, P.L. 104-191, Sec. 511(a), amended subsec. (a) ... Sec. 511(b)(1), deleted subsec. (d) and redesignated subsec. (c) as subsec. (d) ... Sec. 511(b)(2), substituted "subsection (d)" for "subsection (c)" in para. (b)(1) ... Sec. 511(c), amended subsec. (d) [as redesignated by Sec. 511(b)(1), of this Act, see above] ... Sec. 511(d)(1), added the sentence to the end of subsec. (b) ... Sec. 511(d)(2), added "(after any reduction in such tax under the last sentence of such subsection)" after "such subsection" in para. (a)(1) ... Sec. 511(f)(1), redesignated subsec. (e) as subsec. (f) and added new subsec. (e), effective as provided in Sec. 511(g) of this Act, which reads as follows:

"(g) Effective date.

"(1) In general. The amendments made by this section shall apply to—

"(A) individuals losing United States citizenship (within the meaning of section 877 of the Internal Revenue Code of 1986) on or after February 6, 1995, and

"(B) long-term residents of the United States with respect to whom an event described in subparagraph (A) or (B) of section 877(e)(1) of such Code occurs on or after February 6, 1995.

"(2) Rulings requests. In no event shall the 1-year period referred to in section 877(c)(1)(B) of such Code, as amended by this section, expire before the date which is 90 days after the date of the enactment of this Act.

"(3) Special rule.

"(A) In general. In the case of an individual who performed an act of expatriation specified in paragraph (1), (2), (3), or (4) of section 349(a) of the Immigration and Nationality Act (8 U.S.C. 1481(a)(1)(4)) before February 6, 1995, but who did not, on or before such date, furnish to the United States Department of State a signed statement of voluntary relinquishment of United States nationality confirming the performance of such act, the amendments made by this section and section 512 shall apply to such individual except that the 10-year period described in section 877(a) of such Code shall not expire before the end of the 10-year period beginning on the date such statement is so furnished.

"(B) Exception. Subparagraph (A) shall not apply if the individual establishes to the satisfaction of the Secretary of the Treasury that such loss of United States citizenship occurred before February 6, 1994."

Prior to amendment, subsec. (a) read as follows:

"(a) In general. Every nonresident alien individual who at any time after March 8, 1965, and within the 10-year period immediately preceding the close of the taxable year lost United States citizenship, unless such loss did not have for one of its principal purposes the avoidance of taxes under this subtitle or subtitle B, shall be taxable for such taxable year in the manner provided in subsection (b) if the tax imposed pursuant to such subsection exceeds the tax which, without regard to this section, is imposed pursuant to section 871."

Prior to deletion, subsec. (d) read as follows:

"(d) Exception for loss of citizenship for certain causes. Subsection (a) shall not apply to a nonresident alien individual whose loss of United States citizenship resulted from the application of section 301(b), 350, or 355 of the Immigration and Nationality Act, as amended (8 U.S.C. 1401(b), 1482, or 1487)."

Prior to amendment, subsec. (d) [as redesignated by Sec. 511(b)(1)] read as follows:

"(d) Special rules of source. For purposes of subsection (b), the following items of gross income shall be treated as income from sources within the United States:

"(1) Sale of property. Gains on the sale or exchange of property (other than stock or debt obligations) located in the United States.

"(2) Stock or debt obligations. Gains on the sale or exchange of stock issued by a domestic corporation or debt obligations of United States persons or of the United States, a State or political subdivision thereof, or the District of Columbia. For purposes of this section, gain on the sale or exchange of property which has a basis determined in whole or in part by reference to property described in paragraph (1) or (2) shall be treated as gain described in paragraph (1) or (2)."

—P.L. 104-188, Sec. 1401(b)(11), substituted "section 1 or 55" for "section 1, 55, or 402(d)(1)" in subsec. (b), effective for tax. yrs. begin. after 12/31/99. Sec. 1401(c)(2) of this Act provides:

"(2) Retention of certain transition rules. The amendments made by this section shall not apply to any distribution for which the taxpayer is eligible to elect the benefits of section 1122(h)(3) or (5) of the Tax Reform Act of 1986. Notwithstanding the preceding sentence, individuals who elect such benefits after December 31, 1999, shall not be eligible for 5-year averaging under section 402(d) of the Internal Revenue Code of 1986 (as in effect immediately before such amendments)."

In 1992, P.L. 102-318, Sec. 521(b)(31), substituted "402(d)(1)" for "402(e)(1)" in subsec. (b), effective for distributions after 12/31/92. For special rule, see Sec. 521(e)(2) of this Act which reads as follows:

"(2) Special rule for partial distributions. For purposes of section 402(a)(5)(D)(i)(II) of the Internal Revenue Code of 1986 (as in effect before the amendments made by this section), a distribution before January 1, 1993, which is made before or at the same time as a series of periodic payments shall not be treated as one of such series if it is not substantially equal in amount to other payments in such series."

In 1986, P.L. 99-514, Sec. 1243(a), added the sentence at the end of subsec. (c), effective for sales or exchanges of property received in exchanges after 9/25/85.

In 1980, P.L. 96-222, Sec. 104(a)(1), substituted "or 402(e)(1)" for "402(e)(1), or section 1201(b)" in subsec. (b) ... Sec. 104(a)(4)(H)(v), substituted "55" for "section 55" in subsec. (b), effective for tax. yrs. begin. after 12/31/78.

In 1978, P.L. 95-600, Sec. 421(e)(5), added ", section 55," after "section 1" in subsec. (b), effective for tax. yrs. begin. after 12/31/78.

In 1976, P.L. 94-455, Sec. 1906(b)(13)(A), substituted "Secretary" for "Secretary or his delegate" each place it appeared in Code Sec. 877, effective for tax. yrs. begin. after 12/31/76.

In 1974, P.L. 93-406, Sec. 2005(c)(8), added ", 402(e)(1)," after "section 1" in subsec. (b), effective for distributions and payments made after 12/31/73, in tax. yrs. begin. after 12/31/73.

In 1966, P.L. 89-809, Sec. 103(f)(1), added Code Sec. 877, effective for tax. yrs. begin. after 12/31/66.

Sec. 877A. Tax responsibilities of expatriation.

(a) General rules.

For purposes of this subtitle—

(1) Mark to market. All property of a covered expatriate shall be treated as sold on the day before the expatriation date for its fair market value.

(2) Recognition of gain or loss. In the case of any sale under paragraph (1)—

(A) notwithstanding any other provision of this title, any gain arising from such sale shall be taken into account for the taxable year of the sale, and

(B) any loss arising from such sale shall be taken into account for the taxable year of the sale to the extent otherwise provided by this title, except that section 1091 shall not apply to any such loss.

Proper adjustment shall be made in the amount of any gain or loss subsequently realized for gain or loss taken into account under the preceding sentence, determined without regard to paragraph (3).

(3) Exclusion for certain gain.

(A) In general. The amount which would (but for this paragraph) be includible in the gross income of any individual by reason of paragraph (1) shall be reduced (but not below zero) by $600,000.

(B) Adjustment for inflation.

(i) In general. In the case of any taxable year beginning in a calendar year after 2008, the dollar amount in subparagraph (A) shall be increased by an amount equal to—

(I) such dollar amount, multiplied by

(II) the cost-of-living adjustment determined under section 1(f)(3) for the calendar year in which the taxable year begins, by substituting "calendar year 2007" for "calendar year 1992" in subparagraph (B) thereof.

(ii) Rounding. If any amount as adjusted under clause (i) is not a multiple of $1,000, such amount shall be rounded to the nearest multiple of $1,000.

(b) Election to defer tax.

(1) In general. If the taxpayer elects the application of this subsection with respect to any property treated as sold by reason of subsection (a), the time for payment of the additional tax attributable to such property shall be extended until the due date of the return for the taxable year in which such property is disposed of (or, in the case of property disposed of in a transaction in which gain is not recognized in whole or in part, until such other date as the Secretary may prescribe).

(2) Determination of tax with respect to property. For purposes of paragraph (1), the additional tax attributable to any property is an amount which bears the same ratio to the additional tax imposed by this chapter for the taxable year solely by reason of subsection (a) as the gain taken into account under subsection (a) with respect to such property bears to the total gain taken into account under subsection (a) with respect to all property to which subsection (a) applies.

(3) Termination of extension. The due date for payment of tax may not be extended under this subsection later than the due date for the return of tax imposed by this chapter for the taxable year which includes the date of death of the expatriate (or, if earlier, the time that the security provided with respect to the property fails to meet the requirements of paragraph (4), unless the taxpayer corrects such failure within the time specified by the Secretary).

(4) Security.

(A) In general. No election may be made under paragraph (1) with respect to any property unless adequate security is provided with respect to such property.

(B) Adequate security. For purposes of subparagraph (A), security with respect to any property shall be treated as adequate security if—

(i) it is a bond which is furnished to, and accepted by, the Secretary, which is conditioned on the payment of tax (and interest thereon), and which meets the requirements of section 6325, or

(ii) it is another form of security for such payment (including letters of credit) that meets such requirements as the Secretary may prescribe.

(5) Waiver of certain rights. No election may be made under paragraph (1) unless the taxpayer makes an irrevocable waiver of any right under any treaty of the United States which would preclude assessment or collection of any tax imposed by reason of this section.

(6) Elections. An election under paragraph (1) shall only apply to property described in the election and, once made, is irrevocable.

(7) Interest. For purposes of section 6601, the last date for the payment of tax shall be determined without regard to the election under this subsection.

(c) Exception for certain property.

Subsection (a) shall not apply to—

(1) any deferred compensation item (as defined in subsection (d)(4)),

(2) any specified tax deferred account (as defined in subsection (e)(2)), and

(3) any interest in a nongrantor trust (as defined in subsection (f)(3)).

(d) Treatment of deferred compensation items.

(1) Withholding on eligible deferred compensation items.

(A) In general. In the case of any eligible deferred compensation item, the payor shall deduct and withhold from any taxable payment to a covered expatriate with respect to such item a tax equal to 30 percent thereof.

(B) Taxable payment. For purposes of subparagraph (A), the term "taxable payment" means with respect to a covered expatriate any payment to the extent it would be includible in the gross income of the covered expatriate if such expatriate continued to be subject to tax as a citizen or resident of the United States. A deferred compensation item shall be taken into account as a payment under the preceding sentence when such item would be so includible.

(2) Other deferred compensation items. In the case of any deferred compensation item which is not an eligible deferred compensation item—

(A)(i) with respect to any deferred compensation item to which clause (ii) does not apply, an amount equal to the present value of the covered expatriate's accrued benefit shall be treated as having been received by such individual on the day before the expatriation date as a distribution under the plan, and

(ii) with respect to any deferred compensation item referred to in paragraph (4)(D), the rights of the covered expatriate to such item shall be treated as becoming transferable and not subject to a substantial risk of forfeiture on the day before the expatriation date,

(B) no early distribution tax shall apply by reason of such treatment, and

(C) appropriate adjustments shall be made to subsequent distributions from the plan to reflect such treatment.

(3) Eligible deferred compensation items. For purposes of this subsection, the term "eligible deferred compensation item" means any deferred compensation item with respect to which—

(A) the payor of such item is—

(i) a United States person, or

(ii) a person who is not a United States person but who elects to be treated as a United States person for purposes of paragraph (1) and meets such requirements as the Secretary may provide to ensure that the payor will meet the requirements of paragraph (1), and

(B) the covered expatriate—
(i) notifies the payor of his status as a covered expatriate, and
(ii) makes an irrevocable waiver of any right to claim any reduction under any treaty with the United States in withholding on such item.

(4) Deferred compensation item. For purposes of this subsection, the term "deferred compensation item" means—

(A) any interest in a plan or arrangement described in section 219(g)(5),
(B) any interest in a foreign pension plan or similar retirement arrangement or program,
(C) any item of deferred compensation, and
(D) any property, or right to property, which the individual is entitled to receive in connection with the performance of services to the extent not previously taken into account under section 83 or in accordance with section 83.

(5) Exception. Paragraphs (1) and (2) shall not apply to any deferred compensation item to the extent attributable to services performed outside the United States while the covered expatriate was not a citizen or resident of the United States.

(6) Special rules.
(A) Application of withholding rules. Rules similar to the rules of subchapter B of chapter 3 shall apply for purposes of this subsection.
(B) Application of tax. Any item subject to the withholding tax imposed under paragraph (1) shall be subject to tax under section 871.
(C) Coordination with other withholding requirements. Any item subject to withholding under paragraph (1) shall not be subject to withholding under section 1441 or chapter 24.

(e) Treatment of specified tax deferred accounts.
(1) Account treated as distributed. In the case of any interest in a specified tax deferred account held by a covered expatriate on the day before the expatriation date—
(A) the covered expatriate shall be treated as receiving a distribution of his entire interest in such account on the day before the expatriation date,
(B) no early distribution tax shall apply by reason of such treatment, and
(C) appropriate adjustments shall be made to subsequent distributions from the account to reflect such treatment.

(2) Specified tax deferred account. For purposes of paragraph (1), the term "specified tax deferred account" means an individual retirement plan (as defined in section 7701(a)(37)) other than any arrangement described in subsection (k) or (p) of section 408, a qualified tuition program (as defined in section 529), a Coverdell education savings account (as defined in section 530), a health savings account (as defined in section 223), and an Archer MSA (as defined in section 220).

(f) Special rules for nongrantor trusts.
(1) In general. In the case of a distribution (directly or indirectly) of any property from a nongrantor trust to a covered expatriate—

(A) the trustee shall deduct and withhold from such distribution an amount equal to 30 percent of the taxable portion of the distribution, and
(B) if the fair market value of such property exceeds its adjusted basis in the hands of the trust, gain shall be recognized to the trust as if such property were sold to the expatriate at its fair market value.

(2) Taxable portion. For purposes of this subsection, the term "taxable portion" means, with respect to any distribution, that portion of the distribution which would be includible in the gross income of the covered expatriate if such expatriate continued to be subject to tax as a citizen or resident of the United States.

(3) Nongrantor trust. For purposes of this subsection, the term "nongrantor trust" means the portion of any trust that the individual is not considered the owner of under subpart E of part I of subchapter J. The determination under the preceding sentence shall be made immediately before the expatriation date.

(4) Special rules relating to withholding. For purposes of this subsection—
(A) rules similar to the rules of subsection (d)(6) shall apply, and
(B) the covered expatriate shall be treated as having waived any right to claim any reduction under any treaty with the United States in withholding on any distribution to which paragraph (1)(A) applies unless the covered expatriate agrees to such other treatment as the Secretary determines appropriate.

(5) Application. This subsection shall apply to a nongrantor trust only if the covered expatriate was a beneficiary of the trust on the day before the expatriation date.

(g) Definitions and special rules relating to expatriation. For purposes of this section—

(1) Covered expatriate.
(A) In general. The term "covered expatriate" means an expatriate who meets the requirements of subparagraph (A), (B), or (C) of section 877(a)(2).
(B) Exceptions. An individual shall not be treated as meeting the requirements of subparagraph (A) or (B) of section 877(a)(2) if—
(i) the individual—
(I) became at birth a citizen of the United States and a citizen of another country and, as of the expatriation date, continues to be a citizen of, and is taxed as a resident of, such other country, and
(II) has been a resident of the United States (as defined in section 7701(b)(1)(A)(ii)) for not more than 10 taxable years during the 15-taxable year period ending with the taxable year during which the expatriation date occurs, or
(ii)
(I) the individual's relinquishment of United States citizenship occurs before such individual attains age 18½, and
(II) the individual has been a resident of the United States (as so defined) for not more than 10 taxable years before the date of relinquishment.
(C) Covered expatriates also subject to tax as citizens or residents. In the case of any covered expatriate who is subject to tax as a citizen or resident of the United States for any period beginning after the expatriation date, such individual shall not be treated as a covered expatriate during such period for purposes of subsections (d)(1) and (f) and section 2801.

(2) **Expatriate.** The term "expatriate" means—
(A) any United States citizen who relinquishes his citizenship, or
(B) any long-term resident of the United States who ceases to be a lawful permanent resident of the United States (within the meaning of section 7701(b)(6)).

(3) **Expatriation date.** The term "expatriation date" means—
(A) the date an individual relinquishes United States citizenship, or
(B) in the case of a long-term resident of the United States, the date on which the individual ceases to be a lawful permanent resident of the United States (within the meaning of section 7701(b)(6)).

(4) **Relinquishment of citizenship.** A citizen shall be treated as relinquishing his United States citizenship on the earliest of—
(A) the date the individual renounces his United States nationality before a diplomatic or consular officer of the United States pursuant to paragraph (5) of section 349(a) of the Immigration and Nationality Act (8 U.S.C. 1481(a)(5)),
(B) the date the individual furnishes to the United States Department of State a signed statement of voluntary relinquishment of United States nationality confirming the performance of an act of expatriation specified in paragraph (1), (2), (3), or (4) of section 349(a) of the Immigration and Nationality Act (8 U.S.C. 1481(a)(1)-(4)),
(C) the date the United States Department of State issues to the individual a certificate of loss of nationality, or
(D) the date a court of the United States cancels a naturalized citizen's certificate of naturalization.

Subparagraph (A) or (B) shall not apply to any individual unless the renunciation or voluntary relinquishment is subsequently approved by the issuance to the individual of a certificate of loss of nationality by the United States Department of State.

(5) **Long-term resident.** The term "long-term resident" has the meaning given to such term by section 877(e)(2).

(6) **Early distribution tax.** The term "early distribution tax" means any increase in tax imposed under section 72(t), 220(e)(4), 223(f)(4), 409A(a)(1)(B), 529(c)(6), or 530(d)(4).

(h) **Other rules.**
(1) **Termination of deferrals, etc.** In the case of any covered expatriate, notwithstanding any other provision of this title—
(A) any time period for acquiring property which would result in the reduction in the amount of gain recognized with respect to property disposed of by the taxpayer shall terminate on the day before the expatriation date, and
(B) any extension of time for payment of tax shall cease to apply on the day before the expatriation date and the unpaid portion of such tax shall be due and payable at the time and in the manner prescribed by the Secretary.

(2) **Step-up in basis.** Solely for purposes of determining any tax imposed by reason of subsection (a), property which was held by an individual on the date the individual first became a resident of the United States (within the meaning of section 7701(b)) shall be treated as having a basis on such date of not less than the fair market value of such property on such date. The preceding sentence shall not apply if the individual elects not to have such sentence apply. Such an election, once made, shall be irrevocable.

(3) **Coordination with section 684.** If the expatriation of any individual would result in the recognition of gain under section 684, this section shall be applied after the application of section 684.

(i) **Regulations.**
The Secretary shall prescribe such regulations as may be necessary or appropriate to carry out the purposes of this section.

In **2008,** P.L. 110-245, Sec. 301(a), added Code Sec. 877A, effective for any individual whose expatriation date (as so defined) is on or after 6/17/2008.

Sec. 878. Foreign educational, charitable, and certain other exempt organizations.

For special provisions relating to foreign educational, charitable, and other exempt organizations, see sections 512(a) and 4948.

In **1969,** P.L. 91-172, Sec. 101(j)(20), deleted "unrelated business income of" after "provisions relating to" and substituted "organizations, see sections 512(a) and 4948" for "trusts, see section 512(a)" in Code Sec. 878, effective for tax. yrs. begin. after 12/31/69.
In **1966,** P.L. 89-809, Sec. 103, redesignated Code Sec. 877 as Code Sec. 878, effective for tax. yrs. begin. after 12/31/66.

Sec. 879. Tax treatment of certain community income in the case of nonresident alien individuals.

(a) **General rule.**

In the case of a married couple 1 or both of whom are nonresident alien individuals and who have community income for the taxable year, such community income shall be treated as follows:

(1) Earned income (within the meaning of section 911(d)(2)), other than trade or business income and a partner's distributive share of partnership income, shall be treated as the income of the spouse who rendered the personal services,

(2) Trade or business income, and a partner's distributive share of partnership income, shall be treated as provided in section 1402(a)(5),

(3) Community income not described in paragraph (1) or (2) which is derived from the separate property (as determined under the applicable community property law) of one spouse shall be treated as the income of such spouse, and

(4) All other such community income shall be treated as provided in the applicable community property law.

(b) **Exception where election under section 6013(g) is in effect.**

Subsection (a) shall not apply for any taxable year for which an election under subsection (g) or (h) of section 6013 (relating to election to treat nonresident alien individual as resident of the United States) is in effect.

(c) **Definitions and special rules.**

For purposes of this section—

(1) **Community income.** The term "community income" means income which, under applicable community property laws, is treated as community income.

(2) **Community property laws.** The term "community property laws" means the community property laws of a State, a foreign country, or a possession of the United States.

(3) **Determination of marital status.** The determination of marital status shall be made under section 7703(a).

In 1986, P.L. 99-514, Sec. 1301(j)(9), substituted "section 7703(a)" for "section 143(a)" in para. (c)(3), effective for bonds issued after 8/15/86.
In 1984, P.L. 98-369, Sec. 139(a), amended the material preceding para. (a)(1) . . . Sec. 139(b)(1), amended the heading of Code Sec. 879, effective for tax. yrs. begin. after 12/31/84.
Prior to amendment, the material preceding para. (a)(1) read as follows:
"(a) General rule.
"In the case of a citizen or resident of the United States who is married to a nonresident alien individual and who has community income for the taxable year, such community income shall be treated as follows:"
Prior to amendment, the heading for Code Sec. 879 read as follows:
"SEC. 879. TAX TREATMENT OF CERTAIN COMMUNITY INCOME IN THE CASE OF A RESIDENT OR CITIZEN OF THE UNITED STATES WHO IS MARRIED TO A NONRESIDENT ALIEN INDIVIDUAL."
In 1981, P.L. 97-34, Sec. 111(b)(4), substituted "section 911(d)(2)" for "section 911(b)" in para. (a)(1), effective for tax. yrs. begin. after 12/31/81.
In 1976, P.L. 94-455, Sec. 1012(b)(1), added Code Sec. 879, effective for tax. yrs. begin. after 12/31/76.

SUBPART B.—FOREIGN CORPORATIONS
Sec.
881. Tax on income of foreign corporations not connected with United States business.
882. Tax on income of foreign corporations connected with United States business.
883. Exclusions from gross income.
884. Branch profits tax.
885. Cross references.

In 1986, P.L. 99-514, Sec. 1241(d), deleted item 884 and added new items 884 and 885.
Prior to deletion, item 884 read as follows:
"884. Cross references."
In 1966, changed item 881 from "Tax on foreign corporations not engaged in business in United States" and item 882 from "Tax on resident foreign corporation."

Sec. 881. Tax on income of foreign corporations not connected with United States business.
(a) Imposition of tax.
Except as provided in subsection (c), there is hereby imposed for each taxable year a tax of 30 percent of the amount received from sources within the United States by a foreign corporation as—
(1) interest (other than original issue discount as defined in section 1273), dividends, rents, salaries, wages, premiums, annuities, compensations, remunerations, emoluments, and other fixed or determinable annual or periodical gains, profits, and income,
(2) gains described in section 631(b) or (c),
(3) in the case of—
(A) a sale or exchange of an original issue discount obligation, the amount of the original issue discount accruing while such obligation was held by the foreign corporation (to the extent such discount was not theretofore taken into account under subparagraph (B)), and
(B) a payment on an original issue discount obligation, an amount equal to the original issue discount accruing while such obligation was held by the foreign corporation (except that such original issue discount shall be taken into account under this subparagraph only to the extent such discount was not theretofore taken into account under this subparagraph and only to the extent that the tax thereon does not exceed the payment less the tax imposed by paragraph (1) thereon), and
(4) gains from the sale or exchange after October 4, 1986, of patents, copyrights, secret processes and formulas, good will, trademarks, trade brands, franchises, and other like property, or of any interest in any such property, to the extent such gains are from payments which are contingent on the productivity, use, or disposition of the property or interest sold or exchanged,
but only to the extent the amount so received is not effectively connected with the conduct of a trade or business within the United States.
(b) Exception for certain possessions.
(1) Guam, American Samoa, the Northern Mariana Islands, and the Virgin Islands. For purposes of this section and section 884, a corporation created or organized in Guam, American Samoa, the Northern Mariana Islands, or the Virgin Islands or under the law of any such possession shall not be treated as a foreign corporation for any taxable year if—
(A) at all times during such taxable year less than 25 percent in value of the stock of such corporation is beneficially owned (directly or indirectly) by foreign persons,
(B) at least 65 percent of the gross income of such corporation is shown to the satisfaction of the Secretary to be effectively connected with the conduct of a trade or business in such a possession or the United States for the 3-year period ending with the close of the taxable year of such corporation (or for such part of such period as the corporation or any predecessor has been in existence), and
(C) no substantial part of the income of such corporation is used (directly or indirectly) to satisfy obligations to persons who are not bona fide residents of such a possession or the United States.
(2) Commonwealth of Puerto Rico.
(A) In general. If dividends are received during a taxable year by a corporation—
(i) created or organized in, or under the law of, the Commonwealth of Puerto Rico, and
(ii) with respect to which the requirements of subparagraphs (A), (B), and (C) of paragraph (1) are met for the taxable year,
subsection (a) shall be applied for such taxable year by substituting "10 percent" for "30 percent".
(B) Applicability. If, on or after the date of the enactment of this paragraph, an increase in the rate of the Commonwealth of Puerto Rico's withholding tax which is generally applicable to dividends paid to United States corporations not engaged in a trade or business in the Commonwealth to a rate greater than 10 percent takes effect, this paragraph shall not apply to dividends received on or after the effective date of the increase.
(3) Definitions.
(A) Foreign person. For purposes of paragraph (1), the term "foreign person" means any person other than—
(i) a United States person, or
(ii) a person who would be a United States person if references to the United States in section 7701 included references to a possession of the United States.
(B) Indirect ownership rules. For purposes of paragraph (1), the rules of section 318(a)(2) shall apply except that "5 percent" shall be substituted for "50 percent" in subparagraph (C) thereof.
(c) Repeal of tax on interest of foreign corporations received from certain portfolio debt investments.
(1) In general. In the case of any portfolio interest received by a foreign corporation from sources within the United States, no tax shall be imposed under paragraph (1) or (3) of subsection (a).

Foreign taxpayers   Code Sec. 881

> • **Caution:** Code Sec. 881(c)(2), following, is effective for obligations issued before 3/19/2012. For Code Sec. 881(c)(2) effective for obligations issued after 3/18/2012, see below.

(2) **Portfolio interest.** For purposes of this subsection, the term "portfolio interest" means any interest (including original issue discount) which would be subject to tax under subsection (a) but for this subsection and which is described in any of the following subparagraphs:

(A) Certain obligations which are not registered. Interest which is paid on any obligation which is described in section 871(h)(2)(A).

(B) Certain registered obligations. Interest which is paid on an obligation—
(i) which is in registered form, and
(ii) with respect to which the person who would otherwise be required to deduct and withhold tax from such interest under section 1442(a) receives a statement which meets the requirements of section 871(h)(5) that the beneficial owner of the obligation is not a United States person.

> • **Caution:** Code Sec. 881(c)(2), following, is effective for obligations issued after 3/18/2012. For Code Sec. 881(c)(2) effective for obligations issued before 3/19/2012, see above.

(2) **Portfolio interest.** For purposes of this subsection, the term "portfolio interest" means any interest (including original issue discount) which—
(A) would be subject to tax under subsection (a) but for this subsection, and
(B) is paid on an obligation—
(i) which is in registered form, and
(ii) with respect to which—
(I) the person who would otherwise be required to deduct and withhold tax from such interest under section 1442(a) receives a statement which meets the requirements of section 871(h)(5) that the beneficial owner of the obligation is not a United States person, or
(II) the Secretary has determined that such a statement is not required in order to carry out the purposes of this subsection.

(3) **Portfolio interest shall not include interest received by certain persons.** For purposes of this subsection, the term "portfolio interest" shall not include any portfolio interest which—
(A) except in the case of interest paid on an obligation of the United States, is received by a bank on an extension of credit made pursuant to a loan agreement entered into in the ordinary course of its trade or business,
(B) is received by a 10-percent shareholder (within the meaning of section 871(h)(3)(B)), or
(C) is received by a controlled foreign corporation from a related person (within the meaning of section 864(d)(4)).

(4) **Portfolio interest not to include certain contingent interest.** For purposes of this subsection, the term "portfolio interest" shall not include any interest which is treated as not being portfolio interest under the rules of section 871(h)(4).

(5) **Special rules for controlled foreign corporations.**
(A) In general. In the case of any portfolio interest received by a controlled foreign corporation, the following provisions shall not apply:
(i) Subparagraph (A) of section 954(b)(3) (relating to exception where foreign base company income is less than 5 percent or $1,000,000).
(ii) Paragraph (4) of section 954(b) (relating to exception for certain income subject to high foreign taxes).
(iii) Clause (i) of section 954(c)(3)(A) (relating to certain income received from related persons).
(B) Controlled foreign corporation. For purposes of this subsection, the term "controlled foreign corporation" has the meaning given to such term by section 957(a).

(6) **Secretary may cease application of this subsection.** Under rules similar to the rules of section 871(h)(6), the Secretary may provide that this subsection shall not apply to payments of interest described in section 871(h)(6).

(7) **Registered form.** For purposes of this subsection, the term "registered form" has the meaning given such term by section 163(f).

(d) **Tax not to apply to certain interest and dividends.** No tax shall be imposed under paragraph (1) or (3) of subsection (a) on any amount described in section 871(i)(2).

(e) **Tax not to apply to certain dividends of regulated investment companies.**

(1) **Interest-related dividends.**
(A) In general. Except as provided in subparagraph (B), no tax shall be imposed under paragraph (1) of subsection (a) on any interest-related dividend (as defined in section 871(k)(1)) received from a regulated investment company.
(B) Exception. Subparagraph (A) shall not apply—
(i) to any dividend referred to in section 871(k)(1)(B), and
(ii) to any interest-related dividend received by a controlled foreign corporation (within the meaning of section 957(a)) to the extent such dividend is attributable to interest received by the regulated investment company from a person who is a related person (within the meaning of section 864(d)(4)) with respect to such controlled foreign corporation.
(C) Treatment of dividends received by controlled foreign corporations. The rules of subsection (c)(5)(A) shall apply to any interest-related dividend received by a controlled foreign corporation (within the meaning of section 957(a)) to the extent such dividend is attributable to interest received by the regulated investment company which is described in clause (ii) of section 871(k)(1)(E) (and not described in clause (i) or (iii) of such section).

(2) **Short-term capital gain dividends.** No tax shall be imposed under paragraph (1) of subsection (a) on any short-term capital gain dividend (as defined in section 871(k)(2)) received from a regulated investment company.

(f) **Cross reference.**
For doubling of tax on corporations of certain foreign countries, see section 891.
For special rules for original issue discount, see section 871(g).

In 2010, P.L. 111-147, Sec. 502(b)(2)(B), amended para. (c)(2), effective for obligations issued after 3/18/2012.
Prior to amendment, para. (c)(2) read as follows:
"(2) Portfolio interest.
"For purposes of this subsection, the term 'portfolio interest' means any interest (including original issue discount) which would be subject to tax under subsection

2,527

(a) but for this subsection and which is described in any of the following subparagraphs:

"(A) Certain obligations which are not registered. Interest which is paid on any obligation which is described in section 871(h)(2)(A).

"(B) Certain registered obligations. Interest which is paid on an obligation—

"(i) which is in registered form, and

"(ii) with respect to which the person who would otherwise be required to deduct and withhold tax from such interest under section 1442(a) receives a statement which meets the requirements of section 871(h)(5) that the beneficial owner of the obligation is not a United States person."

In 2005, P.L. 109-135, Sec. 412(jj), added "interest-related dividend received by a controlled foreign corporation" after "shall apply to any" in subpara. (e)(2)(C), effective 12/21/2005.

In 2004, P.L. 108-357, Sec. 411(a)(2), redesignated subsec. (e) as subsec. (f) and added subsec. (e), effective for dividends with respect to tax. yrs. of regulated investment companies begin. after 12/31/2004.

—P.L. 108-357, Sec. 420(a), redesignated para. (b)(2) as (3) and added para. (b)(2) . . . Sec. 420(c)(1), substituted "possessions" for "Guam and Virgin Islands corporations" in the heading of subsec. (b) . . . Sec. 420(c)(2), substituted "Guam, American Samoa, the Northern Mariana Islands, and the Virgin Islands" for "In general" in the heading of para. (b)(1), effective for dividends paid after 10/22/2004.

In 1993, P.L. 103-66, Sec. 13237(a)(2), redesignated paras. (c)(4), (5), and (6) as paras. (c)(5), (6), and (7) and added new para. (c)(4) . . . Sec. 13237(c)(2), substituted "section 871(h)(5)" for "section 871(h)(4)" in clause (c)(2)(B)(ii) . . . Sec. 13237(c)(3), substituted "section 871(h)(6)" for "section 871(h)(5)" each place it appeared in para. (c)(6) [as redesignated by Sec. 13237(a)(2) of this Act, see above], effective for interest received after 12/31/93.

In 1988, P.L. 100-647, Sec. 1012(g)(1)(A), amended Sec. 1214(d)(1) of P.L. 99-514, the effective date for amendments made by Sec. 1214(c)(1) of P.L. 99-514, by substituting "payments made in a taxable year of the payor beginning after December 31, 1986" for "payments after December 31, 1986", see below. Sec. 1012(g)(1)(B) of this Act provides:

"(B) A taxpayer may elect not to have the amendment made by subparagraph (A) apply and to have section 1214(d)(1) of the Reform Act apply as in effect before such amendment. Such election shall be made at such time and in such manner as the Secretary of the Treasury or his delegate may prescribe."

—P.L. 100-647, Sec. 1012(i)(17), amended clauses (c)(4)(A)(ii) and (c)(4)(A)(iii), and deleted clauses (c)(4)(A)(iv) and (c)(4)(A)(v), effective for tax. yrs. of foreign corporations begin. after 12/31/86.

Prior to amendment, clauses (c)(4)(A)(ii) and (c)(4)(A)(iii) read as follows:

"(ii) Paragraph (4) of section 954(b) relating to corporations not formed or availed of to avoid tax).

"(iii) Subparagraph (B) of section 954(c)(3) (relating to certain income derived in active conduct of trade or business)."

Prior to deletion, clauses (c)(4)(A)(iv) and (c)(4)(A)(v) read as follows:

"(iv) Subparagraph (C) of section 954(c)(3) (relating to certain income derived by an insurance company).

"(v) Subparagraphs (A) and (B) of section 954(c)(4) (relating to exception for certain income received from related persons)."

—P.L. 100-647, Sec. 1012(aa)(3)(A) and (D), and (4), provide:

"(3) Certain amendments not to apply to the extent inconsistent with treaties.— The following amendments made by the Reform Act shall not apply to the extent the application of such amendments would be contrary to any treaty obligation of the United States in effect on the date of the enactment of the Reform Act:"

"(A) The amendments made by section 1211 of the Reform Act to the extent—

"(i) such amendments apply in the case of an individual treated as a resident of a foreign country under a treaty obligation of the United States as so in effect, or

"(ii) such amendments relate to income of a non-resident from the sale or exchange of inventory property which would otherwise be sourced under section 865(e)(2) of the 1986 Code.

* * *

"(D) The amendments made by section 1214 of the Reform Act; except for purposes of determining the amount of the foreign tax credit."

* * *

"(4) Treatment of technical corrections. For purposes of paragraphs (2) and (3), any amendment made by this title shall be treated as if it had been included in the provision of the Reform Act to which such amendment relates."

In 1986, P.L. 99-514, Sec. 1211(b)(6), substituted "sold or exchanged" for "sold or exchanged, or from payments which are treated as being so contingent under section 871(c)," in para. (a)(4), effective [as amended by Sec. 1012(g)(1) of P.L. 100-642, see above] for payments made in a tax yr. of the payor begin. after 12/31/86, [Sec. 1012' of P.L. 100-647(aa)(3)(A) and (4) above] except as provided at Sec. 1211(c)(2) of this Act:

"(2) Special rule for foreign persons. In the case of any foreign person other than any controlled foreign corporations (within the meaning of section 957(a) of the Internal Revenue Code of 1954), the amendments made by this section shall apply to transactions entered into after March 18,1986."

—P.L. 99-514, Sec. 1214(c)(2), redesignated subsec. (d) as subsec. (e), and added new subsec. (d), effective for payments made in a tax. yr. of the payor begin. after 12/31/86, except as provided in Sec. 1214(d)(2)-(d)(4) of this Act reproduced at Code Sec. 861 [See Sec. 1012 of P.L. 100-647(aa)(3)(D) and (4), above].

—P.L. 99-514, Sec. 1223(b)(2), substituted "less than 5 percent or $1,000,000" for "less than 10 percent" in clause (c)(4)(A)(i), effective for tax. yrs. begin. after 12/31/86.

—P.L. 99-514, Sec. 1273(b)(1), amended para. (b)(1), and deleted para. (b)(2) . . . Sec. 1273(b)(2)(A), redesignated para. (b)(3) as para. (b)(2), and deleted para. (b)(4), effective for tax. yrs. begin. after 12/31/86, except as provided by Secs. 1271 and 1277(b) and (f) [added by Sec. 1012(Z)(1) of P.L. 100-647] of this Act, reproduced in note following Code Sec. 931.

Prior to amendment, para. (b)(1) read as follows:

"(1) In general. For purposes of this section, a corporation created or organized in Guam or the Virgin Islands or under the law of Guam or the Virgin Islands shall not be treated as a foreign corporation for any taxable year if—

"(A) at all times during such taxable year less than 25 percent in value of the stock of such corporation is owned (directly or indirectly) by foreign persons, and

"(B) at least 20 percent of the gross income of such corporation is shown to the satisfaction of the Secretary to have been derived from sources within Guam or the Virgin Islands (as the case may be) for the 3-year period ending with the close of the preceding taxable year of such corporation (or for such part of such period as the corporation has been in existence)."

Prior to deletion, para. (b)(2) [as amended by Sec. 1899A(22) of this Act, see below] read as follows:

"(2) Paragraph (1) not to apply to tax imposed in Guam. For purposes of applying this subsection with respect to income tax liability incurred to Guam—

"(A) paragraph (1) shall not apply, and

"(B) for purposes of this section, the term 'foreign corporation' does not include a corporation created or organized in Guam or under the law of Guam."

Prior to deletion, para. (b)(4) read as follows:

"(4) Cross reference. For tax imposed in the Virgin Islands, see sections 934 and 934A."

—P.L. 99-514, Sec. 1810(d)(1)(B), substituted "which would be subject to tax under subsection (a) but for this subsection and which is described in" for "which is described in" in para. (c)(2) . . . Sec. 1810(d)(3)(C), substituted "receives" for "has received" in clause (c)(2)(B)(ii), effective for interest received after 7/18/84 for obligations issued after 7/18/84, in tax. yrs. end. after 7/18/84. For special rule see Sec. 127(g)(3) of P.L. 98-369 reproduced in note following Code Sec. 864.

—P.L. 99-514, Sec. 1810(e)(2)(B), amended para. (a)(3), effective for payments made on or after 9/16/84 for obligations issued after 3/31/72.

Prior to amendment, para. (a)(3) read as follows:

"(3) in the case of—

"(A) a sale or exchange of an original issue discount obligation, the amount of any gain not in excess of the original issue discount accruing while such obligation was held by the foreign corporation (to the extent such discount was not therefore taken into account under subparagraph (B)), and

"(B) the payment of interest on an original issue discount obligation, an amount equal to the original issue discount accrued on such obligation since the last payment of interest thereon (except that such original issue discount shall be taken into account under this subparagraph only to the extent that the tax thereon does not exceed the interest payment less than tax imposed by paragraph (1) thereon), and"

—P.L. 99-514, Sec. 1899A(22), substituted "paragraph" for "Paragraph" in subpara. (b)(2)(A) . . . Sec. 1899A(23), substituted "section 864(d)(4))" for "section 864(d)(4)" in subpara. (c)(3)(C), effective 10/22/86.

In 1984, P.L. 98-369, Sec. 42(a)(10), substituted "section 1273" for "section 1232(b)" in para. (a)(1), effective for tax. yrs. end. after 7/18/84.

—P.L. 98-369, Sec. 127(b)(1), redesignated subsec. (c) as subsec. (d) and added new subsec. (c) . . . Sec. 127(b)(2), substituted "Except as provided in subsection (c), there" for "There" in subsec. (a), effective for interest received after 7/18/84 for obligations issued after 7/18/84, in tax. yrs. end. after 7/18/84. Sec. 127(g)(3) of the Act provides a special rule, see note following Code Sec. 864.

—P.L. 98-369, Sec. 128(b)(1), amended para. (a)(3) . . . Sec. 128(b)(2), amended subsec. (c) (before redesignation by Sec. 127(b)(1) of the Act, see above), effective for payments made on or after 9/16/84 for obligations issued after 3/31/72.

Prior to amendment, para. (a)(3) read as follows:

"(3) in the case of—

"(A) bonds or other evidences of indebtedness issued after September 28, 1965, and before April 1, 1972, amounts which under section 1232(a)(2)(B) are considered as ordinary income, and, in the case of corporate obligations issued after May 27, 1969, and before April 1, 1972, amounts which would be so considered but for the fact the obligations were issued after May 27, 1969, or

"(B) bonds or other evidences of indebtedness issued after March 31, 1972, and payable more than six months from the date of original issue (without regard to the period held by the taxpayer), amounts which under section 1232(a)(2)(B) would be considered as ordinary income but for the fact such obligations were issued after May 27, 1969, and

"(C) the payment of interest on an obligation described in subparagraph (B), an amount equal to the original issue discount (but not in excess of such interest less the tax imposed by paragraph (1) thereon) accrued on such obligations since the last payment of interest thereon, and"

Prior to amendment, subsec. (c) (before redesignation by Sec. 127(b)(1)) read as follows:

"(c) Doubling of tax.

"For doubling of tax on corporations of certain foreign countries, see section 891."

—P.L. 98-369, Sec. 130(a), amended subsec. (b), effective for payments made after 3/1/84, in tax. yrs. end. after 3/1/84.

Prior to amendment, subsec. (b) read as follows:

"(b) Exception for Guam corporations.

"For purposes of this section, the term 'foreign corporation' does not include a corporation created or organized in Guam or under the law of Guam."

In 1976, P.L. 94-455, Sec. 1901(b)(3)(I), substituted "ordinary income" for "gain from the sale or exchange of property which is not a capital asset" each place it appeared in subparas. (a)(3)(A) and (a)(3)(B), effective for tax. yrs. begin. after 12/31/76.

In 1972, P.L. 92-606, Sec. 1(e)(1), redesignated subsec. (b) as subsec. (c) and added new subsec. (b), effective for tax. yrs. begin. after 12/31/71.

In 1971, P.L. 92-178, Sec. 313(a), added "(other than original issue discount as defined in section 1232(b))" after "interest" in para. (a)(1) . . . Sec. 313(c), amended para. (a)(3), effective for tax. yrs. begin. after 12/31/66.

Prior to amendment para. (a)(3) read as follows:

"(3) in the case of bonds or other evidences of indebtedness issued after September 28, 1965, amounts which under section 1232 are considered as gains from the sale or exchange of property which is not a capital asset,"

In 1966, P.L. 89-809, Sec. 104(a), amended Code Sec. 881, effective for tax. yrs. begin. after 12/31/66.

Prior to amendment, Code Sec. 881 read as follows:

"SEC. 881. TAX ON FOREIGN CORPORATIONS NOT ENGAGED IN BUSINESS IN UNITED STATES.

"(a) *Imposition of tax.*

"In the case of every foreign corporation not engaged in trade or business within the United States, there is hereby imposed for each taxable year, in lieu of the taxes imposed by section 11, 55, 59A, or 1201(a) on its taxable income which is effectively connected with the conduct of a trade or business within the United States as interest (except interest on deposits with persons carrying on the banking business), dividends, rents, salaries, wages, premiums, annuities, compensations, remunerations, emoluments, or other fixed or determinable annual or periodical gains, profits, and income (including amounts described in section 631 (b) and (c) which are considered to be gains from the sale or exchange of capital assets).

"(b) *Doubling of tax.*

"For doubling of tax on corporations of certain foreign countries, see section 891."

Sec. 882. Tax on income of foreign corporations connected with United States business.

(a) Imposition of tax.

(1) In general. A foreign corporation engaged in trade or business within the United States during the taxable year shall be taxable as provided in section 11, 55, 59A, or 1201(a) on its taxable income which is effectively connected with the conduct of a trade or business within the United States.

(2) Determination of taxable income. In determining taxable income for purposes of paragraph (1), gross income includes only gross income which is effectively connected with the conduct of a trade or business within the United States.

(3) For special tax treatment of gain or loss from the disposition by a foreign corporation of a United States real property interest, see section 897.

(b) Gross income.

In the case of a foreign corporation, except where the context clearly indicates otherwise, gross income includes only—

(1) gross income which is derived from sources within the United States and which is not effectively connected with the conduct of a trade or business within the United States, and

(2) gross income which is effectively connected with the conduct of a trade or business within the United States.

(c) Allowance of deductions and credits.

(1) Allocation of deductions.

(A) General rule. In the case of a foreign corporation, the deductions shall be allowed only for purposes of subsection (a) and (except as provided by subparagraph (B)) only if and to the extent that they are connected with income which is effectively connected with the conduct of a trade or business within the United States; and the proper apportionment and allocation of the deductions for this purpose shall be determined as provided in regulations prescribed by the Secretary.

(B) Charitable contributions. The deduction for charitable contributions and gifts provided by section 170 shall be allowed whether or not connected with income which is effectively connected with the conduct of a trade or business within the United States.

(2) Deductions and credits allowed only if return filed. A foreign corporation shall receive the benefit of the deductions and credits allowed to it in this subtitle only by filing or causing to be filed with the Secretary a true and accurate return, in the manner prescribed in subtitle F, including therein all the information which the Secretary may deem necessary for the calculation of such deductions and credits. The preceding sentence shall not apply for purposes of the tax imposed by section 541 (relating to personal holding company tax), and shall not be construed to deny the credit provided by section 33 for tax withheld at source or the credit provided by section 34 for certain uses of gasoline.

(3) Foreign tax credit. Except as provided by section 906, foreign corporations shall not be allowed the credit against the tax for taxes of foreign countries and possessions of the United States allowed by section 901.

(4) Cross reference. For rule that certain foreign taxes are not to be taken into account in determining deduction or credit, see section 906(b)(1).

(d) Election to treat real property income as income connected with United States business.

(1) In general. A foreign corporation which during the taxable year derives any income—

(A) from real property located in the United States, or from any interest in such real property, including (i) gains from the sale or exchange of real property or an interest therein, (ii) rents or royalties from mines, wells or other natural deposits, and (iii) gains described in section 631(b) or (c), and

(B) which, but for this subsection, would not be treated as income effectively connected with the conduct of a trade or business within the United States,

may elect for such taxable year to treat all such income as income which is effectively connected with the conduct of a trade or business within the United States. In such case, such income shall be taxable as provided in subsection (a)(1) whether or not such corporation is engaged in trade or business within the United States during the taxable year. An election under this paragraph for any taxable year shall remain in effect for all subsequent taxable years, except that it may be revoked with the consent of the Secretary with respect to any taxable year.

(2) Election after revocation, etc. Paragraphs (2) and (3) of section 871(d) shall apply in respect of elections under this subsection in the same manner and to the same extent as they apply in respect of elections under section 871(d).

(e) Interest on United States obligations received by banks organized in possessions.

In the case of a corporation created or organized in, or under the law of, a possession of the United States which is carrying on the banking business in a possession of the United States, interest on obligations of the United States which is not portfolio interest (as defined in section 881(c)(2)) shall—

(1) for purposes of this subpart, be treated as income which is effectively connected with the conduct of a trade or business within the United States, and

(2) shall be taxable as provided in subsection (a)(1) whether or not such corporation is engaged in trade or business within the United States during the taxable year.

(f) Returns of tax by agent.

If any foreign corporation has no office or place of business in the United States but has an agent in the United

Code Sec. 882(f)

States, the return required under section 6012 shall be made by the agent.

In 1988, P.L. 100-647, Sec. 1012(s)(2)(B), substituted "the case of a foreign corporation, except where the context clearly indicates otherwise" for "the case of a foreign corporation" in subsec. (b), effective for distributions after 12/31/87 (or, if earlier, the effective date) (which shall not be earlier than 1/1/87) of the initial regulations issued under Code Sec. 1446.
— P.L. 100-647, Sec. 2001(c)(2), added "59A," after "55" in para. (a)(1), effective for tax. yrs. begin. after 12/31/86.
— P.L. 100-647, Sec. 6133(a)(1), added "which is not portfolio interest (as defined in section 881(c)(2))" before "shall" in subsec. (e)... Sec. 6133(a)(2), deleted the last sentence of subsec. (e), effective for tax. yrs. begin. after 12/31/88. Prior to deletion the last sentence of subsec. (e) read as follows:
"The preceding sentence shall not apply to any Guam corporation which is treated as not being a foreign corporation by section 881(b)(1) for the taxable year.".
In 1986, P.L. 99-514, Sec. 701(e)(4)(F), substituted ", 55, or 1201(a)" for " or 1201(a)" in para. (a)(1), effective for tax. yrs. begin after 12/31/86.
— P.L. 99-514, Sec. 1236(a), added the last sentence to subsec. (e), effective for tax. yrs. begin. after 11/16/85. For study of U.S. reinsurance industry, see Sec. 1244 of this Act reproduced in note following Code Sec. 881.
In 1984, P.L. 98-369, Sec. 474(r)(19), substituted "33" for "32" and substituted "section 34" for "section 39" in para. (c)(2), effective for tax. yrs. begin. after 12/31/83, and for carrybacks from tax. yrs. begin. after 12/31/83.
In 1983, P.L. 97-424, Sec. 515(b)(6)(F), deleted "and lubricating oil" after "gasoline" in para. (c)(2), effective for articles sold after 1/6/83.
In 1980, P.L. 96-499, Sec. 1122(c)(2), added para. (a)(3), effective for dispositions after 6/18/80.
In 1978, P.L. 95-600, Sec. 301(b)(13), substituted "Imposition of tax." for "Normal tax and surtax." in the heading of subsec. (a), substituted "In general." for "Imposition of tax." in the heading of para. (a)(1), effective for tax. yrs. begin. after 12/31/78.
In 1976, P.L. 94-455, Sec. 1906(b)(13)(A), substituted "Secretary" for "Secretary or his delegate" each time it appeared in subsec. (c), for tax. yrs. begin. after '76.
In 1966, P.L. 89-809, Sec. 104, amended Code Sec. 882, effective for tax. yrs. begin. after 12/31/66.
Prior to amendment, Code Sec. 882 read as follows:
"SEC. 882. TAX ON RESIDENT FOREIGN CORPORATIONS.
"(a) Imposition of tax. A foreign corporation engaged in trade or business within the United States shall be taxable as provided in section 11.
"(b) Gross income. In the case of a foreign corporation, gross income includes only the gross income from sources within the United States.
"(c) Allowance of deductions and credits.
"(1) Deductions allowed only if return filed. A foreign corporation shall receive the benefit of the deductions allowed to it in this subtitle only by filing or causing to be filed with the Secretary or his delegate a true and accurate return of its total income received from all sources in the United States, in the manner prescribed in subtitle F, including therein all the information which the Secretary or his delegate may deem necessary for this calculation of such deductions.
"(2) Allocation of deductions. In the case of a foreign corporation the deductions shall be allowed only if and to the extent that they are connected with income from sources within the United States; and the proper apportionment and allocation of the deductions with respect to sources within and without the United States shall be determined as provided in part I, under regulations prescribed by the Secretary or his delegate.
"(3) Charitable contributions. The deduction for charitable contributions and gifts provided by section 170 shall be allowed whether or not connected with income from sources within the United States.
"(4) Foreign tax credit. Foreign corporations shall not be allowed the credits against the tax for taxes of foreign countries and possessions of the United States allowed by section 901.
"(d) Returns of tax by agent. If any foreign corporation has no office or place of business in the United States but has an agent in the United States, the return required under section 6012 shall be made by the agent."

Sec. 883. Exclusions from gross income.
(a) Income of foreign corporations from ships and aircraft.
The following items shall not be included in gross income of a foreign corporation, and shall be exempt from taxation under this subtitle:

(1) Ships operated by certain foreign corporations. Gross income derived by a corporation organized in a foreign country from the international operation of a ship or ships if such foreign country grants an equivalent exemption to corporations organized in the United States.

(2) Aircraft operated by certain foreign corporations. Gross income derived by a corporation organized in a foreign country from the international operation of aircraft if such foreign country grants an equivalent exemption to corporations organized in the United States.

Foreign taxpayers

(3) Railroad rolling stock of foreign corporations. Earnings derived from payments by a common carrier for the use on a temporary basis (not expected to exceed a total of 90 days in any taxable year) of railroad rolling stock owned by a corporation of a foreign country which grants an equivalent exemption to corporations organized in the United States.

(4) Special rules. The rules of paragraphs (6), (7), and (8) of section 872(b) shall apply for purposes of this subsection.

(5) Special rule for countries which tax on residence basis. For purposes of this subsection, there shall not be taken into account any failure of a foreign country to grant an exemption to a corporation organized in the United States if such corporation is subject to tax by such foreign country on a residence basis pursuant to provisions of foreign law which meets such standards (if any) as the Secretary may prescribe.

(b) Earnings derived from communications satellite system.
The earnings derived from the ownership or operation of a communications satellite system by a foreign entity designated by a foreign government to participate in such ownership or operation shall be exempt from taxation under this subtitle, if the United States, through its designated entity, participates in such system pursuant to the Communications Satellite Act of 1962 (47 U.S.C. 701 and following).

(c) Treatment of certain foreign corporations.

(1) In general. Paragraph (1) or (2) of subsection (a) (as the case may be) shall not apply to any foreign corporation if 50 percent or more of the value of the stock of such corporation is owned by individuals who are not residents of such foreign country or another foreign country meeting the requirements of such paragraph.

(2) Treatment of controlled foreign corporations. Paragraph (1) shall not apply to any foreign corporation which is a controlled foreign corporation (as defined in section 957(a)).

(3) Special rules for publicly traded corporations.

(A) Exception. Paragraph (1) shall not apply to any corporation which is organized in a foreign country meeting the requirements of paragraph (1) or (2) of subsection (a) (as the case may be) and the stock of which is primarily and regularly traded on an established securities market in such foreign country, another foreign country meeting the requirements of such paragraph, or the United States.

(B) Treatment of stock owned by publicly traded corporation. Any stock in another corporation which is owned (directly or indirectly) by a corporation meeting the requirements of subparagraph (A) shall be treated as owned by individuals who are residents of the foreign country in which the corporation meeting the requirements of subparagraph (A) is organized.

(4) Stock ownership through entities. For purposes of paragraph (1), stock owned (directly or indirectly) by or for a corporation, partnership, trust, or estate shall be treated as being owned proportionately by its shareholders, partners, or beneficiaries. Stock considered to be owned by a person by reason of the application of the preceding sentence shall, for purposes of applying such sentence, be treated as actually owned by such person.

In 2004, P.L. 108-357, Sec. 419(b), substituted "(6), (7), and (8)" for "(5), (6), and (7)" in para. (a)(4), effective for wagers made after 10/22/2004.
In 1988, P.L. 100-647, Sec. 1012(e)(1)(A), amended para. (c)(3)... Sec. 1012(e)(1)(B), substituted "Paragraph (1) or (2) of subsection (a) (as the case may be)" for "Paragraphs (1) and (2) of subsection (a)" and substituted "such para-

2,530

Foreign taxpayers   Code Sec. 884(d)(2)(E)

graph" for "such paragraphs (1) and (2)" in para. (c)(1) . . . Sec. 1012(e)(2)(A), deleted "to citizens of the United States and" before "to corporations" in paras. (a)(1) and (2) . . . Sec. 1012(e)(5), substituted "international operation" for "operation" in paras. (a)(1) and (2), effective for tax. yrs. begin. after 12/31/86.

Prior to amendment para. (c)(3) read as follows:

"(3) Exception for publicly traded corporations. Paragraph (1) shall not apply to any foreign corporation—

"(A) the stock of which is primarily and regularly traded on an established securities market in the foreign country in which such corporation is organized, or

"(B) which is wholly owned (either directly or indirectly) by another corporation meeting the requirements of subparagraph (A) and is organized in the same foreign country as such other corporation."

—P.L. 100-647, Sec. 1012(aa)(3)(C) and (4), provides:

"(3) Certain amendments not to apply to the extent inconsistent with treaties. The following amendments made by the Reform Act shall not apply to the extent the application of such amendments would be contrary to any treaty obligation of the United States in effect on the date of the enactment of the Reform Act:

"(C) The amendments made by subsections (b) and (c) of section 1212 of the Reform Act."

* * *

"(4) Treatment of technical corrections. For purposes of paragraphs (2) and (3), any amendment made by this title shall be treated as if it had been included in the provision of the Reform Act to which such amendment relates."

In **1986,** P.L. 99-514, Sec. 1212(c)(3), amended paras. (a)(1) and (a)(2) . . . Sec. 1212(c)(4), added para. (a)(4) . . . Sec. 1212(c)(5), added subsec. (c), effective for tax. yrs. begin. after 12/31/86 [see Sec. 1012 of P.L. 100-647(aa)(3)(C) and (4), above].

Prior to amendment, paras. (a)(1) and (a)(2) read as follows:

"(1) Ships under foreign flag. Earnings derived from the operation of a ship or ships documented under the laws of a foreign country which grants an equivalent exemption to citizens of the United States and to corporations organized in the United States.

"(2) Aircraft of foreign registry. Earnings derived from the operation of aircraft registered under the laws of a foreign country which grants an equivalent exemption to citizens of the United States and to corporations organized in the United States."

In **1975,** P.L. 94-164, Sec. 6(a), added para. (a)(3), effective for payments made after 11/18/74.

In **1968,** P.L. 90-622, designated existing provisions as subsec. (a), added the heading in subsec. (a), and added subsec. (b), effective for tax. yrs. begin. after 12/31/66.

Sec. 884. Branch profits tax.
(a) Imposition of tax.

In addition to the tax imposed by section 882 for any taxable year, there is hereby imposed on any foreign corporation a tax equal to 30 percent of the dividend equivalent amount for the taxable year.

(b) Dividend equivalent amount.

For purposes of subsection (a), the term "dividend equivalent amount" means the foreign corporation's effectively connected earnings and profits for the taxable year adjusted as provided in this subsection:

(1) Reduction for increase in U.S. net equity. If—

(A) the U.S. net equity of the foreign corporation as of the close of the taxable year, exceeds

(B) the U.S. net equity of the foreign corporation as of the close of the preceding taxable year,

the effectively connected earnings and profits for the taxable year shall be reduced (but not below zero) by the amount of such excess.

(2) Increase for decrease in net equity.

(A) In general. If—

(i) the U.S. net equity of the foreign corporation as of the close of the preceding taxable year, exceeds

(ii) the U.S. net equity of the foreign corporation as of the close of the taxable year,

the effectively connected earnings and profits for the taxable year shall be increased by the amount of such excess.

(B) Limitation.

(i) In general. The increase under subparagraph (A) for any taxable year shall not exceed the accumulated effectively connected earnings and profits as of the close of the preceding taxable year.

(ii) Accumulated effectively connected earnings and profits. For purposes of clause (i), the term "accumulated effectively connected earnings and profits" means the excess of—

(I) the aggregate effectively connected earnings and profits for preceding taxable years beginning after December 31, 1986, over

(II) the aggregate dividend equivalent amounts determined for such preceding taxable years.

(c) U.S. net equity.

For purposes of this section—

(1) In general. The term "U.S. net equity" means—

(A) U.S. assets, reduced (including below zero) by

(B) U.S. liabilities.

(2) U.S. assets and U.S. liabilities. For purposes of paragraph (1)—

(A) U.S. assets. The term "U.S. assets" means the money and aggregate adjusted bases of property of the foreign corporation treated as connected with the conduct of a trade or business in the United States under regulations prescribed by the Secretary. For purposes of the preceding sentence, the adjusted basis of any property shall be its adjusted basis for purposes of computing earnings and profits.

(B) U.S. liabilities. The term "U.S. liabilities" means the liabilities of the foreign corporation treated as connected with the conduct of a trade or business in the United States under regulations prescribed by the Secretary.

(C) Regulations to be consistent with allocation of deductions. The regulations prescribed under subparagraphs (A) and (B) shall be consistent with the allocation of deductions under section 882(c)(1).

(d) Effectively connected earnings and profits.

For purposes of this section—

(1) In general. The term "effectively connected earnings and profits" means earnings and profits (without diminution by reason of any distributions made during the taxable year) which are attributable to income which is effectively connected (or treated as effectively connected) with the conduct of a trade or business within the United States.

(2) Exception for certain income. The term "effectively connected earnings and profits" shall not include any earnings and profits attributable to—

(A) income not includible in gross income under paragraph (1) or (2) of section 883(a),

(B) income treated as effectively connected with the conduct of a trade or business within the United States under section 921(d) or 926(b) (as in effect before their repeal by the FSC Repeal and Extraterritorial Income Exclusion Act of 2000),

(C) gain on the disposition of a United States real property interest described in section 897(c)(1)(A)(ii),

(D) income treated as effectively connected with the conduct of a trade or business within the United States under section 953(c)(3)(C), or

(E) income treated as effectively connected with the conduct of a trade or business within the United States under section 882(e).

Property and liabilities of the foreign corporation treated as connected with such income under regulations prescribed by the Secretary shall not be taken into account in determining the U.S. assets or U.S. liabilities of the foreign corporation.

(e) Coordination with income tax treaties; etc.
(1) Limitation on treaty exemption. No treaty between the United States and a foreign country shall exempt any foreign corporation from the tax imposed by subsection (a) (or reduce the amount thereof) unless—
(A) such treaty is an income tax treaty, and
(B) such foreign corporation is a qualified resident of such foreign country.

(2) Treaty modifications. If a foreign corporation is a qualified resident of a foreign country with which the United States has an income tax treaty—
(A) the rate of tax under subsection (a) shall be the rate of tax specified in such treaty—
(i) on branch profits if so specified, or
(ii) if not so specified, on dividends paid by a domestic corporation to a corporation resident in such country which wholly owns such domestic corporation, and
(B) any other limitations under such treaty on the tax imposed by subsection (a) shall apply.

(3) Coordination with withholding tax.
(A) In general. If a foreign corporation is subject to the tax imposed by subsection (a) for any taxable year (determined after the application of any treaty), no tax shall be imposed by section 871(a), 881(a), 1441, or 1442 on any dividends paid by such corporation out of its earnings and profits for such taxable year.
(B) Limitation on certain treaty benefits. If—
(i) any dividend described in section 861(a)(2)(B) is received by a foreign corporation, and
(ii) subparagraph (A) does not apply to such dividend,
rules similar to the rules of subparagraphs (A) and (B) of subsection (f)(3) shall apply to such dividend.

(4) Qualified resident. For purposes of this subsection—
(A) In general. Except as otherwise provided in this paragraph, the term "qualified resident" means, with respect to any foreign country, any foreign corporation which is a resident of such foreign country unless—
(i) 50 percent or more (by value) of the stock of such foreign corporation is owned (within the meaning of section 883(c)(4)) by individuals who are not residents of such foreign country and who are not United States citizens or resident aliens, or
(ii) 50 percent or more of its income is used (directly or indirectly) to meet liabilities to persons who are not residents of such foreign country or citizens or residents of the United States.
(B) Special rule for publicly traded corporations. A foreign corporation which is a resident of a foreign country shall be treated as a qualified resident of such foreign country if—
(i) the stock of such corporation is primarily and regularly traded on an established securities market in such foreign country, or
(ii) such corporation is wholly owned (either directly or indirectly) by another foreign corporation which is organized in such foreign country and the stock of which is so traded.
(C) Corporations owned by publicly traded domestic corporations. A foreign corporation which is a resident of a foreign country shall be treated as a qualified resident of such foreign country if—
(i) such corporation is wholly owned (directly or indirectly) by a domestic corporation, and
(ii) the stock of such domestic corporation is primarily and regularly traded on an established securities market in the United States.
(D) Secretarial authority. The Secretary may, in his sole discretion, treat a foreign corporation as being a qualified resident of a foreign country if such corporation establishes to the satisfaction of the Secretary that such corporation meets such requirements as the Secretary may establish to ensure that individuals who are not residents of such foreign country do not use the treaty between such foreign country and the United States in a manner inconsistent with the purposes of this subsection.

(5) Exception for international organizations. This section shall not apply to an international organization (as defined in section 7701(a)(18)).

(f) Treatment of interest allocable to effectively connected income.
(1) In general. In the case of a foreign corporation engaged in a trade or business in the United States (or having gross income treated as effectively connected with the conduct of a trade or business in the United States), for purposes of this subtitle—
(A) any interest paid by such trade or business in the United States shall be treated as if it were paid by a domestic corporation, and
(B) to the extent that the allocable interest exceeds the interest described in subparagraph (A), such foreign corporation shall be liable for tax under section 881(a) in the same manner as if such excess were interest paid to such foreign corporation by a wholly owned domestic corporation on the last day of such foreign corporation's taxable year.
To the extent provided in regulations, subparagraph (A) shall not apply to interest in excess of the amounts reasonably expected to be allocable interest.

(2) Allocable interest. For purposes of this subsection, the term "allocable interest" means any interest which is allocable to income which is effectively connected (or treated as effectively connected) with the conduct of a trade or business in the United States.

(3) Coordination with treaties.
(A) Payor must be qualified resident. In the case of any interest described in paragraph (1) which is paid or accrued by a foreign corporation, no benefit under any treaty between the United States and the foreign country of which such corporation is a resident shall apply unless—
(i) such treaty is an income tax treaty, and
(ii) such foreign corporation is a qualified resident of such foreign country.
(B) Recipient must be qualified resident. In the case of any interest described in paragraph (1) which is received or accrued by any corporation, no benefit under any treaty between the United States and the foreign country of which such corporation is a resident shall apply unless—
(i) such treaty is an income tax treaty, and
(ii) such foreign corporation is a qualified resident of such foreign country.

(g) Regulations.
The Secretary shall prescribe such regulations as may be necessary or appropriate to carry out the purposes of this section, including regulations providing for appropriate adjustments in the determination of the dividend equivalent amount in connection with the distribution to shareholders or transfer to a controlled corporation of the taxpayer's U.S. as-

sets and other adjustments in such determination as are necessary or appropriate to carry out the purposes of this section.

In 2007, P.L. 110-172, Sec. 11(g)(8), added "(as in effect before their repeal by the FSC Repeal and Extraterritorial Income Exclusion Act of 2000)" before the comma in subpara. (d)(2)(B), enacted 12/29/2007.

In 1996, P.L. 104-188, Sec. 1704(f)(3)(A)(i), substituted "to the extent that the allocable interest exceeds the interested described in subparagraph (A)" for "to the extent the amount of interest allowable as a deduction under section 882 in computing the effectively connected taxable income of such foreign corporation exceeds the interest described in subparagraph (A)" in subpara. (f)(1)(B) . . . Sec. 1704(f)(3)(A)(ii), substituted "reasonably expected to be allocable interest." for "reasonably expected to be deductible under section 882 in computing the effectively connected taxable income of such foreign corporation." at the end of para. (f)(1) . . . Sec. 1704(f)(3)(A)(iii), amended para. (f)(2), effective for tax. yrs. begin. after 12/31/86, except as provided in Sec. 1012(aa)(3)(E), (G) and (aa)(4) of P.L. 100-647, see below].

Prior to amendment, para. (f)(2) read as follows:

"(2) Effectively connected taxable income. For purposes of this subsection, the term 'effectively connected taxable income' means taxable income which is effectively connected (or treated as effectively connected) with the conduct of a trade or business within the United States."

In 1989, P.L. 101-239, Sec. 7811(i)(5), amended Sec. 1012(q)(1)(B) of P.L. 100-647 [reproduced below] by substituting "1021(c)(2)(C)" for "1021(e)(2)(C)", and by substituting "832(b)(4)(C)" for "823(b)(4)(C)", see below.

In 1988, P.L. 100-647, Sec. 1012(q)(1)(A), amended subpara. (b)(2)(B) . . . Sec. 1012(q)(2)(A), amended para. (e)(1) . . . Sec. 1012(q)(2)(B), amended para. (e)(3) . . . Sec. 1012(q)(2)(C)(i), deleted the second sentence of para. (f)(1) . . . Sec. 1012(q)(2)(C)(ii), added para. (f)(3) . . . Sec. 1012(q)(3)(A), substituted "this subtitle" for "sections 871, 881, 1441 and 1442" in para. (f)(1) . . . Sec. 1012(q)(3)(B), added the last sentence of para. (f)(1) . . . Sec. 1012(q)(4), redesignated subpara. (e)(4)(C) as subpara. (e)(4)(D) and added new subpara. (e)(4)(C) . . . Sec. 1012(q)(5)(A), substituted "50 percent or more" for "more than 50 percent" in clause (e)(4)(A)(i) . . . Sec. 1012(q)(5)(B), substituted "in the United States" in clause (e)(4)(A)(ii) . . . Sec. 1012(q)(6), added para. (e)(5) . . . Sec. 1012(q)(14), added "(or having gross income treated as effectively connected with the conduct of a trade or business in the United States)" after "United States" in the material preceding subpara. (f)(1)(A), effective for tax. yrs. begin. after 12/31/86.

Prior to amendment, subpara. (b)(2)(B) read as follows:

"(B) Limitation. The increase under subparagraph (A) for any taxable year shall not exceed the aggregate reductions under paragraph (1) for prior taxable years to the extent not previously taken into account under subparagraph (A)."

Prior to amendment, para. (e)(1) read as follows:

"(1) Limitation on treaty exemption. No income tax treaty between the United States and a foreign country shall exempt any foreign corporation from the tax imposed by subsection (a) (or reduce the amount thereof) unless—

"(A) such foreign corporation is a qualified resident of such foreign country, or

"(B) such foreign corporation is not a qualified resident of such foreign country but such income tax treaty permits a withholding tax on dividends described in section 861(a)(2)(B) which are paid by such foreign corporation."

Prior to amendment para. (e)(3) read as follows:

"(3) Coordination with 2nd tier withholding tax.

"(A) In general. If a foreign corporation is not exempt for any taxable year from the tax imposed by subsection (a) by reason of clause (i), no tax shall be imposed by section 871(a), 881(a), 1441, or 1442 on any dividends paid by such corporation during the taxable year.

"(B) Limitation on certain treaty benefits. No foreign corporation which is not a qualified resident of a foreign country shall be entitled to claim benefits under any income tax treaty between the United States and such foreign country with respect to dividends.—

"(i) which are paid by such foreign corporation and with respect to which such foreign corporation is otherwise required to deduct and withhold tax under section 1441 or 1442, or

"(ii) which are received by such foreign corporation and are described in section 861(a)(2)(B)."

Prior to deletion the second sentence of para. (f)(1) read as follows:
"Rules similar to the rules of subsection (e)(3)(B) shall apply to interest described in the preceding sentence."

—P.L. 100-647, Sec. 1012(q)(1)(B), [as amended by Sec. 7811(i)(5) of P.L. 101-239, see above] of this Act provides:

"(B) For purposes of applying section 884 of the 1986 Code, the earnings and profits of any corporation shall be determined without regard to any increase in earnings and profits under sections 1023(e)(3)(C) and 1021(c)(2)(C) of the Reform Act or arising from section 832(b)(4)(C) of the 1986 Code."

—P.L. 100-647, Sec. 1012(aa)(3)(E), (G) and (aa)(4), provide:

"(3) Certain amendments not to apply to the extent inconsistent with treaties.— The following amendments made by the Reform Act shall not apply to the extent the application of such amendments would be contrary to any treaty obligation of the United States in effect on the date of the enactment of the Reform Act:

* * *

"(E) The amendment made by section 1241(a) of the Reform Act to the extent that, under a treaty obligation of the United States, interest described in section 884(f)(1)(A) of the 1986 Code (as added by such amendment) which is in excess of amounts deducted would be treated as other than United States source."

* * *

"(G) The amendment made by section 1241(a) of the Reform Act to the extent such amendment relates to section 884(f)(1)(B) of the 1986 Code."

* * *

"(4) Treatment of technical corrections.—For purposes of paragraphs (2) and (3), any amendment made by this title shall be treated as if it had been included in the provision of the Reform Act to which such amendment relates."

—P.L. 100-647, Sec. 6133(b), deleted "or" at the end of subpara. (d)(2)(C), substituted ", or" for the period at the end of subpara. (d)(2)(D) and added subpara. (d)(2)(E), effective for tax. yrs. begin. after 12/31/88.

In 1986, P.L. 99-514, Sec. 1241(a), added Code Sec. 884, effective for tax. yrs. begin. after 12/31/86 [see Sec. 1012 of P.L. 100-647(aa)(3)(E) and (G) and (4), above].

Sec. 885. Cross references.

(1) For special provisions relating to foreign corporations carrying on an insurance business within the United States, see section 842.

(2) For rules applicable in determining whether any foreign corporation is engaged in trade or business within the United States, see section 864(b).

(3) For adjustment of tax in case of corporations of certain foreign countries, see section 896.

(4) For allowance of credit against the tax in case of a foreign corporation having income effectively connected with the conduct of a trade or business within the United States, see section 906.

(5) For withholding at source of tax on income of foreign corporations, see section 1442.

In 1986, P.L. 99-514, Sec. 1241(a), redesignated Code Sec. 884 as Code Sec. 885, effective for tax. yrs. begin. after 12/31/86.

In 1969, P.L. 91-172, Sec. 101(j)(21), deleted para. (1) and redesignated paras. (2), (3), (4), (5), and (6) as paras. (1), (2), (3), (4), and (5), effective for tax. yrs. begin. after 12/31/69.

Prior to amendment para. (1) read as follows:

"(1) For special provisions relating to unrelated business income of foreign educational, charitable, and certain other exemption organizations see section 512(a)."

In 1966, P.L. 89-809, Sec. 104, amended Code Sec. 884, effective for tax. yrs. begin. after 12/31/66.

Prior to amendment, Code Sec. 884 read as follows:
"SEC. 884. CROSS REFERENCES.

"(1) For withholding at source of tax on income of foreign corporations, see section 1442.

"(2) For rules applicable in determining whether any foreign corporation is engaged in trade or business within the United States, see section 871(c).

"(3) For special provisions relating to foreign insurance companies, see subchapter L (sec. 801 and following).

"(4) For special provisions relating to unrelated business income of foreign educational, charitable, and certain other exempt organizations, see section 512(a)."

SUBPART C.—TAX ON GROSS TRANSPORTATION INCOME

Sec.

887. Imposition of tax on gross transportation income of nonresident aliens and foreign corporations.

In 1986, P.L. 99-514, Sec. 1212(b)(1), added subpart C.

Sec. 887. Imposition of tax on gross transportation income of nonresident aliens and foreign corporations.

(a) Imposition of tax.

In the case of any nonresident alien individual or foreign corporation, there is hereby imposed for each taxable year a tax equal to 4 percent of such individual's or corporation's United States source gross transportation income for such taxable year.

(b) United States source gross transportation income.

(1) In general. Except as provided in paragraphs (2) and (3), the term "United States source gross transportation income" means any gross income which is transportation income (as defined in section 863(c)(3)) to the extent such income is treated as from sources in the United States under section 863(c)(2). To the extent provided in regulations, such term does not include any income of a kind to which an exemption under paragraph (1) or (2) of section 883(a) would not apply.

(2) Exception for certain income effectively connected with business in the United States. The term "United States source gross transportation income" shall not include any income taxable under section 871(b) or 882.

(3) Exception for certain income taxable in possessions. The term "United States source gross transportation income" does not include any income taxable in a possession of the United States under the provisions of this title as made applicable in such possession.

(4) Determination of effectively connected income. For purposes of this chapter, United States source gross transportation income of any taxpayer shall not be treated as effectively connected with the conduct of a trade or business in the United States unless—

(A) the taxpayer has a fixed place of business in the United States involved in the earning of United States source gross transportation income, and

(B) substantially all of the United States source gross transportation income (determined without regard to paragraph (2)) of the taxpayer is attributable to regularly scheduled transportation (or, in the case of income from the leasing of a vessel or aircraft, is attributable to a fixed place of business in the United States).

(c) Coordination with other provisions. Any income taxable under this section shall not be taxable under section 871, 881, or 882.

In **1989**, P.L. 101-239, Sec. 7811(i)(8)(A), redesignated para. (b)(3) as para. (b)(4) and added new para. (b)(3) . . . Sec. 7811(i)(8)(B), substituted "paragraphs (2) and (3)" for "paragraph (2)" in para. (b)(1) . . . Sec. 7811(i)(9), substituted "United States source gross transportation income" for "transportation income" the first two places it appeared in para. (b)(4) (as redesignated), effective for tax. yrs. begin. after 12/31/86.

In **1988**, P.L. 100-647, Sec. 1012(e)(6)(A), substituted "under section 863(c)(2)" for "under section 863(c)" in para. (b)(1) . . . Sec. 1012(e)(6)(B), added the sentence at the end of para. (b)(1), effective for tax. yrs. begin. after 12/31/86.

—P.L. 100-647, Sec. 1012(aa)(3)(C) and (4), provides:

"(3) Certain amendments not to apply to the extent inconsistent with treaties.— The following amendments made by the Reform Act [P.L. 99-514] shall not apply to the extent the application of such amendments would be contrary to any treaty obligation of the United States in effect on 10/22/86:"

* * *

"(C) The amendments made by subsections (b) and (c) of section 1212 of the Reform Act."

* * *

"(4) Treatment of technical corrections. For purposes of paragraphs (2) and (3), any amendment made by this title shall be treated as if it had been included in the provision of the Reform Act to which such amendment relates."

In **1986**, P.L. 99-514, Sec. 1212(b)(1), added Code Sec. 887 as part of Subpart C of Part II of subchapter N of chapter 1, effective for tax. yrs. begin. after 12/31/86 [see Sec. 1012 of P.L. 100-647(aa)(3)(C) and (4), above].

SUBPART D.— MISCELLANEOUS PROVISIONS

Sec.
891. Doubling of rates of tax on citizens and corporations of certain foreign countries.
892. Income of foreign governments and of international organizations.
893. Compensation of employees of foreign governments or international organizations.
894. Income affected by treaty.
895. Income derived by a foreign central bank of issue from obligations of the United States or from bank deposits.
896. Adjustment of tax on nationals, residents, and corporations of certain foreign countries.
897. Disposition of investment in United States real property.
898. Taxable year of certain foreign corporations.

In **1989**, P.L. 101-239, Sec. 7401(c), added item 898.
In **1986**, P.L. 99-514, Sec. 1212(b)(1), redesignated subpart C as subpart D.
In **1980**, P.L. 96-499, Sec. 1122(b), added item 897.
In **1966**, P.L. 89-809, Sec. 102 and 105, changed item 894 from "Income exempt under treaty," added "or bank deposits" in item 895, and added item 896.
In **1961**, added item 895.

Sec. 891. Doubling of rates of tax on citizens and corporations of certain foreign countries.

Whenever the President finds that, under the laws of any foreign country, citizens or corporations of the United States are being subjected to discriminatory or extraterritorial taxes, the President shall so proclaim and the rates of tax imposed by section 1, 3, 11, 801, 831, 852, 871, and 881 shall, for the taxable year during which such proclamation is made and for each taxable year thereafter, be doubled in the case of each citizen and corporation of such foreign country; but the tax at such doubled rate shall be considered as imposed by such sections as the case may be. In no case shall this section operate to increase the taxes imposed by such sections (computed without regard to this section) to an amount in excess of 80 percent of the taxable income of the taxpayer (computed without regard to the deductions allowable under section 151 and under part VIII of subchapter B). Whenever the President finds that the laws of any foreign country with respect to which the President has made a proclamation under the preceding provisions of this section have been modified so that discriminatory and extraterritorial taxes applicable to citizens and corporations of the United States have been removed, he shall so proclaim, and the provisions of this section providing for doubled rates of tax shall not apply to any citizen or corporation of such foreign country with respect to any taxable year beginning after such proclamation is made.

In **1986**, P.L. 99-514, Sec. 1024(c)(13), deleted "821," after "801" in Code Sec. 891, effective for tax. yrs. begin. after 12/31/86.
In **1984**, P.L. 98-369, Sec. 211(b)(12), substituted "801" for "802" in Code Sec. 891, effective for tax. yrs. begin. after 12/31/83.
In **1959**, P.L. 86-69, Sec. 3(f)(1), deleted "811" after "802" in Code Sec. 891, effective for tax. yrs. begin. after 12/31/57.
In **1956**, P.L. 429, Sec. 5(8), added "811" after "802" in Code Sec. 891, effective for tax. yrs. begin. after 12/31/54.

Sec. 892. Income of foreign governments and of international organizations.

(a) Foreign governments.

(1) In general. The income of foreign governments received from—

(A) investments in the United States in—

(i) stocks, bonds, or other domestic securities owned by such foreign governments, or

(ii) financial instruments held in the execution of governmental financial or monetary policy, or

(B) interest on deposits in banks in the United States of moneys belonging to such foreign governments,

shall not be included in gross income and shall be exempt from taxation under this subtitle.

(2) Income received directly or indirectly from commercial activities.

(A) In general. Paragraph (1) shall not apply to any income—

(i) derived from the conduct of any commercial activity (whether within or outside the United States),

(ii) received by a controlled commercial entity or received (directly or indirectly) from a controlled commercial entity, or

(iii) derived from the disposition of any interest in a controlled commercial entity.

(B) Controlled commercial entity. For purposes of subparagraph (A), the term "controlled commercial entity" means any entity engaged in commercial activities (whether within or outside the United States) if the government—

(i) holds (directly or indirectly) any interest in such entity which (by value or voting interest) is 50 percent or more of the total of such interests in such entity, or

(ii) holds (directly or indirectly) any other interest in such entity which provides the foreign government with effective control of such entity.

For purposes of the preceding sentence, a central bank of issue shall be treated as a controlled commercial entity only if engaged in commercial activities within the United States.

(3) Treatment as resident. For purposes of this title, a foreign government shall be treated as a corporate resident of its country. A foreign government shall be so treated for purposes of any income tax treaty obligation of the United States if such government grants equivalent treatment to the Government of the United States.

(b) International organizations.

The income of international organizations received from investments in the United States in stocks, bonds, or other domestic securities owned by such international organizations, or from interest on deposits in banks in the United States of moneys belonging to such international organizations, or from any other source within the United States, shall not be included in gross income and shall be exempt from taxation under this subtitle.

(c) Regulations.

The Secretary shall prescribe such regulations as may be necessary or appropriate to carry out the purposes of this section.

In 1990, P.L. 101-508, Sec. 11704(a)(35), amended Sec. 1012(t)(1) of P.L. 100-647 by substituting ", or" for the period at the end of clause (a)(2)(A)(ii) [as amended by Sec. 1012(t)(2) of P.L. 100-647].

In 1988, P.L. 100-647, Sec. 1012(t)(1)(A), deleted "or" at the end of clause (a)(2)(A)(i), substituted ", or" for the period at the end of clause (a)(2)(A)(ii) [as amended by Sec. 1012(t)(2) of this Act] and added new clause (a)(2)(A)(iii) . . . Sec. 1012(t)(2), [as amended by Sec. 11704(a)(35) of P.L. 101-508, see above] amended clause (a)(2)(A)(ii) . . . Sec. 1012(t)(3), added para. (a)(3), effective for amounts received on or after 7/1/86, except that no amount shall be required to be deducted or withheld by reason of the amendment made by Sec. 1247(a) of P.L. 99-514 from any payment made before 10/22/86.

Prior to amendment clause (a)(2)(A)(ii) read as follows:

"(ii) received from or by a controlled commercial entity.

—P.L. 100-647, Sec. 1012(aa)(3)(I) and (4), provides:

"(3) Certain amendments not to apply to the extent inconsistent with treaties.—The following amendments made by the Reform Act [P.L. 99-514] shall not apply to the extent the application of such amendments would be contrary to any treaty obligation of the United States in effect on the date of the enactment of the Reform Act [10/22/86]:"

* * *

"(I) The amendment made by section 1247(a) of the Reform Act.

* * *

"(4) Treatment of technical corrections—For purposes of paragraphs (2) and (3), any amendment made by this title shall be treated as if it had been included in the provision of the Reform Act to which such amendment relates."

In 1986, P.L. 99-514, Sec. 1247(a), amended Code Sec. 892, effective for amounts received on or after 7/1/86, except that no amount shall be required to be deducted or withheld by reason of the amendment made by Sec. 1247(a) of this Act from any payment made before 10/22/86 [See Sec. 1012 of P.L. 100-647(aa)(3)(I) and (4), above].

Prior to amendment, Code Sec. 892 read as follows:

"SEC. 892. INCOME OF FOREIGN GOVERNMENTS AND OF INTERNATIONAL ORGANIZATIONS.

"The income of foreign governments or international organizations received from investments in the United States in stocks, bonds, or other domestic securities, owned by such foreign governments or by international organizations, or from interest on deposits in banks in the United States of moneys belonging to such foreign governments or international organizations, or from any other source within the United States, shall not be included in gross income and shall be exempt from taxation under this subtitle."

Sec. 893. Compensation of employees of foreign governments or international organizations.

(a) Rule for exclusion.

Wages, fees, or salary of any employee of a foreign government or of an international organization (including a consular or other officer, or a nondiplomatic representative), received as compensation for official services to such government or international organization shall not be included in gross income and shall be exempt from taxation under this subtitle if—

(1) such employee is not a citizen of the United States, or is a citizen of the Republic of the Philippines (whether or not a citizen of the United States); and

(2) in the case of an employee of a foreign government, the services are of a character similar to those performed by employees of the Government of the United States in foreign countries; and

(3) in the case of an employee of a foreign government, the foreign government grants an equivalent exemption to employees of the Government of the United States performing similar services in such foreign country.

(b) Certificate by Secretary of State.

The Secretary of State shall certify to the Secretary of the Treasury the names of the foreign countries which grant an equivalent exemption to the employees of the Government of the United States performing services in such foreign countries, and the character of the services performed by employees of the Government of the United States in foreign countries.

(c) Limitation on exclusion.

Subsection (a) shall not apply to—

(1) any employee of a controlled commercial entity (as defined in section 892(a)(2)(B)), or

(2) any employee of a foreign government whose services are primarily in connection with a commercial activity (whether within or outside the United States) of the foreign government.

In 1988, P.L. 100-647, Sec. 1012(t)(4), added subsec. (c), effective for amounts received on or after 7/1/86, except that no amount shall be required to be deducted and withheld by reason of the amendment made by Sec. 1247(a) of P.L. 99-514 from any payment made before 10/22/86.

Sec. 894. Income affected by treaty.

(a) Treaty provisions.

(1) In general. The provisions of this title shall be applied to any taxpayer with due regard to any treaty obligation of the United States which applies to such taxpayer.

(2) Cross reference. For relationship between treaties and this title, see section 7852(d).

(b) Permanent establishment in United States.

For purposes of applying any exemption from, or reduction of, any tax provided by any treaty to which the United States is a party with respect to income which is not effectively connected with the conduct of a trade or business within the United States, a nonresident alien individual or a foreign corporation shall be deemed not to have a permanent establishment in the United States at any time during the taxable year. This subsection shall not apply in respect of the tax computed under section 877(b).

(c) Denial of treaty benefits for certain payments through hybrid entities.

(1) Application to certain payments. A foreign person shall not be entitled under any income tax treaty of the United States with a foreign country to any reduced rate of any withholding tax imposed by this title on an item of income derived through an entity which is treated as a partnership (or is otherwise treated as fiscally transparent) for purposes of this title if—

(A) such item is not treated for purposes of the taxation laws of such foreign country as an item of income of such person,

(B) the treaty does not contain a provision addressing the applicability of the treaty in the case of an item of income derived through a partnership, and

(C) the foreign country does not impose tax on a distribution of such item of income from such entity to such person.

(2) Regulations. The Secretary shall prescribe such regulations as may be necessary or appropriate to determine the extent to which a taxpayer to which paragraph (1) does not apply shall not be entitled to benefits under any income tax treaty of the United States with respect to any payment received by, or income attributable to any activities of, an entity organized in any jurisdiction (including the United States) that is treated as a partnership or is otherwise treated as fiscally transparent for purposes of this title (including a common investment trust under section 584, a grantor trust, or an entity that is disregarded for purposes of this title) and is treated as fiscally nontransparent for purposes of the tax laws of the jurisdiction of residence of the taxpayer.

In 1997, P.L. 105-34, Sec. 1054(a), added subsec. (c), effective 8/5/97.

In 1988, P.L. 100-647, Sec. 1012(aa)(6), amended subsec. (a), effective for any tax. period for which the time for assessment of any deficiency has not expired by reason of any law or rule of law before 11/10/88.

Prior to amendment, subsec. (a) read as follows:

"(a) Income exempt under treaty.

"Income of any kind, to the extent required by any treaty obligation of the United States, shall not be included in gross income and shall be exempt form taxation under this subtitle."

—P.L. 100-647, Sec. 6139(a), and (b) provide:

"SEC. 6139. SUNSET OF TREATY PROVISIONS.

"(a) In general.

"No provisions of the Tax Convention with the United Kingdom (on behalf of Bermuda) or the Tax Convention with Barbados, whether entered into on, before, or after the date of enactment of this Act shall prevent application of any provision of the Internal Revenue Code of 1986 imposing insurance excise taxes. In the case of a treaty entered into after the date of enactment of this Act, the preceding sentence shall not apply if such treaty by specific reference to this section of this Act clearly expresses the intent to override the provisions of this section.

"(b) Special rule for certain treaties.

"In the case of any treaty in effect on December 31, 1989, subsection (a) shall not apply to any premium allocable to insurance coverage for periods before January 1, 1990."

In 1966, P.L. 89-809, Sec. 105, designated existing provisions as subsec. (a) and added subsec. (b), effective for tax. yrs. begin. after 12/31/66.

Sec. 895. Income derived by a foreign central bank of issue from obligations of the United States or from bank deposits.

Income derived by a foreign central bank of issue from obligations of the United States or of any agency or instrumentality thereof (including beneficial interests, participations, and other instruments issued under section 302(c) of the Federal National Mortgage Association Charter Act (12 U.S.C. 1717)) which are owned by such foreign central bank of issue, or derived from interest on deposits with persons carrying on the banking business, shall not be included in gross income and shall be exempt from taxation under this subtitle unless such obligations or deposits are held for, or used in connection with, the conduct of commercial banking functions or other commercial activities. For purposes of the preceding sentence the Bank for International Settlements shall be treated as a foreign central bank of issue.

In 1966, P.L. 89-809, Sec. 102, amended Code Sec. 895, effective for tax. yrs. begin. after 12/31/66.

Prior to amendment, Code Sec. 895 read as follows:

"SEC. 895. INCOME DERIVED BY A FOREIGN CENTRAL BANK OF ISSUE FROM OBLIGATIONS OF THE UNITED STATES.

"Income derived by a foreign central bank of issue from obligations of the United States owned by such foreign central bank of issue shall not be included in gross income and shall be exempt from taxation under this subtitle unless such obligations are held for, or used in connection with, the conduct of commercial banking functions or other commercial activities."

In 1961, P.L. 87-29, Sec. 1(a), added Code Sec. 895 for tax. yrs. begin. after '60.

Sec. 896. Adjustment of tax on nationals, residents, and corporations of certain foreign countries.

(a) Imposition of more burdensome taxes by foreign country.

Whenever the President finds that—

(1) under the laws of any foreign country, considering the tax system of such foreign country, citizens of the United States not residents of such foreign country or domestic corporations are being subjected to more burdensome taxes, on any item of income received by such citizens or corporations from sources within such foreign country, than taxes imposed by the provisions of this subtitle on similar income derived from sources within the United States by residents or corporations of such foreign country,

(2) such foreign country, when requested by the United States to do so, has not acted to revise or reduce such taxes so that they are no more burdensome than taxes imposed by the provisions of this subtitle on similar income derived from sources within the United States by residents or corporations of such foreign country, and

(3) it is in the public interest to apply pre-1967 tax provisions in accordance with the provisions of this subsection to residents or corporations of such foreign country,

the President shall proclaim that the tax on such similar income derived from sources within the United States by residents or corporations of such foreign country shall, for taxable years beginning after such proclamation, be determined under this subtitle without regard to amendments made to this subchapter and chapter 3 on or after the date of enactment of this section.

(b) Imposition of discriminatory taxes by foreign country.

Whenever the President finds that—

(1) under the laws of any foreign country, citizens of the United States or domestic corporations (or any class of such citizens or corporations) are, with respect to any item of income, being subjected to a higher effective rate of tax than are nationals, residents, or corporations of such foreign country (or a similar class of such nationals, residents, or corporations) under similar circumstances;

(2) such foreign country, when requested by the United States to do so, has not acted to eliminate such higher effective rate of tax; and

(3) it is in the public interest to adjust, in accordance with the provisions of this subsection, the effective rate of tax imposed by this subtitle on similar income of nationals, residents, or corporations of such foreign country (or such similar class of such nationals, residents, or corporations),

the President shall proclaim that the tax on similar income of nationals, residents, or corporations of such foreign country (or such similar class of such nationals, residents, or corporations) shall, for taxable years beginning after such proclamation, be adjusted so as to cause the effective rate of tax imposed by this subtitle on such similar income to be substantially equal to the effective rate of tax imposed by such foreign country on such item of income of citizens of the

United States or domestic corporations (or such class of citizens or corporations). In implementing a proclamation made under this subsection, the effective rate of tax imposed by this subtitle on an item of income may be adjusted by the disallowance, in whole or in part, of any deduction, credit, or exemption which would otherwise be allowed with respect to that item of income or by increasing the rate of tax otherwise applicable to that item of income.

(c) Alleviation of more burdensome or discriminatory taxes.

Whenever the President finds that—

(1) the laws of any foreign country with respect to which the President has made a proclamation under subsection (a) have been modified so that citizens of the United States not residents of such foreign country or domestic corporations are no longer subject to more burdensome taxes on the item of income derived by such citizens or corporations from sources within such foreign country, or

(2) the laws of any foreign country with respect to which the President has made a proclamation under subsection (b) have been modified so that citizens of the United States or domestic corporations (or any class of such citizens or corporations) are no longer subject to a higher effective rate of tax on the item of income,

he shall proclaim that the tax imposed by this subtitle on the similar income of nationals, residents, or corporations of such foreign country shall, for any taxable year beginning after such proclamation, be determined under this subtitle without regard to such subsection.

(d) Notification of Congress required.

No proclamation shall be issued by the President pursuant to this section unless, at least 30 days prior to such proclamation, he has notified the Senate and the House of Representatives of his intention to issue such proclamation.

(e) Implementation by regulations.

The Secretary shall prescribe such regulations as he deems necessary or appropriate to implement this section.

In 1976, P.L. 94-455, Sec. 1906(b)(13)(A), substituted "Secretary" for "Secretary or his delegate" in subsec. (e), effective for tax. yrs. begin. after 12/31/76.

In 1966, P.L. 89-809, Sec. 105, added Code Sec. 896, effective for tax. yrs. begin. after 12/31/66.

Sec. 897. Disposition of investment in United States real property.

(a) General rule.

(1) Treatment as effectively connected with United States trade or business. For purposes of this title, gain or loss of a nonresident alien individual or a foreign corporation from the disposition of a United States real property interest shall be taken into account—

(A) in the case of a nonresident alien individual, under section 871([b])(1), or

(B) in the case of a foreign corporation, under section 882(a)(1),

as if the taxpayer were engaged in a trade or business within the United States during the taxable year and as if such gain or loss were effectively connected with such trade or business.

(2) Minimum tax on nonresident alien individuals.

(A) In general. In the case of any nonresident alien individual, the taxable excess for purposes of section 55(b)(1)(A) shall not be less than the lesser of—

(i) the individual's alternative minimum taxable income (as defined in section 55(b)(2)) for the taxable year, or

(ii) the individual's net United States real property gain for the taxable year.

(B) Net United States real property gain. For purposes of subparagraph (A), the term "net United States real property gain" means the excess of—

(i) the aggregate of the gains for the taxable year from dispositions of United States real property interests, over

(ii) the aggregate of the losses for the taxable year from dispositions of such interests.

(b) Limitation on losses of individuals.

In the case of an individual, a loss shall be taken into account under subsection (a) only to the extent such loss would be taken into account under section 165(c) (determined without regard to subsection (a) of this section).

(c) United States real property interest.

For purposes of this section—

(1) United States real property interest.

(A) In general. Except as provided in subparagraph (B), the term "United States real property interest" means—

(i) an interest in real property (including an interest in a mine, well, or other natural deposit) located in the United States or the Virgin Islands, and

(ii) any interest (other than an interest solely as a creditor) in any domestic corporation unless the taxpayer establishes (at such time and in such manner as the Secretary by regulations prescribes) that such corporation was at no time a United States real property holding corporation during the shorter of—

(I) the period after June 18, 1980, during which the taxpayer held such interest, or

(II) the 5-year period ending on the date of the disposition of such interest.

(B) Exclusion for interest in certain corporations. The term "United States real property interest" does not include any interest in a corporation if—

(i) as of the date of the disposition of such interest, such corporation did not hold any United States real property interests, and

(ii) all of the United States real property interests held by such corporation at any time during the shorter of the periods described in subparagraph (A)(ii)—

(I) were disposed of in transactions in which the full amount of the gain (if any) was recognized, or

(II) ceased to be United States real property interests by reason of the application of this subparagraph to 1 or more other corporations.

(2) United States real property holding corporation. The term "United States real property holding corporation" means any corporation if—

(A) the fair market value of its United States real property interests equals or exceeds 50 percent of

(B) the fair market value of—

(i) its United States real property interests,

(ii) its interests in real property located outside the United States, plus

(iii) any other of its assets which are used or held for use in a trade or business.

(3) Exception for stock regularly traded on established securities markets. If any class of stock of a corporation is regularly traded on an established securities market, stock of such class shall be treated as a United States real property interest only in the case of a person who, at some time during the shorter of the periods described in paragraph (1)(A)(ii), held more than 5 percent of such class of stock.

(4) Interests held by foreign corporations and by partnerships, trusts, and estates. For purposes of determining whether any corporation is a United States real property holding corporation—

(A) Foreign corporations. Paragraph (1)(A)(ii) shall be applied by substituting "any corporation (whether foreign or domestic)" for "any domestic corporation".

(B) Assets held by partnerships, etc. Under regulations prescribed by the Secretary, assets held by a partnership, trust, or estate shall be treated as held proportionately by its partners or beneficiaries. Any asset treated as held by a partner or beneficiary by reason of this subparagraph which is used or held for use by the partnership, trust, or estate in a trade or business shall be treated as so used or held by the partner or beneficiary. Any asset treated as held by a partner or beneficiary by reason of this subparagraph shall be so treated for purposes of applying this subparagraph successively to partnerships, trusts, or estates which are above the first partnership, trust, or estate in a chain thereof.

(5) Treatment of controlling interests.

(A) In general. Under regulations, for purposes of determining whether any corporation is a United States real property holding corporation, if any corporation (hereinafter in this paragraph referred to as the "first corporation") holds a controlling interest in a second corporation—

(i) the stock which the first corporation holds in the second corporation shall not be taken into account,

(ii) the first corporation shall be treated as holding a portion of each asset of the second corporation equal to the percentage of the fair market value of the stock of the second corporation represented by the stock held by the first corporation, and

(iii) any asset treated as held by the first corporation by reason of clause (ii) which is used or held for use by the second corporation in a trade or business shall be treated as so used or held by the first corporation.

Any asset treated as held by the first corporation by reason of the preceding sentence shall be so treated for purposes of applying the preceding sentence successively to corporations which are above the first corporation in a chain of corporations.

(B) Controlling interest. For purposes of subparagraph (A), the term "controlling interest" means 50 percent or more of the fair market value of all classes of stock of a corporation.

(6) Other special rules.

(A) Interest in real property. The term "interest in real property" includes fee ownership and co-ownership of land or improvements thereon, leaseholds of land or improvements thereon, options to acquire land or improvements thereon, and options to acquire leaseholds of land or improvements thereon.

(B) Real property includes associated personal property. The term "real property" includes movable walls, furnishings, and other personal property associated with the use of the real property.

(C) Constructive ownership rules. For purposes of determining under paragraph (3) whether any person holds more than 5 percent of any class of stock and of determining under paragraph (5) whether a person holds a controlling interest in any corporation, section 318(a) shall apply (except that paragraphs (2)(C) and (3)(C) of section 318(a) shall be applied by substituting "5 percent" for "50 percent").

(d) Treatment of distributions by foreign corporations.

(1) In general. Except to the extent otherwise provided in regulations, notwithstanding any other provision of this chapter, gain shall be recognized by a foreign corporation on the distribution (including a distribution in liquidation or redemption) of a United States real property interest in an amount equal to the excess of the fair market value of such interest (as of the time of the distribution) over its adjusted basis.

(2) Exceptions. Gain shall not be recognized under paragraph (1)—

(A) if—

(i) at the time of the receipt of the distributed property, the distributee would be subject to taxation under this chapter on a subsequent disposition of the distributed property, and

(ii) the basis of the distributed property in the hands of the distributee is no greater than the adjusted basis of such property before the distribution, increased by the amount of gain (if any) recognized by the distributing corporation, or

(B) if such nonrecognition is provided in regulations prescribed by the Secretary under subsection (e)(2).

(e) Coordination with nonrecognition provisions.

(1) In general. Except to the extent otherwise provided in subsection (d) and paragraph (2) of this subsection, any nonrecognition provision shall apply for purposes of this section to a transaction only in the case of an exchange of a United States real property interest for an interest the sale of which would be subject to taxation under this chapter.

(2) Regulations. The Secretary shall prescribe regulations (which are necessary or appropriate to prevent the avoidance of Federal income taxes) providing—

(A) the extent to which nonrecognition provisions shall, and shall not, apply for purposes of this section, and

(B) the extent to which—

(i) transfers of property in reorganization, and

(ii) changes in interests in, or distributions from, a partnership, trust, or estate,

shall be treated as sales of property at fair market value.

(3) Nonrecognition provision defined. For purposes of this subsection, the term "nonrecognition provision" means any provision of this title for not recognizing gain or loss.

(f) Repealed.

(g) Special rule for sales of interest in partnerships, trusts, and estates.

Under regulations prescribed by the Secretary, the amount of any money, and the fair market value of any property, received by a nonresident alien individual or foreign corporation in exchange for all or part of its interest in a partnership, trust, or estate shall, to the extent attributable to United States real property interests, be considered as an amount received from the sale or exchange in the United States of such property.

(h) Special rules for certain investment entities.

For purposes of this section—

(1) Look-through of distributions. Any distribution by a qualified investment entity to a nonresident alien individual, a foreign corporation, or other qualified investment entity shall, to the extent attributable to gain from sales or exchanges by the qualified investment entity of United States real property interests, be treated as gain recognized by such nonresident alien individual, foreign corporation, or other qualified investment entity from the sale or exchange of a United States real property interest. Notwithstanding the preceding sentence, any distribution by a qualified investment entity to a nonresident alien individual or a foreign corporation with respect to any class of stock which is regularly traded on an established securities market located in the United States shall not be treated as gain recognized from the sale or exchange of a United States real property interest if such individual or corporation did not own more than 5 percent of such class of stock at any time during the 1-year period ending on the date of such distribution.

(2) Sale of stock in domestically controlled entity not taxed. The term "United States real property interest" does not include any interest in a domestically controlled qualified investment entity.

(3) Distributions by domestically controlled qualified investment entities. In the case of a domestically controlled qualified investment entity, rules similar to the rules of subsection (d) shall apply to the foreign ownership percentage of any gain.

(4) Definitions.

(A) Qualified investment entity.

(i) In general. The term "qualified investment entity" means—

(I) any real estate investment trust, and

(II) any regulated investment company which is a United States real property holding corporation or which would be a United States real property holding corporation if the exceptions provided in subsections (c)(3) and (h)(2) did not apply to interests in any real estate investment trust or regulated investment company.

(ii) Termination. Clause (i)(II) shall not apply after December 31, 2011. Notwithstanding the preceding sentence, an entity described in clause (i)(II) shall be treated as a qualified investment entity for purposes of applying paragraphs (1) and (5) and section 1445 with respect to any distribution by the entity to a nonresident alien individual or a foreign corporation which is attributable directly or indirectly to a distribution to the entity from a real estate investment trust.

(B) Domestically controlled. The term "domestically controlled qualified investment entity" means any qualified investment entity in which at all times during the testing period less than 50 percent in value of the stock was held directly or indirectly by foreign persons.

(C) Foreign ownership percentage. The term "foreign ownership percentage" means that percentage of the stock of the qualified investment entity which was held (directly or indirectly) by foreign persons at the time during the testing period during which the direct and indirect ownership of stock by foreign persons was greatest.

(D) Testing period. The term "testing period" means whichever of the following periods is the shortest:

(i) the period beginning on June 19, 1980, and ending on the date of the disposition or of the distribution, as the case may be,

(ii) the 5-year period ending on the date of the disposition or of the distribution, as the case may be, or

(iii) the period during which the qualified investment entity was in existence.

(5) Treatment of certain wash sale transactions.

(A) In general. If an interest in a domestically controlled qualified investment entity is disposed of in an applicable wash sale transaction, the taxpayer shall, for purposes of this section, be treated as having gain from the sale or exchange of a United States real property interest in an amount equal to the portion of the distribution described in subparagraph (B) with respect to such interest which, but for the disposition, would have been treated by the taxpayer as gain from the sale or exchange of a United States real property interest under paragraph (1).

(B) Applicable wash sales transaction. For purposes of this paragraph—

(i) In general. The term "applicable wash sales transaction" means any transaction (or series of transactions) under which a nonresident alien individual, foreign corporation, or qualified investment entity—

(I) disposes of an interest in a domestically controlled qualified investment entity during the 30-day period preceding the ex-dividend date of a distribution which is to be made with respect to the interest and any portion of which, but for the disposition, would have been treated by the taxpayer as gain from the sale or exchange of a United States real property interest under paragraph (1), and

(II) acquires, or enters into a contract or option to acquire, a substantially identical interest in such entity during the 61-day period beginning with the 1st day of the 30-day period described in subclause (I).

For purposes of subclause (II), a nonresident alien individual, foreign corporation, or qualified investment entity shall be treated as having acquired any interest acquired by a person related (within the meaning of section 267(b) or 707(b)(1)) to the individual, corporation, or entity, and any interest which such person has entered into any contract or option to acquire.

(ii) Application to substitute dividend and similar payments. Subparagraph (A) shall apply to—

(I) any substitute dividend payment (within the meaning of section 861), or

(II) any other similar payment specified in regulations which the Secretary determines necessary to prevent avoidance of the purposes of this paragraph.

The portion of any such payment treated by the taxpayer as gain from the sale or exchange of a United States real property interest under subparagraph (A) by reason of this clause shall be equal to the portion of the distribution such payment is in lieu of which would have been so treated but for the transaction giving rise to such payment.

(iii) Exception where distribution actually received. A transaction shall not be treated as an applicable wash sales transaction if the nonresident alien individual, foreign corporation, or qualified investment entity receives the distribution described in clause (i)(I) with respect to either the interest which was disposed of, or acquired, in the transaction.

(iv) Exception for certain publicly traded stock. A transaction shall not be treated as an applicable wash sales transaction if it involves the disposition of any class of stock in a qualified investment entity which is regularly traded on an established securities market within the United States but only if the nonresident alien individual, foreign corporation, or qualified investment entity did not own more than 5 percent of such class of stock at any time during the 1-year period ending on the date of the distribution described in clause (i)(I).

Code Sec. 897(i)

(i) Election by foreign corporation to be treated as domestic corporation.
(1) In general. If—
(A) a foreign corporation holds a United States real property interest, and
(B) under any treaty obligation of the United States the foreign corporation is entitled to nondiscriminatory treatment with respect to that interest,

then such foreign corporation may make an election to be treated as a domestic corporation for purposes of this section, section 1445, and section 6039C.

(2) Revocation only with consent. Any election under paragraph (1), once made, may be revoked only with the consent of the Secretary.

(3) Making of election. An election under paragraph (1) may be made only—
(A) if all of the owners of all classes of interests (other than interests solely as a creditor) in the foreign corporation at the time of the election consent to the making of the election and agree that gain, if any, from the disposition of such interest after June 18, 1980, which would be taken into account under subsection (a) shall be taxable notwithstanding any provision to the contrary in a treaty to which the United States is a party, and
(B) subject to such other conditions as the Secretary may prescribe by regulations with respect to the corporation or its shareholders.

In the case of a class of interest (other than an interest solely as a creditor) which is regularly traded on an established securities market, the consent described in subparagraph (A) need only be made by any person if such person held more than 5 percent of such class of interest at some time during the shorter of the periods described in subsection (c)(1)(A)(ii). The constructive ownership rules of subsection (c)(6)(C) shall apply in determining whether a person held more than 5 percent of a class of interest.

(4) Exclusive method of claiming nondiscrimination. The election provided by paragraph (1) shall be the exclusive remedy for any person claiming discriminatory treatment with respect to this section, section 1445, and section 6039C.

(j) Certain contributions to capital.
Except to the extent otherwise provided in regulations, gain shall be recognized by a nonresident alien individual or foreign corporation on the transfer of a United States real property interest to a foreign corporation if the transfer is made as paid in surplus or as a contribution to capital, in the amount of the excess of—
(1) the fair market value of such property transferred, over
(2) the sum of—
(A) the adjusted basis of such property in the hands of the transferor, plus
(B) the amount of gain, if any, recognized to the transferor under any other provision at the time of the transfer.

In 2010, P.L. 111-312, Sec. 749(a), substituted "December 31, 2011" for "December 31, 2009" in clause (h)(4)(A)(ii), effective 1/1/2010. Sec. 749(b) of this Act read as follows:

"(b) Effective Date.

"(1) In general. The amendment made by subsection (a) shall take effect on January 1, 2010. Notwithstanding the preceding sentence, such amendment shall not apply with respect to the withholding requirement under section 1445 of the Internal Revenue Code of 1986 for any payment made before the date of the enactment of this Act.

"(2) Amounts withheld on or before date of enactment. In the case of a regulated investment company—

"(A) which makes a distribution after December 31, 2009, and before the date of the enactment of this Act; and

"(B) which would (but for the second sentence of paragraph (1)) have been required to withhold with respect to such distribution under section 1445 of such Code,

"such investment company shall not be liable to any person to whom such distribution was made for any amount so withheld and paid over to the Secretary of the Treasury."

In 2008, P.L. 110-343, Sec. 208(a)DivC, substituted "December 31, 2009" for "December 31, 2007" in clause (h)(4)(A)(ii), effective 1/1/2008.

In 2006, P.L. 109-222, Sec. 504(a), added "which is a United States real property holding corporation or which would be a United States real property holding corporation if the exceptions provided in subsections (c)(3) and (h)(2) did not apply to interests in any real estate investment trust or regulated investment company" after "regulated investment company" in subclause (h)(4)(A)(i)(II), effective after 12/31/2004, as if included in Sec. 411 of the American Jobs Creation Act of 2004 [P.L. 108-357].

—P.L. 109-222, Sec. 505(a)(1)(A), substituted "a nonresident alien individual, a foreign corporation, or other qualified investment entity" for "a nonresident alien individual or a foreign corporation" in para. (h)(1) . . . Sec. 505(a)(1)(B), substituted "such nonresident alien individual, foreign corporation, or other qualified investment entity" for "such nonresident alien individual or foreign corporation" in para. (h)(1) . . . Sec. 505(a)(1)(C), substituted "Notwithstanding the preceding sentence, any distribution by a qualified investment entity to a nonresident alien individual or a foreign corporation with respect to any class of stock which is regularly traded on an established securities market located in the United States shall not be treated as gain recognized from the sale or exchange of a United States real property interest if such individual or corporation did not own more than 5 percent of such class of stock at any time during the 1 year period ending on the date of such distribution." for "Notwithstanding the preceding sentence, any distribution by a real estate investment trust with respect to any class of stock which is regularly traded on an established securities market located in the United States shall not be treated as gain recognized from the sale or exchange of a United States real property interest if the shareholder did not own more than 5 percent of such class of stock at any time during the 1-year period ending on the date of the distribution." in para. (h)(1) . . . Sec. 505(a)(2), added "Notwithstanding the preceding sentence, an entity described in clause (i)(II) shall be treated as a qualified investment entity for purposes of applying paragraphs (1) and (5) and section 1445 with respect to any distribution by the entity to a nonresident alien individual or a foreign corporation which is attributable directly or indirectly to a distribution to the entity from a real estate investment trust." at the end of clause (h)(4)(A)(ii), effective for tax. yrs. of qualified investment entities begin. after 12/31/2005, except that no amount shall be required to be withheld under Code Secs. 1441, 1442, or 1445 with respect to any distribution before the 5/17/2006 if such amount was not otherwise required to be withheld under any such section as in effect before such amendments.

—P.L. 109-222, Sec. 506(a), added para. (h)(5), effective for tax. yrs. begin. after 12/31/2005, except that such amendments shall not apply to any distribution, or substitute dividend payment, occurring before the date that is 30 days after 5/17/2006.

In 2005, P.L. 109-135, Sec. 403(p)(1)(A), substituted "any distribution by a real estate investment trust with respect to any class of stock" for "any distribution by a REIT with respect to any class of stock" in para. (h)(1) . . . Sec. 403(p)(1)(B), substituted "the 1-year period ending on the date of the distribution" for "the taxable year" in para. (h)(1), effective as provided by Sec. 418(c) of P.L. 108-357 [as amended by Sec. 403(p)(2) of this Act, see below].

—P.L. 109-135, Sec. 403(p)(2), amended Sec. 418(c) of P.L. 108-357 [see below] to read as follows:

"(c) Effective date. The amendments made by this section shall apply to—

"(1) any distribution by a real estate investment trust which is treated as a deduction for a taxable year of such trust beginning after the date of the enactment of this Act, and

"(2) any distribution by a real estate investment trust made after such date which is treated as a deduction under section 860 for a taxable year of such trust beginning on or before such date."

Prior to amendment, Sec. 418(c) of P.L. 108-357 [see below] read as follows:

"(c) Effective date. The amendments made by this section shall apply to taxable years beginning after the date of the enactment of this Act."

In 2004, P.L. 108-357, Sec. 411(c)(1), substituted "qualified investment entity" for "REIT" each place it appeared in para. (h)(1), effective for dividends with respect to tax. yrs. of regulated investment companies begin. after 12/31/2004.

—P.L. 108-357, Sec. 411(c)(2), amended paras. (h)(2) and (3) . . . Sec. 411(c)(3), amended subparas. (h)(4)(A) and (B) . . . Sec. 411(c)(4), substituted "qualified investment entity" for "REIT" in subparas. (h)(4)(C) and (D) . . . Sec. 411(c)(5), substituted "certain investment entities" for "REITs" in the heading of subsec. (h), effective after 12/31/2004.

Prior to amendment, paras. (h)(2) and (3) read as follows:

"(2) Sale of stock in domestically-controlled REIT not taxed. The term 'United States real property interest' does not include any interest in a domestically-controlled REIT.

"(3) Distributions by domestically-controlled REITS. In the case of a domestically-controlled REIT, rules similar to the rules of subsection (d) shall apply to the foreign ownership percentage of any gain."

Prior to amendment, subparas. (h)(4)(A) and (B) read as follows:

"(A) REIT. The term 'REIT' means a real estate investment trust.

"(B) Domestically-controlled REIT. The term 'domestically-controlled REIT' means a REIT in which at all times during the testing period less than 50 percent in value of the stock was held directly or indirectly by foreign persons."

—P.L. 108-357, Sec. 418(a), added "Notwithstanding the preceding sentence, any distribution by a REIT with respect to any class of stock which is regularly

Foreign taxpayers Code Sec. 897

traded on an established securities market located in the United States shall not be treated as gain recognized from the sale or exchange of a United States real property interest if the shareholder did not own more than 5 percent of such class of stock at any time during the taxable year." at the end of para. (h)(1), effective as provided by Sec. 418(c) of this Act [as amended by Sec. 403(p)(2) of P.L. 109-135, see above], which reads as follows:

"*(c) Effective date.* The amendments made by this section shall apply to—

"(1) any distribution by a real estate investment trust which is treated as a deduction for a taxable year of such trust beginning after the date of the enactment of this Act, and

"(2) any distribution by a real estate investment trust made after such date which is treated as a deduction under section 860 for a taxable year of such trust beginning on or before such date."

In 1996, P.L. 104-188, Sec. 1702(g)(2), deleted subsec. (f), effective 11/5/90, except as provided in Sec. 11821(b) of P.L. 101-508 [reproduced at note to Code Sec. 861].

Prior to deletion, subsec. (f) read as follows:

"(f) Distributions by domestic corporations to foreign shareholders. If a domestic corporation distributes a United States real property interest to a nonresident alien individual or a foreign corporation in a distribution to which section 301 applies, notwithstanding any other provision of this chapter, the basis of such United States real property interest in the hands of such nonresident alien individual or foreign corporation shall not exceed—

"(1) the adjusted basis of such property before the distribution, increased by

"(2) the sum of —

"(A) any gain recognized by the distributing corporation on the distribution, and

"(B) any tax paid under this chapter by the distributee on such distribution."

In 1993, P.L. 103-66, Sec. 13203(c)(2)(A), substituted "the taxable excess for purposes of section 55(b)(1)(A) shall not be less than" for "the amount determined under section 55(b)(1)(A) shall not be less than 21 percent of" in subpara. (a)(2)(A) . . . Sec. 13203(c)(2)(B), deleted "21-percent" from the heading of para. (a)(2), effective for tax. yrs. begin. after 12/31/92.

In 1990, P.L. 101-508, Sec. 11801(a)(30), deleted subsec. (k), effective 11/5/90 except as provided in Sec. 11821(b) of this Act, reproduced in note following Code Sec. 861.

Prior to deletion, subsec. (k) read as follows:

"(k) Foreign corporations acquired before enactment. If—

"(1) a foreign corporation adopts, or has adopted, a plan of liquidation described in section 334(b)(2)(A), and

"(2) the 12-month period described in section 334(b)(2)(B) for the acquisition by purchase of the stock of the foreign corporation, began after December 31, 1979, and before November 26, 1980.

then such foreign corporation may make an election to be treated, for the period following June 18, 1980, as a domestic corporation pursuant to section 897(i)(1). Notwithstanding an election under the preceding sentence, any selling shareholder of such corporation shall be considered to have sold the stock of a foreign corporation."

In 1988, P.L. 100-647, Sec. 1006(e)(19), deleted subsec. (l), effective for any distribution incomplete liquidation, and any sale or exchange, made by a corporation after 7/31/86, unless such corporation is completely liquidated before 1/1/87. For special rules, see Sec. 633(c), (d)(1)-(6), (e), (f), (g) of P.L. 99-514 reproduced in note following Code Sec. 336.

Prior to deletion, subsec. (l) read as follows:

"(l) Special rule for certain United States shareholders of liquidating foreign corporations. If a corporation adopts a plan of complete liquidation and if, solely by reason of section 897(d), section 337(a) does not apply to sales or exchanges, or section 336 does not apply to distributions, of United States real property interests by such corporation, then, in the case of any shareholder who is a United States citizen or resident and who has held stock in such corporation continuously since June 18, 1980, for the first taxable year of such shareholder in which he receives a distribution in complete liquidation with respect to such stock—

"(1) the amount realized by such shareholder on the distribution shall be increased by his proportionate share of the amount by which the tax imposed by this subtitle on such corporation would have been reduced if section 897(d) had not been applicable, and

"(2) for purposes of this title, such shareholder shall be deemed to have paid, on the last day prescribed by law for the payment of the tax imposed by this subtitle on such shareholder for such taxable year, an amount of tax equal to the amount of the increase described in paragraph (1)."

—P.L. 100-647, Sec. 1012(m)(1), deleted "and" at the end of Sec. 1228(a)(3) of P.L. 99-514, amended Sec. 1228(a)(4) of P.L. 99-514 and added Secs. 1228(a)(5) through (a)(6) of P.L. 99-514 and added the sentence at the end of Sec. 1228(a) of P.L. 99-514 . . . Sec. 1012(m)(2), repealed Sec. 1228(c) of P.L. 99-514. Amendments above apply to the special rules for applying Code Sec. 897, reproduced below.

Prior to amendment, Sec. 1228(a)(4) of P.L. 99-514 read as follows:

"(4) an election under this section applies to such transfer, sale, exchange, or other disposition."

Prior to repeal, Sec. 1228(c) of P.L. 99-514 read as follows:

"(c) Election. An election under this section shall be made at such time and in such manner as the Secretary of the Treasury or his delegate may prescribe, and an election under this section may only be made with respect to 1 transfer, sale, exchange, or other disposition."

In 1986, P.L. 99-514, Sec. 631(e)(12)(A), deleted para. (d)(2) . . . Sec. 631(e)(12)(B), deleted the heading of para. (d)(1) . . . Sec. 631(e)(12)(C), redesignated subpara. (d)(1)(A) as para. (d)(1), redesignated subpara. (d)(1)(B) as para. (d)(2), redesignated clause (d)(1)(B)(i) as subpara. (d)(2)(A), redesignated subclauses (d)(1)(B)(i)(I) and (II) as clauses (d)(2)(A)(i) and (ii), redesignated clause (d)(1)(B)(ii) as subpara. (d)(2)(B) . . . Sec. 631(e)(12)(D), substituted "paragraph (1)" for "subparagraph (A)" in para. (d)(2) [as redesignated by Sec. 631(e)(12)(C) of this Act, see above] . . . Sec. 631(e)(12)(E), deleted ", etc.," after "distributions" in heading of subsec. (d), effective as provided in Secs. 633(c), (d)(1) - (d)(6), (e), (f) and (g) of this Act, reproduced in note following Code Sec. 336, and as provided in Sec. 633(a) of this Act which reads as follows:

"(a) General rule.

Except as otherwise provided in this section, the amendments made by this subtitle shall apply to—

"(1) any distribution in complete liquidation, and any sale or exchange, made by a corporation after July 31, 1986, unless such corporation is completely liquidated before January 1, 1987,

"(2) any transaction described in section 338 of the Internal Revenue Code of 1986 for which the acquisition date occurs after December 31, 1986, and

"(3) any distribution (not in complete liquidation) made after December 31, 1986."

Prior to deletion, para. (d)(2) read as follows:.

"(2) Section 337 not to apply. Section 337 shall not apply to any sale or exchange of a United States real property interest by a foreign corporation."

Prior to deletion, the heading of para. (d)(1) read as follows:

"(1) Distributions."

—P.L. 99-514, Sec. 701(e)(4)(G), amended the heading of para. (a)(2) and subpara. (a)(2)(A), effective for tax. yrs. begin. after 12/31/86.

Prior to amendment, the heading of para. (a)(2) and subpara. (a)(2)(A) read as follows:

"(2) 20-Percent minimum tax on nonresident alien individuals.

"(A) In General. In the case of any nonresident alien individual, the amount determined under section 55(a)(1) for the taxable year shall not be less than 20 percent of the lesser of—

"(i) the individual's alternative minimum taxable income (as defined in section 55(b)) for the taxable year, or

"(ii) the individual's net United States real property gain for the taxable year."

—P.L. 99-514, Sec. 1228, [as amended by Secs. 1012(m)(1) and 1012(m)(2) of P.L. 100-647, see above], provides as follows:

"Sec. 1228. Special rule for applying section 897.

"(a) In general.

"For purposes of section 897 of the Internal Revenue Code of 1986, gain shall not be recognized on the transfer, sale, exchange, or other disposition, of shares of stock of a United States real property holding company, if—

"(1) such United States real property holding company is a Delaware corporation incorporated on January 17, 1984,

"(2) the transfer, sale, exchange, or other disposition is to any member of a qualified ownership group,

"(3) the recipient of the share of stock elects, for purposes of such section 897, a carryover basis in the transferred shares, and

"(4) the transfer, sale, exchange, or other disposition is part of a single integrated plan, whereby the stock of the corporation described in paragraph (1) becomes owned directly by the 2 corporations specifically referred to in subsection (b) or by such 2 corporations and by 1 or both of their jointly owned direct subsidiaries,

"(5) within 20 days after each transfer sale, exchange, or other disposition, the person making such transfer, sale, exchange, or other disposition notifies the Internal Revenue Service of the transaction, the date of the transaction, the basis of the stock involved, the holding period for such stock, and such other information as the Internal Revenue Service may require, and

"(6) the integrated plan is completed before the date 4 years after the date of the enactment of the Technical and Miscellaneous Revenue Act of 1988. In the case of any underpayment attributable to a failure to meet any requirement of this subsection, the period during which such underpayment may be assessed shall in no event expire before the date 5 years after the date of the enactment of the Technical and Miscellaneous Revenue Act of 1988.

"(b) Member of a qualified ownership group.

For purposes of this section, the term 'member of a qualified ownership group' means a corporation incorporated on June 16, 1890, under the laws of the Netherlands or a corporation incorporated on October 18, 1897, under the laws of the United Kingdom or any corporation owned directly or indirectly by either or both such corporations.

"(c) Election.— [Repealed by Sec. 1012(m)(2) of P.L. 100-647, see above]

"(d) Effective date.

"The provisions of this section shall take effect on the date of the enactment of this section."

—P.L. 99-514, Sec. 1810(f)(1)(A), substituted ", section 1445, and section 6039C" for "and section 6039C" in para. (i)(1) . . . Sec. 1810(f)(1)(B), substituted "this section, section 1445, and section 6039C" for "this section and section 6039C" in para. (i)(4), effective for any disposition on or after 1/1/85.

In 1983, P.L. 97-448, Sec. 306(a)(1)(A)(i), redesignated the second Sec. 201(c) of P.L. 97-248 as Sec. 201(d) of P.L. 97-248, see below.

In 1982, P.L. 97-248, Sec. 201(d)(6), [as redesignated by Sec. 306(a)(1)(A)(i) of P.L. 97-448, see above] amended subpara. (a)(2)(A), effective for tax. yrs. begin. after 12/31/82.

Prior to amendment, subpara. (a)(2)(A) read as follows:

"(A) In general. In the case of any nonresident alien individual, the amount determined under section 55(a)(1)(A) for the taxable year shall not be less than 20 percent of whichever of the following is the least:

"(i) the individual's alternative minimum taxable income (as defined in section 55(b)(1)) for the taxable year,

2,541

"(ii) the individual's net United States real property gain for the taxable year, or (iii) $60,000.

In 1981, P.L. 97-34, Sec. 831(a)(1), substituted "United States or the Virgin Islands" for "United States" in clause (c)(1)(A)(i) . . . Sec. 831(b), amended subpara. (c)(4)(B) . . . Sec. 831(c), amended subpara. (d)(1)(B) . . . Sec. 831(d), amended subsec. (i) . . . Sec. 831(f), added subsec. (j) . . . Sec. 831(g), added subsecs. (k) and (l) . . . Sec. 831(h), amended Sec. 1125[(c)](2)(B) of P.L. 96-499 [part of the effective date for amendment made by Sec. 1122(a) of P.L. 96-499, see below] effective for dispositions after 6/18/80 in tax. yrs. end. after 6/18/80.
Prior to amendment, subpara. (c)(4)(B) read as follows:
"(B) Interests held by partnerships, etc. United States real property interests held by a partnership, trust, or estate shall be treated as owned proportionately by its partners or beneficiaries."
Prior to amendment, subpara. (d)(1)(B) read as follows:
"(B) Exception where there is a carryover basis. Subparagraph (A) shall not apply if the basis of the distributed property in the hands of the distributee is the same as the adjusted basis of such property before the distribution increased by the amount of any gain recognized by the distributing corporation."
Prior to amendment, subsec. (i) read as follows:
"(i) Election by foreign corporation to be treated as domestic corporation.
"(1) In general. If—
"(A) a foreign corporation has a permanent establishment in the United States, and
"(B) under any treaty, such permanent establishment may not be treated less favorably than domestic corporations carrying on the same activities,
then such foreign corporation may make an election to be treated as a domestic corporation for purposes of this section and section 6039C.
"(2) Revocation only with consent. An election under paragraph (1), once made, may be revoked only with the consent of the Secretary.
"(3) Making of election. An election under paragraph (1) may be made only subject to such conditions as may be prescribed by the Secretary."
Prior to amendment, Sec. 1125(c)(2)(B) of P.L. 96-499 read as follows:
"(B) the new treaty is signed before January 1, 1985, then paragraph (1) shall be applied with respect to obligations under the old treaty by substituting for 'December 31, 1984' the date (not later than 2 years after the new treaty was signed) specified in the new treaty (or accompanying exchange of notes)."

In 1980, P.L. 96-499, Sec. 1122(a), added Code Sec. 897, effective for dispositions after 6/18/80. Secs. 1125(c) [as amended by Sec. 831(h) of P.L. 97-34, see above] and (d) of this Act provide:
"(c) Special rule for treaties.
"(1) In general. Except as provided in paragraph (2), after December 31, 1984, nothing in section 894(a) or 7852(d) of the Internal Revenue Code of 1954 or in any other provision of law shall be treated as requiring, by reason of any treaty obligation of the United States, an exemption from (or reduction of) any tax imposed by section 871 or 882 of such Code on a gain described in section 897 of such Code.
"(2) Special rule for treaties renegotiated before 1985. If—
"(A) any treaty (hereinafter in this paragraph referred to as the 'old treaty') is renegotiated to resolve conflicts between such treaty and the provisions of section 897 of the Internal Revenue Code of 1954, and
"(B) the new treaty is signed on or after January 1, 1981, and before January 1, 1985,
then paragraph (1) shall be applied with respect to obligations under the old treaty by substituting for 'December 31, 1984' the date (not later than 2 years after the new treaty was signed) specified in the new treaty (or accompanying exchange of notes)."
"(d) Adjustment in basis for certain transactions between related persons.
"(1) In general. In the case of any disposition after December 31, 1979, of a United States real property interest (as defined in section 897(c) of the Internal Revenue Code of 1954) to a related person (within the meaning of section 453(f)(1) of such Code), the basis of the interest in the hands of the person acquiring it shall be reduced by the amount of any nontaxed gain.
"(2) Nontaxed gain. For purposes of paragraph (1), the term 'nontaxed gain' means any gain which is not subject to tax under section 871(b)(1) or 882(a)(1) of such Code—
"(A) because the disposition occurred before June 19, 1980, or
"(B) because of any treaty obligation of the United States."

Sec. 898. Taxable year of certain foreign corporations.
(a) General rule.
For purposes of this title, the taxable year of any specified foreign corporation shall be the required year determined under subsection (c).
(b) Specified foreign corporation.
For purposes of this section—
(1) **In general.** The term "specified foreign corporation" means any foreign corporation—
(A) which is treated as a controlled foreign corporation for any purpose under subpart F of part III of this subchapter, and
(B) with respect to which the ownership requirements of paragraph (2) are met.

(2) **Ownership requirements.**
(A) In general. The ownership requirements of this paragraph are met with respect to any foreign corporation if a United States shareholder owns, on each testing day, more than 50 percent of—
(i) the total voting power of all classes of stock of such corporation entitled to vote, or
(ii) the total value of all classes of stock of such corporation.
(B) Ownership. For purposes of subparagraph (A), the rules of subsections (a) and (b) of section 958 shall apply in determining ownership.
(3) **United States shareholder.** The term "United States shareholder" has the meaning given to such term by section 951(b), except that, in the case of a foreign corporation having related person insurance income (as defined in section 953(c)(2)), the Secretary may treat any person as a United States shareholder for purposes of this section if such person is treated as a United States shareholder under section 953(c)(1).
(c) Determination of required year.
(1) **In general.** The required year is—
(A) the majority U.S. shareholder year, or
(B) if there is no majority U.S. shareholder year, the taxable year prescribed under regulations.
(2) **1-month deferral allowed.** A specified foreign corporation may elect, in lieu of the taxable year under paragraph (1)(A), a taxable year beginning 1 month earlier than the majority U.S. shareholder year.
(3) **Majority U.S. shareholder year.**
(A) In general. For purposes of this subsection, the term "majority U.S. shareholder year" means the taxable year (if any) which, on each testing day, constituted the taxable year of—
(i) each United States shareholder described in subsection (b)(2)(A), and
(ii) each United States shareholder not described in clause (i) whose stock was treated as owned under subsection (b)(2)(B) by any shareholder described in such clause.
(B) Testing day. The testing days shall be—
(i) the first day of the corporation's taxable year (determined without regard to this section), or
(ii) the days during such representative period as the Secretary may prescribe.

In 2004, P.L. 108-357, Sec. 413(c)(13)(A), amended subpara. (b)(1)(A) . . . Sec. 413(c)(13)(B), deleted "and sections 551(f) and 554, whichever are applicable," after "of section 958" in subpara. (b)(2)(B) . . . Sec. 413(c)(13)(C), amended para. (b)(3) . . . Sec. 413(c)(13)(D), amended subsec. (c), effective for tax. yrs. of foreign corporations begin. after 12/31/2004, and for tax. yrs. of United States shareholders with or within which such tax. yrs. of foreign corporations end.
Prior to amendment, subpara. (b)(1)(A) read as follows:
"(A) which is—
"(i) treated as a controlled foreign corporation for any purpose under subpart F of part III of this subchapter, or
"(ii) a foreign personal holding company (as defined in section 552), and"
Prior to amendment, para. (b)(3) read as follows:
"(3) United States shareholder.
"(A) In general. The term 'United States shareholder' has the meaning given to such term by section 951(b), except that, in the case of a foreign corporation having related person insurance income (as defined in section 953(c)(2)), the Secretary may treat any person as a United States shareholder for purposes of this section if such person is treated as a United States shareholder under section 953(c)(1).
"(B) Foreign personal holding companies. In the case of any foreign personal holding company (as defined in section 552) which is not a specified foreign corporation by reason of paragraph (1)(A)(i), the term 'United States shareholder' means any person who is treated as a United States shareholder under section 551."
Prior to amendment, subsec. (c) read as follows:
"(c) Determination of required year.
"(1) Controlled foreign corporations.

Income from foreign sources — Code Sec. 901(b)(5)

"(A) In general. In the case of a specified foreign corporation described in subsection (b)(1)(A)(i), the required year is—
"(i) the majority U.S. shareholder year, or
"(ii) if there is no majority U.S. shareholder year, the taxable year prescribed under regulations.
"(B) 1-month deferral allowed. A specified foreign corporation may elect, in lieu of the taxable year under subparagraph (A)(i), a taxable year beginning 1 month earlier than the majority U.S. shareholder year.
"(C) Majority U.S. shareholder year.
"(i) In general. For purposes of this subsection, the term 'majority U.S. shareholder year' means the taxable year (if any) which, on each testing day, constituted the taxable year of—
"(I) each United States shareholder described in subsection (b)(2)(A), and
"(II) each United States shareholder not described in subclause (I) whose stock was treated as owned under subsection (b)(2)(B) by any shareholder described in such subclause.
"(ii) Testing day. The testing days shall be—
"(I) the first day of the corporation's taxable year (determined without regard to this section), or
"(II) the days during such representative period as the Secretary may prescribe.
"(2) Foreign personal holding companies. In the case of a foreign personal holding company described in subsection (b)(3)(B), the required year shall be determined under paragraph (1), except that subparagraph (B) of paragraph (1) shall not apply."

In 1989, P.L. 101-239, Sec. 7401(a), added Code Sec. 898, effective for tax. yrs. of foreign corporations begin. after 7/10/89. Sec. 7401(d)(2) of this Act provides:
"(2) Special rules.— If any foreign corporation is required by the amendments made by this section to change its taxable year for its first taxable year beginning after July 10, 1989—
"(A) such change shall be treated as initiated by the taxpayer,
"(B) such change shall be treated as having been made with the consent of the Secretary of the Treasury or his delegate, and
"(C) if, by reason of such change, any United States person is required to include in gross income for 1 taxable year amounts attributable to 2 taxable years of such foreign corporation, the amount which would otherwise be required to be included in gross income for such 1 taxable year by reason of the short taxable year of the foreign corporation resulting from such change shall be included in gross income ratably over the 4-taxable-year period beginning with such 1 taxable year."

PART III.— INCOME FROM SOURCES WITHOUT THE UNITED STATES

Subpart
A. Foreign tax credit.
B. Earned income of citizens or residents of United States.
C. [Repealed] Taxation of foreign sales corporations.
D. Possessions of the United States.
E. [Repealed] Qualifying foreign trade income.
F. Controlled foreign corporations.
G. Export trade corporations.
H. [Repealed] Income of certain nonresident United States citizens subject to foreign community property laws.
I. Admissibility of documentation maintained in foreign countries.
J. Foreign currency transactions.

In 2004, P.L. 108-357, Sec. 101(b)(2), deleted the heading for subpart E.
In 1984, P.L. 98-369, Sec. 802(c)(4), added the heading for subpart C.
In 1982, P.L. 97-248, Sec. 337(b), added the heading of subpart I.
In 1976, P.L. 94-455, Sec. 1052(c)(7), deleted the heading for subpart C.
In 1966, P.L. 89-809, Sec. 105, added the heading of subpart H.
In 1962, added the headings of subparts F and G.

SUBPART A.— FOREIGN TAX CREDIT

Sec.
901. Taxes of foreign countries and of possessions of United States.
902. Deemed paid credit where domestic corporation owns 10 percent or more of voting stock of foreign corporation.
903. Credit for taxes in lieu of income, etc., taxes.
904. Limitation on credit.
905. Applicable rules.
906. Nonresident alien individuals and foreign corporations.
907. Special rules in case of foreign oil and gas income.
908. Reduction of credit for participation in or cooperation with an international boycott.
909. Suspension of taxes and credits until related income taken into account.

In 2010, P.L. 111-226, Sec. 211(b), added item 909.
In 1986, P.L. 99-514, Sec. 1202(d), amended item 902.
Prior to amendment, item 902 read as follows:
"902. Credit for corporate stockholder in foreign corporation."
In 1976, P.L. 94-455, Sec. 1031(b), added item 908.
In 1975, P.L. 94-12, Sec. 602(a), added item 907.
In 1966, P.L. 89-809, Sec. 106, added item 906.

Sec. 901. Taxes of foreign countries and of possessions of United States.

(a) Allowance of credit.

If the taxpayer chooses to have the benefits of this subpart, the tax imposed by this chapter shall, subject to the limitation of section 904, be credited with the amounts provided in the applicable paragraph of subsection (b) plus, in the case of a corporation, the taxes deemed to have been paid under sections 902 and 960. Such choice for any taxable year may be made or changed at any time before the expiration of the period prescribed for making a claim for credit or refund of the tax imposed by this chapter for such taxable year. The credit shall not be allowed against any tax treated as a tax not imposed by this chapter under section 26(b).

(b) Amount allowed.

Subject to the limitation of section 904, the following amounts shall be allowed as the credit under subsection (a):

(1) Citizens and domestic corporations. In the case of a citizen of the United States and of a domestic corporation, the amount of any income, war profits, and excess profits taxes paid or accrued during the taxable year to any foreign country or to any possession of the United States; and

(2) Resident of the United States or Puerto Rico. In the case of a resident of the United States and in the case of an individual who is a bona fide resident of Puerto Rico during the entire taxable year, the amount of any such taxes paid or accrued during the taxable year to any possession of the United States; and

(3) Alien resident of the United States or Puerto Rico. In the case of an alien resident of the United States and in the case of an alien individual who is a bona fide resident of Puerto Rico during the entire taxable year, the amount of any such taxes paid or accrued during the taxable year to any foreign country; and

(4) Nonresident alien individuals and foreign corporations. In the case of any nonresident alien individual not described in section 876 and in the case of any foreign corporation, the amount determined pursuant to section 906; and

(5) Partnerships and estates. In the case of any person described in paragraph (1), (2), (3), or (4), who is a member of a partnership or a beneficiary of an estate or trust, the amount of his proportionate share of the taxes (described in such paragraph) of the partnership or the estate or trust paid or accrued during the taxable year to a foreign country or to any possession of the United States, as the case may be. Under rules or regulations prescribed by the Secretary, in the case of any foreign trust of which the settlor or another person would be treated as owner of any portion of the trust under subpart E but for section 672(f), the allocable amount of any income, war profits, and excess profits taxes imposed by any foreign country or possession of the United States on the settlor or such other person in respect of trust income.

(c) Similar credit required for certain alien residents.
Whenever the President finds that—

(1) a foreign country, in imposing income, war profits, and excess profits taxes, does not allow to citizens of the United States residing in such foreign country a credit for any such taxes paid or accrued to the United States or any foreign country, as the case may be, similar to the credit allowed under subsection (b)(3),

(2) such foreign country, when requested by the United States to do so, has not acted to provide such a similar credit to citizens of the United States residing in such foreign country, and

(3) it is in the public interest to allow the credit under subsection (b)(3) to citizens or subjects of such foreign country only if it allows such a similar credit to citizens of the United States residing in such foreign country,

the President shall proclaim that, for taxable years beginning while the proclamation remains in effect, the credit under subsection (b)(3) shall be allowed to citizens or subjects of such foreign country only if such foreign country, in imposing income, war profits, and excess profits taxes, allows to citizens of the United States residing in such foreign country such a similar credit.

(d) Treatment of dividends from a DISC or former DISC.
For purposes of this subpart, dividends from a DISC or former DISC (as defined in section 992(a)) shall be treated as dividends from a foreign corporation to the extent such dividends are treated under part I as income from sources without the United States.

(e) Foreign taxes on mineral income.

(1) **Reduction in amount allowed.** Notwithstanding subsection (b), the amount of any income, war profits, and excess profits taxes paid or accrued during the taxable year to any foreign country or possession of the United States with respect to foreign mineral income from sources within such country or possession which would (but for this paragraph) be allowed under such subsection shall be reduced by the amount (if any) by which—

(A) the amount of such taxes (or, if smaller, the amount of the tax which would be computed under this chapter with respect to such income determined without the deduction allowed under section 613), exceeds

(B) the amount of the tax computed under this chapter with respect to such income.

(2) **Foreign mineral income defined.** For purposes of paragraph (1), the term "foreign mineral income" means income derived from the extraction of minerals from mines, wells, or other natural deposits, the processing of such minerals into their primary products, and the transportation, distribution, or sale of such minerals or primary products. Such term includes, but is not limited to—

(A) dividends received from a foreign corporation in respect of which taxes are deemed paid by the taxpayer under section 902, to the extent such dividends are attributable to foreign mineral income, and

(B) that portion of the taxpayer's distributive share of the income of partnerships attributable to foreign mineral income.

(f) Certain payments for oil or gas not considered as taxes.
Notwithstanding subsection (b) and sections 902 and 960, the amount of any income, or profits, and excess profits taxes paid or accrued during the taxable year to any foreign country in connection with the purchase and sale of oil or gas extracted in such country is not to be considered as tax for purposes of section 275(a) and this section if—

(1) the taxpayer has no economic interest in the oil or gas to which section 611(a) applies, and

(2) either such purchase or sale is at a price which differs from the fair market value for such oil or gas at the time of such purchase or sale.

(g) Certain taxes paid with respect to distributions from possessions corporations.

(1) **In general.** For purposes of this chapter, any tax of a foreign country or possession of the United States which is paid or accrued with respect to any distribution from a corporation—

(A) to the extent that such distribution is attributable to periods during which such corporation is a possessions corporation, and

(B)(i) if a dividends received deduction is allowable with respect to such distribution under part VIII of subchapter B, or

(ii) to the extent that such distribution is received in connection with a liquidation or other transaction with respect to which gain or loss is not recognized,

shall not be treated as income, war profits, or excess profits taxes paid or accrued to a foreign country or possession of the United States, and no deduction shall be allowed under this title with respect to any amount so paid or accrued.

(2) **Possessions corporation.** For purposes of paragraph (1), a corporation shall be treated as a possessions corporation for any period during which an election under section 936 applied to such corporation, during which section 931 (as in effect on the day before the date of the enactment [10/4/76] of the Tax Reform Act of 1976) applied to such corporation, or during which section 957(c) (as in effect on the day before the date of the enactment [10/22/86] of the Tax Reform Act of 1986) applied to such corporation.

(h) Repeal.

(i) Taxes used to provide subsidies.
Any income, war profits, or excess profits tax shall not be treated as a tax for purposes of this title to the extent—

(1) the amount of such tax is used (directly or indirectly) by the country imposing such tax to provide a subsidy by any means to the taxpayer, a related person (within the meaning of section 482), or any party to the transaction or to a related transaction, and

(2) such subsidy is determined (directly or indirectly) by reference to the amount of such tax, or the base used to compute the amount of such tax.

(j) Denial of foreign tax credit, etc., with respect to certain foreign countries.

(1) **In general.** Notwithstanding any other provision of this part—

(A) no credit shall be allowed under subsection (a) for any income, war profits, or excess profits taxes paid or accrued (or deemed paid under section 902 or 960) to any country if such taxes are with respect to income attributable to a period during which this subsection applies to such country, and

(B) subsections (a), (b), and (c) of section 904 and sections 902 and 960 shall be applied separately with respect to income attributable to such a period from sources within such country.

(2) **Countries to which subsection applies.**

(A) In general. This subsection shall apply to any foreign country—

(i) the government of which the United States does not recognize, unless such government is otherwise eligible to purchase defense articles or services under the Arms Export Control Act,
(ii) with respect to which the United States has severed diplomatic relations,
(iii) with respect to which the United States has not severed diplomatic relations but does not conduct such relations, or
(iv) which the Secretary of State has, pursuant to section 6(j) of the Export Administration Act of 1979, as amended, designated as a foreign country which repeatedly provides support for acts of international terrorisms.
(B) Period for which subsection applies. This subsection shall apply to any foreign country described in subparagraph (A) during the period—
(i) beginning on the later of—
(I) January 1, 1987, or
(II) 6 months after such country becomes a country described in subparagraph (A), and
(ii) ending on the date the Secretary of State certifies to the Secretary of the Treasury that such country is no longer described in subparagraph (A).
(3) **Taxes allowed as a deduction, etc.** Sections 275 and 78 shall not apply to any tax which is not allowable as a credit under subsection (a) by reason of this subsection.
(4) **Regulations.** The Secretary shall prescribe such regulations as may be necessary or appropriate to carry out the purposes of this subsection, including regulations which treat income paid through 1 or more entities as derived from a foreign country to which this subsection applies if such income was, without regard to such entities, derived from such country.
(5) **Waiver of denial.**
(A) In general. Paragraph (1) shall not apply with respect to taxes paid or accrued to a country if the President —
(i) determines that a waiver of the application of such paragraph is in the national interest of the United States and will expand trade and investment opportunities for United States companies in such country; and
(ii) reports such waiver under subparagraph (B).
(B) Report. Not less than 30 days before the date on which a waiver is granted under this paragraph, the President shall report to Congress—
(i) the intention to grant such waiver; and
(ii) the reason for the determination under subparagraph (A)(i).
(k) **Minimum holding period for certain taxes on dividends.**
(1) **Withholding taxes.**
(A) In general. In no event shall a credit be allowed under subsection (a) for any withholding tax on a dividend with respect to stock in a corporation if—
(i) such stock is held by the recipient of the dividend for 15 days or less during the 31-day period beginning on the date which is 15 days before the date on which such share becomes ex-dividend with respect to such dividend, or
(ii) to the extent that the recipient of the dividend is under an obligation (whether pursuant to a short sale or otherwise) to make related payments with respect to positions in substantially similar or related property.

(B) Withholding tax. For purposes of this paragraph, the term "withholding tax" includes any tax determined on a gross basis; but does not include any tax which is in the nature of a prepayment of a tax imposed on a net basis.
(2) **Deemed paid taxes.** In the case of income, war profits, or excess profits taxes deemed paid under section 853, 902, or 960 through a chain of ownership of stock in 1 or more corporations, no credit shall be allowed under subsection (a) for such taxes if—
(A) any stock of any corporation in such chain (the ownership of which is required to obtain credit under subsection (a) for such taxes) is held for less than the period described in paragraph (1)(A)(i), or
(B) the corporation holding the stock is under an obligation referred to in paragraph (1)(A)(ii).
(3) **45-day rule in the case of certain preference dividends.** In the case of stock having preference in dividends and dividends with respect to such stock which are attributable to a period or periods aggregating in excess of 366 days, paragraph (1)(A)(i) shall be applied—
(A) by substituting "45 days" for "15 days" each place it appears, and
(B) by substituting "91-day period" for "31-day period".
(4) **Exception for certain taxes paid by securities dealers.**
(A) In general. Paragraphs (1) and (2) shall not apply to any qualified tax with respect to any security held in the active conduct in a foreign country of a business as a securities dealer of any person—
(i) who is registered as a securities broker or dealer under section 15(a) of the Securities Exchange Act of 1934,
(ii) who is registered as a Government securities broker or dealer under section 15C(a) of such Act, or
(iii) who is licensed or authorized in such foreign country to conduct securities activities in such country and is subject to bona fide regulation by a securities regulating authority of such country.
(B) Qualified tax. For purposes of subparagraph (A), the term "qualified tax" means a tax paid to a foreign country (other than the foreign country referred to in subparagraph (A)) if—
(i) the dividend to which such tax is attributable is subject to taxation on a net basis by the country referred to in subparagraph (A), and
(ii) such country allows a credit against its net basis tax for the full amount of the tax paid to such other foreign country.
(C) Regulations. The Secretary may prescribe such regulations as may be appropriate to carry out this paragraph, including regulations to prevent the abuse of the exception provided by this paragraph and to treat other taxes as qualified taxes.
(5) **Certain rules to apply.** For purposes of this subsection, the rules of paragraphs (3) and (4) of section 246(c) shall apply.
(6) **Treatment of bona fide sales.** If a person's holding period is reduced by reason of the application of the rules of section 246(c)(4) to any contract for the bona fide sale of stock, the determination of whether such person's holding period meets the requirements of paragraph (2) with respect to taxes deemed paid under section 902 or 960 shall be made as of the date such contract is entered into.

2,545

(7) Taxes allowed as deduction, etc. Sections 275 and 78 shall not apply to any tax which is not allowable as a credit under subsection (a) by reason of this subsection.

(l) Minimum holding period for withholding taxes on gain and income other than dividends etc.

(1) In general. In no event shall a credit be allowed under subsection (a) for any withholding tax (as defined in subsection (k)) on any item of income or gain with respect to any property if—

(A) such property is held by the recipient of the item for 15 days or less during the 31-day period beginning on the date which is 15 days before the date on which the right to receive payment of such item arises, or

(B) to the extent that the recipient of the item is under an obligation (whether pursuant to a short sale or otherwise) to make related payments with respect to positions in substantially similar or related property.

This paragraph shall not apply to any dividend to which subsection (k) applies.

(2) Exception for taxes paid by dealers.

(A) In general. Paragraph (1) shall not apply to any qualified tax with respect to any property held in the active conduct in a foreign country of a business as a dealer in such property.

(B) Qualified tax. For purposes of subparagraph (A), the term "qualified tax" means a tax paid to a foreign country (other than the foreign country referred to in subparagraph (A)) if—

(i) the item to which such tax is attributable is subject to taxation on a net basis by the country referred to in subparagraph (A), and

(ii) such country allows a credit against its net basis tax for the full amount of the tax paid to such other foreign country.

(C) Dealer. For purposes of subparagraph (A), the term "dealer" means—

(i) with respect to a security, any person to whom paragraphs (1) and (2) of subsection (k) would not apply by reason of paragraph (4) thereof, and

(ii) with respect to any other property, any person with respect to whom such property is described in section 1221(a)(1).

(D) Regulations. The Secretary may prescribe such regulations as may be appropriate to carry out this paragraph, including regulations to prevent the abuse of the exception provided by this paragraph and to treat other taxes as qualified taxes.

(3) Exceptions. The Secretary may by regulation provide that paragraph (1) shall not apply to property where the Secretary determines that the application of paragraph (1) to such property is not necessary to carry out the purposes of this subsection.

(4) Certain rules to apply. Rules similar to the rules of paragraphs (5), (6), and (7) of subsection (k) shall apply for purposes of this subsection.

(5) Determination of holding period. Holding periods shall be determined for purposes of this subsection without regard to section 1235 or any similar rule.

(m) Denial of foreign tax credit with respect to foreign income not subject to United States taxation by reason of covered asset acquisitions.

(1) In general. In the case of a covered asset acquisition, the disqualified portion of any foreign income tax determined with respect to the income or gain attributable to the relevant foreign assets—

(A) shall not be taken into account in determining the credit allowed under subsection (a), and

(B) in the case of a foreign income tax paid by a section 902 corporation (as defined in section 909(d)(5)), shall not be taken into account for purposes of section 902 or 960.

(2) Covered asset acquisition. For purposes of this section, the term "covered asset acquisition" means—

(A) a qualified stock purchase (as defined in section 338(d)(3)) to which section 338(a) applies,

(B) any transaction which—

(i) is treated as an acquisition of assets for purposes of this chapter, and

(ii) is treated as the acquisition of stock of a corporation (or is disregarded) for purposes of the foreign income taxes of the relevant jurisdiction,

(C) any acquisition of an interest in a partnership which has an election in effect under section 754, and

(D) to the extent provided by the Secretary, any other similar transaction.

(3) Disqualified portion. For purposes of this section—

(A) In general. The term "disqualified portion" means, with respect to any covered asset acquisition, for any taxable year, the ratio (expressed as a percentage) of—

(i) the aggregate basis differences (but not below zero) allocable to such taxable year under subparagraph (B) with respect to all relevant foreign assets, divided by

(ii) the income on which the foreign income tax referred to in paragraph (1) is determined (or, if the taxpayer fails to substantiate such income to the satisfaction of the Secretary, such income shall be determined by dividing the amount of such foreign income tax by the highest marginal tax rate applicable to such income in the relevant jurisdiction).

(B) Allocation of basis difference. For purposes of subparagraph (A)(i)—

(i) In general. The basis difference with respect to any relevant foreign asset shall be allocated to taxable years using the applicable cost recovery method under this chapter.

(ii) Special rule for disposition of assets. Except as otherwise provided by the Secretary, in the case of the disposition of any relevant foreign asset—

(I) the basis difference allocated to the taxable year which includes the date of such disposition shall be the excess of the basis difference with respect to such asset over the aggregate basis difference with respect to such asset which has been allocated under clause (i) to all prior taxable years, and

(II) no basis difference with respect to such asset shall be allocated under clause (i) to any taxable year thereafter.

(C) Basis difference.

(i) In general. The term "basis difference" means, with respect to any relevant foreign asset, the excess of—

(I) the adjusted basis of such asset immediately after the covered asset acquisition, over

(II) the adjusted basis of such asset immediately before the covered asset acquisition.

(ii) Built-in loss assets. In the case of a relevant foreign asset with respect to which the amount described in clause (i)(II) exceeds the amount described in clause (i)(I), such excess shall be taken into account under this subsection as a basis difference of a negative amount.

Income from foreign sources   Code Sec. 901

(iii) Special rule for section 338 elections. In the case of a covered asset acquisition described in paragraph (2)(A), the covered asset acquisition shall be treated for purposes of this subparagraph as occurring at the close of the acquisition date (as defined in section 338(h)(2)).

(4) Relevant foreign assets. For purposes of this section, the term "relevant foreign asset" means, with respect to any covered asset acquisition, any asset (including any goodwill, going concern value, or other intangible) with respect to such acquisition if income, deduction, gain, or loss attributable to such asset is taken into account in determining the foreign income tax referred to in paragraph (1).

(5) Foreign income tax. For purposes of this section, the term "foreign income tax" means any income, war profits, or excess profits tax paid or accrued to any foreign country or to any posses7 sion of the United States.

(6) Taxes allowed as a deduction, etc. Sections 275 and 78 shall not apply to any tax which is not allowable as a credit under subsection (a) by reason of this subsection.

(7) Regulations. The Secretary may issue such regulations or other guidance as is necessary or appropriate to carry out the purposes of this sub15 section, including to exempt from the application of this subsection certain covered asset acquisitions, and relevant foreign assets with respect to which the basis difference is de minimis.

(n) Cross reference.

(1) For deductions of income, war profits, and excess profits taxes paid to a foreign country or a possession of the United States, see sections 164 and 275.

(2) For right of each partner to make election under this section, see section 703(b).

(3) For right of estate or trust to the credit for taxes imposed by foreign countries and possessions of the United States under this section, see section 642(a).

(4) For reduction of credit for failure of a United States person to furnish certain information with respect to a foreign corporation or partnership controlled by him, see section 6038.

In 2010, P.L. 111-226, Sec. 212(a), redesignated subsec. (m) as subsec. (n) and added new subsec. (m), effective to covered asset acquisitions (as defined in section 901(m)(2) of the Internal Revenue Code of 1986, as added by this section) after 12/31/2010. . . . Sec. 212(b)(2), of this Act, reads as follows:

"(2) TRANSITION RULE. The amendments made by this section shall not apply to any covered asset acquisition (as so defined) with respect to which the transferor and the transferee are not related if such acquisition is—

"(A) made pursuant to a written agreement which was binding on January 1, 2011, and at all times thereafter,

"(B) described in a ruling request submitted to the Internal Revenue Service on or before July 29, 2010, or

"(C) described on or before January 1, 2011, in a public announcement or in a filing with the Securities and Exchange Commission.

"(3) RELATED PERSONS. For purposes of this subsection, a person shall be treated as related to another person if the relationship between such persons is described in section 267 or 707(b) of the Internal Revenue Code of 1986."

In 2007, P.L. 110-172, Sec. 11(g)(9), deleted subsec. (h), enacted 12/29/2007. Prior to deletion, subsec. (h) read as follows:

"(h) Taxes paid with respect to foreign trade income.

"No credit shall be allowed under this section for any income, war profits, and excess profits taxes paid or accrued with respect to the foreign trade income (within the meaning of section 923(b)) of a FSC, other than section 923(a)(2) non-exempt income (within the meaning of section 927(d)(6))."

In 2005, P.L. 109-135, Sec. 403(aa)(2), deleted "if such security were stock" after "paragraph (4) thereof" in clause (l)(2)(C)(i), effective for amounts paid or accrued more than 30 days after 10/22/2004 as if included in Sec. 832 of the American Jobs Creation Act of 2004, P.L. 108-357.

In 2004, P.L. 108-357, Sec. 405(b), substituted "any person" for "any individual" in para. (b)(5), effective for taxes of foreign corporations for tax. yrs. of such corporations begin. after 10/22/2004.

—P.L. 108-357, Sec. 832(a), redesignated subsec. (l) as (m) and added subsec. (l) . . . Sec. 832(b), added "on dividends" after "taxes" in the heading of subsec. (k), effective for amounts paid or accrued more than 30 days after 10/22/2004.

—P.L. 108-311, Sec. 406(g)(1), substituted "31-day period" for "30-day period" in clause (k)(1)(A)(i) . . . Sec. 406(g)(2)(A), substituted "91-day period" for "90-day period" in subpara. (k)(3)(B) . . . Sec. 406(g)(2)(B), substituted "31-day period" for "30-day period" in subpara. (k)(3)(B), effective for dividends paid or accrued more than 30 days after 8/5/97 as if included in Sec. 1053 of the Taxpayer Relief Act of 1997, P.L. 105-34.

In 2000, P.L. 106-200, Sec. 601(a), added para. (j)(5), effective on or after 2/1/2001.

In 1998, P.L. 105-206, Sec. 6010(k)(3), substituted "business as a securities dealer" for "securities business" in subpara. (k)(4)(A), effective for dividends paid or accrued more than 30 days after 8/5/97.

In 1997, P.L. 105-34, Sec. 1053(a), redesignated subsec. (k) as subsec. (l) and added a new subsec. (k), effective for dividends paid or accrued more than 30 days after 8/5/97.

—P.L. 105-34, Sec. 1142(e)(4), substituted "foreign corporation or partnership" for "foreign corporation" in para. (k)(4) [before redesignation by Sec. 1053(a) of this Act, see above], effective for annual accounting periods begin. after 8/5/97.

In 1996, P.L. 104-188, Sec. 1904(b)(2), added the sentence at the end of para. (b)(5), effective as provided in Secs. 1904(d) and (e) of this Act, which read as follows:

"(d) Effective date.

"(1) In general. Except as provided by paragraph (2), the amendments made by this section shall take effect on the date of the enactment of this Act.

"(2) Exception for certain trusts. The amendments made by this section shall not apply to any trust—

"(A) which is treated as owned by the grantor under section 676 or 677 (other than subsection (a)(3) thereof) of the Internal Revenue Code of 1986, and

"(B) which is in existence on September 19, 1995.

The preceding sentence shall not apply to the portion of any such trust attributable to any transfer to such trust after September 19, 1995.

"(e) Transitional rule. If—

"(1) by reason of the amendments made by this section, any person other than a United States person ceases to be treated as the owner of a portion of a domestic trust, and

"(2) before January 1, 1997, such trust becomes a foreign trust, or the assets of such trust are transferred to a foreign trust,

no tax shall be imposed by section 1491 of the Internal Revenue Code of 1986 by reason of such trust becoming a foreign trust or the assets of such trust being transferred to a foreign trust."

In 1993, P.L. 103-149, Sec. 4(b)(8)(A), deleted subpara. (j)(2)(C), effective 11/23/93.

Prior to deletion, subpara. (j)(2)(C) read as follows:

"(C) Special rule for South Africa.

"(i) In general. In addition to any period during which this subsection would otherwise apply to South Africa, this subsection shall apply to South Africa during the period—

"(I) beginning on January 1, 1988, and

"(II) ending on the date the Secretary of State certifies to the Secretary of the Treasury that South Africa meets the requirements of section 311(a) of the Comprehensive Anti-Apartheid Act of 1986 (as in effect on the date of the enactment of this subparagraph).

"(ii) South Africa defined. For purposes of clause (i), the term 'South Africa' has the meaning given to such term by paragraph (6) of section 3 of the Comprehensive Anti-Apartheid Act of 1986 (as so in effect)."

—P.L. 103-149, Sec. 4(b)(8)(B), of this Act, provides:

"(B) Subparagraph (A) shall not be construed as affecting any of the transitional rules contained in Revenue Ruling 92-62 which apply by reason of the termination of the period for which section 901(j) of the Internal Revenue Code of 1986 was applicable to South Africa."

In 1988, P.L. 100-647, Sec. 1012(j), substituted "section 957(c) (as in effect on the day before the date of the enactment of the Tax Reform Act of 1986)" for "section 957(c)" in para. (g)(2), effective for tax. yrs. of foreign corporations begin. after 12/31/86, except that for purposes of applying Code Secs. 951(a)(1)(B) and 956, such amendments shall take effect on 8/16/86. For transitional rules see Sec. 1224(b)(2) of P.L. 99-514 reproduced at Code Sec. 957.

—P.L. 100-647, Sec. 2003(c)(1)(A), substituted "Sections 275 and 78" for "Section 275" in para. (j)(3) . . . Sec. 2003(c)(1)(B), added ", etc." after "deduction" in the heading of para. (j)(3), effective on 1/1/87.

In 1987, P.L. 100-203, Sec. 10231(a), added subpara. (j)(2)(C) . . . Sec. 10231(b)(1), substituted "during which" for "to which" in subpara. (j)(1)(A) . . . Sec. 10231(b)(2), substituted "such country" for "any country so identified" in subpara. (j)(1)(B), effective for tax. yrs. begin. after 12/31/87.

In 1986, P.L. 99-514, Sec. 112(b)(3), substituted "642(a)" for "642(a)(1)" in para. (i)(3), effective for tax. yrs. begin. after 12/31/86.

—P.L. 99-514, Sec. 1204(a), redesignated subsec. (i) as subsec. (j) [redesignated as subsec. (k) by Sec. 8041(a) of P.L. 99-509, below] and added new subsec. (i), effective for foreign taxes paid or accrued in tax. yrs. begin. after 12/31/86.

—P.L. 99-514, Sec. 1876(p)(2), substituted "section 927(d)(6))" for "section 927(d)(6)", in subsec. (h), effective for transactions made after 12/31/84, in tax. yrs. end. after 12/31/84.

—P.L. 99-509, Sec. 8041(a), redesignated subsec. (j) [as redesignated by Sec. 1204(a) of P.L. 99-514, above] as subsec. (k) and added new subsec. (j), effective 1/1/87.

In 1984, P.L. 98-369, Sec. 474(r)(20), amended the last sentence of subsec. (a), effective for tax. yrs. begin. after 12/31/83, and to carrybacks from tax. yrs. begin. after 12/31/83.

2,547

Code Sec. 901 — Income from foreign sources

Prior to amendment, the last sentence of of subsec. (a) read as follows:

"The credit shall not be allowed against the tax imposed by section 56 (relating to corporate minimum tax), against the tax imposed for the taxable year under section 72(m)(5)(B) (relating to 10 percent tax on premature distributions to key employees) section 72(q)(1) (relating to 5-percent tax on premature distributions under annuity contracts), against the tax imposed by section 402(e) (relating to tax on lump sum distributions), against the tax imposed for the taxable year by section 408(f) (relating to additional tax on income from certain retirement accounts), against the tax imposed by section 531 (relating to the tax on accumulated earnings), against the additional tax imposed for the taxable year under section 1351 (relating to recoveries of foreign expropriation losses), or against the personal holding company tax imposed by section 541."

—P.L. 98-369, Sec. 612(e)(1), substituted "section 26(b)" for "section 25(b)" in subsec. (a) as amended by Sec. 474(r)(20) of this Act, effective for interest paid or accrued after 12/31/84, on indebtedness incurred after 12/31/84.

—P.L. 98-369, Sec. 632, provided various exceptions to the amendments made by Title VI of this Act. See note following Code Sec. 103A.

—P.L. 98-369, Sec. 713(c)(1)(C), substituted "tax on premature distributions to key employees" for "tax on premature distributions to owner-employees", in subsec. (a), effective for tax. yrs. begin. after 12/31/83.

—P.L. 98-369, Sec. 801(d)(1), redesignated subsec. (h) as subsec. (i) and added new subsec. (h), effective for transactions made after 12/31/84, in tax. yrs. end. after 12/31/84.

In 1983, P.L. 97-448, Sec. 306(a)(1)(A)(i), redesignated the second Sec. 201(c) of P.L. 97-248 as Sec. 201(d) of P.L. 97-248, see below.

In 1982, P.L. 97-248, Sec. 201(d)(8)(A), substituted "(relating to corporate minimum tax)" for "(relating to minimum tax for tax preferences)" in subsec. (a), effective for tax. yrs. begin. after 12/31/82.

—P.L. 97-248, Sec. 265(b)(2)(A)(iv), added "section 72(q)(1) (relating to 5-percent tax on premature distributions under annuity contracts)" after "owner employees)" in subsec. (a), effective for distributions after 12/31/82.

In 1978, P.L. 95-600, Sec. 701(u)(1)(A), amended para. (g)(1), effective for tax. yrs. begin. after 12/31/75, except as provided in Sec. 1051(i)(2) of P.L. 94-455, see below.

Prior to amendment, para. (g)(1) read as follows:

"(1) In general. For purposes of this chapter, any tax of a foreign country or possession of the United States which is paid or accrued with respect to any distribution from a corporation, to the extent such distribution is attributable to periods during which such corporation is a possessions corporation, shall not be treated as income, war profits, or excess profits taxes paid or accrued to a foreign country or possession of the United States, and no deduction shall be allowed under this title with respect to any amount so paid or accrued."

—P.L. 95-600, Sec. 701(u)(1)(B), substituted ", during which section 931" for "or during which section 931" in para. (g)(2), and added ", or during which section 957(c) applied to such corporation" before the period at the end of para. (g)(2), effective for distributions made after 11/6/78 in tax. yrs. end. after 11/6/78.

In 1976, P.L. 94-455, Sec. 1031(b)(1), substituted "limitation" for "applicable limitation" in subsecs. (a) and (b), effective for tax. yrs. begin. after 12/31/75.

—P.L. 94-455, Sec. 1051(d)(1), amended subsec. (d), effective for tax. yrs. begin. after 12/31/75.

Prior to amendment, subsec. (d) read as follows:

"(d) Corporations treated as foreign.

"For purposes of this subpart, the following corporations shall be treated as foreign corporations:

"(1) a corporation entitled to the benefits of section 931, by reason of receiving a large percentage of its gross income from sources within a possession of the United States; and

"(2) a corporation organized under the China Trade Act, 1922 (15 U. S. C., chapter 4), and entitled to the deduction provided in section 941.

For purposes of this subpart, dividends from a DISC or former DISC (as defined in section 992(a)) shall be treated as dividends from a foreign corporation to the extent such dividends are treated under part I as income from sources without the United States."

—P.L. 94-455, Sec. 1051(d)(2), redesignated subsec. (g) as subsec. (h), and added new subsec. (g), effective for tax. yrs. begin. after 12/31/75. Sec. 1051(i)(2) of the Act provided as follows:

"(2) The amendment made by subsection (d)(2) shall not apply to any tax imposed by a possession of the United States with respect to the complete liquidation occurring before January 1, 1979, of a corporation to the extent that such tax is attributable to earnings and profits accumulated by such corporation during periods ending before January 1, 1976."

—P.L. 94-455, Sec. 1901(b)(1)(H)(iii), substituted "section 642(a)(1)" for "section 642(a)(2)" in para. (g)(3), [sic ; presumably meaning (h)(3)] as amended by this Act, effective for tax. yrs. begin. after 12/31/76.

—P.L. 94-455, Sec. 1901(b)(37)(A), deleted "under section 1333 (relating to war loss recoveries) or", after "against the additional tax imposed for the taxable year", in subsec. (a), effective for tax. yrs. begin. after 12/31/76.

In 1975, P.L. 94-12, Sec. 601(b), redesignated subsec. (f) as subsec. (g), and added new subsec. (f), effective for tax. yrs. end. after 12/31/74.

In 1974, P.L. 93-406, Sec. 2001(g)(2)(C), substituted "tax preferences", against the tax imposed for the taxable year under section 72(m)(5)(B) (relating to 10 percent tax on premature distributions to owner-employees)," for "tax preferences)", in the third sentence of subsec. (a), as amended by Sec. 2005(c)(5) of this Act, effective for distributions made in tax. yrs. begin. after 12/31/74.

—P.L. 93-406, Sec. 2002(g)(3), added "against the tax imposed for the taxable year by section 408(f) (relating to additional tax on income from certain retirement accounts)," before "against the tax imposed by section 531" in the third sentence of subsec. (a), as amended by Sec. 2005(c)(5) of this Act, effective 1/1/75.

—P.L. 93-406, Sec. 2005(c)(5), added "against the tax imposed by section 402(e) (relating to tax on lump sum distributions)," before "against the tax imposed by section 531" in the third sentence of subsec. (a), effective for distributions or payments made after 12/31/73, in tax. yrs. begin. after 12/31/73.

In 1971, P.L. 92-178, Sec. 502(b)(1), added a sentence to the end of subsec. (d), effective for tax. yrs. end. after 12/31/71, except that a corporation may not be a DISC for any tax. yr. begin. before 1/1/72.

In 1969, P.L. 91-172, Sec. 301(b)(9), added "against the tax imposed by section 56 (relating to minimum tax for tax preferences)," after "not be allowed" in the last sentence of subsec. (a), effective for tax. yrs. end. after 12/31/69.

—P.L. 91-172, Sec. 506(a)(1), redesignated subsec. (e) as subsec. (f) and added subsec. (e), effective for tax. yrs. begin. after 12/31/69.

In 1966, P.L. 89-809, Sec. 106, deleted "if the foreign country of which such alien resident is a citizen or subject, in imposing such taxes, allows a similar credit to citizens of the United States residing in such country" in para. (b)(3), added para. (b)(4), redesignated para. (b)(4) as para. (b)(5), substituted "(3), or (4)" for "or (3)", in para. (b)(5) [as redesignated], added subsec. (c), and redesignated subsecs. (c) and (d) as subsecs. (d) and (e), effective for tax. yrs. begin. after 12/31/66.

—P.L. 89-384, Sec. 1(c), added "or under section 1351 (relating to recoveries of foreign expropriation losses)" after "section 1333 (relating to war loss recoveries)" in the last sentence of subsec. (a), effective for amounts received after 12/31/64, in respect of foreign expropriation losses (as defined in Code Sec. 1351(b)) sustained after 12/31/58.

In 1964, P.L. 88-272, Sec. 207(b)(7), substituted "sections 164 and 275" for "section 164" in para. (d)(1), effective for tax. yrs. begin. after 12/31/63.

In 1962, P.L. 87-834, Sec. 9(d)(3), added subsec. (d)(4) . . . Sec. 12(b)(1), substituted "sections 902 and 960" for "section 902" in subsec. (a), effective for tax. yrs. begin. after 12/31/62.

In 1960, P.L. 86-780, Sec. 3(a), added "applicable" before "limitation" in subsecs. (a) and (b), effective for tax. yrs. begin. after 12/31/60.

—P.L. 86-780, Sec. 3(b), substituted "Such choice for any taxable year may be made or changed at any time before the expiration of the period prescribed for making a claim for credit or refund of the tax imposed by this chapter for such taxable year" for "Such choice may be made or changed at any time prior to the expiration of the period prescribed for making a claim for credit or refund of the tax against which the credit is allowable", effective for tax. yrs. begin. after 12/31/53, and end. after 8/16/54.

Sec. 902. Deemed paid credit where domestic corporation owns 10 percent or more of voting stock of foreign corporation.

(a) Taxes paid by foreign corporation treated as paid by domestic corporation.

For purposes of this subpart, a domestic corporation which owns 10 percent or more of the voting stock of a foreign corporation from which it receives dividends in any taxable year shall be deemed to have paid the same proportion of such foreign corporation's post-1986 foreign income taxes as—

(1) the amount of such dividends (determined without regard to section 78), bears to

(2) such foreign corporation's post-1986 undistributed earnings.

(b) Deemed taxes increased in case of certain lower tier corporations.

(1) **In general.** If—

(A) any foreign corporation is a member of a qualified group, and

(B) such foreign corporation owns 10 percent or more of the voting stock of another member of such group from which it receives dividends in any taxable year,

such foreign corporation shall be deemed to have paid the same proportion of such other member's post-1986 foreign income taxes as would be determined under subsection (a) if such foreign corporation were a domestic corporation.

(2) **Qualified group.** For purposes of paragraph (1), the term "qualified group" means—

(A) the foreign corporation described in subsection (a), and

(B) any other foreign corporation if—

(i) the domestic corporation owns at least 5 percent of the voting stock of such other foreign corporation

Income from foreign sources   Code Sec. 902

indirectly through a chain of foreign corporations connected through stock ownership of at least 10 percent of their voting stock,

(ii) the foreign corporation described in subsection (a) is the first tier corporation in such chain, and

(iii) such other corporation is not below the sixth tier in such chain.

The term "qualified group" shall not include any foreign corporation below the third tier in the chain referred to in clause (i) unless such foreign corporation is a controlled foreign corporation (as defined in section 957) and the domestic corporation is a United States shareholder (as defined in section 951(b)) in such foreign corporation. Paragraph (1) shall apply to those taxes paid by a member of the qualified group below the third tier only with respect to periods during which it was a controlled foreign corporation.

(c) Definitions and special rules.

For purposes of this section—

(1) Post-1986 undistributed earnings. The term "post-1986 undistributed earnings" means the amount of the earnings and profits of the foreign corporation (computed in accordance with sections 964(a) and 986) accumulated in taxable years beginning after December 31, 1986—

(A) as of the close of the taxable year of the foreign corporation in which the dividend is distributed, and

(B) without diminution by reason of dividends distributed during such taxable year.

(2) Post-1986 foreign income taxes. The term "post-1986 foreign income taxes" means the sum of—

(A) the foreign income taxes with respect to the taxable year of the foreign corporation in which the dividend is distributed, and

(B) the foreign income taxes with respect to prior taxable years beginning after December 31, 1986, to the extent such foreign taxes were not attributable to dividends distributed by the foreign corporation in prior taxable years.

(3) Special rule where foreign corporation first qualifies after December 31, 1986.

(A) In general. If the 1st day on which the requirements of subparagraph (B) are met with respect to any foreign corporation is in a taxable year of such corporation beginning after December 31, 1986, the post-1986 undistributed earnings and the post-1986 foreign income taxes of such foreign corporation shall be determined by taking into account only periods beginning on and after the 1st day of the 1st taxable year in which such requirements are met.

(B) Ownership requirements. The requirements of this subparagraph are met with respect to any foreign corporation if—

(i) 10 percent or more of the voting stock of such foreign corporation is owned by a domestic corporation, or

(ii) the requirements of subsection (b)(2) are met with respect to such foreign corporation.

(4) Foreign income taxes.

(A) In general. The term "foreign income taxes" means any income, war profits, or excess profits taxes paid by the foreign corporation to any foreign country or possession of the United States.

(B) Treatment of deemed taxes. Except for purposes of determining the amount of the post-1986 foreign income taxes of a sixth tier foreign corporation referred to in subsection (b)(2), the term "foreign income taxes" includes any such taxes deemed to be paid by the foreign corporation under this section.

(5) Accounting periods. In the case of a foreign corporation the income, war profits, and excess profits taxes of which are determined on the basis of an accounting period of less than 1 year, the word "year" as used in this subsection shall be construed to mean such accounting period.

(6) Treatment of distributions from earnings before 1987.

(A) In general. In the case of any dividend paid by a foreign corporation out of accumulated profits (as defined in this section as in effect on the day before the date of the enactment [10/22/86] of the Tax Reform Act of 1986) for taxable years beginning before the 1st taxable year taken into account in determining the post-1986 undistributed earnings of such corporation—

(i) this section (as amended by the Tax Reform Act of 1986) shall not apply, but

(ii) this section (as in effect on the day before the date of the enactment of such Act) shall apply.

(B) Dividends paid first out of post-1986 earnings. Any dividend in a taxable year beginning after December 31, 1986, shall be treated as made out of post-1986 undistributed earnings to the extent thereof.

(7) Constructive ownership through partnerships. Stock owned, directly or indirectly, by or for a partnership shall be considered as being owned proportionately by its partners. Stock considered to be owned by a person by reason of the preceding sentence shall, for purposes of applying such sentence, be treated as actually owned by such person. The Secretary may prescribe such regulations as may be necessary to carry out the purposes of this paragraph, including rules to account for special partnership allocations of dividends, credits, and other incidents of ownership of stock in determining proportionate ownership.

(8) Regulations. The Secretary shall provide such regulations as may be necessary or appropriate to carry out the provisions of this section and section 960, including provisions which provide for the separate application of this section and section 960 to reflect the separate application of section 904 to separate types of income and loss.

(d) Cross references.

(1) For inclusion in gross income of an amount equal to taxes deemed paid under subsection (a), see section 78.

(2) For application of subsections (a) and (b) with respect to taxes deemed paid in a prior taxable year by a United States shareholder with respect to a controlled foreign corporation, see section 960.

(3) For reduction of credit with respect to dividends paid out of post-1986 undistributed earnings for years for which certain information is not furnished, see section 6038.

In 2004, P.L. 108-357, Sec. 405(a), redesignated para. (c)(7) as (c)(8) and added para. (c)(7), effective for taxes of foreign corporations for tax. yrs. of such corporations begin. after 10/22/2004.

In 1997, P.L. 105-34, Sec. 1113(a)(1), amended subsec. (b) ... Sec. 1113(a)(2)(A), added "or" at the end of clause (c)(3)(B)(i), deleted clauses (c)(3)(B)(ii) and (iii) and added new clause (c)(3)(B)(ii) ... Sec. 1113(a)(2)(B), substituted "sixth tier foreign corporation" for "3rd foreign corporation" in subpara. (c)(4)(B) ... Sec. 1113(a)(2)(C), substituted "where foreign corporation first qualifies" for "where domestic corporation acquires 10 percent of foreign corporation" in the heading of para. (c)(3) ... Sec. 1113(a)(2)(D), removed "ownership" before "requirements" each place it appeared in para. (c)(3), effective for taxes of foreign corporations for tax. yrs. of such corporations begin. after 8/5/97. Sec. 1113(c)(2) of this Act provides:

"(2) Special rule. In the case of any chain of foreign corporations described in clauses (i) and (ii) of section 902(b)(2)(B) of the Internal Revenue Code of 1986 (as amended by this section), no liquidation, reorganization, or similar transaction in a taxable year beginning after the date of the enactment of this Act shall have the effect of permitting taxes to be taken into account under section 902 of the Internal Revenue Code of 1986 which could not have been taken into account under such section but for such transaction."

Prior to amendment, subsec. (b) read as follows:

"(b) Deemed taxes increased in case of certain 2nd and 3rd tier foreign corporations.

"(1) 2nd tier. If the foreign corporation described in subsection (a) (hereinafter in this section referred to as the '1st tier corporation') owns 10 percent or more of the voting stock of a 2nd foreign corporation from which it receives dividends in any taxable year, the 1st tier corporation shall be deemed to have paid the same proportion of such 2nd foreign corporation's post-1986 foreign income taxes as would be determined under subsection (a) if such 1st tier corporation were a domestic corporation.

"(2) 3rd tier. If such 1st tier corporation owns 10 percent or more of the voting stock of a 2nd foreign corporation which, in turn, owns 10 percent or more of the voting stock of a 3rd foreign corporation from which the 2nd corporation receives dividends in any taxable year, such 2nd foreign corporation shall be deemed to have paid the same proportion of such 3rd foreign corporation's post-1986 foreign income taxes as would be determined under subsection (a) if such 2nd foreign corporation were a domestic corporation.

"(3) 5 percent stock requirement. For purposes of this subpart—

"(A) For 2nd tier. Paragraph (1) shall not apply unless the percentage of voting stock owned by the domestic corporation in the 1st tier corporation and the percentage of voting stock owned by the 1st tier corporation in the 2nd foreign corporation when multiplied together equal at least 5 percent.

"(B) For 3rd tier. Paragraph (2) shall not apply unless the percentage arrived at for purposes of applying paragraph (1) when multiplied by the percentage of voting stock owned by the 2nd foreign corporation in the 3rd foreign corporation is equal to at least 5 percent."

Prior to deletion, clauses (c)(3)(B)(ii) and (iii) read as follows:

"(ii) the requirements of subsection (b)(3)(A) are met with respect to such foreign corporation and 10 percent or more of the voting stock of such foreign corporation is owned by another foreign corporation described in clause (i), or

"(iii) the requirements of subsection (b)(3)(B) are met with respect to such foreign corporation and 10 percent or more of the voting stock of such foreign corporation is owned by another foreign corporation described in clause (ii)."

—P.L. 105-34, Sec. 1163(a), substituted "attributable to" for "deemed paid with respect to" in subpara. (c)(2)(B), effective 8/5/97.

In 1988, P.L. 100-647, Sec. 1012(b)(1)(A), substituted "section 960" for "secton 960" in para. (c)(7) . . . Sec. 1012(b)(1)(B), substituted "this section and section 960" for "this section" the second time it appears in para. (c)(7) . . . Sec. 1012(b)(2), substituted "sections 964(a) and 986" for "sections 964 and 986", in para. (c)(1) effective for distributions by foreign corporations out of, and to inclusions under Code Sec. 951(a) attributable to earnings and profits for tax. yrs. begin. after 12/31/86.

—P.L. 100-647, Sec. 1012(b)(3), provides:

"(3) For purposes of sections 902 and 960 of the 1986 Code, the increase in earnings and profits of any foreign corporation under section 1023(e)(3)(C) [reproduced in note following Code Sec. 832] of the Reform Act [P.L. 99-514] shall be taken into account ratably over the 10-year period beginning with the corporation's first taxable year beginning after December 31, 1986."

In 1986, P.L. 99-514, Sec. 1202(a), amended Code Sec. 902, effective for distributions by foreign corporations out of, and to inclusions under Code Sec. 951(a) attributable to, earnings and profits for tax. yrs. begin. after 12/31/86.

Prior to amendment, Code Sec. 902 read as follows:

"SEC. 902. CREDIT FOR CORPORATE STOCKHOLDER IN FOREIGN CORPORATION.

"(a) Treatment of taxes paid by foreign corporation.

"For purposes of this subpart, a domestic corporation which owns at least 10 percent of the voting stock of a foreign corporation from which it receives dividends in any taxable year shall be deemed to have paid the same proportion of any income, war profits, or excess profits taxes paid or deemed to be paid by such foreign corporation to any foreign country or to any possession of the United States, on or with respect to the accumulated profits of such foreign corporation from which such dividends were paid, which the amount of such dividends (determined without regard to section 78) bears to the amount of such accumulated profits in excess of such income, war profits, and excess profits taxes (other than those deemed paid).

"(b) Foreign subsidiary of first and second foreign corporation.

"(1) One tier. If the foreign corporation described in subsection (a) (hereinafter in this subsection referred to as the 'first foreign corporation') owns 10 percent or more of the voting stock of a second foreign corporation from which it receives dividends in any taxable year, it shall be deemed to have paid the same proportion of any income, war profits, or excess profits taxes paid or deemed to be paid by such second foreign corporation to any foreign country or to any possession of the United States, on or with respect to the accumulated profits of such second foreign corporation from which such dividends were paid, which the amount of such dividends bears to the amount of such accumulated profits in excess of such income, war profits, and excess profits taxes (other than those deemed paid).

"(2) Two tiers. If such first foreign corporation owns 10 percent or more of the voting stock of a second foreign corporation which, in turn, owns 10 percent or more of the voting stock of a third foreign corporation from which the second foreign corporation receives dividends in any taxable year, the second foreign corporation shall be deemed to have paid the same proportion of any income, war profits, or excess profits taxes paid by such third foreign corporation to any foreign country or to any possession of the United States, on or with respect to the accumulated profits of such third foreign corporation from which such dividends were paid, which the amount of such dividends bears to the amount of such accumulated profits in excess of such income, war profits, and excess profits taxes.

"(3) Voting stock requirement. For purposes of this subpart—

"(A) paragraph (1) shall not apply unless the percentage of voting stock owned by the domestic corporation in the first foreign corporation and the percentage of voting stock owned by the first foreign corporation in the second foreign corporation when multiplied together equal at least 5 percent, and

"(B) paragraph (2) shall not apply unless the percentage arrived at for purposes of applying paragraph (1) when multiplied by the percentage of voting stock owned by the second foreign corporation in the third foreign corporation is equal to at least 5 percent.

"(c) Applicable rules.

"(1) Accumulated profits defined. For purposes of this section, the term 'accumulated profits' means, with respect to any foreign corporation, the amount of its gains, profits, or income computed without reduction by the amount of the income, war profits, and excess profits taxes imposed on or with respect to such profits or income by any foreign country or by any possession of the United States. The Secretary shall have full power to determine from the accumulated profits of what year or years such dividends were paid, treating dividends paid in the first 60 days of any year as having been paid from the accumulated profits of the preceding year or years (unless to his satisfaction shown otherwise), and in other respects treating dividends as having been paid from the most recently accumulated gains, profits, or earnings.

"(2) Accounting periods. In the case of a foreign corporation the income, war profits, and excess profits taxes of which are determined on the basis of an accounting period of less than 1 year, the word 'year' as used in this subsection, shall be construed to mean such accounting period.

"(d) Cross references.

"(1) For inclusion in gross income of an amount equal to taxes deemed paid under subsection (a), see section 78.

"(2) For application of subsections (a) and (b) with respect to taxes deemed paid in a prior taxable year by a United States shareholder with respect to a controlled foreign corporation, see section 960.

"(3) For reduction of credit with respect to dividends paid out of accumulated profits for years for which certain information is not furnished, see section 6038."

In 1976, P.L. 94-455, Sec. 1033(a), amended Code Sec. 902. Sec. 1033(c) of the Act provided as follows:

"(c) Effective dates.

The amendments made by this section shall apply—

"(1) in respect of any distribution received by a domestic corporation after December 31, 1977, and

"(2) in respect of any distribution received by a domestic corporation before January 1, 1978, in a taxable year of such corporation beginning after December 31, 1975, but only to the extent that such distribution is made out of the accumulated profits of a foreign corporation for a taxable year (of such foreign corporation) beginning after December 31, 1975.

For purposes of paragraph (2), a distribution made by a foreign corporation out of its profits which are attributable to a distribution received from a foreign corporation to which section 902(b) of the Internal Revenue Code of 1954 applies shall be treated as made out of the accumulated profits of a foreign corporation for a taxable year beginning before January 1, 1976, to the extent that such distribution was paid out of the accumulated profits of such foreign corporation for a taxable year beginning before January 1, 1976."

Prior to amendment, Code Sec. 902 read as follows:

"SEC. 902. CREDIT FOR CORPORATE STOCKHOLDER IN FOREIGN CORPORATION.

"(a) Treatment of taxes paid by foreign corporation.

"For purposes of this subpart, a domestic corporation which owns at least 10 percent of the voting stock of a foreign corporation from which it receives dividends in any taxable year shall—

"(1) to the extent such dividends are paid by such foreign corporation out of accumulated profits (as defined in subsection (c)(1)(A)) of a year for which such foreign corporation is not a less developed country corporation, be deemed to have paid the same proportion of any income, war profits, or excess profits taxes paid or deemed to be paid by such foreign corporation to any foreign country or to any possession of the United States on or with respect to such accumulated profits, which the amount of such dividends (determined without regard to section 78) bears to the amount of such accumulated profits in excess of such income, war profits, and excess profits taxes (other than those deemed paid); and

"(2) to the extent such dividends are paid by such foreign corporation out of accumulated profits (as defined in subsection (c)(1)(B)) of a year for which such foreign corporation is a less developed country corporation, be deemed to have paid the same proportion of any income, war profits, or excess profits taxes paid or deemed to be paid by such foreign corporation to any foreign country or to any possession of the United States on or with respect to such accumulated profits, which the amount of such dividends bears to the amount of such accumulated profits.

"(b) Foreign subsidiary of first and second foreign corporation.

"(1) If the foreign corporation described in subsection (a) (hereinafter in this subsection referred to as the 'first foreign corporation') owns 10 percent or more of the voting stock of a second foreign corporation from which it receives dividends in any taxable year, it shall be deemed to have paid the same proportion of any income, war profits, or excess profits taxes paid or deemed to be paid by such second foreign corporation to any foreign country or to any possession of the United States on or with respect to the accumulated profits of the corporation from which such dividends were paid which—

"(A) for purposes of applying subsection (a)(1), the amount of such dividends bears to the amount of the accumulated profits (as defined in subsection (c)(1)(A)) of such second foreign corporation from which such dividends were paid in excess of such income, war profits, and excess profits taxes, or

Income from foreign sources — Code Sec. 902

"(B) for purposes of applying subsection (a)(2), the amount of such dividends bears to the amount of the accumulated profits (as defined in subsection (c)(1)(B)) of such second foreign corporation from which such dividends were paid.

"(2) If such first foreign corporation owns 10 percent or more of the voting stock of a second foreign corporation which, in turn, owns 10 percent or more of the voting stock of a third foreign corporation from which the second foreign corporation receives dividends in any taxable year, the second foreign corporation shall be deemed to have paid the same proportion of any income, war profits, or excess profits taxes paid by such third foreign corporation to any foreign country or to any possession of the United States on or with respect to the accumulated profits of the corporation from which such dividends were paid which—

"(A) for purposes of applying subsection (a)(1), the amount of such dividends bears to the amount of the accumulated profits (as defined in subsection (c)(1)(A)) of such third foreign corporation from which such dividends were paid in excess of such income, war profits, and excess profits taxes, or

"(B) for purposes of applying subsection (a)(2), the amount of such dividends bears to the amount of the accumulated profits (as defined in subsection (c)(1)(B)) of such third foreign corporation from which such dividends were paid.

"(3) For purposes of this subpart, subsection (b)(1) shall not apply unless the percentage of voting stock owned by the domestic corporation in the first foreign corporation and the percentage of voting stock owned by the first foreign corporation in the second foreign corporation when multiplied together equal at least 5 percent, and for purposes of this subpart, subsection (b)(2) shall not apply unless the percentage arrived at for purposes of applying subsection (b)(1) when multiplied by the percentage of voting stock owned by the second foreign corporation in the third foreign corporation is equal to at least 5 percent.

"(c) Applicable rules.

"(1) Accumulated profits defined. For purposes of this section, the term 'accumulated profits' means with respect to any foreign corporation—

"(A) for purposes of subsections (a)(1), (b)(1)(A), and (b)(2)(A), the amount of its gains, profits or income computed without reduction by the amount of the income, war profits, and excess profits taxes imposed on or with respect to such profits or income by any foreign country or any possession of the United States; and

"(B) for purposes of subsections (a)(2), (b)(1)(B), and (b)(2)(B), the amount of its gains, profits, or income in excess of the income, war profits, and excess profits taxes imposed on or with respect to such profits or income.

The Secretary or his delegate shall have full power to determine from the accumulated profits of what year or years such dividends were paid, treating dividends paid in the first 60 days of any year as having been paid from the accumulated profits of the preceding year or years (unless to his satisfaction shown otherwise), and in other respects treating dividends as having been paid from the most recently accumulated gains, profits, or earnings.

"(2) Accounting periods. In the case of a foreign corporation, the income, war profits, and excess profits taxes of which are determined on the basis of an accounting period of less than 1 year, the word 'year' as used in this subsection shall be construed to mean such accounting period.

"(d) Less developed country corporation defined.

"For purposes of this section, the term 'less developed country corporation' means—

"(1) a foreign corporation which, for its taxable year, is a less developed country corporation within the meaning of paragraph (3) or (4), and

"(2) a foreign corporation which owns 10 percent or more of the total combined voting power of all classes of stock entitled to vote of a foreign corporation which is a less developed country corporation within the meaning of paragraph (3), and—

"(A) 80 percent or more of the gross income of which for its taxable year meets the requirement of paragraph (3)(A), and

"(B) 80 percent or more in value of the assets of which on each day of such year consists of property described in paragraph (3)(B).

A foreign corporation which is a less developed country corporation for its first taxable year beginning after December 31, 1962, shall, for purposes of this section, be treated as having been a less developed country corporation for each of its taxable years beginning before January 1, 1963.

"(3) The term 'less developed country corporation' means a foreign corporation which during the taxable year is engaged in the active conduct of one or more trades or businesses and—

"(A) 80 percent or more of the gross income of which for the taxable year is derived from sources within less developed countries; and

"(B) 80 percent or more in value of the assets of which on each day of the taxable year consists of—

"(i) property used in such trades or businesses and located in less developed countries,

"(ii) money, and deposits with persons carrying on the banking business,

"(iii) stock, and obligations which, at the time of their acquisition, have a maturity of one year or more, of any other less developed country corporation,

"(iv) an obligation of a less developed country,

"(v) an investment which is required because of restrictions imposed by a less developed country, and

"(vi) property described in section 956(b)(2).

For purposes of subparagraph (A), the determination as to whether income is derived from sources within less developed countries shall be made under regulations prescribed by the Secretary or his delegate.

"(4) The term 'less developed country corporation' also means a foreign corporation—

"(A) 80 percent or more of the gross income of which for the taxable year consists of—

"(i) gross income derived from, or in connection with, the using (or hiring or leasing for use) in foreign commerce of aircraft or vessels registered under the laws of a less developed country, or from, or in connection with, the performance of services directly related to use of such aircraft or vessels, or from the sale or exchange of such aircraft or vessels, and

"(ii) dividends and interest received from foreign corporations which are less developed country corporations within the meaning of this paragraph and 10 percent or more of the total combined voting power of all classes of stock of which are owned by the foreign corporation, and gain from the sale or exchange of stock or obligations of foreign corporations which are such less developed country corporations, and

"(B) 80 percent or more of the assets of which on each day of the taxable year consists of (i) assets used, or held for use, for or in connection with the production of income described in subparagraph (A), and (ii) property described in section 956(b)(2).

"(5) The term 'less developed country' means (in respect to any foreign corporation) any foreign country (other than an area within the Sino-Soviet bloc) or any possession of the United States with respect to which, on the first day of the taxable year, there is in effect an Executive order by the President of the United States designating such country or possession as an economically less developed country for purposes of this section. For purposes of the preceding sentence, an overseas territory, department, province, or possession may be treated as a separate country. No designation shall be made under this paragraph with respect to—

Australia	Luxembourg
Austria	Monaco
Belgium	Netherlands
Canada	New Zealand
Denmark	Norway
France	Union of South Africa
Germany (Federal Republic)	San Marino
Hong Kong	Sweden
Italy	Switzerland
Japan	United Kingdom
Liechtenstein	

After the President has designated any foreign country or any possession of the United States as an economically less developed country for purposes of this section, he shall not terminate such designation (either by issuing an Executive order for that purpose or by issuing an Executive order under the first sentence of this paragraph which has the effect of terminating such designation) unless, at least 30 days prior to such termination, he has notified the Senate and the House of Representatives of his intention to terminate such designation. Any designation in effect on March 26, 1975, under section 955(c)(3) (as in effect before the enactment of the Tax Reduction Act of 1975) shall be treated as made under this paragraph.

"(e) Cross references.

"(1) For inclusion in gross income of an amount equal to taxes deemed paid under subsection (a)(1), see section 78.

"(2) For application of subsections (a) and (b) with respect to taxes deemed paid in a prior taxable year by a United States shareholder with respect to a controlled foreign corporation, see section 960.

"(3) For reduction of credit with respect to dividends paid out of accumulated profits for years for which certain information is not furnished, see section 6038."

In 1975, P.L. 94-12, Sec. 602(c)(6), amended subsec. (d), effective for tax. yrs. of foreign corporations begin. after 12/31/75, and for tax. yrs. of U.S. shareholders (within the meaning of Code Sec. 951(b)) within which or with which such tax. yrs. of such foreign corporations end.

Prior to amendment, subsec. (d) read as follows:

"(d) Less developed country corporation defined.

"For purposes of this section, the term 'less developed country corporation' means—

"(1) a foreign corporation which, for its taxable year, is a less developed country corporation within the meaning of section 955(c)(1) or (2), and

"(2) a foreign corporation which owns 10 percent or more of the total combined voting power of all classes of stock entitled to vote of a foreign corporation which is a less developed country corporation within the meaning of section 955(c)(1), and—

"(A) 80 percent or more of the gross income of which for its taxable year meets the requirements of section 955(c)(1)(A); and

"(B) 80 percent or more in value of the assets of which on each day of such year consists of property described in section 955(c)(1)(B).

A foreign corporation which is a less developed country corporation for its first taxable year beginning after December 31, 1962, shall, for purposes of this section, be treated as having been a less developed country corporation for each of its taxable years beginning before January 1, 1963."

In 1971, P.L. 91-684, Sec. 1, amended subsec. (b)... Sec. 2, substituted "(b)(1)(A), and (b)(2)(A)" for "and (b)(1)," in subpara. (c)(1)(A) and substituted "(b)(1)(B), and (b)(2)(B)," for "and (b)(2)," in subpara. (c)(1)(B), effective for all tax. yrs. of domestic corporations, end. after 1/12/71, but only in respect of dividends paid by one corporation to another corporation after 1/12/71.

Prior to amendment, subsec. (b) read as follows:

"(b) Foreign subsidiary of a foreign corporation.

"If such foreign corporation owns 50 percent or more of the voting stock of another foreign corporation from which it receives dividends in any taxable year, it shall be deemed to have paid the same proportion of any income, war profits, or excess profits taxes paid by such other foreign corporation to any foreign country or to any possession of the United States, on or with respect to the accumulated profits of the corporation from which such dividends were paid which—

2,551

"(1) for purposes of applying subsection (a)(1), the amount of such dividends bears to the amount of the accumulated profits (as defined in subsection (c)(1)(A)) of such other foreign corporation from which such dividends were paid in excess of such income, war profits, and excess profits taxes, or

"(2) for purposes of applying subsection (a)(2), the amount of such dividends bears to the amount of the accumulated profits (as defined in subsection (c)(1)(B)) of such other foreign corporation from which such dividends were paid."

In 1962, P.L. 87-834, Sec. 9(a), amended Code Sec. 902, effective for any distribution received by a domestic corporation after 12/31/64 and any distribution received by a domestic corporation before 1/1/65, in a tax. yr. of such corporation beginning after 12/31/62, but only to the extent that such distribution is made out of the accumulated profits of a foreign corporation for a tax. yr. (of such foreign corporation) begin. after 12/31/62.

"For purposes of paragraph (2), a distribution made by a foreign corporation out of its profits which are attributable to a distribution received from a foreign subsidiary to which section 902(b) applies shall be treated as made out of the accumulated profits of a foreign corporation for a taxable year beginning before January 1, 1963, to the extent that such distribution was paid out of the accumulated profits of such foreign subsidiary for a taxable year beginning before January 1, 1963."

Prior to amendment, Code Sec. 902 read as follows:

"SEC. 902. CREDIT FOR CORPORATE STOCKHOLDER IN FOREIGN CORPORATION.

"(a) Treatment of taxes paid by foreign corporation.

"For purposes of this subpart, a domestic corporation which owns at least 10 percent of the voting stock of a foreign corporation from which it receives dividends in any taxable year shall be deemed to have paid the same proportion of any income, war profits, or excess profits taxes paid or deemed to be paid by such foreign corporation to any foreign country or to any possession of the United States, on or with respect to the accumulated profits of such foreign corporation from which such dividends were paid, which the amount of such dividends bears to the amount of such accumulated profits.

"(b) Foreign subsidiary of foreign corporation.

"If such foreign corporation owns 50 percent or more of the voting stock of another foreign corporation from which it receives dividends in any taxable year, it shall be deemed to have paid the same proportion of any income, war profits, or excess profits taxes paid by such other foreign corporation to any foreign country or to any possession of the United States, on or with respect to the accumulated profits of the corporation from which such dividends were paid, which the amount of such dividends bears to the amount of such accumulated profits.

"(c) Applicable rules.

"(1) The term 'accumulated profits', when used in this section in reference to a foreign corporation, means the amount of its gains, profits, or income in excess of the income, war profits, and excess profits taxes imposed on or with respect to such profits or income; and the Secretary or his delegate shall have full power to determine from the accumulated profits of what year or years such dividends were paid, treating dividends paid in the first 60 days of any year as having been paid from the accumulated profits of the preceding year or years (unless to his satisfaction shown otherwise), and in other respects, treating dividends as having been paid from the most recently accumulated gains, profits, or earnings.

"(2) In the case of a foreign corporation, the income, war profits, and excess profits taxes of which are determined on the basis of an accounting period of less than 1 year, the word 'year' as used in this subsection shall be construed to mean such accounting period.

"(d) Special rules for certain wholly-owned foreign corporations.

"For purposes of this subtitle, if—

"(1) a domestic corporation owns, directly or indirectly, 100 percent of all classes of outstanding stock of a foreign corporation engaged in manufacturing, production, or mining,

"(2) such domestic corporation receives property in the form of a royalty or compensation from such foreign corporation pursuant to any form of contractual arrangement under which the domestic corporation agrees to furnish services or property in consideration for the property so received, and

"(3) such contractual arrangement provides that the property so received by such domestic corporation shall be accepted by such domestic corporation in lieu of dividends and that such foreign corporation shall neither declare nor pay any dividends of any kind in any calendar year in which such property is paid to such domestic corporation by such foreign corporation,

"then the excess of the fair market value of such property so received by such domestic corporation over the cost to such domestic corporation of the property and services so furnished by such domestic corporation shall be treated as a distribution by such foreign corporation to such domestic corporation, and, for purposes of section 301, the amount of such distribution shall be such excess, in lieu of any amount otherwise determined under section 301 without regard to this subsection; and the basis of such property so received by such domestic corporation shall be the fair market value of such property, in lieu of the basis otherwise determined under section 301(d) without regard to this subsection.

"(e) Cross reference.

"For reduction of credit with respect to dividends paid out of accumulated profits for years for which certain information is not furnished, see section 6038."

In 1960, P.L. 86-870, Sec. 0, added subsec. (e), for tax. yrs. begin. after '60.

Sec. 903. Credit for taxes in lieu of income, etc., taxes.

For purposes of this part and of sections 164(a) and 275(a), the term "income, war profits, and excess profits taxes" shall include a tax paid in lieu of a tax on income, war profits, or excess profits otherwise generally imposed by any foreign country or by any possession of the United States.

In 2006, P.L. 109-222, Sec. 513(a), amended Sec. 5(c)(1) of P.L. 106-519 [see below] . . . Sec. 513(b), repealed Sec. 101(f) of P.L. 108-357 [see below], effective for tax. yrs. begin. after 5/17/2006.

Prior to amendment, Sec. 5(c)(1) of P.L. 106-519 read as follows:

"(1) In general. In the case of a FSC (as so defined) in existence on September 30, 2000, and at all times thereafter, the amendments made by this Act shall not apply to any transaction in the ordinary course of trade or business involving a FSC which occurs—

"(A) before January 1, 2002; or

"(B) after December 31, 2001, pursuant to a binding contract—

"(i) which is between the FSC (or any related person) and any person which is not a related person; and

"(ii) which is in effect on September 30, 2000, and at all times thereafter.

For purposes of this paragraph, a binding contract shall include a purchase option, renewal option, or replacement option which is included in such contract and which is enforceable against the seller or lessor."

Prior to repeal, Sec. 101(f) of P.L. 108-357 read as follows:

"(f) Binding contracts. The amendments made by this section shall not apply to any transaction in the ordinary course of a trade or business which occurs pursuant to a binding contract—

"(1) which is between the taxpayer and a person who is not a related person (as defined in section 943(b)(3) of such Code, as in effect on the day before the date of the enactment of this Act), and

"(2) which is in effect on September 17, 2003, and at all times thereafter.

"For purposes of this subsection, a binding contract shall include a purchase option, renewal option, or replacement option which is included in such contract and which is enforceable against the seller or lessor."

In 2004, P.L. 108-357, Sec. 101(b)(7), substituted "164(a)" for "114, 164(a)," in Code Sec. 903, effective for transactions after 12/31/2004. Sec. 101(d)-(f) [subsec. (f) was repealed by Sec. 513(b) of P.L. 109-222, see above] of this Act, reads as follows:

"(d) Transitional rule for 2005 and 2006.

"(1) In general. In the case of transactions during 2005 or 2006, the amount includible in gross income by reason of the amendments made by this section shall not exceed the applicable percentage of the amount which would have been so included but for this subsection.

"(2) Applicable percentage. For purposes of paragraph (1), the applicable percentage shall be as follows:

"(A) For 2005, the applicable percentage shall be 20 percent.

"(B) For 2006, the applicable percentage shall be 40 percent.

"(e) Revocation of election to be treated as domestic corporation. If, during the 1-year period beginning on the date of the enactment of this Act, a corporation for which an election is in effect under section 943(e) of the Internal Revenue Code of 1986 revokes such election, no gain or loss shall be recognized with respect to property treated as transferred under clause (ii) of section 943(e)(4)(B) of such Code to the extent such property—

"(1) was treated as transferred under clause (i) thereof, or

"(2) was acquired during a taxable year to which such election applies and before May 1, 2003, in the ordinary course of its trade or business.

The Secretary of the Treasury (or such Secretary's delegate) may prescribe such regulations as may be necessary to prevent the abuse of the purposes of this subsection.

"(f) [Repealed by Sec. 513(b) of P.L. 109-222, see above]

In 2000, P.L. 106-519, Sec. 4(4), substituted '114, 164(a),' for '164(a)', effective for transactions after 9/30/2000. Sec. 5(b)-(d) [para. (c)(1) as amended by Sec. 513(a) of P.L. 109-222, see above] of this Act, provides:

"(b) No new FSCs; termination of inactive FSCs—

"(1) No new FSCs. No corporation may elect after September 30, 2000, to be a FSC (as defined in section 922 of the Internal Revenue Code of 1986, as in effect before the amendments made by this Act).

"(2) Termination of inactive FSCs. If a FSC has no foreign trade income (as defined in section 923(b) of such Code, as so in effect) for any period of 5 consecutive taxable years beginning after December 31, 2001, such FSC shall cease to be treated as a FSC for purposes of such Code for any taxable year beginning after such period.

"(c) Transition period for existing Foreign Sales Corporations.

"(1) In general. In the case of a FSC (as so defined) in existence on September 30, 2000, and at all times thereafter, the amendments made by this Act shall not apply to any transaction in the ordinary course of trade or business involving a FSC which occurs before January 1, 2002.

"(2) Election to have amendments apply earlier. A taxpayer may elect to have the amendments made by this Act apply to any transaction by a FSC or any related person to which such amendments would apply but for the application of paragraph (1). Such election shall be effective for the taxable year for which made and all subsequent taxable years, and, once made, may be revoked only with the consent of the Secretary of the Treasury.

"(3) Exception for old earnings and profits of certain corporations.

"(A) In general. In the case of a foreign corporation to which this paragraph applies—

"(i) earnings and profits of such corporation accumulated in taxable years ending before October 1, 2000, shall not be included in the gross income of the persons holding stock in such corporation by reason of section 943(e)(4)(B)(i), and "(ii) rules similar to the rules of clauses (ii), (iii), and (iv) of section 953(d)(4)(B) shall apply with respect to such earnings and profits.

The preceding sentence shall not apply to earnings and profits acquired in a transaction after September 30, 2000, to which section 381 applies unless the distributor or transferor corporation was immediately before the transaction a foreign corporation to which this paragraph applies.

"(B) Existing FSCs. This paragraph shall apply to any controlled foreign corporation (as defined in section 957) if—

"(i) such corporation is a FSC (as so defined) in existence on September 30, 2000,

"(ii) such corporation is eligible to make the election under section 943(e) by reason of being described in paragraph (2)(B) of such section, and

"(iii) such corporation makes such election not later than for its first taxable year beginning after December 31, 2001.

"(C) Other corporations. This paragraph shall apply to any controlled foreign corporation (as defined in section 957), and such corporation shall (notwithstanding any provision of section 943(e)) be treated as an applicable foreign corporation for purposes of section 943(e), if—

"(i) such corporation is in existence on September 30, 2000;

"(ii) as of such date, such corporation is wholly owned (directly or indirectly) by a domestic corporation (determined without regard to any election under section 943(e));

"(iii) for each of the 3 taxable years preceding the first taxable year to which the election under section 943(e) by such controlled foreign corporation applies—

"(I) all of the gross income of such corporation is subpart F income (as defined in section 952), including by reason of section 954(b)(3)(B); and

"(II) in the ordinary course of such corporation's trade or business, such corporation regularly sold (or paid commissions) to a FSC which on September 30, 2000, was a related person to such corporation;

"(iv) such corporation has never made an election under section 922(a)(2) (as in effect before the date of the enactment of this paragraph) to be treated as a FSC; and

"(v) such corporation makes the election under section 943(e) not later than for its first taxable year beginning after December 31, 2001.

The preceding sentence shall cease to apply as of the date that the domestic corporation referred to in clause (ii) ceases to wholly own (directly or indirectly) such controlled foreign corporation.

"(4) Related person. For purposes of this subsection, the term 'related person' has the meaning given to such term by section 943(b)(3).

"(5) Section references. Except as otherwise expressly provided, any reference in this subsection to a section or other provision shall be considered to be a reference to a section or other provision of the Internal Revenue Code of 1986, as amended by this Act.

"(d) Special rules relating to leasing transactions.

"(1) Sales income. If foreign trade income in connection with the lease or rental of property described in section 927(a)(1)(B) of such Code (as in effect before the amendments made by this Act) is treated as exempt foreign trade income for purposes of section 921(a) of such Code (as so in effect), such property shall be treated as property described in section 941(c)(1)(B) of such Code (as added by this Act) for purposes of applying section 941(c)(2) of such Code (as so added) to any subsequent transaction involving such property to which the amendments made by this Act apply.

"(2) Limitation on use of gross receipts method. If any person computed its foreign trade income from any transaction with respect to any property on the basis of a transfer price determined under the method described in section 925(a)(1) of such Code (as in effect before the amendments made by this Act), then the qualifying foreign trade income (as defined in section 941(a) of such Code, as in effect after such amendment) of such person (or any related person) with respect to any other transaction involving such property (and to which the amendments made by this Act apply) shall be zero."

In **1988**, P.L. 100-647, Sec. 1012(v)(9), substituted "this part" for "this subpart", in Code Sec. 903, effective for tax. yrs. begin. after 12/31/86.

In **1964**, P.L. 88-272, Sec. 207(b)(8), substituted "sections 164(a) and 275(a)" for "section 164(b)", effective for tax. yrs. begin. after 12/31/63.

Sec. 904. Limitation on credit.
(a) Limitation.

The total amount of the credit taken under section 901(a) shall not exceed the same proportion of the tax against which such credit is taken which the taxpayer's taxable income from sources without the United States (but not in excess of the taxpayer's entire taxable income) bears to his entire taxable income for the same taxable year.

(b) Taxable income for purpose of computing limitation.

(1) **Personal exemptions.** For purposes of subsection (a), the taxable income in the case of an individual, estate, or trust shall be computed without any deduction for personal exemptions under section 151 or 642(b).

(2) **Capital gains.** For purposes of this section—

(A) In general. Taxable income from sources outside the United States shall include gain from the sale or exchange of capital assets only to the extent of foreign source capital gain net income.

(B) Special rules where capital gain rate differential. In the case of any taxable year for which there is a capital gain rate differential—

(i) in lieu of applying subparagraph (A), the taxable income from sources outside the United States shall include gain from the sale or exchange of capital assets only in an amount equal to foreign source capital gain net income reduced by the rate differential portion of foreign source net capital gain,

(ii) the entire taxable income shall include gain from the sale or exchange of capital assets only in an amount equal to capital gain net income reduced by the rate differential portion of net capital gain, and

(iii) for purposes of determining taxable income from sources outside the United States, any net capital loss (and any amount which is a short-term capital loss under section 1212(a)) from sources outside the United States to the extent taken into account in determining capital gain net income for the taxable year shall be reduced by an amount equal to the rate differential portion of the excess of net capital gain from sources within the United States over net capital gain.

(C) Coordination with capital gains rates. The Secretary may by regulations modify the application of this paragraph and paragraph (3) to the extent necessary to properly reflect any capital gain rate differential under section 1(h) or 1201(a) and the computation of net capital gain.

(3) **Definitions.** For purposes of this subsection—

(A) Foreign source capital gain net income. The term "foreign source capital gain net income" means the lesser of—

(i) capital gain net income from sources without the United States, or

(ii) capital gain net income.

(B) Foreign source net capital gain. The term "foreign source net capital gain" means the lesser of—

(i) net capital gain from sources without the United States, or

(ii) net capital gain.

(C) Section 1231 gains. The term "gain from the sale or exchange of capital assets" includes any gain so treated under section 1231.

(D) Capital gain rate differential. There is a capital gain rate differential for any taxable year if—

(i) in the case of a taxpayer other than a corporation, subsection (h) of section 1 applies to such taxable year, or

(ii) in the case of a corporation, any rate of tax imposed by section 11, 511, or 831(a) or (b) (whichever applies) exceeds the alternative rate of tax under section 1201(a) (determined without regard to the last sentence of section 11(b)(1)).

(E) Rate differential portion.

(i) In general. The rate differential portion of foreign source net capital gain, net capital gain, or the excess of net capital gain from sources within the United States over net capital gain, as the case may be, is the same proportion of such amount as—

(I) the excess of the highest applicable tax rate over the alternative tax rate, bears to

(II) the highest applicable tax rate.

(ii) Highest applicable tax rate. For purposes of clause (i), the term "highest applicable tax rate" means—

(I) in the case of a taxpayer other than a corporation, the highest rate of tax set forth in subsection (a), (b), (c), (d), or (e) of section 1 (whichever applies), or

(II) in the case of a corporation, the highest rate of tax specified in section 11(b).

(iii) Alternative tax rate. For purposes of clause (i), the term "alternative tax rate" means—

(I) in the case of a taxpayer other than a corporation, the alternative rate of tax determined under section 1(h), or

(II) in the case of a corporation, the alternative rate of tax under section 1201(a).

(4) Coordination with section 936. For purposes of subsection (a), in the case of a corporation, the taxable income shall not include any portion thereof taken into account for purposes of the credit (if any) allowed by section 936 (without regard to subsections (a)(4) and (i) thereof).

(c) Carryback and carryover of excess tax paid.

Any amount by which all taxes paid or accrued to foreign countries or possessions of the United States for any taxable year for which the taxpayer chooses to have the benefits of this subpart exceed the limitation under subsection (a) shall be deemed taxes paid or accrued to foreign countries or possessions of the United States in the first preceding taxable year and in any of the first 10 succeeding taxable years, in that order and to the extent not deemed taxes paid or accrued in a prior taxable year, in the amount by which the limitation under subsection (a) for such preceding or succeeding taxable year exceeds the sum of the taxes paid or accrued to foreign countries or possessions of the United States for such preceding or succeeding taxable year and the amount of the taxes for any taxable year earlier than the current taxable year which shall be deemed to have been paid or accrued in such preceding or subsequent taxable year (whether or not the taxpayer chooses to have the benefits of this subpart with respect to such earlier taxable year). Such amount deemed paid or accrued in any year may be availed of only as a tax credit and not as a deduction and only if the taxpayer for such year chooses to have the benefits of this subpart as to taxes paid or accrued for that year to foreign countries or possessions of the United States.

(d) Separate application of section with respect to certain categories of income.

(1) In general. The provisions of subsections (a), (b), and (c) and sections 902, 907, and 960 shall be applied separately with respect to—

(A) passive category income, and

(B) general category income.

(2) Definitions and special rules. For purposes of this subsection—

(A) Categories.

(i) Passive category income. The term "passive category income" means passive income and specified passive category income.

(ii) General category income. The term "general category income" means income other than passive category income.

(B) Passive income.

(i) In general. Except as otherwise provided in this subparagraph, the term "passive income" means any income received or accrued by any person which is of a kind which would be foreign personal holding company income (as defined in section 954(c)).

(ii) Certain amounts included. Except as provided in clause (iii), the term "passive income" includes, except as provided in subparagraph (E)(iii) or paragraph (3)(I), any amount includible in gross income under section 1293 (relating to certain passive foreign investment companies).

(iii) Exceptions. The term "passive income" shall not include—

(I) any export financing interest, and

(II) any high-taxed income.

(iv) Clarification of application of section 864(d)(6). In determining whether any income is of a kind which would be foreign personal holding company income, the rules of section 864(d)(6) shall apply only in the case of income of a controlled foreign corporation.

(v) Specified passive category income. The term "specified passive category income" means—

(I) dividends from a DISC or former DISC (as defined in section 992(a)) to the extent such dividends are treated as income from sources without the United States, and

(II) distributions from a former FSC (as defined in section 922) out of earnings and profits attributable to foreign trade income (within the meaning of section 923(b)) or interest or carrying charges (as defined in section 927(d)(1)) derived from a transaction which results in foreign trade income (as defined in section 923(b)).

Any reference in subclause II to section 922, 923, or 927 shall be treated as a reference to such section as in effect before its repeal by the FSC Repeal and Extraterritorial Income Exclusion Act of 2000.

(C) Treatment of financial services income and companies.

(i) In general. Financial services income shall be treated as general category income in the case of—

(I) a member of a financial services group, and

(II) any other person if such person is predominantly engaged in the active conduct of a banking, insurance, financing, or similar business.

(ii) Financial services group. The term "financial services group" means any affiliated group (as defined in section 1504(a) without regard to paragraphs (2) and (3) of section 1504(b)) which is predominantly engaged in the active conduct of a banking, insurance, financing, or similar business. In determining whether such a group is so engaged, there shall be taken into account only the income of members of the group that are—

(I) United States corporations, or

(II) controlled foreign corporations in which such United States corporations own, directly or indirectly, at least 80 percent of the total voting power and value of the stock.

(iii) Pass-thru entities. The Secretary shall by regulation specify for purposes of this subparagraph the treatment of financial services income received or accrued by partnerships and by other pass-thru entities which are not members of a financial services group.

(D) Financial services income.

(i) In general. Except as otherwise provided in this subparagraph, the term "financial services income" means any income which is received or accrued by any person predominantly engaged in the active con-

duct of a banking, insurance, financing, or similar business, and which is—
  (I) described in clause (ii), or
  (II) passive income (determined without regard to subparagraph (B)(iii)(II)).
(ii) General description of financial services income. Income is described in this clause if such income is—
  (I) derived in the active conduct of a banking, financing, or similar business,
  (II) derived from the investment by an insurance company of its unearned premiums or reserves ordinary and necessary for the proper conduct of its insurance business, or
  (III) of a kind which would be insurance income as defined in section 953(a) determined without regard to those provisions of paragraph (1)(A) of such section which limit insurance income to income from countries other than the country in which the corporation was created or organized.
(E) Noncontrolled section 902 corporation.
  (i) In general. The term "noncontrolled section 902 corporation" means any foreign corporation with respect to which the taxpayer meets the stock ownership requirements of section 902(a) (or, for purposes of applying paragraph (3) or (4), the requirements of section 902(b)). A controlled foreign corporation shall not be treated as a noncontrolled section 902 corporation with respect to any distribution out of its earnings and profits for periods during which it was a controlled foreign corporation.
  (ii) Treatment of inclusions under section 1293. If any foreign corporation is a non-controlled section 902 corporation with respect to the taxpayer, any inclusion under section 1293 with respect to such corporation shall be treated as a dividend from such corporation.
(F) High-taxed income. The term "high-taxed income" means any income which (but for this subparagraph) would be passive income if the sum of—
  (i) the foreign income taxes paid or accrued by the taxpayer with respect to such income, and
  (ii) the foreign income taxes deemed paid by the taxpayer with respect to such income under section 902 or 960,
exceeds the highest rate of tax specified in section 1 or 11 (whichever applies) multiplied by the amount of such income (determined with regard to section 78). For purposes of the preceding sentence, the term "foreign income taxes" means any income, war profits, or excess profits tax imposed by any foreign country or possession of the United States.
(G) Export financing interest. For purposes of this paragraph, the term "export financing interest" means any interest derived from financing the sale (or other disposition) for use or consumption outside the United States of any property—
  (i) which is manufactured, produced, grown, or extracted in the United States by the taxpayer or a related person, and
  (ii) not more than 50 percent of the fair market value of which is attributable to products imported into the United States.
For purposes of clause (ii), the fair market value of any property imported into the United States shall be its appraised value, as determined by the Secretary under section 402 of the Tariff Act of 1930 (19 U.S.C. 1401a) in connection with its importation.
(H) Treatment of income tax base differences.
  (i) In general. In the case of taxable years beginning after December 31, 2006, tax imposed under the law of a foreign country or possession of the United States on an amount which does not constitute income under United States tax principles shall be treated as imposed on income described in paragraph (1)(B).
  (ii) Special rule for years before 2007.
    (I) In general. In the case of taxes paid or accrued in taxable years beginning after December 31, 2004, and before January 1, 2007, a taxpayer may elect to treat tax imposed under the law of a foreign country or possession of the United States on an amount which does not constitute income under United States tax principles as tax imposed on income described in subparagraph (C) or (I) of paragraph (1).
    (II) Election irrevocable. Any such election shall apply to the taxable year for which made and all subsequent taxable years described in subclause (I) unless revoked with the consent of the Secretary.
(I) Related person. For purposes of this paragraph, the term "related person" has the meaning given such term by section 954(d)(3), except that such section shall be applied by substituting "the person with respect to whom the determination is being made" for "controlled foreign corporation" each place it appears.
(J) Transitional rule. For purposes of paragraph (1)—
  (i) taxes paid or accrued in a taxable year beginning before January 1, 1987, with respect to income which was described in subparagraph (A) of paragraph (1) (as in effect on the day before the date of the enactment [10/22/86] of the Tax Reform Act of 1986) shall be treated as taxes paid or accrued with respect to income described in subparagraph (A) of paragraph (1) (as in effect after such date),
  (ii) taxes paid or accrued in a taxable year beginning before January 1, 1987, with respect to income which was described in subparagraph (E) of paragraph (1) (as in effect on the day before the date of the enactment [10/22/86] of the Tax Reform Act of 1986) shall be treated as taxes paid or accrued with respect to income described in subparagraph (I) of paragraph (1) (as in effect after such date) except that—
    (I) such taxes shall be treated as paid or accrued with respect to shipping income to the extent the taxpayer establishes to the satisfaction of the Secretary that such taxes were paid or accrued with respect to such income,
    (II) in the case of a person described in subparagraph (C)(i), such taxes shall be treated as paid or accrued with respect to financial services income to the extent the taxpayer establishes to the satisfaction of the Secretary that such taxes were paid or accrued with respect to such income, and
    (III) such taxes shall be treated as paid or accrued with respect to high withholding tax interest to the extent the taxpayer establishes to the satisfaction of the Secretary that such taxes were paid or accrued with respect to such income, and
  (iii) taxes paid or accrued in a taxable year beginning before January 1, 1987, with respect to income described in any other subparagraph of paragraph (1) (as so in effect before such date) shall be treated as

taxes paid or accrued with respect to income described in the corresponding subparagraph of paragraph (1) (as so in effect after such date).

(K) Transitional rules for 2007 changes. For purposes of paragraph (1)—

(i) taxes carried from any taxable year beginning before January 1, 2007, to any taxable year beginning on or after such date, with respect to any item of income, shall be treated as described in the subparagraph of paragraph (1) in which such income would be described were such taxes paid or accrued in a taxable year beginning on or after such date, and

(ii) the Secretary may by regulations provide for the allocation of any carryback of taxes with respect to income from a taxable year beginning on or after January 1, 2007, to a taxable year beginning before such date for purposes of allocating such income among the separate categories in effect for the taxable year to which carried.

(3) Look-thru in case of controlled foreign corporations.

(A) In general. Except as otherwise provided in this paragraph, dividends, interest, rents, and royalties received or accrued by the taxpayer from a controlled foreign corporation in which the taxpayer is a United States shareholder shall not be treated as passive category income.

(B) Subpart F inclusions. Any amount included in gross income under section 951(a)(1)(A) shall be treated as passive category income to the extent the amount so included is attributable to passive category income.

(C) Interest, rents, and royalties. Any interest, rent, or royalty which is received or accrued from a controlled foreign corporation in which the taxpayer is a United States shareholder shall be treated as passive category income to the extent it is properly allocable (under regulations prescribed by the Secretary) to passive category income of the controlled foreign corporation.

(D) Dividends. Any dividend paid out of the earnings and profits of any controlled foreign corporation in which the taxpayer is a United States shareholder shall be treated as passive category income in proportion to the ratio of—

(i) the portion of the earnings and profits attributable to passive category income, to

(ii) the total amount of earnings and profits.

(E) Look-thru applies only where subpart F applies. If a controlled foreign corporation meets the requirements of section 954(b)(3)(A) (relating to de minimis rule) for any taxable year, for purposes of this paragraph, none of its foreign base company income (as defined in section 954(a) without regard to section 954(b)(5)) and none of its gross insurance income (as defined in section 954(b)(3)(C)) for such taxable year shall be treated as passive category income, except that this sentence shall not apply to any income which (without regard to this sentence) would be treated as financial services income. Solely for purposes of applying subparagraph (D), passive income of a controlled foreign corporation shall not be treated as passive category income if the requirements of section 954(b)(4) are met with respect to such income.

(F) Coordination with high-taxed income provisions.

(i) In determining whether any income of a controlled foreign corporation is passive category income, subclause (II) of paragraph (2)(B)(iii) shall not apply.

(ii) Any income of the taxpayer which is treated as passive category income under this paragraph shall be so treated notwithstanding any provision of paragraph (2); except that the determination of whether any amount is high-taxed income shall be made after the application of this paragraph.

(G) Dividend. For purposes of this paragraph, the term "dividend" includes any amount included in gross income in section 951(a)(1)(B). Any amount included in gross income under section 78 to the extent attributable to amounts included in gross income in section 951(a)(1)(A) shall not be treated as a dividend but shall be treated as included in gross income under section 951(a)(1)(A).

(H) Look-thru applies to passive foreign investment company inclusion. If—

(i) a passive foreign investment company is a controlled foreign corporation, and

(ii) the taxpayer is a United States shareholder in such controlled foreign corporation,

any amount included in gross income under section 1293 shall be treated as income in a separate category to the extent such amount is attributable to income in such category.

(4) Look-thru applies to dividends from noncontrolled section 902 corporations.

(A) In general. For purposes of this subsection, any dividend from a noncontrolled section 902 corporation with respect to the taxpayer shall be treated as income described in a subparagraph of paragraph (1) in proportion to the ratio of—

(i) the portion of earnings and profits attributable to income described in such subparagraph, to

(ii) the total amount of earnings and profits.

(B) Earnings and profits of controlled foreign corporations. In the case of any distribution from a controlled foreign corporation to a United States shareholder, rules similar to the rules of subparagraph (A) shall apply in determining the extent to which earnings and profits of the controlled foreign corporation which are attributable to dividends received from a noncontrolled section 902 corporation may be treated as income in a separate category.

(C) Special rules. For purposes of this paragraph—

(i) Earnings and profits.

(I) In general. The rules of section 316 shall apply.

(II) Regulations. The Secretary may prescribe regulations regarding the treatment of distributions out of earnings and profits for periods before the taxpayer's acquisition of the stock to which the distributions relate.

(ii) Inadequate substantiation. If the Secretary determines that the proper subparagraph of paragraph (1) in which a dividend is described has not been substantiated, such dividend shall be treated as income described in paragraph (1)(A).

(iii) Coordination with high-taxed income provisions. Rules similar to the rules of paragraph (3)(F) shall apply for purposes of this paragraph.

(iv) Look-thru with respect to carryover of credit. Rules similar to subparagraph (A) also shall apply to any carryforward under subsection (c) from a taxable year beginning before January 1, 2003, of tax allocable to a dividend from a noncontrolled section 902 corporation with respect to the taxpayer. The Secretary may by regulations provide for the allocation of any carryback of tax allocable to a dividend from a noncontrolled section 902 corporation from a taxable year beginning on or after January 1, 2003, to a taxable year beginning before such date for purposes of allocating such dividend among the separate categories in effect for the taxable year to which carried.

(5) Controlled foreign corporation; United States shareholder. For purposes of this subsection—

(A) Controlled foreign corporation. The term "controlled foreign corporation" has the meaning given such term by section 957 (taking into account section 953(c)).

(B) United States shareholder. The term "United States shareholder" has the meaning given such term by section 951(b) (taking into account section 953(c)).

(6) Separate application to items resourced under treaties.

(A) In general. If—

(i) without regard to any treaty obligation of the United States, any item of income would be treated as derived from sources within the United States,

(ii) under a treaty obligation of the United States, such item would be treated as arising from sources outside the United States, and

(iii) the taxpayer chooses the benefits of such treaty obligation, subsections (a), (b), and (c) of this section and sections 902, 907, and 960 shall be applied separately with respect to each such item.

(B) Coordination with other provisions. This paragraph shall not apply to any item of income to which subsection (h)(10) or section 865(h) applies.

(C) Regulations. The Secretary may issue such regulations or other guidance as is necessary or appropriate to carry out the purposes of this paragraph, including regulations or other guidance which provides that related items of income may be aggregated for purposes of this paragraph.

(7) Regulations. The Secretary shall prescribe such regulations as may be necessary or appropriate for the purposes of this subsection, including regulations—

(A) for the application of paragraph (3) and subsection (f)(5) in the case of income paid (or loans made) through 1 or more entities or between 2 or more chains of entities,

(B) preventing the manipulation of the character of income the effect of which is to avoid the purposes of this subsection, and

(C) providing that rules similar to the rules of paragraph (3)(C) shall apply to interest, rents, and royalties received or accrued from entities which would be controlled foreign corporations if they were foreign corporations.

(e) Repealed.

(f) Recapture of overall foreign loss.

(1) General rule. For purposes of this subpart and section 936, in the case of any taxpayer who sustains an overall foreign loss for any taxable year, that portion of the taxpayer's taxable income from sources without the United States for each succeeding taxable year which is equal to the lesser of—

(A) the amount of such loss (to the extent not used under this paragraph in prior taxable years), or

(B) 50 percent (or such larger percent as the taxpayer may choose) of the taxpayer's taxable income from sources without the United States for such succeeding taxable year,

shall be treated as income from sources within the United States (and not as income from sources without the United States).

(2) Overall foreign loss defined. For purposes of this subsection, the term "overall foreign loss" means the amount by which the gross income for the taxable year from sources without the United States (whether or not the taxpayer chooses the benefits of this subpart for such taxable year) for such year is exceeded by the sum of the deductions properly apportioned or allocated thereto, except that there shall not be taken into account—

(A) any net operating loss deduction allowable for such year under section 172(a), and

(B) any—

(i) foreign expropriation loss for such year, as defined in section 172(h) (as in effect on the day before the date of the enactment [11/5/90] of the Revenue Reconciliation Act of 1990), or

(ii) loss for such year which arises from fire, storm, shipwreck, or other casualty, or from theft,

to the extent such loss is not compensated for by insurance or otherwise.

(3) Dispositions.

(A) In general. For purposes of this chapter, if property which has been used predominantly without the United States in a trade or business is disposed of during any taxable year—

(i) the taxpayer, notwithstanding any other provision of this chapter (other than paragraph (1)), shall be deemed to have received and recognized taxable income from sources without the United States in the taxable year of the disposition, by reason of such disposition, in an amount equal to the lesser of the excess of the fair market value of such property over the taxpayer's adjusted basis in such property or the remaining amount of the overall foreign losses which were not used under paragraph (1) for such taxable year or any prior taxable year, and

(ii) paragraph (1) shall be applied with respect to such income by substituting "100 percent" for "50 percent."

In determining for purposes of this subparagraph whether the predominant use of any property has been without the United States, there shall be taken into account use during the 3-year period ending on the date of the disposition (or, if shorter, the period during which the property has been used in the trade or business).

(B) Disposition defined and special rules.

(i) For purposes of this subsection, the term "disposition" includes a sale, exchange, distribution, or gift of property whether or not gain or loss is recognized on the transfer.

(ii) Any taxable income recognized solely by reason of subparagraph (A) shall have the same characterization it would have had if the taxpayer had sold or exchanged the property.

(iii) The Secretary shall prescribe such regulations as he may deem necessary to provide for adjustments to the basis of property to reflect taxable income recognized solely by reason of subparagraph (A).

(C) Exceptions. Notwithstanding subparagraph (B), the term "disposition" does not include—

(i) a disposition of property which is not a material factor in the realization of income by the taxpayer, or

(ii) a disposition of property to a domestic corporation in a distribution or transfer described in section 381(a).

(D) Application to certain dispositions of stock in controlled foreign corporation.

(i) In general. This paragraph shall apply to an applicable disposition in the same manner as if it were a disposition of property described in subparagraph (A), except that the exception contained in subparagraph (C)(i) shall not apply.

(ii) Applicable disposition. For purposes of clause (i), the term "applicable disposition" means any disposition of any share of stock in a controlled foreign corporation in a transaction or series of transactions if, immediately before such transaction or series of transactions, the taxpayer owned more than 50 percent (by vote or value) of the stock of the controlled foreign corporation. Such term shall not include a disposition described in clause (iii) or (iv), except that clause (i) shall apply to any gain recognized on any such disposition.

(iii) Exception for certain exchanges where ownership percentage retained. A disposition shall not be treated as an applicable disposition under clause (ii) if it is part of a transaction or series of transactions—

(I) to which section 351 or 721 applies, or under which the transferor receives stock in a foreign corporation in exchange for the stock in the controlled foreign corporation and the stock received is exchanged basis property (as defined in section 7701(a)(44)), and

(II) immediately after which, the transferor owns (by vote or value) at least the same percentage of stock in the controlled foreign corporation (or, if the controlled foreign corporation is not in existence after such transaction or series of transactions, in another foreign corporation stock in which was received by the transferor in exchange for stock in the controlled foreign corporation) as the percentage of stock in the controlled foreign corporation which the taxpayer owned immediately before such transaction or series of transactions.

(iv) Exception for certain asset acquisitions. A disposition shall not be treated as an applicable disposition under clause (ii) if it is part of a transaction or series of transactions in which the taxpayer (or any member of an affiliated group of corporations filing a consolidated return under section 1501 which includes the taxpayer) acquires the assets of a controlled foreign corporation in exchange for the shares of the controlled foreign corporation in a liquidation described in section 332 or a reorganization described in section 368(a)(1).

(v) Controlled foreign corporation. For purposes of this subparagraph, the term "controlled foreign corporation" has the meaning given such term by section 957.

(vi) Stock ownership. For purposes of this subparagraph, ownership of stock shall be determined under the rules of subsections (a) and (b) of section 958.

(4) Accumulation distributions of foreign trust. For purposes of this chapter, in the case of amounts of income from sources without the United States which are treated under section 666 (without regard to subsections (b) and (c) thereof if the taxpayer chose to take a deduction with respect to the amounts described in such subsections under section 667(d)(1)(B)) as having been distributed by a foreign trust in a preceding taxable year, that portion of such amounts equal to the amount of any overall foreign loss sustained by the beneficiary in a year prior to the taxable year of the beneficiary in which such distribution is received from the trust shall be treated as income from sources within the United States (and not income from sources without the United States) to the extent that such loss was not used under this subsection in prior taxable years, or in the current taxable year, against other income of the beneficiary.

(5) Treatment of separate limitation losses.

(A) In general. The amount of the separate limitation losses for any taxable year shall reduce income from sources within the United States for such taxable year only to the extent the aggregate amount of such losses exceeds the aggregate amount of the separate limitation incomes for such taxable year.

(B) Allocation of losses. The separate limitation losses for any taxable year (to the extent such losses do not exceed the separate limitation incomes for such year) shall be allocated among (and operate to reduce) such incomes on a proportionate basis.

(C) Recharacterization of subsequent income. If—

(i) a separate limitation loss from any income category (hereinafter in this subparagraph referred to as "the loss category") was allocated to income from any other category under subparagraph (B), and

(ii) the loss category has income for a subsequent taxable year,

such income (to the extent it does not exceed the aggregate separate limitation losses from the loss category not previously recharacterized under this subparagraph) shall be recharacterized as income from such other category in proportion to the prior reductions under subparagraph (B) in such other category not previously taken into account under this subparagraph. Nothing in the preceding sentence shall be construed as recharacterizing any tax.

(D) Special rules for losses from sources in the United States. Any loss from sources in the United States for any taxable year (to the extent such loss does not exceed the separate limitation incomes from such year) shall be allocated among (and operate to reduce) such incomes on a proportionate basis. This subparagraph shall be applied after subparagraph (B).

(E) Definitions. For purposes of this paragraph—

(i) Income category. The term "income category" means each separate category of income described in subsection (d)(1).

(ii) Separate limitation income. The term "separate limitation income" means, with respect to any income category, the taxable income from sources outside the United States, separately computed for such category.

(iii) Separate limitation loss. The term "separate limitation loss" means, with respect to any income category, the loss from such category determined under the principles of section 907(c)(4)(B).

(F) Dispositions. If any separate limitation loss for any taxable year is allocated against any separate limitation income for such taxable year, except to the extent provided in regulations, rules similar to the rules of paragraph (3) shall apply to any disposition of property if gain from such disposition would be in the income category with respect to which there was such separate limitation loss.

Income from foreign sources — Code Sec. 904(h)(7)

(g) Recharacterization of overall domestic loss.

(1) General rule. For purposes of this subpart and section 936, in the case of any taxpayer who sustains an overall domestic loss for any taxable year beginning after December 31, 2006, that portion of the taxpayer's taxable income from sources within the United States for each succeeding taxable year which is equal to the lesser of—

(A) the amount of such loss (to the extent not used under this paragraph in prior taxable years), or

(B) 50 percent of the taxpayer's taxable income from sources within the United States for such succeeding taxable year,

shall be treated as income from sources without the United States (and not as income from sources within the United States).

(2) Overall domestic loss. For purposes of this subsection—

(A) In general. The term "overall domestic loss" means—

(i) with respect to any qualified taxable year, the domestic loss for such taxable year to the extent such loss offsets taxable income from sources without the United States for the taxable year or for any preceding qualified taxable year by reason of a carryback, and

(ii) with respect to any other taxable year, the domestic loss for such taxable year to the extent such loss offsets taxable income from sources without the United States for any preceding qualified taxable year by reason of a carryback.

(B) Domestic loss. For purposes of subparagraph (A), the term "domestic loss" means the amount by which the gross income for the taxable year from sources within the United States is exceeded by the sum of the deductions properly apportioned or allocated thereto (determined without regard to any carryback from a subsequent taxable year).

(C) Qualified taxable year. For purposes of subparagraph (A), the term "qualified taxable year" means any taxable year for which the taxpayer chose the benefits of this subpart.

(3) Characterization of subsequent income.

(A) In general. Any income from sources within the United States that is treated as income from sources without the United States under paragraph (1) shall be allocated among and increase the income categories in proportion to the loss from sources within the United States previously allocated to those income categories.

(B) Income category. For purposes of this paragraph, the term "income category" has the meaning given such term by subsection (f)(5)(E)(i).

(4) Coordination with subsection (f). The Secretary shall prescribe such regulations as may be necessary to coordinate the provisions of this subsection with the provisions of subsection (f).

(h) Source rules in case of United States-owned foreign corporations.

(1) In general. The following amounts which are derived from a United States-owned foreign corporation and which would be treated as derived from sources outside the United States without regard to this subsection shall, for purposes of this section, be treated as derived from sources within the United States to the extent provided in this subsection:

(A) Any amount included in gross income under—

(i) section 951(a) (relating to amounts included in gross income of United States shareholders), or

(ii) section 1293 (relating to current taxation of income from qualified funds).

(B) Interest.

(C) Dividends.

(2) Subpart F and passive foreign investment company inclusions. Any amount described in subparagraph (A) of paragraph (1) shall be treated as derived from sources within the United States to the extent such amount is attributable to income of the United States-owned foreign corporation from sources within the United States.

(3) Certain interest allocable to United States source income. Any interest which—

(A) is paid or accrued by a United States-owned foreign corporation during any taxable year,

(B) is paid or accrued to a United States shareholder (as defined in section 951(b)) or a related person (within the meaning of section 267(b)) to such a shareholder, and

(C) is properly allocable (under regulations prescribed by the Secretary) to income of such foreign corporation for the taxable year from sources within the United States,

shall be treated as derived from sources within the United States.

(4) Dividends.

(A) In general. The United States source ratio of any dividend paid or accrued by a United States-owned foreign corporation shall be treated as derived from sources within the United States.

(B) United States source ratio. For purposes of subparagraph (A), the term "United States source ratio" means, with respect to any dividend paid out of the earnings and profits for any taxable year, a fraction—

(i) the numerator of which is the portion of the earnings and profits for such taxable year from sources within the United States, and

(ii) the denominator of which is the total amount of earnings and profits for such taxable year.

(5) Exception where United States-owned foreign corporation has small amount of United States source income. Paragraph (3) shall not apply to interest paid or accrued during any taxable year (and paragraph (4) shall not apply to any dividends paid out of the earnings and profits for such taxable year) if—

(A) the United States-owned foreign corporation has earnings and profits for such taxable year, and

(B) less than 10 percent of such earnings and profits is attributable to sources within the United States.

For purposes of the preceding sentence, earnings and profits shall be determined without any reduction for interest described in paragraph (3) (determined without regard to subparagraph (C) thereof).

(6) United States-owned foreign corporation. For purposes of this subsection, the term "United States-owned foreign corporation" means any foreign corporation if 50 percent or more of—

(A) the total combined voting power of all classes of stock of such corporation entitled to vote, or

(B) the total value of the stock of such corporation,

is held directly (or indirectly through applying paragraphs (2) and (3) of section 958(a) and paragraph (4) of section 318(a)) by United States persons (as defined in section 7701(a)(30)).

(7) Dividend. For purposes of this subsection, the term "dividend" includes any gain treated as ordinary income under section 1246 or as a dividend under section 1248.

(8) Coordination with subsection (f). This subsection shall be applied before subsection (f).

(9) Treatment of certain domestic corporations. In the case of any dividend treated as not from sources within the United States under section 861(a)(2)(A), the corporation paying such dividend shall be treated for purposes of this subsection as a United States-owned foreign corporation.

(10) Coordination with treaties.

(A) In general. If—

(i) any amount derived from a United States-owned foreign corporation would be treated as derived from sources within the United States under this subsection by reason of an item of income of such United States-owned foreign corporation,

(ii) under a treaty obligation of the United States (applied without regard to this subsection and by treating any amount included in gross income under section 951(a)(1) as a dividend), such amount would be treated as arising from sources outside the United States, and

(iii) the taxpayer chooses the benefits of this paragraph,

this subsection shall not apply to such amount to the extent attributable to such item of income (but subsections (a), (b), and (c) of this section and sections 902, 907, and 960 shall be applied separately with respect to such amount to the extent so attributable).

(B) Special rule. Amounts included in gross income under section 951(a)(1) shall be treated as a dividend under subparagraph (A)(ii) only if dividends paid by each corporation (the stock in which is taken into account in determining whether the shareholder is a United States shareholder in the United States-owned foreign corporation), if paid to the United States shareholder, would be treated under a treaty obligation of the United States as arising from sources outside the United States (applied without regard to this subsection).

(11) Regulations. The Secretary shall prescribe such regulations as may be necessary or appropriate for purposes of this subsection, including—

(A) regulations for the application of this subsection in the case of interest or dividend payments through 1 or more entities, and

(B) regulations providing that this subsection shall apply to interest paid or accrued to any person (whether or not a United States shareholder).

• *Caution:* Code Sec. 904(i), following, reflects amendments made by Sec. 10909, P.L. 111-148. As provided in Sec. 10909(c), P.L. 111-148 as amended by Sec. 101(b)(1), P.L. 111-312, Code Sec. 904(i) will read as if those amendments had never been enacted, effective for tax. yrs. begin. after 12/31/2011. For Code Sec. 904(i) as it will read for tax. yrs. begin. after 12/31/2011, see below.

(i) Coordination with nonrefundable personal credits.
In the case of any taxable year of an individual to which section 26(a)(2) does not apply, for purposes of subsection (a), the tax against which the credit is taken is such tax reduced by the sum of the credits allowable under subpart A of part IV of subchapter A of this chapter (other than sections 24, 25A(i), 25B, 30, 30B, and 30D).

• *Caution:* Code Sec. 904(i), following, is effective for tax. yrs. begin. after 12/31/2011, and reflects the sunset of the amendments made by Sec. 10909, P.L. 111-148. For details of those amendments, effective date and sunset provisions, see the history for this Code Sec. For Code Sec. 904(i), effective for tax. yrs. begin. before 1/1/2012, see above.

(i) Coordination with nonrefundable personal credits.
In the case of any taxable year of an individual to which section 26(a)(2) does not apply, for purposes of subsection (a), the tax against which the credit is taken is such tax reduced by the sum of the credits allowable under subpart A of part IV of subchapter A of this chapter (other than sections 23, 24, 25A(i), 25B, 30, 30B, and 30D).

(j) Limitation on use of deconsolidation to avoid foreign tax credit limitations.

If 2 or more domestic corporations would be members of the same affiliated group if—

(1) section 1504(b) were applied without regard to the exceptions contained therein, and

(2) the constructive ownership rules of section 1563(e) applied for purposes of section 1504(a),

the Secretary may by regulations provide for resourcing the income of any of such corporations or for modifications to the consolidated return regulations to the extent that such resourcing or modifications are necessary to prevent the avoidance of the provisions of this subpart.

(k) Certain individuals exempt.

(1) In general. In the case of an individual to whom this subsection applies for any taxable year—

(A) the limitation of subsection (a) shall not apply,

(B) no taxes paid or accrued by the individual during such taxable year may be deemed paid or accrued under subsection (c) in any other taxable year, and

(C) no taxes paid or accrued by the individual during any other taxable year may be deemed paid or accrued under subsection (c) in such taxable year.

(2) Individuals to whom subsection applies. This subsection shall apply to an individual for any taxable year if—

(A) the entire amount of such individual's gross income for the taxable year from sources without the United States consists of qualified passive income,

(B) the amount of the creditable foreign taxes paid or accrued by the individual during the taxable year does not exceed $300 ($600 in the case of a joint return), and

(C) such individual elects to have this subsection apply for the taxable year.

(3) Definitions. For purposes of this subsection—

(A) Qualified passive income. The term "qualified passive income" means any item of gross income if—

(i) such item of income is passive income (as defined in subsection (d)(2)(B) without regard to clause (iii) thereof), and

(ii) such item of income is shown on a payee statement furnished to the individual.

(B) Creditable foreign taxes. The term "creditable foreign taxes" means any taxes for which a credit is allowable under section 901; except that such term shall not include any tax unless such tax is shown on a payee statement furnished to such individual.

(C) Payee statement. The term "payee statement" has the meaning given to such term by section 6724(d)(2).

(D) Estates and trusts not eligible. This subsection shall not apply to any estate or trust.

Income from foreign sources   Code Sec. 904

(l) Cross references.

(1) For increase of limitation under subsection (a) for taxes paid with respect to amounts received which were included in the gross income of the taxpayer for a prior taxable year as a United States shareholder with respect to a controlled foreign corporation, see section 960(b).

(2) For modification of limitation under subsection (a) for purposes of determining the amount of credit which can be taken against the alternative minimum tax, see section 59(a).

In 2010, P.L. 111-312, Sec. 101(a)(1), substituted "December 31, 2012" for "December 31, 2010" both places it appears in Sec. 901 of P.L. 107-16, effective as if included in the enactment of P.L. 107-16, EGTRRA, 6/7/2001.

—P.L. 111-312, Sec. 101(b)(1), amended Sec. 10909(c) of P.L. 111-148 to read as follows:

"(c) Sunset provision. Each provision of law amended by this section is amended to read as such provision would read if this section had never been enacted. The amendments made by the preceding sentence shall apply to taxable years beginning after December 31, 2011."

—P.L. 111-312, Sec. 101(b)(2), substituted "Except as provided in subsection (c), the amendments" for "The amendments" in Sec. 10909(d) of P.L. 111-148 (the effective date section for amendments made by Sec. 10909 of P.L. 111-148) [see below].

Prior to amendment, Sec. 10909(d) of P.L. 111-148 read as follows:

"(d) Effective date. The amendments made by this section shall apply to taxable years beginning after December 31, 2009."

—P.L. 111-312, Sec. 103(b)(1), substituted "2009, 2010, 2011, and 2012" for "2009 and 2010" in the heading of para. (d)(4) . . . Sec. 103(b)(2), substituted ", 2010, 2011, or 2012" for "or 2010" in para. (d)(4), effective for tax. yrs. begin. after 12/31/2010.

—P.L. 111-148, Sec. 10909(b)(2)(K), deleted "23," in subsec. (i), effective for tax. yrs. begin. after 12/31/2009, except as provided in Sec. 10909(c), see below. As provided in Sec. 10909(c) of this Act, as amended by Sec. 101(b)(1), P.L. 111-312. These amendments will be repealed as if never enacted effective for tax. yrs. begin. after 12/31/2011.

—P.L. 111-148, Sec. 10909(c), of this Act, relating to the application and extension of the EGTRRA sunset, provides:

"(c) Application and Extension of EGTRRA Sunset. Notwithstanding section 901 of the Economic Growth and Tax Relief Reconciliation Act of 2001, such section shall apply to the amendments made by this section and the amendments made by section 202 of such Act by substituting 'December 31, 2011' for 'December 31, 2010' in subsection (a)(1) thereof."

—P.L. 111-148, Sec. 10909(d), [as amended by Sec. 101(b)(2), P.L. 111-312, see above] reads as follows:

"(d) Effective date. Except as provided in subsection (c), the amendments made by this section shall apply to taxable years beginning after December 31, 2009."

—P.L. 111-226, Sec. 213(a), redsignated para. (d)(6) as para. (d)(7) and added new para. (d)(6), effective for tax. yrs. begin. after 8/10/2010. . . . Sec. 217(c)(2), amended para. (h)(9), effective for tax. yrs. begin. after 12/31/2010.

Prior to amendment, para. (h)(9) read as follows:

"(9) Treatment of certain domestic corporations.

"For purposes of this subsection—

"(A) in the case of interest treated as not from sources within the United States under section 861(a)(1)(A), the corporation paying such interest shall be treated as a United States-owned foreign corporation, and

"(B) in the case of any dividend treated as not from sources within the United States under section 861(a)(2)(A), the corporation paying such dividend shall be treated as a United States-owned foreign corporation."

Sec. 217(d)(2) of this Act reads as follows:

"(2) Grandfather rule for outstanding debt obligations.

"(A) In general. The amendments made by this section shall not apply to payments of interest on obligations issued before the date of the enactment of this Act.

"(B) Exception for related party debt. Subparagraph (A) shall not apply to any interest which is payable to a related person (determined under rules similar to the rules of section 954(d)(3)).

"(C) Significant modifications treated as new issues. For purposes of subparagraph (A), a significant modification of the terms of any obligation (including any extension of the term of such obligation) shall be treated as a new issue."

—P.L. 111-148, Sec. 10909(b)(2)(K), deleted "23," before "24," in subsec. (i), effective for tax. yrs. begin. after 12/31/2009.

—P.L. 111-148, Sec. 10909(c), of this Act, relating to the application and extension of the EGTRRA sunset, provides:

"(c) Application and Extension of EGTRRA Sunset. Notwithstanding section 901 of the Economic Growth and Tax Relief Reconciliation Act of 2001, such section shall apply to the amendments made by this section and the amendments made by section 202 of such Act by substituting 'December 31, 2011' for 'December 31, 2010' in subsection (a)(1) thereof."

In 2009, P.L. 111-5, Sec. 1004(b)(5), added "25A(i)," after "24," in subsec. (i), effective for tax. yrs. begin. after 12/31/2008.

—P.L. 111-5, Sec. 1142(b)(1)(E), substituted "25B, 30, and 30D" for "and 25B" in subsec. (i) [as amended by Sec. 1004(b)(5) of this Act, see above], effective for vehicles acquired after 2/17/2009.

—P.L. 111-5, Sec. 1144(b)(1)(E), added "30B," after "30" in subsec. (i) [as amended by Secs. 1004(b)(5) and 1142(b)(1)(E) of this Act, see above], effective for tax. yrs. begin. after 12/31/2008.

In 2007, P.L. 110-172, Sec. 11(f)(3), substituted "an affiliated group" for "a controlled group" in clause (f)(3)(D)(iv), effective for dispositions after 10/22/2004.

—P.L. 110-172, Sec. 11(g)(10)(A), added "and" at the end of subcl. (d)(2)(B)(v)(I), deleted subcl. (d)(2)(B)(v)(II) and redesignated subcl.(d)(2)(B)(v)(III) as (II) . . . Sec. 11(g)(10)(B), substituted "a former FSC (as defined in section 922)" for "a FSC (or a former FSC)" in subcl. (d)(2)(B)(v)(II) [as redesignated by Sec. 11(g)(10)(A) of this Act, see above] . . . Sec. 11(g)(10)(C), added a sentence at the end of clause (d)(2)(B)(v), enacted 12/29/2007.

Prior to deletion, subcl. (d)(2)(B)(v)(II) read as follows:

"(II) taxable income attributable to foreign trade income (within the meaning of section 923(b))," and"

In 2006, P.L. 109-280, Sec. 811, of this Act [relating to Sec. 901 of P.L. 107-16, see below], provides:

"Sec. 811. Pensions and individual retirement arrangement provisions of Economic Growth and Tax Relief Reconciliation Act of 2001 made permanent.

"Title IX of the Economic Growth and Tax Relief Reconciliation Act of 2001 shall not apply to the provisions of, and amendments made by, subtitles A through F of title VI of such Act (relating to pension and individual retirement arrangement provisions)."

In 2005, P.L. 109-135, Sec. 402(i)(3)(G), amended subsec. (i), effective for tax. yrs. begin. after 12/31/2005.

Prior to amendment, subsec. (i) read as follows:

"(i) Coordination with nonrefundable personal credits. In the case of an individual, for purposes of subsection (a), the tax against which the credit is taken is such tax reduced by the sum of the credits allowable under subpart A of part IV of subchapter A of this chapter. This subsection shall not apply to taxable years beginning during 2000, 2001, 2002, 2003, 2004, or 2005."

—P.L. 109-135, Sec. 402(i)(3)(H), of this Act, reads as follows:

"(H) Application of EGTRRA sunset. The amendments made by this paragraph (and each part thereof) shall be subject to title IX of the Economic Growth and Tax Relief Reconciliation Act of 2001 [Sec. 901 of P.L. 107-16] in the same manner as the provisions of such Act to which such amendment (or part thereof) relates."

—P.L. 109-135, Sec. 403(k), amended para. (g)(2), effective for tax. yrs. begin. after 12/31/2006 as if included in Sec. 402 of the American Jobs Creation Act of 2004, P.L. 108-357.

Prior to amendment, para. (g)(2) read as follows:

"(2) Overall domestic loss defined. For purposes of this subsection—

"(A) In general. The term 'overall domestic loss' means any domestic loss to the extent such loss offsets taxable income from sources without the United States for the taxable year or for any preceding taxable year by reason of a carryback. For purposes of the preceding sentence, the term 'domestic loss' means the amount by which the gross income for the taxable year from sources within the United States is exceeded by the sum of the deductions properly apportioned or allocated thereto (determined without regard to any carryback from a subsequent taxable year).

"(B) Taxpayer must have elected foreign tax credit for year of loss. The term 'overall domestic loss' shall not include any loss for any taxable year unless the taxpayer chose the benefits of this subpart for such taxable year."

—P.L. 109-135, Sec. 403(l), added Sec. 403(d) of P.L. 108-357 [see below].

—P.L. 109-135, Sec. 403(o), added "as in effect before its repeal" after "section 954(f)" in subpara. (d)(2)(D), effective for tax. yrs. of foreign corporations begin. after 12/31/2004, and for tax. yrs. of U.S. shareholders with or within which such tax. yrs. of foreign corporations end.

In 2004, P.L. 108-357, Sec. 402(a), redesignated clauses (g)-(k) as (h)-(l) and added clause (g), effective for tax. yrs. begin. after 12/31/2006.

—P.L. 108-357, Sec. 403(a), amended para. (d)(4) . . . Sec. 403(b)(1), deleted subpara. (d)(1)(E) . . . Sec. 403(b)(2), added "and" at the end of subclause (d)(2)(C)(iii)(I), deleted subclause (d)(2)(C)(iii)(II) and redesignated subclause (d)(2)(C)(iii)(III) as (II) . . . Sec. 403(b)(3), substituted "Such term does not include any financial services income." for "Such term does not include any dividend from a noncontrolled section 902 corporation out of earnings and profits accumulated in taxable years beginning before January 1, 2003 and does not include any financial services income." in subpara. (d)(2)(D) . . . Sec. 403(b)(4)(A), added "or (4)" after "paragraph (3)" in clause (d)(2)(E)(i) . . . Sec. 403(b)(4)(B), deleted clauses (d)(2)(E)(ii) and (iv) and redesignated clause (d)(2)(E)(iii) as (ii) . . . Sec. 403(b)(5), substituted "or (D)" for "(D), or (E)" in clause (d)(3)(F)(i), effective for tax. yrs. begin. after 12/31/2002.

Prior to deletion, subpara. (d)(1)(E) read as follows:

"(E) in the case of a corporation, dividends from noncontrolled section 902 corporations out of earnings and profits accumulated in taxable years beginning before January 1, 2003,"

Prior to deletion, subclause (d)(2)(C)(iii)(II) read as follows:

"(II) any dividend from a noncontrolled section 902 corporation out of earnings and profits accumulated in taxable years beginning before January 1, 2003, and"

Prior to deletion, clause (d)(2)(E)(ii) read as follows:

"(ii) Special rule for taxes on high-withholding tax interest. If a foreign corporation is a noncontrolled section 902 corporation with respect to the taxpayer, taxes on high withholding tax interest (to the extent imposed at a rate in excess of 5 percent) shall not be treated as foreign taxes for purposes of determining the amount of foreign taxes deemed paid by the taxpayer under section 902."

Prior to deletion, clause (d)(2)(E)(iv) read as follows:

"(iv) All non-PFICs treated as one. All noncontrolled section 902 corporations which are not passive foreign investment companies (as defined in section 1297) shall be treated as one noncontrolled section 902 corporation for purposes of paragraph (1)."

Prior to amendment, para. (d)(4) read as follows:

"(4) Look-thru applies to dividends from noncontrolled section 902 corporations.

"(A) In general. For purposes of this subsection, any applicable dividend shall be treated as income in a separate category in proportion to the ratio of—

"(i) the portion of the earnings and profits described in subparagraph (B)(ii) attributable to income in such category, to

"(ii) the total amount of such earnings and profits.

"(B) Applicable dividend. For purposes of subparagraph (A), the term 'applicable dividend' means any dividend—

"(i) from a noncontrolled section 902 corporation with respect to the taxpayer, and

"(ii) paid out of earnings and profits accumulated in taxable years beginning after December 31, 2002.

"(C) Special rules.

"(i) In general. Rules similar to the rules of paragraph (3)(F) shall apply for purposes of this paragraph.

"(ii) Earnings and profits. For purposes of this paragraph and paragraph (1)(E)—

"(I) In general. The rules of section 316 shall apply.

"(II) Regulations. The Secretary may prescribe regulations regarding the treatment of distributions out of earnings and profits for periods prior to the taxpayer's acquisition of such stock."

—P.L. 108-357, Sec. 403(d), [as added by Sec. 403(l) of P.L. 109-135, see above] reads as follows:

"(d) Transition rule. If the taxpayer elects (at such time and in such form and manner as the Secretary of the Treasury may prescribe) to have the rules of this subsection apply—

"(1) the amendments made by this section shall not apply to taxable years beginning after December 31, 2002, and before January 1, 2005, or

"(2) in the case of taxable years beginning after December 31, 2004, clause (iv) of section 904(d)(4)(C) of the Internal Revenue Code of 1986 (as amended by this section) shall be applied by substituting 'January 1, 2005' for 'January 1, 2003' both places it appears."

—P.L. 108-357, Sec. 404(a), amended para. (d)(1)... Sec. 404(b), deleted subpara. (d)(2)(B), redesignated subpara. (d)(2)(A) as (d)(2)(B) and added subpara. (d)(2)(A)... Sec. 404(c), added clause (d)(2)(B)(v) [as redesignated by Sec. 404(b) of this Act, see above]... Sec. 404(d), deleted subpara. (d)(2)(D), redesignated subpara. (d)(2)(C) as (d)(2)(D) and added subpara. (d)(2)(C), effective for tax. yrs. begin. after 12/31/2006.

Prior to amendment, para. (d)(1) read as follows:

"(1) In general. The provisions of subsections (a), (b), and (c) and sections 902, 907, and 960 shall be applied separately with respect to each of the following items of income:

"(A) passive income,

"(B) high withholding tax interest,

"(C) financial services income,

"(D) shipping income,

"(E) Repealed.

"(F) dividends from a DISC or former DISC (as defined in section 992(a)) to the extent such dividends are treated as income from sources without the United States,

"(G) taxable income attributable to foreign trade income (within the meaning of section 923(b)),

"(H) distributions from a FSC (or a former FSC) out of earnings and profits attributable to foreign trade income (within the meaning of section 923(b)) or interest or carrying charges (as defined in section 927(d)(1)) derived from a transaction which results in foreign trade income (as defined in section 923(b)), and

"(I) income other than income described in any of the preceding subparagraphs."

Prior to deletion, subpara. (d)(2)(B) read as follows:

"(B) High withholding tax interest.

"(i) In general. Except as otherwise provided in this subparagraph, the term 'high withholding tax interest' means any interest if—

"(I) such interest is subject to a withholding tax of a foreign country or possession of the United States (or other tax determined on a gross basis), and

"(II) the rate of such tax applicable to such interest is at least 5 percent.

"(ii) Exception for export financing. The term 'high withholding tax interest' shall not include any export financing interest.

"(iii) Regulations. The Secretary may by regulations provide that—

"(I) amounts (not otherwise high withholding tax interest) shall be treated as high withholding tax interest where necessary to prevent avoidance of the purposes of this subparagraph, and

"(II) a tax shall not be treated as a withholding tax or other tax imposed on a gross basis if such tax is in the nature of a prepayment of a tax imposed on a net basis."

Prior to deletion, subpara. (d)(2)(D) read as follows:

"(D) Shipping income. The term 'shipping income' means any income received or accrued by any person which is of a kind which would be foreign base company shipping income (as defined in section 954(f)). Such term does not include any dividend from a noncontrolled section 902 corporation out of earnings and profits accumulated in taxable years beginning before January 1, 2003 and does not include any financial services income."

—P.L. 108-357, Sec. 404(e), redesignated subparas. (d)(2)(H)-(I) as (d)(2)(I)-(J) and added subpara. (d)(2)(H), effective for tax. yrs. begin. after 12/31/2006, except as provided in Sec. 404(g)(2) of this Act, which reads as follows:

"(2) Transitional rule relating to income tax base difference. Section 904(d)(2)(H)(ii) of the Internal Revenue Code of 1986, as added by subsection (e), shall apply to taxable years beginning after December 31, 2004."

—P.L. 108-357, Sec. 404(f)(1), deleted subclause (d)(2)(B)(iii)(I) [as redesignated by Sec. 404(b) of this Act, see above] and redesignated subclauses (d)(2)(B)(iii)(II)-(III) as (d)(2)(B)(iii)(I)-(II) [as redesignated by Sec. 404(b) of this Act, see above]... Sec. 404(f)(2), added "or" at the end of subclause (d)(2)(D)(i)(I) [as redesignated by Sec. 404(d) of this Act, see above], deleted subclauses (d)(2)(D)(i)(II)-(III) [as redesignated by Sec. 404(d) of this Act, see above] and added subclause (d)(2)(D)(i)(II) [as redesignated by Sec. 404(d) of this Act, see above]... Sec. 404(f)(3), deleted clause (d)(2)(D)(iii) [as redesignated by Sec. 404(d) of this Act, see above]... Sec. 404(f)(4), amended para. (d)(3)... Sec. 404(f)(5), added subpara. (d)(2)(K)... Sec. 404(f)(6), substituted "subsection (d)(2)(B)" for "subsection (d)(2)(A)" in clause (j)(3)(A)(i) [sic (k)(3)(A)(i)] [redesignated as clause (k)(3)(A)(i) by Sec. 402(a) of tis Act, see above], effective for tax. yrs. begin. after 12/31/2006.

Prior to deletion, subclause (d)(2)(B)(iii)(II) [as redesignated by Sec. 404(b) of this Act, see above] read as follows:

"(I) any income described in a subparagraph of paragraph (1) other than subparagraph (A),"

Prior to deletion, subclauses (d)(2)(D)(i)(II)-(III) [as redesignated by Sec. 404(d) of this Act, see above] read as follows:

"(II) passive income (determined without regard to subclauses (I) and (III) of subparagraph (A)(iii)), or

"(III) export financing interest which (but for subparagraph (B)(ii)) would be high withholding tax interest."

Prior to deletion, clause (d)(2)(D)(iii) [as redesignated by Sec. 404(d) of this Act, see above] read as follows:

"(iii) Exceptions. The term 'financial services income' does not include—

"(I) any high withholding tax interest,

"(II) any dividend from a noncontrolled section 902 corporation out of earnings and profits accumulated in taxable years beginning before January 1, 2003, and

"(III) any export financing interest not described in clause (i)(III)."

Prior to amendment, para. (d)(3) read as follows:

"(3) Look-thru in case of controlled foreign corporations.

"(A) In general. Except as otherwise provided in this paragraph, dividends, interest, rents, and royalties received or accrued by the taxpayer from a controlled foreign corporation in which the taxpayer is a United States shareholder shall not be treated as income in a separate category.

"(B) Subpart F inclusions. Any amount included in gross income under section 951(a)(1)(A) shall be treated as income in a separate category to the extent the amount so included is attributable to income in such category.

"(C) Interest, rents, and royalties. Any interest, rent, or royalty which is received or accrued from a controlled foreign corporation in which the taxpayer is a United States shareholder shall be treated as income in a separate category to the extent it is properly allocable (under regulations prescribed by the Secretary) to income of the controlled foreign corporation in such category.

"(D) Dividends. Any dividend paid out of the earnings and profits of any controlled foreign corporation in which the taxpayer is a United States shareholder shall be treated as income in a separate category in proportion to the ratio of—

"(i) the portion of the earnings and profits attributable to income in such category, to

"(ii) the total amount of earnings and profits.

"(E) Look-thru applies only where subpart F applies. If a controlled foreign corporation meets the requirements of section 954(b)(3)(A) (relating to de minimis rule) for any taxable year, for purposes of this paragraph, none of its foreign base company income (as defined in section 954(a) without regard to section 954(b)(5)) and none of its gross insurance income (as defined in section 954(b)(3)(C)) for such taxable year shall be treated as income in a separate category, except that this sentence shall not apply to any income which (without regard to this sentence) would be treated as financial services income. Solely for purposes of applying subparagraph (D), passive income of a controlled foreign corporation shall not be treated as income in a separate category if the requirements of section 954(b)(4) are met with respect to such income.

"(F) Separate category. For purposes of this paragraph—

"(i) In general. Except as provided in clause (ii), the term 'separate category' means any category of income described in subparagraph (A), (B), (C), (D), or (E) of paragraph (1).

"(ii) Coordination with high-taxed income provisions.

"(I) In determining whether any income of a controlled foreign corporation is in a separate category, subclause (III) of paragraph (2)(A)(iii) shall not apply.

"(II) Any income of the taxpayer which is treated as income in a separate category under this paragraph shall be so treated notwithstanding any provision of paragraph (2); except that the determination of whether any amount is high-taxed income shall be made after the application of this paragraph.

"(G) Dividend. For purposes of this paragraph, the term 'dividend' includes any amount included in gross income in section 951(a)(1)(B). Any amount included in gross income under section 78 to the extent attributable to amounts included in gross income in section 951(a)(1)(A) shall not be treated as a dividend but shall be included as included in gross income under section 951(a)(1)(A).

"(H) Exception for certain high withholding tax interest. This paragraph shall not apply to any amount which—

"(i) without regard to this paragraph, is high withholding tax interest (including any amount treated as high withholding tax interest under paragraph (2)(B)(iii)), and

Income from foreign sources Code Sec. 904

"(ii) would (but for this subparagraph) be treated as financial services income under this paragraph.

The amount to which this paragraph does not apply by reason of the preceding sentence shall not exceed the interest or equivalent income of the controlled foreign corporation taken into account in determining financial services income without regard to this subparagraph.

"(I) Look-thru applies to passive foreign investment company inclusion if—

"(i) a passive foreign investment company is a controlled foreign corporation, and

"(ii) the taxpayer is a United States shareholder in such controlled foreign corporation,

any amount included in gross income under section 1293 shall be treated as income in a separate category to the extent such amount is attributable to income in such category."

—P.L. 108-357, Sec. 413(c)(14), amended clause (d)(2)(A)(ii) [(d)(2)(B)(ii)]... Sec. 413(c)(15)(A), added "or" at the end of clause (h)(1)(A)(i) [as redesignated by Sec. 402(a) of this Act, see above], deleted clause (h)(1)(A)(ii) [as redesignated by Sec. 402(a) of this Act, see above] and redesignated clause (h)(1)(A)(iii) as (h)(1)(A)(ii) [as redesignated by Sec. 402(a) of this Act, see above]... Sec. 413(c)(15)(B), deleted "foreign personal holding or" after "Subpart F and" in the heading of para. (h)(2) [as redesignated by Sec. 402(a) of this Act, see above], effective for tax. yrs. of foreign corporations begin. after 12/31/2004, and for tax. yrs. of U.S. shareholders with or within which such tax. yrs. of foreign corporations end.

Prior to amendment, clause (d)(2)(A)(ii) [sic (d)(2)(B)(ii)] read as follows:

"(ii) Certain amounts included. Except as provided in clause (iii), the term 'passive income' includes any amount includible in gross income under section 551 or, except as provided in subparagraph (E)(iii) or paragraph (3)(I), section 1293 (relating to certain passive foreign investment companies)."

Prior to deletion, clause (h)(1)(A)(ii) [as redesignated by Sec. 402(a) of this Act, see above] read as follows:

"(ii) section 551 (relating to foreign personal holding company income taxed to United States shareholders), or"

—P.L. 108-357, Sec. 417(a)(1), deleted "in the second preceding taxable year," before " in the first preceding taxable year" in subsec. (c), effective for excess foreign taxes arising in tax. yrs. begin. after 10/22/2004.

—P.L. 108-357, Sec. 417(a)(2), substituted "and in any of the first 10" for ", and in the first, second, third, fourth, or fifth" in subsec. (c), effective for excess foreign taxes which (without regard to the amendments made by Sec. 417 of this Act) may be carried to any tax. yr. end. after 10/22/2004.

—P.L. 108-357, Sec. 895(a), added subpara. (f)(3)(D), effective for dispositions after 10/22/2004.

—P.L. 108-311, Sec. 312(b)(1), substituted "2003, 2004, or 2005" for "or 2003" in subsec. (h), effective for tax. yrs. begin. after 12/31/2003.

—P.L. 108-311, Sec. 312(b)(2), of this Act, provides:

"(2) The amendments made by sections 201(b), 202(f), and 618(b) of the Economic Growth and Tax Relief Reconciliation Act of 2001 [P.L. 107-16] shall not apply to taxable years beginning during 2004 or 2005."

In 2002, P.L. 107-358, Sec. 2, added subsec. (c) in Sec. 901 of P.L. 107-16 [see below], effective 12/17/2002.

—P.L. 107-147, Sec. 601(b)(1), substituted "during 2000, 2001, 2002, or 2003" for "during 2000 or 2001" in subsec. (h), effective for tax. yrs. begin. after 12/31/2001.

—P.L. 107-147, Sec. 601(b)(2), of this Act, provides:

"(2) The amendments made by sections 201(b), 202(f), and 618(b) of the Economic Growth and Tax Relief Reconciliation Act of 2001 shall not apply to taxable years beginning during 2002 and 2003."

In 2001, P.L. 107-16, Sec. 201(b)(2)(G), added "(other than section 24)" after "chapter" in subsec. (h), effective for tax. yrs. begin. after 12/31/2001. For special provision, see Sec. 601(b)(2) of P.L. 107-147 and Sec. 312(b)(2) of 108-311, above.

—P.L. 107-16, Sec. 202(f)(2)(C), substituted "sections 23 and 24" for "section 24" in subsec. (h) [as amended by Sec. 201(b)(2)(G) of this Act, see above], effective for tax. yrs. begin. after 12/31/2001. For special provision, see Sec. 601(b)(2) of P.L. 107-147, above.

—P.L. 107-16, Sec. 618(b)(2)(D), substituted ", 24, and 25B" for "and 24" in subsec. (h) [as amended by Sec. 201(b)(2)(G) and Sec. 202(f)(2)(C) of this Act, see above], effective for tax. yrs. begin. after 12/31/2001. For special provision, see Sec. 601(b)(2) of P.L. 107-147 and Sec. 312(b)(2) of 108-311, above.

—P.L. 107-16, Sec. 901, of this Act [as amended by Sec. 2 of P.L. 107-358, and Sec. 101(a)(1) of P.L. 111-312, and as related to Sec. 811 of P.L. 109-280, see above], reads as follows:

"Sec. 901. Sunset of provisions of Act.

"(a) In general. All provisions of, and amendments made by, this Act shall not apply—

"(1) to taxable, plan, or limitation years beginning after December 31, 2012, or

"(2) in the case of title V, to estates of decedents dying, gifts made, or generation skipping transfers, after December 31, 2012.

"(b) Application of certain laws. The Internal Revenue Code of 1986 and the Employee Retirement Income Security Act of 1974 shall be applied and administered to years, estates, gifts, and transfers described in subsection (a) as if the provisions and amendments described in subsection (a) had never been enacted.

"(c) Exception. Subsection (a) shall not apply to section 803 (relating to no federal income tax on restitution received by victims of the Nazi regime or their heirs or estates)."

In 1999, P.L. 106-170, Sec. 501(b)(2), added a sentence at the end of subsec. (h), effective for tax. yrs. begin. after 12/31/98.

In 1997, P.L. 105-34, Sec. 311(c)(3), added subpara. (b)(2)(C), effective for tax. yrs. end. after 5/6/97.

—P.L. 105-34, Sec. 1101(a), redesignated subsec. (j) as subsec. (k) and added new subsec. (j), effective for tax. yrs. begin. after 12/31/97.

—P.L. 105-34, Sec. 1105(a)(1), amended subpara. (d)(1)(E)... Sec. 1105(a)(2), added clause (d)(2)(E)(iv)... Sec. 1105(a)(3), added "out of earnings and profits accumulated in taxable years beginning before January 1, 2003" after "corporation" in subclause (d)(2)(C)(iii)(II) and subpara. (d)(2)(D)... Sec. 1105(b), redesignated paras. (d)(4) and (5) as paras. (d)(5) and (6), and added a new para. (d)(4), effective for tax. yrs. begin. after 12/31/2002.

Prior to amendment, subpara. (d)(1)(E) read as follows:

"(E) in the case of a corporation, dividends from each noncontrolled section 902 corporation,"

—P.L. 105-34, Sec. 1111(b), deleted "and except as provided in regulations, the taxpayer was a United States shareholder in such corporation" at the end of clause (d)(2)(E)(i), effective for distributions after 8/5/97.

—P.L. 105-34, Sec. 1163(b), substituted "subclauses (I) and (III)" for "subclause (I)" in subclause (d)(2)(C)(ii)(II), effective 8/5/97.

In 1996, P.L. 104-188, Sec. 1501(b)(1), substituted "section 951(a)(1)(B)" for "subparagraph (B) or (C) of section 951(a)(1)" in subpara. (d)(3)(G) [as amended by Sec. 1703(i)(i) of this Act, see below]... Sec. 1501(b)(11), substituted "section 951(a)(1)(B)" for "subparagraph (B) or (C) of section 951(a)(1)" in subpara. (d)(3)(G) [same amendment as Sec. 1501(b)(1) of this Act, see above], effective for tax. yrs. of foreign corporations begin. after 12/31/96, and for tax. yrs. of U.S. shareholders within which or with which such tax. yrs. of foreign corporations end.

—P.L. 104-188, Sec. 1703(i)(1), substituted "subparagraph (B) or (C) of section 951(a)(1)" for "section 951(a)(1)(B)" in subpara. (d)(3)(G), effective for tax. yrs. of foreign corporations begin. after 9/30/93, and to tax. yrs. of U.S. shareholders in which or with which such tax. yrs. of foreign corporations end.

—P.L. 104-188, Sec. 1704(t)(36), added "(as in effect on the day before the date of the enactment of the Revenue Reconciliation Act of 1990)" after "section 172(h)" in clause (f)(2)(B)(i), effective 8/20/96.

In 1993, P.L. 103-66, Sec. 13227(d), added "(without regard to subsections (a)(4) and (i) thereof)" before the period at the end of para. (b)(4), effective for tax. yrs. begin. after 12/31/93.

—P.L. 103-66, Sec. 13235(a)(2), added "and" at the end of subclause (d)(2)(A)(iii)(II), substituted a period for ", and" at the end of subclause (d)(2)(A)(iii)(III), and deleted subclause (d)(2)(A)(iii)(IV), effective for tax. yrs. begin. after 12/31/92.

Prior to amendment, subclause (d)(2)(A)(iii)(IV) read as follows:

"(IV) any foreign oil and gas extraction income (as defined in section 907(c))."

In 1990, P.L. 101-508, Sec. 11101(d)(5)(A), substituted "subsection (h)" for "subsection (j)" in clause (b)(3)(D)(i)... Sec. 11101(d)(5)(B), substituted "section 1(h)" for "section 1(j)" in subclause (b)(3)(E)(iii)(I), effective for tax. yrs. begin. after 12/31/90.

—P.L. 101-508, Sec. 11801(a)(31), repealed subsec. (e), effective 11/5/90 except as provided in Sec. 11821(b) of this Act, which reads as follows:

"(b) Savings provision. If—

"(1) any provision amended or repealed by this part applied to—

"(A) any transaction occurring before the date of the enactment of this act [11/5/90],

"(B) any property acquired before such date of enactment [11/5/90], or

"(C) any item of income, loss, deduction, or credit taken into account before such date of enactment [11/5/90], and

"(2) the treatment of such transaction, property, or item under such provision would (without regard to the amendments made by this part) affect liability for tax for periods ending after such date of enactment [11/5/90],

nothing in the amendments made by this part shall be construed to affect the treatment of such transaction, property, or item for purposes of determining liability for tax for periods ending after such date of enactment [11/5/90]."

Prior to repeal, subsec. (e) read as follows:

"(e) Transitional rules for carrybacks and carryovers for taxpayers on the per-country limitation.

"(1) Application of subsection. This subsection shall apply only to a taxpayer who is on the per-country limitation for his last taxable year beginning before January 1, 1976.

"(2) Carryovers to years beginning after December 31, 1975. In the case of any taxpayer to whom this subsection applies, any carryover from a taxable year beginning before January 1, 1976, may be used in taxable years beginning after December 31, 1975, to the extent provided in subsection (c), but only to the extent such carryover could have been used in such succeeding taxable years if the per-country limitation continued to apply to all taxable years beginning after December 31, 1975.

"(3) Carrybacks to years beginning before January 1, 1976. In the case of any taxpayer to whom this subsection applies, any carryback from a taxable year beginning after December 31, 1975, may be used in taxable years beginning before January 1, 1976, to the extent provided in subsection (c), but only to the extent such carryback could have been used in such preceding taxable year if the per-country limitation continued to apply to all taxable years beginning after December 31, 1975.

"(4) Application of limitations. For purposes of this subsection—

"(A) the overall limitation shall be applied before the per-country limitation, and

"(B) where the amount of any carryback or carryover is reduced by the overall limitation, the reduction shall be allocated to the amounts carried from each coun-

2,563

try or possession in the proportion to the taxes paid or accrued to such country or possession in the taxable year from which such amount is being carried."

In 1989, P.L. 101-239, Sec. 7402(a), redesignated subsec. (i) as subsec. (j) and added new subsec. (i), effective for tax. yrs. begin. after 7/10/89.

—P.L. 101-239, Sec. 7404(a), repealed Sec. 1201(e)(2) of P.L. 99-514, [part of the effective date for amendments made by Sec. 1201 of P.L. 99-514, see below] effective for tax. yrs. begin. after 12/31/89. Sec. 7404(c) of this Act provides special rules as follows:

"(c) Exception for certain taxpayers with substantial loan reserves.

"(1) In general. The repeal made by subsection (a) shall not apply to any taxpayer if, on any financial statement filed by such taxpayer for regulatory purposes with respect to any quarter ending during the period beginning on March 31, 1989 and ending on December 31, 1989, such taxpayer showed loss reserves against its qualified loans equal to at least 25 percent of the amount of such loans.

"(2) Definitions and special rules. For purposes of this subsection—

"(A) Qualified loan. The term 'qualified loan' has the meaning given such term by section 1201(e)(2)(H) of the Tax Reform Act of 1986 (as in effect before its repeal by subsection (a)).

"(B) Parent-subsidiary controlled groups. In the case of any taxpayer which is a member of a parent-subsidiary controlled group (as defined in section 585(c)(5)(A)), this subsection shall be applied by treating all members of such group as 1 taxpayer."

Prior to repeal, Sec. 1201(e)(2) [as amended by Sec. 1012(a)(5) of P.L. 100-647, see below] of P.L. 99-514 read as follows:

"(2) Qualified loans.

"(A) In general. The following shall not be treated as high withholding tax interest for purposes of applying section 904(d) of the Internal Revenue Code of 1986 (as amended by this section):

"(i) Any interest received or accrued by any taxpayer during any taxable year beginning after December 31, 1986, and before January 1, 1990, on any pre-1990 qualified loan, and

"(ii) The phase-out percentage of any interest received or accrued by any taxpayer during any taxable year beginning after December 31, 1989 on any post-1989 qualified loan.

"(B) Phase-out percentage. For purposes of subparagraph (A) the phase-out percentage is—

"In the case of the following taxable years beginning after 12/31/89:	The phase out percentage is:
1st	80
2nd	60
3rd	40
4th	20
5th or succeeding	0

"(C) Pre-1990 qualified loan. For purposes of subparagraph (A), the term 'pre-1990 qualified loan' means, with respect to any taxable year beginning before January 1, 1990, any qualified loan outstanding at any time during such taxable year to the extent that the total amount of foreign taxes which would be creditable (without regard to the limitation of section 904 of the Internal Revenue Code of 1986) with respect to all qualified loans outstanding at any time during such taxable year does not exceed the applicable credit limit for such taxable year.

"(D) Post-1989 qualified loans. For purposes of subparagraph (A), the term 'post-1989 qualified loan' means any qualified loan outstanding as of the close of the 1st taxable year of the taxpayer beginning after December 31, 1988, to the extent that the total amount of foreign taxes which would be creditable (without regard to the limitation of section 904 of the Internal Revenue Code of 1986) with respect to all qualified loans outstanding as of the close of such taxable year does not exceed the applicable credit limit for post-1989 qualified loans.

"(E) Classification of qualified loans. For purposes of this paragraph, if the foreign taxes creditable for any taxable year beginning before January 1, 1990, with respect to any qualified loan, when added to the aggregate amount of foreign taxes creditable for such taxable year with respect to qualified loans entered into by the taxpayer before the date on which such qualified loan was entered into, exceed the applicable credit limit, then that portion of a qualified loan which causes the taxpayer to exceed the applicable credit limit shall not be treated as a pre-1990 or post-1989 qualified loan, as the case may be.

"(F) Applicable credit limit.

"(i) In general. The applicable credit limit shall be equal to—

"(I) except as provided in subclause (II), 110 percent of the base credit amount multiplied by the applicable interest rate adjustment for the taxable year, and

"(II) in the case of post-1989 qualified loans, the amount determined under subclause (I) (without regard to the interest rate adjustment) multiplied by the interest rate adjustment for post-1989 qualified loans.

"(ii) Base credit amount. The base credit amount of a taxpayer shall be an amount equal to the principal amount of qualified loans held by such taxpayer on November 16, 1985, multiplied by the product of—

"(I) the interest rate applicable to such loan on November 16, 1985, and

"(II) the foreign withholding tax rate applicable to interest payable with respect to such loan on November 16, 1985.

"(G) Interest rate adjustment.

"(i) In general. Except as provided in clause (ii), the applicable interest rate adjustment shall equal the ratio of the weighted average 6-month London Interbank Offered Rate (LIBOR) for the taxable year in question to LIBOR on November 15, 1985.

"(ii) Post-1989 qualified loans. The applicable interest rate adjustment for post-1989 qualified loans shall be equal to the ratio of LIBOR on the last day of the taxpayer's 1st taxable year beginning after December 31, 1988 to LIBOR on November 15, 1985.

"(H) Qualified loan. For purposes of this subsection, the term 'qualified loan' means any loan made by the taxpayer to any of the following countries or any resident thereof for use in such country:

"(i) Argentina.
"(ii) Bolivia.
"(iii) Brazil.
"(iv) Chile.
"(v) Columbia.
"(vi) Costa Rica.
"(vii) The Dominican Republic.
"(viii) Ecuador.
"(ix) Guyana.
"(x) Honduras.
"(xi) The Ivory Coast.
"(xii) Jamaica.
"(xiii) Liberia.
"(xiv) Madagascar.
"(xv) Malawi.
"(xvi) Mexico.
"(xvii) Morocco.
"(xviii) Mozambique.
"(xix) Niger.
"(xx) Nigeria.
"(xxi) Panama.
"(xxii) Peru.
"(xxiii) The Philippines.
"(xxiv) Romania.
"(xxv) Senegal.
"(xxvi) Sierra Leone.
"(xxvii) The Sudan.
"(xxviii) Togo.
"(xxix) Uruguay.
"(xxx) Venezuela.
"(xxxi) Yugoslavia.
"(xxxii) Zaire.
"(xxxiii) Zambia.

"(I) No benefit for increased withholding taxes. No benefit shall be allowable by reason of this paragraph for any foreign withholding tax imposed on interest payable with respect to any qualified loan to the extent the rate of such tax exceeds the foreign withholding tax rate applicable to interest payable with respect to such loan on November 16, 1985.

"(J) Treatment of affiliated group filing consolidated return. For purposes of this paragraph, all members of an affiliated group of corporations filing a consolidated return shall be treated as 1 corporation."

—P.L. 101-239, Sec. 7811(i)(1), substituted "interest or carrying charges (as defined in section 927(d)(1)) derived from a transaction which results in foreign trade income (as defined in section 923(b))" for "qualified interest and carrying charges (as defined in section 245(c))" in subpara. (d)(1)(H), effective for transactions after 12/31/84, in tax. yrs. end. after 12/31/84.

In 1988, P.L. 100-647, Sec. 1003(b)(2)(A), amended para. (b)(2) ... Sec. 1003(b)(2)(B), amended subpara. (b)(3)(D) and added subpara. (b)(3)(E), effective for tax. yrs. begin. after 12/31/86.

Prior to amendment, para. (b)(2) read as follows:

"(2) Capital gains. For purposes of this section—

"(A) Corporations. In the case of a corporation—

"(i) the taxable income of such corporation from sources without the United States shall include gain from the sale or exchange of capital assets only in an amount equal to foreign source capital gain net income reduced by the rate differential portion of foreign source net capital gain.

"(ii) the entire taxable income of such corporation shall include gain from the sale or exchange of capital assets only in an amount equal to capital gain net income reduced by the rate differential portion of net capital gain, and

"(iii) for purposes of determining taxable income from sources without the United States, any net capital loss (and any amount which is a short-term capital loss under section 1212(a)) from sources without the United States to the extent taken into account in determining capital gain net income for the taxable year shall be reduced by an amount equal to the rate differential portion of the excess of net capital gain from sources within the United States over net capital gain.

"(B) Other taxpayers. In the case of a taxpayer other than a taxpayer described in subparagraph (A), taxable income from sources without the United States shall include gain from the sale or exchange of capital assets only to the extent of foreign source capital gain net income."

Prior to amendment, subpara. (b)(3)(D) read as follows:

"(D) Rate differential portion. The 'rate differential portion' of foreign source net capital gain, net capital gain, or the excess of net capital gain from sources within the United States over net capital gain, as the case may be, is the same proportion of such amount as the excess of the highest rate of tax specified in section 11(b) over the alternative rate of tax under section 1201(a) bears to the highest rate of tax specified in section 11(b)."

—P.L. 100-647, Sec. 1012(a)(1)(A), amended subpara. (d)(2)(C) ... Sec. 1012(a)(2), added the sentence at the end of subpara. (d)(2)(D) ... Sec. 1012(a)(3), added subpara. (d)(3)(H) ... Sec. 1012(a)(4)(A), amended the sentence at the beginning of subpara. (d)(3)(E) ... Sec. 1012(a)(4)(B), substituted "passive income" for "income (other than high withholding tax interest and dividends from a noncontrolled section 902 corporation)" in subpara. (d)(3)(E) ... Sec. 1012(a)(6)(A), substituted "Except as provided in clause (iii), the term" for "The term" in subpara. (d)(2)(A) ... Sec. 1012(a)(6)(B), added clause (d)(2)(A)(iv) ... Sec. 1012(a)(7), amended subpara. (d)(3)(F) ... Sec. 1012(a)(8), amended clause (d)(2)(B)(iii) ... Sec. 1012(a)(9), amended clause (d)(2)(I)(ii) ... Sec. 1012(a)(10), substituted "during which it was a controlled foreign corporation and except as provided in regulations, the taxpayer was a United States shareholder in such corporation" for "during which it was a controlled foreign corporation" in clause (d)(2)(E)(i) ... Sec. 1012(a)(11), substituted "in the case of a corporation, dividends" for "dividends" in subpara. (d)(1)(E), effective for tax. yrs. begin. after 12/31/86 and as provided in Secs. 1201(c)(2) and (3) of P.L. 99-514, [as amended by Sec. 1012(a)(5) of this Act, see below, and as amended by Sec. 7404(a) of P.L. 101-239, see above], reproduced below.

Prior to amendment, subpara. (d)(2)(C) read as follows:

"(C) Financial services income.

"(i) In general. Except as otherwise provided in this subparagraph, the term 'financial services income' means income received or accrued by any person which is not passive income (determined without regard to subparagraph (A)(iii)(I) and which—

"(I) is derived in the active conduct of a banking, financing, or similar business, or derived from the investment by an insurance company of its unearned premiums or reserves ordinary and necessary for the proper conduct of its insurance business, or

"(II) is of a kind which would be insurance income as defined in section 953(a) determined without regard to those provisions of paragraph (1)(A) of such section which limit insurance income to income from countries other than the country in which the corporation was created or organized.

"(ii) Special rule if entity predominantly engaged in banking, etc., business. If, for any taxable year, an entity is predominantly engaged in the active conduct of a banking, insurance, financing, or similar business, the term 'financial services income' includes any passive income (determined without regard to subparagraph (A)(iii)(I) of such corporation for such taxable year. In the case of any entity described in the preceding sentence, the term 'shipping income' shall not include any income treated as financial services income under the preceding sentence.

"(iii) Exception for export financing. The term 'financial services income' does not include any export financing interest.

"(iv) High withholding tax interest. The term 'financial services income' does not include any high withholding tax interest."

Prior to amendment, the sentence at the beginning of subpara. (d)(3)(E) read as follows:

"If a controlled foreign corporation meets the requirements of section 954(b)(3)(A) (relating to de minimis rule for any taxable year for purpose of this paragraph, none of its income for such taxable year shall be treated as income in a separate category."

Prior to amendment, subpara. (d)(3)(F) read as follows:

"(F) Separate category. For purposes of this paragraph, the term 'separate category' means any category of income described in subparagraph (A), (B), (C), (D), or (E) of paragraph (1)."

Prior to amendment, clause (d)(2)(B)(iii) read as follows:

"(iii) Regulations. The Secretary may by regulations provide that amounts (not otherwise high withholding tax interest) shall be treated as high withholding tax interest where necessary to prevent avoidance of the purposes of this subparagraph."

Prior to amendment, of clause (d)(2)(I)(ii) read as follows:

"(ii) taxes paid or accrued in a taxable year beginning before January 1, 1987, with respect to income which was described in subparagraph (E) of paragraph (1) (as in effect on the day before the date of the enactment of the Tax Reform Act of 1986) shall be treated as taxes paid or accrued with respect to income described in subparagraph (I) of paragraph (1) (as in effect after such date) except to the extent that—

"(I) the taxpayer establishes to the satisfaction of the Secretary that such taxes were paid or accrued with respect to shipping income, or

"(II) in the case of an entity meeting the requirements of subparagraph (C)(ii), the taxpayer establishes to the satisfaction of the Secretary that such taxes were paid or accrued with respect to financial services income, and"

—P.L. 100-647, Sec. 1012(a)(5), added Sec. 1201(e)(2)(J) to P.L. 99-514 [part of the effective date for amendments made by Sec. 1201 of P.L. 99-514, see below].

—P.L. 100-647, Sec. 1012(c), added subpara. (f)(5)(F), effective for losses incurred in tax. yrs. begin. after 12/31/86.

—P.L. 100-647, Sec. 1012(p)(11), added subpara. (d)(3)(I) . . . Sec. 1012(p)(29)(A), substituted "or, except as provided in subparagraph (E)(iii) or paragraph (3)(I), section 1293" for "or section 1293" in clause (d)(2)(A)(ii) . . . Sec. 1012(p)(29)(B), added clause (d)(2)(E)(iii), effective for tax. yrs. of foreign corporations begin. after 12/31/86.

—P.L. 100-647, Sec. 1012(q)(12), substituted "861(a)(1)(A)" for "861(a)(1)(B)" in subpara. (g)(9)(A), effective for tax. yrs. begin. after 12/31/86.

—P.L. 100-647, Sec. 1012(aa)(2), (3)(A) and (4), provide:

"(2) Certain amendments to apply notwithstanding treaties. The following amendments made by the Reform Act shall apply notwithstanding any treaty obligation of the United States in effect on the date of the enactment of the Reform Act:

"(A) The amendments made by section 1201 of the Reform Act.

"(B) The amendments made by title VII of the Reform Act to the extent such amendments relate to the alternative minimum tax foreign tax credit.

"(3) Certain amendments not to apply to the extent inconsistent with treaties. The following amendments made by the Reform Act shall not apply to the extent the application of such amendments would be contrary to any treaty obligation of the United States in effect on the date of the enactment of the Reform Act:

"(A) The amendments made by section 1211 of the Reform Act to the extent—

"(i) such amendments apply in the case of an individual treated as a resident of a foreign country under a treaty obligation of the United States as so in effect, or

"(ii) such amendments relate to income of a non-resident from the sale or exchange of inventory property which would otherwise be sourced under section 865(e)(2) of the 1986 Code."

"(4) Treatment of technical corrections. For purposes of paragraphs (2) and (3), any amendment made by this title shall be treated as if it had been included in the provision of the Reform Act to which such amendment relates."

—P.L. 100-647, Sec. 1012(bb)(4)(A), redesignated para. (g)(10) as para. (g)(11) and added new para. (g)(10), effective 7/18/84 except as provided in Secs. 121(b)(1)-(6) of P.L. 98-369, see below.

—P.L. 100-647, Sec. 1018(g)(1), substituted "section 121(b)(5)" for "section 125(b)(5)" each place it appeared in Sec. 1810(a)(5) of P.L. 99-514, reproduced below.

—P.L. 100-647, Sec. 2004(1), substituted "section 11(b)(1)" for "section 11(b)" in clause (b)(3)(D)(ii), effective for tax. yrs. begin. after 12/31/87.

In 1986, P.L. 99-514, Sec. 104(b)(13), deleted the sentence at the end of subsec. (a) . . . Sec. 701(e)(4)(H), substituted "against the alternative minimum tax, see section 59(a)." for "by an individual against the alternative minimum tax, see section 55(c)." in para. (i)(2), effective for tax. yrs. begin. after 12/31/86.

Prior to deletion, the sentence at the end of subsec. (a) read as follows:

"For purposes of the preceding sentence in the case of an individual the entire taxable income shall be reduced by an amount equal to the zero bracket amount."

—P.L. 99-514, Sec. 1201(a), deleted subpara. (d)(1)(A), redesignated subparas. (d)(1)(B), (C), (D), and (E) as subparas. (d)(1)(F), (G), (H), and (I), respectively, and added new subparas. (d)(1)(A), (B), (C), (D), and (E) . . . Sec. 1201(b), amended paras. (d)(2) and (3), and added paras. (d)(4) and (5) . . . Sec. 1201(d)(1). amended the heading of subsec. (d) . . . Sec. 1201(d)(2), substituted "in any of the preceding subparagraphs" for "in subparagraph (A), (B), (C), or (D)" in subpara. (d)(1)(I) [as redesignated by Sec. 1201(a) of this Act, see above] . . . Sec. 1201(d)(3), added "and sections 902, 907, and 960" to para. (d)(1), effective for tax. yrs. begin. after 12/31/86 [see Sec. 1012 of P.L. 100-647(aa)(2)(A), reproduced above].

—P.L. 99-514, Sec. 1201(e)(2), [as amended by Sec. 1012(a)(5) of P.L. 100-647, see above], was repealed by Sec. 7404(a) of P.L. 101-239, see above

—P.L. 99-514, Sec. 1201(e)(3), of this Act provides:

"(3) Special rule for taxpayer with overall foreign loss.

"(A) In general. If a taxpayer incorporated on June 20, 1928, the principal headquarters of which is in Minneapolis, Minnesota, sustained an overall foreign loss (as defined in section 904(f)(2) of the Internal Revenue Code of 1954) in taxable years beginning before January 1, 1986, in connection with 2 separate trades or businesses which the taxpayer had, during 1985, substantially disposed of in tax-free transactions pursuant to section 355 of such Code, then an amount, not to exceed $40,000,000 of foreign source income, which, but for this paragraph, would not be treated as overall limitation income, shall be so treated.

"(B) Substantial disposition. For purposes of this paragraph, a taxpayer shall be treated as having substantially disposed of a trade or business if the retained portion of such business had sales of less than 10 percent of the annual sales of such business for taxable years ending in 1985."

Prior to deletion, subpara. (d)(1)(A) read as follows:

"(A) the interest income described in paragraph (2),"

Prior to amendment, paras. (d)(2) and (3) [as amended by Secs. 1810(b)(1), (2), (3) and (4)(A) of this Act, see below] read as follows:

"(2) Interest income to which applicable. For purposes of this subsection, the interest income described in this paragraph is interest other than interest—

"(A) derived from any transaction which is directly related to the active conduct by the taxpayer of a trade or business in a foreign country or a possession of the United States,

"(B) derived in the conduct by the taxpayer of a banking, financing, or similar business,

"(C) received from a corporation in which the taxpayer (or one or more includible corporations in an affiliated group, as defined in section 1504, of which the taxpayer is a member) owns, directly or indirectly, at least 10 percent of the voting stock, or

"(D) received on obligations acquired as a result of the disposition of a trade or business actively conducted by the taxpayer in a foreign country or possession of the United States or as a result of the disposition of stock or obligations of a corporation in which the taxpayer owned at least 10 percent of the voting stock.

For purposes of subparagraph (C), stock owned, directly or indirectly, by or for a foreign corporation, shall be considered as being proportionately owned by its shareholders. For purposes of this subsection, interest (after the operation of section 904(d)(3)) received from a designated payor corporation described in section 904(d)(3)(E)(iii) by a taxpayer which owns directly or indirectly less than 10 percent of the voting stock of such designated payor corporation shall be treated as interest described in subparagraph (A) to the extent such interest would have been so treated had such taxpayer received it from other than a designated payor corporation.

"(3) Certain amounts attributable to United States-owned foreign corporations, etc., treated as interest.

"(A) In general. For purposes of this subsection, dividends and interests—

"(i) paid or accrued by a designated payor corporation, and

"(ii) attributable to any taxable year of such corporation,

shall be treated as interest income described in paragraph (2) to the extent that the aggregate amount of such dividends and interest does not exceed the separate limitation interests of the designated payor corporation for such taxable year.

"(B) Separate limitation interest. For purposes of this subsection, the term 'separate limitation interest' means, with respect to any taxable year—

"(i) the aggregate amount of the interest income described in paragraph (2) (including amounts treated as so described by reason of this paragraph) which is received or accrued by the designated payor corporation during the taxable year, reduced by

"(ii) the deductions properly allocable (under regulations prescribed by the Secretary) to such income.

"(C) Exception where designated corporation has small amount of separate limitation interest. Subparagraph (A) shall not apply to any amount attributable to the taxable year of a designated payor corporation if—

"(i) such corporation has earnings and profits for such taxable year, and

"(ii) less than 10 percent of such earnings and profits is attributable to separate limitation interest.

The preceding sentence shall not apply to any amount includible in gross income under section 551 or 951.

"(D) Treatment of certain interest. For purposes of this paragraph, the amount of the separate limitation interest and the earnings and profits of any designated payor corporation shall be determined without any reduction for interest paid or accrued to a United States shareholder (as defined in section 951(b)) or a related person (within the meaning of section 267(b)) to such a shareholder.

"(E) Designated payor corporation. For purposes of this paragraph, the term 'designated payor corporation' means—

"(i) any United States-owned foreign corporation (within the meaning of subsection (g)(6)),

"(ii) any other foreign corporation in which a United States person is a United States shareholder (as defined in section 951(b)) at any time during the taxable year of such foreign corporation,

"(iii) any regulated investment company, and

"(iv) any other corporation formed or availed of for purposes of avoiding the provisions of this paragraph.

For purposes of this paragraph, the rules of paragraph (9) of subsection (g) shall apply.

"(F) Determination of year to which amount is attributable. For purposes of determining whether an amount is attributable to a taxable year of a designated payor corporation—

"(i) any amount includible in gross income under section 551 or 951 in respect of such taxable year,

"(ii) any interest paid or accrued by such corporation during such taxable year, and

"(iii) any dividend paid out of the earnings and profits of such corporation for such taxable year,

shall be treated as attributable to such taxable year.

"(G) Ordering rules. Subparagraph (A) shall be applied to amounts described therein in the order in which such amounts are described in subparagraph (F).

"(H) Dividend. For purposes of this paragraph, the term 'dividend' includes—

"(i) any amount includible in gross income under section 551 or 951, and

"(ii) any gain treated as ordinary income under section 1246 or as a dividend under section 1248.

"(I) Interest and dividends from members of same affiliated group. For purposes of this paragraph, dividends and interest received or accrued by the designated payor corporation from another member of the same affiliated group (determined under section 1504 without regard to subsection (b)(3) thereof) shall be treated as separate limitation interest if (and only if) such amounts are attributable (directly or indirectly) to separate limitation interest of any other member of such group.

"(J) Distributions through other entities. The Secretary shall prescribe such regulations as may be necessary to carry out the purposes of this paragraph in the case of distributions or payments through 1 or more entities."

Prior to amendment, the heading of subsec. (d) read as follows:

"(d) Separate application of section with respect to certain interest income and income from DISC, former FSC, or former FSC."

—P.L. 99-514, Sec. 1203(a), added para. (f)(5), effective for losses incurred in tax. yrs. begin. after 12/31/86. Sec. 1205 of this Act provides as follows:

SEC. 1205. LIMITATION ON CARRYBACK OF FOREIGN TAX CREDITS TO TAXABLE YEARS BEGINNING BEFORE 1987.

"(a) Determination of excess credits.

"(1) In general. Any taxes paid or accrued in a taxable year beginning after 1986 may be treated under section 904(c) of the Internal Revenue Code of 1954 as paid or accrued in a taxable year beginning before 1987 only to the extent such taxes would be so treated if the tax imposed by chapter 1 of such Code for the taxable year beginning after 1986 were determined by applying section 1 or 11 of such Code (as the case may be) as in effect on the day before the date of the enactment of this Act.

"(2) Adjustments. Under regulations prescribed by the Secretary of the Treasury or his delegate proper adjustments shall be made in the application of paragraph (1) to take into account—

"(A) the repeal of the zero bracket amount, and

"(B) the changes in the treatment of capital gains.

"(b) Coordination with separate baskets. Any taxes paid or accrued in a taxable year beginning after 1986 which (after the application of subsection (a)) are treated as paid or accrued in a taxable year beginning before 1987 shall be treated as imposed on income described in section 904(d)(1)(E) of the Internal Revenue Code of 1954 (as in effect on the day before the date of the enactment of this Act). No taxes paid or accrued in a taxable year beginning after 1986 with respect to high withholding tax interest (as defined in section 904(d)(2)(B) of the Internal Revenue Code of 1986 as amended by this Act) may be treated as paid or accrued in a taxable year beginning before 1987."

—P.L. 99-514, Sec. 1211(b)(3), deleted subparas. (b)(3)(C) and (D), and redesignated subparas. (b)(3)(E) and (F) as (b)(3)(C) and (D), effective for tax. yrs. begin. after 12/31/86 except as provided in Sec. 1012(aa)(3)(A) of P.L. 99-647 [reproduced above] and Sec. 1211(c)(2) of this Act, which reads as follows:

"(2) Special rule for foreign persons. In the case of any foreign person other than any controlled foreign corporations (within the meaning of section 957(a) of the Internal Revenue Code of 1954), the amendments made by this section shall apply to transactions entered into after March 18, 1986."

Prior to deletion, subparas. (b)(3)(C) and (D) read as follows:

"(C) Exception for gain from the sale of certain personal property. There shall be included as gain from sources within the United States any gain from sources without the United States from the sale or exchange of a capital asset which is personal property which—

"(i) in the case of an individual, is sold or exchanged outside of the country (or possession) of the individual's residence,

"(ii) in the case of a corporation, is stock in a second corporation sold or exchanged other than in a country (or possession) in which such second corporation derived more than 50 percent of its gross income for the 3-year period ending with the close of such second corporation's taxable year immediately preceding the year during which the sale or exchange occurred, or

"(iii) in the case of any taxpayer, is personal property (other than stock in a corporation) sold or exchanged other than in a country (or possession) in which such property is used in a trade or business of the taxpayer or in which such taxpayer derived more than 50 percent of its gross income for the 3-year period ending with the close of its taxable year immediately preceding the year during which the sale or exchange occurred,

unless such gain is subject to an income, war profits, or excess profits tax of a foreign country or possession of the United States, and the rate of tax applicable to such gain is 10 percent or more of the gain from the sale or exchange (computed under this chapter).

"(D) Gain from liquidation of certain foreign corporations. Subparagraphs (C) shall not apply with respect to a distribution in liquidation of a foreign corporation to which part II of subchapter C applies if such corporation derived less than 50 percent of its gross income from sources within the United States for the 3-year period ending with the close of such corporation's taxable year immediately preceding the year during which the distribution occurred."

—P.L. 99-514, Sec. 1235(f)(4)(A), deleted "or" at the end of clause (g)(1)(A)(i), substituted ", or" for the period at the end of clause (g)(1)(A)(ii), and added clause (g)(1)(A)(iii) ... Sec. 1235(f)(4)(B), substituted "holding or passive foreign investment company" for "holding company" in the heading of para. (g)(2), effective for tax. yrs. of foreign corporations begin. after 12/31/86.

—P.L. 99-514, Sec. 1810(a)(1)(A), redesignated para. (g)(9) as para. (g)(10) and added new para. (g)(9), effective as provided in Sec. 1810(a)(1)(B) of this Act, which reads as follows:

"(B) Effective date. The amendment made by subparagraph (A) [Sec. 1810(a)(1)(A)] shall take effect on March 28, 1985. In the case of any taxable year ending after such date of any corporation treated as a United States-owned foreign corporation by reason of the amendment made by subparagraph (A) [Sec. 1810(a)(1)(A)]—

"(i) only income received or accrued by such corporation after such date shall be taken into account under section 904(g) of the Internal Revenue Code of 1954; except that

"(ii) paragraph (5) of such section 904(g) shall be applied by taking into account all income received or accrued by such corporation during such taxable year."

—P.L. 99-514, Sec. 1810(a)(2), added Sec. 121(b)(2)(E)(iii) to P.L. 98-369 [part of the effective date for amendments made by Sec. 121(a) of P.L. 98-369, reproduced below] ... Sec. 1810(a)(3), substituted "(or short-term borrowing from nonaffiliated persons) and lending the proceeds of such obligations (or such borrowing) to affiliates." for "or the holding of short-term obligations and lending the proceeds of such obligations to affiliates." in Sec. 121(b)(2)(D)(ii) of P.L. 98-369 [part of the effective date for amendments made by Sec. 121(a) of P.L. 98-369, reproduced below]. Secs. 1810(a)(4) and (5) of this Act [as amended by Sec. 1018(g)(1) of P.L. 100-647, see above] provide special rules as follows:

"(4) Coordination with treaty obligations. Section 904(g) of the Internal Revenue Code of 1954 shall apply notwithstanding any treaty obligation of the United States to the contrary (whether entered into on, before, or after the date of the enactment of this Act) unless (in the case of a treaty entered into after the date of the enactment of this Act) such treaty by specific reference to such section 904(g) clearly expresses the intent to override the provisions of such section.

"(5) Transitional rule related to section 121(b)(5) of the act. For purposes of section 121(b)(5) of the Tax Reform Act of 1984 (relating to separate application of section 904 in case of income covered by transitional rules), any carryover under section 904(c) of the Internal Revenue Code of 1954 allowed to a taxpayer which was incorporated on August 31, 1962, attributable to taxes paid or accrued in taxable years beginning in 1981, 1982, 1983, or 1984, with respect to amounts included in gross income under section 951 of such Code in respect of a controlled foreign corporation which was incorporated on May 27, 1977, shall be treated as taxes paid or accrued on income separately treated under such section 121(b)(5)."

—P.L. 99-514, Sec. 1810(b)(1), added the sentence at the end of subpara. (d)(3)(C) [before deletion by Sec. 1201(b) of this Act, see above] ... Sec. 1810(b)(2), deleted subpara. (d)(3)(J), redesignated subpara. (d)(3)(I) as (J), and added new subpara. (d)(3)(I) [before deletion by Sec. 1201(b) of this Act, see above] ... Sec. 1810(b)(3), added the sentence at the end of para. (d)(2) [before deletion by Sec. 1201(b) of this Act, see above], effective 7/18/84, except as provided in Sec. 122(b)(2)-(3) of P.L. 98-369, see below.

Prior to deletion, subpara. (d)(3)(J) read as follows:

"(J) Interest from members of same affiliated group. For purposes of this paragraph, interest received or accrued by the designated payor corporation from another member of the same affiliated group (determined under section 1504 without regard to subsection (b)(3) thereof) shall not be treated as separate limitation interest, unless such interest is attributable directly or indirectly to separate limitation interest of such other member."

—P.L. 99-514, Sec. 1810(b)(4)(A), deleted "and" at the end of clause (d)(3)(E)(ii), substituted ", and" for the period at the end of clause (d)(3)(E)(iii), and added clause (d)(3)(E)(iv) and the sentence at the end of subpara. (d)(3)(E) [before deletion by Sec. 1201(b) of this Act, see above], effective as provided in Sec. 1810(b)(4)(B) of this Act, which reads as follows:

"(B) Effective dates.

"(i) The amendment made by subparagraph (A) insofar as it adds the last sentence to subparagraph (E) of section 905(d)(3) [sic 904(d)(3)] shall take effect on March 28, 1985. In the case of any taxable year ending after such date of any corporation treated as a designated payor corporation by reason of the amendment made by subparagraph (A)—

Income from foreign sources Code Sec. 904

"(I) only income received or accrued by such corporation after such date shall be taken into account under section 904(d)(3) of the Internal Revenue Code of 1954; except that

"(II) subparagraph (C) of such section 904(d)(3) shall be applied by taking into account all income received or accrued by such corporation during such taxable year.

"(ii) The amendment made by subparagraph (A) insofar as it adds clause (iv) to subparagraph (E) of section 904(d)(3) shall take effect on December 31, 1985. For purposes of such amendment, the rule of the second sentence of clause (i) shall be applied by taking into account December 31, 1985, in lieu of March 28, 1985."

—P.L. 99-514, Sec. 1876(d)(2), amended subpara. (d)(1)(D) [before redesignation as (d)(1)(H) by Sec. 1201(a) of this Act, see above], effective for transactions after 12/31/84, in tax. yrs. end. after 12/31/84.

Prior to amendment, subpara. (d)(1)(D) read as follows:

"(D) distributions from a FSC (or former FSC) out of earnings and profits attributable to foreign trade income (within the meaning of section 923(b))," and

—P.L. 99-514, Sec. 1899A(24), corrected the spelling in the heading of para. (d)(1), effective 10/22/86.

In 1984, P.L. 98-369, Sec. 121(a), redesignated subsecs. (g) and (h) as subsecs. (h) and (i), respectively, and added new subsec. (g), effective as provided in Sec. 121(b) [as amended by Secs. 1810(a)(2) and (3) of P.L. 99-514, see above] which reads as follows:

"(b) Effective date.

"(1) In general. Except as otherwise provided in this subsection, the amendment made by subsection (a) shall take effect on the date of the enactment of this Act. In the case of any taxable year of any United States-owned foreign corporation ending after the date of the enactment of this Act—

"(A) only income received or accrued by such foreign corporation after such date of enactment shall be taken into account under section 904(g) of the Internal Revenue Code of 1954 (as added by subsection (a)); except that

"(B) paragraph (5) of such section 904(g) (relating to exception where small amount of United States source income) shall be applied by taking into account all income received or accrued by such foreign corporation during such taxable year.

"(2) Special rule for applicable CFC.

"(A) In general. In the case of qualified interest received or accrued by an applicable CFC before January 1, 1992—

"(i) such interest shall not be taken into account under section 904(g) of the Internal Revenue Code of 1954 (as added by subsection (a)), except that

"(ii) such interest shall be taken into account for purposes of applying paragraph (5) of such section 904(g) (relating to exception where small amount of United States source income).

"(B) Qualified interest. For purposes of subparagraph (A), the term 'qualified interest' means—

"(i) the aggregate amount of interest received or accrued during any taxable year by an applicable CFC on United States affiliate obligations held by such applicable CFC, multiplied by,

"(ii) a fraction (not in excess of 1)—

"(I) the numerator of which is the sum of the aggregate principal amount of United States affiliate obligations held by the applicable CFC on March 31, 1984, but not in excess of the applicable limit, and

"(II) the denominator of which is the average daily principal amount of United States affiliate obligations held by such applicable CFC during the taxable year. Proper adjustments shall be made to the numerator described in clause (ii)(I) for original issue discount accruing after March 31, 1984, on CFC obligations and United States affiliate obligations.

"(C) Adjustment for retirement of CFC obligations. The amount described in subparagraph (B)(ii)(I) for any taxable year shall be reduced by the sum of—

"(i) the excess of (I) the aggregate principal amount of CFC obligations which are outstanding on March 31, 1984, but only with respect to obligations issued before March 8, 1984, or issued after March 7, 1984, by the applicable CFC pursuant to a binding commitment in effect on March 7, 1984, over (II) the average daily outstanding principal amount during the taxable year of the CFC obligations described in subclause (I), and

"(ii) the portion of the equity of such applicable CFC allocable to the excess described in clause (i) (determined on the basis of the debt-equity ratio of such applicable CFC on March 31, 1984).

"(D) Applicable CFC. For purposes of this paragraph, the term 'applicable CFC' means any controlled foreign corporation (within the meaning of section 957)—

"(i) which was in existence on March 31, 1984, and

"(ii) the principal purpose of which on such date consisted of the issuing of CFC obligations (or short-term borrowing from nonaffiliated persons) and lending the proceeds of such obligations (or such borrowing) to affiliates.

"(E) Affiliates; United States affiliates. For purposes of this paragraph—

"(i) Affiliate. The term 'affiliate' means any person who is a related person (within the meaning of section 482 of the Internal Revenue Code of 1954) to the applicable CFC.

"(ii) United States affiliate. The term 'United States affiliates' means any United States person which is an affiliate of the applicable CFC.

"(iii) Treatment of certain foreign corporations engaged in business in United States.—For purposes of clause (ii), a foreign corporation shall be treated as a United States person with respect to any interest payment made by such corporation if—

"(I) at least 50 percent of the gross income from all sources of such corporation for the 3-year period ending with the close of its last taxable year ending on or before March 31, 1984, was effectively connected with the conduct of a trade or business within the United States, and

"(II) at least 50 percent of the gross income from all sources of such corporation for the 3-year period ending with the close of its taxable year preceding the payment of such interest was effectively connected with the conduct of a trade or business within the United States.

"(F) United States affiliate obligations. For purposes of this paragraph, the term 'United States affiliate obligations' means any obligation of (and payable by) a United States affiliate.

"(G) CFC obligation. For purposes of this paragraph, the term 'CFC obligation' means any obligation of (and issued by) a CFC if—

"(i) the requirements of clause (i) of section 163(f)(2)(B) of the Internal Revenue Code of 1954 are met with respect to such obligation, and

"(ii) in the case of an obligation issued after December 31, 1982, the requirements of clause (ii) of such section 163(f)(2)(B) are met with respect to such obligation.

"(H) Treatment of obligations with original issue discount. For purposes of this paragraph, in the case of any obligation with original issue discount, the principal amount of such obligation as of any day shall be treated as equal to the revised issue price as of such day (as defined in section 1278(a)(4) of the Internal Revenue Code of 1954).

"(I) Applicable limit. For purposes of subparagraph (B)(ii)(I), the term 'applicable limit' means the sum of—

"(i) the equity of the applicable CFC on March 31, 1984, and

"(ii) the aggregate principal amount of CFC obligations outstanding on March 31, 1984, which were issued by an applicable CFC—

"(I) before March 8, 1984, or

"(II) after March 7, 1984, pursuant to a binding commitment in effect on March 7, 1984.

"(3) Exception for certain term obligations. The amendments made by subsection (a) shall not apply to interest on any term obligations held by a foreign corporation on March 7, 1984. The preceding sentence shall not apply to any United States affiliate obligation (as defined in paragraph (2)(F)) held by an applicable CFC (as defined in paragraph (2)(D)).

"(4) Definitions. Any term used in this subsection which is also used in section 904(g) of the Internal Revenue Code of 1954 (as added by subsection (a)) shall have the meaning given such term by such section 904(g).

"(5) Separate application of section 904 in case of income covered by transitional rules. Subsections (a), (b), and (c) of section 904 of the Internal Revenue Code of 1954 shall be applied separately to any amount not treated as income derived from sources within the United States but which (but for the provisions of paragraph (2) or (3) of this subsection) would be so treated under the amendments made by subsection (a). Any such separate application shall be made before any separate application required under section 904(d) of such Code.

"(6) Application of paragraph (5) delayed in certain cases. In the case of a foreign corporation—

"(A) which is a subsidiary of a domestic corporation which has been engaged in manufacturing for more than 50 years, and

"(B) which issued certificates with respect to obligations on—

"(i) September 24, 1979, denominated in French francs,

"(ii) September 10, 1981, denominated in Swiss francs,

"(iii) July 14, 1982, denominated in Swiss francs, and

"(iv) December 1, 1982, denominated in United States dollars,

with a total principal amount of less than 200,000,000 United States dollars, then paragraph (5) shall not apply to the proceeds from relending such obligations or related capital before January 1, 1986."

—P.L. 98-369, Sec. 122(a), added para. (d)(3), effective 7/18/84. Secs. 122(b)(2) and (3) of this Act provide special rules as follows:

"(2) Special rules for interest income.

"(A) In general. Interest income received or accrued by a designated payor corporation shall be taken into account for purposes of the amendment made by subsection (a) only in taxable years beginning after the date of the enactment of this Act.

"(B) Exception for investment after June 22, 1984. Notwithstanding subparagraph (A), the amendment made by subsection (a) shall apply to interest income received or accrued by a designated payor corporation after the date of enactment of this Act if it is attributable to investment in the designated payor corporation after June 22, 1984.

"(3) Term obligations of designated payor corporation which is not applicable CFC. In the case of any designated payor corporation which is not an applicable CFC (as defined in section 121(b)(2)(D)), any interest received or accrued by such corporation on a term obligation held by such corporation on March 7, 1984, shall not be taken into account."

—P.L. 98-369, Sec. 474(r)(21), amended subsec. (h) [as redesignated by Sec. 121(a) of this Act, see above], effective for tax. yrs. begin. after 12/31/83, and for carrybacks from 12/31/83.

Prior to amendment, subsec. (h) read as follows:

"(h) Coordination with credit for the elderly. In the case of an individual, for purposes of subsection (a) the tax against which the credit is taken is such tax reduced by the amount of the credit (if any) for the taxable year allowable under section 37 (relating to credit for the elderly and the permanently and totally disabled)."

—P.L. 98-369, Sec. 712(e), substituted "the eight-year period (or such shorter period as the taxpayer may select" for "the eight-year period" in Sec. 211(e)(2)(A) of P.L. 97-248 [part of the effective date for amendments made by Sec. 211(c)(2) of P.L. 97-248, see below], reproduced below.

2,567

—P.L. 98-369, Sec. 801(d)(2)(A), deleted "and" at the end of subpara. (d)(1)(B) ... Sec. 801(d)(2)(B), amended subpara. (d)(1)(C) and added subparas. (d)(1)(D) and (E) ... Sec. 801(d)(2)(C), amended the heading of subsec. (d), effective for transactions after 12/31/84.

Prior to amendment, subpara. (d)(1)(C) read as follows:

"(C) income other than the interest income described in paragraph (2) and dividends described in subparagraph (B)"

Prior to amendment, the heading of subsec. (d) read as follows:

"(d) Application of section in case of certain interest income and dividends from a DISC or former DISC."

In 1983, P.L. 98-21, Sec. 122(c)(1), substituted "relating to credit for the elderly and the permanently and totally disabled" for "relating to credit for the elderly" in subsec. (g), effective for tax. yrs. begin. after 12/31/83.

—P.L. 97-448, Sec. 306(a)(5), amended Sec. 211(e)(2) of P.L. 97-248, part of the effective date for changes made by Sec. 211 of P.L. 97-248 [reproduced below].

Prior to amendment, Sec. 211(e)(2) of P.L. 97-248 read as follows:

"(2) Retention of old sections 907(b) and 904(f)(4) where taxpayer had foreign loss from an activity not related to oil and gas. If, after applying old sections 907(b) and 904(f)(4) to a taxable year beginning before January 1, 1983, the taxpayer had a foreign loss attributable to activities not taken into account in determining foreign oil related income (as defined in old section 907(c)(2)), such loss shall not be recaptured from foreign oil related income more rapidly than ratably over the 8-year period beginning with the first taxable year beginning after December 31, 1982. For purposes of the preceding sentence, and 'old' section is such section as in effect on the day before the date of the enactment of this Act."

In 1982, P.L. 97-248, Sec. 211(c)(2), deleted para. (f)(4) and redesignated paras. (f)(5) and (f)(6) [sic , no para. (f)(6)] as paras. (f)(4) and (f)(5), effective for tax. yrs. begin. after 12/31/82. Sec. 211(e)(2) [as amended by Sec. 306(a)(5) of P.L. 97-448 and Sec. 712(e) of P.L. 98-369, see above] provides as follows:

"(2) Retention of old sections 907(b) and 904(f)(4) where taxpayer had separate basket foreign loss.

"(A) In general. If, after applying old sections 907(b) and 904(f)(4) to a taxable year beginning before January 1, 1983, the taxpayer had a separate basket foreign loss, such loss shall not be recaptured from income of a kind not taken into account in computing the amount of such separate basket foreign loss more rapidly than ratably over the 8-year period (or such shorter period as the taxpayer may select) beginning with the first taxable year beginning after December 31, 1982.

"(B) Definitions. For purposes of this paragraph—

"(i) The term 'separate basket foreign loss' means any foreign loss attributable to activities taken into account (or not taken into account) in determining foreign oil related income (as defined in old section 907(c)(2)).

"(ii) An 'old' section is such section as in effect on the day before the date of the enactment of this Act."

Prior to deletion, para. (f)(4) read as follows:

"(4) Determination of foreign oil related loss where section 907 applies. In making the separate computation under this subsection with respect to foreign oil related income which is required by section 907(b), the foreign oil related loss shall be the amount by which the gross income for the taxable year from sources without the United States and its possessions (whether or not the taxpayer chooses the benefits of this subpart for such taxable year) taken into account in determining the foreign oil related income for such year is exceeded by the sum of the deductions properly apportioned or allocated thereto, except that there shall not be taken into account—

"(A) any net operating loss deduction allowable for such year under section 172(a), and

"(B) any—

"(i) foreign expropriation loss for such year, as defined in section 172(h), or

"(ii) loss for such year which arises from fire, storm, shipwreck, or other casualty, or from theft,

to the extent such loss is not compensated for by insurance or otherwise."

In 1980, P.L. 96-222, Sec. 104(a)(3)(D)(i), redesignated subpara. (b)(3)(E) [as added by Sec. 403(c)(4)(B) of P.L. 95-600, see below] as subpara. (b)(3)(F), effective 11/6/78.

—P.L. 96-222, Sec. 104(a)(3)(D)(ii), substituted "adding at the end of paragraph (3)" for "striking the period at the end of subparagraph (D) of paragraph (3), inserting in lieu thereof a comma, and inserting immediately thereafter" in Sec. 403(c)(4)(B) of P.L. 95-600 [see below].

In 1978, P.L. 95-600, Sec. 403(c)(4)(A), substituted "the rate differential portion" for "three-eighths" each place it appeared in subsec. (b) ... Sec. 403(c)(4)(B), [as amended by Sec. 104(a)(3)(D)(ii) of P.L. 96-222, see above], added subpara. (b)(3)(E), effective 11/6/78.

—P.L. 95-600, Sec. 421(e)(6), amended subsec. (h), effective for tax. yrs. begin. after 12/31/78.

Prior to amendment, subsec. (h) read as follows:

"(h) Cross reference. For increase of limitation under subsection (a) for taxes paid with respect to amounts received which were included in the gross income of the taxpayer for a prior taxable year as a United States shareholder with respect to a controlled foreign corporation, see section 960(b)."

—P.L. 95-600, Sec. 701(q)(2), added para. (f)(5), effective as provided in Sec. 1032(c) of P.L. 94-455, [as amended by Sec. 701(U)(5)(A) of P.L. 95-600] reproduced below.

—P.L. 95-600, Sec. 701(u)(2)(A), substituted "For purposes of this section—" for "For purposes of subsection (a)—" in para. (b)(2) ... Sec. 701(u)(2)(B), substituted "There" for "For purposes of this paragraph, there" in subpara. (b)(3)(C) ... Sec. 701(u)(2)(C), redesignated subpara. (b)(3)(D) as subpara. (b)(3)(E) and added new subpara. (b)(3)(D) ... Sec. 701(u)(3)(A), substituted "for purposes of

determining taxable income from sources without the United States, any net capital loss (and any amount which is a short-term capital loss under section 1212(a))" for "any net capital loss" in clause (b)(2)(A)(iii), effective for tax. yrs. begin. after 12/31/75.

—P.L. 95-600, Sec. 701(u)(4)(A), deleted "or any capital loss carrybacks and carryovers to such year under section 1212" following "section 172(a)" in subpara. (f)(2)(A) ... Sec. 701(u)(4)(B), deleted "or any capital loss carrybacks and carryovers to such year under section 1212" following "section 172(a)" in subpara. (f)(4)(A), effective for overall foreign losses sustained in tax. yrs. begin. after 12/31/75, and for foreign oil related losses sustained in tax. yrs. ending after 12/31/75.

—P.L. 95-600, Sec. 701(u)(5)(A), amended Sec. 1032(c)(1) of P.L. 94-455 [part of the effective dates for amendments made by Sec. 1032(a) of P.L. 94-455, reproduced below] ... Sec. 701(u)(5)(B), added Sec. 1032(c)(5) [part of the effective dates for amendments made by Sec. 1032(a) of P.L. 94-455, reproduced below].

Prior to amendment, Sec. 1032(c)(1) of P.L. 94-455 read as follows:

"(1) In general. Except as provided in paragraphs (2) and (3), the amendments made by subsections (a) and (b)(2) shall apply to losses sustained in taxable years beginning after December 31, 1975, and the amendment made by subsection (b)(1) shall apply to taxable years beginning after December 31, 1975."

—P.L. 95-600, Sec. 701(u)(6), amended the second sentence in Sec. 1031(c)(2) of P.L. 94-455 [part of the effective dates for amendments made by Sec. 1031(a) of P.L. 94-455, reproduced below].

Prior to amendment, the second sentence in Sec. 1031(c)(2) of P.L. 94-455 read as follows:

"In the case of losses sustained in taxable years beginning before January 1, 1979, by any corporation to which this paragraph applies, the provisions of section 904(f) of such Code shall be applied with respect to such losses under the principles of section 904(a)(1) of such Code as in effect before the enactment of this Act."

—P.L. 95-600, Sec. 701(u)(7)(A), added the sentence at the end of Sec. 1032(c)(4) of P.L. 94-455 [part of the effective dates for amendments made by Sec. 1032(a) of P.L. 94-455, reproduced below] ... Sec. 701(u)(7)(B)(i), added Sec. 1032(c)(6) to P.L. 94-455 [part of the effective dates for amendments made by Sec. 1032(a) of P.L. 94-455, reproduced below].

—P.L. 95-600, Sec. 701(u)(7)(B)(ii), deleted the sentence at the end of Sec. 1031(c)(3) [part of the effective dates for amendments made by Sec. 1031(a) of P.L. 94-455, reproduced below].

Prior to deletion, the sentence at the end of Sec. 1031(c)(3) read as follows:

"In the case of losses sustained in a possession of the United States in taxable years beginning before January 1, 1979, the provisions of section 904(f) of such Code shall be applied with respect to such losses under the principles of section 904(a)(1) of such Code as in effect before the enactment of this Act."

—P.L. 95-600, Sec. 701(u)(8)(C), substituted "In making the separate computation under this subsection with respect to foreign oil related income which is required by section 907(b)" for "In the case of a corporation to which section 907(b)(1) applies" in para. (f)(4) effective as provided in Sec. 701(u)(8)(D) of this Act, which reads as follows:

"(D) Effective dates.

"(i) The amendments made by this paragraph shall apply, in the case of individuals, to taxable years ending after December 31, 1974, and, in the case of corporations, to taxable years ending after December 31, 1976.

"(ii) In the case of any taxable year ending after December 31, 1975, with respect to foreign oil related income (within the meaning of section 907(c) of the Internal Revenue Code of 1954), the overall limitation provided by section 904(a)(2) of such Code shall apply and the per-country limitation provided by section 904(a)(1) of such Code shall not apply."

In 1977, P.L. 95-30, Sec. 102(b)(11), added the sentence at the end of subsec. (a), effective for tax. yrs. begin. after 12/31/76.

—P.L. 95-30, Sec. 403, provided the following:

"SEC. 403. ELECTION OF FORMER RETIREMENT INCOME CREDIT PROVISIONS FOR 1976.

"A taxpayer may elect (at such time and in such manner as the Secretary of the Treasury or his delegate shall prescribe) to determine the amount of his credit under section 37 of the Internal Revenue Code of 1954 for his first taxable year beginning in 1976 under the provisions of such section as they existed before the amendment made by section 503 of the Tax Reform Act of 1976."

In 1976, P.L. 94-455, Sec. 503(b)(1), redesignated subsec. (g) [as amended by this Act] as subsec. (h), and added new subsec. (g), effective for tax. yrs begin. after 12/31/75.

—P.L. 94-455, Sec. 1031(a), amended Code Sec. 904. Sec. 1031(c) [as amended by Sec. 701(u)(6) and Sec. 701(a)(7)(B)(ii) of P.L. 95-600, see above] of this Act, provides as follows:

"(c) Effective dates.

"(1) In general. Except as provided in paragraphs (2) and (3), the amendments made by this section shall apply to taxable years beginning after December 31, 1975.

"(2) Exception for certain mining operations. In the case of a domestic corporation or includible corporation in an affiliated group (as defined in section 1504 of the Internal Revenue Code of 1954) which has as of October 1, 1975—

"(A) been engaged in the active conduct of the trade or business of the extraction of minerals (of a character with respect to which a deduction for depletion is allowable under section 613 of such Code) outside the United States or its possessions for less than 5 years preceding the date of enactment of this Act,

"(B) had deductions properly apportioned or allocated to its gross income from such trade or business in excess of such gross income in at least 2 taxable years,

"(C) 80 percent of its gross receipts are from the sale of such minerals, and

"(D) made commitments for substantial expansion of such mineral extraction activities,
the amendments made by this section shall apply to taxable years beginning after December 31, 1978. In the case of losses sustained in taxable years beginning before January 1, 1979, by any corporation to which this paragraph applies, the provisions of section 904(f) of such Code shall be applied with respect to such losses under the principles of section 904(a)(1) of such Code as in effect before the enactment of this Act.

"(3) Exception for income from possessions. In the case of gross income from sources within a possession of the United States (and the deductions properly apportioned or allocated thereto), the amendments made by this section shall apply to taxable years beginning after December 31, 1978. In the case of losses sustained in a possession of the United States in taxable years beginning before January 1, 1979, the provisions of section 904(f) of such Code shall be applied with respect to such losses under the principles of section 904(a)(1) of such Code as in effect before the enactment of this Act.

"(4) Carrybacks and carryovers in the case of mining operations and income from a possession. In the case of a taxpayer to whom paragraph (2) or (3) of this subsection applies, section 904(e) of such Code shall apply except that 'January 1, 1979' shall be substituted for 'January 1, 1976' each place it appears therein. If such a taxpayer elects the overall limitation for a taxable year beginning before January 1, 1979, such section 904(e) shall be applied by substituting 'the January 1, of the last year for which such taxpayer is on the per-country limitation' for 'January 1, 1976' each place it appears therein."

Prior to amendment, Code Sec. 904 read as follows:

"SEC. 904. LIMITATION ON CREDIT.

"(a) Alternative limitations.

"(1) Per-country limitation. In the case of any taxpayer who does not elect the limitation provided by paragraph (2), the amount of the credit in respect of the tax paid or accrued to any foreign country or possession of the United States shall not exceed the same proportion of the tax against which such credit is taken which the taxpayer's taxable income from sources within such country or possession (but not in excess of the taxpayer's entire taxable income) bears to his entire taxable income for the same taxable year.

"(2) Overall limitation. In the case of any taxpayer who elects the limitation provided by this paragraph, the total amount of the credit in respect of taxes paid or accrued to all foreign countries and possessions of the United States shall not exceed the same proportion of the tax against which such credit is taken which the taxpayer's taxable income from sources without the United States (but not in excess of the taxpayer's entire taxable income) bears to his entire taxable income for the same taxable year.

"(b) Election of overall limitation.

"(1) In general. A taxpayer may elect the limitation provided by subsection (a)(2) for any taxable year beginning after December 31, 1960. An election under this paragraph for any taxable year shall remain in effect for all subsequent taxable years, except that it may be revoked (A) with the consent of the Secretary or his delegate with respect to any taxable year or (B) for the taxpayer's first taxable year beginning after December 31, 1969.

"(2) Election after revocation. Except in a case to which paragraph (1)(B) applies, if the taxpayer has made an election under paragraph (1) and such election has been revoked, such taxpayer shall not be eligible to make a new election under paragraph (1) for any taxable year, unless the Secretary or his delegate consents to such new election.

"(3) Form and time of election and revocation. An election under paragraph (1), and any revocation of such an election, may be made only in such manner as the Secretary or his delegate may by regulations prescribe. Such an election or revocation with respect to any taxable year may be made or changed at any time before the expiration of the period prescribed for making a claim for credit or refund of the tax imposed by this chapter for such taxable year.

"(c) Taxable income for purpose of computing limitation. For purposes of computing the applicable limitation under subsection (a), the taxable income in the case of an individual, estate, or trust shall be computed without any deduction for personal exemptions under section 151 or 642(b).

"(d) Carryback and carryover of excess tax paid. Any amount by which any such tax paid or accrued to any foreign country or possession of the United States for any taxable year beginning after December 31, 1957, for which the taxpayer chooses to have the benefits of this subpart exceeds the applicable limitation under subsection (a) shall be deemed tax paid or accrued to such foreign country or possession of the United States in the second preceding taxable year, in the first preceding taxable year, and in the first, second, third, fourth, or fifth succeeding taxable years, in that order and to the extent not deemed tax paid or accrued in a prior taxable year, in the amount by which the applicable limitation under subsection (a) for such preceding or succeeding taxable year exceeds the sum of the tax paid or accrued to such foreign country or possession for such preceding or succeeding taxable year and the amount of the tax for any taxable year earlier than the current taxable year which shall be deemed to have been paid or accrued in such preceding or subsequent taxable year (whether or not the taxpayer chooses to have the benefits of this subpart with respect to such earlier taxable year). Such amount deemed paid or accrued in any year may be availed of only as a tax credit and not as a deduction and only if taxpayer for such year chooses to have the benefits of this subpart as to taxes paid or accrued for that year to foreign countries or possessions. For purposes of this subsection, the terms 'second preceding taxable year' and 'first preceding taxable year' do not include any taxable year beginning before January 1, 1958.

"(e) Carrybacks and carryovers where overall limitation is elected.

"(1) Foreign taxes to be aggregated for purposes of subsection (d). With respect to each taxable year of the taxpayer to which the limitation provided by subsection (a)(2) applies, the taxes referred to in the first sentence of subsection (d) shall, for purposes of applying such first sentence, be aggregated on an overall basis (rather than taken into account on a per-country basis).

"(2) Foreign taxes may not be carried from per-country year to overall year or from overall year to per-country year. No amount paid or accrued for any taxable year to which the limitation provided by subsection (a)(1) applies shall (except for purposes of determining the number of taxable years which have elapsed) be deemed paid or accrued under subsection (d) in any taxable year to which the limitation provided by subsection (a)(2) applies. No amount paid or accrued for any taxable year to which the limitation provided by subsection (a)(2) applies shall (except for purposes of determining the number of taxable years which have elapsed) be deemed paid or accrued under subsection (d) in any taxable year to which the limitation provided by subsection (a)(1) applies.

"(f) Application of section in case of certain interest income and dividends from a DISC or former DISC.

"(1) In general. The provisions of subsections (a), (c), (d), and (e) of this section shall be applied separately with respect to each of the following items of income—

"(A) the interest income described in paragraph (2),

"(B) dividends from a DISC or former DISC (as defined in section 992(a)) to the extent such dividends are treated as income from sources without the United States, and

"(C) income other than the interest income described in paragraph (2) and dividends described in subparagraph (B).

"(2) Interest income to which applicable. For purposes of this subsection, the interest income described in this paragraph is interest other than interest—

"(A) derived from any transaction which is directly related to the active conduct of a trade or business in a foreign country or a possession of the United States,

"(B) derived in the conduct of a banking, financing, or similar business,

"(C) received from a corporation in which the taxpayer (or one or more includible corporations in an affiliated group, as defined in section 1504, of which the taxpayer is a member) owns, directly or indirectly, at least 10 percent of the voting stock, or

"(D) received on obligations acquired as a result of the disposition of a trade or business actively conducted by the taxpayer in a foreign country or possession of the United States or as a result of the disposition of stock or obligations of a corporation in which the taxpayer owned at least 10 percent of the voting stock.

For purposes of subparagraph (C), stock owned, directly or indirectly, by or for a foreign corporation shall be considered as being proportionately owned by its shareholders.

"(3) Overall limitation not to apply. The limitation provided by subsection (a)(2) shall not apply with respect to the interest income described in paragraph (2) or to dividends described in paragraph (1)(B). The Secretary or his delegate shall by regulations prescribe the manner of application of subsection (e) with respect to cases in which the limitation provided by subsection (a)(2) applies with respect to income described in paragraph (1)(B) and (C).

"(4) Transitional rules for carrybacks and carryovers.

"(A) Carrybacks to years prior to Revenue Act of 1962. Where, under the provisions of subsection (d), taxes (i) paid or accrued to any foreign country or possession of the United States in any taxable year beginning after the date of the enactment of the Revenue Act of 1962 are deemed (ii) paid or accrued in one or more taxable years beginning on or before the date of enactment of the Revenue Act of 1962, the amount of such taxes deemed paid or accrued shall be determined without regard to the provisions of this subsection. To the extent the taxes paid or accrued to a foreign country or possession of the United States in any taxable year described in clause (i) are not, with the application of the preceding sentence, deemed paid or accrued in any taxable year described in clause (ii), such taxes shall, for purposes of applying subsection (d), be deemed paid or accrued in a taxable year beginning after the date of the enactment of the Revenue Act of 1962, with respect to interest income described in paragraph (2), and with respect to income other than interest income described in paragraph (2), in the same ratios as the amount of such taxes paid or accrued with respect to interest income described in paragraph (2), and the amount of such taxes paid or accrued with respect to income other than interest income described in paragraph (2), respectively, bear to the total amount of such taxes paid or accrued to such foreign country or possession of the United States.

"(B) Carryovers to years after Revenue Act of 1962. Where, under the provisions of subsection (d), taxes (i) paid or accrued to any foreign country or possession of the United States in any taxable year beginning on or before the date of the enactment of the Revenue Act of 1962 are deemed (ii) paid or accrued in one or more taxable years beginning after the date of the enactment of the Revenue Act of 1962, the amount of such taxes deemed paid or accrued in any year described in clause (ii) shall, with respect to interest income described in paragraph (2), be an amount which bears the same ratio to the amount of such taxes deemed paid or accrued as the amount of the taxes paid or accrued to such foreign country or possession for such year with respect to interest income described in paragraph (2) bears to the total amount of the taxes paid or accrued to such foreign country or possession for such year; and the amount of such taxes deemed paid or accrued in any year described in clause (ii) with respect to income other than interest income described in paragraph (2) shall be an amount which bears the same ratio to the amount of such taxes deemed paid or accrued for such year as the amount of taxes paid or accrued to such foreign country or possession for such year with respect to income other than interest income described in paragraph (2) bears to the total amount of the taxes paid or accrued to such foreign country or possession for such year.

"(5) DISC dividends aggregated for purpose of per-country limitation. In the case of a taxpayer who for the taxable year has dividends described in paragraph

"(1)(B) from more than one corporation, the limitation provided by subsection (a)(1) shall be applied with respect to the aggregate of such dividends.
"(g) Cross reference.
"(1) For increase of applicable limitation under subsection (a) for taxes paid with respect to amounts received which were included in the gross income of the taxpayer for a prior taxable year as a United States shareholder with respect to a controlled foreign corporation, see section 960(b).
"(2) For special rule relating to the application of the credit provided by section 901 in the case of affiliated groups which include Western Hemisphere trade corporations for years in which the limitation provided by subsection (a)(2) applies, see section 1503(b)."

—P.L. 94-455, Sec. 1032(a), redesignated subsec. (f) as subsec. (g), [as redesignated by Sec. 1031(a) of this Act, see above] and added new subsec. (f), effective as provided in Sec. 1032(c) of this Act [as amended by Secs. 701(u)(5)(A), (u)(5)(B), (u)(7)(A) and (u)(7)(B)(i) of P.L. 95-600, see above], which reads as follows:

"(c) Effective dates.
"(1) In general. Except as provided in paragraphs (2), (3), and (5), the amendment made by subsection (a) shall apply to losses sustained in taxable years beginning after December 31, 1975. The amendment made by subsection (b)(1) shall apply to taxable years beginning after December 31, 1975. The amendment made by subsection (b)(2) shall apply to losses sustained in taxable years ending after December 31, 1975.
"(2) Obligations of foreign governments. The amendments made by subsection (a) shall not apply to losses on the sale, exchange, or other disposition of bonds, notes, or other evidences of indebtedness issued before May 14, 1976, by a foreign government or instrumentality thereof for the acquisition of property located in that country or stock of a corporation (created or organized in or under the laws of that foreign country) or indebtedness of such corporation.
"(3) Substantial worthlessness before enactment. The amendments made by subsection (a) shall not apply to losses incurred on the loss from stock or indebtedness of a corporation in which the taxpayer owned at least 10 percent of the voting stock and which has sustained losses in 3 out of the last 5 taxable years beginning before January 1, 1975, which has sustained an overall loss for those 5 years, and with respect to which the taxpayer has terminated or will terminate all operations by reason of sale, liquidation, or other disposition before January 1, 1977, of such corporation or its assets.
"(4) Limitation based on deficit in earnings and profits. If paragraph (3) would apply to a taxpayer but for the fact that the loss is sustained after December 31, 1975, and if the loss is sustained in a taxable year beginning before January 1, 1979, the amendments made by subsection (a) shall not apply to such loss to the extent that there was on December 31, 1975, a deficit in earnings and profits in the corporation from which the loss arose. For purposes of the preceding sentence, there shall be taken into account only earnings and profits of the corporation which (A) were accumulated in taxable years of the corporation beginning after December 31, 1962, and during the period in which the stock of such corporation from which the loss arose was held by the taxpayer and (B) are attributable to such stock.
"(5) foreign oil related losses. The amendment made by subsection (a) shall apply to foreign oil related losses sustained in taxable years ending after December 31, 1975.
"(6) Recapture of possession losses during transitional period where taxpayer is on a per-country basis.
"(A) Application of paragraph. This paragraph shall apply if—
"(i) the taxpayer sustained a loss in a possession of the United States in a taxable year beginning after December 31, 1975, and before January 1, 1979,
"(ii) such loss is attributable to a trade or business engaged in by the taxpayer in such possession on January 1, 1976, and
"(iii) the taxpayer chooses to have the benefits of subpart A of part III of subchapter N apply for such taxable year and section 904(a)(1) of the Internal Revenue Code of 1954 (as in effect before the enactment of this Act) applies with respect to such taxable year.
"(B) No recapture during transition period.—In any case to which this paragraph applies, for purposes of determining the liability for tax of the taxpayer for taxable years beginning before January 1, 1979, section 904(f) of the Internal Revenue Code of 1954 shall not apply with respect to the loss described in subparagraph (A)(i).
"(C) Recapture of loss after the transition period. In any case to which this paragraph applies—
"(i) for purposes of determining the liability for tax of the taxpayer for taxable years beginning after December 31, 1978, section 904(f) of the Internal Revenue Code of 1954 shall be applied with respect to the loss described in subparagraph (A)(i) under the principles of section 904(a)(1) of such Code (as in effect before the enactment of this Act); but
"(ii) in the case of any taxpayer and any possession, the aggregate amount to which such section 904(f) applies by reason of clause (i) shall not exceed the sum of the net incomes of all affiliated corporations from such possession for taxable years of such affiliated corporations beginning after December 31, 1975, and before January 1, 1979.
"(D) Taxpayers not engaged in trade on [sic or] business on January 1, 1976. In any case to which this paragraph applies but for the fact that the taxpayer was not engaged in a trade or business in such possession on January 1, 1976, for purposes of determining the liability for tax of the taxpayer for taxable years beginning before January 1, 1979; if section 904(a)(1) of such Code (as in effect before the enactment of this Act) applies with respect to such taxable year, the provisions of section 904(f) of such Code shall be applied with respect to the loss described in subparagraph (A)(i) under the principles of such section 904(a)(1).

"(E) Affiliated corporation defined. For purposes of subparagraph (C)(ii), the term 'affiliated corporation' means a corporation which, for the taxable year for which the net income is being determined, was not a member of the same affiliated group (within the meaning of section 1504 of the Internal Revenue Code of 1954) as the taxpayer but would have been a member of such group but for the application of subsection (b) of such section 1504."

—P.L. 94-455, Sec. 1034(a), amended subsec. (b) [as amended by Sec. 1031(a) of this Act, see above], effective as provided in Sec. 1034(b) of this Act, which reads as follows:

"(b) Effective dates. The amendment made by this section shall apply to taxable years beginning after December 31, 1975, except that the provisions of section 904(b)(3)(C) shall only apply to sales or exchanges made after November 12, 1975."

Prior to amendment, subsec. (b) as amended by Sec. 1031(a) of this Act, see above] read as follows:

"(b) Taxable income for purposes of computing limitation.
"For purposes of subsection (a), the taxable income in the case of an individual, estate, or trust shall be computed without any deduction for personal exemptions under section 151 or 642(b)."

—P.L. 94-455, Sec. 1051(e), added para. (b)(4) [as amended by Secs. 1031(a) and 1034(a) of this Act, see above], effective for tax. yrs. begin. after 12/31/75.

—P.L. 94-455, Sec. 1901(b)(10)(B), substituted "section 172(h)" for "section 172(k)(1)" in clauses (f)(2)(B)(i) and (f)(4)(B)(i), [as amended by Sec. 1031(a) of this Act, see above], effective for tax. yrs. end. after 10/4/76.

In 1971, P.L. 92-178, Sec. 502(b)(2), amended the heading of subsec. (f) and para. (f)(1)... Sec. 502(b)(3), amended para. (f)(3)... Sec. 502(b)(4), added para. (f)(5), effective as provided in Sec. 507 of this Act, which reads as follows:
"Sec. 507. General effective date of title.
Except as provided in section 505 of this title, the amendments made by sections 501 through 504 of this title shall apply with respect to taxable year ending after December 31, 1971, except that a corporation may not be a DISC (as defined in section 992(a) of the Internal Revenue Code of 1954, added by section 501 of this title) for any taxable year beginning before January 1, 1972."

Prior to amendment, the heading of subsec. (f) and para. (f)(1) read as follows:
"(f) Application of section in case of certain interest income.
"(1) In general. The provisions of subsections (a), (c), (d), and (e) of this section shall be applied separately with respect to—
"(A) The interest income described in paragraph (2), and
"(B) income other than the interest income described in paragraph (2)"

Prior to amendment, para. (f)(3) read as follows:
"(3) Overall limitation not to apply. The limitation provided by subsection (a)(2) shall not apply with respect to the interest income described in paragraph (2). The Secretary or his delegate shall by regulations prescribe the manner of application of subsection (e) with respect to cases in which the limitation provided by subsection (a)(2) applies with respect to income other than the interest income described in paragraph (2)."

In 1969, P.L. 91-172, Sec. 506(b)(1), substituted "(A) with the consent of the Secretary or his delegate with respect to any taxable year or (B) for the taxpayer's first taxable year beginning after December 31, 1969" for "with the consent of the Secretary or his delegate with respect to any taxable year" in para. (b)(1)... Sec. 506(b)(2), substituted "Except in a case to which paragraph (1)(B) applies, if the taxpayer" in para. (b)(2), effective for "If a taxpayer" in para. (b)(2), effective for tax. yrs. begin. after 12/31/69.

In 1966, P.L. 89-809, Sec. 106(c)(1), amended subpara. (f)(2)(C) and added the sentence at the end of para. (f)(2), effective for interest received after 12/31/65 in tax. yrs. end. after 12/31/65.

Prior to amendment, subpara. (f)(2)(C) read as follows:
"(C) received from a corporation in which the taxpayer owns at least 10 percent of the voting stock, or"

In 1964, P.L. 88-272, Sec. 234(b)(6), substituted "section 1503(b)" for "section 1503(d)" in para. (g)(2), effective for tax. yrs. begin. after 12/31/63.

In 1962, P.L. 87-834, Sec. 10(a), redesignated subsec. (f) as subsec. (g) and added new subsec. (f), effective for tax. yrs. begin. after 10/16/62, but only for interest resulting from transactions consummated after 4/2/62.

—P.L. 87-834, Sec. 12(b)(2), amended subsec. (g) [as redesignated by Sec. 10(a) of this Act, see above], effective for tax. yrs. of foreign corporations begin. after 12/31/62, and to tax. yrs. of U.S. shareholders within which or with which such tax. yrs. of foreign corporations end.

Prior to amendment, subsec. (g) [as redesignated by Sec. 10(a) of this Act, see above] read as follows:
"(g) Cross reference. For special rule relating to the application of the credit provided by section 901 in the case of affiliated groups which include Western Hemisphere trade corporations for years in which the limitation provided by subsection (a)(2) applies, see section 1503(d)."

In 1960, P.L. 86-780, Sec. [1](a), amended subsec. (a), and added new subsec. (b)... Sec. [1](b)(1), redesignated subsec. (b) [before amendment by Sec. [1](a) of this Act, see above] as subsec. (c)... Sec. [1](b)(2), substituted "the applicable limitation under subsection (a)" for "the limitation under subsection (a)" each place it appeared in the sentence at the beginning of subsec. (c) [as redesignated by Sec. [1](b)(1) of this Act, see above]... Sec. [1](c)(1), redesignated subsec. (c) [before amendment by Sec. [1](b)(1) of this Act, see above] as subsec. (d)... Sec. [1](c)(2), substituted "the applicable limitation under subsection (a)" for "the limitation under subsection (a)" each place it appeared in the sentence at the beginning of subsec. (d) [as redesignated by Sec. [1](c)(1) of this Act, see above]... Sec. [1](d), added subsecs. (e) and (f), effective for tax. yrs. begin. after 12/31/60.

Prior to amendment, subsec. (a) read as follows:

Income from foreign sources — Code Sec. 905

"(a) Limitation. The amount of the credit in respect of the tax paid or accrued to any country shall not exceed the same proportion of the tax against which such credit is taken which the taxpayer's taxable income from sources with such country (but not in excess of the taxpayer's entire taxable income) bears to his entire taxable income for the same taxable year."

In **1958**, P.L. 85-866, Sec. 42(c), added subsec. (c), effective for tax. yrs. begin. after 12/31/57.

Sec. 905. Applicable rules.

(a) Year in which credit taken.

The credits provided in this subpart may, at the option of the taxpayer and irrespective of the method of accounting employed in keeping his books, be taken in the year in which the taxes of the foreign country or the possession of the United States accrued, subject, however, to the conditions prescribed in subsection (c). If the taxpayer elects to take such credits in the year in which the taxes of the foreign country or the possession of the United States accrued, the credits for all subsequent years shall be taken on the same basis, and no portion of any such taxes shall be allowed as a deduction in the same or any succeeding year.

(b) Proof of credits.

The credits provided in this subpart shall be allowed only if the taxpayer establishes to the satisfaction of the Secretary—

(1) the total amount of income derived from sources without the United States, determined as provided in part I,

(2) the amount of income derived from each country, the tax paid or accrued to which is claimed as a credit under this subpart, such amount to be determined under regulations prescribed by the Secretary, and

(3) all other information necessary for the verification and computation of such credits.

(c) Adjustments to accrued taxes.

(1) In general. If—

(A) accrued taxes when paid differ from the amounts claimed as credits by the taxpayer,

(B) accrued taxes are not paid before the date 2 years after the close of the taxable year to which such taxes relate, or

(C) any tax paid is refunded in whole or in part,

the taxpayer shall notify the Secretary, who shall redetermine the amount of the tax for the year or years affected. The Secretary may prescribe adjustments to the pools of post-1986 foreign income taxes and the pools of post-1986 undistributed earnings under sections 902 and 960 in lieu of the redetermination under the preceding sentence.

(2) Special rule for taxes not paid within 2 years.

(A) In general. Except as provided in subparagraph (B), in making the redetermination under paragraph (1), no credit shall be allowed for accrued taxes not paid before the date referred to in subparagraph (B) of paragraph (1).

(B) Taxes subsequently paid. Any such taxes if subsequently paid—

(i) shall be taken into account—

(I) in the case of taxes deemed paid under section 902 or section 960, for the taxable year in which paid (and no redetermination shall be made under this section by reason of such payment), and

(II) in any other case, for the taxable year to which such taxes relate, and

(ii) shall be translated as provided in section 986(a)(2)(A).

(3) Adjustments. The amount of tax (if any) due on any redetermination under paragraph (1) shall be paid by the taxpayer on notice and demand by the Secretary, and the amount of tax overpaid (if any) shall be credited or refunded to the taxpayer in accordance with subchapter B of chapter 66 (section 6511 et seq.).

(4) **Bond requirements.** In the case of any tax accrued but not paid, the Secretary, as a condition precedent to the allowance of the credit provided in this subpart, may require the taxpayer to give a bond, with sureties satisfactory to and approved by the Secretary, in such sum as the Secretary may require, conditioned on the payment by the taxpayer of any amount of tax found due on any such redetermination. Any such bond shall contain such further conditions as the Secretary may require.

(5) **Other special rules.** In any redetermination under paragraph (1) by the Secretary of the amount of tax due from the taxpayer for the year or years affected by a refund, the amount of the taxes refunded for which credit has been allowed under this section shall be reduced by the amount of any tax described in section 901 imposed by the foreign country or possession of the United States with respect to such refund; but no credit under this subpart, or deduction under section 164, shall be allowed for any taxable year with respect to any such tax imposed on the refund. No interest shall be assessed or collected on any amount of tax due on any redetermination by the Secretary, resulting from a refund to the taxpayer, for any period before the receipt of such refund, except to the extent interest was paid by the foreign country or possession of the United States on such refund for such period.

In **1997**, P.L. 105-34, Sec. 1102(a)(2), amended subsec. (c), effective for taxes which relate to tax. yrs. begin. after 12/31/97.

Prior to amendment, subsec. (c) read as follows:

"(c) Adjustments on payment of accrued taxes.

"If accrued taxes when paid differ from the amounts claimed as credits by the taxpayer, or if any tax paid is refunded in whole or in part, the taxpayer shall notify the Secretary, who shall redetermine the amount of the tax for the year or years affected. The amount of tax due on such redetermination, if any, shall be paid by the taxpayer on notice and demand by the Secretary, or the amount of tax overpaid, if any, shall be credited or refunded to the taxpayer in accordance with subchapter B of chapter 66 (sec. 6511 and following). In the case of such a tax accrued but not paid, the Secretary, as a condition precedent to the allowance of this credit, may require the taxpayer to give a bond, with sureties satisfactory to and to be approved by the Secretary, in such sum as the Secretary may require, conditioned on the payment by the taxpayer of any amount of tax found due on any such redetermination; and the bond herein prescribed shall contain such further conditions as the Secretary may require. In such redetermination by the Secretary of the amount of tax due from the taxpayer for the year or years affected by a refund, the amount of the taxes refunded for which credit has been allowed under this section shall be reduced by the amount of any tax described in section 901 imposed by the foreign country or possession of the United States with respect to such refund; but no credit under this subpart, and no deduction under section 164 (relating to deduction for taxes) shall be allowed for any taxable year with respect to such tax imposed on the refund. No interest shall be assessed or collected on any amount of tax due on any redetermination by the Secretary, resulting from a refund to the taxpayer, for any period before the receipt of such refund, except to the extent interest was paid by the foreign country or possession of the United States on such refund for such period."

In **1982**, P.L. 97-248, Sec. 343(a), deleted the last sentence of subsec. (c), effective as if this sentence had never been enacted.

Prior to deletion, the last sentence of subsec. (c) read as follows:

"The preceding sentence shall not apply (with respect to any period after the refund or adjustment in the foreign taxes) if the taxpayer fails to notify the Secretary (on or before the date prescribed by regulations for giving such notice) unless it is shown that such failure is due to reasonable cause and not due to willful neglect."

In **1980**, P.L. 96-603, Sec. 2(c)(1), added the last sentence of subsec. (c), effective for employer contributions or accruals for tax. yrs. begin. after 12/31/79. For special election see Sec. 2(e)(2) of this Act reproduced in note following Code Sec. 404A.

In **1976**, P.L. 94-455, Sec. 1901(a)(114), deleted the last sentence of subsec. (b), effective tax. yrs. begin. after 12/31/76.

Prior to deletion, the last sentence of subsec. (b) read as follows:

"For purposes of this subpart, the recipient of a royalty or other amount paid or accrued as consideration for the use of, or for the privilege of using, copyrights, patents, designs, secret processes and formulas, trademarks, and other like property, and derived from sources within the United Kingdom of Great Britain and Northern Ireland, shall be deemed to have paid or accrued any income, war-profits and excess-profits taxes paid or accrued to the United Kingdom with respect to such royalty or other amount (including the amount by which the payor's United Kingdom tax was increased by inability to deduct such royalty or other amount) if

such recipient elects to include in its gross income the amount of such United Kingdom tax."
—P.L. 94-455, Sec. 1906(b)(13)(A), substituted "Secretary" for "Secretary or his delegate" each place it appeared in subsecs. (b) and (c), effective for tax. yrs. begin. after 12/31/76.

In 1958, P.L. 85-866, Sec. 103(b), added last sentence in subsec. (b), effective for tax. yrs. begin. after 12/31/53.

Sec. 906. Nonresident alien individuals and foreign corporations.
(a) Allowance of credit.

A nonresident alien individual or a foreign corporation engaged in trade or business within the United States during the taxable year shall be allowed a credit under section 901 for the amount of any income, war profits, and excess profits taxes paid or accrued during the taxable year (or deemed, under section 902, paid or accrued during the taxable year) to any foreign country or possession of the United States with respect to income effectively connected with the conduct of a trade or business within the United States.

(b) Special rules.

(1) For purposes of subsection (a) and for purposes of determining the deductions allowable under sections 873(a) and 882(c), in determining the amount of any tax paid or accrued to any foreign country or possession there shall not be taken into account any amount of tax to the extent the tax so paid or accrued is imposed with respect to income from sources within the United States which would not be taxed by such foreign country or possession but for the fact that—

(A) in the case of a nonresident alien individual, such individual is a citizen or resident of such foreign country or possession, or

(B) in the case of a foreign corporation, such corporation was created or organized under the law of such foreign country or possession or is domiciled for tax purposes in such country or possession.

(2) For purposes of subsection (a), in applying section 904 the taxpayer's taxable income shall be treated as consisting only of the taxable income effectively connected with the taxpayer's conduct of a trade or business within the United States.

(3) The credit allowed pursuant to subsection (a) shall not be allowed against any tax imposed by section 871(a) (relating to income of nonresident alien individual not connected with United States business) or 881 (relating to income of foreign corporations not connected with United States business).

(4) For purposes of sections 902(a) and 78, a foreign corporation choosing the benefits of this subpart which receives dividends shall, with respect to such dividends, be treated as a domestic corporation.

(5) For purposes of section 902, any income, war profits, and excess profits taxes paid or accrued (or deemed paid or accrued) to any foreign country or possession of the United States with respect to income effectively connected with the conduct of a trade or business within the United States shall not be taken into account, and any accumulated profits attributable to such income shall not be taken into account.

(6) No credit shall be allowed under this section against the tax imposed by section 884.

In 2007, P.L. 110-172, Sec. 11(g)(11), deleted para. (b)(5) and redesignated paras. (b)(6) and (7) as paras. (b)(5) and (6), enacted 12/29/2007.
Prior to deletion, para. (b)(5) read as follows:
"(5) No credit shall be allowed under this section for any income, war profits, and excess profits taxes paid or accrued with respect to the foreign trade income (within the meaning of section 923(b)) of a FSC."

In 1988, P.L. 100-647, Sec. 1012(q)(10), redesignated para. (b)(6) [added by Sec. 1241(c) of 99-514] as para. (b)(7), effective for tax. yrs. begin. after 12/31/86.
In 1986, P.L. 99-514, Sec. 1241(c), added para. (b)(6) [sic (b)(7)], effective for tax. yrs. begin. after 12/31/86.
—P.L. 99-514, Sec. 1876(d)(3), added para. (b)(6), effective for transactions after 12/31/84, in tax. yrs. end. after 12/31/84.
In 1984, P.L. 98-369, Sec. 801(d)(3), added para. (b)(5), effective for transactions after 12/31/84, in tax. yrs. end. after 12/31/84.
In 1966, P.L. 89-809, Sec. 106, added Code Sec. 906, effective for tax. yrs. begin. after 12/31/66. Sec. 106(a)(6) of this Act provides:
"In applying section 904 of the Internal Revenue Code of 1954 with respect to section 906 of such Code, no amount may be carried from or to any taxable year beginning before January 1, 1967, and no such year shall be taken into account."

Sec. 907. Special rules in case of foreign oil and gas income.
(a) Reduction in amount allowed as foreign tax under section 901.

In applying section 901, the amount of any foreign oil and gas taxes paid or accrued (or deemed to have been paid) during the taxable year which would (but for this subsection) be taken into account for purposes of section 901 shall be reduced by the amount (if any) by which the amount of such taxes exceeds the product of—

(1) the amount of the combined foreign oil and gas income for the taxable year,

(2) multiplied by—

(A) in the case of a corporation, the percentage which is equal to the highest rate of tax specified under section 11(b), or

(B) in the case of an individual, a fraction the numerator of which is the tax against which the credit under section 901(a) is taken and the denominator of which is the taxpayer's entire taxable income.

(b) Combined foreign oil and gas income; foreign oil and gas taxes.

For purposes of this section—

(1) **Combined foreign oil and gas income.** The term "combined foreign oil and gas income" means, with respect to any taxable year, the sum of—

(A) foreign oil and gas extraction income, and

(B) foreign oil related income.

(2) **Foreign oil and gas taxes.** The term "foreign oil and gas taxes" means, with respect to any taxable year, the sum of—

(A) oil and gas extraction taxes, and

(B) any income, war profits, and excess profits taxes paid or accrued (or deemed to have been paid or accrued under section 902 or 960) during the taxable year with respect to foreign oil related income (determined without regard to subsection (c)(4)) or loss which would be taken into account for purposes of section 901 without regard to this section.

(c) Foreign income definitions and special rules.

For purposes of this section—

(1) **Foreign oil and gas extraction income.** The term "foreign oil and gas extraction income" means the taxable income derived from sources without the United States and its possessions from—

(A) the extraction (by the taxpayer or any other person) of minerals from oil or gas wells, or

(B) the sale or exchange of assets used by the taxpayer in the trade or business described in subparagraph (A).

Such term does not include any dividend or interest income which is passive income (as defined in section 904(d)(2)(A)).

(2) **Foreign oil related income.** The term "foreign oil related income" means the taxable income derived from sources outside the United States and its possessions from—

(A) the processing of minerals extracted (by the taxpayer or by any other person) from oil or gas wells into their primary products,
(B) the transportation of such minerals or primary products,
(C) the distribution or sale of such minerals or primary products,
(D) the disposition of assets used by the taxpayer in the trade or business described in subparagraph (A), (B), or (C), or
(E) the performance of any other related service.

Such term does not include any dividend or interest income which is passive income (as defined in section 904(d)(2)(A)).

(3) Dividends, interest, partnership distribution, etc. The term "foreign oil and gas extraction income" and the term "foreign oil related income" include—
(A) dividends and interest from a foreign corporation in respect of which taxes are deemed paid by the taxpayer under section 902,
(B) amounts with respect to which taxes are deemed paid under section 960(a), and
(C) the taxpayer's distributive share of the income of partnerships,
to the extent such dividends, interest, amounts, or distributive share is attributable to foreign oil and gas extraction income, or to foreign oil related income, as the case may be; except that interest described in subparagraph (A) shall not be taken into account in computing foreign oil and gas extraction income but shall be taken into account in computing foreign oil-related income.

(4) Recapture of foreign oil and gas losses by recharacterizing later combined foreign oil and gas income.
(A) In general. The combined foreign oil and gas income of a taxpayer for a taxable year (determined without regard to this paragraph) shall be reduced—
(i) first by the amount determined under subparagraph (B), and
(ii) then by the amount determined under subparagraph (C).

The aggregate amount of such reductions shall be treated as income (from sources without the United States) which is not combined foreign oil and gas income.
(B) Reduction for pre-2009 foreign oil extraction losses. The reduction under this paragraph shall be equal to the lesser of—
(i) the foreign oil and gas extraction income of the taxpayer for the taxable year (determined without regard to this paragraph), or
(ii) the excess of—
(I) the aggregate amount of foreign oil extraction losses for preceding taxable years beginning after December 31, 1982, and before January 1, 2009, over
(II) so much of such aggregate amount as was recharacterized under this paragraph (as in effect before and after the date of the enactment of the Energy Improvement and Extension Act of 2008) [10/3/2008] for preceding taxable years beginning after December 31, 1982.
(C) Reduction for post-2008 foreign oil and gas losses. The reduction under this paragraph shall be equal to the lesser of—
(i) the combined foreign oil and gas income of the taxpayer for the taxable year (determined without regard to this paragraph), reduced by an amount equal to the reduction under subparagraph (A) for the taxable year, or
(ii) the excess of—
(I) the aggregate amount of foreign oil and gas losses for preceding taxable years beginning after December 31, 2008, over
(II) so much of such aggregate amount as was recharacterized under this paragraph for preceding taxable years beginning after December 31, 2008.
(D) Foreign oil and gas loss defined.
(i) In general. For purposes of this paragraph, the term "foreign oil and gas loss" means the amount by which—
(I) the gross income for the taxable year from sources without the United States and its possessions (whether or not the taxpayer chooses the benefits of this subpart for such taxable year) taken into account in determining the combined foreign oil and gas income for such year, is exceeded by
(II) the sum of the deductions properly apportioned or allocated thereto.
(ii) Net operating loss deduction not taken into account. For purposes of clause (i), the net operating loss deduction allowable for the taxable year under section 172(a) shall not be taken into account.
(iii) Expropriation and casualty losses not taken into account. For purposes of clause (i), there shall not be taken into account—
(I) any foreign expropriation loss (as defined in section 172(h) (as in effect on the day before the date of the enactment of the Revenue Reconciliation Act of 1990)) for the taxable year, or
(II) any loss for the taxable year which arises from fire, storm, shipwreck, or other casualty, or from theft,
to the extent such loss is not compensated for by insurance or otherwise.
(iv) Foreign oil extraction loss.—For purposes of subparagraph (B)(ii)(I), foreign oil extraction losses shall be determined under this paragraph as in effect on the day before the date of the enactment of the Energy Improvement and Extension Act of 2008.

(5) Oil and gas extraction taxes. The term "oil and gas extraction taxes" means any income, war profits, and excess profits tax paid or accrued (or deemed to have been paid under section 902 or 960) during the taxable year with respect to foreign oil and gas extraction income (determined without regard to paragraph (4)) or loss which would be taken into account for purposes of section 901 without regard to this section.

(d) Disregard of certain posted prices, etc.

For purposes of this chapter, in determining the amount of taxable income in the case of foreign oil and gas extraction income, if the oil or gas is disposed of, or is acquired other than from the government of a foreign country, at a posted price (or other pricing arrangement) which differs from the fair market value for such oil or gas, such fair market value shall be used in lieu of such posted price (or other pricing arrangement).

(e) Repealed.

(f) Carryback and carryover of disallowed credits.
(1) In general. If the amount of the foreign oil and gas taxes paid or accrued during any taxable year exceeds the limitation provided by subsection (a) for such taxable year

(hereinafter in this subsection referred to as the "unused credit year"), such excess shall be deemed to be foreign oil and gas taxes paid or accrued in the first preceding taxable year and in any of the first 10 succeeding taxable year, in that order and to the extent not deemed tax paid or accrued in a prior taxable year by reason of the limitation imposed by paragraph (2). Such amount deemed paid or accrued in any taxable year may be availed of only as a tax credit and not as a deduction and only if the taxpayer for such year chooses to have the benefits of this subpart as to taxes paid or accrued for that year to foreign countries or possessions.

(2) Limitation. The amount of the unused foreign oil and gas taxes which under paragraph (1) may be deemed paid or accrued in any preceding or succeeding taxable year shall not exceed the lesser of—

(A) the amount by which the limitation provided by subsection (a) for such taxable year exceeds the sum of—

(i) the foreign oil and gas taxes paid or accrued during such taxable year, plus

(ii) the amounts of the foreign oil and gas taxes which by reason of this subsection are deemed paid or accrued in such taxable year and are attributable to taxable years preceding the unused credit year; or

(B) the amount by which the limitation provided by section 904 for such taxable year exceeds the sum of—

(i) the taxes paid or accrued (or deemed to have been paid under section 902 or 960) to all foreign countries and possessions of the United States during such taxable year,

(ii) the amount of such taxes which were deemed paid or accrued in such taxable year under section 904(c) and which are attributable to taxable years preceding the unused credit year, plus

(iii) the amount of the foreign oil and gas taxes which by reason of this subsection are deemed paid or accrued in such taxable year and are attributable to taxable years preceding the unused credit year.

(3) Special rules.

(A) In the case of any taxable year which is an unused credit year under this subsection and which is an unused credit year under section 904(c), the provisions of this subsection shall be applied before section 904(c).

(B) For purposes of determining the amount of taxes paid or accrued in any taxable year which may be deemed paid or accrued in a preceding or succeeding taxable year under section 904(c), any tax deemed paid or accrued in such preceding or succeeding taxable year under this subsection shall be considered to be tax paid or accrued in such preceding or succeeding taxable year.

(4) Transition rules for pre-2009 and 2009 disallowed credits.

(A) Pre-2009 credits. In the case of any unused credit year beginning before January 1, 2009, this subsection shall be applied to any unused oil and gas extraction taxes carried from such unused credit year to a year beginning after December 31, 2008—

(i) by substituting "oil and gas extraction taxes" for "foreign oil and gas taxes" each place it appears in paragraphs (1), (2), and (3), and

(ii) by computing, for purposes of paragraph (2)(A), the limitation under subparagraph (A) for the year to which such taxes are carried by substituting "foreign oil and gas extraction income" for "foreign oil and gas income" in subsection (a).

(B) 2009 credits. In the case of any unused credit year beginning in 2009, the amendments made to this subsection by the Energy Improvement and Extension Act of 2008 shall be treated as being in effect for any preceding year beginning before January 1, 2009, solely for purposes of determining how much of the unused foreign oil and gas taxes for such unused credit year may be deemed paid or accrued in such preceding year.

In 2008, P.L. 110-343, Sec. 402(a)DivB, amended subsec. (a) and (b) . . . Sec. 402(b)DivB, amended para. (c)(4) . . . Sec. 402(c)(1)DivB, substituted "foreign oil and gas taxes" for "oil and gas extraction taxes" each place it appeared in subsec. (f) . . . Sec. 402(c)(2)DivB, added para. (f)(4), effective for tax. yrs. begin. after 12/31/2008.

Prior to amendment subsecs. (a) and (b) read as follows:

"(a) Reduction in amount allowed as foreign tax under section 901.

"In applying section 901, the amount of any oil and gas extraction taxes paid or accrued (or deemed to have been paid) during the taxable year which would (but for this subsection) be taken into account for purposes of section 901 shall be reduced by the amount (if any) by which the amount of such taxes exceeds the product of—

"(1) the amount of the foreign oil and gas extraction income for the taxable year,

"(2) multiplied by—

"(A) in the case of a corporation, the percentage which is equal to the highest rate of tax specified under section 11(b), or

"(B) in the case of an individual, a fraction the numerator of which is the tax against which the credit under section 901(a) is taken and the denominator of which is the taxpayer's entire taxable income."

"(b) Foreign taxes on foreign oil related income.

"For purposes of this subtitle, in the case of taxes paid or accrued to any foreign country with respect to foreign oil related income, the term 'income, war profits, and excess profits taxes' shall not include any amount paid or accrued after December 31, 1982, to the extent that the Secretary determines that the foreign law imposing such amount of tax is structured, or in fact operates, so that the amount of tax imposed with respect to foreign oil related income will generally be materially greater, over a reasonable period of time, than the amount generally imposed on income that is neither foreign oil related income nor foreign oil and gas extraction income. In computing the amount not treated as tax under this subsection, such amount shall be treated as a deduction under the foreign law.

Prior to amendment para. (c)(4) read as follows:

"(4) Recapture of foreign oil and gas extraction losses by recharacterizing later extraction income.

"(A) In general. That portion of the income of the taxpayer for the taxable year which (but for this paragraph) would be treated as foreign oil and gas extraction income shall be treated as income (from sources without the United States) which is not foreign oil and gas extraction income to the extent of the excess of—

"(i) the aggregate amount of foreign oil extraction losses for preceding taxable years beginning after December 31, 1982, over

"(ii) so much of such aggregate amount as was recharacterized under this subparagraph for preceding taxable years beginning after December 31, 1982.

"(B) Foreign oil extraction loss defined.

"(i) In general. For purposes of this paragraph, the term 'foreign oil extraction loss' means the amount by which—

"(I) the gross income for the taxable year from sources without the United States and its possessions (whether or not the taxpayer chooses the benefits of this subpart for such taxable year) taken into account in determining the foreign oil and gas extraction income for such year, is exceeded by

"(II) the sum of the deductions properly apportioned or allocated thereto.

"(ii) Net operating loss deduction not taken into account. For purposes of clause (i), the net operating loss deduction allowable for the taxable year under section 172(a) shall not be taken into account.

"(iii) Expropriation and casualty losses not taken into account. For purposes of clause (i), there shall not be taken into account—

"(I) any foreign expropriation loss (as defined in section 172(h) (as in effect on the day before the date of the enactment [11/5/90] of the Revenue Reconciliation Act of 1990)) for the taxable year, or

"(II) any loss for the taxable year which arises from fire, storm, shipwreck, or other casualty, or from theft,

"to the extent such loss is not compensated for by insurance or otherwise."

In 2004, P.L. 108-357, Sec. 417(b)(1), deleted "in the second preceding taxable year," before "in the first preceding taxable year" in para. (f)(1), effective for excess foreign taxes arising in tax. yrs. begin. after 10/22/2004.

—P.L. 108-357, Sec. 417(b)(2), substituted "and in any of the first 10" for ", and in the first, second, third, fourth, or fifth" in para. (f)(1), effective for excess foreign taxes which (without regard to the amendments made by this section) may be carried to any tax. yr. end. after 10/22/2004.

—P.L. 108-357, Sec. 417(b)(3), deleted "For purposes of this subsection, the terms 'second preceding taxable year', and 'first preceding taxable year' do not include any taxable year ending before January 1, 1975." before the period in para. (f)(1), effective 10/22/2004

In 1996, P.L. 104-188, Sec. 1704(t)(36), added "(as in effect on the day before the date of the enactment of the Revenue Reconciliation Act of 1990)" after "section 172(h)" in subclause (c)(4)(B)(iii)(I), effective 8/20/96.

Income from foreign sources Code Sec. 907

In 1993, P.L. 103-66, Sec. 13235(a)(1)(A), added the flush sentence at the end of para. (c)(1) . . . Sec. 13235(a)(1)(B), added the flush sentence at the end of para. (c)(2), effective for tax. yrs. begin. after 12/31/92.

In 1990, P.L. 101-508, Sec. 11801(a)(32), deleted subsec. (e) and subpara. (f)(3)(C), effective 11/5/90 except as provided in Sec. 11821(b) of this Act, reproduced in note following Code Sec. 421.

Prior to deletion, subsec. (e) read as follows:

"(e) Transitional rules.

"(1) Credits arising in taxable years beginning before January 1, 1983. The amount of taxes paid or accrued in any taxable year beginning before January 1, 1983 (hereinafter in this paragraph referred to as the 'excess credit year') which under section 904(c) or 907(f) may be deemed paid or accrued in a taxable year beginning after December 31, 1982, shall not exceed the amount which could have been deemed paid or accrued if sections 907(b), 907(f), and 904(f)(4) (as in effect on the day before the date of the enactment of the Tax Equity and Fiscal Responsibility Act of 1982) remained in effect for taxable years beginning after December 31, 1982.

"(2) Carryback of credits arising in taxable years beginning after December 31, 1982. The amount of the taxes paid or accrued in a taxable year beginning after December 31, 1982, which may be deemed paid or accrued under section 904(c) or 907(f) in a taxable year beginning before January 1, 1983, shall not exceed the amount which could have been deemed paid or accrued if sections 907(b), 907(f), and 904(f)(4) (as in effect on the day before the date of the enactment of the Tax Equity and Fiscal Responsibility Act of 1982) remained in effect for taxable years beginning after December 31, 1982."

Prior to deletion, subpara. (f)(3)(C) read as follows:

"(C) For purposes of determining the amount of the unused oil and gas extraction taxes which under paragraph (1) may be deemed paid or accrued in any taxable year ending before January 1, 1977, subparagraph (A) of paragraph (2) shall be applied as if the amendment made by section 1035(a) of the Tax Reform Act of 1976 applied to such taxable year."

In 1988, P.L. 100-647, Sec. 1012(g)(6)(A), deleted subpara. (c)(3)(B) and redesignated subparas. (c)(3)(C) and (D) as subparas. (c)(3)(B) and (C) . . . Sec. 1012(g)(6)(B), deleted "and dividends deducted in subparagraph (B)" before "shall not be taken into account" in para. (c)(3), effective for payments before 12/31/86.

Prior to deletion subpara. (c)(3)(B) read as follows:

"(B) dividends from a domestic corporation which are treated under section 861(a)(2)(A) as income from sources without the United States,"

In 1984, P.L. 98-369, Sec. 712(e), substituted "the 8-year period (or shorter period as the taxpayer may select)" for "the 8-year period" in Sec. 211(e)(2)(A) of P.L. 97-248 [part of the effective date for amendments made by Sec. 211 of P.L. 97-248, reproduced below].

In 1983, P.L. 97-448, Sec. 306(a)(5), amended Sec. 211(e)(2) of P.L. 97-248 [part of the effective date for amendments made by Sec. 211 of P.L. 97-248, reproduced below].

Prior to amendment, Sec. 211(e)(2) of P.L. 97-248 read as follows:

"(2) Retention of old sections 907(b) and 904(f)(4) where taxpayer had foreign loss from an activity not related to oil and gas.—If, after applying old sections 907(b) and 904(f)(4) to a taxable year beginning before January 1, 1983, the taxpayer had a foreign loss attributable to activities not taken into account in determining foreign oil related income (as defined in old section 907(c)(2)), such loss shall not be recaptured from foreign oil related income more rapidly than ratably over the 8-year period beginning with the first taxable year beginning after December 31, 1982. For purposes of the preceding sentence, and 'old' section is such section as in effect on the day before the date of the enactment of this Act."

In 1982, P.L. 97-248, Sec. 211(a), amended para. (c)(4) . . . Sec. 211(b), amended para. (c)(2) . . . Sec. 211(c)(1), amended subsec. (b) . . . Sec. 211(d)(1), amended subsec. (e) . . . Sec. 211(d)(2)(A)(i), substituted "such excess" for "so much of such excess as does not exceed 2 percent of foreign oil and gas extraction income for such taxable year" in para. (f)(1) . . . Sec. 211(d)(2)(A)(ii), deleted the sentence at the end of para. (f)(1) . . . Sec. 211(d)(2)(B)(i)(I), deleted "on taxes paid or accrued with respect to foreign oil related income" after "by section 904" in subpara. (f)(2)(B) . . . Sec. 211(d)(2)(B)(i)(II), deleted "with respect to such income" after "of the United States" in clause (f)(2)(B)(i) . . . Sec. 211(d)(2)(B)(ii), deleted "with respect to oil-related income" after "section 904(c)" in subpara. (f)(3)(A) . . . Sec. 211(d)(2)(B)(iii), deleted "oil-related" after "determining the amount of" in subpara. (f)(3)(B), effective for tax. yrs. begin. after 12/31/82. Sec. 211(c)(2) of this Act [as amended by Sec. 712(e) of P.L. 98-369, and Sec. 306(a)(5) of P.L. 97-448, see above] provides special rules as follows:

"(2) Retention of old sections 907(b) and 904(f)(4) where taxpayer had separate basket foreign loss.

"(A) In general. If, after applying old sections 907(b) and 904(f)(4) to a taxable year beginning before January 1, 1983, the taxpayer had a separate basket foreign loss, such loss shall not be recaptured from income of a kind not taken into account in computing the amount of such separate basket foreign loss more rapidly than ratably over the 8-year period (or such shorter period as the taxpayer may select) beginning with the first taxable year beginning after December 31, 1982.

"(B) Definitions. For purposes of this paragraph—

"(i) The term 'separate basket foreign loss' means any foreign loss attributable to activities taken into account (or not taken into account) in determining foreign oil related income (as defined in old section 907(c)(2)).

"(ii) An 'old' section is such section as in effect on the day before the date of the enactment of this Act."

Prior to amendment, para. (c)(4) read as follows:

"(4) Certain losses. If for any foreign country for any taxable year the taxpayer would have a net operating loss if only items from sources within such country (including deductions properly apportioned or allocated thereto) which relate to the extraction of minerals from oil or gas wells were taken into account, such items—

"(A) shall not be taken into account in computing foreign oil and gas extraction income for such year, but

"(B) shall be taken into account in computing foreign oil related income for such year."

Prior to amendment, para. (c)(2) read as follows:

"(2) Foreign oil related income. The term 'foreign oil related income' means the taxable income derived from sources outside the United States and its possessions from—

"(A) the extraction (by the taxpayer or any other person) of minerals from oil or gas wells,

"(B) the processing of such minerals into their primary products,

"(C) the transportation of such minerals or primary products,

"(D) the distribution or sale of such minerals or primary products, or

"(E) the sale or exchange of assets used by the taxpayer in the trade or business described in subparagraph (A), (B), (C), or (D)."

Prior to amendment, subsec. (b) read as follows:

"(b) Application of section 904 limitation.

"The provisions of section 904 shall be applied separately with respect to—

"(1) foreign oil related income, and

"(2) other taxable income."

Prior to amendment, subsec. (e) read as follows:

"(e) Transitional rules.

"(1) Taxable years ending after December 31, 1974. In applying subsections (d) and (e) of section 904 (as in effect on the day before the date of the enactment of the Tax Reform Act of 1976 [date of enactment: 10/4/76]) for purposes of determining the amount which may be carried over from a taxable year ending before January 1, 1975, to any taxable year ending after December 31, 1974—

"(A) subsection (a) of this section shall be deemed to have been in effect for such prior taxable year and for all taxable years thereafter, and

"(B) the carryover from such prior year shall be divided (effective as of the first day of the first taxable year ending after December 31, 1974) into—

"(i) a foreign oil related carryover, and

"(ii) another carryover,

on the basis of the proportionate share of the foreign oil related income, or the other taxable income, as the case may be, of the total taxable income taken into account in computing the amount of such carryover.

"(2) Taxable years ending after December 31, 1975. In applying subsections (d) and (e) of section (04 (as in effect on the day before the date of enactment of the Tax Reform Act of 1976 [date of enactment: 10/4/76]) for purposes of determining the amount which may be carried over from a taxable year ending before January 1, 1976, to any taxable year ending after December 31, 1975, if the per-country limitation provided by section 904(a)(1) (as so in effect) applied to such prior taxable year and to the taxpayer's last taxable year ending before January 1, 1976, then in the case of any foreign oil related carryover—

"(A) the first sentence of section 904(e)(2) (as so in effect) shall not apply, but

"(B) such amount may not exceed the amount which could have been used in such succeeding taxable year if the per-country limitation continued to apply."

Prior to deletion, the sentence at the end of para. (f)(1) read as follows:

"For purposes of determining the amount of such taxes which may be deemed paid or accrued in any taxable year ending in 1975, 1976, or 1977, the first sentence of this paragraph shall be applied by substituting 'such excess' for 'so much of such excess as does not exceed 2 percent of the foreign oil and gas extraction income for such taxable year'."

In 1978, P.L. 95-600, Sec. 301(b)(14), amended para. (a)(2), effective for tax. yrs. begin. after 12/31/78.

Prior to amendment, para. (a)(2) read as follows:

"(2) the percentage which is the sum of the normal tax rate and the surtax rate for the taxable year specified in section 11."

—P.L. 95-600, Sec. 701(u)(8)(A), amended subsec. (a) [as amended by Sec. 301(b)(14) of this Act, see above] . . . Sec. 701(u)(8)(B), amended subsec. (b), effective as provided in Sec. 701(u)(8)(D) of this Act, which reads as follows:

"(D) Effective dates.

"(i) The amendments made by this paragraph shall apply, in the case of individuals, to taxable years ending after December 31, 1974, and, in the case of corporations, to taxable years ending after December 31, 1976.

"(ii) In the case of any taxable year ending after December 31, 1975, with respect to foreign oil related income (within the meaning of section 907(c) of the Internal Revenue Code of 1954), the overall limitation provided by section 904(a)(2) of such Code shall apply and the per-country limitation provided by section 904(a)(1) of such Code shall not apply."

Prior to amendment, subsecs. (a) and (b) read as follows:

"(a) Reduction in amount allowed as foreign tax under section 901.

"In applying section 901, the amount of any oil and gas extraction taxes paid or accrued (or deemed to have been paid) during the taxable year which would (but for this subsection) be taken into account for purposes of section 901 shall be reduced by the amount (if any) by which the amount of such taxes exceeds the product of—

"(1) the amount of the foreign oil and gas extraction income for the taxable year, multiplied by

"(2) the percentage which is equal to the highest rate of tax specified in section 11(b).

"(b) Application of section 904 limitation.

"(1) Corporations. In the case of a corporation, the provisions of section 904 shall be applied separately with respect to—

Code Sec. 907   Income from foreign sources

"(A) foreign oil related income, and
"(B) other taxable income.
"(2) Other taxpayers. In the case of a taxpayer other than a corporation, the provisions of subsection (a) shall not apply and the provisions of section 904 shall be applied separately with respect to—
"(A) foreign oil and gas extraction income, and
"(B) other taxable income (including other foreign oil related income)."

—P.L. 95-600, Sec. 701(u)(9), amended the second sentence of Sec. 1035(c)(3) of P.L. 94-455 [part of the effective dates for amendments made by Sec. 1035(a) of P.L. 94-455, reproduced below].

Prior to amendment, the second sentence of Sec. 1035(c)(3) of P.L. 94-455 read as follows:

"No such contract shall be taken into account for any taxable year ending after December 31, 1977."

—P.L. 95-600, Sec. 703(h)(1)(A), added "(as defined in section 907(c) of such Code)" after "gas extraction income" in Sec. 1035(c)(2)(A) of P.L. 94-455 [part of the effective dates for amendments made by Sec. 1035(a) of P.L. 94-455, reproduced below] . . . Sec. 703(h)(1)(B), substituted "(as so defined)" for "(as defined in section 907(c)(1) of such Code)" in Sec. 1035(c)(2)(B) of P.L. 94-455 [part of the effective dates for amendments made by Sec. 1035(a) of P.L. 94-455, reproduced below], effective 10/4/76.

In 1976, P.L. 94-455, Sec. 1031(b)(6)(A), substituted "(d) and (e) of section 904 (as in effect on the day before the date of the enactment of the Tax Reform Act of 1976)" for "(d) and (e) of section 904" in paras. (e)(1) and (2) . . . Sec. 1031(b)(6)(B), substituted "section 904(a)(1) (as so in effect)" for "section 904(a)(1)" in para. (e)(2) . . . Sec. 1031(b)(6)(C), substituted "section 904(e)(2) (as so in effect)" for "section 904(e)(2)" in subpara. (e)(2)(A), effective for tax. yrs. begin. after 12/31/75, except as provided in Secs. 1031(c)(2), (3) and (4) of this Act reproduced in note following Code Sec. 904.

—P.L. 94-455, Sec. 1032(b)(1), deleted the sentence at the end of subsec. (b) [as amended by Sec. 1035(b) of this Act, see below], effective for tax. yrs. begin. after 12/31/75.

Prior to deletion, the sentence at the end of subsec. (b) [as amended by Sec. 1035(b) of this Act, see below] read as follows:

"In the case of a corporation, with respect to foreign oil-related income, and in the case of a taxpayer other than a corporation, with respect to foreign oil and gas extraction income, the overall limitation provided by section 904(a)(2) shall apply and the per-country limitation provided by subsection (a)(1) shall not apply."

—P.L. 94-455, Sec. 1032(b)(2), deleted subsec. (f) and redesignated subsec. (g) as subsec. (f), effective for losses sustained in tax. yrs. begin. after 12/31/75.

Prior to amendment, subsec. (f) read as follows:

"(f) Recapture of foreign oil related loss.
"(1) General rule. For purposes of this subpart, in the case of any taxpayer who sustains a foreign oil related loss for any taxable year—
"(A) that portion of the foreign oil related income for each succeeding taxable year which is equal to the lesser of—
"(i) the amount of such loss (to the extent not used under this paragraph in prior years), or
"(ii) 50 percent of the foreign oil related income for such succeeding taxable year,
shall be treated as income from sources within the United States (and not as income from sources without the United States), and
"(B) the amount of the income, war profits, and excess profits taxes paid or accrued (or deemed to have been paid) to a foreign country for such succeeding taxable year with respect to foreign oil related income shall be reduced by an amount which bears the same proportion to the total amount of such foreign taxes as the amount treated as income from sources within the United States under subparagraph (A) nears to the total foreign oil related income for such succeeding taxable year.

For purposes of this chapter, the amount of any foreign taxes for which credit is denied under subparagraph (B) of the preceding sentence shall not be allowed as a deduction for any taxable year. For purposes of this subsection, foreign oil related income shall be determined without regard to this subsection.

"(2) Foreign oil related loss defined. For purposes of this subsection, the term 'foreign oil related loss' means the amount by which the gross income for the taxable year from sources without the United States and its possessions (whether or not the taxpayer chooses the benefits of this subpart for such taxable year) taken into account in determining the foreign oil related income for such year is exceeded by the sum of the deductions properly apportioned or allocated thereto, except that there shall not be taken into account—
"(A) any net operating loss deduction allowable for such year under section 172(a) or any capital loss carrybacks and carryovers to such year under section 1212, and
"(B) any—
"(i) foreign expropriation loss for such year, as defined in section 172(k)(1), or
"(ii) loss for such year which arises from fire, storm, shipwreck, or other casualty, or from theft,
to the extent such loss is not compensated for by insurance or otherwise.
"(3) Dispositions.
"(A) In general. For purposes of this chapter, if property used in a trade or business described in subparagraph (A), (B), (C), or (D) of subsection (c)(2) is disposed of during any taxable year—
"(i) the taxpayer notwithstanding any other provision of this chapter (other than paragraph (1)) shall be deemed to have received and recognized foreign oil related income in the taxable year of the disposition, by reason of such disposition, in an amount equal to the lesser of the excess of the fair market value of such property over the taxpayer's adjusted basis in such property or the remaining amount of the foreign oil related losses which were not used under paragraph (1) for such taxable year or any prior taxable year, and
"(ii) paragraph (1) shall be applied with respect to such income by substituting '100 percent' for '50 percent'.
"(B) Disposition defined. For purposes of this subsection, the term 'disposition' includes a sale, exchange, distribution, or gift of property, whether or not gain or loss is recognized on the transfer.
"(C) Exceptions. Notwithstanding subparagraph (B), the term 'disposition' does not include—
"(i) a disposition of property which is not a material factor in the realization of income by the taxpayer, or
"(ii) a disposition of property to a domestic corporation in a distribution or transfer described in section 381(a),".

—P.L. 94-455, Sec. 1035(a), amended subsec. (a), effective for tax. yrs. end. after 12/31/76. Sec. 1035(c) of this Act [as amended by Secs. 701(u)(9), 703(h)(1)(A) and (B) of P.L. 95-600, see above] provides as follows:

"(c) Tax credit for production-sharing contracts.
"(1) For purposes of section 901 of the Internal Revenue Code of 1954, there shall be treated as income, war profits, and excess profits taxes to be taken into account under section 907(a) of such Code amounts designated as income taxes of a foreign government by such government (which otherwise would not be treated as taxes for purposes of section 901 of such Code) with respect to production-sharing contracts for the extraction of foreign oil or gas.
"(2) The amounts specified in paragraph (1) shall not exceed the lesser of—
"(A) the product of the foreign oil and gas extraction income (as defined in section 907(c) of such Code) with respect to all such production-sharing contracts multiplied by the sum of the normal tax rate and the surtax rate for the taxable year specified in section 11 of such Code, or
"(B) the excess of the total amount of foreign oil and gas extraction income (as so defined) for the taxable year multiplied by the sum of the normal tax rate and the surtax rate for the taxable year specified in section 11 of such Code over the amount of any income, war profits, and excess profits taxes paid or accrued (or deemed to have been paid) without regard to paragraph (1) during the taxable year with respect to foreign oil and gas extraction income.
"(3) The production-sharing contracts taken into account for purposes of paragraph (1) shall be those contracts which were entered into before April 8, 1976, for the sharing of foreign oil and gas production with a foreign government (or an entity owned by such government) with respect to which amounts claimed as taxes paid or accrued to such foreign government for taxable years beginning before June 30, 1976, will not be disallowed as such taxes. A contract described in the preceding sentence shall be taken into account under paragraph (1) only with respect to amounts (A) paid or accrued to the foreign government before January 1, 1978, and (B) attributable to income earned before such date."

Prior to amendment, subsec. (a) read as follows:

"(a) Reduction in amount allowed as foreign tax under section 901.
"In applying section 901, the amount of any income, war profits, and excess profits taxes paid or accrued (or deemed to have been paid) during the taxable year with respect to foreign oil and gas extraction income which would (but for this subsection) be taken into account for purposes of section 901 shall be reduced by the amount (if any) by which the amount of such taxes exceeds the product of—
"(1) the amount of the foreign oil and gas extraction income for the taxable year, multiplied by
"(2) the percentage which is—
"(A) in taxable years ending in 1975, 110 percent of,
"(B) in taxable years ending in 1976, 105 percent of, and
"(C) in taxable years ending after 1976, 2 percentage points above, the sum of the normal tax rate and the surtax rate for the taxable year specified in section 11."

—P.L. 94-455, Sec. 1035(b), amended subsec. (b), [prior to amendment by Sec. 1032(b)(1) of this Act, see above], effective for tax. yrs. end. after 12/31/74, except for the sentence at the end of subsec. (b) [deleted by Sec. 1032(b)(1) of this Act, see above], which applies only for tax. yrs. end. after 12/31/75.

Prior to amendment, subsec. (b) read as follows:

"(b) Application of section 904 limitation.
"The provisions of section 904 shall be applied separately with respect to—
"(1) foreign oil related income, and
"(2) other taxable income.

With respect to foreign oil related income, the overall limitation provided by section 901(a)(2) shall apply and the per-country limitation provided by section 904(a)(1) shall not apply."

—P.L. 94-455, Sec. 1035(d)(1), redesignated subsec. (f) as subsec. (g), [as redesignated by Sec. 1032(b)(2) of this Act, see above], and added new subsec. (f) . . . Sec. 1035(d)(2), added para. (c)(5), for taxes paid or accrued during tax. yrs. end. after 10/4/76.

—P.L. 94-455, Sec. 1052(c)(4), deleted subsec. (g), effective for tax. yrs. begin. after 12/31/79.

Prior to deletion, subsec. (g) read as follows:

"(g) Western Hemisphere trade corporations which are members of an affiliated group. If a Western Hemisphere trade corporation is a member of an affiliated group for the taxable year, then in applying section 901, the amount of any income, war profits, and excess profits taxes paid or accrued (or deemed to have been paid) during the taxable year with respect to foreign oil and gas extraction income which would (but for this section and section 1503(b)) be taken into account for purposes of section 901 shall be reduced by the greater of—
"(1) the reduction with respect to such taxes provided by subsection (a) of this section, or

2,576

"(2) the reduction determined under section 1503(b) by applying section 1503(b) separately with respect to such taxes, but not by both such reductions."

In 1975, P.L. 94-12, Sec. 601(a), added Code Sec. 907, effective as provided in Sec. 601(d) of this Act, which reads as follows:

"(d) Effective Dates. The amendments made by this section shall apply to taxable years ending after December 31, 1974; except that—

"(1) the second sentence of section 907(b) shall apply to taxable years ending after December 31, 1975, and

"(2) the provisions of section 907(f) shall apply to losses sustained in taxable years ending after December 31, 1975."

Sec. 908. Reduction of credit for participation in or cooperation with an international boycott.

(a) In general.

If a person, or a member of a controlled group (within the meaning of section 993(a)(3)) which includes such person, participates in or cooperates with an international boycott during the taxable year (within the meaning of section 999(b)), the amount of the credit allowable under section 901 to such person, or under section 902 or 960 to United States shareholders of such person, for foreign taxes paid during the taxable year shall be reduced by an amount equal to the product of—

(1) the amount of the credit which, but for this section, would be allowed under section 901 for the taxable year, multiplied by

(2) the international boycott factor (determined under section 999).

(b) Application with sections 275(a)(4) and 78.

Section 275(a)(4) and section 78 shall not apply to any amount of taxes denied credit under subsection (a).

In 1976, P.L. 94-455, Sec. 1061(a), added Code Sec. 908, effective for participation in or cooperation with an international boycott more than 30 days after 10/4/76. For participation in or cooperation with an international boycott carried out in accordance with terms of a binding contract entered into before 9/2/76, Code Sec. 908 applies after 12/31/77.

Sec. 909. Suspension of taxes and credits until related income taken into account.

(a) In general.

If there is a foreign tax credit splitting event with respect to a foreign income tax paid or accrued by the taxpayer, such tax shall not be taken into account for purposes of this title before the taxable year in which the related income is taken into account under this chapter by the taxpayer.

(b) Special rules with respect to section 902 corporations.

If there is a foreign tax credit splitting event with respect to a foreign income tax paid or accrued by a section 902 corporation, such tax shall not be taken into account—

(1) for purposes of section 902 or 960, or

(2) for purposes of determining earnings and profits under section 964(a), before the taxable year in which the related income is taken into account under this chapter by such section 902 corporation or a domestic corporation which meets the ownership requirements of subsection (a) or (b) of section 902 with respect to such section 902 corporation.

(c) Special rules.

For purposes of this section—

(1) Application to partnerships, etc. In the case of a partnership, subsections (a) and (b) shall be applied at the partner level. Except as otherwise provided by the Secretary, a rule similar to the rule of the preceding sentence shall apply in the case of any S corporation or trust.

(2) Treatment of foreign taxes after suspension. In the case of any foreign income tax not taken into account by reason of subsection (a) or (b), except as otherwise provided by the Secretary, such tax shall be so taken into account in the taxable year referred to in such subsection (other than for purposes of section 986(a)) as a foreign income tax paid or accrued in such taxable year.

(d) Definitions.

For purposes of this section—

(1) Foreign tax credit splitting event. There is a foreign tax credit splitting event with respect to a foreign income tax if the related income is (or will be) taken into account under this chapter by a covered person.

(2) Foreign income tax. The term "foreign income tax" means any income, war profits, or excess profits tax paid or accrued to any foreign country or to any possession of the United States.

(3) Related income. The term "related income" means, with respect to any portion of any foreign income tax, the income (or, as appropriate, earnings and profits) to which such portion of foreign income tax relates.

(4) Covered person. The term "covered person" means, with respect to any person who pays or accrues a foreign income tax (hereafter in this paragraph referred to as the "payor")—

(A) any entity in which the payor holds, directly or indirectly, at least a 10 percent ownership interest (determined by vote or value),

(B) any person which holds, directly or indirectly, at least a 10 percent ownership interest (determined by vote or value) in the payor,

(C) any person which bears a relationship to the payor described in section 267(b) or 707(b), and

(D) any other person specified by the Secretary for purposes of this paragraph.

(5) Section 902 corporation. The term "section 902 corporation" means any foreign corporation with respect to which one or more domestic corporations meets the ownership requirements of subsection (a) or (b) of section 902.

(e) Regulations.

The Secretary may issue such regulations or other guidance as is necessary or appropriate to carry out the purposes of this section, including regulations or other guidance which provides—

(1) appropriate exceptions from the provisions of this section, and

(2) for the proper application of this section with respect to hybrid instruments.

In 2010, P.L. 111-226, Sec. 211(b), added Code Sec. 909, effective for foreign income taxes (as defined in section 909(d) of the Internal Revenue Code of 1986, as added by this section) paid or accrued in tax. yrs. begin. after 12/31/2010. . . . Sec. 211(c)(2), of this Act reads as follows:

"(2) foreign income taxes (as so defined) paid or accrued by a section 902 corporation (as so defined) in taxable years beginning on or before such date (and not deemed paid under section 902(a) or 960 of such Code on or before such date), but only for purposes of applying sections 902 and 960 with respect to periods after such date.

"Section 909(b)(2) of the Internal Revenue Code of 1986, as added by this section, shall not apply to foreign income taxes described in paragraph (2)."

SUBPART B.—EARNED INCOME OF CITIZENS OR RESIDENTS OF UNITED STATES

Sec.

911. Citizens or residents of the United States living abroad.

912. Exemption for certain allowances.

913. Repealed.

In 1981, P.L. 97-34, Sec. 111(b)(1), amended item 911 . . . Sec. 112(b)(1), repealed item 913.

Prior to amendment, item 911 read as follows:

"911. Income earned by individuals in certain camps from charitable services."

Prior to repeal, item 913 read as follows:

"913. Deduction for certain expenses of living abroad."

In 1980, P.L. 96-595, Sec. 4(c)(2), added "or from charitable services" after "camps" in item 911.
—P.L. 96-222, Sec. 108(a)(1)(A), redesignated Sec. 202(f) of P.L. 95-600 as Sec. 202(g) [see below].
In 1978, P.L. 95-615, Sec. 202(g)(2), amended the item for Code Sec. 911. Prior to amendment the item for Code Sec. 911 read as follows:
"911. Earned income from sources without the United States."
—P.L. 95-615, Sec. 203(c), added the item for Code Sec. 913.

Sec. 911. Citizens or residents of the United States living abroad.

(a) Exclusion from gross income.

At the election of a qualified individual (made separately with respect to paragraphs (1) and (2)), there shall be excluded from the gross income of such individual, and exempt from taxation under this subtitle, for any taxable year—

(1) the foreign earned income of such individual, and

(2) the housing cost amount of such individual.

(b) Foreign earned income.

(1) **Definition.** For purposes of this section—

(A) In general. The term "foreign earned income" with respect to any individual means the amount received by such individual from sources within a foreign country or countries which constitute earned income attributable to services performed by such individual during the period described in subparagraph (A) or (B) of subsection (d)(1), whichever is applicable.

(B) Certain amounts not included in foreign earned income. The foreign earned income for an individual shall not include amounts—

(i) received as a pension or annuity,

(ii) paid by the United States or an agency thereof to an employee of the United States or an agency thereof,

(iii) included in gross income by reason of section 402(b) (relating to taxability of beneficiary of nonexempt trust) or section 403(c) (relating to taxability of beneficiary under a nonqualified annuity), or

(iv) received after the close of the taxable year following the taxable year in which the services to which the amounts are attributable are performed.

(2) **Limitation on foreign earned income.**

(A) In general. The foreign earned income of an individual which may be excluded under subsection (a)(1) for any taxable year shall not exceed the amount of foreign earned income computed on a daily basis at an annual rate equal to the exclusion amount for the calendar year in which such taxable year begins.

(B) Attribution to year in which services are performed. For purposes of applying subparagraph (A), amounts received shall be considered received in the taxable year in which the services to which the amounts are attributable are performed.

(C) Treatment of community income. In applying subparagraph (A) with respect to amounts received from services performed by a husband or wife which are community income under community property laws applicable to such income, the aggregate amount which may be excludable from the gross income of such husband and wife under subsection (a)(1) for any taxable year shall equal the amount which would be so excludable if such amounts did not constitute community income.

(D) Exclusion amount.

(i) In general. The exclusion amount for any calendar year is the exclusion amount determined in accordance with the following table (as adjusted by clause (ii)):

For calendar year—	The exclusion amount is—
1998	$72,000
1999	74,000
2000	76,000
2001	78,000
2002 and thereafter	80,000

(ii) Inflation adjustment. In the case of any taxable year beginning in a calendar year after 2005, the $80,000 amount in clause (i) shall be increased by an amount equal to the product of—

(I) such dollar amount, and

(II) the cost-of-living adjustment determined under section 1(f)(3) for the calendar year in which the taxable year begins, determined by substituting "2004" for "1992" in subparagraph (B) thereof.

If any increase determined under the preceding sentence is not a multiple of $100, such increase shall be rounded to the next lowest multiple of $100.

(c) Housing cost amount.

For purposes of this section—

(1) **In general.** The term "housing cost amount" means an amount equal to the excess of—

(A) the housing expenses of an individual for the taxable year to the extent such expenses do not exceed the amount determined under paragraph (2), over

(B) an amount equal to the product of—

(i) 16 percent of the amount (computed on a daily basis) in effect under subsection (b)(2)(D) for the calendar year in which such taxable year begins, multiplied by

(ii) the number of days of such taxable year within the applicable period described in subparagraph (A) or (B) of subsection (d)(1).

(2) **Limitation.**

(A) In general. The amount determined under this paragraph is an amount equal to the product of—

(i) 30 percent (adjusted as may be provided under subparagraph (B)) of the amount (computed on a daily basis) in effect under subsection (b)(2)(D) for the calendar year in which the taxable year of the individual begins, multiplied by

(ii) the number of days of such taxable year within the applicable period described in subparagraph (A) or (B) of subsection (d)(1).

(B) Regulations. The Secretary may issue regulations or other guidance providing for the adjustment of the percentage under subparagraph (A)(i) on the basis of geographic differences in housing costs relative to housing costs in the United States.

(3) **Housing expenses.**

(A) In general. The term "housing expenses" means the reasonable expenses paid or incurred during the taxable year by or on behalf of an individual for housing for the individual (and, if they reside with him, for his spouse and dependents) in a foreign country. The term—

(i) includes expenses attributable to the housing (such as utilities and insurance), but

(ii) does not include interest and taxes of the kind deductible under section 163 or 164 or any amount allowable as a deduction under section 216(a).

Housing expenses shall not be treated as reasonable to the extent such expenses are lavish or extravagant under the circumstances.

(B) Second foreign household.

(i) In general. Except as provided in clause (ii), only housing expenses incurred with respect to that abode which bears the closest relationship to the tax home of the individual shall be taken into account under paragraph (1).

(ii) Separate household for spouse and dependents. If an individual maintains a separate abode outside the United States for his spouse and dependents and they do not reside with him because of living conditions which are dangerous, unhealthful, or otherwise adverse, then—

(I) the words "if they reside with him" in subparagraph (A) shall be disregarded, and

(II) the housing expenses incurred with respect to such abode shall be taken into account under paragraph (1).

(4) Special rules where housing expenses not provided by employer.

(A) In general. To the extent the housing cost amount of any individual for any taxable year is not attributable to employer provided amounts, such amount shall be treated as a deduction allowable in computing adjusted gross income to the extent of the limitation of subparagraph (B).

(B) Limitation. For purposes of subparagraph (A), the limitation of this subparagraph is the excess of—

(i) the foreign earned income of the individual for the taxable year, over

(ii) the amount of such income excluded from gross income under subsection (a) for the taxable year.

(C) 1-year carryover of housing amounts not allowed by reason of subparagraph (B).

(i) In general. The amount not allowable as a deduction for any taxable year under subparagraph (A) by reason of the limitation of subparagraph (B) shall be treated as a deduction allowable in computing adjusted gross income for the succeeding taxable year (and only for the succeeding taxable year) to the extent of the limitation of clause (ii) for such succeeding taxable year.

(ii) Limitation. For purposes of clause (i), the limitation of this clause for any taxable year is the excess of—

(I) the limitation of subparagraph (B) for such taxable year, over

(II) amounts treated as a deduction under subparagraph (A) for such taxable year.

(D) Employer provided amounts. For purposes of this paragraph, the term "employer provided amounts" means any amount paid or incurred on behalf of the individual by the individual's employer which is foreign earned income included in the individual's gross income for the taxable year (without regard to this section).

(E) Foreign earned income. For purposes of this paragraph, an individual's foreign earned income for any taxable year shall be determined without regard to the limitation of subparagraph (A) of subsection (b)(2).

(d) Definitions and special rules.

For purposes of this section—

(1) Qualified individual. The term "qualified individual" means an individual whose tax home is in a foreign country and who is—

(A) a citizen of the United States and establishes to the satisfaction of the Secretary that he has been a bona fide resident of a foreign country or countries for an uninterrupted period which includes an entire taxable year, or

(B) a citizen or resident of the United States and who, during any period of 12 consecutive months, is present in a foreign country or countries during at least 330 full days in such period.

(2) Earned income.

(A) In general. The term "earned income" means wages, salaries, or professional fees, and other amounts received as compensation for personal services actually rendered, but does not include that part of the compensation derived by the taxpayer for personal services rendered by him to a corporation which represents a distribution of earnings or profits rather than a reasonable allowance as compensation for the personal services actually rendered.

(B) Taxpayer engaged in trade or business. In the case of a taxpayer engaged in a trade or business in which both personal services and capital are material income-producing factors, under regulations prescribed by the Secretary, a reasonable allowance as compensation for the personal services rendered by the taxpayer, not in excess of 30 percent of his share of the net profits of such trade or business, shall be considered as earned income.

(3) Tax home. The term "tax home" means, with respect to any individual, such individual's home for purposes of section 162(a)(2) (relating to traveling expenses while away from home). An individual shall not be treated as having a tax home in a foreign country for any period for which his abode is within the United States.

(4) Waiver of period of stay in foreign country. Notwithstanding paragraph (1), an individual who—

(A) is a bona fide resident of, or is present in, a foreign country for any period,

(B) leaves such foreign country after August 31, 1978—

(i) during any period during which the Secretary determines, after consultation with the Secretary of State or his delegate, that individuals were required to leave such foreign country because of war, civil unrest, or similar adverse conditions in such foreign country which precluded the normal conduct of business by such individuals, and

(ii) before meeting the requirements of such paragraph (1), and

(C) establishes to the satisfaction of the Secretary that such individual could reasonably have been expected to have met such requirements but for the conditions referred to in clause (i) of subparagraph (B),

shall be treated as a qualified individual with respect to the period described in subparagraph (A) during which he was a bona fide resident of, or was present in, the foreign country, and in applying subsections (b)(2)(A), (c)(1)(B)(ii), and (c)(2)(A)(ii) with respect to such individual, only the days within such period shall be taken into account.

(5) Test of bona fide residence. If—

(A) an individual who has earned income from sources within a foreign country submits a statement to the authorities of that country that he is not a resident of that country, and

(B) such individual is held not subject as a resident of that country to the income tax of that country by its authorities with respect to such earnings, then such individual shall not be considered a bona fide resident of that country for purposes of paragraph (1)(A).

(6) Denial of double benefits. No deduction or exclusion from gross income under this subtitle or credit against the tax imposed by this chapter (including any credit or deduction for the amount of taxes paid or accrued to a foreign country or possession of the United States) shall be allowed to the extent such deduction, exclusion, or credit is properly allocable to or chargeable against amounts excluded from gross income under subsection (a).

(7) Aggregate benefit cannot exceed foreign earned income. The sum of the amount excluded under subsection (a) and the amount deducted under subsection (c)(4)(A) for the taxable year shall not exceed the individual's foreign earned income for such year.

(8) Limitation on income earned in restricted country.

(A) In general. If travel (or any transaction in connection with such travel) with respect to any foreign country is subject to the regulations described in subparagraph (B) during any period—

(i) the term "foreign earned income" shall not include any income from sources within such country attributable to services performed during such period,

(ii) the term "housing expenses" shall not include any expenses allocable to such period for housing in such country or for housing of the spouse or dependents of the taxpayer in another country while the taxpayer is present in such country, and

(iii) an individual shall not be treated as a bona fide resident of, or as present in, a foreign country for any day during which such individual was present in such country during such period.

(B) Regulations. For purposes of this paragraph, regulations are described in this subparagraph if such regulations—

(i) have been adopted pursuant to the Trading With the Enemy Act (50 U.S.C. App. 1 *et seq.*), or the International Emergency Economic Powers Act (50 U.S.C. 1701 *et seq.*), and

(ii) include provisions generally prohibiting citizens and residents of the United States from engaging in transactions related to travel to, from, or within a foreign country.

(C) Exception. Subparagraph (A) shall not apply to any individual during any period in which such individual's activities are not in violation of the regulations described in subparagraph (B).

(9) Regulations. The Secretary shall prescribe such regulations as may be necessary or appropriate to carry out the purposes of this section, including regulations providing rules—

(A) for cases where a husband and wife each have earned income from sources outside the United States, and

(B) for married individuals filing separate returns.

(e) Election.

(1) In general. An election under subsection (a) shall apply to the taxable year for which made and to all subsequent taxable years unless revoked under paragraph (2).

(2) Revocation. A taxpayer may revoke an election made under paragraph (1) for any taxable year after the taxable year for which such election was made. Except with the consent of the Secretary, any taxpayer who makes such a revocation for any taxable year may not make another election under this section for any subsequent taxable year before the 6th taxable year after the taxable year for which such revocation was made.

(f) Determination of tax liability.

(1) In general. If, for any taxable year, any amount is excluded from gross income of a taxpayer under subsection (a), then, notwithstanding sections 1 and 55—

(A) if such taxpayer has taxable income for such taxable year, the tax imposed by section 1 for such taxable year shall be equal to the excess (if any) of—

(i) the tax which would be imposed by section 1 for such taxable year if the taxpayer's taxable income were increased by the amount excluded under subsection (a) for such taxable year, over

(ii) the tax which would be imposed by section 1 for such taxable year if the taxpayer's taxable income were equal to the amount excluded under subsection (a) for such taxable year, and

(B) if such taxpayer has a taxable excess (as defined in section 55(b)(1)(A)(ii)) for such taxable year, the amount determined under the first sentence of section 55(b)(1)(A)(i) for such taxable year shall be equal to the excess (if any) of—

(i) the amount which would be determined under such sentence for such taxable year (subject to the limitation of section 55(b)(3)) if the taxpayer's taxable excess (as so defined) were increased by the amount excluded under subsection (a) for such taxable year, over

(ii) the amount which would be determined under such sentence for such taxable year if the taxpayer's taxable excess (as so defined) were equal to the amount excluded under subsection (a) for such taxable year.

(2) Special rules.

(A) Regular tax. In applying section 1(h) for purposes of determining the tax under paragraph (1)(A)(i) for any taxable year in which, without regard to this subsection, the taxpayer's net capital gain exceeds taxable income (hereafter in this subparagraph referred to as the capital gain excess)—

(i) the taxpayer's net capital gain (determined without regard to section 1(h)(11)) shall be reduced (but not below zero) by such capital gain excess,

(ii) the taxpayer's qualified dividend income shall be reduced by so much of such capital gain excess as exceeds the taxpayer's net capital gain (determined without regard to section 1(h)(11) and the reduction under clause (i)), and

(iii) adjusted net capital gain, unrecaptured section 1250 gain, and 28-percent rate gain shall each be determined after increasing the amount described in section 1(h)(4)(B) by such capital gain excess.

(B) Alternative minimum tax. In applying section 55(b)(3) for purposes of determining the tax under paragraph (1)(B)(i) for any taxable year in which, without regard to this subsection, the taxpayer's net capital gain exceeds the taxable excess (as defined in section 55(b)(1)(A)(ii))—

(i) the rules of subparagraph (A) shall apply, except that such subparagraph shall be applied by substituting "the taxable excess (as defined in section 55(b)(1)(A)(ii))" for "taxable income", and

(ii) the reference in section 55(b)(3)(B) to the excess described in section 1(h)(1)(B) shall be treated as a reference to such excess as determined under the

Income from foreign sources — Code Sec. 911

rules of subparagraph (A) for purposes of determining the tax under paragraph (1)(A)(i).

(C) Definitions. Terms used in this paragraph which are also used in section 1(h) shall have the respective meanings given such terms by section 1(h), except that in applying subparagraph (B) the adjustments under part VI of subchapter A shall be taken into account.

(g) Cross references.

For administrative and penal provisions relating to the exclusions provided for in this section, see sections 6001, 6011, 6012(c), and the other provisions of subtitle F.

In 2007, P.L. 110-172, Sec. 4(c), amended subsec. (f), effective for tax. yrs. begin. after 12/31/2006.

Prior to amendment, subsec. (f) read as follows:

1. "(f) Determination of tax liability on nonexcluded amounts. For purposes of this chapter, if any amount is excluded from the gross income of a taxpayer under subsection (a) for any taxable year, then, notwithstanding section 1 or 55—

"(1) the tax imposed by section 1 on the taxpayer for such taxable year shall be equal to the excess (if any) of—

"(A) the tax which would be imposed by section 1 for the taxable year if the taxpayer's taxable income were increased by the amount excluded under subsection (a) for the taxable year, over

"(B) the tax which would be imposed by section 1 for the taxable year if the taxpayer's taxable income were equal to the amount excluded under subsection (a) for the taxable year, and

"(2) the tentative minimum tax under section 55 for such taxable year shall be equal to the excess (if any) of—

"(A) the amount which would be such tentative minimum tax for the taxable year if the taxpayer's taxable excess were increased by the amount excluded under subsection (a) for the taxable year, over

"(B) the amount which would be such tentative minimum tax for the taxable year if the taxpayer's taxable excess were equal to the amount excluded under subsection (a) for the taxable year.

For purposes of this subsection, the amount excluded under subsection (a) shall be reduced by the aggregate amount of any deductions or exclusions disallowed under subsection (d)(6) with respect to such excluded amount."

In 2006, P.L. 109-222, Sec. 515(a)(1), substituted "2005" for "2007" in clause (b)(2)(D)(ii) . . . Sec. 515(a)(2), substituted "2004" for "2006" in subclause (b)(2)(D)(ii)(II) . . . Sec. 515(b)(1), amended clause (c)(1)(B)(i) . . . Sec. 515(b)(2)(A), added "to the extent such expenses do not exceed the amount determined under paragraph (2)" after "the taxable year" in subpara. (c)(1)(A) . . . Sec. 515(b)(2)(B), redesignated paras. (c)(2) and (3) as paras. (c)(3) and (4), and added para. (c)(2) . . . Sec. 515(b)(2)(C)(i), substituted ", (c)(1)(B)(ii), and (c)(1)(A)(ii)" for "and (c)(1)(B)(ii)" in para. (d)(4) . . . Sec. 515(b)(2)(C)(ii), substituted "subsection (c)(4)" for "subsection (c)(3)" in para. (d)(7) . . . Sec. 515(c), redesignated subsec. (f) as (g) and added subsec. (f), effective for tax. yrs. begin. after 12/31/2005.

Prior to amendment, clause (c)(1)(B)(i) read as follows:

"(i) 16 percent of the salary (computed on a daily basis) of an employee of the United States who is compensated at a rate equal to the annual rate paid for step 1 of grade GS-14, multiplied by"

In 1997, P.L. 105-34, Sec. 1172(a)(1), substituted "equal to the exclusion amount for the calendar year in which such taxable year begins" for "of $70,000" in subpara. (b)(2)(A) . . . Sec. 1102(a)(2), added subpara. (b)(2)(D), effective for tax. yrs. begin. after 12/31/97.

In 1990, P.L. 101-508, Sec. 11833(a), amended Sec. 208(a) of P.L. 95-615] as amended by Sec. 114 of P.L. 97-34] by substituting "(a) General rule. As soon as practicable after December 31, 1993, and as soon as practicable after the close of each fifth calendar year thereafter," for "(a) General rule. As soon as practicable after the date of the enactment of the Economic Recovery Tax Act of 1981, and as soon as practicable after the close of the fourth calendar year thereafter," . . . Sec. 11833(b), amended Sec. 208(b) of P.L. 95-615 [as amended by Sec. 114 of P.L. 97-34] by substituting "shall keep such records and furnish" for "shall furnish."

In 1986, P.L. 99-514, Sec. 1232(a), provides:

"Sec. 1232. Treatment of certain persons in Panama.

"(a) General rule. —

"Nothing in the Panama Canal Treaty (or in any agreement implementing such Treaty) shall be construed as exempting (in whole or in part) any citizen or resident of the United States from any tax under the Internal Revenue Code of 1954 or 1986. The preceding sentence shall apply to all taxable years whether beginning before, on, or after the date of the enactment of this Act (or in the case of any tax not imposed with respect to a taxable year, to taxable events after the date of enactment of this Act.)"

— P.L. 99-514, Sec. 1233(a), amended subpara. (b)(2)(A) . . . Sec. 1233(b), redesignated para. (d)(8) as (d)(9), and added new para. (d)(8), effective for tax. yrs. begin. after 12/31/86.

Prior to amendment, subpara. (b)(2)(A) read as follows:

"(A) In general. The foreign earned income of an individual which may be excluded under subsection (a)(1) for any taxable year shall not exceed the amount of foreign earned income computed on a daily basis at the annual rate set forth in the following table for each day of the taxable year within the applicable period described in subparagraph (A) or (B) of subsection (d)(1):

"In the case of taxable years beginning in:	The annual rate is:
1983, 1984, 1985, 1986, or 1987	$80,000
1988	85,000
1989	90,000
1990 and thereafter	95,000."

In 1984, P.L. 98-369, Sec. 17, amended the table contained in subpara. (b)(2)(A), effective for tax. yrs. end. after 12/31/83.

Prior to amendment, the table in subpara. (b)(2)(A) read as follows:

"In the case of taxable years beginning in:	The annual rate is:
1982	$ 75,000
1983	80,000
1984	85,000
1985	90,000
1986 and thereafter	95,000."

In 1983, P.L. 97-448, Sec. 101(c)(1), redesignated para. (d)(7) as para. (d)(8) and added new para. (d)(7) . . . Sec. 101(c)(2), substituted "subsection (a)" for "subsection (a)(1)" in clause (c)(3)(B)(ii), effective for tax. yrs. begin. after 12/31/81.

In 1981, P.L. 97-34, Sec. 111(a), amended Code Sec. 911, effective for tax. yrs. begin. after 12/31/81.

Prior to amendment, Code Sec. 911 read as follows:

"Sec. 911. Income earned by individuals in certain camps or from charitable services.

"(a) General rule.

"In the case of an individual described in section 913(a) who, because of his employment, resides in a camp located in a hardship area, or who performs qualified charitable services in a lesser developed country, the following items shall not be included in gross income and shall be exempt from taxation under this subtitle:

"(1) Bona fide resident of foreign country. If such individual is described in section 913(a)(1), amounts received from sources within a foreign country or countries (except amounts paid by the United States or any agency thereof) which constitute earned income attributable to services performed during the period of bona fide residence. The amount excluded under this paragraph for any taxable year shall be computed by applying the special rules contained in subsection (c).

"(2) Presence in foreign country for 17 months. If such individual is described in section 913(a)(2), amounts received from sources within a foreign country or countries (except amounts paid by the United States or any agency thereof) which constitute earned income attributable to services performed during the 18-month period. The amount excluded under this paragraph for any taxable year shall be computed by applying the special rules contained in subsection (c).

An individual shall not be allowed as a deduction from his gross income any deduction or as a credit against the tax imposed by this chapter any credit for the amount of taxes paid or accrued to a foreign country or possession of the United States, to the extent that such deduction or credit is properly allocable to or chargeable against amounts excluded from gross income under this subsection, other than the deduction allowed by section 217 (relating to moving expenses).

"(b) Definition of earned income.

"For purposes of this section, the term 'earned income' means wages, salaries, or professional fees, and other amounts received as compensation for personal services actually rendered, but does not include that part of the compensation derived by the taxpayer for personal services rendered by him to a corporation which represents a distribution of earnings or profits rather than a reasonable allowance as compensation for the personal services actually rendered. In the case of a taxpayer engaged in a trade or business in which both personal services and capital are material income-producing factors, under regulations prescribed by the Secretary, a reasonable allowance as compensation for the personal services rendered by the taxpayer, not in excess of 30 percent of his share of the net profits of such trade or business, shall be considered as earned income.

"(c) Special rules.

"For purposes of computing the amount excludable under subsection (a), the following rules shall apply:

"(1) Limitations on amount of exclusion.

"(A) Dollar limitations —

"(i) Camp residents. In the case of an individual who resides in a camp located in a hardship area, the amount excluded from the gross income of the individual under subsection (a) for the taxable year shall not exceed an amount which shall be computed on a daily basis at an annual rate of $20,000 for days during which he resides in a camp.

"(ii) Employees of charitable organizations. If any individual performs qualified charitable services in a lesser developed country during any taxable year, the amount of the earned income attributable to such services excluded from the gross income of the individual under subsection (a) for the taxable year shall not exceed an amount which shall be computed on a daily basis at an annual rate of $20,000.

"(iii) Special rule. If any individual performs qualified charitable services in a lesser developed country and performs other services while residing in a camp located in a hardship area during any taxable year, the amount of the earned income attributable to such other services excluded from the gross income of the individual under subsection (a) for the taxable year shall not (after the application of clause (i) with respect to such earned income) exceed $20,000 reduced by the amount of the earned income attributable to qualified charitable services excluded from gross income under subsection (a) for the taxable year.

"(B) Camp. For purposes of this section, an individual shall not be considered to reside in a camp because of his employment unless the camp constitutes substandard lodging which is—

"(i) provided by or on behalf of the employer for the convenience of the employer because the place at which such individual renders services is in a remote area where satisfactory housing is not available on the open market;

"(ii) located, as near as practicable, in the vicinity of the place at which such individual renders services, and

"(iii) furnished in a common area (or enclave) which is not available to the public and which normally accommodates 10 or more employees.

"(C) Hardship area. For purposes of this section, the term 'hardship area' has the same meaning as in section 913(h).

"(D) Qualified charitable services. For purposes of this subsection, the term 'qualified charitable services' means services performed by an employee for an employer which—

"(i) meets the requirements of section 501(c)(3), and

"(ii) is not a private foundation (within the meaning of section 509(a)).

"(E) Lesser developed country. The term 'lesser developed country' means any foreign country other than—

"(i) a country listed in the first sentence of section 502(b) of the Trade Act of 1974 (19 U.S.C. 2462), or

"(ii) a country designated by the President as not being a lesser developed country.

"(2) Attribution to year in which services are performed. For purposes of applying paragraph (1), amounts received shall be considered received in the taxable year in which the services to which the amounts are attributable are performed.

"(3) Treatment of community income. In applying paragraph (1) with respect to amounts received for services performed by a husband or wife which are community income under community property laws applicable to such income, the aggregate amount excludable under subsection (a) from the gross income of such husband and wife shall equal the amount which would be excludable if such amounts did not constitute such community income.

"(4) Requirement as to time of receipt. No amount received after the close of the taxable year following the taxable year in which the services to which the amounts are attributable are performed may be excluded under subsection (a).

"(5) Certain amounts not excludable. No amount—

"(A) received as a pension or annuity, or

"(B) included in gross income by reason of section 402(b) (relating to taxability of beneficiary of non-exempt trust), section 403(c) (relating to taxability of beneficiary under a non-qualified annuity), or section 403(d) (relating to taxability of beneficiary under certain forfeitable contracts purchased by exempt organizations), may be excluded under subsection (a).

"(6) Test of bona fide residence. A statement by an individual who has earned income from sources within a foreign country to the authorities of that country that he is not a resident of that country, if he is held not subject as a resident of that country to the income tax of that country by its authorities with respect to such earnings, shall be conclusive evidence with respect to such earnings that he is not a bona fide resident of that country for purposes of subsection (a)(1).

"(7) Business premises of the employer. In the case of an individual residing in a camp who elects the exclusion provided in this section for a taxable year, the camp shall be considered to be part of the business premises of the employer for purposes of section 119 for such taxable year.

"(d) Section not to apply.

"An individual entitled to the benefits of this section for a taxable year may elect, in such manner and at such time as shall be prescribed by the Secretary, not to have the provisions of this section apply for the taxable year.

"(e) Cross reference.

"(1) For administrative and penal provisions relating to the exclusion provided for in this section, see sections 6001, 6011, 6012(c), and the other provisions of subtitle F.

"(2) For elections as to treatment of income subject to foreign community property laws, see section 981."

—P.L. 97-34, Sec. 114, amended Sec. 208 of P.L. 95-615 [reproduced below]. Prior to amendment, Sec. 208 of P.L. 95-615 read as follows:

"SEC. 208. REPORTS BY SECRETARY.

"(a) General rule.

"As soon as practicable after the close of the calendar year 1979 and after the close of each second calendar year thereafter, the Secretary of the Treasury shall transmit a report to the Committee on Ways and Means of the House of Representatives and to the Committee on Finance of the Senate setting forth with respect to the preceding 2 calendar years—

"(1) the number, country of residence, and other pertinent characteristics of persons claiming the benefits of sections 911, 912, and 913 of the Internal Revenue Code of 1954,

"(2) the revenue cost and economic effects of the provisions of such sections 911, 912, and 913, and

"(3) a detailed description of the manner in which the provisions of such sections 911, 912, and 913 have been administered during the preceding 2 calendar years.

"(b) Information from federal agencies.

"Each agency of the Federal Government which pays allowances excludable from gross income under section 912 of such Code shall furnish to the Secretary of the Treasury such information as he determines to be necessary to carry out his responsibility under subsection (a)."

In 1980, P.L. 96-608, Sec. 1(b)(2), provides:

"(2) Application for purposes of section 911. In the case of an individual who leaves the foreign country after August 31, 1978, rules similar to the rules of section 913(j)(4) of the Internal Revenue Code of 1954 (as added by subsection (a)) shall apply for purposes of applying section 911 of such Code for taxable years beginning in 1977 or 1978."

—P.L. 96-595, Sec. 4(a), added "or who performs qualified charitable services in a lesser developed country," after "hardship area" in subsec. (a) . . . Sec. 4(b)(1), amended subpara. (c)(1)(A) . . . Sec. 4(b)(2), added subparas. (c)(1)(D) and (c)(1)(E), effective for tax. yrs. begin. after 12/31/78.

Prior to amendment, subpara. (c)(1)(A) read as follows:

"(A) In general. The amount excluded from the gross income of an individual under subsection (a) for any taxable year shall not exceed an amount which shall be computed on a daily basis at an annual rate of $20,000 for days during which he resides in a camp."

—P.L. 96-222, Sec. 107(a)(1)(B), amended Sec. 701(u)(10)(B) of P.L. 95-600 [the effective date for amendments made by Sec. 701(u)(10)(a) of P.L. 95-600, see below] . . . P.L. 96-222, Sec. 107(a)(3)(B), repealed Sec. 703(e) of P.L. 95-600 [see below]. Prior to amendment, Sec. 701(u)(10)(B) of P.L. 95-600 read as follows:

"(B) Effective date. The amendment made by subparagraph (A) shall apply to taxable years beginning after December 31, 1976."

Prior to repeal, Sec. 703(e) of P.L. 95-600 read as follows:

"(e) Amendment of section 911. Subsection (c) of section 911 is amended by redesignating paragraph (8) as paragraph (7)."

—P.L. 96-222, Sec. 108(a)(1)(C), substituted "a foreign country or" for "qualified foreign" in para. (a)(2) . . . Sec. 108(a)(1)(D), added "any deduction" after "his gross income" and substituted "deduction allowed by section 217" for "deductions allowed by sections 217" in the sentence at the end of subsec. (a), effective for tax. yrs. begin after 12/31/77.

In 1978, P.L. 95-615, Sec. 4(a), submitted "December 31, 1977" for "December 31, 1976" in Sec. 1011(b) of P.L. 94-455 [the effective date for amendments made by Sec. 1011 of P.L. 94-455, see below, as amended by Sec. 302 of P.L. 95-30, see below]. Sec. 4(b) of this Act provides transitional rules as follows:

"(b) Transitional rule. If for any taxable year beginning in 1977—

"(1) an individual is entitled to the benefits of section 911 of the Internal Revenue Code of 1954, and

"(2) such individual chooses to take to any extent the benefits of section 901 of such Code,

then such individual shall be treated for such taxable year as an individual for whom an unused zero bracket amount computation is provided by section 63(e) of such Code."

—P.L. 95-615, Sec. 202(a), amended subsec. (a) . . . Sec. 202(b), amended para. (c)(1) . . . Sec. 202(c), added para. (c)(7) . . . Sec. 202(d)(1), amended subsec. (d) and repealed subsec. (e) . . . Sec. 202(d)(2), redesignated subsec. (f) as subsec. (d) . . . Sec. 202(e), repealed para. (c)(8) . . . Sec. 202(f)(1), amended the heading of Code Sec. 911, effective for tax. yrs. begin. after 12/31/77. Sec. 209(c) of this Act provides as follows:

"(c) Election of prior law. —

"(1) A taxpayer may elect not to have the amendments made by this title apply with respect to any taxable year beginning after December 31, 1977, and before January 1, 1979.

"(2) An election under this subsection shall be filed with a taxpayer's timely filed return for the first taxable year beginning after December 31, 1977."

—P.L. 95-615, Sec. 208, [as amended by Sec. 114 of P.L. 97-34 and Sec. 11833 of P.L. 101-508, see above] provides as follows:

"SEC. 208. REPORTS BY SECRETARY.

"(a) General rule.

"As soon as practicable after December 31, 1993, and as soon as practicable after the close of each fifth calendar year thereafter, the Secretary of the Treasury shall transmit a report to the Committee on Ways and Means of the House of Representatives and to the Committee on Finance of the Senate on the operation and effects of sections 911 and 912 of the Internal Revenue Code of 1954.

"(b) Information from federal agencies.

"Each agency of the Federal Government which pays allowances excludable from gross income under section 912 of such Code shall keep such record and furnish to the Secretary of the Treasury such information as he determines to be necessary to carry out his responsibility under subsection (a)."

Prior to amendment, subsec. (a) read as follows:

"(a) General rule.

The following items shall not be included in gross income and shall be exempt from taxation under this subtitle:

"(1) Bona fide resident of foreign country. In the case of an individual citizen of the United States who establishes to the satisfaction of the Secretary that he has been a bona fide resident of a foreign country or countries for an uninterrupted period which includes an entire taxable year, amounts received from sources without the United States (except amounts paid by the United States or any agency thereof) which constitute earned income attributable to services performed during such uninterrupted period. The amount excluded under this paragraph for any taxable year shall be computed by applying the special rules contained in subsection (c).

"(2) Presence in foreign country for 17 months. In the case of an individual citizen of the United States who during any period of 18 consecutive months is present in a foreign country or countries during at least 510 full days in such period, amounts received from sources without the United States (except amounts paid by the United States or any agency thereof) which constitute earned income attributable to services performed during such 18-month period. The amount excluded under this paragraph for any taxable year shall be computed by applying the special rules contained in subsection (c).

An individual shall not be allowed as a deduction from his gross income any deductions (other than those allowed by section 151, relating to personal exemptions), to the extent that such deductions are properly allocable to or chargeable against amounts excluded from gross income under this subsection. For purposes of this title, the amount of the income, war profits, and excess profits taxes paid or accrued by any individual to a foreign country or possession of the United States for any taxable year shall be reduced by an amount determined by multiplying the amount of such taxes by a fraction—

"(A) the numerator of which is the tax determined under subsection (d)(1)(B), and

"(B) the denominator of which is the sum of the amount referred to in subparagraph (A), plus the limitation imposed for the taxable year by section 904(a)."

Prior to amendment, para. (c)(1) read as follows:

"(1) Limitations on amount of exclusion.

"(A) In general. Except as provided in subparagraphs (B) and (C), the amount excluded from the gross income of an individual under subsection (a) for any taxable year shall not exceed an amount which shall be computed on a daily basis at an annual rate of $15,000.

"(B) Employees of charitable organizations. If any individual performs qualified charitable services during any taxable year, the amount of the earned income attributable to such services excluded from the gross income of the individual under subsection (a) for the taxable year shall not exceed an amount which shall be computed on a daily basis at an annual rate of $20,000.

"(C) Special rule. If any individual performs qualified charitable services and other services during any taxable year, the amount of the earned income attributable to such other services excluded from the gross income of the individual under subsection (a) for the taxable year shall not (after the application of subparagraph (A) with respect to such earned income) exceed $15,000 reduced by the amount of the earned income attributable to qualified charitable services excluded from gross income under subsection (a) for the taxable year.

"(D) Qualified charitable services. For purposes of this subsection, the term 'qualified charitable services' means services performed by an employee for an employer created or organized in the United States, or under the law of the United States, any State, or the District of Columbia, which meets the requirements of section 501(c)(3)."

Prior to amendment, subsec. (d) read as follows:

"(d) Amount excluded under subsection (a) included in computation of tax.

"(1) Computation of tax. If for any taxable year an individual has earned income which is excluded from gross income under subsection (a), the tax imposed by section 1 shall be the excess of—

"(A) the tax imposed by section 1 (whichever is applicable) on the amount of net taxable income, over

"(B) the tax imposed by section 1 on the sum of—

"(i) the amount of net excluded earned income, and

"(ii) the zero bracket amount.

"(2) Definitions. For purposes of this subsection—

"(A) the term 'net taxable income' means an amount equal to the sum of the amount of taxable income for the taxable year plus the amount of net excluded earned income of such individual for such taxable year; and

"(B) the term 'net excluded earned income' means the excess of the amount of earned income excluded under subsection (a) for the taxable year over the amount of the deductions disallowed with respect to such excluded earned income for such taxable year under subsection (a)."

Prior to repeal, subsec. (e) read as follows:

"(e) Section not to apply.

"(1) In general. An individual entitled to the benefits of this section for a taxable year may elect, in such manner and at such time as shall be prescribed by the Secretary, not to have the provisions of this section apply.

"(2) Effect of election. An election under paragraph (1) shall apply to the taxable year for which made and to all subsequent taxable years. Such election may not be revoked except with the consent of the Secretary."

Prior to repeal, para. (c)(8) read as follows:

"(8) Business premises of the employer. In the case of an individual residing in a camp who elects the exclusion provided in this section for a taxable year, the camp shall be considered to be part of the business premises of the employer for purposes of section 119 for such taxable year."

—P.L. 95-600, Sec. 401(b)(4)(A), substituted "section 1" for "section 1 or section 1201" each place it appeared in para. (d)(1) . . . Sec. 401(b)(4)(B), deleted "(whichever is applicable)" each place it appears in para. (d)(1), effective for tax. yrs. begin. after 12/31/78.

—P.L. 95-600, Sec. 701(u)(10)(A), amended the sentence at the end of subsec. (a), effective [as amended by Sec. 107(a)(1)(B) of P.L. 96-222, see above] for tax. yrs. begin. in calendar year 1978, but only in the case of taxpayers who make an election under Sec. 209(c) of P.L. 95-615.

Prior to amendment, the sentence at the end of subsec. (a) read as follows:

"An individual shall not be allowed as a deduction from his gross income any deductions (other than those allowed by section 151, relating to personal exemptions), or as a credit against the tax imposed by this chapter any credit for the amount of taxes paid or accrued to a foreign country or possession of the United States, to the extent that such deductions or credit is properly allocable to or chargeable against amounts excluded from gross income under this subsection."

—P.L. 95-600, Sec. 703(e), redesignated para. (c)(8) as para. (c)(7), effective 10/4/76, [Sec. 703(e) was repealed by Sec. 107(a)(3)(B) of P.L. 96-222, see above].

In 1977, P.L. 95-30, Sec. 102(b)(12), amended subpara. (d)(1)(B), effective for tax. yrs. begin. after 12/31/76.

Prior to amendment, subpara. (d)(1)(B) read as follows:

"(B) the tax imposed by section 1 or section 1201 (whichever is applicable) on the amount of net excluded earned income."

—P.L. 95-30, Sec. 302, substituted "December 31, 1976" for "December 31, 1975" in Sec. 1011(d) of P.L. 94-455 [the effective date for amendments made by Sec. 1011 of P.L. 94-455, see below].

In 1976, P.L. 94-455, Sec. 1011(a), amended para. (c)(1) . . . Sec. 1011(b)(1), amended the sentence at the end of subsec. (a) . . . Sec. 1011(b)(2), added para. (c)(8) . . . Sec. 1011(b)(3), redesignated subsec. (d) as subsec. (f), added new subsec. (d) and added subsec. (e), effective [as amended by Sec. 302 of P.L. 95-30, and Sec. 4(a) of P.L. 95-615 see above] for tax. yrs. begin. after 12/31/77.

Prior to amendment, para. (c)(1) read as follows:

"(1) Limitations on amount of exclusion. The amount excluded from the gross income of an individual under subsection (a) for any taxable year shall not exceed an amount which shall be computed on a daily basis at an annual rate of—

"(A) except as provided in subparagraph (B), $20,000 in the case of an individual who qualifies under subsection (a), or

(B) $25,000 in the case of an individual who qualifies under subsection (a)(1), but only with respect to that portion of such taxable year occurring after such individual has been a bona fide resident of a foreign country or countries for an uninterrupted period of 3 consecutive years."

Prior to amendment, the sentence at the end of subsec. (a) read as follows:

"An individual shall not be allowed, as a deduction from his gross income, any deductions (other than those allowed by section 151, relating to personal exemptions) properly allocable to or chargeable against amounts excluded from gross income under this subsection."

—P.L. 94-455, Sec. 1901(a)(115), deleted para. (c)(7) . . . Sec. 1906(b)(13)(A), substituted "Secretary" for "Secretary or his delegate" each place it appeared in Code Sec. 911, effective for tax. yrs. begin. after 12/31/76.

Prior to amendment, para. (c)(7) read as follows:

"(7) Certain noncash remuneration. If an individual who qualifies under subsection (a)(1) receives compensation from sources without the United States (except from the United States or any agency thereof) in the form of the right to use property or facilities, the limitation under paragraph (1) applicable with respect to such individual—

"(A) for a taxable year ending in 1963, shall be increased by an amount equal to the amount of such compensation so received during such taxable year;

"(B) for a taxable year ending in 1964, shall be increased by an amount equal to two-thirds of such compensation so received during such taxable year; and

"(C) for a taxable year ending in 1965, shall be increased by an amount equal to one-third of such compensation so received during such taxable year."

In 1964, P.L. 88-272, Sec. 237(a), substituted "$25,000" for "$35,000" in subpara. (c)(1)(B), effective for tax. yrs. begin. after 12/31/64.

In 1962, P.L. 87-834, Sec. 11(a), amended Code Sec. 911, effective as provided in Sec. 11(c)(1) of this Act, which reads as follows:

"(1) Amendment to section 911. The amendment made by subsection (a) shall apply to taxable years ending after September 4, 1962, but only with respect to amounts—

"(A) received after March 12, 1962, which are attributable to services performed after December 31, 1962, or

"(B) received after December 31, 1962, which are attributable to services performed on or before December 31, 1962, unless on March 12, 1962, there existed a right (whether forfeitable or nonforfeitable) to receive such amounts."

Prior to amendment, Code Sec. 911 read as follows:

"(a) General rule.

"The following items shall not be included in gross income and shall be exempt from taxation under this subtitle:

"(1) Bona fide resident of foreign country. In the case of an individual citizen of the United States, who establishes to the satisfaction of the Secretary or his delegate that he has been a bona fide resident of a foreign country or countries for an uninterrupted period which includes an entire taxable year, amounts received from sources without the United States (except amounts paid by the United States or any agency thereof) if such amounts constitute earned income (as defined in subsection (b)) attributable to such period; but such individual shall not be allowed as a deduction from his gross income any deductions (other than those allowed by section 151, relating to personal exemptions) properly allocable to or chargeable against amounts excluded from gross income under this paragraph.

"(2) Presence in foreign country for 17 months. In the case of an individual citizen of the United States, who during any period of 18 consecutive months is present in a foreign country or countries during at least 510 full days in such period, amounts received from sources without the United States (except amounts paid by the United States or an agency thereof) if such amounts constitute earned income (as defined in subsection (b)) attributable to such period; but such individual shall not be allowed as a deduction from his gross income any deductions (other than those allowed by section 151, relating to personal exemptions) properly allocable to or chargeable against amounts excluded from gross income under this paragraph. If the 18-month period includes the entire taxable year, the amount excluded under this paragraph for such taxable year shall not exceed $20,000. If the 18-month period does not include the entire taxable year, the amount excluded under this paragraph for such taxable year shall not exceed an amount which bears the same ratio to $20,000 as the number of days in the part of the taxable year within the 18-month period bears to the total number of days in such year.

"(b) Definition of earned income. For purposes of this section, the term 'earned income' means wages, salaries, or professional fees, and other amounts received as compensation for personal services actually rendered, but does not include that part of the compensation derived by the taxpayer for personal services rendered by him to a corporation which represents a distribution of earnings or profits rather than a reasonable allowance as compensation for the personal services actually rendered. In the case of a taxpayer engaged in a trade or business in which both personal services and capital are material income-producing factors, under regulations prescribed by the Secretary or his delegate, a reasonable allowance as compensation for the personal services rendered by the taxpayer, not in excess of 30 percent of his share of the net profits of such trade or business, shall be considered as earned income.

"(c) Cross references. For administrative and penal provisions relating to the exclusion provided for in this section, see sections 6001, 6011, 6012(c), and the other provisions of subtitle F."

In **1958**, P.L. 85-866, Sec. 72(b), added subsec. (c), effective for tax. yrs. begin. after 12/31/57.

Sec. 912. Exemption for certain allowances.

The following items shall not be included in gross income, and shall be exempt from taxation under this subtitle:

(1) Foreign areas allowances. In the case of civilian officers and employees of the Government of the United States, amounts received as allowances or otherwise (but not amounts received as post differentials) under—

(A) chapter 9 of title I of the Foreign Service Act of 1980,

(B) section 4 of the Central Intelligence Agency Act of 1949, as amended (50 U.S.C., sec. 403e),

(C) title II of the Overseas Differentials and Allowances Act, or

(D) subsection (e) or (f) of the first section of the Administrative Expenses Act of 1946, as amended, or section 22 of such Act.

(2) Cost-of-living allowances. In the case of civilian officers or employees of the Government of the United States stationed outside the continental United States (other than Alaska), amounts (other than amounts received under title II of the Overseas Differentials and Allowances Act) received as cost-of-living allowances in accordance with regulations approved by the President (or in the case of judicial officers or employees of the United States, in accordance with rules similar to such regulations).

(3) Peace Corps allowances. In the case of an individual who is a volunteer or volunteer leader within the meaning of the Peace Corps Act and members of his family, amounts received as allowances under section 5 or 6 of the Peace Corps Act other than amounts received as—

(A) termination payments under section 5(c) or section 6(1) of such Act,

(B) leave allowances,

(C) if such individual is a volunteer leader training in the United States, allowances to members of his family, and

(D) such portion of living allowances as the President may determine under the Peace Corps Act as constituting basic compensation.

In **1988**, P.L. 100-647, Sec. 6137(a), added "(or in the case of judicial officers or employees of the United States, in accordance with rules similar to such regulations)" after "President" in para. (2), effective for allowances received after 10/12/87, in tax. yrs. ending after such date.

In **1986**, P.L. 99-514, Sec. 1232(b), provides:

"SEC. 1232. TREATMENT OF CERTAIN PERSONS IN PANAMA.

"(b) Treatment of Employees of Panama Canal Commission and Department of Defense for Purposes of Section 912.

"Employees of the Panama Canal Commission and civilian employees of the Defense Department of the United States stationed in Panama may exclude from gross income allowances which are comparable to the allowances excludable under section 912(1) of the Internal Revenue Code of 1986 by employees of the State Department of the United States stationed in Panama. The preceding sentence shall apply to taxable years beginning after December 31, 1986."

In **1980**, P.L. 96-465, Sec. 2206(e)(3), amended para. (1)(A), effective 2/15/81. Prior to amendment, para. (1)(A) read as follows:

"(A) title IX of the Foreign Service Act of 1946, as amended (22 U.S.C., sec. 1131 and following),"

In **1978**, P.L. 95-615, Sec. 208, provides for reports by Secretary [reproduced in note following Code Sec. 911.]

In **1961**, P.L. 87-293, Sec. 201(a), added para. (3) effective for tax. yrs. end. after 3/1/61.

In **1960**, P.L. 86-707, Sec. 523(a), amended paras. (1) and (2), effective for amounts received on or after 9/6/60, in tax. yrs. end. after 9/6/60.

Prior to amendment, paras. (1) and (2) read as follows:

"(1) Cost-of-living allowances.— In the case of civilian officers or employees of the Government of the United States stationed outside continental United States, amounts received as cost-of-living allowances in accordance with regulations approved by the President.

"(2) Foreign service allowances.— In the case of an officer or employee of the Foreign Service of the United States, amounts received by such officer or employee as allowances or otherwise under the terms of title IX of the Foreign Service Act of 1946 (22 U. S. C. 1131– 1158)."

Sec. 913. Repealed.

In **1981**, P.L. 97-34, Sec. 112(a), repealed Code Sec. 913 for tax yrs. begin. after 12/31/81.

Prior to repeal, Code Sec. 913 read as follows:

"SEC. 913. DEDUCTION FOR CERTAIN EXPENSES OF LIVING ABROAD.

"(a) Allowance of deduction.

"In the case of an individual who is —

"(1) Bona fide resident of foreign country. A citizen of the United States and who establishes to the satisfaction of the Secretary that he has been a bona fide resident of a foreign country or countries for an uninterrupted period which includes an entire taxable year, or

"(2) Presence in foreign country for 17 months. A citizen or resident of the United States and who during any period of 18 consecutive months is present in a foreign country or countries during at least 510 full days in such period,

there shall be allowed as a deduction for such taxable year or for any taxable year which contains part of such period, the sum of the amounts set forth in subsection (b).

"(b) Amounts.

"The amounts referred to in this subsection are:

"(1) The qualified cost-of-living differential.

"(2) The qualified housing expenses.

"(3) The qualified schooling expenses.

"(4) The qualified home leave travel expenses.

"(5) The qualified hardship area deduction.

"(c) Deduction not to exceed net foreign source earned income.

"(1) In general. The deduction allowed by subsection (a) to any individual for the taxable year shall not exceed—

"(A) such individual's earned income from sources outside the United States for the portion of the taxable year in which such individual's tax home is in a foreign country, reduced by

"(B) the sum of—

"(i) any earned income referred to in subparagraph (A) which is excluded from gross income under section 119, and

"(ii) the allocable deductions.

"(2) Allocable deductions defined. For purposes of paragraph (1)(B)(ii), the term 'allocable deductions' means the deductions properly allocable to or chargeable against the earned income referred to in paragraph (1)(A), other than the deduction allowed by this section.

"(d) Qualified cost-of-living differential.

"(1) In general. For purposes of this section, the term 'qualified cost-of-living differential' means a reasonable amount determined under tables (or under another method) prescribed by the Secretary establishing the amount (if any) by which the general cost of living in the foreign place in which the individual's tax home is located exceeds the general cost of living for the metropolitan area in the continental United States (excluding Alaska) having the highest general cost of living. The tables (or other methods) so prescribed shall be revised at least once during each calendar year.

"(2) Special rules. For purposes of paragraph (1)—

"(A) Computation on daily basis. The differential shall be computed on a daily basis for the period during which the individual's tax home is in a foreign country.

"(B) Differential to be based on daily living expenses. An individual's cost-of-living differential shall be determined by reference to reasonable daily living expenses (excluding housing and schooling expenses).

"(C) Basis of comparison. The differential prescribed for any foreign place —

"(i) shall vary depending on the composition of the family (spouse and dependents) residing with the individual (or at a qualified second household), and

"(ii) shall reflect the costs of living of a family whose income is equal to the salary of an employee of the United States who is compensated at a rate equal to the annual rate paid for step 1 of grade GS-14.

"(D) State department's index may be taken into account. The Secretary, in determining the qualified cost-of-living differential for any foreign place, may take into account the Department of State's Local Index of Living Costs Abroad as it relates to such place.

"(E) No differential for periods during which individual is eligible under section 119. Except as provided in subsection (i)(1)(A)(ii) an individual shall not be entitled to any qualified cost-of-living differential for any period for which such individual's meals and lodging are excluded from gross income under section 119.

"(e) Qualified housing expenses.

"(1) In general. For purposes of this section, the term 'qualified housing expenses' means the excess of—

"(A) the individual's housing expenses, over

"(B) the individual's base housing amount.

"(2) Housing expenses.

"(A) In general. For purposes of paragraph (1), the term 'housing expenses' means the reasonable expenses paid or incurred during the taxable year by or on behalf of the individual for housing for the individual (and, if they reside with him, for his spouse and dependents) in a foreign country. Such term—

"(i) except as provided in clause (ii), includes expenses attributable to the housing (such as utilities and insurance), and

"(ii) does not include interest and taxes of the kind deductible under section 163 or 164 or any amount allowable as a deduction under section 216(a).

"(B) Portion which is lavish or extravagant not allowed. For purposes of subparagraph (A), housing expenses shall not be treated as reasonable to the extent such expenses are lavish or extravagant under the circumstances.

"(3) Base housing amount. For purposes of paragraph (1)—

"(A) In general. The term 'base housing amount' means 20 percent of the excess of—

"(i) the individual's housing income (reduced by the deductions properly allocable to or chargeable against such housing income (other than the deduction allowed by this section)), over

"(ii) the sum of—

"(I) the housing expenses taken into account under paragraphs (1)(A) of this subsection,

"(II) the qualified cost-of-living differential,

"(III) the qualified school expenses,

"(IV) the qualified home leave travel expenses, and

"(V) the qualified hardship area deduction.

"(B) Base housing amount to be zero in certain cases. If, because of adverse living conditions, the individual maintains a household for his spouse and dependents at a foreign place other than his tax home which is in addition to the household he maintains as his tax home, and if his tax home is in a hardship area as defined in subsection (h), the base housing amount for the household maintained at his tax home shall be zero.

"(4) Periods taken into account.

"(A) In general. The expenses taken into account under this subsection shall be only those which are attributable to housing during periods for which—

"(i) the individual's tax home is in a foreign country, and

"(ii) except as provided in subsection (i)(1)(B)(iii), the value of the individual's housing is not excluded under section 119.

"(B) Determination of base housing amount. The base housing amount shall be determined for the periods referred to in subparagraph (A) (as modified by subsection (i)(1)(B)(iii)).

"(5) Only one house per period. If, but for this paragraph, housing expenses for any individual would be taken into account under paragraph (2) of subsection (b) with respect to more than one abode for any period, only housing expenses with respect to that abode which bears the closest relationship to the individual's tax home shall be taken into account under such paragraph (2) for such period.

"(6) Housing income. For purposes of this subsection, the term 'housing income' has the meaning given to the term 'earned income' by section 911(b) (determined with the rule set forth in paragraph (3) of section 911(c)).

"(7) Recapture of excess housing deductions attributable to treatment of after-received compensation.

"(A) In general. There shall be included in the gross income of the individual for the taxable year in which any after-received compensation is received an amount equal to any excess housing deduction determined for such year.

"(B) Excess housing deduction. For purposes of subparagraph (A), the excess housing deduction determined for any taxable year is the excess (if any) of

"(i) the aggregate amount which has been allowed as a housing deduction (for such taxable year and all prior taxable years), over

"(ii) the aggregate amount which would have been allowable as a housing deduction (for such taxable year and all prior taxable years for which a housing deduction has been allowed), by taking after-received compensation into account under this subsection as if it had been received in the taxable year in which the services were performed.

"In applying the preceding sentence to any taxable year, proper adjustment shall be made for the effect of applying such sentence for purposes of all prior taxable years.

"(C) Treatment of amount included in income. Any amount included in gross income under subparagraph (A) shall not be treated as income for purposes of applying subsection (c) of this section.

"(D) Definitions. For purposes of this paragraph

"(i) Housing deduction. The term 'housing deduction' means that portion of the deduction allowable under subsection (a) for any taxable year which is attributable to qualified housing expenses. For such purpose, qualified housing expenses shall be taken into account after all other amounts described in subsection (b).

"(ii) After-received compensation. The term 'after-received compensation' means compensation received by an individual in a taxable year which is attributable to services performed by such individual in the third preceding, second preceding, or first preceding taxable year.

"(f) Qualified schooling expenses.

"(1) In general. For purposes of this section, the term 'qualified schooling expenses' means the reasonable schooling expenses paid or incurred by or on behalf of the individual during the taxable year for the education of each dependent of the individual at the elementary or secondary level. For purposes of the preceding sentence, the elementary or secondary level means education which is the equivalent of education from the kindergarten through the 12th grade in a United States-type school.

"(2) Expenses included. For purposes of paragraph (1), the term 'schooling expenses' means the cost of tuition, fees, books, and local transportation and of other expenses required by the school. Except as provided in paragraph (3), such term does not include expenses of room and board or expenses of transportation other than local transportation.

"(3) Room, board, and travel allowed in certain cases. If an adequate United States-type school is not available within a reasonable commuting distance of the individual's tax home, the expenses of room and board of the dependent and the expenses of the transportation of the dependent each school year between such tax home and the location of the school shall be treated as schooling expenses.

"(4) Determination of reasonable expenses. If—

"(A) there is an adequate United States-type school available within a reasonable commuting distance of the individual's tax home, and

"(B) the dependent attends a school other than the school referred to in subparagraph (A),

"then the amount taken into account under paragraph (2) shall not exceed the aggregate amount which would be charged for the period by the school referred to in subparagraph (A).

"(5) Period taken into account. An amount shall be taken into account as a qualified schooling expense only if it is attributable to education for a period during which the individual's tax home is in a foreign country.

"(g) Qualified home leave travel expenses.

"(1) In general. For purposes of this section, the term 'qualified home leave travel expenses' means the reasonable amounts paid or incurred by or on behalf of an individual for the transportation of such individual, his spouse, and each dependent

"(A) from a point of outside the United States to the individual's principal domestic residence, and

"(B) from the individual's principal domestic residence to a point outside the United States.

"(2) Limitation to cost between tax home and place of residence. The amount taken into account under subparagraph (A) or (B) of paragraph (1) with respect to any transportation shall not exceed the reasonable amount for transportation between the location of the individual's tax home outside the United States and the individual's principal domestic residence.

"(3) Substitution of nearest port of entry in certain cases. With respect to any person whose travel in the United States is not travel to and from the individual's principal domestic residence, paragraphs (1) and (2) shall be applied by substituting the nearest port of entry in the United States for the individual's principal domestic residence.

"(4) Nearest port of entry. For purposes of paragraph (3), the nearest port of entry in the United States shall not include a nearest port of entry located in Alaska or Hawaii unless the individual elects to have such port of entry taken into account.

"(5) Principal domestic residence defined. For purposes of this subsection, an individual's principal domestic residence is the location of such individual's present (or, if none, most recent) principal residence in the United States.

"(6) 1 round trip per 12-month period abroad. Amounts may be taken into account under paragraph (4) of subsection (b) only with respect to 1 trip to the United States, and 1 trip from the United States, per person for each continuous period of 12 months for which the individual's tax home is in a foreign country.

"(h) Qualified hardship area deduction.

"(1) In general. For purposes of this section, the term 'qualified hardship area deduction' means an amount computed on a daily basis at an annual rate of $5,000 for days during which the individual's tax home is in a hardship area.

"(2) Hardship area defined. For purposes of this section, the term 'hardship area' means any foreign place designated by the Secretary of State as a hardship post where extraordinarily difficult living conditions, notably unhealthful conditions, or excessive physical hardships exist and for which a post differential of 15 percent or more—

"(A) is provided under section 5925 of title 5, United States Code, or

"(B) would be so provided if officers and employees of the Government of the United States were present at that place.

"(i) Special rules where individual maintains separate household for spouse and dependents because of adverse living conditions at tax home.

"(1) In general. For any period during which an individual maintains a qualified second household—

"(A) Qualified cost-of-living differential.

"(i) Allowance determined by reference to location of qualified second household. Paragraph (1) of subsection (d) shall be applied by substituting 'the qualified second household' for 'the individual's tax home'.

"(ii) Disregard of section 119 rule. Subparagraph (E) of subsection (d)(2) shall not apply with respect to the spouse and dependents.

"(B) Qualified housing expenses.

"(i) Expenses with respect to qualified second household taken into account. For purposes of subsection (e), the expenses for housing of an individual's spouse and dependents at the qualified second household shall be treated as housing expenses if they would meet the requirements of subsection (e)(2) if the individual resided at such household.

"(ii) Separate application of subsection (e). Subsection (e) shall be applied separately with respect to the housing expenses for the qualified second household; except that, in determining the base housing amount, the housing expenses (if any) of the individual for housing at his tax home shall also be taken into account under subsection (e)(3)(A)(ii).

"(iii) Certain rules not to apply. Paragraphs (4)(A)(ii) and (5)of subsection (e) shall not apply with respect to housing expenses for the qualified second household.

"(C) Requirement that spouse and dependents reside with individual for purposes of schooling and home leave.

"(i) In general. The requirement of subsection (j)(3) that the dependent or spouse of the individual (as the case may be) reside with the individual at his tax home shall be treated as met if such spouse or dependent resides at the qualified second household.

"(ii) Substitution of household for tax home. In any case where clause (i) applies, paragraphs (3) and (4) of subsection (f), and subsection (g), shall be applied with respect to amounts paid or incurred for the spouse or dependent by substituting the location of the qualified second household for the individual's tax home.

"(2) Definition of qualified second household. For purposes of this section, the term 'qualified second household' means any household maintained in a foreign country by an individual for the spouse and dependents of such individual at a place other than the tax home of such individual because of adverse living conditions at the individual's tax home.

"(j) Other definitions and special rules.

"(1) Definitions. For purposes of this section—

"(A) Earned income. The term 'earned income' has the meaning given to such term by section 911(b) (determined with the rules set forth in paragraphs (2), (3), (4), and (5) of section 911(c)), except that such term does not include amounts paid by the United States or any agency thereof.

"(B) Tax home. The term 'tax home' means, with respect to any individual, such individual's home for purposes of section 162(a)(2) (relating to traveling expenses while away from home). An individual shall not be treated as having a tax home in a foreign country for any period for which his abode is within the United States.

"(C) Residence at tax home. A household or residence shall be treated as at the tax home of an individual if such household or residence is within a reasonable commuting distance of such tax home.

"(D) Adverse living conditions. The term 'adverse living conditions' means living conditions which are dangerous, unhealthful, or otherwise adverse.

"(E) United States. The term 'United States', when used in a geographical sense, includes the possessions of the United States and the areas set forth in paragraph (1) of section 638 and so much of paragraph (2) of section 638 as relates to the possessions of the United States.

"(2) Limitation to coach or economy fare. The amount taken into account under this section for any transportation by air shall not exceed the lowest coach or economy rate of such transportation charged by a commercial airline for such transportation during the calendar month in which such transportation is furnished. If there is no such coach or economy rate or if the individual is required to use first-class transportation because of a physical impairment, the preceding sentence shall be applied by substituting 'first-class' for 'coach or economy'.

"(3) Requirement that spouse and dependents reside with individual for purposes of schooling and home leave. Except as provided in subsections (i)(1)(C)(i), amounts may be taken into account under subsection (f) with respect to any dependent of the individual, and under subsection (g) with respect to the individual's spouse or any dependent of the individual, only for the period that such spouse or dependent (as the case may be) resides with the individual at his tax home.

"(4) Waiver of period of stay in foreign country. For purposes of paragraphs (1) and (2) of subsection (a), an individual who—

"(A) for any period is a bona fide resident of or is present in a foreign country,

"(B) leaves such foreign country after August 31, 1978—

"(i) during any period during which the Secretary determines, after consultation with the Secretary of State or his delegate, that individuals were required to leave such foreign country because of war, civil unrest, or similar adverse conditions in such foreign country which precluded the normal conduct of business by such individuals, and

"(ii) before meeting the requirements of such paragraphs (1) and (2), and

"(C) establishes to the satisfaction of the Secretary that he could reasonably have been expected to have met such requirements but for the conditions referred to in clause (i) of subparagraph (B),

shall be treated as having met such requirements with respect to the period described in subparagraph (A) during which he was a bona fide resident or was present in the foreign country.

"(k) Certain double benefits disallowed.

"An individual shall not be allowed—

"(1) as a deduction (other than the deduction under section 151),

"(2) as an exclusion, or

"(3) as a credit under section 44A (relating to household and dependent care services),

any amount to the extent that such amount is taken into account under subsection (d), (e), (f), or (g).

"(l) Application with section 911.

"An individual shall not be allowed the deduction allowed by subsection (a) for any taxable year with respect to which he elects the exclusion provided in section 911.

"(m) Regulations.

"The Secretary shall prescribe such regulations as may be necessary or appropriate to carry out the purposes of this section, including regulations providing rules—

"(1) for cases where a husband and wife each have earned income from sources outside the United States, and

"(2) for married individuals filing separate returns."

In 1980, P.L. 96-608, Sec. 1(a), added new para. (4), for tax. yrs. begin. after 12/31/77.

—P.L. 96-222, Sec. 108(a)(1)(B)(i), substituted "housing income" for "earned income" each place it appeared in subpara. (e)(3)(A) ... Sec. 108(a)(1)(B)(ii), added new paras. (e)(6) and (e)(7) ... Sec. 108(a)(1)(F)(i), amended subsec. (g) ... Sec. 108(a)(1)(F)(ii), substituted ", and subsection (g)," for ", and paragraph (1) of subsection (g)," in clause (i)(1)(C)(ii), for tax. yrs. begin. after '77.

Prior to amendment, subsec. (g) read as follows:

"(g) Qualified home leave travel expenses.

"(1) In general. For purposes of this section, the term 'qualified home leave travel expenses' means the reasonable amounts paid or incurred by or on behalf of an individual for the transportation of such individual, his spouse, and each dependent from the location of the individual's tax home outside the United States to—

"(A) the individual's present (or, if none, most recent) principal residence in the United States, or

"(B) if subparagraph (A) does not apply to the individual, the nearest port of entry in the continental United States (excluding Alaska)

and return.

"(2) One trip per 12-month period abroad. Amounts may be taken into account under paragraph (4) of subsection (b) only with respect to one round trip per person for each continuous period of 12 months for which the individual's tax home is in a foreign country."

In 1978, P.L. 95-615, Sec. 203(a), added Code Sec. 913, for tax. yrs. begin. after '77.

SUBPART C.—TAXATION OF FOREIGN SALES CORPORATIONS [REPEALED]

In 2000, P.L. 106-519, Sec. 2, deleted the table for subpart C.
Prior to deletion, the table for subpart C read as follows:
"SUBPART C.—TAXATION OF FOREIGN SALES CORPORATIONS
"Sec.
"921. Exempt foreign trade income excluded from gross income.
"922. FSC defined.
"923. Exempt foreign trade income.
"924. Foreign trading gross receipts.
"925. Transfer pricing rules.
"926. Distributions to shareholders.
"927. Other definitions and special rules."

In 1984, P.L. 98-369, Sec. 801(a), added the heading for subpart C and the items for Code Secs. 921–927.

In 1976, P.L. 94-455, Sec. 1052(c)(7), deleted the table for Subpart C, for tax. yrs. begin after '79.

Prior to amendment, Subpart C read as follows:
"SUBPART C.—WESTERN HEMISPHERE TRADE CORPORATIONS
"Sec.
"921. Definition of Western Hemisphere trade corporations.
"922. Special deduction."

Sec. 921. Repealed.

In 2000, P.L. 106-519, Sec. 2, repealed Code Sec. 921, effective for transactions after 9/30/2000. Sec. 5(b)–(d) of this Act, provides:

"(b) No new FSCs; termination of inactive FSCs—

"(1) No new FSCs. No corporation may elect after September 30, 2000, to be a FSC (as defined in section 922 of the Internal Revenue Code of 1986, as in effect before the amendments made by this Act).

"(2) Termination of inactive FSCs. If a FSC has no foreign trade income (as defined in section 923(b) of such Code, as so in effect) for any period of 5 consecutive taxable years beginning after December 31, 2001, such FSC shall cease to be treated as a FSC for purposes of such Code for any taxable year beginning after such period.

"(c) Transition period for existing Foreign Sales Corporations.

"(1) In general. In the case of a FSC (as so defined) in existence on September 30, 2000, and at all times thereafter, the amendments made by this Act shall not apply to any transaction in the ordinary course of trade or business involving a FSC which occurs—

"(A) before January 1, 2002; or

"(B) after December 31, 2001, pursuant to a binding contract—

"(i) which is between the FSC (or any related person) and any person which is not a related person; and

"(ii) which is in effect on September 30, 2000, and at all times thereafter.

For purposes of this paragraph, a binding contract shall include a purchase option, renewal option, or replacement option which is included in such contract and which is enforceable against the seller or lessor.

"(2) Election to have amendments apply earlier. A taxpayer may elect to have the amendments made by this Act apply to any transaction to a FSC or any related person to which such amendments would apply but for the application of paragraph (1). Such election shall be effective for the taxable year for which made and all subsequent taxable years, and, once made, may be revoked only with the consent of the Secretary of the Treasury.

"(3) Exception for old earnings and profits of certain corporations.

"(A) In general. In the case of a foreign corporation to which this paragraph applies—

"(i) earnings and profits of such corporation accumulated in taxable years ending before October 1, 2000, shall not be included in the gross income of the persons holding stock in such corporation by reason of section 943(e)(4)(B)(i), and

"(ii) rules similar to the rules of clauses (ii), (iii), and (iv) of section 953(d)(4)(B) shall apply with respect to such earnings and profits.

Income from foreign sources

The preceding sentence shall not apply to earnings and profits acquired in a transaction after September 30, 2000, to which section 381 applies unless the distributor or transferor corporation was immediately before the transaction a foreign corporation to which this paragraph applies.

"(B) Existing FSCs. This paragraph shall apply to any controlled foreign corporation (as defined in section 957) if—

"(i) such corporation is a FSC (as so defined) in existence on September 30, 2000,

"(ii) such corporation is eligible to make the election under section 943(e) by reason of being described in paragraph (2)(B) of such section, and

"(iii) such corporation makes such election not later than for its first taxable year beginning after December 31, 2001.

"(C) Other corporations. This paragraph shall apply to any controlled foreign corporation (as defined in section 957), and such corporation shall (notwithstanding any provision of section 943(e)) be treated as an applicable foreign corporation for purposes of section 943(e), if—

"(i) such corporation is in existence on September 30, 2000;

"(ii) as of such date, such corporation is wholly owned (directly or indirectly) by a domestic corporation (determined without regard to any election under section 943(e));

"(iii) for each of the 3 taxable years preceding the first taxable year to which the election under section 943(e) by such controlled foreign corporation applies—

"(I) all of the gross income of such corporation is subpart F income (as defined in section 952), including by reason of section 954(b)(3)(B); and

"(II) in the ordinary course of such corporation's trade or business, such corporation regularly sold (or paid commissions) to a FSC which on September 30, 2000, was a related person to such corporation;

"(iv) such corporation has never made an election under section 922(a)(2) (as in effect before the date of the enactment of this paragraph) to be treated as a FSC; and

"(v) such corporation makes the election under section 943(e) not later than for its first taxable year beginning after December 31, 2001.

The preceding sentence shall cease to apply as of the date that the domestic corporation referred to in clause (ii) ceases to wholly own (directly or indirectly) such controlled foreign corporation.

"(4) Related person. For purposes of this subsection, the term 'related person' has the meaning given to such term by section 943(b)(3).

"(5) Section references. Except as otherwise expressly provided, any reference in this subsection to a section or other provision shall be considered to be a reference to a section or other provision of the Internal Revenue Code of 1986, as amended by this Act.

"(d) Special rules relating to leasing transactions.

"(1) Sales income. If foreign trade income in connection with the lease or rental of property described in section 927(a)(1)(B) of such Code (as in effect before the amendments made by this Act) is treated as exempt foreign trade income for purposes of section 921(a) of such Code (as so in effect), such property shall be treated as property described in section 941(c)(1)(A) of such Code (as added by this Act) for purposes of applying section 941(c)(2) of such Code (as so added) to any subsequent transaction involving such property to which the amendments made by this Act apply.

"(2) Limitation on use of gross receipts method. If any person computed its foreign trade income from any transaction with respect to any property on the basis of a transfer price determined under the method described in section 925(a)(1) of such Code (as in effect before the amendments made by this Act), then the qualifying foreign trade income (as defined in section 941(a) of such Code, as in effect after such amendment) of such person (or any related person) with respect to any other transaction involving such property (and to which the amendments made by this Act apply) shall be zero."

Prior to repeal, Code Sec. 921 read as follows:

"SEC. 921. EXEMPT FOREIGN TRADE INCOME EXCLUDED FROM GROSS INCOME.

"(a) Exclusion. Exempt foreign trade income of a FSC shall be treated as foreign source income which is not effectively connected with the conduct of a trade or business within the United States.

"(b) Proportionate allocation of deductions to exempt foreign trade income. Any deductions of the FSC properly apportioned and allocated to the foreign trade income derived by a FSC from any transaction shall be allocated between—

"(1) the exempt foreign trade income derived from such transaction, and

"(2) the foreign trade income (other than exempt foreign trade income) derived from such transaction, on a proportionate basis.

"(c) Denial of credits. Notwithstanding any other provision of this chapter, no credit (other than a credit allowable under section 27(a), 33, or 34) shall be allowed under this chapter to any FSC.

"(d) Foreign trade income, investment income, and carrying charges treated as effectively connected with United States business. For purposes of this chapter—

"(1) all foreign trade income of a FSC other than—

"(A) exempt foreign trade income, and

"(B) section 923(a)(2) non-exempt income,

"(2) all interest, dividends, royalties, and other investment income received or accrued by a FSC, and

"(3) all carrying charges received or accrued by a FSC, shall be treated as income effectively connected with a trade or business conducted through a permanent establishment of such corporation within the United States. Income described in paragraph (1) shall be treated as derived from sources within the United States."

In 1988, P.L. 100-647, Sec. 6252(b)(2)(A), amended Sec. 804(a) of P.L. 98-369 [reproduced below], by substituting "shall, during 1990 and each fourth calendar year thereafter, submit a report to the Congress (using the most recent information available) setting forth" for "shall, for calendar year 1985 and each second calendar year thereafter, submit a report to the Congress within 27½ months following the close of such calendar year setting forth", effective 7/18/84.

In 1984, P.L. 98-369, Sec. 801(a), added Code Sec. 921, effective for transactions after 12/31/84, in tax. yrs. end. after 12/31/84. Sec. 804(a) [as amended by Sec. 6252(b)(2)(A) of P.L. 100-647, see above] of this Act provides:

"(a) In general.— The Secretary of the Treasury shall, during 1990 and each fourth calendar year thereafter, submit a report to the Congress (using the most recent information available) setting forth an analysis of the operation and effect of the provisions of this title."

Sec. 922. Repealed.

In 2000, P.L. 106-519, Sec. 2, repealed Code Sec. 922, effective for transactions after 9/30/2000. Sec. 5(b)–(d) of this Act, provides:

"(b) No new FSCs; termination of inactive FSCs—

"(1) No new FSCs. No corporation may elect after September 30, 2000, to be a FSC (as defined in section 922 of the Internal Revenue Code of 1986, as in effect before the amendments made by this Act).

"(2) Termination of inactive FSCs. If a FSC has no foreign trade income (as defined in section 923(b) of such Code, as so in effect) for any period of 5 consecutive taxable years beginning after December 31, 2001, such FSC shall cease to be treated as a FSC for purposes of such Code for any taxable year beginning after such period.

"(c) Transition period for existing Foreign Sales Corporations.

"(1) In general. In the case of a FSC (as so defined) in existence on September 30, 2000, and at all times thereafter, the amendments made by this Act shall not apply to any transaction in the ordinary course of trade or business involving a FSC which occurs—

"(A) before January 1, 2002; or

"(B) after December 31, 2001, pursuant to a binding contract—

"(i) which is between the FSC (or any related person) and any person which is not a related person; and

"(ii) which is in effect on September 30, 2000, and at all times thereafter.

For purposes of this paragraph, a binding contract shall include a purchase option, renewal option, or replacement option which is included in such contract and which is enforceable against the seller or lessor.

"(2) Election to have amendments apply earlier. A taxpayer may elect to have the amendments made by this Act apply to any transaction by a FSC or any related person to which such amendments would apply but for the application of paragraph (1). Such election shall be effective for the taxable year for which made and all subsequent taxable years, and, once made, may be revoked only with the consent of the Secretary of the Treasury.

"(3) Exception for old earnings and profits of certain corporations.

"(A) In general. In the case of a foreign corporation to which this paragraph applies—

"(i) earnings and profits of such corporation accumulated in taxable years ending before October 1, 2000, shall not be included in the gross income of the persons holding stock in such corporation by reason of section 943(e)(4)(B)(i), and

"(ii) rules similar to the rules of clauses (ii), (iii), and (iv) of section 953(d)(4)(B) shall apply with respect to such earnings and profits.

The preceding sentence shall not apply to earnings and profits acquired in a transaction after September 30, 2000, to which section 381 applies unless the distributor or transferor corporation was immediately before the transaction a foreign corporation to which this paragraph applies.

"(B) Existing FSCs. This paragraph shall apply to any controlled foreign corporation (as defined in section 957) if—

"(i) such corporation is a FSC (as so defined) in existence on September 30, 2000,

"(ii) such corporation is eligible to make the election under section 943(e) by reason of being described in paragraph (2)(B) of such section, and

"(iii) such corporation makes such election not later than for its first taxable year beginning after December 31, 2001.

"(C) Other corporations. This paragraph shall apply to any controlled foreign corporation (as defined in section 957), and such corporation shall (notwithstanding any provision of section 943(e)) be treated as an applicable foreign corporation for purposes of section 943(e), if—

"(i) such corporation is in existence on September 30, 2000;

"(ii) as of such date, such corporation is wholly owned (directly or indirectly) by a domestic corporation (determined without regard to any election under section 943(e));

"(iii) for each of the 3 taxable years preceding the first taxable year to which the election under section 943(e) by such controlled foreign corporation applies—

"(I) all of the gross income of such corporation is subpart F income (as defined in section 952), including by reason of section 954(b)(3)(B); and

"(II) in the ordinary course of such corporation's trade or business, such corporation regularly sold (or paid commissions) to a FSC which on September 30, 2000, was a related person to such corporation;

"(iv) such corporation has never made an election under section 922(a)(2) (as in effect before the date of the enactment of this paragraph) to be treated as a FSC; and

"(v) such corporation makes the election under section 943(e) not later than for its first taxable year beginning after December 31, 2001.

The preceding sentence shall cease to apply as of the date that the domestic corporation referred to in clause (ii) ceases to wholly own (directly or indirectly) such controlled foreign corporation.

Code Sec. 922 — Income from foreign sources

"(4) Related person. For purposes of this subsection, the term 'related person' has the meaning given to such term by section 943(b)(3).

"(5) Section references. Except as otherwise expressly provided, any reference in this subsection to a section or other provision shall be considered to be a reference to a section or other provision of the Internal Revenue Code of 1986, as amended by this Act.

"(d) Special rules relating to leasing transactions.

"(1) Sales income. If foreign trade income in connection with the lease or rental of property described in section 927(a)(1)(B) of such Code (as in effect before the amendments made by this Act) is treated as exempt foreign trade income for purposes of section 921(a) of such Code (as so in effect), such property shall be treated as property described in section 941(c)(1)(B) of such Code (as added by this Act) for purposes of applying section 941(c)(2) of such Code (as so added) to any subsequent transaction involving such property to which the amendments made by this Act apply.

"(2) Limitation on use of gross receipts method. If any person computed its foreign trade income from any transaction with respect to any property on the basis of a transfer price determined under the method described in section 925(a)(1) of such Code (as in effect before the amendments made by this Act), then the qualifying foreign trade income (as defined in section 941(a) of such Code, as in effect after such amendment) of such person (or any related person) with respect to any other transaction involving such property (and to which the amendments made by this Act apply) shall be zero."

Prior to repeal, Code Sec. 922 read as follows:

"SEC. 922. FSC DEFINED.

"(a) FSC defined. For purposes of this title, the term 'FSC' means any corporation—

"(1) which—

"(A) was created or organized—

"(i) under the laws of any foreign country which meets the requirements of section 927(e)(3), or

"(ii) under the laws applicable to any possession of the United States,

"(B) has no more than 25 shareholders at any time during the taxable year,

"(C) does not have any preferred stock outstanding at any time during the taxable year,

"(D) during the taxable year—

"(i) maintains an office located outside the United States in a foreign country which meets the requirements of section 927(e)(3) or in any possession of the United States,

"(ii) maintains a set of the permanent books of account (including invoices) of such corporation at such office, and

"(iii) maintains at a location within the United States the records which such corporation is required to keep under section 6001,

"(E) at all times during the taxable year, has a board of directors which includes at least one individual who is not a resident of the United States, and

"(F) is not a member, at any time during the taxable year, of any controlled group of corporations of which a DISC is a member, and

"(2) which has made an election (at the time and in the manner provided in section 927(f)(1)) which is in effect for the taxable year to be treated as a FSC.

"(b) Small FSC defined. For purposes of this title, a FSC is a small FSC with respect to any taxable year if—

"(1) such corporation has made an election (at the time and in the manner provided in section 927(f)(1)) which is in effect for the taxable year to be treated as a small FSC, and

"(2) such corporation is not a member, at any time during the taxable year, of a controlled group of corporations which includes a FSC unless such other FSC has also made an election under paragraph (1) which is in effect for such year."

In **1984**, P.L. 98-369, Sec. 801(a), added Code Sec. 922, effective for transactions after 12/31/84, in tax. yrs. end. after 12/31/84.

Sec. 923. Repealed.

In **2000**, P.L. 106-519, Sec. 2, repealed Code Sec. 923, effective for transactions after 9/30/2000. Sec. 5(b)–(d) of this Act, provides:

"(b) No new FSCs; termination of inactive FSCs—

"(1) No new FSCs. No corporation may elect after September 30, 2000, to be a FSC (as defined in section 922 of the Internal Revenue Code of 1986, as in effect before the amendments made by this Act).

"(2) Termination of inactive FSCs. If a FSC has no foreign trade income (as defined in section 923(b) of such Code, as so in effect) for any period of 5 consecutive taxable years beginning after December 31, 2001, such FSC shall cease to be treated as a FSC for purposes of such Code for any taxable year beginning after such period.

"(c) Transition period for existing Foreign Sales Corporations.

"(1) In general. In the case of a FSC (as so defined) in existence on September 30, 2000, and at all times thereafter, the amendments made by this Act shall not apply to any transaction in the ordinary course of trade or business involving a FSC which occurs—

"(A) before January 1, 2002; or

"(B) after December 31, 2001, pursuant to a binding contract—

"(i) which is between the FSC (or any related person) and any person which is not a related person; and

"(ii) which is in effect on September 30, 2000, and at all times thereafter.

For purposes of this paragraph, a binding contract shall include a purchase option, renewal option, or replacement option which is included in such contract and which is enforceable against the seller or lessor.

"(2) Election to have amendments apply earlier. A taxpayer may elect to have the amendments made by this Act apply to any transaction by a FSC or any related person to which such amendments would apply but for the application of paragraph (1). Such election shall be effective for the taxable year for which made and all subsequent taxable years, and, once made, may be revoked only with the consent of the Secretary of the Treasury.

"(3) Exception for old earnings and profits of certain corporations.

"(A) In general. In the case of a foreign corporation to which this paragraph applies—

"(i) earnings and profits of such corporation accumulated in taxable years ending before October 1, 2000, shall not be included in the gross income of the persons holding stock in such corporation by reason of section 943(e)(4)(B)(i), and

"(ii) rules similar to the rules of clauses (ii), (iii), and (iv) of section 953(d)(4)(B) shall apply with respect to such earnings and profits.

The preceding sentence shall not apply to earnings and profits acquired in a transaction after September 30, 2000, to which section 381 applies unless the distributor or transferor corporation was immediately before the transaction a foreign corporation to which this paragraph applies.

"(B) Existing FSCs. This paragraph shall apply to any controlled foreign corporation (as defined in section 957) if—

"(i) such corporation is a FSC (as so defined) in existence on September 30, 2000,

"(ii) such corporation is eligible to make the election under section 943(e) by reason of being described in paragraph (2)(B) of such section, and

"(iii) such corporation makes such election not later than for its first taxable year beginning after December 31, 2001.

"(C) Other corporations. This paragraph shall apply to any controlled foreign corporation (as defined in section 957), and such corporation shall (notwithstanding any provision of section 943(e)) be treated as an applicable foreign corporation for purposes of section 943(e), if—

"(i) such corporation is in existence on September 30, 2000;

"(ii) as of such date, such corporation is wholly owned (directly or indirectly) by a domestic corporation (determined without regard to any election under section 943(e));

"(iii) for each of the 3 taxable years preceding the first taxable year to which the election under section 943(e) by such controlled foreign corporation applies—

"(I) all of the gross income of such corporation is subpart F income (as defined in section 952), including by reason of section 954(b)(3)(B); and

"(II) in the ordinary course of such corporation's trade or business, such corporation regularly sold (or paid commissions) to a FSC which on September 30, 2000, was a related person to such corporation;

"(iv) such corporation has never made an election under section 922(a)(2) (as in effect before the date of the enactment of this paragraph) to be treated as a FSC; and

"(v) such corporation makes the election under section 943(e) not later than for its first taxable year beginning after December 31, 2001.

The preceding sentence shall cease to apply as of the date that the domestic corporation referred to in clause (ii) ceases to wholly own (directly or indirectly) such controlled foreign corporation.

"(4) Related person. For purposes of this subsection, the term 'related person' has the meaning given to such term by section 943(b)(3).

"(5) Section references. Except as otherwise expressly provided, any reference in this subsection to a section or other provision shall be considered to be a reference to a section or other provision of the Internal Revenue Code of 1986, as amended by this Act.

"(d) Special rules relating to leasing transactions.

"(1) Sales income. If foreign trade income in connection with the lease or rental of property described in section 927(a)(1)(B) of such Code (as in effect before the amendments made by this Act) is treated as exempt foreign trade income for purposes of section 921(a) of such Code (as so in effect), such property shall be treated as property described in section 941(c)(1)(B) of such Code (as added by this Act) for purposes of applying section 941(c)(2) of such Code (as so added) to any subsequent transaction involving such property to which the amendments made by this Act apply.

"(2) Limitation on use of gross receipts method. If any person computed its foreign trade income from any transaction with respect to any property on the basis of a transfer price determined under the method described in section 925(a)(1) of such Code (as in effect before the amendments made by this Act), then the qualifying foreign trade income (as defined in section 941(a) of such Code, as in effect after such amendment) of such person (or any related person) with respect to any other transaction involving such property (and to which the amendments made by this Act apply) shall be zero."

Prior to repeal, Code Sec. 923 read as follows:

"SEC. 923. EXEMPT FOREIGN TRADE INCOME.

"(a) Exempt foreign trade income. For purposes of this subpart—

"(1) In general. The term 'exempt foreign trade income' means the aggregate amount of all foreign trade income of a FSC for the taxable year which is described in paragraph (2) or (3).

"(2) Income determined without regard to administrative pricing rules. In the case of any transaction to which paragraph (3) does not apply, 32 percent of the foreign trade income derived from such transaction shall be treated as described in this paragraph. For purposes of the preceding sentence, foreign trade income shall not include any income properly allocable to excluded property described in subparagraph (B) of section 927(a)(2) (relating to intangibles).

"(3) Income determined with regard to administrative pricing rules. In the case of any transaction with respect to which paragraph (1) or (2) of section 925(a) (or the corresponding provisions of the regulations prescribed under section 925(b))

Income from foreign sources Code Sec. 924

applies, 16/23 of the foreign trade income derived from such transaction shall be treated as described in this paragraph.

"(4) Special rule for foreign trade income allocable to a cooperative.

"(A) In general. In any case in which a qualified cooperative is a shareholder of a FSC, paragraph (3) shall be applied with respect to that portion of the foreign trade income of such FSC for any taxable year which is properly allocable to the marketing of agricultural or horticultural products (or the providing of related services) by such cooperative by substituting '100 percent' for '16/23'.

"(B) Paragraph only to apply to amounts FSC distributes. Subparagraph (A) shall not apply for any taxable year unless the FSC distributes to the qualified cooperative the amount which (but for such subparagraph) would not be treated as exempt foreign trade income. Any distribution under this subparagraph for any taxable year—

"(i) shall be made before the due date for filing the return of tax for such taxable year, but

"(ii) shall be treated as made on the last day of such taxable year.

"(5) Special rule for military property. Under regulations prescribed by the Secretary, that portion of the foreign trading gross receipts of the FSC for the taxable year attributable to the disposition of, or services relating to, military property (within the meaning of section 995(b)(3)(B)) which may be treated as exempt foreign trade income shall equal 50 percent of the amount which (but for this paragraph) would be treated as exempt foreign trade income.

"(6) Cross reference. For reduction in amount of exempt foreign trade income, see section 291(a)(4).

"(b) Foreign trade income defined. For purposes of this subpart, the term 'foreign trade income' means the gross income of a FSC attributable to foreign trading gross receipts."

In 1986, P.L. 99-514, Sec. 1876(b)(3), added para. (a)(6), effective for transactions after 12/31/84, in tax. yrs. end. after 12/31/84.

In 1984, P.L. 98-369, Sec. 801(a), added Code Sec. 923, effective for transactions after 12/31/84, in tax. yrs. end. after 12/31/84.

Sec. 924. Repealed.

In 2000, P.L. 106-519, Sec. 2, repealed Code Sec. 924, effective for transactions after 9/30/2000. Sec. 5(b)–(d) of this Act, provides:

"(b) No new FSCs; termination of inactive FSCs—

"(1) No new FSCs. No corporation may elect after September 30, 2000, to be a FSC (as defined in section 922 of the Internal Revenue Code of 1986, as in effect before the amendments made by this Act).

"(2) Termination of inactive FSCs. If a FSC has no foreign trade income (as defined in section 923(b) of such Code, as so in effect) for any period of 5 consecutive taxable years beginning after December 31, 2001, such FSC shall cease to be treated as a FSC for purposes of such Code for any taxable year beginning after such period.

"(c) Transition period for existing Foreign Sales Corporations.

"(1) In general. In the case of a FSC (as so defined) in existence on September 30, 2000, and at all times thereafter, the amendments made by this Act shall not apply to any transaction in the ordinary course of trade or business involving a FSC which occurs—

"(A) before January 1, 2002; or

"(B) after December 31, 2001, pursuant to a binding contract—

"(i) which is between the FSC (or any related person) and any person which is not a related person; and

"(ii) which is in effect on September 30, 2000, and at all times thereafter.

For purposes of this paragraph, a binding contract shall include a purchase option, renewal option, or replacement option which is included in such contract and which is enforceable against the seller or lessor.

"(2) Election to have amendments apply earlier. A taxpayer may elect to have the amendments made by this Act apply to any transaction by a FSC or any related person to which such amendments would apply but for the application of paragraph (1). Such election shall be effective for the taxable year for which made and all subsequent taxable years, and, once made, may be revoked only with the consent of the Secretary of the Treasury.

"(3) Exception for old earnings and profits of certain corporations.

"(A) In general. In the case of a foreign corporation to which this paragraph applies—

"(i) earnings and profits of such corporation accumulated in taxable years ending before October 1, 2000, shall not be included in the gross income of the persons holding stock in such corporation by reason of section 943(e)(4)(B)(i), and

"(ii) rules similar to the rules of clauses (ii), (iii), and (iv) of section 953(d)(4)(B) shall apply with respect to such earnings and profits.

The preceding sentence shall not apply to earnings and profits acquired in a transaction after September 30, 2000, to which section 381 applies unless the distributor or transferor corporation was immediately before the transaction a foreign corporation to which this paragraph applies.

"(B) Existing FSCs. This paragraph shall apply to any controlled foreign corporation (as defined in section 957) if—

"(i) such corporation is a FSC (as so defined) in existence on September 30, 2000,

"(ii) such corporation is eligible to make the election under section 943(e) by reason of being described in paragraph (2)(B) of such section, and

"(iii) such corporation makes such election not later than for its first taxable year beginning after December 31, 2001.

"(C) Other corporations. This paragraph shall apply to any controlled foreign corporation (as defined in section 957), and such corporation shall (notwithstanding any provision of section 943(e)) be treated as an applicable foreign corporation for purposes of section 943(e), if—

"(i) such corporation is in existence on September 30, 2000;

"(ii) as of such date, such corporation is wholly owned (directly or indirectly) by a domestic corporation (determined without regard to any election under section 943(e));

"(iii) for each of the 3 taxable years preceding the first taxable year to which the election under section 943(e) by such controlled foreign corporation applies—

"(I) all of the gross income of such corporation is subpart F income (as defined in section 952), including by reason of section 954(b)(3)(B); and

"(II) in the ordinary course of such corporation's trade or business, such corporation regularly sold (or paid commissions) to a FSC which on September 30, 2000, was a related person to such corporation;

"(iv) such corporation has never made an election under section 922(a)(2) (as in effect before the date of the enactment of this paragraph) to be treated as a FSC; and

"(v) such corporation makes the election under section 943(e) not later than for its first taxable year beginning after December 31, 2001.

The preceding sentence shall cease to apply as of the date that the domestic corporation referred to in clause (ii) ceases to wholly own (directly or indirectly) such controlled foreign corporation.

"(4) Related person. For purposes of this subsection, the term 'related person' has the meaning given to such term by section 943(b)(3).

"(5) Section references. Except as otherwise expressly provided, any reference in this subsection to a section or other provision shall be considered to be a reference to a section or other provision of the Internal Revenue Code of 1986, as amended by this Act.

"(d) Special rules relating to leasing transactions.

"(1) Sales income. If foreign trade income in connection with the lease or rental of property described in section 927(a)(1)(B) of such Code (as in effect before the amendments made by this Act) is treated as exempt foreign trade income for purposes of section 921(a) of such Code (as so in effect), such property shall be treated as property described in section 941(c)(1)(B) of such Code (as added by this Act) for purposes of applying section 941(c)(2) of such Code (as so added) to any subsequent transaction involving such property to which the amendments made by this Act apply.

"(2) Limitation on use of gross receipts method. If any person computed its foreign trade income from any transaction with respect to any property on the basis of a transfer price determined under the method described in section 925(a)(1) of such Code (as in effect before the amendments made by this Act), then the qualifying foreign trade income (as defined in section 941(a) of such Code, as in effect after such amendment) of such person (or any related person) with respect to any other transaction involving such property (and to which the amendments made by this Act apply) shall be zero."

Prior to repeal, Code Sec. 924 read as follows:

"SEC. 924. FOREIGN TRADING GROSS RECEIPTS.

"(a) In general. Except as otherwise provided in this section, for purposes of this subpart, the term 'foreign trading gross receipts' means the gross receipts of any FSC which are—

"(1) from the sale, exchange, or other disposition of export property,

"(2) from the lease or rental of export property for use by the lessee outside the United States,

"(3) for services which are related and subsidiary to—

"(A) any sale, exchange, or other disposition of export property by such corporation, or

"(B) any lease or rental of export property described in paragraph (2) by such corporation,

"(4) for engineering or architectural services for construction projects located (or proposed for location) outside the United States, or

"(5) for the performance of managerial services for an unrelated FSC or DISC in furtherance of the production of foreign trading gross receipts described in paragraph (1), (2), or (3).

Paragraph (5) shall not apply to a FSC for any taxable year unless at least 50 percent of its gross receipts for such taxable year is derived from activities described in paragraph (1), (2), or (3).

"(b) Foreign management and foreign economic process requirements.

"(1) In general. Except as provided in paragraph (2)—

"(A) a FSC shall be treated as having foreign trading gross receipts for the taxable year only if the management of such corporation during such taxable year takes place outside the United States as required by subsection (c), and

"(B) a FSC has foreign trading gross receipts from any transaction only if economic processes with respect to such transaction take place outside the United States as required by subsection (d).

"(2) Exception for small FSC.

"(A) In general. Paragraph (1) shall not apply with respect to any small FSC.

"(B) Limitation on amount of foreign trading gross receipts of small FSC taken into account.

"(i) In general. Any foreign trading gross receipts of a small FSC for the taxable year which exceed $5,000,000 shall not be taken into account in determining the exempt foreign trade income of such corporation and shall not be taken into account under any other provision of this subpart.

"(ii) Allocation of limitation. If the foreign trading gross receipts of a small FSC exceed the limitation of clause (i), the corporation may allocate such limitation among such gross receipts in such manner as it may select (at such time and in such manner as may be prescribed in regulations).

2,589

Code Sec. 924 — Income from foreign sources

"(iii) Receipts of controlled group aggregated. For purposes of applying clauses (i) and (ii), all small FSC's which are members of the same controlled group of corporations shall be treated as a single corporation.

"(iv) Allocation of limitation among members of controlled group. The limitation under clause (i) shall be allocated among the foreign trading gross receipts of small FSC's which are members of the same controlled group of corporations in a manner provided in regulations prescribed by the Secretary.

"(c) Requirement that FSC be managed outside the United States. The management of a FSC meets the requirements of this subsection for the taxable year if—

"(1) all meetings of the board of directors of the corporation, and all meetings of the shareholders of the corporation, are outside the United States,

"(2) the principal bank account of the corporation is maintained in a foreign country which meets the requirements of section 927(e)(3) or in a possession of the United States at all times during the taxable year, and

"(3) all dividends, legal and accounting fees, and salaries of officers and members of the board of directors of the corporation disbursed during the taxable year are disbursed out of bank accounts of the corporation maintained outside the United States.

"(d) Requirement that economic processes take place outside the United States.

"(1) In general. The requirements of this subsection are met with respect to the gross receipts of a FSC derived from any transaction if—

"(A) such corporation (or any person acting under a contract with such corporation) has participated outside the United States in the solicitation (other than advertising), the negotiation, or the making of the contract relating to such transaction, and

"(B) the foreign direct costs incurred by the FSC attributable to the transaction equal or exceed 50 percent of the total direct costs attributable to the transaction.

"(2) Alternative 85-percent test. A corporation shall be treated as satisfying the requirements of paragraph (1)(B) with respect to any transaction if, with respect to each of at least 2 paragraphs of subsection (e), the foreign direct costs incurred by such corporation attributable to activities described in such paragraph equal or exceed 85 percent of the total direct costs attributable to activities described in such paragraph.

"(3) Definitions. For purposes of this subsection—

"(A) Total direct costs. The term 'total direct costs' means, with respect to any transaction, the total direct costs incurred by the FSC attributable to activities described in subsection (e) performed at any location by the FSC or any person acting under a contract with such FSC.

"(B) Foreign direct costs. The term 'foreign direct costs' means, with respect to any transaction, the portion of the total direct costs which are attributable to activities performed outside the United States.

"(4) Rules for commissions, etc. The Secretary shall prescribe such regulations as may be necessary to carry out the purposes of this subsection and subsection (e) in the case of commissions, rentals, and furnishing of services.

"(e) Activities relating to disposition of export property. The activities referred to in subsection (d) are—

"(1) advertising and sales promotion,

"(2) the processing of customer orders and the arranging for delivery of the export property,

"(3) transportation from the time of acquisition by the FSC (or, in the case of a commission relationship, from the beginning of such relationship for such transaction) to the delivery to the customer,

"(4) the determination and transmittal of a final invoice or statement of account and the receipt of payment, and

"(5) the assumption of credit risk.

"(f) Certain receipts not included in foreign trading gross receipts.

"(1) Certain receipts excluded on basis of use; subsidized receipts and receipts from related parties excluded. The term 'foreign trading gross receipts' shall not include receipts of a FSC from a transaction if—

"(A) the export property or services—

"(i) are for ultimate use in the United States, or

"(ii) are for use by the United States or any instrumentality thereof and such use of export property or services is required by law or regulation,

"(B) such transaction is accomplished by a subsidy granted by the United States or any instrumentality thereof, or

"(C) such receipts are from another FSC which is a member of the same controlled group of corporations of which such corporation is a member. In the case of gross receipts of a FSC from a transaction involving any property, subparagraph (C) shall not apply if such FSC (and all other FSC's which are members of the same controlled group and which receive gross receipts from a transaction involving such property) do not use the pricing rules under paragraph (1) of section 925(a) (or the corresponding provisions of the regulations prescribed under section 925(b)) with respect to any transaction involving such property.

"(2) Investment income; carrying charges. The term 'foreign trading gross receipts' shall not include any investment income or carrying charges."

In **1986**, P.L. 99-514, Sec. 1876(e)(2), amended para. (c)(2), effective for periods after 3/28/85.

—P.L. 99-514, Sec. 1876(f), added the last sentence to para. (f)(1), effective for transactions after 12/31/84, in tax. yrs. end. after 12/31/84. For special rules, see Sec. 805(a)(2) of P.L. 98-369, reproduced below.

Prior to amendment, para. (c)(2) read as follows:

"(2) the principal bank account of the corporation is maintained outside the United States at all times during the taxable year, and"

—P.L. 99-514, Sec. 1876(o), amended Sec. 805(a)(2) of P.L. 98-369 [reproduced below], transitional rules for changes made by Sec. 801(a) of P.L. 98-369, see below.

Prior to amendment, Sec. 805(a)(2) of P.L. 98-369 read as follows:

"(2) Special rule for certain contracts. To the extent provided in regulations prescribed by the Secretary, subsections (c) and (d) of section 924 of the Internal Revenue Code of 1954 (as added by this title shall not apply to—

"(A) any contract with respect to which the DISC or a related party uses the completed contract method of accounting and which—

"(i) was entered into before March 16, 1984, or

"(ii) was entered into after March 15, 1984, and before January 1, 1985, pursuant to a written plan to enter into such contract which was in effect on March 15, 1984,

"(B) any contract which was entered into before March 16, 1984, except that this subparagraph shall only apply to the first 2 taxable years of the FSC ending after January 1, 1985, or such later taxable years as the Secretary of the Treasury may designate, or

"(C) any contract which was entered into after March 15, 1984, and before January 1, 1985, except that this subparagraph shall only apply to the first taxable year of the FSC ending after January 1, 1985, or such later taxable years as the Secretary of the Treasury may designate."

—P.L. 99-514, Sec. 1876(p)(4), amended Sec. 805(a)(2)(A) of P.L. 98-369 [before amendment by Sec. 1876(o) of this Act] by substituting "the DISC or a related party" for "the taxpayer" [reproduced above].

In **1984**, P.L. 98-369, Sec. 801(a), added Code Sec. 924, effective for transactions after 12/31/84, in tax. yrs. end. after 12/31/84. Sec. 805(a)(2) of this Act [as amended by P.L. 99-514, Secs. 1876(p)(4) and 1876(o), see above], provides:

"(2) Special rule for certain contracts. To the extent provided in regulations prescribed by the Secretary of the Treasury or his delegate, any event or activity required to occur or required to be performed, before January 1, 1985, by section 924(c) or (d) or 925(c) of the Internal Revenue Code of 1954 shall be treated as meeting the requirements of such section if such event or activity is with respect to—

"(A) any lease of more than 3 years duration which was entered into before January 1, 1985,

"(B) any contract with respect to which the taxpayer uses the completed contract method of accounting which was entered into before January 1, 1985, or

"(C) in the case of any contract other than a lease or contract described in subparagraph (A) or (B), any contract which was entered into before January 1, 1985; except that this subparagraph shall only apply to the first 3 taxable years of the FSC ending after January 1, 1985, or such later taxable years as the Secretary of the Treasury or his delegate may prescribe."

Sec. 925. Repealed.

In **2000**, P.L. 106-519, Sec. 2, repealed Code Sec. 925, effective for transactions after 9/30/2000. Sec. 5(b)–(d) of this Act, provides:

"(b) No new FSCs; termination of inactive FSCs—

"(1) No new FSCs. No corporation may elect after September 30, 2000, to be a FSC (as defined in section 922 of the Internal Revenue Code of 1986, as in effect before the amendments made by this Act).

"(2) Termination of inactive FSCs. If a FSC has no foreign trade income (as defined in section 923(b) of such Code, as so in effect) for any period of 5 consecutive taxable years beginning after December 31, 2001, such FSC shall cease to be treated as a FSC for purposes of such Code for any taxable year beginning after such period.

"(c) Transition period for existing Foreign Sales Corporations.

"(1) In general. In the case of a FSC (as so defined) in existence on September 30, 2000, and at all times thereafter, the amendments made by this Act shall not apply to any transaction in the ordinary course of trade or business involving a FSC which occurs—

"(A) before January 1, 2002; or

"(B) after December 31, 2001, pursuant to a binding contract—

"(i) which is between the FSC (or any related person) and any person which is not a related person; and

"(ii) which is in effect on September 30, 2000, and at all times thereafter.

For purposes of this paragraph, a binding contract shall include a purchase option, renewal option, or replacement option which is included in such contract and which is enforceable against the seller or lessor.

"(2) Election to have amendments apply earlier. A taxpayer may elect to have the amendments made by this Act apply to any transaction by a FSC or any related person to which such amendments would apply but for the application of paragraph (1). Such election shall be effective for the taxable year for which made and all subsequent taxable years, and, once made, may be revoked only with the consent of the Secretary of the Treasury.

"(3) Exception for old earnings and profits of certain corporations.

"(A) In general. In the case of a foreign corporation to which this paragraph applies—

"(i) earnings and profits of such corporation accumulated in taxable years ending before October 1, 2000, shall not be included in the gross income of the persons holding stock in such corporation by reason of section 943(e)(4)(B)(i), and

"(ii) rules similar to the rules of clauses (ii), (iii), and (iv) of section 953(d)(4)(B) shall apply with respect to such earnings and profits.

The preceding sentence shall not apply to earnings and profits acquired in a transaction after September 30, 2000, to which section 381 applies unless the distributor or transferor corporation was immediately before the transaction a foreign corporation to which this paragraph applies.

"(B) Existing FSCs. This paragraph shall apply to any controlled foreign corporation (as defined in section 957) if—

"(i) such corporation is a FSC (as so defined) in existence on September 30, 2000,

Income from foreign sources   Code Sec. 926

"(ii) such corporation is eligible to make the election under section 943(e) by reason of being described in paragraph (2)(B) of such section, and

"(iii) such corporation makes such election not later than for its first taxable year beginning after December 31, 2001.

"(C) Other corporations. This paragraph shall apply to any controlled foreign corporation (as defined in section 957), and such corporation shall (notwithstanding any provision of section 943(e)) be treated as an applicable foreign corporation for purposes of section 943(e), if —

"(i) such corporation is in existence on September 30, 2000;

"(ii) as of such date, such corporation is wholly owned (directly or indirectly) by a domestic corporation (determined without regard to any election under section 943(e));

"(iii) for each of the 3 taxable years preceding the first taxable year to which the election under section 943(e) by such controlled foreign corporation applies —

"(I) all of the gross income of such corporation is subpart F income (as defined in section 952), including by reason of section 954(b)(3)(B); and

"(II) in the ordinary course of such corporation's trade or business, such corporation regularly sold (or paid commissions) to a FSC which on September 30, 2000, was a related person to such corporation;

"(iv) such corporation has never made an election under section 922(a)(2) (as in effect before the date of the enactment of this paragraph) to be treated as a FSC; and

"(v) such corporation makes the election under section 943(e) not later than for its first taxable year beginning after December 31, 2001.

The preceding sentence shall cease to apply as of the date that the domestic corporation referred to in clause (ii) ceases to wholly own (directly or indirectly) such controlled foreign corporation.

"(4) Related person. For purposes of this subsection, the term 'related person' has the meaning given to such term by section 943(b)(3).

"(5) Section references. Except as otherwise expressly provided, any reference in this subsection to a section or other provision shall be considered to be a reference to a section or other provision of the Internal Revenue Code of 1986, as amended by this Act.

"(d) Special rules relating to leasing transactions.

"(1) Sales income. If foreign trade income in connection with the lease or rental of property described in section 927(a)(1)(B) of such Code (as in effect before the amendments made by this Act) is treated as exempt foreign trade income for purposes of section 921(a) of such Code (as so in effect), such property shall be treated as property described in section 941(c)(1)(B) of such Code (as added by this Act) for purposes of applying section 941(c)(2) of such Code (as so added) to any subsequent transaction involving such property to which the amendments made by this Act apply.

"(2) Limitation on use of gross receipts method. If any person computed its foreign trade income from any transaction with respect to any property on the basis of a transfer price determined under the method described in section 925(a)(1) of such Code (as in effect before the amendments made by this Act), then the qualifying foreign trade income (as defined in section 941(a) of such Code, as in effect after such amendment) of such person (or any related person) with respect to any other transaction involving such property (and to which the amendments made by this Act apply) shall be zero."

Prior to repeal, Code Sec. 925 read as follows:

"SEC. 925. TRANSFER PRICING RULES.

"(a) In general. In the case of a sale of export property to a FSC by a person described in section 482, the taxable income of such FSC and such person shall be based upon a transfer price which would allow such FSC to derive taxable income attributable to such sale (regardless of the sales price actually charged) in an amount which does not exceed the greatest of —

"(1) 1.83 percent of the foreign trading gross receipts derived from the sale of such property by such FSC,

"(2) 23 percent of the combined taxable income of such FSC and such person which is attributable to the foreign trading gross receipts derived from the sale of such property by such FSC, or

"(3) taxable income based upon the sale price actually charged (but subject to the rules provided in section 482).

Paragraphs (1) and (2) shall apply only if the FSC meets the requirements of subsection (c) with respect to the sale.

"(b) Rules for commissions, rentals, and marginal costing. The Secretary shall prescribe regulations setting forth —

"(1) rules which are consistent with the rules set forth in subsection (a) for the application of this section in the case of commissions, rentals, and other income, and

"(2) rules for the allocation of expenditures in computing combined taxable income under subsection (a)(2) in those cases where a FSC is seeking to establish or maintain a market for export property.

"(c) Requirements for use of administrative pricing rules. A sale by a FSC meets the requirements of this subsection if —

"(1) all of the activities described in section 924(e) attributable to such sale, and

"(2) all of the activities relating to the solicitation (other than advertising), negotiation, and making of the contract for such sale, have been performed by such FSC (or by another person acting under a contract with such FSC).

"(d) Limitation on gross receipts pricing rule. The amount determined under subsection (a)(1) with respect to any transaction shall not exceed 2 times the amount which would be determined under subsection (a)(2) with respect to such transaction.

"(e) Taxable income. For purposes of this section, the taxable income of a FSC shall be determined without regard to section 921.

"(f) Special rule for cooperatives. In any case in which a qualified cooperative sells export property to a FSC, in computing the combined taxable income of such FSC and such organization for purposes of subsection (a)(2) , there shall not be taken into account any deduction allowable under subsection (b) or (c) of section 1382 (relating to patronage dividends, per-unit retain allocations, and nonpatronage distributions)."

In 1984, P.L. 98-369, Sec. 801(a), added Code Sec. 925, effective for transactions after 12/31/84, in tax. yrs. end. after 12/31/84. See Sec. 805(a)(2) of this Act, providing transitional rules reproduced in the note following Code Sec. 924.

Sec. 926. Repealed.

In 2000, P.L. 106-519, Sec. 2, repealed Code Sec. 926, effective for transactions after 9/30/2000. Sec. 5(b)–(d) of this Act, provides:

"(b) No new FSCs; termination of inactive FSCs —

"(1) No new FSCs. No corporation may elect after September 30, 2000, to be a FSC (as defined in section 922 of the Internal Revenue Code of 1986, as in effect before the amendments made by this Act).

"(2) Termination of inactive FSCs. If a FSC has no foreign trade income (as defined in section 923(b) of such Code, as so in effect) for any period of 5 consecutive taxable years beginning after December 31, 2001, such FSC shall cease to be treated as a FSC for purposes of such Code for any taxable year beginning after such period.

"(c) Transition period for existing Foreign Sales Corporations.

"(1) In general. In the case of a FSC (as so defined) in existence on September 30, 2000, and at all times thereafter, the amendments made by this Act shall not apply to any transaction in the ordinary course of trade or business involving a FSC which occurs —

"(A) before January 1, 2002; or

"(B) after December 31, 2001, pursuant to a binding contract —

"(i) which is between the FSC (or any related person) and any person which is not a related person; and

"(ii) which is in effect on September 30, 2000, and at all times thereafter.

For purposes of this paragraph, a binding contract shall include a purchase option, renewal option, or replacement option which is included in such contract and which is enforceable against the seller or lessor.

"(2) Election to have amendments apply earlier. A taxpayer may elect to have the amendments made by this Act apply to any transaction by a FSC or any related person to which such amendments would apply but for the application of paragraph (1). Such election shall be effective for the taxable year for which made and all subsequent taxable years, and, once made, may be revoked only with the consent of the Secretary of the Treasury.

"(3) Exception for old earnings and profits of certain corporations.

"(A) In general. In the case of a foreign corporation to which this paragraph applies —

"(i) earnings and profits of such corporation accumulated in taxable years ending before October 1, 2000, shall not be included in the gross income of the persons holding stock in such corporation by reason of section 943(e)(4)(B)(i), and

"(ii) rules similar to the rules of clauses (ii), (iii), and (iv) of section 953(d)(4)(B) shall apply with respect to such earnings and profits.

The preceding sentence shall not apply to earnings and profits acquired in a transaction after September 30, 2000, to which section 381 applies unless the distributor or transferor corporation was immediately before the transaction a foreign corporation to which this paragraph applies.

"(B) Existing FSCs. This paragraph shall apply to any controlled foreign corporation (as defined in section 957) if —

"(i) such corporation is a FSC (as so defined) in existence on September 30, 2000,

"(ii) such corporation is eligible to make the election under section 943(e) by reason of being described in paragraph (2)(B) of such section, and

"(iii) such corporation makes such election not later than for its first taxable year beginning after December 31, 2001.

"(C) Other corporations. This paragraph shall apply to any controlled foreign corporation (as defined in section 957), and such corporation shall (notwithstanding any provision of section 943(e)) be treated as an applicable foreign corporation for purposes of section 943(e), if —

"(i) such corporation is in existence on September 30, 2000;

"(ii) as of such date, such corporation is wholly owned (directly or indirectly) by a domestic corporation (determined without regard to any election under section 943(e));

"(iii) for each of the 3 taxable years preceding the first taxable year to which the election under section 943(e) by such controlled foreign corporation applies —

"(I) all of the gross income of such corporation is subpart F income (as defined in section 952), including by reason of section 954(b)(3)(B); and

"(II) in the ordinary course of such corporation's trade or business, such corporation regularly sold (or paid commissions) to a FSC which on September 30, 2000, was a related person to such corporation;

"(iv) such corporation has never made an election under section 922(a)(2) (as in effect before the date of the enactment of this paragraph) to be treated as a FSC; and

"(v) such corporation makes the election under section 943(e) not later than for its first taxable year beginning after December 31, 2001.

The preceding sentence shall cease to apply as of the date that the domestic corporation referred to in clause (ii) ceases to wholly own (directly or indirectly) such controlled foreign corporation.

"(4) Related person. For purposes of this subsection, the term 'related person' has the meaning given to such term by section 943(b)(3).

"(5) Section references. Except as otherwise expressly provided, any reference in this subsection to a section or other provision shall be considered to be a reference to a section or other provision of the Internal Revenue Code of 1986, as amended by this Act.

"(d) Special rules relating to leasing transactions.

"(1) Sales income. If foreign trade income in connection with the lease or rental of property described in section 927(a)(1)(B) of such Code (as in effect before the amendments made by this Act) is treated as exempt foreign trade income for purposes of section 921(a) of such Code (as so in effect), such property shall be treated as property described in section 941(c)(1)(B) of such Code (as added by this Act) for purposes of applying section 941(c)(2) of such Code (as so added) to any subsequent transaction involving such property to which the amendments made by this Act apply.

"(2) Limitation on use of gross receipts method. If any person computed its foreign trade income from any transaction with respect to any property on the basis of a transfer price determined under the method described in section 925(a)(1) of such Code (as in effect before the amendments made by this Act), then the qualifying foreign trade income (as defined in section 941(a) of such Code, as in effect after such amendment) of such person (or any related person) with respect to any other transaction involving such property (and to which the amendments made by this Act apply) shall be zero."

Prior to repeal, Code Sec. 926 read as follows:

"SEC. 926. DISTRIBUTIONS TO SHAREHOLDERS.

"(a) Distributions made first out of foreign trade income. For purposes of this title, any distribution to a shareholder of a FSC by such FSC which is made out of earnings and profits shall be treated as made—

"(1) first, out of earnings and profits attributable to foreign trade income, to the extent thereof, and

"(2) then, out of any other earnings and profits.

"(b) Distributions by FSC to nonresident aliens and foreign corporations treated as United States connected. For purposes of this title, any distribution by a FSC which is made out of earnings and profits attributable to foreign trade income to any shareholder of such corporation which is a foreign corporation or a nonresident alien individual shall be treated as a distribution—

"(1) which is effectively connected with the conduct of a trade or business conducted through a permanent establishment of such shareholder within the United States, and

"(2) of income which is derived from sources within the United States.

"(c) FSC includes former FSC. For purposes of this section, the term 'FSC' includes a former FSC."

In 1984, P.L. 98-369, Sec. 801(a), added Code Sec. 926, effective for transactions after 12/31/84, in tax. yrs. end. after 12/31/84.

Sec. 927. Repealed.

In 2000, P.L. 106-519, Sec. 2, repealed Code Sec. 927, effective for transactions after 9/30/2000. Sec. 5(b)–(d) of this Act, provides:

"(b) No new FSCs; termination of inactive FSCs—

"(1) No new FSCs. No corporation may elect after September 30, 2000, to be a FSC (as defined in section 922 of the Internal Revenue Code of 1986, as in effect before the amendments made by this Act).

"(2) Termination of inactive FSCs. If a FSC has no foreign trade income (as defined in section 923(b) of such Code, as so in effect) for any period of 5 consecutive taxable years beginning after December 31, 2001, such FSC shall cease to be treated as a FSC for purposes of such Code for any taxable year beginning after such period.

"(c) Transition period for existing Foreign Sales Corporations.

"(1) In general. In the case of a FSC (as so defined) in existence on September 30, 2000, and at all times thereafter, the amendments made by this Act shall not apply to any transaction in the ordinary course of trade or business involving a FSC which occurs—

"(A) before January 1, 2002; or

"(B) after December 31, 2001, pursuant to a binding contract—

"(i) which is between the FSC (or any related person) and any person which is not a related person; and

"(ii) which is in effect on September 30, 2000, and at all times thereafter.

For purposes of this paragraph, a binding contract shall include a purchase option, renewal option, or replacement option which is included in such contract and which is enforceable against the seller or lessor.

"(2) Election to have amendments apply earlier. A taxpayer may elect to have the amendments made by this Act apply to any transaction by a FSC or any related person to which such amendments would apply but for the application of paragraph (1). Such election shall be effective for the taxable year for which made and all subsequent taxable years, and, once made, may be revoked only with the consent of the Secretary of the Treasury.

"(3) Exception for old earnings and profits of certain corporations.

"(A) In general. In the case of a foreign corporation to which this paragraph applies—

"(i) earnings and profits of such corporation accumulated in taxable years ending before October 1, 2000, shall not be included in the gross income of the persons holding stock in such corporation by reason of section 943(e)(4)(B)(i), and

"(ii) rules similar to the rules of clauses (ii), (iii), and (iv) of section 953(d)(4)(B) shall apply with respect to such earnings and profits.

The preceding sentence shall not apply to earnings and profits acquired in a transaction after September 30, 2000, to which section 381 applies unless the distributor or transferor corporation was immediately before the transaction a foreign corporation to which this paragraph applies.

"(B) Existing FSCs. This paragraph shall apply to any controlled foreign corporation (as defined in section 957) if—

"(i) such corporation is a FSC (as so defined) in existence on September 30, 2000,

"(ii) such corporation is eligible to make the election under section 943(e) by reason of being described in paragraph (2)(B) of such section, and

"(iii) such corporation makes such election not later than for its first taxable year beginning after December 31, 2001.

"(C) Other corporations. This paragraph shall apply to any controlled foreign corporation (as defined in section 957), and such corporation shall (notwithstanding any provision of section 943(e)) be treated as an applicable foreign corporation for purposes of section 943(e), if—

"(i) such corporation is in existence on September 30, 2000;

"(ii) as of such date, such corporation is wholly owned (directly or indirectly) by a domestic corporation (determined without regard to any election under section 943(e));

"(iii) for each of the 3 taxable years preceding the first taxable year to which the election under section 943(e) by such controlled foreign corporation applies—

"(I) all of the gross income of such corporation is subpart F income (as defined in section 952), including by reason of section 954(b)(3)(B); and

"(II) in the ordinary course of such corporation's trade or business, such corporation regularly sold (or paid commissions) to a FSC which on September 30, 2000, was a related person to such corporation;

"(iv) such corporation has never made an election under section 922(a)(2) (as in effect before the date of the enactment of this paragraph) to be treated as a FSC; and

"(v) such corporation makes the election under section 943(e) not later than for its first taxable year beginning after December 31, 2001.

The preceding sentence shall cease to apply as of the date that the domestic corporation referred to in clause (ii) ceases to wholly own (directly or indirectly) such controlled foreign corporation.

"(4) Related person. For purposes of this subsection, the term 'related person' has the meaning given to such term by section 943(b)(3).

"(5) Section references. Except as otherwise expressly provided, any reference in this subsection to a section or other provision shall be considered to be a reference to a section or other provision of the Internal Revenue Code of 1986, as amended by this Act.

"(d) Special rules relating to leasing transactions.

"(1) Sales income. If foreign trade income in connection with the lease or rental of property described in section 927(a)(1)(B) of such Code (as in effect before the amendments made by this Act) is treated as exempt foreign trade income for purposes of section 921(a) of such Code (as so in effect), such property shall be treated as property described in section 941(c)(1)(B) of such Code (as added by this Act) for purposes of applying section 941(c)(2) of such Code (as so added) to any subsequent transaction involving such property to which the amendments made by this Act apply.

"(2) Limitation on use of gross receipts method. If any person computed its foreign trade income from any transaction with respect to any property on the basis of a transfer price determined under the method described in section 925(a)(1) of such Code (as in effect before the amendments made by this Act), then the qualifying foreign trade income (as defined in section 941(a) of such Code, as in effect after such amendment) of such person (or any related person) with respect to any other transaction involving such property (and to which the amendments made by this Act apply) shall be zero."

Prior to repeal, Code Sec. 927 read as follows:

"SEC. 927. OTHER DEFINITIONS AND SPECIAL RULES.

"(a) Export property. For purposes of this subpart—

"(1) In general. The term 'export property' means property

"(A) manufactured, produced, grown, or extracted in the United States by a person other than a FSC,

"(B) held primarily for sale, lease, or rental, in the ordinary course of trade or business, by, or to, a FSC, for direct use, consumption, or disposition outside the United States, and

"(C) not more than 50 percent of the fair market value of which is attributable to articles imported into the United States.

For purposes of subparagraph (C), the fair market value of any article imported into the United States shall be its appraised value, as determined by the Secretary under section 402 of the Tariff Act of 1930 (19 U.S.C. 1401a) in connection with its importation.

"(2) Excluded property. The term 'export property' shall not include—

"(A) property leased or rented by a FSC for use by any member of a controlled group of corporations of which such FSC is a member,

"(B) patents, inventions, models, designs, formulas, or processes whether or not patented, copyrights (other than films, tapes, records, or similar reproductions, and other than computer software (whether or not patented), for commercial or home use), good will, trademarks, trade brands, franchises, or other like property,

"(C) oil or gas (or any primary product thereof),

"(D) products the export of which is prohibited or curtailed to effectuate the policy set forth in paragraph (2)(C) of section 3 of the Export Administration Act of 1979 (relating to the protection of the domestic economy), or

"(E) any unprocessed timber which is a softwood.

For purposes of subparagraph (E), the term 'unprocessed timber' means any log, cant, or similar form of timber.

"(3) Property in short supply. If the President determines that the supply of any property described in paragraph (1) is insufficient to meet the requirements of the domestic economy, he may by Executive order designate the property as in short supply. Any property so designated shall not be treated as export property during

Income from foreign sources Code Sec. 927

the period beginning with the date specified in the Executive order and ending with the date specified in an Executive order setting forth the President's determination that the property is no longer in short supply.

"(4) Qualified cooperative. The term 'qualified cooperative' means any organization to which part I of subchapter T applies which is engaged in the marketing of agricultural or horticultural products.

"(b) Gross receipts.

"(1) In general. For purposes of this subpart, the term 'gross receipts' means —

"(A) the total receipts from the sale, lease, or rental of property held primarily for sale, lease, or rental in the ordinary course of trade or business, and

"(B) gross income from all other sources.

"(2) Gross receipts taken into account in case of commissions. In the case of commissions on the sale, lease, or rental of property, the amount taken into account for purposes of this subpart as gross receipts shall be the gross receipts on the sale, lease, or rental of the property on which such commissions arose.

"(c) Investment income. For purposes of this subpart, the term 'investment income' means —

"(1) dividends,

"(2) interest,

"(3) royalties,

"(4) annuities,

"(5) rents (other than rents from the lease or rental of export property for use by the lessee outside of the United States),

"(6) gains from the sale or exchange of stock or securities,

"(7) gains from futures transactions in any commodity on, or subject to the rules of, a board of trade or commodity exchange (other than gains which arise out of a bona fide hedging transaction reasonably necessary to conduct the business of the FSC in the manner in which such business is customarily conducted by others),

"(8) amounts includible in computing the taxable income of the corporation under part I of subchapter J, and

"(9) gains from the sale or other disposition of any interest in an estate or trust.

"(d) Other definitions. For purposes of this subpart —

"(1) Carrying charges. The term 'carrying charges' means —

"(A) carrying charges, and

"(B) under regulations prescribed by the Secretary, any amount in excess of the price for an immediate cash sale and any other unstated interest.

"(2) Transaction.

"(A) In general. The term 'transaction' means —

"(i) any sale, exchange, or other disposition,

"(ii) any lease or rental, and

"(iii) any furnishing of services.

"(B) Grouping of transactions. To the extent provided in regulations, any provision of this subpart which, but for this subparagraph, would be applied on a transaction-by-transaction basis may be applied by the taxpayer on the basis of groups of transactions based on product lines or recognized industry or trade usage. Such regulations may permit different groupings for different purposes.

"(3) United States defined. The term 'United States' includes the Commonwealth of Puerto Rico.

"(4) Controlled group of corporations. The term 'controlled group of corporations' has the meaning given to such term by section 1563(a), except that —

"(A) 'more than 50 percent' shall be substituted for 'at least 80 percent' each place it appears therein, and

"(B) section 1563(b) shall not apply.

"(5) Possessions. The term 'possession of the United States' means Guam, American Samoa, the Commonwealth of the Northern Mariana Islands, and the Virgin Islands of the United States.

"(6) Section 923(A)(2) non-exempt income. The term 'section 923(a)(2) non-exempt income' means any foreign trade income from a transaction with respect to which paragraph (1) or (2) of section 925(a) does not apply and which is not exempt foreign trade income. Such term shall not include any income which is effectively connected with the conduct of a trade or business within the United States (determined without regard to this subpart).

"(e) Special rules.

"(1) Source rules for related persons. Under regulations, the income of a person described in section 482 from a transaction giving rise to foreign trading gross receipts of a FSC which is treated as from sources outside the United States shall not exceed the amount which would be treated as foreign source income earned by such person if the pricing rule under section 994 which corresponds to the rule used under section 925 with respect to such transaction applied to such transaction.

"(2) Participation in international boycotts, etc. Under regulations prescribed by the Secretary, the exempt foreign trade income of a FSC for any taxable year shall be limited under rules similar to the rules of clauses (ii) and (iii) of section 995(b)(1)(F).

"(3) Exchange of information requirements. For purposes of this title, the term 'FSC' shall not include any corporation which was created or organized under the laws of any foreign country unless there is in effect between such country and the United States —

"(A) a bilateral or multilateral agreement described in section 274(h)(6)(C) (determined by treating any reference to a beneficiary country as being a reference to any foreign country and by applying such section without regard to clause (ii) thereof), or

"(B) an income tax treaty which contains an exchange of information program —

"(i) which the Secretary certifies (and has not revoked such certification) is satisfactory in practice for purposes of this title, and

"(ii) to which the FSC is subject.

"(4) Disallowance of treaty benefits. Any corporation electing to be treated as a FSC under subsection (f)(1) may not claim any benefits under any income tax treaty between the United States and any foreign country.

"(5) Coordination with possessions taxation.

"(A) Exemption. No tax shall be imposed by any possession of the United States on any foreign trade income derived before January 1, 1987. The preceding sentence shall not apply to any income attributable to the sale of property or the performance of services for ultimate use, consumption, or disposition within the possession.

"(B) Clarification that possession may exempt certain income from tax. Nothing in any provision of law shall be construed as prohibiting any possession of the United States from exempting from tax any foreign trade income of a FSC or any other income of a FSC described in paragraph (2) or (3) of section 921(d).

"(C) No cover over of taxes imposed on FSC. Nothing in any provision of law shall be construed as requiring any tax imposed by this title on a FSC to be covered over (or otherwise transferred) to any possession of the United States.

"(f) Election of status as FSC (and as small FSC).

"(1) Election.

"(A) Time for making. An election by a corporation under section 922(a)(2) to be treated as a FSC, and an election under section 922(b)(1) to be a small FSC, shall be made by such corporation for a taxable year at some time during the 90-day period immediately preceding the beginning of the taxable year, except that the Secretary may give his consent to the making of an election at such other times as he may designate.

"(B) Manner of election. An election under subparagraph (A) shall be made in such manner as the Secretary shall prescribe and shall be valid only if all persons who are shareholders in such corporation on the first day of the first taxable year for which such election is effective consent to such election.

"(2) Effect of election. If a corporation makes an election under paragraph (1), then the provisions of this subpart shall apply to such corporation for the taxable year of the corporation for which made and for all succeeding taxable years.

"(3) Termination of election.

"(A) Revocation. An election under this subsection made by any corporation may be terminated by revocation of such election for any taxable year of the corporation after the first taxable year of the corporation for which the election is effective. A termination under this paragraph shall be effective with respect to such election —

"(i) for the taxable year in which made, if made at any time during the first 90 days of such taxable year, or

"(ii) for the taxable year following the taxable year in which made, if made after the close of such 90 days, and for all succeeding taxable years of the corporation. Such termination shall be made in such manner as the Secretary shall prescribe by regulations.

"(B) Continued failure to be a FSC. If a corporation is not a FSC for each of any 5 consecutive taxable years of the corporation for which an election under this subsection is effective, the election to be a FSC shall be terminated and not be in effect for any taxable year of the corporation after such 5th year.

"(g) Treatment of shared FSC's.

"(1) In general. Except as provided in paragraph (2) , each separate account referred to in paragraph (3) maintained by a shared FSC shall be treated as a separate corporation for purposes of this subpart.

"(2) Certain requirements applied at shared FSC level. Paragraph (1) shall not apply —

"(A) for purposes of

"(i) subparagraphs (A), (B), (D), and (E) of section 922(a)(1),

"(ii) paragraph (2) of section 922(a),

"(iii) subsections (b), (c), and (e) of section 924, and

"(iv) subsection (f) of this section, and

"(B) for such other purposes as the Secretary may by regulations prescribe.

"(3) Shared FSC. For purposes of this subsection , the term 'shared FSC' means any corporation if —

"(A) such corporation maintains a separate account for transactions with each shareholder (and persons related to such shareholder),

"(B) distributions to each shareholder are based on the amounts in the separate account maintained with respect to such shareholder, and

"(C) such corporation meets such other requirements as the Secretary may by regulations prescribe."

In 1997, P.L. 105-34, Sec. 1171(a), added ", and other than computer software (whether or not patented)" before ", for commercial or home use" in subpara. (a)(2)(B), effective for gross receipts attributable to periods after 12/31/97, in tax. yrs. end. 12/31/97.

In 1993, P.L. 103-66, Sec. 13239(a), deleted "or" at the end of subpara. (a)(2)(C), substituted ", or" for the period at the end of subpara. (a)(2)(D), added subpara. (a)(2)(E), and the flush sentence at the end of para. (a)(2), effective for sales, exchanges, or other dispositions after 8/10/93.

In 1990, P.L. 101-508, Sec. 11704(a)(10), substituted "prescribe" for "prescribed", in subpara. (g)(2)(B), effective 11/5/90.

In 1988, P.L. 100-647, Sec. 1012(bb)(8)(A), added subsec. (g), effective for transactions after 12/31/84, in tax. yrs. end. after 12/31/84.

In 1986, P.L. 99-514, Sec. 1876(a)(1), added the last sentence to para. (d)(6) . . . Sec. 1876(e)(1)(A), substituted "unless there is" for "unless, at the same time such corporation was created or organized, there was" in para. (e)(3) . . . Sec. 1876(e)(1)(B), amended subpara. (e)(3)(A) . . . Sec. 1876(e)(1)(C), amended subpara. (e)(3)(B) . . . Sec. 1876(f)(1), amended para. (e)(3) . . . Sec. 1876(p)(5), substituted "clauses (ii) and (iii)" for "clauses (i) and (ii)" in para. (e)(2), effective for transactions after 12/31/84, in tax. yrs. end. after 12/31/84.

2,593

Prior to amendment, subpara. (e)(3)(A) read as follows:
"(A) a bilateral or multilateral agreement described in section 274(h)(6)(C), or"
Prior to amendment, subpara. (e)(3)(B) read as follows:
"(B) an income tax treaty with respect to which the Secretary certifies that the exchange of information program with such country under such treaty carries out the purposes of this paragraph."
Prior to amendment, para. (e)(5) read as follows:
"(5) Exemption from certain other taxes. No tax shall be imposed by any jurisdiction described in subsection (d)(5) on any foreign trade income derived before January 1, 1987."
In **1984**, P.L. 98-369, Sec. 801(a), added Code Sec. 927, effective for transactions after 12/31/84, in tax. yrs. end. after 12/31/84.

SUBPART D.—POSSESSIONS OF THE UNITED STATES
Sec.
931. Income from sources within Guam, American Samoa, or the Northern Mariana Islands.
932. Coordination of United States and Virgin Islands income taxes.
933. Income from sources within Puerto Rico.
934. Limitation on reduction in income tax liability incurred to the Virgin Islands.
936. Puerto Rico and possession tax credit.
937. Residence and source rules involving possessions.

In **2004**, P.L. 108-357, Sec. 908(c)(6), added item 937.
In **1986**, P.L. 99-514, Sec. 1272(d)(12), amended item 931 . . . Sec. 1272(d)(12), deleted item 932 . . . Sec. 1274(d), added item 932 . . . Sec. 1275(c)(8), deleted item 934A . . . Sec. 1272(d)(12), deleted item 935.
Prior to amendment, items 931, 932, 934A and 935 read as follows:
"931. Income from sources within posessions of the United States."
"932. Citizens of possessions of the United States."
"934A. Income tax rate on Virgin Islands source income."
"935. Coordination of United States and Guam individual income taxes."
In **1983**, P.L. 97-455, Sec. 1(d)(1), added item. 934A.
In **1976**, P.L. 94-455, Sec. 1051(b), added Code Sec. 936, but did not add a provision to add the heading to the above table. Congress apparently meant to do so; the heading has been added thusly above.
In **1972**, P.L. 92-606, Sec. 1(f)(5), added item 935.
In **1960**, added item 934.

Sec. 931. Income from sources within Guam, American Samoa, or the Northern Mariana Islands.

(a) General rule.

In the case of an individual who is a bona fide resident of a specified possession during the entire taxable year, gross income shall not include—

(1) income derived from sources within any specified possession, and

(2) income effectively connected with the conduct of a trade or business by such individual within any specified possession.

(b) Deductions, etc. allocable to excluded amounts not allowable.

An individual shall not be allowed—

(1) as a deduction from gross income any deductions (other than the deduction under section 151, relating to personal exemptions), or

(2) any credit,

properly allocable or chargeable against amounts excluded from gross income under this section.

(c) Specified possession.

For purposes of this section, the term "specified possession" means Guam, American Samoa, and the Northern Mariana Islands.

(d) Employees of the United States.

Amounts paid for services performed as an employee of the United States (or any agency thereof) shall be treated as not described in paragraph (1) or (2) of subsection (a).

In **2004**, P.L. 108-357, Sec. 908(c)(1), amended subsec. (d), effective for tax. yrs. end. after 10/22/2004.
Prior to amendment, subsec. (d) read as follows:
"(d) Special rules. For purposes of this section —
"(1) Employees of the United States. Amounts paid for services performed as an employee of the United States (or any agency thereof) shall be treated as not described in paragraph (1) or (2) of subsection (a).
"(2) Determination of source, etc. The determination as to whether income is described in paragraph (1) or (2) of subsection (a) shall be made under regulations prescribed by the Secretary.
"(3) Determination of residency. For purposes of this section and section 876, the determination of whether an individual is a bona fide resident of Guam, American Samoa, or the Northern Mariana Islands shall be made under regulations prescribed by the Secretary.
In **1988**, P.L. 100-647, Sec. 1012(z)(1), amended Sec. 1277 of P.L. 99-514 by adding Sec. 1277(f) of P.L. 99-514 [reproduced below] . . . Sec. 1012(z)(2), substituted "Not withstanding subsection (b), the preceding sentence" for "The preceding sentence" in Sec. 1277(e) of P.L. 99-514, reproduced below . . . Sec. 6140, of this Act provides:
"SEC. 6140. TREATMENT OF CERTAIN AWARDS BY THE DISTRICT COURT OF GUAM.
"For purposes of the internal revenue laws of the United States and Guam, gross income shall not include any amount received pursuant to any claim over which the District Court of Guam has jurisdiction by reason of Sec. 204 of P.L. 95-134 (commonly referred to as the Omnibus Territories Act of 1977). This section shall be effective for taxable years beginning December 31, 1985."
In **1986**, P.L. 99-514, Sec. 1272(a), amended Code Sec. 931, effective for tax. yrs. begin. after 12/31/86. Secs. 1277(b), (d), (e) and (f) [as amended by P.L. 100-647, Secs. 1012(z)(1) and (2), see above] provides the following special rule:
"(b) Special rule for Guam, American Samoa, and the Northern Mariana Islands. The amendments made by this subtitle shall apply with respect to Guam, American Samoa, or the Northern Mariana Islands (and to residents thereof and corporations created or organized therein) only if (and so long as) an implementing agreement under section 1271 [Sec. 1271 of P.L. 99-514, reproduced below] is in effect between the United States and such possession."
"(d) Report on implementing agreements. If during the 1-year period beginning on the date of the enactment of this Act, [11/10/88] any implementing agreement described in subsection (b) or (c) is not executed, the Secretary of the Treasury or his delegate shall report to the Committee on Finance of the United States Senate, the Committee on Ways and Means, and the Committee on Interior and Insular Affairs of the House of Representatives with respect to—
"(1) the status of such negotiations, and
"(2) the reason why such agreement has not been executed."
"(e) Treatment of certain United States persons. Except as otherwise provided in regulations prescribed by the Secretary of the Treasury or his delegate, if a United States person becomes a resident of Guam, American Samoa, or the Northern Mariana Islands, the rules of section 877(c) of the Internal Revenue Code of 1954 shall apply to such person during the 10-year period beginning when such person became such a resident. Notwithstanding subsection (b), the preceding sentence shall apply to dispositions after December 31, 1985, in taxable years ending after such date.
"(f) Exemption from withholding. Notwithstanding subsection (b), the modification of section 884 of the Internal Revenue Code of 1986 by reason of the amendment to section 881 of such Code by section 1273(b)(1) of this Act shall apply to taxable years beginning after December 31, 1986."
Sec. 1271 of this Act provides:
"SEC. 1271. AUTHORITY OF GUAM, AMERICAN SAMOA, AND THE NORTHERN MARIANA ISLANDS TO ENACT REVENUE LAWS.
"(a) In general. Except as provided in subsection (b), nothing in the laws of the United States shall prevent Guam, American Samoa, or the Northern Mariana Islands from enacting tax laws (which shall apply in lieu of the mirror system) with respect to income—
"(1) from sources within, or effectively connected with the conduct of a trade or business within, any such possession, or
"(2) received or accrued by any resident of such possession.
"(b) Agreements to alleviate certain problems relating to tax administration. Subsection (a) shall apply to Guam, American Samoa, or the Northern Mariana Islands only if (and so long as) an implementing agreement is in effect between the United States and such possession with respect to—
"(1) the elimination of double taxation involving taxation by such possession and taxation by the United States,
"(2) the establishment of rules under which the evasion or avoidance of United States income tax shall not be permitted or facilitated by such possession,
"(3) the exchange of information between such possession and the United States for purposes of tax administration, and
"(4) the resolution of other problems arising in connection with the administration of the tax laws of such possession or the United States.
Any such implementing agreement shall be executed on behalf of the United States by the Secretary of the Treasury after consultation with the Secretary of the Interior.
"(c) Revenues not to decrease. The total amount of the revenue received by any possession referred to in subsection (a) pursuant to its tax laws during the implementation year and each of the 4 fiscal years thereafter shall not be less than the revenue (adjusted for inflation) which was received by such possession pursuant to tax laws for its last fiscal year before the implementation year.

"(d) Nondiscriminatory treatment required. Nothing in any tax law of a possession referred to in subsection (a) may discriminate against any United States person or any resident (corporate or otherwise) of any other possession.

"(e) Enforcement.

"(1) In general. If the Secretary of the Treasury (after consultation with the Secretary of the Interior) determines that any possession has failed to comply with subsection (c) or (d), the Secretary of the Treasury shall so notify the Governor of such possession in writing. If such possession does not comply with subsection (c) or (d) (as the case may be) within 90 days of such notification, the Secretary of the Treasury shall notify the Congress of such noncompliance. Unless the Congress by law provides otherwise, the mirror system of taxation shall be reinstated in such possession and shall be in full force and effect for taxable years beginning after such notification to the Congress.

"(2) Special rule for revenue requirements. If the failure to comply with subsection (c) is for good cause and does not jeopardize the fiscal integrity of the possession, the Secretary may waive the requirements of subsection (c) for such period as he determines appropriate.

"(f) Definitions and special rules.

"(1) Implementation year. For purposes of this section, the term 'implementation year' means the 1st fiscal year of the possession in which the tax laws authorized by subsection (a) take effect.

"(2) Mirror system. For purposes of this section, the mirror system of taxation consists of the provisions of law (in effect on the day before the date of the enactment of this Act) which make the provisions of the income tax laws of the United States (as in effect from time to time) in effect in a possession of the United States.

"(3) Special rule for Northern Mariana Islands. Notwithstanding the provisions of the last clause of Sec. 601(a) of P.L. 94-241, the Commonwealth of the Northern Mariana Islands may elect to continue its mirror system of taxation without regard to whether Guam enacts tax laws under the authority provided in subsection (a)."

Prior to amendment, Code Sec. 931 read as follows:

"SEC. 931. INCOME FROM SOURCES WITHIN POSSESSIONS OF THE UNITED STATES.

"(a) General rule. In the case of individual citizens of the United States, gross income means only gross income from sources within the United States if the conditions of both paragraph (1) and paragraph (2) are satisfied:

"(1) 3-year period. If 80 percent or more of the gross income of such citizen (computed without the benefit of this section) for the 3-year period immediately preceding the close of the taxable year (or for such part of such period immediately preceding the close of such taxable year as may be applicable) was derived from sources within a possession of the United States; and

"(2) Trade or business. If 50 percent or more of his gross income (computed without the benefit of this section) for such period or such part thereof was derived from the active conduct of a trade or business within a possession of the United States either on his own account or as an employee or agent of another.

"(b) Amounts received in United States. Notwithstanding subsection (a), there shall be included in gross income all amounts received by such citizens or corporations within the United States, whether derived from sources within or without the United States.

"(c) Definition. For purposes of this section, the term 'possession of the United States' does not include the Commonwealth of Puerto Rico, the Virgin Islands of the United States, or Guam.

"(d) Deductions.

"(1) General rule. Except as otherwise provided in this subsection and subsection (e), in the case of a citizen of the United States entitled to the benefits of this section the deductions shall be allowed only if and to the extent that they are connected with income from sources within the United States; and the proper apportionment and allocation of the deductions with respect to sources of income within and without the United States shall be determined as provided in part I, under regulations prescribed by the Secretary.

"(2) Exceptions. The following deductions shall be allowed whether or not they are connected with income from sources within the United States:

"(A) The deduction, for losses not connected with the trade or business if incurred in transactions entered into for profit, allowed by section 165(c)(2), but only if the profit, if such transaction had resulted in a profit, would be taxable under this subtitle.

"(B) The deduction for losses allowed by section 165(c)(3), but only if the loss is of property within the United States.

"(C) The deduction for charitable contributions and gifts allowed by section 170.

"(e) Deduction for personal exemption. A citizen of the United States entitled to the benefits of this section shall be allowed a deduction for only one exemption under section 151.

"(f) Allowance of deductions and credits. A citizen of the United States entitled to the benefits of this section shall receive the benefit of the deductions and credits allowed to them in this subtitle only by filing or causing to be filed with the Secretary a true and accurate return of their total income received from all sources in the United States, in the manner prescribed in subtitle F, including therein all the information which the Secretary may deem necessary for the calculation of such deductions and credits.

"(g) Foreign tax credit. Persons entitled to the benefits of this section shall not be allowed the credits against the tax for taxes of foreign countries and possessions of the United States allowed by section 901.

"(h) Employees of the United States. For purposes of this section, amounts paid for services performed by a citizen of the United States as an employee of the United States or any agency thereof shall be deemed to be derived from sources within the United States."

In **1984,** P.L. 98-369, Sec. 711(c)(2)(A)(iv), substituted "for losses" for ", for losses of property not connected with the trade or business if arising from certain casualties or theft," in subpara. (d)(2)(B), effective for tax. yrs. begin. after 12/31/83.

In **1977,** P.L. 95-30, Sec. 101(d)(12), deleted para. (d)(3), effective for tax. yrs. begin. after 12/31/76.

Prior to amendment, para. (d)(3) read as follows:

"(3) Deduction disallowed. For disallowance of standard deduction, see section 142(b)(2)."

In **1976,** P.L. 94-455, Sec. 1051(c)(1), amended subsec. (a), effective for tax. yrs. begin. after 12/31/75.

Prior to amendment, subsec. (a) read as follows:

"(a) General rule. In the case of citizens of the United States or domestic corporations, gross income means only gross income from sources within the United States if the conditions of both paragraph (1) and paragraph (2) are satisfied:

"(1) Three-year period. If 80 percent or more of the gross income of such citizen or domestic corporation (computed without the benefit of this section) for the 3-year period immediately preceding the close of the taxable year (or for such part of such period immediately preceding the close of such taxable year as may be applicable) was derived from sources within a possession of the United States; and

"(2) Trade or business. If—

"(A) in the case of such corporation, 50 percent or more of its gross income (computed without the benefit of this section) for such period or such part thereof was derived from the active conduct of a trade or business within a possession of the United States; or

"(B) in the case of such citizen, 50 percent or more of his gross income (computed without the benefit of this section) for such period or such part thereof was derived from the active conduct of a trade or business within a possession of the United States either on his own account or as an employee or agent of another. This section shall not apply in the case of a corporation for a taxable year for which it is a DISC or in which it owns at any time stock in a DISC or former DISC (as defined in section 992(a))."

—P.L. 94-455, Sec. 1051(c)(2), amended subsec. (c), effective for tax. yrs. begin. after 12/31/75.

Prior to amendment, subsec. (c) read as follows:

"(c) Definition. For the purposes of this section, the term 'possession of the United States' does not include the Virgin Islands of the United States, and such term when used with respect to citizens of the United States does not include Puerto Rico or Guam."

—P.L. 94-455, Sec. 1051(c)(3), substituted "a citizen of the United States" for "persons" in para. (d)(1) and subsec. (f), effective for tax. yrs. begin. after 12/31/75.

—P.L. 94-455, Sec. 1901(a)(117), deleted subsec. (h) and redesignated subsec. (i) as subsec. (h), effective for tax. yrs. begin. after 12/31/76.

Prior to amendment, subsec. (h) read as follows:

"(h) Internees. In the case of a citizen of the United States interned by the enemy while serving as an employee within a possession of the United States—

"(1) if such citizen was confined in any place not within a possession of the United States, such place of confinement shall, for purposes of this section, be considered as within a possession of the United States; and

"(2) subsection (b) shall not apply to any compensation received within the United States by such citizen attributable to the period of time during which such citizen was interned by the enemy."

—P.L. 94-455, Sec. 1906(b)(13)(A), substituted "Secretary" for "Secretary or his delegate" each place it appeared in para. (d)(1) and subsec. (f), effective for tax. yrs. begin. after 12/31/76. (But Sec. 1908 of the Act makes this effective date to be for tax. yrs. begin. after '75.)

In **1972,** P.L. 92-606, Sec. 1(f)(i), added "or Guam" after "Puerto Rico" in subsec. (c), effective for tax. yrs. begin. after 12/31/72.

In **1971,** P.L. 92-178, Sec. 502(d), added a sentence to the end of subsec. (a), effective for tax. yrs. end. after 12/31/71, except that a corporation may not be a DISC for any tax. yr. begin. before 1/1/72.

In **1966,** P.L. 89-809, Sec. 107, amended subsec. (d) effective for tax. yrs. begin. after 12/31/66.

Prior to amendment, subsec. (d) read as follows:

"(d) Deductions.

"(1) Citizens of the United States entitled to the benefits of this section shall have the same deductions as are allowed by section 873 in the case of a nonresident alien individual engaged in trade or business within the United States.

"(2) Domestic corporations entitled to the benefits of this section shall have the same deductions as are allowed by section 882(c) in the case of a foreign corporation engaged in trade or business within the United States."

Sec. 932. Coordination of United States and Virgin Islands income taxes.

(a) Treatment of United States residents.

(1) Application of subsection. This subsection shall apply to an individual for the taxable year if—

(A) such individual—

(i) is a citizen or resident of the United States (other than a bona fide resident of the Virgin Islands during the entire taxable year, and

(ii) has income derived from sources within the Virgin Islands, or effectively connected with the conduct of a trade or business within such possession, for the taxable year, or

(B) such individual files a joint return for the taxable year with an individual described in subparagraph (A).

(2) Filing requirement. Each individual to whom this subsection applies for the taxable year shall file his income tax return for the taxable year with both the United States and the Virgin Islands.

(3) Extent of income tax liability. In the case of an individual to whom this subsection applies in a taxable year for purposes of so much of this title (other than this section and section 7654) as relates to the taxes imposed by this chapter, the United States shall be treated as including the Virgin Islands.

(b) Portion of United States tax liability payable to the Virgin Islands.

(1) In general. Each individual to whom subsection (a) applies for the taxable year shall pay the applicable percentage of the taxes imposed by this chapter for such taxable year (determined without regard to paragraph (3)) to the Virgin Islands.

(2) Applicable percentage.

(A) In general. For purposes of paragraph (1), the term "applicable percentage" means the percentage which Virgin Islands adjusted gross income bears to adjusted gross income.

(B) Virgin Islands adjusted gross income. For purposes of subparagraph (A), the term "Virgin Islands adjusted gross income" means adjusted gross income determined by taking into account only income derived from sources within the Virgin Islands and deductions properly apportioned or allocable thereto.

(3) Amounts paid allowed as credit. There shall be allowed as a credit against the tax imposed by this chapter for the taxable year an amount equal to the taxes required to be paid to the Virgin Islands under paragraph (1) which are so paid.

(c) Treatment of Virgin Islands residents.

(1) Application of subsection. This subsection shall apply to an individual for the taxable year if—

(A) such individual is a bona fide resident of the Virgin Islands during the entire taxable year, or

(B) such individual files a joint return for the taxable year with an individual described in subparagraph (A).

(2) Filing requirement. Each individual to whom this subsection applies for the taxable year shall file an income tax return for the taxable year with the Virgin Islands.

(3) Extent of income tax liability. In the case of an individual to whom this subsection applies in a taxable year for purposes of so much of this title (other than this section and section 7654) as relates to the taxes imposed by this chapter, the Virgin Islands shall be treated as including the United States.

(4) Residents of the Virgin Islands. In the case of an individual—

(A) who is a bona fide resident of the Virgin Islands during the entire taxable year,

(B) who, on his return of income tax to the Virgin Islands, reports income from all sources and identifies the source of each item shown on such return, and

(C) who fully pays his tax liability referred to in section 934(a) to the Virgin Islands with respect to such income,

for purposes of calculating income tax liability to the United States, gross income shall not include any amount included in gross income on such return, and allocable deductions and credits shall not be taken into account.

(d) Special rule for joint returns.

In the case of a joint return, this section shall be applied on the basis of the residence of the spouse who has the greater adjusted gross income (determined without regard to community property laws) for the taxable year.

(e) Special rule for applying section to tax imposed in Virgin Islands.

In applying this section for purposes of determining income tax liability incurred to the Virgin Islands, the provisions of this section shall not be affected by the provisions of Federal law referred to in section 934(a).

In 2004, P.L. 108-357, Sec. 908(c)(2), substituted "during the entire taxable year" for "at the close of the taxable year" each place it appeared in Code Sec. 932, effective for tax. yrs. end. after 10/22/2004.

In 1988, P.L. 100-647, Sec. 1012(w)(1), amended subsec. (e) . . . Sec. 1012(w)(2), amended para. (c)(4) . . . Sec. 1012(w)(3), substituted "an income tax return" for "his income tax return" in para. (c)(2), effective for tax. yrs. begin. after 12/31/86, except as provided in Secs. 1274(b) and (c) of P.L. 99-514 [as amended by this Act] reproduced below.

Prior to amendment subsec. (e) read as follows:

"(e) Section not to apply to tax imposed in Virgin Islands. This section shall not apply for purposes of determining income tax liability incurred to the Virgin Islands."

Prior to amendment para. (c)(4) read as follows:

"(4) Residents of the Virgin Islands. In the case of an individual who is a bona fide resident of the Virgin Islands at the close of the taxable year and who, on his return of income tax to the Virgin Islands, reports income from all sources and identifies the source of each item shown on such return, for purposes of calculating income tax liability to the United States gross income shall not include any amount included in gross income on such return."

—P.L. 100-647, Sec. 1012(w)(4), amended Sec. 1274(c) [reproduced below] of P.L. 99-514, part of the effective date for changes made by Sec. 1274(a) of P.L. 99-514, by substituting "the Internal Revenue Code of 1986" for "this title", see below.

In 1986, P.L. 99-514, Sec. 1272(d)(1), repealed Code Sec. 932, effective for tax. yrs. begin. after 12/31/86.

Prior to repeal, Code Sec. 932 read as follows:

"SEC. 932. CITIZENS OF POSSESSIONS OF THE UNITED STATES.

"(a) General rule. Any individual who is a citizen of any possession of the United States (but not otherwise a citizen of the United States) and who is not a resident of the United States shall be subject to taxation under this subtitle in the same manner and subject to the same conditions as in the case of a nonresident alien individual. This section shall have no application in the case of a citizen of Puerto Rico or Guam.

"(b) Virgin Islands. Nothing in this section shall be construed to alter or amend the Act entitled 'An Act making appropriations for the naval service for the fiscal year ending June 30, 1922, and for other purposes', approved July 12, 1921 (48 U.S.C. 1397), relating to the imposition of income taxes in the Virgin Islands of the United States.

"(c) Taxation of social security benefits. If, for purposes of an income tax imposed in the possession, any social security benefit (as defined in section 86(d)) received by an individual described in subsection (a) is treated in a manner equivalent to that provided by section 86, then—

"(1) such benefit shall be exempt from the tax imposed by section 871, and

"(2) no amount shall be deducted and withheld from such benefit under section 1441.

Any income tax imposed in a possession which treats social security benefits (as defined in section 86(d)) in a manner equivalent to section 86, and which first becomes effective within 15 months after the date of the enactment of this subsection, shall, for purposes of this section, be deemed to have been in effect as of January 1, 1984.

"(d) Guam. For provisions relating to the individual income tax in the case of Guam, see sections 935 and 7654; see also sections 30 and 31 of the Act of August 1, 1950 (48 U.S.C., secs. 1421h and 1421i)."

—P.L. 99-514, Sec. 1274(a), added Code Sec. 932 to Subpart D of part III of subchapter N, effective for tax. yrs. begin. after 12/31/86, except as provided in Sec. 1274(b) and (c) [as amended by Sec. 1012(w)(4) of P.L. 100-647] and Sec. 1277(b) of this Act which read:

"(b) Authority to impose nondiscriminatory local income taxes. Nothing in any provision of Federal law shall prevent the Virgin Islands from imposing on any person nondiscriminatory local income taxes. Any taxes so imposed shall be treated in the same manner as State and local income taxes under section 164 of the Internal Revenue Code of 1954 and shall not be treated as taxes to which section 901 of such Code applies."

Sec. 1274(c) [as amended by Sec. 1012(w)(4) of P.L. 100-647] of this Act provides:

"(c) Regulations on application of mirror system. The Secretary of the Treasury or his delegate shall prescribe such regulations as may be necessary or appropriate for applying the Internal Revenue Code of 1986, for purposes of determining tax liability incurred to the Virgin Islands."

Income from foreign sources   Code Sec. 934

Sec. 1277(b) of this Act, see note following Code Sec. 931.

—P.L. 99-272, Sec. 12103(a), redesignated subsec. (c) as subsec. (d) and added new subsec. (c), effective for benefits received after 12/31/83 in tax. yrs. end. after 12/31/83.

In **1972**, P.L. 92-606, Sec. 1(f)(2), added "or Guam" after "Puerto Rico" in the second sentence of subsec. (a), . . . Sec. 1(f)(3), amended subsec. (c), effective for tax. yrs. begin. after 12/31/72.

Prior to amendment subsec. (c) read as follows:

"*(c) Guam.* For applicability of United States income tax laws in Guam, see section 31 of the Act of August 1, 1950 (48 U.S.C. 1421i); for disposition of the proceeds of such taxes, see section 30 of such Act (48 U.S.C. 1421h)."

In **1966**, P.L. 89-809, Sec. 103, deleted "only as to income derived from sources within the United States, and in such case the tax shall be computed and paid" after "subtitle" and substituted "a nonresident alien individual for 'other persons who are taxable only as to income derived from such sources' in the first sentence of subsec. (a), effective for tax. yrs. begin. after 12/31/66."

Sec. 933. Income from sources within Puerto Rico.

The following items shall not be included in gross income and shall be exempt from taxation under this subtitle:

(1) Resident of Puerto Rico for entire taxable year. In the case of an individual who is a bona fide resident of Puerto Rico during the entire taxable year, income derived from sources within Puerto Rico (except amounts received for services performed as an employee of the United States or any agency thereof); but such individual shall not be allowed as a deduction from his gross income any deductions (other than the deduction under section 151, relating to personal exemptions), or any credit, properly allocable to or chargeable against amounts excluded from gross income under this paragraph.

(2) Taxable year of change of residence from Puerto Rico. In the case of an individual citizen of the United States who has been a bona fide resident of Puerto Rico for a period of at least 2 years before the date on which he changes his residence from Puerto Rico, income derived from sources therein (except amounts received for services performed as an employee of the United States or any agency thereof) which is attributable to that part of such period of Puerto Rican residence before such date; but such individual shall not be allowed as a deduction from his gross income any deductions (other than the deduction for personal exemptions under section 151), or any credit, properly allocable to or chargeable against amounts excluded from gross income under this paragraph.

In **1986**, P.L. 99-514, Sec. 1272(d)(3), added ", or any credit," after "relating to personal exemptions)" in para. (1) and after "section 151)" in para. (2), effective for tax. yrs. begin. after 12/31/86. For special rules, see Sec. 1277(b) and 1277(d)-(f) reproduced in note following Code Sec. 46.

Sec. 934. Limitation on reduction in income tax liability incurred to the Virgin Islands.

(a) General rule.

Tax liability incurred to the Virgin Islands pursuant to this subtitle, as made applicable in the Virgin Islands by the Act entitled "An Act making appropriations for the naval service for the fiscal year ending June 30, 1922, and for other purposes", approved July 12, 1921 (48 U.S.C. 1397), or pursuant to section 28(a) of the Revised Organic Act of the Virgin Islands, approved July 22, 1954 (48 U.S.C. 1642), shall not be reduced or remitted in any way, directly or indirectly, whether by grant, subsidy, or other similar payment, by any law enacted in the Virgin Islands, except to the extent provided in subsection (b).

(b) Reductions permitted with respect to certain income.

(1) In general. Except as provided in paragraph (2), subsection (a) shall not apply with respect to so much of the tax liability referred to in subsection (a) as is attributable to income derived from sources within the Virgin Islands or income effectively connected with the conduct of a trade or business within the Virgin Islands.

(2) Exception for liability paid by citizens or residents of the United States. Paragraph (1) shall not apply to any liability payable to the Virgin Islands under section 932(b).

(3) Special rule for non-United States income of certain foreign corporations.

(A) In general. In the case of a qualified foreign corporation, subsection (a) shall not apply with respect to so much of the tax liability referred to in subsection (a) as is attributable to income which is derived from sources outside the United States and which is not effectively connected with the conduct of a trade or business within the United States.

(B) Qualified foreign corporation. For purposes of subparagraph (A), the term "qualified foreign corporation" means any foreign corporation if less than 10 percent of—

(i) the total voting power of the stock of such corporation, and

(ii) the total value of the stock of such corporation,

is owned or treated as owned (within the meaning of section 958) by 1 or more United States persons.

(4) Determination of income source, etc. The determination as to whether income is derived from sources within the United States or is effectively connected with the conduct of a trade or business within the United States shall be made under regulations prescribed by the Secretary.

In **2004**, P.L. 108-357, Sec. 908(c)(3), deleted "the Virgin Islands or" each place it appeared in para. (b)(4), effective for tax. yrs. end. after 10/22/2004.

In **1988**, P.L. 100-647, Sec. 6252(b)(1), amended Sec. 441(a) of P.L. 98-369 [reproduced below], by substituting "shall, during 1988 and each fourth calendar year thereafter, submit a report to the Congress (using the most recent information available) setting forth" for "shall, for the calendar year 1981 and each second calendar year thereafter, submit a report to the Congress within 24 months following the close of such calendar year setting forth", effective for reports for calendar years after 1982.

In **1986**, P.L. 99-514, Sec. 1275(a)(2)(A), deleted subsecs. (e) and (f), effective for tax. yrs. begin. after 12/31/86.

Prior to deletion, subsecs. (e) and (f) read as follows:

"*(e) Tax treatment of intangible property income of certain domestic corporations.*

"(1) In general.

"(A) Income attributable to shareholder. The intangible property income (within the meaning of section 936(h)(3)) for any taxable year of any domestic corporation which is described in subsection (b) and which is an inhabitant of the Virgin Islands (within the meaning of section 28(a) of the Revised Organic Act of the Virgin Islands (48 U.S.C. 1642)), shall be included on a pro rata basis in the gross income of all shareholders of such corporation at the close o the taxable year of such corporation as income from sources within the United States for the taxable year of such shareholder in which or with which the taxable year of such corporation ends.

"(B) Exclusion from the income of the corporation. Any intangible property income of a corporation described in subparagraph (A) which is included in the gross income of a shareholder of such corporation by reason of subparagraph (A) shall be excluded from the gross income of such corporation.

"(2) Foreign shareholders; shareholders not subject to tax; inhabitants of the Virgin Islands.

"(A) In general. Paragraph (1)(A) shall not apply with respect to any shareholder—

"(i) who is not a United States person,

"(ii) who is not subject to tax under this title on intangible property income which would be allocated to such shareholder (but for this subparagraph), or

"(iii) who is an inhabitant of the Virgin Islands.

"(B) Treatment of nonallocated intangible property income. For purposes of this subtitle, intangible property income of a corporation described in paragraph (1)(A) which is not included in the gross income of a shareholder of such corporation by reason of subparagraph (A)—

"(i) shall be treated as income from sources within the United States, and

"(ii) shall not be taken into account for purposes of determining whether the conditions specified in paragraph (1) or (2) of subsection (b) are satisfied.

"(3) Distribution to meet qualification requirements—

"(A) In general. If the Secretary determines that a corporation does not satisfy a condition specified in paragraph (1) or (2) of subsection (b) for any taxable year by reason of the exclusion from gross income under paragraph (1)(B), such corporation shall nevertheless be treated as satisfying such condition for such year if it makes a pro rata distribution of property after the close of such taxable year to its

2,597

shareholders (designated at the time of such distribution as a distribution to meet qualification requirements) with respect to their stock in an amount which is equal to—

"(i) if the condition of subsection (b)(1) is not satisfied, that portion of the gross income for the period described in subsection (b)(1)—

"(I) which was not derived from sources within the Virgin Islands, and

"(II) which exceeds the amount of such income for such period which would enable such corporation to satisfy the condition of subsection (b)(1).

"(ii) if the condition of subsection (b0(2) is not satisfied, that portion of the aggregate gross income for such period—

"(I) which was not derived from the active conduct of a trade or business within the Virgin Islands, and

"(II) which exceeds the amount of such income for such period which would enable such corporations to satisfy the conditions of subsection (b)(2), or

"(iii) if neither of such conditions is satisfied, that portion of the gross income which exceeds the amount of gross income for such period which would enable such corporation to satisfy the conditions of paragraphs (1) and (2) of subsection (b).

"(B) Effectively connected income. In the case of a shareholder who is a nonresident alien individual, an inhabitant of the Virgin Islands, or a foreign corporation, trust, or estate, any distribution described in subparagraph (A) shall be treated as income which is effectively connected with the conduct of a trade or business conducted through a permanent establishment of such shareholder within the United States.

"(C) Distribution denied in case of fraud or willful neglect. Subparagraph (A) shall not apply to a corporation if the determination of the Secretary described in subparagraph (A) contains a finding that the failure of such corporation to satisfy the conditions in subsection (b) was due in whole or in part to fraud with intent to evade tax or willful neglect on the part of such corporation.

"(4) Certain provisions of section 936 to apply.

"(A) In general. The rules contained in paragraphs (5), (6), and (7) of section 936(h) shall apply to a domestic corporation described in paragraph (1)(A) of this subsection.

"(B) Certain modifications. For purposes of subparagraph (A), section 936(h) shall be applied by substituting wherever appropriate—

"(i) 'Virgin Islands' for 'possession', and

"(ii) qualification under paragraphs (1) and (2) of subsection (b) for qualification under section 936(a)(2).

"(f) Transitional rule.

"In applying subsection (b)(2) with respect to taxable years beginning after December 31, 1982, and before January 1, 1985, the following percentage shall be substituted for '65 percent'.

For taxable years beginning in calendar year:	The percentage is:
1983	55
1984	60."

—P.L. 99-514, Sec. 1275(c)(1), deleted subsecs. (b), (c) and (d), ... Sec. 1275(c)(2)(A), deleted "or (c) or in section 934A" after "subsection (b)" in subsec. (a) ... Sec. 1275(c)(2)(B), added new subsec. (b), effective for tax. yrs. begin. after 12/31/86. Sec. 1277(c)(1) of this Act provides:

"(c) Special rules for the Virgin Islands.

"(1) In general. The amendments made by section 1275(c) shall apply with respect to the Virgin Islands (and residents thereof and corporations created or organized therein) only if (and so long as) an implementing agreement is in effect between the United States and the Virgin Islands with respect to the establishment of rules under which the evasion or avoidance of United States income tax shall not be permitted or facilitated by such possession. Any such implementing agreement shall be executed on behalf of the United States by the Secretary of the Treasury, after consultation with the Secretary of the Interior."

Prior to deletion, subsecs. (b), (c) and (d) read as follows:

"(b) Exception for certain domestic and Virgin Islands corporations.

"In the case of a domestic corporation or a Virgin Islands corporation, subsection (a) shall not apply (if the information required by subsection (d) is supplied) to the extent such corporation derived its income from sources without the United States if the conditions of both paragraph (1) and paragraph (2) are satisfied:

"(1) Three-year period. If 80 percent or more of the gross income of such corporation for the 3-year period immediately preceding the close of the taxable year (or for such part of such period immediately preceding the close of such taxable year as may be applicable) was derived from sources within the Virgin Islands; and

"(2) Trade or business. If 65 percent or more of the gross income of such corporation for such period or such part thereof was derived from the active conduct of a trade or business within the Virgin Islands.

For purposes of the preceding sentence, the gross income of a Virgin Islands corporation, and the sources from which the income of such corporation is derived, shall be determined as if such corporation were a domestic corporation.

"(c) Exception for certain residents of the Virgin Islands.

"Subsection (a) shall not apply in the case of an individual citizen of the United States who is a bona fide resident of the Virgin Islands during the entire taxable year (if the information required by subsection (d) is supplied) to the extent his income is derived from sources within the Virgin Islands (except that subsection (a) shall apply in the case of amounts received for services performed as an employee of the United States or any agency thereof). For purposes of the preceding sentence, gain or loss from the sale or exchange of any security (as defined in section 165(g)(2)) shall not be treated as derived from sources within the Virgin Islands.

"(d) Requirement to supply information.

"Subsections (b) and (c) shall apply only in the case of persons who supply (at such time and in such manner as the Secretary may by regulations prescribe) such information as the Secretary may by regulations prescribe for purposes of determining the applicability of such subsections."

—P.L. 99-514, Sec. 1876(f)(2), deleted subsec. (f) [sic (g)] (as added by Sec. 801(d)(7) of P.L. 98-369), effective for transactions after 12/31/84, in tax. yrs. end. after 12/31/84.

Prior to deletion, subsec. (f) [sic (g)] read as follows:

"(f) [sic , (g)] FSC.

"Subsection (a) shall not apply in the case of a Virgin Islands corporation which is a FSC."

In 1984, P.L. 98-369, Sec. 441(a), [as amended by Sec. 6252(b)(1) of P.L. 100-647, see above], provides:

"SEC. 441. SIMPLIFICATION OF CERTAIN REPORTING REQUIREMENTS.

"(a) Report on possessions corporations.— The Secretary of the Treasury shall, during 1988 and each fourth calendar year thereafter, submit a report to the Congress (using the most recent information available) setting forth an analysis of the operation and effect of sections 936 and 934(b) of the Internal Revenue Code of 1954."

—P.L. 98-369, Sec. 801(d)(7), added new subsec. (f) [sic (g)], effective for transactions after 12/31/84, in tax. yrs. end. after 12/31/84.

In 1983, P.L. 97-455, Sec. 1(c), added "or in section 934A" before the period at the end of subsec. (a), effective for amounts received after 1/12/83, in tax. yrs. end. after 1/12/83.

In 1982, P.L. 97-248, Sec. 213(b)(1), substituted "65 percent" for "50 percent" in para. (2) ... Sec. 213(b)(2), added subsecs. (e) and (f), effective for tax. yrs. begin. after 12/31/82. Sec. 213(e)(2) of this Act provides as follows:

"(2) Certain sales made after July 1, 1982. Paragraph (6) of section 936(h) of the Internal Revenue Code of 1954, and so much of section 934 to which such paragraph applies by reason of section 934(e)(4) of such Code, shall apply to taxable years ending after July 1, 1982."

In 1976, P.L. 94-455, Sec. 1901(a)(118), deleted the last sentence of subsec. (b), effective for tax. yrs. begin. after 12/31/76.

Prior to amendment, the last sentence in subsec. (b) read as follows:

"For the purposes of this subsection, all amounts received by such corporation within the United States, whether derived from sources within or without the United States, shall be considered as being derived from sources within the United States."

—P.L. 94-455, Sec. 1906(b)(13)(A), substituted "Secretary" for "Secretary or his delegate" each place it appeared in subsec. (d), effective for tax. yrs. begin. after 12/31/76.

In 1960, P.L. 86-779, Sec. 4(a), added Code Sec. 934, effective for tax. yrs. begin. on or after 1/1/60.

Sec. 934A. Repealed.

In 1986, P.L. 99-514, Sec. 1275(c)(3), repealed Code Sec. 934A, effective for tax. yrs. begin. after 12/31/86. For special rules, see Sec. 1277(c)(1) of this Act, reproduced in note following Code Sec. 934.

Prior to repeal, Code Sec. 934A read as follows:

"SEC. 934A. INCOME TAX RATE ON VIRGIN ISLANDS SOURCE INCOME.

"(a) General rule.

"For purposes of determining the tax liability incurred by citizens and resident alien individuals of the United States, and corporations organized in the United States, to the Virgin Islands pursuant to this title with respect to amounts received from sources within the Virgin Islands—

"(1) the taxes imposed by sections 871(a)(1) and 881 (as made applicable to the Virgin Islands) shall apply except that '10 percent' shall be substituted for '30 percent', and

"(2) subsection (a) of section 934 shall not apply to such taxes.

"(b) Subsection (a) rates not to apply to pre-effective date earnings.

"(1) In general. Any change under subsection (a)(1), and any reduction under section 934 pursuant to subsection (a)(2), in a rate of tax imposed by section 871(a)(1) or 881 shall not apply to dividends paid out of earnings and profits accumulated for taxable years beginning before the effective date of the change or reduction.

"(2) Ordering rule. For purposes of paragraph (1), dividends shall be treated as first being paid out of earnings and profits accumulated for taxable years beginning before the effective date of the change or reduction (to the extent thereof)."

In 1983, P.L. 97-455, Sec. 1(a), added Code Sec. 934A, effective for amounts received after 1/12/83 in tax. yrs. end. after 1/12/83.

Sec. 935. Repealed.

In 2004, P.L. 108-357, Sec. 908(c)(4)(A), substituted "who, during the entire taxable year" for "for the taxable year who" in subsec. (a) ... Sec. 908(c)(4)(B), added "bona fide" before "resident" in para. (a)(1) ... Sec. 908(c)(4)(C)(i), added "(other [than] a bona fide resident of Guam during the entire taxable year)" after "United States" in subpara. (b)(1)(A) ... Sec. 908(c)(4)(C)(ii), added "bona fide" before "resident" in subpara. (b)(1)(B) ... Sec. 908(c)(4)(D), deleted "residence and" after "determinations of" in para. (b)(2), effective for tax. yrs. end. after 10/22/2004. Note: These amendments are to be applied to Code Sec. 935 prior to its repeal by Sec. 1272(d)(2) of P.L. 99-514, see below.

Income from foreign sources

In 1986, P.L. 99-514, Sec. 1272(d)(2), repealed Code Sec. 935, effective for tax. yrs. begin. after 12/31/86. For special rule see Sec. 1277(b) of this Act reproduced in note following Code Sec. 931.

Prior to repeal, Code Sec. 935 read as follows:

"SEC. 935. COORDINATION OF UNITED STATES AND GUAM INDIVIDUAL INCOME TAXES.

"(a) Application of section.

"This section shall apply to any individual who, during the entire taxable year [as amended by Sec. 908(c)(4)(A) of P.L. 108-357, see above]—

"(1) is a bona fide [as amended by Sec. 908(c)(4)(B) of P.L. 108-357, see above] resident of Guam,

"(2) is a citizen of Guam but not otherwise a citizen of the United States,

"(3) has income derived from Guam for the taxable year and is a citizen or resident of the United States, or

"(4) files a joint return for the taxable year with an individual who satisfies paragraph (1), (2), or (3) for the taxable year.

"(b) Filing requirement.

"(1) In general. Each individual to whom this section applies for the taxable year shall file his income tax return for the taxable year—

"(A) with the United States (other [than] a bona fide resident of Guam during the entire taxable year) [as amended by Sec. 908(c)(4)(C)(i) of P.L. 108-357, see above], if he is a resident of the United States,

"(B) with Guam, if he is a bona fide [as amended by Sec. 908(c)(4)(C)(ii) of P.L. 108-357, see above] resident of Guam, and

"(C) if neither subparagraph (A) nor subparagraph (B) applies—

"(i) with Guam, if he is a citizen of Guam but not otherwise a citizen of the United States, or

"(ii) with the United States, if clause (i) does not apply.

"(2) Determination date. For purposes of this section, determinations of [as amended by Sec. 908(c)(4)(D) of P.L. 108-357, see above] citizenship for the taxable year shall be made as of the close of the taxable year.

"(3) Special rule for joint returns. In the case of a joint return, this subsection shall be applied on the basis of the residence and citizenship of the spouse who has the greater adjusted gross income (determined without regard to community property laws) for the taxable year.

"(c) Extent of income tax liability.

"In the case of any individual to whom this section applies for the taxable year—

"(1) for the purposes of so much of this title (other than this section and section 7654) as relates to the taxes imposed by this chapter, the United States shall be treated as including Guam.

"(2) for purposes of the Guam territorial income tax, Guam shall be treated as including the United States, and

"(3) such individual is hereby relieved of liability for income tax for such year to the jurisdiction (the United States or Guam) other than the jurisdiction with which he is required to file under subsection (b).

"(d) Special rules for estimated income tax.

"If there is reason to believe that this section will apply to an individual for the taxable year, then—

"(1) he shall file any declaration of estimated income tax (and all amendments thereto) with the jurisdiction with which he would be required to file a return for such year under subsection (b) if his taxable year closed on the date he is required to file such declaration,

"(2) he is hereby relieved of any liability to file a declaration of estimated income tax (and amendments thereto) for such taxable year to the other jurisdiction, and

"(3) his liability for underpayments of estimated income tax shall be to the jurisdiction with which he is required to file his return for the taxable year (determined under subsection (b))."

In 1972, P.L. 92-606, Sec. 1(a), added Code Sec. 935, effective for tax. yrs. begin. after 12/31/72.

Sec. 936. Puerto Rico and possession tax credit.

(a) Allowance of credit.

(1) In general. Except as otherwise provided in this section, if a domestic corporation elects the application of this section and if the conditions of both subparagraph (A) and subparagraph (B) of paragraph (2) are satisfied, there shall be allowed as a credit against the tax imposed by this chapter an amount equal to the portion of the tax which is attributable to the sum of—

(A) the taxable income, from sources without the United States, from—

(i) the active conduct of a trade or business within a possession of the United States, or

(ii) the sale or exchange of substantially all of the assets used by the taxpayer in the active conduct of such trade or business, and

(B) the qualified possession source investment income.

(2) Conditions which must be satisfied. The conditions referred to in paragraph (1) are:

(A) 3-year period. If 80 percent or more of the gross income of such domestic corporation for the 3-year period immediately preceding the close of the taxable year (or for such part of such period immediately preceding the close of such taxable year as may be applicable) was derived from sources within a possession of the United States (determined without regard to subsections (f) and (g) of section 904); and

(B) Trade or business. If 75 percent or more of the gross income of such domestic corporation for such period or such part thereof was derived from the active conduct of a trade or business within a possession of the United States.

(3) Credit not allowed against certain taxes. The credit provided by paragraph (1) shall not be allowed against the tax imposed by—

(A) section 59A (relating to environmental tax),

(B) section 531 (relating to the tax on accumulated earnings),

(C) section 541 (relating to personal holding company tax), or

(D) section 1351 (relating to recoveries of foreign expropriation losses).

(4) Limitations on credit for active business income.

(A) In general. The amount of the credit determined under paragraph (1) for any taxable year with respect to income referred to in subparagraph (A) thereof shall not exceed the sum of the following amounts:

(i) 60 percent of the sum of—

(I) the aggregate amount of the possession corporation's qualified possession wages for such taxable year, plus

(II) the allocable employee fringe benefit expenses of the possession corporation for the taxable year.

(ii) The sum of—

(I) 15 percent of the depreciation allowances for the taxable year with respect to short-life qualified tangible property,

(II) 40 percent of the depreciation allowances for the taxable year with respect to medium-life qualified tangible property, and

(III) 65 percent of the depreciation allowances for the taxable year with respect to long-life qualified tangible property.

(iii) If the possession corporation does not have an election to use the method described in subsection (h)(5)(C)(ii) (relating to profit split) in effect for the taxable year, the amount of the qualified possession income taxes for the taxable year allocable to non-sheltered income.

(B) Election to take reduced credit.

(i) In general. If an election under this subparagraph applies to a possession corporation for any taxable year—

(I) subparagraph (A), and the provisions of subsection (i), shall not apply to such possession corporation for such taxable year, and

(II) the credit determined under paragraph (1) for such taxable year with respect to income referred to in subparagraph (A) thereof shall be the applicable percentage of the credit which would otherwise have been determined under such paragraph with respect to such income.

Notwithstanding subclause (I), a possession corporation to which an election under this subparagraph applies shall be entitled to the benefits of subsection (i)(3)(B) for taxes allocable (on a pro rata basis) to taxable income the tax on which is not offset by reason of this subparagraph.

(ii) Applicable percentage. The term "applicable percentage" means the percentage determined in accordance with the following table:

In the case of taxable years beginning in:	The percentage is:
1994	60
1995	55
1996	50
1997	45
1998 and thereafter	40.

(iii) Election.

(I) In general. An election under this subparagraph by any possession corporation may be made only for the corporation's first taxable year beginning after December 31, 1993, for which it is a possession corporation.

(II) Period of election. An election under this subparagraph shall apply to the taxable year for which made and all subsequent taxable years unless revoked.

(III) Affiliated groups. If, for any taxable year, an election is not in effect for any possession corporation which is a member of an affiliated group, any election under this subparagraph for any other member of such group is revoked for such taxable year and all subsequent taxable years. For purposes of this subclause, members of an affiliated group shall be determined without regard to the exceptions contained in section 1504(b) and as if the constructive ownership rules of section 1563(e) applied for purposes of section 1504(a). The Secretary may prescribe regulations to prevent the avoidance of this subclause through deconsolidation or otherwise.

(C) Cross reference. For definitions and special rules applicable to this paragraph, see subsection (i).

(b) Amounts received in United States.

In determining taxable income for purposes of subsection (a), there shall not be taken into account as income from sources without the United States any gross income which was received by such domestic corporation within the United States, whether derived from sources within or without the United States. This subsection shall not apply to any amount described in subsection (a)(1)(A)(i) received from a person who is not a related person (within the meaning of subsection (h)(3) but without regard to subparagraphs (D)(ii) and (E)(i) thereof) with respect to the domestic corporation.

(c) Treatment of certain foreign taxes.

For purposes of this title, any tax of a foreign country or a possession of the United States which is paid or accrued with respect to taxable income which is taken into account in computing the credit under subsection (a) shall not be treated as income, war profits, or excess profits taxes paid or accrued to a foreign country or possession of the United States, and no deduction shall be allowed under this title with respect to any amounts so paid or accrued.

(d) Definitions and special rules.

For purposes of this section—

(1) Possession. The term "possession of the United States" includes the Commonwealth of Puerto Rico, and the Virgin Islands.

(2) Qualified possession source investment income. The term "qualified possession source investment income" means gross income which—

(A) is from sources within a possession of the United States in which a trade or business is actively conducted, and

(B) the taxpayer establishes to the satisfaction of the Secretary is attributable to the investment in such possession (for use therein) of funds derived from the active conduct of a trade or business in such possession, or from such investment,

less the deductions properly apportioned or allocated thereto.

(3) Carryover basis property.

(A) In general. Income from the sale or exchange of any asset the basis of which is determined in whole or in part by reference to its basis in the hands of another person shall not be treated as income described in subparagraph (A) or (B) of subsection (a)(1).

(B) Exception for possessions corporations, etc. For purposes of subparagraph (A), the holding of any asset by another person shall not be taken into account if throughout the period for which such asset was held by such person section 931, this section, or section 957(c) (as in effect on the day before the date of the enactment [10/22/86] of the Tax Reform Act of 1986) applied to such person.

(4) Investment in qualified Caribbean Basin countries.

(A) In general. For purposes of paragraph (2)(B), an investment in a financial institution shall, subject to such conditions as the Secretary may prescribe by regulations, be treated as for use in Puerto Rico to the extent used by such financial institution (or by the Government Development Bank for Puerto Rico or the Puerto Rico Economic Development Bank)—

(i) for investment, consistent with the goals and purposes of the Caribbean Basin Economic Recovery Act, in—

(I) active business assets in a qualified Caribbean Basin country, or

(II) development projects in a qualified Caribbean Basin country, and

(ii) in accordance with a specific authorization granted by the Commissioner of Financial Institutions of Puerto Rico pursuant to regulations issued by such Commissioner.

A similar rule shall apply in the case of a direct investment in the Government Development Bank for Puerto Rico or the Puerto Rico Economic Development Bank.

(B) Qualified Caribbean Basin country. For purposes of this subsection, the term "qualified Caribbean Basin country" means any beneficiary country (within the meaning of section 212(a)(1)(A) of the Caribbean Basin Economic Recovery Act) which meets the requirements of clauses (i) and (ii) of section 274(h)(6)(A) and the Virgin Islands.

(C) Additional requirements. Subparagraph (A) shall not apply to any investment made by a financial institution (or by the Government Development Bank for Puerto Rico or the Puerto Rico Economic Development Bank) unless—

(i) the person in whose trade or business such investment is made (or such other recipient of the investment) and the financial institution or such Bank certify to the Secretary and the Commissioner of Financial Institutions of Puerto Rico that the proceeds of the loan will be promptly used to acquire active business assets or to make other authorized expenditures, and

(ii) the financial institution (or the Government Development Bank for Puerto Rico or the Puerto Rico Economic Development Bank) and the recipient of the investment funds agree to permit the Secretary and the Commissioner of Financial Institutions of Puerto Rico to examine such of their books and records as may be necessary to ensure that the requirements of this paragraph are met.

(D) Requirement for investment in Caribbean Basin countries.

(i) In general. For each calendar year, the government of Puerto Rico shall take such steps as may be necessary to ensure that at least $100,000,000 of qualified Caribbean Basin country investments are made during such calendar year.

(ii) Qualified Caribbean Basin country investment. For purposes of clause (i), the term "qualified Caribbean Basin country investment" means any investment if—

(I) the income from such investment is treated as qualified possession source investment income by reason of subparagraph (A), and

(II) such investment is not (directly or indirectly) a refinancing of a prior investment (whether or not such prior investment was a qualified Caribbean Basin country investment).

(e) Election.

(1) Period of election. The election provided in subsection (a) shall be made at such time and in such manner as the Secretary may by regulations prescribe. Any such election shall apply to the first taxable year for which such election was made and for which the domestic corporation satisfied the conditions of subparagraphs (A) and (B) of subsection (a)(2) and for each taxable year thereafter until such election is revoked by the domestic corporation under paragraph (2). If any such election is revoked by the domestic corporation under paragraph (2), such domestic corporation may make a subsequent election under subsection (a) for any taxable year thereafter for which such domestic corporation satisfies the conditions of subparagraphs (A) and (B) of subsection (a)(2) and any such subsequent election shall remain in effect until revoked by such domestic corporation under paragraph (2).

(2) Revocation. An election under subsection (a)—

(A) may be revoked for any taxable year beginning before the expiration of the 9th taxable year following the taxable year for which such election first applies only with the consent of the Secretary; and

(B) may be revoked for any taxable year beginning after the expiration of such 9th taxable year without the consent of the Secretary.

(f) Limitation on credit for DISC's and FSC's.

No credit shall be allowed under this section to a corporation for any taxable year—

(1) for which it is a DISC or former DISC, or

(2) in which it owns at any time stock in a—

(A) DISC or former DISC, or

(B) former FSC.

(g) Exception to accumulated earnings tax.

(1) For purposes of section 535, the term "accumulated taxable income" shall not include taxable income entitled to the credit under subsection (a).

(2) For purposes of section 537, the term "reasonable needs of the business" includes assets which produce income eligible for the credit under subsection (a).

(h) Tax treatment of intangible property income.

(1) In general.

(A) Income attributable to shareholders. The intangible property income of a corporation electing the application of this section for any taxable year shall be included on a pro rata basis in the gross income of all shareholders of such electing corporation at the close of the taxable year of such electing corporation as income from sources within the United States for the taxable year of such shareholder in which or with which the taxable year of such electing corporation ends.

(B) Exclusion from the income of an electing corporation. Any intangible property income of a corporation electing the application of this section which is included in the gross income of a shareholder of such corporation by reason of subparagraph (A) shall be excluded from the gross income of such corporation.

(2) Foreign shareholders; shareholders not subject to tax.

(A) In general. Paragraph (1)(A) shall not apply with respect to any shareholder—

(i) who is not a United States person, or

(ii) who is not subject to tax under this title on intangible property income which would be allocated to such shareholder (but for this subparagraph).

(B) Treatment of nonallocated intangible property income. For purposes of this subtitle, intangible property income of a corporation electing the application of this section which is not included in the gross income of a shareholder of such corporation by reason of subparagraph (A)—

(i) shall be treated as income from sources within the United States, and

(ii) shall not be taken into account under subsection (a)(2).

(3) Intangible property income. For purposes of this subsection—

(A) In general. The term "intangible property income" means the gross income of a corporation attributable to any intangible property other than intangible property which has been licensed to such corporation since prior to 1948 and is in use by such corporation on the date of the enactment of this subparagraph.

(B) Intangible property. The term "intangible property" means any—

(i) patent, invention, formula, process, design, pattern, or know-how;

(ii) copyright, literary, musical, or artistic composition;

(iii) trademark, trade name, or brand name;

(iv) franchise, license, or contract;

(v) method, program, system, procedure, campaign, survey, study, forecast, estimate, customer list, or technical data; or

(vi) any similar item,

which has substantial value independent of the services of any individual.

(C) Exclusion of reasonable profit. The term "intangible property income" shall not include any portion of the income from the sale, exchange or other disposition of any product, or from the rendering of services, by a corporation electing the application of this section which is determined by the Secretary to be a reasonable profit on the direct and indirect costs incurred by such electing corporation which are attributable to such income.

(D) Related person.

(i) In general. A person (hereinafter referred to as the "related person") is related to any person if—

(I) the related person bears a relationship to such person specified in section 267(b) or section 707(b)(1), or

(II) the related person and such person are members of the same controlled group of corporations.

(ii) Special rule. For purposes of clause (i), section 267(b) and section 707(b)(1) shall be applied by substituting "10 percent" for "50 percent".

(E) Controlled group of corporations. The term "controlled group of corporations" has the meaning given to such term by section 1563(a), except that—

(i) "more than 10 percent" shall be substituted for "at least 80 percent" and "more than 50 percent" each place either appears in section 1563(a), and

(ii) the determination shall be made without regard to subsections (a)(4), (b)(2), and (e)(3)(C) of section 1563.

(4) Distributions to meet qualification requirements.

(A) In general. If the Secretary determines that a corporation does not satisfy a condition specified in subparagraph (A) or (B) of subsection (a)(2) for any taxable year by reason of the exclusion from gross income under paragraph (1)(B), such corporation shall nevertheless be treated as satisfying such condition for such year if it makes a pro rata distribution of property after the close of such taxable year to its shareholders (designated at the time of such distribution as a distribution to meet qualification requirements) with respect to their stock in an amount which is equal to—

(i) if the condition of subsection (a)(2)(A) is not satisfied, that portion of the gross income for the period described in subsection (a)(2)(A)—

(I) which was not derived from sources within a possession, and

(II) which exceeds the amount of such income for such period which would enable such corporation to satisfy the condition of subsection (a)(2)(A),

(ii) if the condition of subsection (a)(2)(B) is not satisfied, that portion of the gross income for such period—

(I) which was not derived from the active conduct of a trade or business within a possession, and

(II) which exceeds the amount of such income for such period which would enable such corporation to satisfy the conditions of subsection (a)(2)(B), or

(iii) if neither of such conditions is satisfied, that portion of the gross income which exceeds the amount of gross income for such period which would enable such corporation to satisfy the conditions of subparagraphs (A) and (B) of subsection (a)(2).

(B) Effectively connected income. In the case of a shareholder who is a nonresident alien individual or a foreign corporation, trust, or estate, any distribution described in subparagraph (A) shall be treated as income which is effectively connected with the conduct of a trade or business conducted through a permanent establishment of such shareholder within the United States.

(C) Distribution denied in case of fraud or willful neglect. Subparagraph (A) shall not apply to a corporation if the determination of the Secretary described in subparagraph (A) contains a finding that the failure of such corporation to satisfy the conditions in subsection (a)(2) was due in whole or in part to fraud with intent to evade tax or willful neglect on the part of such corporation.

(5) Election out.

(A) In general. The rules contained in paragraphs (1) through (4) do not apply for any taxable year if an election pursuant to subparagraph (F) is in effect to use one of the methods specified in subparagraph (C).

(B) Eligibility.

(i) Requirement of significant business presence. An election may be made to use one of the methods specified in subparagraph (C) with respect to a product or type of service only if an electing corporation has a significant business presence in a possession with respect to such product or type of service. An election may remain in effect with respect to such product or type of service for any subsequent taxable year only if such electing corporation maintains a significant business presence in a possession with respect to such product or type of service in such subsequent taxable year. If an election is not in effect for a taxable year because of the preceding sentence, the electing corporation shall be deemed to have revoked the election on the first day of such taxable year.

(ii) Definition. For purposes of this subparagraph, an electing corporation has a "significant business presence" in a possession for a taxable year with respect to a product or type of service if:

(I) the total production costs (other than direct material costs and other than interest excluded by regulations prescribed by the Secretary) incurred by the electing corporation in the possession in producing units of that product sold or otherwise disposed of during the taxable year by the affiliated group to persons who are not members of the affiliated group are not less than 25 percent of the difference between (a) the gross receipts from sales or other dispositions during the taxable year by the affiliated group to persons who are not members of the affiliated group of such units of the product produced, in whole or in part, by the electing corporation in the possession, and (b) the direct material costs of the purchase of materials for such units of that product by all members of the affiliated group from persons who are not members of the affiliated group; or

(II) no less than 65 percent of the direct labor costs of the affiliated group for units of the product produced during the taxable year in whole or in part by the electing corporation or for the type of service rendered by the electing corporation during the taxable year, is incurred by the electing corporation and is compensation for services performed in the possession; or

(III) with respect to purchases and sales by an electing corporation of all goods not produced in whole or in part by any member of the affiliated group and sold by the electing corporation to persons other than members of the affiliated group, no less than 65 percent of the total direct labor costs of the affiliated group in connection with all purchases and sales of such goods sold during the taxable year by such electing corporation is incurred by such electing corporation and is compensation for services performed in the possession.

Notwithstanding satisfaction of one of the foregoing tests, an electing corporation shall not be treated as having a significant business presence in a possession with respect to a product produced in whole or in part by the electing corporation in the possession, for purposes of an election to use the method specified in subparagraph (C)(ii), unless such product is manufactured or produced in the possession by the electing corporation within the meaning of subsection (d)(1)(A) of section 954.

(iii) Special rules.

(I) An electing corporation which produces a product or renders a type of service in a possession on the date of the enactment of this clause is not required to meet the significant business presence test in a possession with respect to such product or type of service for its taxable years beginning before January 1, 1986.

(II) For purposes of this subparagraph, the costs incurred by an electing corporation or any other member of the affiliated group in connection with contract manufacturing by a person other than a member of the affiliated group, or in connection with a similar arrangement thereto, shall be treated as direct labor costs of the affiliated group and shall not be treated as production costs incurred by the electing corporation in the possession or as direct material costs or as compensation for services performed in the possession, except to the extent as may be otherwise provided in regulations prescribed by the Secretary.

(iv) Regulations. The Secretary may prescribe regulations setting forth:

(I) an appropriate transitional (but not in excess of three taxable years) significant business presence test for commencement in a possession of operations with respect to products or types of service after the date of the enactment of this clause and not described in subparagraph (B)(iii)(I),

(II) a significant business presence test for other appropriate cases, consistent with the tests specified in subparagraph (B)(ii),

(III) rules for the definition of a product or type of service, and

(IV) rules for treating components produced in whole or in part by a related person as materials, and the costs (including direct labor costs) related thereto as a cost of materials, where there is an independent resale price for such components or where otherwise consistent with the intent of the substantial business presence tests.

(C) Methods of computation of taxable income. If an election of one of the following methods is in effect pursuant to subparagraph (F) with respect to a product or type of service, an electing corporation shall compute its income derived from the active conduct of a trade or business in a possession with respect to such product or type of service in accordance with the method which is elected.

(i) Cost sharing.

(I) Payment of cost sharing. If an election of this method is in effect, the electing corporation must make a payment for its share of the cost (if any) of product area research which is paid or accrued by the affiliated group during that taxable year. Such share shall not be less than the same proportion of 110 percent of the cost of such product area research which the amount of "possession sales" bears to the amount of "total sales" of the affiliated group. The cost of product area research paid or accrued solely by the electing corporation in a taxable year (excluding amounts paid directly or indirectly to or on behalf of related persons and excluding amounts paid under any cost sharing agreements with related persons) will reduce (but not below zero) the amount of the electing corporation's cost sharing payment under this method for that year. In the case of intangible property described in subsection (h)(3)(B)(i) which the electing corporation is treated as owning under subclause (II), in no event shall the payment required under this subclause be less than the inclusion or payment which would be required under section 367(d)(2)(A)(ii) or section 482 if the electing corporation were a foreign corporation.

(a) Product area research. For purposes of this section, the term "product area research" includes (notwithstanding any provision to the contrary) the research, development and experimental costs, losses, expenses and other related deductions—including amounts paid or accrued for the performance of research or similar activities by another person; qualified research expenses within the meaning of section 41(b); amounts paid or accrued for the use of, or the right to use, research or any of the items specified in subsection (h)(3)(B)(i); and a proper allowance for amounts incurred for the acquisition of any of the items specified in subsection (h)(3)(B)(i)—which are properly apportioned or allocated to the same product area as that in which the electing corporation conducts its activities, and a ratable part of any such costs, losses, expenses and other deductions which cannot definitely be allocated to a particular product area.

(b) Affiliated group. For purposes of this subsection, the term "affiliated group" shall mean the electing corporation and all other organizations, trades or businesses (whether or not incorporated, whether or not organized in the United States, and whether or not affiliated) owned or controlled directly or indirectly by the same interests, within the meaning of section 482.

(c) Possession sales. For purposes of this section, the term "possession sales" means the aggregate sales or other dispositions for the taxable year to persons who are not members of the affiliated group by members of the affiliated group of products produced, in whole or in part, by the electing corporation in the possession which are in the same product area as is used for determining the amount of product area research, and of services rendered, in whole or in part, in the possession in such product area to persons who are not members of the affiliated group.

(d) Total sales. For purposes of this section, the term "total sales" means the aggregate sales or other dispositions for the taxable year to persons who are not members of the affiliated group by members of the affiliated group of all products in the same product area as is used for determining the amount of product area research, and of services rendered in such product area to persons who are not members of the affiliated group.

(e) Product area. For purposes of this section, the term "product area" shall be defined by reference to the three-digit classification of the Standard Industrial Classification code. The Secretary may provide for the aggregation of two or more three-digit classifications where appropriate, and for a classification system other than the Standard Industrial Classification code in appropriate cases.

(II) Effect of election. For purposes of determining the amount of its gross income derived from the active conduct of a trade or business in a possession with respect to a product produced by, or type of service rendered by, the electing corporation for a taxable year, if an election of this method is in effect, the electing corporation shall be treated as the owner (for purposes of obtaining a return thereon) of intangible property described in subsection (h)(3)(B)(i) which is related to the units of the product produced, or type of service rendered, by the electing corporation. Such electing corporation shall not be treated as the owner (for purposes of obtaining a return thereon) of any intangible property described in subsection (h)(3)(B)(ii) through (v) (to the extent not described in subsection (h)(3)(B)(i)) or of any other nonmanufacturing intangible. Notwithstanding the preceding sentence, an electing corporation shall be treated as the owner (for purposes of obtaining a return thereon) of (a) intangible property which was developed solely by such corporation in a possession and is owned by such corporation, (b) intangible property described in subsection (h)(3)(B)(i) acquired by such corporation from a person who was not related to such corporation (or to any person related to such corporation) at the time of, or in connection with, such acquisition, and (c) any intangible property described in subsection (h)(3)(B)(ii) through (v) (to the extent not described in subsection (h)(3)(B)(i)) and other nonmanufacturing intangibles which relate to sales of units of products, or services rendered, to unrelated persons for ultimate consumption or use in the possession in which the electing corporation conducts its trade or business.

(III) Payment provisions.

(a) The cost sharing payment determined under subparagraph (C)(i)(I) for any taxable year shall be made to the person or persons specified in subparagraph (C)(i)(IV)(a) not later than the time prescribed by law for filing the electing corporation's return for such taxable year (including any extensions thereof). If all or part of such payment is not timely made, the amount of the cost sharing payment required to be paid shall be increased by the amount of interest that would have been due under section 6601(a) had the portion of the cost sharing payment that is not timely made been an amount of tax imposed by this title and had the last date prescribed for payment been the due date of the electing corporations return (determined without regard to any extension thereof). The amount by which a cost sharing payment determined under subparagraph (C)(i)(I) is increased by reason of the preceding sentence shall not be treated as a cost sharing payment or as interest. If failure to make timely payment is due in whole or in part to fraud or willful neglect, the electing corporation shall be deemed to have revoked the election made under subparagraph (A) on the first day of the taxable year for which the cost sharing payment was required.

(b) For purposes of this title, any tax of a foreign country or possession of the United States which is paid or accrued with respect to the payment or receipt of a cost sharing payment determined under subparagraph (C)(i)(I) or of an amount of increase referred to in subparagraph (C)(i)(III)(a) shall not be treated as income, war profits, or excess profits taxes paid or accrued to a foreign country or possession of the United States, and no deduction shall be allowed under this title with respect to any amounts of such tax so paid or accrued.

(IV) Special rules.

(a) The amount of the cost sharing payment determined under subparagraph (C)(i)(I), and any increase in the amount thereof in accordance with subparagraph (C)(i)(III)(a), shall not be treated as income of the recipient, but shall reduce the amount of the deductions (and the amount of reductions in earnings and profits) otherwise allowable to the appropriate domestic member or members (other than an electing corporation) of the affiliated group, or, if there is no such domestic member, to the foreign member or members of such affiliated group as the Secretary may provide under regulations.

(b) If an election of this method is in effect, the electing corporation shall determine its intercompany pricing under the appropriate section 482 method, provided, however, that an electing corporation shall not be denied use of the resale price method for purposes of such intercompany pricing merely because the reseller adds more than an insubstantial amount to the value of the product by the use of intangible property.

(c) The amount of qualified research expenses, within the meaning of section 41, of any member of the controlled group of corporations (as defined in section 41(f)) of which the electing corporation is a member shall not be affected by the cost sharing payment required under this method.

(ii) Profit split.

(I) General rule. If an election of this method is in effect, the electing corporation's taxable income derived from the active conduct of a trade or business in a possession with respect to units of a product produced or type of service rendered, in whole or in part, by the electing corporation shall be equal to 50 percent of the combined taxable income of the affiliated group (other than foreign affiliates) derived from covered sales of units of the product produced or type of service rendered, in whole or in part, by the electing corporation in a possession.

(II) Computation of combined taxable income. Combined taxable income shall be computed separately for each product produced or type of service rendered, in whole or in part, by the electing corporation in a possession. Combined taxable income shall be computed (notwithstanding any provision to the contrary) for each such product or type of service rendered by deducting from the gross income of the affiliated group (other than foreign affiliates) derived from covered sales of such product or type of service all expenses, losses, and other deductions properly apportioned or allocated to gross income from such sales or services, and a ratable part of all expenses, losses, or other deductions which cannot definitely be allocated to some item or class of gross income, which are incurred by the affiliated group (other than foreign affiliates). Notwithstanding any other provision to the contrary, in computing the combined taxable income for each such product or type of service rendered, the research, development, and experimental costs, expenses and related deductions for the taxable year which would otherwise be apportioned or allocated to the gross income of the affiliated group (other than foreign affiliates) derived from covered sales of such product produced or type of service rendered, in whole or in part, by the electing corporation in a possession, shall not be less than the same proportion of the amount of the share of product area research determined under subparagraph (C)(i)(I) (without regard to the third and fourth sentences thereof, but substituting "120 percent" for "110 percent" in the second sentence thereof) in the product area which includes such product or type of service, that such gross income from the product or type of service bears to such gross income from all products and types of services, within such product area, produced or rendered, in whole or part, by the electing corporation in a possession.

(III) Division of combined taxable income. 50 percent of the combined taxable income computed as provided in subparagraph (C)(ii)(II) shall be allocated to the electing corporation. Combined taxable income, computed without regard to the last sentence of subparagraph (C)(ii)(II), less the amount allocated to the electing corporation under the preceding sentence, shall be allocated to the appropriate domestic member or members (other than any electing corporation) of the affiliated group and shall be treated as income from sources within the United States, or, if there is no such domestic member, to a foreign member or members of such affiliated group as the Secretary may provide under regulations.

(IV) Covered sales. For purposes of this paragraph, the term "covered sales" means sales by members of the affiliated group (other than foreign affiliates) to persons who are not members of the affiliated group or to foreign affiliates.

(D) Unrelated person. For purposes of this paragraph, the term "unrelated person" means any person other than a person related within the meaning of paragraph (3)(D) to the electing corporation.

(E) Electing corporation. For purposes of this subsection, the term "electing corporation" means a domestic corporation for which an election under this section is in effect.

(F) Time and manner of election; revocation.

(i) In general. An election under subparagraph (A) to use one of the methods under subparagraph (C) shall be made only on or before the due date prescribed by law (including extensions) for filing the tax return of the electing corporation for its first taxable year beginning after December 31, 1982. If an election of one of such methods is made, such election shall be binding on the electing corporation and such method must be used for each taxable year thereafter until such election is revoked by the electing corporation under subparagraph (F)(iii). If any such election is revoked by the electing corporation under subparagraph (F)(iii), such electing corporation may make a subsequent election under subparagraph (A) only with the consent of the Secretary.

(ii) Manner of making election. An election under subparagraph (A) to use one of the methods under subparagraph (C) shall be made by filing a statement to such effect with the return referred to in subparagraph (F)(i) or in such other manner as the Secretary may prescribe by regulations.

(iii) Revocation.

(I) Except as provided in subparagraph (F)(iii)(II), an election may be revoked for any taxable year only with the consent of the Secretary.

(II) An election shall be deemed revoked for the year in which the electing corporation is deemed to have revoked such election under subparagraph (B)(i) or (C)(i)(III)(a).

(iv) Aggregation.

(I) Where more than one electing corporation in the affiliated group produces any product or renders any services in the same product area, all such electing corporations must elect to compute their taxable income under the same method under subparagraph (C).

(II) All electing corporations in the same affiliated group that produce any products or render any services in the same product area may elect, subject to such terms and conditions as the Secretary may prescribe by regulations, to compute their taxable income from export sales under a different method from that used for all other sales and services. For this purpose, export sales means all sales by the electing corporation of products to foreign persons for use or consumption outside the United States and its possessions, provided such products are manufactured or produced in the possession within the meaning of subsection (d)(1)(A) of section 954, and further provided (except to the extent otherwise provided by regulations) the income derived by such foreign person on resale of such products (in the same state or in an altered state) is not included in foreign base company income for purposes of section 954(a).

(III) All members of an affiliated group must consent to an election under this subsection at such time and in such manner as shall be prescribed by the Secretary by regulations.

(6) Treatment of certain sales made after July 1, 1982.
(A) In general. For purposes of this section, in the case of a disposition of intangible property made by a corporation after July 1, 1982, any gain or loss from such disposition shall be treated as gain or loss from sources within the United States to which paragraph (5) does not apply.

(B) Exception. Subparagraph (A) shall not apply to any disposition by a corporation of intangible property if

2,605

such disposition is to a person who is not a related person to such corporation.

(C) Paragraph does not affect eligibility. This paragraph shall not apply for purposes of determining whether the corporation meets the requirements of subsection (a)(2).

(7) **Section 864(e)(1) not to apply.** This subsection shall be applied as if section 864(e)(1) (relating to treatment of affiliated groups) had not been enacted.

(8) **Regulations.** The Secretary shall prescribe such regulations as may be necessary or appropriate to carry out the purposes of this subsection, including rules for the application of this subsection to income from leasing of products to unrelated persons.

(i) Definitions and special rules relating to limitations of subsection (a)(4).

(1) **Qualified possession wages.** For purposes of this section—

(A) In general. The term "qualified possession wages" means wages paid or incurred by the possession corporation during the taxable year in connection with the active conduct of a trade or business within a possession of the United States to any employee for services performed in such possession, but only if such services are performed while the principal place of employment of such employee is within such possession.

(B) Limitation on amount of wages taken into account.
(i) In general. The amount of wages which may be taken into account under subparagraph (A) with respect to any employee for any taxable year shall not exceed 85 percent of the contribution and benefit base determined under section 230 of the Social Security Act for the calendar year in which such taxable year begins.

(ii) Treatment of part-time employees, etc. If—
(I) any employee is not employed by the possession corporation on a substantially full-time basis at all times during the taxable year, or
(II) the principal place of employment of any employee with the possession corporation is not within a possession at all times during the taxable year,

the limitation applicable under clause (i) with respect to such employee shall be the appropriate portion (as determined by the Secretary) of the limitation which would otherwise be in effect under clause (i).

(C) Treatment of certain employees. The term "qualified possession wages" shall not include any wages paid to employees who are assigned by the employer to perform services for another person, unless the principal trade or business of the employer is to make employees available for temporary periods to other persons in return for compensation. All possession corporations treated as 1 corporation under paragraph (5) shall be treated as 1 employer for purposes of the preceding sentence.

(D) Wages.
(i) In general. Except as provided in clause (ii), the term "wages" has the meaning given to such term by subsection (b) of section 3306 (determined without regard to any dollar limitation contained in such section). For purposes of the preceding sentence, such subsection (b) shall be applied as if the term "United States" included all possession of the United States.

(ii) Special rule for agricultural labor and railway labor. In any case to which subparagraph (A) or (B) of paragraph (1) of section 51(h) applies, the term "wages" has the meaning given to such term by section 51(h)(2).

(2) **Allocable employee fringe benefit expenses.**
(A) In general. The allocable employee fringe benefit expenses of any possession corporation for any taxable year is an amount which bears the same ratio to the amount determined under subparagraph (B) for such taxable year as—
(i) the aggregate amount of the possession corporation's qualified possession wages for such taxable year, bears to
(ii) the aggregate amount of the wages paid or incurred by such possession corporation during such taxable year.

In no event shall the amount determined under the preceding sentence exceed 15 percent of the amount referred to in clause (i).

(B) Expenses taken into account. For purposes of subparagraph (A), the amount determined under this subparagraph for any taxable year is the aggregate amount allowable as a deduction under this chapter to the possession corporation for such taxable year with respect to—
(i) employer contributions under a stock bonus, pension, profit-sharing, or annuity plan,
(ii) employer-provided coverage under any accident or health plan for employees, and
(iii) the cost of life or disability insurance provided to employees.

Any amount treated as wages under paragraph (1)(D) shall not be taken into account under this subparagraph.

(3) **Treatment of possession taxes.**
(A) Amount of credit for possession corporations not using profit split.
(i) In general. For purposes of subsection (a)(4)(A)(iii), the amount of the qualified possession income taxes for any taxable year allocable to non-sheltered income shall be an amount which bears the same ratio to the possession income taxes for such taxable years as—
(I) the increase in the tax liability of the possession corporation under this chapter for the taxable year by reason of subsection (a)(4)(A) (without regard to clause (iii) thereof), bears to
(II) the tax liability of the possession corporation under this chapter for the taxable year determined without regard to the credit allowable under this section.

(ii) Limitation on amount of taxes taken into account. Possession income taxes shall not be taken into account under clause (i) for any taxable year to the extent that the amount of such taxes exceeds 9 percent of the amount of the taxable income for such taxable year.

(B) Deduction for possession corporations using profit split. Notwithstanding subsection (c), if a possession corporation is not described in subsection (a)(4)(A)(iii) for the taxable year, such possession corporation shall be allowed a deduction for such taxable year in an amount which bears the same ratio to the possession income taxes for such taxable year as—
(i) the increase in the tax liability of the possession corporation under this chapter for the taxable year by reason of subsection (a)(4)(A), bears to
(ii) the tax liability of the possession corporation under this chapter for the taxable year determined

without regard to the credit allowable under this section.

In determining the credit under subsection (a) and in applying the preceding sentence, taxable income shall be determined without regard to the preceding sentence.

(C) Possession income taxes. For purposes of this paragraph, the term "possession income taxes" means any taxes of a possession of the United States which are treated as not being income, war profits, or excess profits taxes paid or accrued to a possession of the United States by reason of subsection (c).

(4) Depreciation rules. For purposes of this section—

(A) Depreciation allowances. The term "depreciation allowances" means the depreciation deductions allowable under section 167 to the possession corporation.

(B) Categories of property.

(i) Qualified tangible property. The term "qualified tangible property" means any tangible property used by the possession corporation in a possession of the United States in the active conduct of a trade or business within such possession.

(ii) Short-life qualified tangible property. The term "short-life qualified tangible property" means any qualified tangible property to which section 168 applies and which is 3-year property or 5-year property for purposes of such section.

(iii) Medium-life qualified tangible property. The term "medium-life qualified tangible property" means any qualified tangible property to which section 168 applies and which is a 7-year property or 10-year property for purposes of such section.

(iv) Long-life qualified tangible property. The term "long-life qualified tangible property" means any qualified tangible property to which section 168 applies and which is not described in clause (ii) or (iii).

(v) Transitional rule. In the case of any qualified tangible property to which section 168 (as in effect on the day before the date of the enactment [10/22/86] of the Tax Reform Act of 1986) applies, any reference in this paragraph to section 168 shall be treated as a reference to such section as so in effect.

(5) Election to compute credit on consolidated basis.

(A) In general. Any affiliated group may elect to treat all possession corporations which would be members of such group but for section 1504(b)(3) or (4) as 1 corporation for purposes of this section. The credit determined under this section with respect to such 1 corporation shall be allocated among such possession corporations in such manner as the Secretary may prescribe.

(B) Election. An election under subparagraph (A) shall apply to the taxable year for which made and all succeeding taxable years unless revoked with the consent of the Secretary.

(6) Possession corporation. The term "possession corporation" means a domestic corporation for which the election provided in subsection (a) is in effect.

(j) Termination.

(1) In general. Except as otherwise provided in this subsection, this section shall not apply to any taxable year beginning after December 31, 1995.

(2) Transition rules for active business income credit. Except as provided in paragraph (3)—

(A) Economic activity credit. In the case of an existing credit claimant—

(i) with respect to a possession other than Puerto Rico, and

(ii) to which subsection (a)(4)(B) does not apply,

the credit determined under subsection (a)(1)(A) shall be allowed for taxable years beginning after December 31, 1995, and before January 1, 2002.

(B) Special rule for reduced credit.

(i) In general. In the case of an existing credit claimant to which subsection (a)(4)(B) applies, the credit determined under subsection (a)(1)(A) shall be allowed for taxable years beginning after December 31, 1995, and before January 1, 1998.

(ii) Election irrevocable after 1997. An election under subsection (a)(4)(B)(iii) which is in effect for the taxpayer's last taxable year beginning before 1997 may not be revoked unless it is revoked for the taxpayer's first taxable year beginning in 1997 and all subsequent taxable years.

(C) Economic activity credit for Puerto Rico. For economic activity credit for Puerto Rico, see section 30A.

(3) Additional restricted credit.

(A) In general. In the case of an existing credit claimant—

(i) the credit under subsection (a)(1)(A) shall be allowed for the period beginning with the first taxable year after the last taxable year to which subparagraph (A) or (B) of paragraph (2), whichever is appropriate, applied and ending with the last taxable year beginning before January 1, 2006, except that

(ii) the aggregate amount of taxable income taken into account under subsection (a)(1)(A) for any such taxable year shall not exceed the adjusted base period income of such claimant.

(B) Coordination with subsection (a)(4). The amount of income described in subsection (a)(1)(A) which is taken into account in applying subsection (a)(4) shall be such income as reduced under this paragraph.

(4) Adjusted base period income. For purposes of paragraph (3)—

(A) In general. The term "adjusted base period income" means the average of the inflation-adjusted possession incomes of the corporation for each base period year.

(B) Inflation-adjusted possession income. For purposes of subparagraph (A), the inflation-adjusted possession income of any corporation for any base period year shall be an amount equal to the sum of—

(i) the possession income of such corporation for such base period year, plus

(ii) such possession income multiplied by the inflation adjustment percentage for such base period year.

(C) Inflation adjustment percentage. For purposes of subparagraph (B), the inflation adjustment percentage for any base period year means the percentage (if any) by which—

(i) the CPI for 1995, exceeds

(ii) the CPI for the calendar year in which the base period year for which the determination is being made ends.

For purposes of the preceding sentence, the CPI for any calendar year is the CPI (as defined in section 1(f)(5)) for such year under section 1(f)(4).

(D) Increase in inflation adjustment percentage for growth during base years. The inflation adjustment percentage (determined under subparagraph (C) without regard to this subparagraph) for each of the 5 taxable

years referred to in paragraph (5)(A) shall be increased by—
(i) 5 percentage points in the case of a taxable year ending during the 1-year period ending on October 13, 1995;
(ii) 10.25 percentage points in the case of a taxable year ending during the 1-year period ending on October 13, 1994;
(iii) 15.76 percentage points in the case of a taxable year ending during the 1-year period ending on October 13, 1993;
(iv) 21.55 percentage points in the case of a taxable year ending during the 1-year period ending on October 13, 1992; and
(v) 27.63 percentage points in the case of a taxable year ending during the 1-year period ending on October 13, 1991.

(5) Base period year. For purposes of this subsection—
(A) In general. The term "base period year" means each of 3 taxable years which are among the 5 most recent taxable years of the corporation ending before October 14, 1995, determined by disregarding—
(i) one taxable year for which the corporation had the largest inflation-adjusted possession income, and
(ii) one taxable year for which the corporation had the smallest inflation-adjusted possession income.
(B) Corporations not having significant possession income throughout 5-year period.
(i) In general. If a corporation does not have significant possession income for each of the most recent 5 taxable years ending before October 14, 1995, then, in lieu of applying subparagraph (A), the term "base period year" means only those taxable years (of such taxable years) for which the corporation has significant possession income; except that, if such corporation has significant possession income for 4 of such 5 taxable years, the rule of subparagraph (A)(ii) shall apply.
(ii) Special rule. If there is no year (of such 5 taxable years) for which a corporation has significant possession income—
(I) the term "base period year" means the first taxable year ending on or after October 14, 1995, but
(II) the amount of possession income for such year which is taken into account under paragraph (4) shall be the amount which would be determined if such year were a short taxable year ending on September 30, 1995.
(iii) Significant possession income. For purposes of this subparagraph, the term "significant possession income" means possession income which exceeds 2 percent of the possession income of the taxpayer for the taxable year (of the period of 6 taxable years ending with the first taxable year ending on or after October 14, 1995) having the greatest possession income.
(C) Election to use one base period year.
(i) In general. At the election of the taxpayer, the term "base period year" means—
(I) only the last taxable year of the corporation ending in calendar year 1992, or
(II) a deemed taxable year which includes the first ten months of calendar year 1995.
(ii) Base period income for 1995. In determining the adjusted base period income of the corporation for the deemed taxable year under clause (i)(II), the possession income shall be annualized and shall be determined without regard to any extraordinary item.
(iii) Election. An election under this subparagraph by any possession corporation may be made only for the corporation's first taxable year beginning after December 31, 1995, for which it is a possession corporation. The rules of subclauses (II) and (III) of subsection (a)(4)(B)(iii) shall apply to the election under this subparagraph.
(D) Acquisitions and dispositions. Rules similar to the rules of subparagraphs (A) and (B) of section 41(f)(3) shall apply for purposes of this subsection.

(6) Possession income. For purposes of this subsection, the term "possession income" means, with respect to any possession, the income referred to in subsection (a)(1)(A) determined with respect to that possession. In no event shall possession income be treated as being less than zero.

(7) Short years. If the current year or a base period year is a short taxable year, the application of this subsection shall be made with such annualizations as the Secretary shall prescribe.

(8) Special rules for certain possessions.
(A) In general. In the case of an existing credit claimant with respect to an applicable possession, this section (other than the preceding paragraphs of this subsection) shall apply to such claimant with respect to such applicable possession for taxable years beginning after December 31, 1995, and before January 1, 2006.
(B) Applicable possession. For purposes of this paragraph, the term "applicable possession" means Guam, American Samoa, and the Commonwealth of the Northern Mariana Islands.

(9) Existing credit claimant. For purposes of this subsection—
(A) In general. The term "existing credit claimant" means a corporation—
(i)(I) which was actively conducting a trade or business in a possession on October 13, 1995, and
(II) with respect to which an election under this section is in effect for the corporation's taxable year which includes October 13, 1995, or
(ii) which acquired all of the assets of a trade or business of a corporation which—
(I) satisfied the requirements of subclause (I) of clause (i) with respect to such trade or business, and
(II) satisfied the requirements of subclause (II) of clause (i).
(B) New lines of business prohibited. If, after October 13, 1995, a corporation which would (but for this subparagraph) be an existing credit claimant adds a substantial new line of business (other than in an acquisition described in subparagraph (A)(ii)), such corporation shall cease to be treated as an existing credit claimant as of the close of the taxable year ending before the date of such addition.
(C) Binding contract exception. If, on October 13, 1995, and at all times thereafter, there is in effect with respect to a corporation a binding contract for the acquisition of assets to be used in, or for the sale of assets to be produced from, a trade or business, the corporation shall be treated for purposes of this paragraph as actively conducting such trade or business on October 13, 1995. The preceding sentence shall not apply if such

Income from foreign sources — Code Sec. 936

trade or business is not actively conducted before January 1, 1996.

(10) Separate application to each possession. For purposes of determining—

(A) whether a taxpayer is an existing credit claimant, and

(B) the amount of the credit allowed under this section, this subsection (and so much of this section as relates to this subsection) shall be applied separately with respect to each possession.

In 2010, P.L. 111-312, Sec. 756(a)(1), substituted "first 6 taxable years" for "first 4 taxable years" in Sec. 119(d), P.L. 109-432, Div. A, reproduced below.... Sec. 756(a)(2), substituted "January 1, 2012" for "January 1, 2010" in Sec. 119(d), P.L. 109-432, Div. A, reproduced below.

In 2008, P.L. 110-343, Sec. 309(a)(1)DivA, substituted "first 4 taxable years" for "first two taxable years" in Sec. 119(d), P.L. 109-432, reproduced below ... Sec. 309(a)(2)DivA, substituted "January 1, 2010" for "January 1, 2008" in Sec. 119(d), P.L. 109-432, reproduced below.

In 2007, P.L. 110-172, Sec. 11(g)(12), deleted "FSC or" before "former FSC" in subpara. (f)(2)(B), enacted 12/29/2007.

In 2006, P.L. 109-432, Sec. 119DivA, of this Act, as amended by Sec. 309(a)(1) Div A, P.L. 110-343 and Sec. 756(a)(1)-(2), P.L. 111-312, [see above] reads as follows:

"Sec. 119. American Samoa Economic Development Credit.

"(a) In general. For purposes of section 30A of the Internal Revenue Code of 1986, a domestic corporation shall be treated as a qualified domestic corporation to which such section applies if such corporation

"(1) is an existing credit claimant with respect to American Samoa, and

"(2) elected the application of section 936 of the Internal Revenue Code of 1986 for its last taxable year beginning before January 1, 2006.

"(b) Special rules for application of Section. The following rules shall apply in applying section 30A of the Internal Revenue Code of 1986 for purposes of this section:

" (1) Amount of credit. Notwithstanding section 30A(a)(1) of such Code, the amount of the credit determined under section 30A(a)(1) of such Code for any taxable year shall be the amount deter-mined under section 30A(d) of such Code, except that section 30A(d) shall be applied without regard to paragraph (3) thereof.

"(2) Separate application. In applying section 30A(a)(3) of such Code in the case of a corporation treated as a qualified domestic corporation by reason of this section, section 30A of such Code (and so much of section 936 of such Code as relates to such section 30A) shall be applied separately with respect to American Samoa.

"(3) Foreign tax credit allowed. Notwithstanding section 30A(e) of such Code, the provisions of section 936(c) of such Code shall not apply with respect to the credit allowed by reason of this section.

"(c) Definitions. For purposes of this section, any term which is used in this section which is also used in section 30A or 936 of such Code shall have the same meaning given such term by such section 30A or 936.

"(d) Application of Section. Notwithstanding section 30A(h) or section 936(j) of such Code, this section (and so much of section 30A and section 936 of such Code as relates to this section) shall apply to the first 6 taxable years of a corporation to which subsection (a) applies which begin after December 31, 2005, and before January 1, 2012. "

In 2004, P.L. 108-357, Sec. 402(b)(2), substituted "subsections (f) and (g) of section 904" for "section 904(f)" in subpara. (a)(2)(A), effective for losses for tax. yrs. begin. after 12/31/2006.

In 1996, P.L. 104-188, Sec. 1601(a), added subsec. (j), effective for tax. yrs. begin. after 12/31/95. Sec. 1601(c)(2) and (3) of this Act provides:

"(2) Special rule for qualified possession source investment income. The amendments made by this section shall not apply to qualified possession source investment income received or accrued before July 1, 1996, without regard to the taxable year in which received or accrued.

"(3) Special transition rule for payment of estimated tax installments. In determining the amount of any installment due under section 6655 of the Internal Revenue Code of 1986 after the date of the enactment of this Act and before October 1, 1996, only ½ of any increase in tax (for the taxable year for which such installment is made) by reason of the amendments made by subsections (a) and (b) shall be taken into account. Any reduction in such installment by reason of the preceding sentence shall be recaptured by increasing the next required installment for such year by the amount of such reduction."

—P.L. 104-188, Sec. 1704(t)(37), substituted "subparagraphs (D)(ii)" for "subparagraphs (D)(i)(I)" in subsec. (b) ... Sec. 1704(t)(80), substituted "depreciation" for "deprecation" in subclause (a)(4)(A)(ii)(I), effective 8/20/96.

In 1993, P.L. 103-66, Sec. 13227(a)(1), substituted "as otherwise provided in this section" for "as provided in paragraph (3)" in para. (a)(1) ... Sec. 13227(a)(2), added para. (a)(4) ... Sec. 13227(b), added subsec. (j), effective for tax. yrs. begin. after 12/31/93.

In 1990, P.L. 101-508, Sec. 11704(a)(11), substituted "subsection (a)(2)" for "subsection (a)(1)", each place it appeared in para. (e)(1), effective 11/5/90.

—P.L. 101-382, Sec. 227(a), added subpara. (d)(4)(D), effective for calendar yrs. after 1989.

In 1988, P.L. 100-647, Sec. 1002(h)(3)(A), substituted "section 41" for "section 30", in subclause (h)(5)(C)(i)(IV)(c) ... Sec. 1002(h)(3)(b), substituted "section 41(f)" for "section 30(f)" in subclause (h)(5)(C)(i)(IV)(c), effective for tax. yrs. begin. after 12/31/85.

—P.L. 100-647, Sec. 1012(h)(2)(B), redesignated para. (h)(7) as para. (h)(8) and added new para. (h)(7), effective for tax. yrs. begin. after 12/31/86, except as provided in Sec. 1215(c)(2)-(6) of P.L. 99-514, reproduced in note following Code Sec. 864.

—P.L. 100-647, Sec. 1012(j), substituted "section 957(c) (as in effect on the day before the date of the enactment of the Tax Reform Act of 1986)" for "section 957(c) in subpara. (d)(3)(B), effective for tax. yrs. of foreign corporations begin. after 12/31/86.

—P.L. 100-647, Sec. 1012(n)(2), amended Sec. 1231(g)(2)(B) of P.L. 99-514, [reproduced below] by substituting 'if any, was made' for 'was made', see below ... Sec. 1012(n)(3), added Sec. 1231(g)(5) of P.L. 99-514, [reproduced below] part of the effective date for changes made by Sec. 1231(a)-(f) see below.... Sec. 1012(n)(4), amended Sec. 1231(a)(1)(B), so that it would add a sentence at the end of the material relating to payment of cost sharing in clause (h)(5)(C)(i)(I), rather than at the end of clause (h)(5)(C)(i)(I), see below.

—P.L. 100-647, Sec. 1012(n)(5)(A), amended clause (d)(4)(A)(ii) ... Sec. 1012(n)(5)(B), substituted 'the Commissioner of Financial Institutions of Puerto Rico' for 'the Secretary of the Treasury of Puerto Rico' in clauses (d)(4)(C)(i) and (ii), effective for tax. yrs. begin. after 12/31/86, except as provided in Secs. 1231(g)(2)(B), (g)(4), and (g)(5) of P.L. 99-514, reproduced below.

Prior to amendment, clause (d)(4)(A)(ii) read as follows:

"(ii) in accordance with a specific authorization granted by the Government Development Bank for Puerto Rico pursuant to regulations issued by the Secretary of the Treasury of Puerto Rico."

—P.L. 100-647, Sec. 6132(a), added "and the Virgin Islands" after "274(h)(6)(A)" in subpara. (d)(4)(B), effective for investments made after 11/10/88.

—P.L. 100-647, Sec. 6252(b)(1), amended Sec. 441(a) of P.L. 98-369 [reproduced below], by substituting "shall, during 1988 and each fourth calendar year thereafter, submit a report to the Congress (using the most recent information available) setting forth" for "shall, for the calendar year 1981 and each second calendar year thereafter, submit a report to the Congress within 24 months following the close of such calendar year setting forth", effective for reports for calendar years after 1982.

In 1986, P.L. 99-514, Sec. 231(d)(3)(G), substituted "section 41(b)" for "section 30(b)", in subclause (h)(5)(C)(i)(I)(a), effective for tax. yrs. begin. after 12/31/85.

—P.L. 99-514, Sec. 701(e)(4)(I), deleted subpara. (a)(3)(A), and redesignated (a)(3)(B), (a)(3)(C), (a)(3)(E), as (a)(3)(A), (a)(3)(B), and (a)(3)(C), respectively, effective for tax. yrs. begin. after 12/31/86.

Prior to deletion, subpara. (a)(3)(A), read as follows:

"(A) section 56 (relating to corporate minimum tax),"

—P.L. 99-514, Sec. 1231(a)(1)(A), substituted "the same proportion of 110 percent of the cost" for "the same proportion of the cost", in subclause (h)(5)(C)(i)(I) ... Sec. 1231(a)(1)(B), [as amended by Sec. 1012(n)(4) of P.L. 100-647, see above], added the sentence at the end of the material relating to the payment of cost sharing in clause (h)(5)(C)(i)(I) ... Sec. 1231(a)(2), substituted "the third and fourth sentences thereof, but substituting '120 percent' for '110 percent' in the second sentence thereof)" for "the third sentence thereof)" in subclause (h)(5)(C)(ii)(II) ... Sec. 1231(b), added the last sentence to subsec. (b) ... Sec. 1231(c), added para. (d)(4) ... Sec. 1231(d)(1), substituted "75 percent" for "65 percent" in subpara. (a)(2)(B) ... Sec. 1231(d)(2), deleted subpara. (a)(2)(C) ... Sec. 1231(f), substituted "all products and types of services, within such product area, produced or rendered" for "all products produced and types of service rendered" in subclause (h)(5)(C)(ii)(II), effective for tax. yrs. begin. after 12/31/86, except as provided in Secs. 1231(g)(2)(B), [amended by Sec. 1012(n)(2) of P.L. 100-647] (g)(4), and (g)(5) [as added by Sec. 1012(n)(3) of P.L. 100-647, see above] of this Act, which reads as follows:

"(B) Special rule for section 936. For purposes of section 936(h)(5)(C) of the Internal Revenue Code of 1986 the amendments made by subsection (e) shall apply to taxable years beginning after December 31, 1986, without regard to when the transfer (or license) if any, was made."

"(4) Transitional Rule. In the case of a corporation—

"(A) with respect to which an election under section 936 of the Internal Revenue Code of 1986 (relating to possessions tax credit) is in effect,

"(B) which produced an end-product form in Puerto Rico on or before September 3, 1982,

"(C) which began manufacturing a component of such product in Puerto Rico in its taxable year beginning in 1983, and

"(D) with respect to which a Puerto Rican tax exemption was granted on June 27, 1983,

such corporation shall treat such component as a separate product for such taxable year for purposes of determining whether such corporation had a significant business presence in Puerto Rico with respect to such product and its income with respect to such product."

"(5) Transitional rule for increase in gross income test.—

"(A) In general. If—

"(i) a corporation fails to meet the requirements of subparagraph (B) of section 936(a)(2) of the Internal Revenue Code of 1986 (as amended by subsection (d)(1)) for any taxable year beginning in 1987 or 1988,

"(ii) such corporation would have met the requirements of such subparagraph (B) if such subparagraph had been applied without regard to the amendment made by subsection (d)(1), and "(iii) 75 percent or more of the gross income of such corporation for such taxable year (or, in the case of a taxable year beginning in 1988, for the period consisting of such taxable year and the preceding taxable year) was derived from the active conduct of a trade or business within a possession of the United States, such corporation shall nevertheless be treated as meeting the requirements of such subparagraph (B) for such taxable year if it elects to reduce the amount of the qualified possession source investment income for the taxable year by the amount of the shortfall determined under subparagraph (B) of this paragraph.

"(B) Determination of shortfall.—The shortfall determined under this subparagraph for any taxable year is an amount equal to the excess of—

"(i) 75 percent of the gross income of the corporation for the 3-year period (or part thereof) referred to in section 936(a)(2)(A) of such Code, over

"(ii) the amount of the gross income of such corporation for such period (or part thereof) which was derived from the active conduct of a trade or business within a possession of the United States.

"(C) Special rule.— Any income attributable to the investment of the amount not treated as qualified possession source investment income under subparagraph (A) shall not be treated as qualified possession source investment income for any taxable year."

Prior to amendment, subpara. (a)(2)(C) read as follows:

"(C) Transitional rule. In applying subparagraph (B) with respect to taxable years beginning after December 31, 1982, and before January 1, 1985, the following percentage shall be substituted for '65 percent':

For taxable years beginning in calendar year:	The percentage is:
1983	55
1984	60"

—P.L. 99-514, Sec. 1275(a)(1), substituted "and the Virgin Islands" for ", but does not include the Virgin Islands of the United States" in para. (d)(1), effective for tax. yrs. begin. after 12/31/86. Sec. 1277(b) of this Act provides the following special rule:

"(b) Special rule for Guam, American Samoa, and the Northern Mariana Islands.

"The amendments made by this subtitle shall apply with respect to Guam, American Samoa, or the Northern Mariana Islands (and to residents thereof and corporations created or organized therein) only if (and so long as) an implementing agreement under section 1271 is in effect between the United States and such possession."

—P.L. 99-514, Sec. 1812(c)(4)(C), amended clause (h)(3)(D)(ii), effective for tax. yrs. begin. after 12/31/83.

Prior to amendment, clause (h)(3)(D)(ii), read as follows:

"(ii) Special rules. For purposes of clause (i)—

"(I) section 267(b) and section 707(b)(1) shall be applied by substituting '10 percent' for '50 percent', and

"(II) section 267(b)(3) shall be applied without regard to whether a person was a personal holding company or a foreign personal holding company."

—P.L. 99-499, Sec. 516(b)(1)(B), redesignated subparas. (a)(3)(A), (a)(3)(B) and (a)(3)(C) as subparas. (a)(3)(B), (a)(3)(C) and (a)(3)(D) respectively (as amended by Sec. 701(e)(4)(I) of P.L. 99-514, see above) and added new subpara. (c)(3)(A), effective for tax. yrs. begin. after 12/31/86.

In 1984, P.L. 98-369, Sec. 441(a), [as amended by Sec. 6252(b)(1) of P.L. 100-647, see above], provides:

"SEC. 441. SIMPLIFICATION OF CERTAIN REPORTING REQUIREMENTS.

"(a) Report on possessions corporations. —The Secretary of the Treasury shall, during 1988 and each fourth calendar year thereafter, submit a report to the Congress (using the most recent information available) setting forth an analysis of the operation and effect of sections 936 and 934(b) of the Internal Revenue Code of 1954."

—P.L. 98-369, Sec. 474(r)(22)(A), substituted "section 30(b)" for "section 44F(b)" in subclause (h)(5)(C)(i)(I)(a) . . . Sec. 474(r)(22)(B)(i), substituted "section 30" for "section 44F" in subclause (h)(5)(C)(i)(IV)(c) . . . Sec. 474(r)(22)(B)(ii), substituted "section 30(f)" for "section 44F(f)" in subclause (h)(5)(C)(i)(IV)(c), effective for tax. yrs. begin. after 12/31/83, and for carrybacks from tax. yrs. begin. after 12/31/83.

—P.L. 98-369, Sec. 712(g), substituted "The percentage is:" for "The percentage tax is:" in the table in subpara. (a)(2)(C), effective for tax. yrs. begin. after 12/31/82.

—P.L. 98-369, Sec. 801(d)(11), amended subsec. (f), effective for transactions after 12/31/84, in tax. yrs. end. after 12/31/84.

Prior to amendment, subsec. (f) read as follows:

"(f) DISC or former DISC corporation ineligible for credit.

"No credit shall be allowed under this section to a corporation for a taxable year for which it is a DISC or former DISC (as defined in section 992(a)) or in which it owns at any time stock in a DISC or former DISC."

In 1983, P.L. 97-448, Sec. 306(a)(1)(A)(i), redesignated the second Sec. 201(c) of P.L. 97-248 as Sec. 201(d) of P.L. 97-248, see below.

In 1982, P.L. 97-248, Sec. 201(d)(8)(B), substituted "(relating to corporate minimum tax)" for "(relating to minimum tax)" in subpara. (a)(3)(A) . . . Sec. 213(a)(1)(A), substituted "65 percent" for "50 percent" in subpara. (a)(2)(B) . . . Sec. 213(a)(1)(B), added subpara. (a)(2)(C) . . . Sec. 213(a)(2), added subsec. (h), effective for tax. yrs. begin. after 12/31/82. Sec. 213(e)(2) of the Act provides as follows:

"(2) Certain sales made after July 1, 1982.— Paragraph (6) of section 936(h) of the Internal Revenue Code of 1954, and so much of section 934 to which such paragraph applies by reason of section 934(e)(4) of such Code, shall apply to taxable years ending after July 1, 1982."

In 1978, P.L. 95-600, Sec. 701(u)(11)(A), redesignated para. (a)(2) as para. (a)(3), and amended so much of para. (a)(1) as preceded subpara. (a)(1)(A) . . . Sec. 701(u)(11)(B)(i), added new para. (d)(3) . . . Sec. 701(u)(11)(B)(ii), substituted "(d) Definitions and special rules—." for "(d) Definitions—." in the heading of subsec. (d), effective as if included in the addition of Code Sec. 936, as made by Sec. 1051(b) of P.L. 94-455, see below.

Prior to amendment, so much of para. (a)(1), as preceded subpara. (a)(1)(A) read as follows:

"(1) In general. Except as provided in paragraph (2), in the case of a domestic corporation which elects the application of this section, there shall be allowed as a credit against the tax imposed by this chapter an amount equal to the portion of the tax which is attributable to taxable income, from sources without the United States, from the active conduct of a trade or business within a possession of the United States, and from qualified possession source investment income, if the conditions of both subparagraph (A) and subparagraph (B) are satisfied:"

In 1976, P.L. 94-455, Sec. 1051(b), added Code Sec. 936, effective for tax. yrs. begin. after 12/31/75, except "qualified possession source investment income," as defined in Code Sec. 936(d)(2), includes income from any source outside the United States if the taxpayer establishes to the satisfaction of the Secretary of the Treasury or his delegate that the income from such sources was earned before 10/1/76.

—P.L. 94-455, Sec. 1901(b)(37)(B)(i), added "or" at the end of subpara. (a)(2)(C) . . . Sec. 1901(b)(37)(B)(ii), deleted subpara. (a)(2)(D), effective for tax. yrs. begin. after 12/31/76.

Prior to amendment, subpara. (a)(2)(D) read as follows:

"(D) section 1333 (relating to war loss recoveries), or"

Sec. 937. Residence and source rules involving possessions.

(a) Bona fide resident.

For purposes of this subpart, section 865(g)(3), section 876, section 881(b), paragraphs (2) and (3) of section 901(b), section 957(c), section 3401(a)(8)(C), and section 7654(a), except as provided in regulations, the term "bona fide resident" means a person—

(1) who is present for at least 183 days during the taxable year in Guam, American Samoa, the Northern Mariana Islands, Puerto Rico, or the Virgin Islands, as the case may be, and

(2) who does not have a tax home (determined under the principles of section 911(d)(3) without regard to the second sentence thereof) outside such specified possession during the taxable year and does not have a closer connection (determined under the principles of section 7701(b)(3)(B)(ii)) to the United States or a foreign country than to such specified possession.

For purposes of paragraph (1), the determination as to whether a person is present for any day shall be made under the principles of section 7701(b).

(b) Source rules.

Except as provided in regulations, for purposes of this title —

(1) except as provided in paragraph (2), rules similar to the rules for determining whether income is income from sources within the United States or is effectively connected with the conduct of a trade or business within the United States shall apply for purposes of determining whether income is from sources within a possession specified in subsection (a)(1) or effectively connected with the conduct of a trade or business within any such possession, and

(2) any income treated as income from sources within the United States or as effectively connected with the conduct of a trade or business within the United States shall not be treated as income from sources within any such possession or as effectively connected with the conduct of a trade or business within any such possession.

(c) Reporting requirement.

(1) In general. If, for any taxable year, an individual takes the position for United States income tax reporting purposes that the individual became, or ceases to be, a bona fide resident of a possession specified in subsection (a)(1), such individual shall file with the Secretary, at such time and in such manner as the Secretary may prescribe, notice of such position.

(2) Transition rule. If, for any of an individual's 3 taxable years ending before the individual's first taxable year ending after the date of the enactment of this subsection, the individual took a position described in paragraph (1), the individual shall file with the Secretary, at such time and in such manner as the Secretary may prescribe, notice of such position.

In 2004, P.L. 108-357, Sec. 908(a), added Code Sec. 937, effective for tax. yrs. end. after 10/22/2004, except as provided in Sec. 908(d)(2) and (3), P.L. 108-357, which reads as follows:

"(2) 183-day rule. Section 937(a)(1) of the Internal Revenue Code of 1986 (as added by this section) shall apply to taxable years beginning after the date of the enactment of this Act.

"(3) Sourcing. Section 937(b)(2) of such Code (as so added) shall apply to income earned after the date of the enactment of this Act."

SUBPART E.—QUALIFYING FOREIGN TRADE INCOME [REPEALED]

Sec.
941. Repealed [Qualifying foreign trade income.]
942. Repealed [Foreign trading gross receipts.]
943. Repealed [Other definitions and special rules.]

In 2004, P.L. 108-357, Sec. 101(b)(2), repealed subpart E, effective for transactions after 12/31/2004.

In 2000, P.L. 106-519, Sec. 4(7), added subpart E, effective for transactions after 9/30/2000.

Sec. 941. Repealed.

In 2006, P.L. 109-222, Sec. 513(a), amended Sec. 5(c)(1) of P.L. 106-519 [see below]... Sec. 513(b), repealed Sec. 101(f) of P.L. 108-357 [see below], effective for tax. yrs. begin. after 5/17/2006.

Prior to amendment, Sec. 5(c)(1) of P.L. 106-519 read as follows:

"(1) In general. In the case of a FSC (as so defined) in existence on September 30, 2000, and at all times thereafter, the amendments made by this Act shall not apply to any transaction in the ordinary course of trade or business involving a FSC which occurs—

"(A) before January 1, 2002; or

"(B) after December 31, 2001, pursuant to a binding contract—

"(i) which is between the FSC (or any related person) and any person which is not a related person; and

"(ii) which is in effect on September 30, 2000, and at all times thereafter.

For purposes of this paragraph, a binding contract shall include a purchase option, renewal option, or replacement option which is included in such contract and which is enforceable against the seller or lessor."

Prior to repeal, Sec. 101(f) of P.L. 108-357 read as follows:

"(f) Binding contracts. The amendments made by this section shall not apply to any transaction in the ordinary course of a trade or business which occurs pursuant to a binding contract—

"(1) which is between the taxpayer and a person who is not a related person (as defined in section 943(b)(3) of such Code, as in effect on the day before the date of the enactment of this Act), and

"(2) which is in effect on September 17, 2003, and at all times thereafter.

"For purposes of this subsection, a binding contract shall include a purchase option, renewal option, or replacement option which is included in such contract and which is enforceable against the seller or lessor."

In 2004, P.L. 108-357, Sec. 101(b)(1), repealed Code Sec. 941, effective for transactions after 12/31/2004. Sec. 101(d)-(f) [subsec. (f) was repealed by Sec. 513(b) of P.L. 109-222, see above] of this Act, reads as follows:

"(d) Transitional rule for 2005 and 2006.

"(1) In general. In the case of transactions during 2005 or 2006, the amount includible in gross income by reason of the amendments made by this section shall not exceed the applicable percentage of the amount which would have been so included but for this subsection.

"(2) Applicable percentage. For purposes of paragraph (1), the applicable percentage shall be as follows:

"(A) For 2005, the applicable percentage shall be 20 percent.

"(B) For 2006, the applicable percentage shall be 40 percent."

"(e) Revocation of election to be treated as domestic corporation. If, during the 1-year period beginning on the date of the enactment of this Act, a corporation for which an election is in effect under section 943(e) of the Internal Revenue Code of 1986 revokes such election, no gain or loss shall be recognized with respect to property treated as transferred under clause (ii) of section 943(e)(4)(B) of such Code to the extent such property—

"(1) was treated as transferred under clause (i) thereof, or

"(2) was acquired during a taxable year to which such election applies and before May 1, 2003, in the ordinary course of its trade or business.

"The Secretary of the Treasury (or such Secretary's delegate) may prescribe such regulations as may be necessary to prevent the abuse of the purposes of this subsection."

"(f) [Repealed by Sec. 513(b), P.L. 109-222, see above.]

Prior to repeal, Code Sec. 941 read as follows:

"SEC. 941. QUALIFYING FOREIGN TRADE INCOME.

"(a) Qualifying foreign trade income. For purposes of this subpart and section 114—

"(1) In general. The term 'qualifying foreign trade income' means, with respect to any transaction, the amount of gross income which, if excluded, will result in a reduction of the taxable income of the taxpayer from such transaction equal to the greatest of—

"(A) 30 percent of the foreign sale and leasing income derived by the taxpayer from such transaction,

"(B) 1.2 percent of the foreign trading gross receipts derived by the taxpayer from the transaction, or

"(C) 15 percent of the foreign trade income derived by the taxpayer from the transaction.

"In no event shall the amount determined under subparagraph (B) exceed 200 percent of the amount determined under subparagraph (C).

"(2) Alternative computation. A taxpayer may compute its qualifying foreign trade income under a subparagraph of paragraph (1) other than the subparagraph which results in the greatest amount of such income.

"(3) Limitation on use of foreign trading gross receipts method. If any person computes its qualifying foreign trade income from any transaction with respect to any property under paragraph (1)(B), the qualifying foreign trade income of such person (or any related person) with respect to any other transaction involving such property shall be zero.

"(4) Rules for marginal costing. The Secretary shall prescribe regulations setting forth rules for the allocation of expenditures in computing foreign trade income under paragraph (1)(C) in those cases where a taxpayer is seeking to establish or maintain a market for qualifying foreign trade property.

"(5) Participation in international boycotts, etc. Under regulations prescribed by the Secretary, the qualifying foreign trade income of a taxpayer for any taxable year shall be reduced (but not below zero) by the sum of—

"(A) an amount equal to such income multiplied by the international boycott factor determined under section 999, and

"(B) any illegal bribe, kickback, or other payment (within the meaning of section 162(c)) paid by or on behalf of the taxpayer directly or indirectly to an official, employee, or agent in fact of a government.

"(b) Foreign trade income. For purposes of this subpart—

"(1) In general. The term 'foreign trade income' means the taxable income of the taxpayer attributable to foreign trading gross receipts of the taxpayer.

"(2) Special rule for cooperatives. In any case in which an organization to which part I of subchapter T applies which is engaged in the marketing of agricultural or horticultural products sells qualifying foreign trade property, in computing the taxable income of such cooperative, there shall not be taken into account any deduction allowable under subsection (b) or (c) of section 1382 (relating to patronage dividends, per-unit retain allocations, and nonpatronage distributions).

"(c) Foreign sale and leasing income. For purposes of this section—

"(1) In general. The term 'foreign sale and leasing income' means, with respect to any transaction—

"(A) foreign trade income properly allocable to activities which—

"(i) are described in paragraph (2)(A)(i) or (3) of section 942(b), and

"(ii) are performed by the taxpayer (or any person acting under a contract with such taxpayer) outside the United States, or

"(B) foreign trade income derived by the taxpayer in connection with the lease or rental of qualifying foreign trade property for use by the lessee outside the United States.

"(2) Special rules for leased property.

"(A) Sales income. The term 'foreign sale and leasing income' includes any foreign trade income derived by the taxpayer from the sale of property described in paragraph (1)(B).

"(B) Limitation in certain cases. Except as provided in regulations, in the case of property which—

"(i) was manufactured, produced, grown, or extracted by the taxpayer, or

"(ii) was acquired by the taxpayer from a related person for a price which was not determined in accordance with the rules of section 482,

"the amount of foreign trade income which may be treated as foreign sale and leasing income under paragraph (1)(B) or subparagraph (A) of this paragraph with respect to any transaction involving such property shall not exceed the amount which would have been determined if the taxpayer had acquired such property for the price determined in accordance with the rules of section 482.

"(3) Special rules.

"(A) Excluded property. Foreign sale and leasing income shall not include any income properly allocable to excluded property described in subparagraph (B) of section 943(a)(3) (relating to intangibles).

"(B) Only direct expenses taken into account. For purposes of this subsection, any expense other than a directly allocable expense shall not be taken into account in computing foreign trade income."

In 2000, P.L. 106-519, Sec. 3(b), added Code Sec. 941 as part of subpart E of part III of subchapter N of chapter 1, effective for transactions after 9/30/2000. Sec. 5(b)–(d) of this Act [para. (c)(1) as amended by Sec. 513(a) of P.L. 109-222, see above], provides:

"(b) No new FSCs; termination of inactive FSCs—

Code Sec. 941

"(1) No new FSCs. No corporation may elect after September 30, 2000, to be a FSC (as defined in section 922 of the Internal Revenue Code of 1986, as in effect before the amendments made by this Act).

"(2) Termination of inactive FSCs. If a FSC has no foreign trade income (as defined in section 923(b) of such Code, as so in effect) for any period of 5 consecutive taxable years beginning after December 31, 2001, such FSC shall cease to be treated as a FSC for purposes of such Code for any taxable year beginning after such period.

"(c) Transition period for existing Foreign Sales Corporations.

"(1) In general. In the case of a FSC (as so defined) in existence on September 30, 2000, and at all times thereafter, the amendments made by this Act shall not apply to any transaction in the ordinary course of trade or business involving a FSC which occurs before January 1, 2002.

"(2) Election to have amendments apply earlier. A taxpayer may elect to have the amendments made by this Act apply to any transaction by a FSC or any related person to which such amendments would apply but for the application of paragraph (1). Such election shall be effective for the taxable year for which made and all subsequent taxable years, and, once made, may be revoked only with the consent of the Secretary of the Treasury.

"(3) Exception for old earnings and profits of certain corporations.

"(A) In general. In the case of a foreign corporation to which this paragraph applies—

"(i) earnings and profits of such corporation accumulated in taxable years ending before October 1, 2000, shall not be included in the gross income of the persons holding stock in such corporation by reason of section 943(e)(4)(B)(i), and

"(ii) rules similar to the rules of clauses (ii), (iii), and (iv) of section 953(d)(4)(B) shall apply with respect to such earnings and profits.

The preceding sentence shall not apply to earnings and profits acquired in a transaction after September 30, 2000, to which section 381 applies unless the distributor or transferor corporation was immediately before the transaction a foreign corporation to which this paragraph applies.

"(B) Existing FSCs. This paragraph shall apply to any controlled foreign corporation (as defined in section 957) if—

"(i) such corporation is a FSC (as so defined) in existence on September 30, 2000,

"(ii) such corporation is eligible to make the election under section 943(e) by reason of being described in paragraph (2)(B) of such section, and

"(iii) such corporation makes such election not later than for its first taxable year beginning after December 31, 2001.

"(C) Other corporations. This paragraph shall apply to any controlled foreign corporation (as defined in section 957), and such corporation shall (notwithstanding any provision of section 943(e)) be treated as an applicable foreign corporation for purposes of section 943(e), if—

"(i) such corporation is in existence on September 30, 2000;

"(ii) as of such date, such corporation is wholly owned (directly or indirectly) by a domestic corporation (determined without regard to any election under section 943(e));

"(iii) for each of the 3 taxable years preceding the first taxable year to which the election under section 943(e) by such controlled foreign corporation applies—

"(I) all of the gross income of such corporation is subpart F income (as defined in section 952), including by reason of section 954(b)(3)(B); and

"(II) in the ordinary course of such corporation's trade or business, such corporation regularly sold (or paid commissions) to a FSC which on September 30, 2000, was a related person to such corporation;

"(iv) such corporation has never made an election under section 922(a)(2) (as in effect before the date of the enactment of this paragraph) to be treated as a FSC; and

"(v) such corporation makes the election under section 943(e) not later than for its first taxable year beginning after December 31, 2001.

The preceding sentence shall cease to apply as of the date that the domestic corporation referred to in clause (ii) ceases to wholly own (directly or indirectly) such controlled foreign corporation.

"(4) Related person. For purposes of this subsection, the term 'related person' has the meaning given to such term by section 943(b)(3).

"(5) Section references. Except as otherwise expressly provided, any reference in this subsection to a section or other provision shall be considered to be a reference to a section or other provision of the Internal Revenue Code of 1986, as amended by this Act.

"(d) Special rules relating to leasing transactions.

"(1) Sales income. If foreign trade income in connection with the lease or rental of property described in section 927(a)(1)(B) of such Code (as in effect before the amendments made by this Act) is treated as exempt foreign trade income for purposes of section 921(a) of such Code (as so in effect), such property shall be treated as property described in section 941(c)(1)(B) of such Code (as added by this Act) for purposes of applying section 941(c)(2) of such Code (as so added) to any subsequent transaction involving such property to which the amendments made by this Act apply.

"(2) Limitation on use of gross receipts method. If any person computed its foreign trade income from any transaction with respect to any property on the basis of a transfer price determined under the method described in section 925(a)(1) of such Code (as in effect before the amendments made by this Act), then the qualifying foreign trade income (as defined in section 941(a) of such Code, as in effect after such amendment) of such person (or any related person) with respect to any other transaction involving such property (and to which the amendments made by this Act apply) shall be zero."

Sec. 942. Repealed.

In 2006, P.L. 109-222, Sec. 513(a), amended Sec. 5(c)(1) of P.L. 106-519 [see below]..., Sec. 513(b), repealed Sec. 101(f) of P.L. 108-357 [see below], effective for tax. yrs. begin. after 5/17/2006.

Prior to amendment, Sec. 5(c)(1) of P.L. 106-519 read as follows:

"(1) In general. In the case of a FSC (as so defined) in existence on September 30, 2000, and at all times thereafter, the amendments made by this Act shall not apply to any transaction in the ordinary course of trade or business involving a FSC which occurs—

"(A) before January 1, 2002; or

"(B) after December 31, 2001, pursuant to a binding contract—

"(i) which is between the FSC (or any related person) and any person which is not a related person; and

"(ii) which is in effect on September 30, 2000, and at all times thereafter.

For purposes of this paragraph, a binding contract shall include a purchase option, renewal option, or replacement option which is included in such contract and which is enforceable against the seller or lessor."

Prior to repeal, Sec. 101(f) of P.L. 108-357 read as follows:

"(f) Binding contracts. The amendments made by this section shall not apply to any transaction in the ordinary course of a trade or business which occurs pursuant to a binding contract—

"(1) which is between the taxpayer and a person who is not a related person (as defined in section 943(b)(3) of such Code, as in effect on the day before the date of the enactment of this Act), and

"(2) which is in effect on September 17, 2003, and at all times thereafter.

"For purposes of this subsection, a binding contract shall include a purchase option, renewal option, or replacement option which is included in such contract and which is enforceable against the seller or lessor."

In 2004, P.L. 108-357, Sec. 101(b)(1), repealed Code Sec. 942, effective for transactions after 12/31/2004. Sec. 101(d)-(f) of this Act [subsec. (f) was repealed by Sec. 513(b) of P.L. 109-222, see above], provides:

"(d) Transitional rule for 2005 and 2006.

"(1) In general. In the case of transactions during 2005 or 2006, the amount includible in gross income by reason of the amendments made by this section shall not exceed the applicable percentage of the amount which would have been so included but for this subsection.

"(2) Applicable percentage. For purposes of paragraph (1), the applicable percentage shall be as follows:

"(A) For 2005, the applicable percentage shall be 20 percent.

"(B) For 2006, the applicable percentage shall be 40 percent.

"(e) Revocation of election to be treated as domestic corporation. If, during the 1-year period beginning on the date of the enactment of this Act, a corporation for which an election is in effect under section 943(e) of the Internal Revenue Code of 1986 revokes such election, no gain or loss shall be recognized with respect to property treated as transferred under clause (ii) of section 943(e)(4)(B) of such Code to the extent such property—

"(1) was treated as transferred under clause (i) thereof, or

"(2) was acquired during a taxable year to which such election applies and before May 1, 2003, in the ordinary course of its trade or business.

"The Secretary of the Treasury (or such Secretary's delegate) may prescribe such regulations as may be necessary to prevent the abuse of the purposes of this subsection."

"(f) [Repealed by Sec. 513(b) of P.L. 109-222, see above.]

Prior to repeal, Code Sec. 942 read as follows:

"SEC. 942. FOREIGN TRADING GROSS RECEIPTS.

"(a) Foreign trading gross receipts.

"(1) In general. Except as otherwise provided in this section, for purposes of this subpart, the term 'foreign trading gross receipts' means the gross receipts of the taxpayer which are—

"(A) from the sale, exchange, or other disposition of qualifying foreign trade property,

"(B) from the lease or rental of qualifying foreign trade property for use by the lessee outside the United States,

"(C) for services which are related and subsidiary to—

"(i) any sale, exchange, or other disposition of qualifying foreign trade property by such taxpayer, or

"(ii) any lease or rental of qualifying foreign trade property described in subparagraph (B) by such taxpayer,

"(D) for engineering or architectural services for construction projects located (or proposed for location) outside the United States, or

"(E) for the performance of managerial services for a person other than a related person in furtherance of the production of foreign trading gross receipts described in subparagraph (A), (B), or (C).

"Subparagraph (E) shall not apply to a taxpayer for any taxable year unless at least 50 percent of its foreign trading gross receipts (determined without regard to this sentence) for such taxable year is derived from activities described in subparagraph (A), (B), or (C).

"(2) Certain receipts excluded on basis of use; subsidized receipts excluded. The term 'foreign trading gross receipts' shall not include receipts of a taxpayer from a transaction if—

"(A) the qualifying foreign trade property or services—

"(i) are for ultimate use in the United States, or

"(ii) are for use by the United States or any instrumentality thereof and such use of qualifying foreign trade property or services is required by law or regulation, or

Income from foreign sources — Code Sec. 943

"(B) such transaction is accomplished by a subsidy granted by the government (or any instrumentality thereof) of the country or possession in which the property is manufactured, produced, grown, or extracted.

"(3) Election to exclude certain receipts. The term 'foreign trading gross receipts' shall not include gross receipts of a taxpayer from a transaction if the taxpayer elects not to have such receipts taken into account for purposes of this subpart.

"(b) Foreign economic process requirements.

"(1) In general. Except as provided in subsection (c), a taxpayer shall be treated as having foreign trading gross receipts from any transaction only if economic processes with respect to such transaction take place outside the United States as required by paragraph (2).

"(2) Requirement.

"(A) In general. The requirements of this paragraph are met with respect to the gross receipts of a taxpayer derived from any transaction if—

"(i) such taxpayer (or any person acting under a contract with such taxpayer) has participated outside the United States in the solicitation (other than advertising), the negotiation, or the making of the contract relating to such transaction, and

"(ii) the foreign direct costs incurred by the taxpayer attributable to the transaction equal or exceed 50 percent of the total direct costs attributable to the transaction.

"(B) Alternative 85-percent test. A taxpayer shall be treated as satisfying the requirements of subparagraph (A)(ii) with respect to any transaction if, with respect to each of at least 2 subparagraphs of paragraph (3), the foreign direct costs incurred by such taxpayer attributable to activities described in such subparagraph equal or exceed 85 percent of the total direct costs attributable to activities described in such subparagraph.

"(C) Definitions. For purposes of this paragraph—

"(i) Total direct costs. The term 'total direct costs' means, with respect to any transaction, the total direct costs incurred by the taxpayer attributable to activities described in paragraph (3) performed at any location by the taxpayer or any person acting under a contract with such taxpayer.

"(ii) Foreign direct costs. The term 'foreign direct costs' means, with respect to any transaction, the portion of the total direct costs which are attributable to activities performed outside the United States.

"(3) Activities relating to qualifying foreign trade property. The activities described in this paragraph are any of the following with respect to qualifying foreign trade property—

"(A) advertising and sales promotion,

"(B) the processing of customer orders and the arranging for delivery,

"(C) transportation outside the United States in connection with delivery to the customer,

"(D) the determination and transmittal of a final invoice or statement of account or the receipt of payment, and

"(E) the assumption of credit risk.

"(4) Economic processes performed by related persons. A taxpayer shall be treated as meeting the requirements of this subsection with respect to any sales transaction involving any property if any related person has met such requirements in such transaction or any other sales transaction involving such property.

"(c) Exception from foreign economic process requirement.

"(1) In general. The requirements of subsection (b) shall be treated as met for any taxable year if the foreign trading gross receipts of the taxpayer for such year do not exceed $5,000,000.

"(2) Receipts of related persons aggregated. All related persons shall be treated as one person for purposes of paragraph (1), and the limitation under paragraph (1) shall be allocated among such persons in a manner provided in regulations prescribed by the Secretary.

"(3) Special rule for pass-thru entities. In the case of a partnership, S corporation, or other pass-thru entity, the limitation under paragraph (1) shall apply with respect to the partnership, S corporation, or entity and with respect to each partner, shareholder, or other owner."

In 2000, P.L. 106-519, Sec. 3(b), added Code Sec. 942 as part of subpart E of part III of subchapter N of chapter 1, effective for transactions after 9/30/2000. Sec. 5(b)–(d) [para. (c)(1) as amended by Sec. 513(a) of P.L. 109-222, see above] of this Act, provides:

"(b) No new FSCs; termination of inactive FSCs—

"(1) No new FSCs. No corporation may elect after September 30, 2000, to be a FSC (as defined in section 922 of the Internal Revenue Code of 1986, as in effect before the amendments made by this Act).

"(2) Termination of inactive FSCs. If a FSC has no foreign trade income (as defined in section 923(b) of such Code, as so in effect) for any period of 5 consecutive taxable years beginning after December 31, 2001, such FSC shall cease to be treated as a FSC for purposes of such Code for any taxable year beginning after such period.

"(c) Transition period for existing Foreign Sales Corporations.

"(1) In general. In the case of a FSC (as so defined) in existence on September 30, 2000, and at all times thereafter, the amendments made by this Act shall not apply to any transaction in the ordinary course of trade or business involving a FSC which occurs before January 1, 2002.

"(2) Election to have amendments apply earlier. A taxpayer may elect to have the amendments made by this Act apply to any transaction by a FSC or any related person to which such amendments would apply but for the application of paragraph (1). Such election shall be effective for the taxable year for which made and all subsequent taxable years, and, once made, may be revoked only with the consent of the Secretary of the Treasury.

"(3) Exception for old earnings and profits of certain corporations.

"(A) In general. In the case of a foreign corporation to which this paragraph applies—

"(i) earnings and profits of such corporation accumulated in taxable years ending before October 1, 2000, shall not be included in the gross income of the persons holding stock in such corporation by reason of section 943(e)(4)(B)(i), and

"(ii) rules similar to the rules of clauses (ii), (iii), and (iv) of section 953(d)(4)(B) shall apply with respect to such earnings and profits.

The preceding sentence shall not apply to earnings and profits acquired in a transaction after September 30, 2000, to which section 381 applies unless the distributor or transferor corporation was immediately before the transaction a foreign corporation to which this paragraph applies.

"(B) Existing FSCs. This paragraph shall apply to any controlled foreign corporation (as defined in section 957) if—

"(i) such corporation is a FSC (as so defined) in existence on September 30, 2000,

"(ii) such corporation is eligible to make the election under section 943(e) by reason of being described in paragraph (2)(B) of such section, and

"(iii) such corporation makes such election not later than for its first taxable year beginning after December 31, 2001.

"(C) Other corporations. This paragraph shall apply to any controlled foreign corporation (as defined in section 957), and such corporation shall (notwithstanding any provision of section 943(e)) be treated as an applicable foreign corporation for purposes of section 943(e), if—

"(i) such corporation is in existence on September 30, 2000;

"(ii) as of such date, such corporation is wholly owned (directly or indirectly) by a domestic corporation (determined without regard to any election under section 943(e));

"(iii) for each of the 3 taxable years preceding the first taxable year to which the election under section 943(e) by such controlled foreign corporation applies—

"(I) all of the gross income of such corporation is subpart F income (as defined in section 952), including by reason of section 954(b)(3)(B); and

"(II) in the ordinary course of such corporation's trade or business, such corporation regularly sold (or paid commissions) to a FSC which on September 30, 2000, was a related person to such corporation;

"(iv) such corporation has never made an election under section 922(a)(2) (as in effect before the date of the enactment of this paragraph) to be treated as a FSC; and

"(v) such corporation makes the election under section 943(e) not later than for its first taxable year beginning after December 31, 2001.

The preceding sentence shall cease to apply as of the date that the domestic corporation referred to in clause (ii) ceases to wholly own (directly or indirectly) such controlled foreign corporation.

"(4) Related person. For purposes of this subsection, the term 'related person' has the meaning given to such term by section 943(b)(3).

"(5) Section references. Except as otherwise expressly provided, any reference in this subsection to a section or other provision shall be considered to be a reference to a section or other provision of the Internal Revenue Code of 1986, as amended by this Act.

"(d) Special rules relating to leasing transactions.

"(1) Sales income. If foreign trade income in connection with the lease or rental of property described in section 927(a)(1)(B) of such Code (as in effect before the amendments made by this Act) is treated as exempt foreign trade income for purposes of section 921(a) of such Code (as so in effect), such property shall be treated as property described in section 941(c)(1)(B) of such Code (as added by this Act) for purposes of applying section 941(c)(2) of such Code (as so added) to any subsequent transaction involving such property to which the amendments made by this Act apply.

"(2) Limitation on use of gross receipts method. If any person computed its foreign trade income from any transaction with respect to any property on the basis of a transfer price determined under the method described in section 925(a)(1) of such Code (as in effect before the amendments made by this Act), then the qualifying foreign trade income (as defined in section 941(a) of such Code, as in effect after such amendment) of such person (or any related person) with respect to any other transaction involving such property (and to which the amendments made by this Act apply) shall be zero."

Sec. 943. Repealed.

In 2006, P.L. 109-222, Sec. 513(a), amended Sec. 5(c)(1) of P.L. 106-519 [see below] . . . Sec. 513(b), repealed Sec. 101(f) of P.L. 108-357 [see below], effective for tax. yrs. begin. after 5/17/2006.

Prior to amendment, Sec. 5(c)(1) of P.L. 106-519 read as follows:

"(1) In general. In the case of a FSC (as so defined) in existence on September 30, 2000, and at all times thereafter, the amendments made by this Act shall not apply to any transaction in the ordinary course of trade or business involving a FSC which occurs—

"(A) before January 1, 2002; or

"(B) after December 31, 2001, pursuant to a binding contract—

"(i) which is between the FSC (or any related person) and any person which is not a related person; and

"(ii) which is in effect on September 30, 2000, and at all times thereafter.

For purposes of this paragraph, a binding contract shall include a purchase option, renewal option, or replacement option which is included in such contract and which is enforceable against the seller or lessor."

Prior to repeal, Sec. 101(f) of P.L. 108-357 read as follows:

"(f) Binding contracts. The amendments made by this section shall not apply to any transaction in the ordinary course of a trade or business which occurs pursuant to a binding contract—

"(1) which is between the taxpayer and a person who is not a related person (as defined in section 943(b)(3) of such Code, as in effect on the day before the date of the enactment of this Act), and

"(2) which is in effect on September 17, 2003, and at all times thereafter.

"For purposes of this subsection, a binding contract shall include a purchase option, renewal option, or replacement option which is included in such contract and which is enforceable against the seller or lessor."

In 2004, P.L. 108-357, Sec. 101(b)(1), repealed Code Sec. 943, effective for transactions after 12/31/2004. Sec. 101(d)-(f) [subsec. (f) was repealed by Sec. 513(b) of P.L. 109-222, see above] of this Act, provides:

"(d) Transitional rule for 2005 and 2006.

"(1) In general. In the case of transactions during 2005 or 2006, the amount includible in gross income by reason of the amendments made by this section shall not exceed the applicable percentage of the amount which would have been so included but for this subsection.

"(2) Applicable percentage. For purposes of paragraph (1), the applicable percentage shall be as follows:

"(A) For 2005, the applicable percentage shall be 20 percent.

"(B) For 2006, the applicable percentage shall be 40 percent.

"(e) Revocation of election to be treated as domestic corporation. If, during the 1-year period beginning on the date of the enactment of this Act, a corporation for which an election is in effect under section 943(e) of the Internal Revenue Code of 1986 revokes such election, no gain or loss shall be recognized with respect to property treated as transferred under clause (ii) of section 943(e)(4)(B) of such Code to the extent such property—

"(1) was treated as transferred under clause (i) thereof, or

"(2) was acquired during a taxable year to which such election applies and before May 1, 2003, in the ordinary course of its trade or business.

"The Secretary of the Treasury (or such Secretary's delegate) may prescribe such regulations as may be necessary to prevent the abuse of the purposes of this subsection."

"(f) [Repealed by Sec. 513(b), P.L. 109-222, see above.]

Prior to repeal, Code Sec. 943 read as follows:

"Sec. 943. Other definitions and special rules.

"(a) Qualifying foreign trade property. For purposes of this subpart—

"(1) In general. The term 'qualifying foreign trade property' means property—

"(A) manufactured, produced, grown, or extracted within or outside the United States,

"(B) held primarily for sale, lease, or rental, in the ordinary course of trade or business for direct use, consumption, or disposition outside the United States, and

"(C) not more than 50 percent of the fair market value of which is attributable to—

"(i) articles manufactured, produced, grown, or extracted outside the United States, and

"(ii) direct costs for labor (determined under the principles of section 263A) performed outside the United States.

"For purposes of subparagraph (C), the fair market value of any article imported into the United States shall be its appraised value, as determined by the Secretary under section 402 of the Tariff Act of 1930 (19 U.S.C. 1401a) in connection with its importation, and the direct costs for labor under clause (ii) do not include costs that would be treated under the principles of section 263A as direct labor costs attributable to articles described in clause (i).

"(2) U.S. taxation to ensure consistent treatment. Property which (without regard to this paragraph) is qualifying foreign trade property and which is manufactured, produced, grown, or extracted outside the United States shall be treated as qualifying foreign trade property only if it is manufactured, produced, grown, or extracted by—

"(A) a domestic corporation,

"(B) an individual who is a citizen or resident of the United States,

"(C) a foreign corporation with respect to which an election under subsection (e) (relating to foreign corporations electing to be subject to United States taxation) is in effect, or

"(D) a partnership or other pass-thru entity all of the partners or owners of which are described in subparagraph (A), (B), or (C).

"Except as otherwise provided by the Secretary, tiered partnerships or pass-thru entities shall be treated as described in subparagraph (D) if each of the partnerships or entities is directly or indirectly wholly owned by persons described in subparagraph (A), (B), or (C).

"(3) Excluded property. The term 'qualifying foreign trade property' shall not include—

"(A) property leased or rented by the taxpayer for use by any related person,

"(B) patents, inventions, models, designs, formulas, or processes whether or not patented, copyrights (other than films, tapes, records, or similar reproductions, and other than computer software (whether or not patented), for commercial or home use), goodwill, trademarks, trade brands, franchises, or other like property,

"(C) oil or gas (or any primary product thereof),

"(D) products the transfer of which is prohibited or curtailed to effectuate the policy set forth in paragraph (2)(C) of Sec. 3 of P.L. 96-72, or

"(E) any unprocessed timber which is a softwood.

"For purposes of subparagraph (E), the term 'unprocessed timber' means any log, cant, or similar form of timber.

"(4) Property in short supply. If the President determines that the supply of any property described in paragraph (1) is insufficient to meet the requirements of the domestic economy, the President may by Executive order designate the property as in short supply. Any property so designated shall not be treated as qualifying foreign trade property during the period beginning with the date specified in the Executive order and ending with the date specified in an Executive order setting forth the President's determination that the property is no longer in short supply.

"(b) Other definitions and rules. For purposes of this subpart—

"(1) Transaction.

"(A) In general. The term 'transaction' means—

"(i) any sale, exchange, or other disposition,

"(ii) any lease or rental, and

"(iii) any furnishing of services.

"(B) Grouping of transactions. To the extent provided in regulations, any provision of this subpart which, but for this subparagraph, would be applied on a transaction-by-transaction basis may be applied by the taxpayer on the basis of groups of transactions based on product lines or recognized industry or trade usage. Such regulations may permit different groupings for different purposes.

"(2) United States defined. The term 'United States' includes the Commonwealth of Puerto Rico. The preceding sentence shall not apply for purposes of determining whether a corporation is a domestic corporation.

"(3) Related person. A person shall be related to another person if such persons are treated as a single employer under subsection (a) or (b) of section 52 or subsection (m) or (o) of section 414, except that determinations under subsections (a) and (b) of section 52 shall be made without regard to section 1563(b).

"(4) Gross and taxable income. Section 114 shall not be taken into account in determining the amount of gross income or foreign trade income from any transaction.

"(c) Source rule. Under regulations, in the case of qualifying foreign trade property manufactured, produced, grown, or extracted within the United States, the amount of income of a taxpayer from any sales transaction with respect to such property which is treated as from sources without the United States shall not exceed—

"(1) in the case of a taxpayer computing its qualifying foreign trade income under section 941(a)(1)(B), the amount of the taxpayer's foreign trade income which would (but for this subsection) be treated as from sources without the United States if the foreign trade income were reduced by an amount equal to 4 percent of the foreign trading gross receipts with respect to the transaction, and

"(2) in the case of a taxpayer computing its qualifying foreign trade income under section 941(a)(1)(C), 50 percent of the amount of the taxpayer's foreign trade income which would (but for this subsection) be treated as from sources without the United States.

"(d) Treatment of withholding taxes.

"(1) In general. For purposes of section 114(d), any withholding tax shall not be treated as paid or accrued with respect to extraterritorial income which is excluded from gross income under section 114(a).

"For purposes of this paragraph, the term 'withholding tax' means any tax which is imposed on a basis other than residence and for which credit is allowable under section 901 or 903.

"(2) Exception. Paragraph (1) shall not apply to any taxpayer with respect to extraterritorial income from any transaction if the taxpayer computes its qualifying foreign trade income with respect to the transaction under section 941(a)(1)(A).

"(e) Election to be treated as domestic corporation.

"(1) In general. An applicable foreign corporation may elect to be treated as a domestic corporation for all purposes of this title if such corporation waives all benefits to such corporation granted by the United States under any treaty. No election under section 1362(a) may be made with respect to such corporation.

"(2) Applicable foreign corporation. For purposes of paragraph (1), the term 'applicable foreign corporation' means any foreign corporation if—

"(A) such corporation manufactures, produces, grows, or extracts property in the ordinary course of such corporation's trade or business, or

"(B) substantially all of the gross receipts of such corporation are foreign trading gross receipts.

"(3) Period of election.

"(A) In general. Except as provided in this paragraph, an election under paragraph (1) shall apply to the taxable year for which made and all subsequent taxable years unless revoked by the taxpayer. Any revocation of such election shall apply to taxable years beginning after such revocation.

"(B) Termination. If a corporation which made an election under paragraph (1) for any taxable year fails to meet the requirements of subparagraph (A) or (B) of paragraph (2) for any subsequent taxable year, such election shall not apply to any taxable year beginning after such subsequent taxable year.

"(C) Effect of revocation or termination. If a corporation which made an election under paragraph (1) revokes such election or such election is terminated under subparagraph (B), such corporation (and any successor corporation) may not make such election for any of the 5 taxable years beginning with the first taxable year for which such election is not in effect as a result of such revocation or termination.

"(4) Special rules.

"(A) Requirements. This subsection shall not apply to an applicable foreign corporation if such corporation fails to meet the requirements (if any) which the Secretary may prescribe to ensure that the taxes imposed by this chapter on such corporation are paid.

"(B) Effect of election, revocation, and termination.

"(i) Election. For purposes of section 367, a foreign corporation making an election under this subsection shall be treated as transferring (as of the first day of the first taxable year to which the election applies) all of its assets to a domestic corporation in connection with an exchange to which section 354 applies.

"(ii) Revocation and termination. For purposes of section 367, if—

"(I) an election is made by a corporation under paragraph (1) for any taxable year, and

Income from foreign sources   Code Sec. 941

"(II) such election ceases to apply for any subsequent taxable year,

"such corporation shall be treated as a domestic corporation transferring (as of the 1st day of the first such subsequent taxable year to which such election ceases to apply) all of its property to a foreign corporation in connection with an exchange to which section 354 applies.

"(C) Eligibility for election. The Secretary may by regulation designate one or more classes of corporations which may not make the election under this subsection.

"(f) Rules relating to allocations of qualifying foreign trade income from shared partnerships.

"(1) In general. If—

"(A) a partnership maintains a separate account for transactions (to which this subpart applies) with each partner,

"(B) distributions to each partner with respect to such transactions are based on the amounts in the separate account maintained with respect to such partner, and

"(C) such partnership meets such other requirements as the Secretary may by regulations prescribe,

"then such partnership shall allocate to each partner items of income, gain, loss, and deduction (including qualifying foreign trade income) from any transaction to which this subpart applies on the basis of such separate account.

"(2) Special rules. For purposes of this subpart, in the case of a partnership to which paragraph (1) applies—

"(A) any partner's interest in the partnership shall not be taken into account in determining whether such partner is a related person with respect to any other partner, and

"(B) the election under section 942(a)(3) shall be made separately by each partner with respect to any transaction for which the partnership maintains separate accounts for each partner.

"(g) Exclusion for patrons of agricultural and horticultural cooperatives. Any amount described in paragraph (1) or (3) of section 1385(a)—

"(1) which is received by a person from an organization to which part I of subchapter T applies which is engaged in the marketing of agricultural or horticultural products, and

"(2) which is allocable to qualifying foreign trade income and designated as such by the organization in a written notice mailed to its patrons during the payment period described in section 1382(d),

shall be treated as qualifying foreign trade income of such person for purposes of section 114. The taxable income of the organization shall not be reduced under section 1382 by reason of any amount to which the preceding sentence applies.

"(h) Special rule for DISCs. Section 114 shall not apply to any taxpayer for any taxable year if, at any time during the taxable year, the taxpayer is a member of any controlled group of corporations (as defined in section 927(d)(4), as in effect before the date of the enactment of this subsection) of which a DISC is a member."

In 2002, P.L. 107-147, Sec. 417(14), adjusted the flush language at the end of subpara. (e)(4)(B) so that it is flush with subpara. (e)(4)(A), rather than with clause (e)(4)(B)(ii).

In 2000, P.L. 106-519, Sec. 3(b), added Code Sec. 943 as part of subpart E of part III of subchapter N of chapter 1, effective for transactions after 9/30/2000. Sec. 5(b)–(d) [para. (c)(1) as amended by Sec. 513(a) of P.L. 109-222, see above] of this Act, provides:

"(b) No new FSCs; termination of inactive FSCs—

"(1) No new FSCs. No corporation may elect after September 30, 2000, to be a FSC (as defined in section 922 of the Internal Revenue Code of 1986, as in effect before the amendments made by this Act).

"(2) Termination of inactive FSCs. If a FSC has no foreign trade income (as defined in section 923(b) of such Code, as so in effect) for any period of 5 consecutive taxable years beginning after December 31, 2001, such FSC shall cease to be treated as a FSC for purposes of such Code for any taxable year beginning after such period.

"(c) Transition period for existing Foreign Sales Corporations.

"(1) In general. In the case of a FSC (as so defined) in existence on September 30, 2000, and at all times thereafter, the amendments made by this Act shall not apply to any transaction in the ordinary course of trade or business involving a FSC which occurs before January 1, 2002.

"(2) Election to have amendments apply earlier. A taxpayer may elect to have the amendments made by this Act apply to any transaction by a FSC or any related person to which such amendments would apply but for the application of paragraph (1). Such election shall be effective for the taxable year for which made and all subsequent taxable years, and, once made, may be revoked only with the consent of the Secretary of the Treasury.

"(3) Exception for old earnings and profits of certain corporations.

"(A) In general. In the case of a foreign corporation to which this paragraph applies—

"(i) earnings and profits of such corporation accumulated in taxable years ending before October 1, 2000, shall not be included in the gross income of the persons holding stock in such corporation by reason of section 943(e)(4)(B)(i), and

"(ii) rules similar to the rules of clauses (ii), (iii), and (iv) of section 953(d)(4)(B) shall apply with respect to such earnings and profits.

The preceding sentence shall not apply to earnings and profits acquired in a transaction after September 30, 2000, to which section 381 applies unless the distributor or transferor corporation was immediately before the transaction a foreign corporation to which this paragraph applies.

"(B) Existing FSCs. This paragraph shall apply to any controlled foreign corporation (as defined in section 957) if—

"(i) such corporation is a FSC (as so defined) in existence on September 30, 2000,

"(ii) such corporation is eligible to make the election under section 943(e) by reason of being described in paragraph (2)(B) of such section, and

"(iii) such corporation makes such election not later than for its first taxable year beginning after December 31, 2001.

"(C) Other corporations. This paragraph shall apply to any controlled foreign corporation (as defined in section 957), and such corporation shall (notwithstanding any provision of section 943(e)) be treated as an applicable foreign corporation for purposes of section 943(e), if—

"(i) such corporation is in existence on September 30, 2000;

"(ii) as of such date, such corporation is wholly owned (directly or indirectly) by a domestic corporation (determined without regard to any election under section 943(e));

"(iii) for each of the 3 taxable years preceding the first taxable year to which the election under section 943(e) by such controlled foreign corporation applies—

"(I) all of the gross income of such corporation is subpart F income (as defined in section 952), including by reason of section 954(b)(3)(B); and

"(II) in the ordinary course of such corporation's trade or business, such corporation regularly sold (or paid commissions) to a FSC which on September 30, 2000, was a related person to such corporation;

"(iv) such corporation has never made an election under section 922(a)(2) (as in effect before the date of the enactment of this paragraph) to be treated as a FSC; and

"(v) such corporation makes the election under section 943(e) not later than for its first taxable year beginning after December 31, 2001.

The preceding sentence shall cease to apply as of the date that the domestic corporation referred to in clause (ii) ceases to wholly own (directly or indirectly) such controlled foreign corporation.

"(4) Related person. For purposes of this subsection, the term 'related person' has the meaning given to such term by section 943(b)(3).

"(5) Section references. Except as otherwise expressly provided, any reference in this subsection to a section or other provision shall be considered to be a reference to a section or other provision of the Internal Revenue Code of 1986, as amended by this Act.

"(d) Special rules relating to leasing transactions.

"(1) Sales income. If foreign trade income in connection with the lease or rental of property described in section 927(a)(1)(B) of such Code (as in effect before the amendments made by this Act) is treated as exempt foreign trade income for purposes of section 921(a) of such Code (as so in effect), such property shall be treated as property described in section 941(c)(1)(B) of such Code (as added by this Act) for purposes of applying section 941(c)(2) of such Code (as so added) to any subsequent transaction involving such property to which the amendments made by this Act apply.

"(2) Limitation on use of gross receipts method. If any person computed its foreign trade income from any transaction with respect to any property on the basis of a transfer price determined under the method described in section 925(a)(1) of such Code (as in effect before the amendments made by this Act), then the qualifying foreign trade income (as defined in section 941(a) of such Code, as in effect after such amendment) of such person (or any related person) with respect to any other transaction involving such property (and to which the amendments made by this Act apply) shall be zero."

SUBPART E.—REPEALED.

In 1976, P.L. 94-455, Sec. 1053(d)(5), deleted the table for subpart E, for tax. yrs. begin. after '77.

Prior to deletion, Subpart E read as follows:
"SUBPART E.—CHINA TRADE ACT CORPORATIONS
"941. Special deduction for China Trade Act corporations.
"942. Disallowance of foreign tax credit.
"943. Exclusion of dividends to residents of Formosa or Hong Kong."

Sec. 941.   Repealed.

In 1976, P.L. 94-455, Sec. 1053(a), added subsec. (d), effective for tax. yrs. begin. after 12/31/75.

—P.L. 94-455, Sec. 1053(c), repealed Code Sec. 941, effective for tax. yrs. begin. after 12/31/77.

Prior to repeal, Code Sec. 941 read as follows:
"Sec. 941. Special deductions for China Trade Act Corporations.
"(a) Allowance of deduction.

"For purposes only of the taxes imposed by section 11, there shall be allowed, in the case of a corporation organized under the China Trade Act, 1922 (15 U.S.C. ch. 4, sec. 141 and following), in addition to the deductions from taxable income otherwise allowed such corporation, a special deduction, in computing the taxable income, of an amount equal to the proportion of the taxable income derived from sources within Formosa and Hong Kong (determined without regard to this section and determined in a similar manner to that provided in part I) which the par value of the shares of stock of the corporation owned on the last day of the taxable year by—

"(1) persons resident in Formosa, Hong Kong, the United States, or possessions of the United States, and

"(2) individual citizens of the United States wherever resident,

bears to the par value of the whole number of shares of stock of the corporation outstanding on such date. In no case shall the diminution, by reason of such special deduction, of the taxes imposed by section 11 (computed without regard to this section) exceed the amount of the special dividend certified under subsection (b) of this section.

"(b) Special dividend.

"The special deduction provided in subsection (a) shall not be allowed unless the Secretary of Commerce has certified to the Secretary of the Treasury or his delegate—

"(1) the amount which, during the year ending on the date fixed by law for filing the return, the corporation has distributed as a special dividend to or for the benefit of such persons as on the last day of the taxable year were resident in Formosa, Hong Kong, the United States, or possessions of the United States, or were individual citizens of the United States, and owned shares of stock of the corporation;

"(2) that such special dividend was in addition to all other amounts, payable or to be payable to such persons or for their benefit, by reason of their interest in the corporation; and

"(3) that such distribution has been made to or for the benefit of such persons in proportion to the par value of the shares of stock of the corporation owned by each; except that if the corporation has more than one class of stock, the certificates shall contain a statement that the articles of incorporation provide a method for the apportionment of such special dividend among such persons, and that the amount certified has been distributed in accordance with the method so provided.

"(c) Ownership of stock.

"For purposes of this section, shares of stock of a corporation shall be considered to be owned by the person in whom the equitable right to the income from such shares is in good faith vested.

"(d) Phaseout of deduction.

"In the case of a taxable year beginning after December 31, 1975, and before January 1, 1978, the amount of the special deduction under subsection (a) (determined without regard to this subsection) shall be reduced by the percentage reduction specified in the following table:

For a taxable year beginning in—	The percentage reduction shall be—
1976	33⅓
1977	66⅔

Sec. 942. Repealed.

In 1976, P.L. 94-455, Sec. 1053(c), repealed Code Sec. 942, effective for tax. yrs. begin. after 12/31/77.
Prior to repeal, Code Sec. 942 read as follows:
"Sec. 942. Disallowance of foreign tax credit.
"A corporation organized under the China Trade Act, 1922, shall not be allowed the credits against the tax for taxes of foreign countries and possessions of the United States allowed by section 901."

Sec. 943. Repealed.

In 1976, P.L. 94-455, Sec. 1053(b), added the last sentence in Code Sec. 943, effective for tax. yrs. begin. after 12/31/75.
—P.L. 94-455, Sec. 1053(c), repealed Code Sec. 943, effective for tax. yrs. begin. after 12/31/77.
Prior to repeal, Code Sec. 943 read as follows:
"Sec. 943. Exclusion of dividends to residents of Formosa or Hong Kong.
"Amounts distributed as dividends to or for the benefit of any person by a corporation organized under the China Trade Act, 1922, shall not be included in gross income and shall be exempt from taxation under this subtitle if, at the time of such distribution, such person is a resident of Formosa or Hong Kong, and the equitable right to the income of the shares of stock of the corporation is in good faith vested in him. In the case of a taxable year beginning after December 31, 1975, and before January 1, 1978, the amount of the distributions which are excludable from gross income under this section (determined without regard to this sentence) shall be reduced by the percentage reduction specified in the following table:

"For a taxable year beginning in—	The percentage reduction shall be—
1976	33⅓
1977	66⅔

SUBPART F.—CONTROLLED FOREIGN CORPORATIONS

Sec.
951. Amounts included in gross income of United States shareholders.
952. Subpart F income defined.
953. Insurance income.
954. Foreign base company income.
955. Withdrawal of previously excluded subpart F income from qualified investment.
956. Investment of earnings in United States property.
957. Controlled foreign corporations; United States persons.
958. Rules for determining stock ownership.
959. Exclusion from gross income of previously taxed earnings and profits.
960. Special rules for foreign tax credit.
961. Adjustments to basis of stock in controlled foreign corporations and of other property.
962. Election by individuals to be subject to tax at corporate rates.
963. [Repealed]
964. Miscellaneous provisions.
965. Temporary dividends received deduction.

In 2004, P.L. 108-357, Sec. 422(c), added item 965.
In 1996, P.L. 104-188, Sec. 1501(c), deleted item 956A.
Prior to deletion, item 956A read as follows:
"Sec. 956A. Earnings invested in excess passive assets."
In 1993, P.L. 103-66, Sec. 13231(b), added item 956A.
In 1986, P.L. 99-514, Sec. 1221(b)(3)(E), substituted "Insurance income" for "Income from insurance of United States risks" in item 953.
In 1975, P.L. 94-12, Sec. 602(a)(3)(A), repealed item 963.
Prior to repeal, item 963 read as follows:
"963. Receipt of minimum distributions by domestic corporations."
In 1962, added the heading of subpart F, and items 951–964.

Sec. 951. Amounts included in gross income of United States shareholders.

(a) Amounts included.

(1) In general. If a foreign corporation is a controlled foreign corporation for an uninterrupted period of 30 days or more during any taxable year, every person who is a United States shareholder (as defined in subsection (b)) of such corporation and who owns (within the meaning of section 958(a)) stock in such corporation on the last day, in such year, on which such corporation is a controlled foreign corporation shall include in his gross income, for his taxable year in which or with which such taxable year of the corporation ends—

(A) the sum of—

(i) his pro rata share (determined under paragraph (2)) of the corporation's subpart F income for such year,

(ii) his pro rata share (determined under section 955(a)(3) as in effect before the enactment of the Tax Reduction Act of 1975) of the corporation's previously excluded subpart F income withdrawn from investment in less developed countries for such year, and

(iii) his pro rata share (determined under section 955(a)(3)) of the corporation's previously excluded subpart F income withdrawn from foreign base company shipping operations for such year; and

(B) the amount determined under section 956 with respect to such shareholder for such year (but only to the extent not excluded from gross income under section 959(a)(2)).

(2) Pro rata share of subpart F income. The pro rata share referred to in paragraph (1)(A)(i) in the case of any United States shareholder is the amount—

(A) which would have been distributed with respect to the stock which such shareholder owns (within the meaning of section 958(a)) in such corporation if on the last day, in its taxable year, on which the corporation is a controlled foreign corporation it had distributed pro rata to its shareholders an amount (i) which bears the same ratio to its subpart F income for the taxable year, as (ii) the part of such year during which the corpora-

Income from foreign sources — Code Sec. 951

tion is a controlled foreign corporation bears to the entire year, reduced by

(B) the amount of distributions received by any other person during such year as a dividend with respect to such stock, but only to the extent of the dividend which would have been received if the distribution by the corporation had been the amount (i) which bears the same ratio to the subpart F income of such corporation for the taxable year, as (ii) the part of such year during which such shareholder did not own (within the meaning of section 958(a)) such stock bears to the entire year.

For purposes of subparagraph (B), any gain included in the gross income of any person as a dividend under section 1248 shall be treated as a distribution received by such person with respect to the stock involved.

(3) Limitation on pro rata share of previously excluded subpart F income withdrawn from investment. For purposes of paragraph (1)(A)(iii), the pro rata share of any United States shareholder of the previously excluded subpart F income of a controlled foreign corporation withdrawn from investment in foreign base company shipping operations shall not exceed an amount—

(A) which bears the same ratio to his pro rata share of such income withdrawn (as determined under section 955(a)(3)) for the taxable year, as

(B) the part of such year during which the corporation is a controlled foreign corporation bears to the entire year.

(b) United States shareholder defined.

For purposes of this subpart, the term "United States shareholder" means, with respect to any foreign corporation, a United States person (as defined in section 957(c)) who owns (within the meaning of section 958(a)), or is considered as owning by applying the rules of ownership of section 958(b), 10 percent or more of the total combined voting power of all classes of stock entitled to vote of such foreign corporation.

(c) Coordination with passive foreign investment company provisions.

If, but for this subsection, an amount would be included in the gross income of a United States shareholder for any taxable year both under subsection (a)(1)(A)(i) and under section 1293 (relating to current taxation of income from certain passive foreign investment companies), such amount shall be included in the gross income of such shareholder only under subsection (a)(1)(A).

In 2007, P.L. 110-172, Sec. 11(g)(13), deleted subsec. (c) and redesignated subsec. (d) as (c), enacted 12/29/2007.

Prior to amendment, subsec. (c) read as follows:

"(c) Foreign trade income not taken into account.

"(1) In general. The foreign trade income of a FSC and any deductions which are apportioned or allocated to such income shall not be taken into account under this subpart.

"(2) Foreign trade income. For purposes of this subsection, the term 'foreign trade income' has the meaning given such term by section 923(b), but does not include section 923(a)(2) non-exempt income (within the meaning of section 927(d)(6))."

In 2004, P.L. 108-357, Sec. 413(c)(16), deleted subsecs. (c) and (d) and redesignated subsecs. (e) and (f) as subsecs. (c) and (d), effective for tax. yrs. of foreign corporations begin. after 12/31/2004, and for tax. yrs. of United States shareholders with or within which such tax. yrs. of foreign corporations end.

Prior to deletion, subsec. (c) read as follows:

"(c) Coordination with election of a foreign investment company to distribute income. A United States shareholder who, for his taxable year, is a qualified shareholder (within the meaning of section 1247(c)) of a foreign investment company with respect to which an election under section 1247 is in effect shall not be required to include in gross income, for such taxable year, any amount under subsection (a) with respect to such company."

Prior to deletion, subsec. (d) read as follows:

"(d) Coordination with foreign personal holding company provisions. If, but for this subsection, an amount would be included in the gross income of a United States shareholder for any taxable year both under subsection (a)(1)(A)(i) and under 551(b) (relating to foreign personal holding company income included in gross income of United States shareholder), such amount shall be included in the gross income of such shareholder only under subsection (a)(1)(A)."

In 1997, P.L. 105-34, Sec. 1112(a)(1), added the sentence at the end of para. (a)(2), effective for dispositions after 8/5/97.

In 1996, P.L. 104-188, Sec. 1501(a)(1), added "and" at the end of subpara. (a)(1)(A), substituted a period for "; and" at the end of subpara. (a)(1)(B), and deleted subpara. (a)(1)(C), effective for tax. yrs. of foreign corporations begin. after 12/31/96, and for tax. yrs. of U.S. shareholders within which or with which such tax. yrs. of foreign corporations end.

Prior to deletion, subpara. (a)(1)(C) read as follows:

"(C) the amount determined under section 956A with respect to such shareholder for such year (but only to the extent not excluded from gross income under section 959(a)(3))."

In 1993, P.L. 103-66, Sec. 13231(a), deleted "and" at the end of subpara. (a)(1)(A), substituted "; and" for the period at the end of subpara. (a)(1)(B), and added subpara. (a)(1)(C), effective for tax. yrs. of foreign corporations begin. after 9/30/93, and for tax. yrs. of U.S. shareholders in which or with which such tax. yrs. of foreign corporations end.

—P.L. 103-66, Sec. 13232(c)(1), amended subpara. (a)(1)(B). . . . Sec. 13232(c)(2), deleted para. (a)(4), effective for tax. yrs. of controlled foreign corporations begin. after 9/30/93, and for tax. yrs. of U.S. shareholders in which or with which such tax. yrs. of controlled foreign corporations end.

Prior to amendment, subpara. (a)(1)(B) read as follows:

"(B) his pro rata share (determined under section 956(a)(2)) of the corporation's increase in earnings invested in United States property for such year (but only to the extent not excluded from gross income under section 959(a)(2)); and"

Prior to deletion, para. (a)(4) read as follows:

"(4) Limitation on pro rata share of investment in United States property. For purposes of paragraph (1)(B), the pro rata share of any United States shareholder in the increase of the earnings of a controlled foreign corporation invested in United States property shall not exceed an amount (A) which bears the same ratio to his pro rata share of such increase (as determined under section 956(a)(2)) for the taxable year, as (B) the part of such year during which the corporation is a controlled foreign corporation bears to the entire year."

In 1988, P.L. 100-647, Sec. 1012(i)(15), substituted "section 957(c)" for "section 957(d)" in subsec. (b), effective for tax. yrs. begin. after 12/31/86. For special rules, see Sec. 1221(g)(2)-(3) of P.L. 99-514, reproduced in the note following Code Sec. 955.

In 1986, P.L. 99-514, Sec. 1235(c), added subsec. (f), effective for tax. yrs. of foreign corporations begin. after 12/31/86.

—P.L. 99-514, Sec. 1876(c)(2), deleted the sentence at the end of para. (e)(1), effective for transactions after 12/31/84 in tax. yrs. end. after 12/31/84.

Prior to deletion, the sentence at the end of para. (e)(1) read as follows:

"For purposes of the preceding sentence, income described in paragraph (2) or (3) of section 921(d) shall be treated as derived from sources within the United States."

In 1984, P.L. 98-369, Sec. 132(c)(1), amended subsec. (d), effective for tax. yrs. of U.S. shareholders begin. after 7/18/84.

Prior to amendment, subsec. (d) read as follows:

"(d) Coordination with foreign personal holding company provisions.

"A United States shareholder who, for his taxable year, is subject to tax under section 551(b) (relating to foreign personal holding company income included in gross income of United States shareholders) on income of a controlled foreign corporation shall not be required to include in gross income, for such taxable year, any amount under subsection (a) with respect to such company."

—P.L. 98-369, Sec. 801(d)(4), added subsec. (e), effective for transactions after 12/31/84, in tax. yrs. end. after 12/31/84.

In 1976, P.L. 94-455, Sec. 1901(a)(119), deleted "beginning after December 31, 1962", after "during any taxable year", in para. (a)(1), effective for tax. yrs. begin. after 12/31/76.

In 1975, P.L. 94-12, Sec. 602(a)(3)(B), deleted "except as provided in section 963." [sic "963,"] before "his pro rata share" in clause (a)(1)(A)(i) . . . Sec. 602(c)(3), substituted "(determined under section 955(a)(3) as in effect before the enactment of the Tax Reduction Act of 1975)" for "(determined under section 955(a)(3))" in clause (a)(1)(A)(ii) . . . Sec. 602(c)(4), deleted para. (a)(3) . . . Sec. 602(d)(2)(A), deleted "and" at the end of clause (a)(1)(A)(i), substituted a comma for the semicolon at the end of clause (a)(1)(A)(ii), and added clause (a)(1)(A)(iii) . . . Sec. 602(d)(2)(B), added para. (a)(3) [as amended by Sec. 602(c)(4) of this Act, see above], effective as provided in Sec. 602(f) of this Act, which reads as follows:

"(f) Effective date. The amendments made by this section shall apply to taxable years of foreign corporation beginning after December 31, 1975, and to taxable years of United States shareholders (within the meaning of 951(b) of the Internal Revenue Code of 1954) within which or with which such taxable years of such foreign corporations end."

Prior to deletion, para. (a)(3) read as follows:

"(3) Limitation on pro rata share of previously excluded subpart F income withdrawn from investment. For purposes of paragraph (1)(A)(ii), the pro rata share of United States shareholder of the previously excluded sub F income of a controlled foreign corporation withdrawn for investment in less developed countries shall not exceed amount (A) which bears the same ratio to his pro rata share of such income withdrawn (as determined under section 955(a)(3)) for the taxable year, as (B) the part of such yield during which the corporation is a controlled foreign corporation bears to the entire year."

Code Sec. 951   Income from foreign sources

In 1962, P.L. 87-834, Sec. 12(a), added Code Sec. 951, effective for tax. yrs. of foreign corporations begin. after 12/31/62 and tax. yrs. of U.S. shareholders within which or with which such tax. yrs. of such foreign corporations end.

Sec. 952. Subpart F income defined.
(a) In general.
For purposes of this subpart, the term "subpart F income" means, in the case of any controlled foreign corporation, the sum of—
  (1) insurance income (as defined under section 953),
  (2) the foreign base company income (as determined under section 954),
  (3) an amount equal to the product of—
    (A) the income of such corporation other than income which—
      (i) is attributable to earnings and profits of the foreign corporation included in the gross income of a United States person under section 951 (other than by reason of this paragraph), or
      (ii) is described in subsection (b),
    multiplied by
    (B) the international boycott factor (as determined under section 999),
  (4) the sum of the amounts of any illegal bribes, kickbacks, or other payments (within the meaning of section 162(c)) paid by or on behalf of the corporation during the taxable year of the corporation directly or indirectly to an official, employee, or agent in fact of a government, and
  (5) the income of such corporation derived from any foreign country during any period during which section 901(j) applies to such foreign country.
The payments referred to in paragraph (4) are payments which would be unlawful under the Foreign Corrupt Practices Act of 1977 if the payor were a United States person. For purposes of paragraph (5), the income described therein shall be reduced, under regulations prescribed by the Secretary, so as to take into account deductions (including taxes) properly allocable to such income.
(b) Exclusion of United States income.
In the case of a controlled foreign corporation, subpart F income does not include any item of income from sources within the United States which is effectively connected with the conduct by such corporation of a trade or business within the United States unless such item is exempt from taxation (or is subject to a reduced rate of tax) pursuant to a treaty obligation of the United States. For purposes of this subsection, any exemption (or reduction) with respect to the tax imposed by section 884 shall not be taken into account.
(c) Limitation.
  (1) In general.
    (A) Subpart F income limited to current earnings and profits. For purposes of subsection (a), the subpart F income of any controlled foreign corporation for any taxable year shall not exceed the earnings and profits of such corporation for such taxable year.
    (B) Certain prior year deficits may be taken into account.
      (i) In general. The amount included in the gross income of any United States shareholder under section 951(a)(1)(A)(i) for any taxable year and attributable to a qualified activity shall be reduced by the amount of such shareholder's pro rata share of any qualified deficit.
      (ii) Qualified deficit. The term "qualified deficit" means any deficit in earnings and profits of the controlled foreign corporation for any prior taxable year which began after December 31, 1986, and for which the controlled foreign corporation was a controlled foreign corporation; but only to the extent such deficit—
        (I) is attributable to the same qualified activity as the activity giving rise to the income being offset, and
        (II) has not previously been taken into account under this subparagraph.
      In determining the deficit attributable to qualified activities described in subclause (II) or (III) of clause (iii), deficits in earnings and profits (to the extent not previously taken into account under this section) for taxable years beginning after 1962 and before 1987 also shall be taken into account. In the case of the qualified activity described in clause (iii)(I), the rule of the preceding sentence shall apply, except that "1982" shall be substituted for "1962".
      (iii) Qualified activity. For purposes of this paragraph, the term "qualified activity" means any activity giving rise to—
        (I) foreign base company oil related income,
        (II) foreign base company sales income,
        (III) foreign base company services income,
        (IV) in the case of a qualified insurance company, insurance income or foreign personal holding company income, or
        (V) in the case of a qualified financial institution, foreign personal holding company income.
      (iv) Pro rata share. For purposes of this paragraph, the shareholder's pro rata share of any deficit for any prior taxable year shall be determined under rules similar to rules under section 951(a)(2) for whichever of the following yields the smaller share:
        (I) the close of the taxable year, or
        (II) the close of the taxable year in which the deficit arose.
      (v) Qualified insurance company. For purposes of this subparagraph, the term "qualified insurance company" means any controlled foreign corporation predominantly engaged in the active conduct of an insurance business in the taxable year and in the prior taxable years in which the deficit arose.
      (vi) Qualified financial institution. For purposes of this paragraph, the term "qualified financial institution" means any controlled foreign corporation predominantly engaged in the active conduct of a banking, financing, or similar business in the taxable year and in the prior taxable year in which the deficit arose.
      (vii) Special rules for insurance income.
        (I) In general. An election may be made under this clause to have section 953(a) applied for purposes of this title without regard to the same country exception under paragraph (1)(A) thereof. Such election, once made, may be revoked only with the consent of the Secretary.
        (II) Special rules for affiliated groups. In the case of an affiliated group of corporations (within the meaning of section 1504 but without regard to section 1504(b)(3) and by substituting "more than 50 percent" for "at least 80 percent" each place it appears), no election may be made under subclause (I) for any controlled foreign corporation unless such election is made for all other controlled foreign corporations who are members of such group and who were created or organized under the laws of the same country as such controlled foreign corporation. For purposes of clause (v), in determin-

ing whether any controlled corporation described in the preceding sentence is a qualified insurance company, all such corporations shall be treated as 1 corporation.

(C) Certain deficits of member of the same chain of corporations may be taken into account.

(i) In general. A controlled foreign corporation may elect to reduce the amount of its subpart F income for any taxable year which is attributable to any qualified activity by the amount of any deficit in earnings and profits of a qualified chain member for a taxable year ending with (or within) the taxable year of such controlled foreign corporation to the extent such deficit is attributable to such activity. To the extent any deficit reduces subpart F income under the preceding sentence, such deficit shall not be taken into account under subparagraph (B).

(ii) Qualified chain member. For purposes of this subparagraph, the term "qualified chain member" means, with respect to any controlled foreign corporation, any other corporation which is created or organized under the laws of the same foreign country as the controlled foreign corporation but only if—

(I) all the stock of such other corporation (other than directors' qualifying shares) is owned at all times during the taxable year in which the deficit arose (directly or through 1 or more corporations other than the common parent) by such controlled foreign corporation, or

(II) all the stock of such controlled foreign corporation (other than directors' qualifying shares) is owned at all times during the taxable year in which the deficit arose (directly or through 1 or more corporations other than the common parent) by such other corporation.

(iii) Coordination. This subparagraph shall be applied after subparagraphs (A) and (B).

(2) Recharacterization in subsequent taxable years. If the subpart F income of any controlled foreign corporation for any taxable year was reduced by reason of paragraph (1)(A), any excess of the earnings and profits of such corporation for any subsequent taxable year over the subpart F income of such foreign corporation for such taxable year shall be recharacterized as subpart F income under rules similar to the rules applicable under section 904(f)(5).

(3) Special rule for determining earnings and profits. For purposes of this subsection, earnings and profits of any controlled foreign corporation shall be determined without regard to paragraphs (4), (5), and (6) of section 312(n). Under regulations, the preceding sentence shall not apply to the extent it would increase earnings and profits by an amount which was previously distributed by the controlled foreign corporation.

(d) Income derived from foreign country.

The Secretary shall prescribe such regulations as may be necessary or appropriate to carry out the purposes of subsection (a)(5), including regulations which treat income paid through 1 or more entities as derived from a foreign country to which section 901(j) applies if such income was, without regard to such entities, derived from such country.

In **2007**, P.L. 110-172, Sec. 11(g)(14), deleted "For purposes of the preceding sentence, income described in paragraph (2) or (3) of section 921(d) shall be treated as derived from sources within the United States." in subsec. (b), enacted 12/29/2007.

In **2005**, P.L. 109-135, Sec. 412(kk)(1), substituted "subclause (II) or (III) of clause (iii)" for "clause (iii)(III) or (IV)" in clause (c)(1)(B)(ii) . . . Sec.

412(kk)(2), substituted "clause (iii)(I)" for "clause (iii)(II)" in clause (c)(1)(B)(ii), effective 12/21/2005.

In **2004**, P.L. 108-357, Sec. 415(c)(1), deleted subclause (c)(1)(B)(iii)(I) and redesignated subclauses (c)(1)(B)(iii)(II)-(VI) as (c)(1)(B)(iii)(I)-(V), effective for tax. yrs. of foreign corporations begin. after 12/31/2004, and for tax. yrs. of United States shareholders with or within which such tax. yrs. of foreign corporations end.

Prior to deletion, subclause (c)(1)(B)(iii)(I) read as follows:

"(I) foreign base company shipping income,"

In **1997**, P.L. 105-34, Sec. 1112(c)(1), added the sentence at the end of subsec. (b), effective for tax. yrs. begin. after 12/31/86.

In **1988**, P.L. 100-647, Sec. 1012(i)(6), provides

"(6) For purposes of applying section 952(c)(1)(A) of the 1986 Code, the earnings and profits of any corporation shall be determined without regard to any increase in earnings and profits under section 1023(e)(3)(C) [P.L. 99-514] of the Reform Act."

—P.L. 100-647, Sec. 1012(i)(13)(A), and (B), amended Sec. 1221(g)(3) of P.L. 99-514 [reproduced below], exceptions to the effective date for changes made by Secs. 1221(b)(3)(A), and (f) of P.L. 99-514, by substituting "June 9" for "July 9", and "November 3, 1981" for "March 31, 1982" in Sec. 1221(g)(3)(C) of P.L. 99-514 and by substituting "under a reinsurance contract" for "as of August 16, 1986, under a reinsurance contract in effect on such date", and by substituting "this subparagraph" for "the preceding sentence" and by adding the last two sentences to Sec. 1221(g)(3)(D) of P.L. 99-514, see below.

—P.L. 100-647, Sec. 1012(i)(16), added para. (c)(3) . . . Sec. 1012(i)(22), substituted "insurance income or foreign personal holding company income," for "insurance income" in subclause (c)(1)(B)(iii)(III) . . . Sec. 1012(i)(23), redesignated subclauses (c)(1)(B)(iii)(III) and (c)(1)(B)(iii)(IV) as subclauses (c)(1)(B)(iii)(V) and (c)(1)(B)(iii)(VI), respectively and added new subclauses (c)(1)(B)(iii)(III) and (c)(1)(B)(iii)(IV) . . . Sec. 1012(i)(24), added last two sentences of clause (c)(1)(B)(ii) . . . Sec. 1012(i)(25)(A), added subpara. (c)(1)(C), effective for tax. yrs. of foreign corporations begin. after 12/31/86, except as provided by Sec. 1221(g)(3) of P.L. 99-514, reproduced below.

—P.L. 100-647, Sec. 6131(a), added clause (c)(1)(B)(vii), effective for tax. yrs. of foreign corporations begin. after 12/31/86, except as provided by Sec. 1221(g)(3) of P.L. 99-514, reproduced below.

In **1986**, P.L. 99-514, Sec. 1221(b)(3)(A), amended para. (a)(1) . . . Sec. 1221(f), amended subsec. (c), and deleted subsec. (d) effective for tax. yrs. of foreign corporations begin. after 12/31/86, except as provided by Sec. 1221(g)(3) [as amended by Sec. 1012(i)(13) of P.L. 100-647, see above] of this Act, which reads as follows:

"(3) Exception for certain reinsurance contracts.—

"(A) In general.—In the case of the last 1st 3 taxable years of a qualified controlled foreign insurer beginning after December 31, 1986, the amendments made by this section shall not apply to the phase-in percentage of any qualified reinsurance income.

"(B) Phase-in percentage.—For purposes of subparagraph (A):

"In the case of taxable years beginning in:	The phase-in percentage is:
1987	75
1988	50
1989	25.

"(C) Qualified controlled foreign insurer.—For purposes of this paragraph, the term 'qualified controlled foreign insurer' means—

"(i) any controlled foreign corporation which on August 16, 1986, was a member of an affiliated group (as defined in section 1504(a) of the Internal Revenue Code of 1986 without regard to subsection (b)(3) thereof) which had as its common parent a corporation incorporated in Delaware on June 9, 1967, with executive offices in New York, New York, or

"(ii) any controlled foreign corporation which on August 16, 1986, was a member of an affiliated group (as so defined) which had as its common parent a corporation incorporated in Delaware on November 3, 1981. with executive offices in Philadelphia, Pennsylvania.

"(D) Qualified reinsurance income.—For purposes of this paragraph, the term 'qualified reinsurance income' means any insurance income attributable to risks (other than risks described in section 953(a) or 954(e) of such Code as in effect on the day before the date of the enactment of this Act) assumed under a reinsurance contract. For purposes of this subparagraph, insurance income shall mean the underwriting income (as defined in section 832(b)(3) of such Code) and investment income derived from an amount of assets (to be segregated and separately identified) equivalent to the ordinary and necessary insurance reserves and necessary surplus equal to ⅓ of earned premium attributable to such contracts.' For purposes of this paragraph, the amount of qualified reinsurance income shall not exceed the amount of insurance income from reinsurance contracts for calendar year 1985. In the case of controlled foreign corporations described in subparagraph (C)(ii), the preceding sentence shall not apply and the qualified reinsurance income of any such corporation shall not exceed such corporation's proportionate share of $27,000,000 (determined on the basis of respective amounts of qualified reinsurance income determined without regard to this subparagraph)."

Prior to amendment, para. (a)(1) read as follows:

"(1) the income derived from the insurance of United States risks (as determined under section 953),"

Prior to amendment, subsec. (c) read as follows:

"(c) Limitation.

"For purposes of subsection (a), the subpart F income of any controlled foreign corporation for any taxable year shall not exceed the earnings and profits of such corporation for such year reduced by the amount (if any) by which—

"(1) an amount equal to—

"(A) the sum of the deficits in earnings and profits for prior taxable years beginning after December 31, 1962, plus

"(B) the sum of the deficits in earnings and profits for taxable years beginning after December 31, 1959, and before January 1, 1963 (reduced by the sum of the earnings and profits for such taxable years); exceeds

"(2) an amount equal to the sum of the earnings and profits for prior taxable years beginning after December 31, 1962, allocated to other earnings and profits under section 959(c)(3).

For purposes of the preceding sentence, any deficit in earnings and profits for any prior taxable year shall be taken into account under paragraph (1) for any taxable year only to the extent it has not been taken into account under such paragraph for any preceding taxable year to reduce earnings and profits of such preceding year."

Prior to deletion, subsec. (d) read as follows:

"(d) Special rule in case of indirect ownership.

"For purposes of subsection (c), if—

"(1) a United States shareholder owns (within the meaning of section 958(a)) stock of a foreign corporation, and by reason of such ownership owns (within the meaning of such section) stock of any other foreign corporation, and

"(2) any of such foreign corporations has a deficit in earning and profits for the taxable year,

then the earnings and profits for the taxable year of each such foreign corporation which is a controlled foreign corporation shall, with respect to such United States shareholder, be properly reduced to take into account any deficit described in paragraph (2) in such manner as the Secretary shall prescribe by regulations."

—P.L. 99-514, Sec. 1876(c)(1), added the last sentence to subsec. (b), effective for tax. yrs. begin. after 12/31/66.

—P.L. 99-509, Sec. 8041(b)(1)(A), deleted "and" at the end of para. (a)(3), substituted ", and" for the period at the end of para. (a)(4) and added para. (a)(5)... Sec. 8041(b)(1)(B), added the last sentence to subsec. (a)... Sec. 8041(b)(2), added subsec. (d) [after the amendments made by P.L. 99-514, see above], effective 1/1/87.

In **1982,** P.L. 97-248, Sec. 288(b)(1), added the last sentence to subsec. (a), for payments made after 9/3/82.

In **1976,** P.L. 94-455, Sec. 1062(a)(1), deleted "and" at the end of para. (a)(1)... Sec. 1062(a)(2), substituted ", and" for the period at the end of para. (a)(2)... Sec. 1062(a)(3), added para. (a)(3), effective for participation in or cooperation with an international boycott more than 30 days after 10/4/76 (date of enactment), except for operations which constitute participation in or cooperation with an international boycott and are carried out in accordance with the terms of a binding contract entered into before 9/2/76, whereby these amendments apply to such participation or cooperation after 12/31/77.

—P.L. 94-455, Sec. 1065(a)(1)(A), deleted "and" at the end of para. (a)(2)... Sec. 1065(a)(1)(B), substituted ", and" for the period at the end of para. (a)(3)... Sec. 1065(a)(1)(C), added para. (a)(4), effective for payments described in Code Sec. 162(c) made more than 30 days after 10/4/76 (date of enactment).

—P.L. 94-455, Sec. 1906(b)(13)(A), substituted "Secretary" for "Secretary or his delegate" in subsec. (d), effective for tax. yrs. begin. after 12/31/76.

In **1966,** P.L. 89-809, Sec. 104(a), amended subsec. (b), effective for tax. yrs. begin. after 12/31/66.

Prior to amendment, subsec. (b) read as follows:

"(b) Exclusion of United States income.

"Subpart F income does not include any item includible in gross income under this chapter (other than this subpart) as income derived from sources within the United States of a foreign corporation engaged in trade or business in the United States."

In **1962,** P.L. 87-834, Sec. 12(a), added Code Sec. 952, effective for tax. yrs. of foreign corporations begin. after 12/31/62 and tax. yrs. of U.S. shareholders within which or with which such tax. yrs. of such foreign corporations end.

Sec. 953. Insurance income.

(a) Insurance income.

(1) In general. For purposes of section 952(a)(1), the term "insurance income" means any income which—

(A) is attributable to the issuing (or reinsuring) of an insurance or annuity contract, and

(B) would (subject to the modifications provided by subsection (b)) be taxed under subchapter L of this chapter if such income were the income of a domestic insurance company.

(2) Exception. Such term shall not include any exempt insurance income (as defined in subsection (e)).

(b) Special rules.

For purposes of subsection (a)—

(1) The following provisions of subchapter L shall not apply:

(A) The small life insurance company deduction.

(B) Section 805(a)(5) (relating to operations loss deduction).

(C) Section 832(c)(5) (relating to certain capital losses).

(2) The items referred to in—

(A) section 803(a)(1) (relating to gross amount of premiums and other considerations),

(B) section 803(a)(2) (relating to net decrease in reserves),

(C) section 805(a)(2) (relating to net increase in reserves), and

(D) section 832(b)(4) (relating to premiums earned on insurance contracts),

shall be taken into account only to the extent they are in respect of any reinsurance or the issuing of any insurance or annuity contract described in subsection (a)(1).

(3) Reserves for any insurance or annuity contract shall be determined in the same manner as under section 954(i).

(4) All items of income, expenses, losses, and deductions shall be properly allocated or apportioned under regulations prescribed by the Secretary.

(c) Special rule for certain captive insurance companies.

(1) In general. For purposes only of taking into account related person insurance income—

(A) the term "United States shareholder" means, with respect to any foreign corporation, a United States person (as defined in section 957(c)) who owns (within the meaning of section 958(a)) any stock of the foreign corporation,

(B) the term "controlled foreign corporation" has the meaning given to such term by section 957(a) determined by substituting "25 percent or more" for "more than 50 percent", and

(C) the pro rata share referred to in section 951(a)(1)(A)(i) shall be determined under paragraph (5) of this subsection.

(2) Related person insurance income. For purposes of this subsection, the term "related person insurance income" means any insurance income (within the meaning of subsection (a)) attributable to a policy of insurance or reinsurance with respect to which the person (directly or indirectly) insured is a United States shareholder in the foreign corporation or a related person to such a shareholder.

(3) Exceptions.

(A) Corporations not held by insureds. Paragraph (1) shall not apply to any foreign corporation if at all times during the taxable year of such foreign corporation—

(i) less than 20 percent of the total combined voting power of all classes of stock of such corporation entitled to vote, and

(ii) less than 20 percent of the total value of such corporation,

is owned (directly or indirectly under the principles of section 883(c)(4)) by persons who are (directly or indirectly) insured under any policy of insurance or reinsurance issued by such corporation or who are related persons to any such person.

(B) De minimis exception. Paragraph (1) shall not apply to any foreign corporation for a taxable year of such corporation if the related person insurance income (determined on a gross basis) of such corporation for such taxable year is less than 20 percent of its insurance income (as so determined) for such taxable year determined without regard to those provisions of subsection (a)(1) which limit insurance income to income from countries other than the country in which the corporation was created or organized.

(C) Election to treat income as effectively connected. Paragraph (1) shall not apply to any foreign corporation for any taxable year if—

(i) such corporation elects (at such time and in such manner as the Secretary may prescribe)—

(I) to treat its related person insurance income for such taxable year as income effectively connected with the conduct of a trade or business in the United States, and

(II) to waive all benefits (other than with respect to section 884) with respect to related person insurance income granted by the United States under any treaty between the United States and any foreign country, and

(ii) such corporation meets such requirements as the Secretary shall prescribe to ensure that the tax imposed by this chapter on such income is paid.

An election under this subparagraph made for any taxable year shall not be effective if the corporation (or any predecessor thereof) was a disqualified corporation for the taxable year for which the election was made or for any prior taxable year beginning after 1986.

(D) Special rules for subparagraph (C).

(i) Period during which election in effect.

(I) In general. Except as provided in subclause (II), any election under subparagraph (C) shall apply to the taxable year for which made and all subsequent taxable years unless revoked with the consent of the Secretary.

(II) Termination. If a foreign corporation which made an election under subparagraph (C) for any taxable year is a disqualified corporation for any subsequent taxable year, such election shall not apply to any taxable year beginning after such subsequent taxable year.

(ii) Exemption from tax imposed by section 4371. The tax imposed by section 4371 shall not apply with respect to any related person insurance income treated as effectively connected with the conduct of a trade or business within the United States under subparagraph (C).

(E) Disqualified corporation. For purposes of this paragraph the term "disqualified corporation" means, with respect to any taxable year, any foreign corporation which is a controlled foreign corporation for an uninterrupted period of 30 days or more during such taxable year (determined without regard to this subsection) but only if a United States shareholder (determined without regard to this subsection) owns (within the meaning of section 958(a)) stock in such corporation at some time during such taxable year.

(4) Treatment of mutual insurance companies. In the case of a mutual insurance company—

(A) this subsection shall apply,

(B) policyholders of such company shall be treated as shareholders, and

(C) appropriate adjustments in the application of this subpart shall be made under regulations prescribed by the Secretary.

(5) Determination of pro rata share.

(A) In general. The pro rata share determined under this paragraph for any United States shareholder is the lesser of—

(i) the amount which would be determined under paragraph (2) of section 951(a) if—

(I) only related person insurance income were taken into account,

(II) stock owned (within the meaning of section 958(a)) by United States shareholders on the last day of the taxable year were the only stock in the foreign corporation, and

(III) only distributions received by United States shareholders were taken into account under subparagraph (B) of such paragraph (2), or

(ii) the amount which would be determined under paragraph (2) of section 951(a) if the entire earnings and profits of the foreign corporation for the taxable year were subpart F income.

(B) Coordination with other provisions. The Secretary shall prescribe regulations providing for such modifications to the provisions of this subpart as may be necessary or appropriate by reason of subparagraph (A).

(6) Related person. For purposes of this subsection—

(A) In general. Except as provided in subparagraph (B), the term "related person" has the meaning given such term by section 954(d)(3).

(B) Treatment of certain liability insurance policies. In the case of any policy of insurance covering liability arising from services performed as a director, officer, or employee of a corporation or as a partner or employee of a partnership, the person performing such services and the entity for which such services are performed shall be treated as related persons.

(7) Coordination with section 1248. For purposes of section 1248, if any person is (or would be but for paragraph (3)) treated under paragraph (1) as a United States shareholder with respect to any foreign corporation which would be taxed under subchapter L if it were a domestic corporation and which is (or would be but for paragraph (3)) treated under paragraph (1) as a controlled foreign corporation—

(A) such person shall be treated as meeting the stock ownership requirements of section 1248(a)(2) with respect to such foreign corporation, and

(B) such foreign corporation shall be treated as a controlled foreign corporation.

(8) Regulations. The Secretary shall prescribe such regulations as may be necessary to carry out the purposes of this subsection, including—

(A) regulations preventing the avoidance of this subsection through cross insurance arrangements or otherwise, and

(B) regulations which may provide that a person will not be treated as a United States shareholder under paragraph (1) with respect to any foreign corporation if neither such person (nor any related person to such person) is (directly or indirectly) insured under any policy of insurance or reinsurance issued by such foreign corporation.

(d) Election by foreign insurance company to be treated as domestic corporation.

(1) In general. If—

(A) a foreign corporation is a controlled foreign corporation (as defined in section 957(a) by substituting "25 percent or more" for "more than 50 percent" and by using the definition of United States shareholder under 953(c)(1)(A)),

(B) such foreign corporation would qualify under part I or II of subchapter L for the taxable year if it were a domestic corporation,

(C) such foreign corporation meets such requirements as the Secretary shall prescribe to ensure that the taxes

2,621

imposed by this chapter on such foreign corporation are paid, and

(D) such foreign corporation makes an election to have this paragraph apply and waives all benefits to such corporation granted by the United States under any treaty,

for purposes of this title, such corporation shall be treated as a domestic corporation.

(2) Period during which election is in effect.

(A) In general. Except as provided in subparagraph (B), an election under paragraph (1) shall apply to the taxable year for which made and all subsequent taxable years unless revoked with the consent of the Secretary.

(B) Termination. If a corporation which made an election under paragraph (1) for any taxable year fails to meet the requirements of subparagraphs (A), (B), and (C), of paragraph (1) for any subsequent taxable year, such election shall not apply to any taxable year beginning after such subsequent taxable year.

(3) Treatment of losses. If any corporation treated as a domestic corporation under this subsection is treated as a member of an affiliated group for purposes of chapter 6 (relating to consolidated returns), any loss of such corporation shall be treated as a dual consolidated loss for purposes of section 1503(d) without regard to paragraph (2)(B) thereof.

(4) Effect of election.

(A) In general. For purposes of section 367, any foreign corporation making an election under paragraph (1) shall be treated as transferring (as of the 1st day of the 1st taxable year to which such election applies) all of its assets to a domestic corporation in connection with an exchange to which section 354 applies.

(B) Exception for pre-1988 earnings and profit.

(i) In general. Earnings and profits of the foreign corporation accumulated in taxable years beginning before January 1, 1988, shall not be included in the gross income of the persons holding stock in such corporation by reason of subparagraph (A).

(ii) Treatment of distributions. For purposes of this title, any distribution made by a corporation to which an election under paragraph (1) applies out of earnings and profits accumulated in taxable years beginning before January 1, 1988, shall be treated as a distribution made by a foreign corporation.

(iii) Certain rules to continue to apply to pre-1988 earnings. The provisions specified in clause (iv) shall be applied without regard to paragraph (1), except that, in the case of a corporation to which an election under paragraph (1) applies, only earnings and profits accumulated in taxable years beginning before January 1, 1988, shall be taken into account.

(iv) Specified provisions. The provisions specified in this clause are:

(I) Section 1248 (relating to gain from certain sales or exchanges of stock in certain foreign corporations).

(II) Subpart F of part III of subchapter N to the extent such subpart relates to earnings invested in United States property or amounts referred to in clause (ii) or (iii) of section 951(a)(1)(A).

(III) Section 884 to the extent the foreign corporation reinvested 1987 earnings and profits in United States assets.

(5) Effect of termination. For purposes of section 367, if—

(A) an election is made by a corporation under paragraph (1) for any taxable year, and

(B) such election ceases to apply for any subsequent taxable year,

such corporation shall be treated as a domestic corporation transferring (as of the 1st day of such subsequent taxable year) all of its property to a foreign corporation in connection with an exchange to which section 354 applies.

(6) Additional tax on corporation making election.

(A) In general. If a corporation makes an election under paragraph (1), the amount of tax imposed by this chapter for the 1st taxable year to which such election applies shall be increased by the amount determined under subparagraph (B).

(B) Amount of tax. The amount of tax determined under this paragraph shall be equal to the lesser of—

(i) 3/4 of 1 percent of the aggregate amount of capital and accumulated surplus of the corporation as of December 31, 1987, or

(ii) $1,500,000.

(e) Exempt insurance income.

For purposes of this section—

(1) Exempt insurance income defined.

(A) In general. The term "exempt insurance income" means income derived by a qualifying insurance company which—

(i) is attributable to the issuing (or reinsuring) of an exempt contract by such company or a qualifying insurance company branch of such company, and

(ii) is treated as earned by such company or branch in its home country for purposes of such country's tax laws.

(B) Exception for certain arrangements. Such term shall not include income attributable to the issuing (or reinsuring) of an exempt contract as the result of any arrangement whereby another corporation receives a substantially equal amount of premiums or other consideration in respect of issuing (or reinsuring) a contract which is not an exempt contract.

(C) Determinations made separately. For purposes of this subsection and section 954(i), the exempt insurance income and exempt contracts of a qualifying insurance company or any qualifying insurance company branch of such company shall be determined separately for such company and each such branch by taking into account—

(i) in the case of the qualifying insurance company, only items of income, deduction, gain, or loss, and activities of such company not properly allocable or attributable to any qualifying insurance company branch of such company, and

(ii) in the case of a qualifying insurance company branch, only items of income, deduction, gain, or loss and activities properly allocable or attributable to such unit.

(2) Exempt contract.

(A) In general. The term "exempt contract" means an insurance or annuity contract issued or reinsured by a qualifying insurance company or qualifying insurance company branch in connection with property in, liability arising out of activity in, or the lives or health of residents of, a country other than the United States.

(B) Minimum home country income required.

(i) In general. No contract of a qualifying insurance company or of a qualifying insurance company branch shall be treated as an exempt contract unless

such company or branch derives more than 30 percent of its net written premiums from exempt contracts (determined without regard to this subparagraph)—
  (I) which cover applicable home country risks, and
  (II) with respect to which no policyholder, insured, annuitant, or beneficiary is a related person (as defined in section 954(d)(3)).
  (ii) Applicable home country risks. The term "applicable home country risks" means risks in connection with property in, liability arising out of activity in, or the lives or health of residents of, the home country of the qualifying insurance company or qualifying insurance company branch, as the case may be, issuing or reinsuring the contract covering the risks.
(C) Substantial activity requirements for cross border risks. A contract issued by a qualifying insurance company or qualifying insurance company branch which covers risks other than applicable home country risks (as defined in subparagraph (B)(ii)) shall not be treated as an exempt contract unless such company or branch, as the case may be—
  (i) conducts substantial activity with respect to an insurance business in its home country, and
  (ii) performs in its home country substantially all of the activities necessary to give rise to the income generated by such contract.
(3) Qualifying insurance company. The term "qualifying insurance company" means any controlled foreign corporation which—
(A) is subject to regulation as an insurance (or reinsurance) company by its home country, and is licensed, authorized, or regulated by the applicable insurance regulatory body for its home country to sell insurance, reinsurance, or annuity contracts to persons other than related persons (within the meaning of section 954(d)(3)) in such home country,
(B) derives more than 50 percent of its aggregate net written premiums from the issuance or reinsurance by such controlled foreign corporation and each of its qualifying insurance company branches of contracts—
  (i) covering applicable home country risks (as defined in paragraph (2)) of such corporation or branch, as the case may be, and
  (ii) with respect to which no policyholder, insured, annuitant, or beneficiary is a related person (as defined in section 954(d)(3)),
except that in the case of a branch, such premiums shall only be taken into account to the extent such premiums are treated as earned by such branch in its home country for purposes of such country's tax laws, and
(C) is engaged in the insurance business and would be subject to tax under subchapter L if it were a domestic corporation.
(4) Qualifying insurance company branch. The term "qualifying insurance company branch" means a qualified business unit (within the meaning of section 989(a)) of a controlled foreign corporation if—
(A) such unit is licensed, authorized, or regulated by the applicable insurance regulatory body for its home country to sell insurance, reinsurance, or annuity contracts to persons other than related persons (within the meaning of section 954(d)(3)) in such home country, and
(B) such controlled foreign corporation is a qualifying insurance company, determined under paragraph (3) as if such unit were a qualifying insurance company branch.

(5) Life insurance or annuity contract. For purposes of this section and section 954, the determination of whether a contract issued by a controlled foreign corporation or a qualified business unit (within the meaning of section 989(a)) is a life insurance contract or an annuity contract shall be made without regard to sections 72(s), 101(f), 817(h), and 7702 if—
(A) such contract is regulated as a life insurance or annuity contract by the corporation's or unit's home country, and
(B) no policyholder, insured, annuitant, or beneficiary with respect to the contract is a United States person.
(6) Home country. For purposes of this subsection, except as provided in regulations—
(A) Controlled foreign corporation. The term "home country" means, with respect to a controlled foreign corporation, the country in which such corporation is created or organized.
(B) Qualified business unit. The term "home country" means, with respect to a qualified business unit (as defined in section 989(a)), the country in which the principal office of such unit is located and in which such unit is licensed, authorized, or regulated by the applicable insurance regulatory body to sell insurance, reinsurance, or annuity contracts to persons other than related persons (as defined in section 954(d)(3)) in such country.
(7) Anti-abuse rules. For purposes of applying this subsection and section 954(i)—
(A) the rules of section 954(h)(7) (other than subparagraph (B) thereof) shall apply,
(B) there shall be disregarded any item of income, gain, loss, or deduction of, or derived from, an entity which is not engaged in regular and continuous transactions with persons which are not related persons,
(C) there shall be disregarded any change in the method of computing reserves a principal purpose of which is the acceleration or deferral of any item in order to claim the benefits of this subsection or section 954(i),
(D) a contract of insurance or reinsurance shall not be treated as an exempt contract (and premiums from such contract shall not be taken into account for purposes of paragraph (2)(B) or (3)) if—
  (i) any policyholder, insured, annuitant, or beneficiary is a resident of the United States and such contract was marketed to such resident and was written to cover a risk outside the United States, or
  (ii) the contract covers risks located within and without the United States and the qualifying insurance company or qualifying insurance company branch does not maintain such contemporaneous records, and file such reports, with respect to such contract as the Secretary may require,
(E) the Secretary may prescribe rules for the allocation of contracts (and income from contracts) among 2 or more qualifying insurance company branches of a qualifying insurance company in order to clearly reflect the income of such branches, and
(F) premiums from a contract shall not be taken into account for purposes of paragraph (2)(B) or (3) if such contract reinsures a contract issued or reinsured by a related person (as defined in section 954(d)(3)).
For purposes of subparagraph (D), the determination of where risks are located shall be made under the principles of section 953.
(8) Coordination with subsection (c). In determining insurance income for purposes of subsection (c), exempt in-

surance income shall not include income derived from exempt contracts which cover risks other than applicable home country risks.

(9) Regulations. The Secretary shall prescribe such regulations as may be necessary or appropriate to carry out the purposes of this subsection and section 954(i).

(10) Application. This subsection and section 954(i) shall apply only to taxable years of a foreign corporation beginning after December 31, 1998, and before January 1, 2012, and to taxable years of United States shareholders with or within which any such taxable year of such foreign corporation ends. If this subsection does not apply to a taxable year of a foreign corporation beginning after December 31, 2011 (and taxable years of United States shareholders ending with or within such taxable year), then, notwithstanding the preceding sentence, subsection (a) shall be applied to such taxable years in the same manner as it would if the taxable year of the foreign corporation began in 1998.

(11) Cross reference. For income exempt from foreign personal holding company income, see section 954(i).

In 2010, P.L. 111-312, Sec. 750(a), substituted "January 1, 2012" for "January 1, 2010" in para. (e)(10) . . . Sec. 750(b), substituted "December 31, 2011" for "December 31, 2009" in para. (e)(10), effective for tax. yrs. of foreign corporations begin. after 12/31/2009, and to tax. yrs. of United States shareholders with or within which any such tax. yr. of such foreign corporation ends.

In 2008, P.L. 110-343, Sec. 303(a)(1)DivC, substitued "January 1, 2010" for "January 1, 2009" in para. (e)(10) . . . Sec. 303(a)(2)DivC, substituted "December 31, 2009" for "December 31, 2008" in para. (e)(10), effective 10/3/2008.

In 2006, P.L. 109-222, Sec. 103(a)(1)(A), substituted "January 1, 2009" for "January 1, 2007" in para. (e)(10) . . . Sec. 103(a)(1)(B), substituted "December 31, 2008" for "December 31, 2006" in para. (e)(10), enacted 5/17/2006.

In 2002, P.L. 107-147, Sec. 614(a)(1)(A), substituted "January 1, 2007" for "January 1, 2002" in para. (e)(10) . . . Sec. 614(a)(1)(B), substituted "December 31, 2006" for "December 31, 2001" in para. (e)(10), effective for tax. yrs. begin. after 12/31/2001.

In 1999, P.L. 106-170, Sec. 503(a)(1), substituted "taxable years" for "the first taxable year" in para. (e)(10) . . . Sec. 503(a)(2), substituted "January 1, 2002" for "January 1, 2000" in para. (e)(10) . . . Sec. 503(a)(3), substituted "within which any such" for "within which such" in para. (e)(10) . . . Sec. 503(b), added a sentence at the end of para. (e)(10), effective for tax. yrs. begin. after 12/31/99.

In 1998, P.L. 105-277, Sec. 1005(b)(1)(A), amended subsec. (a) . . . Sec. 1005(b)(1)(B), added subsec. (e) . . . Sec. 1005(b)(3), redesignated para. (b)(3) as (b)(4) and added para. (b)(3), effective 10/21/98.

Prior to amendment, subsec. (a) read as follows:

"(a) General rule. For purposes of section 952(a)(1), the term 'insurance income' means any income which—

"(1) is attributable to the issuing (or reinsuring) of any insurance or annuity contract—

"(A) in connection with property in, liability arising out of activity in, or in connection with the lives or health of residents of, a country other than the country under the laws of which the controlled foreign corporation is created or organized, or

"(B) in connection with risks not described in subparagraph (A) as the result of any arrangement whereby another corporation receives a substantially equal amount of premiums or other consideration in respect of issuing (or reinsuring) a contract described in subparagraph (A), and

"(2) would (subject to the modifications provided by paragraphs (1) and (2) of subsection (b)) be taxed under subchapter L of this chapter if such income were the income of a domestic insurance company."

In 1989, P.L. 101-239, Sec. 7816(p), substituted "for purposes of section 1503(d) without regard to paragraph (2)(B) thereof" for "(as defined in section 1503(d))" in para. (d)(3), effective for tax yrs. begin. after 12/31/87.

In 1988, P.L. 100-647, Sec. 1012(i)(1)(A), added the last sentence of subpara. (c)(3)(C) . . . Sec. 1012(i)(1)(B), amended clause (c)(3)(D)(i) . . . Sec. 1012(i)(1)(C), added subpara. (c)(3)(E) . . . Sec. 1012(i)(2)(A), deleted "and" at end of subpara. (c)(1)(A), substituted ", and" for the period at end of subpara. (c)(1)(B), and added subpara. (c)(1)(C) . . . Sec. 1012(i)(2)(B), redesignated para. (c)(5) as (c)(6) and added new para. (c)(5) . . . Sec. 1012(i)(4)(A), redesignated para. (c)(6) [as redesignated by Sec. 1012(i)(4)(B) of this Act] as (c)(7) and added new para. (c)(6) . . . Sec. 1012(i)(4)(B), deleted "(within the meaning of section 954(d)(3))" after "related persons" in para. (c)(2) and subpara. (c)(3)(A) . . . Sec. 1012(i)(5), substituted "insurance income (within the meaning of subsection (a)) attributable" for "insurance income attributable" in para. (c)(2) . . . Sec. 1012(i)(7)(A), deleted para. (b)(1) and redesignated paras. (b)(2)-(4) as (b)(1)-(3) . . . Sec. 1012(i)(7)(B), amended subpara. (b)(1)(A) (as redesignated) . . . Sec. 1012(i)(7)(C), deleted "(other than those taken into account under paragraph (3))" after "deductions" in para. (b)(3) . . . Sec. 1012(i)(8)(A), and (B), substituted "related person insurance income (determined on a gross basis)" for "related person insurance income" and substituted "its insurance income (as so determined)" for "its insurance income" in subpara. (c)(3)(B) . . . Sec. 1012(i)(9)(A), and (B), substituted "all benefits (other than with respect to section 884)" for "all benefits" and substituted "granted by the United States under any treaty" for "under any income tax treaty" in clause (c)(3)(C)(i)(II) . . . Sec. 1012(i)(21), deleted para. (c)(7) and added new paras. (c)(7) and (8), effective for tax. yrs. of foreign corporations begin. after 12/31/86, except as provided by Sec. 1221(g)(3) of P.L. 99-514, reproduced below.

Prior to amendment, clause (c)(3)(D)(i) read as follows:

"(i) Election irrevocable.

Any election under subparagraph (C) shall apply to the taxable year for which made and all subsequent taxable years unless revoked with the consent of the Secretary."

Prior to amendment, para. (b)(1) read as follows:

"(1) A corporation which would, if it were a domestic insurance corporation, be taxable under part II of subchapter L shall apply subsection (a) as if it were taxable under part III of subchapter L."

Prior to amendment subpara. (b)(1)(A) (as redesignated) read as follows:

"(A) The special life insurance company deduction and the small life insurance company deduction."

Prior to deletion para. (c)(7) (as redesignated) read as follows:

"(7) Regulations. The Secretary shall prescribe such regulations as may be necessary to carry out the purposes of this subsection, including regulations preventing the avoidance of this subsection through cross insurance arrangements or otherwise."

— P.L. 100-647, Sec. 1012(i)(3)(A), substituted "with respect to which the person (directly or indirectly) insured is" for "with respect to which the primary insured is" in para. (c)(2) . . . Sec. 1012(i)(3)(B), substituted "persons who are (directly or indirectly) insured" for "persons who are the primary insured", and "to any such person" for "to any such primary insured" in subpara. (c)(3)(A), effective to the extent such amendments add the phrase "(directly or indirectly)" only for tax. yrs. begin. after 12/31/87.

— P.L. 100-647, Sec. 1012(i)(13)(A), and (B), amended Sec. 1221(g)(3) of P.L. 99-514 [reproduced below] part of the effective date for changes made by Secs. 1221(b)(1)-(b)(3) of P.L. 99-514, by substituting "June 9" for "July 9", and "November 3, 1981" for "March 31, 1982" in Sec. 1221(g)(3)(C) of P.L. 99-514, by substituting "under a reinsurance contract" for "as of August 16, 1986, under a reinsurance contract in effect on such date" and "this subparagraph" for "the preceding sentence" in Sec. 1221(g)(3)(D) of P.L. 99-514 and by adding the last two sentences of Sec. 1221(g)(3)(D) of P.L. 99-514, see below.

— P.L. 100-647, Sec. 6135(a), added subsec. (d), effective for tax. yrs. begin. after 12/31/87.

In 1986, P.L. 99-514, Sec. 1221(b)(1), amended subsec. (a) . . . Sec. 1221(b)(2), added subsec. (c) . . . Sec. 1221(b)(3)(D), substituted "Insurance income" for "Income from insurance of United States risks" in the heading of Code Sec. 953, effective for tax. yrs. of foreign corporations begin. after 12/31/86, except as provided by Sec. 1221(g)(3) of this Act [as amended by Secs. 1012(i)(13)(A) and (B) of P.L. 100-647]:

"(3) Exception for certain reinsurance contracts.—

"(A) In general.— In the case of the 1st 3 taxable years of a qualified controlled foreign insurer beginning after December 31,1986, the amendments made by this section shall not apply to the phase-in percentage of any qualified reinsurance income.

"(B) Phase-in percentage.— For purposes of subparagraph (A):

"In the case of taxable years beginning in:	The phase-in percentage is:
1987	75
1988	50
1989	25.

"(C) Qualified controlled foreign insurer.— For purposes of this paragraph, the term 'qualified controlled foreign insurer' means—

"(i) any controlled foreign corporation which on August 16, 1986, was a member of an affiliated group (as defined in section 1504(a) of the Internal Revenue Code of 1986 without regard to subsection (b)(3) thereof) which had as its common parent a corporation incorporated in Delaware on June 9, 1967, with executive offices in New York, New York, or

"(ii) any controlled foreign corporation which on August 16, 1986, was a member of an affiliated group (as so defined) which had as its common parent a corporation incorporated in Delaware on November 3, 1981, with executive offices in Philadelphia, Pennsylvania.

"(D) Qualified reinsurance income.— For purposes of this paragraph, the term 'qualified reinsurance income' means any insurance income attributable to risks (other than risks described in section 953(a) or 954(e) of such Code as in effect on the day before the date of the enactment of this Act) assumed under a reinsurance contract. For purposes of this subparagraph insurance income shall mean the underwriting income (as defined in section 832(b)(3) of such Code) and investment income derived from an amount of assets (to be segregated and separately identified) equivalent to the ordinary and necessary insurance reserves and necessary surplus equal to ⅓ of earned premium attributable to such contracts.' For purposes of this paragraph, the amount of qualified reinsurance income shall not exceed the amount of insurance income from reinsurance contracts for calendar year 1985. In the case of controlled foreign corporations described in subparagraph (C)(ii), the preceding sentence shall not apply and the qualified reinsurance income of any such corporation shall not exceed such corporation's proportionate share of $27,000,000 (determined on the basis of respective amounts of qualified reinsurance income determined without regard to this subparagraph).

Income from foreign sources Code Sec. 954(c)(1)(B)(i)

Prior to amendment, subsec. (a) read as follows:
"*(a) General rule.*

"For purposes of section 952(a)(1), the term 'income derived from the insurance of United States risks' means that income which—

"(1) is attributable to the reinsurance or the issuing of any insurance or annuity contract—

"(A) in connection with property in, or liability arising out of activity in, or in connection with the lives or health of residents of, the United States, or

"(B) in connection with risks not included in subparagraph (A) as the result of any arrangement whereby another corporation receives a substantially equal amount of premiums or other consideration in respect to any reinsurance or the issuing of any insurance or annuity contract in connection with property in, or liability arising out of activity in, or in connection with the lives or health of residents of, the United States, and

"(2) would (subject to the modifications provided by paragraphs (1) and (2) of subsection (b)) be taxed under subchapter L of this chapter if such income were the income of a domestic insurance corporation.

This section shall apply only in the case of a controlled foreign corporation which receives, during any taxable year, premiums or other consideration in respect of the reinsurance, and the issuing, of insurance and annuity contracts described in paragraph (1) in excess of 5 percent of the total of premiums and other consideration received during such taxable year in respect of all reinsurance and issuing of insurance and annuity contracts."

In **1984**, P.L. 98-369, Sec. 211(b)(13)(A), deleted para. (b)(1) and redesignated paras. (b)(2), (3), (4) and (5) as paras. (b)(1), (2), (3) and (4), respectively. . . . Sec. 211(b)(13)(B), amended para. (b)(2) (as redesignated by Sec. 211(b)(13)(A)) . . . Sec. 211(b)(13)(C)(i)-(iii), substituted "section 803(a)(1)" for "section 809(c)(1)", substituted "section 803(a)(2)" for "section 809(c)(2)", and substituted "section 805(a)(2)" for "section 809(d)(2)" in para. (b)(3) (as redesignated by Sec. 211(b)(13)(A)) . . . Sec. 211(b)(13)(D), substituted "and (2)" for ", (2), and (3)" in para. (a)(2) . . . Sec. 211(b)(13)(E), substituted "paragraph (3)" for "paragraph (4)" in para. (b)(4) (as redesignated by Sec. 211(b)(13)(A)), effective for tax. yrs. begin. after 12/31/83.

Prior to deletion, para. (b)(1) read as follows:

"(1) In the application of part I of subchapter L, life insurance company taxable income in the gain from operations as defined in section 809(b)."

Prior to amendment, para. (b)(2) (as redesignated) read as follows:

"(2) The following provisions of subchapter L shall not apply:

"(A) Section 809(d)(4) (operations loss deduction).

"(B) Section 809(d)(5) (certain nonparticipating contracts).

"(C) Section 809(d)(6) (group life, accident, and health insurance).

"(D) Section 809(d)(10) (small business deduction).

"(E) Section 817(b) (gain on property held on December 31, 1958, and certain substituted property acquired after 1958).

"(F) Section 832(c)(5) (certain capital losses)."

In **1976**, P.L. 94-455, Sec. 1906(b)(13)(A), substituted "Secretary" for "Secretary or his delegate" in para. (b)(5), effective for tax. yrs. begin. after 12/31/76.

In **1966**, P.L. 89-809, Sec. 104, substituted "832(c)(5)" for "832(b)(5)" in subpara. (b)(3)(F), effective for tax. yrs. begin. after 12/31/66.

In **1962**, P.L. 87-834, Sec. 12, added Code Sec. 953 for tax. yrs. of foreign corporations begin. after '62 and tax. yrs. of U.S. shareholders within which or with which such tax. yrs. of such foreign corporations end.

Sec. 954. Foreign base company income.
(a) Foreign base company income.

For purposes of section 952(a)(2), the term "foreign base company income" means for any taxable year the sum of—

(1) the foreign personal holding company income for the taxable year (determined under subsection (c) and reduced as provided in subsection (b)(5)),

(2) the foreign base company sales income for the taxable year (determined under subsection (d) and reduced as provided in subsection (b)(5)),

(3) the foreign base company services income for the taxable year (determined under subsection (e) and reduced as provided in subsection (b)(5)),

(4) Repealed.

(5) the foreign base company oil related income for the taxable year (determined under subsection (g) and reduced as provided in subsection (b)(5)).

(b) Exclusions and special rules.
  (1) Repealed.
  (2) Repealed.
  (3) De minimis, etc., rules. For purposes of subsection (a) and section 953—

  (A) De minimis rule. If the sum of foreign base company income (determined without regard to paragraph (5)) and the gross insurance income for the taxable year is less than the lesser of—

    (i) 5 percent of gross income, or
    (ii) $1,000,000,

no part of the gross income for the taxable year shall be treated as foreign base company income or insurance income.

(B) Foreign base company income and insurance income in excess of 70 percent of gross income. If the sum of the foreign base company income (determined without regard to paragraph (5)) and the gross insurance income for the taxable year exceeds 70 percent of gross income, the entire gross income for the taxable year shall, subject to the provisions of paragraphs (4) and (5), be treated as foreign base company income or insurance income (whichever is appropriate).

(C) Gross insurance income. For purposes of subparagraphs (A) and (B), the term "gross insurance income" means any item of gross income taken into account in determining insurance income under section 953.

(4) Exception for certain income subject to high foreign taxes. For purposes of subsection (a) and section 953, foreign base company income and insurance income shall not include any item of income received by a controlled foreign corporation if the taxpayer establishes to the satisfaction of the Secretary that such income was subject to an effective rate of income tax imposed by a foreign country greater than 90 percent of the maximum rate of tax specified in section 11. The preceding sentence shall not apply to foreign base company oil-related income described in subsection (a)(5).

(5) Deductions to be taken into account. For purposes of subsection (a), the foreign personal holding company income, the foreign base company sales income, the foreign base company services income, and the foreign base company oil related income shall be reduced, under regulations prescribed by the Secretary, so as to take into account deductions (including taxes) properly allocable to such income. Except to the extent provided in regulations prescribed by the Secretary, any interest which is paid or accrued by the controlled foreign corporation to any United States shareholder in such corporation (or any controlled foreign corporation related to such a shareholder) shall be allocated first to foreign personal holding company income which is passive income (within the meaning of section 904(d)(2)) of such corporation to the extent thereof. The Secretary may, by regulations, provide that the preceding sentence shall apply also to interest paid or accrued to other persons.

(6) Foreign base company oil related income not treated as another kind of base company income. Income of a corporation which is foreign base company oil related income shall not be considered foreign base company income of such corporation under paragraph (2), or (3) of subsection (a).

(c) Foreign personal holding company income.

(1) In general. For purposes of subsection (a)(1), the term "foreign personal holding company income" means the portion of the gross income which consists of:

  (A) Dividends, etc. Dividends, interest, royalties, rents, and annuities.

  (B) Certain property transactions. The excess of gains over losses from the sale or exchange of property—

    (i) which gives rise to income described in subparagraph (A) (after application of paragraph (2)(A)) other than property which gives rise to income not treated as foreign personal holding company income by reason of subsection (h) or (i) for the taxable year,

2,625

(ii) which is an interest in a trust, partnership, or REMIC, or

(iii) which does not give rise to any income.

Gains and losses from the sale or exchange of any property which, in the hands of the controlled foreign corporation, is property described in section 1221(a)(1) shall not be taken into account under this subparagraph.

(C) Commodities transactions. The excess of gains over losses from transactions (including futures, forward, and similar transactions) in any commodities. This subparagraph shall not apply to gains or losses which—

(i) arise out of commodity hedging transactions (as defined in paragraph (5)(A)),

(ii) are active business gains or losses from the sale of commodities, but only if substantially all of the controlled foreign corporation's commodities are property described in paragraph (1), (2), or (8) of section 1221(a), or

(iii) are foreign currency gains or losses (as defined in section 988(b)) attributable to any section 988 transactions.

(D) Foreign currency gains. The excess of foreign currency gains over foreign currency losses (as defined in section 988(b)) attributable to any section 988 transactions. This subparagraph shall not apply in the case of any transaction directly related to the business needs of the controlled foreign corporation.

(E) Income equivalent to interest. Any income equivalent to interest, including income from commitment fees (or similar amounts) for loans actually made.

(F) Income from notional principal contracts.

(i) In general. Net income from notional principal contracts.

(ii) Coordination with other categories of foreign personal holding company income.—Any item of income, gain, deduction, or loss from a notional principal contract entered into for purposes of hedging any item described in any preceding subparagraph shall not be taken into account for purposes of this subparagraph but shall be taken into account under such other subparagraph.

(G) Payments in lieu of dividends. Payments in lieu of dividends which are made pursuant to an agreement to which section 1058 applies.

(H) Personal service contracts.

(i) Amounts received under a contract under which the corporation is to furnish personal services if—

(I) some person other than the corporation has the right to designate (by name or by description) the individual who is to perform the services, or

(II) the individual who is to perform the services is designated (by name or by description) in the contract, and

(ii) amounts received from the sale or other disposition of such a contract.

This subparagraph shall apply with respect to amounts received for services under a particular contract only if at some time during the taxable year 25 percent or more in value of the outstanding stock of the corporation is owned, directly or indirectly, by or for the individual who has performed, is to perform, or may be designated (by name or by description) as the one to perform, such services.

(2) Exception for certain amounts.

(A) Rents and royalties derived in active business. Foreign personal holding company income shall not include rents and royalties which are derived in the active conduct of a trade or business and which are received from a person other than a related person (within the meaning of subsection (d)(3)). For purposes of the preceding sentence, rents derived from leasing an aircraft or vessel in foreign commerce shall not fail to be treated as derived in the active conduct of a trade or business if, as determined under regulations prescribed by the Secretary, the active leasing expenses are not less than 10 percent of the profit on the lease.

(B) Certain export financing. Foreign personal holding company income shall not include any interest which is derived in the conduct of a banking business and which is export financing interest (as defined in section 904(d)(2)(G)).

(C) Exception for dealers. Except as provided by regulations, in the case of a regular dealer in property which is property described in paragraph (1)(B), forward contracts, option contracts, or similar financial instruments (including notional principal contracts and all instruments referenced to commodities), there shall not be taken into account in computing foreign personal holding company income—

(i) any item of income, gain, deduction, or loss (other than any item described in subparagraph (A), (E), or (G) of paragraph (1)) from any transaction (including hedging transactions and transactions involving physical settlement) entered into in the ordinary course of such dealer's trade or business as such a dealer, and

(ii) if such dealer is a dealer in securities (within the meaning of section 475), any interest or dividend or equivalent amount described in subparagraph (E) or (G) of paragraph (1) from any transaction (including any hedging transaction or transaction described in section 956(c)(2)(I)) entered into in the ordinary course of such dealer's trade or business as such a dealer in securities, but only if the income from the transaction is attributable to activities of the dealer in the country under the laws of which the dealer is created or organized (or in the case of a qualified business unit described in section 989(a), is attributable to activities of the unit in the country in which the unit both maintains its principal office and conducts substantial business activity).

(3) Certain income received from related persons.

(A) In general. Except as provided in subparagraph (B), the term "foreign personal holding company income" does not include—

(i) dividends and interest received from a related person which (I) is a corporation created or organized under the laws of the same foreign country under the laws of which the controlled foreign corporation is created or organized, and (II) has a substantial part of its assets used in its trade or business located in such same foreign country, and

(ii) rents and royalties received from a corporation which is a related person for the use of, or the privilege of using, property within the country under the laws of which the controlled foreign corporation is created or organized.

To the extent provided in regulations, payments made by a partnership with 1 or more corporate partners shall be treated as made by such corporate partners in proportion to their respective interests in the partnership.

(B) Exception not to apply to items which reduce subpart F income. Subparagraph (A) shall not apply in the case of any interest, rent, or royalty to the extent such interest, rent, or royalty reduces the payor's subpart F income or creates (or increases) a deficit which under section 952(c) may reduce the subpart F income of the payor or another controlled foreign corporation.

(C) Exception for certain dividends. Subparagraph (A)(i) shall not apply to any dividend with respect to any stock which is attributable to earnings and profits of the distributing corporation accumulated during any period during which the person receiving such dividend did not hold such stock either directly, or indirectly through a chain of one or more subsidiaries each of which meets the requirements of subparagraph (A)(i).

(4) Look-thru rule for certain partnership sales.

(A) In general. In the case of any sale by a controlled foreign corporation of an interest in a partnership with respect to which such corporation is a 25-percent owner, such corporation shall be treated for purposes of this subsection as selling the proportionate share of the assets of the partnership attributable to such interest. The Secretary shall prescribe such regulations as may be appropriate to prevent abuse of the purposes of this paragraph, including regulations providing for coordination of this paragraph with the provisions of subchapter K.

(B) 25-percent owner. For purposes of this paragraph, the term "25-percent owner" means a controlled foreign corporation which owns directly 25 percent or more of the capital or profits interest in a partnership. For purposes of the preceding sentence, if a controlled foreign corporation is a shareholder or partner of a corporation or partnership, the controlled foreign corporation shall be treated as owning directly its proportionate share of any such capital or profits interest held directly or indirectly by such corporation or partnership. If a controlled foreign corporation is treated as owning a capital or profits interest in a partnership under constructive ownership rules similar to the rules of section 958(b), the controlled foreign corporation shall be treated as owning such interest directly for purposes of this subparagraph.

(5) Definition and special rules relating to commodity transactions.

(A) Commodity hedging transactions. For purposes of paragraph (1)(C)(i), the term "commodity hedging transaction" means any transaction with respect to a commodity if such transaction—

  (i) is a hedging transaction as defined in section 1221(b)(2), determined—

    (I) without regard to subparagraph (A)(ii) thereof,

    (II) by applying subparagraph (A)(i) thereof by substituting "ordinary property or property described in section 1231(b)" for "ordinary property", and

    (III) by substituting "controlled foreign corporation" for "taxpayer" each place it appears, and

  (ii) is clearly identified as such in accordance with section 1221(a)(7).

(B) Treatment of dealer activities under paragraph (1)(C). Commodities with respect to which gains and losses are not taken into account under paragraph (2)(C) in computing a controlled foreign corporation's foreign personal holding company income shall not be taken into account in applying the substantially all test under paragraph (1)(C)(ii) to such corporation.

(C) Regulations. The Secretary shall prescribe such regulations as are appropriate to carry out the purposes of paragraph (1)(C) in the case of transactions involving related parties.

(6) Look-thru rule for related controlled foreign corporations.

(A) In general. For purposes of this subsection, dividends, interest, rents, and royalties received or accrued from a controlled foreign corporation which is a related person shall not be treated as foreign personal holding company income to the extent attributable or properly allocable (determined under rules similar to the rules of subparagraphs (C) and (D) of section 904(d)(3)) to income of the related person which is neither subpart F income nor income treated as effectively connected with the conduct of a trade or business in the United States. For purposes of this subparagraph, interest shall include factoring income which is treated as income equivalent to interest for purposes of paragraph (1)(E). The Secretary shall prescribe such regulations as may be necessary or appropriate to carry out this paragraph, including such regulations as may be necessary or appropriate to prevent the abuse of the purposes of this paragraph.

(B) Exception. Subparagraph (A) shall not apply in the case of any interest, rent, or royalty to the extent such interest, rent, or royalty creates (or increases) a deficit which under section 952(c) may reduce the subpart F income of the payor or another controlled foreign corporation.

(C) Application. Subparagraph (A) shall apply to taxable years of foreign corporations beginning after December 31, 2005, and before January 1, 2012, and to taxable years of United States shareholders with or within which such taxable years of foreign corporations end.

(d) Foreign base company sales income.

(1) In general. For purposes of subsection (a)(2), the term "foreign base company sales income" means income (whether in the form of profits, commissions, fees, or otherwise) derived in connection with the purchase of personal property from a related person and its sale to any person, the sale of personal property to any person on behalf of a related person, the purchase of personal property from any person and its sale to a related person, or the purchase of personal property from any person on behalf of a related person where—

(A) the property which is purchased (or in the case of property sold on behalf of a related person, the property which is sold) is manufactured, produced, grown, or extracted outside the country under the laws of which the controlled foreign corporation is created or organized, and

(B) the property is sold for use, consumption, or disposition outside such foreign country, or, in the case of property purchased on behalf of a related person, is purchased for use, consumption, or disposition outside such foreign country.

For purposes of this subsection, personal property does not include agricultural commodities which are not grown in the United States in commercially marketable quantities.

(2) Certain branch income. For purposes of determining foreign base company sales income in situations in which the carrying on of activities by a controlled foreign corporation through a branch or similar establishment outside the country of incorporation of the controlled foreign corporation has substantially the same effect as if such branch or similar establishment were a wholly owned subsidiary corporation deriving such income, under regulations prescribed by the Secretary the income attributable to the carrying on of such activities of such branch or similar establishment shall be treated as income derived by a wholly owned subsidiary of the controlled foreign corporation and shall constitute foreign base company sales income of the controlled foreign corporation.

(3) Related person defined. For purposes of this section, a person is a related person with respect to a controlled foreign corporation, if—

(A) such person is an individual, corporation, partnership, trust, or estate which controls, or is controlled by, the controlled foreign corporation, or

(B) such person is a corporation, partnership, trust, or estate which is controlled by the same person or persons which control the controlled foreign corporation.

For purposes of the preceding sentence, control means, with respect to a corporation, the ownership, directly or indirectly, of stock possessing more than 50 percent of the total voting power of all classes of stock entitled to vote or of the total value of stock of such corporation. In the case of a partnership, trust, or estate, control means the ownership, directly or indirectly, of more than 50 percent (by value) of the beneficial interests in such partnership, trust, or estate. For purposes of this paragraph, rules similar to the rules of section 958 shall apply.

(4) Special rule for certain timber products. For purposes of subsection (a)(2), the term "foreign base company sales income" includes any income (whether in the form of profits, commissions, fees, or otherwise) derived in connection with—

(A) the sale of any unprocessed timber referred to in section 865(b), or

(B) the milling of any such timber outside the United States.

Subpart G shall not apply to any amount treated as subpart F income by reason of this paragraph.

(e) Foreign base company services income.

(1) In general. For purposes of subsection (a)(3), the term "foreign base company services income" means income (whether in the form of compensation, commissions, fees, or otherwise) derived in connection with the performance of technical, managerial, engineering, architectural, scientific, skilled, industrial, commercial, or like services which—

(A) are performed for or on behalf of any related person (within the meaning of subsection (d)(3)), and

(B) are performed outside the country under the laws of which the controlled foreign corporation is created or organized.

(2) Exception. Paragraph (1) shall not apply to income derived in connection with the performance of services which are directly related to—

(A) the sale or exchange by the controlled foreign corporation of property manufactured, produced, grown, or extracted by it and which are performed before the time of the sale or exchange, or

(B) an offer or effort to sell or exchange such property.

Paragraph (1) shall also not apply to income which is exempt insurance income (as defined in section 953(e)) or which is not treated as foreign personal holding income by reason of subsection (c)(2)(C)(ii), (h), or (i).

(f) Repealed.

(g) Foreign base company oil related income.

For purposes of this section—

(1) In general. Except as otherwise provided in this subsection, the term "foreign base company oil related income" means foreign oil related income (within the meaning of paragraphs (2) and (3) of section 907(c)) other than income derived from a source within a foreign country in connection with—

(A) oil or gas which was extracted from an oil or gas well located in such foreign country, or

(B) oil, gas, or a primary product of oil or gas which is sold by the foreign corporation or a related person for use or consumption within such country or is loaded in such country on a vessel or aircraft as fuel for such vessel or aircraft.

Such term shall not include any foreign personal holding company income (as defined in subsection (c)).

(2) Paragraph (1) applies only where corporation has produced 1,000 barrels per day or more.

(A) In general. The term "foreign base company oil related income" shall not include any income of a foreign corporation if such corporation is not a large oil producer for the taxable year.

(B) Large oil producer. For purposes of subparagraph (A), the term "large oil producer" means any corporation if, for the taxable year or for the preceding taxable year, the average daily production of foreign crude oil and natural gas of the related group which includes such corporation equaled or exceeded 1,000 barrels.

(C) Related group. The term "related group" means a group consisting of the foreign corporation and any other person who is a related person with respect to such corporation.

(D) Average daily production of foreign crude oil and natural gas. For purposes of this paragraph, the average daily production of foreign crude oil or natural gas of any related group for any taxable year (and the conversion of cubic feet of natural gas into barrels) shall be determined under rules similar to the rules of section 613A except that only crude oil or natural gas from a well located outside the United States shall be taken into account.

(h) Special rule for income derived in the active conduct of banking, financing, or similar businesses.

(1) In general. For purposes of subsection (c)(1), foreign personal holding company income shall not include qualified banking or financing income of an eligible controlled foreign corporation.

(2) Eligible controlled foreign corporation. For purposes of this subsection—

(A) In general. The term "eligible controlled foreign corporation" means a controlled foreign corporation which—

(i) is predominantly engaged in the active conduct of a banking, financing, or similar business, and

(ii) conducts substantial activity with respect to such business.

(B) Predominantly engaged. A controlled foreign corporation shall be treated as predominantly engaged in the active conduct of a banking, financing, or similar business if—

(i) more than 70 percent of the gross income of the controlled foreign corporation is derived directly from the active and regular conduct of a lending or finance business from transactions with customers which are not related persons,

(ii) it is engaged in the active conduct of a banking business and is an institution licensed to do business as a bank in the United States (or is any other corporation not so licensed which is specified by the Secretary in regulations), or

(iii) it is engaged in the active conduct of a securities business and is registered as a securities broker or dealer under section 15(a) of the Securities Exchange Act of 1934 or is registered as a Government securities broker or dealer under section 15C(a) of such Act (or is any other corporation not so registered which is specified by the Secretary in regulations).

(3) Qualified banking or financing income. For purposes of this subsection—

(A) In general. The term "qualified banking or financing income" means income of an eligible controlled foreign corporation which—

(i) is derived in the active conduct of a banking, financing, or similar business by—

(I) such eligible controlled foreign corporation, or

(II) a qualified business unit of such eligible controlled foreign corporation,

(ii) is derived from one or more transactions—

(I) with customers located in a country other than the United States, and

(II) substantially all of the activities in connection with which are conducted directly by the corporation or unit in its home country, and

(iii) is treated as earned by such corporation or unit in its home country for purposes of such country's tax laws.

(B) Limitation on nonbanking and nonsecurities businesses. No income of an eligible controlled foreign corporation not described in clause (ii) or (iii) of paragraph (2)(B) (or of a qualified business unit of such corporation) shall be treated as qualified banking or financing income unless more than 30 percent of such corporation's or unit's gross income is derived directly from the active and regular conduct of a lending or finance business from transactions with customers which are not related persons and which are located within such corporation's or unit's home country.

(C) Substantial activity requirement for cross border income. The term "qualified banking or financing income" shall not include income derived from 1 or more transactions with customers located in a country other than the home country of the eligible controlled foreign corporation or a qualified business unit of such corporation unless such corporation or unit conducts substantial activity with respect to a banking, financing, or similar business in its home country.

(D) Determinations made separately. For purposes of this paragraph, the qualified banking or financing income of an eligible controlled foreign corporation and each qualified business unit of such corporation shall be determined separately for such corporation and each such unit by taking into account—

(i) in the case of the eligible controlled foreign corporation, only items of income, deduction, gain, or loss and activities of such corporation not properly allocable or attributable to any qualified business unit of such corporation, and

(ii) in the case of a qualified business unit, only items of income, deduction, gain, or loss and activities properly allocable or attributable to such unit.

(E) Direct conduct of activities. For purposes of subparagraph (A)(ii)(II), an activity shall be treated as conducted directly by an eligible controlled foreign corporation or qualified business unit in its home country if the activity is performed by employees of a related person and—

(i) the related person is an eligible controlled foreign corporation the home country of which is the same as the home country of the corporation or unit to which subparagraph (A)(ii)(II) is being applied,

(ii) the activity is performed in the home country of the related person, and

(iii) the related person is compensated on an arm's-length basis for the performance of the activity by its employees and such compensation is treated as earned by such person in its home country for purposes of the home country's tax laws.

(4) Lending or finance business. For purposes of this subsection, the term "lending or finance business" means the business of—

(A) making loans,

(B) purchasing or discounting accounts receivable, notes, or installment obligations,

(C) engaging in leasing (including entering into leases and purchasing, servicing, and disposing of leases and leased assets),

(D) issuing letters of credit or providing guarantees,

(E) providing charge and credit card services, or

(F) rendering services or making facilities available in connection with activities described in subparagraphs (A) through (E) carried on by—

(i) the corporation (or qualified business unit) rendering services or making facilities available, or

(ii) another corporation (or qualified business unit of a corporation) which is a member of the same affiliated group (as defined in section 1504, but determined without regard to section 1504(b)(3)).

(5) Other definitions. For purposes of this subsection—

(A) Customer. The term "customer" means, with respect to any controlled foreign corporation or qualified business unit, any person which has a customer relationship with such corporation or unit and which is acting in its capacity as such.

(B) Home country. Except as provided in regulations—

(i) Controlled foreign corporation. The term "home country" means, with respect to any controlled foreign corporation, the country under the laws of which the corporation was created or organized.

(ii) Qualified business unit. The term "home country" means, with respect to any qualified business unit, the country in which such unit maintains its principal office.

(C) Located. The determination of where a customer is located shall be made under rules prescribed by the Secretary.

(D) Qualified business unit. The term "qualified business unit" has the meaning given such term by section 989(a).

(E) Related person. The term "related person" has the meaning given such term by subsection (d)(3).

(6) Coordination with exception for dealers. Paragraph (1) shall not apply to income described in subsection (c)(2)(C)(ii) of a dealer in securities (within the meaning of section 475) which is an eligible controlled foreign corporation described in paragraph (2)(B)(iii).

(7) Anti-abuse rules. For purposes of applying this subsection and subsection (c)(2)(C)(ii)—

(A) there shall be disregarded any item of income, gain, loss, or deduction with respect to any transaction or series of transactions one of the principal purposes of which is qualifying income or gain for the exclusion under this section, including any transaction or series of transactions a principal purpose of which is the acceleration or deferral of any item in order to claim the benefits of such exclusion through the application of this subsection,

(B) there shall be disregarded any item of income, gain, loss, or deduction of an entity which is not engaged in regular and continuous transactions with customers which are not related persons,

(C) there shall be disregarded any item of income, gain, loss, or deduction with respect to any transaction or series of transactions utilizing, or doing business with—

(i) one or more entities in order to satisfy any home country requirement under this subsection, or

(ii) a special purpose entity or arrangement, including a securitization, financing, or similar entity or arrangement,

if one of the principal purposes of such transaction or series of transactions is qualifying income or gain for the exclusion under this subsection, and

(D) a related person, an officer, a director, or an employee with respect to any controlled foreign corporation (or qualified business unit) which would otherwise be treated as a customer of such corporation or unit with respect to any transaction shall not be so treated if a principal purpose of such transaction is to satisfy any requirement of this subsection.

(8) Regulations. The Secretary shall prescribe such regulations as may be necessary or appropriate to carry out the purposes of this subsection, subsection (c)(1)(B)(i), subsection (c)(2)(C)(ii), and the last sentence of subsection (e)(2).

(9) Application. This subsection, subsection (c)(2)(C)(ii), and the last sentence of subsection (e)(2) shall apply only to taxable years of a foreign corporation beginning after December 31, 1998, and before January 1, 2012, and to taxable years of United States shareholders with or within which any such taxable year of such foreign corporation ends.

(i) Special rule for income derived in the active conduct of insurance business.

(1) In general. For purposes of subsection (c)(1), foreign personal holding company income shall not include qualified insurance income of a qualifying insurance company.

(2) Qualified insurance income. The term "qualified insurance income" means income of a qualifying insurance company which is—

(A) received from a person other than a related person (within the meaning of subsection (d)(3)) and derived from the investments made by a qualifying insurance company or a qualifying insurance company branch of its reserves allocable to exempt contracts or of 80 percent of its unearned premiums from exempt contracts (as both are determined in the manner prescribed under paragraph (4)), or

(B) received from a person other than a related person (within the meaning of subsection (d)(3)) and derived from investments made by a qualifying insurance company or a qualifying insurance company branch of an amount of its assets allocable to exempt contracts equal to—

(i) in the case of property, casualty, or health insurance contracts, one-third of its premiums earned on such insurance contracts during the taxable year (as defined in section 832(b)(4)), and

(ii) in the case of life insurance or annuity contracts, 10 percent of the reserves described in subparagraph (A) for such contracts.

(3) Principles for determining insurance income. Except as provided by the Secretary, for purposes of subparagraphs (A) and (B) of paragraph (2)—

(A) in the case of any contract which is a separate account-type contract (including any variable contract not meeting the requirements of section 817), income credited under such contract shall be allocable only to such contract, and

(B) income not allocable under subparagraph (A) shall be allocated ratably among contracts not described in subparagraph (A).

(4) Methods for determining unearned premiums and reserves. For purposes of paragraph (2)(A)—

(A) Property and casualty contracts. The unearned premiums and reserves of a qualifying insurance company or a qualifying insurance company branch with respect to property, casualty, or health insurance contracts shall be determined using the same methods and interest rates which would be used if such company or branch were subject to tax under subchapter L, except that—

(i) the interest rate determined for the functional currency of the company or branch, and which, except as provided by the Secretary, is calculated in the same manner as the Federal mid-term rate under section 1274(d), shall be substituted for the applicable Federal interest rate, and

(ii) such company or branch shall use the appropriate foreign loss payment pattern.

(B) Life insurance and annuity contracts.

(i) In general. Except as provided in clause (ii), the amount of the reserve of a qualifying insurance company or qualifying insurance company branch for any life insurance or annuity contract shall be equal to the greater of—

(I) the net surrender value of such contract (as defined in section 807(e)(1)(A)), or

(II) the reserve determined under paragraph (5).

(ii) Ruling request, etc. The amount of the reserve under clause (i) shall be the foreign statement reserve for the contract (less any catastrophe, deficiency, equalization, or similar reserves), if, pursuant to a ruling request submitted by the taxpayer or as provided in published guidance, the Secretary determines that the factors taken into account in determining the foreign statement reserve provide an appropriate means of measuring income.

(C) Limitation on reserves. In no event shall the reserve determined under this paragraph for any contract as of any time exceed the amount which would be taken into account with respect to such contract as of such time in determining foreign statement reserves (less any catastrophe, deficiency, equalization, or similar reserves).

(5) Amount of reserve. The amount of the reserve determined under this paragraph with respect to any contract shall be determined in the same manner as it would be determined if the qualifying insurance company or qualifying insurance company branch were subject to tax under subchapter L, except that in applying such subchapter—

(A) the interest rate determined for the functional currency of the company or branch, and which, except as provided by the Secretary, is calculated in the same manner as the Federal mid-term rate under section 1274(d), shall be substituted for the applicable Federal interest rate,

(B) the highest assumed interest rate permitted to be used in determining foreign statement reserves shall be

Income from foreign sources — Code Sec. 954

substituted for the prevailing State assumed interest rate, and

(C) tables for mortality and morbidity which reasonably reflect the current mortality and morbidity risks in the company's or branch's home country shall be substituted for the mortality and morbidity tables otherwise used for such subchapter.

The Secretary may provide that the interest rate and mortality and morbidity tables of a qualifying insurance company may be used for 1 or more of its qualifying insurance company branches when appropriate.

(6) Definitions. For purposes of this subsection, any term used in this subsection which is also used in section 953(e) shall have the meaning given such term by section 953.

In 2010, P.L. 111-312, Sec. 750(a), substituted "January 1, 2012" for "January 1, 2010" in para. (h)(9), effective for taxable yrs. of foreign corporations begin. after 12/31/2009, and to tax. yrs. of United States shareholders with or within which any such tax. year of such foreign corporation ends.

— P.L. 111-312, Sec. 751(a), substituted "January 1, 2012" for "January 1, 2010" in subpara. (c)(6)(C), effective for tax. yrs. of foreign corporations beginning after 12/31/2009, and to tax. yrs. of United States shareholders with or within which any such tax. year of such foreign corporation ends.

In 2008, P.L. 110-343, Sec. 303(b)DivC, substituted "January 1, 2010" for "January 1, 2009" in para. (h)(9), effective 10/3/2008.

— P.L. 110-343, Sec. 304(a)DivC, substituted "January 1, 2010" for "January 1, 2009" in subpara. (c)(6)(C), effective for tax. yrs. of foreign corporations beginning after 12/31/2007, and to tax. yrs. of United States shareholders with or within which such tax. yrs. of foreign corporations end.

In 2007, P.L. 110-172, Sec. 11(a)(19), amended subpara. (c)(1)(F)... Sec. 11(a)(20), redesignated subpara. (c)(1)(I) as subpara. (c)(1)(H)... Sec. 11(g)(15)(B), substituted "section 956(c)(2)(I)" for "section 956(c)(2)(J)" in clause (c)(2)(C)(ii), enacted 12/29/2007

Prior to amendment, subpara. (c)(1)(F) read as follows:

"(F) Income from notional principal contracts. Any item of income, gain, deduction, or loss from a notional principal contract entered into for purposes of hedging any item described in any preceding subparagraph shall not be taken into account for purposes of this subparagraph but shall be taken into account under such other subparagraph."

— P.L. 110-172, Sec. 4(a), redesignated subpara. (c)(6)(B) as subpara. (c)(6)(C) and added subpara. (c)(6)(B), effective for tax. yrs. of foreign corporations begin. after 12/31/2005, and for tax. yrs. of United States shareholders with or within which such tax. yrs. of foreign corporations end.

In 2006, P.L. 109-432, Sec. 426(a)(1)(A), substituted "which is neither subpart F income nor income treated as effectively connected with the conduct of a trade or business in the United States" for "which is not subpart F income" in subpara. (c)(6)(A)... Sec. 426(a)(1)(B), substituted "The Secretary shall prescribe such regulations as may be necessary or appropriate to carry out this paragraph, including such regulations as may be necessary or appropriate to prevent the abuse of the purposes of this paragraph." for "The Secretary shall prescribe such regulations as may be appropriate to prevent the abuse of the purposes of this paragraph." in subpara. (c)(6)(A), effective for tax. yrs. of foreign corporations begin. after 12/31/2005, and for tax. yrs. of United States shareholders with or within which such tax. yrs. of foreign corporations end.

— P.L. 109-222, Sec. 103(a)(2), substituted "January 1, 2009" for "January 1, 2007" in para. (h)(9), enacted 5/17/2006.

— P.L. 109-222, Sec. 103(b)(1), added para. (c)(6), effective for tax. yrs. of foreign corporations begin. after 12/31/2005, and for tax. yrs. of United States shareholders with or within which such tax. yrs. of foreign corporations end.

In 2005, P.L. 109-135, Sec. 403(m), added "If a controlled foreign corporation is treated as owning a capital or profits interest in a partnership under constructive ownership rules similar to the rules of section 958(b), the controlled foreign corporation shall be treated as owning such interest directly for purposes of this subparagraph." at the end of subpara. (c)(4)(B), effective for tax. yrs. of foreign corporations begin. after 12/31/2004, and for tax. yrs. of United States shareholders with or within which such tax. yrs. of foreign corporations end, as if included in Sec. 412 of the American Jobs Creation Act of 2004, P.L. 108-357.

— P.L. 109-135, Sec. 412(ll), substituted "paragraph (5)(A)" for "paragraph (4)(A)" in clause (c)(1)(C)(i)... Sec. 412(mm), deleted "Net income from notional principal contracts." after "Income from notional principal contracts." in subpara. (c)(1)(F), effective 12/21/2005.

In 2004, P.L. 108-357, Sec. 412(a), added para. (c)(4), effective for tax. yrs. of foreign corporations begin. after 12/31/2004, and for tax. yrs. of United States shareholders with or within which such tax. yrs. of foreign corporations end.

— P.L. 108-357, Sec. 413(b)(2), added subpara. (c)(1)(I) [sic (H)], effective for tax. yrs. of foreign corporations begin. after 12/31/2004, and for tax. yrs. of United States shareholders with or within which such tax. yrs. of foreign corporations end.

— P.L. 108-357, Sec. 414(a), amended clauses (c)(1)(C)(i) and (ii)... Sec. 414(b), added para. (c)(5)... Sec. 414(c), added "and transactions involving physical settlement" after "(including hedging transactions" in clause (c)(2)(C)(i), effective for transactions entered into after 12/31/2004.

Prior to amendment, clauses (c)(1)(C)(i) and (ii) read as follows:

"(i) arise out of bona fide hedging transactions reasonably necessary to the conduct of any business by a producer, processor, merchant, or handler of a commodity in the manner in which such business is customarily and usually conducted by others,

"(ii) are active business gains or losses from the sale of commodities, but only if substantially all of the controlled foreign corporation's business is as an active producer, processor, merchant, or handler of commodities, or"

— P.L. 108-357, Sec. 415(a)(1), deleted para. (a)(4)... Sec. 415(a)(2), deleted subsec. (f)... Sec. 415(b), added "For purposes of the preceding sentence, rents derived from leasing an aircraft or vessel in foreign commerce shall not fail to be treated as derived in the active conduct of a trade or business if, as determined under regulations prescribed by the Secretary, the active leasing expenses are not less than 10 percent of the profit on the lease." at the end of subpara. (c)(2)(A)... Sec. 415(c)(2)(A), deleted "the foreign base company shipping income," after "foreign base company services income" in para. (b)(5)... Sec. 415(c)(2)(B), deleted paras. (b)(6) and (7)... Sec. 415(c)(2)(C), redesignated para. (b)(8) as (6), effective for tax. yrs. of foreign corporations begin. after 12/31/2004, and for tax. yrs. of United States shareholders with or within which such tax. yrs. of foreign corporations end.

Prior to deletion, para. (a)(4) read as follows:

"(4) the foreign base company shipping income for the taxable year (determined under subsection (f) and reduced as provided in subsection (b)(5)), and"

Prior to deletion, subsec. (f) read as follows:

"(f) Foreign base company shipping income. For purposes of subsection (a)(4), the term 'foreign base company shipping income' means income derived from, or in connection with, the use (or hiring or leasing for use) of any aircraft or vessel in foreign commerce, or from, or in connection with, the performance of services directly related to the use of any such aircraft, or vessel, or from the sale, exchange, or other disposition of any such aircraft or vessel. Such term includes, but is not limited to—

"(1) dividends and interest received from a foreign corporation in respect of which taxes are deemed paid under section 902, and gain from the sale, exchange, or other disposition of stock or obligations of such a foreign corporation to the extent that such dividends, interest, and gains are attributable to foreign base company shipping income, and

"(2) that portion of the distributive share of the income of a partnership attributable to foreign base company shipping income.

Such term includes any income derived from a space or ocean activity (as defined in section 863(d)(2)). Except as provided in paragraph (1), such term shall not include any dividend or interest income which is foreign personal holding company income (as defined in subsection (c))."

Prior to deletion, paras. (b)(6) and (7) read as follows:

"(6) Special rules for foreign base company shipping income. Income of a corporation which is foreign base company shipping income under paragraph (4) of subsection (a)—

"(A) shall not be considered foreign base company income of such corporation under any other paragraph of subsection (a) and

"(B) if distributed through a chain of ownership described under section 958(a), shall not be included in foreign base company income of another controlled foreign corporation in such chain.

"(7) Special exclusion for foreign base company shipping income. Income of a corporation which is foreign base company shipping income under paragraph (4) of subsection (a) shall be excluded from foreign base company income if derived by a controlled foreign corporation from, or in connection with, the use (or hiring or leasing for use) of an aircraft or vessel in foreign commerce between two points within the foreign country in which such corporation is created or organized and such aircraft or vessel is registered."

— P.L. 108-357, Sec. 416(a), added subpara. (h)(3)(E), effective for tax. yrs. of such foreign corporations begin. after 12/31/2004, and for tax. yrs. of United States shareholders with or within which such tax. yrs. of such foreign corporations end.

In 2002, P.L. 107-147, Sec. 417(24)(B)(ii), substituted "954(c)(1)(B)" for "954(c)(1)(B)(iii)" in Sec. 532(c)(2)(Q) of P.L. 106-170 [see below], effective 3/9/2002.

— P.L. 107-147, Sec. 614(a)(2), substituted "January 1, 2007" for "January 1, 2002" in para. (h)(9)... Sec. 614(b)(1), amended subpara. (i)(4)(B), effective for tax. yrs. begin. after 12/31/2001.

Prior to amendment, subpara. (i)(4)(B) read as follows:

"(B) Life insurance and annuity contracts. The amount of the reserve of a qualifying insurance company or qualifying insurance company branch for any life insurance or annuity contract shall be equal to the greater of—

"(i) the net surrender value of such contract (as defined in section 807(e)(1)(A)), or

"(ii) the reserve determined under paragraph (5)."

In 1999, P.L. 106-170, Sec. 503(a)(1), substituted "taxable years" for "the first taxable year" in para. (h)(9)... Sec. 503(a)(2), substituted "January 1, 2002" for "January 1, 2000" in para. (h)(9)... Sec. 503(a)(3), substituted "within which any such" for "within which such" in para. (h)(9), effective for tax. yrs. begin. after 12/31/99.

— P.L. 106-170, Sec. 532(c)(2)(Q), [as amended by Sec. 417(24)(B)(ii), P.L. 107-147, see above] substituted "section 1221(a)(1)" for "section 1221(1)" in subpara. (c)(1)(B), effective for any instrument held, acquired, or entered into, any transaction entered into, and supplies held or acquired on or after 12/17/99.

Code Sec. 954 — Income from foreign sources

In 1998, P.L. 105-277, Sec. 1005(a), amended subsec. (h) . . . Sec. 1005(b)(2), added subsec. (i) . . . Sec. 1005(c), amended subpara. (c)(2)(C) . . . Sec. 1005(d), added "or" at the end of subpara. (e)(2)(A), substituted a period for ", or" at the end of subpara. (e)(2)(B), deleted subpara. (e)(2)(C) [as amended by Sec. 403(j) of this Act, see below], and added a flush sentence at the end of para. (e)(2) . . . Sec. 1005(e), added "other than property which gives rise to income not treated as foreign personal holding company income by reason of subsection (h) or (i) for the taxable year" before the comma at the end of clause (c)(1)(B)(i), effective 10/21/98..

Prior to amendment, subpara. (c)(2)(C) read as follows:

"(C) Exception for dealers. Except as provided in subparagraph (A), (E), or (G) of paragraph (1) or by regulations, in the case of a regular dealer in property (within the meaning of paragraph (1)(B)), forward contracts, option contracts, or similar financial instruments (including notional principal contracts and all instruments referenced to commodities), there shall not be taken into account in computing foreign personal holding income any item of income, gain, deduction, or loss from any transaction (including hedging transactions) entered into in the ordinary course of such dealer's trade or business as such a dealer."

Prior to deletion, subpara. (e)(2)(C) [as amended by Sec. 403(j) of this Act, see below] read as follows:

"(C) In the case of taxable years described in subsection (h)(9), the active conduct by a controlled foreign corporation of a banking, financing, insurance, or similar business, but only if the corporation is predominantly engaged in the active conduct of such business (within the meaning of subsection (h)(3)) or is a qualifying insurance company."

Prior to amendment, subsec. (h) read as follows:

"(h) Special rule for income derived in the active conduct of banking, financing, or similar businesses.

"(1) In general. For purposes of subsection (c)(1), foreign personal holding company income shall not include income which is—

"(A) derived in the active conduct by a controlled foreign corporation of a banking, financing, or similar business, but only if the corporation is predominantly engaged in the active conduct of such business,

"(B) received from a person other than a related person (within the meaning of subsection (d)(3)) and derived from the investments made by a qualifying insurance company of its reserves or of 80 percent of its unearned premiums (as both are determined in the manner prescribed under paragraph (4)), or

"(C) received from a person other than a related person (within the meaning of subsection (d)(3)) and derived from investments made by a qualifying insurance company of an amount of its assets equal to—

"(i) in the case of contracts regulated in the country in which sold as property, casualty, or health insurance contracts, one-third of its premiums earned on such insurance contracts during the taxable year (as defined in section 832(b)(4)), and

"(ii) in the case of contracts regulated in the country in which sold as life insurance or annuity contracts, the greater of—

"(I) 10 percent of the reserves described in subparagraph (B) for such contracts, or

"(II) in the case of a qualifying insurance company which is a start-up company, $10,000,000.

"(2) Principles for determining applicable income.

"(A) Banking and financing income. The determination as to whether income is described in paragraph (1)(A) shall be made—

"(i) except as provided in clause (ii), in accordance with the applicable principles of section 904(d)(2)(C)(ii), except that such income shall include income from all leases entered into in the ordinary course of the active conduct of a banking, financing, or similar business, and

"(ii) in the case of a corporation described in paragraph (3)(B), in accordance with the applicable principles of section 1296(b) (as in effect on the day before the enactment of the Taxpayer Relief Act of 1997) for determining what is not passive income.

"(B) Insurance income. Under rules prescribed by the Secretary, for purposes of paragraphs (1)(B) and (C)—

"(i) in the case of contracts which are separate account-type contracts (including variable contracts not meeting the requirements of section 817), only income specifically allocable to such contracts shall be taken into account, and

"(ii) in the case of other contracts, income not allocable under clause (i) shall be allocated ratably among such contracts.

"(C) Look-thru rules. The Secretary shall prescribe regulations consistent with the principles of section 904(d)(3) which provide that dividends, interest, income equivalent to interest, rents, or royalties received or accrued from a related person (within the meaning of subsection (d)(3)) shall be subject to look-thru treatment for purposes of this subsection.

"(3) Predominantly engaged. For purposes of paragraph (1)(A), a corporation shall be deemed predominantly engaged in the active conduct of a banking, financing, or similar business only if—

"(A) more than 70 percent of its gross income is derived from such business from transactions with persons which are not related persons (as defined in subsection (d)(3)) and which are located within the country under the laws of which the controlled foreign corporation is created or organized, or

"(B) the corporation is—

"(i) engaged in the active conduct of a banking or securities business (within the meaning of section 1296(b), as in effect before the enactment of the Taxpayer Relief Act of 1997), or

"(ii) a qualified bank affiliate or a qualified securities affiliate within the meaning of the proposed regulations under such section 1296(b)).

"(4) Methods for determining unearned premiums and reserves. For purposes of paragraph (1)(B)—

"(A) Property and casualty contracts. The unearned premiums and reserves of a qualifying insurance company with respect to property, casualty, or health insurance contracts shall be determined using the same methods and interest rates which would be used if such company were subject to tax under subchapter L.

"(B) Life insurance and annuity contracts. The reserves of a qualifying insurance company with respect to life insurance or annuity contracts shall be determined under the method described in paragraph (5) which such company elects to apply for purposes of this paragraph. Such election shall be made at such time and in such manner as the Secretary may prescribe and, once made, shall be irrevocable without the consent of the Secretary.

"(C) Limitation on reserves. In no event shall the reserve determined under this paragraph for any contract as of any time exceed the amount which would be taken into account with respect to such contract as of such time in determining foreign annual statement reserves (less any catastrophe or deficiency reserves).

"(5) Methods. The methods described in this paragraph are as follows:

"(A) U.S. method. The method which would apply if the qualifying insurance company were subject to tax under subchapter L, except that the interest rate used shall be an interest rate determined for the foreign country in which such company is created or organized and which is calculated in the same manner as the Federal mid-term rate under section 1274(d).

"(B) Foreign method. A preliminary term method, except that the interest rate used shall be the interest rate determined for the foreign country in which such country is created or organized and which is calculated in the same manner as the Federal mid-term rate under section 1274(d). If a qualifying insurance company uses such a preliminary term method with respect to contracts insuring risks located in such foreign country, such method shall apply if such company elects the method under this clause.

"(C) Cash surrender value. A method under which reserves are equal to the net surrender value (as defined in section 807(e)(1)(A)) of the contract.

"(6) Definitions. For purposes of this subsection—

"(A)(i) Qualifying insurance company. The term 'qualifying insurance company' means an entity which—

"(I) is subject to regulation as an insurance company under the laws of its country of incorporation.

"(II) realizes at least 50 percent of its net written premiums from the insurance or reinsurance of risks located within the country in which such entity is created or organized, and

"(III) is engaged in the active conduct of an insurance business and would be subject to tax under subchapter L if it were a domestic corporation.

"(ii) Start-up company. A qualifying insurance company shall be treated as a start-up company if such company (and any predecessor) has not been engaged in the active conduct of an insurance business for more than 5 years as of the beginning of the taxable year of such company.

"(B) Located. For purposes of paragraph (3)(A)—

"(i) In general. A person shall be treated as located—

"(I) except as provided in subclause (II), within the country in which it maintains an office or other fixed place of business through which it engages in a trade or business and by which the transaction is effected, or

"(II) in the case of a natural person, within the country in which such person is physically located when such person enters into a transaction.

"(ii) Special rule for qualified business units. Gross income derived by a corporation's qualified business unit (within the meaning of section 989(a)) from transactions with persons which are not related persons (as defined in subsection (d)(3)) and which are located in the country in which the qualified business unit both maintains its principal office and conducts substantial business activity shall be treated as derived from transactions with persons which are not related persons (as defined in subsection (d)(3)) and which are located within the country under the laws of which the controlled foreign corporation is created or organized.

"(7) Anti-abuse rules. For purposes of applying this subsection, there shall be disregarded any item of income, gain, loss, or deduction with respect to any transaction or series of transactions one of the principal purposes of which is qualifying income or gain for the exclusion under this section, including any change in the method of computing reserves or any other transaction or series of transactions a principal purposes of which is the acceleration or deferral of any item in order to claim the benefits of such exclusion through the application of this subsection.

"(8) Coordination with section 953. This subsection shall not apply to investment income allocable to contracts that insure related party risks or risks located in an foreign country other than the country in which the qualifying insurance company is created or organized.

"(9) Application. This subsection shall apply to the first full taxable year of a foreign corporation beginning after December 31, 1997, and before January 1, 1999, and to taxable years of United States shareholders with or within which such taxable year of such foreign corporation ends."

—P.L. 105-277, Sec. 4003(j), substituted "subsection (h)(9)" for "subsection (h)(8)" in subpara. (e)(2)(C) [prior to deletion by Sec. 105(d), of this Act, see above], effective for the first full tax. yr. of a foreign corporation begin. after 12/31/97, and before 1/1/99, and for tax. yrs. of U.S. shareholders with or within which such tax. yr. of such foreign corporation ends.

In 1997, P.L. 105-34, Sec. 1051(a)(1), added subparas. (c)(1)(F) and (G) . . . Sec. 1051(a)(2)(A), deleted "In the case of any regular dealer in property, gains and losses from the sale or exchange of any such property or arising out of bona fide hedging transactions reasonably necessary to the conduct of the business of being a dealer in such property shall not be taken into account under this subparagraph." from the beginning of the flush language after clause (iii) in subpara. (c)(1)(B) . . . Sec. 1051(a)(2)(B), deleted "also" after "section 1221(1)" in subpara. (c)(1)(B) . . . Sec. 1051(b), added subpara. (c)(2)(C), effective for tax. yrs. begin. after 8/5/97.

Income from foreign sources Code Sec. 954

—P.L. 105-34, Sec. 1175(a), added subsec. (h)... Sec. 1175(b), deleted "or" at the end of subpara. (e)(2)(A), substituted ", or" for the period at the end of subpara. (e)(2)(B), and added subpara. (e)(2)(C), effective for the first full tax. yr. of a foreign corporation begin. after 12/31/97, and before 1/1/99, and for tax. yrs. of U.S. shareholders with or within which such tax. yr. of such foreign corporation ends.

In 1996, P.L. 104-188, Sec. 1704(t)(25), amended Sec. 7811(i)(3)(A) of P.L. 101-239, by adding "the first place it appears" before "in clause (i)", see below.

In 1993, P.L. 103-66, Sec. 13233(a)(1), added subpara. (c)(3)(C), effective for tax. yrs. of controlled foreign corporations begin. after 9/30/93, and for tax. yrs. of U.S. shareholders in which or with which such tax. yrs. of controlled foreign corporations end.

—P.L. 103-66, Sec. 13235(a)(3)(A), added "Except as provided in paragraph (1), such term shall not include any foreign personal holding company income (as defined in subsection (c))." at the end of para. (g)(1)... Sec. 13235(a)(3)(B), deleted "(1)," after "paragraph" in para. (b)(8)... Sec. 13235(b), added a sentence at the end of subsec. (f), effective for tax. yrs. begin. after 12/31/92.

—P.L. 103-66, Sec. 13239(d), added para. (d)(4), effective for sales, exchanges, or other dispositions after 8/10/93.

In 1989, P.L. 101-239, Sec. 7811(i)(3)(A), [as amended by Sec. 1704(t)(25) of P.L. 104-188, see above] substituted "is a corporation created" for "is created" the first place it appeared in clause (c)(3)(A)(i)... Sec. 7811(i)(3)(B), substituted "from a corporation which is a related person" for "from a related person" in clause (c)(3)(A)(ii)... Sec. 7811(i)(3)(C), added the sentence at the end of subpara. (c)(3)(A), effective for tax. yrs. of foreign corporations begin. after 12/31/86 with exceptions provided by Sec. 1221(g)(3) of P.L. 99-514, reproduced below.

In 1988, P.L. 100-647, Sec. 1012(i)(12), deleted "(determined without regard to the exclusion under paragraph (2) of this subsection)", after "subsection (a)" in paras (b)(6) and (7) effective for tax. yrs. begin. after 12/31/86.

—P.L. 100-647, Sec. 1012(i)(13)(A)(i), substituted "June 9" for "July 9" in Sec. 1221(g)(3)(C) of P.L. 99-514 [reproduced below]... Sec. 1012(i)(13)(A)(ii), substituted "November 3, 1981" for "March 31, 1982" in Sec. 1221(g)(3)(C) of P.L. 99-514 [reproduced below]... Sec. 1012(i)(13)(B)(i), substituted "under a reinsurance contract" for "as of August 16, 1986, under a reinsurance contract in effect on such date" in Sec. 1221(g)(3)(D) of P.L. 99-514 [reproduced below]... Sec. 1012(i)(13)(B)(ii), substituted "this subparagraph" for "the preceding sentence" in Sec. 1221(g)(3)(D) of P.L. 99-514 [reproduced below]... Sec. 1012(i)(13)(B)(iii), added the two sentences at the end of Sec. 1221(g)(3)(D) of P.L. 99-514 [reproduced below]. The above amendments apply to part of the effective date for amendments made by Sec. 1221 of P.L. 99-514, see below.

—P.L. 100-647, Sec. 1012(i)(14)(A), substituted "more than 50 percent" for "50 percent or more" each place it appeared in para. (d)(3)... Sec. 1012(i)(18), deleted "or" at the end of clause (c)(1)(B)(i), redesignated clause (c)(1)(B)(ii) as clause (c)(1)(B)(iii) and added new clause (c)(1)(B)(ii)... Sec. 1012(i)(20), amended the sentence at the end of subpara. (c)(1)(B)... Sec. 1012(i)(25)(B), added "or creates (or increases) a deficit which under section 952(c) may reduce the subpart F income of the payor or another controlled foreign corporation" before the period at the end of subpara. (c)(3)(B), effective for tax. yrs. of foreign corporations begin. after 12/31/86 with exceptions provided by Sec. 1221(g)(3) of P.L. 99-514, reproduced below.

Prior to amendment, the sentence at the end of subpara. (c)(1)(B) read as follows: "This subparagraph shall not apply to gain from the sale or exchange of any property which, in the hands of the taxpayer, is property described in section 1221(1) or to gain from the sale or exchange of any property by a regular dealer in such property."

—P.L. 100-647, Sec. 1012(aa)(2)(A) and (4), of this Act provide:

"(2) Certain amendments to apply notwithstanding treaties. The following amendments made by the Reform Act P.L. 99-514 shall apply notwithstanding any treaty obligation of the United States in effect on the date of the enactment of the Reform Act [10/22/86]:

* * *

"(4) Treatment of technical corrections. For purposes of paragraphs (2) and (3), any amendment made by this title shall be treated as if it had been included in the provision of the Reform Act to which such amendment relates."

"(A) The amendments made by section 1201 of the Reform Act."

—P.L. 100-647, Sec. 1018(u)(38), clarified that para. (e)(3) was deleted by Sec. 1221(b)(3)(B) of P.L. 99-514, see below.

In 1986, P.L. 99-514, Sec. 1201(c), added two sentences to the end of para. (b)(5), effective for tax. yrs. begin. after 12/31/86. [See Sec. 1012(aa)(2)(A) and (4) of P.L. 100-647, above]

—P.L. 99-514, Sec. 1221(a)(1), amended subsec. (c)... Sec. 1221(b)(3)(B), deleted para. (e)(3) [as amended by Sec. 1810(k) of this Act, see below, and as clarified by Sec. 1018(u)(38) of P.L. 100-647, see above]... Sec. 1221(c)(1), deleted para. (b)(2)... Sec. 1221(c)(2), added the sentence at the end of subsec. (f)... Sec. 1221(c)(3)(A)(i), deleted subsec. (g) and redesignated subsec. (h) as subsec. (g)... Sec. 1221(c)(3)(A)(ii), substituted "determined under subsection (g)" for "determined under subsection (h)" in para. (a)(5)... Sec. 1221(d), amended para. (b)(4)... Sec. 1221(e)(1), amended subparas. (d)(3)(A) and (B), and deleted subpara. (d)(3)(C)... Sec. 1221(e)(2), substituted three sentences for the two sentences at the end of para. (d)(3), effective for tax. yrs. of foreign corporations begin. after 12/31/86. Secs. 1221(g)(2) and (3) [as amended by Sec. 1012(i)(13) of P.L. 100-647, see above] provide special rules as follows:

"(2) Special rule for repeal of exclusion for reinvestment shipping income.

"(A) In general. In the case of any qualified controlled foreign corporation

"(i) the amendments made by subsection (c) shall apply to taxable years ending on or after January 1, 1992, and

"(ii) sections 955(a)(l)(A) and 955(a)(2)(A) of the Internal Revenue Code of 1986 (as amended by subsection (c)(3)) shall be applied by substituting 'ending before 1992' for 'beginning before 1987'.

"(B) Qualified controlled foreign corporation. For purposes of subparagraph (A), the term 'qualified controlled foreign corporation' means any controlled foreign corporation (as defined in section 957 of such Code)

"(i) if the United States agent of such corporation is a domestic corporation incorporated on March 13, 1951, and

"(ii) if

"(I) the certificate of incorporation of such corporation is dated July 23, 1963, and

"(II) such corporation has a wholly owned subsidiary and its certificate of incorporation is dated November 2, 1965."

"(3) Exception for certain reinsurance contracts.

"(A) In general. In the case of the 1st 3 taxable years of a qualified controlled foreign insurer beginning after December 31, 1986, the amendments made by this section shall not apply to the phase-in percentage of any qualified reinsurance income.

"(B) Phase-in percentage. For purposes of subparagraph (A):

In the case of taxable years beginning in:	The phase-in percentage is:
1987	75
1988	50
1989	25.

"(C) Qualified controlled foreign insurer. For purposes of this paragraph, the term 'qualified controlled foreign insurer' means

"(i) any controlled foreign corporation which on August 16, 1986, was a member of an affiliated group (as defined in section 1504(a) of the Internal Revenue Code of 1986 without regard to subsection (b)(3) thereof) which had as its common parent a corporation incorporated in Delaware on June 9, 1967, with executive offices in New York, New York, or

"(ii) any controlled foreign corporation which on August 16, 1986, was a member of an affiliated group (as so defined) which had as its common parent a corporation incorporated in Delaware on November 3, 1981, with executive offices in Philadelphia, Pennsylvania.

"(D) Qualified reinsurance income. For purposes of this paragraph, the term 'qualified reinsurance income' means any insurance income attributable to risks (other than risks described in section 953(a) or 954(c) of such Code) as in effect on the day before the date of the enactment of this Act) assumed under a reinsurance contract. For purposes of this subparagraph, insurance income shall mean the underwriting income (as defined in section 832(b)(3) of such Code) and investment income derived from an amount of assets (to be segregated and separately identified) equivalent to the ordinary and necessary insurance reserves and necessary surplus equal to 1/3 of earned premium attributable to such contracts

For purposes of this paragraph, the amount of qualified reinsurance income shall not exceed the amount of insurance income from reinsurance contracts for calendar year 1985. In the case of controlled foreign corporations described in subparagraph (C)(ii), the preceding sentence shall not apply and the qualified reinsurance income of any such corporation shall not exceed such corporation's proportionate share of $27,000,000 (determined on the basis of respective amounts of qualified reinsurance income determined without regard to this subparagraph)."

Prior to amendment, subsec. (c) read as follows:

"(c) Foreign personal holding company income.

"(1) In general. For purposes of subsection (a)(1), the term 'foreign personal holding company income' means the foreign personal holding company income (as defined in section 553), modified and adjusted as provided in paragraphs (2), (3), and (4).

"(2) Rents included without regard to 50 percent limitation. For purposes of paragraph (1), all rents shall be included in foreign personal holding company income without regard to whether or not such rents constitute 50 percent or more of gross income.

"(3) Certain income derived in active conduct of trade or business. For purposes of paragraph (1), foreign personal holding company income does not include

"(A) rents and royalties which are derived in the active conduct of a trade or business and which are received from a person other than a related person (within the meaning of subsection (d)(3)),

"(B) dividends, interest, and gains from the sale or exchange of stock or securities derived in the conduct of a banking, financing, or similar business, or derived from the investments made by an insurance company of its unearned premiums or reserves ordinary and necessary for the proper conduct of its insurance business, and which are received from a person other than a related person (within the meaning of subsection (d)(3)), or

"(C) dividends, interest, and gains from the sale or exchange of stock or securities received from a person other than a related person (within the meaning of subsection (d)(3)) derived from investments made by an insurance company of an amount of its assets equal to one-third of its premiums earned on insurance contracts (other than life insurance and annuity contracts) during the taxable year (as defined in section 832(b)(4)) which are not directly or indirectly attributable to the insurance or reinsurance of risks of persons who are related persons (within the meaning of subsection (d)(3)).

"(4) Certain income received from related persons. For purposes of paragraph (1), foreign personal holding company income does not include

"(A) dividends and interest received from a related person which (i) is created or organized under the laws of the same foreign country under the laws of which the controlled foreign corporation is created or organized, and (ii) has a substan-

2,633

tial part of its assets used in its trade or business located in such same foreign country;

"(B) interest received in the conduct of a banking, financing, or similar business from a related person engaged in the conduct of a banking, financing, or similar business if the businesses of the recipient and the payor are predominantly with persons other than related persons; and

"(C) rents, royalties, and similar amounts received from a related person for the use of, or the privilege of using, property within the country under the laws of which the controlled foreign corporation is created or organized."

Prior to deletion, para. (e)(3) [as added by Sec. 1810(k) of this Act, see below] read as follows:

"(3) Treatment of certain insurance contracts. For purposes of paragraph (1), in the case of any services performed with respect to any policy of insurance or reinsurance with respect to which the primary insured is a related person (within the meaning of section 864(d)(4))

"(A) such primary insured shall be treated as a related person for purposes of paragraph (1)(A) (whether or not the requirements of subsection (d)(3) are met),

"(B) such services shall be treated as performed in the country within which the insured hazards, risks, losses, or liabilities occur, and

"(C) except as otherwise provided in regulations by the Secretary, rules similar to the rules of section 953(b) shall be applied in determining the income from such services."

Prior to deletion, para. (b)(2) read as follows:

"(2) Exclusion for reinvested shipping income. For purposes of subsection (a), foreign base company income does not include foreign base company shipping income to the extent that the amount of such income does not exceed the increase for the taxable year in qualified investments in foreign base company shipping operations of the controlled foreign corporation (as determined under subsection (g))."

Prior to deletion, subsec. (g) read as follows:

"(g) Increase in qualified investments in foreign base company shipping operations.

"For purposes of subsection (b)(2), the increase for any taxable year in qualified investments in foreign base company shipping operations of any controlled foreign corporation is the amount by which

"(1) the qualified investments in foreign base company shipping operations (as defined in section 955(b)) of the controlled foreign corporation at the close of the taxable year, exceed

"(2) the qualified investments in foreign base company shipping operations (as so defined) of the controlled foreign corporation at the close of the preceding taxable year."

Prior to amendment, para. (b)(4) read as follows:

"(4) Exception for foreign corporations not availed of to reduce taxes. For purposes of subsection (a), foreign base company income does not include any item of income received by a controlled foreign corporation if it is established to the satisfaction of the Secretary that neither

"(A) the creation or organization of such controlled foreign corporation under the laws of the foreign country in which it is incorporated (or, in the case of controlled foreign corporation which is an acquired corporation, the acquisition of such corporation created or organized under the laws of the foreign country in which it is incorporated), nor

"(B) the effecting of the transaction giving rise to such income through the controlled foreign corporation, has as one of its significant purposes a substantial reduction of income, war profits, or excess profits or similar taxes. The preceding sentence shall not apply to foreign base company oil related income described in subsection (a)(5)."

Prior to amendment, subparas. (d)(3)(A) and (B) read as follows:

"(A) such person is an individual, partnership, trust, or estate which controls the controlled foreign corporation;

"(B) such person is a corporation which controls, or is controlled by, the controlled foreign corporation; or"

Prior to deletion, subpara. (d)(3)(C) read as follows:

"(C) such person is a corporation which is controlled by the same person or persons which control the controlled foreign corporation."

Prior to substitution, the two sentences at the end of para. (d)(3) read as follows: "For purposes on the preceding sentence, control means the ownership, directly or indirectly, of stock possessing more than 50 percent of the total combined voting power of all classes of stock entitled to vote. For purposes of this paragraph, the rules for determining ownership of stock prescribed by section 958 shall apply."

—P.L. 99-514, Sec. 1223(a), amended para. (b)(3), effective for tax. yrs. begin. after 12/31/86.

Prior to amendment, para. (b)(3) read as follows:

"(3) Special rule where foreign base company income is less than 10 percent or more than 70 percent of gross income. For purposes of subsection (a)—

"(A) if the foreign base company income (determined without regard to paragraphs (2) and (5)) is less than 10 percent of gross income, no part of the gross income of the taxable year shall be treated as foreign base company income.

"(B) if the foreign base company income (determined without regard to paragraphs (2) and (5)) exceeds 70 percent of gross income, the entire gross income of the taxable year shall, subject to the provisions of paragraph (2), (4), and (5), be treated as foreign base company income."

—P.L. 99-514, Sec. 1227, provides a special rule as follows:

"SEC. 1227. SPECIAL RULE FOR APPLICATION OF SECTION 954 TO CERTAIN DIVIDENDS. "(a) In general.

"For purposes of section 954(c)(3)(A) of the Internal Revenue Code of 1986, any dividends received by a qualified controlled foreign corporation (within the meaning of section 951 of such Code) during any of its 1st 5 taxable years beginning after December 31, 1986, with respect to its 32.7 percent interest in a Brazilian corporation shall be treated as if such Brazilian corporation were a related person to the qualified controlled foreign corporation to the extent the Brazilian corporation's income is attributable to its interest in the trade or business of mining in Brazil.

"(b) Qualified controlled foreign corporation.

"For purposes of this section, a qualified controlled foreign corporation is a corporation the greater than 99 percent shareholder of which is a company originally incorporated in Montana on July 9, 1951 (the name of which was changed on August 10, 1966).

"(c) Effective date.

"The amendment made by this section shall apply to dividends received after December 31, 1986."

—P.L. 99-514, Sec. 1810(k), amended subsec. (e) [before amendment by Sec. 1221(b)(3)(B) of this Act, see above], effective for tax. yrs. of controlled foreign corporations begin. after 7/18/84.

Prior to amendment, subsec. (e) read as follows:

"(e) Foreign base company services income.

"For purposes of subsection (a)(3), the term 'foreign base company services income' means income (whether in the form of compensation, commissions, fees, or otherwise) derived in connection with the performance of technical, managerial, engineering, architectural, scientific, skilled, industrial, commercial, or like services which—

"(1) are performed for or on behalf of any related person (within the meaning of subsection (d)(3)), and

"(2) are performed outside the country under the laws of which the controlled foreign corporation is created or organized.

The preceding sentence shall not apply to income derived in connection with the performance of services which are directly related to the sale or exchange by the controlled foreign corporation of property manufactured, produced, grown, or extracted by it and which are performed prior to the time of the sale or exchange, or of services directly related to an offer or effort to sell or exchange such property. For purposes of paragraph (2), any services performed with respect to any policy of insurance or reinsurance with respect to which the primary insured is a related person (within the meaning of section 864(d)(4)) shall be treated as having been performed in the country within which the insured hazards, risks, losses, or liabilities occur, and except as provided in regulations prescribed by the Secretary, rules similar to the rules of section 953(b) shall be applied in determining the income from such services."

In 1984, P.L. 98-369, Sec. 137(a), added the sentence at the end of subsec. (e), effective for tax. yrs. of controlled foreign corporations begin. after 7/18/84.

—P.L. 98-369, Sec. 712(f), substituted "paragraphs (2) and (3) of section 907(c)" for "section 907(c)(2)" in para. (h)(1), effective for tax. yrs. of foreign corporations begin. after 12/31/82, and to tax. yrs. of United States shareholders in which, or with which, such tax. yrs. of foreign corporations end.

In 1982, P.L. 97-248, Sec. 212(a), added para. (a)(5) . . . Sec. 212(b)(1), substituted ", the foreign base company shipping income, and the foreign base company oil related income" for "and the foreign base company shipping income" in para. (b)(5) . . . Sec. 212(b)(2), added para. (b)(8) . . . Sec. 212(c), added subsec. (h) . . . Sec. 212(d), added the sentence at the end of para. (b)(4) . . . Sec. 212(e), deleted "and" at the end of para. (a)(3), and substituted ", and" for the period at the end of para. (a)(4), effective for tax. yrs. of foreign corporations begin. after 12/31/82, and to tax. yrs. of United States shareholders in which, or with which, such tax. yrs. of foreign corporations end.

In 1976, P.L. 94-455, Sec. 1023(a), deleted "or" at the end of subpara. (c)(3)(A), substituted ", or" for the period at the end of subpara. (c)(3)(B), and added subpara. (c)(3)(C) . . . Sec. 1024(a), added para. (b)(7), effective for tax. yrs. of foreign corps. begin. after '75, and for tax. yrs. of United States shareholders, within the meaning of subsec. 951(b), within which or with which such tax. yrs. of such foreign corps. end.

—P.L. 94-455, Sec. 1906(b)(13)(A), substituted "Secretary" for "Secretary or his delegate" each place it appeared in Code Sec. 954, effective for tax. yrs. begin. after 12/31/76.

In 1975, P.L. 94-12, Sec. 602(b), added the sentence at the end of para. (d)(1) . . . Sec. 602(c)(1), deleted para. (b)(1) . . . Sec. 602(c)(2), deleted subsec. (f) . . . Sec. 602(d)(1)(A), deleted "and" at the end of para. (a)(2), substituted ", and" for the period at the end of (a)(3), and added para. (a)(4) . . . Sec. 602(d)(1)(B), amended para. (b)(2) . . . Sec. 602(d)(1)(C), substituted "paragraphs (2) and (5)" for "paragraphs (1) and (5)" in subparas. (b)(3)(A) and (B) . . . Sec. 602(d)(1)(D), substituted "paragraph (2)," for "paragraphs (1), (2)," in subpara. (b)(3)(B) . . . Sec. 602(d)(1)(E), substituted "the foreign base company services income, and the foreign base company shipping income" for "and the foreign base company services income" in para. (b)(5) . . . Sec. 602(d)(1)(F), added para. (b)(6) . . . Sec. 602(d)(1)(G), added subsecs. (f) [after repeal by Sec. 602(c)(2) of this Act, see above] and (g) . . . Sec. 602(e), substituted "10 percent" for "30 percent" each place it appeared in para. (b)(3), effective for tax. yrs. of foreign corporations begin. after 12/31/75, and to tax. yrs. of U.S. shareholders (within the meaning of '54 Code Sec. 951(b)) within which or with which such tax. yrs. of such foreign corporations end.

Prior to deletion, para. (b)(1) read as follows:

"(1) Exclusion of certain dividends, interest, and gains from qualified investments in less developed countries. For purposes of subsection (a), foreign base company income does not include

"(A) dividends and interest received during the taxable year from investments which at the time of receipt are qualified investments in less developed countries (as defined in section 955(b)), or

"(B) if the gains from the sale or exchange during the taxable year of investments which at the time of sale or exchange are qualified investments in less de-

Income from foreign sources — Code Sec. 955(b)(4)

veloped countries exceed the losses from the sale or exchange during the taxable year of such qualified investments the amount by which such gains exceed such losses.

The preceding sentence shall apply only to the extent that the sum of the dividends and interest described in subparagraph (A) and the amount described in subparagraph (B) does not exceed the increase for the taxable year in qualified investments in less developed countries of the controlled foreign corporation (as determined under subsection (f)).''

Prior to deletion, subsec. (f) read as follows:

"(f) Increase in qualified investments in less developed countries.

"For purposes of subsection (b)(1), the increase for any taxable year in qualified investment in less developed countries of any controlled foreign corporation is the amount by which

"(1) the qualified investments in less developed countries (as defined in section 955(b)) of the controlled foreign corporation at the close of the taxable year, exceeds

"(2) the qualified investments in less developed countries (as so defined) of the controlled foreign corporations at the close of the preceding taxable year."

Prior to amendment, para. (b)(2) read as follows:

"(2) Exclusion of certain shipping income. For purposes of subsection (a), foreign base company income does not include income derived from, or in connection with, the use (or hiring or leasing for use) of any aircraft or vessel in foreign commerce, or the performance of services directly related to the use of any such aircraft or vessel."

In 1969, P.L. 91-172, Sec. 909(a), amended para. (b)(4), effective for tax. yrs. ending after 10/9/69.

Prior to amendment, para. (b)(4) read as follows:

"(4) Exception for foreign corporations not availed of to reduce taxes. For purposes of subsection (a), foreign base company income does not include any item of income received by a controlled foreign corporation if it is established to the satisfaction of the Secretary or his delegate with respect to such item that the creation or organization of the controlled foreign corporation receiving such item under the laws of the foreign country in which it is incorporated does not have the effect of substantial reduction of income, war profits, or excess profits taxes or similar taxes."

In 1962, P.L. 87-834, Sec. 12(a), added Code Sec. 954, effective for tax. yrs. of foreign corporations begin. after 12/31/62 and tax. yrs. of U.S. shareholders within which or with which such tax. yrs. of such foreign corporations end.

Sec. 955. Withdrawal of previously excluded subpart F income from qualified investment.

(a) General rules.

(1) Amount withdrawn. For purposes of this subpart, the amount of previously excluded subpart F income of any controlled foreign corporation withdrawn from investment in foreign base company shipping operations for any taxable year is an amount equal to the decrease in the amount of qualified investments in foreign base company shipping operations of the controlled foreign corporation for such year, but only to the extent that the amount of such decrease does not exceed an amount equal to—

(A) the sum of the amounts excluded under section 954(b)(2) from the foreign base company income of such corporation for all prior taxable years beginning before 1987, reduced by

(B) the sum of the amounts of previously excluded subpart F income withdrawn from investment in foreign base company shipping operations of such corporation determined under this subsection for all prior taxable years.

(2) Decrease in qualified investments. For purposes of paragraph (1), the amount of the decrease in qualified investments in foreign base company shipping operations of any controlled foreign corporation for any taxable year is the amount by which—

(A) the amount of qualified investments in foreign base company shipping operations of the controlled foreign corporation as of the close of the last taxable year beginning before 1987 (to the extent such amount exceeds the sum of the decreases in qualified investments determined under this paragraph for prior taxable years beginning after 1986), exceeds

(B) the amount of qualified investments in foreign base company shipping operations of the controlled foreign corporation at the close of the taxable year, to the extent that the amount of such decrease does not exceed the sum of the earnings and profits for the taxable year and the earnings and profits accumulated for prior taxable years beginning after December 31, 1975, and the amount of previously excluded subpart F income invested in less developed country corporations described in section 955(c)(2) (as in effect before the enactment of the Tax Reduction Act of 1975) to the extent attributable to earnings and profits accumulated for taxable years beginning after December 31, 1962. For purposes of this paragraph, if qualified investments in foreign base company shipping operations are disposed of by the controlled foreign corporation during the taxable year, the amount of the decrease in qualified investments in foreign base company shipping operations of such controlled foreign corporation for such year shall be reduced by an amount equal to the amount (if any) by which the losses on such dispositions during such year exceed the gains on such dispositions during such year.

(3) Pro rata share of amount withdrawn. In the case of any United States shareholder, the pro rata share of the amount of previously excluded subpart F income of any controlled foreign corporation withdrawn from investment in foreign base company shipping operations for any taxable year is his pro rata share of the amount determined under paragraph (1).

(b) Qualified investments in foreign base company shipping operations.

(1) In general. For purposes of this subpart, the term "qualified investments in foreign base company shipping operations" means investments in—

(A) any aircraft or vessel used in foreign commerce, and

(B) other assets which are used in connection with the performance of services directly related to the use of any such aircraft or vessel.

Such term includes, but is not limited to, investments by a controlled foreign corporation in stock or obligations of another controlled foreign corporation which is a related person (within the meaning of section 954(d)(3)) and which holds assets described in the preceding sentence, but only to the extent that such assets are so used.

(2) Qualified investments by related persons. For purposes of determining the amount of qualified investments in foreign base company shipping operations, an investment (or a decrease in investment) in such operations by one or more controlled foreign corporations may, under regulations prescribed by the Secretary, be treated as an investment (or a decrease in investment) by another corporation which is a controlled foreign corporation and is a related person (as defined in section 954(d)(3)) with respect to the corporation actually making or withdrawing the investment.

(3) Special rule. For purposes of this subpart, a United States shareholder of a controlled foreign corporation may, under regulations prescribed by the Secretary, elect to make the determinations under subsection (a)(2) of this section and under subsection (g) of section 954 as of the close of the years following the years referred to in such subsections, or as of the close of such longer period of time as such regulations may permit, in lieu of on the last day of such years. Any election under this paragraph made with respect to any taxable year shall apply to such year and to all succeeding taxable years unless the Secretary consents to the revocation of such election.

(4) Amount attributable to property. The amount taken into account under this subpart with respect to any prop-

erty described in paragraph (1) shall be its adjusted basis, reduced by any liability to which such property is subject.
(5) Income excluded under prior law. Amounts invested in less developed country corporations described in section 955(c)(2) (as in effect before the enactment of the Tax Reduction Act of 1975) shall be treated as qualified investments in foreign base company shipping operations and shall not be treated as investments in less developed countries for purposes of section 951(a)(1)(A)(ii).

In **1988,** P.L. 100-647, Sec. 1012(i)(11), substituted "beginning before 1987 (to the extent such amount exceeds the sum of the decreases in qualified investments determined under this paragraph for prior taxable years beginning after 1986)" for "beginning before 1987" in subpara. (a)(2)(A), effective for tax. yrs. of foreign corporations begin. after 12/31/86, and as provided by Secs. 1221(g)(2) and (3) of P.L. 99-514, reproduced in note following Code Sec. 954.

In **1986,** P.L. 99-514, Sec. 1221(c)(3)(B), substituted "all prior taxable years beginning before 1987" for "all prior taxable years" in subpara. (a)(1)(A), . . . Sec. 1221(c)(3)(C), substituted "as of the close of the last taxable year beginning before 1987" for "at the close of the preceding taxable year" in subpara. (a)(2)(A) effective for tax. yrs. of foreign corporations begin. after 12/31/86 and as provided by Secs. 1221(g)(2) and (3) of this Act, reproduced in note following Code Sec. 954.

In **1976,** P.L. 94-455, Sec. 1906(b)(13)(A), substituted "Secretary" for "Secretary or his delegate" each place it appeared in Code Sec. 955, effective for tax. yrs. begin. after 12/31/76.

In **1975,** P.L. 94-12, Sec. 602(c)(5), repealed Code Sec. 955. . . Sec. 602(d)(3)(A), added new Code Sec. 955, effective for tax. yrs. of foreign corporations begin. after 12/31/75 and for tax. yrs. of U.S. shareholders (within the meaning of '54 Code Sec. 951 (b)) within which or with which such tax. yrs. of such foreign corporations end.

Prior to amendment, Code Sec. 955 read as follows:
SEC. 955. WITHDRAWAL OF PREVIOUSLY EXCLUDED SUBPART F INCOME FROM QUALIFIED INVESTMENT.
"(a) General rules.
"(1) Amount withdrawn. For purposes of this subpart, the amount of previously excluded subpart F income of any controlled foreign corporation withdrawn from investment in less developed countries for any taxable year is an amount equal to the decrease in the amount of qualified investments in less developed countries of the controlled foreign corporation for such year, but only to the extent that the amount of such decrease does not exceed an amount equal to—
"(A) the sum of the amounts excluded under section 954(b)(1) from the foreign base company income of such corporation for all prior taxable years, reduced by
"(B) the sum of the amounts of previously excluded subpart F income withdrawn from investment in less developed countries of such corporation determined under this subsection for all prior taxable years.
"(2) Decrease in qualified investments. For purposes of paragraph (1), the amount of the decrease in qualified investments in less developed countries of any controlled foreign corporation for any taxable year is the amount of which—
"(A) the amount of qualified investments in less developed countries of the controlled foreign corporation at the close of the preceding taxable year, exceeds
"(B) the amount of qualified investments in less developed countries of the controlled foreign corporation at the close of the taxable year,
to the extent the amount of such decrease does not exceed the sum of the earnings and profits for the taxable year and the earnings and profits accumulated for prior taxable years beginning after December 31, 1962. For purposes of this paragraph, if qualified investments in less developed countries are disposed of by the controlled foreign corporation during the taxable year, the amount of the decrease in qualified investments in less developed countries of such controlled foreign corporation for such year shall be reduced by an amount equal to the amount (if any) by which the losses on such dispositions during such year exceed the gains on such dispositions during such year.
"(3) Pro rata share of amount withdrawn. In the case of any United States shareholder, the pro rata share of the amount of previously excluded subpart F income of any controlled foreign corporation withdrawn from investment in less developed countries for any taxable year is his pro rata share of the amount determined under paragraph (1).
"(b) Qualified investments in less developed countries.
"(1) In general. For purposes of this subpart, the term 'qualified investments in less developed countries' means property which is—
"(A) stock of a less developed country corporation held by the controlled foreign corporation but only if the controlled foreign corporation owns 10 percent or more of the total combined voting power of all classes of stock of such less developed country corporation;
"(B) an obligation of a less developed country corporation held by the controlled foreign corporation, which, at the time of its acquisition by the controlled foreign corporation, has a maturity of one year or more, but only if the controlled foreign corporation owns 10 percent or more of the total combined voting power of all classes of stock of such less developed country corporation; or
"(C) an obligation of a less developed country.
"(2) Country ceases to be less developed country. For purposes of this subpart, property which would be a qualified investment in less developed countries, but for the fact that a foreign country has, after the acquisition of such property by the controlled foreign corporation, ceased to be a less developed country, shall be treated as a qualified investment in less developed countries.
"(3) Special rule. For purposes of this subpart, a United States shareholder of a controlled foreign corporation may, under regulations prescribed by the Secretary or his delegate, make the determinations under subsection (a)(2) of this section and under subsection (f) of section 954 as of the close of the years following the years referred to in such subsection, or as of the close of such longer period of time as such regulations may permit, in lieu of on the last day of such years. Any election under this paragraph made with respect to any taxable year shall apply to such year and to all succeeding taxable years unless the Secretary or his delegate consents to the revocation of such election.
"(4) Exception. For purposes of this subpart, property shall not constitute qualified investments in less developed countries if such property is disposed of within 6 months after the date of its acquisition.
"(5) Amount attributable to property. For amount taken into account under this subpart with respect to any property described in paragraph (1) or (2) shall be its adjusted basis, reduced by any liability to which such property is subject.
"(c) Less developed country corporations.
"(1) In general. For purposes of this subpart, the term 'less developed country corporation' means a foreign corporation which during the taxable year is engaged in the active conduct of one or more trades or businesses and—
"(A) 80 percent or more of the gross income of which for the taxable year is derived from sources within less developed countries; and
"(B) 80 percent or more in value of the assets of which on each day of the taxable year consists of—
"(i) property used in such trades or businesses and located in less developed countries,
"(ii) money, and deposits with persons carrying on the banking business,
"(iii) stock, and obligations which, at the time of their acquisition, have a maturity of one year or more, of any other less developed country corporation,
"(iv) an obligation of a less developed country,
"(v) an investment which is required because of restrictions imposed by a less developed country, and
"(vi) property described in section 956(b)(2).
For purposes of subparagraph (A), the determination as to whether income is derived from sources within less developed countries shall be made under regulations prescribed by the Secretary or his delegate.
"(2) Shipping companies. For purposes of this subpart, the term 'less developed country corporation' also means a foreign corporation—
"(A) 80 percent or more of the gross income of which for the taxable year consists of—
"(i) gross income derived from, or in connection with, the using (or hiring or leasing for use) in foreign commerce of aircraft or vessels registered under the laws of a less developed country, or from, or in connection with, the performance of services directly related to use of such aircraft or vessels, or from the sale or exchange of such aircraft or vessels, and
"(ii) dividends and interest received from foreign corporations which are less developed country corporations within the meaning of this paragraph and 10 percent or more of the total combined voting power of all classes of stock of which are owned by the foreign corporation, and gain from the sale or exchange of stock or obligations of foreign corporations which are such less developed country corporations, and
"(B) 80 percent or more of the assets of which on each day of the taxable year consists of (i) assets used, or held for use, for or in connection with the production of income described in subparagraph (A), and (ii) property described in section 956(b)(2).
"(3) Less developed country defined. For purposes of this subpart, the term 'less developed country' means (in respect of any foreign corporation) any foreign country (other than an area within the Sino-Soviet bloc) or any possession of the United States with respect to which, on the first day of the taxable year, there is in effect an Executive order by the President of the United States designating such country or possession as an economically less developed country for purposes of this subpart. For purposes of the preceding sentence, an overseas territory, department, province, or possession may be treated as a separate country. No designation shall be made under this paragraph with respect to—

Australia	Luxembourg
Austria	Monaco
Belgium	Netherlands
Canada	New Zealand
Denmark	Norway
France	Union of South Africa
Germany (Federal Republic)	San Marino
Hong Kong	Sweden
Italy	Switzerland
Japan	United Kingdom
Liechtenstein	

"After the President has designated any foreign country or any possession of the United States as an economically less developed country for purposes of this subpart, he shall not terminate such designation (either by issuing an Executive order for that purpose or by issuing an Executive order under the first sentence of this paragraph which has the effect of terminating such designation) unless, at least 30 days prior to such termination, he has notified the Senate and the House of Representatives of his intention to terminate such designation."
In **1962,** P.L. 87-834, Sec. 12(a), added Code Sec. 955, effective for tax. yrs. of foreign corporations begin. after 12/31/62 and tax. yrs. of U.S. shareholders within which or with which such tax. yrs. of such foreign corporations end.

Income from foreign sources

Sec. 956. Investment of earnings in United States property.

(a) General rule.

In the case of any controlled foreign corporation, the amount determined under this section with respect to any United States shareholder for any taxable year is the lesser of—

(1) the excess (if any) of—

(A) such shareholder's pro rata share of the average of the amounts of United States property held (directly or indirectly) by the controlled foreign corporation as of the close of each quarter of such taxable year, over

(B) the amount of earnings and profits described in section 959(c)(1)(A) with respect to such shareholder, or

(2) such shareholder's pro rata share of the applicable earnings of such controlled foreign corporation.

The amount taken into account under paragraph (1) with respect to any property shall be its adjusted basis as determined for purposes of computing earnings and profits, reduced by any liability to which the property is subject.

(b) Special rules.

(1) **Applicable earnings.** For purposes of this section, the term "applicable earnings" means, with respect to any controlled foreign corporation, the sum of—

(A) the amount (not including a deficit) referred to in section 316(a)(1) to the extent such amount was accumulated in prior taxable years, and

(B) the amount referred to in section 316(a)(2),

but reduced by distributions made during the taxable year and by earnings and profits described in section 959(c)(1).

(2) **Special rule for U.S. property acquired before corporation is a controlled foreign corporation.** In applying subsection (a) to any taxable year, there shall be disregarded any item of United States property which was acquired by the controlled foreign corporation before the first day on which such corporation was treated as a controlled foreign corporation. The aggregate amount of property disregarded under the preceding sentence shall not exceed the portion of the applicable earnings of such controlled foreign corporation which were accumulated during periods before such first day.

(3) **Special rule where corporation ceases to be controlled foreign corporation.** If any foreign corporation ceases to be a controlled foreign corporation during any taxable year—

(A) the determination of any United States shareholder's pro rata share shall be made on the basis of stock owned (within the meaning of section 958(a)) by such shareholder on the last day during the taxable year on which the foreign corporation is a controlled foreign corporation,

(B) the average referred to in subsection (a)(1)(A) for such taxable year shall be determined by only taking into account quarters ending on or before such last day, and

(C) in determining applicable earnings, the amount taken into account by reason of being described in paragraph (2) of section 316(a) shall be the portion of the amount so described which is allocable (on a pro rata basis) to the part of such year during which the corporation is a controlled foreign corporation.

(c) United States property defined.

(1) **In general.** For purposes of subsection (a), the term "United States property" means any property acquired after December 31, 1962, which is—

(A) tangible property located in the United States;

(B) stock of a domestic corporation;

(C) an obligation of a United States person; or

(D) any right to the use in the United States of—

(i) a patent or copyright,

(ii) an invention, model, or design (whether or not patented),

(iii) a secret formula or process, or

(iv) any other similar property right,

which is acquired or developed by the controlled foreign corporation for use in the United States.

(2) **Exceptions.** For purposes of subsection (a), the term "United States property" does not include—

(A) obligations of the United States, money, or deposits with—

(i) any bank (as defined by section 2(c) of the Bank Holding Company Act of 1956 (12 U.S.C. 1841(c)), without regard to subparagraphs (C) and (G) of paragraph (2) of such section), or

(ii) any corporation not described in clause (i) with respect to which a bank holding company (as defined by section 2(a) of such Act) or financial holding company (as defined by section 2(p) of such Act) owns directly or indirectly more than 80 percent by vote or value of the stock of such corporation;

(B) property located in the United States which is purchased in the United States for export to, or use in, foreign countries;

(C) any obligation of a United States person arising in connection with the sale or processing of property if the amount of such obligation outstanding at no time during the taxable year exceeds the amount which would be ordinary and necessary to carry on the trade or business of both the other party to the sale or processing transaction and the United States person had the sale or processing transaction been made between unrelated persons;

(D) any aircraft, railroad rolling stock, vessel, motor vehicle, or container used in the transportation of persons or property in foreign commerce and used predominantly outside the United States;

(E) an amount of assets of an insurance company equivalent to the unearned premiums or reserves ordinary and necessary for the proper conduct of its insurance business attributable to contracts which are not contracts described in section 953(a)(1);

(F) the stock or obligations of a domestic corporation which is neither a United States shareholder (as defined in section 951(b)) of the controlled foreign corporation, nor a domestic corporation, 25 percent or more of the total combined voting power of which, immediately after the acquisition of any stock in such domestic corporation by the controlled foreign corporation, is owned, or is considered as being owned, by such United States shareholders in the aggregate;

(G) any movable property (other than a vessel or aircraft) which is used for the purpose of exploring for, developing, removing, or transporting resources from ocean waters or under such waters when used on the Continental Shelf of the United States;

(H) an amount of assets of the controlled foreign corporation equal to the earnings and profits accumulated after December 31, 1962, and excluded from subpart F income under section 952(b);

(I) deposits of cash or securities made or received on commercial terms in the ordinary course of a United States or foreign person's business as a dealer in securities or in commodities, but only to the extent such deposits are made or received as collateral or margin for

(i) a securities loan, notional principal contract, options contract, forward contract, or futures contract, or (ii) any other financial transaction in which the Secretary determines that it is customary to post collateral or margin;

(J) an obligation of a United States person to the extent the principal amount of the obligation does not exceed the fair market value of readily marketable securities sold or purchased pursuant to a sale and repurchase agreement or otherwise posted or received as collateral for the obligation in the ordinary course of its business by a United States or foreign person which is a dealer in securities or commodities;

(K) securities acquired and held by a controlled foreign corporation in the ordinary course of its business as a dealer in securities if—

(i) the dealer accounts for the securities as securities held primarily for sale to customers in the ordinary course of business, and

(ii) the dealer disposes of the securities (or such securities mature while held by the dealer) within a period consistent with the holding of securities for sale to customers in the ordinary course of business; and

(L) an obligation of a United States person which—

(i) is not a domestic corporation, and

(ii) is not—

(I) a United States shareholder (as defined in section 951(b)) of the controlled foreign corporation, or

(II) a partnership, estate, or trust in which the controlled foreign corporation, or any related person (as defined in section 954(d)(3)), is a partner, beneficiary, or trustee immediately after the acquisition of any obligation of such partnership, estate, or trust by the controlled foreign corporation.

For purposes of subparagraphs (I), (J), and (K) the term "dealer in securities" has the meaning given such term by section 475(c)(1), and the term "dealer in commodities" has the meaning given such term by section 475(e), except that such term shall include a futures commission merchant.

(3) Certain trade or service receivables acquired from related United States persons.

(A) In general. Notwithstanding paragraph (2) (other than subparagraph (H) thereof), the term "United States property" includes any trade or service receivable if—

(i) such trade or service receivable is acquired (directly or indirectly) from a related person who is a United States person, and

(ii) the obligor under such receivable is a United States person.

(B) Definitions. For purposes of this paragraph, the term "trade or service receivable" and "related person" have the respective meanings given to such terms by section 864(d).

(d) Pledges and guarantees.

For purposes of subsection (a), a controlled foreign corporation shall, under regulations prescribed by the Secretary, be considered as holding an obligation of a United States person if such controlled foreign corporation is a pledgor or guarantor of such obligation.

(e) Regulations.

The Secretary shall prescribe such regulations as may be necessary to carry out the purposes of this section, including regulations to prevent the avoidance of the provisions of this section through reorganizations or otherwise.

In 2007, P.L. 110-172, Sec. 11(g)(15)(A)(i), deleted subparas. (c)(2)(I) and redes. subpara. (c)(2)(J)-(M) as subparas. (c)(2)(I)-(L)... Sec. 11(g)(15)(A)(ii), substituted "subparagraphs (I), (J), and (K)" for "subparagraphs (J), (K), and (L)" in para. (c)(2), enacted 12/29/2007.

Prior to deletion, subpara. (c)(2)(I) read as follows:

"(I) to the extent provided in regulations prescribed by the Secretary, property which is otherwise United States property which is held by a FSC and which is related to the export activities of such FSC;"

In 2004, P.L. 108-357, Sec. 407(a), deleted "and" at the end of subpara. (c)(2)(J), substituted a semicolon for the period at the end of subpara. (c)(2)(K), and added subparas. (c)(2)(L) and (M)... Sec. 407(b), substituted ", (K), and (L)" for "and (K)" in para. (c)(2), effective for tax. yrs. of foreign corporations begin. after 12/31/2004, and for tax. yrs. of U.S. shareholders with or within which such tax. yrs. of foreign corporations end.

—P.L. 108-357, Sec. 837(a), amended subpara. (c)(2)(A), effective 10/22/2004.

Prior to amendment, subpara. (c)(2)(A) read as follows:

"(A) obligations of the United States, money, or deposits with persons carrying on the banking business;"

In 1997, P.L. 105-34, Sec. 1173(a), deleted "and" at the end of subpara. (c)(2)(H), substituted a semicolon for the period at the end of subpara. (c)(2)(I), and added subparas. (c)(2)(J) and (K) and flush language at the end of para. (c)(2), effective for tax. yrs. of foreign corporations begin. after 12/31/97, and for tax. yrs. of U.S. shareholders with or within which such tax. yrs. of foreign corporations end.

—P.L. 105-34, Sec. 1601(e), added "to the extent such amount was accumulated in prior taxable years" after "section 316(a)(1)" in subpara. (b)(1)(A), effective for tax. yrs. of foreign corporations begin. after 12/31/96, and for tax. yrs. of U.S. shareholders within which or with which such tax. yrs. of foreign corporations end.

In 1996, P.L. 104-188, Sec. 1501(b)(1), [the second 1501(b)(1) appearing in this Act] amended para. (b)(1)... Sec. 1501(b)(2), amended para. (b)(3), effective for tax. yrs. of foreign corporations begin. after 12/31/96, and for tax. yrs. of U.S. shareholders within which or with which such tax. yrs. of foreign corporations end.

Prior to amendment, para. (b)(1) read as follows:

"(1) Applicable earnings. For purposes of this section, the term 'applicable earnings' has the meaning given to such term by section 956A(b), except that the provisions of such section excluding earnings and profits accumulated in taxable years beginning before October 1, 1993, shall be disregarded."

Prior to amendment, para. (b)(3) read as follows:

"(3) Special rule where corporation ceases to be controlled foreign corporation. Rules similar to the rules of section 956A(e) shall apply for purposes of this section."

In 1993, P.L. 103-66, Sec. 13232(a)(1), redesignated subsecs. (b) and (c) as subsecs. (c) and (d)... Sec. 13232(a)(2), deleted subsec. (a) and added new subsecs. (a) and (b)... Sec. 13232(b), added subsec. (e), effective for tax. yrs. of controlled foreign corporations begin. after 9/30/93, and for tax. yrs. of U.S. shareholders in which or with which such tax. yrs. of controlled foreign corporations end.

Prior to deletion, subsec. (a) read as follows:

"(a) General rules.

"For purposes of this subpart—

"(1) Amount of investment. The amount of earnings of a controlled foreign corporation invested in United States property at the close of any taxable year is the aggregate amount of such property held, directly or indirectly, by the controlled foreign corporation at the close of the taxable year, to the extent such amount would have constituted a dividend (determined after the application of section 955(a)) if it had been distributed.

"(2) Pro rata share of increase for year. In the case of any United States shareholder, the pro rata share of the increase for any taxable year in the earnings of a controlled foreign corporation invested in United States property is the amount determined by subtracting his pro rata share of—

"(A) the amount determined under paragraph (1) for the close of the preceding taxable year, reduced by amounts paid during such preceding taxable year to which section 959(c)(1) applies, from

"(B) the amount determined under paragraph (1) for the close of the taxable year.

The determinations under subparagraphs (A) and (B) shall be made on the basis of stock owned (within the meaning of section 958(a)) by such United States shareholder on the last day during the taxable year on which the foreign corporation is a controlled foreign corporation.

"(3) Amount attributable to property. The amount taken into account under paragraph (1) or (2) with respect to any property shall be its adjusted basis, reduced by any liability to which the property is subject."

In 1986, P.L. 99-514, Sec. 1810(c)(1), substituted "paragraph (2) (other than subparagraph (H) thereof)" for "paragraph (2)" in subpara. (b)(3)(A), effective for accounts receivable and evidences of indebtedness transferred after 3/1/85, in tax. yrs. end. after 3/1/84. Sec. 123(c)(2) of P.L. 98-369 provides a transitional rule, reproduced below.

In 1984, P.L. 98-369, Sec. 123(b), added para. (b)(3), effective for accounts receivable and evidences of indebtedness transferred after 3/1/84, in tax. yrs. end. after 3/1/84. Sec. 123(c)(2) of this Act provides the following transitional rule:

"(2) Transitional rule—The amendments made by this section shall not apply to accounts receivable and evidences of indebtedness acquired after March 1, 1984, and before March 1, 1994, by a Belgian corporation in existence on March 1, 1984, in any taxable year ending after such date, but only to the extent that the

Income from foreign sources

amount includible in gross income by reason of section 956 of the Internal Revenue Code of 1954 with respect to such corporation for all such taxable years is not reduced by reason of this paragraph by more than the lesser of—
"(A) $15,000,000 or
"(B) the amount of the Belgian corporation's adjusted basis on March 1, 1984, in stock of a foreign corporation formed to issue bonds outside the United States to the public."
—P.L. 98-369, Sec. 801(d)(8), deleted "and" at the end of subpara. (b)(2)(G), substituted "; and" for the period at the end of subpara. (b)(2)(H), and added subpara. (b)(2)(I), effective for transactions after 12/31/84, in tax. yrs. end. after 12/31/84.

In 1976, P.L. 94-455, Sec. 1021(a), deleted "and" at the end of subpara. (b)(2)(E), redesignated subpara. (b)(2)(F) as subpara. (b)(2)(H), and added new subparas. (b)(2)(F) and (G), effective for tax. yrs. of foreign corps. begin. after 12/31/75, and for tax yrs. of United States shareholders, within the meaning of subsec. 951(b), within which or with which such tax. yrs. of such foreign corps. end. In determining for purposes of any tax. yr. referred to in the preceding sentence the amount referred to in subpara. (a)(2)(A) for the last tax. yr. of a corp. begin. before 1/1/76, the amendments made here also apply to such last tax. yr.
—P.L. 94-455, Sec. 1906(b)(13)(A), substituted "Secretary" for "Secretary or his delegate" in Code Sec. 956, effective for tax. yrs. begin. after 12/31/76.

In 1962, P.L. 87-834, Sec. 12, added Code Sec. 956, effective for tax. yrs. of foreign corporations begin. after 12/31/62 and tax. yrs. of U.S. shareholders within which or with which such tax. yrs. of such foreign corporations end.

Sec. 956A. Repealed.

In 1996, P.L. 104-188, Sec. 1501(a)(2), repealed Code Sec. 956A, effective for tax. yrs. of foreign corporations begin. after 12/31/96, and for tax. yrs. of U.S. shareholders within which or with which such tax. yrs. of foreign corporations end.

Prior to repeal, Code Sec. 956A read as follows:
"956A. EARNINGS INVESTED IN EXCESS PASSIVE ASSETS.
"(a) General rule. In the case of any controlled foreign corporation, the amount determined under this section with respect to any United States shareholder for any taxable year is the lesser of—
"(1) the excess (if any) of—
"(A) such shareholder's pro rata share of the amount of the controlled foreign corporation's excess passive assets for such taxable year, over
"(B) the amount of earnings and profits described in section 959(c)(1)(B) with respect to such shareholder, or
"(2) such shareholder's pro rata share of the applicable earnings of such controlled foreign corporation determined after the application of section 951(a)(1)(B).
"(b) Applicable earnings. For purposes of this section, the term 'applicable earnings' means, with respect to any controlled foreign corporation, the sum of—
"(1) the amount (not including a deficit) referred to in section 316(a)(1) to the extent such amount was accumulated in prior taxable years beginning after September 30, 1993, and
"(2) the amount referred to in section 316(a)(2),
but reduced by distributions made during the taxable year and reduced by the earnings and profits described in section 959(c)(1) to the extent that the earnings and profits so described were accumulated in taxable years beginning after September 30, 1993.
"(c) Excess passive assets. For purposes of this section—
"(1) In general. The excess passive assets of any controlled foreign corporation for any taxable year is the excess (if any) of—
"(A) the average of the amounts of passive assets held by such corporation as of the close of each quarter of such taxable year, over
"(B) 25 percent of the average of the amounts of total assets held by such corporation as of the close of each quarter of such taxable year.
For purposes of the preceding sentence, the amount taken into account with respect to any asset shall be its adjusted basis as determined for purposes of computing earnings and profits.
"(2) Passive asset.
"(A) In general. Except as otherwise provided in this section, the term 'passive asset' means any asset held by the controlled foreign corporation which produces passive income (as defined in section 1296(b)) or is held for the production of such income.
"(B) Coordination with section 956. The term 'passive asset' shall not include any United States property (as defined in section 956).
"(3) Certain rules to apply. For purposes of this subsection, the rules of the following provisions shall apply:
"(A)Section 1296(c) (relating to look-thru rules).
"(B) Section 1297(d) (relating to leasing rules).
"(C) Section 1297(e) (relating to intangible property).
"(d) Treatment of certain groups of controlled foreign corporations.
"(1) In general. For purposes of applying subsection (c)—
"(A) all controlled foreign corporations which are members of the same CFC group shall be treated as 1 controlled foreign corporation, and
"(B) the amount of the excess passive assets determined with respect to such 1 corporation shall be allocated among the controlled foreign corporations which are members of such group in proportion to their respective amounts of applicable earnings.
"(2) CFC group. For purposes of paragraph (1), the term 'CFC group' means 1 or more chains of controlled foreign corporations connected through stock ownership with a top tier corporation which is a controlled foreign corporation, but only if—
"(A) the top tier corporation owns directly more than 50 percent (by vote or value) of the stock of at least 1 of the other controlled foreign corporations, and
"(B) more than 50 percent (by vote or value) of the stock of each of the controlled foreign corporations (other than the top tier corporation) is owned (directly or indirectly) by one or more other members of the group.
"(e) Special rule where corporation ceases to be controlled foreign corporation during taxable year. If any foreign corporation ceases to be a controlled foreign corporation during any taxable year—
"(1) the determination of any United States shareholder's pro rata share shall be made on the basis of stock owned (within the meaning of section 958(a)) by such shareholder on the last day during the taxable year on which the foreign corporation is a controlled foreign corporation, and
"(2) the amount of such corporation's excess passive assets for such taxable year shall be determined by only taking into account quarters ending on or before such last day, and
"(3) in determining applicable earnings, the amount taken into account by reason of being described in paragraph (2) of section 316(a) shall be the portion of the amount so described which is allocable (on a pro rata basis) to the part of such year during which the corporation is a controlled foreign corporation.
"(f) Regulations. The Secretary shall prescribe such regulations as may be necessary to carry out the purposes of this section, including regulations to prevent the avoidance of the provisions of this section through reorganizations or otherwise and regulations coordinating the provisions of subsections (c)(3)(A) and (d)."
—P.L. 104-188, Sec. 1703(i)(2), amended para. (b)(1) . . . Sec. 1703(i)(3), added "and regulations coordinating the provisions of subsections (c)(3)(A) and (d)" before the period at the end of subsec. (f), effective for tax. yrs. of foreign corporations begin. after 9/30/93, and for tax. yrs. of U.S. shareholders in which or with which such tax. yrs. of foreign corporations end.

Prior to amendment, para. (b)(1) read as follows:
"(1) the amount referred to in section 316(a)(1) to the extent such amount was accumulated in taxable years beginning after September 30, 1993, and"

In 1993, P.L. 103-66, Sec. 13231(b), added Code Sec. 956A, effective for tax. yrs. of foreign corporations begin. after 9/30/93, and for tax. yrs. of U.S. shareholders in which or with which such tax. yrs. of foreign corporations end.

Sec. 957. Controlled foreign corporations; United States persons.

(a) General rule.

For purposes of this subpart, the term "controlled foreign corporation" means any foreign corporation if more than 50 percent of—

(1) the total combined voting power of all classes of stock of such corporation entitled to vote, or

(2) the total value of the stock of such corporation,

is owned (within the meaning of section 958(a)), or is considered as owned by applying the rules of ownership of section 958(b), by United States shareholders on any day during the taxable year of such foreign corporation.

(b) Special rule for insurance.

For purposes only of taking into account income described in section 953(a) (relating to insurance income), the term "controlled foreign corporation" includes not only a foreign corporation as defined by subsection (a) but also one of which more than 25 percent of the total combined voting power of all classes of stock (or more than 25 percent of the total value of stock) is owned (within the meaning of section 958(a)), or is considered as owned by applying the rules of ownership of section 958(b), by United States shareholders on any day during the taxable year of such corporation, if the gross amount of premiums or other consideration in respect of the reinsurance or the issuing of insurance or annuity contracts described in section 953(a)(1) exceeds 75 percent of the gross amount of all premiums or other consideration in respect of all risks.

(c) United States person.

For purposes of this subpart, the term "United States person" has the meaning assigned to it by section 7701(a)(30) except that—

(1) with respect to a corporation organized under the laws of the Commonwealth of Puerto Rico, such term does not include an individual who is a bona fide resident of Puerto Rico, if a dividend received by such individual during the taxable year from such corporation would, for purposes of section 933(1), be treated as income derived from sources within Puerto Rico, and

(2) with respect to a corporation organized under the laws of Guam, American Samoa, or the Northern Mariana Islands—

(A) 80 percent or more of the gross income of which for the 3-year period ending at the close of the taxable year (or for such part of such period as such corporation or any predecessor has been in existence) was derived from sources within such a possession or was effectively connected with the conduct of a trade or business in such a possession, and

(B) 50 percent or more of the gross income of which for such period (or part) was derived from the active conduct of a trade or business within such a possession,

such term does not include an individual who is a bona fide resident of Guam, American Samoa, or the Northern Mariana Islands.

For purposes of subparagraphs (A) and (B) of paragraph (2), the determination as to whether income was derived from the active conduct of a trade or business within a possession shall be made under regulations prescribed by the Secretary.

In 2004, P.L. 108-357, Sec. 908(c)(5)(A), substituted "active conduct of a" for "conduct of an active" in subpara. (c)(2)(B) . . . Sec. 908(c)(5)(B), deleted "derived from sources within a possession, was effectively connected with the conduct of a trade or business within a possession, or" after "whether income was" in the last sentence of subsec. (c), effective for tax. yrs. end. after 10/22/2004.

In 1986, P.L. 99-514, Sec. 1221(b)(3)(C), substituted "insurance income" for "income derived from insurance of United States risks" in subsec. (b), effective for tax. yrs. of foreign corporations begin. after 12/31/86.

—P.L. 99-514, Sec. 1222(a)(1), amended subsec. (a) . . . Sec. 1221(a)(2), substituted "all classes of stock (or more than 25 percent of the total value of stock)" for "all classes of stock" in subsec. (b) . . . Sec. 1224(a), deleted subsec. (c) and redesignated subsec. (d) as subsec. (c), effective for tax. yrs. of foreign corporations begin. after 12/31/86 except that for purposes of applying '86 Code Secs. 951(a)(1)(B) and 956, such amendments shall take effect on 8/16/86.

Secs. 1222(c)(2) and (c)(3) of this Act provide:

"(2) Transitional rule. In the case of any corporation treated as a controlled foreign corporation by reason of the amendments made by this section, property acquired before August 16, 1986, shall not be taken into account under section 956(b) of the Internal Revenue Code of 1986.

"(3) Special rule for beneficiary of trust. In the case of an individual —

"(A) who is a beneficiary of a trust which was established on December 7, 1979, under the laws of a foreign jurisdiction, and

"(B) who was not a citizen or resident of the United States on the date the trust was established,

amounts which are included in the gross income of such beneficiary under section 951(a) of the Internal Revenue Code of 1986 with respect to stock held by the trust (and treated as distributed to the trust) shall be treated as the first amounts which are distributed by the trust to such beneficiary and as amounts to which section 959(a) of such Code applies."

Sec. 1224(b)(2) of this Act provides:

"(2) Transitional rule. In the case of any corporation treated as a controlled foreign corporation by reason of the amendment made by subsection (a), property acquired before August 16, 1986, shall not be taken into account under section 956(b) of the Internal Revenue Code of 1986."

Prior to amendment, subsec. (a) read as follows:

"(a) General rule.

"For purposes of this subpart, the term 'controlled foreign corporation' means any foreign corporation of which more than 50 percent of the total combined voting power of all classes of stock entitled to vote is owned (within the meaning of section 958(a)), or is considered as owned by applying the rules of ownership of section 958(b), by United States shareholders on any day during the taxable year of such foreign corporation."

Prior to deletion, subsec. (c) read as follows:

"(c) Corporations organized in United States possessions.

"For purposes of this subpart, the term 'controlled foreign corporation' does not include any corporation created or organized in the Commonwealth of Puerto Rico or a possession of the United States or under the laws of the Commonwealth of Puerto Rico or a possession of the United States if—

"(1) 80 percent or more of the gross income of such corporation for the 3-year period immediately preceding the close of the taxable year (or for such part of such period immediately preceding the close of such taxable year as may be applicable) was derived from sources within the Commonwealth of Puerto Rico or a possession of the United States; and

"(2) 50 percent or more of the gross income of such corporation for such period, or for such part thereof, was derived from the active conduct within the Commonwealth of Puerto Rico or a possession of the United States of any trades or businesses constituting the manufacture or processing of goods, wares, mer-

chandise, or other tangible personal property; the processing of agricultural or horticultural products or commodities (including but not limited to livestock, poultry, or fur-bearing animals); the catching or taking of any kind of fish or the mining or extraction of natural resources, or any manufacturing or processing of any products or commodities obtained from such activities; or the ownership or operation of hotels.

For purposes of paragraphs (1) and (2), the determination as to whether income was derived from sources within the Commonwealth of Puerto Rico or a possession of the United States and was derived from the active conduct of a described trade or business within the Commonwealth of Puerto Rico or a possession of the United States shall be made under regulations prescribed by the Secretary."

—P.L. 99-514, Sec. 1273(a), added and at the end of para. (c)(1), deleted paras. (c)(2) and (c)(3) [as redesignated by Sec. 1224(a)] and added new para. (c)(2), effective for tax. yrs. begin. after 12/31/86. For special rules see Secs. 1271 and 1277(b) of this Act, reproduced in note following Code Sec. 931.

Prior to amendment, paras. (c)(2) and (c)(3) read as follows:

"(2) with respect to a corporation organized under the laws of the Virgin Islands, such term does not include an individual who is a bona fide resident of the Virgin Islands and whose income tax obligation under this subtitle for the taxable year is satisfied pursuant to section 28(a) of the Revised Organic Act of the Virgin Islands, approved July 22, 1954 (48 U.S.C. 1642), by paying tax on income derived from all sources both within and outside the Virgin Islands into the treasury of the Virgin Islands, and

"(3) with respect to a corporation organized under the laws of any other possession of the United States, such term does not include an individual who is a bona fide resident of any such other possession and whose income derived from sources within possessions of the United States is not, by reason of section 931(a), includible in gross income under this subtitle for the taxable year."

In 1962, P.L. 87-834, Sec. 12, added Code Sec. 957 for tax. yrs. of foreign corporations begin. after '62 and tax. yrs. of U.S. shareholders within which or with which such tax. yrs. of such foreign corporations end.

Sec. 958. Rules for determining stock ownership.

(a) Direct and indirect ownership.

(1) General rule. For purposes of this subpart (other than section 960(a)(1), stock owned means—

(A) stock owned directly, and

(B) stock owned with the application of paragraph (2).

(2) Stock ownership through foreign entities. For purposes of subparagraph (B) of paragraph (1), stock owned, directly or indirectly, by or for a foreign corporation, foreign partnership, or foreign trust or foreign estate (within the meaning of section 7701(a)(31)) shall be considered as being owned proportionately by its shareholders, partners, or beneficiaries. Stock considered to be owned by a person by reason of the application of the preceding sentence shall, for purposes of applying such sentence, be treated as actually owned by such person.

(3) Special rule for mutual insurance companies. For purposes of applying paragraph (1) in the case of a foreign mutual insurance company, the term "stock" shall include any certificate entitling the holder to voting power in the corporation.

(b) Constructive ownership.

For purposes of sections 951(b), 954(d)(3), 956(c)(2), and 957, section 318(a) (relating to constructive ownership of stock) shall apply to the extent that the effect is to treat any United States person as a United States shareholder within the meaning of section 951(b), to treat a person as a related person within the meaning of section 954(d)(3), to treat the stock of a domestic corporation as owned by a United States shareholder of the controlled foreign corporation for purposes of section 956(c)(2), or to treat a foreign corporation as a controlled foreign corporation under section 957, except that—

(1) In applying paragraph (1)(A) of section 318(a), stock owned by a nonresident alien individual (other than a foreign trust or foreign estate) shall not be considered as owned by a citizen or by a resident alien individual.

(2) In applying subparagraphs (A), (B), and (C) of section 318(a)(2), if a partnership, estate, trust, or corporation owns, directly or indirectly, more than 50 percent of the total combined voting power of all classes of stock entitled to vote of a corporation, it shall be considered as owning all the stock entitled to vote.

(3) In applying subparagraph (C) of section 318(a)(2), the phrase "10 percent" shall be substituted for the phrase "50 percent" used in subparagraph (C).

(4) Subparagraphs (A), (B), and (C) of section 318(a)(3) shall not be applied so as to consider a United States person as owning stock which is owned by a person who is not a United States person.

Paragraphs (1) and (4) shall not apply for purposes of section 956(c)(2) to treat stock of a domestic corporation as not owned by a United States shareholder.

In 1996, P.L. 104-188, Sec. 1703(i)(4), substituted "956(c)(2)" for "956(b)(2)" each place it appeared in subsec. (b), effective for tax. yrs. of controlled foreign corporations begin. after 9/30/93, and for tax. yrs. of U.S. shareholders in which or with which such tax. yrs. of controlled foreign corporations end.
—P.L. 104-188, Sec. 1704(t)(7), substituted "section 960(a)(1)" for "sections 955(b)(1)(A) and (B), 955(c)(2)(A)(ii), and 960(a)(1)" in para. (a)(1), effective 8/20/96.

In 1976, P.L. 94-455, Sec. 1021(b), substituted "954(d)(3), 956(b)(2)," for "954(d)(3)," the first place it appeared in subsec. (b), substituted "954(d)(3), to treat the stock of a domestic corporation as owned by a United States shareholder of the controlled foreign corporation for purposes of section 956(b)(2)," for "954(d)(3)," the second place it appeared in subsec. (b), and added the sentence at the end of subsec. (b), effective for tax. yrs. of foreign corps. begin. after 12/31/75, and for tax. yrs. of United States shareholders, within the meaning of subsec. 951(b), within which or with which such tax. yrs. of such foreign corps. end. In determining for purposes of any tax. yr. referred to in the preceding sentence the amount referred to in subpara. 956(a)(2)(A) for the last tax. yr. of a corp. begin. before '76, the amendments made here apply to such last tax. yr.

In 1964, P.L. 88-554, Sec. 4(b)(5)(A), substituted "subparagraphs (A), (B), and (C)" for "the first sentence of subparagraphs (A) and (B), and in applying clause (i) of subparagraph (C)," in para. (b)(2) . . . Sec. 4(b)(5)(B), deleted para. (b)(3) . . . Sec. 4(b)(5)(C), redesignated para. (b)(4) as new para. (b)(3), and substituted "In applying subparagraph (C)" for "In applying clause (i) of subparagraph (C)" in para. (b)(3) [as redesignated, see above] . . . Sec. 4(b)(5)(D), redesignated para. (b)(5) as new para. (b)(4), and substituted "Subparagraphs (A), (B), and (C) of section 318(a)(3)" for "The second sentence of subparagraphs (A) and (B), and clause (ii) of subparagraph (C), of section 318(a)(2)" in para. (b)(4) [as redesignated, see above], effective as provided in Sec. 4(c) of this Act, which reads as follows:

"(c) The amendments made by this section shall take effect on the date of the enactment of this Act, except that, for purposes of sections 302 and 304 of the Internal Revenue Code of 1954, such amendments shall not apply with respect to distributions in payment for stock acquisitions or redemptions, if such acquisitions or redemptions occurred before the date of the enactment of this Act."

Prior to deletion, para. (b)(3) read as follows:

"(3) Stock owned by a partnership, estate, trust, or corporation, by reason of the application of the second sentence of subparagraphs (A) and (B), and the application of clause (ii) of subparagraph (C), of section 318(a)(2), shall not be considered as owned by such partnership, estate, trust, or corporation, for purposes of applying the first sentence of subparagraphs (A) and (B), and in applying clause (i) of subparagraph (C), of section 318(a)(2)."

In 1962, P.L. 87-834, Sec. 12(a), added Code Sec. 958, effective for tax. yrs. of foreign corporations begin. after 12/31/62 and tax. yrs. of U.S. shareholders within which or with which such tax. yrs. of such foreign corporations end.

Sec. 959. Exclusion from gross income of previously taxed earnings and profits.

(a) Exclusion from gross income of United States persons.

For purposes of this chapter, the earnings and profits of a foreign corporation attributable to amounts which are, or have been, included in the gross income of a United States shareholder under section 951(a) shall not, when—

(1) such amounts are distributed to, or

(2) such amounts would, but for this subsection, be included under section 951(a)(1)(B) in the gross income of, such shareholder (or any other United States person who acquires from any person any portion of the interest of such United States shareholder in such foreign corporation, but only to the extent of such portion, and subject to such proof of the identity of such interest as the Secretary may by regulations prescribe) directly or indirectly through a chain of ownership described under section 958(a), be again included in the gross income of such United States shareholder (or of such other United States person). The rules of subsection (c) shall apply for purposes of paragraph (1) of this subsection and the rules of subsection (f) shall apply for purposes of paragraph (2) of this subsection.

(b) Exclusion from gross income of certain foreign subsidiaries.

For purposes of section 951(a), the earnings and profits of a controlled foreign corporation attributable to amounts which are, or have been, included in the gross income of a United States shareholder under section 951(a), shall not, when distributed through a chain of ownership described under section 958(a), be also included in the gross income of another controlled foreign corporation in such chain for purposes of the application of section 951(a) to such other controlled foreign corporation with respect to such United States shareholder (or to any other United States shareholder who acquires from any person any portion of the interest of such United States shareholder in the controlled foreign corporation, but only to the extent of such portion, and subject to such proof of identity of such interest as the Secretary may prescribe by regulations).

(c) Allocation of distributions.

For purposes of subsections (a) and (b), section 316(a) shall be applied by applying paragraph (2) thereof, and then paragraph (1) thereof—

(1) first to the aggregate of—

(A) earnings and profits attributable to amounts included in gross income under section 951(a)(1)(B) (or which would have been included except for subsection (a)(2) of this section), and

(B) earnings and profits attributable to amounts included in gross income under section 951(a)(1)(C) (or which would have been included except for subsection (a)(3) of this section),

with any distribution being allocated between earnings and profits described in subparagraph (A) and earnings and profits described in subparagraph (B) proportionately on the basis of the respective amounts of such earnings and profits,

(2) then to earnings and profits attributable to amounts included in gross income under section 951(a)(1)(A) (but reduced by amounts not included under subparagraph (B) or (C) of section 951(a)(1) because of the exclusions in paragraphs (2) and (3) of subsection (a) of this section), and

(3) then to other earnings and profits.

References in this subsection to section 951(a)(1)(C) and subsection (a)(3) shall be treated as references to such provisions as in effect on the day before the date of the enactment [8/20/96] of the Small Business Job Protection Act of 1996.

(d) Distributions excluded from gross income not to be treated as dividends.

Except as provided in section 960(a)(3), any distribution excluded from gross income under subsection (a) shall be treated, for purposes of this chapter, as a distribution which is not a dividend; except that such distributions shall immediately reduce earnings and profits.

(e) Coordination with amounts previously taxed under section 1248.

For purposes of this section and section 960(b), any amount included in the gross income of any person as a dividend by reason of subsection (a) or (f) of section 1248 shall be treated as an amount included in the gross income of such person (or, in any case to which section 1248(e) applies, of the domestic corporation referred to in section 1248(e)(2)) under section 951(a)(1)(A).

Code Sec. 959(f) — Income from foreign sources

(f) Allocation rules for certain inclusions.
   (1) In general. For purposes of this section, amounts that would be included under subparagraph (B) of section 951(a)(1) (determined without regard to this section) shall be treated as attributable first to earnings described in subsection (c)(2), and then to earnings described in subsection (c)(3).
   (2) Treatment of distributions. In applying this section, actual distributions shall be taken into account before amounts that would be included under section 951(a)(1)(B) (determined without regard to this section).

In 1996, P.L. 104-188, Sec. 1501(b)(3), added "or" at the end of para. (a)(1), deleted "or" at the end of para. (a)(2), and deleted para. (a)(3)... Sec. 1501(b)(4), substituted "paragraph (2)" for "paragraphs (2) and (3)" in the last sentence of subsec. (a)... Sec. 1501(b)(5), added the sentence at the end of subsec. (c)... Sec. 1501(b)(6), amended para. (f)(1)... Sec. 1501(b)(7), substituted "section 951(a)(1)(B)" for "subparagraph (B) or (C) of section 951(a)(1)" in para. (f)(2), effective for tax. yrs. of foreign corporations begin. after 12/31/96, and for tax. yrs. of U.S. shareholders within which or with which such tax. yrs. of foreign corporations end.

Prior to deletion, para. (a)(3) read as follows:
"(3) such amounts would, but for this subsection, be included under section 951(a)(1)(C) in the gross income of,"
Prior to amendment, para. (f)(1) read as follows:
"(1) In general. For purposes of this section—
"(A) amounts that would be included under subparagraph (B) of section 951(a)(1) (determined without regard to this section) shall be treated as attributable first to earnings described in subsection (c)(2), and then to earnings described in subsection (c)(3), and
"(B) amounts that would be included under subparagraph (C) of section 951(a)(1) (determined without regard to this section) shall be treated as attributable first to earnings described in subsection (c)(2) to the extent the earnings so described were accumulated in taxable years beginning after September 30, 1993, and then to earnings described in subsection (c)(3)."

In 1993, P.L. 103-66, Sec. 13231(c)(1), deleted "or" at the end of para. (a)(1), added "or" at the end of para. (a)(2), and added para. (a)(3)... Sec. 13231(c)(2)(A), added "The rules of subsection (c) shall apply for purposes of paragraph (1) of this subsection and the rules of subsection (f) shall apply for purposes of paragraphs (2) and (3) of this subsection." at the end of subsec. (a)... Sec. 13231(c)(2)(B), added subsec. (f)... Sec. 13231(c)(2)(C), amended para. (c)(1)... Sec. 13231(c)(4)(A), substituted "earnings and profits" for "earnings and profits for a taxable year" in subsecs. (a) and (b)... Sec. 13231(c)(4)(B), amended para. (c)(2), effective for tax. yrs. of foreign corporations begin. after 9/30/93, and for tax. yrs. of U.S. shareholders in which or with which such tax. yrs. of foreign corporations end.

Prior to amendment, para. (c)(1) read as follows:
"(1) first to earnings and profits attributable to amounts included in gross income under section 951(a)(1)(B) (or which would have been included except for subsection (a)(2) of this section),"
Prior to amendment, para. (c)(2) read as follows:
"(2) then to earnings and profits attributable to amounts included in gross income under section 951(a)(1)(A) (but reduced by amounts not included under section 951(a)(1)(B) because of the exclusion in subsection (a)(2) of this section), and"

In 1988, P.L. 100-647, Sec. 1012(bb)(7)(A), substituted "such person (or, in any case to which section 1248(e) applies, of the domestic corporation referred to in section 1248(e)(2)) under" for "such person under" in subsec. (e), effective for transactions to which Code Sec. 1248(e) applies and which occur after 12/31/86.
In 1986, P.L. 99-514, Sec. 1226(b), substituted "; except that such distributions shall immediately reduce earnings and profits." for the period at the end of subsec. (d), effective for distributions made after 10/22/86.
In 1984, P.L. 98-369, Sec. 133(b)(1), added subsec. (e), effective for transactions to which subsec. (a) or (f) of Code Sec. 1248 applies occurring after 7/18/84.
In 1976, P.L. 94-455, Sec. 1906(b)(13)(A), substituted "Secretary" for "Secretary or his delegate" each place it appeared in Code Sec. 959, effective for tax. yrs. begin. after 12/31/76.
In 1962, P.L. 87-834, Sec. 12, added Code Sec. 959, effective for tax. yrs. of foreign corporations begin. after '62 and tax. yrs. of U.S. shareholders within which or with which such tax. yrs. of such foreign corporations end.

Sec. 960. Special rules for foreign tax credit.
(a) Taxes paid by a foreign corporation.
   (1) Deemed paid credit. For purposes of subpart A of this part, if there is included under section 951(a) in the gross income of a domestic corporation any amount attributable to earnings and profits of a foreign corporation which is a member of a qualified group (as defined in section 902(b)) with respect to the domestic corporation, then, except to the extent provided in regulations, section 902 shall be applied as if the amount so included were a dividend paid by such foreign corporation (determined by applying section 902(c) in accordance with section 904(d)(3)(B)).
   (2) Taxes previously deemed paid by domestic corporation. If a domestic corporation receives a distribution from a foreign corporation, any portion of which is excluded from gross income under section 959, the income, war profits, and excess profits taxes paid or deemed paid by such foreign corporation to any foreign country or to any possession of the United States in connection with the earnings and profits of such foreign corporation from which such distribution is made shall not be taken into account for purposes of section 902, to the extent such taxes were deemed paid by a domestic corporation under paragraph (1) for any prior taxable year.
   (3) Taxes paid by foreign corporation and not previously deemed paid by domestic corporation. Any portion of a distribution from a foreign corporation received by a domestic corporation which is excluded from gross income under section 959(a) shall be treated by the domestic corporation as a dividend, solely for purposes of taking into account under section 902 any income, war profits, or excess profits taxes paid to any foreign country or to any possession of the United States, on or with respect to the accumulated profits of such foreign corporation from which such distribution is made, which were not deemed paid by the domestic corporation under paragraph (1) for any prior taxable year.
(b) Special rules for foreign tax credit in year of receipt of previously taxed earnings and profits.
   (1) Increase in section 904 limitation. In the case of any taxpayer who—
      (A) either (i) chose to have the benefits of subpart A of this part for a taxable year beginning after September 30, 1993, in which he was required under section 951(a) to include any amount in his gross income, or (ii) did not pay or accrue for such taxable year any income, war profits, or excess profits taxes to any foreign country or to any possession of the United States,
      (B) chooses to have the benefits of subpart A of this part for any taxable year in which he receives 1 or more distributions or amounts which are excludable from gross income under section 959(a) and which are attributable to amounts included in his gross income for taxable years referred to in subparagraph (A), and
      (C) for the taxable year in which such distributions or amounts are received, pays, or is deemed to have paid, or accrues income, war profits, or excess profits taxes to a foreign country or to any possession of the United States with respect to such distributions or amounts,
the limitation under section 904 for the taxable year in which such distributions or amounts are received shall be increased by the lesser of the amount of such taxes paid, or deemed paid, or accrued with respect to such distributions or amounts or the amount in the excess limitation account as of the beginning of such taxable year.
   (2) Excess limitation account.
      (A) Establishment of account. Each taxpayer meeting the requirements of paragraph (1)(A) shall establish an excess limitation account. The opening balance of such account shall be zero.
      (B) Increases in account. For each taxable year beginning after September 30, 1993, the taxpayer shall increase the amount in the excess limitation account by the excess (if any) of—

Income from foreign sources — Code Sec. 960

(i) the amount by which the limitation under section 904(a) for such taxable year was increased by reason of the total amount of the inclusions in gross income under section 951(a) for such taxable year, over

(ii) the amount of any income, war profits, and excess profits taxes paid, or deemed paid, or accrued to any foreign country or possession of the United States which were allowable as a credit under section 901 for such taxable year and which would not have been allowable but for the inclusions in gross income described in clause (i).

Proper reductions in the amount added to the account under the preceding sentence for any taxable year shall be made for any increase in the credit allowable under section 901 for such taxable year by reason of a carryback if such increase would not have been allowable but for the inclusions in gross income described in clause (i).

(C) Decreases in account. For each taxable year beginning after September 30, 1993, for which the limitation under section 904 was increased under paragraph (1), the taxpayer shall reduce the amount in the excess limitation account by the amount of such increase.

(3) Distributions of income previously taxed in years beginning before October 1, 1993. If the taxpayer receives a distribution or amount in a taxable year beginning after September 30, 1993, which is excluded from gross income under section 959(a) and is attributable to any amount included in gross income under section 951(a) for a taxable year beginning before October 1, 1993, the limitation under section 904 for the taxable year in which such amount or distribution is received shall be increased by the amount determined under this subsection as in effect on the day before the date of the enactment [8/10/93] of the Revenue Reconciliation Act of 1993.

(4) Cases in which taxes not to be allowed as deduction. In the case of any taxpayer who—

(A) chose to have the benefits of subpart A of this part for a taxable year in which he was required under section 951(a) to include in his gross income an amount in respect of a controlled foreign corporation, and

(B) does not choose to have the benefits of subpart A of this part for the taxable year in which he receives a distribution or amount which is excluded from gross income under section 959(a) and which is attributable to earnings and profits of the controlled foreign corporation which was included in his gross income for the taxable year referred to in subparagraph (A),

no deduction shall be allowed under section 164 for the taxable year in which such distribution or amount is received for any income, war profits, or excess profits taxes paid or accrued to any foreign country or to any possession of the United States on or with respect to such distribution or amount.

(5) Insufficient taxable income. If an increase in the limitation under this subsection exceeds the tax imposed by this chapter for such year, the amount of such excess shall be deemed an overpayment of tax for such year.

⌐
• **Caution:** Code Sec. 960(c), following, is effective to acquisitions of United States property (as defined in section 956(c) of the Internal Revenue Code of 1986) after 12/31/2010.
⌐

(c) Limitation with respect to Section 956 inclusions.

(1) In general. If there is included under section 951(a)(1)(B) in the gross income of a domestic corporation any amount attributable to the earnings and profits of a foreign corporation which is a member of a qualified group (as defined in section 902(b)) with respect to the domestic corporation, the amount of any foreign income taxes deemed to have been paid during the taxable year by such domestic corporation under section 902 by reason of subsection (a) with respect to such inclusion in gross income shall not exceed the amount of the foreign income taxes which would have been deemed to have been paid during the taxable year by such domestic corporation if cash in an amount equal to the amount of such inclusion in gross income were distributed as a series of distributions (determined without regard to any foreign taxes which would be imposed on an actual distribution) through the chain of ownership which begins with such foreign corporation and ends with such domestic corporation.

(2) Authority to prevent abuse. The Secretary shall issue such regulations or other guidance as is necessary or appropriate to carry out the purposes of this subsection, including regulations or other guidance which prevent the inappropriate use of the foreign corporation's foreign income taxes not deemed paid by reason of paragraph (1).

In 2010, P.L. 111-226, Sec. 214(a), added subsec. (c), effective to acquisitions of United States property (as defined in section 956(c) of the Internal Revenue Code of 1986) after 12/31/2010.

In 1997, P.L. 105-34, Sec. 1113(b), amended para. (a)(1), effective for taxes of foreign corporations for tax. yrs. of such corporations begin. after 8/5/97. Sec. 1113(c)(2) of this Act provides:

"(2) Special rule. In the case of any chain of foreign corporations described in clauses (i) and (ii) of section 902(b)(2)(B) of the Internal Revenue Code of 1986 (as amended by this section), no liquidation, reorganization, or similar transactions in a taxable year beginning after the date of enactment [8/5/97] of this act shall have the effect of permitting taxes to be taken into account under section 902 of the Internal Revenue Code of 1986 which could not have been taken into account under such section but for such transaction."

Prior to amendment, para. (a)(1) read as follows:

"(1) General rule. For purposes of subpart A of this part, if there is included, under section 951(a), in the gross income of a domestic corporation any amount attributable to earnings and profits—

"(A) of a foreign corporation (hereafter in this subsection referred to as the 'first foreign corporation') at least 10 percent of the voting stock of which is owned by such domestic corporation, or

"(B) of a second foreign corporation (hereinafter in this subsection referred to as the 'second foreign corporation') at least 10 percent of the voting stock of which is owned by the first foreign corporation, or

"(C) of a third foreign corporation (hereinafter in this subsection referred to as the 'third foreign corporation') at least 10 percent of the voting stock of which is owned by the second foreign corporation,

then, except to the extent provided in regulations, such domestic corporation shall be deemed to have paid a portion of such foreign corporation's post-1986 foreign income taxes determined under section 902 in the same manner as if the amount so included were a dividend paid by such foreign corporation (determined by applying section 902(c) in accordance with section 904(d)(3)(B)). This paragraph shall not apply with respect to any amount included in the gross income of such domestic corporation attributable to earnings and profits of the second foreign corporation or of the third foreign corporation unless, in the case of the second foreign corporation, the percentage-of-voting-stock requirement of section 902(b)(3)(A) is satisfied, and in the case of the third foreign corporation, the percentage-of-voting-stock requirement of section 902(b)(3)(B) is satisfied."

In 1993, P.L. 103-66, Sec. 13233(b)(1)(A), redesignated paras. (b)(3) and (4) as paras. (b)(4) and (5) . . . Sec. 13233(b)(1)(B), repealed paras. (b)(1) and (2) and added new paras. (b)(1), (2), and (3), effective for tax. yrs. begin. after 9/30/93. Prior to deletion, paras. (b)(1) and (2) read as follows:

"(1) Increase in section 904 limitation. In the case of any taxpayer who—

"(A) either (i) chose to have the benefits of subpart A of this part for a taxable year in which he was required under section 951(a) to include in his gross income an amount in respect of a controlled foreign corporation, or (ii) did not pay or accrue for such taxable year any income, war profits, or excess profits taxes to any foreign country or to any possession of the United States, and

"(B) chooses to have the benefits of subpart A of this part for the taxable year in which he receives a distribution or amount which is excluded from gross income under section 959(a) and which is attributable to earnings and profits of the controlled foreign corporation which was included in his gross income for the taxable year referred to in subparagraph (A), and

"(C) for the taxable year in which such distribution or amount is received, pays, or is deemed to have paid, or accrues income, war profits, or excess profits taxes to a foreign country or to any possession of the United States with respect to such distribution or amount,

the limitation under section 904 for the taxable year in which such distribution or amount is received shall be increased as provided in paragraph (2), but such increase shall not exceed the amount of such taxes paid, or deemed paid, or accrued with respect to such distribution or amount.

"(2) Amount of increase. The amount of increase of the limitation under section 904(a) for the taxable year in which the distribution or amount referred to in paragraph (1)(B) is received shall be an amount equal to—

"(A) the amount by which the limitation under section 904(a) for the taxable year referred to in paragraph (1)(A) was increased by reason of the inclusion in gross income under section 951(a) of the amount in respect of the controlled foreign corporation, reduced by

"(B) the amount of any income, war profits, and excess profits taxes paid, or deemed paid, or accrued to any foreign country or possession of the United States which were allowable as a credit under section 901 for the taxable year referred to in paragraph (1)(A) and which would not have been allowable but for the inclusion in gross income of the amount described in subparagraph (A)."

In **1988**, P.L. 100-647, Sec. 1012(b)(3), provides:

"(3) For purposes of sections 902 and 960 of the 1986 Code, the increase in earnings and profits of any foreign corporation under section 1023(e)(3)(C) [reproduced in note following Code Sec. 832] of the Reform Act [P.L. 99-514] shall be taken into account ratably over the 10-year period beginning with the corporation's first taxable year beginning after December 31, 1986."

In **1986**, P.L. 99-514, Sec. 1202(b), substituted "then, except to the extent provided in regulations, such domestic corporation shall be deemed to have paid a portion of such foreign corporation's post-1986 foreign income taxes determined under section 902 in the same manner as if the amount so included were a dividend paid by such foreign corporation (determined by applying section 902(c) in accordance with section 904(d)(3)(B))." for "then, under regulations prescribed by the Secretary, such domestic corporation shall be deemed to have paid the same proportion of the total income, war profits, and excess profits taxes paid (or deemed paid) by such foreign corporation to a foreign country or possession of the United States for the taxable year on or with respect to the earnings and profits of such foreign corporation which the amount of earnings and profits of such foreign corporation so included in gross income of the domestic corporation bears to the entire amount of the earnings and profits of such corporation for such taxable year. This paragraph shall not apply with respect to any amount included in the gross income of such domestic corporation attributable to earnings and profits of the second foreign corporation or of the third foreign corporation unless, in the case of the second foreign corporation, the percentage-of-voting-stock requirement of section 902(b)(3)(A) is satisfied, and in the case of the third foreign corporation, the percentage-of-voting-stock requirement of section 902(b)(3)(B) is satisfied.", in the first sentence of para. (a)(1), effective for distributions by foreign corporations out of, and to inclusions under '86 Code Sec. 951(a) attributable to earnings and profits for tax. yrs. begin. after 12/31/86.

In **1976**, P.L. 94-455, Sec. 1031(b)(1), substituted "limitation" for "applicable limitation" each place it appeared in subsec. (b), for tax. yrs. begin. after '75.

—P.L. 94-455, Sec. 1033(b)(2), substituted "bears to the entire amount of the earnings and profits of such foreign corporation for such taxable year." for "bears to—" and all that followed to the end of para. (a)(1). Sec. 1033(c) of the Act provided as follows:

"(c) Effective dates. The amendments made by this section shall apply—

"(1) in respect of any distribution received by a domestic corporation after December 31, 1977, and

"(2) in respect of any distribution received by a domestic corporation before January 1, 1978, in a taxable year of such corporation beginning after December 31, 1975, but only to the extent that such distribution is made out of the accumulated profits of a foreign corporation for a taxable year (of such foreign corporation) beginning after December 31, 1975.

For purposes of paragraph (2), a distribution made by a foreign corporation out of its profits which are attributable to a distribution received from a foreign corporation to which section 902(b) of the Internal Revenue Code of 1954 applies shall be treated as made out of the accumulated profits of a foreign corporation for a taxable year beginning before January 1, 1976, to the extent that such distribution was paid out of the accumulated profits of such foreign corporation for a taxable year beginning before January 1, 1976."

Prior to amendment, the part of para. (a)(1) amended by Sec. 1033(b)(2) of the Act read as follows:

"bears to—

"(C) if the foreign corporation at least 10 percent of the voting stock of which is owned by such domestic corporation referred to in subparagraph (A) or (B) is not a less developed country corporation (as defined in section 902(d)) for such taxable year, the entire amount of the earnings and profits of such foreign corporation for such taxable year, or

"(D) if the foreign corporation at least 10 percent of the voting stock of which is owned by such domestic corporation referred to in subparagraph (A) or (B) is a less developed country corporation (as defined in section 902(d)) for such taxable year, the sum of the entire amount of the earnings and profits of such foreign corporation for such taxable year and the total income, war profits, and excess profits paid by such foreign corporation to foreign countries or possessions of the United States for such taxable year."

—P.L. 94-455, Sec. 1037(a), amended para. (a)(1), as previously amended by this Act, effective with respect to earnings and profits of a foreign corp. included, under subsec. 951(a), in the gross income of a domestic corp. in tax. yrs. begin. after '76.

Prior to amendment, para. (a)(1) read as follows:

"(1) General rule. For purposes of subpart A of this part, if there is included, under section 951(a), in the gross income of a domestic corporation any amount attributable to earnings and profits—

"(A) of a foreign corporation at least 10 percent of the voting stock of which is owned by such domestic corporation, or

"(B) of a foreign corporation at least 50 percent of the voting stock of which is owned by such domestic corporation at least 10 percent of the voting stock of which is in turn owned by such domestic corporation,

then, under regulations prescribed by the Secretary or his delegate, such domestic corporation shall be deemed to have paid the same proportion of the total income, war profits, and excess profits taxes paid (or deemed paid) by such foreign corporation to a foreign country or possession of the United States for the taxable year on or with respect to the earnings and profits of such foreign corporation which the amount of earnings and profits of such foreign corporation so included in gross income of the domestic corporation bears to the entire amount of the earnings and profits of such foreign corporation for such taxable year."

In **1962**, P.L. 87-834, Sec. 12, added Code Sec. 960, effective for tax. yrs. of foreign corporations begin. after '62 and tax. yrs. of U.S. shareholders within which or with which such tax. yrs. of such foreign corporations end.

Sec. 961. Adjustments to basis of stock in controlled foreign corporations and of other property.

(a) Increase in basis.

Under regulations prescribed by the Secretary, the basis of a United States shareholder's stock in a controlled foreign corporation, and the basis of property of a United States shareholder by reason of which he is considered under section 958(a)(2) as owning stock of a controlled foreign corporation, shall be increased by the amount required to be included in his gross income under section 951(a) with respect to such stock or with respect to such property, as the case may be, but only to the extent to which such amount was included in the gross income of such United States shareholder. In the case of a United States shareholder who has made an election under section 962 for the taxable year, the increase in basis provided by this subsection shall not exceed an amount equal to the amount of tax paid under this chapter with respect to the amounts required to be included in his gross income under section 951(a).

(b) Reduction in basis.

(1) In general. Under regulations prescribed by the Secretary, the adjusted basis of stock or other property with respect to which a United States shareholder or a United States person receives an amount which is excluded from gross income under section 959(a) shall be reduced by the amount so excluded. In the case of a United States shareholder who has made an election under section 962 for any prior taxable year, the reduction in basis provided by this paragraph shall not exceed an amount equal to the amount received which is excluded from gross income under section 959(a) after the application of section 962(d).

(2) Amount in excess of basis. To the extent that an amount excluded from gross income under section 959(a) exceeds the adjusted basis of the stock or other property with respect to which it is received, the amount shall be treated as gain from the sale or exchange of property.

(c) Basis adjustments in stock held by foreign corporations.

Under regulations prescribed by the Secretary, if a United States shareholder is treated under section 958(a)(2) as owning stock in a controlled foreign corporation which is owned by another controlled foreign corporation, then adjustments similar to the adjustments provided by subsections (a) and (b) shall be made to—

(1) the basis of such stock, and

(2) the basis of stock in any other controlled foreign corporation by reason of which the United States shareholder is considered under section 958(a)(2) as owning the stock described in paragraph (1),

Income from foreign sources — Code Sec. 963

but only for the purposes of determining the amount included under section 951 in the gross income of such United States shareholder (or any other United States shareholder who acquires from any person any portion of the interest of such United States shareholder by reason of which such shareholder was treated as owning such stock, but only to the extent of such portion, and subject to such proof of identity of such interest as the Secretary may prescribe by regulations). The preceding sentence shall not apply with respect to any stock to which a basis adjustment applies under subsection (a) or (b).

In 2005, P.L. 109-135, Sec. 409(b), amended subsec. (c), effective for purposes of determining inclusions for tax. yrs. of United States shareholders begin. after 12/31/97 as if included in Sec. 1112 of the Taxpayer Relief Act of 1997, P.L. 105-34.
Prior to amendment, subsec. (c) read as follows:
"(c) Basis adjustments in stock held by foreign corporations. Under regulations prescribed by the Secretary, if a United States shareholder is treated under section 958(a)(2) as owning any stock in a controlled foreign corporation which is actually owned by another controlled foreign corporation, adjustments similar to the adjustments provided by subsections (a) and (b) shall be made to the basis of such stock in the hands of such other controlled foreign corporation, but only for the purposes of determining the amount included under section 951 in the gross income of such United States shareholder (or any other United States shareholder who acquires from any person any portion of the interest of such United States shareholder by reason of which such shareholder was treated as owning such stock, but only to the extent of such portion, and subject to such proof of identity of such interest as the Secretary may prescribe by regulations)."
In 1997, P.L. 105-34, Sec. 1112(b)(1), added subsec. (c), effective for purposes of determining inclusions for tax. yrs. of United States shareholders begin. after 12/31/97.
In 1976, P.L. 94-455, Sec. 1906(b)(13)(A), substituted "Secretary" for "Secretary or his delegate" each place it appeared in Code Sec. 961, effective for tax. yrs. begin. after 12/31/76.
In 1962, P.L. 87-834, Sec. 12, added Code Sec. 961, effective for tax. yrs. of foreign corporations begin. after '62 and tax. yrs. of U.S. shareholders within which or with which such tax. yrs. of such foreign corporations end.

Sec. 962. Election by individuals to be subject to tax at corporate rates.

(a) General rule.

Under regulations prescribed by the Secretary, in the case of a United States shareholder who is an individual and who elects to have the provisions of this section apply for the taxable year—

(1) the tax imposed under this chapter on amounts which are included in his gross income under section 951(a) shall (in lieu of the tax determined under sections 1 and 55) be an amount equal to the tax which would be imposed under sections 11 and 55 if such amounts were received by a domestic corporation, and

(2) for purposes of applying the provisions of section 960 (relating to foreign tax credit) such amounts shall be treated as if they were received by a domestic corporation.

(b) Election.

An election to have the provisions of this section apply for any taxable year shall be made by a United States shareholder at such time and in such manner as the Secretary shall prescribe by regulations. An election made for any taxable year may not be revoked except with the consent of the Secretary.

(c) Pro ration of each section 11 bracket amount.

For purposes of applying subsection (a)(1), the amount in each taxable income bracket in the tax table in section 11(b) shall not exceed an amount which bears the same ratio to such bracket amount as the amount included in the gross income of the United States shareholder under section 951(a) for the taxable year bears to such shareholder's pro rata share of the earnings and profits for the taxable year of all controlled foreign corporations with respect to which such shareholder includes any amount in gross income under section 951(a).

(d) Special rule for actual distributions.

The earnings and profits of a foreign corporation attributable to amounts which were included in the gross income of a United States shareholder under section 951(a) and with respect to which an election under this section applied shall, when such earnings and profits are distributed, notwithstanding the provisions of section 959(a)(1), be included in gross income to the extent that such earnings and profits so distributed exceed the amount of tax paid under this chapter on the amounts to which such election applied.

In 1988, P.L. 100-647, Sec. 1007(g)(11)(A), substituted "sections 1 and 55" for "section 1" in para. (a)(1)... Sec. 1007(g)(11)(B), substituted "sections 11 and 55" for "section 11" in para. (a)(1), effective for tax. yrs. begin. after 12/31/86.
In 1978, P.L. 95-600, Sec. 301(b)(16), amended subsec. (c), effective for tax. yrs. begin. after 12/31/78.
Prior to amendment, subsec. (c) read as follows:
"(c) Surtax exemption.
"For purposes of applying subsection (a)(1), the surtax exemption provided by section 11(c) shall not exceed, in the case of any United States shareholder, an amount which bears the same ratio to the surtax exemption as the amounts included in his gross income under section 951(a) for the taxable year bears to his pro rata share of the earnings and profits for the taxable year of all controlled foreign corporations with respect to which such United States shareholder includes any amount in gross income under section 951(a)."
In 1976, P.L. 94-455, Sec. 1906(b)(13)(A), substituted "Secretary" for "Secretary or his delegate" each place it appeared in Code Sec. 962, effective for tax. yrs. begin. after 12/31/76.
In 1975, P.L. 94-164, Sec. 4(d)(1), substituted "the surtax exemption" for "$25,000" in subsec. (c), effective for tax. yrs. end. after 12/31/75.
—P.L. 94-12, Sec. 303(c)(3), substituted "$50,000" for "$25,000" in subsec. (c), effective for tax. yrs. end. after 12/31/74 and before 1/1/76.
In 1962, P.L. 87-834, Sec. 12(a), added Code Sec. 962, effective for tax. yrs. of foreign corporations begin. after 12/31/62 and tax. yrs. of U.S. shareholders within which or with which such tax. yrs. of such foreign corporations end.

Sec. 963. Repealed.

In 1975, P.L. 94-12, Sec. 602(a)(1), repealed Code Sec. 963, effective for tax. yrs. of foreign corporations begin. after 12/31/75, and for tax. yrs. of U.S. shareholders (within the meaning of Code Sec. 951(b)) within which or with which such tax. yrs. of such foreign corporations end.
Prior to repeal, Code Sec. 963 read as follows:
"SEC. 963. RECEIPT OF MINIMUM DISTRIBUTIONS BY DOMESTIC CORPORATIONS.
"(a) General rule.
"In the case of a United States shareholder which is a domestic corporation and which consents to all the regulations prescribed by the Secretary or his delegate under this section prior to the last day prescribed by law for filing its return of the tax imposed by this chapter for the taxable year, no amount shall be included in gross income under section 951(a)(1)(A)(i) for the taxable year with respect to the subpart F income of a controlled foreign corporation, if—
"(1) in the case of a controlled foreign corporation described in subsection (c)(1), the United States shareholder receives a minimum distribution of the earnings and profits for the taxable year of such controlled foreign corporation;
"(2) in the case of controlled foreign corporations described in subsection (c)(2), the United States shareholder receives a minimum distribution with respect to the consolidated earnings and profits for the taxable year of all such controlled foreign corporations; or
"(3) in the case of controlled foreign corporations described in subsection (c)(3), the United States shareholder receives a minimum distribution of the consolidated earnings and profits for the taxable year of all such controlled foreign corporations.
"(b) Minimum distributions.
"For purposes of this section, a minimum distribution with respect to the earnings and profits for the taxable year of any controlled foreign corporation or corporations shall, in the case of any United States shareholder, be its pro rata share of an amount determined in accordance with whichever of the following tables applies to the taxable year:
"(1) Taxable years beginning in 1963 and taxable years entirely within the surcharge period ending before January 1, 1970.

If the effective foreign tax rate is (percentage)—	"The required minimum distribution of earnings and profits is (percentage)—
Under 10	90
10 or over but less than 20	86
20 or over but less than 28	82
28 or over but less then 34	75
34 or over but less than 39	68
39 or over but less than 42	55
42 or over but less than 44	40
44 or over but less than 46	27

2,645

Code Sec. 963 — Income from foreign sources

46 or over but less than 47	14
47 or over	0

"(2) Taxable years beginning in 1964 and taxable years beginning in 1969 and ending in 1970 to the extent subparagraph (B) applies.

"If the effective foreign tax rate is (percentage)—	"The required minimum distribution of earnings and profits is (percentage)—
Under 10	87
10 or over but less than 19	83
19 or over but less than 27	79
27 or over but less than 33	72
33 or over but less than 37	65
37 or over but less than 40	53
40 or over but less than 42	38
42 or over but less than 44	26
44 or over but less than 45	13
45 or over	0

"(3) Taxable years beginning after 1964 (except taxable years which include any part of the surcharge period).

"If the effective foreign tax rate is (percentage)—	"The required minimum distribution of earnings and profits is (percentage)—
Under 9	83
9 or over but less than 18	79
18 or over but less than 26	76
26 or over but less than 32	69
32 or over but less than 36	63
36 or over but less than 39	51
39 or over but less than 41	37
41 or over but less than 42	25
42 or over but less than 43	13
43 or over	0

"In the case of a taxable year beginning before the surcharge period and ending within the surcharge period, or beginning within the surcharge period and ending after the surcharge period, or beginning before January 1, 1970, and ending after December 31, 1969, the required minimum distribution shall be equal to the sum of—

"(A) that portion of the minimum distribution which would be required if the provisions of paragraph (1) were applicable to the taxable year, which the number of days in such taxable year which are within the surcharge period and before January 1, 1970, bears to the total number of days in such taxable year,

"(B) that portion of the minimum distribution which would be required if the provisions of paragraph (2) were applicable to such taxable year, which the number of days in such taxable year which are within the surcharge period and after December 31, 1969, bears to the total number of days in such taxable year, and

"(C) that portion of the minimum distribution which would be required if the provisions of paragraph (3) were applicable to such taxable year, which the number of days in such taxable year which are not within the surcharge period bears to the total number of days in such taxable year.

"As used in this subsection, the term 'surcharge period' means the period beginning January 1, 1968, and ending June 30, 1970.

"(c) Amounts to which section applies.

"(1) Foreign subsidiaries. Subsection (a)(1) shall apply to amounts which (but for the provisions of this section) would be included in the gross income of the United States shareholder under section 951(a)(1)(A)(i) by reason of its ownership, within the meaning of section 958(a)(1)(A), of stock of a controlled foreign corporation.

"(2) Chain of controlled foreign corporations. Subsection (a)(2) shall apply to amounts which (but for the provisions of this section) would be included in the gross income of the United States shareholder under section 951(a)(1)(A)(i)—

"(A) by reason of its ownership, within the meaning of section 958(a)(1)(A), of stock of a controlled foreign corporation, and

"(B) to the extent that the United States shareholder so elects, by reason of its ownership, within the meaning of section 958(a)(2), of stock of any other controlled foreign corporation (on account of its ownership of the stock described in subparagraph (A) or of stock described in this subparagraph), but only if there is taken into account the earnings and profits of each foreign corporation, whether or not a controlled foreign corporation, by reason of which the United States shareholder owns, within the meaning of section 958(a)(2), stock of such controlled foreign corporation.

"(3) All controlled foreign corporations. Except as provided in paragraph (4), subsection (a)(3) shall apply to amounts which (but for the provisions of this section) would be included in the gross income of the United States shareholder under section 951(a)(1)(A)(i)—

"(A) by reason of its ownership, within the meaning of section 958(a)(1)(A), of stock of all controlled foreign corporations in which it owns stock within the meaning of such section, and

"(B) by reason of its ownership, within the meaning of section 958(a)(2), of stock of all controlled foreign corporations in which it owns stock within the meaning of such section, but only if there is taken into account the earnings and profits of each foreign corporation, whether or not a controlled foreign corporation, by reason of which the United States shareholder owns, within the meaning of section 958(a), stock of any of such controlled foreign corporations.

"(4) Exceptions and special rules.

"(A) Less developed country corporations. If the United States shareholder so elects, subsection (a)(3) and paragraph (3) of this subsection shall not apply to amounts which would be included in the gross income of such shareholder under section 951(a)(1)(A)(i) by reason of its ownership, within the meaning of section 958(a), of stock of controlled foreign corporations which are less developed country corporations, as defined in section 955(c). This subparagraph shall not apply with respect to a less developed country corporation if, by reason of the ownership of the stock of such corporation, the United States shareholder owns, within the meaning of section 958(a)(2), stock of any other controlled foreign corporation which is not a less developed country corporation. Except as provided in the preceding sentence, an election under this subparagraph may be made only with respect to all controlled foreign corporations which are less developed country corporations and with respect to which the domestic corporation making the election is a United States shareholder.

"(B) Foreign branches. In applying subsection (a)(3) and paragraph (3) of this subsection, if a United States shareholder so elects, all branches maintained by such shareholder in foreign countries, the Commonwealth of Puerto Rico, or possessions of the United States shall, under regulations prescribed by the Secretary or his delegate, be treated as wholly owned subsidiary corporations of such shareholder organized under the laws of such foreign countries, the Commonwealth of Puerto Rico, or possessions of the United States, as the case may be. Each branch so treated shall, for purposes of this section, be considered to have distributed to the United States shareholder all of its earnings and profits for the taxable year. This subparagraph shall not apply to a branch maintained by a United States shareholder in the Commonwealth of Puerto Rico or a possession of the United States unless—

"(i) such branch would be a controlled foreign corporation (as defined in section 957) if it were incorporated under the laws of the Commonwealth of Puerto Rico or the possession of the United States, as the case may be, and

"(ii) the gross income of the United States shareholder for the taxable year includes income derived from sources within the Commonwealth of Puerto Rico and possessions of the United States.

"(C) Blocked foreign income. If a United States shareholder so elects, the provisions of subsection (a)(3) and paragraph (3) of this subsection shall not apply with respect to any foreign corporation, if it is established to the satisfaction of the Secretary or his delegate that the earnings and profits of such foreign corporation could not have been distributed to United States shareholders who own (within the meaning of section 958(a)) stock of such foreign corporation because of currency or other restrictions or limitations imposed under the laws of any foreign country.

"(d) Effective foreign tax rate.

"For purposes of this section, the term 'effective foreign tax rate' means—

"(1) with respect to a single controlled foreign corporation, the percentage which—

"(A) the income, war profits, or excess profits taxes paid or accrued to foreign countries or possessions of the United States by the controlled foreign corporation for the taxable year on or with respect to its earnings and profits for the taxable year, is of

"(B) the sum of (i) the earnings and profits of the controlled foreign corporation described in subparagraph (A) and (ii) the taxes described in subparagraph (A); and

"(2) with respect to two or more foreign corporations, the percentage which—

"(A) the total income, war profits, or excess profits taxes paid or accrued to foreign countries or possessions of the United States by such foreign corporations for the taxable year on or with respect to the consolidated earnings and profits of such foreign corporations for the taxable year, is of

"(B) the sum of (i) the consolidated earnings and profits of such foreign corporations described in subparagraph (A) and (ii) the taxes described in subparagraph (A).

"For purposes of the preceding sentence, in the case of any United States shareholder, the computation of the effective foreign tax rate applicable with respect to any controlled foreign corporation or corporations shall be made without regard to distributions made by such controlled foreign corporation or corporations to such United States shareholder.

"(e) Special rules.

"(1) Year from which distributions are made. For purposes of this section, the second sentence of section 902(c)(1) shall apply in determining from the earnings and profits of what year distributions are made by any foreign corporation, except that the Secretary or his delegate may by regulations provide a period in excess of 60 days in lieu of the 60-day period prescribed in such section.

"(2) Insufficient distributions. If—

"(A) a United States shareholder, in making its return of the tax imposed by this chapter for any taxable year, applies the provisions of this section with respect to any controlled foreign corporation,

"(B) it is subsequently determined that this section did not apply with respect to such controlled foreign corporation for such taxable year due to the failure of the United States shareholder to receive a minimum distribution with respect to such controlled foreign corporation, and

"(C) such failure is due to reasonable cause, then a subsequent distribution made with respect to such controlled foreign corporation may, if made at a time and in a manner prescribed by the Secretary or his delegate by regulations, be treated, for purposes of this chapter, as having been made for, and received in, the taxable year of the United States shareholder for which such shareholder applied the provisions of this section.

"(3) Affiliated groups of corporations. An affiliated group of corporations which makes a consolidated return under section 1501 for the taxable year, may,

Income from foreign sources

if it so elects, be treated as a single United States shareholder for purposes of applying this section for the taxable year.

"(f) Regulations.

"The Secretary or his delegate shall prescribe such regulations as he may deem necessary to carry out the provisions of this section, including regulations for the determination of the amount of foreign tax credit in the case of distributions with respect to the earnings and profits of two or more foreign corporations."

In 1969, P.L. 91-172, Sec. 701(b)(1), substituted "surcharge period ending before January 1, 1970" for "surcharge period" in the heading of para. (b)(1)... Sec. 701(b)(2), substituted "1964 and taxable years beginning in 1969 and ending in 1970 to the extent subparagraph (B) applies" for "1964" in the heading of para. (b)(2)... Sec. 701(b)(3), amended the last two sentences in subsec. (b), effective for tax. yrs. end. after 12/31/69, and begin. before 7/1/70.

Prior to amendment, the last two sentences of subsec. (b) read as follows:

"In the case of a taxable year beginning before the surcharge period and ending within the surcharge period, or beginning within the surcharge period and ending after the surcharge period, the required minimum distribution shall be an amount equal to the sum of—

"(A) that portion of the minimum distribution which would be required if the provisions of paragraph (1) were applicable to the taxable year, which the number of days in such taxable year which are within the surcharge period bears to the total number of days in such taxable year, plus

"(B) that portion of the minimum distribution which would be required if the provisions of paragraph (3) were applicable to such taxable year, which the number of days in such taxable year which are not within the surcharge period bears to the total number of days in such taxable year.

As used in this subsection, the term 'surcharge period' means the period beginning January 1, 1968, and ending June 30, 1969."

In 1968, P.L. 90-364, Sec. 102(b)(1), amended the heading of para. (b)(1)... Sec. 102(b)(2), amended the heading of para. (b)(3)... Sec. 102(b)(3), added the material immediately following the table in para. (b)(3), and added subparas. (b)(3)(A) and (B), and added the sentence following subpara. (b)(3)(A), effective as provided in Sec. 102(e) of this Act, which reads as follows:

"(e) Effective date.

"Except as provided by section 104, the amendments made by this section (other than subsection (c)) shall apply—

"(1) Insofar as they relate to taxpayers other than corporations, to taxable years ending after March 31, 1968, and beginning before July 1, 1969."

"(2) Insofar as they relate to corporations, to taxable years ending after December 31, 1967, and beginning before July 1, 1969."

For special provisions, see Sec. 104 of this Act reproduced in note following Code Sec. 6425.

Prior to amendment, the heading of para. (b)(1) read as follows:

"(1) Taxable years beginning in 1963.—"

Prior to amendment, the heading of para. (b)(3) read as follows:

"(3) Taxable years beginning after December 31, 1964.—"

In 1964, P.L. 88-272, Sec. 123(b), amended subsec. (b), effective for tax. yrs. begin. after 12/31/63.

Prior to amendment, subsec. (b) read as follows:

"(b) Minimum distributions. For purposes of this section, a minimum distribution with respect to the earnings and profits for the taxable year of any controlled foreign corporation or corporations shall, in the case of any United States shareholder, be its pro rata share of an amount determined in accordance with the following table:

If the effective foreign tax rate is (percentage)—	The required minimum distribution of earnings and profits is (percentage)—
Under 10	90
10 or over but less than 20	86
20 or over but less than 28	82
28 or over but less than 34	75
34 or over but less than 39	68
39 or over but less than 42	55
42 or over but less than 44	40
44 or over but less than 46	27
46 or over but less than 47	14
47 or over	0"

In 1962, P.L. 87-834, Sec. 12(a), added Code Sec. 963, effective for tax. yrs. of foreign corporations begin. after 12/31/62 and tax. yrs. of U.S. share-holders within which or with which such tax. yrs. of such foreign corporations end.

Sec. 964. Miscellaneous provisions.

(a) Earnings and profits.

Except as provided in section 312(k)(4), for purposes of this subpart the earnings and profits of any foreign corporation, and the deficit in earnings and profits of any foreign corporation, for any taxable year shall be determined according to rules substantially similar to those applicable to domestic corporations, under regulations prescribed by the Secretary. In determining such earnings and profits, or the deficit in such earnings and profits, the amount of any illegal bribe, kickback, or other payment (within the meaning of section 162(c)) shall not be taken into account to decrease such earnings and profits or to increase such deficit. The payments referred to in the preceding sentence are payments which would be unlawful under the Foreign Corrupt Practices Act of 1977 if the payor were a United States person.

(b) Blocked foreign income.

Under regulations prescribed by the Secretary, no part of the earnings and profits of a controlled foreign corporation for any taxable year shall be included in earnings and profits for purposes of sections 952, 955, and 956, if it is established to the satisfaction of the Secretary that such part could not have been distributed by the controlled foreign corporation to United States shareholders who own (within the meaning of section 958(a)) stock of such controlled foreign corporation because of currency or other restrictions or limitations imposed under the laws of any foreign country.

(c) Records and accounts of United States shareholders.

(1) Records and accounts to be maintained. The Secretary may by regulations require each person who is, or has been, a United States shareholder of a controlled foreign corporation to maintain such records and accounts as may be prescribed by such regulations as necessary to carry out the provisions of this subpart and subpart G.

(2) Two or more persons required to maintain or furnish the same records and accounts with respect to the same foreign corporation. Where, but for this paragraph, two or more United States persons would be required to maintain or furnish the same records and accounts as may by regulations be required under paragraph (1) with respect to the same controlled foreign corporation for the same period, the Secretary may by regulations provide that the maintenance or furnishing of such records and accounts by only one such person shall satisfy the requirements of paragraph (1) for such other persons.

(d) Treatment of certain branches.

(1) In general. For purposes of this chapter, section 6038, section 6046, and such other provisions as may be specified in regulations—

(A) a qualified insurance branch of a controlled foreign corporation shall be treated as a separate foreign corporation created under the laws of the foreign country with respect to which such branch qualifies under paragraph (2), and

(B) except as provided in regulations, any amount directly or indirectly transferred or credited from such branch to one or more other accounts of such foreign corporation shall be treated as a dividend paid to such controlled foreign corporation.

(2) Qualified insurance branch. For purposes of paragraph (1), the term "qualified insurance branch" means any branch of a controlled foreign corporation which is licensed and predominantly engaged on a permanent basis in the active conduct of an insurance business in a foreign country if—

(A) separate books and accounts are maintained for such branch,

(B) the principal place of business of such branch is in such foreign country,

(C) such branch would be taxable under subchapter L if it were a separate domestic corporation, and

(D) an election under this paragraph applies to such branch.

An election under this paragraph shall apply to the taxable year for which made and all subsequent taxable years unless revoked with the consent of the Secretary.

(3) Regulations. The Secretary shall prescribe such regulations as may be necessary or appropriate to carry out the purposes of this subsection.

(e) Gain on certain stock sales by controlled foreign corporations treated as dividends.

(1) In general. If a controlled foreign corporation sells or exchanges stock in any other foreign corporation, gain recognized on such sale or exchange shall be included in the gross income of such controlled foreign corporation as a dividend to the same extent that it would have been so included under section 1248(a) if such controlled foreign corporation were a United States person. For purposes of determining the amount which would have been so includible, the determination of whether such other foreign corporation was a controlled foreign corporation shall be made without regard to the preceding sentence.

(2) Same country exception not applicable. Clause (i) of section 954(c)(3)(A) shall not apply to any amount treated as a dividend by reason of paragraph (1).

(3) Clarification of deemed sales. For purposes of this subsection, a controlled foreign corporation shall be treated as having sold or exchanged any stock if, under any provision of this subtitle, such controlled foreign corporation is treated as having gain from the sale or exchange of such stock.

In 1997, P.L. 105-34, Sec. 1111(a), added subsec. (e), effective for gain recognized on transactions occurring after 8/5/97.

In 1988, P.L. 100-647, Sec. 6129(a), added subsec. (d), effective for tax. yrs. of foreign corporations begin. after 12/31/88.

In 1982, P.L. 97-248, Sec. 288(b)(2), added the last sentence to subsec. (a), effective for payments made after 9/3/82.

In 1981, P.L. 97-34, Sec. 206(c), substituted "section 312(k)(4)" for "section 312(k)(3)" in subsec. (a), effective for property placed in service after 12/31/80, in tax. yrs. ending after 12/31/80.

In 1976, P.L. 94-455, Sec. 1065(b), added the last sentence to subsec. (a), effective for payments described in Code Sec. 162(c) made more than 30 days after 10/14/76.

—P.L. 94-455, Sec. 1901(b)(32)(B)(iii), substituted "312(k)(3)" for "312(m)(3)" in subsec. (a), . . . Sec. 1906(b)(13)(A), substituted "Secretary" for "Secretary or his delegate" each place it appeared in Code Sec. 964, effective for tax. yrs. begin. after 12/31/76.

In 1969, P.L. 91-172, Sec. 442(b)(1), substituted "Except as provided in section 312(m)(3), for" for "For" in subsec. (a).

In 1962, P.L. 87-834, Sec. 12, added Code Sec. 964 for tax. yrs. of foreign corporations begin. after '62 and tax. yrs. of U. S. shareholders within which or with which such tax. yrs. of such foreign corporations end.

Sec. 965. Temporary dividends received deduction.

(a) Deduction.

(1) In general. In the case of a corporation which is a United States shareholder and for which the election under this section is in effect for the taxable year, there shall be allowed as a deduction an amount equal to 85 percent of the cash dividends which are received during such taxable year by such shareholder from controlled foreign corporations.

(2) Dividends paid indirectly from controlled foreign corporations. If, within the taxable year for which the election under this section is in effect, a United States shareholder receives a cash distribution from a controlled foreign corporation which is excluded from gross income under section 959(a), such distribution shall be treated for purposes of this section as a cash dividend to the extent of any amount included in income by such United States shareholder under section 951(a)(1)(A) as a result of any cash dividend during such taxable year to—

(A) such controlled foreign corporation from another controlled foreign corporation that is in a chain of ownership described in section 958(a), or

(B) any other controlled foreign corporation in such chain of ownership from another controlled foreign corporation in such chain of ownership, but only to the extent of cash distributions described in section 959(b) which are made during such taxable year to the controlled foreign corporation from which such United States shareholder received such distribution.

(b) Limitations.

(1) In general. The amount of dividends taken into account under subsection (a) shall not exceed the greater of—

(A) $500,000,000,

(B) the amount shown on the applicable financial statement as earnings permanently reinvested outside the United States, or

(C) in the case of an applicable financial statement which fails to show a specific amount of earnings permanently reinvested outside the United States and which shows a specific amount of tax liability attributable to such earnings, the amount equal to the amount of such liability divided by 0.35.

The amounts described in subparagraphs (B) and (C) shall be treated as being zero if there is no such statement or such statement fails to show a specific amount of such earnings or liability, as the case may be.

(2) Dividends must be extraordinary. The amount of dividends taken into account under subsection (a) shall not exceed the excess (if any) of—

(A) the cash dividends received during the taxable year by such shareholder from controlled foreign corporations, over

(B) the annual average for the base period years of—

(i) the dividends received during each base period year by such shareholder from controlled foreign corporations,

(ii) the amounts includible in such shareholders gross income for each base period year under section 951(a)(1)(B) with respect to controlled foreign corporations, and

(iii) the amounts that would have been included for each base period year but for section 959(a) with respect to controlled foreign corporations.

The amount taken into account under clause (iii) for any base period year shall not include any amount which is not includible in gross income by reason of an amount described in clause (ii) with respect to a prior taxable year. Amounts described in subparagraph (B) for any base period year shall be such amounts as shown on the most recent return filed for such year; except that amended returns filed after June 30, 2003, shall not be taken into account.

(3) Reduction of benefit if increase in related party indebtedness. The amount of dividends which would (but for this paragraph) be taken into account under subsection (a) shall be reduced by the excess (if any) of—

(A) the amount of indebtedness of the controlled foreign corporation to any related person (as defined in section 954(d)(3)) as of the close of the taxable year for which the election under this section is in effect, over

(B) the amount of indebtedness of the controlled foreign corporation to any related person (as so defined) as of the close of October 3, 2004.

All controlled foreign corporations with respect to which the taxpayer is a United States shareholder shall be treated as 1 controlled foreign corporation for purposes of this paragraph. The Secretary may prescribe such regulations as may be necessary or appropriate to prevent the avoidance of the purposes of this paragraph, including regulations which provide that cash dividends shall not be taken into account under subsection (a) to the extent such dividends are attributable to the direct or indirect transfer (including through the use of intervening entities or capital contributions) of cash or other property from a related person (as so defined) to a controlled foreign corporation.

(4) Requirement to invest in United States. Subsection (a) shall not apply to any dividend received by a United States shareholder unless the amount of the dividend is invested in the United States pursuant to a domestic reinvestment plan which—

(A) is approved by the taxpayer's president, chief executive officer, or comparable official before the payment of such dividend and subsequently approved by the taxpayer's board of directors, management committee, executive committee, or similar body, and

(B) provides for the reinvestment of such dividend in the United States (other than as payment for executive compensation), including as a source for the funding of worker hiring and training, infrastructure, research and development, capital investments, or the financial stabilization of the corporation for the purposes of job retention or creation.

(c) Definitions and special rules.

For purposes of this section—

(1) Applicable financial statement. The term "applicable financial statement" means—

(A) with respect to a United States shareholder which is required to file a financial statement with the Securities and Exchange Commission (or which is included in such a statement so filed by another person), the most recent audited annual financial statement (including the notes which form an integral part of such statement) of such shareholder (or which includes such shareholder)—

(i) which was so filed on or before June 30, 2003, and

(ii) which was certified on or before June 30, 2003, as being prepared in accordance with generally accepted accounting principles, and

(B) with respect to any other United States shareholder, the most recent audited financial statement (including the notes which form an integral part of such statement) of such shareholder (or which includes such shareholder)—

(i) which was certified on or before June 30, 2003, as being prepared in accordance with generally accepted accounting principles, and

(ii) which is used for the purposes of a statement or report—

(I) to creditors,

(II) to shareholders, or

(III) for any other substantial nontax purpose.

(2) Base period years.

(A) In general. The base period years are the 3 taxable years—

(i) which are among the 5 most recent taxable years ending on or before June 30, 2003, and

(ii) which are determined by disregarding—

(I) 1 taxable year for which the sum of the amounts described in clauses (i), (ii), and (iii) of subsection (b)(2)(B) is the largest, and

(II) 1 taxable year for which such sum is the smallest.

(B) Shorter period. If the taxpayer has fewer than 5 taxable years ending on or before June 30, 2003, then in lieu of applying subparagraph (A), the base period years shall include all the taxable years of the taxpayer ending on or before June 30, 2003.

(C) Mergers, acquisitions, etc.

(i) In general. Rules similar to the rules of subparagraphs (A) and (B) of section 41(f)(3) shall apply for purposes of this paragraph.

(ii) Spin-offs, etc. If there is a distribution to which section 355 (or so much of section 356 as relates to section 355) applies during the 5-year period referred to in subparagraph (A)(i) and the controlled corporation (within the meaning of section 355) is a United States shareholder—

(I) the controlled corporation shall be treated as being in existence during the period that the distributing corporation (within the meaning of section 355) is in existence, and

(II) for purposes of applying subsection (b)(2) to the controlled corporation and the distributing corporation, amounts described in subsection (b)(2)(B) which are received or includible by the distributing corporation or controlled corporation (as the case may be) before the distribution referred to in subclause (I) from a controlled foreign corporation shall be allocated between such corporations in proportion to their respective interests as United States shareholders of such controlled foreign corporation immediately after such distribution.

Subclause (II) shall not apply if neither the controlled corporation nor the distributing corporation is a United States shareholder of such controlled foreign corporation immediately after such distribution.

(3) Dividend. The term "dividend" shall not include amounts includible in gross income as a dividend under section 78, 367, or 1248. In the case of a liquidation under section 332 to which section 367(b) applies, the preceding sentence shall not apply to the extent the United States shareholder actually receives cash as part of the liquidation.

(4) Coordination with dividends received deduction. No deduction shall be allowed under section 243 or 245 for any dividend for which a deduction is allowed under this section.

(5) Controlled groups.

(A) In general. All United States shareholders which are members of an affiliated group filing a consolidated return under section 1501 shall be treated as one United States shareholder.

(B) Application of $500,000,000 limit. All corporations which are treated as a single employer under section 52(a) shall be limited to one $500,000,000 amount in subsection (b)(1)(A), and such amount shall be divided among such corporations under regulations prescribed by the Secretary.

(C) Permanently reinvested earnings. If a financial statement is an applicable financial statement for more than 1 United States shareholder, the amount applicable under subparagraph (B) or (C) of subsection (b)(1) shall be divided among such shareholders under regulations prescribed by the Secretary.

(d) Denial of foreign tax credit; denial of certain expenses.

(1) Foreign tax credit. No credit shall be allowed under section 901 for any taxes paid or accrued (or treated as paid or accrued) with respect to the deductible portion of—

   (A) any dividend, or

   (B) any amount described in subsection (a)(2) which is included in income under section 951(a)(1)(A).

No deduction shall be allowed under this chapter for any tax for which credit is not allowable by reason of the preceding sentence.

(2) **Expenses.** No deduction shall be allowed for expenses directly allocable to the deductible portion described in paragraph (1).

(3) **Deductible portion.** For purposes of paragraph (1), unless the taxpayer otherwise specifies, the deductible portion of any dividend or other amount is the amount which bears the same ratio to the amount of such dividend or other amount as the amount allowed as a deduction under subsection (a) for the taxable year bears to the amount described in subsection (b)(2)(A) for such year.

(4) **Coordination with section 78.** Section 78 shall not apply to any tax which is not allowable as a credit under section 901 by reason of this subsection.

(e) **Increase in tax on included amounts not reduced by credits, etc.**

(1) **In general.** Any tax under this chapter by reason of nondeductible CFC dividends shall not be treated as tax imposed by this chapter for purposes of determining—

   (A) the amount of any credit allowable under this chapter, or

   (B) the amount of the tax imposed by section 55.

Subparagraph (A) shall not apply to the credit under section 53 or to the credit under section 27(a) with respect to taxes which are imposed by foreign countries and possessions of the United States and are attributable to such dividends.

(2) **Limitation on reduction in taxable income, etc.**

   (A) In general. The taxable income of any United States shareholder for any taxable year shall in no event be less than the amount of nondeductible CFC dividends received during such year.

   (B) Coordination with section 172. The nondeductible CFC dividends for any taxable year shall not be taken into account—

      (i) in determining under section 172 the amount of any net operating loss for such taxable year, and

      (ii) in determining taxable income for such taxable year for purposes of the 2nd sentence of section 172(b)(2).

(3) **Nondeductible CFC dividends.** For purposes of this subsection, the term "nondeductible CFC dividends" means the excess of the amount of dividends taken into account under subsection (a) over the deduction allowed under subsection (a) for such dividends.

(f) **Election.**

The taxpayer may elect to apply this section to—

(1) the taxpayer's last taxable year which begins before the date of the enactment of this section, or

(2) the taxpayer's first taxable year which begins during the 1-year period beginning on such date.

Such election may be made for a taxable year only if made on or before the due date (including extensions) for filing the return of tax for such taxable year.

In 2005, P.L. 109-135, Sec. 403(q)(1), added "from another controlled foreign corporation in such chain of ownership" before ", but only to the extent" in subpara. (a)(2)(B)... Sec. 403(q)(2), added "cash" before "dividends" in subpara. (b)(2)(A)... Sec. 403(q)(3), added "The Secretary may prescribe such regulations as may be necessary or appropriate to prevent the avoidance of the purposes of this paragraph, including regulations which provide that cash dividends shall not be taken into account under subsection (a) to the extent such dividends are attributable to the direct or indirect transfer (including through the use of intervening entities or capital contributions) of cash or other property from a related person (as so defined) to a controlled foreign corporation." at the end of para. (b)(3)... Sec. 403(q)(4), amended para. (c)(1)... Sec. 403(q)(5), substituted "directly allocable" for "properly allocated and apportioned" in para. (d)(2)... Sec. 403(q)(6), added para. (d)(4)... Sec. 403(q)(7), added "which are imposed by foreign countries and possessions of the United States and are" after "taxes" in para. (e)(1) ... Sec. 403(q)(8), added "on or" before "before the due date" in subsec. (f), effective for tax. yrs. end. on or after 10/22/2004 as if included in Sec. 422 of the American Jobs Creation Act of 2004, P.L. 108-357.

Prior to amendment, para. (c)(1) read as follows:

"(1) Applicable financial statement. The term 'applicable financial statement' means, with respect to a United States shareholder, the most recently audited financial statement (including notes and other documents which accompany such statement) which includes such shareholder—

"(A) which is certified on or before June 30, 2003, as being prepared in accordance with generally accepted accounting principles, and

"(B) which is used for the purposes of a statement or report—

"(i) to creditors,

"(ii) to shareholders, or

"(iii) for any other substantial nontax purpose.

"In the case of a corporation required to file a financial statement with the Securities and Exchange Commission, such term means the most recent such statement filed on or before June 30, 2003."

In 2004, P.L. 108-357, Sec. 422(a), added Code Sec. 965, effective for tax. yrs. end. on or after 10/22/2004.

SUBPART G.—EXPORT TRADE CORPORATIONS

Sec.

970. Reduction of subpart F income of export trade corporations.

971. Definitions.

972. Repealed.

In 1976, P.L. 94-455, Sec. 1901(b)(27)(B), deleted the item for Code Sec. 972. Prior to repeal, that item read as follows:

"972. Consolidation of group of export trade corporations."

In 1962, added the heading of subpart G, and items 970–972.

Sec. 970. Reduction of subpart F income of export trade corporations.

(a) **Export trade income constituting foreign base company income.**

(1) **In general.** In the case of a controlled foreign corporation (as defined in section 957) which for the taxable year is an export trade corporation, the subpart F income (determined without regard to this subpart) of such corporation for such year shall be reduced by an amount equal to so much of the export trade income (as defined in section 971(b)) of such corporation for such year as constitutes foreign base company income (as defined in section 954), but only to the extent that such amount does not exceed whichever of the following amounts is the lesser:

   (A) an amount equal to 1½ times so much of the export promotion expenses (as defined in section 971(d)) of such corporation for such year as is properly allocable to the export trade income which constitutes foreign base company income of such corporation for such year, or

   (B) an amount equal to 10 percent of so much of the gross receipts for such year (or, in the case of gross receipts arising from commissions, fees, or other compensation for its services, so much of the gross amount upon the basis of which such commissions, fees, or other compensation is computed) accruing to such export trade corporation from the sale, installation, operation, maintenance, or use of property in respect of which such corporation derives export trade income as is properly allocable to the export trade income which constitutes foreign base company income of such corporation for such year.

The allocations with respect to export trade income which constitutes foreign base company income under subpara-

Income from foreign sources   Code Sec. 970

graphs (A) and (B) shall be made under regulations prescribed by the Secretary.

(2) Overall limitation. The reduction under paragraph (1) for any taxable year shall not exceed an amount which bears the same ratio to the increase in the investments in export trade assets (as defined in section 971(c)) of such corporation for such year as the export trade income which constitutes foreign base company income of such corporation for such year bears to the entire export trade income of such corporation for such year.

(b) Inclusion of certain previously excluded amounts.

Each United States shareholder of a controlled foreign corporation which for any prior taxable year was an export trade corporation shall include in his gross income under section 951(a)(1)(A)(ii), as an amount to which section 955 (relating to withdrawal of previously excluded subpart F income from qualified investment) applies, his pro rata share of the amount of decrease in the investments in export trade assets of such corporation for such year, but only to the extent that his pro rata share of such amount does not exceed an amount equal to—

(1) his pro rata share of the sum of (A) the amounts by which the subpart F income of such corporation was reduced for all prior taxable years under subsection (a), and (B) the amounts not included in subpart F income (determined without regard to this subpart) for all prior taxable years by reason of the treatment (under section 972 as in effect before the date of the enactment [10/4/76] of the Tax Reform Act of 1976) of two or more controlled foreign corporations which are export trade corporations as a single controlled foreign corporation, reduced by

(2) the sum of the amounts which were included in his gross income under section 951(a)(1)(A)(ii) under the provisions of this subsection for all prior taxable years.

(c) Investments in export trade assets.

(1) Amount of investments. For purposes of this section, the amount taken into account with respect to any export trade asset shall be its adjusted basis, reduced by any liability to which the asset is subject.

(2) Increase in investments in export trade assets. For purposes of subsection (a), the amount of increase in investments in export trade assets of any controlled foreign corporation for any taxable year is the amount by which—

(A) the amount of such investments at the close of the taxable year, exceeds

(B) the amount of such investments at the close of the preceding taxable year.

(3) Decrease in investments in export trade assets. For purposes of subsection (b), the amount of decrease in investments in export trade assets of any controlled foreign corporation for any taxable year is the amount by which—

(A) the amount of such investments at the close of the preceding taxable year (reduced by an amount equal to the amount of net loss sustained during the taxable year with respect to export trade assets), exceeds

(B) the amount of such investments at the close of the taxable year.

(4) Special rule. A United States shareholder of an export trade corporation may, under regulations prescribed by the Secretary, make the determinations under paragraphs (2) and (3) as of the close of the 75th day after the close of the years referred to in such paragraphs in lieu of on the last day of such years. A United States shareholder of an export trade corporation may, under regulations prescribed by the Secretary, make the determinations under paragraphs (2) and (3) with respect to export trade assets described in section 971(c)(3) as of the close of the years following the years referred to in such paragraphs, or as of the close of such longer period of time as such regulations may permit, in lieu of on the last day of such years and in lieu of on the day prescribed in the preceding sentence. Any election under this paragraph made with respect to any taxable year shall apply to such year and to all succeeding taxable years unless the Secretary consents to the revocation of such election.

In **1976**, P.L. 94-455, Sec. 1906(b)(13)(A), substituted "Secretary" for "Secretary or his delegate" each place it appeared in Code Sec. 970 . . . Sec. 1901(b)(27)(A), substituted "treatment (under section 972 as in effect before the date of the enactment of the Tax Reform Act of 1976) of two or more controlled foreign corporations which are export trade corporations as a single controlled foreign corporation" for "application of section 972" in para. (b)(1), effective for tax. yrs. begin. after 12/31/76.

In **1971**, P.L. 92-178, Sec. 505, provided as follows:

"SEC. 505. EXPORT TRADE CORPORATIONS.

"(a) Use of terms.

"Except as otherwise expressly provided, whenever in this section a reference is made to a section, chapter, or other provision, the reference shall be considered to be made to a section, chapter, or other provision of the Internal Revenue Code of 1954, and terms used in this section shall have the same meaning as when used in such Code.

"(b) Transfer to a DISC of assets of export trade corporation.

"(1) In general.—If a corporation (hereinafter in this section called 'parent') owns all of the outstanding stock of an export trade corporation (as defined in section 971), and the export trade corporation, during a taxable year beginning before January 1, 1976, transfers property, without receiving consideration, to a DISC (as defined in section 992(a)) all of whose outstanding stock is owned by the parent, and if the amount transferred by the export trade corporation is not less than the amount of its untaxed subpart F income (as defined in paragraph (2) of this subsection) at the time of such transfer, then—

"(A) notwithstanding section 367 or any other provision of chapter 1, no gain or loss to the export trade corporation, the parent, or the DISC shall be recognized by reason of such transfer;

"(B) the earnings and profits of the DISC shall be increased by the amount transferred to it by the export trade corporation and such amount shall be included in accumulated DISC income, and for purposes of section 861(a)(2)(D) shall be considered to be qualified export receipts;

"(C) the adjusted basis of the assets transferred to the DISC shall be the same in the hands of the DISC as in the hands of the export trade corporation;

"(D) the earnings and profits of the export trade corporation shall be reduced by the amount transferred to the DISC, to the extent thereof, with the reduction being applied first to the untaxed subpart F income and then to the other earnings and profits in the order in which they were most recently accumulated;

"(E) the basis of the parent's stock in the export trade corporation shall be decreased by the amount obtained by multiplying its basis in such stock by a fraction the numerator of which is the amount transferred to the DISC and the denominator of which is the aggregate adjusted basis of all the assets of the export trade corporation immediately before such transfer;

"(F) the basis of the parent's stock in the DISC shall be increased by the amount of the reduction under subparagraph (E) of its basis in the stock of the export trade corporation;

"(G) the property transferred to the DISC shall not be considered to reduce the investments of the export trade corporation in export trade assets for purposes of applying section 970(b); and

"(H) any foreign income taxes which would have been deemed under section 902 to have been paid by the parent if the transfer had been made to the parent shall be treated as foreign income taxes paid by the DISC.

"For purposes of this section, the amount transferred by the export trade corporation to the DISC shall be the aggregate of the adjusted basis of the properties transferred, with proper adjustments for any indebtedness secured by such property or assumed by the DISC in connection with the transfer. For purposes of this section, a foreign corporation which qualified as an export trade corporation for any 3 taxable years beginning before November 1, 1971, shall be treated as an export trade corporation.

"(2) Definition of untaxed subpart F income.— For purposes of this section, the term 'untaxed subpart F income' means with respect to an export trade corporation the amount by which—

"(A) the sum of the amounts by which the subpart F income of such corporation was reduced for the taxable year and all prior taxable years under section 970(a) and the amounts not included in subpart F income (determined without regard to subpart G of subchapter N of chapter 1) for all prior taxable years by reason of the application of section 972, exceeds

"(B) the sum of the amounts which were included in the gross income of the shareholders of such corporation under section 951(a)(1)(A)(ii) and under the provision of section 970(b) for all prior taxable years, determined without regard to the transfer of property described in paragraph (1) of this subsection.

"(3) Special cases.— If the provisions of paragraph (1) of this subsection are not applicable solely because the export trade corporation or the DISC, or both, are not owned in the manner prescribed in such paragraph, the provisions shall

2,651

nevertheless be applicable in such cases to the extent, and in accordance with such rules, as may be prescribed by the Secretary or his delegate.

"(4) Treatment of Export Trade Assets.—If the provisions of this subsection are applicable, accounts receivable held by an export trade corporation and transferred to a DISC, to the extent such receivables were export trade assets in the hands of the export trade corporation, shall be treated as qualified export assets for purposes of section 993(b)."

In 1962, P.L. 87-834, Sec. 12, added Code Sec. 970, effective for tax. yrs. of foreign corporations begin. after '62 and tax. yrs. of U. S. shareholders within which or with which such tax. yrs. of such foreign corporations end.

Sec. 971. Definitions.

(a) Export trade corporations.

For purposes of this subpart, the term "export trade corporation" means—

(1) **In general.** A controlled foreign corporation (as defined in section 957) which satisfies the following conditions:

(A) 90 percent or more of the gross income of such corporation for the 3-year period immediately preceding the close of the taxable year (or such part of such period subsequent to the effective date of this subpart during which the corporation was in existence) was derived from sources without the United States, and

(B) 75 percent or more of the gross income of such corporation for such period constituted gross income in respect of which such corporation derived export trade income.

(2) **Special rule.** If 50 percent or more of the gross income of a controlled foreign corporation in the period specified in subsection (a)(1)(A) is gross income in respect of which such corporation derived export trade income in respect of agricultural products grown in the United States, it may qualify as an export trade corporation although it does not meet the requirements of subsection (a)(1)(B).

(3) **Limitation.** No controlled foreign corporation may qualify as an export trade corporation for any taxable year beginning after October 31, 1971, unless it qualified as an export trade corporation for any taxable year beginning before such date. If a corporation fails to qualify as an export trade corporation for a period of any 3 consecutive taxable years beginning after such date, it may not qualify as an export trade corporation for any taxable year beginning after such period.

(b) Export trade income.

For the purposes of this subpart, the term "export trade income" means net income from—

(1) the sale to an unrelated person for use, consumption, or disposition outside the United States of export property (as defined in subsection (e)), or from commissions, fees, compensation, or other income from the performance of commercial, industrial, financial, technical, scientific, managerial, engineering, architectural, skilled, or other services in respect of such sales or in respect of the installation or maintenance of such export property;

(2) commissions, fees, compensation, or other income from commercial, industrial, financial, technical, scientific, managerial, engineering, architectural, skilled, or other services performed in connection with the use by an unrelated person outside the United States of patents, copyrights, secret processes and formulas, goodwill, trademarks, trade brands, franchises, and other like property acquired or developed and owned by the manufacturer, producer, grower, or extractor of export property in respect of which the export trade corporation earns export trade income under paragraph (1);

(3) commissions, fees, rentals, or other compensation or income attributable to the use of export property by an unrelated person or attributable to the use of export property in the rendition of technical, scientific, or engineering services to an unrelated person; and

(4) interest from export trade assets described in subsection (c)(4).

For purposes of paragraph (3), if a controlled foreign corporation receives income from an unrelated person attributable to the use of export property in the rendition of services to such unrelated person together with income attributable to the rendition of other services to such unrelated person, including personal services, the amount of such aggregate income which shall be considered to be attributable to the use of the export property shall (if such amount cannot be established by reference to transactions between unrelated persons) be that part of such aggregate income which the cost of the export property consumed in the rendition of such services (including a reasonable allowance for depreciation) bears to the total costs and expenses attributable to such aggregate income.

(c) Export trade assets.

For purposes of this subpart, the term "export trade assets" means—

(1) working capital reasonably necessary for the production of export trade income,

(2) inventory of export property held for use, consumption, or disposition outside the United States,

(3) facilities located outside the United States for the storage, handling, transportation, packaging, or servicing of export property, and

(4) evidences of indebtedness executed by persons, other than related persons, in connection with payment for purchases of export property for use, consumption, or disposition outside the United States, or in connection with the payment for services described in subsections (b)(2) and (3).

(d) Export promotion expenses.

For purposes of this subpart, the term "export promotion expenses" means the following expenses paid or incurred in the receipt or production of export trade income—

(1) a reasonable allowance for salaries or other compensation for personal services actually rendered for such purpose,

(2) rentals or other payments for the use of property actually used for such purpose,

(3) a reasonable allowance for the exhaustion, wear and tear, or obsolescence of property actually used for such purpose, and

(4) any other ordinary and necessary expenses of the corporation to the extent reasonably allocable to the receipt or production of export trade income.

No expense incurred within the United States shall be treated as an export promotion expense within the meaning of the preceding sentence, unless at least 90 percent of each category of expenses described in such sentence is incurred outside the United States.

(e) Export property.

For purposes of this subpart, the term "export property" means any property or any interest in property manufactured, produced, grown, or extracted in the United States.

(f) Unrelated person.

For purposes of this subpart, the term "unrelated person" means a person other than a related person as defined in section 954(d)(3).

In 1986, P.L. 99-514, Sec. 1876(m), provides:

"(m) *Treatment of certain former export trade corporations.*—

"If

Income from foreign sources — Code Sec. 982(a)

"(1) a corporation which is not an export trading corporation for its most recent taxable year ending before the date of the enactment of the Tax Reform Act of 1984 but was an export trading corporation for any prior taxable year, and

"(2)(A) such corporation may not qualify as an export trade corporation for any taxable year beginning after December 31, 1984, by reason of section 971(a)(3) of the Internal Revenue Code of 1954, or (B) such corporation makes an election, before the date 6 months after the date of the enactment of this Act, not to be treated as an export trade corporation with respect to taxable years beginning after December 31, 1984,

rules similar to the rules of paragraphs (2) and (4) of section 805(b) of the Tax Reform Act of 1984 shall apply to such corporation. For purposes of the preceding sentence, the term 'export trade corporation' has the meaning given such term by section 971 of such Code."

In 1971, P.L. 92-178, Sec. 505(c), added para. (a)(3).

In 1962, P.L. 87-834, Sec. 12, added Code Sec. 971, effective for tax. yrs. of foreign corporations begin. after '62 and tax. yrs. of U.S. shareholders within which or with which such tax. yrs. of such foreign corporations end.

Sec. 972. Repealed.

In 1976, P.L. 94-455, Sec. 1901(a)(120), repealed Code Sec. 972, for tax. yrs. begin. after '76.

Prior to repeal, Code Sec. 972 read as follows:

"SEC. 972. CONSOLIDATION OF GROUP OF EXPORT TRADE CORPORATIONS.

"For purposes of this subpart and subpart F of this part, a United States shareholder of a controlled foreign corporation which is an export trade corporation may, under regulations prescribed by the Secretary or his delegate, treat as a single controlled foreign corporation—

"(1) such controlled foreign corporation,

"(2) all controlled foreign corporations which are export trade corporations and 80 percent or more of the total combined voting power of all classes of stock entitled to vote of which is owned by such controlled foreign corporation; and

"(3) all controlled foreign corporations which are export trade corporations and 80 percent or more of the total combined voting power of all classes of stock entitled to vote of which is owned by controlled foreign corporations described in paragraph (2)."

In 1962, P.L. 87-834, Sec. 12, added Code Sec. 972 for tax. yrs. of foreign corporations begin. after '62 and tax. yrs. of U. S. shareholders within which or with which such tax. yrs. of such foreign corporations end.

SUBPART H.—[REPEALED] INCOME OF CERTAIN NONRESIDENT UNITED STATES CITIZENS SUBJECT TO FOREIGN COMMUNITY PROPERTY LAWS

Sec.
981. [Repealed.]

In 1976, P.L. 94-455, Sec. 1012(b)(3)(B), repealed subpart H and item 981.

Prior to repeal subpart H and item 981 read as follows:

"Subpart H—Income of Certain Nonresident United States Citizens Subject to Foreign Community Property Laws
"Sec.
"981. Election as to treatment of income subject to foreign community property laws."

In 1966, added subpart H and item 981.

In 1976, P.L. 94-455, Sec. 1901(b)(2), repealed Code Sec. 981, for tax. yrs. begin. after '76.

Prior to repeal Code Sec. 981 read as follows:

"SEC. 981. ELECTION AS TO TREATMENT OF INCOME SUBJECT TO FOREIGN COMMUNITY PROPERTY LAWS.

"(a) General rule.

"In the case of any taxable year beginning after December 31, 1966, if—

"(1) an individual is (A) a citizen of the United States, (B) a bona fide resident of a foreign country or countries during the entire taxable year, and (C) married at the close of the taxable year to a spouse who is a nonresident alien during the entire taxable year, and

"(2) such individual and his spouse elect to have subsection (b) apply to their community income under foreign community property laws

"then subsection (b) shall apply to such income of such individual and such spouse for the taxable year and for all subsequent taxable years for which the requirements of paragraph (1) are met, unless the Secretary or his delegate consents to a termination of the election.

"(b) Treatment of community income.

"For any taxable year to which an election made under subsection (a) applies, the community income under foreign community property laws of the husband and wife making the election shall be treated as follows:

"(1) Earned income (within the meaning of the first sentence of section 911(b)), other than trade or business income and a partner's distributive share of partnership income, shall be treated as the income of the spouse who rendered the personal services.

"(2) Trade or business income, and a partner's distributive share of partnership income, shall be treated as provided in section 1402(a)(5).

"(3) Community income not described in paragraph (1) or (2) which is derived from the separate property (as determined under the applicable foreign community property law) of one spouse shall be treated as the income of such spouse.

"(4) All other such community income shall be treated as provided in the applicable foreign community property law.

"(c) Election for pre-1967 years.

"(1) Election. If an individual meets the requirements of subsections (a)(1)(A) and (C) for any taxable year beginning before January 1, 1967, and if such individual and the spouse referred to in subsection (a)(1)(C) elect under this subsection, then paragraph (2) of this subsection shall apply to their community income under foreign community property laws for all open taxable years beginning before January 1, 1967 (whether under this chapter, the corresponding provisions of the Internal Revenue Code of 1939, or the corresponding provisions of prior revenue laws), for which the requirements of subsection (a)(1)(A) and (C) are met.

"(2) Effect of election. For any taxable year to which an election made under this subsection applies, the community income under foreign community property laws of the husband and wife making the election shall be treated as provided by subsection (b), except that the other community income described in paragraph (4) of subsection (b) shall be treated as the income of the spouse who, for such taxable year, had gross income under paragraphs (1), (2), and (3) of subsection (b), plus separate gross income, greater than that of the other spouse.

"(d) Time for making elections; period of limitations; etc.

"(1) Time. An election under subsection (a) or (c) for a taxable year may be made at any time while such year is still open, and shall be made in such manner as the Secretary or his delegate shall by regulations prescribe.

"(2) Extension of period for assessing deficiencies and making refunds. If any taxable year to which an election under subsection (a) or (c) applies is open at the time such election is made, the period for assessing a deficiency against, and the period for filing claim for credit or refund of any overpayment by, the husband and wife for such taxable year, to the extent such deficiency or overpayment is attributable to such an election, shall not expire before 1 year after the date of such election.

"(3) Alien spouse need not join in subsection (c) election in certain cases. If the Secretary or his delegate determines—

"(A) that an election under subsection (c) would not effect the liability for Federal income tax of the spouse referred to in subsection (a)(1)(C) for any taxable year, or

"(B) that the effect on such liability for tax cannot be ascertained and that to deny the election to the citizen of the United States would be inequitable and cause undue hardship,

"such spouse shall not be required to join in such election, and paragraph (2) of this subsection shall not apply with respect to such spouse.

"(4) Interest. To the extent that any overpayment or deficiency for a taxable year is attributable to an election made under this section, no interest shall be allowed or paid for any period before the day which is 1 year after the date of such election.

"(e) Definitions and special rules.

"For purposes of this section—

"(1) Deductions. Deductions shall be treated in a manner consistent with the manner provided by this section for the income to which they relate.

"(2) Open years. A taxable year of a citizen of the United States and his spouse shall be treated as 'open' if the period for assessing a deficiency against such citizen for such year has not expired before the date of the election under subsection (a) or (c), as the case may be.

"(3) Elections in case of decedents. If a husband or wife is deceased his election under this section may be made by his executor, administrator, or other person charged with his property.

"(4) Death of spouse during taxable year. In applying subsection (a)(1)(C), and in determining under subsection (c)(2) which spouse has the greater income for a taxable year, if a husband or wife dies the taxable year of the surviving spouse shall be treated as ending on the date of such death."

In 1966, P.L. 89-808, Sec. 105, added Code Sec. 981 on Nov. 13, '66.

SUBPART I.—ADMISSIBILITY OF DOCUMENTATION MAINTAINED IN FOREIGN COUNTRIES

Sec.
982. Admissibility of documentation maintained in foreign countries.

In 1982, P.L. 97-248, Sec. 337(a), added Subpart I.

Sec. 982. Admissibility of documentation maintained in foreign countries.

(a) General Rule.

If the taxpayer fails to substantially comply with any formal document request arising out of the examination of the tax treatment of any item (hereinafter in this section referred to as the "examined item") before the 90th day after the date of the mailing of such request on motion by the Secretary, any court having jurisdiction of a civil proceeding in which the tax treatment of the examined item is an issue shall prohibit the introduction by the taxpayer of any foreign-based documentation covered by such request.

(b) Reasonable cause exception.

(1) In general. Subsection (a) shall not apply with respect to any documentation if the taxpayer establishes that the failure to provide the documentation as requested by the Secretary is due to reasonable cause.

(2) Foreign nondisclosure law not reasonable cause. For purposes of paragraph (1), the fact that a foreign jurisdiction would impose a civil or criminal penalty on the taxpayer (or any other person) for disclosing the requested documentation is not reasonable cause.

(c) Formal document request.

For purposes of this section—

(1) Formal document request. The term "formal document request" means any request (made after the normal request procedures have failed to produce the requested documentation) for the production of foreign-based documentation which is mailed by registered or certified mail to the taxpayer at his last known address and which sets forth—

(A) the time and place for the production of the documentation,

(B) a statement of the reason the documentation previously produced (if any) is not sufficient,

(C) a description of the documentation being sought, and

(D) the consequences to the taxpayer of the failure to produce the documentation described in subparagraph (C).

(2) Proceeding to quash.

(A) In general. Notwithstanding any other law or rule of law, any person to whom a formal document request is mailed shall have the right to begin a proceeding to quash such request not later than the 90th day after the day such request was mailed. In any such proceeding, the Secretary may seek to compel compliance with such request.

(B) Jurisdiction. The United States district court for the district in which the person (to whom the formal document request is mailed) resides or is found shall have jurisdiction to hear any proceeding brought under subparagraph (A). An order denying the petition shall be deemed a final order which may be appealed.

(C) Suspension of 90-day period. The running of the 90-day period referred to in subsection (a) shall be suspended during any period during which a proceeding brought under subparagraph (A) is pending.

(d) Definitions and special rules.

For purposes of this section—

(1) Foreign-based documentation. The term "foreign-based documentation" means any documentation which is outside the United States and which may be relevant or material to the tax treatment of the examined item.

(2) Documentation. The term "documentation" includes books and records.

(3) Authority to extend 90-day period. The Secretary, and any court having jurisdiction over a proceeding under subsection (c)(2), may extend the 90-day period referred to in subsection (a).

(e) Suspension of statute of limitations.

If any person takes any action as provided in subsection (c)(2), the running of any period of limitations under section 6501 (relating to the assessment and collection of tax) or under section 6531 (relating to criminal prosecutions) with respect to such person shall be suspended for the period during which the proceeding under such subsection, and appeals therein, are pending.

In 1984, P.L. 98-369, Sec. 714(k), deleted para. (d)(3) and redesignated para. (d)(4) as para. (d)(3), effective for document requests (as defined in Code Sec. 982(c)(1)) mailed after 9/3/82.
Prior to deletion, para. (d)(3) read as follows:
"(3) Foreign-connected. An item shall be treated as foreign-connected if—
"(A) such item is directly or indirectly from a source outside the United States, or
"(B) such item (in whole or in part)—
"(i) purports to arise outside the United States, or
"(ii) is otherwise dependent on transactions occurring outside the United States."
In 1982, P.L. 97-248, Sec. 337(a), added Code Sec. 982, effective for document requests (as defined in Code Sec. 982(c)(1)) mailed after 9/3/82.

SUBPART J.—FOREIGN CURRENCY TRANSACTIONS

Sec.
985. Functional currency.
986. Determination of foreign taxes and foreign corporation's earnings and profits.
987. Branch transactions.
988. Treatment of certain foreign currency transactions.
989. Other definitions and special rules.

In 1988, P.L. 100-647, Sec. 1012(v)(1)(C), amended item 986.
Prior to amendment, item 986 read as follows:
"986. Determination of foreign corporation's earnings and profits and foreign taxes."
In 1986, P.L. 99-514, Sec. 126(a), added Subpart J to Part III of subchapter N of chapter 1, effective for tax. years begin. after 12/31/86.

Sec. 985. Functional currency.

(a) In general.

Unless otherwise provided in regulations, all determinations under this subtitle shall be made in the taxpayer's functional currency.

(b) Functional currency.

(1) In general. For purposes of this subtitle, the term "functional currency" means—

(A) except as provided in subparagraph (B), the dollar, or

(B) in the case of a qualified business unit, the currency of the economic environment in which a significant part of such unit's activities are conducted and which is used by such unit in keeping its books and records.

(2) Functional currency where activities primarily conducted in dollars. The functional currency of any qualified business unit shall be the dollar if activities of such unit are primarily conducted in dollars.

(3) Election. To the extent provided in regulations, the taxpayer may elect to use the dollar as the functional currency for any qualified business unit if—

(A) such unit keeps its books and records in dollars, or

(B) the taxpayer uses a method of accounting that approximates a separate transactions method.

Any such election shall apply to the taxable year for which made and all subsequent taxable years unless revoked with the consent of the Secretary.

(4) Change in functional currency treated as a change in method of accounting. Any change in the functional currency shall be treated as a change in the taxpayer's method of accounting for purposes of section 481 under procedures to be established by the Secretary.

In 1986, P.L. 99-514, Sec. 1261(a), added Code Sec. 985, as part of Subpart J to Part III of subchapter N of chapter 1, effective for tax. yrs. begin. after 12/31/86.

Income from foreign sources

Sec. 986. Determination of foreign taxes and foreign corporation's earnings and profits.

(a) Foreign income taxes.

(1) Translation of accrued taxes.

(A) In general. For purposes of determining the amount of the foreign tax credit, in the case of a taxpayer who takes foreign income taxes into account when accrued, the amount of any foreign income taxes (and any adjustment thereto) shall be translated into dollars by using the average exchange rate for the taxable year to which such taxes relate.

(B) Exception for certain taxes. Subparagraph (A) shall not apply to any foreign income taxes—

(i) paid after the date 2 years after the close of the taxable year to which such taxes relate, or

(ii) paid before the beginning of the taxable year to which such taxes relate.

(C) Exception for inflationary currencies. Subparagraph (A) shall not apply to any foreign income taxes the liability for which is denominated in any inflationary currency (as determined under regulations).

(D) Elective exception for taxes paid other than in functional currency.

(i) In general. At the election of the taxpayer, subparagraph (A) shall not apply to any foreign income taxes the liability for which is denominated in any currency other than in the taxpayer's functional currency.

(ii) Application to qualified business units. An election under this subparagraph may apply to foreign income taxes attributable to a qualified business unit in accordance with regulations prescribed by the Secretary.

(iii) Election. Any such election shall apply to the taxable year for which made and all subsequent taxable years unless revoked with the consent of the Secretary.

(E) Special rule for regulated investment companies. In the case of a regulated investment company which takes into account income on an accrual basis, subparagraphs (A) through (D) shall not apply and foreign income taxes paid or accrued with respect to such income shall be translated into dollars using the exchange rate as of the date the income accrues.

(F) Cross reference. For adjustments where tax is not paid within 2 years, see section 905(c).

(2) Translation of taxes to which paragraph (1) does not apply. For purposes of determining the amount of the foreign tax credit, in the case of any foreign income taxes to which subparagraph (A) or (E) of paragraph (1) does not apply—

(A) such taxes shall be translated into dollars using the exchange rates as of the time such taxes were paid to the foreign country or possession of the United States, and

(B) any adjustment to the amount of such taxes shall be translated into dollars using—

(i) except as provided in clause (ii), the exchange rate as of the time when such adjustment is paid to the foreign country or possession, or

(ii) in the case of any refund or credit of foreign income taxes, using the exchange rate as of the time of the original payment of such foreign income taxes.

(3) Authority to permit use of average rates. To the extent prescribed in regulations, the average exchange rate for the period (specified in such regulations) during which the taxes or adjustment is paid may be used instead of the exchange rate as of the time of such payment.

(4) Foreign income taxes. For purposes of this subsection, the term "foreign income taxes" means any income, war profits, or excess profits taxes paid or accrued to any foreign country or to any possession of the United States.

(b) Earnings and profits and distributions.

For purposes of determining the tax under this subtitle—

(1) of any shareholder of any foreign corporation, the earnings and profits of such corporation shall be determined in the corporation's functional currency, and

(2) in the case of any United States person, the earnings and profits determined under paragraph (1) (when distributed, deemed distributed, or otherwise taken into account under this subtitle) shall (if necessary) be translated into dollars using the appropriate exchange rate.

(c) Previously taxed earnings and profits.

(1) In general. Foreign currency gain or loss with respect to distributions of previously taxed earnings and profits (as described in section 959 or 1293(c)) attributable to movements in exchange rates between the times of deemed and actual distribution shall be recognized and treated as ordinary income or loss from the same source as the associated income inclusion.

(2) Distributions through tiers. The Secretary shall prescribe regulations with respect to the treatment of distributions of previously taxed earnings and profits through tiers of foreign corporations.

In 2004, P.L. 108-357, Sec. 408(a), redesignated subpara. (a)(1)(D) as (a)(1)(E) and added subpara. (a)(1)(D)...Sec. 408(b)(1), redesignated subpara. (a)(1)(E) as (a)(1)(F) [as redesignated by Sec. 408(a) of this Act, see above] and added subpara. (a)(1)(E)...Sec. 408(b)(2), added "or (E)" after "subparagraph (A)" in para. (a)(2), effective for tax. yrs. begin. after 12/31/2004.

In 1997, P.L. 105-34, Sec. 1102(a)(1), amended subsec. (a)...Sec. 1102(b)(1), redesignated para. (a)(3) as para. (a)(4) [as amended by Sec. 1104(a)(1) of this Act, see above] and added para. (a)(3), effective for taxes paid or accrued in tax. yrs. begin. after 12/31/97.

Prior to amendment, subsec. (a) read as follows:

"(a) Foreign taxes.

"(1) In general. For purposes of determining the amount of the foreign tax credit—

"(A) any foreign income taxes shall be translated into dollars using the exchange rates as of the time such taxes were paid to the foreign country or possession of the United States, and

"(B) any adjustment to the amount of foreign income taxes shall be translated into dollars using—

"(i) except as provided in clause (ii), the exchange rate as of the time when such adjustment is paid to the foreign country or possession, or

"(ii) in the case of any refund or credit of foreign income taxes, using the exchange rate as of the time of original payment of such foreign income taxes.

"(2) Foreign income taxes. For purposes of paragraph (1), 'foreign income taxes' means any income, war profits, or excess profits taxes paid to any foreign country or to any possession of the United States."

In 1988, P.L. 100-647, Sec. 1012(v)(1)(A), amended all that preceded subsec. (c), effective for tax. yrs. begin. after 12/31/86.

Prior to amendment, all of Codes Sec. 986 that preceded Subsec. (c), read as follows:

"SEC. 986. DETERMINATION OF FOREIGN CORPORATION'S EARNINGS AND PROFITS AND FOREIGN TAXES.

"(a) Earnings and profits and distributions.

For purposes of determining the tax under this subtitle—

"(1) of any shareholder of any foreign corporation, the earnings and profits of such corporation shall be determined in the corporation's functional currency, and

"(2) in the case of any United States person, the earnings and profits determined under paragraph (1) (when distributed, deemed distributed, or otherwise taken into account under this subtitle) shall (if necessary) be translated into dollars using the appropriate exchange rate.

"(b) Foreign taxes.

"(1) In general. In determining the amount of foreign taxes deemed paid under section 902 or 960—

"(A) any foreign income taxes paid by a foreign corporation shall be translated into dollars using the exchange rates as of the time of payment, and

"(B) any adjustment to the amount of foreign income taxes paid by a foreign corporation shall be translated into dollars using—

"(i) except as provided in clause (ii), the appropriate exchange rate as of when such adjustment is made, and "(ii) in the case of any refund or credit of foreign taxes, using the exchange rate as of the time of original payment of such foreign income taxes.

"(2) Foreign income taxes. For purposes of paragraph (1), 'foreign income taxes' means any income, war profits, or excess profits taxes paid to any foreign country or to any possession of the United States."

In 1986, P.L. 99-514, Sec. 1261(a), added Code Sec. 986, as part of Subpart J to Part III of Subchapter N of chapter 1, effective for taxable years begin. after 12/31/86.

Sec. 987. Branch transactions.

In the case of any taxpayer having 1 or more qualified business units with a functional currency other than the dollar, taxable income of such taxpayer shall be determined—

(1) by computing the taxable income or loss separately for each such unit in its functional currency,

(2) by translating the income or loss separately computed under paragraph (1) at the appropriate exchange rate, and

(3) by making proper adjustments (as prescribed by the Secretary) for transfers of property between qualified business units of the taxpayer having different functional currencies, including—

(A) treating post-1986 remittances from each such unit as made on a pro rata basis out of post-1986 accumulated earnings, and

(B) treating gain or loss determined under this paragraph as ordinary income or loss, respectively, and sourcing such gain or loss by reference to the source of the income giving rise to post-1986 accumulated earnings.

In 1988, P.L. 100-647, Sec. 1012(v)(1)(B), added "and" at the end of para. (2), substituted a period for ", and" at the end of para. (3), and deleted para. (4), effective for tax. yrs. begin. after 12/31/86.

Prior to deletion, para. (4) read as follows:

"(4) by translating foreign income taxes paid by each qualified business unit of the taxpayer in the same manner as provided under section 986(b)."

In 1986, P.L. 99-514, Sec. 1261(a), added Code Sec. 987, as part of Subpart J to Part III of Subchapter N of chapter 1, effective for tax. yrs. begin. after 12/31/86.

Sec. 988. Treatment of certain foreign currency transactions.

(a) General rule.

Notwithstanding any other provision of this chapter—

(1) Treatment as ordinary income or loss.

(A) In general. Except as otherwise provided in this section, any foreign currency gain or loss attributable to a section 988 transaction shall be computed separately and treated as ordinary income or loss (as the case may be).

(B) Special rule for forward contracts, etc. Except as provided in regulations, a taxpayer may elect to treat any foreign currency gain or loss attributable to a forward contract, a futures contract, or option described in subsection (c)(1)(B)(iii) which is a capital asset in the hands of the taxpayer and which is not a part of a straddle (within the meaning of section 1092(c), without regard to paragraph (4) thereof) as capital gain or loss (as the case may be) if the taxpayer makes such election and identifies such transaction before the close of the day on which such transaction is entered into (or such earlier time as the Secretary may prescribe).

(2) Gain or loss treated as interest for certain purposes. To the extent provided in regulations, any amount treated as ordinary income or loss under paragraph (1) shall be treated as interest income or expense (as the case may be).

(3) Source.

(A) In general. Except as otherwise provided in regulations, in the case of any amount treated as ordinary income or loss under paragraph (1) (without regard to paragraph (1)(B)), the source of such amount shall be determined by reference to the residence of the taxpayer or the qualified business unit of the taxpayer on whose books the asset, liability, or item of income or expense is properly reflected.

(B) Residence. For purposes of this subpart—

(i) In general. The residence of any person shall be—

(I) in the case of an individual, the country in which such individual's tax home (as defined in section 911(d)(3)) is located,

(II) in the case of any corporation, partnership, trust, or estate which is a United States person (as defined in section 7701(a)(30)), the United States, and

(III) in the case of any corporation, partnership, trust, or estate which is not a United States person, a country other than the United States.

If an individual does not have a tax home (as so defined), the residence of such individual shall be the United States if such individual is a United States citizen or a resident alien and shall be a country other than the United States if such individual is not a United States citizen or a resident alien.

(ii) Exception. In the case of a qualified business unit of any taxpayer (including an individual), the residence of such unit shall be the country in which the principal place of business of such qualified business unit is located.

(iii) Special rule for partnerships. To the extent provided in regulations, in the case of a partnership, the determination of residence shall be made at the partner level.

(C) Special rule for certain related party loans. Except to the extent provided in regulations, in the case of a loan by a United States person or a related person to a 10-percent owned foreign corporation which is denominated in a currency other than the dollar and bears interest at a rate at least 10 percentage points higher than the Federal mid-term rate (determined under section 1274(d)) at the time such loan is entered into, the following rules shall apply:

(i) For purposes of section 904 only, such loan shall be marked to market on an annual basis.

(ii) Any interest income earned with respect to such loan for the taxable year shall be treated as income from sources within the United States to the extent of any loss attributable to clause (i).

For purposes of this subparagraph, the term "related person" has the meaning given such term by section 954(d)(3), except that such section shall be applied by substituting "United States person" for "controlled foreign corporation" each place such term appears.

(D) 10-percent owned foreign corporation. The term "10-percent owned foreign corporation" means any foreign corporation in which the United States person owns directly or indirectly at least 10 percent of the voting stock.

(b) Foreign currency gain or loss.

For purposes of this section—

(1) Foreign currency gain. The term "foreign currency gain" means any gain from a section 988 transaction to the extent such gain does not exceed gain realized by reason of changes in exchange rates on or after the booking date and before the payment date.

(2) Foreign currency loss. The term "foreign currency loss" means any loss from a section 988 transaction to the extent such loss does not exceed the loss realized by rea-

son of changes in exchange rates on or after the booking date and before the payment date.

(3) Special rule for certain contracts, etc. In the case of any section 988 transaction described in subsection (c)(1)(B)(iii), any gain or loss from such transaction shall be treated as foreign currency gain or loss (as the case may be).

(c) Other definitions.

For purposes of this section—

(1) Section 988 transaction.

(A) In general. The term "section 988 transaction" means any transaction described in subparagraph (B) if the amount which the taxpayer is entitled to receive (or is required to pay) by reason of such transaction—

(i) is denominated in terms of a nonfunctional currency, or

(ii) is determined by reference to the value of 1 or more nonfunctional currencies.

(B) Description of transactions. For purposes of subparagraph (A), the following transactions are described in this subparagraph:

(i) The acquisition of a debt instrument or becoming the obligor under a debt instrument.

(ii) Accruing (or otherwise taking into account) for purposes of this subtitle any item of expense or gross income or receipts which is to be paid or received after the date on which so accrued or taken into account.

(iii) Entering into or acquiring any forward contract, futures contract, option, or similar financial instrument.

The Secretary may prescribe regulations excluding from the application of clause (ii) any class of items the taking into account of which is not necessary to carry out the purposes of this section by reason of the small amounts or short periods involved, or otherwise.

(C) Special rules for disposition of nonfunctional currency.

(i) In general. In the case of any disposition of any nonfunctional currency—

(I) such disposition shall be treated as a section 988 transaction, and

(II) any gain or loss from such transaction shall be treated as foreign currency gain or loss (as the case may be).

(ii) Nonfunctional currency. For purposes of this section, the term "nonfunctional currency" includes coin or currency, and nonfunctional currency denominated demand or time deposits or similar instruments issued by a bank or other financial institution.

(D) Exception for certain instruments marked to market.

(i) In general. Clause (iii) of subparagraph (B) shall not apply to any regulated futures contract or nonequity option which would be marked to market under section 1256 if held on the last day of the taxable year.

(ii) Election out.

(I) In general. The taxpayer may elect to have clause (i) not apply to such taxpayer. Such an election shall apply to contracts held at any time during the taxable year for which such election is made or any succeeding taxable year unless such election is revoked with the consent of the Secretary.

(II) Time for making election. Except as provided in regulations, an election under subclause (I) for any taxable year shall be made on or before the 1st day of such taxable year (or, if later, on or before the 1st day during such year on which the taxpayer holds a contract described in clause (i)).

(III) Special rule for partnerships, etc. In the case of a partnership, an election under subclause (I) shall be made by each partner separately. A similar rule shall apply in the case of an S corporation.

(iii) Treatment of certain partnerships. This subparagraph shall not apply to any income or loss of a partnership for any taxable year if such partnership made an election under subparagraph (E)(iii)(V) for such year or any preceding year.

(E) Special rules for certain funds.

(i) In general. In the case of a qualified fund, clause (iii) of subparagraph (B) shall not apply to any instrument which would be marked to market under section 1256 if held on the last day of the taxable year (determined after the application of clause (iv)).

(ii) Special rule where electing partnership does not qualify. If any partnership made an election under clause (iii)(V) for any taxable year and such partnership has a net loss for such year or any succeeding year from instruments referred to in clause (i), the rules of clauses (i) and (iv) shall apply to any such loss year whether or not such partnership is a qualified fund for such year.

(iii) Qualified fund defined. For purposes of this subparagraph, the term "qualified fund" means any partnership if—

(I) at all times during the taxable year (and during each preceding taxable year to which an election under subclause (V) applied), such partnership has at least 20 partners and no single partner owns more than 20 percent of the interests in the capital or profits of the partnership,

(II) the principal activity of such partnership for such taxable year (and each such preceding taxable year) consists of buying and selling options, futures, or forwards with respect to commodities,

(III) at least 90 percent of the gross income of the partnership for the taxable year (and for each such preceding taxable year) consisted of income or gains described in subparagraph (A), (B), or (G) of section 7704(d)(1) or gain from the sale or disposition of capital assets held for the production of interest or dividends,

(IV) no more than a de minimis amount of the gross income of the partnership for the taxable year (and each such preceding taxable year) was derived from buying and selling commodities, and

(V) an election under this subclause applies to the taxable year.

An election under subclause (V) for any taxable year shall be made on or before the 1st day of such taxable year (or, if later, on or before the 1st day during such year on which the partnership holds an instrument referred to in clause (i)). Any such election shall apply to the taxable year for which made and all succeeding taxable years unless revoked with the consent of the Secretary.

(iv) Treatment of certain currency contracts.

(I) In general. Except as provided in regulations, in the case of a qualified fund, any bank forward contract, any foreign currency futures contract traded on a foreign exchange, or to the extent provided in regulations any similar instrument, which is not otherwise a section 1256 contract shall be treated as a section 1256 contract for purposes of section 1256.

(II) Gains and losses treated as short-term. In the case of any instrument treated as a section 1256 contract under subclause (I), subparagraph (A) of section 1256(a)(3) shall be applied by substituting "100 percent" for "40 percent" (and subparagraph (B) of such section shall not apply).

(v) Special rules for clause (iii)(I).

(I) Certain general partners. The interest of a general partner in the partnership shall not be treated as failing to meet the 20-percent ownership requirements of clause (iii)(I) for any taxable year of the partnership if, for the taxable year of the partner in which such partnership taxable year ends, such partner (and each corporation filing a consolidated return with such partner) had no ordinary income or loss from a section 988 transaction which is foreign currency gain or loss (as the case may be).

(II) Treatment of incentive compensation. For purposes of clause (iii)(I), any income allocable to a general partner as incentive compensation based on profits rather than capital shall not be taken into account in determining such partner's interest in the profits of the partnership.

(III) Treatment of tax-exempt partners. Except as provided in regulations, the interest of a partner in the partnership shall not be treated as failing to meet the 20-percent ownership requirements of clause (iii)(I) if none of the income of such partner from such partnership is subject to tax under this chapter (whether directly or through 1 or more pass-thru entities).

(IV) Look-thru rule. In determining whether the requirements of clause (iii)(I) are met with respect to any partnership, except to the extent provided in regulations, any interest in such partnership held by another partnership shall be treated as held proportionately by the partners in such other partnership.

(vi) Other special rules. For purposes of this subparagraph—

(I) Related persons. Interests in the partnership held by persons related to each other (within the meaning of sections 267(b) and 707(b)) shall be treated as held by 1 person.

(II) Predecessors. References to any partnership shall include a reference to any predecessor thereof.

(III) Inadvertent terminations. Rules similar to the rules of section 7704(e) shall apply.

(IV) Treatment of certain Debt Instruments. For purposes of clause (iii)(IV), any debt instrument which is a section 988 transaction shall be treated as a commodity.

(2) Booking date. The term "booking date" means—

(A) in the case of a transaction described in paragraph (1)(B)(i), the date of acquisition or on which the taxpayer becomes the obligor, or

(B) in the case of a transaction described in paragraph (1)(B)(ii), the date on which accrued or otherwise taken into account.

(3) Payment date. The term "payment date" means the date on which the payment is made or received.

(4) Debt instrument. The term "debt instrument" means a bond, debenture, note, or certificate or other evidence of indebtedness. To the extent provided in regulations, such term shall include preferred stock.

(5) Special rules where taxpayer takes or makes delivery. If the taxpayer takes or makes delivery in connection with any section 988 transaction described in paragraph (1)(B)(iii), any gain or loss (determined as if the taxpayer sold the contract, option, or instrument on the date on which he took or made delivery for its fair market value on such date) shall be recognized in the same manner as if such contract, option, or instrument were so sold.

(d) Treatment of 988 hedging transactions.

(1) In general. To the extent provided in regulations, if any section 988 transaction is part of a 988 hedging transaction, all transactions which are part of such 988 hedging transaction shall be integrated and treated as a single transaction or otherwise treated consistently for purposes of this subtitle. For purposes of the preceding sentence, the determination of whether any transaction is a section 988 transaction shall be determined without regard to whether such transaction would otherwise be marked-to-market under section 475 or 1256 and such term shall not include any transaction with respect to which an election is made under subsection (a)(1)(B). Sections 475, 1092, and 1256 shall not apply to a transaction covered by this subsection.

(2) 988 hedging transaction. For purposes of paragraph (1), the term "988 hedging transaction" means any transaction—

(A) entered into by the taxpayer primarily—

(i) to manage risk of currency fluctuations with respect to property which is held or to be held by the taxpayer, or

(ii) to manage risk of currency fluctuations with respect to borrowings made or to be made, or obligations incurred or to be incurred, by the taxpayer, and

(B) identified by the Secretary or the taxpayer as being a 988 hedging transaction.

(e) Application to individuals.

(1) In general. The preceding provisions of this section shall not apply to any section 988 transaction entered into by an individual which is a personal transaction.

(2) Exclusion for certain personal transactions. If—

(A) nonfunctional currency is disposed of by an individual in any transaction, and

(B) such transaction is a personal transaction,

no gain shall be recognized for purposes of this subtitle by reason of changes in exchange rates after such currency was acquired by such individual and before such disposition. The preceding sentence shall not apply if the gain which would otherwise be recognized on the transaction exceeds $200.

(3) Personal transactions. For purposes of this subsection, the term "personal transaction" means any transaction entered into by an individual, except that such term shall not include any transaction to the extent that expenses properly allocable to such transaction meet the requirements of—

(A) section 162 (other than traveling expenses described in subsection (a)(2) thereof), or

(B) section 212 (other than that part of section 212 dealing with expenses incurred in connection with taxes).

In 1999, P.L. 106-170, Sec. 532(b)(3), substituted "to manage" for "to reduce" in clause (d)(2)(A)(i) and (ii), effective for any instrument held, acquired, or entered into, any transaction entered into, and supplies held or acquired on or after 12/17/99.

In 1997, P.L. 105-34, Sec. 1104(a), amended subsec. (e), effective for tax. yrs. begin. after 12/31/97.

Prior to amendment, subsec. (e) read as follows:

"(e) Application to individuals.

"This section shall apply to section 988 transactions entered into by an individual only to the extent expenses properly allocable to such transactions meet the requirements of section 162 or 212 (other than that part of section 212 dealing with expenses incurred in connection with taxes)."

In 1993, P.L. 103-66, Sec. 13223(b)(1)(A), substituted "section 475 or 1256" for "section 1256" in para. (d)(1)... Sec. 13223(b)(1)(B), substituted "section 475, 1092, and 1256" for "section 1092 and 1256" in para. (d)(1), effective for tax. yrs. end. on or after 12/31/93. Sec. 13223(c)(2) and (3) of this Act provides:

"(2) Change in method of accounting. In the case of any taxpayer required by this section to change its method of accounting for any taxable year—

"(A) such change shall be treated as initiated by the taxpayer,

"(B) such change shall be treated as made with the consent of the Secretary, and

"(C) except as provided in paragraph (3), the net amount of the adjustments required to be taken into account by the taxpayer under section 481 of the Internal Revenue Code of 1986 shall be taken into account ratably over the 5-taxable year period beginning with the first taxable year ending on or after December 31, 1993.

"(3) Special rule for floor specialists and market makers.

"(A) In general. If—

"(i) a taxpayer (or any predecessor) used the last-in first-out (LIFO) method of accounting with respect to any qualified securities for the 5-taxable year period ending with its last taxable year ending before December 31, 1993, and

"(ii) any portion of the net amount described in paragraph (2)(C) is attributable to the use of such method of accounting,

then paragraph (2)(C) shall be applied by taking such portion into account ratably over the 15-taxable year period beginning with the first taxable year ending on or after December 31, 1993.

"(B) Qualified security. For purposes of this paragraph, the term 'qualified security' means any security acquired—

"(i) by a floor specialist (as defined in section 1236(d)(2) of the Internal Revenue Code of 1986) in connection with the specialist's duties as a specialist on an exchange, but only if the security is one in which the specialist is registered with the exchange, or

"(ii) by a taxpayer who is a market maker in connection with the taxpayer's duties as a market maker, but only if—

"(I) the security is included on the National Association of Security Dealers Automated Quotation System,

"(II) the taxpayer is registered as a market maker in such security with the National Association of Security Dealers, and

"(III) as of the last day of the taxable year preceding the taxpayer's first taxable year ending on or after December 31, 1993, the taxpayer (or any predecessor) has been actively and regularly engaged as a market maker in such security for the 2-year period ending on such date (or, if shorter, the period beginning 61 days after the security was listed in such quotation system and ending on such date)."

In 1989, P.L. 101-239, Sec. 7811(i)(7), added "Notwithstanding any other provision of this chapter—" after the heading of subsec. (a), effective for tax. yrs. begin. after 12/31/86.

In 1988, P.L. 100-647, Sec. 1012(v)(2)(A), added para. (c)(5), effective as provided in Sec. 1012(v)(2)(B) of this Act, which reads as follows:

"(B) The amendment made by subparagraph (A) shall not apply in any case in which the taxpayer takes or makes delivery before June 11, 1987."

—P.L. 100-647, Sec. 1012(v)(3)(A), added para. (b)(3)... Sec. 1012(v)(3)(B), amended clause (c)(1)(B)(i)(II)... Sec. 1012(v)(3)(C), added "or" at the end of subpara. (c)(2)(A), substituted the period for ", or" at the end of subpara. (c)(2)(B), and deleted subpara. (c)(2)(C)... Sec. 1012(v)(3)(D), amended para. (c)(3)... Sec. 1012(v)(4), substituted "this subtitle" for "this section" in para. (d)(1)... Sec. 1012(v)(6), amended clause (c)(1)(B)(iii)... Sec. 1012(v)(7), added clause (a)(3)(B)(iii)... Sec. 1012(v)(8), added the last sentence of clause (a)(3)(B)(i), effective for tax. yrs. begin. after 12/31/86.

Prior to amendment, subclause (c)(1)(B)(i)(II) read as follows:

"(II) for purposes of determining the foreign currency gain or loss from such transaction, paragraphs (1) and (2) of subsection (b) shall be applied by substituting 'acquisition date' for 'booking date' and 'disposition' for 'payment date'".

Prior to deletion, subpara. (c)(2)(C) read as follows:

"(C) in the case of a transaction described in paragraph (1)(B)(iii), the date on which the position is entered into or acquired."

Prior to amendment, para. (c)(3) read as follows:

"(3) Payment date. The term 'payment date' means—

"(A) in the case of a transaction described in paragraph (1)(B)(i) or (ii), the date on which payment is made or received, or

"(B) in the case of a transaction described in paragraph (1)(B)(iii), the date payment is made or received or the date the taxpayer's rights with respect to the position are terminated."

Prior to amendment, clause (c)(1)(B)(iii) read as follows:

"(iii) Entering into or acquiring any forward contract, futures contract, option, or similar financial instrument if such instrument is not marked to market at the close of the taxable year under section 1256."

—P.L. 100-647, Sec. 6130(a), deleted "unless such instrument would be marked to market under section 1256 if held on the last day of the taxable year" at the end of clause (c)(1)(B)(iii) [as amended by Sec. 1012(v)(6) of this Act]... Sec. 6130(b), added subparas. (c)(1)(D) and (c)(1)(E), effective as provided by Sec. 6130(d) of this Act which reads as follows:

"(d) Effective date.

"(1) In general.—The amendments made by this section shall apply with respect to forward contracts, future contracts, options, and similar instruments entered into or acquired after October 21, 1988.

"(2) Time for making election.—The time for making any election under subparagraph (D) or (E) of section 988(c)(1) of the 1986 Code shall not expire before the date 30 days after the date of the enactment of this Act.

"(3) Transitional rules.—

"(A) The requirements of subclause (IV) of section 988(c)(1)(E)(iii) of the 1986 Code (as added by subsection (b)) shall not apply to periods before the date of the enactment of this Act.

"(b) In the case of any partner in an existing partnership, the 20-percent ownership requirements of subclause (I) of such section 988(c)(1)(E)(iii) shall be treated as met during any period during which such partner does not own a percentage interest in the capital or profits of such partnership greater than 33⅓ percent (or, if lower, the lowest such percentage interest of such partner during any prior period after October 21, 1988, during which such partnership is in existence). For purposes of the preceding sentence, the term 'existing partnership' means any partnership if—

"(i) such partnership was in existence on October 21, 1988, and principally engaged on such date in buying and selling options, futures, or forwards with respect to commodities, or

"(ii) a registration statement was filed with respect to such partnership with the Securities and Exchange Commission on or before such date and such registration statement indicated that the principal activity of such partnership will consist of buying and selling instruments referred to in clause (i)."

In 1986, P.L. 99-514, Sec. 1261(a), added Code Sec. 988, as part of Subpart J to Part III of Subchapter N of chapter 1, effective for tax. yrs. begin. after 12/31/86.

Sec. 989. Other definitions and special rules.

(a) Qualified business unit.

For purposes of this subpart, the term "qualified business unit" means any separate and clearly identified unit of a trade or business of a taxpayer which maintains separate books and records.

(b) Appropriate exchange rate.

Except as provided in regulations, for purposes of this subpart, the term "appropriate exchange rate" means—

(1) in the case of an actual distribution of earnings and profits, the spot rate on the date such distribution is included in income,

(2) in the case of an actual or deemed sale or exchange of stock in a foreign corporation treated as a dividend under section 1248, the spot rate on the date the deemed dividend is included in income,

(3) in the case of any amounts included in income under section 951(a)(1)(A) or 1293(a), the average exchange rate for the taxable year of the foreign corporation, or

(4) in the case of any other qualified business unit of a taxpayer, the average exchange rate for the taxable year of such qualified business unit.

For purposes of the preceding sentence, any amount included in income under section 951(a)(1)(B) shall be treated as an actual distribution made on the last day of the taxable year for which such amount was so included.

(c) Regulations

The Secretary shall prescribe such regulations as may be necessary or appropriate to carry out the purposes of this subpart including regulations—

(1) setting forth procedures to be followed by taxpayers with qualified business units using a net worth method of accounting before the enactment of this subpart,

(2) limiting the recognition of foreign currency loss on certain remittances from qualified business units,

(3) providing for the recharacterization of interest and principal payments with respect to obligations denominated in certain hyperinflationary currencies,

(4) providing for alternative adjustments to the application of section 905(c),

(5) providing for the appropriate treatment of related party transactions (including transactions between qualified business units of the same taxpayer), and

(6) setting forth procedures for determining the average exchange rate for any period.

In 2004, P.L. 108-357, Sec. 413(c)(17), deleted ", 551(a),", after "951(a)(1)(A)" in para. (b)(3), effective for tax. yrs. of foreign corporations begin. after 12/31/2004, and for tax. yrs. of United States shareholders with or within which such tax. yrs. of foreign corporations end.

In 1997, P.L. 105-34, Sec. 1102(b)(2), deleted "and" at the end of para. (c)(4), substituted ", and" for the period at the end of para. (c)(5), and added para. (c)(6) ... Sec. 1102(b)(3), deleted "weighted" before "average exchange rate" each place it appeared in paras. (b)(3) and (4), effective for taxes paid or accrued in tax. yrs. begin. after 12/31/97.

In 1996, P.L. 104-188, Sec. 1501(b)(8), substituted "section 951(a)(1)(B)" for "subparagraph (B) or (C) of section 951(a)(1)" in subsec. (b), effective for tax. yrs. of foreign corporations begin. after 12/31/96, and for tax. yrs. of U.S. shareholders in which or with which such tax. yrs. of foreign corporations end.

In 1993, P.L. 103-66, Sec. 13231(c)(4)(C), substituted "subparagraph (B) or (C) of section 951(a)(1)" for "section 951(a)(1)(B)" in subsec. (b), effective for tax. yrs. of foreign corporations begin. after 9/30/93, and for tax. yrs. of U.S. shareholders in which or with which such tax. yrs. of foreign corporations end.

In 1988, P.L. 100-647, Sec. 1012(v)(5)(A), substituted "951(a)(1)(A)" for "951(a)" in para. (b)(3) ... Sec. 1012(v)(5)(B), added the last sentence in subsec. (b), effective for tax. yrs. begin. after 12/31/86.

In 1986, P.L. 99-514, Sec. 1261(a), added Code Sec. 989, as part of Subpart J of Part III of Subchapter N of chapter 1, effective for tax. yrs. begin. after 12/31/86.

PART IV.—DOMESTIC INTERNATIONAL SALES CORPORATIONS

Subpart

A. Treatment of qualifying corporations.

B. Treatment of distributions to shareholders.

SUBPART A.—TREATMENT OF QUALIFYING CORPORATIONS

Sec.

991. Taxation of a domestic international sales corporation.

992. Requirements of a domestic international sales corporation.

993. Definitions.

994. Inter-company pricing rules.

In 1971, P.L. 92-178, Sec. 501, added Part IV.

Sec. 991. Taxation of a domestic international sales corporation.

For purposes of the taxes imposed by this subtitle upon a DISC (as defined in section 992(a)), a DISC shall not be subject to the taxes imposed by this subtitle.

In 1998, P.L. 105-206, Sec. 6011(e)(1), deleted "except for the tax imposed by chapter 5" before the period at the end of Code Sec. 991, effective 8/5/97.

In 1986, P.L. 99-514, Sec. 1876(h), added the last sentence to Sec. 805(b)(2)(A) of P.L. 98-369, reproduced below ... Sec. 1876(n), added subpara. (c) to Sec. 805(b)(2) of P.L. 98-369, reproduced below.

In 1984, P.L. 98-369, Sec. 805(b), [as amended by P.L. 99-514, Secs. 1876(h) and (n), see above] provides:

"(b) Transition rules for DISC's.—

"(1) Close of 1984 taxable years of disc's.—

"(A) In general.— For purposes of applying the Internal Revenue Code of 1954, the taxable year of each DISC which begins before January 1, 1985, and which (but for this paragraph) would include January 1, 1985, shall close on December 31, 1984. For purposes of such Code, the requirements of section 992(a)(1)(B) of such Code (relating to percentage of qualified export assets on last day of the taxable year) shall not apply to any taxable year ending on December 31, 1984.

"(B) Underpayments of estimated tax.— To the extent provided in regulations prescribed by the Secretary of the Treasury or his delegate, no addition to tax shall be made under section 6654 or 6655 of such Code with respect to any underpayment of any installment required to be paid before April 13, 1985, to the extent the underpayment was created or increased by reason of subparagraph (A).

"(2) Exemption of accumulated disc income from tax.—

"(A) In general.— For purposes of applying the Internal Revenue Code of 1954 with respect to actual distributions made after December 31, 1984, by a DISC or former DISC which was a DISC on December 31, 1984, any accumulated DISC income of a DISC or former DISC (within the meaning of section 996(f)(1) of such Code) which is derived before January 1, 1985, shall be treated as previously taxed income (within the meaning of section 996(f)(2) of such Code) with respect to which there had previously been a deemed distribution to which section 996(e)(1) of such Code applied. For purposes of the preceding sentence, the term 'actual distribution' includes a distribution in liquidation, and the earnings and profits of any corporation receiving a distribution not included in gross income by reason of the preceding sentence shall be increased by the amount of such distribution.

"(B) Exception for distribution of amounts previously disqualified.— Subparagraph (A) shall not apply to the distribution of any accumulated DISC income of a DISC or former DISC to which section 995(b)(2) of such Code applied by reason of any revocation or disqualification (other than a revocation which under regulations prescribed by the Secretary results solely from the provisions of this title.

"(C) Treatment of distribution of accumulated DISC income received by cooperatives.— In the case of any actual distribution received by an organization described in section 1381 of such Code and excluded from the gross income of such corporation by reason of subparagraph (A)—

"(i) such amount shall not be included in the gross income of any member of such organization when distributed in the form of a patronage dividend or otherwise, and

"(ii) no deduction shall be allowed to such organization by reason of any such distribution.

"(3) Installment treatment of certain deemed distributions of shareholders.—

"(A) In general.— Notwithstanding section 995(b) of such Code, if a shareholder of a DISC elects the application of this paragraph, any qualified distribution shall be treated, for purposes of such Code, as received by such shareholder in 10 equal installments on the last day of each of the 10 taxable years of such shareholder which begins after the first taxable year of such shareholder beginning in 1984. The preceding sentence shall apply without regard to whether the DISC exists after December 31, 1984.

"(B) Qualified distribution.— The term 'qualified distribution' means any distribution which a shareholder is deemed to have received by reason of section 995(b) of such Code with respect to income derived by the DISC in the first taxable year of the DISC beginning—

"(i) in 1984, and

"(ii) after the date in 1984 on which the taxable year of such shareholder begins.

"(C) Shorter period for installments.— The Secretary of the Treasury or his delegate may by regulations provide for the election by any shareholder to be treated as receiving a qualified distribution over such shorter period as the taxpayer may elect.

"(D) Elections.— Any election under this paragraph shall be made at such time and in such manner as the Secretary of the Treasury or his delegate may prescribe.

"(4) Treatment of transfers from disc to fsc.— Except to the extent provided in regulations, section 367 of such Code shall not apply to transfers made before January 1, 1986 (or, if later, the date 1 year after the date on which the corporation ceases to be a DISC), to a FSC of qualified export assets (as defined in section 993(b) of such Code) held on August 4, 1983, by a DISC in a transaction described in section 351 or 368(a)(1) of such Code.

"(5) Deemed termination of a disc.— Under regulations prescribed by the Secretary, if any controlled group of corporations of which a DISC is a member establishes a FSC, then any DISC which is a member of such group shall be treated as having terminated its DISC status.

"(6) Definitions.— For purposes of this subsection, the terms 'DISC' and 'former DISC' have the respective meanings given to such terms by section 992 of such Code."

In 1971, P.L. 92-178, Sec. 501, added Code Sec. 991, effective for tax. yrs. end. 12/31/71, except that a corporation may not be a DISC for any tax. yr. begin. before 1/1/72.

—P.L. 92-178, Sec. 506, provided as follows:

"SEC 506. SUBMISSION OF ANNUAL REPORTS TO CONGRESS.

"The Secretary of the Treasury shall, commencing for the calendar year 1972, submit an annual report to the Congress within 15½ months following the close of each calendar year setting forth an analysis of the operation and effect of the provisions of this title."

Sec. 992. Requirements of a domestic international sales corporation.

(a) Definition of "DISC" and "Former DISC".

(1) DISC. For purposes of this title, the term "DISC" means, with respect to any taxable year, a corporation which is incorporated under the laws of any State and satisfies the following conditions for the taxable year:

(A) 95 percent or more of the gross receipts (as defined in section 993(f)) of such corporation consist of qualified export receipts (as defined in section 993(a)),

(B) the adjusted basis of the qualified export assets (as defined in section 993(b)) of the corporation at the close of the taxable year equals or exceeds 95 percent of the sum of the adjusted basis of all assets of the corporation at the close of the taxable year,

(C) such corporation does not have more than one class of stock and the par or stated value of its outstanding stock is at least $2,500 on each day of the taxable year, and

(D) the corporation has made an election pursuant to subsection (b) to be treated as a DISC and such election is in effect for the taxable year.

(2) Status as DISC after having filed a return as a DISC. The Secretary shall prescribe regulations setting forth the conditions under and the extent to which a corporation which has filed a return as a DISC for a taxable year shall be treated as a DISC for such taxable year for all purposes of this title, notwithstanding the fact that the corporation has failed to satisfy the conditions of paragraph (1).

(3) "Former DISC". For purposes of this title, the term "former DISC" means, with respect to any taxable year, a corporation which is not a DISC for such year but was a DISC in a preceding taxable year and at the beginning of the taxable year has undistributed previously taxed income or accumulated DISC income.

(b) Election.

(1) Election.

(A) An election by a corporation to be treated as a DISC shall be made by such corporation for a taxable year at any time during the 90-day period immediately preceding the beginning of the taxable year, except that the Secretary may give his consent to the making of an election at such other times as he may designate.

(B) Such election shall be made in such manner as the Secretary shall prescribe and shall be valid only if all persons who are shareholders in such corporation on the first day of the first taxable year for which such election is effective consent to such election.

(2) Effect of election. If a corporation makes an election under paragraph (1), then the provisions of this part shall apply to such corporation for the taxable year of the corporation for which made and for all succeeding taxable years and shall apply to each person who at any time is a shareholder of such corporation for all periods on or after the first day of the first taxable year of the corporation for which the election is effective.

(3) Termination of election.

(A) Revocation. An election under this subsection made by any corporation may be terminated by revocation of such election for any taxable year of the corporation after the first taxable year of the corporation for which the election is effective. A termination under this paragraph shall be effective with respect to such election—

(i) for the taxable year in which made, if made at any time during the first 90 days of such taxable year, or

(ii) for the taxable year following the taxable year in which made, if made after the close of such 90 days,

and for all succeeding taxable years of the corporation. Such termination shall be made in such manner as the Secretary shall prescribe by regulations.

(B) Continued failure to be DISC.—If a corporation is not a DISC for each of any 5 consecutive taxable years of the corporation for which an election under this subsection is effective, the election shall be terminated and not be in effect for any taxable year of the corporation after such 5th year.

(c) Distributions to meet qualification requirements.

(1) In general. Subject to the conditions provided by paragraph (2), a corporation which for a taxable year does not satisfy a condition specified in paragraph (1)(A) (relating to gross receipts) or (1)(B) (relating to assets) of subsection (a) shall nevertheless be deemed to satisfy such condition for such year if it makes a pro rata distribution of property after the close of the taxable year to its shareholders (designated at the time of such distribution as a distribution to meet qualification requirements) with respect to their stock in an amount which is equal to—

(A) if the condition of subsection (a)(1)(A) is not satisfied, the portion of such corporation's taxable income attributable to its gross receipts which are not qualified export receipts for such year,

(B) if the condition of subsection (a)(1)(B) is not satisfied, the fair market value of those assets which are not qualified export assets on the last day of such taxable year, or

(C) if neither of such conditions is satisfied, the sum of the amounts required by subparagraphs (A) and (B).

(2) Reasonable cause for failure. The conditions under paragraph (1) shall be deemed satisfied in the case of a distribution made under such paragraph—

(A) if the failure to meet the requirements of subsection (a)(1)(A) or (B), and the failure to make such distribution prior to the date on which made, are due to reasonable cause; and

(B) the corporation pays, within the 30-day period beginning with the day on which such distribution is made, to the Secretary, if such corporation makes such distribution after the 15th day of the 9th month after the close of the taxable year, an amount determined by multiplying (i) the amount equal to 4½ percent of such distribution, by (ii) the number of its taxable years which begin after the taxable year with respect to which such distribution is made and before such distribution is made. For purposes of this title, any payment made pursuant to this paragraph shall be treated as interest.

(3) Certain distributions made within 8½ months after close of taxable year deemed for reasonable cause. A distribution made on or before the 15th day of the 9th month after the close of the taxable year shall be deemed for reasonable cause for purposes of paragraph (2)(A) if—

(A) at least 70 percent of the gross receipts of such corporation for such taxable year consist of qualified export receipts, and

(B) the adjusted basis of the qualified export assets held by the corporation on the last day of each month of the taxable year equals or exceeds 70 percent of the sum of the adjusted basis of all assets held by the corporation on such day.

(d) Ineligible corporations.

The following corporations shall not be eligible to be treated as a DISC—

(1) a corporation exempt from tax by reason of section 501,

(2) a personal holding company (as defined in section 542),

(3) a financial institution to which section 581 applies,

(4) an insurance company subject to the tax imposed by subchapter L,

(5) a regulated investment company (as defined in section 851(a)),

(6) a China Trade Act corporation receiving the special deduction provided in section 941(a), or

(7) an S corporation.

(e) Coordination with personal holding company provisions in case of certain produced film rents.

If—

(1) a corporation (hereinafter in this subsection referred to as "subsidiary") was established to take advantage of the provisions of this part, and

(2) a second corporation (hereinafter in this subsection referred to as "parent") throughout the taxable year owns directly at least 80 percent of the stock of the subsidiary,

then, for purposes of applying subsection (d)(2) and section 541 (relating to personal holding company tax) to the subsidiary for the taxable year, there shall be taken into account under section 543(a)(5) (relating to produced film rents) any interest in a film acquired by the parent and transferred to the subsidiary as if such interest were acquired by the subsidiary at the time it was acquired by the parent.

In 2007, P.L. 110-172, Sec. 11(g)(16), added "and" at the end of subpara. (a)(1)(C), substituted a period for ", and" at the end of subpara. (a)(1)(D), and deleted subpara. (a)(1)(E), enacted 12/29/2007.
Prior to deletion, subpara. (a)(1)(E) read as follows:
"(E) such corporation is not a member of any controlled group of which a FSC is a member."
In 1996, P.L. 104-188, Sec. 1616(b)(11), deleted "or 593" after "581" in para. (d)(3), effective for tax. yrs. begin. after 12/31/95.
In 1984, P.L. 98-369, Sec. 802(c)(1)(A)-(C), deleted "and" from the end of subpara. (a)(1)(C), substituted ", and" for the period at the end of subpara. (a)(1)(D), and added new subpara. (a)(1)(E), effective for transactions after 12/31/84, in tax. yrs. end. after 12/31/84.
In 1982, P.L. 97-354, Sec. 5(a)(32), amended para. (d)(7), effective for tax. yrs. begin. after 12/31/82.
Prior to amendment, para. (d)(7) read as follows:
"(7) an electing small business corporation (as defined in section 1371(b))."
In 1976, P.L. 94-455, Sec. 1906(b)(13)(A), substituted "Secretary" for "Secretary or his delegate" each place it appeared in Code Sec. 992, effective for tax. yrs. begin. after 12/31/76.
In 1971, P.L. 92-178, Sec. 501, added Code Sec. 992, effective for tax. yrs. end. 12/31/71, except that a corporation may not be a DISC for any tax. yr. begin. before 1/1/72, as provided in Sec. 507.

Sec. 993. Definitions.
(a) Qualified Export Receipts.

(1) General rule. For purposes of this part, except as provided by regulations under paragraph (2), the qualified export receipts of a corporation are—

(A) gross receipts from the sale, exchange, or other disposition of export property,

(B) gross receipts from the lease or rental of export property, which is used by the lessee of such property outside the United States,

(C) gross receipts for services which are related and subsidiary to any qualified sale, exchange, lease, rental, or other disposition of export property by such corporation,

(D) gross receipts from the sale, exchange, or other disposition of qualified export assets (other than export property),

(E) dividends (or amounts includible in gross income under section 951) with respect to stock of a related foreign export corporation (as defined in subsection (e)),

(F) interest on any obligation which is a qualified export asset,

(G) gross receipts for engineering or architectural services for construction projects located (or proposed for location) outside the United States, and

(H) gross receipts for the performance of managerial services in furtherance of the production of other qualified export receipts of a DISC.

(2) Excluded receipts. The Secretary may under regulations designate receipts from the sale, exchange, lease, rental, or other disposition of export property, and from services, as not being receipts described in paragraph (1) if he determines that such sale, exchange, lease, rental, or other disposition, or furnishing of services—

(A) is for ultimate use in the United States;

(B) is accomplished by a subsidy granted by the United States or any instrumentality thereof;

(C) is for use by the United States or any instrumentality thereof where the use of such export property or services is required by law or regulation.

For purposes of this part, the term "qualified export receipts" does not include receipts from a corporation which is a DISC for its taxable year in which the receipts arise and which is a member of a controlled group (as defined in paragraph (3)) which includes the recipient corporation.

(3) Definition of controlled group. For purposes of this part, the term "controlled group" has the meaning assigned to the term "controlled group of corporations" by section 1563(a), except that the phrase "more than 50 percent" shall be substituted for the phrase "at least 80 percent" each place it appears therein, and section 1563(b) shall not apply.

(b) Qualified export assets.

For purposes of this part, the qualified export assets of a corporation are—

(1) export property (as defined in subsection (c));

(2) assets used primarily in connection with the sale, lease, rental, storage, handling, transportation, packaging, assembly, or servicing of export property, or the performance of engineering or architectural services described in subparagraph (G) of subsection (a)(1) or managerial services in furtherance of the production of qualified export receipts described in subparagraphs (A), (B), (C), and (G) of subsection (a)(1);

(3) accounts receivable and evidences of indebtedness which arise by reason of transactions of such corporation or of another corporation which is a DISC and which is a member of a controlled group which includes such corporation described in subparagraph (A), (B), (C), (D), (G), or (H), of subsection (a)(1);

(4) money, bank deposits, and other similar temporary investments, which are reasonably necessary to meet the working capital requirements of such corporation;

(5) obligations arising in connection with a producer's loan (as defined in subsection (d));

(6) stock or securities of a related foreign export corporation (as defined in subsection (e));

(7) obligations issued, guaranteed, or insured, in whole or in part, by the Export-Import Bank of the United States or the Foreign Credit Insurance Association in those cases where such obligations are acquired from such Bank or Association or from the seller or purchaser of the goods or services with respect to which such obligations arose;

(8) obligations issued by a domestic corporation organized solely for the purpose of financing sales of export property pursuant to an agreement with the Export-Import Bank of the United States under which such corporation makes export loans guaranteed by such bank; and

(9) amounts (other than reasonable working capital) on deposit in the United States that are utilized during the period provided for in, and otherwise in accordance with, regulations prescribed by the Secretary to acquire other qualified export assets.

(c) Export property.

(1) In general. For purposes of this part, the term "export property" means property—

(A) manufactured, produced, grown, or extracted in the United States by a person other than a DISC,

(B) held primarily for sale, lease, or rental, in the ordinary course of trade or business, by, or to, a DISC, for direct use, consumption, or disposition outside the United States, and

(C) not more than 50 percent of the fair market value of which is attributable to articles imported into the United States.

In applying subparagraph (C), the fair market value of any article imported into the United States shall be its appraised value, as determined by the Secretary under section 402 of the Tariff Act of 1930 (19 U.S.C. 1401a) in connection with its importation.

(2) Excluded property. For purposes of this part, the term "export property" does not include—

(A) property leased or rented by a DISC for use by any member of a controlled group (as defined in subsection (a)(3)) which includes the DISC,

(B) patents, inventions, models, designs, formulas, or processes, whether or not patented, copyrights (other than films, tapes, records, or similar reproductions, for commercial or home use), good will, trademarks, trade brands, franchises, or other like property,

(C) products of a character with respect to which a deduction for depletion is allowable (including oil, gas, coal, or uranium products) under section 613 or 613A,

(D) products the export of which is prohibited or curtailed under section 7(a) of the Export Administration Act of 1979 to effectuate the policy set forth in paragraph (2)(C) of section 3 of such Act (relating to the protection of the domestic economy), or

(E) any unprocessed timber which is a softwood.

Subparagraph (C) shall not apply to any commodity or product at least 50 percent of the fair market value of which is attributable to manufacturing or processing, except that subparagraph (C) shall apply to any primary product from oil, gas, coal, or uranium. For purposes of the preceding sentence, the term "processing" does not include extracting or handling, packing, packaging, grading, storing, or transporting. For purposes of subparagraph (E), the term "unprocessed timber" means any log, cant, or similar form of timber.

(3) Property in short supply. If the President determines that the supply of any property described in paragraph (1) is insufficient to meet the requirements of the domestic economy, he may by Executive order designate the property as in short supply. Any property so designated shall be treated as property not described in paragraph (1) during the period beginning with the date specified in the Executive order and ending with the date specified in an Executive order setting forth the President's determination that the property is no longer in short supply.

(d) Producer's loans.

(1) In general. An obligation, subject to the rules provided in paragraphs (2) and (3), shall be treated as arising out of a producer's loan if—

(A) the loan, when added to the unpaid balance of all other producer's loans made by the DISC, does not exceed the accumulated DISC income at the beginning of the month in which the loan is made;

(B) the obligation is evidenced by a note (or other evidence of indebtedness) with a stated maturity date not more than 5 years from the date of the loan;

(C) the loan is made to a person engaged in the United States in the manufacturing, production, growing, or extraction of export property determined without regard to subparagraph (C) or (D) of subsection (c)(2), (referred to hereinafter as the "borrower"); and

(D) at the time of such loan it is designated as a producer's loan.

(2) Limitation. An obligation shall be treated as arising out of a producer's loan only to the extent that such loan, when added to the unpaid balance of all other producer's loans to the borrower outstanding at the time such loan is made, does not exceed an amount determined by multiplying the sum of—

(A) the amount of the borrower's adjusted basis determined at the beginning of the borrower's taxable year in which the loan is made, in plant, machinery, and equipment, and supporting production facilities in the United States;

(B) the amount of the borrower's property held primarily for sale, lease, or rental, to customers in the ordinary course of trade or business, at the beginning of such taxable year; and

(C) the aggregate amount of the borrower's research and experimental expenditures (within the meaning of section 174) in the United States during all preceding taxable years beginning after December 31, 1971,

by the percentage which the borrower's receipts, during the 3 taxable years immediately preceding the taxable year (but not including any taxable year commencing prior to 1972) in which the loan is made, from the sale, lease, or rental outside the United States of property which would be export property (determined without regard to subparagraph (C) or (D) of subsection (c)(2)) if held by a DISC is of the gross receipts during such 3 taxable years from the sale, lease, or rental of property held by such borrower primarily for sale, lease, or rental to customers in the ordinary course of the trade or business of such borrower.

(3) Increased investment requirement. An obligation shall be treated as arising out of a producer's loan in a taxable year only to the extent that such loan, when added to the unpaid balance of all other producer's loans to the borrower made during such taxable year, does not exceed an amount equal to—

(A) the amount by which the sum of the adjusted basis of assets described in paragraph (2)(A) and (B) on the last day of the taxable year in which the loan is made exceeds the sum of the adjusted basis of such assets on the first day of such taxable year; plus

(B) the aggregate amount of the borrower's research and experimental expenditures (within the meaning of section 174) in the United States during such taxable year.

(4) Special limitation in the case of domestic film maker.

(A) In general. In the case of a borrower who is a domestic film maker and who incurs an obligation to a DISC for the making of a film, and such DISC is engaged in the trade or business of selling, leasing, or renting films which are export property, the limitation described in paragraph (2) may be determined (to the extent provided under regulations prescribed by the Secretary) on the basis of—

(i) the sum of the amounts described in subparagraphs (A), (B), and (C) thereof plus reasonable estimates of all such amounts to be incurred at any time by the borrower with respect to films which are commenced within the taxable year in which the loan is made, and

(ii) the percentage which, based on the experience of producers of similar films, the annual receipts of such producers from the sale, lease, or rental of such films outside the United States is of the annual gross receipts of such producers from the sale, lease, or rental of such films.

Code Sec. 993(d)(4)(B) — DISC

(B) Domestic film maker. For purposes of this paragraph, a borrower is a domestic film maker with respect to a film if—

(i) such borrower is a United States person within the meaning of section 7701(a)(30), except that with respect to a partnership, all of the partners must be United States persons, and with respect to a corporation, all of its officers and at least a majority of its directors must be United States persons;

(ii) such borrower is engaged in the trade or business of making the film with respect to which the loan is made;

(iii) the studio, if any, used or to be used for the taking of photographs and the recording of sound incorporated into such film is located in the United States;

(iv) the aggregate playing time of portions of such film photographed outside the United States does not or will not exceed 20 percent of the playing time of such film; and

(v) not less than 80 percent of the total amount paid or to be paid for services performed in the making of such film is paid or to be paid to persons who are United States persons at the time such services are performed or consists of amounts which are fully taxable by the United States.

(C) Special rules for application of subparagraph (B)(v). For purposes of clause (v) of subparagraph (B)—

(i) there shall not be taken into account any amount which is contingent upon receipts or profits of the film and which is fully taxable by the United States (within the meaning of clause (ii)); and

(ii) any amount paid or to be paid to a United States person, to a non-resident alien individual, or to a corporation which furnishes the services of an officer or employee to the borrower with respect to the making of a film, shall be treated as fully taxable by the United States only if the total amount received by such person, individual, officer, or employee for services performed in the making of such film is fully included in gross income for purposes of this chapter.

(e) Related foreign export corporation.

In determining whether a corporation (hereinafter in this subsection referred to as "the domestic corporation") is a DISC—

(1) **Foreign international sales corporation.** A foreign corporation is a related foreign export corporation if—

(A) stock possessing more than 50 percent of the total combined voting power of all classes of stock entitled to vote is owned directly by the domestic corporation,

(B) 95 percent or more of such foreign corporation's gross receipts for its taxable year ending with or within the taxable year of the domestic corporation consists of qualified export receipts described in subparagraphs (A), (B), (C), and (D) of subsection (a)(1) and interest on any obligation described in paragraphs (3) and (4) of subsection (b), and

(C) the adjusted basis of the qualified export assets (described in paragraphs (1), (2), (3), and (4) of subsection (b)) held by such foreign corporation at the close of such taxable year equals or exceeds 95 percent of the sum of the adjusted basis of all assets held by it at the close of such taxable year.

(2) **Real property holding company.** A foreign corporation is a related foreign export corporation if—

(A) stock possessing more than 50 percent of the total combined voting power of all classes of stock entitled to vote is owned directly by the domestic corporation, and

(B) its exclusive function is to hold real property for the exclusive use (under a lease or otherwise) of the domestic corporation.

(3) **Associated foreign corporation.** A foreign corporation is a related foreign export corporation if—

(A) less than 10 percent of the total combined voting power of all classes of stock entitled to vote of such foreign corporation is owned (within the meaning of section 1563(d) and (e)) by the domestic corporation or by a controlled group of corporations (within the meaning of section 1563) of which the domestic corporation is a member, and

(B) the ownership of stock or securities in such foreign corporation by the domestic corporation is determined (under regulations prescribed by the Secretary) to be reasonably in furtherance of a transaction or transactions giving rise to qualified export receipts of the domestic corporation.

(f) Gross receipts.

For purposes of this part, the term "gross receipts" means the total receipts from the sale, lease, or rental of property held primarily for sale, lease, or rental in the ordinary course of trade or business, and gross income from all other sources. In the case of commissions on the sale, lease, or rental of property, the amount taken into account for purposes of this part as gross receipts shall be the gross receipts on the sale, lease, or rental of the property on which such commissions arose.

(g) United States defined.

For purposes of this part, the term "United States" includes the Commonwealth of Puerto Rico and the possessions of the United States.

In 1993, P.L. 103-66, Sec. 13239(b)(1), deleted "or" at the end of subpara. (c)(2)(C), substituted ", or" for the period at the end of subpara. (c)(2)(D), and added subpara. (c)(2)(E)... Sec. 13239(b)(2), added the last sentence at the end of para. (c)(2), effective for sales, exchanges, or other dispositions after 8/10/93.

In 1984, P.L. 98-369, Sec. 802(c)(2), substituted "the term 'controlled group of corporations' by" for "such term by" in para. (a)(3), effective for transactions after 12/31/84, in tax. yrs. end. after 12/31/84.

In 1979, P.L. 96-72, Sec. 22(c)(1), substituted "7(a) of the Export Administration Act of 1979" for "4(b) of the Export Administration Act of 1969 (50 U.S.C. App. 2403(b))" in subpara. (c)(2)(D)... Sec. 22(c)(2), substituted "(C)" for "(A)" after "paragraph (2)" in subpara. (c)(2)(D), effective upon the expiration of the Export Administration Act of 1969.

—P.L. 96-39, Sec. 202(c)(2), substituted "of the Tariff Act of 1930 (19 U.S.C. 1401a)" for "or 402a of the Tariff Act of 1930 (19 U.S.C., sec. 1401a or 1402)" in para. (c)(1), effective 1/1/81.

In 1976, P.L. 94-455, Sec. 1101(b)(1), deleted "or" at the end of subpara. (c)(2)(B)... Sec. 1101(b)(2), substituted "under section 613 or 613A" for "under section 611" in subpara. (c)(2)(C), effective for sales, exchanges, and other dispositions made after 3/18/75, in tax. yrs. end. after 3/18/75.

—P.L. 94-455, Sec. 1101(c)(1), added "determined without regard to subparagraph (C) or (D) of subsection (c)(2),", after "export property", in subpara. (d)(1)(C)... Sec. 1101(c)(2), added "(determined without regard to subparagraph (C) or (D) of subsection (c)(2))", after "of property which would be export property", in para. (d)(2), effective for tax. yrs. end. after 3/18/75.

—P.L. 94-455, Sec. 1101(f), amended the effective date for changes made by Sec. 603(a) of P.L. 94-12, by adding Sec. 603(b)(2) of P.L. 94-12, which provides exceptions to the effective date, see below.

—P.L. 94-455, Sec. 1906(b)(13)(A), substituted "Secretary" for "Secretary or his delegate" each place it appeared in Code Sec. 993, effective for tax. yrs. begin. after 12/31/76.

In 1975, P.L. 94-12, Sec. 603(a), struck out "or" at the end of subpara. (c)(2)(A), substituted ", or" for the period at the end of subpara. (c)(2)(B), and added new subparas. (c)(2)(C) and (D), effective with respect to sales, exchanges, and other dispositions made after 3/18/75, in tax. yrs. end. after 3/18/75, except as provided in Sec. 603(b)(2) [added by Sec. 1101(f) of P.L. 94-455] which reads:

"(2) Binding contract. — The amendments made by subsection (a) shall not apply to sales, exchanges, and other dispositions made after March 18, 1975, but before March 19, 1980, if such sales, exchanges, and other dispositions are made pursuant to a fixed contract. The term 'fixed contract' means a contract which was, on March 18, 1975, and is at all times thereafter binding on the DISC or a taxpayer which was a member of the same controlled group (within the meaning of section 993(a)(3) of the Internal Revenue Code of 1954) as the DISC, which was entered into after the date on which the DISC qualified as a DISC and the DISC and the taxpayer became members of the same controlled group, and under which the price and quantity of the products sold, exchanged, or otherwise disposed of cannot be increased."

In 1974, P.L. 93-482, Sec. 3(a), substituted "such corporation or of another corporation which is a DISC and which is a member of a controlled group which includes such corporation" for "such corporation" in para. (b)(3), effective with respect to tax. yrs. begin. after 12/31/73, or, at the election of the taxpayer made within 90 days after 10/26/74, with respect to any tax. yr. begin. after 12/31/71, and before 1/1/74.

In 1971, P.L. 92-178, Sec. 501, added Code Sec. 993, effective for tax. yrs. end. 12/31/71, except that a corporation may not be a DISC for any tax. yr. begin. before 1/1/72, as provided in Sec. 507.

Sec. 994. Inter-company pricing rules.
(a) In general.

In the case of a sale of export property to a DISC by a person described in section 482, the taxable income of such DISC and such person shall be based upon a transfer price which would allow such DISC to derive taxable income attributable to such sale (regardless of the sales price actually charged) in an amount which does not exceed the greatest of—

(1) 4 percent of the qualified export receipts on the sale of such property by the DISC plus 10 percent of the export promotion expenses of such DISC attributable to such receipts,

(2) 50 percent of the combined taxable income of such DISC and such person which is attributable to the qualified export receipts on such property derived as the result of a sale by the DISC plus 10 percent of the export promotion expenses of such DISC attributable to such receipts, or

(3) taxable income based upon the sale price actually charged (but subject to the rules provided in section 482).

(b) Rules for commissions, rentals, and marginal costing.

The Secretary shall prescribe regulations setting forth—

(1) rules which are consistent with the rules set forth in subsection (a) for the application of this section in the case of commissions, rentals, and other income, and

(2) rules for the allocation of expenditures in computing combined taxable income under subsection (a)(2) in those cases where a DISC is seeking to establish or maintain a market for export property.

(c) Export promotion expenses.

For purposes of this section, the term "export promotion expenses" means those expenses incurred to advance the distribution or sale of export property for use, consumption, or distribution outside of the United States, but does not include income taxes. Such expenses shall also include freight expenses to the extent of 50 percent of the cost of shipping export property aboard airplanes owned and operated by United States persons or ships documented under the laws of the United States in those cases where law or regulations does not require that such property be shipped aboard such airplanes or ships.

In 1976, P.L. 94-455, Sec. 1906(b)(13)(A), substituted "Secretary" for "Secretary or his delegate" in subsec. (b), effective for tax. yrs. begin. after 12/31/76.

In 1971, P.L. 92-178, Sec. 501, added Code Sec. 994, effective for tax. yrs. end. 12/31/71, except that a corporation may not be a DISC for any tax. yr. begin. before 1/1/72.

SUBPART B.—TREATMENT OF DISTRIBUTIONS TO SHAREHOLDERS

Sec.
995. Taxation of DISC income to shareholders.
996. Rules for allocation in the case of distributions and losses.
997. Special subchapter C rules.

Sec. 995. Taxation of DISC income to shareholders.
(a) General rule.

A shareholder of a DISC or former DISC shall be subject to taxation on the earnings and profits of a DISC as provided in this chapter, but subject to the modifications of this subpart.

(b) Deemed distributions.

(1) **Distributions in qualified years.** A shareholder of a DISC shall be treated as having received a distribution taxable as a dividend with respect to his stock in an amount which is equal to his pro rata share of the sum (or, if smaller, the earnings and profits for the taxable year) of—

(A) the gross interest derived during the taxable year from producer's loans,

(B) the gain recognized by the DISC during the taxable year on the sale or exchange of property, other than property which in the hands of the DISC is a qualified export asset, previously transferred to it in a transaction in which gain was not recognized in whole or in part, but only to the extent that the transferor's gain on the previous transfer was not recognized,

(C) the gain (other than the gain described in subparagraph (B)) recognized by the DISC during the taxable year on the sale or exchange of property (other than property which in the hands of the DISC is stock in trade or other property described in section 1221(a)(1)) previously transferred to it in a transaction in which gain was not recognized in whole or in part, but only to the extent that the transferor's gain on the previous transfer was not recognized and would have been treated as ordinary income if the property had been sold or exchanged rather than transferred to the DISC,

(D) 50 percent of the taxable income of the DISC for the taxable year attributable to military property,

(E) the taxable income of the DISC attributable to qualified export receipts of the DISC for the taxable year which exceed $10,000,000,

(F) the sum of—

(i) in the case of a shareholder which is a C corporation, one-seventeenth of the excess of taxable income of the DISC for the taxable year, before the reduction for any distributions during the year, over the sum of the amounts deemed distributed for the taxable year under subparagraphs (A), (B), (C), (D), and (E),

(ii) an amount equal to $16/17$ of the excess referred to in clause (i), multiplied by the international boycott factor determined under section 999, and

(iii) any illegal bribe, kickback, or other payment (within the meaning of section 162(c)) paid by or on behalf of the DISC directly or indirectly to an official, employee, or agent in fact of a government, and

(G) the amount of foreign investment attributable to producer's loans (as defined in subsection (d)) of a DISC for the taxable year.

Distributions described in this paragraph shall be deemed to be received on the last day of the taxable year of the DISC in which the income was derived. In the case of a distribution described in subparagraph (G), earnings and profits for the taxable year shall include accumulated earnings and profits.

(2) **Distributions upon disqualification.**

(A) A shareholder of a corporation which revoked its election to be treated as a DISC or failed to satisfy the conditions of section 992(a)(1) for a taxable year shall be deemed to have received (at the time specified in subparagraph (B)) a distribution taxable as a dividend equal to his pro rata share of the DISC income of such corporation accumulated during the immediately preceding consecutive taxable years for which the corporation was a DISC.

(B) Distributions described in subparagraph (A) shall be deemed to be received in equal installments on the last day of each of the 10 taxable years of the corporation following the year of the termination or disqualification described in subparagraph (A) (but in no case over more than twice the number of immediately preceding consecutive taxable years during which the corporation was a DISC).

(3) **Taxable income attributable to military property.**

(A) In general. For purposes of paragraph (1)(D), taxable income of a DISC for the taxable year attributable to military property shall be determined by only taking into account—

(i) the gross income of the DISC for the taxable year which is attributable to military property, and

(ii) the deductions which are properly apportioned or allocated to such income.

(B) Military property. For purposes of subparagraph (A), the term "military property" means any property which is an arm, ammunition, or implement of war designated in the munitions list published pursuant to section 38 of the Arms Export Control Act (22 U.S.C. 2778).

(4) **Aggregation of qualified export receipts.**

(A) In general. For purposes of applying paragraph (1)(E), all DISC's which are members of the same controlled group shall be treated as a single corporation.

(B) Allocation. The dollar amount under paragraph (1)(E) shall be allocated among the DISC's which are members of the same controlled group in a manner provided in regulations prescribed by the Secretary.

(c) **Gain on disposition of stock in a DISC.**

(1) In general. If—

(A) a shareholder disposes of stock in a DISC or former DISC any gain recognized on such disposition shall be included in gross income as a dividend to the extent provided in paragraph (2), or

(B) stock of a DISC or former DISC is disposed of in a transaction in which the separate corporate existence of the DISC or former DISC is terminated other than by a mere change in place of organization, however effected, any gain realized on the disposition of such stock in the transaction shall be recognized notwithstanding any other provision of this title to the extent provided in paragraph (2) and to the extent so recognized shall be included in gross income as a dividend.

(2) **Amount included.** The amounts described in paragraph (1) shall be included in gross income as a dividend to the extent of the accumulated DISC income of the DISC or former DISC which is attributable to the stock disposed of and which was accumulated in taxable years of such corporation during the period or periods the stock disposed of was held by the shareholder which disposed of such stock.

(d) **Foreign investment attributable to DISC earnings.**

For the purposes of this part—

(1) In general. The amount of foreign investment attributable to producer's loans of a DISC for a taxable year shall be the smallest of—

(A) the net increase in foreign assets by members of the controlled group (as defined in section 993(a)(3)) which includes the DISC,

(B) the actual foreign investment by domestic members of such group, or

(C) the amount of outstanding producer's loans by such DISC to members of such controlled group.

(2) **Net increase in foreign assets.** The term "net increase in foreign assets" of a controlled group means the excess of—

(A) the amount incurred by such group to acquire assets (described in section 1231(b)) located outside the United States over,

(B) the sum of—

(i) the depreciation with respect to assets of such group located outside the United States;

(ii) the outstanding amount of stock or debt obligations of such group issued after December 31, 1971, to persons other than the United States persons or any member of such group;

(iii) one-half the earnings and profits of foreign members of such group and foreign branches of domestic members of such group;

(iv) one-half the royalties and fees paid by foreign members of such group to domestic members of such group; and

(v) the uncommitted transitional funds of the group as determined under paragraph (4).

For purposes of this paragraph, assets which are qualified export assets of a DISC (or would be qualified export assets if owned by a DISC) shall not be taken into account. Amounts described in this paragraph (other than in subparagraphs (B)(ii) and (v)) shall be taken into account only to the extent they are attributable to taxable years beginning after December 31, 1971.

(3) **Actual foreign investment.** The term "actual foreign investment" by domestic members of a controlled group means the sum of—

(A) contributions to capital of foreign members of the group by domestic members of the group after December 31, 1971,

(B) the outstanding amount of stock or debt obligations of foreign members of such group (other than normal trade indebtedness) issued after December 31, 1971, to domestic members of such group,

(C) amounts transferred by domestic members of the group after December 31, 1971, to foreign branches of such members, and

(D) one-half the earnings and profits of foreign members of such group and foreign branches of domestic members of such group for taxable years beginning after December 31, 1971.

As used in this subsection, the term "domestic member" means a domestic corporation which is a member of a controlled group (as defined in section 993(a)(3)), and the term "foreign member" means a foreign corporation which is a member of such a controlled group.

(4) **Uncommitted transitional funds.** The uncommitted transitional funds of the group shall be an amount equal to the sum of—

(A) the excess of—

(i) the amount of stock or debt obligations of domestic members of such group outstanding on December 31, 1971, and issued on or after January 1, 1968, to persons other than United States persons or any members of such group, but only to the extent the taxpayer establishes that such amount constitutes a long-term borrowing for purposes of the foreign direct investment program, over

(ii) the net amount of actual foreign investment by domestic members of such group during the period that such stock or debt obligations have been outstanding; and

(B) the amount of liquid assets to the extent not included in subparagraph (A) held by foreign members of such group and foreign branches of domestic members of such group on October 31, 1971, in excess of their reasonable working capital needs on such date.

For purposes of this paragraph, the term "liquid assets" means money, bank deposits (not including time deposits), and indebtedness of 2 years or less to maturity on the date of acquisition and the actual foreign investment shall be determined under paragraph (3) without regard to the date in subparagraph (A) of such paragraph and without regard to subparagraph (D) of such paragraph.

(5) Special rule. Under regulations prescribed by the Secretary the determinations under this subsection shall be made on a cumulative basis with proper adjustments for amounts previously taken into account.

(e) Certain transfers of DISC assets.

If—

(1) a corporation owns, directly or indirectly, all of the stock of a subsidiary and a DISC,

(2) the subsidiary has been engaged in the active conduct of a trade or business (within the meaning of section 355(b)) throughout the 5-year period ending on the date of the transfer and continues to be so engaged thereafter, and

(3) during the taxable year of the subsidiary in which its stock is transferred and its preceding taxable year, such trade or business gives rise to qualified export receipts of the subsidiary and the DISC,

then, under such terms and conditions as the Secretary by regulations shall prescribe, transfers of assets, stock, or both, will be deemed to be a reorganization within the meaning of section 368, a transaction to which section 355 applies, an exchange of stock to which section 351 applies, or a combination thereof. The preceding sentence shall apply only to the extent that the transfer or transfers involved are for the purpose of preventing the separation of the ownership of the stock in the DISC from the ownership of the trade or business which (during the base period) produced the export gross receipts of the DISC.

(f) Interest on DISC-related deferred tax liability.

(1) In general. A shareholder of a DISC shall pay for each taxable year interest in an amount equal to the product of—

(A) the shareholder's DISC-related deferred tax liability for such year, and

(B) the base period T-bill rate.

(2) Shareholder's DISC-related deferred tax liability. For purposes of this subsection—

(A) In general. The term "shareholder's DISC-related deferred tax liability" means, with respect to any taxable year of a shareholder of a DISC, the excess of—

(i) the amount which would be the tax liability of the shareholder for the taxable year if the deferred DISC income of such shareholder for such taxable year were included in gross income as ordinary income, over

(ii) the actual amount of the tax liability of such shareholder for such taxable year.

Determinations under the preceding sentence shall be made without regard to carrybacks to such taxable year.

(B) Adjustments for losses, credits, and other items. The Secretary shall prescribe regulations which provide such adjustments—

(i) to the accounts of the DISC, and

(ii) to the amount of any carryover or carryback of the shareholder,

as may be necessary or appropriate in the case of net operating losses, credits, and carryovers, and carrybacks of losses and credits.

(C) Tax liability. The term "tax liability" means the amount of the tax imposed by this chapter for the taxable year reduced by credits allowable against such tax (other than credits allowable under sections 31, 32, and 34).

(3) Deferred DISC income. For purposes of this subsection—

(A) In general. The term "deferred DISC income" means, with respect to any taxable year of a shareholder, the excess of—

(i) the shareholder's pro rata share of accumulated DISC income (for periods after 1984) of the DISC as of the close of the computation year, over

(ii) the amount of the distributions-in-excess-of-income for the taxable year of the DISC following the computation year.

(B) Computation year. For purposes of applying subparagraph (A) with respect to any taxable year of a shareholder, the computation year is the taxable year of the DISC which ends with (or within) the taxable year of the shareholder which precedes the taxable year of the shareholder for which the amount of deferred DISC income is being determined.

(C) Distributions-in-excess-of-income. For purposes of subparagraph (A), the term "distributions-in-excess-of-income" means, with respect to any taxable year of a DISC, the excess (if any) of—

(i) the amount of actual distributions to the shareholder out of accumulated DISC income, over

(ii) the shareholder's pro rata share of the DISC income for such taxable year.

(4) Base period T-bill rate. For purposes of this subsection, the term "base period T-bill rate" means the annual rate of interest determined by the Secretary to be equivalent to the average of the 1-year constant maturity Treasury yields, as published by the Board of Governors of the Federal Reserve System, for the 1-year period ending on September 30 of the calendar year ending with (or of the most recent calendar year ending before) the close of the taxable year of the shareholder.

(5) Short years. The Secretary shall prescribe such regulations as may be necessary for the application of this subsection to short years of the DISC, the shareholder, or both.

(6) Payment and assessment and collection of interest. The interest accrued during any taxable year which a shareholder is required to pay under paragraph (1) shall be treated, for purposes of this title, as interest payable under section 6601 and shall be paid by the shareholder at the time the tax imposed by this chapter for such taxable year is required to be paid.

(7) DISC includes former DISC. For purposes of this subsection, the term "DISC" includes a former DISC.

(g) Treatment of tax-exempt shareholders.

If any organization described in subsection (a)(2) or (b)(2) of section 511 (or any other person otherwise subject to tax under section 511) is a shareholder in a DISC—

(1) any amount deemed distributed to such shareholder under subsection (b),

(2) any actual distribution to such shareholder which under section 996 is treated as out of accumulated DISC income, and

(3) any gain which is treated as a dividend under subsection (c),

shall be treated as derived from the conduct of an unrelated trade or business (and the modifications of section 512(b) shall not apply). The rules of the preceding sentence shall apply also for purposes of determining any such shareholder's DISC-related deferred tax liability under subsection (f).

In 2002, P.L. 107-147, Sec. 417(15), substituted "Arms Export Control Act" for "International Security Assistance and Arms Export Control Act of 1976" in subpara. (b)(3)(B), effective 3/9/2002.

In 2000, P.L. 106-554, Sec. 1(a)(7), [which enacted into law Sec. 307(c) of P.L. 106-554] substituted "the average of the 1-year constant maturity Treasury yields, as published by the Board of Governors of the Federal Reserve System, for the 1-year period" for "the average investment yield of United States Treasury bills with maturities of 52 weeks which were auctioned during the 1-year period" in para. (f)(4), effective 12/21/2000.

—P.L. 106-554, Sec. 1(a)(7), [which enacted into law Sec. 319(12) of P.L. 106-554] substituted "section 38 of the International Security Assistance and Arms Export Control Act of 1976 (22 U.S.C. 2778)" for "the Military Security Act of 1954 (22 U.S.C. 1934)" in subpara. (b)(3)(B), effective 12/21/2000.

In 1999, P.L. 106-170, Sec. 532(c)(2)(R), substituted "section 1221(a)(1)" for "section 1221(1)" in subpara. (b)(1)(C), effective for any instrument held, acquired, or entered into, any transaction entered into, and supplies held or acquired on or after 12/17/99.

In 1989, P.L. 101-239, Sec. 7811(i)(12), substituted "section 511 (or any other person otherwise subject to tax under section 511)" for "section 511", in subsec. (g), effective for tax. yrs. begin. after 12/31/87.

In 1988, P.L. 100-647, Sec. 1006(e)(15), added "or" at the end of subpara. (c)(1)(A), substituted the period for ", or" at the end of subpara. (c)(1)(B), and deleted subpara. (c)(1)(C) and the sentence thereafter, effective as provided by Sec. 633(a) and (c) of P.L. 99-514 which reads as follows:

"(a) General rule. Except as otherwise provided in this section, the amendments made by this subtitle shall apply to—

"(1) any distribution in complete liquidation, and any sale or exchange, made by a corporation after July 31, 1986, unless such corporation is completely liquidated before January 1, 1987,

"(2) any transaction described in section 338 of the Internal Revenue Code of 1986 for which the acquisition date occurs after December 31, 1986, and

"(3) any distribution (not in complete liquidation) made after December 31, 1986.

"(c) Exception for certain plans of liquidation and binding contracts.

"(1) In general. The amendments made by this subtitle shall not apply to—

"(A) any distribution or sale or exchange made pursuant to a plan of liquidation adopted before August 1, 1986, if the liquidating corporation is completely liquidated before January 1, 1988,

"(B) any distribution or sale or exchange made by any corporation if 50 percent or more of the voting stock (by value) of such corporation is acquired on or after August 1, 1986, pursuant to a written binding contract in effect before such date and if such corporation is completely liquidated before January 1, 1988,

"(C) any distribution or sale or exchange made by any corporation if substantially all of the assets of such corporation are sold on or after August 1, 1986, pursuant to 1 or more written binding contracts in effect before such date and if such corporation is completely liquidated before January 1, 1988, or

"(D) any transaction described in section 338 of the Internal Revenue Code of 1986 with respect to any target corporation if a qualified stock purchase of such target corporation is made on or after August 1, 1986, pursuant to a written binding contract in effect before such date and the acquisition date (within the meaning of such section 338) is before January 1, 1988.

"(2) Special rule for certain actions taken before November 20, 1985. For purposes of paragraph (1), transaction shall be treated as pursuant to a plan of liquidation adopted before August 1, 1986, if—

"(A) before November 20, 1985—

"(i) the board of directors of the liquidating corporation adopted a resolution to solicit shareholder approval for a transaction of a kind described in section 336 or 337, or

"(ii) the shareholders or board of directors have approved such a transaction,

"(B) before November 20, 1985—

"(i) there has been an offer to purchase a majority of the voting stock of the liquidating corporation, or

"(ii) the board of directors of the liquidating corporation has adopted a resolution approving an acquisition or recommending the approval of an acquisition to the shareholders, or

"(C) before November 20, 1985, a ruling request was submitted to the Secretary of the Treasury or his delegate with respect to a transaction of a kind described in section 336 or 337 of the Internal Revenue Code of 1954 (as in effect before the amendments made by this subtitle).

For purposes of the preceding sentence, any action taken by the board of directors or shareholders of a corporation with respect to any subsidiary of such corporation shall be treated as taken by the board of directors or shareholders of such subsidiary."

Prior to deletion, subpara. (c)(1)(C) and the sentence thereafter read as follows:

"(C) a shareholder distributes, sells, or exchanges stock in a DISC or former DISC in a transaction to which section 311, 336, or 337 applies. Then an amount equal to the excess of the fair market value of such stock over its adjusted basis in the hands of the shareholder shall, notwithstanding any other provision of this title, be included in gross income of the shareholder as a dividend to the extent provided in paragraph (2).

Subparagraph (C) shall not apply if the person receiving the stock in the disposition has a holding period for the stock which includes the period for which the stock was held by the shareholder disposing of such stock."

—P.L. 100-647, Sec. 1012(bb)(6)(A), added subsec. (g), effective for tax. yrs. begin. after 12/31/87.

In 1986, P.L. 99-514, Sec. 1876(b)(2)(A), added "in the case of a shareholder which is a C corporation," before "one-seventeenth" in clause (b)(1)(F)(i) . . . Sec. 1876(b)(2)(B), substituted "¹⁹⁄₁₇ of the excess referred to in clause (i)," for "the amount determined under clause (i)" in clause (b)(1)(F)(ii), effective for tax yrs. begin. after 12/31/84.

—P.L. 99-514, Sec. 1876(g), added para. (f)(7) . . . Sec. 1876(p)(1), redesignated the paragraphs following para. (f)(3) as paras. (f)(4), (5) and (6), effective for transactions after 12/31/84.

In 1984, P.L. 98-369, Sec. 68(d), substituted "one-seventeenth" for "one-half" in clause (b)(1)(F)(i), effective for tax. yrs. begin. after 12/31/84.

—P.L. 98-369, Sec. 802(a)(1)-(3), deleted subsecs. (e) and (f), redesignated subsec. (g) as subsec. (e), and added new subsec. (f) . . . Sec. 802(b)(1), amended subpara. (b)(1)(E) . . . Sec. 802(b)(2), added para. (b)(4), effective for transactions after 12/31/84, in tax. yrs. end. after 12/31/84.

Prior to deletion, subsecs. (e) and (f) read as follows:

"(e) Definitions and special rules relating to computation of taxable income attributable to base period export gross receipts.

"(1) Taxable income attributable to base period export gross receipts. For purposes of this section, the taxable income attributable to base period export gross receipts shall be an amount equal to that portion of the adjusted taxable income of a DISC which—

"(A) the amount of the adjusted base period export gross receipts, bears to

"(B) the amount of the export gross receipts of the DISC for the taxable year.

"(2) Adjusted taxable income. For purposes of this section, the term 'adjusted taxable income' means the income of a DISC for the taxable year, reduced by the amounts described in subparagraphs (A), (B), (C), and (D) of paragraph (1) of subsection (b).

"(3) Adjusted base period export gross receipts. For purposes of this section, the term 'adjusted base period export gross receipts' means 67 percent of the average of the export gross receipts of the DISC for taxable years during the base period (as defined in paragraph (5)). For purposes of the preceding sentence, if any property would not qualify during the taxable year as export property by reason of section 993(c)(2), gross receipts from such property shall be excluded from export gross receipts during the taxable years in the base period.

"(4) Export gross receipts. For purposes of this section, the term 'export gross receipts' means—

"(A) qualified export receipts described in subparagraphs (A), (B), (C), (G), and (H) of section 993(a)(1), reduced by

"(B) 50 percent of such qualified export receipts which are attributable to military property (as defined in subsection (b)(3)(B)).

"(5) Base period. For purposes of paragraph (3)—

"(A) for any taxable year beginning before 1980, the base period shall be the taxable years beginning in 1972, 1973, 1974, and 1975, and

"(B) for any taxable year beginning in any calendar year after 1979, the base period shall be the taxable years beginning in the fourth, fifth, sixth, and seventh calendar years preceding such calendar year.

"(6) No base period year. If a DISC did not have a taxable year beginning in a calendar year specified in paragraph (5), then, for purposes of computing the adjusted base period export gross receipts, such DISC is deemed to have a taxable year and export gross receipts of zero for that year.

"(7) Short taxable year. The Secretary shall prescribe such regulations as he deems necessary with respect to a short taxable year for purposes of computing base period export gross receipts of a DISC, or a short taxable year in which deemed distributions (as described in subsection (b)) are made, including the circumstances under which the short taxable year shall be annualized, and the proper method of annualization.

"(8) Controlled group. If more than one member of a controlled group (as defined in section 993(a)(3)) for the taxable year qualifies as a DISC, then subsection (b)(1)(E), this subsection, and subsection (f) shall each be applied in a manner provided by regulations prescribed by the Secretary by aggregating the export gross receipts and taxable income of such DISCs for the taxable year and by aggregating the export gross receipts of such DISCs for each taxable year in the base period.

"(9) Special rule where the ownership of DISC stock and the trade or business giving rise to export gross receipts of the DISC are separated.

"(A) In general. If, at any time after the beginning of the base period, there has been a separation of the ownership of the stock in the DISC from the ownership of the trade or business which (during the base period) produced the export gross receipts of the DISC, then the persons who own the trade or business during the taxable year shall be treated as having had additional export gross receipts during the base period attributable to such trade or business.

"(B) Exceptions. Subparagraph (A) shall not apply—

DISC

Code Sec. 996(b)(3)

"(i) where the stock in the DISC and the trade or business are owned throughout the taxable year by members of the same controlled group, and

"(ii) to the extent that the taxpayer's ownership of the stock in the DISC for the taxable year is proportionate to his ownership during the taxable year of the trade or business.

"(10) DISC base period attributed through shareholders in certain cases.

"(A) In general. If—

"(i) any person owns 5 percent or more of the stock of a DISC (hereinafter in this paragraph referred to as 'first DISC'), and

"(ii) such person at any time during the base period of the first DISC owned 5 percent or more of the stock of a second DISC,

then, to the extent provided in such regulations as the Secretary may prescribe to prevent circumvention of the application of subsection (b)(1)(E), an amount equal to such shareholder's share of the base period export gross receipts of the second DISC shall be added to the base period export gross receipts of the first DISC.

"(B) Ownership of stock. For purposes of subparagraph (A), the ownership of stock shall be determined under section 318.

"(f) Small DISCs.

"(1) Adjusted taxable income of $100,000 or less. If a DISC has adjusted taxable income of $100,000 or less for a taxable year, subsection (b)(1)(E) shall not apply with respect to such year.

"(2) Special rule. If a DISC has adjusted taxable income of more than $100,000 for a taxable year, then the amount taken into account under subsection (b)(1)(E) shall be deemed to be an amount equal to the excess (if any) of—

"(A) the amount which would (but for this paragraph) be taken into account under subsection (b)(1)(E), over

"(B) twice the excess (if any) of $150,000 over the adjusted taxable income."

Prior to amendment, subpara. (b)(1)(E) read as follows:

"(E) the taxable income for the taxable year attributable to base period export gross receipts (as defined in subsection (e)),"

In 1978, P.L. 95-600, Sec. 701(u)(12)(A), changed the effective dates for amendments made by Sec. 1101(d)(1) of P.L. 94-455, see below, from effective for sales, exchanges or dispositions after 12/31/75, in tax years ending after 12/31/75, to effective for sales, exchanges or dispositions after 12/31/76, in tax years ending after 12/31/76.

—P.L. 95-600, Sec. 701(u)(12)(B), added a new sentence to the end of para. (c)(1), effective for dispositions made after 12/31/76, in tax. yrs. ending after 12/31/76.

—P.L. 95-600, Sec. 703(i)(1), substituted "income" for "gross income (taxable income in the case of subparagraph (D))" in the material following subpara. (G) of para. (b)(1) . . . substituted "subparagraph (G)" for "subparagraph (E)" in the last sentence of para. (b)(1) . . . Sec. 703(i)(2), substituted "subsection (d)" for "subsection (D)" in subpara. (b)(1)(G) . . . Sec. 703(i)(4), amended the effective date for changes made by Sec. 1101(g)(5) of P.L. 94-455, by substituting "section 995(e)(3)" for "section 993(e)(3)", see below, effective 10/4/76.

In 1976, P.L. 94-455, Sec. 1063(a), amended subpara. (b)(1)(D), for participation in or cooperation with an international boycott after 11/4/76. For operations which constitute participation in or cooperation with an international boycott and are carried out in accordance with the terms of a binding contract entered into before 9/2/76, this amendment applies to such participation or cooperation after 12/31/77. Prior to amendment, subpara. (b)(1)(D) read as follows:

"(D) one-half of the excess of the taxable income of the DISC for the taxable year, before reduction for any distributions during the year, over the sum of the amounts deemed distributed for the taxable year under subparagraphs (A), (B), and (C), and"

—P.L. 94-455, Sec. 1065(a)(2), deleted "and" at the end of clause (b)(1)(D)(i), as amended by this Act, and added clause (b)(1)(D)(iii), for payments described in Code Sec. 162(c) made more than 30 days after 10/4/76.

—P.L. 94-455, Sec. 1101(a), redesignated subparas. (b)(1)(D) and (b)(1)(E) as subparas. (b)(1)(F) and (b)(1)(G), substituted "(C), (D), and (E)" for "and (C)" in redesignated subpara. (b)(1)(F), added new subparas. (b)(1)(D) and (b)(1)(E), substituted "more than twice the number" for "more than the number" in subpara. (b)(2)(B), added para. (b)(3) and added subsecs. (e), (f) and (g), effective for tax. yrs. begin. after 12/31/75. Sec. 1101(g)(5) of the Act provided as follows:

"(5) Proration of base period in case of fixed contracts.—

"For purposes of determining adjusted base period export gross receipts (under section 995(e)(3) of the Internal Revenue Code of 1954, as amended by this section), if any DISC has export gross receipts from export property by reason of paragraph (2) of section 603(b) of the Tax Reduction Act of 1975, then the export gross receipts of such DISC for the taxable years of the base period shall be increased by an amount equal to the amount of gross receipts which were excluded from export gross receipts during each taxable year of the base period by reason of the last sentence of section 993(e)(3) of such Code multiplied by a fraction, the numerator of which is the amount of the gross receipts in the taxable year which are export gross receipts by reason of paragraph (2) of section 603(b) of the Tax Reduction Act of 1975 and the denominator of which is the amount of total gross receipts which are excluded from export gross receipts in the taxable year by reason of subparagraph (C) or (D) of paragraph (2) of section 993(c) (determined without regard to paragraph (2) of section 603(b) of the Tax Reduction Act of 1975)."

—P.L. 94-455, Sec. 1101(d)(1), amended subsec. (c), effective for sales, exchanges, or other dispositions after 12/31/76, in tax. yrs. end. after 12/31/76.

Prior to amendment, subsec. (c) read as follows:

"(c) Gain on disposition of stock in a DISC.

"If a shareholder disposes of stock in a DISC or former DISC, any gain recognized on such disposition shall be included in gross income as dividend to the extent of the accumulated DISC income of such DISC or former DISC which is attributable to such stock and which was accumulated in taxable years of such corporation during the period or periods the stock disposed of was held by such shareholder. If stock of the DISC or former DISC is disposed of in a transaction in which the separate corporate existence of the DISC or former DISC is terminated other than by a mere change in place of organization, however effected, any gain realized on the disposition of such stock in the transaction shall be recognized notwithstanding any other provision of this title to the extent of the accumulated DISC income of such DISC or former DISC which is attributable to such stock and which was accumulated in taxable years of such corporation during the period or periods the stock disposed of was held by the stockholder which disposed of such stock, and such gain shall be included in gross income as a dividend."

—P.L. 94-455, Sec. 1901(b)(3)(K), substituted "ordinary income" for "gain from the sale or exchange of property which is neither a capital asset nor property described in section 1231" in subpara. (b)(1)(C), effective for tax. yrs. begin. after 12/31/76.

—P.L. 94-455, Sec. 1906(b)(13)(A), substituted "Secretary" for "Secretary or his delegate" in para. (d)(5), effective for tax. yrs. begin. after 12/31/76.

In 1971, P.L. 92-178, Sec. 501, added Code Sec. 995, effective for tax. yrs. end. 12/31/71, except that a corporation may not be a DISC for any tax. yr. begin. before 1/1/72, as provided in Sec. 507.

Sec. 996. Rules for allocation in the case of distributions and losses.

(a) Rules for actual distributions and certain deemed distributions.

(1) In general. Any actual distribution (other than a distribution described in paragraph (2) or to which section 995(c) applies) to a shareholder by a DISC (or former DISC) which is made out of earnings and profits shall be treated as made—

(A) first, out of previously taxed income, to the extent thereof,

(B) second, out of accumulated DISC income, to the extent thereof, and

(C) finally, out of other earnings and profits.

(2) Qualifying distributions. Any actual distribution made pursuant to section 992(c) (relating to distributions to meet qualification requirements), and any deemed distribution pursuant to section 995(b)(1)(G) (relating to foreign investment attributable to producer's loans), shall be treated as made—

(A) first, out of accumulated DISC income, to the extent thereof,

(B) second, out of the earnings and profits described in paragraph (1)(C), to the extent thereof, and

(C) finally, out of previously taxed income.

In the case of any amount of any actual distribution to a C corporation made pursuant to section 992(c) which is required to satisfy the condition of section 992(a)(1)(A), the preceding sentence shall apply to 16/17ths of such amount and paragraph (1) shall apply to the remaining 1/17th of such amount.

(3) Exclusion from gross income. Amounts distributed out of previously taxed income shall be excluded by the distributee from gross income except for gains described in subsection (e)(2), and shall reduce the amount of the previously taxed income.

(b) Ordering rules for losses.

If for any taxable year a DISC, or a former DISC, incurs a deficit in earnings and profits, such deficit shall be chargeable—

(1) first, to earnings and profits described in subsection (a)(1)(C), to the extent thereof,

(2) second, to accumulated DISC income, to the extent thereof, and

(3) finally, to previously taxed income, except that a deficit in earnings and profits shall not be applied against accumulated DISC income which has been determined is to be deemed distributed to the shareholders (pursuant to section 995(b)(2)(A)) as a result of a revocation of election or other disqualification.

2,669

(c) Priority of distributions.

Any actual distribution made during a taxable year shall be treated as being made subsequent to any deemed distribution made during such year. Any actual distribution made pursuant to section 992(c) (relating to distributions to meet qualification requirements) shall be treated as being made before any other actual distributions during the taxable year.

(d) Subsequent effect of previous disposition of DISC stock.

(1) **Shareholder previously taxed income adjustment.** If—

(A) gain with respect to a share of stock of a DISC or former DISC is treated under section 995(c) as a dividend or as ordinary income, and

(B) any person subsequently receives an actual distribution made out of accumulated DISC income, or a deemed distribution made pursuant to section 995(b)(2), with respect to such share,

such person shall treat such distribution in the same manner as a distribution from previously taxed income to the extent that (i) the gain referred to in subparagraph (A), exceeds (ii) any other amounts with respect to such share which were treated under this paragraph as made from previously taxed income. In applying this paragraph with respect to a share of stock in a DISC or former DISC, gain on the acquisition of such share by the DISC or former DISC or gain on a transaction prior to such acquisition shall not be considered gain referred to in subparagraph (A).

(2) **Corporate adjustment upon redemption.** If section 995(c) applies to a redemption of stock in a DISC or former DISC, the accumulated DISC income shall be reduced by an amount equal to the gain described in section 995(c) with respect to such stock which is (or has been) treated as ordinary income, except to the extent distributions with respect to such stock have been treated under paragraph (1).

(e) Adjustment to basis.

(1) **Additions to basis.** Amounts representing deemed distributions as provided in section 995(b) shall increase the basis of the stock with respect to which the distribution is made.

(2) **Reductions of basis.** The portion of an actual distribution made out of previously taxed income shall reduce the basis of the stock with respect to which it is made, and to the extent that it exceeds the adjusted basis of such stock, shall be treated as gain from the sale or exchange of property. In the case of stock includible in the gross estate of a decedent for which an election is made under section 2032 (relating to alternate valuation), this paragraph shall not apply to any distribution made after the date of the decedent's death and before the alternate valuation date provided by section 2032.

(f) Definitions of divisions of earnings and profits.

For purposes of this part:

(1) **DISC income.** The earnings and profits derived by a corporation during a taxable year in which such corporation is a DISC, before reduction for any distributions during the year, but reduced by amounts deemed distributed under section 995(b)(1), shall constitute the DISC income for such year. The earnings and profits of a DISC for a taxable year include any amounts includible in such DISC's gross income pursuant to section 951(a) for such year. Accumulated DISC income shall be reduced by deemed distributions under section 995(b)(2).

(2) **Previously taxed income.** Earnings and profits deemed distributed under section 995(b) for a taxable year shall constitute previously taxed income for such year.

(3) **Other earnings and profits.** The earnings and profits for a taxable year which are described in neither paragraph (1) nor (2) shall constitute the other earnings and profits for such year.

(g) Effectively connected income.

In the case of a shareholder who is a nonresident alien individual or a foreign corporation, trust, or estate, gains referred to in section 995(c) and all distributions out of accumulated DISC income including deemed distributions shall be treated as gains and distributions which are effectively connected with the conduct of a trade or business conducted through a permanent establishment of such shareholder within the United States and which are derived from sources within the United States.

In **1986,** P.L. 99-514, Sec. 1876(k), amended the last sentence of para. (a)(2), effective for distributions on or after 6/22/84.
Prior to amendment, the last sentence of para (a)(2) read as follows:
"In the case of any amount of any actual distribution made pursuant to section 992(c) which is required to satisfy the condition of section 992(a)(1)(A), the preceding sentence shall apply to one-half of such amount, and paragraph (1) shall apply to the remaining one-half of such amount"
In **1984,** P.L. 98-369, Sec. 801(d)(10), added "and which are derived from sources with the United States" after "United States" in subsec. (g), effective for distributions on or after 6/22/84.
In **1978,** P.L. 95-600, Sec. 703(i)(3), substituted "section 995(b)(1)(G)" for "section 995(b)(1)(E)" in para. (a)(2), effective 10/4/76.
In **1976,** P.L. 94-455, Sec. 1101(e), added the last sentence of para. (a)(2), effective for tax. yrs. begin. after 12/31/75.
— P.L. 94-455, Sec. 1901(b)(3)(I), substituted "ordinary income" for "gain from the sale or exchange of property which is not a capital asset" in paras. (d)(1) and (d)(2), effective for tax. yrs. begin. after 12/31/76.
In **1971,** P.L. 92-178, Sec. 501, added Code Sec. 996, effective for tax. yrs. end. 12/31/71, except that a corporation may not be a DISC for any tax. yr. begin. before 1/1/72, as provided in Sec. 507.

Sec. 997. Special subchapter C rules.

For purposes of applying the provisions of subchapter C of chapter 1, any distribution in property to a corporation by a DISC or former DISC which is made out of previously taxed income or accumulated DISC income shall—

(1) be treated as a distribution in the same amount as if such distribution of property were made to an individual, and

(2) have a basis, in the hands of the recipient corporation, equal to the amount determined under paragraph (1).

In **1971,** P.L. 92-178, Sec. 501, added Code Sec. 997, effective for tax. yrs. end. after 12/31/71, except that a corporation may not be a DISC (as defined in Code Sec. 992(a)) for any tax. yr. begin. before 1/1/72.

PART V.—INTERNATIONAL BOYCOTT DETERMINATIONS

Sec.
999. Reports by taxpayers; determinations.

Sec. 999. Reports by taxpayers; determinations.

(a) International boycott reports by taxpayers.

(1) **Report required.** If any person, or a member of a controlled group (within the meaning of section 993(a)(3)) which includes that person, has operations in, or related to—

(A) a country (or with the government, a company, or a national of a country) which is on the list maintained by the Secretary under paragraph (3), or

(B) any other country (or with the government, a company, or a national of that country) in which such person or such member had operations during the taxable year if such person (or, if such person is a foreign corporation, any United States shareholder of that corporation) knows or has reason to know that participation in

International boycotts Code Sec. 999(d)

or cooperation with an international boycott is required as a condition of doing business within such country or with such government, company, or national, that person or shareholder (within the meaning of section 951(b)) shall report such operations to the Secretary at such time and in such manner as the Secretary prescribes, except that in the case of a foreign corporation such report shall be required only of a United States shareholder (within the meaning of such section) of such corporation.

(2) Participation and cooperation; request therefor. A taxpayer shall report whether he, a foreign corporation of which he is a United States shareholder, or any member of a controlled group which includes the taxpayer or such foreign corporation has participated in or cooperated with an international boycott at any time during the taxable year, or has been requested to participate in or cooperate with such a boycott, and, if so, the nature of any operation in connection with which there was participation in or cooperation with such boycott (or there was a request to participate or cooperate).

(3) List to be maintained. The Secretary shall maintain and publish not less frequently than quarterly a current list of countries which require or may require participation in or cooperation with an international boycott (within the meaning of subsection (b)(3)).

(b) Participation in or cooperation with an international boycott.

(1) General rule. If the person or a member of a controlled group (within the meaning of section 993(a)(3)) which includes the person participates in or cooperates with an international boycott in the taxable year, all operations of the taxpayer or such group in that country and in any other country which requires participation in or cooperation with the boycott as a condition of doing business within that country, or with the government, a company, or a national of that country, shall be treated as operations in connection with which such participation of cooperation occurred, except to the extent that the person can clearly demonstrate that a particular operation is a clearly separate and identifiable operation in connection with which there was no participation in or cooperation with an international boycott.

(2) Special rule.

(A) Nonboycott operations. A clearly separate and identifiable operation of a person, or of a member of the controlled group (within the meaning of section 993(a)(3)) which includes that person, in or related to any country within the group of countries referred to in paragraph (1) shall not be treated as an operation in or related to a group of countries associated in carrying out an international boycott if the person can clearly demonstrate that he, or that such member, did not participate in or cooperate with the international boycott in connection with that operation.

(B) Separate and identifiable operations. A taxpayer may show that different operations within the same country, or operations in different countries, are clearly separate and identifiable operations.

(3) Definition of boycott participation and cooperation. For purposes of this section, a person participates in or cooperates with an international boycott if he agrees—

(A) as a condition of doing business directly or indirectly within a country or with the government, a company, or a national of a country—

(i) to refrain from doing business with or in a country which is the object of the boycott or with the government, companies, or nationals of that country;

(ii) to refrain from doing business with any United States person engaged in trade in a country which is the object of the boycott or with the government, companies, or nationals of that country;

(iii) to refrain from doing business with any company whose ownership or management is made up, all or in part, of individuals of a particular nationality, race, or religion, or to remove (or refrain from selecting) corporate directors who are individuals of a particular nationality, race, or religion; or

(iv) to refrain from employing individuals of a particular nationality, race, or religion; or

(B) as a condition of the sale of a product to the government, a company, or a national of a country, to refrain from shipping or insuring that product on a carrier owned, leased, or operated by a person who does not participate in or cooperate with an international boycott (within the meaning of subparagraph (A)).

(4) Compliance with certain laws. This section shall not apply to any agreement by a person (or such member)—

(A) to meet requirements imposed by a foreign country with respect to an international boycott if United States law or regulations, or an Executive Order, sanctions participation in, or cooperation with, that international boycott,

(B) to comply with a prohibition on the importation of goods produced in whole or in part in any country which is the object of an international boycott, or

(C) to comply with a prohibition imposed by a country on the exportation of products obtained in such country to any country which is the object of an international boycott.

(c) International boycott factor.

(1) International boycott factor. For purposes of sections 908(a), 952(a)(3), and 995(b)(1)(F)(ii), the international boycott factor is a fraction, determined under regulations prescribed by the Secretary, the numerator of which reflects the world-wide operations of a person (or, in the case of a controlled group (within the meaning of section 993(a)(3)) which includes that person, of the group) which are operations in or related to a group of countries associated in carrying out an international boycott in or with which that person or a member of that controlled group has participated or cooperated in the taxable year, and the denominator of which reflects the world-wide operations of that person or group.

(2) Specifically attributable taxes and income. If the taxpayer clearly demonstrates that the foreign taxes paid and income earned for the taxable year are attributable to specific operations, then, in lieu of applying the international boycott factor for such taxable year, the amount of the credit disallowed under section 908(a), the addition to subpart F income under section 952(a)(3), and the amount of deemed distribution under section 995(b)(1)(F)(ii) for the taxable year, if any, shall be the amount specifically attributable to the operations in which there was participation in or cooperation with an international boycott under section 999(b)(1).

(3) World-wide operations. For purposes of this subsection, the term "world-wide operations" means operations in or related to countries other than the United States.

(d) Determinations with respect to particular operations.

Upon a request made by the taxpayer, the Secretary shall issue a determination with respect to whether a particular operation of a person, or of a member of a controlled group which includes that person, constitutes participation in or cooperation with an international boycott. The Secretary may

2,671

issue such a determination in advance of such operation in cases which are of such a nature that an advance determination is possible and appropriate under the circumstances. If the request is made before the operation is commenced, or before the end of a taxable year in which the operation is carried out, the Secretary may decline to issue such a determination before close of the taxable year.

(e) Participation or cooperation by related persons.

If a person controls (within the meaning of section 304(c)) a corporation—

(1) participation in or cooperation with an international boycott by such corporation shall be presumed to be such participation or cooperation by such person, and

(2) participation in or cooperation with such a boycott by such person shall be presumed to be such participation or cooperation by such corporation.

(f) Willful failure to report.

Any person (within the meaning of section 6671(b)) required to report under this section who willfully fails to make such report shall, in addition to other penalties provided by law, be fined not more than $25,000, imprisoned for not more than one year, or both.

In 2006, P.L. 109-222, Sec. 513(a), amended Sec. 5(c)(1) of P.L. 106-519 [see below]... Sec. 513(b), repealed Sec. 101(f) of P.L. 108-357 [see below], effective for tax. yrs. begin. after 5/17/2006.

Prior to amendment, Sec. 5(c)(1) of P.L. 106-519 read as follows:

"(1) In general. In the case of a FSC (as so defined) in existence on September 30, 2000, and at all times thereafter, the amendments made by this Act shall not apply to any transaction in the ordinary course of trade or business involving a FSC which occurs—

"(A) before January 1, 2002; or

"(B) after December 31, 2001, pursuant to a binding contract—

"(i) which is between the FSC (or any related person) and any person which is not a related person; and

"(ii) which is in effect on September 30, 2000, and at all times thereafter.

For purposes of this paragraph, a binding contract shall include a purchase option, renewal option, or replacement option which is included in such contract and which is enforceable against the seller or lessor."

Prior to repeal, Sec. 101(f) of P.L. 108-357 read as follows:

"(f) Binding contracts. The amendments made by this section shall not apply to any transaction in the ordinary course of a trade or business which occurs pursuant to a binding contract—

"(1) which is between the taxpayer and a person who is not a related person (as defined in section 943(b)(3) of such Code, as in effect on the day before the date of the enactment of this Act), and

"(2) which is in effect on September 17, 2003, and at all times thereafter.

"For purposes of this subsection, a binding contract shall include a purchase option, renewal option, or replacement option which is included in such contract and which is enforceable against the seller or lessor."

In 2004, P.L. 108-357, Sec. 101(b)(8), deleted "941(a)(5)," after "908(a)," in para. (c)(1), effective for transactions after 12/31/2004. Sec. 101(d) of this Act, provides:

"(d) Transitional rule for 2005 and 2006.

"(1) In general. In the case of transactions during 2005 or 2006, the amount includible in gross income by reason of the amendments made by this section shall not exceed the applicable percentage of the amount which would have been so included but for this subsection.

"(2) Applicable percentage. For purposes of paragraph (1), the applicable percentage shall be as follows:

"(A) For 2005, the applicable percentage shall be 20 percent.

"(B) For 2006, the applicable percentage shall be 40 percent."

—P.L. 108-357, Sec. 101(f), of this Act [prior to repeal by Sec. 513(b) of P.L. 109-222, see above] read as follows:

"(f) Binding contracts. The amendments made by this section shall not apply to any transaction in the ordinary course of a trade or business which occurs pursuant to a binding contract—

"(1) which is between the taxpayer and a person who is not a related person (as defined in section 943(b)(3) of such Code, as in effect on the day before the date of the enactment of this Act), and

"(2) which is in effect on September 17, 2003, and at all times thereafter.

"For purposes of this subsection, a binding contract shall include a purchase option, renewal option, or replacement option which is included in such contract and which is enforceable against the seller or lessor."

In 2000, P.L. 106-519, Sec. 4(5), added "941(a)(5)," after "908(a)," in para. (c)(1), effective for transactions after 9/30/2000. Sec. 5(b)–(d) [para. (c)(1) as amended by Sec. 513(a) of P.L. 109-222, see above] of this Act, provides:

"(b) No new FSCs; termination of inactive FSCs—

"(1) No new FSCs. No corporation may elect after September 30, 2000, to be a FSC (as defined in section 922 of the Internal Revenue Code of 1986, as in effect before the amendments made by this Act).

"(2) Termination of inactive FSCs. If a FSC has no foreign trade income (as defined in section 923(b) of such Code, as so in effect) for any period of 5 consecutive taxable years beginning after December 31, 2001, such FSC shall cease to be treated as a FSC for purposes of such Code for any taxable year beginning after such period.

"(c) Transition period for existing Foreign Sales Corporations.

"(1) In general. In the case of a FSC (as so defined) in existence on September 30, 2000, and at all times thereafter, the amendments made by this Act shall not apply to any transaction in the ordinary course of trade or business involving a FSC which occurs before January 1, 2002.

"(2) Election to have amendments apply earlier. A taxpayer may elect to have the amendments made by this Act apply to any transaction by a FSC or any related person to which such amendments would apply but for the application of paragraph (1). Such election shall be effective for the taxable year for which made and all subsequent taxable years, and, once made, may be revoked only with the consent of the Secretary of the Treasury.

"(3) Exception for old earnings and profits of certain corporations.

"(A) In general. In the case of a foreign corporation to which this paragraph applies—

"(i) earnings and profits of such corporation accumulated in taxable years ending before October 1, 2000, shall not be included in the gross income of the persons holding stock in such corporation by reason of section 943(e)(4)(B)(i), and

"(ii) rules similar to the rules of clauses (ii), (iii), and (iv) of section 953(d)(4)(B) shall apply with respect to such earnings and profits.

The preceding sentence shall not apply to earnings and profits acquired in a transaction after September 30, 2000, to which section 381 applies unless the distributor or transferor corporation was immediately before the transaction a foreign corporation to which this paragraph applies.

"(B) Existing FSCs. This paragraph shall apply to any controlled foreign corporation (as defined in section 957) if—

"(i) such corporation is a FSC (as so defined) in existence on September 30, 2000,

"(ii) such corporation is eligible to make the election under section 943(e) by reason of being described in paragraph (2)(B) of such section, and

"(iii) such corporation makes such election not later than for its first taxable year beginning after December 31, 2001.

"(C) Other corporations. This paragraph shall apply to any controlled foreign corporation (as defined in section 957), and such corporation shall (notwithstanding any provision of section 943(e)) be treated as an applicable foreign corporation for purposes of section 943(e), if—

"(i) such corporation is in existence on September 30, 2000;

"(ii) as of such date, such corporation is wholly owned (directly or indirectly) by a domestic corporation (determined without regard to any election under section 943(e));

"(iii) for each of the 3 taxable years preceding the first taxable year to which the election under section 943(e) by such controlled foreign corporation applies—

"(I) all of the gross income of such corporation is subpart F income (as defined in section 952), including by reason of section 954(b)(3)(B); and

"(II) in the ordinary course of such corporation's trade or business, such corporation regularly sold (or paid commissions) to a FSC which on September 30, 2000, was a related person to such corporation;

"(iv) such corporation has never made an election under section 922(a)(2) (as in effect before the date of the enactment of this paragraph) to be treated as a FSC; and

"(v) such corporation makes the election under section 943(e) not later than for its first taxable year beginning after December 31, 2001.

The preceding sentence shall cease to apply as of the date that the domestic corporation referred to in clause (ii) ceases to wholly own (directly or indirectly) such controlled foreign corporation.

"(4) Related person. For purposes of this subsection, the term 'related person' has the meaning given to such term by section 943(b)(3).

"(5) Section references. Except as otherwise expressly provided, any reference in this subsection to a section or other provision shall be considered to be a reference to a section or other provision of the Internal Revenue Code of 1986, as amended by this Act.

"(d) Special rules relating to leasing transactions.

"(1) Sales income. If foreign trade income in connection with the lease or rental of property described in section 927(a)(1)(B) of such Code (as in effect before the amendments made by this Act) is treated as exempt foreign trade income for purposes of section 921(a) of such Code (as so in effect), such property shall be treated as property described in section 941(c)(1)(B) of such Code (as added by this Act) for purposes of applying section 941(c)(2) of such Code (as so added) to any subsequent transaction involving such property to which the amendments made by this Act apply.

"(2) Limitation on use of gross receipts method. If any person computed its foreign trade income from any transaction with respect to any property on the basis of a transfer price determined under the method described in section 925(c)(1) of such Code (as in effect before the amendments made by this Act), then the qualifying foreign trade income (as defined in section 941(a) of such Code, as in effect after such amendment) of such person (or any related person) with respect to any other transaction involving such property (and to which the amendments made by this Act apply) shall be zero."

In 1986, P.L. 99-514, Sec. 1876(p)(3), repealed Sec. 802(c)(3) of P.L. 98-369, which substituted "995(b)(1)(F)(i)" for "995(b)(1)(F)(ii)" each time it appeared

Basis Code Sec. 1001(e)(3)

in subsec. (c), effective for transactions after 12/31/84, in tax. yrs. end. after 12/31/84.

In 1984, P.L. 98-369, Sec. 441(c)(2), amended Sec. 1067 of P.L. 94-455 (reproduced below) effective for reports or periods after 12/31/81.

Prior to amendment. Sec. 1067 of P.L. 94-455 read as follows:

"SEC. 1067. REPORTS BY SECRETARY.

"(a) Reports to the Congress. As soon after the close of each calendar year as the data become available, the Secretary shall transmit a report to the Committee on Ways and Means of the House of Representatives and to the Committee on Finance of the Senate setting forth, for that calendar year—

"(1) the number of reports filed under section 999(a) of the Internal Revenue Code of 1954 for taxable years ending with or within such taxable year,

"(2) the number of such reports on which the taxpayer indicated international boycott participation or cooperation (within the meaning of section 999(b)(3) of such Code), and

"(3) a detailed description of the manner in which the provisions of such Code relating to international boycott activity have been administered during such calendar year.

"(b) Initial list. The Secretary of the Treasury shall publish an initial list of those countries which may require participation in or cooperation with an international boycott as a condition of doing business within such country, or with the government, a company, or a national of such country (within the meaning of section 999(b) of the Internal Revenue Code of 1954) within 30 days after the enactment of this Act."

—P.L. 98-369, Sec. 802(c)(3), substituted "995(b)(1)(F)(i)" for "995(b)(1)(F)(ii)" each place it appeared in subsec. (c), effective for transactions after 12/31/84, in tax. yrs. end. after 12/31/84. [This provision repealed by Sec. 1876(p)(3) of P.L. 99-514, see below]

In 1978, P.L. 95-600, Sec. 703(h)(2), substituted "995(b)(1)(F)(ii)" for "995(b)(3)" in para. (c)(1) . . . Sec. 703(h)(3), substituted "995(b)(1)(F)(ii)" for "995(b)(1)(D)(ii)" in para. (c)(2), effective 10/4/76.

In 1976, P.L. 94-455, Sec. 1064(a), added Code Sec. 999, for participation in or cooperation with an international boycott more than 30 days after 10/4/76. Sec. 1066(a)(2) of the Act provided the following with respect to existing contracts:

"(2) Existing contracts. In the case of operations which constitute participation in or cooperation with an international boycott and which are carried out in accordance with the terms of a binding contract entered into before September 2, 1976, the amendments made by this part (other than by section 1065) apply to such participation or cooperation after December 31, 1977."

Sec. 1067 of the Act provided as follows:

"SEC. 1067. REPORTS BY THE SECRETARY.

"(a) General rule. As soon after the close of each 4-year period as the data become available, the Secretary shall transmit a report to the Committee on Ways and Means of the House of Representatives and to the Committee on Finance of the Senate setting forth for such 4-year period—

"(1) the number of reports filed under section 999(a) of the Internal Revenue Code of 1954 for taxable years ending with or within each calendar year in such 4-year period,

"(2) the number of such reports with respect to each such calendar year on which the taxpayer indicated international boycott participation or cooperation (within the meaning of section 999(b)(3) of such Code), and

"(3) a detailed description of the manner in which the provisions of such Code relating to international boycott activity have been administered during such 4-year period.

"(b) 4-year period. For purposes of subsection (a), the term '4-year period' means the period consisting of 4 calendar years beginning with calendar year 1982 and each subsequent fourth calendar year."

Subchapter O.—Gain or Loss on Disposition of Property

Part
- I. Determination of amount of and recognition of gain or loss.
- II. Basis rules of general application.
- III. Common nontaxable exchanges.
- IV. Special rules.
- V. [Repealed] Changes to effectuate F.C.C. policy.
- VI. Exchanges in obedience to S.E.C. orders.
- VII. Wash sales; straddles.
- VIII. [Repealed] Distributions pursuant to Bank Holding Company Act.
- IX. [Repealed] Distributions pursuant to orders enforcing the antitrust laws.

In 1990, P.L. 101-508, Sec. 11801(b)(a), deleted the item for Part VIII.
Prior to deletion, the item for Part VIII read as follows:
"VIII. Distributions pursuant to Bank Holding Company Act."
In 1981, P.L. 97-24, Sec. 501(d)(3), amended item VII.
Prior to amendment, item VII read as follows:
"VII. Wash sales of stock or securities."

In 1976, P.L. 94-455, Sec. 1901(b)(32)(I), deleted the item for Part IX.
Prior to repeal, that item read as follows:
"IX. Distributions pursuant to orders enforcing the antitrust laws."
—P.L. 94-452, Sec. (2)(c), deleted "of 1956" at the end of the item for Part VIII.
In 1962, added the heading of Part IX.
In 1956, added Part VIII.

PART I.—DETERMINATION OF AMOUNT OF AND RECOGNITION OF GAIN OR LOSS

Sec.
1001. Determination of amount of and recognition of gain or loss.
1002. Repealed.

In 1976, P.L. 94-455, Sec. 1901(b)(28)(B)(ii), deleted item 1002.
Prior to deletion, the item read as follows:
"1002. Recognition of gain or loss."

Sec. 1001. Determination of amount of and recognition of gain or loss.

(a) Computation of gain or loss.

The gain from the sale or other disposition of property shall be the excess of the amount realized therefrom over the adjusted basis provided in section 1011 for determining gain, and the loss shall be the excess of the adjusted basis provided in such section for determining loss over the amount realized.

(b) Amount realized.

The amount realized from the sale or other disposition of property shall be the sum of any money received plus the fair market value of the property (other than money) received. In determining the amount realized—

(1) there shall not be taken into account any amount received as reimbursement for real property taxes which are treated under section 164(d) as imposed on the purchaser, and

(2) there shall be taken into account amounts representing real property taxes which are treated under section 164(d) as imposed on the taxpayer if such taxes are to be paid by the purchaser.

(c) Recognition of gain or loss.

Except as otherwise provided in this subtitle, the entire amount of the gain or loss, determined under this section, on the sale or exchange of property shall be recognized.

(d) Installment sales.

Nothing in this section shall be construed to prevent (in the case of property sold under contract providing for payment in installments) the taxation of that portion of any installment payment representing gain or profit in the year in which such payment is received.

(e) Certain term interests.

(1) **In general.** In determining gain or loss from the sale or other disposition of a term interest in property, that portion of the adjusted basis of such interest which is determined pursuant to section 1014, 1015, or 1041 (to the extent that such adjusted basis is a portion of the entire adjusted basis of the property) shall be disregarded.

(2) **Term interest in property defined.** For purposes of paragraph (1), the term "term interest in property" means—

(A) a life interest in property,

(B) an interest in property for a term of years, or

(C) an income interest in a trust.

(3) **Exception.** Paragraph (1) shall not apply to a sale or other disposition which is a part of a transaction in which the entire interest in property is transferred to any person or persons.

2,673

Code Sec. 1001 — Basis

In 1993, P.L. 103-66, Sec. 13213(a)(2)(E), deleted subsec. (f), effective for expenses incurred after 12/31/93.
Prior to deletion, subsec. (f) read as follows:
"(f) Cross reference. For treatment of certain expenses incident to the sale of a residence which were deducted as moving expenses by the taxpayer or his spouse under section 217(a), see section 217(e)."

In 1984, P.L. 98-369, Sec. 421(b)(4), substituted "section 1014, 1015, or 1041" for "section 1014 or 1015" in para. (e)(1), effective for transfers after 7/18/84 in tax. yrs. end. after 7/18/84. Secs. 421(d)(2)–(4) of this Act provide:

"(2) Election to have amendments apply to transfers after 1983.—If both spouses or former spouses make an election under this paragraph, the amendments made by this section shall apply to all transfers made by such spouses (or former spouses) after December 31, 1983.

"(3) Exception for transfers pursuant to existing decrees.—Except in the case of an election under paragraph (2), the amendments made by this section shall not apply to transfers under any instrument in effect on or before the date of the enactment of this Act unless both spouses (or former spouses) elect to have such amendments apply to transfers under such instrument.

"(4) Election.—Any election under paragraph (2) or (3) shall be made in such manner, at such time, and subject to such conditions, as the Secretary of the Treasury or his delegate may by regulations prescribe."

In 1980, P.L. 96-223, repealed Sec. 702(c)(9) of P.L. 95-600, and the amendment made by Sec. 702(c)(9) [see below], effective for decedents dying after 12/31/76. Sec. 401(b) of P.L. 96-223 provides as follows:
"(b) Revival of prior law.
"Except to the extent necessary to carry out subsection (d), the Internal Revenue Code of 1954 shall be applied and administered as if the provisions repealed by subsection (a), and the amendments made by those provisions, had not been enacted."

In 1978, P.L. 95-600, Sec. 702(c)(9), [repealed by Sec. 401(a) of P.L. 96-223 see above], substituted "section 1014, 1015, or 1023" for "section 1014 or 1015" in para. (e)(1), effective for tax. yrs. begin. after 12/31/76.

In 1976, P.L. 94-455, Sec. 1901(a)(121), amended subsec. (c), effective for tax. yrs. begin. after 12/31/76.
Prior to amendment, subsec. (c) read as follows:
"(c) Recognition of gain or loss.
"In the case of a sale or exchange of property, the extent to which the gain or loss determined under this section shall be recognized for purposes of this subtitle shall be determined under section 1002."

In 1969, P.L. 91-172, Sec. 231(c)(2), added subsec. (f), effective for tax. yrs. begin. after 12/31/69, except that Sec. 231(f)(2) provides that: "the amendments made by this section shall not apply (at the election of the taxpayer made at such time and manner as the Secretary of the Treasury or his delegate prescribes) with respect to moving expenses paid or incurred before July 1, 1970, in connection with the commencement of work by the taxpayer as an employee at a new principal place of work of which the taxpayer had been notified by his employer on or before December 19, 1969."
—P.L. 91-172, Sec. 516(a), added subsec. (e), effective for sales or other dispositions after 10/9/69.

Sec. 1002. Repealed.

In 1976, P.L. 94-455, Sec. 1901(b)(28)(B)(i), repealed Code Sec. 1002, effective for tax. yrs. begin. after 12/31/76.
Prior to repeal, Code Sec. 1002 read as follows:
"Sec. 1002. Recognition of gain or loss.
"Except as otherwise provided in this subtitle, on the sale or exchange of property the entire amount of the gain or loss, determined under section 1001, shall be recognized."

PART II.—BASIS RULES OF GENERAL APPLICATION

Sec.
1011. Adjusted basis for determining gain or loss.
1012. Basis of property—cost.
1013. Basis of property included in inventory.
1014. Basis of property acquired from a decedent.
1015. Basis of property acquired by gifts and transfers in trust.
1016. Adjustments to basis.
1017. Discharge of indebtedness.
1018. Repealed.
1019. Property on which lessee has made improvements.
1020. Repealed.
1021. Sale of annuities.
1022. Treatment of property acquired from a decedent dying after December 31, 2009.
1023. Cross references.

In 2001, P.L. 107-16, Sec. 542(e)(6), added item 1022.
In 1980, P.L. 96-589, Sec. 6(h)(2), repealed the item for 1018.
—P.L. 96-223, Sec. 401(a), Sec. 2005(e)(1) of P.L. 94-455 and the amendment made by Sec. 2005(e)(1) [see below].
In 1978, P.L. 95-600, Sec. 515(5), substituted "December 31, 1979" for "December 31, 1976" in the item for Code Sec. 1023. [inoperative]
In 1976, P.L. 94-455, Sec. 1901(b)(29)(B), repealed the item for Code Sec. 1020.
—P.L. 94-455, Sec. 1901(b)(30)(C), repealed the item for Code Sec. 1022.
—P.L. 94-455, Sec. 2005(e)(1), redesignated the item for Code Sec. 1023 as 1024 ... added a new item for Code Sec. 1023, but Sec. 2005(e)(1) of P.L. 94-455 was repealed by Sec. 401(a) of P.L. 96-223 [see above]. The item for Code Sec. 1023 added by Sec. 2005(e)(1) read as follows:
"1023. CARRYOVER BASIS FOR CERTAIN PROPERTY ACQUIRED FROM A DECEDENT DYING AFTER DECEMBER 31, 1976."
In 1964, added item 1022, and redesignated former item 1022 as 1023.

Sec. 1011. Adjusted basis for determining gain or loss.
(a) General rule.
The adjusted basis for determining the gain or loss from the sale or other disposition of property, whenever acquired, shall be the basis (determined under section 1012 or other applicable sections of this subchapter and subchapters C (relating to corporate distributions and adjustments), K (relating to partners and partnerships), and P (relating to capital gains and losses)), adjusted as provided in section 1016.
(b) Bargain sale to a charitable organization.
If a deduction is allowable under section 170 (relating to charitable contributions) by reason of a sale, then the adjusted basis for determining the gain from such sale shall be that portion of the adjusted basis which bears the same ratio to the adjusted basis as the amount realized bears to the fair market value of the property.

In 1969, P.L. 91-172, Sec. 201(f), added "(a) General rule." before "The adjusted basis" and added subsec. (b), effective for sales made after 12/19/69.

Sec. 1012. Basis of property—cost.
(a) In general.
The basis of property shall be the cost of such property, except as otherwise provided in this subchapter and subchapters C (relating to corporate distributions and adjustments), K (relating to partners and partnerships), and P (relating to capital gains and losses).
(b) Special rule for apportioned real estate taxes.
The cost of real property shall not include any amount in respect of real property taxes which are treated under section 164(d) as imposed on the taxpayer.
(c) Determinations by account.
(1) In general. In the case of the sale, exchange, or other disposition of a specified security on or after the applicable date, the conventions prescribed by regulations under this section shall be applied on an account by account basis.

(2) Application to certain funds.
(A) In general. Except as provided in subparagraph (B), any stock for which an average basis method is permissible under section 1012 which is acquired before January 1, 2012, shall be treated as a separate account from any such stock acquired on or after such date.
(B) Election fund for treatment as single account. If a fund described in subparagraph (A) elects to have this subparagraph apply with respect to one or more of its stock holders—
(i) subparagraph (A) shall not apply with respect to any stock in such fund held by such stockholders, and
(ii) all stock in such fund which is held by such stockholders shall be treated as covered securities described in section 6045(g)(3) without regard to the date of the acquisition of such stock.

A rule similar to the rule of the preceding sentence shall apply with respect to a broker holding such stock as a nominee.

(3) Definitions. For purposes of this section, the terms "specified security" and "applicable date" shall have the meaning given such terms in section 6045(g).

(d) Average basis for stock acquired pursuant to a dividend reinvestment plan.

(1) In general. In the case of any stock acquired after December 31, 2010, in connection with a dividend reinvestment plan, the basis of such stock while held as part of such plan shall be determined using one of the methods which may be used for determining the basis of stock in an open-end fund.

(2) Treatment after transfer. In the case of the transfer to another account of stock to which paragraph (1) applies, such stock shall have a cost basis in such other account equal to its basis in the dividend reinvestment plan immediately before such transfer (properly adjusted for any fees or other charges taken into account in connection with such transfer).

(3) Separate accounts; election for treatment as single account. Rules similar to the rules of subsection (c)(2) shall apply for purposes of this subsection.

(4) Dividend reinvestment plan. For purposes of this subsection—

(A) In general. The term "dividend reinvestment plan" means any arrangement under which dividends on any stock are reinvested in stock identical to the stock with respect to which the dividends are paid.

(B) Initial stock acquisition treated as acquired in connection with plan. Stock shall be treated as acquired in connection with a dividend reinvestment plan if such stock is acquired pursuant to such plan or if the dividends paid on such stock are subject to such plan.

In 2008, P.L. 110-343, Sec. 403(b)(1)DivB, substituted "(a) In general. The basis of property" for "The basis of property" in Code Sec. 1012... Sec. 403(b)(2)DivB, substituted "(b) Special rule for apportioned real estate taxes. The cost of real property" for "The cost of real property" in Code Sec. 1012... Sec. 403(b)(3)DivB, added subsec. (c) and subsec. (d), effective 1/1/2011.

Sec. 1013. Basis of property included in inventory.

If the property should have been included in the last inventory, the basis shall be the last inventory value thereof.

Sec. 1014. Basis of property acquired from a decedent.

(a) In general.

Except as otherwise provided in this section, the basis of property in the hands of a person acquiring the property from a decedent or to whom the property passed from a decedent shall, if not sold, exchanged, or otherwise disposed of before the decedent's death by such person, be—

(1) the fair market value of the property at the date of the decedent's death,

(2) in the case of an election under either section 2032 or section 811(j) of the Internal Revenue Code of 1939 where the decedent died after October 21, 1942, its value at the applicable valuation date prescribed by those sections,

(3) in the case of an election under section 2032A, its value determined under such section, or

(4) to the extent of the applicability of the exclusion described in section 2031(c), the basis in the hands of the decedent.

(b) Property acquired from the decedent.

For purposes of subsection (a), the following property shall be considered to have been acquired from or to have passed from the decedent:

(1) Property acquired by bequest, devise, or inheritance, or by the decedent's estate from the decedent;

(2) Property transferred by the decedent during his lifetime in trust to pay the income for life to or on the order or direction of the decedent, with the right reserved to the decedent at all times before his death to revoke the trust;

(3) In the case of decedents dying after December 31, 1951, property transferred by the decedent during his lifetime in trust to pay the income for life to or on the order or direction of the decedent with the right reserved to the decedent at all times before his death to make any change in the enjoyment thereof through the exercise of a power to alter, amend, or terminate the trust;

(4) Property passing without full and adequate consideration under a general power of appointment exercised by the decedent by will;

(5) In the case of decedents dying after August 26, 1937, and before January 1, 2005, property acquired by bequest, devise, or inheritance or by the decedent's estate from the decedent, if the property consists of stock or securities of a foreign corporation, which with respect to its taxable year next preceding the date of the decedent's death was, under the law applicable to such year, a foreign personal holding company. In such case, the basis shall be the fair market value of such property at the date of the decedent's death or the basis in the hands of the decedent, whichever is lower;

(6) In the case of decedents dying after December 31, 1947, property which represents the surviving spouse's one-half share of community property held by the decedent and the surviving spouse under the community property laws of any State, or possession of the United States or any foreign country, if at least one-half of the whole of the community interest in such property was includible in determining the value of the decedent's gross estate under chapter 11 of subtitle B (section 2001 and following, relating to estate tax) or section 811 of the Internal Revenue Code of 1939;

(7) In the case of decedents dying after October 21, 1942, and on or before December 31, 1947, such part of any property, representing the surviving spouse's one-half share of property held by a decedent and the surviving spouse under the community property laws of any State, or possession of the United States or any foreign country, as was included in determining the value of the gross estate of the decedent, if a tax under chapter 3 of the Internal Revenue Code of 1939 was payable on the transfer of the net estate of the decedent. In such case, nothing in this paragraph shall reduce the basis below that which would exist if the Revenue Act of 1948 had not been enacted;

(8) In the case of decedents dying after December 31, 1950, and before January 1, 1954, property which represents the survivor's interest in a joint and survivor's annuity if the value of any part of such interest was required to be included in determining the value of decedent's gross estate under section 811 of the Internal Revenue Code of 1939;

(9) In the case of decedents dying after December 31, 1953, property acquired from the decedent by reason of death, form of ownership, or other conditions (including property acquired through the exercise or non-exercise of a power of appointment), if by reason thereof the property is required to be included in determining the value of the decedent's gross estate under chapter 11 of subtitle B or under the Internal Revenue Code of 1939. In such case, if the property is acquired before the death of the decedent, the basis shall be the amount determined under subsection

Code Sec. 1014(b)(9)   **Basis**

(a) reduced by the amount allowed to the taxpayer as deductions in computing taxable income under this subtitle or prior income tax laws for exhaustion, wear and tear, obsolescence, amortization, and depletion on such property before the death of the decedent. Such basis shall be applicable to the property commencing on the death of the decedent. This paragraph shall not apply to—

  (A) annuities described in section 72;

  (B) property to which paragraph (5) would apply if the property had been acquired by bequest; and

  (C) property described in any other paragraph of this subsection.

(10) Property includible in the gross estate of the decedent under section 2044 (relating to certain property for which marital deduction was previously allowed). In any such case, the last 3 sentences of paragraph (9) shall apply as if such property were described in the first sentence of paragraph (9).

(c) Property representing income in respect of a decedent.

This section shall not apply to property which constitutes a right to receive an item of income in respect of a decedent under section 691.

(d) Special rule with respect to DISC stock.

If stock owned by a decedent in a DISC or former DISC (as defined in section 992(a)) acquires a new basis under subsection (a), such basis (determined before the application of this subsection) shall be reduced by the amount (if any) which would have been included in gross income under section 995(c) as a dividend if the decedent had lived and sold the stock at its fair market value on the estate tax valuation date. In computing the gain the decedent would have had if he had lived and sold the stock, his basis shall be determined without regard to the last sentence of section 996(e)(2) (relating to reductions of basis of DISC stock). For purposes of this subsection, the estate tax valuation date is the date of the decedent's death or, in the case of an election under section 2032, the applicable valuation date prescribed by that section.

(e) Appreciated property acquired by decedent by gift within 1 year of death.

  (1) In general. In the case of a decedent dying after December 31, 1981, if—

    (A) appreciated property was acquired by the decedent by gift during the 1-year period ending on the date of the decedent's death, and

    (B) such property is acquired from the decedent by (or passes from the decedent to) the donor of such property (or the spouse of such donor),

the basis of such property in the hands of such donor (or spouse) shall be the adjusted basis of such property in the hands of the decedent immediately before the death of the decedent.

  (2) Definitions. For purposes of paragraph (1)—

    (A) Appreciated property. The term "appreciated property" means any property if the fair market value of such property on the day it was transferred to the decedent by gift exceeds its adjusted basis.

    (B) Treatment of certain property sold by estate. In the case of any appreciated property described in subparagraph (A) of paragraph (1) sold by the estate of the decedent or by a trust of which the decedent was the grantor, rules similar to the rules of paragraph (1) shall apply to the extent the donor of such property (or the spouse of such donor) is entitled to the proceeds from such sale.

• **Caution:** Code Sec. 1014(f), was added by Sec. 541, P.L. 107-16, EGTRRA. As provided in Sec. 301(a), P.L. 111-312, this amendment will apply as if never enacted, effective for estates of decedents dying, and transfers made, after 12/31/2009.

(f) Termination.

This section shall not apply with respect to decedents dying after December 31, 2009.

In 2010, P.L. 111-312, Sec. 101(a)(1), substituted "December 31, 2012" for "December 31, 2010" both places it appeared in Sec. 901, P.L. 107-16 [see below], effective as if included in the enactment of P.L. 107-16, EGTRRA, 6/7/2001.

—P.L. 111-312, Sec. 301(a), provides that Code Sec. 1014, as amended by Sec. 541, P.L. 107-16, (added subsec. (f), see below) will read as if such provision had never been enacted, effective for estates of decedents dying, and transfers made, after 12/31/2009.

Sec. 301(a), P.L. 111-312, provides:

"(a) In general. Each provision of law amended by subtitle A or E of title V of the Economic Growth and Tax Relief Reconciliation Act of 2001 is amended to read as such provision would read if such subtitle had never been enacted."

Prior to the enactment of Sec. 301(a) of P.L. 111-312, subsec. (f) read as follows:

"(f) Termination. This section shall not apply with respect to decedents dying after December 31, 2009."

—P.L. 111-312, Sec. 301(c), of this Act, provides

"(c) Special election with respect to estates of decedents dying in 2010. Notwithstanding subsection (a), in the case of an estate of a decedent dying after December 31, 2009, and before January 1, 2011, the executor (within the meaning of section 2203 of the Internal Revenue Code of 1986) may elect to apply such Code as though the amendments made by subsection (a) do not apply with respect to chapter 11 of such Code and with respect to property acquired or passing from such decedent (within the meaning of section 1014(b) of such Code). Such election shall be made at such time and in such manner as the Secretary of the Treasury or the Secretary's delegate shall provide. Such an election once made shall be revocable only with the consent of the Secretary of the Treasury or the Secretary's delegate. For purposes of section 2652(a)(1) of such Code, the determination of whether any property is subject to the tax imposed by such chapter 11 shall be made without regard to any election made under this subsection."

—P.L. 111-312, Sec. 301(d), of this Act, provides

" (d) Extension of time for performing certain acts.

" (1) Estate tax. In the case of the estate of a decedent dying after December 31, 2009, and before the date of the enactment of this Act, the due date for—

" (A) filing any return under section 6018 of the Internal Revenue Code of 1986 (including any election required to be made on such a return) as such section is in effect after the date of the enactment of this Act without regard to any election under subsection (c),

" (B) making any payment of tax under chapter 11 of such Code, and

" (C) making any disclaimer described in section 2518(b) of such Code of an interest in property passing by reason of the death of such decedent, shall not be earlier than the date which is 9 months after the date of the enactment of this Act.

" (2) Generation-skipping tax. In the case of any generation-skipping transfer made after December 31, 2009, and before the date of the enactment of this Act, the due date for filing any return under section 2662 of the Internal Revenue Code of 1986 (including any election required to be made on such a return) shall not be earlier than the date which is 9 months after the date of the enactment of this Act."

In 2004, P.L. 108-357, Sec. 413(c)(18), added "and before January 1, 2005," after "August 26, 1937," in para. (b)(5), effective for tax. yrs. of foreign corporations begin. after 12/31/2004, and for tax. yrs. of United States shareholders with or within which such tax. yrs. of foreign corporations end.

In 2002, P.L. 107-358, Sec. 2, added subsec. (c) in Sec. 901 of P.L. 107-16 [see below], effective 12/17/2002.

In 2001, P.L. 107-16, Sec. 541, added subsec. (f), effective 6/7/2001.

—P.L. 107-16, Sec. 901, of this Act [as amended by Sec. 2, P.L. 107-358, and Sec. 101(a)(1), P.L. 111-312, see above], reads as follows:

"Sec. 901. Sunset of provisions of Act.

"(a) In general. All provisions of, and amendments made by, this Act shall not apply—

"(1) to taxable, plan, or limitation years beginning after December 31, 2012, or

"(2) in the case of title V, to estates of decedents dying, gifts made, or generation skipping transfers, after December 31, 2012.

"(b) Application of certain laws. The Internal Revenue Code of 1986 and the Employee Retirement Income Security Act of 1974 shall be applied and administered to years, estates, gifts, and transfers described in subsection (a) as if the provisions and amendments described in subsection (a) had never been enacted.

"(c) Exception. Subsection (a) shall not apply to section 803 (relating to no federal income tax on restitution received by victims of the Nazi regime or their heirs or estates)."

In 1997, P.L. 105-34, Sec. 508(b), deleted "or" at the end of paras. (a)(1) and (2), substituted ", or" for the period at the end of para. (a)(3), and added para. (a)(4), effective for estates of decedents dying after 12/31/97.

In 1983, P.L. 97-448, Sec. 104(a)(1)(A), added para. (b)(10), effective for estates of decedents dying after 12/31/81.

Basis   Code Sec. 1014

In **1981**, P.L. 97-34, Sec. 425(a), added subsec. (e), effective for property acquired after 8/13/81 by decedents dying after 12/31/81.

In **1980**, P.L. 96-223, Sec. 401(a), repealed Sec. 2005(a)(1) of P.L. 94-455 which amended subsec. (d), effective for decedents dying after 12/31/76. [see below].

Sec. 401(b) of P.L. 96-223 provides as follows:

"(b) Revival of prior law. Except to the extent necessary to carry out subsection (d), the Internal Revenue Code of 1954 shall be applied and administered as if the provisions repealed by subsection (a), and the amendments made by those provisions, had not been enacted."

—P.L. 96-223, Sec. 401(d), provides:

"(d) Election of carryover basis rules by certain estates. Notwithstanding any other provision of law, in the case of a decedent dying after December 31, 1976, and before November 7, 1978, the executor (within the meaning of section 2203 of the Internal Revenue Code of 1954) of such decedent's estate may irrevocably elect, within 120 days following the date of enactment of this Act and in such manner as the Secretary of the Treasury or his delegate shall prescribe, to have the basis of all property acquired from or passing from the decedent (within the meaning of section 1014(b) of the Internal Revenue Code of 1954) determined for all purposes under such Code as though the provisions of section 2005 of the Tax Reform Act of 1976 (as amended by the provisions of section 702(c) of the Revenue Act of 1978) applied to such property acquired or passing from such decedent."

Sec. 2005(a)(1), (a)(2) (as amended by Sec. 702(c)(2), (3), (4), (6), (7) and (8) of P.L. 95-600) (a)(3), (a)(5) and (d) of P.L. 94-455 reads as follows:

"SEC. 2005. CARRYOVER BASIS.

"(a) General rule.

"(1) Amendment of section 1014. Subsection (d) of section 1014 (relating to basis of property acquired from a decedent) is amended to read as follows:

"(d) Decedents dying after December 31, 1976. In the case of a decedent dying after December 31, 1976, the section shall not apply to any property for which a carryover basis is provided by section 1023.'

"(2) Carryover basis. Part II of subchapter O of chapter 1 (relating to basis rules of general application) is amended by redesignating section 1023 as section 1024 and by inserting after section 1022 the following new section:

"SEC. 1023. CARRYOVER BASIS FOR CERTAIN PROPERTY ACQUIRED FROM A DECEDENT DYING AFTER DECEMBER 31, 1976.

"(a) General rule.

"(1) Carryover basis. Except as otherwise provided in this section, the basis of carryover basis property acquired from a decedent dying after December 31, 1979, in the hands of the person so acquiring it shall be the adjusted basis of the property immediately before the death of the decedent, further adjusted as provided in this section.

"(2) Loss on personal and household effects. In the case of any carryover basis property which, in the hands of the decedent, was a personal or household effect, for purposes of determining loss, the basis of such property in the hands of the person acquiring such property from the decedent shall not exceed its fair market value.

"(b) Carryover basis property defined.

"(1) In general. For purposes of this section, the term 'carryover basis property' means any property which is acquired from or passed from a decedent (within the meaning of section 1014(b)) and which is not excluded pursuant to paragraph (2) or (3).

"(2) Certain property not carryover basis property. The term 'carryover basis property' does not include—

"(A) any item of gross income in respect of a decedent described in section 691;

"(B) property described in section 2042 (relating to proceeds of life insurance);

"(C) a joint and survivor annuity under which the surviving annuitant is taxable under section 72, and payments and distributions under a deferred compensation plan described in part I of subchapter D of chapter 1 to the extent such payments and distributions are taxable to the decedent's beneficiary under chapter 1;

"(D) property included in the decedent's gross estate by reason of section 2035, 2038, or 2041 which has been disposed of before the decedent's death in a transaction in which gain or loss is recognizable for purposes of chapter 1;

"(E) stock or a stock option passing from the decedent to the extent income in respect of such stock or stock option is includable in gross income under section 422(c)(1), 423(c), or 424(c)(1); and

"(F) property described in section 1014(b)'(5).

"(3) $10,000 exclusion for certain assets.

"(A) Exclusion. The term 'carryover basis property' does not include any asset—

"(i) which, in the hands of the decedent, was a personal or household effect, and

"(ii) with respect to which the executor has made an election under this paragraph.

"(B) Limitation. The fair market value of all assets designated under this subsection with respect to any decedent shall not exceed $10,000.

"(C) Election. An election under this paragraph with respect to any asset shall be made by the executor not later than the date prescribed by section 6075(a) for filing the return of the tax imposed by section 2001 or 2101 (including extension thereof), and shall be made in such manner as the Secretary shall by regulations prescribe.

"(c) Increase in basis for Federal and State estate taxes attributable to appreciation.

"(1) Federal estate taxes. The basis of appreciated carryover basis property (determined after any adjustment under subsection (h)) which is subject to the tax imposed by section 2001 or 2101 in the hands of the person acquiring it from the decedent shall be increased by an amount which bears the same ratio to the Federal estate taxes as—

"(A) the net appreciation in value of such property, bears to

"(B) the fair market value of all property which is subject to the tax imposed by section 2001 or 2101.

"(2) State estate taxes. The basis of appreciated carryover basis property (determined after any adjustment under subsection (h)) which is subject to State estate taxes in the hands of the person acquiring it from the decedent shall be increased by an amount which bears the same ratio to the State estate taxes as—

"(A) the net appreciation in value of such property, bears to

"(B) the fair market value of all property which is subject to the State estate taxes.

"(d) $60,000 minimum for bases of carryover basis properties.

"(1) In general. If $60,000 exceeds the aggregate bases (as determined after any adjustment under subsection (h) or (c)) of all carryover basis property, the basis of each appreciated carryover basis property (after any adjustment under subsection (h) or (c)) shall be increased by an amount which bears the same ratio to the amount of such excess as—

"(A) the net appreciation in value of such property, bears to

"(B) the net appreciation in value of all such property.

"(2) Special rule for personal or household effect. For purposes of paragraph (1), the basis of any property which is a personal or household effect shall be treated as not greater than the fair market value of such property.

"(3) Nonresident not citizen. This subsection shall not apply to any carryover basis property acquired from any decedent who was (at the time of his death) a nonresident not a citizen of the United States.

"(e) Further increase in basis for certain state succession tax paid by transferee of property. If—

"(1) any person acquires appreciated carryover basis property from a decedent, and

"(2) such person actually pays an amount of estate, inheritance, legacy, or succession taxes with respect to such property to any State or the District of Columbia,

then the basis of such property (after any adjustment under subsection (h), (c), or (d)) shall be increased by an amount which bears the same ratio to the aggregate amount of all such taxes paid by such person as—

"(A) the net appreciation in value of such property, bears to

"(B) the fair market value of all property acquired by such person which is subject to such taxes.

"(f) Special rules and definitions for application of subsections (c), (d), and (e).

"(1) Fair market value limitation. The adjustments under subsections (c), (d), and (e) shall not increase the basis of property above its fair market value.

"(2) Net appreciation. For purposes of this section, the net appreciation in value of any property is the amount by which the fair market value of such property exceeds the adjusted basis of such property immediately before the death of the decedent (as determined after any adjustment under subsection (h)). For purposes of paragraph (2) of subsection (c), such adjusted basis shall be increased by the amount of any adjustment under paragraph (1) of subsection (c), for purposes of subsection (d), such adjusted basis shall be increased by the amount of any adjustment under subsection (c), and, for purposes of subsection (e), such adjusted basis shall be increased by the amount of any adjustment under subsection (c) or (d).

"(3) Federal and State estate taxes. For purposes of subsection (c)—

"(A) Federal estate taxes. The term 'Federal estate taxes' means the tax imposed by section 2001 or 2101, reduced by the credits against such tax.

"(B) State estate taxes. The term 'State estate taxes' means any estate, inheritance, legacy, or succession taxes, for which the estate is liable, actually paid by the estate to any State or the District of Columbia.

"(4) Certain marital and charitable deduction property treated as not subject to tax. For purposes of subsections (c) and (e), property shall be treated as not subject to a tax—

"(A) with respect to the tax imposed by section 2001 or 2101, to the extent that a deduction is allowable with respect to such property under section 2055 or 2056 or under section 2106(a)(2), and

"(B) with respect to State estate taxes and with respect to the State taxes referred to in subsection (e)(2), to the extent that such property is not subject to such taxes.

"(5) Appreciated carryover basis property. For purposes of this section, the term 'appreciated carryover basis property' means any carryover basis property if the fair market value of such property exceeds the adjusted basis of such property immediately before the death of the decedent.

"(g) Other special rules and definitions.

"(1) Fair market value. For purposes of this section, when not otherwise distinctly expressed, the term 'fair market value' means value as determined under chapter 11 (without regard to whether there is a mortgage on, or indebtedness in respect of, the property).

"(2) Property passing from the decedent. For purposes of this section, property passing from the decedent shall be treated as property acquired from the decedent.

"(3) Decedent's basis unknown. If the facts necessary to determine the basis (unadjusted) of carryover basis property immediately before the death of the decedent are unknown and cannot be reasonably ascertained, such basis shall be treated as being the fair market value of such property as of the date (or approximate date) at which such property was acquired by the decedent or by the last preceding owner in whose hands it did not have a basis determined in whole or in part by reference to its basis in the hands of a prior holder.

"(h) Adjustment to basis for December 31, 1976, fair market value.

"(1) Marketable bonds and securities. If the adjusted basis immediately before the death of the decedent of any property which is carryover basis property reflects the adjusted basis of any marketable bond or security on December 31, 1976, and if the fair market value of such bond or security on December 31, 1976, exceeded its adjusted basis on such date, then, for purposes of determining gain and applying this section, the adjusted basis of such property shall be increased by the amount of such excess.

"(2) Property other than marketable bonds and securities.

"(A) In general. If —

"(i) the adjusted basis immediately before the death of the decedent of any property which is carryover basis property reflects the adjusted basis on December 31, 1976, of any property other than a marketable bond or security, and

"(ii) the value of such carryover basis property (as determined with respect to the estate of the decedent without regard to section 2032) exceeds the adjusted basis of such property immediately before the death of the decedent (determined without regard to this subsection),

then, for purposes of determining gain and applying this section, the adjusted basis of such property immediately before the death of the decedent (determined without regard to this subsection) shall be increased by the amount determined under subparagraph (B).

"(B) Amount of increase. The amount of the increase under this subparagraph for any property is the sum of —

"(i) the excess referred to in subparagraph (A)'(ii), reduced by an amount equal to all adjustments for depreciation, amortization, or depletion for the holding period of such property, and then multiplied by the applicable fraction determined under subparagraph (C), and

"(ii) the adjustments to basis for depreciation, amortization, or depletion which are attributable to that portion of the holding period for such property which occurs before January 1, 1977.

"(C) Applicable fraction. For purposes of subparagraph (B)'(i), the term 'applicable fraction' means, with respect to any property, a fraction —

"(i) the numerator of which is the number of days in the holding period with respect to such property which occurs before January 1, 1977, and

"(ii) the denominator of which is the total number of days in such holding period.

"(D) Substantial improvements. Under regulations prescribed by the Secretary, if there is a substantial improvement of any property, such substantial improvement shall be treated as a separate property for purposes of this paragraph.

"(E) Definitions. For purposes of this paragraph —

"(i) The term 'marketable bond or security' means any security for which, as of December 1976, there was a market on a stock exchange, in an over-the-counter market, or otherwise.

"(ii) The term 'holding period' means, with respect to any carryover basis property, the period during which the decedent (or, if any other person held such property immediately before the death of the decedent, such other person) held such property as determined under section 1223; except that such period shall end on the date of the decedent's death.

"(3) Minimum basis for tangible personal property.

"(A) In general. If the holding period for any carryover basis property which is tangible personal property includes December 31, 1976, then, for purposes of determining gain and applying this section, the adjusted basis of such property immediately before the death of the decedent shall be treated as being not less than the amount determined under subparagraph (B).

"(B) Amount. The amount determined under this subparagraph for any property is —

"(i) the value of such property (as determined with respect to the estate of the decedent without regard to section 2032), divided by

"(ii) 1.0066 to the nth power where n equals the number of full calendar months which have elapsed between December 31, 1976, and the date of the decedent's death.

"(4) Only one fresh start. There shall be no increase in basis under this subsection by reason of the death of any decedent if the adjusted basis of the property in the hands of such decedent reflects the adjusted basis of property which was carryover basis property with respect to a prior decedent.

"(i) Regulations. The Secretary shall prescribe such regulations as may be necessary to carry out the purposes of this section."

"(3) Amendment of section 1016. Section 1016(a) (relating to adjustments to basis) is amended by striking out the period at the end thereof and by inserting in lieu thereof a semicolon and by adding at the end thereof the following new paragraph:

"(23) to the extent provided in section 1023, relating to carryover basis for certain property acquired from a decedent dying after December 31, 1976.

"(5) Repeal of section 1246(e). — Section 1246 (relating to gain on foreign investment company stock) is amended by striking out subsection (e) and by redesignating subsections (f) and (g) as subsections (e) and (f), respectively.

"(d) Information requirement. —

"(1) In general. — Subpart A of part III of subchapter A of chapter 61 (relating to information concerning persons subject to special provisions) is amended by inserting after section 6039 the following new section:

"Sec. 6039A. Information regarding carryover basis property acquired from a decedent.

"(a) In general.

"Every executor (as defined in section 2203) shall furnish the secretary such information with respect to carryover basis property to which section 1023 applies as the Secretary may by regulations prescribe.

"(b) Statements to be furnished to persons who acquire property from a decedent.

"Every executor who is required to furnish information under subsection (a) shall furnish in writing to each person acquiring an item of such property from the decedent (or to whom the item passes from the decedent) the adjusted basis of such item.

"(2) Penalties. — Subchapter B of chapter 68 (relating to assessable penalties) is amended by adding at the end thereof the following new section:

"Sec. 6694. Failure to file information with respect to carryover basis property.

"(a) Information required to be furnished to the secretary.

"Any executor who fails to furnish information required under subsection (a) of section 6039A on the date prescribed therefor (determined with regard to any extension of time for filing), unless it is shown that such failure is due to reasonable cause and not to willful neglect, shall pay a penalty of $100 for each such failure, but the total amount imposed for all such failures shall not exceed $5,000.

"(b) Information required to be furnished to beneficiaries.

"Any executor who fails to furnish in writing to each person described in subsection (b) of section 6039A the information required under such subsection, unless it is shown that such failure is due to reasonable cause and not to willful neglect, shall pay a penalty of $50 for each such failure, but the total amount imposed for all such failures shall not exceed $2,500."

—P.L. 96-222, Sec. 107(a)(2)(A), substituted "section 2032A" for "section 2032.1" in para. (a)(3), effective for decedents dying after '79.

In **1978**, P.L. 95-600, Sec. 515(1), substituted "December 31, 1979" for "December 31, 1976" in the heading and text of subsec. (d), [as amended by repealed Sec. 2005(a)(1) of P.L. 94-455] effective 11/6/78.

—P.L. 95-600, Sec. 515(6), extended the effective date for changes made by Sec. 2005(a) of P.L. 94-445 to apply to decedents dying after '79.

Prior to amendment the effective date applies to decedents dying after '76. [inoperative]

—P.L. 95-600, Sec. 702(c)(1)(A), amended subsec. (a), effective for decedents dying after '79.

Prior to amendment subsec. (a) read as follows:

"(a) In general.

"Except as otherwise provided in this section, the basis of property in the hands of a person acquiring the property from a decedent or to whom the property passed from a decedent shall, if not sold, exchanged, or otherwise disposed of before the decedent's death by such person, be the fair market value of the property at the date of the decedent's death, or, in the case of an election under either section 2032 or section 811(j) of the Internal Revenue Code of 1939 where the decedent died after October 21, 1942, its value at the applicable valuation date prescribed by those sections."

In **1976**, P.L. 94-455, Sec. 1901(c)(8), deleted "Territory," after "State," in paras. (b)(6) and (b)(7), effective for tax. yrs. begin. after 12/31/76.

—P.L. 94-455, Sec. 2005(a)(1), amended subsec. (d), effective for decedent's dying after 12/31/79, but Sec. 2005(a)(1) was repealed by Sec. 401(a) of P.L. 96-223 [see above]. For subsec. (d) as amended by Sec. 2005(a)(1) see Sec. 401(d) of P.L. 96-223, above.

In **1971**, P.L. 92-178, Sec. 502(f), added subsec. (d), effective for tax. yrs. end. after 12/31/71, except that a corporation may not be a DISC for any tax. yr. begin. before 1/1/72.

In **1958**, P.L. 85-320, Sec. 2, deleted subsec. (d), effective for tax. yrs. end. after 12/31/56, but only in the case of employees dying after 12/31/56.

Prior to deletion, subsec. (d) read as follows:

"(d) Employee stock options. This section shall not apply to restricted stock options described in Section 421 which the employee has not exercised at death."

Sec. 1015. Basis of property acquired by gifts and transfers in trust.

(a) Gifts after December 31, 1920.

If the property was acquired by gift after December 31, 1920, the basis shall be the same as it would be in the hands of the donor or the last preceding owner by whom it was not acquired by gift, except that if such basis (adjusted for the period before the date of the gift as provided in section 1016) is greater than the fair market value of the property at the time of the gift, then for the purpose of determining loss the basis shall be such fair market value. If the facts necessary to determine the basis in the hands of the donor or the last preceding owner are unknown to the donee, the Secretary shall, if possible, obtain such facts from such donor or last preceding owner, or any other person cognizant thereof. If the Secretary finds it impossible to obtain such facts, the basis in the hands of such donor or last preceding owner shall be the fair market value of such property as found by the Secretary as of the date or approximate date at which, according to the best information that the Secretary is able to obtain, such property was acquired by such donor or last preceding owner.

(b) Transfer in trust after December 31, 1920.

If the property was acquired after December 31, 1920, by a transfer in trust (other than by a transfer in trust by a gift, bequest, or devise), the basis shall be the same as it would be in the hands of the grantor increased in the amount of gain or decreased in the amount of loss recognized to the grantor on such transfer under the law applicable to the year in which the transfer was made.

(c) Gift or transfer in trust before January 1, 1921.

If the property was acquired by gift or transfer in trust on or before December 31, 1920, the basis shall be the fair market value of such property at the time of such acquisition.

(d) Increased basis for gift tax paid.

(1) In general. If—

(A) the property is acquired by gift on or after September 2, 1958, the basis shall be the basis determined under subsection (a), increased (but not above the fair market value of the property at the time of the gift) by the amount of gift tax paid with respect to such gift, or

(B) the property was acquired by gift before September 2, 1958, and has not been sold, exchanged, or otherwise disposed of before such date, the basis of the property shall be increased on such date by the amount of gift tax paid with respect to such gift, but such increase shall not exceed an amount equal to the amount by which the fair market value of the property at the time of the gift exceeded the basis of the property in the hands of the donor at the time of the gift.

(2) Amount of tax paid with respect to gift. For purposes of paragraph (1), the amount of gift tax paid with respect to any gift is an amount which bears the same ratio to the amount of gift tax paid under chapter 12 with respect to all gifts made by the donor for the calendar year (or preceding calendar period) in which such gift is made as the amount of such gift bears to the taxable gifts (as defined in section 2503(a) but computed without the deduction allowed by section 2521) made by the donor during such calendar year or period. For purposes of the preceding sentence, the amount of any gift shall be the amount included with respect to such gift in determining (for the purposes of section 2503(a)) the total amount of gifts made during the calendar year or period, reduced by the amount of any deduction allowed with respect to such gift under section 2522 (relating to charitable deduction) or under section 2523 (relating to marital deduction).

(3) Gifts treated as made one-half by each spouse. For purposes of paragraph (1), where the donor and his spouse elected, under section 2513 to have the gift considered as made one-half by each, the amount of gift tax paid with respect to such gift under chapter 12 shall be the sum of the amounts of tax paid with respect to each half of such gift (computed in the manner provided in paragraph (2)).

(4) Treatment as adjustment to basis. For purposes of section 1016(b), an increase in basis under paragraph (1) shall be treated as an adjustment under section 1016(a).

(5) Application to gifts before 1955. With respect to any property acquired by gift before 1955, references in this subsection to any provision of this title shall be deemed to refer to the corresponding provision of the Internal Revenue Code of 1939 or prior revenue laws which was effective for the year in which such gift was made.

(6) Special rule for gifts made after December 31, 1976.

(A) In general. In the case of any gift made after December 31, 1976, the increase in basis provided by this subsection with respect to any gift for the gift tax paid under chapter 12 shall be an amount (not in excess of the amount of tax so paid) which bears the same ratio to the amount of tax so paid as—

(i) the net appreciation in value of the gift, bears to

(ii) the amount of the gift.

(B) Net appreciation. For purposes of paragraph (1), the net appreciation in value of any gift is the amount by which the fair market value of the gift exceeds the donor's adjusted basis immediately before the gift.

(e) Gifts between spouses.

In the case of any property acquired by gift in a transfer described in section 1041(a), the basis of such property in the hands of the transferee shall be determined under section 1041(b)(2) and not this section.

In 1984, P.L. 98-369, Sec. 421(b)(5), added subsec. (e), effective for transfers after 7/18/84 in tax. yrs. end. after 7/18/84. Sec. 421(d)(2)–(4) of this Act provide:

"(2) Election to have amendments apply to transfers after 1983.—If both spouses or former spouses make an election under this paragraph, the amendments made by this section shall apply to all transfers made by such spouses (or former spouses) after December 31, 1983.

"(3) Exception for transfers pursuant to existing decrees.—Except in the case of an election under paragraph (2), the amendments made by this section shall not apply to transfers made under any instrument in effect on or before the date of the enactment of this Act unless both spouses (or former spouses) elect to have such amendments apply to transfers under such instrument.

"(4) Election.— Any election under paragraph (2) or (3) shall be made in such manner, at such time, and subject to such conditions, as the Secretary of the Treasury or his delegate may by regulations prescribe."

In 1981, P.L. 97-34, Sec. 442(d)(1)(A), substituted "calendar year (or preceding calendar period)" for "calendar quarter (or calendar year if the gift was made before January 1, 1971)" in para. (d)(2) . . . Sec. 442(d)(1)(B), substituted "calendar year or period" for "calendar quarter or year" each place it appeared in para. (d)(2), effective for gifts made after 12/31/81.

In 1976, P.L. 94-455, Sec. 1901(a)(122), substituted "September 2, 1958" for "the date of the enactment of the Technical Amendments Act of 1958" in subparas. (d)(1)(A) and (B), effective for tax. begin. after 12/31/76.

—P.L. 94-455, Sec. 1906(b)(13)(A), substituted "Secretary" for "Secretary or his delegate" each place it appeared in subsec. (a), effective for tax. yrs. begin. after 12/31/76.

—P.L. 94-455, Sec. 2005(c), added para. (d)(6), effective for gifts made after 12/31/76.

In 1970, P.L. 91-614, Sec. 102(d)(1), substituted "calendar quarter (or calendar year if the gift was made before January 1, 1971)" for "calendar year" the first place it appeared in para. (d)(2) and substituted "calendar quarter or year" for "calendar year" every other place it appeared in para. (d)(2), effective for gifts made after 12/31/70.

In 1958, P.L. 85-866, Sec. 43(a), added subsec. (d), effective for tax. yrs. begin. after 12/31/53 and end. after 8/16/54.

Sec. 1016. Adjustments to basis.

(a) General rule.

Proper adjustment in respect of the property shall in all cases be made—

(1) for expenditures, receipts, losses, or other items, properly chargeable to capital account, but no such adjustment shall be made—

(A) for taxes or other carrying charges described in section 266, or

(B) for expenditures described in section 173 (relating to circulation expenditures),

for which deductions have been taken by the taxpayer in determining taxable income for the taxable year or prior taxable years;

(2) in respect of any period since February 28, 1913, for exhaustion, wear and tear, obsolescence, amortization, and depletion, to the extent of the amount—

(A) allowed as deductions in computing taxable income under this subtitle or prior income tax laws, and

(B) resulting (by reason of the deductions so allowed) in a reduction for any taxable year of the taxpayer's taxes under this subtitle (other than chapter 2, relating to tax on self-employment income), or prior income, war-profits, or excess-profits tax laws,

but not less than the amount allowable under this subtitle or prior income tax laws. Where no method has been adopted under section 167 (relating to depreciation deduction), the amount allowable shall be determined under the straight line method. Subparagraph (B) of this paragraph shall not apply in respect of any period since February 28,

1913, and before January 1, 1952, unless an election has been made under section 1020 (as in effect before the date of the enactment of the Tax Reform Act of 1976). Where for any taxable year before the taxable year 1932 the depletion allowance was based on discovery value or a percentage of income, then the adjustment for depletion for such year shall be based on the depletion which would have been allowable for such year if computed without reference to discovery value or a percentage of income;

(3) in respect of any period—
   (A) before March 1, 1913,
   (B) since February 28, 1913, during which such property was held by a person or an organization not subject to income taxation under this chapter or prior income tax laws,
   (C) since February 28, 1913, and before January 1, 1958, during which such property was held by a person subject to tax under part I of subchapter L (or the corresponding provisions of prior income tax laws), to the extent that paragraph (2) does not apply, and
   (D) since February 28, 1913, during which such property was held by a person subject to tax under part II of subchapter L (or the corresponding provisions of prior income tax laws), to the extent that paragraph (2) does not apply,

for exhaustion, wear and tear, obsolescence, amortization, and depletion, to the extent sustained;

(4) in the case of stock (to the extent not provided for in the foregoing paragraphs) for the amount of distributions previously made which, under the law applicable to the year in which the distribution was made, either were tax-free or were applicable in reduction of basis (not including distributions made by a corporation which was classified as a personal service corporation under the provisions of the Revenue Act of 1918 (40 Stat. 1057), or the Revenue Act of 1921 (42 Stat. 227), out of its earnings or profits which were taxable in accordance with the provisions of section 218 of the Revenue Act of 1918 or 1921);

(5) in the case of any bond (as defined in section 171(d)) the interest on which is wholly exempt from the tax imposed by this subtitle, to the extent of the amortizable bond premium disallowable as a deduction pursuant to section 171(a)(2), and in the case of any other bond (as defined in section 171(d)) to the extent of the deductions allowable pursuant to section 171(a)(1) (or the amount applied to reduce interest payments under section 171(e)(2)) with respect thereto;

(6) in the case of any municipal bond (as defined in section 75(b)), to the extent provided in section 75(a)(2);

(7) in the case of a residence the acquisition of which resulted, under section 1034 (as in effect on the day before the date of enactment [8/5/97] of the Taxpayer Relief Act of 1997), in the nonrecognition of any part of the gain realized on the sale, exchange, or involuntary conversion of another residence, to the extent provided in section 1034(e) (as so in effect);

(8) in the case of property pledged to the Commodity Credit Corporation, to the extent of the amount received as a loan from the Commodity Credit Corporation and treated by the taxpayer as income for the year in which received pursuant to section 77, and to the extent of any deficiency on such loan with respect to which the taxpayer has been relieved from liability;

(9) for amounts allowed as deductions as deferred expenses under section 616(b) (relating to certain expenditures in the development of mines) and resulting in a reduction of the taxpayer's taxes under this subtitle, but not less than the amounts allowable under such section for the taxable year and prior years;

(10) Repealed.

(11) for deductions to the extent disallowed under section 268 (relating to sale of land with unharvested crops), notwithstanding the provisions of any other paragraph of this subsection;

(12) to the extent provided in section 28(h) of the Internal Revenue Code of 1939 in the case of amounts specified in a shareholder's consent made under section 28 of such code;

(13) Repealed.

(14) for amounts allowed as deductions as deferred expenses under section 174(b)(1) (relating to research and experimental expenditures) and resulting in a reduction of the taxpayers' taxes under this subtitle, but not less than the amounts allowable under such section for the taxable year and prior years;

(15) for deductions to the extent disallowed under section 272 (relating to disposal of coal or domestic iron ore), notwithstanding the provisions of any other paragraph of this subsection;

(16) in the case of any evidence of indebtedness referred to in section 811(b) (relating to amortization of premium and accrual of discount in the case of life insurance companies), to the extent of the adjustments required under section 811(b) (or the corresponding provisions of prior income tax laws) for the taxable year and all prior taxable years;

(17) to the extent provided in section 1367 in the case of stock of, and indebtedness owed to, shareholders of an S corporation;

(18) to the extent provided in section 961 in the case of stock in controlled foreign corporations (or foreign corporations which were controlled foreign corporations) and of property by reason of which a person is considered as owning such stock;

(19) to the extent provided in section 50(c), in the case of expenditures with respect to which a credit has been allowed under section 38;

(20) for amounts allowed as deductions under section 59(e) (relating to optional 10-year writeoff of certain tax preferences);

(21) to the extent provided in section 1059 (relating to reduction in basis for extraordinary dividends);

(22) in the case of qualified replacement property the acquisition of which resulted under section 1042 in the nonrecognition of any part of the gain realized on the sale or exchange of any property, to the extent provided in section 1042(d),

(23) in the case of property the acquisition of which resulted under section 1043, 1044, 1045, or 1397B in the nonrecognition of any part of the gain realized on the sale of other property, to the extent provided in section 1043(c), 1044(d), 1045(b)(3), or 1397B(b)(4), as the case may be,

(24) to the extent provided in section 179A(e)(6)(A),

(25) to the extent provided in section 30(e)(1), [Ed. Note: Sec. 1141(b)(3), P.L. 111-5, 2/17/2009, says to amend Code Sec. 1016(a)(25). However, this amendment cannot be made to Code Sec. 1016(a)(25). We believe the intention of Congress was to amend Code Sec. 1016(a)(37), see below.]

Basis   Code Sec. 1016(c)(5)(B)

> • **Caution:** Code Sec. 1016(a)(26), following, reflects amendments made by Sec. 10909, P.L. 111-148. As provided in Sec. 10909(c), P.L. 111-148 as amended by Sec. 101(b)(1), P.L. 111-312, Code Sec. 1016(a)(26) will read as if those amendments had never been enacted, effective for tax. yrs. begin. after 12/31/2011. For Code Sec. 1016(a)(26) as it will read for tax. yrs. begin. after 12/31/2011, see below.

(26) to the extent provided in sections 36C(g) and 137(e),

> • **Caution:** Code Sec. 1016(a)(26), following, following, is effective for tax. yrs. begin. after 12/31/2011, and reflects the sunset of the amendments made by Sec. 10909, P.L. 111-148. For details of those amendments, effective date and sunset provisions, see the history for this Code Sec. For Code Sec. 1016(a)(26), effective for tax. yrs. begin. before 1/1/2012, see above.

(26) to the extent provided in sections 23(g) and 137(e),

> • **Caution:** Code Sec. 1016(a)(26), and Code Sec. 1016(a)(27) were amended, and Code Sec. 1016(a)(28) was added by P.L. 107-16, the Economic Growth and Tax Relief Reconciliation Act of 2001 (EGTRRA). These provisions generally sunset for tax years beginning after 12/31/2012. For specific sunset provisions, see Sec. 901, P.L. 107-16 (as amended) reproduced in history notes for this Code Sec.

(26) to the extent provided in sections 36C(g) and 137(e),
(27) in the case of a residence with respect to which a credit was allowed under section 1400C, to the extent provided in section 1400C(h),
(28) in the case of a facility with respect to which a credit was allowed under section 45F, to the extent provided in section 45F(f)(1),
(29) in the case of railroad track with respect to which a credit was allowed under section 45G, to the extent provided in section 45G(e)(3),
(30) to the extent provided in section 179B(c),
(31) to the extent provided in section 179D(e),
(32) to the extent provided in section 45L(e), in the case of amounts with respect to which a credit has been allowed under section 45L,
(33) to the extent provided in section 25C(f), in the case of amounts with respect to which a credit has been allowed under section 25C,
(34) to the extent provided in section 25D(f), in the case of amounts with respect to which a credit has been allowed under section 25D,
(35) to the extent provided in section 30B(h)(4),
(36) to the extent provided in section 30C(e)(1), and
(37) to the extent provided in section 30D(e)(4) [sic section 30D(f)(1)] [Ed. Note. Sec. 1141(b)(3), P.L. 111-5, says to substitute "section 30D(f)(1)" for "section 30D(e)(4)" in Code Sec. 1016(a)(25). However, we believe it was the intent of Congress to make that amendment to Code Sec. 1016(a)(37). The amendment is effective for vehicles acquired after 12/31/2009.].

(b) Substituted basis.

Whenever it appears that the basis of property in the hands of the taxpayer is a substituted basis, then the adjustments provided in subsection (a) shall be made after first making in respect of such substituted basis proper adjustments of a similar nature in respect of the period during which the property was held by the transferor, donor, or grantor, or during which the other property was held by the person for whom the basis is to be determined. A similar rule shall be applied in the case of a series of substituted bases.

(c) Increase in basis of property on which additional estate tax is imposed.

(1) Tax imposed with respect to entire interest. If an additional estate tax is imposed under section 2032A(c)(1) with respect to any interest in property and the qualified heir makes an election under this subsection with respect to the imposition of such tax, the adjusted basis of such interest shall be increased by an amount equal to the excess of—

(A) the fair market value of such interest on the date of the decedent's death (or the alternate valuation date under section 2032, if the executor of the decedent's estate elected the application of such section), over

(B) the value of such interest determined under section 2032A(a).

(2) Partial dispositions.

(A) In general. In the case of any partial disposition for which an election under this subsection is made, the increase in basis under paragraph (1) shall be an amount—

(i) which bears the same ratio to the increase which would be determined under paragraph (1) (without regard to this paragraph) with respect to the entire interest, as

(ii) the amount of the tax imposed under section 2032A(c)(1) with respect to such disposition bears to the adjusted tax difference attributable to the entire interest (as determined under section 2032A(c)(2)(B)).

(B) Partial disposition. For purposes of subparagraph (A), the term "partial disposition" means any disposition or cessation to which subsection (c)(2)(D), (h)(1)(B), or (i)(1)(B) of section 2032A applies.

(3) Time adjustment made. Any increase in basis under this subsection shall be deemed to have occurred immediately before the disposition or cessation resulting in the imposition of the tax under section 2032A(c)(1).

(4) Special rule in the case of substituted property. If the tax under section 2032A(c)(1) is imposed with respect to qualified replacement property (as defined in section 2032A(h)(3)(B)) or qualified exchange property (as defined in section 2032A(i)(3)), the increase in basis under paragraph (1) shall be made by reference to the property involuntarily converted or exchanged (as the case may be).

(5) Election.

(A) In general. An election under this subsection shall be made at such time and in such manner as the Secretary shall by regulations prescribe. Such an election, once made, shall be irrevocable.

(B) Interest on recaptured amount. If an election is made under this subsection with respect to any additional estate tax imposed under section 2032A(c)(1), for purposes of section 6601 (relating to interest on underpayments), the last date prescribed for payment of such tax shall be deemed to be the last date prescribed for payment of the tax imposed by section 2001with respect to the estate of the decedent (as determined for purposes of section 6601).

(d) Reduction in basis of automobile on which gas guzzler tax was imposed.

If—

(1) the taxpayer acquires any automobile with respect to which a tax was imposed by section 4064, and

(2) the use of such automobile by the taxpayer begins not more than 1 year after the date of the first sale for ultimate use of such automobile,

the basis of such automobile shall be reduced by the amount of the tax imposed by section 4064 with respect to such automobile. In the case of importation, if the date of entry or withdrawal from warehouse for consumption is later than the date of the first sale for ultimate use, such later date shall be substituted for the date of such first sale in the preceding sentence.

(e) Cross reference.

For treatment of separate mineral interests as one property, see section 614.

In 2010, P.L. 111-312, Sec. 101(a)(1), substituted "December 31, 2012" for "December 31, 2010" both places it appeared in Sec. 901, P.L. 107-16, effective as if included in the enactment of P.L. 107-16, EGTRRA, 6/7/2001.

—P.L. 111-312, Sec. 101(b)(1), amended Sec. 10909(c), P.L. 111-148.

Prior to amendment, Sec. 10909(c), P.L. 111-148 read as follows:

"(c) Application and Extension of EGTRRA Sunset. Notwithstanding section 901 of the Economic Growth and Tax Relief Reconciliation Act of 2001, such section shall apply to the amendments made by this section and the amendments mad by section 202 of such Act by substituting 'December 31, 2011' for 'December 31, 2010' in subsection (a)(1) therof."

—P.L. 111-312, Sec. 101(b)(2), substituted "Except as provided in subsection (c), the amendments" for "the amendments" in Sec. 10909(d), P.L. 111-148 (the effective date section for amendments made by Sec. 10909, P.L. 111-148)

Prior to amendment, Sec. 10909(d), P.L. 111-148 read as follows:

"(d) Effective Date. The amendments made by this section shall apply to taxable years beginning after December 31, 2009."

—P.L. 111-148, Sec. 10909(b)(2)(L), substituted "36C(g)" for "23(g)" in para. (a)(26), effective for tax. yrs. begin. after 12/31/2009, except as provided in Sec. 10909(c), see below.

—P.L. 111-148, Sec. 10909(c), of this Act, relating to the application and extension of the EGTRRA sunset, provides, as amended by Sec. 101(b)(1), P.L. 111-312, reads as follows:

"(c) Sunset provision. Each provision of law amended by this section is amended to read as such provision would read if this section had never been enacted. The amendments made by the preceding sentence shall apply to taxable years beginning after December 31, 2011."

In 2009, P.L. 111-5, Sec. 1141(b)(3), says to substitute "section 30D(f)(1)" for "section 30D(e)(4) in para. (a)(25). However, the amendment cannot be made to para. (a)(25). We believe it was the intent of Congress to make the amendment to para. (a)(37), effective for vehicles acquired after 12/31/2009.

—P.L. 111-5, Sec. 1142(b)(6), substituted 'section 30(e)(1)' for 'section 30(d)(1)' in para. (a)(25), effective for vehicles acquired after 2/17/2009.

In 2008, P.L. 110-343, Sec. 205(d)(2)DivB, deleted 'and' at the end of para. (a)(35), substituted ', and' for the period at the end of para. (a)(36), and added para. (a)(37), effective for tax. yrs. begin. after 12/31/2008.

In 2007, P.L. 110-172, Sec. 7(a)(1)(C), deleted para. (a)(31) and redesignated paras. (a)(32) through (a)(37) as paras. (a)(31) through (a)(36), respectively, effective for expenses paid or incurred after 12/31/2002, in tax. yrs. end. after 12/31/2002.

—P.L. 110-172, Sec. 11(a)(21), substituted 'section 25C(f)' for 'section 25C(e)' in para. (a)(33) [as redes. by Sec. 7(a)(1)(C) of this Act, see above]... Sec. 11(a)(22), substituted 'section 30C(e)(1)' for 'section 30C(f)' in para. (a)(36) [as redes. by Sec. 7(a)(1)(C) of this Act, see above], enacted 12/29/2007.

Prior to amendment, para. (a)(31) read as follows:

"(31) in the case of a facility with respect to which a credit was allowed under section 45H, to the extent provided in section 45H(d),"

In 2005, P.L. 109-135, Sec. 412(nn), substituted "1045(b)(3)" for "1045(b)(4)" in para. (a)(23), effective 12/21/2005.

—P.L. 109-58, Sec. 1331(b)(1), deleted "and" at the end of para. (a)(30), substituted ", and" for the period at the end of para. (a)(31), and added para. (a)(32), effective for property placed in service after 12/31/2005.

—P.L. 109-58, Sec. 1332(c), deleted "and" at the end of para. (a)(31) [as amended by Sec. 1331(b)(1) of this Act, see above], substituted ", and" for the period at the end of para. (a)(32) [as added by Sec. 1331(b)(1) of this Act, see above], and added para. (a)(33), effective for qualified new energy efficient homes acquired after 12/31/2005, in tax. yrs. end. after 12/31/2005.

—P.L. 109-58, Sec. 1333(b)(1), deleted "and" at the end of para. (a)(32) [as added by Sec. 1331(b)(1) and amended by Sec. 1332(c) of this Act, see above], substituted ", and" for the period at the end of para. (a)(33) [as added by Sec. 1332(c) of this Act, see above], and added para. (a)(34), effective for property placed in service after 12/31/2005.

—P.L. 109-58, Sec. 1335(b)(4), deleted "and" at the end of para. (a)(33) [as added by Sec. 1332(c) and amended by Sec. 1333(b)(1) of this Act, see above], substituted ", and" for the period at the end of para. (a)(34) [as added by Sec. 1333(b)(1) of this Act, see above], and added para. (a)(35), effective for property placed in service after 12/31/2005, in tax. yrs. end. after 12/31/2005.

—P.L. 109-58, Sec. 1341(b)(2), deleted "and" at the end of para. (a)(34) [as added by Sec. 1333(b)(1) and amended by Sec. 1335(b)(4) of this Act, see above], substituted ", and" for the period at the end of para. (a)(35) [as added by Sec. 1335(b)(4) of this Act, see above], and added para. (a)(36), effective for property placed in service after 12/31/2005, in tax. yrs. end. after 12/31/2005.

—P.L. 109-58, Sec. 1342(b)(2), deleted "and" at the end of para. (a)(35) [as added by Sec. 1335(b)(4) and amended by Sec. 1341(b)(2) of this Act, see above], substituted ", and" for the period at the end of para. (a)(36) [as added by Sec. 1341(b)(2) of this Act, see above], and added para. (a)(37), effective for property placed in service after 12/31/2005, in tax. yrs. end. after 12/31/2005.

In 2004, P.L. 108-357, Sec. 245(c)(2), deleted "and" at the end of para. (a)(27), substituted ", and" for the period at the end of para. (a)(28), and added para. (a)(29), effective for tax. yrs. begin. after 12/31/2004.

—P.L. 108-357, Sec. 338(b)(4), deleted "and" at the end of para. (a)(28) [as amended by Sec. 245(c)(2) of this Act, see above], substituted ", and" for the period at the end of para. (a)(29) [as added by Sec. 245(c)(2) of this Act, see above], and added para. (a)(30), effective for expenses paid or incurred after 12/31/2002, in tax. yrs. end. after 12/31/2002.

—P.L. 108-357, Sec. 339(d), deleted "and" at the end of para. (a)(29) [as added by Sec. 245(c)(2) and amended by Sec. 338(b)(4) of this Act, see above], substituted ", and" for the period at the end of para. (a)(30) [as added by Sec. 338(b)(4) of this Act, see above], and added para. (a)(31), effective for expenses paid or incurred after 12/31/2002, in tax. yrs. end. after 12/31/2002.

—P.L. 108-357, Sec. 413(c)(19), deleted para. (a)(13), effective for tax. yrs. of foreign corporations begin. after 12/31/2004, and for tax. yrs. of United States shareholders with or within which tax. yrs. of foreign corporations end.

Prior to deletion, para. (a)(13) read as follows:

"(13) to the extent provided in section 551(e) in the case of the stock of United States shareholders in a foreign personal holding company;"

In 2002, P.L. 107-358, Sec. 2, added subsec. (c) in Sec. 901 of P.L. 107-16 [see below], effective 12/17/2002.

In 2001, P.L. 107-16, Sec. 205(b)(3), deleted "and" at the end of para. (a)(26), substituted ", and" for the period at the end of para. (a)(27), and added para. (a)(28), effective for tax. yrs. begin. after 12/31/2001.

—P.L. 107-16, Sec. 901, of this Act [as amended by Sec. 2, P.L. 107-358, and Sec. 101(a)(1), P.L. 111-312, see above], reads as follows:

"Sec. 901. Sunset of provisions of Act.

"(a) In general. All provisions of, and amendments made by, this Act shall not apply—

"(1) to taxable, plan, or limitation years beginning after December 31, 2012, or

"(2) in the case of title V, to estates of decedents dying, gifts made, or generation skipping transfers, after December 31, 2012.

"(b) Application of certain laws. The Internal Revenue Code of 1986 and the Employee Retirement Income Security Act of 1974 shall be applied and administered to years, estates, gifts, and transfers described in subsection (a) as if the provisions and amendments described in subsection (a) had never been enacted.

"(c) Exception. Subsection (a) shall not apply to section 803 (relating to no federal income tax on restitution received by victims of the Nazi regime or their heirs or estates)."

In 2000, P.L. 106-554, Sec. 1(a)(7), [which enacted into law Sec. 116(b)(1)(A) of P.L. 106-554] substituted "1045, or 1397B" for "or 1045" in para. (a)(23)... Sec. 1(a)(7), [which enacted into law Sec. 116(b)(1)(B) of P.L. 106-554] substituted "1045(b)(4), or 1397B(b)(4)" for "or 1045(b)(4)" in para. (a)(23), effective for qualified empowerment zone assets acquired after 12/21/2000.

In 1998, P.L. 105-206, Sec. 6005(e)(3), added "on or" before "before" each place it appeared in the heading and text of Sec. 312(d)(2)[sic (e)] of P.L. 105-34, see below.

In 1997, P.L. 105-34, Sec. 312(d)(6), added "(as in effect on the day before the date of enactment of the Taxpayer Relief Act of 1997)" after "1034" in para. (a)(7) and added "(as so in effect)" after "1034(e)" in para. (a)(7), effective for sales and exchanges after 5/6/97. Sec. 312(d)(2)-(4) [sic (e)(2)-(4)] of this Act [as amended by Sec. 6005(e)(3), 105-206, see above], reads as follows:

"(2) Sales on or before date of enactment. At the election of the taxpayer, the amendments made by this section shall not apply to any sale or exchange on or before the date of the enactment of this Act.

"(3) Certain sales within 2 years after date of enactment. Section 121 of the Internal Revenue Code of 1986 (as amended by this section) shall be applied without regard to subsection (c)(2)(B) thereof in the case of any sale or exchange of property during the 2-year period beginning on the date of the enactment of this Act if the taxpayer held such property on the date of the enactment of this Act and fails to meet the ownership and use requirements of subsection (a) thereof with respect to such property.

"(4) Binding contracts. At the election of the taxpayer, the amendments made by this section shall not apply to a sale or exchange after the date of the enactment of this Act, if—

"(A) such sale or exchange is pursuant to a contract which was binding on such date, or

Basis   Code Sec. 1016

"(B) without regard to such amendments, gain would not be recognized under section 1034 of the Internal Revenue Code of 1986 (as in effect on the day before the date of the enactment of this Act) on such sale or exchange by reason of a new residence acquired on or before such date or with respect to the acquisition of which by the taxpayer a binding contract was in effect on such date.

This paragraph shall not apply to any sale or exchange by an individual if the treatment provided by section 877(a)(1) of the Internal Revenue Code of 1986 applies to such individual."

—P.L. 105-34, Sec. 313(b)(1)(A), substituted ", 1044, or 1045" for "or 1044" in para. (a)(23) . . . Sec. 313(b)(1)(B), substituted ", 1044(d), or 1045(b)(4)" for "or 1044(d)" in para. (a)(23), effective for sales after 8/5/97.

—P.L. 105-34, Sec. 701(b)(2), deleted "and" at the end of para. (a)(25), substituted ", and" for the period at the end of para. (a)(26), and added para. (a)(27), effective 8/5/97.

In 1996, P.L. 104-188, Sec. 1703(l), substituted "by the taxpayer or a related person" for "by the taxpayer" in Sec. 13261(g)(2)(A)(iii) of P.L. 103-66 [see below].

—P.L. 104-188, Sec. 1704(t)(56), substituted "Paragraph (20) of section 1016(a), as redesignated by section 11801" for "Paragraph (21) of section 1016(a)" in Sec. 11813(b)(19) of P.L. 101-508 [see below].

—P.L. 104-188, Sec. 1807(c)(5), deleted "and" at the end of para. (a)(24), substituted ", and" for the period at the end of para. (a)(25), and added para. (a)(26), effective for tax. yrs. begin. after 12/31/96.

In 1993, P.L. 103-66, Sec. 13114(b)(1), substituted "section 1043 or 1044" for "section 1043" in para. (a)(24) [before redesignation by Sec. 13261(f)(3) of this Act, see below] . . . Sec. 13114(b)(2), substituted "section 1043(c) or 1044(d), as the case may be" for "section 1043(c)" in para. (a)(24) [before redesignation by Sec. 13261(f)(3) of this Act, see below], effective for sales on and after 8/10/93, in tax. yrs. end. on and after 8/10/93.

—P.L. 103-66, Sec. 13213(a)(2)(F), amended subsec. (e), effective for expenses incurred after 12/31/93.

Prior to amendment, subsec. (e) read as follows:

"(e) Cross references.

"(1) For treatment of certain expenses incident to the purchase of a residence which were deducted as moving expenses by the taxpayer or his spouse under section 217(a), see section 217(e).

"(2) For treatment of separate mineral interests as one property, see section 614."

—P.L. 103-66, Sec. 13261(f)(3), deleted para. (a)(19) and redesignated paras. (a)(20) through (a)(26) as paras. (a)(19) through (a)(25), effective for property acquired after 8/10/93, except as provided in Sec. 13261(g)(2) and (3) of this Act [amended by Sec. 1703(l) of P.L. 104-188, see above] which reads as follows:

"(2) Election to have amendments apply to property acquired after July 25, 1991.

"(A) In general. If an election under this paragraph applies to the taxpayer—

"(i) the amendments made by this section shall apply to property acquired by the taxpayer after July 25, 1991,

"(ii) subsection (c)(1)(A) of section 197 of the Internal Revenue Code of 1986 (as added by this section) (and so much of subsection (f)(9)(A) of such section 197 as precedes clause (i) thereof) shall be applied with respect to the taxpayer by treating July 25, 1991, as the date of the enactment of such section, and

"(iii) in applying subsection (f)(9) of such section, with respect to any property acquired by the taxpayer or a related person on or before the date of the enactment of this Act, only holding or use on July 25, 1991, shall be taken into account.

"(B) Election. An election under this paragraph shall be made at such time and in such manner as the Secretary of the Treasury or his delegate may prescribe. Such an election by any taxpayer, once made—

"(i) may be revoked only with the consent of the Secretary, and

"(ii) shall apply to the taxpayer making such election and any other taxpayer under common control with the taxpayer (within the meaning of subparagraphs (A) and (B) of section 41(f)(1) of such Code) at any time after August 2, 1993, and on or before the date on which such election is made.

"(3) Elective binding contract exception.

"(A) In general. The amendments made by this section shall not apply to any acquisition of property by the taxpayer if—

"(i) such acquisition is pursuant to a written binding contract in effect on the date of the enactment of this Act and at all times thereafter before such acquisition,

"(ii) an election under paragraph (2) does not apply to the taxpayer, and

"(iii) the taxpayer makes an election under this paragraph with respect to such contract.

"(B) Election. An election under this paragraph shall be made at such time and in such manner as the Secretary of the Treasury or his delegate shall prescribe. Such an election, once made—

"(i) may be revoked only with the consent of the Secretary, and

"(ii) shall apply to all property, acquired pursuant to the contract with respect to which such election was made."

Prior to deletion, para. (a)(19) read as follows:

"(19) for amounts allowed as deductions for payments made on account of transfers of franchises, trademarks, and trade names under section 1253(d)(2);"

In 1992, P.L. 102-486, Sec. 1913(a)(3)(A), deleted "and" at the end of para. (a)(23), substituted ", and" for the period at the end of para. (a)(24), and added para. (a)(25) . . . Sec. 1913(b)(2)(B), deleted "and" at the end of para. (a)(24) [as amended by Sec. 1913(a)(3)(A)], substituted ", and" for the period at the end of para. (a)(25) [as added by Sec. 1913(A)(3)(A)], and added para. (a)(26) effective for property placed in service after 6/30/93.

In 1990, P.L. 101-508, Sec. 11801(c)(1), deleted para. (a)(20) and redesignated paras. (a)(21)-(a)(25) as paras. (a)(20)-(a)(24), effective 11/5/90 except as provided in Sec. 11821(b) of this Act, reproduced in note following Code Sec. 23.

Prior to deletion, para. (a)(20) read as follows:

"(20) to the extent provided in section 23(e), in the case of property with respect to which a credit has been allowed under section 23;"

—P.L. 101-508, Sec. 11812(b)(10), substituted "under the straight line method" for "under section 167(b)(1)", in para. (a)(2), effective for property placed in service after 11/5/90, except as provided in Sec. 11812(c)(2) and (3) of this Act, reproduced in note following Code Sec. 42.

—P.L. 101-508, Sec. 11813(b)(19), substituted "section 50(c)" for "section 48(q)", in para. (a)(20) [amended by Sec. 1704(t)(56) of P.L. 104-188, see above], effective for property placed in service after 12/31/90, except as provided in Sec. 11813(c)(2) of this Act reproduced in note following Code Sec. 46.

In 1989, P.L. 101-194, Sec. 502(b)(2), deleted "and" at the end of para. (a)(23), substituted ", and" for the period at the end of para. (a)(24) and added para. (a)(25), effective for sales after 11/30/89.

In 1988, P.L. 100-647, Sec. 1006(j)(1)(B), substituted "allowable pursuant to section 171(a)(1) (or the amount applied to reduce interest payments under section 171(e)(2))" for "allowable pursuant to section 171(a)(1)", in para. (a)(5), effective for obligations acquired after 12/31/87, except that the taxpayer may elect to have such amendment apply to obligations acquired after 10/22/86.

—P.L. 100-647, Sec. 1018(u)(22), deleted paras. (a)(23)-(a)(26), and added new paras. (a)(21)-(a)(24) effective 10/22/86.

Prior to deletion, paragraphs (a)(23)-(a)(26) read as follows.

"(23) to the extent provided in section 48(q), in the case of expenditures with respect to which a credit has been allowed under section 38;

"(24) for amounts allowed as deductions under section 59(d) (relating to optional 10-year writeoff of certain tax preferences);

"(25) to the extent provided in section 1059 (relating to reduction in basis for extraordinary dividends); and

"(26) in the case of qualified replacement property, the acquisition of which resulted under section 1042 in the nonrecognition of any part of the gain realized on the sale or exchange of any property, to the extent provided in section 1042(c)."

In 1986, P.L. 99-514, Sec. 241(b)(2), deleted para. (a)(16) and redesignated paras. (a)(17)-(a)(27) as paras. (a)(16)-(a)(26), effective for expenditures paid or incurred after 12/31/86. Sec. 241(c)(2) of this Act provides:

"(2) Transitional rule. The amendments made by this section shall not apply to any expenditure incurred—

"(A) pursuant to a binding contract entered into before March 2, 1986, or

"(B) with respect to the development, protection, expansion, registration, or defense of a trademark or trade name commenced before March 2, 1986, but only if not less than the lesser of $1,000,000 or 5 percent of the aggregate cost of such development, protection, expansion, registration, or defense has been incurred or committed before such date.

The preceding sentence shall not apply to any expenditure with respect to a trademark or trade name placed in service after December 31, 1987."

Prior to deletion, para. (a)(16) read as follows:

"(16) for amounts allowed as deductions for expenditures treated as deferred expenses under section 177 (relating to trademark and trade name expenditures) and resulting in a reduction of the taxpayer's taxes under this subtitle, but not less than the amounts allowable under such section for the taxable year and prior years."

—P.L. 99-514, Sec. 701(e)(4)(D), substituted "section 59(d)" for "section 58(i)" in para. (a)(24), effective for tax. yrs. begin. after 12/31/86.

—P.L. 99-514, Sec. 1303(b)(3), deleted para. (a)(22) and redesignated paragraphs (a)(23)[sic]-(27) as paragraphs (a)(22)[sic]-(26), effective on 10/22/86.

Prior to deletion, para. (a)(22) read as follows:

"(22) to the extent provided in section 1395 in the case of stock of shareholders of a general ownership corporation (as defined in section 1391) which makes the election provided by section 1392;"

—P.L. 99-514, Sec. 1899A(25), amended paragraphs (a)(23)-(a)(26) (before redesignation by Secs. 241 and 1303 of this Act) by substituting a semicolon for the comma at the end of each paragraph, effective 10/22/86.

In 1984, P.L. 98-369, Sec. 43(a)(2), deleted the last sentence from subsec. (b), effective for tax. yrs. end. after 7/18/84.

Prior to deletion, the last sentence of subsec. (b) read as follows:

"The term 'substituted basis' as used in this section means a basis determined under any provision of this subchapter and subchapters C (relating to corporate distributions and adjustments), K (relating to partners and partnerships), and P (relating to capital gains and losses), or under any corresponding provision of a prior income tax law, providing that the basis shall be determined—

"(1) by reference to the basis in the hands of a transferor, donor, or grantor, or

"(2) by reference to other property held at any time by the person for whom the basis is to be determined."

—P.L. 98-369, Sec. 53(d)(3), deleted "and" from the end of para. (a)(24), substituted ", and" for the period at the end of para. (a)(25), and added para. (a)(26), effective for distributions after 3/1/84, in tax. yrs. end. after 3/1/84.

—P.L. 98-369, Sec. 211(b)(14), substituted "section 811(b)" for "section 818(b)" each place it appeared in para. (a)(17), effective for tax. yrs. begin. after 12/31/83.

—P.L. 98-369, Sec. 474(r)(23)(A), substituted "section 23(e)" for "section 44C(e)" in para. (a)(21) . . . Sec. 474(r)(23)(B), substituted "section 23" for "section 44C" in para. (a)(21), effective for tax. yrs. begin. after 12/31/83, and for carrybacks from such years.

—P.L. 98-369, Sec. 541(b)(2), deleted "and" from the end of para. (a)(25), substituted ", and" for the period at the end of para. (a)(26) (as added by Sec.

53(d)(3)], and added para. (a)(27), effective for sales of securities in tax. yrs. begin. after 7/18/84.

In 1982, P.L. 97-354, Sec. 5(a)(33), amended para. (a)(18), effective for tax. yrs. begin. after 12/31/82.

Prior to amendment, para. (a)(18) read as follows:

"(18) to the extent provided in section 1376 in the case of stock of, and indebtedness owing, shareholders of an electing small business corporation (as defined in section 1371(b));"

—P.L. 97-248, Sec. 201(c)(2), deleted "and" at the end of para. (a)(23) [sic , (a)(22)], substituted ", and" for the period at the end of para. (a)(24), and added para. (a)(25), effective for tax. yrs. begin. after 12/31/82.

—P.L. 97-248, Sec. 205(a)(5)(B), substituted "section 48(q)" for "section 48(g)(5)" in para. (a)(24), effective for periods after 12/31/82 under rules similar to the rules of Code Sec. 48(m). For exceptions see Sec. 205(c)(1)(B)-(E) of this Act reproduced in note following Code Sec. 48.

In 1981, P.L. 97-34, Sec. 212(d)(2)(G), deleted "and" at the end of para. (a)(22) [sic], substituted ", and" for the period at the end of para. (a)(23) [sic , (a)(24)] and added para. (a)(24), effective for expenditures incurred after 12/31/81, in tax. yrs. end. after 12/31/81. For transitional rule see Sec. 212(e)(2) of this Act reproduced in note following Code Sec. 46.

—P.L. 97-34, Sec. 421(g), amended subsec. (c), effective for estates of decedents dying after 12/31/81.

Prior to amendment, subsec. (c) read as follows:

"(c) Increase in basis in the case of certain involuntary conversions.

"(1) In general. If—

"(A) there is a compulsory or involuntary conversion (within the meaning of section 1033) of any property, and

"(B) an additional estate tax is imposed on such conversion under section 2032A(c),

then the adjusted basis of such property shall be increased by the amount of such tax.

"(2) Time adjustment made. Any adjustment under paragraph (1) shall be deemed to have occurred immediately before the compulsory or involuntary conversion."

In 1980, P.L. 96-487, Sec. 1408, provides:

"Basis in the land

"Sec. 1408. Section 21(c) of the Alaska Native Claims Settlement Act is amended to read as follows:

"(c) The receipt of land or any interest therein pursuant to this Act or of cash in order to equalize the values of properties exchanged pursuant to subsection 22(f) shall not be subject to any form of Federal, State, or local taxation. The basis for determining gain or loss from the sale or other disposition of such land or interest in land shall be the fair value of such land or interest in land at the time of receipt, adjusted as provided in section 1016 of the Internal Revenue Code of 1954, as amended:

Provided, however, That the basis of any such land or interest therein attributable to an interest in a mine, well, other natural deposit, or block of timber shall be not less than the fair value of such mine, well, natural deposit, or block of timber (or such interest therein as the Secretary shall convey) at the time of the first commercial development thereof, adjusted as provided in section 1016 of such Code. For purposes of this subsection, the time of receipt of land or any interest therein shall be the time of the conveyance by the Secretary of such land or interest (whether by interim conveyance or patent)."

—P.L. 96-223, Sec. 401(a), repealed Sec. 2005(a)(3) of P.L. 94-455 and Sec. 702(r)(3) of P.L. 95-600 and the amendments made by Sec. 2005(a)(3) and Sec. 702(r)(3), effective for decedents dying after '76 [see below], Sec. 401(b) of P.L. 96-223 provides as follows:

"(b) Revival of prior law.

"Except to the extent necessary to carry out subsection (d), the Internal Revenue Code of 1954 shall be applied and administered as if the provisions repealed by subsection (a), and the amendments made by those provisions, had not been enacted."

—P.L. 96-223, Sec. 401(c)(1), amended subsec. (c), effective for decedents dying after '76.

Prior to amendment, subsec. (c) read as follows:

"(c) Increase in basis in the case of involuntary conversions.

"(1) In general. If there is a compulsory or involuntary conversion (within the meaning of section 1033) of any property the basis of which is determined under section 1023 and an additional estate tax is imposed on such conversion under section 2032A(c), then the adjusted basis of such property shall be increased by an amount which bears the same ratio to such tax with respect to the conversion of that property as—

"(A) the net appreciation in value of such property, bears to

"(B) the excess of—

"(i) the value of such property for purposes of chapter 11 as determined with respect to the estate of the decedent without regard to section 2032A; over

"(ii) the value of such property for purposes of chapter 11 as determined with respect to the estate of the decedent with regard to section 2032A.

"(2) Net appreciation in value. For purposes of this subsection, the net appreciation in value of any property shall be determined in accordance with section 1023(f)(2) except that—

"(A) the adjusted basis taken into account shall be increased by any adjustment under section 1023,

"(B) the fair market value of such property shall be determined without regard to section 2032A, and

"(C) any net appreciation in value in excess of the amount determined under paragraph (1)(B) shall be disregarded.

"(3) Time adjustment made. Any adjustment under paragraph (1) shall be deemed to have occurred immediately before the compulsory or involuntary conversion."

—P.L. 96-222, Sec. 106(a)(2), redesignated para. (a)(21) as added by Sec. 601(b)(3) of P.L. 95-600, as para. (a)(22), effective for corporations chartered after 12/31/78 and before 1/1/84 . . . Sec. 106(a)(3), corrected Sec. 601(b)(3) of P.L. 95-600 by inserting para. (a)(21) before para. (a)(23).

—P.L. 96-222, Sec. 107(a)(2)(C), repealed Sec. 702(r)(3) of P.L. 95-600.

In 1978, P.L. 95-618, Sec. 101(b)(3), added para. (a)(21), effective for tax. yrs. end. on or after 4/20/77.

—P.L. 95-618, Sec. 201(b), redesignated subsec. (d) as subsec. (e) . . . added new subsec. (d), effective with respect to 1980 and later model year automobiles (as defined in Code Sec. 4064(b)).

—P.L. 95-600, Sec. 515(2), substituted "December 31, 1979" for "December 31, 1976" in para. (a)(23), [as amended by repealed Sec. 2005(a)(3) of P.L. 94-455] effective 11/6/78.

—P.L. 95-600, Sec. 515(6), extended the effective date for amendments made by Sec. 2005(a)(3) of P.L. 94-455 to apply to decedents dying after '79.

Prior to amendment the effective date applied to decedents dying after '76. [inoperative]

—P.L. 95-600, Sec. 601(b)(3), added para. (a)(21) before para. (a)(23), effective for corporations chartered after 12/31/78 and before 1/1/84.

—P.L. 95-600, Sec. 702(r)(3), redesignated para. (a)(23) as para. (a)(21), effective for decedents dying after 12/31/76, but Sec. 702(r) was repealed by Sec. 401(a) of P.L. 96-223 [see above] .

—P.L. 95-472, Sec. 4(b), redesignated subsec. (c) as subsec. (d) and added new subsec. (c), for involuntary conversions after 12/31/76.

In 1976, P.L. 94-455, Sec. 1901(a)(123), deleted para. (a)(19), effective for tax. yrs. begin. after 12/31/76.

Prior to amendment, para. (a)(19) read as follows:

"(19) to the extent provided in section 48(g) and in section 203(a)(2) of the Revenue Act of 1964, in the case of property which is or has been section 38 property (as defined in section 48(a));"

—P.L. 94-455, Sec. 1901(b)(1)(F)(ii), substituted "section 551(e)" for "section 551(f)" following "to the extent provided in" in para. (a)(13), effective for tax. yrs. begin. after 12/31/76.

—P.L. 94-455, Sec. (b)(21)(G), deleted para. (a)(10), effective for tax. yrs. begin. after 12/31/76.

Prior to deletion, para. (a)(10) read as follows:

"(10) for amounts allowed as deduction as deferred expenses under section 615(b) (relating to certain pre-1970 exploration expenditures) and resulting in a reduction of the taxpayer's taxes under this subtitle but not less than the amounts allowable under such section for the taxable year and prior years;"

—P.L. 94-455, Sec. 1901(b)(29)(A), substituted "under section 1020 (as in effect before the date of enactment of the Tax Reform Act of 1976)" for "under section 1020" in the third sentence of subsec. (a), effective for tax. yrs. begin. after 12/31/76.

—P.L. 94-455, Sec. 1901(b)(30)(A)(i), deleted para. (a)(21), effective for stock or securities acquired from a decedent dying after 10/4/76.

—P.L. 94-455, Sec. 1901(b)(3)(A)(ii), redesignated paras. (a)(20) and (a)(22) as (a)(19) and (a)(20), effective for tax. yrs. begin. after 12/31/76.

Prior to amendment, para. (a)(21) read as follows:

"(21) to the extent provided in section 1022, relating to increase in basis for certain foreign personal holding company stock or securities,"

—P.L. 94-455, Sec. 2005(a)(3), substituted a semicolon for the period at the end of subsec. (a) and added para. (a)(23), effective for decedent's dying after 12/31/76, but Sec. 2005(a)(3) was repealed by Sec. 401(a) of P.L. 96-223 [see above]. For para. (a)(23) added by Sec. 2005(a)(3) see note for Sec. 401(d) of P.L. 96-223 following Code Sec. 1014.

In 1969, P.L. 91-172, Sec. 231(c)(3), amended subsec. (c), for tax. yrs. begin. after 12/31/69, except that Sec. 231(d)(2) provides that "the amendments made by this section shall not apply (at the election of the taxpayer made at such time and manner as the Secretary of the Treasury or his delegate prescribes) with respect to moving expenses paid or incurred before July 1, 1970, in connection with the commencement of work by the taxpayer as an employee at a new principal place of work of which the taxpayer had been notified by his employer on or before December 19, 1969.

Prior to amendment, subsec. (c) read as follows:

"(c) Separate mineral interests treated as one property.

"For treatment of separate mineral interests as one property, see section 614."

—P.L. 91-172, Sec. 516(c)(2)(B), deleted the period at the end of para. (a)(21) and added a semicolon and added para. (a)(22), effective for transfers after 12/31/69.

—P.L. 91-172, Sec. 504(c)(4), added "pre-1970" after "certain" in para. (a)(10), effective for exploration expenditures paid or incurred after 12/31/69.

In 1964, P.L. 88-272, Sec. 203(a)(3)(C), amended para. (a)(19), effective for property placed in service after 12/31/63, for tax. yrs. end. after 12/31/63 and for property placed in service before 1/1/64, for tax. yrs. begin. after 12/31/63.

—P.L. 88-272, Sec. 225(j)(2), substituted a semicolon for the period at the end of para. (a)(20) and added para. (a)(21), effective for decedents dying after 12/31/63.

—P.L. 88-272, Sec. 227(b)(5), added "or domestic iron ore" after "coal" in para. (a)(15), effective for amounts received or accrued in tax. yrs. begin after 12/31/63, attributable to iron ore mined in such tax. yrs.

In **1962**, P.L. 87-834, Sec. 2(f)(1), substituted a semicolon for the period at the end of para. (a)(18) . . . Sec. 2(f)(2), added para. (a)(19), effective for tax. yrs. end. after 12/31/61.

—P.L. 87-834, Sec. 8(g)(2), deleted "and" at the end of subpara. (a)(3)(B), added "and" at the end of subpara. (a)(3)(C) and added subpara. (a)(3)(D), effective for tax. yrs. begin after 12/31/62.

—87-834, Sec. 12(b)(4), added para. (a)(20), effective for tax. yrs. of foreign corporations begin. after 12/31/62, and for tax. yrs. of U.S. shareholders within which or with which such tax. yrs. of such foreign corporations end.

In **1959**, P.L. 86-69, Sec. 3(d), deleted "and" at the end of subpara. (a)(3)(A), added "and" at the end of subpara. (a)(3)(B), added subpara. (a)(3)(C), and added para. (a)(17), effective for tax. yrs. begin. after 12/31/57.

In **1958**, P.L. 85-866, Sec. 2, deleted "short term" preceding "municipal bond" in para. (a)(6), effective for tax. yrs. end. after 12/31/57, but only with respect to obligations acquired after 12/31/57.

—P.L. 85-866, Sec. 64, added para. (a)(18), effective for tax. yrs. begin. after 12/31/57.

—P.L. 85-66, Sec. 94, provided for change from retirement to straight line method of computing depreciation in certain cases as follows:

"(a) Short title.

"This section may be cited as the 'Retirement-Straight Line Adjustment Act of 1958'.

"(b) Making of election.

"Any taxpayer who held retirement-straight line property on his 1956 adjustment date may elect to have this section apply. Such an election shall be made at such time and in such manner as the Secretary shall prescribe. Any election under this section shall be irrevocable and shall apply to all retirement-straight line property as hereinafter provided in this section (including such property for periods when held by predecessors of the taxpayer).

"(c) Retirement-straight line property defined.

"For purposes of this section, the term 'retirement-straight line property' means any property of a kind or class with respect to which the taxpayer or a predecessor (under the terms and conditions prescribed for him by the Commissioner) for any taxable year beginning after December 31, 1940, and before January 1, 1956, changed from the retirement to the straight line method of computing the allowance of deductions for depreciation.

"(d) Basis adjustments as of 1956 adjustment date.

"If the taxpayer has made an election under this section, then in determining the adjusted basis on his 1956 adjustment date of all retirement-straight line property held by the taxpayer, in lieu of the adjustments for depreciation provided in section 1016(a)(2) and (3) of the Internal Revenue Code of 1954, the following adjustments shall be made (effective as of his 1956 adjustment date) in respect of all periods before the 1956 adjustment date:

"(1) Depreciation sustained before March 1, 1913.—For depreciation sustained before March 1, 1913, on retirement-straight line property held by the taxpayer or a predecessor on such date for which cost was or is claimed as basis and which either—

"(A) Retired before changeover.—Was retired by the taxpayer or a predecessor before the changeover date, but only if (i) a deduction was allowed in computing net income by reason of such retirement, and (ii) such deduction was computed on the basis of cost without adjustment for depreciation sustained before March 1, 1913. In the case of any such property retired during any taxable year beginning after December 31, 1929, the adjustment under this subparagraph shall not exceed that portion of the amount attributable to depreciation sustained before March 1, 1913, which resulted (by reason of the deduction so allowed) in a reduction in taxes under the Internal Revenue Code of 1954 or prior income, war-profits, or excess-profits tax laws.

"(B) Held on changeover date.—Was held by the taxpayer or a predecessor on the changeover date. This subparagraph shall not apply to property to which paragraph (2) applies.

"The adjustment determined under this paragraph shall be allocated (in the manner prescribed by the Secretary) among all retirement-straight line property held by the taxpayer on his 1956 adjustment date.

"(2) Property disposed of after changeover and before 1956 adjustment date.—For that portion of the reserve prescribed by the Commissioner in connection with the changeover which was applicable to property—

"(A) sold, or

"(B) with respect to which a deduction was allowed for Federal income tax purposes by reason of casualty or 'abnormal' retirement in the nature of special obsolescence, if such sale occurred in, or such deduction was allowed for, a period on or after the changeover date and before the taxpayer's 1956 adjustment date.

"(3) Depreciation allowable from changeover to 1956 adjustment date.—For depreciation allowable, under the terms and conditions prescribed by the Commissioner in connection with the changeover, for all periods on and after the changeover date and before the taxpayer's 1956 adjustment date.

"This subsection shall apply only with respect to taxable years beginning after December 31, 1955.

"(e) Effect on period from changeover to 1956 adjustment date.

"If the taxpayer has made an election under this section, then in determining the adjusted basis of any retirement-straight line property as of any time on or after the changeover date and before the taxpayer's 1956 adjustment date, in lieu of the adjustments for depreciation provided in section 1016(a)(2) and (3) of the Internal Revenue Code of 1954 and the corresponding provisions of prior revenue laws, the following adjustments shall be made:

"(1) For prescribed reserve.—For the amount of the reserve prescribed by the Commissioner in connection with the changeover.

"(2) For allowable depreciation.—For the depreciation allowable under the terms and conditions prescribed by the Commissioner in connection with the changeover.

"This subsection shall not apply in determining adjusted basis for purposes of section 437(c) of the Internal Revenue Code of 1939. This subsection shall apply only with respect to taxable years beginning on or after the changeover date and before the taxpayer's 1956 adjustment date.

"(f) Equity invested capital, etc.

"If an election is made under this section, then (not withstanding the terms and conditions prescribed by the Commissioner in connection with the changeover)—

"(1) Equity invested capital.—In determining equity invested capital under sections 458 and 718 of the Internal Revenue Code of 1939, accumulated earnings and profits as of the changeover date, and as of the beginning of each taxable year thereafter, shall be reduced by the depreciation sustained before March 1, 1913, as computed under subsection (d)(1)(B); and

"(2) Definition of equity capital.—In determining the adjusted basis of assets for the purpose of section 437(c) of the Internal Revenue Code of 1939 (and in addition to any other adjustments required by such Code), the basis shall be reduced by depreciation sustained before March 1, 1913 (as computed under subsection (d)), together with any depreciation allowable under subsection (e)(2) for any period before the year for which the excess profits credit is being computed.

"(g) Definitions.

"For purposes of this section—

"(1) Depreciation.—The term 'depreciation' means exhaustion, wear and tear, and obsolescence.

"(2) Changeover.—The term 'changeover' means a change from the retirement to the straight line method of computing the allowance of deductions for depreciation.

"(3) Changeover date.—The term 'changeover date' means the first day of the first taxable year for which the changeover was effective.

"(4) 1956 adjustment date.—The term '1956 adjustment date' means, in the case of any taxpayer, the first day of his first taxable year beginning after December 31, 1955.

"(5) Predecessor.—The term 'predecessor' means any person from whom property of a kind or class to which this section refers was acquired, if the basis of such property is determined by reference to its basis in the hands of such person. Where a series of transfers of property has occurred and where in each instance the basis of the property was determined by reference to its basis in the hands of the prior holder, the term includes each such prior holder.

"(6) The term 'Secretary' means the Secretary of the Treasury or his delegate.

"(7) The term 'Commissioner' means the Commissioner of Internal Revenue."

In **1956**, ch. 464, Sec. 4(c), added para. (a)(16).

Sec. 1017. Discharge of indebtedness.
(a) General rule.

If—

(1) an amount is excluded from gross income under subsection (a) of section 108 (relating to discharge of indebtedness), and

(2) under subsection (b)(2)(E), (b)(5), or (c)(1) of section 108, any portion of such amount is to be applied to reduce basis,

then such portion shall be applied in reduction of the basis of any property held by the taxpayer at the beginning of the taxable year following the taxable year in which the discharge occurs.

(b) Amount and properties determined under regulations.

(1) In general. The amount of reduction to be applied under subsection (a) (not in excess of the portion referred to in subsection (a)), and the particular properties the bases of which are to be reduced, shall be determined under regulations prescribed by the Secretary.

(2) Limitation in title 11 case or insolvency. In the case of a discharge to which subparagraph (A) or (B) of section 108(a)(1) applies, the reduction in basis under subsection (a) of this section shall not exceed the excess of—

(A) the aggregate of the bases of the property held by the taxpayer immediately after the discharge, over

(B) the aggregate of the liabilities of the taxpayer immediately after the discharge.

The preceding sentence shall not apply to any reduction in basis by reason of an election under section 108(b)(5).

(3) Certain reductions may only be made in the basis of depreciable property.

(A) In general. Any amount which under subsection (b)(5) or (c)(1) of section 108 is to be applied to reduce basis shall be applied only to reduce the basis of depreciable property held by the taxpayer.

(B) **Depreciable property.** For purposes of this section, the term "depreciable property" means any property of a character subject to the allowance for depreciation, but only if a basis reduction under subsection (a) will reduce the amount of depreciation or amortization which otherwise would be allowable for the period immediately following such reduction.

(C) **Special rule for partnership interests.** For purposes of this section, any interest of a partner in a partnership shall be treated as depreciable property to the extent of such partner's proportionate interest in the depreciable property held by such partnership. The preceding sentence shall apply only if there is a corresponding reduction in the partnership's basis in depreciable property with respect to such partner.

(D) **Special rule in case of affiliated group.** For purposes of this section, if—

(i) a corporation holds stock in another corporation (hereinafter in this subparagraph referred to as the "subsidiary"), and

(ii) such corporations are members of the same affiliated group which file a consolidated return under section 1501 for the taxable year in which the discharge occurs,

then such stock shall be treated as depreciable property to the extent that such subsidiary consents to a corresponding reduction in the basis of its depreciable property.

(E) **Election to treat certain inventory as depreciable property.**

(i) **In general.** At the election of the taxpayer, for purposes of this section, the term "depreciable property" includes any real property which is described in section 1221(a)(1).

(ii) **Election.** An election under clause (i) shall be made on the taxpayer's return for the taxable year in which the discharge occurs or at such other time as may be permitted in regulations prescribed by the Secretary. Such an election, once made, may be revoked only with the consent of the Secretary.

(F) **Special rules for qualified real property business indebtedness.** In the case of any amount which under section 108(c)(1) is to be applied to reduce basis—

(i) depreciable property shall only include depreciable real property for purposes of subparagraphs (A) and (C),

(ii) subparagraph (E) shall not apply, and

(iii) in the case of property taken into account under section 108(c)(2)(B), the reduction with respect to such property shall be made as of the time immediately before disposition if earlier than the time under subsection (a).

(4) Special rules for qualified farm indebtedness.

(A) **In general.** Any amount which under subsection (b)(2)(E) of section 108 is to be applied to reduce basis and which is attributable to an amount excluded under subsection (a)(1)(C) of section 108—

(i) shall be applied only to reduce the basis of qualified property held by the taxpayer, and

(ii) shall be applied to reduce the basis of qualified property in the following order:

(I) First the basis of qualified property which is depreciable property.

(II) Second the basis of qualified property which is land used or held for use in the trade or business of farming.

(III) Then the basis of other qualified property.

(B) **Qualified property.** For purposes of this paragraph, the term "qualified property" has the meaning given to such term by section 108(g)(3)(C).

(C) **Certain rules made applicable.** Rules similar to the rules of subparagraphs (C), (D), and (E) of paragraph (3) shall apply for purposes of this paragraph and section 108(g).

(c) Special rules.

(1) Reduction not to be made in exempt property. In the case of an amount excluded from gross income under section 108(a)(1)(A), no reduction in basis shall be made under this section in the basis of property which the debtor treats as exempt property under section 522 of title 11 of the United States Code.

(2) Reductions in basis not treated as dispositions. For purposes of this title, a reduction in basis under this section shall not be treated as a disposition.

(d) Recapture of reductions.

(1) In general. For purposes of sections 1245 and 1250—

(A) any property the basis of which is reduced under this section and which is neither section 1245 property nor section 1250 property shall be treated as section 1245 property, and

(B) any reduction under this section shall be treated as a deduction allowed for depreciation.

(2) Special rule for section 1250. For purposes of section 1250(b), the determination of what would have been the depreciation adjustments under the straight line method shall be made as if there had been no reduction under this section.

In **1999**, P.L. 106-170, Sec. 532(c)(2)(S), substituted "section 1221(a)(1)" for "section 1221(1)" in clause (b)(3)(E)(i), effective for any instrument held, acquired, or entered into, any transaction entered into, and supplies held or acquired on or after 12/17/99.

In **1998**, P.L. 105-206, Sec. 6023(11), substituted "(b)(2)(E)" for "(b)(2)(D)" in para. (a)(2), effective 7/22/98.

In **1996**, P.L. 104-188, Sec. 1703(n)(5), substituted "subsection (b)(2)(E)" for "subsection (b)(2)(D)" in subpara. (b)(4)(A), effective for discharges of indebtedness in tax. yrs. begin. after 12/31/93.

In **1993**, P.L. 103-66, Sec. 13150(c)(6), substituted ", (b)(5), or (c)(1)" for "or (b)(5)" in para. (a)(2) . . . Sec. 13150(c)(7), added "or (c)(1)" after "subsection (b)(5)" in subpara. (b)(3)(A) . . . Sec. 13150(c)(8), added subpara. (b)(3)(F), effective for discharges after 12/31/92, in tax. yrs. end. after 12/31/92.

In **1990**, P.L. 101-508, Sec. 11704(a)(12), substituted "subparagraphs" for "subparagraph" in subpara. (b)(4)(C), effective 11/5/90.

In **1988**, P.L. 100-647, Sec. 1004(a)(5), amended para. (b)(4), effective for discharges of indebtedness occurring after 4/9/86, in tax. yrs. end. after 4/9/86.

Prior to amendment, para. (b)(4) read as follows:

"(4) Ordering rule in the case of qualified farm indebtedness. Any amount which is excluded from gross income under section 108(a) by reason of the discharge of qualified farm indebtedness (within the meaning of section 108(g)(2)) and which under subsection (b) of section 108 is to be applied to reduce basis shall be applied—

"(A) first to reduce the tax attributes described in section 108(b)(2) (other than subparagraph (D) thereof),

"(B) then to reduce basis of property other than property described in subparagraph (C), and

"(C) then to reduce the basis of land used or held for use in the trade or business of farming."

In **1986**, P.L. 99-514, Sec. 405(b), added para. (b)(4), effective for discharges of indebtedness occurring after 4/9/86, in tax. yrs. end. after 4/9/86.

—P.L. 99-514, Sec. 822(b)(4), substituted "or (b)(5)" for ", (b)(5), or (c)(1)(A)" in para. (a)(2) . . . Sec. 822(b)(5), deleted "or (c)(1)(A)" after "subsection (b)(5)" in subpara. (b)(3)(A), effective for discharges after 12/31/86.

In **1980**, P.L. 96-589, Sec. 2(b), amended Code Sec. 1017. Sec. 7(a)(1) makes this amendment effective for any transaction which occurs after 12/31/80, other than a transaction which occurs in a proceeding in a bankruptcy case of similar judicial proceeding (or in a proceeding under the Bankruptcy Act) begun on or before 12/31/80. Sec. 7(a)(2) of this Act provides:

"(2) Transitional rule. In the case of any discharge of indebtedness to which subparagraph (A) or (B) of section 108(a)(1) of the Internal Revenue Code of

Basis   Code Sec. 1022(b)(2)(B)

1954 (relating to exclusion from gross income), as amended by section 2, applies and which occurs before January 1, 1982, or which occurs in a proceeding in a bankruptcy case or similar judicial proceedings commencing before January 1, 1982, then—

"(A) section 108(b)(2) of the such Code (relating to reduction of tax attributes), as so amended, shall be applied without regard to subparagraphs (A), (B), (C), and (E) thereof, and

"(B) the basis of any property shall not be reduced under section 1017 of such Code (relating to reduction in basis in connection with discharges of indebtedness), as so amended, below the fair market value of such property on the date the debt is discharged."

Sec. 7(f) and (g) of this Act provides:

"(f) *Election to substitute September 30, 1979, for December 31, 1980.*—

"(1) In general. The debtor (or debtors) in a bankruptcy case or similar judicial proceeding may (with the approval of the court) elect to apply [Subsection 7(a) of this Act] by substituting 'September 30, 1979' for 'December 31, 1980' each place it appears in such subsections.

"(2) Effect of election. Any election made under paragraph (1) with respect to any proceeding shall apply to all parties to the proceeding.

"(3) Revocation only with consent. Any election under this subsection may be revoked only with the consent of the Secretary of the Treasury or his delegate.

"(4) Time and manner of election. Any election under this subsection shall be made at such time, and in such manner, as the Secretary of the Treasury or his delegate may by regulations prescribe.

"(g) *Definitions.*

"For purposes of this section—

"(1) Bankruptcy case. The term 'bankruptcy case' means any case under title 11 of the United States Code (as recodified by P.L. 95-598).

"(2) Similar judicial proceeding. The term 'similar judicial proceeding' means a receivership, foreclosure, or similar proceeding in a Federal or State court (as modified by section 368(a)(3)(D) of the Internal Revenue Code of 1954)."

Prior to amendment Code Sec. 1017 read as follows:

"Sec. 1017. Discharge of Indebtedness.

"Where any amount is excluded from gross income under section 108 (relating to income from discharge of indebtedness) on account of the discharge of indebtedness the whole or a part of the amount so excluded from gross income shall be applied in reduction of the basis of any property held (whether before or after the time of the discharge) by the taxpayer during any portion of the taxable year in which such discharge occurred. The amount to be so applied (not in excess of the amount so excluded from gross income, reduced by the amount of any deduction disallowed under section 108) and the particular properties to which the reduction shall be allocated, shall be determined under regulations (prescribed by the Secretary) in effect at the time of the filing of the consent by the taxpayer referred to in section 108. The reduction shall be made as of the first day of the taxable year in which the discharge occurred, except in the case of property not held by the taxpayer on such first day, in which case it shall take effect as of the time the holding of the taxpayer began."

In 1976, P.L. 94-455, Sec. 1906(b)(13)(A), substituted "Secretary" for "Secretary or his delegate" in Code Sec. 1017, effective for tax. yrs. begin. after 12/31/76.

—P.L. 94-455, Sec. 1951(c)(1), substituted "section 108" for "section 108(a)" each time it appeared in Code Sec. 1017, effective for tax. yrs. begin. after 12/31/76.

Sec. 1018. Repealed.

In 1980, P.L. 96-589, Sec. 6(h)(1), repealed Code Sec. 1018, effective 10/1/79, except for any proceeding under the Bankruptcy Act begun before 10/1/79. Sec. 7(g) of this Act provides:

"(g) *Definitions.*

"For purposes of this section—

"(1) Bankruptcy case. The term 'bankruptcy case' means any case under title 11 of the United States Code (as recodified by P.L. 95-598).

"(2) Similar judicial proceeding. The term 'similar judicial proceeding' means a receivership, foreclosure, or similar proceeding in a Federal or State court (as modified by section 368(a)(3)(D) of the Internal Revenue Code of 1954)."

Prior to repeal, Code Sec. 1018 read as follows:

"Sec. 1018. Adjustment of Capital Structure Before September 22, 1938.

"Where a plan of reorganization of a corporation, approved by the court in a proceeding under section 77B of the National Bankruptcy Act, as amended (48 Stat. 912), is consummated by adjustment of the capital or debt structure of such corporation without the transfer of its assets to another corporation, and a final judgment or decree in such proceeding has been entered before September 22, 1938, then the provisions of section 270 of the Bankruptcy Act, as amended (11 U.S.C. 670), shall not apply in respect of the property of such corporation. For purposes of this section, the term 'reorganization' shall not be limited by the definition of such term in section 112(g) of the Internal Revenue Code of 1939."

In 1976, P.L. 94-455, Sec. 1901(a)(124), deleted "54 Stat. 709;" after "as amended" in Code Sec. 1018, effective for tax. yrs. begin. after 12/31/76.

Sec. 1019. Property on which lessee has made improvements.

Neither the basis nor the adjusted basis of any portion of real property shall, in the case of the lessor of such property, be increased or diminished on account of income derived by the lessor in respect of such property and excludable from gross income under section 109 (relating to improvements by lessee on lessor's property). If an amount representing any part of the value of real property attributable to buildings erected or other improvements made by a lessee in respect of such property was included in gross income of the lessor for any taxable year beginning before January 1, 1942, the basis of each portion of such property shall be properly adjusted for the amount so included in gross income.

Sec. 1020. Repealed.

In 1976, P.L. 94-455, Sec. 1901(a)(125), repealed Code Sec. 1020, effective for tax. yrs. begin. after 12/31/76.

Prior to repeal, Code Sec. 1020 read as follows:

"Sec. 1020. Election in Respect of Depreciation, etc., Allowed Before 1952.

"Any person may elect to have subparagraph (B) of section 1016(a)(2) apply in respect of periods since February 28, 1913, and before January 1, 1952. Such an election shall be made in such manner as the Secretary or his delegate may by regulations prescribe and shall be irrevocable when made, except that an election made on or before December 31, 1952, may be revoked at any time before January 1, 1955. A revocation of an election shall be made in such manner as the Secretary or his delegate may by regulations prescribe, and no election may be made by any person after he has so revoked an election. The election shall apply in respect of all property held by the person making the election at any time on or before December 31, 1952, and in respect of all periods since February 28, 1913, and before January 1, 1952, during which such person held such property or for which adjustments must be made under section 1016(b). An election or a revocation of an election by a transferor, donor, or grantor made after the date of the transfer, gift, or grant of property shall not affect the basis of such property in the hands of the transferee, donee, or grantee. No election may be made under this section after December 31, 1954."

Sec. 1021. Sale of annuities.

In case of the sale of an annuity contract, the adjusted basis shall in no case be less than zero.

• **Caution:** Code Sec. 1022, following, was added by Sec. 542(a), P.L. 107-16, the Economic Growth and Tax Relief Reconciliation Act of 2001 (EGTRRA). As provided in Sec. 301(a), P.L. 111-312, this amendment will apply as if never enacted, effective for estates for decedents dying, and transfers made, after 12/31/2009.

Sec. 1022. Treatment of property acquired from a decedent dying after December 31, 2009.

(a) In general.

Except as otherwise provided in this section—

(1) property acquired from a decedent dying after December 31, 2009, shall be treated for purposes of this subtitle as transferred by gift, and

(2) the basis of the person acquiring property from such a decedent shall be the lesser of—

(A) the adjusted basis of the decedent, or

(B) the fair market value of the property at the date of the decedent's death.

(b) Basis increase for certain property.

(1) In general. In the case of property to which this subsection applies, the basis of such property under subsection (a) shall be increased by its basis increase under this subsection.

(2) Basis increase. For purposes of this subsection—

(A) In general. The basis increase under this subsection for any property is the portion of the aggregate basis increase which is allocated to the property pursuant to this section.

(B) Aggregate basis increase. In the case of any estate, the aggregate basis increase under this subsection is $1,300,000.

(C) Limit increased by unused built-in losses and loss carryovers. The limitation under subparagraph (B) shall be increased by—
(i) the sum of the amount of any capital loss carryover under section 1212(b), and the amount of any net operating loss carryover under section 172, which would (but for the decedent's death) be carried from the decedent's last taxable year to a later taxable year of the decedent, plus
(ii) the sum of the amount of any losses that would have been allowable under section 165 if the property acquired from the decedent had been sold at fair market value immediately before the decedent's death.

(3) **Decedent nonresidents who are not citizens of the United States.** In the case of a decedent nonresident not a citizen of the United States—
(A) paragraph (2)(B) shall be applied by substituting "$60,000" for "$1,300,000", and
(B) paragraph (2)(C) shall not apply.

(c) **Additional basis increase for property acquired by surviving spouse.**
(1) **In general.** In the case of property to which this subsection applies and which is qualified spousal property, the basis of such property under subsection (a) (as increased under subsection (b)) shall be increased by its spousal property basis increase.
(2) **Spousal property basis increase.** For purposes of this subsection—
(A) In general. The spousal property basis increase for property referred to in paragraph (1) is the portion of the aggregate spousal property basis increase which is allocated to the property pursuant to this section.
(B) Aggregate spousal property basis increase. In the case of any estate, the aggregate spousal property basis increase is $3,000,000.
(3) **Qualified spousal property.** For purposes of this subsection, the term "qualified spousal property" means—
(A) outright transfer property, and
(B) qualified terminable interest property.
(4) **Outright transfer property.** For purposes of this subsection—
(A) In general. The term "outright transfer property" means any interest in property acquired from the decedent by the decedent's surviving spouse.
(B) Exception. Subparagraph (A) shall not apply where, on the lapse of time, on the occurrence of an event or contingency, or on the failure of an event or contingency to occur, an interest passing to the surviving spouse will terminate or fail—
(i)(I) if an interest in such property passes or has passed (for less than an adequate and full consideration in money or money's worth) from the decedent to any person other than such surviving spouse (or the estate of such spouse), and
(II) if by reason of such passing such person (or his heirs or assigns) may possess or enjoy any part of such property after such termination or failure of the interest so passing to the surviving spouse, or
(ii) if such interest is to be acquired for the surviving spouse, pursuant to directions of the decedent, by his executor or by the trustee of a trust.
For purposes of this subparagraph, an interest shall not be considered as an interest which will terminate or fail merely because it is the ownership of a bond, note, or similar contractual obligation, the discharge of which would not have the effect of an annuity for life or for a term.
(C) Interest of spouse conditional on survival for limited period. For purposes of this paragraph, an interest passing to the surviving spouse shall not be considered as an interest which will terminate or fail on the death of such spouse if—
(i) such death will cause a termination or failure of such interest only if it occurs within a period not exceeding 6 months after the decedent's death, or only if it occurs as a result of a common disaster resulting in the death of the decedent and the surviving spouse, or only if it occurs in the case of either such event, and
(ii) such termination or failure does not in fact occur.
(5) **Qualified terminable interest property.** For purposes of this subsection—
(A) In general. The term "qualified terminable interest property" means property—
(i) which passes from the decedent, and
(ii) in which the surviving spouse has a qualifying income interest for life.
(B) Qualifying income interest for life. The surviving spouse has a qualifying income interest for life if—
(i) the surviving spouse is entitled to all the income from the property, payable annually or at more frequent intervals, or has a usufruct interest for life in the property, and
(ii) no person has a power to appoint any part of the property to any person other than the surviving spouse.
Clause (ii) shall not apply to a power exercisable only at or after the death of the surviving spouse. To the extent provided in regulations, an annuity shall be treated in a manner similar to an income interest in property (regardless of whether the property from which the annuity is payable can be separately identified).
(C) Property includes interest therein. The term "property" includes an interest in property.
(D) Specific portion treated as separate property. A specific portion of property shall be treated as separate property. For purposes of the preceding sentence, the term "specific portion" only includes a portion determined on a fractional or percentage basis.

(d) **Definitions and special rules for application of subsections (b) and (c).**
(1) **Property to which subsections (b) and (c) apply.**
(A) In general. The basis of property acquired from a decedent may be increased under subsection (b) or (c) only if the property was owned by the decedent at the time of death.
(B) Rules relating to ownership.
(i) Jointly held property. In the case of property which was owned by the decedent and another person as joint tenants with right of survivorship or tenants by the entirety—
(I) if the only such other person is the surviving spouse, the decedent shall be treated as the owner of only 50 percent of the property,
(II) in any case (to which subclause (I) does not apply) in which the decedent furnished consideration for the acquisition of the property, the decedent shall be treated as the owner to the extent of the portion of the property which is proportionate to such consideration, and

(III) in any case (to which subclause (I) does not apply) in which the property has been acquired by gift, bequest, devise, or inheritance by the decedent and any other person as joint tenants with right of survivorship and their interests are not otherwise specified or fixed by law, the decedent shall be treated as the owner to the extent of the value of a fractional part to be determined by dividing the value of the property by the number of joint tenants with right of survivorship.

(ii) Revocable trusts. The decedent shall be treated as owning property transferred by the decedent during life to a qualified revocable trust (as defined in section 645(b)(1)).

(iii) Powers of appointment. The decedent shall not be treated as owning any property by reason of holding a power of appointment with respect to such property.

(iv) Community property. Property which represents the surviving spouse's one-half share of community property held by the decedent and the surviving spouse under the community property laws of any State or possession of the United States or any foreign country shall be treated for purposes of this section as owned by, and acquired from, the decedent if at least one-half of the whole of the community interest in such property is treated as owned by, and acquired from, the decedent without regard to this clause.

(C) Property acquired by decedent by gift within 3 years of death.

(i) In general. Subsections (b) and (c) shall not apply to property acquired by the decedent by gift or by inter vivos transfer for less than adequate and full consideration in money or money's worth during the 3-year period ending on the date of the decedent's death.

(ii) Exception for certain gifts from spouse. Clause (i) shall not apply to property acquired by the decedent from the decedent's spouse unless, during such 3-year period, such spouse acquired the property in whole or in part by gift or by inter vivos transfer for less than adequate and full consideration in money or money's worth.

(D) Stock of certain entities. Subsections (b) and (c) shall not apply to—

(i) stock or securities of a foreign personal holding company,

(ii) stock of a DISC or former DISC,

(iii) stock of a foreign investment company, or

(iv) stock of a passive foreign investment company unless such company is a qualified electing fund (as defined in section 1295) with respect to the decedent.

(2) Fair market value limitation. The adjustments under subsections (b) and (c) shall not increase the basis of any interest in property acquired from the decedent above its fair market value in the hands of the decedent as of the date of the decedent's death.

(3) Allocation rules.

(A) In general. The executor shall allocate the adjustments under subsections (b) and (c) on the return required by section 6018.

(B) Changes in allocation. Any allocation made pursuant to subparagraph (A) may be changed only as provided by the Secretary.

(4) Inflation adjustment of basis adjustment amounts.

(A) In general. In the case of decedents dying in a calendar year after 2010, the $1,300,000, $60,000, and $3,000,000 dollar amounts in subsections (b) and (c)(2)(B) shall each be increased by an amount equal to the product of—

(i) such dollar amount, and

(ii) the cost-of-living adjustment determined under section 1(f)(3) for such calendar year, determined by substituting "2009" for "1992" in subparagraph (B) thereof.

(B) Rounding. If any increase determined under subparagraph (A) is not a multiple of—

(i) $100,000 in the case of the $1,300,000 amount,

(ii) $5,000 in the case of the $60,000 amount, and

(iii) $250,000 in the case of the $3,000,000 amount,

such increase shall be rounded to the next lowest multiple thereof.

(e) Property acquired from the decedent.

For purposes of this section, the following property shall be considered to have been acquired from the decedent:

(1) Property acquired by bequest, devise, or inheritance, or by the decedent's estate from the decedent.

(2) Property transferred by the decedent during his lifetime—

(A) to a qualified revocable trust (as defined in section 645(b)(1)), or

(B) to any other trust with respect to which the decedent reserved the right to make any change in the enjoyment thereof through the exercise of a power to alter, amend, or terminate the trust.

(3) Any other property passing from the decedent by reason of death to the extent that such property passed without consideration.

(f) Coordination with section 691.

This section shall not apply to property which constitutes a right to receive an item of income in respect of a decedent under section 691.

(g) Certain liabilities disregarded.

(1) In general. In determining whether gain is recognized on the acquisition of property—

(A) from a decedent by a decedent's estate or any beneficiary other than a tax-exempt beneficiary, and

(B) from the decedent's estate by any beneficiary other than a tax-exempt beneficiary,

and in determining the adjusted basis of such property, liabilities in excess of basis shall be disregarded.

(2) Tax-exempt beneficiary. For purposes of paragraph (1), the term "tax-exempt beneficiary" means—

(A) the United States, any State or political subdivision thereof, any possession of the United States, any Indian tribal government (within the meaning of section 7871), or any agency or instrumentality of any of the foregoing,

(B) an organization (other than a cooperative described in section 521) which is exempt from tax imposed by chapter 1,

(C) any foreign person or entity (within the meaning of section 168(h)(2)), and

(D) to the extent provided in regulations, any person to whom property is transferred for the principal purpose of tax avoidance.

(h) Regulations.

The Secretary shall prescribe such regulations as may be necessary to carry out the purposes of this section.

Code Sec. 1022 — Basis

In 2010, P.L. 111-312, Sec. 101(a)(1), substituted "December 31, 2012" for "December 31, 2010" both places it appeared in Sec. 901, P.L. 107-16 [see below], effective as if included in the enactment of P.L. 107-16, EGTRRA, 6/7/2001.

—P.L. 111-312, Sec. 301(a), amended Code Sec. 1022 [as added by Sec. 542(a), P.L. 107-16, EGTRRA, 6/7/2001] to read as if such provision had never been enacted, effective for estates of decedents dying, and transfers made, after 12/31/2009.

Sec. 301(a), P.L. 111-312, 12/17/2010, provides:

"(a) In general. Each provision of law amended by subtitle A or E of title V of the Economic Growth and Tax Relief Reconciliation Act of 2001 [P.L. 107-16, see below] is amended to read as such provision would read if such subtitle had never been enacted."

—P.L. 111-312, Sec. 301(c), of this Act, provides

"(c) Special election with respect to estates of decedents dying in 2010. Notwithstanding subsection (a), in the case of an estate of a decedent dying after December 31, 2009, and before January 1, 2011, the executor (within the meaning of section 2203 of the Internal Revenue Code of 1986) may elect to apply such Code as though the amendments made by subsection (a) do not apply with respect to chapter 11 of such Code and with respect to property acquired or passing from such decedent (within the meaning of section 1014(b) of such Code). Such election shall be made at such time and in such manner as the Secretary of the Treasury or the Secretary's delegate shall provide. Such an election once made shall be revocable only with the consent of the Secretary of the Treasury or the Secretary's delegate. For purposes of section 2652(a)(1) of such Code, the determination of whether any property is subject to the tax imposed by such chapter 11 shall be made without regard to any election made under this subsection."

—P.L. 111-312, Sec. 301(d), of this Act, provides

" (d) Extension of time for performing certain acts.

" (1) Estate tax. In the case of the estate of a decedent dying after December 31, 2009, and before the date of the enactment of this Act, the due date for—

" (A) filing any return under section 6018 of the Internal Revenue Code of 1986 (including any election required to be made on such a return) as such section is in effect after the date of the enactment of this Act without regard to any election under subsection (c),

" (B) making any payment of tax under chapter 11 of such Code, and

" (C) making any disclaimer described in section 2518(b) of such Code of an interest in property passing by reason of the death of such decedent, shall not be earlier than the date which is 9 months after the date of the enactment of this Act.

" (2) Generation-skipping tax. In the case of any generation-skipping transfer made after December 31, 2009, and before the date of the enactment of this Act, the due date for filing any return under section 2662 of the Internal Revenue Code of 1986 (including any election required to be made on such a return) shall not be earlier than the date which is 9 months after the date of the enactment of this Act."

In 2002, P.L. 107-358, Sec. 2, added subsec. (c) in Sec. 901 of P.L. 107-16 [see below], effective 12/17/2002.

In 2001, P.L. 107-16, Sec. 542(a), added Code Sec. 1022, effective for estates of decedents dying after 12/31/2009.

—P.L. 107-16, Sec. 901, of this Act [as amended by Sec. 2 of P.L. 107-358, and Sec. 101(a)(1), P.L. 111-312, see above], reads as follows:

"SEC. 901. SUNSET OF PROVISIONS OF ACT.

"(a) In general. All provisions of, and amendments made by, this Act shall not apply—

"(1) to taxable, plan, or limitation years beginning after December 31, 2012, or

"(2) in the case of title V, to estates of decedents dying, gifts made, or generation skipping transfers, after December 31, 2012.

"(b) Application of certain laws. The Internal Revenue Code of 1986 and the Employee Retirement Income Security Act of 1974 shall be applied and administered to years, estates, gifts, and transfers described in subsection (a) as if the provisions and amendments described in subsection (a) had never been enacted.

"(c) Exception. Subsection (a) shall not apply to section 803 (relating to no federal income tax on restitution received by victims of the Nazi regime or their heirs or estates)."

Sec. 1022. Repealed.

In 1976, P.L. 94-455, Sec. 1901(a)(126)(A), repealed Code Sec. 1022, effective for stock or securities acquired from a decedent dying after 10/4/76.

Prior to repeal, Code Sec. 1022 read as follows:

"Sec. 1022. Increase in basis with respect to certain foreign personal holding company stock or securities.

"(a) General rule.

"The basis (determined under section 1014(b)(5), relating to basis of stock or securities in a foreign personal holding company) of a share of stock or a security, acquired from a decedent dying after December 31, 1963, of a corporation which was a foreign personal holding company for its most recent taxable year ending before the date of the decedent's death shall be increased by its proportionate share of any Federal estate tax attributable to the net appreciation in value of all of such shares and securities determined as provided in this section.

"(b) Proportionate share.

"For purposes of subsection (a), the proportionate share of a share of stock or of a security is that amount which bears the same ratio to the aggregate increase determined under subsection (c)(2) as the appreciation in value of such share or security bears to the aggregate appreciation in value of all such shares and securities having appreciation in value.

"(c) Special rules and definitions.

"For purposes of this section—

"(1) Federal estate tax. The term 'Federal estate tax' means only the tax imposed by section 2001 or 2101, reduced by any credit allowable with respect to a tax on prior transfers by section 2013 or 2102.

"(2) Federal estate tax attributable to net appreciation in value. The Federal estate tax attributable to the net appreciation in value of all shares of stock and securities to which subsection (a) applies is that amount which bears the same ratio to the Federal estate tax as the net appreciation in value of all of such shares and securities bears to the value of the gross estate as determined under chapter 11 (including section 2032, relating to alternate valuation).

"(3) Net appreciation. The net appreciation in value of all shares and securities to which subsection (a) applies is the amount by which the fair market value of all such shares and securities exceeds the adjusted basis of such property in the hands of the decedent.

"(4) Fair market value. For purposes of this section, the term 'fair market value' means fair market value determined under chapter 11 (including section 2032, relating to alternate valuation).

"(d) Limitations.

"This section shall not apply to any foreign personal holding company referred to in section 342(a)(2)."

In 1964, P.L. 88-272, Sec. 225(j), added Code Sec. 1022, effective for decedents dying after 12/31/63.

Sec. 1023. Cross references.

(1) For certain distributions by a corporation which are applied in reduction of basis of stock, see section 301(c)(2).

(2) For basis in case of construction of new vessels, see chapter 533 of title 46, United States Code.

In 2006, P.L. 109-304, Sec. 17(e)(4), substituted "chapter 533 of title 46, United States Code" for "section 511 of the Merchant Marine Act, 1936, as amended (46 U.S.C. 1161)" in para. (2), enacted 10/6/2006.

In 1980, P.L. 96-589, Sec. 6(i)(4), deleted para. (2) and redesignated para. (3) as para. (2), effective 10/1/79, except for any proceeding under the Bankruptcy Act begun before 10/1/79. Sec. 7(g) of this Act provides:

"(g) Definitions.

"For purposes of this section—

"(1) Bankruptcy case. The term 'bankruptcy case' means any case under title 11 of the United States Code (as recodified by P.L. 95-598).

"(2) Similar judicial proceeding. The term 'similar judicial proceeding' means a receivership, foreclosure, or similar proceeding in a Federal or State court (as modified by section 368(a)(3)(D) of the Internal Revenue Code of 1954)."

Prior to deletion para. (2) read as follows:

"(2) For basis of property in case of certain reorganizations and arrangements under the Bankruptcy Act, see sections 270, 396, and 522 of that Act, as amended (11 U. S. C. 670, 796, 922)."

—P.L. 96-223, Sec. 401(a), repealed Sec. 2005(a)(2) of P.L. 94-455 and the amendment made by Sec. 2005(a)(2), effective for decedents dying after '76 [see below]. Sec. 401(b) of P.L. 96-223 provides as follows:

"(b) Revival of prior law.

"Except to the extent necessary to carry out subsection (d), the Internal Revenue Code of 1954 shall be applied and administered as if the provisions repealed by subsection (a), and the amendments made by those provisions, had not been enacted."

In 1976, P.L. 94-455, Sec. 1901(a)(127), deleted para. (4), effective for tax. yrs. begin. after '76.

Prior to deletion, para. (4) read as follows:

"(4) For rules applicable in case of payments in violation of Defense Production Act of 1950, as amended see section 405 of that Act.

—P.L. 94-455, Sec. 2005(a)(2), redesignated Code Sec. 1023 as Code Sec. 1024 and added new Code Sec. 1023, but Sec. 2005(a)(2) was repealed by Sec. 401(a) of P.L. 96-223 [see above]. For Code Sec. 1023 added by Sec. 2005(a)(2) see note for Sec. 401(d) of P.L. 96-223 following Code Sec. 1014.

In 1964, P.L. 88-272, Sec. 225(j)(1), redesignated Code Sec. 1022 as Code Sec. 1023.

PART III.—COMMON NONTAXABLE EXCHANGES

Sec.

1031. Exchange of property held for productive use or investment.

1032. Exchange of stock for property.

1033. Involuntary conversions.

1034. Repealed.

1035. Certain exchanges of insurance policies.

1036. Stock for stock of same corporation.

1037. Certain exchanges of United States obligations.

1038. Certain reacquisitions of real property.

1039. Repealed.
1040. Transfer of certain farm, etc., real property [effective before 1/1/2010].
1040. Use of appreciated carryover basis property to satisfy pecuniary bequest [effective after 12/31/2009].
1041. Transfers of property between spouses or incident to divorce.
1042. Sales of stock to employee stock ownership plans or certain cooperatives.
1043. Sale of property to comply with conflict-of-interest requirements.
1044. Rollover of publicly traded securities gain into specialized small business investment companies.
1045. Rollover of gain from qualified small business stock to another qualified small business stock.

In 2001, P.L. 107-16, Sec. 542(d)(2), amended item 1040.
Prior to amendment, item 1040 read as follows:
"1040. Transfer of certain farm, etc., real property."
In 1997, P.L. 105-34, Sec. 312(d)(15), deleted item 1034 ... Sec. 313(b)(3), added item 1045.
In 1993, P.L. 103-66, Sec. 13114(c), added item 1044.
In 1990, P.L. 101-508, Sec. 11801(b)(8), deleted item 1039.
Prior to deletion, item 1039 read as follows:
"1039. Certain sales of low-income housing projects."
In 1989, P.L. 101-194, Sec. 502(b)(3), added item 1043.
In 1986, P.L. 99-514, Sec. 1854(a)(12), amended item 1042.
Prior to amendment, item 1042 read as follows:
"1042. Sales of stock to stock ownership plans or certain cooperatives."
In 1984, P.L. 98-369, Sec. 421(c), added item 1041 ... Sec. 541(a), added item 1042.
In 1981, P.L. 97-34, Sec. 421(j)(2)(C), amended item 1040.
Prior to amendment, item 1040 read as follows:
"1040. Use of farm, etc., real property to satisfy pecuniary bequest."
In 1980, P.L. 96-223, Sec. 401(c)(2)(B), revised Table, part III, Subch O, ch. 1 to read "Sec. 1040. Use of farm, etc., real property to satisfy pecuniary bequest.", in respect of decedents dying after 12/31/76.
Prior to revision the table read as follows:
"1040. Use of certain appreciated carryover basis property to satisfy pecuniary request."
In 1978, P.L. 95-600, Sec. 405(c)(2), amended item 1034.
Prior to amendment item 1034 read as follows:
"Sale or exchange of residence."
In 1976, P.L. 94-455, Sec. 2005(e)(2), added item 1040.
In 1969, P.L. 91-172, Sec. 910(c), added item 1039.
In 1964, inserted item 1038.
In 1959, added item 1037.

Sec. 1031. Exchange of property held for productive use or investment.

(a) Nonrecognition of gain or loss from exchanges solely in kind.

(1) In general. No gain or loss shall be recognized on the exchange of property held for productive use in a trade or business or for investment if such property is exchanged solely for property of like kind which is to be held either for productive use in a trade or business or for investment.

(2) Exception. This subsection shall not apply to any exchange of—

(A) stock in trade or other property held primarily for sale,

(B) stocks, bonds, or notes,

(C) other securities or evidences of indebtedness or interest,

(D) interests in a partnership,

(E) certificates of trust or beneficial interests, or

(F) choses in action.

For purposes of this section, an interest in a partnership which has in effect a valid election under section 761(a) to be excluded from the application of all of subchapter K shall be treated as an interest in each of the assets of such partnership and not as an interest in a partnership.

(3) Requirement that property be identified and that exchange be completed not more than 180 days after transfer of exchanged property. For purposes of this subsection, any property received by the taxpayer shall be treated as property which is not like-kind property if—

(A) such property is not identified as property to be received in the exchange on or before the day which is 45 days after the date on which the taxpayer transfers the property relinquished in the exchange, or

(B) such property is received after the earlier of—

(i) the day which is 180 days after the date on which the taxpayer transfers the property relinquished in the exchange, or

(ii) the due date (determined with regard to extension) for the transferor's return of the tax imposed by this chapter for the taxable year in which the transfer of the relinquished property occurs.

(b) Gain from exchanges not solely in kind.

If an exchange would be within the provisions of subsection (a), of section 1035(a), of section 1036(a), or of section 1037(a), if it were not for the fact that the property received in exchange consists not only of property permitted by such provisions to be received without the recognition of gain, but also of other property or money, then the gain, if any, to the recipient shall be recognized, but in an amount not in excess of the sum of such money and the fair market value of such other property.

(c) Loss from exchanges not solely in kind.

If an exchange would be within the provisions of subsection (a), of section 1035(a), of section 1036(a), or of section 1037(a), if it were not for the fact that the property received in exchange consists not only of property permitted by such provisions to be received without the recognition of gain or loss, but also of other property or money, then no loss from the exchange shall be recognized.

(d) Basis.

If property was acquired on an exchange described in this section, section 1035(a), section 1036(a), or section 1037(a), then the basis shall be the same as that of the property exchanged, decreased in the amount of any money received by the taxpayer and increased in the amount of gain or decreased in the amount of loss to the taxpayer that was recognized on such exchange. If the property so acquired consisted in part of the type of property permitted by this section, section 1035(a), section 1036(a), or section 1037(a), to be received without the recognition of gain or loss, and in part of other property, the basis provided in this subsection shall be allocated between the properties (other than money) received, and for the purpose of the allocation there shall be assigned to such other property an amount equivalent to its fair market value at the date of the exchange. For purposes of this section, section 1035(a), and section 1036(a), where as part of the consideration to the taxpayer another party to the exchange assumed (as determined under section 357(d)) a liability of the taxpayer, such assumption shall be considered as money received by the taxpayer on the exchange.

(e) Exchanges of livestock of different sexes.

For purposes of this section, livestock of different sexes are not property of a like kind.

(f) Special rules for exchanges between related persons.

(1) In general. If—

(A) a taxpayer exchanges property with a related person,

(B) there is nonrecognition of gain or loss to the taxpayer under this section with respect to the exchange of such property (determined without regard to this subsection), and

(C) before the date 2 years after the date of the last transfer which was part of such exchange—

(i) the related person disposes of such property, or

(ii) the taxpayer disposes of the property received in the exchange from the related person which was of like kind to the property transferred by the taxpayer, there shall be no nonrecognition of gain or loss under this section to the taxpayer with respect to such exchange; except that any gain or loss recognized by the taxpayer by reason of this subsection shall be taken into account as of the date on which the disposition referred to in subparagraph (C) occurs.

(2) Certain dispositions not taken into account. For purposes of paragraph (1)(C), there shall not be taken into account any disposition—

(A) after the earlier of the death of the taxpayer or the death of the related person,

(B) in a compulsory or involuntary conversion (within the meaning of section 1033) if the exchange occurred before the threat or imminence of such conversion, or

(C) with respect to which it is established to the satisfaction of the Secretary that neither the exchange nor such disposition had as one of its principal purposes the avoidance of Federal income tax.

(3) Related person. For purposes of this subsection, the term "related person" means any person bearing a relationship to the taxpayer described in section 267(b) or 707(b)(1).

(4) Treatment of certain transactions. This section shall not apply to any exchange which is part of a transaction (or series of transactions) structured to avoid the purposes of this subsection.

(g) Special rule where substantial diminution of risk.

(1) In general. If paragraph (2) applies to any property for any period, the running of the period set forth in subsection (f)(1)(C) with respect to such property shall be suspended during such period.

(2) Property to which subsection applies. This paragraph shall apply to any property for any period during which the holder's risk of loss with respect to the property is substantially diminished by—

(A) the holding of a put with respect to such property,

(B) the holding by another person of a right to acquire such property, or

(C) a short sale or any other transaction.

(h) Special rules for foreign real and personal property. For purposes of this section—

(1) Real property. Real property located in the United States and real property located outside the United States are not property of a like kind.

(2) Personal property.

(A) In general. Personal property used predominantly within the United States and personal property used predominantly outside the United States are not property of a like kind.

(B) Predominant use. Except as provided in subparagraphs (C) and (D), the predominant use of any property shall be determined based on—

(i) in the case of the property relinquished in the exchange, the 2-year period ending on the date of such relinquishment, and

(ii) in the case of the property acquired in the exchange, the 2-year period beginning on the date of such acquisition.

(C) Property held for less than 2 years. Except in the case of an exchange which is part of a transaction (or series of transactions) structured to avoid the purposes of this subsection—

(i) only the periods the property was held by the person relinquishing the property (or any related person) shall be taken into account under subparagraph (B)(i), and

(ii) only the periods the property was held by the person acquiring the property (or any related person) shall be taken into account under subparagraph (B)(ii).

(D) Special rule for certain property. Property described in any subparagraph of section 168(g)(4) shall be treated as used predominantly in the United States.

(i) Special rules for mutual ditch, reservoir, or irrigation company stock.

For purposes of subsection (a)(2)(B), the term "stocks" shall not include shares in a mutual ditch, reservoir, or irrigation company if at the time of the exchange—

(1) the mutual ditch, reservoir, or irrigation company is an organization described in section 501(c)(12)(A) (determined without regard to the percentage of its income that is collected from its members for the purpose of meeting losses and expenses), and

(2) the shares in such company have been recognized by the highest court of the State in which such company was organized or by applicable State statute as constituting or representing real property or an interest in real property.

In 2008, P.L. 110-246, Sec. 4, Repeals the duplicative enactment and provides effective date provisions of the Act entitled "An Act to provide for the continuation of agricultural programs through fiscal year 2012, and for other purposes" Sec. 4, P.L. 110-246 reads as follows:

"Sec. 4. Repeal of duplicative enactment.

"(a) In General- The Act entitled 'An Act to provide for the continuation of agricultural programs through fiscal year 2012, and for other purposes' (H.R. 2419 of the 110th Congress), and the amendments made by that Act, are repealed, effective on the date of enactment of that Act.

"(b) Effective Date- Except as otherwise provided in this Act, this Act and the amendments made by this Act shall take effect on the earlier of--

"(1) the date of enactment of this Act; or

"(2) the date of the enactment of the Act entitled 'An Act to provide for the continuation of agricultural programs through fiscal year 2012, and for other purposes' (H.R. 2419 of the 110th Congress)."

—P.L. 110-246, Sec. 15342(a), added subsec. (i), effective for exchanges completed after 5/22/2008. [Ed. Note: May 22, 2008 was the date of enactment for H.R. 2419 (PL 110-234), which was repealed by (2008 Farm Act § 4(a)) (PL 110-246, 6/18/2008), in connection with the reenactment of the farm bill to correct a technical deficiency in its original passage.]

In 2005, P.L. 109-135, Sec. 412(pp), substituted "subparagraphs" for "subparagraph" in subpara. (h)(2)(B), effective 12/21/2005.

In 1999, P.L. 106-36, Sec. 3001(c)(2)(A), substituted "assumed (as determined under section 357(d)) a liability of the taxpayer" for "assumed a liability of the taxpayer or acquired from the taxpayer property subject to a liability" in subsec. (d) . . . Sec. 3001(c)(2)(B), deleted "or acquisition (in the amount of the liability)" after "such assumption" in subsec. (d), effective for transfers after 10/31/98.

In 1997, P.L. 105-34, Sec. 1052(a), amended subsec. (h), effective for transfers after 6/8/97, in tax. yrs. end. after 6/8/97. Sec. 1052(b)(2) of this Act provides:

"(2) Binding contracts. The amendment made by this section shall not apply to any transfer pursuant to a written binding contract in effect on June 8, 1997, and at all times thereafter before the disposition of property. A contract shall not fail to meet the requirements of the preceding sentence solely because—

"(A) it provides for a sale in lieu of an exchange, or

"(B) the property to be acquired as replacement property was not identified under such contract before June 9, 1997."

Prior to amendment, subsec. (h) read as follows:

"(h) Special rule for foreign real property.

"For purposes of this section, real property located in the United States and real property located outside the United States are not property of a like kind."

In 1990, P.L. 101-508, Sec. 11701(h), substituted "section 267(b) or 707(b)(1)" for "section 267(b)", in para. (f)(3), effective for transfers after 8/3/90.

—P.L. 101-508, Sec. 11703(d)(1), added the last sentence to para. (a)(2), effective for transfers after 7/18/84.

In 1989, P.L. 101-239, Sec. 7601(a), added subsecs. (f)-(h), effective for transfers after 7/10/89, in tax. yrs. end. after 7/10/89, except as provided in Sec. 7601(b)(2) of this Act, which reads as follows:

"(2) Binding contract.— The amendments made by this section shall not apply to any transfer pursuant to a written binding contract in effect on July 10, 1989, and at all times thereafter before the transfer."

Nontaxable exchanges   Code Sec. 1033(a)(2)(D)

In 1986, P.L. 99-514, Sec. 1805(d), substituted "on or before the day" for "before the day" in subpara. (a)(3)(A), effective for transfers made after 7/18/84 in tax. yrs. end. after 7/18/84. Special rules and exceptions are provided by Sec. 77(b)(2)-(5) of P.L. 98-369, see below.

In 1984, P.L. 98-369, Sec. 77(a), amended subsec. (a), effective for transfers made after 7/18/84 in tax. yrs. end. after 7/18/84. Sec. 77(b)(2)-(5) of this Act provide the following exception, requirement and special rules:

"(2) Binding contract exception for transfer of partnership interests.—Paragraph (2)(D) of section 1031(a) of the Internal Revenue Code of 1954 (as amended by subsection (a)) shall not apply in the case of any exchange pursuant to a binding contract in effect on March 1, 1984, and at all times thereafter before the exchange.

"(3) Requirement that property be identified within 45 days and that exchange be completed within 180 days.—Paragraph (3) of section 1031(a) of the Internal Revenue Code of 1954 (as amended by subsection (a)) shall apply—

"(A) to transfers after the date of the enactment of this Act, and

"(B) to transfers on or before such date of enactment if the property to be received in the exchange is not received before January 1, 1987.

In the case of any transfer on or before the date of the enactment of this Act which the taxpayer treated as part of a like-kind exchange, the period for assessing any deficiency of tax attributable to the amendment made by subsection (a) shall not expire before January 1, 1988.

"(4) Special rule where property identified in binding contract.—If the property to be received in the exchange is identified in a binding contract in effect on June 13, 1984, and at all times thereafter before the transfer, paragraph (3) shall be applied—

"(A) by substituting 'January 1, 1989' for 'January 1, 1987', and

"(B) by substituting 'January 1, 1990' for 'January 1, 1988'.

"(5) Special rule for like-kind exchange of partnership interests.—Paragraph (2)(D) of section 1031(a) of the Internal Revenue Code of 1954 (as amended by subsection (a)) shall not apply to any exchange of an interest as general partner pursuant to a plan of reorganization of ownership interest under a contract which took effect on March 29, 1984, and which was executed on or before March 31, 1984, but only if all the exchanges contemplated by the reorganization plan are completed on or before December 31, 1987."

Prior to amendment, subsec. (a) read as follows:

"(a) Nonrecognition of gain or loss from exchanges solely in kind.

"No gain or loss shall be recognized if property held for productive use in trade or business or for investment (not including stock in trade or other property held primarily for sale, nor stocks, bonds, notes, chooses in action, certificates of trust, or beneficial interest, or other securities or evidences of indebtedness or interest) is exchanged solely for property of a like kind to be held either for productive use in trade or business or for investment."

In 1969, P.L. 91-172, Sec. 212(c), added subsec. (e), effective for tax. yrs. to which the Internal Revenue Code of 1954 applies.

In 1959, P.L. 86-346, Sec. 201(c), substituted "the provisions of subsection (a) of section 1035(a), of section 1036(a), or of section 1037(a)," for "the provisions of subsection (a) of section 1035(a), or of section 1036(a)," in subsec. (b) . . . Sec. 201(d), substituted "the provisions of subsection (a), of section 1035(a), of section 1036(a), or of section 1037(a)" for "the provisions of subsection (a), of section 1035(a), or of section 1036(a)" in subsec. (c) . . . Sec. 201(e), substituted "this section, section 1035(a), section 1036(a), or section 1037(a)," for "this section, section 1035(a), or section 1036(a)" each place it appeared in the first two sentences of subsec. (d), effective for tax. yrs. end. after 9/22/59.

In 1958, P.L. 85-866, Sec. 44(a), amended the first sentence of subsec. (d) . . . Sec. 44(b), substituted "subsection" for "paragraph" in subsec. (d), effective for tax. yrs. begin. after 12/31/53, and ending after 8/16/54.

Sec. 1032. Exchange of stock for property.
(a) Nonrecognition of gain or loss.

No gain or loss shall be recognized to a corporation on the receipt of money or other property in exchange for stock (including treasury stock) of such corporation. No gain or loss shall be recognized by a corporation with respect to any lapse or acquisition of an option, or with respect to a securities futures contract (as defined in section 1234B), to buy or sell its stock (including treasury stock).

(b) Basis.

For basis of property acquired by a corporation in certain exchanges for its stock, see section 362.

In 2000, P.L. 106-554, Sec. 1(a)(7), [which enacted into law Sec. 401(c) of P.L. 106-554] added ", or with respect to a securities futures contract (as defined in section 1234B)," after "an option" in subsec. (a), effective 12/21/2000.

In 1984, P.L. 98-369, Sec. 57(a), added a sentence to the end of subsec. (a), effective for options acquired or lapsed after 7/18/84, in tax. yrs. end. after 7/18/84.

Sec. 1033. Involuntary conversions.
(a) General rule.

If property (as a result of its destruction in whole or in part, theft, seizure, or requisition or condemnation or threat or imminence thereof) is compulsorily or involuntarily converted—

(1) Conversion into similar property. Into property similar or related in service or use to the property so converted, no gain shall be recognized.

(2) Conversion into money. Into money or into property not similar or related in service or use to the converted property, the gain (if any) shall be recognized except to the extent hereinafter provided in this paragraph:

(A) Nonrecognition of gain. If the taxpayer during the period specified in subparagraph (B), for the purpose of replacing the property so converted, purchases other property similar or related in service or use to the property so converted, or purchases stock in the acquisition of control of a corporation owning such other property, at the election of the taxpayer the gain shall be recognized only to the extent that the amount realized upon such conversion (regardless of whether such amount is received in one or more taxable years) exceeds the cost of such other property or such stock. Such election shall be made at such time and in such manner as the Secretary may by regulations prescribe. For purposes of this paragraph—

(i) no property or stock acquired before the disposition of the converted property shall be considered to have been acquired for the purpose of replacing such converted property unless held by the taxpayer on the date of such disposition; and

(ii) the taxpayer shall be considered to have purchased property or stock only if, but for the provisions of subsection (b) of this section, the unadjusted basis of such property or stock would be its cost within the meaning of section 1012.

(B) Period within which property must be replaced. The period referred to in subparagraph (A) shall be the period beginning with the date of the disposition of the converted property, or the earliest date of the threat or imminence of requisition or condemnation of the converted property, whichever is the earlier, and ending—

(i) 2 years after the close of the first taxable year in which any part of the gain upon the conversion is realized, or

(ii) subject to such terms and conditions as may be specified by the Secretary, at the close of such later date as the Secretary may designate on application by the taxpayer. Such application shall be made at such time and in such manner as the Secretary may by regulations prescribe.

(C) Time for assessment of deficiency attributable to gain upon conversion. If a taxpayer has made the election provided in subparagraph (A), then—

(i) the statutory period for the assessment of any deficiency, for any taxable year in which any part of the gain on such conversion is realized, attributable to such gain shall not expire prior to the expiration of 3 years from the date the Secretary is notified by the taxpayer (in such manner as the Secretary may by regulations prescribe) of the replacement of the converted property or of an intention not to replace, and

(ii) such deficiency may be assessed before the expiration of such 3-year period notwithstanding the provisions of section 6212(c) or the provisions of any other law or rule of law which would otherwise prevent such assessment.

(D) Time for assessment of other deficiencies attributable to election. If the election provided in subparagraph (A) is made by the taxpayer and such other property or such stock was purchased before the beginning of the last taxable year in which any part of the gain upon such conversion is realized, any deficiency, to the extent resulting from such election, for any taxable year ending before such last taxable year may be assessed (notwithstanding the provisions of section 6212(c) or 6501 or the provisions of any other law or rule of law which would otherwise prevent such assessment) at any time before the expiration of the period within which a deficiency for such last taxable year may be assessed.

(E) Definitions. For purposes of this paragraph—

(i) Control. The term "control" means the ownership of stock possessing at least 80 percent of the total combined voting power of all classes of stock entitled to vote and at least 80 percent of the total number of shares of all other classes of stock of the corporation.

(ii) Disposition of the converted property. The term "disposition of the converted property" means the destruction, theft, seizure, requisition, or condemnation of the converted property, or the sale or exchange of such property under threat or imminence of requisition or condemnation.

(b) Basis of property acquired through involuntary conversion.

(1) Conversions described in subsection (a)(1). If the property was acquired as the result of a compulsory or involuntary conversion described in subsection (a)(1), the basis shall be the same as in the case of the property so converted—

(A) decreased in the amount of any money received by the taxpayer which was not expended in accordance with the provisions of law (applicable to the year in which such conversion was made) determining the taxable status of the gain or loss upon such conversion, and

(B) increased in the amount of gain or decreased in the amount of loss to the taxpayer recognized upon such conversion under the law applicable to the year in which such conversion was made.

(2) Conversions described in subsection (a)(2). In the case of property purchased by the taxpayer in a transaction described in subsection (a)(2) which resulted in the nonrecognition of any part of the gain realized as the result of a compulsory or involuntary conversion, the basis shall be the cost of such property decreased in the amount of the gain not so recognized; and if the property purchased consists of more than 1 piece of property, the basis determined under this sentence shall be allocated to the purchased properties in proportion to their respective costs.

(3) Property held by corporation the stock of which is replacement property.

(A) In general. If the basis of stock in a corporation is decreased under paragraph (2), an amount equal to such decrease shall also be applied to reduce the basis of property held by the corporation at the time the taxpayer acquired control (as defined in subsection (a)(2)(E)) of such corporation.

(B) Limitation. Subparagraph (A) shall not apply to the extent that it would (but for this subparagraph) require a reduction in the aggregate adjusted bases of the property of the corporation below the taxpayer's adjusted basis of the stock in the corporation (determined immediately after such basis is decreased under paragraph (2)).

(C) Allocation of basis reduction. The decrease required under subparagraph (A) shall be allocated—

(i) first to property which is similar or related in service or use to the converted property,

(ii) second to depreciable property (as defined in section 1017(b)(3)(B)) not described in clause (i), and

(iii) then to other property.

(D) Special rules.

(i) Reduction not to exceed adjusted basis of property. No reduction in the basis of any property under this paragraph shall exceed the adjusted basis of such property (determined without regard to such reduction).

(ii) Allocation of reduction among properties. If more than 1 property is described in a clause of subparagraph (C), the reduction under this paragraph shall be allocated among such property in proportion to the adjusted bases of such property (as so determined).

(c) Property sold pursuant to reclamation laws.

For purposes of this subtitle, if property lying within an irrigation project is sold or otherwise disposed of in order to conform to the acreage limitation provisions of Federal reclamation laws, such sale or disposition shall be treated as an involuntary conversion to which this section applies.

(d) Livestock destroyed by disease.

For purposes of this subtitle, if livestock are destroyed by or on account of disease, or are sold or exchanged because of disease, such destruction or such sale or exchange shall be treated as an involuntary conversion to which this section applies.

(e) Livestock sold on account of drought, flood, or other weather-related conditions.

(1) In general. For purposes of this subtitle, the sale or exchange of livestock (other than poultry) held by a taxpayer for draft, breeding, or dairy purposes in excess of the number the taxpayer would sell if he followed his usual business practices shall be treated as an involuntary conversion to which this section applies if such livestock are sold or exchanged by the taxpayer solely on account of drought, flood, or other weather-related conditions.

(2) Extension of replacement period.

(A) In general. In the case of drought, flood, or other weather-related conditions described in paragraph (1) which result in the area being designated as eligible for assistance by the Federal Government, subsection (a)(2)(B) shall be applied with respect to any converted property by substituting "4 years" for "2 years".

(B) Further extension by Secretary. The Secretary may extend on a regional basis the period for replacement under this section (after the application of subparagraph (A)) for such additional time as the Secretary determines appropriate if the weather-related conditions which resulted in such application continue for more than 3 years.

(f) Replacement of livestock with other farm property in certain cases.

For purposes of subsection (a), if, because of drought, flood, or other weather-related conditions, or soil contamination or other environmental contamination, it is not feasible for the taxpayer to reinvest the proceeds from compulsorily or involuntarily converted livestock in property similar or related in use to the livestock so converted, other property (including real property in the case of soil contamination or other environmental contamination) used for farming purposes shall be treated as property similar or related in service or use to the livestock so converted.

(g) Condemnation of real property held for productive use in trade or business or for investment.

(1) Special rule. For purposes of subsection (a), if real property (not including stock in trade or other property held primarily for sale) held for productive use in trade or business or for investment is (as the result of its seizure, requisition, or condemnation, or threat or imminence thereof) compulsorily or involuntarily converted, property of a like kind to be held either for productive use in trade or business or for investment shall be treated as property similar or related in service or use to the property so converted.

(2) Limitation. Paragraph (1) shall not apply to the purchase of stock in the acquisition of control of a corporation described in subsection (a)(2)(A).

(3) Election to treat outdoor advertising displays as real property.

(A) In general. A taxpayer may elect, at such time and in such manner as the Secretary may prescribe, to treat property which constitutes an outdoor advertising display as real property for purposes of this chapter. The election provided by this subparagraph may not be made with respect to any property with respect to which an election under section 179(a) (relating to election to expense certain depreciable business assets) is in effect.

(B) Election. An election made under subparagraph (A) may not be revoked without the consent of the Secretary.

(C) Outdoor advertising display. For purposes of this paragraph, the term "outdoor advertising display" means a rigidly assembled sign, display, or device permanently affixed to the ground or permanently attached to a building or other inherently permanent structure constituting, or used for the display of, a commercial or other advertisement to the public.

(D) Character of replacement property. For purposes of this subsection, an interest in real property purchased as replacement property for a compulsorily or involuntarily converted outdoor advertising display defined in subparagraph (C) (and treated by the taxpayer as real property) shall be considered property of a like kind as the property converted without regard to whether the taxpayer's interest in the replacement property is the same kind of interest the taxpayer held in the converted property.

(4) Special rule. In the case of a compulsory or involuntary conversion described in paragraph (1), subsection (a)(2)(B)(i) shall be applied by substituting "3 years" for "2 years".

(h) Special rules for property damaged by federally declared disasters.

(1) Principal residences. If the taxpayer's principal residence or any of its contents is located in a disaster area and is compulsorily or involuntarily converted as a result of a federally declared disaster—

(A) Treatment of insurance proceeds.

(i) Exclusion for unscheduled personal property. No gain shall be recognized by reason of the receipt of any insurance proceeds for personal property which was part of such contents and which was not scheduled property for purposes of such insurance.

(ii) Other proceeds treated as common fund. In the case of any insurance proceeds (not described in clause (i)) for such residence or contents—

(I) such proceeds shall be treated as received for the conversion of a single item of property, and

(II) any property which is similar or related in service or use to the residence so converted (or contents thereof) shall be treated for purposes of subsection (a)(2) as property similar or related in service or use to such single item of property.

(B) Extension of replacement period. Subsection (a)(2)(B) shall be applied with respect to any property so converted by substituting "4 years" for "2 years".

(2) Trade or business and investment property. If a taxpayer's property held for productive use in a trade or business or for investment located in a disaster area and compulsorily or involuntarily converted as a result of a federally declared disaster, tangible property of a type held for productive use in a trade or business shall be treated for purposes of subsection (a) as property similar or related in service or use to the property so converted.

(3) Federally declared disaster; disaster area. The terms "federally declared disaster" and "disaster area" shall have the respective meaning given such terms by section 165(h)(3)(C).

(4) Principal residence. For purposes of this subsection, the term "principal residence" has the same meaning as when used in section 121, except that such term shall include a residence not treated as a principal residence solely because the taxpayer does not own the residence.

(i) Replacement property must be acquired from unrelated person in certain cases.

(1) In general. If the property which is involuntarily converted is held by a taxpayer to which this subsection applies, subsection (a) shall not apply if the replacement property or stock is acquired from a related person. The preceding sentence shall not apply to the extent that the related person acquired the replacement property or stock from an unrelated person during the period applicable under subsection (a)(2)(B).

(2) Taxpayers to which subsection applies. This subsection shall apply to—

(A) a C corporation,

(B) a partnership in which 1 or more C corporations own, directly or indirectly (determined in accordance with section 707(b)(3)), more than 50 percent of the capital interest, or profits interest, in such partnership at the time of the involuntary conversion, and

(C) any other taxpayer if, with respect to property which is involuntarily converted during the taxable year, the aggregate of the amount of realized gain on such property on which there is realized gain exceeds $100,000.

In the case of a partnership, subparagraph (C) shall apply with respect to the partnership and with respect to each partner. A similar rule shall apply in the case of an S corporation and its shareholders.

(3) Related person. For purposes of this subsection, a person is related to another person if the person bears a relationship to the other person described in section 267(b) or 707(b)(1).

(j) Sales or exchanges to implement microwave relocation policy.

(1) In general. For purposes of this subtitle, if a taxpayer elects the application of this subsection to a qualified sale or exchange, such sale or exchange shall be treated as an involuntary conversion to which this section applies.

(2) Qualified sale or exchange. For purposes of paragraph (1), the term "qualified sale or exchange" means a sale or exchange before January 1, 2000, which is certified by the Federal Communications Commission as having been made by a taxpayer in connection with the relo-

Code Sec. 1033(j)(2) — Nontaxable exchanges

cation of the taxpayer from the 1850-1990MHz spectrum by reason of the Federal Communications Commission's reallocation of that spectrum for use for personal communications services. The Commission shall transmit copies of certifications under this paragraph to the Secretary.

(k) Sales or exchanges under certain hazard mitigation programs.

For purposes of this subtitle, if property is sold or otherwise transferred to the Federal Government, a State or local government, or an Indian tribal government to implement hazard mitigation under the Robert T. Stafford Disaster Relief and Emergency Assistance Act (as in effect on the date of the enactment of this subsection) or the National Flood Insurance Act (as in effect on such date), such sale or transfer shall be treated as an involuntary conversion to which this section applies.

(l) Cross references.

(1) For determination of the period for which the taxpayer has held property involuntarily converted, see section 1223.

(2) For treatment of gains from involuntary conversions as capital gains in certain cases, see section 1231(a).

(3) For exclusion from gross income of gain from involuntary conversion of principal residence, see section 121.

In 2008, P.L. 110-343, Sec. 702DivC, Sec. 702(a)-(c), P.L. 110-343, provide: apply for the temporary tax relief for areas damaged by 2008 Midwestern storms, tornados, and flooding. Sec. 702(a)-(c) Div C read as follows:

"Sec. 702. Temporary tax relief for areas damaged by 2008 Midwestern severe storms, tornados, and flooding.

"(a) In general. Subject to the modifications described in this section, the following provisions of or relating to the Internal Revenue Code of 1986 shall apply to any Midwestern disaster area in addition to the areas to which such provisions otherwise apply:

"(1) GO Zone benefits.

"(A) Section 1400N (relating to tax benefits) other than subsections (b), (d), (e), (i), (j), (m), and (o) thereof.

"(B) Section 1400O (relating to education tax benefits).

"(C) Section 1400P (relating to housing tax benefits).

"(D) Section 1400Q (relating to special rules for use of retirement funds).

"(E) Section 1400R(a) (relating to employee retention credit for employers).

"(F) Section 1400S (relating to additional tax relief) other than subsection (d) thereof.

"(G) Section 1400T (relating to special rules for mortgage revenue bonds).

"(2) Other benefits included in Katrina Emergency Tax Relief Act of 2005. Sections 302, 303, 304, 401, and 405 of the Katrina Emergency Tax Relief Act of 2005.

"(b) Midwestern disaster area.

"(1) In general. For purposes of this section and for applying the substitutions described in subsections (d) and (e), the term 'Midwestern disaster area' means an area—

"(A) with respect to which a major disaster has been declared by the President on or after May 20, 2008, and before August 1, 2008, under section 401 of the Robert T. Stafford Disaster Relief and Emergency Assistance Act by reason of severe storms, tornados, or flooding occurring in any of the States of Arkansas, Illinois, Indiana, Iowa, Kansas, Michigan, Minnesota, Missouri, Nebraska, and Wisconsin, and

"(B) determined by the President to warrant individual or individual and public assistance from the Federal Government under such Act with respect to damages attributable to such severe storms, tornados, or flooding.

"(2) Certain benefits available to areas eligible only for public assistance. For purposes of applying this section to benefits under the following provisions, paragraph (1) shall be applied without regard to subparagraph (B):

"(A) Sections 1400Q, 1400S(b), and 1400S(d) of the Internal Revenue Code of 1986.

"(B) Sections 302, 401, and 405 of the Katrina Emergency Tax Relief Act of 2005.

"(c) References.

"(1) Area. Any reference in such provisions to the Hurricane Katrina disaster area or the Gulf Opportunity Zone shall be treated as a reference to any Midwestern disaster area and any reference to the Hurricane Katrina disaster area or the Gulf Opportunity Zone within a State shall be treated as a reference to all Midwestern disaster areas within the State.

"(2) Items attributable to disaster. Any reference in such provisions to any loss, damage, or other item attributable to Hurricane Katrina shall be treated as a reference to any loss, damage, or other item attributable to the severe storms, tornados, or flooding giving rise to any Presidential declaration described in subsection (b)(1)(A).

"(3) Applicable disaster date. For purposes of applying the substitutions described in subsections (d) and (e), the term 'applicable disaster date' means, with respect to any Midwestern disaster area, the date on which the severe storms, tornados, or flooding giving rise to the Presidential declaration described in subsection (b)(1)(A) occurred.

—P.L. 110-343, Sec. 702(e)(5)DivC, following applies to Sec. 405, P.L. 109-73, see below, for the temporary tax relief for areas damaged by 2008 Midwestern storms, tornados, and flooding. Sec. 702(e)(5) Div C, 110-343 reads as follows:

"(e) Modifications to Katrina Emergency Tax Relief Act of 2005. The following provisions of the Katrina Emergency Tax Relief Act of 2005 shall be applied with the following modifications:

* * * * * * * * * *

"(5) Extension of replacement period for nonrecognition of gain. Section 405, by substituting 'on or after the applicable disaster date' for 'on or after August 25, 2005'.

—P.L. 110-343, Sec. 706(a)(2)(D)(i)DivC, amended subsec. (h) preceding subpara. (h)(1)(A) . . . Sec. 706(a)(2)(D)(ii)DivC, substituted 'investment located in a disaster area and compulsorily or involuntarily converted as a result of a federally declared disaster' for 'investment is compulsorily or involuntarily converted as a result of a Presidentially declared disaster' in para. (h)(2) . . . Sec. 706(a)(2)(D)(ii)DivC, amended para. (h)(3), effective for disasters declared in tax. yrs. begin. after 12/31/2007.

Prior to amendment, subsec. (h) preceding subpara. (h)(1)(A), read as follows:

"(h) Special rules for property damaged by Presidentially declared disasters.

"(1) Principal residences. If the taxpayer's principal residence or any of its contents is compulsorily or involuntarily converted as a result of a Presidentially declared disaster—"

Prior to amendment, para. (h)(3) read as follows:

"(3) Presidentially declared disaster. For purposes of this subsection , the term 'Presidentially declared disaster' means any disaster which, with respect to the area in which the property is located, resulted in a subsequent determination by the President that such area warrants assistance by the Federal Government under the Robert T. Stafford Disaster Relief and Emergency Assistance Act."

—P.L. 110-234, Sec. 15345(a)(10), relating to Sec. 405 of P.L. 109-73 [see below] provides:

"Sec. 15345. Temporary tax relief for Kiowa County, Kansas and surrounding area. (a) In general. Subject to the modifications described in this section, the following provisions of or relating to the Internal Revenue Code of 1986 shall apply to the Kansas disaster area in addition to the areas to which such provisions otherwise apply:

"(10) Section 405 of the Katrina Emergency Tax Relief Act of 2005 (relating to extension of replacement period for nonrecognition of gain)."

—P.L. 110-234, Sec. 15345(d)(8), substituted "on or after May 4, 2007" for "on or after August 25, 2005" in Sec. 405 of P.L. 109-73, [see below].

In 2005, P.L. 109-73, Sec. 405, of this Act [as amended by Sec. 15345(d)(8) of P.L. 110-234, see above], provides:

"SEC. 405. EXTENSION OF REPLACEMENT PERIOD FOR NONRECOGNITION OF GAIN FOR PROPERTY LOCATED IN HURRICANE KATRINA DISASTER AREA.

"Clause (i) of section 1033(a)(2)(B) of the Internal Revenue Code of 1986 shall be applied by substituting '5 years' for '2 years' with respect to property in the Hurricane Katrina disaster area which is compulsorily or involuntarily converted on or after May 4, 2007, by reason of Hurricane Katrina, but only if substantially all of the use of the replacement property is in such area."

—P.L. 109-7, Sec. 1(b), redesignated subsec. (k) as (l) and added subsec. (k), effective for sales or other dispositions before, on, or after 4/15/2005.

In 2004, P.L. 108-357, Sec. 311(a)(1), added "drought, flood, or other weather-related conditions, or" after "because of" in subsec. (f) . . . Sec. 311(a)(2), added "in the case of soil contamination or other environmental contamination" after "including real property" in subsec. (f) . . . Sec. 311(a)(3), substituted "in certain cases" for "where there has been environmental contamination" in the heading of subsec. (f) . . . Sec. 311(b)(1), substituted "conditions. (1) In general. For purposes" for "conditions. For purposes" in subsec. (e) . . . Sec. 311(b)(2), added para. (e)(2), effective for any tax. yr. with respect to which the due date (without regard to extensions) for the return is after 12/31/2002.

—P.L. 108-311, Sec. 408(a)(7)(C), added "Robert T. Stafford" before "Disaster Relief and Emergency Assistance Act" in para. (h)(3), enacted 10/4/2004.

In 1998, P.L. 105-206, Sec. 6005(e)(3), added "on or" before "before" each place it appeared in the heading and text of Sec. 312(d)(2)[sic (e)] of P.L. 105-34, see below.

In 1997, P.L. 105-34, Sec. 312(d)(1), substituted "section 121" for "section 1034" in para. (h)(4) . . . Sec. 312(d)(7), amended para. (k)(3), effective for sales and exchanges after 5/6/97. Sec. 312(d)(2)-(4) [sic (d)(2)-(4)] of this Act [as amended by Sec. 6005(e)(3), 105-206, see above] provides:

"(2) Sales on or before date of enactment. At the election of the taxpayer, the amendments made by this section shall not apply to any sale or exchange on or before the date of the enactment of this Act.

"(3) Certain sales within 2 years after date of enactment. Section 121 of the Internal Revenue Code of 1986 (as amended by this section) shall be applied without regard to subsection (c)(2)(B) thereof in the case of any sale or exchange of property during the 2-year period beginning on the date of the enactment of this Act if the taxpayer held such property on the date of the enactment of this Act and fails to meet the ownership and use requirements of subsection (a) thereof with respect to such property.

"(4) Binding contracts. At the election of the taxpayer, the amendments made by this section shall not apply to a sale or exchange after the date of the enactment of this Act, if—

"(A) such sale or exchange is pursuant to a contract which was binding on such date, or

"(B) without regard to such amendments, gain would not be recognized under section 1034 of the Internal Revenue Code of 1986 (as in effect on the day before the date of the enactment of this Act) on such sale or exchange by reason of a new residence acquired on or before such date or with respect to the acquisition of which by the taxpayer a binding contract was in effect on such date.

This paragraph shall not apply to any sale or exchange by an individual if the treatment provided by section 877(a)(1) of the Internal Revenue Code of 1986 applies to such individual."

Prior to amendment para. (k)(3) read as follows:

"(3) For one-time exclusion from gross income of gain from involuntary conversion of principal residence by individual who has attained age 55, see section 121."

—P.L. 105-34, Sec. 913(b)(1), added ", flood, or other weather-related conditions" before the period at the end of subsec. (e) . . . Sec. 913(b)(2), added ", flood, or other weather-related conditions" after "drought" in the heading of subsec. (e), effective for sales and exchanges after 12/31/96.

—P.L. 105-34, Sec. 1087(a), amended subsec. (i), effective for involuntary conversions occurring after 6/8/97.

Prior to amendment, subsec. (i) read as follows:

"(i) Nonrecognition not to apply if corporation acquires replacement property from related person.

"(1) In general. In the case of—

"(A) a C corporation, or

"(B) a partnership in which 1 or more C corporations own, directly or indirectly (determined in accordance with section 707(b)(3)), more than 50 percent of the capital interest, or profits interest, in such partnership at the time of the involuntary conversion,

subsection (a) shall not apply if the replacement property or stock is acquired from a related person. The preceding sentence shall not apply to the extent that the related person acquired the replacement property or stock from an unrelated person during the period described in subsection (a)(2)(B).'

"(2) Related person. For purposes of this subsection, a person is related to another person if the person bears a relationship to the other person described in section 267(b) or 707(b)(1)."

In 1996, P.L. 104-188, Sec. 1119(a), redesignated paras. (h)(2) and (3) as (h)(3) and (4), and added new para. (h)(2) . . . Sec. 1119(b)(1), substituted "property" for "residence" in para. (h)(3) [as redesignated by Sec. 1119(a)(1) of this Act, see above] . . . Sec. 1119(b)(2), substituted "property" for "principal residences" in the heading of subsec. (h) . . . Sec. 1119(b)(3), substituted "(1) Principal residences" for "(1) In general" in para. (h)(1) , effective for disasters declared after 12/31/94, in tax. yrs. end. after 12/31/94.

—P.L. 104-188, Sec. 1610(a), amended subsec. (b), effective for involuntary conversions occurring after 8/20/96.

Prior to amendment, subsec. (b) read as follows:

"(b) Basis of property acquired through involuntary conversion. If the property was acquired, after February 28, 1913, as the result of a compulsory or involuntary conversion described in subsection (a)(1) or section 112(f)(2) of the Internal Revenue Code of 1939, the basis shall be the same as in the case of the property so converted, decreased in the amount of any money received by the taxpayer which was not expended in accordance with the provisions of law (applicable to the year in which such conversion was made) determining the taxable status of the gain or loss upon such conversion, and increased in the amount of gain or decreased in the amount of loss to the taxpayer recognized upon such conversion under the law applicable to the year in which such conversion was made. This subsection shall not apply in respect of property acquired as a result of a compulsory or involuntary conversion of property used by the taxpayer as his principal residence if the destruction, theft, seizure, requisition, or condemnation of such residence, or the sale or exchange of such residence under threat or imminence thereof, occurred after December 31, 1950, and before January 1, 1954. In the case of property purchased by the taxpayer in a transaction described in subsection (a)(3)[(2)] which resulted in the nonrecognition of any part of the gain realized as the result of a compulsory or involuntary conversion, the basis shall be the cost of such property decreased in the amount of the gain not so recognized; and if the property purchased consists of more than one piece of property, the basis determined under this sentence shall be allocated to the purchased properties in proportion to their respective costs."

In 1995, P.L. 104-7, Sec. 3(a)(1), redesignated subsec. (i) as subsec. (j) and added new subsec. (i), effective for involuntary conversions occurring on or after 2/6/95.

—P.L. 104-7, Sec. 3(b)(1), redesignated subsec. (j) [as redesignated by Sec. 3(a)(1) of this Act] as subsec. (k) and added new subsec. (j), effective for sales or exchanges after 3/14/95.

In 1993, P.L. 103-66, Sec. 13431(a), redesignated subsec. (h) as subsec. (i) and added new subsec. (h), effective for property compulsorily or involuntarily converted as a result of disasters for which the determination referred to in Code Sec. 1033(h)(2) (as added by this section) is made on or after 9/1/91, and for tax. yrs. end. on or after such date.

In 1990, P.L. 101-508, Sec. 11813(b)(20), deleted "with respect to which the investment credit determined under section 46(a) is or has been claimed or" after "with respect to any property" in subpara. (g)(3)(A), effective for property placed in service after 12/31/90 except as provided in Sec. 11813(c)(2) of this Act, reproduced in note following Code Sec. 46.

In 1984, P.L. 98-369, Sec. 474(r)(24), substituted "the investment credit determined under section 46(a)" for "the credit allowed by section 38 (relating to investment in certain depreciable property)" in subpara. (g)(3)(A), effective for tax. yrs. begin. after 12/31/83, and for carrybacks from tax. yrs. begin. after 12/31/83.

In 1981, P.L. 97-34, Sec. 202(d)(2), substituted "(relating to election to expense certain depreciable business assets)" for "(relating to additional first-year depreciation allowance for small business)" in subpara. (g)(3)(A), effective for property placed in service after 12/31/80, in tax. yrs. end. after 12/31/80.

In 1980, P.L. 96-601, Sec. 5, provides:

"SEC. 5. RHODE ISLAND INDIAN CLAIMS SETTLEMENT ACT.

"(a) In general.

The Rhode Island Indian Claims Settlement Act (P.L. 95-395) is amended by adding at the end thereof the following new title:

"TITLE II—TAX TREATMENT

"EXEMPTION FROM TAXATION

"Sec. 201. (a) Except as otherwise provided in subsections (b) and (c), the settlement lands received by the State Corporation shall not be subject to any form of Federal, State, or local taxation while held by the State Corporation.

"(b) The exemption provided in subsection (a) shall not apply to any income-producing activities occurring on the settlement lands.

"(c) Nothing in this Act shall prevent the making of payments in lieu of taxes by the State Corporation for services provided in connection with the settlement lands.

"DEFERRAL OF CAPITAL GAINS

"Sec. 202. For purposes of the Internal Revenue Code of 1954, any sale or disposition of private settlement lands pursuant to the terms and conditions of the settlement agreement shall be treated as an involuntary conversion within the meaning of section 1033 of the Internal Revenue Code of 1954.".

"(b) Effective date.

"The amendment made by subsection (a) shall take effect on September 30, 1978."

In 1978, P.L. 95-600, Sec. 404(c)(4), amended para. (g)(3), effective for sales or exchange after 7/26/78, in tax. yrs. end. after 7/26/78.

Prior to amendment, para. (g)(3) read as follows:

"(3) For exclusion from gross income of certain gain from involuntary conversion of residence of taxpayer who has attained age 65, see section 121."

—P.L. 95-600, Sec. 542(a), redesignated subsecs. (f) and (g) as subsecs. (g) and (h) and added new subsec. (f), effective for tax. yrs. begin. after 12/31/74.

—P.L. 95-600, Sec. 703(j)(5), substituted "subsection (b)" for "subsection (c)" in clause (a)(2)(A)(ii), effective 10/4/76.

In 1976, P.L. 94-455, Sec. 1901(a)(128)(A), deleted para. (a)(2) and redesignated para. (a)(3) as (a)(2) . . . Sec. 1901(a)(128)(B)(i), deleted "where disposition occurred after 1950" in the heading of para. (a)(2) [as redesignated by Sec. 1901(a)(128)(A) of this Act, see above] . . . Sec. 1901(a)(128)(B)(ii), substituted "(h)" for "(g)" each place it appeared in para. (a)(2) [as redesignated, see above] . . . Sec. 1901(a)(128)(B)(iii), deleted "and the disposition of the converted property (as defined in paragraph (2)) occurred after December 31, 1950," in para. (a)(2) [as redesignated, see above] . . . Sec. 1901(a)(128)(B)(iv), added subpara. (a)(2)(E) [as redesignated, see above] . . . Sec. 1901(a)(128)(C), deleted subsec. (b) and redesignated subsecs. (c), (d), (e), (f), (g) and (h) as subsecs. (b), (c), (d), (e), (f) and (g) . . . Sec. 1901(a)(128)(D), substituted "or section 112(f)(2) of the Internal Revenue Code of 1939" for "or (2)" in the first sentence of subsec. (b) [as redesignated by Sec. 1901(a)(128)(C) of this Act, see above] . . . Sec. 1901(a)(128)(E), amended para. (f)(2) [as redesignated by Sec. 1901(a)(128)(C) of this Act, see above] . . . Sec. 1901(a)(128)(F), substituted "(a)(2)(B)(i)" for "(a)(3)(B)(i)" in para. (g)(4) [as redesignated by Sec. 1901(a)(128)(C) of this Act, see above, and as added by Sec. 2140(a) of this Act, see below] . . . Sec. 1906(b)(13)(A), substituted "Secretary" for "Secretary or his delegate" each place it appeared in Code Sec. 1033, effective for tax. yrs. begin. after 12/31/76.

Prior to deletion, para. (a)(2) read as follows:

"(2) Conversion into money where disposition occurred prior to 1951. Into money, and the disposition of the converted property occurred before January 1, 1951, no gain shall be recognized if such money is forthwith in good faith, under regulations prescribed by the Secretary or his delegate, expended in the acquisition of other property similar or related in service or use to the property so converted, or in the acquisition of control of a corporation owning such other property, or in the establishment of a replacement fund. If any part of the money is not so expended, the gain shall be recognized to the extent of the money which is not so expended (regardless of whether such money is received in one or more taxable years and regardless of whether or not the money which is not so expended constitutes gain). For purposes of this paragraph and paragraph (3), the term 'disposition of the converted property' means the destruction, theft, seizure, requisition, or condemnation of the converted property, or the sale or exchange of such property under threat or imminence of requisition or condemnation. For purposes of this paragraph and paragraph (3), the term 'control' means the ownership of stock possessing at least 80 percent of the total combined voting power of all classes of stock entitled to vote and at least 80 percent of the total number of shares of all other classes of stock of the corporation."

Prior to deletion, subsec. (b) read as follows:

"(b) Residence of taxpayer. Subsection (a) shall not apply, in the case of property used by the taxpayer as his principal residence, if the destruction, theft, seizure, requisition, or condemnation of the residence, or the sale or exchange of such residence under threat or imminence thereof, occurred after December 31, 1950, and before January 1, 1954."

Prior to amendment, para. (f)(2) [as redesignated by Sec. 1901(a)(128)(C) of this Act, see above] read as follows:

"(2) Limitations.

"(A) Purchase of stock. Paragraph (1) shall not apply to the purchase of stock in the acquisition of control of a corporation described in subsection (a)(3)(A).

"(B) Conversions before January 1, 1958. Paragraph (1) shall apply with respect to the compulsory or involuntary conversion of any real property only if the disposition of the converted property (within the meaning of subsection (a)(2)) occurs after December 31, 1957."

Code Sec. 1033

—P.L. 94-455, Sec. 2127(a), added para. (g)(3), effective for tax. yrs. begin. after 12/31/70.

—P.L. 94-455, Sec. 2140(a), added para. (g)(4), effective for any disposition of converted property (within the meaning of '54 Code Sec. 1033(a)(2)) after 12/31/74, unless a condemnation proceeding for such property began before 10/4/76.

In 1969, P.L. 91-172, Sec. 915(a), substituted "2 years" for "one year" in clause (a)(3)(B)(i), effective only if the disposition of the converted property (within the meaning of '54 Code Sec. 1033(a)(2)) occurs after 12/30/69.

In 1964, P.L. 88-272, Sec. 206(c)(3), added para. (h)(3), effective for dispositions after 12/31/63 in tax. yrs. end. after 12/31/63.

In 1958, P.L. 85-866, Sec. 45, added the sentence at the end of para. (a)(2)... Sec. 46(a), redesignated subsec. (g) as subsec. (h), and added new subsec. (g), effective for tax. yrs. begin. after 12/31/53 and end. after 8/16/54.

In 1956, P.L. 629, Sec. 5(a), redesignated subsec. (f) as subsec. (g), and added new subsec. (f), effective for tax. yrs. end. after 12/31/55, but only for sales and exchanges of livestock after 12/31/55.

Sec. 1034. Repealed.

In 1998, P.L. 105-206, Sec. 6005(e)(3), added "on or" before "before" each place it appeared in the heading and text of Sec. 312(d)(2)[sic (e)] of P.L. 105-34, see below.

In 1997, P.L. 105-34, Sec. 312(b), repealed Code Sec. 1034, effective for sales and exchanges after 5/6/97, except for as provided in Secs. 312(d)(2)-(4) [sic (e)(2)-(4)] of this Act [as amended by Sec. 6005(e)(3), 105-206, see above], which read as follows:

"(2) Sales on or before date of enactment. — At the election of the taxpayer, the amendments made by this section shall not apply to any sale or exchange on or before the date of the enactment of this Act.

"(3) Certain sales within 2 years after date of enactment. Section 121 of the Internal Revenue Code of 1986 (as amended by this section) shall be applied without regard to subsection (c)(2)(B) thereof in the case of any sale or exchange of property during the 2-year period beginning on the date of the enactment of this Act if the taxpayer held such property on the date of the enactment of this Act and fails to meet the ownership and use requirements of subsection (a) thereof with respect to such property.

"(4) Binding contracts. — At the election of the taxpayer, the amendments made by this section shall not apply to a sale or exchange after the date of the enactment of this Act, if—

"(A) such sale or exchange is pursuant to a contract which was binding on such date, or

"(B) without regard to such amendments, gain would not be recognized under section 1034 of the Internal Revenue Code of 1986 (as in effect on the day before the date of the enactment of this Act) on such sale or exchange by reason of a new residence acquired on or before such date or with respect to the acquisition of which by the taxpayer a binding contract was in effect on such date.

This paragraph shall not apply to any sale or exchange by an individual if the treatment provided by section 877(a)(1) of the Internal Revenue Code of 1986 applies to such individual."

Prior to repeal, Code Sec. 1034 read as follows:

"Sec. 1034. Rollover of gain on sale of principal residence.

"(a) Nonrecognition of gain.

"If property (in this section called 'old residence') used by the taxpayer as his principal residence is sold by him and, within a period beginning 2 years before the date of such sale and ending 2 years after such date, property (in this section called 'new residence') is purchased and used by the taxpayer as his principal residence, gain (if any) from such sale shall be recognized only to the extent that the taxpayer's adjusted sales price (as defined in subsection (b)) of the old residence exceeds the taxpayer's cost of purchasing the new residence.

"(b) Adjusted sales price defined.

"(1) In general. For purposes of this section, the term 'adjusted sales price' means the amount realized, reduced by the aggregate of the expenses for work performed on the old residence in order to assist in its sale.

"(2) Limitations. The reduction provided in paragraph (1) applies only to expenses —

"(A) for work performed during the 90-day period ending on the day on which the contract to sell the old residence is entered into;

"(B) which are paid on or before the 30th day after the date of the sale of the old residence; and

"(C) which are —

"(i) not allowable as deductions in computing taxable income under section 63 (defining taxable income), and

"(ii) not taken into account in computing the amount realized from the sale of the old residence.

"(c) Rules for application of section.

"For purposes of this section:

"(1) An exchange by the taxpayer of his residence for other property shall be treated as a sale of such residence, and the acquisition of a residence on the exchange of property shall be treated as a purchase of such residence.

"(2) A residence any part of which was constructed or reconstructed by the taxpayer shall be treated as purchased by the taxpayer. In determining the taxpayer's cost of purchasing a residence, there shall be included only so much of his cost as is attributable to the acquisition, construction, reconstruction, and improvements made which are properly chargeable to capital account, during the period specified in subsection (a).

Nontaxable exchanges

"(3) If a residence is purchased by the taxpayer before the date of his sale of the old residence, the purchased residence shall not be treated as his new residence if sold or otherwise disposed of by him before the date of the sale of the old residence.

"(4) If the taxpayer, during the period described in subsection (a), purchases more than one residence which is used by him as his principal residence at some time within 2 years after the date of the sale of the old residence, only the last of such residences so used by him after the date of such sale shall constitute the new residence. If a principal residence is sold in a sale to which subsection (d)(2) applies within 2 years after the sale of the old residence, for purposes of applying the preceding sentence with respect to the old residence, the principal residence so sold shall be treated as the last residence used during such 2-year period.

"(d) Limitation.

"(1) In general. Subsection (a) shall not apply with respect to the sale of the taxpayer's residence if within 2 years before the date of such sale the taxpayer sold at a gain other property used by him as his principal residence, and any part of such gain was not recognized by reason of subsection (a).

"(2) Subsequent sale connected with commencing work at new place. Paragraph (1) shall not apply with respect to the sale of the taxpayer's residence if —

"(A) such sale was in connection with the commencement of work by the taxpayer as an employee or as a self-employed individual at a new principal place of work, and

"(B) if the residence so sold is treated as the former residence for purposes of section 217 (relating to moving expenses), the taxpayer would satisfy the conditions of subsection (c) of section 217 (as modified by the other subsections of such section).

"(e) Basis of new residence.

"Where the purchase of a new residence results, under subsection (a) or under section 112(n) of the Internal Revenue Code of 1939, in the nonrecognition of gain on the sale of an old residence, in determining the adjusted basis of the new residence as of any time following the sale of the old residence, the adjustments to basis shall include a reduction by an amount equal to the amount of the gain not so recognized on the sale of the old residence. For this purpose, the amount of the gain not so recognized on the sale of the old residence includes only so much of such gain as is not recognized by reason of the cost, up to such time, of purchasing the new residence.

"(f) Tenant-stockholder in a cooperative housing corporation.

"For purposes of this section, section 1016 (relating to adjustments to basis), and section 1223 (relating to holding period), references to property used by the taxpayer as his principal residence, and references to the residence of a taxpayer, shall include stock held by a tenant-stockholder (as defined in section 216, relating to deduction for amounts representing taxes and interest paid to a cooperative housing corporation) in a cooperative housing corporation (as defined in such section) if —

"(1) in the case of stock sold, the house or apartment which the taxpayer was entitled to occupy as such stockholder was used by him as his principal residence, and

"(2) in the case of stock purchased, the taxpayer used as his principal residence the house or apartment which he was entitled to occupy as such stockholder.

"(g) Husband and wife.

"If the taxpayer and his spouse, in accordance with regulations which shall be prescribed by the Secretary pursuant to this subsection, consent to the application of paragraph (2) of this subsection, then —

"(1) for purposes of this section —

"(A) the taxpayer's adjusted sales price of the old residence is the adjusted sales price (of the taxpayer, or of the taxpayer and his spouse) of the old residence, and

"(B) the taxpayer's cost of purchasing the new residence is the cost (to the taxpayer, his spouse, or both) of purchasing the new residence (whether held by the taxpayer, his spouse, or the taxpayer and his spouse); and

"(2) so much of the gain on the sale of the old residence as is not recognized solely by reason of subsection, and so much of the adjustment under subsection (e) to the basis of the new residence as results solely from this subsection shall be allocated between the taxpayer and his spouse as provided in such regulations.

This subsection shall apply only if the old residence and the new residence are each used by the taxpayer and his spouse as their principal residence. In case the taxpayer and his spouse do not consent to the application of paragraph (2) of this subsection then the recognition of gain on the sale of the old residence shall be determined under this section without regard to the rules provided in this subsection. For purposes of this subsection, except to the extent provided in regulations, in the case of an individual who dies after the date of the sale of the old residence and is married on the date of death, consent to the application of paragraph (2) by such individual's spouse and use of the new residence as the principal residence of such spouse shall be treated as consent and use by such individual.

"(h) Members of Armed Forces.

"(1) In general. The running of any period of time specified in subsection (a) or (c) (other than the 2 years referred to in subsection (c)(4)) shall be suspended during any time that the taxpayer (or his spouse if the old residence and the new residence are each used by the taxpayer and his spouse as their principal residence) serves on extended active duty with the Armed Forces of the United States after the date of the sale of the old residence, except that any such period of time as so suspended shall not extend beyond the date 4 years after the date of the sale of the old residence.

"(2) Members stationed outside the United States or required to reside in government quarters. In the case of any taxpayer who, during any period of time the running of which is suspended by paragraph (1) —

"(A) is stationed outside the United States, or

"(B) after returning from a tour of duty outside of the United States and pursuant to a determination by the Secretary of Defense that adequate off-base housing is not available at a remote base site, is required to reside in on-base Government quarters,

any such period of time as so suspended shall not expire before the day which is 1 year after the last day described in subparagraph (A) or (B), as the case may be, except that any such period of time as so suspended shall not extend beyond the date which is 8 years after the date of the sale of the old residence.

"(3) Extended active duty defined. For purposes of this subsection, the term 'extended active duty' means any period of active duty pursuant to a call or order to such duty for a period in excess of 90 days or for an indefinite period.

"(i) Special rule for condemnation.

"In the case of the seizure, requisition, or condemnation of a residence, or the sale or exchange of a residence under threat or imminence thereof, the provisions of this section, in lieu of section 1033 (relating to involuntary conversions), shall be applicable if the taxpayer so elects. If such election is made, such seizure, requisition, or condemnation shall be treated as the sale of the residence. Such election shall be made at such time and in such manner as the Secretary shall prescribe by regulations.

"(j) Statute of limitations.

"If the taxpayer during a taxable year sells at a gain property used by him as his principal residence, then—

"(1) the statutory period for the assessment of any deficiency attributable to any part of such gain shall not expire before the expiration of 3 years from the date the Secretary is notified by the taxpayer (in such manner as the Secretary may by regulations prescribe) of—

"(A) the taxpayer's cost of purchasing the new residence which the taxpayer claims results in nonrecognition of any part of such gain,

"(B) the taxpayer's intention not to purchase a new residence within the period specified in subsection (a), or

"(C) a failure to make such purchase within such period; and

"(2) such deficiency may be assessed before the expiration of such 3-year period notwithstanding the provisions of any other law or rule of law which would otherwise prevent such assessment.

"(k) Individual whose tax home is outside the United States.

"The running of any period of time specified in subsection (a) or (c) (other than the 2 years referred to in subsection (c)(4)) shall be suspended during any time that the taxpayer (or his spouse if the old residence and the new residence are each used by the taxpayer and his spouse as their principal residence) has a tax home (as defined in section 911(d)(3)) outside the United States after the date of the sale of the old residence; except that any such period of time as so suspended shall not extend beyond the date 4 years after the date of the sale of the old residence.

"(l) Cross reference.

"For one-time exclusion from gross income of gain from sale of principal residence by individual who has attained age 55, see section 121."

In 1988, P.L. 100-647, Sec. 6002(a), added the sentence at the end of subsec. (g), effective for sales and exchanges of old residences (within the meaning of Code Sec. 1034 of the 1986 Code) after 12/31/84, in tax. yrs. ending after 12/31/84.

In 1986, P.L. 99-514, Sec. 1878(g), substituted "before the day which is 1 year after the last day described" for "before the last day described" in para. (h)(2), effective for sales of old residences (within the meaning of Code Sec. 1034) after 7/18/84.

In 1984, P.L. 98-369, Sec. 1053(a), amended subsec. (h), effective for sales of old residences (within the meaning of Code Sec. 1034) after 7/18/84.

Prior to amendment, subsec. (h) read as follows:

"(h) Members of Armed Forces.

"The running of any period of time specified in subsection (a) or (c) (other than the 2 years referred to in subsection (c)(4)) shall be suspended during any time that the taxpayer (or his spouse if the old residence and the new residence are each used by the taxpayer and his spouse as their principal residence) serves on extended active duty with the Armed Forces of the United States after the date of the sale of the old residence except that any such period of time as so suspended shall not extend beyond the date 4 years after the date of the sale of the old residence. For purposes of this subsection, the term 'extended active duty' means any period of active duty pursuant to a call or order to such duty for a period in excess of 90 days or for an indefinite period."

In 1983, P.L. 97-448, Sec. 101(d), added the two sentences at the end of Sec. 122(c) of P.L. 97-34, [the effective date for changes made by Sec. 122 of P.L. 97-34, see below].

In 1981, P.L. 97-34, Sec. 112(b)(4), substituted "section 911(d)(3)" for "section 913(j)(1)(B)" in subsec. (k), effective for tax. yrs. begin. after 12/31/81.

—P.L. 97-34, Sec. 122(a), substituted "2 years" for "18 months" each place it appeared in Code Sec. 1034 ... Sec. 122(b)(1), substituted "2-year" for "18-month" in para. (c)(4) ... Sec. 122(b)(2), repealed para. (c)(5), effective as provided in Sec. 122(c) of this Act [as amended by Sec. 101(d) of P.L. 97-448, see above] which reads as follows:

"(c) Effective date.

"The amendments made by this section shall apply to old residences (within the meaning of section 1034 of the Internal Revenue Code of 1954) sold or exchanged—

"(1) after July 20, 1981, or

"(2) on or before such date, if the rollover period under such section (determined without regard to the amendments made by this section) expires on or after such date.

Notwithstanding the preceding sentence, the taxpayer may elect to have the amendments made by this section not apply to any old residence sold or exchanged on or before August 13, 1981. Such an election shall be made at such time and in such manner as the Secretary of the Treasury or his delegate shall by regulations prescribe."

Prior to repeal, para. (c)(5) read as follows:

"(5) In the case of a new residence the construction of which was commenced by the taxpayer before the expiration of 18months after the date of the sale of the old residence, the period specified in subsection (a), and the 18 months referred to in paragraph (4) of this subsection, shall be treated as including a period of 2 years beginning with the date of the sale of the old residence."

In 1980, P.L. 96-598, Sec. 2, provides:

"SEC. 2. NONRECOGNITION OF GAIN ON SALE OF PRINCIPAL RESIDENCE.

"(a) In general.

"In the case of an individual—

"(1) who sold his principal residence (within the meaning of section 1034 of the Internal Revenue Code of 1954) in 1977,

"(2) who purchased property on which to construct a new principal residence (within the meaning of such section)—

"(A) the construction of which commenced during such year, and

"(B) the construction of which was terminated before completion,

"(3) who brought an action, and obtained a judgment, against the builder who commenced construction of the new residence but failed to complete it,

"(4) who suspended construction of such residence so that the partially constructed residence could be used as evidence in connection with the prosecution of the builder (without regard to whether it was so used), and

"(5) who failed to meet the requirements of such section with respect to occupancy of the new principal residence because of such suspension of construction, the Secretary of the Treasury, in the administration of section 1034(c) of the Internal Revenue Code of 1954 (relating to rules for application of section 1034), shall apply paragraph (5) of such section as if '5 years' were substituted for '2 years' where it appears in the last sentence of such paragraph.

"(b) Effective date.

" The provisions of the first section of this Act shall apply with respect to taxable years beginning after December 31, 1976, and before January 1, 1983."

In 1978, P.L. 95-615, Sec. 206, redesignated subsec. (k) as subsec. (l) and added new subsec. (k), effective for tax. yrs. begin. after 12/31/77. Sec. 209(c) of this Act provides as follows:

"(c) Election of prior law.—

"(1) A taxpayer may elect not to have the amendments made by this title apply with respect to any taxable year beginning after December 31, 1977, and before January 1, 1979.

"(2) An election under this subsection shall be filed with a taxpayer's timely filed return for the first taxable year beginning after December 31, 1977."

—P.L. 95-600, Sec. 404(c)(5), amended subsec. (k), for sales or exchanges after 7/26/78, in tax. yrs. ending after 7/26/78.

Prior to amendment, subsec. (k) read as follows:

"(k) Cross reference.

"For exclusion from gross income of certain gain from sale or exchange of residence of taxpayer who has attained age 65, see section 121."

—P.L. 95-600, Sec. 405(a), amended subsec. (d) ... Sec. 405(b), added the sentence at the end of para. (c)(4) ... Sec. 405(c)(1), amended the heading of Code Sec. 1034, effective for sales and exchanges of residences after 7/26/78, in tax. yrs. end. after 7/26/78.

Prior to amendment, the heading of Code Sec. 1034 read as follows:

"SEC. 1034. SALE OR EXCHANGE OF RESIDENCE."

Prior to amendment, subsec. (d) read as follows:

"(d) Limitation.

"Subsection (a) shall not apply with respect to the sale of the taxpayer's residence if within 18 months before the date of such sale the taxpayer sold at a gain other property used by him as his principal residence, and any part of such gain was not recognized by reason of subsection (a)."

In 1977, P.L. 95-30, Sec. 102(b)(13), substituted "section 63" for "section 63(a)" in clause (b)(2)(C)(i), effective for tax. yrs. begin. after 12/31/76.

In 1976, P.L. 94-455, Sec. 1901(a)(129)(A), deleted "after December 31, 1953," after "is sold by him" in subsec. (a) ... Sec. 1901(a)(129)(B), deleted para. (b)(3) ... Sec. 1901(a)(129)(C), deleted "or section 112(n) of the Internal Revenue Code of 1939" after "subsection (a)" in subsec. (d) ... Sec. 1901(a)(129)(D), amended subsec. (i) ... Sec. 1901(a)(129)(E), deleted "after December 31, 1950," after "If" in subsec. (j), effective for tax. yrs. begin. after 12/31/76.

Prior to deletion, para. (b)(3) read as follows:

"(3) Effective date. The reduction provided in paragraph (1) applies to expenses for work performed in any taxable year (whether beginning before, on, or after January 1, 1954), but only in the case of a sale or exchange of an old residence which occurs after December 31, 1953."

Prior to amendment, subsec. (i) read as follows:

"(i) Special rule for involuntary conversions.

"(1) In general. For purposes of this section, the destruction, theft, seizure, requisition, or condemnation of property, or the sale or exchange of property under threat or imminence thereof—

"(A) if occurring after December 31, 1950, and before January 1, 1954, shall be treated as the sale of such property; and

"(B) if occurring after December 31, 1953, shall not be treated as the sale of such property.

"(2) Condemnations after December 31, 1957. For purposes of this section, the seizure, requisition, or condemnation of property, or the sale or exchange of property under threat or imminence thereof, if occurring after December 31, 1957, shall, at the election of the taxpayer, be treated as the sale of such property. Such election shall be made at such time and in such manner as the Secretary or his delegate shall prescribe by regulations.

"(3) Cross reference. For treatment of residences involuntarily converted after December 31, 1953, see section 1033 (relating to involuntary conversions)."

—P.L. 94-455, Sec. 1906(b)(13)(A), substituted "Secretary" for "Secretary or his delegate" in subsecs. (g) and (j), effective for tax. yrs. begin. after 12/31/76.

In 1975, P.L. 94-12, Sec. 207(a)(1), substituted "18 months" for "1 year" each place it appeared in subsecs. (a), (d) and (h) and paras. (c)(4) and (c)(5)... Sec. 207(a)(2), substituted "18 months" for "one year" in para. (c)(5)... Sec. 207(b), substituted "2 years" for "18 months" in para. (c)(5), effective for old residences (within the meaning of Code Sec. 1034) sold or exchanged after 12/31/74 in tax. yrs. end. after 12/31/74.

In 1975, P.L. 93-597, Sec. 6(a), deleted "and during an induction period (as defined in section 112(c)(5))" following "sale of the old residence" in subsec. (h), effective 7/1/73.

In 1964, P.L. 88-272, Sec. 206(b)(4), added subsec. (k), effective for dispositions after 12/31/63 in tax. yrs. end. after 12/31/63.

In 1958, P.L. 85-866, Sec. 46(b), redesignated para. (i)(2) as para. (i)(3) and added new para. (i)(3), effective for tax. yrs. begin. after 12/31/53 and end. after 8/16/54.

Sec. 1035. Certain exchanges of insurance policies.
(a) General rules.

No gain or loss shall be recognized on the exchange of—

(1) a contract of life insurance for another contract of life insurance or for an endowment or annuity contract or for a qualified long-term care insurance contract; or

(2) a contract of endowment insurance (A) for another contract of endowment insurance which provides for regular payments beginning at a date not later than the date payments would have begun under the contract exchanged, or (B) for an annuity contract, or (C) for a qualified long-term care insurance contract;

(3) an annuity contract for an annuity contract or for a qualified long-term care insurance contract; or

(4) a qualified long-term care insurance contract for a qualified long-term care insurance contract.

(b) Definitions.

For the purpose of this section—

(1) Endowment contract. A contract of endowment insurance is a contract with an insurance company which depends in part on the life expectancy of the insured, but which may be payable in full in a single payment during his life.

(2) Annuity contract. An annuity contract is a contract to which paragraph (1) applies but which may be payable during the life of the annuitant only in installments. For purposes of the preceding sentence, a contract shall not fail to be treated as an annuity contract solely because a qualified long-term care insurance contract is a part of or a rider on such contract.

(3) Life insurance contract. A contract of life insurance is a contract to which paragraph (1) applies but which is not ordinarily payable in full during the life of the insured. For purposes of the preceding sentence, a contract shall not fail to be treated as a life insurance contract solely because a qualified long-term care insurance contract is a part of or a rider on such contract.

(c) Exchanges involving foreign persons.

To the extent provided in regulations, subsection (a) shall not apply to any exchange having the effect of transferring property to any person other than a United States person.

(d) Cross references.

(1) For rules relating to recognition of gain or loss where an exchange is not solely in kind, see subsections (b) and (c) of section 1031.

(2) For rules relating to the basis of property acquired in an exchange described in subsection (a), see subsection (d) of section 1031.

In 2006, P.L. 109-280, Sec. 844(b)(1), added "For purposes of the preceding sentence, a contract shall not fail to be treated as an annuity contract solely because a qualified long-term care insurance contract is a part of or a rider on such contract." at the end of para. (b)(2)... Sec. 844(b)(2), added "For purposes of the preceding sentence, a contract shall not fail to be treated as a life insurance contract solely because a qualified long-term care insurance contract is a part of or a rider on such contract." at the end of para. (b)(3)... Sec. 844(b)(3)(A), added "or for a qualified long-term care insurance contract" before the semicolon at the end of para. (a)(1)... Sec. 844(b)(3)(B), added ", or (C) for a qualified long-term care insurance contract" before the semicolon at the end of para. (a)(2)... Sec. 844(b)(3)(C), added "or for a qualified long-term care insurance contract" before the period at the end of para. (a)(3)... Sec. 844(b)(4), deleted "or" at the end of para. (a)(2 [as amended by Sec. 844(b)(3)(B), of this Act, see above] substituted "; or" for " " at the end of para. (a)(3) [as amended by Sec. 844(b)(3)(C) of this Act, see above], and added para. (a)(4), effective for exchanges occurring after 12/31/2009.

In 1997, P.L. 105-34, Sec. 1131(b)(1) [sic (c)(1)], redesignated subsec. (c) as (d) and added new subsec. (c), effective 8/5/97.

In 1986, P.L. 99-514, Sec. 1828, deleted "subject to tax under subchapter L" after "with an insurance company" in para. (b)(1), effective for all exchanges whether before, on, or after 7/18/84.

In 1984, P.L. 98-369, Sec. 211(b)(15), substituted "section 816" for "section 801" in para. (b)(1), effective for tax. yrs. begin. after 12/31/83. [see Sec. 224(a) of this Act, below.]

—P.L. 98-369, Sec. 224(a), substituted "an insurance company subject to tax under subchapter L" for "a life insurance company as defined in section 801" [sic 816], effective for all exchanges whether before, on, or after 7/18/84.

Sec. 1036. Stock for stock of same corporation.
(a) General rule.

No gain or loss shall be recognized if common stock in a corporation is exchanged solely for common stock in the same corporation, or if preferred stock in a corporation is exchanged solely for preferred stock in the same corporation.

(b) Nonqualified preferred stock not treated as stock.

For purposes of this section, nonqualified preferred stock (as defined in section 351(g)(2)) shall be treated as property other than stock.

(c) Cross references.

(1) For rules relating to recognition of gain or loss where an exchange is not solely in kind, see subsections (b) and (c) of section 1031.

(2) For rules relating to the basis of property acquired in an exchange described in subsection (a), see subsection (d) of section 1031.

In 1997, P.L. 105-34, Sec. 1014(e)(3), redesignated subsec. (b) as (c) and added a new subsec. (b), effective for transactions after 6/8/97. Sec. 1014(f)(2) of this Act reads as follows:

"(2) Transition rule. The amendments made by this section shall not apply to any transaction after June 8, 1997, if such transaction is—

"(A) made pursuant to a written agreement which was binding on such date and at all times thereafter,

"(B) described in a ruling request submitted to the Internal Revenue Service on or before such date, or

"(C) described on or before such date in a public announcement or in a filing with the Securities and Exchange Commission required solely by reason of the transaction."

Sec. 1037. Certain exchanges of United States obligations.
(a) General rule.

When so provided by regulations promulgated by the Secretary in connection with the issue of obligations of the United States, no gain or loss shall be recognized on the surrender to the United States of obligations of the United States issued under chapter 31 of title 31 in exchange solely for other obligations issued under such chapter.

(b) Application of original issue discount rules.

(1) Exchanges involving obligations issued at a discount. In any case in which gain has been realized but not recognized because of the provisions of subsection (a) (or so much of section 1031(b) as relates to subsection (a) of this section), to the extent such gain is later recognized by reason of a disposition or redemption of an obligation re-

Nontaxable exchanges   Code Sec. 1038(e)(1)

ceived in an exchange subject to such provisions, the first sentence of section 1271(c)(2) shall apply to such gain as though the obligation disposed of or redeemed were the obligation surrendered to the Government in the exchange rather than the obligation actually disposed of or redeemed. For purposes of this paragraph and subpart A of part V of subchapter P, if the obligation surrendered in the exchange is a nontransferable obligation described in subsection (a) or (c) of section 454—

(A) the aggregate amount considered, with respect to the obligation surrendered, as ordinary income shall not exceed the difference between the issue price and the stated redemption price which applies at the time of the exchange, and

(B) the issue price of the obligation received in the exchange shall be considered to be the stated redemption price of the obligation surrendered in the exchange, increased by the amount of other consideration (if any) paid to the United States as a part of the exchange.

(2) Exchanges of transferable obligations issued at not less than par. In any case in which subsection (a) (or so much of section 1031(b) or (c) as relates to subsection (a) of this section) has applied to the exchange of a transferable obligation which was issued at not less than par for another transferable obligation, the issue price of the obligation received from the Government in the exchange shall be considered for purposes of applying subpart A of part V of subchapter P to be the same as the issue price of the obligation surrendered to the Government in the exchange, increased by the amount of other consideration (if any) paid to the United States as a part of the exchange.

(c) Cross references.

(1) For rules relating to the recognition of gain or loss in a case where subsection (a) would apply except for the fact that the exchange was not made solely for other obligations of the United States, see subsections (b) and (c) of section 1031.

(2) For rules relating to the basis of obligations of the United States acquired in an exchange for other obligations described in subsection (a), see subsection (d) of section 1031.

In 1984, P.L. 98-369, Sec. 42(a)(11)(A)-(C), substituted "section 1271(c)(2)" for "section 1232(a)(2)(B)" in para. (b)(1), substituted "subpart A of part V of subchapter P" for "section 1232" in paras. (b)(1) and (2), and substituted "Original issue discount rules" for "Section 1232" in the subsec. (b) heading, effective for tax. yrs. end. after 7/18/84.

In 1983, P.L. 97-452, Sec. 1037(a), substituted "chapter 31 of title 31" for "the Second Liberty Bond Act" in subsec. (a) and substituted "chapter" for "Act" in subsec. (a).

In 1976, P.L. 94-455, Sec. 1901(a)(130), substituted "section 1232(a)(2)(B)" for "section 1232(a)(2)(A)" in para. (b)(1), effective for tax. yrs. begin. after 12/31/76.

—P.L. 94-455, Sec. 1901(b)(3)(I), substituted "ordinary income" for "gain from the sale or exchange of property which is not a capital asset" in subpara. (b)(1)(A), effective for tax. yrs. begin. after 12/31/76.

In 1959, P.L. 86-346, Sec. 201(a), added Code Sec. 1037, effective for tax. yrs. end. after 9/22/59.

Sec. 1038. Certain reacquisitions of real property.

(a) General rule.

If—

(1) a sale of real property gives rise to indebtedness to the seller which is secured by the real property sold, and

(2) the seller of such property reacquires such property in partial or full satisfaction of such indebtedness,

then, except as provided in subsections (b) and (d), no gain or loss shall result to the seller from such reacquisition, and no debt shall become worthless or partially worthless as a result of such reacquisition.

(b) Amount of gain resulting.

(1) In general. In the case of a reacquisition of real property to which subsection (a) applies, gain shall result from such reacquisition to the extent that—

(A) the amount of money and the fair market value of other property (other than obligations of the purchaser) received, prior to such reacquisition, with respect to the sale of such property, exceeds

(B) the amount of the gain on the sale of such property returned as income for periods prior to such reacquisition.

(2) Limitation. The amount of gain determined under paragraph (1) resulting from a reacquisition during any taxable year beginning after the date of the enactment of this section shall not exceed the amount by which the price at which the real property was sold exceeded its adjusted basis, reduced by the sum of—

(A) the amount of the gain on the sale of such property returned as income for periods prior to the reacquisition of such property, and

(B) the amount of money and the fair market value of other property (other than obligations of the purchaser received with respect to the sale of such property) paid or transferred by the seller in connection with the reacquisition of such property.

For purposes of this paragraph, the price at which real property is sold is the gross sales price reduced by the selling commissions, legal fees, and other expenses incident to the sale of such property which are properly taken into account in determining gain or loss on such sale.

(3) Gain recognized. Except as provided in this section, the gain determined under this subsection resulting from a reacquisition to which subsection (a) applies shall be recognized, notwithstanding any other provision of this subtitle.

(c) Basis of reacquired real property.

If subsection (a) applies to the reacquisition of any real property, the basis of such property upon such reacquisition shall be the adjusted basis of the indebtedness to the seller secured by such property (determined as of the date of reacquisition), increased by the sum of—

(1) the amount of the gain determined under subsection (b) resulting from such reacquisition, and

(2) the amount described in subsection (b)(2)(B).

If any indebtedness to the seller secured by such property is not discharged upon the reacquisition of such property, the basis of such indebtedness shall be zero.

(d) Indebtedness treated as worthless prior to reacquisition.

If, prior to a reacquisition of real property to which subsection (a) applies, the seller has treated indebtedness secured by such property as having become worthless or partially worthless—

(1) such seller shall be considered as receiving, upon the reacquisition of such property, an amount equal to the amount of such indebtedness treated by him as having become worthless, and

(2) the adjusted basis of such indebtedness shall be increased (as of the date of reacquisition) by an amount equal to the amount so considered as received by such seller.

(e) Principal residences.

If—

(1) subsection (a) applies to a reacquisition of real property with respect to the sale of which gain was not recognized under section 121 (relating to gain on sale of principal residence); and

(2) within 1 year after the date of the reacquisition of such property by the seller, such property is resold by him, then, under regulations prescribed by the Secretary, subsections (b), (c), and (d) of this section shall not apply to the reacquisition of such property and, for purposes of applying section 121, the resale of such property shall be treated as a part of the transaction constituting the original sale of such property.

(f) Repealed.

(g) Acquisition by estate, etc., of seller.

Under regulations prescribed by the Secretary, if an installment obligation is indebtedness to the seller which is described in subsection (a), and if such obligation is, in the hands of the taxpayer, an obligation with respect to which section 691(a)(4)(B) applies, then—

(1) for purposes of subsection (a), acquisition of real property by the taxpayer shall be treated as reacquisition by the seller, and

(2) the basis of the real property acquired by the taxpayer shall be increased by an amount equal to the deduction under section 691(c) which would (but for this subsection) have been allowable to the taxpayer with respect to the gain on the exchange of the obligation for the real property.

In 1998, P.L. 105-206, Sec. 6005(e)(3), added "on or" before "before" each place it appeared in the heading and text of Sec. 312(d)(2)[sic (e)] of P.L. 105-34, see below.

In 1997, P.L. 105-34, Sec. 312(d)(8), amended subsec. (e), effective for sales and exchanges after 5/6/97, except as provided by Sec. 312(d)(2)-(4) [sic (e)(2)-(4)] of this Act [as amended by Sec. 6005(e)(3) of P.L. 105-206, see above], which read as follows:

"(2) Sales on or before date of enactment. At the election of the taxpayer, the amendments made by this section shall not apply to any sale or exchange on or before the date of the enactment of this Act.

"(3) Certain sales within 2 years after date of enactment. Section 121 of the Internal Revenue Code of 1986 (as amended by this section) shall be applied without regard to subsection (c)(2)(B) thereof in the case of any sale or exchange of property during the 2-year period beginning on the date of the enactment of this Act if the taxpayer held such property on the date of the enactment of this Act and fails to meet the ownership and use requirements of subsection (a) thereof with respect to such property.

"(4) Binding contracts. At the election of the taxpayer, the amendments made by this section shall not apply to a sale or exchange after the date of the enactment of this Act, if—

"(A) such sale or exchange is pursuant to a contract which was binding on such date, or

"(B) without regard to such amendments, gain would not be recognized under section 1034 of the Internal Revenue Code of 1986 (as in effect on the day before the date of the enactment of this Act) on such sale or exchange by reason of a new residence acquired on or before such date or with respect to the acquisition of which by the taxpayer a binding contract was in effect on such date.

This paragraph shall not apply to any sale or exchange by an individual if the treatment provided by section 877(a)(1) of the Internal Revenue Code of 1986 applies to such individual."

Prior to amendment, subsec. (e) read as follows:

"(e) Principal residences.

"If—

"(1) subsection (a) applies to a reacquisition of real property with respect to the sale of which—

"(A) an election under section 121 (relating to one-time exclusion of gain from sale of principal residence by individual who has attained age 55) is in effect, or

"(B) gain was not recognized under section 1034 (relating to rollover of gain on sale of principal residence); and

"(2) within one year after the date of the reacquisition of such property by the seller, such property is resold by him,

then, under regulations prescribed by the Secretary, subsections (b), (c), and (d) of this section shall not apply to the reacquisition of such property and, for purposes of applying sections 121 and 1034, the resale of such property shall be treated as a part of the transaction constituting the original sale of such property."

In 1996, P.L. 104-188, Sec. 1616(b)(12), deleted subsec. (f), effective for tax. yrs. begin. after 12/31/95.

Prior to deletion, subsec. (f) read as follows:

"(f) Reacquisitions by domestic building and loan associations.

This section shall not apply to a reacquisition of real property by an organization described in section 593(a) (relating to domestic building and loan associations, etc.)."

In 1980, P.L. 96-471, Sec. 4, added subsec. (g), effective for acquisitions of real property by the taxpayer after 10/19/80.

In 1978, P.L. 95-600, Sec. 404(c)(6), substituted "relating to one-time exclusion of gain from sale of principal residence by individual who has attained age 55" for "relating to gain from sale or exchange of residence of an individual who has attained age 65" in subpara. (e)(1)(A), effective for sales or exchanges after 7/26/78, in tax. yrs. end. after 7/26/78.

—P.L. 95-600, Sec. 405(c)(3), substituted "(relating to rollover of gain on sale of principal residence)" for "(relating to sale or exchange of residence)" in subpara. (e)(1)(B), effective for sales and exchanges of residences after 7/26/78, in tax. yrs. end. after 7/26/78.

In 1976, P.L. 94-455, Sec. 1906(b)(13)(A), substituted "Secretary" for "Secretary or his delegate" each place it appeared in Code Sec. 1038, effective for tax. yrs. begin. after 12/31/76.

In 1964, P.L. 88-570, Sec. 2(a), added Code Sec. 1038, effective for tax. yrs. begin. after 9/2/64. Secs. 2(c)(2) and (3) of this Act provide special rules as follows:

"(2) If the taxpayer makes an election under this paragraph, the amendments made by this section [adding Code Sec. 1038] shall also apply to taxable years beginning after December 31, 1957, except that such amendments shall not apply with respect to any reacquisition of real property in a taxable year for which the assessment of a deficiency, or the credit or refund of an overpayment, is prevented on the date of the enactment of this Act [9/2/64] by the operation of any law or rule of law. An election under this paragraph shall be made within one year after the date of the enactment of this Act and shall be made in such form and manner as the Secretary of the Treasury or his delegate shall prescribe by regulations.

"(3) If an election is made by the taxpayer under paragraph (2), and if the assessment of a deficiency, or the credit or refund of an overpayment, for any taxable year to which such election applies is not prevented on the date of the enactment of this Act by the operation of any law or rule of law—

"(A) the period within which a deficiency for such taxable year may be assessed (to the extent such deficiency is attributable to the application of the amendments made by this section) shall not expire prior to one year after the date of such election; and

"(B) the period within which a claim for credit or refund of an overpayment for such taxable year may be filed (to the extent such overpayment is attributable to the application of such amendments) shall not expire prior to one year after the date of such election.

No interest shall be payable with respect to any deficiency attributable to the application of such amendments, and no interest shall be allowed with respect to any credit or refund of any overpayment attributable to the application of such amendments, for any period prior to the date of the enactment of this Act. An election by a taxpayer under paragraph (2) shall be deemed a consent to the application of this paragraph."

Sec. 1039. Repealed.

In 1990, P.L. 101-508, Sec. 11801(a)(33), repealed Code Sec. 1039, effective 11/5/90 except as provided in Sec. 11821(b) of this Act, which reads as follows:

"(b) Savings provision.

"If—

"(1) any provision amended or repealed by this part applied to

"(A) any transaction occurring before the date of the enactment of this Act [11/5/90],

"(B) any property acquired before such date of enactment [11/5/90],

"(C) any item of income, loss, deduction, or credit taken into account before such date of enactment] 11/5/90], and

"(2) the treatment of such transaction, property, or item under such provision would (without regard to the amendments made by this part) affect liability for tax for periods ending after such date of enactment [11/5/90],

nothing in the amendments made by this part shall be construed to affect the treatment of such transaction, property, or item for purposes of determining liability for tax for periods ending after such date of enactment."

Prior to repeal, Code Sec. 1039 read as follows:

"SEC. 1039. CERTAIN SALES OF LOW-INCOME HOUSING PROJECTS.

"(a) Nonrecognition of gain.

"If—

"(1) a qualified housing project is sold or disposed of by the taxpayer in an approved disposition, and

"(2) within the reinvestment period the taxpayer constructs, reconstructs, or acquires another qualified housing project,

then, at the election of the taxpayer, gain from such approved disposition shall be recognized only to the extent that the net amount realized on such approved disposition exceeds the cost of such other qualified housing project. An election under this subsection shall be made at such time and in such manner as the Secretary prescribes by regulations.

"(b) Definitions.

"For purposes of this section—

"(1) Qualified housing project. The term 'qualified housing project' means a project to provide rental or cooperative housing for lower income families—

"(A) with respect to which a mortgage is insured under section 221(d)(3) or 236 of the National Housing Act, and

"(B) with respect to which the owner is, under such sections or regulations issued thereunder—

"(i) limited as to the rate of return on his investment in the project, and

"(ii) limited as to rentals or occupancy charges for units in the project.

"(2) Approved disposition. The term 'approved disposition' means a sale or other disposition of a qualified housing project to the tenants or occupants of units in such project, or to a cooperative or other nonprofit organization formed solely

Nontaxable exchanges Code Sec. 1040

for the benefit of such tenants or occupants, which sale or disposition is approved by the Secretary of Housing and Urban Development under section 221(d)(3) or 236 of the National Housing Act or regulations issued under such sections.

"(3) Reinvestment period. The reinvestment period, with respect to an approved disposition of a qualified housing project, is the period beginning one year before the date of such approved disposition and ending—

"(A) one year after the close of the first taxable year in which any part of the gain from such approved disposition is realized, or

"(B) subject to such terms and conditions as may be specified by the Secretary, at the close of such later date as the Secretary may designate on application by the taxpayer. Such application shall be made at such time and in such manner as the Secretary prescribes by regulations.

"(4) Net amount realized. The net amount realized on an approved disposition of a qualified housing project is the amount realized reduced by—

"(A) the expenses paid or incurred which are directly connected with such approved disposition, and

"(B) the amount of taxes (other than income taxes) paid or incurred which are attributable to such approved disposition.

"(c) Special rules.

"For purposes of applying subsection (a)(2) with respect to an approved disposition—

"(1) no property acquired by the taxpayer before the date of the approved disposition shall be taken into account unless such property is held by the taxpayer on such date, and

"(2) no property acquired by the taxpayer shall be taken into account unless, except as provided in subsection (d), the unadjusted basis of such property is its cost within the meaning of section 1012.

"(d) Basis of other qualified housing project.

"If the taxpayer makes an election under subsection (a) with respect to an approved disposition, the basis of the qualified housing project described in subsection (a)(2) shall be its cost reduced by an amount equal to the amount of gain not recognized by reason of the application of subsection (a).

"(e) Assessment of deficiencies.

"(1) Deficiency attributable to gain. If the taxpayer has made an election under subsection (a) with respect to an approved disposition—

"(A) the statutory period for the assessment of any deficiency, for any taxable year in which any part of the gain on such approved disposition is realized, attributable to the gain on such approved disposition shall not expire prior to the expiration of 3 years from the date the Secretary is notified by the taxpayer (in such manner as the Secretary may by regulations prescribe) of the construction, reconstruction, or acquisition of another qualified housing project or of the failure to construct, reconstruct, or acquire another qualified housing project, and

"(B) such deficiency may be assessed before the expiration of such 3-year period notwithstanding the provisions of section 6212(c) or the provision of any other law or rule of law which would otherwise prevent such assessment.

"(2) Time for assessment of other deficiencies attributable to election. If a taxpayer has made an election under subsection (a) with respect to an approved disposition and another qualified housing project is constructed, reconstructed, or acquired before the beginning of the last taxable year in which any part of the gain upon such disposition is realized, any deficiency, to the extent resulting from such election, for any taxable year ending before such last taxable year may be assessed (notwithstanding the provisions of section 6212(c) or 6501 or the provisions of any other law or rule of law which would otherwise prevent such assessment) at any time before the expiration of the period within which a deficiency for such last taxable year may be assessed."

In 1976, P.L. 94-455, Sec. 1906(b)(13)(A), substituted "Secretary" for "Secretary or his delegate" each place it appeared in Code Sec. 1039, effective for tax. yrs. begin. after 12/31/76.

In 1969, P.L. 91-172, Sec. 910(a), added Code Sec. 1039, effective for approved dispositions of qualified housing projects (within the meaning of 1954 Code Sec. 1039) after 10/9/69.

> • **Caution:** Sec. 301(a), P.L. 111-312, (reproduced in the history notes following this Code Sec.) provides that the amendments made by Sec. 542(d)(1), P.L. 107-16, EGTRRA, will apply as if never enacted. Code Sec. 1040, following, reflects the removal of these amendments, effective for estates of decedents dying, and transfers made, after 12/31/2009.

Sec. 1040. Transfer of certain farm, etc., real property.
(a) General rule.

If the executor of the estate of any decedent transfers to a qualified heir (within the meaning of section 2032A(e)(1)) any property with respect to which an election was made under section 2032A, then gain on such transfer shall be recognized to the estate only to the extent that, on the date of such transfer, the fair market value of such property exceeds the value of such property for purposes of chapter 11 (determined without regard to section 2032A).

(b) Similar rule for certain trusts.

To the extent provided in regulations prescribed by the Secretary, a rule similar to the rule provided in subsection (a) shall apply where the trustee of a trust (any portion of which is included in the gross estate of the decedent) transfers property with respect to which an election was made under section 2032A.

(c) Basis of property acquired in transfer described in subsection (a) or (b).

The basis of property acquired in a transfer with respect to which gain realized is not recognized by reason of subsection (a) or (b) shall be the basis of such property immediately before the transfer increased by the amount of the gain recognized to the estate or trust on the transfer.

> • **Caution:** Code Sec. 1040, following, reflects amendments made by Sec. 542(d)(1), P.L. 107-16, EGTRRA. As provided in Sec. 301(a), P.L. 111-312, these amendments will apply as if never enacted, effective for estates of decedents dying, and transfers made, after 12/31/2009.

Sec. 1040. Use of appreciated carryover basis property to satisfy pecuniary bequest.
(a) In general.

If the executor of the estate of any decedent satisfies the right of any person to receive a pecuniary bequest with appreciated property, then gain on such exchange shall be recognized to the estate only to the extent that, on the date of such exchange, the fair market value of such property exceeds such value on the date of death.

(b) Similar rule for certain trusts.

To the extent provided in regulations prescribed by the Secretary, a rule similar to the rule provided in subsection (a) shall apply where—

(1) by reason of the death of the decedent, a person has a right to receive from a trust a specific dollar amount which is the equivalent of a pecuniary bequest, and

(2) the trustee of a trust satisfies such right with property.

(c) Basis of property acquired in exchange described in subsection (a) or (b).

The basis of property acquired in an exchange with respect to which gain realized is not recognized by reason of subsection (a) or (b) shall be the basis of such property immediately before the exchange increased by the amount of the gain recognized to the estate or trust on the exchange.

In 2010, P.L. 111-312, Sec. 101(a)(1), substituted "December 31, 2012" for "December 31, 2010" both places it appeared in Sec. 901 of P.L. 107-16 [see below], effective as if included in the enactment of P.L. 107-16, EGTRRA, 6/7/2001.

—P.L. 111-312, Sec. 301(a), provides that Code Sec. 1040, as amended by Sec. 542(d)(1) [see below] will read as if such provisions had never been enacted, effective for estates of decedents dying, and transfers made, after 12/31/2009.

Sec. 301(a) P.L. 111-312, 12/17/2010, provides:

"(a) In general. Each provision of law amended by subtitle A or E of title V of the Economic Growth and Tax Relief Reconciliation Act of 2001 is amended to read as such provision would read if such subtitle had never been enacted."

Prior to the enactment of Sec. 301(a), P.L. 111-312, Code Sec. 1040 read as follows:

"Code Sec. 1040. Use of appreciated carryover basis property to satisfy pecuniary bequest.

"(a) In general. If the executor of the estate of any decedent satisfies the right of any person to receive a pecuniary bequest with appreciated property, then gain on such exchange shall be recognized to the estate only to the extent that, on the date of such exchange, the fair market value of such property exceeds such value on the date of death.

2,703

"(b) Similar rule for certain trusts. To the extent provided in regulations prescribed by the Secretary, a rule similar to the rule provided in subsection (a) shall apply where—

"(1) by reason of the death of the decedent, a person has a right to receive from a trust a specific dollar amount which is the equivalent of a pecuniary bequest, and

"(2) the trustee of a trust satisfies such right with property.

"(c) Basis of property acquired in exchange described in subsection (a) or (b).

"The basis of property acquired in an exchange with respect to which gain realized is not recognized by reason of subsection (a) or (b) shall be the basis of such property immediately before the exchange increased by the amount of the gain recognized to the estate or trust on the exchange."

—P.L. 111-312, Sec. 301(c), of this Act, provides:

"(c) Special election with respect to estates of decedents dying in 2010. Notwithstanding subsection (a), in the case of an estate of a decedent dying after December 31, 2009, and before January 1, 2011, the executor (within the meaning of section 2203 of the Internal Revenue Code of 1986) may elect to apply such Code as though the amendments made by subsection (a) do not apply with respect to chapter 11 of such Code and with respect to property acquired or passing from such decedent (within the meaning of section 1014(b) of such Code). Such election shall be made at such time and in such manner as the Secretary of the Treasury or the Secretary's delegate shall provide. Such an election once made shall be revocable only with the consent of the Secretary of the Treasury or the Secretary's delegate. For purposes of section 2652(a)(1) of such Code, the determination of whether any property is subject to the tax imposed by such chapter 11 shall be made without regard to any election made under this subsection."

—P.L. 111-312, Sec. 301(d), of this Act, provides:

"(d) Extension of time for performing certain acts.

"(1) Estate tax. In the case of the estate of a decedent dying after December 31, 2009, and before the date of the enactment of this Act, the due date for—

"(A) filing any return under section 6018 of the Internal Revenue Code of 1986 (including any election required to be made on such a return) as such section is in effect after the date of the enactment of this Act without regard to any election under subsection (c),

"(B) making any payment of tax under chapter 11 of such Code, and

"(C) making any disclaimer described in section 2518(b) of such Code of an interest in property passing by reason of the death of such decedent, shall not be earlier than the date which is 9 months after the date of the enactment of this Act.

"(2) Generation-skipping tax. In the case of any generation-skipping transfer made after December 31, 2009, and before the date of the enactment of this Act, the due date for filing any return under section 2662 of the Internal Revenue Code of 1986 (including any election required to be made on such a return) shall not be earlier than the date which is 9 months after the date of the enactment of this Act."

In 2002, P.L. 107-358, Sec. 2, added subsec. (c) in Sec. 901 of P.L. 107-16 [see below], effective 12/17/2002.

In 2001, P.L. 107-16, Sec. 542(d)(1), amended Code Sec. 1040, effective for estates of decedents dying after 12/31/2009.

Prior to amendment, Code Sec. 1040 read as follows:

"SEC. 1040. TRANSFER OF CERTAIN FARM, ETC., REAL PROPERTY.

"(a) General rule. If the executor of the estate of any decedent transfers to a qualified heir (within the meaning of section 2032A(e)(1)) any property with respect to which an election was made under section 2032A, then gain on such transfer shall be recognized to the estate only to the extent that, on the date of such transfer, the fair market value of such property exceeds the value of such property for purposes of chapter 11 (determined without regard to section 2032A).

"(b) Similar rule for certain trusts. To the extent provided in regulations prescribed by the Secretary, a rule similar to the rule provided in subsection (a) shall apply where the trustee of a trust (any portion of which is included in the gross estate of the decedent) transfers property with respect to which an election was made under section 2032A.

"(c) Basis of property acquired in transfer described in subsection (a) or (b). The basis of property acquired in a transfer with respect to which gain realized is not recognized by reason of subsection (a) or (b) shall be the basis of such property immediately before the transfer increased by the amount of the gain recognized to the estate or trust on the transfer."

—P.L. 107-16, Sec. 901, of this Act [as amended by Sec. 2 of P.L. 107-358, and Sec. 101(a)(1) of P.L. 111-312, see above], reads as follows:

"SEC. 901. SUNSET OF PROVISIONS OF ACT.

"(a) In general. All provisions of, and amendments made by, this Act shall not apply—

"(1) to taxable, plan, or limitation years beginning after December 31, 2012, or

"(2) in the case of title V, to estates of decedents dying, gifts made, or generation skipping transfers, after December 31, 2012.

"(b) Application of certain laws. The Internal Revenue Code of 1986 and the Employee Retirement Income Security Act of 1974 shall be applied and administered to years, estates, gifts, and transfers described in subsection (a) as if the provisions and amendments described in subsection (a) had never been enacted.

"(c) Exception. Subsection (a) shall not apply to section 803 (relating to no federal income tax on restitution received by victims of the Nazi regime or their heirs or estates)."

In 1983, P.L. 97-448, Sec. 104(b)(3)(A), substituted "such transfer" for "such exchange" in subsec. (a) . . . Sec. 104(b)(3)(B)(i)-(iii), substituted "a transfer" for "an exchange" in subsec. (c), substituted "the transfer" for "the exchange" each place it appeared in subsec. (c), and substituted "transfer" for "exchange" in the heading of subsec. (c); effective for the estates of decedents dying after 12/31/76.

—P.L. 97-448, Sec. 104(b)(4)(B), amended the second sentence of Sec. 421(k)(5)(B) of P.L. 97-34 [reproduced below].

Prior to amendment, the second sentence of Sec. 421(k)(5)(B) of P.L. 97-34 read as follows: "If the time for making an election would have otherwise expired after July 28, 1980, the time for making such election shall not expire before the date 6 months after the date of the enactment of his Act."

—P.L. 97-448, Sec. 104(b)(4)(C)(i), amended Sec. 421(k)(5)(C) of P.L. 97-34 [reproduced below] by substituting "at any time before February 17, 1982" for "within 6 months after the date of the enactment of this Act" . . . Sec. 104(b)(4)(C)(ii), amended Sec. 421(k)(5)(D) of P.L. 97-34 [reproduced below] by substituting "before February 17, 1982" for "within 6 months after such date of enactment" and substituting "February 17, 1982" for "the date 6 months after such date of enactment".

In 1981, P.L. 97-34, Sec. 421(j)(2)(B), amended the heading of Code Sec. 1040 and subsecs. (a) and (b), effective for the estates of decedents dying after 12/31/76. Sec. 421(k)(5)(B), (C) and (D) of this Act provide:

"(B) Timely election required. Subparagraph (A) shall only apply in the case of an estate if a timely election under section 2032A was made with respect to such estate. If the time for making an election under section 2032A with respect to any estate would have otherwise expired after July 28, 1980, the time for making such election shall not expire before the close of February 16, 1982.

"(C) Reinstatement of elections. If any election under section 2032A was revoked before the date of the enactment of this Act, such election may be reinstated at any time before February 17, 1982.

"(D) Statute of limitations. If on the date of the enactment of this Act (or at any time within 6 months after such date of enactment) the making of a credit or refund of any overpayment of tax resulting from the amendments described in subparagraph (A) is barred by any law or rule of law, such credit or refund shall nevertheless be made if claim therefor is made before February 17, 1982."

Prior to amendment, the heading of Code Sec. 1040 and subsecs. (a) and (b) read as follows:

"SEC. 1040. USE OF FARM, ETC., REAL PROPERTY TO SATISFY PECUNIARY BEQUEST.

"(a) General rule.

"If the executor of the estate of any decedent satisfies the right of a qualified heir (within the meaning of section 2032A(e)(1)) to receive a pecuniary bequest with property with respect to which an election was made under section 2032A, then gain on such exchange shall be recognized to the estate only to the extent that, on the date of such exchange, the fair market value of such property exceeds the value of such property for purposes of chapter 11 (determined without regard to section 2032A).

"(b) Similar rule for certain trusts.

"To the extent provided in regulations prescribed by the Secretary, a rule similar to the rule provided in subsection (a) shall apply where

"(1) by reason of the death of the decedent, a qualified heir has a right to receive from a trust a specific dollar amount which is the equivalent of a pecuniary bequest, and

"(2) the trustee of the trust satisfies such right with property with respect to which an election was made under section 2302A."

In 1980, P.L. 96-223, Sec. 401(c)(2)(A), amended Code Sec. 1040, effective decedents dying after 12/31/76.

Prior to amendment, Code Sec. 1040 read as follows:

"SEC. 1040. USE OF CERTAIN APPRECIATED CARRYOVER BASES PROPERTY TO SATISFY PECUNIARY REQUEST.

"(a) General rule.

"If the executor of the estate of any decedent satisfies the right of any person to receive a pecuniary bequest with appreciated carryover basis property (as defined in section 1023(f)(5)), then gain on such exchange shall be recognized to the estate only to the extent that, on the date of such exchange, the fair market value of such property exceeds the value of such property for purposes of chapter 11. (determined without regard to section 2032A).

"(b) Similar rule for certain trusts.

"To the extent provided in regulations prescribed by the Secretary, a rule similar to the rule provided in subsection (a) shall apply where—

"(1) by reason of the death of the decedent, a person has a right to receive from a trust a specific dollar amount which is the equivalent of a pecuniary bequest, and

"(2) the trustee of the trust satisfies such right with carryover basis property to which section 1023 applies.

"(c) Basis of property acquired in exchange described in subsection (a) or (b).

"The basis of property acquired in an exchange with respect to which gain realized is not recognized by reason of subsection (a) or (b) shall be the basis of such property immediately before the exchange, increased by the amount of the gain recognized to the estate or trust on the exchange.

"(d) Application to section 2032A property.

"For purposes of this section, references to carryover basis property shall be treated as including a reference to property the valuation of which is determined under section 2032A."

—P.L. 96-222, Sec. 105(a)(5)(A), added subsec. (d) [reproduced in note following P.L. 96-223, above], effective with respect to decedents dying after '76.

—P.L. 96-222, Sec. 105(a)(5)(B), provides as follows:

"(B) Period for which section 1040 applies. Notwithstanding section 515 of the Revenue Act of 1978, section 1040 of the Internal Revenue Code of 1954 (as amended by subparagraph (A)) shall apply with respect to the estates of decedents dying after December 31, 1976."

In 1978, P.L. 95-600, Sec. 515(6), changed the effective date for amendments made by Sec. 2005(b) of P.L. 94-455 to be effective to decedents dying after 12/31/79, from effective for decedents dying after 12/31/76.

Nontaxable exchanges Code Sec. 1042(c)(2)(D)

—P.L. 95-600, Sec. 702(d)(3), added "(determined without regard to section 2032A)" at the end of subsec. (a), effective for estates of decedents dying after 12/31/76.

In 1976, P.L. 94-455, Sec. 2005(b), added Code Sec. 1040, effective [as amended by Sec. 515(6) of P.L. 95-600, see above] for decedents dying after 12/31/79.

Sec. 1041. Transfers of property between spouses or incident to divorce.

(a) General rule.

No gain or loss shall be recognized on a transfer of property from an individual to (or in trust for the benefit of)—

(1) a spouse, or

(2) a former spouse, but only if the transfer is incident to the divorce.

(b) Transfer treated as gift; transferee has transferor's basis.

In the case of any transfer of property described in subsection (a)—

(1) for purposes of this subtitle, the property shall be treated as acquired by the transferee by gift, and

(2) the basis of the transferee in the property shall be the adjusted basis of the transferor.

(c) Incident to divorce.

For purposes of subsection (a)(2), a transfer of property is incident to the divorce if such transfer—

(1) occurs within 1 year after the date on which the marriage ceases, or

(2) is related to the cessation of the marriage.

(d) Special rule where spouse is nonresident alien.

Subsection (a) shall not apply if the spouse (or former spouse) of the individual making the transfer is a nonresident alien.

(e) Transfers in trust where liability exceeds basis.

Subsection (a) shall not apply to the transfer of property in trust to the extent that—

(1) the sum of the amount of the liabilities assumed, plus the amount of the liabilities to which the property is subject, exceeds

(2) the total of the adjusted basis of the property transferred.

Proper adjustment shall be made under subsection (b) in the basis of the transferee in such property to take into account gain recognized by reason of the preceding sentence.

In **1988**, P.L. 100-647, Sec. 1018(1)(3)(A) and (B), substituted "Subsection (a)" for "Paragraph (1) of subsection (a)" and substituted "the spouse (or former spouse)" for "the spouse" in subsec. (d), effective for transfers after 6/21/88.

In **1986**, P.L. 99-514, Sec. 1842(b), added subsec. (e), effective for transfers after 7/18/84, in tax. yrs. end. after 7/18/84, except as provided by Sec. 421(d)(2)-(4) of P.L. 98-369, reproduced below.

In **1984**, P.L. 98-369, Sec. 421(a), added Code Sec. 1041, for transfers after 7/18/84, in tax. yrs. end. after 7/18/84, except as provided in Sec. 421(d)(2) through (4) of the this Act which read as follows:

"(2) Election to have amendments apply to transfers after 1983. If both spouses or former spouses make an election under this paragraph, the amendments made by this section shall apply to all transfers made by such spouses (or former spouses) after December 31, 1983.

"(3) Exception for transfers pursuant to existing decrees. Except in the case of an election under paragraph (2), the amendments made by this section shall not apply to transfers under any instrument in effect on or before the date of the enactment of this Act unless both spouses (or former spouses) elect to have such amendments apply to transfers under such instrument.

"(4) Election. Any election under paragraph (2) or (3) shall be made in such manner, at such time, and subject to such conditions, as the Secretary of the Treasury or his delegate may by regulations prescribe."

Sec. 1042. Sales of stock to employee stock ownership plans or certain cooperatives.

(a) Nonrecognition of gain.

If—

(1) the taxpayer or executor elects in such form as the Secretary may prescribe the application of this section with respect to any sale of qualified securities,

(2) the taxpayer purchases qualified replacement property within the replacement period, and

(3) the requirements of subsection (b) are met with respect to such sale,

then the gain (if any) on such sale which would be recognized as long-term capital gain shall be recognized only to the extent that the amount realized on such sale exceeds the cost to the taxpayer of such qualified replacement property.

(b) Requirements to qualify for nonrecognition.

A sale of qualified securities meets the requirements of this subsection if—

(1) Sale to employee organizations. The qualified securities are sold to—

(A) an employee stock ownership plan (as defined in section 4975(e)(7)), or

(B) an eligible worker-owned cooperative.

(2) Plan must hold 30 percent of stock after sale. The plan or cooperative referred to in paragraph (1) owns (after application of section 318(a)(4)), immediately after the sale, at least 30 percent of—

(A) each class of outstanding stock of the corporation (other than stock described in section 1504(a)(4)) which issued the qualified securities, or

(B) the total value of all outstanding stock of the corporation (other than stock described in section 1504(a)(4)).

(3) Written statement required.

(A) In general. The taxpayer files with the Secretary the written statement described in subparagraph (B).

(B) Statement. A statement is described in this subparagraph if it is a verified written statement of—

(i) the employer whose employees are covered by the plan described in paragraph (1), or

(ii) any authorized officer of the cooperative described in paragraph (1),

consenting to the application of sections 4978 and 4979A with respect to such employer or cooperative.

(4) 3-year holding period. The taxpayer's holding period with respect to the qualified securities is at least 3 years (determined as of the time of the sale).

(c) Definitions; special rules.

For purposes of this section—

(1) Qualified securities. The term "qualified securities" means employer securities (as defined in section 409(1)) which—

(A) are issued by a domestic C corporation that has no stock outstanding that is readily tradable on an established securities market, and

(B) were not received by the taxpayer in—

(i) a distribution from a plan described in section 401(a), or

(ii) a transfer pursuant to an option or other right to acquire stock to which section 83, 422, or 423 applied (or to which section 422 or 424 (as in effect on the day before the date of the enactment [11/5/90] of the Revenue Reconciliation Act of 1990) applied).

(2) Eligible worker-owned cooperative. The term "eligible worker-owned cooperative" means any organization—

(A) to which part I of subchapter T applies,

(B) a majority of the membership of which is composed of employees of such organization,

(C) a majority of the voting stock of which is owned by members,

(D) a majority of the board of directors of which is elected by the members on the basis of 1 person 1 vote, and

2,705

(E) a majority of the allocated earnings and losses of which are allocated to members on the basis of—
(i) patronage,
(ii) capital contributions, or
(iii) some combination of clauses (i) and (ii).

(3) Replacement period. The term "replacement period" means the period which begins 3 months before the date on which the sale of qualified securities occurs and which ends 12 months after the date of such sale.

(4) Qualified replacement property.
(A) In general. The term "qualified replacement property" means any security issued by a domestic operating corporation which—
(i) did not, for the taxable year preceding the taxable year in which such security was purchased, have passive investment income (as defined in section 1362(d)(3)(C)) in excess of 25 percent of the gross receipts of such corporation for such preceding taxable year, and
(ii) is not the corporation which issued the qualified securities which such security is replacing or a member of the same controlled group of corporations (within the meaning of section 1563(a)(1)) as such corporation.

For purposes of clause (i), income which is described in section 954(c)(3) (as in effect immediately before the Tax Reform Act of 1986) shall not be treated as passive investment income.

(B) Operating corporation. For purposes of this paragraph—
(i) In general. The term "operating corporation" means a corporation more than 50 percent of the assets of which were, at the time the security was purchased or before the close of the replacement period, used in the active conduct of the trade or business.
(ii) Financial institutions and insurance companies. The term "operating corporation" shall include—
(I) any financial institution described in section 581, and
(II) an insurance company subject to tax under subchapter L.

(C) Controlling and controlled corporations treated as 1 corporation.
(i) In general. For purposes of applying this paragraph, if—
(I) the corporation issuing the security owns stock representing control of 1 or more other corporations,
(II) 1 or more other corporations own stock representing control of the corporation issuing the security, or
(III) both,
then all such corporations shall be treated as 1 corporation.
(ii) Control. For purposes of clause (i), the term "control" has the meaning given such term by section 304(c). In determining control, there shall be disregarded any qualified replacement property of the taxpayer with respect to the section 1042 sale being tested.

(D) Security defined. For purposes of this paragraph, the term "security" has the meaning given such term by section 165(g)(2), except that such term shall not include any security issued by a government or political subdivision thereof.

(5) Securities sold by underwriter. No sale of securities by an underwriter to an employee stock ownership plan or eligible worker-owned cooperative in the ordinary course of his trade or business as an underwriter, whether or not guaranteed, shall be treated as a sale for purposes of subsection (a).

(6) Time for filing election. An election under subsection (a) shall be filed not later than the last day prescribed by law (including extensions thereof) for filing the return of tax imposed by this chapter for the taxable year in which the sale occurs.

(7) Section not to apply to gain of C corporation. Subsection (a) shall not apply to any gain on the sale of any qualified securities which is includible in the gross income of any C corporation.

(d) Basis of qualified replacement property.
The basis of the taxpayer in qualified replacement property purchased by the taxpayer during the replacement period shall be reduced by the amount of gain not recognized by reason of such purchase and the application of subsection (a). If more than one item of qualified replacement property is purchased, the basis of each of such items shall be reduced by an amount determined by multiplying the total gain not recognized by reason of such purchase and the application of subsection (a) by a fraction—
(1) the numerator of which is the cost of such item of property, and
(2) the denominator of which is the total cost of all such items of property.

Any reduction in basis under this subsection shall not be taken into account for purposes of section 1278(a)(2)(A)(ii) (relating to definition of market discount).

(e) Recapture of gain on disposition of qualified replacement property.
(1) In general. If a taxpayer disposes of any qualified replacement property, then, notwithstanding any other provision of this title, gain (if any) shall be recognized to the extent of the gain which was not recognized under subsection (a) by reason of the acquisition by such taxpayer of such qualified replacement property.

(2) Special rule for corporations controlled by the taxpayer. If—
(A) a corporation issuing qualified replacement property disposes of a substantial portion of its assets other than in the ordinary course of its trade or business, and
(B) any taxpayer owning stock representing control (within the meaning of section 304(c)) of such corporation at the time of such disposition holds any qualified replacement property of such corporation at such time,
then the taxpayer shall be treated as having disposed of such qualified replacement property at such time.

(3) Recapture not to apply in certain cases. Paragraph (1) shall not apply to any transfer of qualified replacement property—
(A) in any reorganization (within the meaning of section 368) unless the person making the election under subsection (a)(1) owns stock representing control in the acquiring or acquired corporation and such property is substituted basis property in the hands of the transferee,
(B) by reason of the death of the person making such election,
(C) by gift, or
(D) in any transaction to which section 1042(a) applies.

(f) Statute of limitations.
If any gain is realized by the taxpayer on the sale or exchange of any qualified securities and there is in effect an

Nontaxable exchanges
Code Sec. 1042

election under subsection (a) with respect to such gain, then—

(1) the statutory period for the assessment of any deficiency with respect to such gain shall not expire before the expiration of 3 years from the date the Secretary is notified by the taxpayer (in such manner as the Secretary may by regulations prescribe) of—

(A) the taxpayer's cost of purchasing qualified replacement property which the taxpayer claims results in non-recognition of any part of such gain,

(B) the taxpayer's intention not to purchase qualified replacement property within the replacement period, or

(C) a failure to make such purchase within the replacement period, and

(2) such deficiency may be assessed before the expiration of such 3-year period notwithstanding the provisions of any other law or rule of law which would otherwise prevent such assessment.

(g) Application of section to sales of stock in agricultural refiners and processors to eligible farm cooperatives.

(1) **In general.** This section shall apply to the sale of stock of a qualified refiner or processor to an eligible farmers' cooperative.

(2) **Qualified refiner or processor.** For purposes of this subsection, the term "qualified refiner or processor" means a domestic corporation—

(A) substantially all of the activities of which consist of the active conduct of the trade or business of refining or processing agricultural or horticultural products, and

(B) which, during the 1-year period ending on the date of the sale, purchases more than one-half of such products to be refined or processed from—

(i) farmers who make up the eligible farmers' cooperative which is purchasing stock in the corporation in a transaction to which this subsection is to apply, or

(ii) such cooperative.

(3) **Eligible farmers' cooperative.** For purposes of this section, the term "eligible farmers' cooperative" means an organization to which part I of subchapter T applies and which is engaged in the marketing of agricultural or horticultural products.

(4) **Special rules.** In applying this section to a sale to which paragraph (1) applies—

(A) the eligible farmers' cooperative shall be treated in the same manner as a cooperative described in subsection (b)(1)(B),

(B) subsection (b)(2) shall be applied by substituting "100 percent" for "30 percent" each place it appears,

(C) the determination as to whether any stock in the domestic corporation is a qualified security shall be made without regard to whether the stock is an employer security or to subsection (c)(1)(A), and

(D) paragraphs (2)(D) and (7) of subsection (c) shall not apply.

In 1997, P.L. 105-34, Sec. 968(a), added subsec. (g), effective for sales after 12/31/97.

In 1996, P.L. 104-188, Sec. 1311(b)(3), substituted "section 1362(d)(3)(C)" for "section 1362(d)(3)(D)" in clause (c)(4)(A)(i), effective for tax. yrs. begin. after 12/31/96.

—P.L. 104-188, Sec. 1316(d)(3), substituted "domestic C corporation" for "domestic corporation" in subpara. (c)(1)(A), effective for tax. yrs. begin. after 12/31/97.

—P.L. 104-188, Sec. 1616(b)(13), deleted "or 593" after "581" in subclause (c)(4)(B)(ii)(I), effective for tax. yrs. begin. after 12/31/95.

—P.L. 104-188, Sec. 1704(t)(50), substituted "section 1042(c)(1)(B)" for "section 1042(c)(2)(B)" in Sec. 11801(c)(9)(H) of P.L. 101-508 [see below], effective 8/20/96.

In 1990, P.L. 101-508, Sec. 11801(c)(9)(H), substituted "section 83, 422, or 423 applied (or to which section 422 or 424 (as in effect on the day before the date of the enactment of the Revenue Reconciliation Act of 1990) applied)" for "section 83, 422, 422A, 423, or 424 applies" in clause (c)(1)(B)(ii) [amended by Sec. 1704(t)(50) of P.L. 104-188, see above], effective 11/5/90 except as provided in Sec. 11821(b) of this Act, reproduced in note following Code Sec. 422.

In 1989, P.L. 101-239, Sec. 7303(a), added para. (b)(4), effective for sales after 7/10/89.

In 1988, P.L. 100-647, Sec. 1018(t)(4)(D), added "(as in effect immediately before the Tax Reform Act of 1986)" after "section 954(c)(3)" in subpara. (c)(4)(A) . . . Sec. 1018(t)(4)(E), substituted "replacement period" for "placement period" in clause (c)(4)(B)(i), effective for sales of securities in tax. yrs. begin. after 7/18/84, and as provided in Sec. 1854(a)(5)(B) of P.L. 99-514, see below.

—P.L. 100-647, Sec. 1018(t)(4)(G), added Sec. 1854(a)(3)(C)(ii) [reproduced below] of P.L. 99-514, part of the effective date for changes made by Sec. 1854(a)(3)(B) of P.L. 99-514, see below.

In 1986, P.L. 99-514, Sec. 1854(a)(1)(A), substituted "gain (if any) on such sale which would be recognized as long-term capital gain" for "gain (if any) on such sale" in subsec. (a) . . . Sec. 1854(a)(1)(B), substituted "the taxpayer or executor elects in such form as the Secretary may prescribe" for "the taxpayer elects" in para. (a)(1), effective for sales of securities in tax. yrs. begin. after 7/18/84.

—P.L. 99-514, Sec. 1854(a)(2)(A), amended para. (b)(2), effective for sales of securities in tax. yrs. begin. after 7/18/84, except as provided in Sec. 1854(a)(2)(B) of this Act, which read as follows:

"(B)(i) The requirement that section 1042(b) of the Internal Revenue Code of 1954 shall be applied with regard to section 318(a)(4) of such Code shall apply to sales after May 6, 1986.

"(ii) In the case of sales after July 18, 1984, and before the date of the enactment of this Act, paragraph (2) of section 1042(b) of such Code shall apply as if it read as follows:

"(2) Employees must own 30 percent of stock after sale. The plan or cooperative referred to in paragraph (1) owns, immediately after the sale, at least 30 percent of the employer securities or 30 percent of the value of employer securities (within the meaning of section 409(l)) outstanding at the time of sale."

Prior to amendment, para. (b)(2) read as follows:

"(2) Employees must own 30 percent of stock after sale. The plan or cooperative referred to in paragraph (1) owns, immediately after the sale, at least 30 percent of the total value of the employer securities (within the meaning of section 409(l)) outstanding as of such time."

—P.L. 99-514, Sec. 1854(a)(3)(B), deleted para. (b)(3) and redesignated para. (b)(4) as para. (b)(3), effective for sales of securities after 10/22/86. Sec 1854(a)(3)(C)(ii) [as added by Sec. 1018(1)(4)(6) of P.L. 100-647] provides:

"(ii) A taxpayer or executor may elect to have section 1042(b)(3) of the Internal Revenue Code of 1954 (as in effect before the amendment made by subparagraph (B)) apply to sales before the date of the enactment of this Act as if such section included the last sentence of section 409(n)(1) of the Internal Revenue Code of 1986 (as added by subparagraph (A))."

Prior to deletion, para. (b)(3) read as follows:

"(3) Plan maintained for benefit of employees. No portion of the assets of the plan or cooperative attributable to employer securities (within the meaning of section 409(l)) acquired by the plan or cooperative described in paragraph (1) accrue under such plan, or are allocated by such cooperative, for the benefit of—

"(A) the taxpayer,

"(B) any person who is a member of the family of the taxpayer (within the meaning of section 267(c)(4)), or

"(C) any other person who owns (after application of section 318(a)) more than 25 percent in value of any class of outstanding employer securities (within the meaning of section 409(l))."

—P.L. 99-514, Sec. 1854(a)(4)(A), substituted "stock outstanding that is" for "securities outstanding that are" in subpara. (c)(1)(A) . . . Sec. 1854(a)(4)(B), added "and" to the end of subpara. (c)(1)(A) . . . Sec. 1854(a)(4)(C), deleted subpara. (c)(1)(B) and redesignated subpara. (c)(1)(C) as subpara. (c)(1)(B), effective for sales of securities in tax. yrs. begin. after 7/18/84.

Prior to deletion, subpara. (c)(1)(B) read as follows:

"(B) at the time of the sale described in subsection (a)(1), have been held by the taxpayer for more than 1 year, and"

—P.L. 99-514, Sec. 1854(a)(5)(A), amended para. (c)(4), effective for sales of securities in tax. yrs. begin. after 7/18/84, and as provided in Sec. 1854(a)(5)(B) of this Act:

"(B) If—

"(i) before January 1, 1987, the taxpayer acquired any security (as defined in section 165(g)(2) of the Internal Revenue Code of 1954) issued by a domestic corporation or by any State or political subdivision thereof,

"(ii) the taxpayer treated such security as qualified replacement property for purposes of section 1042 of such Code, and

"(iii) such property does not meet the requirements of section 1042(c)(4) of such Code (as amended by subparagraph (A) [Sec. 1854(a)(5)(A)]),

then, with respect to so much of any gain which the taxpayer treated as not recognized under section 1042(a) by reason of the acquisition of such property, the replacement period for purposes of such section shall not expire before January 1, 1987."

Prior to amendment, para. (c)(4) read as follows:

"(4) Qualified replacement property. The term 'qualified replacement property' means any securities (as defined in section 165(g)(2)) issued by a domestic corpo-

2,707

ration which does not, for the taxable year in which such stock is issued, have passive investment income (as defined in section 1362(d)(3)(D)) that exceeds 25 percent of the gross receipts of such corporation for such taxable year."
—P.L. 99-514, Sec. 1854(a)(6)(A), added para. (c)(7), effective as provided in Sec. 1854(a)(6)(B)-(D) of this Act:

"(B) The amendment made by subparagraph (A) shall apply to sales after March 28, 1985, except that such amendment shall not apply to sales made before July 1, 1985, if made pursuant to a binding contract in effect on March 28, 1985, and at all times thereafter.

"(C) The amendment made by subparagraph (A) shall not apply to any sale occurring on December 20, 1985, with respect to which—

"(i) a commitment letter was issued by a bank on October 31, 1984, and
"(ii) a final purchase agreement was entered into on November 5, 1985.

"(D) In the case of a sale on September 27, 1985, with respect to which a preliminary commitment letter was issued by a bank on April 10, 1985, and with respect to which a commitment letter was issued by a bank on June 28, 1985, the amendment made by subparagraph (A) shall apply but such sale shall be treated as having occurred on September 27, 1986."

—P.L. 99-514, Sec. 1854(a)(7), added a sentence to the end of subsec. (d), effective for sales of securities in tax. yrs. begin. after 7/18/84.

—P.L. 99-514, Sec. 1854(a)(8)(A), redesignated subsec. (e) as subsec. (f) and added new subsec. (e), effective for dispositions after 10/22/86, in tax. yrs. end. after 10/22/86.

—P.L. 99-514, Sec. 1854(a)(9)(B), substituted "sections 4978 and 4979A" for "section 4978(a)" in subpara. (b)(3)(B), effective for sales of securities after 10/22/86.

—P.L. 99-514, Sec. 1854(a)(10)(A), substituted "sale" for "acquisition" in para. (c)(5) . . . Sec. 1854(a)(10)(B), added "to an employee stock ownership plan or eligible worker-owned cooperative" before "in" in para. (c)(5) . . . Sec. 1854(a)(10)(C), substituted "sold" for "acquired" in the heading of para. (c)(5) . . . Sec. 1854(a)(11), added "employee" before "stock" in the heading of Code Sec. 1042, effective for sales of securities in tax. yrs. begin. after 7/18/84.

—P.L. 99-514, Sec. 1854(f)(3)(B), added "and 4979A" after "section 4978(a)" in subpara. (b)(3)(B), effective 10/22/86.

—P.L. 99-514, Sec. 1899A(26), substituted "this section—" for "this section.—" in subsec. (c), effective 10/22/86.

In **1984**, P.L. 98-369, Sec. 541(a), added Code Sec. 1042, effective for sales of securities in tax. yrs. begin. after 7/18/84.

Sec. 1043. Sale of property to comply with conflict-of-interest requirements.
(a) Nonrecognition of gain.

If an eligible person sells any property pursuant to a certificate of divestiture, at the election of the taxpayer, gain from such sale shall be recognized only to the extent that the amount realized on such sale exceeds the cost (to the extent not previously taken into account under this subsection) of any permitted property purchased by the taxpayer during the 60-day period beginning on the date of such sale.

(b) Definitions.

For purposes of this section—

(1) Eligible person. The term "eligible person" means—

(A) an officer or employee of the executive branch, or a judicial officer, of the Federal Government, but does not mean a special Government employee as defined in section 202 of title 18, United States Code, and

(B) any spouse or minor or dependent child whose ownership of any property is attributable under any statute, regulation, rule, judicial canon, or executive order referred to in paragraph (2) to a person referred to in subparagraph (A).

(2) Certificate of divestiture. The term "certificate of divestiture" means any written determination—

(A) that states that divestiture of specific property is reasonably necessary to comply with any Federal conflict of interest statute, regulation, rule, judicial canon, or executive order (including section 208 of title 18, United States Code), or requested by a congressional committee as a condition of confirmation,

(B) that has been issued by the President or the Director of the Office of Government Ethics, in the case of executive branch officers or employees, or by the Judicial Conference of the United States (or its designee), in the case of judicial officers, and

(C) that identifies the specific property to be divested.

(3) Permitted property. The term "permitted property" means any obligation of the United States or any diversified investment fund approved by regulations issued by the Office of Government Ethics.

(4) Purchase. The taxpayer shall be considered to have purchased any permitted property if, but for subsection (c), the unadjusted basis of such property would be its cost within the meaning of section 1012.

(5) Special rule for trusts. For purposes of this section, the trustee of a trust shall be treated as an eligible person with respect to property which is held in the trust if—

(A) any person referred to in paragraph (1)(A) has a beneficial interest in the principal or income of the trust, or

(B) any person referred to in paragraph (1)(B) has a beneficial interest in the principal or income of the trust and such interest is attributable under any statute, regulation, rule, judicial canon, or executive order referred to in paragraph (2) to a person referred to in paragraph (1)(A).

(6) Judicial officer. The term "judicial officer" means the Chief Justice of the United States, the Associate Justices of the Supreme Court, and the judges of the United States courts of appeals, United States district courts, including the district courts in Guam, the Northern Mariana Islands, and the Virgin Islands, Court of Appeals for the Federal Circuit, Court of International Trade, Tax Court, Court of Federal Claims, Court of Appeals for Veterans Claims, United States Court of Appeals for the Armed Forces, and any court created by Act of Congress, the judges of which are entitled to hold office during good behavior.

(c) Basis adjustments.

If gain from the sale of any property is not recognized by reason of subsection (a), such gain shall be applied to reduce (in the order acquired) the basis for determining gain or loss of any permitted property which is purchased by the taxpayer during the 60-day period described in subsection (a).

In **2006**, P.L. 109-432, Sec. 418(a)(1)(A), added ", or a judicial officer," after "an officer or employee of the executive branch" in subpara. (b)(1)(A) . . . Sec. 418(a)(1)(B), added ",judicial canon," after "any statute, regulation, rule," in subpara. (b)(1)(B) . . . Sec. 418(a)(2)(A), added ",judicial canon," after "any Federal conflict of interest statute, regulation, rule," in subpara. (b)(2)(A) . . . Sec. 418(b)(2)(B), added ",in the case of executive branch officers or employers, or by the Judicial Conference of the United States (or its designee), in the case of judicial officers," after "the Director of the Office of Government Ethics" in subpara. (b)(2)(B) . . . Sec. 418(a)(3), added ",judicial canon," after "any statute, regulation, rule," in subpara. (b)(5)(B). . . . Sec. 418(b), added para. (b)(6), effective for sales after 12/20/2006.

In **1990**, P.L. 101-508, Sec. 11703(a)(1), substituted "to the extent not previously taken into account under this subsection" for "reduced by any basis adjustment under subsection (c) attributable to a prior sale" in subsec. (a), effective for sales after 11/30/89.

—P.L. 101-280, Sec. 6(a)(1), added para. (b)(5), effective for sales after 11/30/89. Sec. 6(a)(2)(A) and (B), of this Act provides:

"(2)(A) For purposes of section 1043 of such Code—

"(i) any property sold before June 19, 1990, shall be treated as sold pursuant to a certificate of divestiture (as defined in subsection (b)(2) thereof) if such a certificate is issued with respect to such sale before such date, and

"(ii) in any such case, the 60-day period referred to in subsection (a) thereof shall not expire before the end of the 60-day period beginning on the date on which the certificate of divestiture was issued.

"(B) Notwithstanding subparagraph (A), section 1043 of such Code shall not apply to any sale before April 19, 1990, unless—

"(i) the sale was made in order to comply with an ethics agreement or pursuant to specific direction from the appropriate agency or confirming committee, and

"(ii) the justification for the sale meets the criteria set forth in subsection (b)(2)(A) thereof as implemented by the interim regulations implementing such section 1043, published on April 18, 1990."

In **1989**, P.L. 101-194, Sec. 502(a), added Code Sec. 1043, effective for sales after 11/30/89.

Sec. 1044. Rollover of publicly traded securities gain into specialized small business investment companies.

Nontaxable exchanges — Code Sec. 1045

(a) Nonrecognition of gain.

In the case of the sale of any publicly traded securities with respect to which the taxpayer elects the application of this section, gain from such sale shall be recognized only to the extent that the amount realized on such sale exceeds—

(1) the cost of any common stock or partnership interest in a specialized small business investment company purchased by the taxpayer during the 60-day period beginning on the date of such sale, reduced by

(2) any portion of such cost previously taken into account under this section.

This section shall not apply to any gain which is treated as ordinary income for purposes of this subtitle.

(b) Limitations.

(1) **Limitation on individuals.** In the case of an individual, the amount of gain which may be excluded under subsection (a) for any taxable year shall not exceed the lesser of—

(A) $50,000, or

(B) $500,000, reduced by the amount of gain excluded under subsection (a) for all preceding taxable years.

(2) **Limitation on C corporations.** In the case of a C corporation, the amount of gain which may be excluded under subsection (a) for any taxable year shall not exceed the lesser of—

(A) $250,000, or

(B) $1,000,000, reduced by the amount of gain excluded under subsection (a) for all preceding taxable years.

(3) **Special rules for married individuals.** For purposes of this subsection—

(A) Separate returns. In the case of a separate return by a married individual, paragraph (1) shall be applied by substituting "$25,000" for "$50,000" and "$250,000" for "$500,000".

(B) Allocation of gain. In the case of any joint return, the amount of gain excluded under subsection (a) for any taxable year shall be allocated equally between the spouses for purposes of applying this subsection to subsequent taxable years.

(C) Marital status. For purposes of this subsection, marital status shall be determined under section 7703.

(4) **Special rules for C corporation.** For purposes of this subsection—

(A) all corporations which are members of the same controlled group of corporations (within the meaning of section 52(a)) shall be treated as 1 taxpayer, and

(B) any gain excluded under subsection (a) by a predecessor of any C corporation shall be treated as having been excluded by such C corporation.

(c) Definitions and special rules.

For purposes of this section—

(1) **Publicly traded securities.** The term "publicly traded securities" means securities which are traded on an established securities market.

(2) **Purchase.** The taxpayer shall be considered to have purchased any property if, but for subsection (d), the unadjusted basis of such property would be its cost within the meaning of section 1012.

(3) **Specialized small business investment company.** The term "specialized small business investment company" means any partnership or corporation which is licensed by the Small Business Administration under section 301(d) of the Small Business Investment Act of 1958 (as in effect on May 13, 1993).

(4) **Certain entities not eligible.** This section shall not apply to any estate, trust, partnership, or S corporation.

(d) Basis adjustments.

If gain from any sale is not recognized by reason of subsection (a), such gain shall be applied to reduce (in the order acquired) the basis for determining gain or loss of any common stock or partnership interest in any specialized small business investment company which is purchased by the taxpayer during the 60-day period described in subsection (a). This subsection shall not apply for purposes of section 1202.

In **1996,** P.L. 104-188, Sec. 1703(a), amended para. (c)(2), effective for sales on and after 8/10/93 in tax yrs. end. after 8/10/93.
Prior to amendment, para. (c)(2) read as follows:
"(2) Purchase. The term 'purchase' has the meaning given such term by section 1043(b)(4)."
In **1993,** P.L. 103-66, Sec. 13114(a), added Code Sec. 1044, effective for sales on and after 8/10/93 in tax yrs. end. after 8/10/93.

Sec. 1045. Rollover of gain from qualified small business stock to another qualified small business stock.

(a) Nonrecognition of gain.

In the case of any sale of qualified small business stock held by a taxpayer other than a corporation for more than 6 months and with respect to which such taxpayer elects the application of this section, gain from such sale shall be recognized only to the extent that the amount realized on such sale exceeds—

(1) the cost of any qualified small business stock purchased by the taxpayer during the 60-day period beginning on the date of such sale, reduced by

(2) any portion of such cost previously taken into account under this section.

This section shall not apply to any gain which is treated as ordinary income for purposes of this title.

(b) Definitions and special rules.

For purposes of this section—

(1) **Qualified small business stock.** The term "qualified small business stock" has the meaning given such term by section 1202(c).

(2) **Purchase.** A taxpayer shall be treated as having purchased any property if, but for paragraph (3), the unadjusted basis of such property in the hands of the taxpayer would be its cost (within the meaning of section 1012).

(3) **Basis adjustments.** If gain from any sale is not recognized by reason of subsection (a), such gain shall be applied to reduce (in the order acquired) the basis for determining gain or loss of any qualified small business stock which is purchased by the taxpayer during the 60-day period described in subsection (a).

(4) **Holding period.** For purposes of determining whether the nonrecognition of gain under subsection (a) applies to stock which is sold—

(A) the taxpayer's holding period for such stock and the stock referred to in subsection (a)(1) shall be determined without regard to section 1223, and

(B) only the first 6 months of the taxpayer's holding period for the stock referred to in subsection (a)(1) shall be taken into account for purposes of applying section 1202(c)(2).

(5) **Certain rules to apply.** Rules similar to the rules of subsections (f), (g), (h), (i), (j), and (k) of section 1202 shall apply.

In **1998,** P.L. 105-206, Sec. 6005(f)(1)(A), substituted "a taxpayer other than a corporation" for "an individual" in subsec. (a) . . . Sec. 6005(f)(1)(B), substituted "such taxpayer" for "such individual" in subsec. (a) . . . Sec. 6005(f)(2), added para. (b)(5), effective for sales after 8/5/97.

Code Sec. 1045

In **1997**, P.L. 105-34, Sec. 313(a), added Code Sec. 1045, effective for sales after 8/5/97.

PART IV.—SPECIAL RULES

Sec.
1051. Property acquired during affiliation.
1052. Basis established by the Revenue Act of 1932 or 1934 or by the Internal Revenue Code of 1939.
1053. Property acquired before March 1, 1913.
1054. Certain stock of Federal National Mortgage Association.
1055. Redeemable ground rents.
1056. Repealed [Basis limitation for player contracts transferred in connection with the sale of a franchise.]
1057. Repealed [Election to treat transfer to foreign trust, etc., as taxable exchange].
1058. Transfers of securities under certain agreements.
1059. Corporate shareholder's basis in stock reduced by nontaxed portion of extraordinary dividends.
1059A. Limitation on taxpayer's basis or inventory cost in property imported from related persons.
1060. Special allocation rules for certain asset acquisitions.
1061. Cross references.

In **2004**, P.L. 108-357, Sec. 886(b)(1)(B), deleted item 1056.
Prior to deletion, item 1056 read as follows:
"1056. Basis limitation for player contracts transferred in connection with the sale of a franchise."
In **1997**, P.L. 105-34, Sec. 1131(c)(5) sic [(d)], deleted item 1057.
Prior to deletion, item 1057 read as follows:
"1057. Election to treat transfer to foreign trust, etc., as taxable exchange."
In **1986**, P.L. 99-514, Sec. 614(b), redesignated item 1060 as 1061 and added new item 1060 . . . Sec. 1248(b), added item 1059A.
In **1984**, P.L. 98-369, Sec. 53(d)(1), redesignated item 1059 as 1060 and added new item 1059.
In **1978**, P.L. 95-345, Sec. 2(d)(2), renumbered former item 1058 as 1059 and added new item 1058.
In **1976**, P.L. 94-455, Sec. 212(a)(2), deleted item 1056 and added new items 1056 and 1057.
Prior to amendment, item 1056 read as follows:
"1056. Cross references."
—P.L. 94-455, Sec. 1015(c), deleted item 1057 and added new items 1057 and 1058.
Prior to amendment, item 1057 read as follows:
"1057. Cross references."
In **1963**, inserted item 1055 and renumbered former item 1055 as 1056.
In **1960**, renumbered former item 1054 as 1055 and inserted new item 1054.

Sec. 1051. Property acquired during affiliation.

In the case of property acquired by a corporation, during a period of affiliation, from a corporation with which it was affiliated, the basis of such property, after such period of affiliation, shall be determined, in accordance with regulations prescribed by the Secretary, without regard to inter-company transactions in respect of which gain or loss was not recognized. For purposes of this section, the term "period of affiliation" means the period during which such corporations were affiliated (determined in accordance with the law applicable thereto) but does not include any taxable year beginning on or after January 1, 1922, unless a consolidated return was made, nor any taxable year after the taxable year 1928.

In **1976**, P.L. 94-455, Sec. 1901(a)(131), deleted the last two sentences in Code Sec. 1051, effective for tax. yrs. begin. after 12/31/76.
Prior to amendment, the last two sentences in Code Sec. 1051 read as follows:
"The basis in case of property acquired by a corporation during any period, in the taxable year 1929 or any subsequent taxable year, in respect of which a consolidated return was made by such corporation under chapter 6 of this subtitle (sec. 1501 and following) or under section 141 of the Internal Revenue Code of 1939 or of the Revenue Act of 1938, 1936, 1934, 1932, or 1928 shall be determined in accordance with regulations prescribed under section 1502 or in accordance with regulations prescribed under the appropriate section 141, as the case may be. The basis in the case of property held by a corporation during any period, in the taxable year 1929 or any subsequent taxable year, in respect of which a consolidated return was made by such corporation under chapter 6 of this subtitle or such section 141 shall be adjusted in respect of any items relating to such period, in accordance with regulations prescribed under section 1502 or in accordance with regulations prescribed under the appropriate section 141, as the case may be."
—P.L. 94-455, Sec. 1906(b)(13)(A), substituted "Secretary" for "Secretary or his delegate" in Code Sec. 1051, effective for tax. yrs. begin. after 12/31/76.

Sec. 1052. Basis established by the Revenue Act of 1932 or 1934 or by the Internal Revenue Code of 1939.

(a) Revenue Act of 1932.

If the property was acquired, after February 28, 1913, in any taxable year beginning before January 1, 1934, and the basis thereof, for purposes of the Revenue Act of 1932 was prescribed by section 113(a)(6), (7), or (9) of such Act (47 Stat. 199), then for purposes of this subtitle the basis shall be the same as the basis therein prescribed in the Revenue Act of 1932.

(b) Revenue Act of 1934.

If the property was acquired, after February 28, 1913, in any taxable year beginning before January 1, 1936, and the basis thereof, for purposes of the Revenue Act of 1934, was prescribed by section 113(a)(6), (7), or (8) of such Act (48 Stat. 706), then for purposes of this subtitle the basis shall be the same as the basis therein prescribed in the Revenue Act of 1934.

(c) Internal Revenue Code of 1939.

If the property was acquired, after February 28, 1913, in a transaction to which the Internal Revenue Code of 1939 applied, and the basis thereof, for purposes of the Internal Revenue Code of 1939, was prescribed by section 113(a)(6), (7), (8), (13), (15), (18), (19), or (23) of such Code, then for purposes of this subtitle the basis shall be the same as the basis therein prescribed in the Internal Revenue Code of 1939.

Sec. 1053. Property acquired before March 1, 1913.

In the case of property acquired before March 1, 1913, if the basis otherwise determined under this subtitle, adjusted (for the period before March 1, 1913) as provided in section 1016, is less than the fair market value of the property as of March 1, 1913, then the basis for determining gain shall be such fair market value. In determining the fair market value of stock in a corporation as of March 1, 1913, due regard shall be given to the fair market value of the assets of the corporation as of that date.

In **1958**, P.L. 85-866, Sec. 47, substituted "subtitle" for "part," effective for tax. yrs. begin. after 12/31/53, and end. after 8/16/54.

Sec. 1054. Certain stock of Federal National Mortgage Association.

In the case of a share of stock issued pursuant to section 303(c) of the Federal National Mortgage Association Charter Act (12 U.S.C., sec. 1718), the basis of such share in the hands of the initial holder shall be an amount equal to the capital contributions evidenced by such share reduced by the amount (if any) required by section 162(d) to be treated (with respect to such share) as ordinary and necessary expenses paid or incurred in carrying on a trade or business.

In **1960**, P.L. 86-779, Sec. 8(b), redesignated Code Sec. 1054 as 1055 and added Code Sec. 1054, effective for tax. yrs. begin. after 12/31/59.

Sec. 1055. Redeemable ground rents.
(a) Character.

For purposes of this subtitle—

(1) a redeemable ground rent shall be treated as being in the nature of a mortgage, and

(2) real property held subject to liabilities under a redeemable ground rent shall be treated as held subject to liabilities under a mortgage.

(b) Application of subsection (a).

(1) In general. Subsection (a) shall take effect on the day after the date of the enactment of this section and shall apply with respect to taxable years ending after such date of enactment.

(2) Basis of holder. In determining the basis of real property held subject to liabilities under a redeemable ground rent, subsection (a) shall apply whether such real property was acquired before or after the enactment of this section.

(3) Basis of reserved redeemable ground rent. In the case of a redeemable ground rent reserved or created on or before the date of the enactment of this section in connection with a transfer of the right to hold real property subject to liabilities under such ground rent, the basis of such ground rent after such date in the hands of the person who reserved or created the ground rent shall be the amount taken into account in respect of such ground rent for Federal income tax purposes as consideration for the disposition of such real property. If no such amount was taken into account, such basis shall be determined as if this section had not been enacted.

(c) Redeemable ground rent defined.

For purposes of this subtitle, the term "redeemable ground rent" means only a ground rent with respect to which—

(1) there is a lease of land which is assignable by the lessee without the consent of the lessor and which (together with periods for which the lease may be renewed at the option of the lessee) is for a term in excess of 15 years,

(2) the leaseholder has a present or future right to terminate, and to acquire the entire interest of the lessor in the land, by payment of a determined or determinable amount, which right exists by virtue of State or local law and not because of any private agreement or privately created condition, and

(3) the lessor's interest in the land is primarily a security interest to protect the rental payments to which the lessor is entitled under the lease.

(d) Cross reference.

For treatment of rentals under redeemable ground rents as interest, see section 163(c).

In **1963**, P.L. 88-9, Sec. 1(b), redesignated Code Sec. 1055 as Code Sec. 1056 and added new Code Sec. 1055, effective for tax. yrs. end. after 4/10/63.

Sec. 1056. Repealed.

In **2004**, P.L. 108-357, Sec. 886(b)(1)(A), repealed Code Sec. 1056, effective for property acquired after 10/22/2004.
Prior to repeal, Code Sec. 1056 read as follows:
"Sec. 1056. BASIS LIMITATION FOR PLAYER CONTRACTS TRANSFERRED IN CONNECTION WITH THE SALE OF A FRANCHISE.
"(a) General rule. If a franchise to conduct any sports enterprise is sold or exchanged, and if, in connection with such sale or exchange, there is a transfer of a contract for the services of an athlete, the basis of such contract in the hands of the transferee shall not exceed the sum of—
"(1) the adjusted basis of such contract in the hands of the transferor immediately before the transfer, plus
"(2) the gain (if any) recognized by the transferor on the transfer of such contract.
"(b) Exceptions. Subsection (a) shall not apply—
"(1) to an exchange described in section 1031 (relating to exchange of property held for productive use or investment), and
"(2) to property in the hands of a person acquiring the property from a decedent or to whom the property passed from a decedent (within the meaning of section 1014(a)).
"(c) Transferor required to furnish certain information. Under regulations prescribed by the Secretary, the transfer[or] shall, at the times and in the manner provided in such regulations, furnish to the Secretary and to the transferee the following information:

"(1) the amount which the transferor believes to be the adjusted basis referred to in paragraph (1) of subsection (a),
"(2) the amount which the transferor believes to be the gain referred to in paragraph (2) of subsection (a), and
"(3) any subsequent modification of either such amount.
To the extent provided in such regulations, the amounts furnished pursuant to the preceding sentence shall be binding on the transferor and on the transferee.
"(d) Presumption as to amount allocable to player contracts. In the case of any sale or exchange described in subsection (a), it shall be presumed that not more than 50 percent of the consideration is allocable to contracts for the services of athletes unless it is established to the satisfaction of the Secretary that a specified amount in excess of 50 percent is properly allocable to such contracts. Nothing in the preceding sentence shall give rise to a presumption that an allocation of less than 50 percent of the consideration to contracts for the services of athletes is a proper allocation."
In **1986**, P.L. 99-514, Sec. 631(e)(13), deleted the last sentence of subsec. (a), effective as provided in Sec. 633(a)(1) of this Act, which read as follows:
"(a) General rule.
"Except as otherwise provided in this section [Sec. 633], the amendments made by this subtitle shall apply to—
"(1) any distribution in complete liquidation, and any sale or exchange, made by a corporation after July 31, 1986, unless such corporation is completely liquidated before January 1, 1987,"
Sec. 633(e) of this Act provides:
"(e) Complete liquidation defined. —
"For purposes of this section, a corporation shall be treated as completely liquidated if all of the assets of such corporation are distributed in complete liquidation, less assets retained to meet claims."
Prior to deletion, the last sentence of subsec. (a) read as follows:
"For purposes of this section, gain realized by the transferor on the transfer of such contract, but not recognized by reason of section 337(a), shall be treated as recognized to the extent recognized by the transferor's shareholders."
In **1976**, P.L. 94-455, Sec. 212(a)(1), added new Code Sec. 1056, effective for sales or exchanges of franchises after 12/31/75 in tax. yrs. end. after 12/31/75.

Sec. 1057. Repealed.

In **1997**, P.L. 105-34, Sec. 1131(c)(2), sic [(d)(2)], repealed Code Sec. 1057, effective 8/5/97.
Prior to its repeal, Code Sec. 1057 read as follows:
"Sec. 1057. ELECTION TO TREAT TRANSFER TO FOREIGN TRUST, ETC., AS TAXABLE EXCHANGE.
"In lieu of payment of the tax imposed by section 1491, the taxpayer may elect (for purposes of this subtitle), at such time and in such manner as the Secretary may prescribe, to treat a transfer described in section 1491 as a sale or exchange of property for an amount equal in value to the fair market value of the property transferred and to recognize as gain the excess of —
"(1) the fair market value of the property so transferred, over
"(2) the adjusted basis (for determining gain) of such property in the hands of the transferor."
In **1976**, P.L. 94-455, Sec. 1015(c), added new Code Sec. 1057, effective for transfers of property after 10/2/75.

Sec. 1058. Transfers of securities under certain agreements.

(a) General rule.

In the case of a taxpayer who transfers securities (as defined in section 1236(c)) pursuant to an agreement which meets the requirements of subsection (b), no gain or loss shall be recognized on the exchange of such securities by the taxpayer for an obligation under such agreement, or on the exchange of rights under such agreement by that taxpayer for securities identical to the securities transferred by that taxpayer.

(b) Agreement requirements.

In order to meet the requirements of this subsection, an agreement shall—

(1) provide for the return to the transferor of securities identical to the securities transferred;

(2) require that payments shall be made to the transferor of amounts equivalent to all interest, dividends, and other distributions which the owner of the securities is entitled to receive during the period beginning with the transfer of the securities by the transferor and ending with the transfer of identical securities back to the transferor;

(3) not reduce the risk of loss or opportunity for gain of the transferor of the securities in the securities transferred; and

(4) meet such other requirements as the Secretary may by regulation prescribe.

(c) Basis.

Property acquired by a taxpayer described in subsection (a), in a transaction described in that subsection, shall have the same basis as the property transferred by that taxpayer.

In 1978, P.L. 95-345, Sec. 2(d)(1), added new Code Sec. 1058, effective for amounts received after 12/31/76, as payments with respect to securities loans (as defined in section 512(a)(5) of this title), and transfers of Securities, under agreements described in Code Sec. 1058 made after 12/31/76.

Sec. 1059. Corporate shareholder's basis in stock reduced by nontaxed portion of extraordinary dividends.

(a) General rule.

If any corporation receives any extraordinary dividend with respect to any share of stock and such corporation has not held such stock for more than 2 years before the dividend announcement date—

(1) Reduction in basis. The basis of such corporation in such stock shall be reduced (but not below zero) by the nontaxed portion of such dividends.

(2) Amounts in excess of basis. If the nontaxed portion of such dividends exceeds such basis, such excess shall be treated as gain from the sale or exchange of such stock for the taxable year in which the extraordinary dividend is received.

(b) Nontaxed portion.

For purposes of this section—

(1) In general. The nontaxed portion of any dividend is the excess (if any) of—

(A) the amount of such dividend, over

(B) the taxable portion of such dividend.

(2) Taxable portion. The taxable portion of any dividend is—

(A) the portion of such dividend includible in gross income, reduced by

(B) the amount of any deduction allowable with respect to such dividend under section 243, 244, or 245.

(c) Extraordinary dividend defined.

For purposes of this section—

(1) In general. The term "extraordinary dividend" means any dividend with respect to a share of stock if the amount of such dividend equals or exceeds the threshold percentage of the taxpayer's adjusted basis in such share of stock.

(2) Threshold percentage. The term "threshold percentage" means—

(A) 5 percent in the case of stock which is preferred as to dividends, and

(B) 10 percent in the case of any other stock.

(3) Aggregation of dividends.

(A) Aggregation within 85-day period. All dividends—

(i) which are received by the taxpayer (or a person described in subparagraph (C)) with respect to any share of stock, and

(ii) which have ex-dividend dates within the same period of 85 consecutive days,

shall be treated as 1 dividend.

(B) Aggregation within 1 year where dividends exceed 20 percent of adjusted basis. All dividends—

(i) which are received by the taxpayer (or a person described in subparagraph (C)) with respect to any share of stock, and

(ii) which have ex-dividend dates during the same period of 365 consecutive days,

shall be treated as extraordinary dividends if the aggregate of such dividends exceeds 20 percent of the taxpayer's adjusted basis in such stock (determined without regard to this section).

(C) Substituted basis transactions. In the case of any stock, a person is described in this subparagraph if—

(i) the basis of such stock in the hands of such person is determined in whole or in part by reference to the basis of such stock in the hands of the taxpayer, or

(ii) the basis of such stock in the hands of the taxpayer is determined in whole or in part by reference to the basis of such stock in the hands of such person.

(4) Fair market value determination. If the taxpayer establishes to the satisfaction of the Secretary the fair market value of any share of stock as of the day before the ex-dividend date, the taxpayer may elect to apply paragraphs (1) and (3) by substituting such value for the taxpayer's adjusted basis.

(d) Special rules.

For purposes of this section—

(1) Time for reduction. Any reduction in basis under subsection (a)(1) shall be treated as occurring at the beginning of the ex-dividend date of the extraordinary dividend to which the reduction relates.

(2) Distributions in kind. To the extent any dividend consists of property other than cash, the amount of such dividend shall be treated as the fair market value of such property (as of the date of the distribution) reduced as provided in section 301(b)(2).

(3) Determination of holding period. For purposes of determining the holding period of stock under subsection (a), rules similar to the rules of paragraphs (3) and (4) of section 246(c) shall apply; except that "2 years" shall be substituted for the number of days specified in subparagraph (B) of section 246(c)(3).

(4) Ex-dividend date. The term "ex-dividend date" means the date on which the share of stock becomes ex-dividend.

(5) Dividend announcement date. The term "dividend announcement date" means, with respect to any dividend, the date on which the corporation declares, announces, or agrees to the amount or payment of such dividend, whichever is the earliest.

(6) Exception where stock held during entire existence of corporation.

(A) In general. Subsection (a) shall not apply to any extraordinary dividend with respect to any share of stock of a corporation if—

(i) such stock was held by the taxpayer during the entire period such corporation was in existence, and

(ii) except as provided in regulations, no earnings and profits of such corporation were attributable to transfers of property from (or earnings and profits of) a corporation which is not a qualified corporation.

(B) Qualified corporation. For purposes of subparagraph (A), the term "qualified corporation" means any corporation (including a predecessor corporation)—

(i) with respect to which the taxpayer holds directly or indirectly during the entire period of such corporation's existence at least the same ownership interest as the taxpayer holds in the corporation distributing the extraordinary dividend, and

(ii) which has no earnings and profits—

(I) which were earned by, or

(II) which are attributable to gain on property which accrued during a period the corporation holding the property was,

a corporation not described in clause (i).

(C) Application of paragraph. This paragraph shall not apply to any extraordinary dividend to the extent such application is inconsistent with the purposes of this section.

(e) **Special rules for certain distributions.**

(1) **Treatment of partial liquidations and certain redemptions.** Except as otherwise provided in regulations—

(A) Redemptions. In the case of any redemption of stock—

(i) which is part of a partial liquidation (within the meaning of section 302(e)) of the redeeming corporation,

(ii) which is not pro rata as to all shareholders, or

(iii) which would not have been treated (in whole or in part) as a dividend if—

(I) any options had not been taken into account under section 318(a)(4), or

(II) section 304(a) had not applied,

any amount treated as a dividend with respect to such redemption shall be treated as an extraordinary dividend to which paragraphs (1) and (2) of subsection (a) apply without regard to the period the taxpayer held such stock. In the case of a redemption described in clause (iii), only the basis in the stock redeemed shall be taken into account under subsection (a).

(B) Reorganizations, etc. An exchange described in section 356 which is treated as a dividend shall be treated as a redemption of stock for purposes of applying subparagraph (A).

(2) **Qualifying dividends.**

(A) In general. Except as provided in regulations, the term "extraordinary dividend" does not include any qualifying dividend (within the meaning of section 243).

(B) Exception. Subparagraph (A) shall not apply to any portion of a dividend which is attributable to earnings and profits which—

(i) were earned by a corporation during a period it was not a member of the affiliated group, or

(ii) are attributable to gain on property which accrued during a period the corporation holding the property was not a member of the affiliated group.

(3) **Qualified preferred dividends.**

(A) In general. In the case of 1 or more qualified preferred dividends with respect to any share of stock—

(i) this section shall not apply to such dividends if the taxpayer holds such stock for more than 5 years, and

(ii) if the taxpayer disposes of such stock before it has been held for more than 5 years, the aggregate reduction under subsection (a)(1) with respect to such dividends shall not be greater than the excess (if any) of—

(I) the qualified preferred dividends paid with respect to such stock during the period the taxpayer held such stock, over

(II) the qualified preferred dividends which would have been paid during such period on the basis of the stated rate of return.

(B) Rate of return. For purposes of this paragraph—

(i) Actual rate of return. The actual rate of return shall be the rate of return for the period for which the taxpayer held the stock, determined—

(I) by only taking into account dividends during such period, and

(II) by using the lesser of the adjusted basis of the taxpayer in such stock or the liquidation preference of such stock.

(ii) Stated rate of return. The stated rate of return shall be the annual rate of the qualified preferred dividend payable with respect to any share of stock (expressed as a percentage of the amount described in clause (i)(II)).

(C) Definitions and special rules. For purposes of this paragraph—

(i) Qualified preferred dividend. The term "qualified preferred dividend" means any fixed dividend payable with respect to any share of stock which—

(I) provides for fixed preferred dividends payable not less frequently than annually, and

(II) is not in arrears as to dividends at the time the taxpayer acquires the stock.

Such term shall not include any dividend payable with respect to any share of stock if the actual rate of return on such stock exceeds 15 percent.

(ii) Holding period. In determining the holding period for purposes of subparagraph (A)(ii), subsection (d)(3) shall be applied by substituting "5 years" for "2 years."

(f) **Treatment of dividends on certain preferred stock.**

(1) **In general.** Any dividend with respect to disqualified preferred stock shall be treated as an extraordinary dividend to which paragraphs (1) and (2) of subsection (a) apply without regard to the period the taxpayer held the stock.

(2) **Disqualified preferred stock.** For purposes of this subsection, the term "disqualified preferred stock" means any stock which is preferred as to dividends if—

(A) when issued, such stock has a dividend rate which declines (or can reasonably be expected to decline) in the future,

(B) the issue price of such stock exceeds its liquidation rights or its stated redemption price, or

(C) such stock is otherwise structured—

(i) to avoid the other provisions of this section, and

(ii) to enable corporate shareholders to reduce tax through a combination of dividend received deductions and loss on the disposition of the stock.

(g) **Regulations.**

The Secretary shall prescribe such regulations as may be appropriate to carry out the purposes of this section, including regulations—

(1) providing for the application of this section in the case of stock dividends, stock splits, reorganizations, and other similar transactions, in the case of stock held by pass-thru entities, and in the case of consolidated groups, and

(2) providing that the rules of subsection (f) shall apply in the case of stock which is not preferred as to dividends in cases where stock is structured to avoid the purposes of this section.

In 1998, P.L. 105-206, Sec. 6010(b), substituted ", in the case of stock held by pass-thru entities, and in the case of consolidated groups" for "and in the case of stock held by pass-thru entities" in para. (g)(1), effective for distributions after 5/3/95. For transitional rules, see Sec. 1011(d)(2)-(3) of P.L. 105-34, reproduced below.

Code Sec. 1059 — Special basis rules

In 1997, P.L. 105-34, Sec. 1011(a), amended para. (a)(2)... Sec. 1011(b), amended para. (e)(1)... Sec. 1011(c), amended para. (d)(1), effective for distributions after 5/3/95. Sec. 1011(d)(2)-(3) of this Act reads as follows:

"(2) Transition rule. The amendments made by this section shall not apply to any distribution made pursuant to the terms of—

"(A) a written binding contract in effect on May 3, 1995, and at all times thereafter before such distribution, or

"(B) a tender offer outstanding on May 3, 1995.

"(3) Certain dividends not pursuant to certain redemptions. In determining whether the amendment made by subsection (a) applies to any extraordinary dividend other than a dividend treated as an extraordinary dividend under section 1059(e)(1) of the Internal Revenue Code of 1986 (as amended by this Act), paragraphs (1) and (2) shall be applied by substituting 'September 13, 1995' for 'May 3, 1995'."

Prior to amendment, para. (a)(2) read as follows:

"(2) Recognition upon sale or disposition in certain cases. In addition to any gain recognized under this chapter, there shall be treated as gain from the sale or exchange of any stock for the taxable year in which the sale or disposition of such stock occurs an amount equal to the aggregate nontaxed portions of any extraordinary dividends with respect to such stock which did not reduce the basis of such stock by reason of the limitation on reducing basis below zero."

Prior to amendment, para. (d)(1) read as follows:

"(1) Time for reduction.

"(A) In general. Except as provided in subparagraph (B), any reduction in basis under subsection (a)(1) shall occur immediately before any sale or disposition of the stock.

"(B) Special rule for computing extraordinary dividend. In determining a taxpayer's adjusted basis for purposes of subsection (c)(1), any reduction in basis under subsection (a)(1) by reason of a prior distribution which was an extraordinary dividend shall be treated as occurring at the beginning of the ex-dividend date for such distribution."

Prior to amendment, para. (e)(1) read as follows:

"(1) Treatment of partial liquidations and non-pro rata redemptions. Except as otherwise provided in regulations, in the case of any redemption of stock which is—

"(A) part of a partial liquidation (within the meaning of section 302(e)) of the redeeming corporation, or

"(B) not pro rata as to all shareholders,

any amount treated as a dividend under section 301 with respect to such redemption shall be treated as an extraordinary dividend to which paragraphs (1) and (2) of subsection (a) apply without regard to the period the taxpayer held such stock."

—P.L. 105-34, Sec. 1013(b), amended clause (e)(1)(A)(iii) [as amended by Sec. 1011(b) of this Act, see above], effective for distributions and acquisitions after 6/8/97. Sec. 1011(d)(2) of this Act reads as follows:

"(2) Transition rule. The amendments made by this section shall not apply to any distribution or acquisition after June 8, 1997, if such distribution or acquisition is—

"(A) made pursuant to a written agreement which was binding on such date and at all times thereafter,

"(B) described in a ruling request submitted to the Internal Revenue Service on or before such date, or

"(C) described in a public announcement or filing with the Securities and Exchange Commission on or before such date."

Prior to amendment, clause (e)(1)(A)(iii) [as amended by Sec. 1011(b) of this Act, see above] read as follows:

"(iii) which would not have been treated (in whole or in part) as a dividend if any options had not been taken into account under section 381(a)(4)."

—P.L. 105-34, Sec. 1604(d), substituted "subsection (a)" for "subsection (a)(2)" in para. (d)(3), effective 8/5/97.

In 1989, P.L. 101-239, Sec. 7206(a), amended subsec. (f) and added subsec. (g), effective for stock issued after 7/10/89, in tax. yrs. end. after 7/10/89, except as provided by Sec. 7206(b)(2), which reads as follows:

"(2) Binding contract.—The amendment made by subsection (a) shall not apply to any stock issued pursuant to a written binding contract in effect on July 10, 1989, and at all times thereafter before the stock is issued."

Prior to amendment, subsec. (f) read as follows:

"(f) Regulations.

The Secretary shall prescribe such regulations as may be appropriate to carry out the purposes of this section, including regulations providing for the application of this section in the case of stock dividends, stock splits, reorganizations, and other similar transactions and in the case of stock held by pass-thru entities."

In 1988, P.L. 100-647, Sec. 1006(c)(1), deleted para. (d)(5) and redesignated paras. (d)(6) and (7) as paras. (d)(5) and... Sec. 1006(c)(2), added "amount or" before "payment" in para. (d)(5) as so redesignated by Sec. 1006(c)(1) of this Act ... Sec. 1006(c)(3), amended para. (d)(6), as so redesignated by Sec. 1006(c)(1) of this Act... Sec. 1006(c)(4), substituted "to which paragraphs (1) and (2) of subsection (a) apply without regard to the period the taxpayer held such stock" for "for purposes of this section (without regard to the holding period of the stock)" in para. (e)(1)... Sec. 1006(c)(5), amended para. (e)(2)... Sec. 1006(c)(6), amended subpara. (e)(3)(A)... Sec. 1006(c)(7)(A), substituted "any fixed dividend payable" for "any dividend payable" in clause (e)(3)(C)(i)... Sec. 1006(c)(7)(B), added a sentence to the end of clause (e)(3)(C)(i)... Sec. 1006(c)(8)(A), substituted "this paragraph" for "subparagraph (A)" in subpara. (e)(3)(B)... Sec. 1006(c)(8)(B), substituted "clause (i)(II))" for "subparagraph (B)(i)(II)" in clause (e)(3)(B)(ii)... Sec. 1006(c)(9), added "and in the case of stock held by pass-thru entities" before the period at the end of subsec. (f), effective for dividends declared after 7/18/86, in tax. yrs. end. after 7/18/86. For special rules see Secs. 614(f)(2) and (f)(3) of P.L. 99-514, reproduced below.

Prior to deletion, para. (d)(5) read as follows:

"(5) Extension to certain property distributions. In the case of any distribution of property (other than cash) to which section 301 applies—

"(A) such distribution shall be treated as a dividend without regard to whether the corporation has earnings and profits, and

"(B) the amount so treated shall be reduced by the amount of any reduction in basis under section 301(c)(2) by reason of such distribution."

Prior to amendment paragraph (d)(6), as so redesignated by Sec. 1006(c)(1) of this Act read as follows:

"(6) Exception where stock held during entire existence of corporation. Subsection (a) shall not apply to any extraordinary dividend with respect to any share of stock of a corporation if—

"(A) such stock was held by the taxpayer during the entire period such corporation (and any predecessor corporation) was in existence.

"(B) except as provided in regulations, the only earnings and profits of such corporation were earnings and profits accumulated by such corporation (or any predecessor corporation) during such period, and

"(C) the application of this paragraph to such dividend is not inconsistent with the purposes of this section."

Prior to amendment paragraph (e)(2) read as follows:

"(2) Qualifying dividends. Except as provided in regulations, the term 'extraordinary dividend' shall not include any qualifying dividend (within the meaning of section 243(b)(1))."

Prior to amendment subparagraph (e)(3)(A) read as follows:

"(3) Qualified preferred dividends.

"(A) In general. A qualified preferred dividend shall be treated as an extraordinary dividend—

"(i) only if the actual rate of return of the taxpayer on the stock with respect to which such dividend was paid exceeds 15 percent, or

"(ii) of clause (i) does not apply, and the taxpayer disposes of such stock before the taxpayer has held such stock for more than 5 years, only to the extent the actual rate of return exceeds the stated rate of return."

In 1986, P.L. 99-514, Sec. 614(a)(1), amended subsec. (a)... Sec. 614(a)(2), added para. (d)(6)... Sec. 614(a)(3), substituted "2 years" for "1 year" in para. (d)(3)... Sec. 614(b), added para. (c)(4)... Sec. 614(c)(1), amended para. (d)(1)... Sec. 614(c)(2), deleted "(determined without regard to this section)" at the end of para. (c)(1)... Sec. 614(d), added para. (d)(7)... Sec. 614(e), redesignated subsec. (e) as subsec. (f) and added new subsec. (e), effective for dividends declared after 7/18/86, in tax. yrs. end. after 7/18/86. Secs. 614(f)(2) and (3) of this Act provide:

"(2) Aggregation. For purposes of section 1059(c)(3) of the Internal Revenue Code of 1986, dividends declared after July 18, 1986, shall not be aggregated with dividends declared on or before July 18, 1986.

"(3) Redemptions. Section 1059(e)(1) of the Internal Revenue Code of 1986 (as added by subsection (e)) shall apply to dividends declared after the date of the enactment of this Act, in taxable years ending after such date."

Prior to amendment, subsec. (a) read as follows:

"(a) General rule.

"If any corporation—

"(1) receives an extraordinary dividend with respect to any share of stock, and

"(2) sells or otherwise disposes of such stock before such stock has been held for more than 1 year,

the basis of such corporation in such stock shall be reduced by the nontaxed portion of such dividend. If the nontaxed portion of such dividend exceeds such basis, such excess shall be treated as gain from the sale or exchange of such stock."

Prior to amendment, para. (d)(1) read as follows:

"(d) Special rules.

"For purposes of this section—

"(1) Time for reduction. Any reduction in basis under subsection (a) by reason of any distribution which is an extraordinary dividend shall occur at the beginning of the ex-dividend date for such distribution."

In 1984, P.L. 98-369, Sec. 53(a), added Code Sec. 1059, effective distributions after 3/1/84, in tax. yrs. end. after 3/1/84.

Sec. 1059A. Limitation on taxpayer's basis or inventory cost in property imported from related persons.

(a) In general.

If any property is imported into the United States in a transaction (directly or indirectly) between related persons (within the meaning of section 482), the amount of any costs—

(1) which are taken into account in computing the basis or inventory cost of such property by the purchaser, and

(2) which are also taken into account in computing the customs value of such property,

shall not, for purposes of computing such basis or inventory cost for purposes of this chapter, be greater than the amount of such costs taken into account in computing such customs value.

Special basis rules — Code Sec. 1060

(b) Customs value; import.
For purposes of this section—
(1) Customs value. The term "customs value" means the value taken into account for purposes of determining the amount of any customs duties or any other duties which may be imposed on the importation of any property.
(2) Import. Except as provided in regulations, the term "import" means the entering, or withdrawal from warehouse, for consumption.

In 1986, P.L. 99-514, Sec. 1248(a), added Code Sec. 1059A, effective for transactions entered into after 3/18/86.

Sec. 1060. Special allocation rules for certain asset acquisitions.

(a) General rule.
In the case of any applicable asset acquisition, for purposes of determining both—
(1) the transferee's basis in such assets, and
(2) the gain or loss of the transferor with respect to such acquisition,
the consideration received for such assets shall be allocated among such assets acquired in such acquisition in the same manner as amounts are allocated to assets under section 338(b)(5). If in connection with an applicable asset acquisition, the transferee and transferor agree in writing as to the allocation of any consideration, or as to the fair market value of any of the assets, such agreement shall be binding on both the transferee and transferor unless the Secretary determines that such allocation (or fair market value) is not appropriate.

(b) Information required to be furnished to Secretary.
Under regulations, the transferor and transferee in an applicable asset acquisition shall, at such times and in such manner as may be provided in such regulations, furnish to the Secretary the following information:
(1) The amount of the consideration received for the assets which is allocated to section 197 intangibles.
(2) Any modification of the amount described in paragraph (1).
(3) Any other information with respect to other assets transferred in such acquisition as the Secretary deems necessary to carry out the provisions of this section.

(c) Applicable asset acquisition.
For purposes of this section, the term "applicable asset acquisition" means any transfer (whether directly or indirectly)—
(1) of assets which constitute a trade or business, and
(2) with respect to which the transferee's basis in such assets is determined wholly by reference to the consideration paid for such assets.
A transfer shall not be treated as failing to be an applicable asset acquisition merely because section 1031 applies to a portion of the assets transferred.

(d) Treatment of certain partnership transactions.
In the case of a distribution of partnership property or a transfer of an interest in a partnership—
(1) the rules of subsection (a) shall apply but only for purposes of determining the value of section 197 intangibles for purposes of applying section 755, and
(2) if section 755 applies, such distribution or transfer (as the case may be) shall be treated as an applicable asset acquisition for purposes of subsection (b).

(e) Information required in case of certain transfers of interests in entities.
(1) In general. If—
(A) a person who is a 10-percent owner with respect to any entity transfers an interest in such entity, and
(B) in connection with such transfer, such owner (or a related person) enters into an employment contract, covenant not to compete, royalty or lease agreement, or other agreement with the transferee,
such owner and the transferee shall, at such time and in such manner as the Secretary may prescribe, furnish such information as the Secretary may require.

(2) 10-percent owner. For purposes of this subsection—
(A) In general. The term "10-percent owner" means, with respect to any entity, any person who holds 10 percent or more (by value) of the interests in such entity immediately before the transfer.
(B) Constructive ownership. Section 318 shall apply in determining ownership of stock in a corporation. Similar principles shall apply in determining the ownership of interests in any other entity.

(3) Related person. For purposes of this subsection, the term "related person" means any person who is related (within the meaning of section 267(b) or 707(b)(1)) to the 10-percent owner.

(f) Cross reference.
For provisions relating to penalties for failure to file a return required by this section, see section 6721.

In 1996, P.L. 104-188, Sec. 1703(l), amended Sec. 13261(g)(2)(A)(iii), P.L. 103-66, by substituting "by the taxpayer or a related person" for "by the taxpayer", see below.
In 1993, P.L. 103-66, Sec. 13261(e)(1), substituted "section 197 intangibles" for "goodwill or going concern value" in para. (b)(1) ... Sec. 13261(e)(2), substituted "section 197 intangibles" for "goodwill or going concern value (or similar items)" in para. (d)(1), effective for property acquired after 8/10/93, except as provided in Sec. 13261(g)(2) [as amended by Sec. 1703(l) of P.L. 104-188, see above] and (3) of this Act which reads as follows:
"(2) Election to have amendments apply to property acquired after July 25, 1991.
"(A) In general. If an election under this paragraph applies to the taxpayer—
"(i) the amendments made by this section shall apply to property acquired by the taxpayer after July 25, 1991,
"(ii) subsection (c)(1)(A) of section 197 of the Internal Revenue Code of 1986 (as added by this section) (and so much of subsection (f)(9)(A) of such section 197 as precedes clause (i) thereof) shall be applied with respect to the taxpayer by treating July 25, 1991, as the date of the enactment of such section, and
"(iii) in applying subsection (f)(9) of such section, with respect to any property acquired by the taxpayer or a related person on or before the date of the enactment of this Act, only holding or use on July 25, 1991, shall be taken into account.
"(B) Election. An election under this paragraph shall be made at such time and in such manner as the Secretary of the Treasury or his delegate may prescribe. Such an election by any taxpayer, once made—
"(i) may be revoked only with the consent of the Secretary, and
"(ii) shall apply to the taxpayer making such election and any other taxpayer under common control with the taxpayer (within the meaning of subparagraphs (A) and (B) of section 41(f)(1) of such Code) at any time after August 2, 1993, and on or before the date on which such election is made.
"(3) Elective binding contract exception.
"(A) In general. The amendments made by this section shall not apply to any acquisition of property by the taxpayer if—
"(i) such acquisition is pursuant to a written binding contract in effect on the date of the enactment of this Act and at all times thereafter before such acquisition,
"(ii) an election under paragraph (2) does not apply to the taxpayer, and
"(iii) the taxpayer makes an election under this paragraph with respect to such contract.
"(B) Election. An election under this paragraph shall be made at such time and in such manner as the Secretary of the Treasury or his delegate shall prescribe. Such an election, once made—
"(i) may be revoked only with the consent of the Secretary, and
"(ii) shall apply to all property acquired pursuant to the contract with respect to which such election was made."
In 1990, P.L. 101-508, Sec. 11323(a), added the sentence to the end of subsec. (a) ... Sec. 11323(b)(1), redesignated subsec. (e) as subsec. (f), and added new subsec. (e), effective for acquisitions after 10/9/90 with the exception of any acquisi-

tion pursuant to a written binding contract in effect on 10/9/90 and at all times thereafter before such acquisition.

In **1988**, P.L. 100-647, Sec. 1006(h)(1), substituted "the Secretary deems necessary" for "the Secretary may find necessary" in para. (b)(3) . . . Sec. 1006(h)(2), added subsec. (d) . . . Sec. 1006(h)(3)(B), added subsec. (e), effective for any acquisition of assets after 5/6/86, unless such acquisition is pursuant to a binding contract which was in effect on 5/6/86 and at all times thereafter.

In **1986**, P.L. 99-514, Sec. 641(a), added Code Sec. 1060, effective for any acquisition of assets after 5/6/86, unless such acquisition is pursuant to a binding contract which was in effect on 5/6/86 and at all times thereafter.

Sec. 1061. Cross references.

(1) For nonrecognition of gain in connection with the transfer of obsolete vessels to the Maritime Administration under chapter 573 of title 46, United States Code, see section 57307 of title 46.

(2) For recognition of gain or loss in connection with the construction of new vessels, see chapter 533 of title 46, United States Code.

In **2006**, P.L. 109-304, Sec. 17(e)(5)(A), substituted "chapter 573 of title 46, United States Code, see section 57307 of title 46" for "section 510 of the Merchant Marine Act, 1936, see subsection (e) of that section, as amended August 4, 1939 (46 U.S.C. App. 1160)" in para. (1) . . . Sec. 17(e)(5)(B), substituted "chapter 533 of title 46, United States Code" for "section 511 of such Act, as amended (46 U.S.C. App. 1161)" in para. (2) . . . Sec. 17(e)(5)(C), deleted para. (3), enacted 10/6/2006.

Prior to deletion, para. (3) read as follows:

"(3) For nonrecognition of gain in connection with vessels exchanged with the Maritime Administration under section 8 of the Merchant Ship Sales Act of 1946, see subsection (a) of that section (50 U.S.C. App. 1741)."

In **1986**, P.L. 99-514, Sec. 641(a), redesignated Code Sec. 1060 as Code Sec. 1061, effective for any acquisition of assets after 5/6/86, unless such acquisition is pursuant to a binding contract which was in effect on 5/6/86 and at all times thereafter.

—P.L. 99-514, Sec. 1899A(27), substituted "46 U.S.C. App." for "46 U.S.C." in paragraphs (1) and (2), effective 10/22/86.

In **1984**, P.L. 98-369, Sec. 53(a), redesignated Code Sec. 1059 as Code Sec. 1060, effective for distributions after 3/1/84, in tax. yrs. end. after 3/1/84.

In **1978**, P.L. 95-345, Sec. 2(d)(1), redesignated Code Sec. 1058 as Code Sec. 1059, effective for transfers of securities, under agreements described in Code Sec. 1058 made after 12/31/76.

In **1976**, P.L. 94-455, Sec. 212(a)(1), redesignated Code Sec. 1056 as Code Sec. 1057, effective for sales or exchanges of franchises after 12/31/75 in tax. yrs. end. after 12/31/75.

—P.L. 94-455, Sec. 1015(c), redesignated Code Sec. 1057 as Code Sec. 1058, effective for transfers of property after 10/2/75.

In **1963**, P.L. 88-9, Sec. 1(b), redesignated Code Sec. 1055 as Code Sec. 1056.

In **1960**, P.L. 86-779, Sec. 8(b), redesignated Code Sec. 1054 as Code Sec 1055.

PART V.—CHANGES TO EFFECTUATE F.C.C. POLICY [REPEALED]

Sec.

1071. Repealed. [Gain from sale or exchange to effectuate policies of F.C.C.]

Sec. 1071. Repealed.

In **1995**, P.L. 104-7, Sec. 2(a), deleted Code Sec. 1071 as part of the repeal of Part V of Subchapter O of Chapter 1, effective as provided in Sec. 2(d) of this Act, which reads as follows:

"(d) Effective date.

"(1) In general. The amendments made by this section shall apply to—

"(A) sales and exchanges on or after January 17, 1995, and

"(B) sales and exchanges before such date if the FCC tax certificate with respect to such sale or exchange is issued on or after such date.

"(2) Binding contracts.

"(A) In general. The amendments made by this section shall not apply to any sale or exchange pursuant to a written contract which was binding on January 16, 1995, and at all times thereafter before the sale or exchange, if the FCC tax certificate with respect to such sale or exchange was applied for, or issued, on or before such date.

"(B) Sales contingent on issuance of certificate.

"(i) In general. A contract shall be treated as non binding for purposes of subparagraph (A) if the sale or exchange pursuant to such contract, were contingent, at any time on January 16, 1995, on the issuance of an FCC tax certificate. The preceding sentence shall not apply if the FCC tax certificate for such sale or exchange is issued on or before January 16, 1995.

"(ii) Material terms. For purposes of clause (i), the material terms of a contract shall not be treated as contingent on the issuance of an FCC tax certificate solely because such terms provide that the sales price would, if such certificate were not issued, be increased by an amount not greater than 10 percent of the sales price otherwise provided in the contract.

"(3) FCC tax certificate. For purposes of this subsection, the term 'FCC tax certificate' means any certificate of the Federal Communications Commission for the effectuation of section 1071 of the Internal Revenue Code of 1986 (as in effect on the day before the date of the enactment of this Act)."

Prior to repeal, Code Sec. 1071 read as follows:

"Sec. 1071. Gain from sale or exchange to effectuate policies of F.C.C.

"(a) Nonrecognition of gain or loss.

"If the sale or exchange of property (including stock in a corporation) is certified by the Federal Communications Commission to be necessary or appropriate to effectuate a change in a policy of, or the adoption of a new policy by, the Commission with respect to the ownership and control of radio broadcasting stations, such sale or exchange shall, if the taxpayer so elects, be treated as an involuntary conversion of such property within the meaning of section 1033. For purposes of such section as made applicable by the provisions of this section, stock of a corporation operating a radio broadcasting station, whether or not representing control of such corporation, shall be treated as property similar or related in service or use to the property so converted. The part of the gain, if any, on such sale or exchange to which section 1033 is not applied shall nevertheless not be recognized, if the taxpayer so elects, to the extent that it is applied to reduce the basis for determining gain or loss on sale or exchange of property, of a character subject to the allowance for depreciation under section 167, remaining in the hands of the taxpayer immediately after the sale or exchange, or acquired in the same taxable year. The manner and amount of such reduction shall be determined under regulations prescribed by the Secretary. Any election made by the taxpayer under this section shall be made by a statement to that effect in his return for the taxable year in which the sale or exchange takes place, and such election shall be binding for the taxable year and all subsequent taxable years.

"(b) Basis.

"For basis of property acquired on a sale or exchange treated as an involuntary conversion under subsection (a), see section 1033(b)."

In **1976**, P.L. 94-455, Sec. 1901(b)(31)(E), substituted "1033(b)" for "1033(c)" in subsec. (b) . . . Sec. 1906(b)(13)(A), substituted "Secretary" for "Secretary or his delegate" each place it appeared in subsec. (a), effective for tax. yrs. begin. after 12/31/76.

In **1958**, P.L. 85-866, Sec. 48(a), substituted "necessary or appropriate to effectuate a change in a policy of, or the adoption of a new policy by, the Commission" for "necessary or appropriate to effectuate the policies of the Commission" in subsec. (a), effective for any sale or exchange after 12/31/57.

PART VI.—Repealed [EXCHANGES IN OBEDIENCE TO S.E.C. ORDERS]

Sec.

1081. Repealed [Nonrecognition of gain or loss on exchanges or distributions in obedience to orders of S.E.C.]

1082. Repealed [Basis for determining gain or loss.]

1083. Repealed [Definitions.]

In **2005**, P.L. 109-135, Sec. 402(a)(1), repealed Part VI of subchapter O of chapter 1.

Prior to repeal Part VI of subchapter O of chapter 1, read as follows:

"VI. EXCHANGES IN OBEDIENCE TO S.E.C. ORDERS

"1081. Nonrecognition of gain or loss on exchanges or distributions in obedience to orders of S.E.C.

"1082. Basis for determining gain or loss.

"1083. Definitions."

Sec. 1081. Repealed.

In **2005**, P.L. 109-135, Sec. 402(a)(1), repealed Code Sec. 1081, effective (as provided by Sec. 1274(a) of P.L. 109-58) 6 months after 8/8/2005 as if included in Sec. 1263 of the Energy Policy Act of 2005, P.L. 109-58. Sec. 1274(b) of P.L. 109-58 provides:

"(b) Compliance with certain rules. If the Commission approves and makes effective any final rulemaking modifying the standards of conduct governing entities that own, operate, or control facilities for transmission of electricity in interstate commerce or transportation of natural gas in interstate commerce prior to the effective date of this subtitle, any action taken by a public-utility company or utility holding company to comply with the requirements of such rulemaking shall not subject such public-utility company or utility holding company to any regulatory requirement applicable to a holding company under the Public Utility Holding Company Act of 1935 (15 U.S.C. 79 et seq.)."

Sec. 402(m)(2) of this Act, provides:

"(2) Repeal of Public Utility Holding Company Act of 1935. The amendments made by subsection (a) shall not apply with respect to any transaction ordered in compliance with the Public Utility Holding Company Act of 1935 before its repeal."

Prior to repeal, Code Sec. 1081 read as follows:

"SEC. 1081. NONRECOGNITION OF GAIN OR LOSS ON EXCHANGES OR DISTRIBUTIONS IN OBEDIENCE TO ORDERS OF S.E.C.

"(a) Exchanges of stock or securities only. No gain or loss shall be recognized to the transferor if stock or securities in a corporation which is a registered holding company or a majority-owned subsidiary company are transferred to such corporation or to an associate company thereof which is a registered holding company or a majority-owned subsidiary company solely in exchange for stock or securities (other than stock or securities which are non-exempt property), and the exchange is made by the transferee corporation in obedience to an order of the Securities and Exchange Commission.

"(b) Exchanges and sales of property by corporations.

"(1) General rule. No gain shall be recognized to a transferor corporation which is a registered holding company or an associate company of a registered holding company, if such corporation, in obedience to an order of the Securities and Exchange Commission, transfers property in exchange for property, and such order recites that such exchange by the transferor corporation is necessary or appropriate to the integration or simplification of the holding company system of which the transferor corporation is a member. Any gain, to the extent that it cannot be applied in reduction of basis under section 1082(a)(2), shall be recognized.

"(2) Nonexempt property. If any such property so received is nonexempt property, gain shall be recognized unless such nonexempt property or an amount equal to the fair market value of such property at the time of the transfer is, within 24 months of the transfer, under regulations prescribed by the Secretary, and in accordance with an order of the Securities and Exchange Commission, expended for property other than nonexempt property or is invested as a contribution to the capital, or as paid-in surplus, of another corporation, and such order recites that such expenditure or investment by the transferor corporation is necessary or appropriate to the integration or simplification of the holding company system of which the transferor corporation is a member. If the fair market value of such nonexempt property at the time of the transfer exceeds the amount expended and the amount invested, as required in the preceding sentence, the gain, if any, to the extent of such excess, shall be recognized.

"(3) Cancellation or redemption of stock or securities. For purposes of this subsection, a distribution in cancellation or redemption (except a distribution having the effect of a dividend) of the whole or a part of the transferor's own stock (not acquired on the transfer) and a payment in complete or partial retirement or cancellation of securities representing indebtedness of the transferor or a complete or partial retirement or cancellation of such securities which is a part of the consideration for the transfer shall be considered an expenditure for property other than nonexempt property, and if, on the transfer, a liability of the transferor is assumed, or property of the transferor is transferred subject to a liability, the amount of such liability shall be considered to be an expenditure by the transferor for property other than nonexempt property.

"(4) Consents. This subsection shall not apply unless the transferor corporation consents, at such time and in such manner as the Secretary may by regulations prescribe to the regulations prescribed under section 1082(a)(2) in effect at the time of filing its return for the taxable year in which the transfer occurs.

"(c) Distribution of stock or securities only. If there is distributed, in obedience to an order of the Securities and Exchange Commission, to a shareholder in a corporation which is a registered holding company or a majority-owned subsidiary company, stock or securities (other than stock or securities which are nonexempt property), without the surrender by such shareholder of stock or securities in such corporation, no gain to the distributee from the receipt of the stock or securities so distributed shall be recognized.

"(d) Transfers within system group.

"(1) General rule. No gain or loss shall be recognized to a corporation which is a member of a system group—

"(A) if such corporation transfers property to another corporation which is a member of the same system group in exchange for other property, and the exchange by each corporation is made in obedience to an order of the Securities and Exchange Commission, or

"(B) if there is distributed to such corporation as a shareholder in a corporation which is a member of the same system group, property, without the surrender by such shareholder of stock or securities in the corporation making the distribution, and the distribution is made and received in obedience to an order of the Securities and Exchange Commission.

If an exchange by or a distribution to a corporation with respect to which no gain or loss is recognized under any of the provisions of this paragraph may also be considered to be within the provisions of subsection (a), (b), or (c), then the provisions of this paragraph only shall apply.

"(2) Sales of stock or securities. If the property received on an exchange which is within any of the provisions of paragraph (1) consists in whole or in part of stock or securities issued by the corporation from which such property was received, and if in obedience to an order of the Securities and Exchange Commission such stock or securities (other than stock which is not preferred as to both dividends and assets) are sold and the proceeds derived therefrom are applied in whole or in part in the retirement or cancellation of stock or of securities of the recipient corporation outstanding at the time of such exchange, no gain or loss shall be recognized to the recipient corporation on the sale of the stock or securities with respect to which such order was made; except that if any part of the proceeds derived from the sale of such stock or securities is not so applied, or if the amount of such proceeds is in excess of the fair market value of such stock or securities at the time of such exchange, the gain, if any, shall be recognized, but in an amount not in excess of the proceeds which are not so applied, or in an amount not more than the amount by which the proceeds derived from such sale exceed such fair market value, whichever is the greater.

"(e) Exchanges not solely in kind.

"(1) General rule. If an exchange (not within any of the provisions of subsection (d)) would be within the provisions of subsection (a) if it were not for the fact that property received in exchange consists not only of property permitted by such subsection to be received without the recognition of gain or loss, but also of other property or money, then the gain, if any, to the recipient shall be recognized, but in an amount not in excess of the sum of such money and the fair market value of such other property, and the loss, if any, to the recipient shall not be recognized.

"(2) Distribution treated as dividend. If an exchange is within the provisions of paragraph (1) and if it includes a distribution which has the effect of the distribution of a taxable dividend, then there shall be taxed as a dividend to each distributee such an amount of the gain recognized under such paragraph as is not in excess of his ratable share of the undistributed earnings and profits of the corporation accumulated after February 28, 1913. The remainder, if any, of the gain recognized under paragraph (1) shall be taxed as a gain from the exchange of property.

"(f) Conditions for application of section. The provisions of this section shall not apply to an exchange, expenditure, investment, distribution, or sale unless—

"(1) the order of the Securities and Exchange Commission in obedience to which such exchange, expenditure, investment, distribution, or sale was made recites that such exchange, expenditure, investment, distribution, or sale is necessary or appropriate to effectuate the provisions of section 11(b) of the Public Utility Holding Company Act of 1935 (15 U.S.C. 79k(b)),

"(2) such order specifies and itemizes the stock and securities and other property which are ordered to be acquired, transferred, received, or sold on such exchange, acquisition, expenditure, distribution, or sale, and, in the case of an investment, the investment to be made, and

"(3) such exchange, acquisition, expenditure, investment, distribution, or sale was made in obedience to such order, and was completed within the time prescribed therefor.

"(g) Nonapplication of other provisions. If an exchange or distribution made in obedience to an order of the Securities and Exchange Commission is within any of the provisions of this part and may also be considered to be within any of the other provisions of this subchapter or subchapter C (sec. 301 and following, relating to corporate distributions and adjustments), then the provisions of this part only shall apply."

In 1976, P.L. 94-455, Sec. 1901(a)(132)(A), amended subsec. (c) . . . Sec. 1901(a)(132)(B), substituted "The provisions" for "Except in the case of a distribution described in subsection (c)(2), the provisions" and deleted "49 Stat. 820;" in subsec. (f) . . . Sec. 1901(a)(132)(C), substituted "If an" for "If a distribution described in subsection (c)(2), or an" and deleted the comma following "Commission" in subsec. (g), for tax. yrs. begin. after 12/31/76.

Prior to amendment, subsec. (c) read as follows:

"(c) Distribution of stock or securities only.

"(1) In general. If there is distributed, in obedience to an order of the Securities and Exchange Commission, to a shareholder in a corporation which is a registered holding company or a majority-owned subsidiary company, stock or securities (other than stock or securities which are nonexempt property), without the surrender by such shareholder of stock or securities in such corporation, no gain to the distributee from the receipt of the stock or securities so distributed shall be recognized.

"(2) Special rule. If—

"(A) there is distributed to a shareholder in a corporation rights to acquire common stock in a second corporation without the surrender by such shareholder of stock in the first corporation,

"(B) such distribution is in accordance with an arrangement forming a ground for an order of the Securities and Exchange Commission issued pursuant to section 3 of the Public Utility Holding Company Act of 1935 (49 Stat. 810; 15 U.S.C. 79c) that such corporation is exempt from any provision or provisions of such Act, and

"(C) before January 1, 1958, the first corporation disposes of all of the common stock in the second corporation which it owns,

then no gain to the distributee from the receipt of the rights so distributed shall be recognized. If the first corporation does not, before January 1, 1958, dispose of all of the common stock which it owns in the second corporation, then the periods of limitation provided in sections 6501 and 6502 on the making of an assessment or the collection by levy or a proceeding in court shall, with respect to any deficiency (including interest and additions to the tax) resulting solely from the receipt of such rights to acquire stock, include one year immediately following the date on which the first corporation notifies the Secretary or his delegate whether or not the requirements of subparagraph (C) of the preceding sentence have been met; and such assessment and collection may be made notwithstanding any provision of law or rule of law which would otherwise prevent such assessment and collection."

—P.L. 94-455, Sec. 1906(b)(13)(A), substituted "Secretary" for "Secretary or his delegate" in paras. (b)(2) and (b)(4), effective for tax. yrs. begin. after 12/31/76.

Sec. 1082. Repealed.

In 2005, P.L. 109-135, Sec. 402(a)(1), repealed Code Sec. 1082, effective (as provided by Sec. 1274(a) of P.L. 109-58) 6 months after 8/8/2005 as if included in Sec. 1263 of the Energy Policy Act of 2005, P.L. 109-58. Sec. 1274(b) of P.L. 109-58 provides:

"(b) Compliance with certain rules. If the Commission approves and makes effective any final rulemaking modifying the standards of conduct governing entities that own, operate, or control facilities for transmission of electricity in interstate commerce or transportation of natural gas in interstate commerce prior to the effective date of this subtitle, any action taken by a public-utility company or utility holding company to comply with the requirements of such rulemaking shall not subject such public-utility company or utility holding company to any regulatory

Code Sec. 1082

requirement applicable to a holding company under the Public Utility Holding Company Act of 1935 (15 U.S.C. 79 et seq.)."

Sec. 402(m)(2) of this Act, provides:

"(2) Repeal of Public Utility Holding Company Act of 1935. The amendments made by subsection (a) shall not apply with respect to any transaction ordered in compliance with the Public Utility Holding Company Act of 1935 before its repeal."

Prior to repeal, Code Sec. 1082 read as follows:

"SEC. 1082. BASIS FOR DETERMINING GAIN OR LOSS.

"(a) Exchanges generally.

"(1) Exchanges subject to the provisions of section 1081(a) or (e). If the property was acquired on an exchange subject to the provisions of section 1081(a) or (e), or the corresponding provisions of prior internal revenue laws, the basis shall be the same as in the case of the property exchanged, decreased in the amount of any money received by the taxpayer, and increased in the amount of gain or decreased in the amount of loss to the taxpayer that was recognized on such exchange under the law applicable to the year in which the exchange was made. If the property so acquired consisted in part of the type of property permitted by section 1081(a) to be received without the recognition of gain or loss, and in part of nonexempt property, the basis provided in this subsection shall be allocated between the properties (other than money) received, and for the purpose of the allocation there shall be assigned to such nonexempt property (other than money) an amount equivalent to its fair market value at the date of the exchange. This subsection shall not apply to property acquired by a corporation by the issuance of its stock or securities as the consideration in whole or in part for the transfer of the property to it.

"(2) Exchanges subject to the provisions of section 1081(b). The gain not recognized on a transfer by reason of section 1081(b) or the corresponding provisions of prior internal revenue laws shall be applied to reduce the basis for determining gain or loss on sale or exchange of the following categories of property in the hands of the transferor immediately after the transfer, and property acquired within 24 months after such transfer by an expenditure or investment to which section 1081(b) relates on account of the acquisition of which gain is not recognized under such subsection, in the following order:

"(A) property of a character subject to the allowance for depreciation under section 167;

"(B) property (not described in subparagraph (A)) with respect to which a deduction for amortization is allowable under section 169;

"(C) property with respect to which a deduction for depletion is allowable under section 611 but not allowable under section 613;

"(D) stock and securities of corporations not members of the system group of which the transferor is a member (other than stock or securities of a corporation of which the transferor is a subsidiary);

"(E) securities (other than stock) of corporations which are members of the system group of which the transferor is a member (other than securities of the transferor or of a corporation of which the transferor is a subsidiary);

"(F) stock of corporations which are members of the system group of which the transferor is a member (other than stock of the transferor or of a corporation of which the transferor is a subsidiary);

"(G) all other remaining property of the transferor (other than stock or securities of the transferor or of a corporation of which the transferor is a subsidiary). The manner and amount of the reduction to be applied to particular property within any of the categories described in subparagraphs (A) to (G), inclusive, shall be determined under regulations prescribed by the Secretary.

"(3) Basis in case of pre-1942 acquisition. Notwithstanding the provisions of paragraph (1) or (2), if the property was acquired in a taxable year beginning before January 1, 1942, in any manner described in section 372 of the Internal Revenue Code of 1939 before its amendment by the Revenue Act of 1942, the basis shall be that prescribed in such section (before its amendment by such Act) with respect to such property.

"(b) Transfers to corporations. If, in connection with a transfer subject to the provisions of section 1081(a), (b), or (e) or the corresponding provisions of prior internal revenue laws, the property was acquired by a corporation, either as paid-in surplus or as a contribution to capital, or in consideration for stock or securities issued by the corporation receiving the property (including cases where part of the consideration for the transfer of such property to the corporation consisted of property or money in addition to such stock or securities), then the basis shall be the same as it would be in the hands of the transferor, increased in the amount of gain or decreased in the amount of loss recognized to the transferor on such transfer under the law applicable to the year in which the transfer was made.

"(c) Distributions of stock or securities. If the stock or securities were received in a distribution subject to the provisions of section 1081(c) or the corresponding provisions of prior internal revenue laws, then the basis in the case of the stock in respect of which the distribution was made shall be apportioned, under regulations prescribed by the Secretary, between such stock and the stock or securities distributed.

"(d) Transfers within system group. If the property was acquired by a corporation which is a member of a system group on a transfer or distribution described in section 1081(d)(1), then the basis shall be the same as it would be in the hands of the transferor; except that if such property is stock or securities issued by the corporation from which such stock or securities were received and they were issued—

"(1) as the sole consideration for the property transferred to such corporation, then the basis of such stock or securities shall be either—

"(A) the same as in the case of the property transferred therefor, or

"(B) the fair market value of such stock or securities at the time of their receipt, whichever is the lower; or

Special basis rules

"(2) as part consideration for the property transferred to such corporation, then the basis of such stock or securities shall be either—

"(A) an amount which bears the same ratio to the basis of the property transferred as the fair market value of such stock or securities at the time of their receipt bears to the total fair market value of the entire consideration received, or

"(B) the fair market value of such stock or securities at the time of their receipt, whichever is the lower."

In 1990, P.L. 101-508, Sec. 11801(c)(6)(D), substituted "169" for "169, 184, or 188" in subpara. (a)(2)(B), effective 11/5/90 except as provided in Sec. 11821(b) of this Act, reproduced in note following Code Sec. 184.

In 1986, P.L. 99-514, Sec. 242(b)(1), deleted ", 185," in subpara. (a)(2)(B), effective for that portion of the basis of any property which is attributable to expenditures paid or incurred after 12/31/86. Sec. 242(c)(2) of this Act provides a transitional rule as follows:

"(2) Transitional rule. The amendments made by this section shall not apply to any expenditure incurred—

"(A) pursuant to a binding contract entered into before March 2, 1986, or

"(B) with respect to any improvement commenced before March 2, 1986, but only if not less than the lesser of $1,000,000 or 5 percent of the aggregate cost of such improvement has been incurred or committed before such date.

The preceding sentence shall not apply to any expenditure with respect to an improvement placed in service after December 31, 1987."

In 1981, P.L. 97-34, Sec. 212(d)(2)(E), substituted "or 188" for "188, or 191", in subpara. (a)(2)(B), effective for expenditures incurred after 12/31/81, in tax. yrs. end after 12/31/81. For transitional rule, see Sec. 212(e)(2) of this Act reproduced in note following Code Sec. 46.

In 1980, P.L. 96-541, Sec. 2(e)(1), repealed Sec. 2124(a)(4) of P.L. 94-455, the effective date for changes made by Sec. 2124(a)(3)(C) of P.L. 94-455, see below. Prior to amendment, Sec. 2124(a)(4) of P.L. 94-455 read as follows:

"(4) Effective date. The amendments made by this subsection shall apply with respect to additions to capital account made after June 14, 1976 and before June 15, 1981."

In 1976, P.L. 94-455, Sec. 1901(b)(11)(C), deleted "187," after "185," in subpara. (a)(2)(B) . . . Sec. 1906(b)(13)(A), substituted "Secretary" for "Secretary or his delegate" each place it appeared in Code Sec. 1082 . . . Sec. 1951(c)(2)(B), deleted "168," after "under section" in subpara. (a)(2)(B), effective for tax. yrs. begin. after 12/31/76.

—P.L. 94-455, Sec. 2124(a)(3)(C), substituted "188, or 191" for "or 188" in subpara. (a)(2)(B). Sec. 2(e)(1) of P.L. 96-541 repealed Sec. 2124(a)(4) of this Act [the effective date for this amendment, see above].

In 1971, P.L. 92-178, Sec. 303(c)(5), substituted "187, or 188" for "or 187" in subpara. (a)(2)(B), effective for tax. yrs. end. after 12/31/71.

In 1969, P.L. 91-172, Sec. 704(b)(3), substituted ", 169, 184, 185, or 187" for "or 169" in subpara. (a)(2)(B), effective for tax. yrs. end. after 12/31/68.

Sec. 1083. Repealed.

In 2005, P.L. 109-135, Sec. 402(a)(1), repealed Code Sec. 1083, effective (as provided by Sec. 1274(a) of P.L. 109-58) 6 months after 8/8/2005 as if included in Sec. 1263 of the Energy Policy Act of 2005, P.L. 109-58. Sec. 1274(b) of P.L. 109-58 provides:

"(b) Compliance with certain rules. If the Commission approves and makes effective any final rulemaking modifying the standards of conduct governing entities that own, operate, or control facilities for transmission of electricity in interstate commerce or transportation of natural gas in interstate commerce prior to the effective date of this subtitle, any action taken by a public-utility company or utility holding company to comply with the requirements of such rulemaking shall not subject such public-utility company or utility holding company to any regulatory requirement applicable to a holding company under the Public Utility Holding Company Act of 1935 (15 U.S.C. 79 et seq.)."

Sec. 402(m)(2) of this Act, provides:

"(2) Repeal of Public Utility Holding Company Act of 1935. The amendments made by subsection (a) shall not apply with respect to any transaction ordered in compliance with the Public Utility Holding Company Act of 1935 before its repeal."

Prior to repeal, Code Sec. 1083 read as follows:

"SEC. 1083. DEFINITIONS.

"(a) Order of Securities and Exchange Commission. For purposes of this part, the term 'order of the Securities and Exchange Commission' means an order issued after May 28, 1938, by the Securities and Exchange Commission which requires, authorizes, permits, or approves transactions described in such order to effectuate section 11(b) of the Public Utility Holding Company Act of 1935 (15 U.S.C. 79k(b)), which has become or becomes final in accordance with law.

"(b) Registered holding company; holding company system; associate company. For purposes of this part, the terms 'registered holding company', 'holding company system', and 'associate company' shall have the meanings assigned to them by section 2 of the Public Utility Holding Company Act of 1935 (15 U.S.C. 79b(a)).

"(c) Majority-owned subsidiary company. For purposes of this part, the term 'majority-owned subsidiary company' of a registered holding company means a corporation, stock of which, representing in the aggregate more than 50 percent of the total combined voting power of all classes of stock of such corporation entitled to vote (not including stock which is entitled to vote only on default or nonpayment of dividends or other special circumstances) is owned wholly by such registered holding company, or partly by such registered holding company and partly by one or more majority-owned subsidiary companies thereof, or by one or more majority-owned subsidiary companies of such registered holding company.

"(d) System group. For purposes of this part, the term 'system group' means one or more chains of corporations connected through stock ownership with a common parent corporation if—

"(1) at least 90 percent of each class of the stock (other than (A) stock which is preferred as to both dividends and assets, and (B) stock which is limited and preferred as to dividends but which is not preferred as to assets but only if the total value of such stock is less than 1 percent of the aggregate value of all classes of stock which are not preferred as to both dividends and assets) of each of the corporations (except the common parent corporation) is owned directly by one or more of the other corporations; and

"(2) the common parent corporation owns directly at least 90 percent of each class of the stock (other than stock, which is preferred as to both dividends and assets) of at least one of the other corporations; and

"(3) each of the corporations is either a registered holding company or a majority-owned subsidiary company.

"(e) Nonexempt property. For purposes of this part, the term 'nonexempt property' means—

"(1) any consideration in the form of evidences of indebtedness owed by the transferor or a cancellation or assumption of debts or other liabilities of the transferor (including a continuance of encumbrances subject to which the property was transferred);

"(2) short-term obligations (including notes, drafts, bills of exchange, and bankers' acceptances) having a maturity at the time of issuance of not exceeding 24 months, exclusive of days of grace;

"(3) securities issued or guaranteed as to principal or interest by a government or subdivision thereof (including those issued by a corporation which is an instrumentality of a government or subdivision thereof);

"(4) stock or securities which were acquired from a registered holding company or an associate company of a registered holding company which acquired such stock or securities after February 28, 1938, unless such stock or securities (other than obligations described as nonexempt property in paragraph (1), (2), or (3)) were acquired in obedience to an order of the Securities and Exchange Commission or were acquired with the authorization or approval of the Securities and Exchange Commission under any section of the Public Utility Holding Company Act of 1935 (15 U.S.C. 79k(b));

"(5) money, and the right to receive money not evidenced by a security other than an obligation described as nonexempt property in paragraph (2) or (3).

"(f) Stock or securities. For purposes of this part, the term 'stock or securities' means shares of stock in any corporation, certificates of stock or interest in any corporation, notes, bonds, debentures, and evidences of indebtedness (including any evidence of an interest in or right to subscribe to or purchase any of the foregoing)."

In 1976, P.L. 94-455, Sec. 1901(a)(133)(A), deleted "49 Stat. 820;" in subsec. (a) . . . Sec. 1901(a)(133)(B), deleted "49 Stat. 804;" in subsec. (b) . . . Sec. 1901(a)(133)(C), deleted "49 Stat. 820;" in para. (e)(4), effective for tax. yrs. begin. after 12/31/76.

PART VII.—WASH SALES; STRADDLES

Sec.
1091. Loss from wash sales of stock or securities.
1092. Straddles.

In 1981, P.L. 97-34, Sec. 501(d)(1), added item 1092.

Sec. 1091. Loss from wash sales of stock or securities.
(a) Disallowance of loss deduction.

In the case of any loss claimed to have been sustained from any sale or other disposition of shares of stock or securities where it appears that, within a period beginning 30 days before the date of such sale or disposition and ending 30 days after such date, the taxpayer has acquired (by purchase or by an exchange on which the entire amount of gain or loss was recognized by law), or has entered into a contract or option so to acquire, substantially identical stock or securities, then no deduction shall be allowed under section 165 unless the taxpayer is a dealer in stock or securities and the loss is sustained in a transaction made in the ordinary course of such business. For purposes of this section, the term "stock or securities" shall, except as provided in regulations, include contracts or options to acquire or sell stock or securities.

(b) Stock acquired less than stock sold.

If the amount of stock or securities acquired (or covered by the contract or option to acquire) is less than the amount of stock or securities sold or otherwise disposed of, then the particular shares of stock or securities the loss from the sale or other disposition of which is not deductible shall be determined under regulations prescribed by the Secretary.

(c) Stock acquired not less than stock sold.

If the amount of stock or securities acquired (or covered by the contract or option to acquire) is not less than the amount of stock or securities sold or otherwise disposed of, then the particular shares of stock or securities the acquisition of which (or the contract or option to acquire which) resulted in the nondeductibility of the loss shall be determined under regulations prescribed by the Secretary.

(d) Unadjusted basis in case of wash sale of stock.

If the property consists of stock or securities the acquisition of which (or the contract or option to acquire which) resulted in the nondeductibility (under this section or corresponding provisions of prior internal revenue laws) of the loss from the sale or other disposition of substantially identical stock or securities, then the basis shall be the basis of the stock or securities so sold or disposed of, increased or decreased, as the case may be, by the difference, if any, between the price at which the property was acquired and the price at which such substantially identical stock or securities were sold or otherwise disposed of.

(e) Certain short sales of stock or securities and securities futures contracts to sell.

Rules similar to the rules of subsection (a) shall apply to any loss realized on the closing of a short sale of (or the sale, exchange, or termination of a securities futures contract to sell) stock or securities if, within a period beginning 30 days before the date of such closing and ending 30 days after such date—

(1) substantially identical stock or securities were sold, or

(2) another short sale of (or securities futures contracts to sell) substantially identical stock or securities was entered into.

For purposes of this subsection, the term "securities futures contract" has the meaning provided by section 1234B(c).

(f) Cash settlement.

This section shall not fail to apply to a contract or option to acquire or sell stock or securities solely by reason of the fact that the contract or option settles in (or could be settled in) cash or property other than such stock or securities.

In 2009, P.L. 111-5, Sec. 1211(c), of this Act, provides:
"(c) ANTI-ABUSE RULES.
"The Secretary of Treasury or the Secretary's designee shall prescribes such rules as are necessary to prevent the abuse of the purposes of the amendments made by this section, including anti-stuffing rules, anti-churning rules (including rules relating to sale-leasebacks), and rules similar to the rules under section 1091 of the Internal Revenue Code of 1986 relating to losses from wash sales."

In 2002, P.L. 107-147, Sec. 412(d)(2)(A), substituted "securities and securities futures contracts to sell." for "securities." in the heading of subsec. (e) . . . Sec. 412(d)(2)(B), added "(or the sale, exchange, or termination of a securities futures contract to sell)" after "closing of a short sale of" in subsec. (e) . . . Sec. 412(d)(2)(C), added "(or securities futures contracts to sell)" after "short sale of" in para. (e)(2) . . . Sec. 412(d)(2)(D), added a flush sentence at the end of subsec. (e), effective 12/21/2000.

In 2000, P.L. 106-554, Sec. 1(a)(7), [which enacted into law Sec. 401(d) of P.L. 106-554] added subsec. (f), effective 12/21/2000.

In 1988, P.L. 100-647, Sec. 5075(a), added the sentence at the end of subsec. (a), effective for any sale after 11/10/88, in tax. yrs. end. after 11/10/88.

In 1984, P.L. 98-369, Sec. 106(a), added subsec. (e), effective for short sales of stock or securities after 7/18/84 in tax. yrs. end. after 7/18/84.

—P.L. 98-369, Sec. 106(b), substituted "no deduction shall be allowed under section 165 unless the taxpayer is a dealer in stock or securities and the loss is sustained in a transaction made in the ordinary course of such business." for "no deduction for the loss shall be allowed under section 165(c)(2); nor shall such deduction be allowed a corporation under section 165(a) unless it is a dealer in stocks or securities, and the loss is sustained in a transaction made in the ordinary course of its business." in subsec. (a), effective for sales after 12/31/84, in tax. yrs. end. after 12/31/84.

In 1976, P.L. 94-455, Sec. 1906(b)(13)(A), substituted "Secretary" for "Secretary or his delegate" each place it appeared in Code Sec. 1091, effective for tax. yrs. begin. after 12/31/76.

Sec. 1092. Straddles.

(a) Recognition of loss in case of straddles, etc.
(1) Limitation on recognition of loss.
(A) In general. Any loss with respect to 1 or more positions shall be taken into account for any taxable year only to the extent that the amount of such loss exceeds the unrecognized gain (if any) with respect to 1 or more positions which were offsetting positions with respect to 1 or more positions from which the loss arose.
(B) Carryover of loss. Any loss which may not be taken into account under subparagraph (A) for any taxable year shall, subject to the limitations under subparagraph (A), be treated as sustained in the succeeding taxable year.

(2) Special rule for identified straddles.
(A) In general. In the case of any straddle which is an identified straddle—
(i) paragraph (1) shall not apply with respect to positions comprising the identified straddle,
(ii) if there is any loss with respect to any position of the identified straddle, the basis of each of the offsetting positions in the identified straddle shall be increased by an amount which bears the same ratio to the loss as the unrecognized gain with respect to such offsetting position bears to the aggregate unrecognized gain with respect to all such offsetting positions,
(iii) if the application of clause (ii) does not result in an increase in the basis of any offsetting position in the identified straddle, the basis of each of the offsetting positions in the identified straddle shall be increased in a manner which—
(I) is reasonable, consistent with the purposes of this paragraph, and consistently applied by the taxpayer, and
(II) results in an aggregate increase in the basis of such offsetting positions which is equal to the loss described in clause (ii), and
(iv) any loss described in clause (ii) shall not otherwise be taken into account for purposes of this title.
(B) Identified straddle. The term "identified straddle" means any straddle—
(i) which is clearly identified on the taxpayer's records as an identified straddle before the earlier of—
(I) the close of the day on which the straddle is acquired, or
(II) such time as the Secretary may prescribe by regulations.
(ii) to the extent provided by regulations, the value of each position of which (in the hands of the taxpayer immediately before the creation of the straddle) is not less than the basis of such position in the hands of the taxpayer at the time the straddle is created, and
(iii) which is not part of a larger straddle.
A straddle shall be treated as clearly identified for purposes of clause (i) only if such identification includes an identification of the positions in the straddle which are offsetting with respect other positions in the straddle.
(C) Application to liabilities and obligations. Except as otherwise provided by the Secretary, rules similar to the rules of clauses (ii) and (iii) of subparagraph (A) shall apply for purposes of this paragraph with respect to any position which is, or has been, a liability or obligation.
(D) Regulations. The Secretary shall prescribe such regulations or other guidance as may be necessary or appropriate to carry out the purposes of this paragraph. Such regulations or other guidance may specify the proper methods for clearly identifying a straddle as an identified straddle (and for identifying the positions comprising such straddle), the rules for the application of this section to a taxpayer which fails to comply with those identification requirements, the rules for the application of this section to a position which is or has been a liability or obligation, methods of loss allocation which satisfy the requirements of subparagraph (A)(iii), and the ordering rules in cases where a taxpayer disposes (or otherwise ceases to be the holder) of any part of any position which is part of an identified straddle.

(3) Unrecognized gain. For purposes of this subsection—
(A) In general. The term "unrecognized gain" means—
(i) in the case of any position held by the taxpayer as of the close of the taxable year, the amount of gain which would be taken into account with respect to such position if such position were sold on the last business day of such taxable year at its fair market value, and
(ii) in the case of any position with respect to which, as of the close of the taxable year, gain has been realized but not recognized, the amount of gain so realized.
(B) Special rule for identified straddles. For purposes of paragraph (2)(A)(ii), the unrecognized gain with respect to any offsetting position shall be the excess of the fair market value of the position at the time of the determination over the fair market value of the position at the time the taxpayer identified the position as a position in an identified straddle.
(C) Reporting of gain.
(i) In general. Each taxpayer shall disclose to the Secretary, at such time and in such manner and form as the Secretary may prescribe by regulations—
(I) each position (whether or not part of a straddle) with respect to which, as of the close of the taxable year, there is unrecognized gain, and
(II) the amount of such unrecognized gain.
(ii) Reports not required in certain cases. Clause (i) shall not apply—
(I) to any position which is part of an identified straddle,
(II) to any position which, with respect to the taxpayer, is property described in paragraph (1) or (2) of section 1221(a) or to any position which is part of a hedging transaction (as defined in section 1256(e)), or
(III) with respect to any taxable year if no loss on a position (including a regulated futures contract) has been sustained during such taxable year or if the only loss sustained on such position is a loss described in subclause (II).

(b) Regulations.
(1) In general. The Secretary shall prescribe such regulations with respect to gain or loss on positions which are a part of a straddle as may be appropriate to carry out the purposes of this section and section 263(g). To the extent consistent with such purposes, such regulations shall include rules applying the principles of subsections (a) and (d) of section 1091 and of subsections (b) and (d) of section 1233.

(2) Regulations relating to mixed straddles.
(A) Elective provisions in lieu of section 1233(d) principles. The regulations prescribed under paragraph (1) shall provide that—
(i) the taxpayer may offset gains and losses from positions which are part of mixed straddles—
(I) by straddle-by-straddle identification, or
(II) by the establishment (with respect to any class of activities) of a mixed straddle account for which gains and losses would be recognized (and offset) on a periodic basis,
(ii) such offsetting will occur before the application of section 1256, and section 1256(a)(3) will only apply to net gain or net loss attributable to section 1256 contracts, and
(iii) the principles of section 1233(d) shall not apply with respect to any straddle identified under clause (i)(I) or part of an account established under clause (i)(II).
(B) Limitation on net gain or net loss from mixed straddle account. In the case of any mixed straddle account referred to in subparagraph (A)(i)(II)—
(i) Not more than 50 percent of net gain may be treated as long-term capital gain. In no event shall more than 50 percent of the net gain from such account for any taxable year be treated as long-term capital gain.
(ii) Not more than 40 percent of net loss may be treated as short-term capital loss. In no event shall more than 40 percent of the net loss from such account for any taxable year be treated as short-term capital loss.
(C) Authority to treat certain positions as mixed straddles. The regulations prescribed under paragraph (1) may treat as a mixed straddle positions not described in section 1256(d)(4).
(D) Timing and character authority. The regulations prescribed under paragraph (1) shall include regulations relating to the timing and character of gains and losses in case of straddles where at least 1 position is ordinary and at least 1 position is capital.

(c) Straddle defined.
For purposes of this section—
(1) In general. The term "straddle" means offsetting positions with respect to personal property.
(2) Offsetting positions.
(A) In general. A taxpayer holds offsetting positions with respect to personal property if there is a substantial diminution of the taxpayer's risk of loss from holding any position with respect to personal property by reason of his holding 1 or more other positions with respect to personal property (whether or not of the same kind).
(B) Special rule for identified straddles. In the case of any position which is not part of an identified straddle (within the meaning of subsection (a)(2)(B)), such position shall not be treated as offsetting with respect to any position which is part of an identified straddle.
(3) Presumption.
(A) In general. For purposes of paragraph (2), 2 or more positions shall be presumed to be offsetting if—
(i) the positions are in the same personal property (whether established in such property or a contract for such property),
(ii) the positions are in the same personal property, even though such property may be in a substantially altered form,
(iii) the positions are in debt instruments of a similar maturity or other debt instruments described in regulations prescribed by the Secretary,
(iv) the positions are sold or marketed as offsetting positions (whether or not such positions are called a straddle, spread, butterfly, or any similar name),
(v) the aggregate margin requirement for such positions is lower than the sum of the margin requirements for each such position (if held separately), or
(vi) there are such other factors (or satisfaction of subjective or objective tests) as the Secretary may by regulations prescribe as indicating that such positions are offsetting.
For purposes of the preceding sentence, 2 or more positions shall be treated as described in clause (i), (ii), (iii), or (vi) only if the value of 1 or more of such positions ordinarily varies inversely with the value of 1 or more other such positions.
(B) Presumption may be rebutted. Any presumption established pursuant to subparagraph (A) may be rebutted.
(4) Exception for certain straddles consisting of qualified covered call options and the optioned stock.
(A) In general. If—
(i) all the offsetting positions making up any straddle consist of 1 or more qualified covered call options and the stock to be purchased from the taxpayer under such options, and
(ii) such straddle is not part of a larger straddle,
such straddle shall not be treated as a straddle for purposes of this section and section 263(g).
(B) Qualified covered call option defined. For purposes of subparagraph (A), the term "qualified covered call option" means any option granted by the taxpayer to purchase stock held by the taxpayer (or stock acquired by the taxpayer in connection with the granting of the option) but only if—
(i) such option is traded on a national securities exchange which is registered with the Securities and Exchange Commission or other market which the Secretary determines has rules adequate to carry out the purposes of this paragraph,
(ii) such option is granted more than 30 days before the day on which the option expires,
(iii) such option is not a deep-in-the-money option,
(iv) such option is not granted by an options dealer (within the meaning of section 1256(g)(8)) in connection with his activity of dealing in options, and
(v) gain or loss with respect to such option is not ordinary income or loss.
(C) Deep-in-the-money option. For purposes of subparagraph (B), the term "deep-in-the-money option" means an option having a strike price lower than the lowest qualified bench mark.
(D) Lowest qualified bench mark.
(i) In general. Except as otherwise provided in this subparagraph, for purposes of subparagraph (C), the term "lowest qualified bench mark" means the highest available strike price which is less than the applicable stock price.
(ii) Special rule where option is for period more than 90 days and strike price exceeds $50. In the case of an option—
(I) which is granted more than 90 days before the date on which such option expires, and
(II) with respect to which the strike price is more than $50,

the lowest qualified bench mark is the second highest available strike price which is less than the applicable stock price.
  (iii) 85 percent rule where applicable stock price $25 or less. If—
    (I) the applicable stock price is $25 or less, and
    (II) but for this clause, the lowest qualified bench mark would be less than 85 percent of the applicable stock price,
  the lowest qualified bench mark shall be treated as equal to 85 percent of the applicable stock price.
  (iv) Limitation where applicable stock price $150 or less. If—
    (I) the applicable stock price is $150 or less, and
    (II) but for this clause, the lowest qualified bench mark would be less than the applicable stock price reduced by $10,
  the lowest qualified bench mark shall be treated as equal to the applicable stock price reduced by $10.
(E) Special year-end rule. Subparagraph (A) shall not apply to any straddle for purposes of section 1092(a) if—
  (i) the qualified covered call options referred to in such subparagraph are closed or the stock is disposed of at a loss during any taxable year,
  (ii) gain on disposition of the stock to be purchased from the taxpayer under such options or gains on such options are includible in gross income for a later taxable year, and
  (iii) such stock or option was not held by the taxpayer for 30 days or more after the closing of such options or the disposition of such stock.
For purposes of the preceding sentence, the rules of paragraphs (3) (other than subparagraph (B) thereof) and (4) of section 246(c) shall apply in determining the period for which the taxpayer holds the stock.
(F) Strike price. For purposes of this paragraph, the term "strike price" means the price at which the option is exercisable.
(G) Applicable stock price. For purposes of subparagraph (D), the term "applicable stock price" means, with respect to any stock for which an option has been granted—
  (i) the closing price of such stock on the most recent day on which such stock was traded before the date on which such option was granted, or
  (ii) the opening price of such stock on the day on which such option was granted, but only if such price is greater than 110 percent of the price determined under clause (i).
(H) Regulations. The Secretary shall prescribe such regulations as may be necessary or appropriate to carry out the purposes of this paragraph. Such regulations may include modifications to the provisions of this paragraph which are appropriate to take account of changes in the practices of option exchanges or to prevent the use of options for tax avoidance purposes.

(d) Definitions and special rules.
For purposes of this section—
(1) **Personal property.** The term "personal property" means any personal property of a type which is actively traded.
(2) **Position.** The term "position" means an interest (including a futures or forward contract or option) in personal property.

(3) **Special rules for stock.** For purposes of paragraph (1)—
  (A) In general. In the case of stock, the term "personal property" includes stock only if—
    (i) such stock is of a type which is actively traded and at least 1 of the positions offsetting such stock is a position with respect to such stock or substantially similar or related property, or
    (ii) such stock is of a corporation formed or availed of to take positions in personal property which offset positions taken by any shareholder.
  (B) Rule for application. For purposes of determining whether subsection (e) applies to any transaction with respect to stock described in subparagraph (A)(ii), all includible corporations of an affiliated group (within the meaning of section 1504(a)) shall be treated as 1 taxpayer.
(4) **Positions held by related persons, etc.**
  (A) In general. In determining whether 2 or more positions are offsetting, the taxpayer shall be treated as holding any position held by a related person.
  (B) Related person. For purposes of subparagraph (A), a person is a related person to the taxpayer if with respect to any period during which a position is held by such person, such person—
    (i) is the spouse of the taxpayer, or
    (ii) files a consolidated return (within the meaning of section 1501) with the taxpayer for any taxable year which includes a portion of such period.
  (C) Certain flowthrough entities. If part or all of the gain or loss with respect to a position held by a partnership, trust, or other entity would properly be taken into account for purposes of this chapter by a taxpayer, then, except to the extent otherwise provided in regulations, such position shall be treated as held by the taxpayer.
(5) **Special rule for section 1256 contracts.**
  (A) General rule. In the case of a straddle at least 1 (but not all) of the positions of which are section 1256 contracts, the provisions of this section shall apply to any section 1256 contract and any other position making up such straddle.
  (B) Special rule for identified straddles. For purposes of subsection (a)(2) (relating to identified straddles), subparagraph (A) and section 1256(a)(4) shall not apply to a straddle all of the offsetting positions of which consist of section 1256 contracts.
(6) **Section 1256 contract.** The term "section 1256 contract" has the meaning given such term by section 1256(b).
(7) **Special rules for foreign currency.**
  (A) Position to include interest in certain debt. For purposes of paragraph (2), an obligor's interest in a nonfunctional currency denominated debt obligation is treated as a position in the nonfunctional currency.
  (B) Actively traded requirement. For purposes of paragraph (1), foreign currency for which there is an active interbank market is presumed to be actively traded.
(8) **Special rules for physically settled positions.** For purposes of subsection (a), if a taxpayer settles a position which is part of a straddle by delivering property to which the position relates (and such position, if terminated, would result in a realization of a loss), then such taxpayer shall be treated as if such taxpayer—
  (A) terminated the position for its fair market value immediately before the settlement, and

(B) sold the property so delivered by the taxpayer at its fair market value.

(e) Exception for hedging transactions.

This section shall not apply in the case of any hedging transaction (as defined in section 1256(e)).

(f) Treatment of gain or loss and suspension of holding period where taxpayer grantor of qualified covered call option.

If a taxpayer holds any stock and grants a qualified covered call option to purchase such stock with a strike price less than the applicable stock price—

(1) Treatment of loss. Any loss with respect to such option shall be treated as long-term capital loss if, at the time such loss is realized, gain on the sale or exchange of such stock would be treated as long-term capital gain.

(2) Suspension of holding period. The holding period of such stock shall not include any period during which the taxpayer is the grantor of such option.

(g) Cross reference.

For provision requiring capitalization of certain interest and carrying charges where there is a straddle, see section 263(g).

In 2007, P.L. 110-172, Sec. 7(d)(1), deleted "and" at the end of clause (a)(2)(A)(ii), redesignated clause (a)(2)(A)(iii) as (iv) and added clause (a)(2)(A)(iii), effective for positions established on or after 10/22/2004.
—P.L. 110-172, Sec. 7(d)(2)(A), added a flush sentence at the end of subpara. (a)(2)(B), effective for straddles acquired after 12/29/2007.
—P.L. 110-172, Sec. 7(d)(2)(B)(i), substituted "positions" for "identified positions" in clause (a)(2)(A)(i) . . . Sec. 7(d)(2)(B)(ii), substituted "position" for "identified position" in clause (a)(2)(A)(ii) . . . Sec. 7(d)(2)(B)(iii), substituted "offsetting positions" for "identified offsetting positions" in clause (a)(2)(A)(ii) . . . Sec. 7(d)(2)(C), substituted "offsetting position" for "identified offsetting position" in subpara. (a)(3)(B) . . . Sec. 7(d)(3), redesignated subpara. (a)(2)(C) as (D) and added subpara. (a)(2)(C) . . . Sec. 7(d)(4), added "the rules for the application of this section to a position which is or has been a liability or obligation, methods of loss allocation which satisfy the requirements of subparagraph (A)(iii)," before "and ordering rules" in subpara. (a)(2)(D) [as redesignated by Sec. 7(d)(3) of this Act, see above], effective for positions established on or after 10/22/2004.

In 2005, P.L. 109-135, Sec. 403(ii), deleted "The Secretary shall prescribe regulations which specify the proper methods for clearly identifying a straddle as an identified straddle (and the positions comprising such straddle), which specify the rules for the application of this section for a taxpayer who fails to properly identify the positions of an identified straddle, and which specify the ordering rules in cases where a taxpayer disposes of less than an entire position which is part of an identified straddle." at the end of para. (a)(2) and added subpara. (a)(2)(C), effective for positions established on or after 10/22/2004 as if included in Sec. 888 of the American Jobs Creation Act of 2004, P.L. 108-357.

In 2004, P.L. 108-357, Sec. 888(a)(1), amended subpara. (a)(2)(A) . . . Sec. 888(a)(2)(A), amended clause (a)(2)(B)(ii) . . . Sec. 888(a)(2)(B), added a flush sentence at the end of subpara. (a)(2)(B) . . . Sec. 888(a)(3), redesignated subpara. (a)(3)(B) as subpara. (a)(3)(C) and added subpara. (a)(3)(B) . . . Sec. 888(a)(4), deleted subpara. (c)(2)(B) and redesignated subpara. (c)(2)(C) as subpara. (c)(2)(B) . . . Sec. 888(b), added para. (d)(8) . . . Sec. 888(c)(1), amended para. (d)(3), effective for positions established on or after 10/22/2004.
Prior to amendment, subpara. (a)(2)(A) read as follows:
"(A) In general. In the case of any straddle which is an identified straddle as of the close of any taxable year—
"(i) paragraph (1) shall not apply for such taxable year, and
"(ii) any loss with respect to such straddle shall be treated as sustained not earlier than the day on which all of the positions making up the straddle are disposed of."
Prior to amendment, clause (a)(2)(B)(ii) read as follows:
"(ii) all of the original positions of which (as identified by the taxpayer) are acquired on the same day and with respect to which—
"(I) all of such positions are disposed of on the same day during the taxable year, or
"(II) none of such positions has been disposed of as of the close of the taxable year, and"
Prior to deletion, subpara. (c)(2)(B) read as follows:
"(B) One side larger than other side. If 1 or more positions offset only a portion of 1 or more other positions, the Secretary shall by regulations prescribe the method for determining the portion of such other positions which is to be taken into account for purposes of this section."
Prior to amendment, para. (d)(3) read as follows:
"(3) Special rules for stock. For purposes of paragraph (1)—
"(A) In general. Except as provided in subparagraph (B), the term 'personal property' does not include stock. The preceding sentence shall not apply to any interest in stock.

"(B) Exceptions. The term 'personal property' includes—
"(i) any stock which is part of a straddle at least 1 of the offsetting positions of which is—
"(I) an option with respect to such stock or substantially identical stock or securities,
"(II) a securities futures contract (as defined in section 1234B) with respect to such stock or substantially identical stock or securities, or
"(III) under regulations, a position with respect to substantially similar or related property (other than stock), and
"(ii) any stock of a corporation formed or availed of to take positions in personal property which offset positions taken by any shareholder.
"(C) Special rules.
"(i) For purposes of subparagraph (B), subsection (c) and paragraph (4) shall be applied as if stock described in clause (i) or (ii) of subparagraph (B) were personal property.
"(ii) For purposes of determining whether subsection (e) applies to any transaction with respect to stock described in clause (ii) of subparagraph (B), all includible corporations of an affiliated group (within the meaning of section 1504(a)) shall be treated as 1 taxpayer."

In 2000, P.L. 106-554, Sec. 1(a)(7), [which enacted into law Sec. 401(e) of P.L. 106-554] deleted "or" at the end of subclause (d)(3)(B)(i)(I), redesignated subclause (d)(3)(B)(i)(II) as (III), and added subclause (d)(3)(B)(i)(II), effective 12/21/2000.

In 1999, P.L. 106-170, Sec. 532(c)(1)(F), substituted "section 1221(a)" for "section 1221" in subclause (a)(3)(B)(ii)(II), effective for any instrument held, acquired, or entered into, any transaction entered into, and supplies held or acquired on or after 12/17/99.

In 1997, P.L. 105-34, Sec. 1271(b)(9), substituted "The" for "Except for purposes of section 851(b)(3), the" in para. (f)(2), effective for tax. yrs. begin. after 8/5/97.

In 1988, P.L. 100-647, Sec. 6130(c), added subpara. (b)(2)(D), effective for forward contracts, future contracts, options, and similar instruments entered into or acquired after 10/21/88.

In 1986, P.L. 99-514, Sec. 331(a)(1), added "or the stock is disposed of at a loss" after "closed" in clause (c)(4)(E)(i) . . . Sec. 331(a)(2), substituted "or gains on such options are" for "is" in clause (c)(4)(E)(ii) . . . Sec. 331(a)(3), added "or option" after "stock" and "or the disposition of such stock" after "options" in clause (c)(4)(E)(iii), effective for positions established on or after 1/1/87.
—P.L. 99-514, Sec. 1261(b), added para. (d)(7), effective for tax. yrs. begin. after 12/31/86. Sec. 1261(e)(2) of this Act provides:
"(2) Special rules for purposes of sections 902 and 960. For purposes of applying sections 902 and 960 of the Internal Revenue Code of 1986, the amendments made by this section shall apply to—
"(A) earnings and profits of the foreign corporation for taxable years beginning after December 31, 1986, and
"(B) foreign taxes paid or accrued by the foreign corporation with respect to such earnings and profits."
—P.L. 99-514, Sec. 1808(c), added the last sentence to subpara. (d)(3)(A), effective for positions established on or after 12/31/83, in tax. yrs. end. after 12/31/83. For special rule, see Sec. 101(e)(2) of P.L. 98-369, reproduced below.
—P.L. 99-514, Sec. 1808(d), amended Sec. 108 of P.L. 98-369, reproduced below, by substituting "if such loss is incurred in a trade or business, or if such transaction entered into for profit though not connected with a trade or business" for "if such position is part of a transaction entered into for profit" in para. (a)(2); by amending Sec. 108(b); by substituting in Sec. 108(c) "(c) Net Losses Allowed." for "(c) Net loss allowed whether or not transaction entered into for profit."; by amending Sec. 108(f) and Sec. 108(h).
Prior to amendment, Sec. 108(b) of P.L. 98-369 read as follows:
"(b) Presumption that transaction entered into for profit.
"For purposes of subsection (a), any position held by a commodities dealer or any person regularly engaged in investing in regulated futures contracts shall be rebuttably presumed to be part of a transaction entered into for profit."
Prior to amendment, Sec. 108(f) of P.L. 98-369 read as follows:
"(f) Commodities dealer.
"For purposes of this section, the term 'commodities dealer' has the meaning given to such term by section 1402(i)(2)(B) of the Internal Revenue Code of 1954 (as added by this subtitle)."
Prior to amendment, Sec. 108(h) of P.L. 98-369 read as follows:
"(h) Syndicates.
"Subsection (b) shall not apply to any syndicate (as defined in section 1256(e)(3)(B) of the Internal Revenue Code of 1954."
—P.L. 99-514, Sec. 1899A(66), added "(as such paragraphs (4) and (5) are amended by this section and section 102)" after "(4), and (5)" [Sec. 101(d) and 102(e)(2) amendments precede Sec. 101(b)(2) amendments] to Sec. 101(b)(2) of P.L. 98-369, which amended subsec. (d), see below.

In 1984, P.L. 98-369, Sec. 101(a)(1), amended para. (d)(2) . . . Sec. 101(a)(2), added para. (c)(4) . . . Sec. 101(b)(1), deleted "(other than stock)" after "personal property" in para. (d)(1) . . . Sec. 101(b)(2), redesignated paras. (d)(3), (d)(4), and (d)(5) [as amended by Sec. 101(d) and 102(e)(2) of this Act, see below] as paras. (d)(4), (d)(5), and (d)(6), and added new para. (d)(3), effective for positions established after 12/31/83, in tax. yrs. end. after 12/31/83. Sec. 101(e)(2) of the Act provides the following special rule:
"(2) Special rule for offsetting position stock.—In the case of any stock of a corporation formed or availed of to take positions in personal property which offset positions taken by any shareholder, the amendments made by this section shall apply to positions established on or after May 23, 1983, in taxable years ending on or after such date."

Code Sec. 1092 — Straddles

Prior to amendment, para. (d)(2) read as follows:

"(2) Position.

"(A) In general. The term 'position' means an interest (including a futures or forward contract or option) in personal property.

"(B) Special rule for stock options. The term 'position' includes any stock option which is a part of a straddle and which is an option to buy or sell stock which is actively traded, but does not include a stock option which—

"(i) is traded on a domestic exchange or on a similar foreign exchange designated by the Secretary, and

"(ii) is of a type with respect to which the maximum period during which such option may be exercised is less than the minimum period for which a capital asset must be held for gain to be treated as long-term capital gain under section 1222(3)."

—P.L. 98-369, Sec. 101(c), redesignated subsec. (f) as subsec. (g) and added new subsec. (f), effective for positions established after 6/30/84, in tax. yrs. end. after 6/30/84.

—P.L. 98-369, Sec. 101(d), amended para. (d)(4) [sic (d)(5), redesignated by Sec. 101(b)(2), see above], effective for positions established after 7/18/84 in tax. yrs. end. after 7/18/84.

Prior to amendment, para. (d)(4) [sic (d)(5)] read as follows:

"(4)[sic (5)] Special rule for regulated futures contracts. In the case of a straddle at least 1 (but not all) of the positions of which are regulated futures contracts, the provisions of this section shall apply to any regulated futures contract and any other position making up such straddle."

—P.L. 98-369, Sec. 102(e)(2), amended para. (d)(5) [before redesignation by Sec. 101(b)(2), see above], effective for positions established after 7/18/84 in tax. yrs. end. after 7/18/84. For special rules and elections, see Sec. 102(g),(h) and (i) of this Act reproduced in note following Code Sec. 1256.

Prior to amendment, para. (d)(5) [sic (d)(6)] read as follows:

"(5)[sic (6)] Regulated futures contract. The term 'regulated futures contract' has the same meaning given such term by section 1256(b)."

—P.L. 98-369, Sec. 103(a), amended subsec. (b), effective as provided by Secs. 103(b) and (c) of this Act, which read as follows:

"(b) Requirement that regulations be issued within 6 months after the date of enactment [7/18/84]. — The Secretary of the Treasury or his delegate shall prescribe initial regulations under section 1092(b) of the Internal Revenue Code of 1954 (including regulations relating to mixed straddles) not later than the date 6 months after the date of the enactment of this Act [7/18/84].

"(c) Effective date of regulations with respect to mixed straddles.— The regulations described in subsection (b) with respect to the application of section 1233 of the Internal Revenue Code of 1954 to mixed straddles shall not apply to mixed straddles all of the positions of which were established before January 1, 1984."

Prior to amendment, subsec. (b) read as follows:

"(b) Character of gain or loss; wash sales.

"Under regulations prescribed by the Secretary, in the case of gain or loss with respect to any position of a straddle, rules which are similar to the rules of subsections (a) and (d) of section 1091 and of subsections (b) and (d) of section 1233 and which are consistent with the purposes of this section shall apply."

—P.L. 98-369, Sec. 107(a), amended clause (a)(2)(B)(i), effective for positions entered into after 7/18/84, in tax. yrs. end. after 7/18/84.

Prior to amendment, clause (a)(2)(B)(i) read as follows:

"(i) which is clearly identified on the taxpayer's records, before the close of the day on which the position is acquired, as an identified straddle."

—P.L. 98-369, Sec. 108, [as amended by Sec. 1808(d) of P.L. 99-514, see above] provides:

"SEC. 108. TREATMENT OF CERTAIN LOSSES ON STRADDLES ENTERED INTO BEFORE EFFECTIVE DATE OF ECONOMIC RECOVERY TAX ACT OF 1981.

"(a) General rule.

"For purposes of the Internal Revenue Code of 1954, in the case of any disposition of 1 or more positions—

"(1) which were entered into before 1982 and form part of a straddle, and

"(2) to which the amendments made by title V of the Economic Recovery Tax Act of 1981 do not apply,

any loss from such disposition shall be allowed for the taxable year of the disposition if such loss is incurred in a trade or business, or if such loss in incurred in a transaction entered into for profit though not connected with a trade or business.

"(b) Loss incurred in a trade or business.

"For purposes of subsection (a), any loss incurred by a commodities dealer in the trading of commodities shall be treated as a loss incurred in a trade or business.

"(c) Net losses allowed.

"If any loss with respect to a position described in paragraphs (1) and (2) of subsection (a) is not allowable as a deduction (after applying subsections (a) and (b)), such loss shall be allowed in determining the gain or loss from dispositions of other positions in the straddle to the extent required to accurately reflect the taxpayer's net gain or loss from all positions in such straddle.

"(d) Other rules.

"Except as otherwise provided in subsections (a) and (c) and in sections 1233 and 1234 of such Code, the determination of whether there is recognized gain or loss with respect to a position, and the amount and timing of such gain or loss, and the treatment of such gain or loss as long-term or short-term shall be made without regard to whether such position constitutes part of a straddle.

"(e) Straddle.

"For purposes of this section, the term 'straddle' has the meaning given to such term by section 1092(c) of the Internal Revenue Code of 1954 as in effect on the day after the date of the enactment of the Economic Recovery Tax Act of 1981,

and shall include a straddle all the positions of which are regulated futures contracts.

"(f) Commodities dealer.

"For purposes of this section, the term 'commodities dealer' means any taxpayer who—

"(1) at any time before January 1, 1982, was an individual described in section 1402(i)(2)(B) of the Internal Revenue Code of 1954 (as added by this subtitle), or

"(2) was a member of the family (within the meaning of section 704(e)(3) of such Code) of an individual described in paragraph (1) to the extent such member engaged in commodities trading through an organization the members of which consisted solely of—

"(A) 1 or more individuals described in paragraph (1), and

"(B) 1 or more members of the families (as so defined) of such individuals.

"(g) Regulated futures contracts.

"For purposes of this section, the term 'regulated futures contracts' has the meaning given to such term by section 1256(b) of the Internal Revenue Code of 1954 (as in effect before the date of enactment of this Act [7/18/84]).

"(h) Syndicates.

"For purposes of this section, any loss incurred by a person (other than a commodities dealer) with respect to an interest in a syndicate (within the meaning of section 1256(e)(3)(B) of the Internal Revenue Code of 1954) shall not be considered to be a loss incurred in a trade or business."

In 1983, P.L. 97-448, Sec. 105(a)(1)(A), substituted "unrecognized gain" for "unrealized gain" in subpara. (a)(1)(A) . . . Sec. 105(a)(1)(B), amended so much of para. (a)(3) as precedes subpara. (a)(3)(B) . . . Sec. 105(a)(1)(C), amended subclauses (a)(3)(B)(i)(I) and (a)(3)(B)(i)(II) . . . Sec. 105(a)(2), amended subpara. (a)(1)(A) . . . Sec. 105(a)(3), amended para. (d)(4) . . . Sec. 105(a)(4), substituted "subsection (a)(2)(B)" for "subsection (a)(3)(B)" in subpara. (c)(2)(C), effective for property acquired and positions established by the taxpayer after 6/23/81, in tax. yrs. end. after 6/23/81.

Prior to amendment, so much of para. (a)(3) as precedes subpara. (a)(3)(B) read as follows:

"(3) Unrealized gain. For purposes of this subsection—

"(A) In general. The term 'unrealized gain' means the amount of gain which would be taken into account with respect to any position held by the taxpayer as of the close of the taxable year if such position were sold on the last business day of such taxable year at its fair market value."

Prior to amendment, subclauses (a)(3)(B)(i)(I) and (a)(3)(B)(i)(II) read as follows:

"(I) each position (whether or not part of a straddle) which is held by such taxpayer as of the close of the taxable year and with respect to which there is unrealized gain, and

"(II) the amount of such unrealized gain."

Prior to amendment, subpara. (a)(1)(A) [as amended by Sec. 105(a)(1)(A) of the Act] read as follows:

"(A) In general. Any loss with respect to 1 or more positions shall be taken into account for any taxable year only to the extent that the amount of such loss exceeds the unrecognized gain (if any) with respect to 1 or more positions which—

"(i) were acquired by the taxpayer before the disposition giving rise to such loss,

"(ii) were offsetting positions with respect to the 1 or more positions from which the loss arose, and

"(iii) were not part of an identified straddle as of the close of the taxable year."

Prior to amendment, para. (d)(4) read as follows:

"(4) Special rule for regulated futures contracts. In the case of a straddle—

"(A) at least 1 (but not all) of the positions of which are regulated futures contracts, and

"(B) with respect to which the taxpayer has elected not to have the provisions of section 1256 apply,

the provisions of this section shall apply to any regulated futures contract and any other position making up such straddle."

In 1981, P.L. 97-34, Sec. 501(a), added Code Sec. 1092, effective for property acquired and positions established by the taxpayer after 6/23/81 in tax. yrs. ending after 6/23/81. Sec. 508(c) of this Act provides:

"(c) Election with respect to property held on June 23, 1981.

"If the taxpayer so elects (at such time and in such manner as the Secretary of the Treasury or his delegate shall prescribe) with respect to all regulated futures contracts or positions held by the taxpayer on June 23, 1981, the amendments made by this title shall apply to all such contracts and positions, effective for periods after such date in taxable years ending after such date. For purposes of the preceding sentence, the term 'regulated futures contract' has the meaning given to such term by section 1256(b) of the Internal Revenue Code of 1954, and the term 'position' has the meaning given to such term by section 1092(d)(2) of such Code."

PART VIII. REPEALED [DISTRIBUTIONS PURSUANT TO BANK HOLDING COMPANY ACT]

Sec.

1101. Repealed [Distributions pursuant to Bank Holding Company Act.]

1102. Repealed [Special rules.]

1103. Repealed [Definitions.]

Special basis rules

Code Sec. 1101

In 1990, P.L. 101-508, Sec. 11801(a)(34), repealed Part VIII of Subchapter O of Chapter 1.
In 1976, P.L. 94-452, Sec. 2(a), added the table of Code Secs. for Part VIII, effective 10/1/77 for distributions after 7/7/70 in tax. yrs. end. after 7/7/70.
Prior to amend. the table read as follows:
"PART VIII.— DISTRIBUTIONS PURSUANT TO BANK HOLDING COMPANY ACT OF 1956
"Sec.
"1101. Distributions pursuant to Bank Holding Company Act of 1956.
"1102. Special rules.
"1103. Definitions."
In 1956, added Part VIII.

Sec. 1101. Repealed.

In 1990, P.L. 101-508, Sec. 11801(a)(34), repealed Code Sec. 1101, as part of the repeal of part VIII of subchapter O of chapter 1, effective 11/5/90 except as provided in Sec. 11821(b) of this Act, which reads as follows:
"(b) Savings provision.
"If—
"(1) any provision amended or repealed by this part applied to—
"(A) any transaction occurring before the date of the enactment of this Act [11/5/90],
"(B) any property acquired before such date of enactment [11/5/90] or
"(C) any item of income, loss, deduction, or credit taken into account before such date of enactment [11/5/90] and
"(2) the treatment of such transaction, property, or item under such provision would (without regard to the amendments made by this part) affect liability for tax for periods ending after such date of enactment [11/5/90],
nothing in the amendments made by this part shall be construed to affect the treatment of such transaction, property or item for purposes of determining liability for tax for periods ending after such date of enactment [11/5/90]."
Prior to repeal, Code Sec. 1101 read as follows:
"SEC. 1101. DISTRIBUTIONS PURSUANT TO BANK HOLDING COMPANY ACT.
"(a) Distributions of certain non-banking property.
"(1) Distributions of prohibited property. If—
"(A) a qualified bank holding corporation distributes prohibited property (other than stock received in an exchange to which subsection (c)(2) applies)—
"(i) to a shareholder (with respect to its stock held by such shareholder), without the surrender by such shareholder of stock in such corporation, or
"(ii) to a shareholder, in exchange for its preferred stock, or
"(iii) to a security holder, in exchange for its securities, and
"(B) the Board has, before the distribution, certified that the distribution of such prohibited property is necessary or appropriate to effectuate section 4 of the Bank Holding Company Act,
then no gain to the shareholder or security holder from the receipt of such property shall be recognized.
"(2) Distributions of stock and securities received in an exchange to which subsection (c)(2) applies. If—
"(A) a qualified bank holding corporation distributes—
"(i) common stock received in an exchange to which subsection (c)(2) applies to a shareholder (with respect to its stock held by such shareholder), without the surrender by such shareholder of stock in such corporation, or
"(ii) common stock received in an exchange to which subsection (c)(2) applies to a shareholder, in exchange for its common stock, or
"(iii) preferred stock or common stock received in an exchange to which subsection (c)(2) applies to a shareholder, in exchange for its preferred stock, or
"(iv) securities or preferred or common stock received in an exchange to which subsection (c)(2) applies to a security holder in exchange for its securities, and
"(B) any preferred stock received has substantially the same terms as the preferred stock exchanged, and any securities received have substantially the same terms as the securities exchanged,
then, except as provided in subsection (f), no gain to the shareholder or security holder from the receipt of such stock or such securities or such stock and securities shall be recognized.
"(3) Pro rata and other requirements.
"(A) In general. Paragraphs (1) and (2) of this subsection, or paragraphs (1) and (2) of subsection (b), as the case may be, shall apply to any distribution to the shareholders of a qualified bank holding corporation only if each distribution—
"(i) which is made by such corporation to its shareholders after July 7, 1970, and on or before the date on which the Board makes its final certification under subsection (e), and
"(ii) to which such paragraph (1) or (2) applies (determined without regard to this paragraph),
meets the requirements of subparagraph (B), (C), or (D).
"(B) Pro rata requirements. A distribution meets the requirements of this subparagraph if the distribution is pro rata with respect to all shareholders of the distributing qualified bank holding corporation or with respect to all shareholders of common stock of such corporation.
"(C) Redemptions when uniform offer is made. A distribution meets the requirements of this subparagraph if the distribution is in exchange for stock of the distributing qualified bank holding corporation and such distribution is pursuant to a good faith offer made on a uniform basis to all shareholders of the distributing qualified bank holding corporation or to all shareholders of common stock of such corporation.

"(D) Non-pro rata distributions from certain closely-held corporations. A distribution meets the requirements of this subparagraph if such distribution is made by a qualified bank holding corporation which does not have more than 10 shareholders (within the meaning of section 1361(b)(1)(A)) and does not have as a shareholder a person (other than an estate) which is not an individual, and if the Board (after consultation with the Secretary) certifies that—
"(i) a distribution which meets the requirements of subparagraph (B) or (C) is not appropriate to effectuate section 4 or the policies of the Bank Holding Company Act, and
"(ii) the distribution being made is necessary or appropriate to effectuate section 4 of the policies of such Act.
"(4) Exception. This subsection shall not apply to any distribution by a corporation if such corporation, a corporation having control of such corporation, or a subsidiary of such corporation has made any distribution pursuant to subsection (b) or has made an election under section 6158 with respect to bank property (as defined in section 6158(f)(3)).
"(5) Distributions involving gift or compensation. In the case of a distribution to which paragraph (1) or (2) applies but which—
"(A) results in a gift, see section 2501 and following, or
"(B) has the effect of the payment of compensation, see section 61.
"(b) Corporation ceasing to be a bank holding company.
"(1) Distributions of property which cause a corporation to be a bank holding company. If—
"(A) a qualified bank holding corporation distributes property (other than stock received in an exchange to which subsection (c)(3) applies)—
"(i) to a shareholder (with respect to its stock held by such shareholder), without the surrender by such shareholder of stock in such corporation, or
"(ii) to a shareholder, in exchange for its preferred stock, or
"(iii) to a security holder, in exchange for its securities, and
"(B) the Board has, before the distribution, certified that—
"(i) such property is all or part of the property by reason of which such corporation controls (within the meaning of section 2(a) of the Bank Holding Company Act) a bank or bank holding company or such property is part of the property by reason of which such corporation did control a bank or a bank holding company before any property of the same kind was distributed under this subsection or exchanged under subsection (c)(3), and
"(ii) the distribution is necessary or appropriate to effectuate the policies of such Act,
then no gain to the shareholder or security holder from the receipt of such property shall be recognized.
"(2) Distributions of stock and securities received in an exchange to which subsection (c)(3) applies. If—
"(A) a qualified bank holding corporation distributes—
"(i) common stock received in an exchange to which subsection (c)(3) applies to a shareholder (with respect to its stock held by such shareholder), without the surrender by such shareholder of stock in such corporation, or
"(ii) common stock received in an exchange to which subsection (c)(3) applies to a shareholder in exchange for its common stock, or
"(iii) preferred stock or common stock received in an exchange to which subsection (c)(3) applies to a shareholder, in exchange for its preferred stock, or
"(iv) securities or preferred or common stock received in an exchange to which subsection (c)(3) applies to a security holder, in exchange for its securities, and
"(B) any preferred stock received has substantially the same terms as the preferred stock exchanged, and any securities received have substantially the same terms as the securities exchanged,
then, except as provided in subsection (f), no gain to the shareholder or security holder from the receipt of such stock or such securities or such stock and securities shall be recognized.
"(3) Pro rata and other requirements. For pro rata and other requirements, see subsection (a)(3).
"(4) Exception. This subsection shall not apply to any distribution by a corporation if such corporation, a corporation having control of such corporation, or a subsidiary of such corporation has made any distribution pursuant to subsection (a) or has made an election under section 6158 with respect to prohibited property.
"(5) Distributions involving gift or compensation. In the case of a distribution to which paragraph (1) or (2) applies but which—
"(A) results in a gift, see section 2501 and following, or
"(B) has the effect of the payment of compensation, see section 61.
"(c) Property acquired after July 7, 1970.
"(1) In general. Except as provided in paragraphs (2) and (3), subsection (a) or (b) shall not apply to—
"(A) any property acquired by the distributing corporation after July 7, 1970, unless (i) gain to such corporation with respect to the receipt of such property was not recognized by reason of subsection (a) or (b), or (ii) such property was received by it in exchange for all of its stock in an exchange to which paragraph (2) or (3) applies, or (iii) such property was acquired by the distributing corporation in a transaction in which gain was not recognized under section 305(a) or section 332, or under section 354 or 356 (but only with respect to property permitted by section 354 or 356 to be received without the recognition of gain or loss) with respect to a reorganization described in section 368(a)(1)(A), (B), (E), or (F), or
"(B) any property which was acquired by the distributing corporation in a distribution with respect to stock acquired by such corporation after July 7, 1970, unless such stock was acquired by such corporation (i) in a distribution (with respect to stock held by it on July 7, 1970, or with respect to stock in respect of which all previous applications of this clause are satisfied) with respect to which gain to it was not recognized by reason of subsection (a) or (b), or (ii) in exchange for all

of its stock in an exchange to which paragraph (2) or (3) applies, or (iii) in a transaction in which gain was not recognized under section 305(a) or section 332, or under section 354 or 356 (but only with respect to property permitted by section 354 or 356 to be received without the recognition of gain or loss) with respect to a reorganization described in section 368(a)(1)(A), (B), (E), or (F), or

"(C) any property acquired by the distributing corporation in a transaction in which gain was not recognized under section 332, unless such property was acquired from a corporation which, if it had been a qualified bank holding corporation, could have distributed such property under subsection (a)(1) or (b)(1), or

"(D) any property acquired by the distributing corporation in a transaction in which gain was not recognized under section 354 or 356 with respect to a reorganization described in section 368(a)(1)(A) or (B), unless such property was acquired by the distributing corporation in exchange for property which the distributing corporation could have distributed under subsection (a)(1) or (b)(1).

"(2) Exchanges involving prohibited property. If—

"(A) any qualified bank holding corporation exchanges (i) property, which, under subsection (a)(1), such corporation could distribute directly to its shareholders or security holders without the recognition of gain to such shareholders or security holders, and other property (except property described in subsection (b)(1)(B)(i)), for (ii) all of the stock of a second corporation created and availed of solely for the purpose of receiving such property.

"(B) immediately after the exchange, the qualified bank holding corporation distributes all of such stock in a manner prescribed in subsection (a)(2)(A), and

"(C) before such distribution, the Board has certified (with respect to the property exchanged which consists of property which, under subsection (a)(1), such corporation could distribute directly to its shareholders or security holders without the recognition of gain) that the exchange and distribution are necessary or appropriate to effectuate section 4 of the Bank Holding Company Act,
then paragraph (1) shall not apply with respect to such distribution.

"(3) Exchanges involving interests in banks. If—

"(A) any qualified bank holding corporation exchanges (i) property which, under subsection (b)(1), such corporation could distribute directly to its shareholders or security holders without the recognition of gain to such shareholders or security holders, and other property (except prohibited property), for (ii) all of the stock of a second corporation created and availed of solely for the purpose of receiving such property.

"(B) immediately after the exchange, the qualified bank holding corporation distributes all of such stock in a manner prescribed in subsection (b)(2)(A), and

"(C) before such distribution, the Board has certified (with respect to the property exchanged which consists of property which, under subsection (b)(1), such corporation could distribute directly to its shareholders or security holders without the recognition of gain) that—

"(i) such property is all or part of the property by reason of which such corporation controls (within the meaning of section 2(a) of the Bank Holding Company Act) a bank or bank holding company, or such property is part of the property by reason of which such corporation did control a bank or a bank holding company before any property of the same kind was distributed under subsection (b)(1) or exchanged under this paragraph, and

"(ii) the exchange and distribution are necessary or appropriate to effectuate the policies of such Act,
then paragraph (1) shall not apply with respect to such distribution.

"(d) Distribution to avoid federal income tax.

"(1) Prohibited property. Subsection (a) shall not apply to a distribution if, in connection with such distribution, the distributing corporation retains, or transfers after July 7, 1970 to any corporation, property (other than prohibited property) as part of a plan one of the principal purposes of which is the distribution of the earnings and profits of any corporation.

"(2) Banking property. Subsection (b) shall not apply to a distribution if, in connection with such distribution, the distributing corporation retains, or transfers after July 7, 1970 to any corporation, property (other than property described in subsection (b)(1)(B)(i)) as part of a plan one of the principal purposes of which is the distribution of the earnings and profits of any corporation.

"(e) Final certification.

"(1) For subsection (a). Subsection (a) shall not apply with respect to any distribution by a corporation unless the Board certifies, before the close of the calendar year following the calendar year in which the last distribution occurred, that the corporation has (before the expiration of the period prohibited property is permitted under the Bank Holding Company Act to be held by a bank holding company) disposed of all of the property the disposition of which is necessary or appropriate to effectuate section 4 of the Bank Holding Company Act.

"(2) For subsection (b). Subsection (b) shall not apply with respect to any distribution by a corporation unless the Board certifies, before the close of the calendar year following the calendar year in which the last distribution occurred, that the corporation has (before the expiration of the period prohibited property is permitted under the Bank Holding Company Act to be held by a bank holding company) ceased to be a bank holding company.

"(f) Certain exchange of securities.

"In the case of an exchange described in subsection (a)(2)(A)(iv) or subsection (b)(2)(A)(iv), subsection (a) or subsection (b) (as the case may be) shall apply only to the extent that the principal amount of the securities received does not exceed the principal amount of the securities exchanged."

In 1982, P.L. 97-354, Sec. 5(a)(34), substituted "section 1361(b)(1)(A)" for "section 1371(a)(1)" in subpara. (a)(3)(D), effective for tax. yrs. begin. after 12/31/82.
In 1976, P.L. 94-455, Sec. 1906(b)(13)(A), substituted "Secretary" for "Secretary or his delegate" in subpara. (a)(3)(D), for tax. yrs. begin. after '76.
—P.L. 94-452, Sec. 2(a), amended Code Sec. 1101, effective 10/1/77 for distributions after 7/7/70 in tax. yrs. end. after 7/7/70, but only in the case of qualified bank holding corporations within the meaning of subsec. 1103(b), as amended by this Act. Secs. 2(d)(2) and (3) of this Act provide special rules as follows:

"(2) Special rule for certifying distributions which have already taken place.—For purposes of sections 1101(a)(1)(B), 1101(a)(3)(D), 1101(b)(1)(B), 1101(c)(2)(C), 1101(c)(3)(C), and 1101(e) of the Internal Revenue Code of 1954 (as amended by subsection (a) of this section), in the case of any distribution which takes place on or before the 90th day after the date of the enactment of this Act, a certification by the Federal Reserve Board described in any such section shall be treated as made before the distribution (or, in the case of section 1101(e), before the close of the calendar year following the calendar year in which the last distribution occurred) if application for such certification is made before the close of the 90th day after the date of the enactment of this Act.

"(3) Period of limitations.—If refund or credit of any overpayment of income tax attributable to the amendment made by subsection (a) is prevented at any time before October 1, 1978, by the operation of any law or rule of law, refund or credit of such overpayment may, nevertheless, be made or allowed if claim therefor is filed before October 1, 1978."
Sec. 3(d) of the Act provided rules for certain successor corps., see note at Code Sec. 1103, as amended by this Act.
Prior to amendment, Code Sec. 1101 read as follows:
"SEC. 1101. DISTRIBUTIONS PURSUANT TO BANK HOLDING COMPANY ACT OF 1956.
"(a) Distributions of certain non-banking property.
"(1) Distributions of prohibited property. If—
"(A) a qualified bank holding corporation distributes prohibited property (other than stock received in an exchange to which subsection (c)(2) applies)—
"(i) to a shareholder (with respect to its stock held by such shareholder), without the surrender by such shareholder of stock in such corporation; or
"(ii) to a shareholder, in exchange for its preferred stock; or
"(iii) to a security holder, in exchange for its securities; and
"(B) the Board has, before the distribution, certified that the distribution of such prohibited property is necessary or appropriate to effectuate section 4 of the Bank Holding Company Act of 1956,
then no gain to the shareholder or security holder from the receipt of such property shall be recognized.
"(2) Distributions of stock and securities received in an exchange to which subsection (c)(2) applies. If—
"(A) a qualified bank holding corporation distributes—
"(i) common stock received in an exchange to which subsection (c)(2) applies to a shareholder (with respect to its stock held by such shareholder), without the surrender by such shareholder of stock in such corporation; or
"(ii) common stock received in an exchange to which subsection (c)(2) applies to a shareholder, in exchange for its common stock; or
"(iii) preferred stock or common stock received in an exchange to which subsection (c)(2) applies to a shareholder, in exchange for its preferred stock; or
"(iv) securities or preferred or common stock received in an exchange to which subsection (c)(2) applies to a security holder, in exchange for its securities; and
"(B) any preferred stock received has substantially the same terms as the preferred stock exchanged, and any securities received have substantially the same terms as the securities exchanged,
then, except as provided in subsection (f), no gain to the shareholder or security holder from the receipt of such stock or such securities or such stock and securities shall be recognized.
"(3) Non pro rata distributions. Paragraphs (1) and (2) shall apply to a distribution whether or not the distribution is pro rata with respect to all of the shareholders of the distributing qualified bank holding corporation.
"(4) Exception. This subsection shall not apply to any distribution by a corporation which has made any distribution pursuant to subsection (b).
"(5) Distributions involving gift or compensation. In the case of a distribution to which paragraph (1) or (2) applies, but which—
"(A) results in a gift, see section 2501, and following, or
"(B) has the effect of the payment of compensation, see section 61(a)(1).
"(b) Corporation ceasing to be a bank holding company.
"(1) Distributions of property which cause a corporation to be a bank holding company. If—
"(A) a qualified bank holding corporation distributes property (other than stock received in an exchange to which subsection (c)(3) applies)—
"(i) to a shareholder (with respect to its stock held by such shareholder), without the surrender by such shareholder of stock in such corporation; or
"(ii) to a shareholder, in exchange for its preferred stock; or
"(iii) to a security holder, in exchange for its securities; and
"(B) the Board has, before the distribution, certified that—
"(i) such property is all or part of the property by reason of which such corporation controls (within the meaning of section 2(a) of the Bank Holding Company Act of 1956) a bank or bank holding company, or such property is part of the property by reason of which such corporation did control a bank or a bank holding company before any property of the same kind was distributed under this subsection or exchanged under subsection (c)(3); and
"(ii) the distribution is necessary or appropriate to effectuate the policies of such Act, then no gain to the shareholder or security holder from the receipt of such property shall be recognized.
"(2) Distributions of stock and securities received in an exchange to which subsection (c)(3) applies. If—
"(A) a qualified bank holding corporation distributes—
"(i) common stock received in an exchange to which subsection (c)(3) applies to a shareholder (with respect to its stock held by such shareholder), without the surrender by such shareholder of stock in such corporation; or

"(ii) common stock received in an exchange to which subsection (c)(3) applies to a shareholder, in exchange for its common stock; or

"(iii) preferred stock or common stock received in an exchange to which subsection (c)(3) applies to a shareholder, in exchange for its preferred stock; or

"(iv) securities or preferred or common stock received in an exchange to which subsection (c)(3) applies to a security holder, in exchange for its securities; and

"(B) any preferred stock received has substantially the same terms as the preferred stock exchanged, and any securities received have substantially the same terms as the securities exchanged,

then, except as provided in subsection (f), no gain to the shareholder or security holder from the receipt of such stock or such securities or such stock and securities shall be recognized.

"(3) Non pro rata distributions. Paragraphs (1) and (2) shall apply to a distribution whether or not the distribution is pro rata with respect to all of the shareholders of the distributing qualified bank holding corporation.

"(4) Exception. This subsection shall not apply to any distribution by a corporation which has made any distribution pursuant to subsection (a).

"(5) Distributions involving gift or compensation. In the case of a distribution to which paragraph (1) or (2) applies, but which—

"(A) results in a gift, see section 2501, and following, or

"(B) has the effect of the payment of compensation, see section 61(a)(1).

"(c) Property acquired after May 15, 1955.

"(1) In general. Except as provided in paragraphs (2) and (3), subsection (a) or (b) shall not apply to—

"(A) any property acquired by the distributing corporation after May 15, 1955, unless (i) gain to such corporation with respect to the receipt of such property was not recognized by reason of subsection (a) or (b), or (ii) such property was received by it in exchange for all of its stock in an exchange to which paragraph (2) or (3) applies, or (iii) such property was acquired by the distributing corporation in a transaction in which gain was not recognized under section 305(a) or section 332, or under section 354 with respect to a reorganization described in section 368(a)(1)(E) or (F), or

"(B) any property which was acquired by the distributing corporation in a distribution with respect to stock acquired by such corporation after May 15, 1955, unless such stock was acquired by such corporation (i) in a distribution (with respect to stock held by it on May 15, 1955, or with respect to stock in respect of which all previous applications of this clause are satisfied) with respect to which gain to it was not recognized by reason of subsection (a) or (b), or (ii) in exchange for all of its stock in an exchange to which paragraph (2) or (3) applies, or (iii) in a transaction in which gain was not recognized under section 305(a) or section 332, or under section 354 with respect to a reorganization described in section 368(a)(1)(E) or (F), or

"(C) any property acquired by the distributing corporation in a transaction in which gain was not recognized under section 332, unless such property was acquired from a corporation which, if it had been a qualified bank holding corporation, could have distributed such property under subsection (a)(1) or (b)(1).

"(2) Exchanges involving prohibited property. If—

"(A) any qualified bank holding corporation exchanges (i) property, which, under subsection (a)(1), such corporation could distribute directly to its shareholders or security holders without the recognition of gain to such shareholders or security holders, and other property (except property described in subsection (b)(1)(B)(i)), for (ii) all of the stock of a second corporation created and availed of solely for the purpose of receiving such property;

"(B) immediately after the exchange, the qualified bank holding corporation distributes all of such stock in a manner prescribed in subsection (a)(2)(A); and

"(C) before such exchange, the Board has certified (with respect to the property exchanged which consists of property which, under subsection (a)(1) such corporation could distribute directly to its shareholders or security holders without the recognition of gain) that the exchange and distribution are necessary or appropriate to effectuate section 4 of the Bank Holding Company Act of 1956,

then paragraph (1) shall not apply with respect to such distribution.

"(3) Exchanges involving interests in banks. If—

"(A) any qualified bank holding corporation exchanges (i) property which, under subsection (b)(1), such corporation could distribute directly to its shareholders or security holders without the recognition of gain to such shareholders or security holders, and other property (except prohibited property), for (ii) all of the stock of a second corporation created and availed of solely for the purpose of receiving such property;

"(B) immediately after the exchange, the qualified bank holding corporation distributes all of such stock in a manner prescribed in subsection (b)(2)(A); and

"(C) before such exchange, the Board has certified (with respect to the property exchanged which consists of property which, under subsection (b)(1), such corporation could distribute directly to its shareholders or security holders without the recognition of gain) that—

"(i) such property is all or part of the property by reason of which such corporation controls (within the meaning of section 2(a) of the Bank Holding Company Act of 1956) a bank or bank holding company, or such property is part of the property by reason of which such corporation did control a bank or a bank holding company before any property of the same kind was distributed under subsection (b)(1) or exchanged under this paragraph; and

"(ii) the exchange and distribution are necessary or appropriate to effectuate the policies of such Act,

then paragraph (1) shall not apply with respect to such distribution.

"(d) Distributions to avoid Federal income tax.

"(1) Prohibited property. Subsection (a) shall not apply to a distribution if, in connection with such distribution, the distributing corporation retains, or transfers after May 15, 1955, to any corporation, property (other than prohibited property) as part of a plan one of the principal purposes of which is the distribution of the earnings and profits of any corporation.

"(2) Banking property. Subsection (b) shall not apply to a distribution if, in connection with such distribution, the distributing corporation retains, or transfers after May 15, 1955, to any corporation, property (other than property described in subsection (b)(1)(B)(i)) as part of a plan one of the principal purposes of which is the distribution of the earnings and profits of any corporation.

"(3) Certain contributions to capital. In the case of a distribution a portion of which is attributable to a transfer which is a contribution to the capital of a corporation, made after May 15, 1955, and prior to the date of the enactment of this part, if subsection (a) or (b) would apply to such distribution but for the fact that, under paragraph (1) or (2) (as the case may be) of this subsection, such contribution to capital is part of a plan one of the principal purposes of which is to distribute the earnings and profits of any corporation, then, notwithstanding paragraph (1) or (2), subsection (a) or (b) (as the case may be) shall apply to that portion of such distribution not attributable to such contribution to capital, and shall not apply to that portion of such distribution attributable to such contribution to capital.

"(e) Final certification.

"(1) For subsection (a). Subsection (a) shall not apply with respect to any distribution by a corporation unless the Board certifies that, before the expiration of the period permitted under section 4(a) of the Bank Holding Company Act of 1956 (including any extensions thereof granted to such corporation under such section 4(a)), the corporation has disposed of all the property the disposition of which is necessary or appropriate to effectuate section 4 of such Act (or would have been so necessary or appropriate if the corporation had continued to be a bank holding company).

"(2) For subsection (b).

"(A) Subsection (b) shall not apply with respect to any distribution by any corporation unless the Board certifies that, before the expiration of the period specified in subparagraph (B), the corporation has ceased to be a bank holding company.

"(B) The period referred to in subparagraph (A) is the period which expires 2 years after the date of the enactment of this part or 2 years after the date on which the corporation becomes a bank holding company, whichever date is later. The Board is authorized, on application by any corporation, to extend such period from time to time with respect to such corporation for not more than one year at a time if, in its judgment, such an extension would not be detrimental to the public interest; except that such period may not in any case be extended beyond the date 5 years after the date of the enactment of this part or 5 years after the date on which the corporation becomes a bank holding company, whichever date is later.

"(f) Certain exchanges of securities.

"In the case of an exchange described in subsection (a)(2)(A)(iv) or subsection (b)(2)(A)(iv), subsection (a) or subsection (b) (as the case may be) shall apply only to the extent that the principal amount of the securities received does not exceed the principal amount of the securities exchanged."

In 1956, P.L. 511, Sec. 10, added Code Sec. 1101, effective for tax. yrs. end. after 5/9/56.

Sec. 1102. Repealed.

In 1990, P.L. 101-508, Sec. 11801(a)(34), repealed Code Sec. 1102, as part of the repeal of part VIII of subchapter O of chapter 1, effective 11/5/90 except as provided in Sec. 11821(b) of this Act, reproduced in note following Code Sec. 1101. Prior to repeal, Code Sec 1102 read as follows:

"SEC. 1102. SPECIAL RULES.

"(a) Basis of property acquired in distributions.

"If, by reason of section 1101, gain is not recognized with respect to the receipt of any property, then, under regulations prescribed by the Secretary—

"(1) if the property is received by a shareholder with respect to stock without the surrender by such shareholder of stock, the basis of the property received and of the stock with respect to which it is distributed shall, in the distributee's hands, be determined by allocating between such property and such stock the adjusted basis of such stock, or

"(2) if the property is received by a shareholder in exchange for stock or by a security holder in exchange for securities, the basis of the property received shall, in the distributee's hands, be the same as the adjusted basis of the stock or securities exchanged, increased by the amount of gain to the taxpayer recognized on the property received.

"(b) Periods of limitation.

"The periods of limitation provided in section 6501 (relating to limitations on assessment and collection) shall not expire, with respect to any deficiency (including interest and additions to the tax) resulting solely from the receipt of property by shareholders in a distribution which is certified by the Board under subsection (a), (b), or (c) of section 1101, until 5 years after the distributing corporation notifies the Secretary (in such manner and with such accompanying information as the Secretary may by regulations prescribe)—

"(1) that the final certification required by subsection (e) of section 1101 has been made, or

"(2) that such final certification will not be made;

and such assessment may be made notwithstanding any provision of law or rule of law which would otherwise prevent such assessment.

"(c) Allocation of earnings and profits.

"(1) Distribution of stock in a controlled corporation. In the case of a distribution by a qualified bank holding corporation under section 1101(a)(1) or (b)(1) of stock in a controlled corporation, proper allocation with respect to the earning and profits of the distributing corporation and the controlled corporation shall be made under regulations prescribed by the Secretary.

"(2) Exchanges described in section 1101(c)(2) or (3). In the case of any exchange described in section 1101(c)(2) or (3), proper allocation with respect to the earnings and profits of the corporation transferring the property and the corporation receiving such property shall be made under regulations prescribed by the Secretary.

"(3) Definition of controlled corporation. For purposes of paragraph (1), the term 'controlled corporation' means a corporation with respect to which at least 80 percent of the total combined voting power of all classes of stock entitled to vote and at least 80 percent of the total number of shares of all other classes of stock is owned by the distributing qualified bank holding corporation.

"(d) Itemization of property.

"In any certification under this part, the Board shall make such specification and itemization of property as may be necessary to carry out the provisions of this part."

In 1976, P.L. 94-452, Sec. 2(a), amended Code Sec. 1102, effective 10/1/77 for distributions after 7/7/70 in tax. yrs. end. after 7/7/70, but only in the case of qualified bank holding corps. within the meaning of subsec. 1103(b), as amended by this Act. Sec. 2(d)(3) of the Act provided as follows:

"(3) Period of limitations. If refund or credit of any overpayment of income tax attributable to the amendment made by subsection (a) is prevented at any time before October 1, 1978, by the operation of any law or rule of law, refund or credit of such overpayment may, nevertheless, be made or allowed if claim therefor is filed before October 1, 1978."

Prior to amendment, Code Sec. 1102 read as follows:

"SEC. 1102. SPECIAL RULES.

"(a) Basis of property acquired in distributions.

"If, by reason of section 1101, gain is not recognized with respect to the receipt of any property, then, under regulations prescribed by the Secretary—

"(1) if the property is received by a shareholder with respect to stock, without the surrender by such shareholder of stock, the basis of the property received and of the stock with respect to which it is distributed shall, in the distributee's hands, be determined by allocating between such property and such stock the adjusted basis of such stock; or

"(2) if the property is received by a shareholder in exchange for stock or by a security holder in exchange for securities, the basis of the property received shall, in the distributee's hands, be the same as the adjusted basis of the stock or securities exchanged, increased by—

"(A) the amount of the property received which was treated as a dividend, and

"(B) the amount of gain to the taxpayer recognized on the property received (not including any portion of such gain which was treated as a dividend).

"(b) Periods of limitation.

"The periods of limitation provided in section 6501 (relating to limitations on assessment and collection) shall not expire, with respect to any deficiency (including interest and additions to the tax) resulting solely from the receipt of property by shareholders in a distribution which is certified by the Board under subsection (a), (b), or (c) of section 1101, until five years after the distributing corporation notifies the Secretary (in such manner and with such accompanying information as the Secretary may by regulations prescribe) that the period (including extensions thereof) prescribed in section 4(a) of the Bank Holding Company Act of 1956, or section 1101(e)(2)(B), whichever is applicable, has expired; and such assessment may be made notwithstanding any provision of law or rule of law which would otherwise prevent such assessment.

"(c) Allocation of earnings and profits.

"(1) Distribution of stock in a controlled corporation. In the case of a distribution by a qualified bank holding corporation under section 1101(a)(1) or (b)(1) of stock in a controlled corporation, proper allocation with respect to the earnings and profits of the distributing corporation and the controlled corporation shall be made under regulations prescribed by the Secretary.

"(2) Exchanges described in section 1101(c)(2) or (3). In the case of any exchange described in section 1101(c)(2) or (3), proper allocation with respect to the earnings and profits of the corporation transferring the property and the corporation receiving such property shall be made under regulations prescribed by the Secretary.

"(3) Definition of controlled corporation. For purposes of paragraph (1), the term 'controlled corporation' means a corporation with respect to which at least 80 percent of the total combined voting power of all classes of stock entitled to vote and at least 80 percent of the total number of shares of all other classes of stock is owned by the distributing qualified bank holding corporation.

"(d) Itemization of property.

"In any certification under this part, the Board shall make such specification and itemization of property as may be necessary to carry out the provisions of this part.

"(e) Certain bank holding companies.

"This part shall apply in respect of any company which becomes a bank holding company as a result of the enactment of the Act entitled 'An Act to amend the Bank Holding Company Act of 1956', approved July 1, 1966 (P.L. 89-485), with the following modifications:

"(1) Subsections (a)(3) and (b)(3) of section 1101 shall not apply.

"(2) Subsections (a)(1) and (2) and (b)(1) and (2) of section 1101 shall apply in respect of distributions to shareholders of the distributing bank holding corporation only if all distributions to each class of shareholders which are made—

"(A) after April 12, 1965, and

"(B) on or before the date on which the Board of Governors of the Federal Reserve System makes its final certification under section 1101(e), are pro rata. For purposes of the preceding sentence, any redemption of stock made in whole or in part with property other than money shall be treated as a distribution.

"(3) In applying subsections (c) and (d) of section 1101 and subsection (b) of section 1103, the date 'April 12, 1965' shall be substituted for the date 'May 15, 1955'.

"(4) In applying subsection (d)(3) of section 1101, the date of the enactment of this subsection shall be treated as being the date of the enactment of this part.

"(5) In applying subsection (b)(2)(A) of section 1103, thereference to the Bank Holding Company Act of 1956 shall be treated as referring to such Act as amended by P.L. 89-485."

—P.L. 94-455, Sec. 1906(b)(13)(A), substituted "Secretary" for "Secretary or his delegate" each place it appeared in Code Sec. 1102, effective for tax. yrs. begin. after 12/31/76.

In 1967, P.L. 90-225, Sec. 1(a), added Code Sec. 1102(e), effective for distributions made after 12/27/67 in tax. yrs. end. after 12/27/67.

In 1956, P.L. 511, Sec. 10, added Code Sec. 1102, effective for tax. yrs. end. after 5/9/56.

Sec. 1103. Repealed.

In 1990, P.L. 101-508, Sec. 11801(a)(34), repealed Code Sec. 1103, as part of the repeal of part VIII of subchapter O of chapter 1, effective 11/5/90 except as provided in Sec. 11821(b) of this Act, reproduced in note following Code Sec. 1101. Prior to repeal, Code Sec. 1103 read as follows:

"SEC. 1103. DEFINITIONS

"(a) Bank holding company; Bank Holding Company Act.

"For purposes of this part—

"(1) Bank holding company. The term 'bank holding company' means—

"(A) a bank holding company within the meaning of section 2(a) of the Bank Holding Company Act, or

"(B) a bank holding company subsidiary within the meaning of section 2(d) of such Act.

"(2) Bank Holding Company Act. The term 'Bank Holding Company Act' means the Bank Holding Company Act of 1956, as amended through December 31, 1970 (12 U.S.C. 1841 et seq.).

"(b) Qualified bank holding corporation.

"(1) In general. Except as provided in paragraph (2), for purposes of this part the term 'qualified bank holding corporation' means any corporation (as defined in section 7701(a)(3)) which is a bank holding company and which holds prohibited property acquired by it—

"(A) on or before July 7, 1970,

"(B) in a distribution in which gain to such corporation with respect to the receipt of such property was not recognized by reason of subsection (a) or (b) of section 1101, or

"(C) in exchange for all of its stock in an exchange described in section 1101(c)(2) or (c)(3).

"(2) Limitations.

"(A) A bank holding company shall not be a qualified bank holding corporation, unless it would have been a bank holding company on July 7, 1970, if the Bank Holding Company Act Amendments of 1970 had been in effect on such date, or unless it is a bank holding company determined solely by reference to—

"(i) property acquired by it on or before July 7, 1970,

"(ii) property acquired by it in a distribution in which gain to such corporation with respect to the receipt of such property was not recognized by reason of subsection (a) or (b) of section 1101, or

"(iii) property acquired by it in exchange for all of its stock in an exchange described in section 1101(c)(2) or (3).

For purposes of this subparagraph, property held by a corporation having control of the corporation or by a subsidiary of the corporation shall be treated as held by the corporation.

"(B) A bank holding company shall not be a qualified bank holding corporation by reason of property described in subparagraph (B) of paragraph (1) or clause (ii) of subparagraph (A) of this paragraph, unless such property was acquired in a distribution with respect to stock, which stock was acquired by such bank holding company—

"(i) on or before July 7, 1970,

"(ii) in a distribution (with respect to stock held by it on July 7, 1970, or with respect to stock in respect of which all previous applications of this clause are satisfied) with respect to which gain to it was not recognized by reason of subsection (a) or (b) of section 1101, or

"(iii) in exchange for all of its stock in an exchange described in section 1101(c)(2) or (3).

"(C) A corporation shall be treated as a qualified bank holding corporation only if the Board certifies that it satisfies the foregoing requirements of this subsection.

"(3) Certain successor corporations. For purposes of this subsection, a successor corporation in a reorganization described in section 368(a)(1)(F) shall succeed to the status of its predecessor corporation as a qualified bank holding corporation.

"(c) Prohibited property.

"For purposes of this part, the term 'prohibited property' means, in the case of any bank holding company, property (other than nonexempt property) the disposition of which would be necessary or appropriate to effectuate section 4 of the Bank Holding Company Act if such company continued to be a bank holding company beyond the period (including any extensions thereof) specified in subsection (a) of such section. The term 'prohibited property' also includes shares of any company not in excess of 5 percent of the outstanding voting shares of such company if the prohibitions of section 4 of such Act apply to the shares of such company in excess of such 5 percent.

"(d) Nonexempt property.

Special basis rules — Part IX

"For purposes of this part, the term 'nonexempt property' means—

"(1) obligations (including notes, drafts, bills of exchange, and bankers' acceptances) having a maturity at the time of issuance of not exceeding 24 months, exclusive of days of grace;

"(2) securities issued by or guaranteed as to principal or interest by a government or subdivision thereof or by any instrumentality of a government or subdivision, or

"(3) money, and the right to receive money not evidenced by a security or obligation (other than a security or obligation described in paragraph (1) or (2)).

"(e) Board.

"For purposes of this part, the term 'Board' means the Board of Governors of the Federal Reserve System.

"(f) Control; subsidiary.

"For purposes of this part—

"(1) Control Except as provided in section 1102(c)(3), a corporation shall be treated as having control of another corporation if such corporation has control (within the meaning of section 2(a)(2) of the Bank Holding Company Act) of such other corporation.

"(2) Subsidiary. The term 'subsidiary' has the meaning given to such term by section 2(d) of the Bank Holding Company Act.

"(g) Election to forego grandfather provision for all property representing pre-June 30, 1968, activities.

"Any bank holding company may elect, for purposes of this part and section 6158, to have the determination of whether property is property described in subsection (c) or is property eligible to be distributed without recognition of gain under section 1101(b)(1) made under the Bank Holding Company Act as if such Act did not contain the proviso of section 4(a)(2) thereof. Any election under this subsection shall apply to all property described in such proviso and shall be made at such time and in such manner as the Secretary may by regulations prescribe. Any such election, once made, shall be irrevocable. An election under this subsection or subsection (h) shall not apply unless the final certification referred to in section 1101(e) or section 6158(c)(2), as the case may be, includes a certification by the Board that the bank holding company has disposed of either all banking property or all nonbanking property.

"(h) Election to divest all banking or nonbanking property in case of certain closely held bank holding companies.

"Any bank holding company may elect, for purposes of this part and section 6158, to have the determination of whether property is property described in subsection (c) or is property eligible to be distributed without recognition of gain under section 1101(b)(1) made under the Bank Holding Company Act as if such Act did not contain clause (ii) of section 4(c) of such Act. Any election under this subsection shall apply to all property described in subsection (c), or to all property eligible to be distributed without recognition of gain under section 1101(b)(1), as the case may be, and shall be made at such time and in such manner as the Secretary may by regulations prescribe. Any such election, once made, shall be irrevocable."

In 1976, P.L. 94-455, Sec. 1906(b)(13)(A), substituted "Secretary" for "Secretary or his delegate" each place it appeared in Code Sec. 1103, effective for tax. yrs. begin. after 12/31/76.

—P.L. 94-452, Sec. 2(a), amended Code Sec. 1103, effective 10/1/77 for distributions after 7/7/70 in tax. yrs. end. after 7/7/70, but only in the case of qualified bank holding corps. within the meaning of subsec. (b). Sec. 2(d)(3) of this Act provides as follows:

"(3) Period of limitations. If refund or credit of any overpayment of income tax attributable to the amendment made by subsection (a) is prevented at any time before October 1, 1978, by the operation of any law or rule of law, refund or credit of such overpayment may, nevertheless, be made or allowed if claim therefor is filed before October 1, 1978."

Sec. 3(d) of this Act provides:

"(d) Applicability to certain successor corporations.

"If, after July 7, 1970, and before August 1, 1974—

"(1) a corporation acquires substantially all of the properties of a qualified bank holding corporation (as defined in section 1103(b) of the Internal Revenue Code of 1954) in a transaction described in sections 368(a)(1)(A) and 368(a)(2)(D), or

"(2) the acquiring corporation (or a corporation in control of the acquiring corporation) acquires beneficial interests in shares described in section 2(g)(2) of the Bank Holding Company Act (as defined in section 1103(a)(2) of the Internal Revenue Code of 1954) in a transaction to which section 351 applies,

then, the acquiring corporation or a corporation which is in control (within the meaning of section 2(a)(2) of such Act) of the acquiring corporation or a subsidiary (within the meaning of section 2(d) of such Act) of the corporation so in control) shall be treated as a qualified bank holding corporation for purposes of section 1103(b) and 6158 of the Internal Revenue Code of 1954 and the shares described in such section 2(g)(2) shall be considered property which is acquired by such corporation, for purposes of section 1101(c)(1)(A)(iii) of the Internal Revenue Code of 1954, after July 7, 1970."

Prior to amendment, Code Sec. 1103 read as follows:

"SEC. 1103. DEFINITIONS.

"(a) Bank holding company.

"For purposes of this part, the term 'bank holding company' has the meaning assigned to such term by section 2 of the Bank Holding Company Act of 1956.

"(b) Qualified bank holding corporation.

"(1) In general. Except as provided in paragraph (2), for purposes of this part the term 'qualified bank holding corporation' means any corporation (as defined in section 7701(a)(3)) which is a bank holding company and which holds prohibited property acquired by it—

"(A) on or before May 15, 1955,

"(B) in a distribution in which gain to such corporation with respect to the receipt of such property was not recognized by reason of subsection (a) or (b) of section 1101, or

"(C) in exchange for all of its stock in an exchange described in section 1101(c)(2) or (c)(3).

"(2) Limitations.

"(A) A bank holding company shall not be a qualified bank holding corporation, unless it would have been a bank holding company on May 15, 1955, if the Bank Holding Company Act of 1956 had been in effect on such date, or unless it is a bank holding company determined solely by reference to—

"(i) property acquired by it on or before May 15, 1955,

"(ii) property acquired by it in a distribution in which gain to such corporation with respect to the receipt of such property was not recognized by reason of subsection (a) or (b) of section 1101, and

"(iii) property acquired by it in exchange for all of its stock in an exchange described in section 1101(c)(2) or (3).

"(B) A bank holding company shall not be a qualified bank holding corporation by reason of property described in subparagraph (B) of paragraph (1) or clause (ii) of subparagraph (A) of this paragraph, unless such property was acquired in a distribution with respect to stock, which stock was acquired by such bank holding company—

"(i) on or before May 15, 1955,

"(ii) in a distribution (with respect to stock held by it on May 15, 1955, or with respect to stock in respect of which all previous applications of this clause are satisfied) with respect to which gain to it was not recognized by reason of subsection (a) or (b) of section 1101, or

"(iii) in exchange for all of its stock in an exchange described in section 1101(c)(2) or (3).

"(C) A corporation shall be treated as a qualified bank holding corporation only if the Board certifies that it satisfies the foregoing requirements of this subsection.

"(c) Prohibited property.

"For the purposes of this part, the term 'prohibited property' means, in the case of any bank holding company, property (other than nonexempt property) the disposition of which would be necessary or appropriate to effectuate section 4 of the Bank Holding Company Act of 1956 if such company continued to be a bank holding company beyond the period (including any extensions thereof) specified in subsection (a) of such section or in section 1101(e)(2)(B) of this part, as the case may be. The term 'prohibited property' does not include shares of any company held by a bank holding company to the extent that the prohibitions of section 4 of the Bank Holding Company Act of 1956 do not apply to the ownership by such bank holding company of such property by reason of subsection (c)(5) of such section.

"(d) Nonexempt property.

"For purposes of this part, the term 'nonexempt property' means—

"(1) obligations (including notes, drafts, bills of exchange, and bankers' acceptances) having a maturity at the time of issuance of not exceeding 24 months, exclusive of days of grace;

"(2) securities issued by or guaranteed as to principal or interest by a government or subdivision thereof or by any instrumentality of a government or subdivision; or

"(3) money, and the right to receive money not evidenced by a security or obligation (other than a security or obligation described in paragraph (1) or (2)).

"(e) Board.

"For purposes of this part, the term 'Board' means the Board of Governors of the Federal Reserve System."

In 1956, P.L. 511, Sec. 10, added Code Sec. 1103, effective for tax. yrs. end. after 5/9/56.

PART IX. Repealed.

In 1976, P.L. 94-455, Sec. 1901(a)(134), repealed Part IX, for tax. yrs. begin. after '76.

Prior to repeal, Part IX read as follows:

"PART IX—DISTRIBUTIONS PURSUANT TO ORDERS ENFORCING THE ANTITRUST LAWS

"Sec.

"1111. Distribution of stock pursuant to order enforcing the antitrust laws.

"SEC. 1111. DISTRIBUTION OF STOCK PURSUANT TO ORDER ENFORCING THE ANTITRUST LAWS.

"(a) General rule.

"Notwithstanding sections 301, 312, and 316, a distribution of divested stock (as defined in subsection (e)), to a qualifying shareholder (as defined in subsection (b)), to which section 301(c)(1) would, but for this section, apply, shall be a distribution which is not out of the earnings and profits of the distributing corporation for purposes of this subtitle.

"(b) Qualifying shareholder.

"For purposes of this section, the term 'qualifying shareholder' means any shareholder other than a corporation which may be allowed a deduction under section 243, 244, or 245 with respect to dividends received.

"(c) Special rules.

"(1) Distributions to avoid federal income tax. Subsection (a) shall not apply to any transaction one of the principal purposes of which is the distribution of the earnings and profits of the distributing corporation or of the corporation whose stock is distributed, or both.

Part IX — Special basis rules

"(2) Stock. For purposes of this section, the term 'stock' includes rights to fractional shares.

"(d) Definition of antitrust order.

"For purposes of this section, the term 'antitrust order' means, in the case of any corporation, a final judgment rendered after January 1, 1961, by a court with respect to such corporation in a court proceeding under the Sherman Act (26 Stat. 209; 15 U.S.C. 1–7) or the Clayton Act (38 Stat. 730; 15 U.S.C. 12–27), or both, to which the United States is a party, if such proceeding was commenced on or before January 1, 1959.

"(e) Definition of divested stock.

"For purposes of this section, the term 'divested stock' means stock meeting the following requirements:

"(1) the stock is the subject of an antitrust order entered after January 1, 1961, which—

"(A) directs the distributing corporation to divest itself of such stock by distributing it to its shareholders (or requires such distribution as an alternative to other action by any person);

"(B) specifies and itemizes the stock to be divested; and

"(C) fixes the period of time within which the distributing corporation must divest itself of all stock to be disposed of by it by reason of the suit, and such period expires not later than 3 years from the date on which such order becomes final (appeal time having run or appeal having been completed); and

"(2) the court finds—

"(A) that the divestiture of such stock, in the manner described in paragraph (1)(A), is necessary or appropriate to effectuate the policies of the Sherman Act, or the Clayton Act, or both;

"(B) that the application of subsection (a) is required to reach an equitable antitrust order in such suit or proceeding; and

"(C) that the period of time for the complete divestiture fixed in the order is the shortest period within which such divestiture can be executed with due regard to the circumstances of the particular case;

"but no stock shall be divested stock if the court finds that its divestiture is required because of an intentional violation of the Sherman Act, or the Clayton Act, or both."

In **1962**, P.L. 87-403, Sec. 1(a), added Code Sec. 1111, for distributions made after 2/2/62.

Subchapter P.— Capital Gains and Losses

Part

  I. Treatment of capital gains.
  II. Treatment of capital losses.
  III. General rules for determining capital gains and losses.
  IV. Special rules for determining capital gains and losses.
  V. Special rules for bonds and other debt instruments.
  VI. Treatment of certain passive foreign investment companies.

In **1984**, P.L. 98-369, Sec. 42(b)(1), added part V.

PART I.— TREATMENT OF CAPITAL GAINS

Sec.
1201. Alternative tax for corporations.
1202. Partial exclusion for gain from certain small business stock.

In **2000**, P.L. 106-554, Sec. 1(a)(7) [which enacted into law Sec. 117(b)(3) of H.R. 5662], amended item 1202.
Prior to amendment, item 1202 read as follows:
"1202. 50-percent exclusion for gain from certain small business stock."
In **1993**, P.L. 103-66, Sec. 13113(d)(6), added item 1202.
In **1986**, P.L. 99-514, Sec. 301(a), deleted item 1202.
Prior to deletion, item 1202 read as follows:
"1202. Deduction for capital gains."
In **1978**, P.L. 95-600, Sec. 401(a)(3), amended item 1201.
Prior to amendment, item 1201 read as follows: "1201. Alternative tax."

Sec. 1201. Alternative tax for corporations.

(a) General rule.

If for any taxable year a corporation has a net capital gain and any rate of tax imposed by section 11, 511, or 831(a) or (b) (whichever is applicable) exceeds 35 percent (determined without regard to the last 2 sentences of section 11(b)(1)), then, in lieu of any such tax, there is hereby imposed a tax (if such tax is less than the tax imposed by such sections) which shall consist of the sum of—

(1) a tax computed on the taxable income reduced by the amount of the net capital gain, at the rates and in the manner as if this subsection had not been enacted, plus

(2) a tax of 35 percent of the net capital gain (or, if less, taxable income).

(b) Special rate for qualified timber gains.

(1) In general. If, for any taxable year ending after the date of the enactment of the Food, Conservation, and Energy Act of 2008 and beginning on or before the date which is 1 year after such date, a corporation has both a net capital gain and qualified timber gain—

  (A) subsection (a) shall apply to such corporation for the taxable year without regard to whether the applicable tax rate exceeds 35 percent, and

  (B) the tax computed under subsection (a)(2) shall be equal to the sum of—

    (i) 15 percent of the least of—

      (I) qualified timber gain,

      (II) net capital gain, or

      (III) taxable income, plus

    (ii) 35 percent of the excess (if any) of taxable income over the sum of the amounts for which a tax was determined under subsection (a)(1) and clause (i).

(2) Qualified timber gain. For purposes of this section, the term "qualified timber gain" means, with respect to any taxpayer for any taxable year, the excess (if any) of—

  (A) the sum of the taxpayer's gains described in subsections (a) and (b) of section 631 for such year, over

  (B) the sum of the taxpayer's losses described in such subsections for such year.

For purposes of subparagraphs (A) and (B), only timber held more than 15 years shall be taken into account.

(3) Computation for taxable years in which rate first applies or ends. In the case of any taxable year which includes either of the dates set forth in paragraph (1), the qualified timber gain for such year shall not exceed the qualified timber gain properly taken into account for—

  (A) in the case of the taxable year including the date of the enactment of the Food, Conservation, and Energy Act of 2008, the portion of the year after such date, and

  (B) in the case of the taxable year including the date which is 1 year after such date of enactment, the portion of the year on or before such later date.

(c) Cross references.

For computation of the alternative tax—

(1) in the case of life insurance companies, see section 801(a)(2),

(2) in the case of regulated investment companies and their shareholders, see section 852(b)(3)(A) and (D), and

(3) in the case of real estate investment trusts, see section 857(b)(3)(A).

In **2008**, P.L. 110-246, Sec. 4, Repeals the duplicative enactment and provides effective date provisions of the Act entitled "An Act to provide for the continuation of agricultural programs through fiscal year 2012, and for other purposes" Sec. 4, P.L. 110-246 reads as follows:

"Sec. 4. Repeal of duplicative enactment.

"(a) In General- The Act entitled 'An Act to provide for the continuation of agricultural programs through fiscal year 2012, and for other purposes' (H.R. 2419 of the 110th Congress), and the amendments made by that Act, are repealed, effective on the date of enactment of that Act.

"(b) Effective Date- Except as otherwise provided in this Act, this Act and the amendments made by this Act shall take effect on the earlier of--

"(1) the date of enactment of this Act; or

"(2) the date of the enactment of the Act entitled 'An Act to provide for the continuation of agricultural programs through fiscal year 2012, and for other purposes' (H.R. 2419 of the 110th Congress)."

—P.L. 110-246, Sec. 15311(a), redesignated subsec. (b) as subsec. (c) and added a new subsec. (b), effective for tax. yrs. end. after 5/22/2008. [Ed. Note: May 22, 2008 was the date of enactment for H.R. 2419 (PL 110-234), which was repealed

Capital gains and losses — Code Sec. 1201

by (2008 Farm Act § 4(a)) (PL 110-246, 6/18/2008), in connection with the reenactment of the farm bill to correct a technical deficiency in its original passage.]

In 1997, P.L. 105-34, Sec. 314(a), added "(or, if less, taxable income)" before the period in para. (a)(2), effective for tax. yrs. end. after 12/31/97.

In 1996, P.L. 104-188, Sec. 1703(f), substituted "last 2 sentences" for "last sentence" in subsec. (a), effective for tax. yrs. begin. on or after 1/1/93.

In 1993, P.L. 103-66, Sec. 13221(c)(2), substituted "35 percent" for "34 percent" each place it appeared in subsec. (a), effective for tax. yrs. begin. on or after 1/1/93.

In 1988, P.L. 100-647, Sec. 1003(c)(1), substituted "831(a) or (b)" for "831(a)" in subsec. (a), effective for tax. yrs. begin. after 12/31/86.

— P.L. 100-647, Sec. 1004(b)(1), added "before October 1, 1987," after "from the sale" in Sec. 406 of P.L. 99-514 [reproduced below] . . . Sec. 1004(b)(2), substituted "to the extent such gain is properly taken into account under the taxpayer's method of accounting during 1987." for "to the extent such gain is properly taken into account under the taxpayer's method of accounting after January 1, 1987, and before September 1, 1987." in Sec. 406 of P.L. 99-514 [reproduced below].

— P.L. 100-647, Sec. 1010(a)(2)(A), substituted "any market discount bond (as defined in section 1278 of the Internal Revenue Code of 1986)" for "any bond" in Sec. 1011(d)(1) of P.L. 99-514 [reproduced below] . . . Sec. 1010(a)(2)(B), substituted "31.6 percent" for "28 percent" in Sec. 1011(d)(1) of P.L. 99-514 [reproduced below] . . . Sec. 1010(a)(2)(C), added the sentence at the end of Sec. 1011(d)(1) of P.L. 99-514 [reproduced below] . . . Sec. 1010(a)(3), amended Sec. 1011(d)(2) of P.L. 99-514 [reproduced below].

Prior to amendment Sec. 1011(d)(2) of P.L. 99-514 read as follows:

"(2) Qualified life insurance company. For purposes of paragraph (1) the term 'qualified life insurance company' means any of the following companies: Aetna, Provident Life and Accident, Massachusetts Mutual, Mutual Benefit, Connecticut Mutual, Phoenix Mutual, John Hancock, New England Life, Pennsylvania Mutual, Transamerica, Northwestern, Provident Mutual, Prudential, Mutual of Omaha, and Metropolitan."

— P.L. 100-647, Sec. 2004(l), substituted "section 11(b)(1)" for "section 11(b)" in subsec. (a), effective for tax. yrs. begin. after 12/31/87.

In 1986, P.L. 99-514, Sec. 311(a), amended Code Sec. 1201 [as amended by Sec. 1024(c)(14) of this Act, see below] effective for tax. yrs. begin. after 12/31/86. Sec. 311(d) of this Act provides transitional rules as follows:

"(d) Transitional rules. —

"(1) Taxable years which begin in 1986 and end in 1987. — In the case of any taxable year which begins before January 1, 1987, and ends on or after such date, paragraph (2) of section 1201(a) of the Internal Revenue Code of 1954, as in effect on the date before the date of enactment of this Act, shall be applied as if it read as follows:

"(2) the sum of —

"(A) 28 percent of the lesser of —

"(i) the net capital gain determined by taking into account only gain or loss which is properly taken into account for the portion of the taxable year before January 1, 1987, or

"(ii) the net capital gain for the taxable year, and

"(B) 34 percent of the excess (if any) of —

"(i) the net capital gain for the taxable year, over

"(ii) the amount of the net capital gain taken into account under subparagraph (A).

"(2) Revocation of elections under section 631(a). — Any election under section 631(a) of the Internal Revenue Code of 1954 made (whether by a corporation or a person other than a corporation) for a taxable year beginning before January 1, 1987, may be revoked by the taxpayer for any taxable year ending after December 31, 1986. For purposes of determining whether the taxpayer may make a further election under such section, such election (and any revocation under this paragraph) shall not be taken into account."

— P.L. 99-514, Sec. 406, [as amended by Secs. 1004(b)(1) and (2) of Sec. 100-647, see above] of this Act provides as follows:

"SEC. 406. RETENTION OF CAPITAL GAINS TREATMENT FOR SALES OF DAIRY CATTLE UNDER MILK PRODUCTION TERMINATION PROGRAM.

"The amendments made by subtitles A and B of title III [Sec. 301 and 302] shall not apply to any gain from the sale before October 1, 1987 of dairy cattle under a valid contract with the United States Department of Agriculture under the milk production termination program to the extent such gain is properly taken into account under the taxpayer's method of accounting during 1987."

Prior to amendment, Code Sec. 1201 [as amended by Sec. 1024(c)(14) of this Act, see below] read as follows:

"SEC. 1201. ALTERNATIVE TAX FOR CORPORATIONS.

"(a) Corporations.

"If for any taxable year a corporation has a net capital gain, then, in lieu of the tax imposed by sections 11, 511, 831(a) or (b), there is hereby imposed a tax (if such tax is less than the tax imposed by such sections) which shall consist of the sum of —

"(1) a tax computed on the taxable income reduced by the amount of the net capital gain, at the rates and in the manner as if this subsection had not been enacted, plus

"(2) a tax of 28 percent of the net capital gain.

"(b) Cross references.

"For computation of the alternative tax —

"(1) in the case of life insurance companies, see section 801(a)(2);

"(2) in the case of regulated investment companies and their shareholders, see section 852(b)(3)(A) and (D); and

"(3) in the case of real estate investment trusts, see section 857(c)(3)(A)."

"(c) Transitional rule.

If for any taxable year ending after December 31, 1978 and beginning before January 1, 1980, a corporation has a net capital gain, then subsection (a) shall be applied by substituting for the language of paragraph (2) the following:

"(2)(A) a tax of 28 percent of the lesser of —

"(i) the net capital gain for the taxable year, or

"(ii) the net capital gain taking into account only gain or loss properly taken into account for the portion of the taxable year after December 31, 1978, plus

"(B) a tax of 30 percent of the excess of —

"(i) the net capital gains for the taxable year, over

"(ii) the amount of net capital gain taken into account under subparagraph (A)."

— P.L. 99-514, Sec. 1011(d), [as amended by Sec. 1010(a)(2) of P.L. 100-647 and (3), see above] provides:

"(d) Treatment of certain market discount bonds. —

"(1) In general. Notwithstanding the amendments made by subtitle B of title III, any gain recognized by a qualified life insurance company on the redemption at maturity of any market discount bond (as defined in section 1278 of the Internal Revenue Code of 1986) which was issued before July 19, 1984, and acquired by such company on or before September 25, 1985, shall be subject to tax at the rate of 31.6 percent. The preceding sentence shall apply only if the tax determined under the preceding sentence is less than the tax which would otherwise be imposed.

"(2) Qualified life insurance company. For purposes of paragraph (1), the term 'qualified life insurance company' means any life insurance company subject to tax under part I of subchapter L of chapter 1 of the Internal Revenue Code of 1986."

— P.L. 99-514, Sec. 1024(c)(14), substituted "831(a) or (b)" for "821(a) or (c) and 831(a)" in subsec. (a) [before amendment by Sec. 311(a) of this Act, see above], effective for tax. yrs. begin. after 12/31/86.

In 1984, P.L. 98-369, Sec. 211(b)(16), substituted "section 801(a)(2)" for "section 802(a)(2)" in para. (b)(1), effective for tax. yrs. begin. after 12/31/83.

In 1983, P.L. 97-448, Sec. 101(aa), amended Sec. 102(b)(1)(B)(ii) of P.L. 97-34 by substituting "qualified net capital gain (or, if lesser, the alternative minimum taxable income within the meaning of section 55(b)(1) of such Code)" for "qualified net capital gain", see below.

In 1981, P.L. 97-34, Sec. 102, provides as follows:

"SEC. 102. 20-PERCENT MAXIMUM RATE ON NET CAPITAL GAIN FOR PORTION OF 1981.

"(a) In general.

"If for any taxable year ending after June 9, 1981, and beginning before January 1, 1982, a taxpayer other than a corporation has qualified net capital gain, then the tax imposed under section 1 of the Internal Revenue Code of 1954 for such taxable year shall be equal to the lesser of —

"(1) the tax imposed under such section determined without regard to this subsection, or

"(2) the sum of —

"(A) the tax imposed under such section on the excess of —

"(i) the taxable income of the taxpayer, over

"(ii) 40 percent of the qualified net capital gain of the taxpayer, and

"(B) 20 percent of the qualified net capital gain.

"(b) Application with alternative minimum tax.

"(1) In general. If subsection (a) applies to any taxpayer for any taxable year, then the amount determined under section 55(a)(1) of the Internal Revenue Code of 1954 for such taxable year shall be equal to the lesser of —

"(A) the amount determined under such section 55(a)(1) determined without regard to this subsection, or

"(B) the sum of —

"(i) the amount which would be determined under such section 55(a)(1) if the alternative minimum taxable income was the excess of —

"(I) the alternative minimum taxable income (within the meaning of section 55(b)(1) of such Code) of the taxpayer, over

"(II) the qualified net capital gain of the taxpayer, and

"(ii) 20 percent of the qualified net capital gain (or, if lesser, the alternative minimum taxable income within the meaning of section 55(b)(1) of such Code).

"(2) No credits allowable. No portion of section 55(c) of such Code, no credit allowable under subpart A of part IV of subchapter A of chapter 1 of such Code (other than section 33(a) of such Code) shall be allowable against the amount described in paragraph (1)(B)(i).

"(c) Qualified net capital gain.

"(1) In general. For purposes of this section, the term 'qualified net capital gain' means the lesser of —

"(A) the net capital gain for the taxable year, or

"(B) the net capital gain for the taxable year taking into account only gain or loss from sales or exchanges occurring after June 9, 1981.

"(2) Net capital gain. For purposes of this subsection, the term 'net capital gain' has the meaning given such term by section 1222(11) of the Internal Revenue Code of 1954.

"(d) Special rule for pass-thru entities.

"(1) In general. In applying subsections (a), (b), and (c) with respect to any pass-thru entity, the determination of when a sale or exchange has occurred shall be made at the entity level.

"(2) Pass-thru entity defined. For purposes of paragraph (1), the term 'pass-thru entity' means —

"(A) a regulated investment company,

"(B) a real estate investment trust,

"(C) an electing small business corporation,

"(D) a partnership,

Code Sec. 1201 — Capital gains and losses

"(E) an estate or trust, and
"(F) a common trust fund."

In 1980, P.L. 96-222, Sec. 104(a)(2)(B)(i), substituted "the excess of the net capital gain over the deduction under section 1202" for "50 percent of the net capital gain" in para. (b)(1) [before amendment by Secs. 401(a)(1) and (2) of P.L. 95-600, see below]... Sec. 104(a)(2)(B)(ii), amended subsec. (c) [before amendment by Secs. 401(a)(1) and (2) of P.L. 95-600, see below], effective for tax. yrs. begin. in 1978. Sec. 104(a)(2)(C) of this Act provides as follows:

"(C) Special rule for pass-through entities.
"(i) In general. In applying sections 1201(c)(2)(A)(ii) and 1202(c)(1)(B) of the Internal Revenue Code of 1954 with respect to any pass-through entity, the determination of the period for which gain or loss is properly taken into account shall be made at the entity level.
"(ii) Pass-through entity defined. For purposes of clause (i), the term 'pass-through entity' means—
"(I) a regulated investment company,
"(II) a real estate investment trust,
"(III) an electing small business corporation,
"(IV) a partnership,
"(V) an estate or trust, and
"(VI) a common trust fund."

—P.L. 96-222, Sec. 104(a)(3)(A)(i), substituted "(c) Transitional rule.—If for any taxable year ending after December 31, 1978, and beginning before January 1, 1980," for "(c) Taxable years which include January 1, 1979. If for any taxable year beginning before January 1, 1979, and ending after December 31, 1978" in subsec. (c)... Sec. 104(a)(3)(A)(ii), amended clause (c)(2)(A)(ii), effective for tax. yrs. end. after 12/31/78.
Prior to amendment, clause (c)(2)(A)(ii) read as follows:
"(ii) the net capital gain taking into account only sales and exchanges after December 31, 1978, plus"

In 1978, P.L. 95-600, Sec. 401(a)(1), deleted subsecs. (b) and (c)... Sec. 401(a)(2), redesignated subsec. (d) as subsec. (b)... Sec. 401(a)(3), amended the heading of Code Sec. 1201, effective for tax. yrs. begin. after 12/31/78.
Prior to amendment, the heading of Code Sec. 1201 read as follows:
"Sec. 1201. ALTERNATIVE TAX."
Prior to deletion, subsecs. (b) and (c) [as amended by Sec. 104(a)(2)(B) of P.L. 96-222, see above] read as follows:
"(b) Other taxpayers. If for any taxable year a taxpayer other than a corporation has a net capital gain, then, in lieu of the tax imposed by sections 1 and 511, there is hereby imposed a tax (if such tax is less than the tax imposed by such sections) which shall consist of the sum of—
"(1) a tax computed on the taxable income reduced by an amount equal to the excess of the net capital gain over the deduction under section 1202, at the rate and in the manner as if this subsection has not been enacted,
"(2) a tax of 25 percent of the lesser of—
"(A) the sum of the long-term capital gains for the taxable year, but not to exceed $50,000 ($25,000 in the case of a married individual filing a separate return), or
"(B) the amount of the net capital gain, and
"(3) if the amount of the net capital gain exceeds the sum referred to in subparagraph (A), a tax computed as provided in subsection (c) on such excess.
"(c) Computation of tax where capital gain exceeds $50,000. The tax computed for purposes of subsection (b)(3) shall be the amount by which a tax determined under section 1 or 511 on an amount equal to the taxable income (but not less than the excess of the net capital gain over the deduction under section 1202) for the taxable year exceeds a tax determined under section 1 or 511 on an amount equal to the sum of
"(1) the amount subject to tax under subsection (b)(1), plus
"(2) an amount determined by multiplying the sum referred to in subsection (b)(2)(A) by a fraction
"(A) the numerator of which is the excess of the net capital gain over the deduction under section 1202, and
"(B) the denominator of which is the net capital gain."
—P.L. 95-600, Sec. 403(a), substituted "28 percent" for "30 percent" in para. (a)(2)... Sec. 403(b), added new subsec. (c), effective for tax. yrs. end. after 12/31/78.

In 1976, P.L. 94-455, Sec. 1901(a)(135)(A), amended subsec. (a)... Sec. 1901(a)(135)(B), amended subsec. (c)... Sec. 1901(a)(135)(C)(i), deleted subsec. (d) and redesignated subsec. (e) as subsec. (d)... Sec. 1901(a)(135)(C)(ii), substituted "the sum of the long-term capital gains for the taxable year, but not to exceed $50,000 ($25,000 in the case of a married individual filing a separate return)" for "the amount of the subsection (d) gain" in subpara. (b)(2)(A)... Sec. 1901(a)(135)(C)(iii), substituted "the sum referred to in subparagraph (A)" for "the amount of the subsection (d) gain" in para. (b)(3)... Sec. 1901(b)(33)(L), substituted "net capital gain" for "net section 1201 gain" each place it appeared in subsec. (b), effective for tax. yrs. begin. after 12/31/76.
Prior to amendment, subsec. (a) read as follows:
"(a) Corporations.
"If for any taxable year a corporation has a net section 1201 gain, then, in lieu of the tax imposed by sections 11, 511, 821(a)or (c), and 831(a), there is hereby imposed a tax (if such tax is less than the tax imposed by such sections) which shall consist of the sum of a tax computed on the taxable income reduced by the amount of the net section 1201 gain, at the rates and in the manner as if this subsection had not been enacted, plus—
"(1) in the case of a taxable year beginning before January 1, 1975—
"(A) a tax of 25 percent of the lesser of—
"(i) the amount of the subsection (d) gain, or

"(ii) the amount of the net section 1201 gain, and
"(B) a tax of 30 percent (28 percent in the case of a taxable year beginning after December 31, 1969, and before January 1, 1971) of the excess (if any) of the net section 1201 gain over the subsection (d) gain; and
"(2) in the case of a taxable year beginning after December 31, 1974, a tax of 30 percent of the net section 1201 gain."
Prior to amendment, subsec. (c) read as follows:
"(c) Computation of tax on capital gain in excess of subsection (d) gain.
"(1) In general. The tax computed for purposes of subsection (b)(3) shall be the amount by which a tax determined under section 1 or 511 on an amount equal to the taxable income (but not less than 50 percent of the net section 1201 gain) for the taxable year exceeds a tax determined under section 1 or 511 on an amount equal to the sum of (A) the amount subject to tax under subsection (b)(1) plus (B) an amount equal to 50 percent of the subsection (d) gain.
"(2) Limitation. Notwithstanding paragraph (1), the tax computed for purposes of subsection (b)(3) shall not exceed an amount equal to the following percentage of the excess of the net section 1201 gain over the subsection (d) gain:
"(A) 29½ percent, in the case of a taxable year beginning after December 31, 1969, and before January 1, 1971, or
"(B) 32½ percent, in the case of a taxable year beginning after December 31, 1970, and before January 1, 1972."
Prior to deletion, subsec. (d) read as follows:
"(d) Subsection (d) gain defined. For purposes of this section, the term 'subsection (d) gain' means the sum of the long-term capital gains for the taxable year arising—
"(1) in the case of amounts received before January 1, 1975, from sales or other dispositions pursuant to binding contracts (other than any gain from a transaction described in section 631 or 1235) entered into on or before October 9, 1969, including sales or other dispositions the income from which is returned on the basis and in the manner prescribed in section 453(a)(1),
"(2) in respect of distributions from a corporation made prior to October 10, 1970, which are pursuant to a plan of complete liquidation adopted on or before October 9, 1969, and
"(3) in the case of a taxpayer other than a corporation, from any other source, but the amount taken into account from such other sources for the purposes of this paragraph shall be limited to an amount equal to the excess (if any) of $50,000 ($25,000 in the case of a married individual filing a separate return) over the sum of the gains to which paragraphs (1) and (2) apply."

In 1969, P.L. 91-172, Sec. 511(b), amended Code Sec. 1201, effective for tax. yrs. begin. after 12/31/69.
Prior to amendment, Code Sec. 1201 read as follows:
"(a) Corporations.
"If for any taxable year the net long-term capital gain of any corporation exceeds the net short-term capital loss, then, in lieu of the tax imposed by sections 11, 511, 821(a) or (c), and 831(a), there is hereby imposed a tax (if such tax is less than the tax imposed by such sections) which shall consist of the sum of—
"(1) a partial tax computed on the taxable income reduced by the amount of such excess, at the rates and in the manner as if this subsection had not been enacted, and
"(2) an amount equal to 25 percent of such excess, or, in the case of a taxable year beginning before April 1, 1954, an amount equal to 26 percent of such excess.
In the case of a taxable year beginning before April 1, 1954, the amount under paragraph (2) shall be determined without regard to section 21 (relating to effect of change of tax rates).
"(b) Other taxpayers.
"If for any taxable year the net long-term capital gain of any taxpayer (other than a corporation) exceeds the net short-term capital loss, then, in lieu of the tax imposed by sections 1 and 511, there is hereby imposed a tax (if such tax is less than the tax imposed by such sections) which shall consist of the sum of—
"(1) a partial tax computed on the table income reduced by an amount equal to 50 percent of such excess, at the rate and in the manner as if this subsection had not been enacted, and
"(2) an amount equal to 25 percent of the excess of the net long-term capital gain over the net short-term capital loss.
"(c) Life insurance companies.
"For alternative tax in case of life insurance companies, see section 802(a)(2)."
In 1962, P.L. 87-834, Sec. 8(g)(3), substituted "821(a) or (c)," for "821(a)(1) or (b)," in subsec. (a), effective for tax. yrs. begin. after 12/31/62
In 1959, P.L. 86-69, Sec. 3(f)(2), deleted "802(a)," after "511," in subsec. (a), and added subsec. (c), effective for tax. yrs. begin. after 12/31/57.
In 1956, P.L. 429, Sec. 5(7), added "802(a)," after "511," in subsec. (a), effective only for tax. yrs. begin. after 12/31/54.

Sec. 1202. Partial exclusion for gain from certain small business stock.

(a) Exclusion.

(1) In general. In the case of a taxpayer other than a corporation, gross income shall not include 50 percent of any gain from the sale or exchange of qualified small business stock held for more than 5 years.

(2) Empowerment zone businesses.

(A) In general. In the case of qualified small business stock acquired after the date of the enactment of this paragraph in a corporation which is a qualified business entity (as defined in section 1397C(b)) during substantially all of the taxpayer's holding period for such stock, paragraph (1) shall be applied by substituting "60 percent" for "50 percent".

(B) Certain rules to apply. Rules similar to the rules of paragraphs (5) and (7) of section 1400B(b) shall apply for purposes of this paragraph.

(C) Gain after 2016 not qualified. Subparagraph (A) shall not apply to gain attributable to periods after December 31, 2016.

(D) Treatment of DC Zone. The District of Columbia Enterprise Zone shall not be treated as an empowerment zone for purposes of this paragraph.

(3) Special rules for 2009 and certain periods in 2010. In the case of qualified small business stock acquired after the date of the enactment of this paragraph and on or before the date of the enactment of the Creating Small Business Jobs Act of 2010.

(A) paragraph (1) shall be applied by substituting "75 percent" for "50 percent", and

(B) paragraph (2) shall not apply.

(4) 100 Percent exclusion for stock acquired during certain periods in 2010 and 2011. In the case of qualified small business stock acquired after the date of the enactment of the Creating Small Business Jobs Act of 2010 and before January 1, 2012—

(A) paragraph (1) shall be applied by substituting "100 percent" for "50 percent",

(B) paragraph (2) shall not apply, and

(C) paragraph (7) of section 57(a) shall not apply.

(b) Per-issuer limitation on taxpayer's eligible gain.

(1) In general. If the taxpayer has eligible gain for the taxable year from 1 or more dispositions of stock issued by any corporation, the aggregate amount of such gain from dispositions of stock issued by such corporation which may be taken into account under subsection (a) for the taxable year shall not exceed the greater of—

(A) $10,000,000 reduced by the aggregate amount of eligible gain taken into account under subsection (a) for prior taxable years and attributable to dispositions of stock issued by such corporation, or

(B) 10 times the aggregate adjusted bases of qualified small business stock issued by such corporation and disposed of by the taxpayer during the taxable year.

For purposes of subparagraph (B), the adjusted basis of any stock shall be determined without regard to any addition to basis after the date on which such stock was originally issued.

(2) Eligible gain. For purposes of this subsection, the term "eligible gain" means any gain from the sale or exchange of qualified small business stock held for more than 5 years.

(3) Treatment of married individuals.

(A) Separate returns. In the case of a separate return by a married individual, paragraph (1)(A) shall be applied by substituting "$5,000,000" for "$10,000,000".

(B) Allocation of exclusion. In the case of any joint return, the amount of gain taken into account under subsection (a) shall be allocated equally between the spouses for purposes of applying this subsection to subsequent taxable years.

(C) Marital status. For purposes of this subsection, marital status shall be determined under section 7703.

(c) Qualified small business stock.

For purposes of this section—

(1) In general. Except as otherwise provided in this section, the term "qualified small business stock" means any stock in a C corporation which is originally issued after the date of the enactment of the Revenue Reconciliation Act of 1993, if—

(A) as of the date of issuance, such corporation is a qualified small business, and

(B) except as provided in subsections (f) and (h), such stock is acquired by the taxpayer at its original issue (directly or through an underwriter)—

(i) in exchange for money or other property (not including stock), or

(ii) as compensation for services provided to such corporation (other than services performed as an underwriter of such stock).

(2) Active business requirement; etc.

(A) In general. Stock in a corporation shall not be treated as qualified small business stock unless, during substantially all of the taxpayer's holding period for such stock, such corporation meets the active business requirements of subsection (e) and such corporation is a C corporation.

(B) Special rule for certain small business investment companies.

(i) Waiver of active business requirement. Notwithstanding any provision of subsection (e), a corporation shall be treated as meeting the active business requirements of such subsection for any period during which such corporation qualifies as a specialized small business investment company.

(ii) Specialized small business investment company. For purposes of clause (i), the term "specialized small business investment company" means any eligible corporation (as defined in subsection (e)(4)) which is licensed to operate under section 301(d) of the Small Business Investment Act of 1958 (as in effect on May 13, 1993).

(3) Certain purchases by corporation of its own stock.

(A) Redemptions from taxpayer or related person. Stock acquired by the taxpayer shall not be treated as qualified small business stock if, at any time during the 4-year period beginning on the date 2 years before the issuance of such stock, the corporation issuing such stock purchased (directly or indirectly) any of its stock from the taxpayer or from a person related (within the meaning of section 267(b) or 707(b)) to the taxpayer.

(B) Significant redemptions. Stock issued by a corporation shall not be treated as qualified business stock if, during the 2-year period beginning on the date 1 year before the issuance of such stock, such corporation made 1 or more purchases of its stock with an aggregate value (as of the time of the respective purchases) exceeding 5 percent of the aggregate value of all of its stock as of the beginning of such 2-year period.

(C) Treatment of certain transactions. If any transaction is treated under section 304(a) as a distribution in redemption of the stock of any corporation, for purposes of subparagraphs (A) and (B), such corporation shall be treated as purchasing an amount of its stock equal to the amount treated as such a distribution under section 304(a).

(d) Qualified small business. For purposes of this section—

(1) In general. The term "qualified small business" means any domestic corporation which is a C corporation if—

(A) the aggregate gross assets of such corporation (or any predecessor thereof) at all times on or after the date of the enactment of the Revenue Reconciliation Act of 1993, and before the issuance did not exceed $50,000,000,

(B) the aggregate gross assets of such corporation immediately after the issuance (determined by taking into account amounts received in the issuance) does not exceed $50,000,000, and

(C) such corporation agrees to submit such reports to the Secretary and to shareholders as the Secretary may require to carry out the purposes of this section.

(2) Aggregate gross assets.

(A) In general. For purposes of paragraph (1), the term "aggregate gross assets" means the amount of cash and the aggregate adjusted bases of other property held by the corporation.

(B) Treatment of contributed property. For purposes of subparagraph (A), the adjusted basis of any property contributed to the corporation (or other property with a basis determined in whole or in part by reference to the adjusted basis of property so contributed) shall be determined as if the basis of the property contributed to the corporation (immediately after such contribution) were equal to its fair market value as of the time of such contribution.

(3) Aggregation rules.

(A) In general. All corporations which are members of the same parent-subsidiary controlled group shall be treated as 1 corporation for purposes of this subsection.

(B) Parent-subsidiary controlled group. For purposes of subparagraph (A), the term "parent-subsidiary controlled group" means any controlled group of corporations as defined in section 1563(a)(1), except that—

(i) "more than 50 percent" shall be substituted for "at least 80 percent" each place it appears in section 1563(a)(1), and

(ii) section 1563(a)(4) shall not apply.

(e) Active business requirement.

(1) In general. For purposes of subsection (c)(2), the requirements of this subsection are met by a corporation for any period if during such period—

(A) at least 80 percent (by value) of the assets of such corporation are used by such corporation in the active conduct of 1 or more qualified trades or businesses, and

(B) such corporation is an eligible corporation.

(2) Special rule for certain activities. For purposes of paragraph (1), if, in connection with any future qualified trade or business, a corporation is engaged in—

(A) start-up activities described in section 195(c)(1)(A),

(B) activities resulting in the payment or incurring of expenditures which may be treated as research and experimental expenditures under section 174, or

(C) activities with respect to in-house research expenses described in section 41(b)(4),

assets used in such activities shall be treated as used in the active conduct of a qualified trade or business. Any determination under this paragraph shall be made without regard to whether a corporation has any gross income from such activities at the time of the determination.

(3) Qualified trade or business. For purposes of this subsection, the term "qualified trade or business" means any trade or business other than—

(A) any trade or business involving the performance of services in the fields of health, law, engineering, architecture, accounting, actuarial science, performing arts, consulting, athletics, financial services, brokerage services, or any other trade or business where the principal asset of such trade or business is the reputation or skill of 1 or more of its employees,

(B) any banking, insurance, financing, leasing, investing, or similar business,

(C) any farming business (including the business of raising or harvesting trees),

(D) any business involving the production or extraction of products of a character with respect to which a deduction is allowable under section 613 or 613A, and

(E) any business of operating a hotel, motel, restaurant, or similar business.

(4) Eligible corporation. For purposes of this subsection, the term "eligible corporation" means any domestic corporation; except that such term shall not include—

(A) a DISC or former DISC,

(B) a corporation with respect to which an election under section 936 is in effect or which has a direct or indirect subsidiary with respect to which such an election is in effect,

(C) a regulated investment company, real estate investment trust, or REMIC, and

(D) a cooperative.

(5) Stock in other corporations.

(A) Look-thru in case of subsidiaries. For purposes of this subsection, stock and debt in any subsidiary corporation shall be disregarded and the parent corporation shall be deemed to own its ratable share of the subsidiary's assets, and to conduct its ratable share of the subsidiary's activities.

(B) Portfolio stock or securities. A corporation shall be treated as failing to meet the requirements of paragraph (1) for any period during which more than 10 percent of the value of its assets (in excess of liabilities) consists of stock or securities in other corporations which are not subsidiaries of such corporation (other than assets described in paragraph (6)).

(C) Subsidiary. For purposes of this paragraph, a corporation shall be considered a subsidiary if the parent owns more than 50 percent of the combined voting power of all classes of stock entitled to vote, or more than 50 percent in value of all outstanding stock, of such corporation.

(6) Working capital. For purposes of paragraph (1)(A), any assets which—

(A) are held as a part of the reasonably required working capital needs of a qualified trade or business of the corporation, or

(B) are held for investment and are reasonably expected to be used within 2 years to finance research and experimentation in a qualified trade or business or increases in working capital needs of a qualified trade or business,

shall be treated as used in the active conduct of a qualified trade or business. For periods after the corporation has been in existence for at least 2 years, in no event may more than 50 percent of the assets of the corporation qualify as used in the active conduct of a qualified trade or business by reason of this paragraph.

Capital gains and losses   Code Sec. 1202(i)(2)

(7) Maximum real estate holdings. A corporation shall not be treated as meeting the requirements of paragraph (1) for any period during which more than 10 percent of the total value of its assets consists of real property which is not used in the active conduct of a qualified trade or business. For purposes of the preceding sentence, the ownership of, dealing in, or renting of real property shall not be treated as the active conduct of a qualified trade or business.

(8) Computer software royalties. For purposes of paragraph (1), rights to computer software which produces active business computer software royalties (within the meaning of section 543(d)(1)) shall be treated as an asset used in the active conduct of a trade or business.

(f) Stock acquired on conversion of other stock.

If any stock in a corporation is acquired solely through the conversion of other stock in such corporation which is qualified small business stock in the hands of the taxpayer—

(1) the stock so acquired shall be treated as qualified small business stock in the hands of the taxpayer, and

(2) the stock so acquired shall be treated as having been held during the period during which the converted stock was held.

(g) Treatment of pass-thru entities.

(1) In general. If any amount included in gross income by reason of holding an interest in a pass-thru entity meets the requirements of paragraph (2)—

(A) such amount shall be treated as gain described in subsection (a), and

(B) for purposes of applying subsection (b), such amount shall be treated as gain from a disposition of stock in the corporation issuing the stock disposed of by the pass-thru entity and the taxpayer's proportionate share of the adjusted basis of the pass-thru entity in such stock shall be taken into account.

(2) Requirements. An amount meets the requirements of this paragraph if—

(A) such amount is attributable to gain on the sale or exchange by the pass-thru entity of stock which is qualified small business stock in the hands of such entity (determined by treating such entity as an individual) and which was held by such entity for more than 5 years, and

(B) such amount is includible in the gross income of the taxpayer by reason of the holding of an interest in such entity which was held by the taxpayer on the date on which such pass-thru entity acquired such stock and at all times thereafter before the disposition of such stock by such pass-thru entity.

(3) Limitation based on interest originally held by taxpayer. Paragraph (1) shall not apply to any amount to the extent such amount exceeds the amount to which paragraph (1) would have applied if such amount were determined by reference to the interest the taxpayer held in the pass-thru entity on the date the qualified small business stock was acquired.

(4) Pass-thru entity. For purposes of this subsection, the term "pass-thru entity" means—

(A) any partnership,
(B) any S corporation,
(C) any regulated investment company, and
(D) any common trust fund.

(h) Certain tax-free and other transfers.

For purposes of this section—

(1) In general. In the case of a transfer described in paragraph (2), the transferee shall be treated as—

(A) having acquired such stock in the same manner as the transferor, and

(B) having held such stock during any continuous period immediately preceding the transfer during which it was held (or treated as held under this subsection) by the transferor.

(2) Description of transfers. A transfer is described in this subsection if such transfer is—

(A) by gift,
(B) at death, or
(C) from a partnership to a partner of stock with respect to which requirements similar to the requirements of subsection (g) are met at the time of the transfer (without regard to the 5-year holding period requirement).

(3) Certain rules made applicable. Rules similar to the rules of section 1244(d)(2) shall apply for purposes of this section.

(4) Incorporations and reorganizations involving non-qualified stock.

(A) In general. In the case of a transaction described in section 351 or a reorganization described in section 368, if qualified small business stock is exchanged for other stock which would not qualify as qualified small business stock but for this subparagraph, such other stock shall be treated as qualified small business stock acquired on the date on which the exchanged stock was acquired.

(B) Limitation. This section shall apply to gain from the sale or exchange of stock treated as qualified small business stock by reason of subparagraph (A) only to the extent of the gain which would have been recognized at the time of the transfer described in subparagraph (A) if section 351 or 368 had not applied at such time. The preceding sentence shall not apply if the stock which is treated as qualified small business stock by reason of subparagraph (A) is issued by a corporation which (as of the time of the transfer described in subparagraph (A)) is a qualified small business.

(C) Successive application. For purposes of this paragraph, stock treated as qualified small business stock under subparagraph (A) shall be so treated for subsequent transactions or reorganizations, except that the limitation of subparagraph (B) shall be applied as of the time of the first transfer to which such limitation applied (determined after the application of the second sentence of subparagraph (B)).

(D) Control test. In the case of a transaction described in section 351, this paragraph shall apply only if, immediately after the transaction, the corporation issuing the stock owns directly or indirectly stock representing control (within the meaning of section 368(c)) of the corporation whose stock was exchanged.

(i) Basis rules.

For purposes of this section—

(1) Stock exchanged for property. In the case where the taxpayer transfers property (other than money or stock) to a corporation in exchange for stock in such corporation—

(A) such stock shall be treated as having been acquired by the taxpayer on the date of such exchange, and

(B) the basis of such stock in the hands of the taxpayer shall in no event be less than the fair market value of the property exchanged.

(2) Treatment of contributions to capital. If the adjusted basis of any qualified small business stock is adjusted by reason of any contribution to capital after the date on which such stock was originally issued, in determining the amount of the adjustment by reason of such contribution,

Code Sec. 1202(i)(2) — Capital gains and losses

the basis of the contributed property shall in no event be treated as less than its fair market value on the date of the contribution.

(j) Treatment of certain short positions.

(1) In general. If the taxpayer has an offsetting short position with respect to any qualified small business stock, subsection (a) shall not apply to any gain from the sale or exchange of such stock unless—

(A) such stock was held by the taxpayer for more than 5 years as of the first day on which there was such a short position, and

(B) the taxpayer elects to recognize gain as if such stock were sold on such first day for its fair market value.

(2) Offsetting short position. For purposes of paragraph (1), the taxpayer shall be treated as having an offsetting short position with respect to any qualified small business stock if—

(A) the taxpayer has made a short sale of substantially identical property,

(B) the taxpayer has acquired an option to sell substantially identical property at a fixed price, or

(C) to the extent provided in regulations, the taxpayer has entered into any other transaction which substantially reduces the risk of loss from holding such qualified small business stock.

For purposes of the preceding sentence, any reference to the taxpayer shall be treated as including a reference to any person who is related (within the meaning of section 267(b) or 707(b)) to the taxpayer.

(k) Regulations.

The Secretary shall prescribe such regulations as may be appropriate to carry out the purposes of this section, including regulations to prevent the avoidance of the purposes of this section through split-ups, shell corporations, partnerships, or otherwise.

In 2010, P.L. 111-312, Sec. 753(b)(1), substituted "December 31, 2016" for "December 31, 2014" in subpara. (a)(2)(C) . . . Sec. 753(b)(2), substituted "2016" for "2014" in the heading of subpara. (a)(2)(C), effective for periods after 12/31/2009. . . . Sec. 760(a)(1), substituted "January 1, 2012" for "January 1, 2011" in para. (a)(4) . . . Sec. 760(a)(2), added "and 2011" after "2010" in the heading of para. (a)(4), effective for stock acquired after 12/31/2010.

—P.L. 111-240, Sec. 2011(a), added para. (a)(4) . . . Sec. 2011(b)(1), added "certain periods" before "2010" in the heading to para. (a)(3) . . . Sec. 2011(b)(2), substituted "on or before the date of the enactment of the Creating Small Business Jobs Act of 2010" for "before January 1, 2011" in para. (a)(3), effective for stock acquired after 9/27/2010.

In 2009, P.L. 111-5, Sec. 1241(a), added para. (a)(3), effective for stock acquired after 2/17/2009.

In 2004, P.L. 108-357, Sec. 835(b)(9), substituted "or REMIC" for "REMIC, or FASIT" in subpara. (e)(4)(C), effective 1/1/2005, except as provided in Sec. 835(c)(2) of this Act, which reads as follows:

"(2) Exception for existing FASITs. Paragraph (1) shall not apply to any FASIT in existence on the date of the enactment of this Act to the extent that regular interests issued by the FASIT before such date continue to remain outstanding in accordance with the original terms of issuance."

In 2000, P.L. 106-554, Sec. 1(a)(7), [which enacted into law Sec. 117(a) of P.L. 106-554] amended subsec. (a), effective for stock acquired after 12/21/2000. . . . Sec. 1(a)(7), [which enacted into law Sec. 117(b)(2) of P.L. 106-554] substituted "Partial" for "50-percent" in the section heading.

Prior to amendment, subsec. (a) read as follows:

"(a) 50-percent exclusion. In the case of a taxpayer other than a corporation, gross income shall not include 50 percent of any gain from the sale or exchange of qualified small business stock held for more than 5 years."

In 1996, P.L. 104-188, Sec. 1621(b)(7), substituted "REMIC, or FASIT" for "or REMIC," in subpara. (e)(4)(C), effective 9/1/97.

In 1993, P.L. 103-66, Sec. 13113(a), added Code Sec. 1202, effective for stock issued after 8/10/93.

Sec. 1202. Repealed.

In 1986, P.L. 99-514, Sec. 301(a), repealed Code Sec. 1202, effective for tax. yrs. begin. after 12/31/86. For rules on retention of capital gains treatment for sales of dairy cattle under milk production termination program, see Sec. 406 of this Act reproduced in note following Code Sec. 1201.

Prior to repeal, Code Sec. 1202 read as follows:

"Sec. 1202. Deduction for capital gains.

"(a) In general.

"If for any taxable year a taxpayer other than a corporation has a net capital gain, 60 percent of the amount of the net capital gain shall be a deduction from gross income.

"(b) Estates and trusts.

"In the case of an estate or trust, the deduction shall be computed by excluding the portion (if any) of the gains for the taxable year from sales or exchanges of capital assets which, under sections 652 and 662 (relating to inclusions of amounts in gross income of beneficiaries of trusts), is includible by the income beneficiaries as gain derived from the sale or exchange of capital assets.

"(c) Transitional rule.

"If for any taxable year ending after October 31, 1978, and beginning before November 1, 1979, a taxpayer other than a corporation has a net capital gain, the deduction under subsection (a) shall be the sum of—

"(1) 60 percent of the lesser of—

"(A) the net capital gain for the taxable year, or

"(B) the net capital gain taking into account only gain or loss properly taken into account for the portion of the taxable year after October 31, 1978, plus

"(2) 50 percent of the excess of—

"(A) the net capital gain for the taxable year, over

"(B) the amount of net capital gain taken into account under paragraph (1)."

In 1980, P.L. 96-222, Sec. 104(a)(2)(A)(i), amended so much of subsec. (c) as precedes "a taxpayer other than a corporation" . . . Sec. 104(a)(2)(A)(ii), amended subpara. (c)(1)(B), effective for tax. yrs. end. after 10/31/78. Sec. 104(a)(2)(C) of this Act provides as follows:

"(C) Special rule for pass-through entities.

"(i) In general. In applying sections 1201(c)(2)(A)(ii) and 1202(c)(1)(B) of the Internal Revenue Code of 1954 with respect to any pass-through entity, the determination of the period for which gain or loss is properly taken into account shall be made at the entity level.

"(ii) Pass-through entity defined. For purposes of clause (i), the term 'pass-through entity' means—

"(I) a regulated investment company,

"(II) a real estate investment trust,

"(III) an electing small business corporation,

"(IV) a partnership,

"(V) an estate or trust, and

"(VI) a common trust fund."

Prior to amendment, so much of subsec. (c) as precedes "a taxpayer other than a corporation" read as follows:

"(c) Taxable years which include November 1, 1978.

"If for any taxable year beginning before November 1, 1978, and ending after October 31, 1978,"

Prior to amendment, subpara. (c)(1)(B) read as follows:

"(B) the net capital gain taking into account only sales and exchanges after October 31, 1978, plus

In 1978, P.L. 95-600, Sec. 402(a), amended Code Sec. 1202, effective for tax. yrs. ending after 10/31/78.

Prior to amendment, Code Sec. 1202 read as follows:

"Sec. 1202. Deduction for capital gains.

"If for any taxable year, a taxpayer other than a corporation has a net capital gain, 50 percent of the amount of the net capital gain shall be a deduction from gross income. In the case of an estate or trust, the deduction shall be computed by excluding the portion (if any), of the gains for the taxable year from sales or exchanges of capital assets, which, under sections 652 and 662 (relating to inclusions of amounts in gross income of beneficiaries of trusts), is includible by the income beneficiaries as gain derived from the sale or exchange of capital assets."

In 1976, P.L. 94-455, Sec. 1901(b)(33)(M), amended the first sentence of Code Sec. 1202, effective for tax. yrs. begin. after 12/31/76.

Prior to amendment, the first sentence of Code Sec. 1202 read as follows:

"In the case of a taxpayer other than a corporation, if for any taxable year the net long-term capital gain exceeds the net short-term capital loss, 50 percent of the amount of such excess shall be a deduction from gross income."

PART II.—TREATMENT OF CAPITAL LOSSES

Sec.

1211. Limitation on capital losses.

1212. Capital loss carrybacks and carryovers.

In 1969, P.L. 91-172, Sec. 512(f)(2), substituted "carrybacks and carryovers" for "carryover" in item 1212.

Sec. 1211. Limitation on capital losses.
(a) Corporations.
In the case of a corporation, losses from sales or exchanges of capital assets shall be allowed only to the extent of gains from such sales or exchanges.
(b) Other taxpayers.
In the case of a taxpayer other than a corporation, losses from sales or exchanges of capital assets shall be allowed only to the extent of the gains from such sales or exchanges, plus (if such losses exceed such gains) the lower of—

(1) $3,000 ($1,500 in the case of a married individual filing a separate return), or

(2) the excess of such losses over such gains.

In 1986, P.L. 99-514, Sec. 301(b)(10), amended subsec. (b), effective for tax. yrs. begin. after 12/31/86. Sec. 406 of this Act provides:
"SEC. 406. RETENTION OF CAPITAL GAINS TREATMENT FOR SALES OF DAIRY CATTLE UNDER MILK PRODUCTION TERMINATION PROGRAM.
"The amendments made by subtitles A and B of title III shall not apply to any gain from the sale of dairy cattle under a valid contract with the United States Department of Agriculture under the milk production termination program to the extent such gain is properly taken into account under the taxpayer's method of accounting after January 1, 1987, and before September 1, 1987."
Prior to amendment, subsec. (b) read as follows:
"(b) Other taxpayers.
"(1) In general. In the case of a taxpayer other than a corporation, losses from sales or exchanges of capital assets shall be allowed only to the extent of the gains from such sales or exchanges, plus (if such losses exceed such gains) whichever of the following is smallest:
"(A) the taxable income for the taxable year reduced (but not below zero) by the zero bracket amount,
"(B) the applicable amount, or
"(C) the sum of—
"(i) the excess of the net short-term capital loss over the net long-term capital gain, and
"(ii) one-half of the excess of the net long-term capital loss over the net short-term capital gain.
"(2) Applicable amount. For purposes of paragraph (1)(B), the term 'applicable amount' means—
"(A) $2,000 in the case of any taxable year beginning in 1977; and
"(B) $3,000 in the case of any taxable year beginning after 1977.
In the case of a separate return by a husband or wife, the applicable amount shall be one-half of the amount determined under the preceding sentence.
"(3) Computation of taxable income. For purposes of paragraph (1), taxable income shall be computed without regard to gains or losses from sales or exchanges of capital assets and without regard to the deductions provided in section 151 (relating to personal exemptions) or any deduction in lieu thereof."
In 1977, P.L. 95-30, Sec. 102(b)(14), amended subpara. (b)(1)(A), effective for tax. yrs. begin. after 12/31/76.
Prior to amendment, subpara. (b)(1)(A) read as follows:
"(A) the taxable income for the taxable year,"
In 1976, P.L. 94-455, Sec. 501(b)(6), deleted the sentence at the end of para. (b)(3), effective for tax. yrs. begin. after 12/31/75.
Prior to amendment, the sentence at the end of para. (b)(3) read as follows:
"If the taxpayer elects to pay the optional tax imposed by section 3, 'taxable income' as used in this subsection shall read as 'adjusted gross income.'"
—P.L. 94-455, Sec. 1401(a), substituted "the applicable amount" for "$1,000" in subpara. (b)(1)(B) . . . Sec. 1401(b), amended para. (b)(2), effective for tax. yrs. begin. after 12/31/76.
Prior to amendment, para. (b)(2) read as follows:
"(2) Married individuals. In the case of a husband or wife who files a separate return, the amount specified in paragraph (1)(B) shall be $500 in lieu of $1,000."
In 1969, P.L. 91-172, Sec. 513(a), amended subsec. (b), effective for tax. yrs. begin. after 12/31/69.
Prior to amendment, subsec. (b) read as follows:
"(b) Other taxpayers.
"In the case of a taxpayer other than a corporation, losses from sales or exchanges of capital assets shall be allowed only to the extent of the gains from such sales or exchanges, plus the taxable income of the taxpayer or $1,000, whichever is smaller. For purposes of this subsection, taxable income shall be computed without regard to gains or losses from sales or exchanges of capital assets and without regard to the deductions provided in section 151 (relating to personal exemptions) or any deduction in lieu thereof. If the taxpayer elects to pay the optional tax imposed by section 3, 'taxable income' as used in this subsection shall be read as 'adjusted gross income'."

Sec. 1212. Capital loss carrybacks and carryovers.
(a) Corporations.
(1) In general. If a corporation has a net capital loss for any taxable year (hereinafter in this paragraph referred to as the "loss year"), the amount thereof shall be—

(A) a capital loss carryback to each of the 3 taxable years preceding the loss year, but only to the extent—

(i) such loss is not attributable to a foreign expropriation capital loss, and

(ii) the carryback of such loss does not increase or produce a net operating loss (as defined in section 172(c)) for the taxable year to which it is being carried back;

(B) except as provided in subparagraph (C), a capital loss carryover to each of the 5 taxable years succeeding the loss year; and

(C) a capital loss carryover to each of the 10 taxable years succeeding the loss year, but only to the extent such loss is attributable to a foreign expropriation loss, and shall be treated as a short-term capital loss in each such taxable year. The entire amount of the net capital loss for any taxable year shall be carried to the earliest of the taxable years to which such loss may be carried, and the portion of such loss which shall be carried to each of the other taxable years to which such loss may be carried shall be the excess, if any, of such loss over the total of the capital gain net income for each of the prior taxable years to which such loss may be carried. For purposes of the preceding sentence, the capital gain net income for any such prior taxable year shall be computed without regard to the net capital loss for the loss year or for any taxable year thereafter. In the case of any net capital loss which cannot be carried back in full to a preceding taxable year by reason of clause (ii) of subparagraph (A), the capital gain net income for such prior taxable year shall in no case be treated as greater than the amount of such loss which can be carried back to such preceding taxable year upon the application of such clause (ii).

(2) Definitions and special rules.

(A) Foreign expropriation capital loss defined. For purposes of this subsection, the term "foreign expropriation capital loss" means, for any taxable year, the sum of the losses taken into account in computing the net capital loss for such year which are—

(i) losses sustained directly by reason of the expropriation, intervention, seizure, or similar taking of property by the government of any foreign country, any political subdivision thereof, or any agency or instrumentality of the foregoing, or

(ii) losses (treated under section 165(g)(1) as losses from the sale or exchange of capital assets) from securities which become worthless by reason of the expropriation, intervention, seizure, or similar taking of property by the government of any foreign country, any political subdivision thereof, or any agency or instrumentality of the foregoing.

(B) Portion of loss attributable to foreign expropriation capital loss. For purposes of paragraph (1), the portion of any net capital loss for any taxable year attributable to a foreign expropriation capital loss is the amount of the foreign expropriation capital loss for such year (but not in excess of the net capital loss for such year).

(C) Priority of application. For purposes of paragraph (1), if a portion of a net capital loss for any taxable year is attributable to a foreign expropriation capital loss, such portion shall be considered to be a separate net capital loss for such year to be applied after the other portion of such net capital loss.

(3) Regulated investment companies.

(A) In general. If a regulated investment company has a net capital loss for any taxable year—

(i) paragraph (1) shall not apply to such loss,

(ii) the excess of the net short-term capital loss over the net long-term capital gain for such year shall be a short-term capital loss arising on the first day of the next taxable year, and

(iii) the excess of the net long-term capital loss over the net short-term capital gain for such year shall be a long-term capital loss arising on the first day of the next taxable year.

(B) Coordination with general rule. If a net capital loss to which paragraph (1) applies is carried over to a taxable year of a regulated investment company—

(i) Losses to which this paragraph applies. Clauses (ii) and (iii) of subparagraph (A) shall be applied without regard to any amount treated as a short-term capital loss under paragraph (1).

(ii) Losses to which general rule applies. Paragraph (1) shall be applied by substituting "net capital loss for the loss year or any taxable year thereafter (other than a net capital loss to which paragraph (3)(A) applies)" for "net capital loss for the loss year or any taxable year thereafter".

(4) **Special rules on carrybacks.** A net capital loss of a corporation shall not be carried back under paragraph (1)(A) to a taxable year—

(A) for which it is a regulated investment company (as defined in section 851), or

(B) for which it is a real estate investment trust (as defined in section 856).

(b) **Other taxpayers.**

(1) **In general.** If a taxpayer other than a corporation has a net capital loss for any taxable year—

(A) the excess of the net short-term capital loss over the net long-term capital gain for such year shall be a short-term capital loss in the succeeding taxable year, and

(B) the excess of the net long-term capital loss over the net short-term capital gain for such year shall be a long-term capital loss in the succeeding taxable year.

(2) **Treatment of amounts allowed under section 1211(b)(1) or (2).**

(A) In general. For purposes of determining the excess referred to in subparagraph (A) or (B) of paragraph (1), there shall be treated as a short-term capital gain in the taxable year an amount equal to the lesser of—

(i) the amount allowed for the taxable year under paragraph (1) or (2) of section 1211(b), or

(ii) the adjusted taxable income for such taxable year.

(B) Adjusted taxable income. For purposes of subparagraph (A), the term "adjusted taxable income" means taxable income increased by the sum of—

(i) the amount allowed for the taxable year under paragraph (1) or (2) of section 1211(b), and

(ii) the deduction allowed for such year under section 151 or any deduction in lieu thereof.

For purposes of the preceding sentence, any excess of the deductions allowed for the taxable year over the gross income for such year shall be taken into account as negative taxable income.

(c) **Carryback of losses from section 1256 contracts to offset prior gains from such contracts.**

(1) **In general.** If a taxpayer (other than a corporation) has a net section 1256 contracts loss for the taxable year and elects to have this subsection apply to such taxable year, the amount of such net section 1256 contracts loss—

(A) shall be a carryback to each of the 3 taxable years preceding the loss year, and

(B) to the extent that, after the application of paragraphs (2) and (3), such loss is allowed as a carryback to any such preceding taxable year—

(i) 40 percent of the amount so allowed shall be treated as a short-term capital loss from section 1256 contracts, and

(ii) 60 percent of the amount so allowed shall be treated as a long-term capital loss from section 1256 contracts.

(2) **Amount carried to each taxable year.** The entire amount of the net section 1256 contracts loss for any taxable year shall be carried to the earliest of the taxable years to which such loss may be carried back under paragraph (1). The portion of such loss which shall be carried to each of the 2 other taxable years to which such loss may be carried back shall be the excess (if any) of such loss over the portion of such loss which, after the application of paragraph (3), was allowed as a carryback for any prior taxable year.

(3) **Amount which may be used in any prior taxable year.** An amount shall be allowed as a carryback under paragraph (1) to any prior taxable year only to the extent—

(A) such amount does not exceed the net section 1256 contract gain for such year, and

(B) the allowance of such carryback does not increase or produce a net operating loss (as defined in section 172(c)) for such year.

(4) **Net section 1256 contracts loss.** For purposes of paragraph (1), the term "net section 1256 contracts loss" means the lesser of—

(A) the net capital loss for the taxable year determined by taking into account only gains and losses from section 1256 contracts, or

(B) the sum of the amounts which, but for paragraph (6)(A), would be treated as capital losses in the succeeding taxable year under subparagraphs (A) and (B) of subsection (b)(1).

(5) **Net section 1256 contract gain.** For purposes of paragraph (1)—

(A) In general. The term "net section 1256 contract gain" means the lesser of—

(i) the capital gain net income for the taxable year determined by taking into account only gains and losses from section 1256 contracts, or

(ii) the capital gain net income for the taxable year.

(B) Special rule. The net section 1256 contract gain for any taxable year before the loss year shall be computed without regard to the net section 1256 contracts loss for the loss year or for any taxable year thereafter.

(6) **Coordination with carryforward provisions of subsection (b)(1).**

(A) Carryforward amount reduced by amount used as carryback. For purposes of applying subsection (b)(1), if any portion of the net section 1256 contracts loss for any taxable year is allowed as a carryback under paragraph (1) to any preceding taxable year—

(i) 40 percent of the amount allowed as a carryback shall be treated as a short-term capital gain for the loss year, and

(ii) 60 percent of the amount allowed as a carryback shall be treated as a long-term capital gain for the loss year.

(B) Carryover loss retains character as attributable to section 1256 contract. Any amount carried forward as a short-term or long-term capital loss to any taxable year under subsection (b)(1) (after the application of subpar-

Capital gains and losses — Code Sec. 1212

agraph (A)) shall, to the extent attributable to losses from section 1256 contracts, be treated as loss from section 1256 contracts for such taxable year.

(7) Other definitions and special rules. For purposes of this subsection—

(A) Section 1256 contract. The term "section 1256 contract" means any section 1256 contract (as defined in section 1256(b)) to which section 1256 applies.

(B) Exclusion for estates and trusts. This subsection shall not apply to any estate or trust.

In **2010**, P.L. 111-325, Sec. 101(b)(1), amended subpara. (a)(1)(C) ... Sec. 101(a), redesignated para. (a)(3) as (4) and added new para. (a)(3), effective for net capital losses for tax. yrs. begin. after 12/22/2010.

Prior to amendment, subpara. (a)(1)(C) read as follows:

"(C) a capital loss carryover—

"(i) in the case of a regulated investment company (as defined in section 851) to each of the 8 taxable years succeeding the loss year, and

"(ii) to the extent such loss is attributable to a foreign expropriation capital loss, to each of the 10 taxable years succeeding the loss year."

In **2004**, P.L. 108-357, Sec. 413(c)(20)(A), amended para. (a)(3), effective for tax. yrs. begin. after 12/31/2004.

Prior to amendment, para. (a)(3) read as follows:

"(3) Special rules on carrybacks. A net capital loss of a corporation shall not be carried back under paragraph (1)(A) to a taxable year—

"(A) for which it is a foreign personal holding company (as defined in section 552);

"(B) for which it is a regulated investment company (as defined in section 851);

"(C) for which it is a real estate investment trust (as defined in section 856); or

"(D) for which an election made by it under section 1247 is applicable (relating to election by foreign investment companies to distribute income currently)."

In **1988**, P.L. 100-647, Sec. 1003(a)(3), amended para. (b)(2), effective for tax. yrs. begin. after 12/31/86. For special rules see Sec. 406 of P.L. 99-514, reproduced below.

Prior to amendment subpara. (b)(2) read as follows:

"(2) Special rule. For purposes of determining the excess referred to in subparagraph (A) or (B) of paragraph (1), an amount equal to the amount allowed for the taxable year under paragraph (1) or (2) of section 1211(b) shall be treated as a short-term capital gain in such year."

In **1986**, P.L. 99-514, Sec. 301(b)(11), amended para. (b)(2), effective for tax. yrs. begin. after 12/31/86. Sec. 406 of this Act provides the following:

"SEC. 406. RETENTION OF CAPITAL GAINS TREATMENT FOR SALES OF DAIRY CATTLE UNDER MILK PRODUCTION TERMINATION PROGRAM.

"The amendments made by subtitles A and B of title III [of P.L. 99-514] shall not apply to any gain from the sale of dairy cattle under a valid contract with the United States Department of Agriculture under the milk production termination program to the extent such gain is properly taken into account under the taxpayer's method of accounting after January 1, 1987, and before September 1, 1987."

Prior to amendment, para. (b)(2) read as follows:

"(2) Special rules.

"(A) For purposes of determining the excess referred to in paragraph (1)(A), an amount equal to the amount allowed for the taxable year under section 1211(b)(1)(A), (B), or (C) shall be treated as a short-term capital gain in such year.

"(B) For purposes of determining the excess referred to in paragraph (1)(B), an amount equal to the sum of—

"(i) the amount allowed for the taxable year under section 1211(b)(1)(A), (B), or (C), and

"(ii) the excess of the amount described in clause (i) over the net short-term capital loss (determined without regard to this subsection) for such year,

shall be treated as a short-term capital gain in such year."

—P.L. 99-514, Sec. 1899A(67), corrected Sec. 102(e)(3)(C) of P.L. 98-369 to amend subpara. (c)(6)(B), see below.

In **1984**, P.L. 98-369, Sec. 102(e)(3)(A), substituted "net section 1256 contracts loss" for "net commodity futures loss" each place it appeared (including any headings) in subsec. (c) ... Sec. 102(e)(3)(B), substituted "section 1256 contracts" for "regulated futures contracts" each place it appears (including any headings) in subsec. (c) ... Sec. 102(e)(3)(C), substituted "section 1256 contract" for "regulated futures contract" each place it appeared (including the headings) in subparas. (c)(6)(B) and (c)(7)(A) ... Sec. 102(e)(3)(D), substituted "net section 1256 contract gain" for "net commodity futures gain" each place it appeared (including any headings) in subsec. (c), effective for positions established after 7/18/84, in tax. yrs. ending after 7/18/84.

—P.L. 98-369, Sec. 1002(a), deleted para. (b)(3), effective for tax. yrs. begin. after 12/31/83.

Prior to deletion, para. (b)(3) read as follows:

"(3) Transitional rule. In the case of any amount which, under paragraph (1) and section 1211(b) (as in effect for taxable years beginning before January 1, 1970), is treated as a capital loss in the first taxable year beginning after December 31, 1969, paragraph (1) and section 1211(b) (as in effect for taxable years beginning before January 1, 1970) shall apply (and paragraph (1) and section 1211(b) as in effect for taxable years beginning after December 31, 1969, shall not apply) to the extent such amount exceeds the total of any net capital gains (determined without regard to this subsection) of taxable years beginning after December 31, 1969."

In **1983**, P.L. 97-448, Sec. 105(c)(7), deleted "and positions to which section 1256 applies" after "from regulated futures contracts" in subpara. (c)(4)(A), for property acquired and positions established by the taxpayer after 6/23/81, in tax. yrs. end. after 6/23/81.

In **1982**, P.L. 97-354, Sec. 5(a)(35), deleted para. (a)(3) and redesignated para. (a)(4) as para. (a)(3), effective for tax. yrs. begin. after 12/31/82.

Prior to deletion, para. (a)(3) read as follows:

"(3) Electing small business corporations. Paragraph (1)(A) shall not apply to the net capital loss of a corporation for any taxable year for which it is an electing small business corporation under subchapter S, and a net capital loss of a corporation (for a year for which it is not such an electing small business corporation) shall not be carried back under paragraph (1)(A) to a taxable year for which it is an electing small business corporation."

In **1981**, P.L. 97-34, Sec. 504, added subsec. (c), effective for property acquired and positions established by the taxpayer after 6/23/81, in tax. yrs. end. after 6/23/81. For election with respect to property held on 6/23/81, see Sec. 508(c) of this Act reproduced in note following Code Sec. 1092.

In **1978**, P.L. 95-600, Sec. 703(k), substituted "succeeding the loss year" for "exceeding the loss year" in clause (a)(1)(C)(ii), effective 10/4/76.

In **1976**, P.L. 94-455, Sec. 1403(a), deleted "and" at the end of subpara. (a)(1)(A) and substituted new subparas. (a)(1)(B) and (C) for subpara. (a)(1)(B), for loss years (within the meaning of Code Sec. 1212(a)(1)) end. on or after 1/1/70.

Prior to amendment, subpara. (a)(1)(B) read as follows:

"(B) a capital loss carryover to each of the 5 taxable years (10 taxable years to the extent such loss is attributable to a foreign expropriation capital loss) succeeding the loss year,"

—P.L. 94-455, Sec. 1901(b)(33)(O), substituted "capital gain net income" for "net capital gain" each place it appeared, and substituted "capital gain net income" for "net capital gains", in para. (a)(1), effective for tax. yrs. begin. after 12/31/76.

In **1971**, P.L. 91-688, Sec. 3(a), ,(b) and (c) provided the following:

"(a) For purposes of applying section 1212(a) of the Internal Revenue Code of 1954 (as amended by section 512 of the Tax Reform Act of 1969) in the case of a corporation which makes an election under subsection (b), any net capital loss sustained in a taxable year beginning after December 31, 1969, may not be carried back to any taxable year beginning before January 1, 1970, for which it was subject to taxation under section 802 of such Code, if the carryback of such loss would result in an increase in such corporation's income tax liability for any such taxable year.

"(b) An election to have the provisions of subsection (a) apply shall be made by a corporation —

"(1) in such form and manner as the Secretary of the Treasury or his delegate may prescribe, and

"(2) not later than the time prescribed by law for filing a claim for credit or refund of overpayment of income tax for the first taxable year beginning after December 31, 1969, in which such corporation sustains a net capital loss.

"(c) The Secretary of the Treasury or his delegate shall prescribe such regulations as he determines necessary to carry out the purposes of this section.

In **1969**, P.L. 91-172, Sec. 512(a), amended subsec. (a)(1) ... Sec. 512(b), added paras. (a)(3) and (4), effective for net capital losses sustained in tax. yrs. begin. after 12/31/69.

Prior to amendment para. (a)(1) read as follows:

"(1) In general. If for any taxable year a corporation has a net capital loss, the amount thereof shall be a short-term capital loss —

"(A) in each of the 5 succeeding taxable years, or

"(B) to the extent such loss is attributable to a foreign expropriation capital loss, in each of the 10 succeeding taxable years,

to the extent such amount exceeds the total of any net capital gains (determined without regard to this paragraph) of any taxable years intervening between the taxable year in which the net capital loss arose and such succeeding taxable year."

—P.L. 91-172, Sec. 512(f)(1), amended the heading of Code Sec. 1212, effective for net capital losses sustained in tax. yrs. begin. after 12/31/69.

—P.L. 91-172, Sec. 513(b), amended subsec. (b), effective for tax. yrs. begin. after 12/31/69.

Prior to amendment subsec. (b) read as follows:

"(1) In general. If a taxpayer other than a corporation has a net capital loss for any taxable year beginning after December 31, 1963 —

"(A) the excess of the net short-term capital loss over the net long-term capital gain in such year shall be a short-term capital loss in the succeeding taxable year, and

"(B) the excess of the net long-term capital loss over the net short-term capital gain for such year shall be a long-term capital loss in the succeeding taxable year. For purposes of this paragraph, in determining such excesses an amount equal to the excess of the sum allowed for the taxable year under section 1211(b) over the gains from sales or exchanges of capital assets (determined without regard to this sentence) shall be treated as a short-term capital gain in such year.

"(2) Transitional rule. In the case of a taxpayer other than a corporation, there shall be treated as a short-term capital loss in the first taxable year beginning after December 31, 1963, any amount which is treated as a short-term capital loss in such year under this subchapter as in effect immediately before the enactment of the Revenue Act of 1964."

In 1964, P.L. 88-571, Sec. 7(a), amended subsec. (a), effective to net capital losses (to the extent attributable to foreign expropriation capital losses, as defined in Code Sec. 1212(a)(2)(A) sustained in tax. yrs. end. after 12/31/58.
Prior to amendment, subsec. (a) read as follows:
"(a) *Corporations.*

"If for any taxable year a corporation has a net capital loss, the amount thereof shall be a short-term capital loss in each of the 5 succeeding taxable years to the extent that such amount exceeds the total of any net capital gains of any taxable years intervening between the taxable year in which the net capital loss arose and such succeeding taxable year. For purposes of this section, a net capital gain shall be computed without regard to such net capital loss or to any net capital losses arising in any such intervening taxable years, and a net capital loss for a taxable year beginning before October 20, 1951, shall be determined under the applicable law relating to the computation of capital gains and losses in effect before such date."

—P.L. 88-272, Sec. 230(a), substituted "(a) Corporations—If for any taxable year a corporation" for "If for any taxable year the taxpayer", in Code Sec. 1212, and added subsec. (b), effective for tax. yrs. begin. after 12/31/63.

PART III.—GENERAL RULES FOR DETERMINING CAPITAL GAINS AND LOSSES

Sec.
1221. Capital asset defined.
1222. Other terms relating to capital gains and losses.
1223. Holding period of property.

Sec. 1221. Capital asset defined.
(a) In general.

For purposes of this subtitle, the term "capital asset" means property held by the taxpayer (whether or not connected with his trade or business), but does not include—

(1) stock in trade of the taxpayer or other property of a kind which would properly be included in the inventory of the taxpayer if on hand at the close of the taxable year, or property held by the taxpayer primarily for sale to customers in the ordinary course of his trade or business;

(2) property, used in his trade or business, of a character which is subject to the allowance for depreciation provided in section 167, or real property used in his trade or business;

(3) a copyright, a literary, musical, or artistic composition, a letter or memorandum, or similar property, held by—

(A) a taxpayer whose personal efforts created such property,

(B) in the case of a letter, memorandum, or similar property, a taxpayer for whom such property was prepared or produced, or

> • *Caution:* Sec. 301(a), P.L. 111-312, (reproduced in the history notes following this Code Sec.) provides that the amendments made by Sec. 542(e)(2)(A), P.L. 107-16, EGTRRA, will apply as if never enacted. Code Sec. 1221(a)(3)(C), following, reflects the removal of these amendments, effective for estates of decedents dying, and transfers made, after 12/31/2009.

(C) a taxpayer in whose hands the basis of such property is determined, for purposes of determining gain from a sale or exchange, in whole or part by reference to the basis of such property in the hands of a taxpayer described in subparagraph (A) or (B);

> • *Caution:* Code Sec. 1221(a)(3)(C), was amended by Sec. 542(e)(2)(A), P.L. 107-16, EGTRRA. As provided in Sec. 301(a), P.L. 111-312, this amendment will apply as if never enacted, effective for estates of decedents dying, and transfers made, after 12/31/2009.

(C) a taxpayer in whose hands the basis of such property is determined (other than by reason of section 1022), for purposes of determining gain from a sale or exchange, in whole or part by reference to the basis of such property in the hands of a taxpayer described in subparagraph (A) or (B);

(4) accounts or notes receivable acquired in the ordinary course of trade or business for services rendered or from the sale of property described in paragraph (1);

(5) a publication of the United States Government (including the Congressional Record) which is received from the United States Government or any agency thereof, other than by purchase at the price at which it is offered for sale to the public, and which is held by—

(A) a taxpayer who so received such publication, or

(B) a taxpayer in whose hands the basis of such publication is determined, for purposes of determining gain from a sale or exchange, in whole or in part by reference to the basis of such publication in the hands of a taxpayer described in subparagraph (A);

(6) any commodities derivative financial instrument held by a commodities derivatives dealer, unless—

(A) it is established to the satisfaction of the Secretary that such instrument has no connection to the activities of such dealer as a dealer, and

(B) such instrument is clearly identified in such dealer's records as being described in subparagraph (A) before the close of the day on which it was acquired, originated, or entered into (or such other time as the Secretary may by regulations prescribe);

(7) any hedging transaction which is clearly identified as such before the close of the day on which it was acquired, originated, or entered into (or such other time as the Secretary may by regulations prescribe); or

(8) supplies of a type regularly used or consumed by the taxpayer in the ordinary course of a trade or business of the taxpayer.

(b) Definitions and special rules.

(1) Commodities derivative financial instruments. For purposes of subsection (a)(6)—

(A) Commodities derivatives dealer. The term "commodities derivatives dealer" means a person which regularly offers to enter into, assume, offset, assign, or terminate positions in commodities derivative financial instruments with customers in the ordinary course of a trade or business.

(B) Commodities derivative financial instrument.

(i) In general. The term "commodities derivative financial instrument" means any contract or financial instrument with respect to commodities (other than a share of stock in a corporation, a beneficial interest in a partnership or trust, a note, bond, debenture, or other evidence of indebtedness, or a section 1256 contract (as defined in section 1256(b))), the value or settlement price of which is calculated by or determined by reference to a specified index.

(ii) Specified index. The term "specified index" means any one or more or any combination of—

(I) a fixed rate, price, or amount, or

(II) a variable rate, price, or amount,

which is based on any current, objectively determinable financial or economic information with respect to commodities which is not within the control of any of the parties to the contract or instrument and is not unique to any of the parties' circumstances.

(2) Hedging transaction.

(A) In general. For purposes of this section, the term "hedging transaction" means any transaction entered into by the taxpayer in the normal course of the taxpayer's trade or business primarily—

(i) to manage risk of price changes or currency fluctuations with respect to ordinary property which is held or to be held by the taxpayer,

(ii) to manage risk of interest rate or price changes or currency fluctuations with respect to borrowings made or to be made, or ordinary obligations incurred or to be incurred, by the taxpayer, or

(iii) to manage such other risks as the Secretary may prescribe in regulations.

(B) Treatment of nonidentification or improper identification of hedging transactions. Notwithstanding subsection (a)(7), the Secretary shall prescribe regulations to properly characterize any income, gain, expense, or loss arising from a transaction—

(i) which is a hedging transaction but which was not identified as such in accordance with subsection (a)(7), or

(ii) which was so identified but is not a hedging transaction.

(3) Sale or exchange of self-created musical works. At the election of the taxpayer, paragraphs (1) and (3) of subsection (a) shall not apply to musical compositions or copyrights in musical works sold or exchanged by a taxpayer described in subsection (a)(3).

(4) Regulations. The Secretary shall prescribe such regulations as are appropriate to carry out the purposes of paragraph (6) and (7) of subsection (a) in the case of transactions involving related parties.

In 2010, P.L. 111-312, Sec. 101(a)(1), substituted "December 31, 2012" for "December 31, 2010" both places it appeared in Sec. 901, P.L. 107-16 [see below], effective as if included in the enactment of P.L. 107-16, EGTRRA, 6/7/2001.

—P.L. 111-312, Sec. 301(a), provides that Code Sec. 1221, as amended by Sec. 542(e)(2)(A), P.L. 107-16, EGTRRA, 6/7/2001 (amended subpara. (a)(3)(C), see below) will read as if such provision had never been enacted, effective for estates of decedents dying, and transfers made, after 12/31/2009.

Sec. 301(a), P.L. 111-312, 12/17/2010, provides:

"(a) In general. Each provision of law amended by subtitle A or E of title V of the Economic Growth and Tax Relief Reconciliation Act of 2001 is amended to read as such provision would read if such subtitle had never been enacted."

Prior to the enactment of Sec. 301(a) of P.L. 111-312, subpara. (a)(3)(C) read as follows:

"(C) a taxpayer in whose hands the basis of such property is determined (other than by reason of section 1022), for purposes of determining gain from a sale or exchange, in whole or part by reference to the basis of such property in the hands of a taxpayer described in subparagraph (A) or (B);

—P.L. 111-312, Sec. 301(c), of this Act, provides

"(c) Special election with respect to estates of decedents dying in 2010. Notwithstanding subsection (a), in the case of an estate of a decedent dying after December 31, 2009, and before January 1, 2011, the executor (within the meaning of section 2203 of the Internal Revenue Code of 1986) may elect to apply such Code as though the amendments made by subsection (a) do not apply with respect to chapter 11 of such Code and with respect to property acquired or passing from such decedent (within the meaning of section 1014(b) of such Code). Such election shall be made at such time and in such manner as the Secretary of the Treasury or the Secretary's delegate shall provide. Such an election once made shall be revocable only with the consent of the Secretary of the Treasury or the Secretary's delegate. For purposes of section 2652(a)(1) of such Code, the determination of whether any property is subject to the tax imposed by such chapter 11 shall be made without regard to any election made under this subsection."

—P.L. 111-312, Sec. 301(d), of this Act, provides

"(d) Extension of time for performing certain acts.

"(1) Estate tax. In the case of the estate of a decedent dying after December 31, 2009, and before the date of the enactment of this Act, the due date for—

"(A) filing any return under section 6018 of the Internal Revenue Code of 1986 (including any election required to be made on such a return) as such section is in effect after the date of the enactment of this Act without regard to any election under subsection (c),

"(B) making any payment of tax under chapter 11 of such Code, and

"(C) making any disclaimer described in section 2518(b) of such Code of an interest in property passing by reason of the death of such decedent, shall not be earlier that the date which is 9 months after the date of the enactment of this Act.

"(2) Generation-skipping tax. In the case of any generation-skipping transfer made after December 31, 2009, and before the date of the enactment of this Act, the due date for filing any return under section 2662 of the Internal Revenue Code of 1986 (including any election required to be made on such a return) shall not be earlier than the date which is 9 months after the date of the enactment of this Act."

In 2006, P.L. 109-432, Sec. 412(a), deleted "before January 1, 2011," after "sold or exchanged" in para. (b)(3), effective for sales and exchanges in tax. yrs. begin. after 5/17/2006.

—P.L. 109-222, Sec. 204(a), redesignated para. (b)(3) as (b)(4) and added para. (b)(3), effective for sales and exchanges in tax. yrs. begin. after 5/17/2006.

In 2002, P.L. 107-358, Sec. 2, added subsec. (c) in Sec. 901 of P.L. 107-16 [see below], effective 12/17/2002.

—P.L. 107-147, Sec. 417(20), substituted "1256(b)))" for "1256(b))" in clause (b)(1)(B)(i), effective 3/9/2002.

In 2001, P.L. 107-16, Sec. 542(e)(2)(A), added "(other than by reason of section 1022)" after "is determined" in subpara. (a)(3)(C), effective for estates of decedents dying after 12/31/2009.

—P.L. 107-16, Sec. 901, of this Act [as amended by Sec. 2 of P.L. 107-358, and Sec. 101(a)(1), P.L. 111-312, see above], reads as follows:

"SEC. 901. SUNSET OF PROVISIONS OF ACT.

"(a) In general. All provisions of, and amendments made by, this Act shall not apply—

"(1) to taxable, plan, or limitation years beginning after December 31, 2012, or

"(2) in the case of title V, to estates of decedents dying, gifts made, or generation skipping transfers, after December 31, 2012.

"(b) Application of certain laws. The Internal Revenue Code of 1986 and the Employee Retirement Income Security Act of 1974 shall be applied and administered to years, estates, gifts, and transfers described in subsection (a) as if the provisions and amendments described in subsection (a) had never been enacted.

"(c) Exception. Subsection (a) shall not apply to section 803 (relating to no federal income tax on restitution received by victims of the Nazi regime or their heirs or estates)."

In 1999, P.L. 106-170, Sec. 532(a)(1), substituted "(a) In general. For purposes" for "For purposes" in Code Sec. 1221 . . . Sec. 532(a)(2), substituted a semicolon for the period at the end of para. (a)(5) . . . Sec. 532(a)(3), added paras. (a)(6)-(8) and subsec. (b), effective for any instrument held, acquired, or entered into, any transaction entered into, and supplies held or acquired on or after 12/17/99.

In 1981, P.L. 97-34, Sec. 505(a), deleted para. (5) and redesignated para. (6) as para. (5), effective for property acquired and positions established by the taxpayer after 6/23/81, in tax. yrs. end. after 6/23/81. For election with respect to property held on 6/23/81, see Sec. 508(c) of this Act reproduced in note following Code Sec. 1092.

Prior to deletion, para. (5) read as follows:

"(5) an obligation of the United States or any of its possessions, or of a State or any political subdivision thereof, or of the District of Columbia, issued on or after March 1, 1941, on a discount basis and payable without interest at a fixed maturity date not exceeding one year from the date of issue; or"

In 1976, P.L. 94-455, Sec. 1901(c)(9), deleted "or Territory," after "or of a State" in para. (5), effective for tax. yrs. begin. after 12/31/76.

—P.L. 94-455, Sec. 2132(a)(1), deleted "or" at the end of para. (4) . . . Sec. 2132(a)(2), substituted "; or" for the period at the end of para. (5) . . . Sec. 2132(a)(3), added para. (6), effective for sales, exchanges and contributions made after 10/4/76.

In 1969, P.L. 91-172, Sec. 514(a), amended para. (3), effective for sales and other dispositions occurring after 7/25/69.

Prior to amendment, para. (3) read as follows:

"(3) a copyright, a literary, musical, or artistic composition, or similar property, held by—

"(A) a taxpayer whose personal efforts created such property, or

"(B) a taxpayer in whose hands the basis of such property is determined, for the purpose of determining gain from a sale or exchange, in whole or in part by reference to the basis of such property in the hands of the person whose personal efforts created such property;"

Sec. 1222. Other terms relating to capital gains and losses.

For purposes of this subtitle—

(1) Short-term capital gain. The term "short-term capital gain" means gain from the sale or exchange of a capital asset held for not more than 1 year , if and to the extent such gain is taken into account in computing gross income.

(2) Short-term capital loss. The term "short-term capital loss" means loss from the sale or exchange of a capital asset held for not more than 1 year , if and to the extent that such loss is taken into account in computing taxable income.

(3) Long-term capital gain. The term "long-term capital gain" means gain from the sale or exchange of a capital asset held for more than 1 year, if and to the extent such gain is taken into account in computing gross income.

(4) Long-term capital loss. The term "long-term capital loss" means loss from the sale or exchange of a capital asset held for more than 1 year, if and to the extent that such loss is taken into account in computing taxable income.

(5) Net short-term capital gain. The term "net short-term capital gain" means the excess of short-term capital gains for the taxable year over the short-term capital losses for such year.

(6) Net short-term capital loss. The term "net short-term capital loss" means the excess of short-term capital losses for the taxable year over the short-term capital gains for such year.

(7) Net long-term capital gain. The term "net long-term capital gain" means the excess of long-term capital gains for the taxable year over the long-term capital losses for such year.

(8) Net long-term capital loss. The term "net long-term capital loss" means the excess of long-term capital losses for the taxable year over the long-term capital gains for such year.

(9) Capital gain net income. The term "capital gain net income" means the excess of the gains from sales or exchanges of capital assets over the losses from such sales or exchanges.

(10) Net capital loss. The term "net capital loss" means the excess of the losses from sales or exchanges of capital assets over the sum allowed under section 1211. In the case of a corporation, for the purpose of determining losses under this paragraph, amounts which are short-term capital losses under section 1212(a)(1) shall be excluded.

(11) Net capital gain. The term "net capital gain" means the excess of the net long-term capital gain for the taxable year over the net short-term capital loss for such year.

For purposes of this subtitle, in the case of futures transactions in any commodity subject to the rules of a board of trade or commodity exchange, the length of the holding period taken into account under this section or under any other section amended by section 1402 of the Tax Reform Act of 1976 shall be determined without regard to the amendments made by subsections (a) and (b) of such section 1402.

In 2010, P.L. 111-325, Sec. 101(b)(2), substituted "section 1212(a)(1)" for "section 1212" in para. (10), effective for net capital losses for tax. yrs. begin. after 12/22/2010.

In 1984, P.L. 98-369, Sec. 1001(a)(1), substituted "6 months" for "1 year" in paras. (1) and (3) . . . Sec. 1001(a)(2), substituted "6 months" for "1 year" in paras. (2) and (4), effective for property acquired after 6/22/84, and before 1/1/88.

In 1976, P.L. 94-455, Sec. 1402(a)(1), substituted "9 months" for "6 months" in paras. (1), (2), (3) and (4), effective for tax. yrs. begin. in 1977.

—P.L. 94-455, Sec. 1402(a)(2), substituted "1 year" for "9 months" in paras. (1), (2), (3) and (4), effective for tax. yrs. begin. after 12/31/77. Sec. 1402(c) of this Act provides as follows:

"(c) Transitional rule for certain installment obligations.

"In the case of amounts received from sales or other dispositions of capital assets pursuant to binding contracts, including sales or other dispositions the income from which is returned on the basis and in the manner prescribed in section 453(a)(1) of the Internal Revenue Code of 1954, if the gain or loss was treated as long-term for the taxable year for which the amount was realized, such gain or loss shall be treated as long-term for the taxable year for which the gain or loss is returned or otherwise recognized."

—P.L. 94-455, Sec. 1402(d), added the sentence at the end of Code Sec. 1222, effective 10/4/76.

—P.L. 94-455, Sec. 1901(a)(136)(A), amended para. (9) . . . Sec. 1901(a)(136)(B), amended para. (11), effective for tax. yrs. begin. after 12/31/76.

Prior to amendment, para. (9) read as follows:

"(9) Net capital gain. The term 'net capital gain' means the excess of the gains from sales or exchanges of capital assets over the losses from such sales or exchanges."

Prior to amendment, para. (11) read as follows:

"(11) Net section 1201 gain. The term 'net section 1201 gain' means the excess of the net long-term capital gain for the taxable year over the net short-term capital loss for such year."

In 1969, P.L. 91-172, Sec. 511(a), added para. (11) . . . Sec. 513(c), substituted "The" for "In the case of a corporation, the" in para. (9), effective for tax. yrs. begin. after 12/31/69.

In 1964, P.L. 88-272, Sec. 230(b)(1), amended para. (9) . . . Sec. 230(b)(2), substituted "In the case of a corporation, for the purpose" for "For the purpose" in the second sentence of para. (10), effective for tax. yrs. begin. after 12/31/63.

Prior to amendment, para. (9) read as follows:

"(9) Net capital gain.—

"(A) Corporations.—In the case of a corporation, the term 'net capital gain' means the excess of the gains from sales or exchanges of capital assets over the losses from such sales or exchanges.

"(B) Other taxpayers.—In the case of a taxpayer other than a corporation, the term 'net capital gain' means the excess of—

"(i) the sum of the gains from sales or exchanges of capital assets, plus taxable income (computed without regard to the deductions provided by section 151, relating to personal exemptions or any deduction in lieu thereof) of the taxpayer or $1,000, whichever is smaller, over

"(ii) the losses from such sales or exchanges. For purposes of this subparagraph, taxable income shall be computed without regard to gains or losses from sales or exchanges of capital assets. If the taxpayer elects to pay the optional tax under section 3, the term 'taxable income' as used in this subparagraph shall be read as 'adjusted gross income.'"

Sec. 1223. Holding period of property.

For purposes of this subtitle—

(1) In determining the period for which the taxpayer has held property received in an exchange, there shall be included the period for which he held the property exchanged if, under this chapter, the property has, for the purpose of determining gain or loss from a sale or exchange, the same basis in whole or in part in his hands as the property exchanged, and, in the case of such exchanges after March 1, 1954, the property exchanged at the time of such exchange was a capital asset as defined in section 1221 or property described in section 1231. For purposes of this paragraph—

(A) an involuntary conversion described in section 1033 shall be considered an exchange of the property converted for the property acquired, and

(B) a distribution to which section 355 (or so much of section 356 as relates to section 355) applies shall be treated as an exchange.

(2) In determining the period for which the taxpayer has held property however acquired there shall be included the period for which such property was held by any other person, if under this chapter such property has, for the purpose of determining gain or loss from a sale or exchange, the same basis in whole or in part in his hands as it would have in the hands of such other person.

(3) In determining the period for which the taxpayer has held stock or securities the acquisition of which (or the contract or option to acquire which) resulted in the nondeductibility (under section 1091 relating to wash sales) of the loss from the sale or other disposition of substantially identical stock or securities, there shall be included the period for which he held the stock or securities the loss from the sale or other disposition of which was not deductible.

(4) In determining the period for which the taxpayer has held stock or rights to acquire stock received on a distribution, if the basis of such stock or rights is determined under section 307 (or under so much of section 1052(c) as refers to section 113(a)(23) of the Internal Revenue Code of 1939), there shall (under regulations prescribed by the Secretary) be included the period for which he held the stock in the distributing corporation before the receipt of such stock or rights upon such distribution.

(5) In determining the period for which the taxpayer has held stock or securities acquired from a corporation by the exercise of rights to acquire such stock or securities, there shall be included only the period beginning with the date on which the right to acquire was exercised.

(6) In determining the period for which the taxpayer has held a residence, the acquisition of which resulted under section 1034 (as in effect on the day before the date of the enactment [8/5/97] of the Taxpayer Relief Act of 1997) in the nonrecognition of any part of the gain realized on the sale or exchange of another residence, there shall be included the period for which such other residence had been held as of the date of such sale or exchange. For purposes of this paragraph, the term "sale or exchange" includes an involuntary conversion occurring after December 31, 1950, and before January 1, 1954.

(7) In determining the period for which the taxpayer has held a commodity acquired in satisfaction of a commodity futures contract (other than a commodity futures contract to which section 1256 applies) there shall be included the period for which he held the commodity futures contract if such commodity futures contract was a capital asset in his hands.

(8) Any reference in this section to a provision of this title shall, where applicable, be deemed a reference to the corresponding provision of the Internal Revenue Code of 1939, or prior internal revenue laws.

(9) In the case of a person acquiring property from a decedent or to whom property passed from a decedent (within the meaning of section 1014(b)), if—

(A) the basis of such property in the hands of such person is determined under section 1014, and

(B) such property is sold or otherwise disposed of by such person within 1 year after the decedent's death,

then such person shall be considered to have held such property for more than 1 year.

(10) If—

(A) property is acquired by any person in a transfer to which section 1040 applies,

(B) such property is sold or otherwise disposed of by such person within 1 year after the decedent's death, and

(C) such sale or disposition is to a person who is a qualified heir (as defined in section 2032A(e)(1)) with respect to the decedent,

then the person making such sale or other disposition shall be considered to have held such property for more than 1 year.

(11) In determining the period for which the taxpayer has held qualified replacement property (within the meaning of section 1042(b)) the acquisition of which resulted under section 1042 in the nonrecognition of any part of the gain realized on the sale of qualified securities (within the meaning of section 1042(b)), there shall be included the period for which such qualified securities had been held by the taxpayer.

(12) In determining the period for which the taxpayer has held property the acquisition of which resulted under section 1043 in the nonrecognition of any part of the gain realized on the sale of other property, there shall be included the period for which such other property had been held as of the date of such sale.

(13) Except for purposes of sections 1202(a)(2), 1202(c)(2)(A), 1400B(b), and 1400F(b), in determining the period for which the taxpayer has held property the acquisition of which resulted under section 1045 or 1397B in the nonrecognition of any part of the gain realized on the sale of other property, there shall be included the period for which such other property has been held as of the date of such sale.

(14) If the security to which a securities futures contract (as defined in section 1234B) relates (other than a contract to which section 1256 applies) is acquired in satisfaction of such contract, in determining the period for which the taxpayer has held such security, there shall be included the period for which the taxpayer held such contract if such contract was a capital asset in the hands of the taxpayer.

(15) Cross reference. For special holding period provision relating to certain partnership distributions, see section 735(b).

In **2005,** P.L. 109-135, Sec. 402(a)(2), deleted para. (3) and redesignated paras. (4)-(16) as paras. (3)-(15), effective 6 months after 8/8/2005 as if included in Sec. 1263 of the Energy Policy Act of 2005, P.L. 109-58. Sec. 1274(b) of P.L. 109-58, provides:

"(b) Compliance with certain rules. If the Commission approves and makes effective any final rulemaking modifying the standards of conduct governing entities that own, operate, or control facilities for transmission of electricity in interstate commerce or transportation of natural gas in interstate commerce prior to the effective date of this subtitle, any action taken by a public-utility company or utility holding company to comply with the requirements of such rulemaking shall not subject such public-utility company or utility holding company to any regulatory requirement applicable to a holding company under the Public Utility Holding Company Act of 1935 (15 U.S.C. 79 et seq.)."

—P.L. 109-135, Sec. 402(m)(2), of this Act, provides:

"(2) Repeal of Public Utility Holding Company Act of 1935. The amendments made by subsection (a) shall not apply with respect to any transaction ordered in compliance with the Public Utility Holding Company Act of 1935 before its repeal."

Prior to deletion, para. (3) read as follows:

"(3) In determining the period for which the taxpayer has held stock or securities received upon a distribution where no gain was recognized to the distributee under section 1081(c) (or under section 112(g) of the Revenue Act of 1928, 45 Stat. 818, or the Revenue Act of 1932, 48 Stat. 705), there shall be included the period for which he held the stock or securities in the distributing corporation before the receipt of the stock or securities on such distribution."

In **2004,** P.L. 108-357, Sec. 413(c)(21), deleted para. (10) and redesignated paras. (11)-(17) as paras. (10)-(16), effective for tax. yrs. of foreign corporations begin. after 12/31/2004, and for tax. yrs. of United States shareholders with or within which such tax. yrs. of foreign corporations end.

Prior to deletion, para. (10) read as follows:

"(10) In determining the period for which the taxpayer has held trust certificates of a trust to which subsection (d) of section 1246 applies, or the period for which the taxpayer has held stock in a corporation to which subsection (d) of section 1246 applies, there shall be included the period for which the trust or corporation (as the case may be) held the stock of foreign investment companies."

In **2000,** P.L. 106-554, Sec. 1(a)(7), [which enacted into law Sec. 116(b)(2) of P.L. 106-554] amended para. (15), effective for qualified empowerment zone assets acquired after 12/21/2000.

Prior to amendment, para. (15) read as follows:

"(15) In determining the period for which the taxpayer has held property the acquisition of which resulted under section 1045 in the nonrecognition of any part of the gain realized on the sale of other property, there shall be included the period for which such other property has been held as of the date of such sale."

—P.L. 106-554, Sec. 1(a)(7), [which enacted into law Sec. 401(h)(1) of P.L. 106-554] redesignated para. (16) as (17) and added para. (16), effective 12/21/2000.

In **1998,** P.L. 105-206, Sec. 5001(a)(5), substituted "1 year" for "18 months" each place it appeared in paras. (11) and (12), effective 1/1/98.

—P.L. 105-206, Sec. 6005(d)(4), substituted "18 months" for "1 year" each place it appeared in paras. (11) and (12), effective for tax. yrs. end. after 5/6/97.

—P.L. 105-206, Sec. 6005(e)(3), added "on or" before "before" in Sec. 312(d)(2) [sic (e)(2)] of P.L. 105-34, see below.

In **1997,** P.L. 105-34, Sec. 312(d)(9), added "(as in effect on the day before the date of the enactment of the Taxpayer Relief Act of 1997)" after "1034" in para. (7), effective for sales and exchanges after 5/6/97, except as provided by Secs. 312(d)(2)-(4) [sic (e)(2)-(4)] of this Act [as amended by Sec. 6005(e)(3) of 105-206, see above], which read as follows:

"(2) Sales on or before date of enactment. At the election of the taxpayer, the amendments made by this section shall not apply to any sale or exchange on or before the date of the enactment of this Act.

"(3) Certain sales within 2 years after date of enactment. Section 121 of the Internal Revenue Code of 1986 (as amended by this section) shall be applied without regard to subsection (c)(2)(B) thereof in the case of any sale or exchange of property during the 2-year period beginning on the date of the enactment of this Act if the taxpayer held such property on the date of the enactment of this Act and fails to meet the ownership and use requirements of subsection (a) thereof with respect to such property.

"(4) Binding contracts. At the election of the taxpayer, the amendments made by this section shall not apply to a sale or exchange after the date of the enactment of this Act, if—

"(A) such sale or exchange is pursuant to a contract which was binding on such date, or

"(B) without regard to such amendments, gain would not be recognized under section 1034 of the Internal Revenue Code of 1986 (as in effect on the day before the date of the enactment of this Act) on such sale or exchange by reason of a new residence acquired on or before such date or with respect to the acquisition of which by the taxpayer a binding contract was in effect on such date. This paragraph shall not apply to any sale or exchange by an individual if the treatment provided by section 877(a)(1) of the Internal Revenue Code of 1986 applies to such individual."

—P.L. 105-34, Sec. 313(b)(2), redesignated para. (15) as para. (16) and added new para. (15), effective for sales after 8/5/97.

In 1989, P.L. 101-194, Sec. 502(b)(1), redesignated para. (14) as para. (15) and added new para. (14), effective for sales after 11/30/89.

In 1988, P.L. 100-647, Sec. 1006(e)(17), amended para. 1223(14), effective for any distribution (not incomplete liquidation) made after 12/31/86.

Prior to amendment para. (14) read as follows:

"(14) Cross references.

"(A) For special holding period provision relating to certain partnership distributions, see section 735(b).

"(B) For special holding period provision relating to distributions of appreciated property to corporations, see section 301(e)."

In 1984, P.L. 98-369, Sec. 54(c), amended para. (13) (prior to redesignation by Sec. 541(b)(1)), effective for distributions after 7/18/84 in tax. yrs. ending after 7/18/84.

Prior to amendment, para. (13) read as follows:

"(13) Cross reference. For special holding period provision relating to certain partnership distributions, see section 735(b)."

—P.L. 98-369, Sec. 541(b)(1), redesignated para. (13) as para. (14) and added new para. (13), effective for sales of securities in tax. yrs. beginning after 7/18/84.

—P.L. 98-369, Sec. 1001(b)(14), substituted "6 months" for "1 year" each place it appeared in paragraphs (11) and (12), effective for property acquired after 6/22/84, and before 1/1/88.

In 1983, P.L. 97-448, Sec. 104(b)(3)(C), redesignated para. (12) as (13) and added para. (12), effective for estates of decedents dying after 12/31/76.

—P.L. 97-448, Sec. 105(c)(4), added "(other than a commodity futures contract to which section 1256 applies)" after "commodity futures contract" the first place it appeared in para. (8), effective for property acquired and positions established by the taxpayer after 6/23/81, in tax. yrs. end. after 6/23/81.

In 1980, P.L. 96-223, Sec. 401(a), repealed Sec. 702(c)(5) of P.L. 96-500 and the amendment made by Sec. 702(c)(5), effective for decedents dying after '76 [see below]. Sec. 401(b) of P.L. 96-223 provides as follows:

"(b) Revival of prior law.

"Except to the extent necessary to carry out subsection (d), the Internal Revenue Code of 1954 shall be applied and administered as if the provisions repealed by subsection (a), and the amendments made by those provisions, had not been enacted."

In 1978, P.L. 95-600, Sec. 702(c)(5), [repealed by Sec. 401(a) of P.L. 96-223, see above] added "or 1023" after "section 1014" in subpara. (11)(A).

In 1976, P.L. 94-455, Sec. 1402(b)(1)(Q), substituted "9 months" for "6 months" each place it appeared in para. (11), effective for tax. yrs. begin. in '77.

—P.L. 94-455, Sec. 1402(b)(2), of the Act substituted "1 year" for "9 months" each place it appeared in para. (11), effective for tax. yrs. begin. after 12/31/77. Sec. 1402(c) of the Act provided a transitional rule for certain installment obligations (see note at Code Sec. 1222).

—P.L. 94-455, Sec. 1906(b)(13)(A), substituted "Secretary" for "Secretary or his delegate" in para. (5), effective for tax. yrs. begin. after 12/31/76.

In 1970, P.L. 91-614, Sec. 101(g), redesignated para. (11) as para. (12) and added new para. (11), effective for decedents dying after 12/31/70.

In 1962, P.L. 87-834, Sec. 14(b)(3), added para. (10) and redesignated para. (10) as para. (11), effective for tax. yrs. begin. after 12/31/62.

PART IV.—SPECIAL RULES FOR DETERMINING CAPITAL GAINS AND LOSSES

Sec.
1231. Property used in the trade or business and involuntary conversions.
1232. Repealed.
1232A. Repealed.
1232B. Repealed.
1233. Gains and losses from short sales.
1234. Options to buy or sell.
1234A. Gains or losses from certain terminations.
1234B. Gains or losses from securities futures contracts.
1235. Sale or exchange of patents.
1236. Dealers in securities.
1237. Real property subdivided for sale.
1238. Repealed.
1239. Gain from sale of depreciable property between certain related taxpayers.
1240. Repealed.
1241. Cancellation of lease or distributor's agreement.
1242. Losses on small business investment company stock.
1243. Loss of small business investment company.
1244. Losses on small business stock.
1245. Gain from dispositions of certain depreciable property.
1246. [Repealed] Gain on foreign investment company stock.
1247. [Repealed] Election by foreign investment companies to distribute income currently.
1248. Gain from certain sales or exchanges of stock in certain foreign corporations.
1249. Gain from certain sales or exchanges of patents, etc., to foreign corporations.
1250. Gain from dispositions of certain depreciable realty.
1251. Repealed.
1252. Gain from the disposition of farm land.
1253. Transfers of franchises, trademarks, and trade names.
1254. Gain from disposition of interest in oil, gas, geothermal, or other mineral properties.
1255. Gain from disposition of section 126 property.
1256. Section 1256 contracts marked to market.
1257. Disposition of converted wetlands or highly erodible croplands.
1258. Recharacterization of gain from certain financial transactions.
1259. Constructive sales treatment for appreciated financial positions.
1260. Gains from constructive ownership transactions.

In 2004, P.L. 108-357, Sec. 413(c)(32), deleted items 1246 and 1247, effective for tax. yrs. of foreign corporations begin. after 12/31/2004, and for tax. yrs. of United States shareholders with or within which such tax. yrs. of foreign corporations end.

Prior to deletion, items 1246 and 1247 read as follows:

"1246. Gain on foreign investment company stock."

"1247. Election by foreign investment companies to distribute income currently."

—P.L. 108-311, Sec. 408(a)(18), amended item 1234B.

Prior to amendment, item 1234B read as follows:

"1234B. Securities futures contracts."

In 2000, P.L. 106-554, Sec. 1(a)(7) [which enacted into law Sec. 401(h)(2) of H.R. 5662], added item 1234B.

In 1999, P.L. 106-170, Sec. 534(b), added item 1260.

In 1997, P.L. 105-34, Sec. 1001(c), added item 1259.

In 1993, P.L. 103-66, Sec. 13206(a)(2), added item 1258.

In 1990, P.L. 101-508, Sec. 11801(b)(10), deleted item 1238.

Prior to deletion, item 1238 read as follows:

"1238. Amortization in excess of depreciation."

In 1988, P.L. 100-647, Sec. 1018(u)(24), amended item 1254.

Prior to amendment, item 1254 read as follows:

"1254. Gain from disposition of interest in oil, gas, or geothermal property."

In 1986, P.L. 99-514, Sec. 403(b), added item 1257.

In 1984, P.L. 98-369, Sec. 42(b)(2), deleted items 1232, 1232A, and 1232B . . . Sec. 102(e)(6), substituted "Section 1256" for "Regulated futures" in item 1256 . . . Sec. 492(c), deleted item 1251.

Prior to deletion the items for 1232, 1232A and 1232B and 1251 read as follows:

"1232. Bonds and other evidences of indebtedness.

"1232A. Original issue discount.

"1232B. Tax treatment of stripped bonds.

"1251. Gain from disposition of property used in farming where farm losses offset non-farm income."

In 1982, P.L. 97-248, Sec. 231(d), added item 1232A.

—P.L. 97-248, Sec. 232(c), added item 1232B.

In 1981, P.L. 97-34, Sec. 507(b), added item 1234A . . . Sec. 503(b), added item 1256.

In 1978, P.L. 95-600, Sec. 543(c)(2), added item 1255.

—P.L. 95-600, Sec. 402(c)(4), amended the item of Code Sec. 1254 by substituting "oil, gas, or geothermal" for "oil or gas."

In 1976, P.L. 94-455, Sec. 205(d), added item 1254.

—P.L. 94-455, Sec. 1901(b)(34), deleted item 1240.

Prior to repeal, item 1240 read as follows:

"1240. Taxability to employee of termination payments."
In 1969, P.L. 91-172, Sec. 211(b)(7), added item 1251.
—P.L. 91-172, Sec. 214(b), added item 1252.
—P.L. 91-172, Sec. 516(c)(1), added item 1253.
In 1964, added item 1250.
In 1962, added items 1245–1249.
In 1958, added items 1242–1244.

Sec. 1231. Property used in the trade or business and involuntary conversions.
(a) General rule.
  (1) Gains exceed losses. If—
    (A) the section 1231 gains for any taxable year, exceed
    (B) the section 1231 losses for such taxable year,
  such gains and losses shall be treated as long-term capital gains or long-term capital losses, as the case may be.
  (2) Gains do not exceed losses. If—
    (A) the section 1231 gains for any taxable year, do not exceed
    (B) the section 1231 losses for such taxable year,
  such gains and losses shall not be treated as gains and losses from sales or exchanges of capital assets.
  (3) Section 1231 gains and losses. For purposes of this subsection—
    (A) Section 1231 gain. The term "section 1231 gain" means—
      (i) any recognized gain on the sale or exchange of property used in the trade or business, and
      (ii) any recognized gain from the compulsory or involuntary conversion (as a result of destruction in whole or in part, theft or seizure, or an exercise of the power of requisition or condemnation or the threat or imminence thereof) into other property or money of—
        (I) property used in the trade or business, or
        (II) any capital asset which is held for more than 1 year and is held in connection with a trade or business or a transaction entered into for profit.
    (B) Section 1231 loss. The term "section 1231 loss" means any recognized loss from a sale or exchange or conversion described in subparagraph (A).
  (4) Special rules. For purposes of this subsection—
    (A) In determining under this subsection whether gains exceed losses—
      (i) the section 1231 gains shall be included only if and to the extent taken into account in computing gross income, and
      (ii) the section 1231 losses shall be included only if and to the extent taken into account in computing taxable income, except that section 1211 shall not apply.
    (B) Losses (including losses not compensated for by insurance or otherwise) on the destruction, in whole or in part, theft or seizure, or requisition or condemnation of—
      (i) property used in the trade or business, or
      (ii) capital assets which are held for more than 1 year and are held in connection with a trade or business or a transaction entered into for profit,
    shall be treated as losses from a compulsory or involuntary conversion.
    (C) In the case of any involuntary conversion (subject to the provisions of this subsection but for this sentence) arising from fire, storm, shipwreck, or other casualty, or from theft, of any—
      (i) property used in the trade or business, or
      (ii) any capital asset which is held for more than 1 year and is held in connection with a trade or business or a transaction entered into for profit,
    this subsection shall not apply to such conversion (whether resulting in gain or loss) if during the taxable year the recognized losses from such conversions exceed the recognized gains from such conversions.
(b) Definition of property used in the trade or business.
  For purposes of this section—
  (1) General rule. The term "property used in the trade or business" means property used in the trade or business, of a character which is subject to the allowance for depreciation provided in section 167, held for more than 1 year, and real property used in the trade or business, held for more than 1 year, which is not—
    (A) property of a kind which would properly be includible in the inventory of the taxpayer if on hand at the close of the taxable year,
    (B) property held by the taxpayer primarily for sale to customers in the ordinary course of his trade or business,
    (C) a copyright, a literary, musical, or artistic composition, a letter or memorandum, or similar property, held by a taxpayer described in paragraph (3) of section 1221(a), or
    (D) a publication of the United States Government (including the Congressional Record) which is received from the United States Government, or any agency thereof, other than by purchase at the price at which it is offered for sale to the public, and which is held by a taxpayer described in paragraph (5) of section 1221(a).
  (2) Timber, coal, or domestic iron ore. Such term includes timber, coal, and iron ore with respect to which section 631 applies.
  (3) Livestock. Such term includes—
    (A) cattle and horses, regardless of age, held by the taxpayer for draft, breeding, dairy, or sporting purposes, and held by him for 24 months or more from the date of acquisition, and
    (B) other livestock, regardless of age, held by the taxpayer for draft, breeding, dairy, or sporting purposes, and held by him for 12 months or more from the date of acquisition.
  Such term does not include poultry.
  (4) Unharvested crop. In the case of an unharvested crop on land used in the trade or business and held for more than 1 year, if the crop and the land are sold or exchanged (or compulsorily or involuntarily converted) at the same time and to the same person, the crop shall be considered as "property used in the trade or business."
(c) Recapture of net ordinary losses.
  (1) In general. The net section 1231 gain for any taxable year shall be treated as ordinary income to the extent such gain does not exceed the non-recaptured net section 1231 losses.
  (2) Non-recaptured net section 1231 losses. For purposes of this subsection, the term "non-recaptured net section 1231 losses" means the excess of—
    (A) the aggregate amount of the net section 1231 losses for the 5 most recent preceding taxable years beginning after December 31, 1981, over
    (B) the portion of such losses taken into account under paragraph (1) for such preceding taxable years.
  (3) Net section 1231 gain. For purposes of this subsection, the term "net section 1231 gain" means the excess of—
    (A) the section 1231 gains, over

(B) the section 1231 losses.

(4) Net section 1231 loss. For purposes of this subsection, the term "net section 1231 loss" means the excess of—

(A) the section 1231 losses, over

(B) the section 1231 gains.

(5) Special rules. For purposes of determining the amount of the net section 1231 gain or loss for any taxable year, the rules of paragraph (4) of subsection (a) shall apply.

In **1999**, P.L. 106-170, Sec. 532(c)(1)(G), substituted "section 1221(a)" for "section 1221" in subpara. (b)(1)(C) and (D), effective for any instrument held, acquired, or entered into, any transaction entered into, and supplies held or acquired on or after 12/17/99.

In **1984**, P.L. 98-369, Sec. 176(a), added subsec. (c), effective for net Code Sec. 1231 gains for tax. yrs. begin. after 12/31/84.

—P.L. 98-369, Sec. 711(c)(2)(A)(iii), amended subsec. (a), effective for tax. yrs. begin. after 12/31/83. Sec. 711(c)(2)(B) of the Act provides:

"(B) Transitional rule. In the case of taxable years beginning before January 1, 1984—

"(i) For purposes of paragraph (1)(B) of section 165(h) of the Internal Revenue Code of 1954, adjusted gross income shall be determined without regard to the application of section 1231 of such Code to any gain or loss from an involuntary conversion of property described in subsection (c)(3) of section 165 of such Code arising from fire, storm, shipwreck, or other casualty or from theft.

"(ii) Section 1231 of such Code shall be applied after the application of paragraph (1) of section 165(h) of such Code."

Prior to amendment, subsec. (a) read as follows:

"(a) General rule.

"If, during the taxable year, the recognized gains on sales or exchanges of property used in the trade or business, plus the recognized gains from the compulsory or involuntary conversion (as a result of destruction in whole or in part, theft or seizure, or an exercise of the power of requisition or condemnation or the threat or imminence thereof) of property used in the trade or business and capital assets held for more than 1 year into other property or money, exceed the recognized losses from such sales, exchanges, and conversions, such gains and losses shall be considered as gains and losses from sales or exchanges of capital assets held for more than 1 year. If such gains do not exceed such losses, such gains and losses shall not be considered as gains and losses from sales or exchanges of capital assets. For purposes of this subsection—

"(1) in determining under this subsection whether gains exceed losses, the gains described therein shall be included only if and to the extent taken into account in computing gross income and the losses described therein shall be included only if and to the extent taken into account in computing taxable income, except that section 1211 shall not apply; and

"(2) losses (including losses not compensated for by insurance or otherwise) upon the destruction, in whole or in part, theft or seizure, or requisition or condemnation of (A) property used in the trade or business or (B) capital assets held for more than 1 year shall be considered losses from a compulsory or involuntary conversion.

In the case of any involuntary conversion (subject to the provisions of this subsection but for this sentence) arising from fire, storm, shipwreck, or other casualty, or from theft, of any property held in the trade or business or of any capital asset held for more than 1 year, this subsection shall not apply to such conversion (whether resulting in gain or loss) if during the taxable year the recognized losses from such conversions exceed the recognized gains from such conversions."

—P.L. 98-369, Sec. 1001(b)(15), substituted "6 months" for "1 year" each place it appeared in Code Sec. 1231, effective for property acquired after 6/22/84, and before 1/1/88.

In **1981**, P.L. 97-34, Sec. 505(c)(1), substituted "paragraph (5)" for "paragraph (6)" in subpara. (b)(1)(D), effective for property acquired and positions established by the taxpayer after 6/23/81, in tax. yrs. end. after 6/23/81. For election with respect to property held on 6/23/81, see Sec. 508(c) of this Act reproduced in note following Code Sec. 1092.

In **1978**, P.L. 95-600, Sec. 701(ee)(1)(A), deleted "or" at the end of subpara. (b)(1)(B) . . . Sec. 701(ee)(1)(B), substituted ", or" for the period at the end of subpara. (b)(1)(C) . . . Sec. 701(ee)(1)(C), added new subpara. (b)(1)(D), effective for sales, exchanges, and contributions made after 10/4/76.

In **1976**, P.L. 94-455, Sec. 1402(b)(1)(R), substituted "9 months" for "6 months" each place it appeared in Code Sec. 1231, effective for tax. yrs. begin. in 1977.

—P.L. 94-455, Sec. 1402(b)(2), substituted "1 year" for "9 months" each place it appeared in Code Sec. 1231, effective for tax. yrs. begin. after 12/31/77. Sec. 1402(c) of the Act provided a transitional rule for certain installment obligations (see note at Code Sec. 1222).

In **1969**, P.L. 91-172, Sec. 212(b)(1), amended para. (b)(3), effective for livestock acquired after 12/31/69.

Prior to amendment, para. (b)(3) read as follows:

"(3) Livestock. Such term also includes livestock, regardless of age, held by the taxpayer for draft, breeding, or dairy purposes, and held by him for 12 months or more from the date of acquisition. Such term does not include poultry."

—P.L. 91-172, Sec. 514(b)(2), added ", a letter or memorandum" before ", or similar property" in subpara. (b)(1)(C), effective for sales and other dispositions occurring after 7/25/69.

—P.L. 91-172, Sec. 516(b), amended all that follows para. (a)(1), effective for tax. yrs. begin. after 12/31/69.

Prior to amendment, all that followed para. (a)(1) read as follows:

"(2) losses upon the destruction, in whole or in part, theft or seizure, or requisition or condemnation of property used in the trade or business or capital assets held for more than 6 months shall be considered losses from a compulsory or involuntary conversion.

In the case of any property used in the trade or business and of any capital asset held for more than 6 months and held for the production of income, this subsection shall not apply to any loss, in respect of which the taxpayer is not compensated for by insurance in any amount, arising from fire, storm, shipwreck, or other casualty, or from theft."

In **1964**, P.L. 88-272, Sec. 227(a)(2), amended para. (b)(2), effective for amounts received or accrued in tax. yrs. begin. after 12/31/63, attributable to iron ore mined in such tax. yrs.

Prior to amendment, para. (b)(2) read as follows:

"(2) Timber or coal, such term includes timber and coal with respect to which section 631 applies."

In **1958**, P.L. 85-866, Sec. 49(a), added a sentence at the end of subsec. (a), effective for tax. yrs. begin. after 12/31/57.

Sec. 1232. Repealed.

In **1984**, P.L. 98-369, Sec. 42(a)(1), repealed Code Sec. 1232 [as amended by Sec. 1001(b)(16) and 1001(d) of this Act], effective for tax. yrs. ending after 7/18/84.

—P.L. 98-369, Sec. 1001(b)(16), substituted "6 months [more than 1 year for property acquired before 6/23/84 and after 12/31/87]" for "1 year" each place it appeared in para. (a)(2), as repealed by Sec. 42(a)(1) of this Act . . . Sec. 1001(d), deleted "held less than 1 year" after "sale or exchange or a capital asset" in subpara. (a)(3)(A), as repealed by Sec. 42(a)(1), of this Act, effective for property acquired after 6/22/84 and before 1/1/88.

Prior to repeal, Code Sec. 1232 read as follows:

"Sec. 1232. BONDS AND OTHER EVIDENCES OF INDEBTEDNESS.

"(a) General rule.

"For purposes of this subtitle, in the case of bonds, debentures, notes, or certificates or other evidences of indebtedness, which are capital assets in the hands of the taxpayer, and which are issued by any corporation, or by any government or political subdivision thereof—

"(1) Retirement. Amounts received by the holder on retirement of such bonds or other evidences of indebtedness shall be considered as amounts received in exchange therefor (except that in the case of bonds or other evidences of indebtedness issued before January 1, 1955, this paragraph shall apply only to those issued with interest coupons or in registered form, or to those in such form on March 1, 1954).

"(2) Sale or exchange.

"(A) Corporate bonds issued after May 27, 1969, and government bonds issued after July 1, 1982. Except as provided in subparagraph (C), on the sale or exchange of bonds or other evidences of indebtedness issued by a corporation after May 27, 1969, or by a government or political subdivision thereof after July 1, 1982 held by the taxpayer more than 6 months [more than 1 year for property acquired before 6/23/84 and after 12/31/87] any gain realized shall (except as provided in the following sentence) be considered gain from the sale or exchange of a capital asset held for more than 6 months [more than 1 year for property acquired before 6/23/84 and after 12/31/87]. If at the time of original issue there was an intention to call the bond or other evidence of indebtedness before maturity, any gain realized on the sale or exchange thereof which does not exceed an amount equal to the original issue discount (as defined in subsection (b)) reduced by the portion of original issue discount previously includible in the gross income of any holder (without regard to subsection (a)(6) or (b)(4) of section 1232A (or the corresponding provisions of prior law)) shall be considered as ordinary income.

"(B) Corporate bonds issued on or before May 27, 1969, and government bonds issued on or before July 1, 1982. Except as provided in subparagraph (C), on the sale or exchange of bonds or other evidences of indebtedness issued by a government or political subdivision thereof after December 31, 1954, and on or before July 1, 1982, or by a corporation after December 31, 1954, and on or before May 27, 1969, held by the taxpayer more than 6 months [more than 1 year for property acquired before 6/23/84 and after 12/31/87], any gain realized which does not exceed—

"(i) an amount equal to the original issue discount (as defined in subsection (b)), or

"(ii) if at the time of original issue there was no intention to call the bond or other evidence of indebtedness before maturity, an amount which bears the same ratio to the original issue discount (as defined in subsection (b)) as the number of complete months that the bond or other evidence of indebtedness was held by the taxpayer bears to the number of complete months from the date of original issue to the date of maturity,

shall be considered as ordinary income. Gain in excess of such amount shall be considered gain from the sale or exchange of a capital asset held more than 6 months [more than 1 year for property acquired before 6/23/84 and after 12/31/87].

"(C) Exceptions. This paragraph shall not apply to—

"(i) obligations the interest on which is not includible in gross income under section 103 (relating to certain governmental obligations), or

"(ii) any holder who has purchased the bond or other evidence of indebtedness at a premium.

"(D) Double inclusion in income not required. This section and sections 1232A and 1232B shall not require the inclusion of any amount previously includible in gross income.

"(3) Certain short-term government obligations.

"(A) In general. On the sale or exchange of any short-term Government obligation, any gain realized which does not exceed an amount equal to the ratable share of the acquisition discount shall be treated as ordinary income. Gain in excess of such amount shall be considered gain from the sale or exchange of a capital asset.

"(B) Short-term government obligation. For purposes of this paragraph, the term 'short-term Government obligation' means any obligation of the United States or any of its possessions, or of a State or any political subdivision thereof, or of the District of Columbia which is issued on a discount basis and payable without interest at a fixed maturity date not exceeding 1 year from the date of issue. Such term does not include any obligation the interest on which is not includible in gross income under section 103 (relating to certain governmental obligations).

"(C) Acquisition discount. For purposes of this paragraph, the term 'acquisition discount' means the excess of the stated redemption price at maturity over the taxpayer's basis for the obligation.

"(D) Ratable share. For purposes of this paragraph, the ratable share of the acquisition discount is an amount which bears the same ratio to such discount as—

"(i) the number of days which the taxpayer held the obligation, bears to

"(ii) the number of days after the date the taxpayer acquired the obligation and up to (and including) the date of its maturity.

"(b) Definitions.

"(1) Original issue discount. For purposes of subsection (a), the term 'original issue discount' means the difference between the issue price and the stated redemption price at maturity. If the original issue discount is less than one-fourth of 1 percent of the redemption price at maturity multiplied by the number of complete years to maturity, then the issue discount shall be considered to be zero. For purposes of this paragraph, the term 'stated redemption price at maturity' means the amount fixed by the last modification of the purchase agreement and includes dividends payable at that time.

"(2) Issue price. In the case of issues of bonds or other evidences of indebtedness registered with the Securities and Exchange Commission, the term 'issue price' means the initial offering price to the public (excluding bond housed and brokers) at which price a substantial amount of such bonds or other evidences of indebtedness were sold. In the case of privately placed issues of bonds or other evidence of indebtedness, the issue price of each such bond or other evidence of indebtedness is the price paid by the first buyer of such bond increased by the amount, if any, of tax paid under section 4911, as in effect before July 1, 1974 (and not credited, refunded, or reimbursed) on the acquisition of such bond or evidence of indebtedness by the first buyer. For purposes of this paragraph, the terms 'initial offering price' and 'price paid by the first buyer' include the aggregate payments made by the purchaser under the purchase agreement, including modifications thereof.

In the case of a bond or other evidence of indebtedness and an option or other security issued together as an investment unit, the issue price for such investment unit shall be determined in accordance with the rules stated in this paragraph. Such issue price attributable to each element of the investment unit shall be that portion thereof which the fair market value of such element bears to the total fair market value of all the elements in the investment unit. The issue price of the bond or other evidence of indebtedness included in such investment unit shall be the portion so allocated to it. In the case of a bond or other evidence of indebtedness, or an investment unit as described in this paragraph, which is issued for property and which—

"(A) is part of an issue a portion of which is traded on an established securities market, or

"(B) is issued for stock or securities which are traded on an established securities market,

the issue price of such bond or other evidence of indebtedness or investment unit, as the case may be, shall be the fair market value of such property. Except in cases to which the preceding sentence applies, the issue price of a bond or other evidence of indebtedness (whether or not issued as a part of an investment unit) which is issued for property (other than money) shall be the stated redemption price at maturity.

"(3) Issue date. In the case of issues of bonds or other evidences of indebtedness registered with the Securities and Exchange Commission, the term 'date of original issue' means the date on which the issue was first sold to the public at the issue price. In the case of privately placed issues of bonds or other evidences of indebtedness, the term 'date of original issue' means the date on which each such bond or other evidence of indebtedness was sold by the issuer.

"(4) Special rule for exchange of bonds in reorganizations.

"(A) In general. If—

"(i) any bond is issued pursuant to a plan of reorganization within the meaning of section 368(a)(1) for another bond (hereinafter in this paragraph referred to as the 'old bond'), and

"(ii) the fair market value of the old bond is less than its adjusted issue price, then, for purposes of the next to the last sentence of paragraph (2), the fair market value of the old bond shall be treated as equal to its adjusted issue price.

"(B) Definitions. For purposes of this paragraph—

"(i) Bond. The term 'bond' includes any other evidence of indebtedness and an investment unit.

"(ii) Adjusted issue price.

"(I) In general. The adjusted issue price of the old bond is its issue price, increased by the portion of any original issue discount previously includible in the gross income of any holder (without regard to subsection (a)(6) or (b)(4) of section 1232A (or the corresponding provisions of prior law)).

"(II) Special rule for applying section 163(e). For purposes of section 163(e), the adjusted issue price of the old bond is its issue price, increased by any original issue discount previously allowed as a deduction.

"(c) Denial of capital gain treatment for gains on certain obligations not in registered form.

"(1) In general. If any registration-required obligation is not in registered form, any gain on the sale or other disposition of such obligation shall be treated as ordinary income (unless the issuance of such obligation was subject to tax under section 4701).

"(2) Definitions. For purposes of this subsection—

"(A) Registration-required obligation. The term 'registration-required obligation' has the meaning given to such term by section 163(f)(2) except that clause (iv) of subparagraph (A), and subparagraph (B), of such section shall not apply.

"(B) Registered form. Term 'registered form' has the same meaning as when used in section 163(f)."

In 1983, P.L. 97-448, Sec. 306(a)(9)(B), redesignated subsec. (d) as subsec. (c).

—P.L. 97-448, Sec. 306(a)(9)(C)(i), deleted "(other than a bond or other evidence of indebtedness or an investment unit issued pursuant to a plan of reorganization within the meaning of section 368(a)(1) or an insolvency reorganization within the meaning of section 371 or 374)" after "described in this paragraph" in the next to the last sentence of para. (b)(2) . . . Sec. 306(a)(9)(C)(ii), added para. (b)(4), effective as provided in Sec. 306(a)(9)(C)(iv) of this Act which reads as follows:

"(iv) The amendments made by this subparagraph [Sec. 306(a)(9)(C) of P.L. 97-448] shall apply to evidences of indebtedness issued after December 13, 1982; except that such amendments shall not apply to any evidence of indebtedness issued after such date pursuant to a written commitment which was binding on such date and at all times thereafter."

—P.L. 97-448, Sec. 306(a)(9)(C)(iii), of this Act provides:

"(iii) For purposes of paragraph (4) of section 1232(b) of the Internal Revenue Code of 1954 (as added by clause (ii) [Sec. 306(a)(9)(C)]), any insolvency reorganization within the meaning of section 371 or 374 of such Code shall be treated as a reorganization within the meaning of section 368(a)(1) of such Code."

In 1982, P.L. 97-248, Sec. 231(c)(1)(A), substituted "by a corporation after May 27, 1969, or by a government or political subdivision thereof after July 1, 1982" for "by a corporation after May 27, 1969" in subpara. (a)(2)(A) . . . Sec. 231(c)(1)(B), substituted "without regard to subsection (a)(6) or (b)(4) of section 1232A (or the corresponding provisions of prior law" for "as provided in paragraph (3)(B)" in subpara. (a)(2)(A) . . . Sec. 231(c)(1)(C), substituted "(A) Corporate bonds issued after May 27, 1969, and government bonds issued after July 1, 1982." for "(A) Corporate bonds issued after May 27, 1969." as the heading for subpara. (a)(2)(A) . . . Sec. 231(c)(2)(A), substituted "by a government or political subdivision thereof after December 31, 1954, and on or before July 1, 1982" for "by a government or political subdivision thereof after December 31, 1954" in subpara. (a)(2)(B) . . . Sec. 231(c)(2)(B), substituted "government bonds issued on or before July 1, 1982" for "government bonds" in the heading of subpara. (a)(2)(B) . . . Sec. 231(c)(3), substituted "This section and sections 1232A and 1232B" for "This section" in subpara. (a)(2)(D) . . . Sec. 231(c)(4), deleted para. (a)(3) and redesignated para. (a)(4) as para. (a)(3), effective 9/3/82. Sec. 231(e) of this Act provides:

"(e) Transitional rule.— For purposes of the amendments made by this section, any evidence of indebtedness issued pursuant to a written commitment which was binding on July 1, 1982, and at all times thereafter shall be treated as issued on July 1, 1982."

Prior to deletion, para. (a)(3) read as follows:

"(3) Inclusion in income of original issue discount on corporate bonds issued after May 27, 1969.

"(A) General rule. There shall be included in the gross income of the holder of any bond or other evidence of indebtedness issued by a corporation after May 27, 1969, the ratable monthly portion of original issue discount multiplied by the number of complete months (plus any fractional part of a month determined in accordance with the last sentence of this subparagraph) such holder held such bond or other evidence of indebtedness during the taxable year. Except as provided in subparagraph (B), the ratable monthly portion of original issued discount shall equal the original issue discount (as defined in subsection (b)) divided by the number of complete months from the date of original issue to the stated maturity date of such bond or other evidence of indebtedness. For purposes of this section, a complete month commences with the date of original issue and the corresponding day of each succeeding calendar month (or the last day of a calendar month in which there is no corresponding day); and, in any case where a bond or other evidence of indebtedness is acquired on any other day, the ratable monthly portion of original issue discount for the complete month in which such acquisition occurs shall be allocated between the transferor and the transferee in accordance with the number of days in such complete month each held the bond or other evidence of indebtedness.

"(B) Reduction in case of any subsequent holder. For purposes of this paragraph, the ratable monthly portion of original issue discount shall not include an amount, determined at the time of any purchase after the original issue of such bond or other evidence of indebtedness, equal to the excess of—

"(i) the cost of such bond or other evidence of indebtedness incurred by such holder, over

"(ii) the issue price of such bond or other evidence of indebtedness increased by the portion of original discount previously includible in the gross income of any holder (computed without regard to this subparagraph), divided by the number of complete months (plus any fractional part of a month commencing with the date of purchase) from the date of such purchase to the stated maturity date of such bond or other evidence of indebtedness.

"(C) Purchase defined. For purposes of subparagraph (B), the term 'purchase' means any acquisition of a bond or other evidence of indebtedness, but only if the basis of the bond or other evidence of indebtedness is not determined in whole or in part by reference to the adjusted basis of such bond or other evidence of indebtedness in the hands of the person from whom acquired, or under section 1014(a) (relating to property acquired from a decedent).

"(D) Exceptions. This paragraph shall not apply to any holder—

"(i) who has purchased the bond or other evidence of indebtedness at a premium, or

"(ii) which is a life insurance company to which section 818(b) applies.

"(E) Basis adjustments. The basis of any bond or other evidence of indebtedness in the hands of the holder thereof shall be increased by the amount included in his gross income pursuant to subparagraph (A)."

—P.L. 97-248, Sec. 232(b), repealed subsecs. (c) and (d), effective 9/3/82.

Prior to repeal, subsecs. (c) and (d) read as follows:

"(c) Bond with unmatured coupons detached.

"If a bond or other evidence of indebtedness issued at any time with interest coupons—

"(1) is purchased after August 16, 1954, and before January 1, 1958, and the purchaser does not receive all the coupons which first become payable more than 12 months after the date of the purchase, or

"(2) is purchased after December 31, 1957, and the purchaser does not receive all the coupons which first become payable after the date of the purchase,

then the gain on the sale or other disposition of such evidence of indebtedness by such purchaser (or by a person whose basis is determined by reference to the basis in the hands of such purchaser) shall be considered as ordinary income to the extent that the fair market value (determined as of the time of the purchase) of the evidence of indebtedness with coupons attached exceeds the purchase price. If this subsection and subsection (a)(2)(A) apply with respect to gain realized on the sale or exchange of any evidence of indebtedness, then subsection (a)(2)(A) shall apply with respect to that part of the gain to which this subsection does not apply.

"(d) Cross reference.

"For special treatment of face-amount certificates on retirement, see section 72."

—P.L. 97-248, Sec. 310(b)(6), redesignated subsec. (d) and subsec. (e) [sic , subsecs. (c) and (d), were repealed by Sec. 232(b) of P.L. 97-248, see above] and added new subsec. (d) [sic c)], for obligations issued after 12/31/82. Sec. 310(d)(3) of this Act provides:

"(3) Exception for certain warrants, etc.— The amendments made by subsection (b) shall not apply to any obligations issued after December 31, 1982, on the exercise of a warrant or the conversion of a convertible obligation if such warrant or obligation was offered or sold outside the United States without registration under the Securities Act of 1933 and was issued before August 10, 1982. A rule similar to the rule of the preceding sentence shall also apply in the case of any regulations issued under section 163(f)(2)(C) of the Internal Revenue Code of 1954 (as added by this section) except that the date on which such regulations take effect shall be substituted for 'August 10, 1982'."

In **1981**, P.L. 97-34, Sec. 505(b), added para. (a)(4), effective for property acquired and positions established by the taxpayer after 6/23/81, in tax. yrs. end. after 6/23/81. For election with respect to property held on 6/23/81, see Sec. 508(c) of this Act reproduced in note following Code Sec. 1092.

In **1976**, P.L. 94-455, Sec. 1402(b)(1)(S), substituted "9 months" for "6 months" each place it appeared in para. (a)(2), effective for tax. yrs. begin. in 1977.

—P.L. 94-455, Sec. 1402(b)(2), substituted "1 year" for "9 months" each place it appeared in para. (a)(2), effective for tax. yrs. begin. after 12/31/77. For transitional rules, see Sec. 1402(c) of this Act, reproduced in note following Code Sec. 1222.

—P.L. 94-455, Sec. 1901(b)(3)(I), substituted "ordinary income" for "gain from the sale or exchange of property which is not a capital asset" each place it appeared in subparas. (a)(2)(A) and (B) and subsec. (c), effective for tax. yrs. begin. after 12/31/76.

—P.L. 94-455, Sec. 1901(b)(14)(D), substituted "section 371 or 374" for "section 371, 373, or 374" in para. (b)(2), effective for tax. yrs. begin. after 12/31/76.

—P.L. 94-455, Sec. 1904(b)(10)(C), substituted "section 4911, as in effect before July 1, 1974" for "section 4911" in para. (b)(2), effective 2/1/77.

In **1969**, P.L. 91-172, Sec. 413(a), amended subsec. (a), effective for bonds and other evidences of indebtedness issued after 5/27/69 (other than evidences issued pursuant to a written commitment which was binding on 5/27/69, and at all times thereafter).

Prior to amendment, subsec. (a) read as follows:

"(a) General rule.

"For purposes of this subtitle, in the case of bonds, debentures, notes, or certificates or other evidences of indebtedness, which are capital assets in the hands of the taxpayer, and which are issued by any corporation, or government or political subdivision thereof—

"(1) Retirement. Amounts received by the holder on retirement of such bonds or other evidences of indebtedness shall be considered as amounts received in exchange therefor (except that in the case of bonds or other evidences of indebtedness issued before January 1, 1955, this paragraph shall apply only to those issued with interest coupons or in registered form, or to those in such form on March 1, 1954).

"(2) Sale or exchange.

"(A) General rule. Except as provided in subparagraph (B), upon sale or exchange of bonds or other evidences of indebtedness issued after December 31, 1954, held by the taxpayer more than 6 months, any gain realized which does not exceed—

"(i) an amount equal to the original issue discount (as defined in subsection (b)), or

"(ii) if at the time of original issue there was no intention to call the bond or other evidence of indebtedness before maturity, an amount which bears the same ratio to the original issue discount (as defined in subsection (b)) as the number of complete months that the bond or other evidence of indebtedness was held by the taxpayer bears to the number of complete months from the date of original issue to the date of maturity, shall be considered as gain from the sale or exchange of property which is not a capital asset. Gain in excess of such amount shall be considered gain from the sale or exchange of a capital asset held more than 6 months.

"(B) Exceptions. This paragraph shall not apply to—

"(i) obligations the interest on which is not includible in gross income under section 103 (relating to certain governmental obligations), or

"(ii) any holder who has purchased the bond or other evidence of indebtedness at a premium.

"(C) Double inclusion in income not required. This section shall not require the inclusion of any amount previously includible in gross income."

—P.L. 91-172, Sec. 413(b), added all that follows the third sentence of para. (b)(2), effective for bonds and other evidences of indebtedness issued after 5/27/69 (other than evidences of indebtedness issued pursuant to a written commitment which was binding on 5/27/69, and at all times thereafter).

In **1964**, P.L. 88-563, Sec. 5, added, "increased by the amount, if any, of tax paid under section 4911 (and not credited, refunded or reimbursed)" on the acquisition of such bond or evidence of indebtedness by the first buyer" at the end of the second sentence of para. (b)(2).

In **1959**, P.L. 86-69, Sec. 3(e), amended subpara. (a)(2)(C), effective for tax. yrs. begin. after 12/31/57.

Prior to amendment, subpara. (a)(2)(C) read as follows:

"(C) Election as to inclusion.— In the case of obligations with respect to which the taxpayer has made an election provided by section 454(a) and (c) (relating to accounting rules for certain obligations issued at a discount), this section shall not require the inclusion of any amount previously includible in gross income."

In **1958**, P.L. 85-866, Sec. 50, substituted "which does not exceed—" for "which does not exceed" in subpara. (a)(2)(A), added clause (1) and designated existing provisions as clause (2), inserting the conditional clause therein, effective for tax. yrs. end. after 12/31/57, but only with respect to dispositions after 12/31/57.

—P.L. 85-866, Sec. 51, amended subsec. (c), effective for tax. yrs. begin. after 12/31/53, and end. after 8/16/54.

Prior to amendment, subsec. (c) read as follows:

"(c) Bond with excess number of coupons detached

"If—

"(1) a bond or other evidence of indebtedness issued at any time with interest coupons is purchased after the date of enactment of this title, and

"(2) the purchaser does not receive all the coupons which first become payable more than 12 months after the date of the purchase, then the gain on the sale or other disposition of such evidence of indebtedness by such purchaser shall be considered as gain from the sale or exchange of property which is not a capital asset to the extent that the market value (determined as of the time of the purchase) of the evidence of indebtedness with coupons attached exceeds the purchase price. If this subsection and subsection (a)(2)(A) apply with respect to gain realized on the retirement of any bond, then subsection (a)(2)(A) shall apply with respect to that part of the gain to which this subsection does not apply."

Sec. 1232A. Repealed.

In **1984**, P.L. 98-369, Sec. 42(a)(1), repealed Code Sec. 1232A [as amended by Sec. 211(b)(17), of this Act], effective for tax. yrs. ending after 7/18/84.

—P.L. 98-369, Sec. 211(b)(17), substituted "section 811(b)" for "section 818(b)" in subpara. (c)(4)(B), (as repealed by Sec. 42(a)(1), of the Act see below), effective for tax. yrs. begin. after 12/31/83.

Prior to repeal, Code Sec. 1232A read as follows:

"SEC. 1232A. ORIGINAL ISSUE DISCOUNT.

"(a) Original issue discount on bonds issued after July 1, 1982, included in income on basis of constant interest rate.

"(1) General rule. For purposes of this subtitle, there shall be included in the gross income of the holder of any bond having an original issue discount issued after July 1, 1982 and which is a capital asset in the hands of the holder) an amount equal to the sum of the daily portions of the original issue discount for each day during the taxable year on which such holder held such bond.

"(2) Exceptions. Paragraph (1) shall not apply to—

"(A) Natural persons. Any obligation issued by a natural person.

"(B) Tax-exempt obligations. Any obligation if—

"(i) the interest on such obligation is not includible in gross income under section 103, or

"(ii) the interest on such obligation is exempt from tax (without regard to the identity of the holder) under any other provision of law.

"(C) Short-term government obligations. Any short-term Government obligation (within the meaning of section 1232(a)(3)).

"(D) United States savings bonds. Any United States savings bond.

"(3) Determination of daily portions. For purposes of paragraph (1), the daily portion of the original issue discount on any bond shall be determined by allocating to each day in any bond period its ratable portion of the increase during such bond period in the adjusted issue price of the bond. For purposes of the preceding

Capital gains and losses

Code Sec. 1232B

sentence, the increase in the adjusted issue price for any bond period shall be an amount equal to the excess (if any) of—
"(A) the product of—
"(i) the adjusted issue price of the bond at the beginning of such bond period, and
"(ii) the yield to maturity (determined on the basis of compounding at the close of each bond period), over
"(B) the sum of the amounts payable as interest on such bond during such bond period.
"(4) Adjusted issue price. For purposes of this subsection, the adjusted issue price of any bond at the beginning of any bond period is the sum of—
"(A) the issue price of such bond, plus
"(B) the adjustments under this subsection to such issue price for all periods before the first day of such bond period.
"(5) Bond period. Except as otherwise provided in regulations prescribed by the Secretary, the term 'bond period' means a 1-year period (or the shorter period to maturity) beginning on the day in the calendar year which corresponds to the date of original issue of the bond.
"(6) Reduction in case of certain subsequent holders. For purposes of this subsection, in the case of any purchase of a bond to which this subsection applies after its original issue, the daily portion shall not include an amount (determined at the time of purchase) equal to the excess (if any) of—
"(A) the cost of such bond incurred by the purchaser, over
"(B) the issue price of such bond, increased by the sum of the daily portions for such bond for all days before the date of purchase (computed without regard to this paragraph),
"divided by the number of days beginning on the date of such purchase and ending on the day before the stated maturity date.
"(7) Regulation authority. The Secretary may prescribe regulations providing that where, by reason of varying rates of interest, put or call options, or other circumstances, the inclusion under paragraph (1) for the taxable year does not accurately reflect the income of the holder, the proper amount of income shall be included for such taxable year (and appropriate adjustments shall be made in the amounts included for subsequent taxable years).
"(b) Ratable inclusion retained for corporate bonds issued before July 2, 1982.
"(1) General rule. There shall be included in the gross income of the holder of any bond issued by corporation after May 27, 1969, and before July 2, 1982 (and which is a capital asset in the hands of the holder)—
"(A) the ratable monthly portion of original issue discount, multiplied by
"(B) the number of complete months (plus any fractional part of a month determined under paragraph (3)) such holder held such bond during the taxable year.
"(2) Determination of ratable monthly portion. Except as provided in paragraph (4), the ratable monthly portion of original issue discount shall equal—
"(A) the original issue discount, divided by
"(B) the number of complete months from the date of original issue to the stated maturity date of the bond.
"(3) Month defined. For purposes of this subsection, a complete month commences with the date of original issue and the corresponding day of each succeeding calendar month (or the last day of a calendar month in which there is no corresponding day). In any case where a bond is acquired on any day other than a day determined under the preceding sentence, the ratable monthly portion of original issue discount for the complete month (or partial month) in which such acquisition occurs shall be allocated between the transferor and the transferee in accordance with the number of days in such complete (or partial) month each held the bond.
"(4) Reduction in case of certain subsequent holders. For purposes of this subsection, the ratable monthly portion of original issue discount shall not include an amount, determined at the time of any purchase after the original issue of the bond, equal to the excess of—
"(A) the cost of such bond incurred by the holder, over
"(B) the issue price of such bond, increased by the portion of original discount previously includible in the gross income of any holder (computed without regard to this paragraph),
"divided by the number of complete months (plus any fractional part of a month) from the date of such purchase to the stated maturity date of such bond.
"(c) Definitions and special rules.
"(1) Bond includes other evidences of indebtedness. For purposes of this section, the term 'bond' means a bond, debenture, note, or certificate or other evidence of indebtedness.
"(2) Purchase defined. For purposes of this section, the term 'purchase' means any acquisition of a bond, but only if the basis of the bond is not determined in whole or in part by reference to the adjusted basis of such bond in the hands of the person from whom acquired, or under section 1014(a) (relating to property acquired from a decedent).
"(3) Original issue discount, etc. For purposes of this section, the terms 'original issue discount', 'issue price', and 'date of original issue' shall have the respective meanings given to such terms by section 1232(b).
"(4) Exceptions. This section shall not apply to any holder—
"(A) who has purchased the bond at a premium, or
"(B) which is a life insurance company to which section 811(b) applies.
"(5) Basis adjustments. The basis of any bond in the hands of the holder thereof shall be increased by the amount included in his gross income pursuant to this section."

In 1982, P.L. 97-248, Sec. 231(a), added Code Sec. 1232A, effective 9/3/82. Sec. 231(e) of this Act provides:
"(e) Transitional rule.

"For purposes of the amendments made by this section, any evidence of indebtedness issued pursuant to a written commitment which was binding on July 1, 1982, and at all times thereafter shall be treated as issued on July 1, 1982."

Sec. 1232B. Repealed.

In 1984, P.L. 98-369, Sec. 42(a)(1), repealed Code Sec. 1232B, effective for tax. yrs. ending after 7/18/84.
Prior to repeal, Code Sec. 1232B read as follows:
"SEC. 1232B. TAX TREATMENT OF STRIPPED BONDS
"(a) Inclusion in income as if bond and coupons were original issue discount bonds.
"If any person purchases after July 1, 1982, a stripped bond or a stripped coupon, then such bond or coupon while held by such purchaser (or by any other person whose basis is determined by reference to the basis in the hands of such purchaser) shall be treated for purposes of section 1232A(a) as a bond originally issued by a corporation on the purchase date and having an original issue discount equal to the excess (if any) of—
"(1) the stated redemption price at maturity (or, in the case of a coupon, the amount payable on the due date of such coupon), over
"(2) such bond's or coupon's ratable share of the purchase price.
For purposes of paragraph (2), ratable shares shall be determined on the basis of their respective fair market values on the date of purchase.
"(b) Tax treatment of person stripping bond.
"For purposes of this subtitle, if any person strips 1 or more coupons from a bond and after July 1, 1982, disposes of the bond or such coupon—
"(1) such person shall include in gross income an amount equal to the interest accrued on such bond before the time that such coupon or bond was disposed of (to the extent such interest has not theretofore been included in such person's gross income),
"(2) the basis of the bond and coupons shall be increased by the amount of the accrued interest described in paragraph (1),
"(3) the basis of the bond and coupons immediately before the disposition (as adjusted pursuant to paragraph (2)) shall be allocated among the items retained by such person and the items disposed of by such person on the basis of their respective fair market values, and
"(4) for purposes of subsection (a), such person shall be treated as having purchased on the date of such disposition each such item which he retains for an amount equal to the basis allocated to such item under paragraph (3).
A rule similar to the rule of paragraph (4) shall apply in the case of any person whose basis in any bond or coupon is determined by reference to the basis of the person described in the preceding sentence.
"(c) Retention of existing law for stripped bonds purchased before July 2, 1982.
"If a bond issued at any time with interest coupons—
"(1) is purchased after August 16, 1954, and before January 1, 1958, and the purchaser does not receive all the coupons which first become payable more than 12 months after the date of the purchase, or
"(2) is purchased after December 31, 1957, and before July 2, 1982, and the purchaser does not receive all the coupons which first become payable after the date of the purchase,
then the gain on the sale or other disposition of such bond by such purchaser (or by a person whose basis is determined by reference to the basis in the hands of such purchaser) shall be considered as ordinary income to the extent that the fair market value (determined as of the time of the purchase) of the bond with coupons attached exceeds the purchase price. If this subsection and section 1232(a)(2)(A) apply with respect to gain realized on the sale or exchange of any evidence of indebtedness, then section 1232(a)(2)(A) shall apply with respect to that part of the gain to which this subsection does not apply.
"(d) Special rules for tax-exempt obligations.
"In the case of any obligation the interest on which is not includible in gross income under section 103 or is exempt from tax (without regard to the identity of the holder) under any other provision of law—
"(1) subsections (a) and (b)(1) shall not apply,
"(2) the rules of subsection (b)(4) shall apply for purposes of subsection (c), and
"(3) subsection (c) shall be applied without regard to the requirement that the bond be purchased before July 2, 1982.
"(e) Definitions and special rules.
"For purposes of this section—
"(1) Bond. The term 'bond' means a bond, debenture, note, or certificate or other evidence of indebtedness.
"(2) Stripped bond. The term 'stripped bond' means a bond issued at any time with interest coupons where there is a separation in ownership between the bond and any coupon which has not yet become payable.
"(3) Stripped coupon. The term 'stripped coupon' means any coupon relating to a stripped bond.
"(4) Stated redemption price at maturity. The term 'stated redemption price at maturity' has the meaning given such term by the third sentence of section 1232(b)(1).
"(5) Coupon. The term 'coupon' includes any right to receive interest on a bond (whether or not evidenced by a coupon). This paragraph shall apply for purposes of subsection (c) only in the case of purchases after July 1, 1982.
"(f) Regulation authority.
"The Secretary may prescribe regulations providing that where, by reason of varying rates of interest, put or call options, extendable maturities, or other circumstances, the tax treatment under this section does not accurately reflect the income of the holder of a stripped coupon or stripped bond, or of the person dispos-

ing of such bond or coupon, as the case may be, for any period, such treatment shall be modified to require that the proper amount of income be included for such period."

In 1982, P.L. 97-248, Sec. 232(a), added Code Sec. 1232B, effective 9/3/82.

Sec. 1233. Gains and losses from short sales.
(a) Capital assets.

For purposes of this subtitle, gain or loss from the short sale of property shall be considered as gain or loss from the sale or exchange of a capital asset to the extent that the property, including a commodity future, used to close the short sale constitutes a capital asset in the hands of the taxpayer.

(b) Short-term gains and holding periods.

If gain or loss from a short sale is considered as gain or loss from the sale or exchange of a capital asset under subsection (a) and if on the date of such short sale substantially identical property has been held by the taxpayer for not more than 1 year (determined without regard to the effect, under paragraph (2) of this subsection, of such short sale on the holding period), or if substantially identical property is acquired by the taxpayer after such short sale and on or before the date of the closing thereof—

(1) any gain on the closing of such short sale shall be considered as a gain on the sale or exchange of a capital asset held for not more than 1 year (notwithstanding the period of time any property used to close such short sale has been held); and

(2) the holding period of such substantially identical property shall be considered to begin (notwithstanding section 1223, relating to the holding period of property) on the date of the closing of the short sale, or on the date of a sale, gift, or other disposition of such property, whichever date occurs first. This paragraph shall apply to such substantially identical property in the order of the dates of the acquisition of such property, but only to so much of such property as does not exceed the quantity sold short.

For purposes of this subsection, the acquisition of an option to sell property at a fixed price shall be considered as a short sale, and the exercise or failure to exercise such option shall be considered as a closing of such short sale.

(c) Certain options to sell.

Subsection (b) shall not include an option to sell property at a fixed price acquired on the same day on which the property identified as intended to be used in exercising such option is acquired and which, if exercised, is exercised through the sale of the property so identified. If the option is not exercised, the cost of the option shall be added to the basis of the property with which the option is identified. This subsection shall apply only to options acquired after August 16, 1954.

(d) Long-term losses.

If on the date of such short sale substantially identical property has been held by the taxpayer for more than 1 year, any loss on the closing of such short sale shall be considered as a loss on the sale or exchange of a capital asset held for more than 1 year (notwithstanding the period of time any property used to close such short sale has been held, and notwithstanding section 1234).

(e) Rules for application of section.

(1) Subsection (b)(1) or (d) shall not apply to the gain or loss, respectively, on any quantity of property used to close such short sale which is in excess of the quantity of the substantially identical property referred to in the applicable subsection.

(2) For purposes of subsections (b) and (d)—

(A) the term "property" includes only stocks and securities (including stocks and securities dealt with on a "when issued" basis), and commodity futures, which are capital assets in the hands of the taxpayer, but does not include any position to which section 1092(b) applies;

(B) in the case of futures transactions in any commodity on or subject to the rules of a board of trade or commodity exchange, a commodity future requiring delivery in 1 calendar month shall not be considered as property substantially identical to another commodity future requiring delivery in a different calendar month;

(C) in the case of a short sale of property by an individual, the term "taxpayer", in the application of this subsection and subsections (b) and (d), shall be read as "taxpayer or his spouse"; but an individual who is legally separated from the taxpayer under a decree of divorce or of separate maintenance shall not be considered as the spouse of the taxpayer;

(D) a securities futures contract (as defined in section 1234B) to acquire substantially identical property shall be treated as substantially identical property; and

(E) entering into a securities futures contract (as so defined) to sell shall be considered to be a short sale, and the settlement of such contract shall be considered to be the closing of such short sale.

(3) Where the taxpayer enters into 2 commodity futures transactions on the same day, one requiring delivery by him in one market and the other requiring delivery to him of the same (or substantially identical) commodity in the same calendar month in a different market, and the taxpayer subsequently closes both such transactions on the same day, subsections (b) and (d) shall have no application to so much of the commodity involved in either such transaction as does not exceed in quantity the commodity involved in the other.

(4)(A) In the case of a taxpayer who is a dealer in securities (within the meaning of section 1236)—

(i) if, on the date of a short sale of stock, substantially identical property which is a capital asset in the hands of the taxpayer has been held for not more than 1 year, and

(ii) if such short sale is closed more than 20 days after the date on which it was made,

subsection (b)(2) shall apply in respect of the holding period of such substantially identical property.

(B) For purposes of subparagraph (A)—

(i) the last sentence of subsection (b) applies; and

(ii) the term "stock" means any share or certificate of stock in a corporation, any bond or other evidence of indebtedness which is convertible into any such share or certificate, or any evidence of an interest in, or right to subscribe to or purchase, any of the foregoing.

(f) Arbitrage operations in securities.

In the case of a short sale which had been entered into as an arbitrage operation, to which sale the rule of subsection (b)(2) would apply except as otherwise provided in this subsection—

(1) subsection (b)(2) shall apply first to substantially identical assets acquired for arbitrage operations held at the close of business on the day such sale is made, and only to the extent that the quantity sold short exceeds the substantially identical assets acquired for arbitrage operations held at the close of business on the day such sale is made, shall the holding period of any other such identical assets held by the taxpayer be affected;

(2) in the event that assets acquired for arbitrage operations are disposed of in such manner as to create a net

short position in assets acquired for arbitrage operations, such net short position shall be deemed to constitute a short sale made on that day;

(3) for the purpose of paragraphs (1) and (2) of this subsection the taxpayer will be deemed as of the close of any business day to hold property which he is or will be entitled to receive or acquire by virtue of any other asset acquired for arbitrage operations or by virtue of any contract he has entered into in an arbitrage operation; and

(4) for the purpose of this subsection arbitrage operations are transactions involving the purchase and sale of assets for the purpose of profiting from a current difference between the price of the asset purchased and the price of the asset sold, and in which the asset purchased, if not identical to the asset sold, is such that by virtue thereof the taxpayer is, or will be, entitled to acquire assets identical to the assets sold. Such operations must be clearly identified by the taxpayer in his records as arbitrage operations on the day of the transaction or as soon thereafter as may be practicable. Assets acquired for arbitrage operations will include stocks and securities and the right to acquire stocks and securities.

(g) Hedging transactions.
This section shall not apply in the case of a hedging transaction in commodity futures.

(h) Short sales of property which becomes substantially worthless.
(1) **In general.** If—
(A) the taxpayer enters into a short sale of property, and
(B) such property becomes substantially worthless,
the taxpayer shall recognize gain in the same manner as if the short sale were closed when the property becomes substantially worthless. To the extent provided in regulations prescribed by the Secretary, the preceding sentence also shall apply with respect to any option with respect to property, any offsetting notional principal contract with respect to property, any futures or forward contract to deliver any property, and any other similar transaction.

(2) **Statute of limitations.** If property becomes substantially worthless during a taxable year and any short sale of such property remains open at the time such property becomes substantially worthless, then—
(A) the statutory period for the assessment of any deficiency attributable to any part of the gain on such transaction shall not expire before the earlier of—
(i) the date which is 3 years after the date the Secretary is notified by the taxpayer (in such manner as the Secretary may by regulations prescribe) of the substantial worthlessness of such property, or
(ii) the date which is 6 years after the date the return for such taxable year is filed, and
(B) such deficiency may be assessed before the date applicable under subparagraph (A) notwithstanding the provisions of any other law or rule of law which would otherwise prevent such assessment.

In 2002, P.L. 107-147, Sec. 412(d)(3)(A), deleted "and" at the end of subpara. (e)(2)(C), substituted "; and" for the period at the end of subpara. (e)(2)(D), and added subpara. (e)(2)(E), effective 12/21/2000.

In 2000, P.L. 106-554, Sec. 1(a)(7), [which enacted into law Sec. 401(f) of P.L. 106-554] deleted "and" at the end of subpara. (e)(2)(B), substituted "; and" for the period at the end of subpara. (e)(2)(C), and added subpara. (e)(2)(D), effective 12/21/2000.

In 1997, P.L. 105-34, Sec. 1003(b)(1), added subsec. (h), effective for property which becomes substantially worthless after 8/5/97.

In 1984, P.L. 98-369, Sec. 1001(b)(17), substituted "6 months" for "1 year" each place it appeared in subsecs. (b) and (d) and in subpara. (e)(4)(A), effective for property acquired after 6/22/84 and before 1/1/88.

In 1981, P.L. 97-34, Sec. 501(c), added ", but does not include any position to which section 1092(b) applies" after "taxpayer" in para. (e)(2), effective for property acquired and positions established by the taxpayer after 6/23/81, in tax. yrs. end. after 6/23/81. For election with respect to property held on 6/23/81, see Sec. 508(c) of this Act reproduced in note following Code Sec. 1092.

In 1976, P.L. 94-455, Sec. 1402(b)(1)(T), substituted "9 months" for "6 months" in subsecs. (b), (d) and (e), effective for tax. yrs. begin. in 1977.
—P.L. 94-455, Sec. 1402(b)(2), substituted "1 year" for "9 months" in subsecs. (b), (d) and (e), effective for tax. yrs. begin. after 12/31/77. For transitional rules, see Sec. 1402(c) of this Act reproduced in note following Code Sec. 1222.
—P.L. 94-455, Sec. 1901(a)(137), substituted "August 16, 1954" for "the date of enactment of this title" in subsec. (c), effective for tax. yrs. begin. after 12/31/76.

In 1958, P.L. 85-866, Sec. 52(a), added para. (e)(4), effective for short sales made after 12/31/57.
—P.L. 85-866, Sec. 52(b), deleted ", other than a hedging transaction in commodity futures," after "sale of property" in subsec. (a), and added subsec. (g), effective for tax. yrs. begin. after 12/31/53 and end. after 8/16/54.

In 1955, P.L. 385, Sec. 1, added subsec. (f), effective for tax. yrs. end. after 8/12/55 and only in the case of a short sale of property made by the taxpayer after such date.

Sec. 1234. Options to buy or sell.
(a) Treatment of gain or loss in the case of the purchaser.
(1) **General rule.** Gain or loss attributable to the sale or exchange of, or loss attributable to failure to exercise, an option to buy or sell property shall be considered gain or loss from the sale or exchange of property which has the same character as the property to which the option relates has in the hands of the taxpayer (or would have in the hands of the taxpayer if acquired by him).

(2) **Special rule for loss attributable to failure to exercise option.** For purposes of paragraph (1), if loss is attributable to failure to exercise an option, the option shall be deemed to have been sold or exchanged on the day it expired.

(3) **Nonapplication of subsection.** This subsection shall not apply to—
(A) an option which constitutes property described in paragraph (1) of section 1221(a);
(B) in the case of gain attributable to the sale or exchange of an option, any income derived in connection with such option which, without regard to this subsection, is treated as other than gain from the sale or exchange of a capital asset; and
(C) a loss attributable to failure to exercise an option described in section 1233(c).

(b) Treatment of grantor of option in the case of stock, securities, or commodities.
(1) **General rule.** In the case of the grantor of the option, gain or loss from any closing transaction with respect to, and gain on lapse of, an option in property shall be treated as a gain or loss from the sale or exchange of a capital asset held not more than 1 year.

(2) **Definitions.** For purposes of this subsection—
(A) Closing transaction. The term "closing transaction" means any termination of the taxpayer's obligation under an option in property other than through the exercise or lapse of the option.
(B) Property. The term "property" means stocks and securities (including stocks and securities dealt with on a "when issued" basis), commodities, and commodity futures.

(3) **Nonapplication of subsection.** This subsection shall not apply to any option granted in the ordinary course of the taxpayer's trade or business of granting options.

(c) Treatment of options on section 1256 contracts and cash settlement options.
(1) **Section 1256 contracts.** Gain or loss shall be recognized on the exercise of an option on a section 1256 contract (within the meaning of section 1256(b)).

(2) Treatment of cash settlement options.
(A) In general. For purposes of subsections (a) and (b), a cash settlement option shall be treated as an option to buy or sell property.
(B) Cash settlement option. For purposes of subparagraph (A), the term "cash settlement option" means any option which on exercise settles in (or could be settled in) cash or property other than the underlying property.

In **1999**, P.L. 106-170, Sec. 532(c)(1)(H), substituted "section 1221" for "section 1221" in subpara. (a)(3)(A), effective for any instrument held, acquired, or entered into, any transaction entered into, and supplies held or acquired on or after 12/17/99.
In **1984**, P.L. 98-369, Sec. 105(a), added subsec. (c), effective for options purchased or granted after 10/31/83, in tax. yrs. end. after 10/31/83.
—P.L. 98-369, Sec. 1001(b)(18), substituted "6 months" for "1 year" in para. (b)(1), effective for property acquired after 6/22/84, and before 1/1/88.
In **1976**, P.L. 94-455, Sec. 1402(b)(1)(U), substituted "9 months" for "6 months" in para. (b)(1) [as amended by Sec. 2136 of this Act, see below], effective for tax. yrs. begin. in 1977.
—P.L. 94-455, Sec. 1402(b)(2), substituted "1 year" for "9 months" in para. (b)(1) [as amended by Sec. 2136 of this Act, see below], effective for tax. yrs. begin. after 12/31/77. For transitional rules, see Sec. 1402(c) of this Act reproduced in note following Code Sec. 1222.
—P.L. 99-455, Sec. 2136, amended Code Sec. 1234, effective for options granted after 9/1/76.
Prior to amendment, Code Sec. 1234 read as follows:
"Sec. 1234. Options to buy or sell.
"(a) Treatment of gain or loss.
"Gain or loss attributable to the sale or exchange of, or loss attributable to failure to exercise, a privilege or option to buy or sell property shall be considered gain or loss from the sale or exchange of property which has the same character as the property to which the option or privilege relates has in the hands of the taxpayer (or would have in the hands of the taxpayer if acquired by him).
"(b) Special rule for loss attributable to failure to exercise option.
"For purposes of subsection (a), if loss is attributable to failure to exercise a privilege or option, the privilege or option shall be deemed to have been sold or exchanged on the day it expired.
"(c) Special rule for grantors of straddles.
"(1) Gain on lapse. In the case of gain on lapse of an option granted by the taxpayer as part of a straddle, the gain shall be deemed to be gain from the sale or exchange of a capital asset held for not more than 6 months on the day that the option expired.
"(2) Exception. This subsection shall not apply to any person who holds securities for sale to customers in the ordinary course of his trade or business.
"(3) Definitions. For purposes of this subsection—
"(A) The term 'straddle' means a simultaneously granted combination of an option to buy, and an option to sell, the same quantity of a security at the same price during the same period of time.
"(B) The term 'security' has the meaning assigned to such term by section 1236(c).
"(d) Non-application of section.
"This section shall not apply to—
"(1) a privilege or option which constitutes property described in paragraph (1) of section 1221;
"(2) in the case of gain attributable to the sale or exchange of a privilege or option, any income derived in connection with such privilege or option which, without regard to this section, is treated as other than gain from the sale or exchange of a capital asset;
"(3) a loss attributable to failure to exercise an option described in section 1233(c); or
"(4) gain attributable to the sale or exchange of a privilege or option acquired by the taxpayer before March 1, 1954, if in the hands of the taxpayer such privilege or option is a capital asset."
In **1966**, P.L. 89-809, Sec. 210, redesignated subsec. (c) as subsec. (d) and added new subsec. (c), effective for straddle transactions entered into after 1/25/65, in tax. yrs. end. after 1/25/65.
In **1958**, P.L. 85-866, Sec. 53, amended Code Sec. 1234, effective for tax. yrs. begin. after 12/31/53 and end. after 8/16/54.
Prior to amendment, Code Sec. 1234 read as follows:
"Sec. 1234. Options to Buy or Sell.
"Gain or loss attributable to the sale or exchange of, or loss on failure to exercise, a privilege or option to buy or sell property which in the hands of the taxpayer constitutes (or if acquired would constitute) a capital asset shall be considered gain or loss from the sale or exchange of a capital asset; and, if the loss is attributable to failure to exercise such privilege or option, the privilege or option shall be deemed to have been sold or exchanged on the day it expired. This section shall not apply to losses on failure to exercise options described in section 1233(c)."

Sec. 1234A. Gains or losses from certain terminations.
Gain or loss attributable to the cancellation, lapse, expiration, or other termination of—
(1) a right or obligation (other than a securities futures contract, as defined in section 1234B) with respect to property which is (or on acquisition would be) a capital asset in the hands of the taxpayer, or
(2) a section 1256 contract (as defined in section 1256) not described in paragraph (1) which is a capital asset in the hands of the taxpayer,
shall be treated as gain or loss from the sale of a capital asset. The preceding sentence shall not apply to the retirement of any debt instrument (whether or not through a trust or other participation agreement).

In **2002**, P.L. 107-147, Sec. 412(d)(1)(A), added "or" at the end of para. (1), deleted "or" at the end of para. (2), and deleted para. (3), effective 12/21/2000.
Prior to deletion, para. (3) read as follows:
"(3) a securities futures contract (as so defined) which is a capital asset in the hands of the taxpayer,"
In **2000**, P.L. 106-554, Sec. 1(a)(7), [which enacted into law Sec. 401(b)(1) of P.L. 106-554] added "(other than a securities futures contract, as defined in section 1234B)" after "right or obligation" in para. (1) . . . Sec. 1(a)(7), [which enacted into law Sec. 401(b)(2) of P.L. 106-554] deleted "or" at the end of para. (1) . . . Sec. 1(a)(7), [which enacted into law Sec. 401(b)(3) of P.L. 106-554] added "or" at the end of para. (2) . . . Sec. 1(a)(7), [which enacted into law Sec. 401(b)(4) of P.L. 106-554] added para. (3), effective 12/21/2000.
In **1997**, P.L. 105-34, Sec. 1003(a)(1), substituted "property" for "personal property (as defined in section 1092(d)(1))" in para. (1), effective for terminations more than 30 days after 8/5/97.
In **1984**, P.L. 98-369, Sec. 102(e)(4), substituted "a section 1256 contract" for "a regulated futures contract" in para. (2), effective for positions established after 7/18/84, in tax. yrs. ending after 7/18/84.
—P.L. 98-369, Sec. 102(e)(9), added "The preceding sentence shall not apply to the retirement of any debt instrument (whether or not through a trust or other participation arrangement)." at the end of Code Sec. 1234(A), effective for property acquired and positions established by the taxpayer after 6/23/81, in tax yrs. end. after 6/23/81.
In **1983**, P.L. 97-448, Sec. 105(e), amended Code Sec. 1234A, effective for property acquired and positions established by the taxpayer after 6/23/81, in tax. yrs. end. after 6/23/81.
Prior to amendment Code Sec. 1234A read as follows:
"SEC. 1234A. GAINS OR LOSSES FROM CERTAIN TERMINATIONS.
"Gain or loss attributable to the cancellation, lapse, expiration, or other termination of a right or obligation with respect to personal property (as defined in section 1092(d)(1)) which is (or on acquisition would be) a capital asset in the hands of the taxpayer shall be treated as gain or loss from the sale of a capital asset."
In **1981**, P.L. 97-34, Sec. 507(a), added Code Sec. 1234A, effective for property acquired and positions established by the taxpayer after 6/23/81, in tax. yrs. end. after 6/23/81. For election with respect to property held on 6/23/81, see Sec. 508(c) of this Act reproduced in note following Code Sec. 1092.

Sec. 1234B. Gains or losses from securities futures contracts.
(a) Treatment of gain or loss.
(1) In general. Gain or loss attributable to the sale, exchange, or termination of a securities futures contract shall be considered gain or loss from the sale or exchange of property which has the same character as the property to which the contract relates has in the hands of the taxpayer (or would have in the hands of the taxpayer if acquired by the taxpayer).
(2) Nonapplication of subsection. This subsection shall not apply to—
(A) a contract which constitutes property described in paragraph (1) or (7) of section 1221(a), and
(B) any income derived in connection with a contract which, without regard to this subsection, is treated as other than gain from the sale or exchange of a capital asset.
(b) Short-term gains and losses.
Except as provided in the regulations under section 1092(b) or this section, or in section 1233, if gain or loss on the sale, exchange, or termination of a securities futures contract to sell property is considered as gain or loss from the

Capital gains and losses Code Sec. 1236(d)(1)(A)

sale or exchange of a capital asset, such gain or loss shall be treated as short-term capital gain or loss.

(c) Securities futures contract.

For purposes of this section, the term "securities futures contract" means any security future (as defined in section 3(a)(55)(A) of the Securities Exchange Act of 1934, as in effect on the date of the enactment [12/21/2000] of this section). The Secretary may prescribe regulations regarding the status of contracts the values of which are determined directly or indirectly by reference to any index which becomes (or ceases to be) a narrow-based security index (as defined for purposes of section 1256(g)(6)).

(d) Contracts not treated as commodity futures contracts.

For purposes of this title, a securities futures contract shall not be treated as a commodity futures contract.

(e) Regulations.

The Secretary shall prescribe such regulations as may be appropriate to provide for the proper treatment of securities futures contracts under this title.

(f) Cross reference.

For special rules relating to dealer securities futures contracts, see section 1256.

In **2004**, P.L. 108-311, Sec. 405(a)(1), added "The Secretary may prescribe regulations regarding the status of contracts the values of which are determined directly or indirectly by reference to any index which becomes (or ceases to be) a narrow-based security index (as defined for purposes of section 1256(g)(6))." at the end of subsec. (c), effective 12/21/2000 as if included in Sec. 401 of the Community Renewal Tax Relief Act of 2000, P.L. 106-554 [P.L. 106-554].

In **2002**, P.L. 107-147, Sec. 412(d)(1)(B)(i), substituted "sale, exchange, or termination" for "sale or exchange" the first place it appeared in para. (a)(1) and subsec. (b)... Sec. 412(d)(1)(B)(ii), added subsec. (f)... Sec. 412(d)(3)(B), added "or in section 1233," after "or this section," in subsec. (b), effective 12/21/2000.

In **2000**, P.L. 106-554, Sec. 1(a)(7), [which enacted into law Sec. 401(a) of P.L. 106-554] added Code Sec. 1234B, effective 12/21/2000.

Sec. 1235. Sale or exchange of patents.

(a) General.

A transfer (other than by gift, inheritance, or devise) of property consisting of all substantial rights to a patent, or an undivided interest therein which includes a part of all such rights, by any holder shall be considered the sale or exchange of a capital asset held for more than 1 year, regardless of whether or not payments in consideration of such transfer are—

(1) payable periodically over a period generally coterminous with the transferee's use of the patent, or

(2) contingent on the productivity, use, or disposition of the property transferred.

(b) "Holder" defined.

For purposes of this section, the term "holder" means—

(1) any individual whose efforts created such property, or

(2) any other individual who has acquired his interest in such property in exchange for consideration in money or money's worth paid to such creator prior to actual reduction to practice of the invention covered by the patent, if such individual is neither—

(A) the employer of such creator, nor

(B) related to such creator (within the meaning of subsection (d)).

(c) Effective date.

This section shall be applicable with regard to any amounts received, or payments made, pursuant to a transfer described in subsection (a) in any taxable year to which this subtitle applies, regardless of the taxable year in which such transfer occurred.

(d) Related persons.

Subsection (a) shall not apply to any transfer, directly or indirectly, between persons specified within any one of the paragraphs of section 267(b) or persons described in section 707(b); except that, in applying section 267(b) and (c) and section 707(b) for purposes of this section—

(1) the phrase "25 percent or more" shall be substituted for the phrase "more than 50 percent" each place it appears in section 267(b) or 707(b), and

(2) paragraph (4) of section 267(c) shall be treated as providing that the family of an individual shall include only his spouse, ancestors, and lineal descendants.

(e) Cross reference.

For special rule relating to nonresident aliens, see section 871(a).

In **1998**, P.L. 105-206, Sec. 5001(a)(5), substituted "1 year" for "18 months" in subsec. (a), effective for tax. yrs. end. after 12/31/97.

—P.L. 105-206, Sec. 6005(d)(4), substituted "18 months" for "1 year" in subsec. (a), effective for tax. yrs. end. after 5/6/97.

In **1984**, P.L. 98-369, Sec. 174(b)(5)(C)(i), substituted "section 267(b) or persons described in section 707(b)" for "section 267(b)" in the matter preceding para. (d)(1) ... Sec. 174(b)(5)(C)(ii), substituted "section 267(b) and (c) and section 707(b)" for "section 267(b) and (c)" in the matter preceding para. (d)(1) ... Sec. 174(b)(5)(C)(iii), substituted "section 267(b) or 707(b)" for "section 267(b)" in para. (d)(1), effective for transactions after 12/31/83, in tax. yrs. ending after 12/31/83.

—P.L. 98-369, Sec. 1001(b)(19), substituted "6 months" for "1 year" in subsec. (a), effective for property acquired after 6/22/84, and before 1/1/88.

In **1976**, P.L. 94-455, Sec. 1402(b)(1)(V), substituted "9 months" for "6 months" in subsec. (a), effective for tax. yrs. begin. in 1977.

—P.L. 94-455, Sec. 1402(b)(2), substituted "1 year" for "9 months" in subsec. (a), effective for tax. yrs. begin. after 12/31/77. For transitional rules, see Sec. 1402(c) of this Act reproduced in note following Code Sec. 1222.

In **1958**, P.L. 85-866, Sec. 54(a), amended subsec. (d), effective for tax. yrs. end. after 9/2/58, but only for transfers after 9/2/58.

Prior to amendment, subsec. (d) read as follows:

"(d) Related persons. Subsection (a) shall not apply to any sale or exchange between an individual and any other related person (as defined in section 267(b)), except brothers and sisters, whether by the whole or half blood."

Sec. 1236. Dealers in securities.

(a) Capital gains.

Gain by a dealer in securities from the sale or exchange of any security shall in no event be considered as gain from the sale or exchange of a capital asset unless—

(1) the security was, before the close of the day on which it was acquired (or such earlier time as the Secretary may prescribe by regulations), clearly identified in the dealer's records as a security held for investment; and

(2) the security was not, at any time after the close of such day (or such earlier time), held by such dealer primarily for sale to customers in the ordinary course of his trade or business.

(b) Ordinary losses.

Loss by a dealer in securities from the sale or exchange of any security shall, except as otherwise provided in section 582(c), (relating to bond, etc., losses of banks), in no event be considered as ordinary loss if at any time after November 19, 1951, the security was clearly identified in the dealer's records as a security held for investment.

(c) Definition of security.

For purposes of this section, the term "security" means any share of stock in any corporation, certificate of stock or interest in any corporation, note, bond, debenture, or evidence of indebtedness, or any evidence of an interest in or right to subscribe to or purchase any of the foregoing.

(d) Special rule for floor specialists.

(1) **In general.** In the case of a floor specialist (but only with respect to acquisitions, in connection with his duties on an exchange, of stock in which the specialist is registered with the exchange), subsection (a) shall be applied—

(A) by inserting "the 7th business day following" before "the day" the first place it appears in paragraph

2,753

(1) and by inserting "7th business" before "day" in paragraph (2), and

(B) by striking the parenthetical phrase in paragraph (1).

(2) Floor specialist. The term "floor specialist" means a person who is—

(A) a member of a national securities exchange,

(B) is registered as a specialist with the exchange, and

(C) meets the requirements for specialists established by the Securities and Exchange Commission.

(e) Special rule for options.

For purposes of subsection (a), any security acquired by a dealer pursuant to an option held by such dealer may be treated as held for investment only if the dealer, before the close of the day on which the option was acquired, clearly identified the option on his records as held for investment. For purposes of the preceding sentence, the term "option" includes the right to subscribe to or purchase any security.

In **1984**, P.L. 98-369, Sec. 107(b)(1), amended para. (a)(1)... Sec. 107(b)(2), added "(or such earlier time)" after "such day" in para. (a)(2), effective for positions entered into after 7/18/84, in tax. yrs. ending after 7/1/8/84.
Prior to amendment, para. (a)(1) read as follows:
"(1) the security was, before the close of the day on which it was acquired (before the close of the following day in the case of an acquisition before January 1, 1982), clearly identified in the dealer's records as a security held for investment or if acquired before October 20, 1951, was so identified before November 20, 1951; and"
In **1983**, P.L. 97-448, Sec. 105(d)(1), added subsec. (e), effective for securities acquired after 9/22/82, in tax. yrs. end. after 9/22/82.
In **1981**, P.L. 97-34, Sec. 506(a), substituted "before the close of the day on which it was acquired (before the close of the following day in the case of an acquisition before January 1, 1982)" for "before the expiration of the 30th day after the date of its acquisition" and substituted "close of such day" for "expiration of such 30th day" in subsec. (a)... Sec. 506(b), added subsec. (d), effective for property acquired by the taxpayer after 8/13/81 in tax. yrs. end. after 8/13/81.
In **1976**, P.L. 94-455, Sec. 1901(b)(3)(E), substituted "an ordinary loss" for "loss from the sale or exchange of property which is not a capital asset" in subsec. (b), effective for tax. yrs. begin. after 12/31/76.

Sec. 1237. Real property subdivided for sale.
(a) General.

Any lot or parcel which is part of a tract of real property in the hands of a taxpayer other than a C corporation shall not be deemed to be held primarily for sale to customers in the ordinary course of trade or business at the time of sale solely because of the taxpayer having subdivided such tract for purposes of sale or because of any activity incident to such subdivision or sale, if—

(1) such tract, or any lot or parcel thereof, had not previously been held by such taxpayer primarily for sale to customers in the ordinary course of trade or business (unless such tract at such previous time would have been covered by this section) and, in the same taxable year in which the sale occurs, such taxpayer does not so hold any other real property; and

(2) no substantial improvement that substantially enhances the value of the lot or parcel sold is made by the taxpayer on such tract while held by the taxpayer or is made pursuant to a contract of sale entered into between the taxpayer and the buyer. For purposes of this paragraph, an improvement shall be deemed to be made by the taxpayer if such improvement was made by—

(A) the taxpayer or members of his family (as defined in section 267(c)(4)), by a corporation controlled by the taxpayer, an S corporation which included the taxpayer as a shareholder, or by a partnership which included the taxpayer as a partner; or

(B) a lessee, but only if the improvement constitutes income to the taxpayer; or

(C) Federal, State, or local government, or political subdivision thereof, but only if the improvement constitutes an addition to basis for the taxpayer; and

(3) such lot or parcel, except in the case of real property acquired by inheritance or devise, is held by the taxpayer for a period of 5 years.

(b) Special rules for application of section.

(1) Gains. If more than 5 lots or parcels contained in the same tract of real property are sold or exchanged, gain from any sale or exchange (which occurs in or after the taxable year in which the sixth lot or parcel is sold or exchanged) of any lot or parcel which comes within the provisions of paragraphs (1), (2) and (3) of subsection (a) of this section shall be deemed to be gain from the sale of property held primarily for sale to customers in the ordinary course of the trade or business to the extent of 5 percent of the selling price.

(2) Expenditures of sale. For the purpose of computing gain under paragraph (1) of this subsection, expenditures incurred in connection with the sale or exchange of any lot or parcel shall neither be allowed as a deduction in computing taxable income, nor treated as reducing the amount realized on such sale or exchange; but so much of such expenditures as does not exceed the portion of gain deemed under paragraph (1) of this subsection to be gain from the sale of property held primarily for sale to customers in the ordinary course of trade or business shall be so allowed as a deduction, and the remainder, if any, shall be treated as reducing the amount realized on such sale or exchange.

(3) Necessary improvements. No improvement shall be deemed a substantial improvement for purposes of subsection (a) if the lot or parcel is held by the taxpayer for a period of 10 years and if—

(A) such improvement is the building or installation of water, sewer, or drainage facilities or roads (if such improvement would except for this paragraph constitute a substantial improvement);

(B) it is shown to the satisfaction of the Secretary that the lot or parcel, the value of which was substantially enhanced by such improvement, would not have been marketable at the prevailing local price for similar building sites without such improvement; and

(C) the taxpayer elects, in accordance with regulations prescribed by the Secretary, to make no adjustment to basis of the lot or parcel, or of any other property owned by the taxpayer, on account of the expenditures for such improvements. Such election shall not make any item deductible which would not otherwise be deductible.

(c) Tract defined.

For purposes of this section, the term "tract of real property" means a single piece of real property, except that 2 or more pieces of real property shall be considered a tract if at any time they were contiguous in the hands of the taxpayer or if they would be contiguous except for the interposition of a road, street, railroad, stream, or similar property. If, following the sale or exchange of any lot or parcel from a tract of real property, no further sales or exchanges of any other lots or parcels from the remainder of such tract are made for a period of 5 years, such remainder shall be deemed a tract.

In **1996**, P.L. 104-188, Sec. 1314(a), substituted "other than a C corporation" for "other than a corporation" in subsec. (a)... Sec. 1314(b), added "an S corporation which included the taxpayer as a shareholder," after "controlled by the taxpayer," in subpara. (a)(2)(A), effective for tax. yrs. begin. after 12/31/96.
In **1976**, P.L. 94-455, Sec. 1901(a)(138), deleted subsec. (d), effective for tax. yrs. begin. after 12/31/76.

Prior to deletion, subsec. (d) read as follows:
"(d) Effective date. This section shall apply only with respect to sales of property occurring after December 31, 1953, except that, for purposes of subsection (c) (defining tract of real property) and for determining the number of sales under paragraph (1) of subsection (b), all sales of lots and parcels from any tract of real property during the period of 5 years before December 31, 1953, shall be taken into account, except as provided in subsection (c)."

—P.L. 94-455, Sec. 1906(b)(13)(A), substituted "Secretary" for "Secretary or his delegate" each place it appeared in Code Sec. 1237, effective for tax. yrs. begin. after 12/31/76.

In 1971, P.L. 91-686, Sec. 2(a)(1), substituted "other than a corporation" for "(including corporations only if no shareholder directly or indirectly holds real property for sale to customers in the ordinary course of trade or business and only in the case of property described in the last sentence of subsection (b)(3))" in subsec. (a)... Sec. 2(a)(2), deleted the last sentence of subsec. (b), effective for tax. yrs. begin. after 1/12/71.

Prior to deletion, the last sentence of subsec. (b) read as follows:
"The requirements of subparagraphs (B) and (C) shall not apply in the case of property acquired through the foreclosure of a lien thereon which secured the payment of an indebtedness to the taxpayer or (in the case of a corporation) to a creditor who has transferred the foreclosure bid to the taxpayer in exchange for all of its stock and other consideration and in the case of property adjacent to such property if 80 percent of the real property owned by the taxpayer is property described in the first part of this sentence."

—P.L. 91-686, Sec. 1, provides:
"(a) for purposes of the Internal Revenue Code of 1954 any lot or parcel of real property sold or exchanged by a corporation which would, but for this Act, be treated as property held primarily for sale to customers in the ordinary course of trade or business shall not, except to the extent provided in (b), be so treated if—
"(1) no shareholder of the corporation directly or indirectly holds real property primarily for sale to customers in the ordinary course of trade or business; and
"(2)(A) such lot or parcel is a part of real property (i) held for more than twenty-five years at the time of sale or exchange, and (ii) acquired before January 1, 1934, by the corporation as a result of the foreclosure of a lien (or liens) thereon which secured the payment of indebtedness held by one or more creditors who transferred one or more foreclosure bids to the corporation in exchange for all its stock (with or without other consideration), or
"(B)(i) such lot or parcel is a part of additional real property acquired before January 1, 1957, by the corporation in the near vicinity of any real property to which subparagraph (A) applies, or
"(ii) such lot or parcel is wholly or to some extent a part of any minor acquisition made after December 31, 1956, by the corporation to adjust boundaries, to fill gaps in previously acquired property, to facilitate the installation of streets, utilities, and other public facilities, or to facilitate the sale of adjacent property, or
"(iii) such lot or parcel is wholly or to some extent a part of a reacquisition by the corporation after December 31, 1956, of property previously owned by the corporation;
but only if at least 80 percent (as measured by area) of the real property sold or exchanged by the corporation within the taxable year is property described in subparagraph (A); and
"(3) there were no acquisitions of real property by the corporation after December 31, 1956, other than—
"(A) acquisitions described in paragraph (2)(B)(ii) and reacquisitions described in paragraph (2)(B)(iii), or
"(B) acquisitions of real property used in a trade or business of the corporation or held for investment by the corporation; and
"(4) the corporation did not after December 31, 1957, sell or exchange (except in condemnation or under threat of condemnation) any residential lot or parcel on which, at the time of the sale or exchange, there existed any substantial improvements (other than improvements in existence at the time the land was acquired by the corporation) except subdivision, clearing, grubbing, and grading, building or installation of water, sewer, and drainage facilities, construction of roads, streets, and sidewalks, and installation of utilities.
In any case in which a corporation referred to in paragraphs (1), (2), (3), and (4) is a member of an affiliated group as defined in section 1504(a) of the Internal Revenue Code of 1954, such affiliated group shall, for purposes of such paragraphs, be treated as a single corporation.
"(b)(1) Gain from any sale or exchange described in subsection (a) shall be deemed, for purposes of such Code, to be gain from the sale of property held primarily for sale to customers in the ordinary course of trade or business to the extent of 5 percent of the selling price.
"(2) For the purpose of computing gain under paragraph (1), expenditures incurred in connection with the sale or exchange of any lot or parcel shall neither be allowed as a deduction in computing taxable income, nor treated as reducing the amount realized on such sale or exchange; but so much of such expenditures as does not exceed the portion of gain deemed under paragraph (1) to be gain from the sale of property held primarily for sale to customers in the ordinary course of trade or business shall be so allowed as a deduction, and the remainder, if any, shall be treated as reducing the amount realized on such sale or exchange.
"(c) The provisions of subsections (a) and (b) shall apply to taxable years beginning after December 31, 1957, and before January 1, 1984."

In 1958, P.L. 85-866, Sec. 55, substituted "and, in the same taxable year" for "or, in the same taxable year" in para. (a)(1), effective for tax. yrs. begin. after 12/31/53 and end. after 8/16/54.

In 1956, P.L. 495, Sec. [1], substituted "(including corporations only if no shareholder directly or indirectly holds real property for sale to customers in the ordinary course of trade or business and only in the case of property described in the last sentence of subsection (b)(3))" for "other than a corporation" in subsec. (a) ... Sec. 2(a), substituted "water, sewer, or drainage facilities" for "water or sewer facilities" in para. (b)(3),... Sec. 2(b), added the last sentence of para. (b)(3), effective for tax. yrs. begin. after 12/31/54.

Sec. 1238. Repealed.

In 1990, P.L. 101-508, Sec. 11801(a)(35), repealed Code Sec. 1238, effective 11/5/90, except as provided in Sec. 11821(b) of this Act, which reads as follows:
"(b) Savings provision. If—
"(1) any provision amended or repealed by this part applied to—
"(A) any transaction occurring before the date of the enactment of this Act [11/5/90],
"(B) any property acquired before such date of enactment [11/5/90], or
"(C) any item of income, loss, deduction, or credit taken into account before such date of enactment [11/5/90], and
"(2) the treatment of such transaction, property, or item under such provision would (without regard to the amendments made by this part) affect liability for tax for periods ending after such date of enactment [11/5/90],
nothing in the amendments made by this part shall be construed to affect the treatment of such transaction, property, or item for purposes of determining liability for tax for periods ending after such date of enactment [11/5/90]."

Prior to repeal, Code Sec. 1238 read as follows:
"SEC. 1238. AMORTIZATION IN EXCESS OF DEPRECIATION.
Gain from the sale or exchange of property, to the extent that the adjusted basis of such property is less than its adjusted basis determined without regard to section 168 (as in effect before its repeal by the Tax Reform Act of 1976), shall be considered as ordinary income."

In 1976, P.L. 94-455, Sec. 1901(b)(3)(K), substituted "ordinary income" for "gain from the sale or exchange of property which is neither a capital asset nor property described in section 1231" in Code Sec. 1238, effective for tax. yrs. begin. after 12/31/76.

—P.L. 94-455, Sec. 1951(c)(2)(A), substituted "(as in effect before its repeal by the Tax Reform Act of 1976)" for "(relating to amortization deduction of emergency facilities)" in Code Sec. 1238, effective for tax. yrs. begin. after 12/31/76.

Sec. 1239. Gain from sale of depreciable property between certain related taxpayers.

(a) Treatment of gain as ordinary income.

In the case of a sale or exchange of property, directly or indirectly, between related persons, any gain recognized to the transferor shall be treated as ordinary income if such property is, in the hands of the transferee, of a character which is subject to the allowance for depreciation provided in section 167.

(b) Related persons.

For purposes of subsection (a), the term "related persons" means—

(1) a person and all entities which are controlled entities with respect to such person,

(2) a taxpayer and any trust in which such taxpayer (or his spouse) is a beneficiary, unless such beneficiary's interest in the trust is a remote contingent interest (within the meaning of section 318(a)(3)(B)(i)), and

(3) except in the case of a sale or exchange in satisfaction of a pecuniary bequest, an executor of an estate and a beneficiary of such estate.

(c) Controlled entity defined.

(1) General rule. For purposes of this section, the term "controlled entity" means, with respect to any person—

(A) a corporation more than 50 percent of the value of the outstanding stock of which is owned (directly or indirectly) by or for such person,

(B) a partnership more than 50 percent of the capital interest or profits interest in which is owned (directly or indirectly) by or for such person, and

(C) any entity which is a related person to such person under paragraph (3), (10), (11), or (12) of section 267(b).

(2) Constructive ownership. For purposes of this section, ownership shall be determined in accordance with rules similar to the rules under section 267(c) (other than paragraph (3) thereof).

(d) Employer and related employee association.

For purposes of subsection (a), the term "related person" also includes—

(1) an employer and any person related to the employer (within the meaning of subsection (b)), and

(2) a welfare benefit fund (within the meaning of section 419(e)) which is controlled directly or indirectly by persons referred to in paragraph (1).

(e) Patent applications treated as depreciable property.

For purposes of this section, a patent application shall be treated as property which, in the hands of the transferee, is of a character which is subject to the allowance for depreciation provided in section 167.

In 1997, P.L. 105-34, Sec. 1308(b), substituted ", and" for the period at the end of para. (b)(2) and added para. (b)(3), effective for tax. yrs. begin. after 8/5/97.

In 1988, P.L. 100-647, Sec. 1006(i)(3), substituted "Transitional" for "Traditional" in the heading of Sec. 642(c)(2) [reproduced below] of P.L. 99-514, part of the transitional rules for changes made by Secs. 642(a)(1)(A), (B) and (C) of P.L. 99-514, see below

In 1986, P.L. 99-514, Sec. 642(a)(1)(A), substituted "controlled" for "80-percent owned" in para. (b)(1)... Sec. 642(a)(1)(B)(i)(I), substituted "controlled" for "80-percent owned" in para. (c)(1)... Sec. 642(a)(1)(B)(i)(II), substituted "more than 50 percent of the value" for "80 percent or more in value" in subpara. (c)(1)(A)... Sec. 642(a)(1)(B)(i)(III), substituted "more than 50 percent" for "80 percent or more" in subpara. (c)(1)(B)... Sec. 642(a)(1)(B)(i)(IV), deleted "and" at the end of subpara. (c)(1)(A), substituted ", and" for the period at the end of subpara. (c)(1)(B), and added subpara. (c)(1)(C)... Sec. 642(a)(1)(B)(ii), substituted "Controlled" for "80-percent owned" in the heading of subsec. (c)... Sec. 642(a)(1)(C), amended para. (c)(2), effective for sales after 10/22/86, in tax. yrs. end. after 10/22/86. Sec. 642(c)(2) [as amended by Sec. 1006(i)(3) of P.L. 100-647, see above] of this Act provides:

"(2) Transitional rule for binding contracts.— The amendments made by this section shall not apply to sales made after August 14, 1986, which are made pursuant to a binding contract in effect on August 14, 1986, and at all times thereafter."

Prior to amendment, para. (c)(2) read as follows:

"(2) Constructive ownership. For purposes of subparagraphs (A) and (B) of paragraph (1), the principles of section 318 shall apply, except that—

"(A) the members of an individual's family shall consist only of such individual and such individual's spouse,

"(B) paragraph (2)(C) of section 318(a) shall be applied without regard to the 50-percent limitation contained therein, and

"(C) paragraph (3) of section 318(a) shall not apply."

In 1984, P.L. 98-369, Sec. 175(a), added subsec. (c)... Sec. 175(b), amended subsec. (b), effective for sales or exchanges after 3/1/84, in tax. yrs. ending after 3/1/84.

Prior to amendment, subsec. (b) read as follows:

"(b) Related persons.

"For purposes of subsection (a), the term 'related persons' means—

"(1) a husband and wife, and

"(2) a person and all entities which are 80-percent owned entities with respect to such person."

—P.L. 98-369, Sec. 421(b)(6)(A), deleted para. (b)(1) and redesignated paras. (b)(2) and (3) as paras. (b)(1) and (2), effective for transfers after 7/18/84 in tax. yrs. ending after 7/18/84. Sec. 421(d) of this Act provides:

"(2) Election to have amendments apply to transfers after 1983.—If both spouses or former spouses make an election under this paragraph, the amendments made by this section shall apply to all transfers made by such spouses (or former spouses) after December 31, 1983.

"(3) Exception for transfers pursuant to existing decrees.—Except in the case of an election under paragraph (2), the amendments made by this section shall not apply to transfers under any instrument in effect on or before the date of the enactment of this Act unless both spouses (or former spouses) elect to have such amendments apply to transfers under such instrument.

"(4) Election.—Any election under paragraph (2) or (3) shall be made in such manner, at such time, and subject to such conditions, as the Secretary of the Treasury or his delegate may by regulations prescribe."

Prior to deletion, para. (b)(1) read as follows:

"(1) a husband and wife,"

—P.L. 98-369, Sec. 557(a), added subsec. (d), effective for sales or exchanges after 7/18/84 in tax. yrs. ending after 7/18/84.

In 1983, P.L. 97-448, Sec. 301(a), amended subsec. (b)... Sec. 301(b), amended subsec. (c), effective for dispositions made after 10/19/80, in tax. yrs. ending after 10/19/80.

Prior to amendment, subsec. (b) read as follows:

"(b) Related persons.

"For purposes of subsection (a), the term 'related persons' means—

"(1) the taxpayer and the taxpayer's spouse,

"(2) the taxpayer and an 80-percent owned entity, or

"(3) two 80-percent owned entities."

Prior to amendment, subsec. (c) read as follows:

"(c) 80-percent owned entity defined.

"(1) General rule. For purposes of this section, the term '80-percent owned entity' means—

"(A) a corporation 80 percent or more in value of the outstanding stock of which is owned (directly or indirectly) by or for the taxpayer, and

"(B) a partnership 80 percent or more of the capital interest or profits interest in which is owned (directly or indirectly) by or for the taxpayer.

"(2) Constructive ownership. For purposes of subparagraphs (A) and (B) of paragraph (1), the principles of section 318 shall apply, except that—

"(A) the members of an individual's family shall consist only of such individual and such individual's spouse, and

"(B) paragraphs (2)(C) and (3)(C) of section 318(a) shall be applied without regard to the 50-percent limitation contained therein."

In 1980, P.L. 96-471, Sec. 5, amended subsecs. (b) and (c), effective for dispositions made after 10/19/80 in tax. yrs. end. after 10/19/80

Prior to amendment, subsecs. (b) and (c) read as follows:

"(b) Related persons.

"For purposes of subsection (a), the term 'related persons' means—

"(1) a husband and wife,

"(2) an individual and a corporation 80 percent or more in value of the outstanding stock of which is owned, directly or indirectly, by or for such individual, or

"(3) two or more corporations 80 percent or more in value of the outstanding stock of each of which is owned, directly or indirectly, by or for the same individual.

"(c) Constructive ownership of stock.

"Section 318 shall apply in determining the ownership of stock for purposes of this section, except that sections 318(a)(2)(C) and 318(a)(3)(C) shall be applied without regard to the 50-percent limitation contained therein."

In 1978, P.L. 95-600, Sec. 701(v)(1), substituted "of a character which is subject to the allowance for depreciation provided in section 167." for "subject to the allowance for depreciation provided in section 167", effective as provided in Sec. 2129(b) of P.L. 94-455, reproduced below

In 1976, P.L. 94-455, Sec. 2129, amended Code Sec. 1239, effective as provided in Sec. 2129(b) of this Act, which reads as follows:

"(b) Effective date.

"The amendment made by this section shall apply to sales or exchanges after the date of enactment [10/4/76] of this act. For purposes of the preceding sentence, a sale or exchange is considered to have occurred on or before such date of enactment if such sale or exchange is made pursuant to a binding contract entered into on or before that date."

Prior to amendment, Code Sec. 1239 read as follows:

"SEC. 1239. GAIN FROM SALE OF CERTAIN PROPERTY BETWEEN SPOUSES OR BETWEEN AN INDIVIDUAL AND A CONTROLLED CORPORATION.

"(a) Treatment of gain as ordinary income.

"In the case of a sale or exchange, directly or indirectly, of property described in subsection (b)—

"(1) between a husband and wife; or

"(2) between an individual and a corporation more than 80 percent in value of the outstanding stock of which is owned by such individual, his spouse, and his minor children and minor grandchildren;

any gain recognized to the transferor from the sale or exchange of such property shall be considered as gain from the sale or exchange of property which is neither a capital asset nor property described in section 1231.

"(b) Section applicable only to sales or exchanges of depreciable property.

"This section shall apply only in the case of a sale or exchange by a transferor of property which in the hands of the transferee is property of a character which is subject to the allowance for depreciation provided in section 167.

"(c) Section not applicable with respect to sales or exchanges made on or before May 3, 1951.

"This section shall apply only in the case of a sale or exchange made after May 3, 1951."

In 1958, P.L. 85-866, Sec. 56, added subsec. (c).

Sec. 1240. Repealed.

In 1976, P.L. 94-455, Sec. 1901(a)(139), repealed Code Sec. 1240, effective for tax. yrs. begin. after 12/31/76.

Prior to repeal Code Sec. 1240 read as follows:

"SEC. 1240. TAXABILITY TO EMPLOYEE OF TERMINATION PAYMENTS.

"Amounts received from the assignment or release by an employee, after more than 20 years' employment, of all his rights to receive, after termination of his employment and for a period of not less than 5 years (or for a period ending with his death), a percentage of future profits or receipts of his employer shall be considered an amount received from the sale or exchange of a capital asset held for more than 6 months if—

"(1) such rights were included in the terms of the employment of such employee for not less than 12 years,

"(2) such rights were included in the terms of the employment of such employee before the date of enactment of this title, and

"(3) the total of the amounts received for such assignment or release is received in one taxable year and after the termination of such employment."

Sec. 1241. Cancellation of lease or distributor's agreement.

Amounts received by a lessee for the cancellation of a lease, or by a distributor of goods for the cancellation of a distributor's agreement (if the distributor has a substantial capital investment in the distributorship), shall be considered as amounts received in exchange for such lease or agreement.

Sec. 1242. Losses on small business investment company stock.

If—

(1) a loss is on stock in a small business investment company operating under the Small Business Investment Act of 1958, and

(2) such loss would (but for this section) be a loss from the sale or exchange of a capital asset,

then such loss shall be treated as an ordinary loss. For purposes of section 172 (relating to the net operating loss deduction) any amount of loss treated by reason of this section as an ordinary loss shall be treated as attributable to a trade or business of the taxpayer.

In 1976, P.L. 94-455, Sec. 1901(b)(3)(F), substituted "an ordinary loss" for "a loss from the sale or exchange of property which is not a capital asset" in para. (2), effective for tax. yrs. begin. after 12/31/76.
In 1958, P.L. 85-866, Sec. 57, added Code Sec. 1242, effective for tax. yrs. begin. after 9/2/58.

Sec. 1243. Loss of small business investment company.

In the case of a small business investment company operating under the Small Business Investment Act of 1958, if—

(1) a loss is on stock received pursuant to the conversion privilege of convertible debentures acquired pursuant to section 304 of the Small Business Investment Act of 1958, and

(2) such loss would (but for this section) be a loss from the sale or exchange of a capital asset,

then such loss shall be treated as an ordinary loss.

In 1976, P.L. 94-455, Sec. 1901(b)(3)(F), substituted "an ordinary loss" for "a loss from the sale or exchange of property which is not a capital asset" in para. (2), effective for tax. yrs. begin. after 12/31/76.
In 1969, P.L. 91-172, Sec. 433(b), amended para. (1), effective for tax. yrs. begin. after 7/11/69, except as provided in Sec. 433(d)(2) of this Act, reproduced in note following Code Sec. 582.
Prior to amendment para. (1) read as follows:
"(1) a loss is on convertible debentures (including stock received pursuant to the conversion privilege) acquired pursuant to section 304 of the Small Business Investment Act of 1958, and"
In 1958, P.L. 85-866, Sec. 57, added Code Sec. 1243, effective for tax. yrs. begin. after 9/2/58.

Sec. 1244. Losses on small business stock.
(a) General rule.

In the case of an individual, a loss on section 1244 stock issued to such individual or to a partnership which would (but for this section) be treated as a loss from the sale or exchange of a capital asset shall, to the extent provided in this section, be treated as an ordinary loss.

(b) Maximum amount for any taxable year.

For any taxable year the aggregate amount treated by the taxpayer by reason of this section as an ordinary loss shall not exceed—

(1) $50,000, or

(2) $100,000, in the case of a husband and wife filing a joint return for such year under section 6013.

(c) Section 1244 stock defined.

(1) **In general.** For purposes of this section, the term "section 1244 stock" means stock in a domestic corporation if—

(A) at the time such stock is issued, such corporation was a small business corporation,

(B) such stock was issued by such corporation for money or other property (other than stock and securities), and

(C) such corporation, during the period of its 5 most recent taxable years ending before the date the loss on such stock was sustained, derived more than 50 percent of its aggregate gross receipts from sources other than royalties, rents, dividends, interests, annuities, and sales or exchanges of stocks or securities.

(2) **Rules for application of paragraph (1)(C).**

(A) Period taken into account with respect to new corporations. For purposes of paragraph (1)(C), if the corporation has not been in existence for 5 taxable years ending before the date the loss on the stock was sustained, there shall be substituted for such 5-year period—

(i) the period of the corporation's taxable years ending before such date, or

(ii) if the corporation has not been in existence for 1 taxable year ending before such date, the period such corporation has been in existence before such date.

(B) Gross receipts from sales of securities. For purposes of paragraph (1)(C), gross receipts from the sales or exchanges of stock or securities shall be taken into account only to the extent of gains therefrom.

(C) Nonapplication where deductions exceed gross income. Paragraph (1)(C) shall not apply with respect to any corporation if, for the period taken into account for purposes of paragraph (1)(C), the amount of the deductions allowed by this chapter (other than by sections 172, 243, 244, and 245) exceeds the amount of gross income.

(3) **Small business corporation defined.**

(A) In general. For purposes of this section, a corporation shall be treated as a small business corporation if the aggregate amount of money and other property received by the corporation for stock, as a contribution to capital, and as paid-in surplus, does not exceed $1,000,000. The determination under the preceding sentence shall be made as of the time of the issuance of the stock in question but shall include amounts received for such stock and for all stock theretofore issued.

(B) Amount taken into account with respect to property. For purposes of subparagraph (A), the amount taken into account with respect to any property other than money shall be the amount equal to the adjusted basis to the corporation of such property for determining gain, reduced by any liability to which the property was subject or which was assumed by the corporation. The determination under the preceding sentence shall be made as of the time the property was received by the corporation.

(d) Special rules.

(1) **Limitations on amount of ordinary loss.**

(A) Contributions of property having basis in excess of value. If—

(i) section 1244 stock was issued in exchange for property,

(ii) the basis of such stock in the hands of the taxpayer is determined by reference to the basis in his hands of such property, and

(iii) the adjusted basis (for determining loss) of such property immediately before the exchange exceeded its fair market value at such time, then in computing the amount of the loss on such stock for purposes of this section the basis of such stock shall be reduced by an amount equal to the excess described in clause (iii).

(B) Increases in basis. In computing the amount of the loss on stock for purposes of this section, any increase in the basis of such stock (through contributions to the capital of the corporation, or otherwise) shall be treated as allocable to stock which is not section 1244 stock.

(2) Recapitalizations, changes in name, etc. To the extent provided in regulations prescribed by the Secretary, stock in a corporation, the basis of which (in the hands of a taxpayer) is determined in whole or in part by reference to the basis in his hands of stock in such corporation which meets the requirements of subsection (c)(1) (other than subparagraph (C) thereof), or which is received in a reorganization described in section 368(a)(1)(F) in exchange for stock which meets such requirements, shall be treated as meeting such requirements. For purposes of paragraphs (1)(C) and (3)(A) of subsection (c), a successor corporation in a reorganization described in section 368(a)(1)(F) shall be treated as the same corporation as its predecessor.

(3) Relationship to net operating loss deduction. For purposes of section 172 (relating to the net operating loss deduction), any amount of loss treated by reason of this section as an ordinary loss shall be treated as attributable to a trade or business of the taxpayer.

(4) Individual defined. For purposes of this section, the term "individual" does not include a trust or estate.

(e) Regulations.
The Secretary shall prescribe such regulations as may be necessary to carry out the purposes of this section.

In 1984, P.L. 98-369, Sec. 481(a), substituted "stock" for "common stock" in paragraphs (c)(1) and (d)(2), effective for stock issued after 7/18/84 in tax. yrs. ending after 7/18/84.

In 1980, P.L. 96-222, Sec. 103(a)(9), amended Sec. 345(e) of P.L. 95-600, the effective date for changes made by Sec. 345 of P.L. 95-600, by adding paras. (e)(2) and (e)(3) [see below].

In 1978, P.L. 95-600, Sec. 345(a), deleted para. (c)(2) and added new para. (c)(3) . . . Sec. 345(b), substituted "$50,000" for "$25,000" in para. (b)(1) and substituted "$100,000" for "$50,000" in para. (b)(2) . . . Sec. 345(c), amended para. (c)(1) and added new para. (c)(2) . . . Sec. 345(d), substituted "subparagraph (C)" for "subparagraph (E)" and substituted "paragraphs (1)(C) and (3)(A)" for "paragraphs (1)(E) and (2)(A)" in para. (d)(2), effective [as amended by Sec. 103(a)(9) of P.L. 96-222, see above] for stock issued after 11/6/78 except as provided in Sec. 345(e)(2) and (3) of this Act, which reads as follows:

"(2) Subsection (b). The amendments made by subsection (b) shall apply to taxable years beginning after 12/31/78."

"(3) Transitional rule for subsection (b). In the case of a taxable year which includes November 6, 1978, the amendments made by subsection (b) shall apply with respect to stock issued after such date."

Prior to amendment, paras. (c)(1) and (2) read as follows:

"(1) In general. For purposes of this section, the term 'section 1244 stock' means common stock in a domestic corporation if—

"(A) such corporation adopted a plan after June 30, 1958, to offer such stock for a period (ending not later than two years after the date such plan was adopted) specified in the plan,

"(B) at the time such plan was adopted, such corporation was a small business corporation,

"(C) at the time such plan was adopted, no portion of a prior offering was outstanding,

"(D) such stock was issued by such corporation, pursuant to such plan, for money or other property (other than stock and securities), and

"(E) such corporation, during the period of its 5 most recent taxable years ending before the date the loss on such stock is sustained (or if such corporation has not been in existence for 5 taxable years ending before such date, during the period of its taxable years ending before such date, or if such corporation has not been in existence for one taxable year ending before such date, during the period such corporation has been in existence before such date), derived more than 50 percent of its aggregate gross receipts from sources other than royalties, rents, dividends, interest, annuities, and sales or exchanges of stock or securities (gross receipts from such sales or exchanges being taken into account for purposes of this subparagraph only to the extent of gains therefrom); except that this subparagraph shall not apply with respect to any corporation if, for the period referred to,

the amount of the deductions allowed by this chapter (other than by sections 172, 243, 244, and 245) exceed the amount of gross income.

Such term does not include stock if issued (pursuant to the plan referred to in subparagraph (A)) after a subsequent offering of stock has been made by the corporation.

"(2) Small business corporation defined. For purposes of this section, a corporation shall be treated as a small business corporation if at the time of the adoption of the plan—

"(A) the sum of—
"(i) the aggregate amount which may be offered under the plan, plus
"(ii) the aggregate amount of money and other property (taken into account in an amount, as of the time received by the corporation, equal to the adjusted basis to the corporation of such property for determining gain, reduced by any liabilities to which the property was subject or which were assumed by the corporation at such time) received by the corporation after June 30, 1958, for stock, as a contribution to capital, and as paid-in surplus,

does not exceed $500,000; and

"(B) the sum of—
"(i) the aggregate amount which may be offered under the plan, plus
"(ii) the equity capital of the corporation (determined on the date of the adoption of the plan),

does not exceed $1,000,000.

For purposes of subparagraph (B), the equity capital of a corporation is the sum of its money and other property (in an amount equal to the adjusted basis of such property for determining gain), less the amount of its indebtedness (other than indebtedness to shareholders)."

In 1976, P.L. 94-455, Sec. 1901(b)(1)(W), substituted "sections 172, 243" for "sections 172, 242, 243" in subpara. (c)(1)(E), effective for tax. yrs. begin. after 12/31/76.

—P.L. 94-455, Sec. 1901(b)(3)(G), substituted "an ordinary loss" for "a loss from the sale or exchange of an asset which is not a capital asset" in subsecs. (a) and (b) and para. (d)(3), effective for tax. yrs. begin. after 12/31/76.

—P.L. 94-455, Sec. 1906(b)(13)(A), substituted "Secretary" for "Secretary or his delegate" in para. (d)(2) and subsec. (e), effective for tax. yrs. begin. after 12/31/76.

In 1958, P.L. 85-866, Sec. 202, added Code Sec. 1244, effective 9/2/58.

Sec. 1245. Gain from dispositions of certain depreciable property.

(a) General rule.

(1) Ordinary income. Except as otherwise provided in this section, if section 1245 property is disposed of the amount by which the lower of—

(A) the recomputed basis of the property, or

(B)(i) in the case of a sale, exchange, or involuntary conversion, the amount realized, or

(ii) in the case of any other disposition, the fair market value of such property,

exceeds the adjusted basis of such property shall be treated as ordinary income. Such gain shall be recognized notwithstanding any other provision of this subtitle.

(2) Recomputed basis. For purposes of this section—

(A) In general. The term "recomputed basis" means, with respect to any property, its adjusted basis recomputed by adding thereto all adjustments reflected in such adjusted basis on account of deductions (whether in respect of the same or other property) allowed or allowable to the taxpayer or to any other person for depreciation or amortization.

(B) Taxpayer may establish amount allowed. For purposes of subparagraph (A), if the taxpayer can establish by adequate records or other sufficient evidence that the amount allowed for depreciation or amortization for any period was less than the amount allowable, the amount added for such period shall be the amount allowed.

(C) Certain deductions treated as amortization. Any deduction allowable under section 179, 179A, 179B, 181, 179C, 179D, 179E, 190, 193, or 194 shall be treated as if it were a deduction allowable for amortization.

(3) Section 1245 property. For purposes of this section, the term "section 1245 property" means any property which is or has been property of a character subject to the allowance for depreciation provided in section 167 and is either—

(A) personal property,

(B) other property (not including a building or its structural components) but only if such other property is tangible and has an adjusted basis in which there are reflected adjustments described in paragraph (2) for a period in which such property (or other property)—
  (i) was used as an integral part of manufacturing, production, or extraction or of furnishing transportation, communications, electrical energy, gas, water, or sewage disposal services,
  (ii) constituted a research facility used in connection with any of the activities referred to in clause (i), or
  (iii) constituted a facility used in connection with any of the activities referred to in clause (i) for the bulk storage of fungible commodities (including commodities in a liquid or gaseous state),
(C) so much of any real property (other than any property described in subparagraph (B)) which has an adjusted basis in which there are reflected adjustments for amortization under section 169, 179, 179A, 179B, 179C, 179D, 179E, 185, 188 (as in effect before its repeal by the Revenue Reconciliation Act of 1990), 190, 193, or 194[,]
(D) a single purpose agricultural or horticultural structure (as defined in section 168(i)(13)),
(E) a storage facility (not including a building or its structural components) used in connection with the distribution of petroleum or any primary product of petroleum, or
(F) any railroad grading or tunnel bore (as defined in section 168(e)(4)).

(b) Exceptions and limitations.
(1) Gifts. Subsection (a) shall not apply to a disposition by gift.
(2) Transfers at death. Except as provided in section 691 (relating to income in respect of a decedent), subsection (a) shall not apply to a transfer at death.
(3) Certain tax-free transactions. If the basis of property in the hands of a transferee is determined by reference to its basis in the hands of the transferor by reason of the application of section 332, 351, 361, 721, or 731, then the amount of gain taken into account by the transferor under subsection (a)(1) shall not exceed the amount of gain recognized to the transferor on the transfer of such property (determined without regard to this section). Except as provided in paragraph (6), this paragraph shall not apply to a disposition to an organization (other than a cooperative described in section 521) which is exempt from the tax imposed by this chapter.
(4) Like kind exchanges; involuntary conversions, etc. If property is disposed of and gain (determined without regard to this section) is not recognized in whole or in part under section 1031 or 1033, then the amount of gain taken into account by the transferor under subsection (a)(1) shall not exceed the sum of—
  (A) the amount of gain recognized on such disposition (determined without regard to this section), plus
  (B) the fair market value of property acquired which is not section 1245 property and which is not taken into account under subparagraph (A).
(5) Property distributed by a partnership to a partner.
  (A) In general. For purposes of this section, the basis of section 1245 property distributed by a partnership to a partner shall be deemed to be determined by reference to the adjusted basis of such property to the partnership.
  (B) Adjustments added back. In the case of any property described in subparagraph (A), for purposes of computing the recomputed basis of such property the amount of the adjustments added back for periods before the distribution by the partnership shall be—
    (i) the amount of the gain to which subsection (a) would have applied if such property had been sold by the partnership immediately before the distribution at its fair market value at such time, reduced by
    (ii) the amount of such gain to which section 751(b) applied.
(6) Transfers to tax-exempt organization where property will be used in unrelated business.
  (A) In general. The second sentence of paragraph (3) shall not apply to a disposition of section 1245 property to an organization described in section 511(a)(2) or 511(b)(2) if, immediately after such disposition, such organization uses such property in an unrelated trade or business (as defined in section 513).
  (B) Later change in use. If any property with respect to the disposition of which gain is not recognized by reason of subparagraph (A) ceases to be used in an unrelated trade or business of the organization acquiring such property, such organization shall be treated for purposes of this section as having disposed of such property on the date of such cessation.
(7) Timber property. In determining, under subsection (a)(2), the recomputed basis of property with respect to which a deduction under section 194 was allowed for any taxable year, the taxpayer shall not take into account adjustments under section 194 to the extent such adjustments are attributable to the amortizable basis of the taxpayer acquired before the 10th taxable year preceding the taxable year in which gain with respect to the property is recognized.
(8) Disposition of amortizable section 197 intangibles.
  (A) In general. If a taxpayer disposes of more than 1 amortizable section 197 intangible (as defined in section 197(c)) in a transaction or a series of related transactions, all such amortizable section 197 intangibles shall be treated as 1 section 1245 property for purposes of this section.
  (B) Exception. Subparagraph (A) shall not apply to any amortizable section 197 intangible (as so defined) with respect to which the adjusted basis exceeds the fair market value.
(c) Adjustments to basis.
The Secretary shall prescribe such regulations as he may deem necessary to provide for adjustments to the basis of property to reflect gain recognized under subsection (a).
(d) Application of section.
This section shall apply notwithstanding any other provision of this subtitle.

In 2006, P.L. 109-432, Sec. 404(b)(3), added "179E," after "179D," in subparas. (a)(2)(C) and (a)(3)(C), effective for costs paid or incurred after 12/20/2006.
In 2005, P.L. 109-135, Sec. 402(a)(6)(A), deleted para. (b)(5) and redesignated paras. (b)(6)-(9) as paras. (b)(5)-(8) . . . Sec. 402(a)(6)(B), substituted "paragraph (6)" for "paragraph (7)" in para. (b)(3), effective for dispositions of property after 8/8/2005 as if included in Sec. 1263 [sic 1363] of the Energy Policy Act of 2005, P.L. 109-58. Sec. 402(m)(2) of this Act, provides:
"(2) Repeal of Public Utility Holding Company Act of 1935. The amendments made by subsection (a) shall not apply with respect to any transaction ordered in compliance with the Public Utility Holding Company Act of 1935 before its repeal."
Prior to deletion,para. (b)(5) read as follows:
"(5) Section 1081 transactions. Under regulations prescribed by the Secretary, rules consistent with paragraphs (3) and (4) of this subsection shall apply in the case of transactions described in section 1081 (relating to exchanges in obedience to SEC orders)."
—P.L. 109-135, Sec. 403(e)(2), added "181," after "179B," in subpara. (a)(2)(C), [Note: The placement of "181" after "179B," in subpara. (a)(2)(C) possibly does not take into account the addition of "179C, 179D" by Secs. 1323(b)(1) and 1331(b)(2) of the Energy Policy Act of 2005, P.L. 109-58.] effec-

tive for qualified film and television productions (as defined in Code Sec. 181(d)(1), as added by Sec. 244 of P.L. 108-357) commencing after 10/22/2004.
—P.L. 109-135, Sec. 403(i)(2), substituted "193, or 194" for "or 193" in subpara. (a)(2)(C), effective for expenditures paid or incurred after 10/22/2004 as if included in Sec. 322 of the American Jobs Creation Act of 2004, P.L. 108-357.
—P.L. 109-58, Sec. 1323(b)(1), added "179C," after "179B," in subparas. (a)(2)(C) and (a)(3)(C), effective for properties placed in service after 8/8/2005.
—P.L. 109-58, Sec. 1331(b)(2), added "179D," after "179C," in subparas. (a)(2)(C) and (a)(3)(C) [as amended by Sec. 1323(b)(1) of this Act, see above], effective for property placed in service after 12/31/2005.
—P.L. 109-58, Sec. 1363(a), added para. (b)(9), effective for dispositions of property after 8/8/2005.
In 2004, P.L. 108-357, Sec. 338(b)(5), added "179B," after "179A," in subparas. (a)(2)(C) and (a)(3)(C), effective for expenses paid or incurred after 12/31/2002, in tax. yrs. end. after 12/31/2002.
—P.L. 108-357, Sec. 886(b)(2), deleted para. (a)(4), effective for franchises acquired after 10/22/2004.
Prior to deletion, para. (a)(4) read as follows:
"(4) Special rule for player contracts.
"(A) In general. For purposes of this section, if a franchise to conduct any sports enterprise is sold or exchanged, and if, in connection with such sale or exchange, there is a transfer of any player contracts, the recomputed basis of such player contracts in the hands of the transferor shall be the adjusted basis of such contracts increased by the greater of—
"(i) the previously unrecaptured depreciation with respect to player contracts acquired by the transferor at the time of acquisition of such franchise, or
"(ii) the previously unrecaptured depreciation with respect to the player contracts involved in such transfer.
"(B) Previously unrecaptured depreciation with respect to initial contracts. For purposes of subparagraph (A)(i), the term 'previously unrecaptured depreciation' means the excess (if any) of—
"(i) the sum of the deduction allowed or allowable to the taxpayer transferor for the depreciation attributable to periods after December 31, 1975, of any player contracts acquired by him at the time of acquisition of such franchise, plus the deduction allowed or allowable for losses incurred after December 31, 1975, with respect to such player contracts acquired at the time of such acquisition, over
"(ii) the aggregate of the amounts described in clause (i) treated as ordinary income by reason of this section with respect to prior dispositions of such player contracts acquired upon acquisition of the franchise.
"(C) Previously unrecaptured depreciation with respect to contracts transferred. For purposes of subparagraph (A)(ii), the term 'previously unrecaptured depreciation' means the amount of any deduction allowed or allowable to the taxpayer transferor for the depreciation of any contracts involved in such transfer.
"(D) Player contract. For purposes of this paragraph, the term 'player contract' means any contract for the services of an athlete which, in the hands of the taxpayer, is of a character subject to the allowance for depreciation provided in section 167."
In 1997, P.L. 105-34, Sec. 1604(a)(3), added "179A," after "179," in subparas. (a)(2)(C) and (a)(3)(C), effective for property placed in service after 6/30/93.
In 1996, P.L. 104-188, Sec. 1703(l), substituted "by the taxpayer or a related person" for "by the taxpayer" in Sec. 13261(g)(2)(A)(iii), P.L. 103-66, see below.
—P.L. 104-188, Sec. 1703(n)(6), amended para. (a)(3) introductory text, effective for property acquired after 8/10/93, except as provided in Sec. 13261(g)(2) and (3) of P.L. 103-66, see below.
Prior to amendment, para. (a)(3) preceding subpara. (a)(3)(A) read as follows:
"(3) Section 1245 property. For purposes of this section, the term 'section 1245 property' means any property which is or has been property of a character subject to the allowance for depreciation provided in section 167 [sic (or subject to the allowance of amortization provided in)] and is either—".
In 1995, P.L. 104-7, Sec. 2(b)(1), deleted "section 1071 (relating to gain from sale or exchange to effectuate policies of FCC) or" after "described in" in para. (b)(5) . . . Sec. 2(b)(2), deleted "1071 and" after "Section" in the heading of para. (b)(5), effective as provided in Sec. 2(d) of this Act, which reads as follows:
"(d) Effective date.
"(1) In general. The amendments made by this section shall apply to—
"(A) sales and exchanges on or after January 17, 1995, and
"(B) sales and exchanges before such date if the FCC tax certificate with respect to such sale or exchange is issued on or after such date.
"(2) Binding contracts.
"(A) In general. The amendments made by this section shall not apply to any sale or exchange pursuant to a written contract which was binding on January 16, 1995, and at all times thereafter before the sale or exchange, if the FCC tax certificate with respect to such sale or exchange was applied for, or issued, on or before such date.
"(B) Sales contingent on issuance of certificate.
"(i) In general. A contract shall be treated as not binding for purposes of subparagraph (A) if the sale or exchange pursuant to such contract, or the material terms of such contract, were contingent, at any time on January 16, 1995, on the issuance of an FCC tax certificate. The preceding sentence shall not apply if the FCC tax certificate for such sale or exchange is issued on or before January 16, 1995.
"(ii) Material terms. For purposes of clause (i), the material terms of a contract shall not be treated as contingent on the issuance of an FCC tax certificate solely because such terms provide that the sales price would, if such certificate were not issued, be increases by an amount not greater than 10 percent of the sales price otherwise provided in the contract.

"(3) FCC tax certificate. For purposes of this subsection, the term 'FCC tax certificate' means any certificate of the Federal Communications Commission for the effectuation of section 1071 of the Internal Revenue Code of 1986 (as in effect on the day before the date of the enactment of this Act)."
In 1993, P.L. 103-66, Sec. 13261(f)(4), substituted "or 193" for "193, 253(d)(2) or (3)" in subpara. (a)(2)(C) . . . Sec. 13261(f)(5), deleted "section 185 or 1253(d)(2) or (3)" [sic (or subject to the allowance of amortization provided in section 185 or 1253(d)(2) or (3))] and added "section 197" in para. (a)(3), effective for property acquired after 8/10/93, except as provided in Sec. 13261(g)(2) and (3) of this Act [as amended by Sec. 1703(l) of P.L. 104-188, see above], which reads as follows:
"(2) Election to have amendments apply to property acquired after July 25, 1991.
"(A) In general. If an election under this paragraph applies to the taxpayer—
"(i) the amendments made by this section shall apply to property acquired by the taxpayer after July 25, 1991,
"(ii) subsection (c)(1)(A) of section 197 of the Internal Revenue Code of 1986 (as added by this section) (and so much of subsection (f)(9)(A) of such section 197 as precedes clause (i) thereof) shall be applied with respect to the taxpayer by treating July 25, 1991, as the date of the enactment of such section, and
"(iii) in applying subsection (f)(9) of such section, with respect to any property acquired by the taxpayer or a related person on or before the date of the enactment of this Act, only holding or use on July 25, 1991, shall be taken into account.
"(B) Election. An election under this paragraph shall be made at such time and in such manner as the Secretary of the Treasury or his delegate may prescribe. Such an election by any taxpayer, once made—
"(i) may be revoked only with the consent of the Secretary, and
"(ii) shall apply to the taxpayer making such election and any other taxpayer under common control with the taxpayer (within the meaning of subparagraphs (A) and (B) of section 41(f)(1) of such Code) at any time after August 2, 1993, and on or before the date on which such election is made.
"(3) Elective binding contract exception.
"(A) In general. The amendments made by this section shall not apply to any acquisition of property by the taxpayer if—
"(i) such acquisition is pursuant to a written binding contract in effect on the date of the enactment of this Act and at all times thereafter before such acquisition,
"(ii) an election under paragraph (2) does not apply to the taxpayer, and
"(iii) the taxpayer makes an election under this paragraph with respect to such contract.
"(B) Election. An election under this paragraph shall be made at such time and in such manner as the Secretary of the Treasury or his delegate shall prescribe. Such an election, once made—
"(i) may be revoked only with the consent of the Secretary, and
"(ii) shall apply to all property, acquired pursuant to the contract with respect to which such election was made."
In 1990, P.L. 101-508, Sec. 11704(a)(13), substituted "or (3))" for "or (3)" in the material preceding subpara. (a)(3)(A), effective 11/5/90.
—P.L. 101-508, Sec. 11801(c)(6)(E), substituted "188 (as in effect before its repeal by the Revenue Reconciliation Act of 1990)," for "188," in subpara. (a)(3)(C) . . . Sec. 11801(c)(8)(H), deleted "371(a), 374(a)," after "application of section 332, 351, 361," in para. (b)(3), effective 11/5/90 except as provided in 11821(b) of this Act, reproduced in note following Code Sec. 184.
—P.L. 101-508, Sec. 11813(b)(21), substituted "section 168(i)(13)" for "section 48(p)" in subpara. (a)(3)(D), effective for property placed in service after 12/31/90 except as provided by Sec. 11813(c)(2) of this Act, reproduced in note following Code Sec. 46.
In 1989, P.L. 101-239, Sec. 7622(b)(2)(A), [sic (d)(2)(A)], substituted "193, or 1253(d)(2) or (3)" for "or 193" in subpara. (a)(2)(C) . . . Sec. 7622(b)(2)(B), [sic (d)(2)(B)], substituted "section 185 or 1253(d)(2) or (3)" for "section 185" in para. (a)(3), effective for transfers after 10/2/89. Sec. 7622(c)(2) [sic (e)(2)] provides:
"(2) Binding contract. The amendments made by this section shall not apply to any transfer pursuant to a written binding contract in effect on October 2, 1989, and at all times thereafter before the transfer."
In 1988, P.L. 100-647, Sec. 1002(c)(1), added a new sentence to the end of Sec. 203(a)(1)(B) [reproduced below] of P.L. 99-514, part of the effective date for changes made by Sec. 201(d)(11) of P.L. 99-514.
—P.L. 100-647, Sec. 1002(c)(3), of this Act provides:
"(3) Notwithstanding section 203 of the Reform Act, the amendments made by section 201 of the Reform Act shall apply to any real property which was acquired before January 1, 1987, and was converted on or after such date from personal use to a use for which depreciation is allowable."
—P.L. 100-647, Sec. 1002(i)(2)(I), deleted the "or" at the end of subpara. (a)(3)(D), substituted ", or" for the period at the end of subpara. (a)(3)(E), added new subpara. (a)(3)(F), effective for that portion of the basis of any property which is attributable to expenditures paid or incurred after 12/31/86. For transitional rules, see Sec. 242(c)(2) of P.L. 99-514 reproduced in note following Code Sec. 185.
In 1986, P.L. 99-514, Sec. 201(d)(11)(A), deleted "during a taxable year beginning after December 31, 1962, or section 1245 recovery property is disposed of after December 31, 1980," before "the amount" in para. (a)(1) . . . Sec. 201(d)(11)(B), amended para. (a)(2) . . . Sec. 201(d)(11)(C), deleted subpara. (a)(3)(C) and redesignated subparas. (a)(3)(D), (E), and (F) as (a)(3)(C), (D), and (E), respectively . . . Sec. 201(d)(11)(D), deleted paras. (a)(5) and (6), effective for property placed in service after 12/31/86, in tax. yrs. end. after 12/31/86 [see Sec.

Capital gains and losses Code Sec. 1245

1002(c)(3) of P.L. 100-647 above]. For transitional rules, see Sec. 203(b)-(e) of this Act reproduced in note following Code Sec. 168. Sec. 203(a)(1)(B) [as amended by Sec. 1002(c)(1) of P.L. 100-647] of this Act provides:

"(B) Election to have amendments made by section 201 apply.

"A taxpayer may elect (at such time and in such manner as the Secretary of the Treasury or his delegate may prescribe) to have the amendments made by section 201 apply to any property placed in service after July 31, 1986, and before January 1, 1987 No election may be made under this subparagraph with respect to property to which section 168 of the Internal Revenue Code of 1986 would not apply by reason of section 168(f)(5) of such Code if such property were placed in service after December 31, 1986."

For transitional and other rules, see Sec. 203(b)-(e) of this Act reproduced in note following Code Sec. 168.

Prior to amendment, para. (a)(2) read as follows:

"(2) Recomputed basis. For purposes of this section, the term 'recomputed basis' means —

"(A) with respect to any property referred to in paragraph (3)(A) or (B), its adjusted basis recomputed by adding thereto all adjustments, attributable to periods after December 31, 1961,

"(B) with respect to any property referred to in paragraph (3)(C), its adjusted basis recomputed by adding thereto all adjustments, attributable to periods after June 30, 1963,

"(C) with respect to livestock, its adjusted basis recomputed by adding thereto all adjustments attributable to periods after December 31, 1969,

"(D) with respect to any property referred to in paragraph (3)(D), its adjusted basis recomputed by adding thereto all adjustments attributable to periods beginning with the first month for which a deduction for amortization is allowed under section 169, 179, 185, 190, 193, or 194, or

"(E) with respect to any section 1245 recovery property, the adjusted basis of such property recomputed by adding thereto all adjustments attributable to periods for which a deduction is allowed under section 168(a) (as added by the Economic Recovery Tax Act of 1981) with respect to such property.

reflected in such adjusted basis on account of deductions (whether in respect of the same or other property) allowed or allowable to the taxpayer or to any other person for depreciation, or for amortization under section 168 (as in effect before its repeal by the Tax Reform Act of 1976), 169, 179, 184, 185, 188, or 190, 193, 194 or (in the case of property described in paragraph (3)(C)) 191 (as in effect before its repeal by the Economic Recovery Tax Act of 1981). For purposes of the preceding sentences, if the taxpayer can establish by adequate records or other sufficient evidence that the amount allowed for depreciation, or for amortization under section 168 (as in effect before its repeal by the Tax Reform Act of 1976), 169, 179, 184, 185, 188, or 190, 193, 194 or (in the case of property described in paragraph (3)(C)) 191 (as in effect before its repeal by the Economic Recovery Tax Act of 1981) for any period was less than the amount allowable, the amount added for such period shall be the amount allowed. For purposes of this section, any deduction allowable under section 179, 190 or 193 shall be treated as if it were a deduction allowable for amortization."

Prior to deletion, subpara. (a)(3)(C) read as follows:

"(C) an elevator or an escalator,"

Prior to deletion, paras. (a)(5) and (6) read as follows:

"(5) Section 1245 recovery property. For purposes of this section, the term 'section 1245 recovery property' means recovery property (within the meaning of section 168) other than —

"(A) 19-year real property and low-income housing which is residential rental property (as defined in section 167(j)(2)(B)),

"(B) 19-year real property and low-income housing which is described in section 168(f)(2),

"(C) 19-year real property and low-income housing with respect to which an election under subsection (b)(3) of section 168 to use a different recovery percentage is in effect, and

"(D) low-income housing (within the meaning of section 168(c)(2)(F)).

If only a portion of a building (or other structure) is section 1245 recovery property, gain from any disposition of such building (or other structure) shall be allocated first to the portion of the building (or other structure) which is section 1245 recovery property (to the extent of the amount which may be treated as ordinary income under this section) and then to the portion of the building or other structure which is not section 1245 recovery property.

"(6) Special rule for qualified leased property. In any case in which —

"(A) the lessor of qualified leased property (within the meaning of section 168(f)(8)(D)) is treated as the owner of such property for purposes of this subtitle under section 168(f)(8), and

"(B) the lessee acquires such property,

the recomputed basis of the lessee under this subsection shall be determined by taking into account any adjustments which would be taken into account in determining the recomputed basis of the lessor."

In 1985, P.L. 99-121, Sec. 103(b)(1)(D), substituted "19-year real property" for "18-year real property" in subparas. (a)(5)(A), (B) and (C), effective for property placed in service by the taxpayer after 5/8/85, except as provided in Sec. 105(b)(2) and (3) of this Act, reproduced in note following Code Sec. 168.

In 1984, P.L. 98-369, Sec. 111(e)(5), substituted "18-year real property and low-income housing" for "15-year real property" in subparagraphs (a)(5)(A), (a)(5)(B) and (a)(5)(C)... Sec. 111(e)(10), amended subpara. (a)(5)(D), effective for property placed in service by the taxpayer after 3/15/84.

Sec. 111(g)(2) and (3) of this Act provide:

"(2) Exception. — The amendments made by this section shall not apply to property placed in service by the taxpayer before January 1, 1987, if —

"(A) the taxpayer or a qualified person entered into a binding contract to purchase or construct such property before March 16, 1984, or

"(B) construction of such property was commenced by or for the taxpayer or a qualified person before March 16, 1984.

For purposes of this paragraph the term 'qualified person' means any person who transfers his rights in such a contract or such property to the taxpayer, but only if such property is not placed in service by such person before such rights are transferred to the taxpayer.

"(3) Special rules for application of paragraph (2). —

"(A) Certain inventory. — In the case of any property which —

"(i) is held by a person as property described in section 1221(1), and

"(ii) is disposed of by such person before January 1, 1985,

such person shall not, for purposes of paragraph (2), be treated as having placed such property in service before such property is disposed of merely because such person rented such property or held such property for rental. No deduction for depreciation or amortization shall be allowed to such person with respect to such property,

"(B) Certain property financed by bonds. — In the case of any property with respect to which —

"(i) bonds were issued to finance such property before 1984, and

"(ii) an architectural contract was entered into before March 16, 1984,

paragraph (2) shall be applied by substituting 'May 2' for 'March 16'."

Prior to amendment, subpara. (a)(5)(D) read as follows:

"(D) 15-year real property which is described in clause (i), (ii), (iii), or (iv) of section 1250(a)(1)(B)."

In 1983, P.L. 97-448, Sec. 102(e)(2)(B), added "(not including a building or its structural components)" after "storage facility" in subpara. (a)(3)(F), effective for property placed in service after 12/31/80, in tax. yrs. ending after 12/31/80.

In 1981, P.L. 97-34, Sec. 201(b), deleted "or" at the end of subpara. (a)(3)(C), deleted the period at the end of subpara. (a)(3)(D), and added subparas. (a)(3)(E) and (F) ... Sec. 202(b)(1), substituted "169, 179, 184" for "169, 184" each place it appeared in para. (a)(2) ... Sec. 202(b)(2), substituted "section 179, 190" for "section 190" in para. (a)(2) ... Sec. 202(b)(3), substituted "169, 179, 185" for "169, 185" in subparas. (a)(2)(D) and (a)(3)(D) ... Sec. 204(a), added "or section 1245 recovery property is disposed of after December 31, 1980," after "December 31, 1962," in para. (a)(1) ... Sec. 204(b), deleted "or" at the end of subpara. (a)(2)(C), added ", or" at the end of subpara. (a)(2)(D), and added a new subpara. (a)(2)(E) ... Sec. 204(c), added para. (a)(5) ... Sec. 204(d), added para. (a)(6), effective for property placed in service after 12/31/80, in tax. yrs. end. after 12/31/80.

— P.L. 97-34, Sec. 212(d)(2)(F), added "(as in effect before its repeal by the Economic Recovery Tax Act of 1981)" after "191" each place it appeared in para. (a)(2), effective for expenditures incurred after 12/31/81, in tax. yrs. end. after 12/31/81. For transitional rule, see Sec. 212(e)(2) of this Act reproduced in note following Code Sec. 46.

In 1980, P.L. 96-541, Sec. 2(e)(1), deleted Sec. 2124(a)(4) of P.L. 94-455, the effective date for changes made by Sec. 2124(a)(2) of P.L. 94-455, see below.

Prior to amendment Sec. 2124(a)(4) of P.L. 94-455 read as follows:

"(4) Effective date. The amendments made by this subsection shall apply with respect to additions to capital account made after June 14, 1976 and before June 15, 1981."

— P.L. 96-451, Sec. 301(c)(1), substituted "190, 193, 194" for "190, 193" each place it appeared in para. (a)(2), substituted "193, or 194" for "or 193" in subparas. (a)(2)(D) and (a)(3)(D), and added para. (b)(8), effective for additions to capital account made after 12/31/79.

— P.L. 96-223, Sec. 251(a)(2)(C)(i), substituted "190, or 193" for "or 190" each place it appeared in subparas. (a)(2)(D) and (a)(3)(D) ... Sec. 251(a)(2)(C)(ii), added "193" after "190" each place it appeared in para. (a)(2) ... Sec. 251(a)(2)(C)(iii), added "or 193" after "190" in the last sentence of para (a)(2), effective for tax. yrs. begin. after 12/31/79.

In 1979, P.L. 96-167, Sec. 9(d), extended the effective date of changes made by Sec. 2122(c) of P.L. 94-455 to tax. yrs. begin. after 1996 and before 1983. See below.

In 1978, P.L. 95-600, Sec. 701(f)(3)(A), substituted "or 190" for "190, or 191" the first place it appeared in para. (a)(2) and substituted "190, or (in the case of property described in paragraph (3)(C)) 191" for "190, of 191" the second and third place it appeared in para. (a)(2) ... Sec. 701(f)(3)(B), substituted "or 190" for "190, or 191" in subpara. (a)(3)(D), effective for additions to capital account made after 6/14/76 and before 6/15/81.

— P.L. 95-600, Sec. 701(w)(1), amended subpara. (a)(4)(C) ... Sec. 701(w)(2), added "attributable to periods after December 31, 1975" after "depreciation" in clause (a)(4)(B)(i) and added "described in clause (i)" after "amounts" in clause (a)(4)(B)(ii), effective for transfers of player contracts in connection with any sale or exchange of a franchise after 12/31/75.

Prior to amendment, subpara. (a)(4)(C) read as follows:

"(C) Previously unrecaptured depreciation with respect to contracts transferred. For purposes of subparagraph (A)(ii), the term 'previously unrecaptured depreciation' means —

"(i) the amount of any deduction allowed or allowable to the taxpayer transferor for the depreciation of any contracts involved in such transfer, over

"(ii) the aggregate of the amounts treated as ordinary income by reason of this section with respect to prior dispositions of such player contracts acquired upon acquisition of the franchise."

In 1976, P.L. 94-455, Sec. 212(b), added para. (a)(6), effective for transfers of player contracts in connection with any sale or exchange of a franchise after 12/31/75.

2,761

—P.L. 94-455, Sec. 1901(a)(140), deleted "such organization acquiring such property," after "business of the organization acquiring such property" in subpara. (b)(7)(B), effective for tax. yrs. begin. after 12/31/76.

—P.L. 94-455, Sec. 1901(b)(3)(K), substituted "ordinary income" for "gain from the sale or exchange of property which is neither a capital asset nor property described in section 1231" in para. (a)(1), effective for tax. yrs. begin. after 12/31/76.

—P.L. 94-455, Sec. 1901(b)(11)(D), deleted "187," each place it appeared in para. (a)(2), effective for tax. yrs. begin. after 12/31/76.

—P.L. 94-455, Sec. 1906(b)(13)(A), substituted "Secretary" for "Secretary or his delegate" in para. (b)(5), and subsec. (c) effective for tax. yrs. begin. after 12/31/76.

—P.L. 94-455, Sec. 1951(c)(2)(C), substituted "168 (as in effect before its repeal by the Tax Reform Act of 1976)," for "168," each place it appeared in para. (a)(2), effective for tax. yrs. begin. after 12/31/76.

—P.L. 94-455, Sec. 2122(b)(3), substituted "188, or 190" for "or 188" each place it appeared in para. (a)(2) and subpara. (a)(3)(D), substituted "185, or 190" for "or 185" in subpara. (a)(2)(D), and added a new sentence at the end of para. (a)(2), effective for tax. yrs. begin. after 12/31/76 and before 1/1/80.

—P.L. 94-455, Sec. 2124(a)(2), substituted "190, or 191" for "or 190", each place it appeared in subsec. (a), effective for additions to capital account made after 6/14/76 and before 6/15/81.

In 1975, P.L. 94-81, Sec. 2(a)(1), substituted "Except as provided in paragraph (7), this" for "This" in the second sentence of para. (b)(3) . . . Sec. 2(a)(2), added para. (b)(7), effective with respect to dispositions after 12/31/69, in tax. yrs. end. after 12/31/69, except as provided in Sec. 2(c)(2) of the Act which reads as follows:

"(2) Election for past transactions.—In the case of any disposition occurring before the date of the enactment [8/9/75] of this Act, the amendments made by this section shall apply only if the organization acquiring the property elects (in the manner provided by regulations prescribed by the Secretary of the Treasury or his delegate) within 1 year after the date of the enactment of this Act to have such amendments apply with respect to such property."

In 1971, P.L. 92-178, Sec. 104(a)(2), struck out "or" at the end of clause (a)(3)(B)(i), deleted clause (a)(3)(B)(ii) and added new clauses (a)(3)(B)(ii) and (iii), effective for property described in Code Sec. 50.

Prior to amendment clause (a)(3)(B)(ii) read as follows:

"(ii) constituted research or storage facilities used in connection with any of the activities referred to in clause (i),".

—P.L. 92-178, Sec. 303(c)(1), substituted "187, or 188" for "or 187" each place it appeared in para. (a)(2) . . . Sec. 303(c)(2), substituted ", 185, or 188", for "or 185", effective for tax. yrs. end. after 12/31/71.

In 1969, P.L. 91-172, Sec. 212(a)(1), deleted out "or" at the end of subpara. (a)(2)(A) and added new subpara. (a)(2)(C), effective for tax. yrs. begin. after 12/31/69.

—P.L. 91-172, Sec. 212(a)(2), deleted "(other than livestock)" after "any property" in para. (a)(3), effective for tax. yrs. begin. after 12/31/69.

—P.L. 91-172, Sec. 704(b)(4), added subpara. (a)(2)(D), substituted "168, 169, 184, 185, or 187" for "168" each time it appeared in para. (a)(2), substituted "section 167 (or subject to the allowance of amortization provided in section 185)" for "section 167" in para. (a)(3), struck out "or" at the end of subparas. (a)(3)(A) and (B), substituted ", or" for the period at the end of subpara. (a)(3)(C) and added new subpara. (a)(3)(D), effective for tax. yrs. end. after 12/31/68.

In 1964, P.L. 88-272, Sec. 203(d), amended para. (a)(2) and added subpara. (a)(3)(C), effective for dispositions after 12/31/63 in tax. yrs. end. after 12/31/63.

Prior to amendment, para. (a)(2) read as follows:

"(2) Recomputed basis.—For purposes of this section, the term 'recomputed basis' means, with respect to any property, its adjusted basis recomputed by adding thereto all adjustments, attributable to periods after December 31, 1961, reflected in such adjusted basis on account of deductions (whether in respect of the same or other property) allowed or allowable to the taxpayer or to any other person for depreciation, or for amortization under section 168. For purposes of the preceding sentence, if the taxpayer can establish by adequate records or other sufficient evidence that the amount allowed for depreciation, or for amortization under section 168, for any period was less than the amount allowable, the amount added for such period shall be the amount allowed."

In 1962, P.L. 87-834, Sec. 13, added Code Sec. 1245, effective for tax. yrs. begin. after 12/31/62.

Sec. 1246. Repealed.

In 2010, P.L. 111-312, Sec. 101(a)(1), substituted "December 31, 2012" for "December 31, 2010" both places it appears in Sec. 901, P.L. 107-16 [see below], effective as if included in the enactment of P.L. 107-16, EGTRRA, 6/7/2001.

—P.L. 111-312, Sec. 301(a), provides that Code Sec. 1246, as amended by Sec. 542(e)(4), P.L. 107-16 EGTRRA, 6/7/2001 (amended subsec. (e), see below) will read as if such provision had never been enacted, effective for estates of decedents dying, and transfers made, after 12/31/2009.

Sec. 301(a), P.L. 111-312, 12/17/2010., provides:

"(a) In general. Each provision of law amended by subtitle A or E of title V of the Economic Growth and Tax Relief Reconciliation Act of 2001 is amended to read as such provision would read if such subtitle had never been enacted."

—P.L. 111-312, Sec. 301(c), of this Act, provides

"(c) Special election with respect to estates of decedents dying in 2010. Notwithstanding subsection (a), in the case of an estate of a decedent dying after December 31, 2009, and before January 1, 2011, the executor (within the meaning of section 2203 of the Internal Revenue Code of 1986) may elect to apply such Code as though the amendments made by subsection (a) do not apply with respect to chapter 11 of such Code and with respect to property acquired or passing from such decedent (within the meaning of section 1014(b) of such Code). Such election shall be made at such time and in such manner as the Secretary of the Treasury or the Secretary's delegate shall provide. Such an election once made shall be revocable only with the consent of the Secretary of the Treasury or the Secretary's delegate. For purposes of section 2652(a)(1) of such Code, the determination of whether any property is subject to the tax imposed by such chapter 11 shall be made without regard to any election made under this subsection."

—P.L. 111-312, Sec. 301(d), of this Act, provides

" (d) Extension of time for performing certain acts.

" (1) Estate tax. In the case of the estate of a decedent dying after December 31, 2009, and before the date of the enactment of this Act, the due date for—

" (A) filing any return under section 6018 of the Internal Revenue Code of 1986 (including any election required to be made on such a return) as such section is in effect after the date of the enactment of this Act without regard to any election under subsection (c),

" (B) making any payment of tax under chapter 11 of such Code, and

" (C) making any disclaimer described in section 2518(b) of such Code of an interest in property passing by reason of the death of such decedent, shall not be earlier than the date which is 9 months after the date of the enactment of this Act.

" (2) Generation-skipping tax. In the case of any generation-skipping transfer made after December 31, 2009, and before the date of the enactment of this Act, the due date for filing any return under section 2662 of the Internal Revenue Code of 1986 (including any election required to be made on such a return) shall not be earlier than the date which is 9 months after the date of the enactment of this Act."

In 2004, P.L. 108-357, Sec. 413(a)(2), repealed Code Sec. 1246, effective for tax. yrs. of foreign corporations begin. after 12/31/2004, and for tax. yrs. of United States shareholders with or within which such tax. yrs. of foreign corporations end.

Prior to repeal, Code Sec. 1246 read as follows:

"SEC. 1246. GAIN ON FOREIGN INVESTMENT COMPANY STOCK.

"(a) Treatment of gain as ordinary income.

"(1) General rule. In the case of a sale or exchange (or a distribution which, under section 302 or 331, is treated as an exchange of stock) after December 31, 1962, of stock in a foreign corporation which was a foreign investment company (as defined in subsection (b)) at any time during the period during which the taxpayer held such stock, any gain shall be treated as ordinary income, to the extent of the taxpayer's ratable share of the earnings and profits of such corporation accumulated for taxable years beginning after December 31, 1962.

"(2) Ratable share. For purposes of this section, the taxpayer's ratable share shall be determined under regulations prescribed by the Secretary, but shall include only his ratable share of the accumulated earnings and profits of such corporation—

"(A) for the period during which the taxpayer held such stock, but

"(B) excluding such earnings and profits attributable to—

"(i) any amount previously included in the gross income of such taxpayer under section 951 (but only to the extent the inclusion of such amount did not result in an exclusion of any other amount from gross income under section 959), or

"(ii) any taxable year during which such corporation was not a foreign investment company but only if—

"(I) such corporation was not a foreign investment company at any time before such taxable year, and

"(II) such corporation was treated as a foreign investment company solely by reason of subsection (b)(2).

"(3) Taxpayer to establish earnings and profits. Unless the taxpayer establishes the amount of the accumulated earnings and profits of the foreign investment company and the ratable share thereof for the period during which the taxpayer held such stock, all the gain from the sale or exchange of stock in such company shall be considered as ordinary income.

"(4) Holding period of stock must be more than 1 year. This section shall not apply with respect to the sale or exchange of stock where the holding period of such stock as of the date of such sale or exchange is 1 year or less.

"(b) Definition of foreign investment company. For purposes of this section, the term 'foreign investment company' means any foreign corporation which, for any taxable year beginning after December 31, 1962, is—

"(1) registered under the Investment Company Act of 1940, as amended (15 U.S.C. 80a-1 to 80b-2), either as a management company or as a unit investment trust, or

"(2) engaged (or holding itself out as being engaged) primarily in the business of investing, reinvesting, or trading in—

"(A) securities (as defined in section 2(a)(36) of the Investment Company Act of 1940, as amended),

"(B) commodities, or

"(C) any interest (including a futures or forward contract or option) in property described in subparagraph (A) or (B),

"at a time when 50 percent or more of the total combined voting power of all classes of stock entitled to vote, or the total value of all classes of stock, was held directly (or indirectly through applying paragraphs (2) and (3) of section 958(a) and paragraph (4) of section 318(a)) by United States persons (as defined in section 7701(a)(30)).

"(c) Stock having transferred or substituted basis. To the extent provided in regulations prescribed by the Secretary, stock in a foreign corporation, the basis of which (in the hands of the taxpayer selling or exchanging such stock) is determined by reference to the basis (in the hands of such taxpayer or any other person) of stock in a foreign investment company, shall be treated as stock of a for-

Capital gains and losses — Code Sec. 1247

eign investment company and held by the taxpayer throughout the holding period for such stock (determined under section 1223).

"(d) Rules relating to entities holding foreign investment company stock. To the extent provided in regulations prescribed by the Secretary—

"(1) trust certificates of a trust to which section 677 (relating to income for benefit of grantor) applies, and

"(2) stock of a domestic corporation,

"shall be treated as stock of a foreign investment company and held by the taxpayer throughout the holding period for such certificates or stock (determined under section 1223) in the same proportion that the investment in stock in a foreign investment company by the trust or domestic corporation bears to the total assets of such trust or corporation.

Ed. Note. Caution: Subsec. (e), following, is effective for estates of decedents dying before 1/1/2010. For subsec. (e), effective for estates of decedents dying after 12/31/2009, see below. For sunset provisions, see Sec. 901 of P.L. 107-16 reproduced in the history of this Code Sec.

"(e) Rules relating to stock acquired from a decedent.

"(1) Basis. In the case of stock of a foreign investment company acquired by bequest, devise, or inheritance (or by the decedent's estate) from a decedent dying after December 31, 1962, the basis determined under section 1014 shall be reduced (but not below the adjusted basis of such stock in the hands of the decedent immediately before his death) by the amount of the decedent's ratable share of the earnings and profits of such company accumulated after December 31, 1962. Any stock so acquired shall be treated as stock described in subsection (c).

"(2) Deduction for estate tax. If stock to which subsection (a) applies is acquired from a decedent, the taxpayer shall, under regulations prescribed by the Secretary be allowed (for the taxable year of the sale or exchange) a deduction from gross income equal to that portion of the decedent's estate tax deemed paid which is attributable to the excess of (A) the value at which such stock was taken into account for purposes of determining the value of the decedent's gross estate, over (B) the value at which it would have been so taken into account if such value had been reduced by the amount described in paragraph (1).

Ed. Note. Caution: Subsec. (e) is repealed, effective for estates of decedents dying after 12/31/2009. For subsec. (e), effective for estates of decedents dying before 1/1/2010, see above. For sunset provisions, see Sec. 901 of P.L. 107-16 reproduced in the history of this Code Sec.

"(e) Repealed.

"(f) Information with respect to certain foreign investment companies. Every United States person who, on the last day of the taxable year of a foreign investment company, owns 5 percent or more in value of the stock of such company shall furnish with respect to such company such information as the Secretary shall by regulations prescribe.

"(g) Coordination with section 1248. This section shall not apply to any gain to the extent such gain is treated as ordinary income under section 1248 (determined without regard to section 1248(g)(2)).

"(h) Cross reference. For special rules relating to the earnings and profits of foreign investment companies, see section 312(j)."

In 2002, P.L. 107-358, Sec. 2, added subsec. (c) in Sec. 901 of P.L. 107-16 [see below], effective 12/17/2002.

In 2001, P.L. 107-16, Sec. 542(e)(5)(A), deleted subsec. (e), effective for estates of decedents dying after 12/31/2009.

Prior to deletion, subsec. (e) read as follows:

"(e) Rules relating to stock acquired from a decedent.

"(1) Basis. In the case of stock of a foreign investment company acquired by bequest, devise, or inheritance (or by the decedent's estate) from a decedent dying after December 31, 1962, the basis determined under section 1014 shall be reduced (but not below the adjusted basis of such stock in the hands of the decedent immediately before his death) by the amount of the decedent's ratable share of the earnings and profits of such company accumulated after December 31, 1962. Any stock so acquired shall be treated as stock described in subsection (c).

"(2) Deduction for estate tax. If stock to which subsection (a) applies is acquired from a decedent, the taxpayer shall, under regulations prescribed by the Secretary be allowed (for the taxable year of the sale or exchange) a deduction from gross income equal to that portion of the decedent's estate tax deemed paid which is attributable to the excess of (A) the value at which such stock was taken into account for purposes of determining the value of the decedent's gross estate, over (B) the value at which it would have been so taken into account if such value had been reduced by the amount described in paragraph (1).".

—P.L. 107-16, Sec. 901, of this Act [as amended by Sec. 2 of P.L. 107-358 and Sec. 101(a)(1), P.L. 111-312, see above], reads as follows:

"SEC. 901. SUNSET OF PROVISIONS OF ACT.

"(a) In general. All provisions of, and amendments made by, this Act shall not apply—

"(1) to taxable, plan, or limitation years beginning after December 31, 2012, or

"(2) in the case of title V, to estates of decedents dying, gifts made, or generation skipping transfers, after December 31, 2012.

"(b) Application of certain laws. The Internal Revenue Code of 1986 and the Employee Retirement Income Security Act of 1974 shall be applied and administered to years, estates, gifts, and transfers described in subsection (a) as if the provisions and amendments described in subsection (a) had never been enacted.

"(c) Exception. Subsection (a) shall not apply to section 803 (relating to no federal income tax on restitution received by victims of the Nazi regime or their heirs or estates)."

In 1988, P.L. 100-647, Sec. 1012(p)(21), redesignated the subsection relating to information with respect to certain foreign investment companies as subsec. (f), redesignated the subsec. relating to coordination with section 1248 as subsec. (g), and redesignated the subsec. relating to cross reference as subsec. (h), effective for tax. yrs. of foreign corporations begin. after 12/31/86.

—P.L. 100-647, Sec. 1018(o)(2), substituted "1248(g)(2)" for "1238(g)(3)" in subsec. (g) (as redes. by Sec. 1012(p)(21)), effective for exchanges after 3/1/86. Sec. 1875(g)(3) of P.L. 99-514 provides:

"(3) Transitional Rule. An exchange shall be treated as occurring on or before March 1, 1986, if—

"(A) on or before such date, the taxpayer adopts a plan of reorganization to which section 356 applies, and

"(B) such plan or reorganization is implemented and distributions pursuant to such plan are completed on or before the date of enactment of this Act."

In 1986, P.L. 99-514, Sec. 1235(b), redesignated subsec. (f) as subsec. (g) and added new subsec. (f), effective for tax. yrs. of foreign corporations begin. after 12/31/86.

In 1984, P.L. 98-369, Sec. 134(a), amended para. (b)(2), effective for sales and exchanges (and distributions) on or after 9/29/83, in tax. yrs. end. on or after 9/29/83. Sec. 134(b)(2) of this Act provides:

"(2) Stock held on September 29, 1983.—In the case of a sale or exchange (or distribution) not later than the date which is 1 year after the date of the enactment of this Act, the amendment made by subsection (a) shall not apply with respect to stock held by the taxpayer continuously from September 29, 1983, to the date of such sale or exchange (or distribution)."

Prior to amendment, para. (b)(2) read as follows:

"(2) engaged (or holding itself out as being engaged) primarily in the business of investing, reinvesting, or trading in securities (within the meaning of section 3(a)(1) of such Act, as limited by paragraphs (2) through (10) (except paragraph (6)(C)) and paragraphs (12) through (15) of section 3(c) of such Act) at a time when more than 50 percent of the total combined voting power of all classes of stock entitled to vote, or of the total value of shares of all classes of stock, was held, directly or indirectly (within the meaning of section 958(a)), by United States persons (as defined in section 7701(a)(30))."

—P.L. 98-369, Sec. 1001(b)(20), substituted "6 months" for "1 year" each place it appeared in para. (a)(4), effective for property acquired after 6/22/84, and before 1/1/88.

In 1981, P.L. 97-34, Sec. 832(a), amended subpara. (a)(2)(B), effective for sales or exchanges after 8/13/81, in tax. yrs. end. after 8/13/81.

Prior to amendment, subpara. (a)(2)(B) read as follows:

"(B) excluding such earnings and profits attributable to any amount previously included in the gross income of such taxpayer under section 951 (but only to the extent the inclusion of such amount did not result in an exclusion of any other amount from gross income under section 959)."

In 1980, P.L. 96-223, Sec. 401(a), repealed Sec. 2005(a)(5) of P.L. 94-455 and the amendment made by Sec. 2005(a)(5), effective for decedents dying after 1976 [see below]. Sec. 401(b) of P.L. 96-223 provides as follows:

"(b) Revival of prior law.

"Except to the extent necessary to carry out subsection (d), the Internal Revenue Code of 1954 shall be applied and administered as if the provisions repealed by subsection (a), and the amendments made by those provisions, had not been enacted."

In 1978, P.L. 95-600, Sec. 515(6), amended the effective date for changes made by Sec. 2005(a) of P.L. 94-455, by substituting "'79" for "'76", see below. [inoperative]

In 1976, P.L. 94-455, Sec. 1402(b)(1)(W), substituted "9 months" for "6 months" each place it appeared in para. (a)(4), effective for tax. yrs. begin. in 12/31/76.

—P.L. 94-455, Sec. 1402(b)(2), of the Act substituted "1 year" for "9 months" each place it appeared in para. (a)(4), effective for tax. yrs. begin. after 12/31/77.

—P.L. 94-455, Sec. 1901(a)(141), deleted "beginning after December 31, 1962", after "foreign investment company", in subsec. (f), effective for tax. yrs. begin. after '76. This is an unworkable amendment for subsec. (f); it was apparently meant for subsec. (e), which was redesignated by this Act.

—P.L. 94-455, Sec. 1901(b)(3)(I), substituted "ordinary income" for "gain from the sale or exchange of property which is not a capital asset" in paras. (a)(1) and (a)(3), effective for tax. yrs. begin. after 12/31/76.

—P.L. 94-455, Sec. 1906(b)(13)(A), substituted "Secretary" for "Secretary or his delegate" each place it appeared in Code Sec. 1246, effective for tax. yrs. begin. after 12/31/76.

—P.L. 94-455, Sec. 1901(b)(32)(B)(ii), substituted "312(j)" for "312(l)" in subsec. (g), for tax. yrs. begin. after '76. This amendment is unworkable for subsec. (g); it was apparently meant for subsec. (f), which was redesignated by this Act.

—P.L. 94-455, Sec. 2005(a)(5), deleted subsec. (e), and redesignated subsecs. (f) and (g) as subsecs. (e) and (f), effective [as amended by Sec. 515(6) of P.L. 95-600, see above] for decedents dying after '79, but Sec. 2005(a)(5) was repealed by Sec. 401(a) of P.L. 96-223 [see above].

In 1962, P.L. 87-834, Sec. 14, added Code Sec. 1246, effective for tax. yrs. begin. after 12/31/62.

Sec. 1247. Repealed.

In 2004, P.L. 108-357, Sec. 413(a)(3), repealed Code Sec. 1247, effective for tax. yrs. of foreign corporations begin. after 12/31/2004, and for tax. yrs. of United States shareholders with or within which such tax. yrs. of foreign corporations end.

Prior to repeal, Code Sec. 1247 read as follows:

"SEC. 1247. ELECTION BY FOREIGN INVESTMENT COMPANIES TO DISTRIBUTE INCOME CURRENTLY.

2,763

Code Sec. 1247 — Capital gains and losses

"(a) Election by foreign investment company.

"(1) In general. If a foreign investment company which is described in section 1246(b)(1) elects (in the manner provided in regulations prescribed by the Secretary) on or before December 31, 1962, with respect to each taxable year beginning after December 31, 1962, to—

"(A) distribute to its shareholders 90 percent or more of what its taxable income would be if it were a domestic corporation;

"(B) designate in a written notice mailed to its shareholders at any time before the expiration of 45 days after the close of its taxable year the pro rata amount of the amount (determined as if such corporation were a domestic corporation) of the net capital gain of the taxable year; and the portion thereof which is being distributed; and

"(C) provide such information as the Secretary deems necessary to carry out the purposes of this section,

"then section 1246 shall not apply with respect to the qualified shareholders of such company during any taxable year to which such election applies.

"(2) Special rules.

"(A) Computation of taxable income. For purposes of paragraph (1)(A), the taxable income of the company shall be computed without regard to—

"(i) the net capital gain referred to in paragraph (1)(B),

"(ii) section 172 (relating to net operating losses), and

"(iii) any deduction provided by part VIII of subchapter B (other than the deduction provided by section 248, relating to organizational expenditures).

"(B) Distributions after the close of the taxable year. For purposes of paragraph (1)(A), a distribution made after the close of the taxable year and on or before the 15th day of the third month of the next taxable year shall be treated as distributed during the taxable year to the extent elected by the company (in accordance with regulations prescribed by the Secretary) on or before the 15th day of such third month.

"(C) Carryover of capital losses from nonelection years denied. In computing the net capital gain referred to in paragraph (1)(B), section 1212 shall not apply to losses incurred in or with respect to taxable years before the first taxable year to which the election applies.

"(b) Years to which election applies. The election of any foreign investment company under this section shall terminate as of the close of the taxable year preceding its first taxable year in which any of the following occurs:

"(1) the company fails to comply with the provisions of subparagraph (A), (B), or (C) of subsection (a)(1), unless it is shown that such failure is due to reasonable cause and not due to willful neglect,

"(2) the company is a foreign personal holding company, or

"(3) the company is not a foreign investment company which is described in section 1246(b)(1).

"(c) Qualified shareholders. For purposes of this section—

"(1) In general. The term 'qualified shareholder' means any shareholder who is a United States person (as defined in section 7701(a)(30)), other than a shareholder described in paragraph (2).

"(2) Certain United States persons excluded from definition. A United States person shall not be treated as a qualified shareholder for the taxable year if for such taxable year (or for any prior taxable year) he did not include, in computing his long-term capital gains in his return for such taxable year, the amount designated by such company pursuant to subsection (a)(1)(B) as his share of the undistributed capital gains of such company for its taxable year ending within or with such taxable year of the taxpayer. The preceding sentence shall not apply with respect to any failure by the taxpayer to treat an amount as provided therein if the taxpayer shows that such failure was due to reasonable cause and not due to willful neglect.

"(d) Treatment of distributed and undistributed capital gains by a qualified shareholder. Every qualified shareholder of a foreign investment company for any taxable year of such company with respect to which an election pursuant to subsection (a) is in effect shall include, in computing his long-term capital gains—

"(1) for his taxable year in which received, his pro rata share of the distributed portion of the net capital gain for such taxable year of such company, and

"(2) for his taxable year in which or with which the taxable year of such company ends, his pro rata share of the undistributed portion of the net capital gain for such taxable year of such company.

"(e) Adjustments. Under regulations prescribed by the Secretary, proper adjustment shall be made—

"(1) in the earnings and profits of the electing foreign investment company and a qualified shareholder's ratable share thereof, and

"(2) in the adjusted basis of stock of such company held by such shareholder,

"to reflect such shareholder's inclusion in gross income of undistributed capital gains.

"(f) Election by foreign investment company with respect to foreign tax credit. A foreign investment company with respect to which an election pursuant to subsection (a) is in effect and more than 50 percent of the value (as defined in section 851(c)(4)) of whose total assets at the close of the taxable year consists of stock or securities in foreign corporations may, for such taxable year, elect the application of this subsection with respect to income, war profits, and excess profits taxes described in section 901(b)(1) which are paid by the foreign investment company during such taxable year to foreign countries and possessions of the United States. If such election is made—

"(1) the foreign investment company—

"(A) shall compute its taxable income, for purposes of subsection (a)(1)(A), without any deductions for income, war profits, or excess profits taxes paid to foreign countries or possessions of the United States, and

"(B) shall treat the amount of such taxes, for purposes of subsection (a)(1)(A), as distributed to its shareholders;

"(2) each qualified shareholder of such foreign investment company—

"(A) shall include in gross income and treat as paid by him his proportionate share of such taxes, and

"(B) shall treat, for purposes of applying subpart A of part III of subchapter N, his proportionate share of such taxes as having been paid to the country in which the foreign investment company is incorporated, and

"(C) shall treat as gross income from sources within the country in which the foreign investment company is incorporated, for purposes of applying subpart A of part III of subchapter N, the sum of his proportionate share of such taxes and any dividend paid to him by such foreign investment company.

"(g) Notice to shareholders. The amounts to be treated by qualified shareholders, for purposes of subsection (f)(2), as their proportionate share of the taxes described in subsection (f)(1)(A) paid by a foreign investment company shall not exceed the amounts so designated by the foreign investment company in a written notice mailed to its shareholders not later than 45 days after the close of its taxable year.

"(h) Manner of making election and notifying shareholders. The election provided in subsection (f) and the notice to shareholders required by subsection (g) shall be made in such manner as the Secretary may prescribe by regulations.

"(i) Loss on sale or exchange of certain stock held less than 1 year. If—

"(1) under this section, any qualified shareholder treats any amount designated under subsection (a)(1)(B) with respect to a share of stock as long-term capital gain, and

"(2) such share is held by the taxpayer for less than 1 year,

"then any loss on the sale or exchange of such share shall, to the extent of the amount described in paragraph (1), be treated as loss from the sale or exchange of a capital asset held for more than 1 year."

In 1984, P.L. 98-369, Sec. 1001(b)(21), substituted "6 months" for "1 year" each place it appeared in subsec. (i), effective for property acquired after 6/22/84, and before 1/1/88.

In 1976, P.L. 94-455, Sec. 1402(b)(1)(X), substituted "9 months" for "6 months" each place it appeared in subsec. (i), effective for tax. yrs. begin. in '77.

—P.L. 94-455, Sec. 1402(b)(2), of the Act substituted "1 year" for "9 months" each place it appeared in subsec. (i), effective for tax. yrs. begin. after 12/31/77.

—P.L. 94-455, Sec. 1901(b)(33)(P), substituted "the amount (determined as if such corporation were a domestic corporation) of the net capital gain" for "the excess (determined as if such corporation were a domestic corporation) of the net long-term capital gain over the net short-term capital loss" in subpara. (a)(1)(B), effective for tax. yrs. begin. after 12/31/76.

—P.L. 94-455, Sec. 1901(b)(33)(R), substituted "the net capital gain" for "the excess of the net long-term capital gain over the net short-term capital loss" in clause (a)(2)(A)(i), subpara. (a)(2)(C), and paras. (d)(1) and (d)(2), effective for tax. yrs. begin. after 12/31/76.

—P.L. 94-455, Sec. 1906(b)(13)(A), substituted "Secretary" for "Secretary or his delegate" each place it appeared in Code Sec. 1247, for tax. yrs. begin. after '76.

In 1962, P.L. 87-834, Sec. 14, added Code Sec. 1247, effective for tax. yrs. begin. after 12/31/62.

Sec. 1248. Gain from certain sales or exchanges of stock in certain foreign corporations.

(a) General rule.

If—

(1) a United States person sells or exchanges stock in a foreign corporation, and

(2) such person owns, within the meaning of section 958(a), or is considered as owning by applying the rules of ownership of section 958(b), 10 percent or more of the total combined voting power of all classes of stock entitled to vote of such foreign corporation at any time during the 5-year period ending on the date of the sale or exchange when such foreign corporation was a controlled foreign corporation (as defined in section 957),

then the gain recognized on the sale or exchange of such stock shall be included in the gross income of such person as a dividend, to the extent of the earnings and profits of the foreign corporation attributable (under regulations prescribed by the Secretary) to such stock which were accumulated in taxable years of such foreign corporation beginning after December 31, 1962, and during the period or periods the stock sold or exchanged was held by such person while such foreign corporation was a controlled foreign corporation. For purposes of this section, a United States person shall be treated as having sold or exchanged any stock if, under any provision of this subtitle, such person is treated as realizing gain from the sale or exchange of such stock.

(b) Limitation on tax applicable to individuals.

In the case of an individual, if the stock sold or exchanged is a capital asset (within the meaning of section 1221) and has been held for more than 1 year, the tax attrib-

utable to an amount included in gross income as a dividend under subsection (a) shall not be greater than a tax equal to the sum of—
  (1) a pro rata share of the excess of—
    (A) the taxes that would have been paid by the foreign corporation with respect to its income had it been taxed under this chapter as a domestic corporation (but without allowance for deduction of, or credit for, taxes described in subparagraph (B)), for the period or periods the stock sold or exchanged was held by the United States person in taxable years beginning after December 31, 1962, while the foreign corporation was a controlled foreign corporation, adjusted for distributions and amounts previously included in gross income of a United States shareholder under section 951, over
    (B) the income, war profits, or excess profits taxes paid by the foreign corporation with respect to such income; and
  (2) an amount equal to the tax that would result by including in gross income, as gain from the sale or exchange of a capital asset held for more than 1 year, an amount equal to the excess of (A) the amount included in gross income as a dividend under subsection (a), over (B) the amount determined under paragraph (1).

(c) **Determination of earnings and profits.**
  (1) **In general.** Except as provided in section 312(k)(4), for purposes of this section the earnings and profits of any foreign corporation for any taxable year shall be determined according to rules substantially similar to those applicable to domestic corporations, under regulations prescribed by the Secretary.
  (2) **Earnings and profits of subsidiaries of foreign corporations.** If—
    (A) subsection (a) or (f) applies to a sale, exchange, or distribution by a United States person of stock of a foreign corporation and, by reason of the ownership of the stock sold or exchanged, such person owned within the meaning of section 958(a)(2) stock of any other foreign corporation; and
    (B) such person owned, within the meaning of section 958(a), or was considered as owning by applying the rules of ownership of section 958(b), 10 percent or more of the total combined voting power of all classes of stock entitled to vote of such other foreign corporation at any time during the 5-year period ending on the date of the sale or exchange when such other foreign corporation was a controlled foreign corporation (as defined in section 957),
  then, for purposes of this section, the earnings and profits of the foreign corporation the stock of which is sold or exchanged which are attributable to the stock sold or exchanged shall be deemed to include the earnings and profits of such other foreign corporation which—
    (C) are attributable (under regulations prescribed by the Secretary) to the stock of such other foreign corporation which such person owned within the meaning of section 958(a)(2) (by reason of his ownership within the meaning of section 958(a)(1)(A) of the stock sold or exchanged) on the date of such sale or exchange (or on the date of any sale or exchange of the stock of such other foreign corporation occurring during the 5-year period ending on the date of the sale or exchange of the stock of such foreign corporation, to the extent not otherwise taken into account under this section but not in excess of the fair market value of the stock of such other foreign corporation sold or exchanged over the basis of such stock (for determining gain) in the hands of the transferor); and
    (D) were accumulated in taxable years of such other corporation beginning after December 31, 1962, and during the period or periods—
      (i) such other corporation was a controlled foreign corporation, and
      (ii) such person owned within the meaning of section 958(a) the stock of such other foreign corporation.

(d) **Exclusions from earnings and profits.**
For purposes of this section, the following amounts shall be excluded, with respect to any United States person, from the earnings and profits of a foreign corporation:
  (1) **Amounts included in gross income under section 951.** Earnings and profits of the foreign corporation attributable to any amount previously included in the gross income of such person under section 951, with respect to the stock sold or exchanged, but only to the extent the inclusion of such amount did not result in an exclusion of an amount from gross income under section 959.
  (2) **Repealed.**
  (3) **Less developed country corporations under prior law.** Earnings and profits of a foreign corporation which were accumulated during any taxable year beginning before January 1, 1976, while such corporation was a less developed country corporation under section 902(d) as in effect before the enactment of the Tax Reduction Act of 1975.
  (4) **United States income.** Any item includible in gross income of the foreign corporation under this chapter—
    (A) for any taxable year beginning before January 1, 1967, as income derived from sources within the United States of a foreign corporation engaged in trade or business within the United States, or
    (B) for any taxable year beginning after December 31, 1966, as income effectively connected with the conduct by such corporation of a trade or business within the United States.
  This paragraph shall not apply with respect to any item which is exempt from taxation (or is subject to a reduced rate of tax) pursuant to a treaty obligation of the United States.
  (5) **Foreign trade income.** Earnings and profits of the foreign corporation attributable to foreign trade income of a FSC (as defined in section 922) other than foreign trade income which—
    (A) is section 923(a)(2) non-exempt income (within the meaning of section 927(d)(6)), or
    (B) would not (but for section 923(a)(4)) be treated as exempt foreign trade income.
  For purposes of the preceding sentence, the terms "foreign trade income" and "exempt foreign trade income" have the respective meanings given such terms by section 923. Any reference in this paragraph to section 922, 923, or 927 shall be treated as a reference to such section as in effect before its repeal by the FSC Repeal and Extraterritorial Income Exclusion Act of 2000.
  (6) **Amounts included in gross income under section 1293.** Earnings and profits of the foreign corporation attributable to any amount previously included in the gross income of such person under section 1293 with respect to the stock sold or exchanged, but only to the extent the inclusion of such amount did not result in an exclusion of an amount under section 1293(c).

Code Sec. 1248(e) — Capital gains and losses

(e) Sales or exchanges of stock in certain domestic corporations.

Except as provided in regulations prescribed by the Secretary, if—

(1) a United States person sells or exchanges stock of a domestic corporation, and

(2) such domestic corporation was formed or availed of principally for the holding, directly or indirectly, of stock of one or more foreign corporations,

such sale or exchange shall, for purposes of this section, be treated as a sale or exchange of the stock of the foreign corporation or corporations held by the domestic corporation.

(f) Certain nonrecognition transactions.

Except as provided in regulations prescribed by the Secretary—

(1) In general. If—

(A) a domestic corporation satisfies the stock ownership requirements of subsection (a)(2) with respect to a foreign corporation, and

(B) such domestic corporation distributes stock of such foreign corporation in a distribution to which section 311(a), 337, 355(c)(1), or 361(c)(1) applies,

then, notwithstanding any other provision of this subtitle, an amount equal to the excess of the fair market value of such stock over its adjusted basis in the hands of the domestic corporation shall be included in the gross income of the domestic corporation as a dividend to the extent of the earnings and profits of the foreign corporation attributable (under regulations prescribed by the Secretary) to such stock which were accumulated in taxable years of such foreign corporation beginning after December 31, 1962, and during the period or periods the stock was held by such domestic corporation while such foreign corporation was a controlled foreign corporation. For purposes of subsections (c)(2), (d), and (h), a distribution of stock to which this subsection applies shall be treated as a sale of stock to which subsection (a) applies.

(2) Exception for certain distributions. In the case of any distribution of stock of a foreign corporation, paragraph (1) shall not apply if such distribution is to a domestic corporation—

(A) which is treated under this section as holding such stock for the period for which the stock was held by the distributing corporation, and

(B) which, immediately after the distribution, satisfies the stock ownership requirements of subsection (a)(2) with respect to such foreign corporation.

(3) Application to cases described in subsection (e). To the extent that earnings and profits are taken into account under this subsection, they shall be excluded and not taken into account for purposes of subsection (e).

(g) Exceptions.

This section shall not apply to—

(1) distributions to which section 303 (relating to distributions in redemption of stock to pay death taxes) applies; or

(2) any amount to the extent that such amount is, under any other provision of this title, treated as—

(A) a dividend (other than an amount treated as a dividend under subsection (f)),

(B) ordinary income, or

(C) gain from the sale of an asset held for not more than 1 year.

(h) Taxpayer to establish earnings and profits.

Unless the taxpayer establishes the amount of the earnings and profits of the foreign corporation to be taken into account under subsection (a) or (f), all gain from the sale or exchange shall be considered a dividend under subsection (a) or (f), and unless the taxpayer establishes the amount of foreign taxes to be taken into account under subsection (b), the limitation of such subsection shall not apply.

(i) Treatment of certain indirect transfers.

(1) In general. If any shareholder of a 10-percent corporate shareholder of a foreign corporation exchanges stock of the 10-percent corporate shareholder for stock of the foreign corporation, such 10-percent corporate shareholder shall recognize in the same manner as if the stock of the foreign corporation received in such exchange had been—

(A) issued to the 10-percent corporate shareholder, and

(B) then distributed by the 10-percent corporate shareholder to such shareholder in redemption or liquidation (whichever is appropriate).

The amount of gain recognized by such 10-percent corporate shareholder under the preceding sentence shall not exceed the amount treated as a dividend under this section.

(2) 10-percent corporate shareholder defined. For purposes of this subsection, the term "10-percent corporate shareholder" means any domestic corporation which, as of the day before the exchange referred to in paragraph (1), satisfies the stock ownership requirements of subsection (a)(2) with respect to the foreign corporation.

(j) Cross reference.

For provision excluding amounts previously taxed under this section from gross income when subsequently distributed, see section 959(e).

In **2007**, P.L. 110-172, Sec. 11(g)(17)(A), added "(as defined in section 922)" after "a FSC" in para. (d)(5) . . . Sec. 11(g)(17)(B), added a sentence at the end of para. (d)(5), enacted 12/29/2007.

In **2004**, P.L. 108-357, Sec. 413(c)(22), deleted para. (d)(5), and redesignated paras. (d)(6) and (7) as paras. (d)(5) and (6), effective for tax. yrs. of foreign corporations begin. after 12/31/2004, and for tax. yrs. of United States shareholders with or within which such tax. yrs. of foreign corporations end.

Prior to deletion, para. (d)(5) read as follows:

"(5) Amounts included in gross income under section 1247. If the United States person whose stock is sold or exchanged was a qualified shareholder (as defined in section 1247(c)) of a foreign corporation which was a foreign investment company (as described in section 1246(b)(1)), the earnings and profits of the foreign corporation for taxable years in which such person was a qualified shareholder."

In **1996**, P.L. 104-188, Sec. 1702(g)(1)(A)(i), deleted ", or if a United States person receives a distribution from a foreign corporation which, under section 302 or 331, is treated as an exchange of stock" after "foreign corporation" in para. (a)(1) . . . Sec. 1702(g)(1)(A)(ii), added a sentence at the end of subsec. (a) . . . Sec. 1702(g)(1)(B), deleted ", or receives a distribution from a domestic corporation which, under section 302 or 331, is treated as an exchange of stock" after "domestic corporation" in para. (e)(1) . . . Sec. 1702(g)(1)(C), substituted "355(c)(1), or 361(c)(1)" for "or 361(c)(1)" in subpara. (f)(1)(B) . . . Sec. 1702(g)(1)(D), amended para. (i)(1), effective 11/5/90.

Prior to amendment, para. (i)(1) read as follows:

"(1) In general. If any shareholder of a 10-percent corporate shareholder of a foreign corporation exchanges stock of the 10-percent corporate shareholder for stock of the foreign corporation, for purposes of this section, the stock of the foreign corporation received in such exchange shall be treated as if it had been—

"(A) issued to the 10-percent corporate shareholder, and

"(B) then distributed by the 10-percent corporate shareholder to such shareholder in redemption or liquidation (whichever is appropriate)."

In **1988**, P.L. 100-647, Sec. 1006(e)(14)(A), deleted para. (d)(2) . . . Sec. 1006(e)(14)(B), amended subpara. (f)(1)(B) . . . Sec. 1006(e)(14)(C), substituted "distribution" for "distribution, sale, or exchange" in para. (f)(1) . . . Sec. 1006(e)(14)(D), deleted para. (f)(3) and redesignated para. (f)(4) as para. (f)(3) . . . Sec. 1006(e)(14)(E), substituted "nonrecognition transactions" for "section 311, 336, or 337 transactions", in the heading of subsec. (f), effective as provided in Sec. 633(a) of P.L. 99-514, reproduced in note following Code Sec. 897 and Sec. 633(c) of P.L. 99-514, reproduced in note following Code Sec. 336.

Prior to deletion, para. (d)(2) read as follows:

"(2) Gain realized from the sale or exchange of property in pursuance of a plan of complete liquidation. If a foreign corporation adopts a plan of complete liquidation in a taxable year of a foreign corporation beginning after December 31, 1962, and if section 337(a) would apply if such foreign corporation were a domestic corporation, earnings and profits of the foreign corporation attributable (under regulations prescribed by the Secretary) to any net gain from the sale or exchange of property."

Prior to amendment, subpara. (f)(1)(B) read as follows:

Capital gains and losses Code Sec. 1249(b)

"(B) such domestic corporation distributes, sells, or exchanges stock of such foreign corporation in a transaction to which section 311, 336, or 337 applies,"
Prior to deletion, para. (f)(3) read as follows:
"(3) Nonapplication of paragraph (1) in certain cases. Paragraph (1) shall not apply to a sale or exchange to which section 337 applies if —
"(A) throughout the period or periods the stock of the foreign corporation was held by the domestic corporation (or predecessor referred to in paragraph (2)) all the stock of such domestic corporation was owned by United States persons who satisfied the 10-percent stock ownership requirements of subsection (a)(2) with respect to such domestic corporation, and
"(B) subsection (a) applies to the proceeds of the sale or exchange and also applied to all transactions described in subsection (e)(1) which took place during the period or periods referred to in subparagraph (A)."
—P.L. 100-647, Sec. 1012(p)(19), added para. (d)(7), effective for tax. yrs. of foreign corporations begin. after 12/31/86.
—P.L. 100-647, Sec. 1018(g)(2), substituted "Tax Reform Act of 1986" for "Tax Reform Act of 1985" in Sec. 133(d)(3)(B)(iii) of P.L. 98-369 [as amended by Sec. 1810(i)(2) of P.L. 99-514, see below]. [Sec. 133(d)(3)(B)(iii) of P.L. 98-369 is part of the effective date for amendments made by Secs. 133(b) and (c) of P.L. 98-369, see below.]
In 1986, P.L. 99-514, Sec. 631(d)(2)(A), substituted "Except as provided in regulations" for "Under regulations" in subsec. (e) . . . Sec. 631(d)(2)(B), added "Except as provided in regulations prescribed by the Secretary — " after the heading of subsec. (f), effective as provided in Sec. 633(a) of this Act, reproduced in note following Code Sec. 897 and Sec. 633(c) of this Act, reproduced in note following Code Sec. 336.
—P.L. 99-514, Sec. 1810(i)(1), substituted "in redemption or liquidation (whichever is appropriate)" for "in redemption of his stock" in subpara. (i)(1)(B), effective for exchanges after 7/18/84, in tax. yrs. end. after 7/18/84. For special rules, see Sec. 133(d)(3) of P.L. 98-369, reproduced below.
—P.L. 99-514, Sec. 1810(i)(2), substituted "the date which is one year after the date of the enactment of the Tax Reform Act of 1985" for "180 days after the date of the enactment of this Act" in Sec. 133(d)(3)(B)(iii) of P.L. 98-369 [part of the effective date for amendments made by Secs. 133(b) and (c) of P.L. 98-369, see below].
—P.L. 99-514, Sec. 1875(g)(1), added "or" at the end of para. (g)(1), deleted para. (g)(2), and redesignated para. (g)(3) as para. (g)(2), effective for exchanges after 3/1/86. Sec. 1875(g)(3) of this Act provides a transitional rule as follows:
"(3) Transitional rule.—An exchange shall be treated as occurring on or before March 1, 1986, if —
"(A) on or before such date, the taxpayer adopts a plan of reorganization to which section 356 applies, and
"(B) such plan or reorganization is implemented and distributions pursuant to such plan are completed on or before the date of enactment of this Act."
Prior to deletion, para. (g)(2) read as follows:
"(2) gain realized on exchanges to which section 356 (relating to receipt of additional consideration in certain reorganizations) applies; or"
—P.L. 99-514, Sec. 1876(a)(2), amended para. (d)(6), effective for transactions after 12/31/84, in tax. yrs. end. after 12/31/84.
Prior to amendment, para. (d)(6) read as follows:
"(6) foreign trade income. Earnings and profits of the foreign corporation attributable to foreign trade income (within the meaning of section 923(b)) of a FSC."
In 1984, P.L. 98-369, Sec. 133(a), added subsec. (i), effective for exchanges after 7/18/84 in tax. yrs. ending after 7/18/84.
—P.L. 98-369, Sec. 133(b)(2), added subsec. (j) . . . Sec. 133(c), substituted "section 958(a)" for "section 958(a)(2)" in subpara. (c)(2)(D), effective for transactions to which subsec. (a) or (f) of Code Sec. 1248 applies occurring after 7/18/84. Sec. 133(d)(3) of this Act [as amended by Sec. 1810(i)(2) of P.L. 99-514 and Sec. 1018(g)(2) of P.L. 100-647, see above] provides special rules as follows:
"(3) Election of earlier date for certain transactions.
"(A) In general. If the appropriate election is made under subparagraph (B), the amendments made by subsection (b) shall apply with respect to transactions to which subsection (a) or (f) of section 1248 of such Code applies occurring after October 9, 1975.
"(B) Election.—
"(i) Subparagraph (A) shall apply with respect to transactions to which subsection (a) of section 1248 of such Code applies if the foreign corporation described in such subsection (or its successor in interest) so elects.
"(ii) Subparagraph (A) shall apply with respect to transactions to which subsection (f) of section 1248 of such Code applies if the domestic corporation described in section 1248(f)(1) of such Code (or its successor) so elects.
"(iii) Any election under clause (i) or (ii) shall be made not later than the date which is 1 year after the date of the enactment of the Tax Reform Act of 1986 and shall be made in such manner as the Secretary of the Treasury or his delegate shall prescribe."
—P.L. 98-369, Sec. 801(d)(6), added para. (d)(6), effective for transactions after 12/31/84, in tax. yrs. end. after 12/31/84.
—P.L. 98-369, Sec. 1001(b)(22), substituted, "6 months" for "1 year" in subsec. (b) and subpara. (g)(3)(C), effective for property acquired after 6/22/84, and before 1/1/88.
In 1983, P.L. 97-448, Sec. 102(c)(1), substituted "section 312(k)(4)" for "section 312(k)(3)" in para. (c)(1), effective for property placed in service after 12/31/80 in tax. yrs. end. after 12/31/80.
In 1976, P.L. 94-455, Sec. 1022(a), amended para. (d)(3), effective for tax. yrs. begin. after 12/31/75.
Prior to amendment, para. (d)(3) read as follows:

"(3) Less developed country corporations. Earnings and profits accumulated by a foreign corporation while it was a less developed country corporation (as defined in section 902(d)), if the stock sold or exchanged was owned for a continuous period of at least 10 years, ending with the date of the sale or exchange, by the United States person who sold or exchanged such stock. In the case of stock sold or exchanged by a corporation, if United States persons who are individuals, estates, or trusts (each of whom owned within the meaning of section 958(a), or were considered as owning by applying the rules of ownership of section 958(b), 10 percent or more of the total combined voting power of all classes of stock entitled to vote of such corporation) owned, or were considered as owning, at any time during the 10-year period ending on the date of the sale or exchange more than 50 percent of the total combined voting power of all classes of stock entitled to vote of such corporation, this paragraph shall apply only if such United States persons owned, or were considered as owning, at all times during the remainder of such 10-year period more than 50 percent of the total combined voting power of all classes of stock entitled to vote of such corporation. For purposes of this paragraph, stock owned by a United States person who is an individual, estate, or trust which was acquired by reason of the death of the predecessor in interest of such United States person shall be considered as owned by such United States person during the period such stock was owned by such predecessor in interest, and during the period such stock was owned by any other predecessor in interest if between such United States person and such other predecessor in interest there was no transfer other than by reason of the death of an individual."
—P.L. 94-455, Sec. 1042(b), substituted "(or on the date of any sale or exchange of the stock of such other foreign corporation occurring during the 5-year period ending on the date of the sale or exchange of the stock of such foreign corporation, to the extent not otherwise taken into account under this section but not in excess of the fair market value of the stock of such other foreign corporation sold or exchanged over the basis of such stock (for determining gain) in the hands of the transferor); and" for "; and" in subpara. (c)(2)(C) . . . Sec. 1042(c)(1), redesignated subsecs. (f) and (g) as subsecs. (g) and (h), and added new subsec. (f) . . . Sec. 1042(c)(3)(A), substituted "subsection (a) or (f) applies to a sale, exchange, or distribution" for "subsection (a) applies to a sale or exchange" in subpara. (c)(2)(A) . . . Sec. 1042(c)(3)(B), amended subpara. (g)(3)(A) [as redesignated by Sec. 1042(c)(1) of this Act, see above] . . . Sec. 1042(c)(3)(C), substituted "subsection (a) of (f)" for "subsection (a)" each place it appeared in subsec. (h) [as redesignated by Sec. 1042(c)(1) of this Act, see above], effective for transfers begin. after 10/9/75, and for sales, exchanges and distributions occurring after 10/9/75.
Prior to amendment, subpara. (g)(3)(A) [as redesignated by Sec. 1042(c)(1) of this Act, see above] read as follows:
"(A) a dividend,"
—P.L. 94-455, Sec. 1402(b)(1)(Y), substituted "9 months" for "6 months" each place it appeared in subsec. (b) and subpara. (f)(3)(C), effective for tax. yrs. begin. in 1977.
—P.L. 94-455, Sec. 1402(b)(2), substituted "1 year" for "9 months" in subsec. (b) and subpara. (f)(3)(C) [as amended by Sec. 1402(b)(1) of this Act, see above], effective for tax. yrs. begin. after 12/31/77.
—P.L. 94-455, Sec. 1901(b)(3)(H), substituted "ordinary income" for "gain from the sale of an asset which is not a capital asset" in subpara. (g)(3)(B) [as redesignated by Sec. 1042(c)(1) of this Act, see above] . . . Sec. 1901(b)(32)(B)(iii), substituted "312(c)(3)" for "312(m)(3)" in para. (c)(1) . . . Sec. 1906(b)(13)(A), substituted "Secretary" for "Secretary or his delegate" each place it appeared in Code Sec. 1248, effective for tax. yrs. begin. after 12/31/76.
In 1969, P.L. 91-172, Sec. 442(b)(2), substituted "Except as provided in section 312(m)(3), for purposes of this section" for "For purposes of this section," in para. (c)(1), effective 12/30/69.
In 1966, P.L. 89-809, Sec. 104(k), amended para. (d)(4), effective for sales or exchanges occurring after 12/31/66.
Prior to amendment, para. (d)(4) read as follows:
"(4) United States income. Any item includible in gross income of the foreign corporation under this chapter as income derived from sources within the United States of a foreign corporation engaged in trade or business in the United States."
In 1962, P.L. 87-834, Sec. 15(a), added Code Sec. 1248, effective for sales or exchanges occurring after 12/31/62.

Sec. 1249. Gain from certain sales or exchanges of patents, etc., to foreign corporations.

(a) General rule.

Gain from the sale or exchange after December 31, 1962, of a patent, an invention, model, or design (whether or not patented), a copyright, a secret formula or process, or any other similar property right to any foreign corporation by any United States person (as defined in section 7701(a)(30)) which controls such foreign corporation shall, if such gain would (but for the provisions of this subsection) be gain from the sale or exchange of a capital asset or of property described in section 1231, be considered as ordinary income.

(b) Control.

For purposes of subsection (a), control means, with respect to any foreign corporation, the ownership, directly or indirectly, of stock possessing more than 50 percent of the total combined voting power of all classes of stock entitled

2,767

to vote. For purposes of this subsection, the rules for determining ownership of stock prescribed by section 958 shall apply.

In 1976, P.L. 94-455, Sec. 1901(b)(3)(K), substituted "ordinary income" for "gain from the sale or exchange of property which is neither a capital asset nor property described in section 1231" in subsec. (a), effective for tax. yrs. begin. after 12/31/76.
In 1966, P.L. 89-809, Sec. 104(m)(3), substituted "Gain" for "Except as provided in subsection (c), gain," in subsec. (a), effective for tax. yrs. begin. after 12/31/66.
In 1962, P.L. 87-834, Sec. 16, added Code Sec. 1249, effective for tax. yrs. begin. after 12/31/62.

Sec. 1250. Gain from dispositions of certain depreciable realty.

(a) General rule.

Except as otherwise provided in this section—

(1) Additional depreciation after December 31, 1975.

(A) In general. If section 1250 property is disposed of after December 31, 1975, then the applicable percentage of the lower of—

(i) that portion of the additional depreciation (as defined in subsection (b)(1) or (4)) attributable to periods after December 31, 1975, in respect of the property, or

(ii) the excess of the amount realized (in the case of a sale, exchange, or involuntary conversion), or the fair market value of such property (in the case of any other disposition), over the adjusted basis of such property,

shall be treated as gain which is ordinary income. Such gain shall be recognized notwithstanding any other provision of this subtitle.

(B) Applicable percentage. For purposes of subparagraph (A), the term "applicable percentage" means—

(i) in the case of section 1250 property with respect to which a mortgage is insured under section 221(d)(3) or 236 of the National Housing Act, or housing financed or assisted by direct loan or tax abatement under similar provisions of State or local laws and with respect to which the owner is subject to the restrictions described in section 1039(b)(1)(B) (as in effect on the day before the date of the enactment [11/5/90] of the Revenue Reconciliation Act of 1990), 100 percent minus 1 percentage point for each full month the property was held after the date the property was held 100 full months;

(ii) in the case of dwelling units which, on the average, were held for occupancy by families or individuals eligible to receive subsidies under section 8 of the United States Housing Act of 1937, as amended, or under the provisions of State or local law authorizing similar levels of subsidy for lower-income families, 100 percent minus 1 percentage point for each full month the property was held after the date the property was held 100 full months;

(iii) in the case of section 1250 property with respect to which a depreciation deduction for rehabilitation expenditures was allowed under section 167(k), 100 percent minus 1 percentage point for each full month in excess of 100 full months after the date on which such property was placed in service;

(iv) in the case of section 1250 property with respect to which a loan is made or insured under title V of the Housing Act of 1949, 100 percent minus 1 percentage point for each full month the property was held after the date the property was held 100 full months; and

(v) in the case of all other section 1250 property, 100 percent.

In the case of a building (or a portion of a building devoted to dwelling units), if, on the average, 85 percent or more of the dwelling units contained in such building (or portion thereof) are units described in clause (ii), such building (or portion thereof) shall be treated as property described in clause (ii). Clauses (i), (ii), and (iv) shall not apply with respect to the additional depreciation described in subsection (b)(4) which was allowed under section 167(k).

(2) Additional depreciation after December 31, 1969, and before January 1, 1976.

(A) In general. If section 1250 property is disposed of after December 31, 1969, and the amount determined under paragraph (1)(A)(ii) exceeds the amount determined under paragraph (1)(A)(i), then the applicable percentage of the lower of—

(i) that portion of the additional depreciation attributable to periods after December 31, 1969, and before January 1, 1976, in respect of the property, or

(ii) the excess of the amount determined under paragraph (1)(A)(ii) over the amount determined under paragraph (1)(A)(i),

shall also be treated as gain which is ordinary income. Such gain shall be recognized notwithstanding any other provision of this subtitle.

(B) Applicable percentage. For purposes of subparagraph (A), the term "applicable percentage" means—

(i) in the case of section 1250 property disposed of pursuant to a written contract which was, on July 24, 1969, and at all times thereafter, binding on the owner of the property, 100 percent minus 1 percentage point for each full month the property was held after the date the property was held 20 full months;

(ii) in the case of section 1250 property with respect to which a mortgage is insured under section 221(d)(3) or 236 of the National Housing Act, or housing financed or assisted by direct loan or tax abatement under similar provisions of State or local laws, and with respect to which the owner is subject to the restrictions described in section 1039(b)(1)(B) (as in effect on the day before the date of the enactment [11/5/90] of the Revenue Reconciliation Act of 1990), 100 percent minus 1 percentage point for each full month the property was held after the date the property was held 20 full months;

(iii) in the case of residential rental property (as defined in section 167(j)(2)(B)) other than that covered by clauses (i) and (ii), 100 percent minus 1 percentage point for each full month the property was held after the date the property was held 100 full months;

(iv) in the case of section 1250 property with respect to which a depreciation deduction for rehabilitation expenditures was allowed under section 167(k), 100 percent minus 1 percentage point for each full month in excess of 100 full months after the date on which such property was placed in service; and

(v) in the case of all other section 1250 property, 100 percent.

Clauses (i), (ii), and (iii) shall not apply with respect to the additional depreciation described in subsection (b)(4).

(3) Additional depreciation before January 1, 1970.

(A) In general. If section 1250 property is disposed of after December 31, 1963, and the amount determined under paragraph (1)(A)(ii) exceeds the sum of the amounts determined under paragraphs (1)(A)(i) and (2)(A)(i), then the applicable percentage of the lower of—

(i) that portion of the additional depreciation attributable to periods before January 1, 1970, in respect of the property, or

(ii) the excess of the amount determined under paragraph (1)(A)(ii) over the sum of the amounts determined under paragraphs (1)(A)(i) and (2)(A)(i),

shall also be treated as gain which is ordinary income. Such gain shall be recognized notwithstanding any other provision of this subtitle.

(B) Applicable percentage. For purposes of subparagraph (A), the term "applicable percentage" means 100 percent minus 1 percentage point for each full month the property was held after the date on which the property was held for 20 full months.

(4) Special rule. For purposes of this subsection, any reference to section 167(k) or 167(j)(2)(B) shall be treated as a reference to such section as in effect on the day before the date of the enactment [11/5/90] of the Revenue Reconciliation Act of 1990.

(5) Cross reference. For reduction in the case of corporations on capital gain treatment under this section, see section 291(a)(1).

(b) Additional depreciation defined.

For purposes of this section—

(1) In general. The term "additional depreciation" means, in the case of any property, the depreciation adjustments in respect of such property; except that, in the case of property held more than one year, it means such adjustments only to the extent that they exceed the amount of the depreciation adjustments which would have resulted if such adjustments had been determined for each taxable year under the straight line method of adjustment.

(2) Property held by lessee. In the case of a lessee, in determining the depreciation adjustments which would have resulted in respect of any building erected (or other improvement made) on the leased property, or in respect of any cost of acquiring the lease, the lease period shall be treated as including all renewal periods. For purposes of the preceding sentence—

(A) the term "renewal period" means any period for which the lease may be renewed, extended, or continued pursuant to an option exercisable by the lessee, but

(B) the inclusion of renewal periods shall not extend the period taken into account by more than ⅔ of the period on the basis of which the depreciation adjustments were allowed.

(3) Depreciation adjustments. The term "depreciation adjustments" means, in respect of any property, all adjustments attributable to periods after December 31, 1963, reflected in the adjusted basis of such property on account of deductions (whether in respect of the same or other property) allowed or allowable to the taxpayer or to any other person for exhaustion, wear and tear, obsolescence, or amortization (other than amortization under section 168 (as in effect before its repeal by the Tax Reform Act of 1976), 169, 185 (as in effect before its repeal by the Tax Reform Act of 1986), 188 (as in effect before its repeal by the Revenue Reconciliation Act of 1990), 190, or 193). For purposes of the preceding sentence, if the taxpayer can establish by adequate records or other sufficient evidence that the amount allowed as a deduction for any period was less than the amount allowable, the amount taken into account for such period shall be the amount allowed.

(4) Additional depreciation attributable to rehabilitation expenditures. The term "additional depreciation" also means, in the case of section 1250 property with respect to which a depreciation or amortization deduction for rehabilitation expenditures was allowed under section 167(k) (as in effect on the day before the date of the enactment [11/5/90] of the Revenue Reconciliation Act of 1990) or 191 (as in effect before its repeal by the Economic Recovery Tax Act of 1981), the depreciation or amortization adjustments allowed under such section to the extent attributable to such property, except that, in the case of such property held for more than one year after the rehabilitation expenditures so allowed were incurred, it means such adjustments only to the extent that they exceed the amount of the depreciation adjustments which would have resulted if such adjustments had been determined under the straight line method of adjustment without regard to the useful life permitted under section 167(k) (as in effect on the day before the date of the enactment [11/5/90] of the Revenue Reconciliation Act of 1990) or 191 (as in effect before its repeal by the Economic Recovery Tax Act of 1981).

(5) Method of computing straight line adjustments. For purposes of paragraph (1), the depreciation adjustments which would have resulted for any taxable year under the straight line method shall be determined—

(A) in the case of property to which section 168 applies, by determining the adjustments which would have resulted for such year if the taxpayer had elected the straight line method for such year using the recovery period applicable to such property, and

(B) in the case any property to which section 168 does not apply, if a useful life (or salvage value) was used in determining the amount allowable as a deduction for any taxable year, by using such life (or value).

(c) Section 1250 property.

For purposes of this section, the term "section 1250 property" means any real property (other than section 1245 property, as defined in section 1245(a)(3)) which is or has been property of a character subject to the allowance for depreciation provided in section 167.

(d) Exceptions and limitations.

(1) Gifts. Subsection (a) shall not apply to a disposition by gift.

(2) Transfers at death. Except as provided in section 691 (relating to income in respect of a decedent), subsection (a) shall not apply to a transfer at death.

(3) Certain tax-free transactions. If the basis of property in the hands of a transferee is determined by reference to its basis in the hands of the transferor by reason of the application of section 332, 351, 361, 721, or 731, then the amount of gain taken into account by the transferor under subsection (a) shall not exceed the amount of gain recognized to the transferor on the transfer of such property (determined without regard to this section). Except as provided in paragraph (9), this paragraph shall not apply to a disposition to an organization (other than a cooperative described in section 521) which is exempt from the tax imposed by this chapter.

(4) Like kind exchanges; involuntary conversions, etc.

(A) Recognition limit. If property is disposed of and gain (determined without regard to this section) is not recognized in whole or in part under section 1031 or 1033, then the amount of gain taken into account by the transferor under subsection (a) shall not exceed the greater of the following:

(i) the amount of gain recognized on the disposition (determined without regard to this section), increased as provided in subparagraph (B), or

(ii) the amount determined under subparagraph (C).

(B) Increase for certain stock. With respect to any transaction, the increase provided by this subparagraph is the amount equal to the fair market value of any stock purchased in a corporation which (but for this paragraph) would result in nonrecognition of gain under section 1033(a)(2)(A).

(C) Adjustment where insufficient section 1250 property is acquired. With respect to any transaction, the amount determined under this subparagraph shall be the excess of—

(i) the amount of gain which would (but for this paragraph) be taken into account under subsection (a), over

(ii) the fair market value (or cost in the case of a transaction described in section 1033(a)(2)) of the section 1250 property acquired in the transaction.

(D) Basis of property acquired. In the case of property purchased by the taxpayer in a transaction described in section 1033(a)(2), in applying section 1033(b)(2), such sentence shall be applied—

(i) first solely to section 1250 properties and to the amount of gain not taken into account under subsection (a) by reason of this paragraph, and

(ii) then to all purchased properties to which such sentence applies and to the remaining gain not recognized on the transaction as if the cost of the section 1250 properties were the basis of such properties computed under clause (i).

In the case of property acquired in any other transaction to which this paragraph applies, rules consistent with the preceding sentence shall be applied under regulations prescribed by the Secretary.

(E) Additional depreciation with respect to property disposed of. In the case of any transaction described in section 1031 or 1033, the additional depreciation in respect of the section 1250 property acquired which is attributable to the section 1250 property disposed of shall be an amount equal to the amount of the gain which was not taken into account under subsection (a) by reason of the application of this paragraph.

(5) Property distributed by a partnership to a partner.

(A) In general. For purposes of this section, the basis of section 1250 property distributed by a partnership to a partner shall be deemed to be determined by reference to the adjusted basis of such property to the partnership.

(B) Additional depreciation. In respect of any property described in subparagraph (A), the additional depreciation attributable to periods before the distribution by the partnership shall be—

(i) the amount of the gain to which subsection (a) would have applied if such property had been sold by the partnership immediately before the distribution at its fair market value at such time and the applicable percentage for the property had been 100 percent, reduced by

(ii) if section 751(b) applied to any part of such gain, the amount of such gain to which section 751(b) would have applied if the applicable percentage for the property had been 100 percent.

(6) Transfers to tax-exempt organization where property will be used in unrelated business.

(A) In general. The second sentence of paragraph (3) shall not apply to a disposition of section 1250 property to an organization described in section 511(a)(2) or 511(b)(2) if, immediately after such disposition, such organization uses such property in an unrelated trade or business (as defined in section 513).

(B) Later change in use. If any property with respect to the disposition of which gain is not recognized by reason of subparagraph (A) ceases to be used in an unrelated trade or business of the organization acquiring such property, such organization shall be treated for purposes of this section as having disposed of such property on the date of such cessation.

(7) Foreclosure dispositions. If any section 1250 property is disposed of by the taxpayer pursuant to a bid for such property at foreclosure or by operation of an agreement or of process of law after there was a default on indebtedness which such property secured, the applicable percentage referred to in paragraph (1)(B), (2)(B), or (3)(B) of subsection (a), as the case may be, shall be determined as if the taxpayer ceased to hold such property on the date of the beginning of the proceedings pursuant to which the disposition occurred, or, in the event there are no proceedings, such percentage shall be determined as if the taxpayer ceased to hold such property on the date, determined under regulations prescribed by the Secretary, on which such operation of an agreement or process of law, pursuant to which the disposition occurred, began.

(e) Holding period.

For purposes of determining the applicable percentage under this section, the provisions of section 1223 shall not apply, and the holding period of section 1250 property shall be determined under the following rules:

(1) Beginning of holding period. The holding period of section 1250 property shall be deemed to begin—

(A) in the case of property acquired by the taxpayer, on the day after the date of acquisition, or

(B) in the case of property constructed, reconstructed, or erected by the taxpayer, on the first day of the month during which the property is placed in service.

(2) Property with transferred basis. If the basis of property acquired in a transaction described in paragraph (1), (2), or (3) of subsection (d) is determined by reference to its basis in the hands of the transferor, then the holding period of the property in the hands of the transferee shall include the holding period of the property in the hands of the transferor.

(3) Repealed.

(f) Special rules for property which is substantially improved.

(1) Amount treated as ordinary income. If, in the case of a disposition of section 1250 property, the property is treated as consisting of more than one element by reason of paragraph (3), then the amount taken into account under subsection (a) in respect of such section 1250 property as ordinary income shall be the sum of the amounts determined under paragraph (2).

(2) Ordinary income attributable to an element. For purposes of paragraph (1), the amount taken into account for any element shall be the sum of a series of amounts determined for the periods set forth in subsection (a), with the amount for any such period being determined by multiplying—

(A) the amount which bears the same ratio to the lower of the amounts specified in clause (i) or (ii) of subsection (a)(1)(A), in clause (i) or (ii) of subsection (a)(2)(A), or in clause (i) or (ii) of subsection (a)(3)(A), as the case may be, for the section 1250 property as the additional depreciation for such element attributable to such period bears to the sum of the additional depreciation for all elements attributable to such period, by

(B) the applicable percentage for such element for such period.

For purposes of this paragraph, determinations with respect to any element shall be made as if it were a separate property.

(3) Property consisting of more than one element. In applying this subsection in the case of any section 1250 property, there shall be treated as a separate element—

(A) each separate improvement,

(B) if, before completion of section 1250 property, units thereof (as distinguished from improvements) were placed in service, each such unit of section 1250 property, and

(C) the remaining property which is not taken into account under subparagraphs (A) and (B).

(4) Property which is substantially improved. For purposes of this subsection—

(A) In general. The term "separate improvement" means each improvement added during the 36-month period ending on the last day of any taxable year to the capital account for the property, but only if the sum of the amounts added to such account during such period exceeds the greatest of—

(i) 25 percent of the adjusted basis of the property,

(ii) 10 percent of the adjusted basis of the property, determined without regard to the adjustments provided in paragraphs (2) and (3) of section 1016(a), or

(iii) $5,000.

For purposes of clauses (i) and (ii), the adjusted basis of the property shall be determined as of the beginning of the first day of such 36-month period, or of the holding period of the property (within the meaning of subsection (e)), whichever is the later.

(B) Exception. Improvements in any taxable year shall be taken into account for purposes of subparagraph (A) only if the sum of the amounts added to the capital account for the property for such taxable year exceeds the greater of—

(i) $2,000, or

(ii) one percent of the adjusted basis referred to in subparagraph (A)(ii), determined, however, as of the beginning of such taxable year.

For purposes of this section, if the amount added to the capital account for any separate improvement does not exceed the greater of clause (i) or (ii), such improvement shall be treated as placed in service on the first day, of a calendar month, which is closest to the middle of the taxable year.

(C) Improvement. The term "improvement" means, in the case of any section 1250 property, any addition to capital account for such property after the initial acquisition or after completion of the property.

(g) Adjustments to basis.

The Secretary shall prescribe such regulations as he may deem necessary to provide for adjustments to the basis of property to reflect gain recognized under subsection (a).

(h) Application of section.

This section shall apply notwithstanding any other provision of this subtitle.

In 2005, P.L. 109-135, Sec. 402(a)(7)(A), deleted para. (d)(5) and redesignated paras. (d)(6)-(8) as paras. (d)(5)-(7) . . . Sec. 402(a)(7)(B), substituted "or (3)" for "(3), or (5)" in para. (e)(2), effective 6 months after 8/8/2005 as if included in Sec. 1263 of the Energy Policy Act of 2005, P.L. 109-58. Sec. 1274(b) of P.L. 109-58, provides:

"(b) Compliance with certain rules. If the Commission approves and makes effective any final rulemaking modifying the standards of conduct governing entities that own, operate, or control facilities for transmission of electricity in interstate commerce or transportation of natural gas in interstate commerce prior to the effective date of this subtitle, any action taken by a public-utility company or utility holding company to comply with the requirements of such rulemaking shall not subject such public-utility company or utility holding company to any regulatory requirement applicable to a holding company under the Public Utility Holding Company Act of 1935 (15 U.S.C. 79 et seq.)."

Prior to deletion, para. (d)(5) read as follows:

"(5) Section 1081 transactions. Under regulations prescribed by the Secretary, rules consistent with paragraphs (3) and (4) of this subsection and with subsections (e) and (f) shall apply in the case of transactions described in section 1081 (relating to exchanges in obedience to SEC orders)."

— P.L. 109-135, Sec. 402(h), deleted "or by section 179D" after ", or 193)" in para. (b)(3), effective for property placed in service after 12/31/2005 as if included in Sec. 1331 of the Energy Policy Act of 2005, P.L. 109-58. Sec. 402(m)(2) of this Act, provides:

"(2) Repeal of Public Utility Holding Company Act of 1935. The amendments made by subsection (a) shall not apply with respect to any transaction ordered in compliance with the Public Utility Holding Company Act of 1935 before its repeal."

— P.L. 109-58, Sec. 1331(b)(3), added "or by section 179D" before the period at the end of the first sentence in para. (b)(3), effective for property placed in service after 12/31/2005.

In 1998, P.L. 105-206, Sec. 6005(e)(3), added "on or" before "before" each place it appeared in Sec. 312(d)(2) [sic (e)(2)] of P.L. 105-34 [see below]

— P.L. 105-206, Sec. 6023(12), substituted "section 1033(b)(2)" for "the last sentence of section 1033(b)" in subpara. (d)(4)(D), effective 7/22/98.

In 1997, P.L. 105-34, Sec. 312(d)(10)(A), deleted para. (d)(7) and redesignated paras. (d)(9) and (10) as paras. (d)(7) and (8) . . . Sec. 312(d)(10)(B), deleted para. (e)(3), effective for sales and exchanges after 5/6/97. Sec. 312(d)(2)-(4) [sic (e)(2)-(4)] of this Act [as amended by Sec. 6005(e)(3) of 105-206, see below] provides:

"(2) Sales on or before date of enactment. At the election of the taxpayer, the amendments made by this section shall not apply to any sale or exchange on or before the date of the enactment of this Act.

"(3) Certain sales within 2 years after date of enactment. Section 121 of the Internal Revenue Code of 1986 (as amended by this section) shall be applied without regard to subsection (c)(2)(B) thereof in the case of any sale or exchange of property during the 2-year period beginning on the date of the enactment of this Act if the taxpayer held such property on the date of the enactment of this Act and fails to meet the ownership and use requirements of subsection (a) thereof with respect to such property.

"(4) Binding contracts. At the election of the taxpayer, the amendments made by this section shall not apply to a sale or exchange after the date of the enactment of this Act, if—

"(A) such sale or exchange is pursuant to a contract which was binding on such date, or

"(B) without regard to such amendments, gain would not be recognized under section 1034 of the Internal Revenue Code of 1986 (as in effect on the day before the date of the enactment of this Act) on such sale or exchange by reason of a new residence acquired on or before such date or with respect to the acquisition of which by the taxpayer a binding contract was in effect on such date.

This paragraph shall not apply to any sale or exchange by an individual if the treatment provided by section 877(a)(1) of the Internal Revenue Code of 1986 applies to such individual."

Prior to deletion, para. (d)(7) read as follows:

"(7) Disposition of principal residence. Subsection (a) shall not apply to a disposition of—

"(A) property to the extent used by the taxpayer as his principal residence (within the meaning of section 1034, relating to rollover of gain on sale of principal residence), and

"(B) property in respect of which the taxpayer meets the age and ownership requirements of section 121 (relating to one-time exclusion of gain from sale of principal residence by individual who has attained age 55) but only to the extent that he meets the use requirements of such section in respect of such property."

Prior to deletion, para. (e)(3) read as follows:

"(3) Principal residence. If the basis of property acquired in a transaction described in paragraph (7) of subsection (d) is determined by reference to the basis in the hands of the taxpayer of other property, then the holding period of the property acquired shall include the holding period of such other property."

In 1996, P.L. 104-188, Sec. 1702(h)(18), repealed para. (e)(4), effective for property placed in service after 11/5/90, except as provided in Sec. 11812(c)(2) of P.L. 101-508 reproduced in note following Code Sec. 42.

Prior to repeal, para. (e)(4) read as follows:

"(4)Qualified low-income housing.

The holding period of any section 1250 property acquired which is described in subsection (d)(8)(E)(i) shall include the holding period of the corresponding element of section 1250 property disposed of."

In 1995, P.L. 104-7, Sec. 2(b)(1), deleted "section 1071 (relating to gain from sale or exchange to effectuate policies of FCC) or" after "described in" in para. (d)(5) . . . Sec. 2(b)(2), deleted "1071 and" after "Section" in the heading of para. (d)(5), effective as provided in Sec. 2(d) of this Act, which reads as follows:

"(d) Effective date.

"(1) In general. The amendments made by this section shall apply to—

"(A) sales and exchanges on or after January 17, 1995, and

2,771

"(B) sales and exchanges before such date if the FCC tax certificate with respect to such sale or exchange is issued on or after such date.

"(2) Binding contracts.

"(A) In general. The amendments made by this section shall not apply to any sale or exchange pursuant to a written contract which was binding on January 16, 1995, and at all times thereafter before the sale or exchange, if the FCC tax certificate with respect to such sale or exchange was applied for, or issued, on or before such date.

"(B) Sales contingent on issuance of certificate.

"(i) In general. A contract shall be treated as not binding for purposes of subparagraph (A) if the sale or exchange pursuant to such contract, or the material terms of such contract, were contingent, at any time on January 16, 1995, on the issuance of an FCC tax certificate. The preceding sentence shall not apply if the FCC tax certificate for such sale or exchange is issued on or before January 16, 1995.

"(ii) Material terms. For purposes of clause (i), the material terms of a contract shall not be treated as contingent on the issuance of an FCC tax certificate solely because such terms provide that the sales price would, if such certificate were not issued, be increases by an amount not greater than 10 percent of the sales price otherwise provided in the contract.

"(3) FCC tax certificate. For purposes of this subsection, the term 'FCC tax certificate' means any certificate of the Federal Communications Commission for the effectuation of section 1071 of the Internal Revenue Code of 1986 (as in effect on the day before the date of the enactment of this Act)."

In **1990**, P.L. 101-508, Sec. 11801(c)(6)(F), substituted "188 (as in effect before its repeal by the Revenue Reconciliation Act of 1990)," for "188," in para. (b)(3) . . . Sec. 11801(c)(8)(I), deleted "371(a), 374(a)," after "351, 361," in para. (d)(3) . . . Sec. 11801(c)(15)(A), added "(as in effect on the day before the date of the enactment of the Revenue Reconciliation Act of 1990)" after "section 1039(b)(1)(B)" in clauses (a)(1)(A)[sic (B)](i) and (a)(2)(B)(ii) . . . Sec. 11801(c)(15)(B), deleted para. (d)(8) . . . Sec. 11801(c)(15)(C), deleted subsec. (g), and redesignated subsecs. (h) and (i) as subsecs. (g) and (h), effective 11/5/90, except as provided in Sec. 11821(b) of this Act, reproduced in note following Code Sec. 1039.

Prior to deletion, para. (d)(8) read as follows:

"(8) Disposition of qualified low-income housing. If section 1250 property is disposed of and gain (determined without regard to this section) is not recognized in whole or in part under section 1039, then—

"(A) Recognition limit. The amount of gain recognized by the transferor under subsection (a) shall not exceed the greater of—

"(i) the amount of gain recognized on the disposition (determined without regard to this section), or

"(ii) the amount determined under subparagraph (B).

"(B) Adjustment where insufficient section 1250 property is acquired. With respect to any transaction, the amount determined under this subparagraph shall be the excess of—

"(i) the amount of gain which would (but for this paragraph) be taken into account under subsection (a), over

"(ii) the cost of the section 1250 property acquired in the transaction.

"(C) Basis of property acquired. The basis of property acquired by the taxpayer, determined under section 1039(d), shall be allocated—

"(i) first to the section 1250 property described in subparagraph (E)(i), in the amount determined under such subparagraph, reduced by the amount of gain not recognized attributable to the section 1250 property disposed of,

"(ii) then to any property (other than section 1250 property) to which section 1039 applies, in the amount of its cost, reduced by the amount of gain not recognized except to the extent taken into account under clause (i), and

"(iii) then to the section 1250 property described in subparagraph (E)(ii), in the amount determined thereunder, reduced by the amount of gain not recognized except to the extent taken into account under clauses (i) and (ii).

"(D) Additional depreciation with respect to property disposed of. The additional depreciation with respect to any property acquired shall include the additional depreciation with respect to the corresponding section 1250 property disposed of, reduced by the amount of gain recognized attributable to such property.

"(E) Property consisting of more than one element. There shall be treated as a separate element of section 1250 property—

"(i) that portion of the section 1250 property acquired the cost of which does not exceed the net amount realized (as defined in section 1039(b)) attributable to the section 1250 property disposed of, reduced by the amount of gain recognized (if any) attributable to such property, and

"(ii) that portion of the section 1250 property acquired the cost of which exceeds the net amount realized (as defined in section 1039(b)) attributable to the section 1250 property disposed of.

"(F) Allocation rules. For purposes of this paragraph—

"(i) the amount of gain recognized attributable to the section 1250 property disposed of shall be the net amount realized with respect to such property, reduced by the greater of the adjusted basis of the section 1250 property disposed of or the cost of the section 1250 property acquired, but shall not exceed the gain recognized in the transaction, and

"(ii) if any section 1250 property is treated as consisting of more than one element by reason of the application of subparagraph (E) to a prior transaction, then the amount of gain recognized, the net amount realized, and the additional depreciation, with respect to each such element shall be allocated in accordance with regulations prescribed by the Secretary."

Prior to deletion, subsec. (g) read as follows:

"(g) Special rules for qualified low-income housing.

"(1) Amount treated as ordinary income. If, in the case of a disposition of section 1250 property, the property is treated as consisting of more than one element by reason of the application of subsection (d)(8)(E), and gain is recognized in whole or in part, then the amount taken into account under subsection (a) as ordinary income shall be the sum of the amounts determined under paragraph (2).

"(2) Ordinary income attributable to an element. For purposes of paragraph (1), the amount taken into account for any element shall be determined in a manner similar to that provided by subsection (f)(2)."

—P.L. 101-508, Sec. 11812(b)(11), redesignated para. (a)(4) as para. (a)(5), and added new para. (a)(4) . . . Sec. 11812(b)(12), substituted "167(k) (as in effect on the day before the date of the enactment of the Revenue Reconciliation Act of 1990)" for "167(k)" each place it appeared in para. (b)(4), effective for property placed in service after 11/5/90, except as provided in Sec. 11812(c)(2) reproduced in note following Code Sec. 42.

In **1989**, P.L. 101-239, Sec. 7831(b)(1), substituted "in the case of property to which section 168 applies" for "in the case of recovery property" in subpara. (b)(5)(A) . . . Sec. 7831(b)(2), substituted "in the case any property to which section 168 does not apply" for "in the case of any property which is not recovery property" in subpara. (b)(5)(B), effective for that portion of the basis of any property which is attributable to expenditures paid or incurred after 12/31/86, except as provided in Sec. 242(c)(2) of P.L. 99-514, reproduced below.

In **1988**, P.L. 100-647, Sec. 1002(a)(1), deleted para. (d)(11), effective for property placed in service after 12/31/86, in tax. yrs. ending after such date.

Prior to deletion, para. (d)(11) read as follows:

"(11) Section 1245 recovery property. Subsection (a) shall not apply to the disposition of property which is section 1245 recovery property (as defined in section 1245(a)(5))."

In **1986**, P.L. 99-514, Sec. 242(b)(2), added "(as in effect before its repeal by the Tax Reform Act of 1986)" after "185" in para. (b)(3), effective for that portion of the basis of any property which is attributable to expenditures paid or incurred after 12/31/86, except as provided in Sec. 242(c)(2), which reads:

"(2) Transitional rule.—The amendments made by this section shall not apply to any expenditure incurred—

"(A) pursuant to a binding contract entered into before March 2, 1986, or

"(B) with respect to any improvement commenced before March 2, 1986, but only if not less than the lesser of $1,000,000 or 5 percent of the aggregate cost of such improvement has been incurred or committed before such date.

The preceding sentence shall not apply to any expenditure with respect to an improvement placed in service after December 31, 1987."

In **1984**, P.L. 98-369, Sec. 712(a)(1)(B), added para. (a)(4), effective for tax. yrs. begin. after 12/31/82.

In **1983**, P.L. 97-448, Sec. 102(a)(7)(A), added para. (b)(5) . . . Sec. 102(a)(7)(B), deleted the last sentence of para. (b)(1), effective for property placed in service after 12/31/80 in tax. yrs. end. after 12/31/80.

Prior to deletion, the last sentence of para. (b)(1) read as follows:

"For purposes of the preceding sentence, if a useful life (or salvage value) was used in determining the amount allowed as a deduction for any taxable year, such life (or value) shall be used in determining the depreciation adjustments which would have resulted for such year under the straight line method."

In **1981**, P.L. 97-34, Sec. 204(e), added para. (d)(11), effective for property placed in service after 12/31/80, in tax. yrs. end. after 12/31/80.

—P.L. 97-34, Sec. 212(d)(2)(F), added "(as in effect before its repeal by the Economic Recovery Tax Act of 1981)" after "191" each place it appeared in para. (b)(4), effective for expenditures incurred after 12/31/81, in tax. yrs. end. after 12/31/81.

Sec. 212(e)(2) of this Act provides as follows:

"(2) Transitional rule. The amendments made by this section shall not apply with respect to any rehabilitation of a building if—

"(A) the physical work on such rehabilitation began before January 1, 1982, and

"(B) such building meets the requirements of paragraph (1) of section 48(g) of the Internal Revenue Code of 1954 (as in effect on the day before the date of enactment of this Act) but does not meet the requirements of such paragraph (1) (as amended by this Act)."

In **1980**, P.L. 96-541, Sec. 2(e)(1), repealed Sec. 2124(a)(4) of P.L. 94-455, the effective date for changes made by Sec. 2124(a)(3)(D) of P.L. 94-455, see below.

Prior to repeal, Sec. 2124(a)(4) of P.L. 94-455 read as follows:

"(4) Effective date. The amendments made by this subsection shall apply with respect to additions to capital account made after June 14, 1976 and before June 15, 1981."

—P.L. 96-223, Sec. 251(a)(2)(D), substituted "190, or 193" for "or 190" in para. (b)(3), effective for tax. yrs. begin. after 12/31/79.

—P.L. 96-222, Sec. 107(a)(1)(D), added "which was allowed under section 167(k)" before the period at the end of subpara. (a)(1)(B), effective for additions to capital account made after 6/14/76 and before 6/15/81.

In **1979**, P.L. 96-167, Sec. 9(c), extended the effective date of changes made by Sec. 2122(b)(4) of P.L. 94-455 [see below] to tax. yrs. begin. after 12/31/76 and before 1/1/83.

In **1978**, P.L. 95-600, Sec. 404(c)(7), substituted "relating to one-time exclusion of gain from sale of principal residence by individual who has attained age 55" for "relating to gains from sale or exchange of residence of individual who has attained the age of 65" in subpara. (d)(7)(B), effective for sales or exchanges after 7/26/78, in tax. yrs. ending after 7/26/78.

—P.L. 95-600, Sec. 405(c)(4), substituted "relating to rollover of gain on sale of principal residence" for "relating to sale or exchange of residence" in subpara. (d)(7)(A), effective for sales and exchanges of residences after 7/26/78, in tax. yrs. ending after 7/26/78.

—P.L. 95-600, Sec. 701(f)(3)(C), substituted "or 190" for "190 or 191" in para. (b)(3) . . . Sec. 701(f)(3)(E), added "or amortization" after "depreciation" the

Capital gains and losses — Code Sec. 1250

second and third place it appeared in para. (b)(4) and added "or 191" after "167(k)" each place it appeared in para. (b)(4), effective for additions to capital account made after 6/14/76 and before 6/15/81.

In 1976, P.L. 94-455, Sec. 202(a), amended subsec. (a), effective for tax. yrs. end. after 12/31/75.

Prior to amendment, subsec. (a) read as follows:

"(a) General rule.

"Except as otherwise provided in this section—

"(1) Additional depreciation after December 31, 1969. If section 1250 property is disposed of after December 31, 1969, the applicable percentage of the lower of—

"(A) that portion of the additional depreciation (as defined in subsection (b)(1) or (4)) attributable to periods after December 31, 1969, in respect of the property, or

"(B) the excess of—

"(i) the amount realized (in the case of a sale, exchange, or involuntary conversion), or the fair market value of such property (in the case of any other disposition), over

"(ii) the adjusted basis of such property,

shall be treated as gain from the sale or exchange of property which is neither a capital asset nor property described in section 1231. Such gain shall be recognized notwithstanding any other provision of this subtitle.

"(C) Applicable percentage. For purposes of paragraph (1), the term 'applicable percentage' means—

"(i) in the case of section 1250 property disposed of pursuant to a written contract which was, on July 24, 1969, and at all times thereafter, binding on the owner of the property, 100 percent minus 1 percentage point for each full month the property was held after the date the property was held 20 full months;

"(ii) in the case of section 1250 property constructed, reconstructed, or acquired by the taxpayer before January 1, 1976, with respect to which a mortgage is insured under section 221(d)(3) or 236 of the National Housing Act, or housing is financed or assisted by direct loan or tax abatement under similar provisions of State or local laws, and with respect to which the owner is subject to the restrictions described in section 1039(b)(1)(B), 100 percent minus one percentage point for each full month the property was held after the date the property was held 20 full months;

"(iii) in the case of residential rental property (as defined in section 167(j)(2)(B)) other than that covered by clauses (i) and (ii), 100 percent minus 1 percentage point for each full month the property was held after the date the property was held 100 full months;

"(iv) in the case of section 1250 property with respect to which a depreciation deduction for rehabilitation expenditures was allowed under section 167(k), 100 percent minus 1 percentage point for each full month in excess of 100 full months after the date on which such property was placed in service; and

"(v) in the case of all other section 1250 property, 100 percent.

Clauses (i), (ii), and (iii) shall not apply with respect to the additional depreciation described in subsection (b)(4).

"(2) Additional depreciation before January 1, 1970.

"(A) In general. If section 1250 property is disposed of after December 31, 1963, and the amount determined under paragraph (1)(B) exceeds the amount determined under paragraph (1)(A), then the applicable percentage of the lower of—

"(i) that portion of the additional depreciation attributable to periods before January 1, 1970, in respect of the property, or

"(ii) the excess of the amount determined under paragraph (1)(B) over the amount determined under paragraph (1)(A),

shall also be treated as gain from the sale or exchange of property which is neither a capital asset nor property described in section 1231. Such gain shall be recognized notwithstanding any other provision of this subtitle.

"(B) Applicable percentage. For purposes of subparagraph (A) the term 'applicable percentage' means 100 percent minus 1 percentage point for each full month the property was held after the date on which the property was held for 20 full months."

—P.L. 94-455, Sec. 202(b), added para. (d)(10), effective for proceedings and operations of law referred to in para. (d)(10) which begin after 12/31/75.

—P.L. 94-455, Sec. 202(c)(1), amended para. (f)(2), . . . Sec. 202(c)(2), amended para. (g)(2), effective for tax. yrs. end. after 12/31/75.

Prior to amendment, para. (f)(2) read as follows:

"(2) Ordinary income attributable to an element. For purposes of paragraph (1), the amount taken into account for any element shall be the sum of—

"(A) the amount (if any) determined by multiplying—

"(i) the amount which bears the same ratio to the lower of the amounts specified in subparagraph (A) or (B) of subsection (a)(1) for the section 1250 property as the additional depreciation for such element attributable to periods after December 31, 1969, bears to the sum of the additional depreciation for all elements *attributable to periods after December 31, 1969, by*

"(ii) the applicable percentage for such element, and

"(B) the amount (if any) determined by multiplying—

"(i) the amount which bears the same ratio to the lower of the amounts specified in subsection (a)(2)(A)(i) or (ii) for the section 1250 property as the additional depreciation for such element attributable to periods before January 1, 1970, bears to the sum of the additional depreciation for all elements attributable to periods before January 1, 1970, by

"(ii) the applicable percentage for such element.

For purposes of this paragraph, determinations with respect to any element shall be made as if it were a separate property."

Prior to amendment, para. (g)(2) read as follows:

"(2) Ordinary income attributable to an element. For purposes of paragraph (1), the amount taken into account for any element shall be the amount determined by multiplying—

"(A) the amount which bears the same ratio to the lower of the additional depreciation or the gain recognized for the section 1250 property disposed of as the additional depreciation for such element bears to the sum of the additional depreciation for all elements disposed of, by

"(B) the applicable percentage for such element.

For purposes of this paragraph, determinations with respect to any element shall be made as if it were a separate property."

—P.L. 94-455, Sec. 1901(b)(3)(K), substituted "ordinary income" for "gain from the sale or exchange of property which is neither a capital asset nor property described in section 1231" in paras. (f)(1) and (g)(1), effective for tax. yrs. begin. after 12/31/76.

—P.L. 94-455, Sec. 1901(b)(31)(A), substituted "1033(a)(2)(A)" for "1033(a)(3)(A)" in subpara. (d)(4)(B) . . . Sec. 1901(b)(31)(B), substituted "1033(a)(2)" for "1033(a)(3)" in subparas. (d)(4)(C) and (D) . . . Sec. 1901(b)(31)(E), substituted "1033(b)" for "1033(c)" in subpara. (d)(4)(D), effective for tax. yrs. begin. after 12/31/76.

—P.L. 94-455, Sec. 1906(b)(13)(A), substituted "Secretary" for "Secretary or his delegate" each place it appeared in Code Sec. 1250, effective for tax. yrs. begin. after 12/31/76.

—P.L. 94-455, Sec. 1951(c)(2)(C), substituted "168 (as in effect before its repeal by the Tax Reform Act of 1976)," for "168," in para. (b)(3), effective for tax. yrs. begin. after 12/31/76.

—P.L. 94-455, Sec. 2122(b)(4), substituted "188, or 190" for "or 188" in para. (b)(3), effective [as amended by Sec. 9(c) of P.L. 96-167, see above] for tax. yrs. begin. after 12/31/76 and before 1/1/83.

—P.L. 94-455, Sec. 2124(a)(3)(D), substituted "190 or 191" for "or 190" in para. (b)(3) [as amended by this Act. See above, effective date repealed by Sec. 2(e)(1) of P.L. 96-541, see above].

In 1975, P.L. 94-81, Sec. 2(b)(1), substituted "Except as provided in paragraph (9), this" for "This" in the second sentence of para. (d)(3) . . . Sec. 2(b)(2), added para. (d)(9), effective for dispositions after 12/31/69, in tax. yrs. end. after 12/31/69, except as provided in Sec. 2(c)(2) of this Act, which reads as follows:

"(2) Election for past transactions.— In the case of any disposition occurring before the date of the enactment [8/9/75] of this Act, the amendments made by this section shall apply only if the organization acquiring the property elects (in the manner provided by regulations prescribed by the Secretary of the Treasury or his delegate) within 1 year after the date of the enactment of this Act to have such amendments apply with respect to such property."

In 1975, P.L. 93-625, Sec. 5(c), substituted "January 1, 1976" for "January 1, 1975" in clause (a)(1)(C)(ii), effective for property placed in service after 12/31/73.

In 1971, P.L. 92-178, Sec. 303(c)(3), substituted ", 185, or 188" for "or 185" in para. (b)(3), effective for tax. yrs. end. after 12/31/71.

In 1969, P.L. 91-172, Sec. 521(b), amended subsec. (a) . . . Sec. 521(c), added para. (b)(4) . . . Sec. 521(e)(1), substituted "subsection (a)" for "subsection (a)(1)" each place it appeared in subsec. (d) . . . Sec. 521(e)(2)(A), substituted "subsection (a)" for "subsection (a)(1)" in subsec. (f) . . . Sec. 521(e)(2)(B), amended para. (f)(2), effective for tax. yrs. end. after 7/24/69.

Prior to amendment, subsec. (a) read as follows:

"(a) General rule.

"(1) Ordinary income. Except as otherwise provided in this section, if section 1250 property is disposed of after December 31, 1963, the applicable percentage of the lower of—

"(A) the additional depreciation (as defined in subsection (b)(1)) in respect of the property, or

"(B) the excess of—

"(i) the amount realized (in the case of a sale, exchange, or involuntary conversion), or the fair market value of such property (in the case of any other disposition), over

"(ii) the adjusted basis of such property, shall be treated as gain from the sale or exchange of property which is neither a capital asset nor property described in section 1231. Such gain shall be recognized notwithstanding any other provision of this subtitle.

"(2) Applicable percentage. For purposes of paragraph (1), the term 'applicable percentage' means 100 percent minus one percentage point for each full month the property was held after the date on which the property was held 20 full months."

Prior to amendment, para. (f)(2) read as follows:

"(2) Ordinary income attributable to an element. For purposes of paragraph (1), the amount taken into account for any element shall be the amount determined by multiplying—

"(A) the amount which bears the same ratio to the lower of the amounts specified in subparagraph (A) or (B) of subsection (a)(1) for the section 1250 property as the additional depreciation for such element bears to the sum of the additional depreciation for all elements, by

"(B) the applicable percentage for such element.

For purposes of this paragraph, determinations with respect to any element shall be made as if it were a separate property."

—P.L. 91-172, Sec. 704(b)(5), substituted "168, 169, or 185" for "168" in para. (b)(3), effective for tax. yrs. end. after 12/31/68.

—P.L. 91-172, Sec. 910(b)(1), added para. (d)(8) . . . Sec. 910(b)(2), added para. (e)(4) . . . Sec. 910(b)(3), redesignated subsecs. (g) and (h) as subsecs. (h) and (i) and added new subsec. (g), effective for approved dispositions of qualified housing projects (within the meaning of Code Sec. 1039) after 10/9/69.

2,773

Code Sec. 1250 — Capital gains and losses

In 1964, P.L. 88-272, Sec. 231(a), added Code Sec. 1250, effective for dispositions after 12/31/63 in tax. yrs. end. after 12/31/63.

Sec. 1251. Repealed.

In 1984, P.L. 98-369, Sec. 492(a), repealed Code Sec. 1251, effective for tax. yrs. begin. after 12/31/83.

—P.L. 98-369, Sec. 1001(b)(23), substituted "6 months [more than 1 year for property acquired before 6/23/84 and after 12/31/87]" for "1 year" in subpara. (e)(1)(A), [as repealed by Sec. 492(a), of this Act], effective for property acquired after 6/22/84 and before 1/1/88.

Prior to repeal, Code Sec. 1251 read as follows:

"Sec. 1251. GAIN FROM DISPOSITION OF PROPERTY USED IN FARMING WHERE FARM LOSSES OFFSET NON-FARM INCOME.

"(a) Circumstances under which section applies.

"This section shall apply with respect to any taxable year only if—

"(1) there is a farm net loss for the taxable year, or

"(2) there is a balance in the excess deductions account as of the close of the taxable year after applying subsection (b)(3)(A).

"(b) Excess deductions account.

"(1) Requirement. Each taxpayer subject to this section shall, for purposes of this section, establish and maintain an excess deductions account.

"(2) Additions to account.

"(A) General rule. There shall be added to the excess deductions account for each taxable year an amount equal to the farm net loss.

"(B) Exceptions. In the case of an individual (other than a trust) and, except as provided in this subparagraph, in the case of an S corporation, subparagraph (A) shall apply for a taxable year—

"(i) only if the taxpayer's nonfarm adjusted gross income for such year exceeds $50,000, and

"(ii) only to the extent the taxpayer's farm net loss for such year exceeds $25,000.

This subparagraph shall not apply to an S corporation for a taxable year if on any day of such year a shareholder of such corporation is an individual who, for his taxable year with which or within which the taxable year of the corporation ends, has a farm net loss or is a shareholder of another S corporation which has a farm net loss for its taxable year ending within such taxable year of the individual. For purposes of clause (i), in the case of an electing S corporation the nonfarm adjusted gross income of the corporation shall be increased by the amount of the nonfarm adjusted gross income of that shareholder (on any day of the corporation's taxable year) who has the highest amount of all such shareholders of nonfarm adjusted gross income for his taxable year with which or within which the taxable year of the corporation ends.

"(C) Married individuals. In the case of a husband or wife who files a separate return, the amount specified in subparagraph (B)(i) shall be $25,000 in lieu of $50,000, and in subparagraph (B)(ii) shall be $12,500 in lieu of $25,000. This subparagraph shall not apply if the spouse of the taxpayer does not have any nonfarm adjusted gross income for the taxable year.

"(D) Nonfarm adjusted gross income. For purposes of this section, the term 'nonfarm adjusted gross income' means adjusted gross income (taxable income, in the case of an S corporation) computed without regard to income or deductions attributable to the business of farming.

"(E) Termination of additions. No amount shall be added to the excess deductions account for any taxable year beginning after December 31, 1975.

"(3) Subtractions from account. If there is any amount in the excess deductions account at the close of any taxable year (determined before any amount is subtracted under this paragraph for such year) there shall be subtracted from the account—

"(A) an amount equal to the farm net income for such year, plus the amount (determined as provided in regulations prescribed by the Secretary) necessary to adjust the account for deductions which did not result in a reduction of the taxpayer's tax under this subtitle for the taxable year or any preceding taxable year, and

"(B) after applying paragraph (2) or subparagraph (A) of this paragraph (as the case may be), an amount equal to the sum of the amounts treated, solely by reason of the application of subsection (c), as ordinary income.

In the case of a corporation which has made or received a transfer described in clause (ii) of paragraph (5)(A), subtractions from the excess deductions account shall be determined, in such manner as the Secretary shall prescribe, applying this paragraph to the farm net income, and the amounts described in subparagraph (B), of the transferor corporation and the transferee corporation on an aggregate basis.

"(4) Exception for taxpayers using certain accounting methods.

"(A) General rule. Except to the extent that the taxpayer has succeeded to an excess deductions account as provided in paragraph (5), additions to the excess deductions account shall not be required by a taxpayer who elects to compute taxable income from farming (i) by using inventories, and (ii) by charging to capital account all expenditures paid or incurred which are properly chargeable to capital account (including such expenditures which the taxpayer may, under this chapter or regulations prescribed thereunder, otherwise treat or elect to treat as expenditures which are not chargeable to capital account).

"(B) Time, manner and effect of election. An election under subparagraph (A) for any taxable year shall be filed within the time prescribed by law (including extensions thereof) for filing the return for such taxable year, and shall be made and filed in such manner as the Secretary shall prescribe by regulations. Such election shall be binding on the taxpayer for such taxable year and for all subsequent taxable years and may not be revoked except with the consent of the Secretary.

"(C) Change of method of accounting, etc. If, in order to comply with the election made under subparagraph (A), a taxpayer changes his method of accounting in computing taxable income from the business of farming, such change shall be treated as having been made with the consent of the Secretary and for purposes of section 481(a)(2) shall be treated as a change not initiated by the taxpayer.

"(5) Transfer of account.

"(A) Certain corporate transactions.

"(i) In the case of a transfer in subsection (d)(3) to which section 371(a), 374(a), or 381 applies, the acquiring corporation shall succeed to and take into account as of the close of the day of distribution or transfer, the excess deductions account of the transferor.

"(ii) In the case of a transfer which is described in subsection (d)(3), which is in connection with a reorganization described in section 368(a)(1)(D), and which is not described in clause (i), the transferee corporation shall be deemed to have an excess deductions account in an amount equal to the amount in the excess deductions account of the transferor. The transferor's excess deductions account shall not be reduced by reason of the preceding sentence.

"(B) Certain gifts. If—

"(i) farm recapture property is disposed of by gift, and

"(ii) the potential gain (as defined in subsection (e)(5)) on farm recapture property disposed of by gift during any one-year period in which any such gift occurs is more than 25 percent of the potential gain on farm recapture property held by the donor immediately prior to the first of such gifts,

each donee of the property shall succeed (at the time the first of such gifts is made, but in an amount determined as of the close of the donor's taxable year in which the first of such gifts is made) to the same proportion of the donor's excess deductions account (determined, after the application of paragraphs (2) and (3) with respect to the donor, as of the close of such taxable year), as the potential gain on the property received by such donee bears to the aggregate potential gain on farm recapture property held by the donor immediately prior to the first of such gifts.

"(6) Joint return. In the case of an addition to an excess deductions account for a taxable year for which a joint return was filed under section 6013, for any subsequent taxable year for which a separate return was filed the Secretary shall provide rules for allocating any remaining amount of such addition in a manner consistent with the purposes of this section.

"(c) Ordinary income.

"(1) General rule. Except as otherwise provided in this section, if farm recapture property (as defined in subsection (e)(1)) is disposed of during a taxable year beginning after December 31, 1969, the amount by which—

"(A) in the case of a sale, exchange, or involuntary conversion, the amount realized, or

"(B) in the case of any other disposition, the fair market value of such property, exceeds the adjusted basis of such property shall be treated as ordinary income. Such gain shall be recognized notwithstanding any other provision of this subtitle.

"(2) Limitation.

"(A) Amount in excess deductions account. The aggregate of the amounts treated under paragraph (1) as ordinary income for any taxable year shall not exceed the amount in the excess deductions account at the close of the taxable year after applying subsection (b)(3)(A).

"(B) Dispositions taken into account. If the aggregate of the amounts to which paragraph (1) applies is limited by the application of subparagraph (A), paragraph (1) shall apply in respect of such dispositions (and in such amounts) as provided under regulations prescribed by the Secretary.

"(C) Special rule for dispositions of land. In applying subparagraph (A), any gain on the sale or exchange of land shall be taken into account only to the extent of its potential gain (as defined in subsection (e)(5)).

"(d) Exceptions and special rules.

"(1) Gifts. Subsection (c) shall not apply to a disposition by gift.

"(2) Transfer at death. Except as provided in section 691 (relating to income in respect of a decedent), subsection (c) shall not apply to a transfer at death.

"(3) Certain corporate transactions. If the basis of property in the hands of a transferee is determined by reference to its basis in the hands of the transferor by reason of the application of sections 332, 351, 361, 371(a), or 374(a), then the amount of gain taken into account by the transferor under subsection (c)(1) shall not exceed the amount of gain recognized to the transferor on the transfer of such property (determined without regard to this section). This paragraph shall not apply to a disposition to an organization (other than a cooperative described in section 521) which is exempt from the tax imposed by this chapter.

"(4) Like kind exchanges; involuntary conversion, etc. If property is disposed of and gain (determined without regard to this section) is not recognized in whole or in part under section 1031 or 1033, then the amount of gain taken into account by the transferor under subsection (c)(1) shall not exceed the sum of—

"(A) the amount of gain recognized on such disposition (determined without regard to this section), plus

"(B) the fair market value of property acquired with respect to which no gain is recognized under subparagraph (A), but which is not farm recapture property.

"(5) Partnerships.

"(A) In general. In the case of a partnership, each partner shall take into account separately his distributive share of the partnership's farm net losses, gains from dispositions of farm recapture property, and other items in applying this section to the partner.

"(B) Transfers to partnerships. If farm recapture property is contributed to a partnership and gain (determined without regard to this section) is not recognized under section 721, then the amount of gain taken into account by the transferor under subsection (c)(1) shall not exceed the excess of the fair market value of farm recapture property transferred over the fair market value of the partnership interest attributable to such property. If the partnership agreement provides for an

Capital gains and losses   Code Sec. 1253(a)

allocation of gain to the contributing partner with respect to farm recapture property contributed to the partnership (as provided in section 704(c)(2)), the partnership interest of the contributing partner shall be deemed to be attributable to such property.

"(6) Property transferred to controlled corporations. Except for transactions described in subsection (b)(5)(A), in the case of a transfer, described in paragraph (3), of farm recapture property to a corporation, stock or securities received by a transferor in the exchange shall be farm recapture property to the extent attributable to the fair market value of the farm recapture property (or, in the case of land, if less, the adjusted basis plus the potential gain (as defined in subsection (e)(5)) on farm recapture property) contributed to the corporation by such transferor.

"(e) Definitions.

"For purposes of this section—

"(1) Farm recapture property. The term 'farm recapture property' means—

"(A) any property (other than section 1250 property) described in paragraph (1) (relating to business property held for more than 6 months [more than 1 year for property acquired before 6/23/84 and after 12/31/87]), (3) (relating to livestock), or (4) (relating to an unharvested crop) of section 1231(b) which is or has been used in the trade or business of farming by the taxpayer or by a transferor in a transaction described in subsection (b)(5), and

"(B) any property the basis of which in the hands of the taxpayer is determined with reference to the adjusted basis of property which was farm recapture property in the hands of the taxpayer within the meaning of subparagraph (A).

"(2) Farm net loss. The term 'farm net loss' means the amount by which—

"(A) the deductions allowed or allowable by this chapter which are directly connected with the carrying on of the trade or business of farming, exceed

"(B) the gross income derived from such trade or business. Gains and losses on the disposition of farm recapture property referred to in section 1231(a) (determined without regard to this section or section 1245(a)) shall not be taken into account.

"(3) Farm net income. The term 'farm net income' means the amount by which the amount referred to in paragraph (2)(B) exceeds the amount referred to in paragraph (2)(A).

"(4) Trade or business of farming.

"(A) Horse racing. In the case of a taxpayer engaged in the raising of horses, the term 'trade or business of farming' includes the racing of horses.

"(B) Several businesses of farming. If a taxpayer is engaged in more than one trade or business of farming, all such trades and businesses shall be treated as one trade or business.

"(5) Potential gain. The term 'potential gain' means an amount equal to the excess of the fair market value of property over its adjusted basis, but limited in the case of land to the extent of the deductions allowable in respect to such land under sections 175 (relating to soil and water conservation expenditures) and 182 (relating to expenditures by farmers for clearing land) for the taxable year and the 4 preceding taxable years."

In **1982**, P.L. 97-354, Sec. 5(a)(36)(A)(i), substituted "an S corporation," for "an electing small business corporation (as defined in section 1371(b))," in subpara. (b)(2)(B) ... Sec. 5(a)(36)(A)(ii), substituted "S corporation" for "electing small business corporation" each place it appeared in the second and third sentences of subpara. (b)(2)(B) ... Sec. 5(a)(36)(B), substituted "an S corporation" for "an electing small business corporation" in subpara. (b)(2)(D), effective for tax. yrs. begin. after 12/31/82.

In **1976**, P.L. 94-455, Sec. 206(a), added subpara. (b)(2)(E) ... Sec. 206(b)(1), amended subpara. (b)(5)(A), effective for transfers occurring after 12/31/75.

Prior to amendment, subpara. (b)(5)(A) read as follows:

"(A) Certain corporate transactions. In the case of a transfer described in subsection (d)(3) to which section 371(a), 374(a), or 381 applies, the acquiring corporation shall succeed to and take into account as of the close of the day of distribution or transfer, the excess deductions account of the transferor."

—P.L. 94-455, Sec. 206(b)(2), added the sentence at the end of para. (b)(3), effective for transfers occurring after 12/31/75.

—P.L. 94-455, Sec. 1402(b)(1)(Z), substituted "9 months" for "6 months" in para. (e)(1), effective for tax. yrs. begin. in 1977.

—P.L. 94-455, Sec. 1402(b)(2), substituted "1 year" for "9 months" in para. (e)(1), effective for tax. yrs. begin. after 12/31/77.

—P.L. 94-455, Sec. 1901(b)(3)(K), substituted "ordinary income" for "gain from the sale or exchange of property which is neither a capital asset nor property described in section 1231" in subparas. (b)(3)(B), (c)(1)(B), and (c)(2)(A), effective for tax. yrs. begin. after 12/31/76.

—P.L. 94-455, Sec. 1906(b)(13)(A), substituted "Secretary" for "Secretary or his delegate" each place it appeared in Code Sec. 1251, effective for tax. yrs. begin. after 12/31/76.

In **1971**, P.L. 92-178, Sec. 305, replaced the last sentence of subpara. (b)(2)(B) with two new sentences, effective for tax. yrs. end. after 12/10/71.

Prior to deletion, the last sentence of subpara. (b)(2)(B) read as follows:

"This subparagraph shall not apply to an electing small business corporation for a taxable year if on any day of such year a shareholder of such corporation is an individual who, for his taxable year with which or within which the taxable year of the corporation ends, has a farm net loss."

In **1969**, P.L. 91-172, Sec. 211(a), added Code Sec. 1251, effective for tax. yrs. begin. after 12/31/69.

Sec. 1252. Gain from disposition of farm land.
(a) General rule.

(1) Ordinary income. Except as otherwise provided in this section, if farm land which the taxpayer has held for less than 10 years is disposed of during a taxable year beginning after December 31, 1969, the lower of—

(A) the applicable percentage of the aggregate of the deductions allowed under sections 175 (relating to soil and water conservation expenditures) and 182 (as in effect on the day before the date of the enactment [10/22/86] of the Tax Reform Act of 1986) for expenditures made by the taxpayer after December 31, 1969, with respect to the farm land, or

(B) the excess of—

(i) the amount realized (in the case of a sale, exchange, or involuntary conversion), or the fair market value of the farm land (in the case of any other disposition), over

(ii) the adjusted basis of such land,

shall be treated as ordinary income. Such gain shall be recognized notwithstanding any other provision of this subtitle.

(2) Farm land. For purposes of this section, the term "farm land" means any land with respect to which deductions have been allowed under sections 175 (relating to soil and water conservation expenditures) or 182 (relating to expenditures by farmers for clearing land).

(3) Applicable percentage. For purposes of this section—

If the farm land is disposed of—	The applicable percentage is—
Within 5 years after the date it was acquired	100 percent.
Within the sixth year after it was acquired	80 percent.
Within the seventh year after it was acquired	60 percent.
Within the eighth year after it was acquired	40 percent.
Within the ninth year after it was acquired	20 percent.
10 years or more years after it was acquired	0 percent.

(b) Special rules.

Under regulations prescribed by the Secretary, rules similar to the rules of section 1245 shall be applied for purposes of this section.

In **1986**, P.L. 99-514, Sec. 402(b)(2), substituted "(as in effect on the day before the date of the enactment of the Tax Reform Act of 1986)" for "(relating to expenditures by farmers for clearing land)", in subpara. (a)(1)(A), effective for amounts paid or incurred after 12/31/85, in tax. yrs. end. after 12/31/85.

In **1984**, P.L. 98-369, Sec. 492(b)(5), deleted ", except that this section shall not apply to the extent section 1251 applies to such gain" after "this subtitle" in para. (a)(1), effective for tax. yrs. begin. after 12/31/83.

In **1976**, P.L. 94-455, Sec. 1901(b)(3)(K), substituted "ordinary income" for "gain from the sale or exchange of property which is neither a capital asset nor property described in section 1231" in clause (a)(1)(B)(ii), effective for tax. yrs. begin. after 12/31/76.

—P.L. 94-455, Sec. 1906(b)(13)(A), substituted "Secretary" for "Secretary or his delegate" in subsec. (b), effective for tax. yrs. begin. after 12/31/76.

In **1969**, P.L. 91-172, Sec. 214(a), added Code Sec. 1252, effective for tax. yrs. begin. after 12/31/69.

Sec. 1253. Transfers of franchises, trademarks, and trade names.
(a) General rule.

A transfer of a franchise, trademark, or trade name shall not be treated as a sale or exchange of a capital asset if the transferor retains any significant power, right, or continuing interest with respect to the subject matter of the franchise, trademark, or trade name.

(b) Definitions.
For purposes of this section—
(1) Franchise. The term "franchise" includes an agreement which gives one of the parties to the agreement the right to distribute, sell, or provide goods, services, or facilities, within a specified area.
(2) Significant power, right, or continuing interest. The term "significant power, right, or continuing interest" includes, but is not limited to, the following rights with respect to the interest transferred:
(A) A right to disapprove any assignment of such interest, or any part thereof.
(B) A right to terminate at will.
(C) A right to prescribe the standards of quality of products used or sold, or of services furnished, and of the equipment and facilities used to promote such products or services.
(D) A right to require that the transferee sell or advertise only products or services of the transferor.
(E) A right to require that the transferee purchase substantially all of his supplies and equipment from the transferor.
(F) A right to payments contingent on the productivity, use, or disposition of the subject matter of the interest transferred, if such payments constitute a substantial element under the transfer agreement.
(3) Transfer. The term "transfer" includes the renewal of a franchise, trademark, or trade name.
(c) Treatment of contingent payments by transferor. Amounts received or accrued on account of a transfer, sale, or other disposition of a franchise, trademark, or trade name which are contingent on the productivity, use, or disposition of the franchise, trademark, or trade name transferred shall be treated as amounts received or accrued from the sale or other disposition of property which is not a capital asset.
(d) Treatment of payments by transferee.
(1) Contingent serial payments.
(A) In general. Any amount described in subparagraph (B) which is paid or incurred during the taxable year on account of a transfer, sale, or other disposition of a franchise, trademark, or trade name shall be allowed as a deduction under section 162(a) (relating to trade or business expenses).
(B) Amounts to which paragraph applies. An amount is described in this subparagraph if it—
(i) is contingent on the productivity, use, or disposition of the franchise, trademark, or trade name, and
(ii) is paid as part of a series of payments—
(I) which are payable not less frequently than annually throughout the entire term of the transfer agreement, and
(II) which are substantially equal in amount (or payable under a fixed formula).
(2) Other payments. Any amount paid or incurred on account of a transfer, sale, or other disposition of a franchise, trademark, or trade name to which paragraph (1) does not apply shall be treated as an amount chargeable to capital account.
(3) Renewals, etc. For purposes of determining the term of a transfer agreement under this section, there shall be taken into account all renewal options (and any other period for which the parties reasonably expect the agreement to be renewed).

(e) Repealed.

In 2004, P.L. 108-357, Sec. 886(b)(3), deleted subsec. (e), effective for property acquired after 10/22/2004.
Prior to deletion, subsec. (e) read as follows:
"(e) Exception. This section shall not apply to the transfer of a franchise to engage in professional football, basketball, baseball, or other professional sport."
In 1996, P.L. 104-188, Sec. 1703(l), amended Sec. 13261(g)(2)(A)(iii), P.L. 103-66, by substituting "by the taxpayer or a related person" for "by the taxpayer", see below.
—P.L. 104-188, Sec. 1704(t)(47), amended Sec. 11701(i) of P.L. 101-508, by substituting "subsection" for "section" in the material to be stricken, see below.
In 1993, P.L. 103-66, Sec. 13261(c), deleted paras. (d)(2), (3), (4), and (5) and added paras. (d)(2) and (3), effective for property acquired after 8/10/93, except as provided in Sec. 13261(g)(2) [as amended by Sec. 1703(l) of P.L. 104-188, see above] and(3) of this Act which reads as follows:
"(2) Election to have amendments apply to property acquired after July 25, 1991.
"(A) In general. If an election under this paragraph applies to the taxpayer—
"(i) the amendments made by this section shall apply to property acquired by the taxpayer after July 25, 1991,
"(ii) subsection (c)(1)(A) of section 197 of the Internal Revenue Code of 1986 (as added by this section) (and so much of subsection (f)(9)(A) of such section 197 as precedes clause (i) thereof) shall be applied with respect to the taxpayer by treating July 25, 1991, as the date of the enactment of such section, and
"(iii) in applying subsection (f)(9) of such section, with respect to any property acquired by the taxpayer or a related person on or before the date of the enactment of this Act, only holding or use on July 25, 1991, shall be taken into account.
"(B) Election. An election under this paragraph shall be made at such time and in such manner as the Secretary of the Treasury or his delegate may prescribe. Such an election by any taxpayer, once made—
"(i) may be revoked only with the consent of the Secretary, and
"(ii) shall apply to the taxpayer making such election and any other taxpayer under common control with the taxpayer (within the meaning of subparagraphs (A) and (B) of section 41(f)(1) of such Code) at any time after August 2, 1993, and on or before the date on which such election is made.
"(3) Elective binding contract exception.
"(A) In general. The amendments made by this section shall not apply to any acquisition of property by the taxpayer if—
"(i) such acquisition is pursuant to a written binding contract in effect on the date of the enactment of this Act and at all times thereafter before such acquisition,
"(ii) an election under paragraph (2) does not apply to the taxpayer, and
"(iii) the taxpayer makes an election under this paragraph with respect to such contract.
"(B) Election. An election under this paragraph shall be made at such time and in such manner as the Secretary of the Treasury or his delegate shall prescribe. Such an election, once made—
"(i) may be revoked only with the consent of the Secretary, and
"(ii) shall apply to all property acquired pursuant to the contract with respect to which such election was made."
Prior to deletion, paras. (d)(2), (3), (4), and (5) read as follows:
"(2) Certain payments in discharge of principal sums.
"(A) In general. If a transfer of a franchise, trademark, or trade name is not (by reason of the application of subsection (a)) treated as a sale or exchange of a capital asset, any payment not described in paragraph (1) which is made in discharge of a principal sum agreed upon in the transfer agreement shall be allowed as a deduction—
"(i) in the case of a single payment made in discharge of such principal sum, ratably over the taxable years in the period beginning with the taxable year in which the payment is made and ending with the ninth succeeding taxable year or ending with the last taxable year beginning in the period of the transfer agreement, whichever period is shorter;
"(ii) in the case of a payment which is one of a series of approximately equal payments made in discharge of such principal sum, which are payable over—
"(I) the period of the transfer agreement, or
"(II) a period of more than 10 taxable years, whether ending before or after the end of the period of the transfer agreement,
in the taxable year in which the payment is made; and
"(iii) in the case of any other payment, in the taxable year or years specified in regulations prescribed by the Secretary, consistently with the preceding provisions of this paragraph.
"(B) $100,000 limitation on deductibility of principal sum. Subparagraph (A) shall not apply if the principal sum referred to in such subparagraph exceeds $100,000. For purposes of the preceding sentence, all payments which are part of the same transaction (or a series of related transactions) shall be taken into account as payments with respect to each such transaction.
"(3) Other payments.
"(A) In general. Any amount paid or incurred on account of a transfer, sale, or other disposition of a franchise, trademark, or trade name to which paragraph (1) or (2) does not apply shall be treated as an amount chargeable to capital account.
"(B) Election to recover amounts over 25 years.
"(i) In general. If the taxpayer elects the application of this subparagraph, an amount chargeable to capital account—
"(I) to which paragraph (1) would apply but for subparagraph (B)(ii) thereof, or

"(II) to which paragraph (2) would apply but for subparagraph (B) thereof, shall be allowed as a deduction ratably over the 25-year period beginning with the taxable year in which the transfer occurs.

"(ii) Consistent treatment. An election under clause (i) shall apply to all amounts which are part of the same transaction (or a series of related transactions).

"(4) Renewals, etc. For purposes of determining the term of a transfer agreement under this section or any period of amortization under this subtitle for any payment described in this section, there shall be taken into account all renewal options (and any other period for which the parties reasonably expect the agreement to be renewed).

"(5) Certain rules made applicable. Rules similar to the rules of section 168(i)(7) shall apply for purposes of this subsection."

In 1990, P.L. 101-508, Sec. 11701(i), [as amended by Sec. 1704(t)(47) of P.L. 104-188, see above] substituted "under this section or any period of amortization under this subtitle for any payment described in this section" for "or any period of amortization under this subsection" in para. (d)(4), effective for transfers after 10/2/89, except as provided in Sec. 7622(c)(2) [sic 7622(e)(2)] of P.L. 101-239, reproduced below.

In 1989, P.L. 101-239, Sec. 7622(a), amended para. (d)(1) . . . Sec. 7622(b)(1), added subpara. (d)(2)(B) . . . Sec. 7622(b)(2)(A), substituted "(2) Certain payments in discharge of principal sums. (A) In general." for "(2) Other payments." in para. (d)(2) . . . Sec. 7622(b)(2)(B), redesignated subparas. (d)(2)(A), (B), and (C) as clauses (d)(2)(A)(i), (ii), and (iii), and redesignated clauses (d)(2)(B)(i) and (ii) as subclauses (d)(2)(A)(ii)(I) and (II) . . . Sec. 7622(c), added paras. (d)(3), (4) and (5), effective for transfers after 10/2/89, except as provided in Sec. 7622(c)(2) [sic 7622(e)(2)] of this Act, which reads as follows:

"(2) Binding contract.—The amendments made by this section [Sec. 7622] shall not apply to any transfer pursuant to a written binding contract in effect on October 2, 1989, and at all times thereafter before the transfer."

Prior to amendment, para. (d)(1) read as follows:

"(1) Contingent payments. Amounts paid or incurred during the taxable year on account of a transfer, sale, or other disposition of a franchise, trademark, or trade name which are contingent on the productivity, use, or disposition of the franchise, trademark, or trade name transferred shall be allowed as a deduction under section 162(a) (relating to trade or business expenses)."

In 1976, P.L. 94-455, Sec. 1906(b)(13)(A), substituted "Secretary" for "Secretary or his delegate" in subpara. (d)(2)(C), effective for tax. yrs. begin. after 12/31/76.

In 1969, P.L. 91-172, Sec. 516(c)(1), added Code Sec. 1253, effective for transfers made after 12/31/69, except that Sec. 516(d)(3) of this Act provides that para. (d)(1) shall, at the election of the taxpayer (made at such time and in such manner as the Secretary or his delegate may by regulations prescribe), apply to transfers before 1/1/70, but only for payments made in tax. yrs. end. after 12/31/69, and begin. before 1/1/80.

Sec. 1254. Gain from disposition of interest in oil, gas, geothermal, or other mineral properties.

(a) General rule.

(1) Ordinary income. If any section 1254 property is disposed of, the lesser of—

(A) the aggregate amount of—

(i) expenditures which have been deducted by the taxpayer or any person under section 263, 616, or 617 with respect to such property and which, but for such deduction, would have been included in the adjusted basis of such property, and

(ii) the deductions for depletion under section 611 which reduced the adjusted basis of such property, or

(B) the excess of—

(i) in the case of—

(I) a sale, exchange, or involuntary conversion, the amount realized, or

(II) in the case of any other disposition, the fair market value of such property, over

(ii) the adjusted basis of such property,

shall be treated as gain which is ordinary income. Such gain shall be recognized notwithstanding any other provision of this subtitle.

(2) Disposition of portion of property. For purposes of paragraph (1)—

(A) In the case of the disposition of a portion of section 1254 property (other than an undivided interest), the entire amount of the aggregate expenditures or deductions described in paragraph (1)(A) with respect to such property shall be treated as allocable to such portion to the extent of the amount of the gain to which paragraph (1) applies.

(B) In the case of the disposition of an undivided interest in a section 1254 property (or a portion thereof), a proportionate part of the expenditures or deductions described in paragraph (1)(A) with respect to such property shall be treated as allocable to such undivided interest to the extent of the amount of the gain to which paragraph (1) applies.

This paragraph shall not apply to any expenditures to the extent the taxpayer establishes to the satisfaction of the Secretary that such expenditures do not relate to the portion (or interest therein) disposed of.

(3) Section 1254 property. The term " section 1254 property" means any property (within the meaning of section 614) if—

(A) any expenditures described in paragraph (1)(A) are properly chargeable to such property, or

(B) the adjusted basis of such property includes adjustments for deductions for depletion under section 611.

(4) Adjustment for amounts included in gross income under section 617(b)(1)(A). The amount of the expenditures referred to in paragraph (1)(A)(i) shall be properly adjusted for amounts included in gross income under section 617(b)(1)(A).

(b) Special rules under regulations.

Under regulations prescribed by the Secretary—

(1) rules similar to the rule of subsection (g) of section 617 and to the rules of subsections (b) and (c) of section 1245 shall be applied for purposes of this section; and

(2) in the case of the sale or exchange of stock in an S corporation, rules similar to the rules of section 751 shall be applied to that portion of the excess of the amount realized over the adjusted basis of the stock which is attributable to expenditures referred to in subsection (a)(1)(A) of this section.

In 1988, P.L. 100-647, Sec. 1004(c), added para. (a)(4), effective for any disposition of property which is placed in service by the taxpayer after 12/31/86, except as provided in Sec. 413(c)(2) of P.L. 99-514, reproduced below.

In 1986, P.L. 99-514, Sec. 413(a), amended Code Sec. 1254, effective for any disposition of property which is placed in service by the taxpayer after 12/31/86. Sec. 413(c)(2) of this Act provides:

"(2) Exception for binding contracts. The amendments made by this section shall not apply to any disposition of property placed in service after December 31, 1986, if such property was acquired pursuant to a written contract which was entered into before September 26, 1985, and which was binding at all times thereafter."

Prior to amendment, Code Sec. 1254 read as follows:

"Sec. 1254. Gain from disposition of interest in oil, gas, or geothermal property.

"(a) General rule.

"(1) Ordinary income. If oil, gas, or geothermal property is disposed of after December 31, 1975, the lower of—

"(A) the aggregate amount of expenditures after December 31, 1975, which are allocable to such property and which have been deducted as intangible drilling and development costs under section 263(c) by the taxpayer or any other person and which (but for being so deducted) would be reflected in the adjusted basis of such property, adjusted as provided in paragraph (4), or

"(B) the excess of—

"(i) the amount realized (in the case of a sale, exchange, or involuntary conversion), or the fair market value of the interest (in the case of any other disposition), over

"(ii) the adjusted basis of such interest,

shall be treated as gain which is ordinary income. Such gain shall be recognized notwithstanding any other provision of this subtitle.

"(2) Disposition of portion of property. For purposes of paragraph (1)—

"(A) In the case of the disposition of a portion of an oil, gas, or geothermal property (other than an undivided interest), the entire amount of the aggregate expenditures described in paragraph (1)(A) with respect to such property shall be treated as allocable to such portion to the extent of the amount of the gain to which paragraph (1) applies.

"(B) In the case of the disposition of an undivided interest in an oil, gas, or geothermal property (or a portion thereof), a proportionate part of the expenditures described in paragraph (1)(A) with respect to such property shall be treated as allocable to such undivided interest to the extent of the amount of the gain to which paragraph (1) applies.

This paragraph shall not apply to any expenditures to the extent the taxpayer establishes to the satisfaction of the Secretary that such expenditures do not relate to the portion (or interest therein) disposed of.

"(3) Oil, gas, or geothermal property. The term 'oil, gas, or geothermal property' means any property (within the meaning of section 614) to which any expenditures described in paragraph (1)(A) are properly chargeable.

"(4) Special rule for paragraph (1)(A). In applying paragraph (1)(A), the amount deducted for intangible drilling and development costs and allocable to the interest disposed of shall be reduced by the amount (if any) by which the deduction for depletion under section 611 with respect to such interest would have been increased if such costs incurred (after December 31, 1975) had been charged to capital account rather than deducted.

"(b) Special rules under regulations.

"Under regulations prescribed by the Secretary—

"(1) rules similar to the rules of subsection (g) of section 617 and to the rules of subsections (b) and (c) of section 1245 shall be applied for purposes of this section; and

"(2) in the case of the sale or exchange of stock in an S corporation rules similar to the rules of section 751 shall be applied to that portion of the excess of the amount realized over the adjusted basis of the stock which is attributable to expenditures referred to in subsection (a)(1)(A) of this section."

In 1982, P.L. 97-354, Sec. 5(a)(37), substituted "an S corporation," for "an electing small business corporation (as defined in section 1371(b))," in para. (b)(2), effective for tax. yrs., begin. after 12/31/82.

In 1978, P.L. 95-618, Sec. 402(c)(1), (2), and (3), substituted "oil, gas, or geothermal" for "oil or gas" in paras. (a)(1), (2) and (3) and in the heading of Code Sec. 1254, effective for wells commenced on or after 10/1/78, in tax. yrs. end. on or after 10/1/78. Sec. 402(e)(2) of the Act provides:

"(2) Election. The taxpayer may elect to capitalize or deduct any costs to which section 263(c) of the Internal Revenue Code of 1954 applies by reason of the amendments made by this section. Any such election shall be made before the expiration of the time for filing claim for credit or refund of any overpayment of tax imposed by chapter 1 of such Code with respect to the taxpayer's first taxable year to which the amendments made by this section apply and for which he pays or incurs costs to which such section 263(c) applies by reason of the amendments made by this section. Any election under this paragraph may be changed or revoked at any time before the expiration of the time referred to in the preceding sentence, but after the expiration of such time such election may not be changed or revoked."

In 1976, P.L. 94-455, Sec. 205(a), added Code Sec. 1254, for tax. yrs. end. after '75.

Sec. 1255. Gain from disposition of section 126 property.

(a) General rule.

(1) Ordinary income. Except as otherwise provided in this section, if section 126 property is disposed of, the lower of—

(A) the applicable percentage of the aggregate payments, with respect to such property, excluded from gross income under section 126, or

(B) the excess of—

(i) the amount realized (in the case of a sale, exchange, or involuntary conversion), or the fair market value of such section 126 property (in the case of any other disposition), over

(ii) the adjusted basis of such property,

shall be treated as ordinary income. Such gain shall be recognized notwithstanding any other provision of this subtitle, except that this section shall not apply to the extent such gain is recognized as ordinary income under any other provision of this part.

(2) Section 126 property. For purposes of this section, "section 126 property" means any property acquired, improved, or otherwise modified by the application of payments excluded from gross income under section 126.

(3) Applicable percentage. For purposes of this section, if section 126 property is disposed of less than 10 years after the date of receipt of payments excluded from gross income under section 126, the applicable percentage is 100 percent. If section 126 property is disposed of more than 10 years after such date, the applicable percentage is 100 percent reduced (but not below zero) by 10 percent for each year or part thereof in excess of 10 years such property was held after the date of receipt of the payments.

(b) Special rules.

Under regulations prescribed by the Secretary—

(1) rules similar to the rules applicable under section 1245 shall be applied for purposes of this section, and

> • **Caution:** Code Sec. 1255(b)(2), following, was amended by Sec. 302(e)(4)(B)(ii), P.L. 108-27. These provisions generally sunset for tax years beginning after 12/31/2012. For specific sunset provisions see Sec. 303, P.L. 108-27, as amended by Sec. 102(a), P.L. 111-312, reproduced in history notes for this Code Sec.

(2) for purposes of sections 170(e) and 751(c), amounts treated as ordinary income under this section shall be treated in the same manner as amounts treated as ordinary income under section 1245.

In 2010, P.L. 111-312, Sec. 102(a), substituted "December 31, 2012" for "December 31, 2010" in Sec. 303 of P.L. 108-27 [see below] effective as if included in the enactment of P.L. 108-27, 5/28/2003.

In 2006, P.L. 109-222, Sec. 102, substituted "December 31, 2010" for "December 31, 2008" in Sec. 303 of P.L. 108-27 [see below], effective 5/17/2006.

In 2004, P.L. 108-311, Sec. 402(a)(6), of this Act [which amended Sec. 302(f)(2) of P.L. 108-27, see below], provides:

"(2) Pass-thru entities. In the case of a pass-thru entity described in subparagraph (A), (B), (C), (D), (E), or (F) of section 1(h)(10) of the Internal Revenue Code of 1986, as amended by this Act, the amendments made by this section shall apply to taxable years ending after December 31, 2002; except that dividends received by such an entity on or before such date shall not be treated as qualified dividend income (as defined in section 1(h)(11)(B) of such Code, as added by this Act)."

In 2003, P.L. 108-27, Sec. 302(e)(4)(B)(ii), deleted ", 341(e)(12)," after "sections 170(e)" in para. (b)(2), effective for tax. yrs. begin. after 12/31/2002. Sec. 302(f)(2), of this Act [prior to amendment by Sec. 402(a)(6) of P.L. 108-311 see above] provides:

"(2) Regulated investment companies and real estate investment trusts. In the case of a regulated investment company or a real estate investment trust, the amendments made by this section shall apply to taxable years ending after December 31, 2002; except that dividends received by such a company or trust on or before such date shall not be treated as qualified dividend income (as defined in section 1(h)(11)(B) of the Internal Revenue Code of 1986, as added by this Act)."

—P.L. 108-27, Sec. 303, of this Act [as amended by Sec. 102, P.L. 109-222, and Sec. 102(a), P.L. 111-312, see above], reads as follows:

"SEC. 303. SUNSET OF TITLE. All provisions of, and amendments made by, this title [Secs. 301 and 302] shall not apply to taxable years beginning after December 31, 2012, and the Internal Revenue Code of 1986 shall be applied and administered to such years as if such provisions and amendments had never been enacted."

In 1988, P.L. 100-647, Sec. 1005(c)(10), deleted "section" before "163(d)," in Sec. 511(d)(2)(A) of P.L. 99-514, see below.

In 1986, P.L. 99-514, Sec. 511(d)(2)(A), [as amended by Sec. 1005(c)(10) of P.L. 100-647, see above] deleted "163(d)," before "170(e)," in para. (b)(2), effective for tax. yrs. begin. after 12/31/86.

—P.L. 99-514, Sec. 631(e)(14), deleted "453B(d)(2)," after "341(e)(12)," in para. (b)(2), effective as provided in Sec. 633(a) of this Act, reproduced in note following Code Sec. 897 and Sec. 633(e) of this Act reproduced in note following Code Sec. 336.

In 1980, P.L. 96-471, Sec. 2(b)(6), substituted "453B(d)(2)" for "453(d)(4)(B)" in para. (b)(2), effective dispositions made after 10/19/80 in tax. yrs. end. after 10/19/80.

—P.L. 96-222, Sec. 105(a)(7)(B), amended clause (a)(1)(B)(ii) and added "shall be treated as ordinary income. Such gain shall be recognized notwithstanding any other provision of this subtitle, except that this section shall not apply to the extent such gain is recognized as ordinary income under any other provision of this part." in subpara. (a)(1)(B) following clause (a)(1)(B)(ii) [as amended by this Sec., above] ... Sec. 105(a)(7)(D), substituted "(2) for purposes of sections 163(d), 170(e), 341(e)(12), 453(d)(4)(B), and 751(c)," for "(2)" in para. (b)(2), effective for grants made under the programs after 9/30/79.

Prior to amendment, clause (a)(1)(B)(ii) read as follows:

"(ii) the adjusted basis of such property shall be treated as ordinary income."

In 1978, P.L. 95-600, Sec. 543(c)(1), added Code Sec. 1255, effective for grants made under the programs after 9/30/79.

Capital gains and losses

Sec. 1256. Section 1256 contracts marked to market.
(a) General rule.
For purposes of this subtitle—
(1) each section 1256 contract held by the taxpayer at the close of the taxable year shall be treated as sold for its fair market value on the last business day of such taxable year (and any gain or loss shall be taken into account for the taxable year),
(2) proper adjustment shall be made in the amount of any gain or loss subsequently realized for gain or loss taken into account by reason of paragraph (1),
(3) any gain or loss with respect to a section 1256 contract shall be treated as—
   (A) short-term capital gain or loss, to the extent of 40 percent of such gain or loss, and
   (B) long-term capital gain or loss, to the extent of 60 percent of such gain or loss, and
(4) if all the offsetting positions making up any straddle consist of section 1256 contracts to which this section applies (and such straddle is not part of a larger straddle), sections 1092 and 263(g) shall not apply with respect to such straddle.

(b) Section 1256 contract defined.
(1) **In general.** For popuse of this section, the term "section 1256 contract" means—
   (A) any regulated futures contract,
   (B) any foreign currency contract,
   (C) any nonequity option,
   (D) any dealer equity option, and
   (E) any dealer securities futures contract.
(2) **Exceptions.** The term "section 1256 contract" shall not include—
   (A) any securities futures contract or option on such a contract unless such contract or option is a dealer securities futures contract, or
   (B) any interest rate swap, currency swap, basis swap, interest rate cap, interest rate floor, commodity swap, equity swap, equity index swap, credit default swap, or similar agreement.

(c) Terminations, etc.
(1) **In general.** The rules of paragraphs (1), (2), and (3) of subsection (a) shall also apply to the termination (or transfer) during the taxable year of the taxpayer's obligation (or rights) with respect to a section 1256 contract by offsetting, by taking or making delivery, by exercise or being exercised, by assignment or being assigned, by lapse, or otherwise.
(2) **Special rule where taxpayer takes delivery on or exercises part of straddle.** If—
   (A) 2 or more section 1256 contracts are part of a straddle (as defined in section 1092(c)), and
   (B) the taxpayer takes delivery under or exercises any of such contracts,
then, for purposes of this section, each of the other such contracts shall be treated as terminated on the day on which the taxpayer took delivery.
(3) **Fair market value taken into account.** For purposes of this subsection, fair market value at the time of the termination (or transfer) shall be taken into account.

(d) Elections with respect to mixed straddles.
(1) **Election.** The taxpayer may elect to have this section not to apply to all section 1256 contracts which are part of a mixed straddle.
(2) **Time and manner.** An election under paragraph (1) shall be made at such time and in such manner as the Secretary may by regulations prescribe.

(3) **Election revocable only with consent.** An election under paragraph (1) shall apply to the taxpayer's taxable year for which made and to all subsequent taxable years, unless the Secretary consents to a revocation of such election.
(4) **Mixed straddle.** For purposes of this subsection, the term "mixed straddle" means any straddle (as defined in section 1092(c))—
   (A) at least 1 (but not all) of the positions of which are section 1256 contracts, and
   (B) with respect to which each position forming part of such straddle is clearly identified, before the close of the day on which the first section 1256 contract forming part of the straddle is acquired (or such earlier time as the Secretary may prescribe by regulations), as being part of such straddle.

(e) Mark to market not to apply to hedging transactions.
(1) **Section not to apply.** Subsection (a) shall not apply in the case of a hedging transaction.
(2) **Definition of hedging transaction.** For purposes of this subsection, the term "hedging transaction" means any hedging transaction (as defined in section 1221(b)(2)(A)) if, before the close of the day on which such transaction was entered into (or such earlier time as the Secretary may prescribe by regulations), the taxpayer clearly identifies such transaction as being a hedging transaction.
(3) **Special rule for syndicates.**
   (A) In general. Notwithstanding paragraph (2), the term "hedging transaction" shall not include any transaction entered into by or for a syndicate.
   (B) Syndicate defined. For purposes of subparagraph (A), the term "syndicate" means any partnership or other entity (other than a corporation which is not an S corporation) if more than 35 percent of the losses of such entity during the taxable year are allocable to limited partners or limited entrepreneurs (within the meaning of section 464(e)(2)).
   (C) Holdings attributable to active management. For purposes of subparagraph (B), an interest in an entity shall not be treated as held by a limited partner or a limited entrepreneur (within the meaning of section 464(e)(2))—
      (i) for any period if during such period such interest is held by an individual who actively participates at all times during such period in the management of such entity,
      (ii) for any period if during such period such interest is held by the spouse, children, grandchildren, and parents of an individual who actively participates at all times during such period in the management of such entity,
      (iii) if such interest is held by an individual who actively participated in the management of such entity for a period of not less than 5 years,
      (iv) if such interest is held by the estate of an individual who actively participated in the management of such entity or is held by the estate of an individual if with respect to such individual such interest was at any time described in clause (ii), or
      (v) if the Secretary determines (by regulations or otherwise) that such interest should be treated as held by an individual who actively participates in the management of such entity, and that such entity and such interest are not used (or to be used) for tax-avoidance purposes.

For purposes of this subparagraph, a legally adopted child of an individual shall be treated as a child of such individual by blood.

(4) Limitation on losses from hedging transactions.

(A) In general.

(i) Limitation. Any hedging loss for a taxable year which is allocable to any limited partner or limited entrepreneur (within the meaning of paragraph (3)) shall be allowed only to the extent of the taxable income of such limited partner or entrepreneur for such taxable year attributable to the trade or business in which the hedging transactions were entered into. For purposes of the preceding sentence, taxable income shall be determined by not taking into account items attributable to hedging transactions.

(ii) Carryover of disallowed loss. Any hedging loss disallowed under clause (i) shall be treated as a deduction attributable to a hedging transaction allowable in the first succeeding taxable year.

(B) Exception where economic loss. Subparagraph (A)(i) shall not apply to any hedging loss to the extent that such loss exceeds the aggregate unrecognized gains from hedging transactions as of the close of the taxable year attributable to the trade or business in which the hedging transactions were entered into.

(C) Exception for certain hedging transactions. In the case of any hedging transaction relating to property other than stock or securities, this paragraph shall apply only in the case of a taxpayer described in section 465(a)(1).

(D) Hedging loss. The term "hedging loss" means the excess of—

(i) the deductions allowable under this chapter for the taxable year attributable to hedging transactions (determined without regard to subparagraph (A)(i)), over

(ii) income received or accrued by the taxpayer during such taxable year from such transactions.

(E) Unrecognized gain. The term "unrecognized gain" has the meaning given to such term by section 1092(a)(3).

(f) Special rules.

(1) Denial of capital gains treatment for property identified as part of a hedging transaction. For purposes of this title, gain from any property shall in no event be considered as gain from the sale or exchange of a capital asset if such property was at any time personal property (as defined in section 1092(d)(1)) identified under subsection (e)(2) by the taxpayer as being part of a hedging transaction.

(2) Subsection (a)(3) not to apply to ordinary income property. Paragraph (3) of subsection (a) shall not apply to any gain or loss which, but for such paragraph, would be ordinary income or loss.

(3) Capital gain treatment for traders in section 1256 contracts.

(A) In general. For purposes of this title, gain or loss from trading of section 1256 contracts shall be treated as gain or loss from the sale or exchange of a capital asset.

(B) Exception for certain hedging transactions. Subparagraph (A) shall not apply to any section 1256 contract to the extent such contract is held for purposes of hedging property if any loss with respect to such property in the hands of the taxpayer would be ordinary loss.

(C) Treatment of underlying property. For purposes of determining whether gain or loss with respect to any property is ordinary income or loss, the fact that the taxpayer is actively engaged in dealing in or trading section 1256 contracts related to such property shall not be taken into account.

(4) Special rule for dealer equity options and dealer securities futures contracts of limited partners or limited entrepreneurs. In the case of any gain or loss with respect to dealer equity options, or dealer securities futures contracts, which are allocable to limited partners or limited entrepreneurs (within the meaning of subsection (e)(3))—

(A) paragraph (3) of subsection (a) shall not apply to any such gain or loss, and

(B) all such gains or losses shall be treated as short-term capital gains or losses, as the case may be.

(5) Special rule related to losses. Section 1091 (relating to loss from wash sales of stock or securities) shall not apply to any loss taken into account by reason of paragraph (1) of subsection (a).

(g) Definitions.

For purposes of this section—

(1) Regulated futures contracts defined. The term "regulated futures contract" means a contract—

(A) with respect to which the amount required to be deposited and the amount which may be withdrawn depends on a system of marking to market, and

(B) which is traded on or subject to the rules of a qualified board or exchange.

(2) Foreign currency contract defined.

(A) Foreign currency contract. The term "foreign currency contract" means a contract—

(i) which requires delivery of, or the settlement of which depends on the value of, a foreign currency which is a currency in which positions are also traded through regulated futures contracts,

(ii) which is traded in the interbank market, and

(iii) which is entered into at arm's length at a price determined by reference to the price in the interbank market.

(B) Regulations. The Secretary shall prescribe such regulations as may be necessary or appropriate to carry out the purposes of subparagraph (A), including regulations excluding from the application of subparagraph (A) any contract (or type of contract) if its application thereto would be inconsistent with such purposes.

(3) Nonequity option. The term "nonequity option" means any listed option which is not an equity option.

(4) Dealer equity option. The term "dealer equity option" means, with respect to an options dealer, any listed option which—

(A) is an equity option,

(B) is purchased or granted by such options dealer in the normal course of his activity of dealing in options, and

(C) is listed on the qualified board or exchange on which such options dealer is registered.

(5) Listed option. The term "listed option" means any option (other than a right to acquire stock from the issuer) which is traded on (or subject to the rules of) a qualified board or exchange.

(6) Equity option. The term "equity option" means any option—

(A) to buy or sell stock, or

(B) the value of which is determined directly or indirectly by reference to any stock or any narrow-based security index (as defined in section 3(a)(55) of the Se-

Capital gains and losses   Code Sec. 1256

curities Exchange Act of 1934, as in effect on the date of the enactment of this paragraph).

The term "equity option" includes such an option on a group of stocks only if such group meets the requirements for a narrow-based security index (as so defined). The Secretary may prescribe regulations regarding the status of options the values of which are determined directly or indirectly by reference to any index which becomes (or ceases to be) a narrow-based security index (as so defined).

(7) Qualified board or exchange. The term "qualified board or exchange" means—

(A) a national securities exchange which is registered with the Securities and Exchange Commission,

(B) a domestic board of trade designated as a contract market by the Commodity Futures Trading Commission, or

(C) any other exchange, board of trade, or other market which the Secretary determines has rules adequate to carry out the purposes of this section.

(8) Options dealer.

(A) In general. The term "options dealer" means any person registered with an appropriate national securities exchange as a market maker or specialist in listed options.

(B) Persons trading in other markets. In any case in which the Secretary makes a determination under subparagraph (C) of paragraph (7), the term "options dealer" also includes any person whom the Secretary determines performs functions similar to the persons described in subparagraph (A). Such determinations shall be made to the extent appropriate to carry out the purposes of this section.

(9) Dealer securities futures contract.

(A) In general. The term "dealer securities futures contract" means, with respect to any dealer, any securities futures contract, and any option on such a contract, which—

(i) is entered into by such dealer (or, in the case of an option, is purchased or granted by such dealer) in the normal course of his activity of dealing in such contracts or options, as the case may be, and

(ii) is traded on a qualified board or exchange.

(B) Dealer. For purposes of subparagraph (A), a person shall be treated as a dealer in securities futures contracts or options on such contracts if the Secretary determines that such person performs, with respect to such contracts or options, as the case may be, functions similar to the functions performed by persons described in paragraph (8)(A). Such determination shall be made to the extent appropriate to carry out the purposes of this section.

(C) Securities futures contract. The term "securities futures contract" has the meaning given to such term by section 1234B.

In 2010, P.L. 111-203, Sec. 1601(a)(1), redesignated para. (b)(1)-(5) as subpara. (b)(1)(A)-(E) (as amended) . . . Sec. 1601(a)(2), substituted "(1) In general. For purposes of" for "For purposes of" in subsec. (b) . . . Sec. 1601(a)(3), deleted the last sentence in subsec. (b) and added para. (b)(2) (as amended), effective for tax. yrs. begin. after 7/21/2010.

Prior to deletion the last sentence in subsec. (b) read as follows:

"The term 'section 1256 contract' shall not include any securities futures contract or option on such a contract unless such contract or option is a dealer securities futures contract."

In 2005, P.L. 109-135, Sec. 412(oo), substituted "subsection (e)(2)" for "subsection (e)(2)(C)" in para. (f)(1), effective 12/21/2005.

In 2004, P.L. 108-311, Sec. 405(a)(2), added "The Secretary may prescribe regulations regarding the status of options the values of which are determined directly or indirectly by reference to any index which becomes (or ceases to be) a narrow-based security index (as so defined)." at the end of para. (g)(6), effective 12/21/2000 as provided in Sec. 401(j) of the Community Renewal Tax Relief Act of 2000, P.L. 106-554 [P.L. 106-554].

In 2002, P.L. 107-147, Sec. 416(b)(1), added para. (f)(5), effective for any sale after 11/10/88, in tax. yrs. end. after 11/10/88.

In 2000, P.L. 106-554, Sec. 1(a)(7), [which enacted into law Sec. 401(g)(1)(A) of P.L. 106-554] deleted "and" at the end of para. (b)(3), substituted ", and" for the period at the end of para. (b)(4), and added para. (b)(5) . . . Sec. 1(a)(7), [which enacted into law Sec. 401(g)(1)(B) of P.L. 106-554] added para. (g)(9) . . . Sec. 1(a)(7), [which enacted into law Sec. 401(g)(2)(A) of P.L. 106-554] added ", or dealer securities futures contracts," after "dealer equity options" in para. (f)(4) . . . Sec. 1(a)(7), [which enacted into law Sec. 401(g)(2)(B) of P.L. 106-554] added "and dealer securities futures contracts" after "dealer equity options" in the heading of para. (f)(4) . . . Sec. 1(a)(7), [which enacted into law Sec. 401(g)(3) of P.L. 106-554] amended para. (g)(6), effective 12/21/2000.

Prior to amendment, para. (g)(6) read as follows:

"(6) Equity option.

"(A) In general. Except as provided in subparagraph (B), the term 'equity option' means any option—

"(i) to buy or sell stock, or

"(ii) the value of which is determined directly or indirectly by reference to any stock (or group of stocks) or stock index.

"(B) Exception for certain options regulated by commodities futures trading commission. The term 'equity option' does not include any option with respect to any group of stocks or stock index if—

"(i) there is in effect a designation by the Commodities Futures Trading Commission of a contract market for a contract based on such group of stocks or index, or

"(ii) the Secretary determines that such option meets the requirements of law for such a designation."

—P.L. 106-554, Sec. 1(a)(7), [which enacted into law Sec. 401(g)(4) of P.L. 106-554] of this Act, reads as follows:

"(4) The Secretary of the Treasury or his delegate shall make the determinations under section 1256(g)(9)(B) of the Internal Revenue Code of 1986, as added by this Act, not later than July 1, 2001."

In 1999, P.L. 106-170, Sec. 532(b)(4), amended para. (e)(2), effective for any instrument held, acquired, or entered into, any transaction entered into, and supplies held or acquired on or after 12/17/99.

Prior to amendment, para. (e)(2) read as follows:

"(2) Definition of hedging transaction. For purposes of this subsection, the term 'hedging transaction' means any transaction if—

"(A) such transaction is entered into by the taxpayer in the normal course of the taxpayer's trade or business primarily—

"(i) to reduce risk of price change or currency fluctuations with respect to property which is held or to be held by the taxpayer, or

"(ii) to reduce risk of interest rate or price changes or currency fluctuations with respect to borrowings made or to be made, or obligations incurred or to be incurred, by the taxpayer,

"(B) the gain or loss on such transactions is treated as ordinary income or loss, and

"(C) before the close of the day on which such transaction was entered into (or such earlier time as the Secretary may prescribe by regulations), the taxpayer clearly identifies such transaction as being a hedging transaction."

In 1986, P.L. 99-514, Sec. 1261(c), deleted para. (e)(4) and redesignated para. (e)(5) as (e)(4), effective for tax. yrs. begin. after 12/31/86.

Prior to deletion, para. (e)(4) read as follows:

"(4) Special rule for banks. In the case of a bank (as defined in section 581), subparagraph (A) of paragraph (2) shall be applied without regard to clause (i) or (ii) thereof."

—P.L. 99-514, Sec. 1808(a)(1), added Sec. 102(j) of P.L. 98-369 [reproduced below], part of the special rules for the effective date of amendments made by Sec. 102 of P.L. 98-369.

In 1984, P.L. 98-369, Sec. 102(a)(1)(A), substituted "section 1256 contract" for "regulated futures contract" each place it appeared in Code Sec. 1256 . . . Sec. 102(a)(1)(B), substituted "section 1256 contracts" for "regulated futures contracts" each place it appeared in Code Sec. 1256 . . . Sec. 102(a)(2), amended subsec. (b) . . . Sec. 102(a)(3), amended subsec. (g) . . . Sec. 102(b), added paras. (f)(3) and (f)(4) . . . Sec. 102(e)(1)(A), substituted "by taking or making delivery, by exercise or being exercised, by assignment or being assigned, by lapse," for "by taking or making delivery," in para. (c)(1) . . . Sec. 102(e)(1)(B), substituted "takes delivery under or exercises" for "takes delivery under" in para. (c)(2) . . . Sec. 102(e)(1)(C), substituted "takes delivery on or exercises" for "takes delivery on" in the heading of para. (c)(2) . . . Sec. 102(e)(5), substituted "Section 1256 contracts" for "Regulated futures contracts" in the heading of Code Sec. 1256, effective for positions established after 7/18/84, in tax. yrs. end. after 7/18/84 and subject to the special rules and elections provided in Secs. 102(f)(2), (g), (h), (i) and (j) of this Act [as amended by Sec. 1808(a)(1) of P.L. 99-514, see above], which reads as follows:

"(f)(2) Special rule for options on regulated futures contracts.—In the case of any option with respect to a regulated futures contract (within the meaning of section 1256 of the Internal Revenue Code of 1954), the amendments made by this section shall apply to positions established after October 31, 1983, in taxable years ending after such date.

"(g) Elections with respect to property held on or before the date of the enactment of this act [7/18/84].—At the election of the taxpayer—

2,781

"(1) the amendments made by this section shall apply to all section 1256 contracts held by the taxpayer on the date of the enactment of this Act [7/18/84], effective for periods after such date in taxable years ending after such date, or

"(2) in lieu of an election under paragraph (1), the amendments made by this section shall apply to all section 1256 contracts held by the taxpayer at any time during the taxable year of the taxpayer which includes the date of the enactment of this Act.

"(h) Elections for installment payment of tax attributable to stock options. —

"(1) In general. — If the taxpayer makes an election under subsection (g)(2) and under this subsection —

"(A) the taxpayer may pay part or all the tax for the taxable year referred to in subsection (g)(2) in 2 or more (but not exceeding 5) equal installments, and

"(B) the maximum amount of tax which may be paid in installments under this subsection shall be the excess of —

"(i) the tax for such taxable year determined by taking into account subsection (g)(2), over

"(ii) the tax for such taxable year determined by taking into account subsection (g)(2) and by treating —

"(I) all section 1256 contracts which are stock options, and

"(II) any stock which was a part of a straddle including any such stock options, as having been acquired for a purchase price equal to their fair market value on the last business day of the preceding taxable year. Stock options and stock shall be taken into account under subparagraph (B)(ii) only if such options or stock were held on the last day of the preceding taxable year and only if income on such options or stock would have been ordinary income if such options or stock were sold at a gain on such last day.

"(2) Date for payment of installment —

"(A) If an election is made under this subsection, the first installment under paragraph (1) shall be paid on or before the due date for filing the return for the taxable year described in paragraph (1), and each succeeding installment shall be paid on or before the date which is 1 year after the date prescribed for payment of the preceding installment.

"(B) If a bankruptcy case or insolvency proceeding involving the taxpayer is commenced before the final installment is paid, the total amount of any unpaid installments shall be treated as due and payable on the day preceding the day on which such case or proceeding is commenced.

"(3) Interest imposed. — For purposes of section 6601 of the Internal Revenue Code of 1954, the time for payment of any tax with respect to which an election is made under this subsection shall be determined without regard to this subsection.

"(4) Form of election. — An election under this subsection shall be made not later than the time for filing the return for the taxable year described in paragraph (1) and shall be made in the manner and form required by regulations prescribed by Secretary of the Treasury or his delegate. The election shall set forth —

"(A) the amount determined under paragraph (1)(B) and the number of installments elected by the taxpayer,

"(B) the property described in paragraph (1)(B)(ii), and the date on which such property was acquired,

"(C) the fair market value of the property described in paragraph (1)(B)(ii) on the last business day of the taxable year preceding the taxable year described in paragraph (1), and

"(D) such other information for purposes of carrying out the provisions of this subsection as may be required by such regulations.

"(5) Delay of identification requirement. — Section 1256(e)(2)(C) of the Internal Revenue Code of 1954 shall not apply to any stock option or stock acquired on or before the 60th day after the date of the enactment of this Act.

"(i) Definitions. — For purposes of subsections (g) and (h) —

"(1) Section 1256 contract. — The term 'section 1256 contract' has the meaning given to such term by section 1256(b) of the Internal Revenue Code of 1954 (as amended by this section).

"(2) Stock option. — The term 'stock option' means any option to buy or sell stock.

"(j) Coordination of election under subsection (d)(3) with elections under subsections (g) and (h). —

"The Secretary of the Treasury or his delegate shall prescribe such regulations as may be necessary to coordinate the election provided by subsection (d)(3) with the elections provided by subsections (g) and (h)."

Prior to amendment, subsec. (b) read as follows:

"(b) Regulated futures contracts defined.

"For purposes of this section, the term 'regulated futures contract' means a contract —

"(1) with respect to which the amount required to be deposited and the amount which may be withdrawn depends on a system of marking to market; and

"(2) which is traded on or subject to the rules of a domestic board of trade designated as a contract market by the Commodity Futures Trading Commission or of any board of trade or exchange which the Secretary determines has rules adequate to carry out the purposes of this section.

Such term includes any foreign currency contract."

Prior to amendment, subsec. (g) read as follows:

"(g) Foreign currency contract defined.

"(1) Foreign currency contract. For purposes of this section, the term 'foreign currency contract' means a contract —

"(A) which requires delivery of, or the settlement of which depends on the value of, a foreign currency which is a currency in which positions are also traded through regulated futures contracts,

"(B) which is traded in the interbank market,

"(C) which is entered into at arm's length at a price determined by reference to the price in the interbank market.

"(2) Regulations. The Secretary shall prescribe such regulations as may be necessary or appropriate to carry out the purposes of paragraph (1), including regulations excluding from the application of paragraph (1) any contract (or type of contract) if its application thereto would be inconsistent with such purposes."

— P.L. 98-369, Sec. 104(a), added para. (e)(5), effective for tax. yrs. begin. after 12/31/84.

— P.L. 98-369, Sec. 107(c), added "(or such earlier time as the Secretary may prescribe by regulations)" after "acquired" in subpara. (d)(4)(B) . . . Sec. 107(d), added "(or such earlier time as the Secretary may prescribe by regulations)" after "entered into" in subpara. (e)(2)(C), effective for positions entered into after 7/18/84, in tax. yrs. end. after 7/18/84.

— P.L. 98-369, Sec. 722(a)(2), added ", or the settlement of which depends on the value of," after "delivery of" in subpara. (g)(1)(A) (before amendment by Sec. 102(a)(3), see above), effective for contracts entered into after 5/11/82.

In 1983, P.L. 97-448, Sec. 105(c)(1), amended subsec. (c) . . . Sec. 105(c)(2), substituted "the first regulated futures contract forming part of the straddle" for "such position" in subpara. (d)(4)(B) . . . Sec. 105(c)(3), added "(by regulations or otherwise)" after "determines" in clause (e)(3)(C)(v) . . . Sec. 105(c)(5)(A), deleted para. (b)(1) and redesignated paras. (b)(2) and (b)(3) as paras. (b)(1) and (b)(2) respectively, effective for property acquired and positions established by the taxpayer after 6/23/81, in tax. yrs. end. after 6/23/81.

Prior to amendment, subsec. (c) read as follows:

"(c) Terminations.

"The rules of paragraphs (1), (2), and (3) of subsection (a) shall also apply to the termination during the taxable year of the taxpayer's obligation with respect to a regulated futures contract by offsetting, by taking or making delivery, or otherwise. For purposes of the preceding sentence, fair market value at the time of the termination shall be taken into account."

Prior to deletion, para. (b)(1) read as follows:

"(1) which requires delivery of personal property (as defined in section 1092(d)(1)) or an interest in such property;"

— P.L. 97-448, Sec. 105(c)(5)(B), added the last sentence to subsec. (b) [as amended by Sec. 105(c)(5)(A) of this Act], see above . . . Sec. 105(c)(5)(C), added subsec. (g), effective for contracts entered into after 5/11/82, except as provided in Sec. 105(c)(5)(D)(ii) and (iii) of this Act which read as follows:

"(ii) Election by taxpayer of retroactive application. —

"(I) Retroactive application. — If the taxpayer so elects, the amendments made by subparagraphs (B) and (C) shall apply as if included within the amendments made by title V of the Economic Recovery Tax Act of 1981.

"(II) Additional choices with respect to 1981. — If the taxpayer held a foreign currency contract after December 31, 1980, and before June 24, 1981, and such taxpayer makes an election under subclause (I), such taxpayer may revoke any election made under section 508(c) or 509(a) of such Act, and may make an election under section 508(c) or 509(a) of such Act.

"(III) Additional choices apply to all regulated futures contracts. — Except as provided in subclause (IV), in the case of any taxpayer who makes an election under subclause (I), any election under section 508(c) or 509(a) of such Act or any revocation of such an election shall apply to all regulated futures contracts (including foreign currency contracts).

"(IV) Section 509(a) (3) and (4) not to apply to foreign currency contracts. — Paragraphs (3) and (4) of section 509(a) of such Act shall not apply to any foreign currency contract.

"(V) Time for making election or revocation. — Any election under subclause (I) and any election or revocation under subclause (II) may be made only within the 90-day period beginning on the date of the enactment of this Act. Any such action, once taken, shall be irrevocable.

"(VI) Definitions. — For purposes of this clause, the terms 'regulated futures contract' and 'foreign currency contract' have the same respective meanings as when used in section 1256 of the Internal Revenue Code of 1954 (as amended by this Act).

"(iii) Election by taxpayer with respect to positions held during taxable years ending after May 11, 1982. — In lieu of the election under clause (ii), a taxpayer may elect to have the amendments made by subparagraphs (B) and (C) applied to all positions held in taxable years ending after May 11, 1982, except that the provisions of section 509(a) (3) and (4) of the Economic Recovery Tax Act of 1981 shall not apply."

— P.L. 97-448, Sec. 105(c)(6), amended Sec. 509(b)(3) of P.L. 97-34, reproduced below.

Prior to amendment, Sec. 509(b)(3) of P.L. 97-34 read as follows:

"(3) the fair market value on the last business day of such taxable year for each regulated futures contract described in subparagraph (B), and"

In 1982, P.L. 97-354, Sec. 5(a)(38), substituted "an S corporation" for "an electing small business corporation within the meaning of section 1371(b)" in subpara. (e)(3)(B), effective for tax. yrs. begin. after 12/31/82.

In 1981, P.L. 97-34, Sec. 503(a), added new Code Sec. 1256, effective for property acquired and positions established by the taxpayer after 6/23/81, in tax. yrs. end. after 6/23/81.

— P.L. 97-34, Sec. 509, provides as follows:

"Sec. 509. Election for extension of time for payment and application of section 1256 for the taxable year including June 23, 1981.

"(a) Election.

"(1) In general. In the case of any taxable year beginning before June 23, 1981, and ending after June 22, 1981, the taxpayer may elect, in lieu of any election under section 508(c), to have this section apply to all regulated futures contracts held during such taxable year.

Capital gains and losses

"(2) Application of section 1256. If a taxpayer elects to have the provisions of this section apply to the taxable year described in paragraph (1).

"(A) the provisions of section 1256 of the Internal Revenue Code of 1954 (other than section 1256(e)(2)(C)) shall apply to regulated futures contracts held by the taxpayer at any time during such taxable year, and

"(B) for purposes of determining the rate of tax applicable to gains and losses from regulated futures contracts held at any time during such year, such gains and losses shall be treated as gain or loss from a sale or exchange occurring in a taxable year beginning in 1982.

"(3) Determination of deferred tax liability. If the taxpayer makes an election under this subsection.

"(A) the taxpayer may pay part or all of the tax for such year in two or more (but not exceeding five) equal installments;

"(B) the maximum amount of tax which may be paid in installments under this section shall be the excess of—

"(i) the tax for such year, determined by taking into account paragraph (2), over

"(ii) the tax for such year, determined by taking into account paragraph (2) and by treating all regulated futures contracts which were held by the taxpayer on the first day of the taxable year described in paragraph (1), and which were acquired before the first day of such taxable year, as having been acquired for a purchase price equal to their fair market value on the last business day of the preceding taxable year.

"(4) Date for payment of installment.

"(A) In the case of an election made under this subsection, the first installment under subsection (a)(3)(A) shall be paid on or before the due date for filing the return for the taxable year described in paragraph (1), and each succeeding installment shall be paid on or before the date which is one year after the date prescribed for payment of the preceding installment.

"(B) If a bankruptcy case or insolvency proceeding involving the taxpayer is commenced before the final installment is paid, the total amount of any unpaid installments shall be treated as due and payable on the day preceding the day on which such case or proceeding is commenced.

"(5) Interest imposed. For purposes of section 6601 of the Internal Revenue Code of 1954, the time for payment of any tax with respect to which an election is made under this subsection shall be determined without regard to this subsection.

"(b) Form of election.

"An election under this section shall be made not later than the time for filing the return for the taxable year made not later than the time for filing the return for the taxable year described in subsection (a)(1) and shall be made in the manner and form required by regulations prescribed by the Secretary. The election shall set forth—

"(1) the amount determined under subsection (a)(3)(B) and the number of installments elected by the taxpayer,

"(2) each regulated futures contract held by the taxpayer on the first day of the taxable year described in subsection (a)(1), and the date such contract was acquired,

"(3) the fair market value on the last business day of the preceding taxable year for each regulated futures contract described in paragraph (2), and

"(4) such other information for purposes of carrying out the provisions of this section as may be required by such regulations."

Sec. 1257. Disposition of converted wetlands or highly erodible croplands.

(a) Gain treated as ordinary income.

Any gain on the disposition of converted wetland or highly erodible cropland shall be treated as ordinary income. Such gain shall be recognized notwithstanding any other provision of this subtitle, except that this section shall not apply to the extent such gain is recognized as ordinary income under any other provision of this part.

(b) Loss treated as long-term capital loss.

Any loss recognized on the disposition of converted wetland or highly erodible cropland shall be treated as a long-term capital loss.

(c) Definitions.

For purposes of this section—

(1) Converted wetland. The term "converted wetland" means any converted wetland (as defined in section 1201(4) of the Food Security Act of 1985 (16 U.S.C. 3801(4))) held—

(A) by the person whose activities resulted in such land being converted wetland, or

(B) by any other person who at any time used such land for farming purposes.

(2) Highly erodible cropland. The term "highly erodible cropland" means any highly erodible cropland (as defined in section 1201(6) of the Food Security Act of 1985 (16 U.S.C. 3801(6))), if at any time the taxpayer used such land for farming purposes (other than the grazing of animals).

(3) Treatment of successors. If any land is converted wetland or highly erodible cropland in the hands of any person, such land shall be treated as converted wetland or highly erodible cropland in the hands of any other person whose adjusted basis in such land is determined (in whole or in part) by reference to the adjusted basis of such land in the hands of such person.

⎡ • *Caution:* Code Sec. 1257(d), following, was amended by Sec. 302(e)(4)(B)(ii), P.L. 108-27. These provisions generally sunset for tax years beginning after 12/31/2012. For specific sunset provisions see Sec. 303, P.L. 108-27, as amended by Sec. 102(a), P.L. 111-312, reproduced in history notes for this Code Sec. ⎦

(d) Special rules.

Under regulations prescribed by the Secretary, rules similar to the rules applicable under section 1245 shall apply for purposes of subsection (a). For purposes of sections 170(e) and 751(c), amounts treated as ordinary income under subsection (a) shall be treated in the same manner as amounts treated as ordinary income under section 1245.

In 2010, P.L. 111-312, Sec. 102(a), substituted "December 31, 2012" for "December 31, 2010" in Sec. 303, P.L. 108-27 [see below], effective as if included in the enactment of P.L. 108-27, 5/28/2003.

In 2006, P.L. 109-222, Sec. 102, substituted "December 31, 2010" for "December 31, 2008" in Sec. 303 of P.L. 108-27 [see below], effective 5/17/2006.

In 2004, P.L. 108-311, Sec. 402(a)(6), of this Act [which amended Sec. 302(f)(2) of P.L. 108-27, see below], provides:

"(2) Pass-thru entities. In the case of a pass-thru entity described in subparagraph (A), (B), (C), (D), (E), or (F) of section 1(h)(10) of the Internal Revenue Code of 1986, as amended by this Act, the amendments made by this section shall apply to taxable years ending after December 31, 2002; except that dividends received by such an entity on or before such date shall not be treated as qualified dividend income (as defined in section 1(h)(11)(B) of such Code, as added by this Act)."

In 2003, P.L. 108-27, Sec. 302(e)(4)(B)(ii), deleted ", 341(e)(12)," after "sections 170(e)" in subsec. (d), effective for tax. yrs. begin. after 12/31/2002. Sec. 302(f)(2), of this Act [prior to amendment by Sec. 402(a)(6) of P.L. 108-311 see above] provides:

"(2) Regulated investment companies and real estate investment trusts. In the case of a regulated investment company or a real estate investment trust, the amendments made by this section shall apply to taxable years ending after December 31, 2002; except that dividends received by such a company or trust on or before such date shall not be treated as qualified dividend income (as defined in section 1(h)(11)(B) of the Internal Revenue Code of 1986, as added by this Act)."

—P.L. 108-27, Sec. 303, of this Act [as amended by Sec. 102 of P.L. 109-222, and Sec. 102(a), P.L. 111-312, see above], reads as follows:

"Sec. 303. Sunset of title. All provisions of, and amendments made by, this title [Secs. 301 and 302] shall not apply to taxable years beginning after December 31, 2012, and the Internal Revenue Code of 1986 shall be applied and administered to such years as if such provisions and amendments had never been enacted."

In 1986, P.L. 99-514, Sec. 403(a), added Code Sec. 1257, effective for dispositions of converted wetland or highly erodible cropland (as defined in Code Sec. 1257(c)) first used for farming after 3/1/86, in tax. yrs. end. after 3/1/86.

Sec. 1258. Recharacterization of gain from certain financial transactions.

(a) General rule.

In the case of any gain—

(1) which (but for this section) would be treated as gain from the sale or exchange of a capital asset, and

(2) which is recognized on the disposition or other termination of any position which was held as part of a conversion transaction,

such gain (to the extent such gain does not exceed the applicable imputed income amount) shall be treated as ordinary income.

2,783

Code Sec. 1258(b) — Capital gains and losses

(b) Applicable imputed income amount.

For purposes of subsection (a), the term "applicable imputed income amount" means, with respect to any disposition or other termination referred to in subsection (a), an amount equal to—

(1) the amount of interest which would have accrued on the taxpayer's net investment in the conversion transaction for the period ending on the date of such disposition or other termination (or, if earlier, the date on which the requirements of subsection (c) ceased to be satisfied) at a rate equal to 120 percent of the applicable rate, reduced by

(2) the amount treated as ordinary income under subsection (a) with respect to any prior disposition or other termination of a position which was held as a part of such transaction.

The Secretary shall by regulations provide for such reductions in the applicable imputed income amount as may be appropriate by reason of amounts capitalized under section 263(g), ordinary income received, or otherwise.

(c) Conversion transaction.

For purposes of this section, the term "conversion transaction" means any transaction—

(1) substantially all of the taxpayer's expected return from which is attributable to the time value of the taxpayer's net investment in such transaction, and

(2) which is—

(A) the holding of any property (whether or not actively traded), and the entering into a contract to sell such property (or substantially identical property) at a price determined in accordance with such contract, but only if such property was acquired and such contract was entered into on a substantially contemporaneous basis,

(B) an applicable straddle,

(C) any other transaction which is marketed or sold as producing capital gains from a transaction described in paragraph (1), or

(D) any other transaction specified in regulations prescribed by the Secretary.

(d) Definitions and special rules.

For purposes of this section—

(1) **Applicable straddle.** The term "applicable straddle" means any straddle (within the meaning of section 1092(c)).

(2) **Applicable rate.** The term "applicable rate" means—

(A) the applicable Federal rate determined under section 1274(d) (compounded semiannually) as if the conversion transaction were a debt instrument, or

(B) if the term of the conversion transaction is indefinite, the Federal short-term rates in effect under section 6621(b) during the period of the conversion transaction (compounded daily).

(3) **Treatment of built-in losses.**

(A) In general. If any position with a built-in loss becomes part of a conversion transaction—

(i) for purposes of applying this subtitle to such position for periods after such position becomes part of such transaction, such position shall be taken into account at its fair market value as of the time it became part of such transaction, except that

(ii) upon the disposition or other termination of such position in a transaction in which gain or loss is recognized, such built-in loss shall be recognized and shall have a character determined without regard to this section.

(B) Built-in loss. For purposes of subparagraph (A), the term "built-in loss" means the loss (if any) which would have been realized if the position had been disposed of or otherwise terminated at its fair value as of the time such position became part of the conversion transaction.

(4) **Position taken into account at fair market value.** In determining the taxpayer's net investment in any conversion transaction, there shall be included the fair market value of any position which becomes part of such transaction (determined as of the time such position became part of such transaction).

(5) **Special rule for options dealers and commodities traders.**

(A) In general. Subsection (a) shall not apply to transactions—

(i) of an options dealer in the normal course of the dealer's trade or business of dealing in options, or

(ii) of a commodities trader in the normal course of the trader's trade or business of trading section 1256 contracts.

(B) Definitions. For purposes of this paragraph—

(i) Options dealer. The term "options dealer" has the meaning given such term by section 1256(g)(8).

(ii) Commodities trader. The term "commodities trader" means any person who is a member (or, except as otherwise provided in regulations, is entitled to trade as a member) of a domestic board of trade which is designated as a contract market by the Commodity Futures Trading Commission.

(C) Limited partners and limited entrepreneurs. In the case of any gain from a transaction recognized by an entity which is allocable to a limited partner or limited entrepreneur (within the meaning of section 464(e)(2)), subparagraph (A) shall not apply if—

(i) substantially all of the limited partner's (or limited entrepreneur's) expected return from the entity is attributable to the time value of the partner's (or entrepreneur's) net investment in such entity,

(ii) the transaction (or the interest in the entity) was marketed or sold as producing capital gains treatment from a transaction described in subsection (c)(1), or

(iii) the transaction (or the interest in the entity) is a transaction (or interest) specified in regulations prescribed by the Secretary.

In 2004, P.L. 108-357, Sec. 888(c)(2), deleted "; except that the term 'personal property' shall include stock" after "section 1092(c)" in para. (d)(1), effective for positions established on or after 10/22/2004.

In 1996, P.L. 104-188, Sec. 1703(n)(11), amended Sec. 13206(a)(3) of P.L. 103-66, the effective date for changes made by Sec. 13206(a)(1), 103-66, see below, by substituting "this subsection" for "this section".

In 1993, P.L. 103-66, Sec. 13206(a)(1), added Code Sec. 1258, effective for conversion transactions entered into after 4/30/93.

Sec. 1259. Constructive sales treatment for appreciated financial positions.

(a) In general.

If there is a constructive sale of an appreciated financial position—

(1) the taxpayer shall recognize gain as if such position were sold, assigned, or otherwise terminated at its fair market value on the date of such constructive sale (and any gain shall be taken into account for the taxable year which includes such date), and

(2) for purposes of applying this title for periods after the constructive sale—

(A) proper adjustment shall be made in the amount of any gain or loss subsequently realized with respect to such position for any gain taken into account by reason of paragraph (1), and

(B) the holding period of such position shall be determined as if such position were originally acquired on the date of such constructive sale.

(b) Appreciated financial position.

For purposes of this section—

(1) In general. Except as provided in paragraph (2), the term "appreciated financial position" means any position with respect to any stock, debt instrument, or partnership interest if there would be gain were such position sold, assigned, or otherwise terminated at its fair market value.

(2) Exceptions. The term "appreciated financial position" shall not include—

(A) any position with respect to debt if—

(i) the position unconditionally entitles the holder to receive a specified principal amount,

(ii) the interest payments (or other similar amounts) with respect to such position meet the requirements of clause (i) of section 860G(a)(1)(B), and

(iii) such position is not convertible (directly or indirectly) into stock of the issuer or any related person,

(B) any hedge with respect to a position described in subparagraph (A), and

(C) any position which is marked to market under any provision of this title or the regulations thereunder.

(3) Position. The term "position" means an interest, including a futures or forward contract, short sale, or option.

(c) Constructive sale.

For purposes of this section—

(1) In general. A taxpayer shall be treated as having made a constructive sale of an appreciated financial position if the taxpayer (or a related person)—

(A) enters into a short sale of the same or substantially identical property,

(B) enters into an offsetting notional principal contract with respect to the same or substantially identical property,

(C) enters into a futures or forward contract to deliver the same or substantially identical property,

(D) in the case of an appreciated financial position that is a short sale or a contract described in subparagraph (B) or (C) with respect to any property, acquires the same or substantially identical property, or

(E) to the extent prescribed by the Secretary in regulations, enters into 1 or more other transactions (or acquires 1 or more positions) that have substantially the same effect as a transaction described in any of the preceding subparagraphs.

(2) Exception for sales of nonpublicly traded property. A taxpayer shall not be treated as having made a constructive sale solely because the taxpayer enters into a contract for sale of any stock, debt instrument, or partnership interest which is not a marketable security (as defined in section 453(f)) if the contract settles within 1 year after the date such contract is entered into.

(3) Exception for certain closed transactions.

(A) In general. In applying this section, there shall be disregarded any transaction (which would otherwise cause a constructive sale) during the taxable year if—

(i) such transaction is closed on or before the 30th day after the close of such taxable year,

(ii) the taxpayer holds the appreciated financial position throughout the 60-day period beginning on the date such transaction is closed, and

(iii) at no time during such 60-day period is the taxpayer's risk of loss with respect to such position reduced by reason of a circumstance which would be described in section 246(c)(4) if references to stock included references to such position.

(B) Treatment of certain closed transactions where risk of loss on appreciated financial position diminished. If—

(i) a transaction, which would otherwise cause a constructive sale of an appreciated financial position, is closed during the taxable year or during the 30 days thereafter, and

(ii) another transaction is entered into during the 60-day period beginning on the date the transaction referred to in clause (i) is closed—

(I) which would (but for this subparagraph) cause the requirement of subparagraph (A)(iii) not to be met with respect to the transaction described in clause (i) of this subparagraph,

(II) which is closed on or before the 30th day after the close of the taxable year in which the transaction referred to in clause (i) occurs, and

(III) which meets the requirements of clauses (ii) and (iii) of subparagraph (A),

the transaction referred to in clause (ii) shall be disregarded for purposes of determining whether the requirements of subparagraph (A)(iii) are met with respect to the transaction described in clause (i).

(4) Related person. A person is related to another person with respect to a transaction if—

(A) the relationship is described in section 267(b) or 707(b), and

(B) such transaction is entered into with a view toward avoiding the purposes of this section.

(d) Other definitions.

For purposes of this section—

(1) Forward contract. The term "forward contract" means a contract to deliver a substantially fixed amount of property (including cash) for a substantially fixed price.

(2) Offsetting notional principal contract. The term "offsetting notional principal contract" means, with respect to any property, an agreement which includes—

(A) a requirement to pay (or provide credit for) all or substantially all of the investment yield (including appreciation) on such property for a specified period, and

(B) a right to be reimbursed for (or receive credit for) all or substantially all of any decline in the value of such property.

(e) Special rules.

(1) Treatment of subsequent sale of position which was deemed sold. If—

(A) there is a constructive sale of any appreciated financial position,

(B) such position is subsequently disposed of, and

(C) at the time of such disposition, the transaction resulting in the constructive sale of such position is open with respect to the taxpayer or any related person,

solely for purposes of determining whether the taxpayer has entered into a constructive sale of any other appreciated financial position held by the taxpayer, the taxpayer shall be treated as entering into such transaction immediately after such disposition. For purposes of the preceding sentence, an assignment or other termination shall be treated as a disposition.

(2) Certain trust instruments treated as stock. For purposes of this section, an interest in a trust which is actively traded (within the meaning of section 1092(d)(1)) shall be treated as stock unless substantially all (by value) of the property held by the trust is debt described in subsection (b)(2)(A).

(3) Multiple positions in property. If a taxpayer holds multiple positions in property, the determination of whether a specific transaction is a constructive sale and, if so, which appreciated financial position is deemed sold shall be made in the same manner as actual sales.

(f) Regulations.

The Secretary shall prescribe such regulations as may be necessary or appropriate to carry out the purposes of this section.

In **2004**, P.L. 108-311, Sec. 406(e)(1), substituted "A taxpayer shall not be treated as having made a constructive sale solely because the taxpayer enters into a contract" for "The term 'constructive sale' shall not include any contract" in para. (c)(2)... Sec. 406(e)(2), substituted "cause a constructive sale" for "be treated as a constructive sale" in subpara. (c)(3)(A) and clause (c)(3)(B)(i)... Sec. 406(e)(3), substituted "on or before" for "before the end of" in clause (c)(3)(A)(i)... Sec. 406(e)(4), deleted "substantially similar" after "another" in clause (c)(3)(B)(ii)... Sec. 406(e)(5), amended subclause (c)(3)(B)(ii)(I)... Sec. 406(e)(6), added "on or" before "before the 30th day" in subclause (c)(3)(B)(ii)(II)... Sec. 406(e)(7), substituted "certain closed transactions where risk of loss on appreciated financial position diminished" for "positions which are reestablished" in the heading of subpara. (c)(3)(B), effective for any constructive sale after 6/8/97, except as provided in Sec. 1001(d)(2)-(4) of the Taxpayer Relief Act of 1997, P.L. 105-34 [as amended by Sec. 6010(a)(4) of P.L. 105-206, which substituted "before the close of the 30th day after" for "within the 30-day period beginning on" in Sec. 1001(d)(3)(C) of P.L. 105-34], which read as follows:

"(2) Exception for sales of positions, etc. held before June 9, 1997. If—

"(A) before June 9, 1997, the taxpayer entered into any transaction which is a constructive sale of any appreciated financial position, and

"(B) before the close of the 30-day period beginning on the date of the enactment of this Act or before such later date as may be specified by the Secretary of the Treasury, such transaction and position are clearly identified in the taxpayer's records as offsetting,

such transaction and position shall not be taken into account in determining whether any other constructive sale after June 8, 1997, has occurred. The preceding sentence shall cease to apply as of the date such transaction is closed or the taxpayer ceases to hold such position.

"(3) Special rule. In the case of a decedent dying after June 8, 1997, if—

"(A) there was a constructive sale on or before such date of any appreciated financial position,

"(B) the transaction resulting in such constructive sale of such position remains open (with respect to the decedent or any related person)—

"(i) for not less than 2 years after the date of such transaction (whether such period is before or after June 8, 1997), and

"(ii) at any time during the 3-year period ending on the date of the decedent's death, and

"(C) such transaction is not closed *before the close of the 30th day after* the date of the enactment of this Act,

then, for purposes of such Code, such position (and the transaction resulting in such constructive sale) shall be treated as property constituting rights to receive an item of income in respect of a decedent under section 691 of such Code. Section 1014(c) of such Code shall not apply to so much of such position's or property's value (as included in the decedent's estate for purposes of chapter 11 of such Code) as exceeds its fair market value as of the date such transaction is closed.

"(4) Election of mark to market by securities traders and traders and dealers in commodities.

"(A) In general. The amendments made by subsection (b) shall apply to taxable years ending after the date of the enactment of this Act.

"(B) 4-year spread of adjustments. In the case of a taxpayer who elects under subsection (e) or (f) of section 475 of the Internal Revenue Code of 1986 (as added by this section) to change its method of accounting for the taxable year which includes the date of the enactment of this Act—

"(i) any identification required under such subsection with respect to securities and commodities held on the date of the enactment of this Act shall be treated as timely made if made on or before the 30th day after such date of enactment, and

"(ii) the net amount of the adjustments required to be taken into account by the taxpayer under section 481 of such Code shall be taken into account ratably over the 4-taxable year period beginning with such first taxable year."

"* Matter in *italics* in Sec. 1001(d)(3)(C) of P.L. 105-34 [above] added by Sec. 6010(a)(4) of P.L. 105-206, which struck out:

*. "within the 30-day period beginning on"

Prior to amendment, subclause (c)(3)(B)(ii)(I) read as follows:

"(I) which also would otherwise be treated as a constructive sale of such position,"

In **1998**, P.L. 105-206, Sec. 6010(a)(1)(A), substituted "position" for "debt" each place it appeared in clauses (b)(2)(A)(i), (ii) and (iii)... Sec. 6010(a)(1)(B), deleted "and" at the end of subpara. (b)(2)(A)... Sec. 6010(a)(1)(C), redesignated subpara. (b)(2)(B) as (C) and added subpara. (b)(2)(B)... Sec. 6010(a)(2), added "(including cash)" after "property" in para. (d)(1), effective for any constructive sale after 6/8/97, except as provided in Secs. 1001(d)(2)-(4) of P.L. 105-34, see below.

—P.L. 105-206, Sec. 6010(a)(4), substituted "before the close of the 30th day after" for "within the 30-day period beginning on" in Sec. 1001(d)(3)(C) of P.L. 105-34 [see below]

In **1997**, P.L. 105-34, Sec. 1001(a), added Code Sec. 1259 as part of part IV of subchapter P of chapter 1, effective for any constructive sale after 6/8/97, except as provided in Secs. 1001(d)(2)-(4) of this Act [as amended by Sec. 6010(a)(4) of 105-206, see above] which read as follows:

"(2) Exception for sales of positions, etc. held before June 9, 1997. If—

"(A) before June 9, 1997, the taxpayer entered into any transaction which is a constructive sale of any appreciated financial position, and

"(B) before the close of the 30-day period beginning on the date of the enactment of this Act or before such later date as may be specified by the Secretary of the Treasury, such transaction and position are clearly identified in the taxpayer's records as offsetting,

such transaction and position shall not be taken into account in determining whether any other constructive sale after June 8, 1997, has occurred. The preceding sentence shall cease to apply as of the date such transaction is closed or the taxpayer ceases to hold such position.

"(3) Special rule. In the case of a decedent dying after June 8, 1997, if—

"(A) there was a constructive sale on or before such date of any appreciated financial position,

"(B) the transaction resulting in such constructive sale of such position remains open (with respect to the decedent or any related person)—

"(i) for not less than 2 years after the date of such transaction (whether such period is before or after June 8, 1997), and

"(ii) at any time during the 3-year period ending on the date of the decedent's death, and

"(C) such transaction is not closed before the close of the 30th day after the date of the enactment of this Act,

then, for purposes of such Code, such position (and the transaction resulting in such constructive sale) shall be treated as property constituting rights to receive an item of income in respect of a decedent under section 691 of such Code. Section 1014(c) of such Code shall not apply to so much of such position's or property's value (as included in the decedent's estate for purposes of chapter 11 of such Code) as exceeds its fair market value as of the date such transaction is closed.

"(4) Election of mark to market by securities traders and traders and dealers in commodities.

"(A) In general. The amendments made by subsection (b) shall apply to taxable years ending after the date of the enactment of this Act.

"(B) 4-year spread of adjustments. In the case of a taxpayer who elects under subsection (e) or (f) of section 475 of the Internal Revenue Code of 1986 (as added by this section) to change its method of accounting for the taxable year which includes the date of the enactment of this Act—

"(i) any identification required under such subsection with respect to securities and commodities held on the date of the enactment of this Act shall be treated as timely made if made on or before the 30th day after such date of enactment, and

"(ii) the net amount of the adjustments required to be taken into account by the taxpayer under section 481 of such Code shall be taken into account ratably over the 4-taxable year period beginning with such first taxable year."

Sec. 1260. Gains from constructive ownership transactions.

(a) In general.

If the taxpayer has gain from a constructive ownership transaction with respect to any financial asset and such gain would (without regard to this section) be treated as a long-term capital gain—

(1) such gain shall be treated as ordinary income to the extent that such gain exceeds the net underlying long-term capital gain, and

(2) to the extent such gain is treated as a long-term capital gain after the application of paragraph (1), the determination of the capital gain rate (or rates) applicable to such gain under section 1(h) shall be determined on the basis of the respective rate (or rates) that would have been applicable to the net underlying long-term capital gain.

(b) Interest charge on deferral of gain recognition.

(1) In general. If any gain is treated as ordinary income for any taxable year by reason of subsection (a)(1), the tax imposed by this chapter for such taxable year shall be increased by the amount of interest determined under paragraph (2) with respect to each prior taxable year during any portion of which the constructive ownership transac-

Capital gains and losses   Code Sec. 1260

tion was open. Any amount payable under this paragraph shall be taken into account in computing the amount of any deduction allowable to the taxpayer for interest paid or accrued during such taxable year.

(2) Amount of interest. The amount of interest determined under this paragraph with respect to a prior taxable year is the amount of interest which would have been imposed under section 6601 on the underpayment of tax for such year which would have resulted if the gain (which is treated as ordinary income by reason of subsection (a)(1)) had been included in gross income in the taxable years in which it accrued (determined by treating the income as accruing at a constant rate equal to the applicable Federal rate as in effect on the day the transaction closed). The period during which such interest shall accrue shall end on the due date (without extensions) for the return of tax imposed by this chapter for the taxable year in which such transaction closed.

(3) Applicable Federal rate. For purposes of paragraph (2), the applicable Federal rate is the applicable Federal rate determined under section 1274(d) (compounded semi-annually) which would apply to a debt instrument with a term equal to the period the transaction was open.

(4) No credits against increase in tax. Any increase in tax under paragraph (1) shall not be treated as tax imposed by this chapter for purposes of determining—

(A) the amount of any credit allowable under this chapter, or

(B) the amount of the tax imposed by section 55.

(c) Financial asset.

For purposes of this section—

(1) In general. The term "financial asset" means—

(A) any equity interest in any pass-thru entity, and

(B) to the extent provided in regulations—

(i) any debt instrument, and

(ii) any stock in a corporation which is not a pass-thru entity.

(2) Pass-thru entity. For purposes of paragraph (1), the term "pass-thru entity" means—

(A) a regulated investment company,

(B) a real estate investment trust,

(C) an S corporation,

(D) a partnership,

(E) a trust,

(F) a common trust fund,

(G) a passive foreign investment company (as defined in section 1297 without regard to subsection (d) thereof), and

(H) a REMIC.

(d) Constructive ownership transaction.

For purposes of this section—

(1) In general. The taxpayer shall be treated as having entered into a constructive ownership transaction with respect to any financial asset if the taxpayer—

(A) holds a long position under a notional principal contract with respect to the financial asset,

(B) enters into a forward or futures contract to acquire the financial asset,

(C) is the holder of a call option, and is the grantor of a put option, with respect to the financial asset and such options have substantially equal strike prices and substantially contemporaneous maturity dates, or

(D) to the extent provided in regulations prescribed by the Secretary, enters into one or more other transactions (or acquires one or more positions) that have substantially the same effect as a transaction described in any of the preceding subparagraphs.

(2) Exception for positions which are marked to market. This section shall not apply to any constructive ownership transaction if all of the positions which are part of such transaction are marked to market under any provision of this title or the regulations thereunder.

(3) Long position under notional principal contract. A person shall be treated as holding a long position under a notional principal contract with respect to any financial asset if such person—

(A) has the right to be paid (or receive credit for) all or substantially all of the investment yield (including appreciation) on such financial asset for a specified period, and

(B) is obligated to reimburse (or provide credit for) all or substantially all of any decline in the value of such financial asset.

(4) Forward contract. The term "forward contract" means any contract to acquire in the future (or provide or receive credit for the future value of) any financial asset.

(e) Net underlying long-term capital gain.

For purposes of this section, in the case of any constructive ownership transaction with respect to any financial asset, the term "net underlying long-term capital gain" means the aggregate net capital gain that the taxpayer would have had if—

(1) the financial asset had been acquired for fair market value on the date such transaction was opened and sold for fair market value on the date such transaction was closed, and

(2) only gains and losses that would have resulted from the deemed ownership under paragraph (1) were taken into account.

The amount of the net underlying long-term capital gain with respect to any financial asset shall be treated as zero unless the amount thereof is established by clear and convincing evidence.

(f) Special rule where taxpayer takes delivery.

Except as provided in regulations prescribed by the Secretary, if a constructive ownership transaction is closed by reason of taking delivery, this section shall be applied as if the taxpayer had sold all the contracts, options, or other positions which are part of such transaction for fair market value on the closing date. The amount of gain recognized under the preceding sentence shall not exceed the amount of gain treated as ordinary income under subsection (a). Proper adjustments shall be made in the amount of any gain or loss subsequently realized for gain recognized and treated as ordinary income under this subsection.

(g) Regulations.

The Secretary shall prescribe such regulations as may be necessary or appropriate to carry out the purposes of this section, including regulations—

(1) to permit taxpayers to mark to market constructive ownership transactions in lieu of applying this section, and

(2) to exclude certain forward contracts which do not convey substantially all of the economic return with respect to a financial asset.

In 2007, P.L. 110-172, Sec. 11(a)(23), added "and" at the end of subpara. (c)(2)(G)... Sec. 11(a)(24)(B), substituted "subsection (d)" for "subsection (e)" in subpara. (c)(2)(G), enacted 12/29/2007.

In 2004, P.L. 108-357, Sec. 413(c)(23), deleted subparas. (c)(2)(H) and (c)(2)(I) and redesignated subpara. (c)(2)(J) as subpara. (c)(2)(H), effective for tax. yrs. of foreign corporations begin. after 12/31/2004, and for tax. yrs. of United States shareholders with or within which such tax. yrs. of foreign corporations end. Prior to deletion, subparas. (c)(2)(H) and (c)(2)(I) read as follows:

"(H) a foreign personal holding company,"
"(I) a foreign investment company (as defined in section 1246(b)), and"

In 1999, P.L. 106-170, Sec. 534(a), added Code Sec. 1260, effective for transactions entered into after 7/11/99.

PART V.— SPECIAL RULES FOR BONDS AND OTHER DEBT INSTRUMENTS

Subpart
A. Original issue discount.
B. Market discount on bonds.
C. Discount on short-term obligations.
D. Miscellaneous provisions.

In 1984, P.L. 98-369, Sec. 41(a), added the heading for part V and the items for subparts A–D.

SUBPART A.— ORIGINAL ISSUE DISCOUNT

Sec.
1271. Treatment of amounts received on retirement or sale or exchange of debt instruments.
1272. Current inclusion in income of original issue discount.
1273. Determination of amount of original issue discount.
1274. Determination of issue price in the case of certain debt instruments issued for property.
1274A. Special rules for certain transactions where stated principal amount does not exceed $2,800,000.
1275. Other definitions and special rules.

In 1985, P.L. 99-121, Sec. 102(d), added the item for 1274A.

Sec. 1271. Treatment of amounts received on retirement or sale or exchange of debt instruments.

(a) General rule.
For purposes of this title—
(1) Retirement. Amounts received by the holder on retirement of any debt instrument shall be considered as amounts received in exchange therefor.
(2) Ordinary income on sale or exchange where intention to call before maturity.
 (A) In general. If at the time of original issue there was an intention to call a debt instrument before maturity, any gain realized on the sale or exchange thereof which does not exceed an amount equal to—
  (i) the original issue discount, reduced by
  (ii) the portion of original issue discount previously includible in the gross income of any holder (without regard to subsection (a)(7) or (b)(4) of section 1272 (or the corresponding provisions of prior law)),
shall be treated as ordinary income.
 (B) Exceptions. This paragraph (and paragraph (2) of subsection (c)) shall not apply to—
  (i) any tax-exempt obligation, or
  (ii) any holder who has purchased the debt instrument at a premium.
(3) Certain short-term Government obligations.
 (A) In general. On the sale or exchange of any short-term Government obligation, any gain realized which does not exceed an amount equal to the ratable share of the acquisition discount shall be treated as ordinary income.
 (B) Short-term government obligation. For purposes of this paragraph, the term "short-term Government obligation" means any obligation of the United States or any of its possessions, or of a State or any political subdivision thereof, or of the District of Columbia, which has a fixed maturity date not more than 1 year from the date of issue. Such term does not include any tax-exempt obligation.
 (C) Acquisition discount. For purposes of this paragraph, the term "acquisition discount" means the excess of the stated redemption price at maturity over the taxpayer's basis for the obligation.
 (D) Ratable share. For purposes of this paragraph, except as provided in subparagraph (E), the ratable share of the acquisition discount is an amount which bears the same ratio to such discount as—
  (i) the number of days which the taxpayer held the obligation, bears to
  (ii) the number of days after the date the taxpayer acquired the obligation and up to (and including) the date of its maturity.
 (E) Election of accrual on basis of constant interest rate. At the election of the taxpayer with respect to any obligation, the ratable share of the acquisition discount is the portion of the acquisition discount accruing while the taxpayer held the obligation determined (under regulations prescribed by the Secretary) on the basis of—
  (i) the taxpayer's yield to maturity based on the taxpayer's cost of acquiring the obligation, and
  (ii) compounding daily.
An election under this subparagraph, once made with respect to any obligation, shall be irrevocable.
(4) Certain short-term nongovernment obligations.
 (A) In general. On the sale or exchange of any short-term nongovernment obligation, any gain realized which does not exceed an amount equal to the ratable share of the original issue discount shall be treated as ordinary income.
 (B) Short-term nongovernment obligation. For purposes of this paragraph, the term "short-term nongovernment obligation" means any obligation which—
  (i) has a fixed maturity date not more than 1 year from the date of the issue, and
  (ii) is not a short-term Government obligation (as defined in paragraph (3)(B) without regard to the last sentence thereof).
 (C) Ratable share. For purposes of this paragraph, except as provided in subparagraph (D), the ratable share of the original issue discount is an amount which bears the same ratio to such discount as—
  (i) the number of days which the taxpayer held the obligation, bears to
  (ii) the number of days after the date of original issue and up to (and including) the date of its maturity.
 (D) Election of accrual on basis of constant interest rate. At the election of the taxpayer with respect to any obligation, the ratable share of the original issue discount is the portion of the original issue discount accruing while the taxpayer held the obligation determined (under regulations prescribed by the Secretary) on the basis of—
  (i) the yield to maturity based on the issue price of the obligation, and
  (ii) compounding daily.
Any election under this subparagraph, once made with respect to any obligation, shall be irrevocable.
(b) Exception for certain obligations.
(1) In general. This section shall not apply to—
 (A) any obligation issued by a natural person before June 9, 1997, and

Original issue discount Code Sec. 1272(a)(4)(B)

(B) any obligation issued before July 2, 1982, by an issuer which is not a corporation and is not a government or political subdivision thereof.

(2) Termination. Paragraph (1) shall not apply to any obligation purchased (within the meaning of section 1272(d)(1)) after June 8, 1997.

(c) Transition rules

(1) Special rule for certain obligations issued before January 1, 1955. Paragraph (1) of subsection (a) shall apply to a debt instrument issued before January 1, 1955, only if such instrument was issued with interest coupons or in registered form, or was in such form on March 1, 1954.

(2) Special rule for certain obligations with respect to which original issue discount not currently includible.

(A) In general. On the sale or exchange of debt instruments issued by a government or political subdivision thereof after December 31, 1954, and before July 2, 1982, or by a corporation after December 31, 1954, and on or before May 27, 1969, any gain realized which does not exceed—

(i) an amount equal to the original issue discount, or

(ii) if at the time of original issue there was no intention to call the debt instrument before maturity, an amount which bears the same ratio to the original issue discount as the number of complete months that the debt instrument was held by the taxpayer bears to the number of complete months from the date of original issue to the date of maturity,

shall be considered as ordinary income.

(B) Subsection (a)(2)(A) not to apply. Subsection (a)(2)(A) shall not apply to any debt instrument referred to in subparagraph (A) of this paragraph.

(C) Cross reference. For current inclusion of original issue discount, see section 1272.

(d) Double inclusion in income not required.

This section and sections 1272 and 1286 shall not require the inclusion of any amount previously includible in gross income.

In 1997, P.L. 105-34, Sec. 1003(c)(1), amended subsec. (b), effective for sales, exchanges and retirements after 8/5/97.
Prior to amendment, subsec. (b) read as follows:
"(b) Exceptions.
"This section shall not apply to—
"(1) Natural persons. Any obligation issued by a natural person.
"(2) Obligations issued before July 2, 1982, by certain issuers. Any obligation issued before July 2, 1982, by an issuer which—
"(A) is not a corporation, and
"(B) is not a government or political subdivision thereof."

In 1988, P.L. 100-647, Sec. 1006(u)(4), substituted "subsection (a)(7)" for "subsection (a)(6)" in clause (a)(2)(A)(ii), effective for debt instruments issued after 12/31/86 in tax. yrs. end. after 12/31/86.

In 1986, P.L. 99-514, Sec. 1803(a)(1)(A), added para. (a)(4) ... Sec. 1803(a)(2)(A), added subpara. (a)(3)(E) ... Sec. 1803(a)(2)(B), substituted "this paragraph, except as provided in subparagraph (E)" for "this paragraph" in subpara. (a)(3)(D) ... Sec. 1803(a)(3), amended subpara. (a)(3)(B), effective for tax. yrs. end. after 7/18/84 and as provided in Sec. 44(j) of P.L. 98-369, reproduced below.
Prior to amendment, subpara. (a)(3)(B) read as follows:
"(B) Short-term government obligation. For purposes of this paragraph, the term 'short-term Government obligation' means any obligation of the United States or any of its possessions, or of a State or any political subdivision thereof, or of the District of Columbia which is—
"(i) issued on a discount basis, and
"(ii) payable without interest at a fixed maturity date not more than 1 year from the date of issue. Such term does not include any tax-exempt obligation."

In 1984, P.L. 98-369, Sec. 41(a), added Code Sec. 1271 for tax. yrs. end. after 7/18/84. Sec. 44(j) of the Act provides:
"(j) Clarification that prior effective date rules not affected.
"Nothing in the amendment made by section 41(a) shall affect the application of any effective date provision (including any transitional rule) for any provision which was a predecessor to any provision contained in part V of subchapter P of chapter 1 of the Internal Revenue Code of 1954 (as added by section 41)."

Sec. 1272. Current inclusion in income of original issue discount.

(a) Original issue discount on debt instruments issued after July 1, 1982, included in income on basis of constant interest rate.

(1) General rule. For purposes of this title, there shall be included in the gross income of the holder of any debt instrument having original issue discount issued after July 1, 1982, an amount equal to the sum of the daily portions of the original issue discount for each day during the taxable year on which such holder held such debt instrument.

(2) Exceptions. Paragraph (1) shall not apply to—

(A) Tax-exempt obligations. Any tax-exempt obligation.

(B) United States savings bonds. Any United States savings bond.

(C) Short-term obligations. Any debt instrument which has a fixed maturity date not more than 1 year from the date of issue.

(D) Obligations issued by natural persons before March 2, 1984. Any obligation issued by a natural person before March 2, 1984.

(E) Loans between natural persons.

(i) In general. Any loan made by a natural person to another natural person if—

(I) such loan is not made in the course of a trade or business of the lender, and

(II) the amount of such loan (when increased by the outstanding amount of prior loans by such natural person to such other natural person) does not exceed $10,000.

(ii) Clause (i) not to apply where tax avoidance a principal purpose. Clause (i) shall not apply if the loan has as 1 of its principal purposes the avoidance of any Federal tax.

(iii) Treatment of husband and wife. For purposes of this subparagraph, a husband and wife shall be treated as 1 person. The preceding sentence shall not apply where the spouses lived apart at all times during the taxable year in which the loan is made.

(3) Determination of daily portions. For purposes of paragraph (1), the daily portion of the original issue discount on any debt instrument shall be determined by allocating to each day in any accrual period its ratable portion of the increase during such accrual period in the adjusted issue price of the debt instrument. For purposes of the preceding sentence, the increase in the adjusted issue price for any accrual period shall be an amount equal to the excess (if any) of—

(A) the product of—

(i) the adjusted issue price of the debt instrument at the beginning of such accrual period, and

(ii) the yield to maturity (determined on the basis of compounding at the close of each accrual period and properly adjusted for the length of the accrual period), over

(B) the sum of the amounts payable as interest on such debt instrument during such accrual period.

(4) Adjusted issue price. For purposes of this subsection, the adjusted issue price of any debt instrument at the beginning of any accrual period is the sum of—

(A) the issue price of such debt instrument, plus

(B) the adjustments under this subsection to such issue price for all periods before the first day of such accrual period.

(5) Accrual period. Except as otherwise provided in regulations prescribed by the Secretary, the term "accrual period" means a 6-month period (or shorter period from the date of original issue of the debt instrument) which ends on a day in the calendar year corresponding to the maturity date of the debt instrument or the date 6 months before such maturity date.

(6) Determination of daily portions where principal subject to acceleration.

(A) In general. In the case of any debt instrument to which this paragraph applies, the daily portion of the original issue discount shall be determined by allocating to each day in any accrual period its ratable portion of the excess (if any) of—

(i) the sum of (I) the present value determined under subparagraph (B) of all remaining payments under the debt instrument as of the close of such period, and (II) the payments during the accrual period of amounts included in the stated redemption price of the debt instrument, over

(ii) the adjusted issue price of such debt instrument at the beginning of such period.

(B) Determination of present value. For purposes of subparagraph (A), the present value shall be determined on the basis of—

(i) the original yield to maturity (determined on the basis of compounding at the close of each accrual period and properly adjusted for the length of the accrual period),

(ii) events which have occurred before the close of the accrual period, and

(iii) a prepayment assumption determined in the manner prescribed by regulations.

(C) Debt instruments to which paragraph applies. This paragraph applies to—

(i) any regular interest in a REMIC or qualified mortgage held by a REMIC,

(ii) any other debt instrument if payments under such debt instrument may be accelerated by reason of prepayments of other obligations securing such debt instrument (or, to the extent provided in regulations, by reason of other events), or

(iii) any pool of debt instruments the yield on which may be affected by reason of prepayments (or to the extent provided in regulations, by reason of other events).

To the extent provided in regulations prescribed by the Secretary, in the case of a small business engaged in the trade or business of selling tangible personal property at retail, clause (iii) shall not apply to debt instruments incurred in the ordinary course of such trade or business while held by such business.

(7) Reduction where subsequent holder pays acquisition premium.

(A) Reduction. For purposes of this subsection, in the case of any purchase after its original issue of a debt instrument to which this subsection applies, the daily portion for any day shall be reduced by an amount equal to the amount which would be the daily portion for such day (without regard to this paragraph) multiplied by the fraction determined under subparagraph (B).

(B) Determination of fraction. For purposes of subparagraph (A), the fraction determined under this subparagraph is a fraction—

(i) the numerator of which is the excess (if any) of—

(I) the cost of such debt instrument incurred by the purchaser, over

(II) the issue price of such debt instrument, increased by the portion of original issue discount previously includible in the gross income of any holder (computed without regard to this paragraph), and

(ii) the denominator of which is the sum of the daily portions for such debt instrument for all days after the date of such purchase and ending on the stated maturity date (computed without regard to this paragraph).

(b) Ratable inclusion retained for corporate debt instruments issued before July 2, 1982.

(1) General rule. There shall be included in the gross income of the holder of any debt instrument issued by a corporation after May 27, 1969, and before July 2, 1982—

(A) the ratable monthly portion of original issue discount, multiplied by

(B) the number of complete months (plus any fractional part of a month determined under paragraph (3)) such holder held such debt instrument during the taxable year.

(2) Determination of ratable monthly portion. Except as provided in paragraph (4), the ratable monthly portion of original issue discount shall equal—

(A) the original issue discount, divided by

(B) the number of complete months from the date of original issue to the stated maturity date of the debt instrument.

(3) Month defined. For purposes of this subsection—

(A) Complete month. A complete month commences with the date of original issue and the corresponding day of each succeeding calendar month (or the last day of a calendar month in which there is no corresponding day).

(B) Transfers during month. In any case where a debt instrument is acquired on any day other than a day determined under subparagraph (A), the ratable monthly portion of original issue discount for the complete month (or partial month) in which such acquisition occurs shall be allocated between the transferor and the transferee in accordance with the number of days in such complete (or partial) month each held the debt instrument.

(4) Reduction where subsequent holder pays acquisition premium.

(A) Reduction. For purposes of this subsection, the ratable monthly portion of original issue discount shall not include its share of the acquisition premium.

(B) Share of acquisition premium. For purposes of subparagraph (A), any month's share of the acquisition premium is an amount (determined at the time of the purchase) equal to—

(i) the excess of—

(I) the cost of such debt instrument incurred by the holder, over

(II) the issue price of such debt instrument, increased by the portion of original issue discount previously includible in the gross income of any holder (computed without regard to this paragraph),

(ii) divided by the number of complete months (plus any fractional part of a month) from the date of such

Original issue discount   Code Sec. 1273(c)(2)(C)

purchase to the stated maturity date of such debt instrument.

(c) Exceptions.

This section shall not apply to any holder—

(1) who has purchased the debt instrument at a premium, or

(2) which is a life insurance company to which section 811(b) applies.

(d) Definition and special rule.

(1) Purchase defined. For purposes of this section, the term "purchase" means—

(A) any acquisition of a debt instrument, where

(B) the basis of the debt instrument is not determined in whole or in part by reference to the adjusted basis of such debt instrument in the hands of the person from whom acquired.

(2) Basis adjustment. The basis of any debt instrument in the hands of the holder thereof shall be increased by the amount included in his gross income pursuant to this section.

In 1997, P.L. 105-34, Sec. 1004(a), deleted "or" at the end of clause (a)(6)(C)(i), substituted ", or" for the period at the end of clause (a)(6)(C)(ii) and added clause (a)(6)(C)(iii) and a flush sentence at the end of subpara. (a)(6)(C), effective for tax. yrs. begin. after 8/5/97. Sec. 1004(b)(2) of this Act provides:

"(2) Change in method of accounting. In the case of any taxpayer required by this section to change its method of accounting for its first taxable year beginning after the date of the enactment [8/5/97] of this Act—

"(A) such change shall be treated as initiated by the taxpayer,

"(B) such change shall be treated as made with the consent of the Secretary of the Treasury, and

"(C) the net amount of the adjustments required to be taken into account by the taxpayer under section 481 of the Internal Revenue Code of 1986 shall be taken into account ratably over the 4-taxable year period beginning with such first taxable year."

In 1986, P.L. 99-514, Sec. 672, redesignated para. (a)(6) as (a)(7) and added new para. (a)(6), effective for debt instruments issued after 12/31/86, in tax. yrs. end. after 12/31/86.

—P.L. 99-514, Sec. 1803(b)(5), amended Sec. 44(g) [reproduced below] of P.L. 98-369, part of the effective date for amendments made by Sec. 41(a) of P.L. 98-369, by substituting "on or before December 31, 1984" for "before December 31, 1984", see below.

In 1984, P.L. 98-369, Sec. 41(a), added Code Sec. 1272, effective for tax. yrs. end. after 7/18/84, except as provided in Sec. 44(g) of this Act [as amended by Sec. 1803(b)(5) of P.L. 99-514, see above] which reads as follows:

"(g) Repeal of capital asset requirement.—

"Section 1272 of such Code (as added by section 41 [of this Act]) shall not apply to any obligation issued on or before December 31, 1984, which is not a capital asset in the hands of the taxpayer."

Secs. 44(i) and 44(j) of the Act provide:

"(i) Other miscellaneous changes.

"(1) Accrual period. In the case of any obligation issued after July 1, 1982, and before January 1, 1985, the accrual period, for purposes of section 1272(a) of the Internal Revenue Code of 1954 (as amended by section 41(a)), shall be a 1-year period (or shorter period to maturity) beginning on the day in the calendar year which corresponds to the date of original issue of the obligation.

"(2) Change in reduction for purchase after original issue. Section 1272(a)(6) of such Code (as so amended) shall not apply to any purchase on or before the date of the enactment of this Act, and the rules of section 1232A(a)(6) of such Code (as in effect on the day before the date of the enactment of this Act) shall continue to apply to such purchase.

"(j) Clarification that prior effective date rules not affected.

"Nothing in the amendment made by section 41(a) shall affect the application of any effective date provision (including any transitional rule) for any provision which was a predecessor to any provision contained in part V of subchapter P of chapter 1 of the Internal Revenue Code of 1954 (as added by section 41)."

Sec. 1273. Determination of amount of original issue discount.

(a) General rule.

For purposes of this subpart—

(1) In general. The term "original issue discount" means the excess (if any) of—

(A) the stated redemption price at maturity, over

(B) the issue price.

(2) Stated redemption price at maturity. The term "stated redemption price at maturity" means the amount fixed by the last modification of the purchase agreement and includes interest and other amounts payable at that time (other than any interest based on a fixed rate, and payable unconditionally at fixed periodic intervals of 1 year or less during the entire term of the debt instrument).

(3) ¼ of 1 percent de minimis rule. If the original issue discount determined under paragraph (1) is less than—

(A) ¼ of 1 percent of the stated redemption price at maturity, multiplied by

(B) the number of complete years to maturity,

then the original issue discount shall be treated as zero.

(b) Issue price.

For purposes of this subpart—

(1) Publicly offered debt instruments not issued for property. In the case of any issue of debt instruments—

(A) publicly offered, and

(B) not issued for property,

the issue price is the initial offering price to the public (excluding bond houses and brokers) at which price a substantial amount of such debt instruments was sold.

(2) Other debt instruments not issued for property. In the case of any issue of debt instruments not issued for property and not publicly offered, the issue price of each such instrument is the price paid by the first buyer of such debt instrument.

(3) Debt instruments issued for property where there is public trading. In the case of a debt instrument which is issued for property and which—

(A) is part of an issue a portion of which is traded on an established securities market, or

(B)(i) is issued for stock or securities which are traded on an established securities market, or

(ii) to the extent provided in regulations, is issued for property (other than stock or securities) of a kind regularly traded on an established market,

the issue price of such debt instrument shall be the fair market value of such property.

(4) Other cases. Except in any case—

(A) to which paragraph (1), (2), or (3) of this subsection applies, or

(B) to which section 1274 applies,

the issue price of a debt instrument which is issued for property shall be the stated redemption price at maturity.

(5) Property. In applying this subsection, the term "property" includes services and the right to use property, but such term does not include money.

(c) Special rules for applying subsection (b).

For purposes of subsection (b)—

(1) Initial offering price; price paid by the first buyer. The terms "initial offering price" and "price paid by the first buyer" include the aggregate payments made by the purchaser under the purchase agreement, including modifications thereof.

(2) Treatment of investment units. In the case of any debt instrument and an option, security, or other property issued together as an investment unit—

(A) the issue price for such unit shall be determined in accordance with the rules of this subsection and subsection (b) as if it were a debt instrument,

(B) the issue price determined for such unit shall be allocated to each element of such unit on the basis of the relationship of the fair market value of such element to the fair market value of all elements in such unit, and

(C) the issue price of any debt instrument, included in such unit shall be the portion of the issue price of the unit allocated to the debt instrument under subparagraph (B).

In 1986, P.L. 99-514, Sec. 1803(a)(10), amended subpara. (b)(3)(B), effective for tax. yrs. end. after 7/18/84. For special rules see Sec. 44(j) of P.L. 98-369, reproduced below.
Prior to amendment, subpara. (b)(3)(B) read as follows:
"(B) is issued for stock or securities which are traded on an established securities market."
In 1984, P.L. 98-369, Sec. 41(a), added Code Sec. 1273, effective for tax. yrs. end. after 7/18/84. Sec. 44(j) of this Act provides:
"(j) *Clarification that prior effective date rules not affected.* — Nothing in the amendment made by section 41(a) shall affect the application of any effective date provision (including any transitional rule) for any provision which was a predecessor to any provision contained in part V of subchapter P of chapter 1 of the Internal Revenue Code of 1954 (as added by section 41)."

Sec. 1274. Determination of issue price in the case of certain debt instruments issued for property.
(a) In general.
In the case of any debt instrument to which this section applies, for purposes of this subpart, the issue price shall be—
   (1) where there is adequate stated interest, the stated principal amount, or
   (2) in any other case, the imputed principal amount.
(b) Imputed principal amount.
For purposes of this section—
   (1) In general. Except as provided in paragraph (3), the imputed principal amount of any debt instrument shall be equal to the sum of the present values of all payments due under such debt instrument.
   (2) Determination of present value. For purposes of paragraph (1), the present value of a payment shall be determined in the manner provided by regulations prescribed by the Secretary—
      (A) as of the date of the sale or exchange, and
      (B) by using a discount rate equal to the applicable Federal rate, compounded semiannually.
   (3) Fair market value rule in potentially abusive situations.
      (A) In general. In the case of any potentially abusive situation, the imputed principal amount of any debt instrument received in exchange for property shall be the fair market value of such property adjusted to take into account other consideration involved in the transaction.
      (B) Potentially abusive situation defined. For purposes of subparagraph (A), the term "potentially abusive situation" means—
         (i) a tax shelter (as defined in section 6662(d)(2)(C)(iii)), and
         (ii) any other situation which, by reason of—
            (I) recent sales transactions,
            (II) nonrecourse financing,
            (III) financing with a term in excess of the economic life of the property, or
            (IV) other circumstances,
      is of a type which the Secretary specifies by regulations as having potential for tax avoidance.
(c) Debt instruments to which section applies.
   (1) In general. Except as otherwise provided in this subsection, this section shall apply to any debt instrument given in consideration for the sale or exchange of property if—
      (A) the stated redemption price at maturity for such debt instrument exceeds—
         (i) where there is adequate stated interest, the stated principal amount, or

         (ii) in any other case, the imputed principal amount of such debt instrument determined under subsection (b), and
      (B) some or all of the payments due under such debt instrument are due more than 6 months after the date of such sale or exchange.
   (2) Adequate stated interest. For purposes of this section, there is adequate stated interest with respect to any debt instrument if the stated principal amount for such debt instrument is less than or equal to the imputed principal amount of such debt instrument determined under subsection (b).
   (3) Exceptions. This section shall not apply to—
      (A) Sales for $1,000,000 or less of farms by individuals or small businesses.
         (i) In general. Any debt instrument arising from the sale or exchange of a farm (within the meaning of section 6420(c)(2))—
            (I) by an individual, estate, or testamentary trust,
            (II) by a corporation which as of the date of the sale or exchange is a small business corporation (as defined in section 1244(c)(3)), or
            (III) by a partnership which as of the date of the sale or exchange meets requirements similar to those of section 1244(c)(3).
         (ii) $1,000,000 limitation. Clause (i) shall apply only if it can be determined at the time of the sale or exchange that the sales price cannot exceed $1,000,000. For purposes of the preceding sentence, all sales and exchanges which are part of the same transaction (or a series of related transactions) shall be treated as 1 sale or exchange.
      (B) Sales of principal residences. Any debt instrument arising from the sale or exchange by an individual of his principal residence (within the meaning of section 121).
      (C) Sales involving total payments of $250,000 or less.
         (i) In general. Any debt instrument arising from the sale or exchange of property if the sum of the following amounts does not exceed $250,000:
            (I) the aggregate amount of the payments due under such debt instrument and all other debt instruments received as consideration for the sale or exchange, and
            (II) the aggregate amount of any other consideration to be received for the sale or exchange.
         (ii) Consideration other than debt instrument taken into account at fair market value. For purposes of clause (i), any consideration (other than a debt instrument) shall be taken into account at its fair market value.
         (iii) Aggregation of transactions. For purposes of this subparagraph, all sales and exchanges which are part of the same transaction (or a series of related transactions) shall be treated as 1 sale or exchange.
      (D) Debt instruments which are publicly traded or issued for publicly traded property. Any debt instrument to which section 1273(b)(3) applies.
      (E) Certain sales of patents. In the case of any transfer described in section 1235(a) (relating to sale or exchange of patents), any amount contingent on the productivity, use, or disposition of the property transferred.
      (F) Sales or exchanges to which section 483(e) applies. Any debt instrument to the extent section 483(e) (relating to certain land transfers between related persons) applies to such instrument.

Original issue discount Code Sec. 1274

(4) **Exception for assumptions.** If any person—
(A) in connection with the sale or exchange of property, assumes any debt instrument, or
(B) acquires any property subject to any debt instrument,
in determining whether this section or section 483 applies to such debt instrument, such assumption (or such acquisition) shall not be taken into account unless the terms and conditions of such debt instrument are modified (or the nature of the transaction is changed) in connection with the assumption (or acquisition).

(d) **Determination of applicable federal rate.**
For purposes of this section—
(1) **Applicable federal rate.**
(A) In general.

In the case of a debt instrument with a term of:	The applicable Federal rate is:
Not over 3 years	The Federal short-term rate.
Over 3 years but not over 9 years	The Federal mid-term rate.
Over 9 years	The Federal long-term rate.

(B) Determination of rates. During each calendar month, the Secretary shall determine the Federal short-term rate, mid-term rate, and long-term rate which shall apply during the following calendar month.
(C) Federal rate for any calendar month. For purposes of this paragraph—
(i) Federal short-term rate. The Federal short-term rate shall be the rate determined by the Secretary based on the average market yield (during any 1-month period selected by the Secretary and ending in the calendar month in which the determination is made) on outstanding marketable obligations of the United States with remaining periods to maturity of 3 years or less.
(ii) Federal mid-term and long-term rates. The Federal mid-term and long-term rate shall be determined in accordance with the principles of clause (i).
(D) Lower rate permitted in certain cases. The Secretary may by regulations permit a rate to be used with respect to any debt instrument which is lower than the applicable Federal rate if the taxpayer establishes to the satisfaction of the Secretary that such lower rate is based on the same principles as the applicable Federal rate and is appropriate for the term of such instrument.

(2) **Lowest 3-month rate applicable to any sale or exchange.**
(A) In general. In the case of any sale or exchange, the applicable Federal rate shall be the lowest 3-month rate.
(B) Lowest 3-month rate. For purposes of subparagraph (A), the term "lowest 3-month rate" means the lowest of the applicable Federal rates in effect for any month in the 3-calendar-month period ending with the 1st calendar month in which there is a binding contract in writing for such sale or exchange.

(3) **Term of debt instrument.** In determining the term of a debt instrument for purposes of this subsection, under regulations prescribed by the Secretary, there shall be taken into account options to renew or extend.

(e) **110 percent rate where sale-leaseback involved.**
(1) **In general.** In the case of any debt instrument to which this subsection applies, the discount rate used under subsection (b)(2)(B) or section 483(b) shall be 110 percent of the applicable Federal rate, compounded semiannually.
(2) **Lower discount rates shall not apply.** Section 1274A shall not apply to any debt instrument to which this subsection applies.
(3) **Debt instruments to which this subsection applies.** This subsection shall apply to any debt instrument given in consideration for the sale or exchange of any property if, pursuant to a plan, the transferor or any related person leases a portion of such property after such sale or exchange.

In **1998,** P.L. 105-206, Sec. 6005(e)(3), added "on or" before "before" each place it appeared in the heading and text of Sec. 312(d)(2)[sic (e)] of P.L. 105-34, see below.

In **1997,** P.L. 105-34, Sec. 312(d)(1), substituted "section 121" for "section 1034" in subpara. (c)(3)(B), effective for sales and exchanges after 5/6/97, except as provided by Sec. 312(d)(2)-(4) [sic (e)(2)-(4)] of this Act [as amended by Sec. 6005(e)(3), 105-206, see above], which reads as follows:
"(2) Sales on or before date of enactment. At the election of the taxpayer, the amendments made by this section shall not apply to any sale or exchange on or before the date of the enactment of this Act.
"(3) Certain sales within 2 years after date of enactment. Section 121 of the Internal Revenue Code of 1986 (as amended by this section) shall be applied without regard to subsection (c)(2)(B) thereof in the case of any sale or exchange of property during the 2-year period beginning on the date of the enactment of this Act if the taxpayer held such property on the date of the enactment of this Act and fails to meet the ownership and use requirements of subsection (a) thereof with respect to such property.
"(4) Binding contracts. At the election of the taxpayer, the amendments made by this section shall not apply to a sale or exchange after the date of the enactment of this Act, if—
"(A) such sale or exchange is pursuant to a contract which was binding on such date, or
"(B) without regard to such amendments, gain would not be recognized under section 1034 of the Internal Revenue Code of 1986 (as in effect on the day before the date of the enactment of this Act) on such sale or exchange by reason of a new residence acquired on or before such date or with respect to the acquisition of which by the taxpayer a binding contract was in effect on such date.
This paragraph shall not apply to any sale or exchange by an individual if the treatment provided by section 877(a)(1) of the Internal Revenue Code of 1986 applies to such individual."

In **1996,** P.L. 104-188, Sec. 1704(t)(78), substituted "section 6662(d)(2)(C)(iii)" for "section 6662(d)(2)(C)(ii)" in clause (b)(3)(B)(i), effective 8/20/96.

In **1989,** P.L. 101-239, Sec. 7721(c)(11), substituted "section 6662(d)(2)(C)(ii)" for "section 6661(b)(2)(C)(ii)" in clause (b)(3)(B)(i), effective for returns the due date for which (determined without regard to extensions) is after 12/31/89.

In **1986,** P.L. 99-514, Sec. 1803(a)(14)(A), substituted "for $1,000,000 or less" for "for less than $1,000,000" in subpara. (c)(4)(A) (as designated before the amendment made by Sec. 101(a)(1)(D) of P.L. 99-121, see below), effective for sales and exchanges after 12/31/84, except for any sale or exchange pursuant to a written contract which was binding on 3/1/84, and at all times thereafter before the sale or exchange. For special rules and exceptions see Sec. 44(b)(4)-(7) of P.L. 98-369, reproduced below.
—P.L. 99-514, Sec. 1803(b)(1)(A), and (B), added "after December 31, 1984, and" before "before July 1, 1985" in subpara. (A) and the paragraph heading, respectively, of Sec. 44(b)(4) of P.L. 98-369 (see below) . . . Sec. 1803(b)(1)(C), added Sec. 44(b)(4)(G) of P.L. 98-369 (see below) . . . Sec. 1803(b)(4), added "not" before "greater than" in Sec. 44(b)(6)(B)(ii) of P.L. 98-369 (see below).

In **1985,** P.L. 99-121, Sec. 101(a)(1)(A), deleted "120 percent of" after "rate equal to" in subpara. (b)(2)(B) . . . Sec. 101(a)(1)(B), amended clause (c)(1)(A)(ii) . . . Sec. 101(a)(1)(C), substituted "the imputed principal amount of such debt instrument determined under subsection (b)" for "the testing amount" in para. (c)(2) . . . Sec. 101(a)(1)(D), deleted para. (c)(3) and redesignated para. (c)(4) as para. (c)(3) . . . Sec. 101(b)(1), amended subparas. (d)(1)(B), (C) and (D) . . . Sec. 101(b)(2), amended para. (d)(2) . . . Sec. 101(c), added subsec. (e) . . . Sec. 102(b), added para. (c)(4), effective as provided in Sec. 105(a) of this Act, which reads as follows:
"(a) Sections 101 and 102.
"(1) In general. Except as provided in paragraph (2), the amendments made by sections 101 and 102 shall apply to sales and exchanges after June 30, 1985, in taxable years ending after such date. The amendment made by Sec. 2 of P.L. 98-612 [see below] shall not apply to sales and exchanges after June 30, 1985, in taxable years ending after such date.
"(2) Regulatory authority to establish lower rate. Section 1274(d)(1)(D) of the Internal Revenue Code of 1954, as added by section 101(b), shall apply as if included in the amendments made by section 41 of the Tax Reform Act of 1984 [P.L. 98-369]."

Prior to amendment, clause (c)(1)(A)(ii) read as follows:
"(ii) in any other case, the testing amount, and"
Prior to deletion, para. (c)(3) read as follows:
"(3) Testing amount. For purposes of this section, the term 'testing amount' means, with respect to any debt instrument, the imputed principal amount of such

2,793

debt instrument which would be determined under subsection (b) (including paragraph (3) thereof) if a discount rate equal to 110 percent of the applicable Federal rate were used."

Prior to amendment, para. (d)(2) read as follows:

"(2) Rate applicable to any sale or exchange. In the case of any sale or exchange, the determination of the applicable Federal rate shall be made as of the first day on which there is a binding contract in writing for the sale or exchange."

Prior to amendment, subparas. (d)(1)(B), (C) and (D) read as follows:

"(B) Determination of rates. Within 15 days after the close of—

"(i) the 6-month period ending on September 30 of any calendar year, or

"(ii) the 6-month period ending on March 31 of any calendar year, the Secretary shall determine the Federal short-term rate, mid-term rate, and long-term rate for such 6-month period.

"(C) Effective date of determination. Any Federal rate determined under subparagraph (A) shall—

"(i) apply during the 6-month period beginning on January 1 of the succeeding calendar year in the case of a determination made under subparagraph (B)(i), and

"(ii) apply during the 6-month period beginning on July 1 of the calendar year in the case of a determination made under subparagraph (B)(ii).

"(D) Federal rate for any 6-month period. For purposes of this paragraph—

"(i) Federal short-term rate. The Federal short-term rate for any 6-month period shall be the rate determined by the Secretary based on the average market yield (during such 6-month period) on outstanding marketable obligations of the United States with remaining periods to maturity of 3 years or less.

"(ii) Federal mid-term and long-term rates. The Federal mid-term rate and long-term rate shall be determined in accordance with the principles of clause (i)."

—P.L. 99-121, Sec. 104, provides:

"Sec. 104. Special Rule for Certain Workouts.

"(a) General rule. Sections 483 and 1274 of the Internal Revenue Code of 1954 shall not apply to the issuance or modification of any written indebtedness if —

"(1) such issuance or modification is in connection with a workout of a specified MLC loan which (as of May 31, 1985) was substantially in arrears, and

"(2) the aggregate principal amount of indebtedness resulting from such workout does not exceed the sum (as of the time of the workout) of the outstanding principal amount of the specified MLC loan and any arrearages on such loan.

"(b) Specified MLC loan. For purposes of subsection (a), the term 'specified MLC loan' means any loan which, in a submission dated June 17, 1985, on behalf of the New York State Mortgage Loan Enforcement and Administration Corporation, had one of the following loan numbers: 001, 005, 007, 012, 025, 038, 041, 042, 043, 049, 053, 064, 068, 090, 141, 180, or 188."

In 1984, P.L. 98-612, Sec. 2, added Sec. 44(b)(4)-(7) of P.L. 98-369 [as amended by Sec. 1803(b)(1)(A) of P.L. 99-514-(C), see above], reproduced below.

—P.L. 98-369, Sec. 41(a), added Code Sec. 1274, effective (as provided by Sec. 44(b)(1) of this Act) for sales and exchanges after 12/31/84, except for any sale or exchange pursuant to a written contract which was binding on 3/1/84, and at all times thereafter before the sale or exchange. For special rules and exceptions Sec. 44(b)(4)-(7) of this Act [added by Sec. 2 of P.L. 98-612, as amended by Sec. 1803(b)(1)(A) of P.L. 99-514-(C), see above] provides:

"(4) Special rules for sales after December 31, 1984, and before July 1, 1985.

"(A) In general.— In the case of any sale or exchange after December 31, 1984, and before July 1, 1985, of property other than new section 38 property—

"(i) sections 483(c)(1)(B) and 1274(c)(3) of the Internal Revenue Code of 1954 shall be applied by substituting the testing rate determined under subparagraph (B) for 110 percent of the applicable Federal rate determined under section 1274(d) of such Code, and

"(ii) sections 483(b) and 1274(b) of such Code shall be applied by substituting the imputation rate determined under subparagraph (C) for 120 percent of the applicable Federal rate determined under section 1274(d) of such Code.

"(B) Testing rate.— For purposes of this paragraph—

"(i) In general.— The testing rate determined under this subparagraph is the sum of—

"(I) 9 percent, plus

"(II) if the borrowed amount exceeds $2,000,000, the excess determined under clause (ii) multiplied by a fraction the numerator of which is the borrowed amount to the extent it exceeds $2,000,000, and the denominator of which is the borrowed amount.

"(ii) Excess.— For purposes of clause (i), the excess determined under this clause is the excess of 110 percent of the applicable Federal rate determined under section 1274(d) of such Code over 9 percent.

"(C) Imputation rate.— For purposes of this paragraph—

"(i) In general.— The imputation rate determined under this subparagraph is the sum of—

"(I) 10 percent, plus

"(II) if the borrowed amount exceeds $2,000,000, the excess determined under clause (ii) multiplied by a fraction the numerator of which is the borrowed amount to the extent it exceeds $2,000,000, and the denominator of which is the borrowed amount.

"(ii) Excess.— For purposes of clause (i), the excess determined under this clause is the excess of 120 percent of the applicable Federal rate determined under section 1274(d) of such Code over 10 percent.

"(D) Borrowed amount.— For purposes of this paragraph, the term 'borrowed amount' means the stated principal amount.

"(E) Aggregation rules.— For purposes of this paragraph—

"(i) all sales or exchanges which are part of the same transaction (or a series of related transactions) shall be treated as one sale or exchange, and

"(ii) all debt instruments arising from the same transaction (or a series of related transactions) shall be treated as one debt instrument.

"(F) Cash method of accounting.— In the case of any sale or exchange before July 1, 1985, of property (other than new section 38 property) used in the active business of farming and in which the borrowed amount does not exceed $2,000,000—

"(i) section 1274 of the Internal Revenue Code of 1954 shall not apply, and

"(ii) interest on the obligation issued in connection with such sale or exchange shall be taken into account by both buyer and seller on the cash receipts and disbursements method of accounting.

The Secretary of the Treasury or his delegate may by regulation prescribe rules to prevent the mismatching of interest income and interest deductions in connection with obligations on which interest is computed on the cash receipts and disbursements method of accounting.

"(G) Clarification of application of this paragraph, etc.— This paragraph and paragraphs (5), (6), and (7) shall apply only in the case of sales or exchanges to which section 1274 or 483 of the Internal Revenue Code of 1954 (as amended by section 41) applies.

"(5) General rule for assumptions of loans.— Except as provided in paragraphs (6) and (7), if any person—

"(A) assumes, in connection with the sale or exchange of property, any debt obligation, or

"(B) acquires any property subject to any debt obligation, sections 1274 and 483 of the Internal Revenue Code of 1954 shall apply to such debt obligation by reason of such assumption (or such acquisition).

"(6) Exception for assumptions of loans made on or before October 15, 1984.—

"(A) In general.— If any person—

"(i) assumes, in connection with the sale or exchange of property, any debt obligation described in subparagraph (B) and issued on or before October 15, 1984, or

"(ii) acquires any property subject to any such debt obligation issued on or before October 15, 1984,

sections 1274 and 483 of the Internal Revenue Code of 1954 shall not be applied to such debt obligation by reason of such assumption (or such acquisition) unless the terms and conditions of such debt obligation are modified in connection with the assumption (or acquisition).

"(B) Obligations described in this subparagraph.— A debt obligation is described in this subparagraph if such obligation—

"(i) was issued on or before October 15, 1984, and

"(ii) was assumed (or property was taken subject to such obligation) in connection with the sale or exchange of property (including a deemed sale under section 338(a)) the sales price of which is not greater than $100,000,000.

"(C) Regulations.— The Secretary shall prescribe such regulations as may be appropriate to effect the purpose of this paragraph and paragraph (5), including regulations relating to tax-exempt obligations, government subsidized loans, or other instruments.

"(D) Certain exempt transactions.— The Secretary shall prescribe regulations under which any transaction shall be exempt from the application of this paragraph if such exemption is not likely to significantly reduce the tax liability of the purchaser by reason of the overstatement of the adjusted basis of the acquired asset.

"(7) Exception for assumptions of loans with respect to certain property.—

"(A) In general.— If any person—

"(i) assumes, in connection with the sale or exchange of property described in subparagraph (B), any debt obligation, or

"(ii) acquires any such property subject to any such debt obligation,

sections 1274 and 483 of the Internal Revenue Code of 1954 shall not be applied to such debt obligation by reason of such assumption (or such acquisition) unless the terms and conditions of such debt obligation are modified in connection with the assumption (or acquisition).

"(B) Sales or exchanges to which this paragraph applies.— This paragraph shall apply to any of the following sales or exchanges:

"(i) Residences.— Any sale or exchange of a residence by an individual, an estate, or a testamentary trust, but only if—

"(I) either—

"(aa) such residence on the date of such sale or exchange (or in the case of an estate or testamentary trust, on the date of death of the decedent) was the principal residence (within the meaning of section 1034) of the individual or decedent, or

"(bb) during the 2-year period ending on such date, no substantial portion of such residence was of a character subject to an allowance under this title for depreciation (or amortization in lieu thereof) in the hands of such individual or decedent, and

"(II) such residence was not at any time, in the hands of such individual, estate, testamentary trust, or decedent, described in section 1221(1), (relating to inventory, etc.).

"(ii) Farms.— Any sale or exchange by a qualified person of—

"(I) real property which was used as a farm (within the meaning of section 6420(c)(2)) at all times during the 3-year period ending on the date of such sale or exchange, or

"(II) tangible personal property which was used in the active conduct of the trade or business of farming on such farm and is sold in connection with the sale of such farm,

but only if such property is sold or exchanged for use in the active conduct of the trade or business of farming by the transferee of such property.

"(iii) Trades or businesses.—

"(I) In general.— Any sale or exchange by a qualified person of any trade or business.

Original issue discount Code Sec. 1274A

"(II) Application with subparagraph (B).—This subparagraph shall not apply to any sale or exchange of any property described in subparagraph (B).

"(III) New section as property.—This subparagraph shall not apply to the sale or exchange of any property which, in the hands of the transferee, is new section 38 property.

"(iv) Sale of business real estate.—Any sale or exchange of any real property used in an active trade or business by a person who would be a qualified person if he disposed of his entire interest.

This subparagraph shall not apply to any transaction described in the last sentence of paragraph (6)(B) (relating to transaction in excess of $100,000,000).

"(C) Definitions.—For purposes of this paragraph—

"(i) Qualified person defined.—The term 'qualified person' means—

"(I) a person who—

"(aa) is an individual, estate, or testamentary trust,

"(bb) is a corporation which immediately prior to the date of the sale or exchange has 35 or fewer shareholders, or

"(cc) is a partnership which immediately prior to the date of the sale or exchange has 35 or fewer partners,

"(II) is a 10-percent owner of a farm or a trade or business,

"(III) pursuant to a plan, disposes of—

"(aa) an interest in a farm or farm property, or

"(bb) his entire interest in a trade or business and all substantially similar trades or businesses, and

"(IV) the ownership interest of whom may be readily established by reason of qualified allocations (of the type described in section 168(j)(9)(B), one class of stock, or the like).

"(ii) 10-percent owner defined.—The term '10-percent owner' means a person having at least a 10-percent ownership interest, applying the attribution rules of section 318 (other than subsection (a)(4)).

"(iii) Trade or business defined.—

"(I) In general.—The term 'trade or business' means any trade or business, including any line of business, qualifying as an active trade or business within the meaning of section 355.

"(II) Rental of real property.—For purposes of this clause, the holding of real property for rental shall not be treated as an active trade or business."

Sec. 44(j) of P.L. 98-369 of this Act provides:

"(j) Clarification that prior effective date rules not affected. Nothing in the amendment made by section 41(a) shall affect the application of any effective date provision (including any transitional rule) for any provision which was a predecessor to any provision contained in part V of subchapter P of chapter 1 of the Internal Revenue Code of 1954 (as added by section 41)."

Sec. 1274A. Special rules for certain transactions where stated principal amount does not exceed $2,800,000.

(a) Lower discount rate.

In the case of any qualified debt instrument, the discount rate used for purposes of sections 483 and 1274 shall not exceed 9 percent, compounded semiannually.

(b) Qualified debt instrument defined.

For purposes of this section, the term "qualified debt instrument" means any debt instrument given in consideration for the sale or exchange of property (other than new section 38 property within the meaning of section 48(b), as in effect on the day before the date of the enactment [11/5/90] of the Revenue Reconciliation Act of 1990) if the stated principal amount of such instrument does not exceed $2,800,000.

(c) Election to use cash method where stated principal amount does not exceed $2,000,000.

(1) In general. In the case of any cash method debt instrument—

(A) section 1274 shall not apply, and

(B) interest on such debt instrument shall be taken into account by both the borrower and the lender under the cash receipts and disbursements method of accounting.

(2) **Cash method debt instrument.** For purposes of paragraph (1), the term "cash method debt instrument" means any qualified debt instrument if—

(A) the stated principal amount does not exceed $2,000,000,

(B) the lender does not use an accrual method of accounting and is not a dealer with respect to the property sold or exchanged,

(C) section 1274 would have applied to such instrument but for an election under this subsection, and

(D) an election under this subsection is jointly made with respect to such debt instrument by the borrower and lender.

(3) **Successors bound by election.**

(A) In general. Except as provided in subparagraph (B), paragraph (1) shall apply to any successor to the borrower or lender with respect to a cash method debt instrument.

(B) Exception where lender transfers debt instrument to accrual method taxpayer. If the lender (or any successor) transfers any cash method debt instrument to a taxpayer who uses an accrual method of accounting, this paragraph shall not apply with respect to such instrument for periods after such transfer.

(4) **Fair market value rule in potentially abusive situations.** In the case of any cash method debt instrument, section 483 shall be applied as if it included provisions similar to the provisions of section 1274(b)(3).

(d) Other special rules.

(1) **Aggregation rules.** For purposes of this section—

(A) all sales or exchanges which are part of the same transaction (or a series of related transactions) shall be treated as 1 sale or exchange, and

(B) all debt instruments arising from the same transaction (or a series of related transactions) shall be treated as 1 debt instrument.

(2) **Inflation adjustments.**

(A) In general. In the case of any debt instrument arising out of a sale or exchange during any calendar year after 1989, each dollar amount contained in the preceding provisions of this section shall be increased by the inflation adjustment for such calendar year. Any increase under the preceding sentence shall be rounded to the nearest multiple of $100 (or, if such increase is a multiple of $50, such increase shall be increased to the nearest multiple of $100).

(B) Inflation adjustment. For purposes of subparagraph (A), the inflation adjustment for any calendar year is the percentage (if any) by which—

(i) the CPI for the preceding calendar year exceeds

(ii) the CPI for calendar year 1988.

For purposes of the preceding sentence, the CPI for any calendar year is the average of the Consumer Price Index as of the close of the 12-month period ending on September 30 of such calendar year.

(e) Regulations.

The Secretary shall prescribe such regulations as may be necessary to carry out the purposes of this subsection, including—

(1) regulations coordinating the provisions of this section with other provisions of this title,

(2) regulations necessary to prevent the avoidance of tax through the abuse of the provisions of subsection (c), and

(3) regulations relating to the treatment of transfers of cash method debt instruments.

In 1996, P.L. 104-188, Sec. 1704(t)(62), substituted "instrument" for "instument" in subpara. (c)(1)(B), effective 8/20/96.

In 1990, P.L. 101-508, Sec. 11813(b)(22), added ", as in effect on the day before the date of the enactment of the Revenue Reconciliation Act of 1990" after "section 48(b)" in subsec. (b), effective for property placed in service after 12/31/90 except as provided in Sec. 11813(c)(2) of this Act, reproduced in note following Code Sec. 46.

In 1985, P.L. 99-121, Sec. 102(a), added Code Sec. 1274A, effective for sales and exchanges after 6/30/85, in tax. yrs. end. after 6/30/85. The amendment made by Sec. 2 of P.L. 98-612 (adding Sec. 44(b)(4)-(7) of P.L. 98-369, reproduced in note following Code Sec. 1274] shall not apply to sales and exchanges after 6/30/85, in tax. yrs. end. after 6/30/85.

Sec. 1275. Other definitions and special rules.
(a) Definitions.
For purposes of this subpart—
(1) Debt instrument.
(A) In general. Except as provided in subparagraph (B), the term "debt instrument" means a bond, debenture, note, or certificate or other evidence of indebtedness.
(B) Exception for certain annuity contracts. The term "debt instrument" shall not include any annuity contract to which section 72 applies and which—
(i) depends (in whole or in substantial part) on the life expectancy of 1 or more individuals, or
(ii) is issued by an insurance company subject to tax under subchapter L (or by an entity described in section 501(c) and exempt from tax under section 501(a) which would be subject to tax under subchapter L were it not so exempt)—
(I) in a transaction in which there is no consideration other than cash or another annuity contract meeting the requirements of this clause,
(II) pursuant to the exercise of an election under an insurance contract by a beneficiary thereof on the death of the insured party under such contract, or
(III) in a transaction involving a qualified pension or employee benefit plan.
(2) Issue date.
(A) Publicly offered debt instruments. In the case of any debt instrument which is publicly offered, the term "date of original issue" means the date on which the issue was first issued to the public.
(B) Issues not publicly offered and not issued for property. In the case of any debt instrument to which section 1273(b)(2) applies, the term "date of original issue" means the date on which the debt instrument was sold by the issuer.
(C) Other debt instruments. In the case of any debt instrument not described in subparagraph (A) or (B), the term "date of original issue" means the date on which the debt instrument was issued in a sale or exchange.
(3) Tax-exempt obligation. The term "tax-exempt obligation" means any obligation if—
(A) the interest on such obligation is not includible in gross income under section 103, or
(B) the interest on such obligation is exempt from tax (without regard to the identity of the holder) under any other provision of law.
(4) Treatment of obligations distributed by corporations. Any debt obligation of a corporation distributed by such corporation with respect to its stock shall be treated as if it had been issued by such corporation for property.
(b) Treatment of borrower in the case of certain loans for personal use.
(1) Sections 1274 and 483 not to apply. In the case of the obligor under any debt instrument given in consideration for the sale or exchange of property, sections 1274 and 483 shall not apply if such property is personal use property.
(2) Original issue discount deducted on cash basis in certain cases. In the case of any debt instrument, if—
(A) such instrument—
(i) is incurred in connection with the acquisition or carrying of personal use property, and
(ii) has original issue discount (determined after the application of paragraph (1)), and
(B) the obligor under such instrument uses the cash receipts and disbursements method of accounting,

notwithstanding section 163(e), the original issue discount on such instrument shall be deductible only when paid.
(3) Personal use property. For purposes of this subsection, the term "personal use property" means any property substantially all of the use of which by the taxpayer is not in connection with a trade or business of the taxpayer or an activity described in section 212. The determination of whether property is described in the preceding sentence shall be made as of the time of issuance of the debt instrument.
(c) Information requirements.
(1) Information required to be set forth on instrument.
(A) In general. In the case of any debt instrument having original issue discount, the Secretary may by regulations require that—
(i) the amount of the original issue discount, and
(ii) the issue date,
be set forth on such instrument.
(B) Special rule for instruments not publicly offered. In the case of any issue of debt instruments not publicly offered, the regulations prescribed under subparagraph (A) shall not require the information to be set forth on the debt instrument before any disposition of such instrument by the first buyer.
(2) Information required to be submitted to secretary. In the case of any issue of publicly offered debt instruments having original issue discount, the issuer shall (at such time and in such manner as the Secretary shall by regulation prescribe) furnish the Secretary the following information:
(A) The amount of the original issue discount.
(B) The issue date.
(C) Such other information with respect to the issue as the Secretary may by regulations require.
For purposes of the preceding sentence, any person who makes a public offering of stripped bonds (or stripped coupons) shall be treated as the issuer of a publicly offered debt instrument having original issue discount.
(3) Exceptions. This subsection shall not apply to any obligation referred to in section 1272(a)(2) (relating to exceptions from current inclusion of original issue discount).
(4) Cross reference. For civil penalty for failure to meet requirements of this subsection, see section 6706.
(d) Regulation authority.
The Secretary may prescribe regulations providing that where, by reason of varying rates of interest, put or call options, indefinite maturities, contingent payments, assumptions of debt instruments, or other circumstances, the tax treatment under this subpart (or section 163(e)) does not carry out the purposes of this subpart (or section 163(e)), such treatment shall be modified to the extent appropriate to carry out the purposes of this subpart (or section 163(e)).

In 2000, P.L. 106-554, Sec. 1(a)(7), [which enacted into law Sec. 318(c)(1) of P.L. 106-554] substituted "subchapter L (or by an entity described in section 501(c) and exempt from tax under section 501(a) which would be subject to tax under subchapter L were it not so exempt)" for "subchapter L" in clause (a)(1)(B)(ii), effective for tax. yrs. ending after 7/18/84.
In 1990, P.L. 101-508, Sec. 11325(a)(2), deleted para. (a)(4) and redesignated para. (a)(5) as para. (a)(4), effective for debt instruments issued, and stock transferred, after 10/9/90, in satisfaction of any indebtedness, except as provided in Sec. 11325(c)(2) of this Act, which reads as follows:
"(2) Exceptions. The amendments made by this section shall not apply to any debt instrument issued, or stock transferred, in satisfaction of any indebtedness if such issuance or transfer (as the case may be)—
"(A) is in a title 11 or similar case (as defined in section 368(a)(3)(A) of the Internal Revenue Code of 1986) which was filed on or before October 9, 1990, or
"(B) is pursuant to a written binding contract in effect on October 9, 1990, and at all times thereafter before such issuance or transfer,

Market discount on bonds — Code Sec. 1276(c)(1)(A)

"(C) is pursuant to a transaction which was described in documents filed with the Securities and Exchange Commission on or before October 9, 1990, or

"(D) is pursuant to a transaction—

"(i) the material terms of which were described in a written public announcement on or before October 9, 1990,

"(ii) which was the subject of a prior filing with the Securities and Exchange Commission, and

"(iii) which is the subject of a subsequent filing with the Securities and Exchange Commission before January 1, 1991."

Prior to deletion, para. (a)(4) read as follows:

"(4) Special rule for determination of issue price in case of exchange of debt instruments in reorganizations.

"(A) In general. If—

"(i) any debt instrument is issued pursuant to a plan or reorganization (within the meaning of section 368(a)(1)) for another debt instrument (hereinafter in this paragraph referred to as the 'old debt instrument'), and

"(ii) the amount which (but for this paragraph) would be the issue price of the debt instrument so issued is less than the adjusted issue price of the old debt instrument,

then the issue price of the debt instrument so issued shall be treated as equal to the adjusted issue price of the old debt instrument,

"(B) Definitions. For purposes of this paragraph—

"(i) Debt instrument. The term 'debt instrument' includes an investment unit.

"(ii) Adjusted issue price.

"(I) In general. The adjusted issue price of the old debt instrument is its issue price, increased by the portion of any original issue discount previously includible in the gross income of any holder (without regard to subsection (a)(7) or (b)(4) of section 1272 (or the corresponding provisions of prior law)).

"(II) Special rule for applying section 163(e). For purposes of section 163(e), the adjusted issue price of the old debt instrument is its issue price, increased by any original issue discount previously allowed as a deduction."

In 1988, P.L. 100-647, Sec. 1006(u)(4), substituted "subsection (a)(7)" for "subsection (a)(6)" in subclause (a)(4)(B)(ii)(I), effective for debt instruments issued after 12/31/86 in tax. yrs. end. after 12/31/86.

In 1986, P.L. 99-514, Sec. 1804(f)(2)(A)(i), redesignated para. (a)(4) (as added by Sec. 61(c)(2) of P.L. 98-369) as para. (a)(5) [see below] . . . Sec. 1804(f)(2)(A)(ii), substituted "by corporations" for "to corporations" in the heading of the paragraph redesignated as (a)(5), effective for distributions declared after 3/15/84, in tax. yrs. end. after 3/15/84.

In 1984, P.L. 98-369, Sec. 41(a), added Code Sec. 1275, for tax. yrs. end. after 7/18/84, except for subsec. (c) of Code Sec. 1275, which is effective 8/17/84. Sec. 44(j) of the Act provides:

"*(j) Clarification that prior effective date rules not affected.* Nothing in the amendment made by section 41(a) shall affect the application of any effective date provision (including any transitional rule) for any provision which was a predecessor to any provision contained in part V of subchapter P of chapter 1 of the Internal Revenue Code of 1954 (as added by section 41)."

—P.L. 98-369, Sec. 61(c)(2), added para. (a)(4) [sic (a)(5)] effective for distributions declared after 3/15/84, in tax. yrs. end. after 3/15/84.

SUBPART B.—MARKET DISCOUNT ON BONDS

Sec.

1276. Disposition gain representing accrued market discount treated as ordinary income.

1277. Deferral of interest deduction allocable to accrued market discount.

1278. Definitions and special rules.

Sec. 1276. Disposition gain representing accrued market discount treated as ordinary income.

(a) Ordinary income.

(1) In general. Except as otherwise provided in this section, gain on the disposition of any market discount bond shall be treated as ordinary income to the extent it does not exceed the accrued market discount on such bond. Such gain shall be recognized notwithstanding any other provision of this subtitle.

(2) Dispositions other than sales, etc. For purposes of paragraph (1), a person disposing of any market discount bond in any transaction other than a sale, exchange, or involuntary conversion shall be treated as realizing an amount equal to the fair market value of the bond.

(3) Treatment of partial principal payments.

(A) In general. Any partial principal payment on a market discount bond shall be included in gross income as ordinary income to the extent such payment does not exceed the accrued market discount on such bond.

(B) Adjustment. If subparagraph (A) applies to any partial principal payment on any market discount bond, for purposes of applying this section to any disposition of (or subsequent partial principal payment on) such bond, the amount of accrued market discount shall be reduced by the amount of such partial principal payment included in gross income under subparagraph (A).

(4) Gain treated as interest for certain purposes. Except for purposes of sections 103, 871(a), 881, 1441, 1442, and 6049 (and such other provisions as may be specified in regulations), any amount treated as ordinary income under paragraph (1) or (3) shall be treated as interest for purposes of this title.

(b) Accrued market discount.

For purposes of this section—

(1) Ratable accrual. Except as otherwise provided in this subsection or subsection (c), the accrued market discount on any bond shall be an amount which bears the same ratio to the market discount on such bond as—

(A) the number of days which the taxpayer held the bond, bears to

(B) the number of days after the date the taxpayer acquired the bond and up to (and including) the date of its maturity.

(2) Election of accrual on basis of constant interest rate (in lieu of ratable accrual).

(A) In general. At the election of the taxpayer with respect to any bond, the accrued market discount on such bond shall be the aggregate amount which would have been includible in the gross income of the taxpayer under section 1272(a) (determined without regard to paragraph (2) thereof) with respect to such bond for all periods during which the bond was held by the taxpayer if such bond had been—

(i) originally issued on the date on which such bond was acquired by the taxpayer,

(ii) for an issue price equal to the basis of the taxpayer in such bond immediately after its acquisition.

(B) Coordination where bond has original issue discount. In the case of any bond having original issue discount, for purposes of applying subparagraph (A)—

(i) the stated redemption price at maturity of such bond shall be treated as equal to its revised issue price, and

(ii) the determination of the portion of the original issue discount which would have been includible in the gross income of the taxpayer under section 1272(a) shall be made under regulations prescribed by the Secretary.

(C) Election irrevocable. An election under subparagraph (A), once made with respect to any bond, shall be irrevocable.

(3) Special rule where partial principal payments. In the case of a bond the principal of which may be paid in 2 or more payments, the amount of accrued market discount shall be determined under regulations prescribed by the Secretary.

(c) Treatment of nonrecognition transactions.

Under regulations prescribed by the Secretary—

(1) Transferred basis property. If a market discount bond is transferred in a nonrecognition transaction and such bond is transferred basis property in the hands of the transferee, for purposes of determining the amount of the accrued market discount with respect to the transferee—

(A) the transferee shall be treated as having acquired the bond on the date on which it was acquired by the

2,797

transferor for an amount equal to the basis of the transferor, and

(B) proper adjustments shall be made for gain recognized by the transferor on such transfer (and for any original issue discount or market discount included in the gross income of the transferor).

(2) Exchanged basis property. If any market discount bond is disposed of by the taxpayer in a nonrecognition transaction and paragraph (1) does not apply to such transaction, any accrued market discount determined with respect to the property disposed of to the extent not theretofore treated as ordinary income under subsection (a)—

(A) shall be treated as accrued market discount with respect to the exchanged basis property received by the taxpayer in such transaction if such property is a market discount bond, and

(B) shall be treated as ordinary income on the disposition of the exchanged basis property received by the taxpayer in such exchange if such property is not a market discount bond.

(3) Paragraph (1) to apply to certain distributions by corporations or partnerships. For purposes of paragraph (1), if the basis of any market discount bond in the hands of a transferee is determined under section 732(a), or 732(b), such property shall be treated as transferred basis property in the hands of such transferee.

(d) Special rules.
Under regulations prescribed by the Secretary—

(1) rules similar to the rules of subsection (b) of section 1245 shall apply for purposes of this section; except that—

(A) paragraph (1) of such subsection shall not apply,

(B) an exchange qualifying under section 354(a), 355(a), or 356(a) (determined without regard to subsection (a) of this section) shall be treated as an exchange described in paragraph (3) of such subsection, and

(C) paragraph (3) of section 1245(b) shall be applied as if it did not contain a reference to section 351, and

(2) appropriate adjustments shall be made to the basis of any property to reflect gain recognized under subsection (a).

In **1993**, P.L. 103-66, Sec. 13206(b)(1)(A), deleted subsec. (e)... Sec. 13206(b)(2)(B)(i), substituted "sections 103, 871(a)," for "sections 871(a)" in para. (a)(4), effective for obligations purchased (within the meaning of Code Sec. 1272(d)(1)) after 4/30/93.
Prior to deletion, subsec. (e) read as follows:
"(e) Section not to apply to market discount bonds issued on or before date of enactment of section. This section shall not apply to any market discount bond issued on or before July 18, 1984."
In **1988**, P.L. 100-647, Sec. 1018(u)(46)(A), added "(3)" before "Special" in the heading of the para. added by Sec. 1803(a)(13)(A)(iii) of P.L. 99-514 [para.(b)(3)] see below... Sec. 1018(u)(46)(B), added a dash after "payments" in the heading of para. (b)(3)... Sec. 1018(u)(46)(C), added a period at the end of para. (b)(3) effective for obligations acquired after 10/22/86.
In **1986**, P.L. 99-514, Sec. 631(e)(15), deleted "334(c)," before "732(a)," in para. (c)(3), effective as provided in Sec. 633(a) of this Act, reproduced in note following Code Sec. 897 and Secs. 633(c), (d)(1)-(d)(6), (e), (f) and (g) of this Act, reproduced in note following Code Sec. 336.
—P.L. 99-514, Sec. 1803(a)(5), deleted "and" at the end of subpara. (d)(1)(A) and added subpara. (d)(1)(C), effective for obligations issued after 7/18/84, in tax. yrs. end. after 7/18/84, and as provided in Sec. 44(j) of P.L. 98-369 reproduced below.
—P.L. 99-514, Sec. 1803(a)(13)(A)(i), redesignated para. (a)(3) as (a)(4) and added new para. (a)(3)... Sec. 1803(a)(13)(A)(ii), substituted "under paragraph (1) or (3)" for "under paragraph (1)" in para. (a)(4) [as redesignated by Sec. 1803(a)(13)(A)(i) of this Act, see above]... Sec. 1803(a)(13)(A)(iii), added a para. [sic para. (b)(3)] to the end of subsec. (b), effective for obligations acquired after 10/22/86.
—P.L. 99-514, Sec. 1899A(28), substituted "July 18, 1984" for "the date of the enactment of this section" in subsec. (e), effective 10/22/86.
In **1984**, P.L. 98-369, Sec. 41(a), added Code Sec. 1276, effective for obligations issued after 7/18/84, in tax. yrs. end. after 7/18/84. Sec. 44(j) of this Act provides as follows:

"(j) Clarification that prior effective date rules not affected. Nothing in the amendment made by section 41(a) shall affect the application of any effective date provision (including any transitional rule) for any provision which was a predecessor to any provision contained in part V of subchapter P of chapter 1 of the Internal Revenue Code of 1954 (as added by section 41)."

Sec. 1277. Deferral of interest deduction allocable to accrued market discount.

(a) General rule.
Except as otherwise provided in this section, the net direct interest expense with respect to any market discount bond shall be allowed as a deduction for the taxable year only to the extent that such expense exceeds the portion of the market discount allocable to the days during the taxable year on which such bond was held by the taxpayer (as determined under the rules of section 1276(b)).

(b) Disallowed deduction allowed for later years.

(1) Election to take into account in later year where net interest income from bond.

(A) In general. If—
(i) there is net interest income for any taxable year with respect to any market discount bond, and
(ii) the taxpayer makes an election under this subparagraph with respect to such bond,
any disallowed interest expense with respect to such bond shall be treated as interest paid or accrued by the taxpayer during such taxable year to the extent such disallowed interest expense does not exceed the net interest income with respect to such bond.

(B) Determination of disallowed interest expense. For purposes of subparagraph (A), the amount of the disallowed interest expense—
(i) shall be determined as of the close of the preceding taxable year, and
(ii) shall not include any amount previously taken into account under subparagraph (A).

(C) Net interest income. For purposes of this paragraph, the term "net interest income" means the excess of the amount determined under paragraph (2) of subsection (c) over the amount determined under paragraph (1) of subsection (c).

(2) Remainder of disallowed interest expense allowed for year of disposition.

(A) In general. Except as otherwise provided in this paragraph, the amount of the disallowed interest expense with respect to any market discount bond shall be treated as interest paid or accrued by the taxpayer in the taxable year in which such bond is disposed of.

(B) Nonrecognition transactions. If any market discount bond is disposed of in a nonrecognition transaction—
(i) the disallowed interest expense with respect to such bond shall be treated as interest paid or accrued in the year of disposition only to the extent of the amount of gain recognized on such disposition, and
(ii) the disallowed interest expense with respect to such property (to the extent not so treated) shall be treated as disallowed interest expense—
(I) in the case of a transaction described in section 1276(c)(1), of the transferee with respect to the transferred basis property, or
(II) in the case of a transaction described in section 1276(c)(2), with respect to the exchanged basis property.

(C) Disallowed interest expense reduced for amounts previously taken into account under paragraph (1). For purposes of this paragraph, the amount of the disallowed interest expense shall not include any amount previously taken into account under paragraph (1).

(3) Disallowed interest expense. For purposes of this subsection, the term "disallowed interest expense" means the aggregate amount disallowed under subsection (a) with respect to the market discount bond.

(c) Net direct interest expense.

For purposes of this section, the term "net direct interest expense" means, with respect to any market discount bond, the excess (if any) of—

(1) the amount of interest paid or accrued during the taxable year on indebtedness which is incurred or continued to purchase or carry such bond, over

(2) the aggregate amount of interest (including original issue discount) includible in gross income for the taxable year with respect to such bond.

In the case of any financial institution which is a bank (as defined in section 585(a)(2)), the determination of whether interest is described in paragraph (1) shall be made under principles similar to the principles of section 291(e)(1)(B)(ii). Under rules similar to the rules of section 265(a)(5), short sale expenses shall be treated as interest for purposes of determining net direct interest expense.

In 1996, P.L. 104-188, Sec. 1616(b)(4), deleted "or to which section 593 applies" after "section 585(a)(2))" in subsec. (c), effective for tax. yrs. begin. after 12/31/95.

In 1993, P.L. 103-66, Sec. 13206(b)(1)(B), deleted subsec. (d), effective for obligations purchased (within the meaning of Code Sec. 1272(d)(1)) after 4/30/93. Prior to deletion, subsec. (d) read as follows:

"(d) Special rule for gain recognized on disposition of market discount bonds issued on or before date of enactment of section. In the case of a market discount bond issued on or before July 18, 1984, any gain recognized by the taxpayer on any disposition of such bond shall be treated as ordinary income to the extent the amount of such gain does not exceed the amount allowable with respect to such bond under subsection (b)(2) for the taxable year in which such bond is disposed of."

In 1988, P.L. 100-647, Sec. 1018(u)(31), added a closing parenthesis after "section 585(a)(2)", in subsec. (c), effective 10/22/86.

In 1986, P.L. 99-514, Sec. 901(d)(4)(F), substituted "which is a bank (as defined in section 585(a)(2)) or to which section 593 applies," for "to which section 585 or 593 applies," in subsec. (c), effective for tax. yrs. begin. after 12/31/86.

—P.L. 99-514, Sec. 902(e)(2), substituted "section 265(a)(5)" for "section 265(5)" in subsec. (c), effective for tax. yrs. end. after 12/31/86.

—P.L. 99-514, Sec. 1899A(29), substituted "this paragraph" for "this paragaph" in subpara. (b)(1)(C) . . . Sec. 1899A(30), substituted "Paragraph (1)," for "Paragraph 1." in subpara. (b)(2)(C) . . . Sec. 1899A(31), substituted "July 18, 1984" for "the date of enactment of this section" in subsec. (d), effective 10/22/86.

In 1984, P.L. 98-369, Sec. 41(a), added Code Sec. 1277, effective for obligations acquired after 7/18/84, in tax. yrs. end. after 7/18/84. Sec. 44(j) of the Act provides:

"*(j) Clarification that prior effective date rules not affected.* Nothing in the amendment made by section 41(a) shall affect the application of any effective date provision (including any transitional rule) for any provision which was a predecessor to any provision contained in part V of subchapter P of chapter 1 of the Internal Revenue Code of 1954 (as added by section 41)."

Sec. 1278. Definitions and special rules.
(a) In general.

For purposes of this part—

(1) Market discount bond.

(A) In general. Except as provided in subparagraph (B), the term "market discount bond" means any bond having market discount.

(B) Exceptions. The term "market discount bond" shall not include—

(i) Short-term obligations. Any obligation with a fixed maturity date not exceeding 1 year from the date of issue.

(ii) United States savings bonds. Any United States savings bond.

(iii) Installment obligations. Any installment obligation to which section 453B applies.

(C) Section 1277 not applicable to tax-exempt obligations. For purposes of section 1277, the term "market discount bond" shall not include any tax-exempt obligation (as defined in section 1275(a)(3)).

(D) Treatment of bonds acquired at original issue.

(i) In general. Except as otherwise provided in this subparagraph or in regulations, the term "market discount bond" shall not include any bond acquired by the taxpayer at its original issue.

(ii) Treatment of bonds acquired for less than issue price. Clause (i) shall not apply to any bond if—

(I) the basis of the taxpayer in such bond is determined under section 1012, and

(II) such basis is less than the issue price of such bond determined under subpart A of this part.

(iii) Bonds acquired in certain reorganizations. Clause (i) shall not apply to any bond issued pursuant to a plan of reorganization (within the meaning of section 368(a)(1)) in exchange for another bond having market discount. Solely for purposes of section 1276, the preceding sentence shall not apply if such other bond was issued on or before July 18, 1984 (the date of the enactment [7/18/84] of section 1276) and if the bond issued pursuant to such plan of reorganization has the same term and the same interest rate as such other bond had.

(iv) Treatment of certain transferred basis property. For purposes of clause (i), if the adjusted basis of any bond in the hands of the taxpayer is determined by reference to the adjusted basis of such bond in the hands of a person who acquired such bond at its original issue, such bond shall be treated as acquired by the taxpayer at its original issue.

(2) Market discount.

(A) In general. The term "market discount" means the excess (if any) of—

(i) the stated redemption price of the bond at maturity, over

(ii) the basis of such bond immediately after its acquisition by the taxpayer.

(B) Coordination where bond has original issue discount. In the case of any bond having original issue discount, for purposes of subparagraph (A), the stated redemption price of such bond at maturity shall be treated as equal to its revised issue price.

(C) De minimis rule. If the market discount is less than ¼ of 1 percent of the stated redemption price of the bond at maturity multiplied by the number of complete years to maturity (after the taxpayer acquired the bond), then the market discount shall be considered to be zero.

(3) Bond. The term "bond" means any bond, debenture, note, certificate, or other evidence of indebtedness.

(4) Revised issue price. The term "revised issue price" means the sum of—

(A) the issue price of the bond, and

(B) the aggregate amount of the original issue discount includible in the gross income of all holders for periods before the acquisition of the bond by the taxpayer (determined without regard to section 1272(a)(7) or (b)(4)) or, in the case of a tax-exempt obligation, the aggregate amount of the original issue discount which accrued in the manner provided by section 1272(a) (determined without regard to paragraph (7) thereof) during periods before the acquisition of the bond by the taxpayer.

(5) Original issue discount, etc. The terms "original issue discount", "stated redemption price at maturity", and "issue price" have the respective meanings given such terms by subpart A of this part.

Code Sec. 1278(b) — Market discount on bonds

(b) Election to include market discount currently.
(1) In general. If the taxpayer makes an election under this subsection—
(A) sections 1276 and 1277 shall not apply, and
(B) market discount on any market discount bond shall be included in the gross income of the taxpayer for the taxable years to which it is attributable (as determined under the rules of subsection (b) of section 1276).
Except for purposes of sections 103, 871(a), 881, 1441, 1442, and 6049 (and such other provisions as may be specified in regulations), any amount included in gross income under subparagraph (B) shall be treated as interest for purposes of this title.
(2) Scope of election. An election under this subsection shall apply to all market discount bonds acquired by the taxpayer on or after the 1st day of the 1st taxable year to which such election applies.
(3) Period to which election applies. An election under this subsection shall apply to the taxable year for which it is made and for all subsequent taxable years, unless the taxpayer secures the consent of the Secretary to the revocation of such election.
(4) Basis adjustment. The basis of any bond in the hands of the taxpayer shall be increased by the amount included in gross income pursuant to this subsection.
(c) Regulations.
The Secretary shall prescribe such regulations as may be necessary to carry out the purposes of this subpart, including regulations providing proper adjustments in the case of a bond the principal of which may be paid in 2 or more payments.

In 1993, P.L. 103-66, Sec. 13206(b)(2)(A)(i), deleted clause (a)(1)(B)(ii) and redesignated clauses (a)(1)(B)(iii) and (iv) as clauses (a)(1)(B)(ii) and (iii) . . . Sec. 13206(b)(2)(A)(ii), redesignated subpara. (a)(1)(C) as subpara. (a)(1)(D) . . . Sec. 13206(b)(2)(A)(iii), added subpara. (a)(1)(C) . . . Sec. 13206(b)(2)(B)(i), substituted "sections 103, 871(a)," for "sections 871(a)" in para. (b)(1) . . . Sec. 13206(b)(2)(B)(ii), added "or, in the case of a tax-exempt obligation, the aggregate amount of the original issue discount which accrued in the manner provided by section 1272(a) (determined without regard to paragraph (7) thereof) during periods before the acquisition of the bond by the taxpayer" before the period at the end of subpara. (a)(4)(B), effective for obligations purchased (within the meaning of Code Sec. 1272(d)(1)) after 4/30/93.
Prior to deletion, clause (a)(1)(B)(ii) read as follows:
"(ii) Tax-exempt obligations. Any tax-exempt obligation (as defined in section 1275(a)(3))."
In 1988, P.L. 100-647, Sec. 1006(u)(2), substituted "1272(a)(7)" for "1272(a)6", in subpara (a)(4)(B), effective for debt instruments issued after 12/31/86, in tax. yrs. end. after such date.
—P.L. 100-647, Sec. 1018(c)(2), added ", including regulations providing proper adjustments in the case of a bond the principal of which may be paid in 2 or more payments" at the end of subsec. (c) . . . Sec. 1018(c)(3), added para. (b)(4), effective for tax. yrs. end. after 7/18/84, and as provided in Sec. 44(j) of P.L. 98-369, reproduced below.
In 1986, P.L. 99-514, Sec. 1803(a)(6), added subpara. (a)(1)(C), effective for tax. yrs. end. after 7/18/84, and as provided in Sec. 44(j) of P.L. 98-369, reproduced below.
—P.L. 99-514, Sec. 1878(a), added Sec. 1001(b)(24) to P.L. 98-369, see below.
—P.L. 99-514, Sec. 1899A(32), substituted "means" for "means of" in para. (a)(4), effective 10/22/86.
In 1984, P.L. 98-369, Sec. 41(a), added Code Sec. 1278 for tax. yrs. end. after 7/18/84. Sec. 44(j) of the Act provides:
"(j) Clarification that prior effective date rules not affected. Nothing in the amendment made by section 41(a) shall affect the application of any effective date provision (including any transitional rule) for any provision which was a predecessor to any provision contained in part V of subchapter P of chapter 1 of the Internal Revenue Code of 1954 (as added by section 41)."
—P.L. 98-369, Sec. 1001(b)(24), substituted "6 months" for "1 year" in clause (a)(1)(B)(i), effective for property acquired after 6/22/84 and before 1/1/88.

SUBPART C.—DISCOUNT ON SHORT-TERM OBLIGATIONS
Sec.
1281. Current inclusion in income of discount on certain short-term obligations.

1282. Deferral of interest deduction allocable to accrued discount.
1283. Definitions and special rules.

Sec. 1281. Current inclusion in income of discount on certain short-term obligations.
(a) General rule.
In the case of any short-term obligation to which this section applies, for purposes of this title—
(1) there shall be included in the gross income of the holder an amount equal to the sum of the daily portions of the acquisition discount for each day during the taxable year on which such holder held such obligation, and
(2) any interest payable on the obligation (other than interest taken into account in determining the amount of the acquisition discount) shall be included in gross income as it accrues.
(b) Short-term obligations to which section applies.
(1) In general. This section shall apply to any short-term obligation which—
(A) is held by a taxpayer using an accrual method of accounting,
(B) is held primarily for sale to customers in the ordinary course of the taxpayer's trade or business,
(C) is held by a bank (as defined in section 581),
(D) is held by a regulated investment company or a common trust fund,
(E) is identified by the taxpayer under section 1256(e)(2) as being part of a hedging transaction, or
(F) is a stripped bond or stripped coupon held by the person who stripped the bond or coupon (or by any other person whose basis is determined by reference to the basis in the hands of such person).
(2) Treatment of obligations held by pass-thru entities.
(A) In general. This section shall apply also to—
(i) any short-term obligation which is held by a pass-thru entity which is formed or availed of for purposes of avoiding the provisions of this section, and
(ii) any short-term obligation which is acquired by a pass-thru entity (not described in clause (i)) during the required accrual period.
(B) Required accrual period. For purposes of subparagraph (A), the term "required accrual period" means the period—
(i) which begins with the first taxable year for which the ownership test of subparagraph (C) is met with respect to the pass-thru entity (or a predecessor), and
(ii) which ends with the first taxable year after the taxable year referred to in clause (i) for which the ownership test of subparagraph (C) is not met and with respect to which the Secretary consents to the termination of the required accrual period.
(C) Ownership test. The ownership test of this subparagraph is met for any taxable year if, on at least 90 days during the taxable year, 20 percent or more of the value of the interests in the pass-thru entity are held by persons described in paragraph (1) or by other pass-thru entities to which subparagraph (A) applies.
(D) Pass-thru entity. The term "pass-thru entity" means any partnership, S corporation, trust, or other pass-thru entity.
(c) Cross reference.
For special rules limiting the application of this section to original issue discount in the case of nongovernmental obligations, see section 1283(c).

Short-term obligations Code Sec. 1283(a)(2)(B)

In 1988, P.L. 100-647, Sec. 1018(c)(1), substituted "December 31, 1985" for "September 27, 1985" in Sec. 1803(a)(8)(A) [reproduced below] of P.L. 99-514, part of the effective date for changes made by Sec. 1803(a)(8)(A) of P.L. 99-514.
In 1986, P.L. 99-514, Sec. 1803(a)(7), deleted "or" at the end of subpara. (b)(1)(D), substituted ",or" for the period at the end of subpara. (b)(1)(E), and added subpara. (b)(1)(F), effective for obligations acquired after 7/18/84, and as provided in Sec. 44(e) and (j) of P.L. 98-369, reproduced below.
—P.L. 99-514, Sec. 1803(a)(8)(A), amended subsec. (a), effective for obligations acquired after 12/31/85 [as amended by Sec. 1018(c)(1) of P.L. 100-647, see above].
Prior to amendment, subsec. (a) read as follows:
"(a) In general.
"In the case of any short-term obligation to which this section applies, for purposes of this title, there shall be included in the gross income of the holder an amount equal to the sum of the daily portions of the acquisition discount for each day during the taxable year on which such holder held such obligation."
In 1984, P.L. 98-369, Sec. 41(a), added Code Sec. 1281, effective for obligations acquired after 7/18/84. Sec. 44(e) of the Act provides:
"(e) 5-year spread of adjustments required by reason of accrual of discount on certain short-term obligations.
"(1) Election to have section 1281 apply to all obligations held during taxable year. A taxpayer may elect for his first taxable year ending after the date of the enactment of this Act to have section 1281 of the Internal Revenue Code of 1954 apply to all short-term obligations described in subsection (b) of such section which were held by the taxpayer at any time during such first taxable year.
"(2) 5-year spread.
"(A) In general. In the case of any taxpayer who makes an election under paragraph (1)—
"(i) the provisions of section 1281 of the Internal Revenue Code of 1954 (as added by section 41) shall be treated as a change in the method of accounting of the taxpayer,
"(ii) such change shall be treated as having been made with the consent of the Secretary, and
"(iii) the net amount of the adjustments required by section 481(a) of such Code to be taken into account by the taxpayer in computing taxable income (hereinafter in this paragraph referred to as the 'net adjustments') shall be taken into account during the spread period with the amount taken into account in each taxable year in such period determined under subparagraph (B).
"(B) Amount taken into account during each year of spread period.
"(i) First year. The amount taken into account for the first taxable year in the spread period shall be the sum of—
"(I) one-fifth of the net adjustments, and
"(II) the excess (if any) of—
"(a) the cash basis income over the accrual basis income, over
"(b) one-fifth of the net adjustments.
"(ii) For subsequent years in spread period. The amount taken into account in the second or any succeeding taxable year in the spread period shall be the sum of—
"(I) the portion of the net adjustments not taken into account in the preceding taxable year of the spread period divided by the number of remaining taxable years in the spread period (including the year for which the determination is being made), and
"(II) the excess (if any) of—
"(a) the excess of the cash basis income over the accrual basis income, over
"(b) one-fifth of the net adjustments, multiplied by 5 minus the number of years remaining in the spread period (not including the current year).
The excess described in subparagraph (B)(ii)(II)(a) shall be reduced by any amount taken into account under this subclause or clause (i)(II) in any prior year.
"(C) Spread period. For purposes of this paragraph, the term 'spread period' means the period consisting of the 5 taxable years beginning with the year for which the election is made under paragraph (1).
"(D) Cash basis income. For purposes of this paragraph, the term 'cash basis income' means for any taxable year the aggregate amount which would be includible in the gross income of the taxpayer with respect to short-term obligations described in subsection (b) of section 1281 of such Code if the provisions of section 1281 of such Code did not apply to such taxable year and all prior taxable years within the spread period.
"(E) Accrual basis income. For purposes of this paragraph, the term 'accrual basis income' means for any taxable year the aggregate amount includible in gross income under section 1281(a) of such Code for such a taxable year and all prior taxable years within the spread period."
Sec. 44(j) of the Act provides:
"(j) Clarification that prior effective date rules not affected.
"Nothing in the amendment made by section 41(a) shall affect the application of any effective date provision (including any transitional rule) for any provision which was a predecessor to any provision contained in part V of subchapter P of chapter 1 of the Internal Revenue Code of 1954 (as added by section 41)."

Sec. 1282. Deferral of interest deduction allocable to accrued discount.
(a) General rule.
Except as otherwise provided in this section, the net direct interest expense with respect to any short-term obligation shall be allowed as a deduction for the taxable year only to the extent such expense exceeds the sum of—
(1) the daily portions of the acquisition discount for each day during the taxable year on which the taxpayer held such obligation, and
(2) the amount of any interest payable on the obligation (other than interest taken into account in determining the amount of the acquisition discount) which accrues during the taxable year while the taxpayer held such obligation (and is not included in the gross income of the taxpayer for such taxable year by reason of the taxpayer's method of accounting).
(b) Section not to apply to obligations to which section 1281 applies.
(1) **In general.** This section shall not apply to any short-term obligation to which section 1281 applies.
(2) **Election to have section 1281 apply to all obligations.**
(A) In general. A taxpayer may make an election under this paragraph to have section 1281 apply to all short-term obligations acquired by the taxpayer on or after the 1st day of the 1st taxable year to which such election applies.
(B) Period to which election applies. An election under this paragraph shall apply to the taxable year for which it is made and for all subsequent taxable years, unless the taxpayer secures the consent of the Secretary to the revocation of such election.
(c) Certain rules made applicable.
Rules similar to the rules of subsections (b) and (c) of section 1277 shall apply for purposes of this section.
(d) Cross reference.
For special rules limiting the application of this section to original issue discount in the case of nongovernmental obligations, see section 1283(c).

In 1986, P.L. 99-514, Sec. 1803(a)(8)(B), amended subsec. (a), effective for obligations acquired after 7/18/84.
Prior to amendment, subsec. (a) read as follows:
"(a) General rule.
"Except as otherwise provided in this section, the net direct interest expense with respect to any short-term obligation shall be allowed as a deduction for the taxable year only to the extent that such expense exceeds the sum of the daily portions of the acquisition discount for each day during the taxable year on which the taxpayer held such obligation."
In 1984, P.L. 98-369, Sec. 41(a), added Code Sec. 1282, effective for obligations acquired after 7/18/84. Sec. 44(j) of the Act provides:
"(j) Clarification that prior effective date rules not affected. Nothing in the amendment made by section 41(a) shall affect theapplication of any effective date provision (including any transitional rule) for any provision which was a predecessor to any provision contained in part V of subchapter P of chapter 1 of the Internal Revenue Code of 1954 (as added by section 41)."

Sec. 1283. Definitions and special rules.
(a) Definitions.
For purposes of this subpart—
(1) **Short-term obligation.**
(A) In general. Except as provided in subparagraph (B), the term "short-term obligation" means any bond, debenture, note, certificate, or other evidence of indebtedness which has a fixed maturity date not more than 1 year from the date of issue.
(B) Exceptions for tax-exempt obligations. The term "short-term obligation" shall not include any tax-exempt obligation (as defined in section 1275(a)(3)).
(2) **Acquisition discount.** The term "acquisition discount" means the excess of—
(A) the stated redemption price at maturity (as defined in section 1273), over
(B) the taxpayer's basis for the obligation.

2,801

(b) Daily portion.
For purposes of this subpart—
  (1) Ratable accrual. Except as otherwise provided in this subsection, the daily portion of the acquisition discount is an amount equal to—
    (A) the amount of such discount, divided by
    (B) the number of days after the day on which the taxpayer acquired the obligation and up to (and including) the day of its maturity.
  (2) Election of accrual on basis of constant interest rate (in lieu of ratable accrual).
    (A) In general. At the election of the taxpayer with respect to any obligation, the daily portion of the acquisition discount for any day is the portion of the acquisition discount accruing on such day determined (under regulations prescribed by the Secretary) on the basis of—
      (i) the taxpayer's yield to maturity based on the taxpayer's cost of acquiring the obligation, and
      (ii) compounding daily.
    (B) Election irrevocable. An election under subparagraph (A), once made with respect to any obligation, shall be irrevocable.
(c) Special rules for nongovernmental obligations.
  (1) In general. In the case of any short-term obligation which is not a short-term Government obligation (as defined in section 1271(a)(3)(B))—
    (A) sections 1281 and 1282 shall be applied by taking into account original issue discount in lieu of acquisition discount, and
    (B) appropriate adjustments shall be made in the application of subsection (b) of this section.
  (2) Election to have paragraph (1) not apply.
    (A) In general. A taxpayer may make an election under this paragraph to have paragraph (1) not apply to all obligations acquired by the taxpayer on or after the first day of the first taxable year to which such election applies.
    (B) Period to which election applies. An election under this paragraph shall apply to the taxable year for which it is made and for all subsequent taxable years, unless the taxpayer secures the consent of the Secretary to the revocation of such election.
(d) Other special rules.
  (1) Basis adjustments. The basis of any short-term obligation in the hands of the holder thereof shall be increased by the amount included in his gross income pursuant to section 1281.
  (2) Double inclusion in income not required. Section 1281 shall not require the inclusion of any amount previously includible in gross income.
  (3) Coordination with other provisions. Section 454(b) and paragraphs (3) and (4) of section 1271(a) shall not apply to any short-term obligation to which section 1281 applies.

In 1986, P.L. 99-514, Sec. 1803(a)(1)(B), substituted "paragraphs (3) and (4) of section 1271(a)" for "section 1271(a)(3)" in para. (d)(3), effective for obligations acquired after 7/18/84, and as provided in Sec. 44(j) of P.L. 98-369, reproduced below.

In 1984, P.L. 98-369, Sec. 41(a), added Code Sec. 1283, effective for obligations acquired after 7/18/84. Sec. 44(j) of the Act provides:

"*(j) Clarification that prior effective date rules not affected.* Nothing in the amendment made by section 41(a) shall affect the application of any effective date provision (including any transitional rule) for any provision which was a predecessor to any provision contained in part V of subchapter P of chapter 1 of the Internal Revenue Code of 1954 (as added by section 41)."

SUBPART D.—MISCELLANEOUS PROVISIONS

Sec.
1286. Tax treatment of stripped bonds.
1287. Denial of capital gain treatment for gains on certain obligations not in registered form.
1288. Treatment of original issue discount on tax-exempt obligations.

Sec. 1286. Tax treatment of stripped bonds.
(a) Inclusion in income as if bond and coupons were original issue discount bonds.
If any person purchases after July 1, 1982, a stripped bond or a stripped coupon, then such bond or coupon while held by such purchaser (or by any other person whose basis is determined by reference to the basis in the hands of such purchaser) shall be treated for purposes of this part as a bond originally issued on the purchase date and having an original issue discount equal to the excess (if any) of—
  (1) the stated redemption price at maturity (or, in the case of coupon, the amount payable on the due date of such coupon), over
  (2) such bond's or coupon's ratable share of the purchase price.
For purposes of paragraph (2), ratable shares shall be determined on the basis of their respective fair market values on the date of purchase.
(b) Tax treatment of person stripping bond.
For purposes of this subtitle, if any person strips 1 or more coupons from a bond and after July 1, 1982, disposes of the bond or such coupon—
  (1) such person shall include in gross income an amount equal to the sum of—
    (A) the interest accrued on such bond while held by such person and before the time such coupon or bond was disposed of (to the extent such interest has not theretofore been included in such person's gross income), and
    (B) the accrued market discount on such bond determined as of the time such coupon or bond was disposed of (to the extent such discount has not theretofore been included in such person's gross income),
  (2) the basis of the bond and coupons shall be increased by the amount included in gross income under paragraph (1),
  (3) the basis of the bond and coupons immediately before the disposition (as adjusted pursuant to paragraph (2)) shall be allocated among the items retained by such person and the items disposed of by such person on the basis of their respective fair market values, and
  (4) for purposes of subsection (a), such person shall be treated as having purchased on the date of such disposition each such item which he retains for an amount equal to the basis allocated to such item under paragraph (3).
A rule similar to the rule of paragraph (4) shall apply in the case of any person whose basis in any bond or coupon is determined by reference to the basis of the person described in the preceding sentence.
(c) Retention of existing law for stripped bonds purchased before July 2, 1982.
If a bond issued at any time with interest coupons—
  (1) is purchased after August 16, 1954, and before January 1, 1958, and the purchaser does not receive all the coupons which first become payable more than 12 months after the date of the purchase, or
  (2) is purchased after December 31, 1957, and before July 2, 1982, and the purchaser does not receive all the cou-

Original issue discount   Code Sec. 1286

pons which first become payable after the date of the purchase,

then the gain on the sale or other disposition of such bond by such purchaser (or by a person whose basis is determined by reference to the basis in the hands of such purchaser) shall be considered as ordinary income to the extent that the fair market value (determined as of the time of the purchase) of the bond with coupons attached exceeds the purchase price. If this subsection and section 1271(a)(2)(A) apply with respect to gain realized on the sale or exchange of any evidence of indebtedness, then section 1271(a)(2)(A) shall apply with respect to that part of the gain to which this subsection does not apply.

(d) Special rules for tax-exempt obligations.

(1) In general. In the case of any tax-exempt obligation (as defined in section 1275(a)(3)) from which 1 or more coupons have been stripped—

(A) the amount of the original issue discount determined under subsection (a) with respect to any stripped bond or stripped coupon—

(i) shall be treated as original issue discount on a tax-exempt obligation to the extent such discount does not exceed the tax-exempt portion of such discount, and

(ii) shall be treated as original issue discount on an obligation which is not a tax-exempt obligation to the extent such discount exceeds the tax-exempt portion of such discount,

(B) subsection (b)(1)(A) shall not apply, and

(C) subsection (b)(2) shall be applied by increasing the basis of the bond or coupon by the sum of—

(i) the interest accrued but not paid before such bond or coupon was disposed of (and not previously reflected in basis), plus

(ii) the amount included in gross income under subsection (b)(1)(B).

(2) Tax-exempt portion. For purposes of paragraph (1), the tax-exempt portion of the original issue discount determined under subsection (a) is the excess of—

(A) the amount referred to in subsection (a)(1), over

(B) an issue price which would produce a yield to maturity as of the purchase date equal to the lower of—

(i) the coupon rate of interest on the obligation from which the coupons were separated, or

(ii) the yield to maturity (on the basis of the purchase price) of the stripped obligation or coupon.

The purchaser of any stripped obligation or coupon may elect to apply clause (i) by substituting "original yield to maturity of" for "coupon rate of interest on."

(e) Definitions and special rules.

For purposes of this section—

(1) Bond. The term "bond" means a bond, debenture, note, or certificate or other evidence of indebtedness.

(2) Stripped bond. The term "stripped bond" means a bond issued at any time with interest coupons where there is a separation in ownership between the bond and any coupon which has not yet become payable.

(3) Stripped coupon. The term "stripped coupon" means any coupon relating to a stripped bond.

(4) Stated redemption price at maturity. The term "stated redemption price at maturity" has the meaning given such term by section 1273(a)(2).

(5) Coupon. The term "coupon" includes any right to receive interest on a bond (whether or not evidenced by a coupon). This paragraph shall apply for purposes of subsection (c) only in the case of purchases after July 1, 1982.

(6) Purchase. The term "purchase" has the meaning given such term by section 1272(d)(1).

(f) Treatment of stripped interests in bond and preferred stock funds, etc.

In the case of an account or entity substantially all of the assets of which consist of bonds, preferred stock, or a combination thereof, the Secretary may by regulations provide that rules similar to the rules of this section and 305(e), as appropriate, shall apply to interests in such account or entity to which (but for this subsection) this section or section 305(e), as the case may be, would not apply.

(g) Regulation authority.

The Secretary may prescribe regulations providing that where, by reason of varying rates of interest, put or call options, or other circumstances, the tax treatment under this section does not accurately reflect the income of the holder of a stripped coupon or stripped bond, or of the person disposing of such bond or coupon, as the case may be, for any period, such treatment shall be modified to require that the proper amount of income be included for such period.

In 2004, P.L. 108-357, Sec. 831(a), redesignated subsec. (f) as subsec. (g) and added subsec. (f), effective for purchases and dispositions after 10/22/2004.

In 1988, P.L. 100-647, Sec. 1018(q)(4)(A), amended subsec. (d), effective as provided in Sec. 1018(q)(4)(B) of this Act which reads:

"(B)(i) Except as provided in clause (ii), the amendment made by subparagraph (A) shall apply to any purchase or sale after June 10, 1987, of any stripped tax-exempt obligation or stripped coupon from such an obligation.

"(ii) If—

"(I) any person held any obligation or coupon in stripped form on June 10, 1987, and

"(II) such obligation or coupon was held by such person on such date for sale in the ordinary course of such person's trade or business,

the amendment made by subparagraph (A) shall not apply to any sale of such obligation or coupon by such person and shall not apply to any such obligation or coupon while held by another person who purchased such obligation or coupon from the person referred to in subclause (I)."

Prior to amendment, subsec. (d) read as follows:

"(d) Special rules for tax-exempt obligations.

"In the case of any tax-exempt obligation (as defined in section 1275(a)(3)) from which 1 or more coupons have been stripped—

"(1) The amount of original issue discount determined under subsection (a) with respect to any stripped bond or stripped coupon from such obligation shall be the amount which produces a yield to maturity (as of the purchase date) equal to the lower of—

"(A) the coupon rate of interest on such obligation before the separation of coupons, or

"(B) the yield to maturity (on the basis of purchase price) of the stripped obligation or coupon,

"(2) the amount of original issue discount determined under paragraph (1) shall be taken into account in determining the adjusted basis of the holder under section 1288,

"(3) subsection (b)(1) shall not apply, and

"(4) subsection (b)(2) shall be applied by increasing the basis of the bond or coupon by the interest accrued but not paid before the time such bond or coupon was disposed of (and not previously reflected in basis)."

In 1986, P.L. 99-514, Sec. 1803(a)(13)(B)(i), amended para. (b)(1) . . . Sec. 1803(a)(13)(B)(ii), amended para. (b)(2), effective for obligations acquired after 10/22/86.

Prior to amendment, paras. (b)(1) and (b)(2) read as follows:

"(1) such person shall include in gross income an amount equal to the interest accrued on such bond while held by such person and before the time that such coupon or bond was disposed of (to the extent such interest has not theretofore been included in such person's gross income),

"(2) the basis of the bond and coupons shall be increased by the amount of the accrued interest described in paragraph (1),"

—P.L. 99-514, Sec. 1879(s)(1), amended subsec. (d), effective for any purchase or sale of any stripped tax-exempt obligation or stripped coupon from such an obligation after 10/22/86.

Prior to amendment, subsec. (d) read as follows:

"(d) Special rules for tax-exempt obligations.

"In the case of any tax-exempt obligation (as defined in section 1275(a)(3))—

"(1) subsections (a) and (b)(1) shall not apply,

"(2) the rules of subsection (b)(4) shall apply for purposes of subsection (c), and

"(3) subsection (c) shall be applied without regard to the requirement that the bond be purchased before July 2, 1982."

In 1984, P.L. 98-369, Sec. 41(a), added Code Sec. 1286, effective for tax. yrs. end. after 7/18/84. Sec. 44(j) of the Act provides:

"(j) Clarification that prior effective date rules not affected. Nothing in the amendment made by section 41(a) shall affect the application of any effective date provision (including any transitional rule) for any provision which was a predecessor to any provision contained in part V of subchapter P of chapter 1 of the Internal Revenue Code of 1954 (as added by section 41)."

Sec. 1287. Denial of capital gain treatment for gains on certain obligations not in registered form.
(a) In general.

If any registration-required obligation is not in registered form, any gain on the sale or other disposition of such obligation shall be treated as ordinary income (unless the issuance of such obligation was subject to tax under section 4701).

(b) Definitions.

For purposes of subsection (a)—

> • *Caution:* Sec. 1287(b)(1), following, is effective for obligations issued before 3/18/2012. For sec. 1287(b)(1), effective for obligations issued after 3/18/2012, see below.

(1) Registration-required obligation. The term "registration-required obligation" has the meaning given to such term by section 163(f)(2) except that clause (iv) of subparagraph (A), and subparagraph (B), of such section shall not apply.

> • *Caution:* Sec. 1287(b)(1), following, is effective for obligations issued after 3/18/2012. For sec. 1287(b)(1), effective for obligations issued before 3/18/2012, see above.

(1) Registration-required obligation. The term "registration-required obligation" has the meaning given to such term by section 163(f)(2).

(2) Registered form. The term "registered form" has the same meaning as when used in section 163(f).

In 2010, P.L. 111-147, Sec. 502(a)(2)(D), deleted "except that clause (iv) of subparagraph (A), and subparagraph (B), of such section shall not apply" before the period at the end of para. (b)(1), effective for obligations issued after 3/18/2012.
In 1984, P.L. 98-369, Sec. 41(a), added Code sec. 1287, effective for tax. yrs. end. after 7/18/84. Sec. 44(j) of the Act provides:

"(j) Clarification that prior effective date rules not affected. Nothing in the amendment made by section 41(a) shall affect the application of any effective date provision (including any transitional rule) for any provision which was a predecessor to any provision contained in part V of subchapter P of chapter 1 of the Internal Revenue Code of 1954 (as added by section 41)."

Sec. 1288. Treatment of original issue discount on tax-exempt obligations.
(a) General rule.

Original issue discount on any tax-exempt obligation shall be treated as accruing—

(1) for purposes of section 163, in the manner provided by section 1272(a) (determined without regard to paragraph (7) thereof), and

(2) for purposes of determining the adjusted basis of the holder, in the manner provided by section 1272(a) (determined with regard to paragraph (7) thereof).

(b) Definitions and special rules.

For purposes of this section—

(1) Original issue discount. The term "original issue discount" has the meaning given to such term by section 1273(a) without regard to paragraph (3) thereof. In applying section 483 or 1274, under regulations prescribed by the Secretary, appropriate adjustments shall be made to the applicable Federal rate to take into account the tax exemption for interest on the obligation.

(2) Tax-exempt obligation. The term "tax-exempt obligation" has the meaning given to such term by section 1275(a)(3).

(3) Short-term obligations. In applying this section to obligations with maturity of 1 year or less, rules similar to the rules of section 1283(b) shall apply.

In 1988, P.L. 100-647, Sec. 1006(u)(3), substituted "paragraph (7)" for "paragraph (6)" each place it appeared in Code Sec. 1288, effective for tax. yrs. begin. after 12/31/86, in tax. yrs. end. after 12/31/86.
In 1984, P.L. 98-369, Sec. 41(a), added Code Sec. 1288, effective for obligations issued after 9/3/82 and acquired after 3/1/84. Sec. 44(j) of this Act provides:

"(j) Clarification that prior effective date rules not affected. Nothing in the amendment made by section 41(a) shall affect the application of any effective date provision (including any transitional rule) for any provision which was a predecessor to any provision contained in part V of subchapter P of chapter 1 of the Internal Revenue Code of 1954 (as added by section 41)."

PART VI.—TREATMENT OF CERTAIN PASSIVE FOREIGN INVESTMENT COMPANIES

Subpart
A. Interest on tax deferral.
B. Treatment of qualified electing funds.
C. Election of mark to market for marketable stock.
D. General provisions.

In 1997, P.L. 105-34, Sec. 1122(d)(6), deleted the item for Subpart C and added new items for Subparts C and D.
Prior to deletion, the item for Subpart C read as follows:
"Subpart C. General provisions."
In 1986, P.L. 99-514, Sec. 1235(a), added Part IV in Subchapter P of chapter 1.

SUBPART A.—INTEREST ON TAX DEFERRAL

Sec.
1291. Interest on tax deferral.

Sec. 1291. Interest on tax deferral.
(a) Treatment of distributions and stock dispositions.

(1) Distributions. If a United States person receives an excess distribution in respect of stock in a passive foreign investment company, then—

(A) the amount of the excess distribution shall be allocated ratably to each day in the taxpayer's holding period for the stock,

(B) with respect to such excess distribution, the taxpayer's gross income for the current year shall include (as ordinary income) only the amounts allocated under subparagraph (A) to—

(i) the current year, or

(ii) any period in the taxpayer's holding period before the 1st day of the 1st taxable year of the company which begins after December 31, 1986, and for which it was a passive foreign investment company, and

(C) the tax imposed by this chapter for the current year shall be increased by the deferred tax amount (determined under subsection (c)).

(2) Dispositions. If the taxpayer disposes of stock in a passive foreign investment company, then the rules of paragraph (1) shall apply to any gain recognized on such disposition in the same manner as if such gain were an excess distribution.

(3) Definitions. For purposes of this section—

(A) Holding period. The taxpayer's holding period shall be determined under section 1223; except that—

Passive foreign investment companies Code Sec. 1291(d)(2)(A)(ii)

(i) for purposes of applying this section to an excess distribution, such holding period shall be treated as ending on the date of such distribution, and

(ii) if section 1296 applied to such stock with respect to the taxpayer for any prior taxable year, such holding period shall be treated as beginning on the first day of the first taxable year beginning after the last taxable year for which section 1296 so applied.

(B) Current year. The term "current year" means the taxable year in which the excess distribution or disposition occurs.

(b) Excess distribution.

(1) In general. For purposes of this section, the term "excess distribution" means any distribution in respect of stock received during any taxable year to the extent such distribution does not exceed its ratable portion of the total excess distribution (if any) for such taxable year.

(2) Total excess distribution. For purposes of this subsection—

(A) In general. The term "total excess distribution" means the excess (if any) of—

(i) the amount of the distributions in respect of the stock received by the taxpayer during the taxable year, over

(ii) 125 percent of the average amount received in respect of such stock by the taxpayer during the 3 preceding taxable years (or, if shorter, the portion of the taxpayer's holding period before the taxable year).

For purposes of clause (ii), any excess distribution received during such 3-year period shall be taken into account only to the extent it was included in gross income under subsection (a)(1)(B).

(B) No excess for 1st year. The total excess distributions with respect to any stock shall be zero for the taxable year in which the taxpayer's holding period in such stock begins.

(3) Adjustments. Under regulations prescribed by the Secretary—

(A) determinations under this subsection shall be made on a share-by-share basis, except that shares with the same holding period may be aggregated,

(B) proper adjustments shall be made for stock splits and stock dividends,

(C) if the taxpayer does not hold the stock during the entire taxable year, distributions received during such year shall be annualized,

(D) if the taxpayer's holding period includes periods during which the stock was held by another person, distributions received by such other person shall be taken into account as if received by the taxpayer,

(E) if the distributions are received in a foreign currency, determinations under this subsection shall be made in such currency and the amount of any excess distribution determined in such currency shall be translated into dollars,

(F) proper adjustment shall be made for amounts not includible in gross income by reason of section 959(a) or 1293(c), and

(G) if a charitable deduction was allowable under section 642(c) to a trust for any distribution of its income, proper adjustments shall be made for the deduction so allowable to the extent allocable to distributions or gain in respect of stock in a passive foreign investment company.

(c) Deferred tax amount.

For purposes of this section—

(1) In general. The term "deferred tax amount" means, with respect to any distribution or disposition to which subsection (a) applies, an amount equal to the sum of—

(A) the aggregate increases in taxes described in paragraph (2), plus

(B) the aggregate amount of interest (determined in the manner provided under paragraph (3)) on such increases in tax.

Any increase in the tax imposed by this chapter for the current year under subsection (a) to the extent attributable to the amount referred to in subparagraph (B) shall be treated as interest paid under section 6601 on the due date for the current year.

(2) Aggregate increases in taxes. For purposes of paragraph (1)(A), the aggregate increases in taxes shall be determined by multiplying each amount allocated under subsection (a)(1)(A) to any taxable year (other than any taxable year referred to in subsection (a)(1)(B)) by the highest rate of tax in effect for such taxable year under section 1 or 11, whichever applies.

(3) Computation of interest.

(A) In general. The amount of interest referred to in paragraph (1)(B) on any increase determined under paragraph (2) for any taxable year shall be determined for the period—

(i) beginning on the due date for such taxable year, and

(ii) ending on the due date for the taxable year with or within which the distribution or disposition occurs,

by using the rates and method applicable under section 6621 for underpayments of tax for such period.

(B) Due date. For purposes of this subsection, the term "due date" means the date prescribed by law (determined without regard to extensions) for filing the return of the tax imposed by this chapter for the taxable year.

(d) Coordination with subparts B and C.

(1) In general. This section shall not apply with respect to any distribution paid by a passive foreign investment company, or any disposition of stock in a passive foreign investment company, if such company is a qualified electing fund with respect to the taxpayer for each of its taxable years—

(A) which begins after December 31, 1986, and for which such company is a passive foreign investment company, and

(B) which includes any portion of the taxpayer's holding period.

Except as provided in section 1296(j), this section also shall not apply if an election under section 1296(k) is in effect for the taxpayer's taxable year. In the case of stock which is marked to market under section 475 or any other provision of this chapter, this section shall not apply, except that rules similar to the rules of section 1296(j) shall apply.

(2) Election to recognize gain where company becomes qualified electing fund.

(A) In general. If—

(i) a passive foreign investment company becomes a qualified electing fund with respect to the taxpayer for a taxable year which begins after December 31, 1986,

(ii) the taxpayer holds stock in such company on the first day of such taxable year, and

Code Sec. 1291(d)(2)(A)(iii) — Passive foreign investment companies

(iii) the taxpayer establishes to the satisfaction of the Secretary the fair market value of such stock on such first day,

the taxpayer may elect to recognize gain as if he sold such stock on such first day for such fair market value.

(B) Additional election for shareholder of controlled foreign corporations.—

(i) In general. If—

(I) a passive foreign investment company becomes a qualified electing fund with respect to the taxpayer for a taxable year which begins after December 31, 1986,

(II) the taxpayer holds stock in such company on the first day of such taxable year, and

(III) such company is a controlled foreign corporation (as defined in section 957(a)),

the taxpayer may elect to include in gross income as a dividend received on such first day an amount equal to the portion of the post-1986 earnings and profits of such company attributable (under regulations prescribed by the Secretary) to the stock in such company held by the taxpayer on such first day. The amount treated as a dividend under the preceding sentence shall be treated as an excess distribution and shall be allocated under subsection (a)(1)(A) only to days during periods taken into account in determining the post-1986 earnings and profits so attributable.

(ii) Post-1986 earnings and profits. For purposes of clause (i), the term "post-1986 earnings and profits" means earnings and profits which were accumulated in taxable years of such company beginning after December 31, 1986, and during the period or periods the stock was held by the taxpayer while the company was a passive foreign investment company.

(iii) Coordination with section 959(e). For purposes of section 959(e), any amount included in gross income under this subparagraph shall be treated as included in gross income under section 1248(a).

(C) Adjustments. In the case of any stock to which subparagraph (A) or (B) applies—

(i) the adjusted basis of such stock shall be increased by the gain recognized under subparagraph (A) or the amount treated as a dividend under subparagraph (B), as the case may be, and

(ii) the taxpayer's holding period in such stock shall be treated as beginning on the first day referred to in such subparagraph.

• **Caution:** Sec. 301(a), P.L. 111-312, (reproduced in the history notes following this Code Sec.) provides that the amendments made by Sec. 542(e)(5)(B)(i)-(ii), P.L. 107-16, EGTRRA, will apply as if never enacted. Code Sec. 1291(e), following, reflects the removal of these amendments, effective for estates of decedents dying, and transfers made, after 12/31/2009.

(e) Certain basis, etc., rules made applicable.

Except to the extent inconsistent with the regulations prescribed under subsection (f), rules similar to the rules of subsections (c) and (d) of section 1246 (as in effect on the day before the date of the enactment of the American Jobs Creation Act of 2004) shall apply for purposes of this section.

• **Caution:** Code Sec. 1291(e), following, was amended by Sec. 542(e)(5)(B)(i)-(ii), P.L. 107-16, EGTRRA. As provided in Sec. 301(a), P.L. 111-312, this amendment will apply as if never enacted, effective for estates of decedents dying, and transfers made, after 12/31/2009.

(e) Certain basis, etc., rules made applicable.

Except to the extent inconsistent with the regulations prescribed under subsection (f), rules similar to the rules of subsections (c), (d), (e), and (f) of section 1246 (as in effect on the day before the date of the enactment of the American Jobs Creation Act of 2004) shall apply for purposes of this section; except that—

(1) the reduction under subsection (e) of such section shall be the excess of the basis determined under section 1014 over the adjusted basis of the stock immediately before the decedent's death, and

(2) such a reduction shall not apply in the case of a decedent who was a nonresident alien at all times during his holding period in the stock.

(f) Recognition of gain.

To the extent provided in regulations, in the case of any transfer of stock in a passive foreign investment company where (but for this subsection) there is not full recognition of gain, the excess (if any) of—

(1) the fair market value of such stock, over

(2) its adjusted basis,

shall be treated as gain from the sale or exchange of such stock and shall be recognized notwithstanding any provision of law. Proper adjustment shall be made to the basis of any such stock for gain recognized under the preceding sentence.

(g) Coordination with foreign tax credit rules.

(1) In general. If there are creditable foreign taxes with respect to any distribution in respect of stock in a passive foreign investment company—

(A) the amount of such distribution shall be determined for purposes of this section with regard to section 78,

(B) the excess distribution taxes shall be allocated ratably to each day in the taxpayer's holding period for the stock, and

(C) to the extent—

(i) that such excess distribution taxes are allocated to a taxable year referred to in subsection (a)(1)(B), such taxes shall be taken into account under section 901 for the current year, and

(ii) that such excess distribution taxes are allocated to any other taxable year, such taxes shall reduce (subject to the principles of section 904(d) and not below zero) the increase in tax determined under subsection (c)(2) for such taxable year by reason of such distribution (but such taxes shall not be taken into account under section 901).

(2) Definitions. For purposes of this subsection—

(A) Creditable foreign taxes. The term "creditable foreign taxes" means, with respect to any distribution—

(i) any foreign taxes deemed paid under section 902 with respect to such distribution, and

(ii) any withholding tax imposed with respect to such distribution,

but only if the taxpayer chooses the benefits of section 901 and such taxes are creditable under section 901 (determined without regard to paragraph (1)(C)(ii)).

(B) Excess distribution taxes. The term "excess distribution taxes" means, with respect to any distribution, the portion of the creditable foreign taxes with respect to such distribution which is attributable (on a pro rata basis) to the portion of such distribution which is an excess distribution.

(C) Section 1248 gain. The rules of this subsection also shall apply in the case of any gain which but for this section would be includible in gross income as a dividend under section 1248.

In 2010, P.L. 111-312, Sec. 101(a)(1), substituted "December 31, 2012" for "December 31, 2010" both places it appeared in Sec. 901, P.L. 107-16 [see below], effective as if included in the enactment of P.L. 107-16, EGTRRA, 6/7/2001.

—P.L. 111-312, Sec. 301(a), provides that Code Sec. 1291, as amended by Sec. 542(e)(5)(B)(i)-(ii), P.L. 107-16 EGTRRA, 6/7/2001 (amended subsec. (e), see below) will read as if such provision had never been enacted, effective for estates of decedents dying, and transfers made, after 12/31/2009.

Sec. 301(a), P.L. 111-312, 12/17/2010, provides:

"(a) In general. Each provision of law amended by subtitle A or E of title V of the Economic Growth and Tax Relief Reconciliation Act of 2001 is amended to read as such provision would read if such subtitle had never been enacted."

—P.L. 111-312, Sec. 301(c), of this Act, provides

"(c) Special election with respect to estates of decedents dying in 2010. Notwithstanding subsection (a), in the case of an estate of a decedent dying after December 31, 2009, and before January 1, 2011, the executor (within the meaning of section 2203 of the Internal Revenue Code of 1986) may elect to apply such Code as though the amendments made by subsection (a) do not apply with respect to chapter 11 of such Code and with respect to property acquired or passing from such decedent (within the meaning of section 1014(b) of such Code). Such election shall be made at such time and in such manner as the Secretary of the Treasury or the Secretary's delegate shall provide. Such an election once made shall be revocable only with the consent of the Secretary of the Treasury or the Secretary's delegate. For purposes of section 2652(a)(1) of such Code, the determination of whether any property is subject to the tax imposed by such chapter 11 shall be made without regard to any election made under this subsection."

—P.L. 111-312, Sec. 301(d), of this Act, provides

" (d) Extension of time for performing certain acts.
" (1) Estate tax. In the case of the estate of a decedent dying after December 31, 2009, and before the date of the enactment of this Act, the due date for—
" (A) filing any return under section 6018 of the Internal Revenue Code of 1986 (including any election required to be made on such a return) as such section is in effect after the date of the enactment of this Act without regard to any election under subsection (c),
" (B) making any payment of tax under chapter 11 of such Code, and
" (C) making any disclaimer described in section 2518(b) of such Code of an interest in property passing by reason of the death of such decedent, shall not be earlier than the date which is 9 months after the date of the enactment of this Act.
" (2) Generation-skipping tax. In the case of any generation-skipping transfer made after December 31, 2009, and before the date of the enactment of this Act, the due date for filing any return under section 2662 of the Internal Revenue Code of 1986 (including any election required to be made on such a return) shall not be earlier than the date which is 9 months after the date of the enactment of this Act."

—P.L. 111-147, Sec. 521(b), substituted "and (d)" for ", (d), and (f)" in subsec. (e), effective 3/18/2010.

In 2004, P.L. 108-357, Sec. 413(c)(24)(A), substituted "959(a)" for "551(d), 959(a)," in subpara. (b)(3)(F)... Sec. 413(c)(24)(B), added "(as in effect on the day before the date of the enactment of the American Jobs Creation Act of 2004)" after "section 1246" in subsec. (e), effective for tax. yrs. of foreign corporations begin. after 12/31/2004, and for tax. yrs. of United States shareholders with or within which such tax. yrs. of foreign corporations end.

In 2002, P.L. 107-358, Sec. 2, added subsec. (c) in Sec. 901 of P.L. 107-16 [see below], effective 12/17/2002.

In 2001, P.L. 107-16, Sec. 542(e)(5)(B)(i), deleted "(e)," after "(d)," in subsec. (e)... Sec. 542(e)(5)(B)(ii), substituted a period for "; except that—(1) the reduction under subsection (e) of such section shall be the excess of the basis determined under section 1014 over the adjusted basis of the stock immediately before the decedent's death, and (2) such a reduction shall not apply in the case of a decedent who was a nonresident alien at all times during his holding period in the stock." in subsec. (e), effective for estates of decedents dying after 12/31/2009.

—P.L. 107-16, Sec. 901, of this Act [as amended by Sec. 2 of P.L. 107-358 and Sec. 101(a)(1), P.L. 111-312, see above], reads as follows:

"SEC. 901. SUNSET OF PROVISIONS OF ACT.

"(a) In general. All provisions of, and amendments made by, this Act shall not apply—
"(1) to taxable, plan, or limitation years beginning after December 31, 2012, or
"(2) in the case of title V, to estates of decedents dying, gifts made, or generation skipping transfers, after December 31, 2012.
"(b) Application of certain laws. The Internal Revenue Code of 1986 and the Employee Retirement Income Security Act of 1974 shall be applied and administered to years, estates, gifts, and transfers described in subsection (a) as if the provisions and amendments described in subsection (a) had never been enacted.
"(c) Exception. Subsection (a) shall not apply to section 803 (relating to no federal income tax on restitution received by victims of the Nazi regime or their heirs or estates)."

In 1998, P.L. 105-206, Sec. 6011(c)(2), added a sentence at the end of para. (d)(1), effective for tax. yrs. of United States persons begin. after 12/31/97, and for

tax. yrs. of foreign corporations ending with or within such tax. yrs. of United States persons.

In 1997, P.L. 105-34, Sec. 1122(b)(1), added a flush sentence at the end of of para. (d)(1)... Sec. 1122(b)(2), substituted "subparts B and C" for "subpart B" in the heading of subsec. (d)... Sec. 1122(b)(3), amended subpara. (a)(3)(A), effective for tax. yrs. of United States persons beginning after 12/31/97, and tax. yrs. of foreign corporations ending with or within such tax. yrs. of United States persons.

Prior to amendment, subpara. (a)(3)(A) read as follows:

"(A) Holding period. The taxpayer's holding period shall be determined under section 1223; except that, for purposes of applying this section to an excess distribution, such holding period shall be treated as ending on the date of such distribution."

In 1988, P.L. 100-647, Sec. 1012(p)(1), amended para. (d)(1)... Sec. 1012(p)(3), deleted "and" at the end of subpara. (b)(3)(D), substituted ", and" for the period at the end of subpara. (b)(3)(E) and added subpara. (b)(3)(F)... Sec. 1012(p)(6)(A), amended subsec. (f)... Sec. 1012(p)(6)(B), substituted "Except to the extent inconsistent with the regulations prescribed under subsection (f), rules similar" for "in the case of an excess distribution" in subpara. (a)(3)(A)... Sec. 1012(p)(28), amended subpara. (d)(2)(B) and added subpara. (d)(2)(C)... Sec. 1012(p)(31), added the last sentence to para. (c)(1)... Sec. 1012(p)(33), deleted "and" at the end of subpara. (b)(3)(E) [as amended by Sec. 1012(p)(3) of this Act], substituted ", and" for the period at the end of subpara. (b)(3)(F) [as added by Sec. 1012(p)(3) of this Act] and added subpara. (b)(3)(G), effective for tax. yrs. of foreign corporations begin. after 12/31/86.

Prior to amendment, para. (d)(1) read as follows:
"(1) In general. This section shall not apply with respect to—
"(A) any distribution paid by a passive foreign investment company during a taxable year for which such company is a qualified electing fund, and
"(B) any disposition of stock in a passive foreign investment company if such company is a qualified electing fund for each of its taxable years—
"(i) which begins after December 31, 1986, and for which such company is a passive foreign investment company, and
"(ii) which includes any portion of the taxpayer's holding period."

Prior to amendment, subsec. (f) read as follows:
"(f) Nonrecognition provisions.
"To the extent provided in regulations, gain shall be recognized on any disposition of stock in a passive foreign investment company."

Prior to deletion, paras. (a)(4) and (5) read as follows:
"(4) Coordination with section 904. Subparagraph (B) of paragraph (1) shall not apply for purposes of section 904.
"(5) Section 902 not to apply. Section 902 shall not apply to any dividend paid by a passive foreign investment company unless such company is a qualified electing fund."

Prior to amendment, clause (a)(1)(B)(ii) read as follows:
"(ii) any period in the taxpayer's holding period before the 1st day of the 1st taxable year of the company for which it was a passive foreign investment company (or, if later, January 1, 1987), and"

Prior to amendment, subpara. (d)(2)(B) read as follows:
"(B) Adjustments. In the case of any stock to which subparagraph (A) applies—
"(i) the adjusted basis of such stock shall be increased by the gain recognized under subparagraph (A), and
"(ii) the taxpayer's holding period in such stock shall be treated as beginning on the first day referred to in subparagraph (A)."

—P.L. 100-647, Sec. 6127(b)(1), substituted "with respect to the taxpayer for each" for "for each" in para. (d)(1) [as amended by Sec. 1012(p)(1) of this Act] ... Sec. 6127(b)(2), substituted "with respect to the taxpayer for a taxable year" for "for a taxable year" in subparas. (d)(2)(A)(i) and (B)(i) [as amended by Sec. 1012(p)(28) of this Act], effective for tax. yrs. of foreign corporations begin. after 12/31/86 except as provided in Sec. 6127(c)(2) of this Act which reads as follows:

"(2) Time for making election. The period during which an election under section 1295(b) of the 1986 Code may be made shall in no event expire before the date 60 days after the date of the enactment of this Act."

In 1986, P.L. 99-514, Sec. 1235(a), added Code Sec. 1291 as part of Part IV of Subchapter P of chapter 1, effective for tax. yrs. of foreign corporations begin. after 12/31/86.

SUBPART B.—TREATMENT OF QUALIFIED ELECTING FUNDS

Sec.

1293. Current taxation of income from qualified electing funds.

1294. Election to extend time for payment of tax on undistributed earnings.

1295. Qualified electing fund.

Sec. 1293. Current taxation of income from qualified electing funds.

(a) Inclusion.

(1) In general. Every United States person who owns (or is treated under section 1298(a) as owning) stock of a qualified electing fund at any time during the taxable year of such fund shall include in gross income—

(A) as ordinary income, such shareholder's pro rata share of the ordinary earnings of such fund for such year, and

(B) as long-term capital gain, such shareholder's pro rata share of the net capital gain of such fund for such year.

(2) Year of inclusion. The inclusion under paragraph (1) shall be for the taxable year of the shareholder in which or with which the taxable year of the fund ends.

(b) Pro rata share.

The pro rata share referred to in subsection (a) in the case of any shareholder is the amount which would have been distributed with respect to the shareholder's stock if, on each day during the taxable year of the fund, the fund had distributed to each shareholder a pro rata share of that day's ratable share of the fund's ordinary earnings and net capital gain for such year. To the extent provided in regulations, if the fund establishes to the satisfaction of the Secretary that it uses a shorter period than the taxable year to determine shareholders' interests in the earnings of such fund, pro rata shares may be determined by using such shorter period.

(c) Previously taxed amounts distributed tax free.

If the taxpayer establishes to the satisfaction of the Secretary that any amount distributed by a passive foreign investment company is paid out of earnings and profits of the company which were included under subsection (a) in the income of any United States person, such amount shall be treated, for purposes of this chapter, as a distribution which is not a dividend; except that such distribution shall immediately reduce earnings and profits. If the passive foreign investment company is a controlled foreign corporation (as defined in section 957(a)), the preceding sentence shall not apply to any United States shareholder (as defined in section 951(b)) in such corporation, and, in applying section 959 to any such shareholder, any inclusion under this section shall be treated as an inclusion under section 951(a)(1)(A).

(d) Basis adjustments.

The basis of the taxpayer's stock in a passive foreign investment company shall be—

(1) increased by any amount which is included in the income of the taxpayer under subsection (a) with respect to such stock, and

(2) decreased by any amount distributed with respect to such stock which is not includible in the income of the taxpayer by reason of subsection (c).

A similar rule shall apply also in the case of any property if by reason of holding such property the taxpayer is treated under section 1298(a) as owning stock in a qualified electing fund.

(e) Ordinary earnings.

For purposes of this section—

(1) Ordinary earnings. The term "ordinary earnings" means the excess of the earnings and profits of the qualified electing fund for the taxable year over its net capital gain for such taxable year.

(2) Limitation on net capital gain. A qualified electing fund's net capital gain for any taxable year shall not exceed its earnings and profits for such taxable year.

(3) Determination of earnings and profits. The earnings and profits of any qualified electing fund shall be determined without regard to paragraphs (4), (5), and (6) of section 312(n). Under regulations, the preceding sentence shall not apply to the extent it would increase earnings and profits by an amount which was previously distributed by the qualified electing fund.

(f) Foreign tax credit allowed in the case of 10-percent corporate shareholder.

For purposes of section 960—

(1) any amount included in the gross income under subsection (a) shall be treated as if it were included under section 951(a), and

(2) any amount excluded from gross income under subsection (c) shall be treated in the same manner as amounts excluded from gross income under section 959.

(g) Other special rules.

(1) Exception for certain income. For purposes of determining the amount included in the gross income of any person under this section, the ordinary earnings and net capital gain of a qualified electing fund shall not include any item of income received by such fund if—

(A) such fund is a controlled foreign corporation (as defined in section 957(a)) and such person is a United States shareholder (as defined in section 951(b)) in such fund, and

(B) such person establishes to the satisfaction of the Secretary that—

(i) such income was subject to an effective rate of income tax imposed by a foreign country greater than 90 percent of the maximum rate of tax specified in section 11, or

(ii) such income is—

(I) from sources within the United States,

(II) effectively connected with the conduct by the qualified electing fund of a trade or business in the United States, and

(III) not exempt from taxation (or subject to a reduced rate of tax) pursuant to a treaty obligation of the United States.

(2) Prevention of double inclusion. The Secretary shall prescribe such adjustment to the provisions of this section as may be necessary to prevent the same item of income of a qualified electing fund from being included in the gross income of a United States person more than once.

In 1997, P.L. 105-34, Sec. 1122(d)(3), substituted "section 1298(a)" for "section 1297(a)" in para. (a)(1) and subsec. (d), effective for tax. yrs. of U.S. persons begin. after 12/31/97, and as provided in Sec. 1124(2) of this Act, which reads as follows:

"(2) taxable years of foreign corporations ending with or within such taxable years of United States persons."

In 1993, P.L. 103-66, Sec. 13231(c)(3), added the sentence at the end of subsec. (c), effective for tax. yrs. of foreign corporations begin. after 9/30/93, and for tax. yrs. of U.S. shareholders in which or with which such tax. yrs. of foreign corporations end.

In 1988, P.L. 100-647, Sec. 1012(p)(15), added the sentence at the end of subsec. (b) . . . Sec. 1012(p)(18), added para. (e)(3) . . . Sec. 1012(p)(23), substituted "shall be treated, for purposes of this chapter, as a distribution which is not a dividend; except that such distribution shall immediately reduce earnings and profits" for "shall be treated as a distribution which is not a dividend" in subsec. (c) . . . Sec. 1012(p)(32), added subsec. (g), effective for tax. yrs. of foreign corporations begin. after 12/31/88.

In 1986, P.L. 99-514, Sec. 1235(a), added Code Sec. 1293 as part of Part IV of Subchapter P of chapter 1, effective for tax. yrs. of foreign corporations begin. after 12/31/86.

Sec. 1294. Election to extend time for payment of tax on undistributed earnings.

(a) Extension allowed by election.
(1) In general. At the election of the taxpayer, the time for payment of any undistributed PFIC earnings tax liability of the taxpayer for the taxable year shall be extended to the extent and subject to the limitations provided in this section.
(2) Election not permitted where amounts otherwise includible under section 951. The taxpayer may not make an election under paragraph (1) with respect to the undistributed PFIC earnings tax liability attributable to a qualified electing fund for the taxable year if any amount is includible in the gross income of the taxpayer under section 951 with respect to such fund for such taxable year.
(b) Definitions.
For purposes of this section—
(1) Undistributed PFIC earnings tax liability. The term "undistributed PFIC earnings tax liability" means, in the case of any taxpayer, the excess of—
(A) the tax imposed by this chapter for the taxable year, over
(B) the tax which would be imposed by this chapter for such year without regard to the inclusion in gross income under section 1293 of the undistributed earnings of a qualified electing fund.
(2) Undistributed earnings. The term "undistributed earnings" means, with respect to any qualified electing fund, the excess (if any) of—
(A) the amount includible in gross income by reason of section 1293(a) for the taxable year, over
(B) the amount not includible in gross income by reason of section 1293(c) for such taxable year.
(c) Termination of extension.
(1) Distributions.
(A) In general. If a distribution is not includible in gross income for the taxable year by reason of section 1293(c), then the extension under subsection (a) for payment of the undistributed PFIC earnings tax liability with respect to the earnings to which such distribution is attributable shall expire on the last date prescribed by law (determined without regard to extensions) for filing the return of tax for such taxable year.
(B) Ordering rule. For purposes of subparagraph (A), a distribution shall be treated as made from the most recently accumulated earnings and profits.
(2) Transfers, etc. If—
(A) stock in a passive foreign investment company is transferred during the taxable year, or
(B) a passive foreign investment company ceases to be a qualified electing fund,
all extensions under subsection (a) for payment of undistributed PFIC earnings tax liability attributable to such stock (or, in the case of such a cessation, attributable to any stock in such company) which had not expired before the date of such transfer or cessation shall expire on the last date prescribed by law (determined without regard to extensions) for filing the return of tax for the taxable year in which such transfer or cessation occurs. To the extent provided in regulations, the preceding sentence shall not apply in the case of a transfer in a transaction with respect to which gain or loss is not recognized (in whole or in part), and the transferee in such transaction shall succeed to the treatment under this section of the transferor.
(3) Jeopardy. If the Secretary believes that collection of an amount to which an extension under this section relates is in jeopardy, the Secretary shall immediately terminate such extension with respect to such amount, and notice and demand shall be made by him for payment of such amount.
(d) Election.
The election under subsection (a) shall be made not later than the time prescribed by law (including extensions) for filing the return of tax imposed by this chapter for the taxable year.
(e) Authority to require bond.
Section 6165 shall apply to any extension under this section as though the Secretary were extending the time for payment of the tax.
(f) Treatment of loans to shareholder.
For purposes of this section and section 1293, any loan by a qualified electing fund (directly or indirectly) to a shareholder of such fund shall be treated as a distribution to such shareholder.
(g) Cross reference.
For provisions providing for interest for the period of the extension under this section, see section 6601.

In **2004**, P.L. 108-357, Sec. 413(c)(25), amended para. (a)(2), effective for tax. yrs. of foreign corporations begin. after 12/31/2004, and for tax. yrs. of United States shareholders with or within which such tax. yrs. of foreign corporations end.
Prior to amendment, para. (a)(2) read as follows:
"(2) Election not permitted where amounts otherwise includible under section 551 or 951. The taxpayer may not make an election under paragraph (1) with respect to the undistributed PFIC earnings tax liability attributable to a qualified electing fund for the taxable year if—
"(A) any amount is includible in the gross income of the taxpayer under section 551 with respect to such fund for such taxable year, or
"(B) any amount is includible in the gross income of the taxpayer under section 951 with respect to such fund for such taxable year."
In **1988**, P.L. 100-647, Sec. 1012(p)(4)(A), substituted "is transferred" for "is disposed of" in subpara. (c)(2)(A) . . . Sec. 1012(p)(4)(B), substituted "such transfer or cessation" for "such disposition or cessation" in subpara. (c)(2)(B) . . . Sec. 1012(p)(4)(C), substituted "Transfers" for "Dispositions" in heading of para. (c)(2) . . . Sec. 1012(p)(8), added subsec. (g) . . . Sec. 1012(p)(25), added subsec. (f) . . . Sec. 1012(p)(34), added the sentence at the end of para. (c)(2), effective for tax. yrs. of foreign corporations begin. after 12/31/86.
In **1986**, P.L. 99-514, Sec. 1235(a), added Code Sec. 1294 as part of Part IV of Subchapter P of Chapter 1, effective for tax. yrs. of foreign corporations begin. after 12/31/86.

Sec. 1295. Qualified electing fund.
(a) General rule.
For purposes of this part, any passive foreign investment company shall be treated as a qualified electing fund with respect to the taxpayer if—
(1) an election by the taxpayer under subsection (b) applies to such company for the taxable year, and
(2) such company complies with such requirements as the Secretary may prescribe for purposes of—
(A) determining the ordinary earnings and net capital gain of such company, and
(B) otherwise carrying out the purposes of this subpart.
(b) Election.
(1) In general. A taxpayer may make an election under this subsection with respect to any passive foreign investment company for any taxable year of the taxpayer. Such an election, once made with respect to any company, shall apply to all subsequent taxable years of the taxpayer with respect to such company unless revoked by the taxpayer with the consent of the Secretary.
(2) When made. An election under this subsection may be made for any taxable year at any time on or before the due date (determined with regard to extensions) for filing the return of tax imposed by this chapter for such taxable year. To the extent provided in regulations, such an election may be made later than as required in the preced-

ing sentence where the taxpayer fails to make a timely election because the taxpayer reasonably believed that the company was not a passive foreign investment company.

In 1988, P.L. 100-647, Sec. 1012(p)(37)(A), added sentence at the end of para. (b)(2), effective for tax. yrs. of foreign corporations begin. after 12/31/86. Sec. 1012(p)(37)(B) of this Act provides:

"(B) The period during which an election under section 1295(b) of the 1986 Code may be made shall in no event expire before the date 60 days after the date of enactment of this Act."

—P.L. 100-647, Sec. 6127(a), amended Code Sec. 1295, effective for tax. yrs. of foreign corporations begin. after 12/31/86. Sec. 6127(c)(2) of this Act provides:

"(2) Time for making election. The period during which an election under section 1295(b) of the 1986 Code may be made shall in no event expire before the date 60 days after the date of the enactment of this Act."

Prior to amendment Code Sec. 1295 read as follows:

"SEC. 1295. QUALIFIED ELECTING FUND.

"(a) General rule.

"For purposes of this part, the term 'qualified electing fund' means any passive foreign investment company if—

"(1) an election under subsection (b) applies to such company for the taxable year, and

"(2) such company complies for such taxable year with such requirements as the Secretary may prescribe for purposes of—

"(A) determining the ordinary earnings and net capital gain of such company for the taxable year,

"(B) ascertaining the ownership of its outstanding stock, and

"(C) otherwise carrying out the purposes of this subpart.

"(b) Election.

"(1) In general. A passive foreign investment company may make an election under this subsection for any taxable year. Such an election, once made, shall apply to all subsequent taxable years of such company for which such company is a passive foreign investment company unless revoked with the consent of the Secretary.

"(2) When made. An election under this subsection may be made for any taxable year at any time before the 15th day of the 3rd month of the following taxable year. To the extent provided in regulations, such an election may be made later than as required by the preceding sentence in cases where the company failed to make a timely election because it reasonably believed it was not a passive foreign investment company."

In 1986, P.L. 99-514, Sec. 1235(a), added Code Sec. 1295 as part of Part IV of Subchapter P of chapter 1, effective for tax. yrs. of foreign corporations begin. after 12/31/86.

SUBPART C.—ELECTION OF MARK TO MARKET FOR MARKETABLE STOCK

Sec.
1296. Election of mark to market for marketable stock.

Sec. 1296. Election of mark to market for marketable stock.

(a) General rule.

In the case of marketable stock in a passive foreign investment company which is owned (or treated under subsection (g) as owned) by a United States person at the close of any taxable year of such person, at the election of such person—

(1) If the fair market value of such stock as of the close of such taxable year exceeds its adjusted basis, such United States person shall include in gross income for such taxable year an amount equal to the amount of such excess.

(2) If the adjusted basis of such stock exceeds the fair market value of such stock as of the close of such taxable year, such United States person shall be allowed a deduction for such taxable year equal to the lesser of—

(A) the amount of such excess, or

(B) the unreversed inclusions with respect to such stock.

(b) Basis adjustments.

(1) In general. The adjusted basis of stock in a passive foreign investment company—

(A) shall be increased by the amount included in the gross income of the United States person under subsection (a)(1) with respect to such stock, and

(B) shall be decreased by the amount allowed as a deduction to the United States person under subsection (a)(2) with respect to such stock.

(2) Special rule for stock constructively owned. In the case of stock in a passive foreign investment company which the United States person is treated as owning under subsection (g)—

(A) the adjustments under paragraph (1) shall apply to such stock in the hands of the person actually holding such stock but only for purposes of determining the subsequent treatment under this chapter of the United States person with respect to such stock, and

(B) similar adjustments shall be made to the adjusted basis of the property by reason of which the United States person is treated as owning such stock.

(c) Character and source rules.

(1) Ordinary treatment.

(A) Gain. Any amount included in gross income under subsection (a)(1), and any gain on the sale or other disposition of marketable stock in a passive foreign investment company (with respect to which an election under this section is in effect), shall be treated as ordinary income.

(B) Loss. Any—

(i) amount allowed as a deduction under subsection (a)(2), and

(ii) loss on the sale or other disposition of marketable stock in a passive foreign investment company (with respect to which an election under this section is in effect) to the extent that the amount of such loss does not exceed the unreversed inclusions with respect to such stock,

shall be treated as an ordinary loss. The amount so treated shall be treated as a deduction allowable in computing adjusted gross income.

(2) Source. The source of any amount included in gross income under subsection (a)(1) (or allowed as a deduction under subsection (a)(2)) shall be determined in the same manner as if such amount were gain or loss (as the case may be) from the sale of stock in the passive foreign investment company.

(d) Unreversed inclusions.

For purposes of this section, the term "unreversed inclusions" means, with respect to any stock in a passive foreign investment company, the excess (if any) of—

(1) the amount included in gross income of the taxpayer under subsection (a)(1) with respect to such stock for prior taxable years, over

(2) the amount allowed as a deduction under subsection (a)(2) with respect to such stock for prior taxable years.

The amount referred to in paragraph (1) shall include any amount which would have been included in gross income under subsection (a)(1) with respect to such stock for any prior taxable year but for section 1291. In the case of a regulated investment company which elected to mark to market the stock held by such company as of the last day of the taxable year preceding such company's first taxable year for which such company elects the application of this section, the amount referred to in paragraph (1) shall include amounts included in gross income under such mark to market with respect to such stock for prior taxable years.

(e) Marketable stock.

For purposes of this section—

(1) In general. The term "marketable stock" means—

(A) any stock which is regularly traded on—

(i) a national securities exchange which is registered with the Securities and Exchange Commission or the national market system established pursuant to section 11A of the Securities and Exchange Act of 1934, or

(ii) any exchange or other market which the Secretary determines has rules adequate to carry out the purposes of this part,

(B) to the extent provided in regulations, stock in any foreign corporation which is comparable to a regulated investment company and which offers for sale or has outstanding any stock of which it is the issuer and which is redeemable at its net asset value, and

(C) to the extent provided in regulations, any option on stock described in subparagraph (A) or (B).

(2) Special rule for regulated investment companies. In the case of any regulated investment company which is offering for sale or has outstanding any stock of which it is the issuer and which is redeemable at its net asset value, all stock in a passive foreign investment company which it owns directly or indirectly shall be treated as marketable stock for purposes of this section. Except as provided in regulations, similar treatment as marketable stock shall apply in the case of any other regulated investment company which publishes net asset valuations at least annually.

(f) Treatment of controlled foreign corporations which are shareholders in passive foreign investment companies.

In the case of a foreign corporation which is a controlled foreign corporation and which owns (or is treated under subsection (g) as owning) stock in a passive foreign investment company—

(1) this section (other than subsection (c)(2)) shall apply to such foreign corporation in the same manner as if such corporation were a United States person, and

(2) for purposes of subpart F of part III of subchapter N—

(A) any amount included in gross income under subsection (a)(1) shall be treated as foreign personal holding company income described in section 954(c)(1)(A), and

(B) any amount allowed as a deduction under subsection (a)(2) shall be treated as a deduction allocable to foreign personal holding company income so described.

(g) Stock owned through certain foreign entities.

Except as provided in regulations—

(1) In general. For purposes of this section, stock owned, directly or indirectly, by or for a foreign partnership or foreign trust or foreign estate shall be considered as being owned proportionately by its partners or beneficiaries. Stock considered to be owned by a person by reason of the application of the preceding sentence shall, for purposes of applying such sentence, be treated as actually owned by such person.

(2) Treatment of certain dispositions. In any case in which a United States person is treated as owning stock in a passive foreign investment company by reason of paragraph (1)—

(A) any disposition by the United States person or by any other person which results in the United States person being treated as no longer owning such stock, and

(B) any disposition by the person owning such stock,

shall be treated as a disposition by the United States person of the stock in the passive foreign investment company.

(h) Coordination with section 851(b).

For purposes of section 851(b)(2), any amount included in gross income under subsection (a) shall be treated as a dividend.

• *Caution:* Sec. 301(a), P.L. 111-312, (reproduced in the history notes following this Code Sec.) provides that the deletion provided by Sec. 542(e)(5)(C), P.L. 107-16, EGTRRA, will apply as if never enacted. Code Sec. 1396(i), following, reflects the removal of this provision, effective for estates of decedents dying, and transfers made, after 12/31/2009.

(i) Stock acquired from a decedent.

In the case of stock of a passive foreign investment company which is acquired by bequest, devise, or inheritance (or by the decedent's estate) and with respect to which an election under this section was in effect as of the date of the decedent's death, notwithstanding section 1014, the basis of such stock in the hands of the person so acquiring it shall be the adjusted basis of such stock in the hands of the decedent immediately before his death (or, if lesser, the basis which would have been determined under section 1014 without regard to this subsection).

• *Caution:* Code Sec. 1296(i), following, was deleted by Sec. 542(e)(5)(C), P.L. 107-16, EGTRRA. As provided in Sec. 301(a), P.L. 111-312, this provision will apply as if never enacted, effective for estates of decedents dying, and transfers made, after 12/31/2009.

(i) Repealed.

(j) Coordination with section 1291 for first year of election.

(1) Taxpayers other than regulated investment companies.

(A) In general. If the taxpayer elects the application of this section with respect to any marketable stock in a corporation after the beginning of the taxpayer's holding period in such stock, and if the requirements of subparagraph (B) are not satisfied, section 1291 shall apply to—

(i) any distributions with respect to, or disposition of, such stock in the first taxable year of the taxpayer for which such election is made, and

(ii) any amount which, but for section 1291, would have been included in gross income under subsection (a) with respect to such stock for such taxable year in the same manner as if such amount were gain on the disposition of such stock.

(B) Requirements. The requirements of this subparagraph are met if, with respect to each of such corporation's taxable years for which such corporation was a passive foreign investment company and which begin after December 31, 1986, and included any portion of the taxpayer's holding period in such stock, such corporation was treated as a qualified electing fund under this part with respect to the taxpayer.

(2) Special rules for regulated investment companies.

(A) In general. If a regulated investment company elects the application of this section with respect to any marketable stock in a corporation after the beginning of the taxpayer's holding period in such stock, then, with respect to such company's first taxable year for which such company elects the application of this section with respect to such stock—

(i) section 1291 shall not apply to such stock with respect to any distribution or disposition during, or amount included in gross income under this section for, such first taxable year, but

(ii) such regulated investment company's tax under this chapter for such first taxable year shall be increased by the aggregate amount of interest which would have been determined under section 1291(c)(3) if section 1291 were applied without regard to this subparagraph.

Clause (ii) shall not apply if for the preceding taxable year the company elected to mark to market the stock held by such company as of the last day of such preceding taxable year.

(B) **Disallowance of deduction.** No deduction shall be allowed to any regulated investment company for the increase in tax under subparagraph (A)(ii).

(k) Election.

This section shall apply to marketable stock in a passive foreign investment company which is held by a United States person only if such person elects to apply this section with respect to such stock. Such an election shall apply to the taxable year for which made and all subsequent taxable years unless—

(1) such stock ceases to be marketable stock, or

(2) the Secretary consents to the revocation of such election.

(l) Transition rule for individuals becoming subject to United States tax.

If any individual becomes a United States person in a taxable year beginning after December 31, 1997, solely for purposes of this section, the adjusted basis (before adjustments under subsection (b)) of any marketable stock in a passive foreign investment company owned by such individual on the first day of such taxable year shall be treated as being the greater of its fair market value on such first day or its adjusted basis on such first day.

In 2010, P.L. 111-312, Sec. 101(a)(1), substituted "December 31, 2012" for "December 31, 2010" both places it appeared in Sec. 901, P.L. 107-16 [see below], effective as if included in the enactment of P.L. 107-16, EGTRRA, 6/7/2001.

—P.L. 111-312, Sec. 301(a), provides that Code Sec. 1296, as amended by Sec. 542(e)(5)(C), P.L. 107-16 EGTRRA, 6/7/2001 (deleting subpara. (i), see below) will read as if such provision had never been enacted, effective for estates of decedents dying, and transfers made, after 12/31/2009.

Sec. 301(a), P.L. 111-312, provides:

"(a) In general. Each provision of law amended by subtitle A or E of title V of the Economic Growth and Tax Relief Reconciliation Act of 2001 is amended to read as such provision would read if such subtitle had never been enacted."

—P.L. 111-312, Sec. 301(c), of this Act, provides

"(c) Special election with respect to estates of decedents dying in 2010. Notwithstanding subsection (a), in the case of an estate of a decedent dying after December 31, 2009, and before January 1, 2011, the executor (within the meaning of section 2203 of the Internal Revenue Code of 1986) may elect to apply such Code as though the amendments made by subsection (a) do not apply with respect to chapter 11 of such Code and with respect to property acquired or passing from such decedent (within the meaning of section 1014(b) of such Code). Such election shall be made at such time and in such manner as the Secretary of the Treasury or the Secretary's delegate shall provide. Such an election once made shall be revocable only with the consent of the Secretary of the Treasury or the Secretary's delegate. For purposes of section 2652(a)(1) of such Code, the determination of whether any property is subject to the tax imposed by such chapter 11 shall be made without regard to any election made under this subsection."

—P.L. 111-312, Sec. 301(d), of this Act, provides

" (d) Extension of time for performing certain acts.

" (1) Estate tax. In the case of the estate of a decedent dying after December 31, 2009, and before the date of the enactment of this Act, the due date for—

" (A) filing any return under section 6018 of the Internal Revenue Code of 1986 (including any election required to be made on such a return) as such section is in effect after the date of the enactment of this Act without regard to any election under subsection (c),

" (B) making any payment of tax under chapter 11 of such Code, and

" (C) making any disclaimer described in section 2518(b) of such Code of an interest in property passing by reason of the death of such decedent, shall be no earlier than the date which is 9 months after the date of the enactment of this Act.

" (2) Generation-skipping tax. In the case of any generation-skipping transfer made after December 31, 2009, and before the date of the enactment of this Act, the due date for filing any return under section 2662 of the Internal Revenue Code of 1986 (including any election required to be made on such a return) shall not be earlier than the date which is 9 months after the date of the enactment of this Act."

In 2004, P.L. 108-311, Sec. 408(a)(19), substituted "section 851(b)(2)" for "paragraphs (2) and (3) of section 851(b)" in subsec. (h), enacted 10/4/2004.

In 2002, P.L. 107-358, Sec. 2, added subsec. (c) in Sec. 901 of P.L. 107-16 [see below], effective 12/17/2002.

In 2001, P.L. 107-16, Sec. 542(e)(5)(C), deleted subsec. (i), effective for estates of decedents dying after 12/31/2009.

Prior to deletion, subsec. (i) read as follows:

"(i) Stock acquired from a decedent. In the case of stock of a passive foreign investment company which is acquired by bequest, devise, or inheritance (or by the decedent's estate) and with respect to which an election under this section was in effect as of the date of the decedent's death, notwithstanding section 1014, the basis of such stock in the hands of the person so acquiring it shall be the adjusted basis of such stock in the hands of the decedent immediately before his death (or, if lesser, the basis which would have been determined under section 1014 without regard to this subsection)."

—P.L. 107-16, Sec. 901, of this Act [as amended by Sec. 2 of P.L. 107-358, and Sec. 101(a)(1), P.L. 111-312, see above], reads as follows:

"SEC. 901. SUNSET OF PROVISIONS OF ACT.

"(a) In general. All provisions of, and amendments made by, this Act shall not apply—

"(1) to taxable, plan, or limitation years beginning after December 31, 2012, or

"(2) in the case of title V, to estates of decedents dying, gifts made, or generation skipping transfers, after December 31, 2012.

"(b) Application of certain laws. The Internal Revenue Code of 1986 and the Employee Retirement Income Security Act of 1974 shall be applied and administered to years, estates, gifts, and transfers described in subsection (a) as if the provisions and amendments described in subsection (a) had never been enacted.

"(c) Exception. Subsection (a) shall not apply to section 803 (relating to no federal income tax on restitution received by victims of the Nazi regime or their heirs or estates)."

In 1998, P.L. 105-206, Sec. 6011(c)(3), added a sentence at the end of subsec. (d), effective for tax. yrs. of U.S. persons begin. after 12/31/97, and tax. yrs. of foreign corporations end. with or within such tax. yrs. of U.S. persons.

In 1997, P.L. 105-34, Sec. 1122(a), added Code Sec. 1296, effective for tax. yrs. of U.S. persons begin. after 12/31/97, and tax. yrs. of foreign corporations end. with or within such tax. yrs. of U.S. persons.

SUBPART D.—GENERAL PROVISIONS

Sec.

1297. Passive foreign investment company.

1298. Special rules.

In 1997, P.L. 105-34, Sec. 1122(a), redesignated subpart C as subpart D and redesignated Code Secs. 1296 and 1297 as Code Secs. 1297 and 1298.

Sec. 1297. Passive foreign investment company.

(a) In general.

For purposes of this part, except as otherwise provided in this subpart, the term "passive foreign investment company" means any foreign corporation if—

(1) 75 percent or more of the gross income of such corporation for the taxable year is passive income, or

(2) the average percentage of assets (as determined in accordance with subsection (e)) held by such corporation during the taxable year which produce passive income or which are held for the production of passive income is at least 50 percent.

(b) Passive income.

For purposes of this section—

(1) **In general.** Except as provided in paragraph (2), the term "passive income" means any income which is of a kind which would be foreign personal holding company income as defined in section 954(c).

(2) **Exceptions.** Except as provided in regulations, the term "passive income" does not include any income—

(A) derived in the active conduct of a banking business by an institution licensed to do business as a bank in the United States (or, to the extent provided in regulations, by any other corporation),

(B) derived in the active conduct of an insurance business by a corporation which is predominantly engaged in an insurance business and which would be subject to tax under subchapter L if it were a domestic corporation,

(C) which is interest, a dividend, or a rent or royalty, which is received or accrued from a related person (within the meaning of section 954(d)(3)) to the extent such amount is properly allocable (under regulations prescribed by the Secretary) to income of such related person which is not passive income, or

(D) which is export trade income of an export trade corporation (as defined in section 971).

For purposes of subparagraph (C), the term "related person" has the meaning given such term by section 954(d)(3) determined by substituting "foreign corporation" for "controlled foreign corporation" each place it appears in section 954(d)(3).

(c) Look-thru in the case of 25-percent owned corporations.

If a foreign corporation owns (directly or indirectly) at least 25 percent (by value) of the stock of another corporation, for purposes of determining whether such foreign corporation is a passive foreign investment company, such foreign corporation shall be treated as if it—

(1) held its proportionate share of the assets of such other corporation, and

(2) received directly its proportionate share of the income of such other corporation.

(d) Exception for United States shareholders of controlled foreign corporations.

(1) **In general.** For purposes of this part, a corporation shall not be treated with respect to a shareholder as a passive foreign investment company during the qualified portion of such shareholder's holding period with respect to stock in such corporation.

(2) **Qualified portion.** For purposes of this subsection, the term "qualified portion" means the portion of the shareholder's holding period—

(A) which is after December 31, 1997, and

(B) during which the shareholder is a United States shareholder (as defined in section 951(b)) of the corporation and the corporation is a controlled foreign corporation.

(3) **New holding period if qualified portion ends.**

(A) In general. Except as provided in subparagraph (B), if the qualified portion of a shareholder's holding period with respect to any stock ends after December 31, 1997, solely for purposes of this part, the shareholder's holding period with respect to such stock shall be treated as beginning as of the first day following such period.

(B) Exception. Subparagraph (A) shall not apply if such stock was, with respect to such shareholder, stock in a passive foreign investment company at any time before the qualified portion of the shareholder's holding period with respect to such stock and no election under section 1298(b)(1) is made.

(4) **Treatment of holders of options.** Paragraph (1) shall not apply to stock treated as owned by a person by reason of section 1298(a)(4) (relating to the treatment of a person that has an option to acquire stock as owning such stock) unless such person establishes that such stock is owned (within the meaning of section 958(a)) by a United States shareholder (as defined in section 951(b)) who is not exempt from tax under this chapter.

(e) Methods for measuring assets.

(1) **Determination using value.** The determination under subsection (a)(2) shall be made on the basis of the value of the assets of a foreign corporation if—

(A) such corporation is a publicly traded corporation for the taxable year, or

(B) paragraph (2) does not apply to such corporation for the taxable year.

(2) **Determination using adjusted bases.** The determination under subsection (a)(2) shall be based on the adjusted bases (as determined for the purposes of computing earnings and profits) of the assets of a foreign corporation if such corporation is not described in paragraph (1)(A) and such corporation—

(A) is a controlled foreign corporation, or

(B) elects the application of this paragraph.

An election under subparagraph (B), once made, may be revoked only with the consent of the Secretary.

(3) **Publicly traded corporation.** For purposes of this subsection, a foreign corporation shall be treated as a publicly traded corporation if the stock in the corporation is regularly traded on—

(A) a national securities exchange which is registered with the Securities and Exchange Commission or the national market system established pursuant to section 11A of the Securities Exchange Act of 1934, or

(B) any exchange or other market which the Secretary determines has rules adequate to carry out the purposes of this subsection.

In 2007, P.L. 110-172, Sec. 11(g)(18), deleted "foreign trade income of a FSC or" in subpara. (b)(2)(D) . . . Sec. 11(a)(24)(A), deleted subsec. (d) and redes. subsecs. (e)-(f) as subsecs. (d)-(e), enacted 12/29/2007.
Prior to deletion, subsec. (d) read as follows:
"(d) Section 1247 corporations. For purposes of this part, the term "passive foreign investment company" does not include any foreign investment company to which section 1247 applies."

In 1998, P.L. 105-206, Sec. 6011(b)(1), added para. (e)(4) . . . Sec. 6011(d), redesignated subsec. (e) [sic f)] as (f), effective for tax. yrs. of U.S. persons begin. after 12/31/97, and tax. yrs. of foreign corporations end. with or within such tax. yrs. of U.S. persons.

In 1997, P.L. 105-34, Sec. 1121, added subsec. (e) . . . Sec. 1122(a), redesignated Code Sec. 1296 as Code Sec. 1297 . . . Sec. 1122(d)(4), deleted para. (b)(3) . . . Sec. 1123(a), added subsec. (e)[sic (f)] . . . Sec. 1123(b)(1), substituted "(as determined in accordance with subsection (e))" for "(by value)" in subsec. (a) . . . Sec. 1123(b)(2), deleted "In the case of a controlled foreign corporation (or any other foreign corporation if such corporation so elects), the determination under paragraph (2) shall be based on the adjusted bases (as determined for purposes of computing earnings and profits) of its assets in lieu of their value. Such an election, once made, may be revoked only with the consent of the Secretary." in subsec (a), effective for tax. yrs. of U.S. persons begin. after 12/31/97, and tax. yrs. of foreign corporations end. with or within such tax. yrs. of U.S. persons.
Prior to deletion, para. (b)(3) read as follows:
"(3) Treatment of certain dealers in securities.
"(A) In general. In the case of any foreign corporation which is a controlled foreign corporation (as defined in section 957(a)), the term 'passive income' does not include any income derived in the active conduct of a securities business by such corporation if such corporation is registered as a securities broker or dealer under section 15(a) of the Securities Exchange Act of 1934 or is registered as a Government securities broker or dealer under section 15C(a) of such Act. To the extent provided in regulations, such term shall not include any income derived in the active conduct of a securities business by a controlled foreign corporation which is not so registered.
"(B) Application of look-thru rules. For purposes of paragraph (2)(C), rules similar to the rules of subparagraph (A) of this paragraph shall apply in determining whether any income of a related person (whether or not a corporation) is passive income.
"(C) Limitation. The preceding provisions of this paragraph shall only apply in the case of persons who are United States shareholders (as defined in section 951(b)) in the controlled foreign corporation."

In 1996, P.L. 104-188, Sec. 1704(r)(1), deleted "or" at the end of subpara. (b)(2)(B), substituted ", or" for the period at the end of subpara. (b)(2)(C), and added subpara. (b)(2)(D), effective for tax. yrs. of foreign corporations begin. after 12/31/86.

Code Sec. 1297

Passive foreign investment companies

In 1993, P.L. 103-66, Sec. 13231(d)(1), substituted "In the case of a controlled foreign corporation (or any other foreign corporation if such corporation so elects), the determination under paragraph (2) shall be based on the adjusted bases (as determined for purposes of computing earnings and profits) of its assets in lieu of their value. Such an election, once made, may be revoked only with the consent of the Secretary." for "A foreign corporation may elect to have the determination under paragraph (2) based on the adjusted bases of its assets in lieu of their value. Such an election, once made, may be revoked only with the consent of the Secretary." in the material following para. (a)(2) . . . Sec. 13231(d)(3), added para. (b)(3), effective for tax. yrs. of foreign corporations begin. after 9/30/93, and for tax. yrs. of U.S. shareholders in which or with which such tax. yrs. of foreign corporations end.

In 1988, P.L. 100-647, Sec. 1012(p)(2), substituted "owns (directly or indirectly) at least" for "owns at least" in subsec. (c) . . . Sec. 1012(p)(5), amended para. (b)(1) . . . Sec. 1012(p)(16), substituted "by a corporation which is predominantly engaged in an insurance business and which" for "by a corporation which" in subpara. (b)(2)(B) . . . Sec. 1012(p)(26)(A), deleted "or" at end of subpara. (b)(2)(A), substituted ", or" for the period at end of subpara. (b)(2)(B) and added subpara. (b)(2)(C) . . . Sec. 1012(p)(26)(B), substituted "Exceptions" for "Exception for certain banks and insurance companies" in the heading of para. (b)(2) . . . Sec. 1012(p)(27), added two sentences to end of subsec. (a) . . . Sec. 1018(a)(40), added a comma after "this subpart" in subsec. (a), effective for tax. yrs. of foreign corporations begin after 12/31/86.

Prior to amendment para. (b)(1) read as follows:

"(1) In general. Except as provided in paragraph (2), the term 'passive income' has the meaning given such term by section 904(d)(2)(A) without regard to the exceptions contained in clause (iii) thereof."

In 1986, P.L. 99-514, Sec. 1235(a), added Code Sec. 1296 as part of Part IV of Subchapter P of chapter 1, effective for tax. yrs. of foreign corporations begin. after 12/31/86.

Sec. 1298. Special rules.

(a) Attribution of ownership.

For purposes of this part—

(1) Attribution to United States persons. This subsection—

(A) shall apply to the extent that the effect is to treat stock of a passive foreign investment company as owned by a United States person, and

(B) except to the extent provided in regulations, shall not apply to treat stock owned (or treated as owned under this subsection) by a United States person as owned by any other person.

(2) Corporations.

(A) In general. If 50 percent or more in value of the stock of a corporation is owned, directly or indirectly, by or for any person, such person shall be considered as owning the stock owned directly or indirectly by or for such corporation in that proportion which the value of the stock which such person so owns bears to the value of all stock in the corporation.

(B) 50-percent limitation not to apply to PFIC. For purposes of determining whether a shareholder of a passive foreign investment company is treated as owning stock owned directly or indirectly by or for such company, subparagraph (A) shall be applied without regard to the 50-percent limitation contained therein. Section 1297(d) shall not apply in determining whether a corporation is a passive foreign investment company for purposes of this subparagraph.

(3) Partnerships, etc. Stock owned, directly or indirectly, by or for a partnership, estate, or trust shall be considered as being owned proportionately by its partners or beneficiaries.

(4) Options. To the extent provided in regulations, if any person has an option to acquire stock, such stock shall be considered as owned by such person. For purposes of this paragraph, an option to acquire such an option, and each one of a series of such options, shall be considered as an option to acquire such stock.

(5) Successive application. Stock considered to be owned by a person by reason of the application of paragraph (2), (3), or (4) shall, for purposes of applying such paragraphs, be considered as actually owned by such person.

(b) Other special rules.

For purposes of this part—

(1) Time for determination. Stock held by a taxpayer shall be treated as stock in a passive foreign investment company if, at any time during the holding period of the taxpayer with respect to such stock, such corporation (or any predecessor) was a passive foreign investment company which was not a qualified electing fund. The preceding sentence shall not apply if the taxpayer elects to recognize gain (as of the last day of the last taxable year for which the company was a passive foreign investment company (determined without regard to the preceding sentence)) under rules similar to the rules of section 1291(d)(2).

(2) Certain corporations not treated as PFIC's during start-up year. A corporation shall not be treated as a passive foreign investment company for the first taxable year such corporation has gross income (hereinafter in this paragraph referred to as the "start-up year") if—

(A) no predecessor of such corporation was a passive foreign investment company,

(B) it is established to the satisfaction of the Secretary that such corporation will not be a passive foreign investment company for either of the 1st 2 taxable years following the start-up year, and

(C) such corporation is not a passive foreign investment company for either of the 1st 2 taxable years following the start-up year.

(3) Certain corporations changing businesses. A corporation shall not be treated as a passive foreign investment company for any taxable year if—

(A) neither such corporation (nor any predecessor) was a passive foreign investment company for any prior taxable year,

(B) it is established to the satisfaction of the Secretary that—

(i) substantially all of the passive income of the corporation for the taxable year is attributable to proceeds from the disposition of 1 or more active trades or businesses, and

(ii) such corporation will not be a passive foreign investment company for either of the 1st 2 taxable years following such taxable year, and

(C) such corporation is not a passive foreign investment company for either of such 2 taxable years.

(4) Separate interests treated as separate corporations. Under regulations prescribed by the Secretary, where necessary to carry out the purposes of this part, separate classes of stock (or other interests) in a corporation shall be treated as interests in separate corporations.

(5) Application of part where stock held by other entity.

(A) In general. Under regulations, in any case in which a United States person is treated as owning stock in a passive foreign investment company by reason of subsection (a)—

(i) any disposition by the United States person or the person owning such stock which results in the United States person being treated as no longer owning such stock, or

(ii) any distribution of property in respect of such stock to the person holding such stock,

shall be treated as a disposition by, or distribution to, the United States person with respect to the stock in the passive foreign investment company.

2,814

Passive foreign investment companies   Code Sec. 1298

(B) Amount treated in same manner as previously taxed income. Rules similar to the rules of section 959(b) shall apply to any amount described in subparagraph (A) and to any amount included in gross income under section 1293(a) (or which would have been so included but for section 951(f)) in respect of stock which the taxpayer is treated as owning under subsection (a).

(6) Dispositions. Except as provided in regulations, if a taxpayer uses any stock in a passive foreign investment company as security for a loan, the taxpayer shall be treated as having disposed of such stock.

(7) Treatment of certain foreign corporations owning stock in 25-percent owned domestic corporation.

(A) In general. If—

(i) a foreign corporation is subject to the tax imposed by section 531 (or waives any benefit under any treaty which would otherwise prevent the imposition of such tax), and

(ii) such foreign corporation owns at least 25 percent (by value) of the stock of a domestic corporation,

for purposes of determining whether such foreign corporation is a passive foreign investment company, any qualified stock held by such domestic corporation shall be treated as an asset which does not produce passive income (and is not held for the production of passive income) and any amount included in gross income with respect to such stock shall not be treated as passive income.

(B) Qualified stock. For purposes of subparagraph (A), the term "qualified stock" means any stock in a C corporation which is a domestic corporation and which is not a regulated investment company or real estate investment trust.

(8) Treatment of certain subpart F inclusions. Any amount included in gross income under section 951(a)(1)(B) shall be treated as a distribution received with respect to the stock.

(c) Treatment of stock held by pooled income fund.

If stock in a passive foreign investment company is owned (or treated as owned under subsection (a)) by a pooled income fund (as defined in section 642(c)(5)) and no portion of any gain from a disposition of such stock may be allocated to income under the terms of the governing instrument of such fund—

(1) section 1291 shall not apply to any gain on a disposition of such stock by such fund if (without regard to section 1291) a deduction would be allowable with respect to such gain under section 642(c)(3),

(2) section 1293 shall not apply with respect to such stock, and

(3) in determining whether section 1291 applies to any distribution in respect of such stock, subsection (d) of section 1291 shall not apply.

(d) Treatment of certain leased property.

For purposes of this part—

(1) In general. Any tangible personal property with respect to which a foreign corporation is the lessee under a lease with a term of at least 12 months shall be treated as an asset actually held by such corporation.

(2) Amount taken into account.

(A) In general. The amount taken into account under section 1296(a)(2) with respect to any asset to which paragraph (1) applies shall be the unamortized portion (as determined under regulations prescribed by the Secretary) of the present value of the payments under the lease for the use of such property.

(B) Present value. For purposes of subparagraph (A), the present value of payments described in subparagraph (A) shall be determined in the manner provided in regulations prescribed by the Secretary—

(i) as of the beginning of the lease term, and

(ii) except as provided in such regulations, by using a discount rate equal to the applicable Federal rate determined under section 1274(d)—

(I) by substituting the lease term for the term of the debt instrument, and

(II) without regard to paragraph (2) or (3) thereof.

(3) Exceptions. This subsection shall not apply in any case where—

(A) the lessor is a related person (as defined in section 954(d)(3)) with respect to the foreign corporation, or

(B) a principal purpose of leasing the property was to avoid the provisions of this part.

(e) Special rules for certain intangibles.

For purposes of this part—

(1) Research expenditures. The adjusted basis of the total assets of a controlled foreign corporation shall be increased by the research or experimental expenditures (within the meaning of section 174) paid or incurred by such foreign corporation during the taxable year and the preceding 2 taxable years. Any expenditure otherwise taken into account under the preceding sentence shall be reduced by the amount of any reimbursement received by the controlled foreign corporation with respect to such expenditure.

(2) Certain licensed intangibles.

(A) In general. In the case of any intangible property (as defined in section 936(h)(3)(B)) with respect to which a controlled foreign corporation is a licensee and which is used by such foreign corporation in the active conduct of a trade or business, the adjusted basis of the total assets of such foreign corporation shall be increased by an amount equal to 300 percent of the payments made during the taxable year by such foreign corporation for the use of such intangible property.

(B) Exceptions. Subparagraph (A) shall not apply to—

(i) any payments to a foreign person if such foreign person is a related person (as defined in section 954(d)(3)) with respect to the controlled foreign corporation, and

(ii) any payments under a license if a principal purpose of entering into such license was to avoid the provisions of this part.

(3) Controlled foreign corporation. For purposes of this subsection, the term "controlled foreign corporation" has the meaning given such term by section 957(a).

(f) Reporting requirement.

Except as otherwise provided by the Secretary, each United States person who is a shareholder of a passive foreign investment company shall file an annual report containing such information as the Secretary may require.

(g) Regulations.

The Secretary shall prescribe such regulations as may be necessary or appropriate to carry out the purposes of this part.

In 2010, P.L. 111-147, Sec. 521(a), redesignated subsec. (f) as subsec. (g) and added new subsec. (f), effective 3/18/2010.

In 2007, P.L. 110-172, Sec. 11(a)(24)(C), substituted "Section 1297(d)" for "Section 1297(e)" in subpara. (a)(2)(B), enacted 12/29/2007.

— P.L. 110-172, Sec. 11(f)(2), deleted para. (b)(7) and redesignated paras. (b)(8)-(9) as (b)(7)-(8), effective for tax. yrs. of foreign corporations begin. after 12/31/2004, and for tax. yrs. of U.S. shareholders with or within which such tax. yrs. of foreign corporations end.

Code Sec. 1298 — Passive foreign investment companies

Prior to deletion, para. (b)(7) read as follows:

"(7) Coordination with section 1246. Section 1246 shall not apply to earnings and profits of any company for any taxable year beginning after December 31, 1986, if such company is a passive foreign investment company for such taxable year."

In 1998, P.L. 105-206, Sec. 6011(b)(2), added a sentence at the end of subpara. (a)(2)(B), effective for tax. yrs. of U.S. persons begin. after 12/31/97, and tax. yrs. of foreign corporations end. with or within such tax. yrs. of U.S. persons.

In 1997, P.L. 105-34, Sec. 1122(a), redesignated Code Sec. 1297 as Code Sec. 1298 . . . Sec. 1122(e), added "(determined without regard to the preceding sentence)" after "investment company" in para. (b)(1), effective for tax. yrs. of U.S. persons begin. after 12/31/97, and tax. yrs. of foreign corporations end. with or within such tax. yrs. of U.S. persons.

In 1996, P.L. 104-188, Sec. 1501(b)(9), substituted "section 951(a)(1)(B)" for "subparagraph (B) or (C) of section 951(a)(1)" in para. (b)(9) . . . Sec. 1501(b)(10), deleted "or section 956A" after "of this part" in subpara. (d)(3)(B) and clause (e)(2)(B)(ii), effective for tax. yrs. of foreign corporations begin. after 12/31/96, and for tax. yrs. of U.S. shareholders within which or with which such tax. yrs. of foreign corporations end.

— P.L. 104-188, Sec. 1703(i)(5)(A), substituted "The amount taken into account under section 1296(a)(2) with respect to any asset" for "The adjusted basis of any asset" in subpara. (d)(2)(A) . . . Sec. 1703(i)(5)(B), amended the heading of para. (d)(2) . . . Sec. 1703(i)(6), added "For purposes of this part —" after subsec. (e) heading, effective for tax. yrs. of foreign corporations begin. after 9/30/93, and for tax. yrs. of U.S. shareholders in which or with which such tax. yrs. of foreign corporations end.

Prior to amendment, the heading of para. (d)(2) read as follows:

"(2) Determination of adjusted basis."

In 1993, P.L. 103-66, Sec. 13231(d)(2), added para. (b)(9) . . . Sec. 13231(d)(4), redesignated subsec. (d) as subsec. (f) and added new subsecs. (d) and (e), effective for tax. yrs. of foreign corporations begin. after 9/30/93, and for tax. yrs. of U.S. shareholders in which or with which such tax. yrs. of foreign corporations end.

In 1989, P.L. 101-239, Sec. 7811(i)(4)(A), added "stock" after "where" in the heading of para. (b)(5) . . . Sec. 7811(i)(4)(B), substituted "any distribution of" for "any disposition of" in clause (b)(5)(A)(ii) . . . Sec. 7811(i)(4)(C), substituted "treated as a disposition by, or distribution to" for "treated as a disposition to" in subpara. (b)(5)(A), effective for tax. yrs. of foreign corporations begin. after 12/31/86.

In 1988, P.L. 100-647, Sec. 1012(p)(10)(A), redesignated para. (a)(4) as para. (a)(5) and added new para. (a)(4) . . . Sec. 1012(p)(10)(B), substituted "paragraph (2), (3), or (4)" for "paragraph (2) or (3)" in para. (a)(5) . . . Sec. 1012(p)(17), amended para. (b)(5) . . . Sec. 1012(p)(20), substituted "Except as provided in regulations, if a" for "If a" in para. (b)(6) . . . Sec. 1012(p)(22), amended subpara. (b)(3)(A) . . . Sec. 1012(p)(24), added new para. (b)(8) . . . Sec. 1012(p)(35), redesignated subsec. (c) as subsec. (d) and added new subsec. (c) . . . Sec. 1012(p)(36), substituted "passive foreign investment company" for "passive foreign investment corporation" in para. (b)(1) effective for tax. yrs. of foreign corporations begin. after 12/31/86.

Prior to amendment, para. (b)(5) read as follows:

"(5) Application of section where stock held by other entity. Under regulations, in any case in which a United States person is treated as holding stock in a passive foreign investment company by reason of subsection (a), any disposition by the United States person or the person holding such stock which results in the United States person being treated as no longer holding such stock, shall be treated as a disposition by the United States person with respect to stock in the passive foreign investment company."

Prior to amendment, subpara. (b)(3)(A) read as follows:

"(A) such corporation (and any predecessor) was not a passive foreign investment corporation for any prior taxable year."

In 1986, P.L. 99-514, Sec. 1235(a), added Code Sec. 1297 as part of Part IV of Subchapter P of chapter 1, effective for tax. yrs. of foreign corporations begin. after 12/31/86.

Subchapter Q. — Readjustment of Tax Between Years and Special Limitations

Part

    I. Income averaging.

    II. Mitigation of effect of limitations and other provisions.

    III. Repealed.

    IV. Repealed.

    V. Claim of right.

    VI. Repealed.

    VII. Recoveries of foreign expropriation losses.

In 1997, P.L. 105-34, Sec. 933(a), added item for Part I.

In 1986, P.L. 99-514, Sec. 141(c), deleted the items relating to part I.

Prior to deletion, part I read as follows:

"PART I — INCOME AVERAGING

"Sec.

"1301. Limitation on tax.

"1302. Definition of averageable income, related definitions.

"1303. Eligible individuals.

"1304. Special rules.

"1305. Regulations."

In 1981, P.L. 97-34, Sec. 101(c)(2)(C), deleted item VI.

Prior to deletion, item VI read as follows:

"VI. Maximum rate on personal service income."

In 1976, P.L. 94-455, Sec. 1901(b)(36)(E), deleted the item for Part III.

Prior to repeal, that item read as follows:

"III. Involuntary liquidation and replacement of LIFO inventories."

— P.L. 94-455, Sec. 1901(b)(37)(F), deleted the item for Part IV.

Prior to repeal, that item read as follows:

"IV. War loss recoveries."

— P.L. 94-455, Sec. 1951(c)(3)(D), amended the item for Part VI.

Prior to amendment Part VI read as follows:

"VI. Other limitations."

In 1966, added Part VII.

In 1964, rewrote Part I.

PART I. Repealed. [INCOME AVERAGING]

Sec.

1301. Repealed. [Limitation on tax.]

1302. Repealed. [Definition of averageable income, related definitions.]

1303. Repealed. [Eligible individuals.]

1304. Repealed. [Special rules.]

1305. Repealed. [Regulations.]

In 1986, P.L. 99-514, Sec. 141(c), repealed part I.

Prior to repeal, part I read as follows:

"PART I — INCOME AVERAGING

"Sec.

"1301. Limitation on tax.

"1302. Definition of averageable income, related definitions.

"1303. Eligible individuals.

"1304. Special rules.

"1305. Regulations."

"Sec. 1301. Limitation on tax.

"If an eligible individual has averageable income for the computation year, and if the amount of such income exceeds $3,000, then the tax imposed by section 1 for the computation year which is attributable to averageable income shall be 4 times the increase in tax under such section which would result from adding 25 percent of such income to 140 percent of average base period income."

In 1986, P.L. 99-514, Sec. 141(a), repealed Code Sec. 1301, effective for tax. yrs. begin. after 12/31/86.

In 1984, P.L. 98-369, Sec. 173(b), substituted "140 percent" for "120 percent" in Code Sec. 1301 . . . Sec. 173(c)(1)(A), substituted "4 times" for "5 times" in Code Sec. 1301 . . . Sec. 173(c)(1)(B), substituted "25 percent" for "20 percent" in Code Sec. 1301, effective for computation yrs. begin. after 12/31/83, and for base period yrs. applicable to such computation yrs.

In 1969, P.L. 91-172, Sec. 311(a), substituted "20 percent of such income to 120 percent of average base period income." for "20 percent of such income to the sum of —

"(1) 133⅓ percent of average base period income, and

"(2) the amount (if any) of the average base period capital gain net income.", effective for computation yrs. (within the meaning of sec. 1302(c)(1) of the Internal Revenue Code of 1954) begin. after 12/31/69, and to base period yrs. (within the meaning of sec. 1302(c)(3) of such Code) applicable to such computation yrs.

In 1964, P.L. 88-272, Sec. 232, substituted a completely new set of Code Secs. 1301 thru 1305 for former Code Secs. 1301 thru 1307, effective for tax. yrs. begin. after 12/31/63. The former provisions are reproduced in a note following Part I.

In making the change, Sec. 232(g) of P.L. 88-272, provided:

"(2) Income from an employment. — If, in a taxable year beginning after December 31, 1963, an individual or partnership receives or accrues compensation from an employment (as defined by section 1301(b) of the Internal Revenue Code of 1954 as in effect immediately before the enactment of this Act [2/26/64] and the employment began before February 6, 1963, the tax attributable to such compensation may, at the election of the taxpayer, be computed under the provisions of sections 1301 and 1307 of such Code as in effect immediately before the enactment of this Act. If a taxpayer so elects (at such time and in such manner as the Secretary of the Treasury or his delegate by regulations prescribes), he may not choose for such taxable year the benefits provided by part I of subchapter Q of chapter 1 of such Code (relating to income averaging) as amended by this Act and (if he elects to have subsection (e) of such section 1307 apply) section 170(b)(5)

Passive foreign investment companies — Part I

of such Code as amended by this Act shall not apply to charitable contributions paid in such taxable year."

"SEC. 1302. DEFINITION OF AVERAGEABLE INCOME; RELATED DEFINITIONS.
"(a) Averageable income.
"(1) In general. For purposes of this part, the term 'averageable income' means the amount by which taxable income for the computation year (reduced as provided in paragraph (2)) exceeds 140 percent of average base period income.
"(2) Reductions. The taxable income for the computation year shall be reduced by—
"(A) the amount (if any) to which section 72(m)(5) or (q)(1) applies, and
"(B) the amounts included in the income of a beneficiary of a trust under section 667(a).
"(b) Average base period income.
"For purposes of this part—
"(1) In general. The term 'average base period income' means ⅓ of the sum of the base period incomes for the base period.
"(2) Base period income. The base period income for any taxable year is the taxable income for such year—
"(A) increased by an amount equal to the excess of—
"(i) the amount excluded from gross income under section 911 (relating to citizens or residents of the United States living abroad) and subpart D of part III of subchapter N (sec. 931 and following, relating to income from sources within possessions of the United States), over
"(ii) the deductions which would have been properly allocable to or chargeable against such amount but for the exclusion of such amount from gross income; and
"(B) decreased by the amounts included in the income
"(3) Transitional rule for determining base period income. The base period income (determined under paragraph (2)) for any taxable year beginning before January 1, 1977, shall be increased by—
"(A) $3,200 in the case of a joint return or a surviving spouse (as defined in section 2(a)),
"(B) $2,200 in the case of an individual who is not married (within the meaning of section 143) and is not a surviving spouse (as so defined), or
"(C) $1,600 in the case of a married individual (within the meaning of section 143) filing a separate return.
"For purposes of this paragraph, filing status shall be determined as of the computation year.
"(c) Other related definitions.
"For purposes of this part—
"(1) Computation year. The term 'computation year' means the taxable year for which the taxpayer chooses the benefits of this part.
"(2) Base period. The term 'base period' means the 3 taxable years immediately preceding the computation year.
"(3) Base period year. The term 'base period year' means any of the 3 taxable years immediately preceding the computation year.
"(4) Joint return. The term 'joint return' means the return of a husband and wife made under section 6013."

In 1986, P.L. 99-514, Sec. 141(a), repealed Code Sec. 1302, effective for tax. yrs. begin. after 12/31/86.
In 1984, P.L. 98-369, Sec. 173(a), substituted "3 taxable years" for "4 taxable years" in para. (c)(2) . . . Sec. 173(c)(2), substituted "140 percent" for "120 percent" in para. (a)(1) . . . Sec. 173(c)(3), substituted "⅓" for "one-fourth" in para. (b)(1) . . . Sec. 173(c)(4), substituted "3 taxable years" for "4 taxable years" in para. c(3), effective for computation yrs. begin. after 12/31/83, and for base period years applicable to such computation years.
In 1982, P.L. 97-248, Sec. 265(b)(2)(B), added "or (q)(1)" after "section 72(m)(5)" in subpara. (a)(2)(A), effective for distributions after 12/31/82.
In 1981, P.L. 97-34, Sec. 111(b)(3), substituted "relating to citizens or residents of the United States living abroad" for "relating to income earned by employees in certain camps", effective for tax. yrs. begin. after 12/31/81.
In 1980, P.L. 96-222, Sec. 108(a)(1)(A), redesignated Sec. 202(f) of P.L. 95-600 as Sec. 202(g) [see above].
In 1978, P.L. 95-615, Sec. 202(g)(5), substituted "relating to income earned by employees in certain camps" for "relating to earned income from sources without the United States" in clause (b)(2)(A)(i), effective for tax. yrs. begin. after 12/31/77.
—P.L. 95-600, Sec. 101(d)(2), amended para. (b)(3), effective for tax. yrs. begin. after 12/31/78.
Prior to amendment, para. (b)(3) read as follows:
"(3) Transitional rule for determining base period income. The base period income (determined under paragraph (2)) for any taxable year beginning before January 1, 1977, shall be increased by the amount of the taxpayer's zero bracket amount for the computation year."
In 1977, P.L. 95-30, Sec. 102(b)(15), added para. (b)(3), effective for tax. yrs. begin. after 12/31/76.
In 1976, P.L. 94-455, Sec. 701(f)(1), substituted "667(a)" for "668(a)" in subparas. (a)(2)(B) and (b)(2)(B), effective for distributions made in tax. yrs. begin. after 12/31/75.
In 1969, P.L. 91-172, Sec. 311(b), amended Code Sec. 1302, effective for computation yrs. (within the meaning of sec. 1302(c)(1) of the Internal Revenue Code of 1954) begin. after 12/31/69, and to base period yrs. (within the meaning of sec. 1302(c)(3) of such Code) applicable to such computation yrs.
Prior to amendment, Code Sec. 1302 read as follows:

"SEC. 1302. DEFINITION OF AVERAGEABLE INCOME; RELATED DEFINITIONS.
"(a) Averageable income.
"For purposes of this part—
"(1) In general. The term 'averageable income' means the amount (if any) by which adjusted taxable income exceeds 133⅓ percent of average base period income.
"(2) Adjustment in certain cases for capital gains. If—
"(A) the average base period capital gain net income, exceeds
"(B) the capital gain net income for the computation year,
then the term 'averageable income' means the amount determined under paragraph (1), reduced by an amount equal to such excess.
"(b) Adjusted taxable income.
"For purposes of this part, the term 'adjusted taxable income' means the taxable income for the computation year, decreased by the sum of the following amounts:
"(1) Capital gain net income for the computation year. The amount (if any) of the capital gain net income for the computation year.
"(2) Income attributable to gifts, bequests, etc.
"(A) In general. The amount of net income attributable to an interest in property where such interest was received by the taxpayer as a gift, bequest, devise, or inheritance during the computation year or any base period year. This paragraph shall not apply to gifts, bequests, devises, or inheritances between husband and wife if they make a joint return, or if one of them makes a return as a surviving spouse (as defined in section 2(b)), for the computation year.
"(B) Amount of net income. Unless the taxpayer otherwise establishes to the satisfaction of the Secretary or his delegate, the amount of net income for any taxable year attributable to an interest described in subparagraph (A) shall be deemed to be 6 percent of the fair market value of such interest (as determined in accordance with the provisions of chapter 11 or chapter 12, as the case may be).
"(C) Limitation. This paragraph shall apply only if the sum of the net incomes attributable to interests described in subparagraph (A) exceeds $3,000.
"(D) Net income. For purposes of this paragraph, the term 'net income' means, with respect to any interest, the excess of—
"(i) items of gross income attributable to such interest, over
"(ii) the deductions properly allocable to or chargeable against such items.
For purposes of computing such net income, capital gains and losses shall not be taken into account.
"(3) Wagering income. The amount (if any) by which the gains from wagering transactions for the computation year exceed the losses from such transactions.
"(4) Certain amounts received by owner-employees. The amount (if any) to which section 72(m)(5) (relating to penalties applicable to certain amounts received by owner-employees) applies.
"(c) Average base period income.
"For purposes of this part—
"(1) In general. The term 'average base period income' means one-fourth of the sum of the base period incomes for the base period.
"(2) Base period income. The base period income for any taxable year is the taxable income for such year first increased and then decreased (but not below zero) in the following order:
"(A) Taxable income shall be increased by an amount equal to the excess of—
"(i) the amount excluded from gross income under section 911 (relating to earned income from sources without the United States) and subpart D of part III of subchapter N (sec. 931 and following, relating to income from sources within possessions of the United States), over
"(ii) the deductions which would have been properly allocable to or chargeable against such amount but for the exclusion of such amount from gross income.
"(B) Taxable income shall be decreased by the capital gain net income.
"(C) If the decrease provided by paragraph (2) of section (b) applies to the computation year, the taxable income shall be decreased under the rules of such paragraph (2) (other than the limitation contained in subparagraph (C) thereof).
"(d) Capital gain net income, etc.
"For purposes of this part—
"(1) Capital gain net income. The term 'capital gain net income' means the amount equal to 50 percent of the excess of the net long-term capital gain over the net short-term capital loss.
"(2) Average base period capital gain net income. The term 'average base period capital gain net income' means one-fourth of the sum of the capital gain net incomes for the base period. For purposes of the preceding sentence, the capital gain net income for any base period year shall not exceed the base period income for such year computed without regard to subsection (c)(2)(B).
"(e) Other related definitions.
"For purposes of this part—
"(1) Computation year. The term 'computation year' means the taxable year for which the taxpayer chooses the benefits of this part.
"(2) Base period. The term 'base period' means the 4 taxable years immediately preceding the computation year.
"(3) Base period year. The term 'base period year' means any of the 4 taxable years immediately preceding the computation year.
"(4) Joint return. The term 'joint return' means the return of a husband and wife made under section 6013."
In 1964, P.L. 88-272, Sec. 232, substituted a completely new set of Code Secs. 1301 thru 1305 for former Code Secs. 1301 thru 1307, effective for tax. yrs. begin. after 12/31/63. But see note following Code Sec. 1301 for special application of prior provisions.
The former provisions are reproduced in a note following Part I.

"SEC. 1303. ELIGIBLE INDIVIDUALS.

"(a) General rule.

"Except as otherwise provided in this section, for purposes of this part the term 'eligible individual' means any individual who is a citizen or resident of the United States throughout the computation year.

"(b) Nonresident alien individuals.

"For purposes of this part, an individual shall not be an eligible individual for the computation year if, at any time during such year or the base period, such individual was a nonresident alien.

"(c) Individuals receiving support from others.

"(1) In general. For purposes of this part, an individual shall not be an eligible individual for the computation year if, for any base period year, such individual (and his spouse) furnished less than one-half of his support.

"(2) Exceptions. Paragraph (1) shall not apply to any computation year if—

"(A) more than one-half of the individual's taxable income for the computation year is attributable to work performed by him in substantial part during 2 or more of the base period years, or

"(B) the individual makes a joint return for the computation year and not more than 25 percent of the aggregate adjusted gross income of such individual and his spouse for the computation year is attributable to such individual.

In applying subparagraph (B), amounts which constitute earned income (within the meaning of section 911(d)(2)) and are community income under community property laws applicable to such income shall be taken into account as if such amounts did not constitute community income.

"(d) Eligible individuals not to include full-time students.

"(1) In general. For purposes of this part, an individual shall not be an eligible individual for the computation year if, at any time during any base period year, such individual was a student.

"(2) Exception for married students providing 25 percent or less of joint income. Paragraph (1) shall not apply to any individual for any computation year if—

"(A) the individual makes a joint return for the computation year, and

"(B) not more than 25 percent of the aggregate adjusted gross income of such individual and the spouse of such individual for such computation year is attributable to such individual. In applying subparagraph (B), amounts which constitute earned income (within the meaning of section 911(d)(2)) and are community income under community property laws applicable to such income shall be taken into account as if such amounts did not constitute community income.

"(3) Student defined. For purposes of this subsection, the term 'student' means, with respect to a taxable year, an individual who during each of 5 calendar months during such taxable year—

"(A) was a full-time student at an educational organization described in section 170(b)(1)(A)(ii); or

"(B) was pursuing a full-time course of institutional on-farm training under the supervision of an accredited agent of an educational organization described in section 170(b)(1)(A)(ii) or of a State or political subdivision of a State."

In 1986, P.L. 99-514, Sec. 141(a), repealed Code Sec. 1303, effective for tax. yrs. begin. after 12/31/86.

—P.L. 99-272, Sec. 13206(a), amended subsec. (d) . . . Sec. 13206(b), deleted subpara. (c)(2)(A), redesignated subparas. (c)(2)(B) and (C) as subparas. (c)(2)(A) and (B) and substituted "subparagraph (B)" for "subparagraph (C)" in the second sentence of para. (c)(2), effective for tax. yrs. begin. after 12/31/85.

Prior to amendment, subsec. (d) read as follows:

"(d) Student defined.

"For purposes of this section, the term 'student' means, with respect to a taxable year, an individual who during each of 5 calendar months during such taxable year—

"(1) was a full-time student at an educational institution (as defined in section 151(e)(4)); or

"(2) was pursuing a full-time course of institutional on farm training under the supervision of an accredited agent of an educational organization described in section 170(b)(1)(A)(ii) or of a State or political subdivision of a State."

Prior to deletion, subpara. (c)(2)(A) read as follows:

"(A) such year ends after the individual attained the age of 25 and, during at least 4 of his taxable years beginning after he attained age 21 and ending with his computation year, he was not a full-time student,"

In 1981, P.L. 97-34, Sec. 111(b)(4), substituted "911(d)(2)" for "911(b)" in para. (c)(2), effective for tax. yrs. begin. after 12/31/81.

In 1976, P.L. 94-455, Sec. 1901(b)(8)(G), substituted "educational organization described in section 170(b)(1)(A)(ii)" for "educational institution (as defined in section 151(e)(4))" in subsec. (d), effective for tax. yrs. begin. after 12/31/76.

In 1969, P.L. 91-172, Sec. 311(d)(1), substituted "taxable income" for "adjusted taxable income" in subpara. (c)(2)(B), effective, for computation yrs. (within the meaning of sec. 1302(c)(1) of the Internal Revenue Code of 1954) begin. after 12/31/69, and to base period yrs. (within the meaning of sec. 1302(c)(3) of such Code) applicable to such computation yrs.

In 1964, P.L. 88-272, Sec. 232, substituted a completely new set of Code Secs. 1301 thru 1305 for former Code Secs. 1301 thru 1307, for tax. yrs. begin. after '63. But see note following Code Sec. 1301 for special application of prior provisions.

The former provisions are reproduced in a note following Part I.

"SEC. 1304. SPECIAL RULES.

"(a) Taxpayer must choose benefits.

"This part shall apply to the taxable year only if the taxpayer chooses to have the benefits of this part for such taxable year. Such choice may be made or changed at any time before the expiration of the period prescribed for making a claim for credit or refund of the tax imposed by this chapter for the taxable year.

"(b) Certain provisions inapplicable.

"If the taxpayer chooses the benefits of this part for the taxable year, the following provisions shall not apply to him for such year:

"(1) section 911 (relating to citizens or residents of the United States living abroad), and

"(2) subpart D of part III of subchapter N (sec. 931 and following, relating to income from sources within possessions of the United States).

"(c) Failure of certain married individuals to make joint return, etc.

"(1) Application of subsection. Paragraphs (2) and (3) of this subsection shall apply in the case of any individual who was married for any base period year or the computation year; except that—

"(A) such paragraphs shall not apply in respect of a base period year if—

"(i) such individual and his spouse make a joint return, or such individual makes a return as a surviving spouse (as defined in section 2(b)[(a)]), for the computation year, and

"(ii) such individual was not married to any other spouse for such base period year, and

"(B) paragraph (3) shall not apply in respect of the computation year if the individual and his spouse make a joint return for such year.

"(2) Minimum base period income. For purposes of this part, the base period income of an individual for any base period year shall not be less than 50 percent of the base period income which would result from combining his income and deductions for such year—

"(A) with the income and deductions for such year of the individual who is his spouse for the computation year, or

"(B) if greater, with the income and deductions for such year of the individual who was his spouse for such base period year.

"(3) Community income attributable to services. In the case of amounts which constitute earned income (within the meaning of section 911(d)(2)) and are community income under community property laws applicable to such income—

"(A) the amount taken into account for any base period year for purposes of determining base period income shall not be less than the amount which would be taken into account if such amounts did not constitute community income, and

"(B) the amount taken into account for purposes of determining taxable income for the computation year shall not exceed the amount which would be taken into account if such amounts did not constitute community income.

"(4) Marital status. For purposes of this subsection, section 143(a) shall apply in determining whether an individual is married for any taxable year.

"(d) Dollar limitations in case of joint returns.

"In the case of a joint return, the $3,000 figure contained in section 1301 shall be applied to the aggregate averageable income.

"(e) Treatment of certain other items.

"(1) Section 72(m)(5) or (q)(1). Section 72(m)(5) (relating to penalties applicable to certain amounts received by owner-employees) or section 72(q)(1) (relating to 5-percent tax on premature distributions under annuity contracts) shall be applied as if this part had not been enacted.

"(2) Other items. Except as otherwise provided in this part, the order and manner in which items of income or limitations on tax shall be taken into account in computing the tax imposed by this chapter on the income of any eligible individual to whom section 1301 applies for any computation year shall be determined under regulations prescribed by the Secretary.

"(f) Short taxable years.

"In the case of any computation year or base period year which is a short taxable year, this part shall be applied in the manner provided in regulations prescribed by the Secretary."

In 1986, P.L. 99-514, Sec. 141(a), repealed Code Sec. 1304, effective for tax. yrs. begin. after 12/31/86.

In 1982, P.L. 97-248, Sec. 265(b)(2)(C)(i), and (ii), added "or section 72(q)(1) (relating to 5-percent tax on premature distributions under annuity contracts)" after "owner-employees)" in para. (e)(1), and added "or (q)(1)" after "Section 72(m)(5) in the heading of para. (e)(1), effective for distributions after 12/31/82.

In 1981, P.L. 97-34, Sec. 101(c)(2)(B), inserted 'and' at the end of para. (b)(1), substituted a period for ', and' at the end of para. (b)(2) and deleted para. (b)(3), effective for tax. yrs. begin. after 12/31/81.

Prior to deletion, para. (b)(3) read as follows:

"(3) section 1348 (relating to 50-percent maximum rate on personal service income)."

—P.L. 97-34, Sec. 111(b)(3), substituted "relating to citizens or residents of the United States living abroad" for "relating to income earned by employees in certain camps" in para. (b)(1) . . . Sec. 111(b)(4), substituted "section 911(d)(2)" for "section 911(b)" in para. (c)(3), effective for tax. yrs. begin. after 12/31/81.

In 1980, P.L. 96-222, Sec. 108(a)(1)(A), redesignated Sec. 202(f) of P.L. 95-600 as Sec. 202(g) [see below].

In 1978, P.L. 95-615, Sec. 202(g)(5), substituted "relating to income earned by employees in certain camps" for "relating to earned income from sources without the United States" in para. (b)(1), effective for tax. yrs. begin. after 12/31/77.

—P.L. 95-600, Sec. 401(b)(5), added "and" at the end of para. (b)(2), deleted para. (b)(3), and redesignated para. (b)(4) as para. (b)(3), effective for tax. yrs. begin. after '78.

Prior to amendment, para. (b)(3) read as follows:

"(3) section 1201(b) (relating to alternative capital gains tax), and"

In 1976, P.L. 94-455, Sec. 302(c), substituted "personal service" for "earned" in para. (b)(5), effective for tax. yrs. begin. after 12/31/76.

Passive foreign investment companies — Part I

— P.L. 94-455, Sec. 501(b)(7), deleted para. (b)(1), and redesignated paras. (b)(2), (3), (4) and (5) as paras. (b)(1), (2), (3) and (4), effective for tax. yrs. begin. after 12/31/75.
Prior to amendment, para. (b)(1) read as follows:
"(1) section 3 (relating to optional tax),"
— P.L. 94-455, Sec. 1906(b)(13)(A), substituted "Secretary" for "Secretary or his delegate" each place it appeared in Code Sec. 1304, effective for tax. yrs. begin. after 12/31/76.
In 1974, P.L. 93-406, Sec. 2005(c)(6), deleted para. (b)(2) and redesignated paras. (b)(3), (4), (5), and (6) as paras. (b)(2), (3), (4), and (5), effective for distributions or payments made after 12/31/73, in tax. yrs. begin. after 12/31/73.
Prior to deletion, para. (b)(2) read as follows:
"(2) section 72(n)(2) (relating to limitation of tax in case of total distribution),"
In 1969, P.L. 91-172, Sec. 311(c), deleted "and" at the end of para. (b)(3), substituted a comma for the period at the end of para. (b)(4) and added paras. (b)(5) and (6), effective for computation yrs. (within the meaning of sec. 1302(c)(1) of the Internal Revenue Code of 1954) begin. after 12/31/69, and to base period yrs. (within the meaning of sec. 1302(c)(3) of such Code) applicable to such computation yrs.
— P.L. 91-172, Sec. 311(d)(2), deleted para (c)(3) and redesignated paras. (c)(4) and (5) as paras. (c)(3) and (4), substituted "Paragraphs (2) and (3)" for "Paragraphs (2), (3), and (4)" in para. (c)(1); substituted "paragraph (3)" for "paragraph (4)" in subpara. (c)(1)(B); deleted "adjusted" in subpara. (c)(3)(B); deleted ", and the $3,000 figure contained in section 1302(b)(2)(C) shall be applied to the aggregate net incomes" in subsec. (d), amended subsec. (e), deleted subsec. (f), and redesignated subsec. (g) as subsec. (f), effective for computation yrs. (within the meaning of Sec. 1302(c)(1) of the Internal Revenue Code of 1954) begin. after 12/31/69, and to lease period yrs. (within the meaning of Sec. 1302(c)(3) of such Code) applicable to such computation years.
Prior to deletion, para. (c)(3) read as follows:
"(3) Minimum base period capital gain net income. For purposes of this part, the capital gain net income of any individual for any base period year shall not be less than 50 percent of the capital gain net income which would result from combining his capital gain net income for such year (determined without regard to this paragraph) with the capital gain net income for such year (similarly determined) of the individual with whom he is required by paragraph (2) to combine his income and deductions for such year."
Prior to amendment, subsec. (e) read as follows:
"(e) Special rules where there are capital gains.
"(1) Treatment of capital gains in computation year. In the case of any taxpayer who has capital gain net income for the computation year, the tax imposed by section 1 for the computation year, which is attributable to the amount of such net income shall be computed—
"(A) by adding so much of the amount thereof as does not exceed average base period capital gain net income above 133⅓ percent of average base period income, and
"(B) by adding the remainder (if any) of such net income above the 20 percent of the averageable income as taken into account for purposes of computing the tax imposed by section 1 (and above the amounts (if any) referred to in subsection (f)(1)).
"(2) Computation of alternative tax. In the case of any taxpayer who has capital gain net income for the computation year, section 1201(b) shall be treated as imposing a tax equal to the tax imposed by section 1, reduced by the amount (if any) by which—
"(A) the tax imposed by section 1 and attributable to the capital gain net income for the computation year (determined under paragraph (1)), exceeds
"(B) an amount equal to 25 percent of the excess of the net long-term capital gain over the net short-term capital loss.
Prior to deletion, subsec. (f) read as follows:
"(f) Treatment of certain other items.
"(1) Gift or wagering income. The tax imposed by section 1 for the computation year which is attributable to the amounts subtracted from the taxable income under paragraphs (2) and (3) of section 1302(b) shall equal the increase in tax under section 1 which results from adding such amounts above the 20 percent of the averageable income as taken into account for purposes of computing the tax imposed thereon by section 1.
"(2) Section 72(m)(5). Section 72(m)(5) (relating to penalties applicable to certain amounts received by owner-employees) shall be applied as if this part had not been enacted.
"(3) Other items. Except as otherwise provided in this part, the order and manner in which items of income shall be taken into account in computing the tax imposed by this chapter on the income of any eligible individual to whom section 1301 applies for any computation year shall be determined under regulations prescribed by the Secretary or his delegate."
— P.L. 91-172, Sec. 515(c)(4), substituted "distribution)," for "distributions with respect to contributions by self-employed individuals," in para. (b)(2), effective for tax. yrs. end. after 12/31/69.
— P.L. 91-172, Sec. 802(c)(5), substituted "section 143(a)" for "section 143" in subsec. (c)(4), for tax. yrs. begin. after 12/31/69.
— P.L. 91-172, Sec. 803(d)(8), deleted "if adjusted gross income is less than $5,000" in para. (c)(1), effective for tax. yrs. begin. after 12/31/69.
In 1964, P.L. 88-272, Sec. 232, substituted a completely new set of Code Secs. 1301 thru 1305 for former Code Secs. 1301 thru 1307, for tax. yrs. begin. after '63. But see note following Code Sec. 1301 for special application of prior provisions.
The former provisions are reproduced in a note following Part I.

"SEC. 1305. REGULATIONS.
"The Secretary shall prescribe such regulations as may be necessary to carry out the purposes of this part."

In 1986, P.L. 99-514, Sec. 141(a), repealed Code Sec. 1305, effective for tax. yrs. begin. after 12/31/86.
In 1976, P.L. 94-455, Sec. 1906(b)(13)(A), substituted "Secretary" for "Secretary or his delegate" in Code Sec. 1305, effective for tax. yrs. begin. after 12/31/76.
In 1964, P.L. 88-272, Sec. 232, substituted a completely new set of Code Secs. 1301 thru 1305 for former Code Secs. 1301 thru 1307, for tax. yrs. begin. after '63. But see note following Code Sec. 1301 for special application of prior provisions.
The former provisions are reproduced in a note following Part I.

In 1964, P.L. 88-272, Sec. 232, amended Part I.
Prior to amendment, part I read as follows:
"Part I— Income Attributable to Several Taxable Years.
Sec.
1301. Compensation from an employment.
1302. Income from an invention or artistic work.
1303. Income from back pay.
1304. Compensatory damages for patent infringement.
1305. Breach of contract damages.
1306. Damages for injuries under the antitrust laws.
1307. Rules applicable to this part."

"SEC. 1301. COMPENSATION FROM AN EMPLOYMENT.
"(a) Limitation on tax.
"If an individual or partnership—
"(1) engages in an employment as defined in subsection (b); and
"(2) the employment covers a period of 36 months or more (from the beginning to the completion of such employment); and
"(3) the gross compensation from the employment received or accrued in the taxable year of the individual or partnership is not less than 80 percent of the total compensation from such employment, then the tax attributable to any part of the compensation which is included in the gross income of any individual shall not be greater than the aggregate of the taxes attributable to such part had it been included in the gross income of such individual ratably over that part of the period which precedes the date of such receipt or accrual.
"(b) Definition of an employment.
"For purposes of this section, the term 'an employment' means an arrangement or series of arrangements for the performance of personal services by an individual or partnership to effect a particular result, regardless of the number of sources from which compensation therefor is obtained.
"(c) Rule with respect to partners.
"An individual who is a member of a partnership receiving or accruing compensation from an employment of the type described in subsection (a) shall be entitled to the benefits of that subsection only if the individual has been a member of the partnership continuously for a period of 36 months or the period of the employment immediately preceding the receipt or accrual. In such a case the tax attributable to the part of the compensation which is includible in the gross income of the individual shall not be greater than the aggregate of the taxes which would have been attributable to that part had it been included in the gross income of the individual ratably over the period in which it was earned or the period during which the individual continuously was a member of the partnership, whichever period is the shorter. For purposes of this subsection, a member of a partnership shall be deemed to have been a member of the partnership for any period, ending immediately prior to becoming such a member, in which he was an employee of such partnership, if during the taxable year he received or accrued compensation attributable to employment by the partnership during such period."

"SEC. 1302. INCOME FROM AN INVENTION OR ARTISTIC WORK.
"(a) Limitation on tax.
"If—
"(1) an individual includes in gross income amounts in respect of a particular invention or artistic work created by the individual; and
"(2) the work on the invention or the artistic work covered a period of 24 months or more (from the beginning to the completion thereof); and
"(3) the amounts in respect to the invention or the artistic work includible in gross income for the taxable year are not less than 80 percent of the gross income in respect of such invention or artistic work in the taxable year plus the gross income here from in previous taxable years and the 12 months immediately succeeding the close of the taxable year,
then the tax attributable to the part of such gross income of the taxable year which is not taxable as a gain from the sale or exchange of a capital asset held for more than 6 months shall not be greater than the aggregate of the taxes attributable to such part had it been received ratably over, in the case of an invention, that part of the period preceding the close of the taxable year or 60 months, whichever is shorter, or, in the case of an artistic work, that part of the period preceding the close of the taxable year but not more than 36 months.
"(b) Definitions.
"For purposes of this section—
"(1) Invention.— The term 'invention' means a patent covering an invention of the individual.

"(2) Artistic work. — The term 'artistic work' means a literary, musical, or artistic composition or a copyright covering a literary, musical, or artistic composition."

"SEC. 1303. INCOME FROM BACK PAY.
"(a) Limitation on tax.
"If the amount of the back pay received or accrued by an individual during the taxable year exceeds 15 percent of the gross income of the individual for such year, the part of the tax attributable to the inclusion of such back pay in gross income for the taxable year shall not be greater than the aggregate of the increases in the taxes which would have resulted from the inclusion of the respective portions of such back pay in gross income for the taxable years to which such portions are respectively attributable, as determined under regulations prescribed by the Secretary or his delegate.
"(b) Definition of back pay.
"For purposes of this section, the term 'back pay' means amounts includible in gross income under this subtitle which are one of the following—
"(1) Remuneration, including wages, salaries, retirement pay, and other similar compensation, which is received or accrued during the taxable year by an employee for services performed before the taxable year for his employer and which would have been paid before the taxable year except for the intervention of one of the following events:
"(A) bankruptcy or receivership of the employer;
"(B) dispute as to the liability of the employer to pay such remuneration, which is determined after the commencement of court proceedings;
"(C) if the employer is the United States, a State, a Territory, or any political subdivision thereof, or the District of Columbia, or any agency or instrumentality of the foregoing, lack of funds appropriated to pay such remuneration; or
"(D) any other event determined to be similar in nature under regulations prescribed by the Secretary or his delegate.
"(2) Wages or salaries which are received or accrued during the taxable year by an employee for services performed before the taxable year for his employer and which constitute retroactive wage or salary increases ordered, recommended, or approved by any Federal or State agency, and made retroactive to any period before the taxable year.
"(3) Payments which are received or accrued during the taxable year as the result of an alleged violation by an employer of any State or Federal law relating to labor standards or practices, and which are determined under regulations prescribed by the Secretary or his delegate to be attributable to a prior taxable year.
"(4) Termination payments under section 5(c) or section 6(1) of the Peace Corps Act which are received or accrued by an individual during the taxable year on account of any period of service, as a volunteer or volunteer leader under the Peace Corps Act, occurring prior to the taxable year."

In 1961, added Code Sec. 1303(a)(4) for tax. yrs. end. after 3/1/61.

"SEC. 1304. COMPENSATORY DAMAGES FOR PATENT INFRINGEMENT.
"If an amount representing compensatory damages is received or accrued by a taxpayer during a taxable year as the result of an award in a civil action for infringement of a patent issued by the United States, then the tax attributable to the inclusion of such amount in gross income for the taxable year shall not be greater than the aggregate of the increases in taxes which would have resulted if such amount had been included in gross income in equal installments for each month during which such infringement occurred."

In 1961, added para. (a)(4), effective for tax. yrs. end. after 3/1/61.
In 1955, added Code Sec. 1304, effective for damages received or accrued after 8/11/55, in tax. yrs. end. after that date as a result of awards made after that date.

"SEC. 1305. BREACH OF CONTRACT DAMAGES.
"(a) General rule.
"If an amount representing damages is received or accrued by a taxpayer during a taxable year as a result of an award in a civil action for breach of contract or breach of a fiduciary duty or relationship, then the tax attributable to the inclusion in gross income for the taxable year of that part of such amount which would have been received or accrued by the taxpayer in a prior taxable year or years but for the breach of contract, or breach of a fiduciary duty or relationship, shall not be greater than the aggregate of the increases in taxes which would have resulted had such part been included in gross income for such prior taxable year or years.
"(b) Credits and deductions allowed in computation of tax.
"The taxpayer in computing said tax shall be entitled to deduct all credits and deductions for depletion, depreciation, and other items to which he would have been entitled, had such income been received or accrued by the taxpayer in the year during which he would have received or accrued it, except for such breach of contract or for such breach of a fiduciary duty or relationship. The credits, deductions, or other items referred to in the prior sentence, attributable to property, shall be allowed only with respect to that part of the award which represents the taxpayer's share of income from the actual operation of such property.
"(c) Limitation.
"Subsection (a) shall not apply unless the amount representing damages is $3,000 or more."

In 1957, added Code Sec. 1305, effective for tax. yrs. end. after '54 but only for amounts received or accrued after '54 as a result of awards after '54.

In 1955, renumbered Code Sec. 1304 as 1305, effective for damages received or accrued after 8/11/55, in tax. yrs. end. after that date as a result of awards made after that date.

"SEC. 1306. DAMAGES FOR INJURIES UNDER THE ANTITRUST LAWS.
"If an amount representing damages is received or accrued during a taxable year as a result of an award in, or settlement of, a civil action brought under section 4 of the Act entitled 'An Act to supplement existing laws against unlawful restraints and monopolies, and for other purposes', approved October 15, 1914 (commonly known as the Clayton Act), for injuries sustained by the taxpayer in his business or property by reason of anything forbidden in the antitrust laws, then the tax attributable to the inclusion of such amount in gross income for the taxable year shall not be greater than the aggregate of the increases in taxes which would have resulted if such amount had been included in gross income in equal installments for each month during the period in which such injuries were sustained by the taxpayer."

In 1958, added Code Sec. 1306, effective for tax. yrs. end. after 9/2/58 but only for amounts received or accrued after that date as a result of awards or settlements after that date.
In 1957, renumbered Code Sec. 1305 as 1306, effective for tax. yrs. end. after '54 but only for amounts received or accrued after '54 as a result of awards after '54.

"SEC. 1307. RULES APPLICABLE TO THIS PART.
"(a) Fractional parts of a month.
"For purposes of this part, a fractional part of a month shall be disregarded unless it amounts to more than half a month, in which case it should be considered as a month.
"(b) Tax on self-employment income.
"This part shall be applied without regard to, and shall not affect, the tax imposed by chapter 2 relating to self-employment income.
"(c) Computation of tax attributable to income allocated to prior period.
"For the purpose of computing the tax attributable to the amount of an item of gross income allocable under this part to a particular taxable year, such amount shall be considered income only of the person who would be required to include the item of gross income in a separate return filed for the taxable year in which such item was received or accrued.
"(d) Effective date of certain subsections.
"Subsection (c) of section 1301 and subsection (c) of this section shall apply only to amounts received or accrued after March 1, 1954. Notwithstanding any other provision of this title, section 107 of the Internal Revenue Code of 1939 shall apply to amounts received or accrued as a partner on or before March 1, 1954, under this section and to the computation of tax on amounts received or accrued on or before March 1, 1954.
"(e) Election with respect to charitable contributions.
"In the case of an individual who elects (in such manner and at such time as the Secretary or his delegate prescribes by regulations) to have the provisions of this subsection apply, an amount received or accrued to which this part applies shall be reduced, for purposes of computing the tax liability of the taxpayer under this part with respect to the amount so received or accrued, by an amount equal to that portion of (1) the amount of charitable contributions made by the taxpayer during the taxable year in which the amount is so received or accrued which are allowable as a deduction for such year under section 170 (determined without regard to this part), as (2) the amount received or accrued to which this part applies is of the adjusted gross income for the taxable year (determined without regard to this part). In any case in which the taxpayer elects to have the provisions of the preceding sentence apply, for purposes of computing the limitation on tax under this part—
"(1) only the same proportion of the amount to which this part applies shall be taken into account for purposes of computing the limitations under section 170(b)(1)(A) and (B) for taxable years before the taxable year in which such amount is received or accrued as (A) the excess of the maximum amount which could, if the taxpayer had made additional contributions described in clause (i), (ii), or (iii) of section 170(b)(1)(A), have been described in clause (I) of the preceding sentence over the amount described in such clause (1), bears to (B) such maximum amount, and
"(2) the portion of the amount of charitable contributions described in the preceding sentence shall not be taken into account in computing the tax for the taxable year in which the amount to which this part applies is received or accrued."

In 1962, added subsec. (e) for amounts received or accrued in tax. yrs. begin. after '61.
In 1958, renumbered Code Sec. 1306 as 1307, effective for tax. yrs. end. after 9/2/58 but only for amounts received or accrued after that date as a result of awards or settlements after that date.

PART I.— INCOME AVERAGING

Sec.
1301. Averaging of farm income.

In 1997, P.L. 105-34, Sec. 933(a), added Part I and item 1301.

Income averaging — Part II

Sec. 1301. Averaging of farm income.
(a) In general.
At the election of an individual engaged in a farming business or fishing business, the tax imposed by section 1 for such taxable year shall be equal to the sum of—
(1) a tax computed under such section on taxable income reduced by elected farm income, plus
(2) the increase in tax imposed by section 1 which would result if taxable income for each of the 3 prior taxable years were increased by an amount equal to one-third of the elected farm income.
Any adjustment under this section for any taxable year shall be taken into account in applying this section for any subsequent taxable year.
(b) Definitions.
In this section—
(1) Elected farm income.
(A) In general. The term "elected farm income" means so much of the taxable income for the taxable year—
(i) which is attributable to any farming business or fishing business; and
(ii) which is specified in the election under subsection (a).
(B) Treatment of gains. For purposes of subparagraph (A), gain from the sale or other disposition of property (other than land) regularly used by the taxpayer in such a farming business or fishing business for a substantial period shall be treated as attributable to such a farming business or fishing business.
(2) Individual. The term "individual" shall not include any estate or trust.
(3) Farming business. The term "farming business" has the meaning given such term by section 263A(e)(4).
(4) Fishing business. The term "fishing business" means the conduct of commercial fishing as defined in section 3 of the Magnuson-Stevens Fishery Conservation and Management Act (16 U.S.C. 1802).
(c) Regulations.
The Secretary shall prescribe such regulations as may be appropriate to carry out the purposes of this section, including regulations regarding—
(1) the order and manner in which items of income, gain, deduction, or loss, or limitations on tax, shall be taken into account in computing the tax imposed by this chapter on the income of any taxpayer to whom this section applies for any taxable year, and
(2) the treatment of any short taxable year.

In **2008**, P.L. 110-343, Sec. 504DivC, Sec. 504 Div C, with respect in income averaging for amounts received in connection with Exxon Valdez litigation, provides:

"Sec. 504. Income averaging for amounts received in connection with the Exxon Valdez litigation.

"(a) INcome averaging of amounts received from the exxon valdez litigation. For purposes of section 1301 of the Internal Revenue Code of 1986—

"(1) any qualified taxpayer who receives any qualified settlement income in any taxable year shall be treated as ngaged in a fishing business (determined without regard to the commercial nature of the business), and

"(2) such qualified settlement income shall be treated as income attributable to such a fishing business for such taxable year.

"(b) Contributions of amounts received to retirement accounts.

"(1) In general. Any qualified taxpayer who receives qualified settlement income during the taxable year may, at any time before the end of the taxable year in which such income was received, make one or more contributions to an eligible retirement plan of which such qualified taxpayer is a beneficiary in an aggregate amount not to exceed the lesser of—

"(A) $100,000 (reduced by the amount of qualified settlement income contributed to an eligible retirement plan in prior taxable years pursuant to this subsection), or

"(B) the amount of qualified settlement income received by the individual during the taxable year.

"(2) Time when contributions deemed made. For purposes of paragraph (1), a qualified taxpayer shall be deemed to have made a contribution to an eligible retirement plan on the last day of the taxable year in which such income is received if the contribution is made on account of such taxable year and is made not later than the time prescribed by law for filing the return for such taxable year (not including extensions thereof).

"(3) Treatment of contributions to eligible retirement plans. For purposes of the Internal Revenue Code of 1986, if a contribution is made pursuant to paragraph (1) with respect to qualified settlement income, then—

"(A) except as provided in paragraph (4)—

"(i) to the extent of such contribution, the qualified settlement income shall not be included in taxable income, and

"(ii) for purposes of section 72 of such Code, such contribution shall not be considered to be investment in the contract,

"(B) the qualified taxpayer shall, to the extent of the amount of the contribution, be treated—

"(i) as having received the qualified settlement income—

"(I) in the case of a contribution to an individual retirement plan (as defined under section 7701(a)(37) of such Code), in a distribution described in section 408(d)(3) of such Code, and

"9 (II) in the case of any other eligible retirement plan, in an eligible rollover distribution (as defined under section 402(f)(2) of such Code), and

" (ii) as having transferred the amount to the eligible retirement plan in a direct trustee to trustee transfer within 60 days of the distribution,

"(C) section 408(d)(3)(B) of the Internal Revenue Code of 1986 shall not apply with respect to amounts treated as a rollover under this paragraph, and

"(D) section 408A(c)(3)(B) of the Internal Revenue Code of 1986 shall not apply with respect to amounts contributed to a Roth IRA (as defined under section 408A(b) of such Code) or a designated Roth contribution to an applicable retirement plan (within the meaning of section 402A of such Code) under this paragraph.

"3 (4) Special rule for Roth IRAs and Roth 401(k)s. For purposes of the Internal Revenue Code of 1986, if a contribution is made pursuant to paragraph (1) with respect to qualified settlement income to a Roth IRA (as defined under section 408A(b) of such Code) or as a designated Roth contribution to an applicable retirement plan (within the meaning of section 402A of such Code), then—

"(A) the qualified settlement income shall be includible in taxable income, and

"(B) for purposes of section 72 of such Code, such contribution shall be considered to be investment in the contract.

"(5) Eligible retirement plan. For purpose of this subsection, the term 'eligible retirement plan' has the meaning given such term under section 402(c)(8)(B) of the Internal Revenue Code of 1986.

"(c) Treatment of qualified settlement income under employment taxes.

"(1) SECA. For purposes of chapter 2 of the Internal Revenue Code of 1986 and section 211 of the Social Security Act, no portion of qualified settlement income received by a qualified taxpayer shall be treated as self-employment income.

"(2) FICA. For purposes of chapter 21 of the Internal Revenue Code of 1986 and section 209 of the Social Security Act, no portion of qualified settlement income received by a qualified taxpayer shall be treated as wages.

"(d) Qualified taxpayer. For purposes of this section, the term 'qualified taxpayereq; means—

"(1) any individual who is a plaintiff in the civil action In re Exxon Valdez, No. 89-095-CV (HRH) (Consolidated) (D. Alaska); or

"(2) any individual who is a beneficiary of the estate of such a plaintiff who—

"(A) acquired the right to receive qualified settlement income from that plaintiff; and

"(B) was the spouse or an immediate relative of that plaintiff.

"(e) Qualified settlement income. For purposes of this section, the term 'qualified settlement income' means any interest and punitive damage awards which are—

"(1) otherwise includible in taxable income, and

"(2) received (whether as lump sums or periodic payments) in connection with the civil action In re Exxon Valdez, No. 89-095-CV (HRH) (Consolidated) (D. Alaska) (whether pre- or post-judgment and whether related to a settlement or judgment)."

In **2004**, P.L. 108-357, Sec. 314(b)(1), substituted "farming business or fishing business" for "farming business" in subsec. (a) . . . Sec. 314(b)(2)(A), added "or fishing business" before the semicolon in clause (b)(1)(A)(i) . . . Sec. 314(b)(2)(B), added "or fishing business" after "farming business" each place it appeared in subpara. (b)(1)(B) . . . Sec. 314(b)(3), added para. (b)(4), effective for tax. yrs. begin. after 12/31/2003.

In **1998**, P.L. 105-277, Sec. 2011, deleted ", and before January 1, 2001" after December 31, 1997' in Sec. 933(c) of P.L. 105-34 [see below].

In **1997**, P.L. 105-34, Sec. 933(a), added Code Sec. 1301 as Part I of Subchapter Q of Chapter 1 of Subtitle A, effective [as amended by Sec. 2011 of P.L. 105-277, see above] for tax. yrs. begin. after 12/31/97.

PART II.—MITIGATION OF EFFECT OF LIMITATIONS AND OTHER PROVISIONS

Sec.
1311. Correction of error.
1312. Circumstances of adjustment.
1313. Definitions.

1314. Amount and method of adjustment.
1315. Repealed.

In **1976**, P.L. 94-455, Sec. 1901(b)(35), deleted item 1315. Prior to repeal, that item read as follows:
"1315. Effective date."

Sec. 1311. Correction of error.
(a) General rule.

If a determination (as defined in section 1313) is described in one or more of the paragraphs of section 1312 and, on the date of the determination, correction of the effect of the error referred to in the applicable paragraph of section 1312 is prevented by the operation of any law or rule of law, other than this part and other than section 7122 (relating to compromises), then the effect of the error shall be corrected by an adjustment made in the amount and in the manner specified in section 1314.

(b) Conditions necessary for adjustment.

(1) Maintenance of an inconsistent position. Except in cases described in paragraphs (3)(B) and (4) of section 1312, an adjustment shall be made under this part only if—

(A) in case the amount of the adjustment would be credited or refunded in the same manner as an overpayment under section 1314, there is adopted in the determination a position maintained by the Secretary, or

(B) in case the amount of the adjustment would be assessed and collected in the same manner as a deficiency under section 1314, there is adopted in the determination a position maintained by the taxpayer with respect to whom the determination is made,

and the position maintained by the Secretary in the case described in subparagraph (A) or maintained by the taxpayer in the case described in subparagraph (B) is inconsistent with the erroneous inclusion, exclusion, omission, allowance, disallowance, recognition, or nonrecognition, as the case may be.

(2) Correction not barred at time of erroneous action.

(A) Determination described in section 1312(3)(B). In the case of a determination described in section 1312(3)(B) (relating to certain exclusions from income), adjustment shall be made under this part only if assessment of a deficiency for the taxable year in which the item is includible or against the related taxpayer was not barred, by any law or rule of law, at the time the Secretary first maintained, in a notice of deficiency sent pursuant to section 6212 or before the Tax Court, that the item described in section 1312(3)(B) should be included in the gross income of the taxpayer for the taxable year to which the determination relates.

(B) Determination described in section 1312(4). In the case of a determination described in section 1312(4) (relating to disallowance of certain deductions and credits), adjustment shall be made under this part only if credit or refund of the overpayment attributable to the deduction or credit described in such section which should have been allowed to the taxpayer or related taxpayer was not barred, by any law or rule of law, at the time the taxpayer first maintained before the Secretary or before the Tax Court, in writing, that he was entitled to such deduction or credit for the taxable year to which the determination relates.

(3) Existence of relationship. In case the amount of the adjustment would be assessed and collected in the same manner as a deficiency (except for cases described in section 1312(3)(B)), the adjustment shall not be made with respect to a related taxpayer unless he stands in such relationship to the taxpayer at the time the latter first maintains the inconsistent position in a return, claim for refund, or petition (or amended petition) to the Tax Court for the taxable year with respect to which the determination is made, or if such position is not so maintained, then at the time of the determination.

In **1976**, P.L. 94-455, Sec. 1901(a)(142), substituted "Tax Court" for "Tax Court of the United States" in subparas. (b)(2)(A) and (B) and para. (b)(3), effective for tax. yrs. begin. after 12/31/76.
—P.L. 94-455, Sec. 1906(b)(13)(A), substituted "Secretary" for "Secretary or his delegate" each place it appeared in Code Sec. 1311, effective for tax. yrs. begin. after 12/31/76.

Sec. 1312. Circumstances of adjustment.

The circumstances under which the adjustment provided in section 1311 is authorized are as follows:

(1) Double inclusion of an item of gross income. The determination requires the inclusion in gross income of an item which was erroneously included in the gross income of the taxpayer for another taxable year or in the gross income of a related taxpayer.

(2) Double allowance of a deduction or credit. The determination allows a deduction or credit which was erroneously allowed to the taxpayer for another taxable year or to a related taxpayer.

(3) Double exclusion of an item of gross income.

(A) Items included in income. The determination requires the exclusion from gross income of an item included in a return filed by the taxpayer or with respect to which tax was paid and which was erroneously excluded or omitted from the gross income of the taxpayer for another taxable year, or from the gross income of a related taxpayer; or

(B) Items not included in income. The determination requires the exclusion from gross income of an item not included in a return filed by the taxpayer and with respect to which the tax was not paid but which is includible in the gross income of the taxpayer for another taxable year or in the gross income of a related taxpayer.

(4) Double disallowance of a deduction or credit. The determination disallows a deduction or credit which should have been allowed to, but was not allowed to, the taxpayer for another taxable year, or to a related taxpayer.

(5) Correlative deductions and inclusions for trusts or estates and legatees, beneficiaries, or heirs. The determination allows or disallows any of the additional deductions allowable in computing the taxable income of estates or trusts, or requires or denies any of the inclusions in the computation of taxable income of beneficiaries, heirs, or legatees, specified in subparts A to E, inclusive (secs. 641 and following, relating to estates, trusts, and beneficiaries) of part I of subchapter J of this chapter, or corresponding provisions of prior internal revenue laws, and the correlative inclusion or deduction, as the case may be, has been erroneously excluded, omitted, or included, or disallowed, omitted, or allowed, as the case may be, in respect of the related taxpayer.

(6) Correlative deductions and credits for certain related corporations. The determination allows or disallows a deduction (including a credit) in computing the taxable income (or, as the case may be, net income, normal tax net income, or surtax net income) of a corporation, and a correlative deduction or credit has been erroneously allowed, omitted, or disallowed, as the case may be, in respect of a related taxpayer described in section 1313(c)(7).

(7) Basis of property after erroneous treatment of a prior transaction.

(A) General rule. The determination determines the basis of property, and in respect of any transaction on which such basis depends, or in respect of any transaction which was erroneously treated as affecting such basis, there occurred, with respect to a taxpayer described in subparagraph (B) of this paragraph, any of the errors described in subparagraph (C) of this paragraph.

(B) Taxpayers with respect to whom the erroneous treatment occurred. The taxpayer with respect to whom the erroneous treatment occurred must be—

(i) the taxpayer with respect to whom the determination is made,

(ii) a taxpayer who acquired title to the property in the transaction and from whom, mediately or immediately, the taxpayer with respect to whom the determination is made derived title, or

(iii) a taxpayer who had title to the property at the time of the transaction and from whom, mediately or immediately, the taxpayer with respect to whom the determination is made derived title, if the basis of the property in the hands of the taxpayer with respect to whom the determination is made is determined under section 1015(a) (relating to the basis of property acquired by gift).

(C) Prior erroneous treatment. With respect to a taxpayer described in subparagraph (B) of this paragraph—

(i) there was an erroneous inclusion in, or omission from, gross income,

(ii) there was an erroneous recognition, or nonrecognition, of gain or loss, or

(iii) there was an erroneous deduction of an item properly chargeable to capital account or an erroneous charge to capital account of an item properly deductible.

In 1958, P.L. 85-866, Sec. 59(a), redesignated para. (6) as para. (7) and added new para. (6), effective for determinations made after 11/14/54

Sec. 1313. Definitions.
(a) Determination.

For purposes of this part, the term "determination" means—

(1) a decision by the Tax Court or a judgment, decree, or other order by any court of competent jurisdiction, which has become final;

(2) a closing agreement made under section 7121;

(3) a final disposition by the Secretary of a claim for refund. For purposes of this part, a claim for refund shall be deemed finally disposed of by the Secretary—

(A) as to items with respect to which the claim was allowed, on the date of allowance of refund or credit or on the date of mailing notice of disallowance (by reason of offsetting items) of the claim for refund, and

(B) as to items with respect to which the claim was disallowed, in whole or in part, or as to items applied by the Secretary in reduction of the refund or credit, on expiration of the time for instituting suit with respect thereto (unless suit is instituted before the expiration of such time); or

(4) under regulations prescribed by the Secretary, an agreement for purposes of this part, signed by the Secretary and by any person, relating to the liability of such person (or the person for whom he acts) in respect of a tax under this subtitle for any taxable period.

(b) Taxpayer.

Notwithstanding section 7701(a)(14), the term "taxpayer" means any person subject to a tax under the applicable revenue law.

(c) Related taxpayer.

For purposes of this part, the term "related taxpayer" means a taxpayer who, with the taxpayer with respect to whom a determination is made, stood, in the taxable year with respect to which the erroneous inclusion, exclusion, omission, allowance, or disallowance was made, in one of the following relationships:

(1) husband and wife,

(2) grantor and fiduciary,

(3) grantor and beneficiary,

(4) fiduciary and beneficiary, legatee, or heir,

(5) decedent and decedent's estate,

(6) partner, or

(7) member of an affiliated group of corporations (as defined in section 1504).

In 1976, P.L. 94-455, Sec. 1906(b)(13)(A), substituted "Secretary" for "Secretary or his delegate" each place it appeared in Code Sec. 1313, effective for tax. yrs. begin. after 12/31/76.

Sec. 1314. Amount and method of adjustment.
(a) Ascertainment of amount of adjustment.

In computing the amount of an adjustment under this part there shall first be ascertained the tax previously determined for the taxable year with respect to which the error was made. The amount of the tax previously determined shall be the excess of—

(1) the sum of—

(A) the amount shown as the tax by the taxpayer on his return (determined as provided in section 6211(b)(1), (3), and (4), relating to the definition of deficiency), if a return was made by the taxpayer and an amount was shown as the tax by the taxpayer thereon, plus

(B) the amounts previously assessed (or collected without assessment) as a deficiency, over—

(2) the amount of rebates, as defined in section 6211(b)(2), made.

There shall then be ascertained the increase or decrease in tax previously determined which results solely from the correct treatment of the item which was the subject of the error (with due regard given to the effect of the item in the computation of gross income, taxable income, and other matters under this subtitle). A similar computation shall be made for any other taxable year affected, or treated as affected, by a net operating loss deduction (as defined in section 172) or by a capital loss carryback or carryover (as defined in section 1212), determined with reference to the taxable year with respect to which the error was made. The amount so ascertained (together with any amounts wrongfully collected as additions to the tax or interest, as a result of such error) for each taxable year shall be the amount of the adjustment for that taxable year.

(b) Method of adjustment.

The adjustment authorized in section 1311(a) shall be made by assessing and collecting, or refunding or crediting, the amount thereof in the same manner as if it were a deficiency determined by the Secretary with respect to the taxpayer as to whom the error was made or an overpayment claimed by such taxpayer, as the case may be, for the taxable year or years with respect to which an amount is ascertained under subsection (a), and as if on the date of the determination one year remained before the expiration of the periods of limitation upon assessment or filing claim for refund for such taxable year or years. If, as a result of a determination described in section 1313(a)(4), an adjustment has been made by the assessment and collection of a deficiency or the refund or credit of an overpayment, and subsequently such determination is altered or revoked, the amount of the adjustment ascertained under subsection (a) of this section shall be redetermined on the basis of such alteration or revocation and any overpayment or deficiency resulting from such redetermination shall be refunded or credited, or assessed and collected, as the case may be, as an adjustment under this part. In the case of an adjustment resulting from an increase or decrease in a net operating loss or net capital loss which is carried back to the year of adjustment, interest shall not be collected or paid for any period prior to the close of the taxable year in which the net operating loss or net capital loss arises.

(c) Adjustment unaffected by other items.

The amount to be assessed and collected in the same manner as a deficiency, or to be refunded or credited in the same manner as an overpayment, under this part, shall not be diminished by any credit or set-off based upon any item other than the one which was the subject of the adjustment. The amount of the adjustment under this part, if paid, shall not be recovered by a claim or suit for refund or suit for erroneous refund based upon any item other than the one which was the subject of the adjustment.

(d) Periods for which adjustments may be made.

No adjustment shall be made under this part in respect of any taxable year beginning prior to January 1, 1932.

(e) Taxes imposed by subtitle C.

This part shall not apply to any tax imposed by subtitle (C) (sec. 3101 and following relating to employment taxes).

In **1976**, P.L. 94-455, Sec. 1906(b)(13)(A), substituted "Secretary" for "Secretary or his delegate" in subsec. (b), effective for tax. yrs. begin. after 12/31/76.

In **1969**, P.L. 91-172, Sec. 512(f)(7), substituted "capital loss carryback or carryover" for "capital loss carryover" in subsec. (a)... Sec. 512(f)(8), added "or net capital loss" to the last sentence of subsec. (b), effective for net capital losses sustained in tax. yrs. begin. after 12/31/69.

In **1965**, P.L. 89-44, Sec. 809, substituted "section 6211(b)(1), (3) and (4)" for "section 6211(b)(1) and (3)" in subpara. (a)(1)(A), effective for tax. yrs. begin. after 6/30/65.

In **1958**, P.L. 85-866, Sec. 59(b), substituted in the second sentence of subsec. (c) "The" for "Other than in the case of an adjustment resulting from a determination under section 1313(a)(4), the" effective for determinations made after 11/14/54.

Sec. 1315. Repealed.

In **1976**, P.L. 94-455, Sec. 1901(a)(143), repealed Code Sec. 1315, effective for tax. yrs. begin. after 12/31/76.
Prior to repeal, Code Sec. 1315 read as follows:
"SEC. 1315. EFFECTIVE DATE.
"(a) In general.
"This part shall apply only to determinations (as defined in section 1313(a)) made after the 90th day after the date of enactment of this title.
"(b) Transitional provision.
"Notwithstanding any other provision of this title, section 3801 of the Internal Revenue Code of 1939 shall apply to determinations (as defined in subsection (a) of such section) made on or before such 90th day as if this title had not been enacted."

PART III. Repealed.

In **1976**, P.L. 94-455, Sec. 1901(a)(144), repealed Part III, for tax. yrs. begin. after '76.
Prior to repeal, Part III read as follows:
"PART III.—INVOLUNTARY LIQUIDATION AND REPLACEMENT OF LIFO INVENTORIES
"Sec.
"1321. Involuntary liquidation of LIFO inventories.
"SEC. 1321. INVOLUNTARY LIQUIDATION OF LIFO INVENTORIES.
"(a) Adjustment of taxable income and resulting tax.

"If, for any taxable year ending after June 30, 1950, and before January 1, 1955, the closing inventory of a taxpayer inventorying goods under the method provided in section 22(d) of the Internal Revenue Code of 1939 reflects a decrease from the opening inventory of such goods for such year, and if the taxpayer elects, at such time and in such manner and subject to such regulations as the Secretary or his delegate may prescribe, to have this section apply, and if it is established to the satisfaction of the Secretary or his delegate, in accordance with such regulations, that such decrease is attributable to the involuntary liquidation of such inventory as defined in section 22(d)(6)(B) of the Internal Revenue Code of 1939 (as modified by subsection (b) of this section), and if the closing inventory of a subsequent taxable year, ending before January 1, 1956, reflects a replacement, in whole or in part, of the goods so previously liquidated, then the taxable income of the taxpayer otherwise determined for the year of such involuntary liquidation shall be increased by an amount equal to the excess, if any, of the aggregate cost of such goods reflected in the opening inventory of the year of involuntary liquidation over the aggregate replacement cost, or decreased by an amount equal to the excess, if any, of the aggregate replacement cost of such goods over the aggregate cost thereof reflected in the opening inventory of the year of the involuntary liquidation. The taxes imposed by this chapter (and by chapters 1 and 2 of the Internal Revenue Code of 1939) for the year of such liquidation, for preceding taxable years, and for all taxable years intervening between the year of liquidation and the year of replacement shall be redetermined, giving effect to such adjustments. Any increase in such taxes resulting from such adjustments shall be assessed and collected as a deficiency but without interest, and any overpayment so resulting shall be credited or refunded to the taxpayer without interest.
"(b) Definitions.
"For purposes of this section, the term 'involuntary liquidation' shall have the meaning given to it in section 22(d)(6)(B) of the Internal Revenue Code of 1939 and, in addition, it shall mean a failure, as referred to in that section, on the part of the taxpayer due, directly and exclusively, to disruption of normal trade relations between countries. For purposes of this section, the words 'enemy' and 'war', as used in such section 22(d)(6)(B), shall be interpreted, pursuant to regulations prescribed by the Secretary or his delegate, in such a way as to apply to circumstances, occurrences and conditions, lacking a state of war, which are similar, by reason of a state of national preparedness, to those which would exist under a state of war.
"(c) Special rules.
"Subparagraphs (C) and (E) of section 22(d)(6) of the Internal Revenue Code of 1939, to the extent that they refer to any taxpayer subject to subparagraph (A) of such section or to the adjustments specified in or resulting from the effect of subparagraph (A) of such section, shall apply to a taxpayer subject to this section or to adjustments specified in or resulting from the effect of this section as though they specifically referred to this section. If, for any taxable year ending after June 30, 1950, and before January 1, 1953, subparagraph (C) of such section 22(d)(6) applies with respect to involuntary liquidations of goods of the same class subject to both subparagraph (A) of such section and to this section, the involuntary liquidations of such goods subject to this section shall be considered for the purpose of such subparagraph (C) as having occurred before the involuntary liquidations of such goods subject to subparagraph (A) of such section 22(d)(6). For the purpose of this subsection, and with respect to the taxable years covered by this section, the reference in subparagraph (E) of such section 22(d)(6) to section 734(d) shall be taken as a reference to section 452(d) of the Internal Revenue Code of 1939, and, with respect to any taxable year to which any provision of the Internal Revenue Code of 1939 may not be applicable, references in such subparagraph to such provision shall, where applicable, be deemed a reference to the corresponding provision of the Internal Revenue Code of 1954."

PART IV. Repealed.

In **1976**, P.L. 94-455, Sec. 1901(a)(145), repealed Part IV, for war loss recoveries in tax. yrs. begin. after '76.
Prior to repeal, Part IV read as follows:
"PART IV.— WAR LOSS RECOVERIES
"Sec.
"1331. War loss recoveries.
"1332. Inclusion in gross income of war loss recoveries.
"1333. Tax adjustment measured by prior benefits.
"1334. Restoration of value of investments referable to destroyed or seized property.
"1335. Election by taxpayer for application of section 1333.
"1336. Basis of recovered property.
"1337. Applicable rules.
"SEC. 1331. WAR LOSS RECOVERIES.
"On the recovery in the taxable year of any money or property in respect of property considered under section 127(a) of the Internal Revenue Code of 1939, as destroyed or seized, the amount of such recovery shall be included in gross income to the extent provided in section 1332, unless section 1333 applies to the taxable year pursuant to an election made by the taxpayer under section 1335.
"SEC. 1332. INCLUSION IN GROSS INCOME OF WAR LOSS RECOVERIES.
"(a) Amount of recovery.
"The amount of the recovery of any money or property in respect of property considered under section 127(a) of the Internal Revenue Code of 1939, as destroyed or seized, shall be an amount equal to the aggregate of such money and the fair market value of such property, determined as of the date of the recovery.
"(b) Amount of gain includible.

"(1) Portion excluded from gross income. To the extent that the amount of the recovery plus the aggregate of the amounts of previous such recoveries do not exceed that part of the aggregate of the allowable deductions in prior taxable years on account of the destruction or seizure of property described in such section 127(a) which did not result in a reduction of any tax of the taxpayer under chapter 1 or 2 of the Internal Revenue Code of 1939, such amount shall not be includible in gross income and shall not be deemed gain on the involuntary conversion of property as a result of its destruction or seizure.

"(2) Portion treated as ordinary income. To the extent that such amount plus the aggregate of the amounts of previous such recoveries exceed that part of the aggregate of such deductions, which did not result in a reduction of any tax of the taxpayer under such chapters and do not exceed that part of the aggregate of such deductions which did result in a reduction of any tax of the taxpayer under such chapters, such amount shall be included in gross income but shall not be deemed a gain on the involuntary conversion of property as a result of its destruction or seizure.

"(3) Portion treated as gain on involuntary conversion. To the extent that such amount plus the aggregate of the amounts of previous such recoveries exceed the aggregate of the allowable deductions in prior taxable years on account of the destruction or seizure of property described in such section 127(a), such amount shall be considered a gain on the involuntary conversion of property as a result of its destruction or seizure and shall be recognized or not recognized as provided in section 1033 (relating to involuntary conversions).

"(4) Obligations not discharged. If for any previous taxable year the taxpayer chose under section 127(b) of the Internal Revenue Code of 1939 to treat any obligations and liabilities as discharged or satisfied out of the property or interest described in such section 127(a), and if such obligations and liabilities were not so discharged or satisfied, the amount of such obligations and liabilities treated as discharged or satisfied under such section 127(b) shall be considered for purposes of this part as a deduction by reason of such section 127(a) which did not result in a reduction of of any tax of the taxpayer under such chapters 1 or 2.

"(5) Allowable deduction not allowed. For purposes of this subsection, an allowable deduction for any taxable year on account of the destruction or seizure of property described in such section 127(a) shall, to the extent not allowed in computing the tax of the taxpayer for such taxable year, be considered an allowable deduction which did not result in a reduction of any tax of the taxpayer under such chapters 1 or 2.

"SEC. 1333. TAX ADJUSTMENT MEASURED BY PRIOR BENEFITS.

"If this section applies to the taxable year pursuant to an election made by the taxpayer under section 1335 or section 127(c)(5) of the Internal Revenue Code of 1939—

"(1) Amount of recovery. The amount of the recovery in the taxable year of any money or property in respect of property considered under section 127(a) of the Internal Revenue Code of 1939 as destroyed or seized, shall be an amount equal to the aggregate of such money and the fair market value of such property, determined as of the date of the recovery. For purposes of this section, in the case of the recovery of the same property or interest considered under such section 127(a) as destroyed or seized, the fair market value of such property or interest shall, at the option of the taxpayer, be considered an amount equal to the adjusted basis (for determining loss) of such property or interest in the hands of the taxpayer on the date such property or interest was considered under such section 127(a) as destroyed or seized. The amount of the recovery determined under this paragraph shall be reduced for purposes of paragraphs (2) and (3) by the amount of the obligations or liabilities with respect to the property considered under such section 127(a) as destroyed or seized in respect of which the recovery was received, if the taxpayer for any previous taxable year chose under section 127(b)(2) of such code to treat such obligations or liabilities as discharged or satisfied out of such property, and such obligations or liabilities were not so discharged or satisfied before the date of the recovery.

"(2) Adjustment for prior tax benefits. That part of the amount of the recovery, in respect of any property considered under such section 127(a) as destroyed or seized, which is not in excess of the allowable deductions in prior taxable years on account of such destruction or seizure of the property (the amount of such allowable deductions being first reduced by the aggregate amount of any prior recoveries in respect of the same property) shall be excluded from gross income for the taxable year of the recovery for purposes of computing the tax under the subtitle; but there shall be added to, and assessed and collected as a part of, the tax under this subtitle for the taxable year of the recovery the total increase in the tax under chapters 1 and 2 of the Internal Revenue Code of 1939 for all taxable years which would result by decreasing, in an amount equal to such part of the recovery so excluded, such deductions allowable in the prior taxable years with respect to the destruction or seizure of the property. Such increase in the tax for each such year so resulting shall be computed in accordance with regulations prescribed by the Secretary or his delegate. Such regulations shall give effect to previous recoveries of any kind (including recoveries described in section 111, relating to recovery of bad debts, etc.) with respect to any prior year, and shall provide for the case where there was no tax for the prior year, but shall otherwise treat the tax previously determined for any year in accordance with the principles set forth in section 1314(a) (relating to corrections of errors). All credits allowable against the tax for any year and all carryovers and carrybacks affected by so decreasing the allowable deductions shall be taken into account in computing the increase in the tax, except that the computation of the excess profits credit under chapter 2E of such code for any taxable year shall not be affected.

"(3) Gain on recovery. The amount of any recovery or part thereof, in respect of property considered under such section 127(a) as destroyed or seized, which is not excluded from gross income under paragraph (2), shall be considered for the taxable year of the recovery as gain on the involuntary conversion of property as a result of its destruction or seizure and shall be recognized or not recognized as provided in section 1033.

"(4) Recoveries treated as gross income for certain purposes. For purposes of section 6012 (relating to persons required to make income tax returns) and section 1312 (relating to circumstances of adjustment), the recovery in the taxable year of any money or property in respect of property considered under such section 127(a) as destroyed or seized in any prior taxable year shall be deemed to be an item includible in gross income for the taxable year in which the recovery is made.

"SEC. 1334. RESTORATION OF VALUE OF INVESTMENTS REFERABLE TO DESTROYED OR SEIZED PROPERTY.

"For purposes of this part, the restoration in whole or in part of the value of any interest described in section 127(a)(3) of the Internal Revenue Code of 1939 by reason of any recovery of money or property in respect of property to which such interest related and which was considered under subsection (a)(1) or (2) of such section 127 as destroyed or seized shall be deemed a recovery of property in respect of property considered under such section 127(a) as destroyed or seized. In applying section 1333, such restoration shall be treated as the recovery of the same interest considered under such section 127(a) as destroyed or seized.

"SEC. 1335. ELECTION BY TAXPAYER FOR APPLICATION OF SECTION 1333.

"If the taxpayer elects to have section 1333 apply to any taxable year in which he recovered any money or property in respect of property considered under section 127(a) of the Internal Revenue Code of 1939, as destroyed or seized, section 1333 shall apply to all taxable years of the taxpayer beginning after December 31, 1941, and such election, once made, shall be irrevocable. The election shall be made in such manner and at such time as the Secretary or his delegate may by regulations prescribe, except that no election under this section may be made unless the taxpayer recovers money or property (in respect of property considered under such section 127(a) as destroyed or seized) during the taxable year for which the election is made. If pursuant to such election section 1333 applies to any taxable year—

"(1) The period of limitations provided in chapter 66 on the making of assessments and the beginning of distraint or a proceeding in court for collection shall not, with respect to—

"(A) the amount to be added to the tax for such taxable year under section 1333, and

"(B) any deficiency for such taxable year or for any other taxable year, to the extent attributable to the basis of the recovered property being determined under section 1336(b),

expire before the expiration of 2 years following the date of the making of such election, and such amount and such deficiency may be assessed at any time before the expiration of such period notwithstanding any law or rule of law which would otherwise prevent such assessment and collection, and

"(2) in case refund or credit of any overpayment resulting from the application of section 1333 to such taxable year is prevented on the date of the making of such election, or within one year from such date, by the operation of any law or rule of law (other than section 7122, relating to compromises), refund or credit of such overpayment may, nevertheless, be made or allowed if claim therefor is filed within one year from such date.

In the case of any taxable year ending before the date of the making by the taxpayer of an election under this section, no interest shall be paid on any overpayment resulting from the application of section 1333 to such taxable year, and no interest shall be assessed or collected with respect to any amount or any deficiency specified in paragraph (1) for any period before the expiration of 6 months following the date of the making of such election by the taxpayer.

"SEC. 1336. BASIS OF RECOVERED PROPERTY.

"(a) In general.

"The unadjusted basis of property recovered in respect of property considered as destroyed or seized under section 127(a) of the Internal Revenue Code of 1939 shall be determined under this section. Such basis shall be an amount equal to the fair market value of such property, determined as of the date of the recovery, reduced by an amount equal to the excess of the aggregate of such fair market value and the amounts of previous recoveries of money or property in respect of property considered under such section 127(a) as destroyed or seized over the aggregate of the allowable deductions in prior taxable years on account of the destruction or seizure of property described in such section 127(a), and increased by that portion of the amount of the recovery which under section 1332 is treated as a recognized gain from the involuntary conversion of property. On application of the taxpayer, the aggregate of the bases (determined under the preceding sentence) of any properties recovered in respect of properties considered under such section 127(a) as destroyed or seized may be allocated among the properties so recovered in such manner as the Secretary or his delegate may determine under regulations prescribed by the Secretary or his delegate, and the amounts so allocated to any such property so recovered shall be the unadjusted basis of such property in lieu of the unadjusted basis of such property determined under the preceding sentence.

"(b) Property recovered in taxable year to which section 1333 applies.

"In the case of a taxpayer who has made an election under section 1335, the basis of property recovered shall be an amount equal to the value at which such property is included in amount of the recovery under section 1333(1) (determined without regard to the last sentence thereof), reduced by such part of the gain under section 1333(3) which is not recognized as provided in section 1033.

"SEC. 1337. APPLICABLE RULES.

"(a) Determination of tax benefits.

"The determination as to whether and to what extent an allowable deduction on account of the destruction or seizure of property described in section 127(a) of the Internal Revenue Code of 1939 did or did not result in a reduction of any tax of the taxpayer under chapter 1 or 2 of such code shall be made in accordance with regulations prescribed by the Secretary or his delegate.

"(b) Partial worthlessness of certain investments treated as war losses under 1939 Code.

"The part of the stock or other interest of the taxpayer treated under subsection (e) of such section 127 as property described in subsection (a)(3) of such section shall be treated in the same manner for purposes of this part."

PART V.—CLAIM OF RIGHT

Sec.
1341. Computation of tax where taxpayer restores substantial amount held under claim of right.
1342. Repealed.

In 1976, P.L. 94-455, Sec. 1901(b)(38), deleted item 1342.
Prior to repeal, item 1342 read as follows:
"1342. Computation of tax where taxpayer recovers substantial amount held by another under claim of right."

Sec. 1341. Computation of tax where taxpayer restores substantial amount held under claim of right.

(a) General rule.
If—
(1) an item was included in gross income for a prior taxable year (or years) because it appeared that the taxpayer had an unrestricted right to such item;
(2) a deduction is allowable for the taxable year because it was established after the close of such prior taxable year (or years) that the taxpayer did not have an unrestricted right to such item or to a portion of such item; and
(3) the amount of such deduction exceeds $3,000,
then the tax imposed by this chapter for the taxable year shall be the lesser of the following:
(4) the tax for the taxable year computed with such deduction; or
(5) an amount equal to—
(A) the tax for the taxable year computed without such deduction, minus
(B) the decrease in tax under this chapter (or the corresponding provisions of prior revenue laws) for the prior taxable year (or years) which would result solely from the exclusion of such item (or portion thereof) from gross income for such prior taxable year (or years).
For purposes of paragraph (5)(B), the corresponding provisions of the Internal Revenue Code of 1939 shall be chapter 1 of such code (other than subchapter E, relating to self-employment income) and subchapter E of chapter 2 of such code.

(b) Special rules.
(1) If the decrease in tax ascertained under subsection (a)(5)(B) exceeds the tax imposed by this chapter for the taxable year (computed without the deduction) such excess shall be considered to be a payment of tax on the last day prescribed by law for the payment of tax for the taxable year, and shall be refunded or credited in the same manner as if it were an overpayment for such taxable year.
(2) Subsection (a) does not apply to any deduction allowable with respect to an item which was included in gross income by reason of the sale or other disposition of stock in trade of the taxpayer (or other property of a kind which would properly have been included in the inventory of the taxpayer if on hand at the close of the prior taxable year) or property held by the taxpayer primarily for sale to customers in the ordinary course of his trade or business. This paragraph shall not apply if the deduction arises out of refunds or repayments with respect to rates made by a regulated public utility (as defined in section 7701(a)(33) without regard to the limitation contained in the last two sentences thereof) if such refunds or repayments are re-quired to be made by the Government, political subdivision, agency, or instrumentality referred to in such section, or by an order of a court, or are made in settlement of litigation or under threat or imminence of litigation.
(3) If the tax imposed by this chapter for the taxable year is the amount determined under subsection (a)(5), then the deduction referred to in subsection (a)(2) shall not be taken into account for any purpose of this subtitle other than this section.
(4) For purposes of determining whether paragraph (4) or paragraph (5) of subsection (a) applies—
(A) in any case where the deduction referred to in paragraph (4) of subsection (a) results in a net operating loss, such loss shall, for purposes of computing the tax for the taxable year under such paragraph (4), be carried back to the same extent and in the same manner as is provided under section 172; and
(B) in any case where the exclusion referred to in paragraph (5)(B) of subsection (a) results in a net operating loss or capital loss for the prior taxable year (or years), such loss shall, for purposes of computing the decrease in tax for the prior taxable year (or years) under such paragraph (5)(B), be carried back and carried over to the same extent and in the same manner as is provided under section 172 or section 1212, except that no carry-over beyond the taxable year shall be taken into account.
(5) For purposes of this chapter, the net operating loss described in paragraph (4)(A) of this subsection, or the net operating loss or capital loss described in paragraph (4)(B) of this subsection, as the case may be, shall (after the application of paragraph (4) or (5)(B) of subsection (a) for the taxable year) be taken into account under section 172 or 1212 for taxable years after the taxable year to the same extent and in the same manner as—
(A) a net operating loss sustained for the taxable year, if paragraph (4) of subsection (a) applied, or
(B) a net operating loss or capital loss sustained for the prior taxable year (or years), if paragraph (5)(B) of subsection (a) applied.

In 1976, P.L. 94-455, Sec. 1901(a)(146), amended para. (b)(2), effective for tax. yrs. begin. after 12/31/76.
Prior to amendment, para. (b)(2) read as follows:
"(2) Subsection (a) does not apply to any deduction allowable with respect to an item which was included in gross income by reason of the sale or other disposition of stock in trade of the taxpayer (or other property of a kind which would properly have been included in the inventory of the taxpayer if on hand at the close of the prior taxable year) or property held by the taxpayer primarily for sale to customers in the ordinary course of his trade or business. This paragraph shall not apply if the deduction arises out of refunds or repayments with respect to rates made by a regulated public utility (as defined in section 7701(a)(33) without regard to the limitation contained in the last two sentences thereof) if such refunds or repayments are required to be made by the Government, political subdivision, agency, or instrumentality referred to in such section, or by an order of a court, or are made in settlement of litigation or under threat or imminence of litigation. This paragraph shall not apply if the deduction arises out of payments or repayments made pursuant to a price redetermination provision in a subcontract entered into before January 1, 1958, between persons other than those bearing the relationship set forth in section 267(b), if the subcontract containing the price redetermination provision is subject to statutory renegotiation and section 1481 (relating to mitigation of effect of renegotiation of Government contracts) does not apply to such payment or repayment solely because such payment or repayment is not paid or repaid to the United States or any agency thereof."
In 1964, P.L. 88-272, Sec. 234(b)(7), substituted "7701(a)(33) without regard to the limitation continued in the last two sentences thereof)" for "1503(c) without regard to paragraph (2) thereof" in para. (b)(2), effective for tax. yrs. begin. after 12/31/63.
In 1962, P.L. 87-863, Sec. 5(a), added paras. (b)(4) and (5), effective for tax. yrs. begin. after 12/31/61.
In 1958, P.L. 85-866, Sec. 60, added "and subchapter E of chapter 2 of such code" in the last sentence of subsec. (a), added last sentence of subsec. (b)(2) and added subsec. (b)(3), for '54 Code years . . . in second sentence of subsec. (b)(2), added "with respect to rates" and added ", or by an order of a court, or are made

Maximum tax

Code Sec. 1348

in settlement of litigation or under threat or imminence of litigation", for tax. yrs. begin. after '57 no interest shall be allowed or paid on any overpayment resulting from the application of the amendment.

Sec. 1342. Repealed.

In 1976, P.L. 94-455, Sec. 1901(a)(147), repealed Code Sec. 1342, effective for tax. yrs. begin. after 12/31/76.
Prior to repeal, Code Sec. 1342 read as follows:
"SEC. 1342. COMPUTATION OF TAX WHERE TAXPAYER RECOVERS SUBSTANTIAL AMOUNT HELD BY ANOTHER UNDER CLAIM OF RIGHT.
"(a) General rule.
"If—
"(1) an item was deducted from gross income for a prior taxable year (or years) because it appeared that another person held an unrestricted right to such item as a result of a court decision in a patent infringement suit (whether or not the taxpayer is a party to such suit); or
"(2) gross income is increased for the taxable year because it was established after the close of such prior taxable year (or years) that such other person did not have an unrestricted right to such item or to a portion of such item because of the subsequent reversal of such court decision on the ground that such decision was induced by fraud or undue influence; and
"(3) the amount of such increase in gross income exceeds $3,000, then the tax imposed by this chapter for the taxable year shall be the lesser of the following:
"(4) the tax for the taxable year computed with the gross income so increased; or
"(5) an amount equal to—
"(A) the tax for the taxable year computed without such increase in gross income, plus
"(B) the increase in tax (including interest) under this chapter (or the corresponding provisions of prior revenue laws) for the prior taxable year (or years) which would result solely from the elimination of such item (or portion thereof) as a deduction from gross income for such prior taxable year (or years).
"(b) Special rule.
"For purposes of subsection (a)(5)(B) interest shall be computed from the due date of the return for such prior taxable year to the due date of the return for the taxable year."
In 1955, ch. 870, Sec. 3, added Code Sec. 1342, effective for tax. yrs. begin. after 12/31/54.

PART VI. Repealed.

Sec.
1346. Repealed.
1347. Repealed.
1348. Repealed.

In 1981, P.L. 97-34, Sec. 101(c)(1), repealed Part VI, Subchapter Q of chapter 1.
Prior to repeal the Table of Sections read as follows:
"PART VI.—MAXIMUM RATE ON PERSONAL SERVICE INCOME.
"Sec.
"1346. Repealed.
"1347. Repealed.
"1348. 50-percent maximum rate on personal service income."
In 1976, P.L. 94-455, Sec. 302(b), amended item 1348.
Prior to amendment, item 1348 read as follows:
"1348. Fifty-percent maximum rate on earned income."
—P.L. 94-455, Sec. 1901(b)(39)(A), deleted item 1346.
Prior to repeal, item 1346 read as follows:
"1346. Recovery of unconstitutional federal taxes."
—P.L. 94-455, Sec. 1951(c)(3)(B), deleted the item for 1347 ... Sec. 1951(c)(3)(C), amended the heading of part VI of subchapter Q of chapter 1.
Prior to amendment item 1347 read as follows:
"1347. Claims against United States involving acquisition of property."
Prior to amendment the heading of part VI of subchapter Q of chapter 1 read as follows:
"PART VI—OTHER LIMITATIONS"
In 1969, P.L. 91-172, Sec. 804(b), added item 1348.

Sec. 1346. Repealed.

In 1976, P.L. 94-455, Sec. 1901(a)(148), repealed Code Sec. 1346, effective for tax. yrs. begin. after 12/31/76.
Prior to repeal, Code Sec. 1346 read as follows:
"SEC. 1346. RECOVERY OF UNCONSTITUTIONAL FEDERAL TAXES.
"Income (excluding interest) attributable to the recovery during the taxable year of a tax imposed by the United States which has been held unconstitutional, and in respect of which a deduction was allowed in a prior taxable year, may be excluded from gross income for the taxable year, and the deduction allowed in respect thereof in such prior taxable year treated as not having been allowable, if—

"(1) the taxpayer elects in writing (at such time and in such manner as may be prescribed by regulations prescribed by the Secretary or his delegate) to treat such deduction as not having been allowable for such prior taxable year, and
"(2) the taxpayer consents in writing to the assessment, within such period as may be agreed on, of any deficiency resulting from such treatment, even though the statutory period for the assessment of any such deficiency had expired before the filing of such consent."

Sec. 1347. Repealed.

In 1976, P.L. 94-455, Sec. 1951(b)(12)(A), repealed Code Sec. 1347, effective for tax. yrs. begin. after 12/31/76, except as provided in Sec. 1951(b)(12)(B) of this Act, which reads as follows:
"(B) Savings provision.—Notwithstanding subparagraph (A), if amounts received in a taxable year beginning after December 31, 1976, would have been subject to the provisions of section 1347 if received in a taxable year beginning before such date, the tax imposed by section 1 attributable to such receipt shall be computed as if section 1347 had not been repealed."
Prior to repeal, Code Sec. 1347 read as follows:
"SEC. 1347. CLAIMS AGAINST UNITED STATES INVOLVING ACQUISITION OF PROPERTY.
"In the case of amounts (other than interest) received by a taxpayer from the United States with respect to a claim against the United States involving the acquisition of property and remaining unpaid for more than 15 years, the tax imposed by section 1 attributable to such receipt shall not exceed 33 percent of the amount (other than interest) so received. This section shall apply only if claim was filed with the United States before January 1, 1958."
In 1969, P.L. 91-172, Sec. 803(d)(5), substituted "tax" for "surtax" and substituted "33 percent" for "30 percent", effective for tax. yrs. begin. after 12/31/70.
In 1958, P.L. 85-866, Sec. 61(a), substituted "surtax" for "tax", for tax. yrs. begin. after '57 ... added sentence "this section shall apply only if claim was filed with the United States before January 1, 1958".

Sec. 1348. Repealed.

In 1981, P.L. 97-34, Sec. 101(c)(1), repealed Code Sec. 1348, effective for tax. yrs. begin. after 12/31/81.
Prior to repeal, Code Sec. 1348 read as follows:
"SEC. 1348. 50-PERCENT MAXIMUM RATE ON PERSONAL SERVICE INCOME.
"(a) General rule.
"If for any taxable year an individual has personal service taxable income which exceeds the amount of taxable income specified in paragraph (1), the tax imposed by section 1 for such year shall, unless the taxpayer chooses the benefits of part I (relating to income averaging), be the sum of—
"(1) the tax imposed by section 1 on the highest amount of taxable income on which the rate of tax does not exceed 50 percent,
"(2) 50 percent of the amount by which his personal service taxable income exceeds the amount of taxable income specified in paragraph (1) of this subsection, and
"(3) the excess of the tax computed under section 1 without regard to this section over the tax so computed with reference solely to his personal service taxable income.
"(b) Definitions.
"For purposes of this section—
"(1) Personal service income.
"(A) In general. The term 'personal service income' means any income which is earned income within the meaning of section 401(c)(2)(C) or section 911(b) or which is an amount received as a pension or annuity which arises from an employer-employee relationship or from tax-deductible contributions to a retirement plan. For purposes of this subparagraph, section 911(b) shall be applied without regard to the phrase ', not in excess of 30 percent of his share of net profits of such trade or business,'.
"(B) Exceptions. The term 'personal service income' does not include any amount—
"(i) to which section 72(m)(5), 402(a)(2), 402(e), 403(a)(2), 408(e)(2), 408(e)(3), 408(e)(4), 408(e)(5), 408(f), or 409(c) applies; or
"(ii) which is includible in gross income under section 409(b) because of the redemption of a bond which was not tendered before the close of the taxable year in which the registered owner attained age 70½.
"(2) Personal service taxable income. The personal service taxable income of an individual is the excess of—
"(A) the amount which bears the same ratio (but not in excess of 100 percent) to his taxable income as his personal service net income bears to his adjusted gross income, over
"(B) the sum of the items of tax preference described in subsection (a) (other than paragraph (9)) of section 57 for the taxable year.
For purposes of subparagraph (A), the term 'personal service net income' means personal service income reduced by any deductions allowable under section 62 which are properly allocable to or chargeable against such personal service income.
"(c) Married individuals.
"This section shall apply to a married individual only if such individual and his spouse make a single return jointly for the taxable year."
In 1980, P.L. 96-222, Sec. 104(a)(5)(A), amended Sec. 441(b)(2) of P.L. 95-600 [reproduced below].
Prior to amendment, Sec. 441(b)(2) of P.L. 95-600 read as follows:

2,827

"(2) Transitional rules, in the case of a taxable year which begins before November 1, 1978, and ends after October 31, 1978, the amendment made by subsection (a) shall apply with respect to so much of the net capital gain of the taxpayer for the taxable year as is attributable to sales or exchanges after October 31, 1978."

—P.L. 96-222, Sec. 104(a)(5)(B), corrected Sec. 441(a) of P.L. 95-600 by substituting "subparagraph (B)" for "subparagraph (b)" [see below].

In **1978**, P.L. 95-600, Sec. 441(a), substituted "items of tax preference described in subsection (a) (other than paragraph (9)) of section 57" for "items of tax preference as defined in section 57)", in subpara. (b)(2)(B), effective for tax. yrs. begin. after 10/31/78. Sec. 441(b)(2) [as amended by Sec. 104(a)(5)(A) of P.L. 96-222, see above] of this Act provides as follows:

"(2) Taxable years which straddle November 1, 1978. In the case of a taxable year which begins before November 1, 1978, and ends after October 31, 1978, the amount taken into account under section 1348(b)(2)(B) of the Internal Revenue Code of 1954 by reason of section 57(a)(9) of such Code shall be 50 percent of the lesser of—

"(A) the net capital gain for the taxable year, or

"(B) the net capital gain taking into account only gain or loss properly taken into account for the portion of the taxable year before November 1, 1978."

—P.L. 95-600, Sec. 442, added the last sentence of subpara. (b)(1)(A), effective for tax. yrs. begin. after 12/31/78.

—P.L. 95-600, Sec. 701(x)(1), substituted "pension or annuity which arises from an employer-employee relationship or from tax-deductible contributions to a retirement plan" for "pension or annuity" in subpara. (b)(1)(A) ... Sec. 701(x)(2), substituted "personal service income" for "earned income" in the last sentence of subsec. (b), effective for tax. yrs. begin. after 12/31/76.

In **1976**, P.L. 94-455, Sec. 302(a), amended Code Sec. 1348, effective for tax. yrs. begin. after 12/31/76.

Prior to amendment, Code Sec. 1348 read as follows:

"SEC. 1348. FIFTY-PERCENT MAXIMUM RATE ON EARNED INCOME.

"(a) General rule.

"If for any taxable year an individual has earned taxable income which exceeds the amount of taxable income specified in paragraph (1), the tax imposed by section 1 for such year shall, unless the taxpayer chooses the benefits of part I (relating to income averaging), be the sum of—

"(1) the tax imposed by section 1 on the lowest amount of taxable income on which the rate of tax under section 1 exceeds 50 percent.

"(2) 50 percent of the amount by which his earned taxable income exceeds the lowest amount of taxable income on which the rate of tax under section 1 exceeds 50 percent, and

"(3) the excess of the tax computed under section 1 without regard to this section over the tax so computed with reference solely to his earned taxable income. In applying this subsection to a taxable year beginning after December 31, 1970, and before January 1, 1972, '60 percent' shall be substituted for '50 percent' each place it appears in paragraphs (1) and (2).

"(b) Definitions.

"For purposes of this section—

"(1) Earned income. The term 'earned income' means any income which is earned income within the meaning of section 401(c)(2)(C) or section 911(b), except that such term does not include any distribution to which section 72(m)(5), 402(a)(2), 402(e), or 403(a)(2)(A) applies or any deferred compensation within the meaning of section 404. For purposes of this paragraph, deferred compensation does not include any amount received before the end of the taxable year following the first taxable year of the recipient in which his right to receive such amount is not subject to a substantial risk of forfeiture within the meaning of section 83(c)(1)).

"(2) Earned taxable income. The earned taxable income of an individual is the excess of—

"(A) the amount which bears the same ratio (but not in excess of 100 percent) to his taxable income as his earned net income bears to his adjusted gross income, over

"(B) the amount by which the greater of—

"(i) one-fifth of the sum of the taxpayer's items of tax preference referred to in section 57 for the taxable year and the 4 preceding taxable years, or

"(ii) the sum of the items of tax preference for the taxable year, exceeds $30,000.

For purposes of subparagraph (A), the term 'earned net income' means earned income reduced by any deductions allowable under section 62 which are properly allocable to or chargeable against such earned income.

"(c) Married individuals.

"This section shall apply to a married individual only if such individual and his spouse make a single return jointly for the taxable year."

In **1974**, P.L. 93-406, Sec. 2005(c)(14), substituted "402(a)(2), 402(e)" for "72(n), 402(a)(2)" in para. (b)(1), effective for distributions or payments made after 12/31/73, in tax. yrs. begin. after 12/31/73.

In **1969**, P.L. 91-172, Sec. 804(a), added Code Sec. 1348, effective for tax. yrs. begin. after 12/31/70.

PART VII.—RECOVERIES OF FOREIGN EXPROPRIATION LOSSES

Sec.

1351. Treatment of recoveries of foreign expropriation losses.

Sec. 1351. Treatment of recoveries of foreign expropriation losses.

(a) Election.

(1) In general. This section shall apply only to a recovery, by a domestic corporation subject to the tax imposed by section 11 or 801, of a foreign expropriation loss sustained by such corporation and only if such corporation was subject to the tax imposed by section 11 or 801, as the case may be, for the year of the loss and elects to have the provisions of this section apply with respect to such loss.

(2) Time, manner, and scope. An election under paragraph (1) shall be made at such time and in such manner as the Secretary may prescribe by regulations. An election made with respect to any foreign expropriation loss shall apply to all recoveries in respect of such loss.

(b) Definition of foreign expropriation loss.

For purposes of this section, the term "foreign expropriation loss" means any loss sustained by reason of the expropriation, intervention, seizure, or similar taking of property by the government of any foreign country, any political subdivision thereof, or any agency or instrumentality of the foregoing. For purposes of the preceding sentence, a debt which becomes worthless shall, to the extent of any deduction allowed under section 166(a), be treated as a loss.

(c) Amount of recovery.

(1) General rule. The amount of any recovery of a foreign expropriation loss is the amount of money and the fair market value of other property received in respect of such loss, determined as of the date of receipt.

(2) Special rule for life insurance companies. The amount of any recovery of a foreign expropriation loss includes, in the case of a life insurance company, the amount of decrease of any item taken into account under section 807(c), to the extent such decrease is attributable to the release, by reason of such loss, of its liabilities with respect to such item.

(d) Adjustment for prior tax benefits.

(1) In general. That part of the amount of a recovery of a foreign expropriation loss to which this section applies which, when added to the aggregate of the amounts of previous recoveries with respect to such loss, does not exceed the allowable deductions in prior taxable years on account of such loss shall be excluded from gross income for the taxable year of the recovery for purposes of computing the tax under this subtitle; but there shall be added to, and assessed and collected as a part of, the tax under this subtitle for such taxable year an amount equal to the total increase in the tax under this subtitle for all taxable years which would result by decreasing, in an amount equal to such part of the recovery so excluded, the deductions allowable in the prior taxable years on account of such loss. For purposes of this paragraph, if the loss to which the recovery relates was taken into account as a loss from the sale or exchange of a capital asset, the amount of the loss shall be treated as an allowable deduction even though there were no gains against which to allow such loss.

(2) Computation. The increase in the tax for each taxable year referred to in paragraph (1) shall be computed in accordance with regulations prescribed by the Secretary. Such regulations shall give effect to previous recoveries of any kind (including recoveries described in section 111, relating to recovery of tax benefit items) with respect to any prior taxable year, but shall otherwise treat the tax previously determined for any taxable year in accordance with the principles set forth in section 1314(a) (relating to

Maximum tax Code Sec. 1352

correction of errors). Subject to the provisions of paragraph (3), all credits allowable against the tax for any taxable year, and all carryovers and carrybacks affected by so decreasing the allowable deductions, shall be taken into account in computing the increase in the tax.

(3) **Foreign taxes.** For purposes of this subsection, any choice made under subpart A of part III of subchapter N (relating to foreign tax credit) for any taxable year may be changed.

(4) **Substitution of current tax rate.** For purposes of this subsection, the rates of tax specified in section 11(b) for the taxable year of the recovery shall be treated as having been in effect for all prior taxable years.

(e) Gain on recovery.

That part of the amount of a recovery of a foreign expropriation loss to which this section applies which is not excluded from gross income under subsection (d)(1) shall be considered for the taxable year of the recovery as gain on the involuntary conversion of property as a result of its destruction or seizure and shall be recognized or not recognized as provided in section 1033.

(f) Basis of recovered property.

The basis of property (other than money) received as a recovery of a foreign expropriation loss to which this section applies shall be an amount equal to its fair market value on the date of receipt, reduced by such part of the gain under subsection (e) which is not recognized as provided in section 1033.

(g) Restoration of value of investments.

For purposes of this section, if the value of any interest in, or with respect to, property (including any interest represented by a security, as defined in section 165(g)(2))—

(1) which became worthless by reason of the expropriation, intervention, seizure, or similar taking of such property by the government of any foreign country, any political subdivision thereof, or any agency or instrumentality of the foregoing, and

(2) which was taken into account as a loss from the sale or exchange of a capital asset or with respect to which a deduction for a loss was allowed under section 165 or a deduction for a bad debt was allowed under section 166,

is restored in whole or in part by reason of any recovery of money or other property in respect of the property which became worthless, the value so restored shall be treated as property received as a recovery in respect of such loss or such bad debt.

(h) Special rule for evidences of indebtedness.

Bonds or other evidences of indebtedness received as a recovery of a foreign expropriation loss to which this section applies shall not be considered to have any original issue discount within the meaning of section 1273(a).

(i) Adjustments for succeeding years.

For purposes of this subtitle, proper adjustment shall be made, under regulations prescribed by the Secretary, in—

(1) the credit under section 27 (relating to foreign tax credit),

(2) the credit under section 38 (relating to general business credit),

(3) the net operating loss deduction under section 172, or the operations loss deduction under section 810,

(4) the capital loss carryover under section 1212(a), and

(5) such other items as may be specified by such regulations,

for the taxable year of a recovery of a foreign expropriation loss to which this section applies, and for succeeding taxable years, to take into account items changed in making the computations under subsection (d) for taxable years prior to the taxable year of such recovery.

In 1986, P.L. 99-514, Sec. 1812(a)(4), substituted "relating to recovery of tax benefit items" for "relating to recovery of bad debts, etc." in para. (d)(2), effective for amounts recovered after 12/31/83 in tax. yrs. end. after 12/31/83.

In 1984, P.L. 98-369, Sec. 42(a)(12), substituted "section 1273(a)" for "section 1232(a)(2)" in subsec. (h), effective for tax. yrs. ending after 7/18/84.

—P.L. 98-369, Sec. 211(b)(18)(A), substituted "801" for "802" each place it appears in para. (a)(1) . . . Sec. 211(b)(18)(B), substituted "section 807(c)" for "section 810(c)" in para. (c)(2) . . . Sec. 211(b)(18)(C), substituted "section 810" for "section 812" in para. (i)(3), effective for tax. yrs. begin. after 12/31/83.

—P.L. 98-369, Sec. 474(r)(25)(A), substituted "section 27" for "section 33" in subsec. (i) . . . Sec. 474(r)(25)(B), substituted "section 38 (relating to general business credit)" for "section 38 (relating to investment credit)" in subsec. (i), effective for tax. yrs. begin. after 12/31/83, and for carrybacks from 12/31/83.

In 1978, P.L. 95-600, Sec. 301(b)(17), amended para. (d)(4), effective for tax. yrs. begin. after 12/31/78.

Prior to amendment, para. (d)(4) read as follows:

"(4) Substitution of current normal tax and surtax rates. For purposes of this subsection, the normal tax rate provided by section 11(b) and the surtax rate provided by section 11(c) which are in effect for the taxable year of the recovery shall be treated as having been in effect for all prior taxable years."

In 1976, P.L. 94-455, Sec. 1031(b)(3), amended para. (d)(3), effective for tax. yrs. begin. after 12/31/75. For special rules, see Sec. 1031(c)(2)-(4) of this Act, reproduced in note following Code Sec. 904.

Prior to amendment, para. (d)(3) read as follows:

"(3) Foreign taxes. For purposes of this subsection—

"(A) any choice made under subpart A of part III of subchapter N (relating to foreign tax credit) for any taxable year may be changed,

"(B) subject to the provisions of section 904(b), an election to have the limitation provided by section 904(a)(2) apply may be made, and

"(C) notwithstanding section 904(b)(1), an election previously made to have the limitation provided by section 904(a)(2) apply may be revoked with respect to any taxable year and succeeding taxable years."

—P.L. 94-455, Sec. 1906(b)(13)(A), substituted "Secretary" for "Secretary or his delegate" each place it appeared in Code Sec. 1351, effective for tax. yrs. begin. after 12/31/76.

In 1966, P.L. 89-384, Sec. 1(a), added Code Sec. 1351, effective for amounts received after 12/31/64 in respect of foreign expropriation losses (as defined by Code Sec. 1351(b)) sustained after 12/31/58.

Subchapter R.— Election To Determine Corporate Tax on Certain International Shipping Activities Using Per Ton Rate

Sec.
1352. Alternative tax on qualifying shipping activities.
1353. Notional shipping income.
1354. Alternative tax election; revocation; termination.
1355. Definitions and special rules.
1356. Qualifying shipping activities.
1357. Items not subject to regular tax; depreciation; interest.
1358. Allocation of credits, income, and deductions.
1359. Disposition of qualifying vessels.

In 2004, P.L. 108-357, Sec. 248(b)(2), added subchapter R of chapter 1 of subtitle A.

Sec. 1352. Alternative tax on qualifying shipping activities.

In the case of an electing corporation, the tax imposed by section 11 shall be the amount equal to the sum of—

(1) the tax imposed by section 11 determined after the application of this subchapter, and

(2) a tax equal to—

(A) the highest rate of tax specified in section 11, multiplied by

(B) the notional shipping income for the taxable year.

In 2004, P.L. 108-357, Sec. 248(a), added Code Sec. 1352, effective for tax. yrs. begin. after 10/22/2004.

Sec. 1353. Notional shipping income.

(a) In general.

For purposes of this subchapter, the notional shipping income of an electing corporation shall be the sum of the amounts determined under subsection (b) for each qualifying vessel operated by such electing corporation.

(b) Amounts.

(1) In general. For purposes of subsection (a), the amount of notional shipping income of an electing corporation for each qualifying vessel for the taxable year shall equal the product of—

(A) the daily notional shipping income, and

(B) the number of days during the taxable year that the electing corporation operated such vessel as a qualifying vessel in United States foreign trade.

(2) Treatment of vessels the income from which is not otherwise subject to tax. In the case of a qualifying vessel any of the income from which is not included in gross income by reason of section 883 or otherwise, the amount of notional shipping income from such vessel for the taxable year shall be the amount which bears the same ratio to such shipping income (determined without regard to this paragraph) as the gross income from the operation of such vessel in the United States foreign trade bears to the sum of such gross income and the income so excluded.

(c) Daily notional shipping income.

For purposes of subsection (b), the daily notional shipping income from the operation of a qualifying vessel is—

(1) 40 cents for each 100 tons of so much of the net tonnage of the vessel as does not exceed 25,000 net tons, and

(2) 20 cents for each 100 tons of so much of the net tonnage of the vessel as exceeds 25,000 net tons.

(d) Multiple operators of vessel.

If for any period 2 or more persons are operators of a qualifying vessel, the notional shipping income from the operation of such vessel for such period shall be allocated among such persons on the basis of their respective ownership, charter, and operating agreement interests in such vessel or on such other basis as the Secretary may prescribe by regulations.

In **2005,** P.L. 109-135, Sec. 403(g)(1)(A), substituted "ownership, charter, and operating agreement interests" for "ownership and charter interests" in subsec. (d), effective for tax. yrs. begin. after 10/22/2004 as if included in Sec. 248 of the American Jobs Creation Act of 2004, P.L. 108-357.

In **2004,** P.L. 108-357, Sec. 248(a), added Code Sec. 1353, effective for tax. yrs. begin. after 10/22/2004.

Sec. 1354. Alternative tax election; revocation; termination.

(a) In general.

A qualifying vessel operator may elect the application of this subchapter.

(b) Time and manner; years for which effective.

An election under this subchapter—

(1) shall be made in such form as prescribed by the Secretary, and

(2) shall be effective for the taxable year for which made and all succeeding taxable years until terminated under subsection (d).

Such election may be effective for any taxable year only if made on or before the due date (including extensions) for filing the corporation's return for such taxable year.

(c) Consistent elections by members of controlled groups.

An election under subsection (a) by a member of a controlled group shall apply to all qualifying vessel operators that are members of such group.

(d) Termination.

(1) By revocation.

(A) In general. An election under subsection (a) may be terminated by revocation.

(B) When effective. Except as provided in subparagraph (C)—

(i) a revocation made during the taxable year and on or before the 15th day of the 3d month thereof shall be effective on the 1st day of such taxable year, and

(ii) a revocation made during the taxable year but after such 15th day shall be effective on the 1st day of the following taxable year.

(C) Revocation may specify prospective date. If the revocation specifies a date for revocation which is on or after the day on which the revocation is made, the revocation shall be effective for taxable years beginning on and after the date so specified.

(2) By person ceasing to be qualifying vessel operator.

(A) In general. An election under subsection (a) shall be terminated whenever (at any time on or after the 1st day of the 1st taxable year for which the corporation is an electing corporation) such corporation ceases to be a qualifying vessel operator.

(B) When effective. Any termination under this paragraph shall be effective on and after the date of cessation.

(C) Annualization. The Secretary shall prescribe such annualization and other rules as are appropriate in the case of a termination under this paragraph.

(e) Election after termination.

If a qualifying vessel operator has made an election under subsection (a) and if such election has been terminated under subsection (d), such operator (and any successor operator) shall not be eligible to make an election under subsection (a) for any taxable year before its 5th taxable year which begins after the 1st taxable year for which such termination is effective, unless the Secretary consents to such election.

In **2005,** P.L. 109-135, Sec. 403(g)(4), added "on or" after "only if made" in subsec. (b), effective for tax. yrs. begin. after 10/22/2004 as if included in Sec. 248 of the American Jobs Creation Act of 2004, P.L. 108-357.

In **2004,** P.L. 108-357, Sec. 248(a), added Code Sec. 1354, effective for tax. yrs. begin. after 10/22/2004.

Sec. 1355. Definitions and special rules.

(a) Definitions.

For purposes of this subchapter—

(1) Electing corporation. The term "electing corporation" means any corporation for which an election is in effect under this subchapter.

(2) Electing group; controlled group.

(A) Electing group. The term "electing group" means a controlled group of which one or more members is an electing corporation.

(B) Controlled group. The term "controlled group" means any group which would be treated as a single employer under subsection (a) or (b) of section 52 if paragraphs (1) and (2) of section 52(a) did not apply.

(3) Qualifying vessel operator. The term "qualifying vessel operator" means any corporation—

(A) who operates one or more qualifying vessels, and

(B) who meets the shipping activity requirement in subsection (c).

(4) Qualifying vessel. The term "qualifying vessel" means a self-propelled (or a combination self-propelled and non-self-propelled) United States flag vessel of not less than 6,000 deadweight tons used exclusively in the

United States foreign trade during the period that the election under this subchapter is in effect.

(5) United States flag vessel. The term "United States flag vessel" means any vessel documented under the laws of the United States.

(6) United States domestic trade. The term "United States domestic trade" means the transportation of goods or passengers between places in the United States.

(7) United States foreign trade. The term "United States foreign trade" means the transportation of goods or passengers between a place in the United States and a foreign place or between foreign places.

(b) Operating a vessel.

For purposes of this subchapter—

(1) In general. Except as provided in paragraph (2), a person is treated as operating any vessel during any period if—

(A)(i) such vessel is owned by, or chartered (including a time charter) to, the person, or

(ii) the person provides services for such vessel pursuant to an operating agreement, and

(B) such vessel is in use as a qualifying vessel during such period.

(2) Bareboat charters. A person is treated as operating and using a vessel that it has chartered out on bareboat charter terms only if—

(A)(i) the vessel is temporarily surplus to the person's requirements and the term of the charter does not exceed 3 years, or

(ii) the vessel is bareboat chartered to a member of a controlled group which includes such person or to an unrelated person who sub-bareboats or time charters the vessel to such a member (including the owner of the vessel), and

(B) the vessel is used as a qualifying vessel by the person to whom ultimately chartered.

(c) Shipping activity requirement.

For purposes of this section—

(1) In general. Except as otherwise provided in this subsection, a corporation meets the shipping activity requirement of this subsection for any taxable year only if the requirement of paragraph (4) is met for each of the 2 preceding taxable years.

(2) Special rule for 1st year of election. A corporation meets the shipping activity requirement of this subsection for the first taxable year for which the election under section 1354(a) is in effect only if the requirement of paragraph (4) is met for the preceding taxable year.

(3) Controlled groups. A corporation who is a member of a controlled group meets the shipping activity requirement of this subsection only if such requirement is met determined by treating all members of such group as 1 person.

(4) Requirement. The requirement of this paragraph is met for any taxable year if, on average during such year, at least 25 percent of the aggregate tonnage of qualifying vessels used by the corporation were owned by such corporation or chartered to such corporation on bareboat charter terms.

(d) Activities carried on partnerships, etc.

In applying this subchapter to a partner in a partnership—

(1) each partner shall be treated as operating vessels operated by the partnership,

(2) each partner shall be treated as conducting the activities conducted by the partnership, and

(3) the extent of a partner's ownership, charter, or operating agreement interest in any vessel operated by the partnership shall be determined on the basis of the partner's interest in the partnership.

A similar rule shall apply with respect to other pass-thru entities.

(e) Effect of temporarily ceasing to operate a qualifying vessel.

(1) In general. For purposes of subsections (b) and (c), an electing corporation shall be treated as continuing to use a qualifying vessel during any period of temporary cessation if the electing corporation gives timely notice to the Secretary stating—

(A) that it has temporarily ceased to operate the qualifying vessel, and

(B) its intention to resume operating the qualifying vessel.

(2) Notice. Notice shall be deemed timely if given not later than the due date (including extensions) for the corporation's tax return for the taxable year in which the temporary cessation begins.

(3) Period disregard in effect. The period of temporary cessation under paragraph (1) shall continue until the earlier of the date on which—

(A) the electing corporation abandons its intention to resume operation of the qualifying vessel, or

(B) the electing corporation resumes operation of the qualifying vessel.

(f) Effect of temporarily operating a qualifying vessel in the United States domestic trade.

(1) In general. For purposes of this subchapter, an electing corporation shall be treated as continuing to use a qualifying vessel in the United States foreign trade during any period of temporary use in the United States domestic trade if the electing corporation gives timely notice to the Secretary stating—

(A) that it temporarily operates or has operated in the United States domestic trade a qualifying vessel which had been used in the United States foreign trade, and

(B) its intention to resume operation of the vessel in the United States foreign trade.

(2) Notice. Notice shall be deemed timely if given not later than the due date (including extensions) for the corporation's tax return for the taxable year in which the temporary cessation begins.

(3) Period disregard in effect. The period of temporary use under paragraph (1) continues until the earlier of the date of which—

(A) the electing corporation abandons its intention to resume operations of the vessel in the United States foreign trade, or

(B) the electing corporation resumes operation of the vessel in the United States foreign trade.

(4) No disregard if domestic trade use exceeds 30 days. Paragraph (1) shall not apply to any qualifying vessel which is operated in the United States domestic trade for more than 30 days during the taxable year.

(g) Great Lakes domestic shipping to not disqualify vessel.

(1) In general. If the electing corporation elects (at such time and in such manner as the Secretary may require) to apply this subsection for any taxable year to any qualifying vessel which is used in qualified zone domestic trade during the taxable year—

(A) solely for purposes of subsection (a)(4), such use shall be treated as use in United States foreign trade (and not as use in United States domestic trade), and
(B) subsection (f) shall not apply with respect to such vessel for such taxable year.

(2) Effect of temporarily operating vessel in United States domestic trade. In the case of a qualifying vessel to which this subsection applies—

(A) In general. An electing corporation shall be treated as using such vessel in qualified zone domestic trade during any period of temporary use in the United States domestic trade (other than qualified zone domestic trade) if the electing corporation gives timely notice to the Secretary stating—

(i) that it temporarily operates or has operated in the United States domestic trade (other than qualified zone domestic trade) a qualifying vessel which had been used in the United States foreign trade or qualified zone domestic trade, and

(ii) its intention to resume operation of the vessel in the United States foreign trade or qualified zone domestic trade.

(B) Notice. Notice shall be deemed timely if given not later than the due date (including extensions) for the corporation's tax return for the taxable year in which the temporary cessation begins.

(C) Period disregard in effect. The period of temporary use under subparagraph (A) continues until the earlier of the date of which—

(i) the electing corporation abandons its intention to resume operations of the vessel in the United States foreign trade or qualified zone domestic trade, or

(ii) the electing corporation resumes operation of the vessel in the United States foreign trade or qualified zone domestic trade.

(D) No disregard if domestic trade use exceeds 30 days. Subparagraph (A) shall not apply to any qualifying vessel which is operated in the United States domestic trade (other than qualified zone domestic trade) for more than 30 days during the taxable year.

(3) Allocation of income and deductions to qualifying shipping activities. In the case of a qualifying vessel to which this subsection applies, the Secretary shall prescribe rules for the proper allocation of income, expenses, losses, and deductions between the qualified shipping activities and the other activities of such vessel.

(4) Qualified zone domestic trade. For purposes of this subsection—

(A) In general. The term "qualified zone domestic trade" means the transportation of goods or passengers between places in the qualified zone if such transportation is in the United States domestic trade.

(B) Qualified zone. The term "qualified zone" means the Great Lakes Waterway and the St. Lawrence Seaway.

(h) Regulations.
The Secretary shall prescribe such regulations as may be necessary or appropriate to carry out the purposes of this section.

In 2006, P.L. 109-432, Sec. 413(a), substituted "6,000" for "10,000 (6,000, in the case of taxable years beginning after December 31, 2005, and ending before January 1, 2011)" in para. (a)(4), effective for tax. yrs. begin. after 12/31/2005.
—P.L. 109-432, Sec. 415(a), added subsec. (g) and redesignated subsec. (g) as (h), effective for tax. yrs. begin. after 12/20/2006.
—P.L. 109-222, Sec. 205(a), added "(6,000, in the case of taxable years beginning after December 31, 2005, and ending before January 1, 2011)" after "10,000" in para. (a)(4), effective for tax. yrs. begin. after 12/31/2005.

In 2005, P.L. 109-135, Sec. 403(g)(1)(B), deleted para. (a)(8) . . . Sec. 403(g)(1)(C), amended para. (b)(1) . . . Sec. 403(g)(1)(D), amended para. (d)(3) . . . Sec. 403(g)(2), substituted "determined by treating all members of such group as 1 person." for "determined—(A) by treating all members of such group as 1 person, and (B) by disregarding vessel charters between members of such group." in para. (c)(3), effective for tax. yrs. begin. after 10/22/2004 as if included in Sec. 248 of the American Jobs Creation Act of 2004, P.L. 108-357.
Prior to deletion, para. (a)(8) read as follows:
"(8) Charter. The term 'charter' includes an operating agreement."
Prior to amendment, para. (b)(1) read as follows:
"(1) In general. Except as provided in paragraph (2), a person is treated as operating any vessel during any period if such vessel is—
"(A) owned by, or chartered (including a time charter) to, the person, and
"(B) is in use as a qualifying vessel during such period."
Prior to amendment, para. (d)(3) read as follows:
"(3) the extent of a partner's ownership or charter interest in any vessel owned by or chartered to the partnership shall be determined on the basis of the partner's interest in the partnership."
In 2004, P.L. 108-357, Sec. 248(a), added Code Sec. 1355, effective for tax. yrs. begin. after 10/22/2004.

Sec. 1356. Qualifying shipping activities.
(a) Qualifying shipping activities.
For purposes of this subchapter, the term "qualifying shipping activities" means—
(1) core qualifying activities,
(2) qualifying secondary activities, and
(3) qualifying incidental activities.
(b) Core qualifying activities.
For purposes of this subchapter, the term "core qualifying activities" means activities in operating qualifying vessels in United States foreign trade.
(c) Qualifying secondary activities.
For purposes of this section—
(1) In general. The term "qualifying secondary activities" means secondary activities but only to the extent that, without regard to this subchapter, the gross income derived by such corporation from such activities does not exceed 20 percent of the gross income derived by the corporation from its core qualifying activities.
(2) Secondary activities. The term "secondary activities" means—
(A) the active management or operation of vessels other than qualifying vessels in the United States foreign trade,
(B) the provision of vessel, barge, container, or cargo-related facilities or services to any person,
(C) other activities of the electing corporation and other members of its electing group that are an integral part of its business of operating qualifying vessels in United States foreign trade, including—
(i) ownership or operation of barges, containers, chassis, and other equipment that are the complement of, or used in connection with, a qualifying vessel in United States foreign trade,
(ii) the inland haulage of cargo shipped, or to be shipped, on qualifying vessels in United States foreign trade, and
(iii) the provision of terminal, maintenance, repair, logistical, or other vessel, barge, container, or cargo-related services that are an integral part of operating qualifying vessels in United States foreign trade, and
(D) such other activities as may be prescribed by the Secretary pursuant to regulations.
Such term shall not include any core qualifying activities.
(d) Qualifying incidental activities.
For purposes of this section, the term "qualified incidental activities" means shipping-related activities if—
(1) they are incidental to the corporation's core qualifying activities,
(2) they are not qualifying secondary activities, and

(3) without regard to this subchapter, the gross income derived by such corporation from such activities does not exceed 0.1 percent of the corporation's gross income from its core qualifying activities.

(e) Application of gross income tests in case of electing group.

In the case of an electing group, subsections (c)(1) and (d)(3) shall be applied as if such group were 1 entity, and the limitations under such subsections shall be allocated among the corporations in such group.

In 2005, P.L. 109-135, Sec. 403(g)(3)(A), deleted para. (c)(3) . . . Sec. 403(g)(3)(B), added a flush sentence at the end of para. (c)(2), effective for tax. yrs. begin. after 10/22/2004 as if included in Sec. 248 of the American Jobs Creation Act of 2004, P.L. 108-357.

Prior to deletion, para. (c)(3) read as follows:

"(3) Coordination with core activities.

"(A) In general. Such term shall not include any core qualifying activities.

"(B) Nonelecting corporations. In the case of a corporation (other than an electing corporation) which is a member of an electing group, any core qualifying activities of the corporation shall be treated as qualifying secondary activities (and not as core qualifying activities)."

In 2004, P.L. 108-357, Sec. 248(a), added Code Sec. 1356, effective for tax. yrs. begin. after 10/22/2004.

Sec. 1357. Items not subject to regular tax; depreciation; interest.

(a) Exclusion from gross income.

Gross income of an electing corporation shall not include its income from qualifying shipping activities.

(b) Electing group member.

Gross income of a corporation (other than an electing corporation) which is a member of an electing group shall not include its income from qualifying shipping activities conducted by such member.

(c) Denial of losses, deductions, and credits.

(1) **General rule.** Subject to paragraph (2), each item of loss, deduction (other than for interest expense), or credit of any taxpayer with respect to any activity the income from which is excluded from gross income under this section shall be disallowed.

(2) **Depreciation.**

(A) In general. Notwithstanding paragraph (1), the adjusted basis (for purposes of determining gain) of any qualifying vessel shall be determined as if the deduction for depreciation had been allowed.

(B) Method.

(i) In general. Except as provided in clause (ii), the straight-line method of depreciation shall apply to qualifying vessels the income from operation of which is excluded from gross income under this section.

(ii) Exception. Clause (i) shall not apply to any qualifying vessel which is subject to a charter entered into before the date of the enactment of this subchapter.

(3) **Interest.**

(A) In general. Except as provided in subparagraph (B), the interest expense of an electing corporation shall be disallowed in the ratio that the fair market value of such corporation's qualifying vessels bears to the fair market value of such corporation's total assets.

(B) Electing group. In the case of a corporation which is a member of an electing group, the interest expense of such corporation shall be disallowed in the ratio that the fair market value of such corporation's qualifying vessels bears to the fair market value of the electing groups total assets.

In 2004, P.L. 108-357, Sec. 248(a), added Code Sec. 1357, effective for tax. yrs. begin. after 10/22/2004.

Sec. 1358. Allocation of credits, income, and deductions.

(a) Qualifying shipping activities.

For purposes of this chapter, the qualifying shipping activities of an electing corporation shall be treated as a separate trade or business activity distinct from all other activities conducted by such corporation.

(b) Exclusion of credits or deductions.

(1) No deduction shall be allowed against the notional shipping income of an electing corporation, and no credit shall be allowed against the tax imposed by section 1352(a)(2).

(2) No deduction shall be allowed for any net operating loss attributable to the qualifying shipping activities of any person to the extent that such loss is carried forward by such person from a taxable year preceding the first taxable year for which such person was an electing corporation.

(c) Transactions not at arm's length.

Section 482 applies in accordance with this subsection to a transaction or series of transactions—

(1) as between an electing corporation and another person, or

(2) as between an [a] person's qualifying shipping activities and other activities carried on by it.

In 2004, P.L. 108-357, Sec. 248(a), added Code Sec. 1358, effective for tax. yrs. begin. after 10/22/2004.

Sec. 1359. Disposition of qualifying vessels.

(a) In general.

If any qualifying vessel operator sells or disposes of any qualifying vessel in an otherwise taxable transaction, at the election of such operator, no gain shall be recognized if any replacement qualifying vessel is acquired during the period specified in subsection (b), except to the extent that the amount realized upon such sale or disposition exceeds the cost of the replacement qualifying vessel.

(b) Period within which property must be replaced.

The period referred to in subsection (a) shall be the period beginning one year prior to the disposition of the qualifying vessel and ending—

(1) 3 years after the close of the first taxable year in which the gain is realized, or

(2) subject to such terms and conditions as may be specified by the Secretary, on such later date as the Secretary may designate on application by the taxpayer.

Such application shall be made at such time and in such manner as the Secretary may by regulations prescribe.

(c) Application of section to noncorporate operators.

For purposes of this section, the term "qualifying vessel operator" includes any person who would be a qualifying vessel operator were such person a corporation.

(d) Time for assessment of deficiency attributable to gain.

If a qualifying vessel operator has made the election provided in subsection (a), then—

(1) the statutory period for the assessment of any deficiency, for any taxable year in which any part of the gain is realized, attributable to such gain shall not expire prior to the expiration of 3 years from the date the Secretary is notified by such operator (in such manner as the Secretary may by regulations prescribe) of the replacement qualifying vessel or of an intention not to replace, and

(2) such deficiency may be assessed before the expiration of such 3-year period notwithstanding the provisions of

section 6212(c) or the provisions of any other law or rule of law which would otherwise prevent such assessment.

(e) Basis of replacement qualifying vessel.

In the case of any replacement qualifying vessel purchased by the qualifying vessel operator which resulted in the nonrecognition of any part of the gain realized as the result of a sale or other disposition of a qualifying vessel, the basis shall be the cost of the replacement qualifying vessel decreased in the amount of the gain not so recognized; and if the property purchased consists of more than one piece of property, the basis determined under this sentence shall be allocated to the purchased properties in proportion to their respective costs.

In 2004, P.L. 108-357, Sec. 248(a), added Code Sec. 1359, effective for tax. yrs. begin. after 10/22/2004.

Subchapter S.—Tax Treatment of S Corporations and Their Shareholders

Part
 I. In general.
 II. Tax treatment of shareholders.
 III. Special rules.
 IV. Definitions; miscellaneous.

In 1982, P.L. 97-354, Sec. 2, amended Subchapter S, for tax. yrs. begin. after 12/31/82.

Prior to amendment, Subchapter S read as follows:

"**Subchapter S.**—**Election of Certain Small Business Corporations as to Taxable Status**

"Sec.

"1371. Definitions.

"1372. Election by small business corporation.

"1373. Corporation undistributed taxable income taxed to shareholders.

"1374. Corporation net operating loss allowed to shareholders.

"1375. Special rules applicable to distributions of electing small business corporations.

"1376. Adjustment to basis of stock of, and indebtedness owing, shareholders.

"1377. Special rules applicable to earnings and profits of electing small business corporations.

"1378. Tax imposed on certain capital gains.

"1379. Certain qualified pensions, etc., plans.

In 1969, P.L. 91-172, Sec. 531(c), added item 1379.

In 1966, added item 1378.

In 1958, added subchapter S.

"SEC. 1371. DEFINITIONS.

"(a) *Small business corporation.*

"For purposes of this subchapter, the term 'small business corporation' means a domestic corporation which is not a member of an affiliated group (as defined in section 1504) and which does not—

"(1) have more than 25 shareholders;

"(2) have as a shareholder a person (other than an estate and other than a trust described in subsection (e)) who is not an individual;

"(3) have a nonresident alien as a shareholder; and

"(4) have more than one class of stock.

"(b) *Electing small business corporation.*

"For purposes of this subchapter, the term 'electing small business corporation' means, with respect to any taxable year, a small business corporation which has made an election under section 1372(a) which, under section 1372, is in effect for such taxable year.

"(c) *Stock owned by husband and wife.*

"For purposes of subsection (a)(1), husband and wife (and their estates) shall be treated as one shareholder.

"(d) *Ownership of certain stock.*

"For purposes of subsection (a), a corporation shall not be considered a member of an affiliated group at any time during any taxable year by reason of the ownership of stock in another corporation if such other corporation—

"(1) has not begun business at any time on or after the date of its incorporation and before the close of such taxable year, and

"(2) does not have taxable income for the period included within such taxable year.

"(e) *Certain trusts permitted as shareholders.*

"(1) In general. For purposes of subsection (a), the following trusts may be shareholders:

"(A) A trust all of which is treated (under subpart E of part I of subchapter J of this chapter) as owned by an individual who is a citizen or resident of the United States.

"(B) A trust which was described in subparagraph (A) immediately before the death of the deemed owner and which continues in existence after such death, but only for the 60-day period beginning on the day of the deemed owner's death. If a trust is described in the preceding sentence and if the entire corpus of the trust is includible in the gross estate of the deemed owner, the preceding sentence shall be applied by substituting '2-year period' for '60-day period'.

"(C) A trust with respect to stock transferred to it pursuant to the terms of a will, but only for the 60-day period beginning on the day on which such stock is transferred to it.

"(D) A trust created primarily to exercise the voting power of stock transferred to it.

"(2) Treatment as shareholders. For purposes of subsection (a)

"(A) In the case of a trust described in subparagraph (A) of paragraph (1), the deemed owner shall be treated as the shareholder.

"(B) In the case of a trust described in subparagraph (B) of paragraph (1), the estate of the deemed owner shall be treated as the shareholder.

"(C) In the case of a trust described in subparagraph (C) of paragraph (1), the estate of the testator shall be treated as the shareholder.

"(D) In the case of a trust described in subparagraph (D) of paragraph (1), each beneficiary of the trust shall be treated as a shareholder.

"(f) *Estate of individual in title 11 case may be shareholder.*

"For purposes of subsection (a)(2), the term 'estate' includes the estate of an individual in a case under title 11 of the United States Code.

"(g) *Special rule for qualified subchapter S trust.*

"(1) In general. In the case of a qualified subchapter S trust with respect to which a beneficiary makes an election under paragraph (2)—

"(A) such trust shall be treated as a trust described in subsection (e)(1)(A), and

"(B) for purposes of section 678(a), the beneficiary of such trust shall be treated as the owner of that portion of the trust which consists of stock in an electing small business corporation with respect to which the election under paragraph (2) is made.

"(2) Election.

"(A) In general. A beneficiary of a qualified subchapter S trust (or his legal representative) may elect to have this subsection apply.

"(B) Manner and time of election. An election under this paragraph shall be made

"(i) separately with respect to each electing small business corporation the stock of which is held by the trust,

"(ii) separately with respect to each successive income beneficiary of the trust, and

"(iii) in such manner and form, and at such time, as the Secretary may prescribe.

"(C) Election irrevocable. An election under this paragraph, once made, may be revoked only with the consent of the Secretary.

"(D) Grace period. An election under this paragraph shall be effective up to 60 days before the date of the election.

"(3) Qualified subchapter S trust. For purposes of this subsection, the term 'qualified subchapter S trust' means a trust—

"(A) which owns stock in 1 or more electing small business corporations,

"(B) all of the income (within the meaning of section 643(b)) of which is distributed (or required to be distributed) currently to 1 individual who is a citizen or resident of the United States, and

"(C) the terms of which require that

"(i) at any time, there shall be only one income beneficiary of the trust,

"(ii) any corpus distributed during the term of the trust may be distributed only to the current income beneficiary thereof,

"(iii) each income interest in the trust shall terminate on the earlier of the death of the income beneficiary or the termination of the trust, and

"(iv) upon the termination of the trust during the life of an income beneficiary, the trust shall distribute all of its assets to such income beneficiary.

"(4) Trust ceasing to be qualified. If a qualified subchapter S trust ceases to meet any requirement under paragraph (3), the provisions of this subsection shall not apply to such trust as of the date it ceases to meet such requirements."

In 1983, P.L. 97-448, Sec. 102(i)(1), amended subpara. (g)(3)(B), effective for tax. yrs. begin. after 12/31/81.

Prior to amendment, subpara. (g)(3)(B) read as follows: "(B) all of the income of which is distributed currently to one individual who is a citizen or resident of the United States, and"

In 1981, P.L. 97-34, Sec. 233(a), substituted "25 shareholders" for "15 shareholders" in para. (a)(1) . . . Sec. 234(a), amended subsec. (e) . . . Sec. 234(b), added subsec. (g), for tax. yrs. begin. after 12/31/81.

Prior to amendment subsec. (e) read as follows:

"(e) *Certain trusts permitted as shareholders.*

"For purposes of subsection (a), the following trusts may be shareholders:

"(1)(A) A trust of all which is treated as owned by the grantor (who is an individual who is a citizen or resident of the United States) under subpart E of part I of subchapter J of this chapter.

"(B) A trust which was described in subparagraph (A) immediately before the death of the grantor and which continues in existence after such death, but only for the 60-day period beginning on the day of the grantor's death. If a trust is described in the preceding sentence and if the entire corpus of the trust is includible in the gross estate of the grantor, the preceding sentence shall be applied by substituting '2-year period' for '60-day period' ".

In 1980, P.L. 96-589, Sec. 5(d), added subsec. (f), effective for any bankruptcy case begun on or after 10/1/79. Sec. 7(g) of this Act provides:

"(g) Definitions.

"For purposes of this section—

"(1) Bankruptcy case. The term 'bankruptcy case' means any case under title 11 of the United States Code (as recodified by P.L. 95-598).

"(2) Similar judicial proceeding. The term 'similar judicial proceeding' means a receivership, foreclosure, or similar proceeding in a Federal or State court (as modified by section 368(a)(3)(D) of the Internal Revenue Code of 1954)."

In 1978, P.L. 95-600, Sec. 341, amended para. (a)(1) . . . deleted subsec. (e) . . . redesignated subsec. (f) as subsec. (e) . . . substituted "subsection (e)" for "subsection (f)" in para. (a)(2), effective for tax. yrs. begin. after '78.

Prior to amendment para. (a)(1) read as follows:

"(1) have (except as provided in subsection (e)) more than 10 shareholders;"

Prior to amendment, subsec. (e) read as follows:

"*(e) Special shareholder rules.*

"(1) A small business corporation which has been an electing small business corporation for a period of five consecutive taxable years may not have more than 15 shareholders.

"(2) If, during the 5-year period set forth in paragraph (1), the number of shareholders of an electing small business corporation increases to an amount in excess of 10 (but not in excess of 15) solely by reason of additional shareholders who acquired their stock through inheritance, the corporation may have a number of additional shareholders equal to the number by which the inheriting shareholders cause the total number of shareholders of such corporation to exceed 10."

— P.L. 95-600, Sec. 342, amended subsec. (c) . . . added "In the case of a trust described in paragraph (1), the grantor shall be treated as the shareholder." after the first sentence in subsec. (e), as redesignated by Sec. 331(b)(1) [sic , 341(b)(1)] of this Act, effective for tax. yrs. begin. after '78.

Prior to amendment, subsec. (c) read as follows:

"*(c) Stock owned by husband and wife.*

"For purposes of subsection (a)(1) stock which—

"(1) is community property of a husband and wife (or the income from which is community income) under the applicable community property law of a State,

"(2) is held by a husband and wife as joint tenants, tenants by the entirety, or tenants in common,

"(3) was, on the date of death of a spouse, stock described in paragraph (1) or (2), and is, by reason of such death, held by the estate of the deceased spouse and the surviving spouse, or by the estate of both spouses (by reason of their deaths on the same date), in the same proportion as held by the spouses before such death, or

"(4) was, on the date of the death of a surviving spouse, stock described in paragraph (3), and is, by reason of such death, held by the estates of both spouses in the same proportion as held by the spouses before their deaths,

shall be treated as owned by one shareholder."

— P.L. 95-600, Sec. 701(y)(1), amended para. (e)(1), as redesignated by this Act, effective for tax. yrs. begin. after '76.

Prior to amendment, para. (e)(1) read as follows:

"(1) A trust all of which is treated as owned by the grantor under subpart E of part I of subchapter J of this chapter."

In 1976, P.L. 94-455, Sec. 902(a)(1), amended para. (a)(1), for tax. yrs. begin. after '76.

Prior to amendment, para. (a)(1) read as follows:

"(1) have more than 10 shareholders;"

— P.L. 94-455, Sec. 902(a)(2), added subsec. (e), for tax. yrs. begin. after '76.

— P.L. 94-455, Sec. 902(c)(1), amended subsec. (c), for tax. yrs. begin. after '76.

Prior to amendment, subsec. (c) read as follows:

"*(c) Stock owned by husband and wife.*

"For purposes of subsection (a)(1) stock which—

"(1) is community property of a husband and wife (or the income from which is community income) under the applicable community property law of a State, or

"(2) is held by a husband and wife as joint tenants, tenants by the entirety, or tenants in common,

shall be treated as owned by one shareholder."

— P.L. 94-455, Sec. 902(c)(2)(A), added subsec. (f), for tax. yrs. begin. after '76.

— P.L. 94-455, Sec. 902(c)(2)(B), substituted "(other than an estate and other than a trust described in subsection (f))" for "(other than an estate)" in para. (a)(2), for tax. yrs. begin. after '76.

In 1964, P.L. 88-272, Sec. 233, added subsec. (d), for tax. yrs. of corporations begin. after '62.

In 1962, P.L. 87-834, Sec. 23, provided for retroactive application of subsec. (c) to tax. yrs. begin. after '57 and before '60 subject to the following:

"*(b) Election and consent by corporations; consents by shareholders.*

"Subsection (a) shall apply with respect to any corporation and its shareholders only if, within one year after the date of the enactment of this Act [10/16/62]—

"(1) such corporation (in such manner as the Secretary of the Treasury or his delegate prescribes by regulations) elects to have the provisions of subsection (a) apply and consents to the application of subsection (c); and

"(2) each person who is a shareholder of such corporation on the date on which such corporation makes such election, and each person who was a shareholder of such corporation during any taxable year of such corporation beginning after December 31, 1957, and ending before the date of such election, consents (in such manner and at such time as the Secretary of the Treasury or his delegate prescribes by regulations) to such election and to the application of subsection (c).

"*(c) Tolling of statutes of limitations.*

"In any case in which a corporation makes an election under subsection (b)—

"(1) if the assessment of any deficiency against the corporation making such election, or any shareholder of such corporation who consents to such election, for any taxable year is prevented, at any time on or before the expiration of one year after the date of such election, by the operation of any law or rule of law, assessment of such deficiency may, nevertheless, be made, to the extent such deficiency is attributable to the application of subsection (a), at any time on or before the expiration of such one-year period; and

"(2) if credit or refund of any overpayment of tax by the corporation making such election, or any shareholder of such corporation who consents to such election, for any taxable year is prevented, at any time on or before the expiration of one year after the date of such election, by the operation of any law or rule of law, credit or refund of such overpayment may, nevertheless, be allowed or made, to the extent such overpayment is attributable to the application of subsection (a), if claim therefor is filed on or before the expiration of such one-year period."

In 1959, added subsec. (c), for tax. yrs. begin. after '59.

In 1958, P.L. 85-866, Sec. 64, added Code Secs. 1371 through 1377, for tax. yrs. begin. after '57.

"SEC. 1372. ELECTION BY SMALL BUSINESS CORPORATION.

"*(a) Eligibility.*

"Except as provided in subsection (f), any small business corporation may elect, in accordance with the provisions of this section, not to be subject to the taxes imposed by this chapter. Such election shall be valid only if all persons who are shareholders in such corporation on the day on which such election is made consent to such election.

"*(b) Effect.*

"If a small business corporation makes an election under subsection (a), then—

"(1) with respect to the taxable years of the corporation for which such election is in effect, such corporation shall not be subject to the taxes imposed by this chapter (other than as provided by section 58(d)(2) and by section 1378) and, with respect to such taxable years and all succeeding taxable years, the provisions of section 1377 shall apply to such corporation, and

"(2) with respect to the taxable years of a shareholder of such corporation in which or with which the taxable years of the corporation for which such election is in effect end, the provisions of sections 1373, 1374, and 1375 shall apply to such shareholder, and with respect to such taxable years and all succeeding taxable years, the provisions of section 1376 shall apply to such shareholder.

"*(c) When and how made.*

"(1) In general. An election under subsection (a) may be made by a small business corporation for any taxable year—

"(A) at any time during the preceding taxable year, or

"(B) at any time during the first 75 days of the taxable year.

"(2) Treatment of certain late elections. If—

"(A) a small business corporation makes an election under subsection (a) for any taxable year, and

"(B) such election is made after the first 75 days of the taxable year and on or before the last day of such taxable year,

then such election shall be treated as made for the following taxable year.

"(3) Manner of making election. An election under subsection (a) shall be made in such manner as the Secretary shall prescribe by regulations.

"*(d) Years for which effective.*

"An election under subsection (a) shall be effective for the taxable year of the corporation for which it is made and for all succeeding taxable years of the corporation, unless it is terminated, with respect to any such taxable year, under subsection (e).

"*(e) Termination.*

"(1) New shareholders.

"(A) An election under subsection (a) made by a small business corporation shall terminate if any person who was not a shareholder in such corporation on the day on which the election is made becomes a shareholder in such corporation and affirmatively refuses (in such manner as the Secretary may by regulations prescribe) to consent to such election on or before the 60th day after the day on which he acquires the stock.

"(B) If the person acquiring the stock is the estate of a decedent, the period under subparagraph (A) for affirmatively refusing to consent to the election shall expire on the 60th day after whichever of the following is the earlier:

"(i) The day on which the executor or administrator of the estate qualifies; or

"(ii) The last day of the taxable year of the corporation in which the decedent died.

"(C) Any termination of an election under subparagraph (A) by reason of the affirmative refusal of any person to consent to such election shall be effective for the taxable year of the corporation in which such person becomes a shareholder in the corporation (or, if later, the first taxable year for which such election would otherwise have been effective) and for all succeeding taxable years of the corporation.

"(2) Revocation. An election under subsection (a) made by a small business corporation may be revoked by it for any taxable year of the corporation after the first taxable year for which the election is effective. An election may be revoked only if all persons who are shareholders in the corporation on the day on which the revocation is made consent to the revocation. A revocation under this paragraph shall be effective—

"(A) for the taxable year in which made, if made before the close of the first month of such taxable year,

"(B) for the taxable year following the taxable year in which made, if made after the close of such first month,

and for all succeeding taxable years of the corporation. Such revocation shall be made in such manner as the Secretary shall prescribe by regulations.

"(3) Ceases to be small business corporation. An election under subsection (a) made by a small business corporation shall terminate if at any time—

"(A) after the first day of the first taxable year of the corporation for which the election is effective, if such election is made on or before such first day, or

"(B) after the day on which the election is made, if such election is made after such first day,

the corporation ceases to be a small business corporation (as defined in section 1371(a)). Such termination shall be effective for the taxable year of the corporation in which the corporation ceases to be a small business corporation and for all succeeding taxable years of the corporation.

"(4) Foreign income. An election under subsection (a) made by a small business corporation shall terminate if for any taxable year of the corporation for which the election is in effect, such corporation derives more than 80 percent of its gross receipts from sources outside the United States. Such termination shall be effective for the taxable year of the corporation in which it derives more than 80 percent of its gross receipts from sources outside the United States, and for all succeeding taxable years of the corporation.

"(5) Passive investment income.

"(A) Except as provided in subparagraph (B), an election under subsection (a) made by a small business corporation shall terminate if, for any taxable year of the corporation for which the election is in effect, such corporation has gross receipts more than 20 percent of which is passive investment income. Such termination shall be effective for the taxable year of the corporation in which it has gross receipts of such amount, and for all succeeding taxable years of the corporation.

"(B) Subparagraph (A) shall not apply with respect to a taxable year in which a small business corporation has gross receipts more than 20 percent of which is passive investment income, if—

"(i) such taxable year is the first taxable year in which the corporation commenced the active conduct of any trade or business or the next succeeding taxable year; and

"(ii) the amount of passive investment income for such taxable year is less than $3,000.

"(C) For purposes of this paragraph, the term 'passive investment income' means gross receipts derived from royalties, rents, dividends, interest, annuities, and sales or exchanges of stock or securities (gross receipts from such sales or exchanges being taken into account for purposes of this paragraph only to the extent of gains therefrom). Gross receipts derived from sales or exchanges of stock or securities for purposes of this paragraph shall not include amounts received by an electing small business corporation which are treated under section 331 (relating to corporate liquidations) as payments in exchange for stock where the electing small business corporation owned more than 50 percent of each class of the stock of the liquidating corporation.

"(f) Election after termination.

"If a small business corporation has made an election under subsection (a) and if such election has been terminated or revoked under subsection (e), such corporation (and any successor corporation) shall not be eligible to make an election under subsection (a) for any taxable year prior to its fifth taxable year which begins after the first taxable year for which such termination or revocation is effective, unless the Secretary consents to such election.

"(g) Consent to election by certain shareholders of stock held as community property.

"If a husband and wife owned stock which was community property (or the income from which was community income) under the applicable community property law of a State, and if either spouse filed a timely consent to an election under subsection (a) for a taxable year beginning before January 1, 1961, the time for filing the consent of the other spouse to such election shall not expire prior to May 15, 1961."

In **1984**, P.L. 98-369, Sec. 721(i), amended Sec. 6(b)(3) of P.L. 97-354, the effective date for para. (e)(5), by adding the last two sentences.

In **1982**, P.L. 97-354, Sec. 6(b)(3)(B), provides:

"(3) New passive income rules apply to taxable years beginning during 1982.—In the case of a taxable year beginning during 1982—

"(A) sections 1362(d)(3), 1366(f)(3), and 1375 of the Internal Revenue Code of 1954 (as amended by this Act) shall apply, and

"(B) section 1372(e)(5) of such Code (as in effect on the day before the date of the enactment of this Act) shall not apply.

The preceding sentence shall not apply in the case of any corporation which elects (at such time and in such manner as the Secretary of the Treasury or his delegate shall prescribe) to have such sentence not apply. Subsection (e) shall not apply to any termination resulting from an election under the preceding sentence."

In **1978**, P.L. 95-628, Sec. 5, made substantially the same amendments as Sec. 343 of P.L. 95-600, except that "having been made" was substituted for "as made" in subpara. (c)(2)(B) . . . "election was made" was substituted for "election is made" in subpara. (e)(1)(A) . . . "would have taken effect" was substituted for "would have been effective" in subpara. (e)(1)(C), for elections made after 1/9/79 for tax. yrs. begin. after 1/9/79. Sec. 5(d) of the Act provides:

"(d) *Retroactive application of preceding taxable year amendment.*—

"(1) In general.—If—

"(A) a small business corporation has treated itself in its return as an electing small business corporation under subchapter S of chapter 1 of the Internal Revenue Code of 1954 for any taxable year beginning before the date 60 days after the date of the enactment of this Act (hereinafter in this subsection referred to as the 'election year'),

"(B) such treatment was pursuant to an election which such corporation made during the taxable year immediately preceding the election year and which, but for this subsection, would not be effective, and

"(C) at such time and in such manner as the Secretary of the Treasury or his delegate may prescribe by regulations—

"(i) such corporation makes an election under this paragraph, and

"(ii) all persons (or their personal representatives) who were shareholders of such corporation at any time beginning with the first day of the election year and ending on the date of the making of such election consent to such election, consent to the application of the amendment made by subsection (a), and consent to the application of paragraph (3) of this subsection,

then paragraph (1) of the first sentence of section 1372(c) of such Code (as amended by subsection (a)) shall apply with respect to the taxable years referred to in paragraph (2) of this subsection.

"(2) Years to which amendment applies. In the case of an election under paragraph (1) by any corporation, the taxable years referred to in this paragraph are—

"(A) the election year,

"(B) all subsequent taxable years of such corporation, and

"(C) in the case of each person who was a shareholder of such corporation at any time during any taxable year described in subparagraph (A) or (B)—

"(i) the first taxable year of such person ending with or within a taxable year described in subparagraph (A) or (B), and

"(ii) all subsequent taxable years of such person.

"(3) Statute of limitations for assessment of deficiency.—In the assessment of any deficiency in income tax resulting from the filing of an election under paragraph (1) for a taxable year ending before the date of such filing would be prevented, but for the application of this paragraph, before the expiration of one year after the date of such filing by any law or rule of law, then such deficiency (to the extent attributable to such election) may be assessed at any time before the expiration of such one-year period not withstanding any law or rule of law which would otherwise prevent such assessment."

—P.L. 95-600, Sec. 343(a), amended subsec. (c), effective for tax. yrs. begin. after '78.

Prior to amendment, subsec. (c) read as follows:

"(c) *Where and how made.*

"An election under subsection (a) may be made by a small business corporation for any taxable year at any time during the first month of such taxable year, or at any time during the month preceding such first month. Such election shall be made in such manner as the Secretary shall prescribe by regulations."

—P.L. 95-600, Sec. 343(b)(1), amended the second sentence in subsec. (a), effective for tax. yrs. begin. after '78.

Prior to amendment, the second sentence of subsec. (a) read as follows:

"Such election shall be valid only if all persons who are shareholders in such corporation—

"(1) on the first day of the first taxable year for which such election is effective, if such election is made on or before such first day, or

"(2) on the day on which the election is made, if the election is made after such first day, consent to such election."

—P.L. 95-600, Sec. 343(b)(2), amended subpara. (e)(1)(A), effective for tax. yrs. begin. after '78.

Prior to amendment, subpara. (e)(1)(A) read as follows:

"(A) An election under subsection (a) made by a small business corporation shall terminate if any person who was not a shareholder in such corporation—

"(i) on the first day of the first taxable year of the corporation for which the election is effective, if such election is made on or before such first day, or

"(ii) on the day on which the election is made, if such election is made after such first day, becomes a shareholder in such corporation and affirmatively refuses (in such manner as the Secretary shall by regulations prescribe) to consent to such election on or before the 60th day after the day on which he acquires the stock."

—P.L. 95-600, Sec. 343(b)(3), added "(or, if later, the first taxable year for which such election would otherwise have been effective)" following "in the corporation" in subpara. (e)(1)(C), effective for tax. yrs. begin. after '78.

In **1976**, P.L. 94-455, Sec. 902(c)(3), amended para. (e)(1), for tax. yrs. begin. after '76.

Prior to amendment, para. (e)(1) read as follows:

"(1) New shareholders. An election under subsection (a) made by a small business corporation shall terminate if any person who was not a shareholder in such corporation—

"(A) on the first day of the first taxable year of the corporation for which the election is effective, if such election is made on or before such first day, or

"(B) on the day on which the election is made, if such election is made after such first day,

becomes a shareholder in such corporation and does not consent to such election within such time as the Secretary or his delegate shall prescribe by regulations. Such termination shall be effective for the taxable year of the corporation in which such person becomes a shareholder in the corporation and for all succeeding taxable years of the corporation."

—P.L. 94-455, Sec. 1901(a)(149), substituted "(other than as provided by section 58(d)(2) and by section 1378)" for "(other than the tax imposed by section 1378)" in para. (b)(1) . . . amended subsec. (c), for tax. yrs. begin. after '76.

Prior to amendment, subsec. (c) read as follows:

"(c) *Where and how made.*

"(1) In general. An election under subsection (a) may be made by a small business corporation for any taxable year at any time during the first month of such taxable year, or at any time during the month preceding such first month. Such election shall be made in such manner as the Secretary or his delegate shall prescribe by regulations.

"(2) Taxable years beginning before date of enactment. An election may be made under subsection (a) by a small business corporation for its first taxable year which begins after December 31, 1957, and on or before the date of the enactment of this subchapter, and ends after such date at any time—

"(A) within the 90-day period beginning on the day after the date of the enactment of this subchapter, or

Maximum tax Subchapter S

"(B) if its taxable year ends within such 90-day period, before the close of such taxable year.
An election may be made pursuant to this paragraph only if the small business corporation has been a small business corporation (as defined in section 1371(a)) on each day after the date of the enactment of this subchapter and before the day of such election."
—P.L. 94-455, Sec. 1906(b)(13)(A), substituted "Secretary" for "Secretary or his delegate" in subsecs. (e) and (f), for tax. yrs. begin. after '76.

In 1971, 1/12/71, added a new sentence to the end of para. (e)(5), effective for tax. yrs. of electing small business corporations begin. after 1/12/71. Such amendment shall also apply with respect to any tax. yr. end. before 1/7/70, but only if—
"(1) on such date the making of a refund or the allowance of a credit to the electing small business corporation is not prevented by any law or rule of law, and
"(2) within one year after the date of enactment of this Act and in such manner as the Secretary of the Treasury or his delegate prescribes by regulations—
"(A) the corporation elects to have such amendment so apply, and
"(B) all persons (or their personal representatives) who were shareholders of such corporation at any time during any taxable year beginning with the first taxable year to which this amendment applies and ending on or before the date of the enactment of this Act consent to such election and to the application of the amendment made by subsection (a).
"If the assessment of any deficiency in income tax resulting from the filing of such election for a taxable year ending before the date of such filing is prevented before the expiration of one year after the date of such filing by any law or rule of law, such deficiency (to the extent attributable to such election) may be assessed at any time prior to the expiration of such one-year period notwithstanding any law or rule of law which would otherwise prevent such assessment.
"If the election of a corporation under subsection (a) of section 1372 of the Internal Revenue Code of 1954 would have been terminated because of the application of subsection (e)(5) of such section (before the amendment made by subsection (a) of this section) but for the election by such corporation under paragraph (2) of subsection (b) (and the consent of shareholders under such paragraph), such election under section 1372(a) of such code shall not be treated as terminated for any year beginning before the date of the enactment of this Act as a result of—
"(1) such corporation filing its income tax return on a form 1120 (instead of a form 1120S), or
"(2) a new shareholder not consenting to such election of such corporation in accordance with the requirements of subsection (e)(1) of such section 1372."

In 1966, amended subsec. (b)(1), by inserting "(other than the tax imposed by section 1378)" for tax. yrs. of electing small business corporations begin. after 4/14/66, but such amendments shall not apply with respect to sales or exchanges occurring before 2/24/66.
—P.L. 89-389, Sec. 3, rewrote subsec. (e)(5), for tax. yrs. of electing small business corporations end. after 4/14/66. The amendment shall also apply to tax. yrs. begin. after '62 and end. on or before 4/14/66 "if (at such time and in such manner as the Secretary of the Treasury or his delegate prescribes by regulations)—
"(1) the corporation elects to have such amendment so apply, and
"(2) all persons (or their personal representatives) who were shareholders of such corporation at any time during any taxable year beginning after December 31, 1962, and ending on or before the date of the enactment of this Act consent to such election and to the application of the amendment made by subsection (a)."
Prior to amendment, Subsec. (e)(5) read as follows:
"(5) Personal holding company income. An election under subsection (a) made by a small business corporation shall terminate if, for any taxable year of the corporation for which the election is in effect, such corporation has gross receipts more than 20 percent of which is derived from royalties, rents, dividends, interest, annuities, and sales or exchanges of stock or securities (gross receipts from such sales or exchanges being taken into account for purposes of this paragraph only to the extent of gains therefrom). Such termination shall be effective for the taxable year of the corporation in which it has gross receipts of such amount, and for all succeeding taxable years of the corporation."

In 1961, added subsec. (g).
In 1958, P.L. 85-866, Sec. 64, added Code Sec. 1372, for tax. yrs. begin. after '57.

"Sec. 1373. Corporation Undistributed Taxable Income Taxed To Shareholders.
"(a) General rule.
"The undistributed taxable income of an electing small business corporation for any taxable year shall be included in the gross income of the shareholders of such corporation in the manner and to the extent set forth in this section.
"(b) Amount included in gross income.
"Each person who is a shareholder of an electing small business corporation on the last day of a taxable year of such corporation shall include in his gross income, for his taxable year in which or with which the taxable year of the corporation ends, the amount he would have received as a dividend, if on such last day there had been distributed pro rata to its shareholders by such corporation an amount equal to the corporation's undistributed taxable income for the corporation's taxable year. For purposes of this chapter, the amount so included shall be treated as an amount distributed as a dividend on the last day of the taxable year of the corporation.
"(c) Undistributed taxable income defined.
"For purposes of this section, the term 'undistributed taxable income' means taxable income (computed as provided in subsection (d)) minus the sum of (1) the taxes imposed by sections 56 and 1378(a) and (2) the amount of money distributed as dividends during the taxable year, to the extent that any such amount is a distribution out of earnings and profits of the taxable year as specified in section 316(a)(2).
"(d) Taxable income.
"For purposes of this subchapter, the taxable income of an electing small business corporation shall be determined without regard to—
"(1) the deduction allowed by section 172 (relating to net operating loss deduction), and
"(2) the deductions allowed by part VIII of subchapter B (other than the deduction allowed by section 248, relating to organization expenditures)."

In 1969, P.L. 91-172, Sec. 301(b)(10), substituted "taxes imposed by sections 56 and 1378(a)" for "tax imposed by section 1378(a)" in subsec. (c) for tax. year. end. after 12/31/69.

In 1966, amended subsec. (c) by inserting "the sum of (1) the tax imposed by section 1378(a) and (2)" for tax. yrs. of electing small business corporation begin. after 4/14/66 but such amendments shall not apply with respect to sales or exchanges occurring before 2/24/66.

In 1958, P.L. 85-866, Sec. 64, added Code Sec. 1373, for tax. yrs. begin. after '57.

"Sec. 1374. Corporation net operating loss allowed to shareholders.
"(a) General rule.
"A net operating loss of an electing small business corporation for any taxable year shall be allowed as a deduction from gross income of the shareholders of such corporation in the manner and to the extent set forth in this section.
"(b) Allowance of deduction.
"Each person who is a shareholder of an electing small business corporation at any time during a taxable year of the corporation in which it has a net operating loss shall be allowed as a deduction from gross income, for his taxable year in which or with which the taxable year of the corporation ends (or for the final taxable year of a shareholder who dies before the end of the corporation's taxable year), an amount equal to his portion of the corporation's net operating loss (as determined under subsection (c)). The deduction allowed by this subsection shall, for purposes of this chapter, be considered as a deduction attributable to a trade or business carried on by the shareholder.
"(c) Determination of shareholder's portion.
"(1) In general. For purposes of this section, a shareholder's portion of the net operating loss of an electing small business corporation is his pro rata share of the corporation's net operating loss (computed as provided in section 172(c), except that the deductions provided in part VIII (except section 248) of subchapter B shall not be allowed) for his taxable year in which or with which the taxable year of the corporation ends. For purposes of this paragraph, a shareholder's pro rata share of the corporation's net operating loss is the sum of the portions of the corporation's daily net operating loss attributable on a pro rata basis to the shares held by him on each day of the taxable year. For purposes of the preceding sentence, the corporation's daily net operating loss is the corporation's net operating loss divided by the number of days in the taxable year.
"(2) Limitation. A shareholder's portion of the net operating loss of an electing small business corporation for any taxable year shall not exceed the sum of—
"(A) the adjusted basis (determined without regard to any adjustment under section 1376 for the taxable year) of the shareholder's stock in the electing small business corporation, determined as of the close of the taxable year of the corporation (or, in respect of stock sold or otherwise disposed of during such taxable year, as of the day before the day of such sale or other disposition), and
"(B) the adjusted basis (determined without regard to any adjustment under section 1376 for the taxable year) of any indebtedness of the corporation to the shareholder, determined as of the close of the taxable year of the corporation (or, if the shareholder is not a shareholder as of the close of such taxable year, as of the close of the last day in such taxable year on which the shareholder was a shareholder in the corporation)."

In 1976, P.L. 94-455, Sec. 1901(a)(150), added the last sentence in subsec. (b) . . . deleted subsec. (d), for tax. yrs. begin. after '76.
Prior to amendment, subsec. (d) read as follows:
"(d) Application with other provisions.
"(1) In general. The deduction allowed by subsection (b) shall, for purposes of this chapter, be considered as a deduction attributable to a trade or business carried on by the shareholder.
"(2) Adjustment of net operating loss carrybacks and carryovers of shareholders. For the purposes of determining under section 172, the net operating loss carrybacks to taxable years beginning before January 1, 1958, from a taxable year of the shareholder for which he is allowed a deduction under subsection (b), such deduction shall be disregarded in determining the net operating loss for such taxable year. In the case of a net operating loss for a taxable year in which a shareholder is allowed a deduction under subsection (b), the determination of the portion of such loss which may be carried to subsequent years shall be made without regard to the preceding sentence and in accordance with section 172(b)(2), but the sum of the taxable incomes for taxable years beginning before January 1, 1958, shall be deemed not to exceed the amount of the net operating loss determined with the application of the preceding sentence."

In 1962, P.L. 87-834, Sec. 30, provided that: "The amendment made in subsec. (b) by P.L. 86-376 in '59 shall take effect on 9/2/58."

In 1959, inserted "(or for the final taxable year of a shareholder who dies before the end of the corporation's taxable year)" following "the taxable year of the corporation ends" in subsec. (b), effect. 9/24/59.

In 1958, P.L. 85-866, Sec. 64, added Code Sec. 1374, for tax. yrs. begin. after '57.

"Sec. 1375. Special rules applicable to distributions of electing small business corporations.
"(a) Capital gains.

2,837

"(1) Treatment in hands of shareholders. The amount includible in the gross income of a shareholder as dividends (including amounts treated as dividends under section 1373(b)) from an electing small business corporation during any taxable year of the corporation, to the extent that such amount is a distribution of property out of earnings and profits of the taxable year as specified in section 316(a)(2), shall be treated as a long-term capital gain to the extent of the shareholder's pro rata share of the corporation's net capital gain for such taxable year. For purposes of this paragraph, such net capital gain shall be deemed not to exceed the corporation's taxable income (computed as provided in section 1373(d)) for the taxable year.

"(2) Determination of shareholder's pro rata share. A shareholder's pro rata share of such gain for any taxable year shall be an amount which bears the same ratio to such gain as the amount of dividends described in paragraph (1) includible in the shareholder's gross income bears to the entire amount of dividends described in paragraph (1) includible in the gross income of all shareholders.

"(3) Reduction for taxes imposed. For purposes of paragraphs (1) and (2), an electing small business corporation's net capital gain for a taxable year shall be reduced by an amount equal to the amount of the taxes imposed by sections 56 and 1378(a) on such corporation for such year.

"(b) Dividends not treated as such for certain purposes.

"The amount includible in the gross income of a shareholder as dividends from an electing small business corporation during any taxable year of the corporation (including any amount treated as a dividend under section 1373(b)) shall not be considered a dividend for purposes of section 37 or section 116 to the extent that such amount is a distribution of property out of earnings and profits of the taxable year as specified in section 316(a)(2). For purposes of this subsection, the earnings and profits of the taxable year shall be deemed not to exceed the corporation's taxable income (computed as provided in section 1373(d)) for the taxable year.

"(c) Treatment of family groups.

"Any dividend received by a shareholder from an electing small business corporation (including any amount treated as a dividend under section 1373(b)) may be apportioned or allocated by the Secretary between or among shareholders of such corporation who are members of such shareholder's family (as defined in section 704(e)(3)), if he determines that such apportionment or allocation is necessary in order to reflect the value of services rendered to the corporation by such shareholders.

"(d) Distributions of undistributed taxable income previously taxed to shareholders.

"(1) Distributions not considered as dividends. An electing small business corporation may distribute, in accordance with regulations prescribed by the Secretary, to any shareholder all or any portion of the shareholder's net share of the corporation's undistributed taxable income for taxable years prior to the taxable year in which such distribution is made. Any such distribution shall, for purposes of this chapter, be considered a distribution which is not a dividend, but the earnings and profits of the corporation shall not be reduced by reason of any such distribution.

"(2) Shareholder's net share of undistributed taxable income. For purposes of this subsection, a shareholder's net share of the undistributed taxable income of an electing small business corporation is an amount equal to—

"(A) the sum of the amounts included in the gross income of the shareholder under section 1373(b) for all prior taxable years (excluding any taxable year to which the provisions of this section do not apply and all taxable years preceding such year), reduced by

"(B) the sum of—

"(i) the amounts allowable under section 1374(b) as a deduction from gross income of the shareholder for all prior taxable years (excluding any taxable year to which the provisions of the section do not apply and all taxable years preceding such year), and

"(ii) all amounts previously distributed during the taxable year and all prior taxable years (excluding any taxable year to which the provisions of this section do not apply and all taxable years preceding such year) to the shareholder which under subsection (f) or paragraph (1) of this subsection were considered distributions which were not dividends.

"(f) Distributions within 2½-month period after close of taxable year.

"(1) Distributions considered as distributions of undistributed taxable income.

"Any distribution of money made by a corporation after the close of a taxable year with respect to which it was an electing small business corporation and on or before the 15th day of the third month following the close of such taxable year to a person who was a shareholder of such corporation at the close of such taxable year shall be treated as a distribution of the corporation's undistributed taxable income for such year, to the extent such distribution (when added to the sum of all prior distributions of money made to such person by such corporation following the close of such year) does not exceed such person's share of the corporation's undistributed taxable income for such year. Any distribution so treated shall, for purposes of this chapter, be considered a distribution which is not a dividend, and the earnings and profits of the corporation shall not be reduced by reason of such distribution.

"(2) Share of undistributed taxable income. For purposes of paragraph (1), a person's share of a corporation's undistributed taxable income for a taxable year is the amount required to be included in his gross income under section 1373(b) as a shareholder of such corporation for his taxable year in which or with which the taxable year of the corporation ends."

In 1978, P.L. 95-600, Sec. 703(j)(6), substituted "such gain" for "such excess" each place it appeared in para. (a)(2), effective 10/4/76.

In 1976, P.L. 94-455, Sec. 1901(a)(151), substituted "not treated as such for certain purposes" for "received credit not allowed" in the heading of subsec. (b) . . . deleted para. (f)(3), for tax. yrs. begin. after '76.

Prior to amendment, para. (f)(3) read as follows:

"(3) Election under subsection (e). Paragraph (1) shall not apply to any distribution with respect to which an election under subsection (e) applies."

—P.L. 94-455, Sec. 1901(b)(33)(Q), substituted "the corporation's net capital gain" for "the excess of the corporation's net long-term capital gain over its net short-term capital loss" following "the shareholder's pro rata share of" in para. (a)(1) . . . substituted "such net capital gain" for "such excess" following "For purposes of this paragraph," in the second sentence of para. (a)(1) . . . substituted "an electing small business corporation's net capital gain" for "the excess of an electing small business corporation's net long-term capital gain over its short-term capital loss" following "paragraphs (1) and (2)," in para. (a)(3), for tax. yrs. begin. after '76.

—P.L. 94-455, Sec. 1906(b)(13)(A), substituted "Secretary" for "Secretary or his delegate" in subsecs. (c) and (d), for tax. yrs. begin. after '76.

In 1969, P.L. 91-172, Sec. 301(b)(11), substituted "taxes imposed" for "tax imposed by section 1378" in the heading of subsec. (a)(3); and substituted "taxes imposed by sections 56 and 1378(a) on" for "tax imposed by subsec. (a)(3)", for tax. yrs. end. after 12/31/69.

In 1966, added subsec. (a)(3), for tax. yrs. of electing small business corporations begin. after 4/14/66, but such amendments shall not apply with respect to sales or exchanges occurring before 2/24/66.

—repealed subsec. (e), for distributions after 4/14/66.

Prior to repeal, subsec. (e) read as follows:

"(e) Certain distributions after close of taxable year.

"(1) In general. For purposes of this chapter, if—

"(A) a corporation makes a distribution of money to its shareholders on or before the 15th day of the third month following the close of a taxable year with respect to which it was an electing small business corporation, and

"(B) such distribution is made pursuant to a resolution of the board of directors of the corporation, adopted before the close of such taxable year, to distribute to its shareholders all or part of the proceeds of one or more sales of capital assets, or of property described in section 1231(b), made during such taxable year, such distribution shall, at the election of the corporation, be treated as a distribution of money made on the last day of such taxable year.

"(2) Shareholders. An election under paragraph (1) with respect to any distribution may be made by a corporation only if each person who is a shareholder on the day the distribution is received—

"(A) owns the same proportion of the stock of the corporation on such day as he owned on the last day of the taxable year of the corporation preceding the distribution, and

"(B) consents to such election at such time and in such manner as the Secretary or his delegate shall prescribe by regulations.

"(3) Manner and time of election. An election under paragraph (1) shall be made in such manner as the Secretary or his delegate shall prescribe by regulations. Such election shall be made not later than the time prescribed by law for filing the return for the taxable year during which the sale was made (including extensions thereof) except that, with respect to any taxable year ending on or before the date of the enactment of the Revenue Act of 1964, such election shall be made within 120 days after such date."

—added in subsec. (d)(2)(B)(ii) "subsection (f) or" and added subsec. (f) for distributions after 4/14/66 except that the amendments "shall also apply with respect to distributions of money (other than distributions with respect to which an election under section 1375(e) of the Internal Revenue Code of 1954 applies) made by a corporation on or before the date of the enactment of this Act and on or after the date of the first distribution of money during the taxable year designated by the corporation if—

"(A) such corporation elects to have such amendments apply to all such distributions made by it, and

"(B) except as otherwise provided by this subsection, all persons (or their personal representatives) who were shareholders of such corporation at any time on or after the date of such first distribution and before the date on which the corporation files the election with the Secretary of the Treasury or his delegate consent to such election and to the application of this subsection.

"(2) An election by a corporation under this subsection, and the consent thereto of the persons who are or were shareholders of such corporation, shall be made in such manner and within such time as the Secretary of the Treasury or his delegate prescribes by regulations, but the period for making such election shall not expire before one year after the date on which the regulations prescribed under this subsection are published in the Federal Register.

"(3) In applying paragraphs (1) and (2), the consent of a person (or his personal representative) shall not be required if, under regulations prescribed under this subsection, it is shown to the satisfaction of the Secretary of the Treasury or his delegate that the liability of such person for Federal income tax for any taxable year cannot be affected by the election of the corporation of which he is or was a shareholder.

"(4) In applying this subsection, the reference in section 1375(f) of the Internal Revenue Code of 1954 (as added by subsection (a)(1)) to the 15th day of the third month following the close of the taxable year shall be treated as referring to the 15th day of the fourth month following the close of the taxable year.

"(5) The statutory period for the assessment of deficiency for any taxable year against the corporation filing the election or any person consenting thereto, to the extent such deficiency is attributable to an election under this subsection, shall not expire before the latest day of the 2-year period beginning on the date on which the regulations prescribed under this subsection are published in the Federal Register; and such deficiency may be assessed at any time before the expiration of such 2-year period, notwithstanding any law or rule of law which would otherwise prevent such assessment.

Maximum tax Subchapter S

"(6) If—

"(A) a credit or refund of the amount of any overpayment for any taxable year attributable to an election under this subsection is not prevented, on the date of the enactment of this Act, by the operation of any law or rule of law, and

"(B) credit or refund of the amount of such overpayment is prevented, by the operation of any law or rule of law (other than chapter 74 of the Internal Revenue Code of 1954, relating to closing agreements and compromises), at any time on or before the expiration of the 2-year period beginning on the date on which the regulations prescribed under this subsection are published in the Federal Register, credit or refund of such overpayment may, nevertheless, be allowed or made, to the extent such overpayment is attributable to such election, if claim therefor is filed before the expiration of such 2-year period.

"(7) If—

"(A)(i) one or more consecutive distributions of money made by the corporation after the close of a taxable year and on or before the 15th day of the fourth month following the close of the taxable year were substantially the same in amount as the undistributed taxable income of such corporation for such year, and

"(ii) it is established to the satisfaction of the Secretary of the Treasury or his delegate that one or more distributions of money made by the corporation during the period described in clause (i) were intended to be distributions of the undistributed taxable income of such corporation for the taxable year preceding such period, and

"(B) credit or refund of the amount of any overpayment for the taxable year in which such distribution or distributions were received is prevented on the date of the enactment of this Act, by the operation of any law or rule of law (other than chapter 74 of the Internal Revenue Code of 1954, relating to closing agreements and compromises),

credit or refund of such overpayment may, nevertheless, be allowed or made, to the extent such overpayment is attributable to an election under this subsection, if claim therefor is filed before the expiration of the 2-year period beginning on the date on which the regulations prescribed under this subsection are published in the Federal Register.

"(8) No interest on any deficiency attributable to an election under this subsection shall be assessed or collected for any period before the expiration of the 2-year period beginning on the date on which the regulations prescribed under this subsection are published in the Federal Register. No interest on any overpayment attributable to an election under this subsection shall be allowed or paid for any period before the expiration of such 2-year period."

In 1964, P.L. 88-272, Sec. 201, deleted "section 34," preceding "section 37" in subsec. (b), for dividends received after '64, in tax. yrs. end. after '64 ... added subsec. (e), for corporation tax. yrs. begin. after '57.

In 1958, P.L. 85-866, Sec. 64, added Code Sec. 1375 for tax. yrs. begin. after '57.

"SEC. 1376. ADJUSTMENT TO BASIS OF STOCK OF, AND INDEBTEDNESS OWING, SHAREHOLDERS.

"(a) *Increase in basis of stock for amounts treated as dividends.*

"The basis of a shareholder's stock in an electing small business corporation shall be increased by the amount required to be included in the gross income of such shareholder under section 1373(b), but only to the extent to which such amount is included in his gross income in his return, increased or decreased by any adjustment of such amount in any redetermination of the shareholder's tax liability.

"(b) *Reduction in basis of stock and indebtedness for shareholder's portion of corporation net operating loss.*

"(1) Reduction in basis of stock. The basis of a shareholder's stock in an electing small business corporation shall be reduced (but not below zero) by an amount equal to the amount of his portion of the corporation's net operating loss for any taxable year attributable to such stock (as determined under section 1374(c)).

"(2) Reduction in basis of indebtedness. The basis of any indebtedness of an electing small business corporation to a shareholder of such corporation shall be reduced (but not below zero) by an amount equal to the amount of the shareholder's portion of the corporation's net operating loss for any taxable year (as determined under section 1374(c), but only to the extent that such amount exceeds the adjusted basis of the stock of such corporation held by the shareholder."

In 1958, P.L. 85-866, Sec. 64, added Code Sec. 1376, for tax. yrs. begin. after '57.

"SEC. 1377. SPECIAL RULES APPLICABLE TO EARNINGS AND PROFITS OF ELECTING SMALL BUSINESS CORPORATIONS.

"(a) *Reduction for undistributed taxable income.*

"The accumulated earnings and profits of an electing small business corporation as of the close of its taxable year shall be reduced to the extent that its undistributed taxable income for such year is required to be included in the gross income of the shareholders of such corporation under section 1373(b).

"(b) *Current earnings and profits not reduced by any amount not allowable as deduction.*

"The earnings and profits of an electing small business corporation for any taxable year (but not its accumulated earnings and profits) shall not be reduced by any amount which is not allowable as a deduction in computing its taxable income (as provided in section 1373(d)) for such taxable year.

"(c) *Earnings and profits not affected by net operating loss.*

"The earnings and profits and the accumulated earnings and profits of an electing small business corporation shall not be affected by any item of gross income or any deduction taken into account in determining the amount of any net operating loss (computed as provided in section 1374(c)) of such corporation.

"(d) *Distributions of undistributed taxable income previously taxed to shareholders.*

"For purposes of determining whether a distribution by an electing small business corporation constitutes a distribution of such corporation's undistributed taxable income previously taxed to shareholders (as provided for in section 1375(d)), the earnings and profits of such corporation for the taxable year in which the distribution is made shall be computed without regard to section 312(k). Such computation shall be made without regard to section 312(k) only for such purposes."

In 1976, P.L. 94-455, Sec. 902(b), added subsec. (d), for tax. yrs. begin. after '75. —P.L. 94-455, Sec. 1901(b)(32)(B)(iv), substituted "312(k)" for "312(m)" in subsec. (d), as previously amended by the Act, for tax. yrs. begin. after '76.

In 1958, P.L. 85-866, Sec. 64, added Code Sec. 1377, for tax. yrs. begin. after '57.

"SEC. 1378. TAX IMPOSED ON CERTAIN CAPITAL GAINS.

"(a) *General rule.*

"If for a taxable year of an electing small business corporation:

"(1) the net capital gain of such corporation exceeds $25,000, and exceeds 50 percent of its taxable income for such year, and

"(2) the taxable income of such corporation for such year exceeds $25,000, there is hereby imposed a tax (computed under subsection (b)) on the income of such corporation.

"(b) *Amount of tax.*

"The tax imposed by subsection (a) shall be the lower of—

"(1) an amount equal to the tax, determined as provided in section 1201(a), on the amount by which the net capital gain of the corporation for the taxable year exceeds $25,000, or

"(2) an amount equal to the tax which would be imposed by section 11 on the taxable income (computed as provided in section 1373(d)) of the corporation for the taxable year if the corporation was not an electing small business corporation. No credit shall be allowable under part IV of subchapter A of this chapter (other than under section 39) against the tax imposed by subsection (a).

"(c) *Exceptions.*

"(1) In general. Subsection (a) shall not apply to an electing small business corporation for any taxable year if the election under section 1372(a) which is in effect with respect to such corporation for such taxable year has been in effect for the 3 immediately preceding taxable years.

"(2) New corporations. Subsection (a) shall not apply to an electing small business corporation if—

"(A) it has been in existence for less than 4 taxable years, and

"(B) an election under section 1372(a) has been in effect with respect to such corporation for each of its taxable years.

"(3) Property with substituted basis. If—

"(A) but for paragraph (1) or (2), subsection (a) would apply for the taxable year,

"(B) any long-term capital gain is attributable to property acquired by the electing small business corporation during the period beginning 3 years before the first day of the taxable year and ending on the last day of the taxable year, and

"(C) the basis of such property is determined in whole or in part by reference to the basis of any property in the hands of another corporation which was not an electing small business corporation throughout all of the period described in subparagraph (B) before the transfer by such other corporation and during which such other corporation was in existence,

then subsection (a) shall apply for the taxable year, but the amount of the tax determined under subsection (b) shall not exceed a tax, determined as provided in section 1201(a), on the net capital gain attributable to property acquired as provided in subparagraph (B) and having a basis described in subparagraph (C)."

In 1976, P.L. 94-455, Sec. 1901(a)(152), deleted the last sentence in subsec. (b), for tax. yrs. begin. after '76.

Prior to amendment, the last sentence read as follows:

"In applying section 1201(a)(1)(A) and (B) for purposes of paragraph (1), the $25,000 limitation shall first be deducted from the amount (determined without regard to this subsection) subject to tax in accordance with section 1201(a)(1)(B), to the extent thereof, and then from the amount (determined without regard to this subsection) subject to tax in accordance with section 1201(a)(1)(A)."

—P.L. 94-455, Sec. 1901(b)(33)(R), substituted "the net capital gain" for "the excess of the net long-term capital gain over the net short-term capital loss" following "(1)" in para. (a)(1) ... following "on the amount by which" in para. (b)(1) ... following "as provided in section 1201(a), on the" in para. (c)(3), for tax. yrs. begin. after '76.

In 1969, P.L. 91-172, Sec. 511(c)(4), substituted "the tax, determined as provided in section 1201(a), on" in subsec. (b)(1) ... added a new sentence to the end of subsec. (b) ... substituted "a tax, determined as provided in section 1201(a), on" for "25 percent of" in subsec. (c)(3), for tax. yrs. begin. after 12/31/69.

In 1966, added Code Sec. 1378, for tax. yrs. of electing small business corporations begin. after 4/14/66 but such amendments shall not apply with respect to sales or exchanges occurring before 2/24/66.

"SEC. 1379. CERTAIN QUALIFIED PENSION, ETC., PLANS.

"(a) *Additional requirements for qualification of stock bonus or profit-sharing plans.*

"A trust forming part of a stock bonus or profit-sharing plan which provides contributions or benefits for employees some or all of whom are shareholder-employees shall not constitute a qualified trust under section 401 (relating to qualified pension, profit-sharing, and stock bonus plans) unless the plan of which such trust is a part provides that forfeitures attributable to contributions deductible under section 404(a)(3) for any taxable year (beginning after December 31, 1970) of the employer with respect to which it is an electing small business corporation may not inure to the benefit of any individual who is a shareholder-employee for such taxable year. A plan shall be considered as satisfying the requirement of this subsection for the period beginning with the first day of a taxable year and ending

2,839

with the 15th day of the third month following the close of such taxable year, if all the provisions of the plan which are necessary to satisfy this requirement are in effect by the end of such period and have been made effective for all purposes with respect to the whole of such period.

"*(b) Taxability of shareholder-employee beneficiaries.*

"(1) Inclusion of excess contributions in gross income. Notwithstanding the provisions of section 402 (relating to taxability of beneficiary of employees' trust), section 403 (relating to taxation of employee annuities), or section 405(d) (relating to taxability of beneficiaries under qualified bond purchase plans), an individual who is a shareholder-employee of an electing small business corporation shall include in gross income, for his taxable year in which or with which the taxable year of the corporation ends, the excess of the amount of contributions paid on his behalf which is deductible under section 404(a)(1), (2), or (3) by the corporation for its taxable year over the lesser of—

"(A) 15 percent of the compensation received or accrued by him from such corporation during its taxable year, or

"(B) $15,000.

"(2) Treatment of amounts included in gross income. Any amount included in the gross income of a shareholder-employee under paragraph (1) shall be treated as consideration for the contract contributed by the shareholder-employee for purposes of section 72 (relating to annuities).

"(3) Deduction for amounts not received as benefits. If—

"(A) amounts are included in the gross income of an individual under paragraph (1), and

"(B) the rights of such individual (or his beneficiaries) under the plan terminate before payments under the plan which are excluded from gross income equal the amounts included in gross income under paragraph (1),

then there shall be allowed as a deduction, for the taxable year in which such rights terminate, an amount equal to the excess of the amounts included in gross income under paragraph (1) over such payments.

"*(c) Carryover of amounts deductible.*

No amount deductible shall be carried forward under the second sentence of section 404(a)(3)(A) (relating to limits on deductible contributions under stock bonus and profit-sharing trusts) to a taxable year of a corporation with respect to which it is not an electing small business corporation from a taxable year (beginning after December 31, 1970) with respect to which it is an electing small business corporation.

"*(d) Shareholder-employee.*

For purposes of this section, the term 'shareholder-employee' means an employee or officer of an electing small business corporation who owns (or is considered as owning within the meaning of section 318(a)(1), on any day during the taxable year of such corporation, more than 5 percent of the outstanding stock of the corporation."

In 1983, P.L. 97-448, Sec. 103(d)(3), corrected Sec. 312(f)(1) of P.L. 97-34, the effective date for changes made by Sec. 312(c)(6) of P.L. 97-34 to "taxable years beginning after December 31, 1981" from "to plans which include employees within the meaning of section 401(c)(1) with respect to taxable years beginning after 12/31/81" [see below].

In 1982, P.L. 97-354, Sec. 6(a), provides that the amendments to Subchapter S by Sec. 2 of this Act apply to tax. yrs. begin. after 12/31/82, but Sec. 6(b)(1) of this Act provides that Code Sec. 1379 as in effect 10/19/82 remain in effect for yrs. begin. before 1/1/84.

—P.L. 97-248, Sec. 238(c)(1), deleted subsecs. (a) and (b) . . . Sec. 238(c)(2), redesignated subsecs. (c) and (d) as subsecs. (a) and (b), for yrs. begin. after 12/31/83.

Prior to amendment, subsecs. (a) and (b) read as follows:

"*(a) Additional requirements for qualification of stock bonus or profit-sharing plans.*

"A trust forming part of a stock bonus or profit-sharing plan which provides contributions or benefits for employees some or all of whom are shareholder-employees shall not constitute a qualified trust under section 401 (relating to qualified pension, profit-sharing, and stock bonus plans) unless the plan of which such trust is a part provides that forfeitures attributable to contributions deductible under section 404(a)(3) for any taxable year (beginning after December 31, 1970) of the employer with respect to which it is an electing small business corporation may not inure to the benefit of any individual who is a shareholder-employee for such taxable year. A plan shall be considered as satisfying the requirement of this subsection for the period beginning with the first day of a taxable year and ending with the 15th day of the third month following the close of such taxable year, if all the provisions of the plan which are necessary to satisfy this requirement are in effect by the end of such period and have been made effective for all purposes with respect to the whole of such period.

"*(b) Taxability of shareholder-employee beneficiaries.*

"(1) Inclusion of excess contributions in gross income. Notwithstanding the provisions of section 402 (relating to taxability of beneficiary of employees' trust), section 403 (relating to taxation of employee annuities), or section 405(d) (relating to taxability of beneficiaries under qualified bond purchase plans), an individual who is a shareholder-employee of an electing small business corporation shall include in gross income, for his taxable year in which or with which the taxable year of the corporation ends, the excess of the amount of contributions paid on his behalf which is deductible under section 404(a)(1), (2), or (3) by the corporation for its taxable year over the lesser of—

"(A) 15 percent of the compensation received or accrued by him from such corporation during its taxable year, or

"(B) $15,000.

"(2) Treatment of amounts included in gross income. Any amount included in the gross income of a shareholder-employee under paragraph (1) shall be treated as consideration for the contract contributed by the shareholder-employee for purposes of section 72 (relating to annuities).

"(3) Deduction for amounts not received as benefits. If—

"(A) amounts are included in the gross income of an individual under paragraph (1), and

"(B) the rights of such individual (or his beneficiaries) under the plan terminate before payments under the plan which are excluded from gross income equal the amounts included in gross income under paragraph (1),

then there shall be allowed as a deduction, for the taxable year in which such rights terminate, an amount equal to the excess of the amounts included in gross income under paragraph (1) over such payments."

In 1981, P.L. 97-34, Sec. 312(c)(6), substituted "$15,000" for "$7,500" in subpara. (b)(1)(B), for tax. yrs. begin. after 12/31/81.

In 1974, P.L. 93-406, Sec. 2001(b)(1), substituted "15 percent" for "10 percent" in subpara. (b)(1)(A), effective for tax. yrs. begin. after 12/31/73.

—P.L. 93-406, Sec. 2001(b)(2), substituted "$7,500" for "$2,500" in subpara. (b)(1)(B), effective for tax. yrs. begin. after 12/31/73.

In 1969, P.L. 91-172, Sec. 531(a), added Code Sec. 1379, for tax. yrs. of electing small business corporations begin. after 12/31/70.

PART I.— IN GENERAL

Sec.

1361. S corporation defined.

1362. Election; revocation; termination.

1363. Effect of election on corporation.

Sec. 1361. S corporation defined.

(a) S corporation defined.

(1) In general. For purposes of this title, the term "S corporation" means, with respect to any taxable year, a small business corporation for which an election under section 1362(a) is in effect for such year.

(2) C corporation. For purposes of this title, the term "C corporation" means, with respect to any taxable year, a corporation which is not an S corporation for such year.

(b) Small business corporation.

(1) In general. For purposes of this subchapter, the term "small business corporation" means a domestic corporation which is not an ineligible corporation and which does not—

(A) have more than 100 shareholders,

(B) have as a shareholder a person (other than an estate, a trust described in subsection (c)(2), or an organization described in subsection (c)(6)) who is not an individual,

(C) have a nonresident alien as a shareholder, and

(D) have more than 1 class of stock.

(2) Ineligible corporation defined. For purposes of paragraph (1), the term "ineligible corporation" means any corporation which is—

(A) a financial institution which uses the reserve method of accounting for bad debts described in section 585,

(B) an insurance company subject to tax under subchapter L,

(C) a corporation to which an election under section 936 applies, or

(D) a DISC or former DISC.

(3) Treatment of certain wholly owned subsidiaries.

(A) In general. Except as provided in regulations prescribed by the Secretary, for purposes of this title—

(i) a corporation which is a qualified subchapter S subsidiary shall not be treated as a separate corporation, and

(ii) all assets, liabilities, and items of income, deduction, and credit of a qualified subchapter S subsidiary shall be treated as assets, liabilities, and such items (as the case may be) of the S corporation.

(B) Qualified subchapter S subsidiary. For purposes of this paragraph, the term "qualified subchapter S subsid-

iary" means any domestic corporation which is not an ineligible corporation (as defined in paragraph (2)), if—
(i) 100 percent of the stock of such corporation is held by the S corporation, and
(ii) the S corporation elects to treat such corporation as a qualified subchapter S subsidiary.
(C) Treatment of terminations of qualified subchapter S subsidiary status.
(i) In general. For purposes of this title, if any corporation which was a qualified subchapter S subsidiary ceases to meet the requirements of subparagraph (B), such corporation shall be treated as a new corporation acquiring all of its assets (and assuming all of its liabilities) immediately before such cessation from the S corporation in exchange for its stock.
(ii) Termination by reason of sale of stock. If the failure to meet the requirements of subparagraph (B) is by reason of the sale of stock of a corporation which is a qualified subchapter S subsidiary, the sale of such stock shall be treated as if—
(I) the sale were a sale of an undivided interest in the assets of such corporation (based on the percentage of the corporation's stock sold), and
(II) the sale were followed by an acquisition by such corporation of all of its assets (and the assumption by such corporation of all of its liabilities) in a transaction to which section 351 applies.
(D) Election after termination. If a corporation's status as a qualified subchapter S subsidiary terminates, such corporation (and any successor corporation) shall not be eligible to make—
(i) an election under subparagraph (B)(ii) to be treated as a qualified subchapter S subsidiary, or
(ii) an election under section 1362(a) to be treated as an S corporation,
before its 5th taxable year which begins after the 1st taxable year for which such termination was effective, unless the Secretary consents to such election.
(E) Information returns. Except to the extent provided by the Secretary, this paragraph shall not apply to part III of subchapter A of chapter 61 (relating to information returns).

(c) Special rules for applying subsection (b).

(1) Members of a family treated as 1 shareholder.
(A) In general. For purposes of subsection (b)(1)(A), there shall be treated as one shareholder—
(i) a husband and wife (and their estates), and
(ii) all members of a family (and their estates).
(B) Members of a family. For purposes of this paragraph—
(i) In general. The term "members of a family" means a common ancestor, any lineal descendant of such common ancestor, and any spouse or former spouse of such common ancestor or any such lineal descendant.
(ii) Common ancestor. An individual shall not be considered to be a common ancestor if, on the applicable date, the individual is more than 6 generations removed from the youngest generation of shareholders who would (but for this subparagraph) be members of the family. For purposes of the preceding sentence, a spouse (or former spouse) shall be treated as being of the same generation as the individual to whom such spouse is (or was) married.
(iii) Applicable date. The term "applicable date" means the latest of—
(I) the date the election under section 1362(a) is made,
(II) the earliest date that an individual described in clause (i) holds stock in the S corporation, or
(III) October 22, 2004.
(C) Effect of adoption, etc. Any legally adopted child of an individual, any child who is lawfully placed with an individual for legal adoption by the individual, and any eligible foster child of an individual (within the meaning of section 152(f)(1)(C)), shall be treated as a child of such individual by blood.

(2) Certain trusts permitted as shareholders.
(A) In general. For purposes of subsection (b)(1)(B), the following trusts may be shareholders:
(i) A trust all of which is treated (under subpart E of part I of subchapter J of this chapter) as owned by an individual who is a citizen or resident of the United States.
(ii) A trust which was described in clause (i) immediately before the death of the deemed owner and which continues in existence after such death, but only for the 2-year period beginning on the day of the deemed owner's death.
(iii) A trust with respect to stock transferred to it pursuant to the terms of a will, but only for the 2-year period beginning on the day on which such stock is transferred to it.
(iv) A trust created primarily to exercise the voting power of stock transferred to it.
(v) An electing small business trust.
(vi) In the case of a corporation which is a bank (as defined in section 581) or a depository institution holding company (as defined in section 3(w)(1) of the Federal Deposit Insurance Act (12 U.S.C. 1813(w)(1)), a trust which constitutes an individual retirement account under section 408(a), including one designated as a Roth IRA under section 408A, but only to the extent of the stock held by such trust in such bank or company as of the date of the enactment of this clause.
This subparagraph shall not apply to any foreign trust.
(B) Treatment as shareholders.—For purposes of subsection (b)(1)—
(i) In the case of a trust described in clause (i) of subparagraph (A), the deemed owner shall be treated as the shareholder.
(ii) In the case of a trust described in clause (ii) of subparagraph (A), the estate of the deemed owner shall be treated as the shareholder.
(iii) In the case of a trust described in clause (iii) of subparagraph (A), the estate of the testator shall be treated as the shareholder.
(iv) In the case of a trust described in clause (iv) of subparagraph (A), each beneficiary of the trust shall be treated as a shareholder.
(v) In the case of a trust described in clause (v) of subparagraph (A), each potential current beneficiary of such trust shall be treated as a shareholder; except that, if for any period there is no potential current beneficiary of such trust, such trust shall be treated as the shareholder during such period.
(vi) In the case of a trust described in clause (vi) of subparagraph (A), the individual for whose benefit the trust was created shall be treated as a shareholder.

(3) Estate of individual in bankruptcy may be shareholder. For purposes of subsection (b)(1)(B), the term "estate" includes the estate of an individual in a case under title 11 of the United States Code.

(4) **Differences in common stock voting rights disregarded.** For purposes of subsection (b)(1)(D), a corporation shall not be treated as having more than 1 class of stock solely because there are differences in voting rights among the shares of common stock.

(5) **Straight debt safe harbor.**

(A) In general. For purposes of subsection (b)(1)(D), straight debt shall not be treated as a second class of stock.

(B) Straight debt defined. For purposes of this paragraph, the term "straight debt" means any written unconditional promise to pay on demand or on a specified date a sum certain in money if—

(i) the interest rate (and interest payment dates) are not contingent on profits, the borrower's discretion, or similar factors,

(ii) there is no convertibility (directly or indirectly) into stock, and

(iii) the creditor is an individual (other than a nonresident alien), an estate, a trust described in paragraph (2), or a person which is actively and regularly engaged in the business of lending money.

(C) Regulations. The Secretary shall prescribe such regulations as may be necessary or appropriate to provide for the proper treatment of straight debt under this subchapter and for the coordination of such treatment with other provisions of this title.

(6) **Certain exempt organizations permitted as shareholders.** For purposes of subsection (b)(1)(B), an organization which is—

(A) described in section 401(a) or 501(c)(3), and

(B) exempt from taxation under section 501(a),

may be a shareholder in an S corporation.

(d) **Special rule for qualified subchapter S trust.**

(1) **In general.** In the case of a qualified subchapter S trust with respect to which a beneficiary makes an election under paragraph (2)—

(A) such trust shall be treated as a trust described in subsection (c)(2)(A)(i),

(B) for purposes of section 678(a), the beneficiary of such trust shall be treated as the owner of that portion of the trust which consists of stock in an S corporation with respect to which the election under paragraph (2) is made, and

(C) for purposes of applying sections 465 and 469 to the beneficiary of the trust, the disposition of the S corporation stock by the trust shall be treated as a disposition by such beneficiary.

(2) **Election.**

(A) In general. A beneficiary of a qualified subchapter S trust (or his legal representative) may elect to have this subsection apply.

(B) Manner and time of election.

(i) Separate election with respect to each corporation. An election under this paragraph shall be made separately with respect to each corporation the stock of which is held by the trust.

(ii) Elections with respect to successive income beneficiaries. If there is an election under this paragraph with respect to any beneficiary, an election under this paragraph shall be treated as made by each successive beneficiary unless such beneficiary affirmatively refuses to consent to such election.

(iii) Time, manner, and form of election. Any election, or refusal, under this paragraph shall be made in such manner and form, and at such time, as the Secretary may prescribe.

(C) Election irrevocable. An election under this paragraph, once made, may be revoked only with the consent of the Secretary.

(D) Grace period. An election under this paragraph shall be effective up to 15 days and 2 months before the date of the election.

(3) **Qualified subchapter S trust.** For purposes of this subsection, the term "qualified subchapter S trust" means a trust—

(A) the terms of which require that—

(i) during the life of the current income beneficiary, there shall be only 1 income beneficiary of the trust,

(ii) any corpus distributed during the life of the current income beneficiary may be distributed only to such beneficiary,

(iii) the income interest of the current income beneficiary in the trust shall terminate on the earlier of such beneficiary's death or the termination of the trust, and

(iv) upon the termination of the trust during the life of the current income beneficiary, the trust shall distribute all of its assets to such beneficiary, and

(B) all of the income (within the meaning of section 643(b)) of which is distributed (or required to be distributed) currently to 1 individual who is a citizen or resident of the United States.

A substantially separate and independent share of a trust within the meaning of section 663(c) shall be treated as a separate trust for purposes of this subsection and subsection (c).

(4) **Trust ceasing to be qualified.**

(A) Failure to meet requirements of paragraph (3)(A). If a qualified subchapter S trust ceases to meet any requirement of paragraph (3)(A), the provisions of this subsection shall not apply to such trust as of the date it ceases to meet such requirement.

(B) Failure to meet requirements of paragraph (3)(B). If any qualified subchapter S trust ceases to meet any requirement of paragraph (3)(B) but continues to meet the requirements of paragraph (3)(A), the provisions of this subsection shall not apply to such trust as of the first day of the first taxable year beginning after the first taxable year for which it failed to meet the requirements of paragraph (3)(B).

(e) **Electing small business trust defined.**

(1) **Electing small business trust.** For purposes of this section—

(A) In general. Except as provided in subparagraph (B), the term "electing small business trust" means any trust if—

(i) such trust does not have as a beneficiary any person other than (I) an individual, (II) an estate, (III) an organization described in paragraph (2), (3), (4), or (5) of section 170(c), or (IV) an organization described in section 170(c)(1) which holds a contingent interest in such trust and is not a potential current beneficiary,

(ii) no interest in such trust was acquired by purchase, and

(iii) an election under this subsection applies to such trust.

(B) Certain trusts not eligible. The term "electing small business trust" shall not include—
 (i) any qualified subchapter S trust (as defined in subsection (d)(3)) if an election under subsection (d)(2) applies to any corporation the stock of which is held by such trust,
 (ii) any trust exempt from tax under this subtitle, and
 (iii) any charitable remainder annuity trust or charitable remainder unitrust (as defined in section 664(d)).
(C) Purchase. For purposes of subparagraph (A), the term "purchase" means any acquisition if the basis of the property acquired is determined under section 1012.

(2) Potential current beneficiary. For purposes of this section, the term "potential current beneficiary" means, with respect to any period, any person who at any time during such period is entitled to, or at the discretion of any person may receive, a distribution from the principal or income of the trust (determined without regard to any power of appointment to the extent such power remains unexercised at the end of such period). If a trust disposes of all of the stock which it holds in a S corporation, then, with respect to such corporation, the term "potential current beneficiary" does not include any person who first met the requirements of the preceding sentence during the 1-year period ending on the date of such disposition.

(3) Election. An election under this subsection shall be made by the trustee. Any such election shall apply to the taxable year of the trust for which made and all subsequent taxable years of such trust unless revoked with the consent of the Secretary.

(4) Cross reference. For special treatment of electing small business trusts, see section 641(c).

(f) Restricted bank director stock.

(1) In general. Restricted bank director stock shall not be taken into account as outstanding stock of the S corporation in applying this subchapter (other than section 1368(f)).

(2) Restricted bank director stock. For purposes of this subsection, the term "restricted bank director stock" means stock in a bank (as defined in section 581) or a depository institution holding company (as defined in section 3(w)(1) of the Federal Deposit Insurance Act (12 U.S.C. 1813(w)(1)), if such stock—
 (A) is required to be held by an individual under applicable Federal or State law in order to permit such individual to serve as a director, and
 (B) is subject to an agreement with such bank or company (or a corporation which controls (within the meaning of section 368(c)) such bank or company) pursuant to which the holder is required to sell back such stock (at the same price as the individual acquired such stock) upon ceasing to hold the office of director.

(3) Cross reference.
For treatment of certain distributions with respect to restricted bank director stock, see section 1368(f).

(g) Special rule for bank required to change from the reserve method of accounting on becoming S corporation.
In the case of a bank which changes from the reserve method of accounting for bad debts described in section 585 or 593 for its first taxable year for which an election under section 1362(a) is in effect, the bank may elect to take into account any adjustments under section 481 by reason of such change for the taxable year immediately preceding such first taxable year.

In 2007, P.L. 110-28, Sec. 8232(a), added subsec. (f), effective for tax. yrs. begin. after 12/31/06, except as provided in Sec. 8232(c)(2) of this Act, which reads as follows:
"(2) Special rule for treatment as second class of stock. In the case of any taxable year beginning after December 31, 1996, restricted bank director stock (as defined in section 1361(f) of the Internal Revenue Code of 1986, as added by this section) shall not be taken into account in determining whether an S corporation has more than 1 class of stock."
—P.L. 110-28, Sec. 8233(a), added subsec. (g), effective for tax. yrs. begin. after 12/31/06.
—P.L. 110-28, Sec. 8234(a)(1), substituted "(i) In general. For purposes of this title," for "For purposes of this title," in para. (b)(3)(C)... P.L. 110-28, Sec. 8234(a)(2), added clause (b)(3)(C)(ii), effective for tax. yrs. begin. after 12/31/06.
—P.L. 110-28, Sec. 8235, of this Act, [relating to Sec. 1311 of P.L. 104-188, see below] provides:
"SEC. 8235. ELIMINATION OF ALL EARNINGS AND PROFITS ATTRIBUTABLE TO PRE-1983 YEARS FOR CERTAIN CORPORATIONS.
"In the case of a corporation which is—
"(1) described in section 1311(a)(1) of the Small Business Job Protection Act of 1996, and
"(2) not described in section 1311(a)(2) of such Act,
"the amount of such corporation's accumulated earnings and profits (for the first taxable year beginning after the date of the enactment of this Act) shall be reduced by an amount equal to the portion (if any) of such accumulated earnings and profits which were accumulated in any taxable year beginning before January 1, 1983, for which such corporation was an electing small business corporation under subchapter S of the Internal Revenue Code of 1986."
In 2005, P.L. 109-135, Sec. 403(b), amended para. (c)(1), effective for tax. yrs. begin. after 12/31/2004 as if included in Sec. 231 of the American Jobs Creation Act of 2004, P.L. 108-357.
Prior to amendment, para. (c)(1) read as follows:
"(1) Members of family treated as 1 shareholder.
"(A) In general. For purpose of subsection (b)(1)(A)—
"(i) except as provided in clause (ii), a husband and wife (and their estates) shall be treated as 1 shareholder, and
"(ii) in the case of a family with respect to which an election is in effect under subparagraph (D), all members of the family shall be treated as 1 shareholder.
"(B) Members of the family. For purpose of subparagraph (A)(ii)—
"(i) In general. The term 'members of the family' means the common ancestor, lineal descendants of the common ancestor, and the spouses (or former spouses) of such lineal descendants or common ancestor.
"(ii) Common ancestor. For purposes of this paragraph, an individual shall not be considered a common ancestor if, as of the later of the effective date of this paragraph or the time the election under section 1362(a) is made, the individual is more than 6 generations removed from the youngest generation of shareholders who would (but for this clause) be members of the family. For purposes of the preceding sentence, a spouse (or former spouse) shall be treated as being of the same generation as the individual to which such spouse is (or was) married.
"(C) Effect of adoption, etc. In determining whether any relationship specified in subparagraph (B) exists, the rules of section 152(b)(2) shall apply.
"(D) Election. An election under subparagraph (A)(ii)—
"(i) may, except as otherwise provided in regulations prescribed by the Secretary, be made by any member of the family, and
"(ii) shall remain in effect until terminated as provided in regulations prescribed by the Secretary."
—P.L. 109-135, Sec. 413(a)(1)(A), added "or a depository institution holding company (as defined in section 3(w)(1) of the Federal Deposit Insurance Act (12 U.S.C. 1813(w)(1))" after "a bank (as defined in section 581)" in clause (c)(2)(A)(vi)... Sec. 413(a)(1)(B), added "or company" after "such bank" in clause (c)(2)(A)(vi), effective 10/22/2004 as if included in Sec. 233 of the American Jobs Creation Act of 2004, P.L. 108-357.
—P.L. 109-135, Sec. 413(c)(1), deleted "and in the case of information returns required under part III of subchapter A of chapter 61" after "prescribed by the Secretary," in subpara. (b)(3)(A)... Sec. 413(c)(2), added subpara. (b)(3)(E), effective for tax. yrs. begin. after 12/31/2004 as if included in Sec. 239 of the American Jobs Creation Act of 2004, P.L. 108-357.
In 2004, P.L. 108-357, Sec. 231(a), amended para. (c)(1), effective for tax. yrs. begin. after 12/31/2004.
Prior to amendment, para. (c)(1) read as follows:
"(1) Husband and wife treated as 1 shareholder. For purposes of subsection (b)(1)(A), a husband and wife (and their estates) shall be treated as 1 shareholder."
—P.L. 108-357, Sec. 232(a), substituted "100" for "75" in subpara. (b)(1)(A), effective for tax. yrs. begin. after 12/31/2004.
—P.L. 108-357, Sec. 233(a), added clause (c)(2)(A)(vi)... Sec. 233(b), added clause (c)(2)(B)(vi), effective 10/22/2004.
—P.L. 108-357, Sec. 234(a)(1), added "(determined without regard to any power of appointment to the extent such power remains unexercised at the end of such period)" after "of the trust" in para. (e)(2)... Sec. 234(a)(2), substituted "1-year" for "60-day" in para. (e)(2), effective for tax. yrs. begin. after 12/31/2004.
—P.L. 108-357, Sec. 236(a)(1), deleted "and" at the end of subpara. (d)(1)(A)... Sec. 236(a)(2), substituted ", and" for the period at the end of subpara. (d)(1)(B)... Sec. 236(a)(3), added subpara. (d)(1)(C), effective for transfers made after 12/31/2004.

Code Sec. 1361 — Subchapter S

—P.L. 108-357, Sec. 239(a), added "and in the case of information returns required under part III of subchapter A of chapter 61" after "Secretary" in subpara. (b)(3)(A), effective for tax. yrs. begin. after 12/31/2004.

In 2000, P.L. 106-554, Sec. 1(a)(7), [which enacted into law Sec. 316(b) of P.L. 106-554] deleted "or" after "an estate," and added "or (IV) an organization described in section 170(c)(1) which holds a contingent interest in such trust and is not a potential current beneficiary," after "section 170(c)," in clause (e)(1)(A)(i), effective for tax. yrs. begin. after 12/31/96.

In 1998, P.L. 105-206, Sec. 6007(f)(3), substituted "section 641(c)" for "section 641(d)" in para. (e)(4), effective for sales or exchanges after 8/5/97.

In 1997, P.L. 105-34, Sec. 1601(c)(1), deleted "and" at the end of clause (e)(1)(B)(i), substituted ", and" for the period at the end of clause (e)(1)(B)(ii), and added clause (e)(1)(B)(iii) . . . Sec. 1601(c)(3), substituted "Except as provided in regulations prescribed by the Secretary, for purposes of this title" for "For purposes of this title" in subpara. (b)(3)(A), effective for tax. yrs. begin. after 12/31/96.

—P.L. 105-34, Sec. 1601(c)(4)(B), redesignated para. (c)(7) as para. (c)(6) . . . Sec. 1601(c)(4)(C), substituted "subsection (c)(6)" for "subsection (c)(7)" in subpara. (b)(1)(B), effective for tax. yrs. begin. after 12/31/97.

In 1996, P.L. 104-188, Sec. 1301, substituted "75 shareholders" for "35 shareholders" in subpara. (b)(1)(A) . . . Sec. 1302(a), added clause (c)(2)(A)(v) . . . Sec. 1302(b), added clause (c)(2)(B)(v) . . . Sec. 1302(c), added subsec. (e) . . . Sec. 1303(1), substituted "2-year period" for "60-day period" each place it appeared in clauses (c)(2)(A)(ii) and (iii) . . . Sec. 1303(2), deleted " If a trust is described in the preceding sentence and if the entire corpus of the trust is includible in the gross estate of the deemed owner, the preceding sentence shall be applied by substituting '2-year period' for '60-day period'." in clause (c)(2)(A)(ii) . . . Sec. 1304, substituted "a trust described in paragraph (2), or a person which is actively and regularly engaged in the business of lending money" for "or a trust described in paragraph (2)" in clause (c)(5)(B)(iii) . . . Sec. 1308(a), deleted subpara. (b)(2)(A) and redesignated paras. (b)(2)(B)–(E) as subparas. (b)(2)(A)–(D) . . . Sec. 1308(b), added para. (b)(3) . . . Sec. 1308(d)(1), deleted para. (c)(6), effective for tax. yrs. begin. after 12/31/96.

Prior to deletion, subpara. (b)(2)(A) read as follows:

"(A) a member of an affiliated group (determined under section 1504 without regard to the exceptions contained in subsection (b) thereof),"

Prior to deletion, para. (c)(6) read as follows:

"(6) Ownership of stock in certain inactive corporations.

For purposes of subsection (b)(2)(A), a corporation shall not be treated as a member of an affiliated group during any period within a taxable year by reason of the ownership of stock in another corporation if such other corporation—

"(A) has not begun business at any time on or before the close of such period, and

"(B) does not have gross income for such period."

—P.L. 104-188, Sec. 1311(a), of this Act, regarding elimination of certain earnings and profits, provides:

"(a) In general. If—

"(1) a corporation was an electing small business corporation under subchapter S of chapter 1 of the Internal Revenue Code 1986 for any taxable year beginning before January 1, 1983, and

"(2) such corporation is an S corporation under subchapter S of chapter 1 of such Code for its first taxable year beginning after December 31, 1996,

the amount of such corporation's accumulated earnings and profits (as of the beginning of such first taxable year) shall be reduced by an amount equal to the portion (if any) of such accumulated earnings and profits which were accumulated in any taxable year beginning before January 1, 1983, for which such corporation was an electing small business corporation under such subchapter S."

—P.L. 104-188, Sec. 1315, amended subpara. (b)(2)(A) [as redesignated by Sec. 1308(a) of this Act, see above, and as amended by Sec. 1616(b)(15) of this Act, see below], effective for tax. yrs. begin. after 12/31/96.

Prior to amendment, subpara. (b)(2)(A) read as follows:

"(A) a financial institution to which section 585 applies (or would apply but for subsection (c) thereof),"

—P.L. 104-188, Sec. 1316(a)(1), amended subpara. (b)(1)(B) . . . Sec. 1316(a)(2), added para. (c)(7) . . . Sec. 1316(e), deleted "which holds a contingent current beneficiary" in clause (e)(1)(A)(i) [as added by Sec. 1302 of this Act, see above], effective for tax. yrs. begin. after 12/31/97.

Prior to amendment, subpara. (b)(1)(B) read as follows:

"(B) have as a shareholder a person (other than an estate and other than a trust described in subsection (c)(2)) who is not an individual,"

—P.L. 104-188, Sec. 1616(b)(15), deleted "or to which section 593 applies" in subpara. (b)(2)(B) but before amendment by Sec. 1315 of this Act, see above., effective for tax. yrs. begin. after 12/31/95.

In 1989, P.L. 101-239, Sec. 7811(c)(6), amended subpara. (b)(2)(B), effective for tax. yrs. begin. after 12/31/86.

Prior to amendment, subpara. (b)(2)(B) read as follows:

"(B) a financial institution which is a bank (as defined in section 585(a)(2)) or to which section 593 applies,"

In 1988, P.L. 100-647, Sec. 1018(q)(2), substituted "within the meaning of section 663(c)" for "treated as a separate trust under section 663(c)" in para. (d)(3), effective for tax. yrs. begin. after 12/31/82.

In 1986, P.L. 99-514, Sec. 901(d)(4)(G), substituted "which is a bank (as defined in section 585(a)(2)) or to which section 593 applies" for "to which section 585 or 593 applies" in subpara. (b)(2)(B), effective for tax. yrs. begin. after 12/31/86.

—P.L. 99-514, Sec. 1879(m)(1)(A), added the flush sentence at the end of para. (d)(3), effective for tax. yrs. begin. after 12/31/82.

In 1984, P.L. 98-369, Sec. 721(c), amended para. (c)(6) . . . Sec. 721(f)(1), substituted "15 days and 2 months" for "60 days" in subpara. (d)(2)(D) . . . Sec. 721(f)(2), deleted paras. (d)(3) and (d)(4) and added new paras. (d)(3) and (d)(4) . . . Sec. 721(f)(3), substituted "corporation" for "S corporation" each place it appeared in clause (d)(2)(B)(i), effective for tax. yrs. begin. after 12/31/82.

Prior to amendment, para. (c)(6) read as follows:

"(6) Ownership of stock in certain inactive corporations. For purposes of subsection (b)(2)(A), a corporation shall not be treated as a member of an affiliated group at any time during any taxable year by reason of the ownership of stock in another corporation if such other corporation—

"(A) has not begun business at any time on or after the date of its incorporation and before the close of such taxable year, and

"(B) does not have taxable income for the period included within such taxable year."

Prior to deletion, paras. (d)(3) and (d)(4) read as follows:

"(3) Qualified subchapter S trust. For purposes of this subsection, the term 'qualified subchapter S trust' means a trust—

"(A) which owns stock in 1 or more S corporations,

"(B) all of the income (within the meaning of section 643(b)) of which is distributed (or required to be distributed) currently to 1 individual who is a citizen or resident of the United States, and

"(C) the terms of which require that—

"(i) during the life of the current income beneficiary there shall be only 1 income beneficiary of the trust,

"(ii) any corpus distributed during the life of the current income beneficiary may be distributed only to such beneficiary,

"(iii) the income interest of the current income beneficiary in the trust shall terminate on the earlier of such beneficiary's death or the termination of the trust, and

"(iv) upon the termination of the trust during the life of the current income beneficiary, the trust shall distribute all of its assets to such beneficiary.

"(4) Trust ceasing to be qualified. If a qualified subchapter S trust ceases to meet any requirement under paragraph (3), the provisions of this subsection shall not apply to such trust as of the date it ceases to meet such requirements."

In 1982, P.L. 97-354, Sec. 2, added Code Sec. 1361 as part of the amendments to Subchapter S, effective for tax. yrs. begin. after 12/31/82 except as provided in Sec. 6(c) of this Act which reads as follows:

"(c) Grandfather Rules.

"(1) Subsidiaries which are foreign corporations or DISC's.—In the case of any corporation which on September 28, 1982, would have been a member of the same affiliated group as an electing small business corporation but for paragraph (3) or (7) of section 1504(b) of the Internal Revenue Code of 1954, subparagraph (A) of section 1361(b)(2) of such Code (as amended by section 2) shall be applied by substituting 'without regard to the exceptions contained in paragraphs (1), (2), (4), (5), and (6) of subsection (b) thereof' for 'without regard to the exceptions contained in subsection (b) thereof'.

"(2) Casualty insurance companies.—

"(A) In general.—In the case of any qualified casualty insurance electing small business corporation—

"(i) the amendments made by this Act shall not apply, and

"(ii) subchapter S (as in effect on July 1, 1982) of chapter 1 of the Internal Revenue Code of 1954 and part III of subchapter L of chapter 1 of such Code shall apply.

"(B) Qualified casualty insurance electing small business corporation.—The term 'qualified casualty insurance electing small business corporation' means any corporation described in section 831(a) of the Internal Revenue Code of 1954 if—

"(i) as of July 12, 1982, such corporation was an electing small business corporation and was described in section 831(a) of such Code,

"(ii) such corporation was formed before April 1, 1982, and proposed (through a written private offering first circulated to investors before such date) to elect to be taxed as a subchapter S corporation and to be operated on an established insurance exchange, or

"(iii) such corporation is approved for membership on an established insurance exchange pursuant to a written agreement entered into before December 31, 1982, and such corporation is described in section 831(a) of such Code as of December 31, 1984.

A corporation shall not be treated as a qualified casualty insurance electing small business corporation unless an election under subchapter S of chapter 1 of such Code is in effect for its first taxable year beginning after December 31, 1984.

"(3) Certain corporations with oil and gas production.—

"(A) In general.—In the case of any qualified oil corporation—

"(i) the amendments made by this Act shall not apply, and

"(ii) subchapter S (as in effect on July 1, 1982) of chapter 1 of the Internal Revenue Code of 1954 shall apply.

"(B) Qualified oil corporation.—For purposes of this paragraph, the term 'qualified oil corporation' means any corporation if—

"(i) as of September 28, 1982, such corporation—

"(I) was an electing small business corporation, or

"(II) was a small business corporation which made an election under section 1372(a) after December 31, 1981, and before September 28, 1982,

"(ii) for calendar year 1982, the combined average daily production of domestic crude oil or natural gas of such corporation and any one of its substantial shareholders exceeds 1,000 barrels, and

"(iii) such corporation makes an election under this subparagraph at such time and in such manner as the Secretary of the Treasury or his delegate shall prescribe.

Subchapter S — Code Sec. 1362(d)(3)(A)(iii)(II)

"(C) Average daily production.—For purposes of subparagraph (B), the average daily production of domestic crude oil or domestic natural gas shall be determined under section 613A(c)(2) of such Code without regard to the last sentence thereof.

"(D) Substantial shareholder.—For purposes of subparagraph (B), the term 'substantial shareholder' means any person who on July 1, 1982, owns more than 40 percent (in value) of the stock of the corporation.

"(4) Continuity required.—

"(A) In general.—This subsection shall cease to apply with respect to any corporation after—

"(i) any termination of the election of the corporation under subchapter S of chapter 1 of such Code, or

"(ii) the first day on which more than 50 percent of the stock of the corporation is newly owned stock within the meaning of section 1378(c)(2) of such Code (as amended by this Act).

"(B) Special rules for paragraph (2).—

"(i) Paragraph (2) shall also cease to apply with respect to any corporation after the corporation ceases to be described in section 831(a) of such Code.

"(ii) For purposes of determining under subparagraph (A)(ii) whether paragraph (2) ceases to apply to any corporation, section 1378(c)(2) of such Code (as amended by this Act) shall be applied by substituting 'December 31, 1984' for 'December 31, 1982' each place it appears therein."

Sec. 1362. Election; revocation; termination.

(a) Election.

(1) In general. Except as provided in subsection (g), a small business corporation may elect, in accordance with the provisions of this section, to be an S corporation.

(2) All shareholders must consent to election. An election under this subsection shall be valid only if all persons who are shareholders in such corporation on the day on which such election is made consent to such election.

(b) When made.

(1) In general. An election under subsection (a) may be made by a small business corporation for any taxable year—

(A) at any time during the preceding taxable year, or

(B) at any time during the taxable year and on or before the 15th day of the 3d month of the taxable year.

(2) Certain elections made during 1st 2 ½ months treated as made for next taxable year. If—

(A) an election under subsection (a) is made for any taxable year during such year and on or before the 15th day of the 3d month of such year, but

(B) either—

(i) on 1 or more days in such taxable year before the day on which the election was made the corporation did not meet the requirements of subsection (b) of section 1361, or

(ii) 1 or more of the persons who held stock in the corporation during such taxable year and before the election was made did not consent to the election,

then such election shall be treated as made for the following taxable year.

(3) Election made after 1st 2 ½ months treated as made for following taxable year. If—

(A) a small business corporation makes an election under subsection (a) for any taxable year, and

(B) such election is made after the 15th day of the 3d month of the taxable year and on or before the 15th day of the 3rd month of the following taxable year,

then such election shall be treated as made for the following taxable year.

(4) Taxable years of 2 ½ months or less. For purposes of this subsection, an election for a taxable year made not later than 2 months and 15 days after the first day of the taxable year shall be treated as timely made during such year.

(5) Authority to treat late elections, etc., as timely. If—

(A) an election under subsection (a) is made for any taxable year (determined without regard to paragraph (3)), after the date prescribed by this subsection for making such election for such taxable year or no such election is made for any taxable year, and

(B) the Secretary determines that there was reasonable cause for the failure to timely make such election,

the Secretary may treat such an election as timely made for such taxable year (and paragraph (3) shall not apply).

(c) Years for which effective.

An election under subsection (a) shall be effective for the taxable year of the corporation for which it is made and for all succeeding taxable years of the corporation, until such election is terminated under subsection (d).

(d) Termination.

(1) By revocation.

(A) In general. An election under subsection (a) may be terminated by revocation.

(B) More than one-half of shares must consent to revocation. An election may be revoked only if shareholders holding more than one-half of the shares of stock of the corporation on the day on which the revocation is made consent to the revocation.

(C) When effective. Except as provided in subparagraph (D)—

(i) a revocation made during the taxable year and on or before the 15th day of the 3d month thereof shall be effective on the 1st day of such taxable year, and

(ii) a revocation made during the taxable year but after such 15th day shall be effective on the 1st day of the following taxable year.

(D) Revocation may specify prospective date. If the revocation specifies a date for revocation which is on or after the day on which the revocation is made, the revocation shall be effective on and after the date so specified.

(2) By corporation ceasing to be small business corporation.

(A) In general. An election under subsection (a) shall be terminated whenever (at any time on or after the 1st day of the 1st taxable year for which the corporation is an S corporation) such corporation ceases to be a small business corporation.

(B) When effective. Any termination under this paragraph shall be effective on and after the date of cessation.

(3) Where passive investment income exceeds 25 percent of gross receipts for 3 consecutive taxable years and corporation has accumulated earnings and profits.

(A) Termination.

(i) In general. An election under subsection (a) shall be terminated whenever the corporation—

(I) has accumulated earnings and profits at the close of each of 3 consecutive taxable years, and

(II) has gross receipts for each of such taxable years more than 25 percent of which are passive investment income.

(ii) When effective. Any termination under this paragraph shall be effective on and after the first day of the first taxable year beginning after the third consecutive taxable year referred to in clause (i).

(iii) Years taken into account. A prior taxable year shall not be taken into account under clause (i) unless—

(I) such taxable year began after December 31, 1981, and

(II) the corporation was an S corporation for such taxable year.

2,845

(B) Gross receipts from the sales of certain assets. For purposes of this paragraph—
  (i) in the case of dispositions of capital assets (other than stock and securities), gross receipts from such dispositions shall be taken into account only to the extent of the capital gain net income therefrom, and
  (ii) in the case of sales or exchanges of stock or securities, gross receipts shall be taken into account only to the extent of the gains therefrom.
(C) Passive investment income defined.
  (i) In general. Except as otherwise provided in this subparagraph, the term "passive investment income" means gross receipts derived from royalties, rents, dividends, interest, and annuities.
  (ii) Exception for interest on notes from sales of inventory. The term "passive investment income" shall not include interest on any obligation acquired in the ordinary course of the corporation's trade or business from its sale of property described in section 1221(a)(1).
  (iii) Treatment of certain lending or finance companies. If the S corporation meets the requirements of section 542(c)(6) for the taxable year, the term "passive investment income" shall not include gross receipts for the taxable year which are derived directly from the active and regular conduct of a lending or finance business (as defined in section 542(d)(1)).
  (iv) Treatment of certain dividends. If an S corporation holds stock in a C corporation meeting the requirements of section 1504(a)(2), the term "passive investment income" shall not include dividends from such C corporation to the extent such dividends are attributable to the earnings and profits of such C corporation derived from the active conduct of a trade or business.
  (v) Exception for banks, etc. In the case of a bank (as defined in section 581) or a depository institution holding company (as defined in section 3(w)(1) of the Federal Deposit Insurance Act (12 U.S.C. 1813(w)(1)), the term "passive investment income" shall not include—
    (I) interest income earned by such bank or company, or
    (II) dividends on assets required to be held by such bank or company, including stock in the Federal Reserve Bank, the Federal Home Loan Bank, or the Federal Agricultural Mortgage Bank or participation certificates issued by a Federal Intermediate Credit Bank.

(e) Treatment of S termination year.
  (1) In general. In the case of an S termination year, for purposes of this title—
    (A) S short year. The portion of such year ending before the 1st day for which the termination is effective shall be treated as a short taxable year for which the corporation is an S corporation.
    (B) C short year. The portion of such year beginning on such 1st day shall be treated as a short taxable year for which the corporation is a C corporation.
  (2) Pro rata allocation. Except as provided in paragraph (3) and subparagraphs (C) and (D) of paragraph (6), the determination of which items are to be taken into account for each of the short taxable years referred to in paragraph (1) shall be made—
    (A) first by determining for the S termination year—
      (i) the amount of each of the items of income, loss, deduction, or credit described in section 1366(a)(1)(A), and
      (ii) the amount of the nonseparately computed income or loss, and
    (B) then by assigning an equal portion of each amount determined under subparagraph (A) to each day of the S termination year.
  (3) Election to have items assigned to each short taxable year under normal tax accounting rules.
    (A) In general. A corporation may elect to have paragraph (2) not apply.
    (B) Shareholders must consent to election. An election under this subsection shall be valid only if all persons who are shareholders in the corporation at any time during the S short year and all persons who are shareholders in the corporation on the first day of the C short year consent to such election.
  (4) S termination year. For purposes of this subsection, the term "S termination year" means any taxable year of a corporation (determined without regard to this subsection) in which a termination of an election made under subsection (a) takes effect (other than on the 1st day thereof).
  (5) Tax for C short year determined on annualized basis.
    (A) In general. The taxable income for the short year described in subparagraph (B) of paragraph (1) shall be placed on an annual basis by multiplying the taxable income for such short year by the number of days in the S termination year and by dividing the result by the number of days in the short year. The tax shall be the same part of the tax computed on the annual basis as the number of days in such short year is of the number of days in the S termination year.
    (B) Section 443(d)(2) to apply. Subsection (d) of section 443 shall apply to the short taxable year described in subparagraph (B) of paragraph (1).
  (6) Other special rules. For purposes of this title—
    (A) Short years treated as 1 year for carryover purposes. The short taxable year described in subparagraph (A) of paragraph (1) shall not be taken into account for purposes of determining the number of taxable years to which any item may be carried back or carried forward by the corporation.
    (B) Due date for S year. The due date for filing the return for the short taxable year described in subparagraph (A) of paragraph (1) shall be the same as the due date for filing the return for the short taxable year described in subparagraph (B) of paragraph (1) (including extensions thereof).
    (C) Paragraph (2) not to apply to items resulting from section 338. Paragraph (2) shall not apply with respect to any item resulting from the application of section 338.
    (D) Pro rata allocation for S termination year not to apply if 50-percent change in ownership. Paragraph (2) shall not apply to an S termination year if there is a sale or exchange of 50 percent or more of the stock in such corporation during such year.

(f) Inadvertent invalid elections or terminations.
  If—
  (1) an election under subsection (a) or section 1361(b)(3)(B)(ii) by any corporation—
    (A) was not effective for the taxable year for which made (determined without regard to subsection (b)(2))

by reason of a failure to meet the requirements of section 1361(b) or to obtain shareholder consents, or

(B) was terminated under paragraph (2) or (3) of subsection (d) or section 1361(b)(3)(C),

(2) the Secretary determines that the circumstances resulting in such ineffectiveness or termination were inadvertent,

(3) no later than a reasonable period of time after discovery of the circumstances resulting in such ineffectiveness or termination, steps were taken—

(A) so that the corporation for which the election was made or the termination occurred is a small business corporation or a qualified subchapter S subsidiary, as the case may be, or

(B) to acquire the required shareholder consents, and

(4) the corporation for which the election was made or the termination occurred, and each person who was a shareholder in such corporation at any time during the period specified pursuant to this subsection, agrees to make such adjustments (consistent with the treatment of such corporation as an S corporation or a qualified subchapter S subsidiary, as the case may be) as may be required by the Secretary with respect to such period,

then, notwithstanding the circumstances resulting in such ineffectiveness or termination, such corporation shall be treated as an S corporation or a qualified subchapter S subsidiary, as the case may be during the period specified by the Secretary.

(g) Election after termination.

If a small business corporation has made an election under subsection (a) and if such election has been terminated under subsection (d), such corporation (and any successor corporation) shall not be eligible to make an election under subsection (a) for any taxable year before its 5th taxable year which begins after the 1st taxable year for which such termination is effective, unless the Secretary consents to such election.

In 2007, P.L. 110-172, Sec. 11(a)(25)(A), substituted "or section 1361(b)(3)(B)(ii)" for ", section 1361(b)(3)(B)(ii), or section 1361(c)(1)(A)(ii)" in subsec. (f)(1) . . . Sec. 11(a)(25)(B), substituted "or section 1361(b)(3)(C)" for ", section 1361(b)(3)(C), or section 1361(c)(1)(D)(iii)" in subsec. (f)(1)(B), enacted 12/29/2007.
—P.L. 110-28, Sec. 8231(a), deleted subparas. (d)(3)(B)-(F) and added subparas. (d)(3)(B)-(C), effective for tax. yrs. begin. after 5/25/2007.
Prior to deletion, subparas. (d)(3)(B)-(F) read as follows:
"(B) Gross receipts from sales of capital assets (other than stock and securities). For purposes of this paragraph, in the case of dispositions of capital assets (other than stock and securities), gross receipts from such dispositions shall be taken into account only to the extent of the capital gain net income therefrom.
"(C) Passive investment income defined. For purposes of this paragraph—
"(i) In general. Except as otherwise provided in this subparagraph, the term 'passive investment income' means gross receipts derived from royalties, rents, dividends, interest, annuities, and sales or exchanges of stock or securities (gross receipts from such sales or exchanges being taken into account for purposes of this paragraph only to the extent of gains therefrom).
"(ii) Exception for interest on notes from sales of inventory. The term 'passive investment income' shall not include interest on any obligation acquired in the ordinary course of the corporation's trade or business from its sale of property described in section 1221(a)(1).
"(iii) Treatment of certain lending or finance companies. If the S corporation meets the requirements of section 542(c)(6) for the taxable year, the term 'passive investment income' shall not include gross receipts for the taxable year which are derived directly from the active and regular conduct of a lending or finance business (as defined in section 542(d)(1)).
"(iv) Treatment of certain liquidations. Gross receipts derived from sales or exchanges of stock or securities shall not include amounts received by an S corporation which are treated under section 331 (relating to corporate liquidations) as payments in exchange for stock where the S corporation owned more than 50 percent of each class of stock of the liquidating corporation.
"(D) Special rule for options and commodity dealings.
"(i) In general. In the case of any options dealer or commodities dealer, passive investment income shall be determined by not taking into account any gain or loss (in the normal course of the taxpayer's activity of dealing in or trading section 1256 contracts) from any section 1256 contract or property related to such a contract.
"(ii) Definitions. For purposes of this subparagraph—
"(I) Options dealer. The term 'options dealer' has the meaning given such term by section 1256(g)(8).
"(II) Commodities dealer. The term 'commodities dealer' means a person who is actively engaged in trading section 1256 contracts and is registered with a domestic board of trade which is designated as a contract market by the Commodities Futures Trading Commission.
"(III) Section 1256 Contract. The term 'section 1256 contract' has the meaning given to such term by section 1256(b).
"(E) Treatment of certain dividends. If an S corporation holds stock in a C corporation meeting the requirements of section 1504(a)(2), the term 'passive investment income' shall not include dividends from such C corporation to the extent such dividends are attributable to the earnings and profits of such C corporation derived from the active conduct of a trade or business.
"(F) Exception for banks; etc. In the case of a bank (as defined in section 581), [or] a depository institution holding company (as defined in section 3(w)(1) of the Federal Deposit Insurance Act (12 U.S.C. 1813(w)(1)), the term 'passive investment income' shall not include—
"(i) interest income earned by such bank or company, or
"(ii) dividends on assets required to be held by such bank or company, including stock in the Federal Reserve Bank, the Federal Home Loan Bank, or the Federal Agricultural Mortgage Bank or participation certificates issued by a Federal Intermediate Credit Bank."
—P.L. 110-28, Sec. 8235, of this Act, [relating to Sec. 1311 of P.L. 104-188, see below] provides:
"Sec. 8235. Elimination Of All Earnings And Profits Attributable To Pre-1983 Years For Certain Corporations.
"In the case of a corporation which is—
"(1) described in section 1311(a)(1) of the Small Business Job Protection Act of 1996, and
"(2) not described in section 1311(a)(2) of such Act,
the amount of such corporation's accumulated earnings and profits (for the first taxable year beginning after the date of the enactment of this Act) shall be reduced by an amount equal to the portion (if any) of such accumulated earnings and profits which were accumulated in any taxable year beginning before January 1, 1983, for which such corporation was an electing small business corporation under subchapter S of the Internal Revenue Code of 1986."

In 2005, P.L. 109-135, Sec. 413(b), substituted "a depository institution holding company (as defined in section 3(w)(1) of the Federal Deposit Insurance Act (12 U.S.C. 1813(w)(1))" for "a bank holding company (within the meaning of section 2(a) of the Bank Holding Company Act of 1956 (12 U.S.C. 1841(a))), or a financial holding company (within the meaning of section 2(p) of such Act)" in subpara. (d)(3)(F), effective for tax. yrs. begin. after 12/31/2004 as if included in Sec. 237 of the American Jobs Creation Act of 2004, P.L. 108-357.

In 2004, P.L. 108-357, Sec. 231(b)(1), added "or section 1361(c)(1)(A)(ii)" after "section 1361(b)(3)(B)(ii)," in para. (f)(1) [as amended by Sec. 238(a)(1) of this Act, see below] . . . Sec. 231(b)(2), added "or section 1361(c)(1)(D)(iii)" after "section 1361(b)(3)(C)," in subpara. (f)(1)(B) [as amended by Sec. 238(a)(2) of this Act, see below], effective for elections and terminations made after 12/31/2004.
—P.L. 108-357, Sec. 237(a), added subpara. (d)(3)(F), effective for tax. yrs. begin. after 12/31/2004.
—P.L. 108-357, Sec. 238(a)(1), added ", section 1361(b)(3)(B)(ii)," after "subsection (a)" in para. (f)(1) . . . Sec. 238(a)(2), added ", section 1361(b)(3)(C)," after "subsection (d)" in subpara. (f)(1)(B) . . . Sec. 238(a)(3), amended subpara. (f)(3)(A) . . . Sec. 238(a)(4), amended para. (f)(4) . . . Sec. 238(a)(5), added "or a qualified subchapter S subsidiary, as the case may be" after "S corporation" in the last sentence of subsec. (f), effective for elections made and terminations made after 12/31/2004.
Prior to amendment, subpara. (f)(3)(A) read as follows:
"(A) so that the corporation is a small business corporation, or"
Prior to amendment, para. (f)(4) read as follows:
"(4) the corporation, and each person who was a shareholder in the corporation at any time during the period specified pursuant to this subsection, agrees to make such adjustments (consistent with the treatment of the corporation as an S corporation) as may be required by the Secretary with respect to such period,"

In 1999, P.L. 106-170, Sec. 532(c)(2)(T), substituted "section 1221(a)(1)" for "section 1221(1)" in clause (d)(3)(C)(ii), effective for any instrument held, acquired, or entered into, any transaction entered into, and supplies held or acquired on or after 12/17/99.

In 1996, P.L. 104-188, Sec. 1305(a), amended subsec. (f) . . . Sec. 1305(b), added para. (b)(5), effective for elections for tax. yrs. begin. after 12/31/82.
Prior to amendment, subsec. (f) read as follows:
"(f) Inadvertent terminations. If—
"(1) an election under subsection (a) by any corporation was terminated under paragraph (2) or (3) of subsection (d),
"(2) the Secretary determines that the termination was inadvertent,
"(3) no later than a reasonable period of time after discovery of the event resulting in such termination, steps were taken so that the corporation is once more a small business corporation, and
"(4) the corporation, and each person who was a share-holder of the corporation at any time during the period specified pursuant to this subsection, agrees to make such adjustments (consistent with the treatment of the corporation as an S corporation) as may be required by the Secretary with respect to such period,

Code Sec. 1362   Subchapter S

then, notwithstanding the terminating event, such corporation shall be treated as continuing to be an S corporation during the period specified by the Secretary."

—P.L. 104-188, Sec. 1308(c), added subpara. (d)(3)(F), effective for tax. yrs. begin. after 12/31/96.

—P.L. 104-188, Sec. 1311(a), of this Act, regarding elimination of certain earnings and profits, is reproduced in note following Code Sec. 1361.

—P.L. 104-188, Sec. 1311(b)(1)(A), substituted "accumulated" for "subchapter C" in the heading of para. (d)(3) . . . Sec. 1311(b)(1)(B), substituted "accumulated" for "subchapter C" in subclause (d)(3)(A)(i)(I) . . . Sec. 1311(b)(1)(C), deleted subpara. (d)(3)(B) and redesignated subparas. (d)(3)(C)-(F) as subparas. (d)(3)(B)-(E), effective for tax. yrs. begin. after 12/31/96.

Prior to deletion, subpara. (d)(3)(B) read as follows:

"(B) Subchapter C earnings and profits. For purposes of subparagraph (A), the term 'subchapter C earnings and profits' means earnings and profits of any corporation for any taxable year with respect to which an election under section 1362(a) (or under section 1372 of prior law) was not in effect."

—P.L. 104-188, Sec. 1317(b), of this Act provides:

"(b) Treatment of certain elections under prior law. For purposes of section 1362(g) of the Internal Revenue Code of 1986 (relating to election after termination), any termination under section 1362(d) of such Code in a taxable year beginning before January 1, 1997, shall not be taken into account."

In 1988, P.L. 100-647, Sec. 1006(f)(6)(A), deleted clause (d)(3)(D)(v) . . . Sec. 1006(f)(6)(B), added subpara. (d)(3)(E), effective for tax. yrs. begin. after 12/31/86, but only in cases where the 1st tax. yr. for which the corporation is an S corporation is pursuant to an election made after 12/31/86. See Sec. 633(d)(8) of P.L. 99-514 reproduced in note following Code Sec. 1374.

Prior to deletion, clause (d)(3)(D)(v) read as follows:

"(v) Special rule for options and commodities dealers. In the case of any options or commodities dealer, passive investment income shall be determined by not taking into account any gain or loss described in section 1374(c)(4)(A)."

—P.L. 100-647, Sec. 1007(g)(9), substituted "Subsection (d)" for "Subsection (d)(2)" in subpara. (e)(5)(B), effective for tax. yrs. begin. after 12/31/86.

In 1986, P.L. 99-514, Sec. 1808(a)(2), amended Sec. 102(d)(3) of P.L. 98-369 [reproduced below], part of the effective date for changes made by Sec. 102(d)(2) of P.L. 98-369, by substituting "(as so defined) or such other day as may be permitted by regulations" for "(as so defined)".

In 1984, P.L. 98-369, Sec. 102(d)(2), added clause (d)(3)(D)(v), for positions established after 7/18/84, in tax. yrs. ending after 7/18/84 and subject to the special rules and elections provided in Sec. 102(f)(2), (g), (h) and (i) of this Act, which read as follows:

"(2) Special rule for options on regulated futures contracts. In the case of any option with respect to a regulated futures contract (within the meaning of section 1256 of the Internal Revenue Code of 1954), the amendments made by this section shall apply to positions established after October 31, 1983, in taxable years ending after such date.

"(g) Elections With Respect to Property Held on or Before the Date of the Enactment of This Act [7/18/84]. At the election of the taxpayer—

"(1) the amendments made by this section shall apply to all section 1256 contracts held by the taxpayer on the date of the enactment of this Act [7/18/84], effective for periods after such date in taxable years ending after such date, or

"(2) in lieu of an election under paragraph (1), the amendments made by this section shall apply to all section 1256 contracts held by the taxpayer at any time during the taxable year of the taxpayer which includes the date of the enactment of this Act.

"(h) Elections for installment payment of tax attributable to stock options.

"(1) In general. If the taxpayer makes an election under subsection (g)(2) and under this subsection—

"(A) the taxpayer may pay part or all the tax for the taxable year referred to in subsection (g)(2) in 2 or more (but not exceeding 5) equal installments, and

"(B) the maximum amount of tax which may be paid in installments under this subsection shall be the excess of—

"(i) the tax for such taxable year determined by taking into account subsection (g)(2), over

"(ii) the tax for such taxable year determined by taking into account subsection (g)(2) and by treating—

"(I) all section 1256 contracts which are stock options, and

"(II) any stock which was a part of a straddle including any such stock options, as having been acquired for a purchase price equal to their fair market value on the last business day of the preceding taxable year. Stock options and stock shall be taken into account under subparagraph (B)(ii) only if such options or stock were held on the last day of the preceding taxable year and only if income on such options or stock would have been ordinary income if such options or stock were sold at a gain on such last day.

"(2) Date for payment of installment—

"(A) If an election is made under this subsection, the first installment under paragraph (1) shall be paid on or before the due date for filing the return for the taxable year described in paragraph (1), and each succeeding installment shall be paid on or before the date which is 1 year after the date prescribed for payment of the preceding installment.

"(B) If a bankruptcy case or insolvency proceeding involving the taxpayer is commenced before the final installment is paid, the total amount of any unpaid installments shall be treated as due and payable on the day preceding the day on which such case or proceeding is commenced.

"(3) Interest imposed. For purposes of section 6601 of the Internal Revenue Code of 1954, the time for payment of any tax with respect to which an election is made under this subsection shall be determined without regard to this subsection.

"(4) Form of election. An election under this subsection shall be made not later than the time for filing the return for the taxable year described in paragraph (1) and shall be made in the manner and form required by regulations prescribed by Secretary of the Treasury or his delegate. The election shall set forth—

"(A) the amount determined under paragraph (1)(B) and the number of installments elected by the taxpayer,

"(B) the property described in paragraph (1)(B)(ii), and the date on which such property was acquired,

"(C) the fair market value of the property described in paragraph (1)(B)(ii) on the last business day of the taxable year preceding the taxable year described in paragraph (1), and

"(D) such other information for purposes of carrying out the provisions of this subsection as may be required by such regulations.

"(5) Delay of identification requirement. Section 1256(e)(2)(C) of the Internal Revenue Code of 1954 shall not apply to any stock option or stock acquired on or before the 60th day after the date of the enactment of this Act.

"(i) Definitions. For purposes of subsections (g) and (h)—

"(1) Section 1256 contract. The term 'section 1256 contract' has the meaning given to such term by section 1256(b) of the Internal Revenue Code of 1954 (as amended by this section).

"(2) Stock option. The term 'stock option' means any option to buy or sell stock."

—P.L. 98-369, Sec. 102(d)(3), of this Act [as amended by Sec. 1808(a)(2) of P.L. 99-514, see above] provides:

"(3) Subchapter S election. If a commodities dealer or an options dealer—

"(A) becomes a small business corporation (as defined in section 1361(b) of the Internal Revenue Code of 1954) at any time before the close of the 75th day after the date of the enactment of this Act, and

"(B) makes the election under section 1362(a) of such Code before the close of such 75th day,

then such dealer shall be treated as having received approval for and adopted a taxable year beginning on the first day during 1984 on which it was a small business corporation (as so defined) or such other day as may be permitted under regulations and ending on the date determined under section 1378 of such Code and such election shall be effective for such taxable year."

—P.L. 98-369, Sec. 721(g)(1), added subpara. (e)(6)(C), effective for tax. yrs. begin. after 12/31/82, except as provided in Sec. 721(y)(3) of this Act which reads as follows:

"(3) Amendment made by subsection (g)(1). If—

"(A) any portion of a qualified stock purchase is pursuant to a binding contract entered into on or after October 19, 1982, and before the date of enactment of this Act, and

"(B) the purchasing corporation establishes by clear and convincing evidence that such contract was negotiated on the contemplation that, with respect to the deemed sale under section 338 of the Internal Revenue Code of 1954, paragraph (2) of section 1362(e) of such Code would apply,

then the amendment made by paragraph (1) of subsection (g) shall not apply to such qualified stock purchase."

—P.L. 98-369, Sec. 721(g)(2), substituted "as provided in paragraph (3) and subparagraphs (C) and (D) of paragraph (6)," for "as provided in paragraph (3)" in para. (e)(2) . . . Sec. 721(h), amended subpara. (e)(3)(B), effective for tax. yrs. begin. after 12/31/82.

Prior to amendment, subpara. (e)(3)(B) read as follows:

"(B) All shareholders must consent to election. An election under this paragraph shall be valid only if all persons who are shareholders in the corporation at any time during the S termination year consent to such election."

—P.L. 98-369, Sec. 721(i), amended Sec. 6(b)(3) of P.L. 97-354, the effective date for para. (d)(3), by adding the last two sentences.

—P.L. 98-369, Sec. 721(k), amended Sec. 6(e) of P.L. 97-354, part of the effective date for changes made by Sec. 2 of P.L. 97-354, by substituting "any termination or revocation" for "any termination", (reproduced below).

—P.L. 98-369, Sec. 721(l)(1), added para. (b)(4) . . . Sec. 721(l)(2), substituted "on or before the 15th day of the 3rd month of the following taxable year" for "on or before the last day of such taxable year" in para. (b)(3), effective for any election under Code Sec. 1362 (or any corresponding provision of prior law) made after 10/19/82.

—P.L. 98-369, Sec. 721(t), added subpara. (e)(6)(D), effective for tax. yrs. begin. after 12/31/82, except as provided in Sec. 721(y)(5) of this Act which reads as follows:

"(5) Amendment made by subsection (t). If—

"(A) on or before the date of the enactment of this Act 50 percent or more of the stock of an S corporation has been sold or exchanged in 1 or more transactions, and

"(B) the person (or persons) acquiring such stock establish by clear and convincing evidence that such acquisitions were negotiated on the contemplation that paragraph (2) of section 1362(e) of the Internal Revenue Code of 1954 would apply to the S termination year in which such sales or exchanges occur,

then the amendment made by subsection (t) shall not apply to such S termination year."

In 1982, P.L. 97-354, Sec. 2, added Code Sec. 1362 as part of the amendments to Subchapter S, effective for tax. yrs. begin. after 12/31/82, except for para. (d)(3) which is effective for tax. yrs. begin. after 12/31/81 as provided in Sec. 6(b)(3)(A) of this Act which reads as follows:

"(3) New passive income rules apply to taxable years beginning during 1982. In the case of a taxable year beginning during 1982—

"(A) sections 1362(d)(3), 1366(f)(3), and 1375 of the Internal Revenue Code of 1954 (as amended by this Act) shall apply, and

"(B) section 1372(e)(5) of such Code (as in effect on the day before the date of the enactment of this Act) shall not apply.
The preceding sentence shall not apply in the case of any corporation which elects (at such time and in such manner as the Secretary of the Treasury or his delegate shall prescribe) to have such sentence not apply. Subsection (e) shall not apply to any termination resulting from an election under the preceding sentence."
—P.L. 97-354, Sec. 6(e), of this Act provides as follows:
"(e) Treatment of certain elections under prior law. For purposes of section 1362(g) of the Internal Revenue Code of 1954, as amended by this Act (relating to no election permitted within 5 years after termination of prior election), any termination or revocation under section 1372(e) of such Code (as in effect on the day before the date of the enactment of this Act [10/18/82] shall not be taken into account."
For exceptions and special rules see Sec. 6(c) of this Act reproduced in note following Code Sec. 1361.

Sec. 1363. Effect of election on corporation.
(a) General rule.
Except as otherwise provided in this subchapter, an S corporation shall not be subject to the taxes imposed by this chapter.

(b) Computation of corporation's taxable income.
The taxable income of an S corporation shall be computed in the same manner as in the case of an individual, except that—
(1) the items described in section 1366(a)(1)(A) shall be separately stated,
(2) the deductions referred to in section 703(a)(2) shall not be allowed to the corporation,
(3) section 248 shall apply, and
(4) section 291 shall apply if the S corporation (or any predecessor) was a C corporation for any of the 3 immediately preceding taxable years.

(c) Elections of the S corporation.
(1) **In general.** Except as provided in paragraph (2), any election affecting the computation of items derived from an S corporation shall be made by the corporation.
(2) **Exceptions.** In the case of an S corporation, elections under the following provisions shall be made by each shareholder separately—
(A) section 617 (relating to deduction and recapture of certain mining exploration expenditures), and
(B) section 901 (relating to taxes of foreign countries and possessions of the United States).

(d) Recapture of LIFO benefits.
(1) **In general.** If—
(A) an S corporation was a C corporation for the last taxable year before the first taxable year for which the election under section 1362(a) was effective, and
(B) the corporation inventoried goods under the LIFO method for such last taxable year,
the LIFO recapture amount shall be included in the gross income of the corporation for such last taxable year (and appropriate adjustments to the basis of inventory shall be made to take into account the amount included in gross income under this paragraph).
(2) **Additional tax payable in installments.**
(A) In general. Any increase in the tax imposed by this chapter by reason of this subsection shall be payable in 4 equal installments.
(B) Date for payment of installments. The first installment under subparagraph (A) shall be paid on or before the due date (determined without regard to extensions) for the return of the tax imposed by this chapter for the last taxable year for which the corporation was a C corporation and the 3 succeeding installments shall be paid on or before the due date (as so determined) for the corporation's return for the 3 succeeding taxable years.
(C) No interest for period of extension. Notwithstanding section 6601(b), for purposes of section 6601, the date prescribed for the payment of each installment under this paragraph shall be determined under this paragraph.
(3) **LIFO recapture amount.** For purposes of this subsection, the term "LIFO recapture amount" means the amount (if any) by which—
(A) the inventory amount of the inventory asset under the first-in, first-out method authorized by section 471, exceeds
(B) the inventory amount of such assets under the LIFO method.
For purposes of the preceding sentence, inventory amounts shall be determined as of the close of the last taxable year referred to in paragraph (1).
(4) **Other definitions.** For purposes of this subsection—
(A) LIFO method. The term "LIFO method" means the method authorized by section 472.
(B) Inventory assets. The term "inventory assets" means stock in trade of the corporation, or other property of a kind which would properly be included in the inventory of the corporation if on hand at the close of the taxable year.
(C) Method of determining inventory amount. The inventory amount of assets under a method authorized by section 471 shall be determined—
(i) if the corporation uses the retail method of valuing inventories under section 472, by using such method, or
(ii) if clause (i) does not apply, by using cost or market, whichever is lower.
(D) Not treated as member of affiliated group. Except as provided in regulations, the corporation referred to in paragraph (1) shall not be treated as a member of an affiliated group with respect to the amount included in gross income under paragraph (1).
(5) **Special rule.** Sections 1367(a)(2)(D) and 1371(c)(1) shall not apply with respect to any increase in the tax imposed by reason of this subsection.

In 2007, P.L. 110-28, Sec. 7235, of this Act, [relating to Sec. 1311 of P.L. 104-188, see below] provides:
"SEC. 7235. ELIMINATION OF ALL EARNINGS AND PROFITS ATTRIBUTABLE TO PRE-1983 YEARS FOR CERTAIN CORPORATIONS.
"In the case of a corporation which is—
"(1) described in section 1311(a)(1) of the Small Business Job Protection Act of 1996, and
"(2) not described in section 1311(a)(2) of such Act,
"the amount of such corporation's accumulated earnings and profits (for the first taxable year beginning after the date of the enactment of this Act) shall be reduced by an amount equal to the portion (if any) of such accumulated earnings and profits which were accumulated in any taxable year beginning before January 1, 1983, for which such corporation was an electing small business corporation under subchapter S of the Internal Revenue Code of 1986."
In 2005, P.L. 109-135, Sec. 411(a), added para. (d)(5), generally effective in the case of elections made after 12/17/87 as if included in Sec. 10227 of the Omnibus Budget Reconciliation Act of 1987, P.L. 100-203. For special exception, see Sec. 10227(b)(2) of such Act, reproduced below.
In 1996, P.L. 104-188, Sec. 1311(a), of this Act, regarding elimination of certain earnings and profits, is reproduced in note following Code Sec. 1361.
In 1988, P.L. 100-647, Sec. 1006(f)(7), deleted subsecs. (d) and (e), effective as provided in Sec. 633 of P.L. 99-514 reproduced below.
Prior to deletion, subsecs. (d) and (e) read as follows:
"(d) Distributions of appreciated property. Except as provided in subsection (e), if—
"(1) an S corporation makes a distribution of property (other than an obligation of such corporation) with respect to its stock, and
"(2) the fair market value of such property exceeds its adjusted basis in the hands of the S corporation,
then, notwithstanding any other provision of this subtitle, gain shall be recognized to the S corporation on the distribution in the same manner as if it had sold such property to the distributee at its fair market value.
"(e) Subsection (d) not to apply to reorganizations, etc. Subsection (d) shall not apply to any distribution to the extent it consists of property permitted by section 354, 355, or 356 to be received without the recognition of gain."

—P.L. 100-647, Sec. 2004(n), added subpara. (d)(4)(D), effective in the case of elections made after 12/17/87, except as provided by Sec. 10227(b)(2) of 100-203, reproduced below.

In 1987, P.L. 100-203, Sec. 10227(a), added new subsec. (d) [sic (f)], effective in the case of elections made after 12/17/87, except as provided by Sec. 10227(b)(2) which reads as follows:

"(2) Exception.— The amendment made by subsection (a) shall not apply in the case of any election made by a corporation after December 17, 1987, and before January 1, 1989, if, on or before December 17, 1987—

"(A) there was a resolution adopted by the board of directors of such corporation to make an election under subchapter S of chapter 1 of the Internal Revenue Code of 1986, or

"(B) there was a ruling request with respect to the business filed with the Internal Revenue Service expressing an intent to make such an election."

In 1986, P.L. 99-514, Sec. 511(d)(2)(C), deleted subpara. (c)(2)(A) and redesignated subparas. (c)(2)(B) and (C) as subparas. (c)(2)(A) and (B), effective for tax. yrs. begin. after 12/31/86.

Prior to deletion, subpara. (c)(2)(A) read as follows:

"(A) section 163(d) (relating to limitation on interest on investment indebtedness),"

—P.L. 99-514, Sec. 632(b), amended subsec. (e), effective as provided in Sec. 633(a)(1) of this Act, which reads as follows:

"(a) General rule.

"Except as otherwise provided in this section, the amendments made by [Subtitle D of Title VI, P.L. 99-514] shall apply to—

"(1) any distribution in complete liquidation, and any sale or exchange, made by a corporation after July 31, 1986, unless such corporation is completely liquidated before January 1, 1987,"

—P.L. 99-514, Sec. 633(e), of this Act provides:

"(d) [sic (e)] Complete liquidation defined.

"For purposes of this section, a corporation shall be treated as completely liquidated if all of the assets of such corporation are distributed in complete liquidation, less assets retained to meet claims."

Prior to amendment, subsec. (e) read as follows:

"(e) Subsection (d) not to apply to complete liquidations and reorganizations.

"Subsection (d) shall not apply to any distribution—

"(1) of property in complete liquidation of the corporation, or

"(2) to the extent it consists of property permitted by section 354, 355, or 356 to be received without the recognition of gain."

—P.L. 99-514, Sec. 701(e)(4)(J), deleted "and in section 58(d)" after "this subchapter" in subsec. (a), effective for tax. yrs. begin. after 12/31/86.

In 1984, P.L. 98-369, Sec. 721(␣)(1), added subsec. (e) ... Sec. 721(a)(2), substituted "Except as provided in subsection (e), if" for "If" in subsec. (d) ... Sec. 721(b)(1), deleted subpara. (c)(2)(A) and redesignated subparas. (c)(2)(B), (c)(2)(C) and (c)(2)(D) as subparas. (c)(2)(A), (c)(2)(B) and (c)(2)(C) ... Sec. 721(p), deleted "and" at the end of para. (b)(2), substituted ", and" for the period in para. (b)(3), added para. (b)(4), effective, generally, for tax. yrs. begin. after 12/31/82.

Prior to deletion, subpara. (c)(2)(A) read as follows:

"(A) subsection (b)(5) or (d)(4) of section 108 (relating to income from discharge of indebtedness),"

In 1982, P.L. 97-354, Sec. 2, added Code Sec. 1363 as part of the amendments to Subchapter S, effective for tax. yrs. begin. after 12/31/82. For exceptions and special rules see Sec. 6(c) of this Act reproduced in note following Code Sec. 1361.

PART II.—TAX TREATMENT OF SHAREHOLDERS

Sec.

1366. Pass-thru of items to shareholders.

1367. Adjustments to basis of stock of shareholders, etc.

1368. Distributions.

Sec. 1366. Pass-thru of items to shareholders.

(a) Determination of shareholder's tax liability.

(1) In general. In determining the tax under this chapter of a shareholder for the shareholder's taxable year in which the taxable year of the S corporation ends (or for the final taxable year of a shareholder who dies, or of a trust or estate which terminates, before the end of the corporation's taxable year), there shall be taken into account the shareholder's pro rata share of the corporation's

(A) items of income (including tax-exempt income), loss, deduction, or credit the separate treatment of which could affect the liability for tax of any shareholder, and

(B) nonseparately computed income or loss.

For purposes of the preceding sentence, the items referred to in subparagraph (A) shall include amounts described in paragraph (4) or (6) of section 702(a).

(2) Nonseparately computed income or loss defined. For purposes of this subchapter, the term "nonseparately computed income or loss" means gross income minus the deductions allowed to the corporation under this chapter, determined by excluding all items described in paragraph (1)(A).

(b) Character passed thru.

The character of any item included in a shareholder's pro rata share under paragraph (1) of subsection (a) shall be determined as if such item were realized directly from the source from which realized by the corporation, or incurred in the same manner as incurred by the corporation.

(c) Gross income of a shareholder.

In any case where it is necessary to determine the gross income of a shareholder for purposes of this title, such gross income shall include the shareholder's pro rata share of the gross income of the corporation.

(d) Special rules for losses and deductions.

(1) Cannot exceed shareholder's basis in stock and debt. The aggregate amount of losses and deductions taken into account by a shareholder under subsection (a) for any taxable year shall not exceed the sum of

(A) the adjusted basis of the shareholder's stock in the S corporation (determined with regard to paragraphs (1) and (2)(A) of section 1367(a) for the taxable year), and

(B) the shareholder's adjusted basis of any indebtedness of the S corporation to the shareholder (determined without regard to any adjustment under paragraph (2) of section 1367(b) for the taxable year).

(2) Indefinite carryover of disallowed losses and deductions.

(A) In general. Except as provided in subparagraph (B), any loss or deduction which is disallowed for any taxable year by reason of paragraph (1) shall be treated as incurred by the corporation in the succeeding taxable year with respect to that shareholder.

(B) Transfers of stock between spouses or incident to divorce. In the case of any transfer described in section 1041(a) of stock of an S corporation, any loss or deduction described in subparagraph (A) with respect such stock shall be treated as incurred by the corporation in the succeeding taxable year with respect to the transferee.

(3) Carryover of disallowed losses and deductions to post-termination transition period.

(A) In general. If for the last taxable year of a corporation for which it was an S corporation a loss or deduction was disallowed by reason of paragraph (1), such loss or deduction shall be treated as incurred by the shareholder on the last day of any post-termination transition period.

(B) Cannot exceed shareholder's basis in stock. The aggregate amount of losses and deductions taken into account by a shareholder under subparagraph (A) shall not exceed the adjusted basis of the shareholder's stock in the corporation (determined at the close of the last day of the post-termination transition period and without regard to this paragraph).

(C) Adjustment in basis of stock. The shareholder's basis in the stock of the corporation shall be reduced by the amount allowed as a deduction by reason of this paragraph.

(D) At-risk limitations. To the extent that any increase in adjusted basis described in subparagraph (B) would have increased the shareholder's amount at risk under section 465 if such increase had occurred on the day preceding the commencement of the post-termination transition period, rules similar to the rules described in subparagraphs (A) through (C) shall apply to any losses disallowed by reason of section 465(a).

(4) Application of limitation on charitable contributions. In the case of any charitable contribution of property to which the second sentence of section 1367(a)(2) applies, paragraph (1) shall not apply to the extent of the excess (if any) of—

(A) the shareholder's pro rata share of such contribution, over

(B) the shareholder's pro rata share of the adjusted basis of such property.

(e) Treatment of family group.

If an individual who is a member of the family (within the meaning of section 704(e)(3)) of one or more shareholders of an S corporation renders services for the corporation or furnishes capital to the corporation without receiving reasonable compensation therefor, the Secretary shall make such adjustments in the items taken into account by such individual and such shareholders as may be necessary in order to reflect the value of such services or capital.

(f) Special rules.

(1) Subsection (a) not to apply to credit allowable under section 34. Subsection (a) shall not apply with respect to any credit allowable under section 34 (relating to certain uses of gasoline and special fuels).

(2) Treatment of tax imposed on built-in gains. If any tax is imposed under section 1374 for any taxable year on an S corporation, for purposes of subsection (a), the amount so imposed shall be treated as a loss sustained by the S corporation during such taxable year. The character of such loss shall be determined by allocating the loss proportionately among the recognized built-in gains giving rise to such tax.

(3) Reduction in pass-thru for tax imposed on excess net passive income. If any tax is imposed under section 1375 for any taxable year on an S corporation, for purposes of subsection (a), each item of passive investment income shall be reduced by an amount which bears the same ratio to the amount of such tax as—

(A) the amount of such item, bears to

(B) the total passive investment income for the taxable year.

In 2007, P.L. 110-172, Sec. 3(b), added para. (d)(4), effective for contributions made in tax. yrs. begin. after 12/31/2005.

—P.L. 110-28, Sec. 7235, of this Act, [relating to Sec. 1311 of P.L. 104-188, see below] provides:

"SEC. 7235. ELIMINATION OF ALL EARNINGS AND PROFITS ATTRIBUTABLE TO PRE-1983 YEARS FOR CERTAIN CORPORATIONS.

"In the case of a corporation which is—

"(1) described in section 1311(a)(1) of the Small Business Job Protection Act of 1996, and

"(2) not described in section 1311(a)(2) of such Act,

"the amount of such corporation's accumulated earnings and profits (for the first taxable year beginning after the date of the enactment of this Act) shall be reduced by an amount equal to the portion (if any) of such accumulated earnings and profits which were accumulated in any taxable year beginning before January 1, 1983, for which such corporation was an electing small business corporation under subchapter S of the Internal Revenue Code of 1986."

In 2005, P.L. 109-135, Sec. 403(c), of this Act, provides:

"(c) Amendment Related to Section 235 of the Act. Subsection (b) of section 235 of the American Jobs Creation Act of 2004 [P.L. 108-357, see below] is amended by striking 'taxable years beginning' and inserting 'transfers'."

In 2004, P.L. 108-357, Sec. 235(a), amended para. (d)(2), effective for transfers after 12/31/2004 [as amended by Sec. 403(c) of P.L. 109-135, see above].

Prior to amendment, para. (d)(2) read as follows:

"(2) Indefinite carryover of disallowed losses and deductions. Any loss or deduction which is disallowed for any taxable year by reason of paragraph (1) shall be treated as incurred by the corporation in the succeeding taxable year with respect to that shareholder."

In 1996, P.L. 104-188, Sec. 1302(e), added ", or of a trust or estate which terminates," after "who dies" in para. (a)(1) . . . Sec. 1307(c)(3)(A), deleted subsec. (g) . . . Sec. 1309(a)(1), substituted "paragraphs (1) and (2)(A)" for "paragraph (1)" in subpara. (d)(1)(A), effective for tax. yrs. begin. after 12/31/96.

Prior to deletion, subsec. (g) read as follows:

"(g) Cross reference. For rules relating to procedures for determining the tax treatment of subchapter S items, see subchapter D of chapter 63."

—P.L. 104-188, Sec. 1311(a), of this Act, regarding elimination of certain earnings and profits, is reproduced in note following Code Sec. 1361.

—P.L. 104-188, Sec. 1312, added subpara. (d)(3)(D), effective for tax. yrs. begin. after 12/31/96.

In 1989, P.L. 101-239, Sec. 7811(c)(7), amended para. (f)(2), effective as provided in Sec. 633(b) of P.L. 99-514, reproduced below.

Prior to amendment, para (f)(2) read as follows:

"(2) Reduction in pass-thru for tax imposed on built-in gains. If any tax is imposed under section 1374 for any taxable year on an S corporation, for purposes of subsection (a), the amount of each recognized built-in gain within the meaning of section 1374 for such taxable year shall be reduced by its proportionate share of such tax."

In 1988, P.L. 100-647, Sec. 1006(f)(5)(E), substituted "within the meaning of section 1374" for "as defined in section 1374(d)(2)" in para. (f)(2), effective as provided in Sec. 633(b) of P.L. 99-514, reproduced below

—P.L. 100-647, Sec. 1006(g)(1), amended Sec. 633(b) of P.L. 99-514, the effective date for changes made by Sec. 632(c)(2) of P.L. 99-514. see below.

Prior to amendment Sec. 633(b) read as follows:

"(b) Built-in gains of S corporations. The amendments made by section 632 (other than subsection (b) thereof) shall apply to taxable years beginning after December 31, 1986, but only in cases where the 1st taxable year for which the corporation is an S corporation is pursuant to an election made after December 31, 1986."

In 1986, P.L. 99-514, Sec. 632(c)(2), amended para. (f)(2), effective as provided in Sec. 633(b) of this Act [as amended by Sec. 1006(g)(1) of P.L. 100-647, see above] which reads:

"(b) Built-in gains of S corporations.

"(1) In general.—The amendments made by section 632 (other than subsection (b) thereof) shall apply to taxable years beginning after December 31, 1986, but only in cases where the return for the taxable year is filed pursuant to an S election made after December 31, 1986.

"(2) Application of prior law.—In the case of any taxable year of an S corporation which begins after December 31, 1986, and to which the amendments made by section 632 (other than subsection (b) thereof) do not apply, paragraph (1) of section 1374(b) of the Internal Revenue Code of 1954 (as in effect on the date before the date of the enactment of this Act) shall be applied as if it read as follows:

"'(1) an amount equal to 34 percent of the amount by which the net capital gain of the corporation for the taxable year exceeds $25,000, or'".

Prior to amendment, para. (f)(2) [as amended by Sec. 701(e)(4)(K) of this Act, see below] read as follows:

"(2) Reduction in pass-thru for tax imposed on capital gain. If any tax is imposed under section 1374 for any taxable year on an S corporation, for purposes of subsection (a).

"(A) the amount of the corporation's long-term capital gains for the taxable year shall be reduced by the amount of such tax, and

"(B) if the amount of such tax exceeds the amount of such long-term capital gains, the corporation's gains from sales or exchanges of property described in section 1231 shall be reduced by the amount of such excess.

For purposes of the preceding sentence, the term 'long-term capital gain' shall not include any gain from the sale or exchange of property described in section 1231."

—P.L. 99-514, Sec. 701(e)(4)(K), deleted "56 or" after "imposed under section" in para. (f)(2) [as in effect before the amendment made by Sec. 632(c)(2) of this Act, see above], effective for tax. yrs. begin. after 12/31/86 [generally inoperable].

In 1984, P.L. 98-369, Sec. 474(r)(26), substituted "section 34" for "section 39" each place it appeared in para. (f)(1), effective for tax. yrs. begin. after 12/31/83, and for carrybacks from tax. yrs. begin. after 12/31/83.

—P.L. 98-369, Sec. 721(i), amended Sec. 6(b)(3) of P.L. 97-354, the effective date for para. (f)(3), by adding the last two sentences.

—P.L. 98-369, Sec. 735(c)(16), substituted "and special fuels" for "special fuels, and lubricating oil" in para. (f)(1), effective for articles sold after 1/6/83.

In 1982, P.L. 97-354, Sec. 2, added Code Sec. 1366, as part of the amendments to Subchapter S, effective for tax. yrs. begin. after 12/31/82 except for para. (f)(3) which is effective for tax. yrs. begin. after 12/31/81 (as provided in Sec. 6(b)(3)(A)) of this Act which reads as follows:

"(3) New passive income rules apply to taxable years beginning during 1982.—In the case of a taxable year beginning during 1982—

"(A) sections 1362(d)(3), 1366(f)(3), and 1375 of the Internal Revenue Code of 1954 (as amended by this Act) shall apply, and

"(B) section 1372(e)(5) of such Code (as in effect on the day before the date of the enactment of this Act) shall not apply.

The preceding sentence shall not apply in the case of any corporation which elects (at such time and in such manner as the Secretary of the Treasury or his delegate shall prescribe) to have such sentence not apply. Subsection (e) shall not apply to any termination resulting from an election under the preceding sentence. For exceptions and special rules, see Sec. 6(c) of this Act reproduced in the note following Code Sec. 1361."

Sec. 1367. Adjustments to basis of stock of shareholders, etc.

(a) General rule.

(1) **Increases in basis.** The basis of each shareholder's stock in an S corporation shall be increased for any period by the sum of the following items determined with respect to that shareholder for such period:

(A) the items of income described in subparagraph (A) of section 1366(a)(1),

(B) any nonseparately computed income determined under subparagraph (B) of section 1366(a)(1), and

(C) the excess of the deductions for depletion over the basis of the property subject to depletion.

(2) **Decreases in basis.** The basis of each shareholder's stock in an S corporation shall be decreased for any period (but not below zero) by the sum of the following items determined with respect to the shareholder for such period:

(A) distributions by the corporation which were not includible in the income of the shareholder by reason of section 1368,

(B) the items of loss and deduction described in subparagraph (A) of section 1366(a)(1),

(C) any nonseparately computed loss determined under subparagraph (B) of section 1366(a)(1),

(D) any expense of the corporation not deductible in computing its taxable income and not properly chargeable to capital account, and

(E) the amount of the shareholder's deduction for depletion for any oil and gas property held by the S corporation to the extent such deduction does not exceed the proportionate share of the adjusted basis of such property allocated to such shareholder under section 613A(c)(11)(B).

The decrease under subparagraph (B) by reason of a charitable contribution (as defined in section 170(c)) of property shall be the amount equal to the shareholder's pro rata share of the adjusted basis of such property. The preceding sentence shall not apply to contributions made in taxable years beginning after December 31, 2011.

(b) Special rules.

(1) **Income items.** An amount which is required to be included in the gross income of a shareholder and shown on his return shall be taken into account under subparagraph (A) or (B) of subsection (a)(1) only to the extent such amount is included in the shareholder's gross income on his return, increased or decreased by any adjustment of such amount in a redetermination of the shareholder's tax liability.

(2) **Adjustments in basis of indebtedness.**

(A) Reduction of basis. If for any taxable year the amounts specified in subparagraphs (B), (C), (D), and (E) of subsection (a)(2) exceed the amount which reduces the shareholder's basis to zero, such excess shall be applied to reduce (but not below zero) the shareholder's basis in any indebtedness of the S corporation to the shareholder.

(B) Restoration of basis. If for any taxable year beginning after December 31, 1982, there is a reduction under subparagraph (A) in the shareholder's basis in the indebtedness of an S corporation to a shareholder, any net increase (after the application of paragraphs (1) and (2) of subsection (a)) for any subsequent taxable year shall be applied to restore such reduction in basis before any of it may be used to increase the shareholder's basis in the stock of the S corporation.

(3) **Coordination with sections 165(g) and 166(d).** This section and section 1366 shall be applied before the application of sections 165(g) and 166(d) to any taxable year of the shareholder or the corporation in which the security or debt becomes worthless.

(4) **Adjustments in case of inherited stock.**

(A) In general. If any person acquires stock in an S corporation by reason of the death of a decedent or by bequest, devise, or inheritance, section 691 shall be applied with respect to any item of income of the S corporation in the same manner as if the decedent had held directly his pro rata share of such item.

(B) Adjustments to basis. The basis determined under section 1014 of any stock in an S corporation shall be reduced by the portion of the value of the stock which is attributable to items constituting income in respect of the decedent.

In 2010, P.L. 111-312, Sec. 752(a), substituted "December 31, 2011" for "December 31, 2009" in para. (a)(2), effective for contributions made in tax. yrs. begin. after 12/31/2009.

In 2008, P.L. 110-343, Sec. 307(a)DivC, substituted "December 31, 2009" for "December 31, 2007" in para. (a)(2), effective for contributions made in tax. yrs. begin. after 12/31/2007.

In 2007, P.L. 110-28, Sec. 7235, of this Act, [relating to Sec. 1311 of P.L. 104-188, see below] provides:

"SEC. 7235. ELIMINATION OF ALL EARNINGS AND PROFITS ATTRIBUTABLE TO PRE-1983 YEARS FOR CERTAIN CORPORATIONS.

"In the case of a corporation which is—

"(1) described in section 1311(a)(1) of the Small Business Job Protection Act of 1996, and

"(2) not described in section 1311(a)(2) of such Act,

"the amount of such corporation's accumulated earnings and profits (for the first taxable year beginning after the date of the enactment of this Act) shall be reduced by an amount equal to the portion (if any) of such accumulated earnings and profits which were accumulated in any taxable year beginning before January 1, 1983, for which such corporation was an electing small business corporation under subchapter S of the Internal Revenue Code of 1986."

In 2006, P.L. 109-280, Sec. 1203(a), added "The decrease under subparagraph (B) by reason of a charitable contribution (as defined in section 170(c)) of property shall be the amount equal to the shareholder's pro rata share of the adjusted basis of such property. The preceding sentence shall not apply to contributions made in taxable years beginning after December 31, 2007." at the end of para. (a)(2), effective for contributions made in tax. yrs. begin. after 12/31/2005.

In 1996, P.L. 104-188, Sec. 1311(a), of this Act, regarding elimination of certain earnings and profits, is reproduced in note following Code Sec. 1361.

—P.L. 104-188, Sec. 1313(a), added para. (b)(4), effective for decedents dying after 8/20/96.

—P.L. 104-188, Sec. 1702(h)(14), substituted "section 613A(c)(11)(B)" for "section 613A(c)(13)(B)" in subpara. (a)(2)(E), effective for transfers after 10/11/90.

In 1984, P.L. 98-369, Sec. 721(d), amended para. (b)(3)... Sec. 721(w), substituted "for any taxable year beginning after December 31, 1982, there is" for "for any taxable year there is" in subpara. (b)(2)(B), effective for tax. yrs. begin. after 12/31/82. For special rules, see Sec. 6(c) of P.L. 97-354 reproduced in note following Code Sec. 1361.

Prior to amendment, para. (b)(3) read as follows:

"(3) Coordination with section 165(g). This section and section 1366 shall be applied before the application of section 165(g) to any taxable year of the shareholder or the corporation in which the stock becomes worthless."

—P.L. 98-369, Sec. 722(e)(2), amended subpara. (a)(2)(E), effective for tax. yrs. begin. after 12/31/82.

Prior to amendment, subpara. (a)(2)(E) read as follows:

"(E) the amount of the shareholder's deduction for depletion under section 611 with respect to oil and gas wells."

In 1982, P.L. 97-354, Sec. 2, added Code Sec. 1367 as part of the amendments to Subchapter S, effective for tax. yrs. begin. after 12/31/82. For exceptions and special rules, see Sec. 6(c) of this Act reproduced in the note following Code Sec. 1361.

Sec. 1368. Distributions.

(a) General rule.

A distribution of property made by an S corporation with respect to its stock to which (but for this subsection) section 301(c) would apply shall be treated in the manner provided in subsection (b) or (c), whichever applies.

(b) S corporation having no earnings and profits.

In the case of a distribution described in subsection (a) by an S corporation which has no accumulated earnings and profits—

(1) Amount applied against basis. The distribution shall not be included in gross income to the extent that it does not exceed the adjusted basis of the stock.

(2) Amount in excess of basis. If the amount of the distribution exceeds the adjusted basis of the stock, such excess shall be treated as gain from the sale or exchange of property.

(c) S corporation having earnings and profits.

In the case of a distribution described in subsection (a) by an S corporation which has accumulated earnings and profits—

(1) Accumulated adjustments account. That portion of the distribution which does not exceed the accumulated adjustments account shall be treated in the manner provided by subsection (b).

(2) Dividend. That portion of the distribution which remains after the application of paragraph (1) shall be treated as a dividend to the extent it does not exceed the accumulated earnings and profits of the S corporation.

(3) Treatment of remainder. Any portion of the distribution remaining after the application of paragraph (2) of this subsection shall be treated in the manner provided by subsection (b).

Except to the extent provided in regulations, if the distributions during the taxable year exceed the amount in the accumulated adjustments account at the close of the taxable year, for purposes of this subsection, the balance of such account shall be allocated among such distributions in proportion to their respective sizes.

(d) Certain adjustments taken into account.

Subsections (b) and (c) shall be applied by taking into account (to the extent proper)—

(1) the adjustments to the basis of the shareholder's stock described in section 1367, and

(2) the adjustments to the accumulated adjustments account which are required by subsection (e)(1).

In the case of any distribution made during any taxable year, the adjusted basis of the stock shall be determined without regard to the adjustments provided in paragraph (1) of section 1367(a) for the taxable year.

(e) Definitions and special rules.

For purposes of this section—

(1) Accumulated adjustments account.

(A) In general. Except as otherwise provided in this paragraph, the term "accumulated adjustments account" means an account of the S corporation which is adjusted for the S period in a manner similar to the adjustments under section 1367 (except that no adjustment shall be made for income (and related expenses) which is exempt from tax under this title and the phrase "(but not below zero)" shall be disregarded in section 1367(a)(2)) and no adjustment shall be made for Federal taxes attributable to any taxable year in which the corporation was a C corporation.

(B) Amount of adjustment in the case of redemptions. In the case of any redemption which is treated as an exchange under section 302(a) or 303(a), the adjustment in the accumulated adjustments account shall be an amount which bears the same ratio to the balance in such account as the number of shares redeemed in such redemption bears to the number of shares of stock in the corporation immediately before such redemption.

(C) Net loss for year disregarded.

(i) In general. In applying this section to distributions made during any taxable year, the amount in the accumulated adjustments account as of the close of such taxable year shall be determined without regard to any net negative adjustment for such taxable year.

(ii) Net negative adjustment. For purposes of clause (i), the term "net negative adjustment" means, with respect to any taxable year, the excess (if any) of—

(I) the reductions in the account for the taxable year (other than for distributions), over

(II) the increases in such account for such taxable year.

(2) S period. The term "S period" means the most recent continuous period during which the corporation has been an S corporation. Such period shall not include any taxable year beginning before January 1, 1983.

(3) Election to distribute earnings first.

(A) In general. An S corporation may, with the consent of all of its affected shareholders, elect to have paragraph (1) of subsection (c) not apply to all distributions made during the taxable year for which the election is made.

(B) Affected shareholder. For purposes of subparagraph (A), the term "affected shareholder" means any shareholder to whom a distribution is made by the S corporation during the taxable year.

(f) Restricted bank director stock.

If a director receives a distribution (not in part or full payment in exchange for stock) from an S corporation with respect to any restricted bank director stock (as defined in section 1361(f)), the amount of such distribution—

(1) shall be includible in gross income of the director, and

(2) shall be deductible by the corporation for the taxable year of such corporation in which or with which ends the taxable year in which such amount in included in the gross income of the director.

In 2007, P.L. 110-28, Sec. 8232(b), added subsec. (f), effective for tax. yrs. begin. after 12/31/2006, except as provided by Sec. 8232(c) of this Act which reads as follows:

"Special rule for treatment as second class of stock. In the case of any taxable year beginning after December 31, 1996, restricted bank director stock (as defined in section 1361(f) of the Internal Revenue Code of 1986, as added by this section) shall not be taken into account in determining whether an S corporation has more than 1 class of stock.

—P.L. 110-28, Sec. 8235, of this Act, [relating to Sec. 1311 of P.L. 104-188, see below] provides:

"SEC. 8235. ELIMINATION OF ALL EARNINGS AND PROFITS ATTRIBUTABLE TO PRE-1983 YEARS FOR CERTAIN CORPORATIONS.

"In the case of a corporation which is—

"(1) described in section 1311(a)(1) of the Small Business Job Protection Act of 1996, and

"(2) not described in section 1311(a)(2) of such Act,

"the amount of such corporation's accumulated earnings and profits (for the first taxable year beginning after the date of the enactment of this Act) shall be reduced by an amount equal to the portion (if any) of such accumulated earnings and profits which were accumulated in any taxable year beginning before January 1, 1983, for which such corporation was an electing small business corporation under subchapter S of the Internal Revenue Code of 1986."

In 1996, P.L. 104-188, Sec. 1309(a)(2), added the sentence at the end of subsec. (d) . . . Sec. 1309(b), added subpara. (e)(1)(C) . . . Sec. 1309(c)(1), substituted "as otherwise provided in this paragraph" for "as provided in subparagraph (B)" in subpara. (e)(1)(A) . . . Sec. 1309(c)(2), substituted "section 1367(a)(2)" for "section 1367(b)(2)(A)" in subpara. (e)(1)(A), effective for tax. yrs. begin. after 12/31/96.

—P.L. 104-188, Sec. 1311(a), of this Act, regarding elimination of certain earnings and profits, is reproduced in note following Code Sec. 1361.

In 1986, P.L. 99-514, Sec. 1879(m)(1)(B), substituted "and no adjustment shall be made for Federal taxes attributable to any taxable year in which the corporation was a C corporation." for the period at the end of subpara. (e)(1)(A), effective for tax. yrs. begin. after 12/31/82.

In 1984, P.L. 98-369, Sec. 721(r)(1), substituted "(except that no adjustment shall be made for income (and related expenses) which is exempt from tax under this title and the phrase '(but not below zero)' shall be disregarded in section

Code Sec. 1368   Subchapter S

1367(b)(2)(A)" for "(except that no adjustment shall be made for income which is exempt from tax under this title and no adjustment shall be made for any expense not deductible in computing the corporation's taxable income and not properly chargeable to capital account)" in subpara. (e)(1)(A) . . . Sec. 721(r)(2), added the last sentence to subsec. (c), effective for tax. yrs. begin. after 12/31/82. For special rules, see Sec. 6(c) of P.L. 97-354 reproduced in note following Code Sec. 1361.

In **1983**, P.L. 97-448, Sec. 305(d)(2), added para. (e)(3), effective 10/19/82.

In **1982**, P.L. 97-354, Sec. 2, added Code Sec. 1368 as part of the amendments to Subchapter S, effective for tax. yrs. begin after 12/31/82. For exceptions and special rules, see Sec. 6(c) of this Act reproduced in the note following Code Sec. 1361.

PART III.— SPECIAL RULES

Sec.

1371. Coordination with subchapter C.
1372. Partnership rules to apply for fringe benefit purposes.
1373. Foreign income.
1374. Tax imposed on certain built-in gains.
1375. Tax imposed when passive investment income of corporation having accumulated earnings and profits exceeds 25 percent of gross receipts.

In **1996**, P.L. 104-188, Sec. 1311(b)(2)(D), substituted "accumulated" for "subchapter C" in item 1375.

In **1986**, P.L. 99-514, Sec. 632(d), substituted "built-in" for "capital" in item 1374.

Sec. 1371.   Coordination with subchapter C.

(a) Application of subchapter C rules.

Except as otherwise provided in this title, and except to the extent inconsistent with this subchapter, subchapter C shall apply to an S corporation and its shareholders.

(b) No carryover between C year and S year.

(1) From C year to S year. No carryforward, and no carryback, arising for a taxable year for which a corporation is a C corporation may be carried to a taxable year for which such corporation is an S corporation.

(2) No carryover from S year. No carryforward, and no carryback, shall arise at the corporate level for a taxable year for which a corporation is an S corporation.

(3) Treatment of S year as elapsed year. Nothing in paragraphs (1) and (2) shall prevent treating a taxable year for which a corporation is an S corporation as a taxable year for purposes of determining the number of taxable years to which an item may be carried back or carried forward.

(c) Earnings and profits.

(1) In general. Except as provided in paragraphs (2) and (3) and subsection (d)(3), no adjustment shall be made to the earnings and profits of an S corporation.

(2) Adjustments for redemptions, liquidations, reorganizations, divisives, etc. In the case of any transaction involving the application of subchapter C to any S corporation, proper adjustment to any accumulated earnings and profits of the corporation shall be made.

(3) Adjustments in case of distributions treated as dividends under section 1368(c)(2). Paragraph (1) shall not apply with respect to that portion of a distribution which is treated as a dividend under section 1368(c)(2).

(d) Coordination with investment credit recapture.

(1) No recapture by reason of election. Any election under section 1362 shall be treated as a mere change in the form of conducting a trade or business for purposes of the second sentence of section 50(a)(4).

(2) Corporation continues to be liable. Notwithstanding an election under section 1362, an S corporation shall continue to be liable for any increase in tax under section 49(b) or 50(a) attributable to credits allowed for taxable years for which such corporation was not an S corporation.

(3) Adjustment to earnings and profits for amount of recapture. Paragraph (1) of subsection (c) shall not apply to any increase in tax under section 49(b) or 50(a) for which the S corporation is liable.

(e) Cash distributions during post-termination transition period.

(1) In general. Any distribution of money by a corporation with respect to its stock during a post-termination transition period shall be applied against and reduce the adjusted basis of the stock, to the extent that the amount of the distribution does not exceed the accumulated adjustments account (within the meaning of section 1368(e)).

(2) Election to distribute earnings first. An S corporation may elect to have paragraph (1) not apply to all distributions made during a post-termination transition period described in section 1377(b)(1)(A). Such election shall not be effective unless all shareholders of the S corporation to whom distributions are made by the S corporation during such post-termination transition period consent to such election.

In **2007**, P.L. 110-28, Sec. 7235, of this Act, [relating to Sec. 1311 of P.L. 104-188, see below] provides:

"SEC. 7235. ELIMINATION OF ALL EARNINGS AND PROFITS ATTRIBUTABLE TO PRE-1983 YEARS FOR CERTAIN CORPORATIONS.

"In the case of a corporation which is—

"(1) described in section 1311(a)(1) of the Small Business Job Protection Act of 1996, and

"(2) not described in section 1311(a)(2) of such Act,

"the amount of such corporation's accumulated earnings and profits (for the first taxable year beginning after the date of the enactment of this Act) shall be reduced by an amount equal to the portion (if any) of such accumulated earnings and profits which were accumulated in any taxable year beginning before January 1, 1983, for which such corporation was an electing small business corporation under subchapter S of the Internal Revenue Code of 1986."

In **1996**, P.L. 104-188, Sec. 1310, amended subsec. (a), effective for tax. yrs. begin. after 12/31/96.

Prior to amendment, subsec. (a) read as follows:

"(a) Application of subchapter C rules.

"(1) In general. Except as otherwise provided in this title, and except to the extent inconsistent with this subchapter, subchapter C shall apply to an S corporation and its shareholders.

"(2) S corporation as shareholder treated like individual. For purposes of subchapter C, an S corporation in its capacity as a shareholder of another corporation shall be treated as an individual."

—P.L. 104-188, Sec. 1311(a), of this Act, regarding elimination of certain earnings and profits, is reproduced in note following Code Sec. 1361.

In **1990**, P.L. 101-508, Sec. 11813(b)(23)(A), substituted "section 50(a)(4)" for "section 47(b)" in para. (d)(1) . . . Sec. 11813(b)(23)(B), substituted "section 49(b) or 50(a)" for "section 47" in paras. (d)(2) and (d)(3), effective for property placed in service after 12/31/90 except as provided in Sec. 11813(c)(2) of this Act, reproduced in note following Code Sec. 46.

In **1986**, P.L. 99-514, Sec. 1899A(33), added "(within the meaning of section 1368(e))" after "accumulated adjustments account" in para. (e)(1) . . . Sec. 1899A(34), deleted "(within the meaning of section 1368(e))" after "such election" in para. (e)(2), effective 10/22/86.

In **1984**, P.L. 98-369, Sec. 721(e)(1), added para. (d)(3) . . . Sec. 721(e)(2), substituted "paragraphs (2) and (3) and subsection (d)(3)" for "paragraphs (2) and (3)" in para. (c)(1) . . . Sec. 721(o); amended subsec. (e) . . . Sec. 721(x)(3), added "(within the meaning of section 1368(e))" before the period at the end of sentence. (e), as amended by Sec. 721(o) of this Act, effective for tax. yrs. begin. after 12/31/82. For special rules, see Sec. 6(c) of P.L. 97-354 reproduced in note following Code Sec. 1361.

Prior to amendment, subsec. (e) read as follows:

"(e) Cash distributions during post-termination transition period.

"Any distribution of money by a corporation with respect to its stock during a post-termination transition period shall be applied against and reduce the adjusted basis of the stock, to the extent that the amount of the distribution does not exceed the accumulated adjustments account."

In **1982**, P.L. 97-354, Sec. 2, added Code Sec. 1371 as part of the amendments to Subchapter S, effective for tax. yrs. begin. after 12/31/82. For exceptions and special rules, see Sec. 6(c) of this Act reproduced in the note following Code Sec. 1361.

2,854

Sec. 1372. Partnership rules to apply for fringe benefit purposes.

(a) General rule.

For purposes of applying the provisions of this subtitle which relate to employee fringe benefits—

(1) the S corporation shall be treated as a partnership, and

(2) any 2-percent shareholder of the S corporation shall be treated as a partner of such partnership.

(b) 2-percent shareholder defined.

For purposes of this section, the term "2-percent shareholder" means any person who owns (or is considered as owning within the meaning of section 318) on any day during the taxable year of the S corporation more than 2 percent of the outstanding stock of such corporation or stock possessing more than 2 percent of the total combined voting power of all stock of such corporation.

In 2007, P.L. 110-28, Sec. 7235, of this Act, [relating to Sec. 1311 of P.L. 104-188, see below] provides:

"SEC. 7235. ELIMINATION OF ALL EARNINGS AND PROFITS ATTRIBUTABLE TO PRE-1983 YEARS FOR CERTAIN CORPORATIONS.

"In the case of a corporation which is—

"(1) described in section 1311(a)(1) of the Small Business Job Protection Act of 1996, and

"(2) not described in section 1311(a)(2) of such Act,

"the amount of such corporation's accumulated earnings and profits (for the first taxable year beginning after the date of the enactment of this Act) shall be reduced by an amount equal to the portion (if any) of such accumulated earnings and profits which were accumulated in any taxable year beginning before January 1, 1983, for which such corporation was an electing small business corporation under subchapter S of the Internal Revenue Code of 1986."

In 1996, P.L. 104-188, Sec. 1311(a), of this Act, regarding elimination of certain earnings and profits, is reproduced in note following Code Sec. 1361.

In 1982, P.L. 97-354, Sec. 2, added Code Sec. 1372, as part of the amendments to Subchapter S, effective for tax. yrs. begin. after 12/31/82. For exceptions and special rules, see Sec. 6(c) of this Act reproduced in the note following Code Sec. 1361. Sec. 6(d) of this Act provides:

"(d) Treatment of existing fringe benefit plans.

"(1) In General.—In the case of existing fringe benefits of a corporation which as of September 28, 1982, was an electing small business corporation, section 1372 of the Internal Revenue Code of 1954 (as added by this Act) shall apply only with respect to taxable years beginning after December 31, 1987.

"(2) Requirements.—This subsection shall cease to apply with respect to any corporation after whichever of the following first occurs:

"(A) the first day of the first taxable year beginning after December 31, 1982, with respect to which the corporation does not meet the requirements of section 1372(e)(5) of such Code (as in effect on the day before the date of the enactment of this Act),

"any termination after December 31, 1982, of the election of the corporation under subchapter S of chapter 1 of such Code, or

"(C) the first day on which more than 50 percent of the stock of the corporation is newly owned stock within the meaning of section 1378(c)(2) of such Code (as amended by this Act).

"(3) Existing fringe benefit.—For purposes of this subsection, the term 'existing fringe benefit' means any employee fringe benefit of a type which the corporation provided to its employees as of September 28, 1982."

In 1978, P.L. 95-628, Sec. 5(a), amended subsec. (c) [amendment made by 5(a) is the same as that of Sec. 343(a) of P.L. 95-600, see below] . . . Sec. 5(b)(1), amended subpara. (e)(1)(A) . . . Sec. 5(b)(2), amended subsec. (a) [amendment made by 5(b)(2) is the same as that of Sec. 343(b)(1) of P.L. 95-600, see below] . . . Sec. 5(b)(3), amended subpara. (e)(1)(C) [amendment made by 5(b)(3) is the same as that of Sec. 343(b)(3) of P.L. 95-600, see below], effective for elections made more than 60 days after 11/10/78 for tax. yrs. begin. more than 60 days after 11/10/78. . . . Sec. 5(d), of this Act, provides:

"(d) Retroactive application of 'preceding taxable year' amendment.

"(1) In general. If—

"(A) a small business corporation has treated itself in its return as an electing small business corporation under subchapter S of chapter 1 of the Internal Revenue Code of 1954 for any taxable year beginning before the date 60 days after the date of the enactment of this Act (hereinafter in this subsection referred to as the 'election year'),

"(B) such treatment was pursuant to an election which such corporation made during the taxable year immediately preceding the election year and which, but for this subsection, would not be effective, and

"(C) at such time and in such manner as the Secretary of the Treasury or his delegate may prescribe by regulations—

"(i) such corporation makes an election under this paragraph, and

"(ii) all persons (or their personal representatives) who were shareholders of such corporation at any time beginning with the first day of the election year and ending on the date of the making of such election consent to such election, consent to the application of the amendment made by subsection (a), and consent to the application of paragraph (3) of this subsection,

"then paragraph (1) of the first sentence of section 1372(c) of such Code (as amended by subsection (a)) shall apply with respect to the taxable years referred to in paragraph (2) of this subsection.

"(2) Years to which amendment applies. In the case of an election under paragraph (1) by any corporation, the taxable years referred to in this paragraph are—

"(A) the election year,

"(B) all subsequent taxable years of such corporation, and

"(C) in the case of each person who was a shareholder of such corporation at any time during any taxable year described in subparagraph (A) or (B)—

"(i) the first taxable year of such person ending with or within a taxable year described in subparagraph (A) or (B), and

"(ii) all subsequent taxable years of such person.

"(3) Statute of limitations for assessment of deficiency. If the assessment of any deficiency in income tax resulting from the filing of an election under paragraph (1) for a taxable year ending before the date of such filing would be prevented, but for the application of this paragraph, before the expiration of one year after the date of such filing by any law or rule of law, then such deficiency (to the extent attributable to such election) may be assessed at any time before the expiration of such one-year period notwithstanding any law or rule of law which would otherwise prevent such assessment."

Prior to amendment, subpara. (e)(1)(A) read as follows:

"(A) An election under subsection (a) made by a small business corporation shall terminate if any person who was not a shareholder in such corporation on the day on which the election is made becomes a shareholder in such corporation and affirmatively refuses (in such manner as the Secretary may by regulations prescribe) to consent to such election on or before the 60th day after the day on which he acquires the stock."

—P.L. 95-600, Sec. 343(a), amended subsec. (c) [see Sec. 5(a) of P.L. 105-628, above] . . . Sec. 343(b)(1), amended subsec. (a) [see Sec. 5(b)(1) of P.L. 105-628, above] . . . Sec. 343(b)(2), amended subpara. (e)(1)(A) . . . Sec. 343(b)(3), added "(or, if later, the first taxable year for which such election would otherwise have been effective)" after "in the corporation." in subpara. (e)(1)(A) [see Sec. 5(b)(3) of P.L. 105-628, above], effective for tax. yrs. begin. after 12/31/78.

Prior to amendment, subsec. (a) read as follows:

"(a) Eligibility. Except as provided in subsection (f), any small business corporation may elect, in accordance with the provisions of this section, not to be subject to the taxes imposed by this chapter. Such election shall be valid only if all persons who are shareholders in such corporation—

"(1) on the first day of the first taxable year for which such election is effective, if such election is made on or before such first day, or

"(2) on the day on which the election is made, if the election is made after such first day, consent to such election."

Prior to amendment, subsec. (c) read as follows:

"(c) Where and how made. An election under subsection (a) may be made by a small business corporation for any taxable year at any time during the first month of such taxable year, or at any time during the month preceding such first month. Such election shall be made in such manner as the Secretary shall prescribe by regulations."

Prior to amendment, subpara. (e)(1)(A) read as follows:

"(A) An election under subsection (a) made by a small business corporation shall terminate if any person who was not a shareholder in such corporation—

"(i) on the first day of the first taxable year of the corporation for which the election is effective, if such election is made on or before such first day, or

"(ii) on the day on which the election is made, if such election is made after such first day,

"becomes a shareholder in such corporation and affirmatively refuses (in such manner as the Secretary shall by regulations prescribe) to consent to such election on or before the 60th day after the day on which he acquires the stock."

In 1976, P.L. 94-455, Sec. 902(c)(3), amended para. (e)(1), effective for tax. yrs. begin. after 12/31/76.

Prior to amendment, para. (e)(1) read as follows:

"(1) New shareholders. An election under subsection (a) made by a small business corporation shall terminate if any person who was not a shareholder in such corporation—

"(A) on the first day of the first taxable year of the corporation for which the election is effective, if such election is made on or before such first day, or

"(B) on the day on which the election is made, if such election is made after such first day,

"becomes a shareholder in such corporation and does not consent to such election within such time as the Secretary or his delegate shall prescribe by regulations. Such termination shall be effective for the taxable year of the corporation in which such person becomes a shareholder in the corporation and for all succeeding taxable years of the corporation."

—P.L. 95-455, Sec. 1901(a)(149)(A), substituted "(other than as provided by section 58(d)(2) and by section 1378)" for "(other than the tax imposed by section 1378)" in para. (b)(1) . . . Sec. 1901(a)(149)(B), amended subsec. (c) . . . Sec. 1901(a)(149)(C), deleted subsec. (g), effective for tax. yrs. begin. after 12/31/76.

Prior to amendment, subsec. (c) read as follows:

"(c) Where and how made.

"(1) In general. An election under subsection (a) may be made by a small business corporation for any taxable year at any time during the first month of such taxable year, or at any time during the month preceding such first month. Such election shall be made in such manner as the Secretary or his delegate shall prescribe by regulations.

"(2) Taxable years beginning before date of enactment. An election may be made under subsection (a) by a small business corporation for its first taxable year which begins after December 31, 1957, and on or before the date of the enactment of this subchapter, and ends after such date at any time—

"(A) within the 90-day period beginning on the day after the date of the enactment of this subchapter, or

"(B) if its taxable year ends within such 90-day period, before the close of such taxable year.

"An election may be made pursuant to this paragraph only if the small business corporation has been a small business corporation (as defined in section 1371(a)) on each day after the date of the enactment of this subchapter and before the day of such election."

Prior to deletion, subsec. (g) read as follows:

"(g) Consent to election by certain shareholders of stock held as community property. If a husband and wife owned stock which was community property (or the income from which was community income) under the applicable community property law of a State, and if either spouse filed a timely consent to an election under subsection (a) for a taxable year beginning before January 1, 1961, the time for filing the consent of the other spouse to such election shall not expire prior to May 15, 1961."

—P.L. 94-455, Sec. 1906(b)(13)(A), amended the Internal Revenue Code of 1954, as amended by this Act, by substituting "Secretary" for "Secretary or his delegate" each place it appeared, effective for tax. yrs. begin. after 12/31/76.

In **1971**, P.L. 91-683, Sec. 1(a), added "Gross receipts derived from sales or exchanges of stock or securities for purposes of this paragraph shall not include amounts received by an electing small business corporation which are treated under section 331 (relating to corporate liquidations) as payments in exchange for stock where the electing small business corporation owned more than 50 percent of each class of the stock of the liquidating corporation." at the end of subpara. (e)(5)(C), effective for tax. yrs. of electing small business corporations end. after 1/12/71. Such amendment shall also apply with respect to any tax. yr. end. before 10/7/70, except as provided by Secs. 1(b)(1)-(d) of this Act:

"(1) on such date the making of a refund or the allowance of a credit to the electing small business corporation is not prevented by any law or rule of law, and

"(2) within one year after the date of enactment of this Act and in such manner as the Secretary of the Treasury or his delegate prescribes by regulations—

"(A) the corporation elects to have such amendment so apply, and

"(B) all persons (or their personal representatives) who were shareholders of such corporation at any time during any taxable year beginning with the first taxable year to which this amendment applies and ending on or before the date of the enactment of this Act consent to such election and to the application of the amendment made by subsection (a).

"(c) If the assessment of any deficiency in income tax resulting from the filing of such election for a taxable year ending before the date of such filing is prevented before the expiration of one year after the date of such filing by any law or rule of law, such deficiency (to the extent attributable to such election) may be assessed at any time prior to the expiration of such one-year period notwithstanding any law or rule of law which would otherwise prevent such assessment.

"(d) If the election of a corporation under subsection (a) of section 1372 of the Internal Revenue Code of 1954 would have been terminated because of the application of subsection (e)(5) of such section (before the amendment made by subsection (a) of this section) but for the election by such corporation under paragraph (2) of subsection (b) (and the consent of shareholders under such paragraph), such election under section 1372(a) of such code shall not be treated as terminated for any year beginning before the date of the enactment of this Act as a result of—

"(1) such corporation filing its income tax return on a form 1120 (instead of a form 1120S), or

"(2) a new shareholder not consenting to such election of such corporation in accordance with the requirements of subsection (e)(1) of such section 1372."

In **1966**, P.L. 89-389, Sec. 2(b), added "(other than the tax imposed by section 1378)" immediately after "this chapter." in para. (b)(1), effective with respect to tax yrs. of electing small business corporations begin. after 4/14/66, but not with respect to sales or exchanges occurring before 2/24/66.

—P.L. 89-389, Sec. 3(a), amended para. (e)(5), effective for tax. yrs. of electing small business corporations ending after 4/14/66. Such amendment shall also apply with respect to tax. yrs. begin. after 12/31/62, and end. on or before 4/14/66, if (at such time and in such manner as the Secretary of the Treasury or his delegate prescribes by regulations)—(1) the corporation elects to have such amendment so apply, and (2) shall persons (or their personal representatives) who were shareholders of such corporation at any time during any taxable year beginning after December 31, 1962, and ending on or before the date of the enactment of this Act consent to such election and to the application of the amendment made by subsection (a).

Prior to amendment, para. (e)(5) read as follows:

"(5) Personal holding company income. An election under subsection (a) made by a small business corporation shall terminate if, for any taxable year of the corporation for which the election is in effect, such corporation has gross receipts more than 20 percent of which is derived from royalties, rents, dividends, interest, annuities, and sales or exchanges of stock or securities (gross receipts from such sales or exchanges being taken into account for purposes of this paragraph only to the extent of gains therefrom). Such termination shall be effective for the taxable year of the corporation in which it has gross receipts of such amount, and for all succeeding taxable years of the corporation."

In **1961**, P.L. 87-29, Sec. 2, added subsec. (g), effective for tax yrs. begin. before 1/1/61, the time for filing the consent not to expire prior to 5/15/61.

In **1958**, P.L. 85-866, Sec. 64(a), added Code Sec. 1372, effective for tax yrs. begin. after 12/31/57.

Sec. 1373. Foreign income.

(a) S corporation treated as partnership, etc.

For purposes of subparts A and F of part III, and part V, of subchapter N (relating to income from sources without the United States)—

(1) an S corporation shall be treated as a partnership, and

(2) the shareholders of such corporation shall be treated as partners of such partnership.

(b) Recapture of overall foreign loss.

For purposes of section 904(f) (relating to recapture of overall foreign loss), the making or termination of an election to be treated as an S corporation shall be treated as a disposition of the business.

In **2007**, P.L. 110-28, Sec. 7235, of this Act, [relating to Sec. 1311 of P.L. 104-188, see below] provides:

"SEC. 7235. ELIMINATION OF ALL EARNINGS AND PROFITS ATTRIBUTABLE TO PRE-1983 YEARS FOR CERTAIN CORPORATIONS.

"In the case of a corporation which is—

"(1) described in section 1311(a)(1) of the Small Business Job Protection Act of 1996, and

"(2) not described in section 1311(a)(2) of such Act,

"the amount of such corporation's accumulated earnings and profits (for the first taxable year beginning after the date of the enactment of this Act) shall be reduced by an amount equal to the portion (if any) of such accumulated earnings and profits which were accumulated in any taxable year beginning before January 1, 1983, for which such corporation was an electing small business corporation under subchapter S of the Internal Revenue Code of 1986."

In **1996**, P.L. 104-188, Sec. 1311(a), of this Act, regarding elimination of certain earnings and profits, is reproduced in note following Code Sec. 1361.

In **1982**, P.L. 97-354, Sec. 2, added Code Sec. 1373 as part of the amendments to Subchapter S, effective for tax. yrs. begin. after 12/31/82. For exceptions and special rules, see Sec. 6(c) of this Act reproduced in the note following Code Sec. 1361.

Sec. 1374. Tax imposed on certain built-in gains.

(a) General rule.

If for any taxable year beginning in the recognition period an S corporation has a net recognized built-in gain, there is hereby imposed a tax (computed under subsection (b)) on the income of such corporation for such taxable year.

(b) Amount of tax.

(1) In general. The amount of the tax imposed by subsection (a) shall be computed by applying the highest rate of tax specified in section 11(b) to the net recognized built-in gain of the S corporation for the taxable year.

(2) Net operating loss carryforwards from C years allowed. Notwithstanding section 1371(b)(1), any net operating loss carryforward arising in a taxable year for which the corporation was a C corporation shall be allowed for purposes of this section as a deduction against the net recognized built-in gain of the S corporation for the taxable year. For purposes of determining the amount of any such loss which may be carried to subsequent taxable years, the amount of the net recognized built-in gain shall be treated as taxable income. Rules similar to the rules of the preceding sentences of this paragraph shall apply in the case of a capital loss carryforward arising in a taxable year for which the corporation was a C corporation.

(3) Credits.

(A) In general. Except as provided in subparagraph (B), no credit shall be allowable under part IV of subchapter A of this chapter (other than under section 34) against the tax imposed by subsection (a).

(B) Business credit carryforwards from C years allowed. Notwithstanding section 1371(b)(1), any business credit carryforward under section 39 arising in a taxable year for which the corporation was a C corporation shall be allowed as a credit against the tax imposed by subsection (a) in the same manner as if it were imposed by section 11. A similar rule shall apply in the case of the minimum tax credit under section 53 to the extent attributable to taxable years for which the corporation was a C corporation.

(4) **Coordination with section 1201(a).** For purposes of section 1201(a)—

(A) the tax imposed by subsection (a) shall be treated as if it were imposed by section 11, and

(B) the amount of the net recognized built-in gain shall be treated as the taxable income.

(c) **Limitations.**

(1) **Corporations which were always S corporations.** Subsection (a) shall not apply to any corporation if an election under section 1362(a) has been in effect with respect to such corporation for each of its taxable years. Except as provided in regulations, an S corporation and any predecessor corporation shall be treated as 1 corporation for purposes of the preceding sentence.

(2) **Limitation on amount of net recognized built-in gain.** The amount of the net recognized built-in gain taken into account under this section for any taxable year shall not exceed the excess (if any) of—

(A) the net unrealized built-in gain, over

(B) the net recognized built-in gain for prior taxable years beginning in the recognition period.

(d) **Definitions and special rules.**

For purposes of this section—

(1) **Net unrealized built-in gain.** The term "net unrealized built-in gain" means the amount (if any) by which—

(A) the fair market value of the assets of the S corporation as of the beginning of its 1st taxable year for which an election under section 1362(a) is in effect, exceeds

(B) the aggregate adjusted bases of such assets at such time.

(2) **Net recognized built-in gain.**

(A) In general. The term "net recognized built-in gain" means, with respect to any taxable year in the recognition period, the lesser of—

(i) the amount which would be the taxable income of the S corporation for such taxable year if only recognized built-in gains and recognized built-in losses were taken into account, or

(ii) such corporation's taxable income for such taxable year (determined as provided in section 1375(b)(1)(B)).

(B) Carryover. If, for any taxable year, the amount referred to in clause (i) of subparagraph (A) exceeds the amount referred to in clause (ii) of subparagraph (A), such excess shall be treated as a recognized built-in gain in the succeeding taxable year. The preceding sentence shall apply only in the case of a corporation treated as an S corporation by reason of an election made on or after March 31, 1988.

(3) **Recognized built-in gain.** The term "recognized built-in gain" means any gain recognized during the recognition period on the disposition of any asset except to the extent that the S corporation establishes that—

(A) such asset was not held by the S corporation as of the beginning of the 1st taxable year for which it was an S corporation, or

(B) such gain exceeds the excess (if any) of—

(i) the fair market value of such asset as of the beginning of such 1st taxable year, over

(ii) the adjusted basis of the asset as of such time.

(4) **Recognized built-in losses.** The term "recognized built-in loss" means any loss recognized during the recognition period on the disposition of any asset to the extent that the S corporation establishes that—

(A) such asset was held by the S corporation as of the beginning of the 1st taxable year referred to in paragraph (3), and

(B) such loss does not exceed the excess of

(i) the adjusted basis of such asset as of the beginning of such 1st taxable year, over

(ii) the fair market value of such asset as of such time.

(5) **Treatment of certain built-in items.**

(A) Income items. Any item of income which is properly taken into account during the recognition period but which is attributable to periods before the 1st taxable year for which the corporation was an S corporation shall be treated as a recognized built-in gain for the taxable year in which it is properly taken into account.

(B) Deduction items. Any amount which is allowable as a deduction during the recognition period (determined without regard to any carryover) but which is attributable to periods before the 1st taxable year referred to in subparagraph (A) shall be treated as a recognized built-in loss for the taxable year for which it is allowable as a deduction.

(C) Adjustment to net unrealized built-in gain. The amount of the net unrealized built-in gain shall be properly adjusted for amounts which would be treated as recognized built-in gains or losses under this paragraph if such amounts were properly taken into account (or allowable as a deduction) during the recognition period.

(6) **Treatment of certain property.** If the adjusted basis of any asset is determined (in whole or in part) by reference to the adjusted basis of any other asset held by the S corporation as of the beginning of the 1st taxable year referred to in paragraph (3)—

(A) such asset shall be treated as held by the S corporation as of the beginning of such 1st taxable year, and

(B) any determination under paragraph (3)(B) or (4)(B) with respect to such asset shall be made by reference to the fair market value and adjusted basis of such other asset as of the beginning of such 1st taxable year.

(7) **Recognition period.**

(A) In general. The term "recognition period" means the 10-year period beginning with the 1st day of the 1st taxable year for which the corporation was an S corporation.

(B) Special rules for 2009, 2010, and 2011. No tax shall be imposed on the net recognized built-in gain of an S corporation—

(i) in the case of any taxable year beginning in 2009 or 2010, if the 7th taxable year in the recognition period preceded such taxable year, or

(ii) in the case of any taxable year beginning in 2011, if the 5th year in the recognition period preceded such taxable year.

The preceding sentence shall be applied separately with respect to any asset to which paragraph (8) applies.

(C) Special rule for distributions to shareholders. For purposes of applying this section to any amount includible in income by reason of distributions to shareholders pursuant to section 593(e)—

(i) subparagraph (A) shall be applied without regard to the phrase "10-year", and

(ii) subparagraph (B) shall not apply.

(8) **Treatment of transfer of assets from C corporation to S corporation.**

Code Sec. 1374(d)(8)(A)

(A) In general. Except to the extent provided in regulations, if
  (i) an S corporation acquires any asset, and
  (ii) the S corporation's basis in such asset is determined (in whole or in part) by reference to the basis of such asset (or any other property) in the hands of a C corporation,

then a tax is hereby imposed on any net recognized built-in gain attributable to any such assets for any taxable year beginning in the recognition period. The amount of such tax shall be determined under the rules of this section as modified by subparagraph (B).

(B) Modifications. For purposes of this paragraph, the modifications of this subparagraph are as follows:
  (i) In general. The preceding paragraphs of this subsection shall be applied by taking into account the day on which the assets were acquired by the S corporation in lieu of the beginning of the 1st taxable year for which the corporation was an S corporation.
  (ii) Subsection (c)(1) not to apply. Subsection (c)(1) shall not apply.

(9) Reference to 1st taxable year. Any reference in this section to the 1st taxable year for which the corporation was an S corporation shall be treated as a reference to the 1st taxable year for which the corporation was an S corporation pursuant to its most recent election under section 1362.

(e) Regulations.

The Secretary shall prescribe such regulations as may be necessary to carry out the purposes of this section including regulations providing for the appropriate treatment of successor corporations.

In 2010, P.L. 111-240, Sec. 2014(a), amended subpara. (d)(7)(B), effective for tax. yrs. begin. after 12/31/2010.
Prior to amendment subpara. (d)(7)(B) read as follows:
"(B) Special rule for 2009 and 2010. In the case of any taxable year beginning in 2009 or 2010, no tax shall be imposed on the net recognized built-in gain of an S corporation if the 7th taxable year in the recognition period preceded such taxable year. The preceding sentence shall be applied separately with respect to any asset to which paragraph (8) applies."
In 2009, P.L. 111-5, Sec. 1251(a), amended para. (d)(7), effective for tax. yrs. begin. after 12/31/2008.
Prior to amendment para. (d)(7) read as follows:
"(7) Recognition period.
"The term 'recognition period' means the 10-year period beginning with the 1st day of the 1st taxable year for which the corporation was an S corporation. For purposes of applying this section to any amount includible in income by reason of section 593(e), the preceding sentence shall be applied without regard to the phrase '10-year'."
In 2007, P.L. 110-28, Sec. 7235, of this Act, [relating to Sec. 1311 of P.L. 104-188, see below] provides:
"SEC. 7235. ELIMINATION OF ALL EARNINGS AND PROFITS ATTRIBUTABLE TO PRE-1983 YEARS FOR CERTAIN CORPORATIONS.
"In the case of a corporation which is—
"(1) described in section 1311(a)(1) of the Small Business Job Protection Act of 1996, and
"(2) not described in section 1311(a)(2) of such Act,
"the amount of such corporation's accumulated earnings and profits (for the first taxable year beginning after the date of the enactment of this Act) shall be reduced by an amount equal to the portion (if any) of such accumulated earnings and profits which were accumulated in any taxable year beginning before January 1, 1983, for which such corporation was an electing small business corporation under subchapter S of the Internal Revenue Code of 1986."
In 1997, P.L. 105-34, Sec. 1601(f)(5)(B), added a sentence to the end of para. (d)(7), effective for tax. yrs. begin. after 12/31/95.
In 1996, P.L. 104-188, Sec. 1311(a), of this Act, regarding elimination of certain earnings and profits, is reproduced in note following Code Sec. 1361.
In 1989, P.L. 101-239, Sec. 7811(c)(4), deleted "(except as provided in subsection (b)(2))" after "year if" in clause (d)(2)(A)(i) . . . Sec. 7811(c)(5)(B)(i), substituted "during the recognition period (determined without regard to any carryover)" for "during the recognition period" in subpara. (d)(5)(B) . . . Sec. 7811(c)(5)(B)(ii), substituted "which would be treated as recognized built-in gains or losses under this paragraph if such amounts were properly taken into account (or allowable as a deduction) during the recognition period" for "treated as recognized built-in gains or losses under this paragraph" in subpara. (d)(5)(C) . . . Sec.

Subchapter S

7811(c)(8), added the last sentence to subpara. (b)(3)(B), effective as provided in Sec 633(b) and (d)(8) of P.L. 99-514, reproduced below.
In 1988, P.L. 100-647, Sec. 1006(f)(1), substituted "a net recognized built-in gain" for "a recognized built-in gain" in subsec. (a) . . . Sec. 1006(f)(2), amended paras. (b)(1) and (2) . . . Sec. 1006(f)(3), amended subpara. (b)(4)(B) . . . Sec. 1006(f)(4), substituted "net recognized built-in gain" for "recognized built-in gains" each place it appeared in para. (c)(2) . . . Sec. 1006(f)(5)(A), deleted paras. (d)(2), (3) and (4) and added new paras. (d)(2)-(9) and subsec. (e), effective as provided in Sec. 633(b) and (d)(8) of P.L. 99-514 reproduced below.
Prior to amendment, paras. (b)(1) and (2) read as follows:
"(1) In general. The tax imposed by subsection (a) shall be a tax computed by applying the highest rate of tax specified in section 11(b) to the lesser of—
"(A) the recognized built-in gains of the S corporation for the taxable year, or
"(B) the amount which would be the taxable income of the corporation for such taxable year if such corporation were not an S corporation.
"(2) Net operating loss carryforwards from C years allowed. Notwithstanding section 1371(b)(1), any net operating loss carryforward arising in a taxable year for which the corporation was a C corporation shall be allowed as a deduction against the lesser of the amounts referred to in subparagraph (A) or (B) of paragraph (1). For purposes of determining the amount of any such loss which may be carried to subsequent taxable years, the lesser of the amounts referred to in subparagraph (A) or (B) of paragraph (1) shall be treated as taxable income."
Prior to amendment, subpara. (b)(4)(B) read as follows:
"(B) the lower of the amounts specified in subparagraphs (A) and (B) of paragraph (1) shall be treated as the taxable income."
Prior to amendment, paras. (d)(2)-(4) read as follows:
"(2) Recognized built-in gain. The term 'recognized built-in gain' means any gain recognized during the recognition period on the disposition of any asset except to the extent that the S corporation establishes that
"(A) such asset was not held by the S corporation as of the beginning of the 1st taxable year referred to in paragraph (1), or
"(B) such gain exceeds the excess (if any) of—
"(i) the fair market value of such asset as of the beginning of such 1st taxable year, over
"(ii) the adjusted basis of the asset as of such time.
"(3) Recognition period. The term 'recognition period' means the 10-year period beginning with the 1st day of the 1st taxable year for which the corporation was an S corporation.
"(4) Taxable income. Taxable income of the corporation shall be determined under section 63(a)—
"(A) without regard to the deductions allowed by part VIII of subchapter B (other than the deduction allowed by section 248, relating to organization expenditures), and
"(B) without regard to the deduction under section 172."
—P.L. 100-647, Sec. 1006(g)(1), amended Sec. 633(b) of P.L. 99-514 [reproduced below], the effective date for changes made by Sec. 632(a) of P.L. 99-514, see below.
Prior to amendment, Sec. 633(b) of P.L. 99-514 read as follows:
"(b) Built-in gains of S Corporations. The amendments made by section 632 (other than subsection (b) thereof) shall apply to taxable years beginning after December 31, 1986, but only in cases where the 1st taxable year for which the corporation is an S corporation is pursuant to an election made after December 31, 1986."
—P.L. 100-647, Sec. 1006(g)(7), amended Sec. 633(d)(8) of P.L. 99-514 [reproduced below], part of the effective date for changes made by Sec. 632(a) of P.L. 99-514, by substituting "makes an election to be an S corporation under section 1362 of such Code before January 1, 1989, without regard to whether such corporation is completely liquidated" for "becomes an S corporation for a taxable year beginning before January 1, 1989", see below.
In 1986, P.L. 99-514, Sec. 632(a), amended Code Sec. 1374, effective as provided in Sec. 633(b) of this Act [as amended by Sec. 1006(g)(1) of P.L. 100-647, see above] which reads as follows:
"(b) Built-in gains of S Corporations.
"(1) In general. The amendments made by section 632 (other than subsection (b) thereof) shall apply to taxable years beginning after December 31, 1986, but only in cases where the return for the taxable year is filed pursuant to an S election made after December 31, 1986.
"(2) Application of prior law.—In the case of any taxable year of an S corporation which begins after December 31, 1986, and to which the amendments made by section 632 (other than subsection (b) thereof) do not apply paragraph (1) of section 1374(b) of the Internal Revenue Code of 1954 (as in effect on the date before the date of the enactment of this Act) shall be applied as if it read as follows:
"'(1) an amount equal to 34 percent of the amount by which the net capital gain of the corporation for the taxable year exceeds $25,000, or'."
Sec. 633(d)(8) [as amended by Sec. 1006(g)(7) of P.L. 100-647, see above] provides:
"(8) Application of section 1374. Rules similar to the rules of this subsection [Sec. 633(d)] shall apply for purposes of applying section 1374 of the Internal Revenue Code of 1986 (as amended by section 632) in the case of a qualified corporation which makes an election to be an S corporation under section 1362 of such Code before January 1, 1989, without regard to whether such corporation is completely liquidated."
For transitional rules, see Sec. 633(d)(1)-(7) of this Act reproduced in note following Code Sec. 336.
Prior to amendment, Code Sec. 1374 read as follows:
"SEC. 1374. TAX IMPOSED ON CERTAIN CAPITAL GAINS.

2,858

Subchapter S

Code Sec. 1375(d)(2)

"(a) General rule.
"If for a taxable year of an S corporation
"(1) the net capital gain of such corporation exceeds $25,000, and exceeds 50 percent of its taxable income for such year, and
"(2) the taxable income of such corporation for such year exceeds $25,000, there is hereby imposed a tax (computed under subsection (b)) on the income of such corporation.
"(b) Amount of tax.
"The tax imposed by subsection (a) shall be the lower of—
"(1) an amount equal to the tax, determined as provided in section 1201(a), on the amount by which the net capital gain of the corporation for the taxable year exceeds $25,000, or
"(2) an amount equal to the tax which would be imposed by section 11 on the taxable income of the corporation for the taxable year if the corporation were not an S corporation.
No credit shall be allowable under part IV of subchapter A of this chapter (other than under section 34) against the tax imposed by subsection (a).
"(c) Exceptions.
"(1) In general. Subsection (a) shall not apply to an S corporation for any taxable year if the election under section 1362(a) which is in effect with respect to such corporation for such taxable year has been in effect for the 3 immediately preceding taxable years.
"(2) New corporations. Subsection (a) shall not apply to an S corporation if—
"(A) it has been in existence for less than 4 taxable years, and
"(B) an election under section 1362(a) has been in effect with respect to such corporation for each of its taxable years.
To the extent provided in regulations, an S corporation and any predecessor corporation shall be treated as 1 corporation for purposes of this paragraph and paragraph (1).
"(3) Property with substituted basis. If—
"(A) but for paragraph (1) or (2), subsection (a) would apply for the taxable year,
"(B) any long-term capital gain is attributable to property acquired by the S corporation during the period beginning 3 years before the first day of the taxable year and ending on the last day of the taxable year, and
"(C) the basis of such property is determined in whole or in part by reference to the basis of any property in the hands of another corporation which was not an S corporation throughout all of the period described in subparagraph (B) before the transfer by such other corporation and during which such other corporation was in existence,
then subsection (a) shall apply for the taxable year, but the amount of the tax determined under subsection (b) shall not exceed a tax, determined as provided in section 1201(a), on the net capital gain attributable to property acquired as provided in subparagraph (B) and having a basis described in subparagraph (C).
"(4) Treatment of certain gains of options and commodities dealers.
"(A) Exclusion of certain capital gains. For purposes of this section, the net capital gain of any options dealer or commodities dealer shall be determined by not taking into account any gain or loss (in the normal course of the taxpayer's activity of dealing in or trading section 1256 contracts) from any section 1256 contract or property related to such a contract.
"(B) Definitions. For purposes of this paragraph—
"(i) Options dealer. The term 'options dealer' has the meaning given to such term by section 1256(g)(8).
"(ii) Commodities dealer. The term 'commodities dealer' means a person who is actively engaged in trading section 1256 contracts and is registered with a domestic board of trade which is designated as a contract market by the Commodities Futures Trading Commission.
"(iii) Section 1256 contracts. The term 'section 1256 contracts' has the meaning given to such term by section 1256(b)."
"(d) Determination of taxable income.
"For purposes of this section taxable income of the corporation shall be determined under section 63(a) without regard to—
"(1) the deduction allowed by section 172 (relating to net operating loss deduction), and
"(2) the deductions allowed by part VIII of subchapter B (other than the deduction allowed by section 248, relating to organization expenditures)."
In 1984, P.L. 98-369, Sec. 102(d)(1), added para. (c)(4), effective for positions established after 7/18/84, in tax. yrs. end. after 7/18/84. For special rules and elections, see Sec. 102(f)(2), (g), (h) and (i) reproduced in note following Code Sec. 1362.
—P.L. 98-369, Sec. 474(r)(27), substituted "section 34" for "section 39" in subsec. (b), effective for tax. yrs. begin. after 12/31/83, and for carrybacks from such years.
—P.L. 98-369, Sec. 721(u)(1), deleted "(and any predecessor corporation)" after "it" in subpara. (c)(2)(A) . . . Sec. 721(u)(2), added a sentence at the end of para. (c)(2), effective for tax. yrs. begin. after 12/31/82.
In 1983, P.L. 97-448, Sec. 305(d)(3), substituted "this section" for "subsections (a)(2) and (b)(2)" in subsec. (d), effective 10/19/82.
In 1982, P.L. 97-354, Sec. 2, added Code Sec. 1374 as part of the amendments to Subchapter S, effective for tax. yrs. begin. after 12/31/82. For exceptions and special rules, see Sec. 6(c) of this Act reproduced in the note following Code Sec. 1361.

Sec. 1375. Tax imposed when passive investment income of corporation having accumulated earnings and profits exceeds 25 percent of gross receipts.

(a) **General rule.**
If for the taxable year an S corporation has—
(1) accumulated earnings and profits at the close of such taxable year, and
(2) gross receipts more than 25 percent of which are passive investment income,
then there is hereby imposed a tax on the income of such corporation for such taxable year. Such tax shall be computed by multiplying the excess net passive income by the highest rate of tax specified in section 11(b).

(b) **Definitions.**
For purposes of this section—
(1) Excess net passive income.
  (A) In general. Except as provided in subparagraph (B), the term "excess net passive income" means an amount which bears the same ratio to the net passive income for the taxable year as
    (i) the amount by which the passive investment income for the taxable year exceeds 25 percent of the gross receipts for the taxable year, bears to
    (ii) the passive investment income for the taxable year.
  (B) Limitation. The amount of the excess net passive income for any taxable year shall not exceed the amount of the corporation's taxable income for such taxable year as determined under section 63(a)—
    (i) without regard to the deductions allowed by part VIII of subchapter B (other than the deduction allowed by section 248, relating to organization expenditures), and
    (ii) without regard to the deduction under section 172.
(2) **Net passive income.** The term "net passive income" means—
  (A) passive investment income, reduced by
  (B) the deductions allowable under this chapter which are directly connected with the production of such income (other than deductions allowable under section 172 and part VIII of subchapter B).
(3) **Passive investment income, etc.** The terms "passive investment income" and "gross receipts" have the same respective meanings as when used in paragraph (3) of section 1362(d).
(4) **Coordination with section 1374.** Notwithstanding paragraph (3), the amount of passive investment income shall be determined by not taking into account any recognized built-in gain or loss of the S corporation for any taxable year in the recognition period. Terms used in the preceding sentence shall have the same respective meanings as when used in section 1374.

(c) **Credits not allowable.**
No credit shall be allowed under part IV of subchapter A of this chapter (other than section 34) against the tax imposed by subsection (a).

(d) **Waiver of tax in certain cases.**
If the S corporation establishes to the satisfaction of the Secretary that—
(1) it determined in good faith that it had no accumulated earnings and profits at the close of a taxable year, and
(2) during a reasonable period of time after it was determined that it did have accumulated earnings and profits at the close of such taxable year such earnings and profits were distributed,
the Secretary may waive the tax imposed by subsection (a) for such taxable year.

Code Sec. 1375 — Subchapter S

In 2007, P.L. 110-28, Sec. 7235, of this Act, [relating to Sec. 1311 of P.L. 104-188, see below] provides:

"SEC. 7235. ELIMINATION OF ALL EARNINGS AND PROFITS ATTRIBUTABLE TO PRE-1983 YEARS FOR CERTAIN CORPORATIONS.

"In the case of a corporation which is—

"(1) described in section 1311(a)(1) of the Small Business Job Protection Act of 1996, and

"(2) not described in section 1311(a)(2) of such Act,

"the amount of such corporation's accumulated earnings and profits (for the first taxable year beginning after the date of the enactment of this Act) shall be reduced by an amount equal to the portion (if any) of such accumulated earnings and profits which were accumulated in any taxable year beginning before January 1, 1983, for which such corporation was an electing small business corporation under subchapter S of the Internal Revenue Code of 1986."

In 2005, P.L. 109-135, Sec. 412(qq), substituted "accumulated" for "subchapter C" in paras. (d)(1) and (2), effective 12/21/2005.

In 1996, P.L. 104-188, Sec. 1311(a), of this Act, regarding elimination of certain earnings and profits, is reproduced in note following Code Sec. 1361.

—P.L. 104-188, Sec. 1311(b)(2)(A), substituted "accumulated" for "subchapter (C)" in para. (a)(1)...Sec. 1311(b)(2)(B), amended para. (b)(3)...Sec. 1311(b)(2)(C), substituted "accumulated" for "subchapter (C)" in the heading of Code Sec. 1375, effective for tax. yrs. after 12/31/96.

Prior to amendment, para. (b)(3) read as follows:

"(3) Passive investment income; etc. The terms 'subchapter C earnings and profits', 'passive investment income', and 'gross receipts' shall have the same respective meanings as when used in paragraph (3) of section 1362(d)."

In 1988, P.L. 100-647, Sec. 1006(f)(5)(A), amended subpara. (b)(1)(B)...Sec. 1006(f)(5)(C), added para. (b)(4)...Sec. 1006(f)(5)(D), amended subsec. (c), effective as provided in Sec. 633(b) of P.L. 99-514 [as amended by Sec. 1006(g)(1) of this Act] reproduced below. In the case of any taxable year of an S corporation which begins after December 31, 1986, and to which the amendments made by section 632 (other than subsection (b) thereof) do not apply, paragraph (1) of section 1374(b) of the Internal Revenue Code of 1954 (as in effect on the date before the date of the enactment of this Act) shall be applied as if it read as follows:

"(1) an amount equal to 34 percent of the amount by which the net capital gain of the corporation for the taxable year exceeds $25,000, or"

Prior to amendment, subpara. (b)(1)(B) read as follows:

"(B) Limitation. The amount of the excess net passive income for any taxable year shall not exceed the corporation's taxable income for the taxable year (determined in accordance with section 1374(d)(4))."

Prior to amendment, subsec. (c) read as follows:

"(c) Special rules.

"(1) Disallowance of credit. No credit shall be allowed under part IV of subchapter A of this chapter (other than section 34) against the tax imposed by subsection (a)."

—P.L. 100-647, Sec. 1006(g)(1), amended Sec. 633(b) [see below] of P.L. 99-514, the effective date for changes made by Sec. 632(c)(3) of P.L. 99-514.

Prior to amendment, Sec. 633(b) of P.L. 99-514 read as follows:

"(b) Built-in gains of S corporations.

"The amendments made by section 632 (other than subsection (b) thereof) shall apply to taxable years beginning after December 31, 1986, but only in cases where the 1st taxable year for which the corporation is an S corporation is pursuant to an election made after December 31, 1986."

In 1986, P.L. 99-514, Sec. 632(c)(3), substituted "1374(d)(4)" for "1374(d)" in subpara. (b)(1)(B), effective as provided in Sec. 633(b) [as amended by Sec. 1006(g)(1) of P.L. 100-647, see above] which reads as follows:

"(b) Built-in gains of S corporations.

"(1) In general. The amendments made by section 632 (other than subsection (b) thereof) shall apply to taxable years beginning after December 31, 1986, but only in cases where the return for the taxable year is filed pursuant to an S election made after December 31, 1986.

"(2) Application of prior law. In the case of any taxable year of an S corporation which begins after December 31, 1986, and to which the amendments made by section 632 (other than subsection (b) thereof) do not apply, paragraph (1) of section 1374(b) of the Internal Revenue Code of 1954 (as in effect on the date before the date of the enactment of this Act) shall be applied as if it read as follows:

"'(1) an amount equal to 34 percent of the amount by which the net capital gain of the corporation for the taxable year exceeds $25,000, or'"

In 1984, P.L. 98-369, Sec. 474(r)(28), substituted "section 34" for "section 39" in para. (c)(1), effective for tax. yrs. begin. after 12/31/83, and for carrybacks from tax. yrs. begin. after 12/31/83.

—P.L. 98-369, Sec. 721(i), amended Sec. 6(b)(3) of P.L. 97-354, the effective date for Code Sec. 1375, by adding the last two sentences.

—P.L. 98-369, Sec. 721(v), added subsec. (d), effective for tax. yrs. begin. after 12/31/81.

In 1982, P.L. 97-354, Sec. 2, added Code Sec. 1375 as part of the amendments to Subchapter S, effective for tax. yrs. begin. after 12/31/81. For exceptions and special rules, see Sec. 6(c) of this Act reproduced in the note following Code Sec. 1361.

—P.L. 97-354, Sec. 6(b)(3), of this Act provides the following transitional rule:

"(3) New passive income rules apply to taxable years beginning during 1982.— In the case of a taxable year beginning during 1982—

"(A) sections 1362(d)(3), 1366(f)(3), and 1375 of the Internal Revenue Code of 1954 (as amended by this Act) shall apply, and

"(B) section 1372(e)(5) of such Code (as in effect on the day before the date of the enactment of this Act) shall not apply.

The preceding sentence shall not apply in the case of any corporation which elects (at such time and in such manner as the Secretary of the Treasury or his delegate shall prescribe) to have such sentence not apply. Subsection (e) shall not apply to any termination resulting from an election under the preceding sentence."

In 1982, P.L. 97-354, Sec. 2, removed Code Sec. 1376 as part of the amendments made to Subchapter S, effective for tax. yrs. begin. after 12/31/82.

Prior to deletion, Code Sec. 1376 read as follows:

"Sec. 1376. Adjustment to basis of stock of, and indebtedness owing, shareholders.

"(a) Increase in basis of stock for amounts treated as dividends.

"The basis of a shareholder's stock in an electing small business corporation shall be increased by the amount required to be included in the gross income of such shareholder under section 1373(b), but only to the extent to which such amount is included in his gross income in his return, increased or decreased by any adjustment of such amount in any redetermination of the shareholder's tax liability.

"(b) Reduction in basis of stock and indebtedness for shareholder's portion of corporation net operating loss.

"(1) Reduction in basis of stock. The basis of a shareholder's stock in an electing small business corporation shall be reduced (but not below zero) by an amount equal to the amount of his portion of the corporation's net operating loss for any taxable year attributable to such stock (as determined under section 1374(c)).

"(2) Reduction in basis of indebtedness. The basis of any indebtedness of an electing small business corporation to a shareholder of such corporation shall be reduced (but not below zero) by an amount equal to the amount of the shareholder's portion of the corporation's net operating loss for any taxable year (as determined under section 1374(c), but only to the extent that such amount exceeds the adjusted basis of the stock of such corporation held by the shareholder."

In 1958, P.L. 85-866, Sec. 64, added Code Sec. 1376, effective for tax. yrs. begin. after 1957.

PART IV.—DEFINITIONS; MISCELLANEOUS

Sec.

1377. Definitions and special rule.

1378. Taxable year of S corporation.

1379. Transitional rules on enactment.

Sec. 1377. Definitions and special rule.

(a) Pro rata share.

For purposes of this subchapter—

(1) In general. Except as provided in paragraph (2), each shareholder's pro rata share of any item for any taxable year shall be the sum of the amounts determined with respect to the shareholder—

(A) by assigning an equal portion of such item to each day of the taxable year, and

(B) then by dividing that portion pro rata among the shares outstanding on such day.

(2) Election to terminate year.

(A) In general. Under the regulations prescribed by the Secretary, if any shareholder terminates the shareholder's interest in the corporation during the taxable year and all affected shareholders and the corporation agree to the application of this paragraph, paragraph (1) shall be applied to the affected shareholders as if the taxable year consisted of 2 taxable years the first of which ends on the date of the termination.

(B) Affected shareholders. For purposes of subparagraph (A), the term "affected shareholders" means the shareholder whose interest is terminated and all shareholders to whom such shareholder has transferred shares during the taxable year. If such shareholder has transferred shares to the corporation, the term "affected shareholders" shall include all persons who are shareholders during the taxable year.

(b) Post-termination transition period.

(1) In general. For purposes of this subchapter, the term "post-termination transition period" means—

(A) the period beginning on the day after the last day of the corporation's last taxable year as an S corporation and ending on the later of—
  (i) the day which is 1 year after such last day, or
  (ii) the due date for filing the return for such last year as an S corporation (including extensions),
(B) the 120-day period beginning on the date of any determination pursuant to an audit of the taxpayer which follows the termination of the corporation's election and which adjusts a subchapter S item of income, loss, or deduction of the corporation arising during the S period (as defined in section 1368(e)(2)), and
(C) the 120-day period beginning on the date of a determination that the corporation's election under section 1362(a) had terminated for a previous taxable year.

(2) **Determination defined.** For purposes of paragraph (1), the term "determination" means—
  (A) a determination as defined in section 1313(a), or
  (B) an agreement between the corporation and the Secretary that the corporation failed to qualify as an S corporation.

(3) **Special rules for audit related post-termination transition periods.**
  (A) No application to carryovers. Paragraph (1)(B) shall not apply for purposes of section 1366(d)(3).
  (B) Limitation on application to distributions. Paragraph (1)(B) shall apply to a distribution described in section 1371(e) only to the extent that the amount of such distribution does not exceed the aggregate increase (if any) in the accumulated adjustments account (within the meaning of section 1368(e)) by reason of the adjustments referred to in such paragraph.

(c) Manner of making elections, etc.
Any election under this subchapter, and any revocation under section 1362(d)(1), shall be made in such manner as the Secretary shall by regulations prescribe.

In 2007, P.L. 110-28, Sec. 7235, of this Act, [relating to Sec. 1311 of P.L. 104-188, see below] provides:
"SEC. 7235. ELIMINATION OF ALL EARNINGS AND PROFITS ATTRIBUTABLE TO PRE-1983 YEARS FOR CERTAIN CORPORATIONS.
"In the case of a corporation which is—
"(1) described in section 1311(a)(1) of the Small Business Job Protection Act of 1996, and
"(2) not described in section 1311(a)(2) of such Act,
"the amount of such corporation's accumulated earnings and profits (for the first taxable year beginning after the date of the enactment of this Act) shall be reduced by an amount equal to the portion (if any) of such accumulated earnings and profits which were accumulated in any taxable year beginning before January 1, 1983, for which such corporation was an electing small business corporation under subchapter S of the Internal Revenue Code of 1986."

In 2004, P.L. 108-311, Sec. 407(a), added para. (b)(3), effective for determinations made after 12/31/96 as if included in Sec. 1307 of the Small Business Job Protection Act of 1996, P.L. 104-188.

In 1997, P.L. 105-34, Sec. 1601(c)(2), of this Act provides:
"(2) Effective date for section 1307. [of P.L. 104-188]
"(A) Notwithstanding section 1317 of the Small Business Job Protection Act of 1996, the amendments made by subsections (a) and (b) of section 1307 of such Act shall apply to determinations made after December 31, 1996.
"(B) In no event shall the 120-day period referred to in section 1377(b)(1)(B) of the Internal Revenue Code of 1986 (as added by such section 1307) expire before the end of the 120-day period beginning on the date of the enactment of this Act."

In 1996, P.L. 104-188, Sec. 1306, amended para. (a)(2) . . . Sec. 1307(a), deleted "and" at the end of subpara. (b)(1)(A), redesignated subpara. (b)(1)(B) as (C), and added a new subpara. (b)(1)(B) . . . Sec. 1307(b), deleted subparas. (b)(2)(A) and (B), redesignated subpara. (b)(2)(C) as (B), and added a new subpara. (b)(2)(A), effective for determinations made after 12/31/96. [Prior to Sec. 1601(c)(2) of P.L. 105-34, the effective date for these provisions was for tax. yrs. begin. after 12/31/96.]

Prior to amendment, para. (a)(2) read as follows:
"(2) Election to terminate year. Under regulations prescribed by the Secretary, if any shareholder terminates his interest in the corporation during the taxable year and all persons who are shareholders during the taxable year agree to the application of this paragraph, paragraph (1) shall be applied as if the taxable year

consisted of 2 taxable years the first of which ends on the date of the termination."
Prior to deletion, subparas. (b)(2)(A) and (B) read as follows:
"(A) a court decision which becomes final,
"(B) a closing agreement, or"
—P.L. 104-188, Sec. 1311(a), of this Act, regarding elimination of certain earnings and profits, is reproduced in note following Code Sec. 1361.

In 1982, P.L. 97-354, Sec. 2, added Code Sec. 1377 as part of the amendments to Subchapter S, effective for tax. yrs. begin. after 12/31/82. For exceptions and special rules, see Sec. 6(c) of this Act reproduced in the note following Code Sec. 1361.

Sec. 1378. Taxable year of S corporation.
(a) General rule
For purposes of this subtitle, the taxable year of an S corporation shall be a permitted year.
(b) Permitted year defined.
For purposes of this section, the term "permitted year" means a taxable year which—
  (1) is a year ending December 31, or
  (2) is any other accounting period for which the corporation establishes a business purpose to the satisfaction of the Secretary.
For purposes of paragraph (2), any deferral of income to shareholders shall not be treated as a business purpose.

In 2007, P.L. 110-28, Sec. 7235, of this Act, [relating to Sec. 1311 of P.L. 104-188, see below] provides:
"SEC. 7235. ELIMINATION OF ALL EARNINGS AND PROFITS ATTRIBUTABLE TO PRE-1983 YEARS FOR CERTAIN CORPORATIONS.
"In the case of a corporation which is—
"(1) described in section 1311(a)(1) of the Small Business Job Protection Act of 1996, and
"(2) not described in section 1311(a)(2) of such Act,
"the amount of such corporation's accumulated earnings and profits (for the first taxable year beginning after the date of the enactment of this Act) shall be reduced by an amount equal to the portion (if any) of such accumulated earnings and profits which were accumulated in any taxable year beginning before January 1, 1983, for which such corporation was an electing small business corporation under subchapter S of the Internal Revenue Code of 1986."

In 1996, P.L. 104-188, Sec. 1311(a), of this Act, regarding elimination of certain earnings and profits, is reproduced in note following Code Sec. 1361.

In 1988, P.L. 100-647, Sec. 1008(e)(7)(A), (B), deleted "(including such short taxable year)" before "beginning after" and substituted "the partner's or shareholder's taxable year with or within which the partnership's or S corporation's short taxable year ends" for "short taxable year" the second place it appeared in Sec. 806(e)(2)(C) of P.L. 99-514 [reproduced below] part of the effective date for changes made by Sec. 806(b) of P.L. 99-514, see below . . . Sec. 1008(e)(8)(A), (B), substituted "the taxpayer's first taxable year beginning after December 31, 1986" for "any taxable year" and substituted "partnership, S corporation, or personal service corporation" for "taxpayer" each place it appeared in Sec. 806(e)(2) of P.L. 99-514 [reproduced below] part of the effective date for changes made by Sec. 806(b) of P.L. 99-514, see below . . . Sec. 1008(e)(9), of this Act provides:
"(9) Nothing in section 806 of the Reform Act or in any legislative history relating thereto shall be construed as requiring the Secretary of the Treasury or his delegate to permit an automatic change of a taxable year." . . . Sec. 1008(e)(10), added Sec. 806(e)(3) of Sec. 99-514 [reproduced below], part of the effective date for changes made by Sec. 806(b) of P.L. 99-514, see below.

In 1986, P.L. 99-514, Sec. 806(b)(1), amended subsec. (a) . . . Sec. 806(b)(2), added the flush sentence at the end of subsec. (b) . . . Sec. 806(b)(3), deleted subsec. (c), generally effective for tax. yrs. begin. after 12/31/86. Sec. 806(e)(2) and (e)(3) [as amended by Secs. 1008(e)(7), (e)(8), and (e)(10) see 1008(e)(10) of P.L. 100-647, reproduced above] of this Act provides:
"(2) Change in accounting period.—In the case of any partnership, S corporation, or personal service corporation required by the amendments made by this section to change its accounting period for the taxpayer's first taxable year beginning after December 31, 1986
"(A) such change shall be treated as initiated by the partnership, S corporation, or personal service corporation
"(B) such change shall be treated as having been made with the consent of the Secretary, and
"(C) with respect to any partner or shareholder of an S corporation which is required to include the items from more than 1 taxable year of the partnership or S corporation in any 1 taxable year, income in excess of expenses of such partnership or corporation for the short taxable year required by such amendments shall be taken into account ratably in each of the first 4 taxable years beginning after December 31, 1986, unless such partner or shareholder elects to include all such income in the partner's or shareholder's taxable year with or within which the partnerships or S corporation's short taxable year ends.
Subparagraph (C) shall apply to a shareholder of an S corporation only if such corporation was an S corporation for a taxable year beginning in 1986.
"(3) Basis, etc. rules.

Code Sec. 1378   **Subchapter S**

"(A) Basis rule. The adjusted basis of any partner's interest in a partnership or shareholder's stock in an S corporation shall be determined as if all of the income to be taken into account ratably in the 4 taxable years referred to in paragraph (2)(C) were included in gross income for the 1st of such taxable years.

"(B) Treatment of dispositions. If any interest in a partnership or stock in an S corporation is disposed of before the last taxable year in the spread periods, all amounts which would be included in the gross income of the partner or shareholder for subsequent taxable years in the spread period under paragraph (2)(C) and attributable to the interest or stock disposed of shall be included in gross income for the taxable year in which the disposition occurs. For purposes of the preceding sentence, the term 'spread period' means the period consisting of the 4 taxable years referred to in paragraph (2)(C)."

Prior to amendment, subsec. (a) read as follows:

"(a) General rule:

"For purposes of this subtitle

"(1) an S corporation shall not change its taxable year to any accounting period other than a permitted year, and

"(2) no corporation may make an election under section 1362(a) for any taxable year unless such taxable year is a permitted year."

Prior to deletion, subsec. (c) read as follows:

"(c) Existing s corporations required to use permitted year after 50-percent shift in ownership.

"(1) In general. A corporation which is an S corporation for a taxable year which includes December 31, 1982 (or which is an S corporation for a taxable year beginning during 1983 by reason of an election made on or before October 19, 1982) shall not be treated as an S corporation for any subsequent taxable year beginning after the first day on which more than 50 percent of the stock is newly owned stock unless such subsequent taxable year is a permitted year.

"(2) Newly owned stock. For purposes of paragraph (1), the stock held by any person on any day shall be treated as newly owned stock to the extent that—

"(A) the percentage of the stock of such corporation owned by such person on such day, exceeds

"(B) the percentage of the stock of such corporation owned by such person on December 31, 1982.

"(3) Stock acquired by reason of death, gift from family member, etc.

"(A) In general. For purposes of paragraph (2), if—

"(i) a person acquired stock in the corporation after December 31, 1982, and

"(ii) such stock was acquired by such person—

"(I) by reason of the death of a qualified transferor,

"(II) by reason of a gift from a qualified transferor who is a member of such person's family, or

"(III) by reason of a qualified buy-sell agreement from a qualified transferor (or his estate) who was a member of such person's family,

then such stock shall be treated as held on December 31 1982, by the person described in clause (i).

"(B) Qualified transferor. For purposes of subparagraph (A), the term 'qualified transferor' means a person—

"(i) who (or whose estate) held the stock in the corporation (or predecessor stock) on December 31, 1982, or

"(ii) who acquired the stock in an acquisition which meets the requirements of subparagraph (A).

"(C) Family. For purposes of subparagraph (A), the term 'family' has the meaning given such term by section 267(c)(4).

"(D) Qualified buy-sell agreement. For purposes of subparagraph (A), the term 'qualified buy-sell agreement' means any agreement which—

"(i) has been continuously in existence since September 28, 1982, and

"(ii) provides that on the death of any party to such agreement, the stock in the S corporation held by such party will be sold to surviving parties to such agreement who were parties to such agreement on September 28, 1982."

In **1984**, P.L. 98-369, Sec. 721(m), substituted "which includes December 31, 1982 (or which is an S corporation for a taxable year beginning during 1983 by reason of an election made on or before October 19, 1982)" for "which includes December 31, 1982" in para. (c)(1) . . . Sec. 721(q), substituted "who (or whose estate) held" for "who held" in clause (c)(3)(B)(i), effective, generally, for tax. yrs. begin. after 12/31/82.

In **1982**, P.L. 97-354, Sec. 2, added Code Sec. 1378 as part of the amendments to Subchapter S, effective for tax. yrs. begin. after 12/31/82. For exceptions and special rules, see Sec. 6(c) of this Act reproduced in the note following Code Sec. 1361.

Sec. 1379. Transitional rules on enactment.
(a) Old elections.

Any election made under section 1372(a) (as in effect before the enactment of the Subchapter S Revision Act of 1982) shall be treated as an election made under section 1362.

(b) References to prior law included.

Any references in this title to a provision of this subchapter shall, to the extent not inconsistent with the purposes of this subchapter, include a reference to the corresponding provision as in effect before the enactment of the Subchapter S Revision Act of 1982.

(c) Distributions of undistributed taxable income.

If a corporation was an electing small business corporation for the last preenactment year, subsections (f) and (d) of section 1375 (as in effect before the enactment of the Subchapter S Revision Act of 1982) shall continue to apply with respect to distributions of undistributed taxable income for any taxable year beginning before January 1, 1983.

(d) Carryforwards.

If a corporation was an electing small business corporation for the last preenactment year and is an S corporation for the 1st postenactment year, any carryforward to the 1st postenactment year which arose in a taxable year for which the corporation was an electing small business corporation shall be treated as arising in the 1st postenactment year.

(e) Preenactment and postenactment years defined.

For purposes of this subsection—

(1) Last preenactment year. The term "last preenactment year" means the last taxable year of a corporation which begins before January 1, 1983.

(2) 1st postenactment year. The term "1st postenactment year" means the 1st taxable year of a corporation which begins after December 31, 1982.

In **2007**, P.L. 110-28, Sec. 7235, of this Act, [relating to Sec. 1311 of P.L. 104-188, see below] provides:

"SEC. 7235. ELIMINATION OF ALL EARNINGS AND PROFITS ATTRIBUTABLE TO PRE-1983 YEARS FOR CERTAIN CORPORATIONS.

"In the case of a corporation which is—

"(1) described in section 1311(a)(1) of the Small Business Job Protection Act of 1996, and

"(2) not described in section 1311(a)(2) of such Act,

"the amount of such corporation's accumulated earnings and profits (for the first taxable year beginning after the date of the enactment of this Act) shall be reduced by an amount equal to the portion (if any) of such accumulated earnings and profits which were accumulated in any taxable year beginning before January 1, 1983, for which such corporation was an electing small business corporation under subchapter S of the Internal Revenue Code of 1986."

In **1996**, P.L. 104-188, Sec. 1311(a), of this Act, regarding elimination of certain earnings and profits, is reproduced in note following Code Sec. 1361.

In **1984**, P.L. 98-369, Sec. 713(d)(8), of this Act provides:

"(8) Coordination of repeals of certain sections. Sections 404(e) and 1379(b) of the Internal Revenue Code of 1954 (as in effect on the day before the date of the enactment of the Tax Equity and Fiscal Responsibility Act of 1982) shall not apply to any plan to which section 401(j) of such Code applies (or would apply but for its repeal)."

— P.L. 98-369, Sec. 721(n), amended subsec. (b), effective generally to tax. yrs. begin. after 12/31/82.

Prior to amendment, subsec. (b) read as follows:

"(b) References to prior law included.

"In applying this subchapter to any taxable year beginning after December 31, 1982, any reference in this subchapter to another provision of this subchapter shall, to the extent not inconsistent with the purposes of this subchapter, include a reference to the corresponding provision as in effect before the enactment of the Subchapter S Revision Act of 1982."

In **1982**, P.L. 97-354, Sec. 2, added Code Sec. 1379 as part of the amendments to Subchapter S, effective for tax. yrs. begin. after 12/31/82. For exceptions and special rules, see Sec. 6(c) of this Act reproduced in the note following Code Sec. 1361.

Subchapter T.—Cooperatives and Their Patrons
Part
   I. Tax treatment of cooperatives.
  II. Tax treatment by patrons of patronage dividends and per-unit retain allocations.
 III. Definitions; special rules.

PART I.—TAX TREATMENT OF COOPERATIVES

Sec.

1381. Organizations to which part applies.

1382. Taxable income of cooperatives.

1383. Computation of tax where cooperative redeems nonqualified written notices of allocation or nonqualified per-unit retain certificates.

In 1966, revised item 1383 to include reference to nonqualified per-unit retain certificates.
In 1962, added Subchapter T, Parts I-III.

Sec. 1381. Organizations to which part applies.
(a) In general.
This part shall apply to—
(1) any organization exempt from tax under section 521 (relating to exemption of farmers' cooperatives from tax), and
(2) any corporation operating on a cooperative basis other than an organization—
  (A) which is exempt from tax under this chapter,
  (B) which is subject to the provisions of—
    (i) part II of subchapter H (relating to mutual savings banks, etc.), or
    (ii) subchapter L (relating to insurance companies), or
  (C) which is engaged in furnishing electric energy, or providing telephone service, to persons in rural areas.

(b) Tax on certain farmers' cooperatives.
An organization described in subsection (a)(1) shall be subject to the taxes imposed by section 11 or 1201.

(c) Cross reference.
For treatment of income from load loss transactions of organizations described in subsection (a)(2)(C), see section 501(c)(12)(H).

In 2004, P.L. 108-357, Sec. 319(d), added subsec. (c), effective for tax. yrs. begin. after 10/22/2004.
In 1962, P.L. 87-834, Sec. 17(a), added Code Sec. 1381, effective as provided in Sec. 17(c), which reads as follows:
"(1) For the cooperatives.—Except as provided in paragraph (3), the amendments made by subsections (a) and (b) shall apply to taxable years of organizations described in Code Sec. 1381(a), beginning after December 31, 1962.
"(2) For the patrons.—Except as provided in paragraph (3), Code Sec. 1385 shall apply with respect to any amount received from any organization described in section 1381(a) of such Code, to the extent that such amount is paid by such organization in a taxable year of such organization beginning after December 31, 1962.
"(3) Application of existing law.—In the case of any money, written notice of allocation, or other property paid by any organization described in section 1381(a)—
"(A) before the first day of the first taxable year of such organization beginning after December 31, 1962, or
"(B) on or after such first day with respect to patronage occurring before such first day,
the tax treatment of such money, written notice of allocation, or other property (including the tax treatment of gain or loss on the redemption, sale, or other disposition of such written notice of allocation) by any person shall be made under the Internal Revenue Code of 1954 without regard to subchapter T of chapter 1 of such Code."

Sec. 1382. Taxable income of cooperatives.
(a) Gross income.
Except as provided in subsection (b), the gross income of any organization to which this part applies shall be determined without any adjustment (as a reduction in gross receipts, an increase in cost of goods sold, or otherwise) by reason of any allocation or distribution to a patron out of the net earnings of such organization or by reason of any amount paid to a patron as a per-unit retain allocation (as defined in section 1388(f)).

(b) Patronage dividends and per-unit retain allocations.
In determining the taxable income of an organization to which this part applies, there shall not be taken into account amounts paid during the payment period for the taxable year—
(1) as patronage dividends (as defined in section 1388(a)), to the extent paid in money, qualified written notices of allocation (as defined in section 1388(c)), or other property (except nonqualified written notices of allocation (as defined in section 1388(d))) with respect to patronage occurring during such taxable year;
(2) in money or other property (except written notices of allocation) in redemption of a nonqualified written notice of allocation which was paid as a patronage dividend during the payment period for the taxable year during which the patronage occurred;
(3) as per-unit retain allocations (as defined in section 1388(f)), to the extent paid in money, qualified per-unit retain certificates (as defined in section 1388(h)), or other property (except nonqualified per-unit retain certificates, as defined in section 1388(i)) with respect to marketing occurring during such taxable year; or
(4) in money or other property (except per-unit retain certificates) in redemption of a nonqualified per-unit retain certificate which was paid as a per-unit retain allocation during the payment period for the taxable year during which the marketing occurred.

For purposes of this title, any amount not taken into account under the preceding sentence shall, in the case of an amount described in paragraph (1) or (2), be treated in the same manner as item of gross income and as a deduction therefrom, and in the case of an amount described in paragraph (3) or (4), be treated as a deduction in arriving at gross income.

(c) Deduction for nonpatronage distributions, etc.
In determining the taxable income of an organization described in section 1381(a)(1), there shall be allowed as a deduction (in addition to other deductions allowable under this chapter)—
(1) amounts paid during the taxable year as dividends on its capital stock; and
(2) amounts paid during the payment period for the taxable year—
  (A) in money, qualified written notices of allocation, or other property (except nonqualified written notices of allocation) on a patronage basis to patrons with respect to its earnings during such taxable year which are derived from business done for the United States or any of its agencies or from sources other than patronage, or
  (B) in money or other property (except written notices of allocation) in redemption of a nonqualified written notice of allocation which was paid, during the payment period for the taxable year during which the earnings were derived, on a patronage basis to a patron with respect to earnings derived from business or sources described in subparagraph (A).

(d) Payment period for each taxable year.
For purposes of subsections (b) and (c)(2), the payment period for any taxable year is the period beginning with the first day of such taxable year and ending with the fifteenth day of the ninth month following the close of such year. For purposes of subsections (b)(1) and (c)(2)(A), a qualified check issued during the payment period shall be treated as an amount paid in money during such period if endorsed and cashed on or before the 90th day after the close of such period.

(e) Products marketed under pooling arrangements.
For purposes of subsection (b), in the case of a pooling arrangement for the marketing of products—
(1) the patronage shall (to the extent provided in regulations prescribed by the Secretary) be treated as patronage occurring during the taxable year in which the pool closes, and
(2) the marketing of products shall be treated as occurring during any of the taxable years in which the pool is open.

(f) Treatment of earnings received after patronage occurred.

If any portion of the earnings from business done with or for patrons is includible in the organization's gross income for a taxable year after the taxable year during which the patronage occurred, then for purposes of applying paragraphs (1) and (2) of subsection (b) to such portion the patronage shall, to the extent provided in regulations prescribed by the Secretary, be considered to have occurred during the taxable year of the organization during which such earnings are includible in gross income.

(g) Use of completed crop pool method of accounting.

(1) In general. An organization described in section 1381(a) which is engaged in pooling arrangements for the marketing of products may compute its taxable income with respect to any pool opened prior to March 1, 1978, under the completed crop pool method of accounting if—

(A) the organization has computed its taxable income under such method for the 10 taxable years ending with its first taxable year beginning after December 31, 1976, and

(B) with respect to the pool, the organization has entered into an agreement with the United States or any of its agencies which includes provisions to the effect that—

(i) the United States or such agency shall provide a loan to the organization with the products comprising the pool serving as collateral for such loan,

(ii) the organization shall use an amount equal to the proceeds of such loan to make price support advances to eligible producers (as determined by the United States or such agency), to defray costs of handling, processing, and storing such products, or to pay all or part of any administrative costs associated with the price support program,

(iii) an amount equal to the net proceeds (as determined under such agreement) from the sale or exchange of the products in the pool shall be used to repay such loan until such loan is repaid in full (or all the products in the pool are disposed of), and

(iv) the net gains (as determined under such agreement) from the sale or exchange of such products shall be distributed to eligible producers, except to the extent that the United States or such agency permits otherwise.

(2) Completed crop pool method of accounting defined. For purposes of this subsection, the term "completed crop pool method of accounting" means a method of accounting under which gain or loss is computed separately for each crop year pool in the year in which the last of the products in the pool are disposed of.

In 1978, P.L. 95-345, Sec. 3, added subsec. (g), effective 8/15/78.

In 1976, P.L. 94-455, Sec. 1906(b)(13)(A), substituted "Secretary" for "Secretary or his delegate" each place it appeared in Code Sec. 1382, effective for tax. yrs. begin. after 12/31/76.

In 1969, P.L. 91-172, Sec. 911(a), amended para. (b)(3), effective for per-unit retain allocations made after 10/9/69.

Prior to amendment, para. (b)(3) read as follows:

"(3) as per-unit allocations, to the extent paid in qualified per-unit retain certificates (as defined in section 1388(h)) with respect to marketing occurring during such taxable year; or"

In 1966, P.L. 89-809, Sec. 211(a)(1), added to the end of subsec. (a) "or by reason of any amount paid to a patron as a per-unit retain allocation (as defined in section 1388(f))" . . . Sec. 211(a)(2), added "and per-unit retain allocations" after "dividends" in the heading of subsec. (b), and added paras. (3) and (4) and added "and in the case of an amount described in paragraph (3) and (4), be treated as a deduction in arriving at gross income" to the last sentence . . . Sec. 211(a)(3), amended subsec. (e) . . . Sec. 211(a)(4), added "paragraphs (1) and (2) of" before "subsection (b)" in subsec. (f), effective for per-unit retain allocations made during tax. yrs. of an organization described in Code Sec. 1381(a) beginning

after 4/30/66, with respect to products delivered during such years. A written agreement between a patron and a cooperative association—

(A) which clearly provides that the patron agrees to treat the stated dollar amounts of all per-unit retain certificates issued to him by the association as representing cash distributions which he has, of his own choice, reinvested in the cooperative association,

(B) which is revocable by the patron at any time after the close of the taxable year in which it was made,

(C) which was entered into after October 14, 1965, and before [11/13/66] the date of the enactment of the Act, and

(D) which is in effect on [11/13/66] the date of the enactment of this Act, and with respect to which a written notice of revocation has not been furnished to the cooperative association, shall be effective (for the period prescribed in the agreement) for purposes of section 1388(h) of the Internal Revenue Code of 1954 as if entered into, pursuant to such section, after the date of the enactment of this Act.

An agreement described in paragraphs (A) and (C) which was included in a by-law of the cooperative association and which is in effect on the date of the enactment of this Act shall be effective for purposes of Code Sec. 1388(h) only for taxable years of the association beginning before 5/1/67.

Prior to amendment, subsec. (e) read as follows:

"(e) Products marketed under pooling arrangements.

For purposes of subsection (b), in the case of a pooling arrangement for the marketing of products, the patronage shall (to the extent provided in regulations prescribed by the Secretary or his delegate) be treated as patronage occurring during the taxable year in which the pool closes."

In 1962, P.L. 87-834, Sec. 17, added Code Sec. 1382, effective as provided in Sec. 17(c) of this Act, reproduced in note following Code Sec. 1381.

Sec. 1383. Computation of tax where cooperative redeems nonqualified written notices of allocation or nonqualified per-unit retain certificates.

(a) General rule.

If, under section 1382(b)(2) or (4), or (c)(2)(B), a deduction is allowable to an organization for the taxable year for amounts paid in redemption of nonqualified written notices of allocation or nonqualified per-unit retain certificates, then the tax imposed by this chapter on such organization for the taxable year shall be the lesser of the following:

(1) the tax for the taxable year computed with such deduction; or

(2) an amount equal to—

(A) the tax for the taxable year computed without such deduction, minus

(B) the decrease in tax under this chapter for any prior taxable year (or years) which would result solely from treating such nonqualified written notices of allocation or nonqualified per-unit retain certificates as qualified written notices of allocation or qualified per-unit retain certificates (as the case may be).

(b) Special rules.

(1) If the decrease in tax ascertained under subsection (a)(2)(B) exceeds the tax for the taxable year (computed without the deduction described in subsection (a)) such excess shall be considered to be a payment of tax on the last day prescribed by law for the payment of tax for the taxable year, and shall be refunded or credited in the same manner as if it were an overpayment for such taxable year.

(2) For purposes of determining the decrease in tax under subsection (a)(2)(B), the stated dollar amount of any nonqualified written notice of allocation or nonqualified per-unit retain certificate which is to be treated under such subsection as a qualified written notice of allocation or qualified per-unit retain certificate (as the case may be) shall be the amount paid in redemption of such written notice of allocation or per-unit retain certificate which is allowable as a deduction under section 1382(b)(2) or (4), or (c)(2)(B) for the taxable year.

(3) If the tax imposed by this chapter for the taxable year is the amount determined under subsection (a)(2), then the deduction described in subsection (a) shall not be taken into account for any purpose of this subtitle other than for purposes of this section.

In 1966, P.L. 89-809, Sec. 211(a), included per-unit retain certificates in the heading of Sec. 1383 and subsecs. (a) and (b)(2) . . . reference to 1382(b)(4) was added in subsecs. (a) and (b)(2), effective for per-unit retain allocations made during tax. yrs. of an organization described in Code Sec. beginning after 4/30/66, with respect to products delivered during such years. See note at end of Code Sec. 1382.

In 1962, P.L. 87-834, Sec. 17, added Code Sec. 1383, effective as provided in Sec. 17(c) of this Act, reproduced in note following Code Sec. 1381.

PART II.—TAX TREATMENT BY PATRONS OF PATRONAGE DIVIDENDS AND PER-UNIT RETAIN ALLOCATIONS

Sec.
1385. Amounts includible in patron's gross income.

In 1966, added to Part II "and per-unit retain allocations".
In 1962, added Part II and item 1385.

Sec. 1385. Amounts includible in patron's gross income.
(a) General rule.

Except as otherwise provided in subsection (b), each person shall include in gross income—

(1) the amount of any patronage dividend which is paid in money, a qualified written notice of allocation, or other property (except a nonqualified written notice of allocation), and which is received by him during the taxable year from an organization described in section 1381(a),

(2) any amount, described in section 1382(c)(2)(A) (relating to certain nonpatronage distributions by tax-exempt farmers' cooperatives), which is paid in money, a qualified written notice of allocation, or other property (except a nonqualified written notice of allocation), and which is received by him during the taxable year from an organization described in section 1381(a)(1), and

(3) the amount of any per-unit retain allocation which is paid in qualified per-unit retain certificates and which is received by him during the taxable year from an organization described in section 1381(a).

(b) Exclusion from gross income.

Under regulations prescribed by the Secretary, the amount of any patronage dividend, and any amount received on the redemption, sale, or other disposition of a nonqualified written notice of allocation which was paid as a patronage dividend, shall not be included in gross income to the extent that such amount—

(1) is properly taken into account as an adjustment to basis of property, or

(2) is attributable to personal, living, or family items.

(c) Treatment of certain nonqualified written notices of allocation and certain nonqualified per-unit retain certificates.

(1) Application of subsection. This subsection shall apply to—

(A) any nonqualified written notice of allocation which—

(i) was paid as a patronage dividend, or

(ii) was paid by an organization described in section 1381(a)(1) on a patronage basis with respect to earnings derived from business or sources described in section 1382(c)(2)(A), and

(B) any nonqualified per-unit retain certificate which was paid as a per-unit retain allocation.

(2) Basis; amount of gain. In the case of any nonqualified written notice of allocation or nonqualified per-unit retain certificate to which this subsection applies, for purposes of this chapter—

(A) the basis of such written notice of allocation or per-unit retain certificate in the hands of the patron to whom such written notice of allocation or per-unit retain certificate was paid shall be zero.

(B) the basis of such written notice of allocation or per-unit retain certificate which was acquired from a decedent shall be its basis in the hands of the decedent, and

(C) gain on the redemption, sale, or other disposition of such written notice of allocation or per-unit retain certificate by any person shall, to the extent that the stated dollar amount of such written notice of allocation or per-unit retain certificate exceeds its basis, be considered as ordinary income.

In 1976, P.L. 94-455, Sec. 1901(b)(3)(I), substituted "ordinary income" for "gain from the sale or exchange of property which is not a capital asset" in subpara. (c)(2)(C), effective for tax. yrs. begin. after 12/31/76.

—P.L. 94-455, Sec. 1906(b)(13)(A), substituted "Secretary" for "Secretary or his delegate" each place it appeared in Code Sec. 1385, effective for tax. yrs. begin. after 12/31/76.

In 1966, P.L. 89-809, Sec. 211(b)(1), added para. (a)(3) . . . Sec. 211(b)(2), amended the heading of subsec. (c) to provide for per-unit retain certificates . . . Sec. 211(b)(3), amended para. (c)(1) to provide for per-unit retain certificates . . . Sec. 211(b)(4), amended para. (c)(2) to provide for per-unit retain certificates, effective for per-unit retain allocations made during tax. yrs. of an organization described in Code Sec. 1381(a) beginning after 4/30/66, with respect to products delivered during such years. See also note at end of Code Sec. 1382.

In 1962, P.L. 87-834, Sec. 17, added Code Sec. 1385, effective as provided in Sec. 17(c) of this Act, reproduced in note following Code Sec. 1381.

PART III.—DEFINITIONS; SPECIAL RULES

Sec.
1388. Definitions; special rules.

In 1962, added Part III and item 1388.

Sec. 1388. Definitions; special rules.
(a) Patronage dividend.

For purposes of this subchapter, the term "patronage dividend" means an amount paid to a patron by an organization to which part I of this subchapter applies—

(1) on the basis of quantity or value of business done with or for such patron,

(2) under an obligation of such organization to pay such amount, which obligation existed before the organization received the amount so paid, and

(3) which is determined by reference to the net earnings of the organization from business done with or for its patrons.

Such term does not include any amount paid to a patron to the extent that (A) such amount is out of earnings other than from business done with or for patrons, or (B) such amount is out of earnings from business done with or for other patrons to whom no amounts are paid, or to whom smaller amounts are paid, with respect to substantially identical transactions. For purposes of paragraph (3), net earnings shall not be reduced by amounts paid during the year as dividends on capital stock or other proprietary capital interests of the organization to the extent that the articles of incorporation or bylaws of such organization or other contract with patrons provide that such dividends are in addition to amounts otherwise payable to patrons which are derived from business done with or for patrons during the taxable year.

(b) Written notice of allocation.

For purposes of this subchapter, the term "written notice of allocation" means any capital stock, revolving fund certificate, retain certificate, certificate of indebtedness, letter of advice, or other written notice, which discloses to the recipient the stated dollar amount allocated to him by the organization and the portion thereof, if any, which constitutes a patronage dividend.

(c) Qualified written notice of allocation.
   (1) Defined. For purposes of this subchapter, the term "qualified written notice of allocation" means—
   (A) a written notice of allocation which may be redeemed in cash at its stated dollar amount at any time within a period beginning on the date such written notice of allocation is paid and ending not earlier than 90 days from such date, but only if the distributee receives written notice of the right of redemption at the time he receives such written notice of allocation; and
   (B) a written notice of allocation which the distributee has consented, in the manner provided in paragraph (2), to take into account at its stated dollar amount as provided in section 1385(a).

Such term does not include any written notice of allocation which is paid as part of a patronage dividend or as part of a payment described in section 1382(c)(2)(A), unless 20 percent or more of the amount of such patronage dividend, or such payment, is paid in money or by qualified check.

   (2) Manner of obtaining consent. A distributee shall consent to take a written notice of allocation into account as provided in paragraph (1)(B) only by—
   (A) making such consent in writing,
   (B) obtaining or retaining membership in the organization after—
      (i) such organization has adopted (after October 16, 1962) a bylaw providing that membership in the organization constitutes such consent, and
      (ii) he has received a written notification and copy of such bylaw, or
   (C) if neither subparagraph (A) nor (B) applies, endorsing and cashing a qualified check, paid as a part of the patronage dividend or payment of which such written notice of allocation is also a part, on or before the 90th day after the close of the payment period for the taxable year of the organization for which such patronage dividend or payment is paid.

   (3) Period for which consent is effective.
   (A) General rule. Except as provided in subparagraph (B)—
      (i) a consent described in paragraph (2)(A) shall be a consent with respect to all patronage of the distributee with the organization occurring (determined with the application of section 1382(e)) during the taxable year of the organization during which such consent is made and all subsequent taxable years of the organization; and
      (ii) a consent described in paragraph (2)(B) shall be a consent with respect to all patronage of the distributee with the organization occurring (determined without the application of section 1382(e)) after he received the notification and copy described in paragraph (2)(B)(ii).
   (B) Revocation, etc.
      (i) Any consent described in paragraph (2)(A) may be revoked (in writing) by the distributee at any time. Any such revocation shall be effective with respect to patronage occurring on or after the first day of the first taxable year of the organization beginning after the revocation is filed with such organization; except that in the case of a pooling arrangement described in section 1382(e), a revocation made by a distributee shall not be effective as to any pool with respect to which the distributee has been a patron before such revocation.
      (ii) Any consent described in paragraph (2)(B) shall not be effective with respect to any patronage occurring (determined without the application of section 1382(e)) after the distributee ceases to be a member of the organization or after the bylaws of the organization cease to contain the provision described in paragraph (2)(B)(i).

   (4) Qualified check. For purposes of this subchapter, the term "qualified check" means only a check (or other instrument which is redeemable in money) which is paid as a part of a patronage dividend, or as a part of a payment described in section 1382(c)(2)(A), to a distributee who has not given consent as provided in paragraph (2)(A) or (B) with respect to such patronage dividend or payment, and on which there is clearly imprinted a statement that the endorsement and cashing of the check (or other instrument) constitutes the consent of the payee to include in his gross income, as provided in the Federal income tax laws, the stated dollar amount of the written notice of allocation which is a part of the patronage dividend or payment of which such qualified check is also a part. Such term does not include any check (or other instrument) which is paid as part of a patronage dividend or payment which does not include a written notice of allocation (other than a written notice of allocation described in paragraph (1)(A)).

(d) Nonqualified written notice of allocation.
For purposes of this subchapter, the term "nonqualified written notice of allocation" means a written notice of allocation which is not described in subsection (c) or a qualified check which is not cashed on or before the 90th day after the close of the payment period for the taxable year for which the distribution of which it is a part is paid.

(e) Determination of amount paid or received.
For purposes of this subchapter, in determining amounts paid or received—
   (1) property (other than a written notice of allocation or a per-unit retain certificate) shall be taken into account at its fair market value, and
   (2) a qualified written notice of allocation or qualified per-unit retain certificate shall be taken into account at its stated dollar amount.

(f) Per-unit retain allocation.
For purposes of this subchapter, the term "per-unit retain allocation" means any allocation, by an organization to which part I of this subchapter applies, to a patron with respect to products marketed for him, the amount of which is fixed without reference to the net earnings of the organization pursuant to an agreement between the organization and the patron.

(g) Per-unit retain certificate.
For purposes of this subchapter, the term "per-unit retain certificate" means any written notice which discloses to the recipient the stated dollar amount of a per-unit retain allocation to him by the organization.

(h) Qualified per-unit retain certificate.
   (1) Defined. For purposes of this subchapter, the term "qualified per-unit retain certificate" means any per-unit retain certificate which the distributee has agreed, in the manner provided in paragraph (2), to take into account at its stated dollar amount as provided in section 1385(a).
   (2) Manner of obtaining agreement. A distributee shall agree to take a per-unit retain certificate into account as provided in paragraph (1) only by—
   (A) making such agreement in writing, or
   (B) obtaining or retaining membership in the organization after—

(i) such organization has adopted (after November 13, 1966) a bylaw providing that membership in the organization constitutes such agreement, and

(ii) he has received a written notification and copy of such by law.

(3) Period for which agreement is effective.

(A) General rule. Except as provided in subparagraph (B)—

(i) an agreement described in paragraph (2)(A) shall be an agreement with respect to all products delivered by the distributee to the organization during the taxable year of the organization during which such agreement is made and all subsequent taxable years of the organization; and

(ii) an agreement described in paragraph (2)(B) shall be an agreement with respect to all products delivered by the distributee to the organization after he received the notification and copy described in paragraph (2)(B)(ii).

(B) Revocation, etc.

(i) Any agreement described in paragraph (2)(A) may be revoked (in writing) by the distributee at any time. Any such revocation shall be effective with respect to products delivered by the distributee on or after the first day of the first taxable year of the organization beginning after the revocation is filed with the organization; except that in the case of a pooling arrangement described in section 1382(e) a revocation made by a distributee shall not be effective as to any products which were delivered to the organization by the distributee before such revocation.

(ii) any agreement described in paragraph (2)(B) shall not be effective with respect to any products delivered after the distributee ceases to be a member of the organization or after the bylaws of the organization cease to contain the provision described in paragraph (2)(B)(i).

(i) Nonqualified per-unit retain certificate.

For purposes of this subchapter, the term "nonqualified per-unit retain certificate" means a per-unit retain certificate which is not described in subsection (h).

(j) Special rules for the netting of gains and losses by cooperatives.

For purposes of this subchapter, in the case of any organization to which part I of this subchapter applies—

(1) Optional netting of patronage gains and losses permitted. The net earnings of such organization may, at its option, be determined by offsetting patronage losses (including any patronage loss carried to such year) which are attributable to 1 or more allocation units (whether such units are functional, divisional, departmental, geographic, or otherwise) against patronage earnings of 1 or more other such allocation units.

(2) Certain netting permitted after section 381 transactions. If such an organization acquires the assets of another such organization in a transaction described in section 381(a), the acquiring organization may, in computing its net earnings for taxable years ending after the date of acquisition, offset losses of 1 or more allocation units of the acquiring or acquired organization against earnings of the acquired or acquiring organization, respectively, but only to the extent—

(A) such earnings are properly allocable to periods after the date of acquisition, and

(B) such earnings could have been offset by such losses if such earnings and losses had been derived from allocation units of the same organization.

(3) Notice requirements.

(A) In general. In the case of any organization which exercises its option under paragraph (1) for any taxable year, such organization shall, on or before the 15th day of the 9th month following the close of such taxable year, provide to its patrons a written notice which—

(i) states that the organization has offset earnings and losses from 1 or more of its allocation units and that such offset may have affected the amount which is being distributed to its patrons,

(ii) states generally the identity of the offsetting allocation units, and

(iii) states briefly what rights, if any, its patrons may have to additional financial information of such organization under terms of its charter, articles of incorporation, or bylaws, or under any provision of law.

(B) Certain information need not be provided. An organization may exclude from the information required to be provided under clause (ii) of subparagraph (A) any detailed or specific data regarding earnings or losses of such units which such organization determines would disclose commercially sensitive information which—

(i) could result in a competitive disadvantage to such organization, or

(ii) could create a competitive advantage to the benefit of a competitor of such organization.

(C) Failure to provide sufficient notice. If the Secretary determines that an organization failed to provide sufficient notice under this paragraph—

(i) the Secretary shall notify such organization, and

(ii) such organization shall, upon receipt of such notification, provide to its patrons a revised notice meeting the requirements of this paragraph.

Any such failure shall not affect the treatment of the organization under any provision of this subchapter or section 521.

(4) Patronage earnings or losses defined. For purposes of this subsection, the terms "patronage earnings" and "patronage losses" means earnings and losses, respectively, which are derived from business done with or for patrons of the organization.

(k) Cooperative marketing includes value-added processing involving animals.

For purposes of section 521 and this subchapter, the marketing of the products of members or other producers shall include the feeding of such products to cattle, hogs, fish, chickens, or other animals and the sale of the resulting animals or animal products.

In **2004,** P.L. 108-357, Sec. 312(a), added "For purposes of paragraph (3), net earnings shall not be reduced by amounts paid during the year as dividends on capital stock or other proprietary capital interests of the organization to the extent that the articles of incorporation or bylaws of such organization or other contract with patrons provide that such dividends are in addition to amounts otherwise payable to patrons which are derived from business done with or for patrons during the taxable year." at the end of subsec. (a), effective for distributions in tax. yrs. begin. after 10/22/2004.

—P.L. 108-357, Sec. 316(a), added subsec. (k), effective for tax. yrs. begin. after 10/22/2004.

In **1990,** P.L. 101-508, Sec. 11813(b)(24), deleted subsec. (k), effective for property placed in service after 12/31/90 except as provided in Sec. 11813(c)(2) of this Act, reproduced in note following Code Sec. 46.

Prior to deletion, subsec. (k) read as follows:

"*(k) Cross reference.*

For provisions relating to the apportionment of the investment credit between cooperative organizations and their patrons, see section 46(h).".

In **1986**, P.L. 99-272, Sec. 13210(a), redesignated subsec. (j) as subsec. (k) and added new subsec. (j), effective for tax. yrs. begin. after 12/31/62 except as provided in Sec. 13210(c)(2) and (3) of this Act, which reads as follows:

"(2) Notification requirement.— The provisions of section 1388(j)(3) of the Internal Revenue Code of 1954 (as added by subsection (a)[Sec. 13210(a)]) shall apply to taxable years beginning on or after the date of the enactment of this Act [4/7/86].

"(3) No inference.— Nothing in the amendments made by this section shall be construed to infer that a change in law is intended as to whether any patronage earnings may or may not be offset by nonpatronage losses, and any determination of such issue shall be made as if such amendments had not been enacted."

In **1978**, P.L. 95-600, Sec. 316(b)(3), added subsec. (j), effective for tax. yrs. ending after 10/31/78.

In **1976**, P.L. 94-455, Sec. 1901(a)(153)(A), substituted "October 16, 1962" for "the date of the enactment of the Revenue Act of 1962" in clause (c)(2)(B)(i) . . . Sec. 1901(a)(153)(B), substituted "November 13, 1966" for "the date of the enactment of this subsection" in clause (h)(2)(B)(i), effective for tax. yrs. begin. after 12/31/76.

In **1969**, P.L. 91-172, Sec. 911(b), deleted "other than by payment in money or other property (except per-unit retain certificates)" after "part I of this subchapter applies", in subsec. (f), effective for per-unit retain allocations made after 10/9/69.

In **1966**, P.L. 89-809, Sec. 211(c)(1)(A), substituted "allocation or a per-unit retain certificate)" for "allocation)" in para. (e)(1) . . . Sec. 211(c)(1)(B), substituted "allocation or qualified per-unit retain certificate" for "allocation" in para. (e)(2) . . . Sec. 211(c)(2), added subsecs. (f), (g), (h) and (i), effective for per-unit retain allocations made during tax. yrs. of an organization described in Code Sec. 1381(a) beginning after 4/30/66, with respect to products delivered during such years. See note at end of Code Sec. 1382.

In **1962**, P.L. 87-834, Sec. 17(a), added Code Sec. 1388. For effective date, see note following Code Sec. 1381.

Subchapter U. Repealed

In **1986**, P.L. 99-514, Sec. 1303(a), repealed Subchapter U.
Prior to repeal, the table of sections for Subchapter U read as follows:
"Subchapter U.— General Stock Ownership Corporations
"Sec.
"1391. Definitions.
"1392. Election by GSOC.
"1393. GSOC taxable income taxed to shareholders.
"1394. Rules applicable to distributions of an electing GSOC.
"1395. Adjustment to basis of stock of shareholders.
"1396. Minimum distributions.
"1397. Special rules applicable to an electing GSOC."

In **1980**, P.L. 96-595, Sec. 3(a)(11), amended the table of sections for Subchapter U.
Prior to amendment, the table of sections for Subchapter U read as follows:
"Subchapter U.— General Stock Ownership Corporations
"Sec.
"1391. Definitions.
"1392. Election by general stock ownership corporation.
"1393. Corporation taxable income taxed to shareholders.
"1394. Rules applicable to distributions of electing general stock ownership corporations.
"1395. Adjustments to basis of stock of shareholders.
"1396. Minimum distribution.
"1397. Special rules applicable to earnings and profits of an electing general stock ownership plan."

In **1978**, P.L. 95-600, Sec. 601(a), added Subchapter U.

Sec. 1391. Repealed.

In **1986**, P.L. 99-514, Sec. 1303(a), repealed Code Sec. 1391, effective 10/22/86.
Prior to repeal, Code Sec. 1391 read as follows:
"SEC. 1391. DEFINITIONS.
"(a) General stock ownership corporation.
"For purposes of this subchapter, the term 'general stock ownership corporation' (hereinafter referred to as 'GSOC') means a domestic corporation which—
"(1) is not a member of an affiliated group (as defined in section 1504);
"(2) is chartered and organized after December 31, 1978, and before January 1, 1984;
"(3) is chartered by an act of a State legislature or as a result of a State-wide referendum;
"(4) has a charter providing—
"(A) for the issuance of only 1 class of stocks,
"(B) for the issuance of shares only to eligible individuals (as defined in subsection (c));
"(C) for the issuance of at least one share to each eligible individual, unless such eligible individual elects within one year after the date of issuance not to receive such share;
"(D) that no share of stock shall be transferable—

"(i) by a shareholder other than by will or the laws of descent and distribution until after the expiration of 5 years from the date such stock is issued by the GSOC except where the shareholder ceases to be a resident of the State;
"(ii) to any person other than a resident individual of the chartering State or the estate of the deceased shareholder; or
"(iii) to any individual who, after the transfer, would own more than 10 shares of the GSOC; and
"(E) that such corporation shall qualify as a GSOC under the Internal Revenue Code; and
"(5) is empowered to invest in properties (but not in properties acquired by it or for its benefit through the right of eminent domain).
For purposes of this subsection, section 1504(a) shall be applied by substituting '20 percent' for '80 percent' whenever it appears.
"(b) Electing GSOC.
"For purposes of this subchapter, the term 'electing GSOC' means a GSOC which files an election under section 1392 which, under section 1392, is in effect for such taxable year.
"(c) Eligible individual.
"For purposes of subsection (a), the term 'eligible individual' means an individual who is, as of a date specified in the State's enabling legislation for the GSOC, a resident of the chartering State and who remains a resident of such State between that date and the date of issuance.
"(d) Treated as private corporation.
"For purposes of this title, a GSOC shall be treated as a private corporation and not as a governmental unit.
"(e) Study of general stock ownership corporations.
"The staff of the Joint Committee on Taxation shall prepare a report on the operation and effects of this subchapter relating to GSOC's. An interim report shall be filed within two years after the first GSOC is formed and a final report shall be filed by September 30, 1983."

In **1980**, P.L. 96-595, Sec. 3(a)(1), added "or the estate of a deceased shareholder" after "State" in clause (a)(4)(D)(ii) . . . Sec. 3(a)(2), substituted "individual" for "individuals" in the heading of subsec. (c), effective for corporations chartered after 12/31/78 and before 1/1/84.

— P.L. 96-222, Sec. 106(a)(4)(A), substituted a semicolon for ", and" at the end of para. (a)(1) . . . Sec. 106(a)(4)(B), added "or" at the end of clause (a)(4)(D)(ii) . . . Sec. 106(a)(4)(C), added "and" at the end of clause (a)(4)(D)(iii) . . . Sec. 106(a)(4)(D), added "and" at the end of subpara. (a)(4)(E), effective for corporations chartered after 12/31/78 and before 1/1/84.

In **1978**, P.L. 95-600, Sec. 601(a), added Code Sec. 1391, effective for corporations chartered after 12/31/78 and before 1/1/84.

Sec. 1392. Repealed.

In **1986**, P.L. 99-514, Sec. 1303(a), repealed Code Sec. 1392, effective 10/22/86.
Prior to repeal, Code Sec. 1392 read as follows:
"SEC. 1392. ELECTION BY GSOC.
"(a) Eligibility.
"Except as provided in section 1396(b), any GSOC may elect, in accordance with the provisions of this section, not to be subject to the taxes imposed by this chapter.
"(b) Effect.
"If a GSOC makes an election under subsection (a) then—
"(1) with respect to the taxable years of the GSOC for which such election is in effect, such corporation shall not be subject to the taxes imposed by this chapter and, with respect to such taxable years, the provisions of section 1396 shall apply to such GSOC, and
"(2) with respect to each such taxable year, the provisions of sections 1393, 1394, and 1395 shall apply to the shareholders of such GSOC.
"(c) When and how made.
"An election under subsection (a) may be made by a GSOC at such time and in such manner as the Secretary shall prescribe by regulations.
"(d) Years for which effective.
"An election under subsection (a) shall be effective for the taxable year of the GSOC for which it is made and for all succeeding taxable years of the GSOC, unless it is terminated under subsection (f).
"(e) Taxable year.
"The taxable year of the GSOC shall end on October 31 unless the Secretary consents to a different taxable year.
"(f) Termination.
"The election of a GSOC under subsection (a) shall terminate for any taxable year during which it ceases to be a GSOC and for all succeeding taxable years. The election of a GSOC under subsection (a) may be terminated at any other time with the consent of the Secretary, effective for the first taxable year with respect to which the Secretary consents and for all succeeding taxable years."

In **1980**, P.L. 96-595, Sec. 3(a)(3), substituted "1396(b)" for "1393" in subsec. (a) . . . Sec. 3(a)(4), deleted "and all succeeding years" [sic, "and all succeeding taxable years"] after "with respect to such taxable years" in para. (b)(1), effective for corporations chartered after 12/31/78 and before 1/1/84.

— P.L. 96-222, Sec. 106(a)(5), substituted "When" for "Where" in subsec. (c), effective for corporations chartered after 12/31/78 and before 1/1/84.

In **1978**, P.L. 95-600, Sec. 601(a), added Code Sec. 1392, effective for corporations chartered after 12/31/78 and before 1/1/84.

Cooperatives — Subchapter U

Sec. 1393. Repealed.

In **1986**, P.L. 99-514, Sec. 1303(a), repealed Code Sec. 1393, effective 10/22/86.
Prior to repeal, Code Sec. 1393 read as follows:
"SEC. 1393. GSOC TAXABLE INCOME TAXED TO SHAREHOLDERS.
"(a) General rule.
"The taxable income of an electing GSOC for any taxable year shall be included in the gross income of the shareholders of such GSOC in the manner and to the extent set forth in this subsection.
"(1) Amount included in gross income. Each shareholder of an electing GSOC on any day of a taxable year of such GSOC shall include in his gross income for the taxable year with or within which the taxable year of the GSOC ends the amount he would have received if, on each day of such taxable year, there had been distributed pro rata to its shareholders by such GSOC an amount equal to the taxable income of the GSOC for its taxable year divided by the number of days in the GSOC's taxable year.
"(2) Taxable income defined. For purposes of this subchapter, the taxable income of an electing GSOC shall be determined without regard to the deductions allowed by part VIII of subchapter B (other than deductions allowed by section 248, relating to organizational expenditures).
"(b) Special rule for investment credit.
"The investment credit of an electing GSOC for any taxable year shall be allowed as a credit to the shareholders of such corporation in the manner and to the extent set forth in this subsection.
"(1) Credit. There shall be apportioned among the shareholders a credit equal to the amount each shareholder would have received if, on each day of such taxable year, there had been distributed pro rata to the shareholders the electing GSOC's net investment credit divided by the number of days in the GSOC's taxable year.
"(2) Net investment credit. For purposes of this paragraph the term 'net investment credit' means the investment credit of the electing GSOC for its taxable year less any tax from recomputing a prior year's investment credit in accordance with section 47.
"(3) Recapture. There shall be apportioned among the shareholders of an electing GSOC, in the manner described in paragraph (1), an additional tax equal to the excess of any tax resulting from recomputing a prior year's investment credit in accordance with section 47 over the investment credit of an electing GSOC for its taxable year."
In **1980**, P.L. 96-595, Sec. 3(a)(5), substituted "subchapter, the taxable income" for "section, the term 'taxable income'" in para. (a)(2) . . . Sec. 3(a)(6), substituted "an electing GSOC" for "a GSOC" in paras. (a)(2) and (b)(3) . . . Sec. 3(a)(8), substituted "an electing GSOC" for "the GSOC" in para. (b)(3), effective for corporations chartered after 12/31/78 and before 1/1/84.
In **1978**, P.L. 95-600, Sec. 601(a), added Code Sec. 1393, effective for corporations chartered after 12/31/78 and before 1/1/84.

Sec. 1394. Repealed.

In **1986**, P.L. 99-514, Sec. 1303(a), repealed Code Sec. 1394, effective 10/22/86.
Prior to repeal, Code Sec. 1394 read as follows:
"SEC. 1394. RULES APPLICABLE TO DISTRIBUTIONS OF AN ELECTING GSOC.
"(a) Shareholder income account.
"An electing GSOC shall establish and maintain a shareholder income account which amount shall be—
"(1) increased at the close of the GSOC's taxable year by an amount equal to the GSOC's taxable income for such year, and
"(2) decreased, but not below zero, on the first day of the GSOC's taxable year by the amount of any GSOC distribution to the shareholders of such GSOC made or treated as made during the prior taxable year.
"(b) Taxation of distributions.
"Distributions by an electing GSOC shall be treated as—
"(1) a distribution of previously taxed income to the extent such distribution does not exceed the balance of the shareholder income account as of the close of the taxable year of the GSOC, and
"(2) a distribution to which section 301(a) applies but only to the extent such distribution exceeds the balance of the shareholder income account as of the close of the taxable year of the GSOC.
"(c) Distributions not treated as a dividend.
"Any amounts includible in the gross income of any individual by reason of ownership of stock in an electing GSOC shall not be considered as a dividend for purposes of section 116.
"(d) Regulations.
"The Secretary shall have authority to prescribe by regulation, rules for treatment of distributions in respect of shares of stock of the GSOC that have been transferred during the taxable year."
In **1980**, P.L. 96-595, Sec. 3(a)(6), substituted "an electing GSOC" for "a GSOC" in subsec. (c) . . . Sec. 3(a)(7), substituted "GSOC" for "GSOC's" in the heading of Code Sec 1394, . . . Sec. 3(a)(8), substituted "an electing GSOC" for "the GSOC" in subsec. (d), effective for corporations chartered after 12/31/78 and before 1/1/84.
In **1978**, P.L. 95-600, Sec. 601(a), added Code Sec. 1394, effective for corporations chartered after 12/31/78 and before 1/1/84.

Sec. 1395. Repealed.

In **1986**, P.L. 99-514, Sec. 1303(a), repealed Code Sec. 1395, effective 10/22/86.
Prior to repeal, Code Sec. 1395 read as follows:
"SEC. 1395. ADJUSTMENT TO BASIS OF STOCK OF SHAREHOLDERS.
"The basis of a shareholder's stock in an electing GSOC shall be increased by the amount includible in the gross income of such shareholder under section 1393, but only to the extent to which such amount is actually included in the gross income of such shareholder."
In **1978**, P.L. 95-600, Sec. 601(a), added Code Sec. 1395, effective for corporations chartered after 12/31/78 and before 1/1/84.

Sec. 1396. Repealed.

In **1986**, P.L. 99-514, Sec. 1303(a), repealed Code Sec. 1396, effective 10/22/86.
Prior to repeal, Code Sec. 1396 read as follows:
"SEC. 1396. MINIMUM DISTRIBUTIONS.
"(a) General rule.
"An electing GSOC shall distribute at least 90 percent of its taxable income for any taxable year by January 31 following the close of such taxable year. Any distribution made on or before January 31 shall be treated as made as of the close of the preceding taxable year.
"(b) Imposition of tax in case of failure to make minimum distributions.
"If an electing GSOC fails to make the minimum distribution requirements described in subsection (a), there is hereby imposed a tax equal to 20 percent of the excess of the amount required to be distributed over the amount actually distributed. Such tax shall be deductible as an ordinary and necessary expense of the corporation under section 162."
In **1980**, P.L. 96-595, Sec. 3(a)(6), substituted "an electing GSOC" for "a GSOC" in subsec. (b) . . . Sec. 3(a)(9), substituted "An electing GSOC" for "A GSOC" in subsec. (a) . . . Sec. 3(a)(10), added the sentence at the end of subsec. (b), effective for corporations chartered after 12/31/78 and before 1/1/84.
In **1978**, P.L. 95-600, Sec. 601(a), added Code Sec. 1396, effective for corporations chartered after 12/31/78 and before 1/1/84.

Sec. 1397. Repealed.

In **1986**, P.L. 99-514, Sec. 1303(a), repealed Code Sec. 1397, effective 10/22/86.
Prior to repeal, Code Sec. 1397 read as follows:
"SEC. 1397. SPECIAL RULES APPLICABLE TO AN ELECTING GSOC.
"(a) General rule.
"The current earnings and profits of an electing GSOC as of the close of its taxable year shall not include the amount of taxable income for such year which is required to be included in the gross income of the shareholders of such GSOC under section 1393(a).
"(b) Special rule for audit adjustments.
"(1) Taxable income. Taxable income of an electing GSOC shall, in the year of final determination, be increased or decreased, as the case might be, by any adjustment to taxable income for a prior taxable year.
"(2) Investment credit. The net investment credit of an electing GSOC shall, in the year of final determination, be increased or decreased, as the case might be, by any adjustment to the net investment credit for a prior taxable year.
"(3) Method of making adjustments. An electing GSOC shall include in gross income for the year of an adjustment the amount described in paragraph (1) and shall take into account the adjustment described in paragraph (2), and shall be liable for payment of interest in the amount that would have been payable by the GSOC under section 6601 (relating to interest on underpayment, nonpayment or extensions of time for payment, of tax) or receivable by the GSOC under section 6611 (relating to interest on overpayments) if such GSOC had been a corporation other than an electing GSOC."
In **1978**, P.L. 95-600, Sec. 601(a), added Code Sec. 1397, effective for corporations chartered after 12/31/78 and before 1/1/84.

Subchapter U.—Designation and Treatment of Empowerment Zones, Enterprise Communities, and Rural Development Investment Areas

Part
    I. Designation
   II. Tax-exempt facility bonds for empowerment zones and enterprise communities
  III. Additional incentives for empowerment zones
  IV. Incentives for education zones
   V. Regulations

In **1997**, P.L. 105-34, Sec. 226(b)(1), deleted item for Part IV, and added new items for Part IV and V.
Prior to deletion, the item for Part IV read as follows:
"Part IV. Regulations."

In 1993, P.L. 103-66, Sec. 13301(a), added new Subchapter U.

PART I.—DESIGNATION

Sec.
1391. Designation procedure.
1392. Eligibility criteria.
1393. Definitions and special rules.

In 1993, P.L. 103-66, Sec. 13301(a), added Part I as part of new Subchapter U.

Sec. 1391. Designation procedure.
(a) In general.
From among the areas nominated for designation under this section, the appropriate Secretaries may designate empowerment zones and enterprise communities.
(b) Number of designations.
   (1) Enterprise communities. The appropriate Secretaries may designate in the aggregate 95 nominated areas as enterprise communities under this section, subject to the availability of eligible nominated areas. Of that number, not more than 65 may be designated in urban areas and not more than 30 may be designated in rural areas.
   (2) Empowerment zones. The appropriate Secretaries may designate in the aggregate 11 nominated areas as empowerment zones under this section, subject to the availability of eligible nominated areas. Of that number, not more than 8 may be designated in urban areas and not more than 3 may be designated in rural areas. If 8 empowerment zones are designated in urban areas, no less than 1 shall be designated in an urban area the most populous city of which has a population of 500,000 or less and no less than 1 shall be a nominated area which includes areas in 2 States and which has a population of 50,000 or less. The Secretary of Housing and Urban Development shall designate empowerment zones located in urban areas in such a manner that the aggregate population of all such zones does not exceed 1,000,000.
(c) Period designations may be made.
A designation may be made under subsection (a) only after 1993 and before 1996.
(d) Period for which designation is in effect.
   (1) In general. Any designation under this section shall remain in effect during the period beginning on the date of the designation and ending on the earliest of—
      (A)(i) in the case of an empowerment zone, December 31, 2011, or
      (ii) in the case of an enterprise community, the close of the 10th calendar year beginning on or after such date of designation,
      (B) the termination date designated by the State and local governments as provided for in their nomination, or
      (C) the date the appropriate Secretary revokes the designation.
   (2) Revocation of designation. The appropriate Secretary may revoke the designation under this section of an area if such Secretary determines that the local government or the State in which it is located—
      (A) has modified the boundaries of the area, or
      (B) is not complying substantially with, or fails to make progress in achieving the benchmarks set forth in, the strategic plan under subsection (f)(2).
(e) Limitations on designations.
No area may be designated under this section unless—
   (1) the area is nominated by 1 or more local governments and the State or States in which it is located for designation under this section,
   (2) such State or States and the local governments have the authority—
      (A) to nominate the area for designation under this section, and
      (B) to provide the assurances described in paragraph (3),
   (3) such State or States and the local governments provide written assurances satisfactory to the appropriate Secretary that the strategic plan described in the application under subsection (f)(2) for such area will be implemented,
   (4) the appropriate Secretary determines that any information furnished is reasonably accurate, and
   (5) such State or States and local governments certify that no portion of the area nominated is already included in an empowerment zone or in an enterprise community or in an area otherwise nominated to be designated under this section.
(f) Application.
No area may be designated under this section unless the application for such designation—
   (1) demonstrates that the nominated area satisfies the eligibility criteria described in section 1392,
   (2) includes a strategic plan for accomplishing the purposes of this subchapter that—
      (A) describes the coordinated economic, human, community, and physical development plan and related activities proposed for the nominated area,
      (B) describes the process by which the affected community is a full partner in the process of developing and implementing the plan and the extent to which local institutions and organizations have contributed to the planning process,
      (C) identifies the amount of State, local, and private resources that will be available in the nominated area and the private/public partnerships to be used, which may include participation by, and cooperation with, universities, medical centers, and other private and public entities,
      (D) identifies the funding requested under any Federal program in support of the proposed economic, human, community, and physical development and related activities,
      (E) identifies baselines, methods, and benchmarks for measuring the success of carrying out the strategic plan, including the extent to which poor persons and families will be empowered to become economically self-sufficient, and
      (F) does not include any action to assist any establishment in relocating from one area outside the nominated area to the nominated area, except that assistance for the expansion of an existing business entity through the establishment of a new branch, affiliate, or subsidiary is permitted if—
         (i) the establishment of the new branch, affiliate, or subsidiary will not result in a decrease in employment in the area of original location or in any other area where the existing business entity conducts business operations, and
         (ii) there is no reason to believe that the new branch, affiliate, or subsidiary is being established with the intention of closing down the operations of the existing business entity in the area of its original location or in any other area where the existing business entity conducts business operation, and
   (3) includes such other information as may be required by the appropriate Secretary.

(g) Additional designations permitted.
(1) In general. In addition to the areas designated under subsection (a), the appropriate Secretaries may designate in the aggregate an additional 20 nominated areas as empowerment zones under this section, subject to the availability of eligible nominated areas. Of that number, not more than 15 may be designated in urban areas and not more than 5 may be designated in rural areas.
(2) Period designations may be made and take effect. A designation may be made under this subsection after the date of the enactment of this subsection and before January 1, 1999.
(3) Modifications to eligibility criteria, etc.
 (A) Poverty rate requirement.
  (i) In general. A nominated area shall be eligible for designation under this subsection only if the poverty rate for each population census tract within the nominated area is not less than 20 percent and the poverty rate for at least 90 percent of the population census tracts within the nominated area is not less than 25 percent.
  (ii) Treatment of census tracts with small populations. A population census tract with a population of less than 2,000 shall be treated as having a poverty rate of not less than 25 percent if—
   (I) more than 75 percent of such tract is zoned for commercial or industrial use, and
   (II) such tract is contiguous to 1 or more other population census tracts which have a poverty rate of not less than 25 percent (determined without regard to this clause).
  (iii) Exception for developable sites. Clause (i) shall not apply to up to 3 noncontiguous parcels in a nominated area which may be developed for commercial or industrial purposes. The aggregate area of noncontiguous parcels to which the preceding sentence applies with respect to any nominated area shall not exceed 2,000 acres.
  (iv) Certain provisions not to apply. Section 1392(a)(4) (and so much of paragraphs (1) and (2) of section 1392(b) as relate to section 1392(a)(4)) shall not apply to an area nominated for designation under this subsection.
  (v) Special rule for rural empowerment zone. The Secretary of Agriculture may designate not more than 1 empowerment zone in a rural area without regard to clause (i) if such area satisfies emigration criteria specified by the Secretary of Agriculture.
 (B) Size limitation.
  (i) In general. The parcels described in subparagraph (A)(iii) shall not be taken into account in determining whether the requirement of subparagraph (A) or (B) of section 1392(a)(3) is met.
  (ii) Special rule for rural areas. If a population census tract (or equivalent division under section 1392(b)(4)) in a rural area exceeds 1,000 square miles or includes a substantial amount of land owned by the Federal, State, or local government, the nominated area may exclude such excess square mileage or governmentally owned land and the exclusion of that area will not be treated as violating the continuous boundary requirement of section 1392(a)(3)(B).
 (C) Aggregate population limitation. The aggregate population limitation under the last sentence of subsection (b)(2) shall not apply to a designation under paragraph (1).
 (D) Previously designated enterprise communities may be included. Subsection (e)(5) shall not apply to any enterprise community designated under subsection (a) that is also nominated for designation under this subsection.
 (E) Indian reservations may be nominated.
  (i) In general. Section 1393(a)(4) shall not apply to an area nominated for designation under this subsection.
  (ii) Special rule. An area in an Indian reservation shall be treated as nominated by a State and a local government if it is nominated by the reservation governing body (as determined by the Secretary of Interior).

(h) Additional designations permitted.
(1) In general. In addition to the areas designated under subsections (a) and (g), the appropriate Secretaries may designate in the aggregate an additional 9 nominated areas as empowerment zones under this section, subject to the availability of eligible nominated areas. Of that number, not more than seven may be designated in urban areas and not more than 2 may be designated in rural areas.
(2) Period designations may be made and take effect. A designation may be made under this subsection after the date of the enactment of this subsection and before January 1, 2002.
(3) Modifications to eligibility criteria, etc. The rules of subsection (g)(3) shall apply to designations under this subsection.
(4) Empowerment zones which become renewal communities. The number of areas which may be designated as empowerment zones under this subsection shall be increased by 1 for each area which ceases to be an empowerment zone by reason of section 1400E(e). Each additional area designated by reason of the preceding sentence shall have the same urban or rural character as the area it is replacing.

In 2010, P.L. 111-312, Sec. 753(a)(1), substituted "December 31, 2011" for "December 31, 2009" in clause (d)(1)(A)(i) . . . Sec. 753(a)(2), deleted the last sentence of para. (h)(2), effective for periods after 12/31/2009.
Prior to deletion, the last sentence of para. (h)(2) read as follows:
"Subject to subparagraphs (B) and (C) of subsection (d)(1), such designations shall remain in effect during the period beginning on January 1, 2002, and ending on December 31, 2009."
—P.L. 111-312, Sec. 753(c), of this Act, provides:
"(c) Treatment of certain termination dates specified in nominations. In the case of a designation of an empowerment zone the nomination for which included a termination date which is contemporaneous with the date specified in subparagraph (A)(i) of section 1391(d)(1) of the Internal Revenue Code of 1986 (as in effect before the enactment of this Act), subparagraph (B) of such section shall not apply with respect to such designation if, after the date of the enactment of this section, the entity which made such nomination amends the nomination to provide for a new termination date in such manner as the Secretary of the Treasury (or the Secretary's designee) may provide."
In 2000, P.L. 106-554, Sec. 1(a)(7), [which enacted into law Sec. 111 of P.L. 106-554] added subsec. (h), effective 12/21/2000.
—P.L. 106-554, Sec. 1(a)(7), [which enacted into law Sec. 112 of P.L. 106-554] amended subpara. (d)(1)(A), effective 12/21/2000.
Prior to amendment, subpara. (d)(1)(A) read as follows:
"(A) the close of the 10th calendar year beginning on or after such date of designation,"
—P.L. 106-554, Sec. 1(a)(7), [which enacted into law Sec. 319(13) of P.L. 106-554] substituted "paragraph (1)" for "paragraph (1)(B)" in subpara. (g)(3)(C), effective 12/21/2000.
In 1997, P.L. 105-34, Sec. 951(a)(1), substituted "11" for "9" in para. (b)(2) . . . Sec. 951(a)(2), substituted "8" for "6" in para. (b)(2) . . . Sec. 951(a)(3), substituted "1,000,000" for "750,000" in para. (b)(2), effective 8/5/97, except that designations of new empowerment zones made pursuant to such amendments shall be made during the 180-day period begin. 8/5/97. No designation to such amendments shall take effect before 1/1/2000.
—P.L. 105-34, Sec. 952(a), added subsec. (g) . . . Sec. 952(d)(1), substituted "this section" for "subsection (a)" in subsecs. (e) and (f) . . . Sec. 952(d)(2), substituted "subsection (a)" for "this section" in subsec. (c), effective 8/5/97.
In 1996, P.L. 104-188, Sec. 1119(c), of this Act, effective 8/20/96, reads as follows:

"(c) Expansion of Oklahoma City Enterprise Community. Notwithstanding sections 1391 and 1392(a)(3)(D) of the Internal Revenue Code of 1986, the boundaries of the enterprise community for Oklahoma City, Oklahoma, designated by the Secretary of Housing and Urban Development on December 21, 1994, may be extended with respect to census tracts located in the area damaged due to the bombing of the Alfred P. Murrah Federal Building in Oklahoma City on April 19, 1995, primarily in the area bounded on the south by Robert S. Kerr Avenue, on the north by North 13th Street, on the east by Oklahoma Avenue, and on the west by Shartel Avenue."

In 1993, P.L. 103-66, Sec. 13301(a), added Code Sec. 1391, effective 8/10/93.

Sec. 1392. Eligibility criteria.
(a) In general.
A nominated area shall be eligible for designation under section 1391 only if it meets the following criteria:
(1) Population. The nominated area has a maximum population of—
(A) in the case of an urban area, the lesser of—
(i) 200,000, or
(ii) the greater of 50,000 or 10 percent of the population of the most populous city located within the nominated area, and
(B) in the case of a rural area, 30,000.
(2) Distress. The nominated area is one of pervasive poverty, unemployment, and general distress.
(3) Size. The nominated area—
(A) does not exceed 20 square miles if an urban area or 1,000 square miles if a rural area,
(B) has a boundary which is continuous, or, except in the case of a rural area located in more than 1 State, consists of not more than 3 noncontiguous parcels,
(C)(i) in the case of an urban area, is located entirely within no more than 2 contiguous States, and
(ii) in the case of a rural area, is located entirely within no more than 3 contiguous States, and
(D) does not include any portion of a central business district (as such term is used for purposes of the most recent Census of Retail Trade) unless the poverty rate for each population census tract in such district is not less than 35 percent (30 percent in the case of an enterprise community).
(4) Poverty Rate. The poverty rate—
(A) for each population census tract within the nominated area is not less than 20 percent,
(B) for at least 90 percent of the population census tracts within the nominated area is not less than 25 percent, and
(C) for at least 50 percent of the population census tracts within the nominated area is not less than 35 percent.
(b) Special rules relating to determination of poverty rate.
For purposes of subsection (a)(4)—
(1) Treatment of census tracts with small populations.
(A) Tracts with no population. In the case of a population census tract with no population—
(i) such tract shall be treated as having a poverty rate which meets the requirements of subparagraphs (A) and (B) of subsection (a)(4), but
(ii) such tract shall be treated as having a zero poverty rate for purposes of applying subparagraph (C) thereof.
(B) Tracts with populations of less than 2,000. A population census tract with a population of less than 2,000 shall be treated as having a poverty rate which meets the requirements of subparagraphs (A) and (B) of subsection (a)(4) if more than 75 percent of such tract is zoned for commercial or industrial use.

(2) Discretion to adjust requirements for enterprise communities. In determining whether a nominated area is eligible for designation as an enterprise community, the appropriate Secretary may, where necessary to carry out the purposes of this subchapter, reduce by 5 percentage points one of the following thresholds for not more than 10 percent of the population census tracts (or, if fewer, 5 population census tracts) in the nominated area:
(A) The 20 percent threshold in subsection (a)(4)(A).
(B) The 25 percent threshold in subsection (a)(4)(B).
(C) The 35 percent threshold in subsection (a)(4)(C).
If the appropriate Secretary elects to reduce the threshold under subparagraph (C), such Secretary may (in lieu of applying the preceding sentence) reduce by 10 percentage points the threshold under subparagraph (C) for 3 population census tracts.
(3) Each noncontiguous area must satisfy poverty rate rule. A nominated area may not include a noncontiguous parcel unless such parcel separately meets (subject to paragraphs (1) and (2)) the criteria set forth in subsection (a)(4).
(4) Areas not within census tracts. In the case of an area which is not tracted for population census tracts, the equivalent county divisions (as defined by the Bureau of the Census for purposes of defining poverty areas) shall be used for purposes of determining poverty rates.
(c) Factors to consider.
From among the nominated areas eligible for designation under section 1391 by the appropriate Secretary, such appropriate Secretary shall make designations of empowerment zones and enterprise communities on the basis of—
(1) the effectiveness of the strategic plan submitted pursuant to section 1391(f)(2) and the assurances made pursuant to section 1391(e)(3), and
(2) criteria specified by the appropriate Secretary.
(d) Special eligibility for nominated areas located in Alaska or Hawaii.
A nominated area in Alaska or Hawaii shall be treated as meeting the requirements of paragraphs (2), (3), and (4) of subsection (a) if for each census tract or block group within such area 20 percent or more of the families have income which is 50 percent or less of the statewide median family income (as determined under section 143).

In 1997, P.L. 105-34, Sec. 954, added subsec. (d), effective 8/5/97.
In 1996, P.L. 104-188, Sec. 1119(c), of this Act, effective 8/20/96, reads as follows:
"(c) Expansion of Oklahoma City Enterprise Community. Notwithstanding sections 1391 and 1392(a)(3)(D) of the Internal Revenue Code of 1986, the boundaries of the enterprise community for Oklahoma City, Oklahoma, designated by the Secretary of Housing and Urban Development on December 21, 1994, may be extended with respect to census tracts located in the area damaged due to the bombing of the Alfred P. Murrah Federal Building in Oklahoma City on April 19, 1995, primarily in the area bounded on the south by Robert S. Kerr Avenue, on the north by North 13th Street, on the east by Oklahoma Avenue, and on the west by Shartel Avenue."
In 1993, P.L. 103-66, Sec. 13301(a), added Code Sec. 1392, effective 8/10/93.

Sec. 1393. Definitions and special rules.
(a) In general.
For purposes of this subchapter—
(1) Appropriate Secretary. The term "appropriate Secretary" means—
(A) the Secretary of Housing and Urban Development in the case of any nominated area which is located in an urban area, and
(B) the Secretary of Agriculture in the case of any nominated area which is located in a rural area.

(2) **Rural area.** The term "rural area" means any area which is—
(A) outside of a metropolitan statistical area (within the meaning of section 143(k)(2)(B)), or
(B) determined by the Secretary of Agriculture, after consultation with the Secretary of Commerce, to be a rural area.
(3) **Urban area.** The term "urban area" means an area which is not a rural area.
(4) **Special rules for Indian reservations.**
(A) In general. No empowerment zone or enterprise community may include any area within an Indian reservation.
(B) Indian reservation defined. The term "Indian reservation" has the meaning given such term by section 168(j)(6).
(5) **Local government.** The term "local government" means—
(A) any county, city, town, township, parish, village, or other general purpose political subdivision of a State, and
(B) any combination of political subdivisions described in subparagraph (A) recognized by the appropriate Secretary.
(6) **Nominated area.** The term "nominated area" means an area which is nominated by 1 or more local governments and the State or States in which it is located for designation under section 1391.
(7) **Governments.** If more than 1 State or local government seeks to nominate an area under this part, any reference to, or requirement of, this subchapter shall apply to all such governments.
(8) **Special rule.** An area shall be treated as nominated by a State and a local government if it is nominated by an economic development corporation chartered by the State.
(9) **Use of census data.** Population and poverty rate shall be determined by the most recent decennial census data available.
(b) **Empowerment zone; enterprise community.**
For purposes of this title, the terms "empowerment zone" and "enterprise community" mean areas designated as such under section 1391.

In 1993, P.L. 103-66, Sec. 13301(a), added Code Sec. 1393, effective 8/10/93.

PART II.—TAX-EXEMPT FACILITY BONDS FOR EMPOWERMENT ZONES AND ENTERPRISE COMMUNITIES
Sec.
1394. Tax-exempt enterprise zone facility bonds.

In 1993, P.L. 103-66, Sec. 13301(a), added Part II as part of new Subchapter U.

Sec. 1394. Tax-exempt enterprise zone facility bonds.
(a) **In general.**
For purposes of part IV of subchapter B of this chapter (relating to tax exemption requirements for State and local bonds), the term "exempt facility bond" includes any bond issued as part of an issue 95 percent or more of the net proceeds (as defined in section 150(a)(3)) of which are to be used to provide any enterprise zone facility.
(b) **Enterprise zone facility.**
For purposes of this subsection—
(1) **In general.** The term "enterprise zone facility" means any qualified zone property the principal user of which is an enterprise zone business, and any land which is functionally related and subordinate to such property.

(2) **Qualified zone property.** The term "qualified zone property" has the meaning given such term by section 1397D; except that—
(A) the references to empowerment zones shall be treated as including references to enterprise communities, and
(B) section 1397D(a)(2) shall be applied by substituting "an amount equal to 15 percent of the adjusted basis" for "an amount equal to the adjusted basis".
(3) **Enterprise zone business.**
(A) In general. Except as modified in this paragraph, the term "enterprise zone business" has the meaning given such term by section 1397C.
(B) Modifications. In applying section 1397C for purposes of this section—
(i) Businesses in enterprise communities eligible. References in section 1397C to empowerment zones shall be treated as including references to enterprise communities.
(ii) Waiver of requirements during startup period. A business shall not fail to be treated as an enterprise zone business during the startup period if—
(I) as of the beginning of the startup period, it is reasonably expected that such business will be an enterprise zone business (as defined in section 1397C as modified by this paragraph) at the end of such period, and
(II) such business makes bona fide efforts to be such a business.
(iii) Reduced requirements after testing period. A business shall not fail to be treated as an enterprise zone business for any taxable year beginning after the testing period by reason of failing to meet any requirement of subsection (b) or (c) of section 1397C if at least 35 percent of the employees of such business for such year are residents of an empowerment zone or an enterprise community. The preceding sentence shall not apply to any business which is not a qualified business by reason of paragraph (1), (4), or (5) of section 1397C(d).
(C) Definitions relating to subparagraph (B). For purposes of subparagraph (B)—
(i) Startup period. The term "startup period" means, with respect to any property being provided for any business, the period before the first taxable year beginning more than 2 years after the later of—
(I) the date of issuance of the issue providing such property, or
(II) the date such property is first placed in service after such issuance (or, if earlier, the date which is 3 years after the date described in subclause (I)).
(ii) Testing period. The term "testing period" means the first 3 taxable years beginning after the startup period.
(D) Portions of business may be enterprise zone business. The term "enterprise zone business" includes any trades or businesses which would qualify as an enterprise zone business (determined after the modifications of subparagraph (B)) if such trades or businesses were separately incorporated.
(c) **Limitation on amount of bonds.**
(1) **In general.** Subsection (a) shall not apply to any issue if the aggregate amount of outstanding enterprise zone facility bonds allocable to any person (taking into account such issue) exceeds—

(A) $3,000,000 with respect to any 1 empowerment zone or enterprise community, or

(B) $20,000,000 with respect to all empowerment zones and enterprise communities.

(2) Aggregate enterprise zone facility bond benefit. For purposes of paragraph (1), the aggregate amount of outstanding enterprise zone facility bonds allocable to any person shall be determined under rules similar to the rules of section 144(a)(10), taking into account only bonds to which subsection (a) applies.

(d) Acquisition of land and existing property permitted. The requirements of sections 147(c)(1)(A) and 147(d) shall not apply to any bond described in subsection (a).

(e) Penalty for ceasing to meet requirements.

(1) Failures corrected. An issue which fails to meet 1 or more of the requirements of subsections (a) and (b) shall be treated as meeting such requirements if—

(A) the issuer and any principal user in good faith attempted to meet such requirements, and

(B) any failure to meet such requirements is corrected within a reasonable period after such failure is first discovered.

(2) Loss of deductions where facility ceases to be qualified. No deduction shall be allowed under this chapter for interest on any financing provided from any bond to which subsection (a) applies with respect to any facility to the extent such interest accrues during the period beginning on the first day of the calendar year which includes the date on which—

(A) substantially all of the facility with respect to which the financing was provided ceases to be used in an empowerment zone or enterprise community, or

(B) the principal user of such facility ceases to be an enterprise zone business (as defined in subsection (b)).

(3) Exception if zone ceases. Paragraphs (1) and (2) shall not apply solely by reason of the termination or revocation of a designation as an empowerment zone or an enterprise community.

(4) Exception for bankruptcy. Paragraphs (1) and (2) shall not apply to any cessation resulting from bankruptcy.

(f) Bonds for empowerment zones designated under section 1391(g).

(1) In general. In the case of a new empowerment zone facility bond—

(A) such bond shall not be treated as a private activity bond for purposes of section 146, and

(B) subsection (c) of this section shall not apply.

(2) Limitation on amount of bonds.

(A) In general. Paragraph (1) shall apply to a new empowerment zone facility bond only if such bond is designated for purposes of this subsection by the local government which nominated the area to which such bond relates.

(B) Limitation on bonds designated. The aggregate face amount of bonds which may be designated under subparagraph (A) with respect to any empowerment zone shall not exceed—

(i) $60,000,000 if such zone is in a rural area,

(ii) $130,000,000 if such zone is in an urban area and the zone has a population of less than 100,000, and

(iii) $230,000,000 if such zone is in an urban area and the zone has a population of at least 100,000.

(C) Special rules.

(i) Coordination with limitation in subsection (c). Bonds to which paragraph (1) applies shall not be taken into account in applying the limitation of subsection (c) to other bonds.

(ii) Current refunding not taken into account. In the case of a refunding (or series of refundings) of a bond designated under this paragraph, the refunding obligation shall be treated as designated under this paragraph (and shall not be taken into account in applying subparagraph (B)) if—

(I) the amount of the refunding bond does not exceed the outstanding amount of the refunded bond, and

(II) the refunded bond is redeemed not later than 90 days after the date of issuance of the refunding bond.

(3) Empowerment zone facility bond. For purposes of this subsection, the term "empowerment zone facility bond" means any bond which would be described in subsection (a) if—

(A) in the case of obligations issued before January 1, 2002, only empowerment zones designated under section 1391(g) were taken into account under sections 1397C and 1397D, and

(B) in the case of obligations issued after December 31, 2001, all empowerment zones (other than the District of Columbia Enterprise Zone) were taken into account under sections 1397C and 1397D.

In 2002, P.L. 107-147, Sec. 417(16), substituted "paragraph (1)" for "subparagraph (A)" in para. (c)(2), effective 3/9/2002.

In 2000, P.L. 106-554, Sec. 1(a)(7), [which enacted into law Sec. 115(a) of P.L. 106-554] amended para. (f)(3), effective for obligations issued after 12/31/2001. Prior to amendment, para. (f)(3) read as follows:

"(3) New empowerment zone facility bond. For purposes of this subsection, the term 'new empowerment zone facility bond' means any bond which would be described in subsection (a) if only empowerment zones designated under section 1391(g) were taken into account under sections 1397B and 1397C."

—P.L. 106-554, Sec. 1(a)(7), [which enacted into law Sec. 116(b)(3)(A) of P.L. 106-554] substituted "section 1397D" for "section 1397C" in para. (b)(2) . . . Sec. 1(a)(7), [which enacted into law Sec. 116(b)(3)(B) of P.L. 106-554] substituted "section 1397D(a)(2)" for "section 1397C(a)(2)" in para. (b)(2) . . . Sec. 1(a)(7), [which enacted into law Sec. 116(b)(4)(A) of P.L. 106-554] substituted "section 1397C" for "section 1397B" each place it appeared in para. (b)(3) . . . Sec. 1(a)(7), [which enacted into law Sec. 116(b)(4)(B) of P.L. 106-554] substituted "section 1397C(d)" for "section 1397B(d)" in para. (b)(3), effective for qualified empowerment zone assets acquired after 12/21/2000.

In 1997, P.L. 105-34, Sec. 953(a), added subsec. (f), effective for obligations issued after 8/5/97.

—P.L. 105-34, Sec. 955(a), amended para. (b)(3) . . . Sec. 955(b), amended para. (b)(2), effective for obligations issued after 8/5/97.

Prior to amendment, para. (b)(2) read as follows:

"(2) Qualified zone property. The term 'qualified zone property' has the meaning given such term by section 1397C; except that the references to empowerment zones shall be treated as including references to enterprise communities."

Prior to amendment, para. (b)(3) read as follows:

"(3) Enterprise zone business. The term 'enterprise zone business' has the meaning given to such term by section 1397B, except that—

"(A) references to empowerment zones shall be treated as including references to enterprise communities, and

"(B) such term includes any trades or businesses which would qualify as an enterprise zone business (determined after the modification of subparagraph (A)) if such trades or businesses were separately incorporated."

In 1996, P.L. 104-188, Sec. 1703(n)(7)(A), substituted "(A)" for "(i)" in para. (e)(2) . . . Sec. 1703(n)(7)(B), substituted "(B)" for "(ii)" in para. (e)(2), effective 8/10/93.

In 1993, P.L. 103-66, Sec. 13301(a), added Code Sec. 1394, effective 8/10/93.

PART III.—ADDITIONAL INCENTIVES FOR EMPOWERMENT ZONES

Subpart.

A. Empowerment Zone Employment Credit

B. Addtional Expensing

C. Nonrecognition of Gain on Rollover of Empowerment Zone Investments

D. General Provisions

Cooperatives   **Code Sec. 1396**

In 2000, P.L. 106-554, Sec. 1(a)(7) [which enacted into law Sec. 116(b)(6) of H.R. 5662], deleted subpart C and added new subparts C and D.
Prior to deletion, subpart C read as follows:
"C. General provisions"
In 1993, P.L. 103-66, Sec. 13301(a), added Part III as part of new Subchapter U.

SUBPART A.—EMPOWERMENT ZONE EMPLOYMENT CREDIT
Sec.
1396. Empowerment zone employment credit.
1397. Other defintions and special rules.

In 1993, P.L. 103-66, Sec. 13301(a), added Subpart A of Part III as part of new Subchapter U.

Sec. 1396. Empowerment zone employment credit.
(a) Amount of credit.
For purposes of section 38, the amount of the empowerment zone employment credit determined under this section with respect to any employer for any taxable year is the applicable percentage of the qualified zone wages paid or incurred during the calendar year which ends with or within such taxable year.
(b) Applicable percentage.
For purposes of this section, the applicable percentage is 20 percent.
(c) Qualified zone wages.
(1) In general. For purposes of this section, the term "qualified zone wages" means any wages paid or incurred by an employer for services performed by an employee while such employee is a qualified zone employee.
(2) Only first $15,000 of wages per year taken into account. With respect to each qualified zone employee, the amount of qualified zone wages which may be taken into account for a calendar year shall not exceed $15,000.
(3) Coordination with work opportunity credit.
(A) In general. The term "qualified zone wages" shall not include wages taken into account in determining the credit under section 51.
(B) Coordination with paragraph (2). The $15,000 amount in paragraph (2) shall be reduced for any calendar year by the amount of wages paid or incurred during such year which are taken into account in determining the credit under section 51.
(d) Qualified zone employee.
For purposes of this section—
(1) In general. Except as otherwise provided in this subsection, the term "qualified zone employee" means, with respect to any period, any employee of an employer if—
(A) substantially all of the services performed during such period by such employee for such employer are performed within an empowerment zone in a trade or business of the employer, and
(B) the principal place of abode of such employee while performing such services is within such empowerment zone.
(2) Certain individuals not eligible. The term "qualified zone employee" shall not include—
(A) any individual described in subparagraph (A), (B), or (C) of section 51(i)(1),
(B) any 5-percent owner (as defined in section 416(i)(1)(B)),
(C) any individual employed by the employer for less than 90 days,
(D) any individual employed by the employer at any facility described in section 144(c)(6)(B), and
(E) any individual employed by the employer in a trade or business the principal activity of which is farming

(within the meaning of subparagraphs (A) or (B) of section 2032A(e)(5)), but only if, as of the close of the taxable year, the sum of—
(i) the aggregate unadjusted bases (or, if greater, the fair market value) of the assets owned by the employer which are used in such a trade or business, and
(ii) the aggregate value of assets leased by the employer which are used in such a trade or business (as determined under regulations prescribed by the Secretary),
exceeds $500,000.
(3) Special rules related to termination of employment.
(A) In general. Paragraph (2)(C) shall not apply to—
(i) a termination of employment of an individual who before the close of the period referred to in paragraph (2)(C) becomes disabled to perform the services of such employment unless such disability is removed before the close of such period and the taxpayer fails to offer reemployment to such individual, or
(ii) a termination of employment of an individual if it is determined under the applicable State unemployment compensation law that the termination was due to the misconduct of such individual.
(B) Changes in form of business. For purposes of paragraph (2)(C), the employment relationship between the taxpayer and an employee shall not be treated as terminated—
(i) by a transaction to which section 381(a) applies if the employee continues to be employed by the acquiring corporation, or
(ii) by reason of a mere change in the form of conducting the trade or business of the taxpayer if the employee continues to be employed in such trade or business and the taxpayer retains a substantial interest in such trade or business.
(e) Repealed.

In 2000, P.L. 106-554, Sec. 1(a)(7), [which enacted into law Sec. 113(a) of P.L. 106-554] amended subsec. (b)... Sec. 1(a)(7), [which enacted into law Sec. 113(b) of P.L. 106-554] deleted subsec. (e), effective for wages paid or incurred after 12/31/2001.
Prior to amendment, subsec. (b) read as follows:
"*(b) Applicable percentage.* For purposes of this section—
"(1) In general. Except as provided in paragraph (2), the term 'applicable percentage' means the percentage determined in accordance with the following table:

In the case of wages paid or incurred during calendar year:	The applicable percentage is:
1994 through 2001	20
2002	15
2003	10
2004	5"

"(2) Special rule. With respect to each empowerment zone designated pursuant to the amendments made by the Taxpayer Relief Act of 1997 to section 1391(b)(2), the following table shall apply in lieu of the table in paragraph (1)

In the case of wages paid or incurred during calendar year:	The applicable percentage is:
2000 through 2004	20
2005	15
2006	10
2007	5"

Prior to deletion, subsec. (e) read as follows:
"*(e) Credit not to apply to empowerment zones designated under section 1391(g).* This section shall be applied without regard to any empowerment zone designated under section 1391(g)."
In 1997, P.L. 105-34, Sec. 951(b)(1), substituted the heading and text of subsec. (b) and para. (b)(1) preceding the table in para. (b)(1) for "Applicable percentage. For purposes of this section, the term 'applicable percentage' means the percentage determined in accordance with the following table:" ... Sec. 951(b)(2), added para. (b)(2), effective date of enactment, except that designations of new empowerment zones made pursuant to such amendments shall be made during the 180-

day period beginning on date of enactment. No designation pursuant to such amendments shall take effect before 1/1/2000.
— P.L. 105-34, Sec. 952(b), added subsec. (e), effective 8/5/97.

In 1996, P.L. 104-188, Sec. 1201(e)(4), substituted "work opportunity credit" for "targeted jobs credit" in the heading of para. (c)(3), effective for individuals who begin work for the employer after 9/30/96.

In 1993, P.L. 103-66, Sec. 13301(a), added Code Sec. 1396 effective 8/10/93.

Sec. 1397. Other definitions and special rules.
(a) Wages.
For purposes of this subpart—
(1) In general. The term "wages" has the same meaning as when used in section 51.
(2) Certain training and educational benefits.
(A) In general. The following amounts shall be treated as wages paid to an employee:
(i) Any amount paid or incurred by an employer which is excludable from the gross income of an employee under section 127, but only to the extent paid or incurred to a person not related to the employer.
(ii) In the case of an employee who has not attained the age of 19, any amount paid or incurred by an employer for any youth training program operated by such employer in conjunction with local education officials.
(B) Related person. A person is related to any other person if the person bears a relationship to such other person specified in section 267(b) or 707(b)(1), or such person and such other person are engaged in trades or businesses under common control (within the meaning of subsections (a) and (b) of section 52. For purposes of the preceding sentence, in applying section 267(b) or 707(b)(1), "10 percent" shall be substituted for "50 percent".
(b) Controlled groups.
For purposes of this subpart—
(1) all employers treated as a single employer under subsection (a) or (b) of section 52 shall be treated as a single employer for purposes of this subpart, and
(2) the credit (if any) determined under section 1396 with respect to each such employer shall be its proportionate share of the wages giving rise to such credit.
(c) Certain other rules made applicable.
For purposes of this subpart, rules similar to the rules of section 51(k) and subsections (c), (d), and (e) of section 52 shall apply.

In 1993, P.L. 103-66, Sec. 13301(a), added Code Sec. 1397, effective 8/10/93.

SUBPART B.— ADDITIONAL EXPENSING
Sec.
1397A. Increase in expensing under section 179.

In 1993, P.L. 103-66, Sec. 13301(a), added Subpart B of Part III as part of new Subchapter U.

Sec. 1397A. Increase in expensing under section 179.
(a) General rule.
In the case of an enterprise zone business, for purposes of section 179—
(1) the limitation under section 179(b)(1) shall be increased by the lesser of—
(A) $35,000, or
(B) the cost of section 179 property which is qualified zone property placed in service during the taxable year, and
(2) the amount taken into account under section 179(b)(2) with respect to any section 179 property which is qualified zone property shall be 50 percent of the cost thereof.

(b) Recapture.
Rules similar to the rules under section 179(d)(10) shall apply with respect to any qualified zone property which ceases to be used in an empowerment zone by an enterprise zone business.
(c) Repealed.

In 2000, P.L. 106-554, Sec. 1(a)(7), [which enacted into law Sec. 114(a) of P.L. 106-554] substituted "$35,000" for "$20,000" in subpara. (a)(1)(A) ... Sec. 1(a)(7), [which enacted into law Sec. 114(b) of P.L. 106-554] deleted subsec. (c), effective for tax. yrs. begin. after 12/31/2001.
Prior to deletion, subsec. (c) read as follows:
"(c) Limitation. For purposes of this section, qualified zone property shall not include any property substantially all of the use of which is in any parcel described in section 1391(g)(2)(A)(iii)."

In 1997, P.L. 105-34, Sec. 952(c), added subsec. (c), effective 8/5/97.
In 1993, P.L. 103-66, Sec. 13301(a), added Code Sec. 1397A, effective 8/10/93.

SUBPART C.— NONRECOGNITION OF GAIN ON ROLLOVER OF EMPOWERMENT ZONE INVESTMENTS

Sec.
1397B. Nonrecognition of gain on rollover of empowerment zone investments.

In 2000, P.L. 106-554, Sec. 116(a)(3), added Subpart C of Part III of Subchapter U.
In 1993, P.L. 103-66, Sec. 13301(a), added Subpart B of Part III as part of new Subchapter U.

Sec. 1397B. Nonrecognition of gain on rollover of empowerment zone investments.
(a) Nonrecognition of gain.
In the case of any sale of a qualified empowerment zone asset held by the taxpayer for more than 1 year and with respect to which such taxpayer elects the application of this section, gain from such sale shall be recognized only to the extent that the amount realized on such sale exceeds—
(1) the cost of any qualified empowerment zone asset (with respect to the same zone as the asset sold) purchased by the taxpayer during the 60-day period beginning on the date of such sale, reduced by
(2) any portion of such cost previously taken into account under this section.
(b) Definitions and special rules.
For purposes of this section—
(1) Qualified empowerment zone asset.
(A) In general. The term "qualified empowerment zone asset" means any property which would be a qualified community asset (as defined in section 1400F) if in section 1400F—
(i) references to empowerment zones were substituted for references to renewal communities,
(ii) references to enterprise zone businesses (as defined in section 1397C) were substituted for references to renewal community businesses, and
(iii) the date of the enactment of this paragraph were substituted for "December 31, 2001" each place it appears.
(B) Treatment of DC zone. The District of Columbia Enterprise Zone shall not be treated as an empowerment zone for purposes of this section.
(2) Certain gain not eligible for rollover. This section shall not apply to—
(A) any gain which is treated as ordinary income for purposes of this subtitle, and
(B) any gain which is attributable to real property, or an intangible asset, which is not an integral part of an enterprise zone business.

(3) Purchase. A taxpayer shall be treated as having purchased any property if, but for paragraph (4), the unadjusted basis of such property in the hands of the taxpayer would be its cost (within the meaning of section 1012).

(4) Basis adjustments. If gain from any sale is not recognized by reason of subsection (a), such gain shall be applied to reduce (in the order acquired) the basis for determining gain or loss of any qualified empowerment zone asset which is purchased by the taxpayer during the 60-day period described in subsection (a). This paragraph shall not apply for purposes of section 1202.

(5) Holding period. For purposes of determining whether the nonrecognition of gain under subsection (a) applies to any qualified empowerment zone asset which is sold—

(A) the taxpayer's holding period for such asset and the asset referred to in subsection (a)(1) shall be determined without regard to section 1223, and

(B) only the first year of the taxpayer's holding period for the asset referred to in subsection (a)(1) shall be taken into account for purposes of paragraphs (2)(A)(iii), (3)(C), and (4)(A)(iii) of section 1400F(b).

In 2000, P.L. 106-554, Sec. 1(a)(7), [which enacted into law Sec. 116(a)(3) of P.L. 106-554] added Code Sec. 1397B, effective for qualified empowerment zone assets acquired after 12/21/2000.

SUBPART D.—GENERAL PROVISIONS
Sec.
1397C. Enterprise zone business defined.
1397D. Qualified zone property defined.

In 2000, P.L. 106-554, Sec. 116(a)(1), redesignated Subpart C as Subpart D and sections 1397B and C as sections 1397C and D.
In 1993, P.L. 103-66, Sec. 13301(a), added Subpart C of Part III as part of new Subchapter U.

Sec. 1397C. Enterprise zone business defined.
(a) In general.

For purposes of this part, the term "enterprise zone business" means—

(1) any qualified business entity, and
(2) any qualified proprietorship.

(b) Qualified business entity.

For purposes of this section, the term "qualified business entity" means, with respect to any taxable year, any corporation or partnership if for such year—

(1) every trade or business of such entity is the active conduct of a qualified business within an empowerment zone,

(2) at least 50 percent of the total gross income of such entity is derived from the active conduct of such business,

(3) a substantial portion of the use of the tangible property of such entity (whether owned or leased) is within an empowerment zone,

(4) a substantial portion of the intangible property of such entity is used in the active conduct of any such business,

(5) a substantial portion of the services performed for such entity by its employees are performed in an empowerment zone,

(6) at least 35 percent of its employees are residents of an empowerment zone,

(7) less than 5 percent of the average of the aggregate unadjusted bases of the property of such entity is attributable to collectibles (as defined in section 408(m)(2)) other than collectibles that are held primarily for sale to customers in the ordinary course of such business, and

(8) less than 5 percent of the average of the aggregate unadjusted bases of the property of such entity is attributable to nonqualified financial property.

(c) Qualified proprietorship.

For purposes of this section, the term "qualified proprietorship" means, with respect to any taxable year, any qualified business carried on by an individual as a proprietorship if for such year—

(1) at least 50 percent of the total gross income of such individual from such business is derived from the active conduct of such business in an empowerment zone,

(2) a substantial portion of the use of the tangible property of such individual in such business (whether owned or leased) is within an empowerment zone,

(3) a substantial portion of the intangible property of such business is used in the active conduct of such business,

(4) a substantial portion of the services performed for such individual in such business by employees of such business are performed in an empowerment zone,

(5) at least 35 percent of such employees are residents of an empowerment zone,

(6) less than 5 percent of the average of the aggregate unadjusted bases of the property of such individual which is used in such business is attributable to collectibles (as defined in section 408(m)(2)) other than collectibles that are held primarily for sale to customers in the ordinary course of such business, and

(7) less than 5 percent of the average of the aggregate unadjusted bases of the property of such individual which is used in such business is attributable to nonqualified financial property.

For purposes of this subsection, the term "employee" includes the proprietor.

(d) Qualified business.

For purposes of this section—

(1) **In general.** Except as otherwise provided in this subsection, the term "qualified business" means any trade or business.

(2) **Rental of real property.** The rental to others of real property located in an empowerment zone shall be treated as a qualified business if and only if—

(A) the property is not residential rental property (as defined in section 168(e)(2)), and

(B) at least 50 percent of the gross rental income from the real property is from enterprise zone businesses.

For purposes of subparagraph (B), the lessor of the property may rely on a lessee's certification that such lessee is an enterprise zone business.

(3) **Rental of tangible personal property.** The rental to others of tangible personal property shall be treated as a qualified business if and only if at least 50 percent of the rental of such property is by enterprise zone businesses or by residents of an empowerment zone.

(4) **Treatment of business holding intangibles.** The term "qualified business" shall not include any trade or business consisting predominantly of the development or holding of intangibles for sale or license.

(5) **Certain businesses excluded.** The term "qualified business" shall not include—

(A) any trade or business consisting of the operation of any facility described in section 144(c)(6)(B), and

(B) any trade or business the principal activity of which is farming (within the meaning of subparagraphs (A) or (B) of section 2032A(e)(5)), but only if, as of the close of the taxable year, the sum of—

(i) the aggregate unadjusted bases (or, if greater, the fair market value) of the assets owned by the taxpayer which are used in such a trade or business, and
(ii) the aggregate value of assets leased by the taxpayer which are used in such a trade or business, exceeds $500,000.

For purposes of subparagraph (B), rules similar to the rules of section 1397(b) shall apply.

(e) Nonqualified financial property.

For purposes of this section, the term "nonqualified financial property" means debt, stock, partnership interests, options, futures contracts, forward contracts, warrants, notional principal contracts, annuities, and other similar property specified in regulations; except that such term shall not include—

(1) reasonable amounts of working capital held in cash, cash equivalents, or debt instruments with a term of 18 months or less, or

(2) debt instruments described in section 1221(a)(4).

(f) Treatment of businesses straddling census tract lines.

For purposes of this section, if—

(1) a business entity or proprietorship uses real property located within an empowerment zone,

(2) the business entity or proprietorship also uses real property located outside the empowerment zone,

(3) the amount of real property described in paragraph (1) is substantial compared to the amount of real property described in paragraph (2), and

(4) the real property described in paragraph (2) is contiguous to part or all of the real property described in paragraph (1),

then all the services performed by employees, all business activities, all tangible property, and all intangible property of the business entity or proprietorship that occur in or is located on the real property described in paragraphs (1) and (2) shall be treated as occurring or situated in an empowerment zone.

In 2000, P.L. 106-554, Sec. 1(a)(7), [which enacted into law Sec. 116(a)(2) of P.L. 106-554] redesignated Code Sec. 1397B as Code Sec. 1397C, effective for qualified empowerment zone assets acquired after 12/21/2000.

In 1999, P.L. 106-170, Sec. 532(c)(4), substituted "section 1221(a)(4)" for "section 1221(4)" in para. (e)(2), effective for any instrument held, acquired, or entered into, any transaction entered into, and supplies held or acquired on or after 12/17/99.

In 1997, P.L. 105-34, Sec. 956(a)(1), substituted "50 percent" for "80 percent" in paras. (b)(2) and (c)(1) . . . Sec. 956(a)(2), substituted "a substantial portion" for "substantially all" each place it appeared in subsecs. (b) and (c) . . . Sec. 956(a)(3), deleted ", and exclusively related to," in paras. (b)(4) and (c)(3) . . . Sec. 956(a)(4), added flush sentence to the end of para. (d)(2) . . . Sec. 956(a)(5), substituted "at least 50 percent" for "substantially all" in para. (d)(3) . . . Sec. 956(a)(6), added subsec. (f), effective for tax. yrs. begin. on or after 8/5/97. For special rule, see Sec. 956(b)(2) of this Act, which provides:

"(2) Special rule for enterprise zone facility bonds. For purposes of section 1394(b) of the Internal Revenue Code of 1986, the amendments made by this section shall apply to obligations issued after the date of the enactment [8/5/97] of this Act."

In 1996, P.L. 104-188, Sec. 1703(m), deleted "preceding" before "taxable year" in subpara. (d)(5)(B), effective 8/10/93.

In 1993, P.L. 103-66, Sec. 13301(a), added Code Sec. 1397B, effective 8/10/93.

Sec. 1397D. Qualified zone property defined

(a) General rule.

For purposes of this part—

(1) In general. The term "qualified zone property" means any property to which section 168 applies (or would apply but for section 179) if—

(A) such property was acquired by the taxpayer by purchase (as defined in section 179(d)(2)) after the date on which the designation of the empowerment zone took effect,

(B) the original use of which in an empowerment zone commences with the taxpayer, and

(C) substantially all of the use of which is in an empowerment zone and is in the active conduct of a qualified business by the taxpayer in such zone.

(2) **Special rule for substantial renovations.** In the case of any property which is substantially renovated by the taxpayer, the requirements of subparagraphs (A) and (B) of paragraph (1) shall be treated as satisfied. For purposes of the preceding sentence, property shall be treated as substantially renovated by the taxpayer if, during any 24-month period beginning after the date on which the designation of the empowerment zone took effect, additions to basis with respect to such property in the hands of the taxpayer exceed the greater of (i) an amount equal to the adjusted basis at the beginning of such 24-month period in the hands of the taxpayer, or (ii) $5,000.

(b) Special rules for sale-leasebacks.

For purposes of subsection (a)(1)(B), if property is sold and leased back by the taxpayer within 3 months after the date such property was originally placed in service, such property shall be treated as originally placed in service not earlier than the date on which such property is used under the leaseback.

In 2000, P.L. 106-554, Sec. 1(a)(7), [which enacted into law Sec. 116(a)(2) of P.L. 106-554] redesignated Code Sec. 1397C as 1397D, effective for qualified empowerment zone assets acquired after 12/21/2000.

In 1993, P.L. 103-66, Sec. 13301(a), added Code Sec. 1397C, effective 8/10/93.

PART IV.—INCENTIVES FOR EDUCATION ZONES

Sec.

1397E. Credit to holders of qualified zone academy bonds.

In 1997, P.L. 105-34, Sec. 226(a), added new Part IV and item 1397E.

Sec. 1397E. Credit to holders of qualified zone academy bonds.

(a) Allowance of credit.

In the case of an eligible taxpayer who holds a qualified zone academy bond on the credit allowance date of such bond which occurs during the taxable year, there shall be allowed as a credit against the tax imposed by this chapter for such taxable year the amount determined under subsection (b).

(b) Amount of credit.

(1) **In general.** The amount of the credit determined under this subsection with respect to any qualified zone academy bond is the amount equal to the product of—

(A) the credit rate determined by the Secretary under paragraph (2) for the month in which such bond was issued, multiplied by

(B) the face amount of the bond held by the taxpayer on the credit allowance date.

(2) **Determination.** During each calendar month, the Secretary shall determine a credit rate which shall apply to bonds issued during the following calendar month. The credit rate for any month is the percentage which the Secretary estimates will permit the issuance of qualified zone academy bonds without discount and without interest cost to the issuer.

(c) Limitation based on amount of tax.

The credit allowed under subsection (a) for any taxable year shall not exceed the excess of—

(1) the sum of the regular tax liability (as defined in section 26(b)) plus the tax imposed by section 55, over

(2) the sum of the credits allowable under part IV of subchapter A (other than subpart C thereof, relating to refundable credits, and subparts H, I, and J thereof).

(d) Qualified zone academy bond.
For purposes of this section—
   (1) In general. The term "qualified zone academy bond" means any bond issued as part of an issue if—
      (A) 95 percent or more of the proceeds of such issue are to be used for a qualified purpose with respect to a qualified zone academy established by an eligible local education agency,
      (B) the bond is issued by a State or local government within the jurisdiction of which such academy is located,
      (C) the issuer—
         (i) designates such bond for purposes of this section,
         (ii) certifies that it has written assurances that the private business contribution requirement of paragraph (2) will be met with respect to such academy, and
         (iii) certifies that it has the written approval of the eligible local education agency for such bond issuance,
      (D) the term of each bond which is part of such issue does not exceed the maximum term permitted under paragraph (3) and,
      (E) the issue meets the requirements of subsections (f), (g), and (h).
   (2) Private business contribution requirement.
      (A) In general. For purposes of paragraph (1), the private business contribution requirement of this paragraph is met with respect to any issue if the eligible local education agency that established the qualified zone academy has written commitments from private entities to make qualified contributions having a present value (as of the date of issuance of the issue) of not less than 10 percent of the proceeds of the issue.
      (B) Qualified contributions. For purposes of subparagraph (A), the term "qualified contribution" means any contribution (of a type and quality acceptable to the eligible local education agency) of—
         (i) equipment for use in the qualified zone academy (including state-of-the-art technology and vocational equipment),
         (ii) technical assistance in developing curriculum or in training teachers in order to promote appropriate market driven technology in the classroom,
         (iii) services of employees as volunteer mentors,
         (iv) internships, field trips, or other educational opportunities outside the academy for students, or
         (v) any other property or service specified by the eligible local education agency.
   (3) Term requirement. During each calendar month, the Secretary shall determine the maximum term permitted under this paragraph for bonds issued during the following calendar month. Such maximum term shall be the term which the Secretary estimates will result in the present value of the obligation to repay the principal on the bond being equal to 50 percent of the face amount of the bond. Such present value shall be determined using as a discount rate the average annual interest rate of tax-exempt obligations having a term of 10 years or more which are issued during the month. If the term as so determined is not a multiple of a whole year, such term shall be rounded to the next highest whole year.
   (4) Qualified zone academy.
      (A) In general. The term "qualified zone academy" means any public school (or academic program within a public school) which is established by and operated under the supervision of an eligible local education agency to provide education or training below the postsecondary level if—
         (i) such public school or program (as the case may be) is designed in cooperation with business to enhance the academic curriculum, increase graduation and employment rates, and better prepare students for the rigors of college and the increasingly complex workforce,
         (ii) students in such public school or program (as the case may be) will be subject to the same academic standards and assessments as other students educated by the eligible local education agency,
         (iii) the comprehensive education plan of such public school or program is approved by the eligible local education agency, and
         (iv)(I) such public school is located in an empowerment zone or enterprise community (including any such zone or community designated after the date of the enactment of this section), or
            (II) there is a reasonable expectation (as of the date of issuance of the bonds) that at least 35 percent of the students attending such school or participating in such program (as the case may be) will be eligible for free or reduced-cost lunches under the school lunch program established under the Richard B. Russell National School Lunch Act.
      (B) Eligible local education agency. The term "eligible local education agency" means any local educational agency as defined in section 9101 of the Elementary and Secondary Education Act of 1965.
   (5) Qualified purpose. The term "qualified purpose" means, with respect to any qualified zone academy—
      (A) rehabilitating or repairing the public school facility in which the academy is established,
      (B) providing equipment for use at such academy,
      (C) developing course materials for education to be provided at such academy, and
      (D) training teachers and other school personnel in such academy.
   (6) Eligible taxpayer. The term "eligible taxpayer" means—
      (A) a bank (within the meaning of section 581),
      (B) an insurance company to which subchapter L applies, and
      (C) a corporation actively engaged in the business of lending money.

(e) Limitation on amount of bonds designated.
   (1) National limitation. There is a national zone academy bond limitation for each calendar year. Such limitation is $400,000,000 for 1998, 1999, 2000, 2001, 2002, 2003, 2004, 2005, 2006, and 2007, and, except as provided in paragraph (4), zero thereafter.
   (2) Allocation of limitation. The national zone academy bond limitation for a calendar year shall be allocated by the Secretary among the States on the basis of their respective populations of individuals below the poverty line (as defined by the Office of Management and Budget). The limitation amount allocated to a State under the preceding sentence shall be allocated by the State education agency to qualified zone academies within such State.
   (3) Designation subject to limitation amount. The maximum aggregate face amount of bonds issued during any calendar year which may be designated under subsection (d)(1) with respect to any qualified zone academy shall

not exceed the limitation amount allocated to such academy under paragraph (2) for such calendar year.

(4) Carryover of unused limitation. If for any calendar year —

(A) the limitation amount for any State, exceeds

(B) the amount of bonds issued during such year which are designated under subsection (d)(1) with respect to qualified zone academies within such State,

the limitation amount for such State for the following calendar year shall be increased by the amount of such excess.

Any carryforward of a limitation amount may be carried only to the first 2 years (3 years for carryforwards from 1998 or 1999) following the unused limitation year. For purposes of the preceding sentence, a limitation amount shall be treated as used on a first-in first-out basis.

(f) Special rules relating to expenditures.

(1) In general. An issue shall be treated as meeting the requirements of this subsection if, as of the date of issuance, the issuer reasonably expects—

(A) at least 95 percent of the proceeds from the sale of the issue are to be spent for 1 or more qualified purposes with respect to qualified zone academies within the 5-year period beginning on the date of issuance of the qualified zone academy bond,

(B) a binding commitment with a third party to spend at least 10 percent of the proceeds from the sale of the issue will be incurred within the 6-month period beginning on the date of issuance of the qualified zone academy bond, and

(C) such purposes will be completed with due diligence and the proceeds from the sale of the issue will be spent with due diligence.

(2) Extension of period. Upon submission of a request prior to the expiration of the period described in paragraph (1)(A), the Secretary may extend such period if the issuer establishes that the failure to satisfy the 5-year requirement is due to reasonable cause and the related purposes will continue to proceed with due diligence.

(3) Failure to spend required amount of bond proceeds within 5 years. To the extent that less than 95 percent of the proceeds of such issue are expended by the close of the 5-year period beginning on the date of issuance (or if an extension has been obtained under paragraph (2), by the close of the extended period), the issuer shall redeem all of the nonqualified bonds within 90 days after the end of such period. For purposes of this paragraph, the amount of the nonqualified bonds required to be redeemed shall be determined in the same manner as under section 142

(g) Special rules relating to arbitrage.

An issue shall be treated as meeting the requirements of this subsection if the issuer satisfies the arbitrage requirements of section 148 with respect to proceeds of the issue.

(h) Reporting.

Issuers of qualified academy zone bonds shall submit reports similar to the reports required under section 149(e).

(i) Other definitions.

For purposes of this section—

(1) Credit allowance date. The term "credit allowance date" means, with respect to any issue, the last day of the 1-year period beginning on the date of issuance of such issue and the last day of each successive 1-year period thereafter.

(2) Bond. The term "bond" includes any obligation.

(3) State. The term "State" includes the District of Columbia and any possession of the United States.

(j) Credit included in gross income.

Gross income includes the amount of the credit allowed to the taxpayer under this section (determined without regard to subsection (c)).

(k) Credit treated as nonrefundable bondholder credit.

For purposes of this title, the credit allowed by this section shall be treated as a credit allowable under subpart H of part IV of subchapter A of this chapter.

(l) S corporations.

In the case of a qualified zone academy bond held by an S corporation which is an eligible taxpayer—

(1) each shareholder shall take into account such shareholder's pro rata share of the credit, and

(2) no basis adjustments to the stock of the corporation shall be made under section 1367 on account of this section.

(m) Termination.

This section shall not apply to any obligation issued after the date of the enactment of the Tax Extenders and Alternative Minimum Tax Relief Act of 2008 [10/3/2008].

In 2009, P.L. 111-5, Sec. 1531(c)(3), substituted ", I, and J" for "and I" in para. (c)(2), effective for obligations issued after 2/17/2009.

In 2008, P.L. 110-343, Sec. 313(b)(3)DivC, added subsec. (m), effective for obligations issued after 10/3/2008.

—P.L. 110-246, Sec. 4, Repeals the duplicative enactment and provides effective date provisions of the Act entitled "An Act to provide for the continuation of agricultural programs through fiscal year 2012, and for other purposes" Sec. 4, P.L. 110-246 reads as follows:

"Sec. 4. Repeal of duplicative enactment.

"(a) In General- The Act entitled 'An Act to provide for the continuation of agricultural programs through fiscal year 2012, and for other purposes' (H.R. 2419 of the 110th Congress), and the amendments made by that Act, are repealed, effective on the date of enactment of that Act.

"(b) Effective Date- Except as otherwise provided in this Act, this Act and the amendments made by this Act shall take effect on the earlier of--

"(1) the date of enactment of this Act; or

"(2) the date of the enactment of the Act entitled 'An Act to provide for the continuation of agricultural programs through fiscal year 2012, and for other purposes' (H.R. 2419 of the 110th Congress)."

—P.L. 110-246, Sec. 15316(c)(2), substituted "subparts H and I" for "subpart H" in para. (c)(2), effective for obligations issued after 5/22/2008. [Ed. Note: May 22, 2008 was the date of enactment for H.R. 2419 (PL 110-234), which was repealed by (2008 Farm Act § 4(a)) (PL 110-246, 6/18/2008), in connection with the reenactment of the farm bill to correct a technical deficiency in its original passage.]

In 2006, P.L. 109-432, Sec. 107(a), substituted "2005, 2006, and 2007" for "and 2005" in para. (e)(1), effective for obligations issued after 12/31/2005.

—P.L. 109-432, Sec. 107(b)(1)(A), deleted "and" at the end of clause (d)(1)(C)(iii), substituted ", and" for the period at the end of subpara. (d)(1)(D), and added subpara. (d)(1)(E), . . . Sec. 107(b)(1)(B), redesignated subsecs. (f), (g), (h), and (i) as subsecs. (i), (j), (k), and (l), and added new subsecs. (f), (g), and (h), effective for obligations issued after 12/20/2006 for allocations of the national zone academy bond limitation for calendar yrs. after 2005.

In 2005, P.L. 109-135, Sec. 402(c)(2), amended Sec. 1303(e) of P.L. 109-58 to read as follows:

"(e) Effective dates.

"(1) In general. Except as provided in paragraph (2), the amendments made by this section shall apply to bonds issued after December 31, 2005.

"(2) Subsection (c). The amendments made by subsection (c) shall apply to taxable years beginning after December 31, 2005."

Prior to amendment, Sec. 1303(e) P.L. 109-58 read as follows:

"(e) Effective date. The amendments made by this section shall apply to bonds issued after December 31, 2005."

—P.L. 109-58, Sec. 1303(c)(2), added ", and subpart H thereof" after "refundable credits" in para. (c)(2) . . . Sec. 1303(c)(3), amended subsec. (h), effective for tax. yrs. begin. after 12/31/2005 [as amended by Sec. 402(c)(2) of P.L. 109-135, see above].

Prior to amendment, subsec. (h) read as follows:

"(h) Credit treated as allowed under part IV of subchapter A. For purposes of subtitle F, the credit allowed by this section shall be treated as a credit allowable under part IV of subchapter A of this chapter."

In 2004, P.L. 108-311, Sec. 304(a), substituted "2003, 2004, and 2005" for "and 2003" in para. (e)(1), effective for obligations issued after 12/31/2003.

—P.L. 108-311, Sec. 406(c), added subsec. (i), effective for obligations issued after 12/31/97 as if included in Sec. 226 of the Taxpayer Relief Act of 1997, P.L. 105-34.

In 2002, P.L. 107-147, Sec. 608(a), substituted "2000, 2001, 2002, and 2003" for "2000, and 2001" in para. (e)(1), effective for obligations issued after 3/9/2002.

—P.L. 107-110, Sec. 1076(t), substituted "9101" for "14101" in subpara. (d)(4)(B), effective 1/8/2002.

In 1999, P.L. 106-170, Sec. 509(a), substituted ", 1999, 2000, and 2001" for "and 1999" in para. (e)(1)... Sec. 509(b), added two flush sentences at the end of para. (e)(4), effective 12/17/99.

In 1998, P.L. 105-206, Sec. 6004(g)(2), substituted "local educational agency as defined" for "local education agency as defined" in subpara. (d)(4)(B)... Sec. 6004(g)(3), added subsec. (h)... Sec. 6004(g)(4), added "(determined without regard to subsection (c))" at the end of subsec. (g), effective for obligations issued after 12/31/97.

In 1997, P.L. 105-34, Sec. 226(a), added Code Sec. 1397E, effective for obligations issued after 12/31/97.

PART V.—REGULATIONS
Sec.
1397F. Regulations.

In 1998, P.L. 105-206, Sec. 6004(g)(1), substituted "1397D" for "1397E" in Sec. 226(a) of P.L. 105-34, see below. Prior to the amendment made by Sec. 6004(g)(1) of this Act, Sec. 226(a) of P.L. 105-34 directed that Code Sec. 1397E be redesignated as Code Sec. 1397F.

In 1997, P.L. 105-34, Sec. 226(a), [as amended by Sec. 6004(g)(1) of P.L. 105-206, see above] redesignated Part IV of Subchapter U of Chapter 1 of Subtitle A as Part V ... Sec. 226(b)(2), amends the table for Part V by redesignating item 1397E as 1397F. [There is no item 1397E. Item 1397D relates to regulations. It appears it was the intent to amend item 1397D to read 1397F]

In 1993, P.L. 103-66, Sec. 13301(a), added Part IV as part of new Subchapter U.

Sec. 1397F. Regulations.

The Secretary shall prescribe such regulations as may be necessary or appropriate to carry out the purposes of parts II and III, including—

(1) regulations limiting the benefit of parts II and III in circumstances where such benefits, in combination with benefits provided under other Federal programs, would result in an activity being 100 percent or more subsidized by the Federal Government,

(2) regulations preventing abuse of the provisions of parts II and III, and

(3) regulations dealing with inadvertent failures of entities to be enterprise zone businesses.

In 1998, P.L. 105-206, Sec. 6004(g)(1), substituted "1397D" for "1397E" in Sec. 226(a) of P.L. 105-34, see below. Prior to the amendment made by Sec. 6004(g)(1) of this Act, Sec. 226(a) of P.L. 105-34 directed that Code Sec. 1397E be redesignated as Code Sec. 1397F.

In 1997, P.L. 105-34, Sec. 226(a), [as amended by Sec. 6004(g)(1), 105-206, see above] redesignated Code Sec. 1397D as 1397F, effective for obligations issued after 12/31/97.

In 1993, P.L. 103-66, Sec. 13301(a), added Code Sec. 1397D, effective 8/10/93.

Subchapter V.—Title 11 Cases
Sec.
1398. Rules relating to individuals' title 11 cases.
1399. No separate taxable entities for partnerships, corporations, etc.

In 1980, P.L. 96-589, Sec. 3(a)(2), added Subchapter V.

Sec. 1398. Rules relating to individuals' title 11 cases.
(a) Cases to which section applies.

Except as provided in subsection (b), this section shall apply to any case under chapter 7 (relating to liquidations) or chapter 11 (relating to reorganizations) of title 11 of the United States Code in which the debtor is an individual.

(b) Exceptions where case is dismissed, etc.

(1) Section does not apply where case is dismissed. This section shall not apply if the case under chapter 7 or 11 of title 11 of the United States Code is dismissed.

(2) Section does not apply at partnership level. For purposes of subsection (a), a partnership shall not be treated as an individual, but the interest in a partnership of a debtor who is an individual shall be taken into account under this section in the same manner as any other interest of the debtor.

(c) Computation and payment of tax; basic standard deduction.

(1) Computation and payment of tax. Except as otherwise provided in this section, the taxable income of the estate shall be computed in the same manner as for an individual. The tax shall be computed on such taxable income and shall be paid by the trustee.

(2) Tax rates. The tax on the taxable income of the estate shall be determined under subsection (d) of section 1.

(3) Basic standard deduction. In the case of an estate which does not itemize deductions, the basic standard deduction for the estate for the taxable year shall be the same as for a married individual filing a separate return for such year.

(d) Taxable year of debtors.

(1) General rule. Except as provided in paragraph (2), the taxable year of the debtor shall be determined without regard to the case under title 11 of the United States Code to which this section applies.

(2) Election to terminate debtor's year when case commences.

(A) In general. Notwithstanding section 442, the debtor may (without the approval of the Secretary) elect to treat the debtor's taxable year which includes the commencement date as 2 taxable years—

(i) the first of which ends on the day before the commencement date, and

(ii) the second of which begins on the commencement date.

(B) Spouse may join in election. In the case of a married individual (within the meaning of section 7703), the spouse may elect to have the debtor's election under subparagraph (A) also apply to the spouse, but only if the debtor and the spouse file a joint return for the taxable year referred to in subparagraph (A)(i).

(C) No election where debtor has no assets. No election may be made under subparagraph (A) by a debtor who has no assets other than property which the debtor may treat as exempt property under section 522 of title 11 of the United States Code.

(D) Time for making election. An election under subparagraph (A) or (B) may be made only on or before the due date for filing the return for the taxable year referred to in subparagraph (A)(i). Any such election, once made, shall be irrevocable.

(E) Returns. A return shall be made for each of the taxable years specified in subparagraph (A).

(F) Annualization. For purposes of subsections (b), (c), and (d) of section 443, a return filed for either of the taxable years referred to in subparagraph (A) shall be treated as a return made under paragraph (1) of subsection (a) of section 443.

(3) Commencement date defined. For purposes of this subsection, the term "commencement date" means the day on which the case under title 11 of the United States Code to which this section applies commences.

(e) Treatment of income, deductions, and credits.

(1) Estate's share of debtor's income. The gross income of the estate for each taxable year shall include the gross income of the debtor to which the estate is entitled under title 11 of the United States Code. The preceding sentence shall not apply to any amount received or accrued by the debtor before the commencement date (as defined in subsection (d)(3)).

(2) Debtor's share of debtor's income. The gross income of the debtor for any taxable year shall not include any item to the extent that such item is included in the gross income of the estate by reason of paragraph (1).

(3) Rule for making determinations with respect to deductions, credits, and employment taxes. Except as otherwise provided in this section, the determination of whether or not any amount paid or incurred by the estate—

(A) is allowable as a deduction or credit under this chapter, or

(B) is wages for purposes of subtitle C,

shall be made as if the amount were paid or incurred by the debtor and as if the debtor were still engaged in the trades and businesses, and in the activities, the debtor was engaged in before the commencement of the case.

(f) Treatment of transfers between debtor and estate.

(1) Transfer to estate not treated as disposition. A transfer (other than by sale or exchange) of an asset from the debtor to the estate shall not be treated as a disposition for purposes of any provision of this title assigning tax consequences to a disposition, and the estate shall be treated as the debtor would be treated with respect to such asset.

(2) Transfer from estate to debtor not treated as disposition. In the case of a termination of the estate, a transfer (other than by sale or exchange) of an asset from the estate to the debtor shall not be treated as a disposition for purposes of any provision of this title assigning tax consequences to a disposition, and the debtor shall be treated as the estate would be treated with respect to such asset.

(g) Estate succeeds to tax attributes of debtor.

The estate shall succeed to and take into account the following items (determined as of the first day of the debtor's taxable year in which the case commences) of the debtor—

(1) Net operating loss carryovers. The net operating loss carryovers determined under section 172.

(2) Charitable contributions carryovers. The carryover of excess charitable contributions determined under section 170(d)(1).

(3) Recovery of tax benefit items. Any amount to which section 111 (relating to recovery of tax benefit items) applies.

(4) Credit carryovers, etc. The carryovers of any credit, and all other items which, but for the commencement of the case, would be required to be taken into account by the debtor with respect to any credit.

(5) Capital loss carryovers. The capital loss carryover determined under section 1212.

(6) Basis, holding period, and character of assets. In the case of any asset acquired (other than by sale or exchange) by the estate from the debtor, the basis, holding period, and character it had in the hands of the debtor.

(7) Method of accounting. The method of accounting used by the debtor.

(8) Other attributes. Other tax attributes of the debtor, to the extent provided in regulations prescribed by the Secretary as necessary or appropriate to carry out the purposes of this section.

(h) Administration, liquidation, and reorganization expenses; carryovers and carrybacks of certain excess expenses.

(1) Administration, liquidation, and reorganization expenses. Any administrative expense allowed under section 503 of title 11 of the United States Code, and any fee or charge assessed against the estate under chapter 123 of title 28 of the United States Code, to the extent not disallowed under any other provision of this title, shall be allowed as a deduction.

(2) Carryback and carryover of excess administrative costs, etc., to estate taxable years.

(A) Deduction allowed. There shall be allowed as a deduction for the taxable year an amount equal to the aggregate of (i) the administrative expense carryovers to such year, plus (ii) the administrative expense carrybacks to such year.

(B) Administrative expense loss, etc. If a net operating loss would be created or increased for any estate taxable year if section 172(c) were applied without the modification contained in paragraph (4) of section 172(d), then the amount of the net operating loss so created (or the amount of the increase in the net operating loss) shall be an administrative expense loss for such taxable year which shall be an administrative expense carryback to each of the 3 preceding taxable years and an administrative expense carryover to each of the 7 succeeding taxable years.

(C) Determination of amount carried to each taxable year. The portion of any administrative expense loss which may be carried to any other taxable year shall be determined under section 172(b)(2), except that for each taxable year the computation under section 172(b)(2) with respect to the net operating loss shall be made before the computation under this paragraph.

(D) Administrative expense deductions allowed only to estate. The deductions allowable under this chapter solely by reason of paragraph (1), and the deduction provided by subparagraph (A) of this paragraph, shall be allowable only to the estate.

(i) Debtor succeeds to tax attributes of estate

In the case of a termination of an estate, the debtor shall succeed to and take into account the items referred to in paragraphs (1), (2), (3), (4), (5), and (6) of subsection (g) in a manner similar to that provided in such paragraphs (but taking into account that the transfer is from the estate to the debtor instead of from the debtor to the estate). In addition, the debtor shall succeed to and take into account the other tax attributes of the estate, to the extent provided in regulations prescribed by the Secretary as necessary or appropriate to carry out the purposes of this section.

(j) Other special rules.

(1) Change of accounting period without approval. Notwithstanding section 442, the estate may change its annual accounting period one time without the approval of the Secretary.

(2) Treatment of certain carrybacks.

(A) Carrybacks from estate. If any carryback year of the estate is a taxable year before the estate's first taxable year, the carryback to such carryback year shall be taken into account for the debtor's taxable year corresponding to the carryback year.

(B) Carrybacks from debtor's activities. The debtor may not carry back to a taxable year before the debtor's taxable year in which the case commences any carryback from a taxable year ending after the case commences.

(C) Carryback and carryback year defined. For purposes of this paragraph—

(i) Carryback. The term "carryback" means a net operating loss carryback under section 172 or a carryback of any credit provided by part IV of subchapter A.

(ii) Carryback year. The term "carryback year" means the taxable year to which a carryback is carried.

In 1986, P.L. 99-514, Sec. 104(b)(14)(A), substituted "basic standard deduction" for "zero bracket amount" in the heading of subsec. (c)... Sec. 104(b)(14)(B), amended para. (c)(3), effective for tax. yrs. begin. after 12/31/86.
Prior to amendment, para. (c)(3) read as follows:
"(3) Amount of zero bracket amount. The amount of the estate's zero bracket amount for the taxable year shall be the same as for a married individual filing a separate return for such year."
— P.L. 99-514, Sec. 1301(j)(8), substituted "section 7703" for "section 143" in subpara. (d)(2)(B), effective for bonds issued after 8/15/86.
— P.L. 99-514, Sec. 1812(a)(5), amended para. (g)(3), effective for amounts recovered after 12/31/63, in tax. yrs. begin. after 12/31/63.
In 1980, P.L. 96-589, Sec. 3(a)(1), added Code Sec. 1398, effective for any bankruptcy case begin. after 3/25/81 [more than 90 days after the date of enactment (12/24/80)]. Sec. 7(g) of this Act provides:
"(g) Definitions.
"For purposes of this section—
"(1) Bankruptcy case. The term 'bankruptcy case' means any case under title 11 of the United States Code (as recodified by P.L. 95-598).
"(2) Similar judicial proceeding. The term 'similar judicial proceeding' means a receivership, foreclosure, or similar proceeding in a Federal or State court (as modified by section 368(a)(3)(D) of the Internal Revenue Code of 1954)."

Sec. 1399. No separate taxable entities for partnerships, corporations, etc.

Except in any case to which section 1398 applies, no separate taxable entity shall result from the commencement of a case under title 11 of the United States Code.

In 1980, P.L. 96-589, Sec. 3(a)(1), added Code Sec. 1399, effective for any bankruptcy case begin. after 3/25/81 [more than 90 days after the date of enactment (12/24/80)]. Sec. 7(g) of this Act provides:
"(g) Definitions.
"For purposes of this section—
"(1) Bankruptcy case. The term 'bankruptcy case' means any case under title 11 of the United States Code (as recodified by P.L. 95-598).
"(2) Similar judicial proceeding. The term similar judicial proceeding means a receivership, foreclosure, or similar proceeding in a Federal or State court (as modified by section 368(a)(3)(D) of the Internal Revenue Code of 1954)."

Subchapter W.—District of Columbia Enterprise Zone
Sec.
1400. Establishment of DC Zone.
1400A. Tax-exempt economic development bonds.
1400B. Zero percent capital gains rate.
1400C. First-time homebuyer credit for District of Columbia.

In 1997, P.L. 105-34, Sec. 701, added subchapter W.

Sec. 1400. Establishment of DC Zone.
(a) In general.
For purposes of this title—
(1) the applicable DC area is hereby designated as the District of Columbia Enterprise Zone, and
(2) except as otherwise provided in this subchapter, the District of Columbia Enterprise Zone shall be treated as an empowerment zone designated under subchapter U.
(b) Applicable DC area.
For purposes of subsection (a), the term "applicable DC area" means the area consisting of—
(1) the census tracts located in the District of Columbia which are part of an enterprise community designated under subchapter U before the date of the enactment of this subchapter, and
(2) all other census tracts—
(A) which are located in the District of Columbia, and
(B) for which the poverty rate is not less than than [sic] 20 percent as determined on the basis of the 1990 census.

(c) District of Columbia Enterprise Zone.
For purposes of this subchapter, the terms "District of Columbia Enterprise Zone" and "DC Zone" mean the District of Columbia Enterprise Zone designated by subsection (a).
(d) Special rule for application of employment credit.
With respect to the DC Zone, section 1396(d)(1)(B) (relating to empowerment zone employment credit) shall be applied by substituting "the District of Columbia" for "such empowerment zone."
(e) Special rule for application of enterprise zone business definition.
For purposes of this subchapter and for purposes of applying subchapter U with respect to the DC Zone, section 1397C shall be applied without regard to subsections (b)(6) and (c)(5) thereof.
(f) Time for which designation applicable.
(1) In general. The designation made by subsection (a) shall apply for the period beginning on January 1, 1998, and ending on December 31, 2011.
(2) Coordination with DC enterprise community designated under subchapter U. The designation under subchapter U of the census tracts referred to in subsection (b)(1) as an enterprise community shall terminate on December 31, 2011.

In 2010, P.L. 111-312, Sec. 754(a), substituted "December 31, 2011" for "December 31, 2009" each place it appeared in subsec. (f), effective for periods after 12/31/2009.
In 2008, P.L. 110-343, Sec. 322(a)(1)DivC, substituted "2009" for "2007" in para. (f)(1) and para (f)(2), effective for periods begin after 12/31/2007.
In 2006, P.L. 109-432, Sec. 110(a)(1), substituted "2007" for "2005" in para. (f)(1) and para (f)(2), effective for periods begin after 12/31/2005.
In 2004, P.L. 108-311, Sec. 310(a), substituted "December 31, 2005" for "December 31, 2003" each place it appeared in subsec. (f), effective 1/1/2004.
In 2000, P.L. 106-554, Sec. 1(a)(7), [which enacted into law Sec. 113(c) of P.L. 106-554] amended subsec. (d), effective for wages paid or incurred after 12/31/2001.
Prior to amendment, subsec. (d) read as follows:
"(d) Special rules for application of employment credit.
"(1) Employees whose principal place of abode is in District of Columbia. With respect to the DC Zone, section 1396(d)(1)(B) (relating to empowerment zone employment credit) shall be applied by substituting 'the District of Columbia' for 'such empowerment zone'.
"(2) No decrease of percentage in 2002. In the case of the DC Zone, section 1396 (relating to empowerment zone employment credit) shall be applied by substituting '20' for '15' in the table contained in section 1396(b). The preceding sentence shall apply only with respect to qualified zone employees, as defined in section 1396(d), determined by treating no area other than the DC Zone as an empowerment zone or enterprise community."
— P.L. 106-554, Sec. 1(a)(7), [which enacted into law Sec. 116(b)(5) of P.L. 106-554] substituted "section 1397C" for "section 1397B" in subsec. (e), effective for qualified empowerment zone assets acquired after 12/21/2000.
— P.L. 106-554, Sec. 1(a)(7), [which enacted into law Sec. 164(a)(1) of P.L. 106-554] substituted "2003" for "2002" each place it appeared in subsec. (f), effective 12/21/2000.
In 1998, P.L. 105-206, Sec. 6008(a), added "as determined on the basis of the 1990 census" after "percent" in subpara. (b)(2)(B), effective 8/5/97.
In 1997, P.L. 105-34, Sec. 701(a), added Code Sec. 1400, effective 8/5/97.

Sec. 1400A. Tax-exempt economic development bonds.
(a) In general.
In the case of the District of Columbia Enterprise Zone, subparagraph (A) of section 1394(c)(1) (relating to limitation on amount of bonds) shall be applied by substituting "$15,000,000" for "$3,000,000" and section 1394(b)(3)(B)(iii) shall be applied without regard to the employee residency requirement.
(b) Period of applicability.
This section shall apply to bonds issued during the period beginning on January 1, 1998, and ending on December 31, 2011.

In 2010, P.L. 111-312, Sec. 754(b), substituted "December 31, 2011" for "December 31, 2009" in subsec. (b), effective for bonds issued after 12/31/2009.
In 2008, P.L. 110-343, Sec. 322(b)(1)DivC, substituted "2009" for "2007" in subsec. (b), effective for bonds issued after 12/31/2007.
In 2006, P.L. 109-432, Sec. 110(b)(1), substituted "2007" for "2005" in subsec. (b), effective for bonds issued after 12/31/2005.
In 2004, P.L. 108-311, Sec. 310(b), substituted "December 31, 2005" for "December 31, 2003" in subsec. (b), effective for obligations issued after 10/4/2004.
In 2000, P.L. 106-554, Sec. 1(a)(7), [which enacted into law Sec. 164(a)(2) of P.L. 106-554] substituted "2003" for "2002" in subsec. (b), effective 12/21/2000.
In 1998, P.L. 105-206, Sec. 6008(c), added "and section 1394(b)(3)(B)(iii) shall be applied without regard to the employee residency requirement" at the end of subsec. (a), effective 8/5/97.
In 1997, P.L. 105-34, Sec. 701(a), added Code Sec. 1400A, effective 8/5/97.

Sec. 1400B. Zero percent capital gains rate.
(a) Exclusion.
Gross income shall not include qualified capital gain from the sale or exchange of any DC Zone asset held for more than 5 years.
(b) DC Zone asset.
For purposes of this section—
  (1) In general. The term "DC Zone asset" means—
    (A) any DC Zone business stock,
    (B) any DC Zone partnership interest, and
    (C) any DC Zone business property.
  (2) DC Zone business stock.
    (A) In general. The term "DC Zone business stock" means any stock in a domestic corporation which is originally issued after December 31, 1997, if—
      (i) such stock is acquired by the taxpayer, before January 1, 2012, at its original issue (directly or through an underwriter) solely in exchange for cash,
      (ii) as of the time such stock was issued, such corporation was a DC Zone business (or, in the case of a new corporation, such corporation was being organized for purposes of being a DC Zone business), and
      (iii) during substantially all of the taxpayer's holding period for such stock, such corporation qualified as a DC Zone business.
    (B) Redemptions. A rule similar to the rule of section 1202(c)(3) shall apply for purposes of this paragraph.
  (3) DC Zone partnership interest. The term "DC Zone partnership interest" means any capital or profits interest in a domestic partnership which is originally issued after December 31, 1997, if—
    (A) such interest is acquired by the taxpayer, before January 1, 2012, from the partnership solely in exchange for cash,
    (B) as of the time such interest was acquired, such partnership was a DC Zone business (or, in the case of a new partnership, such partnership was being organized for purposes of being a DC Zone business), and
    (C) during substantially all of the taxpayer's holding period for such interest, such partnership qualified as a DC Zone business.
  A rule similar to the rule of paragraph (2)(B) shall apply for purposes of this paragraph.
  (4) DC Zone business property.
    (A) In general. The term "DC Zone business property" means tangible property if—
      (i) such property was acquired by the taxpayer by purchase (as defined in section 179(d)(2)) after December 31, 1997, and before January 1, 2012
      (ii) the original use of such property in the DC Zone commences with the taxpayer, and
      (iii) during substantially all of the taxpayer's holding period for such property, substantially all of the use of such property was in a DC Zone business of the taxpayer.
    (B) Special rule for buildings which are substantially improved.
      (i) In general. The requirements of clauses (i) and (ii) of subparagraph (A) shall be treated as met with respect to—
        (I) property which is substantially improved by the taxpayer before January 1, 2012, and
        (II) any land on which such property is located.
      (ii) Substantial improvement. For purposes of clause (i), property shall be treated as substantially improved by the taxpayer only if, during any 24-month period beginning after December 31, 1997, additions to basis with respect to such property in the hands of the taxpayer exceed the greater of—
        (I) an amount equal to the adjusted basis of such property at the beginning of such 24-month period in the hands of the taxpayer, or
        (II) $5,000.
  (5) Treatment of DC Zone termination. The termination of the designation of the DC Zone shall be disregarded for purposes of determining whether any property is a DC Zone asset.
  (6) Treatment of subsequent purchasers, etc. The term "DC Zone asset" includes any property which would be a DC Zone asset but for paragraph (2)(A)(i), (3)(A), or (4)(A)(i) or (ii) in the hands of the taxpayer if such property was a DC Zone asset in the hands of a prior holder.
  (7) 5-year safe harbor. If any property ceases to be a DC Zone asset by reason of paragraph (2)(A)(iii), (3)(C), or (4)(A)(iii) after the 5-year period beginning on the date the taxpayer acquired such property, such property shall continue to be treated as meeting the requirements of such paragraph; except that the amount of gain to which subsection (a) applies on any sale or exchange of such property shall not exceed the amount which would be qualified capital gain had such property been sold on the date of such cessation.
(c) DC Zone business.
For purposes of this section, the term "DC Zone business" means any enterprise zone business (as defined in section 1397C), determined—
  (1) after the application of section 1400(e),
  (2) by substituting "80 percent" for "50 percent" in subsections (b)(2) and (c)(1) of section 1397C, and
  (3) by treating no area other than the DC Zone as an empowerment zone or enterprise community.
(d) Treatment of Zone as including census tracts with 10 percent poverty rate.
For purposes of applying this section (and for purposes of applying this subchapter and subchapter U with respect to this section), the DC Zone shall be treated as including all census tracts—
  (1) which are located in the District of Columbia, and
  (2) for which the poverty rate is not less than 10 percent as determined on the basis of the 1990 census.
(e) Other definitions and special rules.
For purposes of this section—
  (1) Qualified capital gain. Except as otherwise provided in this subsection, the term "qualified capital gain" means any gain recognized on the sale or exchange of—
    (A) a capital asset, or
    (B) property used in the trade or business (as defined in section 1231(b)).

(2) Gain before 1998 or after 2016 not qualified. The term "qualified capital gain" shall not include any gain attributable to periods before January 1, 1998, or after December 31, 2016.

(3) Certain gain not qualified. The term "qualified capital gain" shall not include any gain which would be treated as ordinary income under section 1245 or under section 1250 if section 1250 applied to all depreciation rather than the additional depreciation.

(4) Intangibles and land not integral part of DC Zone business. The term "qualified capital gain" shall not include any gain which is attributable to real property, or an intangible asset, which is not an integral part of a DC Zone business.

(5) Related party transactions. The term "qualified capital gain" shall not include any gain attributable, directly or indirectly, in whole or in part, to a transaction with a related person. For purposes of this paragraph, persons are related to each other if such persons are described in section 267(b) or 707(b)(1).

(f) Certain other rules to apply.

Rules similar to the rules of subsections (g), (h), (i)(2), and (j) of section 1202 shall apply for purposes of this section.

(g) Sales and exchanges of interests in partnerships and S corporations which are DC Zone businesses.

In the case of the sale or exchange of an interest in a partnership, or of stock in an S corporation, which was a DC Zone business during substantially all of the period the taxpayer held such interest or stock, the amount of qualified capital gain shall be determined without regard to—

(1) any gain which is attributable to real property, or an intangible asset, which is not an integral part of a DC Zone business, and

(2) any gain attributable to periods before January 1, 1998, or after December 31, 2016.

In 2010, P.L. 111-312, Sec. 754(c)(1), substituted "January 1, 2012" for "January 1, 2010" in clause (b)(2)(A)(i), subpara. (b)(3)(A), clause (b)(4)(A)(i), and subcl. (b)(4)(B)(i)(I) . . . Sec. 754(c)(2)(A)(i), substituted "December 31, 2016" for "December 31, 2014" in para. (e)(2) . . . Sec. 754(c)(2)(A)(ii), substituted "2016" for "2014" in the heading of para. (e)(2) . . . Sec. 754(c)(2)(B), substituted "December 31, 2016" for "December 31, 2014" in para. (g)(2), effective for property acquired or substantially improved after 12/31/2009.

In 2008, P.L. 110-343, Sec. 322(c)(1)DivC, substituted "2010" for "2008" each place it appears in subsec. (b), effective for acquisitions after 12/31/2007.

—P.L. 110-343, Sec. 322(c)(2)(A)(i)DivC, substituted "2014" for "2012" in para. (e)(2) . . . Sec. 322(c)(2)(A)(ii)DivC, substituted "2014" for "2012" in in the heading of para. (e)(2) . . . Sec. 322(c)(2)(B)DivC, substituted "2014" for "2012" in para. (g)(2), effective 10/3/2008.

In 2006, P.L. 109-432, Sec. 110(c)(1), substituted "2008" for "2005" each place it appeared in subsec. (b), effective for acquisitions after 12/31/2005.

—P.L. 109-432, Sec. 110(c)(2)(A)(i), substituted "2012" for "2010" in para. (e)(2) . . . Sec. 110(c)(2)(A)(ii), substituted "2012" for "2010" in the heading of para. (e)(2) . . . Sec. 110(c)(2)(B), substituted "2012" for "2010" in para. (g)(2), effective 12/20/2006.

In 2004, P.L. 108-311, Sec. 310(c)(1), substituted "January 1, 2006" for "January 1, 2004" each place it appeared in subsec. (b) . . . Sec. 310(c)(2)(A)(i), substituted "December 31, 2010" for "December 31, 2008" in para. (e)(2) . . . Sec. 310(c)(2)(A)(ii), substituted "2010" for "2008" in the heading of para. (e)(2) . . . Sec. 310(c)(2)(B), substituted "December 31, 2010" for "December 31, 2008" in para. (g)(2), effective 1/1/2004.

In 2000, P.L. 106-554, Sec. 1(a)(7), [which enacted into law Sec. 116(b)(5) of P.L. 106-554] substituted "section 1397C" for "section 1397B" each place it appeared in subsec. (c), effective for qualified empowerment zone assets acquired after 12/21/2000.

—P.L. 106-554, Sec. 1(a)(7), [which enacted into law Sec. 164(b)(1) of P.L. 106-554] substituted "2004" for "2003" each place it appeared in subsec. (b) . . . Sec. 1(a)(7), [which enacted into law Sec. 164(b)(2) of P.L. 106-554] substituted "2008" for "2007" each place it appeared in para. (e)(2) and (g)(2), effective 12/21/2000.

In 1998, P.L. 105-206, Sec. 6008(c)(1), added para. (b)(5) . . . Sec. 6008(c)(2), substituted "(4)(A)(i) or (ii)" for "(4)(A)(ii)" in para. (b)(6) . . . Sec. 6008(c)(3), deleted "entity which is an" before "enterprise zone business" in subsec. (c) . . . Sec. 6008(c)(4), added "as determined on the basis of the 1990 census" at the end of para. (d)(2), effective 8/5/97.

In 1997, P.L. 105-34, Sec. 701(a), added Code Sec. 1400B, effective 8/5/97.

Sec. 1400C. First-time homebuyer credit for District of Columbia.

(a) Allowance of credit.

In the case of an individual who is a first-time homebuyer of a principal residence in the District of Columbia during any taxable year, there shall be allowed as a credit against the tax imposed by this chapter for the taxable year an amount equal to so much of the purchase price of the residence as does not exceed $5,000.

(b) Limitation based on modified adjusted gross income.

(1) In general. The amount allowable as a credit under subsection (a) (determined without regard to this subsection and subsection (d)) for the taxable year shall be reduced (but not below zero) by the amount which bears the same ratio to the credit so allowable as—

(A) the excess (if any) of—

(i) the taxpayer's modified adjusted gross income for such taxable year, over

(ii) $70,000 ($110,000 in the case of a joint return), bears to

(B) $20,000.

(2) Modified adjusted gross income. For purposes of paragraph (1), the term "modified adjusted gross income" means the adjusted gross income of the taxpayer for the taxable year increased by any amount excluded from gross income under section 911, 931, or 933.

(c) First-time homebuyer.

For purposes of this section—

(1) In general. The term "first-time homebuyer" means any individual if such individual (and if married, such individual's spouse) had no present ownership interest in a principal residence in the District of Columbia during the 1-year period ending on the date of the purchase of the principal residence to which this section applies.

(2) One-time only. If an individual is treated as a first-time homebuyer with respect to any principal residence, such individual may not be treated as a first-time homebuyer with respect to any other principal residence.

(3) Principal residence. The term "principal residence" has the same meaning as when used in section 121.

• **Caution:** Code Sec. 1400C(d), following, reflects amendments made by Sec. 10909(b)(2)(M) of P.L. 111-148. As provided in Sec. 10909(c), P.L. 111-148 as amended by Sec. 101(b)(1), P.L. 111-312, Code Sec. 1400C(d) will read as if those amendments had never been enacted, effective for tax. yrs. begin. after 12/31/2011. For Code Sec. 1400C(d) as it will read for tax. yrs. begin. after 12/31/2011, see below.

(d) Carryforward of unused credit.

(1) Rule for years in which all personal credits allowed against regular and alternative minimum tax. In the case of a taxable year to which section 26(a)(2) applies, if the credit allowable under subsection (a) exceeds the limitation imposed by section 26(a)(2) for such taxable year reduced by the sum of the credits allowable under subpart A of part IV of subchapter A (other than this section and section 25D), such excess shall be carried to the succeeding taxable year and added to the credit allowable under subsection (a) for such taxable year.

(2) Rule for other years. In the case of a taxable year to which section 26(a)(2) does not apply, if the credit allowable under subsection (a) exceeds the limitation imposed by section 26(a)(1) for such taxable year reduced by the sum of the credits allowable under subpart A of part IV of subchapter A (other than this section and sections 24, 25A(i), 25B, 25D, 30, and 30B, and 30D), such excess shall be carried to the succeeding taxable year and added to the credit allowable under subsection (a) for such taxable year.

> • **Caution:** Code Sec. 1400C(d), following, is effective for tax. yrs. begin. after 12/31/2011, and reflects the sunset of the amendments made by Sec. 10909, P.L. 111-148. For details of those amendments, effective date and sunset provisions, see the history for this Code Sec. For Code Sec. 1400C(d), effective for tax. yrs. begin. before 1/1/2012, see above.

(d) Carryforward of unused credit.
(1) Rule for years in which all personal credits allowed against regular and alternative minimum tax. In the case of a taxable year to which section 26(a)(2) applies, if the credit allowable under subsection (a) exceeds the limitation imposed by section 26(a)(2) for such taxable year reduced by the sum of the credits allowable under subpart A of part IV of subchapter A (other than this section and section 25D), such excess shall be carried to the succeeding taxable year and added to the credit allowable under subsection (a) for such taxable year.
(2) Rule for other years. In the case of a taxable year to which section 26(a)(2) does not apply, if the credit allowable under subsection (a) exceeds the limitation imposed by section 26(a)(1) for such taxable year reduced by the sum of the credits allowable under subpart A of part IV of subchapter A (other than this section and sections 23, 24, 25A(i), 25B, 25D, 30, and 30B, and 30D), such excess shall be carried to the succeeding taxable year and added to the credit allowable under subsection (a) for such taxable year.
(e) Special rules.
For purposes of this section—
  (1) Allocation of dollar limitation.
    (A) Married individuals filing separately. In the case of a married individual filing a separate return, subsection (a) shall be applied by substituting "$2,500" for "$5,000".
    (B) Other taxpayers. If 2 or more individuals who are not married purchase a principal residence, the amount of the credit allowed under subsection (a) shall be allocated among such individuals in such manner as the Secretary may prescribe, except that the total amount of the credits allowed to all such individuals shall not exceed $5,000.
  (2) Purchase.
    (A) In general. The term "purchase" means any acquisition, but only if—
      (i) the property is not acquired from a person whose relationship to the person acquiring it would result in the disallowance of losses under section 267 or 707(b) (but, in applying section 267(b) and (c) for purposes of this section, paragraph (4) of section 267(c) shall be treated as providing that the family of an individual shall include only his spouse, ancestors, and lineal descendants), and
      (ii) the basis of the property in the hands of the person acquiring it is not determined—

        (I) in whole or in part by reference to the adjusted basis of such property in the hands of the person from whom acquired, or
        (II) under section 1014(a) (relating to property acquired from a decedent).
    (B) Construction. A residence which is constructed by the taxpayer shall be treated as purchased by the taxpayer on the date the taxpayer first occupies such residence.
  (3) Purchase price. The term "purchase price" means the adjusted basis of the principal residence on the date such residence is purchased.
  (4) Coordination with national first-time homebuyers credit. No credit shall be allowed under this section to any taxpayer with respect to the purchase of a residence after December 31, 2008 if a credit under section 36 is allowable to such taxpayer (or the taxpayer's spouse) with respect to such purchase.
(f) Reporting.
If the Secretary requires information reporting under section 6045 by a person described in subsection (e)(2) thereof to verify the eligibility of taxpayers for the credit allowable by this section, the exception provided by section 6045(e)(5) shall not apply.
(g) Credit treated as nonrefundable personal credit.
For purposes of this title, the credit allowed by this section shall be treated as a credit allowable under subpart A of part IV of subchapter A of this chapter.
(h) Basis adjustment.
For purposes of this subtitle, if a credit is allowed under this section with respect to the purchase of any residence, the basis of such residence shall be reduced by the amount of the credit so allowed.
(i) Application of section.
This section shall apply to property purchased after August 4, 1997, and before January 1, 2012.

In 2010, P.L. 111-312, Sec. 101(a)(1), substituted "December 31, 2012" for "December 31, 2010" both places it appeared in Sec. 901 of P.L. 107-16 [see below], effective as if included in the enactment of P.L. 107-16, EGTRRA, 6/7/2001.
—P.L. 111-312, Sec. 101(b)(1), amended Sec. 10909(c), P.L. 111-148 [see below].
Prior to amendment, Sec. 10909(c), P.L. 111-148, read as follows:
"(c) Application and Extension of EGTRRA Sunset. Notwithstanding section 901 of the Economic Growth and Tax Relief Reconciliation Act of 2001, such section shall apply to the amendments made by this section and the amendments made by section 202 of such Act by substituting 'December 31, 2011' for 'December 31, 2010' in subsection (a)(1) thereof."
—P.L. 111-312, Sec. 101(b)(2), substituted "Except as provided in subsection (c), the amendments" for "The amendments" in Sec. 10909(d), P.L. 111-148 (the effective date section for amendments made by Sec. 10909, P.L. 111-148) [see below].
Prior to amendment, Sec. 10909(d), P.L. 111-148, read as follows:
"(d) Effective date. The amendments made by this section shall apply to taxable years beginning after December 31, 2009."
—P.L. 111-312, Sec. 754(2), substituted "January 1, 2012" for "January 1, 2010" in subsec. (i), effective for homes purchased after 12/31/2009.
—P.L. 111-148, Sec. 10909(b)(2)(M), deleted "23, " before "24," in subsec. (d) effective for tax. yrs. begin. after 12/31/2009, except as provided in Sec. 10909(c), [see below].
—P.L. 111-148, Sec. 10909(c), of this Act, relating to the application and extension of the EGTRRA sunset provisions [as amended by Sec. 101(b)(1), P.L. 111-312, see above], reads as follows:
"(c) Sunset provision. Each provision of law amended by this section is amended to read as such provision would read if this section had never been enacted. The amendments made by the preceding sentence shall apply to taxable years beginning after December 31, 2011."
—P.L. 111-148, Sec. 10909(d), of this Act, [as amended by Sec. 101(b)(2), P.L. 111-312, see above] reads as follows:
"(d) Effective date. Except as provided in subsection (c) [Sec. 10909(c), of this Act, see above], the amendments made by this section shall apply to taxable years beginning after December 31, 2011."
In 2009, P.L. 111-92, Sec. 11(i), deleted "and before December 1, 2009," in para. (e)(4), effective for residences purchased after 11/30/2009.
—P.L. 111-5, Sec. 1004(b)(6), added "25A(i)," after "24," in para. (d)(2), effective for tax. yrs. begin. after 12/31/2008.

Renewal communities

—P.L. 111-5, Sec. 1006(c)(1), added para. (e)(4), effective for residences purchased after 12/31/2008.
—P.L. 111-5, Sec. 1142(b)(1)(F), substituted "25D, and 30" for "and 25D" in para. (d)(2) [as amended by Sec. 1004(b)(6) of this Act, see above] [Note: It was the intention of the legislature to make this amendment to the existing text of para. (d)(2).], effective for vehicles acquired after 2/17/2009.
—P.L. 111-5, Sec. 1144(b)(1)(F), substituted "30, and 30B" for "and 30" in para. (d)(2) [as amended by Secs. 1004(b)(6) and 1142(b)(1)(F) of this Act, see above], effective for tax. yrs. begin. after 12/31/2008.
In 2008, P.L. 110-343, Sec. 205(d)(1)(E)DivB, substituted "25D, and 30D" for "and 25D" in para. (d)(2), effective for tax. yrs. begin. after 12/31/2008.
—P.L. 110-343, Sec. 322(d)(1)DivC, substituted "2010" for "2008" in subsec. (i), effective for property purchased after 12/31/2007.
In 2006, P.L. 109-432, Sec. 110(d)(1), substituted "2008" for "2006" in subsec. (i), effective for property purchased after December 31, 2005.
—P.L. 109-280, Sec. 811, of this Act [relating to Sec. 901 of P.L. 107-16, see below], provides:
"Sec. 811. Pensions and individual retirement arrangement provisions of Economic Growth and Tax Relief Reconciliation act of 2001 made permanent."
"Title IX of the Economic Growth and Tax Relief Reconciliation Act of 2001 shall not apply to the provisions of, and amendments made by, subtitles A through F of title VI of such Act (relating to pension and individual retirement arrangement provisions)."
In 2005, P.L. 109-135, Sec. 402(i)(3)(F), amended subsec. (d), effective for tax. yrs. begin. after 12/31/2005.
Prior to amendment, subsec. (d) read as follows:
"*(d) Carryover of credit.* If the credit allowable under subsection (a) exceeds the limitation imposed by section 26(a) for such taxable year reduced by the sum of the credits allowable under subpart A of part IV of subchapter A (other than this section and sections 23, 24, and 25B), such excess shall be carried to the succeeding taxable year and added to the credit allowable under subsection (a) for such taxable year."
—P.L. 109-135, Sec. 402(i)(3)(H), of this Act, reads as follows:
"(H) Application of EGTRRA sunset. The amendments made by this paragraph (and each part thereof) shall be subject to title IX of the Economic Growth and Tax Relief Reconciliation Act of 2001 [Sec. 901 of P.L. 107-16] in the same manner as the provisions of such Act to which such amendment (or part thereof) relates."
—P.L. 109-135, Sec. 402(i)(4), repealed Sec. 1335(b)(3) of P.L. 109-58, effective for property placed in service after 12/31/2005, in tax. yrs. end. after 12/31/2005.
Prior to repeal, Sec. 1335(b)(3) of P.L. 109-58 read as follows:
"(3) Section 1400C(d) is amended by striking 'this section' and inserting 'this section and section 25D'."
In 2004, P.L. 108-311, Sec. 310(d), substituted "January 1, 2006" for "January 1, 2004" in subsec. (i), effective 1/1/2004.
—P.L. 108-311, Sec. 312(b)(2), of this Act, provides:
"(2) The amendments made by sections 201(b), 202(f), and 618(b) of the Economic Growth and Tax Relief Reconciliation Act of 2001 [P.L. 107-16] shall not apply to taxable years beginning during 2004 or 2005."
In 2002, P.L. 107-358, Sec. 2, added subsec. (c) in Sec. 901 of P.L. 107-16 [see below], effective 12/17/2002.
—P.L. 107-147, Sec. 601(b)(2), of this Act, provides:
"(2) The amendments made by sections 201(b), 202(f), and 618(b) of the Economic Growth and Tax Relief Reconciliation Act of 2001 shall not apply to taxable years beginning during 2002 and 2003."
In 2001, P.L. 107-16, Sec. 201(b)(2)(H), added "and section 24" after "this section" in subsec. (d), effective for tax. yrs. begin. after 12/31/2001. For special provisions, see Sec. 601(b)(2) of P.L. 107-147 and Sec. 312(b)(2) of 108-311, above.
—P.L. 107-16, Sec. 202(f)(2)(C), substituted "sections 23 and 24" for "section 24" in subsec. (d), [as amended by Sec. 201(b)(2)(H) of this Act, see above] effective for tax. yrs. begin. after 12/31/2001. For special provision, see Sec. 601(b)(2) of P.L. 107-147, above.
—P.L. 107-16, Sec. 618(b)(2)(E), substituted ", 24, and 25B" for "and 24" in subsec. (d), [as amended by Sec. 201(b)(2)(H) and Sec. 202(f)(2)(C) of this Act, see above] effective for tax. yrs. begin. after 12/31/2001. For special provisions, see Sec. 601(b)(2) of P.L. 107-147 and Sec. 312(b)(2) of 108-311, above.
—P.L. 107-16, Sec. 901, of this Act [as amended by Sec. 2 of P.L. 107-358, and Sec. 101(a)(1) of P.L. 111-312, see above], reads as follows:
"Sec. 901. Sunset of provisions of Act.
"(a) In general. All provisions of, and amendments made by, this Act shall not apply—
"(1) to taxable, plan, or limitation years beginning after December 31, 2012, or
"(2) in the case of title V, to estates of decedents dying, gifts made, or generation skipping transfers, after December 31, 2012.
"(b) Application of certain laws. The Internal Revenue Code of 1986 and the Employee Retirement Income Security Act of 1974 shall be applied and administered to years, estates, gifts, and transfers described in subsection (a) as if the provisions and amendments described in subsection (a) had never been enacted.
"(c) Exception. Subsection (a) shall not apply to section 803 (relating to no federal income tax on restitution received by victims of the Nazi regime or their heirs or estates)."
In 2000, P.L. 106-554, Sec. 1(a)(7), [which enacted into law Sec. 163 of P.L. 106-554] substituted "2004" for "2002" in subsec. (i), effective 12/21/2000.
In 1999, P.L. 106-170, Sec. 510, substituted "2002" for "2001" in subsec. (i), effective 12/17/99.

In 1998, P.L. 105-206, Sec. 6008(d)(1), added "and subsection (d)" after "this subsection" in para. (b)(1) . . . Sec. 6008(d)(2), amended para. (c)(1) . . . Sec. 6008(d)(3), added "on the date the taxpayer first occupies such residence" at the end of subpara. (e)(2)(B) . . . Sec. 6008(d)(4), substituted "on the date such residence is purchased." for "on the date of acquisition (within the meaning of section 72(t)(8)(D)(iii))." in para. (e)(3) . . . Sec. 6008(d)(5), amended subsec. (i), effective 8/5/97.
Prior to amendment, para. (c)(1) read as follows:
"(1) In general. The term 'first-time homebuyer' has the same meaning as when used in section 72(t)(8)(D)(i), except that 'principal residence in the District of Columbia during the 1-year period' shall be substituted for 'principal residence during the 2-year period' in subclause (I) thereof."
Prior to amendment, subsec. (i) read as follows:
"(i) Termination. This section shall not apply to any property purchased after December 31, 2000."
In 1997, P.L. 105-34, Sec. 701(a), added Code Sec. 1400C, effective 8/5/97.

Subchapter X.—Renewal Communities
Part
  I. Designation
 II. Renewal community capital gain; renewal community business
III. Additional incentives

In 2000, P.L. 106-554, Sec. 1(a)(7) [which enacted into law Sec. 101(a) of H.R. 5662], added subchapter X.

PART I.—DESIGNATION
Sec.
1400E. Designation of renewal communities.

In 2000, P.L. 106-554, Sec. 1(a)(7) [which enacted into law Sec. 101(a) of H.R. 5662], added Part I as part of new Subchapter X.

Sec. 1400E. Designation of renewal communities.
(a) Designation.
  (1) Definitions. For purposes of this title, the term "renewal community" means any area—
    (A) which is nominated by 1 or more local governments and the State or States in which it is located for designation as a renewal community (hereafter in this section referred to as a "nominated area"), and
    (B) which the Secretary of Housing and Urban Development designates as a renewal community, after consultation with—
      (i) the Secretaries of Agriculture, Commerce, Labor, and the Treasury; the Director of the Office of Management and Budget, and the Administrator of the Small Business Administration, and
      (ii) in the case of an area on an Indian reservation, the Secretary of the Interior.
  (2) Number of designations.
    (A) In general. Not more than 40 nominated areas may be designated as renewal communities.
    (B) Minimum designation in rural areas. Of the areas designated under paragraph (1), at least 12 must be areas—
      (i) which are within a local government jurisdiction or jurisdictions with a population of less than 50,000,
      (ii) which are outside of a metropolitan statistical area (within the meaning of section 143(k)(2)(B)), or
      (iii) which are determined by the Secretary of Housing and Urban Development, after consultation with the Secretary of Commerce, to be rural areas.
  (3) Areas designated based on degree of poverty, etc.
    (A) In general. Except as otherwise provided in this section, the nominated areas designated as renewal communities under this subsection shall be those nominated areas with the highest average ranking with respect to the criteria described in subparagraphs (B), (C),

and (D) of subsection (c)(3). For purposes of the preceding sentence, an area shall be ranked within each such criterion on the basis of the amount by which the area exceeds such criterion, with the area which exceeds such criterion by the greatest amount given the highest ranking.

(B) Exception where inadequate course of action, etc. An area shall not be designated under subparagraph (A) if the Secretary of Housing and Urban Development determines that the course of action described in subsection (d)(2) with respect to such area is inadequate.

(C) Preference for enterprise communities and empowerment zones. With respect to the first 20 designations made under this section, a preference shall be provided to those nominated areas which are enterprise communities or empowerment zones (and are otherwise eligible for designation under this section).

(4) Limitation on designations.

(A) Publication of regulations. The Secretary of Housing and Urban Development shall prescribe by regulation no later than 4 months after the date of the enactment [12/21/2000] of this section, after consultation with the officials described in paragraph (1)(B)—

(i) the procedures for nominating an area under paragraph (1)(A),

(ii) the parameters relating to the size and population characteristics of a renewal community, and

(iii) the manner in which nominated areas will be evaluated based on the criteria specified in subsection (d).

(B) Time limitations. The Secretary of Housing and Urban Development may designate nominated areas as renewal communities only during the period beginning on the first day of the first month following the month in which the regulations described in subparagraph (A) are prescribed and ending on December 31, 2001.

(C) Procedural rules. The Secretary of Housing and Urban Development shall not make any designation of a nominated area as a renewal community under paragraph (2) unless—

(i) the local governments and the States in which the nominated area is located have the authority—

(I) to nominate such area for designation as a renewal community,

(II) to make the State and local commitments described in subsection (d), and

(III) to provide assurances satisfactory to the Secretary of Housing and Urban Development that such commitments will be fulfilled,

(ii) a nomination regarding such area is submitted in such a manner and in such form, and contains such information, as the Secretary of Housing and Urban Development shall by regulation prescribe, and

(iii) the Secretary of Housing and Urban Development determines that any information furnished is reasonably accurate.

(5) Nomination process for Indian reservations. For purposes of this subchapter, in the case of a nominated area on an Indian reservation, the reservation governing body (as determined by the Secretary of the Interior) shall be treated as being both the State and local governments with respect to such area.

(b) Period for which designation is in effect.

(1) In general. Any designation of an area as a renewal community shall remain in effect during the period beginning on January 1, 2002, and ending on the earliest of—

(A) December 31, 2009,

(B) the termination date designated by the State and local governments in their nomination, or

(C) the date the Secretary of Housing and Urban Development revokes such designation.

(2) Revocation of designation. The Secretary of Housing and Urban Development may revoke the designation under this section of an area if such Secretary determines that the local government or the State in which the area is located—

(A) has modified the boundaries of the area, or

(B) is not complying substantially with, or fails to make progress in achieving, the State or local commitments, respectively, described in subsection (d).

(3) Earlier termination of certain benefits if earlier termination of designation. If the designation of an area as a renewal community terminates before December 31, 2009, the day after the date of such termination shall be substituted for "January 1, 2010" each place it appears in sections 1400F and 1400J with respect to such area.

(c) Area and eligibility requirements.

(1) In general. The Secretary of Housing and Urban Development may designate a nominated area as a renewal community under subsection (a) only if the area meets the requirements of paragraphs (2) and (3) of this subsection.

(2) Area requirements. A nominated area meets the requirements of this paragraph if—

(A) the area is within the jurisdiction of one or more local governments,

(B) the boundary of the area is continuous, and

(C) the area—

(i) has a population of not more than 200,000 and at least—

(I) 4,000 if any portion of such area (other than a rural area described in subsection (a)(2)(B)(i)) is located within a metropolitan statistical area (within the meaning of section 143(k)(2)(B)) which has a population of 50,000 or greater, or

(II) 1,000 in any other case, or

(ii) is entirely within an Indian reservation (as determined by the Secretary of the Interior).

(3) Eligibility requirements. A nominated area meets the requirements of this paragraph if the State and the local governments in which it is located certify in writing (and the Secretary of Housing and Urban Development, after such review of supporting data as he deems appropriate, accepts such certification) that—

(A) the area is one of pervasive poverty, unemployment, and general distress,

(B) the unemployment rate in the area, as determined by the most recent available data, was at least 1 ½ times the national unemployment rate for the period to which such data relate,

(C) the poverty rate for each population census tract within the nominated area is at least 20 percent, and

(D) in the case of an urban area, at least 70 percent of the households living in the area have incomes below 80 percent of the median income of households within the jurisdiction of the local government (determined in the same manner as under section 119(b)(2) of the Housing and Community Development Act of 1974).

(4) Consideration of other factors. The Secretary of Housing and Urban Development, in selecting any nominated area for designation as a renewal community under this section—

(A) shall take into account—

(i) the extent to which such area has a high incidence of crime, or

(ii) if such area has census tracts identified in the May 12, 1998, report of the Government Accountability Office regarding the identification of economically distressed areas, and

(B) with respect to 1 of the areas to be designated under subsection (a)(2)(B), may, in lieu of any criteria described in paragraph (3), take into account the existence of outmigration from the area.

(d) Required State and local commitments.

(1) In general. The Secretary of Housing and Urban Development may designate any nominated area as a renewal community under subsection (a) only if—

(A) the local government and the State in which the area is located agree in writing that, during any period during which the area is a renewal community, such governments will follow a specified course of action which meets the requirements of paragraph (2) and is designed to reduce the various burdens borne by employers or employees in such area, and

(B) the economic growth promotion requirements of paragraph (3) are met.

(2) Course of action.

(A) In general. A course of action meets the requirements of this paragraph if such course of action is a written document, signed by a State (or local government) and neighborhood organizations, which evidences a partnership between such State or government and community-based organizations and which commits each signatory to specific and measurable goals, actions, and timetables. Such course of action shall include at least 4 of the following:

(i) A reduction of tax rates or fees applying within the renewal community.

(ii) An increase in the level of efficiency of local services within the renewal community.

(iii) Crime reduction strategies, such as crime prevention (including the provision of crime prevention services by non governmental entities).

(iv) Actions to reduce, remove, simplify, or streamline governmental requirements applying within the renewal community.

(v) Involvement in the program by private entities, organizations, neighborhood organizations, and community groups, particularly those in the renewal community, including a commitment from such private entities to provide jobs and job training for, and technical, financial, or other assistance to, employers, employees, and residents from the renewal community.

(vi) The gift (or sale at below fair market value) of surplus real property (such as land, homes, and commercial or industrial structures) in the renewal community to neighborhood organizations, community development corporations, or private companies.

(B) Recognition of past efforts. For purposes of this section, in evaluating the course of action agreed to by any State or local government, the Secretary of Housing and Urban Development shall take into account the past efforts of such State or local government in reducing the various burdens borne by employers and employees in the area involved.

(3) Economic growth promotion requirements. The economic growth promotion requirements of this paragraph are met with respect to a nominated area if the local government and the State in which such area is located certify in writing that such government and State (respectively) have repealed or reduced, will not enforce, or will reduce within the nominated area at least 4 of the following:

(A) Licensing requirements for occupations that do not ordinarily require a professional degree.

(B) Zoning restrictions on home-based businesses which do not create a public nuisance.

(C) Permit requirements for street vendors who do not create a public nuisance.

(D) Zoning or other restrictions that impede the formation of schools or child care centers.

(E) Franchises or other restrictions on competition for businesses providing public services, including taxicabs, jitneys, cable television, or trash hauling.

This paragraph shall not apply to the extent that such regulation of businesses and occupations is necessary for and well-tailored to the protection of health and safety.

(e) Coordination with treatment of empowerment zones and enterprise communities.

For purposes of this title, the designation under section 1391 of any area as an empowerment zone or enterprise community shall cease to be in effect as of the date that the designation of any portion of such area as a renewal community takes effect.

(f) Definitions and special rules.

For purposes of this subchapter—

(1) Governments. If more than one government seeks to nominate an area as a renewal community, any reference to, or requirement of, this section shall apply to all such governments.

(2) Local government. The term "local government" means—

(A) any county, city, town, township, parish, village, or other general purpose political subdivision of a State, and

(B) any combination of political subdivisions described in subparagraph (A) recognized by the Secretary of Housing and Urban Development.

(3) Application of rules relating to census tracts. The rules of section 1392(b)(4) shall apply.

(4) Census data. Population and poverty rate shall be determined by using 1990 census data.

(g) Expansion of designated area based on 2000 census.

(1) In general. At the request of all governments which nominated an area as a renewal community, the Secretary of Housing and Urban Development may expand the area of such community to include any census tract if—

(A)(i) at the time such community was nominated, such community would have met the requirements of this section using 1990 census data even if such tract had been included in such community, and

(ii) such tract has a poverty rate using 2000 census data which exceeds the poverty rate for such tract using 1990 census data, or

(B)(i) such community would be described in subparagraph (A)(i) but for the failure to meet one or more of the requirements of paragraphs (2)(C)(i), (3)(C), and (3)(D) of subsection (c) using 1990 census data,

(ii) such community, including such tract, has a population of not more than 200,000 using either 1990 census data or 2000 census data,

(iii) such tract meets the requirement of subsection (c)(3)(C) using 2000 census data, and

(iv) such tract meets the requirement of subparagraph (A)(ii).

(2) Exception for certain census tracts with low population in 1990. In the case of any census tract which did not have a poverty rate determined by the Bureau of the Census using 1990 census data, paragraph (1)(B) shall be applied without regard to clause (iv) thereof.

(3) Special rule for certain census tracts with low population in 2000. At the request of all governments which nominated an area as a renewal community, the Secretary of Housing and Urban Development may expand the area of such community to include any census tract if—

(A) either—

(i) such tract has no population using 2000 census data, or

(ii) no poverty rate for such tract is determined by the Bureau of the Census using 2000 census data,

(B) such tract is one of general distress, and

(C) such community, including such tract, meets the requirements of subparagraphs (A) and (B) of subsection (c)(2).

(4) Period in effect. Any expansion under this subsection shall take effect as provided in subsection (b).

In 2005, P.L. 109-135, Sec. 412(rr)(1), substituted "Government Accountability Office" for "General Accounting Office" in clause (c)(4)(A)(ii), effective 12/21/2005.

In 2004, P.L. 108-357, Sec. 222(a), added subsec. (g), effective 12/21/2000 as if included in Sec. 101 of the Community Renewal Tax Relief Act of 2000, P.L. 106-554 [P.L. 106-554].

In 2000, P.L. 106-554, Sec. 1(a)(7), [which enacted into law Sec. 101(a) of P.L. 106-554] added Code Sec. 1400E, effective 12/21/2000.

PART II.—RENEWAL COMMUNITY CAPITAL GAIN; RENEWAL COMMUNITY BUSINESS

Sec.
1400F. Renewal community capital gain.
1400G. Renewal community business defined.

In 2000, P.L. 106-554, Sec. 1(a)(7) [which enacted into law Sec. 101(a) of H.R. 5662], added Part II as part of new Subchapter X.

Sec. 1400F.   Renewal community capital gain.
(a) General rule.
Gross income does not include any qualified capital gain from the sale or exchange of a qualified community asset held for more than 5 years.

(b) Qualified community asset.
For purposes of this section—

(1) In general. The term "qualified community asset" means—

(A) any qualified community stock,

(B) any qualified community partnership interest, and

(C) any qualified community business property.

(2) Qualified community stock.

(A) In general. Except as provided in subparagraph (B), the term "qualified community stock" means any stock in a domestic corporation if—

(i) such stock is acquired by the taxpayer after December 31, 2001, and before January 1, 2010, at its original issue (directly or through an underwriter) from the corporation solely in exchange for cash,

(ii) as of the time such stock was issued, such corporation was a renewal community business (or, in the case of a new corporation, such corporation was being organized for purposes of being a renewal community business), and

(iii) during substantially all of the taxpayer's holding period for such stock, such corporation qualified as a renewal community business.

(B) Redemptions. A rule similar to the rule of section 1202(c)(3) shall apply for purposes of this paragraph.

(3) Qualified community partnership interest. The term "qualified community partnership interest" means any capital or profits interest in a domestic partnership if—

(A) such interest is acquired by the taxpayer after December 31, 2001, and before January 1, 2010, from the partnership solely in exchange for cash,

(B) as of the time such interest was acquired, such partnership was a renewal community business (or, in the case of a new partnership, such partnership was being organized for purposes of being a renewal community business), and

(C) during substantially all of the taxpayer's holding period for such interest, such partnership qualified as a renewal community business.

A rule similar to the rule of paragraph (2)(B) shall apply for purposes of this paragraph.

(4) Qualified community business property.

(A) In general. The term "qualified community business property" means tangible property if—

(i) such property was acquired by the taxpayer by purchase (as defined in section 179(d)(2)) after December 31, 2001, and before January 1, 2010,

(ii) the original use of such property in the renewal community commences with the taxpayer, and

(iii) during substantially all of the taxpayer's holding period for such property, substantially all of the use of such property was in a renewal community business of the taxpayer.

(B) Special rule for substantial improvements. The requirements of clauses (i)and (ii) of subparagraph (A) shall be treated as satisfied with respect to—

(i) property which is substantially improved by the taxpayer before January 1, 2010, and

(ii) any land on which such property is located.

The determination of whether a property is substantially improved shall be made under clause (ii) of section 1400B(b)(4)(B), except that "December 31, 2001" shall be substituted for "December 31, 1997" in such clause.

(c) Qualified capital gain.

For purposes of this section—

(1) In general. Except as otherwise provided in this subsection, the term "qualified capital gain" means any gain recognized on the sale or exchange of—

(A) a capital asset, or

(B) property used in the trade or business (as defined in section 1231(b)).

(2) Gain before 2002 or after 2014 not qualified. The term "qualified capital gain" shall not include any gain attributable to periods before January 1, 2002, or after December 31, 2014.

(3) Certain rules to apply. Rules similar to the rules of paragraphs (3), (4), and (5) of section 1400B(e) shall apply for purposes of this subsection.

(d) Certain rules to apply.

For purposes of this section, rules similar to the rules of paragraphs (5), (6), and (7) of subsection (b), and subsections (f) and (g), of section 1400B shall apply; except that for such purposes section 1400B(g)(2) shall be applied by substituting "January 1, 2002" for "January 1, 1998" and "December 31, 2014" for "December 31, 2014".

(e) Regulations.

The Secretary shall prescribe such regulations as may be appropriate to carry out the purposes of this section, including regulations to prevent the abuse of the purposes of this section.

In 2008, P.L. 110-343, Sec. 322(c)(2)(C)DivB, substituted "2014" for "2012" in subsec. (d), effective 10/3/2008.
In 2006, P.L. 109-432, Sec. 110(c)(2)(C), substituted "2012" for "2010" in subsec. (d), effective 12/20/2006.
In 2004, P.L. 108-311, Sec. 310(c)(2)(C), substituted "December 31, 2010" for "December 31, 2008" in subsec. (d), effective 1/1/2004.
In 2000, P.L. 106-554, Sec. 1(a)(7), [which enacted into law Sec. 101(a) of P.L. 106-554] added Code Sec. 1400F, effective 12/21/2000.

Sec. 1400G. Renewal community business defined.

For purposes of this subchapter, the term "renewal community business" means any entity or proprietorship which would be a qualified business entity or qualified proprietorship under section 1397C if references to renewal communities were substituted for references to empowerment zones in such section.

In 2000, P.L. 106-554, Sec. 1(a)(7), [which enacted into law Sec. 101(a) of P.L. 106-554] added Code Sec. 1400G, effective 12/21/2000.

PART III.— ADDITIONAL INCENTIVES
Sec.
1400H. Renewal community employment credit.
1400I. Commercial revitalization deduction.
1400J. Increase in expensing under section 179.

In 2000, P.L. 106-554, Sec. 1(a)(7) [which enacted into law Sec. 101(a) of H.R. 5662], added Part III as part of new Subchapter X.

Sec. 1400H. Renewal community employment credit.
(a) In general.
Subject to the modification in subsection (b), a renewal community shall be treated as an empowerment zone for purposes of section 1396 with respect to wages paid or incurred after December 31, 2001.
(b) Modification.
In applying section 1396 with respect to renewal communities—
(1) the applicable percentage shall be 15 percent, and
(2) subsection (c) thereof shall be applied by substituting "$10,000" for "$15,000" each place it appears.

In 2000, P.L. 106-554, Sec. 1(a)(7), [which enacted into law Sec. 101(a) of P.L. 106-554] added Code Sec. 1400H, effective 12/21/2000.

Sec. 1400I. Commercial revitalization deduction.
(a) General rule.
At the election of the taxpayer, either—
(1) one-half of any qualified revitalization expenditures chargeable to capital account with respect to any qualified revitalization building shall be allowable as a deduction for the taxable year in which the building is placed in service, or
(2) a deduction for all such expenditures shall be allowable ratably over the 120-month period beginning with the month in which the building is placed in service.
(b) Qualified revitalization buildings and expenditures.
For purposes of this section—
(1) **Qualified revitalization building.** The term "qualified revitalization building" means any building (and its structural components) if—
(A) the building is placed in service by the taxpayer in a renewal community and the original use of the building begins with the taxpayer, or
(B) in the case of such building not described in subparagraph (A), such building—
(i) is substantially rehabilitated (within the meaning of section 47(c)(1)(C) by the taxpayer, and
(ii) is placed in service by the taxpayer after the rehabilitation in a renewal community.
(2) **Qualified revitalization expenditure.**
(A) In general. The term "qualified revitalization expenditure" means any amount properly chargeable to capital account for property for which depreciation is allowable under section 168 (without regard to this section) and which is—
(i) nonresidential real property (as defined in section 168(e)), or
(ii) section 1250 property (as defined in section 1250(c)) which is functionally related and subordinate to property described in clause (i).
(B) Certain expenditures not included.
(i) Acquistion cost. In the case of a building described in paragraph (1)(B), the cost of acquiring the building or interest therein shall be treated as a qualified revitalization expenditure only to the extent that such cost does not exceed 30 percent of the aggregate qualified revitalization expenditures (determined without regard to such cost) with respect to such building.
(ii) Credits. The term "qualified revitalization expenditure" does not include any expenditure which the taxpayer may take into account in computing any credit allowable under this title unless the taxpayer elects to take the expenditure into account only for purposes of this section.
(c) Dollar limitation.
The aggregate amount which may be treated as qualified revitalization expenditures with respect to any qualified revitalization building shall not exceed the lesser of—
(1) $10,000,000, or
(2) the commercial revitalization expenditure amount allocated to such building under this sectionby the commercial revitalization agency for the State in which the building is located.
(d) Commercial revitalization expenditure amount.
(1) **In general.** The aggregate commercial revitalization expenditure amount which a commercial revitalization agency may allocate for any calendar year is the amount of the State commercial revitalization expenditure ceiling determined under this paragraph for such calendar year for such agency.
(2) **State commercial revitalization expenditure ceiling.** The State commercial revitalization expenditure ceiling applicable to any State—
(A) for each calendar year after 2001 and before 2010 is $12,000,000 for each renewal community in the State, and
(B) for each calendar year thereafter is zero.
(3) **Commercial revitalization agency.** For purposes of this section, the term "commercial revitalization agency" means any agency authorized by a State to carry out this section.
(4) **Time and manner of allocations.** Allocations under this section shall be made at the same time and in the same manner as under paragraphs (1) and (7) of section 42(h).
(e) Responsibilities of commercial revitalization agencies.
(1) **Plans for allocation.** Notwithstanding any other provision of this section, the commercial revitalization expenditure amount with respect to any building shall be zero unless—
(A) such amount was allocated pursuant to a qualified allocation plan of the commercial revitalization agency which is approved (in accordance with rules similar to

the rules of section 147(f)(2) (other than subparagraph (B)(ii) thereof)) by the governmental unit of which such agency is a part, and

(B) such agency notifies the chief executive officer (or its equivalent) of the local jurisdiction within which the building is located of such allocation and provides such individual a reasonable opportunity to comment on the allocation.

(2) **Qualified allocation plan.** For purposes of this subsection, the term "qualified allocation plan" means any plan—

(A) which sets forth selection criteria to be used to determine priorities of the commercial revitalization agency which are appropriate to local conditions,

(B) which considers—

(i) the degree to which a project contributes to the implementation of a strategic plan that is devised for a renewal community through a citizen participation process,

(ii) the amount of any increase in permanent, full-time employment by reason of any project, and

(iii) the active involvement of residents and nonprofit groups within the renewal community, and

(C) which provides a procedure that the agency (or its agent) will follow in monitoring compliance with this section.

(f) **Special rules.**

(1) **Deduction in lieu of depreciation.** The deduction provided by this section for qualified revitalization expenditures shall—

(A) with respect to the deduction determined under subsection (a)(1), be in lieu of any depreciation deduction otherwise allowable on account of one-half of such expenditures, and

(B) with respect to the deduction determined under subsection (a)(2), be in lieu of any depreciation deduction otherwise allowable on account of all of such expenditures.

(2) **Basis adjustment, etc.** For purposes of sections 1016 and 1250, the deduction under this section shall be treated in the same manner as a depreciation deduction. For purposes of section 1250(b)(5), the straight line method of adjustment shall be determined without regard to this section.

(3) **Substantial rehabilitations treated as separate buildings.** A substantial rehabilitation (within the meaning of section 47(c)(1)(C)) of a building shall be treated as a separate building for purposes of subsection (a).

(4) **Clarification of allowance of deduction under minimum tax.** Notwithstanding section 56(a)(1), the deduction under this section shall be allowed in determining alternative minimum taxable income under section 55.

(g) **termination.**

This section shall not apply to any building placed in service after December 31, 2009.

In 2000, P.L. 106-554, Sec. 1(a)(7), [which enacted into law Sec. 101(a) of P.L. 106-554] added Code Sec. 1400I, effective 12/21/2000.

Sec. 1400J. Increase in expensing under section 179.

(a) **In general.**

For purposes of section 1397A—

(1) a renewal community shall be treated as an empowerment zone,

(2) a renewal community business shall be treated as an enterprise zone business, and

(3) qualified renewal property shall be treated as qualified zone property.

(b) **Qualified renewal property.**

For purposes of this section—

(1) **In general.** The term "qualified renewal property" means any property to which section 168 applies (or would apply but for section 179) if—

(A) such property was acquired by the taxpayer by purchase (as defined in section 179(d)(2)) after December 31, 2001, and before January 1, 2010, and

(B) such property would be qualified zone property (as defined in section 1397D) if references to renewal communities were substituted for references to empowerment zones in section 1397D.

(2) **Certain rules to apply.** The rules of subsections (a)(2) and (b) of section 1397D shall apply for purposes of this section.

In 2000, P.L. 106-554, Sec. 1(a)(7), [which enacted into law Sec. 101(a) of P.L. 106-554] added Code Sec. 1400J, effective 12/21/2000.

Subchapter Y.—Short-Term Regional Benefits
Part
 I. Tax Benefits for New York Liberty Zone
 II. Tax Benefits for GO Zones
 III. Recovery Zone Bonds.

In 2009, P.L. 111-5, Sec. 1401(b), added item part III, effective for obligations issued after 2/17/2009

In 2005, P.L. 109-135, Sec. 101(b)(3), amended subchapter Y of chapter 1 of subtitle A as precedes Code Sec. 1400L.

Prior to amendment, subchapter Y of chapter 1 of subtitle A as precedes Code Sec. 1400L read as follows:
"Y. New York Liberty Zone Benefits
"1400L. Tax benefits for New York Liberty Zone."

In 2002, P.L. 107-147, Sec. 301(a), added subchapter Y as part of chapter 1 of subtitle A, effective 3/9/2002.

PART I.—TAX BENEFITS FOR NEW YORK LIBERTY ZONE
Sec.
1400L. Tax benefits for New York Liberty Zone.

In 2005, P.L. 109-135, Sec. 101(b)(3), added part I of subchapter Y of chapter 1 of subtitle A, incorporating Code Sec. 1400L therein. Secs. 101(b)(3), 102(a), 103(a), and 201(a) of this Act added Code Secs. 1400M-1400T as part II of subchapter Y of chapter 1 of subtitle A.

Sec. 1400L. Tax benefits for New York Liberty Zone.

(a) **Expansion of work opportunity tax credit.**

(1) **In general.** For purposes of section 51, a New York Liberty Zone business employee shall be treated as a member of a targeted group.

(2) **New York Liberty Zone business employee.** For purposes of this subsection—

(A) **In general.** The term "New York Liberty Zone business employee" means, with respect to any period, any employee of a New York Liberty Zone business if substantially all the services performed during such period by such employee for such business are performed in the New York Liberty Zone.

(B) Inclusion of certain employees outside the New York Liberty Zone.

(i) **In general.** In the case of a New York Liberty Zone business described in subclause (II) of subparagraph (C)(i), the term "New York Liberty Zone business employee" includes any employee of such business (not described in subparagraph (A)) if substantially all the services performed during such period by such employee for such business are performed in the City of New York, New York.

(ii) Limitation. The number of employees of such a business that are treated as New York Liberty Zone business employees on any day by reason of clause (i) shall not exceed the excess of—

(I) the number of employees of such business on September 11, 2001, in the New York Liberty Zone, over

(II) the number of New York Liberty Zone business employees (determined without regard to this subparagraph) of such business on the day to which the limitation is being applied.

The Secretary may require any trade or business to have the number determined under subclause (I) verified by the New York State Department of Labor.

(C) New York Liberty Zone business.

(i) In general. The term "New York Liberty Zone business" means any trade or business which is—

(I) located in the New York Liberty Zone, or

(II) located in the City of New York, New York, outside the New York Liberty Zone, as a result of the physical destruction or damage of such place of business by the September 11, 2001, terrorist attack.

(ii) Credit not allowed for large businesses. The term "New York Liberty Zone business" shall not include any trade or business for any taxable year if such trade or business employed an average of more than 200 employees on business days during the taxable year.

(D) Special rules for determining amount of credit. For purposes of applying subpart F of part IV of subchapter A of this chapter to wages paid or incurred to any New York Liberty Zone business employee—

(i) section 51(a) shall be applied by substituting "qualified wages" for "qualified first-year wages",

(ii) the rules of section 52 shall apply for purposes of determining the number of employees under this paragraph,

(iii) subsections (c)(4) and (i)(2) of section 51 shall not apply, and

(iv) in determining qualified wages, the following shall apply in lieu of section 51(b):

(I) Qualified wages. The term "qualified wages" means wages paid or incurred by the employer to individuals who are New York Liberty Zone business employees of such employer for work performed during calendar year 2002 or 2003.

(II) Only first $6,000 of wages per calendar year taken into account. The amount of the qualified wages which may be taken into account with respect to any individual shall not exceed $6,000 per calendar year.

(b) Special allowance for certain property acquired after September 10, 2001.

(1) Additional allowance. In the case of any qualified New York Liberty Zone property—

(A) the depreciation deduction provided by section 167(a) for the taxable year in which such property is placed in service shall include an allowance equal to 30 percent of the adjusted basis of such property, and

(B) the adjusted basis of the qualified New York Liberty Zone property shall be reduced by the amount of such deduction before computing the amount otherwise allowable as a depreciation deduction under this chapter for such taxable year and any subsequent taxable year.

(2) Qualified New York Liberty Zone property. For purposes of this subsection—

(A) In general. The term "qualified New York Liberty Zone property" means property—

(i) (I) which is described in section 168(k)(2)(A)(i), or

(II) which is nonresidential real property, or residential rental property, which is described in subparagraph (B),

(ii) substantially all of the use of which is in the New York Liberty Zone and is in the active conduct of a trade or business by the taxpayer in such Zone,

(iii) the original use of which in the New York Liberty Zone commences with the taxpayer after September 10, 2001,

(iv) which is acquired by the taxpayer by purchase (as defined in section 179(d)) after September 10, 2001, but only if no written binding contract for the acquisition was in effect before September 11, 2001, and

(v) which is placed in service by the taxpayer on or before the termination date.

The term "termination date" means December 31, 2006 (December 31, 2009, in the case of nonresidential real property and residential rental property).

(B) Eligible real property. Nonresidential real property or residential rental property is described in this subparagraph only to the extent it rehabilitates real property damaged, or replaces real property destroyed or condemned, as a result of the September 11, 2001, terrorist attack. For purposes of the preceding sentence, property shall be treated as replacing real property destroyed or condemned if, as part of an integrated plan, such property replaces real property which is included in a continuous area which includes real property destroyed or condemned.

(C) Exceptions.

(i) Bonus depreciation property under section 168(k). Such term shall not include property to which section 168(k) applies.

(ii) Alternative depreciation property. The term "qualified New York Liberty Zone property" shall not include any property described in section 168(k)(2)(D)(i).

(iii) Qualified New York Liberty Zone leasehold improvement property. Such term shall not include any qualified New York Liberty Zone leasehold improvement property.

(iv) Election out. For purposes of this subsection, rules similar to the rules of section 168(k)(2)(D)(iii) shall apply.

(D) Special rules. For purposes of this subsection, rules similar to the rules of section 168(k)(2)(E) shall apply, except that clause (i) thereof shall be applied without regard to "and before January 1, 2013", and clause (iv) thereof shall be applied by substituting "qualified New York Liberty Zone property" for "qualified property".

(E) Allowance against alternative minimum tax. For purposes of this subsection, rules similar to the rules of section 168(k)(2)(G) shall apply.

(c) 5-year recovery period for depreciation of certain leasehold improvements.

(1) In general. For purposes of section 168, the term "5-year property" includes any qualified New York Liberty Zone leasehold improvement property.

(2) Qualified New York Liberty Zone leasehold improvement property. For purposes of this section, the

term "qualified New York Liberty Zone leasehold improvement property" means qualified leasehold improvement property (as defined in section 168(k)(3)) if—

(A) such building is located in the New York Liberty Zone,

(B) such improvement is placed in service after September 10, 2001, and before January 1, 2007, and

(C) no written binding contract for such improvement was in effect before September 11, 2001.

(3) Requirement to use straight line method. The applicable depreciation method under section 168 shall be the straight line method in the case of qualified New York Liberty Zone leasehold improvement property.

(4) 9-year recovery period under alternative system. For purposes of section 168(g), the class life of qualified New York Liberty Zone leasehold improvement property shall be 9 years.

(5) Election out. For purposes of this subsection, rules similar to the rules of section 168(k)(2)(D)(iii) shall apply.

(d) Tax-exempt bond financing.

(1) In general. For purposes of this title, any qualified New York Liberty Bond shall be treated as an exempt facility bond.

(2) Qualified New York Liberty Bond. For purposes of this subsection, the term "qualified New York Liberty Bond" means any bond issued as part of an issue if—

(A) 95 percent or more of the net proceeds (as defined in section 150(a)(3)) of such issue are to be used for qualified project costs,

(B) such bond is issued by the State of New York or any political subdivision thereof,

(C) the Governor or the Mayor designates such bond for purposes of this section, and

(D) such bond is issued after the date of the enactment of this section and before January 1, 2012.

(3) Limitations on amount of bonds.

(A) Aggregate amount designated. The maximum aggregate face amount of bonds which may be designated under this subsection shall not exceed $8,000,000,000, of which not to exceed $4,000,000,000 may be designated by the Governor and not to exceed $4,000,000,000 may be designated by the Mayor.

(B) Specific limitations. The aggregate face amount of bonds issued which are to be used for—

(i) costs for property located outside the New York Liberty Zone shall not exceed $2,000,000,000,

(ii) residential rental property shall not exceed $1,600,000,000, and

(iii) costs with respect to property used for retail sales of tangible property and functionally related and subordinate property shall not exceed $800,000,000.

The limitations under clauses (i), (ii), and (iii) shall be allocated proportionately between the bonds designated by the Governor and the bonds designated by the Mayor in proportion to the respective amounts of bonds designated by each.

(C) Movable property. No bonds shall be issued which are to be used for movable fixtures and equipment.

(4) Qualified project costs. For purposes of this subsection—

(A) In general. The term "qualified project costs" means the cost of acquisition, construction, reconstruction, and renovation of—

(i) nonresidential real property and residential rental property (including fixed tenant improvements associated with such property) located in the New York Liberty Zone, and

(ii) public utility property (as defined in section 168(i)(10)) located in the New York Liberty Zone.

(B) Costs for certain property outside zone included. Such term includes the cost of acquisition, construction, reconstruction, and renovation of nonresidential real property (including fixed tenant improvements associated with such property) located outside the New York Liberty Zone but within the City of New York, New York, if such property is part of a project which consists of at least 100,000 square feet of usable office or other commercial space located in a single building or multiple adjacent buildings.

(5) Special rules. In applying this title to any qualified New York Liberty Bond, the following modifications shall apply:

(A) Section 146 (relating to volume cap) shall not apply.

(B) Section 147(d) (relating to acquisition of existing property not permitted) shall be applied by substituting "50 percent" for "15 percent" each place it appears.

(C) Section 148(f)(4)(C) (relating to exception from rebate for certain proceeds to be used to finance construction expenditures) shall apply to the available construction proceeds of bonds issued under this section.

(D) Repayments of principal on financing provided by the issue—

(i) may not be used to provide financing, and

(ii) must be used not later than the close of the 1st semiannual period beginning after the date of the repayment to redeem bonds which are part of such issue.

The requirement of clause (ii) shall be treated as met with respect to amounts received within 10 years after the date of issuance of the issue (or, in the case of a refunding bond, the date of issuance of the original bond) if such amounts are used by the close of such 10 years to redeem bonds which are part of such issue.

(E) Section 57(a)(5) shall not apply.

(6) Separate issue treatment of portions of an issue. This subsection shall not apply to the portion of an issue which (if issued as a separate issue) would be treated as a qualified bond or as a bond that is not a private activity bond (determined without regard to paragraph (1)), if the issuer elects to so treat such portion.

(e) Advance refundings of certain tax-exempt bonds.

(1) In general. With respect to a bond described in paragraph (2) issued as part of an issue 90 percent (95 percent in the case of a bond described in paragraph (2)(C)) or more of the net proceeds (as defined in section 150(a)(3)) of which were used to finance facilities located within the City of New York, New York (or property which is functionally related and subordinate to facilities located within the City of New York for the furnishing of water), one additional advanced refunding after the date of the enactment [3/9/2002] of this section and before January 1, 2006, shall be allowed under the applicable rules of section 149(d) if—

(A) the Governor or the Mayor designates the advance refunding bond for purposes of this subsection, and

(B) the requirements of paragraph (4) are met.

(2) Bonds described. A bond is described in this paragraph if such bond was outstanding on September 11, 2001, and is—

Gulf Opportunity Zone   Code Sec. 1400M(2)

(A) a State or local bond (as defined in section 103(c)(1)) which is a general obligation of the City of New York, New York,

(B) a State or local bond (as so defined) other than a private activity bond (as defined in section 141(a)) issued by the New York Municipal Water Finance Authority or the Metropolitan Transportation Authority of the State of New York or the Municipal Assistance Corporation, or

(C) a qualified 501(c)(3) bond (as defined in section 145(a)) which is a qualified hospital bond (as defined in section 145(c)) issued by or on behalf of the State of New York or the City of New York, New York.

(3) Aggregate limit. For purposes of paragraph (1), the maximum aggregate face amount of bonds which may be designated under this subsection by the Governor shall not exceed $4,500,000,000 and the maximum aggregate face amount of bonds which may be designated under this subsection by the Mayor shall not exceed $4,500,000,000.

(4) Additional requirements. The requirements of this paragraph are met with respect to any advance refunding of a bond described in paragraph (2) if—

(A) no advance refundings of such bond would be allowed under any provision of law after September 11, 2001,

(B) the advance refunding bond is the only other outstanding bond with respect to the refunded bond, and

(C) the requirements of section 148 are met with respect to all bonds issued under this subsection.

(f) Increase in expensing under section 179.

(1) In general. For purposes of section 179—

(A) the limitation under section 179(b)(1) shall be increased by the lesser of—

(i) $35,000, or

(ii) the cost of section 179 property which is qualified New York Liberty Zone property placed in service during the taxable year, and

(B) the amount taken into account under section 179(b)(2) with respect to any section 179 property which is qualified New York Liberty Zone property shall be 50 percent of the cost thereof.

(2) Qualified New York Liberty Zone property. For purposes of this subsection, the term "qualified New York Liberty Zone property" has the meaning given such term by subsection (b)(2), determined without regard to subparagraph (C)(i) thereof.

(3) Recapture. Rules similar to the rules under section 179(d)(10) shall apply with respect to any qualified New York Liberty Zone property which ceases to be used in the New York Liberty Zone.

(g) Extension of replacement period for nonrecognition of gain.

Notwithstanding subsections (g) and (h) of section 1033, clause (i) of section 1033(a)(2)(B) shall be applied by substituting "5 years" for "2 years" with respect to property which is compulsorily or involuntarily converted as a result of the terrorist attacks on September 11, 2001, in the New York Liberty Zone but only if substantially all of the use of the replacement property is in the City of New York, New York.

(h) New York Liberty Zone.

For purposes of this section, the term "New York Liberty Zone" means the area located on or south of Canal Street, East Broadway (east of its intersection with Canal Street), or Grand Street (east of its intersection with East Broadway) in the Borough of Manhattan in the City of New York, New York.

(i) References to Governor and Mayor.

For purposes of this section, the terms "Governor" and "Mayor" mean the Governor of the State of New York and the Mayor of the City of New York, New York, respectively.

In 2010, P.L. 111-312, Sec. 401(d)(6), substituted "January 1, 2013" for "January 1, 2011" in subpara. (b)(2)(D), effective for property placed in service after 12/31/2010, in tax. yrs. end. after such date. . . . Sec. 761(a), substituted "January 1, 2012" for "January 1, 2010" in subpara. (d)(2)(D), effective for bonds issued after 12/31/2009.

—P.L. 111-240, Sec. 2022(b)(6), substituted "January 1, 2011" for "January 1, 2010" in subpara. (b)(2)(D), effective for property placed in service after 12/31/2009, in tax. yrs. ending after 12/31/2009.

In 2008, P.L. 110-185, Sec. 103(c)(8), substituted "January 1, 2010" for "January 1, 2005" in subpara. (b)(2)(D), effective for property placed in service after December 31, 2007, in tax. yrs. ending after 2/13/2008.

In 2005, P.L. 109-135, Sec. 405(a)(2), substituted "January 1, 2005" for "September 11, 2004" in subpara. (b)(2)(D), effective for tax. yrs. end. after 5/5/2003 as if included in Sec. 201 of the Jobs and Growth Tax Relief and Reconciliation Act of 2003, P.L. 108-27.

—P.L. 109-135, Sec. 412(ss)(1), substituted "section 168(k)(2)(D)(i)" for "section 168(k)(2)(C)(i)" in clause (b)(2)(C)(ii) . . . Sec. 412(ss)(2), substituted "section 168(k)(2)(D)(iii)" for "section 168(k)(2)(C)(iii)" in clause (b)(2)(C)(iv) . . . Sec. 412(ss)(3), substituted "secton 168(k)(2)(E)" for "section 168(k)(2)(D)" in subpara. (b)(2)(D) . . . Sec. 412(ss)(4), substituted "secton 168(k)(2)(G)" for "section 168(k)(2)(F)" in subpara. (b)(2)(E) . . . Sec. 412(ss)(5), substituted "section 168(k)(2)(D)(iii)" for "section 168(k)(2)(C)(iii)" in para. (c)(5), effective 12/21/2005.

In 2004, P.L. 108-311, Sec. 309(a), substituted "2010" for "2005" in subpara. (d)(2)(D) . . . Sec. 309(b), substituted "2006" for "2005" in para. (e)(1), effective 10/4/2004.

—P.L. 108-311, Sec. 309(c), substituted "or the Municipal Assistance Corporation, or" for ", or" in subpara. (e)(2)(B), effective 3/9/2002 as if included in Sec. 301 of the Job Creation and Worker Assistance Act of 2002, P.L. 107-147.

—P.L. 108-311, Sec. 403(c)(1)(A), substituted "subchapter A" for "subchapter B" in subpara. (a)(2)(D) . . . Sec. 403(c)(1)(B), substituted "this paragraph" for "subparagraph (B)" in clause (a)(2)(D)(ii) . . . Sec. 403(c)(2), added ", and clause (iv) thereof shall be applied by substituting 'qualified New York Liberty Zone property' for 'qualified property'" before the period at the end of subpara. (b)(2)(D) . . . Sec. 403(c)(3), added para. (c)(5) . . . Sec. 403(c)(4), added ", determined without regard to subparagraph (C)(i) thereof" before the period at the end of para. (f)(2), effective 3/9/2002 as if included in Sec. 301 of the Job Creation and Worker Assistance Act of 2002, P.L. 107-147.

In 2003, P.L. 108-27, Sec. 201(c)(2), substituted "Bonus depreciation property under section 168(k)" for "30-percent additional allowance property" in the heading of clause (b)(2)(C)(i), effective for tax. yrs. end. after 5/5/2003.

In 2002, P.L. 107-147, Sec. 301(a), added Code Sec. 1400L as part of new subchapter Y of chapter 1 of subtitle A, enacted 3/9/2002.

PART II.—TAX BENEFITS FOR GO ZONES

Sec.

1400M. Definitions

1400N. Tax benefits for Gulf Opportunity Zone.

1400O. Education tax benefits.

1400P. Housing tax benefits.

1400Q. Special rules for use of retirement funds.

1400R. Employment relief.

1400S. Additional tax relief provisions.

1400T. Special rules for mortgage revenue bonds.

In 2005, P.L. 109-135, Sec. 101(b)(3), added part II and items 1400M and 1400N . . . Sec. 102(a), added item 1400O. . . . Sec. 103(a), added item 1400P . . . Sec. 201(a), added items 1400Q-1400T.

Sec. 1400M. Definitions.

For purposes of this part—

(1) Gulf Opportunity Zone. The terms "Gulf Opportunity Zone" and "GO Zone" mean that portion of the Hurricane Katrina disaster area determined by the President to warrant individual or individual and public assistance from the Federal Government under the Robert T. Stafford Disaster Relief and Emergency Assistance Act by reason of Hurricane Katrina.

(2) Hurricane Katrina disaster area. The term "Hurricane Katrina disaster area" means an area with respect to

2,895

which a major disaster has been declared by the President before September 14, 2005, under section 401 of such Act by reason of Hurricane Katrina.

(3) Rita GO Zone. The term "Rita GO Zone" means that portion of the Hurricane Rita disaster area determined by the President to warrant individual or individual and public assistance from the Federal Government under such Act by reason of Hurricane Rita.

(4) Hurricane Rita disaster area. The term "Hurricane Rita disaster area" means an area with respect to which a major disaster has been declared by the President before October 6, 2005, under section 401 of such Act by reason of Hurricane Rita.

(5) Wilma GO Zone. The term "Wilma GO Zone" means that portion of the Hurricane Wilma disaster area determined by the President to warrant individual or individual and public assistance from the Federal Government under such Act by reason of Hurricane Wilma.

(6) Hurricane Wilma disaster area. The term "Hurricane Wilma disaster area" means an area with respect to which a major disaster has been declared by the President before November 14, 2005, under section 401 of such Act by reason of Hurricane Wilma.

In 2005, P.L. 109-135, Sec. 101(a), added Code Sec. 1400M, effective for tax. yrs. end. on or after 8/28/2005.

Sec. 1400N. Tax benefits for Gulf Opportunity Zone.

• *Caution:* For application of this section to the Kansas Disaster Area storms beginning on May 4, 2007, see history for this Code Sec.

(a) Tax-exempt bond financing.
 (1) In general. For purposes of this title—
  (A) any qualified Gulf Opportunity Zone Bond described in paragraph (2)(A)(i) shall be treated as an exempt facility bond, and
  (B) any qualified Gulf Opportunity Zone Bond described in paragraph (2)(A)(ii) shall be treated as a qualified mortgage bond.
 (2) Qualified Gulf Opportunity Zone Bond. For purposes of this subsection, the term "qualified Gulf Opportunity Zone Bond" means any bond issued as part of an issue if—
  (A)(i) 95 percent or more of the net proceeds (as defined in section 150(a)(3)) of such issue are to be used for qualified project costs, or
  (ii) such issue meets the requirements of a qualified mortgage issue, except as otherwise provided in this subsection,
  (B) such bond is issued by the State of Alabama, Louisiana, or Mississippi, or any political subdivision thereof,
  (C) such bond is designated for purposes of this section by—
   (i) in the case of a bond which is required under State law to be approved by the bond commission of such State, such bond commission, and
   (ii) in the case of any other bond, the Governor of such State,
  (D) such bond is issued after the date of the enactment of this section and before January 1, 2012, and
  (E) no portion of the proceeds of such issue is to be used to provide any property described in section 144(c)(6)(B).

 (3) Limitations on bonds.
  (A) Aggregate amount designated. The maximum aggregate face amount of bonds which may be designated under this subsection with respect to any State shall not exceed the product of $2,500 multiplied by the portion of the State population which is in the Gulf Opportunity Zone (as determined on the basis of the most recent census estimate of resident population released by the Bureau of Census before August 28, 2005).
  (B) Movable property. No bonds shall be issued which are to be used for movable fixtures and equipment.
 (4) Qualified project costs. For purposes of this subsection, the term "qualified project costs" means—
  (A) the cost of any qualified residential rental project (as defined in section 142(d)) located in the Gulf Opportunity Zone, and
  (B) the cost of acquisition, construction, reconstruction, and renovation of—
   (i) nonresidential real property (including fixed improvements associated with such property) located in the Gulf Opportunity Zone, and
   (ii) public utility property (as defined in section 168(i)(10)) located in the Gulf Opportunity Zone.
 (5) Special rules. In applying this title to any qualified Gulf Opportunity Zone Bond, the following modifications shall apply:
  (A) Section 142(d)(1) (defining qualified residential rental project) shall be applied—
   (i) by substituting "60 percent" for "50 percent" in subparagraph (A) thereof, and
   (ii) by substituting "70 percent" for "60 percent" in subparagraph (B) thereof.
  (B) Section 143 (relating to mortgage revenue bonds: qualified mortgage bond and qualified veterans' mortgage bond) shall be applied—
   (i) only with respect to owner-occupied residences in the Gulf Opportunity Zone,
   (ii) by treating any such residence in the Gulf Opportunity Zone as a targeted area residence,
   (iii) by applying subsection (f)(3) thereof without regard to subparagraph (A) thereof, and
   (iv) by substituting "$150,000" for "$15,000" in subsection (k)(4) thereof.
  (C) Except as provided in section 143, repayments of principal on financing provided by the issue of which such bond is a part may not be used to provide financing.
  (D) Section 146 (relating to volume cap) shall not apply.
  (E) Section 147(d)(2) (relating to acquisition of existing property not permitted) shall be applied by substituting "50 percent" for "15 percent" each place it appears.
  (F) Section 148(f)(4)(C) (relating to exception from rebate for certain proceeds to be used to finance construction expenditures) shall apply to the available construction proceeds of bonds which are part of an issue described in paragraph (2)(A)(i).
  (G) Section 57(a)(5) (relating to tax-exempt interest) shall not apply.
 (6) Separate issue treatment of portions of an issue. This subsection shall not apply to the portion of an issue which (if issued as a separate issue) would be treated as a qualified bond or as a bond that is not a private activity bond (determined without regard to paragraph (1)), if the issuer elects to so treat such portion.

(7) **Special rule for repairs and reconstructions.**
 (A) In general. For purposes of section 143 and this subsection, any qualified GO Zone repair or reconstruction shall be treated as a qualified rehabilitation.
 (B) Qualified GO Zone repair or reconstruction. For purposes of subparagraph (A), the term "qualified GO Zone repair or reconstruction" means any repair of damage caused by Hurricane Katrina, Hurricane Rita, or Hurricane Wilma to a building located in the Gulf Opportunity Zone, the Rita GO Zone, or the Wilma GO Zone (or reconstruction of such building in the case of damage constituting destruction) if the expenditures for such repair or reconstruction are 25 percent or more of the mortgagor's adjusted basis in the residence. For purposes of the preceding sentence, the mortgagor's adjusted basis shall be determined as of the completion of the repair or reconstruction or, if later, the date on which the mortgagor acquires the residence.
 (C) Termination. This paragraph shall apply only to owner-financing provided after the date of the enactment of this paragraph and before January 1, 2012.
(8) **Inclusion of certain counties.** For purposes of this subsection, the Gulf Opportunity Zone includes Colbert County, Alabama and Dallas County, Alabama.

(b) **Advance refundings of certain tax-exempt bonds.**
(1) **In general.** With respect to a bond described in paragraph (3), one additional advance refunding after the date of the enactment of this section and before January 1, 2011, shall be allowed under the applicable rules of section 149(d) if—
 (A) the Governor of the State designates the advance refunding bond for purposes of this subsection, and
 (B) the requirements of paragraph (5) are met.
(2) **Certain private activity bonds.** With respect to a bond described in paragraph (3) which is an exempt facility bond described in paragraph (1) or (2) of section 142(a), one advance refunding after the date of the enactment of this section and before January 1, 2011, shall be allowed under the applicable rules of section 149(d) (notwithstanding paragraph (2) thereof) if the requirements of subparagraphs (A) and (B) of paragraph (1) are met.
(3) **Bonds described.** A bond is described in this paragraph if such bond was outstanding on August 28, 2005, and is issued by the State of Alabama, Louisiana, or Mississippi, or a political subdivision thereof.
(4) **Aggregate limit.** The maximum aggregate face amount of bonds which may be designated under this subsection by the Governor of a State shall not exceed—
 (A) $4,500,000,000 in the case of the State of Louisiana,
 (B) $2,250,000,000 in the case of the State of Mississippi, and
 (C) $1,125,000,000 in the case of the State of Alabama.
(5) **Additional requirements.** The requirements of this paragraph are met with respect to any advance refunding of a bond described in paragraph (3) if—
 (A) no advance refundings of such bond would be allowed under this title on or after August 28, 2005,
 (B) the advance refunding bond is the only other outstanding bond with respect to the refunded bond, and
 (C) the requirements of section 148 are met with respect to all bonds issued under this subsection.
(6) **Use of proceeds requirement.** This subsection shall not apply to any advance refunding of a bond which is issued as part of an issue if any portion of the proceeds of such issue (or any prior issue) was (or is to be) used to provide any property described in section 144(c)(6)(B).

(c) **Low-income housing credit.**
(1) **Additional housing credit dollar amount for Gulf Opportunity Zone.**
 (A) In general. For purposes of section 42, in the case of calendar years 2006, 2007, and 2008, the State housing credit ceiling of each State, any portion of which is located in the Gulf Opportunity Zone, shall be increased by the lesser of—
  (i) the aggregate housing credit dollar amount allocated by the State housing credit agency of such State to buildings located in the Gulf Opportunity Zone for such calendar year, or
  (ii) the Gulf Opportunity housing amount for such State for such calendar year.
 (B) Gulf Opportunity housing amount. For purposes of subparagraph (A), the term "Gulf Opportunity housing amount" means, for any calendar year, the amount equal to the product of $18.00 multiplied by the portion of the State population which is in the Gulf Opportunity Zone (as determined on the basis of the most recent census estimate of resident population released by the Bureau of Census before August 28, 2005).
 (C) Allocations treated as made first from additional allocation amount for purposes of determining carryover. For purposes of determining the unused State housing credit ceiling under section 42(h)(3)(C) for any calendar year, any increase in the State housing credit ceiling under subparagraph (A) shall be treated as an amount described in clause (ii) of such section.
(2) **Additional housing credit dollar amount for Texas and Florida.** For purposes of section 42, in the case of calendar year 2006, the State housing credit ceiling of Texas and Florida shall each be increased by $3,500,000.
(3) **Difficult development area.**
 (A) In general. For purposes of section 42, in the case of property placed in service during the period beginning on January 1, 2006, and ending on December 31, 2010 the Gulf Opportunity Zone, the Rita GO Zone, and the Wilma GO Zone—
  (i) shall be treated as difficult development areas designated under subclause (I) of section 42(d)(5)(C)(iii), and
  (ii) shall not be taken into account for purposes of applying the limitation under subclause (II) of such section.
 (B) Application. Subparagraph (A) shall apply only to—
  (i) housing credit dollar amounts allocated during the period beginning on January 1, 2006, and ending on December 31, 2008, and
  (ii) buildings placed in service during the period described in subparagraph (A) to the extent that paragraph (1) of section 42(h) does not apply to any building by reason of paragraph (4) thereof, but only with respect to bonds issued after December 31, 2005.
(4) **Special rule for applying income tests.** In the case of property placed in service—
 (A) during 2006, 2007, or 2008,
 (B) in the Gulf Opportunity Zone, and
 (C) in a nonmetropolitan area (as defined in section 42(d)(5)(C)(iv)(IV)),
section 42 shall be applied by substituting "national nonmetropolitan median gross income (determined under rules similar to the rules of section 142(d)(2)(B))" for "area median gross income" in subparagraphs (A) and (B) of section 42(g)(1).

(5) Time for making low-income housing credit allocations. Section 42(h)(1)(B) shall not apply to an allocation of housing credit dollar amount to a building located in the Gulf Opportunity Zone, the Rita GO Zone, or the Wilma GO Zone, if such allocation is made in 2006, 2007, or 2008, and such building is placed in service before January 1, 2012.

(6) Community development block grants not taken into account in determining if buildings are federally subsidized. For purpose of applying section 42(i)(2)(D) to any building which is placed in service in the Gulf Opportunity Zone, the Rita GO Zone, or the Wilma GO Zone during the period beginning on January 1, 2006, and ending on December 31, 2010, a loan shall not be treated as a below market Federal loan solely by reason of any assistance provided under section 106, 107, or 108 of the Housing and Community Development Act of 1974 by reason of section 122 of such Act or any provision of the Department of Defense Appropriations Act, 2006, or the Emergency Supplemental Appropriations Act for Defense, the Global War on Terror, and Hurricane Recovery, 2006.

(7) Definitions. Any term used in this subsection which is also used in section 42 shall have the same meaning as when used in such section.

(d) Special allowance for certain property acquired on or after August 28, 2005.

(1) Additional allowance. In the case of any qualified Gulf Opportunity Zone property—

(A) the depreciation deduction provided by section 167(a) for the taxable year in which such property is placed in service shall include an allowance equal to 50 percent of the adjusted basis of such property, and

(B) the adjusted basis of the qualified Gulf Opportunity Zone property shall be reduced by the amount of such deduction before computing the amount otherwise allowable as a depreciation deduction under this chapter for such taxable year and any subsequent taxable year.

(2) Qualified Gulf Opportunity Zone property. For purposes of this subsection—

(A) In general. The term "qualified Gulf Opportunity Zone property" means property—

(i) (I) which is described in section 168(k)(2)(A)(i), or

(II) which is nonresidential real property or residential rental property,

(ii) substantially all of the use of which is in the Gulf Opportunity Zone and is in the active conduct of a trade or business by the taxpayer in such Zone,

(iii) the original use of which in the Gulf Opportunity Zone commences with the taxpayer on or after August 28, 2005,

(iv) which is acquired by the taxpayer by purchase (as defined in section 179(d)) on or after August 28, 2005, but only if no written binding contract for the acquisition was in effect before August 28, 2005, and

(v) which is placed in service by the taxpayer on or before December 31, 2007 (December 31, 2008, in the case of nonresidential real property and residential rental property).

(B) Exceptions.

(i) Alternative depreciation property. Such term shall not include any property described in section 168(k)(2)(D)(i).

(ii) Tax-exempt bond-financed property. Such term shall not include any property any portion of which is financed with the proceeds of any obligation the interest on which is exempt from tax under section 103.

(iii) Qualified revitalization buildings. Such term shall not include any qualified revitalization building with respect to which the taxpayer has elected the application of paragraph (1) or (2) of section 1400I(a).

(iv) Election out. If a taxpayer makes an election under this clause with respect to any class of property for any taxable year, this subsection shall not apply to all property in such class placed in service during such taxable year.

(3) Special rules. For purposes of this subsection, rules similar to the rules of subparagraph (E) of section 168(k)(2) shall apply, except that such subparagraph shall be applied—

(A) by substituting "August 27, 2005" for "December 31, 2007" each place it appears therein,

(B) without regard to "and before January 1, 2013" in clause (i) thereof, and

(C) by substituting "qualified Gulf Opportunity Zone property" for "qualified property" in clause (iv) thereof.

(4) Allowance against alternative minimum tax. For purposes of this subsection, rules similar to the rules of section 168(k)(2)(G) shall apply.

(5) Recapture. For purposes of this subsection, rules similar to the rules under section 179(d)(10) shall apply with respect to any qualified Gulf Opportunity Zone property which ceases to be qualified Gulf Opportunity Zone property.

(6) Extension for certain property.

(A) In general. In the case of any specified Gulf Opportunity Zone extension property, paragraph (2)(A) shall be applied without regard to clause (v) thereof.

(B) Specified Gulf Opportunity Zone extension property. For purposes of this paragraph, the term "specified Gulf Opportunity Zone extension property" means property—

(i) substantially all of the use of which is in one or more specified portions of the GO Zone, and

(ii) which is—

(I) nonresidential real property or residential rental property which is placed in service by the taxpayer on or before December 31, 2011, or

(II) in the case of a taxpayer who places a building described in subclause (I) in service on or before December 31, 2011, property described in section 168(k)(2)(A)(i) if substantially all of the use of such property is in such building and such property is placed in service by the taxpayer not later than 90 days after such building is placed in service.

(C) Specified portions of the GO Zone. For purposes of this paragraph, the term "specified portions of the GO Zone" means those portions of the GO Zone which are in any county or parish which is identified by the Secretary as being a county or parish in which hurricanes occurring during 2005 damaged (in the aggregate) more than 60 percent of the housing units in such county or parish which were occupied (determined according to the 2000 Census).

(D) Only pre-January 1, 2012, basis of real property eligible for additional allowance. In the case of property which is qualified Gulf Opportunity Zone property solely by reason of subparagraph (B)(ii)(I), paragraph (1) shall apply only to the extent of the adjusted basis thereof attributable to manufacture, construction, or production before January 1, 2012.

(E) Exception for bonus depreciation property under section 168(k). The term "specified Gulf Opportunity

Zone extension property" shall not include any property to which section 168(k) applies.

(e) Increase in expensing under section 179.
  (1) In general. For purposes of section 179—
    (A) the dollar amount in effect under section 179(b)(1) for the taxable year shall be increased by the lesser of—
      (i) $100,000, or
      (ii) the cost of qualified section 179 Gulf Opportunity Zone property placed in service during the taxable year, and
    (B) the dollar amount in effect under section 179(b)(2) for the taxable year shall be increased by the lesser of—
      (i) $600,000, or
      (ii) the cost of qualified section 179 Gulf Opportunity Zone property placed in service during the taxable year.
  (2) Qualified section 179 Gulf Opportunity Zone property. For purposes of this subsection—
    (A) In general. The term "qualified section 179 Gulf Opportunity Zone property" means section 179 property (as defined in section 179(d)) which is qualified Gulf Opportunity Zone property (as defined in subsection (d)(2) without regard to subsection (d)(6)).
    (B) Extension for certain property. In the case of property substantially all of the use of which is in one or more specified portions of the GO Zone (as defined by subsection (d)(6)), such term shall include section 179 property (as so defined) which is described in subsection (d)(2), determined—
      (i) without regard to subsection (d)(6), and
      (ii) by substituting "2008" for "2007" in subparagraph (A)(v) thereof.
  (3) Coordination with empowerment zones and renewal communities. For purposes of sections 1397A and 1400J, qualified section 179 Gulf Opportunity Zone property shall not be treated as qualified zone property or qualified renewal property, unless the taxpayer elects not to take such qualified section 179 Gulf Opportunity Zone property into account for purposes of this subsection.
  (4) Recapture. For purposes of this subsection, rules similar to the rules under section 179(d)(10) shall apply with respect to any qualified section 179 Gulf Opportunity Zone property which ceases to be qualified section 179 Gulf Opportunity Zone property.

(f) Expensing for certain demolition and clean-up costs.
  (1) In general. A taxpayer may elect to treat 50 percent of any qualified Gulf Opportunity Zone clean-up cost as an expense which is not chargeable to capital account. Any cost so treated shall be allowed as a deduction for the taxable year in which such cost is paid or incurred.
  (2) Qualified Gulf Opportunity Zone clean-up cost. For purposes of this subsection, the term "qualified Gulf Opportunity Zone clean-up cost" means any amount paid or incurred during the period beginning on August 28, 2005, and ending on December 31, 2007, for the removal of debris from, or the demolition of structures on, real property which is located in the Gulf Opportunity Zone and which is—
    (A) held by the taxpayer for use in a trade or business or for the production of income, or
    (B) property described in section 1221(a)(1) in the hands of the taxpayer.
  For purposes of the preceding sentence, amounts paid or incurred shall be taken into account only to the extent that such amount would (but for paragraph (1)) be chargeable to capital account.

(g) Extension of expensing for environmental remediation costs.
With respect to any qualified environmental remediation expenditure (as defined in section 198(b)) paid or incurred on or after August 28, 2005, in connection with a qualified contaminated site located in the Gulf Opportunity Zone, section 198 (relating to expensing of environmental remediation costs) shall be applied—
  (1) in the case of expenditures paid or incurred on or after August 28, 2005, and before January 1, 2008, by substituting "December 31, 2007" for the date contained in section 198(h), and
  (2) except as provided in section 198(d)(2), by treating petroleum products (as defined in section 4612(a)(3)) as a hazardous substance.

(h) Increase in rehabilitation credit.
In the case of qualified rehabilitation expenditures (as defined in section 47(c)) paid or incurred during the period beginning on August 28, 2005, and ending on December 31, 2011, with respect to any qualified rehabilitated building or certified historic structure (as defined in section 47(c)) located in the Gulf Opportunity Zone, subsection (a) of section 47 (relating to rehabilitation credit) shall be applied—
  (1) by substituting "13 percent" for "10 percent" in paragraph (1) thereof, and
  (2) by substituting "26 percent" for "20 percent" in paragraph (2) thereof.

(i) Special rules for small timber producers.
  (1) Increased expensing for qualified timber property. In the case of qualified timber property any portion of which is located in the Gulf Opportunity Zone, in that portion of the Rita GO Zone which is not part of the Gulf Opportunity Zone, or in the Wilma GO Zone, the limitation under subparagraph (B) of section 194(b)(1) shall be increased by the lesser of—
    (A) the limitation which would (but for this subsection) apply under such subparagraph, or
    (B) the amount of reforestation expenditures (as defined in section 194(c)(3)) paid or incurred by the taxpayer with respect to such qualified timber property during the specified portion of the taxable year.
  (2) 5 year NOL carryback of certain timber losses. For purposes of determining any farming loss under section 172(i), income and deductions which are allocable to the specified portion of the taxable year and which are attributable to qualified timber property any portion of which is located in the Gulf Opportunity Zone, in that portion of the Rita GO Zone which is not part of the Gulf Opportunity Zone, or in the Wilma GO Zone shall be treated as attributable to farming businesses.
  (3) Rules not applicable to certain entities. Paragraphs (1) and (2) shall not apply to any taxpayer which—
    (A) is a corporation the stock of which is publicly traded on an established securities market, or
    (B) is a real estate investment trust.
  (4) Rules not applicable to large timber producers.
    (A) Expensing. Paragraph (1) shall not apply to any taxpayer if such taxpayer holds more than 500 acres of qualified timber property at any time during the taxable year.
    (B) NOL carryback. Paragraph (2) shall not apply with respect to any qualified timber property unless—
      (i) such property was held by the taxpayer—

(I) on August 28, 2005, in the case of qualified timber property any portion of which is located in the Gulf Opportunity Zone,

(II) on September 23, 2005, in the case of qualified timber property (other than property described in subclause (I)) any portion of which is located in that portion of the Rita GO Zone which is not part of the Gulf Opportunity Zone, or

(III) on October 23, 2005, in the case of qualified timber property (other than property described in subclause (I) or (II)) any portion of which is located in the Wilma GO Zone, and

(ii) such taxpayer held not more than 500 acres of qualified timber property on such date.

(5) Definitions. For purposes of this subsection—

(A) Specified portion.

(i) In general. The term "specified portion" means—

(I) in the case of qualified timber property any portion of which is located in the Gulf Opportunity Zone, that portion of the taxable year which is on or after August 28, 2005, and before the termination date,

(II) in the case of qualified timber property (other than property described in clause (i)) any portion of which is located in the Rita GO Zone, that portion of the taxable year which is on or after September 23, 2005, and before the termination date, or

(III) in the case of qualified timber property (other than property described in clause (i) or (ii)) any portion of which is located in the Wilma GO Zone, that portion of the taxable year which is on or after October 23, 2005, and before the termination date.

(ii) Termination date. The term "termination date" means—

(I) for purposes of paragraph (1), January 1, 2008, and

(II) for purposes of paragraph (2), January 1, 2007.

(B) Qualified timber property. The term "qualified timber property" has the meaning given such term in section 194(c)(1).

(j) Special rule for Gulf Opportunity Zone public utility casualty losses.

(1) In general. The amount described in section 172(f)(1)(A) for any taxable year shall be increased by the Gulf Opportunity Zone public utility casualty loss for such taxable year.

(2) Gulf Opportunity Zone public utility casualty loss. For purposes of this subsection, the term "Gulf Opportunity Zone public utility casualty loss" means any casualty loss of public utility property (as defined in section 168(i)(10)) located in the Gulf Opportunity Zone if—

(A) such loss is allowed as a deduction under section 165 for the taxable year,

(B) such loss is by reason of Hurricane Katrina, and

(C) the taxpayer elects the application of this subsection with respect to such loss.

(3) Reduction for gains from involuntary conversion. The amount of any Gulf Opportunity Zone public utility casualty loss which would (but for this paragraph) be taken into account under paragraph (1) for any taxable year shall be reduced by the amount of any gain recognized by the taxpayer for such year from the involuntary conversion by reason of Hurricane Katrina of public utility property (as so defined) located in the Gulf Opportunity Zone.

(4) Coordination with general disaster loss rules. Subsection (k) and section 165(i) shall not apply to any Gulf Opportunity Zone public utility casualty loss to the extent such loss is taken into account under paragraph (1).

(5) Election. Any election under paragraph (2)(C) shall be made in such manner as may be prescribed by the Secretary and shall be made by the due date (including extensions of time) for filing the taxpayer's return for the taxable year of the loss. Such election, once made for any taxable year, shall be irrevocable for such taxable year.

(k) Treatment of net operating losses attributable to Gulf Opportunity Zone losses.

(1) In general. If a portion of any net operating loss of the taxpayer for any taxable year is a qualified Gulf Opportunity Zone loss, the following rules shall apply:

(A) Extension of carryback period. Section 172(b)(1) shall be applied with respect to such portion—

(i) by substituting "5 taxable years" for "2 taxable years" in subparagraph (A)(i), and

(ii) by not taking such portion into account in determining any eligible loss of the taxpayer under subparagraph (F) thereof for the taxable year.

(B) Suspension of 90 percent AMT limitation. Section 56(d)(1) shall be applied by increasing the amount determined under subparagraph (A)(ii)(I) thereof by the sum of the carrybacks and carryovers of any net operating loss attributable to such portion.

(2) Qualified Gulf Opportunity Zone loss. For purposes of paragraph (1), the term "qualified Gulf Opportunity Zone loss" means the lesser of—

(A) the excess of—

(i) the net operating loss for such taxable year, over

(ii) the specified liability loss for such taxable year to which a 10-year carryback applies under section 172(b)(1)(C), or

(B) the aggregate amount of the following deductions to the extent taken into account in computing the net operating loss for such taxable year:

(i) Any deduction for any qualified Gulf Opportunity Zone casualty loss.

(ii) Any deduction for moving expenses paid or incurred after August 27, 2005, and before January 1, 2008, and allowable under this chapter to any taxpayer in connection with the employment of any individual—

(I) whose principal place of abode was located in the Gulf Opportunity Zone before August 28, 2005,

(II) who was unable to remain in such abode as the result of Hurricane Katrina, and

(III) whose principal place of employment with the taxpayer after such expense is located in the Gulf Opportunity Zone.

For purposes of this clause, the term "moving expenses" has the meaning given such term by section 217(b), except that the taxpayer's former residence and new residence may be the same residence if the initial vacating of the residence was as the result of Hurricane Katrina.

(iii) Any deduction allowable under this chapter for expenses paid or incurred after August 27, 2005, and before January 1, 2008, to temporarily house any employee of the taxpayer whose principal place of employment is in the Gulf Opportunity Zone.

(iv) Any deduction for depreciation (or amortization in lieu of depreciation) allowable under this chapter with respect to any qualified Gulf Opportunity Zone property (as defined in subsection (d)(2), but without regard to subparagraph (B)(iv) thereof)) for the taxable year such property is placed in service.

(v) Any deduction allowable under this chapter for repair expenses (including expenses for removal of debris) paid or incurred after August 27, 2005, and before January 1, 2008, with respect to any damage attributable to Hurricane Katrina and in connection with property which is located in the Gulf Opportunity Zone.

(3) Qualified Gulf Opportunity Zone casualty loss.

(A) In general. For purposes of paragraph (2)(B)(i), the term "qualified Gulf Opportunity Zone casualty loss" means any uncompensated section 1231 loss (as defined in section 1231(a)(3)(B)) of property located in the Gulf Opportunity Zone if—

(i) such loss is allowed as a deduction under section 165 for the taxable year, and

(ii) such loss is by reason of Hurricane Katrina.

(B) Reduction for gains from involuntary conversion. The amount of qualified Gulf Opportunity Zone casualty loss which would (but for this subparagraph) be taken into account under subparagraph (A) for any taxable year shall be reduced by the amount of any gain recognized by the taxpayer for such year from the involuntary conversion by reason of Hurricane Katrina of property located in the Gulf Opportunity Zone.

(C) Coordination with general disaster loss rules. Section 165(i) shall not apply to any qualified Gulf Opportunity Zone casualty loss to the extent such loss is taken into account under this subsection.

(4) Special rules. For purposes of paragraph (1), rules similar to the rules of paragraphs (2) and (3) of section 172(i) shall apply with respect to such portion.

(l) Credit to holders of Gulf tax credit bonds.

(1) Allowance of credit. If a taxpayer holds a Gulf tax credit bond on one or more credit allowance dates of the bond occurring during any taxable year, there shall be allowed as a credit against the tax imposed by this chapter for the taxable year an amount equal to the sum of the credits determined under paragraph (2) with respect to such dates.

(2) Amount of credit.

(A) In general. The amount of the credit determined under this paragraph with respect to any credit allowance date for a Gulf tax credit bond is 25 percent of the annual credit determined with respect to such bond.

(B) Annual credit. The annual credit determined with respect to any Gulf tax credit bond is the product of—

(i) the credit rate determined by the Secretary under subparagraph (C) for the day on which such bond was sold, multiplied by

(ii) the outstanding face amount of the bond.

(C) Determination. For purposes of subparagraph (B), with respect to any Gulf tax credit bond, the Secretary shall determine daily or cause to be determined daily a credit rate which shall apply to the first day on which there is a binding, written contract for the sale or exchange of the bond. The credit rate for any day is the credit rate which the Secretary or the Secretary's designee estimates will permit the issuance of Gulf tax credit bonds with a specified maturity or redemption date without discount and without interest cost to the issuer.

(D) Credit allowance date. For purposes of this subsection, the term "credit allowance date" means March 15, June 15, September 15, and December 15. Such term also includes the last day on which the bond is outstanding.

(E) Special rule for issuance and redemption. In the case of a bond which is issued during the 3-month period ending on a credit allowance date, the amount of the credit determined under this paragraph with respect to such credit allowance date shall be a ratable portion of the credit otherwise determined based on the portion of the 3-month period during which the bond is outstanding. A similar rule shall apply when the bond is redeemed or matures.

(3) Limitation based on amount of tax. The credit allowed under paragraph (1) for any taxable year shall not exceed the excess of—

(A) the sum of the regular tax liability (as defined in section 26(b)) plus the tax imposed by section 55, over

(B) the sum of the credits allowable under part IV of subchapter A (other than subparts C I, and J and this subsection).

(4) Gulf tax credit bond. For purposes of this subsection—

(A) In general. The term "Gulf tax credit bond" means any bond issued as part of an issue if—

(i) the bond is issued by the State of Alabama, Louisiana, or Mississippi,

(ii) 95 percent or more of the proceeds of such issue are to be used to—

(I) pay principal, interest, or premiums on qualified bonds issued by such State or any political subdivision of such State, or

(II) make a loan to any political subdivision of such State to pay principal, interest, or premiums on qualified bonds issued by such political subdivision,

(iii) the Governor of such State designates such bond for purposes of this subsection,

(iv) the bond is a general obligation of such State and is in registered form (within the meaning of section 149(a)),

(v) the maturity of such bond does not exceed 2 years, and

(vi) the bond is issued after December 31, 2005, and before January 1, 2007.

(B) State matching requirement. A bond shall not be treated as a Gulf tax credit bond unless—

(i) the issuer of such bond pledges as of the date of the issuance of the issue an amount equal to the face amount of such bond to be used for payments described in subclause (I) of subparagraph (A)(ii), or loans described in subclause (II) of such subparagraph, as the case may be, with respect to the issue of which such bond is a part, and

(ii) any such payment or loan is made in equal amounts from the proceeds of such issue and from the amount pledged under clause (i).

The requirement of clause (ii) shall be treated as met with respect to any such payment or loan made during the 1-year period beginning on the date of the issuance (or any successor 1-year period) if such requirement is met when applied with respect to the aggregate amount of such payments and loans made during such period.

(C) Aggregate limit on bond designations. The maximum aggregate face amount of bonds which may be designated under this subsection by the Governor of a State shall not exceed—

(i) $200,000,000 in the case of the State of Louisiana,
(ii) $100,000,000 in the case of the State of Mississippi, and
(iii) $50,000,000 in the case of the State of Alabama.
(D) Special rules relating to arbitrage. A bond which is part of an issue shall not be treated as a Gulf tax credit bond unless, with respect to the issue of which the bond is a part, the issuer satisfies the arbitrage requirements of section 148 with respect to proceeds of the issue and any loans made with such proceeds.

(5) **Qualified bond.** For purposes of this subsection—
(A) In general. The term "qualified bond" means any obligation of a State or political subdivision thereof which was outstanding on August 28, 2005.
(B) Exception for private activity bonds. Such term shall not include any private activity bond.
(C) Exception for advance refundings. Such term shall not include any bond with respect to which there is any outstanding refunded or refunding bond during the period in which a Gulf tax credit bond is outstanding with respect to such bond.
(D) Use of proceeds requirement. Such term shall not include any bond issued as part of an issue if any portion of the proceeds of such issue was (or is to be) used to provide any property described in section 144(c)(6)(B).

(6) **Credit included in gross income.** Gross income includes the amount of the credit allowed to the taxpayer under this subsection (determined without regard to paragraph (3)) and the amount so included shall be treated as interest income.

(7) **Other definitions and special rules.** For purposes of this subsection—
(A) Bond. The term "bond" includes any obligation.
(B) Partnership; S corporation; and other pass-thru entities.
(i) In general. Under regulations prescribed by the Secretary, in the case of a partnership, trust, S corporation, or other pass-thru entity, rules similar to the rules of section 41(g) shall apply with respect to the credit allowable under paragraph (1).
(ii) No basis adjustment. In the case of a bond held by a partnership or an S corporation, rules similar to the rules under section 1397E(l) shall apply.
(C) Bonds held by regulated investment companies. If any Gulf tax credit bond is held by a regulated investment company, the credit determined under paragraph (1) shall be allowed to shareholders of such company under procedures prescribed by the Secretary.
(D) Reporting. Issuers of Gulf tax credit bonds shall submit reports similar to the reports required under section 149(e).
(E) Credit treated as nonrefundable bondholder credit. For purposes of this title, the credit allowed by this subsection shall be treated as a credit allowable under subpart H of part IV of subchapter A of this chapter.

(m) **Application of new markets tax credit to investments in community development entities serving Gulf Opportunity Zone.**
For purposes of section 45D—
(1) a qualified community development entity shall be eligible for an allocation under subsection (f)(2) thereof of the increase in the new markets tax credit limitation described in paragraph (2) only if a significant mission of such entity is the recovery and redevelopment of the Gulf Opportunity Zone,

(2) the new markets tax credit limitation otherwise determined under subsection (f)(1) thereof shall be increased by an amount equal to—
(A) $300,000,000 for 2005 and 2006, to be allocated among qualified community development entities to make qualified low-income community investments within the Gulf Opportunity Zone, and
(B) $400,000,000 for 2007, to be so allocated, and
(3) subsection (f)(3) thereof shall be applied separately with respect to the amount of the increase under paragraph (2).

(n) **Treatment of representations regarding income eligibility for purposes of qualified residential rental project requirements.**
For purposes of determining if any residential rental project meets the requirements of section 142(d)(1) and if any certification with respect to such project meets the requirements under section 142(d)(7), the operator of the project may rely on the representations of any individual applying for tenancy in such project that such individual's income will not exceed the applicable income limits of section 142(d)(1) upon commencement of the individual's tenancy if such tenancy begins during the 6-month period beginning on and after the date such individual was displaced by reason of Hurricane Katrina.

(o) **Treatment of public utility property disaster losses.**
(1) **In general.** Upon the election of the taxpayer, in the case of any eligible public utility property loss—
(A) section 165(i) shall be applied by substituting "the fifth taxable year immediately preceding" for "the taxable year immediately preceding",
(B) an application for a tentative carryback adjustment of the tax for any prior taxable year affected by the application of subparagraph (A) may be made under section 6411, and
(C) section 6611 shall not apply to any overpayment attributable to such loss.

(2) **Eligible public utility property loss.** For purposes of this subsection—
(A) In general. The term "eligible public utility property loss" means any loss with respect to public utility property located in the Gulf Opportunity Zone and attributable to Hurricane Katrina.
(B) Public utility property. The term "public utility property" has the meaning given such term by section 168(i)(10) without regard to the matter following subparagraph (D) thereof.

(3) **Waiver of limitations.** If refund or credit of any overpayment of tax resulting from the application of paragraph (1) is prevented at any time before the close of the 1-year period beginning on the date of the enactment of this section by the operation of any law or rule of law (including res judicata), such refund or credit may nevertheless be made or allowed if claim therefor is filed before the close of such period.

(p) **Tax benefits not available with respect to certain property.**
(1) **Qualified Gulf Opportunity Zone property.** For purposes of subsections (d), (e), and (k)(2)(B)(iv), the term "qualified Gulf Opportunity Zone property" shall not include any property described in paragraph (3).
(2) **Qualified Gulf Opportunity Zone casualty losses.** For purposes of subsection (k)(2)(B)(i), the term "qualified Gulf Opportunity Zone casualty loss" shall not include any loss with respect to any property described in paragraph (3).

(3) Property described.

(A) In general. For purposes of this subsection, property is described in this paragraph if such property is—

(i) any property used in connection with any private or commercial golf course, country club, massage parlor, hot tub facility, suntan facility, or any store the principal business of which is the sale of alcoholic beverages for consumption off premises, or

(ii) any gambling or animal racing property.

(B) Gambling or animal racing property. For purposes of subparagraph (A)(ii)—

(i) In general. The term "gambling or animal racing property" means—

(I) any equipment, furniture, software, or other property used directly in connection with gambling, the racing of animals, or the on-site viewing of such racing, and

(II) the portion of any real property (determined by square footage) which is dedicated to gambling, the racing of animals, or the on-site viewing of such racing.

(ii) De minimis portion. Clause (i)(II) shall not apply to any real property if the portion so dedicated is less than 100 square feet.

In 2010, P.L. 111-312, Sec. 401(d)(7), substituted "January 1, 2013" for "January 1, 2011" in subpara. (d)(3)(B), effective for property placed in service after 12/31/2010, in tax. yrs. ending after such date.

—P.L. 111-312, Sec. 762(a), substituted "December 31, 2011" for "December 31, 2009" in subsec. (h), effective for amounts paid or incurred after 12/31/2009.

—P.L. 111-312, Sec. 763, substituted "January 1, 2012" for "January 1, 2011" in para. (c)(5) . . . Sec. 764(a), substituted "January 1, 2012" for "January 1, 2011" in subparas. (a)(2)(D) and (a)(7)(C), effective 12/17/2010.

—P.L. 111-312, Sec. 764(b), substituted "January 1, 2012" for "January 1, 2011" in Sec. 702(d)(1) and Sec. 704(a), P.L. 110-343 [see below], effective as if included in the enactment of P.L. 110-343, 10/3/2008.

—P.L. 111-312, Sec. 765(a)(1), substituted "December 31, 2011" for "December 31, 2010" in subcls. (d)(6)(B)(ii)(I) and (d)(6)(B)(ii)(II) . . . Sec. 765(a)(2), substituted "January 1, 2012" for "January 1, 2010" in the heading and text of subpara. (d)(6)(D), effective for property placed in service after 12/31/2009.

—P.L. 111-240, Sec. 2022(b)(7), substituted "January 1, 2011" for "January 1, 2010" in subpara. (d)(3)(B), effective for property placed in service after 12/31/2009, in tax. yrs. ending after such date.

In 2009, P.L. 111-5, Sec. 1201(a)(2)(E), substituted "January 1, 2010" for "January 1, 2009" in subpara. (d)(3)(B), effective for property placed in service after 12/31/2008, in tax. yrs. ending after such date.

—P.L. 111-5, Sec. 1531(c)(3), substituted ", I, and J" for "and I" in subpara. (l)(3)(B), effective for obligations issued after 2/17/2009.

In 2008, P.L. 110-343, Sec. 320(a)DivC, substituted "December 31, 2009" for "December 31, 2008" in subsec. (h), effective for expenditures paid or incurred after 10/3/2008.

—P.L. 110-343, Sec. 702DivC, of this Act [as amended by Sec. 764(b), P.L. 111-312, see above], applies to this Code Sec. 1400N for the temporary tax relief for areas damaged by 2008 Midwestern storms, tornados, and flooding, as specifically outlined in Sec. 702(a)-(c) Div C, and 702(d)(1)-(7) DivC, 110-343, which read as follows:

"Sec. 702. Temporary tax relief for areas damaged by 2008 Midwestern severe storms, tornados, and flooding.

"(a) In general. Subject to the modifications described in this section, the following provisions of or relating to the Internal Revenue Code of 1986 shall apply to any Midwestern disaster area in addition to the areas to which such provisions otherwise apply:

"(1) GO Zone benefits.

"(A) Section 1400N (relating to tax benefits) other than subsections (b), (d), (e), (i), (j), (m), and (o) thereof.

"(B) Section 1400O (relating to education tax benefits).

"(C) Section 1400P (relating to housing tax benefits).

"(D) Section 1400Q (relating to special rules for use of retirement funds).

"(E) Section 1400R(a) (relating to employee retention credit for employers).

"(F) Section 1400S (relating to additional tax relief) other than subsection (d) thereof.

"(G) Section 1400T (relating to special rules for mortgage revenue bonds).

"(2) Other benefits included in Katrina Emergency Tax Relief Act of 2005. Sections 302, 303, 304, 401, and 405 of the Katrina Emergency Tax Relief Act of 2005.

"(b) Midwestern disaster area.

"(1) In general. For purposes of this section and for applying the substitutions described in subsections (d) and (e), the term 'Midwestern disaster area' means an area—

"(A) with respect to which a major disaster has been declared by the President on or after May 20, 2008, and before August 1, 2008, under section 401 of the Robert T. Stafford Disaster Relief and Emergency Assistance Act by reason of severe storms, tornados, or flooding occurring in any of the States of Arkansas, Illinois, Indiana, Iowa, Kansas, Michigan, Minnesota, Missouri, Nebraska, and Wisconsin, and

"(B) determined by the President to warrant individual or individual and public assistance from the Federal Government under such Act with respect to damages attributable to such severe storms, tornados, or flooding.

"(2) Certain benefits available to areas eligible only for public assistance. For purposes of applying this section to benefits under the following provisions, paragraph (1) shall be applied without regard to subparagraph (B):

"(A) Sections 1400Q, 1400S(b), and 1400S(d) of the Internal Revenue Code of 1986.

"(B) Sections 302, 401, and 405 of the Katrina Emergency Tax Relief Act of 2005.

"(c) References.

"(1) Area. Any reference in such provisions to the Hurricane Katrina disaster area or the Gulf Opportunity Zone shall be treated as a reference to any Midwestern disaster area and any reference to the Hurricane Katrina disaster area or the Gulf Opportunity Zone within a State shall be treated as a reference to all Midwestern disaster areas within the State.

"(2) Items attributable to disaster. Any reference in such provisions to any loss, damage, or other item attributable to Hurricane Katrina shall be treated as a reference to any loss, damage, or other item attributable to the severe storms, tornados, or flooding giving rise to any Presidential declaration described in subsection (b)(1)(A).

"(3) Applicable disaster date. For purposes of applying the substitutions described in subsections (d) and (e), the term 'applicable disaster date' means, with respect to any Midwestern disaster area, the date on which the severe storms, tornados, or flooding giving rise to the Presidential declaration described in subsection (b)(1)(A) occurred.

"(d) Modifications to 1986 Code. The following provisions of the Internal Revenue Code of 1986 shall be applied with the following modifications:

"(1) Tax-exempt bond financing. Section 1400N(a)—

"(A) by substituting 'Qalified Midwestern disaster area bond' for 'qualified Gulf Opportunity Zone Bond' each place it appears, except that in determining whether a bond is a qualified Midwestern disaster area bond—

"(i) paragraph (2)(A)(i) shall be applied by only treating costs as qualified 5 project costs if—

"(I) in the case of a project involving a private business use (as defined in section 141(b)(6)), either the person using the property suffered a loss in a trade or business attributable to the severe storms, tornados, or flooding giving rise to any Presidential declaration described in subsection (b)(1)(A) or is a person designated for purposes of this section by the Governor of the State in which the project is located as a person carrying on a trade or business replacing a trade or business with respect to which another person suffered such a loss, and

"(II) in the case of a project relating to public utility property, the project involves repair or reconstruction of public utility property damaged by such severe storms, tornados, or flooding, and

"(ii) paragraph (2)(A)(ii) shall be applied by treating an issue as a qualified mortgage issue only if 95 percent or more of the net proceeds (as defined in section 150(a)(3)) of the issue are to be used to provide financing for mortgagors who suffered damages to their principal residences attributable to such severe storms, tornados, or flooding.

"(B) by substituting 'any State in which a Midwestern disaster area is located' for 'the State of Alabama, Louisiana, or Mississippi' in paragraph (2)(B),

"(C) by substituting 'designated for purposes of this section (on the basis of providing assistance to areas in the order in which such assistance is most needed)' for 'designated for purposes of this section' in paragraph (2)(C),

"(D) by substituting 'January 1, 2013' for 'January 1, 2012' in paragraph (2)(D),

"(E) in paragraph (3)(A)—

"(i) by substituting '$1,000' for '$2,500', and

"(ii) by substituting 'before the earliest applicable disaster date for Midwestern disaster areas within the State' for 'before August 28, 2005',

"(F) by substituting 'qualified Midwestern disaster area repair or construction' for 'qualified GO Zone repair or construction' each place it appears,

"(G) by substituting 'after the date of the enactment of the Heartland Disaster Tax Relief Act of 2008 and before January 1, 2013' for 'after the date of the enactment of this paragraph and before January 1, 2012' in paragraph (7)(C), and

"(H) by disregarding paragraph (8) thereof.

"(2) Low-income housing credit. Section 1400N(c)—

"(A) only with respect to calendar years 2008, 2009, and 2010,

"(B) by substituting 'Disaster Recovery Assistance housing amount' for 'Gulf Opportunity housing amount' each place it appears,

"(C) in paragraph (1)(B)—

"(i) by substituting '$8.00' for '$18.00', and

"(ii) by substituting 'before the earliest applicable disaster date for Midwestern disaster areas within the State' for 'before August 28, 2005', and

"(D) determined without regard to paragraphs (2), (3), (4), (5), and (6) thereof.

"(3) Expensing for certain demolition and clean-up costs. Section 1400N(f)—

"(A) by substituting 'qualified Disaster Recovery Assistance clean-up cost' for 'qualified Gulf Opportunity Zone clean-up cost' each place it appears,

"(B) by substituting 'beginning on the applicable disaster date and ending on December 31, 2010' for 'beginning on August 28, 2005, and ending on December 31, 2007' in paragraph (2), and

"(C) by treating costs as qualified Disaster Recovery Assistance clean-up costs only if the removal of debris or demolition of any structure was necessary due to damage attributable to the severe storms, tornados, or flooding giving rise to any Presidential declaration described in subsection (b)(1)(A).

"(4) Extension of expensing for environmental remediation costs. Section 1400N(g)—

"(A) by substituting 'the applicable disaster date' for 'August 28, 2005' each place it appears,

"(B) by substituting 'January 1, 2011' for 'January 1, 2008' in paragraph (1),

"(C) by substituting 'December 31, 2010' for 'December 31, 2007' in paragraph (1), and

"(D) by treating a site as a qualified contaminated site only if the release (or threat of release) or disposal of a hazardous substance at the site was attributable to the severe storms, tornados, or flooding giving rise to any Presidential declaration described in subsection (b)(1)(A).

"(5) Increase in rehabilitation credit. Section 1400N(h), as amended by this Act—

"(A) by substituting 'the applicable disaster date' for 'August 28, 2005',

"(B) by substituting 'December 31, 2011' for 'December 31, 2009' in paragraph (1), and

"(C) by only applying such subsection to qualified rehabilitation expenditures with respect to any building or structure which was damaged or destroyed as a result of the severe storms, tornados, or flooding giving rise to any Presidential declaration described in subsection (b)(1)(A).

"(6) Treatment of net operating losses attributable to disaster losses. Section 1400N(k)—

"(A) by substituting 'qualified Disaster Recovery Assistance loss' for 'qualified Gulf Opportunity Zone loss' each place it appears,

"(B) by substituting 'after the day before the applicable disaster date, and before January 1, 2012' for 'after August 27, 2005, and before January 1, 2008' each place it appears,

"(C) by substituting 'the applicable disaster date' for 'August 28, 2005' in paragraph (2)(B)(ii)(I),

"(D) by substituting 'qualified Disaster Recovery Assistance property' for 'qualified Gulf Opportunity Zone property' in paragraph (2)(B)(iv), and

"(E) by substituting 'qualified Disaster Recovery Assistance casualty loss' for 'qualified Gulf Opportunity Zone casualty loss' each place it appears.

"(7) Credit to holders of tax credit bonds. Section 1400N(l)—

"(A) by substituting 'Midwestern tax credit bond' for 'Gulf tax credit bond' each place it appears,

"(B) by substituting 'any State in which a Midwestern disaster area is located or any instrumentality of the State' for 'the State of Alabama, Louisiana, or Mississippi' in paragraph (4)(A)(i),

"(C) by substituting 'after December 31, 2008 and before January 1, 2010' for 'after December 31, 2005, and before January 1, 2007',

"(D) by substituting 'shall not exceed $100,000,000 for any State with an aggregate population located in all Midwestern disaster areas within the State of at least 2,000,000, $50,000,000 for any State with an aggregate population located in all Midwestern disaster areas within the State of at least 1,000,000 but less than 2,000,000, and zero for any other State. The population of a State within any area shall be determined on the basis of the most recent census estimate of resident population released by the Bureau of Census before the earliest applicable disaster date for Midwestern disaster areas within the State.' for 'shall not exceed' and all that follows in paragraph (4)(C), and

"(E) by substituting 'the earliest applicable disaster date for Midwestern disaster areas within the State' for 'August 28, 2005' in paragraph (5)(A)."

* * * * * * * * * * *

—P.L. 110-343, Sec. 704(a)DivC, of this Act [as amended by Sec. 764(b), P.L. 111-312, see above], applies to this Code Sec. 1400N for the temporary tax relief for areas damaged by 2008 Midwestern storms, tornados, and flooding, which read as follows:

"Sec. 704. Temporary tax-exempt bond financing and low-income housing tax relief for areas damaged by Hurricane Ike.

"(a) Tax-Exempt Bond Financing. Section 1400N(a) of the Internal Revenue Code of 1986 shall apply to any Hurricane Ike disaster area in addition to any other area referenced in such section, but with the following modifications:

"(1) By substituting 'qualified Hurricane Ike disaster area bond' for 'qualified Gulf Opportunity Zone Bond' each place it appears, except that in determining whether a bond is a qualified Hurricane Ike disaster area bond—

"(A) paragraph (2)(A)(i) shall be applied by only treating costs as qualified project costs if—

"(i) in the case of a project involving a private business use (as defined in section 141(b)(6)), either the person using the property suffered a loss in a trade or business attributable to Hurricane Ike or is a person designated for purposes of this section by the Governor of the State in which the project is located as a person carrying on a trade or business replacing a trade or business with respect to which another person suffered such a loss, and

"(ii) in the case of a project relating to public utility property, the project involves repair or reconstruction of public utility property damaged by Hurricane Ike, and

"(B) paragraph (2)(A)(ii) shall be applied by treating an issue as a qualified mortgage issue only if 95 percent or more of the net proceeds (as defined in section 150(a)(3)) of the issue are to be used to provide financing for mortgagors who suffered damages to their principal residences attributable to Hurricane Ike.

"(2) By substituting 'any State in which any Hurricane Ike disaster area is located' for 'the State of Alabama, Louisiana, or Mississippi' in paragraph (2)(B).

"(3) By substituting 'designated for purposes of this section (on the basis of providing assistance to areas in the order in which such assistance is most needed)' for 'designated for purposes of this section' in paragraph (2)(C).

"(4) By substituting 'January 1, 2013' for 'January 1, 2012' in paragraph (2)(D).

"(5) By substituting the following for subparagraph (A) of paragraph (3):

"'(A) Aggregate amount designated. The maximum aggregate face amount of bonds which may be designated under this subsection with respect to any State shall not exceed the product of $2,000 multiplied by the portion of the State population which is in—

"(i) in the case of Texas, the counties of Brazoria, Chambers, Galveston, Jefferson, and Orange, and

"(ii) in the case of Louisiana, the parishes of Calcasieu and Cameron,

"(as determined on the basis of the most recent census estimate of resident population released by the Bureau of Census before September 13, 2008).'.

"(6) By substituting 'qualified Hurricane Ike disaster area repair or construction' for 'qualified GO Zone repair or construction' each place it appears.

"(7) By substituting 'after the date of the enactment of the Heartland Disaster Tax Relief Act of 2008 and before January 1, 2013' for 'after the date of the enactment of this paragraph and before January 1, 2012' in paragraph (7)(C).

"(8) By disregarding paragraph (8) thereof.

"(9) By substituting 'any Hurricane Ike disaster area' for 'the Gulf Opportunity Zone' each place it appears."

—P.L. 110-289, Sec. 3082(a), of this Act, provides:

"Sec. 3082. Certain GO Zone Incentives.

"(a) Use of amended income tax returns to take into account receipt of certain hurricane-related casualty loss grants by disallowing previously taken casualty loss deductions.

"(1) In general. Notwithstanding any other provision of the Internal Revenue Code of 1986, if a taxpayer claims a deduction for any taxable year with respect to a casualty loss to a principal residence (within the meaning of section 121 of such Code) resulting from Hurricane Katrina, Hurricane Rita, or Hurricane Wilma and in a subsequent taxable year receives a grant under Public Law 109-148, 109-234, or 110-116 as reimbursement for such loss, such taxpayer may elect to file an amended income tax return for the taxable year in which such deduction was allowed (and for any taxable year to which such deduction is carried) and reduce (but not below zero) the amount of such deduction by the amount of such reimbursement.

"(2) Time of filing amended return. Paragraph (1) shall apply with respect to any grant only if any amended income tax returns with respect to such grant are filed not later than the later of—

"(A) the due date for filing the tax return for the taxable year in which the taxpayer receives such grant, or

"(B) the date which is 1 year after the date of the enactment of this Act.

"(3) Waiver of penalties and interest. Any underpayment of tax resulting from the reduction under paragraph (1) of the amount otherwise allowable as a deduction shall not be subject to any penalty or interest under such Code if such tax is paid not later than 1 year after the filing of the amended return to which such reduction relates."

—P.L. 110-289, Sec. 3082(b)(1), amended subpara. (d)(3)(B), effective for property placed in service after 12/31/2007.

Prior to amendment, subpara. (d)(3)(B) read as follows:

"(B) by substituting 'January 1, 2008' for 'January 1, 2009' in clause (i) thereof, and"

—P.L. 110-289, Sec. 3082(c)(1), added para. (a)(8), effective for tax. yrs. end. on or after 8/28/2005, except as provided in Sec. 101(c)(2) of the Gulf Opportunity Zone Act of 2005 [P.L. 109-135], [see below].

—P.L. 110-246, Sec. 4, Repeals the duplicative enactment and provides effective date provisions of the Act entitled "An Act to provide for the continuation of agricultural programs through fiscal year 2012, and for other purposes" Sec. 4, P.L. 110-246 reads as follows:

"Sec. 4. Repeal of duplicative enactment.

"(a) In General- The Act entitled 'An Act to provide for the continuation of agricultural programs through fiscal year 2012, and for other purposes' (H.R. 2419 of the 110th Congress), and the amendments made by that Act, are repealed, effective on the date of enactment of that Act.

"(b) Effective Date- Except as otherwise provided in this Act, this Act and the amendments made by this Act shall take effect on the earlier of--

"(1) the date of enactment of this Act; or

"(2) the date of the enactment of the Act entitled 'An Act to provide for the continuation of agricultural programs through fiscal year 2012, and for other purposes' (H.R. 2419 of the 110th Congress)."

—P.L. 110-246, Sec. 15316(c)(1), substituted "subparts C and I" for "subpart C" in subpara. (l)(3)(B), effective for obligations issued after 5/22/2008.

—P.L. 110-246, Sec. 15345, applies to this Code Sec. 1400N for the Kansas Disaster Area storms beginning on May 4, 2007 as specifically outlined in Sec. 15345(a)(1)-(6), (b), (c), (d)(1)-(4), P.L. 110-246, which read as follows:

"Sec. 15345. Temporary tax relief for Kiowa County, Kansas and surrounding area.

"(a) In General. Subject to the modifications described in this section, the following provisions of or relating to the Internal Revenue Code of 1986 shall apply to the Kansas disaster area in addition to the areas to which such provisions otherwise apply:

"(1) Section 1400N(d) of such Code (relating to special allowance for certain property).

"(2) Section 1400N(e) of such Code (relating to increase in expensing under section 179).

"(3) Section 1400N(f) of such Code (relating to expensing for certain demolition and clean-up costs).

"(4) Section 1400N(k) of such Code (relating to treatment of net operating losses attributable to storm losses).

"(5) Section 1400N(n) of such Code (relating to treatment of representations regarding income eligibility for purposes of qualified rental project requirements).

"(6) Section 1400N(o) of such Code (relating to treatment of public utility property disaster losses).

* * * * * * * * * * *

Sec. 15345(b), defining Kansas Disaster Area, provides:

"(b) Kansas Disaster Area. For purposes of this section, the term 'Kansas disaster area' means an area with respect to which a major disaster has been declared by the President under section 401 of the Robert T. Stafford Disaster Relief and Emergency Assistance Act (FEMA-1699-DR, as in effect on the date of the enactment of this Act) by reason of severe storms and tornados beginning on May 4, 2007, and determined by the President to warrant individual or individual and public assistance from the Federal Government under such Act with respect to damages attributable to such storms and tornados."

Sec. 15345(c), referring to area or loss provides:

"(c) References to Area or Loss—

"(1) Area. Any reference in such provisions to the Katrina disaster area or the Gulf Opportunity Zone shall be treated as a reference to the Kansas disaster area.

"(2) Loss. Any reference in such provisions to any loss or damage attributable to Hurricane Katrina shall be treated as a reference to any loss or damage attributable to the May 4, 2007, storms and tornados."

Sec. 15345(d)(1) through (4), following, provide detailed information on dates and special allowances for certain property acquired on or after May 5, 2007.

"(d) References to Dates, etc.

"(1) Special allowance for certain property acquired on or after May 5, 2007. Section 1400N(d) of such Code—

"(A) by substituting 'qualified Recovery Assistance property' for 'qualified Gulf Opportunity Zone property' each place it appears,.

"(B) by substituting 'May 5, 2007' for 'August 28, 2005' each place it appears,

"(C) by substituting 'December 31, 2008' for 'December 31, 2007' in paragraph (2)(A)(v),

"(D) by substituting 'December 31, 2009' for 'December 31, 2008' in paragraph (2)(A)(v),

"(E) by substituting 'May 4, 2007' for 'August 27, 2005' in paragraph (3)(A),

"(F) by substituting 'January 1, 2009' for 'January 1, 2008' in paragraph (3)(B), and

"(G) determined without regard to paragraph (6) thereof.

"(2) Increase in expensing under section 179. Section 1400N(e) of such Code, by substituting 'qualified section 179 Recovery Assistance property' for 'qualified section 179 Gulf Opportunity Zone property' each place it appears.

"(3) Expensing for certain demolition and clean-up costs. Section 1400N(f) of such Code—

"(A) by substituting 'qualified Recovery Assistance clean-up cost' for 'qualified Gulf Opportunity Zone clean-up cost' each place it appears, and

"(B) by substituting 'beginning on May 4, 2007, and ending on December 31, 2009' for 'beginning on August 28, 2005, and ending on December 31, 2007' in paragraph (2) thereof.

"(4) Treatment of net operating losses attributable to storm losses. Section 1400N(k) of such Code—

"(A) by substituting 'qualified Recovery Assistance loss' for 'qualified Gulf Opportunity Zone loss' each place it appears,

"(B) by substituting 'after May 3, 2007, and before January 1, 2010' for 'after August 27, 2005, and before January 1, 2008' each place it appears,

"(C) by substituting 'May 4, 2007' for 'August 28, 2005' in paragraph (2)(B)(ii)(I) thereof,

"(D) by substituting 'qualified Recovery Assistance property' for 'qualified Gulf Opportunity Zone property' in paragraph (2)(B)(iv) thereof, and

"(E) by substituting 'qualified Recovery Assistance casualty loss' for 'qualified Gulf Opportunity Zone casualty loss' each place it appears."

—P.L. 110-185, Sec. 103(c)(9)(A), substituted "December 31, 2007" for "September 10, 2001" in subpara. (d)(3)(A) . . . Sec. 103(c)(9)(B), substituted "January 1, 2009" for "January 1, 2005" in subpara. (d)(3)(B) . . . Sec. 103(c)(10), added subpara. (d)(6)(E), effective for property placed in service after December 31, 2007, in tax. yrs. ending after 2/13/2008.

In 2007, P.L. 110-28, Sec. 8221(1), substituted "this subsection—(A) IN GENERAL.—The term" for "this subsection, the term" . . . Sec. 8221(2), added subpara. (e)(2)(B) . . . Sec. 8222(a), redesignated para. (c)(5) as para. (c)(6) and added new para. (c)(5) . . . Sec. 8222(b)(1), substituted "the period beginning on January 1, 2006, and ending on December 31, 2010" for "2006, 2007, or 2008" . . . Sec. 8222(b)(2), substituted "the period described in subparagraph (A)" for "such period" . . . Sec. 8222(c), redesignated para. (c)(6) as para. (c)(7) and added new para. (c)(6) . . . Sec. 8223, added para. (a)(7), effective 5/25/2007

In 2006, P.L. 109-432, Sec. 107(b)(2), substituted "section 1397E(I)" for "section 1397E(i)" in clause (l)(7)(B)(ii) effective for obligations issued after 12/20/2006 for allocations of the national zone academy bond limitation for calendar years after 2005.

—P.L. 109-432, Sec. 120(a), added para. (d)(6) . . . Sec. 120(b), added "without regard to subsection (d)(6)" after "subsection (d)(2)" in para. (e)(2), effective for tax. yrs. end. on or after 8/28/2005, except as provided in Sec. 101(c)(2) of P.L. 109-35, reproduced below.

In 2005, P.L. 109-135, Sec. 101(a), added Code Sec. 1400N, effective for tax. yrs. end. on or after 8/28/2005, except as provided in Sec. 101(c)(2) of this Act, which reads as follows: "(2) Carrybacks. Subsections (i)(2), (j), and (k) of section 1400N of the Internal Revenue Code of 1986 (as added by this section) shall apply to losses arising in such taxable years."

⸻

| • **Caution:** For temporary tax relief provisions for areas damaged by 2008 Midwestern severe storms, tornados, and flooding, see History for this Code Sec.

Sec. 1400O. Education tax benefits.

In the case of an individual who attends an eligible educational institution (as defined in section 25A(f)(2)) located in the Gulf Opportunity Zone for any taxable year beginning during 2005 or 2006—

(1) in applying section 25A, the term "qualified tuition and related expenses" shall include any costs which are qualified higher education expenses (as defined in section 529(e)(3)),

(2) each of the dollar amounts in effect under subparagraphs (A) and (B) of section 25A(b)(1) shall be twice the amount otherwise in effect before the application of this subsection, and

(3) section 25A(c)(1) shall be applied by substituting "40 percent" for "20 percent".

⸻

In 2008, P.L. 110-343, Sec. 702(a)DivC, through Sec. 702(c) Div C, P.L. 110-343, relating to tax relief for areas damaged by 2008 Midwestern storms, reads as follows:

"Sec. 702. Temporary tax relief for areas damaged by 2008 Midwestern severe storms, tornados, and flooding.

"(a) In general. Subject to the modifications described in this section, the following provisions of or relating to the Internal Revenue Code of 1986 shall apply to any Midwestern disaster area in addition to the areas to which such provisions otherwise apply:

"(1) GO Zone benefits.

"(A) Section 1400N (relating to tax benefits) other than subsections (b), (d), (e), (i), (j), (m), and (o) thereof.

"(B) Section 1400O (relating to education tax benefits).

"(C) Section 1400P (relating to housing tax benefits).

"(D) Section 1400Q (relating to special rules for use of retirement funds).

"(E) Section 1400R(a) (relating to employee retention credit for employers).

"(F) Section 1400S (relating to additional tax relief) other than subsection (d) thereof.

"(G) Section 1400T (relating to special rules for mortgage revenue bonds).

"(2) Other benefits included in Katrina Emergency Tax Relief Act of 2005. Sections 302, 303, 304, 401, and 405 of the Katrina Emergency Tax Relief Act of 2005.

"(b) Midwestern disaster area.

"(1) In general. For purposes of this section and for applying the substitutions described in subsections (d) and (e), the term 'Midwestern disaster area' means an area—

"(A) with respect to which a major disaster has been declared by the President on or after May 20, 2008, and before August 1, 2008, under section 401 of the Robert T. Stafford Disaster Relief and Emergency Assistance Act by reason of severe storms, tornados, or flooding occurring in any of the States of Arkansas, Illinois, Indiana, Iowa, Kansas, Michigan, Minnesota, Missouri, Nebraska, and Wisconsin, and

"(B) determined by the President to warrant individual or individual and public assistance from the Federal Government under such Act with respect to damages attributable to such severe storms, tornados, or flooding.

"(2) Certain benefits available to areas eligible only for public assistance. For purposes of applying this section to benefits under the following provisions, paragraph (1) shall be applied without regard to subparagraph (B):

"(A) Sections 1400Q, 1400S(b), and 1400S(d) of the Internal Revenue Code of 1986.

"(B) Sections 302, 401, and 405 of the Katrina Emergency Tax Relief Act of 2005.

"(c) References.

"(1) Area. Any reference in such provisions to the Hurricane Katrina disaster area or the Gulf Opportunity Zone shall be treated as a reference to any Midwestern disaster area and any reference to the Hurricane Katrina disaster area or the Gulf Opportunity Zone within a State shall be treated as a reference to all Midwestern disaster areas within the State.

"(2) Items attributable to disaster. Any reference in such provisions to any loss, damage, or other item attributable to Hurricane Katrina shall be treated as a reference to any loss, damage, or other item attributable to the severe storms, tornados, or flooding giving rise to any Presidential declaration described in subsection (b)(1)(A).

"(3) **Applicable disaster date.** For purposes of applying the substitutions described in subsections (d) and (e), the term 'applicable disaster date' means, with respect to any Midwestern disaster area, the date on which the severe storms, tornados, or flooding giving rise to the Presidential declaration described in subsection (b)(1)(A) occurred.

—P.L. 110-343, Sec. 702(d)(8)DivC, relating to temporary tax relief for areas damaged by 2008 Midwestern severe storms, tornados, and flooding, applies the following modifications to Code Sec. 1400O:

"(d) **Modifications to 1986 Code.** The following provisions of the Internal Revenue Code of 1986 shall be applied with the following modifications:

* * * * * * * * * *

"(8) Education tax benefits. Section 1400O, by substituting '2008 or 2009' for '2005 or 2006'.

* * * * * * * * * *

In 2007, P.L. 110-172, Sec. 11(a)(26), substituted 'under' for 'under of' in para. (2), enacted 12/29/2007.

In 2005, P.L. 109-135, Sec. 102(a), added Code Sec. 1400O, effective 12/21/2005.

• *Caution:* For temporary tax relief for areas damaged by 2008 Midwestern severe storms, tornados, and flooding, see History for this Code Sec.

Sec. 1400P. Housing tax benefits.

(a) Exclusion of employer provided housing for individual affected by Hurricane Katrina.

(1) **In general.** Gross income of a qualified employee shall not include the value of any lodging furnished in-kind to such employee (and such employee's spouse or any of such employee's dependents) by or on behalf of a qualified employer for any month during the taxable year.

(2) **Limitation.** The amount which may be excluded under paragraph (1) for any month for which lodging is furnished during the taxable year shall not exceed $600.

(3) **Treatment of exclusion.** The exclusion under paragraph (1) shall be treated as an exclusion under section 119 (other than for purposes of sections 3121(a)(19) and 3306(b)(14)).

(b) Employer credit for housing employees affected by Hurricane Katrina.

For purposes of section 38, in the case of a qualified employer, the Hurricane Katrina housing credit for any month during the taxable year is an amount equal to 30 percent of any amount which is excludable from the gross income of a qualified employee of such employer under subsection (a) and not otherwise excludable under section 119.

(c) Qualified employee.

For purposes of this section, the term 'qualified employee' means, with respect to any month, an individual—

(1) who had a principal residence (as defined in section 121) in the Gulf Opportunity Zone on August 28, 2005, and

(2) who performs substantially all employment services—

(A) in the Gulf Opportunity Zone, and

(B) for the qualified employer which furnishes lodging to such individual.

(d) Qualified employer.

For purposes of this section, the term 'qualified employer' means any employer with a trade or business located in the Gulf Opportunity Zone.

(e) Certain rules to apply.

For purposes of this subsection, rules similar to the rules of sections 51(i)(1) and 52 shall apply.

(f) Application of section.

This section shall apply to lodging furnished during the period—

(1) beginning on the first day of the first month beginning after the date of the enactment of this section, and

(2) ending on the date which is 6 months after the first day described in paragraph (1).

In 2008, P.L. 110-343, Sec. 702(a)DivC, through Sec. 702(c) Div C, P.L. 110-343, relating to tax relief for areas damaged by 2008 Midwestern severe storms, tornados, and flooding, reads as follows:

"Sec. 702. Temporary tax relief for areas damaged by 2008 Midwestern severe storms, tornados, and flooding.

"(a) **In general.** Subject to the modifications described in this section, the following provisions of or relating to the Internal Revenue Code of 1986 shall apply to any Midwestern disaster area in addition to the areas to which such provisions otherwise apply:

"(1) GO Zone benefits.

"(A) Section 1400N (relating to tax benefits) other than subsections (b), (d), (e), (i), (j), (m), and (o) thereof.

"(B) Section 1400O (relating to education tax benefits).

"(C) Section 1400P (relating to housing tax benefits).

"(D) Section 1400Q (relating to special rules for use of retirement funds).

"(E) Section 1400R(a) (relating to employee retention credit for employers).

"(F) Section 1400S (relating to additional tax relief) other than subsection (d) thereof.

"(G) Section 1400T (relating to special rules for mortgage revenue bonds).

"(2) Other benefits included in Katrina Emergency Tax Relief Act of 2005. Sections 302, 303, 304, 401, and 405 of the Katrina Emergency Tax Relief Act of 2005.

"(b) **Midwestern disaster area.**

"(1) **In general.** For purposes of this section and for applying the substitutions described in subsections (d) and (e), the term 'Midwestern disaster area' means an area—

"(A) with respect to which a major disaster has been declared by the President on or after May 20, 2008, and before August 1, 2008, under section 401 of the Robert T. Stafford Disaster Relief and Emergency Assistance Act by reason of severe storms, tornados, or flooding occurring in any of the States of Arkansas, Illinois, Indiana, Iowa, Kansas, Michigan, Minnesota, Missouri, Nebraska, and Wisconsin, and

"(B) determined by the President to warrant individual or individual and public assistance from the Federal Government under such Act with respect to damages attributable to such severe storms, tornados, or flooding.

"(2) Certain benefits available to areas eligible only for public assistance. For purposes of applying this section to benefits under the following provisions, paragraph (1) shall be applied without regard to subparagraph (B):

"(A) Sections 1400Q, 1400S(b), and 1400S(d) of the Internal Revenue Code of 1986.

"(B) Sections 302, 401, and 405 of the Katrina Emergency Tax Relief Act of 2005.

"(c) **References.**

"(1) **Area.** Any reference in such provisions to the Hurricane Katrina disaster area or the Gulf Opportunity Zone shall be treated as a reference to any Midwestern disaster area and any reference to the Hurricane Katrina disaster area or the Gulf Opportunity Zone within a State shall be treated as a reference to all Midwestern disaster areas within the State.

"(2) **Items attributable to disaster.** Any reference in such provisions to any loss, damage, or other item attributable to Hurricane Katrina shall be treated as a reference to any loss, damage, or other item attributable to the severe storms, tornados, or flooding giving rise to any Presidential declaration described in subsection (b)(1)(A).

"(3) **Applicable disaster date.** For purposes of applying the substitutions described in subsections (d) and (e), the term 'applicable disaster date' means, with respect to any Midwestern disaster area, the date on which the severe storms, tornados, or flooding giving rise to the Presidential declaration described in subsection (b)(1)(A) occurred.

—P.L. 110-343, Sec. 702(d)(9)DivC, relating to temporary tax relief for areas damaged by 2008 Midwestern severe storms, tornados, and flooding, applies the following modifications to Code Sec. 1400P:

"(d) **Modifications to 1986 Code.** The following provisions of the Internal Revenue Code of 1986 shall be applied with the following modifications:

* * * * * * * * * *

"(9) Housing tax benefits. Section 1400P, by substituting 'the applicable disaster date' for 'August 28, 2005' in subsection (c)(1).

In 2005, P.L. 109-135, Sec. 103(a), added Code Sec. 1400P, effective 12/21/2005.

Sec. 1400Q. Special rules for use of retirement funds.

• *Caution:* For temporary tax relief provisions for areas damaged by 2008 Midwestern severe storms, tornados, and flooding and for application of this section to the Kansas Disaster Area storms beginning on May 4, 2007, see History for this Code Sec.

Gulf Opportunity Zone

(a) Tax-favored withdrawals from retirement plans.

(1) **In general.** Section 72(t) shall not apply to any qualified hurricane distribution.

(2) **Aggregate dollar limitation.**

(A) In general. For purposes of this subsection, the aggregate amount of distributions received by an individual which may be treated as qualified hurricane distributions for any taxable year shall not exceed the excess (if any) of—

(i) $100,000, over

(ii) the aggregate amounts treated as qualified hurricane distributions received by such individual for all prior taxable years.

(B) Treatment of plan distributions. If a distribution to an individual would (without regard to subparagraph (A)) be a qualified hurricane distribution, a plan shall not be treated as violating any requirement of this title merely because the plan treats such distribution as a qualified hurricane distribution, unless the aggregate amount of such distributions from all plans maintained by the employer (and any member of any controlled group which includes the employer) to such individual exceeds $100,000.

(C) Controlled group. For purposes of subparagraph (B), the term 'controlled group' means any group treated as a single employer under subsection (b), (c), (m), or (o) of section 414.

(3) **Amount distributed may be repaid.**

(A) In general. Any individual who receives a qualified hurricane distribution may, at any time during the 3-year period beginning on the day after the date on which such distribution was received, make one or more contributions in an aggregate amount not to exceed the amount of such distribution to an eligible retirement plan of which such individual is a beneficiary and to which a rollover contribution of such distribution could be made under section 402(c), 403(a)(4), 403(b)(8), 408(d)(3), or 457(e)(16), as the case may be.

(B) Treatment of repayments of distributions from eligible retirement plans other than IRAs. For purposes of this title, if a contribution is made pursuant to subparagraph (A) with respect to a qualified hurricane distribution from an eligible retirement plan other than an individual retirement plan, then the taxpayer shall, to the extent of the amount of the contribution, be treated as having received the qualified hurricane distribution in an eligible rollover distribution (as defined in section 402(c)(4)) and as having transferred the amount to the eligible retirement plan in a direct trustee to trustee transfer within 60 days of the distribution.

(C) Treatment of repayments for distributions from IRAs. For purposes of this title, if a contribution is made pursuant to subparagraph (A) with respect to a qualified hurricane distribution from an individual retirement plan (as defined by section 7701(a)(37)), then, to the extent of the amount of the contribution, the qualified hurricane distribution shall be treated as a distribution described in section 408(d)(3) and as having been transferred to the eligible retirement plan in a direct trustee to trustee transfer within 60 days of the distribution.

(4) **Definitions.** For purposes of this subsection—

(A) Qualified hurricane distribution. Except as provided in paragraph (2), the term 'qualified hurricane distribution' means—

(i) any distribution from an eligible retirement plan made on or after August 25, 2005, and before January 1, 2007, to an individual whose principal place of abode on August 28, 2005, is located in the Hurricane Katrina disaster area and who has sustained an economic loss by reason of Hurricane Katrina,

(ii) any distribution (which is not described in clause (i)) from an eligible retirement plan made on or after September 23, 2005, and before January 1, 2007, to an individual whose principal place of abode on September 23, 2005, is located in the Hurricane Rita disaster area and who has sustained an economic loss by reason of Hurricane Rita, and

(iii) any distribution (which is not described in clause (i) or (ii)) from an eligible retirement plan made on or after October 23, 2005, and before January 1, 2007, to an individual whose principal place of abode on October 23, 2005, is located in the Hurricane Wilma disaster area and who has sustained an economic loss by reason of Hurricane Wilma.

(B) Eligible retirement plan. The term 'eligible retirement plan' shall have the meaning given such term by section 402(c)(8)(B).

(5) **Income inclusion spread over 3-year period.**

(A) In general. In the case of any qualified hurricane distribution, unless the taxpayer elects not to have this paragraph apply for any taxable year, any amount required to be included in gross income for such taxable year shall be so included ratably over the 3-taxable year period beginning with such taxable year.

(B) Special rule. For purposes of subparagraph (A), rules similar to the rules of subparagraph (E) of section 408A(d)(3) shall apply.

(6) **Special rules.**

(A) Exemption of distributions from trustee to trustee transfer and withholding rules. For purposes of sections 401(a)(31), 402(f), and 3405, qualified hurricane distributions shall not be treated as eligible rollover distributions.

(B) Qualified hurricane distributions treated as meeting plan distribution requirements. For purposes of this title, a qualified hurricane distribution shall be treated as meeting the requirements of sections 401(k)(2)(B)(i), 403(b)(7)(A)(ii), 403(b)(11), and 457(d)(1)(A).

(b) Recontributions of withdrawals for home purchases.

(1) **Recontributions.**

(A) In general. Any individual who received a qualified distribution may, during the applicable period, make one or more contributions in an aggregate amount not to exceed the amount of such qualified distribution to an eligible retirement plan (as defined in section 402(c)(8)(B)) of which such individual is a beneficiary and to which a rollover contribution of such distribution could be made under section 402(c), 403(a)(4), 403(b)(8), or 408(d)(3), as the case may be.

(B) Treatment of repayments. Rules similar to the rules of subparagraphs (B) and (C) of subsection (a)(3) shall apply for purposes of this subsection.

(2) **Qualified distribution.** For purposes of this subsection—

(A) In general. The term 'qualified distribution' means any qualified Katrina distribution, any qualified Rita distribution, and any qualified Wilma distribution.

(B) Qualified Katrina distribution. The term 'qualified Katrina distribution' means any distribution—

(i) described in section 401(k)(2)(B)(i)(IV), 403(b)(7)(A)(ii), (but only to the extent such distribution relates to financial hardship), 403(b)(11)(B), or 72(t)(2)(F),

(ii) received after February 28, 2005, and before August 29, 2005, and

(iii) which was to be used to purchase or construct a principal residence in the Hurricane Katrina disaster area, but which was not so purchased or constructed on account of Hurricane Katrina.

(C) Qualified Rita distribution. The term 'qualified Rita distribution' means any distribution (other than a qualified Katrina distribution)—

(i) described in section 401(k)(2)(B)(i)(IV), 403(b)(7)(A)(ii) (but only to the extent such distribution relates to financial hardship), 403(b)(11)(B), or 72(t)(2)(F),

(ii) received after February 28, 2005, and before September 24, 2005, and

(iii) which was to be used to purchase or construct a principal residence in the Hurricane Rita disaster area, but which was not so purchased or constructed on account of Hurricane Rita.

(D) Qualified Wilma distribution. The term 'qualified Wilma distribution' means any distribution (other than a qualified Katrina distribution or a qualified Rita distribution)—

(i) described in section 401(k)(2)(B)(i)(IV), 403(b)(7)(A)(ii) (but only to the extent such distribution relates to financial hardship), 403(b)(11)(B), or 72(t)(2)(F),

(ii) received after February 28, 2005, and before October 24, 2005, and

(iii) which was to be used to purchase or construct a principal residence in the Hurricane Wilma disaster area, but which was not so purchased or constructed on account of Hurricane Wilma.

(3) Applicable period. For purposes of this subsection, the term 'applicable period' means—

(A) with respect to any qualified Katrina distribution, the period beginning on August 25, 2005, and ending on February 28, 2006,

(B) with respect to any qualified Rita distribution, the period beginning on September 23, 2005, and ending on February 28, 2006, and

(C) with respect to any qualified Wilma distribution, the period beginning on October 23, 2005, and ending on February 28, 2006.

(c) **Loans from qualified plans.**

(1) **Increase in limit on loans not treated as distributions.** In the case of any loan from a qualified employer plan (as defined under section 72(p)(4)) to a qualified individual made during the applicable period—

(A) clause (i) of section 72(p)(2)(A) shall be applied by substituting '$100,000' for '$50,000', and

(B) clause (ii) of such section shall be applied by substituting 'the present value of the nonforfeitable accrued benefit of the employee under the plan' for 'one-half of the present value of the nonforfeitable accrued benefit of the employee under the plan'.

(2) **Delay of repayment.** In the case of a qualified individual with an outstanding loan on or after the qualified beginning date from a qualified employer plan (as defined in section 72(p)(4))—

(A) if the due date pursuant to subparagraph (B) or (C) of section 72(p)(2) for any repayment with respect to such loan occurs during the period beginning on the qualified beginning date and ending on December 31, 2006, such due date shall be delayed for 1 year,

(B) any subsequent repayments with respect to any such loan shall be appropriately adjusted to reflect the delay in the due date under paragraph (1) and any interest accruing during such delay, and

(C) in determining the 5-year period and the term of a loan under subparagraph (B) or (C) of section 72(p)(2), the period described in subparagraph (A) shall be disregarded.

(3) **Qualified individual.** For purposes of this subsection—

(A) In general. The term 'qualified individual' means any qualified Hurricane Katrina individual, any qualified Hurricane Rita individual, and any qualified Hurricane Wilma individual.

(B) Qualified Hurricane Katrina individual. The term 'qualified Hurricane Katrina individual' means an individual whose principal place of abode on August 28, 2005, is located in the Hurricane Katrina disaster area and who has sustained an economic loss by reason of Hurricane Katrina.

(C) Qualified Hurricane Rita individual. The term 'qualified Hurricane Rita individual' means an individual (other than a qualified Hurricane Katrina individual) whose principal place of abode on September 23, 2005, is located in the Hurricane Rita disaster area and who has sustained an economic loss by reason of Hurricane Rita.

(D) Qualified Hurricane Wilma individual. The term 'qualified Hurricane Wilma individual' means an individual (other than a qualified Hurricane Katrina individual or a qualified Hurricane Rita individual) whose principal place of abode on October 23, 2005, is located in the Hurricane Wilma disaster area and who has sustained an economic loss by reason of Hurricane Wilma.

(4) **Applicable period; qualified beginning date.** For purposes of this subsection—

(A) Hurricane Katrina. In the case of any qualified Hurricane Katrina individual—

(i) the applicable period is the period beginning on September 24, 2005, and ending on December 31, 2006, and

(ii) the qualified beginning date is August 25, 2005.

(B) Hurricane Rita. In the case of any qualified Hurricane Rita individual—

(i) the applicable period is the period beginning on the date of the enactment of this subsection and ending on December 31, 2006, and

(ii) the qualified beginning date is September 23, 2005.

(C) Hurricane Wilma. In the case of any qualified Hurricane Wilma individual—

(i) the applicable period is the period beginning on the date of the enactment of this subparagraph and ending on December 31, 2006, and

(ii) the qualified beginning date is October 23, 2005.

(d) **Provisions relating to plan amendments.**

(1) **In general.** If this subsection applies to any amendment to any plan or annuity contract, such plan or contract shall be treated as being operated in accordance with the terms of the plan during the period described in paragraph (2)(B)(i).

(2) **Amendments to which subsection applies.**

(A) In general. This subsection shall apply to any amendment to any plan or annuity contract which is made—

(i) pursuant to any provision of this section, or pursuant to any regulation issued by the Secretary or the

Secretary of Labor under any provision of this section, and

(ii) on or before the last day of the first plan year beginning on or after January 1, 2007, or such later date as the Secretary may prescribe.

In the case of a governmental plan (as defined in section 414(d)), clause (ii) shall be applied by substituting the date which is 2 years after the date otherwise applied under clause (ii).

(B) Conditions. This subsection shall not apply to any amendment unless—

(i) during the period—

(I) beginning on the date that this section or the regulation described in subparagraph (A)(i) takes effect (or in the case of a plan or contract amendment not required by this section or such regulation, the effective date specified by the plan), and

(II) ending on the date described in subparagraph (A)(ii) (or, if earlier, the date the plan or contract amendment is adopted),

the plan or contract is operated as if such plan or contract amendment were in effect; and

(ii) such plan or contract amendment applies retroactively for such period.

In 2008, P.L. 110-343, Sec. 702(a)DivC, through Sec. 702(c) Div C, P.L. 110-343, relating to tax relief for areas damaged by 2008 Midwestern severe storms, tornados, and flooding, reads as follows:

"Sec. 702. Temporary tax relief for areas damaged by 2008 Midwestern severe storms, tornados, and flooding.

"(a) In general. Subject to the modifications described in this section, the following provisions of or relating to the Internal Revenue Code of 1986 shall apply to any Midwestern disaster area in addition to the areas to which such provisions otherwise apply:

"(1) GO Zone benefits.

"(A) Section 1400N (relating to tax benefits) other than subsections (b), (d), (e), (i), (j), (m), and (o) thereof.

"(B) Section 1400O (relating to education tax benefits).

"(C) Section 1400P (relating to housing tax benefits).

"(D) Section 1400Q (relating to special rules for use of retirement funds).

"(E) Section 1400R(a) (relating to employee retention credit for employers).

"(F) Section 1400S (relating to additional tax relief other than subsection (d) thereof.

"(G) Section 1400T (relating to special rules for mortgage revenue bonds).

"(2) Other benefits included in Katrina Emergency Tax Relief Act of 2005. Sections 302, 303, 304, 401, and 405 of the Katrina Emergency Tax Relief Act of 2005.

"(b) Midwestern disaster area.

"(1) In general. For purposes of this section and for applying the substitutions described in subsections (d) and (e), the term 'Midwestern disaster area' means an area—

"(A) with respect to which a major disaster has been declared by the President on or after May 20, 2008, and before August 1, 2008, under section 401 of the Robert T. Stafford Disaster Relief and Emergency Assistance Act by reason of severe storms, tornados, or flooding occurring in any of the States of Arkansas, Illinois, Indiana, Iowa, Kansas, Michigan, Minnesota, Missouri, Nebraska, and Wisconsin, and

"(B) determined by the President to warrant individual or individual and public assistance from the Federal Government under such Act with respect to damages attributable to such severe storms, tornados, or flooding.

"(2) Certain benefits available to areas eligible only for public assistance. For purposes of applying this section to benefits under the following provisions, paragraph (1) shall be applied without regard to subparagraph (B):

"(A) Sections 1400Q, 1400S(b), and 1400S(d) of the Internal Revenue Code of 1986.

"(B) Sections 302, 401, and 405 of the Katrina Emergency Tax Relief Act of 2005.

"(c) References.

"(1) Area. Any reference in such provisions to the Hurricane Katrina disaster area or the Gulf Opportunity Zone shall be treated as a reference to any Midwestern disaster area and any reference to the Hurricane Katrina disaster area or the Gulf Opportunity Zone within a State shall be treated as a reference to all Midwestern disaster areas within the State.

"(2) Items attributable to disaster. Any reference in such provisions to any loss, damage, or other item attributable to Hurricane Katrina shall be treated as a reference to any loss, damage, or other item attributable to the severe storms, tornados, or flooding giving rise to any Presidential declaration described in subsection (b)(1)(A).

"(3) Applicable disaster date. For purposes of applying the substitutions described in subsections (d) and (e), the term 'applicable disaster date' means, with respect to any Midwestern disaster area, the date on which the severe storms, tornados, or flooding giving rise to the Presidential declaration described in subsection (b)(1)(A) occurred.

—P.L. 110-343, Sec. 702(d)(10)DivC, relating to temporary tax relief for areas damaged by 2008 Midwestern severe storms, tornados, and flooding, applies the following modifications to Code Sec. 1400Q:

"(d) Modifications to 1986 Code. The following provisions of the Internal Revenue Code of 1986 shall be applied with the following modifications:

* * * * * * * * * *

" (10) Special rules for use of retirement funds. Section 1400Q—

"(A) by substituting 'qualified Disaster Recovery Assistance distribution' for 'qualified hurricane distribution' each place it appears,

"(B) by substituting 'on or after the applicable disaster date and before January 1, 2010' for 'on or after August 25, 2005, and before January 1, 2007' in subsection (a)(4)(A)(i),

"(C) by substituting 'the applicable disaster date' for 'August 28, 2005' in subsections (a)(4)(A)(i) and (c)(3)(B),

"(D) by disregarding clauses (ii) and (iii) of subsection (a)(4)(A) thereof,

"(E) by substituting 'qualified storm damage distribution' for 'qualified Katrina distribution' each place it appears,

"(F) by substituting 'after the date which is 6 months before the applicable disaster date and before the date which is the day after the applicable disaster date' for 'after February 28, 2005, and before August 29, 2005' in subsection (b)(2)(B)(ii),

"(G) by substituting 'the Midwestern disaster area, but not so purchased or constructed on account of severe storms, tornados, or flooding giving rise to the designation of the area as a disaster area' for 'the Hurricane Katrina disaster area, but not so purchased or constructed on account of Hurricane Katrina' in subsection (b)(2)(B)(iii),

"(H) by substituting 'beginning on the applicable disaster date and ending on the date which is 5 months after the date of the enactment of the Heartland Disaster Tax Relief Act of 2008' for 'beginning on August 25, 2005, and ending on February 28, 2006' in subsection (b)(3)(A),

"(I) by substituting 'qualified storm damage individual' for 'qualified Hurricane Katrina individual' each place it appears,

"(J) by substituting 'December 31, 2009' for 'December 31, 2006' in subsection (c)(2)(A),

"(K) by disregarding subparagraphs (C) and (D) of subsection (c)(3) thereof,

"(L) by substituting 'beginning on the date of the enactment of the Heartland Disaster Tax Relief Act of 2008 and ending on December 31, 2009' for 'beginning on September 24, 2005, and ending on December 31, 2006' in subsection (c)(4)(A)(i),

"(M) by substituting 'the applicable disaster date' for 'August 25, 2005' in subsection (c)(4)(A)(ii), and

"(N) by substituting 'January 1, 2010' for 'January 1, 2007' in subsection (d)(2)(A)(ii).

* * * * * * * * * *

—P.L. 110-246, Sec. 4, Repeals the duplicative enactment and provides effective date provisions of the Act entitled 'An Act to provide for the continuation of agricultural programs through fiscal year 2012, and for other purposes' Sec. 4, P.L. 110-246 reads as follows:

"Sec. 4. Repeal of duplicative enactment.

"(a) In General- The Act entitled 'An Act to provide for the continuation of agricultural programs through fiscal year 2012, and for other purposes' (H.R. 2419 of the 110th Congress), and the amendments made by that Act, are repealed, effective on the date of enactment of that Act.

"(b) Effective Date- Except as otherwise provided in this Act, this Act and the amendments made by this Act shall take effect on the earlier of--

"(1) the date of enactment of this Act; or

"(2) the date of the enactment of the Act entitled 'An Act to provide for the continuation of agricultural programs through fiscal year 2012, and for other purposes' (H.R. 2419 of the 110th Congress)."

—P.L. 110-246, Sec. 15345, applies to this Code Sec. 1400Q for the Kansas Disaster Area storms beginning on May 4, 2007 as specifically outlined in Sec. 15345(a)(7), (b), (c), (d)(5), P.L. 110-246, which read as follows:

"Sec. 15345. Temporary tax relief for Kiowa County, Kansas and surrounding area.

"(a) In General. Subject to the modifications described in this section, the following provisions of or relating to the Internal Revenue Code of 1986 shall apply to the Kansas disaster area in addition to the areas to which such provisions otherwise apply:

* * * * * * * * * *

"(7) Section 1400Q of such Code (relating to special rules for use of retirement funds)."

* * * * * * * * * *

Sec. 15345(b), defining Kansas Disaster Area, provides:

"(b) Kansas Disaster Area. For purposes of this section, the term 'Kansas disaster area' means an area with respect to which a major disaster has been declared by the President under section 401 of the Robert T. Stafford Disaster Relief and Emergency Assistance Act (FEMA-1699-DR, as in effect on the date of the enactment of this Act) by reason of severe storms and tornados beginning on May 4, 2007, and determined by the President to warrant individual or individual and public assistance from the Federal Government under such Act with respect to damages attributable to such storms and tornados."

Sec. 15345(c), referring to area or loss provides:

"(c) References to Area or Loss—

"(1) Area. Any reference in such provisions to the Katrina disaster area or the Gulf Opportunity Zone shall be treated as a reference to the Kansas disaster area.

"(2) Loss. Any reference in such provisions to any loss or damage attributable to Hurricane Katrina shall be treated as a reference to any loss or damage attributable to the May 4, 2007, storms and tornados."

Sec. 15345(d)(5), following, provides detailed information on dates and special allowances for certain property acquired on or after May 5, 2007.

"(d) References to Dates, etc.

* * * * * * * * * * * *

"(5) Special rules for use of retirement funds. Section 1400Q of such Code.

"(A) by substituting 'qualified Recovery Assistance distribution' for 'qualified hurricane distribution' each place it appears,

"(B) by substituting 'on or after May 4, 2007, and before January 1, 2009' for 'on or after August 25, 2005, and before January 1, 2007' in subsection (a)(4)(A)(i),

"(C) by substituting 'May 4, 2007' for 'August 28, 2005' in subsections (a)(4)(A)(i) and (c)(3)(B),

"(D) disregarding clauses (ii) and (iii) of subsection (a)(4)(A),

"(E) by substituting 'qualified storm distribution' for 'qualified Katrina distribution' each place it appears,

"(F) by substituting 'after November 4, 2006, and before May 5, 2007' for 'after February 28, 2005, and before August 29, 2005' in subsection (b)(2)(B)(ii),

"(G) by substituting 'the Kansas disaster area (as defined in section 15345(b) of the Food, Conservation, and Energy Act of 2008) but which was not so purchased or constructed on account of the May 4, 2007, storms and tornados' for 'the Hurricane Katrina disaster area, but not so purchased or constructed on account of Hurricane Katrina' in subsection (b)(2)(B)(iii),

"(H) by substituting 'beginning on May 4, 2007, and ending on the date which is 5 months after the date of the enactment of the Heartland, Habitat, Harvest, and Horticulture Act of 2008' for 'beginning on August 25, 2005, and ending on February 28, 2006' in subsection (b)(3)(A),

"(I) by substituting 'qualified storm individual' for 'qualified Hurricane Katrina individual' each place it appears,

"(J) by substituting 'December 31, 2008' for 'December 31, 2006' in subsection (c)(2)(A),

"(K) by substituting 'beginning on the date of the enactment of the Food, Conservation, and Energy Act of 2008 and ending on December 31, 2008' for 'beginning on September 24, 2005, and ending on December 31, 2006' in subsection (c)(4)(A)(i),

"(L) by substituting 'May 4, 2007' for 'August 25, 2005' in subsection (c)(4)(A)(ii), and

"(M) by substituting 'January 1, 2009' for 'January 1, 2007' in subsection (d)(2)(A)(ii)." [Ed. Note: May 22, 2008 was the date of enactment for H.R. 2419 (PL 110-234), which was repealed by (2008 Farm Act § 4(a)) (PL 110-246, 6/18/2008), in connection with the reenactment of the farm bill to correct a technical deficiency in its original passage.]

In 2005, P.L. 109-135, Sec. 201(a), added Code Sec. 1400Q, effective 12/21/2005. . . . Sec. 201(b)(4)(A), Repealed Secs. 101, 102, 103 and 104 of P.L. 109-73, relating to special rules for use of retirement funds, effective 12/21/2005. These rules are similar to those enacted in new Code Sec. 1400Q, as added by Sec. 201(a) of P.L. 109-135, see above.

Prior to repeal, Secs. 101, 102, 103 and 104 of P.L. 109-73 read as follows:

"SEC. 101. TAX-FAVORED WITHDRAWALS FROM RETIREMENT PLANS FOR RELIEF RELATING TO HURRICANE KATRINA.

"(a) In general. Section 72(t) of the Internal Revenue Code of 1986 shall not apply to any qualified Hurricane Katrina distribution.

"(b) Aggregate dollar limitation.

"(1) In general. For purposes of this section, the aggregate amount of distributions received by an individual which may be treated as qualified Hurricane Katrina distributions for any taxable year shall not exceed the excess (if any) of—

"(A) $100,000, over

"(B) the aggregate amounts treated as qualified Hurricane Katrina distributions received by such individual for all prior taxable years.

"(2) Treatment of plan distributions. If a distribution to an individual would (without regard to paragraph (1)) be a qualified Hurricane Katrina distribution, a plan shall not be treated as violating any requirement of the Internal Revenue Code of 1986 merely because the plan treats such distributions as a qualified Hurricane Katrina distribution, unless the aggregate amount of such distributions from all plans maintained by the employer (and any member of any controlled group which includes the employer) to such individual exceeds $100,000.

"(3) Controlled group. For purposes of paragraph (2), the term 'controlled group' means any group treated as a single employer under subsection (b), (c), (m), or (o) of section 414 of such Code.

"(c) Amount distributed may be repaid.

"(1) In general. Any individual who receives a qualified Hurricane Katrina distribution may, at any time during the 3-year period beginning on the day after the date on which such distribution was received, make one or more contributions in an aggregate amount not to exceed the amount of such distribution to an eligible retirement plan of which such individual is a beneficiary and to which a rollover contribution of such distribution could be made under section 402(c), 403(a)(4), 403(b)(8), 408(d)(3), or 457(e)(16) of such Code, as the case may be.

"(2) Treatment of repayments of distributions from eligible retirement plans other than IRAs. For purposes of such Code, if a contribution is made pursuant to paragraph (1) with respect to a qualified Hurricane Katrina distribution from an eligible retirement plan other than an individual retirement plan, then the taxpayer shall, to the extent of the amount of the contribution, be treated as having received the qualified Hurricane Katrina distribution in an eligible rollover distribution (as defined in section 402(c)(4) of such Code) and as having transferred the amount to the eligible retirement plan in a direct trustee to trustee transfer within 60 days of the distribution.

"(3) Treatment of repayments for distributions from IRAs. For purposes of such Code, if a contribution is made pursuant to paragraph (1) with respect to a qualified Hurricane Katrina distribution from an individual retirement plan (as defined by section 7701(a)(37) of such Code), then, to the extent of the amount of the contribution, the qualified Hurricane Katrina distribution shall be treated as a distribution described in section 408(d)(3) of such Code and as having been transferred to the eligible retirement plan in a direct trustee to trustee transfer within 60 days of the distribution.

"(d) Definitions. For purposes of this section—

"(1) Qualified Hurricane Katrina distribution. Except as provided in subsection (b), the term 'qualified Hurricane Katrina distribution' means any distribution from an eligible retirement plan made on or after August 25, 2005, and before January 1, 2007, to an individual whose principal place of abode on August 28, 2005, is located in the Hurricane Katrina disaster area and who has sustained an economic loss by reason of Hurricane Katrina.

"(2) Eligible retirement plan. The term 'eligible retirement plan' shall have the meaning given such term by section 402(c)(8)(B) of such Code.

"(e) Income inclusion spread over 3 year period for qualified Hurricane Katrina distributions.

"(1) In general. In the case of any qualified Hurricane Katrina distribution, unless the taxpayer elects not to have this subsection apply for any taxable year, any amount required to be included in gross income for such taxable year shall be so included ratably over the 3-taxable year period beginning with such taxable year.

"(2) Special rule. For purposes of paragraph (1), rules similar to the rules of subparagraph (E) of section 408A(d)(3) of such Code shall apply.

"(f) Special rules.

"(1) Exemption of distributions from trustee to trustee transfer and withholding rules. For purposes of sections 401(a)(31), 402(f), and 3405 of such Code, qualified Hurricane Katrina distributions shall not be treated as eligible rollover distributions.

"(2) Qualified Hurricane Katrina distributions treated as meeting plan distribution requirements. For purposes of such Code, a qualified Hurricane Katrina distribution shall be treated as meeting the requirements of sections 401(k)(2)(B)(i), 403(b)(7)(A)(ii), 403(b)(11), and 457(d)(1)(A) of such Code."

"SEC. 102. RECONTRIBUTIONS OF WITHDRAWALS FOR HOME PURCHASES CANCELLED DUE TO HURRICANE KATRINA.

"(a) Recontributions.

"(1) In general. Any individual who received a qualified distribution may, during the period beginning on August 25, 2005, and ending on February 28, 2006, make one or more contributions in an aggregate amount not to exceed the amount of such qualified distribution to an eligible retirement plan (as defined in section 402(c)(8)(B) of the Internal Revenue Code of 1986) of which such individual is a beneficiary and to which a rollover contribution of such distribution could be made under section 402(c), 403(a)(4), 403(b)(8), or 408(d)(3) of such Code, as the case may be.

"(2) Treatment of repayments. Rules similar to the rules of paragraphs (2) and (3) of section 101(c) of this Act shall apply for purposes of this section.

"(b) Qualified distribution defined. For purposes of this section, the term 'qualified distribution' means any distribution—

"(1) described in section 401(k)(2)(B)(i)(IV), 403(b)(7)(A)(ii) (but only to the extent such distribution relates to financial hardship), 403(b)(11)(B), or 72(t)(2)(F) of such Code,

"(2) received after February 28, 2005, and before August 29, 2005, and

"(3) which was to be used to purchase or construct a principal residence in the Hurricane Katrina disaster area, but which was not so purchased or constructed on account of Hurricane Katrina."

"SEC. 103. LOANS FROM QUALIFIED PLANS FOR RELIEF RELATING TO HURRICANE KATRINA.

"(a) Increase in limit on loans not treated as distributions. In the case of any loan from a qualified employer plan (as defined under section 72(p)(4) of the Internal Revenue Code of 1986) to a qualified individual made after the date of enactment of this Act and before January 1, 2007—

"(1) clause (i) of section 72(p)(2)(A) of such Code shall be applied by substituting '$100,000' for '$50,000', and

"(2) clause (ii) of such subsection shall be applied by substituting 'the present value of the nonforfeitable accrued benefit of the employee under the plan' for 'one-half of the present value of the nonforfeitable accrued benefit of the employee under the plan'.

"(b) Delay of repayment. In the case of a qualified individual with an outstanding loan on or after August 25, 2005, from a qualified employer plan (as defined in section 72(p)(4) of such Code)—

"(1) if the due date pursuant to subparagraph (B) or (C) of section 72(p)(2) of such Code for any repayment with respect to such loan occurs during the period beginning on August 25, 2005, and ending on December 31, 2006, such due date shall be delayed for 1 year,

"(2) any subsequent repayments with respect to any such loan shall be appropriately adjusted to reflect the delay in the due date under paragraph (1) and any interest accruing during such delay, and

"(3) in determining the 5-year period and the term of a loan under subparagraph (B) or (C) of section 72(p)(2) of such Code, the period described in paragraph (1) shall be disregarded.

"(c) Qualified individual. For purposes of this section, the term 'qualified individual' means an individual whose principal place of abode on August 28, 2005, is located in the Hurricane Katrina disaster area and who has sustained an economic loss by reason of Hurricane Katrina."

"SEC. 104. PROVISIONS RELATING TO PLAN AMENDMENTS.

"(a) In general. If this section applies to any amendment to any plan or annuity contract, such plan or contract shall be treated as being operated in accordance with the terms of the plan during the period described in subsection (b)(2)(A).

"(b) Amendments to which section applies.

"(1) In general. This section shall apply to any amendment to any plan or annuity contract which is made—

"(A) pursuant to any amendment made by this title, or pursuant to any regulation issued by the Secretary of the Treasury or the Secretary of Labor under this title, and

"(B) on or before the last day of the first plan year beginning on or after January 1, 2007, or such later date as the Secretary of the Treasury may prescribe. In the case of a governmental plan (as defined in section 414(d) of the Internal Revenue Code of 1986), subparagraph (B) shall be applied by substituting the date which is 2 years after the date otherwise applied under subparagraph (B).

"(2) Conditions. This section shall not apply to any amendment unless—

"(A) during the period—

"(i) beginning on the date the legislative or regulatory amendment described in paragraph (1)(A) takes effect (or in the case of a plan or contract amendment not required by such legislative or regulatory amendment, the effective date specified by the plan), and

"(ii) ending on the date described in paragraph (1)(B) (or, if earlier, the date the plan or contract amendment is adopted),

the plan or contract is operated as if such plan or contract amendment were in effect; and

"(B) such plan or contract amendment applies retroactively for such period."

- *Caution:* For temporary tax relief provisions for areas damaged by 2008 Midwestern severe storms, tornados, and flooding and for application of this section to the Kansas Disaster Area storms beginning on May 4, 2007, see History for this Code Sec.

Sec. 1400R. Employment relief.

(a) Employee retention credit for employers affected by Hurricane Katrina.

(1) In general. For purposes of section 38, in the case of an eligible employer, the Hurricane Katrina employee retention credit for any taxable year is an amount equal to 40 percent of the qualified wages with respect to each eligible employee of such employer for such taxable year. For purposes of the preceding sentence, the amount of qualified wages which may be taken into account with respect to any individual shall not exceed $6,000.

(2) Definitions. For purposes of this subsection—

(A) Eligible employer. The term "eligible employer" means any employer—

(i) which conducted an active trade or business on August 28, 2005, in the GO Zone, and

(ii) with respect to whom the trade or business described in clause (i) is inoperable on any day after August 28, 2005, and before January 1, 2006, as a result of damage sustained by reason of Hurricane Katrina.

(B) Eligible employee. The term "eligible employee" means with respect to an eligible employer an employee whose principal place of employment on August 28, 2005, with such eligible employer was in the GO Zone.

(C) Qualified wages. The term "qualified wages" means wages (as defined in section 51(c)(1), but without regard to section 3306(b)(2)(B)) paid or incurred by an eligible employer with respect to an eligible employee on any day after August 28, 2005, and before January 1, 2006, which occurs during the period—

(i) beginning on the date on which the trade or business described in subparagraph (A) first became inoperable at the principal place of employment of the employee immediately before Hurricane Katrina, and

(ii) ending on the date on which such trade or business has resumed significant operations at such principal place of employment.

Such term shall include wages paid without regard to whether the employee performs no services, performs services at a different place of employment than such principal place of employment, or performs services at such principal place of employment before significant operations have resumed.

(3) Certain rules to apply. For purposes of this subsection, rules similar to the rules of sections 51(i)(1) and 52 shall apply.

(4) Employee not taken into account more than once. An employee shall not be treated as an eligible employee for purposes of this subsection for any period with respect to any employer if such employer is allowed a credit under section 51 with respect to such employee for such period.

(b) Employee retention credit for employers affected by Hurricane Rita.

(1) In general. For purposes of section 38, in the case of an eligible employer, the Hurricane Rita employee retention credit for any taxable year is an amount equal to 40 percent of the qualified wages with respect to each eligible employee of such employer for such taxable year. For purposes of the preceding sentence, the amount of qualified wages which may be taken into account with respect to any individual shall not exceed $6,000.

(2) Definitions. For purposes of this subsection—

(A) Eligible employer. The term "eligible employer" means any employer—

(i) which conducted an active trade or business on September 23, 2005, in the Rita GO Zone, and

(ii) with respect to whom the trade or business described in clause (i) is inoperable on any day after September 23, 2005, and before January 1, 2006, as a result of damage sustained by reason of Hurricane Rita.

(B) Eligible employee. The term "eligible employee" means with respect to an eligible employer an employee whose principal place of employment on September 23, 2005, with such eligible employer was in the Rita GO Zone.

(C) Qualified wages. The term "qualified wages" means wages (as defined in section 51(c)(1), but without regard to section 3306(b)(2)(B)) paid or incurred by an eligible employer with respect to an eligible employee on any day after September 23, 2005, and before January 1, 2006, which occurs during the period—

(i) beginning on the date on which the trade or business described in subparagraph (A) first became inoperable at the principal place of employment of the employee immediately before Hurricane Rita, and

(ii) ending on the date on which such trade or business has resumed significant operations at such principal place of employment.

Such term shall include wages paid without regard to whether the employee performs no services, performs services at a different place of employment than such principal place of employment, or performs services at such principal place of employment before significant operations have resumed.

(3) Certain rules to apply. For purposes of this subsection, rules similar to the rules of sections 51(i)(1) and 52 shall apply.

(4) Employee not taken into account more than once. An employee shall not be treated as an eligible employee for purposes of this subsection for any period with respect to any employer if such employer is allowed a credit under subsection (a) or section 51, with respect to such employee for such period.

(c) Employee retention credit for employers affected by Hurricane Wilma.

(1) In general. For purposes of section 38, in the case of an eligible employer, the Hurricane Wilma employee retention credit for any taxable year is an amount equal to 40 percent of the qualified wages with respect to each eligible employee of such employer for such taxable year. For purposes of the preceding sentence, the amount of qualified wages which may be taken into account with respect to any individual shall not exceed $6,000.

(2) Definitions. For purposes of this subsection—

(A) Eligible employer. The term "eligible employer" means any employer—

(i) which conducted an active trade or business on October 23, 2005, in the Wilma GO Zone, and

(ii) with respect to whom the trade or business described in clause (i) is inoperable on any day after October 23, 2005, and before January 1, 2006, as a result of damage sustained by reason of Hurricane Wilma.

(B) Eligible employee. The term "eligible employee" means with respect to an eligible employer an employee whose principal place of employment on October 23, 2005, with such eligible employer was in the Wilma GO Zone.

(C) Qualified wages. The term "qualified wages" means wages (as defined in section 51(c)(1), but without regard to section 3306(b)(2)(B)) paid or incurred by an eligible employer with respect to an eligible employee on any day after October 23, 2005, and before January 1, 2006, which occurs during the period—

(i) beginning on the date on which the trade or business described in subparagraph (A) first became inoperable at the principal place of employment of the employee immediately before Hurricane Wilma, and

(ii) ending on the date on which such trade or business has resumed significant operations at such principal place of employment.

Such term shall include wages paid without regard to whether the employee performs no services, performs services at a different place of employment than such principal place of employment, or performs services at such principal place of employment before significant operations have resumed.

(3) Certain rules to apply. For purposes of this subsection, rules similar to the rules of sections 51(i)(1) and 52 shall apply.

(4) Employee not taken into account more than once. An employee shall not be treated as an eligible employee for purposes of this subsection for any period with respect to any employer if such employer is allowed a credit under subsection (a) or (b) or section 51 with respect to such employee for such period.

"(A) Section 1400N (relating to tax benefits) other than subsections (b), (d), (e), (i), (j), (m), and (o) thereof.
"(B) Section 1400O (relating to education tax benefits).
"(C) Section 1400P (relating to housing tax benefits).
"(D) Section 1400Q (relating to special rules for use of retirement funds).
"(E) Section 1400R(a) (relating to employee retention credit for employers).
"(F) Section 1400S (relating to additional tax relief) other than subsection (d) thereof.
"(G) Section 1400T (relating to special rules for mortgage revenue bonds).
"(2) Other benefits included in Katrina Emergency Tax Relief Act of 2005. Sections 302, 303, 304, 401, and 405 of the Katrina Emergency Tax Relief Act of 2005.
"(b) Midwestern disaster area.
"(1) In general. For purposes of this section and for applying the substitutions described in subsections (d) and (e), the term 'Midwestern disaster area' means an area—
"(A) with respect to which a major disaster has been declared by the President on or after May 20, 2008, and before August 1, 2008, under section 401 of the Robert T. Stafford Disaster Relief and Emergency Assistance Act by reason of severe storms, tornados, or flooding occurring in any of the States of Arkansas, Illinois, Indiana, Iowa, Kansas, Michigan, Minnesota, Missouri, Nebraska, and Wisconsin, and
"(B) determined by the President to warrant individual or individual and public assistance from the Federal Government under such Act with respect to damages attributable to such severe storms, tornados, or flooding.
"(2) Certain benefits available to areas eligible only for public assistance. For purposes of applying this section to benefits under the following provisions, paragraph (1) shall be applied without regard to subparagraph (B):
"(A) Sections 1400Q, 1400S(b), and 1400S(d) of the Internal Revenue Code of 1986.
"(B) Sections 302, 401, and 405 of the Katrina Emergency Tax Relief Act of 2005.
"(c) References.
"(1) Area. Any reference in such provisions to the Hurricane Katrina disaster area or the Gulf Opportunity Zone shall be treated as a reference to any Midwestern disaster area and any reference to the Hurricane Katrina disaster area or the Gulf Opportunity Zone within a State shall be treated as a reference to all Midwestern disaster areas within the State.
"(2) Items attributable to disaster. Any reference in such provisions to any loss, damage, or other item attributable to Hurricane Katrina shall be treated as a reference to any loss, damage, or other item attributable to the severe storms, tornados, or flooding giving rise to any Presidential declaration described in subsection (b)(1)(A).
"(3) Applicable disaster date. For purposes of applying the substitutions described in subsections (d) and (e), the term 'applicable disaster date' means, with respect to any Midwestern disaster area, the date on which the severe storms, tornados, or flooding giving rise to the Presidential declaration described in subsection (b)(1)(A) occurred.
—P.L. 110-343, Sec. 702(d)(11)DivC, relating to temporary tax relief for areas damaged by 2008 Midwestern severe storms, tornados, and flooding, applies the following modifications to Code Sec. 1400R:
"(d) Modifications to 1986 Code. The following provisions of the Internal Revenue Code of 1986 shall be applied with the following modifications:
* * * * * * * * * *
"(11) Employee retention credit for employers affected by severe storms, tornados, and flooding. Section 1400R(a)—
"(A) by substituting 'the applicable disaster date' for 'August 28, 2005' each place it appears,
"(B) by substituting 'January 1, 2009' for 'January 1, 2006' both places it appears, and
"(C) only with respect to eligible employers who employed an average of not more than 200 employees on business days during the taxable year before the applicable disaster date.
* * * * * * * * * *
—P.L. 110-246, Sec. 4, Repeals the duplicative enactment and provides effective date provisions of the Act entitled 'An Act to provide for the continuation of agricultural programs through fiscal year 2012, and for other purposes' Sec. 4, P.L. 110-246 reads as follows:
"Sec. 4. Repeal of duplicative enactment.
"(a) In General- The Act entitled 'An Act to provide for the continuation of agricultural programs through fiscal year 2012, and for other purposes' (H.R. 2419 of the 110th Congress), and the amendments made by that Act, are repealed, effective on the date of enactment of that Act.
"(b) Effective Date- Except as otherwise provided in this Act, this Act and the amendments made by this Act shall take effect on the earlier of--
"(1) the date of enactment of this Act; or
"(2) the date of the enactment of the Act entitled 'An Act to provide for the continuation of agricultural programs through fiscal year 2012, and for other purposes' (H.R. 2419 of the 110th Congress)."
—P.L. 110-246, Sec. 15345, applies to this Code Sec. 1400R for the Kansas Disaster Area storms beginning on May 4, 2007 as specifically outlined in Sec. 15345(a)(8) (b), (c), (d)(6), P.L. 110-246, which read as follows:
"Sec. 15345. Temporary tax relief for Kiowa County, Kansas and surrounding area.
"(a) In General. Subject to the modifications described in this section, the following provisions of or relating to the Internal Revenue Code of 1986 shall apply

In 2008, P.L. 110-343, Sec. 702(a)DivC, through Sec. 702(c) Div C, P.L. 110-343, relating to tax relief for areas damaged by 2008 Midwestern severe storms, tornados and flooding reads as follows:
"Sec. 702. Temporary tax relief for areas damaged by 2008 Midwestern severe storms, tornados, and flooding.
"(a) In general. Subject to the modifications described in this section, the following provisions of or relating to the Internal Revenue Code of 1986 shall apply to any Midwestern disaster area in addition to the areas to which such provisions otherwise apply:
"(1) GO Zone benefits.

Gulf Opportunity Zone

to the Kansas disaster area in addition to the areas to which such provisions otherwise apply:

* * * * * * * * * * * *

"(8) Section 1400R(a) of such Code (relating to employee retention credit for employers)."

Sec. 15345(b), defining Kansas Disaster Area, provides:

"(b) Kansas Disaster Area. For purposes of this section, the term 'Kansas disaster area' means an area with respect to which a major disaster has been declared by the President under section 401 of the Robert T. Stafford Disaster Relief and Emergency Assistance Act (FEMA-1699-DR, as in effect on the date of the enactment of this Act) by reason of severe storms and tornados beginning on May 4, 2007, and determined by the President to warrant individual or individual and public assistance from the Federal Government under such Act with respect to damages attributable to such storms and tornados."

Sec. 15345(c), referring to area or loss provides:

"(c) References to Area or Loss—

"(1) Area. Any reference in such provisions to the Katrina disaster area or the Gulf Opportunity Zone shall be treated as a reference to the Kansas disaster area.

"(2) Loss. Any reference in such provisions to any loss or damage attributable to Hurricane Katrina shall be treated as a reference to any loss or damage attributable to the May 4, 2007, storms and tornados."

Sec. 15345(d)(6), following, provides detailed information on dates and special allowances for certain property acquired on or after May 5, 2007.

"(6) Employee retention credit for employers affected by may 4 storms and tornados. Section 1400R(a) of the Internal Revenue Code of 1986—

"(A) by substituting 'May 4, 2007' for 'August 28, 2005' each place it appears,

"(B) by substituting 'January 1, 2008' for 'January 1, 2006' both places it appears, and

"(C) only with respect to eligible employers who employed an average of not more than 200 employees on business days during the taxable year before May 4, 2007." [Ed. Note: May 22, 2008 was the date of enactment for H.R. 2419 (PL 110-234), which was repealed by (2008 Farm Act § 4(a)) (PL 110-246, 6/18/2008), in connection with the reenactment of the farm bill to correct a technical deficiency in its original passage.]

In 2005, P.L. 109-135, Sec. 201(a), added Code Sec. 1400R, effective 12/21/2005.

—P.L. 109-135, Sec. 201(b)(4)(B), Repealed Sec. 202 of P.L. 109-73, relating to employee retention credit for employers affected by Hurricane Katrina, effective 12/21/2005. These rules are similar to those enacted in Code Sec. 1400R, as added by Sec. 201(a) of P.L. 109-135, see above.

Prior to repeal, Sec. 202 of P.L. 109-73 read as follows:

"SEC. 202. EMPLOYEE RETENTION CREDIT FOR EMPLOYERS AFFECTED BY HURRICANE KATRINA.

"(a) In general. In the case of an eligible employer, there shall be allowed as a credit against the tax imposed by chapter 1 of the Internal Revenue Code of 1986 for the taxable year an amount equal to 40 percent of the qualified wages with respect to each eligible employee of such employer for such taxable year. For purposes of the preceding sentence, the amount of qualified wages which may be taken into account with respect to any individual shall not exceed $6,000.

"(b) Definitions. For purposes of this section—

"(1) Eligible employer. The term 'eligible employer' means any employer—

"(A) which conducted an active trade or business on August 28, 2005, in a core disaster area, and

"(B) with respect to whom the trade or business described in subparagraph (A) is inoperable on any day after August 28, 2005, and before January 1, 2006, as a result of damage sustained by reason of Hurricane Katrina.

"(2) Eligible employee. The term 'eligible employee' means with respect to an eligible employer an employee whose principal place of employment on August 28, 2005, with such eligible employer was in a core disaster area.

"(3) Qualified wages. The term 'qualified wages' means wages (as defined in section 51(c)(1) of such Code, but without regard to section 3306(b)(2)(B) of such Code) paid or incurred by an eligible employer with respect to an eligible employee on any day after August 28, 2005, and before January 1, 2006, which occurs during the period—

"(A) beginning on the date on which the trade or business described in paragraph (1) first became inoperable at the principal place of employment of the employee immediately before Hurricane Katrina, and

"(B) ending on the date on which such trade or business has resumed significant operations at such principal place of employment.

Such term shall include wages paid without regard to whether the employee performs no services, performs services at a different place of employment than such principal place of employment, or performs services at such principal place of employment before significant operations have resumed.

"(c) Credit not allowed for large businesses. The term 'eligible employer' shall not include any trade or business for any taxable year if such trade or business employed an average of more than 200 employees on business days during the taxable year.

"(d) Certain rules to apply. For purposes of this section, rules similar to the rules of sections 51(i)(1), 52, and 280C(a) of such Code shall apply.

"(e) Employee not taken into account more than once. An employee shall not be treated as an eligible employee for purposes of this section for any period with respect to any employer if such employer is allowed a credit under section 51 of such Code with respect to such employee for such period.

"(f) Credit to be part of general business credit. The credit allowed under this section shall be added to the current year business credit under section 38(b) of such Code and shall be treated as a credit allowed under subpart D of part IV of subchapter A of chapter 1 of such Code."

> • **Caution:** For temporary tax relief provisions for areas damaged by 2008 Midwestern severe storms, tornados, and flooding and for application of this section to the Kansas Disaster Area storms beginning on May 4, 2007, see History for this Code Sec.

Sec. 1400S. Additional tax relief provisions.

(a) Temporary suspension of limitations on charitable contributions.

(1) In general. Except as otherwise provided in paragraph (2), section 170(b) shall not apply to qualified contributions and such contributions shall not be taken into account for purposes of applying subsections (b) and (d) of section 170 to other contributions.

(2) Treatment of excess contributions. For purposes of section 170—

(A) Individuals. In the case of an individual—

(i) Limitation. Any qualified contribution shall be allowed only to the extent that the aggregate of such contributions does not exceed the excess of the taxpayer's contribution base (as defined in subparagraph (G) of section 170(b)(1)) over the amount of all other charitable contributions allowed under section 170(b)(1).

(ii) Carryover. If the aggregate amount of qualified contributions made in the contribution year (within the meaning of section 170(d)(1)) exceeds the limitation of clause (i), such excess shall be added to the excess described in the portion of subparagraph (A) of such section which precedes clause (i) thereof for purposes of applying such section.

(B) Corporations. In the case of a corporation—

(i) Limitation. Any qualified contribution shall be allowed only to the extent that the aggregate of such contributions does not exceed the excess of the taxpayer's taxable income (as determined under paragraph (2) of section 170(b)) over the amount of all other charitable contributions allowed under such paragraph.

(ii) Carryover. Rules similar to the rules of subparagraph (A)(ii) shall apply for purposes of this subparagraph.

(3) Exception to overall limitation on itemized deductions. So much of any deduction allowed under section 170 as does not exceed the qualified contributions paid during the taxable year shall not be treated as an itemized deduction for purposes of section 68.

(4) Qualified contributions.

(A) In general. For purposes of this subsection, the term "qualified contribution" means any charitable contribution (as defined in section 170(c)) if—

(i) such contribution is paid during the period beginning on August 28, 2005, and ending on December 31, 2005, in cash to an organization described in section 170(b)(1)(A) (other than an organization described in section 509(a)(3)),

(ii) in the case of a contribution paid by a corporation, such contribution is for relief efforts related to Hurricane Katrina, Hurricane Rita, or Hurricane Wilma, and

(iii) the taxpayer has elected the application of this subsection with respect to such contribution.
(B) Exception. Such term shall not include a contribution if the contribution is for establishment of a new, or maintenance in an existing, segregated fund or account with respect to which the donor (or any person appointed or designated by such donor) has, or reasonably expects to have, advisory privileges with respect to distributions or investments by reason of the donor's status as a donor.
(C) Application of election to partnerships and S corporations. In the case of a partnership or S corporation, the election under subparagraph (A)(iii) shall be made separately by each partner or shareholder.

(b) Suspension of certain limitations on personal casualty losses.
Paragraphs (1) and (2)(A) of section 165(h) shall not apply to losses described in section 165(c)(3)—
(1) which arise in the Hurricane Katrina disaster area on or after August 25, 2005, and which are attributable to Hurricane Katrina,
(2) which arise in the Hurricane Rita disaster area on or after September 23, 2005, and which are attributable to Hurricane Rita, or
(3) which arise in the Hurricane Wilma disaster area on or after October 23, 2005, and which are attributable to Hurricane Wilma.
In the case of any other losses, section 165(h)(2)(A) shall be applied without regard to the losses referred to in the preceding sentence.

(c) Required exercise of authority under section 7508A.
In the case of any taxpayer determined by the Secretary to be affected by the Presidentially declared disaster relating to Hurricane Katrina, Hurricane Rita, or Hurricane Wilma, any relief provided by the Secretary under section 7508A shall be for a period ending not earlier than February 28, 2006.

(d) Special rule for determining earned income.
(1) In general. In the case of a qualified individual, if the earned income of the taxpayer for the taxable year which includes the applicable date is less than the earned income of the taxpayer for the preceding taxable year, the credits allowed under sections 24(d) and 32 may, at the election of the taxpayer, be determined by substituting—
(A) such earned income for the preceding taxable year, for
(B) such earned income for the taxable year which includes the applicable date.
(2) Qualified individual. For purposes of this subsection—
(A) In general. The term "qualified individual" means any qualified Hurricane Katrina individual, any qualified Hurricane Rita individual, and any qualified Hurricane Wilma individual.
(B) Qualified Hurricane Katrina individual. The term "qualified Hurricane Katrina individual" means any individual whose principal place of abode on August 25, 2005, was located—
(i) in the GO Zone, or
(ii) in the Hurricane Katrina disaster area (but outside the GO Zone) and such individual was displaced from such principal place of abode by reason of Hurricane Katrina.
(C) Qualified Hurricane Rita individual. The term "qualified Hurricane Rita individual" means any individual (other than a qualified Hurricane Katrina individual) whose principal place of abode on September 23, 2005, was located—
(i) in the Rita GO Zone, or
(ii) in the Hurricane Rita disaster area (but outside the Rita GO Zone) and such individual was displaced from such principal place of abode by reason of Hurricane Rita.
(D) Qualified Hurricane Wilma individual. The term "qualified Hurricane Wilma individual" means any individual whose principal place of abode on October 23, 2005, was located—
(i) in the Wilma GO Zone, or
(ii) in the Hurricane Wilma disaster area (but outside the Wilma GO Zone) and such individual was displaced from such principal place of abode by reason of Hurricane Wilma.
(3) Applicable date. For purposes of this subsection, the term "applicable date" means—
(A) in the case of a qualified Hurricane Katrina individual, August 25, 2005,
(B) in the case of a qualified Hurricane Rita individual, September 23, 2005, and
(C) in the case of a qualified Hurricane Wilma individual, October 23, 2005.
(4) Earned income. For purposes of this subsection, the term "earned income" has the meaning given such term under section 32(c).
(5) Special rules.
(A) Application to joint returns. For purposes of paragraph (1), in the case of a joint return for a taxable year which includes the applicable date—
(i) such paragraph shall apply if either spouse is a qualified individual, and
(ii) the earned income of the taxpayer for the preceding taxable year shall be the sum of the earned income of each spouse for such preceding taxable year.
(B) Uniform application of election. Any election made under paragraph (1) shall apply with respect to both sections 24(d) and section 32.
(C) Errors treated as mathematical error. For purposes of section 6213, an incorrect use on a return of earned income pursuant to paragraph (1) shall be treated as a mathematical or clerical error.
(D) No effect on determination of gross income, etc. Except as otherwise provided in this subsection, this title shall be applied without regard to any substitution under paragraph (1).

(e) Secretarial authority to make adjustments regarding taxpayer and dependency status.
With respect to taxable years beginning in 2005 or 2006, the Secretary may make such adjustments in the application of the internal revenue laws as may be necessary to ensure that taxpayers do not lose any deduction or credit or experience a change of filing status by reason of temporary relocations by reason of Hurricane Katrina, Hurricane Rita, or Hurricane Wilma. Any adjustments made under the preceding sentence shall ensure that an individual is not taken into account by more than one taxpayer with respect to the same tax benefit.

In 2008, P.L. 110-343, Sec. 702(a)DivC, through Sec. 702(c) Div C, P.L. 110-343, relating to tax relief for areas damaged by 2008 Midwestern severe storms, tornados, and flooding, reads as follows:

"Sec. 702. Temporary tax relief for areas damaged by 2008 Midwestern severe storms, tornados, and flooding.

"(a) In general. Subject to the modifications described in this section, the following provisions of or relating to the Internal Revenue Code of 1986 shall apply to any Midwestern disaster area in addition to the areas to which such provisions otherwise apply:

"(1) GO Zone benefits.

"(A) Section 1400N (relating to tax benefits) other than subsections (b), (d), (e), (i), (j), (m), and (o) thereof.
"(B) Section 1400O (relating to education tax benefits).
"(C) Section 1400P (relating to housing tax benefits).
"(D) Section 1400Q (relating to special rules for use of retirement funds).
"(E) Section 1400R(a) (relating to employee retention credit for employers).
"(F) Section 1400S (relating to additional tax relief) other than subsection (d) thereof.
"(G) Section 1400T (relating to special rules for mortgage revenue bonds).
"(2) Other benefits included in Katrina Emergency Tax Relief Act of 2005. Sections 302, 303, 304, 401, and 405 of the Katrina Emergency Tax Relief Act of 2005.
"(b) Midwestern disaster area.
"(1) In general. For purposes of this section and for applying the substitutions described in subsections (d) and (e), the term 'Midwestern disaster area' means an area—
"(A) with respect to which a major disaster has been declared by the President on or after May 20, 2008, and before August 1, 2008, under section 401 of the Robert T. Stafford Disaster Relief and Emergency Assistance Act by reason of severe storms, tornadoes, or flooding occurring in any of the States of Arkansas, Illinois, Indiana, Iowa, Kansas, Michigan, Minnesota, Missouri, Nebraska, and Wisconsin, and
"(B) determined by the President to warrant individual or individual and public assistance from the Federal Government under such Act with respect to damages attributable to such severe storms, tornadoes, or flooding.
"(2) Certain benefits available to areas eligible only for public assistance. For purposes of applying this section to benefits under the following provisions, paragraph (1) shall be applied without regard to subparagraph (B):
"(A) Sections 1400Q, 1400S(b), and 1400S(d) of the Internal Revenue Code of 1986.
"(B) Sections 302, 401, and 405 of the Katrina Emergency Tax Relief Act of 2005.
"(c) References.
"(1) Area. Any reference in such provisions to the Hurricane Katrina disaster area or the Gulf Opportunity Zone shall be treated as a reference to any Midwestern disaster area and any reference to the Hurricane Katrina disaster area or the Gulf Opportunity Zone within a State shall be treated as a reference to all Midwestern disaster areas within the State.
"(2) Items attributable to disaster. Any reference in such provisions to any loss, damage, or other item attributable to Hurricane Katrina shall be treated as a reference to any loss, damage, or other item attributable to the severe storms, tornadoes, or flooding giving rise to any Presidential declaration described in subsection (b)(1)(A).
"(3) Applicable disaster date. For purposes of applying the substitutions described in subsections (d) and (e), the term 'applicable disaster date' means, with respect to any Midwestern disaster area, the date on which the severe storms, tornadoes, or flooding giving rise to the Presidential declaration described in subsection (b)(1)(A) occurred.
—P.L. 110-343, Sec. 702(d)(12)DivC, through Sec. 702(d)(15) Div C, P.L. 110-343, relating to tax relief for areas damaged by 2008 Midwestern severe storms, tornadoes, and flooding applies the following modifications to Code Sec. 1400S:
"(d) Modifications to 1986 Code. The following provisions of the Internal Revenue Code of 1986 shall be applied with the following modifications:
* * * * * * * * * * *
"(12) Temporary suspension of limitations on charitable contributions. Section 1400S(a), by substituting the following paragraph for paragraph (4) thereof:
"'(4) Qualified contributions.
"'(A) In general. For purposes of this subsection, the term 'qualified contribution' means any charitable contribution (as defined in section 170(c)) if—
"'(i) such contribution—
"'(I) is paid during the period beginning on the earliest applicable disaster date for all States and ending on December 31, 2008, in cash to an organization described in section 170(b)(1)(A), and
"'(II) is made for relief efforts in 1 or more Midwestern disaster areas, '(ii) the taxpayer obtains from such organization contemporaneous written acknowledgment (within the meaning of section 170(f)(8)) that such contribution was used (or is to be used) for relief efforts in 1 or more Midwestern disaster areas, and
" '(iii) the taxpayer has elected the application of this subsection with respect to such contribution.
"'(B) Exception. Such term shall not include a contribution by a donor if the contribution is—
"'(i) to an organization described in section 509(a)(3), or
" ' (ii) for establishment of a new, or maintenance of an existing, donor advised fund (as defined in section 4966(d)(2)).
"'(C) Application of election to partnerships and S corporations. In the case of a partnership or S corporation, the election under subparagraph (A)(iii) shall be made separately by each partner or shareholder.'.
"(13) Suspension of certain limitations on personal casualty losses. Section 1400S(b)(1), by substituting 'the applicable disaster date' for 'August 25, 2005'.
"(14) Special rule for determining earned income. Section 1400S(d)—
"(A) by treating an individual as a qualified individual if such individual's principal place of abode on the applicable disaster date was located in a Midwestern disaster area,
"(B) by treating the applicable disaster date with respect to any such individual as the applicable date for purposes of such subsection, and

"(C) by treating an area as described in paragraph (2)(B)(ii) thereof if the area is a Midwestern disaster area only by reason of subsection (b)(2) of this section (relating to areas eligible only for public assistance).
"(15) Adjustments regarding taxpayer and dependency status. Section 1400S(e), by substituting '2008 or 2009' for '2005 or 2006'.
* * * * * * * * * * *
—P.L. 110-246, Sec. 4, Repeals the duplicative enactment and provides effective date provisions of the Act entitled 'An Act to provide for the continuation of agricultural programs through fiscal year 2012, and for other purposes' Sec. 4, P.L. 110-246 reads as follows:
"Sec. 4. Repeal of duplicative enactment.
"(a) In General- The Act entitled 'An Act to provide for the continuation of agricultural programs through fiscal year 2012, and for other purposes' (H.R. 2419 of the 110th Congress), and the amendments made by that Act, are repealed, effective on the date of enactment of that Act.
"(b) Effective Date- Except as otherwise provided in this Act, this Act and the amendments made by this Act shall take effect on the earlier of--
"(1) the date of enactment of this Act; or
"(2) the date of the enactment of the Act entitled 'An Act to provide for the continuation of agricultural programs through fiscal year 2012, and for other purposes' (H.R. 2419 of the 110th Congress)."
—P.L. 110-246, Sec. 15345, applies to this Code Sec. 1400S for the Kansas Disaster Area storms beginning on May 4, 2007 as specifically outlined in Sec. 15345(a)(9), (b), (c), (d)(7), P.L. 110-246, which read as follows:
"Sec. 15345. Temporary tax relief for Kiowa County, Kansas and surrounding area.
"(a) In General. Subject to the modifications described in this section, the following provisions of or relating to the Internal Revenue Code of 1986 shall apply to the Kansas disaster area in addition to the areas to which such provisions otherwise apply:
* * * * * * * * * * *
"(9) Section 1400S(b) of such Code (relating to suspension of certain limitations on personal casualty losses)."
* * * * * * * * * * *
Sec. 15345(b), defining Kansas Disaster Area, provides:
"(b) Kansas Disaster Area. For purposes of this section, the term 'Kansas disaster area' means an area with respect to which a major disaster has been declared by the President under section 401 of the Robert T. Stafford Disaster Relief and Emergency Assistance Act (FEMA-1699-DR, as in effect on the date of the enactment of this Act) by reason of severe storms and tornadoes beginning on May 4, 2007, and determined by the President to warrant individual or individual and public assistance from the Federal Government under such Act with respect to damages attributable to such storms and tornadoes."
Sec. 15345(c), referring to area or loss provides:
"(c) References to Area or Loss—
"(1) Area. Any reference in such provisions to the Katrina disaster area or the Gulf Opportunity Zone shall be treated as a reference to the Kansas disaster area.
"(2) Loss. Any reference in such provisions to any loss or damage attributable to Hurricane Katrina shall be treated as a reference to any loss or damage attributable to the May 4, 2007, storms and tornadoes."
Sec. 15345(d)(7), following, provides detailed information on dates and special allowances for certain property acquired on or after May 5, 2007.
"(d) References to Dates, etc.
* * * * * * * * * * *
"(7) Suspension of certain limitations on personal casualty losses. Section 1400S(b)(1) of the Internal Revenue Code of 1986, by substituting 'May 4, 2007' for 'August 25, 2005'. [Ed. Note: May 22, 2008 was the date of enactment for H.R. 2419 (PL 110-234), which was repealed by (2008 Farm Act § 4(a)) (PL 110-246, 6/18/2008), in connection with the reenactment of the farm bill to correct a technical deficiency in its original passage.]
—P.L. 110-185, Sec. 103(c)(9)(A), substituted 'December 31, 2007' for 'September 10, 2001' in subpara. (d)(3)(A) . . . Sec. 103(c)(9)(B), substituted 'January 1, 2009' for 'January 1, 2005' in subpara. (d)(3)(B) . . . Sec. 103(c)(10), added subpara. (d)(6)(E), effective for property placed in service after December 31, 2007, in tax. yrs. ending after 2/13/2008.
In 2007, P.L. 110-172, Sec. 11(a)(14)(C), substituted 'subparagraph (G)' for 'subparagraph (F)' in clause (a)(2)(A)(i), enacted 12/29/2007.
In 2005, P.L. 109-135, Sec. 201(a), added Code Sec. 1400S, effective 12/21/2005.
—P.L. 109-135, Sec. 201(b)(4)(B), Repealed Secs. 301, 402, 403(b), and 406 of P.L. 109-73.

- **Caution:** For temporary tax relief provisions for areas damaged by 2008 Midwestern severe storms, tornadoes, and flooding, see history for this Code Sec.

Sec. 1400T. Special rules for mortgage revenue bonds.
(a) In general.

In the case of financing provided with respect to owner-occupied residences in the GO Zone, the Rita GO Zone, or the Wilma GO Zone, section 143 shall be applied—

(1) by treating any such residence in the Rita GO Zone or the Wilma GO Zone as a targeted area residence,
(2) by applying subsection (f)(3) thereof without regard to subparagraph (A) thereof, and
(3) by substituting '$150,000' for '$15,000' in subsection (k)(4) thereof.

(b) Application.
Subsection (a) shall not apply to financing provided after December 31, 2010.

In **2008**, P.L. 110-343, Sec. 702(a)DivC, through Sec. 702(c) Div C, P.L. 110-343, relating to tax relief for areas damaged by 2008 Midwestern severe storms, tornados, and flooding, reads as follows:
"Sec. 702. Temporary tax relief for areas damaged by 2008 Midwestern severe storms, tornados, and flooding.
"(a) In general. Subject to the modifications described in this section, the following provisions of or relating to the Internal Revenue Code of 1986 shall apply to any Midwestern disaster area in addition to the areas to which such provisions otherwise apply:
"(1) GO Zone benefits.
"(A) Section 1400N (relating to tax benefits) other than subsections (b), (d), (e), (i), (j), (m), and (o) thereof.
"(B) Section 1400O (relating to education tax benefits).
"(C) Section 1400P (relating to housing tax benefits).
"(D) Section 1400Q (relating to special rules for use of retirement funds).
"(E) Section 1400R(a) (relating to employee retention credit for employers).
"(F) Section 1400S (relating to additional tax relief) other than subsection (d) thereof.
"(G) Section 1400T (relating to special rules for mortgage revenue bonds).
"(2) Other benefits included in Katrina Emergency Tax Relief Act of 2005. Sections 302, 303, 304, 401, and 405 of the Katrina Emergency Tax Relief Act of 2005.
"(b) Midwestern disaster area.
"(1) In general. For purposes of this section and for applying the substitutions described in subsections (d) and (e), the term 'Midwestern disaster area' means an area—
"(A) with respect to which a major disaster has been declared by the President on or after May 20, 2008, and before August 1, 2008, under section 401 of the Robert T. Stafford Disaster Relief and Emergency Assistance Act by reason of severe storms, tornados, or flooding occurring in any of the States of Arkansas, Illinois, Indiana, Iowa, Kansas, Michigan, Minnesota, Missouri, Nebraska, and Wisconsin, and
"(B) determined by the President to warrant individual or individual and public assistance from the Federal Government under such Act with respect to damages attributable to such severe storms, tornados, or flooding.
"(2) Certain benefits available to areas eligible only for public assistance. For purposes of applying this section to benefits under the following provisions, paragraph (1) shall be applied without regard to subparagraph (B):
"(A) Sections 1400Q, 1400S(b), and 1400S(d) of the Internal Revenue Code of 1986.
"(B) Sections 302, 401, and 405 of the Katrina Emergency Tax Relief Act of 2005.
"(c) References.
"(1) Area. Any reference in such provisions to the Hurricane Katrina disaster area or the Gulf Opportunity Zone shall be treated as a reference to any Midwestern disaster area and any reference to the Hurricane Katrina disaster area or the Gulf Opportunity Zone within a State shall be treated as a reference to all Midwestern disaster areas within the State.
"(2) Items attributable to disaster. Any reference in such provisions to any loss, damage, or other item attributable to Hurricane Katrina shall be treated as a reference to any loss, damage, or other item attributable to the severe storms, tornados, or flooding giving rise to any Presidential declaration described in subsection (b)(1)(A).
"(3) Applicable disaster date. For purposes of applying the substitutions described in subsections (d) and (e), the term 'applicable disaster date' means, with respect to any Midwestern disaster area, the date on which the severe storms, tornados, or flooding giving rise to the Presidential declaration described in subsection (b)(1)(A) occurred.
* * * * * * * * * *

In **2005**, P.L. 109-135, Sec. 201(a), added Code Sec. 1400T, effective 12/21/2005.

PART III.—RECOVERY ZONE BONDS
Sec.
1400U-1. Allocation of recovery zone bonds.
1400U-2. Recovery zone economic development bonds.
1400U-3. Recovery zone facility bonds.

In **2009**, P.L. 111-5, Sec. 1401(a), added part III and items 1400U-1, 1400U-2 and 1400U-3.

Sec. 1400U-1. Allocation of recovery zone bonds.
(a) Allocations.
 (1) In general.
  (A) General allocation. The Secretary shall allocate the national recovery zone economic development bond limitation and the national recovery zone facility bond limitation among the States in the proportion that each such State's 2008 State employment decline bears to the aggregate of the 2008 State employment declines for all of the States.
  (B) Minimum allocation. The Secretary shall adjust the allocations under subparagraph (A) for any calendar year for each State to the extent necessary to ensure that no State receives less than 0.9 percent of the national recovery zone economic development bond limitation and 0.9 percent of the national recovery zone facility bond limitation.
 (2) 2008 State employment decline. For purposes of this subsection, the term '2008 State employment decline' means, with respect to any State, the excess (if any) of—
  (A) the number of individuals employed in such State determined for December 2007, over
  (B) the number of individuals employed in such State determined for December 2008.
 (3) Allocations by States.
  (A) In general. Each State with respect to which an allocation is made under paragraph (1) shall reallocate such allocation among the counties and large municipalities in such State in the proportion to each such county's or municipality's 2008 employment decline bears to the aggregate of the 2008 employment declines for all the counties and municipalities in such State. A county or municipality may waive any portion of an allocation made under this subparagraph.
  (B) Large municipalities. For purposes of subparagraph (A), the term 'large municipality' means a municipality with a population of more than 100,000.
  (C) Determination of local employment declines. For purposes of this paragraph, the employment decline of any municipality or county shall be determined in the same manner as determining the State employment decline under paragraph (2), except that in the case of a municipality any portion of which is in a county, such portion shall be treated as part of such municipality and not part of such county.
 (4) National limitations.
  (A) Recovery zone economic development bonds. There is a national recovery zone economic development bond limitation of $10,000,000,000.
  (B) Recovery zone facility bonds. There is a national recovery zone facility bond limitation of $15,000,000,000.
(b) Recovery zone.
For purposes of this part, the term 'recovery zone' means—
 (1) any area designated by the issuer as having significant poverty, unemployment, rate of home foreclosures, or general distress,
 (2) any area designated by the issuer as economically distressed by reason of the closure or realignment of a military installation pursuant to the Defense Base Closure and Realignment Act of 1990, and
 (3) any area for which a designation as an empowerment zone or renewal community is in effect.

Self-employment tax

In 2009, P.L. 111-5, Sec. 1401(a), added Code Sec. 1400U-1, effective for obligations issued after 2/17/2009.

Sec. 1400U-2. Recovery zone economic development bonds.

(a) In general.

In the case of a recovery zone economic development bond—

(1) such bond shall be treated as a qualified bond for purposes of section 6431, and

(2) subsection (b) of such section shall be applied by substituting '45 percent' for '35 percent'.

(b) Recovery zone economic development bond.

(1) **In general.** For purposes of this section, the term 'recovery zone economic development bond' means any build America bond (as defined in section 54AA(d)) issued before January 1, 2011, as part of issue if—

(A) 100 percent of the excess of—

(i) the available project proceeds (as defined in section 54A) of such issue, over

(ii) the amounts in a reasonably required reserve (within the meaning of section 150(a)(3)) with respect to such issue,

are to be used for one or more qualified economic development purposes, and

(B) the issuer designates such bond for purposes of this section.

(2) **Limitation on amount of bonds designated.** The maximum aggregate face amount of bonds which may be designated by any issuer under paragraph (1) shall not exceed the amount of the recovery zone economic development bond limitation allocated to such issuer under section 1400U-1.

(c) Qualified economic development purpose.

For purposes of this section, the term 'qualified economic development purpose' means expenditures for purposes of promoting development or other economic activity in a recovery zone, including—

(1) capital expenditures paid or incurred with respect to property located in such zone,

(2) expenditures for public infrastructure and construction of public facilities, and

(3) expenditures for job training and educational programs.

In 2009, P.L. 111-5, Sec. 1401(a), added Code Sec. 1400U-2, effective for obligations issued after 2/17/2009.

—P.L. 111-5, Sec. 1601(5), of this Act, provides:

"SEC. 1601. APPLICATION OF CERTAIN LABOR STANDARDS TO PROJECTS FINANCED WITH CERTAIN TAX-FAVORED BONDS.

"Subchapter IV of chapter 31 of the title 40, United States Code, shall apply to projects financed with the proceeds of—

* * * * * *

"(5) any recovery zone economic development bond (as defined in section 1400U-2 of the Internal Revenue Code of 1986)."

Sec. 1400U-3. Recovery zone facility bonds.

(a) In general.

For purposes of part IV of subchapter B (relating to tax exemption requirements for State and local bonds), the term "exempt facility bond" includes any recovery zone facility bond.

(b) Recovery zone facility bond.

(1) **In general.** For purposes of this section, the term "recovery zone facility bond" means any bond issued as part of an issue if—

(A) 95 percent or more of the net proceeds (as defined in section 150(a)(3)) of such issue are to be used for recovery zone property,

(B) such bond is issued before January 1, 2011, and

(C) the issuer designates such bond for purposes of this section.

(2) **Limitation on amount of bonds designated.** The maximum aggregate face amount of bonds which may be designated by any issuer under paragraph (1) shall not exceed the amount of recovery zone facility bond limitation allocated to such issuer under section 1400U-1.

(c) Recovery zone property.

For purposes of this section—

(1) **In general.** The term "recovery zone property" means any property to which section 168 applies (or would apply but for section 179) if—

(A) such property was constructed, reconstructed, renovated, or acquired by purchase (as defined in section 179(d)(2)) by the taxpayer after the date on which the designation of the recovery zone took effect,

(B) the original use of which in the recovery zone commences with the taxpayer, and

(C) substantially all of the use of which is in the recovery zone and is in the active conduct of a qualified business by the taxpayer in such zone.

(2) **Qualified business.** The term "qualified business" means any trade or business except that—

(A) the rental to others of real property located in a recovery zone shall be treated as a qualified business only if the property is not residential rental property (as defined in section 168(e)(2)), and

(B) such term shall not include any trade or business consisting of the operation of any facility described in section 144(c)(6)(B).

(3) **Special rules for substantial renovations and saleleaseback.** Rules similar to the rules of subsections (a)(2) and (b) of section 1397D shall apply for purposes of this subsection.

(d) Nonapplication of certain rules.

Sections 146 (relating to volume cap) and 147(d) (relating to acquisition of existing property not permitted) shall not apply to any recovery zone facility bond.

In 2009, P.L. 111-5, Sec. 1401(a), added Code Sec. 1400U-3, effective for obligations issued after 2/17/2009.

CHAPTER 2.—TAX ON SELF-EMPLOYMENT INCOME

Sec.

1401. Rate of tax.
1402. Definitions.
1403. Miscellaneous provisions.

Sec. 1401. Rate of tax.

(a) Old-age, survivors, and disability insurance.

In addition to other taxes, there shall be imposed for each taxable year, on the self-employment income of every individual, a tax equal to the following percent of the amount of the self-employment income for such taxable year:

In the case of a taxable year		
Beginning after:	And before:	Percent:
December 31, 1983	January 1, 1988	11.40
December 31, 1987	January 1, 1990	12.12
December 31, 1989		12.40

• **Caution:** Code Sec. 1401(b), following, is effective with respect to remuneration received, and tax. yrs. begin., before 1/1/2013. For Code Sec. 1401(b), effective with re-

Code Sec. 1401(a) — Self-employment tax

spect to remuneration received, and tax. yrs. begin., after 12/31/2012, see below.

(b) Hospital insurance.
In addition to the tax imposed by the preceding subsection, there shall be imposed for each taxable year, on the self-employment income of every individual, a tax equal to the following percent of the amount of the self-employment income for such taxable year:

In the case of a taxable year		
Beginning after:	And before:	Percent:
December 31, 1983	January 1, 1985	2.60
December 31, 1984	January 1, 1986	2.70
December 31, 1985		2.90

• *Caution:* Code Sec. 1401(b), following, is effective with respect to remuneration received, and tax. yrs. begin., after 12/31/2012. For Code Sec. 1401(b), effective with respect to remuneration received, and tax. yrs. begin., before 1/1/2013, see above.

(b) Hospital insurance.
 (1) **In general.** In addition to the tax imposed by the preceding subsection, there shall be imposed for each taxable year, on the self-employment income of every individual, a tax equal to the following percent of the amount of the self-employment income for such taxable year:

In the case of a taxable year		
Beginning after:	And before:	Percent:
December 31, 1983	January 1, 1985	2.60
December 31, 1984	January 1, 1986	2.70
December 31, 1985		2.90

 (2) **Additional tax.**
 (A) In general. In addition to the tax imposed by paragraph (1) and the preceding subsection, there is hereby imposed on every taxpayer (other than a corporation, estate, or trust) for each taxable year beginning after December 31, 2012, a tax equal to 0.9 percent of the self-employment income for such taxable year which is in excess of—
  (i) in the case of a joint return, $250,000,
  (ii) in the case of a married taxpayer (as defined in section 7703) filing a separate return, ½ of the dollar amount determined under clause (i), and
  (iii) in any other case, $200,000.
 (B) Coordination with FICA. The amounts under clause (i), (ii), or (iii) which ever is applicable) of subparagraph (A) shall be reduced (but not below zero) by the amount of wages taken into account in determining the tax imposed under section 3121(b)(2) with respect to the taxpayer.

(c) Relief from taxes in cases covered by certain international agreements.
During any period in which there is in effect an agreement entered into pursuant to section 233 of the Social Security Act with any foreign country, the self-employment income of an individual shall be exempt from the taxes imposed by this section to the extent that such self-employment income is subject under such agreement exclusively to the laws applicable to the social security system of such foreign country.

In 2010, P.L. 111-312, Sec. 601, of this Act, provides:
"SEC. 601. TEMPORARY EMPLOYEE PAYROLL TAX CUT.
 "(a) In general. Notwithstanding any other provision of law, —
 "(1) with respect to any taxable year which begins in the payroll tax holiday period, the rate of tax under section 1401(a) of the Internal Revenue Code of 1986 shall be 10.40 percent, and
 "(2) with respect to remuneration received during the payroll tax holiday period, the rate of tax under 3101(a) of such Code shall be 4.2 percent (including for purposes of determining the applicable percentage under sections 3201(a) and 3211(a)(1) of such Code).
 "(b) Coordination with deductions for employment taxes.
 "(1) Deduction in computing net earnings from self-employment. For purposes of applying section 1402(a)(12) of the Internal Revenue Code of 1986, the rate of tax imposed by subsection 1401(a) of such Code shall be determined without regard to the reduction in such rate under this section.
 "(2) Individual deduction. In the case of the taxes imposed by section 1401 of such Code for any taxable year which begins in the payroll tax holiday period, the deduction under section 164(f) with respect to such taxes shall be equal to the sum of—
 "(A) 59.6 percent of the portion of such taxes attributable to the tax imposed by section 1401(a) (determined after the application of this section), plus
 "(B) one-half of the portion of such taxes attributable to the tax imposed by section 1401(b).
 "(c) Payroll tax holiday period. The term 'payroll tax holiday period' means calendar year 2011.
 "(d) Employer notification. The Secretary of the Treasury shall notify employers of the payroll tax holiday period in any manner the Secretary deems appropriate.
 "(e) Transfers of funds.
 "(1) Transfers to Federal Old-Age and Survivors Insurance Trust Fund. There are hereby appropriated to the Federal Old-Age and Survivors Trust Fund and the Federal Disability Insurance Trust Fund established under section 201 of the Social Security Act (42 U.S.C. 401) amounts equal to the reduction in revenues to the Treasury by reason of the application of subsection (a). Amounts appropriated by the preceding sentence shall be transferred from the general fund at such times and in such manner as to replicate to the extent possible the transfers which would have occurred to such Trust Fund had such amendments not been enacted.
 "(2) Transfers to Social Security Equivalent Benefit Account. There are hereby appropriated to the Social Security Equivalent Benefit Account established under section 15A(a) of the Railroad Retirement Act of 1974 (45 U.S.C. 231n-1(a)) amounts equal to the reduction in revenues to the Treasury by reason of the application of subsection (a)(2). Amounts appropriated by the preceding sentence shall be transferred from the general fund at such times and in such manner as to replicate to the extent possible the transfers which would have occurred to such Account had such amendments not been enacted.
 "(3) Coordination with other Federal laws. For purposes of applying any provision of Federal law other than the provisions of the Internal Revenue Code of 1986, the rate of tax in effect under section 3101(a) of such Code shall be determined without regard to the reduction in such rate under this section."
—P.L. 111-152, Sec. 1402(b)(1)(B)(i), deleted "and" at the end of clause (b)(2)(A)(i), added clause (b)(2)(A)(ii) and redesignated clause (b)(2)(A)(ii) as (b)(2)(A)(iii) . . . Sec. 1402(b)(1)(B)(ii), substituted "under clause (i), (ii), or (iii) (whichever is applicable)" for "under clauses (i) and (ii)" in subpara. (b)(2)(B), effective with respect to remuneration received, and tax. yrs. begin. after, 12/31/2012.
—P.L. 111-148, Sec. 9015(b)(1)(A), substituted "(1) In general. In addition" for "In addition" in subsec. (b) . . . Sec. 9015(b)(1)(B), added para. (b)(2), effective with respect to remuneration received, and tax. yrs. begin., after 12/31/2012.
—P.L. 111-148, Sec. 10906(b), substituted "0.9 percent" for "0.5 percent" in subpara. (b)(2)(A) [as added by Sec. 9015(b)(1)(B) of this Act, see above], effective with respect to remuneration received, and tax. yrs. begin., after 12/31/2012.
In 2004, P.L. 108-203, Sec. 415, substituted "exclusively to the laws applicable to" for "to taxes or contributions for similar purposes under" in subsec. (c), effective 3/2/2004.
In 1990, P.L. 101-508, Sec. 11801(a)(36), deleted subsec. (c) . . . Sec. 11801(c)(16), redesignated subsec. (d) as subsec. (c), effective 11/5/90 except as provided in Sec. 11821(b) of this Act, which reads as follows:
"(b) Savings provision.
 "If—
 "(1) any provision amended or repealed by this part applied to—
 "(A) any transaction occurring before the date of the enactment of this Act [11/5/90],
 "(B) any property acquired before such date of enactment [11/5/90], or
 "(C) any item of income, loss, deduction, or credit taken into account before such date of enactment [11/5/90], and
 "(2) the treatment of such transaction, property, or item under such provision would (without regard to the amendments made by this part) affect liability for tax for periods ending after such date of enactment [11/5/90],
nothing in the amendments made by this part shall be construed to affect the treatment of such transaction, property, or item for purposes of determining liability for tax for periods ending after such date of enactment [11/5/90]."
Prior to deletion, subsec. (c) read as follows:
"(c) Credit against taxes imposed by this section.
 "(1) In general. In the case of a taxable year beginning before 1990, there shall be allowed as a credit against the taxes imposed by this section for any taxable

Self-employment tax   Code Sec. 1401

year an amount equal to the applicable percentage of the self-employment income of the individual for such taxable year.

"(2) Applicable percentage. For purposes of paragraph (1), the applicable percentage shall be determined in accordance with the following table:

In the case of taxable years beginning in:	The applicable percentage is:
1984	2.7
1985	2.3
1986, 1987, 1988, or 1989	2.0"

In 1983, P.L. 98-21, Sec. 124(a), amended subsecs. (a) and (b) . . . Sec. 124(b), redesignated subsec. (c) as subsec. (d) and added new subsec. (c), effective for tax. yrs. begin. after 12/31/83.

Prior to amendment, subsecs. (a) and (b) read as follows:

"(a) Old-age, survivors, and disability insurance.

"In addition to other taxes, there shall be imposed for each taxable year, on the self-employment income of every individual, a tax as follows:

"(1) in the case of any taxable year beginning before January 1, 1978, the tax shall be equal to 7.0 percent of the amount of the self-employment income for such taxable year;

"(2) in the case of any taxable year beginning after December 31, 1977, and before January 1, 1979, the tax shall be equal to 7.10 percent of the amount of the self-employment income for such taxable year;

"(3) in the case of any taxable year beginning after December 31, 1978, and before January 1, 1981, the tax shall be equal to 7.05 percent of the amount of the self-employment income for such taxable year;

"(4) in the case of any taxable year beginning after December 31, 1980, and before January 1, 1982, the tax shall be equal to 8.00 percent of the amount of the self-employment income for such taxable year;

"(5) in the case of any taxable year beginning after December 31, 1981, and before January 1, 1985, the tax shall be equal to 8.05 percent of the amount of the self-employment income for such taxable year;

"(6) in the case of any taxable year beginning after December 31, 1984, and before January 1, 1990, the tax shall be equal to 8.55 percent of the amount of the self-employment income for such taxable year; and

"(7) in the case of any taxable year beginning after December 31, 1989, the tax shall be equal to 9.30 percent of the amount of the self-employment income for such taxable year.

"(b) Hospital insurance.

"In addition to the tax imposed by the preceding subsection, there shall be imposed for each taxable year, on the self-employment income of every individual, a tax as follows:

"(1) in the case of any taxable year beginning after December 31, 1973, and before January 1, 1978, the tax shall be equal to 0.90 percent of the amount of the self-employment income for such taxable year;

"(2) in the case of any taxable year beginning after December 31, 1977, and before January 1, 1979, the tax shall be equal to 1.00 percent of the amount of the self-employment income for such taxable year;

"(3) in the case of any taxable year beginning after December 31, 1978, and before January 1, 1981, the tax shall be equal to 1.05 percent of the amount of the self-employment income for such taxable year;

"(4) in the case of any taxable year beginning after December 31, 1980, and before January 1, 1985, the tax shall be equal to 1.30 percent of the amount of the self-employment income for such taxable year;

"(5) in the case of any taxable year beginning after December 31, 1984, and before January 1, 1986, the tax shall be equal to 1.35 percent of the amount of the self-employment income for such taxable year; and

"(6) in the case of any taxable year beginning after December 31, 1985, the tax shall be equal to 1.45 percent of the amount of the self-employment income for such taxable year."

In 1977, P.L. 95-216, Sec. 101(a)(3), amended subsec. (a), effective for remunerations paid or received, and tax. yrs. begin. after '77.

Prior to amendment, subsec. (a) read as follows:

"(a) Old-Age, survivors, and disability insurance.

"In addition to other taxes, there shall be imposed for each taxable year, on the self-employment income of every individual, a tax equal to 7.0 percent of the amount of the self-employment income for such taxable year."

—P.L. 95-216, Sec. 101(b)(3), amended paras. (b)(1)-(4), and added paras. (b)(5) and (6), effective for remunerations paid or received, and tax. yrs. begin. after '77.

Prior to amendment, paras. (b)(1)-(4) read as follows:

"(1) in the case of any taxable year beginning after December 31, 1973, and before January 1, 1978, the tax shall be equal to 0.90 percent of the amount of the self-employment income for such taxable year;

"(2) in the case of any taxable year beginning after December 31, 1977, and before January 1, 1981, the tax shall be equal to 1.10 percent of the amount of the self-employment income for such taxable year;

"(3) in the case of any taxable year beginning after December 31, 1980, and before January 1, 1986, the tax shall be equal to 1.35 percent of the amount of the self-employment income for such taxable year; and

"(4) in the case of any taxable year beginning after December 31, 1985, the tax shall be equal to 1.50 percent of the self-employment income for such taxable year."

—P.L. 95-216, Sec. 317(b)(1), added subsec. (c), effective for 12/20/77 [date of enactment].

Sec. 317(b)(4), effective 12/20/77 [date of enactment], provided as follows:

"(4) Notwithstanding any other provision of law, taxes paid by any individual to any foreign country with respect to any period of employment or self-employment which is covered under the social security system of such foreign country in accordance with the terms of an agreement entered into pursuant to section 233 of the Social Security Act shall not, under the income tax laws of the United States, be deductible by, or creditable against the income tax of, any such individual."

In 1976, P.L. 94-455, Sec. 1901(a)(154)(A), amended subsec. (a) . . . Sec. 1901(a)(154)(B), deleted paras. (b)(1) and (2) and redesignated paras. (b)(3), (4), (5) and (6) as paras. (b)(1), (2), (3) and (4), effective for tax. yrs. begin. after 12/31/76.

Prior to amendment, subsec. (a) read as follows:

"(a) Old-age, survivors, and disability insurance.

"In addition to other taxes, there shall be imposed for each taxable year, on the self-employment income of every individual, a tax as follows:

"(1) in the case of any taxable year beginning after December 31, 1967, and before January 1, 1969, the tax shall be equal to 5.8 percent of the amount of the self-employment income for such taxable year;

"(2) in the case of any taxable year beginning after December 31, 1968, and before January 1, 1971, the tax shall be equal to 6.3 percent of the amount of the self-employment income for such taxable year;

"(3) in the case of any taxable year beginning after December 31, 1970, and before January 1, 1973, the tax shall be equal to 6.9 percent of the amount of the self-employment income for such taxable year;

"(4) in the case of any taxable year beginning after December 31, 1972, the tax shall be equal to 7.0 percent of the amount of the self-employment income for such taxable year."

Prior to deletion, paras. (b)(1) and (2) read as follows:

"(1) in the case of any taxable year beginning after December 31, 1967, and before January 1, 1973, the tax shall be equal to 0.60 percent of the amount of the self-employment income for such taxable year;

"(2) in the case of any taxable year beginning after December 31, 1972, and before January 1, 1974, the tax shall be equal to 1.0 percent of the amount of the self-employment income for such taxable year;"

In 1973, P.L. 93-233, Sec. 6(b)(1), amended paras. (b)(2) through (5) and added para. (b)(6), effective for tax. yrs. begin. after 12/31/73.

Prior to amendment, paras. (b)(2) through (b)(5) read as follows:

"(2) in the case of any taxable year beginning after December 31, 1972, and before January 1, 1978, the tax shall be equal to 1.0 percent of the amount of the self-employment income for such taxable year;

"(3) in the case of any taxable year beginning after December 31, 1977, and before January 1, 1981, the tax shall be equal to 1.25 percent of the amount of the self-employment income for such taxable year;

"(4) in the case of any taxable year beginning after December 31, 1980, and before January 1, 1986, the tax shall be equal to 1.35 percent of the amount of the self-employment income for such taxable year;

"(5) in the case of any taxable year beginning after December 31, 1985, the tax shall be equal to 1.45 percent of the amount of the self-employment income for such taxable year."

In 1972, P.L. 92-603, Sec. 135(a)(1), substituted "1973" for "1978" in para. (a)(3), amended para. (a)(4) and deleted para. (a)(5), effective only for tax yrs. begin. after 12/31/72.

Prior to amendment, paras. (a)(4) and (a)(5) read as follows:

"(4) in the case of any taxable year beginning after December 31, 1977, and before January 1, 2011, the tax shall be equal to 6.7 percent of the amount of the self-employment income for such taxable year; and

"(5) in the case of any taxable year beginning after December 31, 2010, the tax shall be equal to 7.0 percent of the amount of the self-employment income for such taxable year."

—P.L. 92-603, Sec. 135(b)(1), amended paras. (b)(2) through (b)(5), effective only for the tax. yrs. begin. after 12/31/72.

Prior to amendment, paras. (b)(2) through (b)(5) read as follows:

"(2) in the case of any taxable year beginning after December 31, 1972, and before January 1, 1978, the tax shall be equal to 0.9 percent of the amount of the self-employment income for such taxable year;

"(3) in the case of any taxable year beginning after December 31, 1977, and before January 1, 1986, the tax shall be equal to 1.0 percent of the amount of the self-employment income for such taxable year;

"(4) in the case of any taxable year beginning after December 31, 1985, and before January 1, 1993, the tax shall be equal to 1.1 percent of the amount of the self-employment income for such taxable year; and

"(5) in the case of any taxable year beginning after December 31, 1992, the tax shall be equal to 1.2 percent of the amount of the self-employment income for such taxable year."

—P.L. 92-336, Sec. 204(a)(1), substituted "January 1, 1978" for "January 1, 1973", in para. (a)(3), deleted "and" from the end of para. (a)(3), amended para. (a)(4) and added para. (a)(5), effective for tax. yrs. begin. after 12/31/72.

Prior to amendment, para. (a)(4) read as follows:

"(4) in the case of any taxable year beginning after December 31, 1972, the tax shall be equal to 7.0 percent of the amount of the self-employment income for such taxable year."

—P.L. 92-336, Sec. 204(b)(1), amended paras. (b)(2) through (5), effective for tax. yrs. begin. after 12/31/72.

Prior to amendment, paras. (b)(2) through (5) read as follows:

"(2) in the case of any taxable year beginning after December 31, 1972, and before January 1, 1976, the tax shall be equal to 0.65 percent of the amount of the self-employment income for such taxable year;

"(3) in the case of any taxable year beginning after December 31, 1975, and before January 1, 1980, the tax shall be equal to 0.70 percent of the amount of the self-employment income for such taxable year;

"(4) in the case of any taxable year beginning after December 31, 1979, and before January 1, 1987, the tax shall be equal to 0.80 percent of the amount of the self-employment income for such taxable year; and

"(5) in the case of any taxable year beginning after December 31, 1986, the tax shall be equal to 0.90 percent of the amount of the self-employment income for such taxable year."

In 1968, P.L. 90-248, Sec. 109(a)(1), substituted "December 31, 1967" and "January 1, 1969" for "December 31, 1965" and "January 1, 1967" in para. (a)(1), "December 31, 1968", "January 1, 1971" and "6.3" for "December 31, 1966", "January 1, 1969", and "5.9" in para. (a)(2), and "December 31, 1970" and "6.9" for "December 31, 1968" and "6.6" in para. (a)(3); and reenacted para. (a)(4) without change.

—P.L. 90-248, Sec. 109(b)(1), deleted para. (b)(1) provision for rate of 0.35 percent of amount of self-employment income for any taxable year beginning after Dec. 31, 1965, and before Jan. 1, 1967, redesignated former paras. (b)(2) to (b)(6) as (b)(1) to (b)(5), substituted "December 31, 1967" for "December 31, 1966" in such para. (b)(1) and increased the rate by 0.10 percent to 0.60, 0.65, 0.70, 0.80, and 0.90 in paras. (b)(1) to (b)(5), respectively.

In 1965, P.L. 89-97, Sec. 321, rewrote Code Sec. 1401 for tax. yrs. begin. after '65 . . . Sec. 111, of the P.L. amended the newly rewritten section by deleting the last sentence which read: "For purposes of the tax imposed by this subsection, the exclusion of employee representatives by section 1402(c)(3) shall not apply."

Prior to amendments, the Code Sec. read as follows:

"Sec. 1401. Rate of tax.

"In addition to other taxes, there shall be imposed for each taxable year, on the self-employment income of every individual, a tax as follows:

"(1) in the case of any taxable year beginning after December 31, 1961, and before January 1, 1963, the tax shall be equal to 4.7 percent of the amount of the self-employment income for such taxable year;

"(2) in the case of any taxable year beginning after December 31, 1962, and before January 1, 1966, the tax shall be equal to 5.4 percent of the amount of the self-employment income for such taxable year;

"(3) in the case of any taxable year beginning after December 31, 1965, and before January 1, 1968, the tax shall be equal to 6.2 percent of the amount of the self-employment income for such taxable year; and

"(4) in the case of any taxable year beginning after December 31, 1967, the tax shall be equal to 6.9 percent of the amount of the self-employment income for such taxable year."

In 1961, P.L. 87-64, increased the rate of tax.

Prior rates were: yrs. begin. in '62 – 4½%; in '63, '64, '65 – 5¼%; in '66, '67, '68 – 6% and after '68 – 6¾%.

In 1958, P.L. 85-840, increased the rate of tax.

Prior rates were: yrs. begin. in '57 thru '59 – 3⅜%; in '60 thru '64 – 4⅛%; in '65 thru '69 – 4⅞%; in '70 thru '74 – 5⅝%; after '74 – 6⅜%.

In 1956, ch. 836, Sec. 202(a), increased the rate of tax.

Prior rates were: yrs. begin. before '60 – 3%; in '60 thru '64 – 3¼%; in '65 thru '69 – 4½%; in '70 thru '74 – 5¼%; after '74 – 6%.

In 1954, ch. 1206, Sec. 208(a), increased the rate of tax.

Prior rates were: yrs. begin. before '60 – 3%; in '60 thru '64 – 3¼%; in '65 thru '69 – 4½%; after '69 – 4⅞%.

Sec. 1402. Definitions.

(a) Net earnings from self-employment.

The term "net earnings from self-employment" means the gross income derived by an individual from any trade or business carried on by such individual, less the deductions allowed by this subtitle which are attributable to such trade or business, plus his distributive share (whether or not distributed) of income or loss described in section 702(a)(8) from any trade or business carried on by a partnership of which he is a member; except that in computing such gross income and deductions and such distributive share of partnership ordinary income or loss—

(1) there shall be excluded rentals from real estate and from personal property leased with the real estate (including such rentals paid in crop shares , and including payments under section 1233(2) of the Food Security Act of 1985 (16 U.S.C. 3833(2)) to individuals receiving benefits under section 202 or 223 of the Social Security Act) together with the deductions attributable thereto, unless such rentals are received in the course of a trade or business as a real estate dealer; except that the preceding provisions of this paragraph shall not apply to any income derived by the owner or tenant of land if (A) such income is derived under an arrangement, between the owner or tenant and another individual, which provides that such other individual shall produce agricultural or horticultural commodities (including livestock, bees, poultry, and fur-bearing animals and wildlife) on such land, and that there shall be material participation by the owner or tenant (as determined without regard to any activities of an agent of such owner or tenant) in the production or the management of the production of such agricultural or horticultural commodities, and (B) there is material participation by the owner or tenant (as determined without regard to any activities of an agent of such owner or tenant) with respect to any such agricultural or horticultural commodity;

(2) there shall be excluded dividends on any share of stock, and interest on any bond, debenture, note, or certificate, or other evidence of indebtedness, issued with interest coupons or in registered form by any corporation (including one issued by a government or political subdivision thereof), unless such dividends and interest are received in the course of a trade or business as a dealer in stocks or securities;

(3) there shall be excluded any gain or loss—

(A) which is considered as gain or loss from the sale or exchange of a capital asset,

(B) from the cutting of timber, or the disposal of timber, coal, or iron ore, if section 631 applies to such gain or loss, or

(C) from the sale, exchange, involuntary conversion, or other disposition of property if such property is neither—

(i) stock in trade or other property of a kind which would properly be includible in inventory if on hand at the close of the taxable year, nor

(ii) property held primarily for sale to customers in the ordinary course of the trade or business;

(4) the deduction for net operating losses provided in section 172 shall not be allowed;

(5) If—

(A) any of the income derived from a trade or business (other than a trade or business carried on by a partnership) is community income under community property laws applicable to such income, the gross income and deductions attributable to such trade or business shall be treated as the gross income and deductions of the spouse carrying on such trade or business or, if such trade or business is jointly operated, treated as the gross income and deductions of each spouse on the basis of their respective distributive share of the gross income and deductions; and

(B) any portion of a partner's distributive share of the ordinary income or loss from a trade or business carried on by a partnership is community income or loss under the community property laws applicable to such share, all of such distributive share shall be included in computing the net earnings from self-employment of such partner, and no part of such share shall be taken into account in computing the net earnings from self-employment of the spouse of such partner;

(6) a resident of Puerto Rico shall compute his net earnings from self-employment in the same manner as a citizen of the United States but without regard to section 933;

(7) the deduction for personal exemptions provided in section 151 shall not be allowed;

(8) an individual who is a duly ordained, commissioned, or licensed minister of a church or a member of a religious order shall compute his net earnings from self-employment derived from the performance of service described in subsection (c)(4) without regard to section 107 (relating to rental value of parsonages), section 119 (relating to meals and lodging furnished for the convenience of the employer), and section 911 (relating to citizens or re-

Self-employment tax   Code Sec. 1402(a)(17)

sidents of the United States living abroad), but shall not include in such net earnings from self-employment the rental value of any parsonage or any parsonage allowance (whether or not excludable under section 107) provided after the individual retires, or any other retirement benefit received by such individual from a church plan (as defined in section 414(e)) after the individual retires;

(9) the exclusion from gross income provided by section 931 shall not apply;

(10) there shall be excluded amounts received by a partner pursuant to a written plan of the partnership, which meets such requirements as are prescribed by the Secretary, and which provides for payments on account of retirement, on a periodic basis, to partners generally or to a class or classes of partners, such payments to continue at least until such partner's death, if—

(A) such partner rendered no services with respect to any trade or business carried on by such partnership (or its successors) during the taxable year of such partnership (or its successors), ending within or with his taxable year, in which such amounts were received, and

(B) no obligation exists (as of the close of the partnership's taxable year referred to in subparagraph (A)) from the other partners to such partner except with respect to retirement payments under such plan, and

(C) such partner's share, if any, of the capital of the partnership has been paid to him in full before the close of the partnership's taxable year referred to in subparagraph (A);

(11) the exclusion from gross income provided by section 911(a)(1) shall not apply;

(12) in lieu of the deduction provided by section 164(f) (relating to deduction for one-half of self-employment taxes), there shall be allowed a deduction equal to the product of—

(A) the taxpayer's net earnings from self-employment for the taxable year (determined without regard to this paragraph), and

> • **Caution:** Code Sec. 1402(a)(12)(B), following, is effective with respect to remuneration received, and tax. yrs. begin., before 1/1/2013. For Code Sec. 1402(a)(12)(B), effective with respect to remuneration received, and tax. yrs. begin., after 12/31/2012, see below.

(B) one-half of the sum of the rates imposed by subsections (a) and (b) of section 1401 for such year;

> • **Caution:** Code Sec. 1402(a)(12)(B), following, is effective with respect to remuneration received, and tax. yrs. begin., after 12/31/2012. For Code Sec. 1402(a)(12)(B), effective with respect to remuneration received, and tax. yrs. begin., before 1/1/2013, see above.

(B) one-half of the sum of the rates imposed by subsections (a) and (b) of section 1401 for such year (determined without regard to the rate imposed under paragraph (2) of section 1401(b));

(13) there shall be excluded the distributive share of any item of income or loss of a limited partner, as such, other than guaranteed payments described in section 707(c) to that partner for services actually rendered to or on behalf of the partnership to the extent that those payments are established to be in the nature of remuneration for those services;

(14) in the case of church employee income, the special rules of subsection (j)(1) shall apply;

(15) in the case of a member of an Indian tribe, the special rules of section 7873 (relating to income derived by Indians from exercise of fishing rights) shall apply;

(16) the deduction provided by section 199 shall not be allowed; and

(17) notwithstanding the preceding provisions of this subsection, each spouse's share of income or loss from a qualified joint venture shall be taken into account as provided in section 761(f) in determining net earnings from self-employment of such spouse.

If the taxable year of a partner is different from that of the partnership, the distributive share which he is required to include in computing his net earnings from self-employment shall be based on the ordinary income or loss of the partnership for any taxable year of the partnership ending within or with his taxable year. In the case of any trade or business which is carried on by an individual or by a partnership and in which, if such trade or business were carried on exclusively by employees, the major portion of the services would constitute agricultural labor as defined in section 3121(g)—

(i) in the case of an individual, if the gross income derived by him from such trade or business is not more than the upper limit, the net earnings from self-employment derived by him from such trade or business may, at his option, be deemed to be 66⅔ percent of such gross income; or

(ii) in the case of an individual, if the gross income derived by him from such trade or business is more than the upper limit and the net earnings from self-employment derived by him from such trade or business (computed under this subsection without regard to this sentence) are less than the lower limit, the net earnings from self-employment derived by him from such trade or business may, at his option, be deemed to be the lower limit; and

(iii) in the case of a member of a partnership, if his distributive share of the gross income of the partnership derived from such trade or business (after such gross income has been reduced by the sum of all payments to which section 707(c) applies) is not more than the upper limit, his distributive share of income described in section 702(a)(8) derived from such trade or business may, at his option, be deemed to be an amount equal to 66⅔ percent of his distributive share of such gross income (after such gross income has been so reduced); or

(iv) in the case of a member of a partnership, if his distributive share of the gross income of the partnership derived from such trade or business (after such gross income has been reduced by the sum of all payments to which section 707(c) applies) is more than the upper limit and his distributive share (whether or not distributed) of income described in section 702(a)(8) derived from such trade or business (computed under this subsection without regard to this sentence) is less than the lower limit, his distributive share of income described in section 702(a)(8) derived from such trade or business may, at his option, be deemed to be the lower limit.

For purposes of the preceding sentence, gross income means—

(v) in the case of any such trade or business in which the income is computed under a cash receipts and disbursements method, the gross receipts from such trade or business reduced by the cost or other basis of property which was purchased and sold in carrying on such trade or business, adjusted (after such reduction) in accordance with the provisions of paragraphs (1) through (7) and paragraph (9) of this subsection; and

(vi) in the case of any such trade or business in which the income is computed under an accrual method, the gross income from such trade or business, adjusted in accordance with the provisions of paragraphs (1) through (7) and paragraph (9) of this subsection;

and, for purposes of such sentence, if an individual (including a member of a partnership) derives gross income from more than one such trade or business, such gross income (including his distributive share of the gross income of any partnership derived from any such trade or business) shall be deemed to have been derived from one trade or business.

The preceding sentence and clauses (i) through (iv) of the second preceding sentence shall also apply in the case of any trade or business (other than a trade or business specified in such second preceding sentence) which is carried on by an individual who is self-employed on a regular basis as defined in subsection (h), or by a partnership of which an individual is a member on a regular basis as defined in subsection (h), but only if such individual's net earnings from self-employment as determined without regard to this sentence in the taxable year are less than the lower limit and less than 66 ⅔ percent of the sum (in such taxable year) of such individual's gross income derived from all trades or businesses carried on by him and his distributive share of the income or loss from all trades or businesses carried on by all the partnerships of which he is a member; except that this sentence shall not apply to more than 5 taxable years in the case of any individual, and in no case in which an individual elects to determine the amount of his net earnings from self-employment for a taxable year under the provisions of the two preceding sentences with respect to a trade or business to which the second preceding sentence applies and with respect to a trade or business to which this sentence applies shall such net earnings for such year exceed the lower limit.

(b) Self-employment income.

The term "self-employment income" means the net earnings from self-employment derived by an individual (other than a nonresident alien individual, except as provided by an agreement under section 233 of the Social Security Act) during any taxable year; except that such term shall not include—

(1) in the case of the tax imposed by section 1401(a), that part of the net earnings from self-employment which is in excess of (i) an amount equal to the contribution and benefit base (as determined under section 230 of the Social Security Act) which is effective for the calendar year in which such taxable year begins, minus (ii) the amount of the wages paid to such individual during such taxable years; or

(2) the net earnings from self-employment, if such net earnings for the taxable year are less than $400.

For purposes of paragraph (1), the term "wages" (A) includes such remuneration paid to an employee for services included under an agreement entered into pursuant to the provisions of section 3121(l) (relating to coverage of citizens of the United States who are employees of foreign affiliates of American employers), as would be wages under section 3121(a) if such services constituted employment under section 3121(b), and (B) includes compensation which is subject to the tax imposed by section 3201 or 3211. An individual who is not a citizen of the United States but who is a resident of the Commonwealth of Puerto Rico, the Virgin Islands, Guam, or American Samoa shall not, for purposes of this chapter be considered to be a nonresident alien individual. In the case of church employee income, the special rules of subsection (j)(2) shall apply for purposes of paragraph (2).

(c) Trade or business.

The term "trade or business", when used with reference to self-employment income or net earnings from self-employment, shall have the same meaning as when used in section 162 (relating to trade or business expenses), except that such term shall not include—

(1) the performance of the functions of a public office, other than the functions of a public office of a State or a political subdivision thereof with respect to fees received in any period in which the functions are performed in a position compensated solely on a fee basis and in which such functions are not covered under an agreement entered into by such State and the Commissioner of Social Security pursuant to section 218 of the Social Security Act;

(2) the performance of service by an individual as an employee, other than—

(A) service described in section 3121(b)(14)(B) performed by an individual who has attained the age of 18,

(B) service described in section 3121(b)(16),

(C) service described in section 3121(b)(11), (12), or (15) performed in the United States (as defined in section 3121(e)(2)) by a citizen of the United States, except service which constitutes "employment" under section 3121(y),

(D) service described in paragraph (4) of this subsection,

(E) service performed by an individual as an employee of a State or a political subdivision thereof in a position compensated solely on a fee basis with respect to fees received in any period in which such service is not covered under an agreement entered into by such State and the Commissioner of Social Security pursuant to section 218 of the Social Security Act,

(F) service described in section 3121(b)(20), and

(G) service described in section 3121(b)(8)(B);

(3) the performance of service by an individual as an employee or employee representative as defined in section 3231;

(4) the performance of service by a duly ordained, commissioned, or licensed minister of a church in the exercise of his ministry or by a member of a religious order in the exercise of duties required by such order;

(5) the performance of service by an individual in the exercise of his profession as a Christian Science practitioner; or

(6) the performance of service by an individual during the period for which an exemption under subsection (g) is effective with respect to him.

The provisions of paragraph (4) or (5) shall not apply to service (other than service performed by a member of a religious order who has taken a vow of poverty as a member of such order) performed by an individual unless an exemption under subsection (e) is effective with respect to him.

(d) Employee and wages.

The term "employee" and the term "wages" shall have the same meaning as when used in chapter 21 (sec. 3101 and following, relating to Federal Insurance Contributions Act).

Self-employment tax

Code Sec. 1402(g)(2)(A)

(e) Ministers, members of religious orders, and Christian Science practitioners.

(1) Exemption. Subject to paragraph (2), any individual who is (A) a duly ordained, commissioned, or licensed minister of a church or a member of a religious order (other than a member of a religious order who has taken a vow of poverty as a member of such order) or (B) a Christian Science practitioner, upon filing an application (in such form and manner, and with such official, as may be prescribed by regulations made under this chapter) together with a statement that either he is conscientiously opposed to, or because of religious principles he is opposed to, the acceptance (with respect to services performed by him as such minister, member, or practitioner) of any public insurance which makes payments in the event of death, disability, old age, or retirement or makes payments toward the cost of, or provides services for, medical care (including the benefits of any insurance system established by the Social Security Act) and, in the case of an individual described in subparagraph (A), that he has informed the ordaining, commissioning, or licensing body of the church or order that he is opposed to such insurance, shall receive an exemption from the tax imposed by this chapter with respect to services performed by him as such minister, member, or practitioner. Notwithstanding the preceding sentence, an exemption may not be granted to an individual under this subsection if he had filed an effective waiver certificate under this section as it was in effect before its amendment in 1967.

(2) Verification of application. The Secretary may approve an application for an exemption filed pursuant to paragraph (1) only if the Secretary has verified that the individual applying for the exemption is aware of the grounds on which the individual may receive an exemption pursuant to this subsection and that the individual seeks exemption on such grounds. The Secretary (or the Commissioner of Social Security under an agreement with the Secretary) shall make such verification by such means as prescribed in regulations.

(3) Time for filing application. Any individual who desires to file an application pursuant to paragraph (1) must file such application on or before whichever of the following dates is later: (A) the due date of the return (including any extension thereof) for the second taxable year for which he has net earnings from self-employment (computed without regard to subsections (c)(4) and (c)(5)) of $400 or more, any part of which was derived from the performance of service described in subsection (c)(4) or (c)(5); or (B) the due date of the return (including any extension thereof) for his second taxable year ending after 1967.

(4) Effective date of exemption. An exemption received by an individual pursuant to this subsection shall be effective for the first taxable year for which he has net earnings from self-employment (computed without regard to subsection (c)(4) and (c)(5)) of $400 or more, any part of which was derived from the performance of service described in subsection (c)(4) or (c)(5), and for all succeeding taxable years. An exemption received pursuant to this subsection shall be irrevocable.

(f) Partner's taxable year ending as the result of death.

In computing a partner's net earnings from self-employment for his taxable year which ends as a result of his death (but only if such taxable year ends within, and not with, the taxable year of the partnership), there shall be included so much of the deceased partner's distributive share of the partnership's ordinary income or loss for the partnership taxable year as is not attributable to an interest in the partnership during any period beginning on or after the first day of the first calendar month following the month in which such partner died. For purposes of this subsection—

(1) in determining the portion of the distributive share which is attributable to any period specified in the preceding sentence, the ordinary income or loss of the partnership shall be treated as having been realized or sustained ratably over the partnership taxable year; and

(2) the term "deceased partner's distributive share" includes the share of his estate or of any other person succeeding, by reason of his death, to rights with respect to his partnership interest.

(g) Members of certain religious faiths.

(1) Exemption. Any individual may file an application (in such form and manner, and with such official, as may be prescribed by regulations under this chapter) for an exemption from the tax imposed by this chapter if he is a member of a recognized religious sect or division thereof and is an adherent of established tenets or teachings of such sect or division by reason of which he is conscientiously opposed to acceptance of the benefits of any private or public insurance which makes payments in the event of death, disability, old-age, or retirement or makes payments toward the cost of, or provides services for, medical care (including the benefits of any insurance system established by the Social Security Act). Such exemption may be granted only if the application contains or is accompanied by—

(A) such evidence of such individual's membership in, and adherence to the tenets or teachings of, the sect or division thereof as the Secretary may require for purposes of determining such individual's compliance with the preceding sentence, and

(B) his waiver of all benefits and other payments under titles II and XVIII of the Social Security Act on the basis of his wages and self-employment income as well as all such benefits and other payments to him on the basis of the wages and self-employment income of any other person,

and only if the Commissioner of Social Security finds that—

(C) such sect or division thereof has the established tenets or teachings referred to in the preceding sentence,

(D) it is the practice, and has been for a period of time which he deems to be substantial, for members of such sect or division thereof to make provision for their dependent members which in his judgment is reasonable in view of their general level of living, and

(E) such sect or division thereof has been in existence at all times since December 31, 1950.

An exemption may not be granted to any individual if any benefit or other payment referred to in subparagraph (B) became payable (or, but for section 203 or 222(b) of the Social Security Act, would have become payable) at or before the time of the filing of such waiver.

(2) Period for which exemption effective. An exemption granted to any individual pursuant to this subsection shall apply with respect to all taxable years beginning after December 31, 1950, except that such exemption shall not apply for any taxable year—

(A) beginning (i) before the taxable year in which such individual first met the requirements of the first sentence of paragraph (1), or (ii) before the time as of which the Commissioner of Social Security finds that the sect or division thereof of which such individual is

2,923

a member met the requirements of subparagraphs (C) and (D), or

(B) ending (i) after the time such individual ceases to meet the requirements of the first sentence of paragraph (1), or (ii) after the time as of which the Commissioner of Social Security finds that the sect or division thereof of which he is a member ceases to meet the requirements of subparagraph (C) or (D).

(3) **Subsection to apply to certain church employees.** This subsection shall apply with respect to services which are described in subparagraph (B) of section 3121(b)(8) (and are not described in subparagraph (A) of such section).

(h) **Regular basis.**

An individual shall be deemed to be self-employed on a regular basis in a taxable year, or to be a member of a partnership on a regular basis in such year, if he had net earnings from self-employment, as defined in the first sentence of subsection (a), of not less than $400 in at least two of the three consecutive taxable years immediately preceding such taxable year from trades or businesses carried on by such individual or such partnership.

(i) **Special rules for options and commodities dealers.**

(1) **In general.** Notwithstanding subsection (a)(3)(A), in determining the net earnings from self-employment of any options dealer or commodities dealer, there shall not be excluded any gain or loss (in the normal course of the taxpayer's activity of dealing in or trading section 1256 contracts) from section 1256 contracts or property related to such contracts.

(2) **Definitions.** For purposes of this subsection—

(A) Options dealer. The term "options dealer" has the meaning given such term by section 1256(g)(8).

(B) Commodities dealer. The term "commodities dealer" means a person who is actively engaged in trading section 1256 contracts and is registered with a domestic board of trade which is designated as a contract market by the Commodities Futures Trading Commission.

(C) Section 1256 contracts. The term "section 1256 contract" has the meaning given to such term by section 1256(b).

(j) **Special rules for certain church employee income.**

(1) **Computation of net earnings.** In applying subsection (a)—

(A) church employee income shall not be reduced by any deduction;

(B) church employee income and deductions attributable to such income shall not be taken into account in determining the amount of other net earnings from self-employment.

(2) **Computation of self-employment income.**

(A) Separate application of subsection (b)(2). Paragraph (2) of subsection (b) shall be applied separately—

(i) to church employee income, and

(ii) to other net earnings from self-employment.

(B) $100 floor. In applying paragraph (2) of subsection (b) to church employee income, "$100" shall be substituted for "$400".

(3) **Coordination with subsection (a)(12).** Paragraph (1) shall not apply to any amount allowable as a deduction under subsection (a)(12), and paragraph (1) shall be applied before determining the amount so allowable.

(4) **Church employee income defined.** For purposes of this section, the term "church employee income" means gross income for services which are described in section 3121(b)(8)(B) (and are not described in section 3121(b)(8)(A)).

(k) **Codification of treatment of certain termination payments received by former insurance salesmen.**

Nothing in subsection (a) shall be construed as including in the net earnings from self-employment of an individual any amount received during the taxable year from an insurance company on account of services performed by such individual as an insurance salesman for such company if—

(1) such amount is received after termination of such individual's agreement to perform such services for such company,

(2) such individual performs no services for such company after such termination and before the close of such taxable year,

(3) such individual enters into a covenant not to compete against such company which applies to at least the 1-year period beginning on the date of such termination, and

(4) the amount of such payment—

(A) depends primarily on policies sold by or credited to the account of such individual during the last year of such agreement or the extent to which such policies remain in force for some period after such termination, or both, and

(B) does not depend to any extent on length of service or overall earnings from services performed for such company (without regard to whether eligibility for payment depends on length of service).

(l) **Upper and lower limits.**

For purposes of subsection (a)—

(1) **Lower limit.** The lower limit for any taxable year is the sum of the amounts required under section 213(d) of the Social Security Act for a quarter of coverage in effect with respect to each calendar quarter ending with or within such taxable year.

(2) **Upper limit.** The upper limit for any taxable year is the amount equal to 150 percent of the lower limit for such taxable year.

In 2010, P.L. 111-312, Sec. 601, of this Act, provides:
"Sec. 601. Temporary Employee Payroll Tax Cut.

"(a) In general. Notwithstanding any other provision of law, —

"(1) with respect to any taxable year which begins in the payroll tax holiday period, the rate of tax under section 1401(a) of the Internal Revenue Code of 1986 shall be 10.40 percent, and

"(2) with respect to remuneration received during the payroll tax holiday period, the rate of tax under 3101(a) of such Code shall be 4.2 percent (including for purposes of determining the applicable percentage under sections 3201(a) and 3211(a)(1) of such Code).

"(b) Coordination with deductions for employment taxes.

"(1) Deduction in computing net earnings from self-employment. For purposes of applying section 1402(a)(12) of the Internal Revenue Code of 1986, the rate of tax imposed by subsection 1401(a) of such Code shall be determined without regard to the reduction in such rate under this section.

"(2) Individual deduction. In the case of the taxes imposed by section 1401 of such Code for any taxable year which begins in the payroll tax holiday period, the deduction under section 164(f) with respect to such taxes shall be equal to the sum of—

"(A) 59.6 percent of the portion of such taxes attributable to the tax imposed by section 1401(a) (determined after the application of this section), plus

"(B) one-half of the portion of such taxes attributable to the tax imposed by section 1401(b).

"(c) Payroll tax holiday period. The term 'payroll tax holiday period' means calendar year 2011.

"(d) Employer notification. The Secretary of the Treasury shall notify employers of the payroll tax holiday period in any manner the Secretary deems appropriate.

"(e) Transfers of funds.

"(1) Transfers to federal old-age and survivors insurance trust fund. There are hereby appropriated to the Federal Old-Age and Survivors Trust Fund and the Federal Disability Insurance Trust Fund established under section 201 of the Social Security Act (42 U.S.C. 401) amounts equal to the reduction in revenues to the Treasury by reason of the application of subsection (a). Amounts appropriated by the preceding sentence shall be transferred from the general fund at such times and in such manner as to replicate to the extent possible the transfers which would have occurred to such Trust Fund had such amendments not been enacted.

"(2) Transfers to social security equivalent benefit account. There are hereby appropriated to the Social Security Equivalent Benefit Account established under section 15A(a) of the Railroad Retirement Act of 1974 (45 U.S.C. 231n-1(a)) amounts equal to the reduction in revenues to the Treasury by reason of the application of subsection (a)(2). Amounts appropriated by the preceding sentence shall be transferred from the general fund at such times and in such manner as to replicate to the extent possible the transfers which would have occurred to such Account had such amendments not been enacted.

"(3) Coordination with other federal laws. For purposes of applying any provision of Federal law other than the provisions of the Internal Revenue Code of 1986, the rate of tax in effect under section 3101(a) of such Code shall be determined without regard to the reduction in such rate under this section."

—P.L. 111-148, Sec. 9015(b)(2)(B), added "(determined without regard to the rate imposed under paragraph (2) of section 1401(b))" after "for such year" in subpara. (a)(12)(B), effective with respect to remuneration received, and tax. yrs. begin., after 12/31/2012.

In 2008, P.L. 110-246, Sec. 4, Repeals the duplicative enactment and provides effective date provisions of the Act entitled "An Act to provide for the continuation of agricultural programs through fiscal year 2012, and for other purposes" Sec. 4, P.L. 110-246 reads as follows:

"Sec. 4. Repeal of duplicative enactment.

"(a) In General- The Act entitled 'An Act to provide for the continuation of agricultural programs through fiscal year 2012, and for other purposes' (H.R. 2419 of the 110th Congress), and the amendments made by that Act, are repealed, effective on the date of enactment of that Act.

"(b) Effective Date- Except as otherwise provided in this Act, this Act and the amendments made by this Act shall take effect on the earlier of--

"(1) the date of enactment of this Act; or

"(2) the date of the enactment of the Act entitled 'An Act to provide for the continuation of agricultural programs through fiscal year 2012, and for other purposes' (H.R. 2419 of the 110th Congress)."

—P.L. 110-246, Sec. 15301(a), added ", and including payments under section 1233(2) of the Food Security Act of 1985 (16 U.S.C. 3833(2)) to individuals receiving benefits under section 202 or 223 of the Social Security Act" after "crop shares" in para. (a)(1), effective for payments made after 12/31/2007. [Ed. Note: May 22, 2008 was the date of enactment for H.R. 2419 (PL 110-234), which was repealed by (2008 Farm Act § 4(a)) (PL 110-246, 6/18/2008), in connection with the reenactment of the farm bill to correct a technical deficiency in its original passage.]

—P.L. 110-234, Sec. 15352(a)(1)(A), substituted "the upper limit" for "$2,400" each place it appeared in para. (a)(17)

—P.L. 110-234, Sec. 15352(a)(1)(B), substituted "the lower limit" for "$1,600" each place it appeared in para. (a)(17)

—P.L. 110-234, Sec. 15352(a)(2), added subsec. (l), effective for tax. yrs. begin. after 12/31/2007.

In 2007, P.L. 110-28, Sec. 8215(b)(1), substituted ";" for ", and" at the end of para. (a)(15), substituted "; and" for "." at the end of para. (a)(16), and added para. (a)(17), effective for tax. yrs. begin. after 12/31/2006.

In 2005, P.L. 109-135, Sec. 403(a)(19), amended Sec. 102(e) of P.L. 108-357 [see below] to read as follows:

"(e) Effective date.

"(1) In general. The amendments made by this section shall apply to taxable years beginning after December 31, 2004.

"(2) Application to pass-thru entities, etc. In determining the deduction under section 199 of the Internal Revenue Code of 1986 (as added by this section), items arising from a taxable year of a partnership, S corporation, estate, or trust beginning before January 1, 2005, shall not be taken into account for purposes of subsection (d)(1) of such section."

In 2004, P.L. 108-357, Sec. 102(d)(7), deleted "and" at the end of para. (a)(14), substituted ", and" for the period at the end of para. (a)(15), and added para. (a)(16), effective for tax. yrs. begin. after 12/31/2004. See also Sec. 403(a)(19) of P.L. 109-135, reproduced above.

—P.L. 108-203, Sec. 425(b), substituted "the gross income and deductions attributable to such trade or business shall be treated as the gross income and deductions of the spouse carrying on such trade or business or, if such trade or business is jointly operated, treated as the gross income and deductions of each spouse on the basis of their respective distributive share of the gross income and deductions; and" for "all of the gross income and deductions attributable to such trade or business shall be treated as the gross income and deductions of the husband unless the wife exercises substantially all of the management and control of such trade or business, in which case all of such gross income and deductions shall be treated as the gross income and deductions of the wife; and" in subpara. (a)(5)(A), effective 3/2/2004.

In 1999, P.L. 106-170, Sec. 403, of this Act, reads as follows:

"Sec. 403. Revocation by members of the clergy of exemption from Social Security coverage.

"(a) In general. Notwithstanding section 1402(e)(4) of the Internal Revenue Code of 1986, any exemption which has been received under section 1402(e)(1) of such Code by a duly ordained, commissioned, or licensed minister of a church, a member of a religious order, or a Christian Science practitioner, and which is effective for the taxable year in which this Act is enacted, may be revoked by filing an application therefor (in such form and manner, and with such official, as may be prescribed by the Commissioner of Internal Revenue), if such application is filed no later than the due date of the Federal income tax return (including any extension thereof) for the applicant's second taxable year beginning after December 31, 1999. Any such revocation shall be effective (for purposes of chapter 2 of the Internal Revenue Code of 1986 and title II of the Social Security Act), as specified in the application, either with respect to the applicant's first taxable year beginning after December 31, 1999, or with respect to the applicant's second taxable year beginning after such date, and for all succeeding taxable years; and the applicant for any such revocation may not thereafter again file application for an exemption under such section 1402(e)(1). If the application is filed after the due date of the applicant's Federal income tax return for a taxable year and is effective with respect to that taxable year, it shall include or be accompanied by payment in full of an amount equal to the total of the taxes that would have been imposed by section 1401 of the Internal Revenue Code of 1986 with respect to all of the applicant's income derived in that taxable year which would have constituted net earnings from self-employment for purposes of chapter 2 of such Code (notwithstanding paragraphs (4) and (5) of section 1402(c)) except for the exemption under section 1402(e)(1) of such Code.

"(b) Effective date. Subsection (a) shall apply with respect to service performed (to the extent specified in such subsection) in taxable years beginning after December 31, 1999, and with respect to monthly insurance benefits payable under title II on the basis of the wages and self-employment income of any individual for months in or after the calendar year in which such individual's application for revocation (as described in such subsection) is effective (and lump-sum death payments payable under such title on the basis of such wages and self-employment income in the case of deaths occurring in or after such calendar year)."

In 1997, P.L. 105-34, Sec. 922(a), added subsec. (k), effective for payments after 12/31/97.

—P.L. 105-34, Sec. 935, of this Act provides:

"Sec. 935 Moratorium on certain regulations.

"No temporary or final regulation with respect to the definition of a limited partner under section 1402(a)(13) of the Internal Revenue Code of 1986 may be issued or made effective before July 1, 1998."

In 1996, P.L. 104-188, Sec. 1456(a), added ", but shall not include in such net earnings from self-employment the rental value of any parsonage or any parsonage allowance (whether or not excludable under section 107) provided after the individual retires, or any other retirement benefit received by such individual from a church plan (as defined in section 414(e)) after the individual retires" before the semicolon at the end of para. (a)(8), effective for yrs. begin. before, on, or after 12/31/94.

In 1994, P.L. 103-296, Sec. 108(h)(1), substituted "Commissioner of Social Security" for "Secretary of Health and Human Services" each place it appeared in para. (c)(1), subpara. (c)(2)(E), para. (e)(2), para. (g)(1) and subparas. (g)(2)(A) and (B), effective 3/31/95.

—P.L. 103-296, Sec. 319(a)(4), added "except service which constitutes "employment" under section 3121(y)," at the end of subpara. (c)(2)(C), effective for service performed after the calendar quarter following the calendar quarter in which the date of enactment [8/15/94] of this Act occurs.

In 1993, P.L. 103-66, Sec. 13207(b)(1)(A), substituted "in the case of the tax imposed by section 1401(a), that part of the net" for "that part of the net" in para. (b)(1) . . . Sec. 13207(b)(1)(B), substituted "contribution and benefit base (as determined under section 230 of the Social Security Act)" for "applicable contribution base (as determined under subsection (k))" in para (b)(1) . . . Sec. 13207(b)(1)(C), added "and" after "section 3121(b)," in subsec. (b) . . . Sec. 13207(b)(1)(D), deleted "and (C) includes but only with respect to the tax imposed by section 1401(b), remuneration paid for medicare qualified government employment (as defined in section 3121(u)(3)) which is subject to the taxes imposed by sections 3101(b) and 3111(b)" after "section 3201 or 3211" in subsec. (b) . . . Sec. 13207(b)(2), deleted subsec. (k), effective for 1994 and later calendar yrs.

Prior to deletion, subsec. (k) read as follows:

"(k) Applicable contribution base.

"For purposes of this chapter—

"(1) Old-age, survivors, and disability insurance. For purposes of the tax imposed by section 1401(a), the applicable contribution base for any calendar year is the contribution and benefit base determined under section 230 of the Social Security Act for such calendar year.

"(2) Hospital insurance. For purposes of the tax imposed by section 1401(b), the applicable contribution base for any calendar year is the applicable contribution base determined under section 3121(x)(2) for such calendar year."

In 1990, P.L. 101-508, Sec. 5123(a)(3), deleted the last undesignated paragraph in subsec. (a), effective for income received for services performed in tax. yrs. begin. after 12/31/90.

Prior to deletion, the last undesignated paragraph in subsec. (a) read as follows:

"Any income of an individual which results from or is attributable to the performance of services by such individual as a director of a corporation during any taxable year shall be deemed to have been derived (and received) by such individual in that year, at the time the services were performed, regardless of when the income is actually paid to or received by such individual (unless it was actually paid and received prior to that year)."

—P.L. 101-508, Sec. 11331(b)(1), substituted "the applicable contribution base (as determined under subsection (k))" for "the contribution and benefit base (as determined under section 230 of the Social Security Act)" in subsec. (b) . . . Sec. 11331(b)(2), added subsec. (k), effective for 1991 and later calendar years.

In 1989, P.L. 101-239, Sec. 10204(a)(1)(A), substituted "to apply" for "not to apply" in the heading of para. (g)(3) . . . Sec. 10204(a)(1)(B), substituted "shall" for "shall not" in para. (g)(3), effective for tax. yrs. begin. after 12/31/89.

In 1988, P.L. 100-647, Sec. 3043(c)(1), deleted "and" at the end of para. (a)(13) and substituted "; and" for the period at the end of para. (a)(14) and added new para. (a)(15), effective for all periods begin. before, on, or after 11/10/88. Sec. 3044(b) of this Act provides:

"(b) No inference created.

"Nothing in the amendments made by this subtitle shall create any inference as to the existence or nonexistence or scope of any exemption from tax for income derived from fishing rights secured as of March 17, 1988, by any treaty, law, or Executive Order."

—P.L. 100-647, Sec. 8007(c)(1), deleted paras. (g)(2) and (4) . . . Sec. 8007(c)(2), redesignated paras. (g)(3) and (5) as paras. (g)(2) and (3), effective for applications for exemptions filed on or after 11/10/88.

Prior to deletion, para. (g)(2) read as follows:

"(2) Time for filing applications. For purposes of this subsection, an application must be filed on or before the time prescribed for filing the return (including any extension thereof) for the first taxable year for which the individual has self-employment income (determined without regard to this subsection or subsection (c)(6)), except that an application filed after such date but on or before the last day of the third calendar month following the calendar month in which the taxpayer is first notified in writing by the Secretary that a timely application for an exemption from the tax imposed by this chapter has not been filed by him shall be deemed to be filed timely."

Prior to deletion, para. (s)(4) read as follows:

"(4) Application by fiduciaries or survivors. In any case where an individual who has self-employment income dies before the expiration of the time prescribed by paragraph (2) for filing an application for exemption pursuant to this subsection, such an application may be filed with respect to such individual within such time by a fiduciary acting for such individual's estate or by such individual's survivor (within the meaning of section 205(c)(1)(C) of the Social Security Act)."

In 1987, P.L. 100-203, Sec. 9022(b), added the undesignated paragraph at the end of subsec. (a), effective with respect to services performed in tax. yrs. begin. on or after 1/1/88.

In 1986, P.L. 99-514, Sec. 301(b)(12), amended para. (i)(1), effective for tax. yrs. begin. after 12/31/86. Sec. 406 of this Act provides the following limitation to this effective date:

"SEC. 406. RETENTION OF CAPITAL GAINS TREATMENT FOR SALES OF DAIRY CATTLE UNDER MILK PRODUCTION TERMINATION PROGRAM.

"The amendments made by subtitles A and B of title III shall not apply to any gain from the sale of dairy cattle under a valid contract with the United States Department of Agriculture under the milk production termination program to the extent such gain is properly taken into account under the taxpayer's method of accounting after January 1, 1987, and before September 1, 1987."

Prior to amendment, para. (i)(1) read as follows:

"(1) In general. In determining the net earnings from self-employment of any options dealer or commodities dealer—

"(A) notwithstanding subsection (a)(3)(A), there shall not be excluded any gain or loss (in the normal course of the taxpayer's activity of dealing in or trading section 1256 contracts) from section 1256 contracts or property related to such contracts, and

"(B) the deduction provided by section 1202 shall not apply."

—P.L. 99-514, Sec. 1272(d)(8), deleted "and section 931 (relating to income from sources within possessions of the United States)" and added "and" after "of the employer)," in para. (a)(8) . . . Sec. 1272(d)(9), amended para. (a)(9), effective for tax. yrs. begin. after 12/31/86.

Prior to amendment, para. (a)(9) read as follows:

"(9) the term 'possession of the United States' as used in sections 931 (relating to income from sources within possessions of the United States) and 932 (relating to citizens of possessions of the United States) shall be deemed not to include the Virgin Islands, Guam, or American Samoa;"

—P.L. 99-514, Sec. 1704(a)(1), added "and, in the case of an individual described in subparagraph (A), that he has informed the ordaining, commissioning, or licensing body of the church or order that he is opposed to such insurance" after "Act" in para. (e)(1) . . . Sec. 1704(a)(2)(A), substituted "Subject to paragraph (2), any individual" for "Any individual" in para. (e)(1) . . . Sec. 1704(a)(2)(B), redesignated paras. (e)(2) and (3) as paras. (e)(3) and (4) . . . Sec. 1704(a)(2)(C), added new para. (e)(2), effective for applications filed after 12/31/86.

—P.L. 99-514, Sec. 1704(b), provides:

"(b) Revocation of exemption—

"(1) In general.—Notwithstanding section 1402(e)(3) of the Internal Revenue Code of 1986, as redesignated by subsection (a)(2)(B) of this section, any exemption which has been received under section 1402(e)(1) of such Code by a duly ordained, commissioned, or licensed minister of a church, a member of a religious order, or a Christian Science practitioner, and which is effective for the taxable year in which this Act is enacted, may be revoked by filing an application therefor (in such form and manner, and with such official, as may be prescribed in regulations made under chapter 2 of subtitle A of such Code), if such application is filed—

"(A) before the applicant becomes entitled to benefits under section 202(a) or 223 of the Social Security Act (without regard to section 202(j)(1) or 223(b) of such Act), and

"(B) no later than the due date of the Federal income tax return (including any extension thereof) for the applicant's first taxable year beginning after the date of the enactment of this Act.

"Any such revocation shall be effective (for purposes of chapter 2 of subtitle A of the Internal Revenue Code of 1986 and title II of the Social Security Act), as specified in the application, either with respect to the applicant's first taxable year ending on or after the date of the enactment of this Act or with respect to the applicant's first taxable year beginning after such date, and for all succeeding taxable years; and the applicant for any such revocation may not thereafter again file application for an exemption under such section 1402(e)(1). If the application is filed on or after the due date of the Federal income tax return for the applicant's first taxable year ending on or after the date of the enactment of this Act and is effective with respect to that taxable year, it shall include or be accompanied by payment in full of an amount equal to the total of the taxes that would have been imposed by section 1401 of the Internal Revenue Code of 1986 with respect to all of the applicant's income derived in that taxable year which would have constituted net earnings from self-employment for purposes of chapter 2 of subtitle A of such Code (notwithstanding paragraph (4) or (5) of section 1402(c) of such Code) but for the exemption under section 1402(e)(1) of such Code.

"(2) Effective date.—Paragraph (1) of this subsection shall apply with respect to service performed (to the extent specified in such paragraph) in taxable years ending on or after the date of the enactment of this Act and with respect to monthly insurance benefits payable under title II of the Social Security Act on the basis of the wages and self-employment income of any individual for months in or after the calendar year in which such individual's application for revocation (as described in such paragraph) is effective (and lump-sum death payments payable under such title on the basis of such wages and self-employment income in the case of deaths occurring in or after such calendar year)."

—P.L. 99-514, Sec. 1882(a), added para. (g)(5) . . . Sec. 1882(b)(1)(A), added subsec. (j) . . . Sec. 1882(b)(1)(B)(i), amended para. (a)(14) . . . Sec. 1882(b)(1)(B)(ii), added the sentence at the end of subsec. (b) . . . Sec. 1882(b)(1)(B)(iii), substituted "paragraph (1)" for "clause (1)", in the second sentence of subsec. (b), effective for remuneration paid or derived in tax. yrs. begin. after 12/31/85.

Prior to amendment, para. (a)(14) read as follows:

"(14) with respect to remuneration for services which are treated as services in a trade or business under subsection (c)(2)(G)—

"(A) no deduction for trade or business expenses provided under this Code (other than the deduction under paragraph (12)) shall apply;

"(B) the provisions of subsection (b)(2) shall not apply; and

"(C) if the amount of such remuneration from an employer for the taxable year is less than $100, such remuneration from that employer shall not be included in self-employment income."

—P.L. 99-514, Sec. 1883(a)(11)(A), indented subpara. (c)(2)(G) two additional ems, so as to align its left margin with those of the other subparas. in para. (c)(2), effective 10/22/86.

—P.L. 99-509, Sec. 9002(b)(1)(B), deleted "under an agreement entered into pursuant to the provisions of section 218 of the Social Security Act (relating to coverage of State employees), or" after "services included" in the flush sentence following para. (b)(2), effective as provided in Sec. 9002(d) of this Act which reads as follows:

"(d) Effective date.—

"The amendments made by this section [Sec. 9002] are effective with respect to payments due with respect to wages paid after December 31, 1986, including wages paid after such date by a State (or political subdivision thereof) that modified its agreement pursuant to the provisions of section 218(e)(2) of the Social Security Act prior to the date of the enactment of this Act; except that in cases where, in accordance with the currently applicable schedule, deposits of taxes due under an agreement entered into pursuant to section 218 of the Social Security Act would be required within 3 days after the close of an eighth-monthly period, such 3-day requirement shall be changed to a 7-day requirement for wages paid prior to October 1, 1987, and to a 5-day requirement for wages paid after September 30, 1987, and prior to October 1, 1988. For wages paid prior to October 1, 1988, the deposit schedule for taxes imposed under sections 3101 and 3111 shall be determined separately from the deposit schedule for taxes withheld under section 3402 if the taxes imposed under sections 3101 and 3111 are due with respect to service included under an agreement entered into pursuant to section 218 of the Social Security Act."

—P.L. 99-272, Sec. 13205(a)(2)(B), substituted "medicare qualified government employment (as defined in section 3121(u)(3))" for "medicare qualified Federal employment (as defined in section 3121(u)(2))" in subsec. (b), effective for services performed after 3/31/86.

In 1984, P.L. 98-369, Sec. 102(c)(1), added subsec. (i), effective for tax. yrs. begin. after 7/18/84. For special rules see Secs. 102(g), (h) and (i) of this Act reproduced in note following Code Sec. 1256.

—P.L. 98-369, Sec. 2603(c)(2), deleted "and" at the end of subpara. (c)(2)(E), substituted ", and" for the semicolon at the end of subpara. (c)(2)(F), and added new subpara. (c)(2)(G) . . . Sec. 2603(d)(2), deleted "and" at the end of para. (a)(12), substituted "; and" for the period at the end of para. (a)(13), and added para. (a)(14), effective for service performed after 12/31/83.

—P.L. 98-369, Sec. 2663(j)(5)(B), substituted "Health and Human Services" for "Health, Education, and Welfare" in para. (c)(1), subpara. (c)(2)(E), para. (g)(1), subpara. (g)(3)(A), and subpara. (g)(3)(B), effective as provided in Sec. 2664(b) of this Act, which reads as follows:

"(b) Except to the extent otherwise specifically provided in this subtitle, the amendments made by section 2663 shall be effective on the date of the enactment of this Act [7/18/84]; but none of such amendments shall be construed as changing or affecting any right, liability, status, or interpretation which existed (under the provisions of law involved) before that date."

In 1983, P.L. 98-21, Sec. 124(c)(2), deleted "and" at the end of para. (a)(11), redesignated para. (a)(12) as (a)(13), and added a new para. (a)(12), effective for tax yrs. begin. after 12/31/89.

—P.L. 98-21, Sec. 321(e)(3), substituted "employees of foreign affiliates of American employers" for "employees of foreign subsidiaries of domestic corporations" in clause (A) of the second sentence of subsec. (b), effective as provided in Sec. 321(f)(1)(A) and (B) which read as follows:

"(f)(1)(A) The amendments made by this section [Sec. 321] (other than subsection (d)) shall apply to agreements entered into after the date of the enactment of this Act [4/20/83].

"(B) At the election of any American employer, the amendments made by this section (other than subsection (d)) shall also apply to any agreement entered into on or before the date of the enactment of this Act. Any such election shall be made at such time and in such manner as the Secretary may by regulations prescribe."

—P.L. 98-21, Sec. 322(b)(2), added ", except as provided by an agreement under section 233 of the Social Security Act" after "non-resident alien individual" in the first sentence of subsec. (b), effective for tax. yrs. begin. on or after 4/20/83.

—P.L. 98-21, Sec. 323(b)(1), deleted "in the case of an individual described in section 911(d)(1)(B)," before "the exclusion" in para. (a)(11), effective for tax. yrs. begin. after 12/31/83.

provides special rules in the case of any land diverted from the production of an agricultural commodity under a 1983 payment-in-kind program. See P.L. 98-4 reproduced in note following Code Sec. 61.

In 1982, P.L. 97-248, Sec. 278(a)(2), deleted "and" before "(B)" and added ", and (C) includes, but only with respect to the tax imposed by section 1401(b), remuneration paid for medicare qualified Federal employment (as defined in section 3121(u)(2)) which is subject to the taxes imposed by sections 3101(b) and 3111(b)" before the period in the second sentence of subsec. (b), effective for remuneration paid after 12/31/82.

In 1981, P.L. 97-34, Sec. 111(b)(3), substituted "relating to citizens or residents of the United States living abroad" for "relating to income earned by employees in certain camps" in para. (a)(8) . . . Sec. 111(b)(5), amended para. (a)(11), effective for tax. yrs. begin. after 12/31/81.

Prior to amendment, para. (a)(11) read as follows:

"(11) in the case of an individual who has been a resident of the United States during the entire taxable year, the exclusion from gross income provided by section 911(a)(2) shall not apply; and"

In 1980, P.L. 96-222, Sec. 108(a)(1)(A), redesignated Sec. 202(f) of P.L. 95-600 as Sec. 202(g) [see below].

In 1978, P.L. 95-615, Sec. 202(g)(5), substituted "relating to income earned by employees in certain camps" for "relating to earned income from sources without the United States" in para. (a)(8), effective for tax. yrs. begin. after 12/31/77.

Sec. 209(c) of this Act provides exception as follows:

"(c) Election of prior law.—

"(1) A taxpayer may elect not to have the amendments made by this title apply with respect to any taxable year beginning after December 31, 1977, and before January 1, 1979.

"(2) An election under this subsection shall be filed with a taxpayer's timely filed return for the first taxable year beginning after December 31, 1977."

—P.L. 95-600, Sec. 701(z)(1), substituted "December 31, 1954" for "December 31, 1971" each place it appeared in Sec. 1207(f)(4) of P.L. 94-455 [the effective date for amendments made by Sec. 1207(e)(1)(B), see below] . . . Sec. 703(j)(8)(A), substituted "subsection (h)" for "subsection (i)" each place it appeared in the last paragraph of subsec. (a) . . . Sec. 703(i)(8)(B), substituted "subsection (g)" for "subsection (h)" in para. (c)(6), effective 10/4/76.

In 1977, P.L. 95-216, Sec. 313(b)(1), deleted "and" at the end of para. (a)(10) . . . Sec. 313(b)(2), substituted "; and" for the period at the end of para. (a)(11) . . . Sec. 313(b)(3), added para. (a)(12), effective for tax. yrs. begin. after 12/31/77.

Sec. 316 of this Act provides special rules as follows:

"Sec. 316

"(a) Notwithstanding section 1402(e)(3) of the Internal Revenue Code of 1954, any exemption which has been received under section 1402(e)(1) of such Code by a duly ordained, commissioned, or licensed minister of a church or a Christian Science practitioner, and which is effective for the taxable year in which this Act is enacted, may be revoked by filing an application therefor (in such form and manner, and with such official, as may be prescribed in regulations made under chapter 2 of such Code), if such application is filed—

"(1) before the applicant becomes entitled to benefits under section 202(a) or 223 of the Social Security Act (without regard to section 202(j)(1) or 223(b) of such Act), and

"(2) no later than the due date of the Federal income tax return (including any extension thereof) for the applicant's first taxable year beginning after the date of the enactment of this Act.

Any such revocation shall be effective (for purposes of chapter 2 of the Internal Revenue Code of 1954 and title II of the Social Security Act), as specified in the application, either with respect to the applicant's first taxable year ending on or after the date of the enactment of this Act or with respect to the applicant's first taxable year beginning after such date, and for all succeeding taxable years; and the applicant for any such revocation may not thereafter again file application for an exemption under such section 1402(c)(1). If the application is filed on or after the due date of the applicant's first taxable year ending on or after the date of the enactment of this Act and is effective with respect to that taxable year, it shall include or be accompanied by payment in full of an amount equal to the total of the taxes that would have been imposed by section 1401 of the Internal Revenue Code of 1954 with respect to all of the applicant's income derived in that taxable year which would have constituted net earnings from self-employment for purposes of chapter 2 of such Code (notwithstanding section 1402(c)(4) or (c)(5) of such Code) except for the exemption under section 1402(e)(1) of such Code.

"(b) Subsection (a) shall apply with respect to service performed (to the extent specified in such subsection) in taxable years ending on or after the date of the enactment of this Act, and with respect to monthly insurance benefits payable under title II of the Social Security Act on the basis of the wages and self-employment income of any individual for months in or after the calendar year in which such individual's application for revocation (as described in such subsection) is filed (and lump-sum death payments payable under such title on the basis of such wages and self-employment income in the case of deaths occurring in or after such calendar year)."

In 1976, P.L. 94-455, Sec. 1207(e)(1)(B), deleted "and" at the end of subpara. (c)(2)(D), substituted ", and" for the semicolon at the end of subpara. (c)(2)(E) and added subpara. (c)(2)(F), effective [as amended by Sec. 701(z)(1) of P.L. 95-600, see above] for tax. yrs. end. after 12/31/54. Sec. 1207(f)(4)(B) [as amended by Sec. 701(z)(1) of P.L. 95-600, see above] provides a special rule as follows:

"(B) Notwithstanding subparagraph (A), if the owner or operator of any boat treated a share of the boat's catch of fish or other aquatic animal life (or a share of the proceeds therefrom) received by an individual after December 31, 1954, and before the date of the enactment of this Act for services performed by such individual after December 31, 1954, on such boat as being subject to the tax under chapter 21 of the Internal Revenue Code of 1954, then the amendments made by paragraphs (1)(A) and (B) and (2) of subsection (e) shall not apply with respect to such services performed by such individual (and the share of the catch, or proceeds therefrom, received by him for such services)."

—P.L. 94-455, Sec. 1901(a)(155)(A), amended para. (b)(1) . . . Sec. 1901(a)(155)(B), repealed subsec. (g) and redesignated subsecs. (h) and (i) as subsecs. (g) and (h) . . . Sec. 1901(a)(155)(C), amended para. (g)(2) [as redesignated by Sec. 1901(a)(155)(B) of this Act, see above] . . . Sec. 1901(b)(1)(I)(iii), substituted "702(a)(8)" for "702(a)(9)" each place it appeared in subsec. (a) . . . Sec. 1901(b)(1)(X), deleted "(other than interest described in section 35)" after "unless such dividends and interest" in para. (a)(2) . . . Sec. 1906(b)(13)(A), substituted "Secretary" for "Secretary of his delegate" each place it appeared in Code Sec. 1402, effective for tax. yrs. begin. after 12/31/76.

Prior to amendment, para. (b)(1) read as follows:

"(1) that part of the net earnings from self-employment which is in excess of—

"(A) for any taxable year ending prior to 1955, (i) $3,600, minus (ii) the amount of the wages paid to such individual during the taxable year; and

"(B) for any taxable year ending after 1954 and before 1959, (i) $4,200, minus (ii) the amount of the wages paid to such individual during the taxable year; and

"(C) for any taxable year ending after 1958 and before 1966, (i) $4,800, minus (ii) the amount of the wages paid to such individual during the taxable year; and

"(D) for any taxable year ending after 1965 and before 1968, (i) $6,600, minus (ii) the amount of the wages paid to such individual during the taxable year; and

"(E) for any taxable year ending after 1967 and beginning before 1972, (i) $7,800 minus (ii) the amount of wages paid to such individual during the taxable year; and

"(F) for any taxable year beginning after 1971 and before 1973, (i) $9,000, minus (ii) the amount of wages paid to such individual during the taxable year; and

"(G) for any taxable year beginning after 1972 and before 1974, (i) $10,800, minus (ii) the amount of the wages paid to such individual during the taxable year;

"(H) for any taxable year beginning after 1973 and before 1975, (i) $13,200, minus (ii) the amount of the wages paid to such individual during the taxable year; and

"(I) for any taxable year beginning in any calendar year after 1974, (i) an amount equal to the contribution and benefit base (as determined under section 230 of the Social Security Act) which is effective for such calendar year, minus (ii) the amount of the wages paid to such individual during such taxable year; or"

Prior to repeal, subsec. (g) read as follows:

"(g) Treatment of certain remuneration erroneously reported as net earnings from self-employment.

"If—

"(1) an amount is erroneously paid as tax under section 1401, for any taxable year ending after 1954 and before 1962, with respect to remuneration for service described in section 3121(b)(8) (other than service described in section 3121(b)(8)(A)), and such remuneration is reported as self-employment income on a return file on or before the due date prescribed for filing such return (including any extension thereof),

"(2) the individual who paid such amount (or a fiduciary acting for such individual or his estate, or his survivor (within the meaning of section 205(c)(1)(C) of the Social Security Act)) requests that such remuneration be deemed to constitute net earnings from self-employment,

"(3) such request is filed after the date of the enactment of this paragraph and on or before April 15, 1962,

"(4) such remuneration was paid to such individual for services performed in the employ of an organization which, on or before the date on which such request is filed, has filed a certificate pursuant to section 3121(k), and

"(5) no credit or refund of any portion of the amount erroneously paid for such taxable year as tax under section 1401 (other than a credit or refund which would be allowable if such tax were applicable with respect to such remuneration) has been obtained before the date on which such request is filed or, if obtained, the amount credited or refunded (including any interest under section 6611) is repaid on or before such date,

then, for purposes of this chapter and chapter 21, any amount of such remuneration which is paid to such individual before the calendar quarter in which such request is filed (or before the succeeding quarter if such certificate first becomes effective with respect to services performed by such individual in such succeeding quarter), and with respect to which no tax (other than an amount erroneously paid as tax) has been paid under chapter 21, shall be deemed to constitute net earnings from self-employment and not remuneration for employment. For purposes of section 3121(b)(8)(B)(ii) and (iii), if the certificate filed by such organization pursuant to section 3121(k) is not effective with respect to services performed by such individual on or before the first day of the calendar quarter in which the request is filed, such individual shall be deemed to have become an employee of such organization (or to have become a member of a group described in section 3121(k)(1)(E)) on the first day of the succeeding quarter."

Prior to amendment, para. (g)(2) [as redesignated by Sec. 1901(a)(155)(B) of this Act, see above] read as follows:

"(2) Time for filing application. For purposes of this subsection, an application must be filed—

"(A) In the case of an individual who has self-employment income (determined without regard to this subsection and subsection (c)(6) for any taxable year ending before December 31, 1967, on or before December 31, 1968, and

"(B) In any other case, on or before the time prescribed for filing the return (including any extension thereof) for the first taxable year ending on or after December 31, 1967, for which he has self-employment income (as so determined), except that an application filed after such date but on or before the last day of the third calendar month following the calendar month in which the taxpayer is first notified in writing by the Secretary or his delegate that a timely application for an exemption from the tax imposed by this chapter has not been filed by him shall be deemed to be filed timely."

In 1975, P.L. 94-92, Sec. 203(a), deleted ", but solely with respect to the tax imposed by section 1401(b)," from item (B) of the second sentence in subsec. (b), effective 1/1/75 for compensation paid for services rendered on or after 1/1/75.

In 1974, P.L. 93-368, Sec. 10(b), added "(as determined without regard to any activities of an agent of such owner or tenant)" after "material participation by the owner or tenant" each place it appeared in para. (a)(1), effective for tax. yrs. begin. after 12/31/73.

In 1973, P.L. 93-66, Sec. 203(b)(1), substituted "$12,600" for "$12,000" in subsec. (h)(1)(H) [sic (b)(1)(H)], effective 7/9/73.

—P.L. 93-233, Sec. 5(b)(1), substituted "$13,200" for "$12,600" in subpara. (b)(1)(H), effective 12/31/73.

In 1972, P.L. 92-603, Sec. 121(b)(1), added the sentence at the end of subsec. (a) . . . Sec. 121(b)(2), added subsec. (i), effective only for tax. yrs. begin. after 12/31/72.

—P.L. 92-603, Sec. 124(b)(1), deleted "and" at the end of para. (a)(9) . . . Sec. 124(b)(2), substituted "; and" for the period at the end of para. (a)(10) . . . Sec. 124(b)(3), added para. (a)(11) . . . Sec. 140(b)(1), substituted ", section 119" for "and section 119" in para. (a)(8) . . . Sec. 140(b)(2), substituted a comma for "and, in addition, if he is a citizen of the United States performing such service as an employee of an American employer (as defined in section 3121(h)) or as a minister in a foreign country who has a congregation which is composed predominantly of citizens of the United States, without regard to" in para. (a)(8), effective for tax. yrs. begin. after 12/31/72.

—P.L. 92-336, Sec. 203(b)(1)(A), added "and before 1973" after "1971" and substituted "; and" for "; or" in subpara. (b)(1)(F) . . . Sec. 203(b)(1)(B), added subparas. (b)(1)(G), (H) and (I), effective only for tax. yrs. begin. after 1972.

In 1971, P.L. 92-5, Sec. 203(b)(1)(A), added "and beginning before 1972" after "1967" and substituted "; and" for "; or" in subpara. (b)(1)(E) . . . Sec. 203(b)(1)(B), added subpara. (b)(1)(F), effective only for tax. yrs. begin. after 1971.

In 1967, P.L. 90-248, Sec. 108(b)(1)(A), added "and before 1968" after "1965" and substituted "; and" for "; or" in subpara. (b)(1)(D) . . . Sec. 108(b)(1)(B), added subpara. (b)(1)(E) . . . Sec. 115(b)(1), amended the sentence at the end of subsec. (c) . . . Sec. 115(b)(2), amended subsec. (e), effective only for tax. yrs. end. after 1967.

Prior to amendment, the sentence at the end of subsec. (c) read as follows:

"The provisions of paragraph (4) or (5) shall not apply to service (other than service performed by a member of a religious order who has taken a vow of poverty as a member of such order) performed by an individual during the period for which a certificate filed by him under subsection (e) is in effect."

Prior to amendment, subsec. (e) read as follows:

"(e) Ministers, members of religious orders, and Christian Science practitioners.

"(1) Waiver certificate. Any individual who is (A) a duly ordained, commissioned, or licensed minister of a church or a member of a religious order (other than a member of a religious order who has taken a vow of poverty as a member of such order) or (B) a Christian Science practitioner may file a certificate (in such form and manner, and with such official, as may be prescribed by regulations made under this chapter) certifying that he elects to have the insurance system established by title II of the Social Security Act extended to service described in subsection (c)(4) or (c)(5) performed by him.

"(2) Time for filing certificate. Any individual who desires to file a certificate pursuant to paragraph (1) must file such certificate on or before whichever of the following dates is later: (A) the due date of the return (including any extension thereof) for his second taxable year ending after 1954 for which he has net earnings from self-employment (computed without regard to subsection (c)(4) and (c)(5)) of $400 or more, any part of which was derived from the performance of service described in subsection (c)(4) or (c)(5); or (B) the due date of the return (including any extension thereof) for his second taxable year ending after 1963.

"(3)(A) Effective date of certificate. A certificate filed pursuant to this subsection shall be effective for the taxable year immediately preceding the earliest taxable year for which, at the time the certificate is filed, the period for filing a return (including any extension thereof) has not expired, and for all succeeding taxable years. An election made pursuant to this subsection shall be irrevocable.

"(B) Notwithstanding the first sentence of subparagraph (A), if an individual filed a certificate on or before the date of enactment of this subparagraph which (but for this subparagraph) is effective only for the first taxable year ending after 1956 and all succeeding taxable years, such certificate shall be effective for his first taxable year ending after 1955 and all succeeding taxable years if—

"(i) such individual files a supplemental certificate after the date of enactment of this subparagraph and on or before April 15, 1962,

"(ii) the tax under section 1401 in respect of all such individual's self-employment income (except for underpayments of tax attributable to errors made in good faith) for his first taxable year ending after 1955 is paid on or before April 15, 1962, and

"(iii) in any case where refund has been made of any such tax which (but for this subparagraph) is an overpayment, the amount refunded (including any interest paid under section 6611) is repaid on or before April 15, 1962.

The provisions of section 6401 shall not apply to any payment or repayment described in this subparagraph.

"(C) Notwithstanding the first sentence of subparagraph (A), if an individual files a certificate after the date of enactment of this subparagraph and on or before the due date of the return (including any extension thereof) for his second taxable year ending after 1962, such certificate shall be effective for his first taxable year ending after 1961 and all succeeding years.

"(D) Notwithstanding the first sentence of subparagraph (A), if an individual files a certificate after the date of the enactment of this subparagraph and on or before the due date of the return (including any extension thereof) for his second taxable year ending after 1963, such certificate shall be effective for his first taxable year ending after 1962 and all succeeding years.

"(E) For purposes of sections 6015 and 6654, a waiver certificate described in paragraph (1) shall be treated as taking effect on the first day of the first taxable year beginning after the date on which such certificate is filed.

"(4) Treatment of certain remuneration paid in 1955 and 1956 as wages.—If

"(A) in 1955 or 1956 an individual was paid remuneration for service described in section 3121(b)(8)(A) which was erroneously treated by the organization employing him (under a certificate filed by such organization pursuant to section 3121(k) or the corresponding section of prior law) as employment (within the meaning of chapter 21), and

"(B) on or before the date of the enactment of this paragraph the taxes imposed by sections 3101 and 3111 were paid (in good faith and upon the assumption that the insurance system established by title II of the Social Security Act had been extended to such service) with respect to any part of the remuneration paid to such individual for such service, then the remuneration with respect to which such taxes were paid, and with respect to which no credit or refund of such taxes (other than a credit or refund which would be allowable if such service had constituted employment) has been obtained on or before the date of the enactment of this paragraph, shall be deemed (for purposes of this chapter and chapter 21) to constitute remuneration paid for employment and not net earnings from self-employment.

"(5) Optional provision for certain certificates filed on or before April 15, 1967.—Notwithstanding any other provision of this section, in any case where an individual has derived earnings in any taxable year ending after 1954 from the performance of service described in subsection (c)(4), or in subsection (c)(5) insofar as it related to the performance of service by an individual in the exercise of his profession as a Christian Science practitioner, and has reported such earnings as self-employment income on a return filed on or before the due date prescribed for filing such return (including any extension thereof)—

"(A) a certificate filed by such individual on or before April 15, 1966, which (but for this subparagraph) is ineffective for the first taxable year ending after 1954 for which such a return was filed shall be effective for such first taxable year and for all succeeding taxable years, provided a supplemental certificate is filed by such individual (or a fiduciary acting for such individual or his estate, or his survivor within the meaning of section 205(c)(1)(C) of the Social Security Act) after the date of enactment of the Social Security Amendments of 1965 and on or before April 15, 1967, and

"(B) a certificate filed after the date of enactment of the Social Security Amendments of 1965 and on or before April 15, 1967, by a survivor (within the meaning of section 205(c)(1)(C) of the Social Security Act) of such an individual who died on or before April 15, 1966, may be effective, at the election of the person filing such a certificate, for the first taxable year ending after 1954 for which such a return was filed and for all succeeding years, but only if—

"(i) the tax under section 1401 in respect to all such individual's self-employment income (except for underpayments of tax attributable to errors made in good faith), for each such year described in subparagraphs (A) and (B) ending before January 1, 1966, is paid on or before April 15, 1967, and

"(ii) in any case where refund has been made of any such tax which (but for this paragraph) is an overpayment, the amount refunded (including any interest paid under section 6611) is repaid on or before April 15, 1967.

The provisions of section 6401 shall not apply to any payment or repayment described in this paragraph."

—P.L. 90-248, Sec. 118(a)(1), deleted "and" at the end of para. (a)(8) . . . Sec. 118(a)(2), substituted "; and" for the period at the end of para. (a)(9) . . . Sec. 118(a)(3), added para. (a)(10), effective only for tax. yrs. end. on or after 12/31/67.

—P.L. 90-248, Sec. 122(b)(1), amended para. (c)(1) . . . Sec. 122(b)(2)(A), deleted "and" at the end of subpara. (c)(2)(C) . . . Sec. 122(b)(2)(B), substituted "; and" for the semicolon at the end of subpara. (c)(2)(D) . . . Sec. 122(b)(2)(C), added subpara. (c)(2)(E), effective for fees received after 1967. Sec. 122(c)(2) of this Act provides as follows:

"(2) Notwithstanding the provisions of subsections (a) and (b) of this section, any individual who in 1968 is in a position to which the amendments made by such subsections apply may make an irrevocable election not to have such amendments apply to the fees he receives in 1968 and every year thereafter, if on or before the due date of his income tax return for 1968 (including any extensions thereof) he files with the Secretary of the Treasury or his delegate, in such manner as the Secretary of the Treasury or his delegate shall by regulations prescribe, a certificate of election of exemption from such amendments."

Prior to amendment, para. (c)(1) read as follows:

"(1) the performance of the functions of a public office;"

—P.L. 90-248, Sec. 501(a), amended para. (h)(2), effective for tax. yrs. begin. after 12/31/50. For such purpose, chapter 2 of the '54 Code shall be treated as applying for all tax. yrs. begin. after 12/31/50. Sec. 501(c) of this Act provides a special rule as follows:

"(c) If refund or credit of any overpayment resulting from the enactment of this section is prevented on the date of the enactment of this Act or at any time on or before December 31, 1968, by the operation of any law or rule of law, refund or credit of such overpayment may, nevertheless, be made or allowed if claim therefor is filed on or before December 31, 1968. No interest shall be allowed or paid on any overpayment resulting from the enactment of this section."

Prior to amendment, para. (h)(2) read as follows:

"(2) Time for filing application. For purposes of this subsection, an application must be filed.

"(A) In the case of an individual who has self-employment income (determined without regard to this subsection and subsection (c)(6)) for any taxable year ending before December 31, 1965, on or before April 15, 1966, and

"(B) In any other case, on or before the time prescribed for filing the return (including any extension thereof) for the first taxable year ending on or after December 31, 1965, for which he has self-employment income as so determined."

—P.L. 90-248, Sec. 502(b)(1)(A), added "(A)" after "'wages'" in the second sentence of subsec. (b) . . . Sec. 501(b)(1)(B), added ", and (B) includes, but solely with respect to the tax imposed by section 1401(b), compensation which is subject to the tax imposed by section 3201 or 3211" before the period in the second sentence of subsec. (b), effective only for tax. yrs. end. on or after 12/31/68.

In 1966, P.L. 89-368, Sec. 102(c), added subpara. (e)(3)(E), effective for tax. yrs. begin. after 12/31/66.

In 1965, P.L. 89-97, Sec. 311(b)(1), amended para. (c)(5) . . . Sec. 311(b)(2), substituted "The provisions of paragraph (4) or (5) shall not apply to service (other than service performed by a member of a religious order who has taken a vow of poverty as a member of such order) performed by an individual during the period for which a certificate filed by him under subsection (e) is in effect." for the two sentences at the end of subsec. (c) . . . Sec. 311(b)(3)(A), substituted "extended to service described in subsection (c)(4) or (c)(5) performed by him." for "extended to service" and all that follows in para. (e)(1) . . . Sec. 311(b)(3)(B), amended subpara. (e)(2)(A), effective only for tax. yrs. end. on or after 12/31/65.

Prior to amendment, para. (c)(5) read as follows:

"(5) the performance of service by an individual in the exercise of his profession as a doctor of medicine, or Christian Science practitioner; or the performance of such service by a partnership."

Prior to amendment, the two sentences at the end of subsec. (c) read as follows:

"The provisions of paragraph (4) shall not apply to service (other than service performed by a member of a religious order who has taken a vow of poverty as a member of such order) performed by an individual during the period for which a certificate filed by such individual under subsection (e) is in effect. The provisions of paragraph (5) shall not apply to service performed by an individual in the exercise of his profession as a Christian Science practitioner during the period for which a certificate filed by him under subsection (e) is in effect."

Prior to amendment, "extended to service" and all that follows in para. (e)(1) read as follows:

"extended to service described in subsection (e)(4), or service described in subsection (e)(5) insofar as it relates to the performance of service by an individual in the exercise of his profession as a Christian Science practitioner, as the case may be, performed by him."

—P.L. 89-97, Sec. 312(b), substituted "$2,400" for "$1,800" and substituted "$1,600" for "$1,200" each place they appeared in the second sentence of para. (a)(9), effective only for tax. yrs. begin. after 12/31/65.

—P.L. 89-97, Sec. 319(a), deleted "or" at the end of para. (c)(4), substituted "; or" for the period at the end of para. (c)(5) and added para. (c)(6) . . . Sec. 319(c), added subsec. (h), effective for tax. yrs. begin. after 12/31/50.

—P.L. 89-97, Sec. 320(b)(1)(A), added "and before 1966" after "1958" and substituted "; and" for "; or" in subpara. (b)(1)(C) . . . Sec. 320(b)(1)(B), added subpara. (b)(1)(D), effective only for tax. yrs. end. after 1965.

—P.L. 89-97, Sec. 331(a), amended para. (e)(5) and repealed para. (e)(6), effective as provided in Secs. 331(b), (c) and (d) of this Act, which read as follows:

"(b) In the case of a certificate or supplemental certificate filed pursuant to section 1402(e)(5) of the Internal Revenue Code of 1954, as amended by subsection (a)—

"(1) for purposes of computing interest, the due date for the payment of the tax under section 1401 of such Code which is due for any taxable year ending before January 1, 1966, solely by reason of the filing of a certificate which is effective under such section 1402(e)(5) shall be April 15, 1967;

"(2) for purposes of section 6501 of such Code, the statutory period for the assessment of any tax for any taxable year for which tax is due solely by reason of the filing of such certificate shall not expire before April 16, 1970; and

"(3) for purposes of section 6651 of such Code (relating to addition to tax for failure to file tax return), the amount of tax required to be shown on the return shall not include tax under section 1401 of such Code which is due for any taxable year ending before January 1, 1966, solely by reason of the filing of a certificate which is effective under section 1402(e)(5).

"(c) notwithstanding any provision of section 205(c)(5)(F) of the Social Security Act, the Secretary of Health, Education, and Welfare may conform, before April 16, 1970, his records to tax returns or statements of earnings which constitute self-employment income solely by reason of the filing of a certificate which is effective under section 1402(e)(5) of such Code.

"(d) The amendments made by this section shall be applicable (except as otherwise specifically provided therein) only to certificates with respect to which supplemental certificates are filed pursuant to section 1402(e)(5)(A) of such Code after the date of the enactment of this Act, and to certificates filed pursuant to section 1402(e)(5)(B) after such date; except that no monthly benefits under title II of the Social Security Act for the month in which this Act is enacted or any prior month shall be payable or increased by reason of such amendments, and no lump-sum death payment under such title shall be payable or increased by reason of such amendments in the case of any individual who died prior to the date of the enactment of this Act. The provisions of section 1402(e)(5) and (6) of the Internal Revenue Code of 1954 which were in effect before the date of enactment of this Act shall be applicable with respect to any certificate filed pursuant thereto before such date if a supplemental certificate is not filed with respect to such certificate as provided in this section."

Prior to amendment, para. (e)(5) read as follows:

"(5) Optional provision for certain certificates filed on or before April 15, 1962.—In any case where an individual has derived earnings, in any taxable year ending after 1954 and before 1960, from the performance of service described in subsection (c)(4), or in subsection (c)(5) (as in effect prior to the enactment of this paragraph) insofar as it related to the performance of service by an individual in the exercise of his profession as a Christian Science practitioner, and has reported such earnings as self-employment income on a return filed on or before the date of the enactment of this paragraph and on or before the due date prescribed for filing such return (including any extension thereof)—

"(A) a certificate filed by such individual (or a fiduciary acting for such individual or his estate, or his survivor within the meaning of section 205(c)(1)(C) of the Social Security Act) after the date of the enactment of this paragraph and on or before April 15, 1962, may be effective, at the election of the person filing such certificate, for the first taxable year ending after 1954 and before 1960 for which such a return was filed, and for all succeeding taxable years, rather than for the period prescribed in paragraph (3), and

"(B) a certificate by such individual on or before the date of the enactment of this paragraph which (but for this subparagraph (is ineffective for the first taxable year ending after 1954 and before 1959 for which such a return was filed shall be effective for such first taxable year, and for all succeeding taxable years, provided a supplemental certificate is filed by such individual (or a fiduciary acting for such individual or his estate, or his survivor within the meaning of section 205(c)(1)(C) of the Social Security Act) after the date of the enactment of this paragraph and on or before April 15, 1962,

but only if—

"(i) the tax under section 1401 in respect of all such individual's self-employment income (except for underpayments of tax attributable to errors made in good faith), for each such year ending before 1960 in the case of a certificate described in subparagraph (a) or of each such year ending before 1959 in the case of a certificate described in subparagraph (B), is paid on or before April 15, 1962, and

"(ii) in any case where refund has been made of any such tax which (but for this paragraph) is an overpayment, the amount refunded (including any interest paid under section 6611) is repaid on or before April 15, 1962.

The provisions of section 6401 shall not apply to any payment or repayment described in this paragraph."

Prior to repeal, para. (e)(6) read as follows:

"(6) Certificate filed by fiduciaries or survivors on or before April 15, 1962.—In any case where an individual, whose death has occurred after September 12, 1960, and before April 16, 1962, derived earnings from the performance of services described in subsection (c)(4), or in subsection (c)(5) insofar as it relates to the performance of service by an individual in the exercise of his profession as a Christian Science practitioner, a certificate may be filed after the date of enactment of this paragraph, and on or before April 15, 1962, by a fiduciary acting for such individual's estate or by such individual's survivor within the meaning of section 205(c)(1)(C) of the Social Security Act. Such certificate shall be effective for the period prescribed in paragraph (3)(A) as if filed by the individual on the day of his death."

—P.L. 89-97, Sec. 341(a), substituted "his second taxable year ending after 1963" for "his second taxable year ending after 1962" in subpara. (e)(2)(B) . . . Sec. 341(b), added subpara. (e)(3)(D), effective only for certificates filed pursuant to Code Sec. 1402(e) of the '54 Code after 7/30/65, except that no monthly benefits under title II of the Social Security Act for the month in which this Act is enacted or any prior month shall be payable or increased by reason of such amendments.

In 1964, P.L. 88-272, amended subpara. (a)(3)(B), effective for amounts received or accrued in tax. yrs. begin. after 12/31/63, attributable to iron ore mined in tax. yrs. begin. after 12/31/63.

Prior to amendment, subpara. (a)(3)(B) read as follows:

"(B) from the cutting of timber, or the disposal of timber or coal, if section 631 applies to such gain or loss, or"

—P.L. 88-650, Sec. 2(a), substituted "his second taxable year ending after 1962" for "his second taxable year ending after 1959" in subpara. (e)(2)(B) . . . Sec. 2(b), added subpara. (e)(3)(C), effective only for certificates filed pursuant to Code Sec. 1402(e) of the '54 Code after 10/13/64, except that no monthly benefits under title II of the Social Security Act for the month in which this Act is enacted or any prior month shall be payable or increased by reason of such amendments.

In 1961, P.L. 87-64, Sec. 202(a), added para. (e)(6), effective 6/30/61, except that no monthly benefits under title II of the Social Security Act for the month in which this Act is enacted or any prior month shall be payable or increased by reason of such amendments, and no lump-sum death payment under such title shall be payable or increased by reason of such amendment in the case of any individual who died prior to 6/30/61.

In 1960, P.L. 86-778, Sec. 101(a), substituted "1959" for "1956" in subpara. (e)(2)(B) . . . Sec. 101(b), amended para. (e)(3) . . . Sec. 101(c), added para. (e)(5), effective only for certificates (and supplemental certificates) filed pursuant to

Code Sec. 1402(e) of the '54 Code after 9/13/60. Sec. 101(d) of this Act provides as follows:

"(d) In the case of a certificate or supplemental certificate filed pursuant to section 1402(e)(3)(B) or (5) of the Internal Revenue Code of 1954—

"(1) for purposes of computing interest, the due date for the payment of the tax under section 1401 which is due for any taxable year ending before 1959 solely by reason of the filing of a certificate which is effective under such section 1402(e)(3)(B) or (5) shall be April 15, 1962;

"(2) the statutory period for the assessment of any tax for any such year which is attributable to the filing of such certificate shall not expire before the expiration of 3 years from such due date; and

"(3) for purposes of section 6651 of such Code (relating to addition to tax for failure to file tax return), the amount of tax required to be shown on the return shall not include such tax under section 1401."

Prior to amendment, para. (e)(3) read as follows:

"(3) Effective date of certificate. A certificate filed pursuant to this subsection shall be effective for the first taxable year with respect to which it is filed (but in no case shall the certificate be effective for a taxable year with respect to which the period for filing a return has expired, or for a taxable year ending prior to 1955) and all succeeding taxable years. An election made pursuant to this subsection shall be irrevocable. Notwithstanding the first sentence of this paragraph:

"(A) A certificate filed by an individual after the date of the enactment of this subparagraph but on or before the due date of the return (including any extension thereof) for his second taxable year ending after 1956 shall be effective for the first taxable year ending after 1955 and all succeeding taxable years.

"(B) If an individual filed a certificate on or before the date of the enactment of this subparagraph which (but for this subparagraph) is effective only for the third or fourth taxable year ending after 1954 and all succeeding taxable years, such certificate shall be effective for his first taxable year ending after 1955 and all succeeding taxable years if such individual files a supplemental certificate after the date of the enactment of this subparagraph and on or before the due date of the return (including any extension thereof) for his second taxable year ending after 1956.

"(C) A certificate filed by an individual after the due date of the return (including any extension thereof) for his second taxable year ending after 1956 shall be effective for the taxable year immediately preceding the taxable year with respect to which it is filed and all succeeding taxable years."

—P.L. 86-778, Sec. 103(k)(1), substituted "; and" for the period at the end of para. (a)(8) and added para. (a)(9) . . . Sec. 103(k)(2), substituted "paragraphs (1) through (7) and paragraph (9)" for "paragraphs (1) through (7)" in clauses (v) and (vi) in the sentence at the end of subsec. (a), effective only in the case of tax. yrs. begin. after 1960, except that, insofar as they involve the nonapplication of Code Sec. 932 of the '54 Code to the Virgin Islands for purposes of chapter 2 of such Code and section 211 of the Social Security Act, such amendments shall be effective for all tax. yrs. for which such chapter 2 (and corresponding provisions of prior law) and such section 211 are applicable.

—P.L. 86-778, Sec. 103(l), substituted "the Commonwealth of Puerto Rico, the Virgin Islands, Guam, or American Samoa" for "the Virgin Islands or a resident of Puerto Rico" in the sentence at the end of subsec. (b), effective only for tax. yrs. begin. after 1960.

—P.L. 86-778, Sec. 105(c)(1), added subsec. (g), effective 9/13/60. Sec. 105(c)(2) of this Act provides as follows:

"(2) Remuneration which is deemed under section 1402(g) of the Internal Revenue Code of 1954 to constitute net earnings from self-employment and not remuneration for employment shall also be deemed, for purposes of title II of the Social Security Act, to constitute net earnings from self-employment and not remuneration for employment. If, pursuant to the last sentence of section 1402(g) of the Internal Revenue Code of 1954, an individual is deemed to have become an employee of an organization (or to have become a member of a group) on the first day of a calendar quarter, such individual shall likewise be deemed, for purposes of clause (ii) or (iii) of section 210(a)(8)(B) of the Social Security Act, to have become an employee of such organization (or to have become a member of such group) on such day."

—P.L. 86-778, Sec. 106(b), amended para. (c)(2), effective only for tax. yrs. end. on or after 12/31/60.

Prior to amendment, para. (c)(2) read as follows:

"(2) the performance of service by an individual as an employee (other than service described in section 3121(b)(14)(B) performed by an individual who has attained the age of 18, service described in section 3121(b)(16), and service described in paragraph (4) of this subsection);".

In 1958, P.L. 85-840, Sec. 402(a)(1), amended subpara. (b)(1)(B) . . . Sec. 402(a)(2), added subpara. (b)(1)(C), effective 8/28/58.

Prior to amendment, subpara. (b)(1)(B) read as follows:

"(B) for any taxable year ending after 1954, (i) $4,200, minus (ii) the amount of the wages paid to such individual during the taxable year; or".

—P.L. 85-840, Sec. 403(a), added subsec. (f), effective only for individuals who die after 8/28/58. Sec. 403(b)(2) of this Act provides an exception as follows:

"(2) In the case of an individual who died after 1955 and on or before the date of the enactment of this Act, the amendment made by subsection (a) shall apply only if—

"(A) before January 1, 1960, there is filed a return (or amended return) of the tax imposed by chapter 2 of the Internal Revenue Code of 1954 for the taxable year ending as a result of his death, and

"(B) in any case where the return is filed solely for the purpose of reporting net earnings from self-employment resulting from the amendment made by subsection (a), the return is accompanied by the amount of tax attributable to such net earnings.

In any case described in the preceding sentence, no interest or penalty shall be assessed or collected on the amount of any tax due under chapter 2 of such Code solely by reason of the operation of section 1402(f) of such Code."

In 1957, P.L. 85-239, Sec. (a)(1), added "whichever of the following dates is later: (A)" after "on or before" in para. (e)(2) . . . Sec. (a)(2), added "; or (B) the due date of the return (including any extension thereof) for his second taxable year ending after 1956" before the period at the end of para. (e)(2) . . . Sec. (b), added "Notwithstanding the first sentence of this paragraph:" to the end of para. (e)(3) and added subparas. (e)(3)(A), (B) and (C), effective as provided in Sec. 4 of this Act, which reads as follows:

"Sec. 4. (a) Section 3, [reproduced below] and the amendments made by the first section of this Act, shall apply with respect to monthly insurance benefits under title II of the Social Security Act for months beginning after, and lump sum death payments under such title in the case of deaths occurring after, the date of the enactment of this Act.

"(b) Notwithstanding subsection (a) in the case of any individual who—

"(1)(A) has remuneration which is deemed, by reason of section 3, to constitute remuneration for employment for purposes of title II of the Social Security Act, or

"(B) has income which constitutes net earnings from self-employment under such title by reason of the filing of a certificate pursuant to section 1402(e)(3)(A) or (B) of the Internal Revenue Code of 1954, and

"(2) was entitled to monthly insurance benefits under title II of the Social Security Act for the month in which this Act is enacted,

section 3 and the amendments made by the first section of this Act shall apply with respect to monthly insurance benefits under such title based on his wages and self-employment income only if he, or any other person entitled to monthly insurance benefits under such title on the basis of such wages and self-employment income, files, on or after the date of enactment of this Act, an application for recomputation by reason of this Act. Such recomputation shall be made in the manner provided in title II of the Social Security Act as in effect at the time of the last previous computation or recomputation of such individual's primary insurance amount and as though the application therefor was filed in the month in which the application for such last previous computation or recomputation was filed. No recomputation under this subsection shall be regarded as a recomputation under section 215(f) of the Social Security Act. Any such recomputation shall be effective for and after the twelfth month before the month in which the application therefor is filed, but in no case for any month which begins on or prior to the date of the enactment of this Act. Any such recomputation shall be effective only if it results in a higher primary insurance amount.

"(c) The preceding provisions of this section shall not render erroneous any monthly insurance benefits under title II of the Social Security Act for the month in which this Act is enacted or any prior month.' Sec. (c) of this Act provides as follows:

"(c) If a certificate filed pursuant to section 1402(e)(3)(A) or (B) of the Internal Revenue Code of 1954 after the due date of the return (including any extension thereof) for any taxable year is effective for such taxable year or for any preceding taxable year, then—

"(1) for purposes of computing interest, the due date for the payment of the increase in tax for such taxable year or years resulting from the filing of such certificate shall be the last day of the sixth month following the month in which such certificate is filed;

"(2) the statutory period for the assessment of any deficiency attributable to such increase in tax shall not expire before the expiration of 3 years from such due date; and

"(3) for purposes of section 6651 of such Code (relating to addition to tax for failure to file tax return), the amount of tax required to be shown on the return shall not include such increase in tax."

—P.L. 85-239, Sec. 2, added para. (e)(4), effective as provided in Sec. 3 of this Act, which reads as follows:

"Sec. 3. Remuneration which is deemed under section 1402(e)(4) of the Internal Revenue Code of 1954 to constitute remuneration for employment shall also be deemed, notwithstanding sections 210(a)(8)(A) and 211(c) of the Social Security Act, to constitute remuneration for employment (and not net earnings from self-employment) for proposes of title II of such Act.' [see also, Sec. 4 of this Act, reproduced above].

—P.L. 85-239, Sec. 5(b), amended para. (a)(8), effective as provided in Sec. 5(c) of this Act, which reads as follows:

"(c) The amendments made by this section shall, except for purposes of section 203 of the Social Security Act, apply only with respect to taxable years ending on or after December 31, 1957. For purposes of section 203 of the Social Security Act (other than subsection (a)), such amendments shall apply only with respect to taxable years beginning after the month in which this Act is enacted. For purposes of subsection (a) of such section 203, such amendments shall apply only with respect to taxable years of the insured individual ending on or after December 31, 1957."

Prior to amendment, para. (a)(8) read as follows:

"(8) an individual who is—

"(A) a duly ordained, commissioned, or licensed minister of a church or a member of a religious order; and

"(B) a citizen of the United States performing service described in subsection (c)(4) as an employee of an American employer (as defined in section 3121 (h)) or as a minister in a foreign country who has a congregation which is composed predominantly of citizens of the United States, shall compute his net earnings from self-employment derived from the performance of service described in subsection (c)(4) without regard to section 911 (relating to earned income from sources without the United States) and section 931 (relating to income from sources within possessions of the United States)."

Sec. 1441. Withholding of tax on nonresident aliens.
(a) General rule.

Except as otherwise provided in subsection (c), all persons, in whatever capacity acting (including lessees or mortgagors of real or personal property, fiduciaries, employers, and all officers and employees of the United States) having the control, receipt, custody, disposal, or payment of any of the items of income specified in subsection (b) (to the extent that any of such items constitutes gross income from sources within the United States), of any nonresident alien individual, or of any foreign partnership shall (except as otherwise provided in regulations prescribed by the Secretary under section 874) deduct and withhold from such items a tax equal to 30 percent thereof, except that in the case of any item of income specified in the second sentence of subsection (b), the tax shall be equal to 14 percent of such item.

(b) Income items.

The items of income referred to in subsection (a) are interest (other than original issue discount as defined in section 1273), dividends, rent, salaries, wages, premiums, annuities, compensations, remunerations, emoluments, or other fixed or determinable annual or periodical gains, profits, and income, gains described in section 631(b) or (c), amounts subject to tax under section 871(a)(1)(C), gains subject to tax under section 871(a)(1)(D), and gains on transfers described in section 1235 made on or before October 4, 1966. The items of income referred to in subsection (a) from which tax shall be deducted and withheld at the rate of 14 percent are amounts which are received by a nonresident alien individual who is temporarily present in the United States as a nonimmigrant under subparagraph (F), (J), (M), or (Q) of section 101(a)(15) of the Immigration and Nationality Act and which are—

  (1) incident to a qualified scholarship to which section 117(a) applies, but only to the extent includible in gross income; or

  (2) in the case of an individual who is not a candidate for a degree at an educational organization described in section 170(b)(1)(A)(ii), granted by—

   (A) an organization described in section 501(c)(3) which is exempt from tax under section 501(a),

   (B) a foreign government,

   (C) an international organization, or a binational or multinational educational and cultural foundation or commission created or continued pursuant to the Mutual Educational and Cultural Exchange Act of 1961, or

   (D) the United States, or an instrumentality or agency thereof, or a State, or a possession of the United States, or any political subdivision thereof, or the District of Columbia,

as a scholarship or fellowship for study, training, or research in the United States.

In the case of a nonresident alien individual who is a member of a domestic partnership, the items of income referred to in subsection (a) shall be treated as referring to items specified in this subsection included in his distributive share of the income of such partnership.

(c) Exceptions.

  (1) Income connected with United States business. No deduction or withholding under subsection (a) shall be required in the case of any item of income (other than compensation for personal services) which is effectively connected with the conduct of a trade or business within the United States and which is included in the gross income of the recipient under section 871(b)(2) for the taxable year.

  (2) Owner unknown. The Secretary may authorize the tax under subsection (a) to be deducted and withheld from the interest upon any securities the owners of which are not known to the withholding agent.

  (3) Bonds with extended maturity dates. The deduction and withholding in the case of interest on bonds, mortgages, or deeds of trust or other similar obligations of a corporation, within subsections (a), (b), and (c) of section 1451 (as in effect before its repeal by the Tax Reform Act of 1984) were it not for the fact that the maturity date of such obligations has been extended on or after January 1, 1934, and the liability assumed by the debtor exceeds 27½ percent of the interest, shall not exceed the rate of 27½ percent per annum.

  (4) Compensation of certain aliens. Under regulations prescribed by the Secretary, compensation for personal services may be exempted from deduction and withholding under subsection (a).

  (5) Special items. In the case of gains described in section 631(b) or (c), gains subject to tax under section 871(a)(1)(D), and gains on transfers described in section 1235 made on or before October 4, 1966, the amount required to be deducted and withheld shall, if the amount of such gain is not known to the withholding agent, be such amount, not exceeding 30 percent of the amount payable, as may be necessary to assure that the tax deducted and withheld shall not be less than 30 percent of such gain.

  (6) Per diem of certain aliens. No deduction or withholding under subsection (a) shall be required in the case of amounts of per diem for subsistence paid by the United States Government (directly or by contract) to any nonresident alien individual who is engaged in any program of training in the United States under the Mutual Security Act of 1954, as amended.

  (7) Certain annuities received under qualified plans. No deduction or withholding under subsection (a) shall be required in the case of any amount received as an annuity if such amount is, under section 871(f), exempt from the tax imposed by section 871(a).

  (8) Original issue discount. The Secretary may prescribe such regulations as may be necessary for the deduction and withholding of the tax on original issue discount subject to tax under section 871(a)(1)(C) including rules for the deduction and withholding of the tax on original issue discount from payments of interest.

  (9) Interest income from certain portfolio debt investments. In the case of portfolio interest (within the meaning of 871(h)), no tax shall be required to be deducted and withheld from such interest unless the person required to deduct and withhold tax from such interest knows, or has reason to know, that such interest is not portfolio interest by reason of section 871(h)(3) or (4).

  (10) Exception for certain interest and dividends. No tax shall be required to be deducted and withheld under subsection (a) from any amount described in section 871(i)(2).

  (11) Certain gambling winnings. No tax shall be required to be deducted and withheld under subsection (a) from any amount exempt from the tax imposed by section 871(a)(1)(A) by reason of section 871(j).

  (12) Certain dividends received from regulated investment companies.

   (A) In general. No tax shall be required to be deducted and withheld under subsection (a) from any amount exempt from the tax imposed by section 871(a)(1)(A) by reason of section 871(k).

(B) Special rule. For purposes of subparagraph (A), clause (i) of section 871(k)(1)(B) shall not apply to any dividend unless the regulated investment company knows that such dividend is a dividend referred to in such clause. A similar rule shall apply with respect to the exception contained in section 871(k)(2)(B).

(d) Exemption of certain foreign partnerships.

Subject to such terms and conditions as may be provided by regulations prescribed by the Secretary, subsection (a) shall not apply in the case of a foreign partnership engaged in trade or business within the United States if the Secretary determines that the requirements of subsection (a) impose an undue administrative burden and that the collection of the tax imposed by section 871(a) on the members of such partnership who are nonresident alien individuals will not be jeopardized by the exemption.

(e) Alien resident of Puerto Rico.

For purposes of this section, the term "nonresident alien individual" includes an alien resident of Puerto Rico.

(f) Continental shelf areas.

For sources of income derived from, or for services performed with respect to, the exploration or exploitation of natural resources on submarine areas adjacent to the territorial waters of the United States, see section 638.

(g) Cross reference.

For provision treating 85 percent of social security benefits as subject to withholding under this section, see section 871(a)(3).

In 2004, P.L. 108-357, Sec. 411(a)(3)(A), added para. (c)(12), effective for dividends with respect to tax. yrs. of regulated investment companies begin. after 12/31/2004.

In 1997, P.L. 105-34, Sec. 1604(g)(3), substituted "85 percent" for "one-half" in subsec. (g), effective 8/5/97.

In 1994, P.L. 103-296, Sec. 320(a)(1)(B), substituted "(J), (M), or (Q)" for "(J), or (M)" in subsec. (b), effective with the calendar quarter following 8/15/94.

In 1993, P.L. 103-66, Sec. 13237(c)(4), substituted "section 871(h)(3) or (4)" for "section 871(h)(3)" in para. (c)(9), effective for interest received after 12/31/93.

In 1992, P.L. 102-318, Sec. 521(b)(32), deleted "402(a)(2), 403(a)(2), or" after "in section" in subsec. (b) . . . Sec. 521(b)(33), deleted "402(a)(2), 403(a)(2), or" after "in section" in para. (c)(5), effective for distributions after 12/31/92. For special rule, see Sec. 521(e)(2) of this Act which reads as follows:

"(2) Special rule for partial distributions. For purposes of section 402(a)(5)(D)(i)(II) of the Internal Revenue Code of 1986 (as in effect before the amendments made by this section), a distribution before January 1, 1993, which is made before or at the same time as a series of periodic payments shall not be treated as one of such series if it is not substantially equal in amount to other payments in such series."

In 1990, P.L. 101-508, Sec. 11704(a)(14), added "section" before "170(b)(1)(A)(ii)" in para. (b)(2), effective 11/5/90.

In 1988, P.L. 100-647, Sec. 1001(d)(2)(A), amended the second sentence of subsec. (b), effective for tax. yrs. begin. after 12/31/86, but only in the case of scholarships and fellowships granted after 8/16/86.

Prior to amendment, the second sentence of subsec. (b) read as follows:

"The items of income referred to in subsection (a) from which tax shall be deducted and withheld at the rate of 14 percent are amounts which are received by a nonresident alien individual who is temporarily present in the United States as a nonimmigrant under subparagraph (F) or (J) of section 101(a)(15) of the Immigration and Nationality Act and which are incident to a qualified scholarship to which section 117(a) applies, but only to the extent such amounts are includible in gross income."

—P.L. 100-647, Sec. 1012(g)(1)(A), amended Sec. 1214(d)(1) of P.L. 99-514 [part of the effective date for amendments made by Sec. 1214(c)(3) of P.L. 99-514, see below]. Sec. 1012(g)(1)(B) of this Act provides a special rule as follows:

"(B) A taxpayer may elect not to have the amendment made by subparagraph (A) apply and to have section 1214(d)(1) of the Reform Act apply as in effect before such amendment. Such election shall be made at such time and in such manner as the Secretary of the Treasury or his delegate may prescribe."

Prior to amendment, Sec. 1214(d)(1) of P.L. 99-514 read as follows:

"(1) In general. The amendments made by this section shall apply to payments after December 31, 1986."

—P.L. 100-647, Sec. 1012(g)(2), substituted "section 904(d)(2)(H)" for "section 904(d)(2)(G)" in Sec. 1214(d)(2)(B) [part of the effective date for amendments made Sec. 1214(c)(3) of P.L. 99-514, see below].

—P.L. 100-647, Sec. 1012(aa)(3)(D), of this Act provides:

"(3) Certain amendments not to apply to the extent inconsistent with treaties. The following amendments made by the Reform Act shall not apply to the extent the application of such amendments would be contrary to any treaty obligation of the United States in effect on the date of the enactment of the Reform Act:"

* * *

"(D) The amendments made by section 1214 of the Reform Act; except for purposes of determining the amount of the foreign tax credit.' [see Sec. 1012(aa)(3) of this Act, reproduced above]"

—P.L. 100-647, Sec. 1012(aa)(4), provides as follows:

"(4) Treatment of technical corrections.—For purposes of paragraphs (2) and (3), any amendment made by this title shall be treated as if it had been included in the provision of the Reform Act to which such amendment relates."

—P.L. 100-647, Sec. 6134(a)(2), added para. (c)(11), effective 11/10/88.

In 1986, P.L. 99-514, Sec. 123(b)(2), amended the second sentence of subsec. (b), effective for tax. yrs. begin. after 12/31/86, but only in the case of scholarships and fellowships granted after 8/16/86.

Prior to amendment, the second sentence of subsec. (b) read as follows:

"The items of income referred to in subsection (a) from which tax shall be deducted and withheld at the rate of 14 percent are —"

Prior to deletion, paras. (b)(1) and (2) read as follows:

"(1) that portion of any scholarship or fellowship grant which is received by a nonresident alien individual who is temporarily present in the United States as a nonimmigrant under subparagraph (F) or (J) of section 101(a)(15) of the Immigration and Nationality Act, as amended, and which is not excluded from gross income under section 117(a)(1) solely by reason of section 117(b)(2)(B); and

"(2) amounts described in subparagraphs (A), (B), (C), and (D) of section 117(a)(2) which are received by any such nonresident alien individual and which are incident to a scholarship or fellowship grant to which section 117(a)(1) applies, but only to the extent such amounts are includible in gross income."

—P.L. 99-514, Sec. 1214(c)(3), added para. (c)(10), effective [as amended by Sec. 1012(g)(1)(A) of P.L. 100-647, see above] for payments made in a tax. yr. of the payor begin. after 12/31/86. [See Sec/ 1012(g)(1)(B) of P.L. 100-647 for a special rule, reproduced above]. Secs. 1214(d)(2)-(d)(4) of this Act [as amended by Sec. 1012(g)(2) of P.L. 100-647, see above] provides as follows:

"(2) Treatment of certain interest.

"(A) In general. The amendments made by this section shall not apply to any interest paid or accrued on any obligation outstanding on December 31, 1985. The preceding sentence shall not apply to any interest paid pursuant to any extension or renewal of such an obligation agreed to after December 31, 1985.

"(B) Special rule for related payee. If the payee of any interest to which subparagraph (A) applies is related (within the meaning of section 904(d)(2)(H) of the Internal Revenue Code of 1986) to the payor, such interest shall be treated for purposes of section 904 of such Code as if the payor were a controlled foreign corporation (within the meaning of section 957(a) of such Code)."

"(3) Transitional rule.

"(A) Years before 1988. In applying the amendments made by this section to any payment made by a corporation in a taxable year of such corporation beginning before January 1, 1988, the requirements of clause (ii) of section 861(c)(1)(B) of the Internal Revenue Code of 1986 (relating to active business requirements), as amended by this section, shall not apply to gross income of such corporation for taxable years beginning before January 1, 1987.

"(B) Years after 1987. In applying the amendments made by this section to any payment made by a corporation in a taxable year of such corporation beginning after December 31, 1987, the testing period for purposes of section 861(c) of such Code (as so amended) shall not include any taxable year beginning before January 1, 1987.

"(4) Certain dividends.

"(A) In general. The amendments made by this section shall not apply to any dividend paid before January 1, 1991, by a qualified corporation with respect to stock which was outstanding on May 31, 1985.

"(B) Qualified corporation. For purposes of subparagraph (A), the term 'qualified corporation' means any business systems corporation which—

"(i) was incorporated in Delaware in February 1979,

"(ii) is headquartered in Garden City, New York, and

"(iii) the parent corporation of which is a resident of Sweden."

—P.L. 99-514, Sec. 1810(d)(3)(D), substituted "section 871(h)" for "871(h)(2)" in para. (c)(9), effective for interest received after 7/18/84 for obligations issued after 7/18/84, in tax. yrs. end. after 7/18/84.

In 1984, P.L. 98-369, Sec. 42(a)(13), substituted "section 1273" for "section 1232(b)" in subsec. (b), effective for tax. yrs. end. after 7/18/84.

—P.L. 98-369, Sec. 127(e)(1), added para. (c)(9), effective for interest received after 7/18/84 for obligations issued after 7/18/84, in tax. yrs. end. after 7/18/84. For special rule, see Sec. 127(g)(3) of this Act reproduced in note following Code Sec. 864.

—P.L. 98-369, Sec. 474(r)(29)(G), deleted "except in the cases provided for in section 1451 and" before "except as otherwise provided") in subsec. (a) . . . Sec. 474(r)(29)(H), substituted "section 1451 (as in effect before its repeal by the Tax Reform Act of 1984)" for "section 1451" in para. (c)(3), effective for tax. yrs. begin. after 12/31/83 and to carrybacks from tax. yrs. end. after 12/31/83. Sec. 475(b) of this Act provides a special rule as follows:

"(b) Tax Free Covenant Bonds.—The amendments made by subsections (j) and (r)(29) of section 474 shall not apply with respect to obligations issued before January 1, 1984."

In 1983, P.L. 98-21, Sec. 121(c)(2), added subsec. (g), effective for benefits received after 12/31/83 in tax. yrs. end. after 12/31/83.

In 1982, P.L. 97-248, Sec. 342, provides as follows:

"SEC. 342. WITHHOLDING OF TAX ON NONRESIDENT ALIENS AND FOREIGN CORPORATIONS.

Withholding on foreign taxpayers — Code Sec. 1442

"Not later than 2 years after the date of the enactment of this Act, the Secretary of the Treasury or his delegate shall prescribe regulations establishing certification procedures, refund procedures, or other procedures which ensure that any benefit of any treaty relating to withholding of tax under sections 1441 and 1442 of the Internal Revenue Code of 1954 is available only to persons entitled to such benefit."

In 1976, P.L. 94-455, Sec. 1906(b)(13)(A), substituted "Secretary" for "Secretary or his delegate" each place it appeared in Code Sec. 1441, effective 2/1/77.

In 1971, P.L. 92-178, Sec. 313(a), added "(other than original issue discount as defined in section 1232(b))" after "interest" in the first sentence of subsec. (b) . . . Sec. 313(d), added para. (c)(8), effective for payments occurring on or after 4/1/72.

In 1969, P.L. 91-172, Sec. 505(b), added subsec. (f), effective 12/30/69.

In 1966, P.L. 89-809, Sec. 103(h)(1), substituted "or of any foreign partnership" for ", or of any partnership not engaged in trade or business within the United States and composed in whole or in part of nonresident aliens," in subsec. (a) . . . Sec. 103(h)(2), deleted "(except interest on deposits with persons carrying on the banking business paid to persons not engaged in business in the United States)" in subsec. (b) . . . Sec. 103(h)(3), substituted "gains described in section 402(a)(2), 403(a)(2), or 631(b) or (c), amounts subject to tax under section 871(a)(1)(C), gains subject to tax under section 871(a)(1)(D), and gains on transfers described in section 1235 made on or before October 4, 1966," for "and amounts described in section 402(a)(2), section 403(a)(2), section 631(b) and (c), and section 1235 which are considered to be gains from the sale or exchange of capital assets," in the first sentence of subsec. (b) . . . Sec. 103(h)(4), added the sentence at the end of subsec. (b) . . . Sec. 103(h)(5), amended para. (c)(1) . . . Sec. 103(h)(6), amended para. (c)(4) . . . Sec. 103(h)(7), substituted "gains described in section 402(a)(2), 403(a)(2), or 631(b) or (c), gains subject to tax under section 871(a)(1)(D), and gains on transfers described in section 1235 made on or before October 4, 1966," for "amounts described in section 402(a)(2), section 403(a)(2), section 631(b) and (c), and section 1235, which are considered to be gains from the sale or exchange of capital assets," in para. (c)(5), and substituted "amount payable," for "proceeds from such sale or exchange," in para. (c)(5) . . . Sec. 103(h)(8), added para. (c)(7) . . . Sec. 103(h)(9), redesignated subsec. (d) as subsec. (e) and added new subsec (d), effective for payments made in tax. yrs. of recipients begin. after 12/31/66.

Prior to amendment, para. (c)(1) read as follows:

"(1) Dividends of foreign corporations.—No deduction or withholding under subsection (a) shall be required in the case of dividends paid by a foreign corporation unless (A) such corporation is engaged in trade or business within the United States, and (B) more than 85 percent of the gross income of such corporation for the 3-year period ending with the close of its taxable year preceding the declaration of such dividends (or for such part of such period as the corporation has been in existence) was derived from sources within the United States as determined under part I of subchapter N of chapter 1."

Prior to amendment, para. (c)(4) read as follows:

"(4) Compensation of certain aliens.—Under regulations prescribed by the Secretary or his delegate, there may be exempted from deduction and withholding under subsection (a) the compensation for personal services of—

"(A) nonresident alien individuals who enter and leave the United States at frequent intervals, and

"(B) a nonresident alien individual for the period he is temporarily present in the United States as a nonimmigrant under subparagraph (F) or (J) of section 101(a)(15) of the Immigration and Nationality Act, as amended."

In 1964, P.L. 88-272, Sec. 302(c), substituted "14 percent" for "18 percent" in subsec. (a) and subsec. (b), effective for payments made after the seventh day following 2/26/64.

In 1961, P.L. 87-256, Sec. 110(d)(1), added ", except that in the case of any item of income specified in the second sentence of subsection (b), the tax shall be equal to 18 percent of such item" before the period at the end of subsec. (a) . . . Sec. 110(d)(2), added "The items of income referred to in subsection (a) from which tax shall be deducted and withheld at the rate of 18 percent are—" to the end of subsec. (b), and added paras. (b)(1) and (2) . . . Sec. 110(d)(3), amended para. (c)(4), effective for payments made after 12/31/61.

Prior to amendment, para. (c)(4) read as follows:

"(4) Compensation of certain aliens.—Under regulations prescribed by the Secretary or his delegate, there may be exempted from deduction and withholding under subsection (a) the compensation for personal services of nonresident alien individuals who enter and leave the United States at frequent intervals."

In 1958, P.L. 85-866, Sec. 40(b), added "section 403(a)(2)," after "section 402(a)(2)," in subsec. (b) and para. (c)(5), effective 9/3/58.

In 1956, P.L. 726, Sec. 11(f), added para. (c)(6), effective 7/18/56.

Sec. 1442. Withholding of tax on foreign corporations.

(a) General rule.

In the case of foreign corporations subject to taxation under this subtitle, there shall be deducted and withheld at the source in the same manner and on the same items of income as is provided in section 1441 a tax equal to 30 percent thereof. For purposes of the preceding sentence, the references in section 1441(b) to sections 871(a)(1)(C) and (D) shall be treated as referring to sections 881(a)(3) and (4), the reference in section 1441(c)(1) to section 871(b)(2) shall be treated as referring to section 842 or section 882(a)(2), as the case may be, the reference in section 1441(c)(5) to section 871(a)(1)(D) shall be treated as referring to section 881(a)(4), the reference in section 1441(c)(8) to section 871(a)(1)(C) shall be treated as referring to section 881(a)(3), the references in section 1441(c)(9) to sections 871(h) and 871(h)(3) or (4) shall be treated as referring to sections 881(c) and 881(c)(3) or (4), the reference in section 1441(c)(10) to section 871(i)(2) shall be treated as referring to section 881(d), and the references in section 1441(c)(12) to sections 871(a) and 871(k) shall be treated as referring to sections 881(a) and 881(e) (except that for purposes of applying subparagraph (A) of section 1441(c)(12), as so modified, clause (ii) of section 881(e)(1)(B) shall not apply to any dividend unless the regulated investment company knows that such dividend is a dividend referred to in such clause).

(b) Exemption.

Subject to such terms and conditions as may be provided by regulations prescribed by the Secretary, subsection (a) shall not apply in the case of a foreign corporation engaged in trade or business within the United States if the Secretary determines that the requirements of subsection (a) impose an undue administrative burden and that the collection of the tax imposed by section 881 on such corporation will not be jeopardized by the exemption.

(c) Exception for certain possessions corporations.

(1) Guam, American Samoa, the Northern Mariana Islands, and the Virgin Islands. For purposes of this section, the term "foreign corporation" does not include a corporation created or organized in Guam, American Samoa, the Northern Mariana Islands, or the Virgin Islands or under the law of any such possession if the requirements of subparagraphs (A), (B), and (C) of section 881(b)(1) are met with respect to such corporation.

(2) Commonwealth of Puerto Rico.

(A) In general. If dividends are received during a taxable year by a corporation—

(i) created or organized in, or under the law of, the Commonwealth of Puerto Rico, and

(ii) with respect to which the requirements of subparagraphs (A), (B), and (C) of section 881(b)(1) are met for the taxable year,

subsection (a) shall be applied for such taxable year by substituting "10 percent" for "30 percent".

(B) Applicability. If, on or after the date of the enactment of this paragraph, an increase in the rate of the Commonwealth of Puerto Rico's withholding tax which is generally applicable to dividends paid to United States corporations not engaged in a trade or business in the Commonwealth to a rate greater than 10 percent takes effect, this paragraph shall not apply to dividends received on or after the effective date of the increase.

In 2004, P.L. 108-357, Sec. 411(a)(3)(B)(i), substituted "the reference in section 1441(c)(10)" for "and the reference in section 1441(c)(10)" in subsec. (a) . . . Sec. 411(a)(3)(B)(ii), added ", and the references in section 1441(c)(12) to sections 871(a) and 871(k) shall be treated as referring to sections 881(a) and 881(e) (except that for purposes of applying subparagraph (A) of section 1441(c)(12), as so modified, clause (ii) of section 881(e)(1)(B) shall not apply to any dividend unless the regulated investment company knows that such dividend is a dividend referred to in such clause)" before the period at the end of subsec. (a), effective for dividends with respect to tax. yrs. of regulated investment companies begin. after 12/31/2004.

—P.L. 108-357, Sec. 420(b)(1), substituted "(1) Guam, American Samoa, the Northern Mariana Islands, and the Virgin Islands. For purposes" for "For purposes" in subsec. (c) . . . Sec. 420(b)(2), added para. (c)(2), effective for dividends paid after 10/22/2004.

In 1993, P.L. 103-66, Sec. 13237(c)(5)(A), substituted "871(h)(3) or (4)" for "871(h)(3)" in subsec. (a) . . . Sec. 13237(c)(5)(B), substituted "881(c)(3) or (4)" for "881(c)(3)" in subsec. (a), effective for interest received after 12/31/93.

In 1988, P.L. 100-647, Sec. 1012(g)(7)(A), substituted "the references in" for "and the references in" in subsec. (a)... Sec. 1012(g)(7)(B), added ", and the reference in section 1441(c)(10) to section 871(i)(2) shall be treated as referring to section 881(d)" before the period at the end of subsec. (a), effective for payments after 12/31/86.

—P.L. 100-647, Sec. 6128(a), added "as such principles are applied in Revenue Ruling 86-6, except that the maximum debt-to-equity ratio described in such Revenue Rulings shall be increased from 5-to-1 to 25-to-1" before the period at the end of Sec. 127(g)(3)(B) of P.L. 98-369 [part of the effective date for amendments made by Sec. 127(e)(2)(A) and (B) of P.L. 98-369, see below], effective for tax. yrs. end. after 11/10/88.

In 1986, P.L. 99-514, Sec. 1273(b)(2)(B), amended subsec. (c), effective for tax. yrs. begin. after 12/31/86, except as provided in Secs. 1277(b) and (d), reproduced in note following Code Sec. 931.

Prior to amendment, subsec. (c) read as follows:

"(c) Exception for certain Guam and Virgin Islands Corporations.

"(1) In general. For purposes of this section, the term 'foreign corporation' does not include a corporation created or organized in Guam or the Virgin Islands or under the law of Guam or the Virgin Islands if the requirements of subparagraphs (A) and (B) of section 881(b)(1) are met with respect to such corporation.

"(2) Paragraph (1) not to apply to tax imposed in Guam. For purposes of applying this subsection with respect to income tax liability incurred to Guam—

"(A) paragraph (1) shall not apply, and

"(B) for purposes of this section, the term 'foreign corporation' does not include a corporation created or organized in Guam or under the law of Guam.

"(3) Cross reference.

"For tax imposed in the Virgin Islands, see sections 934 and 934A."

—P.L. 99-514, Sec. 1810(d)(3)(E)(i), substituted "sections 871(h)" for "sections 871(h)(2)" in subsec. (a)... Sec. 1810(d)(3)(E)(ii), substituted "sections 881(c)" for "sections 881(c)(2)" in subsec. (a)... Sec. 1810(d)(3)(E)(iii), substituted "section 1441(c)(9)" for "section 1449(c)(9)" in subsec. (a), effective for interest received after 7/18/84 in tax. yrs. end. after 7/18/84. Sec. 127(g)(3) of P.L. 98-369 [as amended by Sec. 6128(a) of P.L. 100-647, see above] provides a special rule, reproduced below.

In 1984, P.L. 98-369, Sec. 127(e)(2)(A), deleted "and" after "section 881(a)(4)," in the sentence at the end of subsec. (a)... Sec. 127(e)(2)(B), added ", and the references in section 1449(c)(9) to sections 871(h)(2) and 871(h)(3) shall be treated as referring to sections 881(c)(2) and 881(c)(3)" before the period in the sentence at the end of subsec. (a), effective for interest received after 7/18/84, for obligations issued after 7/18/84, in tax. yrs. end. after 7/18/84. Sec. 127(g)(3) of this Act [as amended by Sec. 6128(a) of P.L. 100-647, see above] provides a special rule as follows:

"(3) Special rule for certain United States affiliate obligations.—

"(A) In general.—For purposes of the Internal Revenue Code of 1954, payments of interest on a United States affiliate obligation to an applicable CFC in existence on or before June 22, 1984, shall be treated as payments to a resident of the country in which the applicable CFC is incorporated.

"(B) Exception.—Subparagraph (A) shall not apply to any applicable CFC which did not meet requirements which are based on the principles set forth in Revenue Rulings 69-501, 69-377, 70-645, and 73-110 as such principles are applied in Revenue Ruling 86-6, except that the maximum debt-to-equity ratio described in such Revenue Rulings shall be increased from 5-to-1 to 25-to-1.

"(C) Definitions.—

"(i) The term 'applicable CFC' has the meaning given such term by section 121(b)(2)(D) of this Act, except that such section shall be applied by substituting 'the date of interest payment' for 'March 31, 1984,' in clause (i) thereof.

"(ii) The term 'United States affiliate obligation' means an obligation described in section 121(b)(2)(F) of this Act which was issued before June 22, 1984."

—P.L. 98-369, Sec. 130(b), amended subsec. (c), effective for payments made after 3/1/84, in tax. yrs. end. after 3/1/84.

Prior to amendment, subsec. (c) read as follows:

"(c) Exception for Guam corporations.

"For purposes of this section, the term 'foreign corporation' does not include a corporation created or organized in Guam or under the law of Guam."

—P.L. 98-369, Sec. 474(r)(29)(I)(i), deleted "or section 1451" after "provided in section 1441" in subsec. (a)... Sec. 474(r)(29)(I)(ii), deleted "; except that, in the case of interest described in section 1451 (relating to tax-free covenant bonds), the deduction and withholding shall be at the rate specified therein" after "30 percent thereof" in subsec. (a), effective for tax. yrs. begin. after 12/31/83 and to carrybacks from tax. yrs. begin. after 12/31/83. Sec. 475(b) of this Act provides a special rule as follows:

"(b) Tax-free covenant bonds. The amendments made by subsections (j) and (r)(29) of section 474 shall not apply with respect to obligations issued before January 1, 1984."

In 1982, P.L. 97-248, Sec. 342, provides:

"SEC. 342. WITHHOLDING OF TAX ON NONRESIDENT ALIENS AND FOREIGN CORPORATIONS.

"Not later than 2 years after the date of the enactment of this Act, the Secretary of the Treasury or his delegate shall prescribe regulations establishing certification procedures, refund procedures, or other procedures which ensure that any benefit of any treaty relating to withholding of tax under sections 1441 and 1442 of the Internal Revenue Code of 1954 is available only to persons entitled to such benefit."

In 1976, P.L. 94-455, Sec. 1906(b)(13)(A), substituted "Secretary" for "Secretary or his delegate" each place it appeared in subsec. (b), effective 2/1/77.

In 1972, P.L. 92-606, Sec. 1(e)(2), added subsec. (d), effective 11/1/72.

In 1971, P.L. 92-178, Sec. 313(c)(1), deleted "and" the last place it appeared in subsec. (a)... Sec. 313(e)(2), added ", and the reference in section 1441(c)(8) to section 871(a)(1)(C) shall be treated as referring to section 881(a)(3)" before the period at the end of subsec. (a), effective for payments occurring on or after 4/1/72.

In 1966, P.L. 89-809, Sec. 104(c), amended Code Sec. 1442, effective for tax. yrs. begin. after 12/31/66.

Prior to amendment, Code Sec. 1442 read as follows:

"Sec. 1442. Withholding of tax on foreign corporations.

"In the case of foreign corporations subject to taxation under this subtitle not engaged in trade or business within the United States, there shall be deducted and withheld at the source in the same manner and on the same items of income as is provided in section 1441 or section 1451 a tax equal to 30 percent thereof; except that, in the case of interest described in section 1451 (relating to tax-free covenant bonds), the deduction and withholding shall be at the rate specified therein."

Sec. 1443. Foreign tax-exempt organizations.

(a) Income subject to section 511.

In the case of income of a foreign organization subject to the tax imposed by section 511, this chapter shall apply to income includible under section 512 in computing its unrelated business taxable income, but only to the extent and subject to such conditions as may be provided under regulations prescribed by the Secretary.

(b) Income subject to section 4948.

In the case of income of a foreign organization subject to the tax imposed by section 4948(a), this chapter shall apply, except that the deduction and withholding shall be at the rate of 4 percent and shall be subject to such conditions as may be provided under regulations prescribed by the Secretary.

In 1976, P.L. 94-455, Sec. 1906(b)(13)(A), substituted "Secretary" for "Secretary or his delegate" each place it appeared in Code Sec. 1443, effective 2/1/77.

In 1969, P.L. 91-172, Sec. 101(j)(22), added the heading of subsec. (a), and added subsec. (b), effective 1/1/70.

—P.L. 91-172, Sec. 121(d)(2)(C), substituted "income" for "rents" in subsec. (a), effective for tax. yrs. begin. after 12/31/69.

Sec. 1444. Withholding on Virgin Islands source income.

For purposes of determining the withholding tax liability incurred in the Virgin Islands pursuant to this title (as made applicable to the Virgin Islands) with respect to amounts received from sources within the Virgin Islands by citizens and resident alien individuals of the United States, and corporations organized in the United States, the rate of withholding tax under sections 1441 and 1442 on income subject to tax under section 871(a)(1) or 881 shall not exceed the rate of tax on such income under section 871(a)(1) or 881, as the case may be.

In 1988, P.L. 100-647, Sec. 1012(x), deleted "(as modified by section 934A)" before "shall not exceed", effective for tax. yrs. begin. after 12/31/86.

In 1983, P.L. 97-455, Sec. 1(b), added Code Sec. 1444, effective for payments made after 1/13/83.

Sec. 1445. Withholding of tax on dispositions of United States real property interests.

(a) General rule.

Except as otherwise provided in this section, in the case of any disposition of a United States real property interest (as defined in section 897(c)) by a foreign person, the transferee shall be required to deduct and withhold a tax equal to 10 percent of the amount realized on the disposition.

(b) Exemptions.

(1) In general. No person shall be required to deduct and withhold any amount under subsection (a) with respect to a disposition if paragraph (2), (3), (4), (5), or (6) applies to the transaction.

(2) Transferor furnishes nonforeign affidavit. Except as provided in paragraph (7), this paragraph applies to the disposition if the transferor furnishes to the transferee an affidavit by the transferor stating, under penalty of perjury, the transferor's United States taxpayer identification number and that the transferor is not a foreign person.

(3) Nonpublicly traded domestic corporation furnishes affidavit that interests in corporation not United States real property interests. Except as provided in paragraph (7), this paragraph applies in the case of a disposition of any interest in any domestic corporation if the domestic corporation furnishes to the transferee an affidavit by the domestic corporation stating, under penalty of perjury, that—

(A) the domestic corporation is not and has not been a United States real property holding corporation (as defined in section 897(c)(2)) during the applicable period specified in section 897(c)(1)(A)(ii), or

(B) as of the date of the disposition, interests in such corporation are not United States real property interests by reason of section 897(c)(1)(B).

(4) Transferee receives qualifying statement.

(A) In general. This paragraph applies to the disposition if the transferee receives a qualifying statement at such time, in such manner, and subject to such terms and conditions as the Secretary may by regulations prescribe.

(B) Qualifying statement. For purposes of subparagraph (A), the term "qualifying statement" means a statement by the Secretary that—

(i) the transferor either—

(I) has reached agreement with the Secretary (or such agreement has been reached by the transferee) for the payment of any tax imposed by section 871(b)(1) or 882(a)(1) on any gain recognized by the transferor on the disposition of the United States real property interest, or

(II) is exempt from any tax imposed by section 871(b)(1) or 882(a)(1) on any gain recognized by the transferor on the disposition of the United States real property interest, and

(ii) the transferor or transferee has satisfied any transferor's unsatisfied withholding liability or has provided adequate security to cover such liability.

(5) Residence where amount realized does not exceed $300,000. This paragraph applies to the disposition if—

(A) the property is acquired by the transferee for use by him as a residence, and

(B) the amount realized for the property does not exceed $300,000.

(6) Stock regularly traded on established securities market. This paragraph applies if the disposition is of a share of a class of stock that is regularly traded on an established securities market.

(7) Special rules for paragraphs (2), (3), and (9). Paragraph (2), (3), or (9) (as the case may be) shall not apply to any disposition—

(A) if—

(i) the transferee or qualified substitute has actual knowledge that the affidavit referred to in such paragraph, or the statement referred to in paragraph (9)(A)(ii), is false, or

(ii) the transferee or qualified substitute receives a notice (as described in subsection (d)) from a transferor's agent, transferee's agent, or qualified substitute that such affidavit or statement is false, or

(B) if the Secretary by regulations requires the transferee or qualified substitute to furnish a copy of such affidavit or statement to the Secretary and the transferee or qualified substitute fails to furnish a copy of such affidavit or statement to the Secretary at such time and in such manner as required by such regulations.

(8) Applicable wash sales transactions. No person shall be required to deduct and withhold any amount under subsection (a) with respect to a disposition which is treated as a disposition of a United States real property interest solely by reason of section 897(h)(5).

(9) Alternative procedure for furnishing nonforeign affidavit. For purposes of paragraphs (2) and (7)—

(A) In general. Paragraph (2) shall be treated as applying to a transaction if, in connection with a disposition of a United States real property interest—

(i) the affidavit specified in paragraph (2) is furnished to a qualified substitute, and

(ii) the qualified substitute furnishes a statement to the transferee stating, under penalty of perjury, that the qualified substitute has such affidavit in his possession.

(B) Regulations. The Secretary shall prescribe such regulations as may be necessary or appropriate to carry out this paragraph.

(c) Limitations on amount required to be withheld.

(1) Cannot exceed transferor's maximum tax liability.

(A) In general. The amount required to be withheld under this section with respect to any disposition shall not exceed the amount (if any) determined under subparagraph (B) as the transferor's maximum tax liability.

(B) Request. At the request of the transferor or transferee, the Secretary shall determine, with respect to any disposition, the transferor's maximum tax liability.

(C) Refund of excess amounts withheld. Subject to such terms and conditions as the Secretary may by regulations prescribe, a transferor may seek and obtain a refund of any amounts withheld under this section in excess of the transferor's maximum tax liability.

(2) Authority of secretary to prescribe reduced amount. At the request of the transferor or transferee, the Secretary may prescribe a reduced amount to be withheld under this section if the Secretary determines that to substitute such reduced amount will not jeopardize the collection of the tax imposed by section 871(b)(1) or 882(a)(1).

(3) Procedural rules.

(A) Regulations. Requests for—

(i) qualifying statements under subsection (b)(4),

(ii) determinations of transferor's maximum tax liability under paragraph (1), and

(iii) reductions under paragraph (2) in the amount required to be withheld,

shall be made at the time and manner, and shall include such information, as the Secretary shall prescribe by regulations.

(B) Requests to be handled within 90 days. The Secretary shall take action with respect to any request described in subparagraph (A) within 90 days after the Secretary receives the request.

(d) Liability of transferor's agents, transferee's agents, or qualified substitutes.

(1) Notice of false affidavit; foreign corporations. If—

(A) the transferor furnishes the transferee or qualified substitute an affidavit described in paragraph (2) of subsection (b) or a domestic corporation furnishes the transferee an affidavit described in paragraph (3) of subsection (b), and

(B) in the case of—

(i) any transferor's agent—

(I) such agent has actual knowledge that such affidavit is false, or

(II) in the case of an affidavit described in subsection (b)(2) furnished by a corporation, such corporation is a foreign corporation, or

(ii) any transferee's agent or qualified substitute, such agent or substitute has actual knowledge that such affidavit is false,

such agent or qualified substitute shall so notify the transferee at such time and in such manner as the Secretary shall require by regulations.

(2) Failure to furnish notice.

(A) In general. If any transferor's agent, transferee's agent, or qualified substitute is required by paragraph (1) to furnish notice, but fails to furnish such notice at such time or times and in such manner as may be required by regulations, such agent or substitute shall have the same duty to deduct and withhold that the transferee would have had if such agent or substitute had complied with paragraph (1).

(B) Liability limited to amount of compensation. An agent's or substitute's liability under subparagraph (A) shall be limited to the amount of compensation the agent or substitute derives from the transaction.

(3) Transferor's agent. For purposes of this subsection, the term "transferor's agent" means any person who represents the transferor—

(A) in any negotiation with the transferee or any transferee's agent related to the transaction, or

(B) in settling the transaction.

(4) Transferee's agent. For purposes of this subsection, the term "transferee's agent" means any person who represents the transferee—

(A) in any negotiation with the transferor or any transferor's agent related to the transaction, or

(B) in settling the transaction.

(5) Settlement officer not treated as transferor's agent. For purposes of this subsection, a person shall not be treated as a transferor's agent or transferee's agent with respect to any transaction merely because such person performs 1 or more of the following acts:

(A) The receipt and the disbursement of any portion of the consideration for the transaction.

(B) The recording of any document in connection with the transaction.

(e) Special rules relating to distributions, etc., by corporations, partnerships, trusts, or estates.

> • *Caution:* Code Sec. 1445(e)(1), following, was amended by Sec. 301(a)(2)(C), P.L. 108-27. These provisions generally sunset for tax year beginning after 12/31/2012. For specific sunset provisions, see Sec. 303, P.L. 108-27, as amended by Sec. 102(a), P.L. 111-312, reproduced in history notes for this Code Sec.

(1) Certain domestic partnerships, trusts, and estates. In the case of any disposition of a United States real property interest as defined in section 897(c) (other than a disposition described in paragraph (4) or 5)) by a domestic partnership, domestic trust, or domestic estate, such partnership, the trustee of such trust, or the executor of such estate (as the case may be) shall be required to deduct and withhold under subsection (a) a tax equal to 35 percent (or, to the extent provided in regulations, 15 percent) of the gain realized to the extent such gain—

(A) is allocable to a foreign person who is a partner or beneficiary of such partnership, trust, or estate, or

(B) is allocable to a portion of the trust treated as owned by a foreign person under subpart E of part I of subchapter J.

(2) Certain distributions by foreign corporations. In the case of any distribution by a foreign corporation on which gain is recognized under subsection (d) or (e) of section 897, the foreign corporation shall deduct and withhold under subsection (a) a tax equal to 35 percent of the amount of gain recognized on such distribution under such subsection.

(3) Distributions by certain domestic corporations to foreign shareholders. If a domestic corporation which is or has been a United States real property holding corporation (as defined in section 897(c)(2)) during the applicable period specified in section 897(c)(1)(A)(ii) distributes property to a foreign person in a transaction to which section 302 or part II of subchapter C applies, such corporation shall deduct and withhold under subsection (a) a tax equal to 10 percent of the amount realized by the foreign shareholder. The preceding sentence shall not apply if, as of the date of the distribution, interests in such corporation are not United States real property interests by reason of section 897(c)(1)(B). Rules similar to the rules of the preceding provisions of this paragraph shall apply in the case of any distribution to which section 301 applies and which is not made out of the earnings and profits of such a domestic corporation.

(4) Taxable distributions by domestic or foreign partnerships, trusts, or estates. A domestic or foreign partnership, the trustee of a domestic or foreign trust, or the executor of a domestic or foreign estate shall be required to deduct and withhold under subsection (a) a tax equal to 10 percent of the fair market value (as of the time of the taxable distribution) of any United States real property interest distributed to a partner of the partnership or a beneficiary of the trust or estate, as the case may be, who is a foreign person in a transaction which would constitute a taxable distribution under the regulations promulgated by the Secretary pursuant to section 897.

(5) Rules relating to dispositions of interest in partnerships, trusts, or estates. To the extent provided in regulations, the transferee of a partnership interest or of a beneficial interest in a trust or estate shall be required to deduct and withhold under subsection (a) a tax equal to 10 percent of the amount realized on the disposition.

(6) Distributions by regulated investment companies and real estate investment trusts. If any portion of a distribution from a qualified investment entity (as defined in section 897(h)(4)) to a nonresident alien individual or a foreign corporation is treated under section 897(h)(1) as gain realized by such individual or corporation from the sale or exchange of a United States real property interest, the qualified investment entity shall deduct and withhold under subsection (a) a tax equal to 35 percent (or, to the extent provided in regulations, 15 percent (20 percent in the case of taxable years beginning after December 31, 2010)) of the amount so treated.

(7) Regulations. The Secretary shall prescribe such regulations as may be necessary to carry out the purposes of this subsection, including regulations providing for exceptions from provisions of this subsection and regulations for the application of this subsection in the case of payments through 1 or more entities.

(f) Definitions.

For purposes of this section—

(1) Transferor. The term "transferor" means the person disposing of the United States real property interest.

(2) Transferee. The term "transferee" means the person acquiring the United States real property interest.

(3) Foreign person. The term "foreign person" means any person other than a United States person.

(4) Transferor's maximum tax liability. The term "transferor's maximum tax liability" means, with respect to the disposition of any interest, the sum of—

(A) the maximum amount which the Secretary determines could be imposed as tax under section 871(b)(1) or 882(a)(1) by reason of the disposition, plus

(B) the amount the Secretary determines to be the transferor's unsatisfied withholding liability with respect to such interest.

(5) Transferor's unsatisfied withholding liability. The term "transferor's unsatisfied withholding liability" means the withholding obligation imposed by this section on the transferor's acquisition of the United States real property interest or on the acquisition of a predecessor interest, to the extent such obligation has not been satisfied.

(6) Qualified substitute. The term "qualified substitute" means, with respect to a disposition of a United States real property interest—

(A) the person (including any attorney or title company) responsible for closing the transaction, other than the transferor's agent, and

(B) the transferee's agent.

In **2010**, P.L. 111-312, Sec. 102(a), substituted "December 31, 2012" for "December 31, 2010" in Sec. 303 of P.L. 108-27 [see below], effective as if included in the enactment of P.L. 108-27, 5/28/2003.

In **2008**, P.L. 110-289, Sec. 3024(a), added para. (b)(9) . . . Sec. 3024(b), added para. (f)(6) . . . Sec. 3024(c)(1), amended para. (b)(7) . . . Sec. 3024(c)(2)(A), amended para. (d)(1) . . . Sec. 3024(c)(2)(B), amended para. (d)(2) . . . Sec. 3024(c)(2)(C), substituted ", transferee's agents, or qualified substitutes" for "or transferee's agents" in the heading of subsec. (d), effective for dispositions of United States real property interests after 7/30/2008.

Prior to amendment, para. (b)(7) read as follows:

"(7) Special rules for paragraphs (2) and (3). Paragraph (2) or (3) (as the case may be) shall not apply to any disposition—

"(A) if—

"(i) the transferee has actual knowledge that the affidavit referred to in such paragraph is false, or

"(ii) the transferee receives a notice (as described in subsection (d)) from a transferor's agent or a transferee's agent that such affidavit is false, or

"(B) if the Secretary by regulations requires the transferee to furnish a copy of such affidavit to the Secretary and the transferee fails to furnish a copy of such affidavit to the Secretary at such time and in such manner as required by such regulations."

Prior to amendment, para. (d)(1) read as follows:

"(1) Notice of false affidavit; foreign corporations. If—

"(A) the transferor furnishes the transferee an affidavit described in paragraph (2) of subsection (b) or a domestic corporation furnishes the transferee an affidavit described in paragraph (3) of subsection (b), and

"(B) in the case of—

"(i) any transferor's agent—

"(I) such agent has actual knowledge that such affidavit is false, or

"(II) in the case of an affidavit described in subsection (b)(2) furnished by a corporation, such corporation is a foreign corporation, or

"(ii) any transferee's agent, such agent has actual knowledge that such affidavit is false,

such agent shall so notify the transferee at such time and in such manner as the Secretary shall require by regulations."

Prior to amendment, para. (d)(2) read as follows:

"(2) Failure to furnish notice.

"(A) In general. If any transferor's agent or transferee's agent is required by paragraph (1) to furnish notice, but fails to furnish such notice at such time or times and in such manner as may be required by regulations, such agent shall have the same duty to deduct and withhold that the transferee would have had if such agent had complied with paragraph (1).

"(B) Liability limited to amount of compensation. An agent's liability under subparagraph (A) shall be limited to the amount of compensation the agent derives from the transaction."

In **2006**, P.L. 109-222, Sec. 102, substituted "December 31, 2010" for "December 31, 2008" in Sec. 303 of P.L. 108-27 [see below], effective 5/17/2006.

—P.L. 109-222, Sec. 505(b), redesignated para. (e)(6) as para. (e)(7), and added para. (e)(6), effective for tax. yrs. of qualified investment entities begin. after 12/31/2005, except that no amount shall be required to be withheld under Code Sec. 1441, 1442, or 1445 with respect to any distribution before 5/17/2006 if such amount was not otherwise required to be withheld under any such section as in effect before such amendments.

—P.L. 109-222, Sec. 506(b), added para. (b)(8), effective for tax. yrs. begin. after 12/31/2005, except that such amendment shall not apply to any distribution, or substitute dividend payment, occurring before the date that is 30 days after 5/17/2006.

In **2003**, P.L. 108-27, Sec. 301(a)(2)(C), substituted "15 percent" for "20 percent" in para. (e)(1), effective for amounts paid after 5/28/2003.

—P.L. 108-27, Sec. 303, of this Act [as amended by Sec. 102, P.L. 109-222, and Sec. 102(a), P.L. 111-312, see above], reads as follows:

"Sec. 303. Sunset of title. All provisions of, and amendments made by, this title [Secs. 301 and 302] shall not apply to taxable years beginning after December 31, 2012, and the Internal Revenue Code of 1986 shall be applied and administered to such years as if such provisions and amendments had never been enacted."

In **1997**, P.L. 105-34, Sec. 311(c)(1), substituted "20 percent" for "28 percent" in para. (e)(1), effective for amounts paid after 8/5/97.

In **1996**, P.L. 104-188, Sec. 1704(c)(1), added sentence to the end of para. (e)(3), effective for distributions after 8/20/96.

In **1993**, P.L. 103-66, Sec. 13221(c)(3), substituted "35 percent" for "34 percent" in paras. (e)(1) and (2), effective 8/10/93.

In **1988**, P.L. 100-647, Sec. 1003(b)(3), substituted "34 percent (or, to the extent provided in regulations, 28 percent)" for "34 percent", in para. (e)(1), effective for tax. yrs. begin. after 12/31/87.

—P.L. 100-647, Sec. 1003(c)(2), amended the effective date for changes made by Sec. 311(b)(4) of P.L. 99-514 [see below], by adding, "except that the amendment made by subsection (b)(4) shall apply to payments made after December 31, 1986" before the period at the end of Sec. 311(c) of P.L. 99-514.

In **1986**, P.L. 99-514, Sec. 311(b)(4), substituted "34 percent" for "28 percent" in paras. (e)(1) [as amended by Sec. 1810(f)(4)(A) of this Act, see below] and (e)(2), effective [as amended by Sec. 1003(c)(2) of P.L. 100-647, see above] for payments made after 12/31/86.

—P.L. 99-514, Sec. 1810(f)(2), amended para. (b)(3) . . . Sec. 1810(f)(3)(A), amended clause (d)(1)(B)(i) . . . Sec. 1810(f)(3)(B), substituted "described in paragraph (2)" for "described in paragraph (2)(A)" in para. (d)(1), effective for any disposition on or after 1/1/85.

Prior to amendment, para. (b)(3) read as follows:

"(3) Nonpublicly traded domestic corporation furnishes affidavit that it is not a United States real property holding corporation. Except as provided in paragraph (7), this paragraph applies in the case of a disposition of any interest in any domestic corporation, if the domestic corporation furnishes to the transferee an affidavit by the domestic corporation stating, under penalty of perjury, that the domestic corporation is not and has not been a United States real property holding corporation (as defined in section 897(c)(2)) during the applicable period specified in section 897(c)(1)(A)(ii)."

Prior to amendment, clause (d)(1)(B)(i) read as follows:

"(i) any transferor's agent, the transferor is a foreign corporation or such agent has actual knowledge that such affidavit is false, or"

—P.L. 99-514, Sec. 1810(f)(4)(A), amended para. (e)(1), effective for dispositions after 11/21/86.

Prior to amendment, para. (e)(1) read as follows:

"(1) Certain domestic partnerships, trusts, and estates. A domestic partnership, the trustee of a domestic trust, or the executor of a domestic estate shall be required to deduct and withhold under subsection (a) a tax equal to 10 percent of any amount of which such partnership, trustee, or executor has custody which is—

"(A) attributable to the disposition of a United States real property interest (as defined in section 897(c), other than a disposition described in paragraph (4) or (5)), and

"(B) either—

"(i) includible in the distributive share of a partner of the partnership who is a foreign person,

"(ii) includible in the income of a beneficiary of the trust or estate who is a foreign person, or

"(iii) includible in the income of a foreign person under the provisions of section 671."

—P.L. 99-514, Sec. 1810(f)(5), added the last sentence to para. (e)(3) . . . Sec. 1810(f)(6), substituted "section 897" for "section 897(g)" in para. (e)(4) . . . Sec. 1810(f)(8), added "and regulations for the application of this subsection in the case of payments through 1 or more entities" before the period at the end of para. (e)(6), effective for any disposition on or after 1/1/85.

In **1984**, P.L. 98-369, Sec. 129(a)(1), added Code Sec. 1445, effective for any disposition on or after 1/1/85.

Sec. 1446. Withholding tax on foreign partners' share of effectively connected income.

(a) General rule.

If—

(1) a partnership has effectively connected taxable income for any taxable year, and

(2) any portion of such income is allocable under section 704 to a foreign partner,

such partnership shall pay a withholding tax under this section at such time and in such manner as the Secretary shall by regulations prescribe.

(b) Amount of withholding tax.

(1) In general. The amount of the withholding tax payable by any partnership under subsection (a) shall be equal to the applicable percentage of the effectively connected taxable income of the partnership which is allocable under section 704 to foreign partners.

(2) Applicable percentage. For purposes of paragraph (1), the term "applicable percentage" means—

(A) the highest rate of tax specified in section 1 in the case of the portion of the effectively connected taxable income which is allocable under section 704 to foreign partners who are not corporations, and

(B) the highest rate of tax specified in section 11(b)(1) in the case of the portion of the effectively connected taxable income which is allocable under section 704 to foreign partners which are corporations.

(c) Effectively connected taxable income.

For purposes of this section, the term "effectively connected taxable income" means the taxable income of the partnership which is effectively connected (or treated as effectively connected) with the conduct of a trade or business in the United States computed with the following adjustments:

(1) Paragraph (1) of section 703(a) shall not apply.

(2) The partnership shall be allowed a deduction for depletion with respect to oil and gas wells but the amount of such deduction shall be determined without regard to sections 613 and 613A.

(3) There shall not be taken into account any item of income, gain, loss, or deduction to the extent allocable under section 704 to any partner who is not a foreign partner.

(d) Treatment of foreign partners.

(1) Allowance of credit. Each foreign partner of a partnership shall be allowed a credit under section 33 for such partner's share of the withholding tax paid by the partnership under this section. Such credit shall be allowed for the partner's taxable year in which (or with which) the partnership taxable year (for which such tax was paid) ends.

(2) Credit treated as distributed to partner. Except as provided in regulations, a foreign partner's share of any withholding tax paid by the partnership under this section shall be treated as distributed to such partner by such partnership on the earlier of—

(A) the day on which such tax was paid by the partnership, or

(B) the last day of the partnership's taxable year for which such tax was paid.

(e) Foreign partner.

For purposes of this section, the term "foreign partner" means any partner who is not a United States person.

(f) Regulations.

The Secretary shall prescribe such regulations as may be necessary to carry out the purposes of this section, including—

(1) regulations providing for the application of this section in the case of publicly traded partnerships, and

(2) regulations providing—

(A) that, for purposes of section 6655, the withholding tax imposed under this section shall be treated as a tax imposed by section 11 and any partnership required to pay such tax shall be treated as a corporation, and

(B) appropriate adjustments in applying section 6655 with respect to such withholding tax.

In **1989,** P.L. 101-239, Sec. 7811(i)(6)(A), substituted "section 11(b)(1)" for "section 11(b)" in subpara. (b)(2)(B) . . . Sec. 7811(i)(6)(B), amended para. (d)(2) . . . Sec. 7811(i)(6)(C), amended subsec. (f), effective as provided in Sec. 1012(s)(1)(D) of P.L. 100-647, reproduced below.

Prior to amendment, para. (d)(2) read as follows:

"(2) Credit treated as distributed to partner. A foreign partner's share of any withholding tax paid by the partnership under this section shall be treated as distributed to such partner by such partnership on the last day of the partnership's taxable year (for which such tax was paid)."

Prior to amendment, subsec. (f) read as follows:

"(f) Regulations.

The Secretary shall prescribe such regulations as may be necessary to carry out the purposes of this section, including regulations providing for the application of this section in the case of publicly traded partnerships."

In **1988,** P.L. 100-647, Sec. 1012(s)(1)(A), amended Code Sec. 1446, effective as provided in Sec. 1012(s)(1)(D) of this Act which reads as follows:

"(D) The amendments made by this paragraph [Sec. 1006(s)(1)] shall apply to taxable years beginning after December 31, 1987. No amount shall be required to be deducted and withheld under section 1446 of the 1986 Code (as in effect before the amendment made by subparagraph (A))."

Prior to amendment Code Sec. 1446 read as follows:

"SEC. 1446. WITHHOLDING TAX ON AMOUNTS PAID BY PARTNERSHIPS TO FOREIGN PARTNERS.

"(a) General rule.

"Except as provided in this section, if a partnership has any income, gain, or loss which is effectively connected or treated as effectively connected with the conduct of a trade or business within the United States, any person described in section 1441(a) shall be required to deduct and withhold a tax equal to 20 percent of any amount distributed to a partner which is not a United States person.

"(b) Limitation if less than 80 percent of gross income is effectively connected with United States trade or business.

"(1) In general. If the effectively connected percentage is less than 80 percent, only the effectively connected percentage of any distribution shall be taken into account under subsection (a).

"(2) Effectively connected percentage. For purposes of paragraph (1) the term 'effectively connected percentage' means the percentage of the gross income of the partnership for the 3 taxable years preceding the taxable year of the distribution which is effectively connected (or treated as effectively connected) with the conduct of a trade or business within the United States.

"(c) Exceptions.

"(1) Amounts on which tax withheld. Subsection (a) shall not apply to that portion of any distribution with respect to which a tax is required to be deducted and withheld under section 1441 or 1442 (or would be required to be deducted and withheld but for a treaty).

"(2) Partnerships with certain allocations. Except as provided in regulations, subsection (a) shall not apply to any partnership with respect to which substantially all income from sources within the United States and substantially all income which is effectively connected with the conduct of a trade or business within the United States is properly allocated to United States persons.

"(3) Coordination with section 1445. Under regulations proper adjustments shall be made in the amount required to be deducted and withheld under subsection (a) for amounts deducted and withheld under section 1445.

"(d) Regulations.

"The Secretary shall prescribe such regulations as may be necessary or appropriate to carry out the purposes of this section."

In **1986,** P.L. 99-514, Sec. 1246(a), added Code Sec. 1446, effective for distributions after 12/31/87, or, if earlier, the effective date (which shall not be earlier than 1/1/87) of the initial regulations issued under such Code Sec. 1446.

Subchapter B. Repealed

Sec.
1451. Repealed.

In **1984,** P.L. 98-369, Sec. 474(r)(29)(A), deleted Subchapter B and the item for Code Sec. 1451.

Prior to deletion Subchapter B read as follows:

"Subchapter B.—Tax-Free Covenant Bonds

Sec.

"1451. Tax-free covenant bonds."

Sec. 1451. Repealed.

In **1984,** P.L. 98-369, Sec. 474(r)(29)(A), repealed Code Sec. 1451, effective for tax. yrs. begin. after 12/31/83 and to carrybacks from tax. yrs. begin. after 12/31/83. Sec. 475(b) of this Act provides a special rule as follows:

"(b) Tax-free covenant bonds.

Withholding on foreign taxpayers — Chapter 4

"The amendments made by subsections (j) and (r)(29) of section 474 shall not apply with respect to obligations issued before January 1, 1984."
Prior to repeal, Code Sec. 1451 read as follows:
"Sec. 1451. Tax-free covenant bonds.
"(a) Requirement of withholding.
"In any case where bonds, mortgages, or deeds of trust, or other similar obligations of a corporation, issued before January 1, 1934, contain a contract or provision by which the obligor agrees to pay any portion of the tax imposed by this subtitle on the obligee, or to reimburse the obligee for any portion of the tax, or to pay the interest without deduction for any tax which the obligor may be required or permitted to pay thereon, or to retain therefrom under any law of the United States, the obligor shall deduct and withhold a tax equal to 2 percent (regardless of whether the liability assumed by the obligor is less than, equal to, or greater than 2 percent) of the interest on such bonds, mortgages, deeds of trust, or other obligations, whether such interest is payable annually or at shorter or longer periods, if payable to—
"(1) an individual,
"(2) a partnership, or
"(3) a foreign corporation not engaged in trade or business within the United States.
"(b) Payments to foreigners.
"Notwithstanding subsection (a), if the liability assumed by the obligor does not exceed 2 percent of the interest, then the deduction and withholding shall be at the rate of 30 percent in the case of—
"(1) a nonresident alien individual,
"(2) any partnership not engaged in trade or business within the United States and composed in whole or in part of nonresident aliens, and
"(3) a foreign corporation not engaged in trade or business within the United States.
"(c) Owner unknown.
"If the owners of such obligations are not known to the withholding agent, the Secretary may authorize such deduction and withholding to be at the rate of 2 percent, or, if the liability assumed by the obligor does not exceed 2 percent of the interest, then at the rate of 30 percent.
"(d) Benefit of personal exemptions.
"Deduction and withholding under this section shall not be required in the case of a citizen or resident entitled to receive such interest, if he files with the withholding agent on or before February 1 a signed notice in writing claiming the benefit of the deduction for personal exemptions provided in section 151; nor in the case of a nonresident alien individual if so provided for in regulations prescribed by the Secretary under section 874.
"(e) Alien residents of Puerto Rico.
"For purposes of this section, the term 'nonresident alien individual' includes an alien resident of Puerto Rico.
"(f) Income of obligor and obligee.
"The obligor shall not be allowed a deduction for the payment of the tax imposed by this subtitle, or any other tax paid pursuant to the tax-free covenant clause, nor shall such tax be included in the gross income of the obligee."
In 1976, P.L. 94-455, Sec. 1906(b)(13)(A), substituted "Secretary" for "Secretary or his delegate" in subsecs. (c) and (d), effective 2/1/77.

Subchapter B.—Application of Withholding Provisions

Sec.
1461. Liability for withheld tax.
1462. Withheld tax as credit to recipient of income.
1463. Tax paid by recipient of income.
1464. Refunds and credits with respect to withheld tax.
1465. Repealed.

In 1986, P.L. 99-514, Sec. 1899A(73), amended item 1461.
Prior to amendment, item 1461 read as follows:
"1461. Return and payment of withheld tax."
In 1984, P.L. 98-369, Sec. 474(r)(29)(A), redesignated subchapter C as B.
In 1976, P.L. 94-455, Sec. 1901(b)(41), deleted item 1465.
Prior to repeal, item 1465 read as follows:
"1465. Definition of withholding agent."

Sec. 1461. Liability for withheld tax.

Every person required to deduct and withhold any tax under this chapter is hereby made liable for such tax and is hereby indemnified against the claims and demands of any person for the amount of any payments made in accordance with the provisions of this chapter.

In 1966, P.L. 89-809, Sec. 103, amended Code Sec. 1461, effective for payments occurring after 12/31/66.
Prior to amendment, Code Sec. 1461 read as follows:
"Sec. 1461. Return and payment of withheld tax.
"Every person required to deduct and withhold any tax under this chapter shall, on or before March 15 of each year, make return thereof and pay the tax to the officer designated in section 6151. Every such person is hereby made liable for such tax and is hereby indemnified against the claims and demands of any person for the amount of any payments made in accordance with the provisions of this chapter."

Sec. 1462. Withheld tax as credit to recipient of income.

Income on which any tax is required to be withheld at the source under this chapter shall be included in the return of the recipient of such income, but any amount of tax so withheld shall be credited against the amount of income tax as computed in such return.

Sec. 1463. Tax paid by recipient of income.

If—
(1) any person, in violation of the provisions of this chapter, fails to deduct and withhold any tax under this chapter, and
(2) thereafter the tax against which such tax may be credited is paid,
the tax so required to be deducted and withheld shall not be collected from such person; but this section shall in no case relieve such person from liability for interest or any penalties or additions to the tax otherwise applicable in respect of such failure to deduct and withhold.

In 1996, P.L. 104-188, Sec. 1704(t)(9, substituted "this section" for "this subsection", in Code Sec. 1463, effective 8/20/96.
In 1989, P.L. 101-239, Sec. 7743(a), amended Code Sec. 1463, effective for failures after 12/31/89.
Prior to amendment, Code Sec. 1463 read as follows:
"Sec. 1463. Tax paid by recipient of income.
"If any tax required under this chapter to be deducted and withheld is paid by the recipient of the income, it shall not be re-collected from the withholding agent; nor in cases in which the tax is so paid shall any penalty be imposed on or collected from the recipient of the income or the withholding agent for failure to return or pay the same, unless such failure was fraudulent and for the purpose of evading payment."

Sec. 1464. Refunds and credits with respect to withheld tax.

Where there has been an overpayment of tax under this chapter, any refund or credit made under chapter 65 shall be made to the withholding agent unless the amount of such tax was actually withheld by the withholding agent.

Sec. 1465. Repealed.

In 1976, P.L. 94-455, Sec. 1901(a)(156), repealed Code Sec. 1465, effective for tax. yrs. begin. after 12/31/76.
Prior to repeal, Code Sec. 1465 read as follows:
"Sec. 1465. Definition of withholding agent.
"The term 'withholding agent' means any person required to deduct and withhold any tax under this chapter."

CHAPTER 4.—Repealed. [RULES APPLICABLE TO RECOVERY OF EXCESSIVE PROFITS ON GOVERNMENT CONTRACTS]

Subchapter
A. Repealed.
B. Repealed [Mitigation of Effect of Renegotiation of Government Contracts].

In 1990, P.L. 101-508, Sec. 11801(a)(37), repealed Chapter 4.
In 1976, P.L. 94-455, Sec. 1951(c)(4), deleted the item for Subchapter A.
Prior to repeal, that item read as follows:
"A. Recovery of Excessive Profits on Government Contracts."

Subpart A. Repealed. [Recovery of Excessive Profits on Government Contracts]

Sec
1471. Repealed [Recovery of excessive profits on government contracts.]

In 1976, P.L. 94-455, Sec. 1951(b)(13)(A), repealed Subchapter A, effective for tax. yrs. begin. after '76, except as provided in Sec. 1951(b)(13)(B) of this Act, which reads as follows:

"(B) Savings provision.—If the amount of profit required to be paid into the Treasury under section 2382 or 7300 of title 10, United States Code, is not voluntarily paid, the Secretary of the Treasury or his delegate shall collect the same under the methods employed to collect taxes under subtitle A. All provisions of law (including penalties) applicable with respect to such taxes and not inconsistent with section 2382 or 7300 of title 10 of such Code, shall apply with respect to the assessment, collection, or payment of excess profits to the Treasury as provided in the preceding sentence, and to refunds by the Treasury of overpayments of excess profits into the Treasury."

Prior to repeal, Subchapter A read as follows:
"Subchapter A.—Recovery of Excessive Profits on Government Contracts
"Sec.
"1471. Recovery of excessive profits on government contracts.

Sec. 1471. Repealed

In 1976, P.L. 94-455, Sec. 1951(b)(13)(A), repealed Code Sec. 1471, effective for tax. yrs. begin. after '76, except as provided in Sec. 1951(b)(13)(B) of this Act, reproduced after Subchapter A.

Prior to repeal, Code Sec. 1471 read as follows:
"SEC. 1471. RECOVERY OF EXCESSIVE PROFITS ON GOVERNMENT CONTRACTS.
"(a) Method of collection.
"If the amount of profit required to be paid into the Treasury under section 3 of the Act of March 27, 1934, as amended (34 U. S. C. 496), with respect to contracts completed within taxable years subject to this code is not voluntarily paid, the Secretary or his delegate shall collect the same under the methods employed to collect taxes under this subtitle.
"(b) Laws applicable.
"All provisions of law (including penalties) applicable with respect to the taxes imposed by this subtitle and not inconsistent with section 3 of the Act of March 27, 1934, as amended, shall apply with respect to the assessment, collection, or payment of excess profits to the Treasury as provided by subsection (a), and to refunds by the Treasury of overpayments of excess profits into the Treasury."

CHAPTER 4.—Taxes to Enforce Reporting on Certain Foreign Accounts

Sec.
1471. Withholdable payments to foreign institutions.
1472. Withholdable payments to other foreign entities.
1473. Definitions.
1474. Special Rules.

In 2010, P.L. 111-147, Sec. 501(a), Added Chapter 4, Subtitle A.

> • **Caution:** Code Sec. 1471, following, is generally effective for payments made after 12/31/2012. For special rules, see Sec. 501(d)(2)-(3), P.L. 111-147, reproduced in notes to this Code Sec.

Sec. 1471. Withholdable payments to foreign financial institutions.

(a) In general.

In the case of any withholdable payment to a foreign financial institution which does not meet the requirements of subsection (b), the withholding agent with respect to such payment shall deduct and withhold from such payment a tax equal to 30 percent of the amount of such payment.

(b) Reporting requirements, etc.

(1) **In general.** The requirements of this subsection are met with respect to any foreign financial institution if an agreement is in effect between such institution and the Secretary under which such institution agrees—

(A) to obtain such information regarding each holder of each account maintained by such institution as is necessary to determine which (if any) of such accounts are United States accounts,

(B) to comply with such verification and due diligence procedures as the Secretary may require with respect to the identification of United States accounts,

(C) in the case of any United States account maintained by such institution, to report on an annual basis the information described in subsection (c) with respect to such account,

(D) to deduct and withhold a tax equal to 30 percent of—

(i) any passthru payment which is made by such institution to a recalcitrant account holder or another foreign financial institution which does not meet the requirements of this subsection, and

(ii) in the case of any passthru payment which is made by such institution to a foreign financial institution which has in effect an election under paragraph (3) with respect to such payment, so much of such payment as is allocable to accounts held by recalcitrant account holders or foreign financial institutions which do not meet the requirements of this subsection,

(E) to comply with requests by the Secretary for additional information with respect to any United States account maintained by such institution, and

(F) in any case in which any foreign law would (but for a waiver described in clause (i)) prevent the reporting of any information referred to in this subsection or subsection (c) with respect to any United States account maintained by such institution—

(i) to attempt to obtain a valid and effective waiver of such law from each holder of such account, and

(ii) if a waiver described in clause (i) is not obtained from each such holder within a reasonable period of time, to close such account.

Any agreement entered into under this subsection may be terminated by the Secretary upon a determination by the Secretary that the foreign financial institution is out of compliance with such agreement.

(2) **Financial institutions deemed to meet requirements in certain cases.** A foreign financial institution may be treated by the Secretary as meeting the requirements of this subsection if—

(A) such institution—

(i) complies with such procedures as the Secretary may prescribe to ensure that such institution does not maintain United States accounts, and

(ii) meets such other requirements as the Secretary may prescribe with respect to accounts of other foreign financial institutions maintained by such institution, or

(B) such institution is a member of a class of institutions with respect to which the Secretary has determined that the application of this section is not necessary to carry out the purposes of this section.

(3) **Election to be withheld upon rather than withhold on payments to recalcitrant account holders and non-participating foreign financial institutions.** In the case of a foreign financial institution which meets the requirements of this subsection and such other requirements as the Secretary may provide and which elects the application of this paragraph—

(A) the requirements of paragraph (1)(D) shall not apply,

(B) the withholding tax imposed under subsection (a) shall apply with respect to any withholdable payment to such institution to the extent such payment is allocable to accounts held by recalcitrant account holders or foreign financial institutions which do not meet the requirements of this subsection, and

(C) the agreement described in paragraph (1) shall—

(i) require such institution to notify the withholding agent with respect to each such payment of the institution's election under this paragraph and such other information as may be necessary for the withholding agent to determine the appropriate amount to deduct and withhold from such payment, and

(ii) include a waiver of any right under any treaty of the United States with respect to any amount deducted and withheld pursuant to an election under this paragraph.

To the extent provided by the Secretary, the election under this paragraph may be made with respect to certain classes or types of accounts of the foreign financial institution.

(c) Information required to be reported on United States accounts.

(1) In general. The agreement described in subsection (b) shall require the foreign financial institution to report the following with respect to each United States account maintained by such institution:

(A) The name, address, and TIN of each account holder which is a specified United States person and, in the case of any account holder which is a United States owned foreign entity, the name, address, and TIN of each substantial United States owner of such entity.

(B) The account number.

(C) The account balance or value (determined at such time and in such manner as the Secretary may provide).

(D) Except to the extent provided by the Secretary, the gross receipts and gross withdrawals or payments from the account (determined for such period and in such manner as the Secretary may provide).

(2) Election to be subject to same reporting as United States financial institutions. In the case of a foreign financial institution which elects the application of this paragraph—

(A) subparagraphs (C) and (D) of paragraph (1) shall not apply, and

(B) the agreement described in subsection (b) shall require such foreign financial institution to report such information with respect to each United States account maintained by such institution as such institution would be required to report under sections 6041, 6042, 6045, and 6049 if—

(i) such institution were a United States person, and

(ii) each holder of such account which is a specified United States person or United States owned foreign entity were a natural person and citizen of the United States.

An election under this paragraph shall be made at such time, in such manner, and subject to such conditions as the Secretary may provide.

(3) Separate requirements for qualified intermediaries. In the case of a foreign financial institution which is treated as a qualified intermediary by the Secretary for purposes of section 1441 and the regulations issued thereunder, the requirements of this section shall be in addition to any reporting or other requirements imposed by the Secretary for purposes of such treatment.

(d) Definitions.

For purposes of this section—

(1) United States account.

(A) In general. The term "United States account" means any financial account which is held by one or more specified United States persons or United States owned foreign entities.

(B) Exception for certain accounts held by individuals. Unless the foreign financial institution elects to not have this subparagraph apply, such term shall not include any depository account maintained by such financial institution if—

(i) each holder of such account is a natural person, and

(ii) with respect to each holder of such account, the aggregate value of all depository accounts held (in whole or in part) by such holder and maintained by the same financial institution which maintains such account does not exceed $50,000.

To the extent provided by the Secretary, financial institutions which are members of the same expanded affiliated group shall be treated for purposes of clause (ii) as a single financial institution.

(C) Elimination of duplicative reporting requirements. Such term shall not include any financial account in a foreign financial institution if—

(i) such account is held by another financial institution which meets the requirements of subsection (b), or

(ii) the holder of such account is otherwise subject to information reporting requirements which the Secretary determines would make the reporting required by this section with respect to United States accounts duplicative.

(2) Financial account. Except as otherwise provided by the Secretary, the term "financial account" means, with respect to any financial institution—

(A) any depository account maintained by such financial institution,

(B) any custodial account maintained by such financial institution, and

(C) any equity or debt interest in such financial institution (other than interests which are regularly traded on an established securities market).

Any equity or debt interest which constitutes a financial account under subparagraph (C) with respect to any financial institution shall be treated for purposes of this section as maintained by such financial institution.

(3) United States owned foreign entity. The term "United States owned foreign entity" means any foreign entity which has one or more substantial United States owners.

(4) Foreign financial institution. The term "foreign financial institution" means any financial institution which is a foreign entity. Except as otherwise provided by the Secretary, such term shall not include a financial institution which is organized under the laws of any possession of the United States.

(5) Financial institution. Except as otherwise provided by the Secretary, the term "financial institution" means any entity that—

(A) accepts deposits in the ordinary course of a banking or similar business,

(B) as a substantial portion of its business, holds financial assets for the account of others, or

(C) is engaged (or holding itself out as being engaged) primarily in the business of investing, reinvesting, or trading in securities (as defined in section 475(c)(2) without regard to the last sentence thereof), partnership interests, commodities (as defined in section 475(e)(2)), or any interest (including a futures or forward contract or option) in such securities, partnership interests, or commodities.

(6) Recalcitrant account holder. The term "recalcitrant account holder" means any account holder which—

(A) fails to comply with reasonable requests for the information referred to in subsection (b)(1)(A) or (c)(1)(A), or

(B) fails to provide a waiver described in subsection (b)(1)(F) upon request.

(7) Passthru payment. The term "passthru payment" means any withholdable payment or other payment to the extent attributable to a withholdable payment.

(e) Affiliated groups.

(1) In general. The requirements of subsections (b) and (c)(1) shall apply—

(A) with respect to United States accounts maintained by the foreign financial institution, and

(B) except as otherwise provided by the Secretary, with respect to United States accounts maintained by each other foreign financial institution (other than any foreign financial institution which meets the requirements of subsection (b)) which is a member of the same expanded affiliated group as such foreign financial institution.

(2) Expanded affiliated group. For purposes of this section, the term "expanded affiliated group" means an affiliated group as defined in section 1504(a), determined—

(A) by substituting "more than 50 percent" for "at least 80 percent" each place it appears, and

(B) without regard to paragraphs (2) and (3) of section 1504(b).

A partnership or any other entity (other than a corporation) shall be treated as a member of an expanded affiliated group if such entity is controlled (within the meaning of section 954(d)(3)) by members of such group (including any entity treated as a member of such group by reason of this sentence).

(f) Exception for certain payments.

Subsection (a) shall not apply to any payment to the extent that the beneficial owner of such payment is—

(1) any foreign government, any political subdivision of a foreign government, or any wholly owned agency or instrumentality of any one or more of the foregoing,

(2) any international organization or any wholly owned agency or instrumentality thereof,

(3) any foreign central bank of issue, or

(4) any other class of persons identified by the Secretary for purposes of this subsection as posing a low risk of tax evasion.

In 2010, P.L. 111-147, Sec. 501(a), added Code Sec. 1471, effective for payments made after 12/31/2012, except as provided in Sec. 501(d)(2)-(3) of this Act which read as follows:

"(2) Grandfathered treatment of outstanding obligations. The amendments made by this section shall not require any amount to be deducted or withheld from any payment under any obligation outstanding on the date which is 2 years after the date of the enactment of this Act or from the gross proceeds from any disposition of such an obligation.

"(3) Interest on overpayments. The amendment made by subsection (b) shall apply—

"(A) in the case of such amendment's application to paragraph (1) of section 6611(e) of the Internal Revenue Code of 1986, to returns the due date for which (determined without regard to extensions) is after the date of the enactment of this Act,

"(B) in the case of such amendment's application to paragraph (2) of such section, to claims for credit or refund of any overpayment filed after the date of the enactment of this Act (regardless of the taxable period to which such refund relates), and

"(C) in the case of such amendment's application to paragraph (3) of such section, to refunds paid after the date of the enactment of this Act (regardless of the taxable period to which such refund relates)."

• **Caution:** Code Sec. 1472, following, is generally effective for payments made after 12/31/2012. For special rules, see Sec. 501(d)(2)-(3), P.L. 111-147, reproduced in notes to this Code Sec.

Sec. 1472. Withholdable payments to other foreign entities.

(a) In general.

In the case of any withholdable payment to a non-financial foreign entity, if—

(1) the beneficial owner of such payment is such entity or any other non-financial foreign entity, and

(2) the requirements of subsection (b) are not met with respect to such beneficial owner,

then the withholding agent with respect to such payment shall deduct and withhold from such payment a tax equal to 30 percent of the amount of such payment.

(b) Requirements for waiver of withholding.

The requirements of this subsection are met with respect to the beneficial owner of a payment if—

(1) such beneficial owner or the payee provides the withholding agent with either—

(A) a certification that such beneficial owner does not have any substantial United States owners, or

(B) the name, address, and TIN of each substantial United States owner of such beneficial owner,

(2) the withholding agent does not know, or have reason to know, that any information provided under paragraph (1) is incorrect, and

(3) the withholding agent reports the information provided under paragraph (1)(B) to the Secretary in such manner as the Secretary may provide.

(c) Exceptions.

Subsection (a) shall not apply to—

(1) except as otherwise provided by the Secretary, any payment beneficially owned by—

(A) any corporation the stock of which is regularly traded on an established securities market,

(B) any corporation which is a member of the same expanded affiliated group (as defined in section 1471(e)(2) without regard to the last sentence thereof) as a corporation described in subparagraph (A),

(C) any entity which is organized under the laws of a possession of the United States and which is wholly owned by one or more bona fide residents (as defined in section 937(a)) of such possession,

(D) any foreign government, any political subdivision of a foreign government, or any wholly owned agency or instrumentality of any one or more of the foregoing,

(E) any international organization or any wholly owned agency or instrumentality thereof,

(F) any foreign central bank of issue, or

(G) any other class of persons identified by the Secretary for purposes of this subsection, and

(2) any class of payments identified by the Secretary for purposes of this subsection as posing a low risk of tax evasion.

(d) Non-financial foreign entity.

For purposes of this section, the term "non-financial foreign entity" means any foreign entity which is not a financial institution (as defined in section 1471(d)(5)).

In 2010, P.L. 111-147, Sec. 501(a), added Code Sec. 1472, effective for payments made after 12/31/2012, except as provided in Sec. 501(d)(2)-(3) of this Act which read as follows:

"(2) Grandfathered treatment of outstanding obligations. The amendments made by this section shall not require any amount to be deducted or withheld from any

Withholding on foreign taxpayers   Code Sec. 1474

payment under any obligation outstanding on the date which is 2 years after the date of the enactment of this Act or from the gross proceeds from any disposition of such an obligation.

"(3) Interest on overpayments. The amendment made by subsection (b) shall apply—

"(A) in the case of such amendment's application to paragraph (1) of section 6611(e) of the Internal Revenue Code of 1986, to returns the due date for which (determined without regard to extensions) is after the date of the enactment of this Act,

"(B) in the case of such amendment's application to paragraph (2) of such section, to claims for credit or refund of any overpayment filed after the date of the enactment of this Act (regardless of the taxable period to which such refund relates), and

"(C) in the case of such amendment's application to paragraph (3) of such section, to refunds paid after the date of the enactment of this Act (regardless of the taxable period to which such refund relates)."

> • *Caution:* Code Sec. 1473, following, is generally effective for payments made after 12/31/2012. For special rules, see Sec. 501(d)(2)-(3), P.L. 111-147, reproduced in notes to this Code Sec.

Sec. 1473. Definitions.

For purposes of this chapter—

(1) Withholdable payment. Except as otherwise provided by the Secretary—

(A) In general. The term "withholdable payment" means—

(i) any payment of interest (including any original issue discount), dividends, rents, salaries, wages, premiums, annuities, compensations, remunerations, emoluments, and other fixed or determinable annual or periodical gains, profits, and income, if such payment is from sources within the United States, and

(ii) any gross proceeds from the sale or other disposition of any property of a type which can produce interest or dividends from sources within the United States.

(B) Exception for income connected with United States business. Such term shall not include any item of income which is taken into account under section 871(b)(1) or 882(a)(1) for the taxable year.

(C) Special rule for sourcing interest paid by foreign branches of domestic financial institutions. Subparagraph (B) of section 861(a)(1) shall not apply.

(2) Substantial United States owner.

(A) In general. The term "substantial United States owner" means—

(i) with respect to any corporation, any specified United States person which owns, directly or indirectly, more than 10 percent of the stock of such corporation (by vote or value),

(ii) with respect to any partnership, any specified United States person which owns, directly or indirectly, more than 10 percent of the profits interests or capital interests in such partnership, and

(iii) in the case of a trust—

(I) any specified United States person treated as an owner of any portion of such trust under subpart E of part I of subchapter J of chapter 1, and

(II) to the extent provided by the Secretary in regulations or other guidance, any specified United States person which holds, directly or indirectly, more than 10 percent of the beneficial interests of such trust.

(B) Special rule for investment vehicles. In the case of any financial institution described in section 1471(d)(5)(C), clauses (i), (ii), and (iii) of subparagraph (A) shall be applied by substituting "0 percent" for "10 percent".

(3) Specified United States person. Except as otherwise provided by the Secretary, the term "specified United States person" means any United States person other than—

(A) any corporation the stock of which is regularly traded on an established securities market,

(B) any corporation which is a member of the same expanded affiliated group (as defined in section 1471(e)(2) without regard to the last sentence thereof) as a corporation the stock of which is regularly traded on an established securities market,

(C) any organization exempt from taxation under section 501(a) or an individual retirement plan,

(D) the United States or any wholly owned agency or instrumentality thereof,

(E) any State, the District of Columbia, any possession of the United States, any political subdivision of any of the foregoing, or any wholly owned agency or instrumentality of any one or more of the foregoing,

(F) any bank (as defined in section 581),

(G) any real estate investment trust (as defined in section 856),

(H) any regulated investment company (as defined in section 851),

(I) any common trust fund (as defined in section 584(a)), and

(J) any trust which—

(i) is exempt from tax under section 664(c), or

(ii) is described in section 4947(a)(1).

(4) Withholding agent. The term "withholding agent" means all persons, in whatever capacity acting, having the control, receipt, custody, disposal, or payment of any withholdable payment.

(5) Foreign entity. The term "foreign entity" means any entity which is not a United States person.

In 2010, P.L. 111-147, Sec. 501(a), added Code Sec. 1473, effective for payments made after 12/31/2012, except as provided in Sec. 501(d)(2)-(3) of this Act which read as follows:

"(2) Grandfathered treatment of outstanding obligations. The amendments made by this section shall not require any amount to be deducted or withheld from any payment under any obligation outstanding on the date which is 2 years after the date of the enactment of this Act or from the gross proceeds from any disposition of such an obligation.

"(3) Interest on overpayments. The amendment made by subsection (b) shall apply—

"(A) in the case of such amendment's application to paragraph (1) of section 6611(e) of the Internal Revenue Code of 1986, to returns the due date for which (determined without regard to extensions) is after the date of the enactment of this Act,

"(B) in the case of such amendment's application to paragraph (2) of such section, to claims for credit or refund of any overpayment filed after the date of the enactment of this Act (regardless of the taxable period to which such refund relates), and

"(C) in the case of such amendment's application to paragraph (3) of such section, to refunds paid after the date of the enactment of this Act (regardless of the taxable period to which such refund relates)."

> • *Caution:* Code Sec. 1474, following, is generally effective for payments made after 12/31/2012. For special rules, see Sec. 501(d)(2)-(3), P.L. 111-147, reproduced in notes to this Code Sec.

Sec. 1474. Special rules.

(a) Liability for withheld tax.

Every person required to deduct and withhold any tax under this chapter is hereby made liable for such tax and is hereby indemnified against the claims and demands of any person for the amount of any payments made in accordance with the provisions of this chapter.

(b) Credits and refunds.

(1) In general. Except as provided in paragraph (2), the determination of whether any tax deducted and withheld under this chapter results in an overpayment by the beneficial owner of the payment to which such tax is attributable shall be made as if such tax had been deducted and withheld under subchapter A of chapter 3.

(2) Special rule where foreign financial institution is beneficial owner of payment.

(A) In general. In the case of any tax properly deducted and withheld under section 1471 from a specified financial institution payment—

(i) if the foreign financial institution referred to in subparagraph (B) with respect to such payment is entitled to a reduced rate of tax with respect to such payment by reason of any treaty obligation of the United States—

(I) the amount of any credit or refund with respect to such tax shall not exceed the amount of credit or refund attributable to such reduction in rate, and

(II) no interest shall be allowed or paid with respect to such credit or refund, and

(ii) if such foreign financial institution is not so entitled, no credit or refund shall be allowed or paid with respect to such tax.

(B) Specified financial institution payment. The term "specified financial institution payment" means any payment if the beneficial owner of such payment is a foreign financial institution.

(3) Requirement to identify substantial United States owners. No credit or refund shall be allowed or paid with respect to any tax properly deducted and withheld under this chapter unless the beneficial owner of the payment provides the Secretary such information as the Secretary may require to determine whether such beneficial owner is a United States owned foreign entity (as defined in section 1471(d)(3)) and the identity of any substantial United States owners of such entity.

(c) Confidentiality of information.

(1) In general. For purposes of this chapter, rules similar to the rules of section 3406(f) shall apply.

(2) Disclosure of list of participating foreign financial institutions permitted. The identity of a foreign financial institution which meets the requirements of section 1471(b) shall not be treated as return information for purposes of section 6103.

(d) Coordination with other withholding provisions.

The Secretary shall provide for the coordination of this chapter with other withholding provisions under this title, including providing for the proper crediting of amounts deducted and withheld under this chapter against amounts required to be deducted and withheld under such other provisions.

(e) Treatment of withholding under agreements.

Any tax deducted and withheld pursuant to an agreement described in section 1471(b) shall be treated for purposes of this title as a tax deducted and withheld by a withholding agent under section 1471(a).

(f) Regulations.

The Secretary shall prescribe such regulations or other guidance as may be necessary or appropriate to carry out the purposes of, and prevent the avoidance of, this chapter.

In 2010, P.L. 111-147, Sec. 501(a), added Code Sec. 1474, effective for payments made after 12/31/2012, except as provided in Sec. 501(d)(2)-(3) of this Act which read as follows:

"(2) Grandfathered treatment of outstanding obligations. The amendments made by this section shall not require any amount to be deducted or withheld from any payment under any obligation outstanding on the date which is 2 years after the date of the enactment of this Act or from the gross proceeds from any disposition of such an obligation.

"(3) Interest on overpayments. The amendment made by subsection (b) shall apply—

"(A) in the case of such amendment's application to paragraph (1) of section 6611(e) of the Internal Revenue Code of 1986, to returns the due date for which (determined without regard to extensions) is after the date of the enactment of this Act,

"(B) in the case of such amendment's application to paragraph (2) of such section, to claims for credit or refund of any overpayment filed after the date of the enactment of this Act (regardless of the taxable period to which such refund relates), and

"(C) in the case of such amendment's application to paragraph (3) of such section, to refunds paid after the date of the enactment of this Act (regardless of the taxable period to which such refund relates)."

Subchapter B. Repealed [Mitigation of Effect of Renegotiation of Government Contracts]

Sec.

1481. Repealed [Mitigation of effect of renegotiation of government contracts].

1482. Repealed [Readjustment for repayments pursuant to price redeterminations].

In 1990, P.L. 101-508, Sec. 11801(a)(37), repealed Chapter 4.
In 1958, added item 1482.

Sec. 1481. Repealed.

In 1990, P.L. 101-508, Sec. 11801(a)(37), repealed Code Sec. 1481 as part of the repeal of Chapter 4, effective 11/5/90 except as provided in Sec. 11821(b) of this Act, which reads as follows:

"(b) Savings provision.

"If—

"(1) any provision amended or repealed by this part applied to—

"(A) any transaction occurring before the date of the enactment of this Act [11/5/90],

"(B) any property acquired before such date of enactment [11/5/90], or

"(C) any item of income, loss, deduction, or credit taken into account before such date of enactment [11/5/90], and

"(2) the treatment of such transaction, property, or item under such provision would (without regard to the amendments made by this part) affect liability for tax periods ending after such date of enactment [11/5/90],

nothing in the amendments made by this part shall be construed to affect the treatment of such transaction, property, or item for purposes of determining liability for tax for periods ending after such date of enactment [11/5/90]."

Prior to repeal, Code Sec. 1481 read as follows:

"Sec. 1481. Mitigation of Effect of Renegotiation of Government Contracts.

"(a) Reduction for prior taxable year.

"(1) Excessive profits eliminated for prior taxable year. In the case of a contract with the United States or any agency thereof, or any subcontract thereunder, which is made by the taxpayer, if a renegotiation is made in respect of such contract or subcontract and an amount of excessive profits received or accrued under such contract or subcontract for a taxable year (referred to in this section as 'prior taxable year') is eliminated and, the taxpayer is required to pay or repay to the United States or any agency thereof the amount of excessive profits eliminated or the amount of excessive profits eliminated is applied as an offset against other amounts due the taxpayer, the part of the contract or subcontract price which was received or was accrued for the prior taxable year shall be reduced by the amount of excessive profits eliminated.

For purposes of this section—

"(A) The term 'renegotiation' includes any transaction which is a renegotiation within the meaning of the Renegotiation Act of 1951, as amended (50 U.S.C. App. 1211 and following), any modification of one or more contracts with the United States or any agency thereof, and any agreement with the United States or any agency thereof in respect of one or more such contracts or subcontracts thereunder.

"(B) The term 'excessive profits' includes any amount which constitutes excessive profits within the meaning assigned to such term by the Renegotiation Act of

Withholding on foreign taxpayers — Code Sec. 1491

1951, as amended, any part of the contract price of a contract with the United States or any agency thereof, any part of the subcontract price of a subcontract under such a contract, and any profits derived from one or more such contracts or subcontracts.

"(C) The term 'subcontract' includes any purchase order or agreement which is a subcontract within the meaning assigned to such term by the Renegotiation Act of 1951, as amended.

"(2) Reduction of reimbursement for prior taxable year. In the case of a cost-plus-a-fixed-fee contract between the United States or any agency thereof and the taxpayer, if an item for which the taxpayer has been reimbursed is disallowed as an item of cost chargeable to such contract and the taxpayer is required to repay the United States or any agency thereof the amount disallowed or the amount disallowed is applied as an offset against other amounts due the taxpayer, the amount of the reimbursement of the taxpayer under the contract for the taxable year in which the reimbursement for such item was received or was accrued shall be reduced by the amount disallowed.

"(3) Deduction disallowed. The amount of the payment, repayment or offset described in paragraph (1) or paragraph (2) shall not constitute a deduction for the year in which paid or incurred.

"(4) Exception. The foregoing provisions of this subsection shall not apply in respect of any contract if the taxpayer shows to the satisfaction of the Secretary that a different method of accounting for the amount of the payment, repayment, or disallowance clearly reflects income, and in such case the payment, repayment, or disallowance shall be accounted for with respect to the taxable year provided for under such method, which for the purposes of subsections (b) and (c) shall be considered a prior taxable year.

"(b) Credit against repayment on account of renegotiation or allowance.

"(1) General rule. There shall be credited against the amount of excessive profits eliminated the amount by which the tax for the prior taxable year under this subtitle is decreased by reason of the application of paragraph (1) of subsection (a); and there shall be credited against the amount disallowed the amount by which the tax for the prior taxable year under this subtitle is decreased by reason of the application of paragraph (2) of subsection (a).

"(2) Credit for barred year. If at the time of the payment, repayment, or offset described in paragraph (1) or paragraph (2) of subsection (a), refund or credit of tax under this subtitle for the prior taxable year is prevented (except for the provisions of section 1311) by any provision of the internal revenue laws other than section 7122, or by rule of law, the amount by which the tax for such year under this subtitle is decreased by the application of paragraph (1) or paragraph (2) of subsection (a) shall be computed under this paragraph. There shall first be ascertained the tax previously determined for the prior taxable year. The amount of the tax previously determined shall be the excess of—

"(A) the sum of—
"(i) the amount shown as the tax by the taxpayer on his return (determined as provided in section 6211(b)(1), (3) and (4)), if a return was made by the taxpayer and an amount was shown as the tax by the taxpayer thereon, plus
"(ii) the amounts previously assessed (or collected without assessment) as a deficiency, over—
"(B) the amount of rebates, as defined in section 6211(b)(2), made.

There shall then be ascertained the decrease in tax previously determined which results solely from the application of paragraph (1) or paragraph (2) of subsection (a) to the prior taxable year. The amount so ascertained, together with any amounts collected as additions to the tax or interest, as a result of paragraph (1) or paragraph (2) of subsection (a) not having been applied to the prior taxable year, shall be the amount by which such tax is decreased.

"(3) Interest. In determining the amount of the credit under this subsection no interest shall be allowed with respect to the amount ascertained under paragraph (1); except that if interest is charged by the United States or the agency thereof on account of the disallowance for any period before the date of the payment, repayment, or offset, the credit shall be increased by an amount equal to interest on the amount ascertained under such paragraph at the same rate and for the period (prior to the date of the payment, repayment, or offset) as interest is so charged.

"(c) Credit in lieu of other credit or refund.
"If a credit is allowed under subsection (b) with respect to a prior taxable year and no other credit or refund under the internal revenue laws founded on the application of subsection (a) shall be made on account of the amount allowed with respect to such taxable year. If the amount allowable as a credit under subsection (b) exceeds the amount allowed under such subsection, the excess shall, for purposes of the internal revenue laws relating to credit or refund of tax, be treated as an overpayment for the prior taxable year which was made at the time the payment, repayment, or offset was made."

In 1976, P.L. 94-455, Sec. 1901(a)(157)(A), substituted "within the meaning of the Renegotiation Act of 1951, as amended (50 U.S.C. App. 1211 and following)" for "within the meaning of the Federal renegotiation act applicable to such transaction" in subpara. (a)(1)(A) . . . Sec. 1901(a)(157)(B), deleted subpara. (a)(1)(D) . . . Sec. 1901(a)(157)(C), substituted "Renegotiation Act of 1951, as amended" for "applicable Federal renegotiation act" in subparas. (a)(1)(B) and (C), effective for tax. yrs. begin. after 12/31/76.
Prior to deletion, subpara. (a)(1)(D) read as follows:
"(D) the term 'Federal renegotiation act' includes section 403 of the Sixth Supplemental National Defense Appropriation Act (Public Law 528, 77th Cong., 2d Sess.), as amended or supplemented, the Renegotiation Act of 1948, as amended or supplemented, and the Renegotiation Act of 1951, as amended or supplemented."

—P.L. 94-455, Sec. 1906(b)(13)(A), substituted "Secretary" for "Secretary or his delegate" each place it appeared in Code Sec. 1481, effective 2/1/77.

—P.L. 94-455, Sec. 1951(b)(14)(A), repealed subsec. (d), effective for tax. yrs. begin. after 12/31/76 except as provided in Sec. 1951(b)(14)(B) of the Act, which reads as follows:
"(B) Savings provision.—If, during a taxable year beginning after December 31, 1976, a recovery of excessive profits through renegotiation which relates to profits of a taxable year subject to the Internal Revenue Code of 1939, the adjustments in respect to such renegotiation shall be made under section 3806 of such Code."
Prior to repeal, subsec. (d) read as follows:
"(d) Renegotiation of Government contracts affecting taxable years prior to 1954.
"If a recovery of excessive profits through renegotiation as described in this section relates to profits of a taxable year subject to the Internal Revenue Code of 1939, the adjustments in respect of such renegotiation shall be made under section 3806 of such code."

In 1965, P.L. 89-44, Sec. 809, substituted "section 6211(b)(1), (3) and (4)" for "section 6211(b)(1) and (3)" in clause (b)(2)(A)(i), effective for tax. yrs. begin. after 6/30/65.

Sec. 1482. Repealed.

In 1990, P.L. 101-508, Sec. 11801(a)(37), repealed Code Sec. 1482 as part of the repeal of Chapter 4, effective 11/5/90, except as provided in Sec. 11821(b) of this Act, reproduced in note following Code Sec. 1481.
Prior to repeal, Code Sec. 1482 read as follows:
"SEC. 1482. READJUSTMENT FOR REPAYMENTS MADE PURSUANT TO PRICE REDETERMINATIONS.
"(a) General rule.
"If pursuant to a price redetermination provision in a subcontract to which this section applies, a repayment with respect to an amount paid under the subcontract is made by one party to the subcontract (hereinafter referred to as the 'payor') to another party to the subcontract (hereinafter referred to as the 'payee') then—
"(1) the tax of the payor for prior taxable years shall be recomputed as if the amount received or accrued by him with respect to which the repayment is made did not include an amount equal to the amount of the repayment, and
"(2) the tax of the payee for prior taxable years shall be recomputed as if the amount paid or incurred by him with respect to which the repayment is made did not include an amount equal to the amount of the repayment.
"(b) Subcontracts to which section applies.
"Subsection (a) shall apply only to a subcontract which is subject to renegotiation under the applicable Federal renegotiation act.
"(c) Limitation.
"Subsection (a) shall not apply only to any repayment to the extent that section 1481 applies to the amount repaid.
"(d) Treatment in year of repayment.
"The amount of any repayment to which subsection (a) applies shall not be taken into account by the payor or payee for the taxable year in which the repayment is made; but any overpayment or underpayment of tax resulting from the application of subsection (a) shall be treated as if it were an overpayment or underpayment for the taxable year in which the repayment is made."

In 1958, P.L. 85-866, Sec. 62(a), added Code Sec. 1482, effective for subcontracts entered into after 12/31/57.

CHAPTER 5.—TAX ON TRANSFERS TO AVOID INCOME TAX [REPEALED]

Sec.
1491. Imposition of tax. [Repealed]
1492. Nontaxable transfers. [Repealed]
1493. Definition of foreign trust. [Repealed]
1494. Payment and collection. [Repealed]

In 1997, P.L. 105-34, Sec. 1131(a), Repealed chapter 5.

Sec. 1491. Repealed.

In 1997, P.L. 105-34, Sec. 1131(a), repealed Code Sec. 1491 as part of the repeal of Chapter 5 of Subtitle A, effective 8/5/97.
Prior to repeal, Code Sec. 1491 read as follows:
"Sec. 1491 Imposition of tax.
"There is hereby imposed on the transfer of property by a citizen or resident of the United States, or by a domestic corporation or partnership, or by an estate or trust which is not a foreign estate or trust, to a foreign corporation as paid-in surplus or as a contribution to capital, or to a foreign estate or trust, or to a foreign partnership, an excise tax equal to 35 percent of the excess of—
"(1) the fair market value of the property so transferred, over
"(2) the sum of—
"(A) the adjusted basis (for determining gain) of such property in the hands of the transferor, plus
"(B) the amount of the gain recognized to the transferor at the time of the transfer.
If a trust which is not a foreign trust becomes a foreign trust, such trust shall be treated for purposes of this section as having transferred, immediately before becoming a foreign trust, all of its assets to a foreign trust."

2,947

In 1996, P.L. 104-188, Sec. 1907(b)(1), added the last sentence to Code Sec. 1491, effective 8/20/96.
In 1978, P.L. 95-600, Sec. 701(u)(14)(A), substituted "estate or trust" for "trust" each place it appeared Code Sec. 1491, effective for transfers after 10/2/75.
In 1976, P.L. 94-455, Sec. 1015(a), amended Code Sec. 1491, effective for transfers of property after 10/2/75.
Prior to amendment, Code Sec. 1491 read as follows:
"SEC. 1491. IMPOSITION OF TAX.
  "There is hereby imposed on the transfer of stock or securities by a citizen or resident of the United States, or by a domestic corporation or partnership, or by a trust which is not a foreign trust, to a foreign corporation as paid-in surplus or as a contribution to capital, or to a foreign trust, or to a foreign partnership, an excise tax equal to 27½ percent of the excess of—
  "(1) the value of the stock or securities so transferred, over
  "(2) its adjusted basis (for determining gain) in the hands of the transferor."

Sec. 1492. Repealed.

In 1997, P.L. 105-34, Sec. 1131(a), repealed Code Sec. 1492 as part of the repeal of Chapter 5 of Subtitle A, effective 8/5/97.
Prior to repeal, Code Sec.1492 read as follows:
"Sec. 1492. Nontaxable transfers.
  "The tax imposed by section 1491 shall not apply—
  "(1) If the transferee is an organization exempt from income tax under part I of subchapter F of chapter 1 (other than an organization described in section 401(a)); or
  "(2) To a transfer—
  "(A) described in section 367, or
  "(B) not described in section 367 but with respect to which the taxpayer elects (before the transfer) the application of principles similar to the principles of section 367, or
  "(3) To a transfer for which an election has been made under section 1057."
In 1984, P.L. 98-369, Sec. 131(f)(1)(A), and (B), deleted paras. (2) and (3), added new para. (2), and redesignated para. (4) as para. (3), effective for transfers or exchanges after 12/31/84, in tax. yrs. end. after 12/31/84. Secs. 131(g)(2) and (3) of this Act provide:
  "(2) Special rule for certain transfers of intangibles.—
  "(A) In general.— If, after June 6, 1984, and before January 1, 1985, a United States person transfers any intangible property (within the meaning of section 936(h)(3)(B) of the Internal Revenue Code of 1954) to a foreign corporation or in a transfer described in section 1491, such transfer shall be treated for purposes of sections 367(a), 1492(2), and 1494(b) of such Code as pursuant to a plan having as 1 of its principal purposes the avoidance of Federal income tax.
  "(B) Waiver.— Subject to such terms and conditions as the Secretary of the Treasury or his delegate may prescribe, the Secretary may waive the application of subparagraph (A) with respect to any transfer.
  "(3) Ruling request before March 1, 1984.— The amendments made by this section (and the provisions of paragraph (2) of this subsection) shall not apply to any transfer or exchange of property described in a request filed before March 1, 1984, under section 367(a), 1492(2), or 1494(b) of the Internal Revenue Code of 1954 (as in effect before such amendments)."
Prior to deletion, paras. (2) and (3) read as follows:
  "(2) If before the transfer it has been established to the satisfaction of the Secretary that such transfer is not in pursuance of a plan having as one of its principal purposes the avoidance of Federal income taxes; or
  "(3) To a transfer described in section 367: or"
In 1978, P.L. 95-600, Sec. 701(u)(14)(B), amended para. (3), effective for transfers after 10/2/75.
Prior to amendment, para. (3) read as follows:
  "(3) To a transfer to which section 367 applies; or"
In 1976, P.L. 94-455, Sec. 1015(b), substituted "section 367 applies; or" for "section 367(d) applies." in para. (3), and added para. (4), effective for transfers of property after 10/2/75.
—P.L. 94-455, Sec. 1906(b)(13)(A), substituted "Secretary" for "Secretary or his delegate" in Code Sec. 1492, effective 2/1/77.
In 1971, P.L. 91-681, Sec. 1(b), deleted the period at end of para. (2) and inserted in lieu thereof "; or" and added new para. (3), effective for transfers made after 12/31/67; except that section 1492 shall apply only with respect to transfers made after 12/31/70.

Sec. 1493. Repealed.

In 1966, P.L. 89-809, Sec. 103, repealed Code Sec. 1493 which defined a foreign trust, effective for tax. yrs. begin. after '66.
Prior to repeal, Code Sec. 1493 read as follows:
"Sec. 1493. Definition of foreign trust.
  "A trust shall be considered a foreign trust within the meaning of this chapter if, assuming a subsequent sale by the trustee, outside the United States and for cash, of the property so transferred, the profit, if any, from such sale would not be included in the gross income of the trust under this subtitle."

Sec. 1494. Repealed.

In 1997, P.L. 105-34, Sec. 1131(a), repealed Code Sec. 1494 as part of the repeal of chapter 5 of subtitle A of title 26, effective 8/5/97.
Prior to repeal, Code Sec. 1494 read as follows:
"SEC. 1494 PAYMENT AND COLLECTION.
  "(a) Time for payment. The tax imposed by section 1491 shall, without assessment or notice and demand, be due and payable by the transferor at the time of the transfer, and shall be assessed, collected, and paid under regulations prescribed by the Secretary.
  "(b) Abatement or refund. Under regulations prescribed by the Secretary, the tax may be abated, remitted, or refunded if the taxpayer, after the transfer, elects the application of principles similar to the principles of section 367.
  "(c) Penalty. In the case of any failure to file a return required by the Secretary with respect to any transfer described in section 1491, the person required to file such return shall be liable for the penalties provided in section 6677 in the same manner as if such failure were a failure to file a notice under section 6048(a)."
In 1996, P.L. 104-188, Sec. 1902(a), added subsec. (c), effective for transfers after 8/20/96.
In 1984, P.L. 98-369, Sec. 131(f)(2), amended subsec. (b), effective for transfers or exchanges after 12/31/84, in tax. yrs. end. after 12/31/84. Secs. 131(g)(2) and (3) of the Act provide:
  "(2) Special rule for certain transfers of intangibles.—
  "(A) In general.— If, after June 6, 1984, and before January 1, 1985, a United States person transfers any intangible property (within the meaning of section 936(h)(3)(B) of the Internal Revenue Code of 1954) to a foreign corporation or in a transfer described in section 1491, such transfer shall be treated for purposes of sections 367(a), 1492(2), and 1494(b) of such Code as pursuant to a plan having as 1 of its principal purposes the avoidance of Federal income tax.
  "(B) Waiver.— Subject to such terms and conditions as the Secretary of the Treasury or his delegate may prescribe, the Secretary may waive the application of subparagraph (A) with respect to any transfer.
  "(3) Ruling request before March 1, 1984.— The amendments made by this section (and the provisions of paragraph (2) of this subsection) shall not apply to any transfer or exchange of property described in a request filed before March 1, 1984, under section 367(a), 1492(2), or 1494(b) of the Internal Revenue Code of 1954 (as in effect before such amendments)."
Prior to amendment, subsec. (b) read as follows:
"(b) Abatement or refund.
  "Under regulations prescribed by the Secretary, the tax may be abated, remitted, or refunded if after the transfer it has been established to the satisfaction of the Secretary or his delegate that such transfer was not in pursuance of a plan having as one of its principal purposes the avoidance of Federal income taxes."
In 1976, P.L. 94-455, Sec. 1906(b)(13)(A), substituted "Secretary" for "Secretary or his delegate" each place it appeared in Code Sec. 1494, effective 2/1/77.

CHAPTER 6.— CONSOLIDATED RETURNS
Subchapter
A. Returns and Payment of Tax.
B. Related Rules.

Subchapter A.— Returns and Payment of Tax
Sec.
1501. Privilege to file consolidated returns.
1502. Regulations.
1503. Computation and payment of tax.
1504. Definitions.
1505. Cross references.

Sec. 1501. Privilege to file consolidated returns.

An affiliated group of corporations shall, subject to the provisions of this chapter, have the privilege of making a consolidated return with respect to the income tax imposed by chapter 1 for the taxable year in lieu of separate returns. The making of a consolidated return shall be upon the condition that all corporations which at any time during the taxable year have been members of the affiliated group consent to all the consolidated return regulations prescribed under section 1502 prior to the last day prescribed by law for the filing of such return. The making of a consolidated return shall be considered as such consent. In the case of a corporation which is a member of the affiliated group for a fractional part of the year, the consolidated return shall include the income of such corporation for such part of the year as it is a member of the affiliated group.

Consolidated returns — Code Sec. 1502

In 1971, P.L. 91-688, Sec. 2(a), and (b) of this Act provide:

"(a) If —

"(1) any insurance company subject to taxation under section 802 of the Internal Revenue Code of 1954 filed a consolidated return under section 1501 of such Code for any taxable year beginning after December 31, 1957, and ending before March 31, 1969, and

"(2) not later than one year after the date of the enactment of this Act—

"(A) such company elects (in such manner as the Secretary of the Treasury or his delegate may prescribe) to have this section apply,

"(B) such company files consents to the application of this section of all companies which at any time during any taxable year beginning after December 31, 1957, and ending before March 13, 1969, were members of the same affiliated group as such company, and

"(C) such company (and each company referred to in subparagraph (B) files a separate return for the first taxable year beginning after December 31, 1957, for which such company filed a consolidated return and for each taxable year thereafter ending before the date of the enactment of this Act,

then not withstanding any law or rule of law the requirement of filing a consolidated return shall be replaced by a requirement of separate returns for each company referred to in paragraph (2)(C) for each taxable year to which paragraph (2)(C) applies with respect to such company. Paragraph (2)(C) shall not apply with respect to any company for any taxable year the allowance of a credit for which is barred on the date of the enactment of this Act by res judicata or through the operation of section 7121 or section 7122 of the Internal Revenue Code of 1954.

"(b) If the making or allowance of any refund or credit, or the assessment of any deficiency, of income tax for any taxable year to which subsection (a)(2)(C) applies is prevented before the expiration of 2 years after the date of the enactment of this Act by any law or rule of law (other than sections 7121 and 7122 of such Code and other than res judicata), such refund or credit may nevertheless be made or allowed, and such deficiency may nevertheless be assessed, at any time before the expiration of such 2-year period, but only to the extent that the overpayment or deficiency is attributable to an election made under this section. No interest shall be allowed on any credit or refund described in the preceding sentence, and no interest shall be assessed with respect to any deficiency described in the preceding sentence, for any period before the day which is one year after the date of the enactment of this Act."

Sec. 1502. Regulations.

The Secretary shall prescribe such regulations as he may deem necessary in order that the tax liability of any affiliated group of corporations making a consolidated return and of each corporation in the group, both during and after the period of affiliation, may be returned, determined, computed, assessed, collected, and adjusted, in such manner as clearly to reflect the income tax liability and the various factors necessary for the determination of such liability, and in order to prevent avoidance of such tax liability. In carrying out the preceding sentence, the Secretary may prescribe rules that are different from the provisions of chapter 1 that would apply if such corporations filed separate returns.

In 2004, P.L. 108-357, Sec. 844(a), added "In carrying out the preceding sentence, the Secretary may prescribe rules that are different from the provisions of chapter 1 that would apply if such corporations filed separate returns." at the end of Code Sec. 1502, effective for tax. yrs. begin. before, on, or after 10/22/2004.
—P.L. 108-357, Sec. 844(b), of this Act, reads as follows:

"(b) Result not overturned. Notwithstanding the amendment made by subsection (a), the Internal Revenue Code of 1986 shall be construed by treating Treasury Regulation § 1.1502-20(c)(1)(iii) (as in effect on January 1, 2001) as being inapplicable to the factual situation in Rite Aid Corporation and Subsidiary Corporations v. United States, 255 F.3d 1357 (Fed. Cir. 2001)."

In 2000, P.L. 106-554, Sec. 1(a)(7), [which enacted into law Sec. 311(c) of P.L. 106-554] of this Act, provides:

"The reference to section 332(b)(1) of the Internal Revenue Code of 1986 in Treasury Regulation section 1.1502-34 shall be deemed to include a reference to section 732(f) of such Code."

In 1987, P.L. 100-647, Sec. 6126, provides:

"SEC. 6126. DUAL RESIDENT COMPANIES

"(a) General rule.

"In the case of a transaction which—

"(1) involves the transfer after the date of the enactment of this Act by a domestic corporation, with respect to which there is a qualified excess loss account, of its assets and liabilities to a foreign corporation in exchange for all of the stock of such foreign corporation, followed by the complete liquidation of the domestic corporation into the common parent, and

"(2) qualifies, pursuant to Revenue Ruling 87-27, as a reorganization which is described in section 368(a)(1)(F) of the 1986 Code,

then, solely for purposes of applying Treasury Regulation section 1.1502-19 to such qualified excess loss account, such foreign corporation shall be treated as a domestic corporation in determining whether such foreign corporation is a member of the affiliated group of the common parent.

"(b) Treatment of income of new foreign corporation.—

"(1) In general. In any case to which subsection (a) applies, for purposes of the 1986 Code —

"(A) the source and character of any item of income of the foreign corporation referred to in subsection (a) shall be determined as if such foreign corporation were a domestic corporation,

"(B) the net amount of any such income shall be treated as subpart F income (without regard to section 952(c) of the 1986 Code), and

"(C) the amount in the qualified excess loss account referred to in subsection (a) shall —

"(i) be reduced by the net amount of any such income, and

"(ii) be increased by the amount of any such income distributed directly or indirectly to the common parent described in subsection (a).

"(2) Limitation. Paragraph (1) shall apply to any item of income only to the extent that the net amount of such income does not exceed the amount in the qualified excess loss account after being reduced under paragraph (1)(C) for prior income.

"(3) Basis adjustments not applicable. To the extent paragraph (1) applies to any item of income, there shall be no increase in basis under section 961(a) of such Code on account of such income (and there shall be no reduction in basis under section 961(b) of such Code on account of an exclusion attributable to the inclusion of such income).

"(4) Recognition of gain. For purposes of paragraph (1), if the foreign corporation referred to in subsection (a) transfers any property acquired by such foreign corporation in the transaction referred to in subsection (a) (or transfers any other property the basis of which is determined in whole or in part by reference to the basis of property so acquired) and (but for this paragraph) there is not full recognition of gain on such transfer, the excess (if any) of—

"(A) the fair market value of the property transferred, over

"(B) its adjusted basis,

shall be treated as gain from the sale or exchange of such property and shall be recognized notwithstanding any other provision of law. Proper adjustment shall be made to the basis of any such property for gain recognized under the preceding sentence.

"(c) Definitions.

"For purposes of this section—

"(1) Common parent. The term 'common parent' means the common parent of the affiliated group which included the domestic corporation referred to in subsection (a)(1).

"(2) Qualified excess loss account. The term 'qualified excess loss account' means any excess loss account (within the meaning of the consolidated return regulations) to the extent such account is attributable—

"(A) to taxable years beginning before January 1, 1988, and

"(B) to periods during which the domestic corporation was subject to an income tax of a foreign country on its income on a residence basis or without regard to whether such income is from sources in or outside of such foreign country.

The amount of such account shall be determined as of immediately after the transaction referred to in subsection (a) and without, except as provided in subsection (b), diminution for any future adjustment.

"(3) Net amount. The net amount of any item of income is the amount of such income reduced by allocable deductions as determined under the rules of section 954(b)(5) of the 1986 Code.

"(4) Second same country corporation may be treated as domestic corporation in certain cases. If—

"(A) another foreign corporation acquires from the common parent stock of the foreign corporation referred to in subsection (a) after the transaction referrred to in subsection (a),

"(B) both of such foreign corporations are subject to the income tax of the same foreign country on a residence basis, and

"(C) such common parent complies with such reporting requirements as the Secretary of the Treasury or his delegate may prescribe for purposes of this paragraph,

such other foreign corporation shall be treated as a domestic corporation in determining whether the foreign corporation referred to in subsection (a) is a member of the affiliated group referred to in subsection (a) (and the rules of subsection (b) shall apply (i) to any gain of such other foreign corporation on any disposition of such stock, and (ii) to any other income of such other foreign corporation except to the extent it establishes to the satisfaction of the Secretary of the Treasury or his delegate that such income is not attributable to property acquired from the foreign corporation referred to in subsection (a))."

In 1986, P.L. 99-514, Sec. 1879(t), provides:

"(t) Disposition of certain subsidiary.

"If for a taxable year of an affiliated group filing a consolidated return ending on or before December 31, 1987, there is 1 disposition of stock of a subsidiary incorporated in Delaware on December 24, 1969, and whose principal place of business is in New Orleans, Louisiana (within the meaning of Treasury Regulation section 1.1502-19), the amount required to be included in income with respect to such disposition under Treasury Regulation section 1.1502-19(a) shall, notwithstanding such section, be included in income ratably over the 15-year period beginning with the taxable year in which the disposition occurs and ending with the 14th succeeding taxable year."

In 1980, P.L. 96-613, Sec. 3(a), effective for tax. yrs. end. after 3/31/76, provides:

"(a) In general.

"For purposes of the consolidated return regulations prescribed under section 1502 of the Internal Revenue Code of 1954, if the determination of whether or not there has been a deemed disposition of stock in a transferor railroad (as de-

fined in section 374(c)(5)(B) of such Code) depends on a determination of final value by the special court under the Regional Rail Reorganization Act of 1973, that deemed disposition shall not be treated as occurring before the earlier of—
"(1) the date on which such determination becomes final, or
"(2) the first date on which there is an actual disposition of the stock or a deemed disposition not described above.",
for tax. yrs. ending after 3/31/76.
In 1976, P.L. 94-455, Sec. 1906(b)(13)(A), substituted "Secretary" for "Secretary or his delegate" in Code Sec. 1502, effective 2/1/77.

Sec. 1503. Computation and payment of tax.
(a) [sic General rule].
In any case in which a consolidated return is made or is required to be made, the tax shall be determined, computed, assessed, collected, and adjusted in accordance with the regulations under section 1502 prescribed before the last day prescribed by law for the filing of such return.
(b) Repealed.
(c) Special rule for application of certain losses against income of insurance companies taxed under section 801.
(1) **In general.** If an election under section 1504(c)(2) is in effect for the taxable year and the consolidated taxable income of the members of the group not taxed under section 801 results in a consolidated net operating loss for such taxable year, then under regulations prescribed by the Secretary, the amount of such loss which cannot be absorbed in the applicable carryback periods against the taxable income of such members not taxed under section 801 shall be taken into account in determining the consolidated taxable income of the affiliated group for such taxable year to the extent of 35 percent of such loss or 35 percent of the taxable income of the members taxed under section 801, whichever is less. The unused portion of such loss shall be available as a carryover, subject to the same limitations (applicable to the sum of the loss for the carryover year and the loss (or losses) carried over to such year), in applicable carryover years.
(2) **Losses of recent nonlife affiliates.** Notwithstanding the provisions of paragraph (1), a net operating loss for a taxable year of a member of the group not taxed under section 801 shall not be taken into account in determining the taxable income of a member taxed under section 801 (either for the taxable year or as a carryover or carryback) if such taxable year precedes the sixth taxable year such members have been members of the same affiliated group (determined without regard to section 1504(b)(2)).
(d) Dual consolidated loss.
(1) **In general.** The dual consolidated loss for any taxable year of any corporation shall not be allowed to reduce the taxable income of any other member of the affiliated group for the taxable year or any other taxable year.
(2) **Dual consolidated loss.** For purposes of this section—
(A) In general. Except as provided in subparagraph (B), the term "dual consolidated loss" means any net operating loss of a domestic corporation which is subject to an income tax of a foreign country on its income without regard to whether such income is from sources in or outside of such foreign country, or is subject to such a tax on a residence basis.
(B) Special rule where loss not used under foreign law. To the extent provided in regulations, the term "dual consolidated loss" shall not include any loss which, under the foreign income tax law, does not offset the income of any foreign corporation.
(3) **Treatment of losses of separate business units.** To the extent provided in regulations, any loss of a separate unit of a domestic corporation shall be subject to the limitations of this subsection in the same manner as if such unit were a wholly owned subsidiary of such corporation.
(4) **Income on assets acquired after the loss.** The Secretary shall prescribe such regulations as may be necessary or appropriate to prevent the avoidance of the purposes of this subsection by contributing assets to the corporation with the dual consolidated loss after such loss was sustained.
(e) Special rule for determining adjustments to basis.
(1) **In general.** Solely for purposes of determining gain or loss on the disposition of intragroup stock and the amount of any inclusion by reason of an excess loss account, in determining the adjustments to the basis of such intragroup stock on account of the earnings and profits of any member of an affiliated group for any consolidated year (and in determining the amount in such account)—
(A) such earnings and profits shall be determined as if section 312 were applied for such taxable year (and all preceding consolidated years of the member with respect to such group) without regard to subsections (k) and (n) thereof, and
(B) earnings and profits shall not include any amount excluded from gross income under section 108 to the extent the amount so excluded was not applied to reduce tax attributes (other than basis in property).
(2) **Definitions.** For purposes of this subsection—
(A) Intragroup stock. The term "intragroup stock" means any stock which—
(i) is in a corporation which is or was a member of an affiliated group of corporations, and
(ii) is held by another corporation which is or was a member of such group.
Such term includes any other property the basis of which is determined (in whole or in part) by reference to the basis of stock described in the preceding sentence.
(B) Consolidated year. The term "consolidated year" means any taxable year for which the affiliated group makes a consolidated return.
(C) Application of section 312(n)(7) not affected. The reference in paragraph (1) to subsection (n) of section 312 shall be treated as not including a reference to paragraph (7) of such subsection.
(3) **Adjustments.** Under regulations prescribed by the Secretary, proper adjustments shall be made in the application of paragraph (1)—
(A) in the case of any property acquired by the corporation before consolidation, for the difference between the adjusted basis of such property for purposes of computing taxable income and its adjusted basis for purposes of computing earnings and profits, and
(B) in the case of any property, for any basis adjustment under section 50(c).
(4) **Elimination of election to reduce basis of indebtedness.** Nothing in the regulations prescribed under section 1502 shall permit any reduction in the amount otherwise included in gross income by reason of an excess loss account if such reduction is on account of a reduction in the basis of indebtedness.
(f) Limitation on use of group losses to offset income of subsidiary paying preferred dividends.
(1) **In general.** In the case of any subsidiary distributing during any taxable year dividends on any applicable preferred stock—
(A) no group loss item shall be allowed to reduce the disqualified separately computed income of such subsidiary for such taxable year, and

(B) no group credit item shall be allowed against the tax imposed by this chapter on such disqualified separately computed income.

(2) **Group items.** For purposes of this subsection—

(A) Group loss item. The term "group loss item" means any of the following items of any other member of the affiliated group which includes the subsidiary:

(i) Any net operating loss and any net operating loss carryover or carryback under section 172.

(ii) Any loss from the sale or exchange of any capital asset and any capital loss carryover or carryback under section 1212.

(B) Group credit item. The term "group credit item" means any credit allowable under part IV of subchapter A of chapter 1 (other than section 34) to any other member of the affiliated group which includes the subsidiary and any carryover or carryback of any such credit.

(3) **Other definitions.** For purposes of this subsection—

(A) Disqualified separately computed income. The term "disqualified separately computed income" means the portion of the separately computed taxable income of the subsidiary which does not exceed the dividends distributed by the subsidiary during the taxable year on applicable preferred stock.

(B) Separately computed taxable income. The term "separately computed taxable income" means the separate taxable income of the subsidiary for the taxable year determined—

(i) by taking into account gains and losses from the sale or exchange of a capital asset and section 1231 gains and losses,

(ii) without regard to any net operating loss or capital loss carryover or carryback, and

(iii) with such adjustments as the Secretary may prescribe.

(C) Subsidiary. The term "subsidiary" means any corporation which is a member of an affiliated group filing a consolidated return other than the common parent.

(D) Applicable preferred stock. The term "applicable preferred stock" means stock described in section 1504(a)(4) in the subsidiary which is—

(i) issued after November 17, 1989, and

(ii) held by a person other than a member of the same affiliated group as the subsidiary.

(4) **Regulations.** The Secretary shall prescribe such regulations as may be necessary or appropriate to carry out the provisions of this subsection, including regulations—

(A) to prevent the avoidance of this subsection through the transfer of built-in losses to the subsidiary,

(B) to provide rules for cases in which the subsidiary owns (directly or indirectly) stock in another member of the affiliated group, and

(C) to provide for the application of this subsection where dividends are not paid currently, where the redemption and liquidation rights of the applicable preferred stock exceed the issue price for such stock, or where the stock is otherwise structured to avoid the purposes of this subsection.

In 1990, P.L. 101-508, Sec. 11802(f)(4), deleted the last two sentences of of para. (c)(1), effective 11/5/90 except as provided in Sec. 11821(b) of this Act, which reads as follows:

"*(b) Savings provision.* If—

"(1) any provision amended or repealed by this part applied to—

"(A) any transaction occurring before the date of the enactment of this Act [11/5/90],

"(B) any property acquired before such date of enactment [11/5/90], or

"(C) any item of income, loss, deduction, or credit taken into account before such date of enactment [11/5/90], and

"(2) the treatment of such transaction, property, or item under such provision would (without regard to the amendments made by this part) affect liability for tax for periods ending after such date of enactment [11/5/90],

nothing in the amendments made by this part shall be construed to affect the treatment of such transaction, property, or item for purposes of determining liability for tax for periods ending after such date of enactment [11/5/90]."

Prior to deletion, the para. (c)(1) read as follows:

"For taxable years ending with or within calendar year 1981, '25 percent' shall be substituted for '35 percent' each place it appears in the first sentence of this subsection. For taxable years ending with or within calendar year 1982, '30 percent' shall be substituted for '35 percent' each place it appears in that sentence."

— P.L. 101-508, Sec. 11813(b)(25), substituted "section 50(c)" for "section 48(q)" in subpara. (e)(3)(B), effective for property placed in service after 12/31/90 except as provided in Sec. 11813(c)(2) of this Act, reproduced in note following Code Sec. 46.

In 1989, P.L. 101-239, Sec. 7201(a), added subsec. (f), effective tax. yrs. end. after 11/17/89, except as provided in Sec. 7201(b)(2)-(6) of this Act which reads as follows:

"(2) Binding contract exception. For purposes of section 1503(f)(3)(D) of the Internal Revenue Code of 1986, stock issued after November 17, 1989, pursuant to a written binding contract in effect on November 17, 1989, and at all times thereafter before such issuance, shall be treated as issued on November 17, 1989.

"(3) Special rule when subsidiary leaves group. If, by reason of a transaction after November 17, 1989, a corporation ceases to be, or becomes, a member of an affiliated group, the stock of such corporation shall be treated, for purposes of section 1503(f)(3)(D) of such Code, as issued on the date of such cessation or commencement, unless such transaction is of a kind which would not result in the recognition of any deferred intercompany gain under the consolidated return regulations by reason of the acquisition of the entire group.

"(4) Retired stock.

"(A) Except as provided in subparagraph (B), if stock issued before November 18, 1989, (or described in paragraph (2)), is retired or acquired after November 17, 1989, by the corporation or another member of the same affiliated group, such stock shall be treated, for purposes of section 1503(f)(3)(D) of such Code, as issued on the date of such retirement or acquisition.

"(B) Subparagraph (A) shall not apply to any retirement or acquisition pursuant to an obligation to reissue under a binding written contract in effect on November 17, 1989, and at all times thereafter before such retirement or acquisition.

"(5) Auction rate preferred. For purposes of section 1503(f)(3)(D) of such Code, auction rate preferred stock shall be treated as issued when the contract requiring the auction became binding.

"(6) Special rule for certain auction rate preferred. For purposes of section 1503(f)(3)(D) of the Internal Revenue Code of 1986, any auction rate preferred stock shall be treated as issued before November 18, 1989, if—

"(A) a subsidiary was incorporated before July 10, 1989 for the special purpose of issuing such stock,

"(B) a rating agency was retained before July 10, 1989, and

"(C) such stock is issued before the date 30 days after the date of the enactment of this Act. [12/19/89]"

— P.L. 101-239, Sec. 7207(a), added para. (e)(4), effective for dispositions after 7/10/89 in tax. yrs. end. after 7/10/89 except as provided in Sec. 7207(b)(2) of this Act which reads as follows:

"(2) Binding contract. The amendment made by subsection (a) shall not apply to any disposition pursuant to a written binding contract in effect on July 10, 1989, and at all times thereafter before such disposition."

— P.L. 101-239, Sec. 7821(c), substituted "another corporation which is or was a member" for "another member" in clause (e)(2)(A)(ii), effective for any intragroup stock disposed of after 12/15/87. For purposes of determining the adjustments to the basis of such stock, [subsec. (e)] shall be deemed to have been [in] effect for all periods before, on, or after 12/15/87, except as provided by Sec. 10222(a)(2)(B) and (C) of P.L. 100-203 reproduced below.

In 1988, P.L. 100-647, Sec. 1012(u), added paras. (d)(3) and (d)(4), effective for net operating losses for tax yrs. begin. after 12/31/86.

— P.L. 100-647, Sec. 2004(j)(1)(A), amended the material preceding subpara. (e)(1)(A) . . . Sec. 2004(j)(2), added para. (e)(3) . . . Sec. 2004(j)(3)(A), added subpara. (e)(2)(C), effective for any intragroup stock disposed of after 12/15/87. For purposes of determining the adjustments to the basis of such stock, [subsec. (e)] shall be deemed to have been [in] effect for all periods before, on, or after 12/15/87, except as provided by Sec. 10222(a)(2)(B) and (C) of P.L. 100-203, reproduced below.

Prior to amendment, the material preceding subpara. (e)(1)(A) read as follows:

"(1) In general. Solely for purposes of determining gain or loss on the disposition of intragroup stock, in determining the adjustments to the basis of such intragroup stock on account of the earnings and profits of any member of an affiliated group for any consolidated year—"

— P.L. 100-647, Sec. 2004(j)(1)(B), added Sec. 10222(a)(2)(C) of P.L. 100-203 [reproduced below], part of the exceptions to the effective date for changes made by Sec. 10222(a)(1) of P.L. 100-203, see below.

— P.L. 100-647, Sec. 6278, provides:

"SEC. 6278. APPLICATION OF SECTION 7503 OF 1986 CODE FOR PURPOSES OF SECTION 10222(B) OF REVENUE ACT OF 1987. Section 7503 of the 1986 Code shall apply for purposes of determining whether any disposition meets the requirements of section 10222(b)(2)(B) of the Revenue Act of 1987. If any disposition meets the requirements of such section by reason of the preceding sentence, for all purposes of the 1986 Code, such disposition shall be deemed to have occurred on December 31, 1988."

In 1987, P.L. 100-203, Sec. 10222(a)(1), added subsec. (e), effective for any intragroup stock disposed of after 12/15/87. For purposes of determining the adjustments to the basis of such stock, [subsec. (e)] shall be deemed to have been [in] effect for all periods before, on, or after 12/15/87, except as provided by Sec. 10222(a)(2)(B) and (C) [as amended by Sec. 2004(j)(1)(B) of P.L. 100-647, see above] which reads as follows:

"(B) Exception. The amendment made by paragraph (1) shall not apply to any intragroup stock disposed of after December 15, 1987, and before January 1, 1989, if such disposition is pursuant to a written binding contract, governmental order, letter of intent or preliminary agreement, or stock acquisition agreement, in effect on or before December 15, 1987.

"(C) Treatment of certain excess loss accounts.

"(i) In general.—If—

"(I) any disposition on or before December 15, 1987, of stock resulted in an inclusion of an excess loss account (or would have so resulted if the amendments made by paragraph (1) had applied to such disposition), and

"(II) there is an unrecaptured amount with respect to such disposition, the portion of such unrecaptured amount allocable to stock disposed of in a disposition to which the amendment made by paragraph (1) applied shall be taken into account as negative basis. To the extent permitted by the Secretary of the Treasury or his delegate, the preceding sentence shall not apply to the extent the taxpayer elects to reduce its basis in indebtedness of the corporation with respect to which there would have been an excess loss account.

"(ii) Special rules. For purposes of this subparagraph—

"(I) Unrecaptured amount. The term 'unrecaptured amount' means the amount by which the inclusion referred to in clause (i)(I) would have been increased if the amendment made by paragraph (1) and applied to the disposition.

"(II) Coordination with binding contract exception. A disposition shall be treated as occurring on or before December 15, 1987, if the amendment made by paragraph (1) does not apply to such disposition by reason of subparagraph (B)."

In 1986, P.L. 99-514, Sec. 1249(a), added subsec. (d), effective for net operating losses for tax. yrs. begin. after 12/31/86.

In 1984, P.L. 98-369, Sec. 211(b)(19)(A), substituted "section 801" for "section 802" each place it appeared in subsec. (c) . . . Sec. 211(b)(19)(B), deleted the third sentence of para. (c)(1) . . . Sec. 211(b)(19)(C), substituted "section 801" for "section 802" in the heading of subsec. (c), effective for tax. yrs. begin. after 12/31/83.

Prior to deletion, the third sentence of para. (c)(1) read as follows:

"For purposes of this subsection, in determining the taxable income of each insurance company subject to tax under section 802, section 802(b)(3) shall not be taken into account."

In 1976, P.L. 94-455, Sec. 1031(b)(4), deleted ", and if for the taxable year an election under section 904(b)(1) (relating to election of overall limitation on foreign tax credit) is in effect" after "defined in section 921)" in para. (b)(1), effective for tax. yrs. begin. after 12/31/75.

—P.L. 94-455, Sec. 1052(c)(5), deleted subsec. (b) and deleted "(a) General rule." at the beginning of subsec. (a), effective for tax. yrs. begin. after '79.

Prior to deletion subsec. (b) read as follows:

"(b) Special rule for application of foreign tax credit when overall limitation applies.

"(1) In general. If the affiliated group includes one or more Western Hemisphere trade corporations (as defined in section 921), then the amount of taxes paid or accrued to foreign countries and possessions of the United States by such Western Hemisphere trade corporations which may be taken into account for purposes of section 901 shall be reduced by the amount (if any) by which—

"(A) the amount of such taxes (or, if smaller, the amount of the tax which would be computed under subsection (a), if such corporations were not Western Hemisphere trade corporations with respect to the portion of the consolidated taxable income attributable to such corporations), exceeds

"(B) the amount of the tax computed under subsection (a) with respect to the portion of the consolidated taxable income attributable to such corporations.

"(2) Adjustment in case of certain public utilities. So much of any reduction under paragraph (1) as is attributable to taxes paid or accrued to foreign countries and possessions of the United States by one or more corporations which are both Western Hemisphere trade corporations and regulated public utilities shall be decreased by the excess of—

"(A) the amount of tax computed under subsection (a) with respect to the portion of the consolidated taxable income attributable to income derived, by the corporations in the affiliated group which are not Western Hemisphere trade corporations, from sources within the foreign countries referred to in paragraph (3)(B), over

"(B) the amount of taxes paid or accrued to such foreign countries by the corporations referred to in subparagraph (A).

"This paragraph shall apply only if the corporations described in subparagraph (A) derive 80 percent or more, of the gross income (computed without regard to capital gains and losses) which they derive from sources within the foreign countries described in paragraph (3)(B), from regulated public utilities and from operations as regulated public utilities.

"(3) Special rules.

"(A) For purposes of paragraph (2), a corporation is a regulated public utility only if it is a regulated public utility within the meaning of subparagraph (A) (other than clauses (ii) and (iii) thereof) or (D) of section 7701(a)(33). For purposes of the preceding sentence, the limitation contained in the last two sentences of section 7701(a)(33) shall be applied as if subparagraphs (A) through (F), inclusive, of section 7701(a)(33) were limited to subparagraphs (A)(i) and (D) thereof.

"(B) For purposes of paragraph (2), the foreign countries referred to in this subparagraph include only any country from which any public utility referred to in the first sentence of paragraph (2) derives the principal part of its income."

—P.L. 94-455, Sec. 1507(b)(3), added subsec. (c), effective for tax. yrs. begin. after 12/31/80.

—P.L. 94-455, Sec. 1901(b)(1)(Y), deleted subpara. (b)(3)(C), effective for tax. yrs. begin. after 12/31/76.

Prior to deletion, subpara. (b)(3)(C) read as follows:

"(C) For purposes of this subsection, the term 'consolidated taxable income' means the consolidated taxable income computed without regard to the deduction provided in section 242 for partially tax-exempt interest."

In 1964, P.L. 88-272, Sec. 234, amended Code Sec. 1503, effective for tax. yrs. begin. after 12/31/63.

Prior to amendment, Code Sec. 1503 read as follows:

"SEC. 1503. COMPUTATION AND PAYMENT OF TAX.

"(a) General rule. In any case in which a consolidated return is made or is required to be made, the tax shall be determined, computed, assessed, collected, and adjusted in accordance with the regulations under section 1502 prescribed prior to the last day prescribed by law for the filing of such return; except that the tax imposed under section 11(c) or section 831 shall be increased for any taxable year by 2 percent of the consolidated taxable income of the affiliated group of includible corporations. For purposes of this section, the term 'consolidated taxable income' means the consolidated taxable income computed without regard to the deduction provided by section 242 for partially tax-exempt interest.

"(b) Limitation. If the affiliated group includes one or more Western Hemisphere trade corporations (as defined in section 921) or one or more regulated public utilities (as defined in subsection (c)), the increase of 2 percent provided in subsection (a) shall be applied only on the amount by which the consolidated taxable income of the affiliated group exceeds the portion (if any) of the consolidated taxable income attributable to the Western Hemisphere trade corporations and regulated public utilities included in such group.

"(c) Regulated public utility defined.

"(1) In general. For purposes of subsection (b), the term 'regulated public utility' means—

"(A) A corporation engaged in the furnishing or sale of—

"(i) electric energy, gas, water, or sewerage disposal services, or

"(ii) transportation (not included in subparagraph (C)) on an intrastate, suburban, municipal, or interurban electric railroad, on an intrastate, municipal, or suburban trackless trolley system, or on a municipal or suburban bus system, or

"(iii) transportation (not included in clause (ii)) by motor vehicle—

if the rates for such furnishing or sale, as the case may be, have been established or approved by a State or political subdivision thereof, by an agency or instrumentality of the United States, by a public service or public utility commission or other similar body of the District of Columbia or of any State or political subdivision thereof, or by a foreign country or an agency or instrumentality or political subdivision thereof.

"(B) A corporation engaged as a common carrier in the furnishing or sale of transportation of gas by pipeline, if subject to the jurisdiction of the Federal Power Commission.

"(C) A corporation engaged as a common carrier (i) in the furnishing or sale of transportation by railroad, if subject to the jurisdiction of the Interstate Commerce Commission, or (ii) in the furnishing or sale of transportation of oil or other petroleum products (including shale oil) by pipeline, if subject to the jurisdiction of the Interstate Commerce Commission or if the rates for such furnishing or sale are subject to the jurisdiction of a public service or public utility commission or other similar body of the District of Columbia or of any State.

"(D) A corporation engaged in the furnishing or sale of telephone or telegraph service, if the rates for such furnishing or sale meet the requirements of subparagraph (A).

"(E) A corporation engaged in the furnishing or sale of transportation as a common carrier by air, subject to the jurisdiction of the Civil Aeronautics Board.

"(F) A corporation engaged in the furnishing or sale of transportation by common carrier by water, subject to the jurisdiction of the Interstate Commerce Commission under part III of the Interstate Commerce Act, or subject to the jurisdiction of the Federal Maritime Board under the Intercoastal Shipping Act, 1933.

"(2) Limitation. For purposes of subsection (b), the term 'regulated public utility' does not (except as provided in paragraph (3)) include a corporation described in paragraph (1) unless 80 percent or more of its gross income (computed without regard to dividends and capital gains and losses) for the taxable year is derived from sources described in paragraph (1). If the taxpayer establishes to the satisfaction of the Secretary or his delegate that—

"(A) its revenue from regulated rates described in paragraph (1)(A) or (D) and its revenue derived from unregulated rates are derived from its operation of a single interconnected and coordinated system or from the operation of more than one such system, and

"(B) the unregulated rates have been and are substantially as favorable to users and consumers as are the regulated rates,

such revenue from such unregulated rates shall be considered, for purposes of this paragraph, as income derived from sources described in paragraph (1)(A) or (D).

"(3) Certain railroad corporations.—

"(A) Lessor, corporation. For purposes of subsection (b), the term 'regulated public utility' shall also include a railroad corporation subject to part I of the Interstate Commerce Act, if (i) substantially all of its railroad properties have been leased to another such railroad corporation or corporations by an agreement or agreements entered into prior to January 1, 1954, (ii) each lease is for a term of more than 20 years, and (iii) at least 80 percent or more of its gross income (computed without regard to dividends and capital gains and losses) for the taxable year is derived from such leases and from sources described in paragraph (1). For purposes of the preceding sentence, an agreement for lease of railroad properties entered into prior to January 1, 1954, shall be considered to be a lease including such term as the total number of years of such agreement may, unless sooner terminated, be renewed or continued under the terms of the agreement, and any such renewal or continuance under such agreement shall be considered part of the lease entered into prior to January 1, 1954.

"(B) Common parent corporation. For purposes of subsection (b), the term 'regulated public utility' also includes a common parent corporation which is a common carrier by railroad subject to part I of the Interstate Commerce Act if at least 80 percent of its gross income (computed without regard to capital gains or losses) is derived directly or indirectly from sources described in paragraph (1). For purposes of the preceding sentence, dividends and interest, and income from leases described in subparagraph (A), received from a regulated public utility shall be considered as derived from sources described in paragraph (1) if the regulated public utility is a member of an affiliated group (as defined in section 1504) which includes the common parent corporation.

"(d) *Special rule for application of foreign tax credit when overall limitation applies.*

"[(1) and (2) same as current (b)(1) and (2)]

"(3) Special rules.

"(A) For purposes of paragraph (2), a corporation is a regulated public utility only if it is a regulated public utility within the meaning of subparagraph (A) (other than clauses (ii) and (iii) thereof) or (D) of subsection (c)(1). For purposes of the preceding sentence, subsection (c)(2) shall be applied as if subsection (c)(1) were limited to subparagraphs (A)(i) and (D) thereof.

"(B) For purposes of paragraph (2), the foreign countries referred to in this subparagraph include only any country from which any public utility referred to in the first sentence of paragraph (2) derives the principal part of its income.

"(C) For purposes of paragraph (1)(A), the amount of tax which would be computed with respect to the portion of the consolidated taxable income attributable to any corporation or corporations shall be determined without regard to the increase of 2 percent provided in subsection (a)."

In 1960, P.L. 86-780, added subsec. (d), effective for tax. yrs. begin. after '60.

Sec. 1504. Definitions.
(a) Affiliated group defined
For purposes of this subtitle—
(1) **In general.** The term "affiliated group" means—
(A) 1 or more chains of includible corporations connected through stock ownership with a common parent corporation which is an includible corporation, but only if—
(B)(i) the common parent owns directly stock meeting the requirements of paragraph (2) in at least 1 of the other includible corporations, and
(ii) stock meeting the requirements of paragraph (2) in each of the includible corporations (except the common parent) is owned directly by 1 or more of the other includible corporations.
(2) **80-percent voting and value test.** The ownership of stock of any corporation meets the requirements of this paragraph if it—
(A) possesses at least 80 percent of the total voting power of the stock of such corporation, and
(B) has a value equal to at least 80 percent of the total value of the stock of such corporation.
(3) **5 years must elapse before reconsolidation.**
(A) In general. If—
(i) a corporation is included (or required to be included) in a consolidated return filed by an affiliated group for a taxable year which includes any period after December 31, 1984, and
(ii) such corporation ceases to be a member of such group in a taxable year beginning after December 31, 1984,
with respect to periods after such cessation, such corporation (and any successor of such corporation) may not be included in any consolidated return filed by the affiliated group (or by another affiliated group with the same common parent or a successor of such common parent) before the 61st month beginning after its first taxable year in which it ceased to be a member of such affiliated group.
(B) Secretary may waive application of subparagraph (A). The Secretary may waive the application of subparagraph (A) to any corporation for any period subject to such conditions as the Secretary may prescribe.
(4) **Stock not to include certain preferred stock.** For purposes of this subsection, the term "stock" does not include any stock which—
(A) is not entitled to vote,
(B) is limited and preferred as to dividends and does not participate in corporate growth to any significant extent,
(C) has redemption and liquidation rights which do not exceed the issue price of such stock (except for a reasonable redemption or liquidation premium), and
(D) is not convertible into another class of stock.
(5) **Regulations.** The Secretary shall prescribe such regulations as may be necessary or appropriate to carry out the purposes of this subsection, including (but not limited to) regulations—
(A) which treat warrants, obligations convertible into stock, and other similar interests as stock, and stock as not stock,
(B) which treat options to acquire or sell stock as having been exercised,
(C) which provide that the requirements of paragraph (2)(B) shall be treated as met if the affiliated group, in reliance on a good faith determination of value, treated such requirements as met,
(D) which disregard an inadvertent ceasing to meet the requirements of paragraph (2)(B) by reason of changes in relative values of different classes of stock,
(E) which provide that transfers of stock within the group shall not be taken into account in determining whether a corporation ceases to be a member of an affiliated group, and
(F) which disregard changes in voting power to the extent such changes are disproportionate to related changes in value.

(b) Definition of "includible corporation".
As used in this chapter, the term "includible corporation" means any corporation except—
(1) Corporations exempt from taxation under section 501.
(2) Insurance companies subject to taxation under section 801.
(3) Foreign corporations.
(4) Corporations with respect to which an election under section 936 (relating to possession tax credit) is in effect for the taxable year.
(5) **Repealed.**
(6) Regulated investment companies and real estate investment trusts subject to tax under subchapter M of chapter 1.
(7) A DISC (as defined in section 992(a)(1)).
(8) An S corporation.

(c) Includible insurance companies.
Notwithstanding the provisions of paragraph (2) of subsection (b)—
(1) Two or more domestic insurance companies each of which is subject to tax under section 801 shall be treated as includible corporations for purposes of applying subsection (a) to such insurance companies alone.
(2)(A) If an affiliated group (determined without regard to subsection (b)(2)) includes one or more domestic insurance companies taxed under section 801, the common parent of such group may elect (pursuant to regulations prescribed by the Secretary) to treat all such companies as includible corporations for purposes of applying subsection (a) except that no such company shall be so

treated until it has been a member of the affiliated group for the 5 taxable years immediately preceding the taxable year for which the consolidated return is filed.

(B) If an election under this paragraph is in effect for a taxable year—

(i) section 243(b)(3) and the exception provided under section 243(b)(2) with respect to subsections (b)(2) and (c) of this section,

(ii) section 542(b)(5), and

(iii) subsection (a)(4) and (b)(2)(D) of section 1563, and the reference to section 1563(b)(2)(D) contained in section 1563(b)(3)(C),

shall not be effective for such taxable year.

(d) Subsidiary formed to comply with foreign law.

In the case of a domestic corporation owning or controlling, directly or indirectly, 100 percent of the capital stock (exclusive of directors' qualifying shares) of a corporation organized under the laws of a contiguous foreign country and maintained solely for the purpose of complying with the laws of such country as to title and operation of property, such foreign corporation may, at the option of the domestic corporation, be treated for the purpose of this subtitle as a domestic corporation.

(e) Includible tax-exempt organizations.

Despite the provisions of paragraph (1) of subsection (b), two or more organizations exempt from taxation under section 501, one or more of which is described in section 501(c)(2) and the others of which derive income from such 501(c)(2) organizations, shall be considered as includible corporations for the purpose of the application of subsection (a) to such organizations alone.

(f) Special rule for certain amounts derived from a corporation previously treated as a DISC.

In determining the consolidated taxable income of an affiliated group for any taxable year beginning after December 31, 1984, a corporation which had been a DISC and which would otherwise be a member of such group shall not be treated as such a member with respect to—

(1) any distribution (or deemed distribution) of accumulated DISC income which was not treated as previously taxed income under section 805(b)(2)(A) of the Tax Reform Act of 1984, and

(2) any amount treated as received under section 805(b)(3) of such Act.

In 1996, P.L. 104-188, Sec. 1308(d)(2), added para. (b)(8), effective for tax. yrs. begin. after 12/31/96.

—P.L. 104-188, Sec. 1702(h)(6), added "section" before "243(b)(2)" in clause (c)(2)(B)(i), effective for tax. yrs. begin. after 12/31/90, except as provided in Sec. 11814(c)(2) of P.L. 101-508, reproduced below.

In 1990, P.L. 101-508, Sec. 11814(b)(1), substituted "section 243(b)(3)" for "section 243(b)(6)" in clause (c)(2)(B)(i) . . . Sec. 11814(b)(2), substituted "243(b)(2)" for "section 243(b)(5)" in clause (c)(2)(B)(i), effective for tax. yrs. begin. after 12/31/90, except as provided in Sec. 11814(c)(2) of this Act, which reads as follows:

"(2) Treatment of old elections. For purposes of section 243(b)(3) of the Internal Revenue Code of 1986 (as amended by subsection (a)), any reference to an election under such section shall be treated as including a reference to an election under section 243(b) of such Code (as in effect on the day before the date of the enactment of this Act)."

In 1989, P.L. 101-239, Sec. 7815(d), amended Sec. 5021(e) of P.L. 100-647, [reproduced below] by substituting "no provision in any law enacted after the date of the enactment of this Act [11/10/88]" for "no provision in any law (whether enacted before, on, or after the date of enactment of this Act)" see below.

In 1988, P.L. 100-647, Sec. 1018(d)(10)(A), amended para. (b)(7) . . . Sec. 1018(d)(10)(B), added new subsec. (f), effective for tax. yrs. begin. after 12/31/84. Prior to amendment, para. (b)(7) read as follows:

"(7) A DISC (as defined in section 992(a)(1)), or any other corporation which has accumulated DISC income which is derived after December 31, 1984."

—P.L. 100-647, Sec. 5021(a)-(e), [as amended by Sec. 7815(b) of P.L. 101-239, see above] of this Act provide:

"SEC. 5021. REPEAL OF RULES PERMITTING LOSS TRANSFERS BY ALASKA NATIVE CORPORATIONS.

"(a) General rule.

"Nothing in section 60(b)(5) of the Tax Reform Act of 1984 (as amended by section 1804(e)(4) of the Tax Reform Act of 1986)—

"(1) shall allow any loss (or credit) of any corporation which arises after April 26, 1988, to be used to offset the income (or tax) of another corporation if such use would not be allowable without regard to such section 60(b)(5) as so amended, or

"(2) shall allow any loss (or credit) of any corporation which arises on or before such date to be used to offset disqualified income (or tax attributable to such income) of another corporation if such use would not be allowable without regard to such section 60(b)(5) as so amended.

"(b) Exception for existing contracts.

"(1) In general. Subsection (a) shall not apply to any loss (or credit) of any corporation if—

"(A) such corporation was in existence on April 26, 1988, and

"(B) such loss (or credit) is used to offset income assigned (or attributable to property contributed) pursuant to a binding contract entered into before July 26, 1988.

"(2) $40,000,000 limitation. The aggregate amount of losses (and the deduction equivalent of credits as determined in the same manner as under section 469(j)(5) of the 1986 Code) to which paragraph (1) applies with respect to any corporation shall not exceed $40,000,000. For purposes of this paragraph, a Native Corporation and all other corporations all of the stock of which is owned directly by such corporation shall be treated as 1 corporation.

"(3) Special rule for corporations under title 11. In the case of a corporation which on April 26, 1988, was under the jurisdiction of a Federal district court under title 11 of the United States Code—

"(A) paragraph (1)(B) shall be applied by substituting the date 1 year after the date of the enactment of this Act for 'July 26, 1988',

"(B) paragraph (1) shall not apply to any loss or credit which arises on or after the date 1 year after the date of the enactment of this Act, and

"(C) paragraph (2) shall be applied by substituting '$99,000,000', for '$40,000,000'.

"(c) Special administrative rules.

"(1) Notice to native corporations of proposed tax adjustments. Notwithstanding section 6103 of the 1986 Code, the Secretary of the Treasury or his delegate shall notify a Native Corporation or its designated representative of any proposed adjustment—

"(A) of the tax liability of a taxpayer which has contracted with the Native Corporation (or other corporation all of the stock of which is owned directly by the Native Corporation) for the use of losses of such Native Corporation (or such other corporation), and

"(B) which is attributable to an asserted overstatement of losses by, or misassignment of income (or income attributable to property contributed) to, an affiliated group of which the Native Corporation (or such other corporation) is a member. Such notice shall only include information with respect to the transaction between the taxpayer and the Native Corporation.

"(2) Rights of Native Corporation.—

"(A) In General. If a Native Corporation receives a notice under paragraph (1), the Native Corporation shall have the right to—

"(i) submit to the Secretary of the Treasury or his delegate a written statement regarding the proposed adjustment, and

"(ii) meet with the Secretary of the Treasury or his delegate with respect to such proposed adjustment.

The Secretary of the Treasury or his delegate may discuss such proposed adjustment with the Native Corporation or its designated representative.

"(B) Extension of statute of limitations. Subparagraph (A) shall not apply if the Secretary of the Treasury or his delegate determines that an extension of the statute of limitation is necessary to permit the participation described in subparagraph (A) and the taxpayer and the Secretary or his delegate have not agreed to such extension.

"(3) Judicial proceedings. In the case of any proceeding in a Federal court or the United States Tax Court involving a proposed adjustment under paragraph (1), the Native Corporation, subject to the rules of such court, may file an amicus brief concerning such adjustment.

"(4) Failures. For purposes of the 1986 Code, any failure by the Secretary of the Treasury or his delegate to comply with the provisions of this subsection shall not affect the validity of the determination of the Internal Revenue Service of any adjustment of tax liability of any taxpayer described in paragraph (1).

"(d) Disqualified income defined.

"For purposes of subsection (a), the term 'disqualified income' means any income assigned (or attributable to property contributed) after April 26, 1988, by a person who is not a Native Corporation or a corporation all the stock of which is owned directly by a Native Corporation.

"(e) Basis determination.

"For purposes of determining basis for Federal tax purposes, no provision in any law enacted after the date of enactment of this Act [11/10/88] shall affect the date on which the transfer to the Native Corporation is made. The preceding sentence shall apply to all taxable years whether beginning before, on, or after such date of enactment."

In 1986, P.L. 99-514, Sec. 1024(c)(15), deleted "or 821" in para. (b)(2) . . . Sec. 1024(c)(16), deleted "or 821" in subpara. (c)(2)(A), effective for tax. yrs. begin. after 12/31/86.

Sec. 1024(d) of this Act provides as follows:

"(d) Transitional rules.—

"(1) Treatment of amounts in protection against loss account. In the case of any insurance company which had a protection against loss account for its last taxable year beginning before January 1, 1987, there shall be included in the gross income of such company for any taxable year beginning after December 31, 1986, the amount which would have been included in gross income for such taxable year under section 824 of the Internal Revenue Code of 1954 (as in effect on the day before the date of the enactment of this Act). For purposes of the preceding sentence, no addition to such account shall be made for any taxable year beginning after December 31, 1986.

"(2) Transitional rule for unused loss carryover under section 825. Any unused loss carryover under section 825 of the Internal Revenue Code of 1954 (as in effect on the day before the date of the enactment of this Act) which—

"(A) is from a taxable year beginning before January 1, 1987, and

"(B) could have been carried under such section to a taxable year beginning after December 31, 1986, but for the repeal made by subsection (a)(1),

shall be included in the net operating loss deduction under section 832(c)(10) of such Code without regard to the limitations of section 844(b) of such Code."

—P.L. 99-514, Sec. 1804(e)(1), amended subpara. (a)(4)(C), effective for tax. yrs. begin. after 12/31/84.

Prior to amendment, subpara. (a)(4)(C) read as follows:

"(C) has redemption and liquidation rights which do not exceed the paid-in capital or par value represented by such stock (except for a reasonable redemption premium in excess of such paid-in capital or par value), and"

—P.L. 99-514, Sec. 1804(e)(2)-(5), amended Sec. 60(b)(2)-(5) of P.L. 98-369 [reproduced below], special rules and exceptions to the effective date for changes made by Sec. 60(a) of P.L. 98-369, by adding the last sentence to Sec. 60(b)(2), by amending Secs. 60(b)(3) and (5), by adding Secs. 60(b)(6)-(9), and by adding the last sentence to Sec. 60(b)(4), see below.

Prior to amendment, Sec. 60(b)(3) and (5) of P.L. 98-369 read as follows:

"(3) Special rule not to apply to sell-downs after June 22, 1984.—If—

"(A) the requirements of subsection (b)(2) are satisfied with respect to a corporation,

"(B) more than a de minimis amount of the stock of such corporation is sold or exchanged (including in a redemption), or issued (other than in the ordinary course of business) after June 22, 1984, and

"(C) the requirements of the amendment made by subsection (a) are not satisfied after such sale, exchange, or issuance, then the amendments made by subsection (a) shall apply for purposes of determining whether such corporation continues to be a member of such group."

"(5) Native corporations.—The amendments made by subsection (a) shall not apply to any Native Corporation established under the Alaska Native Claims Settlement Act (43 U.S.C. 1601 *et seq.*) during any taxable year beginning before 1992 or any part thereof in which such Corporation is subject to the provisions of section 7(h)(1) of such Act (43 U.S.C. 1606(h)(1))."

—P.L. 99-514, Sec. 1804(e)(10), amended para. (b)(7), effective for tax. yrs. begin. after 12/31/87.

Prior to amendment, para. (b)(7) read as follows:

"(7) A DISC or former DISC (as defined in section 992(a))."

—P.L. 99-514, Sec. 1899A(35), substituted "subsection (b)(2)) includes" for "subsection (b)(2) includes" in subpara. (c)(2)(A), effective 10/22/86.

In 1984, P.L. 98-369, Sec. 60(a), amended subsec. (a), effective for tax. yrs. begin. after 12/31/84. Secs. 60(b)(2)–(9) [as amended by Sec. 1804(e)(2)-(5) of P.L. 99-514, see above] of this Act provide the following special rules and exceptions:

"(2) Special rule for corporations, affiliated on June 22, 1984.—In the case of a corporation which on June 22, 1984, is a member of an affiliated group which files a consolidated return for such corporation's taxable year which includes June 22, 1984, for purposes of determining whether such corporation continues to be a member of such group for taxable years beginning before January 1, 1988, the amendment made by subsection (a) shall not apply. The preceding sentence shall cease to apply as of the first day after June 22, 1984, on which such corporation does not qualify as a member of such group under section 1504(a) of the Internal Revenue Code of 1954 (as in effect on the day before the date of the enactment of this Act).

"(3) Special rule not to apply to certain sell-downs after June 22, 1984.—If—

"(A) the requirements of paragraph (2) are satisfied with respect to a corporation,

"(B) more than a de minimis amount of the stock of such corporation—

"(i) is sold or exchanged (including in a redemption), or

"(ii) is issued,

after June 22, 1984 (other than in the ordinary course of business), and

"(C) the requirements of the amendment made by subsection (a) are not satisfied after such sale, exchange, or issuance,

then the amendment made by subsection (a) shall apply for purposes of determining whether such corporation continues to be a member of the group. The preceding sentence shall not apply to any transaction if such transaction does not reduce the percentage of the fair market value of the stock of the corporation referred to in the preceding sentence held by members of the group determined without regard to this paragraph.

"(4) Exception for certain sell-downs.— Subsection (b)(2) (and not subsection (b)(3)) will apply to a corporation if such corporation issues or sells stock after June 22, 1984, pursuant to a registration statement filed with the Securities and Exchange Commission on or before June 22, 1984, but only if the requirements of the amendment made by subsection (a) (substituting 'more than 50 percent' for 'at least 80 percent' in paragraph (2)(B) of section 1504(a) of the Internal Revenue Code of 1954) are satisfied immediately after such issuance or sale and at all times thereafter until the first day of the first taxable year beginning after December 31, 1987. For purposes of the preceding sentence, if there is a letter of intent between a corporation and a securities underwriter entered into on or before June 22, 1984, and the subsequent issuance or sale is effected pursuant to a registration statement filed with the Securities and Exchange Commission, such stock shall be treated as issued or sold pursuant to a registration statement filed with the Securities and Exchange Commission on or before June 22, 1984.

"(5) Native corporations.—

"(A) In the case of a Native Corporation established under the Alaska Native Claims Settlement Act (43 U.S.C. 1601 *et seq.*), or a corporation all of whose stock is owned directly by such a corporation, during any taxable year (beginning after the effective date of these amendments and before 1992), or any part thereof, in which the Native Corporation is subject to the provisions of section 7(h)(1) of such Act (43 U.S.C. 1606(h)(1))—

"(i) the amendment made by subsection (a) shall not apply, and

"(ii) the requirements for affiliation under section 1504(a) of the Internal Revenue Code of 1986 before the amendment made by subsection (a) shall be applied solely according to the provisions expressly contained therein, without regard to escrow arrangements, redemption rights, or similar provisions.

"(B) Except as provided in subparagraph (C), during the period described in subparagraph (A), no provision of the Internal Revenue Code of 1986 (including sections 269 and 482) or principle of law shall apply to deny the benefit or use of losses incurred or credits earned by a corporation described in subparagraph (A) to the affiliated group of which the Native Corporation is the common parent.

"(C) Losses incurred or credits earned by a corporation described in subparagraph (A) shall be subject to the general consolidated return regulations, including the provisions relating to separate return limitation years, and to sections 382 and 383 of the Internal Revenue Code of 1986.

"(D) Losses incurred and credits earned by a corporation which is affiliated with a corporation described in subparagraph (A) shall be treated as having been incurred or earned in a separate return limitation year, unless the corporation incurring the losses or earning the credits satisfies the affiliation requirements of section 1504(a) without application of subparagraph (A).

"(6) Treatment of certain corporations affiliated on June 22, 1984.—In the case of an affiliated group which—

"(A) has as its common parent a Minnesota corporation incorporated on April 23, 1940, and

"(B) has a member which is a New York corporation incorporated on November 13, 1969,

for purposes of determining whether such New York corporation continues to be a member of such group, paragraph (2) shall be applied by substituting for 'January 1, 1988,' the earlier of January 1, 1994, or the date on which the voting power of the preferred stock in such New York corporation terminates.

"(7) Election to have amendments apply for years beginning after 1983.—If the common parent of any group makes an election under this paragraph, notwithstanding any other provision of this subsection, the amendments made by subsection (a) shall apply to such group for taxable years beginning after December 31, 1983. Any such election, once made, shall be irrevocable.

"(8) Treatment of certain affiliated groups.— If—

"(A) a corporation (hereinafter in this paragraph referred to as the 'parent') was incorporated in 1968 and filed consolidated returns as the parent of an affiliated group for each of its taxable years ending after 1969 and before 1985,

"(B) another corporation (hereinafter in this paragraph referred to as the 'subsidiary') became a member of the parent's affiliated group in 1978 by reason of a recapitalization pursuant to which the parent increased its voting interest in the subsidiary from not less than 56 percent to not less than 85 percent, and

"(C) such subsidiary is engaged (or was on September 27, 1985, engaged) in manufacturing and distributing a broad line of business systems and related supplies for binding, laminating, shredding, graphics, and providing secure identification,

then, for purposes of determining whether such subsidiary corporation is a member of the parent's affiliated group under section 1504(a) of the Internal Revenue Code of 1954 (as amended by subsection (a)), paragraph (2)(B) of such section 1504(a) shall be applied by substituting '55 percent' for '80 percent'.

"(9) Treatment of certain corporations affiliated during 1971.—In the case of a group of corporations which filed a consolidated Federal income tax return for the taxable year beginning during 1971 and which—

"(A) included as a common parent on December 31, 1971, a Delaware corporation incorporated on August 26, 1969, and

"(B) included as a member thereof a Delaware corporation incorporated on November 8, 1971,

for taxable years beginning after December 31, 1970, and ending before January 1, 1988, the requirements for affiliation for each member of such group under section 1504(a) of the Internal Revenue Code of 1954 (before the amendment made by subsection (a)) shall be limited solely to the provisions expressly contained therein and by reference to stock issued under State law as common or preferred stock. During the period described in the preceding sentence, no provision of the Internal Revenue Code of 1986 (including sections 269 and 482) or principle of law, except the general consolidated return regulations (including the provisions relating to separate return limitation years) and sections 382 and 383 of such Code, shall apply to deny the benefit or use of losses incurred or credits earned by members of such group."

Prior to amendment, subsec. (a) read as follows:

"(a) Definition of 'affiliated group.'

"As used in this chapter, the term 'affiliated group' means one or more chains of includible corporations connected through stock ownership with a common parent corporation which is an includible corporation if—

"(1) Stock possessing at least 80 percent of the voting power of all classes of stock and at least 80 percent of each class of the nonvoting stock of each of the includible corporations (except the common parent corporation) is owned directly by one or more of the other includible corporations; and

"(2) The common parent corporation owns directly stock possessing at least 80 percent of the voting power of all classes of stock and at least 80 percent of each class of the nonvoting stock of at least one of the other includible corporations. As used in this subsection, the term 'stock' does not include nonvoting stock which is limited and preferred as to dividends, employer securities (within the meaning for section 409A(1) while such securities are held under an a tax credit employee stock ownership plan, or qualifying employer securities (within the meaning of section 4975(e)(8)) while such securities are held under a employee stock ownership plan which meets the requirements of section 4975(e)(7)."
—P.L. 98-369, Sec. 211(b)(20), substituted "section 801" for "section 802" in para. (b)(2), para. (c)(1), and subpara. (c)(2)(A), effective for tax. yrs. begin. after 12/31/83.

In 1980, P.L. 96-222, Sec. 101(a)(7)(B), amended Sec. 141(g) of P.L. 95-600, effective date for amendments made by Sec. 141(f)(4) of P.L. 95-600 [see below].
Prior to amendment, Sec. 141(g) of P.L. 95-600 read as follows:
"(g) Effective dates.
"(1) In general. The amendments made by this section (other than by subsection (f)(3)) shall apply with respect to qualified investment for taxable years beginning after December 31, 1978."
—P.L. 96-222, Sec. 101(a)(7)(L)(i)(VIII), substituted "tax credit employee stock ownership plan" for "an ESOP" in subsec. (a)... Sec. 101(a)(7)(L)(iv)(II), substituted "employee" for "leveraged employee" in subsec. (a), effective for estates of decedents dying after 4/1/80.

In 1978, P.L. 95-600, Sec. 141(f)(4), amended the last sentence of subsec. (a), effective [as amended by Sec. 101(a)(7)(B) of P.L. 96-222, see above] for qualified investments in tax. yrs. begin. after 12/31/78. Sec. 141(g)(2) of this Act [as amended by Sec. 101(a)(7)(B) of P.L. 96-222, see above] provides as follows:
"(2) Election to have amendments apply during 1978. At the election of the taxpayer, paragraph (1) shall be applied by substituting 'December 31, 1977' for 'December 31, 1978'; except that in the case of a plan in existence before December 31, 1978, any such election shall not affect the required allocation of employer securities attributable to qualified investment for taxable years beginning before January 1, 1979. An election under the preceding sentence shall be made at such time and in such manner as the Secretary of the Treasury or his delegate shall prescribe. Such an election, once made, shall be irrevocable."
Prior to amendment, the last sentence of subsec. (a) read as follows:
As used in this subsection, the term "stock" does not include nonvoting stock which is limited and preferred as to dividends, employer securities (within the meaning of section 301(d)(9)(A) of the Tax Reduction Act of 1975, or qualifying employer securities within the meaning of section 4975(e)(8) while such securities are held under an employee stock ownership plan which meets the requirements of section 301(d) of such Act or section 4975(e)(7), respectively."

In 1976, P.L. 94-455, Sec. 803(b)(3), substituted "dividends, employer securities within the meaning of section 301(d)(9)(A) of the Tax Reduction Act of 1975, or qualifying employer securities within the meaning of section 4975(e)(8) while such securities are held under an employee stock ownership plan which meets the requirements of section 301(d) of such Act or section 4975(e)(7), respectively." for "dividends," in subsec. (a), effective for tax. yrs. begin. after 12/31/74.
—P.L. 94-455, Sec. 1051(g), amended para. (b)(4), effective for tax. yrs. begin. after 12/31/75, except that "qualified possession source investment income" as defined in section 936(d)(2) of the Internal Revenue Code of 1954 shall include income from any source outside the United States if the taxpayer establishes to the satisfaction of the Secretary of the Treasury or his delegate that the income from such sources was earned before 10/1/76.
Prior to amendment, para. (b)(4) read as follows:
"(4) Corporations entitled to the benefits of section 931, by reason of receiving a large percentage of their income from sources within possessions of the United States."
—P.L. 94-455, Sec. 1053(d)(2), deleted para. (b)(5), effective for tax. yrs. begin. after 12/31/77.
Prior to deletion, para. (b)(5) read as follows:
"(5) Corporations organized under the China Trade Act, 1922."
—P.L. 94-455, Sec. 1507(a), amended subsec. (c), effective for tax. yrs. begin. after 12/31/80. Sec. 1507(c)(2) of this Act provides the following:
"(2) Transition rules with respect to carryovers or carrybacks relating to preelection taxable years and nontermination of group.—
"(A) Limitations on carryovers or carrybacks for groups electing under section 1504(c)(2).—If an affiliated group elects to file a consolidated return pursuant to section 1504(c)(2) of the Internal Revenue Code of 1954, a carryover of a loss or credit from a taxable year ending before January 1, 1981, and losses or credits which may be carried back to taxable years ending before such date, shall be taken into account as if this section had not been enacted.
"(B) Nontermination of affiliated group.—The mere election to file a consolidated return pursuant to such section 1504(c)(2) shall not cause the termination of an affiliated group filing consolidated returns."
Prior to amendment, subsec. (c) read as follows:
"(c) Includible insurance companies.
"Despite the provisions of paragraph (2) of subsection (b), two or more domestic insurance companies each of which is subject to taxation under the same section of this subtitle shall be considered as includible corporations for the purpose of the application of subsection (a) to such insurance companies alone."

In 1971, P.L. 92-178, Sec. 502(e), added para. (b)(7), effective for tax. yrs. end. after 12/31/71, except that a corporation may not be a DISC (as defined in Code Sec. 992(a) as added by Sec. 501 of this Act) for any tax. yr. begin. before 1/1/72.

In 1969, P.L. 91-172, Sec. 121(a)(4), added subsec. (e), effective for tax. yrs. begin. after 12/31/69.

In 1966, P.L. 89-389, Sec. 4(b)(3), deleted para. (b)(7), effective 1/1/69.
Prior to deletion, para. (b)(7) read as follows:
"(7) Unincorporated business enterprises subject to tax as corporations under section 1361."
In 1960, P.L. 86-779, Sec. 10(3), added "and real estate investment trusts" after "Regulated investment companies" in para. (b)(6), effective for tax. yrs. begin. after 12/31/60.
In 1959, P.L. 86-69, Sec. 3(f)(1), deleted ", 811," in para. (b)(2), effective only for tax. yrs. begin. after 12/31/57.
—P.L. 86-376, Sec. 2(c), deleted para. (b)(8), effective 9/24/59.
Prior to deletion, para. (b)(8) read as follows:
"(8) An electing small business corporation (as defined in section 1371(b))."
In 1958, P.L. 85-866, Sec. 64(d)(3), added para. (b)(8), effective for tax. yrs. begin. after 12/31/57.
In 1956, P.L. 429, Sec. 5(8), substituted "802, 811, or 821" for "802 or 821" in para. (b)(2), effective only for tax. yrs. begin. after 12/31/54.

Sec. 1505. Cross references.

(1) For suspension of running of statute of limitations when notice in respect of a deficiency is mailed to one corporation, see section 6503(a)(1).

(2) For allocation of income and deductions of related trades or businesses, see section 482.

Subchapter B.—Related Rules

Part

I. In general.

II. Certain controlled corporations.

PART I.—IN GENERAL

Sec.

1551. Disallowance of the benefits of the graduated corporate rates and accumulated earnings credit.

1552. Earnings and profits.

In 1978, P.L. 95-600, Sec. 301(b)(18)(B), amended item 1551.
Prior to amendment item 1551 read as follows:
"1551. Disallowance or surtax exemption and accumulated earnings credit."
In 1964, inserted the table of parts, and the heading to Part I.

Sec. 1551. Disallowance of the benefits of the graduated corporate rates and accumulated earnings credit.

(a) In general.

If—

(1) any corporation transfers, on or after January 1, 1951, and on or before June 12, 1963, all or part of its property (other than money) to a transferee corporation,

(2) any corporation transfers, directly or indirectly, after June 12, 1963, all or part of its property (other than money) to a transferee corporation, or

(3) five or fewer individuals who are in control of a corporation transfer, directly or indirectly, after June 12, 1963, property (other than money) to a transferee corporation,

and the transferee corporation was created for the purpose of acquiring such property or was not actively engaged in business at the time of such acquisition, and if after such transfer the transferor or transferors are in control of such transferee corporation during any part of the taxable year of such transferee corporation, then for such taxable year of such transferee corporation the Secretary may (except as may be otherwise determined under subsection (c)) disallow the benefits of the rates contained in section 11(b) which are lower than the highest rate specified in such section, or the accumulated earnings credit provided in paragraph (2) or (3) of section 535(c), unless such transferee corporation shall establish by the clear preponderance of the evidence that the securing of such benefits or credit was not a major purpose of such transfer.

Affiliated corporations Part II

(b) Control.

For purposes of subsection (a), the term "control" means—

(1) With respect to a transferee corporation described in subsection (a)(1) or (2), the ownership by the transferor corporation, its shareholders, or both, of stock possessing at least 80 percent of the total combined voting power of all classes of stock entitled to vote or at least 80 percent of the total value of shares of all classes of the stock; or

(2) With respect to each corporation described in subsection (a)(3), the ownership by the five or fewer individuals described in such subsection of stock possessing—

(A) at least 80 percent of the total combined voting power of all classes of stock entitled to vote or at least 80 percent of the total value of shares of all classes of the stock of each corporation, and

(B) more than 50 percent of the total combined voting power of all classes of stock entitled to vote or more than 50 percent of the total value of shares of all classes of stock of each corporation, taking into account the stock ownership of each such individual only to the extent such stock ownership is identical with respect to each such corporation.

For purposes of this subsection, section 1563(e) shall apply in determining the ownership of stock.

(c) Authority of the Secretary under this section.

The provisions of section 269(c), and the authority of the Secretary under such section, shall, to the extent not inconsistent with the provisions of this section, be applicable to this section.

In 1986, P.L. 99-514, Sec. 1899A(36), substituted "296(c)" for "296(b)" in subsec. (c), effective 10/22/86.
In 1981, P.L. 97-34, Sec. 232(b)(2), deleted "$150,000" before "accumulated earnings credit" in subsec. (a), effective for tax. yrs. begin. after 12/31/81.
In 1978, P.L. 95-600, Sec. 301(b)(18)(A)(i), substituted "disallow the benefits of the rates contained in section 11(b) which are lower than the highest rate specified in such section" for "disallow the surtax exemption (as defined in section 11(d)" in subsec. (a) . . . Sec. 301(b)(18)(B)(ii), substituted "such benefits or" for "such exemption or" in subsec. (a) . . . Sec. 301(b)(18)(B), amended the heading of Code Sec. 1551, effective for tax. yrs. begin. after 12/31/78.
Prior to amendment, the heading of Code Sec. 1551 read as follows:
"SEC. 1551. DISALLOWANCE OF SURTAX EXEMPTION AND ACCUMULATED EARNINGS CREDIT."
In 1976, P.L. 94-455, Sec. 1901(a)(158), substituted "subsection (c)" for "subsection (d)" in subsec. (a), effective for tax. yrs. begin. after 12/31/76.
—P.L. 94-455, Sec. 1906(b)(13)(A), substituted "Secretary" for "Secretary or his delegate" in subsec. (a), effective for tax. yrs. begin. after 12/31/76.
In 1975, P.L. 94-12, Sec. 304(b), substituted "$150,000" for "$100,000" in subsec. (a), effective for tax. yrs. begin. after 12/31/74.
In 1964, P.L. 88-272, Sec. 235(b), amended Code Sec. 1551, effective for transfers made after 6/12/63.
Prior to amendment, Code Sec. 1551 read as follows:
"SEC. 1551. DISALLOWANCE OF SURTAX EXEMPTION AND ACCUMULATED EARNINGS CREDIT.

"If any corporation transfers, on or after January 1, 1951, all or part of its property (other than money) to another corporation which was created for the purpose of acquiring such property or which was not actively engaged in business at the time of such acquisition, and if after such transfer the transferor corporation or its stockholders, or both, are in control of such transferee corporation during any part of the taxable year of such transferee corporation, then such transferee corporation shall not for such taxable year (except as may be otherwise determined under section 269(b)) be allowed either the $25,000 exemption from surtax provided in section 11(c) or the $100,000 accumulated earnings credit provided in paragraph (2) or (3) of section 535(c), unless such transferee corporation shall establish by the clear preponderance of the evidence that the securing of such exemption or credit was not a major purpose of such transfer. For purposes of this section, control means the ownership of stock possessing at least 80 percent of the total combined voting power of all classes of stock entitled to vote or at least 80 percent of the total value of shares of all classes of stock of the corporation. In determining the ownership of stock for the purpose of this section, the ownership of stock shall be determined in accordance with the provisions of section 544, except that constructive ownership under section 544(a)(2) shall be determined only with respect to the individual's spouse and minor children. The provisions of section 269(b), and the authority of the Secretary under such section, shall, to the extent not inconsistent with the provisions of this section, be applicable to this section."

In 1958, P.L. 85-866, Sec. 205(a), substituted "$100,000" for "$60,000", effective for tax. yrs. begin. after 12/31/57.

Sec. 1552. Earnings and profits.
(a) General rule.

Pursuant to regulations prescribed by the Secretary the earnings and profits of each member of an affiliated group required to be included in a consolidated return for such group filed for a taxable year shall be determined by allocating the tax liability of the group for such year among the members of the group in accord with whichever of the following methods the group shall elect in its first consolidated return filed for such a taxable year:

(1) The tax liability shall be apportioned among the members of the group in accordance with the ratio which that portion of the consolidated taxable income attributable to each member of the group having taxable income bears to the consolidated taxable income.

(2) The tax liability of the group shall be allocated to the several members of the group on the basis of the percentage of the total tax which the tax of such member if computed on a separate return would bear to the total amount of the taxes for all members of the group so computed.

(3) The tax liability of the group (excluding the tax increases arising from the consolidation) shall be allocated on the basis of the contribution of each member of the group to the consolidated taxable income of the group. Any tax increases arising from the consolidation shall be distributed to the several members in direct proportion to the reduction in tax liability resulting to such members from the filing of the consolidated return as measured by the difference between their tax liabilities determined on a separate return basis and their tax liabilities based on their contributions to the consolidated taxable income.

(4) The tax liability of the group shall be allocated in accord with any other method selected by the group with the approval of the Secretary.

(b) Failure to elect.

If no election is made in such first return, the tax liability shall be allocated among the several members of the group pursuant to the method prescribed in subsection (a)(1).

In 1976, P.L. 94-455, Sec. 1901(a)(159), deleted "beginning after December 31, 1953, and ending after the date of enactment of this title," after "for such group filed for a taxable year" in the first sentence of subsec. (a), effective for tax. yrs. begin. after 12/31/76.
—P.L. 94-455, Sec. 1906(b)(13)(A), substituted "Secretary" for "Secretary or his delegate" each place it appeared in Code Sec. 1552, effective for tax. yrs. begin. after 12/31/76.
In 1964, P.L. 88-272, Sec. 234(b)(8), deleted "(determined without regard to the 2 percent increase provided by section 1503(a))", before "based on their contributions" in para. (a)(3), effective for tax. yrs. begin. after 12/31/63.

PART II.—CERTAIN CONTROLLED CORPORATIONS

Sec.
1561. Limitations on certain multiple tax benefits in the case of certain controlled corporations.
1562. Repealed.
1563. Definitions and special rules.

In 1990, P.L. 101-508, Sec. 11801(b)(12), deleted item 1564.
Prior to deletion, item 1564 read as follows:
"1564. Transitional rules in the case of certain controlled corporations."
In 1969, P.L. 91-172, Sec. 401(a)(3), substituted new item 1561 for old 1561 and 1562 dealing with surtax exemptions in case of certain controlled corporations, and the privilege of groups to elect multiple surtax exemptions, respectively.
—P.L. 91-172, Sec. 401(b)(2)(E), added item 1564.
In 1964, added the designation of Part II, and items 1561– 1563.

2,957

Code Sec. 1561 — Affiliated corporations

Sec. 1561. Limitations on certain multiple tax benefits in the case of certain controlled corporations.

(a) General rule.

The component members of a controlled group of corporations on a December 31 shall, for their taxable years which include such December 31, be limited for purposes of this subtitle to—

(1) amounts in each taxable income bracket in the tax table in section 11(b)(1) which do not aggregate more than the maximum amount in such bracket to which a corporation which is not a component member of a controlled group is entitled,

(2) one $250,000 ($150,000 if any component member is a corporation described in section 535(c)(2)(B)) amount for purposes of computing the accumulated earnings credit under section 535(c)(2) and (3),

(3) one $40,000 exemption amount for purposes of computing the amount of the minimum tax, and

(4) one $2,000,000 amount for purposes of computing the tax imposed by section 59A.

The amounts specified in paragraph (1), the amount specified in paragraph (3), and the amount specified in paragraph (4) shall be divided equally among the component members of such group on such December 31 unless all of such component members consent (at such time and in such manner as the Secretary shall by regulations prescribe) to an apportionment plan providing for an unequal allocation of such amounts. The amounts specified in paragraph (2) shall be divided equally among the component members of such group on such December 31 unless the Secretary prescribes regulations permitting an unequal allocation of such amounts. Notwithstanding paragraph (1), in applying the last 2 sentences of section 11(b)(1) to such component members, the taxable income of all such component members shall be taken into account and any increase in tax under such last 2 sentences shall be divided among such component members in the same manner as amounts under paragraph (1). In applying section 55(d)(3), the alternative minimum taxable income of all component members shall be taken into account and any decrease in the exemption amount shall be allocated to the component members in the same manner as under paragraph (3).

(b) Certain short taxable years.

If a corporation has a short taxable year which does not include a December 31 and is a component member of a controlled group of corporations with respect to such taxable year, then for purposes of this subtitle—

(1) the amount in each taxable income bracket in the tax table in section 11(b), and

(2) the amount to be used in computing the accumulated earnings credit under section 535(c)(2) and (3),

of such corporation for such taxable year shall be the amount specified in subsection (a)(1) or (2), as the case may be, divided by the number of corporations which are component members of such group on the last day of such taxable year. For purposes of the preceding sentence, section 1563(b) shall be applied as if such last day were substituted for December 31.

In 1996, P.L. 104-188, Sec. 1703(f), substituted "last 2 sentences" for "last sentence" each place it appeared in subsec. (a), effective for tax. yrs. begin. on or after 1/1/93.

In 1988, P.L. 100-647, Sec. 2004(1), substituted "11(b)(1)" for "11(b)" in subsec. (a), effective for tax. yrs. begin. after 12/31/87.

In 1986, P.L. 99-514, Sec. 701(e)(2)(A), deleted "and" at the end of para. (a)(1), substituted ", and" for the period at the end of para. (a)(2), and added para. (a)(3) . . . Sec. 701(e)(2)(B), substituted "specified in paragraph (1) (and the amount specified in paragraph (3))" for "specified in paragraph (1)" in subsec. (a) . . .

Sec. 701(e)(2)(C), added the sentence at the end of subsec. (a), effective for tax. yrs. begin. after 12/31/86.
— P.L. 99-499, Sec. 516(b)(3)(A), deleted "and" from the end of para. (a)(2), and substituted ", and" for the period at the end of para. (a)(3), and added para. (a)(4) . . . Sec. 516(b)(3)(B), substituted ", the amount specified in paragraph (3), and the amount specified in paragraph (4)" for "(and the amount specified in paragraph (3))" in subsec. (a), effective for tax. yrs. begin. after 12/31/86.

In 1984, P.L. 98-369, Sec. 66(b), added the sentence at the end of subsec. (a), effective for tax. yrs. begin. after 12/31/83, except as provided in Sec. 66(c)(2) of this Act, which reads as follows:

"(2) Amendments not treated as changed in rate of tax.—The amendments made by this subsection shall not be treated as a change in a rate of tax for purposes of section 21 of the Internal Revenue Code of 1954."
— P.L. 98-369, Sec. 211(b)(21)(A)(i), deleted paras. (a)(3) and (4), added "and" at the end of para. (a)(1), and substituted a period for the comma at the end of para. (a)(2) . . . Sec. 211(b)(21)(A)(ii), substituted "paragraph (2)" for "paragraphs (2), (3), and (4)" in the last sentence of subsec. (a) . . . Sec. 211(b)(21)(B)(i), and (ii), deleted paras. (b)(3) and (4), added "and" at the end of para. (b)(1), and substituted "or (2)" for ", (2), (3), or (4)" in subsec. (b), effective for tax. yrs. begin. after 12/31/83.

Prior to deletion, paras. (a)(3) and (4) read as follows:

"(3) one $25,000 amount for purposes of computing the limitation on the small business deduction of life insurance companies under sections 804(a)(3) and 809(d)(10).

"(4) one of $1,000,000 amount (adjusted as provided in section 809(f)(3)) for purposes of computing the limitation under paragraph (1) or (2) of section 809(f)."

Prior to deletion, paras. (b)(3) and (4) read as follows:

"(3) the amount to be used in computing the limitation on the small business deduction of life insurance companies under sections 804(a)(3) and 809(d)(10) and

"(4) the amount (adjusted as provided in section 809(f)(3)) to be used in computing the limitation under paragraph (1) or (2) of section 809(f)."

In 1982, P.L. 97-248, Sec. 259(b)(1), deleted "and" at the end of para. (a)(2) . . . Sec. 259(b)(2), substituted "and" for the period at the end of para. (a)(3) . . . Sec. 259(b)(3), added para. (a)(4) . . . Sec. 259(b)(4), substituted "(2), (3), and (4)" for "(2) and (3)" in subsec. (a) . . . Sec. 259(c)(1), deleted "and" at the end of para. (b)(2) . . . Sec. 259(c)(2), substituted "and" for the period at the end of para. (b)(3) . . . Sec. 259(c)(3), added para. (b)(4) . . . Sec. 259(c)(4), substituted "(2), (3), or (4)" for "(2) or (3)" in subsec. (b), effective for tax. yrs. begin. after 12/31/81 and before 1/1/84.

In 1981, P.L. 97-34, Sec. 232(b)(3), substituted "$250,000 ($150,000 if any component member is a corporation described in section 535(c)(2)(B))" for "$150,000" in para. (a)(2), effective for tax. yrs. begin. after 12/31/81.

In 1978, P.L. 95-600, Sec. 301(b)(19)(A)(i), amended para. (a)(1) . . . Sec. 301(b)(19)(A)(ii), substituted "amounts" for "amount" each place it appeared in the second sentence of subsec. (a) . . . Sec. 301(b)(19)(A)(iii), deleted the last sentence of subsec. (a) . . . Sec. 301(b)(19)(B), amended para. (b)(1), effective for tax. yrs. begin. after 12/31/78.

Prior to amendment, para. (a)(1) effective read as follows:

"(1) one surtax exemption under section 11(d),"

Prior to amendment, the last sentence of subsec. (a) read as follows:

"In applying section 11(b)(2), the first $25,000 of taxable income and the second $25,000 of taxable income shall each be allocated among the component members of a controlled group of corporations in the same manner as the surtax exemption is allocated."

Prior to amendment, para. (b)(1) read as follows:

"(1) the surtax exemption under section 11(d),"
— P.L. 95-600, Sec. 703(j)(7), substituted "804(a)(3)" for "804(a)(4)" in para. (b)(3), effective 10/4/76.

In 1976, P.L. 94-455, Sec. 901(c)(1), added the last sentence of subsec. (a), effective for tax. yrs. end. after 12/31/75.
— P.L. 94-455, Sec. 1901(b)(1)(J)(v), substituted "sections 804(a)(3)" for "sections 804(a)(4)" in para. (a)(3), effective for tax. yrs. begin. after 12/31/76.
— P.L. 94-455, Sec. 1906(b)(13)(A), substituted "Secretary" for "Secretary or his delegate" each place it appeared in Code Sec. 1561, effective 2/1/77.

In 1975, P.L. 94-164, Sec. 4(d)(1), deleted "$25,000" from para. (a)(1), as in effect for tax. yrs. end. after 12/31/75, effective for tax. yrs. begin. after 12/31/75.

Prior to amendment, para. (a)(1) read as follows:

"(1) one $25,000 surtax exemption under section 11(d),"
— P.L. 94-12, Sec. 303(c)(1), substituted "$50,000" for "$25,000" in para. (a)(1), effective for tax. yrs. end. after 12/31/74 and before 1/1/76. Sec. 303(c)(1) states that in applying Code Sec. 11(b)(2), "the first $25,000 of taxable income and the second $25,000 of taxable income shall each be allocated among the component members of a controlled group of corporations in the same manner as the surtax exemption is allocated."
— P.L. 94-12, Sec. 304(b), substituted "$150,000" for "$100,000" in para. (a)(2), effective for tax. yrs. begin. after 12/31/74.

In 1969, P.L. 91-172, Sec. 401(a)(1), amended Code Sec. 1561, effective for tax. yrs. begin. after 12/31/74.

Prior to amendment, Code Sec. 1561 read as follows:

"SEC. 1561. SURTAX EXEMPTIONS IN CASE OF CERTAIN CONTROLLED CORPORATIONS.

"(a) General rule.

"If a corporation is a component member of a controlled group of corporations on a December 31, then for purposes of this subtitle the surtax exemption of such corporation for the taxable year which includes such December 31 shall be an amount equal to—

Affiliated corporations — Code Sec. 1562

"(1) $25,000 divided by the number of corporations which are component members of such group on such December 31, or

"(2) if all such component members consent (at such time and in such manner as the Secretary or his delegate shall by regulations prescribe) to an apportionment plan, such portion of $25,000 as is apportioned to such member in accordance with such plan.

The sum of the amounts apportioned under paragraph (2) among the component members of any controlled group shall not exceed $25,000.

"(b) Certain short taxable years.

"If a corporation—

"(1) has a short taxable year which does not include a December 31, and

"(2) is a component member of a controlled group of corporations with respect to such taxable year,

then for purposes of this subtitle the surtax exemption of such corporation for such taxable year shall be an amount equal to $25,000 divided by the number of corporations which are component members of such group on the last day of such taxable year. For purposes of the preceding sentence, section 1563(b) shall be applied as if such last day were substituted for December 31."

In 1964, P.L. 88-272, Sec. 235, added Code Sec. 1561, effective for tax. yrs. end. after 12/31/63.

Sec. 1562.   Repealed.

In 1969, P.L. 91-172, Sec. 401(a)(2), repealed Code Sec. 1562, effective for tax. yrs. begin. after 12/31/74.

Prior to repeal, Code Sec. 1562 read as follows:

"SEC. 1562. PRIVILEGE OF GROUPS TO ELECT MULTIPLE SURTAX EXEMPTIONS.

"(a) Election of multiple surtax exemptions.

"(1) In general. A controlled group of corporations shall (subject to the provisions of this section) have the privilege of electing to have each of its component members make its returns without regard to section 1561. Such election shall be made with respect to a specified December 31 and shall be valid only if—

"(A) each corporation which is a component member of such group on such December 31, and

"(B) each other corporation which is a component member of such group on any succeeding December 31, before the day on which the election is filed, consents to such election.

"(2) Years for which effective. An election by a controlled group of corporations under paragraph (1) shall be effective with respect to the taxable year of each component member of such group which includes the specified December 31, and each taxable year of each corporation which is a component member of such group (or a successor group) on a succeeding December 31 included within such taxable year, unless the election is terminated under subsection (c).

"(3) Effect of election. If an election by a controlled group of corporations under paragraph (1) is effective with respect to any taxable year of a corporation—

"(A) section 1561 shall not apply to such corporation for such taxable year, but

"(B) the additional tax imposed by subsection (b) shall apply to such corporation for such taxable year.

"(b) Additional tax imposed.

"(1) General rule. If an election under subsection (a)(1) by a controlled group of corporations is effective with respect to the taxable year of a corporation, there is hereby imposed for such taxable year on the taxable income of such corporation a tax equal to 6 percent of so much of such corporation's taxable income for such taxable year as does not exceed the amount of such corporation's surtax exemption for each taxable year. This paragraph shall not apply to the taxable year of a corporation if—

"(A) such corporation is the only component member of such controlled group on the December 31 included in such corporation's taxable year which has taxable income for a taxable year including such December 31, or

"(B) such corporation's surtax exemption is disallowed for such taxable year under any provision of this subtitle.

"(2) Tax treated as imposed by section 11, etc. For the taxable year of a corporation a tax is imposed by section 11 on the taxable income of such corporation, the additional tax imposed by this subsection shall be treated for purposes of this title as a tax imposed by section 11. If for the taxable year of a corporation a tax is imposed on the taxable income of such corporation which is computed under any other section by reference to section 11, the additional tax imposed by this subsection shall be treated for purposes of this title as imposed by such other section.

"(3) Taxable income defined. For purposes of this subsection, the term 'taxable income' means—

"(A) in the case of a corporation subject to tax under section 511, its unrelated business taxable income (within the meaning of section 512);

"(B) in the case of a life insurance company, its life insurance company taxable income (within the meaning of section 802(b));

"(C) in the case of a regulated investment company, its investment company taxable income (within the meaning of section 852(b)(2)); and

"(D) in the case of a real estate investment trust, its real estate investment trust taxable income (within the meaning of section 857(b)(2)).

"(4) Special rules. If for the taxable year an additional tax is imposed on the taxable income of a corporation by this subsection, then sections 244 (relating to dividends received on certain preferred stock), 247 (relating to dividends paid on certain preferred stock of public utilities), 804(a)(3) (relating to deduction for partially tax-exempt interest in the case of a life insurance company), and 922 (relating to special deduction for Western Hemisphere trade corporations) shall be applied without regard to the additional tax imposed by this subsection.

"(c) Termination of election.

"An election by a controlled group of corporations under subsection (a) shall terminate with respect to such group—

"(1) Consent of the members. If such group files a termination of such election with respect to a specified December 31, and—

"(A) each corporation which is a component member of such group on such December 31, and

"(B) each other corporation which is a component member of such group on any succeeding December 31 before the day on which the termination is filed, consents to such termination.

"(2) Refusal by new member to consent. If on December 31 of any year such group includes a component member which—

"(A) on the immediately preceding January 1 was not a member of such group, and

"(B) within the time and in the manner provided by regulations prescribed by the Secretary or his delegate, files a statement that it does not consent to the election.

"(3) Consolidated returns. If—

"(A) a corporation is a component member determined without regard to section 1563(b)(3) of such group on a December 31 included within a taxable year ending on or after January 1, 1964, and

"(B) such corporation is a member of an affiliated group of corporations which makes a consolidated return under this chapter (sec. 1501 and following) for such taxable year.

"(4) Controlled group no longer in existence. If such group is considered as no longer in existence with respect to any December 31.

Such determination shall be effective with respect to the December 31 referred to in paragraph (1)(A), (2), (3), or (4), as the case may be.

"(d) Election after termination.

"If an election by a controlled group of corporations is terminated under subsection (c), such group (and any successor group) shall not be eligible to make an election under subsection (a) with respect to any December 31 before the sixth December 31 after the December 31 with respect to which such termination was effective.

"(e) Manner and time of giving consent and making election, etc.

"An election under subsection (a)(1) or a termination under subsection (c)(1) (and the consent of each member of a controlled group of corporations which is required with respect to such election or termination) shall be made in such manner as the Secretary or his delegate shall by regulations prescribe, and shall be made at any time before the expiration of 3 years after—

"(1) in the case of such an election, the date when the income tax return for the taxable year of the component member of the controlled group which has the taxable year ending first on or after the specified December 31 is required to be filed (without regard to any extensions of time), and

"(2) in the case of such a termination, the specified December 31 with respect to which such termination was made.

Any consent to such an election or termination, and a failure by a component member to file a statement that it does not consent to an election under this section, shall be deemed to be a consent to the application of subsection (g)(1) (relating to tolling of statute of limitations on assessment of deficiencies).

"(f) Special rules.

"For purposes of this section—

"(1) Continuing and successor controlled groups. The determination of whether a controlled group of corporations—

"(A) is considered as no longer in existence with respect to any December 31, or

"(B) is a successor to another controlled group of corporations (and the effect of such determination with respect to any election or termination), shall be made under regulations prescribed by the Secretary or his delegate. For purposes of subparagraph (B), such regulations shall be based on the continuation (or termination) of predominant equitable ownership.

"(2) Certain short taxable years. If one or more corporations have short taxable years which do not include a December 31 and are component members of a controlled group of corporations with respect to such taxable years (determined by applying section 1563(b) as if the last day of each such taxable year were substituted for December 31), then an election by such group under this section apply with respect to such corporations with respect to such taxable years if—

"(A) such election is in effect with respect to both the December 31 immediately preceding such taxable years and the December 31 immediately succeeding such taxable years, or

"(B) such election is in effect with respect to the December 31 immediately preceding or succeeding such taxable years and each such corporation files a consent to the application of such election to its short taxable year at such time and in such manner as the Secretary or his delegate shall prescribe by regulations.

"(g) Tolling of statute of limitations.

"In any case in which a controlled group of corporations makes an election or termination under this section, the statutory period—

"(1) for assessment of any deficiency against a corporation which is a component member of such group for any taxable year, to the extent such deficiency is attributable to the application of this part, shall not expire before the expiration of one year after the date such election or termination is made; and

"(2) for allowing or making credit or refund of any overpayment of tax by a corporation which is a component member of such group for any taxable year, to the extent such credit or refund is attributable to the application of this part, shall not expire before the expiration of one year after the date such election or termination is made."

Code Sec. 1562　　　　　　　　　　　　　　　　　　　　　　　　　　Affiliated corporations

—P.L. 91-172, Sec. 401(b)(2)(A), substituted "the amount of such corporation's surtax exemption for such taxable year" for "$25,000" in subsec. (b)(1), effective for tax. yrs. begin. after 12/31/69.

—P.L. 91-172, Sec. 401(g), of this Act provides:

"(g) Retroactive termination of section 1562 elections.— If an affiliated group of corporations makes a consolidated return for the taxable year which includes December 31, 1970 (hereinafter in this subsection referred to as '1970 consolidated return year'), then on or before the due date prescribed by law (including any extensions thereof) for filing such consolidated return such affiliated group of corporations may terminate the election under section 1562 of the Internal Revenue Code of 1954 with respect to any prior December 31 which is included in a taxable year of any of such corporations from which there is a net operating loss carryover to the 1970 consolidated return year. A termination of an election under this subsection shall be valid only if it meets the requirements of sections 1562(c)(1) and 1562(e) of such Code (other than making the termination before the expiration of the 3-year period specified in section 1562(e))."

In 1964, P.L. 88-272, Sec. 235, added Code Sec. 1562, effective for tax. yrs. end. after 12/31/63.

Sec. 1563. Definitions and special rules.
(a) Controlled group of corporations.

For purposes of this part, the term "controlled group of corporations" means any group of—

(1) Parent-subsidiary controlled group. One or more chains of corporations connected through stock ownership with a common parent corporation if—

(A) stock possessing at least 80 percent of the total combined voting power of all classes of stock entitled to vote or at least 80 percent of the total value of shares of all classes of stock of each of the corporations, except the common parent corporation, is owned (within the meaning of subsection (d)(1)) by one or more of the other corporations; and

(B) the common parent corporation owns (within the meaning of subsection (d)(1)) stock possessing at least 80 percent of the total combined voting power of all classes of stock entitled to vote or at least 80 percent of the total value of shares of all classes of stock of at least one of the other corporations, excluding, in computing such voting power or value, stock owned directly by such other corporations.

(2) Brother-sister controlled group. Two or more corporations if 5 or fewer persons who are individuals, estates, or trusts own (within the meaning of subsection (d)(2)) stock possessing more than 50 percent of the total combined voting power of all classes of stock entitled to vote or more than 50 percent of the total value of shares of all classes of stock of each corporation, taking into account the stock ownership of each such person only to the extent such stock ownership is identical with respect to each such corporation.

(3) Combined group. Three or more corporations each of which is a member of a group of corporations described in paragraph (1) or (2), and one of which—

(A) is a common parent corporation included in a group of corporations described in paragraph (1), and also

(B) is included in a group of corporations described in paragraph (2).

(4) Certain insurance companies. Two or more insurance companies subject to taxation under section 801 which are members of a controlled group of corporations described in paragraph (1), (2), or (3). Such insurance companies shall be treated as a controlled group of corporations separate from any other corporations which are members of the controlled group of corporations described in paragraph (1), (2), or (3).

(b) Component member.

(1) General rule. For purposes of this part, a corporation is a component member of a controlled group of corporations on a December 31 of any taxable year (and with respect to the taxable year which includes such December 31) if such corporation—

(A) is a member of such controlled group of corporations on the December 31 included in such year and is not treated as an excluded member under paragraph (2), or

(B) is not a member of such controlled group of corporations on the December 31 included in such year but is treated as an additional member under paragraph (3).

(2) Excluded members. A corporation which is a member of a controlled group of corporations on December 31 of any taxable year shall be treated as an excluded member of such group for the taxable year including such December 31 if such corporation—

(A) is a member of such group for less than one-half the number of days in such taxable year which precede such December 31,

(B) is exempt from taxation under section 501(a) (except a corporation which is subject to tax on its unrelated business taxable income under section 511) for such taxable year,

(C) is a foreign corporation subject to tax under section 881 for such taxable year,

(D) is an insurance company subject to taxation under section 801 (other than an insurance company which is a member of a controlled group described in subsection (a)(4)), or

(E) is a franchised corporation, as defined in subsection (f)(4).

(3) Additional members. A corporation which—

(A) was a member of a controlled group of corporations at any time during a calendar year,

(B) is not a member of such group on December 31 of such calendar year, and

(C) is not described, with respect to such group, in subparagraph (B), (C), (D), or (E) of paragraph (2),

shall be treated as an additional member of such group on December 31 for its taxable year including such December 31 if it was a member of such group for one-half (or more) of the number of days in such taxable year which precede such December 31.

(4) Overlapping groups. If a corporation is a component member of more than one controlled group of corporations with respect to any taxable year, such corporation shall be treated as a component member of only one controlled group. The determination as to the group of which such corporation is a component member shall be made under regulations prescribed by the Secretary which are consistent with the purposes of this part.

(c) Certain stock excluded.

(1) General rule. For purposes of this part, the term "stock" does not include—

(A) nonvoting stock which is limited and preferred as to dividends,

(B) treasury stock, and

(C) stock which is treated as "excluded stock" under paragraph (2).

(2) Stock treated as "excluded stock".

(A) Parent-subsidiary controlled group. For purposes of subsection (a)(1), if a corporation (referred to in this paragraph as "parent corporation") owns (within the meaning of subsections (d)(1) and (e)(4)), 50 percent or more of the total combined voting power of all classes of stock entitled to vote or 50 percent or more of the total value of shares of all classes of stock in another corporation (referred to in this paragraph as "subsidiary corporation"), the following stock of the subsidiary corporation shall be treated as excluded stock—

(i) stock in the subsidiary corporation held by a trust which is part of a plan of deferred compensation for the benefit of the employees of the parent corporation or the subsidiary corporation,

(ii) stock in the subsidiary corporation owned by an individual (within the meaning of subsection (d)(2)) who is a principal stockholder or officer of the parent corporation. For purposes of this clause, the term "principal stockholder" of a corporation means an individual who owns (within the meaning of subsection (d)(2)) 5 percent or more of the total combined voting power of all classes of stock entitled to vote or 5 percent or more of the total value of shares of all classes of stock in such corporation,

(iii) stock in the subsidiary corporation owned (within the meaning of subsection (d)(2)) by an employee of the subsidiary corporation if such stock is subject to conditions which run in favor of such parent (or subsidiary) corporation and which substantially restrict or limit the employee's right (or if the employee constructively owns such stock, the direct owner's right) to dispose of such stock, or

(iv) stock in the subsidiary corporation owned (within the meaning of subsection (d)(2)) by an organization (other than the parent corporation) to which section 501 (relating to certain educational and charitable organizations which are exempt from tax) applies and which is controlled directly or indirectly by the parent corporation or subsidiary corporation, by an individual, estate, or trust that is a principal stockholder (within the meaning of clause (ii)) of the parent corporation, by an officer of the parent corporation, or by any combination thereof.

(B) Brother-sister controlled group. For purposes of subsection (a)(2), if 5 or fewer persons who are individuals, estates, or trusts (referred to in this subparagraph as "common owners") own (within the meaning of subsection (d)(2)), 50 percent or more of the total combined voting power of all classes of stock entitled to vote or 50 percent or more of the total value of shares of all classes of stock in a corporation, the following stock of such corporation shall be treated as excluded stock—

(i) stock in such corporation held by an employees' trust described in section 401(a) which is exempt from tax under section 501(a), if such trust is for the benefit of the employees of such corporation,

(ii) stock in such corporation owned (within the meaning of subsection (d)(2)) by an employee of the corporation if such stock is subject to conditions which run in favor of any of such common owners (or such corporation) and which substantially restrict or limit the employee's right (or if the employee constructively owns such stock, the direct owner's right) to dispose of such stock. If a condition which limits or restricts the employee's right (or the direct owner's right) to dispose of such stock also applies to the stock held by any of the common owners pursuant to a bona fide reciprocal stock purchase arrangement, such condition shall not be treated as one which restricts or limits the employee's right to dispose of such stock, or

(iii) stock in such corporation owned (within the meaning of subsection (d)(2)) by an organization to which section 501 (relating to certain educational and charitable organizations which are exempt from tax) applies and which is controlled directly or indirectly by such corporation, by an individual, estate, or trust that is a principal stockholder (within the meaning of subparagraph (A)(ii)) of such corporation, by an officer of such corporation, or by any combination thereof.

(d) Rules for determining stock ownership.

(1) Parent-subsidiary controlled group. For purposes of determining whether a corporation is a member of a parent-subsidiary controlled group of corporations (within the meaning of subsection (a)(1)), stock owned by a corporation means—

(A) stock owned directly by such corporation, and

(B) stock owned with the application of paragraphs (1), (2), and (3) of subsection (e).

(2) Brother-sister controlled group. For purposes of determining whether a corporation is a member of a brother-sister controlled group of corporations (within the meaning of subsection (a)(2)), stock owned by a person who is an individual, estate, or trust means—

(A) stock owned directly by such person, and

(B) stock owned with the application of subsection (e).

(e) Constructive ownership.

(1) Options. If any person has an option to acquire stock, such stock shall be considered as owned by such person. For purposes of this paragraph, an option to acquire such an option, and each one of a series of such options, shall be considered as an option to acquire such stock.

(2) Attribution from partnerships. Stock owned, directly or indirectly, by or for a partnership shall be considered as owned by any partner having an interest of 5 percent or more in either the capital or profits of the partnership in proportion to his interest in capital or profits, whichever such proportion is the greater.

(3) Attribution from estates or trusts.

(A) Stock owned, directly or indirectly, by or for an estate or trust shall be considered as owned by any beneficiary who has an actuarial interest of 5 percent or more in such stock, to the extent of such actuarial interest. For purposes of this subparagraph, the actuarial interest of each beneficiary shall be determined by assuming the maximum exercise of discretion by the fiduciary in favor of such beneficiary and the maximum use of such stock to satisfy his rights as a beneficiary.

(B) Stock owned, directly or indirectly, by or for any portion of a trust of which a person is considered the owner under subpart E of part I of subchapter J (relating to grantors and others treated as substantial owners) shall be considered as owned by such person.

(C) This paragraph shall not apply to stock owned by any employees' trust described in section 401(a) which is exempt from tax under section 501(a).

(4) Attribution from corporations. Stock owned, directly or indirectly, by or for a corporation shall be considered as owned by any person who owns (within the meaning of subsection (d)) 5 percent or more in value of its stock in that proportion which the value of the stock which such person so owns bears to the value of all the stock in such corporation.

(5) Spouse. An individual shall be considered as owning stock in a corporation owned, directly or indirectly, by or for his spouse (other than a spouse who is legally separated from the individual under a decree of divorce whether interlocutory or final, or a decree of separate maintenance), except in the case of a corporation with re-

spect to which each of the following conditions is satisfied for its taxable year—

(A) The individual does not, at any time during such taxable year, own directly any stock in such corporation;

(B) The individual is not a director or employee and does not participate in the management of such corporation at any time during such taxable year;

(C) Not more than 50 percent of such corporation's gross income for such taxable year was derived from royalties, rents, dividends, interest, and annuities; and

(D) Such stock in such corporation is not, at any time during such taxable year, subject to conditions which substantially restrict or limit the spouse's right to dispose of such stock and which run in favor of the individual or his children who have not attained the age of 21 years.

(6) Children, grandchildren, parents, and grandparents.

(A) Minor children. An individual shall be considered as owning stock owned, directly or indirectly, by or for his children who have not attained the age of 21 years, and, if the individual has not attained the age of 21 years, the stock owned, directly or indirectly, by or for his parents.

(B) Adult children and grandchildren. An individual who owns (within the meaning of subsection (d)(2), but without regard to this subparagraph) more than 50 percent of the total combined voting power of all classes of stock entitled to vote or more than 50 percent of the total value of shares of all classes of stock in a corporation shall be considered as owning the stock in such corporation owned, directly or indirectly, by or for his parents, grandparents, grandchildren, and children who have attained the age of 21 years.

(C) Adopted child. For purposes of this section, a legally adopted child of an individual shall be treated as a child of such individual by blood.

(f) Other definitions and rules.

(1) Employee defined. For purposes of this section the term "employee" has the same meaning such term is given by paragraphs (1) and (2) of section 3121(d).

(2) Operating rules.

(A) In general. Except as provided in subparagraph (B), stock constructively owned by a person by reason of the application of paragraph (1), (2), (3), (4), (5), or (6) of subsection (e) shall, for purposes of applying such paragraphs, be treated as actually owned by such person.

(B) Members of family. Stock constructively owned by an individual by reason of the application of paragraph (5) or (6) of subsection (e) shall not be treated as owned by him for purposes of again applying such paragraphs in order to make another the constructive owner of such stock.

(3) Special rules. For purposes of this section—

(A) If stock may be considered as owned by a person under subsection (e)(1) and under any other paragraph of subsection (e), it shall be considered as owned by him under subsection (e)(1).

(B) If stock is owned (within the meaning of subsection (d)) by two or more persons, such stock shall be considered as owned by the person whose ownership of such stock results in the corporation being a component member of a controlled group. If by reason of the preceding sentence, a corporation would (but for this sentence) become a component member of two controlled groups, it shall be treated as a component member of one controlled group. The determination as to the group of which such corporation is a component member shall be made under regulations prescribed by the Secretary which are consistent with the purposes of this part.

(C) If stock is owned by a person within the meaning of subsection (d) and such ownership results in the corporation being a component member of a controlled group, such stock shall not be treated as excluded stock under subsection (c)(2), if by reason of treating such stock as excluded stock the result is that such corporation is not a component member of a controlled group of corporations.

(4) Franchised corporation. If—

(A) a parent corporation (as defined in subsection (c)(2)(A)), or a common owner (as defined in subsection (c)(2)(B)), of a corporation which is a member of a controlled group of corporations is under a duty (arising out of a written agreement) to sell stock of such corporation (referred to in this paragraph as "franchised corporation") which is franchised to sell the products of another member, or the common owner, of such controlled group;

(B) such stock is to be sold to an employee (or employees) of such franchised corporation pursuant to a bona fide plan designed to eliminate the stock ownership of the parent corporation or of the common owner in the franchised corporation;

(C) such plan—

(i) provides a reasonable selling price for such stock, and

(ii) requires that a portion of the employee's share of the profits of such corporation (whether received as compensation or as a dividend) be applied to the purchase of such stock (or the purchase of notes, bonds, debentures or other similar evidence of indebtedness of such franchised corporation held by such parent corporation or common owner);

(D) such employee (or employees) owns directly more than 20 percent of the total value of shares of all classes of stock in such franchised corporation;

(E) more than 50 percent of the inventory of such franchised corporation is acquired from members of the controlled group, the common owner, or both; and

(F) all of the conditions contained in subparagraphs (A), (B), (C), (D), and (E) have been met for one-half (or more) of the number of days preceding the December 31 included within the taxable year (or if the taxable year does not include December 31, the last day of such year) of the franchised corporation.

then such franchised corporation shall be treated as an excluded member of such group, under subsection (b)(2), for such taxable year.

(5) Brother-sister controlled group definition for provisions other than this part.

(A) In general. Except as specifically provided in an applicable provision, subsection (a)(2) shall be applied to an applicable provision as if it read as follows:

"(2) Brother-sister controlled group. Two or more corporations if 5 or fewer persons who are individuals, estates, or trusts own (within the meaning of subsection (d)(2) stock possessing—

"(A) at least 80 percent of the total combined voting power of all classes of stock entitled to vote, or at least 80 percent of the total value of shares of all classes of stock, of each corporation, and

Affiliated corporations Code Sec. 1564

"(B) more than 50 percent of the total combined voting power of all classes of stock entitled to vote or more than 50 percent of the total value of shares of all classes of stock of each corporation, taking into account the stock ownership of each such person only to the extent such stock ownership is identical with respect to each such corporation."

   (B) Applicable provision. For purposes of this paragraph, an applicable provision is any provision of law (other than this part) which incorporates the definition of controlled group of corporations under subsection (a).

In 2004, P.L. 108-357, Sec. 900(a), substituted "possessing" for "possessing—(A) at least 80 percent of the total combined voting power of all classes of stock entitled to vote or at least 80 percent of the total value of shares of all classes of the stock of each corporation, and (B)" in para. (a)(2) . . . Sec. 900(b), added para. (f)(5), effective for tax. yrs. begin. after 10/22/2004.
In 1988, P.L. 100-647, Sec. 1018(s)(3)(A), substituted "paragraphs (1), (2), and (3) of subsection (e)" for "subsection (e)(1)" in subpara. (d)(1)(B), effective for tax. yrs. begin. after 11/10/88.
In 1986, P.L. 99-514, Sec. 1024(c)(17), substituted "section 801" for "section 801 or section 821" in subpara. (b)(2)(D), effective for tax. yrs. begin. after 12/31/86.
In 1984, P.L. 98-369, Sec. 211(b)(22), substituted "section 801" for "section 802" in para. (a)(4) and subpara. (b)(2)(D), effective for tax. yrs. begin. after 12/31/83.
In 1976, P.L. 94-455, Sec. 1906(b)(13)(A), substituted "Secretary" for "Secretary or his delegate" each place it appeared in Code Sec. 1563, effective for tax. yrs. begin. after 12/31/76.
In 1970, P.L. 91-373, Sec. 102(b), 8/10/70, substituted in para. (f)(1) "by paragraphs (1) and (2) of section 3121(d)" for "in section 3306(i)."
In 1969, P.L. 91-172, Sec. 401(c), amended para. (a)(2), effective for tax. yrs. end. on or after 12/31/70.
Prior to amendment, para. (a)(2) read as follows:
"(2) Brother-sister controlled group. Two or more corporations if stock possessing at least 80 percent of the total combined voting power of all classes of stock entitled to vote or at least 80 percent of the total value of shares of all classes of stock of each of the corporations is owned (within the meaning of subsection (d)(2)) by one person who is an individual, estate, or trust."
—P.L. 91-172, Sec. 401(d)(1), deleted "or" at the end of clause (c)(2)(A)(ii), substituted "stock, or" for "stock." at the end of clause (c)(2)(A)(iii) and added new clause (c)(2)(A)(iv), effective for tax. yrs. end. on or after 12/31/70.
—P.L. 91-172, Sec. 401(d)(2), substituted "5 or fewer persons who are individuals, estates, or trusts (referred to in this subparagraph as 'common owners') own" for "a person who is an individual, estate or trust (referred to in this paragraph as 'common owner') owns", in the material preceding clause (c)(2)(B)(i) struck out "or" at the end of clause (c)(2)(B)(i), substituted "any of such common owners", "any of the common owners", and "stock, or" for "such common owner", "the common owners", and "stock.", respectively in clause (c)(2)(B)(ii), and added new clause (c)(2)(B)(iii), effective for tax. yrs. end. on or after 12/31/70.
In 1964, P.L. 88-272, Sec. 235, added Code Sec. 1563, effective for tax. yrs. end. after 12/31/63.

Sec. 1564. Repealed.

In 1990, P.L. 101-508, Sec. 11801(a)(38), repealed Code Sec. 1564, effective 11/5/90 except as provided in Sec. 11821(b) of this Act, which reads as follows:
"(b) Savings provision.—
"If—
"(1) any provision amended or repealed by this part applied to—
"(A) any transaction occurring before the date of the enactment of this Act [11/5/90],
"(B) any property acquired before such date of enactment [11/5/90], or
"(C) any item of income, loss, deduction, or credit taken into account before such date of enactment [11/5/90], and
"(2) the treatment of such transaction, property, or item under such provision would (without regard to the amendments made by this part) affect liability for tax for periods ending after such date of enactment [11/5/90],
nothing in the amendments made by this part shall be construed to affect the treatment of such transaction, property, or item for purposes of determining liability for tax for periods ending after such date of enactment [11/5/90]."
Prior to repeal, Code Sec. 1564 read as follows:
"Sec. 1564. Transitional rules in the case of certain controlled corporations.
"(a) Limitation on additional benefits.
"(1) In general. With respect to any December 31 after 1969 and before 1975, the amount of—
"(A) each additional $25,000 surtax exemption under section 1562 in excess of the first such exemption,
"(B) each additional $100,000 amount under section 535(c)(2) and (3) in excess of the first such amount, and

"(C) each additional $25,000 limitation on the small business deduction of life insurance companies under sections 804(a)(3) and 809(d)(10) in excess of the first such limitation,
otherwise allowed to the component members of a controlled group of corporations for their taxable years which include such December 31 shall be reduced to the amount set forth in the following schedule:

Taxable years including—	Surtax exemption	Amount under sec. 535(c)(2) and (3)	Small business deduction limitation
Dec. 31, 1970	$20,833	$83,333	$20,833
Dec. 31, 1971	16,667	66,667	16,667
Dec. 31, 1972	12,500	50,000	12,500
Dec. 31, 1973	8,333	33,333	8,333
Dec. 31, 1974	4,167	16,667	4,167

"(2) Election. With respect to any December 31 after 1969 and before 1975, the component members of a controlled group of corporations shall elect (at such time and in such manner as the Secretary shall by regulations prescribe) which component member of such group shall be allowed for its taxable year which includes such December 31 the surtax exemption, the amount under section 535(c)(2) and (3), or the small business deduction limitation which is not reduced under paragraph (1).
"(b) Dividends received by corporations.
"(1) General rule. If—
"(A) an election of a controlled group of corporations (as defined in paragraph (1), or in so much of paragraph (4) as relates to paragraph (1), of section 1563(a)) under section 1562(a) (relating to privilege of a controlled group of corporations to elect to have each of its component members make its returns without regard to section 1561) was made on or before April 22, 1969, and
"(B) such election is effective with respect to the taxable year of each component member of such group which includes December 31, 1969,
then, with respect to a dividend distributed on or before December 31, 1977, out of earnings and profits of a taxable year which includes a December 31 after 1969 and before 1975, subsections (a)(3) and (b) of section 243 (relating to dividends received by corporations) shall be applied to such component members comprising an affiliated group (as defined in section 243(b)(5)) in the manner set forth in paragraph (2).
"(2) Special rules.
"(A) An election under section 243(b)(2) may be made for a taxable year which includes a December 31 after 1969 and before 1975, notwithstanding that an election under section 1562(a) is in effect for the taxable year.
"(B) Section 243(b)(1)(B)(ii) shall not apply with respect to a dividend distributed on or before December 31, 1977, out of earnings and profits of a taxable year which includes a December 31 after 1969 and before 1975 for which an election under section 1562(a) is in effect, and in lieu of the percentage specified in section 243(a)(3) with respect to such dividend, the percentage shall be the percentage set forth in the following schedule:

"If the dividend is distributed out of the earnings and profits of the distributing corporation's taxable year which includes—	The percentage shall be—
December 31, 1970	87 ½ percent.
December 31, 1971	90 percent.
December 31, 1972	92 ½ percent.
December 31, 1973	95 percent.
December 31, 1974	97 ½ percent.

"(C) For taxable years which include a December 31 after 1969 for which an election under section 1562(a) is in effect, [sic] section 243(b)(3)(C)(iv) shall not be applied to limit the number of surtax exemptions.
"(c) Certain short taxable years.
If—
"(1) a corporation has a short taxable year beginning after December 31, 1969, and ending before December 31, 1974, which does not include a December 31, and
"(2) such corporation is a component member of a controlled group of corporations with respect to such taxable year (determined by applying section 1563(b) as if the last day of such taxable year were substituted for December 31),
then subsections (a) and (b) shall be applied as if the last day of such taxable year were the nearest December 31 to such day."
In 1976, P.L. 94-455, Sec. 1901(b)(1)(J)(vi), substituted "sections 804(a)(3)" for "sections 804(a)(4)" in subpara. (a)(1)(C), effective for tax. yrs. begin. after 12/31/76.
—P.L. 94-455, Sec. 1901(b)(21)(A)(ii), substituted "[sic] section 243(b)(3)(C)(iv)" for "section 243(b)(3)(C)(v)" in subpara. (b)(2)(C), effective for tax. yrs. begin. after 12/31/76.
—P.L. 94-455, Sec. 1906(b)(13)(A), substituted "Secretary" for "Secretary or his delegate" in para. (a)(2), effective for tax. yrs. begin. after 12/31/76.
In 1969, P.L. 91-172, Sec. 401(b)(1), added Code Sec. 1564, effective for tax. yrs. begin. after 12/31/69.

Subtitle B.—Estate and Gift Taxes

Chapter
11. Estate tax.
12. Gift tax.
13. Tax on generation-skipping transfers.
14. Special valuation rules.
15. Gifts and bequests from expatriates.

In 2008, P.L. 110-245, Sec. 301(b)(2), added the item for Chapter 15.
In 1990, P.L. 101-508, Sec. 11602(c), added the item for Chapter 14.
In 1986, P.L. 99-514, Sec. 1431(b), amended the item for Chapter 13. Prior to amendment, the item for Chapter 13 read as follows:
"13. Tax on certain generation-skipping transfers."
In 1976, P.L. 94-455, Sec. 2006(b)(1), added the item for Chapter 13.

CHAPTER 11.—ESTATE TAX

Subchapter
A. Estates of citizens or residents.
B. Estates of nonresidents not citizens.
C. Miscellaneous.

Subchapter A.—Estates of Citizens or Residents

Part
 I. Tax imposed.
 II. Credits against tax.
 III. Gross estate.
 IV. Taxable estate.

PART I.—TAX IMPOSED

Sec.
2001. Imposition and rate of tax.
2002. Liability for payment.

In 1976, P.L. 94-455, Sec. 2001(c)(1)(N)(i), amended Sec. 2001 to read "Imposition and rate of tax."

Sec. 2001. Imposition and rate of tax.

(a) Imposition.

A tax is hereby imposed on the transfer of the taxable estate of every decedent who is a citizen or resident of the United States.

(b) Computation of tax.

The tax imposed by this section shall be the amount equal to the excess (if any) of—

(1) a tentative tax computed under subsection (c) on the sum of—

(A) the amount of the taxable estate, and

(B) the amount of the adjusted taxable gifts, over

(2) the aggregate amount of tax which would have been payable under chapter 12 with respect to gifts made by the decedent after December 31, 1976, if the modifications described in subsection (g) had been applicable at the time of such gifts.

For purposes of paragraph (1)(B), the term "adjusted taxable gifts" means the total amount of the taxable gifts (within the meaning of section 2503) made by the decedent after December 31, 1976, other than gifts which are includible in the gross estate of the decedent.

• **Caution:** Code Sec. 2001(c), following, was amended by P.L. 107-16, the Economic Growth and Tax Relief Reconciliation Act of 2001 (EGTRRA) and further amended by Sec. 302, P.L. 111-312. These provisions generally sunset for tax years beginning after 12/31/2012. For sunset provisions, see Sec. 901, P.L. 107-16 reproduced in history notes for this Code Sec.

(c) Rate schedule.

If the amount with respect to which the tentative tax to be computed is:	the tentative tax is:
Not over $10,000	18 percent of such amount.
Over $10,000 but not over $20,000	$1,800, plus 20 percent of the excess of such amount over $10,000.
Over $20,000 but not over $40,000	$3,800, plus 22 percent of the excess of such amount over $20,000.
Over $40,000 but not over $60,000	$8,200, plus 24 percent of the excess of such amount over $40,000.
Over $60,000 but not over $80,000	$13,000, plus 26 percent of the excess of such amount over $60,000.
Over $80,000 but not over $100,000	$18,200, plus 28 percent of the excess of such amount over $80,000.
Over $100,000 but not over $150,000	$23,800, plus 30 percent of the excess of such amount over $100,000.
Over $150,000 but not over $250,000	$38,800, plus 32 percent of the excess of such amount over $150,000.
Over $250,000 but not over $500,000	$70,800, plus 34 percent of the excess of such amount over $250,000.
Over $500,000	$155,800, plus 35 percent of the excess of such amount over $500,000.

(2) Repealed.

(d) Adjustment for gift tax paid by spouse.

For purposes of subsection (b)(2), if—

(1) the decedent was the donor of any gift one-half of which was considered under section 2513 as made by the decedent's spouse, and

(2) the amount of such gift is includible in the gross estate of the decedent,

any tax payable by the spouse under chapter 12 on such gift (as determined under section 2012(d)) shall be treated as a tax payable with respect to a gift made by the decedent.

(e) Coordination of sections 2513 and 2035.

If—

(1) the decedent's spouse was the donor of any gift one-half of which was considered under section 2513 as made by the decedent, and

(2) the amount of such gift is includible in the gross estate of the decedent's spouse by reason of section 2035,

such gift shall not be included in the adjusted taxable gifts of the decedent for purposes of subsection (b)(1)(B), and the aggregate amount determined under subsection (b)(2) shall be reduced by the amount (if any) determined under subsection (d) which was treated as a tax payable by the decedent's spouse with respect to such gift.

(f) Valuation of gifts.

(1) In general. If the time has expired under section 6501 within which a tax may be assessed under chapter 12 (or under corresponding provisions of prior laws) on—

(A) the transfer of property by gift made during a preceding calendar period (as defined in section 2502(b)); or

(B) an increase in taxable gifts required under section 2701(d),

the value thereof shall, for purposes of computing the tax under this chapter, be the value as finally determined for purposes of chapter 12.

(2) Final determination. For purposes of paragraph (1), a value shall be treated as finally determined for purposes of chapter 12 if—

(A) the value is shown on a return under such chapter and such value is not contested by the Secretary before the expiration of the time referred to in paragraph (1) with respect to such return;

(B) in a case not described in subparagraph (A), the value is specified by the Secretary and such value is not timely contested by the taxpayer; or

(C) the value is determined by a court or pursuant to a settlement agreement with the Secretary.

For purposes of subparagraph (A), the value of an item shall be treated as shown on a return if the item is disclosed in the return, or in a statement attached to the return, in a manner adequate to apprise the Secretary of the nature of such item.

(g) Modifications to gift tax payable to reflect different tax rates.

For purposes of applying subsection (b)(2) with respect to 1 or more gifts, the rates of tax under subsection (c) in effect at the decedent's death shall, in lieu of the rates of tax in effect at the time of such gifts, be used both to compute—

(1) the tax imposed by chapter 12 with respect to such gifts, and

(2) the credit allowed against such tax under section 2505, including in computing—

(A) the applicable credit amount under section 2505(a)(1), and

(B) the sum of the amounts allowed as a credit for all preceding periods under section 2505(a)(2).

In 2010, P.L. 111-312, Sec. 101(a)(1), substituted "December 31, 2012" for "December 31, 2010" both places it appeared in Sec. 901 of P.L. 107-16, [see below] effective as if included in the enactment of P.L. 107-16, EGTRRA, 6/7/2001.

—P.L. 111-312, Sec. 302(a)(2)(A), substituted "Over $500,000 ..... $155,800, plus 35 percent of the excess of such amount over $500,000." for "Over $500,000 but not over $750,000 .....$155,800, plus 37 percent of the excess of such amount over $500,000. Over $750,000 but not over $1,000,000 ..... $248,300, plus 39 percent of the excess of such amount over $750,000. Over $1,000,000 but not over $1,250,000 ..... $345,800 plus 41 percent of the excess of such amount over $1,000,000. Over $1,250,000 but not over $1,500,000 ..... $448,300, plus 43 percent of the excess of such amount over $1,250,000. Over $1,500,000 but not over $2,000,000 ..... $555,800, plus 45 percent of the excess of such amount over $1,500,000. Over $2,000,000 but not over $2,500,000 ..... $780,800, plus 49 percent of the excess of such amount over $2,000,000. Over $2,500,000 ..... $1,025,800, plus 50% of the excess over $2,500,000." in the table in para. (c)(1) ... Sec. 302(a)(2)(B), deleted "(1) In general." in subsec. (c) ... Sec. 302(a)(2)(C), deleted para. (c)(2) ... Sec. 302(d)(1)(A), substituted "if the modifications described in subsection (g)" for "if the provisions of subsection (c) (as in effect at the decedent's death)" in para. (b)(2) ... Sec. 302(d)(1)(B), added subsec. (g), effective for estates of decedents dying, generation-skipping transfers, and gifts made, after 12/31/2009.

Prior to amendment [by Sec. 302(a)(2)(A)-(C) of this Act], subsec. (c) read as follows:

"(c) Rate schedule.

"(1) In general.

If the amount with respect to which the tentative tax to be computed is:	the tentative tax is:
Not over $10,000	18 percent of such amount.
Over $10,000 but not over $20,000	$1,800, plus 20 percent of the excess of such amount over $10,000.
Over $20,000 but not over $40,000	$3,800, plus 22 percent of the excess of such amount over $20,000.
Over $40,000 but not over $60,000	$8,200, plus 24 percent of such amount over $40,000.
Over $60,000 but not over $80,000	$13,000, plus 26 percent of the excess of such amount over $60,000.
Over $80,000 but not over $100,000	$18,200, plus 28 percent of the excess of such amount over $80,000.
Over $100,000 but not over $150,000	$23,800, plus 30 percent of the excess of such amount over $100,000.
Over $150,000 but not over $250,000	$38,800, plus 32 percent of the excess of such amount over $150,000.
Over $250,000 but not over $500,000	$70,800, plus 34 percent of the excess of such amount over $250,000.
Over $500,000 but not over $750,000	$155,800, plus 37 percent of the excess of such amount over $500,000.
Over $750,000 but not over $1,000,000	$248,300, plus 39 percent of the excess of such amount over $750,000.
Over $1,000,000 but not over $1,250,000	$345,800 plus 41 percent of the excess of such amount over $1,000,000.
Over $1,250,000 but not over $1,500,000	$448,300, plus 43 percent of the excess of such amount over $1,250,000.
Over $1,500,000 but not over $2,000,000	$555,800, plus 45 percent of the excess of such amount over $1,500,000.
Over $2,000,000 but not over $2,500,000	$780,800, plus 49 percent of the excess of such amount over $2,000,000.
Over $2,500,000	$1,025,800, plus 50% of the excess over $2,500,000.

"(2) Phasedown of maximum rate of tax.

"(A) In general. In the case of estates of decedents dying, and gifts made, in calendar years after 2002 and before 2010, the tentative tax under this subsection shall be determined by using a table prescribed by the Secretary (in lieu of using the table contained in paragraph (1)) which is the same as such table; except that—

"(i) the maximum rate of tax for any calendar year shall be determined in the table under subparagraph (B), and

"(ii) the brackets and the amounts setting forth the tax shall be adjusted to the extent necessary to reflect the adjustments under subparagraph (A).

"(B) Maximum rate.

In calendar year:	The maximum rate is:
2003	49 percent
2004	48 percent
2005	47 percent
2006	46 percent
2007, 2008, and 2009	45 percent"

—P.L. 111-312, Sec. 304, of this Act, provides:

"Sec. 304. Application of EGTRRA sunset to this title..

"Section 901 of the Economic Growth and Tax Relief Reconciliation Act of 2001 [P.L. 107-16, see below] shall apply to the amendments made by this title."

In 2002, P.L. 107-358, Sec. 2, added subsec. (c) in Sec. 901 of P.L. 107-16 [see below], effective 12/17/2002.

In 2001, P.L. 107-16, Sec. 511(a), amended para. (c)(1) ... Sec. 511(b), deleted para. (c)(2), effective for estates of decedents dying, and gifts made, after 12/31/2001.

Prior to amendment, para. (c)(1) read as follows:

"(1) In general.

If the amount with respect to which the tentative tax to be computed is:	the tentative tax is:
Not over $10,000	18 percent of such amount.
Over $10,000 but not over $20,000	$1,800, plus 20 percent of the excess of such amount over $10,000.
Over $20,000 but not over $40,000	$3,800, plus 22 percent of the excess of such amount over $20,000.
Over $40,000 but not over $60,000	$8,200, plus 24 percent of the excess of such amount over $40,000.

Over $60,000 but not over $80,000	$13,000, plus 26 percent of the excess of such amount over $60,000.
Over $80,000 but not over $100,000	$18,200, plus 28 percent of the excess of such amount over $80,000.
Over $100,000 but not over $150,000	$23,800, plus 30 percent of the excess of such amount over $100,000.
Over $150,000 but not over $250,000	$38,800, plus 32 percent of the excess of such amount over $150,000.
Over $250,000 but not over $500,000	$70,800, plus 34 percent of the excess of such amount over $250,000.
Over $500,000 but not over $750,000	$155,800, plus 37 percent of the excess of such amount over $500,000.
Over $750,000 but not over $1,000,000	$248,300, plus 39 percent of the excess of such amount over $750,000.
Over $1,000,000 but not over $1,250,000	$345,800 plus 41 percent of the excess of such amount over $1,000,000.
Over $1,250,000 but not over $1,500,000	$448,300, plus 43 percent of the excess of such amount over $1,250,000.
Over $1,500,000 but not over $2,000,000	$555,800, plus 45 percent of the excess of such amount over $1,500,000.
Over $2,000,000 but not over $2,500,000	$780,800, plus 49 percent of the excess of such amount over $2,000,000.
Over $2,500,000 but not over $3,000,000	$1,025,800, plus 53% of the excess over $2,500,000.
Over $3,000,000............	$1,290,800, plus 55% of the excess over $3,000,000."

Prior to deletion, para. (c)(2) read as follows:

"(2) Phaseout of graduated rates and unified credit. The tentative tax determined under paragraph (1) shall be increased by an amount equal to 5 percent of so much of the amount (with respect to which the tentative tax is to be computed) as exceeds $10,000,000, but the amount does not exceed the amount at which the average tax rate under this section is 55 percent."

—P.L. 107-16, Sec. 511(c), added para. (c)(2), effective for estates of decedents dying, and gifts made, after 12/31/2002.

—P.L. 107-16, Sec. 901, of this Act [as amended by Sec. 2 of P.L. 107-358 and Sec. 101(a)(1) of P.L. 111-312, see above], reads as follows:

"Sec. 901. Sunset of provisions of Act.

"(a) In general. All provisions of, and amendments made by, this Act shall not apply—

"(1) to taxable, plan, or limitation years beginning after December 31, 2012, or

"(2) in the case of title V, to estates of decedents dying, gifts made, or generation-skipping transfers, after December 31, 2012.

"(b) Application of certain laws. The Internal Revenue Code of 1986 and the Employee Retirement Income Security Act of 1974 shall be applied and administered to years, estates, gifts, and transfers described in subsection (a) as if the provisions and amendments described in subsection (a) had never been enacted.

"(c) Exception. Subsection (a) shall not apply to section 803 (relating to no federal income tax on restitution received by victims of the Nazi regime or their heirs or estates)."

In **1998**, P.L. 105-277, Sec. 4003(c), added a sentence at the end of para. (f)(2), effective for gifts made after 8/5/97.

—P.L. 105-206, Sec. 6007(e)(2)(B), amended subsec. (f), effective for gifts made after 8/5/97.

Prior to amendment, subsec. (f) read as follows:

"(f) Valuation of gifts. If—

"(1) the time has expired within which a tax may be assessed under chapter 12 (or under corresponding provisions of prior laws) on the transfer of property by gift made during a preceding calendar period (as defined in section 2502(b)), and

"(2) the value of such gift is shown on the return for such preceding calendar period or is disclosed in such return, or in a statement attached to the return, in a manner adequate to apprise the Secretary of the nature of such gift,

the value of such gift shall, for purposes of computing the tax under this chapter, be the value of such gift as finally determined for purposes of chapter 12."

In **1997**, P.L. 105-34, Sec. 501(a)(1)(D), substituted "the amount at which the average tax rate under this section is 55 percent" for "$21,040,000" in para. (c)(2), effective for estates of decedents dying, and gifts made, after 12/31/97.

—P.L. 105-34, Sec. 506(a), added subsec. (f), effective for gifts made after 8/5/97.

In **1993**, P.L. 103-66, Sec. 13208(a), substituted

"Over $2,500,000 but not over $3,000,000	$1,025,800, plus 53% of the excess over $2,500,000.
Over $3,000,000............	$1,290,800, plus 55% of the excess over $3,000,000.
"Over $2,500,000.	$1,025,800, plus 50 percent of the excess over $2,500,000."

in para. (c)(1)

—P.L. 103-66, Sec. 13208(b)(1), deleted para. (c)(2) and redesignated para. (c)(3) as (c)(2)... Sec. 13208(b)(2), deleted "($18,340,000 in the case of decedents dying, and gifts made, after 1992" after "$21,040,000" in para. (c)(2) [as redesignated by Sec. 13208(b)(1)], effective for decedents dying and gifts made after 12/31/92.

Prior to deletion, para. (c)(2) read as follows:

"(2) Phase-in of 50 percent maximum rate.

"(A) In General. In the case of decedents dying, and gifts made, before 1993, there shall be substituted for the last item in the schedule contained in paragraph (1) the items determined under this paragraph.

"(B) For 1982. In the case of decedents dying, and gifts made, in 1982, the substitution under this paragraph shall be as follows:

Over $2,500,000 but not over $3,000,000	$1,025,800, plus 53% of the excess over $2,500,000.
Over $3,000,000 but not over $3,500,000	$1,290,800, plus 57% of the excess over $3,000,000.
Over $3,500,000 but not over $4,000,000	$1,575,800, plus 61% of the excess over $3,500,000.
Over $4,000,000............	$1,880,800, plus 65% of the excess over $4,000,000.

"(C) For 1983. In the case of decedents dying, and gifts made, in 1983, the substitution under this paragraph shall be as follows:

Over $2,500,000 but not over $3,000,000	$1,025,800, plus 53% of the excess over $2,500,000.
Over $3,000,000 but not over $3,500,000	$1,290,800, plus 57% of the excess over $3,000,000.
Over $3,500,000............	$1,575,800, plus 60% of the excess over $3,500,000.

"(D) After 1983 and before 1993. In the case of decedents dying, and gifts made, after 1983 and before 1993 the substitution under this paragraph shall be as follows:

Over $2,500,000 but not over $3,000,000	$1,025,800, plus 53% of the excess over $2,500,000.
Over $3,000,000............	$1,290,800, plus 55% of the excess over $3,000,000.

In **1987**, P.L. 100-203, Sec. 10401(a)(1), substituted "1993" for "1988" in subpara. (c)(2)(A)... Sec. 10401(a)(2), substituted "after 1983 and before 1993" for "in 1984, 1985, 1986, or 1987" in subpara. (c)(2)(D)... Sec. 10401(a)(3), amended the heading of subpara. (c)(2)(D)... Sec. 10401(b)(1), added para. (c)(3) ... Sec. 10401(b)(2)(A)(i), substituted "under subsection (c)" for "in accordance with the rate schedule set forth in subsection (c)" in para. (b)(1)... Sec. 10401(b)(2)(A)(ii), substituted "the provisions of subsection (c) (as in effect at the decedent's death)" for "the rate schedule set forth in subsection (c) (as in effect at the decedent's death)" in para. (b)(2), effective for decedents dying, and gifts made, after 12/31/87.

Prior to amendment, the heading for subpara. (c)(2)(D) read:

"(D) For 1984, 1985, 1986, or 1987."

In **1984**, P.L. 98-369, Sec. 21(a)(1), and (2), substituted "1988" for "1985" in subpara. (c)(2)(A), and substituted "1984, 1985, 1986, or 1987" for "1984" each place it appears in subpara. (c)(2)(D), effective for the estates of decedents dying after, and gifts made after 12/31/83.

—P.L. 98-369, Sec. 641 and 642, provide:

"SEC. 641. CLARIFICATION OF TREATMENT OF CERTAIN EXEMPTIONS FOR PURPOSES OF THE FEDERAL ESTATE AND GIFT TAXES.

"(a) *General rule.*—Nothing in any provision of law exempting any property (or interest therein) from taxation shall exempt the transfer of such property (or interest therein) from Federal estate, gift, and generation-skipping transfer taxes. In the case of any provision of law enacted after the date of the enactment of this Act, such provision shall not be treated as exempting the transfer of property from Federal estate, gift, and generation-skipping transfer taxes unless it refers to the appropriate provisions of the Internal Revenue Code of 1954.

"(b) *Effective date.*—

"(1) In general.—The provisions of subsection (a) shall apply to the estates of decedents dying, gifts made, and transfers made on or after June 19, 1984.

"(2) Treatment of certain transfers treated as taxable.—The provisions of subsection (a) shall also apply in the case of any transfer of property (or interest therein) if at any time there was filed an estate or gift tax return showing such transfer as subject to Federal estate or gift tax.

"(3) No inference.—No inference shall arise from paragraphs (1) and (2) that any transfer of property (or interest therein) before June 19, 1984, is exempt from Federal estate and gift taxes.

"SEC. 642. REPORTS WITH TRANSFERS OF PUBLIC HOUSING BONDS.

"(a) *General rule.*—With respect to transfers of public housing bonds occurring after December 31, 1983, and before June 19, 1984, the taxpayer shall report the date and amount of such transfer and such other information as the Secretary of the Treasury or his delegate shall prescribe by regulations to allow the determination of the tax and interest due if it is ultimately determined that such transfers are subject to estate, gift, or generation-skipping tax."

In **1981**, P.L. 97-34, Sec. 402(a), substituted "Over $2,500,000 .... $1,025,800, plus 50% of the excess over $2,500,000" for "Over $2,500,000" and all that follows in subsec. (c)... Sec. 402(b)(1), substituted "(c) Rate Schedule.— (1) In General.—" for "(c) Rate Schedule." in subsec. (c)... Sec. 402(b)(2), added

for

Estate taxes   Code Sec. 2002

para. (c)(2)... Sec. 402(c), amended para. (b)(2), effective for estates of decedents dying, and gifts made after 12/31/81.
Prior to amendments subsec. (c) read as follows:
"(c) Rate schedule.

"If the amount with respect to which the tentative tax to be computed is:	the tentative tax is:
Not over $10,000	18 percent of such amount.
Over $10,000 but not over $20,000	$1,800, plus 20 percent of the excess of such amount over $10,000.
Over $20,000 but not over $40,000	$3,800, plus 22 percent of the excess of such amount over $20,000.
Over $40,000 but not over $60,000	$8,200, plus 24 percent of the excess of such amount over $40,000.
Over $60,000 but not over $80,000	$13,000, plus 26 percent of the excess of such amount over $60,000.
Over $80,000 but not over $100,000	$18,200, plus 28 percent of the excess of such amount over $80,000.
Over $100,000 but not over $150,000	$23,800, plus 30 percent of the excess of such amount over $100,000.
Over $150,000 but not over $250,000	$38,800, plus 32 percent of the excess of such amount over $150,000.
Over $250,000 but not over $500,000	$70,800, plus 34 percent of the excess of such amount over $250,000.
Over $500,000 but not over $750,000	$155,800, plus 37 percent of the excess of such amount over $500,000.
Over $750,000 but not over $1,000,000	$248,300, plus 39 percent of the excess of such amount over $750,000.
Over $1,000,000 but not over $1,250,000	$345,800, plus 41 percent of the excess of such amount over $1,000,000.
Over $1,250,000 but not over $1,500,000	$448,300, plus 43 percent of the excess of such amount over $1,250,000.
Over $1,500,000 but not over $2,000,000	$555,800, plus 45 percent of the excess of such amount over $1,500,000.
Over $2,000,000 but not over $2,500,000	$780,800, plus 49 percent of the excess of such amount over $2,000,000.
Over $2,500,000 but not over $3,000,000	$1,025,800, plus 53 percent of the excess of such amount over $2,500,000.
Over $3,000,000 but not over $3,500,000	$1,290,800, plus 57 percent of the excess of such amount over $3,000,000.
Over $3,500,000 but not over $4,000,000	$1,575,800, plus 61 percent of the excess of such amount over $3,500,000.
Over $4,000,000 but not over $4,500,000	$1,880,800, plus 65 percent of the excess of such amount over $4,000,000.
Over $4,500,000 but not over $5,000,000	$2,205,800, plus 69 percent of of the excess of such amount over $4,500,000.
Over $5,000,000	$2,550,800, plus 70 percent of the excess of such amount over $5,000,000."

Prior to amendment para. (b)(2) read as follows:
"(2) the aggregate amount of tax payable under chapter 12 with respect to gifts made by the decedent after December 31, 1976."

In 1978, P.L. 95-600, Sec. 702(h)(1), added subsec. (e), effective for estates of decedents dying after 12/31/76, except for transfers made before 1/1/77.

In 1976, P.L. 94-455, Sec. 2001(a)(1), amended Code Sec. 2001, effective for estates of decedents dying after 12/31/76.
Prior to amendment, Code Sec. 2001 read as follows:
"Sec. 2001. Rate of tax.

"A tax computed in accordance with the following table is hereby imposed on the transfer of the taxable estate, determined as provided in section 2051, of every decedent, citizen or resident of the United States dying after the date of enactment of this title:

"If the taxable estate is:	The tax shall be:
Not over $5,000	3% of the taxable estate.
Over $5,000 but not over $10,000.	$150, plus 7% of excess over $5,000.
Over $10,000 but not over $20,000.	$500, plus 11% of excess over $10,000.
Over $20,000 but not over $30,000.	$1,600, plus 14% of excess over $20,000.
Over $30,000 but not over $40,000.	$3,000, plus 18% of excess over $30,000.
Over $40,000 but not over $50,000.	$4,800, plus 22% of excess over $40,000.
Over $50,000 but not over $60,000.	$7,000, plus 25% of excess over $50,000.
Over $60,000 but not over $100,000.	$9,500, plus 28% of excess over $60,000.
Over $100,000 but not over $250,000.	$20,700, plus 30% of excess over $100,000.
Over $250,000 but not over $500,000.	$65,700, plus 32% of excess over $250,000.
Over $500,000 but not over $750,000.	$145,700, plus 35% of excess over $500,000.
Over $750,000 but not over $1,000,000.	$233,200, plus 37% of excess over $750,000.
Over $1,000,000 but not over $1,250,000.	$325,700, plus 39% of excess over $1,000,000.
Over $1,250,000 but not over $1,500,000.	$423,200, plus 42% of excess over $1,250,000.
Over $1,500,000 but not over $2,000,000.	$528,200, plus 45% of excess over $1,500,000.
Over $2,000,000 but not over $2,500,000.	$753,200, plus 49% of excess over $2,000,000.
Over $2,500,000 but not over $3,000,000.	$998,200, plus 53% of excess over $2,500,000.
Over $3,000,000 but not over $3,500,000.	$1,263,200, plus 56% of excess over $3,000,000.
Over $3,500,000 but not over $4,000,000.	$1,543,200, plus 59% of excess over $3,500,000.
Over $4,000,000 but not over $5,000,000.	$1,838,200, plus 63% of excess over $4,000,000.
Over $5,000,000 but not over $6,000,000.	$2,468,200, plus 67% of excess over $5,000,000.
Over $6,000,000 but not over $7,000,000.	$3,138,200, plus 70% of excess over $6,000,000.
Over $7,000,000 but not over $8,000,000.	$3,838,200, plus 73% of excess over $7,000,000.
Over $8,000,000 but not over $10,000,000.	$4,568,200, plus 76% of excess over $8,000,000.
Over $10,000,000	$6,088,200, plus 77% of excess over $10,000,000."

Sec. 2002. Liability for payment.

The tax imposed by this chapter shall be paid by the executor.

In 1989, P.L. 101-239, Sec. 7304(b)(2)(A), substituted "The" for "Except as provided in section 2210, the", effective for estates of decedents dying after 7/12/89.
In 1984, P.L. 98-369, Sec. 544(b)(1), amended Code Sec. 2002, effective for those estates of decedents which are required to file returns on a date (including any extensions) after 7/18/84.
Prior to amendment, Code Sec. 2002 read as follows:
"Sec. 2002. Liability for payment.

"The tax imposed by this chapter shall be paid by the executor."
In 1976, P.L. 94-455, Sec. 2010, provided as follows:
"Sec. 2010. Credit against certain estate taxes
"(a) In general.

"Subject to the provisions of subsections (b), (c), and (d), credit against the tax imposed by chapter 11 of the Internal Revenue Code of 1954 (relating to estate tax) with respect to the estate of La Vere Redfield shall be allowed by the Secretary of the Treasury or his delegate for the conveyance of real property located within the boundaries of the Toiyabe National Forest.
"(b) Amount of credit.

"The amount treated as a credit shall be equal to the fair market value of the real property transferred as of the valuation date used for purposes of the tax imposed (and interest thereon) by chapter 11 of the Internal Revenue Code of 1954.
"(c) Deed requirements.

"The provisions of this section shall apply only if the executrixes of the estate execute a deed (in accordance with the laws of the State in which such real estate is situated) transferring title to the United States which is satisfactory to the Attorney General or his designee.
"(d) Acceptance as National Forest.

"The provisions of this section shall apply only if the real property transferred is accepted by the Secretary of Agriculture and added to the Toiyabe National Forest. The lands shall be transferred to the Secretary of Agriculture without reimbursement or payment from the Department of Agriculture.
"(e) Interest.

"Unless the Secretary of Agriculture determines and certifies to the Secretary of the Treasury that there has been an expeditious transfer of the real property under this section, no interest payable with respect to the tax imposed by chapter 11 of

2,967

Code Sec. 2002 — Estate taxes

the Internal Revenue Code of 1954 shall be deemed to be waived by reason of the provisions of this section for any period before the date of such transfer.

"(f) Effective date.

"The provisions of this section shall be effective on the date of the enactment of this Act [10/4/76]."

PART II.—CREDITS AGAINST TAX

Sec.
2010. Unified credit against estate tax.
2011. Credit for State death taxes.
2012. Credit for gift tax.
2013. Credit for tax on prior transfers.
2014. Credit for foreign death taxes.
2015. Credit for death taxes on remainders.
2016. Recovery of taxes claimed as credit.

In 2004, P.L. 108-311, Sec. 408(a)(20), added item 2011.
In 2001, P.L. 107-16, Sec. 532(c)(13), [Caution] deleted item 2011. Sec. 532(a) of this Act provides that Code Sec. 2011 shall not apply to the estates of decedents dying after 12/31/2004. Item 2011 was reinstated by Sec. 408(a)(20) of P.L. 108-311, see above.
In 1976, P.L. 94-455, Sec. 2001(c)(1)(N)(ii), added the item for Code Sec. 2010.

Sec. 2010. Unified credit against estate tax.
(a) General rule.

A credit of the applicable credit amount shall be allowed to the estate of every decedent against the tax imposed by section 2001.

(b) Adjustment to credit for certain gifts made before 1977.

The amount of the credit allowable under subsection (a) shall be reduced by an amount equal to 20 percent of the aggregate amount allowed as a specific exemption under section 2521 (as in effect before its repeal by the Tax Reform Act of 1976) with respect to gifts made by the decedent after September 8, 1976.

⌐
• **Caution:** Code Sec. 2010(c), following, was amended by Secs. 302 and 303 of P.L. 111-312, and P.L. 107-16, EGTRRA. These provisions generally sunset for tax years beginning after 12/31/2012. For specific sunset provisions, see Sec. 901, P.L. 107-16 (as amended) reproduced in history notes for this Code Sec.
⌐

(c) Applicable credit amount.

(1) In general. For purposes of this section, the applicable credit amount is the amount of the tentative tax which would be determined under section 2001(c) if the amount with respect to which such tentative tax is to be computed were equal to the applicable exclusion amount.

(2) Applicable exclusion amount. For purposes of this subsection, the applicable exclusion amount is the sum of—

(A) the basic exclusion amount, and
(B) in the case of a surviving spouse, the deceased spousal unused exclusion amount.

(3) Basic exclusion amount.

(A) In general. For purposes of this subsection, the basic exclusion amount is $5,000,000.

(B) Inflation adjustment. In the case of any decedent dying in a calendar year after 2011, the dollar amount in subparagraph (A) shall be increased by an amount equal to—

(i) such dollar amount, multiplied by
(ii) the cost-of-living adjustment determined under section 1(f)(3) for such calendar year by substituting "calendar year 2010" for "calendar year 1992" in subparagraph (B) thereof.

If any amount as adjusted under the preceding sentence is not a multiple of $10,000, such amount shall be rounded to the nearest multiple of $10,000.

(4) Deceased spousal unused exclusion amount. For purposes of this subsection, with respect to a surviving spouse of a deceased spouse dying after December 31, 2010, the term "deceased spousal unused exclusion amount" means the lesser of—

(A) the basic exclusion amount, or
(B) the excess of—
(i) the basic exclusion amount of the last such deceased spouse of such surviving spouse, over
(ii) the amount with respect to which the tentative tax is determined under section 2001(b)(1) on the estate of such deceased spouse.

(5) Special rules.

(A) Election required. A deceased spousal unused exclusion amount may not be taken into account by a surviving spouse under paragraph (2) unless the executor of the estate of the deceased spouse files an estate tax return on which such amount is computed and makes an election on such return that such amount may be so taken into account. Such election, once made, shall be irrevocable. No election may be made under this subparagraph if such return is filed after the time prescribed by law (including extensions) for filing such return.

(B) Examination of prior returns after expiration of period of limitations with respect to deceased spousal unused exclusion amount. Notwithstanding any period of limitation in section 6501, after the time has expired under section 6501 within which a tax may be assessed under chapter 11 or 12 with respect to a deceased spousal unused exclusion amount, the Secretary may examine a return of the deceased spouse to make determinations with respect to such amount for purposes of carrying out this subsection.

(6) Regulations. The Secretary shall prescribe such regulations as may be necessary or appropriate to carry out this subsection.

(d) Limitation based on amount of tax.

The amount of the credit allowed by subsection (a) shall not exceed the amount of the tax imposed by section 2001.

In 2010, P.L. 111-312, Sec. 101(a)(1), substituted "December 31, 2012" for "December 31, 2010" both places it appeared in Sec. 901, P.L. 107-16 [see below], effective as if included in the enactment of P.L. 107-16, EGTRRA, 6/7/2001.
—P.L. 111-312, Sec. 302(a)(1), amended subsec. (c), effective for estates of decedents dying, generation-skipping transfers, and gifts made, after 12/31/2009.
Prior to amendment, subsec. (c) read as follows:

"(c) Applicable credit amount.

"For purposes of this section, the applicable credit amount is the amount of the tentative tax which would be determined under the rate schedule set forth in section 2001(c) if the amount with respect to which such tentative tax is to be computed were the applicable exclusion amount determined in accordance with the following table:

In the case of estates of decedents dying during:	The applicable exclusion amount is:
2002 and 2003	$1,000,000
2004 and 2005	$1,500,000
2006, 2007, and 2008	$2,000,000
2009	$3,500,000

"

—P.L. 111-312, Sec. 303(a), deleted para. (c)(2) [as added by Sec. 302(a)(1), see above] and added paras. (c)(2)-(6), effective for estates of decedents dying and gifts made after 12/31/2010.
Prior to deletion, para. (c)(2) read as follows:
""(2) Applicable exclusion amount.

2,968

Estate taxes

"(A) In general. For purposes of this subsection, the applicable exclusion amount is $5,000,000.

"(B) Inflation adjustment. In the case of any decedent dying in a calendar year after 2011, the dollar amount in subparagraph (A) shall be increased by an amount equal to—

"(i) such dollar amount, multiplied by

"(ii) the cost-of-living adjustment determined under section 1(f)(3) for such calendar year by substituting "calendar year 2010" for "calendar year 1992" in subparagraph (B) thereof.

"If any amount as adjusted under the preceding sentence is not a multiple of $10,000, such amount shall be rounded to the nearest multiple of $10,000."

—P.L. 111-312, Sec. 304, of this Act, provides:

"Sec. 304. Application of EGTRRA sunset to this title.

"Section 901 of the Economic Growth and Tax Relief Reconciliation Act of 2001 shall apply to the amendments made by this title."

In 2002, P.L. 107-358, Sec. 2, added subsec. (c) in Sec. 901 of P.L. 107-16 [see below], effective 12/17/2002.

In 2001, P.L. 107-16, Sec. 521(a), amended the table in subsec. (c), effective for estates of decedents dying, and gifts made, after 12/31/2001.

Prior to amendment, the table in subsec. (c) read as follows:

"In the case of estates of decedents dying, and gifts made, during:	The applicable exclusion amount is:
1998	$ 625,000
1999	$ 650,000
2000 and 2001	$ 675,000
2002 and 2003	$ 700,000
2004	$ 850,000
2005	$ 950,000
2006 or thereafter	$1,000,000."

—P.L. 107-16, Sec. 901, of this Act [as amended by Sec. 2 of P.L. 107-358, and Sec. 101(a)(1), P.L. 111-312, see above], reads as follows:

"Sec. 901. Sunset of provisions of Act.

"(a) In general. All provisions of, and amendments made by, this Act shall not apply—

"(1) to taxable, plan, or limitation years beginning after December 31, 2012, or

"(2) in the case of title V, to estates of decedents dying, gifts made, or generation skipping transfers, after December 31, 2012.

"(b) Application of certain laws. The Internal Revenue Code of 1986 and the Employee Retirement Income Security Act of 1974 shall be applied and administered to years, estates, gifts, and transfers described in subsection (a) as if the provisions and amendments described in subsection (a) had never been enacted.

"(c) Exception. Subsection (a) shall not apply to section 803 (relating to no federal income tax on restitution received by victims of the Nazi regime or their heirs or estates)."

In 1997, P.L. 105-34, Sec. 501(a)(1)(A), substituted "the applicable credit amount" for "$192,800" in subsec. (a) . . . Sec. 501(a)(1)(B), redesignated subsec. (c) as subsec. (d) and added new subsec. (c), effective for estates of decedents dying, and gifts made, after 12/31/97.

In 1990, P.L. 101-508, Sec. 11801(a)(39), deleted subsec. (b) . . . Sec. 11801(c)(19)(A), redesignated subsecs. (c) and (d) as (b) and (c), effective 11/5/90, except as provided in Sec. 11821(b) of this Act, which reads as follows:

"(b) Savings provision. If

"(1) any provision amended or repealed by this part applied to—

"(A) any transaction occurring before the date of the enactment of this Act [11/5/90],

"(B) any property acquired before such date of enactment [11/5/90],

"(C) any item of income, loss, deduction, or credit taken into account before such date of enactment [11/5/90],

"(2) the treatment of such transaction, property, or item under such provision would (without regard to the amendments made by this part) affect liability for tax for periods ending after such date of enactment [11/5/90],

nothing in the amendments made by this part shall be construed to affect the treatment of such transaction, property, or item for purposes of determining liability for tax for periods ending after such date of enactment [11/5/90]."

Prior to deletion, subsec. (b) read as follows:

"(b) Phase-in of credit.

"In the case of decedents dying in:	Subsection (a) shall be applied by substituting for "$192,800" the following amount:
1982	$ 62,800
1983	79,300
1984	96,300
1985	121,800
1986	155,800."

In 1981, P.L. 97-34, Sec. 401(a)(1), substituted "$192,800" for "$47,000" in subsec. (a) . . . Sec. 401(a)(2), amended subsec. (b), effective for estates of decedents dying after 12/31/81.

Prior to amendment, subsec. (b) read as follows:

"(b) Phase-in of $47,000 credit.

"In the case of decedents dying in:	Subsection (a) shall be applied by substituting for "$47,000" the following amount:
1977	$ 30,000
1978	34,000
1979	38,000
1980	42,500"

In 1976, P.L. 94-455, Sec. 2001(a)(2), added Code Sec. 2010, effective for estates of decedents dying after 12/31/76.

Sec. 2011. Credit for State death taxes.

(a) In general.

The tax imposed by section 2001 shall be credited with the amount of any estate, inheritance, legacy, or succession taxes actually paid to any State or the District of Columbia, in respect of any property included in the gross estate (not including any such taxes paid with respect to the estate of a person other than the decedent).

> • **Caution:** Code Sec. 2011(b), following, was amended by P.L. 107-16, the Economic Growth and Tax Relief Reconciliation Act of 2001 (EGTRRA). These provisions generally sunset for tax years beginning after 12/31/2012. For specific sunset provisions, see Sec. 901, P.L. 107-16 (as amended) reproduced in history notes for this Code Sec.

(b) Amount of credit.

(1) In general. Except as provided in paragraph (2), the credit allowed by this section shall not exceed the appropriate amount stated in the following table:

If the adjusted taxable estate is:	The maximum tax credit shall be:
Not over $90,000	8/10ths of 1% of the amount by which the adjusted taxable estate exceeds $40,000.
Over $90,000 but not over $140,000.	$400 plus 1.6% of the excess over $90,000.
Over $140,000 but not over $240,000.	$1,200 plus 2.4% of the excess over $140,000.
Over $240,000 but not over $440,000.	$3,600 plus 3.2% of the excess over $240,000.
Over $440,000 but not over $640,000.	$10,000 plus 4% of the excess over $440,000.
Over $640,000 but not over $840,000.	$18,000 plus 4.8% of the excess over $640,000.
Over $840,000 but not over $1,040,000.	$27,600 plus 5.6% of the excess over $840,000.
Over $1,040,000 but not over $1,540,000.	$38,800 plus 6.4% of the excess over $1,040,000.
Over $1,540,000 but not over $2,040,000.	$70,800 plus 7.2% of the excess over $1,540,000.
Over $2,040,000 but not over $2,540,000.	$106,800 plus 8% of the excess over $2,040,000.
Over $2,540,000 but not over $3,040,000.	$146,800 plus 8.8% of the excess over $2,540,000.
Over $3,040,000 but not over $3,540,000.	$190,800 plus 9.6% of the excess over $3,040,000.
Over $3,540,000 but not over $4,040,000.	$238,800 plus 10.4% of the excess over $3,540,000.
Over $4,040,000 but not over $5,040,000.	$290,800 plus 11.2% of the excess over $4,040,000.
Over $5,040,000 but not over $6,040,000.	$402,800 plus 12% of the excess over $5,040,000.

Over $6,040,000 but not over $7,040,000.	$522,800 plus 12.8% of the excess over $6,040,000.
Over $7,040,000 but not over $8,040,000.	$650,800 plus 13.6% of the excess over $7,040,000.
Over $8,040,000 but not over $9,040,000.	$786,800 plus 14.4% of the excess over $8,040,000.
Over $9,040,000 but not over $10,040,000.	$930,800 plus 15.2% of the excess over $9,040,000.
Over $10,040,000	$1,082,800 plus 16% of the excess over $10,040,000.

(2) Reduction of maximum credit.
(A) In general. In the case of estates of decedents dying after December 31, 2001, the credit allowed by this section shall not exceed the applicable percentage of the credit otherwise determined under paragraph (1).
(B) Applicable percentage.

In the case of estates of decedents dying during:	The applicable percentage is:
2002	75 percent
2003	50 percent
2004	25 percent

(3) Adjusted taxable estate. For purposes of this section, the term "adjusted taxable estate" means the taxable estate reduced by $60,000.

(c) Period of limitations on credit.
The credit allowed by this section shall include only such taxes as were actually paid and credit therefor claimed within 4 years after the filing of the return required by section 6018, except that—
(1) If a petition for redetermination of a deficiency has been filed with the Tax Court within the time prescribed in section 6213(a), then within such 4-year period or before the expiration of 60 days after the decision of the Tax Court becomes final.
(2) If, under section 6161 or 6166, an extension of time has been granted for payment of the tax shown on the return, or of a deficiency, then within such 4-year period or before the date of the expiration of the period of the extension.
(3) If a claim for refund or credit of an overpayment of tax imposed by this chapter has been filed within the time prescribed in section 6511, then within such 4-year period or before the expiration of 60 days from the date of mailing by certified mail or registered mail by the Secretary to the taxpayer of a notice of the disallowance of any part of such claim, or before the expiration of 60 days after a decision by any court of competent jurisdiction becomes final with respect to a timely suit instituted upon such claim, whichever is later.
Refund based on the credit may (despite the provisions of sections 6511 and 6512) be made if claim therefor is filed within the period above provided. Any such refund shall be made without interest.

(d) Limitation in cases involving deduction under section 2053(d).
In any case where a deduction is allowed under section 2053(d) for an estate, succession, legacy, or inheritance tax imposed by a State or the District of Columbia upon a transfer for public, charitable, or religious uses described in section 2055 or 2106(a)(2), the allowance of the credit under this section shall be subject to the following conditions and limitations:
(1) The taxes described in subsection (a) shall not include any estate, succession, legacy, or inheritance tax for which such deduction is allowed under section 2053(d).
(2) The credit shall not exceed the lesser of—
(A) the amount stated in subsection (b) on an adjusted taxable estate determined by allowing such deduction authorized by section 2053(d), or
(B) that proportion of the amount stated in subsection (b) on an adjusted taxable estate determined without regard to such deduction authorized by section 2053(d) as (i) the amount of the taxes described in subsection (a), as limited by the provisions of paragraph (1) of this subsection, bears to (ii) the amount of the taxes described in subsection (a) before applying the limitation contained in paragraph (1) of this subsection.
(3) If the amount determined under subparagraph (B) of paragraph (2) is less than the amount determined under subparagraph (A) of that paragraph, then for purposes of subsection (d) such lesser amount shall be the maximum credit provided by subsection (b).

(e) Limitation based on amount of tax.
The credit provided by this section shall not exceed the amount of the tax imposed by section 2001, reduced by the amount of the unified credit provided by section 2010.

• *Caution:* Code Sec. 2011(f), following, was originally added as subsec. (g) by P.L. 107-16, the Economic Growth and Tax Relief Reconciliation Act of 2001 (EGTRRA). These provisions generally sunset for tax years beginning after 12/31/2012. For specific sunset provisions, see Sec. 901, P.L. 107-16 (as amended) reproduced in history notes for this Code Sec.

(f) Termination.
This section shall not apply to the estates of decedents dying after December 31, 2004.

In 2010, P.L. 111-312, Sec. 101(a)(1), substituted "December 31, 2012" for "December 31, 2010" both places it appeared in Sec. 901, P.L. 107-16 [see below], effective as if included in the enactment of P.L. 107-16, EGTRRA, 6/7/2001.
In 2002, P.L. 107-358, Sec. 2, added subsec. (c) in Sec. 901 of P.L.107-16 [see below], effective 12/17/2002.
—P.L. 107-134, Sec. 103(b)(1), deleted subsec. (d) and redesignated subsecs. (e), (f) and (g) as subsecs. (d), (e) and (f), respectively, effective as provided in Sec. 103(d) of this Act, which reads as follows:
"(d) Effective date; waiver of limitations—
"(1) Effective date. The amendments made by this section shall apply to estates of decedents—
"(A) dying on or after September 11, 2001, and
"(B) in the case of individuals dying as a result of the April 19, 1995, terrorist attack, dying on or after April 19, 1995.
"(2) Waiver of limitations. If refund or credit of any overpayment of tax resulting from the amendments made by this section is prevented at any time before the close of the 1-year period beginning on the date of the enactment of this Act by the operation of any law or rule of law (including res judicata), such refund or credit may nevertheless be made or allowed if claim therefor is filed before the close of such period."
Prior to deletion, subsec. (d) read as follows:
"(d) Basic estate tax.
"The basic estate tax and the estate tax imposed by the Revenue Act of 1926 shall be 125 percent of the amount determined to be the maximum credit provided by subsection (b). The additional estate tax shall be the difference between the tax imposed by section 2001 or 2101 and the basic estate tax."
In 2001, P.L. 107-16, Sec. 531(a)(1), substituted "credit. (1) In general. Except as provided in paragraph (2), the credit allowed" for "credit. The credit allowed" in the heading and opening sentence of subsec. (b)...Sec. 531(a)(2), substituted "(3) Adjustable taxable estate. For purposes" for "For purposes" in the last sentence of subsec. (b)...Sec. 531(a)(3), added para. (b)(2), effective for estates of decedents dying after 12/31/2001.

—P.L. 107-16, Sec. 532(a), added subsec. (g) [prior to redesignation as subsec. (f) by Sec. 103(b)(1) of P.L. 107-134, see above], effective for estates of decedents dying, and generation-skipping transfers, after 12/31/2004.

—P.L. 107-16, Sec. 901, of this Act [as amended by Sec. 2, P.L. 107-358, and Sec. 101(a)(1), P.L. 111-312, see above], reads as follows:

"SEC. 901. SUNSET OF PROVISIONS OF ACT.

"(a) In general. All provisions of, and amendments made by, this Act shall not apply—

"(1) to taxable, plan, or limitation years beginning after December 31, 2012, or

"(2) in the case of title V, to estates of decedents dying, gifts made, or generation skipping transfers, after December 31, 2012.

"(b) Application of certain laws. The Internal Revenue Code of 1986 and the Employee Retirement Income Security Act of 1974 shall be applied and administered to years, estates, gifts, and transfers described in subsection (a) as if the provisions and amendments described in subsection (a) had never been enacted.

"(c) Exception. Subsection (a) shall not apply to section 803 (relating to no federal income tax on restitution received by victims of the Nazi regime or their heirs or estates)."

In **1981**, P.L. 97-34, Sec. 422(e)(2), substituted "6161 or 6166" for "6161, 6166 or 6166A" in para. (c)(2), effective for estates of decedents dying after 12/31/81.

In **1978**, P.L. 95-600, Sec. 703(j)(12), amended the effective date for changes made by Sec. 1902(a)(12)(B) of P.L. 94-455 to apply to estates of decedents dying after 10/4/76. See below.

In **1976**, P.L. 94-455, Sec. 1902(a)(12)(B), deleted "or Territory" from subsecs. (a) and (e), effective for gifts made after 12/31/76.

—P.L. 94-455, Sec. 1906(b)(13)(A), substituted "Secretary" for "Secretary or his delegate" in Code Sec. 2011, effective 2/1/77.

—P.L. 94-455, Sec. 2001(c)(1)(A), substituted "adjusted taxable estate" for "taxable estate" each place it appeared in subsec. (b), added the last sentence to subsec. (b), substituted "adjusted taxable estate" for "taxable estate" each place it appeared in subsec. (e), and added subsec. (f), effective for estates of decedents dying after 12/31/76.

—P.L. 94-455, Sec. 2004(f)(3), substituted "section 6161, 6166 or 6166A" for "section 6161" in para. (c)(2), effective for estates of decedents dying after 12/31/76.

In **1959**, P.L. 86-175, Sec. 3, substituted "imposed by a State or Territory or the District of Columbia upon a transfer" for "imposed upon a transfer" in subsec. (e), "such deduction" for "a deduction" in para. (e)(1), and substituted "such deduction" for "the deduction" each place it appeared in para. (e)(2), effective for decedents dying after 7/1/55.

In **1958**, P.L. 85-866, Sec. 102, deleted "or any possession of the United States," after "District of Columbia," in subsec. (a), effective for estates of decedents dying after 9/2/58.

—P.L. 85-866, Sec. 65, added para. (c)(3), effective for estates of decedents dying after 8/16/54.

In **1956**, P.L. 414, Sec. 2, added subsec. (e), effective for estates of decedents dying after 12/31/53.

Sec. 2012. Credit for gift tax.

• *Caution:* Code Sec. 2012(a), following, was amended by P.L. 107-16, EGTRRA. These provisions generally sunset for tax years beginning after 12/31/2012. For specific sunset provisions, see Sec. 901, P.L. 107-16 (as amended) reproduced in history notes for this Code Sec.

(a) In general.

If a tax on a gift has been paid under chapter 12 (sec. 2501 and following), or under corresponding provisions of prior laws, and thereafter on the death of the donor any amount in respect of such gift is required to be included in the value of the gross estate of the decedent for purposes of this chapter, then there shall be credited against the tax imposed by section 2001 the amount of the tax paid on a gift under chapter 12, or under corresponding provisions of prior laws, with respect to so much of the property which constituted the gift as is included in the gross estate, except that the amount of such credit shall not exceed an amount which bears the same ratio to the tax imposed by section 2001 (after deducting from such tax the unified credit provided by section 2010) as the value (at the time of the gift or at the time of the death, whichever is lower) of so much of the property which constituted the gift as is included in the gross estate bears to the value of the entire gross estate reduced by the aggregate amount of the charitable and marital deductions allowed under sections 2055, 2056, and 2106(a)(2).

(b) Valuation reductions.

In applying, with respect to any gift, the ratio stated in subsection (a), the value at the time of the gift or at the time of the death, referred to in such ratio, shall be reduced—

(1) by such amount as will properly reflect the amount of such gift which was excluded in determining (for purposes of section 2503(a)), or of corresponding provisions of prior laws, the total amount of gifts made during the calendar quarter (or calendar year if the gift was made before January 1, 1971) in which the gift was made;

(2) if a deduction with respect to such gift is allowed under section 2056(a) (relating to marital deduction), then by the amount of such value, reduced as provided in paragraph (1); and

(3) if a deduction with respect to such gift is allowed under sections 2055 or 2106(a)(2) (relating to charitable deduction), then by the amount of such value, reduced as provided in paragraph (1) of this subsection.

(c) Where gift considered made one-half by spouse.

Where the decedent was the donor of the gift but, under the provisions of section 2513, or corresponding provisions of prior laws, the gift was considered as made one-half by his spouse—

(1) the term "the amount of the tax paid on a gift under chapter 12", as used in subsection (a), includes the amounts paid with respect to each half of such gift, the amount paid with respect to each being computed in the manner provided in subsection (d); and

(2) in applying, with respect to such gift, the ratio stated in subsection (a), the value at the time of the gift or at the time of the death, referred to in such ratio, includes such value with respect to each half of such gift, each such value being reduced as provided in paragraph (1) of subsection (b).

(d) Computation of amount of gift tax paid.

(1) **Amount of tax.** For purposes of subsection (a), the amount of tax paid on a gift under chapter 12, or under corresponding provisions of prior laws, with respect to any gift shall be an amount which bears the same ratio to the total tax paid for the calendar quarter (or calendar year if the gift was made before January 1, 1971) in which the gift was made as the amount of such gift bears to the total amount of taxable gifts (computed without deduction of the specific exemption) for such quarter or year.

(2) **Amount of gift.** For purposes of paragraph (1), the "amount of such gift" shall be the amount included with respect to such gift in determining (for the purposes of section 2503(a), or of corresponding provisions of prior laws) the total amount of gifts made during such quarter or year, reduced by the amount of any deduction allowed with respect to such gift under section 2522, or under corresponding provisions of prior laws (relating to charitable deduction), or under section 2523 (relating to marital deduction).

(e) Section inapplicable to gifts made after December 31, 1976.

No credit shall be allowed under this section with respect to the amount of any tax paid under chapter 12 on any gift made after December 31, 1976.

In **2010**, P.L. 111-312, Sec. 101(a)(1), substituted "December 31, 2012" for "December 31, 2010" both places it appeared in Sec. 901, P.L. 107-16 [see below], effective as if included in the enactment of P.L. 107-16, EGTRRA, 6/7/2001.

In **2002**, P.L. 107-358, Sec. 2, added subsec. (c) in Sec. 901 of P.L. 107-16 [see below], effective 12/17/2002.

In **2001**, P.L. 107-16, Sec. 532(c)(1), deleted "the credit for State death taxes provided by section 2011 and" after "deducting from such tax" in subsec. (a), effective for estates of decedents dying, and generation-skipping transfers, after 12/31/2004.

—P.L. 107-16, Sec. 901, of this Act [as amended by Sec. 2, P.L. 107-358, and Sec. 101(a)(1), P.L. 111-312, see above], reads as follows:

"SEC. 901. SUNSET OF PROVISIONS OF ACT.

"(a) In general. All provisions of, and amendments made by, this Act shall not apply—

"(1) to taxable, plan, or limitation years beginning after December 31, 2012, or

"(2) in the case of title V, to estates of decedents dying, gifts made, or generation skipping transfers, after December 31, 2012.

"(b) Application of certain laws. The Internal Revenue Code of 1986 and the Employee Retirement Income Security Act of 1974 shall be applied and administered to years, estates, gifts, and transfers described in subsection (a) as if the provisions and amendments described in subsection (a) had never been enacted.

"(c) Exception. Subsection (a) shall not apply to section 803 (relating to no federal income tax on restitution received by victims of the Nazi regime or their heirs or estates)."

In **1981**, P.L. 97-34, Sec. 403(a)(2)(A), amended para. (b)(2), effective for estates of decedents dying after 12/31/81.

Prior to amendment, para. (b)(2) read as follows:

"(2) if a deduction with respect to such gift is allowed under section 2056(a) (relating to marital deduction), then by an amount which bears the same ratio to such value (reduced as provided in paragraph (1) of this subsection) as the aggregate amount of the marital deductions allowed under section 2056(a) bears to the aggregate amount of such marital deductions computed without regard to subsection (c) thereof; and"

In **1976**, P.L. 94-455, Sec. 1902(a)(1), added the heading for subsec. (b) ... substituted "deduction", then" for "deduction—then" in paras. (b)(2) and (b)(3) ... added the heading for subsec. (c) ... added the headings for subsec. (d) and para. (d)(1) ... added the heading for para. (d)(2), effective for estates of decedents dying after 10/4/76.

—P.L. 94-455, Sec. 2001(a)(3), added subsec. (e), effective for estates of decedents dying after 12/31/76.

—P.L. 94-455, Sec. 2001(c)(1)(B), substituted "provided by section 2011 and the unified credit provided by section 2010" for "provided by section 2011" in subsec. (a), effective for estates of decedents dying after 12/31/76.

In **1970**, P.L. 91-614, Sec. 102(d)(2)(A), substituted "the calendar quarter (or calendar year if the gift was made before January 1, 1971)" for "the year" in paras. (b)(1) and (d)(1) ... Sec. 102(d)(2)(B), substituted "such quarter or year" for "such year," in subsec. (d), effective for gifts made after 12/31/70.

Sec. 2013. Credit for tax on prior transfers.

(a) General rule.

The tax imposed by section 2001 shall be credited with all or a part of the amount of the Federal estate tax paid with respect to the transfer of property (including property passing as a result of the exercise or non-exercise of a power of appointment) to the decedent by or from a person (herein designated as a "transferor") who died within 10 years before, or within 2 years after, the decedent's death. If the transferor died within 2 years of the death of the decedent, the credit shall be the amount determined under subsections (b) and (c). If the transferor predeceased the decedent by more than 2 years, the credit shall be the following percentage of the amount so determined—

(1) 80 percent, if within the third or fourth years preceding the decedent's death;

(2) 60 percent, if within the fifth or sixth years preceding the decedent's death;

(3) 40 percent, if within the seventh or eighth years preceding the decedent's death; and

(4) 20 percent, if within the ninth or tenth years preceding the decedent's death.

(b) Computation of credit.

Subject to the limitation prescribed in subsection (c), the credit provided by this section shall be an amount which bears the same ratio to the estate tax paid (adjusted as indicated hereinafter) with respect to the estate of the transferor as the value of the property transferred bears to the taxable estate of the transferor (determined for purposes of the estate tax) decreased by any death taxes paid with respect to such estate. For purposes of the preceding sentence, the estate tax paid shall be the Federal estate tax paid increased by any credits allowed against such estate tax under section 2012, or corresponding provisions of prior laws, on account of gift tax, and for any credits allowed against such estate tax under this section on account of prior transfers where the transferor acquired property from a person who died within 10 years before the death of the decedent.

(c) Limitation on credit.

(1) In general. The credit provided in this section shall not exceed the amount by which—

> • **Caution:** Code Sec. 2013(c)(1)(A), following, was amended by P.L. 107-16, EGTRRA. These provisions generally sunset for tax years beginning after 12/31/2012. For specific sunset provisions, see Sec. 901, P.L. 107-16 (as amended) reproduced in history notes for this Code Sec.

(A) the estate tax imposed by section 2001 or section 2101 (after deducting the credits provided for in sections 2010, 2012, and 2014) computed without regard to this section, exceeds

(B) such tax computed by excluding from the decedent's gross estate the value of such property transferred and, if applicable, by making the adjustment hereinafter indicated.

If any deduction is otherwise allowable under section 2055 or section 2106(a)(2) (relating to charitable deduction) then, for the purpose of the computation indicated in subparagraph (B), the amount of such deduction shall be reduced by that part of such deduction which the value of such property transferred bears to the decedent's entire gross estate reduced by the deductions allowed under sections 2053 and 2054, or section 2106(a)(1) (relating to deduction for expenses, losses, etc.). For purposes of this section, the value of such property transferred shall be the value as provided for in subsection (d) of this section.

(2) Two or more transferors. If the credit provided in this section relates to property received from 2 or more transferors, the limitation provided in paragraph (1) of this subsection shall be computed by aggregating the value of the property so transferred to the decedent. The aggregate limitation so determined shall be apportioned in accordance with the value of the property transferred to the decedent by each transferor.

(d) Valuation of property transferred.

The value of property transferred to the decedent shall be the value used for the purpose of determining the Federal estate tax liability of the estate of the transferor but—

(1) there shall be taken into account the effect of the tax imposed by section 2001 or 2101, or any estate, succession, legacy, or inheritance tax, on the net value to the decedent of such property;

(2) where such property is encumbered in any manner, or where the decedent incurs any obligation imposed by the transferor with respect to such property, such encumbrance or obligation shall be taken into account in the same manner as if the amount of a gift to the decedent of such property was being determined; and

(3) if the decedent was the spouse of the transferor at the time of the transferor's death, the net value of the property transferred to the decedent shall be reduced by the amount allowed under section 2056 (relating to marital deductions) as a deduction from the gross estate of the transferor.

Estate taxes

(e) Property defined.

For purposes of this section, the term "property" includes any beneficial interest in property, including a general power of appointment (as defined in section 2041).

(f) Treatment of additional tax imposed under section 2032A.

If section 2032A applies to any property included in the gross estate of the transferor and an additional tax is imposed with respect to such property under section 2032A(c) before the date which is 2 years after the date of the decedent's death, for purposes of this section—

(1) the additional tax imposed by section 2032A(c) shall be treated as a Federal estate tax payable with respect to the estate of the transferor; and

(2) the value of such property and the amount of the taxable estate of the transferor shall be determined as if section 2032A did not apply with respect to such property.

In 2010, P.L. 111-312, Sec. 101(a)(1), substituted "December 31, 2012" for "December 31, 2010" both places it appeared in Sec. 901, P.L. 107-16 [see below], effective as if included in the enactment of P.L. 107-16, EGTRRA, 6/7/2001.

In 2002, P.L. 107-358, Sec. 2, added subsec. (c) in Sec. 901 of P.L. 107-16 [see below], effective 12/17/2002.

In 2001, P.L. 107-16, Sec. 532(c)(2), deleted "2011," after "2010," in subpara. (c)(1)(A), effective for estates of decedents dying, and generation-skipping transfers, after 12/31/2004.

—P.L. 107-16, Sec. 901, of this Act [as amended by Sec. 2, P.L. 107-358, and Sec. 101(a)(1), P.L. 111-312, see above], reads as follows:

"SEC. 901. SUNSET OF PROVISIONS OF ACT.

"(a) In general. All provisions of, and amendments made by, this Act shall not apply—

"(1) to taxable, plan, or limitation years beginning after December 31, 2012, or

"(2) in the case of title V, to estates of decedents dying, gifts made, or generation skipping transfers, after December 31, 2012.

"(b) Application of certain laws. The Internal Revenue Code of 1986 and the Employee Retirement Income Security Act of 1974 shall be applied and administered to years, estates, gifts, and transfers described in subsection (a) as if the provisions and amendments described in subsection (a) had never been enacted.

"(c) Exception. Subsection (a) shall not apply to section 803 (relating to no federal income tax on restitution received by victims of the Nazi regime or their heirs or estates)."

In 1997, P.L. 105-34, Sec. 1073(b)(2), deleted subsec. (g), effective for estates of decedents dying after 12/31/96.

Prior to deletion, subsec. (g) read as follows:

"(g) Treatment of additional tax under section 4980A.

"For purposes of this section, the estate tax paid shall not include any portion of such tax attributable to section 4980A(d)."

In 1988, P.L. 100-647, Sec. 1011A(g)(7), added subsec. (g), effective for distributions made after 12/31/86. For special rules, see Sec. 1133(c)(3) of P.L. 99-514, which reads:

"(3) Plan terminations before 1987.—The amendments made by this section shall not apply to distributions before January 1, 1988, which are made on account of the termination of a qualified employer plan if such termination occurred before January 1, 1987."

In 1986, P.L. 99-514, Sec. 1432(c)(2), deleted subsec. (g), effective for any generation-skipping transfer (within the meaning of Code Sec. 2611) made after 10/22/86. For special rules and transitional rules, see Sec. 1433(b)-(d) reproduced in note following Code Sec. 2601.

Prior to deletion, subsec. (g) read as follows:

"(g) Treatment of tax imposed on certain generation-skipping transfers. If any property was transferred to the decedent in a transfer which is taxable under section 2601 (relating to tax imposed on generation-skipping transfers) and if the deemed transferor (as defined in section 2612) is not alive at the time of such transfer, for purposes of this section—

"(1) such property shall be deemed to have passed to the decedent from the deemed transferor;

"(2) the tax payable under section 2601 on such transfer shall be treated as a Federal estate tax payable with respect to the estate of the deemed transferor; and

"(3) the amount of the taxable estate of the deemed transferor shall be increased by the value of such property as determined for purposes of the tax imposed by section 2601 on the transfer."

In 1981, P.L. 97-34, Sec. 428, amended Sec. 2006(c)(2)(B) of P.L. 94-455 (as amended by Sec. 702(n)(1) of P.L. 95-600) by substituting "January 1, 1983" for "January 1, 1982" [see below].

In 1978, P.L. 95-600, Sec. 702(n)(1), amended Sec. 2006(c) of P.L. 94-455 by substituting "June 11, 1976" for "April 30, 1976" each place it appears [see below].

In 1976, P.L. 94-455, Sec. 1902(a)(2), deleted ", or the corresponding provision of prior law," after "marital deductions)", in para. (d)(3), effective for estates of decedents dying after 12/31/76.

—P.L. 94-455, Sec. 2001(c)(1)(C), amended subsec. (b) and subpara. (c)(1)(A), effective for estates of decedents dying after 12/31/76. P.L. 94-455 ordered an inoperative amendment for "Subparagraph (A) of section 2013(e)(1)" which, for the purposes of this edition, has been amended at subpara. (c)(1)(A).

Prior to amendment, subsec. (b) read as follows:

"(b) Computation of credit.

"Subject to the limitation prescribed in subsection (c), the credit provided by this section shall be an amount which bears the same ratio to the estate tax paid (adjusted as indicated hereinafter) with respect to the estate of the transferor as the value of the property transferred bears to the taxable estate of the transferor (determined for purposes of the estate tax) decreased by any death taxes paid with respect to such estate and increased by the exemption provided for by section 2052 or section 2106(a)(3), or the corresponding provisions of prior laws, in determining the taxable estate of the transferor for purposes of the estate tax. For purposes of the preceding sentence, the estate tax paid shall be the Federal estate tax paid increased by any credits allowed against such estate tax under section 2012, or corresponding provisions of prior laws, on account of gift tax, and for any credits allowed against such estate tax under this section on account of prior transfers where the transferor acquired property from a person who died within 10 years before the death of the decedent."

Prior to amendment, subpara. (c)(1)(A) read as follows:

"(A) the estate tax imposed by section 2001 or section 2101 (after deducting the credits for State death taxes, gift tax, and foreign death taxes provided for in sections 2011, 2012, and 2014) computed without regard to this section, exceeds"

—P.L. 94-455, Sec. 2003(c), added subsec. (f), effective for estates of decedents dying after 12/31/76.

—P.L. 94-455, Sec. 2006(b)(2), added subsec. (g). Sec. 2006(c) of the Act provided as follows:

"(c) Effective dates.—

"(1) In general.—Except as provided in paragraph (2), the amendments made by this section shall apply to any generation-skipping transfer (within the meaning of section 2611(a) of the Internal Revenue Code of 1954) made after June 11, 1976.

"(2) Exceptions.—The amendments made by this section shall not apply to any generation-skipping transfer—

"(A) under a trust which was irrevocable on June 11, 1976, but only to the extent that the transfer is not made out of corpus added to the trust after June 11, 1976, or

"(B) in the case of a decedent dying before January 1, 1983, pursuant to a will (or revocable trust) which was in existence on June 11, 1976, and was not amended at any time after that date in any respect which will result in the creation of, or increasing the amount of, any generation-skipping transfer.

For purposes of subparagraph (B), if the decedent on June 11, 1976, was under a mental disability to change the disposition of his property, the period set forth in such subparagraph shall not expire before the date which is 2 years after the date on which he first regains his competence to dispose of such property.

"(3) Trust equivalents.—For purposes of paragraph (2), in the case of a trust equivalent within the meaning of subsection (d) of section 2611 of the Internal Revenue Code of 1954, the provisions of such subsection (d) shall apply."

Sec. 2014. Credit for foreign death taxes.

(a) In general.

The tax imposed by section 2001 shall be credited with the amount of any estate, inheritance, legacy, or succession taxes actually paid to any foreign country in respect of any property situated within such foreign country and included in the gross estate (not including any such taxes paid with respect to the estate of a person other than the decedent). The determination of the country within which property is situated shall be made in accordance with the rules applicable under subchapter B (sec. 2101 and following) in determining whether property is situated within or without the United States.

(b) Limitations on credit.

The credit provided in this section with respect to such taxes paid to any foreign country—

(1) shall not, with respect to any such tax, exceed an amount which bears the same ratio to the amount of such tax actually paid to such foreign country as the value of property which is—

(A) situated within such foreign country,

(B) subjected to such tax, and

(C) included in the gross estate

bears to the value of all property subjected to such tax; and

Code Sec. 2014(b)(1)(C) Estate taxes

> • *Caution:* Code Sec. 2014(b)(2), following, was amended by P.L. 107-16, EGTRRA. These provisions generally sunset for tax years beginning after 12/31/2012. For specific sunset provisions, see Sec. 901, P.L. 107-16 (as amended) reproduced in history notes for this Code Sec.

(2) shall not, with respect to all such taxes, exceed an amount which bears the same ratio to the tax imposed by section 2001 (after deducting from such tax the credits provided by sections 2010 and 2012) as the value of property which is—

(A) situated within such foreign country,
(B) subjected to the taxes of such foreign country, and
(C) included in the gross estate

bears to the value of the entire gross estate reduced by the aggregate amount of the deductions allowed under sections 2055 and 2056.

(c) Valuation of property.

(1) The values referred to in the ratio stated in subsection (b)(1) are the values determined for purposes of the tax imposed by such foreign country.

(2) The values referred to in the ratio stated in subsection (b)(2) are the values determined under this chapter; but, in applying such ratio, the value of any property described in subparagraphs (A), (B), and (C) thereof shall be reduced by such amount as will properly reflect, in accordance with regulations prescribed by the Secretary, the deductions allowed in respect of such property under sections 2055 and 2056 (relating to charitable and marital deductions).

(d) Proof of credit.

The credit provided in this section shall be allowed only if the taxpayer establishes to the satisfaction of the Secretary—

(1) the amount of taxes actually paid to the foreign country,

(2) the amount and date of each payment thereof,

(3) the description and value of the property in respect of which such taxes are imposed, and

(4) all other information necessary for the verification and computation of the credit.

(e) Period of limitation.

The credit provided in this section shall be allowed only for such taxes as were actually paid and credit therefor claimed within 4 years after the filing of the return required by section 6018, except that—

(1) If a petition for redetermination of a deficiency has been filed with the Tax Court within the time prescribed in section 6213(a), then within such 4-year period or before the expiration of 60 days after the decision of the Tax Court becomes final.

(2) If, under section 6161, an extension of time has been granted for payment of the tax shown on the return, or of a deficiency, then within such 4-year period or before the date of the expiration of the period of the extension.

Refund based on such credit may (despite the provisions of sections 6511 and 6512) be made if claim therefor is filed within the period above provided. Any such refund shall be made without interest.

(f) Additional limitation in cases involving a deduction under section 2053(d).

In any case where a deduction is allowed under section 2053(d) for an estate, succession, legacy, or inheritance tax imposed by and actually paid to any foreign country upon a transfer by the decedent for public, charitable, or religious uses described in section 2055, the property described in subparagraphs (A), (B), and (C) of paragraphs (1) and (2) of subsection (b) of this section shall not include any property in respect of which such deduction is allowed under section 2053(d).

(g) Possession of United States deemed a foreign country.

For purposes of the credits authorized by this section, each possession of the United States shall be deemed to be a foreign country.

(h) Similar credit required for certain alien residents.

Whenever the President finds that—

(1) a foreign country, in imposing estate, inheritance, legacy, or succession taxes, does not allow to citizens of the United States resident in such foreign country at the time of death a credit similar to the credit allowed under subsection (a),

(2) such foreign country, when requested by the United States to do so has not acted to provide such a similar credit in the case of citizens of the United States resident in such foreign country at the time of death, and

(3) it is in the public interest to allow the credit under subsection (a) in the case of citizens or subjects of such foreign country only if it allows such a similar credit in the case of citizens of the United States resident in such foreign country at the time of death,

the President shall proclaim that, in the case of citizens or subjects of such foreign country dying while the proclamation remains in effect, the credit under subsection (a) shall be allowed only if such foreign country allows such a similar credit in the case of citizens of the United States resident in such foreign country at the time of death.

In **2010**, P.L. 111-312, Sec. 101(a)(1), substituted "December 31, 2012" for "December 31, 2010" both places it appeared in Sec. 901, P.L. 107-16 [see below], effective as if included in the enactment of P.L. 107-16, EGTRRA, 6/7/2001.

In **2002**, P.L. 107-358, Sec. 2, added subsec. (c) in Sec. 901 of P.L. 107-16 [see below], effective 12/17/2002.

In **2001**, P.L. 107-16, Sec. 532(c)(3), deleted ", 2011," after "sections 2010" in para. (b)(2), effective for estates of decedents dying, and generation-skipping transfers, after 12/31/2004.

—P.L. 107-16, Sec. 901, of this Act [as amended by Sec. 2, P.L. 107-358, and Sec. 101(a)(1), P.L. 111-312, see above], reads as follows:

"SEC. 901. SUNSET OF PROVISIONS OF ACT.

"(a) In general. All provisions of, and amendments made by, this Act shall not apply—

"(1) to taxable, plan, or limitation years beginning after December 31, 2012, or

"(2) in the case of title V, to estates of decedents dying, gifts made, or generation skipping transfers, after December 31, 2012.

"(b) Application of certain laws. The Internal Revenue Code of 1986 and the Employee Retirement Income Security Act of 1974 shall be applied and administered to years, estates, gifts, and transfers described in subsection (a) as if the provisions and amendments described in subsection (a) had never been enacted.

"(c) Exception. Subsection (a) shall not apply to section 803 (relating to no federal income tax on restitution received by victims of the Nazi regime or their heirs or estates)."

In **1976**, P.L. 94-455, Sec. 1906(b)(13)(A), substituted "Secretary" for "Secretary or his delegate" each place it appeared in Code Sec. 2014, effective 2/1/77.

—P.L. 94-455, Sec. 2001(c)(1)(G), substituted "sections 2010, 2011, and 2012" for "sections 2011 and 2012" in para. (b)(2), effective for estates of decedents dying after 12/31/76.

In **1966**, P.L. 89-809, Sec. 106, deleted the second sentence of subsec. (a) and added subsec. (h), effective for decedents dying after 11/13/66.

Prior to deletion, the second sentence of subsec. (a) read as follows:

"If the decedent at the time of his death was not a citizen of the United States, credit shall not be allowed under this section unless the foreign country of which such decedent was a citizen or subject, in imposing such taxes, allows a similar credit in the case of a citizen of the United States resident in such country."

In **1959**, P.L. 86-175, Sec. 2, redesignated subsec. (f) as subsec. (g) and added new subsec. (f), effective for estates of decedents dying after 6/30/55.

In **1958**, P.L. 85-866, Sec. 102(c), added subsec. (f), effective for estates of decedents dying after 9/2/58.

Estate taxes   Part III

Sec. 2015. Credit for death taxes on remainders.

⌐ • *Caution:* Code Sec. 2015, following, was amended by P.L. 107-16, the Economic Growth and Tax Relief Reconciliation Act of 2001 (EGTRRA). These provisions generally sunset for tax years beginning after 12/31/2012. For specific sunset provisions, see Sec. 901, P.L. 107-16 (as amended) reproduced in history notes for this Code Sec. ⌐

Where an election is made under section 6163(a) to postpone payment of the tax imposed by section 2001, or 2101, such part of any estate, inheritance, legacy, or succession taxes allowable as a credit under section 2014, as is attributable to a reversionary or remainder interest may be allowed as a credit against the tax attributable to such interest, subject to the limitations on the amount of the credit contained in such sections, if such part is paid, and credit therefor claimed, at any time before the expiration of the time for payment of the tax imposed by section 2001 or 2101 as postponed and extended under section 6163.

In 2010, P.L. 111-312, Sec. 101(a)(1), substituted "December 31, 2012" for "December 31, 2010" both places it appeared in Sec. 901, P.L. 107-16, see below, effective as if included in the enactment of P.L. 107-16, EGTRRA, 6/7/2001.
In 2002, P.L. 107-358, Sec. 2, added subsec. (c) in Sec. 901 of P.L. 107-16 [see below], effective 12/17/2002.
In 2001, P.L. 107-16, Sec. 532(c)(4), deleted "2011 or" after "as a credit under section" in Code Sec. 2015, effective for estates of decedents dying, and generation-skipping transfers, after 12/31/2004.
—P.L. 107-16, Sec. 901, of this Act [as amended by Sec. 2, P.L. 107-358, and Sec. 101(a)(1), P.L. 111-312, see above], reads as follows:
"SEC. 901. SUNSET OF PROVISIONS OF ACT.
"(a) In general. All provisions of, and amendments made by, this Act shall not apply—
"(1) to taxable, plan, or limitation years beginning after December 31, 2012, or
"(2) in the case of title V, to estates of decedents dying, gifts made, or generation skipping transfers, after December 31, 2012.
"(b) Application of certain laws. The Internal Revenue Code of 1986 and the Employee Retirement Income Security Act of 1974 shall be applied and administered to years, estates, gifts, and transfers described in subsection (a) as if the provisions and amendments described in subsection (a) had never been enacted.
"(c) Exception. Subsection (a) shall not apply to section 803 (relating to no federal income tax on restitution received by victims of the Nazi regime or their heirs or estates)."
In 1958, P.L. 85-866, Sec. 66(a), substituted "the time for payment of the tax imposed by section 2001 or 2101 as postponed and extended under section 6163" for "60 days after the termination of the precedent interest or interests in the property", effective for any reversionary or remainder interest in property only if the precedent interest or interests in the property did not terminate before the beginning of the 60-day period which ends on 9/2/58.

Sec. 2016. Recovery of taxes claimed as credit.

⌐ • *Caution:* Code Sec. 2016 was amended by P.L. 107-16, the Economic Growth and Tax Relief Reconciliation Act of 2001 (EGTRRA). These provisions generally sunset for tax years beginning after 12/31/2012. For specific sunset provisions, see Sec. 901, P.L. 107-16 (as amended) reproduced in history notes for this Code Sec. ⌐

If any tax claimed as a credit under section 2014 is recovered from any foreign country, the executor, or any other person or persons recovering such amount, shall give notice of such recovery to the Secretary at such time and in such manner as may be required by regulations prescribed by him, and the Secretary shall (despite the provisions of section 6501) redetermine the amount of the tax under this chapter and the amount, if any, of the tax due on such redetermination, shall be paid by the executor or such person or persons, as the case may be, on notice and demand. No interest shall be assessed or collected on any amount of tax due on any redetermination by the Secretary resulting from a refund to the executor of tax claimed as a credit under section 2014, for any period before the receipt of such refund, except to the extent interest was paid by the foreign country on such refund.

In 2010, P.L. 111-312, Sec. 101(a)(1), substituted "December 31, 2012" for "December 31, 2010" both places it appears in Sec. 901, P.L. 107-16, see below, effective as if included in the enactment of P.L. 107-16, EGTRRA, 6/7/2001.
In 2002, P.L. 107-358, Sec. 2, added subsec. (c) in Sec. 901 of P.L. 107-16 [see below], effective 12/17/2002.
—P.L. 107-147, Sec. 411(h), deleted "any State, any possession of the United States, or the District of Columbia," after "foreign country," in Code Sec. 2016, effective for estates of decedents dying, and generation-skipping transfers, after 12/31/2004.
In 2001, P.L. 107-16, Sec. 532(c)(4), deleted "2011 or" after "credit under section" in Code Sec. 2016, effective for estates of decedents dying, and generation-skipping transfers, after 12/31/2004.
—P.L. 107-16, Sec. 901, of this Act [as amended by Sec. 2, P. L. 107-358, Sec. 101(a)(1), P.L. 111-312 see above], reads as follows:
"SEC. 901. SUNSET OF PROVISIONS OF ACT.
"(a) In general. All provisions of, and amendments made by, this Act shall not apply—
"(1) to taxable, plan, or limitation years beginning after December 31, 2012, or
"(2) in the case of title V, to estates of decedents dying, gifts made, or generation skipping transfers, after December 31, 2012.
"(b) Application of certain laws. The Internal Revenue Code of 1986 and the Employee Retirement Income Security Act of 1974 shall be applied and administered to years, estates, gifts, and transfers described in subsection (a) as if the provisions and amendments described in subsection (a) had never been enacted.
"(c) Exception. Subsection (a) shall not apply to section 803 (relating to no federal income tax on restitution received by victims of the Nazi regime or their heirs or estates)."
In 1978, P.L. 95-600, Sec. 703(j)(12), amended the effective date for changes made by Sec. 1902(a)(12)(C) of P.L. 94-455 [see below] to apply to estates of decedents dying after 10/4/76.
In 1976, P.L. 94-455, Sec. 1902(a)(12)(C), deleted "Territory or", after "any State, any", in Code Sec. 2016, effective [as amended by Sec. 703(j)(12) of P.L. 95-600, see above] for estates of decedents dying after 10/4/76.
—P.L. 94-455, Sec. 1906(b)(13)(A), substituted "Secretary" for "Secretary or his delegate" each place it appeared in Code Sec. 2016, effective 2/1/77.

PART III.—GROSS ESTATE
Sec.
2031. Definition of gross estate.
2032. Alternate valuation.
2032A. Valuation of certain farm, etc., real property.
2033. Property in which the decedent had an interest.
2034. Dower or curtesy interests.
2035. Adjustments for certain gifts made within 3 years of decedent's death.
2036. Transfers with retained life estate.
2037. Transfers taking effect at death.
2038. Revocable transfers.
2039. Annuities.
2040. Joint interests.
2041. Powers of appointment.
2042. Proceeds of life insurance.
2043. Transfers for insufficient consideration.
2044. Certain property for which marital deduction was previously allowed.
2045. Prior interests.
2046. Disclaimers.

In 1998, P.L. 105-206, Sec. 6007(b)(1)(E), deleted item 2033A.
Prior to deletion, item 2033A read as follows:
"2033A. Family-owned business exclusion."
In 1997, P.L. 105-34, Sec. 502(b), added item 2033A.

In **1981,** P.L. 97-34, Sec. 403(d)(3)(A)(ii), redesignated items 2044 and 2045 as 2045 and 2046, respectively, and added new item 2044.
In **1976,** P.L. 94-455, Sec. 2001(c)(1)(N)(iii), amended item 2035.
Prior to amendment, item 2035 read as follows:
"2035. Transactions in contemplation of death."
—P.L. 94-455, Sec. 2003(d)(1), added item 2032A.
—P.L. 94-455, Sec. 2009(b)(3)(B), added item 2045.

Sec. 2031. Definition of gross estate.
(a) General.
The value of the gross estate of the decedent shall be determined by including to the extent provided for in this part, the value at the time of his death of all property, real or personal, tangible or intangible, wherever situated.

(b) Valuation of unlisted stock and securities.
In the case of stock and securities of a corporation the value of which, by reason of their not being listed on an exchange and by reason of the absence of sales thereof, cannot be determined with reference to bid and asked prices or with reference to sales prices, the value thereof shall be determined by taking into consideration, in addition to all other factors, the value of stock or securities of corporations engaged in the same or a similar line of business which are listed on an exchange.

(c) Estate tax with respect to land subject to a qualified conservation easement.
(1) **In general.** If the executor makes the election described in paragraph (6), then, except as otherwise provided in this subsection, there shall be excluded from the gross estate the lesser of—
(A) the applicable percentage of the value of land subject to a qualified conservation easement, reduced by the amount of any deduction under section 2055(f) with respect to such land, or
(B) the exclusion limitation.

• *Caution:* Code Sec. 2031(c)(2), following, was amended by P.L. 107-16, the Economic Growth and Tax Relief Reconciliation Act of 2001 (EGTRRA). These provisions generally sunset for tax years beginning after 12/31/2012. For specific sunset provisions, see Sec. 901, P.L. 107-16 (as amended) reproduced in history notes for this Code Sec.

(2) **Applicable percentage.** For purposes of paragraph (1), the term "applicable percentage" means 40 percent reduced (but not below zero) by 2 percentage points for each percentage point (or fraction thereof) by which the value of the qualified conservation easement is less than 30 percent of the value of the land (determined without regard to the value of such easement and reduced by the value of any retained development right (as defined in paragraph (5)). The values taken into account under the preceding sentence shall be such values as of the date of the contribution referred to in paragraph (8)(B).
(3) **Exclusion limitation.** For purposes of paragraph (1), the exclusion limitation is the limitation determined in accordance with the following table:

In the case of estates of decedents dying during:	The exclusion limitation is:
1998	$100,000
1999	$200,000
2000	$300,000
2001	$400,000
2002 or thereafter	$500,000

(4) **Treatment of certain indebtedness.**
(A) In general. The exclusion provided in paragraph (1) shall not apply to the extent that the land is debt-financed property.
(B) Definitions. For purposes of this paragraph—
(i) Debt-financed property. The term "debt-financed property" means any property with respect to which there is an acquisition indebtedness (as defined in clause (ii)) on the date of the decedent's death.
(ii) Acquisition indebtedness. The term "acquisition indebtedness" means, with respect to debt-financed property, the unpaid amount of—
(I) the indebtedness incurred by the donor in acquiring such property,
(II) the indebtedness incurred before the acquisition of such property if such indebtedness would not have been incurred but for such acquisition,
(III) the indebtedness incurred after the acquisition of such property if such indebtedness would not have been incurred but for such acquisition and the incurrence of such indebtedness was reasonably foreseeable at the time of such acquisition, and
(IV) the extension, renewal, or refinancing of an acquisition indebtedness.

(5) **Treatment of retained development right.**
(A) In general. Paragraph (1) shall not apply to the value of any development right retained by the donor in the conveyance of a qualified conservation easement.
(B) Termination of retained development right. If every person in being who has an interest (whether or not in possession) in the land executes an agreement to extinguish permanently some or all of any development rights (as defined in subparagraph (D)) retained by the donor on or before the date for filing the return of the tax imposed by section 2001, then any tax imposed by section 2001 shall be reduced accordingly. Such agreement shall be filed with the return of the tax imposed by section 2001. The agreement shall be in such form as the Secretary shall prescribe.
(C) Additional tax. Any failure to implement the agreement described in subparagraph (B) not later than the earlier of—
(i) the date which is 2 years after the date of the decedent's death, or
(ii) the date of the sale of such land subject to the qualified conservation easement,
shall result in the imposition of an additional tax in the amount of the tax which would have been due on the retained development rights subject to such agreement. Such additional tax shall be due and payable on the last day of the 6th month following such date.
(D) Development right defined. For purposes of this paragraph, the term "development right" means any right to use the land subject to the qualified conservation easement in which such right is retained for any commercial purpose which is not subordinate to and directly supportive of the use of such land as a farm for farming purposes (within the meaning of section 2032A(e)(5)).

(6) **Election.** The election under this subsection shall be made on or before the due date (including extensions) for filing the return of tax imposed by section 2001 and shall be made on such return.

(7) **Calculation of estate tax due.** An executor making the election described in paragraph (6) shall, for purposes

of calculating the amount of tax imposed by section 2001, include the value of any development right (as defined in paragraph (5)) retained by the donor in the conveyance of such qualified conservation easement. The computation of tax on any retained development right prescribed in this paragraph shall be done in such manner and on such forms as the Secretary shall prescribe.

(8) Definitions. For purposes of this subsection—

(A) Land subject to a qualified conservation easement. The term "land subject to a qualified conservation easement" means land—

> • **Caution:** Code Sec. 2031(c)(8)(A)(i), following, reflects amendments made by Sec. 551(a), P.L. 107-16, the Economic Growth and Tax Relief Reconciliation Act of 2001 (EGTRRA). These provisions generally sunset for tax years beginning after 12/31/2012. For specific sunset provisions see Sec. 901, P.L. 107-16 (as amended) reproduced in history notes for this Code Sec. For Code Sec. 2031(c)(8)(A)(i) as it will read for tax. yrs. begin. after 12/31/2011, see below.

(i) which is located in the United States or any possession of the United States,

> • **Caution:** Code Sec. 2031(c)(8)(A)(i), following, is effective for tax. yrs. begin. after 12/31/2011, and reflects the sunset of the amendments made by Sec. 551(a), P.L. 107-16. For details of those amendments, effective date and sunset provisions, see the history for this Code Sec. For Code Sec. 2031(c)(8)(A)(i), effective for tax. yrs. begin. before 1/1/2012, see above.

(i) which is located—

(I) in or within 25 miles of an area which, on the date of the decedent's death, is a metropolitan area (as defined by the Office of Management and Budget),

(II) in or within 25 miles of an area which, on the date of the decedent's death, is a national park or wilderness area designated as part of the National Wilderness Preservation System (unless it is determined by the Secretary that land in or within 25 miles of such a park or wilderness area is not under significant development pressure), or

(II) in or within 10 miles of an area which, on the date of the decedent's death, is an Urban National Forest (as designated by the Forest Service),

(ii) which was owned by the decedent or a member of the decedent's family at all times during the 3-year period ending on the date of the decedent's death, and

(iii) with respect to which a qualified conservation easement has been made by an individual described in subparagraph (C), as of the date of the election described in paragraph (6).

(B) Qualified conservation easement. The term "qualified conservation easement" means a qualified conservation contribution (as defined in section 170(h)(1)) of a qualified real property interest (as defined in section 170(h)(2)(C)), except that clause (iv) of section 170(h)(4)(A) shall not apply, and the restriction on the use of such interest described in section 170(h)(2)(C) shall include a prohibition on more than a de minimis use for a commercial recreational activity.

(C) Individual described. An individual is described in this subparagraph if such individual is—

(i) the decedent,

(ii) a member of the decedent's family,

(iii) the executor of the decedent's estate, or

(iv) the trustee of a trust the corpus of which includes the land to be subject to the qualified conservation easement.

(D) Member of family. The term "member of the decedent's family" means any member of the family (as defined in section 2032A(e)(2)) of the decedent.

(9) Treatment of easements granted after death. In any case in which the qualified conservation easement is granted after the date of the decedent's death and on or before the due date (including extensions) for filing the return of tax imposed by section 2001, the deduction under section 2055(f) with respect to such easement shall be allowed to the estate but only if no charitable deduction is allowed under chapter 1 to any person with respect to the grant of such easement.

(10) Application of this section to interests in partnerships, corporations, and trusts. This section shall apply to an interest in a partnership, corporation, or trust if at least 30 percent of the entity is owned (directly or indirectly) by the decedent, as determined under the rules described in section 2057(e)(3).

(d) Cross reference.

For executor's right to be furnished on request a statement regarding any valuation made by the Secretary within the gross estate, see section 7517.

In 2010, P.L. 111-312, Sec. 101(a)(1), substituted "December 31, 2012" for "December 31, 2010" both places it appears in Sec. 901, P.L. 107-16, see below, effective as if included in the enactment of P.L. 107-16, EGTRRA, 6/7/2001.

In 2002, P.L. 107-358, Sec. 2, added subsec. (c) in Sec. 901 of P.L. 107-16 [see below], effective 12/17/2002.

In 2001, P.L. 107-16, Sec. 551(a), amended clause (c)(8)(A)(i) ... Sec. 551(b), added "The values taken into account under the preceding sentence shall be such values as of the date of the contribution referred to in paragraph (8)(B)." after "paragraph (5))" at the end of para. (c)(2), effective for estates of decedents dying after 12/31/2000.

Prior to amendment, clause (c)(8)(A)(i) read as follows:

"(i) which is located—

"(I) in or within 25 miles of an area which, on the date of the decedent's death, is a metropolitan area (as defined by the Office of Management and Budget),

"(II) in or within 25 miles of an area which, on the date of the decedent's death, is a national park or wilderness area designated as part of the National Wilderness Preservation System (unless it is determined by the Secretary that land in or within 25 miles of such a park or wilderness area is not under significant development pressure), or

"(III) in or within 10 miles of an area which, on the date of the decedent's death, is an Urban National Forest (as designated by the Forest Service),"

—P.L. 107-16, Sec. 901, of this Act [as amended by Sec. 2, P.L. 107-358, and Sec. 101(a)(1), P.L. 111-312, see above], reads as follows:

"Sec. 901. Sunset of provisions of Act.

"(a) In general. All provisions of, and amendments made by, this Act shall not apply—

"(1) to taxable, plan, or limitation years beginning after December 31, 2012, or

"(2) in the case of title V, to estates of decedents dying, gifts made, or generation skipping transfers, after December 31, 2012.

"(b) Application of certain laws. The Internal Revenue Code of 1986 and the Employee Retirement Income Security Act of 1974 shall be applied and administered to years, estates, gifts, and transfers described in subsection (a) as if the provisions and amendments described in subsection (a) had never been enacted.

"(c) Exception. Subsection (a) shall not apply to section 803 (relating to no federal income tax on restitution received by victims of the Nazi regime or their heirs or estates)."

In 1998, P.L. 105-277, Sec. 4006(c)(3), substituted "section 2057(e)(3)" for "section 2033A(e)(3)" in para. (c)(10), effective 10/21/98.

—P.L. 105-206, Sec. 6007(g)(1), redesignated para. (c)(9) as (c)(10) and added para. (c)(9) . . . Sec. 6007(g)(2), substituted "on or before the due date (including extensions) for filing the return of tax imposed by section 2001 and shall be made on such return." for "on the return of the tax imposed by section 2001. Such an election, once made, shall be irrevocable." in para. (c)(6), effective for estates of decedents dying after 12/31/97.

In 1997, P.L. 105-34, Sec. 508(a), redesignated subsec. (c) as subsec. (d) and added new subsec. (c), effective for estates of decedents dying after 12/31/97.

In 1976, P.L. 94-455, Sec. 2008(a)(2)(A), added subsec. (c), for estates of decedents dying after '76.

In 1962, P.L. 87-834, Sec. 18(a)(1), deleted ", except real property situated outside of the United States" effective for estates of decedents dying after 10/16/62, except as provided in Sec. 18(b)(2) of this Act which reads as follows:

"(2) In the case of a decedent dying after the date of the enactment of this Act [10/16/62] and before July 1, 1964, the value of real property situated outside of the United States shall not be included in the gross estate (as defined in section 2031(a)) of the decedent—

"(A) under section 2033, 2034, 2035(a), 2036(a), 2037(a), or 2038(a) to the extent the real property, or the decedent's interest in it, was acquired by the decedent before February 1, 1962;

"(B) under section 2040 to the extent such property or interest was acquired by the decedent before February 1, 1962, or was held by the decedent and the survivor in a joint tenancy or tenancy by the entirety before February 1, 1962; or

"(C) under section 2041(a) to the extent that before February 1, 1962, such property or interest was subject to a general power of appointment (as defined in section 2041) possessed by the decedent.

In the case of real property, or an interest therein, situated outside of the United States including a general power of appointment in respect of such property or interest, and including property held by the decedent and the survivor in a joint tenancy or tenancy by the entirety) which was acquired by the decedent after January 31, 1962, by gift within the meaning of section 2511, or from a prior decedent by devise or inheritance, or by reason of death, form of ownership, or other conditions (including the exercise or nonexercise of a power of appointment), for purposes of this paragraph such property or interest therein shall be deemed to have been acquired by the decedent before February 1, 1962, if before that date the donor or prior decedent had acquired the property or his interest therein or had possessed a power of appointment in respect of the property or interest."

Sec. 2032. Alternate valuation.
(a) General.

The value of the gross estate may be determined, if the executor so elects, by valuing all the property included in the gross estate as follows:

(1) In the case of property distributed, sold, exchanged, or otherwise disposed of, within 6 months after the decedent's death such property shall be valued as of the date of distribution, sale, exchange, or other disposition.

(2) In the case of property not distributed, sold, exchanged, or otherwise disposed of, within 6 months after the decedent's death such property shall be valued as of the date 6 months after the decedent's death.

(3) Any interest or estate which is affected by mere lapse of time shall be included at its value as of the time of death (instead of the later date) with adjustment for any difference in its value as of the later date not due to mere lapse of time.

(b) Special rules.

No deduction under this chapter of any item shall be allowed if allowance for such item is in effect given by the alternate valuation provided by this section. Wherever in any other subsection or section of this chapter reference is made to the value of property at the time of the decedent's death, such reference shall be deemed to refer to the value of such property used in determining the value of the gross estate. In case of an election made by the executor under this section, then—

(1) for purposes of the charitable deduction under section 2055 or 2106(a)(2), any bequest, legacy, devise, or transfer enumerated therein, and

(2) for the purpose of the marital deduction under section 2056, any interest in property passing to the surviving spouse,

shall be valued as of the date of the decedent's death with adjustment for any difference in value (not due to mere lapse of time or the occurrence or nonoccurrence of a contingency) of the property as of the date 6 months after the decedent's death (substituting, in the case of property distributed by the executor or trustee, or sold, exchanged, or otherwise disposed of, during such 6-month period, the date thereof).

(c) Election must decrease gross estate and estate tax.

No election may be made under this section with respect to an estate unless such election will decrease—

(1) the value of the gross estate, and

(2) the sum of the tax imposed by this chapter and the tax imposed by chapter 13 with respect to property includible in the decedent's gross estate (reduced by credits allowable against such taxes).

(d) Election.

(1) In general. The election provided for in this section shall be made by the executor on the return of the tax imposed by this chapter. Such election, once made, shall be irrevocable.

(2) Exception. No election may be made under this section if such return is filed more than 1 year after the time prescribed by law (including extensions) for filing such return.

In 1986, P.L. 99-514, Sec. 1432(c)(1), amended para. (c)(2), effective for any generation-skipping transfer (within the meaning of Code Sec. 2611) made after 10/22/86. For special rules and transitional rules see Sec. 1433(b)-(d) of this Act, reproduced in note following Code Sec. 2601.

Prior to amendment, para. (c)(2) read as follows:

"(2) the amount of the tax imposed by this chapter (reduced by credits allowable against such tax)."

In 1984, P.L. 98-369, Sec. 1023(a), redesignated subsec. (c) as subsec. (d) and added new subsec. (c) . . . Sec. 1024(a), amended subsec. (d) (as redesignated by Sec. 1023(a) of the Act), effective for estates of decedents dying after 7/18/84. Sec. 1024(b)(2) provides the following transitional rule:

"(2) Transitional rule.—In the case of an estate of a decedent dying before the date of the enactment of this Act if—

"(A) a credit or refund of the tax imposed by chapter 11 of the Internal Revenue Code of 1954 is not prevented on the date of the enactment of this Act by the operation of any law or rule of law,

"(B) the election under section 2032 of the Internal Revenue Code of 1954 would have met the requirements of such section (as amended by this section and section 1023) had the decedent died after the date of the enactment of this Act, and

"(C) a claim for credit or refund of such tax with respect to such estate is filed not later than the 90th day after the date of the enactment of this Act,

then such election shall be treated as a valid election under such section 2032. The statutory period for the assessment of any deficiency which is attributable to an election under this paragraph shall not expire before the close of the 2-year period beginning on the date of the enactment of this Act."

Prior to amendment, subsec. (d) read as follows:

"(d) Time of election.

"The election provided for in this section shall be exercised by the executor on his return if filed within the time prescribed by law or before the expiration of any extension of time granted pursuant to law for the filing of the return."

In 1970, P.L. 91-614, Sec. 101(a), substituted "6 months" for "1 year" each place it appeared and "6-month" for "1-year," in Code Sec. 2032, effective for decedents dying after 12/31/70.

Sec. 2032A. Valuation of certain farm, etc., real property.
(a) Value based on use under which property qualifies.

(1) General rule. If—

(A) the decedent was (at the time of his death) a citizen or resident of the United States, and

(B) the executor elects the application of this section and files the agreement referred to in subsection (d)(2),

then, for purposes of this chapter, the value of qualified real property shall be its value for the use under which it qualifies, under subsection (b), as qualified real property.

(2) Limitation on aggregate reduction in fair market value. The aggregate decrease in the value of qualified real property taken into account for purposes of this chapter which results from the application of paragraph (1) with respect to any decedent shall not exceed $750,000.

(3) Inflation adjustment. In the case of estates of decedents dying in a calendar year after 1998, the $750,000 amount contained in paragraph (2) shall be increased by an amount equal to—

(A) $750,000, multiplied by

(B) the cost-of-living adjustment determined under section 1(f)(3) for such calendar year by substituting "calendar year 1997" for "calendar year 1992" in subparagraph (B) thereof.

If any amount as adjusted under the preceding sentence is not a multiple of $10,000, such amount shall be rounded to the next lowest multiple of $10,000.

(b) Qualified real property.

(1) In general. For purposes of this section, the term "qualified real property" means real property located in the United States which was acquired from or passed from the decedent to a qualified heir of the decedent and which, on the date of the decedent's death, was being used for a qualified use by the decedent or a member of the decedent's family, but only if—

(A) 50 percent or more of the adjusted value of the gross estate consists of the adjusted value of real or personal property which—

(i) on the date of the decedent's death, was being used for a qualified use by the decedent or a member of the decedent's family, and

(ii) was acquired from or passed from the decedent to a qualified heir of the decedent.

(B) 25 percent or more of the adjusted value of the gross estate consists of the adjusted value of real property which meets the requirements of subparagraphs (A)(ii) and (C),

(C) during the 8-year period ending on the date of the decedent's death there have been periods aggregating 5 years or more during which—

(i) such real property was owned by the decedent or a member of the decedent's family and used for a qualified use by the decedent or a member of the decedent's family, and

(ii) there was material participation by the decedent or a member of the decedent's family in the operation of the farm or other business, and

(D) such real property is designated in the agreement referred to in subsection (d)(2).

(2) Qualified use. For purposes of this section, the term "qualified use" means the devotion of the property to any of the following:

(A) use as a farm for farming purposes, or

(B) use in a trade or business other than the trade or business of farming.

(3) Adjusted value. For purposes of paragraph (1), the term "adjusted value" means—

(A) in the case of the gross estate, the value of the gross estate for purposes of this chapter (determined without regard to this section), reduced by any amounts allowable as a deduction under paragraph (4) of section 2053(a), or

(B) in the case of any real or personal property, the value of such property for purposes of this chapter (determined without regard to this section), reduced by any amounts allowable as a deduction in respect of such property under paragraph (4) of section 2053(a).

(4) Decedents who are retired or disabled.

(A) In general. If, on the date of the decedent's death, the requirements of paragraph (1)(C)(ii) with respect to the decedent for any property are not met, and the decedent—

(i) was receiving old-age benefits under title II of the Social Security Act for a continuous period ending on such date, or

(ii) was disabled for a continuous period ending on such date,

then paragraph (1)(C)(ii) shall be applied with respect to such property by substituting "the date on which the longer of such continuous periods began" for "the date of the decedent's death" in paragraph (1)(C).

(B) Disabled defined. For purposes of subparagraph (A), an individual shall be disabled if such individual has a mental or physical impairment which renders him unable to materially participate in the operation of the farm or other business.

(C) Coordination with recapture. For purposes of subsection (c)(6)(B)(i), if the requirements of paragraph (1)(C)(ii) are met with respect to any decedent by reason of subparagraph (A), the period ending on the date on which the continuous period taken into account under subparagraph (A) began shall be treated as the period immediately before the decedent's death.

(5) Special rules for surviving spouses.

(A) In general. If property is qualified real property with respect to a decedent (hereinafter in this paragraph referred to as the "first decedent") and such property was acquired from or passed from the first decedent to the surviving spouse of the first decedent, for purposes of applying this subsection and subsection (c) in the case of the estate of such surviving spouse, active management of the farm or other business by the surviving spouse shall be treated as material participation by such surviving spouse in the operation of such farm or business.

(B) Special rule. For the purposes of subparagraph (A), the determination of whether property is qualified real property with respect to the first decedent shall be made without regard to subparagraph (D) of paragraph (1) and without regard to whether an election under this section was made.

(C) Coordination with paragraph (4). In any case in which to do so will enable the requirements of paragraph (1)(C)(ii) to be met with respect to the surviving spouse, this subsection and subsection (c) shall be applied by taking into account any application of paragraph (4).

(c) Tax treatment of dispositions and failures to use for qualified use.

(1) Imposition of additional estate tax. If, within 10 years after the decedent's death and before the death of the qualified heir—

(A) the qualified heir disposes of any interest in qualified real property (other than by a disposition to a member of his family), or

(B) the qualified heir ceases to use for the qualified use the qualified real property which was acquired (or passed) from the decedent,

then there is hereby imposed an additional estate tax.

(2) Amount of additional tax.

(A) In general. The amount of the additional tax imposed by paragraph (1) with respect to any interest shall be the amount equal to the lesser of—

(i) the adjusted tax difference attributable to such interest, or

(ii) the excess of the amount realized with respect to the interest (or, in any case other than a sale or exchange at arm's length, the fair market value of the interest) over the value of the interest determined under subsection (a).

(B) Adjusted tax difference attributable to interest. For purposes of subparagraph (A), the adjusted tax difference attributable to an interest is the amount which bears the same ratio to the adjusted tax difference with respect to the estate (determined under subparagraph (C)) as—

(i) the excess of the value of such interest for purposes of this chapter (determined without regard to subsection (a)) over the value of such interest determined under subsection (a), bears to

(ii) a similar excess determined for all qualified real property.

(C) Adjusted tax difference with respect to the estate. For purposes of subparagraph (B), the term "adjusted tax difference with respect to the estate" means the excess of what would have been the estate tax liability but for subsection (a) over the estate tax liability. For purposes of this subparagraph, the term "estate tax liability" means the tax imposed by section 2001 reduced by the credits allowable against such tax.

(D) Partial dispositions. For purposes of this paragraph, where the qualified heir disposes of a portion of the interest acquired by (or passing to) such heir (or a predecessor qualified heir) or there is a cessation of use of such a portion—

(i) the value determined under subsection (a) taken into account under subparagraph (A)(ii) with respect to such portion shall be its pro rata share of such value of such interest, and

(ii) the adjusted tax difference attributable to the interest taken into account with respect to the transaction involving the second or any succeeding portion shall be reduced by the amount of the tax imposed by this subsection with respect to all prior transactions involving portions of such interest.

(E) Special rule for disposition of timber. In the case of qualified woodland to which an election under subsection (e)(13)(A) applies, if the qualified heir disposes of (or severs) any standing timber on such qualified woodland—

(i) such disposition (or severance) shall be treated as a disposition of a portion of the interest of the qualified heir in such property, and

(ii) the amount of the additional tax imposed by paragraph (1) with respect to such disposition shall be an amount equal to the lesser of—

(I) the amount realized on such disposition (or, in any case other than a sale or exchange at arm's length, the fair market value of the portion of the interest disposed or severed), or

(II) the amount of additional tax determined under this paragraph (without regard to this subparagraph) if the entire interest of the qualified heir in the qualified woodland had been disposed of, less the sum of the amount of the additional tax imposed with respect to all prior transactions involving such woodland to which this subparagraph applied.

For purposes of the preceding sentence, the disposition of a right to sever shall be treated as the disposition of the standing timber. The amount of additional tax imposed under paragraph (1) in any case in which a qualified heir disposes of his entire interest in the qualified woodland shall be reduced by any amount determined under this subparagraph with respect to such woodland.

(3) Only 1 additional tax imposed with respect to any 1 portion. In the case of an interest acquired from (or passing from) any decedent, if subparagraph (A) or (B) of paragraph (1) applies to any portion of an interest, subparagraph (B) or (A), as the case may be, of paragraph (1) shall not apply with respect to the same portion of such interest.

(4) Due date. The additional tax imposed by this subsection shall become due and payable on the day which is 6 months after the date of the disposition or cessation referred to in paragraph (1).

(5) Liability for tax; furnishing of bond. The qualified heir shall be personally liable for the additional tax imposed by this subsection with respect to his interest unless the heir has furnished bond which meets the requirements of subsection (e)(11).

(6) Cessation of qualified use. For purposes of paragraph (1)(B), real property shall cease to be used for the qualified use if—

(A) such property ceases to be used for the qualified use set forth in subparagraph (A) or (B) of subsection (b)(2) under which the property qualified under subsection (b), or

(B) during any period of 8 years ending after the date of the decedent's death and before the date of death of the qualified heir, there had been periods aggregating more than 3 years during which—

(i) in the case of periods during which the property was held by the decedent, there was no material participation by the decedent or any member of his family in the operation of the farm or other business, and

(ii) in the case of periods during which the property was held by any qualified heir, there was no material participation by such qualified heir or any member of his family in the operation of the farm or other business.

(7) Special rules.

(A) No tax if use begins within 2 years. If the date on which the qualified heir begins to use the qualified real property (hereinafter in this subparagraph referred to as the commencement date) is before the date 2 years after the decedent's death—

(i) no tax shall be imposed under paragraph (1) by reason of the failure by the qualified heir to so use such property before the commencement date, and

(ii) the 10-year period under paragraph (1) shall be extended by the period after the decedent's death and before the commencement date.

(B) Active management by eligible qualified heir treated as material participation. For purposes of paragraph (6)(B)(ii), the active management of a farm or other business by—

(i) an eligible qualified heir, or

(ii) a fiduciary of an eligible qualified heir described in clause (ii) or (iii) of subparagraph (C),

shall be treated as material participation by such eligible qualified heir in the operation of such farm or business. In the case of an eligible qualified heir described in clause (ii), (iii), or (iv) of subparagraph (C), the preceding sentence shall apply only during periods during which such heir meets the requirements of such clause.

(C) Eligible qualified heir. For purposes of this paragraph, the term "eligible qualified heir" means a qualified heir who—

(i) is the surviving spouse of the decedent,
(ii) has not attained the age of 21,
(iii) is disabled (within the meaning of subsection (b)(4)(B)), or
(iv) is a student.

(D) Student. For purposes of subparagraph (C), an individual shall be treated as a student with respect to periods during any calendar year if (and only if) such individual is a student (within the meaning of section 152(f)(2)) for such calendar year.

(E) Certain rents treated as qualified use. For purposes of this subsection, a surviving spouse or lineal descendant of the decedent shall not be treated as failing to use qualified real property in a qualified use solely because such spouse or descendant rents such property to a member of the family of such spouse or descendant on a net cash basis. For purposes of the preceding sentence, a legally adopted child of an individual shall be treated as the child of such individual by blood.

(8) Qualified conservation contribution is not a disposition. A qualified conservation contribution (as defined in section 170(h)) by gift or otherwise shall not be deemed a disposition under subsection (c)(1)(A).

(d) Election; agreement.

(1) Election. The election under this section shall be made on the return of the tax imposed by section 2001. Such election shall be made in such manner as the Secretary shall by regulations prescribe. Such an election, once made, shall be irrevocable.

(2) Agreement. The agreement referred to in this paragraph is a written agreement signed by each person in being who has an interest (whether or not in possession) in any property designated in such agreement consenting to the application of subsection (c) with respect to such property.

(3) Modification of election and agreement to be permitted. The Secretary shall prescribe procedures which provide that in any case in which the executor makes an election under paragraph (1) (and submits the agreement referred to in paragraph (2)) within the time prescribed therefor, but—

(A) the notice of election, as filed, does not contain all required information, or
(B) signatures of 1 or more persons required to enter into the agreement described in paragraph (2) are not included on the agreement as filed, or the agreement does not contain all required information,

the executor will have a reasonable period of time (not exceeding 90 days) after notification of such failures to provide such information or signatures.

(e) Definitions; special rules.

For purposes of this section—

(1) Qualified heir. The term "qualified heir" means, with respect to any property, a member of the decedent's family who acquired such property (or to whom such property passed) from the decedent. If a qualified heir disposes of any interest in qualified real property to any member of his family, such member shall thereafter be treated as the qualified heir with respect to such interest.

(2) Member of family. The term "member of the family" means, with respect to any individual, only—

(A) an ancestor of such individual,
(B) the spouse of such individual,
(C) a lineal descendant of such individual, of such individual's spouse, or of a parent of such individual, or
(D) the spouse of any lineal descendant described in subparagraph (C).

For purposes of the preceding sentence, a legally adopted child of an individual shall be treated as the child of such individual by blood.

(3) Certain real property included. In the case of real property which meets the requirements of subparagraph (C) of subsection (b)(1), residential buildings and related improvements on such real property occupied on a regular basis by the owner or lessee of such real property or by persons employed by such owner or lessee for the purpose of operating or maintaining such real property, and roads, buildings, and other structures and improvements functionally related to the qualified use shall be treated as real property devoted to the qualified use.

(4) Farm. The term "farm" includes stock, dairy, poultry, fruit, furbearing animal, and truck farms, plantations, ranches, nurseries, ranges, greenhouses or other similar structures used primarily for the raising of agricultural or horticultural commodities, and orchards and woodlands.

(5) Farming purposes. The term "farming purposes" means—

(A) cultivating the soil or raising or harvesting any agricultural or horticultural commodity (including the raising, shearing, feeding, caring for, training, and management of animals) on a farm;
(B) handling, drying, packing, grading, or storing on a farm any agricultural or horticultural commodity in its unmanufactured state, but only if the owner, tenant, or operator of the farm regularly produces more than one-half of the commodity so treated; and
(C)(i) the planting, cultivating, caring for, or cutting of trees, or
(ii) the preparation (other than milling) of trees for market.

(6) Material participation. Material participation shall be determined in a manner similar to the manner used for purposes of paragraph (1) of section 1402(a) (relating to net earnings from self-employment).

(7) Method of valuing farms.

(A) In general. Except as provided in subparagraph (B), the value of a farm for farming purposes shall be determined by dividing—

(i) the excess of the average annual gross cash rental for comparable land used for farming purposes and located in the locality of such farm over the average annual State and local real estate taxes for such comparable land, by
(ii) the average annual effective interest rate for all new Federal Land Bank loans.

For purposes of the preceding sentence, each average annual computation shall be made on the basis of the 5 most recent calendar years ending before the date of the decedent's death.

(B) Value based on net share rental in certain cases.

(i) In general. If there is no comparable land from which the average annual gross cash rental may be determined but there is comparable land from which the average net share rental may be determined, subparagraph (A)(i) shall be applied by substituting "average annual net share rental" for "average annual gross cash rental".
(ii) Net share rental. For purposes of this paragraph, the term "net share rental" means the excess of—

(I) the value of the produce received by the lessor of the land on which such produce is grown, over

(II) the cash operating expenses of growing such produce which, under the lease, are paid by the lessor.

(C) Exception. The formula provided by subparagraph (A) shall not be used—

(i) where it is established that there is no comparable land from which the average annual gross cash rental may be determined and that there is no comparable land from which the average net share rental may be determined, or

(ii) where the executor elects to have the value of the farm for farming purposes determined and that there is no comparable land from which the average net share rental may be determined under paragraph (8).

(8) Method of valuing closely held business interests, etc. In any case to which paragraph (7)(A) does not apply, the following factors shall apply in determining the value of any qualified real property:

(A) The capitalization of income which the property can be expected to yield for farming or closely held business purposes over a reasonable period of time under prudent management using traditional cropping patterns for the area, taking into account soil capacity, terrain configuration, and similar factors,

(B) The capitalization of the fair rental value of the land for farm land or closely held business purposes,

(C) Assessed land values in a State which provides a differential or use value assessment law for farmland or closely held business,

(D) Comparable sales of other farm or closely held business land in the same geographical area far enough removed from a metropolitan or resort area so that nonagricultural use is not a significant factor in the sales price, and

(E) Any other factor which fairly values the farm or closely held business value of the property.

(9) Property acquired from decedent. Property shall be considered to have been acquired from or to have passed from the decedent if—

(A) such property is so considered under section 1014(b) (relating to basis of property acquired from a decedent),

(B) such property is acquired by any person from the estate, or

(C) such property is acquired by any person from a trust (to the extent such property is includible in the gross estate of the decedent).

(10) Community property. If the decedent and his surviving spouse at any time held qualified real property as community property, the interest of the surviving spouse in such property shall be taken into account under this section to the extent necessary to provide a result under this section with respect to such property which is consistent with the result which would have obtained under this section if such property had not been community property.

(11) Bond in lieu of personal liability. If the qualified heir makes written application to the Secretary for determination of the maximum amount of the additional tax which may be imposed by subsection (c) with respect to the qualified heir's interest, the Secretary (as soon as possible, and in any event within 1 year after the making of such application) shall notify the heir of such maximum amount. The qualified heir, on furnishing a bond in such amount and for such period as may be required, shall be discharged from personal liability for any additional tax imposed by subsection (c) and shall be entitled to a receipt or writing showing such discharge.

(12) Active management. The term "active management" means the making of the management decisions of a business (other than the daily operating decisions).

(13) Special rules for woodlands.

(A) In general. In the case of any qualified woodland with respect to which the executor elects to have this subparagraph apply, trees growing on such woodland shall not be treated as a crop.

(B) Qualified woodland. The term "qualified woodland" means any real property which—

(i) is used in timber operations, and

(ii) is an identifiable area of land such as an acre or other area for which records are normally maintained in conducting timber operations.

(C) Timber operations. The term "timber operations" means—

(i) the planting, cultivating, caring for, or cutting of trees, or

(ii) the preparation (other than milling) of trees for market.

(D) Election. An election under subparagraph (A) shall be made on the return of the tax imposed by section 2001. Such election shall be made in such manner as the Secretary shall by regulations prescribe. Such an election, once made, shall be irrevocable.

(14) Treatment of replacement property acquired in section 1031 or 1033 transactions.

(A) In general. In the case of any qualified replacement property, any period during which there was ownership, qualified use, or material participation with respect to the replaced property by the decedent or any member of his family shall be treated as a period during which there was such ownership, use, or material participation (as the case may be) with respect to the qualified replacement property.

(B) Limitation. Subparagraph (A) shall not apply to the extent that the fair market value of the qualified replacement property (as of the date of its acquisition) exceeds the fair market value of the replaced property (as of the date of its disposition).

(C) Definitions. For purposes of this paragraph—

(i) Qualified replacement property. The term "qualified replacement property" means any real property which is—

(I) acquired in an exchange which qualifies under section 1031, or

(II) the acquisition of which results in the nonrecognition of gain under section 1033.

Such term shall only include property which is used for the same qualified use as the replaced property was being used before the exchange.

(ii) Replaced property. The term "replaced property" means—

(I) the property transferred in the exchange which qualifies under section 1031, or

(II) the property compulsorily or involuntarily converted (within the meaning of section 1033).

(f) Statute of limitations.

If qualified real property is disposed of or ceases to be used for a qualified use, then—

(1) the statutory period for the assessment of any additional tax under subsection (c) attributable to such disposition or cessation shall not expire before the expiration of 3 years from the date the Secretary is notified (in such manner as the Secretary may by regulations prescribe) of such disposition or cessation (or if later in the case of an involuntary conversion or exchange to which subsection (h) or (i) applies, 3 years from the date the Secretary is notified of the replacement of the converted property or of an intention not to replace or of the exchange of property), and

(2) such additional tax may be assessed before the expiration of such 3-year period notwithstanding the provisions of any other law or rule of law which would otherwise prevent such assessment.

(g) Application of this section and section 6324B to interests in partnerships, corporations, and trusts.

The Secretary shall prescribe regulations setting forth the application of this section and section 6324B in the case of an interest in a partnership, corporation, or trust which, with respect to the decedent, is an interest in a closely held business (within the meaning of paragraph (1) of section 6166(b)). For purposes of the preceding sentence, an interest in a discretionary trust all the beneficiaries of which are qualified heirs shall be treated as a present interest.

(h) Special rules for involuntary conversions of qualified real property.

(1) Treatment of converted property.

(A) In general. If there is an involuntary conversion of an interest in qualified real property—

(i) no tax shall be imposed by subsection (c) on such conversion if the cost of the qualified replacement property equals or exceeds the amount realized on such conversion, or

(ii) if clause (i) does not apply, the amount of the tax imposed by subsection (c) on such conversion shall be the amount determined under subparagraph (B).

(B) Amount of tax where there is not complete reinvestment. The amount determined under this subparagraph with respect to any involuntary conversion is the amount of the tax which (but for this subsection) would have been imposed on such conversion reduced by an amount which—

(i) bears the same ratio to such tax, as

(ii) the cost of the qualified replacement property bears to the amount realized on the conversion.

(2) Treatment of replacement property. For purposes of subsection (c)—

(A) any qualified replacement property shall be treated in the same manner as if it were a portion of the interest in qualified real property which was involuntarily converted; except that with respect to such qualified replacement property the 10-year period under paragraph (1) of subsection (c) shall be extended by any period, beyond the 2-year period referred to in section 1033(a)(2)(B)(i), during which the qualified heir was allowed to replace the qualified real property,

(B) any tax imposed by subsection (c) on the involuntary conversion shall be treated as a tax imposed on a partial disposition, and

(C) paragraph (6) of subsection (c) shall be applied—

(i) by not taking into account periods after the involuntary conversion and before the acquisition of the qualified replacement property, and

(ii) by treating material participation with respect to the converted property as material participation with respect to the qualified replacement property.

(3) Definitions and special rules. For purposes of this subsection—

(A) Involuntary conversion. The term "involuntary conversion" means a compulsory or involuntary conversion within the meaning of section 1033.

(B) Qualified replacement property. The term "qualified replacement property" means—

(i) in the case of an involuntary conversion described in section 1033(a)(1), any real property into which the qualified real property is converted, or

(ii) in the case of an involuntary conversion described in section 1033(a)(2), any real property purchased by the qualified heir during the period specified in section 1033(a)(2)(B) for purposes of replacing the qualified real property.

Such term only includes property which is to be used for the qualified use set forth in subparagraph (A) or (B) of subsection (b)(2) under which the qualified real property qualified under subsection (a).

(4) Certain rules made applicable. The rules of the last sentence of section 1033(a)(2)(A) shall apply for purposes of paragraph (3)(B)(ii).

(i) Exchanges of qualified real property.

(1) Treatment of property exchanged.

(A) Exchanges solely for qualified exchange property. If an interest in qualified real property is exchanged solely for an interest in qualified exchange property in a transaction which qualifies under section 1031, no tax shall be imposed by subsection (c) by reason of such exchange.

(B) Exchanges where other property received. If an interest in qualified real property is exchanged for an interest in qualified exchange property and other property in a transaction which qualifies under section 1031, the amount of the tax imposed by subsection (c) by reason of such exchange shall be the amount of tax which (but for this subparagraph) would have been imposed on such exchange under subsection (c)(1), reduced by an amount which—

(i) bears the same ratio to such tax, as

(ii) the fair market value of the qualified exchange property bears to the fair market value of the qualified real property exchanged.

For purposes of clause (ii) of the preceding sentence, fair market value shall be determined as of the time of the exchange.

(2) Treatment of qualified exchange property. For purposes of subsection (c)—

(A) any interest in qualified exchange property shall be treated in the same manner as if it were a portion of the interest in qualified real property which was exchanged,

(B) any tax imposed by subsection (c) by reason of the exchange shall be treated as a tax imposed on a partial disposition, and

(C) paragraph (6) of subsection (c) shall be applied by treating material participation with respect to the exchanged property as material participation with respect to the qualified exchange property.

(3) Qualified exchange property. For purposes of this subsection, the term "qualified exchange property" means real property which is to be used for the qualified use set forth in subparagraph (A) or (B) of subsection (b)(2) under which the real property exchanged therefor originally qualified under subsection (a).

In 2004, P.L. 108-311, Sec. 207(22), substituted "section 152(f)(2)" for "section 151(c)(4)" in subpara. (c)(7)(D), effective for tax. yrs. begin. after 12/31/2004.

In 2001, P.L. 107-16, Sec. 581, of this Act, reads as follows:

Code Sec. 2032A — Estate taxes

"SEC. 581. WAIVER OF STATUTE OF LIMITATION FOR TAXES ON CERTAIN FARM VALUATIONS. If on the date of the enactment of this Act (or at any time within 1 year after the date of the enactment) a refund or credit of any overpayment of tax resulting from the application of section 2032A(c)(7)(E) of the Internal Revenue Code of 1986 is barred by any law or rule of law, the refund or credit of such overpayment shall, nevertheless, be made or allowed if claim therefor is filed before the date 1 year after the date of the enactment of this Act."

In 1997, P.L. 105-34, Sec. 501(b), added para. (a)(3), effective for estates of decedents dying, and gifts made, after 12/31/97.

—P.L. 105-34, Sec. 504(a), added subpara. (c)(7)(E)... Sec. 504(b), deleted "For purposes of subsection (c), such surviving spouse shall not be treated as failing to use such property in a qualified use solely because such spouse rents such property to a member of such spouse's family on a net cash basis." at the end of subpara. (b)(5)(A), effective for leases entered into after 12/31/76.

—P.L. 105-34, Sec. 508(c), added para. (c)(8), effective for easements granted after 12/31/97.

—P.L. 105-34, Sec. 1313(a), amended para. (d)(3), effective for estates of decedents dying after 8/5/97.

Prior to amendment, para. (d)(3) read as follows:

"(3) Modification of election and agreement to be permitted. The Secretary shall prescribe procedures which provide that in any case in which—

"(A) the executor makes an election under paragraph (1) within the time prescribed for filing such election, and

"(B) substantially complies with the regulations prescribed by the Secretary with respect to such election, but—

"(i) the notice of election, as filed, does not contain all required information, or

"(ii) signatures of 1 or more persons required to enter into the agreement described in paragraph (2) are not included on the agreement as filed, or the agreement does not contain all required information,

the executor will have a reasonable period of time (not exceeding 90 days) after notification of such failures to provide such information or agreements."

In 1990, P.L. 101-508, Sec. 11802(f)(5), amended para. (a)(2), effective 11/5/90 except as provided in Sec. 11821(b) of this Act, which reads as follows:

"(b) Savings provision.

"If—

"(1) any provision amended or repealed by this part applied to—

"(A) any transaction occurring before the date of the enactment of this Act [11/5/90],

"(B) any property acquired before such date of enactment [11/5/90], or

"(C) any item of income, loss, deduction, or credit taken into account before such date of enactment [11/5/90], and

"(2) the treatment of such transaction, property, or item under such provision would (without regard to the amendments made by this part) affect liability for tax for periods ending after such date of enactment [11/5/90],

nothing in the amendments made by this part shall be construed to affect the treatment of such transaction, property, or item for purposes of determining liability for tax for periods ending after such date of enactment [11/5/90].

Prior to amendment, para. (a)(2) read as follows:

"(2) Limit on aggregate reduction in fair market value. The aggregate decrease in the value of qualified real property taken into account for purposes of this chapter which results from the application of paragraph (1) with respect to any decedent shall not exceed the applicable limit set forth in the following table:

In the case of decedents dying in:	The applicable limit is:
1981	$ 600,000
1982	700,000
1983 or thereafter	750,000."

In 1988, P.L. 100-647, Sec. 1014(f), amended Sec. 1421(a) of P.L. 99-514, [reproduced below] by deleting "within the time prescribed by filing such return (including extensions thereof)" after "section 2001 of such Code", see below.

—P.L. 100-647, Sec. 6151(a), added a sentence to end of subpara. (b)(5)(A), effective with respect to rentals occurring after 12/31/76.

Sec. 6151(b)(2) of this Act provides:

"(2) Waiver of statute of limitations.—If on the date of the enactment of this Act (or at any time within 1 year after such date of enactment) refund or credit of any overpayment of tax resulting from the application of the amendment made by subsection (a) is barred by any law or rule of law, refund or credit of such overpayment shall, nevertheless, be made or allowed if claim therefore is filed before the date 1 year after the date of the enactment of this Act [11/10/88]."

In 1986, P.L. 99-514, Sec. 104(b)(3), substituted "section 151(c)(4)" for "section 151(e)(4)" in subpara. (c)(7)(D), effective for tax. yrs. begin. after 12/31/86.

—P.L. 99-514, Sec. 1421(a), [as amended by Sec. 1014(f) of P.L. 100-647, see above.] provides:

"SEC. 1421. INFORMATION NECESSARY FOR VALID SPECIAL USE VALUATION ELECTION.

"(a) In General.

"In the case of any decedent dying before January 1, 1986, if the executor—

"(1) made an election under section 2032A of the Internal Revenue Code of 1954 on the return of tax imposed by section 2001 of such Code, and

"(2) provided substantially all the information with respect to such return required on such return of tax,

such election shall be a valid election for purposes of section 2032A of such Code.

"(b) Executor must provide information.

"An election described in subsection (a) shall not be valid if the Secretary of the Treasury or his delegate after the date of the enactment of this Act requests information from the executor with respect to such election and the executor does not provide such information within 90 days of receipt of such request.

"(c) Effective date.

"The provisions of this section shall not apply to the estate of any decedent if before the date of the enactment of this Act the statute of limitations has expired with respect to—

"(1) the return of tax imposed by section 2001 of the Internal Revenue Code of 1954, and

"(2) the period during which a claim for credit or refund may be timely filed.

"(d) Special rule for certain estate.

"Notwithstanding subsection (a)(2), the provisions of this section shall apply to the estate of an individual who died on January 30, 1984, and with respect to which—

"(1) a Federal estate tax return was filed on October 30, 1984, electing current use valuation, and

"(2) the agreement required under section 2032A was filed on November 9, 1984."

In 1984, P.L. 98-369, Sec. 1025(a), added new para. (d)(3), for estates of decedents dying after 12/31/76. Sec. 1025(b)(2) of the Act provides:

"(2) Refund or credit of overpayment barred by statute of limitations.—Notwithstanding section 6511(a) of the Internal Revenue Code of 1954 or any other period of limitation or lapse of time, a claim for credit or refund of overpayment of the tax imposed by such Code which arises by reason of this section may be filed by any person at any time within the 1-year period beginning on the date of the enactment of this Act. Sections 6511(b) and 6514 of such Code shall not apply to any claim for credit or refund filed under this subsection within such 1-year period."

In 1983, P.L. 97-448, Sec. 104(b)(1), added subpara. (b)(5)(C)... Sec. 104(b)(2)(A), substituted "the qualified exchange property" for "the other property" in clause (i)(1)(B)(ii)... Sec. 104(b)(2)(B), substituted "subparagraph (A) or (B)" for "subparagraph (A), (B), or (C)" in para. (i)(3), effective for estates of decedents dying after 12/31/81.

provides special rules in the case of any land diverted from the production of an agricultural commodity under a 1983 payment-in-kind program. See P.L. 98-4 reproduced in note following Code Sec. 61.

—P.L. 97-448, Sec. 104(b)(4)(A), amended Sec. 421(k)(5)(A), so that the amendments made by Sec. 421(c)(2) are generally effective for estates of decedents dying after 12/31/81, and that Code Sec. 2032A(c)(7)(A), as added by Sec. 421(c)(2)(A) of P. L. 97-34, is effective for estates of decedents dying after 12/31/76, see below.

—P.L. 97-448, Sec. 104(b)(4)(B), amended the second sentence of Sec. 421(k)(5)(B) of P.L. 97-34 [reproduced below].

Prior to amendment, the second sentence of Sec. 421(k)(5)(B) of P.L. 97-34 read as follows: "If the time for making an election would have otherwise expired after July 28, 1980, the time for making such election shall not expire before the date 6 months after the date of the enactment of his Act."

—P.L. 97-448, Sec. 104(b)(4)(C)(i), amended Sec. 421(k)(5)(C) of P.L. 97-34 [reproduced below] by substituting "at any time before February 17, 1982" for "within 6 months after the date of the enactment of this Act"... Sec. 104(b)(4)(C)(ii), amended Sec. 421(k)(5)(D) of P.L. 97-34 [reproduced below] by substituting "before February 17, 1982" for "within 6 months after such date of enactment" and substituting "February 17, 1982" for "the date 6 months after such date of enactment".

In 1981, P.L. 97-34, Sec. 421(a), amended para. (a)(2), effective for estates of decedents dying after 12/31/80.

Prior to amendment, para. (a)(2) read as follows:

"(2) Limitation. The aggregate decrease in the value of qualified real property taken into account for purposes of this chapter which results from the application of paragraph (1) with respect to any decedent shall not exceed $500,000."

—P.L. 97-34, Sec. 421(b)(1), added "by the decedent or member of decedent's family" after "qualified use" each place it appeared in para. (b)(1), effective for estates of decedents dying after 12/31/76. Sec. 421(k)(5)(B) thru (D), as amended by Sec. 104(b)(4)(B) of P.L. 97-448 and (C) [see above] of this Act provides:

"(B) Timely election required. Subparagraph (A) shall only apply in the case of an estate if a timely election under section 2032A was made with respect to such estate. If the estate of any decedent would not qualify under section 2032A of the Internal Revenue Code of 1954 but for the amendments described in subparagraph (A) and the time for making an election under section 2032A with respect to such estate would (but for this sentence) expire after July 28, 1980, the time for making such election shall not expire before the close of February 16, 1982.

"(C) Reinstatement of elections. If any election under section 2032A was revoked before the date of the enactment of this Act, such election may be reinstated at any time before February 17, 1982.

"(D) Statute of limitations. If on the date of the enactment of this Act (or at any time before February 17, 1982) the making of a credit or refund of any overpayment of tax resulting from the amendments described in subparagraph (A) is barred by any law or rule of law, such credit or refund shall nevertheless be made if claim therefor is made before February 17, 1982."

—P.L. 97-34, Sec. 421(b)(2), added new paras. (b)(4) and (b)(5)... Sec. 421(c)(1)(A), substituted "10 years" for "15 years" in para. (c)(1)... Sec. 421(c)(1)(B)(i), deleted para. (c)(3) and redesignated paras. (c)(4), (c)(5), (c)(6) and (c)(7) as (c)(3), (c)(4), (c)(5) and (c)(6)... Sec. 421(c)(1)(B)(ii), amended subpara. (h)(2)(A)... Sec. 421(c)(1)(B)(iii), substituted "(6)" for "(7)" in subpara. (h)(2)(C), effective for estates of decedents dying after 12/31/81.

Prior to amendment, para. (c)(3) read as follows:

"(3) Phaseout of additional tax between 10th and 15th years. If the date of the disposition or cessation referred to in paragraph (1) occurs more than 120 months

Estate taxes

and less than 180 months after the date of the death of the decedent, the amount of the tax imposed by this subsection shall be reduced (but not below zero) by an amount determined by multiplying the amount of such tax (determined without regard to this paragraph) by a fraction—

"(A) the numerator of which is the number of full months after such death in excess of 120, and

"(B) the denominator of which is 60."

Prior to amendment subpara. (h)(2)(A) read as follows:

"(A) any qualified replacement property shall be treated in the same manner as if it were a portion of the interest in qualified real property which was involuntarily converted, except that with respect to such qualified replacement property—

"(i) the 15-year period under paragraph (1) of subsection (c) shall be extended by any period, beyond the 2-year period referred to in section 1033(a)(2)(B)(i), during which the qualified heir was allowed to replace the qualified real property, and

"(ii) the phaseout period under paragraph (3) of subsection (c) shall be appropriately adjusted to take into account the extension referred to in clause (i)."

—P.L. 97-34, Sec. 421(c)(2)(A), added para. (c)(7) . . . Sec. 421(c)(2)(B)(i), added para. (e)(12) . . . Sec. 421(c)(2)(B)(ii), substituted "more than 3 years" for "3 years or more" in para. (c)(6) effective [as amended by Sec. 104(b)(4) of P.L. 97-448, see above] for estates of decedents dying after 12/31/81, except that subpara. (c)(7)(A) as added by Sec. 421(c)(2)(A) of this Act, is effective for estates of decedents dying after 12/31/76. For special rules provided by Sec. 421(k)(5)(B) thru (D), as amended by Sec. 104(b)(4)(B) and (C) of P.L. 97-448 [see above] of this Act, see above.

—P.L. 97-34, Sec. 421(d)(1), added subsec. (i) . . . Sec. 421(d)(2)(A), added "or exchange" after "conversion", added "or (i)" after "(h)" and added "or of the exchange of property" after "replace" in para. (f)(1), effective for exchanges after 12/31/81.

—P.L. 97-34, Sec. 421(e)(1)(A), deleted "and the qualified heir makes an election under this subsection" after "real property" in subpara. (h)(1)(A) . . . Sec. 421(e)(1)(B), deleted para. (h)(5) . . . Sec. 421(e)(2), substituted "to which subsection (h)" for "to which an election under subsection (h)" in para. (f)(1), for involuntary conversions after 12/31/81.

Prior to deletion, para. (h)(5) read as follows:

"(5) Election. Any election under this subsection shall be made at such time and in such manner as the Secretary may by regulations prescribe."

—P.L. 97-34, Sec. 421(f)(1), redesignated subpara. (e)(7)(B) as (e)(7)(C), and added new subpara. (e)(7)(B) . . . Sec. 421(f)(2), added "and that there is no comparable land from which the average net share rental may be determined" after "determined" in subpara. (e)(7)(C) [as redesignated by Sec. 421(f)(1) of the Act] . . . Sec. 421(h)(1), added para. (e)(13) . . . Sec. 421(h)(2), added subpara. (c)(2)(E) . . . Sec. 421(i), amended para. (e)(2), for estates of decedents dying after 12/31/81.

Prior to amendment, para. (e)(2) read as follows:

"(2) Member of family. The term 'member of the family' means, with respect to any individual, only such individual's ancestor or lineal descendant, a lineal descendant of a grandparent of such individual, the spouse of such individual, or the spouse of any such descendant. For purposes of the preceding sentence, a legally adopted child of an individual shall be treated as a child of such individual by blood."

—P.L. 97-34, Sec. 421(j)(1), added the last sentence to the end of subsec. (g) . . . Sec. 421(j)(2)(A), amended para. (e)(9), for estates of decedents dying after 12/31/76. For special rules provided by Sec. 421(k)(5)(B) thru (D), as amended by Sec. 104(b)(4)(B) and (C) of P. L. 97-448 [see above] of this Act, see above.

Prior to amendment, para. (e)(9) read as follows:

"(9) Property acquired from decedent. Property shall be considered to have been acquired from or to have passed from the decedent if—

"(A) such property is so considered under section 1014(b) (relating to basis of property acquired from a decedent),

"(B) such property is acquired by any person from the estate in satisfaction of the right of such person to a pecuniary bequest, or

"(C) such property is acquired by any person from a trust in satisfaction of a right (which such person has by reason of the death of the decedent) to receive from the trust a specific dollar amount which is the equivalent of a pecuniary bequest."

—P.L. 97-34, Sec. 421(j)(3), amended para. (d)(1) . . . Sec. 421(j)(4), added para. (e)(14), for estates of decedents dying after 12/31/81.

Prior to amendment, para. (d)(1) read as follows:

"(1) Election. The election under this section shall be made not later than the time prescribed by section 6075(a) for filing the return of tax imposed by section 2001 (including extensions thereof), and shall be made in such manner as the Secretary shall by regulations prescribe."

In 1978, P.L. 95-600, Sec. 702(d)(1), added "which was acquired from or passed from the decedent to a qualified heir of the decedent and" following "real property located in the United States" in para. (b)(1) . . . Sec. 702(d)(2), added para. (e)(9) . . . Sec. 702(d)(4), added para. (e)(10) . . . Sec. 702(d)(5)(A), amended para. (c)(6) . . . Sec. 702(d)(5)(B), added para. (e)(11), effective for estates of decedents dying after 12/31/76.

Prior to amendment, para. (c)(6) read as follows:

"(6) Liability for tax. The qualified heir shall be personally liable for the additional tax imposed by this subsection with respect to his interest."

—P.L. 95-472, Sec. 4(a), added subsec. (h) . . . Sec. 4(c), added "(or if later in the case of an involuntary conversion to which an election under subsection (h) applies, 3 years from the date the Secretary is notified of the replacement of the converted property or of an intention not to replace)" before ", and" in para. (f)(1), for involuntary conversions after 12/31/76.

In 1976, P.L. 94-455, Sec. 2003(a), added Code Sec. 2032A, for estates of decedents dying after '76.

Sec. 2033. Property in which the decedent had an interest.

The value of the gross estate shall include the value of all property to the extent of the interest therein of the decedent at the time of his death.

In 1962, P.L. 87-834, Sec. 18(a)(2), deleted "(except real property situated outside of the United States)" in Code Sec. 2033, effective for estates of decedents dying after 10/16/62, except as provided in Sec. 18(b) of this Act, reproduced in note following Code Sec. 2031.

Sec. 2034. Dower or curtesy interests.

The value of the gross estate shall include the value of all property to the extent of any interest therein of the surviving spouse, existing at the time of the decedent's death as dower or curtesy, or by virtue of a statute creating an estate in lieu of dower or curtesy.

In 1962, P.L. 87-834, Sec. 18(a)(2), deleted "(except real property situated outside of the United States)" in Code Sec. 2034, effective for estates of decedents dying after 10/16/62, except as provided in Sec. 18(b) of this Act, reproduced in note following Code Sec. 2031.

Sec. 2035. Adjustments for certain gifts made within 3 years of decedent's death.

(a) Inclusion of certain property in gross estate.

If—

(1) the decedent made a transfer (by trust or otherwise) of an interest in any property, or relinquished a power with respect to any property, during the 3-year period ending on the date of the decedent's death, and

(2) the value of such property (or an interest therein) would have been included in the decedent's gross estate under section 2036, 2037, 2038, or 2042 if such transferred interest or relinquished power had been retained by the decedent on the date of his death,

the value of the gross estate shall include the value of any property (or interest therein) which would have been so included.

(b) Inclusion of gift tax on gifts made during 3 years before decedent's death.

The amount of the gross estate (determined without regard to this subsection) shall be increased by the amount of any tax paid under chapter 12 by the decedent or his estate on any gift made by the decedent or his spouse during the 3-year period ending on the date of the decedent's death.

(c) Other rules relating to transfers within 3 years of death.

(1) In general. For purposes of—

(A) section 303(b) (relating to distributions in redemption of stock to pay death taxes),

(B) section 2032A (relating to special valuation of certain farms, etc., real property), and

(C) subchapter C of chapter 64 (relating to lien for taxes),

the value of the gross estate shall include the value of all property to the extent of any interest therein of which the decedent has at any time made a transfer, by trust or otherwise, during the 3-year period ending on the date of the decedent's death.

(2) Coordination with section 6166. An estate shall be treated as meeting the 35 percent of adjusted gross estate requirement of section 6166(a)(1) only if the estate meets such requirement both with and without the application of subsection (a).

(3) Marital and small transfers. Paragraph (1) shall not apply to any transfer (other than a transfer with respect to

Code Sec. 2035(c)(3) Estate taxes

a life insurance policy) made during a calendar year to any donee if the decedent was not required by section 6019 (other than by reason of section 6019(2)) to file any gift tax return for such year with respect to transfers to such donee.

(d) Exception.

Subsection (a) and paragraph (1) of subsection (c) shall not apply to any bona fide sale for an adequate and full consideration in money or money's worth.

(e) Treatment of certain transfers from revocable trusts.

For purposes of this section and section 2038, any transfer from any portion of a trust during any period that such portion was treated under section 676 as owned by the decedent by reason of a power in the grantor (determined without regard to section 672(e)) shall be treated as a transfer made directly by the decedent.

In 2000, P.L. 106-554, Sec. 1(a)(7), [which enacted into law Sec. 319(14)(A) of P.L. 106-554] substituted "subsection (a)" for "paragraph (1)" in para. (c)(2)... Sec. 1(a)(7), [which enacted into law Sec. 319(14)(B) of P.L. 106-554] added "and paragraph (1) of subsection (c)" after "Subsection (a)" in subsec. (d), effective 12/21/2000.

In 1997, P.L. 105-34, Sec. 1310(a), amended Code Sec. 2035, effective for the estates of decedents dying after 8/5/97.

Prior to amendment, Sec. 2035 read as follows:

"Sec. 2035 Adjustments for gifts made within 3 years of decedent's death.

"(a) Inclusion of gifts made by decedent. Except as provided in subsection (b), the value of the gross estate shall include the value of all property to the extent of any interest therein of which the decedent has at any time made a transfer, by trust or otherwise, during the 3-year period ending on the date of the decedent's death.

"(b) Exceptions. Subsection (a) shall not apply—

"(1) to any bona fide sale for an adequate and full consideration in money or money's worth, and

"(2) to any gift to a donee made during a calendar year if the decedent was not required by section 6019 (other than by reason of section 6019(2)) to file any gift tax return for such year with respect to gifts to such donee.

Paragraph (2) shall not apply to any transfer with respect to a life insurance policy.

"(c) Inclusion of gift tax on certain gifts made during 3 years before decedent's death. The amount of the gross estate (determined without regard to this subsection) shall be increased by the amount of any tax paid under chapter 12 by the decedent or his estate on any gift made by the decedent or his spouse after December 31, 1976, and during the 3-year period ending on the date of the decedent's death.

"(d) Decedents dying after 1981.

"(1) In general. Except as otherwise provided in this subsection, subsection (a) shall not apply to the estate of a decedent dying after December 31, 1981.

"(2) Exceptions for certain transfers. Paragraph (1) of this subsection and paragraph (2) of subsection (b) shall not apply to a transfer of an interest in property which is included in the value of the gross estate under section 2036, 2037, 2038, or 2042 or would have been included under any of such sections if such interest had been retained by the decedent.

"(3) 3-year rule retained for certain purposes. Paragraph (1) shall not apply for purposes of—

"(A) section 303(b) (relating to distributions in redemption of stock to pay death taxes),

"(B) section 2032A (relating to special valuation of certain farm, etc., real property), and

"(C) subchapter C of chapter 64 (relating to lien for taxes).

"(4) Coordination of 3-year rule with section 6166(a)(1). An estate shall be treated as meeting the 35-percent of adjusted gross estate requirement of section 6166(a)(1) only if the estate meets such requirement both with and without the application of paragraph (1)."

In 1983, P.L. 97-448, Sec. 104(a)(9), substituted "section 6019 (2)" for "section 6019(a)(2)" in para. (b)(2)... Sec. 104(d)(1)(A), added para. (d)(4)... Sec. 104(d)(1)(C), deleted subpara. (d)(3)(C), added "and" at the end of subpara. (d)(3)(B), and redesignated subpara. (d)(3)(D) as subpara. (d)(3)(C)... Sec. 104(d)(2)(A), added "of this subsection and paragraph (2) of subsection (b)" after "Paragraph (1)" in para. (d)(2)... Sec. 104(d)(2)(B), deleted "2041," after "2038," in para. (d)(2), effective for estates of decedents dying after 12/31/82.

—P.L. 97-448, Sec. 104(d)(3)(A)-(C), provides:

"(3) Election to have amendments not apply.—

"(A) In the case of any decedent—

"(i) who dies before August 13, 1984, and

"(ii) who made a gift (before August 13, 1981, and during the 3-year period ending on the date of the decedent's death) on which tax imposed by chapter 12 of the Internal Revenue Code of 1954 has been paid before April 16, 1982, such decedent's executor may make an election to have subtitle B of such Code (relating to estate and gift taxes) applied with respect to such decedent without regard to any of the amendments made by title IV of the Economic Recovery Tax Act of 1981.

"(B) An election under subparagraph (A) shall be made at such time and in such manner as the Secretary of the Treasury or his delegate shall prescribe.

"(C) An election under subparagraph (A), once made, shall be irrevocable."

Prior to deletion, subpara. (d)(3)(C) read as follows:

"(C) section 6166 (relating to extension of time for payment of estate tax where estate consists largely of interest in closely held business), and"

In 1981, P.L. 97-34, Sec. 403(b)(3)(B), added "(other than by reason of section 6019(a)(2))" after "section 6019" in para. (b)(2)... Sec. 424(a), added subsec. (d), effective for estates of decedents dying after 12/31/81.

In 1980, P.L. 96-222, Sec. 107(a)(2)(F), provides:

"(F)(i) If the executor elects the benefits of this subparagraph with respect to any estate, section 2035(b) of the Internal Revenue Code of 1954 (relating to adjustments for gifts made within 3 years of decedent's death) shall be applied with respect to transfers made by the decedent during 1977 as if paragraph (2) of such section 2035(b) read as follows:

"(2) to any gift to a donee made during 1977 to the extent of the amount of such gift which was excludable in computing taxable gifts by reason of section 2503(b) (relating to $3,000 annual exclusion for purposes of the gift tax) determined without regard to section 2513(a).

"(ii) The election under clause (i) with respect to any estate shall be made on or before the later of—

"(I) the due date for filing the estate tax return, or

"(II) the day which is 120 days after the date of the enactment of this Act."

In 1978, P.L. 95-600, Sec. 702(f)(1), amended subsec. (b), effective for estates of decedents dying after 12/31/76, except for transfers made before 1/1/77.

Prior to amendment, subsec. (b) read as follows:

"(b) Exceptions.

"Subsection (a) shall not apply to—

"(1) any bona fide sale for an adequate and full consideration in money or money's worth, and

"(2) any gift excludable in computing taxable gifts by reason of section 2503(b) (relating to $3,000 annual exclusion for purposes of the gift tax) determined without regard to section 2513(a)."

In 1976, P.L. 94-455, Sec. 2001(a)(5), amended Code Sec. 2035, effective for estates of decedents dying after 12/31/76, except that it does not apply to transfers made before 1/1/77.

Prior to amendment, Code Sec. 2035 read as follows:

"Sec. 2035. Transactions in contemplation of death.

"(a) General rule.

"The value of the gross estate shall include the value of all property to the extent of any interest therein of which the decedent has at any time made a transfer (except in case of a bona fide sale for an adequate and full consideration in money or money's worth), by trust or otherwise, in contemplation of his death.

"(b) Application of general rule.

"If the decedent within a period of 3 years ending with the date of his death (except in case of a bona fide sale for an adequate and full consideration in money or money's worth) transferred an interest in property, relinquished a power, or exercised or released a general power of appointment, such transfer, relinquishment, exercise, or release shall, unless shown to the contrary, be deemed to have been made in contemplation of death within the meaning of this section and sections 2038 and 2041 (relating to revocable transfers and powers of appointment); but no such transfer, relinquishment, exercise, or release made before such 3-year period shall be treated as having been made in contemplation of death."

In 1962, P.L. 87-834, Sec. 18(a)(2)(C), deleted "(except real property situated outside of the United States)" in subsec. (a), effective for estates of decedents dying after 10/16/62, except as provided in Sec. 18(b)(2) of this Act reproduced in note following Code Sec. 2031.

Sec. 2036. Transfers with retained life estate.

(a) General rule.

The value of the gross estate shall include the value of all property to the extent of any interest therein of which the decedent has at any time made a transfer (except in case of a bona fide sale for an adequate and full consideration in money or money's worth), by trust or otherwise, under which he has retained for his life or for any period not ascertainable without reference to his death or for any period which does not in fact end before his death—

(1) the possession or enjoyment of, or the right to the income from, the property, or

(2) the right, either alone or in conjunction with any person, to designate the persons who shall possess or enjoy the property or the income therefrom.

(b) Voting rights.

(1) In general. For purposes of subsection (a)(1), the retention of the right to vote (directly or indirectly) shares of stock of a controlled corporation shall be considered to be a retention of the enjoyment of transferred property.

Estate taxes — Code Sec. 2036

(2) Controlled corporation. For purposes of paragraph (1), a corporation shall be treated as a controlled corporation if, at any time after the transfer of the property and during the 3-year period ending on the date of the decedent's death, the decedent owned (with the application of section 318), or had the right (either alone or in conjunction with any person) to vote, stock possessing at least 20 percent of the total combined voting power of all classes of stock.

(3) Coordination with section 2035. For purposes of applying section 2035 with respect to paragraph (1), the relinquishment or cessation of voting rights shall be treated as a transfer of property made by the decedent.

(c) Limitation on application of general rule.

This section shall not apply to a transfer made before March 4, 1931; nor to a transfer made after March 3, 1931, and before June 7, 1932, unless the property transferred would have been includible in the decedent's gross estate by reason of the amendatory language of the joint resolution of March 3, 1931 (46 Stat. 1516).

In 1990, P.L. 101-508, Sec. 11601(a), deleted subsec. (c), and redesignated subsec. (d) as subsec. (c), effective for property transferred after 12/17/87.
Prior to deletion, subsec. (c) read as follows:

"(c) Inclusion related to valuation freezes.

"(1) In general. For purposes of subsection (a), if—

"(A) any person holds a substantial interest in an enterprise, and

"(B) such person in effect transfers after December 17, 1987, property having a disproportionately large share of the potential appreciation in such person's interest in the enterprise while retaining an interest in the income of, or rights in, the enterprise,

then the retention of the retained interest shall be considered to be a retention of the enjoyment of the transferred property.

"(2) Special rules for consideration furnished by family members.

"(A) In general. The exception contained in subsection (a) for a bona fide sale shall not apply to a transfer described in paragraph (1) if such transfer is to a member of the transferor's family.

"(B) Treatment of consideration.

"(i) In general. In the case of a transfer described in paragraph (1), if—

"(I) a member of the transferor's family provides consideration in money or money's worth for such member's interest in the enterprise, and

"(II) it is established to the satisfaction of the Secretary that such consideration originally belonged to such member and was never received or acquired (directly or indirectly) by such member from the transferor for less than full and adequate consideration in money or money's worth,

paragraph (1) shall not apply to the applicable fraction of the portion of the enterprise which would (but for this subparagraph) have been included in the gross estate of the transferor by reason of this subsection (determined without regard to any reduction under paragraph (5) for the value of the retained interest).

"(ii) Applicable fraction. For purposes of clause (i), the applicable fraction is a fraction—

"(I) the numerator of which is the amount of the consideration referred to in clause (i), and

"(II) the denominator of which is the value of the portion referred to in clause (i) immediately after the transfer described in paragraph (1).

"(iii) Section 2043 not to apply. The provisions of this subparagraph shall be in lieu of any adjustment under section 2043.

"(3) Definitions. For purposes of this subsection—

"(A) Substantial interest. A person holds a substantial interest in an enterprise if such person owns (directly or indirectly) 10 percent or more of the voting power or income stream, or both, in such enterprise. For purposes of the preceding sentence, an individual shall be treated as owning any interest in an enterprise which is owned (directly or indirectly) by any member of such individual's family.

"(B) Family. The term 'family' means, with respect to any individual, such individual's spouse, any lineal descendant of such individual or of such individual's spouse, any parent or grandparent of such individual, and any spouse of any of the foregoing. For purposes of the preceding sentence, a relationship by legal adoption shall be treated as a relationship by blood.

"(C) Treatment of spouse. Except as provided in regulations, an individual and such individual's spouse shall be treated as 1 person.

"(4) Treatment of certain transfers.

"(A) In general. For purposes of this subtitle, if, before the death of the original transferor—

"(i) the original transferor transfers all (or any portion of) the retained interest referred to in paragraph (1), or

"(ii) the original transferee transfers all (or any portion of) the transferred property referred to in paragraph (1) to a person who is not a member of the original transferor's family, the original transferor shall be treated as having made a transfer by gift of property to the original transferee equal to the paragraph (1) inclusion (or proportionate amount thereof). Proper adjustments shall be made in the amount treated as a gift by reason of the preceding sentence to take into account prior transfers to which this subparagraph applied and take into account any right of recovery (whether or not exercised) under section 2207B.

"(B) Coordination with paragraph (1). In any case to which subparagraph (A) applies, nothing in paragraph (1) or section 2035(d)(2) shall require the inclusion of the transferred property (or proportionate amount thereof).

"(C) Special rule where property retransferred. In the case of a transfer described in subparagraph (A)(ii) from the original transferee to the original transferor, the paragraph (1) inclusion (or proportion thereof) shall be reduced by the excess (if any) of—

"(i) the fair market value of the property so transferred, over

"(ii) the amount of the consideration paid by the original transferor in exchange for such property.

"(D) Definitions. For purposes of this paragraph—

"(i) Original transferor. The term 'original transferor' means the person making the transfer referred to in paragraph (1).

"(ii) Original transferee. The term 'original transferee' means the person to whom the transfer referred to in paragraph (1) is made. Such term includes any member of the original transferor's family to whom the property is subsequently transferred.

"(iii) Paragraph (1) inclusion. The term 'paragraph (1) inclusion' means the amount which would have been included in the gross estate of the original transferor under subsection (a) by reason of paragraph (1) (determined without regard to sections 2032 and 2032A) if the original transferor died immediately before the transfer referred to in subparagraph (A). The amount determined under the preceding sentence shall be reduced by the amount (if any) of the taxable gift resulting from the transfer referred to in paragraph (1)(B).

"(iv) Transfers to include terminations, etc. Terminations, lapses, and other changes in any interest in property of the original transferor or original transferee shall be treated as transfers.

"(E) Continuing interest in transferred property may not be retained. A transfer (to which subparagraph (A) would otherwise apply) shall not be taken into account under subparagraph (A) if the original transferor or the original transferee (as the case may be) retains a direct or indirect continuing interest in the property transferred in such transfer.

"(5) Adjustments. Appropriate adjustments shall be made in the amount included in the gross estate by reason of this subsection for the value of the retained interest, extraordinary distributions, and changes in the capital structure of the enterprise after the transfer described in paragraph (1).

"(6) Treatment of certain grantor retained interest trusts.

"(A) In general. For purposes of this subsection, any retention of a qualified trust income interest shall be disregarded and the property with respect to which such interest exists shall be treated as held by the transferor while such income interest continues.

"(B) Qualified trust income interest. For purposes of subparagraph (A) the term 'qualified trust income interest' means any right to receive amounts determined solely by reference to the income from property held in trust if—

"(i) such right is for a period not exceeding 10 years,

"(ii) the person holding such right transferred the property to the trust, and

"(iii) such person is not a trustee of such trust.

"(7) Exceptions.

"(A) In general. Paragraph (1) shall not apply to a transaction solely by reason of 1 or more of the following:

"(i) The receipt (or retention) of qualified debt.

"(ii) Except as provided in regulations, the existence of an agreement for the sale or lease of goods or other property to be used in the enterprise or the providing of services and—

"(I) the agreement is an arm's length agreement for fair market value, and

"(II) the agreement does not otherwise involve any change in interests in the enterprise.

"(iii) An option or other agreement to buy or sell property at the fair market value of such property as of the time the option is (or the rights under the agreement are) exercised.

"(B) Limitations.

"(i) Services performed after transfer. In the case of compensation for services performed after the transfer referred to in paragraph (1)(B), clause (ii) of subparagraph (A) shall not apply if such services were performed under an agreement providing for the performance of services over a period greater than 3 years after the date of the transfer. For purposes of the preceding sentence, the term of any agreement includes any period for which the agreement may be extended at the option of the service provider.

"(ii) Amounts must not be contingent on profits, etc. Clause (ii) of subparagraph (A) shall not apply to any amount determined (in whole or in part) by reference to gross receipts, income, profits, or similar items of the enterprise.

"(C) Qualified debt. For purposes of this paragraph, except as provided in subparagraph (D), the term 'qualified debt' means any indebtedness if—

"(i) such indebtedness—

"(I) unconditionally requires the payment of a sum certain in money in 1 or more fixed payments on specified dates, and

"(II) has a fixed maturity date not more than 15 years from the date of issue (or, in the case of indebtedness secured by real property, not more than 30 years from the date of issue).

"(ii) the only other amount payable under such indebtedness is interest determined at—

"(I) a fixed rate, or

"(II) a rate which bears a fixed relationship to a specified market interest rate,

"(iii) the interest payment dates are fixed,

"(iv) such indebtedness is not by its terms subordinated to the claims of general creditors,

"(v) except in a case where such indebtedness is in default as to interest or principal, such indebtedness does not grant voting rights to the person to whom the debt is owed or place any limitation on the exercise of voting rights by others, and

"(vi) such indebtedness—

"(I) is not (directly or indirectly) convertible into an interest in the enterprise which would not be qualified debt, and

"(II) does not otherwise grant any right to acquire such an interest.

The requirement of clause (i)(I) that the principal be payable on 1 or more specified dates and the requirement of clause (i)(II) shall not apply to indebtedness payable on demand if such indebtedness is issued in return for cash to be used to meet normal business needs of the enterprise.

"(D) Special rule for startup debt.

"(i) In general. For purposes of this paragraph, the term 'qualified debt' includes any qualified startup debt.

"(ii) Qualified startup debt. For purposes of clause (i), the term 'qualified startup debt' means any indebtedness if—

"(I) such indebtedness unconditionally requires the payment of a sum certain in money,

"(II) such indebtedness was received in exchange for cash to be used in any enterprise involving the active conduct of a trade or business,

"(III) the person to whom the indebtedness is owed has not at any time (whether before, on, or after the exchange referred to in subclause (II)) transferred any property (including goodwill) which was not cash to the enterprise or transferred customers or other business opportunities to the enterprise,

"(IV) the person to whom the indebtedness is owed has not at any time (whether before, on, or after the exchange referred to in subclause (II)) held any interest in the enterprise (including an interest as an officer, director, or employee) which was not qualified startup debt,

"(V) any person who (but for subparagraph (A)(i)) would have been an original transferee (as defined in paragraph (4)(C)) participates in the active management (as defined in section 2032A(e)(12)) of the enterprise, and

"(VI) such indebtedness meets the requirements of clauses (v) and (vi) of subparagraph (C).

"(8) Regulations. The Secretary shall prescribe such regulations as may be necessary or appropriate to carry out the purposes of this subsection, including such regulations as may be necessary or appropriate to prevent avoidance of the purposes of this subsection through distributions or otherwise."

In **1988**, P.L. 100-647, Sec. 3031(a)(1), amended para. (c)(4), effective in cases where the transfer referred to in Code Sec. 2036 (c)(1)(B) is on or after 6/21/88. Sec. 3031(h)(5) of this Act provides:

"(5) Clarification of effective date.— For purposes of section 10402(b) of the Revenue Act of 1987, with respect to property transferred on or before December 17, 1987—

"(A) any failure to exercise a right of conversion,

"(B) any failure to pay dividends, and

"(C) failures to exercise other rights specified in regulations, shall not be treated as a subsequent transfer."

Prior to amendment, para. (c)(4) read as follows:

"(4) Coordination with section 2035. For purposes of applying section 2035, any transfer of the retained interest referred to in paragraph (1) shall be treated as a transfer of an interest in the transferred property referred to in paragraph (1)."

—P.L. 100-647, Sec. 3031(b), added para. (c)(6)... Sec. 3031, (b [sic c]), added paras. (c)(7) and (8)... Sec. 3031(d), substituted "Except as provided in regulations, an individual" for "An individual" in subpara. (c)(3)(C), effective with respect to estates of decedents dying after 12/31/87, but only in the case of property transferred after 12/17/87. For clarification of effective date, see Sec. 3031(h)(5) of this Act, reproduced above.

—P.L. 100-647, Sec. 3031(e), substituted "while retaining an interest in the income of, or rights in, the enterprise," for "while retaining a disproportionately large share in the income of, rights in, the enterprise," in subpara. (c)(1)(B), effective with respect to estates of decedents dying after 12/17/87, but only in the case of property transferred after 12/17/87. Sec. 3031(h)(4) of this Act provides:

"(4) Correction period.— If section 2036(c)(1) of the 1986 Code would (but for this paragraph) apply to any interest arising from a transaction entered into during the period beginning after December 17, 1987, and ending before January 1, 1990, such section shall not apply to such interest if—

"(A) during such period, such actions are taken as are necessary to have such section 2036(c)(1) not apply to such transaction (and any such interest), or

"(B) the original transferor and his spouse on January 1, 1990 (or, if earlier, the date of the original transferor's death), does not hold any interest in the enterprise involved."

—P.L. 100-647, Sec. 3031(g)(1), amended para. (c)(2)... Sec. 3031(g)(2), amended para. (c)(5), effective with respect to estates of decedents dying after 12/17/87, but only in the case of property transferred after 12/17/87. For clarification of effective date, see Sec. 3031(h)(5) of this Act, reproduced above.

Prior to amendment, para. (c)(2) read as follows:

"(2) Special rule for sales to family members. The exception contained in subsection (a) for a bona fide sale shall not apply to a transfer described in paragraph (1) if such transfer is to a member of the transferor's family."

Prior to amendment, para (c)(5) read as follows:

"(5) Coordination with section 2043. In lieu of applying section 2043, appropriate adjustments shall be made for the value of the retained interest."

In **1987**, P.L. 100-203, Sec. 10402(a), redesignated subsec. (c) as subsec. (d) and added new subsec. (c), effective for estates of decedents dying after 12/31/87, but only in the case of property transferred after 12/17/87.

In **1978**, P.L. 95-600, Sec. 702(i)(1), redesignated subsec. (b) as subsec. (c) and added new subsec. (b)... Sec. 702(i)(2), deleted the last sentence in subsec. (a), effective for transfers made after 6/22/76.

Prior to deletion, the last sentence in subsec. (a) read as follows:

"For purposes of paragraph (1), the retention of voting rights in retained stock shall be considered to be a retention of the enjoyment of such stock."

In **1976**, P.L. 94-455, Sec. 2009(a), added a sentence to the end of subsec. (a), effective for transfers made after 6/22/76.

In **1962**, P.L. 87-834, Sec. 18(a)(2)(D), deleted "(except real property situated outside of the United States)" in subsec. (a), effective for estates of decedents dying after 10/16/62, except as provided in Sec. 18(b) at note following Code Sec. 2031.

Sec. 2037. Transfers taking effect at death.

(a) General rule.

The value of the gross estate shall include the value of all property to the extent of any interest therein of which the decedent has at any time after September 7, 1916, made a transfer (except in case of a bona fide sale for an adequate and full consideration in money or money's worth), by trust or otherwise, if—

(1) possession or enjoyment of the property can, through ownership of such interest, be obtained only by surviving the decedent, and

(2) the decedent has retained a reversionary interest in the property (but in the case of a transfer made before October 8, 1949, only if such reversionary interest arose by the express terms of the instrument of transfer), and the value of such reversionary interest immediately before the death of the decedent exceeds 5 percent of the value of such property.

(b) Special rules.

For purposes of this section, the term "reversionary interest" includes a possibility that property transferred by the decedent—

(1) may return to him or his estate, or

(2) may be subject to a power of disposition by him,

but such term does not include a possibility that the income alone from such property may return to him or become subject to a power of disposition by him. The value of a reversionary interest immediately before the death of the decedent shall be determined (without regard to the fact of the decedent's death) by usual methods of valuation, including the use of tables of mortality and actuarial principles, under regulations prescribed by the Secretary. In determining the value of a possibility that property may be subject to a power of disposition by the decedent, such possibility shall be valued as if it were a possibility that such property may return to the decedent or his estate. Notwithstanding the foregoing, an interest so transferred shall not be included in the decedent's gross estate under this section if possession or enjoyment of the property could have been obtained by any beneficiary during the decedent's life through the exercise of a general power of appointment (as defined in section 2041) which in fact was exercisable immediately before the decedent's death.

In **1976**, P.L. 94-455, Sec. 1906(b)(13)(A), substituted "Secretary" for "Secretary or his delegate" in subsec. (b), effective 2/1/77.

In **1962**, P.L. 87-834, Sec. 18(a)(2), deleted "(except real property situated outside of the United States)" in subsec. (a), effective for estates of decedents dying after 10/16/62 except as provided in Sec. 18(b), reproduced in note following Code Sec. 2031.

Sec. 2038. Revocable transfers.

(a) In general.

The value of the gross estate shall include the value of all property—

Estate taxes
Code Sec. 2039

(1) Transfers after June 22, 1936. To the extent of any interest therein of which the decedent has at any time made a transfer (except in case of a bona fide sale for an adequate and full consideration in money or money's worth), by trust or otherwise, where the enjoyment thereof was subject at the date of his death to any change through the exercise of a power (in whatever capacity exercisable) by the decedent alone or by the decedent in conjunction with any other person (without regard to when or from what source the decedent acquired such power), to alter, amend, revoke, or terminate, or where any such power is relinquished during the 3-year period ending on the date of the decedent's death.

(2) Transfers on or before June 22, 1936. To the extent of any interest therein of which the decedent has at any time made a transfer (except in case of a bona fide sale for an adequate and full consideration in money or money's worth), by trust or otherwise, where the enjoyment thereof was subject at the date of his death to any change through the exercise of a power, either by the decedent alone or in conjunction with any person, to alter, amend, or revoke, or where the decedent relinquished any such power during the 3-year period ending on the date of the decedent's death. Except in the case of transfers made after June 22, 1936, no interest of the decedent of which he has made a transfer shall be included in the gross estate under paragraph (1) unless it is includible under this paragraph.

(b) Date of existence of power.

For purposes of this section, the power to alter, amend, revoke, or terminate shall be considered to exist on the date of the decedent's death even though the exercise of the power is subject to a precedent giving of notice or even though the alteration, amendment, revocation, or termination takes effect only on the expiration of a stated period after the exercise of the power, whether or not on or before the date of the decedent's death notice has been given or the power has been exercised. In such cases proper adjustment shall be made representing the interests which would have been excluded from the power if the decedent had lived, and for such purpose, if the notice has not been given or the power has not been exercised on or before the date of his death, such notice shall be considered to have been given, or the power exercised, on the date of his death.

In 1976, P.L. 94-455, Sec. 1902(a)(3), deleted subsec. (c), effective for estates of decedents dying after 10/4/76.
Prior to deletion, subsec. (c) read as follows:
"(c) Effect of disability in certain cases.
"For purposes of this section, in the case of a decedent who was (for a continuous period beginning not less than 3 months before December 31, 1947, and ending with his death) under a mental disability to relinquish a power, the term 'power' shall not include a power the relinquishment of which on or after January 1, 1940, and on or before December 31, 1947, would, by reason of section 1000(e) of the Internal Revenue Code of 1939, be deemed not to be a transfer of property for purposes of chapter 4 of the Internal Revenue Code of 1939."
—P.L. 94-455, Sec. 2001(c)(1)(K), substituted "during the 3-year period ending on the date of the decedent's death" for "in contemplation of decedent's death" in para. (a)(1), and substituted "during the 3-year period ending on the date of the decedent's death" for "in contemplation of his death" in para. (a)(2), effective for estates of decedents dying after 12/31/76, but does not apply to transfers made before 1/1/77.

In 1962, P.L. 87-834, Sec. 18(a)(2), deleted "(except real property situated outside of the United States)" in subsec. (a), effective for estates of decedents dying after 10/16/62, except as provided in Sec. 18(b)(2) of this Act, reproduced in note following Code Sec. 2031.

In 1959, P.L. 86-141, Sec. 1, added subsec. (c), effective for estates of decedents dying after 8/16/54, and that no interest shall be allowed or paid on any overpayment resulting from the application of the amendment made by the first section of this Act with respect to any payment made before the date of the enactment of this Act [8/7/59].

Sec. 2039. Annuities.
(a) General.

The gross estate shall include the value of an annuity or other payment receivable by any beneficiary by reason of surviving the decedent under any form of contract or agreement entered into after March 3, 1931 (other than as insurance under policies on the life of the decedent), if, under such contract or agreement, an annuity or other payment was payable to the decedent, or the decedent possessed the right to receive such annuity or payment, either alone or in conjunction with another for his life or for any period not ascertainable without reference to his death or for any period which does not in fact end before his death.

(b) Amount includible.

Subsection (a) shall apply to only such part of the value of the annuity or other payment receivable under such contract or agreement as is proportionate to that part of the purchase price therefor contributed by the decedent. For purposes of this section, any contribution by the decedent's employer or former employer to the purchase price of such contract or agreement (whether or not to an employee's trust or fund forming part of a pension, annuity, retirement, bonus or profit sharing plan) shall be considered to be contributed by the decedent if made by reason of his employment.

In 1986, P.L. 99-514, Sec. 1848(d), deleted "or a bond described in paragraph (3)", after "described in paragraph (2)" in the second sentence of subsec. (e) [repealed by Sec. 525(a) of P.L. 98-369, see below], effective for estates of decedents dying after 12/31/84.
—P.L. 99-514, Sec. 1852(e)(1)(A), deleted subsec. (c), effective for estates of decedents dying after 10/22/86.
Prior to deletion, subsec. (c) read:
"(c) Exception of certain annuity interests created by community property laws.
"(1) In general. In the case of an employee on whose behalf contributions or payments were made by his employer or former employer under a trust, plan, or contract to which this subsection applies, if the spouse of such employee predeceases such employee, then notwithstanding any provision of law, there shall be excluded from the gross estate of such spouse the value of any interest of such spouse in such trust, plan, or contract, to the extent such interest—
"(A) is attributable to such contributions or payments, and
"(B) arises solely by reason of such spouse's interest in community income under the community property laws of a State.
"(2) Trusts, plans, and contracts to which subsection applies. This subsection shall apply to—
"(A) any trust, plan, or contract which at the time of the decedent's separation from employment (by death or otherwise), or if earlier, at the time of termination of the plan—
"(i) formed part of a plan which met the requirements of section 401(a), or
"(ii) was purchased pursuant to a plan described in section 403(a), or
"(B) a retirement annuity contract purchased for an employee by an employer which is—
"(i) an organization referred to in clause (ii) or (vi) of section 170(b)(1)(A), or
"(ii) a religious organization (other than a trust) exempt from taxation under section 501(a).
"(3) Amount contributed by employee.—For purposes of this subsection—
"(A) contributions or payments made by the decedent's employer or former employer under a trust, plan, or contract described in paragraph (2)(A) shall not be considered to be contributed by the decedent, and
"(B) contributions or payments made by the decedent's employer or former employer toward the purchase of an annuity contract described in paragraph (2)(B) shall not be considered to be contributed by the decedent to the extent excludable from gross income under section 403(b)."
—P.L. 99-514, Sec. 1852(e)(3), added Sec. 525(b)(4) [reproduced below] to P.L. 98-369, exceptions to the effective date for changes made by Sec. 525(a) of P.L. 98-369, see below.

In 1984, P.L. 98-369, Sec. 491(d)(34)(A)-(E), deleted para. (e)(3), substituted a period for ", or" at the end of para. (e)(2), added "or" at the end of para. (e)(1), substituted "or 408(d)(3)" for "405(d)(3), 408(d)(3), or 409(b)(3)(C)" in subsec. (e), and substituted "or annuity" for ", annuity, or bond" each place it appeared in subsec. (e), effective for obligations issued after 12/31/83.
Prior to deletion, para. (e)(3) read as follows:
"(3) a retirement bond described in section 409(a)."
—P.L. 98-369, Sec. 525(a), deleted subsecs. (d), (e), (f), and (g) and amended subsec. (c), effective for estates of decedents dying after 12/31/84, with the following exception, as provided by Sec. 525(b)(2) and (4) of this Act [as amended by Sec. 1852(e)(3) of P.L. 99-514, see above]:
"(2) Exception for participants in pay status. The amendments made by this section shall not apply to the estate of any decedent who—
"(A) was a participant in any plan who was in pay status on December 31, 1984, and

2,989

"(B) irrevocably elected the form of the benefit before the date of the enactment of this Act."

"(4) Irrevocable election. For purposes of paragraph (2) and section 245(c) of the Tax Equity and Fiscal Responsibility Act of 1982, an individual who—

"(A) separated from service before January 1, 1985, with respect to paragraph (2), or January 1, 1983, with respect to section 245(c) of the Tax Equity and Fiscal Responsibility Act of 1982, and

"(B) meets the requirements of such paragraph or such section other than the requirement that there be an irrevocable election, and that the individual be in pay status,

shall be treated as having made an irrevocable election and as being in pay status within the time prescribed with respect to a form of benefit if such individual does not change such form of benefit before death."

Prior to deletion, subsecs. (d), (e), (f), and (g) read as follows:

"(d) Exemption of certain annuity interests created by community property laws.

"In the case of an employee on whose behalf contributions or payments were made by his employer or former employer under a trust or plan described in subsection (c)(1) or (2), or toward the purchase of a contract described in subsection (c)(3), which under subsection (c) are not considered as contributed by the employee, if the spouse of such employee predeceases him, then, notwithstanding the provisions of this section or of any other provision of law, there shall be excluded from the gross estate of such spouse the value of any interest of such spouse in such trust or plan or such contract, to the extent such interest—

"(1) is attributable to such contributions or payments, and

"(2) arises solely by reason of such spouse's interest in community income under the community property laws of a State.

"(e) Exclusion of individual retirement accounts, etc.

"Subject to the limitation of subsection (g), notwithstanding any other provision of this section or of any other provision of law, there shall be excluded from the value of the gross estate the value of an annuity receivable by any beneficiary (other than the executor) under—

"(1) an individual retirement account described in section 408(a), or

"(2) an individual retirement annuity described in section 408(b).

If any payment to an account described in paragraph (1) or for an annuity described in paragraph (2) was not allowable as a deduction under section 219 and was not a rollover contribution described in section 402(a)(5), 403(a)(4), section 403(b)(8) (but only to the extent such contribution is attributable to a distribution from a contract described in subsection (c)(3)), or 408(d)(3), the preceding sentence shall not apply to that portion of the value of the amount receivable under such account or annuity (as the case may be) which bears the same ratio to the total value of the amount so receivable as the total amount which was paid to or for such account or annuity and which was not allowable as a deduction under section 219 and was not such a rollover contribution bears to the total amount paid to or for such account or annuity. For purposes of this subsection, the term 'annuity' means an annuity contract or other arrangement providing for a series of substantially equal periodic payments to be made to a beneficiary (other than the executor) for his life or over a period extending for at least 36 months after the date of the decedent's death.

"(f) Lump sum distributions.

"(1) In general. An amount is described in this subsection if—

"(A) it is a lump sum distribution described in section 402(e)(4) (determined without regard to the third sentence of section 402(e)(4)(A)), or

"(B) it is an amount attributable to accumulated deductible employee contributions (as defined in section 72(o)(5)(B)) in any plan taken into account for purposes of determining whether the distribution described in subparagraph (A) qualifies as a lump sum distribution.

"(2) Exception where recipient elects not to take 10-year averaging. An amount described in paragraph (1) shall be treated as not described in this subsection if the recipient elects irrevocably (at such time and in such manner as the Secretary may by regulations prescribe) to treat the distribution as taxable under section 402(a) (without the application of paragraph (2) thereof), except to the extent that section 402(e)(4)(J) applies to such distribution.

"(g) $100,000 limitation on exclusions under subsections (c) and (e).

"The aggregate amount excluded from the gross estate of any decedent under subsections (c) and (e) of this section shall not exceed $100,000."

Prior to amendment, subsec. (c) read as follows:

"(c) Exemption of annuities under certain trusts and plans.

"Subject to the limitation of subsection (g), notwithstanding any other provision of this section or of any provision of law, there shall be excluded from the gross estate the value of an annuity or other payment (other than an amount described in subsection (f)) receivable by any beneficiary (other than the executor) under—

"(1) an employees' trust (or under a contract purchased by an employees' trust) forming part of a pension, stock bonus, or profit-sharing plan which, at the time of the decedent's separation from employment (whether by death or otherwise), or at the time of termination of the plan if earlier, met the requirements of section 401(a);

"(2) a retirement annuity contract purchased by an employer (and not by an employees' trust) pursuant to a plan which, at the time of decedent's separation from employment (by death or otherwise), or at the time of termination of the plan if earlier, was a plan described in section 403(a);

"(3) a retirement annuity contract purchased for an employee by an employer which is an organization referred to in section 170(b)(1)(A)(ii) or (vi), or which is a religious organization (other than a trust), and which is exempt from tax under section 501(a); or

"(4) chapter 73 of title 10 of the United States Code.

If such amounts payable after the death of the decedent under a plan described in paragraph (1) or (2), under a contract described in paragraph (3), or under chapter 73 of title 10 of the United States Code are attributable to any extent to payments or contributions made by the decedent, no exclusion shall be allowed for that part of the value of such amounts in the proportion that the total payments or contributions made by the decedent bears to the total payments or contributions made. For purposes of this subsection, contributions or payments made by the decedent's employer or former employer under a trust or plan described in paragraph (1) or (2) shall not be considered to be contributed by the decedent, and contributions or payments made by the decedent's employer or former employer toward the purchase of an annuity contract described in paragraph (3) shall, to the extent excludable from gross income under section 403(b), not be considered to be contributed by the decedent. This subsection shall apply to all decedents dying after December 31, 1953. For purposes of this subsection, contributions or payments on behalf of the decedent while he was an employee within the meaning of section 401(c)(1) made under a trust or plan described in paragraph (1) or (2) shall, to the extent allowable as a deduction under section 404, be considered to be made by a person other than the decedent and, to the extent not so allowable, shall be considered to be made by the decedent. For purposes of this subsection, amounts payable under chapter 73 of title 10 of the United States Code are attributable to payments or contributions made by the decedent only to the extent of amounts deposited by him pursuant to section 1438 or 1452(d) of such title 10. For purposes of this subsection, any deductible employee contributions (within the meaning of paragraph (5) of section 72(o)) shall be considered as made by a person other than the decedent."

—P.L. 98-369, Sec. 525(b)(3), amended Sec. 245(c) of P.L. 97-248, the effective date for changes made by Sec. 245(a) and (b) (see below), by adding ", except that such amendments shall not apply to the estate of any decedent who was a participant in any plan who was in pay status on December 31, 1982, and irrevocably elected before January 1, 1983, the form of benefit".

In 1983, P.L. 97-448, Sec. 103(c)(9)(A), amended para. (f)(1), effective for tax yrs. begin. after 12/31/81.

Prior to amendment, para. (f)(1) read as follows:

"(1) In general. An amount is described in this subsection if it is a lump sum distribution described in section 402(e)(4) (determined without regard to the next to the last sentence of section 402(e)(4)(A))."

—P.L. 97-448, Sec. 103(c)(9)(B), substituted "An amount" for "A lump sum distribution" in para. (f)(2), effective for tax yrs. begin. after 12/31/81.

—P.L. 97-448, Sec. 103(c)(11), by adding Sec. 311(i)(5)(A) of P. L. 97-34, changed the effective date for amendments made by Sec. 311(d)(1) and Sec. 311(h)(4) of P. L. 97-34, from effective for tax. yrs. begin. after 12/31/81, to effective for estates of decedents dying after 12/31/81, see below.

In 1982, P.L. 97-248, Sec. 245(a), added subsec. (g) . . . Sec. 245(b), substituted "Subject to the limitation of subsection (g), notwithstanding any other provision of this section" for "Not-withstanding the provisions of this section" in subsecs. (c) and (e), effective [as amended by Sec. 525(b)(3) of P.L. 98-369, see above] for estates of decedents dying after 12/31/82, except that such amendments shall not apply to the estate of any decedent who was a participant in any plan, who was in pay status on 12/31/82, and irrevocably elected before 1/1/83.

In 1981, P.L. 97-34, Sec. 311(d)(1), added the sentence at the end of subsec. (c) . . . Sec. 311(h)(4), substituted "section 219" for "section 219 or 220" in subsec. (e), effective [as amended by Sec. 103(c)(11) of P. L. 97-448, see above] for estates of decedents dying after 12/31/81. For transitional rule, see Sec. 311(i)(2) of this Act reproduced in note following Code Sec. 219.

—P.L. 97-34, Sec. 313(b)(3), added "405(d)(3)," after "a contract described in subsection (c)(3)),", in subsec. (e), effective for redemptions after 8/13/81, in tax. yrs. end. after 8/31/81.

In 1980, P.L. 96-222, Sec. 101(a)(8)(B), substituted "(without the application of paragraph (2) thereof), except to the extent that section 402(e)(4)(J) applies to such distribution" for "without the application of paragraph (2) thereof" in para. (f)(2), effective for estates of decedents dying after 12/31/78.

—P.L. 96-222, Sec. 101(a)(13)(A), amended the effective date for changes made by Sec. 156(c)(4) of P.L. 95-600, from distributions or transfers made after 12/31/78, in tax. yrs. begin after 12/31/78, to distributions or transfers made after 12/31/77, in tax, yrs. begin after 12/31/77 [see below].

In 1978, P.L. 95-600, Sec. 142(a), substituted "(other than an amount described in subsection (f))" for "(other than a lump sum distribution described in section 402(e)(4), determined without regard to the next to the last sentence of section 402(e)(4)(A))" in subsec (c) . . . Sec. 142(b), added subsec. (f), effective for estates of decedents dying after 12/31/78.

—P.L. 95-600, Sec. 156(c)(4), added "section 403(b)(8) (but only to the extent such contribution is attributable to a distribution from a contract described in subsection (c)(3))," following "403(a)(4)," in subsec. (e), effective [as amended by Sec. 101(a)(13)(A) of P.L. 96-222, see above] for distributions or transfers made after 12/31/77, only in tax. yrs. begin. after 12/31/77.

—P.L. 95-600, Sec. 702(j)(1), substituted "section 219 or 220" for "section 219" each place it appeared in subsec. (e), effective for estates of decedents dying after '76.

In 1976, P.L. 94-455, Sec. 2009(c)(1), added subsec. (e) . . . Sec. 2009(c)(2), and (3), amended subsec. (c), effective for estates of decedents dying after 12/31/76.

Prior to amendment, subsec. (c) read as follows:

"(c) Exemption of annuities under certain trusts and plans.

"Notwithstanding the provisions of this section or of any provision of law, there shall be excluded from the gross estate the value of an annuity or other payment receivable by any beneficiary (other than the executor) under—

"(1) and employees' trust (or under a contract purchased by an employees' trust) forming part of a pension, stock bonus, or profit-sharing plan which, at the time of the decedent's separation from employment (whether by death or otherwise), or at the time of termination of the plan if earlier, met the requirements of section 401(a);

Estate taxes
Code Sec. 2040

"(2) a retirement annuity contract purchased by an employer (and not by an employees' trust) pursuant to a plan which, at the time of decedent's separation from employment (by death or otherwise), or at the time of termination of the plan if earlier, was a plan described in section 403(a);

"(3) a retirement annuity contract purchased for an employee by an employer which is an organization referred to in section 170(b)(1)(A)(ii) or (vi), or which is a religious organization (other than a trust), and which is exempt from tax under section 501(a); or

"(4) chapter 73 of title 10 of the United States Code.

If such amounts payable after the death of the decedent under a plan described in paragraph (1) or (2), under a contract described in paragraph (3), or under chapter 73 of title 10 of the United States Code are attributable to any extent to payments or contributions made by the decedent, no exclusion shall be allowed for that part of the value of such amounts in the proportion that the total payments or contributions made by the decedent bears to the total payments or contributions made. For purposes of this subsection, contributions or payments made by the decedent's employer or former employer under a trust or plan described in paragraph (1) or (2) shall not be considered to be contributed by the decedent, and contributions or payments made by the decedent's employer or former employer toward the purchase of an annuity contract described in paragraph (3) shall, to the extent excludable from gross income under section 403(b), not be considered to be contributed by the decedent. This subsection shall apply to all decedents dying after December 31, 1953. For purposes of this subsection, contributions or payments on behalf of the decedent while he was an employee within the meaning of section 401(c)(1) made under a trust or plan described in paragraph (1) or (2) shall be considered to be contributions or payments made by the decedent. For purposes of this subsection, amounts payable under chapter 73 of title 10 of the United States Code are attributable to payments or contributions made by the decedent only to the extent of amounts deposited by him pursuant to section 1438 or 1452(d) of such title 10."

In 1974, P.L. 93-406, Sec. 2008(b)(4), substituted "section 1438 or 1452(d)" for "section 1438" in subsec. (c), effective for individuals dying on or after 9/21/72.

In 1972, P.L. 92-580, Sec. 2, added subsec. (d), effective for estates of decedents for which the period prescribed by the Internal Revenue Code of 1954 for filing of a claim for credit or refund of an overpayment of estate tax ends on or after 10/27/72. No interest shall be allowed or paid on any overpayment of estate tax resulting from the application of the amendment made by subsection (a) for any period prior to the expiration of the one hundred and eightieth day following 10/27/72.

In 1969, P.L. 91-172, Sec. 101(j)(23), substituted "170(b)(1)(A)(ii) or (vi), or which is a religious organization (other than a trust)," for "503(b)(1), (2), or (3)" in para. (c)(3), effective 1/1/70.

In 1966, P.L. 89-365, Sec. 2, deleted "or" at the end of para. (c)(2), substituted "; or" for the period at the end of para. (c)(3), added para. (c)(4), substituted ", under a contract described in paragraph (3), or under chapter 73 of title 10 of the United States Code" for "or under a contract described in paragraph (3)" in the second sentence of subsec. (c), and added the sentence at the end of subsec. (c), effective for decedents dying after 12/31/65.

In 1962, P.L. 87-792, Sec. 7, substituted "was a plan described in section 403(a)" for "met the requirements of section 401(a)(3), (4), (5), and (6)" in para. (c)(2), and added in subsec. (c) a sentence providing, for purposes of this subsection, that contributions or payments on behalf of the decedent while he was an employee within the meaning of section 401(c)(1) made under a trust or plan described in paragraph (1) or (2) shall be considered to be contributions or payments made by the decedent, effective for tax. yrs. begin. after 12/31/62.

In 1958, P.L. 85-866, Sec. 67, added "(4), (5), and (6)" after "section 401(a)(3)" in para. (c)(2), effective for estates of decedents dying after 12/31/53.

—P.L. 85-866, Sec. 23, added para. (c)(3), added "or under contract described in paragraph (3)" in second sentence of subsec. (c), and substituted "paragraph (1) or (2) shall not be considered to be contributed by the decedent, and contributions or payments made by the decedent's employer or former employer toward the purchase of an annuity contract described in paragraph (3) shall, to the extent excludable from gross income under section 403(b)," for "this subsection shall" in third sentence of subsec. (c), effective for decedents dying after 12/31/57.

Sec. 2040. Joint interests.
(a) General rule.

The value of the gross estate shall include the value of all property to the extent of the interest therein held as joint tenants with right of survivorship by the decedent and any other person, or as tenants by the entirety by the decedent and spouse, or deposited, with any person carrying on the banking business, in their joint names and payable to either or the survivor, except such part thereof as may be shown to have originally belonged to such other person and never to have been received or acquired by the latter from the decedent for less than an adequate and full consideration in money or money's worth: *Provided,* That where such property or any part thereof, or part of the consideration with which such property was acquired, is shown to have been at any time acquired by such other person from the decedent for less than an adequate and full consideration in money or money's worth, there shall be excepted only such part of the value of such property as is proportionate to the consideration furnished by such other person: *Provided further,* That where any property has been acquired by gift, bequest, devise, or inheritance, as a tenancy by the entirety by the decedent and spouse, then to the extent of one-half of the value thereof, or, where so acquired by the decedent and any other person as joint tenants with right of survivorship and their interests are not otherwise specified or fixed by law, then to the extent of the value of a fractional part to be determined by dividing the value of the property by the number of joint tenants with right of survivorship.

(b) Certain joint interests of husband and wife.

(1) Interests of spouse excluded from gross estate. Notwithstanding subsection (a), in the case of any qualified joint interest, the value included in the gross estate with respect to such interest by reason of this section is one-half of the value of such qualified joint interest.

(2) Qualified joint interest defined. For purposes of paragraph (1), the term "qualified joint interest" means any interest in property held by the decedent and the decedent's spouse as—

(A) tenants by the entirety, or

(B) joint tenants with right of survivorship, but only if the decedent and the spouse of the decedent are the only joint tenants.

In 1990, P.L. 101-508, Sec. 11701(1)(3), amended Sec. 7815(d)(16) of P.L. 101-239 [reproduced below] by adding "(or would have been so treated if the donor were a citizen of the United States" after "of such Code", see below.

In 1989, P.L. 101-239, Sec. 7815(d)(16), [as amended by Sec. 1170(1)(3) of P.L. 101-508, see above] of this Act provides:

"(d) Amendments related to section 5033 of the 1988 Act.

* * * * *

"(16) For purposes of applying section 2040(a) of the Internal Revenue Code of 1986 with respect to any joint interest to which section 2040(b) of such Code does not apply solely by reason of section 2056(d)(1)(B) of such Code, any consideration furnished before July 14, 1988, by the decedent for such interest to the extent treated as a gift to the spouse of the decedent for purposes of chapter 12 of such Code (or would have been so treated if the donor were a citizen of the United States) shall be treated as consideration originally belonging to such spouse and never acquired by such spouse from the decedent."

In 1981, P.L. 97-34, Sec. 403(c)(1), amended para. (b)(2)... Sec. 403(c)(3), added "with right of survivorship" after "joint tenants" each place it appeared in subsec. (a)... Sec. 403(c)(3)(A), deleted subsecs. (c), (d) & (e), effective for estates of decedents dying after 12/31/81.

Prior to amendment, para. (b)(2) read as follows:

"(2) Qualified joint interest defined. For purposes of paragraph (1), the term 'qualified joint interest' means any interest in property held by the decedent and the decedent's spouse as joint tenants or as tenants by the entirety, but only if —

"(A) such joint interest was created by the decedent, the decedent's spouse, or both,

"(B)(i) in the case of personal property, the creation of such joint interest constituted in whole or in part a gift for purposes of chapter 12, or

"(ii) in the case of real property, an election under section 2515 applies with respect to the creation of such joint interest, and

"(C) in the case of a joint tenancy, only the decedent and the decedent's spouse are joint tenants."

Prior to deletion, subsecs. (c), (d) and (e) read as follows:

"(c) Value, where spouse of decedent materially participated in farm or other business.

"(1) In general. Notwithstanding subsections (a), in the case of an eligible joint interest in section 2040(c) property, the value included in the gross estate with respect to such interest by reason of this section shall be—

"(A) the value of such interest, reduced by

"(B) the sum of—

"(i) the section 2040(c) value of such interest, and

"(ii) the adjusted consideration furnished by the decedent's spouse.

"(2) Limitations.

"(A) At least 50 percent of value to be included. Paragraph (1) shall in no event result in the inclusion in the decedent's gross estate of less than 50 percent of the value of the eligible joint interest.

"(B) Aggregate reduction. The aggregate decrease in the value of the decedent's gross estate resulting from the application of this subsection shall not exceed $500,000.

"(C) Aggregate adjusted consideration must be less than value. Paragraph (1) shall not apply if the sum of

"(i) the adjusted consideration furnished by the decedent, and "(ii) the adjusted consideration furnished by the decedent's spouse, equals or exceeds the value of the interest.

"(3) Eligible joint interest defined. For purposes of paragraph (1) the term 'eligible joint interest' means any interest in property held by the decedent and the decedent's spouse as joint tenants or as tenants by the entirety, but only if—

"(A) such joint interest was created by the decedent, the decedent's spouse, or both, and

"(B) in the case of a joint tenancy, only the decedent and the decedent's spouse are joint tenants.

"(4) Section 2040(c) property defined. For purposes of paragraph (1), the term 'section 2040(c) property' means any interest in any real or tangible personal property which is devoted to use as a farm or used for farming purposes (within the meaning of paragraphs (4) and (5) of section 2032A(e)) or is used in any other trade or business.

"(5) Section 2040(c) value. For purposes of paragraph (1), the term 'section 2040(c) value' means—

"(A) the excess of the value of the eligible joint interest over the adjusted consideration furnished by the decedent, the decedent's spouse, or both, multiplied by

"(B) 2 percent for each taxable year in which the spouse materially participated in the operation of the farm or other trade or business but not to exceed 50 percent.

"(6) Adjusted consideration. For the purpose of this subsection, the term 'adjusted consideration' means—

"(A) the consideration furnished by the individual concerned (not taking into account any consideration in the form of income or gain from the business of which the section 2040(c) property is a part) determined under rules similar to the rules set forth in subsection (a), and

"(B) an amount equal to the amount of interest which the consideration referred to in subparagraph (A) would have earned over the period in which it was invested in the farm or other business if it had been earning interest throughout such period at 6 percent simple interest.

"(7) Material participation. For purposes of paragraph (1), material participation shall be determined in a manner similar to the manner used for purposes of paragraph (1) of section 1402(a) (relating to net earnings from self-employment).

"(8) Value. For purposes of this subsection, except where the context clearly indicates otherwise, the term 'value' means value determined without regard to this subsection.

"(9) Election to have subsection apply. This subsection shall apply with respect to a joint interest only if the estate of the decedent elects to have this subsection apply to such interest. Such an election shall be made not later than the time prescribed by section 6075(a) for filing the return of tax imposed by section 2001 (including extensions thereof), and shall be made in such manner as the Secretary shall by regulations prescribe.

"(d) Joint interests of husband and wife created before 1977. Under regulations prescribed by the Secretary—

"(1) In general. In the case of any joint interest created before January 1, 1977, which (if created after December 31, 1976) would have constituted a qualified joint interest under subsection (b)(2) (determined without regard to clause (ii) of subsection (b)(2)(B)), the donor may make an election under this subsection to have paragraph (1) of subsection (b) apply with respect to such joint interest.

"(2) Time for making election. An election under this subsection with respect to any property shall be made for the calendar quarter in 1977, 1978, or 1979 selected by the donor in a gift tax return filed within the time prescribed by law for filing a gift tax return for such quarter. Such an election may be made irrespective of whether or not the amount involved exceeds the exclusion provided by section 2503(b); but no election may be made under this subsection after the death of the donor.

"(3) Tax effects of election. In the case of any property with respect to which an election has been made under this subsection, for purposes of title—

"(A) the donor shall be treated as having made a gift at the close of the calendar quarter selected under paragraph (2), and

"(B) the amount of the gift shall be determined under paragraph (4).

"(4) Amount of gift. For purposes of paragraph (3)(B), the amount of any gift is one-half of the amount—

"(A) which bears the same ratio to the excess of (i) the value of the property on the date of the deemed making of the gift under paragraph (3)(A), over (ii) the value of such property on the date of the creation of the joint interest, as

"(B) the excess of (i) the consideration furnished by the donor at the time of the creation of the joint interest, over (ii) the consideration furnished at such time by the donor's spouse, bears to the total consideration furnished by both spouses at such time.

"(5) Special rule for paragraph (4)(A). For purposes of paragraph (4)(A)—

"(A) in the case of real property, if the creation was not treated as a gift at the time of the creation, or

"(B) in the case of personal property, if the gift was required to be included on a gift tax return but was not so included, and the period of limitations on assessment under section 6501 has expired with respect to the tax (if any) on such gift, then the value of the property on the date of the creation of the joint interest shall be treated as zero.

"(6) Substantial improvements. For purposes of this subsection, a substantial improvement of any property shall be treated as the creation of a separate joint interest.

"(e) Treatment of certain post-1976 terminations.

"(1) In general. If—

"(A) before January 1, 1977, a husband and wife had a joint interest in property with right of survivorship,

"(B) after December 31, 1976, such joint interest was terminated, and

"(C) after December 31, 1976, a joint interest of such husband and wife in such property (or in property the basis of which in whole or in part reflects the basis of such property) was created,

then paragraph (1) of subsection (b) shall apply to the joint interest described in subparagraph (C) only if an election is made under subsection (d).

"(2) Special rules. For purposes of applying subsection (d) to property described in paragraph (1) of this subsection—

"(A) if the creation described in paragraph (1)(C) occurs after December 31, 1979, the election may be made only with respect to the calendar quarter in which such creation occurs, and

"(B) the creation of the joint interest described in paragraphs (4) and (5) of subsection (d) is the creation of the joint interest described in paragraph (1)(A) of this subsection."

In 1980, P.L. 96-222, Sec. 105(a)(3)(A), added new subpara. (c)(2)(C) . . . Sec. 105(a)(3)(B), substituted "subsection (a)" for "subsections (a)" in para. (c)(1), effective for estates of decedents dying after 12/31/78.

In 1978, P.L. 95-600, Sec. 511(a), added subsec. (c), effective for estates of decedents dying after 12/31/78.

—P.L. 95-600, Sec. 702(k)(2), added subsecs. (d) and (e), effective 11/6/78.

In 1976, P.L. 94-455, Sec. 2002(c)(1), and (c)(3), added subsec. (b) and substituted "(a) General rule. The value" for "The value" in Code Sec. 2040, effective for joint interests created after 12/31/76.

In 1962, P.L. 87-834, Sec. 18(a)(2)(G), eliminated provisions which excepted real property situated outside of the U. S., effective for estates of decedents dying after 10/16/62, except as provided in Sec. 18(b) at note following Code Sec. 2031.

Sec. 2041. Powers of appointment.

(a) In general.

The value of the gross estate shall include the value of all property—

(1) Powers of appointment created on or before October 21, 1942. To the extent of any property with respect to which a general power of appointment created on or before October 21, 1942, is exercised by the decedent—

(A) by will, or

(B) by a disposition which is of such nature that if it were a transfer of property owned by the decedent, such property would be includible in the decedent's gross estate under sections 2035 to 2038, inclusive;

but the failure to exercise such a power or the complete release of such a power shall not be deemed an exercise thereof. If a general power of appointment created on or before October 21, 1942, has been partially released so that it is no longer a general power of appointment, the exercise of such power shall not be deemed to be the exercise of a general power of appointment if—

(i) such partial release occurred before November 1, 1951, or

(ii) the donee of such power was under a legal disability to release such power on October 21, 1942, and such partial release occurred not later than 6 months after the termination of such legal disability.

(2) Powers created after October 21, 1942. To the extent of any property with respect to which the decedent has at the time of his death a general power of appointment created after October 21, 1942, or with respect to which the decedent has at any time exercised or released such a power of appointment by a disposition which is of such nature that if it were a transfer of property owned by the decedent, such property would be includible in the decedent's gross estate under sections 2035 to 2038, inclusive. For purposes of this paragraph (2), the power of appointment shall be considered to exist on the date of the decedent's death even though the exercise of the power is subject to a precedent giving of notice or even though the exercise of the power takes effect only on the expiration of a stated period after its exercise, whether or not on or before the date of the decedent's death notice has been given or the power has been exercised.

(3) Creation of another power in certain cases. To the extent of any property with respect to which the decedent—

(A) by will, or

(B) by a disposition which is of such nature that if it were a transfer of property owned by the decedent such property would be includible in the decedent's gross estate under section 2035, 2036, or 2037,

exercises a power of appointment created after October 21, 1942, by creating another power of appointment which under the applicable local law can be validly exercised so as to postpone the vesting of any estate or interest in such property, or suspend the absolute ownership or power of alienation of such property, for a period ascertainable without regard to the date of the creation of the first power.

(b) Definitions.

For purposes of subsection (a)—

(1) General power of appointment. The term "general power of appointment" means a power which is exercisable in favor of the decedent, his estate, his creditors, or the creditors of his estate; except that—

(A) A power to consume, invade, or appropriate property for the benefit of the decedent which is limited by an ascertainable standard relating to the health, education, support, or maintenance of the decedent shall not be deemed a general power of appointment.

(B) A power of appointment created on or before October 21, 1942, which is exercisable by the decedent only in conjunction with another person shall not be deemed a general power of appointment.

(C) In the case of a power of appointment created after October 21, 1942, which is exercisable by the decedent only in conjunction with another person—

(i) If the power is not exercisable by the decedent except in conjunction with the creator of the power—such power shall not be deemed a general power of appointment.

(ii) If the power is not exercisable by the decedent except in conjunction with a person having a substantial interest in the property, subject to the power, which is adverse to exercise of the power in favor of the decedent—such power shall not be deemed a general power of appointment. For the purposes of this clause a person who, after the death of the decedent, may be possessed of a power of appointment (with respect to the property subject to the decedent's power) which he may exercise in his own favor shall be deemed as having an interest in the property and such interest shall be deemed adverse to such exercise of the decedent's power.

(iii) If (after the application of clauses (i) and (ii)) the power is a general power of appointment and is exercisable in favor of such other person—such power shall be deemed a general power of appointment only in respect of a fractional part of the property subject to such power, such part to be determined by dividing the value of such property by the number of such persons (including the decedent) in favor of whom such power is exercisable.

For purposes of clauses (ii) and (iii), a power shall be deemed to be exercisable in favor of a person if it is exercisable in favor of such person, his estate, his creditors, or the creditors of his estate.

(2) Lapse of power. The lapse of a power of appointment created after October 21, 1942, during the life of the individual possessing the power shall be considered a release of such power. The preceding sentence shall apply with respect to the lapse of powers during any calendar year only to the extent that the property, which could have been appointed by exercise of such lapsed powers, exceeded in value, at the time of such lapse, the greater of the following amounts:

(A) $5,000, or

(B) 5 percent of the aggregate value, at the time of such lapse, of the assets out of which, or the proceeds of which, the exercise of the lapsed powers could have been satisfied.

(3) Date of creation of power. For purposes of this section, a power of appointment created by a will executed on or before October 21, 1942, shall be considered a power created on or before such date if the person executing such will dies before July 1, 1949, without having republished such will, by codicil or otherwise, after October 21, 1942.

In 1976, P.L. 94-455, Sec. 2009(b)(4)(A), deleted the second sentence of para. (a)(2), effective for transfers creating an interest in the person disclaiming made after 12/31/76.
Prior to amendment, the second sentence of para. (a)(2) read as follows:
"A disclaimer or renunciation of such a power of appointment shall not be deemed a release of such power."
In 1962, P.L. 87-834, Sec. 18(a)(2), deleted "(except real property situated outside of the United States)" in Code Sec. 2041, effective for estates of decedents dying after 10/16/62, except as provided in Sec. 18(b) of this Act, reproduced in note following Code Sec. 2031.

Sec. 2042. Proceeds of life insurance.

The value of the gross estate shall include the value of all property—

(1) Receivable by the executor. To the extent of the amount receivable by the executor as insurance under policies on the life of the decedent.

(2) Receivable by other beneficiaries. To the extent of the amount receivable by all other beneficiaries as insurance under policies on the life of the decedent with respect to which the decedent possessed at his death any of the incidents of ownership, exercisable either alone or in conjunction with any other person. For purposes of the preceding sentence, the term "incident of ownership" includes a reversionary interest (whether arising by the express terms of the policy or other instrument or by operation of law) only if the value of such reversionary interest exceeded 5 percent of the value of the policy immediately before the death of the decedent. As used in this paragraph, the term "reversionary interest" includes a possibility that the policy, or the proceeds of the policy, may return to the decedent or his estate, or may be subject to a power of disposition by him. The value of a reversionary interest at any time shall be determined (without regard to the fact of the decedent's death) by usual methods of valuation, including the use of tables of mortality and actuarial principles, pursuant to regulations prescribed by the Secretary. In determining the value of a possibility that the policy or proceeds thereof may be subject to a power of disposition by the decedent, such possibility shall be valued as if it were a possibility that such policy or proceeds may return to the decedent or his estate.

In 1976, P.L. 94-455, Sec. 1906(b)(13)(A), substituted "Secretary" for "Secretary or his delegate" in Code Sec. 2042, effective 2/1/77.

Sec. 2043. Transfers for insufficient consideration.

(a) In general.

If any one of the transfers, trusts, interests, rights, or powers enumerated and described in sections 2035 to 2038, inclusive, and section 2041 is made, created, exercised, or relinquished for a consideration in money or money's worth, but is not a bona fide sale for an adequate and full consideration in money or money's worth, there shall be included in the gross estate only the excess of the fair market value at

Code Sec. 2043(a) — Estate taxes

the time of death of the property otherwise to be included on account of such transaction, over the value of the consideration received therefor by the decedent.

(b) Marital rights not treated as consideration.

(1) In general. For purposes of this chapter, a relinquishment or promised relinquishment of dower or curtesy, or of a statutory estate created in lieu of dower or curtesy, or of other marital rights in the decedent's property or estate, shall not be considered to any extent a consideration "in money or money's worth".

(2) Exception. For purposes of section 2053 (relating to expenses, indebtedness, and taxes), a transfer of property which satisfies the requirements of paragraph (1) of section 2516 (relating to certain property settlements) shall be considered to be made for an adequate and full consideration in money or money's worth.

In **1984**, P.L. 98-369, Sec. 425(a)(1), amended subsec. (b), effective for estates of decedents dying after 7/18/84.
Prior to amendment, subsec. (b) read as follows:
"*(b) Marital rights not treated as consideration.*
"For purposes of this chapter, a relinquishment or promised relinquishment of dower or curtesy, or of a statutory estate created in lieu of dower or curtesy, or of other marital rights in the decedent's property or estate, shall not be considered to any extent a consideration 'in money or money's worth.'"

Sec. 2044. Certain property for which marital deduction was previously allowed.

(a) General rule.
The value of the gross estate shall include the value of any property to which this section applies in which the decedent had a qualifying income interest for life.

(b) Property to which this section applies.
This section applies to any property if—
 (1) a deduction was allowed with respect to the transfer of such property to the decedent—
  (A) under section 2056 by reason of subsection (b)(7) thereof, or
  (B) under section 2523 by reason of subsection (f) thereof, and
 (2) section 2519 (relating to dispositions of certain life estates) did not apply with respect to a disposition by the decedent of part or all of such property.

(c) Property treated as having passed from decedent.
For purposes of this chapter and chapter 13, property includible in the gross estate of the decedent under subsection (a) shall be treated as property passing from the decedent.

In **1983**, P.L. 97-448, Sec. 104(a)(1)(B), added subsec. (c), effective for estates of decedents dying after 12/31/81.
In **1981**, P.L. 97-34, Sec. 403(d)(3)(A), added Code Sec. 2044, effective for estates of decedents dying after 12/31/81.

Sec. 2045. Prior interests.

Except as otherwise specifically provided by law, sections 2034 to 2042, inclusive, shall apply to the transfers, trusts, estates, interests, rights, powers, and relinquishment of powers, as severally enumerated and described therein, whenever made, created, arising, existing, exercised, or relinquished.

In **1981**, P.L. 97-34, Sec. 403(d)(3)(A)(i), redesignated Code Sec. 2044 as 2045, effective for estates of decedents dying after 12/31/81.
In **1976**, P.L. 94-455, Sec. 2001(c)(1)(M), substituted "specifically provided by law" for "specifically provided therein" in Code Sec. 2044, effective for estates of decedents dying after 12/31/76.

Sec. 2046. Disclaimers.

For provisions relating to the effect of a qualified disclaimer for purposes of this chapter, see section 2518.

In **1981**, P.L. 97-34, Sec. 403(d)(3)(A)(i), redesignated Code Sec. 2045 as Code Sec. 2046, effective for estates of decedents dying after 12/31/81.
In **1976**, P.L. 94-455, Sec. 2009(b)(2), added Code Sec. 2045, effective for transfers creating an interest in the person disclaiming made after 12/31/76.

PART IV.—TAXABLE ESTATE

Sec.
2051. Definition of taxable estate.
2052. Repealed.
2053. Expenses, indebtedness, and taxes.
2054. Losses.
2055. Transfers for public, charitable, and religious uses.
2056. Bequests, etc., to surviving spouse.
2056A. Qualified domestic trust.
2057. Family-owned business interests.
2058. State death taxes.

In **2001**, P.L. 107-16, Sec. 532(c)(14), added item 2058.
In **1998**, P.L. 105-206, Sec. 6007(b)(1)(F), added item 2057.
In **1990**, P.L. 101-508, Sec. 11704(a)(16), substituted "trust" for "trusts" in item 2056A.
In **1989**, P.L. 101-239, Sec. 7304(a)(2)(E), deleted item 2057.
Prior to deletion, item 2057 read as follows:
"2057. Sales of employer securities to employee stock ownership plans or worker-owned cooperatives."
In **1988**, P.L. 100-647, Sec. 5033(a)(3), added item 2056A.
In **1986**, P.L. 99-514, Sec. 1172(b)(3), added item 2057.
In **1981**, P.L. 97-34, Sec. 427(b), deleted item 2057.
Prior to deletion, item 2057 read as follows: "2057. Bequests, etc., to certain minor children."
In **1976**, P.L. 94-455, Sec. 2001(c)(1)(N)(iv), deleted the item for Code Sec. 2052.
Prior to repeal, the item read as follows:
"2052. Exemption."
—P.L. 94-455, Sec. 2007(b), added the item for Code Sec. 2057.

Sec. 2051. Definition of taxable estate.

For purposes of the tax imposed by section 2001, the value of the taxable estate shall be determined by deducting from the value of the gross estate the deductions provided for in this part.

In **1978**, P.L. 95-600, Sec. 702(r)(2), deleted "exemption and" after "value of the gross estate the" in Code Sec. 2051, effective for estates of decedents dying after 12/31/76.

Sec. 2052. Repealed.

In **1976**, P.L. 94-455, Sec. 2001(a)(4), repealed Code Sec. 2052, effective for estates of decedents dying after 12/31/76.
Prior to repeal, Code Sec. 2052 read as follows:
"SEC. 2052. EXEMPTION.
"For purposes of the tax imposed by section 2001, the value of the taxable estate shall be determined by deducting from the value of the gross estate an exemption of $60,000."

Sec. 2053. Expenses, indebtedness, and taxes.

(a) General rule.
For purposes of the tax imposed by section 2001, the value of the taxable estate shall be determined by deducting from the value of the gross estate such amounts—
 (1) for funeral expenses,
 (2) for administration expenses,
 (3) for claims against the estate, and
 (4) for unpaid mortgages on, or any indebtedness in respect of, property where the value of the decedent's interest therein, undiminished by such mortgage or indebtedness, is included in the value of the gross estate,
as are allowable by the laws of the jurisdiction, whether within or without the United States under which the estate is being administered.

Estate taxes

Code Sec. 2053

(b) Other administration expenses.

Subject to the limitations in paragraph (1) of subsection (c), there shall be deducted in determining the taxable estate amounts representing expenses incurred in administering property not subject to claims which is included in the gross estate to the same extent such amounts would be allowable as a deduction under subsection (a) if such property were subject to claims, and such amounts are paid before the expiration of the period of limitation for assessment provided in section 6501.

(c) Limitations.

(1) Limitations applicable to subsections (a) and (b).

(A) Consideration for claims. The deduction allowed by this section in the case of claims against the estate, unpaid mortgages, or any indebtedness shall, when founded on a promise or agreement, be limited to the extent that they were contracted bona fide and for an adequate and full consideration in money or money's worth; except that in any case in which any such claim is founded on a promise or agreement of the decedent to make a contribution or gift to or for the use of any donee described in section 2055 for the purposes specified therein, the deduction for such claims shall not be so limited, but shall be limited to the extent that it would be allowable as a deduction under section 2055 if such promise or agreement constituted a bequest.

(B) Certain taxes. Any income taxes on income received after the death of the decedent, or property taxes not accrued before his death, or any estate, succession, legacy, or inheritance taxes, shall not be deductible under this section.

(C) Certain claims by remaindermen. No deduction shall be allowed under this section for a claim against the estate by a remainderman relating to any property described in section 2044.

(D) Section 6166 interest. No deduction shall be allowed under this section for any interest payable under section 6601 on any unpaid portion of the tax imposed by section 2001 for the period during which an extension of time for payment of such tax is in effect under section 6166.

(2) Limitations applicable only to subsection (a). In the case of the amounts described in subsection (a), there shall be disallowed the amount by which the deductions specified therein exceed the value, at the time of the decedent's death, of property subject to claims, except to the extent that such deductions represent amounts paid before the date prescribed for the filing of the estate tax return. For purposes of this section, the term "property subject to claims" means property includible in the gross estate of the decedent which, or the avails of which, would under the applicable law, bear the burden of the payment of such deductions in the final adjustment and settlement of the estate, except that the value of the property shall be reduced by the amount of the deduction under section 2054 attributable to such property.

• *Caution:* Code Sec. 2053(d), reflects amendments made by P.L. 107-16, the Economic Growth and Tax Relief Reconciliation Act of 2001 (EGTRRA). These provisions generally sunset for tax years beginning after 12/31/2012. For specific sunset provisions, see Sec. 901, P.L. 107-16 (as amended) reproduced in history notes for this Code Sec.

(d) Certain foreign death taxes.

(1) In general. Notwithstanding the provisions of subsection (c)(1)(B), for purposes of the tax imposed by section 2001, the value of the taxable estate may be determined, if the executor so elects before the expiration of the period of limitation for assessment provided in section 6501, by deducting from the value of the gross estate the amount (as determined in accordance with regulations prescribed by the Secretary) of any estate, succession, legacy, or inheritance tax imposed by and actually paid to any foreign country, in respect of any property situated within such foreign country and included in the gross estate of a citizen or resident of the United States, upon a transfer by the decedent for public, charitable, or religious uses described in section 2055. The determination under this paragraph of the country within which property is situated shall be made in accordance with the rules applicable under subchapter B (sec. 2101 and following) in determining whether property is situated within or without the United States. Any election under this paragraph shall be exercised in accordance with regulations prescribed by the Secretary.

(2) Condition for allowance of deduction. No deduction shall be allowed under paragraph (1) for a foreign death tax specified therein unless the decrease in the tax imposed by section 2001 which results from the deduction provided in paragraph (1) will inure solely for the benefit of the public, charitable, or religious transferees described in section 2055 or section 2106(a)(2). In any case where the tax imposed by section 2001 is equitably apportioned among all the transferees of property included in the gross estate, including those described in sections 2055 and 2106(a)(2) (taking into account any exemptions, credits, or deductions allowed by this chapter), in determining such decrease, there shall be disregarded any decrease in the Federal estate tax which any transferees other than those described in sections 2055 and 2106(a)(2) are required to pay.

(3) Effect on credit for foreign death taxes of deduction under this subsection.

(A) Election. An election under this subsection shall be deemed a waiver of the right to claim a credit, against the Federal estate tax, under a death tax convention with any foreign country for any tax or portion thereof in respect of which a deduction is taken under this subsection.

(B) Cross reference. See section 2014(f) for the effect of a deduction taken under this paragraph on the credit for foreign death taxes.

(e) Marital rights.

For provisions treating certain relinquishments of marital rights as consideration in money or money's worth, see section 2043(b)(2).

In 2010, P.L. 111-312, Sec. 101(a)(1), substituted "December 31, 2012" for "December 31, 2010" both places it appears in Sec. 901, P.L. 107-16, see below, effective as if included in the enactment of P.L. 107-16, EGTRRA, 6/7/2001.

In 2002, P.L. 107-358, Sec. 2, added subsec. (c) in Sec. 901 of P.L. 107-16 [see below], effective 12/17/2002.

—P.L. 107-134, Sec. 103(b)(2), substituted "section 2011(d)" for "section 2011(e)" in subpara. (d)(3)(B), [Ed note: As in effect prior to the amendment of subsec. (d) by P.L. 107-16.] effective as provided by Sec. 103(d) of this Act, which reads as follows:

"(d) Effective date; waiver of limitations.

"(1) Effective date. The amendments made by this section shall apply to estates of decedents—

"(A) dying on or after September 11, 2001, and

"(B) in the case of individuals dying as a result of the April 19, 1995, terrorist attack, dying on or after April 19, 1995.

"(2) Waiver of limitations. If refund or credit of any overpayment of tax resulting from the amendments made by this section is prevented at any time before the close of the 1-year period beginning on the date of the enactment of this Act by the operation of any law or rule of law (including res judicata), such refund or credit may nevertheless be made or allowed if claim therefor is filed before the close of such period."

In 2001, P.L. 107-16, Sec. 532(c)(5), amended subsec. (d), effective for estates of decedents dying, and generation-skipping transfers, after 12/31/2004.

Prior to amendment, subsec. (d) read as follows:

"(d) Certain State and foreign death taxes.

"(1) General rule. Notwithstanding the provisions of subsection (c)(1)(B) of this section, for purposes of the tax imposed by section 2001 the value of the taxable estate may be determined, if the executor so elects before the expiration of the period of limitation for assessment provided in section 6501, by deducting from the value of the gross estate the amount (as determined in accordance with regulations prescribed by the Secretary) of—

"(A) any estate, succession, legacy, or inheritance tax imposed by a State or the District of Columbia upon a transfer by the decedent for public, charitable, or religious uses described in section 2055 or 2106(a)(2), and

"(B) any estate, succession, legacy, or inheritance tax imposed by and actually paid to any foreign country, in respect of any property situated within such foreign country and included in the gross estate of a citizen or resident of the United States, upon a transfer by the decedent for public, charitable, or religious uses described in section 2055.

"The determination under subparagraph (B) of the country within which property is situated shall be made in accordance with the rules applicable under subchapter B (sec. 2101 and following) in determining whether property is situated within or without the United States. Any election under this paragraph shall be exercised in accordance with regulations prescribed by the Secretary.

"(2) Condition for allowance of deduction. No deduction shall be allowed under paragraph (1) for a State death tax or a foreign death tax specified therein unless the decrease in the tax imposed by section 2001 which results from the deduction provided in paragraph (1) will inure solely for the benefit of the public, charitable, or religious transferees described in section 2055 or section 2106(a)(2). In any case where the tax imposed by section 2001 is equitably apportioned among all the transferees of property included in the gross estate, including those described in sections 2055 and 2106(a)(2) (taking into account any exemptions, credits, or deductions allowed by this chapter), in determining such decrease, there shall be disregarded any decrease in the Federal estate tax which any transferees other than those described in sections 2055 and 2106(a)(2) are required to pay.

"(3) Effect on credits for State and foreign death taxes of deduction under this subsection.

"(A) Election. An election under this subsection shall be deemed a waiver of the right to claim a credit, against the Federal estate tax, under a death tax convention with any foreign country for any tax or portion thereof in respect of which a deduction is taken under this subsection.

"(B) Cross references. See section 2011(e) for the effect of a deduction taken under this subsection on the credit for State death taxes, and see section 2014(f) for the effect of a deduction taken under this subsection on the credit for foreign death taxes."

—P.L. 107-16, Sec. 901, of this Act [as amended by Sec. 2, P.L. 107-358, and Sec. 101(a)(1), P.L. 111-312, see above], reads as follows:

"SEC. 901. SUNSET OF PROVISIONS OF ACT.

"(a) In general. All provisions of, and amendments made by, this Act shall not apply—

"(1) to taxable, plan, or limitation years beginning after December 31, 2012, or

"(2) in the case of title V, to estates of decedents dying, gifts made, or generation skipping transfers, after December 31, 2012.

"(b) Application of certain laws. The Internal Revenue Code of 1986 and the Employee Retirement Income Security Act of 1974 shall be applied and administered to years, estates, gifts, and transfers described in subsection (a) as if the provisions and amendments described in subsection (a) had never been enacted.

"(c) Exception. Subsection (a) shall not apply to section 803 (relating to no federal income tax on restitution received by victims of the Nazi regime or their heirs or estates)."

In 1997, P.L. 105-34, Sec. 503(b)(1), added subpara. (c)(1)(D), effective for estates of decedents dying after 12/31/97. Sec. 503(d)(2) of this Act provides:

"(2) Election.— In the case of the estate of any decedent dying before January 1, 1998, with respect to which there is an election under section 6166 of the Internal Revenue Code of 1986, the executor of the estate may elect to have the amendments made by this section apply with respect to installments due after the effective date of the election; except that the 2-percent portion of such installments shall be equal to the amount which would be the 4-percent portion of such installments without regard to such election. Such an election shall be made before January 1, 1999 in the manner prescribed by the Secretary of the Treasury and, once made, is irrevocable."

—P.L. 105-34, Sec. 1073(b)(3), deleted "This subparagraph shall not apply to any increase in the tax imposed by this chapter by reason of section 4980A(d)." from the end of subpara. (c)(1)(B), effective for estates of decedents dying after 12/31/96.

In 1988, P.L. 100-647, Sec. 1011A(g)(11), added the sentence at the end of subpara. (c)(1)(B), effective in distributions made after 12/31/86, except as provided in Secs 1133(c)(2) and (3) of P. L. 99-514, reproduced in note following Code Sec. 4980A.

In 1984, P.L. 98-369, Sec. 425(a)(2), amended subsec. (e), effective for estates of decedents dying after 7/18/84.

Prior to amendment, subsec. (e) read as follows:

"(e) Marital rights.

"For provisions that relinquishment of marital rights shall not be deemed a consideration 'in money or money's worth,' see section 2043(b)."

—P.L. 98-369, Sec. 1027(b), added subpara. (c)(1)(C), effective for estates of decedents dying after 12/31/81.

In 1978, P.L. 95-600, Sec. 703(j)(12), amended the effective date for changes made by Sec. 1902(a)(12)(B) of P. L. 94-455 to apply to estates of decedents dying after 10/4/76. See below.

In 1976, P.L. 94-455, Sec. 1902(a)(12)(B), deleted "or Territory", after "imposed by a State", in subpara. (d)(1)(A), effective for gifts made after 12/31/76 [sic].

—P.L. 94-455, Sec. 1906(b)(13)(A), substituted "Secretary" for "Secretary or his delegate" each place it appeared in Code Sec. 2053, effective 2/1/77.

In 1959, P.L. 86-175, Sec. 1, amended subsec. (d), effective for estates of decedents dying after 6/30/55.

Prior to amendment, subsec. (d) read as follows:

"(d) Certain State death taxes.

"(1) General rule.— Notwithstanding the provisions of subsection (c)(1)(B) of this section, for purposes of the tax imposed by section 2001 the value of the taxable estate may be determined, if the executor so elects before the expiration of the period of limitation for assessment provided in section 6501, by deducting from the value of the gross estate the amount (as determined in accordance with regulations prescribed by the Secretary or his delegate) of any estate, succession, legacy or inheritance tax imposed by a State or Territory or the District of Columbia, upon a transfer by the decedent for public, charitable, or religious uses described in section 2055 or 2106(a)(2). The election shall be exercised in accordance with regulations prescribed by the Secretary or his delegate.

"(2) Condition for allowance of deduction.— No deduction shall be allowed under paragraph (1) for a State death tax specified therein unless the decrease in the tax imposed by section 2001 which results from the deduction provided in paragraph (1) will inure solely for the benefit of the public, charitable, or religious transferees described in section 2055 or section 2106(a)(2). In any case where the tax imposed by section 2001 is equitably apportioned among all the transferees of property included in the gross estate, including those described in sections 2055 and 2106(a)(2) (taking into account any exemptions, credits, or deductions allowed by this chapter), in determining such decrease, there shall be disregarded any decrease in the Federal estate tax which any transferees other than those described in sections 2055 and 2106(a)(2) are required to pay.

"(3) Effect of deduction on credit for state death taxes.— See section 2011(e) for the effect of a deduction taken under this subsection on the credit for State death taxes."

In 1958, P.L. 85-866, Sec. 102(c), deleted "or any possession of the United States," after "District of Columbia," in para. (d)(1), effective for for estates of decedents dying after 9/2/58.

In 1956, ch. 63, Sec. 2, redesignated subsec. (d) as subsec. (e), and added new subsec. (d), effective for estates of decedents dying after 12/31/53.

Sec. 2054. Losses.

For purposes of the tax imposed by section 2001, the value of the taxable estate shall be determined by deducting from the value of the gross estate losses incurred during the settlement of estates arising from fires, storms, shipwrecks, or other casualties, or from theft, when such losses are not compensated for by insurance or otherwise.

Sec. 2055. Transfers for public, charitable, and religious uses.

(a) In general.

For purposes of the tax imposed by section 2001, the value of the taxable estate shall be determined by deducting from the value of the gross estate the amount of all bequests, legacies, devises, or transfers—

(1) to or for the use of the United States, any State, any political subdivision thereof, or the District of Columbia, for exclusively public purposes;

(2) to or for the use of any corporation organized and operated exclusively for religious, charitable, scientific, literary, or educational purposes, including the encouragement of art, or to foster national or international amateur sports competition (but only if no part of its activities involve the provision of athletic facilities or equipment), and the prevention of cruelty to children or animals, no part of the net earnings of which inures to the benefit of any private stockholder or individual, which is not disqualified for tax exemption under section 501(c)(3) by reason of attempting to influence legislation, and which does not participate in, or intervene in (including the publishing or distributing of statements), any political campaign on behalf of (or in opposition to) any candidate for public office;

(3) to a trustee or trustees, or a fraternal society, order, or association operating under the lodge system, but only if such contributions or gifts are to be used by such trustee or trustees, or by such fraternal society, order, or association, exclusively for religious, charitable, scientific, literary, or educational purposes, or for the prevention of cruelty to children or animals, such trust, fraternal society, order, or association would not be disqualified for tax exemption under section 501(c)(3) by reason of attempting to influence legislation, and such trustee or trustees, or such fraternal society, order, or association, does not participate in, or intervene in (including the publishing or distributing of statements), any political campaign on behalf of (or in opposition to) any candidate for public office;

(4) to or for the use of any veterans' organization incorporated by Act of Congress, or of its departments or local chapters or posts, no part of the net earnings of which inures to the benefit of any private shareholder or individual ; or

(5) to an employee stock ownership plan if such transfer qualifies as a qualified gratuitous transfer of qualified employer securities within the meaning of section 664(g).

For purposes of this subsection, the complete termination before the date prescribed for the filing of the estate tax return of a power to consume, invade, or appropriate property for the benefit of an individual before such power has been exercised by reason of the death of such individual or for any other reason shall be considered and deemed to be a qualified disclaimer with the same full force and effect as though he had filed such qualified disclaimer. Rules similar to the rules of section 501(j) shall apply for purposes of paragraph (2).

(b) Powers of appointment.

Property includible in the decedent's gross estate under section 2041 (relating to powers of appointment) received by a donee described in this section shall, for purposes of this section, be considered a bequest of such decedent.

(c) Death taxes payable out of bequests.

If the tax imposed by section 2001, or any estate, succession, legacy, or inheritance taxes, are, either by the terms of the will, by the law of the jurisdiction under which the estate is administered, or by the law of the jurisdiction imposing the particular tax, payable in whole or in part out of the bequests, legacies, or devises otherwise deductible under this section, then the amount deductible under this section shall be the amount of such bequests, legacies, or devises reduced by the amount of such taxes.

(d) Limitation on deduction.

The amount of the deduction under this section for any transfer shall not exceed the value of the transferred property required to be included in the gross estate.

(e) Disallowance of deductions in certain cases.

(1) No deduction shall be allowed under this section for a transfer to or for the use of an organization or trust described in section 508(d) or 4948(c)(4) subject to the conditions specified in such sections.

(2) Where an interest in property (other than an interest described in section 170(f)(3)(B)) passes or has passed from the decedent to a person, or for a use, described in subsection (a), and an interest (other than an interest which is extinguished upon the decedent's death) in the same property passes or has passed (for less than an adequate and full consideration in money or money's worth) from the decedent to a person, or for a use, not described in subsection (a), no deduction shall be allowed under this section for the interest which passes or has passed to the person, or for the use, described in subsection (a) unless—

(A) in the case of a remainder interest, such interest is in a trust which is a charitable remainder annuity trust or a charitable remainder unitrust (described in section 664) or a pooled income fund (described in section 642(c)(5)), or

(B) in the case of any other interest, such interest is in the form of a guaranteed annuity or is a fixed percentage distributed yearly of the fair market value of the property (to be determined yearly).

(3) Reformations to comply with paragraph (2).

(A) In general. A deduction shall be allowed under subsection (a) in respect of any qualified reformation.

(B) Qualified reformation. For purposes of this paragraph, the term "qualified reformation" means a change of a governing instrument by reformation, amendment, construction, or otherwise which changes a reformable interest into a qualified interest but only if—

(i) any difference between—

(I) the actuarial value (determined as of the date of the decedent's death) of the qualified interest, and

(II) the actuarial value (as so determined) of the reformable interest,

does not exceed 5 percent of the actuarial value (as so determined) of the reformable interest,

(ii) in the case of—

(I) a charitable remainder interest, the nonremainder interest (before and after the qualified reformation) terminated at the same time, or

(II) any other interest, the reformable interest and the qualified interest are for the same period, and

(iii) such change is effective as of the date of the decedent's death.

A nonremainder interest (before reformation) for a term of years in excess of 20 years shall be treated as satisfying subclause (I) of clause (ii) if such interest (after reformation) is for a term of 20 years.

(C) Reformable interest. For purposes of this paragraph—

(i) In general. The term "reformable interest" means any interest for which a deduction would be allowable under subsection (a) at the time of the decedent's death but for paragraph (2).

(ii) Beneficiary's interest must be fixed. The term "reformable interest" does not include any interest unless, before the remainder vests in possession, all payments to persons other than an organization described in subsection (a) are expressed either in specified dollar amounts or a fixed percentage of the fair market value of the property. For purposes of determining whether all such payments are expressed as a fixed percentage of the fair market value of the property, section 664(d)(3) shall be taken into account.

(iii) Special rule where timely commencement of reformation. Clause (ii) shall not apply to any interest if a judicial proceeding is commenced to change such interest into a qualified interest not later than the 90th day after—

(I) if an estate tax return is required to be filed, the last date (including extensions) for filing such return, or

(II) if no estate tax return is required to be filed, the last date (including extensions) for filing the income tax return for the 1st taxable year for which such a return is required to be filed by the trust.

(iv) Special rule for will executed before January 1, 1979, etc. In the case of any interest passing under a will executed before January 1, 1979, or under a trust created before such date, clause (ii) shall not apply.

(D) Qualified interest. For purposes of this paragraph, the term "qualified interest" means an interest for which a deduction is allowable under subsection (a).

(E) Limitation. The deduction referred to in subparagraph (A) shall not exceed the amount of the deduction which would have been allowable for the reformable interest but for paragraph (2).

(F) Special rule where income beneficiary dies. If (by reason of the death of any individual, or by termination or distribution of a trust in accordance with the terms of the trust instrument) by the due date for filing the estate tax return (including any extension thereof) a reformable interest is in a wholly charitable trust or passes directly to a person or for a use described in subsection (a), a deduction shall be allowed for such reformable interest as if it had met the requirements of paragraph (2) on the date of the decedent's death. For purposes of the preceding sentence, the term "wholly charitable trust" means a charitable trust which, upon the allowance of a deduction, would be described in section 4947(a)(1).

(G) Statute of limitations. The period for assessing any deficiency of any tax attributable to the application of this paragraph shall not expire before the date 1 year after the date on which the Secretary is notified that such reformation (or other proceeding pursuant to subparagraph (J) has occurred.

(H) Regulations. The Secretary shall prescribe such regulations as may be necessary to carry out the purposes of this paragraph, including regulations providing such adjustments in the application of the provisions of section 508 (relating to special rules relating to section 501(c)(3) organizations), subchapter J (relating to estates, trusts, beneficiaries, and decedents), and chapter 42 (relating to private foundations) as may be necessary by reason of the qualified reformation.

(I) Reformations permitted in case of remainder interests in residence or farm, pooled income funds, etc. The Secretary shall prescribe regulations (consistent with the provisions of this paragraph) permitting reformations in the case of any failure—

(i) to meet the requirements of section 170(f)(3)(B) (relating to remainder interests in personal residence or farm, etc.), or

(ii) to meet the requirements of section 642(c)(5).

(J) Void or reformed trust in cases of insufficient remainder interests. In the case of a trust that would qualify (or could be reformed to qualify pursuant to subparagraph (B)) but for failure to satisfy the requirement of paragraph (1)(D) or (2)(D) of section 664(d), such trust may be—

(i) declared null and void ab initio, or

(ii) changed by reformation, amendment, or otherwise to meet such requirement by reducing the payout rate or the duration (or both) of any noncharitable beneficiary's interest to the extent necessary to satisfy such requirement,

pursuant to a proceeding that is commenced within the period required in subparagraph (C)(iii). In a case described in clause (i), no deduction shall be allowed under this title for any transfer to the trust and any transactions entered into by the trust prior to being declared void shall be treated as entered into by the transferor.

(4) Works of art and their copyrights treated as separate properties in certain cases.

(A) In general. In the case of a qualified contribution of a work of art, the work of art and the copyright on such work of art shall be treated as separate properties for purposes of paragraph (2).

(B) Work of art defined. For purposes of this paragraph, the term "work of art" means any tangible personal property with respect to which there is a copyright under Federal law.

(C) Qualified contribution defined. For purposes of this paragraph, the term "qualified contribution" means any transfer of property to a qualified organization if the use of the property by the organization is related to the purpose or function constituting the basis for its exemption under section 501.

(D) Qualified organization defined. For purposes of this paragraph, the term "qualified organization" means any organization described in section 501(c)(3) other than a private foundation (as defined in section 509). For purposes of the preceding sentence, a private operating foundation (as defined in section 4942(j)(3)) shall not be treated as a private foundation.

(5) Contributions to donor advised funds. A deduction otherwise allowed under subsection (a) for any contribution to a donor advised fund (as defined in section 4966(d)(2)) shall only be allowed if—

(A) the sponsoring organization (as defined in section 4966(d)(1)) with respect to such donor advised fund is not—

(i) described in paragraph (3) or (4) of subsection (a), or

(ii) a type III supporting organization (as defined in section 4943(f)(5)(A)) which is not a functionally integrated type III supporting organization (as defined in section 4943(f)(5)(B)), and

(B) the taxpayer obtains a contemporaneous written acknowledgment (determined under rules similar to the rules of section 170(f)(8)(C)) from the sponsoring organization (as so defined) of such donor advised fund that such organization has exclusive legal control over the assets contributed.

(f) Special rule for irrevocable transfers of easements in real property.

A deduction shall be allowed under subsection (a) in respect of any transfer of a qualified real property interest (as defined in section 170(h)(2)(C)) which meets the requirements of section 170(h) (without regard to paragraph (4)(A) thereof).

(g) Cross references.

(1) For option as to time for valuation for purpose of deduction under this section, see section 2032.

(2) For treatment of certain organizations providing child care, see section 501(k).

(3) For exemption of gifts and bequests to or for the benefit of Library of Congress, see section 5 of the Act of March 3, 1925, as amended (2 U.S.C. 161).

(4) For treatment of gifts and bequests for the benefit of the Naval Historical Center as gifts or bequests to or for the use of the United States, see section 7222 of title 10, United States Code.

(5) For treatment of gifts and bequests to or for the benefit of National Park Foundation as gifts or bequests to or

Estate taxes   Code Sec. 2055

for the use of the United States, see section 8 of the Act of December 18, 1967 (16 U.S.C. 191).

(6) For treatment of gifts, devises, or bequests accepted by the Secretary of State, the Director of the International Communication Agency, or the Director of the United States International Development Cooperation Agency as gifts, devises, or bequests to or for the use of the United States, see section 25 of the State Department Basic Authorities Act of 1956.

(7) For treatment of gifts or bequests of money accepted by the Attorney General for credit to "Commissary Funds, Federal Prisons," as gifts or bequests to or for the use of the United States, see section 4043 of title 18, United States Code.

(8) For payment of tax on gifts and bequests of United States obligations to the United States, see section 3113(e) of title 31, United States Code.

(9) For treatment of gifts and bequests for benefit of the Naval Academy as gifts or bequests to or for the use of the United States, see section 6973 of title 10, United States Code.

(10) For treatment of gifts and bequests for benefit of the Naval Academy Museum as gifts or bequests to or for the use of the United States, see section 6974 of title 10, United States Code.

(11) For exemption of gifts and bequests received by National Archives Trust Fund Board, see section 2308 of title 44, United States Code.

(12) For treatment of gifts and bequests to or for the use of Indian tribal governments (or their subdivisions), see section 7871.

In **2007**, P.L. 110-172, Sec. 3(d)(1), deleted subsec. (g) and redesignated subsec. (h) as (g), effective for contributions, bequests, and gifts made after 8/17/2006.
Prior to deletion, subsec. (g) read as follows:
"(g) Valuation of subsequent gifts.
"(1) In general. In the case of any additional contribution, the fair market value of such contribution shall be determined by using the lesser of—
"(A) the fair market value of the property at the time of the initial fractional contribution, or
"(B) the fair market value of the property at the time of the additional contribution.
"(2) Definitions. For purposes of this paragraph—
"(A) Additional contribution. The term 'additional contribution' means a bequest, legacy, devise, or transfer described in subsection (a) of any interest in a property with respect to which the decedent had previously made an initial fractional contribution.
"(B) Initial fractional contribution. The term 'initial fractional contribution' means, with respect to any decedent, any charitable contribution of an undivided portion of the decedent's entire interest in any tangible personal property for which a deduction was allowed under section 170."
In **2006**, P.L. 109-280, Sec. 1218(b), redesignated subsec. (g) as (h) and added subsec. (g), effective for contributions, bequests, and gifts made after 8/17/2006.
— P.L. 109-280, Sec. 1234(b), added para. (e)(5), effective for contributions made after the date which is 180 days after 8/17/2006.
In **1997**, P.L. 105-34, Sec. 1089(b)(3), added subpara. (e)(3)(J) . . . Sec. 1089(b)(5), added "(or other proceeding pursuant to subparagraph (J)" after "reformation" in subpara. (e)(3)(G), effective for transfers in trust after 7/28/97. For exceptions, see Sec. 1089(b)(6)(B) of this Act, which provides:
"(B) Special rule for certain decedents. The amendments made by this subsection shall not apply to transfers in trust under the terms of a will (or other testamentary instrument) executed on or before July 28, 1997, if the decedent—
"(i) dies before January 1, 1999, without having republished the will (or amended such instrument) by codicil or otherwise, or
"(ii) was on July 28, 1997, under a mental disability to change the disposition of his property and did not regain his competence to dispose of such property before the date of his death."
— P.L. 105-34, Sec. 1530(c)(7)(i) [sic (c)(7)(A)], deleted "or" at the end of para. (a)(3) . . . Sec. 1503(c)(7)(ii) [sic (c)(7)(B)], substituted "; or" for the period at the end of para. (a)(4) . . . Sec. 1530(c)(7)(iii) [sic (c)(7)(C)], added para. (a)(5), effective for transfers made by trusts to, or for the use of, an employee stock ownership plan after 8/5/97.
In **1996**, P.L. 104-201, Sec. 1073(b)(3), amended para. (g)(4), effective 9/23/96.
Prior to amendment, para. (g)(4) read as follows:
" (4) For treatment of gifts and bequests for the benefit of the Office of Naval Records and History as gifts or bequests to or for the use of the United States, see section 7222 of title 10, United States Code."

In **1987**, P.L. 100-203, Sec. 10711(a)(3), substituted "on behalf of (or in opposition to) any candidate" for "on behalf of any candidate" in paras. (a)(2) and (a)(3), effective for activities after 12/22/87.
In **1986**, P.L. 99-514, Sec. 1422(a), redesignated subsec. (f) as (g) and added new subsec. (f), effective for transfers and contributions made after 12/31/86.
— P.L. 99-514, Sec. 1422(d), provides:
"Special donations.—If the Secretary of the Interior acquires by donation after December 31, 1986, a conservation easement (within the meaning of section 2(h) of S. 720, 99th Congress, 1st Session, as in effect on August 16, 1986), such donation shall qualify for treatment under section 2055(f) or 2522(d) of the Internal Revenue Code of 1954, as added by this section."
In **1984**, P.L. 98-369, Sec. 1022(a), amended para. (e)(3), effective as provided by Secs. 1022(e)(1) and (3) of this Act, which read as follows:
"(1) Subsections (a), (b), and (c).—The amendments made by subsections (a), (b), and (c) shall apply to reformations after December 31, 1978; except that such amendments shall not apply to any reformation to which section 2055(e)(3) of the Internal Revenue Code of 1954 (as in effect on the day before the date of the enactment [7/18/84] of this Act) applies. For purposes of applying clause (iii) of section 2055(e)(3)(C) of such Code (as amended by this section), the 90th day described in such clause shall be treated as not occurring before the 90th day after the date of the enactment of this Act.
"(3) Statute of limitations.—
"(A) In general.—If on the date of the enactment [7/18/84] of this Act (or at any time before the date 1 year after such date of enactment [7/18/84]), credit or refund of any overpayment of tax attributable to the amendments made by this section is barred by any law or rule of law, such credit or refund of such overpayment may nevertheless be made if claim therefor is filed before the date 1 year after the date of the enactment of this Act.
"(B) No interest where statute closed on date of enactment.—In any case where the making of the credit or refund of the overpayment described in subparagraph (A) is barred on the date of the enactment of this Act, no interest shall be allowed with respect to such overpayment (or any related adjustment) for the period before the date 180 days after the date on which the Secretary of the Treasury (or his delegate) is notified that the reformation has occurred."
Prior to amendment, para. (e)(3) read as follows:
"(3) In the case of a will executed before December 31, 1978, or a trust created before such date, if a deduction is not allowable at the time of the decedent's death because of the failure of an interest in property which passes from the decedent to a person, or for a use, described in subsection (a) to meet the requirements of subparagraph (A) or (B) of paragraph (2) of this subsection, and if the governing instrument is amended or conformed on or before December 31, 1981, or, if later, on or before the 30th day after the date on which judicial proceedings begun on or before December 31, 1981 (which are required to amend or conform the governing instrument), become final, so that the interest is in a trust which meets the requirements of such subparagraph (A) or (B) (as the case may be), a deduction shall nevertheless be allowed. The Secretary may, by regulation, provide for the application of the provisions of this paragraph to trusts whose governing instruments are amended or conformed in accordance with this paragraph, and such regulations may provide for any adjustments in the application of the provisions of section 508 (relating to special rules with respect to section 501(c)(3) organizations), subchapter J (relating to estates, trusts, beneficiaries, and decedents), and chapter 42 (relating to private foundations), to such trusts made necessary by the application of this paragraph. If, by the due date for the filing of an estate tax return (including any extension thereof), the interest is in a charitable trust which, upon allowance of a deduction, would be described in section 4947(a)(1), or the interest passes directly to a person or for a use described in subsection (a), a deduction shall be allowed as if the governing instrument was amended or conformed under this paragraph. If the amendment or conformation of the governing instrument is made after the due date for the filing of the estate tax return (including any extension thereof), the deduction shall be allowed upon the filing of a timely claim for credit or refund (as provided for in section 6511) of an overpayment resulting from the application of this paragraph. In the case of a credit refund as a result of an amendment or conformation made pursuant to this paragraph, no interest shall be allowed for the period prior to the expiration of the 180th day after the date on which the claim for credit or refund is filed."
— P.L. 98-369, Sec. 1032(b)(2), redesignated paras. (f)(3)–(11) as paras. (f)(4)–(12), respectively, and added new para. (f)(2), effective for tax. yrs. begin. after 7/18/84.
— P.L. 98-369, Sec. 1065(a)(1), amended Sec. 204 of P. L. 97-473, the effective date for changes made by Sec. 202(b)(5) of P. L. 97-473 (see below), by deleting "and before January 1, 1985" where it first appeared.
In **1983**, P.L. 97-473, Sec. 202(b)(5), added para. (f)(11), effective for estates of decedents dying after 12/31/82 [as amended by Sec. 1065(a)(1) of P. L. 98-369, see above].
In **1982**, P.L. 97-258, Sec. 3(f)(1), substituted "section 4043 of title 18, United States Code" for "section 2 of the Act of May 15, 1952, as amended by the Act of July 9, 1952 (31 U.S.C. 725s-4)" in para. (f)(6) . . . Sec. 3(f)(2), substituted "section 3113(e) of title 31, United States Code" for "section 24 of the Second Liberty Bond Act (31 U.S.C. 757e)" in para. (f)(7), effective 9/13/82.
— P.L. 97-248, Sec. 286(b)(2), added the last sentence to subsec. (a), effective 10/5/76.
In **1981**, P.L. 97-34, Sec. 423(a), added para. (e)(4), for estates of decedents dying after 12/31/81.
In **1980**, P.L. 96-605, Sec. 301(a), substituted "December 31, 1978" for "December 31, 1977" and "December 31, 1981" for "December 31, 1978" in para. (e)(3), effective in the case of decedents dying after 12/31/69. Sec. 301(b)(2) provides:

"(2) Charitable lead trusts and charitable remainder trusts in the case of income and gift taxes. Section 514(b) (and section 514(c) insofar as it relates to section 514(b)) of the Revenue Act of 1978 shall be applied as if the amendment made by subsection (a) had been included in the amendment made by section 514(a) of such Act."

—P.L. 96-541, Sec. 6(c), amended the effective date for changes made by Sec. 2124(e)(2) of P. L. 94-455 (as amended by Sec. 309(b)(2) of P. L. 95-30) from contributions or transfers made after 6/13/76 and before 6/14/81 to contributions or transfers made after 6/13/76 [see below].

—P.L. 96-465, Sec. 2206(e)(4), amended para. (f)(5), effective 2/15/81.

Prior to amendment, para. (f)(5) read as follows:

"(5) For treatment of gifts, devises, or bequests accepted by the Secretary of State under the Foreign Service Act of 1946 as gifts, devices, or bequests to or for the use of the United States, see section 1021(e) of that Act (22 U.S.C. 809(e))."

—P.L. 96-222, Sec. 105(a)(4)(A)(i), substituted "(A) or (B)" for "(a) or (B)" in para. (e)(3) . . . Sec. 105(a)(4)(A)(ii), substituted "so that the interest" for "so that interest" in para. (e)(3), effective for decedents dying after 12/31/69.

—P.L. 96-222, Sec. 105(a)(4)(B), added Sec. 514(c) of P. L. 95-600 which provided the effective date for changes made by Sec. 514(a) of P. L. 95-600, see below.

In 1978, P.L. 95-600, Sec. 514(a), amended the first sentence of para. (e)(3), effective for decedents dying after 12/31/69.

Prior to amendment, the first sentence of para. (e)(3) read as follows:

"In the case of a will executed before December 31, 1977, or a trust created before such date, if a deduction is not allowable at the time of the decedent's death because of the failure of an interest in property which passes from the decedent to a person, or for a use, described in subsection (a), to meet the requirements of subparagraph (A) of paragraph (2) of this subsection, and if the governing instrument is amended or conformed on or before December 31, 1977, or, if later, on or before the 30th day after the date on which judicial proceedings begun on or before December 31, 1977 (which are required to amend or conform the governing instrument), become final, so that the interest is in a trust which is a charitable remainder annuity trust, a charitable remainder unitrust (described in section 664), or a pooled income fund (described in section 642(c)(5)), a deduction shall nevertheless be allowed."

—P.L. 95-600, Sec. 514(b), which provides special provisions is reproduced at note following Code Sec. 2522.

—P.L. 95-600, Sec. 703(j)(12), amended the effective date for changes made by Sec. 1902(a)(12)(A) of P. L. 94-455 to apply to estates of decedents dying after 10/4/76. See below.

In 1977, P.L. 95-30, Sec. 309(b)(2), [as amended by Sec. 6(c) of P. L. 96-541, see above], amended the effective date for amendments made by Sec. 2124(e)(2) of P. L. 94-455, from contributions or transfers made after 6/13/76 and before 6/14/77 to contributions or transfers made after 6/13/76 and before 6/14/81. [see below].

In 1976, P.L. 94-455, Sec. 1304(a), substituted "December 31, 1977," for "September 21, 1974," . . . substituted "December 31, 1977" for "December 31, 1975" each place it appeared in para. (e)(3), for decedents dying after '69. Sec. 1304(b) of the Act provided as follows:

"(b) Extension of period for filing claim for refund of estate tax paid.

"A claim for refund or credit of an overpayment of the tax imposed by section 2001 of the Internal Revenue Code of 1954 allowable under section 2055(e)(3) of such Code (as amended by subsection (a)) shall not be denied because of the expiration of the time for filing such a claim under section 6511(a) if such claim is filed not later than June 30, 1978."

—P.L. 94-455, Sec. 1307(d)(1)(B)(ii), substituted "which is not disqualified for tax exemption under section 501(c)(3) by reason of attempting to influence legislation," for "no substantial part of the activities of which is carrying on propaganda, or otherwise attempting, to influence legislation," in para. (a)(2), effective for estates of decedents dying after 12/31/76.

—P.L. 94-455, Sec. 1307(d)(1)(C), substituted "such trust, fraternal society, order, or association would not be disqualified for tax exemption under section 501(c)(3) by reason of attempting to influence legislation," for "no substantial part of the activities of such trustee or trustees, or of such fraternal society, order, or association, is carrying on propaganda, or otherwise attempting, to influence legislation," for estates of decedents dying after 12/31/76.

—P.L. 94-455, Sec. 1313(b)(2), added ", or to foster national or international amateur sports competition (but only if no part of its activities involve the provision of athletic facilities or equipment)," after "the encouragement of art", effective 10/5/76. . . . Sec. 1313(c), of the Act provides that "an organization which (without regard to the amendments made by this section) is an organization described in section . . . 2055(a)(2) . . . of the Internal Revenue Code of 1954 shall not be treated as an organization not so described as a result of the amendments made by this section."

—P.L. 94-455, Sec. 1902(a)(4)(A), amended subsec. (b), effective for estates of decedents dying after 10/4/76.

Prior to amendment, subsec. (b) read as follows:

"(b) Powers of appointment.

"(1) General rule. Property includible in the decedent's gross estate under section 2041 (relating to powers of appointment) received by a donee described in this section shall, for purposes of this section, be considered a bequest of such decedent.

"(2) Special rule for certain bequests subject to power of appointment. For purposes of this section, in the case of a bequest in trust, if the surviving spouse of the decedent is entitled for life to all of the net income from the trust and such surviving spouse has a power of appointment over the corpus of such trust exercisable by will in favor of, among others, organizations described in subsection (a)(2), such bequest in trust, reduced by the value of the life estate, shall, to the extent such power is exercised in favor of such organizations, be deemed a transfer to such organizations by the decedent if—

"(A) no part of the corpus of such trust is distributed to a beneficiary during the life of the surviving spouse;

"(B) such surviving spouse was over 80 years of age at the date of the decedent's death;

"(C) such surviving spouse by affidavit executed within 6 months after the death of the decedent specifies the organizations described in subsection (a)(2) in favor of which he intends to exercise the power of appointment and indicates the amount or proportion each such organization is to receive; and

"(D) the power of appointment is exercised in favor of such organizations and in the amounts or proportions specified in the affidavit required under subparagraph (C).

The affidavit referred to in subparagraph (C), shall be attached to the estate tax return of the decedent and shall constitute a sufficient basis for the allowance of the deduction under this paragraph in the first instance subject to a later disallowance of the deduction if the conditions herein specified are not complied with."

—P.L. 94-455, Sec. 1902(a)(4)(B), amended subsec. (f), for estates of decedents dying after 10/4/76.

Prior to amendment, subsec. (f) read as follows:

"(f) Other cross references.

"(1) For option as to time for valuation for purpose of deduction under this section, see section 2032.

"(2) For exemption of bequests to or for benefit of Library of Congress, see section 5 of the Act of March 3, 1925, as amended (56 Stat. 765; 2 U.S.C. 161).

"(3) For construction of bequests for benefit of the library of the Post Office Department as bequests to or for the use of the United States, see section 2 of the Act of August 8, 1946 (60 Stat. 924; 5 U.S.C. 393).

"(4) For exemption of bequests for benefit of Office of Naval Records and Library, Navy Department, see section 2 of the Act of March 4, 1937 (50 Stat. 25; 5 U.S.C. 419b).

"(5) For exemption of bequests to or for benefit of National Park Service, see section 5 of the Act of July 10, 1935 (49 Stat. 478; 16 U.S.C. 19c).

"(6) For construction of devises or bequests accepted by the Secretary of State under the Foreign Service Act of 1946 as devises or bequests to or for the use of the United States, see section 1021(e) of that Act (60 Stat. 1032; 32 U.S.C. 809).

"(7) For construction of gifts or bequests of money accepted by the Attorney General for credit to 'Commissary Funds, Federal Prisons' as gifts or bequests to or for the use of the United States, see section 2 of the Act of May 15, 1952, 66 Stat. 73, as amended by the Act of July 9, 1952, 66 Stat. 479 (31 U.S.C. 725s-4).

"(8) For payment of tax on bequests of United States obligations to the United States, see section 24 of the Second Liberty Bond Act, as amended (59 Stat. 48, § 4; 31 U.S.C. 757e).

"(9) For construction of bequests for benefit of or use in connection with the Naval Academy as bequests to or for the use of the United States, see section 3 of the Act of March 31, 1944 (58 Stat. 135; 34 U.S.C. 1115b).

"(10) For exemption of bequests for benefit of Naval Academy Museum, see section 4 of the Act of March 26, 1938 (52 Stat. 119; 34 U.S.C. 1119).

"(11) For exemption of bequests received by National Archives Trust Fund Board, see section 7 of the National Archives Trust Fund Board Act (55 Stat. 582; 44 U.S.C. 300gg)."

—P.L. 94-455, Sec. 1902(a)(12)(A), deleted "Territory,", which followed "any State," in para. (a)(1), for gifts made after 12/31/76.

—P.L. 94-455, Sec. 1906(b)(13)(A), substituted "Secretary" for "Secretary or his delegate" in para. (e)(3), effective 2/1/77.

—P.L. 94-455, Sec. 2009(b)(4)(B), amended so much of subsec. (a) as precedes para. (a)(1), effective with respect to transfers creating an interest in the person disclaiming made after 12/31/76.

Prior to amendment, that part of subsec. (a) read as follows:

"(a) In general.

"For purposes of the tax imposed by section 2001, the value of the taxable estate shall be determined by deducting from the value of the gross estate the amount of all bequests, legacies, devises, or transfers (including the interest which falls into any such bequest, legacy, devise, or transfer as a result of an irrevocable disclaimer of a bequest, legacy, devise, transfer, or power, if the disclaimer is made before the date prescribed for the filing of the estate tax return)—"

—P.L. 94-455, Sec. 2009(b)(4)(C), substituted "a qualified" for "an irrevocable" and "such qualified" for "such irrevocable" in the second sentence of subsec. (a), effective with respect to transfers creating an interest in the person disclaiming made after 12/31/76.

—P.L. 94-455, Sec. 2124(e)(2), substituted "(other than an interest described in section 170(f)(3)(B))" for "(other than a remainder interest in a personal residence or farm or an undivided portion of the decedent's entire interest in property)" in para. (e)(2), effective with respect to contributions or transfers made after 6/13/76 [as amended by Sec. 309(b)(2) of P. L. 95-30, see above, and as amended by Sec. 6(c) of P. L. 96-541, see above].

In 1974, P.L. 93-483, Sec. 3(a), added para. (3) to subsec. (e), effective with respect to estates of decedents dying after 12/31/69.

In 1972, P.L. 92-603, Sec. 132, made bequests to one of the Social Security funds a public bequest. See note following Code Sec. 170.

In 1970, P.L. 91-614, Sec. 101(c), substituted "6 months" for "one year," in subpara. (b)(2)(C), effective for decedents dying after 12/31/70.

In 1969, P.L. 91-172, Sec. 201(d)(1), amended subsec. (e) effective as provided in Sec. 201(g)(4)(A), (B) and (C) which reads as follows:

"(4)(A) Except as provided in subparagraphs (B) and (C), the amendments made by paragraphs (1) and (2) of subsection (d) shall apply in the case of decedents dying after December 31, 1969.

Estate taxes Code Sec. 2056(b)(6)

"(B) Such amendments shall not apply in the case of property passing under the terms of a will executed on or before October 9, 1969—

"(i) if the decedent dies before October 9, 1972, without having republished the will after October 9, 1969, by codicil or otherwise,

"(ii) if the decedent at no time after October 9, 1969, had the right to change the portions of the will which pertain to the passing of the property to, or for the use of, an organization described in section 2055(a), or

"(iii) if the will is not republished by codicil or otherwise before October 9, 1972, and the decedent is on such date and at all times thereafter under a mental disability to republish the will by codicil or otherwise.

"(C) Such amendments shall not apply in the case of property transferred in trust on or before October 9, 1969—

"(i) if the decedent dies before October 9, 1972, without having amended after October 9, 1969, the instrument governing the disposition of the property,

"(ii) if the property transferred was an irrevocable interest to, or for the use of, an organization described in section 2055(a), or

"(iii) if the instrument governing the disposition of the property was not amended by the decedent before October 9, 1972, and the decedent is on such date and at all times thereafter under a mental disability to change the disposition of the property."

Prior to amendment, subsec. (e) read as follows:

"(e) Disallowance of deductions in certain cases.

"For disallowance of certain charitable, etc., deductions otherwise allowable under this section, see sections 503 and 681."

—P.L. 91-172, Sec. 201(d)(4)(A), deleted "and" before "no substantial part" in para. (2) and added before the semicolon at the end of such paragraph ", and which does not participate in, or intervene in (including the publishing or distributing of statements), any political campaign on behalf of any candidate for public office", and deleted "and" before "no substantial part" in para. (3) and added before the semicolon at the end of such paragraph ", and such trustee or trustees, or such fraternal society, order, or association, does not participate in, or intervene in (including the publishing or distributing of statements), any political campaign on behalf of any candidate for public office" in subsec. (a), effective for gifts and transfers made after 12/31/69.

In **1958**, P.L. 85-866, Sec. 30(d), substituted "503" for "504" in subsec. (e).

In **1956**, P.L. 1011, Sec. 1, designated original paragraph as "(1) General rule." and added par. (2) for decedents dying after 8/16/54.

Sec. 2056. Bequests, etc., to surviving spouse.
(a) Allowance of marital deduction.

For purposes of the tax imposed by section 2001, the value of the taxable estate shall, except as limited by subsection (b), be determined by deducting from the value of the gross estate an amount equal to the value of any interest in property which passes or has passed from the decedent to his surviving spouse, but only to the extent that such interest is included in determining the value of the gross estate.

(b) Limitation in the case of life estate or other terminable interest.

(1) General rule. Where, on the lapse of time, on the occurrence of an event or contingency, or on the failure of an event or contingency to occur, an interest passing to the surviving spouse will terminate or fail, no deduction shall be allowed under this section with respect to such interest—

(A) if an interest in such property passes or has passed (for less than an adequate and full consideration in money or money's worth) from the decedent to any person other than such surviving spouse (or the estate of such spouse); and

(B) if by reason of such passing such person (or his heirs or assigns) may possess or enjoy any part of such property after such termination or failure of the interest so passing to the surviving spouse;

and no deduction shall be allowed with respect to such interest (even if such deduction is not disallowed under subparagraphs (A) and (B))—

(C) if such interest is to be acquired for the surviving spouse, pursuant to directions of the decedent, by his executor or by the trustee of a trust.

For purposes of this paragraph, an interest shall not be considered as an interest which will terminate or fail merely because it is the ownership of a bond, note, or similar contractual obligation, the discharge of which would not have the effect of an annuity for life or for a term.

(2) Interest in unidentified assets. Where the assets (included in the decedent's gross estate) out of which, or the proceeds of which, an interest passing to the surviving spouse may be satisfied include a particular asset or assets with respect to which no deduction would be allowed if such asset or assets passed from the decedent to such spouse, then the value of such interest passing to such spouse shall, for purposes of subsection (a), be reduced by the aggregate value of such particular assets.

(3) Interest of spouse conditional on survival for limited period. For purposes of this subsection, an interest passing to the surviving spouse shall not be considered as an interest which will terminate or fail on the death of such spouse if—

(A) such death will cause a termination or failure of such interest only if it occurs within a period not exceeding 6 months after the decedent's death, or only if it occurs as a result of a common disaster resulting in the death of the decedent and the surviving spouse, or only if it occurs in the case of either such event; and

(B) such termination or failure does not in fact occur.

(4) Valuation of interest passing to surviving spouse. In determining for purposes of subsection (a) the value of any interest in property passing to the surviving spouse for which a deduction is allowed by this section—

(A) there shall be taken into account the effect which the tax imposed by section 2001, or any estate, succession, legacy, or inheritance tax, has on the net value to the surviving spouse of such interest; and

(B) where such interest or property is encumbered in any manner, or where the surviving spouse incurs any obligation imposed by the decedent with respect to the passing of such interest, such encumbrance or obligation shall be taken into account in the same manner as if the amount of a gift to such spouse of such interest were being determined.

(5) Life estate with power of appointment in surviving spouse. In the case of an interest in property passing from the decedent, if his surviving spouse is entitled for life to all the income from the entire interest, or all the income from a specific portion thereof, payable annually or at more frequent intervals, with power in the surviving spouse to appoint the entire interest, or such specific portion (exercisable in favor of such surviving spouse, or of the estate of such surviving spouse, or in favor of either, whether or not in each case the power is exercisable in favor of others), and with no power in any other person to appoint any part of the interest, or such specific portion, to any person other than the surviving spouse—

(A) the interest or such portion thereof so passing shall, for purposes of subsection (a), be considered as passing to the surviving spouse, and

(B) no part of the interest so passing shall, for purposes of paragraph (1)(A), be considered as passing to any person other than the surviving spouse.

This paragraph shall apply only if such power in the surviving spouse to appoint the entire interest, or such specific portion thereof, whether exercisable by will or during life, is exercisable by such spouse alone and in all events.

(6) Life insurance or annuity payments with power of appointment in surviving spouse. In the case of an interest in property passing from the decedent consisting of proceeds under a life insurance, endowment, or annuity contract, if under the terms of the contract such proceeds are payable in installments or are held by the insurer subject to an agreement to pay interest thereon (whether the proceeds, on the termination of any interest payments, are

3,001

payable in a lump sum or in annual or more frequent installments), and such installment or interest payments are payable annually or at more frequent intervals, commencing not later than 13 months after the decedent's death, and all amounts, or a specific portion of all such amounts, payable during the life of the surviving spouse are payable only to such spouse, and such spouse has the power to appoint all amounts, or such specific portion, payable under such contract (exercisable in favor of such surviving spouse, or of the estate of such surviving spouse, or in favor of either, whether or not in each case the power is exercisable in favor of others), with no power in any other person to appoint such amounts to any person other than the surviving spouse—

(A) such amounts shall, for purposes of subsection (a), be considered as passing to the surviving spouse, and

(B) no part of such amounts shall, for purposes of paragraph (1)(A), be considered as passing to any person other than the surviving spouse.

This paragraph shall apply only if, under the terms of the contract, such power in the surviving spouse to appoint such amounts, whether exercisable by will or during life, is exercisable by such spouse alone and in all events.

(7) Election with respect to life estate for surviving spouse.

(A) In general. In the case of qualified terminable interest property—

(i) for purposes of subsection (a), such property shall be treated as passing to the surviving spouse, and

(ii) for purposes of paragraph (1)(A), no part of such property shall be treated as passing to any person other than the surviving spouse.

(B) Qualified terminable interest property defined. For purposes of this paragraph—

(i) In general. The term "qualified terminable interest property" means property—

(I) which passes from the decedent,

(II) in which the surviving spouse has a qualifying income interest for life, and

(III) to which an election under this paragraph applies.

(ii) Qualifying income interest for life. The surviving spouse has a qualifying income interest for life if—

(I) the surviving spouse is entitled to all the income from the property, payable annually or at more frequent intervals, or has a usufruct interest for life in the property, and

(II) no person has a power to appoint any part of the property to any person other than the surviving spouse.

Subclause (II) shall not apply to a power exercisable only at or after the death of the surviving spouse. To the extent provided in regulations, an annuity shall be treated in a manner similar to an income interest in property (regardless of whether the property from which the annuity is payable can be separately identified).

(iii) Property includes interest therein. The term "property" includes an interest in property.

(iv) Specific portion treated as separate property. A specific portion of property shall be treated as separate property.

(v) Election. An election under this paragraph with respect to any property shall be made by the executor on the return of tax imposed by section 2001. Such an election, once made, shall be irrevocable.

(C) Treatment of survivor annuities. In the case of an annuity included in the gross estate of the decedent under section 2039 (or, in the case of an interest in an annuity arising under the community property laws of a State, included in the gross estate of the decedent under section 2033) where only the surviving spouse has the right to receive payments before the death of such surviving spouse—

(i) the interest of such surviving spouse shall be treated as a qualifying income interest for life, and

(ii) the executor shall be treated as having made an election under this subsection with respect to such annuity unless the executor otherwise elects on the return of tax imposed by section 2001.

An election under clause (ii), once made, shall be irrevocable.

(8) Special rule for charitable remainder trusts.

(A) In general. If the surviving spouse of the decedent is the only beneficiary of a qualified charitable remainder trust who is not a charitable beneficiary nor an ESOP beneficiary, paragraph (1) shall not apply to any interest in such trust which passes or has passed from the decedent to such surviving spouse.

(B) Definitions. For purposes of subparagraph (A)—

(i) Charitable beneficiary. The term "charitable beneficiary" means any beneficiary which is an organization described in section 170(c).

(ii) ESOP beneficiary. The term "ESOP beneficiary" means any beneficiary which is an employee stock ownership plan (as defined in section 4975(e)(7)) that holds a remainder interest in qualified employer securities (as defined in section 664(g)(4)) to be transferred to such plan in a qualified gratuitous transfer (as defined in section 664(g)(1)).

(iii) Qualified charitable remainder trust. The term "qualified charitable remainder trust" means a charitable remainder annuity trust or charitable remainder unitrust (described in section 664).

(9) Denial of double deduction. Nothing in this section or any other provision of this chapter shall allow the value of any interest in property to be deducted under this chapter more than once with respect to the same decedent.

(10) Specific portion. For purposes of paragraphs (5), (6), and (7)(B)(iv), the term "specific portion" only includes a portion determined on a fractional or percentage basis.

(c) Definition.

For purposes of this section, an interest in property shall be considered as passing from the decedent to any person if and only if—

(1) such interest is bequeathed or devised to such person by the decedent;

(2) such interest is inherited by such person from the decedent;

(3) such interest is the dower or curtesy interest (or statutory interest in lieu thereof) of such person as surviving spouse of the decedent;

(4) such interest has been transferred to such person by the decedent at any time;

(5) such interest was, at the time of the decedent's death, held by such person and the decedent (or by them and any other person) in joint ownership with right of survivorship;

(6) the decedent had a power (either alone or in conjunction with any person) to appoint such interest and if he appoints or has appointed such interest to such person, or if such person takes such interest in default on the release or nonexercise of such power; or

(7) such interest consists of proceeds of insurance on the life of the decedent receivable by such person.

Except as provided in paragraph (5) or (6) of subsection (b), where at the time of the decedent's death it is not possible to ascertain the particular person or persons to whom an interest in property may pass from the decedent, such interest shall, for purposes of subparagraphs (A) and (B) of subsection (b)(1), be considered as passing from the decedent to a person other than the surviving spouse.

(d) **Disallowance of marital deduction where surviving spouse not United States citizen.**

(1) **In general.** Except as provided in paragraph (2), if the surviving spouse of the decedent is not a citizen of the United States—

(A) no deduction shall be allowed under subsection (a), and

(B) section 2040(b) shall not apply.

(2) **Marital deduction allowed for certain transfers in trust.**

(A) In general. Paragraph (1) shall not apply to any property passing to the surviving spouse in a qualified domestic trust.

(B) Special rule. If any property passes from the decedent to the surviving spouse of the decedent, for purposes of subparagraph (A), such property shall be treated as passing to such spouse in a qualified domestic trust if—

(i) such property is transferred to such a trust before the date on which the return of the tax imposed by this chapter is made, or

(ii) such property is irrevocably assigned to such a trust under an irrevocable assignment made on or before such date which is enforceable under local law.

(3) **Allowance of credit to certain spouses.** If—

(A) property passes to the surviving spouse of the decedent (hereinafter in this paragraph referred to as the "first decedent"),

(B) without regard to this subsection, a deduction would be allowable under subsection (a) with respect to such property, and

(C) such surviving spouse dies and the estate of such surviving spouse is subject to the tax imposed by this chapter,

the Federal estate tax paid (or treated as paid under section 2056A(b)(7)) by the first decedent with respect to such property shall be allowed as a credit under section 2013 to the estate of such surviving spouse and the amount of such credit shall be determined under such section without regard to when the first decedent died and without regard to subsection (d)(3) of such section.

(4) **Special rule where resident spouse becomes citizen.** Paragraph (1) shall not apply if—

(A) the surviving spouse of the decedent becomes a citizen of the United States before the day on which the return of the tax imposed by this chapter is made, and

(B) such spouse was a resident of the United States at all times after the date of the death of the decedent and before becoming a citizen of the United States.

(5) **Reformations permitted.**

(A) In general. In the case of any property with respect to which a deduction would be allowable under subsection (a) but for this subsection, the determination of whether a trust is a qualified domestic trust shall be made—

(i) as of the date on which the return of the tax imposed by this chapter is made, or

(ii) if a judicial proceeding is commenced on or before the due date (determined with regard to extensions) for filing such return to change such trust into a trust which is a qualified domestic trust, as of the time when the changes pursuant to such proceeding are made.

(B) Statute of limitations. If a judicial proceeding described in subparagraph (A)(ii) is commenced with respect to any trust, the period for assessing any deficiency of tax attributable to any failure of such trust to be a qualified domestic trust shall not expire before the date 1 year after the date on which the Secretary is notified that the trust has been changed pursuant to such judicial proceeding or that such proceeding has been terminated.

In **1997**, P.L. 105-34, Sec. 1311(a), added "(or, in the case of an interest in an annuity arising under the community property laws of a State, included in the gross estate of the decedent under section 2033)" after "section 2039" in subpara. (b)(7)(C), effective for estates of decedents dying after 8/5/97.

—P.L. 105-34, Sec. 1530(c)(8), amended para. (b)(8), effective for transfers made by trusts to, or for the use of, an employee stock ownership plan after 8/5/97.

Prior to amendment, para. (b)(8) read as follows:

"(8) Special rule for charitable remainder trusts.

"(A) In general. If the surviving spouse of the decedent is the only noncharitable beneficiary of a qualified charitable remainder trust, paragraph (1) shall not apply to any interest in such trust which passes or has passed from the decedent to such surviving spouse.

"(B) Definitions. For purposes of subparagraph (A)—

"(i) Noncharitable beneficiary. The term 'noncharitable beneficiary' means any beneficiary of the qualified charitable remainder trust other than an organization described in section 170(c).

"(ii) Qualified charitable remainder trust. The term 'qualified charitable remainder trust' means a charitable remainder annuity trust or charitable remainder unitrust (described in section 664)."

In **1992**, P.L. 102-486, Sec. 1941(a), added para. (b)(10), effective for estates of decedents dying after 10/24/92 except as provided in Sec. 1941(c)(1)(B) of this Act, which read as follows:

"(B) Exception. The amendment made by subsection (a) shall not apply to any interest in property which passes (or has passed) to the surviving spouse of the decedent pursuant to a will (or revocable trust) in existence on the date of the enactment of this Act if—

"(i) the decedent dies on or before the date 3 years after such date of enactment, or

"(ii) the decedent was, on such date of enactment, under a mental disability to change the disposition of his property and did not regain his competence to dispose of such property before the date of his death.

The preceding sentence shall not apply if such will (or revocable trust) is amended at any time after such date of enactment in any respect which will increase the amount of the interest which so passes or alters the terms of the transfer by which the interest so passes."

In **1990**, P.L. 101-508, Sec. 11701(l)(1), redesignated para. (d)(4) [added by Sec. 7815(d)(8) of P. L. 101-239, see below] relating to reformations permitted, as para. (d)(5), effective for the estates of decedents dying after 11/10/88, except as provided in Sec. 7815(d)(4)(B) and (d)(14) of P. L. 101-239, reproduced below.

—P.L. 101-508, Sec. 11701(l)(2), provides the following:

"(2) The period during which a proceeding may be commenced under section 2056(d)(5)(A)(ii) of the Internal Revenue Code of 1986 (as redesignated by paragraph (1) [of Sec. 11701(l) of this Act]) shall not expire before the date 6 months after the date of the enactment of this Act."

—P.L. 101-508, Sec. 11702(g)(5), substituted "section 2056A(b)(7) for 'section 2056A(b)(6)" in para. (d)(3), effective for the estates of decedents dying after 11/10/88.

In **1989**, P.L. 101-239, Sec. 7815(d)(4)(A), amended subpara. (d)(2)(B) . . . Sec. 7815(d)(5), added para. (d)(4) . . . Sec. 7815(d)(6)(A), substituted 'this chapter' for 'section 2001' in para. (d)(3) . . . Sec. 7815(d)(6)(B), added 'and without regard to subsection (d)(3) of such section' before the period at the end of para. (d)(3) . . . Sec. 7815(d)(8), added para. (d)(4)[sic (d)(5)], effective for the estates of decedents dying after 11/10/88, except as provided in Secs. 7815(d)(4)(B) and (d)(14) of this Act which reads as follows:

"(B) In the case of the estate of a decedent dying before the date of the enactment of this Act, the period during which the transfer (or irrevocable assignment) referred to in section 2056(d)(2)(B) of the Internal Revenue Code of 1986 (as amended by subparagraph (A)) may be made shall not expire before the date 1 year after such date of enactment."

* * *

"(14) In the case of the estate of, or gift by, an individual who was not a citizen or resident of the United States but was a resident of a foreign country with which the United States has a tax treaty with respect to estate, inheritance, or gift taxes, the amendments made by section 5033 of the 1988 Act [P. L. 100-647] shall not apply to the extent such amendments would be inconsistent with the provisions of such treaty relating to estate, inheritance, or gift tax marital deductions. In the case of the estate of an individual dying before the date 3 years after the date of the enactment of this Act [11/10/88], or a gift by an individual before the date 3 years after the date of the enactment of this Act [11/10/88], the requirement of the preceding sentence that the individual not be a citizen or resident of the United States shall not apply."

Prior to amendment, subpara. (d)(2)(B) read as follows:

"(B) Property passing outside of probate estate. If any property passes from the decedent to the surviving spouse of the decedent outside of the decedent's probate estate, for purposes of subparagraph (A), such property shall be treated as passing to such spouse in a qualified domestic trust if such property is transferred to such a trust before the day on which the return of the tax imposed by section 2001 is made."

—P.L. 101-239, Sec. 7816(q), substituted "an annuity included in the gross estate of the decedent under section 2039" for "an annuity" in subpara. (b)(7)(C), effective for decedents dying after 12/31/81, except as provided in Secs. 6152(c)(2) and (3) of P. L. 100-647 reproduced below.

In 1988, P.L. 100-647, Sec. 5033(a)(1), added subsec. (d), effective for the estates of decedents dying after 11/10/88.

—P.L. 100-647, Sec. 6152(a), added subpara. (b)(7)(C), effective for decedents dying after 12/31/81, except as provided in Secs. 6152(c)(2) and (3) of this Act which read as follows:

"(2) Not to apply to extent inconsistent with prior return. In the case of any estate or gift tax return filed before the date of the enactment of this Act, the amendments made by this section shall not apply to the extent such amendments would be inconsistent with the treatment of the annuity on such return unless the executor or donor (as the case may be) otherwise elects under this paragraph before the day 2 years after the date of the enactment of this Act.

"(3) Extension of time for election out. The time for making an election under section 2056(b)(7)(C)(ii) or 2523(f)(6)(B) of the 1986 Code (as added by this subsection [Sec. 6152(a)]) shall not expire before the day 2 years after the date of the enactment of this Act (and, if such election is made within the time permitted under this paragraph, the requirement of such section 2056(b)(7)(C)(ii) that it be made on the return shall not apply)."

In 1984, P.L. 98-369, Sec. 1027(a), added ", or has a usufruct interest for life in the property" after "intervals" in subclause (b)(7)(B)(ii)(I), effective for estates of decedents dying after 12/31/81.

In 1983, P.L. 97-448, Sec. 104(a)(2)(A), added para. (b)(9) . . . Sec. 104(a)(8), added a sentence at the end of clause (b)(7)(B)(ii), effective for estates of decedents dying after 12/31/81.

In 1981, P.L. 97-34, Sec. 403(a)(1)(A), deleted subsec. (c) and redesignated subsec. (d) as subsec. (c) . . . Sec. 403(a)(1)(B), substituted "subsection (b)" for "subsections (b) and (c)" in subsec. (a), effective for estates of decedents dying after 12/31/81. Sec. 403(e)(3) of this Act provides:

"(3) If—

"(A) the decedent dies after December 31, 1981,

"(B) by reason of the death of the decedent property passes from the decedent or is acquired from the decedent under a will executed before the date which is 30 days after the date of the enactment of this Act, or a trust created before such date, which contains a formula expressly providing that the spouse is to receive the maximum amount of property qualifying for the marital deduction allowable by Federal law,

"(C) the formula referred to in subparagraph (B) was not amended to refer specifically to an unlimited marital deduction at any time after the date which is 30 days after the date of enactment of this Act, and before the death of the decedent, and

"(D) the State does not enact a statute applicable to such estate which construes this type of formula as referring to the marital deduction allowable by Federal law as amended by subsection (a),

then the amendment made by subsection (a) shall not apply to the estate of such decedent."

Prior to deletion, subsec. (c) read as follows:

"(c) Limitation on aggregate of deductions.

"(1) Limitation.

"(A) In general. The aggregate amount of the deductions allowed under this section (computed without regard to this subsection) shall not exceed the greater of—

"(i) $250,000, or

"(ii) 50 percent of the value of the adjusted gross estate (as defined in paragraph (2)).

"(B) Adjustment for certain gifts to spouse. If a deduction is allowed to the decedent under section 2523 with respect to any gift made to his spouse after December 31, 1976, the limitation provided by subparagraph (A) (determined without regard to this subparagraph) shall be reduced (but not below zero) by the excess (if any) of—

"(i) the aggregate of the deductions allowed to the decedent under section 2523 with respect to gifts made after December 31, 1976, over

"(ii) the aggregate of the deductions which would have been allowable under section 2523 with respect to gifts made after December 31, 1976, if the amount deductible under such section with respect to any gift required to be included in a gift tax return were 50 percent of its value.

For purposes of this subparagraph, a gift which is includible in the gross estate of the donor by reason of section 2035 shall not be taken into account.

"(C) Community property adjustment. The $250,000 amount set forth in subparagraph (A)(i) shall be reduced by the excess (if any) of—

"(i) the amount of the subtraction determined under clauses (i), (ii), and (iii) of paragraph (2)(B), over

"(ii) the excess of the aggregate of the deductions allowed under sections 2053 and 2054 over the amount taken into account with respect to such deductions under clause (iv) of paragraph (2)(B).

"(2) Computation of adjusted gross estate.

"(A) General rule. Except as provided in subparagraph (B) of this paragraph, the adjusted gross estate shall, for purposes of subsection (c)(1), be computed by subtracting from the entire value of the gross estate the aggregate amount of the deductions allowed by sections 2053 and 2054.

"(B) Special rule in cases involving community property. If the decedent and his surviving spouse at any time, held property as community property under the law of any State, or possession of the United States, or of any foreign country, then the adjusted gross estate shall, for purposes of subsection (c)(1), be determined by subtracting from the entire value of the gross estate the sum of—

"(i) the value of property which is at the time of the death of the decedent held as such community property;

"(ii) the value of property transferred by the decedent during his life, if at the time of such transfer the property was held as such community property; and

"(iii) the amount receivable as insurance under policies on the life of the decedent, to the extent purchased with premiums or other consideration paid out of property held as such community property; and

"(iv) an amount which bears the same ratio to the aggregate of the deductions allowed under sections 2053 and 2054 which the value of the property included in the gross estate, diminished by the amount subtracted under clauses (i), (ii), and (iii) of this subparagraph, bears to the entire value of the gross estate.

For purposes of clauses (i), (ii), and (iii), community property (except property which is considered as community property solely by reason of the provisions of subparagraph (C) of this paragraph) shall be considered as not 'held as such community property' as of any moment of time, if, in case of the death of the decedent at such moment, such property (and not merely one-half thereof) would be or would have been includible in determining the value of his gross estate without regard to the provisions of section 402(b) of the Revenue Act of 1942. The amount to be subtracted under clauses (i), (ii), or (iii) shall not exceed the value of the interest in the property described therein which is included in determining the value of the gross estate.

"(C) Community property — conversion into separate property.

"(i) After December 31, 1941. If after December 31, 1941, property held as such community property (unless considered by reason of subparagraph (B) of this paragraph as not so held) was by the decedent and the surviving spouse converted, by one transaction or a series of transactions, into separate property of the decedent and his spouse (including any form of coownership by them), the separate property so acquired by the decedent and any property acquired at any time by the decedent in exchange therefor (by one exchange or a series of exchanges) shall, for the purposes of clauses (i), (ii), and (iii) of subparagraph (B), be considered as 'held as such community property.'

"(ii) Limitation. Where the value (at the time of such conversion) of the separate property so acquired by the decedent exceeded the value (at such time) of the separate property so acquired by the decedent's spouse, the rule in clause (i) shall be applied only with respect to the same portion of such separate property of the decedent as the portion which the value (as of such time) of such separate property so acquired by the decedent's spouse is of the value (as of such time) of the separate property so acquired by the decedent."

—P.L. 97-34, Sec. 403(d)(1), added paras. (b)(7) and (8), effective for estates of decedents dying after 12/31/81.

In 1978, P.L. 95-600, Sec. 702(g), added the last sentence in subpara. (c)(1)(B), and added "required to be included in a gift tax return" after "with respect to any gift" in clause (c)(1)(B)(ii), effective for estates of decedents dying after 12/31/76.

—P.L. 95-600, Sec. 703(j)(12), amended the effective date for changes made by Sec. 1902(a)(12)(A) of P. L. 94-455 to apply to estates of decedents dying after 10/4/76. See below.

In 1976, P.L. 94-455, Sec. 1902(a)(12)(A), deleted "Territory," which followed "law of any State," in subpara. (c)(2)(B), effective for gifts made after '76 [sic].

—P.L. 94-455, Sec. 2002(a), amended para. (c)(1), effective for estates of decedents dying after 12/31/76, except as provided in Sec. 2002(d)(1)(B) of this Act which provides:

"(B) If—

"(i) the decedent dies after December 31, 1976, and before January 1, 1979,

"(ii) by reason of the death of the decedent property passes from the decedent or is acquired from the decedent under a will executed before January 1, 1977, or a trust created before such date, which contains a formula expressly providing that the spouse is to receive the maximum amount of property qualifying for the marital deduction allowable by Federal law,

"(iii) the formula referred to in clause (ii) was not amended at any time after December 31, 1976, and before the death of the decedent, and

"(iv) the State does not enact a statute applicable to such estate which construes this type of formula as referring to the marital deduction allowable by Federal law as amended by subsection (a),

then the amendment made by subsection (a) shall not apply to the estate of such decedent."

Prior to amendment, para. (c)(1) read as follows:

"(1) General rule. The aggregate amount of the deductions allowed under this section (computed without regard to this subsection) shall not exceed 50 percent of the value of the adjusted gross estate, as defined in paragraph (2)."

—P.L. 94-455, Sec. 2009(b)(4)(D), deleted subsec. (d) and redesignated subsec. (e) as subsec. (d) . . . Sec. 2009(b)(4)(E), substituted "subsections (b) and (c)" for

"subsections (b), (c), and (d)" in subsec. (a), effective for transfers creating an interest in the person disclaiming made after 12/31/76.
Prior to deletion, subsec. (d) read as follows:
"(d) Disclaimers.
"(1) By surviving spouse. If under this section an interest would, in the absence of a disclaimer by the surviving spouse, be considered as passing from the decedent to such spouse, and if a disclaimer of such interest is made by such spouse, then such interest shall, for the purposes of this section, be considered as passing to the person or persons entitled to receive such interest as a result of the disclaimer.
"(2) By any other person. If under this section an interest would, in the absence of a disclaimer by any person other than the surviving spouse, be considered as passing from the decedent to such person, and if a disclaimer of such interest is made by such person and as a result of such disclaimer the surviving spouse is entitled to receive such interest, then—
"(A) if the disclaimer of such interest is made by such person before the date prescribed for the filing of the estate tax return and if such person does not accept such interest before making the disclaimer, such interest shall, for purposes of this section, be considered as passing from the decedent to the surviving spouse, and
"(B) if subparagraph (A) does not apply, such interest shall, for purposes of this section, be considered as passing, not to the surviving spouse, but to the person who made the disclaimer, in the same manner as if the disclaimer had not been made."
In 1966, P.L. 89-621, Sec. 1(a), amended the last part of para. (d)(2) by inserting (A) and the material following, up to and including "(B) if subparagraph (A) does not apply," to the existing section, effective for the estates of decedents dying after, 10/3/66 except
"In the case of the estate of a decedent dying before [10/4/66] for which the date prescribed for the filing of the estate tax return (determined without regard to any extension of time for filing) occurs on or after January 1, 1965, if, under section 2056 of the Internal Revenue Code of 1954, an interest would, in the absence of a disclaimer by any person other than the surviving spouse, be considered as passing from the decedent to such person, and if a disclaimer of such interest is made by such person and as a result of such disclaimer the surviving spouse is entitled to receive such interest, then such interest shall, for purposes of such section, be considered as passing from the decedent to the surviving spouse, if—
"(1) the interest disclaimed was bequeathed or devised to such person,
"(2) before the date prescribed for the filing of the estate tax return such person disclaimed all bequests and devises under such will, and
"(3) such person did not accept any property under any such bequest or devise before making the disclaimer.
The amount of the deductions allowable under section 2056 of such Code by reason of this subsection, when added to the amount of the deductions allowable under such section without regard to this subsection, shall not exceed the greater of (A) the amount of the deductions which would be allowable under such section without regard to the disclaimer if the surviving spouse elected to take against the will, or (B) an amount equal to one-third of the adjusted gross estate (within the meaning of subsection (c)(2) of such section)."

Sec. 2056A. Qualified domestic trust.
(a) Qualified domestic trust defined.
For purposes of this section and section 2056(d), the term "qualified domestic trust" means, with respect to any decedent, any trust if—
(1) the trust instrument—
(A) except as provided in regulations prescribed by the Secretary, requires that at least 1 trustee of the trust be an individual citizen of the United States or a domestic corporation, and
(B) provides that no distribution (other than a distribution of income) may be made from the trust unless a trustee who is an individual citizen of the United States or a domestic corporation has the right to withhold from such distribution the tax imposed by this section on such distribution,
(2) such trust meets such requirements as the Secretary may by regulations prescribe to ensure the collection of any tax imposed by subsection (b), and
(3) an election under this section by the executor of the decedent applies to such trust.
(b) Tax treatment of trust.
(1) Imposition of estate tax. There is hereby imposed an estate tax on—
(A) any distribution before the date of the death of the surviving spouse from a qualified domestic trust, and
(B) the value of the property remaining in a qualified domestic trust on the date of the death of the surviving spouse.

(2) Amount of tax.
(A) In general. In the case of any taxable event, the amount of the estate tax imposed by paragraph (1) shall be the amount equal to—
(i) the tax which would have been imposed under section 2001 on the estate of the decedent if the taxable estate of the decedent had been increased by the sum of—
(I) the amount involved in such taxable event, plus
(II) the aggregate amount involved in previous taxable events with respect to qualified domestic trusts of such decedent, reduced by
(ii) the tax which would have been imposed under section 2001 on the estate of the decedent if the taxable estate of the decedent had been increased by the amount referred to in clause (i)(II).
(B) Tentative tax where tax of decedent not finally determined.
(i) In general. If the tax imposed on the estate of the decedent under section 2001 is not finally determined before the taxable event, the amount of the tax imposed by paragraph (1) on such event shall be determined by using the highest rate of tax in effect under section 2001 as of the date of the decedent's death.
(ii) Refund of excess when tax finally determined. If—
(I) the amount of the tax determined under clause (i), exceeds
(II) the tax determined under subparagraph (A) on the basis of the final determination of the tax imposed by section 2001 on the estate of the decedent,
such excess shall be allowed as a credit or refund (with interest) if claim therefor is filed not later than 1 year after the date of such final determination.
(C) Special rule where decedent has more than 1 qualified domestic trust. If there is more than 1 qualified domestic trust with respect to any decedent, the amount of the tax imposed by paragraph (1) with respect to such trusts shall be determined by using the highest rate of tax in effect under section 2001 as of the date of the decedent's death (and the provisions of paragraph (3)(B) shall not apply) unless, pursuant to a designation made by the decedent's executor, there is 1 person—
(i) who is an individual citizen of the United States or a domestic corporation and is responsible for filing all returns of tax imposed under paragraph (1) with respect to such trusts and for paying all tax so imposed, and
(ii) who meets such requirements as the Secretary may by regulations prescribe.
(3) Certain lifetime distributions exempt from tax.
(A) Income distributions. No tax shall be imposed by paragraph (1)(A) on any distribution of income to the surviving spouse.
(B) Hardship exemption. No tax shall be imposed by paragraph (1)(A) on any distribution to the surviving spouse on account of hardship.
(4) Tax where trust ceases to qualify. If any qualified domestic trust ceases to meet the requirements of paragraphs (1) and (2) of subsection (a), the tax imposed by paragraph (1) shall apply as if the surviving spouse died on the date of such cessation.
(5) Due date.
(A) Tax on distributions. The estate tax imposed by paragraph (1)(A) shall be due and payable on the 15th

day of the 4th month following the calendar year in which the taxable event occurs; except that the estate tax imposed by paragraph (1)(A) on distributions during the calendar year in which the surviving spouse dies shall be due and payable not later than the date on which the estate tax imposed by paragraph (1)(B) is due and payable.

(B) Tax at death of spouse. The estate tax imposed by paragraph (1)(B) shall be due and payable on the date 9 months after the date of such death.

(6) Liability for tax. Each trustee shall be personally liable for the amount of the tax imposed by paragraph (1). Rules similar to the rules of section 2204 shall apply for purposes of the preceding sentence.

(7) Treatment of tax. For purposes of section 2056(d), any tax paid under paragraph (1) shall be treated as a tax paid under section 2001 with respect to the estate of the decedent.

(8) Lien for tax. For purposes of section 6324, any tax imposed by paragraph (1) shall be treated as an estate tax imposed under this chapter with respect to a decedent dying on the date of the taxable event (and the property involved shall be treated as the gross estate of such decedent).

(9) Taxable event. The term "taxable event" means the event resulting in tax being imposed under paragraph (1).

(10) Certain benefits allowed.

> • *Caution:* Code Sec. 2056A(b)(10)(A), following, was amended by Sec. 532(c)(6)(A)-(B), P.L. 107-16, the Economic Growth and Tax Relief Reconciliation Act of 2001 (EGTRRA). These provisions generally sunset for tax years beginning after 12/31/2012. For specific sunset provisions, see Sec. 901, P.L. 107-16 (as amended) reproduced in history notes for this Code Sec.

(A) In general. If any property remaining in the qualified domestic trust on the date of the death of the surviving spouse is includible in the gross estate of such spouse for purposes of this chapter (or would be includible if such spouse were a citizen or resident of the United States), any benefit which is allowable (or would be allowable if such spouse were a citizen or resident of the United States) with respect to such property to the estate of such spouse under section 2014, 2032, 2032A, 2055, 2056, 2058, or 6166 shall be allowed for purposes of the tax imposed by paragraph (1)(B).

(B) Section 303. If the estate of the surviving spouse meets the requirements of section 303 with respect to any property described in subparagraph (A), for purposes of section 303, the tax imposed by paragraph (1)(B) with respect to such property shall be treated as a Federal estate tax payable with respect to the estate of the surviving spouse.

(C) Section 6161(a)(2). The provisions of section 6161(a)(2) shall apply with respect to the tax imposed by paragraph (1)(B), and the reference in such section to the executor shall be treated as a reference to the trustees of the trust.

(11) Special rule where distribution tax paid out of trust. For purposes of this subsection, if any portion of the tax imposed by paragraph (1)(A) with respect to any distribution is paid out of the trust, an amount equal to the portion so paid shall be treated as a distribution described in paragraph (1)(A).

(12) Special rule where spouse becomes citizen. If the surviving spouse of the decedent becomes a citizen of the United States and if—

(A) such spouse was a resident of the United States at all times after the date of the death of the decedent and before such spouse becomes a citizen of the United States,

(B) no tax was imposed by paragraph (1)(A) with respect to any distribution before such spouse becomes such a citizen, or

(C) such spouse elects—

(i) to treat any distribution on which tax was imposed by paragraph (1)(A) as a taxable gift made by such spouse for purposes of—

(I) section 2001, and

(II) determining the amount of the tax imposed by section 2501 on actual taxable gifts made by such spouse during the year in which the spouse becomes a citizen or any subsequent year, and

(ii) to treat any reduction in the tax imposed by paragraph (1)(A) by reason of the credit allowable under section 2010 with respect to the decedent as a credit allowable to such surviving spouse under section 2505 for purposes of determining the amount of the credit allowable under section 2505 with respect to taxable gifts made by the surviving spouse during the year in which the spouse becomes a citizen or any subsequent year,

paragraph (1)(A) shall not apply to any distributions after such spouse becomes such a citizen (and paragraph (1)(B) shall not apply).

(13) Coordination with section 1015. For purposes of section 1015, any distribution on which tax is imposed by paragraph (1)(A) shall be treated as a transfer by gift, and any tax paid under paragraph (1)(A) shall be treated as a gift tax.

(14) Coordination with terminable interest rules. Any interest in a qualified domestic trust shall not be treated as failing to meet the requirements of paragraph (5) or (7) of section 2056(b) merely by reason of any provision of the trust instrument permitting the withholding from any distribution of an amount to pay the tax imposed by paragraph (1) on such distribution.

(15) No tax on certain distributions. No tax shall be imposed by paragraph (1) on any distribution to the surviving spouse to the extent such distribution is to reimburse such surviving spouse for any tax imposed by subtitle A on any item of income of the trust to which such surviving spouse is not entitled under the terms of the trust.

(c) Definitions.

For purposes of this section—

(1) Property includes interest therein. The term "property" includes an interest in property.

(2) Income. Except as provided in regulations, the term "income" has the meaning given to such term by section 643(b).

(3) Trust. To the extent provided in regulations prescribed by the Secretary, the term "trust" includes other arrangements which have substantially the same effect as a trust.

(d) Election.

An election under this section with respect to any trust shall be made by the executor on the return of the tax imposed by section 2001. Such an election, once made, shall be irrevocable. No election may be made under this section on any return if such return is filed more than one year after

Estate taxes

Code Sec. 2057(b)(2)(A)

the time prescribed by law (including extensions) for filing such return.

(e) Regulations.

The Secretary shall prescribe such regulations as may be necessary or appropriate to carry out the purposes of this section, including regulations under which there may be treated as a qualified domestic trust any annuity or other payment which is includible in the decedent's gross estate and is by its terms payable for life or a term of years.

In 2010, P.L. 111-312, Sec. 101(a)(1), substituted "December 31, 2012" for "December 31, 2010" both places it appears in Sec. 901, P.L. 107-16, see below, effective as if included in the enactment of P.L. 107-16, EGTRRA, 6/7/2001.

In 2002, P.L. 107-358, Sec. 2, added subsec. (c) in Sec. 901 of P. L. 107-16 [see below], effective 12/17/2002.

In 2001, P.L. 107-16, Sec. 532(c)(6)(A), deleted "2011," after "spouse under section" in subpara. (b)(10)(A) . . . Sec. 532(c)(6)(B), added "2058," after "2056," in subpara. (b)(10)(A), effective for estates of decedents dying, and generation-skipping transfers, after 12/31/2004.

—P.L. 107-16, Sec. 901, of this Act [as amended by Sec. 2, P. L. 107-358, and Sec. 101(a)(1), P.L. 111-312, see above], reads as follows:

"SEC. 901. SUNSET OF PROVISIONS OF ACT.

"(a) In general. All provisions of, and amendments made by, this Act shall not apply—

"(1) to taxable, plan, or limitation years beginning after December 31, 2012, or

"(2) in the case of title V, to estates of decedents dying, gifts made, or generation-skipping transfers, after December 31, 2012.

"(b) Application of certain laws. The Internal Revenue Code of 1986 and the Employee Retirement Income Security Act of 1974 shall be applied and administered to years, estates, gifts, and transfers described in subsection (a) as if the provisions and amendments described in subsection (a) had never been enacted.

"(c) Exception. Subsection (a) shall not apply to section 803 (relating to no federal income tax on restitution received by victims of the Nazi regime or their heirs or estates)."

In 1997, P.L. 105-34, Sec. 1303(a), of this Act, effective for estates of decedents dying after 11/10/88, provides:

"(a) General rule. In the case of any trust created under an instrument executed before the date of the enactment of the Revenue Reconciliation Act of 1990, such trust shall be treated as meeting the requirements of paragraph (1) of section 2056A(a) of the Internal Revenue Code of 1986 if the trust instrument requires that all trustees of the trust be individual citizens of the United States or domestic corporations."

—P.L. 105-34, Sec. 1315(a), added para. (c)(3), effective for estates of decedents dying after 8/5/97.

—P.L. 105-34, Sec. 1317(a), added "except as provided in regulations prescribed by the Secretary," before "requires that at least" in subpara. (a)(1)(A), effective for estates of decedents dying after 8/5/97.

In 1990, P.L. 101-508, Sec. 11702(g)(2)(A), amended para. (a)(1) . . . Sec. 11702(g)(2)(B), added paras. (b)(14) and (b)(15), effective for estates of decedents dying after 11/10/88.

Prior to amendment, para. (a)(1) read as follows:

"(1) the trust instrument requires that at least 1 trustee of the trust be an individual citizen of the United States or a domestic corporation and that no distribution from the trust may be made without the approval of such a trustee,"

—P.L. 101-508, Sec. 11702(g)(3)(A), added a sentence to the end of subsec. (d), effective for any election made after 6 months after 11/5/90.

—P.L. 101-508, Sec. 11702(g)(4), substituted "section 2011, 2014, 2032" for "section 2032" in subpara. (b)(10)(A), effective for estates of decedents dying after 11/10/88.

—P.L. 101-508, Sec. 11704(a)(15), substituted "therefor" for "therefore" in clause (b)(2)(B)(ii), effective 11/5/90.

In 1989, P.L. 101-239, Sec. 7815(d)(7)(A)(i), amended para. (a)(1) . . . Sec. 7815(d)(7)(A)(ii), deleted para. (a)(2) and redesignated paras. (a)(3) and (4) as paras. (a)(2) and (3) . . . Sec. 7815(d)(7)(B), redesignated paras. (b)(3) through (b)(8) as paras. (b)(4) through (b)(9) and added new para. (b)(3) . . . Sec. 7815(d)(7)(C), deleted "other than a distribution of income required under subsection (a)(2)" after "trust" in subpara. (b)(1)(A) . . . Sec. 7815(d)(7)(D), amended para. (b)(4) [as redesignated by Sec. 7815(d)(7)(B) of this Act] . . . Sec. 7815(d)(9), added paras. (b)(10) through (b)(13) . . . Sec. 7815(d)(10), substituted "Except as provided in regulations, the term" for "The term" in para. (c)(2) . . . Sec. 7815(d)(11), substituted "as a credit or refund (with interest)" for "as a credit or refund" in clause (b)(2)(B)(ii) . . . Sec. 7815(d)(12), added subpara. (b)(2)(C) . . . Sec. 7815(d)(13), added subsec. (e) . . . Sec. 7815(d)(15), amended para. (b)(5) [as redesignated by Sec. 7815(d)(7)(B) of this Act], effective for estates of decedents dying after 11/10/88. Sec. 7815(d)(14) of this Act provides:

"(14) In the case of the estate of, or gift by, an individual who was not a citizen or resident of the United States but was a resident of a foreign country with which the United States has a tax treaty with respect to estate, inheritance, or gift taxes, the amendments made by section 5033 of the 1988 Act [P. L. 100-647] shall not apply to the extent such amendments would be inconsistent with the provisions of such treaty relating to estate, inheritance, or gift tax marital deductions. In the case of the estate of an individual dying before the date 3 years after the date of the enactment of this Act [11/10/88], or a gift by an individual before the date 3 years after the date of the enactment of this Act [11/10/88], the requirement of the preceding sentence that the individual not be a citizen or resident of the United States shall not apply."

Prior to amendment, para. (a)(1) read as follows:

"(1) the trust instrument requires that all trustees of the trust be individual citizens of the United States or domestic corporations,"

Prior to deletion, para. (a)(2) read as follows:

"(2) the surviving spouse of the decedent is entitled to all the income from the property in such trust, payable annually or at more frequent intervals,"

Prior to amendment, para. (b)(4) [as redesignated by Sec. 7815(d)(7)(B) of this Act] read as follows:

"(4) Tax imposed where trust ceases to qualify. If any person other than an individual citizen of the United States or a domestic corporation becomes a trustee of a qualified domestic trust (or such trust ceases to meet the requirements of subsection (a)(3)), the tax imposed by paragraph (1) shall apply as if the surviving spouse died on the date on which such person became such a trustee or the date of such cessation, as the case may be."

Prior to amendment, para. (b)(5) [as redesignated by Sec. 7815(d)(7)(B) of this Act] read as follows:

"(5) Due date. The estate tax imposed by paragraph (1) shall be due and payable on the 15th day of the 4th month following the calendar year in which the taxable event occurs."

In 1988, P.L. 100-647, Sec. 5033(a)(2), added Code Sec. 2056A, effective for estates of decedents dying after 11/10/88.

Sec. 2057. Family-owned business interests.

(a) General rule.

(1) Allowance of deduction. For purposes of the tax imposed by section 2001, in the case of an estate of a decedent to which this section applies, the value of the taxable estate shall be determined by deducting from the value of the gross estate the adjusted value of the qualified family-owned business interests of the decedent which are described in subsection (b)(2).

(2) Maximum deduction. The deduction allowed by this section shall not exceed $675,000.

(3) Coordination with unified credit.

(A) In general. Except as provided in subparagraph (B), if this section applies to an estate, the applicable exclusion amount under section 2010 shall be $625,000.

(B) Increase in unified credit if deduction is less than $675,000. If the deduction allowed by this section is less than $675,000, the amount of the applicable exclusion amount under section 2010 shall be increased (but not above the amount which would apply to the estate without regard to this section) by the excess of $675,000 over the amount of the deduction allowed.

(b) Estates to which section applies.

(1) In general. This section shall apply to an estate if—

(A) the decedent was (at the date of the decedent's death) a citizen or resident of the United States,

(B) the executor elects the application of this section and files the agreement referred to in subsection (h),

(C) the sum of—

(i) the adjusted value of the qualified family-owned business interests described in paragraph (2), plus

(ii) the amount of the gifts of such interests determined under paragraph (3),

exceeds 50 percent of the adjusted gross estate, and

(D) during the 8-year period ending on the date of the decedent's death there have been periods aggregating 5 years or more during which—

(i) such interests were owned by the decedent or a member of the decedent's family, and

(ii) there was material participation (within the meaning of section 2032A(e)(6)) by the decedent or a member of the decedent's family in the operation of the business to which such interests relate.

(2) Includible qualified family-owned business interests. The qualified family-owned business interests described in this paragraph are the interests which—

(A) are included in determining the value of the gross estate, and

(B) are acquired by any qualified heir from, or passed to any qualified heir from, the decedent (within the meaning of section 2032A(e)(9)).

(3) Includible gifts of interests. The amount of the gifts of qualified family-owned business interests determined under this paragraph is the sum of—

(A) the amount of such gifts from the decedent to members of the decedent's family taken into account under section 2001(b)(1)(B), plus

(B) the amount of such gifts otherwise excluded under section 2503(b),

to the extent such interests are continuously held by members of such family (other than the decedent's spouse) between the date of the gift and the date of the decedent's death.

(c) Adjusted gross estate.

For purposes of this section, the term "adjusted gross estate" means the value of the gross estate—

(1) reduced by any amount deductible under paragraph (3) or (4) of section 2053(a), and

(2) increased by the excess of—

(A) the sum of—

(i) the amount of gifts determined under subsection (b)(3), plus

(ii) the amount (if more than de minimis) of other transfers from the decedent to the decedent's spouse (at the time of the transfer) within 10 years of the date of the decedent's death, plus

(iii) the amount of other gifts (not included under clause (i) or (ii)) from the decedent within 3 years of such date, other than gifts to members of the decedent's family otherwise excluded under section 2503(b), over

(B) the sum of the amounts described in clauses (i), (ii), and (iii) of subparagraph (A) which are otherwise includible in the gross estate.

For purposes of the preceding sentence, the Secretary may provide that de minimis gifts to persons other than members of the decedent's family shall not be taken into account.

(d) Adjusted value of the qualified family-owned business interests.

For purposes of this section, the adjusted value of any qualified family-owned business interest is the value of such interest for purposes of this chapter (determined without regard to this section), reduced by the excess of—

(1) any amount deductible under paragraph (3) or (4) of section 2053(a), over

(2) the sum of—

(A) any indebtedness on any qualified residence of the decedent the interest on which is deductible under section 163(h)(3), plus

(B) any indebtedness to the extent the taxpayer establishes that the proceeds of such indebtedness were used for the payment of educational and medical expenses of the decedent, the decedent's spouse, or the decedent's dependents (within the meaning of section 152, determined without regard to subsections (b)(1), (b)(2), and (d)(1)(B) thereof), plus

(C) any indebtedness not described in subparagraph (A) or (B), to the extent such indebtedness does not exceed $10,000.

(e) Qualified family-owned business interest.

(1) In general. For purposes of this section, the term "qualified family-owned business interest" means—

(A) an interest as a proprietor in a trade or business carried on as a proprietorship, or

(B) an interest in an entity carrying on a trade or business, if—

(i) at least—

(I) 50 percent of such entity is owned (directly or indirectly) by the decedent and members of the decedent's family,

(II) 70 percent of such entity is so owned by members of 2 families, or

(III) 90 percent of such entity is so owned by members of 3 families, and

(ii) for purposes of subclause (II) or (III) of clause (i), at least 30 percent of such entity is so owned by the decedent and members of the decedent's family.

For purposes of the preceding sentence, a decedent shall be treated as engaged in a trade or business if any member of the decedent's family is engaged in such trade or business.

(2) Limitation. Such term shall not include—

(A) any interest in a trade or business the principal place of business of which is not located in the United States,

(B) any interest in an entity, if the stock or debt of such entity or a controlled group (as defined in section 267(f)(1)) of which such entity was a member was readily tradable on an established securities market or secondary market (as defined by the Secretary) at any time within 3 years of the date of the decedent's death,

(C) any interest in a trade or business not described in section 542(c)(2), if more than 35 percent of the adjusted ordinary gross income of such trade or business for the taxable year which includes the date of the decedent's death would qualify as personal holding company income (as defined in section 543(a) without regard to paragraph (2)(B) thereof) if such trade or business were a corporation,

(D) that portion of an interest in a trade or business that is attributable to—

(i) cash or marketable securities, or both, in excess of the reasonably expected day-to-day working capital needs of such trade or business, and

(ii) any other assets of the trade or business (other than assets used in the active conduct of a trade or business described in section 542(c)(2)), which produce, or are held for the production of, personal holding company income (as defined in subparagraph (C)) or income described in section 954(c)(1) (determined without regard to subparagraph (A) thereof and by substituting "trade or business" for "controlled foreign corporation").

In the case of a lease of property on a net cash basis by the decedent to a member of the decedent's family, income from such lease shall not be treated as personal holding company income for purposes of subparagraph (C), and such property shall not be treated as an asset described in subparagraph (D)(ii), if such income and property would not be so treated if the lessor had engaged directly in the activities engaged in by the lessee with respect to such property.

(3) Rules regarding ownership.

(A) Ownership of entities. For purposes of paragraph (1)(B) —

(i) Corporations. Ownership of a corporation shall be determined by the holding of stock possessing the appropriate percentage of the total combined voting power of all classes of stock entitled to vote and the appropriate percentage of the total value of shares of all classes of stock.

Estate taxes Code Sec. 2057(i)(3)(A)

(ii) Partnerships. Ownership of a partnership shall be determined by the owning of the appropriate percentage of the capital interest in such partnership.

(B) Ownership of tiered entities. For purposes of this section, if by reason of holding an interest in a trade or business, a decedent, any member of the decedent's family, any qualified heir, or any member of any qualified heir's family is treated as holding an interest in any other trade or business—

(i) such ownership interest in the other trade or business shall be disregarded in determining if the ownership interest in the first trade or business is a qualified family-owned business interest, and

(ii) this section shall be applied separately in determining if such interest in any other trade or business is a qualified family-owned business interest.

(C) Individual ownership rules. For purposes of this section, an interest owned, directly or indirectly, by or for an entity described in paragraph (1)(B) shall be considered as being owned proportionately by or for the entity's shareholders, partners, or beneficiaries. A person shall be treated as a beneficiary of any trust only if such person has a present interest in such trust.

(f) Tax treatment of failure to materially participate in business or dispositions of interests.

(1) In general. There is imposed an additional estate tax if, within 10 years after the date of the decedent's death and before the date of the qualified heir's death—

(A) the material participation requirements described in section 2032A(c)(6)(B) are not met with respect to the qualified family-owned business interest which was acquired (or passed) from the decedent,

(B) the qualified heir disposes of any portion of a qualified family-owned business interest (other than by a disposition to a member of the qualified heir's family or through a qualified conservation contribution under section 170(h)),

(C) the qualified heir loses United States citizenship (within the meaning of section 877) or with respect to whom an event described in subparagraph (A) or (B) of section 877(e)(1) occurs, and such heir does not comply with the requirements of subsection (g), or

(D) the principal place of business of a trade or business of the qualified family-owned business interest ceases to be located in the United States.

(2) Additional estate tax.

(A) In general. The amount of the additional estate tax imposed by paragraph (1) shall be equal to—

(i) the applicable percentage of the adjusted tax difference attributable to the qualified family-owned business interest, plus

(ii) interest on the amount determined under clause (i) at the underpayment rate established under section 6621 for the period beginning on the date the estate tax liability was due under this chapter and ending on the date such additional estate tax is due.

(B) Applicable percentage. For purposes of this paragraph, the applicable percentage shall be determined under the following table:

If the event described in paragraph (1) occurs in the following year of material participation:	The applicable percentage is:
1 through 6	100
7	80
8	60
9	40
10	20

(C) Adjusted tax difference. For purposes of subparagraph (A)—

(i) In general. The adjusted tax difference attributable to a qualified family-owned business interest is the amount which bears the same ratio to the adjusted tax difference with respect to the estate (determined under clause (ii)) as the value of such interest bears to the value of all qualified family-owned business interests described in subsection (b)(2).

(ii) Adjusted tax difference with respect to the estate. For purposes of clause (i), the term "adjusted tax difference with respect to the estate" means the excess of what would have been the estate tax liability but for the election under this section over the estate tax liability. For purposes of this clause, the term "estate tax liability" means the tax imposed by section 2001 reduced by the credits allowable against such tax.

(3) Use in trade or business by family members. A qualified heir shall not be treated as disposing of an interest described in subsection (e)(1)(A) by reason of ceasing to be engaged in a trade or business so long as the property to which such interest relates is used in a trade or business by any member of such individual's family.

(g) Security requirements for noncitizen qualified heirs.

(1) In general. Except upon the application of subparagraph (F) of subsection (i)(3), if a qualified heir is not a citizen of the United States, any interest under this section passing to or acquired by such heir (including any interest held by such heir at a time described in subsection (f)(1)(C)) shall be treated as a qualified family-owned business interest only if the interest passes or is acquired (or is held) in a qualified trust.

(2) Qualified trust. The term "qualified trust" means a trust—

(A) which is organized under, and governed by, the laws of the United States or a State, and

(B) except as otherwise provided in regulations, with respect to which the trust instrument requires that at least 1 trustee of the trust be an individual citizen of the United States or a domestic corporation.

(h) Agreement.

The agreement referred to in this subsection is a written agreement signed by each person in being who has an interest (whether or not in possession) in any property designated in such agreement consenting to the application of subsection (f) with respect to such property.

(i) Other definitions and applicable rules.

For purposes of this section—

(1) Qualified heir. The term "qualified heir"—

(A) has the meaning given to such term by section 2032A(e)(1), and

(B) includes any active employee of the trade or business to which the qualified family-owned business interest relates if such employee has been employed by such trade or business for a period of at least 10 years before the date of the decedent's death.

(2) Member of the family. The term "member of the family" has the meaning given to such term by section 2032A(e)(2).

(3) Applicable rules. Rules similar to the following rules shall apply:

(A) Section 2032A(b)(4) (relating to decedents who are retired or disabled).

(B) Section 2032A(b)(5) (relating to special rules for surviving spouses).
(C) Section 2032A(c)(2)(D) (relating to partial dispositions).
(D) Section 2032A(c)(3) (relating to only 1 additional tax imposed with respect to any 1 portion).
(E) Section 2032A(c)(4) (relating to due date).
(F) Section 2032A(c)(5) (relating to liability for tax; furnishing of bond).
(G) Section 2032A(c)(7) (relating to no tax if use begins within 2 years; active management by eligible qualified heir treated as material participation).
(H) Paragraphs (1) and (3) of section 2032A(d) (relating to election; agreement).
(I) Section 2032A(e)(10) (relating to community property).
(J) Section 2032A(e)(14) (relating to treatment of replacement property acquired in section 1031 or 1033 transactions).
(K) Section 2032A(f) (relating to statute of limitations).
(L) Section 2032A(g) (relating to application to interests in partnerships, corporations, and trusts).
(M) Subsections (h) and (i) of section 2032A.
(N) Section 6166(b)(3) (relating to farmhouses and certain other structures taken into account).
(O) Subparagraphs (B), (C), and (D) of section 6166(g)(1) (relating to acceleration of payment).
(P) Section 6324B (relating to special lien for additional estate tax).

⌐
• **Caution:** Code Sec. 2057(j), following, was added by Sec. 521(d), P.L. 107-16, the Economic Growth and Tax Relief Reconciliation Act of 2001 (EGTRRA). These provisions generally sunset for tax years beginning after 12/31/2012. For specific sunset provisions, see Sec. 901, P.L. 107-16 (as amended) reproduced in history notes for this Code Sec.
⌐

(j) Termination.
This section shall not apply to the estates of decedents dying after December 31, 2003.

In 2010, P.L. 111-312, Sec. 101(a)(1), substituted "December 31, 2012" for "December 31, 2010" both places it appears in Sec. 901, P.L. 107-16, see below, effective as if included in the enactment of P.L. 107-16, EGTRRA, 6/7/2001.
In 2004, P.L. 108-311, Sec. 207(23), added ", determined without regard to subsections (b)(1), (b)(2), and (d)(1)(B) thereof" after "section 152" in subpara. (d)(2)(B), effective for tax. yrs. begin. after 12/31/2004.
In 2002, P.L. 107-358, Sec. 2, added subsec. (c) in Sec. 901 of P. L. 107-16 [see below], effective 12/17/2002.
In 2001, P.L. 107-16, Sec. 521(d), added subsec. (j), effective for estates of decedents dying, and generation-skipping transfers, after 12/31/2003.
—P.L. 107-16, Sec. 901, of this Act [as amended by Sec. 2, P. L. 107-358, and Sec. 101(a)(1), P.L. 111-312, see above], reads as follows:
"SEC. 901. SUNSET OF PROVISIONS OF ACT.
"(a) In general. All provisions of, and amendments made by, this Act shall not apply—
"(1) to taxable, plan, or limitation years beginning after December 31, 2012, or
"(2) in the case of title V, to estates of decedents dying, gifts made, or generation skipping transfers, after December 31, 2012.
"(b) Application of certain laws. The Internal Revenue Code of 1986 and the Employee Retirement Income Security Act of 1974 shall be applied and administered to years, estates, gifts, and transfers described in subsection (a) as if the provisions and amendments described in subsection (a) had never been enacted.
"(c) Exception. Subsection (a) shall not apply to section 803 (relating to no federal income tax on restitution received by victims of the Nazi regime or their heirs or estates)."
In 1998, P.L. 105-206, Sec. 6007(b)(1)(A), redesignated Code Sec. 2033A as Code Sec. 2057 . . . Sec. 6007(b)(1)(B), amended Code Sec. 2057 heading [as redesignated by Sec. 6007(b)(1)(A) of this Act, see above] and subsec. (a) . . . Sec. 6007(b)(1)(C), deleted "(without regard to this section)" after "gross estate" in subpara. (b)(2)(A) . . . Sec. 6007(b)(1)(D), deleted "(determined without regard to this section)" after "gross estate" in subsec. (c) . . . Sec. 6007(b)(2), amended para. (b)(3) . . . Sec. 6007(b)(3)(A), substituted "(as defined in section 543(a) without regard to paragraph (2)(B) thereof) if such trade or business were a corporation" for "(as defined in section 543(a))" in subpara. (e)(2)(C) . . . Sec. 6007(b)(3)(B), substituted "personal holding company income (as defined in subparagraph (C)) or income described" for "income of which is described in section 543(a) or" in clause (e)(2)(D)(ii) . . . Sec. 6007(b)(3)(C), added a flush sentence at the end of para. (e)(2) . . . Sec. 6007(b)(4)(A), deleted "(as determined under rules similar to the rules of section 2032A(c)(2)(B))" after "business interest" in clause (f)(2)(A)(i) . . . Sec. 6007(b)(4)(B), added subpara. (f)(2)(C) . . . Sec. 6007(b)(5)(A), added a flush sentence at the end of para. (e)(1) . . . Sec. 6007(b)(5)(B), added para. (f)(3) . . . Sec. 6007(b)(6), deleted "or (M)" after "subparagraph (F)" in para. (g)(1) . . . Sec. 6007(b)(7), redesignated subparas. (i)(3)(L)-(N) as (i)(3)(N)-(P) and added subparas. (i)(3)(L) and (M), effective for estates of decedents dying after December 31, 1997.
Prior to amendment, Code Sec. 2057 heading and subsec. (a) read as follows:
"SEC. 2057. FAMILY-OWNED BUSINESS EXCLUSION.
"(a) In general. In the case of an estate of a decedent to which this section applies, the value of the gross estate shall not include the lesser of—
"(1) the adjusted value of the qualified family-owned business interests of the decedent otherwise includible in the estate, or
"(2) the excess of $1,300,000 over the applicable amount under section 2010(c) with respect to such estate."
Prior to amendment, para. (b)(3) read as follows:
"(3) Includible gifts of interests. The amount of the gifts of qualified family-owned business interests determined under this paragraph is the excess of—
"(A) the sum of—
"(i) the amount of such gifts from the decedent to members of the decedent's family taken into account under subsection 2001(b)(1)(B), plus
"(ii) the amount of such gifts otherwise excluded under section 2503(b),
to the extent such interests are continuously held by members of such family (other than the decedent's spouse) between the date of the gift and the date of the decedent's death, over
"(B) the amount of such gifts from the decedent to members of the decedent's family otherwise included in the gross estate."
Prior to amendment, para. (b)(3) read as follows:
"(3) Includible gifts of interests. The amount of the gifts of qualified family-owned business interests determined under this paragraph is the excess of—
"(A) the sum of—
"(i) the amount of such gifts from the decedent to members of the decedent's family taken into account under subsection 2001(b)(1)(B), plus
"(ii) the amount of such gifts otherwise excluded under section 2503(b),
to the extent such interests are continuously held by members of such family (other than the decedent's spouse) between the date of the gift and the date of the decedent's death, over
"(B) the amount of such gifts from the decedent to members of the decedent's family otherwise included in the gross estate."
In 1997, P.L. 105-34, Sec. 502(a), added Code Sec. 2033A, effective for estates of decedents dying after December 31, 1997.

Sec. 2057. Repealed.

In 1989, P.L. 101-239, Sec. 7304(a)(1), repealed Code Sec. 2057, effective for estates of decedents dying 12/19/89.
Prior to repeal Code Sec. 2057 read as follows:
"SEC. 2057. SALES OF EMPLOYER SECURITIES TO EMPLOYEE STOCK OWNERSHIP PLANS OR WORKER-OWNED COOPERATIVES.
"(a) General rule.
"For purposes of the tax imposed by section 2001, the value of the taxable estate shall be determined by deducting from the value of the gross estate an amount equal to 50 percent of the proceeds of any sale of any qualified employer securities to—
"(1) an employee stock ownership plan, or
"(2) an eligible worker-owned cooperative.
"(b) Limitations.
"(1) Maximum reduction in tax liability. The amount allowable as a deduction under subsection (a) shall not exceed the amount which would result in an aggregate reduction in the tax imposed by section 2001 (determined without regard to any credit allowable against such tax) equal to $750,000.
"(2) Deduction shall not exceed 50 percent of taxable estate. The amount of the deduction allowable under subsection (a) shall not exceed 50 percent of the taxable estate (determined without regard to this section).
"(c) Limitations on proceeds which may be taken into account.
"(1) Dispositions by plan or cooperative within 1 year of sale.
"(A) In general. Proceeds from a sale which are taken into account under subsection (a) shall be reduced (but not below zero) by the net sale amount.
"(B) Net sale amount. For purposes of subparagraph (A), the term 'net sale amount' means the excess (if any) of—
"(i) the proceeds of the plan or cooperative from the disposition of employer securities during the 1-year period immediately preceding such sale, over
"(ii) the cost of employer securities purchased by such plan or cooperative during such 1-year period.
"(C) Exceptions. For purposes of subparagraph (B)(i), there shall not be taken into account any proceeds of a plan or cooperative from a disposition described in section 4978A(e).

"(D) Aggregation rules. For purposes of this paragraph, all employee stock ownership plans maintained by an employer shall be treated as 1 plan.

"(2) Securities must be acquired by plan from assets which are not transferred assets.

"(A) In general. Proceeds from a sale shall not be taken into account under subsection (a) to the extent that such proceeds (as reduced under paragraph (1)) are attributable to transferred assets. For purposes of the preceding sentence, all assets of plan or cooperative (other than qualified employer securities) shall be treated as first acquired out of transferred assets.

"(B) Transferred assets. For purposes of subparagraph (A)—

"(i) In general. The term 'transferred assets' means assets of an employee stock ownership plan which—

"(I) are attributable to assets held by a plan exempt from tax under section 501(a) and meeting the requirements of section 401(a) (other than an employee stock ownership plan of the employer), or

"(II) were held by the plan when it was not an employee stock ownership plan.

"(ii) Exception for assets held on February 26, 1987. The term 'transferred assets' shall not include any asset held by the employee stock ownership plan on February 26, 1987.

"(iii) Secretarial authority to waive treatment as transferred asset. The Secretary may provide that assets or a class of assets shall not be treated as transferred assets if the Secretary finds such treatment is not necessary to carry out the purposes of this paragraph.

"(3) Other proceeds. The following proceeds shall not be taken into account under subsection (a):

"(A) Proceeds from sale after due date for return. Any proceeds from a sale which occurs after the date on which the return of the tax imposed by section 2001 is required to be filed (determined by taking into account any extension of time for filing).

"(B) Proceeds from sale of certain securities. Any proceeds from a sale of employer securities which were received by the decedent—

"(i) in a distribution from a plan exempt from tax under section 501(a) and meeting the requirements of section 401(a), or

"(ii) as a transfer pursuant to an option or other right to acquire stock to which section 83, 422, 422A, 423, or 424 applies.

Any employer security the basis of which is determined by reference to any employer security described in the preceding sentence shall be treated as an employer security to which this subparagraph applies.

"(d) Qualified employer securities.

"(1) In general. The term 'qualified employer securities' means employer securities—

"(A) which are issued by a domestic corporation which has no stock outstanding which is readily tradable on an established securities market,

"(B) which are includible in the gross estate of the decedent,

"(C) which would have been includible in the gross estate of the decedent if the decedent had died at any time during the shorter of—

"(i) the 5-year period ending on the date of death, or

"(ii) the period beginning on October 22, 1986, and ending on the date of death, and

"(D) with respect to which the executor elects the application of this section.

Subparagraph (C) shall not apply if the decedent died on or before October 22, 1986.

"(2) Certain assets held by spouse. For purposes of paragraph (1)(C), any employer security which would have been includible in the gross estate of the spouse of a decedent during any period if the spouse had died during such period shall be treated as includible in the gross estate of the decedent during such period.

"(3) Periods during which decedent not at risk. For purposes of paragraph (1)(C), employer securities shall not be treated as includible in the gross estate of the decedent during any period described in section 246(c)(4).

"(e) Written statement required.

"(1) In general. No deduction shall be allowed under subsection (a) unless the executor of the estate of the decedent files with the Secretary the statement described in paragraph (2).

"(2) Statement. A statement is described in this paragraph if it is a verified written statement—

"(A) which is made by—

"(i) the employer whose employees are covered by the employee stock ownership plan, or

"(ii) any authorized officer of the eligible worker-owned cooperative, and

"(B) which—

"(i) acknowledges that the sale of employer securities to the plan or cooperative is a sale to which sections 4978A and 4979A apply, and

"(ii) certifies—

"(I) the net sale amount for purposes of subsection (c)(1), and

"(II) the amount of assets which are not transferred assets for purposes of subsection (c)(2).

"(f) Other definitions and special rules.

"For purposes of this section—

"(1) Employer securities. The term 'employer securities' has the meaning given such term by section 409(l).

"(2) Employee stock ownership plan. The term 'employee stock ownership plan' means—

"(A) a tax credit employee stock ownership plan (within the meaning of section 409(a)), or

"(B) a plan described in section 4975(e)(7).

"(3) Eligible worker-owned cooperative. The term 'eligible worker-owned cooperative' has the meaning given such term by section 1042(c).

"(4) Employer. Except to the extent provided in regulations, the term 'employer' includes any person treated as an employer under subsections (b), (c), (m), and (o) of section 414.

"(g) Termination.

"This section shall not apply to any sale after December 31, 1991."

In 1988, P.L. 100-647, Sec. 1011B(g)(3), deleted "is" after "plan" in para. (b)(1) before amend. by P. L. 100-203, see below.

In 1987, P.L. 100-203, Sec. 10412(a), amended Code Sec. 2057, effective as provided in Sec. 10412(b) of the Act which reads:

"(b) Effective dates.

"(1) In general. — Except as provided in this subsection, the amendments made by this section shall apply to sales after February 26, 1987.

"(2) Provisions taking effect as if included in the tax reform act of 1986. — The following provisions shall take effect as if included in the amendments made by section 1172 of the Tax Reform Act of 1986:

"(A) Section 2057(f)(2) of the Internal Revenue Code of 1986, as added by this section.

"(B) The repeal of the requirement that a sale be made by the executor of an estate to qualify for purposes of section 2057 of such Code.

"(3) Direct ownership requirement. — If the requirements of section 2057(d)(1)(B) of such Code (as modified by section 2057(d)(2) of such Code), as in effect after the amendments made by this section, are met with respect to any employer securities sold after October 22, 1986, and before February 27, 1987, such securities shall be treated as having been directly owned by the decedent for purposes of section 2057 of such Code, as in effect before such amendments.

"(4) Reduction for sales on or before February 26, 1987. — In applying the limitations of subsection (b) of section 2057 of such Code to sales after February 26, 1987, there shall be taken into account sales on or before February 26, 1987, to which section 2057 of such Code applied."

Prior to amendment, Code Sec. 2057 read as follows:

"SEC. 2057. SALES OF EMPLOYER SECURITIES TO EMPLOYEE STOCK OWNERSHIP PLANS OR WORKER-OWNED COOPERATIVES.

"(a) General rule.

"For purposes of the tax imposed by section 2001, the value of the taxable estate shall be determined by deducting from the value of the gross estate an amount equal to 50 percent of the qualified proceeds of a qualified sale of employer securities.

"(b) Qualified sale.

"For purposes of this section, the term 'qualified sale' means any sale of employer securities by the executor of an estate to—

"(1) an employee stock ownership plan described in section 4975(e)(7), or

"(2) an eligible worker-owned cooperative (within the meaning of section 1042(c)).

"(c) Qualified proceeds.

"For purposes of this section—

"(1) In general. The term 'qualified proceeds' means the amount received by the estate from the sale of employer securities at any time before the date on which the return of the tax imposed by section 2001 is required to be filed (including any extensions).

"(2) Proceeds from certain securities not qualified. The term 'qualified proceeds' shall not include the proceeds from the sale of any employer securities if such securities were received by the decedent—

"(A) in a distribution from a plan exempt from tax under section 501(a) which meets the requirements of section 401(a), or

"(B) as a transfer pursuant to an option or other right to acquire stock to which section 83, 422, 422A, 423, or 424 applies.

"(d) Qualified proceeds from qualified sales.

"(1) In general. For purposes of this section, the proceeds of a sale of employer securities by an executor to an employee stock ownership plan or an eligible worker-owned cooperative shall not be treated as qualified proceeds from a qualified sale unless—

"(A) the decedent directly owned the securities immediately before death, and

"(B) after the sale, the employer securities—

"(i) are allocated to participants, or

"(ii) are held for future allocation in connection with—

"(I) an exempt loan under the rules of section 4975, or

"(II) a transfer of assets under the rules of section 4980(c)(3).

"(2) No substitution permitted. For purposes of paragraph (1)(B), except in the case of a bona fide business transaction (e.g., a substitution of employer securities in connection with a merger of employers), employer securities shall not be treated as allocated or held for future allocation to the extent that such securities are allocated or held for future allocation in substitution of other employer securities that had been allocated or held for future allocation.

"(e) Written statement required.

"(1) In general. No deduction shall be allowed under subsection (a) unless the executor of the estate of the decedent files with the Secretary the statement described in paragraph (2).

"(2) Statement. A statement is described in this paragraph if it is a verified written statement of—

"(A) the employer whose employees are covered by the plan described in subsection (b)(1), or

"(B) any authorized officer of the cooperative described in subsection (b)(2) "consenting to the application of section 4979A with respect to such employer or cooperative.

"(f) Employer securities.

"For purposes of this section, the term 'employer securities' has the meaning given such term by section 409(1)."
"(g) Termination.
"This section shall not apply to any sale after December 31, 1991."
—P.L. 100-203, Sec. 10411(a), redesignated subsecs. (d)-(f) as subsecs. (e)-(g) and added new subsec. (d), effective as provided in Sec. 1172(c) of P. L. 99-514, see below.
In 1986, P.L. 99-514, Sec. 1172(a), added Code Sec. 2057, effective as provided in Sec. 1172(c) of this Act, which reads as follows:
"Effective date.—The amendments made by this section [Sec. 1172] shall apply to sales after the date of the enactment of this Act [10/22/86] with respect to which an election is made by the executor of an estate who is required to file the return of the tax imposed by the Internal Revenue Code of 1986 on a date (including extensions) after the date of the enactment of this Act [10/22/86]."

Sec. 2057. Repealed.

In 1981, P.L. 97-34, Sec. 427(a), repealed Code Sec. 2057, for estates of decedents dying after 12/31/81.
Prior to repeal, Code Sec. 2057 read as follows:
"SEC. 2057. BEQUESTS, ETC., TO CERTAIN MINOR CHILDREN.
"(a) Allowance of deduction.
"For purposes of the tax imposed by section 2001, if—
"(1) the decedent does not have a surviving spouse, and
"(2) the decedent is survived by a minor child who, immediately after the death of the decedent, has no known parent,
then the value of the taxable estate shall be determined by deducting from the value of the gross estate an amount equal to the value of any interest in property which passes or has passed from the decedent to such child, but only to the extent that such interest is included in determining the value of the gross estate.
"(b) Limitation.
"The aggregate amount of the deductions allowed under this section (computed without regard to this subsection) with respect to interests in property passing to any minor child shall not exceed an amount equal to $5,000 multiplied by the excess of 21 over the age (in years) which such child has attained on the date of the decedent's death.
"(c) Limitation in the case of life estate or other terminable interest.
"A deduction shall be allowed under this section with respect to any interest in property passing to a minor child only to the extent that a deduction would have been allowable under section 2056(b) if such interest had passed to a surviving spouse of the decedent. For purposes of this subsection, an interest shall not be treated as terminable solely because the property will pass to another person if the child dies before the youngest child of the decedent attains age 23.
"(d) Qualified minors' trust.
"(1) In general. For purposes of subsection (a), the interest of a minor child in a qualified minors' trust shall be treated as an interest in property which passes or has passed from the decedent to such child.
"(2) Qualified minors' trust. For purpose of paragraph (1), the term 'qualified minors' trust' means a trust—
"(A) except as provided in subparagraph (D), all of the beneficiaries of which are minor children of the decedent,
"(B) the corpus of which is property which passes or has passed from the decedent to such trust,
"(C) except as provided in paragraph (3), all distributions from which to the beneficiaries of the trust before the termination of their interests will be pro rata,
"(D) on the death of any beneficiary of which before the termination of the trust, the beneficiary's pro rata share of the corpus and accumulated income remains in the trust for the benefit of the minor children of the decedent who survive the beneficiary or vests in any person, and
"(E) on the termination of which, each beneficiary will receive a pro rata share of the corpus and accumulated income.
"(3) Certain disproportionate distributions permitted. A trust shall not be treated as failing to meet the requirements of paragraph (2)(C) solely by reason of the fact that the governing instrument of the trust permits the making of disproportionate distributions which are limited by an ascertainable standard relating to the health, education, support, or maintenance of the beneficiaries.
"(4) Trustee may accumulate income. A trust which otherwise qualifies as a qualified minors' trust shall not be disqualified solely by reason of the fact that the trustee has power to accumulate income.
"(5) Coordination with subsection (c). In applying subsection (c) to a qualified minors' trust, those provisions of section 2056(b) which are inconsistent with paragraph (3) or (4) of this subsection shall not apply.
"(6) Death of beneficiary before youngest child reaches age 23. Nothing in this subsection shall be treated as disqualifying interest of a minor child in a trust solely because such interest will pass to another person if the child dies before the youngest child of the decedent attains age 23.
"(e) Definitions.
"For purposes of this section—
"(1) Minor child. The term 'minor child' means any child of the decedent who has not attained the age of 21 before the date of the decedent's death.
"(2) Adopted children. A relationship by legal adoption shall be treated as replacing a relationship by blood.
"(3) Property passing from the decedent. The determination of whether an interest in property passes from the decedent to any person shall be made in accordance with section 2056(d)."

In 1978, P.L. 95-600, Sec. 702(l)(1), redesignated subsec. (d) as subsec. (e) and added new subsec. (d) . . . Sec. 702(l)(2), substituted "23" for "21" in the last sentence of subsec. (c), effective for estates of decedents dying after 12/31/76.
In 1976, P.L. 94-455, Sec. 2007(a), added Code Sec. 2057, effective for estates of decedents dying after 12/31/76.

Sec. 2058. State death taxes.

> • **Caution:** Code Sec. 2058, following, was added by P.L. 107-16, the Economic Growth and Tax Relief Reconciliation Act of 2001 (EGTRRA). These provisions generally sunset for tax years beginning after 12/31/2012. For specific sunset provisions, see Sec. 901, P.L. 107-16 (as amended) reproduced in history notes for this Code Sec.

(a) Allowance of deduction.
For purposes of the tax imposed by section 2001, the value of the taxable estate shall be determined by deducting from the value of the gross estate the amount of any estate, inheritance, legacy, or succession taxes actually paid to any State or the District of Columbia, in respect of any property included in the gross estate (not including any such taxes paid with respect to the estate of a person other than the decedent).

(b) Period of limitations.
The deduction allowed by this section shall include only such taxes as were actually paid and deduction therefor claimed before the later of—
(1) 4 years after the filing of the return required by section 6018, or
(2) if—
(A) a petition for redetermination of a deficiency has been filed with the Tax Court within the time prescribed in section 6213(a), the expiration of 60 days after the decision of the Tax Court becomes final,
(B) an extension of time has been granted under section 6161 or 6166 for payment of the tax shown on the return, or of a deficiency, the date of the expiration of the period of the extension, or
(C) a claim for refund or credit of an overpayment of tax imposed by this chapter has been filed within the time prescribed in section 6511, the latest of the expiration of—
(i) 60 days from the date of mailing by certified mail or registered mail by the Secretary to the taxpayer of a notice of the disallowance of any part of such claim,
(ii) 60 days after a decision by any court of competent jurisdiction becomes final with respect to a timely suit instituted upon such claim, or
(iii) 2 years after a notice of the waiver of disallowance is filed under section 6532(a)(3).
Notwithstanding sections 6511 and 6512, refund based on the deduction may be made if the claim for refund is filed within the period provided in the preceding sentence. Any such refund shall be made without interest.

In 2010, P.L. 111-312, Sec. 101(a)(1), substituted "December 31, 2012" for "December 31, 2010" both places it appears in Sec. 901, P.L. 107-16, see below, effective as if included in the enactment of P.L. 107-16, EGTRRA, 6/7/2001.
In 2002, P.L. 107-358, Sec. 2, added subsec. (c) in Sec. 901 of P. L. 107-16 [see below], effective 12/17/2002.
In 2001, P.L. 107-16, Sec. 532(b), added Code Sec. 2058, effective for estates of decedents dying, and generation-skipping transfers, after 12/31/2004.
—P.L. 107-16, Sec. 901, of this Act [as amended by Sec. 2, P. L. 107-358, and Sec.101(a)(1), P.L. 111-312, see above], reads as follows:
"SEC. 901. SUNSET OF PROVISIONS OF ACT.
"(a) In general. All provisions of, and amendments made by, this Act shall not apply—

Estate taxes

Code Sec. 2102(b)(3)(A)

"(1) to taxable, plan, or limitation years beginning after December 31, 2012, or
"(2) in the case of title V, to estates of decedents dying, gifts made, or generation skipping transfers, after December 31, 2012.
"(b) Application of certain laws. The Internal Revenue Code of 1986 and the Employee Retirement Income Security Act of 1974 shall be applied and administered to years, estates, gifts, and transfers described in subsection (a) as if the provisions and amendments described in subsection (a) had never been enacted.
"(c) Exception. Subsection (a) shall not apply to section 803 (relating to no federal income tax on restitution received by victims of the Nazi regime or their heirs or estates)."

Subchapter B.—Estates of Nonresidents Not Citizens

Sec.
2101. Tax imposed.
2102. Credits against tax.
2103. Definition of gross estate.
2104. Property within the United States.
2105. Property without the United States.
2106. Taxable estate.
2107. Expatriation to avoid tax.
2108. Application of pre-1967 estate tax provisions.

In **1966**, added items 2107 and 2108.

Sec. 2101. Tax imposed.
(a) Imposition.
Except as provided in section 2107, a tax is hereby imposed on the transfer of the taxable estate (determined as provided in section 2106) of every decedent nonresident not a citizen of the United States.
(b) Computation of tax.
The tax imposed by this section shall be the amount equal to the excess (if any) of—
  (1) a tentative tax computed under section 2001(c) on the sum of—
    (A) the amount of the taxable estate, and
    (B) the amount of the adjusted taxable gifts, over
  (2) a tentative tax computed under section 2001(c) on the amount of the adjusted taxable gifts.
(c) Adjustments for taxable gifts.
  (1) Adjusted taxable gifts defined. For purposes of this section, the term "adjusted taxable gifts" means the total amount of the taxable gifts (within the meaning of section 2503 as modified by section 2511) made by the decedent after December 31, 1976, other than gifts which are includible in the gross estate of the decedent.
  (2) Adjustment for certain gift tax. For purposes of this section, the rules of section 2001(d) shall apply.

In **2002**, P.L. 107-147, Sec. 411(g)(2), deleted "For purposes of the preceding sentence, there shall be appropriate adjustments in the application of section 2001(c)(2) to reflect the difference between the amount of the credit provided under section 2102(c) and the amount of the credit provided under section 2010." after "taxable gifts." at the end of subsec. (b), effective for estates of decedents dying, and gifts made, after 12/31/2001.
In **1993**, P.L. 103-66, Sec. 13208(b)(3), substituted "section 2001(c)(2)" for "section 2001(c)(3)" in the last sentence of subsec. (b), effective in the case of decedents dying and gifts made after 12/31/92.
In **1989**, P.L. 101-239, Sec. 7815(c), added the sentence at the end of subsec. (b), effective for the estates of decedents dying after 11/10/88.
In **1988**, P.L. 100-647, Sec. 5032(a), substituted "a tentative tax computed under section 2001(c)" for "a tentative tax computed in accordance with the rate schedule set forth in subsection (d)" each place it appeared in subsec. (b)... Sec. 5032(c), deleted subsec. (d), effective for the estates of decedents dying after 11/10/88.
Prior to deletion, subsec. (d) read as follows:
"(d) Rate schedule.

If the amount with respect to which the tentative tax to be computed is:	The tentative tax is:
Not over $100,000	6% of such amount.
Over $100,000 but not over $500,000	$6,000, plus 12% of excess over $100,000.
Over $500,000 but not over $1,000,000	$54,000, plus 18% of excess over $500,000.
Over $1,000,000 but not over $2,000,000	$144,000, plus 24% of excess over $1,000,000.
Over $2,000,000	$384,000, plus 30% of excess over $2,000,000."

In **1976**, P.L. 94-455, Sec. 2001(c)(1)(D), amended Code Sec. 2101, effective for estates of decedents dying after 12/31/76.
Prior to amendment, Code Sec. 2101 read as follows:
"SEC. 2101. TAX IMPOSED.
"(a) Rate of tax.
"Except as provided in section 2107, a tax computed in accordance with the following table is hereby imposed on the transfer of the taxable estate, determined as provided in section 2106, of every decedent nonresident not a citizen of the United States:

"If the taxable estate is:	The tax shall be:
Not over $100,000	5% of the taxable estate.
Over $100,000 but not over $500,000	$5,000, plus 10% of excess over $100,000.
Over $500,000, but not over $1,000,000	$45,000, plus 15% of excess over $500,000.
Over $1,000,000 but not over $2,000,000	$120,000, plus 20% of excess over $1,000,000.
Over $2,000,000	$320,000 plus 25% of excess over $2,000,000.

"(b) Property held by alien property custodian.
"For taxes in connection with property or interests transferred to or vested in the Alien Property Custodian, see section 36 of the Trading with the Enemy Act, as added by the act of August 8, 1946 (60 Stat. 929; 50 U.S.C. App. 36.)"
In **1966**, P.L. 89-809, Sec. 108, amended subsec. (a), effective for estates of decedents dying after 11/13/66.
Prior to amendment, subsec. (a) read as follows:
"(a) In general.
"A tax computed in accordance with the table contained in section 2001 is hereby imposed on the transfer of the taxable estate, determined as provided in section 2106, of every decedent nonresident not a citizen of the United States dying after the date of enactment of this title."

Sec. 2102. Credits against tax.

> • *Caution:* Code Secs. 2102(a)-(b), following, were amended by P.L. 107-16, EGTRRA. These provisions generally sunset for tax years beginning after 12/31/2012. For specific sunset provisions, see Sec. 901, P.L. 107-16 (as amended) reproduced in history notes for this Code Sec.

(a) In general.
The tax imposed by section 2101 shall be credited with the amounts determined in accordance with sections 2012 and 2013 (relating to gift tax and tax on prior transfers).
(b) Unified credit.
  (1) In general. A credit of $13,000 shall be allowed against the tax imposed by section 2101.
  (2) Residents of possessions of the United States. In the case of a decedent who is considered to be a "nonresident not a citizen of the United States" under section 2209, the credit under this subsection shall be the greater of—
    (A) $13,000, or
    (B) that proportion of $46,800 which the value of that part of the decedent's gross estate which at the time of his death is situated in the United States bears to the value of his entire gross estate wherever situated.
  (3) Special rules.
    (A) Coordination with treaties. To the extent required under any treaty obligation of the United States, the credit allowed under this subsection shall be equal to

3,013

the amount which bears the same ratio to the applicable credit amount in effect under section 2010(c) for the calendar year which includes the date of death as the value of the part of the decedent's gross estate which at the time of his death is situated in the United States bears to the value of his entire gross estate wherever situated. For purposes of the preceding sentence, property shall not be treated as situated in the United States if such property is exempt from the tax imposed by this subchapter under any treaty obligation of the United States.

(B) Coordination with gift tax unified credit. If a credit has been allowed under section 2505 with respect to any gift made by the decedent, each dollar amount contained in paragraph (1) or (2) or subparagraph (A) of this paragraph (whichever applies) shall be reduced by the amount so allowed.

(4) Limitation based on amount of tax. The credit allowed under this subsection shall not exceed the amount of the tax imposed by section 2101.

(5) Application of other credits. For purposes of subsection (a), sections 2012 and 2013 shall be applied as if the credit allowed under this subsection were allowed under section 2010.

In 2010, P.L. 111-312, Sec. 101(a)(1), substituted "December 31, 2012" for "December 31, 2010" both places it appeared in Sec. 901, P.L. 107-16 [see below], effective as if included in the enactment of P.L. 107-16, EGTRRA, 6/7/2001.

In 2002, P.L. 107-358, Sec. 2, added subsec. (c) in Sec. 901 of P. L. 107-16 [see below], effective 12/17/2002.

In 2001, P.L. 107-16, Sec. 532(c)(7)(A), amended subsec. (a) . . . Sec. 532(c)(7)(B), deleted subsec. (b) and redesignated subsec. (c) as (b) . . . Sec. 532(c)(7)(C), substituted "2012 and 2013" for "2011 to 2013, inclusive," in para. (b)(5) [as redesignated by Sec. 532(c)(7)(B), see above], effective for estates of decedents dying, and generation-skipping transfers, after 12/31/2004.

Prior to amendment, subsec. (a) read as follows:

"(a) In general. The tax imposed by section 2101 shall be credited with the amounts determined in accordance with sections 2011 to 2013, inclusive (relating to State death taxes, gift tax, and tax on prior transfers), subject to the special limitation provided in subsection (b)."

Prior to deletion, subsec. (b) read as follows:

"(b) Special limitation. The maximum credit allowed under section 2011 against the tax imposed by section 2101 for State death taxes paid shall be an amount which bears the same ratio to the credit computed as provided in section 2011(b) as the value of the property, as determined for purposes of this chapter, upon which State death taxes were paid and which is included in the gross estate under section 2103 bears to the value of the total gross estate under section 2103. For purposes of this subsection, the term 'State death taxes' means the taxes described in section 2011(a)."

—P.L. 107-16, Sec. 901, of this Act [as amended by Sec. 2, P. L. 107-358, and Sec. 101(a)(1), P.L. 111-312, see above], reads as follows:

"SEC. 901. SUNSET OF PROVISIONS OF ACT.

"(a) In general. All provisions of, and amendments made by, this Act shall not apply—

"(1) to taxable, plan, or limitation years beginning after December 31, 2012, or

"(2) in the case of title V, to estates of decedents dying, gifts made, or generation skipping transfers, after December 31, 2012.

"(b) Application of certain laws. The Internal Revenue Code of 1986 and the Employee Retirement Income Security Act of 1974 shall be applied and administered to years, estates, gifts, and transfers described in subsection (a) as if the provisions and amendments described in subsection (a) had never been enacted.

"(c) Exception. Subsection (a) shall not apply to section 803 (relating to no federal income tax on restitution received by victims of the Nazi regime or their heirs or estates)."

In 1997, P.L. 105-34, Sec. 501(a)(1)(E), substituted "the applicable credit amount in effect under section 2010(c) for the calendar year which includes the date of death" for "$192,800" in subpara. (c)(3)(A), effective for the estates of decedents dying, and gifts made, after 12/31/97.

In 1996, P.L. 104-188, Sec. 1704(f)(1), added sentence to the end of subpara. (c)(3)(A), effective 8/20/96.

In 1988, P.L. 100-647, Sec. 5032(b)(1)(A), substituted "$13,000" for "$3,600" in para. (c)(1) and subpara. (c)(2)(A) . . . Sec. 5032(b)(1)(B), substituted "$46,800" for "$15,075" in subpara. (c)(2)(B) . . . Sec. 5032(b)(2), amended para. (c)(3), effective for the estates of decedents dying after 11/10/88.

Prior to amendment, para. (c)(3) read as follows:

"(3) Phase-in of paragraph (2)(B) amount. In the case of a decedent dying before 1981, paragraph (2)(B) shall be applied—

"(A) in the case of a decedent dying during 1977, by substituting '$8,480' for '$15,075',

"(B) in the case of a decedent dying during 1978, by substituting '$10,080' for '$15,075',

"(C) in the case of a decedent dying during 1979, by substituting '$11,680' for '$15,075', and

"(D) in the case of a decedent dying during 1980, by substituting '$13,388' for '$15,075'."

In 1976, P.L. 94-455, Sec. 2001(c)(1)(E)(i), added subsec. (c), effective for estates of decedents dying after 12/31/76.

In 1966, P.L. 89-809, Sec. 108, designated Code Sec. 2102 as subsec. (a) and added subsec. (b), effective for estates of decedents dying after 11/13/66.

Sec. 2103. Definition of gross estate.

For the purpose of the tax imposed by section 2101, the value of the gross estate of every decedent nonresident not a citizen of the United States shall be that part of his gross estate (determined as provided in section 2031) which at the time of his death is situated in the United States.

Sec. 2104. Property within the United States.

(a) Stock in corporation.

For purposes of this subchapter shares of stock owned and held by a nonresident not a citizen of the United States shall be deemed property within the United States only if issued by a domestic corporation.

(b) Revocable transfers and transfers within 3 years of death.

For purposes of this subchapter, any property of which the decedent has made a transfer, by trust or otherwise, within the meaning of sections 2035 to 2038, inclusive, shall be deemed to be situated in the United States, if so situated either at the time of the transfer or at the time of the decedent's death.

(c) Debt obligations.

For purposes of this subchapter, debt obligations of—

(1) a United States person, or

(2) the United States, a State or any political subdivision thereof, or the District of Columbia,

owned and held by a nonresident not a citizen of the United States shall be deemed property within the United States. With respect to estates of decedents dying after December 31, 1969, deposits with a domestic branch of a foreign corporation, if such branch is engaged in the commercial banking business, shall, for purposes of this subchapter, be deemed property within the United States. This subsection shall not apply to a debt obligation to which section 2105(b) applies.

In 2010, P.L. 111-226, Sec. 217(c)(3), substituted a period for "or to a debt obligation of a domestic corporation if any interest on such obligation, were such interest received by the decedent at the time of his death, would be treated by reason of section 861(a)(1)(A) as income from sources without the United States." in subsec. (c), effective for tax. yrs. begin. after 12/31/2010. Sec. 217(d)(2) of this Act reads as follows:

"(2) Grandfather rule for outstanding debt obligations.

"(A) In general. The amendments made by this section shall not apply to payments of interest on obligations issued before the date of the enactment of this Act.

"(B) Exception for related party debt. Subparagraph (A) shall not apply to any interest which is payable to a related person (determined under rules similar to the rules of section 954(d)(3)).

"(C) Significant modifications treated as new issues. For purposes of subparagraph (A), a significant modification of the terms of any obligation (including any extension of the term of such obligation) shall be treated as a new issue."

In 1996, P.L. 104-188, Sec. 1704(t)(38), substituted "section 861(a)(1)(A)" for "subparagraph (A), (C), or (D) of section 861(a)(1)" in subsec. (c), effective 8/20/96.

In 1988, P.L. 100-647, Sec. 1012(q)(11), substituted "subparagraph (A), (C), or (D) of section 861(a)(1)" for "section 861(a)(1)(B), section 861(a)(1)(G), or section 861(a)(1)(H)", in subsec. (c), effective for tax. yrs. begin. after 12/31/86.

In 1976, P.L. 94-455, Sec. 2001(c)(1)(L), substituted "and transfers within 3 years of death" for "and transfers in contemplation of death" in the heading for subsec. (b), effective for estates of decedents dying after 12/31/76, but does not apply to transfers made before 1/1/77.

In 1975, P.L. 93-625, Sec. 9(b), substituted ", section 861(a)(1)(G), or section 861(a)(1)(H)" for "or section 861(a)(1)(G)" in subsec. (c), effective for estates of decedents dying after 1/3/75.

Estate taxes   Code Sec. 2106(a)(1)

In 1973, P.L. 93-17, Sec. 3(a)(1), added "or section 861(a)(1)(G)" after "by reason of section 861(a)(1)(B)" in the last sentence of subsec. (c), effective for estates of for decedents dying after 12/31/72, except that in the case of the assumption of a debt obligation of a foreign corporation which is treated as issued under section 4912(c)(2) after 12/31/72, and before 1/1/74, this amendment shall apply for estates of decedents dying after 12/31/73.

In 1969, P.L. 91-172, Sec. 435(b), substituted "1969" for "1972" in subsec. (c).

In 1966, P.L. 89-809, Sec. 108, added subsec. (c), effective for estates of decedents dying after 11/13/66.

Sec. 2105. Property without the United States.
(a) Proceeds of life insurance.

For purposes of this subchapter, the amount receivable as insurance on the life of a nonresident not a citizen of the United States shall not be deemed property within the United States.

(b) Bank deposits and certain other debt obligations.

For purposes of this subchapter, the following shall not be deemed property within the United States—

(1) amounts described in section 871(i)(3), if any interest thereon would not be subject to tax by reason of section 871(i)(1) were such interest received by the decedent at the time of his death,

(2) deposits with a foreign branch of a domestic corporation or domestic partnership, if such branch is engaged in the commercial banking business,

(3) debt obligations, if, without regard to whether a statement meeting the requirements of section 871(h)(5) has been received, any interest thereon would be eligible for the exemption from tax under section 871(h)(1) were such interest received by the decedent at the time of his death, and

(4) obligations which would be original issue discount obligations as defined in section 871(g)(1) but for subparagraph (B)(i) thereof, if any interest thereon (were such interest received by the decedent at the time of his death) would not be effectively connected with the conduct of a trade or business within the United States.

Notwithstanding the preceding sentence, if any portion of the interest on an obligation referred to in paragraph (3) would not be eligible for the exemption referred to in paragraph (3) by reason of section 871(h)(4) if the interest were received by the decedent at the time of his death, then an appropriate portion (as determined in a manner prescribed by the Secretary) of the value (as determined for purposes of this chapter) of such debt obligation shall be deemed property within the United States.

(c) Works of art on loan for exhibition.

For purposes of this subchapter, works of art owned by a nonresident not a citizen of the United States shall not be deemed property within the United States if such works of art are—

(1) imported into the United States solely for exhibition purposes,

(2) loaned for such purposes, to a public gallery or museum, no part of the net earnings of which inures to the benefit of any private stockholder or individual, and

(3) at the time of the death of the owner, on exhibition, or en route to or from exhibition, in such a public gallery or museum.

(d) Stock in a RIC.

(1) In general. For purposes of this subchapter, stock in a regulated investment company (as defined in section 851) owned by a nonresident not a citizen of the United States shall not be deemed property within the United States in the proportion that, at the end of the quarter of such investment company's taxable year immediately preceding a decedent's date of death (or at such other time as the Secretary may designate in regulations), the assets of the investment company that were qualifying assets with respect to the decedent bore to the total assets of the investment company.

(2) Qualifying assets. For purposes of this subsection, qualifying assets with respect to a decedent are assets that, if owned directly by the decedent, would have been—

(A) amounts, deposits, or debt obligations described in subsection (b) of this section,

(B) debt obligations described in the last sentence of section 2104(c), or

(C) other property not within the United States.

(3) Termination. This subsection shall not apply to estates of decedents dying after December 31, 2011.

In 2010, P.L. 111-312, Sec. 726(a), substituted "December 31, 2011" for "December 31, 2009" in para. (d)(3), effective for estates of decedents dying after 12/31/2009.

In 2008, P.L. 110-343, Sec. 207(a)DivC, substituted "December 31, 2009" for "December 31, 2007" in para. (d)(3), effective for decedents dying after 12/31/2007.

In 2004, P.L. 108-357, Sec. 411(b), added subsec. (d), effective for estates of decedents dying after 12/31/2004.

In 1997, P.L. 105-34, Sec. 1304(a), deleted "and" at the end of para. (b)(2), substituted ", and" for the period at the end of para. (b)(3) and added para. (b)(4), effective for estates of decedents dying after 8/5/97.

In 1993, P.L. 103-66, Sec. 13237(b)(1), substituted "this subchapter, the following shall not be deemed property within the United States" for "this subchapter" in subsec. (b) . . . Sec. 13237(b)(2), substituted para. (b)(3) and all that followed with new para (b)(3), effective for estates of decedents dying after 12/31/93.

Prior to amendment, para. (b)(3) and all that followed through the end of subsec. (b) read as follows:

"(3) debt obligations, if, without regard to whether a statement meeting the requirements of section 871(h)(4) has been received, any interest thereon would be eligible for the exemption from tax under section 871(h)(1) were such interest received by the decedent at the time of his death,

shall not be deemed property within the United States."

In 1988, P.L. 100-647, Sec. 1012(g)(4), substituted "section 871(i)(3), if any interest thereon would not be subject to tax by reason of section 871(i)(1)" for "section 861(c), if any interest thereon would be treated by reason of section 861(a)(1)(A) as income from sources without the United States" in para. (b)(1), effective for payments after 12/31/86. For special rules, see Secs. 1214(d)(2)-(4) of P. L. 99-514 reproduced in note following Code Sec. 861.

In 1984, P.L. 98-369, Sec. 127(d), amended subsec. (b), effective for obligations issued after 7/18/84, for the estates of decedents dying after 7/18/84.

Prior to amendment, subsec. (b) read as follows:

"(b) Certain bank deposits, etc.

"For purposes of this subchapter—

"(1) amounts described in section 861(c) if any interest thereon, were such interest received by the decedent at the time of his death, would be treated by reason of section 861(a)(1)(A) as income from sources without the United States, and

"(2) deposits with a foreign branch of a domestic corporation or domestic partnership, if such branch is engaged in the commercial banking business,

shall not be deemed property within the United States."

In 1966, P.L. 89-809, Sec. 108, amended subsec. (b), effective for estates of decedents dying after 11/13/66.

Prior to amendment, subsec. (b) read as follows:

"(b) Bank deposits.

"For purposes of this subchapter, any moneys deposited with any person carrying on the banking business, by or for a nonresident not a citizen of the United States who was not engaged in business in the United States at the time of his death shall not be deemed property within the United States."

Sec. 2106. Taxable estate.
(a) Definition of taxable estate.

For purposes of the tax imposed by section 2101, the value of the taxable estate of every decedent nonresident not a citizen of the United States shall be determined by deducting from the value of that part of his gross estate which at the time of his death is situated in the United States—

(1) Expenses, losses, indebtedness, and taxes. That proportion of the deductions specified in sections 2053 and 2054 (other than the deductions described in the following sentence) which the value of such part bears to the value of his entire gross estate, wherever situated. Any deduction allowable under section 2053 in the case of a claim against the estate which was founded on a promise or agreement but was not contracted for an adequate and full

3,015

consideration in money or money's worth shall be allowable under this paragraph to the extent that it would be allowable as a deduction under paragraph (2) if such promise or agreement constituted a bequest.

(2) Transfers for public, charitable, and religious uses.

(A) In general. The amount of all bequests, legacies, devises, or transfers (including the interest which falls into any such bequest, legacy, devise, or transfer as a result of an irrevocable disclaimer of a bequest, legacy, devise, transfer, or power, if the disclaimer is made before the date prescribed for the filing of the estate tax return)—

(i) to or for the use of the United States, any State, any political subdivision thereof, or the District of Columbia, for exclusively public purposes;

(ii) to or for the use of any domestic corporation organized and operated exclusively for religious, charitable, scientific, literary, or educational purposes, including the encouragement of art and the prevention of cruelty to children or animals, no part of the net earnings of which inures to the benefit of any private stockholder or individual, which is not disqualified for tax exemption under section 501(c)(3) by reason of attempting to influence legislation, and which does not participate in, or intervene in (including the publishing or distributing of statements), any political campaign on behalf of (or in opposition to) any candidate for public office; or

(iii) to a trustee or trustees, or a fraternal society, order, or association operating under the lodge system, but only if such contributions or gifts are to be used within the United States by such trustee or trustees, or by such fraternal society, order, or association, exclusively for religious, charitable, scientific, literary, or educational purposes, or for the prevention of cruelty to children or animals, such trust, fraternal society, order, or association would not be disqualified for tax exemption under section 501(c)(3) by reason of attempting to influence legislation, and such trustee or trustees, or such fraternal society, order, or association, does not participate in, or intervene in (including the publishing or distributing of statements), any political campaign on behalf of (or in opposition to) any candidate for public office;

(B) Powers of appointment. Property includible in the decedent's gross estate under section 2041 (relating to powers of appointment) received by a donee described in this paragraph shall, for purposes of this paragraph, be considered a bequest of such decedent.

(C) Death taxes payable out of bequests. If the tax imposed by section 2101, or any estate, succession, legacy, or inheritance taxes, are, either by the terms of the will, by the law of the jurisdiction under which the estate is administered, or by the law of the jurisdiction imposing the particular tax, payable in whole or in part out of the bequests, legacies, or devises otherwise deductible under this paragraph, then the amount deductible under this paragraph shall be the amount of such bequests, legacies, or devises reduced by the amount of such taxes.

(D) Limitation on deduction. The amount of the deduction under this paragraph for any transfer shall not exceed the value of the transferred property required to be included in the gross estate.

(E) Disallowance of deductions in certain cases. The provisions of section 2055(e) shall be applied in the determination of the amount allowable as a deduction under this paragraph.

(F) Cross references.

(i) For option as to time for valuation for purposes of deduction under this section, see section 2032.

(ii) For exemption of certain bequests for the benefit of the United States and for rules of construction for certain bequests, see section 2055(g).

(iii) For treatment of gifts and bequests to or for the use of Indian tribal governments (or their subdivisions), see section 7871.

(3) Marital deduction. The amount which would be deductible with respect to property situated in the United States at the time of the decedent's death under the principles of section 2056.

• *Caution:* Code Sec. 2106(a)(4), following, was added by P.L. 107-16, EGTRRA. These provisions generally sunset for tax years beginning after 12/31/2012. For specific sunset provisions, see Sec. 901, P.L. 107-16 (as amended) reproduced in history notes for this Code Sec.

(4) State death taxes. The amount which bears the same ratio to the State death taxes as the value of the property, as determined for purposes of this chapter, upon which State death taxes were paid and which is included in the gross estate under section 2103 bears to the value of the total gross estate under section 2103. For purposes of this paragraph, the term "State death taxes" means the taxes described in section 2011(a).

(b) Condition of allowance of deductions.

No deduction shall be allowed under paragraphs (1) and (2) of subsection (a) in the case of a nonresident not a citizen of the United States unless the executor includes in the return required to be filed under section 6018 the value at the time of his death of that part of the gross estate of such nonresident not situated in the United States.

In 2010, P.L. 111-312, Sec. 101(a)(1), substituted "December 31, 2012" for "December 31, 2010" both places it appeared in Sec. 901, P.L. 107-16 [see below], effective as if included in the enactment of P.L. 107-16, EGTRRA, 6/7/2001.

In 2002, P.L. 107-358, Sec. 2, added subsec. (c) in Sec. 901 of P. L. 107-16 [see below], effective 12/17/2002.

In 2001, P.L. 107-16, Sec. 532(c)(8), added para. (a)(4), effective for estates of decedents dying, and generation-skipping transfers, after 12/31/2004.

—P.L. 107-16, Sec. 901, of this Act [as amended by Sec. 2, P. L. 107-358, and Sec. 101(a)(1), P.L. 111-312, see above], reads as follows:

"Sec. 901. Sunset of provisions of Act.

"(a) In general. All provisions of, and amendments made by, this Act shall not apply—

"(1) to taxable, plan, or limitation years beginning after December 31, 2012, or

"(2) in the case of title V, to estates of decedents dying, gifts made, or generation skipping transfers, after December 31, 2012.

"(b) Application of certain laws. The Internal Revenue Code of 1986 and the Employee Retirement Income Security Act of 1974 shall be applied and administered to years, estates, gifts, and transfers described in subsection (a) as if the provisions and amendments described in subsection (a) had never been enacted.

"(c) Exception. Subsection (a) shall not apply to section 803 (relating to no federal income tax on restitution received by victims of the Nazi regime or their heirs or estates)."

In 1989, P.L. 101-239, Sec. 7815(d)(3), deleted "allowed where spouse is citizen" which followed "deduction" from the heading of para. (a)(3), effective for the estates of decedents dying after 11/10/88.

—P.L. 101-239, Sec. 7815(d)(14), of this Act provides:

"(14) In the case of the estate of, or gift by, an individual who was not a citizen or resident of the United States but was a resident of a foreign country with which the United States has a tax treaty with respect to estate, inheritance, or gift taxes, the amendments made by section 5033 of the 1988 Act [P. L. 100-647] shall not apply to the extent such amendments would be inconsistent with the provisions of such treaty relating to estate, inheritance, or gift tax marital deductions. In the case of the estate of an individual dying before the date 3 years after the

Estate taxes   Code Sec. 2107(b)(1)

date of the enactment of this Act or a gift by an individual before the date 3 years after the date of the enactment of this Act, the requirement of the preceding sentence that the individual not be a citizen or resident of the United States shall not apply."

In **1988**, P.L. 100-647, Sec. 5033(c), added para. (a)(3), effective for the estates of decedents dying after 11/10/88.

In **1987**, P.L. 100-203, Sec. 10711(a)(4), substituted "on behalf of (or in opposition to) any candidate" for "on behalf of any candidate" in clauses (a)(2)(A)(ii) and (a)(2)(A)(iii), effective with respect to activities after 12/22/87.

In **1986**, P.L. 99-514, Sec. 1422(c), substituted "section 2055(g)" for "section 2055(f)" in clause (a)(2)(F)(ii), effective for transfers and contributions made after 12/31/86.

In **1984**, P.L. 98-369, Sec. 1065(a)(1), amended Sec. 204 of P. L. 97-473, the effective date for changes made by Sec. 202(b)(6) of P. L. 97-473 (see below), by deleting "and before January 1, 1985" each place it appeared.

In **1983**, P.L. 97-473, Sec. 202(b)(6), amended subpara. (a)(2)(F), effective [as amended by Sec. 1065(a)(1) of P. L. 98-369, see above] for estates of decedents dying after 12/31/82.

Prior to amendment, subpara. (a)(2)(F) read as follows:

"(F) Cross references.

"(1) For option as to time for valuation for purposes of deduction under this section, see section 2032.

"(2) For exemption of certain bequests for the benefit of the United States and for rules of construction for certain bequests, see section 2055(f)."

In **1976**, P.L. 94-455, Sec. 1307(d)(1)(B)(iii), substituted "which is not disqualified for tax exemption under section 501(c)(3) by reason of attempting to influence legislation," for "no substantial part of the activities of which is carrying on propaganda, or otherwise attempting to influence legislation," in clause (a)(2)(A)(ii) . . . Sec. 1307(d)(1)(C), substituted "such trust, fraternal society, order, or association would not be disqualified for tax exemption under section 501(c)(3) by reason of attempting to influence legislation," for "no substantial part of the activities of such trustee or trustees, or of such fraternal society, order, or association, is carrying on propaganda, or otherwise attempting, to influence legislation," in clause (a)(2)(A)(iii), effective for estates of decedents dying after 12/31/76.

—P.L. 94-455, Sec. 1902(a)(5)(A), amended subpara. (a)(2)(F), effective for estates of decedents dying after 10/4/76.

Prior to amendment, subpara. (a)(2)(F) read as follows:

"(F) Other cross references.

"(1) For option as to time for valuation for purpose of deduction under this paragraph [sic], see section 2032.

"(2) For exemption of bequests to or for benefit of Library of Congress, see section 5 of the Act of March 3, 1925, as amended (56 Stat. 765; 2 U.S.C. 161).

"(3) For construction of bequests for benefit of the library of the Post Office Department as bequests to or for the use of the United States, see section 2 of the Act of August 8, 1946 (60 Stat. 924; 5 U.S.C. 393).

"(4) For exemption of bequests for benefit of Office of Naval Records and Library, Navy Department, see section 2 of the Act of March 4, 1937 (50 Stat. 25; 5 U.S.C. 419b).

"(5) For exemption of bequests to or for benefit of National Park Service, see section 5 of the Act of July 10, 1935 (49 Stat. 478; 16 U.S.C. 19c).

"(6) For construction of devises or bequests accepted by the Secretary of State under the Foreign Service Act of 1946 as devises or bequests to or for the use of the United States, see section 1021(e) of that Act (60 Stat. 1032; 22 U.S.C. 809).

"(7) For construction of gifts or bequests of money accepted by the Attorney General for credit to 'Commissary Funds, Federal Prisons' as gifts or bequests to or for the use of the United States, see section 2 of the Act of May 15, 1952, 66 Stat. 73, as amended by the Act of July 9, 1952, 66 Stat. 479 (31 U.S.C. 725s-4).

"(8) For payment of tax on bequests of United States obligations to the United States, see section 24 of the Second Liberty Bond Act, as amended (59 Stat. 48, § 4; 31 U.S.C. 757c).

"(9) For construction of bequests for benefit of or use in connection with the Naval Academy as bequests to or for the use of the United States, see section 3 of the Act of March 31, 1944 (58 Stat. 135; 34 U.S.C. 1115b).

"(10) For exemption of bequests for benefit of Naval Academy Museum, see section 4 of the Act of March 26, 1938 (52 Stat. 119; 34 U.S.C. 1119).

"(11) For exemption of bequests received by National Archives Trust Fund Board, see section 7 of the National Archives Trust Fund Board Act (55 Stat. 582; 44 U.S.C. 300gg)."

—P.L. 94-455, Sec. 1902(a)(5)(B), deleted subsec. (c), effective for estates of decedent dying after 10/4/76.

Prior to deletion, subsec. (c) read as follows:

"(c) United States bonds.

"For purposes of section 2103, the value of the gross estate (determined as provided in section 2031) of a decedent who was not engaged in business in the United States at the time of his death—

"(1) shall not include obligations issued by the United States before March 1, 1941; and

"(2) shall include obligations issued by the United States on or after March 1, 1941."

—P.L. 94-455, Sec. 1902(a)(12)(A), deleted "Territory,", which followed "any State," in clause (a)(2)(A)(i), effective for gifts made after 12/31/76.

—P.L. 94-455, Sec. 2001(c)(1)(F), deleted para. (a)(3) effective for estates of decedents dying after 12/31/76.

Prior to deletion, para. (a)(3) read as follows:

"(3) Exemption.

"(A) General rule. An exemption of $30,000.

"(B) Resident of possessions of the United States. In the case of a decedent who is considered to be a 'non-resident not a citizen of the United States' under the provisions of section 2209, the exemption shall be the greater of (i) $30,000, or (ii) that proportion of the exemption authorized by section 2052 which the value of that part of the decedent's gross estate which at the time of his death is situated in the United States bears to the value of his entire gross estate wherever situated."

In **1969**, P.L. 91-172, Sec. 201(d)(2), amended subpara. (a)(2)(E), effective as provided in Sec. 201 (g)(4)(A), (B) and (C) of this Act, which reads as follows:

"(4)(A) Except as provided in subparagraphs (B) and (C), the amendments made by paragraphs (1) and (2) of subsection (d) shall apply in the case of decedents dying after December 31, 1969.

"(B) Such amendments shall not apply in the case of property passing under the terms of a will executed on or before October 9, 1969—

"(i) if the decedent dies before October 9, 1972, without having republished the will after October 9, 1969, by codicil or otherwise,

"(ii) if the decedent at no time after October 9, 1969, had the right to change the portions of the will which pertain to the passing of the property to, or for the use of, an organization described in section 2055(a), or

"(iii) if the will is not republished by codicil or otherwise before October 9, 1972, and the decedent is on such date and at all times thereafter under a mental disability to republish the will by codicil or otherwise.

"(C) Such amendments shall not apply in the case of property transferred in trust on or before October 9, 1969—

"(i) if the decedent dies before October 9, 1972, without having amended after October 9, 1969, the instrument governing the disposition of the property,

"(ii) if the property transferred was an irrevocable interest to, or for the use of, an organization described in section 2055(a), or

"(iii) if the instrument governing the disposition of the property was not amended by the decedent before October 9, 1972, and the decedent is on such date and at all times thereafter under a mental disability to change the disposition of the property."

Prior to amendment subsec. (a)(2)(E) read as follows:

"(E) Disallowance of deductions in certain cases. For disallowance of certain charitable, etc., deductions otherwise allowable under this paragraph, see sections 503 and 681."

—P.L. 91-172, Sec. 201(d)(4)(B)(i), deleted "and" before "no substantial part" in clause (a)(2)(A)(ii) and added ", and which does not participate in, or intervene in (including the publishing or distributing of statements), any political campaign on behalf of any candidate for public office" before the semicolon at the end of clause (a)(2)(A)(ii) . . . Sec. 201(d)(4)(B)(ii), deleted "and" before "no substantial part" in clause (a)(2)(A)(iii) and added ", and such trustee or trustees, or such fraternal society, order, or association, does not participate in, or intervene in (including the publishing or distributing of statements), any political campaign on behalf of any candidate for public office" before the semicolon at the end of clause (a)(2)(A)(iii), effective for gifts and transfers made after 12/31/69.

In **1966**, P.L. 89-809, Sec. 108(e), amended para. (a)(3), effective for estates of decedents dying after 11/13/66.

Prior to amendment, para. (a)(3) read as follows:

"(3) Exemption.—

"(A) General rule. An exemption of $2,000.

"(B) Residents of Possessions of the United States. In the case of a decedent who is considered to be a 'nonresident not a citizen of the United States' under the provisions of section 2209, the exemption shall be the greater of (i) $2,000, or (ii) that proportion of the exemption authorized by section 2052 which the value of that part of the decedent's gross estate which at the time of his death is situated in the United States bears to the value of this entire gross estate wherever situated."

In **1960**, P.L. 86-779, Sec. 4(c), amended para. (a)(3), effective for estates of decedents dying after 9/14/60.

Prior to amendment, para. (a)(3) read as follows:

"(3) Exemption. An exemption of $2,000."

In **1958**, P.L. 85-866, Sec. 30(d), substituted "503" for "504" in subpara. (a)(2)(E).

Sec. 2107. Expatriation to avoid tax.
(a) Treatment of expatriates.

A tax computed in accordance with the table contained in section 2001 is hereby imposed on the transfer of the taxable estate, determined as provided in section 2106, of every decedent nonresident not a citizen of the United States if the date of death occurs during a taxable year with respect to which the decedent is subject to tax under section 877(b).

(b) Gross estate.

For purposes of the tax imposed by subsection (a), the value of the gross estate of every decedent to whom subsection (a) applies shall be determined as provided in section 2103, except that—

(1) if such decedent owned (within the meaning of section 958(a)) at the time of his death 10 percent or more of the total combined voting power of all classes of stock entitled to vote of a foreign corporation, and

3,017

(2) if such decedent owned (within the meaning of section 958(a)), or is considered to have owned (by applying the ownership rules of section 958(b)), at the time of his death, more than 50 percent of—

(A) the total combined voting power of all classes of stock entitled to vote of such corporation, or

(B) the total value of the stock of such corporation,

then that proportion of the fair market value of the stock of such foreign corporation owned (within the meaning of section 958(a)) by such decedent at the time of his death, which the fair market value of any assets owned by such foreign corporation and situated in the United States, at the time of his death, bears to the total fair market value of all assets owned by such foreign corporation at the time of his death, shall be included in the gross estate of such decedent. For purposes of the preceding sentence, a decedent shall be treated as owning stock of a foreign corporation at the time of his death if, at the time of a transfer, by trust or otherwise, within the meaning of sections 2035 to 2038, inclusive, he owned such stock.

(c) Credits.

(1) Unified credit.

(A) In general. A credit of $13,000 shall be allowed against the tax imposed by subsection (a).

(B) Limitation based on amount of tax. The credit allowed under this paragraph shall not exceed the amount of the tax imposed by subsection (a).

(2) Credit for foreign death taxes.

(A) In general. The tax imposed by subsection (a) shall be credited with the amount of any estate, inheritance, legacy, or succession taxes actually paid to any foreign country in respect of any property which is included in the gross estate solely by reason of subsection (b).

(B) Limitation on credit. The credit allowed by subparagraph (A) for such taxes paid to a foreign country shall not exceed the lesser of—

(i) the amount which bears the same ratio to the amount of such taxes actually paid to such foreign country as the value of the property subjected to such taxes by such foreign country and included in the gross estate solely by reason of subsection (b) bears to the value of all property subjected to such taxes by such foreign country, or

(ii) such property's proportionate share of the excess of—

(I) the tax imposed by subsection (a), over

(II) the tax which would be imposed by section 2101 but for this section.

(C) Proportionate share. In the case of property which is included in the gross estate solely by reason of subsection (b), such property's proportionate share is the percentage which the value of such property bears to the total value of all property included in the gross estate solely by reason of subsection (b).

⸻

• **Caution:** Code Sec. 2107(c)(3), following, was amended by P.L. 107-16, EGTRRA. These provisions generally sunset for tax years beginning after 12/31/2012. For specific sunset provisions, see Sec. 901, P.L. 107-16 (as amended) reproduced in history notes for this Code Sec.

⸻

(3) Other credits. The tax imposed by subsection (a) shall be credited with the amounts determined in accordance with subsections (a) and (b) of section 2102. For purposes of subsection (a) of section 2102, sections 2012 and 2013 shall be applied as if the credit allowed under paragraph (1) were allowed under section 2010.

(d) Burden of proof.

If the Secretary establishes that it is reasonable to believe that an individual's loss of United States citizenship would, but for this section, result in a substantial reduction in the estate, inheritance, legacy, and succession taxes in respect of the transfer of his estate, the burden of proving that such loss of citizenship did not have for one of its principal purposes the avoidance of taxes under this subtitle or subtitle A shall be on the executor of such individual's estate.

(e) Cross reference.

For comparable treatment of long-term lawful permanent residents who ceased to be taxed as residents, see section 877(e).

In 2010, P.L. 111-312, Sec. 101(a)(1), substituted "December 31, 2012" for "December 31, 2010" both places it appeared in Sec. 901, P.L. 107-16 [see below], effective as if included in the enactment of P.L. 107-16, EGTRRA, 6/7/2001.

In 2004, P.L. 108-357, Sec. 804(a)(3), amended subsec. (a), effective for individuals who expatriate after 6/3/2004.

Prior to amendment, subsec. (a) read as follows:

"(a) Treatment of expatriates.

"(1) Rate of tax. A tax computed in accordance with the table contained in section 2001 is hereby imposed on the transfer of the taxable estate, determined as provided in section 2106, of every decedent nonresident not a citizen of the United States if, within the 10-year period ending with the date of the death, such decedent lost United States citizenship, unless such loss did not have for 1 of its principal purposes the avoidance of taxes under this subtitle or subtitle A.

"(2) Certain individuals treated as having tax avoidance purpose.

"(A) In general. For purposes of paragraph (1), an individual shall be treated as having a principal purpose to avoid such taxes if such individual is so treated under section 877(a)(2).

"(B) Exception. Subparagraph (A) shall not apply to a decedent meeting the requirements of section 877(c)(1)."

In 2002, P.L. 107-358, Sec. 2, added subsec. (c) in Sec. 901 of P. L. 107-16 [see below], effective 12/17/2002.

In 2001, P.L. 107-16, Sec. 532(c)(7)(C), substituted "2012 and 2013" for "2011 to 2013, inclusive," in para. (c)(3), effective for estates of decedents dying, and generation-skipping transfers, after 12/31/2004.

—P.L. 107-16, Sec. 901, of this Act [as amended by Sec. 2, P. L. 107-358, and Sec. 101(a)(1), P.L. 111-312, see above], reads as follows:

"SEC. 901. SUNSET OF PROVISIONS OF ACT.

"(a) In general. All provisions of, and amendments made by, this Act shall not apply—

"(1) to taxable, plan, or limitation years beginning after December 31, 2012, or

"(2) in the case of title V, to estates of decedents dying, gifts made, or generation skipping transfers, after December 31, 2012.

"(b) Application of certain laws. The Internal Revenue Code of 1986 and the Employee Retirement Income Security Act of 1974 shall be applied and administered to years, estates, gifts, and transfers described in subsection (a) as if the provisions and amendments described in subsection (a) had never been enacted.

"(c) Exception. Subsection (a) shall not apply to section 803 (relating to no federal income tax on restitution received by victims of the Nazi regime or their heirs or estates)."

In 1997, P.L. 105-34, Sec. 1602(g)(6)(A), substituted "such foreign country as the value of the property subjected to such taxes by such foreign country and" for "such foreign country in respect of property included in the gross estate as the value of the property" in clause (c)(2)(B)(i) . . . Sec. 1602(g)(6)(B), amended subpara. (c)(2)(C), effective as provided in Sec. 511(g) of P. L. 104-191, [see below].

Prior to amendment, subpara. (c)(2)(C) read as follows:

"(C) Proportionate share. For purposes of subparagraph (B), a property's proportionate share is the percentage of the value of the property which is included in the gross estate solely by reason of subsection (b) bears to the total value of the gross estate."

In 1996, P.L. 104-191, Sec. 511(e)(1)(A), amended subsec. (a) . . . Sec. 511(e)(1)(B), redesignated para. (c)(2) as para. (c)(3) and added a new para. (c)(2) . . . Sec. 511(e)(1)(C), substituted "more than 50 percent of—" and subparas. (b)(2)(A) and (b)(2)(B) for "more than 50 percent of the total combined voting power of all classes of stock entitled to vote for such foreign corporation," in para. (b)(2) . . . Sec. 511(f)(2)(A), deleted subsec. (d), redesignated subsec. (e) as subsec. (d) and added a new subsec. (e), effective as provided in Sec. 511(g) of this Act, which reads as follows:

"(g) Effective date.

"(1) In general. The amendments made by this section shall apply to—

"(A) individuals losing United States citizenship (within the meaning of section 877 of the Internal Revenue Code of 1986) on or after February 6, 1995, and

"(B) long-term residents of the United States with respect to whom an event described in subparagraph (A) or (B) of section 877(e)(1) of such Code occurs on or after February 6, 1995.

Estate taxes Subchapter C

"(2) Rulings requests. In no event shall the 1-year period referred to in section 877(c)(1)(B) of such Code, as amended by this section, expire before the date which is 90 days after the date of the enactment of this Act.
 "(3) Special rule.
 "(A) In general. In the case of an individual who performed an act of expatriation specified in paragraph (1), (2), (3), or (4) of section 349(a) of the Immigration and Nationality Act (8 U.S.C. 1481(a)(1)(4)) before February 6, 1995, but who did not, on or before such date, furnish to the United States Department of State a signed statement of voluntary relinquishment of United States nationality confirming the performance of such act, the amendments made by this section and section 512 shall apply to such individual except that the 10-year period described in section 877(a) of such Code shall not expire before the end of the 10-year period beginning on the date such statement is so furnished.
 "(B) Exception. Subparagraph (A) shall not apply if the individual establishes to the satisfaction of the Secretary of the Treasury that such loss of United States citizenship occurred before February 6, 1994."
Prior to amendment, subsec. (a) read as follows:
 "(a) Rate of tax. A tax computed in accordance with the table contained in section 2001 is hereby imposed on the transfer of the taxable estate, determined as provided in section 2106, of every decedent nonresident not a citizen of the United States dying after November 13, 1966, if after March 8, 1965, and within the 10-year period ending with the date of death such decedent lost United States citizenship, unless such loss did not have for one of its principal purposes the avoidance of taxes under this subtitle or subtitle A."
Prior to deletion, subsec. (d) read as follows:
 "(d) Exception for loss of citizenship for certain causes. Subsection (a) shall not apply to the transfer of the estate of a decedent whose loss of United States citizenship resulted from the application of section 301(b), 350, or 355 of the Immigration and Nationality Act, as amended (8 U.S.C. 1401 (b), 1482, or 1487)."
In 1976, P.L. 94-455, Sec. 1902(a)(6), substituted "November 13, 1966" for "the date of enactment of this section" in subsec. (a), effective for estates of decedents dying after 10/4/76.
 —P.L. 94-455, Sec. 1906(b)(13)(A), substituted "Secretary" for "Secretary or his delegate" each place it appeared in subsec. (e), effective 2/1/77.
 —P.L. 94-455, Sec. 2001(c)(1)(E)(ii), amended subsec. (c), effective for estates of decedents dying after 12/31/76.
Prior to amendment, subsec. (c) read as follows:
 "(c) Credits.
 "The tax imposed by subsection (a) shall be credited with the amounts determined in accordance with section 2102."
In 1966, P.L. 89-809, Sec. 108(f), added Code Sec. 2107, effective for estates of decedents dying after 11/13/66.

Sec. 2108. Application of pre-1967 estate tax provisions.
(a) Imposition of more burdensome tax by foreign country.
 Whenever the President finds that—
 (1) under the laws of any foreign country, considering the tax system of such foreign country, a more burdensome tax is imposed by such foreign country on the transfer of estates of decedents who were citizens of the United States and not residents of such foreign country than the tax imposed by this subchapter on the transfer of estates of decedents who were residents of such foreign country,
 (2) such foreign country, when requested by the United States to do so, has not acted to revise or reduce such tax so that it is no more burdensome than the tax imposed by this subchapter on the transfer of estates of decedents who were residents of such foreign country, and
 (3) it is in the public interest to apply pre-1967 tax provisions in accordance with this section to the transfer of estates of decedents who were residents of such foreign country,
the President shall proclaim that the tax on the transfer of the estate of every decedent who was a resident of such foreign country at the time of his death shall, in the case of decedents dying after the date of such proclamation, be determined under this subchapter without regard to amendments made to sections 2101 (relating to tax imposed), 2102 (relating to credits against tax), 2106 (relating to taxable estate), and 6018 (relating to estate tax returns) on or after November 13, 1966.
(b) Alleviation of more burdensome tax.
 Whenever the President finds that the laws of any foreign country with respect to which the President has made a proclamation under subsection (a) have been modified so that the tax on the transfer of estates of decedents who were citizens of the United States and not residents of such foreign country is no longer more burdensome than the tax imposed by this subchapter on the transfer of estates of decedents who were residents of such foreign country, he shall proclaim that the tax on the transfer of the estate of every decedent who was a resident of such foreign country at the time of his death shall, in the case of decedents dying after the date of such proclamation, be determined under this subchapter without regard to subsection (a).
(c) Notification of Congress required.
 No proclamation shall be issued by the President pursuant to this section unless, at least 30 days prior to such proclamation, he has notified the Senate and the House of Representatives of his intention to issue such proclamation.
(d) Implementation by regulations.
 The Secretary shall prescribe such regulations as may be necessary or appropriate to implement this section.

In 1976, P.L. 94-455, Sec. 1902(a)(6), substituted "November 13, 1966" for "the date of enactment of this section" in subsec. (a), effective for estates of decedents dying after 10/4/76.
 —P.L. 94-455, Sec. 1906(b)(13)(A), substituted "Secretary" for "Secretary or his delegate" in subsec. (d), effective 2/1/77.
In 1966, P.L. 89-809, Sec. 108, added Code Sec. 2108, effective for estates of decedents dying after 11/13/66.

Subchapter C.—Miscellaneous
Sec.
2201. Combat zone-related deaths of members of the Armed Forces, deaths of astronauts, and deaths of victims of certain terrorist attacks.
2202. [Repealed.]
2203. Definition of executor.
2204. Discharge of fiduciary from personal liability.
2205. Reimbursement out of estate.
2206. Liability of life insurance beneficiaries.
2207. Liability of recipient of property over which decedent had power of appointment.
2207A. Right of recovery in the case of certain marital deduction property.
2207B. Right of recovery where decedent retained interest.
2208. Certain residents of possessions considered citizens of the United States.
2209. Certain residents of possessions considered nonresidents not citizens of the United States.
2210. Termination.

In 2003, P.L. 108-121, Sec. 110(c)(2)(B), amended item 2201.
Prior to amendment, item 2201 read as follows:
 "Sec. 2201. Combat zone-related deaths of members of the Armed Forces and deaths of victims of certain terrorist attacks."
In 2002, P.L. 107-134, Sec. 103(c), amended item 2201.
Prior to amendment, item 2201 read as follows:
 "Sec. 2201. Members of the Armed Forces dying in combat zone or by reason of combat-zone-incurred wounds, etc."
In 2001, P.L. 107-16, Sec. 501(c)(1), added item 2210.
In 1989, P.L. 101-239, Sec. 7304(b)(2)(C), deleted item 2210.
Prior to deletion item 2210 read as follows:
 "2210. Liability for payment in case of transfer of employer securities to an employee stock ownership plan or a worker-owned cooperative."
In 1988, P.L. 100-647, Sec. 3031(f)(2), added item 2207B.
In 1984, P.L. 98-369, Sec. 544(b)(2), added item 2210.
In 1981, P.L. 97-34, Sec. 403(d)(4)(B), added item 2207A.
In 1976, P.L. 94-455, Sec. 1902(b)(1), deleted the item for Code Sec. 2202.
Prior to repeal, the item read as follows:
 "2202. Missionaries in foreign service."
In 1975, P.L. 93-597, Sec. 6(b)(3), amended item 2201.
Prior to amendment, item 2201 read as follows:
 "2201. Members of the Armed Forces dying during an induction period."

3,019

Subchapter C — Estate taxes

In 1970, P.L. 91-614, Sec. 102(d)(1)(A), substituted "fiduciary" for "executor" in head of item 2204.
In 1960, added item 2209.
In 1958, added item 2208.

Sec. 2201. Combat zone-related deaths of members of the Armed Forces, deaths of astronauts, and deaths of victims of certain terrorist attacks.

(a) In general.
Unless the executor elects not to have this section apply, in applying sections 2001 and 2101 to the estate of a qualified decedent, the rate schedule set forth in subsection (c) shall be deemed to be the rate schedule set forth in section 2001(c).

(b) Qualified decedent.
For purposes of this section, the term "qualified decedent" means—
  (1) any citizen or resident of the United States dying while in active service of the Armed Forces of the United States, if such decedent—
    (A) was killed in action while serving in a combat zone, as determined under section 112(c), or
    (B) died as a result of wounds, disease, or injury suffered while serving in a combat zone (as determined under section 112(c)), and while in the line of duty, by reason of a hazard to which such decedent was subjected as an incident of such service,
  (2) any specified terrorist victim (as defined in section 692(d)(4)), and
  (3) any astronaut whose death occurs in the line of duty.

(c) Rate schedule.

If the amount with respect to which the tentative tax to be computed is:	The tentative tax is:
Not over $150,000	1 percent of the amount by which such amount exceeds $100,000.
Over $150,000 but not over $200,000	$500 plus 2 percent of the excess over $150,000.
Over $200,000 but not over $300,000	$1,500 plus 3 percent of the excess over $200,000.
Over $300,000 but not over $500,000	$4,500 plus 4 percent of the excess over $300,000.
Over $500,000 but not over $700,000	$12,500 plus 5 percent of the excess over $500,000.
Over $700,000 but not over $900,000	$22,500 plus 6 percent of the excess over $700,000.
Over $900,000 but not over $1,100,000	$34,500 plus 7 percent of the excess over $900,000.
Over $1,100,000 but not over $1,600,000	$48,500 plus 8 percent of the excess over $1,100,000.
Over $1,600,000 but not over $2,100,000	$88,500 plus 9 percent of the excess over $1,600,000.
Over $2,100,000 but not over $2,600,000	$133,500 plus 10 percent of the excess over $2,100,000.
Over $2,600,000 but not over $3,100,000	$183,500 plus 11 percent of the excess over $2,600,000.
Over $3,100,000 but not over $3,600,000	$238,500 plus 12 percent of the excess over $3,100,000.
Over $3,600,000 but not over $4,100,000	$298,500 plus 13 percent of the excess over $3,600,000.
Over $4,100,000 but not over $5,100,000	$363,500 plus 14 percent of the excess over $4,100,000.
Over $5,100,000 but not over $6,100,000	$503,500 plus 15 percent of the excess over $5,100,000.
Over $6,100,000 but not over $7,100,000	$653,500 plus 16 percent of the excess over $6,100,000.
Over $7,100,000 but not over $8,100,000	$813,500 plus 17 percent of the excess over $7,100,000.
Over $8,100,000 but not over $9,100,000	$983,500 plus 18 percent of the excess over $8,100,000.
Over $9,100,000 but not over $10,100,000	$1,163,500 plus 19 percent of the excess over $9,100,000.
Over $10,100,000	$1,353,500 plus 20 percent of the excess over $10,100,000.

(d) Determination of unified credit.
In the case of an estate to which this section applies, subsection (a) shall not apply in determining the credit under section 2010.

In 2010, P.L. 111-312, Sec. 101(a)(1), substituted "December 31, 2012" for "December 31, 2010" both places it appeared in Sec. 901 of P.L. 107-16 [see below], effective as if included in the enactment of P.L. 107-16, EGTRRA, 6/7/2001.
In 2003, P.L. 108-121, Sec. 110(c)(1), deleted "and" at the end of subpara. (b)(1)(B), substituted ", and" for the period at the end of para. (b)(2), and added para. (b)(3) . . . Sec. 110(c)(2)(A), added ", deaths of astronauts," after "Forces" in the heading of Code Sec. 2201, effective for estates of decedents dying after 12/31/2002.
In 2002, P.L. 107-358, Sec. 2, added subsec. (c) in Sec. 901 of P. L. 107-16 [see below], effective 12/17/2002.
—P.L. 107-134, Sec. 103(a), amended Code Sec. 2201 . . . Sec. 103(b)(3), deleted Sec. 532(c)(9) of P. L. 107-16 [see below]. Sec. 103(d) of this Act, reads as follows:
  "(d) Effective date; Waiver of limitations.
  "(1) Effective date. The amendments made by this section shall apply to estates of decedents—
    "(A) dying on or after September 11, 2001, and
    "(B) in the case of individuals dying as a result of the April 19, 1995, terrorist attack, dying on or after April 19, 1995.
  "(2) Waiver of limitations. If refund or credit of any overpayment of tax resulting from the amendments made by this section is prevented at any time before the close of the 1-year period beginning on the date of the enactment of this Act by the operation of any law or rule of law (including res judicata), such refund or credit may nevertheless be made or allowed if claim therefor is filed before the close of such period."
Prior to amendment, Code Sec. 2201 read as follows:
  "Sec. 2201. Members of the Armed Forces dying in combat zone or by reason of combat-zone-incurred wounds, etc. The additional estate tax as defined in section 2011(d) shall not apply to the transfer of the taxable estate of a citizen or resident of the United States dying while in active service as a member of the Armed Forces of the United States, if such decedent—
  "(1) was killed in action while serving in a combat zone, as determined under section 112(c); or
  "(2) died as a result of wounds, disease, or injury suffered, while serving in a combat zone (as determined under section 112(c)), and while in the line of duty, by reason of a hazard to which he was subjected as an incident of such service."
In 2001, P.L. 107-16, Sec. 532(c)(9)(A), deleted "as defined in section 2011(d)" after "The additional estate tax" in Code Sec. 2201 . . . Sec. 532(c)(9)(B), [as repealed by Sec. 103(b)(3) of P. L. 107-134, see above] added a flush sentence at

Estate taxes — Code Sec. 2204

the end of Code Sec. 2201, effective for estates of decedents dying, and generation-skipping transfers, after 12/31/2004.

—P.L. 107-16, Sec. 901, of this Act [as amended by Sec. 2 of P.L. 107-358, and Sec. 101(a)(1) of P.L. 111-312, see above], reads as follows:

"SEC. 901. SUNSET OF PROVISIONS OF ACT.

"(a) In general. All provisions of, and amendments made by, this Act shall not apply—

"(1) to taxable, plan, or limitation years beginning after December 31, 2012, or

"(2) in the case of title V, to estates of decedents dying, gifts made, or generation skipping transfers, after December 31, 2012.

"(b) Application of certain laws. The Internal Revenue Code of 1986 and the Employee Retirement Income Security Act of 1974 shall be applied and administered to years, estates, gifts, and transfers described in subsection (a) as if the provisions and amendments described in subsection (a) had never been enacted.

"(c) Exception. Subsection (a) shall not apply to section 803 (relating to no federal income tax on restitution received by victims of the Nazi regime or their heirs or estates)."

In 1996, P.L. 104-117, Sec. 1(a)(1) and (b), of this Act, regarding treatment of certain individuals performing services in certain hazardous duty areas, effective 11/21/95, provides:

"(a) General rule. For purposes of the following provisions of the Internal Revenue Code of 1986, a qualified hazardous duty area shall be treated in the same manner as if it were a combat zone (as determined under section 112 of such Code):

* * *

"(4) Section 2201 (relating to members of the Armed Forces dying in combat zone or by reason of combat-zone-incurred wounds, etc.).

* * *

"(b) Qualified hazardous duty area. For purposes of this section, the term 'qualified hazardous duty area' means Bosnia and Herzegovina, Croatia, or Macedonia, if as of the date of the enactment [3/20/96] of this section any member of the Armed Forces of the United States is entitled to special pay under section 310 of title 37, United States Code (relating to special pay; duty subject to hostile fire or imminent danger) for services performed in such country. Such term includes any such country only during the period such entitlement is in effect. Solely for purposes of applying section 7508 of the Internal Revenue Code of 1986, in the case of an individual who is performing services as part of Operation Joint Endeavor outside the United States while deployed away from such individual's permanent duty station, the term 'qualified hazardous duty area' includes, during the period for which such entitlement is in effect, any area in which such services are performed."

In 1975, P.L. 93-597, Sec. 6(b), amended the heading of Code Sec. 2201, and deleted "during an induction period (as defined in section 112(c)(5))," after "resident of the United States dying", effective 7/1/73.

Prior to amendment, the heading to Code Sec. 2201 read as follows:

"Sec. 2201. Members of the Armed Forces dying during an induction period."

Sec. 2202. Repealed.

In 1976, P.L. 94-455, Sec. 1902(a)(8), repealed Code Sec. 2202, effective for estates of decedents dying after 10/4/76.

Prior to repeal, Code Sec. 2202 read as follows:

"SEC. 2202. MISSIONARIES IN FOREIGN SERVICE.

"Missionaries duly commissioned and serving under boards of foreign missions of the various religious denominations in the United States, dying while in the foreign missionary service of such boards, shall not, by reason merely of their intention to permanently remain in such foreign service, be deemed nonresidents of the United States, but shall be presumed to be residents of the State, or the District of Columbia wherein they respectively resided at the time of their commission and their departure for such foreign service."

In 1960, P.L. 86-624, Sec. 18(b), substituted "the State or the District of Columbia" for "the State, the District of Columbia, or Hawaii." effective 8/21/59.

In 1959, P.L. 86-70, Sec. 22(a), deleted "Alaska," before "or Hawaii" effective 1/3/59.

Sec. 2203. Definition of executor.

The term "executor" wherever it is used in this title in connection with the estate tax imposed by this chapter means the executor or administrator of the decedent, or, if there is no executor or administrator appointed, qualified, and acting within the United States, then any person in actual or constructive possession of any property of the decedent.

Sec. 2204. Discharge of fiduciary from personal liability.

(a) General rule.

If the executor makes written application to the Secretary for determination of the amount of the tax and discharge from personal liability therefor, the Secretary (as soon as possible, and in any event within 9 months after the making of such application, or, if the application is made before the return is filed, then within 9 months after the return is filed, but not after the expiration of the period prescribed for the assessment of the tax in section 6501) shall notify the executor of the amount of the tax. The executor, on payment of the amount of which he is notified (other than any amount the time for payment of which is extended under section 6161, 6163, or 6166), and on furnishing any bond which may be required for any amount for which the time for payment is extended, shall be discharged from personal liability for any deficiency in tax thereafter found to be due and shall be entitled to a receipt or writing showing such discharge.

(b) Fiduciary other than the executor.

If a fiduciary (not including a fiduciary in respect of the estate of a nonresident decedent) other than the executor makes written application to the Secretary for determination of the amount of any estate tax for which the fiduciary may be personally liable, and for discharge from personal liability therefor, the Secretary upon the discharge of the executor from personal liability under subsection (a), or upon the expiration of 6 months after the making of such application by the fiduciary, if later, shall notify the fiduciary (1) of the amount of such tax for which it has been determined the fiduciary is liable, or (2) that it has been determined that the fiduciary is not liable for any such tax. Such application shall be accompanied by a copy of the instrument, if any, under which such fiduciary is acting, a description of the property held by the fiduciary, and such other information for purposes of carrying out the provisions of this section as the Secretary may require by regulations. On payment of the amount of such tax for which it has been determined the fiduciary is liable (other than any amount the time for payment of which has been extended under section 6161, 6163, or 6166), and on furnishing any bond which may be required for any amount for which the time for payment has been extended, or on receipt by him of notification of a determination that he is not liable for any such tax, the fiduciary shall be discharged from personal liability for any deficiency in such tax thereafter found to be due and shall be entitled to a receipt or writing evidencing such discharge.

(c) Special lien under section 6324A.

For purposes of the second sentence of subsection (a) and the last sentence of subsection (b), an agreement which meets the requirements of section 6324A (relating to special lien for estate tax deferred under section 6166) shall be treated as the furnishing of bond with respect to the amount for which the time for payment has been extended under section 6166.

(d) Good faith reliance of gift tax returns.

If the executor in good faith relies on gift tax returns furnished under section 6103(e)(3) for determining the decedent's adjusted taxable gifts, the executor shall be discharged from personal liability with respect to any deficiency of the tax imposed by this chapter which is attributable to adjusted taxable gifts which—

(1) are made more than 3 years before the date of the decedent's death, and

(2) are not shown on such returns.

In 1981, P.L. 97-34, Sec. 422(e)(1), deleted "or 6166A" after "section 6166" each place it appeared in subsec. (c) . . . Sec. 422(e)(3), substituted "or 6166" for "6166 or 6166A" in subsecs. (a) and (b), effective for estates of decedents dying after 12/31/81.

In 1978, P.L. 95-600, Sec. 702(p)(1), added subsec. (d), effective for estates of decedents dying after 12/31/76.

—P.L. 95-600, Sec. 703(j)(12), amended the effective date for changes made by Sec. 1902(a)(9) of P. L. 94-455 to apply to estates of decedents dying after 12/31/70.

In 1976, P.L. 94-455, Sec. 1902(a)(9), substituted "has been" for "has not been" in the last sentence of subsec. (b), effective for estates of decedents dying after 10/4/76.

3,021

Code Sec. 2204 — **Estate taxes**

In 1976, P.L. 94-455, Sec. 1906(b)(13)(A), substituted "Secretary" for "Secretary or his delegate" each place it appeared in Code Sec. 2204, effective 2/1/77.
— P.L. 94-455, Sec. 2004(d)(2), added subsec. (c), effective for estates of decedent dying after 12/31/76.
— P.L. 94-455, Sec. 2004(f)(4), substituted "has been extended under" for "has not been extended under" in subsec. (b), effective for estates of decedents dying after 12/31/76.
— P.L. 94-455, Sec. 2004(f)(6), substituted "6166 or 6166A" for "or 6166" in subsecs. (a) and (b), effective for estates of decedents dying after 12/31/76.
In 1970, P.L. 91-614, Sec. 101(d)(1), amended Code Sec. 2204, effective for decedents dying after 12/31/70.
Prior to amendment, Code Sec. 2204 read as follows:
"SEC. 2204. DISCHARGE OF EXECUTOR FROM PERSONAL LIABILITY.
"If the executor makes written application to the Secretary or his delegate for determination of the amount of the tax and discharge from personal liability therefor, the Secretary or his delegate (as soon as possible, and in any event within 1 year after the making of such application, or, if the application is made before the return is filed, then within 1 year after the return is filed, but not after the expiration of the period prescribed for the assessment of the tax in section 6501) shall notify the executor of the amount of the tax. The executor, on payment of the amount of which he is notified, shall be discharged from personal liability for any deficiency in tax thereafter found to be due and shall be entitled to a receipt or writing showing such discharge."
— P.L. 91-614, Sec. 101(f), substituted "9 months" for "1 year" in subsec. (a), effective for estates of decedents dying after 12/31/73.

Sec. 2205. Reimbursement out of estate.

If the tax or any part thereof is paid by, or collected out of, that part of the estate passing to or in the possession of any person other than the executor in his capacity as such, such person shall be entitled to reimbursement out of any part of the estate still undistributed or by a just and equitable contribution by the persons whose interest in the estate of the decedent would have been reduced if the tax had been paid before the distribution of the estate or whose interest is subject to equal or prior liability for the payment of taxes, debts, or other charges against the estate, it being the purpose and intent of this chapter that so far as is practicable and unless otherwise directed by the will of the decedent the tax shall be paid out of the estate before its distribution.

Sec. 2206. Liability of life insurance beneficiaries.

Unless the decedent directs otherwise in his will, if any part of the gross estate on which tax has been paid consists of proceeds of policies of insurance on the life of the decedent receivable by a beneficiary other than the executor, the executor shall be entitled to recover from such beneficiary such portion of the total tax paid as the proceeds of such policies bear to the taxable estate. If there is more than one such beneficiary, the executor shall be entitled to recover from such beneficiaries in the same ratio. In the case of such proceeds receivable by the surviving spouse of the decedent for which a deduction is allowed under section 2056 (relating to marital deduction), this section shall not apply to such proceeds except as to the amount thereof in excess of the aggregate amount of the marital deductions allowed under such section.

In 1976, P.L. 94-455, Sec. 2001(c)(1)(H), substituted "the taxable estate" for "the sum of the taxable estate and the amount of the exemption allowed in computing the taxable estate, determined under section 2051" in the first sentence of Code Sec. 2206, effective for estates of decedents dying after 12/31/76.

Sec. 2207. Liability of recipient of property over which decedent had power of appointment.

Unless the decedent directs otherwise in his will, if any part of the gross estate on which the tax has been paid consists of the value of property included in the gross estate under section 2041, the executor shall be entitled to recover from the person receiving such property by reason of the exercise, nonexercise, or release of a power of appointment such portion of the total tax paid as the value of such property bears to the taxable estate. If there is more than one such person, the executor shall be entitled to recover from such persons in the same ratio. In the case of such property received by the surviving spouse of the decedent for which a deduction is allowed under section 2056 (relating to marital deduction), this section shall not apply to such property except as to the value thereof reduced by an amount equal to the excess of the aggregate amount of the marital deductions allowed under section 2056 over the amount of proceeds of insurance upon the life of the decedent receivable by the surviving spouse for which proceeds a marital deduction is allowed under such section.

In 1976, P.L. 94-455, Sec. 2001(c)(1)(I), substituted "the taxable estate" for "the sum of the taxable estate and the amount of the exemption allowed in computing the taxable estate, determined under section 2052, or section 2106(a), as the case may be" in the first sentence of Code Sec. 2207, effective for estates of decedents dying after 12/31/76.

Sec. 2207A. Right of recovery in the case of certain marital deduction property.

(a) Recovery with respect to estate tax.

(1) In general. If any part of the gross estate consists of property the value of which is includible in the gross estate by reason of section 2044 (relating to certain property for which marital deduction was previously allowed), the decedent's estate shall be entitled to recover from the person receiving the property the amount by which—

(A) the total tax under this chapter which has been paid, exceeds

(B) the total tax under this chapter which would have been payable if the value of such property had not been included in the gross estate.

(2) Decedent may otherwise direct. Paragraph (1) shall not apply with respect to any property to the extent that the decedent in his will (or a revocable trust) specifically indicates an intent to waive any right of recovery under this subchapter with respect to such property.

(b) Recovery with respect to gift tax.

If for any calendar year tax is paid under chapter 12 with respect to any person by reason of property treated as transferred by such person under section 2519, such person shall be entitled to recover from the person receiving the property the amount by which—

(1) the total tax for such year under chapter 12, exceeds

(2) the total tax which would have been payable under such chapter for such year if the value of such property had not been taken into account for purposes of chapter 12.

(c) More than one recipient of property.

For purposes of this section, if there is more than one person receiving the property, the right of recovery shall be against each such person.

(d) Taxes and interest.

In the case of penalties and interest attributable to additional taxes described in subsections (a) and (b), rules similar to subsections (a), (b), and (c) shall apply.

In 1997, P.L. 105-34, Sec. 1302(a), amended para. (a)(2), effective for estates of decedents dying after 8/5/97.
Prior to amendment, para. (a)(2) read as follows:
"(2) Decedent may otherwise direct by will. Paragraph (1) shall not apply if the decedent otherwise directs by will."
In 1983, P.L. 97-448, Sec. 114(a)(10), changed Sec. 403(e)(2) of P. L. 97-34, the effective date for amendments made by Sec. 403(d)(4)(A) of P. L. 97-34, to effective for gifts made after 12/31/81 (to the extent related to the tax imposed by chapter 12 of the '54 Internal Revenue Code), from effective for estates of decedents dying after 12/31/81 [see below].
In 1981, P.L. 97-34, Sec. 403(d)(4)(A), added Code Sec. 2207A, effective for gifts made after 12/31/81 (to the extent related to the tax imposed by chapter 12 of the '54 Code).

Estate taxes

Sec. 2207B. Right of recovery where decedent retained interest.

(a) Estate tax.

(1) In general. If any part of the gross estate on which tax has been paid consists of the value of property included in the gross estate by reason of section 2036 (relating to transfers with retained life estate), the decedent's estate shall be entitled to recover from the person receiving the property the amount which bears the same ratio to the total tax under this chapter which has been paid as—

(A) the value of such property, bears to

(B) the taxable estate.

(2) Decedent may otherwise direct. Paragraph (1) shall not apply with respect to any property to the extent that the decedent in his will (or a revocable trust) specifically indicates an intent to waive any right of recovery under this subchapter with respect to such property.

(b) More than one recipient.

For purposes of this section, if there is more than 1 person receiving the property, the right of recovery shall be against each such person.

(c) Penalties and interest.

In the case of penalties and interest attributable to the additional taxes described in subsection (a), rules similar to the rules of subsections (a) and (b) shall apply.

(d) No right of recovery against charitable remainder trusts.

No person shall be entitled to recover any amount by reason of this section from a trust to which section 664 applies (determined without regard to this section).

In **1997**, P.L. 105-34, Sec. 1302(b), amended para. (a)(2), effective for estates of decedents dying after 8/5/97.
Prior to amendment, para. (a)(2) read as follows:
"(2) Decedent may otherwise direct by will. Paragraph (1) shall not apply if the decedent otherwise directs in a provision of his will (or a revocable trust) specifically referring to this section."
In **1990**, P.L. 101-508, Sec. 11601(b)(1)(A), deleted subsec. (b), and redesignated subsecs. (c), (d) and (e) as subsecs. (b), (c) and (d) . . . Sec. 11601(b)(1)(B), substituted "subsection (a)" for "subsections (a) and (b)" in subsec. (c) [as redesignated] . . . Sec. 11601(b)(1)(C), substituted "subsections (a) and (b)" for "subsections (a), (b), and (c)" in subsec. (c) [as redesignated], effective for property transferred after 12/17/87.
Prior to deletion, subsec. (b) read as follows:
"(b) Gift tax.
If for any calendar year tax is paid under chapter 12 with respect to any person by reason of property treated as transferred by such person under section 2036(c)(4), such person shall be entitled to recover from the original transferee (as defined in section 2036(c)(4)(C)(ii)) the amount which bears the same ratio to the total tax for such year under chapter 12 as—
"(1) the value of such property for purposes of chapter 12, bears to
"(2) the total amount of the taxable gifts for such year."
In **1988**, P.L. 100-647, Sec. 3031(f)(1), added Code Sec. 2207B, effective for estates of decedents dying after 12/31/87, but only in the case of property transferred after 12/17/87. Sec. 3031(h)(3) of this Act provides:
"(3) Subsection (f) [3031(f)].— If an amount is included in the gross estate of a decedent under section 2036 of the 1986 Code other than solely by reason of section 2036(c) of the 1986 Code, the amendments made by subsection (f) [3031(f)] shall apply to such amount only with respect to property transferred after the date of the enactment of this Act [11/10/88]."

Sec. 2208. Certain residents of possessions considered citizens of the United States.

A decedent who was a citizen of the United States and a resident of a possession thereof at the time of his death shall, for purposes of the tax imposed by this chapter, be considered a "citizen" of the United States within the meaning of that term wherever used in this title unless he acquired his United States citizenship solely by reason of (1) his being a citizen of such possession of the United States, or (2) his birth or residence within such possession of the United States.

In **1958**, P.L. 85-866, Sec. 102(a), added Code Sec. 2208, effective for estates of decedents dying after 9/2/58.

Sec. 2209. Certain residents of possessions considered nonresidents not citizens of the United States.

A decedent who was a citizen of the United States and a resident of a possession thereof at the time of his death shall, for purposes of the tax imposed by this chapter, be considered a "nonresident not a citizen of the United States" within the meaning of that term wherever used in this title, but only if such person acquired his United States citizenship solely by reason of (1) his being a citizen of such possession of the United States, or (2) his birth or residence within such possession of the United States.

In **1960**, P.L. 86-779, Sec. 4(b), added Code Sec. 2209, effective for estates of decedents dying after 9/14/60.

- *Caution:* Code Sec. 2210, following, was added by Sec. 501(a), P.L. 107-16, EGTRRA. As provided in Sec. 301(a), P.L. 111-312, this amendment will apply as if never enacted, effective for estates of decedents dying, and transfers made, after 12/31/2009.

Sec. 2210. Termination.

(a) In general.

Except as provided in subsection (b), this chapter shall not apply to the estates of decedents dying after December 31, 2009.

(b) Certain distributions from qualified domestic trusts.

In applying section 2056A with respect to the surviving spouse of a decedent dying before January 1, 2010—

(1) section 2056A(b)(1)(A) shall not apply to distributions made after December 31, 2020, and

(2) section 2056A(b)(1)(B) shall not apply after December 31, 2009.

In **2010**, P.L. 111-312, Sec. 101(a)(1), substituted "December 31, 2012" for "December 31, 2010" both places it appeared in Sec. 901, P.L. 107-16 [see below], effective as if included in the enactment of P.L. 107-16, EGTRRA, 6/7/2001.
— P.L. 111-312, Sec. 301(a), provides that Code Sec. 2210 [as added by Sec. 501(a), P.L. 107-16, see below], will read as if such amendment had never been enacted, effective for estates of decedents dying, and transfers made, after 12/31/2009.
Sec. 301(a) of P.L. 111-312, provides:
"(a) In general. Each provision of law amended by subtitle A or E of title V of the Economic Growth and Tax Relief Reconciliation Act of 2001 [P.L. 107-16, see below] is amended to read as such provision would read if such subtitle had never been enacted."
Prior to the enactment of Sec. 301(a) of P.L. 111-312, Code Sec. 2210 read as follows:
"Sec. 2210. Termination.
"(a) In general. Except as provided in subsection (b) , this chapter shall not apply to the estates of decedents dying after December 31, 2009.
"(b) Certain distributions from qualified domestic trusts. In applying section 2056A with respect to the surviving spouse of a decedent dying before January 1, 2010—
"(1) section 2056A(b)(1)(A) shall not apply to distributions made after December 31, 2020, and
"(2) section 2056A(b)(1)(B) shall not apply after December 31, 2009."
— P.L. 111-312, Sec. 301(c), of this Act, provides:
"(c) Special election with respect to estates of decedents dying in 2010. Notwithstanding subsection (a), in the case of an estate of a decedent dying after December 31, 2009, and before January 1, 2011, the executor (within the meaning of section 2203 of the Internal Revenue Code of 1986) may elect to apply such Code as though the amendments made by subsection (a) do not apply with respect to chapter 11 of such Code and with respect to property acquired or passing from such decedent (within the meaning of section 1014(b) of such Code). Such election shall be made at such time and in such manner as the Secretary of the Treasury or the Secretary's delegate shall provide. Such an election once made shall be revocable only with the consent of the Secretary of the Treasury or the Secre-

tary's delegate. For purposes of section 2652(a)(1) of such Code, the determination of whether any property is subject to the tax imposed by such chapter 11 shall be made without regard to any election made under this subsection."

—P.L. 111-312, Sec. 301(d), of this Act, provides:

"(d) Extension of time for performing certain acts.

"(1) Estate tax. In the case of the estate of a decedent dying after December 31, 2009, and before the date of the enactment of this Act, the due date for—

"(A) filing any return under section 6018 of the Internal Revenue Code of 1986 (including any election required to be made on such a return) as such section is in effect after the date of the enactment of this Act without regard to any election under subsection (c),

"(B) making any payment of tax under chapter 11 of such Code, and

"(C) making any disclaimer described in section 2518(b) of such Code of an interest in property passing by reason of the death of such decedent, shall not be earlier than the date which is 9 months after the date of the enactment of this Act.

"(2) Generation-skipping tax. In the case of any generation-skipping transfer made after December 31, 2009, and before the date of the enactment of this Act, the due date for filing any return under section 2662 of the Internal Revenue Code of 1986 (including any election required to be made on such a return) shall not be earlier than the date which is 9 months after the date of the enactment of this Act."

In 2002, P.L. 107-358, Sec. 2, added subsec. (c) in Sec. 901 of P. L. 107-16 [see below], effective 12/17/2002.

In 2001, P.L. 107-16, Sec. 501(a), added Code Sec. 2210, effective for estates of decedents dying, and generation-skipping transfers, after 12/31/2009.

—P.L. 107-16, Sec. 901, of this Act [as amended by Sec. 2 of P.L. 107-358, and Sec. 101(a)(1), P.L. 111-312, see above], reads as follows:

"SEC. 901. SUNSET OF PROVISIONS OF ACT.

"(a) In general. All provisions of, and amendments made by, this Act shall not apply—

"(1) to taxable, plan, or limitation years beginning after December 31, 2012, or

"(2) in the case of title V, to estates of decedents dying, gifts made, or generation skipping transfers, after December 31, 2012.

"(b) Application of certain laws. The Internal Revenue Code of 1986 and the Employee Retirement Income Security Act of 1974 shall be applied and administered to years, estates, gifts, and transfers described in subsection (a) as if the provisions and amendments described in subsection (a) had never been enacted.

"(c) Exception. Subsection (a) shall not apply to section 803 (relating to no federal income tax on restitution received by victims of the Nazi regime or their heirs or estates)."

Sec. 2210. Repealed.

In 1989, P.L. 101-239, Sec. 7304(b)(1), repealed Code Sec. 2210, for estates of decedents dying after 7/12/89.

Prior to repeal, Code Sec. 2210 read as follows:

"SEC. 2210. LIABILITY FOR PAYMENT IN CASE OF TRANSFER OF EMPLOYER SECURITIES TO AN EMPLOYEE STOCK OWNERSHIP PLAN OR A WORKER-OWNED COOPERATIVE.

"(a) In general.

"If

"(1) employer securities

"(A) are acquired from the decedent by an employee stock ownership plan or by an eligible worker-owned cooperative from any decedent,

"(B) pass from the decedent to such a plan or cooperative, or

"(C) are transferred by the executor to such a plan or cooperative,

"(2) the executor of the estate of the decedent may (without regard to this section) make an election under section 6166 with respect to that portion of the tax imposed by section 2001 which is attributable to employer securities, and

"(3) the executor elects the application of this section and files the agreements described in subsection (e) before the due date (including extensions) for filing the return of tax imposed by section 2001,

then the executor is relieved of liability for payment of that portion of the tax imposed by section 2001 which such employee stock ownership plan or cooperative is required to pay under subsection (b).

"(b) Payment of tax by employee stock ownership plan or cooperative.

"(1) In general. An employee stock ownership plan or eligible worker-owned cooperative

"(A) which has acquired employer securities from the decedent, or to which such securities have passed from the decedent, or been transferred by the executor, and

"(B) with respect to which an agreement described in subsection (e)(1) is in effect,

shall pay that portion of the tax imposed by section 2001 with respect to the taxable estate of the decedent which is described in paragraph (2).

"(2) Amount of tax to be paid. The portion of the tax imposed by section 2001 with respect to the taxable estate of the decedent that is referred to in paragraph (1) is equal to the lesser of

"(A) the value of the employer securities described in subsection (a)(1) which is included in the gross estate of the decedent, or

"(B) the tax imposed by section 2001 with respect to such taxable estate reduced by the sum of the credits allowable against such tax.

"(c) Installment payments.

"(1) In general. If

"(A) the executor of the estate of the decedent (without regard to this section) elects to have the provisions of section 6166 (relating to extensions of time for payment of estate tax where estate consists largely of interest in closely held business) apply to payment of that portion of the tax imposed by section 2001 with respect to such estate which is attributable to employer securities, and

"(B) the plan administrator or the cooperative provides to the executor the agreement described in subsection (e)(1),

then the plan administrator or any authorized officer of the cooperative may elect, before the due date (including extensions) for filing the return of such tax, to pay all or part of the tax described in subsection (b)(2) in installments under the provisions of section 6166.

"(2) Interest on installments. In determining the 4-percent portion for purposes of section 6601(j)

"(A) the portion of the tax imposed by section 2001 with respect to an estate for which the executor is liable, and

"(B) the portion of such tax for which an employee stock ownership plan or an eligible worker-owned cooperative is liable.

shall be aggregated.

"(3) Special rules for application of section 6166(g). In the case of any transfer of employer securities to an employee stock ownership plan or eligible worker-owned cooperative to which this section applies—

"(A) Transfer does not trigger acceleration. Such transfer shall not be treated as a disposition or withdrawal to which section 6166(g) applies.

"(B) Separate application to estate and plan interests. Section 6166(g) shall be applied separately to the interests held after such transfer by the estate and such plan or cooperative.

"(C) Required distribution not taken into account. In the case of any distribution of such securities by such plan which is described in section 4978(d)(1)

"(i) such distribution shall not be treated as disposition or withdrawal for purposes of section 6166(g), and

"(ii) such securities shall not be taken into account in applying section 6166(g) to any subsequent disposition or withdrawal.

"(d) Guarantee of payments.

"Any employer

"(1) whose employees are covered by an employee stock ownership plan, and

"(2) who has entered into an agreement described in subsection (e)(2) which is in effect,

and any eligible worker-owned cooperative shall guarantee (in such manner as the Secretary may prescribe) the payment of any amount such plan or cooperative, respectively, is required to pay under subsection (b).

"(e) Agreements.

"The agreements described in this subsection are as follows:

"(1) A written agreement signed by the plan administrator, or by any authorized officer of the eligible worker-owned cooperative, consenting to the application of subsection (b) to such plan or cooperative.

"(2) A written agreement signed by the employer whose employees are covered by the plan described in subsection (b) consenting to the application of subsection (d).

"(f) Exemption from tax on prohibited transactions.

"The assumption described in this section by an employee stock ownership plan of any portion of the liability for the tax imposed by section 2001 shall be treated as a loan described in section 4975(d)(3).

"(g) Definitions.

"For purposes of this section

"(1) Employer securities. The term 'employer securities' has the meaning given such term by section 409(1).

"(2) Employee stock ownership plan. The term 'employee stock ownership plan' has the meaning given such term by section 4975(e)(7).

"(3) Eligible worker-owned cooperative. The term 'eligible worker-owned cooperative' has the meaning given to such term by section 1042(c)(2).

"(4) Plan administrator. The term 'plan administrator' has the meaning given such term by section 414(g).

"(5) Tax imposed by section 2001. The term 'tax imposed by section 2001' includes any interest, penalty, addition to tax, or additional amount relating to any tax imposed by section 2001."

In 1986, P.L. 99-514, Sec. 1854(d)(1)(A), deleted "and" from the end of para. (a)(1), redesignated para. (a)(2) as para. (a)(3), and added new para. (a)(2), effective for the estates of decedents dying after 9/27/85.

—P.L. 99-514, Sec. 1854(d)(2), added para. (c)(3) . . . Sec. 1854(d)(3), added para. (g)(5) . . . Sec. 1854(d)(4), added "any authorized officer of" before "the cooperative" in the matter following subpara. (c)(1)(B) . . . Sec. 1854(d)(5), added "and any eligible worker-owned cooperative" before "shall guarantee", and "or cooperative, respectively," after "such plan", and deleted ", including any interest payable under section 6601 which is attributable to such amount" in the matter following para. (d)(2) . . . Sec. 1854(d)(6), substituted "1042(c)(2)" for "1041(b)(2)" in para. (g)(3), effective for estates of decedents which are required to file returns on a date (including any extensions) after 7/18/84.

—P.L. 99-514, Sec. 1899A(37), substituted "may prescribe" for "may prescibe" in the matter following para. (d)(2), effective 10/22/86.

In 1984, P.L. 98-369, Sec. 544(a), added Code Sec. 2210, effective for estates of decedents which are required to file returns on a date (including any extensions) after 7/18/84.

CHAPTER 12.—GIFT TAX

Subchapter

A. Determination of tax liability.

B. Transfers.

C. Deductions.

Gift taxes   Code Sec. 2501

Subchapter A.—Determination of Tax Liability
Sec.
2501. Imposition of tax.
2502. Rate of tax.
2503. Taxable gifts.
2504. Taxable gifts for preceding calendar periods.
2505. Unified credit against gift tax.

In **1981**, P.L. 97-34, Sec. 442(a)(4)(E), substituted "preceding calendar periods" for "preceding years and quarters," in item 2504.
In **1976**, P.L. 94-455, Sec. 2001(c)(2)(B)(i), added the item for Code Sec. 2505.
In **1970**, P.L. 71-614, Sec. 102(a)(4), added "and quarters" to the end of item 2504.

Sec. 2501. Imposition of tax.
(a) Taxable transfers.

(1) **General rule.** A tax, computed as provided in section 2502, is hereby imposed for each calendar year on the transfer of property by gift during such calendar year by any individual, resident or nonresident.

(2) **Transfers of intangible property.** Except as provided in paragraph (3), paragraph (1) shall not apply to the transfer of intangible property by a nonresident not a citizen of the United States.

(3) **Exception.**

(A) Certain individuals. Paragraph (2) shall not apply in the case of a donor to whom section 877(b) applies for the taxable year which includes the date of the transfer.

(B) Credit for foreign gift taxes. The tax imposed by this section solely by reason of this paragraph shall be credited with the amount of any gift tax actually paid to any foreign country in respect of any gift which is taxable under this section solely by reason of this paragraph.

(4) **Transfers to political organizations.** Paragraph (1) shall not apply to the transfer of money or other property to a political organization (within the meaning of section 527(e)(1)) for the use of such organization.

(5) **Transfers of certain stock.**

(A) In general. In the case of a transfer of stock in a foreign corporation described in subparagraph (B) by a donor to whom section 877(b) applies for the taxable year which includes the date of the transfer—

(i) section 2511(a) shall be applied without regard to whether such stock is situated within the United States, and

(ii) the value of such stock for purposes of this chapter shall be its U.S.-asset value determined under subparagraph (C).

(B) Foreign corporation described. A foreign corporation is described in this subparagraph with respect to a donor if—

(i) the donor owned (within the meaning of section 958(a)) at the time of such transfer 10 percent or more of the total combined voting power of all classes of stock entitled to vote of the foreign corporation, and

(ii) such donor owned (within the meaning of section 958(a)), or is considered to have owned (by applying the ownership rules of section 958(b)), at the time of such transfer, more than 50 percent of—

(I) the total combined voting power of all classes of stock entitled to vote of such corporation, or

(II) the total value of the stock of such corporation.

(C) U.S.-asset value. For purposes of subparagraph (A), the U.S.-asset value of stock shall be the amount which bears the same ratio to the fair market value of such stock at the time of transfer as—

(i) the fair market value (at such time) of the assets owned by such foreign corporation and situated in the United States, bears to

(ii) the total fair market value (at such time) of all assets owned by such foreign corporation.

(b) Certain residents of possessions considered citizens of the United States.

A donor who is a citizen of the United States and a resident of a possession thereof shall, for purposes of the tax imposed by this chapter, be considered a "citizen" of the United States within the meaning of that term wherever used in this title unless he acquired his United States citizenship solely by reason of (1) his being a citizen of such possession of the United States, or (2) his birth or residence within such possession of the United States.

(c) Certain residents of possessions considered nonresidents not citizens of the United States.

A donor who is a citizen of the United States and a resident of a possession thereof shall, for purposes of the tax imposed by this chapter, be considered a "nonresident not a citizen of the United States" within the meaning of that term wherever used in this title, but only if such donor acquired his United States citizenship solely by reason of (1) his being a citizen of such possession of the United States, or (2) his birth or residence within such possession of the United States.

(d) Cross references.

(1) For increase in basis of property acquired by gift for gift tax paid, see section 1015(d).

(2) For exclusion of transfers of property outside the United States by a nonresident who is not a citizen of the United States, see section 2511(a).

In **2004**, P.L. 108-357, Sec. 804(d)(1), deleted paras. (a)(3) and (4), added para. (a)(3), and redesignated para. (a)(5) as para. (a)(4)... Sec. 804(d)(2), added para. (a)(5), effective for individuals who expatriate after 6/3/2004.
Prior to deletion, para. (a)(3) read as follows:

"(3) Exception.

"(A) Certain individuals. Paragraph (2) shall not apply in the case of a donor who, within the 10-year period ending with the date of transfer, lost United States citizenship unless such loss did not have for 1 of its principal purposes the avoidance of taxes under this subtitle or subtitle A.

"(B) Certain individuals treated as having tax avoidance purpose. For purposes of subparagraph (A), an individual shall be treated as having a principal purpose to avoid such taxes if such individual is so treated under section 877(a)(2).

"(C) Exception for certain individuals. Subparagraph (B) shall not apply to a donor meeting the requirements of section 877(c)(1).

"(D) Credit for foreign gift taxes. The tax imposed by this section solely by reason of this paragraph shall be credited with the amount of any gift tax actually paid to any foreign country in respect of any gift which is taxable under this section solely by reason of this paragraph.

"(E) Cross reference. For comparable treatment of long-term lawful permanent residents who ceased to be taxed as residents, see section 877(e)."
Prior to deletion, para. (a)(4) read as follows:

"(4) Burden of proof. If the Secretary establishes that it is reasonable to believe that an individual's loss of United States citizenship would, but for paragraph (3), result in a substantial reduction for the calendar year in the taxes on the transfer of property by gift, the burden of proving that such loss of citizenship did not have for one of its principal purposes the avoidance of taxes under this subtitle or subtitle A shall be on such individual."

In **1997**, P.L. 105-34, Sec. 1602(g)(5), substituted "donor" for "decedent" in subpara. (a)(3)(C), effective as provided in Sec. 511(g) of P. L. 104-191, reproduced below.

In **1996**, P.L. 104-191, Sec. 511(e)(2)(A), amended para. (a)(3)... Sec. 511(f)(2)(B), added subpara. (a)(3)(E) [as amended], effective as provided in Sec. 511(g) of this Act, which reads as follows:

"(g) Effective date.

"(1) In general. The amendments made by this section shall apply to—

"(A) individuals losing United States citizenship (within the meaning of section 877 of the Internal Revenue Code of 1986) on or after February 6, 1995, and

"(B) long-term residents of the United States with respect to whom an event described in subparagraph (A) or (B) of section 877(e)(1) of such Code occurs on or after February 6, 1995.

3,025

Code Sec. 2501 — Gift taxes

"(2) Ruling requests. In no event shall the 1-year period referred to in section 877(c)(1)(B) of such Code, as amended by this section, expire before the date which is 90 days after the date of the enactment of this Act.

"(3) Special rule.

"(A) In general. In the case of an individual who performed an act of expatriation specified in paragraph (1), (2), (3), or (4) of section 349(a) of the Immigration and Nationality Act (8 U.S.C. 1481(a)(1)-(4)) before February 6, 1995, but who did not, on or before such date, furnish to the United States Department of State a signed statement of voluntary relinquishment of United States nationality confirming the performance of such act, the amendments made by this section and section 512 shall apply to such individual except that the 10-year period described in section 877(a) of such Code shall not expire before the end of the 10-year period beginning on the date such statement is so furnished.

"(B) Exception. Subparagraph (A) shall not apply if the individual establishes to the satisfaction of the Secretary of the Treasury that such loss of United States citizenship occurred before February 6, 1994."

Prior to amendment, para. (a)(3) read as follows:

"(3) Exceptions. Paragraph (2) shall not apply in the case of a donor who at any time after March 8, 1965, and within the 10-year period ending with the date of transfer lost United States citizenship unless —

"(A) such donor's loss of United States citizenship resulted from the application of section 301(b), 350, or 355 of the Immigration and Nationality Act, as amended (8 U.S.C. 1401(b), 1482, or 1487), or

"(B) such loss did not have for one of its principal purposes the avoidance of taxes under this subtitle or subtitle A."

In 1990, P.L. 101-508, Sec. 11601(b)(2), deleted para. (d)(3), effective for the case of property transferred after 12/17/87.

Prior to deletion, para. (d)(3) read as follows:

"(3) For treatment of certain transfers related to estate tax valuation freezes as gifts to which this chapter applies, see section 2036(c)(4)."

In 1988, P.L. 100-647, Sec. 3031(a)(2), added para (d)(3), effective as provided in Sec. 3031(h)(2) of this Act, which reads as follows:

"(h) Effective date.

"(2) Subsection (a). — The amendments made by subsection (a) shall apply in cases where the transfer referred to in section 2036(c)(1)(B) of the 1986 Code is on or after June 21, 1988."

In 1981, P.L. 97-34, Sec. 442(a)(1), substituted "calendar year" for "calendar quarter" each place it appeared in subsec. (a), effective for gifts made after 12/31/81.

In 1978, P.L. 95-600, Sec. 703(j)(12), amended the effective date for changes made by Sec. 1902(a)(10) of P. L. 94-455, from effective for estates of decedents dying after 10/4/76, to effective for gifts made after 12/31/76, see below.

In 1976, P.L. 94-455, Sec. 1902(a)(10), amended para. (a)(1), effective [as amended by Sec. 703(j)(12) of P. L. 95-600, see above] for gifts made after 12/31/76.

Prior to amendment, para. (a)(1) read as follows:

"(1) General rule. For the first calendar quarter of calendar year 1971 and each calendar quarter thereafter a tax, computed as provided in section 2502, is hereby imposed on the transfer of property by gift during such calendar year by an individual, resident or nonresident."

—P.L. 94-455, Sec. 1906(b)(13)(A), substituted "Secretary" for "Secretary or his delegate" each place it appeared in Code Sec. 2501, effective 2/1/77.

In 1975, P.L. 93-625, Sec. 14(a), added para. (a)(5), effective for transfers made after 5/7/74.

In 1970, P.L. 91-614, Sec. 102(a)(1), amended para. (a)(1) and substituted "calendar quarter" for "calendar year" in para. (a)(4), effective for gifts made after 12/31/70.

Prior to amendment, para. (a)(1) read as follows:

"(1) General rule. For the calendar year 1955 and each calendar year thereafter a tax, computed as provided in section 2502, is hereby imposed on the transfer of property by gift during such calendar year by any individual, resident or nonresident."

In 1966, P.L. 89-809, Sec. 109, amended subsec. (a), effective for the calendar yr. 1967 and all calendar years thereafter.

Prior to amendment, subsec. (a) read as follows:

"(a) General rule.

"For the calendar year 1955 and each calendar year thereafter a tax, computed as provided in section 2502, is hereby imposed on the transfer of property by gift during such calendar year by any individual, resident or nonresident, except transfers of intangible property by a nonresident not a citizen of the United States who was not engaged in business in the United States during such calendar year."

In 1960, P.L. 86-779, Sec. 4(d)(2), deleted "who is" preceding "not a citizen" in subsec. (a) . . . Sec. 4(d)(1), redesignated subsec. (c) as subsec. (d) and added subsec. (c), effective for gifts made after 9/14/60.

In 1958, P.L. 85-866, Sec. 102, redesignated subsec. (b) as (c), and added new subsec. (b), effective for gifts made after 9/2/58.

—P.L. 85-866, Sec. 43(b), made the catchline read in the plural, designated existing provisions as para. (b)(2) and added para. (b)(1) for '54 Code yrs.

Sec. 2502. Rate of tax.

• **Caution:** Code Sec. 2502(a), following, was amended by Sec. 511(d) of P.L. 107-16, the Economic Growth and Tax Relief Reconciliation Act of 2001 (EGTRRA). These provisions generally sunset for tax years beginning after 12/31/2012. For specific sunset provisions, see Sec. 302(b)(2) of P.L. 111-312 and Sec. 901, P.L. 107-16 (as amended) reproduced in the history of this Code Sec.

(a) Computation of tax.

(1) In general. The tax imposed by section 2501 for each calendar year shall be an amount equal to the excess of—

(A) a tentative tax, computed under paragraph (2), on the aggregate sum of the taxable gifts for such calendar year and for each of the preceding calendar periods, over

(B) a tentative tax, computed under paragraph (2), on the aggregate sum of the taxable gifts for each of the preceding calendar periods.

(2) Rate schedule.

If the amount with respect to which the tentative tax to be computed is:	The tentative tax is:
Not over $10,000	18% of such amount
Over $10,000 but not over $20,000	$1,800, plus 20% of the excess over $10,000
Over $20,000 but not over $40,000	$3,800, plus 22% of the excess over $20,000
Over $40,000 but not over $60,000	$8,200, plus 24% of the excess over $40,000
Over $60,000 but not over $80,000	$13,000, plus 26% of the excess over $60,000
Over $80,000 but not over $100,000	$18,200, plus 28% of the excess over $80,000
Over $100,000 but not over $150,000	$23,800, plus 30% of the excess over $100,000
Over $150,000 but not over $250,000	$38,800, plus 32% of the excess over $150,000
Over $250,000 but not over $500,000	$70,800, plus 34% of the excess over $250,000
Over $500,000	$155,800, plus 35% of the excess over $500,000

• **Caution:** Code Sec. 2502(a), following, reflects the sunset of the amendments made by Sec. 511(d) of P.L. 107-16, the Economic Growth and Tax Relief Reconciliation Act of 2001 (EGTRRA). For specific sunset provisions, see Sec. 302(b)(2) of P.L. 111-312 and Sec. 901 of P.L. 107-16 (as amended) reproduced in the history of this Code Sec.

(a) Computation of tax.

The tax imposed by section 2501 for each calendar year shall be an amount equal to the excess of—

(1) a tentative tax, computed under section 2001(c), on the aggregate sum of the taxable gifts for such calendar year and for each of the preceding calendar periods, over

(2) a tentative tax, computed under such section, on the aggregate sum of the taxable gifts for each of the preceding calendar periods.

(b) Preceding calendar period.

Whenever used in this title in connection with the gift tax imposed by this chapter, the term "preceding calendar period" means—

(1) calendar years 1932 and 1970 and all calendar years intervening between calendar year 1932 and calendar year 1970,

(2) the first calendar quarter of calendar year 1971 and all calendar quarters intervening between such calendar quarter and the first calendar quarter of calendar year 1982, and

(3) all calendar years after 1981 and before the calendar year for which the tax is being computed.

For purposes of paragraph (1), the term "calendar year 1932" includes only that portion of such year after June 6, 1932.

(c) Tax to be paid by donor.

The tax imposed by section 2501 shall be paid by the donor.

In 2010, P.L. 111-312, Sec. 101(a)(1), substituted "December 31, 2012" for "December 31, 2010" both places it appeared in Sec. 901 of P.L. 107-16 [see below], effective as if included in the enactment of P.L. 107-16, EGTRRA, 6/7/2001.

—P.L. 111-312, Sec. 302(b)(2), of this Act [relating to the amendment by Sec. 511(d) of P.L. 107-16, see below], provides:

"(2) Modification of gift tax rate. On and after January 1, 2011, subsection (a) of section 2502 is amended to read as such subsection would read if section 511(d) of the Economic Growth and Tax Relief Reconciliation Act of 2001 [P.L. 107-16, see below] had never been enacted."

—P.L. 111-312, Sec. 304, of this Act, provides:

SEC. 304. APPLICATION OF EGTRRA SUNSET TO THIS TITLE.

"Section 901 of the Economic Growth and Tax Relief Reconciliation Act of 2001 shall apply to the amendments made by this title."

In 2002, P.L. 107-358, Sec. 2, added subsec. (c) in Sec. 901 of P. L. 107-16 [see below], effective 12/17/2002.

In 2001, P.L. 107-16, Sec. 511(d), amended subsec. (a), effective for gifts made after 12/31/2009.

Prior to amendment, subsec. (a) read as follows:

"(a) Computation of tax. The tax imposed by section 2501 for each calendar year shall be an amount equal to the excess of—

"(1) a tentative tax, computed under section 2001(c), on the aggregate sum of the taxable gifts for such calendar year and for each of the preceding calendar periods, over

"(2) a tentative tax, computed under such section, on the aggregate sum of the taxable gifts for each of the preceding calendar periods."

—P.L. 107-16, Sec. 901, of this Act [as amended by Sec. 2 of P.L. 107-358, and Sec. 101(a)(1) of P.L. 111-312, see above], reads as follows:

"SEC. 901. SUNSET OF PROVISIONS OF ACT.

"(a) In general. All provisions of, and amendments made by, this Act shall not apply—

"(1) to taxable, plan, or limitation years beginning after December 31, 2012, or

"(2) in the case of title V, to estates of decedents dying, gifts made, or generation skipping transfers, after December 31, 2012.

"(b) Application of certain laws. The Internal Revenue Code of 1986 and the Employee Retirement Income Security Act of 1974 shall be applied and administered to years, estates, gifts, and transfers described in subsection (a) as if the provisions and amendments described in subsection (a) had never been enacted.

"(c) Exception. Subsection (a) shall not apply to section 803 (relating to no federal income tax on restitution received by victims of the Nazi regime or their heirs or estates)."

In 1987, P.L. 100-203, Sec. 10401(b)(2)(B)(i), substituted "under section 2001(c)" for "in accordance with the rate schedule set forth in section 2001(c)" in para. (a)(1) . . . Sec. 10401(b)(2)(B)(ii), substituted "under such section" for "in accordance with such rate schedule" in para. (a)(2), effective in the case of decedents dying, and gifts made, after 12/31/87.

In 1981, P.L. 97-34, Sec. 442(a)(2), amended Code Sec. 2502, effective for gifts made after 12/31/81.

Prior to amendment, Code Sec. 2502 read as follows:

"SEC. 2502. RATE OF TAX.

"(a) Computation of tax.

"The tax imposed by section 2501 for each calendar quarter shall be an amount equal to the excess of—

"(1) a tentative tax, computed in accordance with the rate schedule set forth in section 2001(c), on the aggregate sum of the taxable gifts for such calendar quarter and for each of the preceding calendar years and calendar quarters, over

"(2) a tentative tax, computed in accordance with such rate schedule, on the aggregate sum of the taxable gifts for each of the preceding calendar years and calendar quarters.

"(b) Calendar quarter.

"Wherever used in this title in connection with the gift tax imposed by this chapter, the term 'calendar quarter' includes only the first calendar quarter of the calendar year 1971 and succeeding calendar quarters.

"(c) Preceding calendar years and quarters.

"Wherever used in this title in connection with the gift tax imposed by this chapter—

"(1) The term 'preceding calendar year' means calendar years 1932 and 1970 and all calendar years intervening between calendar year 1932 and calendar year 1970. The term 'calendar year 1932' includes only the portion of such year after June 6, 1932.

"(2) The term 'preceding calendar quarters' means the first calendar quarter of calendar year 1971 and all calendar quarters intervening between such calendar quarter and the calendar quarter for which the tax is being computed.

"(d) Tax to be paid by donor.

"The tax imposed by section 2501 shall be paid by the donor."

In 1976, P.L. 94-455, Sec. 2001(b)(1), amended subsec. (a), effective for gifts made after 12/31/76.

Prior to amendment, subsec. (a) read as follows:

"(a) Computation of tax.

"The tax imposed by section 2501 for each calendar quarter shall be an amount equal to the excess of—

"(1) a tax, computed in accordance with the rate schedule set forth in this subsection, on the aggregate sum of the taxable gifts for such calendar quarter and for each of the preceding calendar years and calendar quarters, over

"(2) a tax, computed in accordance with such rate schedule, on the aggregate sum of the taxable gifts for each of the preceding calendar years and calendar quarters.

RATE SCHEDULE

If the taxable gifts are:	The tax shall be:
Not over $5,000	2 ¼% of the taxable gifts.
Over $5,000 but not over $10,000.	$112.50, plus 5 ¼% of excess over $5,000.
Over $10,000 but not over $20,000.	$375, plus 8 ¼% of excess over $10,000.
Over $20,000 but not over $30,000.	$1,200, plus 10 ½% of excess over $20,000.
Over $30,000 but not over $40,000.	$2,250, plus 13 ½% of excess over $30,000.
Over $40,000 but not over $50,000.	$3,600, plus 16 ½% of excess over $40,000.
Over $50,000 but not over $60,000.	$5,250, plus 18 ¾% of excess over $50,000.
Over $60,000 but not over $100,000.	$7,125, plus 21% of excess over $60,000.
Over $100,000 but not over $250,000.	$15,525, plus 22 ½% of excess over $100,000.
Over $250,000 but not over $500,000.	$49,275, plus 24% of excess over $250,000.
Over $500,000 but not over $750,000.	$109,275, plus 26 ¼% of excess over $500,000.
Over $750,000 but not over $1,000,000.	$174,900, plus 27 ¾% of excess over $750,000.
Over $1,000,000 but not over $1,250,000.	$244,275, plus 29 ¼% of excess over $1,000,000.
Over $1,250,000 but not over $1,500,000.	$317,400, plus 31 ½% of excess over $1,250,000.
Over $1,500,000 but not over $2,000,000.	$396,150, plus 33 ¾% of excess over $1,500,000.
Over $2,000,000 but not over $2,500,000.	$564,900, plus 36 ¾% of excess over $2,000,000.
Over $2,500,000 but not over $3,000,000.	$748,650, plus 39 ¾% of excess over $2,500,000.
Over $3,000,000 but not over $3,500,000.	$947,400, plus 42% of excess over $3,000,000.
Over $3,500,000 but not over $4,000,000.	$1,157,400, plus 44 ¼% of excess over $3,500,000.
Over $4,000,000 but not over $5,000,000.	$1,378,650, plus 47 ¼% of excess over $4,000,000.
Over $5,000,000 but not over $6,000,000.	$1,851,150, plus 50 ¼% of excess over $5,000,000.
Over $6,000,000 but not over $7,000,000.	$2,353,650, plus 52 ½% of excess over $6,000,000.
Over $7,000,000 but not over $8,000,000.	$2,878,650, plus 54 ¾% of excess over $7,000,000.
Over $8,000,000 but not over $10,000,000.	$3,426,150, plus 57% of excess over $8,000,000.
Over $10,000,000	$4,566,150, plus 57 ¾% of excess over $10,000,000."

In 1970, P.L. 91-614, Sec. 102(a)(2)(A), amended so much of subsec. (a) as preceded the tax rate schedule . . . Sec. 102(a)(2)(B), amended subsecs. (b) and (c), effective for gifts made after 12/31/70.

Prior to amendment, so much of subsec. as preceded the tax rate schedule read as follows:

"The tax imposed by section 2501 for each calendar year shall be an amount equal to the excess of—

"(1) a tax, computed in accordance with the rate schedule set forth in this subsection, on the aggregate sum of the taxable gifts for such calendar year and for each of the preceding calendar year, over

"(2) a tax, computed in accordance with such rate schedule, on the aggregate sum of the taxable gifts for each of the preceding calendar years."

Prior to amendment, subsecs (b) and (c) read as follows:

"(b) Calendar year.

"The term 'calendar year' includes only the calendar year 1932 and succeeding calendar years, and, in the case of the calendar year 1932, includes only the portion of such year after June 6, 1932.

"(c) Preceding calendar years.

"The term 'preceding calendar years' means the calendar year 1932 and all calendar years intervening between the calendar year 1932 and the calendar year for which the tax is being computed."

Sec. 2503. Taxable gifts.
(a) General definition.
The term "taxable gifts" means the total amount of gifts made during the calendar year, less the deductions provided in subchapter C (section 2522 and following).

(b) Exclusions from gifts.
(1) In general. In the case of gifts (other than gifts of future interests in property) made to any person by the donor during the calendar year, the first $10,000 of such gifts to such person shall not, for purposes of subsection (a), be included in the total amount of gifts made during such year. Where there has been a transfer to any person of a present interest in property, the possibility that such interest may be diminished by the exercise of a power shall be disregarded in applying this subsection, if no part of such interest will at any time pass to any other person.

(2) Inflation adjustment. In the case of gifts made in a calendar year after 1998, the $10,000 amount contained in paragraph (1) shall be increased by an amount equal to—
(A) $10,000, multiplied by
(B) the cost-of-living adjustment determined under section 1(f)(3) for such calendar year by substituting "calendar year 1997" for "calendar year 1992" in subparagraph (B) thereof.

If any amount as adjusted under the preceding sentence is not a multiple of $1,000, such amount shall be rounded to the next lowest multiple of $1,000.

(c) Transfer for the benefit of minor.
No part of a gift to an individual who has not attained the age of 21 years on the date of such transfer shall be considered a gift of a future interest in property for purposes of subsection (b) if the property and the income therefrom—
(1) may be expended by, or for the benefit of, the donee before his attaining the age of 21 years, and
(2) will to the extent not so expended—
(A) pass to the donee on his attaining the age of 21 years, and
(B) in the event the donee dies before attaining the age of 21 years, be payable to the estate of the donee or as he may appoint under a general power of appointment as defined in section 2514(c).

(d) Repealed.

(e) Exclusion for certain transfers for educational expenses or medical expenses.
(1) In general. Any qualified transfer shall not be treated as a transfer of property by gift for purposes of this chapter.
(2) Qualified transfer. For purposes of this subsection, the term "qualified transfer" means any amount paid on behalf of an individual—
(A) as tuition to an educational organization described in section 170(b)(1)(A)(ii) for the education or training of such individual, or
(B) to any person who provides medical care (as defined in section 213(d)) with respect to such individual as payment for such medical care.

(f) Waiver of certain pension rights.
If any individual waives, before the death of a participant, any survivor benefit, or right to such benefit, under section 401(a)(11) or 417, such waiver shall not be treated as a transfer of property by gift for purposes of this chapter.

(g) Treatment of certain loans of artworks.
(1) In general. For purposes of this subtitle, any loan of a qualified work of art shall not be treated as a transfer (and the value of such qualified work of art shall be determined as if such loan had not been made) if—
(A) such loan is to an organization described in section 501(c)(3) and exempt from tax under section 501(c) (other than a private foundation), and
(B) the use of such work by such organization is related to the purpose or function constituting the basis for its exemption under section 501.
(2) Definitions. For purposes of this section—
(A) Qualified work of art. The term "qualified work of art" means any archaeological, historic, or creative tangible personal property.
(B) Private foundation. The term "private foundation" has the meaning given such term by section 509, except that such term shall not include any private operating foundation (as defined in section 4942(j)(3)).

In 1997, P.L. 105-34, Sec. 501(c)(1), redesignated the text of subsec. (b) as para. (b)(1), and added the heading of para. (b)(1) . . . Sec. 501(c)(3), added para. (b)(2), effective for estates of decedents dying, and gifts made, after 12/31/97.

In 1989, P.L. 101-239, Sec. 7811(m)(1), redesignated subsec. (f) as added by Sec. 1018(s)(2)(A) of P. L. 100-647, as subsec. (g), effective for loans after 7/31/69.

In 1988, P.L. 100-647, Sec. 1018(s)(2)(A), added new subsec. (f) [sic (g)], effective for loans after 7/31/69.

—P.L. 100-647, Sec. 1018(u)(52), substituted "section 213(d)" for "section 213(e)" in subpara. (e)(2)(B), effective for tax. yrs. begin. after 12/31/83.

In 1986, P.L. 99-514, Sec. 1898(h)(1)(B), added subsec. (f), effective for plan years begin. after 12/31/84. For special rules and transitional rules, see Sec. 303 of P. L. 98-397, reproduced in the note following Code Sec. 401.

In 1983, P.L. 97-448, Sec. 103(c)(11), added para. (i)(5) to Sec. 311 of P. L. 97-34, the effective date for changes made by Sec. 311(h)(5) of P. L. 97-34, see below.

In 1981, P.L. 97-34, Sec. 311(h)(5), deleted subsec. (d), effective for transfers after 12/31/81. Sec. 311(i)(2) of this Act provides:

"(2) Transitional rule. For purposes of the Internal Revenue Code of 1954, any amount allowed as a deduction under section 220 of such Code (as in effect before its repeal by this Act) shall be treated as if it were allowed by section 219 of such Code."

Prior to deletion, subsec. (d) read as follows:

"(d) Individual retirement accounts, etc., for spouse. For purposes of subsection (b), any payment made by an individual for the benefit of his spouse—
"(1) to an individual retirement account described in section 408(a),
"(2) for an individual retirement annuity described in section 408(b), or
"(3) for a retirement bond described in section 409, shall not be considered a gift of a future interest in property to the extent that such payment is allowable as a deduction under section 220."

—P.L. 97-34, Sec. 441(a), substituted "$10,000" for "$3,000" in subsec. (b), effective for transfers after 12/31/81. Sec. 441(c)(2) of this Act provides:

"(2) Transitional rule. If—
"(A) an instrument executed before the date which is 30 days after the date of the enactment of this Act provides for a power of appointment which may be exercised during any period after December 31, 1981,
"(B) such power of appointment is expressly defined in terms of, or by reference to, the amount of the gift tax exclusion under section 2503(b) of the Internal Revenue Code of 1954 (or the corresponding provision of prior law),
"(C) the instrument described in subparagraph (A) has not been amended on or after the date which is 30 days after the date of the enactment of this Act, and
"(D) the State has not enacted a statute applicable to such gift under which such power of appointment is to be construed as being defined in terms of, or by reference to, the amount of the exclusion under such section 2503(b) after its amendment by subsection (a),
then the amendment made by subsection [441](a) shall not apply to such gift."

—P.L. 97-34, Sec. 441(b), added subsec. (e), effective for transfers after 12/31/81.

—P.L. 97-34, Sec. 442(a)(3)(A), amended subsec. (a) . . . Sec. 442(a)(3)(B), amended the first sentence of subsec. (b), effective for gifts made after 12/31/81. Prior to amendment subsec. (a) read as follows:

"(a) General definition. The term 'taxable gifts' means, in the case of gifts made after December 31, 1970, the total amount of gifts made during the calendar quarter, less the deductions provided in subchapter C (sec. 2521 and following). In the case of gifts made before January 1, 1971, such term means the total amount of gifts made during the calendar year, less the deductions provided in subchapter C."

Prior to amendment, the first sentence of subsec. (b) read as follows:

"In computing taxable gifts for the calendar quarter, in the case of gifts (other than gifts of future interests in property) made to any person by the donor during the calendar year 1971 and subsequent calendar years, $3,000 of such gifts to

Gift taxes   Code Sec. 2505(a)

such person less the aggregate of the amounts of such gifts to such person during all preceding quarters of the calendar year shall not, for purposes of subsection (a), be included in the total amount of gifts made during such quarter."

In 1978, P.L. 95-600, Sec. 702(j)(2), added subsec. (d), effective for transfers made after 12/31/76.

In 1970, P.L. 91-614, Sec. 102(a)(3), amended subsec. (a) and (b), effective for gifts made after 12/31/70.

Prior to amendment, subsec. (a) and (b) read as follows:

"(a) General definition. The term 'taxable gifts' means the total amount of gifts made during the calendar year, less the deductions provided in subchapter C (sec. 2521 and following).

"(b) Exclusions from gifts. In the case of gifts (other than gifts of future interests in property) made to any person by the donor during the calendar year 1955 and subsequent calendar years, the first $3,000 of such gifts to such persons shall not, for purposes of subsection (a), be included in the total amount of gifts made during such year. Where there has been a transfer to any person of a present interest in property, the possibility that such interest may be diminished by the exercise of a power shall be disregarded in applying this subsection, if no part of such interest will at any time pass to any other person."

Sec. 2504. Taxable gifts for preceding calendar periods.
(a) In general.

In computing taxable gifts for preceding calendar periods for purposes of computing the tax for any calendar year—

(1) there shall be treated as gifts such transfers as were considered to be gifts under the gift tax laws applicable to the calendar period in which the transfers were made,

(2) there shall be allowed such deductions as were provided for under such laws, and

(3) the specific exemption in the amount (if any) allowable under section 2521 (as in effect before its repeal by the Tax Reform Act of 1976) shall be applied in all computations in respect of preceding calendar periods ending before January 1, 1977, for purposes of computing the tax for any calendar year.

(b) Exclusions from gifts for preceding calendar periods.

In the case of gifts made to any person by the donor during preceding calendar periods, the amount excluded, if any, by the provisions of gift tax laws applicable to the periods in which the gifts were made shall not, for purposes of subsection (a), be included in the total amount of the gifts made during such preceding calendar periods.

(c) Valuation of gifts.

If the time has expired under section 6501 within which a tax may be assessed under this chapter 12 (or under corresponding provisions of prior laws) on—

(1) the transfer of property by gift made during a preceding calendar period (as defined in section 2502(b)); or

(2) an increase in taxable gifts required under section 2701(d),

the value thereof shall, for purposes of computing the tax under this chapter, be the value as finally determined (within the meaning of section 2001(f)(2)) for purposes of this chapter.

(d) Net gifts.

The term "net gifts" as used in corresponding provisions of prior laws shall be read as "taxable gifts" for purposes of this chapter.

In 1998, P.L. 105-206, Sec. 6007(e)(1), substituted ", (c), and (d)" for "and (c)" in Sec. 506(e)(1) of P. L. 105-34, the effective date for amendments made by Sec. 506(a), (c), and (d) [see below].

—P.L. 105-206, Sec. 6007(e)(2)(B), [sic (C)] amended subsec. (c), effective for gifts made after 8/5/97.

Prior to amendment, subsec. (c) read as follows:

"(c) Valuation of certain gifts for preceding calendar periods. If the time has expired within which a tax may be assessed under this chapter or under corresponding provisions of prior laws on the transfer of property by gift made during a preceding calendar period, as defined in section 2502(b), the value of such gift made in such preceding calendar period shall, for purposes of computing the tax under this chapter for any calendar year, be the value of such gift which was used in computing the tax for the last preceding calendar period for which a tax under this chapter or under corresponding provisions of prior laws was assessed or paid."

In 1997, P.L. 105-34, Sec. 506(d), deleted ", and if a tax under this chapter or under corresponding provisions of prior laws has been assessed or paid for such preceding calendar period" after "section 2502(b)" in subsec. (c), effective [as amended by Sec. 6007(e)(1) of 105-206, see above] for gifts made after 8/5/97.

In 1981, P.L. 97-34, Sec. 442(a)(4)(A), amended subsec. (a) . . . Sec. 442(a)(4)(B), substituted "preceding calendar periods" for "preceding calendar years and calendar quarters", substituted "the periods" for "the years and calendar quarters", substituted "such preceding calendar periods" for "such years and calendar quarters" in subsec. (b), and substituted "preceding calendar periods" for "preceding years and quarters" in the heading of subsec. (b) . . . Sec. 442(a)(4)(C), substituted "preceding calendar period" for "preceding calendar year or calendar quarter" each place it appeared, in subsec. (c), substituted "under this chapter for any calendar year" for "under this chapter for any calendar quarter", substituted "section 2502(b)" for "section 2502(c)" in subsec. (c) and, substituted "preceding calendar periods" for "preceding calendar years and quarters" in the heading of subsec. (c) . . . Sec. 442(a)(4)(D), substituted "preceding calendar periods" for "preceding years and quarters" in the heading of Code Sec. 2504, effective for gifts made after 12/31/81.

Prior to amendment subsec. (a) read as follows:

"(a) In general. In computing taxable gifts for preceding calendar years or calendar quarters for the purpose of computing the tax for any calendar quarter, there shall be treated as gifts such transfers as were considered to be gifts under the gift tax laws applicable to the years or calendar quarters in which the transfers were made and there shall be allowed such deductions as were produced for under such laws; except that the specific exemption in the amount, if any, allowable under section 2521 (as in effect before its repeal by the Tax Reform Act of 1976) shall be applied in all computations in respect of calendar years or calendar quarters ending before January 1, 1977, for purposes of computing the tax for any calendar quarter."

In 1976, P.L. 94-455, Sec. 2001(c)(2)(A), amended subsec. (a), effective for gifts made after 12/31/76.

Prior to amendment, subsec. (a) read as follows:

"(a) In general. In computing taxable gifts for preceding calendar years or calendar quarters for the purpose of computing the tax for any calendar quarter, there shall be treated as gifts such transfers as were considered to be gifts under the gift tax laws applicable to the years or calendar quarters in which the transfers were made and there shall be allowed such deductions as were provided for under such laws; except that the specific exemption in the amount, if any, allowable under section 2521 shall be applied in all computations in respect of previous calendar years or calendar quarters for the purpose of computing the tax for any calendar year or calendar quarter."

In 1970, P.L. 91-614, Sec. 102(a)(4), amended Code Sec. 2504, effective for gifts made after 12/31/70.

Prior to amendment, Code Sec. 2504 read as follows:

SEC. 2504. TAXABLE GIFTS FOR PRECEDING YEARS.

"(a) In general. In computing taxable gifts for the calendar year 1954 and preceding calendar years for the purpose of computing the tax for the calendar year 1955 or any calendar year thereafter, there shall be treated as gifts such transfers as were considered to be gifts under the gift tax laws applicable to the years in which the transfers were made and there shall be allowed such deductions as were provided for under such laws, except that specific exemption in the amount, if any, allowable under section 2521 shall be applied in all computations in respect of the calendar year 1954 and previous calendar years for the purpose of computing the tax for the calendar year 1955 or any calendar year thereafter.

"(b) Exclusions from gifts for preceding years. In the case of gifts made to any person by the donor during the calendar year 1954 and preceding calendar years, the amount excluded, if any, by the provisions of gift tax laws applicable to the years in which the gifts were made shall not, for purposes of subsection (a), be included in the total amount of the gifts made during such year.

"(c) Valuation of certain gifts for preceding calendar years. If the time has expired within which a tax may be assessed under this chapter or under corresponding provisions of prior laws, on the transfer of property by gift made during a preceding calendar year, as defined in section 2502(c), and if a tax under this chapter or under corresponding provisions of prior laws has been assessed or paid for such preceding calendar year, the value of such gift made in such preceding calendar year shall, for purposes of computing the tax under this chapter for the calendar year 1955 and subsequent calendar years, be the value of such gift which was used in computing the tax for the last preceding calendar year, for which a tax under this chapter or under corresponding provisions of prior laws was assessed or paid.

"(d) Net gifts. For years before the calendar year 1955, the term 'net gifts' as used in corresponding provisions of prior laws shall be read as 'taxable gifts' for purposes of this chapter."

Sec. 2505. Unified credit against gift tax.
(a) General rule.

In the case of a citizen or resident of the United States, there shall be allowed as a credit against the tax imposed by section 2501 for each calendar year an amount equal to—

> • **Caution:** Code Sec. 2505(a)(1), following, reflects amendments made by Sec. 521(b)(2), P.L. 107-16, EGTRRA. These provisions will sunset as provided in Sec. 301(b), P.L. 111-312, and will apply as if never enacted,

3,029

Code Sec. 2505(a) — Gift taxes

effective on and after 1/1/2011. For Code Sec. 2505(a)(1), as it will read on and after 1/1/2011, see below.

(1) the amount of the tentative tax which would be determined under the rate schedule set forth in section 2502(a)(2) if the amount with respect to which such tentative tax is to be computed were $1,000,000, reduced by the applicable credit amount

- **Caution:** Code Sec. 2505(a)(1), following, is effective on and after 1/1/2011, and reflects the sunset of the amendments made by Sec. 521(b)(2), P.L. 107-16, EGTRRA, and includes amendments made by Sec. 302(b)(1)(A), (d)(2) and Sec. 303(b)(1) of P.L.111-312. For details of those amendments, effective date, and sunset provisions, see the history notes for this Code Sec.

(1) the applicable credit amount in effect under section 2010(c) which would apply if the donor died as of the end of the calendar year, reduced by

(2) the sum of the amounts allowable as a credit to the individual under this section for all preceding calendar periods.

For purposes of applying paragraph (2) for any calendar year, the rates of tax in effect under section 2502(a)(2) for such calendar year shall, in lieu of the rates of tax in effect for preceding calendar periods, be used in determining the amounts allowable as a credit under this section for all preceding calendar periods.

(b) Adjustment to credit for certain gifts made before 1977.

The amount allowable under subsection (a) shall be reduced by an amount equal to 20 percent of the aggregate amount allowed as a specific exemption under section 2521 (as in effect before its repeal by the Tax Reform Act of 1976) with respect to gifts made by the individual after September 8, 1976.

(c) Limitation based on amount of tax.

The amount of the credit allowed under subsection (a) for any calendar year shall not exceed the amount of the tax imposed by section 2501 for such calendar year.

In 2010, P.L. 111-312, Sec. 101(a)(1), substituted "December 31, 2012" for "December 31, 2010" both places it appeared in Sec. 901, P.L. 107-16 [see below], effective as if included in the enactment of P.L. 107-16, EGTRRA, 6/7/2001.

—P.L. 111-312, Sec. 301(b), amended Code Sec. 2505(a)(1) [as amended by Sec. 521(b)(2) of P.L. 107-16, EGTRRA, 6/7/2001] to read as if such provision had never been enacted.

Sec. 301(b), P.L. 111-312, reads as follows:

"(b) Conforming amendment. On and after January 1, 2011, paragraph (1) of section 2505(a) of the Internal Revenue Code of 1986 is amended to read as such paragraph would read if section 521(b)(2) of the Economic Growth and Tax Relief Reconciliation Act of 2001 [P.L. 107-16, see below] had never been enacted."

Prior to repeal of amendment by P.L. 111-312, Sec. 301(b) [see above], para. (a)(1) read as follows:

"(1) the amount of the tentative tax which would be determined under the rate schedule set forth in section 2502(a)(2) if the amount with respect to which such tentative tax is to be computed were $1,000,000, reduced by"

—P.L. 111-312, Sec. 302(b)(1)(A), deleted "(determined as if the applicable exclusion amount were $1,000,000)" after "calendar year" in para. (a)(1) [subsequently amended by Sec. 303(b)(1) of this Act, see below], effective for gifts made after 12/31/2010.

—P.L. 111-312, Sec. 302(d)(2), added "For purposes of applying paragraph (2) for any calendar year, the rates of tax in effect under section 2502(a)(2) for such calendar year shall, in lieu of the rates of tax in effect for preceding calendar periods, be used in determining the amounts allowable as a credit under this section for all preceding calendar periods." at the end of subsec. (a), effective for estates of decedents dying, generation-skipping transfers, and gifts made, after 12/31/2009.

—P.L. 111-312, Sec. 303(b)(1), amended para. (a)(1) [as amended by Sec. 302(b)(1)(A) of this Act, see above], effective for estates of decedents dying and gifts made after 12/31/2010.

Prior to amendment, para. (a)(1) read as follows:

"(1) the applicable credit amount in effect under section 2010(c) for such calendar year, reduced by"

—P.L. 111-312, Sec. 304, of this Act, provides:

"Sec. 304. Application of EGTRRA sunset to this title.

"Section 901 of the Economic Growth and Tax Relief Reconciliation Act of 2001 shall apply to the amendments made by this title."

In 2002, P.L. 107-358, Sec. 2, added subsec. (c) in Sec. 901 of P. L. 107-16 [see below], effective 12/17/2002.

In 2001, P.L. 107-16, Sec. 521(b)(1), added "(determined as if the applicable exclusion amount were $1,000,000)" after "calendar year" in para. (a)(1), effective for estates of decedents dying, and gifts made, after 12/31/2001.

—P.L. 107-16, Sec. 521(b)(2), amended para. (a)(1) [as amended by Sec. 521(b)(1) of this Act, see below], effective for gifts made after 12/31/2009.

Prior to amendment para. (a)(1) [as amended by Sec. 521(b)(1) of this Act, see above] read as follows:

"(1) the applicable credit amount in effect under section 2010(c) for such calendar year (determined as if the applicable exclusion amount were $1,000,000), reduced by"

—P.L. 107-16, Sec. 901, of this Act [as amended by Sec. 2 of P.L. 107-358, and Sec. 101(a)(1), P.L. 111-312, see above], reads as follows:

"Sec. 901. Sunset of provisions of Act.

"(a) In general. All provisions of, and amendments made by, this Act shall not apply—

"(1) to taxable, plan, or limitation years beginning after December 31, 2012, or

"(2) in the case of title V, to estates of decedents dying, gifts made, or generation skipping transfers, after December 31, 2012.

"(b) Application of certain laws. The Internal Revenue Code of 1986 and the Employee Retirement Income Security Act of 1974 shall be applied and administered to years, estates, gifts, and transfers described in subsection (a) as if the provisions and amendments described in subsection (a) had never been enacted.

"(c) Exception. Subsection (a) shall not apply to section 803 (relating to no federal income tax on restitution received by victims of the Nazi regime or their heirs or estates)."

In 1997, P.L. 105-34, Sec. 501(a)(2), substituted "the applicable credit amount in effect under section 2010(c) for such calendar year" for "$192,800" in para. (a)(1), effective for estates of decedents dying, and gifts made, after 12/31/97.

In 1990, P.L. 101-508, Sec. 11801(a)(40), deleted subsec. (b) ... Sec. 11801(c)(19)(B), redesignated subsecs. (c) and (d) as subsecs. (b) and (c), effective 11/5/90, except as provided in Sec. 11821(b) of this Act, which reads as follows:

"(b) Savings provision.

"If—

"(1) any provision amended or repealed by this part applied to—

"(A) any transaction occurring before the date of

"(B) any property acquired before such date of enactment [11/5/90], or

"(C) any item of income, loss, deduction, or credit taken into account before such date of enactment, [11/5/90], and

"(2) the treatment of such transaction, property, or item under such provision would (without regard to the amendments made by this part) affect liability for tax for periods ending after such date of enactment [11/5/90],

nothing in the amendments made by this part shall be construed to affect the treatment of such transaction, property, or item for purposes of determining liability for tax for periods ending after such date of enactment [11/5/90]."

Prior to deletion, subsec. (b) read as follows:

"(b) Phase-in of credit.

In the case of gifts made in:	Subsection (a)(1) shall be applied by substituting for "$192,800" the following amount:
1982	$ 62,800
1983	79,300
1984	96,300
1985	121,800
1986	155,800."

In 1981, P.L. 97-34, Sec. 401(b)(1), substituted "$192,800" for "$47,000" in subsec. (a) ... Sec. 401(b)(2), amended subsec. (b)

Prior to amendment, subsec. (b) read as follows:

"(b) Phase-in of $47,000 credit.

"In the case of gifts made	Subsection (a)(1) shall be applied by substituting for '$47,000' the following amount:
"After December 31, 1976, and before July 1, 1977	$ 6,000
"After June 30, 1977, and before January 1, 1978	$ 30,000
"After December 31, 1977, and before January 1, 1979	$ 34,000

Gift taxes — Code Sec. 2513(a)(1)

"After December 31, 1978, and before January 1, 1980	$ 38,000
"After December 31, 1978, and before January 1, 1980	$ 38,000
"After December 31, 1979, and before January 1, 1981	$42,500"

—P.L. 97-34, Sec. 442(a)(5)(A), substituted "each calendar year" for "each calendar quarter", and substituted "preceding calendar periods" for "preceding calendar quarters" in subsec. (a)... P.L. 442(a)(5)(B), substituted "calendar year" for "calendar quarter" each place it appeared in subsec. (d), effective for gifts made after 12/31/81.

In **1976**, P.L. 94-455, Sec. 2001(b)(2), added Code Sec. 2505, effective for gifts made after 12/31/76.

Subchapter B.—Transfers

Sec.
2511. Transfers in general.
2512. Valuation of gifts.
2513. Gift by husband or wife to third party.
2514. Powers of appointment.
2515. Treatment of generation-skipping transfer tax.
2516. Certain property settlements.
2517. Repealed.
2518. Disclaimers.
2519. Dispositions of certain life estates.

In **1986**, P.L. 99-514, Sec. 1432(d)(2), added item 2515... Sec. 1852(e)(2)(B), deleted item 2517.
Prior to deletion, item 2517 read as follows:
"2517. Certain annuities under qualified plans."
In **1981**, P.L. 97-34, Sec. 403(c)(3)(C), deleted items 2515 and 2515A... Sec. 403(d)(3)(B)(ii), added item 2519.
Prior to deletion, items 2515 and 2515A read as follows:
"2515. Tenancies by the entirety in real property.
"2515A. Tenancies by the entirety in personal property."
In **1978**, P.L. 95-600, Sec. 702(k)(1)(C), amended item 2515 and added item 2515A.
Prior to amendment, item 2515 read as follows:
"2515. Tenancies by the entirety."
In **1976**, P.L. 94-455, Sec. 2009(b)(3)(A), added the item for Code Sec. 2518.
In **1958**, added item 2517.

Sec. 2511. Transfers in general.
(a) Scope.

Subject to the limitations contained in this chapter, the tax imposed by section 2501 shall apply whether the transfer is in trust or otherwise, whether the gift is direct or indirect, and whether the property is real or personal, tangible or intangible; but in the case of a nonresident not a citizen of the United States, shall apply to a transfer only if the property is situated within the United States.

(b) Intangible property.

For purposes of this chapter, in the case of a nonresident not a citizen of the United States who is excepted from the application of section 2501(a)(2)—

(1) shares of stock issued by a domestic corporation, and
(2) debt obligations of—
 (A) a United States person, or
 (B) the United States, a State or any political subdivision thereof, or the District of Columbia,
which are owned and held by such nonresident shall be deemed to be property situated within the United States.

⌐ **• Caution:** Code Sec. 2511(c), following, was added by Sec. 511(e), P.L. 107-16, EGTRRA, and subsequently deleted by Sec. 302(e), P.L. 111-312. The provisions by P.L. 107-16 generally sunset for tax years beginning after 12/31/2012. For specific sunset provisions, see Sec. 901, ⌐

P.L. 107-16 (as amended) reproduced in history notes for this Code Sec. ⌐

(c) Repealed.

In **2010**, P.L. 111-312, Sec. 101(a)(1), substituted "December 31, 2012" for "December 31, 2010" both places it appeared in Sec. 901 of P.L. 107-16 [see below], effective as if included in the enactment of P.L. 107-16, EGTRRA, 6/7/2001.
—P.L. 111-312, Sec. 302(e), deleted subsec. (c), effective for estates of decedents dying, generation-skipping transfers, and gifts made, after 12/31/2009.
Prior to deletion, subsec. (c) read as follows:
"(c) Treatment of certain transfers in trust.
Notwithstanding any other provision of this section and except as provided in regulations, a transfer in trust shall be treated as a transfer of property by gift, unless the trust is treated as wholly owned by the donor or the donor's spouse under subpart E of part I of subchapter J of chapter 1."
—P.L. 111-312, Sec. 304, of this Act provides:
"SEC. 304. APPLICATION OF EGTRRA SUNSET TO THIS TITLE.
"Section 901 of the Economic Growth and Tax Relief Reconciliation Act of 2001 shall apply to the amendments made by this title."
In **2002**, P.L. 107-358, Sec. 2, added subsec. (c) in Sec. 901 of P. L. 107-16 [see below], effective 12/17/2002.
—P.L. 107-147, Sec. 411(g)(1), substituted "transfer of property by gift," for "taxable gift under section 2503," in subsec. (c), effective for gifts made after 12/31/2009.
In **2001**, P.L. 107-16, Sec. 511(e), added subsec. (c), effective for gifts made after 12/31/2009.
—P.L. 107-16, Sec. 901, of this Act [as amended by Sec. 2, P.L. 107-358 and Sec. 101(a)(1), P.L. 111-312, see above], reads as follows:
"Sec. 901. Sunset of provisions of Act.
"(a) In general. All provisions of, and amendments made by, this Act shall not apply—
"(1) to taxable, plan, or limitation years beginning after December 31, 2012, or
"(2) in the case of title V, to estates of decedents dying, gifts made, or generation skipping transfers, after December 31, 2012.
"(b) Application of certain laws. The Internal Revenue Code of 1986 and the Employee Retirement Income Security Act of 1974 shall be applied and administered to years, estates, gifts, and transfers described in subsection (a) as if the provisions and amendments described in subsection (a) had never been enacted.
"(c) Exception. Subsection (a) shall not apply to section 803 (relating to no federal income tax on restitution received by victims of the Nazi regime or their heirs or estates)."
In **1966**, P.L. 89-809, Sec. 109, amended subsec. (b) , effective for the calendar year 1967 and all calendar years thereafter.
Prior to amendment, subsec. (b) read as follows:
"(b) Stock in corporation.
"Shares of stock owned and held by a nonresident not a citizen of the United States shall be deemed property within the United States only if issued by a domestic corporation."

Sec. 2512. Valuation of gifts.
(a) If the gift is made in property, the value thereof at the date of the gift shall be considered the amount of the gift.
(b) Where property is transferred for less than an adequate and full consideration in money or money's worth, then the amount by which the value of the property exceeded the value of the consideration shall be deemed a gift, and shall be included in computing the amount of gifts made during the calendar year.
(c) Cross reference.

For individual's right to be furnished on request a statement regarding any valuation made by the Secretary of a gift by that individual, see section 7517.

In **1981**, P.L. 97-34, Sec. 442(b)(1), substituted "calendar year" for "calendar quarter" in subsec. (b), effective for gifts made after 12/31/81.
In **1976**, P.L. 94-455, Sec. 2008(a)(2)(B), added subsec. (c), effective for gifts made after 12/31/76.
In **1970**, P.L. 91-614, Sec. 102(b)(1), substituted "calendar quarter" for "calendar year" in subsec. (b), effective for gifts made after 12/31/70.

Sec. 2513. Gift by husband or wife to third party.
(a) Considered as made one-half by each.

(1) **In general.** A gift made by one spouse to any person other than his spouse shall, for the purposes of this chapter, be considered as made one-half by him and one-half by his spouse, but only if at the time of the gift each spouse is a citizen or resident of the United States. This

3,031

paragraph shall not apply with respect to a gift by a spouse of an interest in property if he creates in his spouse a general power of appointment, as defined in section 2514(c), over such interest. For purposes of this section, an individual shall be considered as the spouse of another individual only if he is married to such individual at the time of the gift and does not remarry during the remainder of the calendar year.

(2) Consent of both spouses. Paragraph (1) shall apply only if both spouses have signified (under the regulations provided for in subsection (b)) their consent to the application of paragraph (1) in the case of all such gifts made during the calendar year by either while married to the other.

(b) Manner and time of signifying consent.

(1) Manner. A consent under this section shall be signified in such manner as is provided under regulations prescribed by the Secretary.

(2) Time. Such consent may be so signified at any time after the close of the calendar year in which the gift was made, subject to the following limitations—

(A) The consent may not be signified after the 15th day of April following the close of such year, unless before such 15th day no return has been filed for such year by either spouse, in which case the consent may not be signified after a return for such year is filed by either spouse.

(B) The consent may not be signified after a notice of deficiency with respect to the tax for such year has been sent to either spouse in accordance with section 6212(a).

(c) Revocation of consent.

Revocation of a consent previously signified shall be made in such manner as is provided under regulations prescribed by the Secretary, but the right to revoke a consent previously signified with respect to a calendar year—

(1) shall not exist after the 15th day of April following the close of such year if the consent was signified on or before such 15th day; and

(2) shall not exist if the consent was not signified until after such 15th day.

(d) Joint and several liability for tax.

If the consent required by subsection (a)(2) is signified with respect to a gift made in any calendar year, the liability with respect to the entire tax imposed by this chapter of each spouse for such year shall be joint and several.

In 1981, P.L. 97-34, Sec. 442(b)(2)(A), substituted "calendar year" for "calendar quarter" each place it appeared in subsec. (a)... Sec. 442(b)(2)(B), substituted "calendar year" for "calendar quarter" in para. (b)(2)... Sec. 442(b)(2)(C), amended subpara. (b)(2)(A)... Sec. 442(b)(2)(D), substituted "The consent" for "the consent" and substituted "such year" for "such calendar quarter" in subpara. (b)(2)(B)... Sec. 442(b)(2)(E), substituted "calendar year" for "calendar quarter", and substituted "15th day of April following the close of such year" for "15th day of the second month following the close of such [sic, calendar] quarter" in subsec. (c)... Sec. 442(b)(2)(F), substituted "any calendar year" for "any calendar quarter", and substituted "such year" for "such calendar quarter", in subsec. (d), effective for gifts made after 12/31/81.

Prior to amendment, subpara. (b)(2)(A) read as follows:

"(A) the consent may not be signified after the 15th day of the second month following the close of such calendar quarter, unless before such 15th day no return has been filed for such calendar quarter, by either spouse, in which case the consent may not be signified after a return for such calendar quarter is filed by either spouse;"

In 1976, P.L. 94-455, Sec. 1906(b)(13)(A), substituted "Secretary" for "Secretary or his delegate" each place it appeared in Code Sec. 2513, effective 2/1/77.

In 1970, P.L. 91-614, Sec. 102(b)(2), substituted "calendar quarter" for "calendar year" each place it appeared in Sec. 2513, substituted "such calendar quarter" for "such year" in subpara. (b)(2)(B) and subsec. (d), substituted "15th day of the second month following the close of such calendar quarter" for "15th day of April following the close of such year" in para. (c)(1), amended subpara. (b)(2)(A), effective for gifts made after 12/31/70.

Prior to amendment, subpara. (b)(2)(A) read as follows:

"(A) the consent may not be signified after the 15th day of April following the close of such year, unless before such 15th day no return has been filed for such year by either spouse, in which case the consent may not be signified after a return for such year is filed by either spouse;"

Sec. 2514. Powers of appointment.

(a) Powers created on or before October 21, 1942.

An exercise of a general power of appointment created on or before October 21, 1942, shall be deemed a transfer of property by the individual possessing such power; but the failure to exercise such a power or the complete release of such a power shall not be deemed an exercise thereof. If a general power of appointment created on or before October 21, 1942, has been partially released so that it is no longer a general power of appointment, the subsequent exercise of such power shall not be deemed to be the exercise of a general power of appointment if—

(1) such partial release occurred before November 1, 1951, or

(2) the donee of such power was under a legal disability to release such power on October 21, 1942, and such partial release occurred not later than six months after the termination of such legal disability.

(b) Powers created after October 21, 1942.

The exercise or release of a general power of appointment created after October 21, 1942, shall be deemed a transfer of property by the individual possessing such power.

(c) Definition of general power of appointment.

For purposes of this section, the term "general power of appointment" means a power which is exercisable in favor of the individual possessing the power (hereafter in this subsection referred to as the "possessor"), his estate, his creditors, or the creditors of his estate; except that—

(1) A power to consume, invade, or appropriate property for the benefit of the possessor which is limited by an ascertainable standard relating to the health, education, support, or maintenance of the possessor shall not be deemed a general power of appointment.

(2) A power of appointment created on or before October 21, 1942, which is exercisable by the possessor only in conjunction with another person shall not be deemed a general power of appointment.

(3) In the case of a power of appointment created after October 21, 1942, which is exercisable by the possessor only in conjunction with another person—

(A) if the power is not exercisable by the possessor except in conjunction with the creator of the power—such power shall not be deemed a general power of appointment;

(B) if the power is not exercisable by the possessor except in conjunction with a person having a substantial interest, in the property subject to the power, which is adverse to exercise of the power in favor of the possessor—such power shall not be deemed a general power of appointment. For the purposes of this subparagraph a person who, after the death of the possessor, may be possessed of a power of appointment (with respect to the property subject to the possessor's power) which he may exercise in his own favor shall be deemed as having an interest in the property and such interest shall be deemed adverse to such exercise of the possessor's power;

(C) if (after the application of subparagraphs (A) and (B)) the power is a general power of appointment and is exercisable in favor of such other person—such power shall be deemed a general power of appointment only in respect of a fractional part of the property subject to such power, such part to be determined by dividing the

Gift taxes
Code Sec. 2516(2)

value of such property by the number of such persons (including the possessor) in favor of whom such power is exercisable.

For purposes of subparagraphs (B) and (C), a power shall be deemed to be exercisable in favor of a person if it is exercisable in favor of such person, his estate, his creditors, or the creditors of his estate.

(d) Creation of another power in certain cases.

If a power of appointment created after October 21, 1942, is exercised by creating another power of appointment which, under the applicable local law, can be validly exercised so as to postpone the vesting of any estate or interest in the property which was subject to the first power, or suspend the absolute ownership or power of alienation of such property, for a period ascertainable without regard to the date of the creation of the first power, such exercise of the first power shall, to the extent of the property subject to the second power, be deemed a transfer of property by the individual possessing such power.

(e) Lapse of power.

The lapse of a power of appointment created after October 21, 1942, during the life of the individual possessing the power shall be considered a release of such power. The rule of the preceding sentence shall apply with respect to the lapse of powers during any calendar year only to the extent that the property which could have been appointed by exercise of such lapsed powers exceeds in value the greater of the following amounts:

(1) $5,000, or

(2) 5 percent of the aggregate value of the assets out of which, or the proceeds of which, the exercise of the lapsed powers could be satisfied.

(f) Date of creation of power.

For purposes of this section a power of appointment created by a will executed on or before October 21, 1942, shall be considered a power created on or before such date if the person executing such will dies before July 1, 1949, without having republished such will, by codicil or otherwise, after October 21, 1942.

In 1976, P.L. 94-455, Sec. 2009(b)(4)(F), deleted the second sentence of subsec. (b), effective for transfers creating an interest in the person disclaiming made after 12/31/76.
Prior to deletion, the second sentence of subsec. (b) read as follows:
"A disclaimer or renunciation of such a power of appointment shall not be deemed a release of such power."

Sec. 2515. Treatment of generation-skipping transfer tax.

In the case of any taxable gift which is a direct skip (within the meaning of chapter 13), the amount of such gift shall be increased by the amount of any tax imposed on the transferor under chapter 13 with respect to such gift.

In 1986, P.L. 99-514, Sec. 1431(d)(1), added Code Sec. 2515, effective for any generation-skipping transfers after 10/22/86. For special rules and transitional rules, see Sec. 1433(b)-(d) of this Act reproduced in note following Code Sec. 2601.

Sec. 2515. Repealed.

In 1981, P.L. 97-34, Sec. 403(c)(3)(B), repealed Code Sec. 2515, effective for gifts made after 12/31/81.
Prior to repeal, Code Sec. 2515 read as follows:
"SEC. 2515. TENANCIES BY THE ENTIRETY IN REAL PROPERTY.
"(a) Creation.
"The creation of a tenancy by the entirety in real property, either by one spouse alone or by both spouses, and additions to the value thereof in the form of improvements, reductions in the indebtedness thereon, or otherwise, shall not be deemed transfers of property for purposes of this chapter, regardless of the proportion of the consideration furnished by each spouse, unless the donor elects to have such creation of a tenancy by the entirety treated as a transfer, as provided in subsection (c).
"(b) Termination.
"In the case of the termination of a tenancy by the entirety, other than by reason of the death of a spouse, the creation of which, or additions to which, were not deemed to be transfers by reason of subsection (a), a spouse shall be deemed to have made a gift to the extent that the proportion of the total consideration furnished by such spouse multiplied by the proceeds of such termination (whether in form of cash, property, or interests in property) exceeds the value of such proceeds of termination received by such spouse.
"(c) Exercise of election.
"(1) In general. The election provided by subsection (a) shall be exercised by including such creation of a tenancy by the entirety as a transfer by gift, to the extent such transfer constitutes a gift (determined without regard to this section), in the gift tax return of the donor for the calendar quarter in which such tenancy by the entirety was created, filed within the time prescribed by law, irrespective of whether or not the gift exceeds the exclusion provided by section 2503(b).
"(2) Subsequent additions in value. If the election provided by subsection (a) has been made with respect to the creation of any tenancy by the entirety, such election shall also apply to each addition made to the value of such tenancy by the entirety.
"(3) Certain actuarial computations not required. In the case of any election under subsection (a) with respect to any property, the retained interest of each spouse shall be treated as one-half of the value of their joint interest.
"(d) Certain joint tenancies included.
"For purposes of this section, the term 'tenancy by the entirety' includes a joint tenancy between husband and wife with right of survivorship."
In 1978, P.L. 95-600, Sec. 702(k)(1)(B), amended the heading of Code Sec. 2515, effective for joint interests created after 12/31/76.
Prior to amendment, the heading of Code Sec. 2515 read as follows:
"SEC. 2515. TENANCIES BY THE ENTIRETY."
In 1976, P.L. 94-455, Sec. 2002(c)(2), amended subsec. (c), effective for joint interest created after 12/31/76.
Prior to amendment, subsec. (c) read as follows:
"(c) Exercise of election.
"The election provided by subsection (a) shall be exercised by including such creation of a tenancy by the entirety or additions made to the value thereof as a transfer by gift, to the extent such transfer constitutes a gift, determined without regard to this section, in the gift tax return of the donor for the calendar quarter in which such tenancy by the entirety was created or additions made to the value thereof, filed within the time prescribed by law, irrespective of whether or not the gift exceeds the exclusion provided by section 2503(b)."
In 1970, P.L. 91-614, Sec. 102(b)(3), substituted "calendar quarter" for "calendar year" in subsec. (c), effective for gifts made after 12/31/70.

Sec. 2515A. Repealed.

In 1981, P.L. 97-34, Sec. 403(c)(3)(B), repealed Code Sec. 2515A, effective for gifts made after 12/31/81.
Prior to repeal, Code Sec. 2515A read as follows:
"SEC. 2515A. TENANCIES BY THE ENTIRETY IN PERSONAL PROPERTY.
"(a) Certain actuarial computations not required.
"In the case of—
"(1) the creation (either by one spouse alone or by both spouses) of a joint interest of a husband and wife in personal property with right of survivorship, or
"(2) additions to the value thereof in the form of improvements, reductions in the indebtedness thereof, or otherwise,
the retained interest of each spouse shall be treated as one-half of the value of their joint interest.
"(b) Exception.
"Subsection (a) shall not apply with respect to any joint interest in property if the fair market value of the interest or of the property (determined as if each spouse had a right to sever) cannot reasonably be ascertained except by reference to the life expectancy of one or both spouses."
In 1978, P.L. 95-600, Sec. 702(k)(1)(A), added Code Sec. 2515A, effective for joint interests created after 12/31/76.

Sec. 2516. Certain property settlements.

Where a husband and wife enter into a written agreement relative to their marital and property rights and divorce occurs within the 3-year period beginning on the date 1 year before such agreement is entered into (whether or not such agreement is approved by the divorce decree), any transfers of property or interests in property made pursuant to such agreement—

(1) to either spouse in settlement of his or her marital or property rights, or

(2) to provide a reasonable allowance for the support of issue of the marriage during minority,

shall be deemed to be transfers made for a full and adequate consideration in money or money's worth.

3,033

In **1984**, P.L. 98-369, Sec. 425(b), substituted

"Where a husband and wife enter into a written agreement relative to their marital and property rights and divorce occurs within the 3-year period beginning on the date 1 year before such agreement is entered into (whether or not such agreement is approved by the divorce decree), any transfers of property or interests in property made pursuant to such agreement—"

for

"Where husband and wife enter into a written agreement relative to their marital and property rights and divorce occurs within 2 years thereafter (whether or not such agreement is approved by the divorce decree), any transfers of property or interests in property made pursuant to such agreement—" before para. (1), effective for transfers after 7/18/84.

Sec. 2517. Repealed.

In **1986**, P.L. 99-514, Sec. 1852(e)(2)(A), repealed Code Sec. 2517, effective for transfers made after 10/22/86.
Prior to repeal, Code Sec. 2517 read as follows:
"SEC. 2517. CERTAIN ANNUITIES UNDER QUALIFIED PLANS.
"*(a) General rule.*

"The exercise or nonexercise by an employee of an election or option whereby an annuity or other payment will become payable to any beneficiary at or after the employee's death shall not be considered a transfer for purposes of this chapter if the option or election and annuity or other payment is provided for under—

"(1) an employees' trust (or under a contract purchased by an employees' trust) forming part of a pension, stock bonus, or profit-sharing plan which, at the time of such exercise or nonexercise, or at the time of termination of the plan if earlier, met the requirements of section 401(a);

"(2) a retirement annuity contract purchased by an employer (and not by an employees' trust) pursuant to a plan which, at the time of such exercise or nonexercise, or at the time of termination of the plan if earlier, was a plan described in section 403(a);

"(3) a retirement annuity contract purchased for an employee by an employer which is an organization referred to in section 170(b)(1)(A)(ii) or (vi), or which is a religious organization (other than a trust), and which is exempt from tax under section 501(a);

"(4) Chapter 73 of title 10 of the United States Code; or

"(5) an individual retirement account described in section 408(a) or an individual retirement annuity described in section 408(b).

"*(b) Transfers attributable to employee contributions.*

"If the annuity or other payment referred to in subsection (a) (other than paragraphs (4) and (5)) is attributable to any extent to payments or contributions made by the employee, then subsection (a) shall not apply to that part of the value of such annuity or other payment which bears the same proportion to the total value of the annuity or other payment as the total payments or contributions made by the employee bear to the total payments or contributions made. For purposes of the preceding sentence, payments or contributions made by the employee's employer or former employer toward the purchase of an annuity contract described in subsection (a)(3) shall, to the extent not excludable from gross income under section 403(b), be considered to have been made by the employee. For purposes of this subsection, contributions or payments on behalf of an individual while he was an employee within the meaning of section 401(c)(1) made under a trust or plan described in paragraph (1) or (2) of subsection (a) shall, to the extent allowable as a deduction under section 404, be considered to be made by a person other than such individual and, to the extent not so allowable, shall be considered to be made by such individual. For purposes of this subsection, any deductible employee contributions (within the meaning of paragraph (5) of section 72(o)) shall be considered as made by a person other than the employee.

"*(c) Exemption of certain annuity interests created by community property laws.*

"Notwithstanding any other provision of law, in the case of an employee on whose behalf contributions or payments are made—

"(1) by his employer or former employer under a trust or plan described in paragraph (1) or (2) of subsection (a), or toward the purchase of a contract described in paragraph (3) of subsection (a), which under subsection (b) are not considered as contributed by the employee, or

"(2) by the employee to a retirement plan described in paragraph (5) of subsection (a),

a transfer of benefits attributable to such contributions or payments shall, for purposes of this chapter, not be considered as a transfer by the spouse of the employee to the extent that the value of any interest of such spouse in such contributions or payments or in such trust or plan or such contract—

"(A) is attributable to such contribution or payments, and

"(B) arises solely by reason of such spouse's interest in community income under the community property laws of the State.

"*(d) Employee defined.*

"For purposes of this section, the term 'employee' includes a former employee. In the case of a retirement plan described in paragraph (5) of subsection (a), such term means the individual for whose benefit the plan was established."

In **1984**, P.L. 98-369, Sec. 491(d)(35), substituted "or an individual retirement annuity described in section 408(b)" for ", an individual retirement annuity described in section 408(b), or a retirement bond described in section 409(a)" in para. (a)(5), effective for obligations issued after 12/31/83.

In **1983**, P.L. 97-448, Sec. 103(c)(11), by adding Sec. 311(i)(5)(B) of P. L. 97-34, changed the effective date for amendments made by Sec. 311(d)(2) of P. L. 97-34, from effective for tax. yrs. begin. after 12/31/81, to effective for transfers after 12/31/81, see below.

In **1981**, P.L. 97-34, Sec. 311(d)(2), added the sentence at the end of subsec. (b), effective [as amended by Sec. 103(c)(11) of P. L. 97-448, see above] for transfers after 12/31/81. For transitional rule, see Sec. 311(i)(2) of this Act reproduced in note following Code Sec. 219.

In **1976**, P.L. 94-455, Sec. 2009(c)(4)(A)(i), deleted "or" at the end of para. (a)(3), substituted "; or" for the period at the end of para. (a)(4), and added para. (a)(5) . . . Sec. 2009(c)(4)(A)(ii), substituted "other than paragraphs (4) and (5)" for "other than paragraph (4)" in subsec. (b) . . . Sec. 2009(c)(4)(A)(iii), added a sentence to the end of subsec. (d), as redesignated by Sec. 2009(c)(5) of the Act, effective for transfers made after 12/31/76.
Prior to amendment, subsec. (c) read as follows:
"*(c) Employee defined.*

"For purposes of this section, the term 'employee' includes a former employee."

—P.L. 94-455, Sec. 2009(c)(4)(B), amended subsec. (b), effective for transfers made after 12/31/76.
Prior to amendment, subsec. (b) read as follows:
"*(b) Transfers attributable to employee contributions.*

"If the annuity or other payment referred to in subsection (a) (other than paragraph 4) is attributable to any extent to payments or contributions made by the employee, then subsection (a) shall not apply to that part of the value of such annuity or other payment which bears the same proportion to the total value of the annuity or other payment as the total payments or contributions made by the employee bear to the total payments or contributions made. For purposes of the preceding sentence, payments or contributions made by the employee's employer or former employer toward the purchase of an annuity contract described in subsection (a)(3) shall, to the extent not excludable from gross income under section 403(b), be considered to have been made by the employee. For purposes of this subsection, payments or contributions on behalf of an individual while he was an employee within the meaning of section 401(c)(1) made under a trust or plan described in subsection (a)(1) or (2) shall be considered to be payments or contributions made by the employee."

—P.L. 94-455, Sec. 2009(c)(5), redesignated subsec. (c) as subsec. (d), and added new subsec. (c), effective for transfers made after 12/31/76.

In **1969**, P.L. 91-172, Sec. 101(j)(24), substituted "170(b)(1)(A)(ii) or (vi), or which is a religious organization (other than a trust)," for "503(b)(1), (2), or (3)," in para. (a)(3), effective 1/1/70.

In **1966**, P.L. 89-365, Sec. 2, deleted "or" at the end of para. (a)(2), substituted "; or" for the period at the end of para. (a)(3), and added para. (a)(4), and added "(other than paragraph (4))" after "referred to in subsec. (a)" in subsec. (b), effective for calendar yrs. after 1965.

In **1962**, P.L. 87-792, Sec. 7, substituted "was a plan described in section 403(a)" for "met the requirements of section 401(a)(3),(4), (5), and (6)" in para. (a)(2) and inserted last sentence in subsec. (b), for tax. yrs. begin. after '62.

In **1958**, P.L. 85-866, Sec. 23, added subsec. (a)(3) and added second sentence in subsec. (b) to the section as added elsewhere in P. L. 85-866, for calendar yrs. after '57.

—P.L. 85-866, Sec. 68, had added Code Sec. 2517 for calendar year 1955 and all calendar years thereafter. "For calendar years before 1955, the determination as to whether the exercise or nonexercise by an employee of an election or option described in section 2517 of the Internal Revenue Code of 1954 (as added by subsection (a)) is a transfer for purposes of chapter 4 of the Internal Revenue Code of 1939 shall be made as if this section had not been enacted and without inferences drawn from the fact that this section is not made applicable with respect to calendar years before 1955."

Sec. 2518. Disclaimers.
(a) General rule.

For purposes of this subtitle, if a person makes a qualified disclaimer with respect to any interest in property, this subtitle shall apply with respect to such interest as if the interest had never been transferred to such person.

(b) Qualified disclaimer defined.

For purposes of subsection (a), the term "qualified disclaimer" means an irrevocable and unqualified refusal by a person to accept an interest in property but only if—

(1) such refusal is in writing,

(2) such writing is received by the transferor of the interest, his legal representative, or the holder of the legal title to the property to which the interest relates not later than the date which is 9 months after the later of—

(A) the day on which the transfer creating the interest in such person is made, or

(B) the day on which such person attains age 21,

(3) such person has not accepted the interest or any of its benefits, and

Gift taxes Code Sec. 2522(a)(2)

(4) as a result of such refusal, the interest passes without any direction on the part of the person making the disclaimer and passes either—
  (A) to the spouse of the decedent, or
  (B) to a person other than the person making the disclaimer.

(c) Other rules.
For purposes of subsection (a)—
(1) Disclaimer of undivided portion of interest. A disclaimer with respect to an undivided portion of an interest which meets the requirements of the preceding sentence shall be treated as a qualified disclaimer of such portion of the interest.
(2) Powers. A power with respect to property shall be treated as an interest in such property.
(3) Certain transfers treated as disclaimers. A written transfer of the transferor's entire interest in the property—
  (A) which meets requirements similar to the requirements of paragraphs (2) and (3) of subsection (b), and
  (B) which is to a person or persons who would have received the property had the transferor made a qualified disclaimer (within the meaning of subsection (b)),
shall be treated as a qualified disclaimer.

In **2010,** P.L. 111-312, Sec. 301(d), of this Act, provides
  "(d) Extension of time for performing certain acts.
  "(1) Estate tax. In the case of the estate of a decedent dying after December 31, 2009, and before the date of the enactment of this Act, the due date for—
  "(A) filing any return under section 6018 of the Internal Revenue Code of 1986 (including any election required to be made on such a return) as such section is in effect after the date of the enactment of this Act without regard to any election under subsection (c),
  "(B) making any payment of tax under chapter 11 of such Code, and
  "(C) making any disclaimer described in section 2518(b) of such Code of an interest in property passing by reason of the death of such decedent, shall not be earlier than the date which is 9 months after the date of the enactment of this Act.
  "(2) Generation-skipping tax. In the case of any generation-skipping transfer made after December 31, 2009, and before the date of the enactment of this Act, the due date for filing any return under section 2662 of the Internal Revenue Code of 1986 (including any election required to be made on such a return) shall not be earlier than the date which is 9 months after the date of the enactment of this Act."
—P.L. 111-312, Sec. 304, of this Act, provides
  "Sec. 304. Application of EGTRRA sunset to this title.
  "Section 901 of the Economic Growth and Tax Relief Reconciliation Act of 2001 shall apply to the amendments made by this section."
In **1983,** P.L. 97-448, Sec. 104(e), substituted "A" for "For purposes of subsection (a), a" in para. (c)(3), effective for transfers creating an interest in the person disclaiming made after 12/31/81.
In **1981,** P.L. 97-34, Sec. 426(a), added para. (c)(3), effective for transfers creating an interest in the person disclaiming made after 12/31/81.
In **1978,** P.L. 95-600, Sec. 702(m)(1), amended para. (b)(4), effective for transfers creating an interest in the person disclaiming made after 12/31/76.
Prior to amendment, para. (b)(4) read as follows:
  "(4) as a result of such refusal, the interest passes to a person other than the person making the disclaimer (without any direction on the part of the person making the disclaimer)."
In **1976,** P.L. 94-455, Sec. 2009(b)(1), added Code Sec. 2518, effective for transfers creating an interest in the person disclaiming made after 12/31/76.

Sec. 2519. Dispositions of certain life estates.
(a) General rule.
For purposes of this chapter and chapter 11, any disposition of all or part of a qualifying income interest for life in any property to which this section applies shall be treated as a transfer of all interests in such property other than the qualifying income interest.
(b) Property to which this subsection applies.
This section applies to any property if a deduction was allowed with respect to the transfer of such property to the donor—
  (1) under section 2056 by reason of subsection (b)(7) thereof, or
  (2) under section 2523 by reason of subsection (f) thereof.

(c) Cross reference.
For right of recovery for gift tax in the case of property treated as transferred under this section, see section 2207A(b).

In **1983,** P.L. 97-448, Sec. 104(a)(3)(A), amended subsec. (a) . . . Sec. 104(a)(7), added subsec. (c), effective for gifts made after 12/31/81.
Prior to amendment, subsec. (a) read as follows:
  "(a) General rule.
  "Any disposition of all or part of a qualifying income interest for life in any property to which this section applies shall be treated as a transfer of such property."
In **1981,** P.L. 97-34, Sec. 403(d)(3)(B)(i), added Code Sec. 2519, effective for gifts made after 12/31/81.

Subchapter C.—Deductions
Sec.
2521. Repealed.
2522. Charitable and similar gifts.
2523. Gift to spouse.
2524. Extent of deductions.

In **1976,** P.L. 94-455, Sec. 2001(c)(2)(B)(ii), deleted the item for Code Sec. 2521.
Prior to repeal, the item read as follows:
"2521. Specific exemption."

Sec. 2521. Repealed.

In **1976,** P.L. 94-455, Sec. 2001(b)(3), repealed Code Sec. 2521, effective for gifts made after 12/31/76.
Prior to repeal, Code Sec. 2521 read as follows:
"SEC. 2521. SPECIFIC EXEMPTION.
  "In computing taxable gifts for the calendar quarter, there shall be allowed as a deduction in the case of a citizen or resident an exemption of $30,000, less the aggregate of the amounts claimed and allowed as specific exemption in the computation of gift taxes for the calendar year 1932 and all calendar years and calendar quarters intervening between that calendar year and the calendar quarter for which the tax is being computed under laws applicable to such years or calendar quarters."
In **1970,** P.L. 91-614, Sec. 102(c)(1), amended Code Sec. 2521, effective for gifts made after 12/31/70.
Prior to amendment, Code Sec. 2521 read as follows:
  "In computing taxable gifts for the calendar year, there shall be allowed a deduction in the case of a citizen or resident an exemption of $30,000, less the aggregate of the amounts claimed and allowed as specific exemption in the computation of gift taxes for the calendar year 1932 and all calendar years intervening between that calendar year and the calendar year for which the tax is being computed under the laws applicable to such years."

Sec. 2522. Charitable and similar gifts.
(a) Citizens or residents.
In computing taxable gifts for the calendar year, there shall be allowed as a deduction in the case of a citizen or resident the amount of all gifts made during such year to or for the use of—
  (1) the United States, any State, or any political subdivision thereof, or the District of Columbia, for exclusively public purposes;
  (2) a corporation, or trust, or community chest, fund, or foundation, organized and operated exclusively for religious, charitable, scientific, literary, or educational purposes, or to foster national or international amateur sports competition (but only if no part of its activities involve the provision of athletic facilities or equipment), including the encouragement of art and the prevention of cruelty to children or animals, no part of the net earnings of which inures to the benefit of any private shareholder or individual, which is not disqualified for tax exemption under section 501(c)(3) by reason of attempting to influence legislation, and which does not participate in, or intervene in (including the publishing or distributing of statements), any political campaign on behalf of (or in opposition to) any candidate for public office;

(3) a fraternal society, order, or association, operating under the lodge system, but only if such gifts are to be used exclusively for religious, charitable, scientific, literary, or educational purposes, including the encouragement of art and the prevention of cruelty to children or animals;

(4) posts or organizations of war veterans, or auxiliary units or societies of any such posts or organizations, if such posts, organizations, units, or societies are organized in the United States or any of its possessions, and if no part of their net earnings inures to the benefit of any private shareholder or individual.

Rules similar to the rules of section 501(j) shall apply for purposes of paragraph (2).

(b) Nonresidents.

In the case of a nonresident not a citizen of the United States, there shall be allowed as a deduction the amount of all gifts made during such year to or for the use of—

(1) the United States, any State, or any political subdivision thereof, or the District of Columbia, for exclusively public purposes;

(2) a domestic corporation organized and operated exclusively for religious, charitable, scientific, literary, or educational purposes, including the encouragement of art and the prevention of cruelty to children or animals, no part of the net earnings of which inures to the benefit of any private shareholder or individual, which is not disqualified for tax exemption under section 501(c)(3) by reason of attempting to influence legislation, and which does not participate in, or intervene in (including the publishing or distributing of statements), any political campaign on behalf of (or in opposition to) any candidate for public office;

(3) a trust, or community chest, fund, or foundation, organized and operated exclusively for religious, charitable, scientific, literary, or educational purposes, including the encouragement of art and the prevention of cruelty to children or animals, no substantial part of the activities of which is carrying on propaganda, or otherwise attempting, to influence legislation, and which does not participate in, or intervene in (including the publishing or distributing of statements), any political campaign on behalf of (or in opposition to) any candidate for public office; but only if such gifts are to be used within the United States exclusively for such purposes;

(4) a fraternal society, order, or association, operating under the lodge system, but only if such gifts are to be used within the United States exclusively for religious, charitable, scientific, literary, or educational purposes, including the encouragement of art and the prevention of cruelty to children or animals;

(5) posts or organizations of war veterans, or auxiliary units or societies of any such posts or organizations, if such posts, organizations, units, or societies are organized in the United States or any of its possessions, and if no part of their net earnings inures to the benefit of any private shareholder or individual.

(c) Disallowance of deductions in certain cases.

(1) No deduction shall be allowed under this section for a gift to or for the use of an organization or trust described in section 508(d) or 4948(c)(4) subject to the conditions specified in such sections.

(2) Where a donor transfers an interest in property (other than an interest described in section 170(f)(3)(B)) to a person, or for a use, described in subsection (a) or (b) and an interest in the same property is retained by the donor, or is transferred or has been transferred (for less than an adequate and full consideration in money or money's worth) from the donor to a person, or for a use, not described in subsection (a) or (b), no deduction shall be allowed under this section for the interest which is, or has been transferred to the person, or for the use, described in subsection (a) or (b), unless—

(A) in the case of a remainder interest, such interest is in a trust which is a charitable remainder annuity trust or a charitable remainder unitrust (described in section 664) or a pooled income fund (described in section 642(c)(5)), or

(B) in the case of any other interest, such interest is in the form of a guaranteed annuity or is a fixed percentage distributed yearly of the fair market value of the property (to be determined yearly).

(3) Rules similar to the rules of section 2055(e)(4) shall apply for purposes of paragraph (2).

(4) Reformations to comply with paragraph (2).

(A) In general. A deduction shall be allowed under subsection (a) in respect of any qualified reformation (within the meaning of section 2055(e)(3)(B)).

(B) Rules similar to section 2055(e)(3) to apply. For purposes of this paragraph, rules similar to the rules of section 2055(e)(3) shall apply.

(5) Contributions to donor advised funds. A deduction otherwise allowed under subsection (a) for any contribution to a donor advised fund (as defined in section 4966(d)(2)) shall only be allowed if—

(A) the sponsoring organization (as defined in section 4966(d)(1)) with respect to such donor advised fund is not—

(i) described in paragraph (3) or (4) of subsection (a), or

(ii) a type III supporting organization (as defined in section 4943(f)(5)(A)) which is not a functionally integrated type III supporting organization (as defined in section 4943(f)(5)(B)), and

(B) the taxpayer obtains a contemporaneous written acknowledgment (determined under rules similar to the rules of section 170(f)(8)(C)) from the sponsoring organization (as so defined) of such donor advised fund that such organization has exclusive legal control over the assets contributed.

(d) Special rule for irrevocable transfers of easements in real property.

A deduction shall be allowed under subsection (a) in respect of any transfer of a qualified real property interest (as defined in section 170(h)(2)(C)) which meets the requirements of section 170(h) (without regard to paragraph (4)(A) thereof).

(e) Special rules for fractional gifts.

(1) Denial of deduction in certain cases.

(A) In general. No deduction shall be allowed for a contribution of an undivided portion of a taxpayer's entire interest in tangible personal property unless all interests in the property are held immediately before such contribution by—

(i) the taxpayer, or

(ii) the taxpayer and the donee.

(B) Exceptions. The Secretary may, by regulation, provide for exceptions to subparagraph (A) in cases where all persons who hold an interest in the property make proportional contributions of an undivided portion of the entire interest held by such persons.

(2) Recapture of deduction in certain cases; addition to tax.

(A) In general. The Secretary shall provide for the recapture of an amount equal to any deduction allowed under this section (plus interest) with respect to any contribution of an undivided portion of a taxpayer's entire interest in tangible personal property—

(i) in any case in which the donor does not contribute all of the remaining interests in such property to the donee (or, if such donee is no longer in existence, to any person described in section 170(c)) on or before the earlier of—

(I) the date that is 10 years after the date of the initial fractional contribution, or

(II) the date of the death of the donor, and

(ii) in any case in which the donee has not, during the period beginning on the date of the initial fractional contribution and ending on the date described in clause (i)—

(I) had substantial physical possession of the property, and

(II) used the property in a use which is related to a purpose or function constituting the basis for the organizations' exemption under section 501.

(B) Addition to tax. The tax imposed under this chapter for any taxable year for which there is a recapture under subparagraph (A) shall be increased by 10 percent of the amount so recaptured.

(C) Initial fractional contribution. For purposes of this paragraph, the term "initial fractional contribution" means, with respect to any donor, the first gift of an undivided portion of the donor's entire interest in any tangible personal property for which a deduction is allowed under subsection (a) or (b).

(f) Cross references.

(1) For treatment of certain organizations providing child care, see section 501(k).

(2) For exemption of certain gifts to or for the benefit of the United States and for rules of construction with respect to certain bequests, see section 2055(f).

(3) For treatment of gifts to or for the use of Indian tribal governments (or their subdivisions), see section 7871.

In 2007, P.L. 110-172, Sec. 3(d)(2)(A), deleted paras. (e)(2) and (4) . . . Sec. 3(d)(2)(B), redesignated para. (e)(3) as (2) . . . Sec. 3(d)(2)(C), added subpara. (e)(2)(C) [as redesignated by Sec. 3(d)(2)(B) of this Act, see above], effective for contributions, bequests, and gifts made after 8/17/2006.

Prior to deletion, para. (e)(2) read as follows:

"(2) Valuation of subsequent gifts. In the case of any additional contribution, the fair market value of such contribution shall be determined by using the lesser of—

"(A) the fair market value of the property at the time of the initial fractional contribution, or

"(B) the fair market value of the property at the time of the additional contribution."

Prior to deletion, para. (e)(4) read as follows:

"(4) Definitions. For purposes of this subsection—

"(A) Additional contribution. The term 'additional contribution' means any gift for which a deduction is allowed under subsection (a) or (b) of any interest in a property with respect to which the donor has previously made an initial fractional contribution.

"(B) Initial fractional contribution. The term 'initial fractional contribution' means, with respect to any donor, the first gift of an undivided portion of the donor's entire interest in any tangible personal property for which a deduction is allowed under subsection (a) or (b)."

—P.L. 110-172, Sec. 3(a)(16)(A), substituted "all interests in the property are" for "all interest n the property is" in subpara. (e)(1)(A) . . . Sec. 3(a)(16)(B)(i), substituted "interests" for "interest" in clause (e)(2)(A)(i) [as redesignated by Sec. 3(d)(2)(B) of this Act, see above] . . . Sec. 3(a)(16)(B)(ii), substituted "on or before" for "before" in clause (e)(2)(A)(i) [as redesignated by Sec. 3(d)(2)(B) of this Act, see above], enacted 12/29/2007.

In 2006, P.L. 109-280, Sec. 1218(f), redesignated subsec. (e) as (f) and added subsec. (e), effective for contributions, bequests, and gifts made after 8/17/2006.

—P.L. 109-280, Sec. 1234(c), added para. (c)(5), effective for contributions made after the date which is 180 days after 8/17/2006.

In 1987, P.L. 100-203, Sec. 10711(a)(5), substituted "on behalf of (or in opposition to) any candidate" for "on behalf of any candidate" in paras. (a)(2) . . . Sec. 10711(a)(6), substituted "on behalf of (or in opposition to) any candidate" for "on behalf of any candidate" in paras. (b)(2) and (b)(3), effective with respect to activities after 12/22/87.

In 1986, P.L. 99-514, Sec. 1422(b), redesignated subsec. (d) as subsec. (e), and added new subsec. (d), effective for transfers and contributions made after 12/31/86.

In 1984, P.L. 98-369, Sec. 1022(c), added para. (c)(4), effective as provided by Secs. 1022(e)(1) and (3) of this Act, as follows

"(e) Effective date.

"(1) Subsections (a), (b), and (c). The amendments made by subsections (a), (b), and (c) shall apply to reformations after December 31, 1978; except that such amendments shall not apply to any reformation to which section 2055(e)(3) of the Internal Revenue Code of 1954 (as in effect on the day before the date of the enactment of this Act) applies. For purposes of applying clause (iii) of section 2055(e)(3)(C) of such Code (as amended by this section), the 90th day described in such clause shall be treated as not occurring before the 90th day after the date of the enactment of this Act [7/18/84].

"(3) Statute of limitations.

"(A) In general. If on the date of the enactment of this Act (or at any time before the date 1 year after such date of enactment [7/18/84]), credit or refund of any overpayment of tax attributable to the amendments made by this section is barred by any law or rule of law, such credit or refund of such overpayment may nevertheless be made if claim therefor is filed before the date 1 year after the date of the enactment of this Act [7/18/84].

"(B) No interest where statute closed on date of enactment. In any case where the making of the credit or refund of the overpayment described in subparagraph (A) is barred on the date of the enactment of this Act [7/18/84], no interest shall be allowed with respect to such overpayment (or any related adjustment) for the period before the date 180 days after the date on which the Secretary of the Treasury (or his delegate) is notified that the reformation has occurred."

—P.L. 98-369, Sec. 1032(b)(3), redesignated paras. (d)(1) and (d)(2) as paras. (d)(2) and (d)(3), respectively, and added new para. (d)(1), effective for tax. yrs. begin. after 7/18/84.

—P.L. 98-369, Sec. 1065(a)(1), amended Sec. 204 of P. L. 98-473, the effective date for changes made by Sec. 202(b)(7) of P. L. 97-473 (see below), by deleting "and before January 1, 1985" each place it appeared.

In 1983, P.L. 97-473, Sec. 202(b)(7), amended subsec. (d), effective for gifts made after 12/31/82.

Prior to amendment subsec. (d) read as follows:

"(d) Cross reference.

"For exemption of certain gifts to or for the benefit of the United States and for rules of construction with respect to certain gifts, see section 2055(f)."

In 1982, P.L. 97-248, Sec. 286(b)(3), added the last sentence to subsec. (a), effective 10/5/76.

In 1981, P.L. 97-34, Sec. 423(b), added para. (c)(3), for transfers after 12/31/81.

—P.L. 97-34, Sec. 442(c), substituted "year" for "quarter" in subsecs. (a) and (b), for gifts made after 12/31/81.

In 1980, P.L. 96-541, Sec. 6(c), amended the effective date for changes made by Sec. 2124(e)(2) of P. L. 94-455 [as amended by Sec. 309(b)(2) of P. L. 95-30, see below] from contributions or transfers made after 6/13/76 and before 6/14/81 to contributions or transfers made after 6/13/76.

—P.L. 96-222, Sec. 105(a)(4)(B), amended Sec. 514 of P. L. 95-600 by adding Sec. 514(c)(2) [reproduced below].

In 1978, P.L. 95-600, Sec. 703(j)(12), amended the effective date for changes made by Sec. 1902(a)(11) of P. L. 94-455 to apply to gifts made after 12/31/76. Sec. 514(b) of this Act provides:

"(b) Charitable lead trusts and charitable remainder trusts in the case of income and gift taxes.

"Under regulations prescribed by the Secretary of the Treasury or his delegate, in the case of trusts created before December 31, 1977, provisions comparable to section 2055(e)(3) of the Internal Revenue Code of 1954 (as amended by subsection (a)) shall be deemed to be included in sections 170 and 2522 of the Internal Revenue Code of 1954."

Sec. 514(c)(2) of this section provides:

"(c) Effective dates.

"(1) For subsection (a). The amendment made by subsection (a) shall apply in the case of decedents dying after December 31, 1969.

"(2) For subsection (b). Subsection (b)

"(A) insofar as it relates to section 170 of the Internal Revenue Code of 1954 shall apply to transfers in trust and contributions made after July 31, 1969, and

"(B) insofar as it relates to section 2522 of the Internal Revenue Code of 1954 shall apply to transfers made after December 31, 1969."

In 1977, P.L. 95-30, Sec. 309(b)(2), amended the effective date for amendments made by Sec. 2124(e)(3) of P.L. 94-455, effective [as amended by Sec. 6(c) of P. L. 96-541, see above] from contributions or transfers made after 6/13/76 and before 6/14/77 to contributions or transfers made after 6/13/76 and before 6/14/81 [see below].

In 1976, P.L. 94-455, Sec. 1307(d)(1)(B)(iv), substituted "which is not disqualified for tax exemption under section 501(c)(3) by reason of attempting to influence legislation," for "no substantial part of the activities of which is carrying on propaganda, or otherwise attempting to influence legislation," in para. (a)(2), effective for gifts in calendar yrs. begin. after 12/31/76.

—P.L. 94-455, Sec. 1307(d)(1)(B)(v), substituted "which is not disqualified for tax exemption under section 501(c)(3) by reason of attempting to influence legislation," for "no substantial part of the activities of which is carrying on propaganda, or otherwise attempting to influence legislation," in para. (b)(2), effective for gifts in calendar yrs. begin. after 12/31/76.

—P.L. 94-455, Sec. 1313(b)(3), added ", or to foster national or international amateur sports competition (but only if no part of its activities involve the provision of athletic facilities or equipment)," after "or educational purposes" in para. (a)(2), effective 10/5/76. Sec. 1313(c) of the Act provided as follows: "An organization which (without regard to the amendments made by this section) is an organization described in section ... 2522(a)(2), of the Internal Revenue Code of 1954 shall not be treated as an organization not so described as a result of the amendments made by this section."

—P.L. 94-455, Sec. 1902(a)(11), amended subsec. (d), for estates of decedents dying after 12/31/70.

Prior to amendment subsec. (d) read as follows:

"(d) Other cross references.

"(1) For exemption of gifts to or for benefit of Library of Congress, see section 5 of the Act of March 3, 1925, as amended (56 Stat. 765; 2 U.S.C. 161).

"(2) For construction of gifts for benefit of library of Post Office Department as gifts to or for the use of the United States, see section 2 of the Act of August 8, 1946 (60 Stat. 924; 5 U.S.C. 393).

"(3) For exemption of gifts for benefit of Office of Naval Records and Library, Navy Department, see section 2 of the Act of March 4, 1937 (50 Stat. 25; 5 U.S.C. 419b).

"(4) For exemption of gifts to or for benefit of National Park Service, see section 5 of the Act of July 10, 1935 (49 Stat. 478; 16 U.S.C. 19c).

"(5) For construction of gifts accepted by the Secretary of State under the Foreign Service Act of 1946 as gifts to or for the use of the United States, see section 1021(e) of that Act (60 Stat. 1032; 22 U.S.C. 809).

"(6) For construction of gifts or bequests of money accepted by the Attorney General for credit to 'Commissary Funds, Federal Prisons' as gifts or bequests to or for the use of the United States, see section 2 of the Act of May 15, 1952, 66 Stat. 73, as amended by the Act of July 9, 1952, 66 Stat. 479 (31 U.S.C. 725s-4).

"(7) For payment of tax on gifts of United States obligations to the United States, see section 24 of the Second Liberty Bond Act, as amended (59 Stat. 48, § 4; 31 U.S.C. 757e).

"(8) For construction of gifts for benefit of or use in connection with Naval Academy as gifts to or for the use of the United States, see section 3 of the Act of March 31, 1944 (58 Stat. 135; 34 U.S.C. 1115h).

"(9) For exemption of gifts for benefit of Naval Academy Museum, see section 4 of the Act of March 26, 1938 (52 Stat. 119; 34 U.S.C. 1119).

"(10) For exemption of gifts received by National Archives Trust Fund Board, see section 7 of the National Archives Trust Fund Board Act (55 Stat. 582; 44 U.S.C. 300gg)."

—P.L. 94-455, Sec. 1902(a)(12)(D), deleted "Territory,", which followed "any State,", in paras. (a)(1) and (b)(1), effective for gifts made after 12/31/76.

—P.L. 94-455, Sec. 2124(e)(3), substituted "(other than an interest described in section 170(f)(3)(B))" for "(other than a remainder interest in a personal residence or farm or an undivided portion of the donor's entire interest in property)" in para. (c)(2), effective [as amended by Sec. 309(b)(2) of P. L. 95-30, see above, and as amended by Sec. 6(c) of P. L. 96-541, see above] for contributions or transfers made after 6/13/76.

In 1972, P.L. 92-603, Sec. 132, made gifts to one of the Social Security funds a public gift. See note following Code Sec. 170.

In 1970, P.L. 91-614, Sec. 102(c)(2), substituted "quarter" for "year" each place it appeared in Sec. 2522, effective for gifts made after 12/31/70.

In 1969, P.L. 91-172, Sec. 201(d)(3), amended subsec. (c). Sec. 201(g)(4)(D) of this Act provides as follows:

"(D) The amendment made by paragraph (3) of subsection (d) shall apply to gifts made after December 31, 1969, except that the amendments made to section 2522(c)(2) of the Internal Revenue Code of 1954 shall apply to gifts made after July 31, 1969."

Prior to amendment subsec. (c) read as follows:

"(c) Disallowance of deductions in certain cases.

"For disallowance of certain charitable, etc., deductions otherwise allowable under this section, see sections 503 and 681."

—P.L. 91-172, Sec. 201(d)(4)(C), deleted "and" before "no substantial part" in para. (2) and added before the semicolon at the end of such paragraph ", and which does not participate in, or intervene in (including the publishing or distributing of statements), any political campaign on behalf of any candidate for public office" in subsec. (a), for gifts and transfers made after 12/31/69. ... Sec. 201(d)(4)(D), deleted "and" before "no substantial part" in para. (2) and added before the semicolon at the end of such paragraph ", and which does not participate in, or intervene in (including the publishing or distributing of statements), any political campaign on behalf of any candidate for public office", and added after "legislation" in para. (3) ", and which does not participate in, or intervene in (including the publishing or distributing of statements), any political campaign on behalf of any candidate for public office" in subsec. (b), effective for gifts and transfers made after 12/31/69.

In 1958, P.L. 85-866, Sec. 30(d), substituted "503" for "504" in subsec. (c).

Sec. 2523. Gift to spouse.
(a) Allowance of deduction.

Where a donor transfers during the calendar year by gift an interest in property to a donee who at the time of the gift is the donor's spouse, there shall be allowed as a deduction in computing taxable gifts for the calendar year an amount with respect to such interest equal to its value.

(b) Life estate or other terminable interest.

Where, on the lapse of time, on the occurrence of an event or contingency, or on the failure of an event or contingency to occur, such interest transferred to the spouse will terminate or fail, no deduction shall be allowed with respect to such interest—

(1) if the donor retains in himself, or transfers or has transferred (for less than an adequate and full consideration in money or money's worth) to any person other than such donee spouse (or the estate of such spouse), an interest in such property, and if by reason of such retention or transfer the donor (or his heirs or assigns) or such person (or his heirs or assigns) may possess or enjoy any part of such property after such termination or failure of the interest transferred to the donee spouse; or

(2) if the donor immediately after the transfer to the donee spouse has a power to appoint an interest in such property which he can exercise (either alone or in conjunction with any person) in such manner that the appointee may possess or enjoy any part of such property after such termination or failure of the interest transferred to the donee spouse. For purposes of this paragraph, the donor shall be considered as having immediately after the transfer to the donee spouse such power to appoint even though such power cannot be exercised until after the lapse of time, upon the occurrence of an event or contingency, or on the failure of an event or contingency to occur.

An exercise or release at any time by the donor, either alone or in conjunction with any person, of a power to appoint an interest in property, even though not otherwise a transfer, shall, for purposes of paragraph (1), be considered as a transfer by him. Except as provided in subsection (e), where at the time of the transfer it is impossible to ascertain the particular person or persons who may receive from the donor an interest in property so transferred by him, such interest shall, for purposes of paragraph (1), be considered as transferred to a person other than the donee spouse.

(c) Interest in unidentified assets.

Where the assets out of which, or the proceeds of which, the interest transferred to the donee spouse may be satisfied include a particular asset or assets with respect to which no deduction would be allowed if such asset or assets were transferred from the donor to such spouse, then the value of the interest transferred to such spouse shall, for purposes of subsection (a), be reduced by the aggregate value of such particular assets.

(d) Joint interests.

If the interest is transferred to the donee spouse as sole joint tenant with the donor or as tenant by the entirety, the interest of the donor in the property which exists solely by reason of the possibility that the donor may survive the donee spouse, or that there may occur a severance of the tenancy, shall not be considered for purposes of subsection (b) as an interest retained by the donor in himself.

(e) Life estate with power of appointment in donee spouse.

Where the donor transfers an interest in property, if by such transfer his spouse is entitled for life to all of the income from the entire interest, or all the income from a specific portion thereof, payable annually or at more frequent intervals, with power in the donee spouse to appoint the entire interest, or such specific portion (exercisable in favor of such donee spouse, or of the estate of such donee spouse, or in favor of either, whether or not in each case the power is exercisable in favor of others), and with no power in any other person to appoint any part of such interest, or such portion, to any person other than the donee spouse—

(1) the interest, or such portion, so transferred shall, for purposes of subsection (a) be considered as transferred to the donee spouse, and

(2) no part of the interest, or such portion, so transferred shall, for purposes of subsection (b)(1), be considered as retained in the donor or transferred to any person other than the donee spouse.

This subsection shall apply only if, by such transfer, such power in the donee spouse to appoint the interest, or such portion, whether exercisable by will or during life, is exercisable by such spouse alone and in all events. For purposes of this subsection, the term "specific portion" only includes a portion determined on a fractional or percentage basis.

(f) Election with respect to life estate for donee spouse.

(1) In general. In the case of qualified terminable interest property—

(A) for purposes of subsection (a), such property shall be treated as transferred to the donee spouse, and

(B) for purposes of subsection (b)(1), no part of such property shall be considered as retained in the donor or transferred to any person other than the donee spouse.

(2) Qualified terminable interest property. For purposes of this subsection, the term "qualified terminable interest property" means any property—

(A) which is transferred by the donor spouse,

(B) in which the donee spouse has a qualifying income interest for life, and

(C) to which an election under this subsection applies.

(3) Certain rules made applicable. For purposes of this subsection, rules similar to the rules of clauses (ii), (iii), and (iv) of section 2056(b)(7)(B) shall apply and the rules of section 2056(b)(10) shall apply.

(4) Election.

(A) Time and manner. An election under this subsection with respect to any property shall be made on or before the date prescribed by section 6075(b) for filing a gift tax return with respect to the transfer (determined without regard to section 6019(2)) and shall be made in such manner as the Secretary shall by regulations prescribe.

(B) Election irrevocable. An election under this subsection, once made, shall be irrevocable.

(5) Treatment of interest retained by donor spouse.

(A) In general. In the case of any qualified terminable interest property—

(i) such property shall not be includible in the gross estate of the donor spouse, and

(ii) any subsequent transfer by the donor spouse of an interest in such property shall not be treated as a transfer for purposes of this chapter.

(B) Subparagraph (A) not to apply after transfer by donee spouse. Subparagraph (A) shall not apply with respect to any property after the donee spouse is treated as having transferred such property under section 2519, or such property is includible in the donee spouse's gross estate under section 2044.

(6) Treatment of joint and survivor annuities. In the case of a joint and survivor annuity where only the donor spouse and donee spouse have the right to receive payments before the death of the last spouse to die—

(A) the donee spouse's interest shall be treated as a qualifying income interest for life,

(B) the donor spouse shall be treated as having made an election under this subsection with respect to such annuity unless the donor spouse otherwise elects on or before the date specified in paragraph (4)(A),

(C) paragraph (5) and section 2519 shall not apply to the donor spouse's interest in the annuity, and

(D) if the donee spouse dies before the donor spouse, no amount shall be includible in the gross estate of the donee spouse under section 2044 with respect to such annuity.

An election under subparagraph (B), once made, shall be irrevocable.

(g) Special rule for charitable remainder trusts.

(1) In general. If, after the transfer, the donee spouse is the only noncharitable beneficiary (other than the donor) of a qualified charitable remainder trust, subsection (b) shall not apply to the interest in such trust which is transferred to the donee spouse.

(2) Definitions. For purposes of paragraph (1), the term "noncharitable beneficiary" and "qualified charitable remainder trust" have the meanings given to such terms by section 2056(b)(8)(B).

(h) Denial of double deduction.

Nothing in this section or any other provision of this chapter shall allow the value of any interest in property to be deducted under this chapter more than once with respect to the same donor.

(i) Disallowance of marital deduction where spouse not citizen.

If the spouse of the donor is not a citizen of the United States—

(1) no deduction shall be allowed under this section,

(2) section 2503(b) shall be applied with respect to gifts which are made by the donor to such spouse and with respect to which a deduction would be allowable under this section but for paragraph (1) by substituting "$100,000" for "$10,000", and

(3) the principles of sections 2515 and 2515A (as such sections were in effect before their repeal by the Economic Recovery Tax Act of 1981) shall apply, except that the provisions of such section 2515 providing for an election shall not apply.

This subsection shall not apply to any transfer resulting from the acquisition of rights under a joint and survivor annuity described in subsection (f)(6).

In 1997, P.L. 105-34, Sec. 1604(g)(4), substituted "qualified charitable remainder trust" for "qualified remainder trust" in para. (g)(1), effective 8/5/97.

In 1992, P.L. 102-486, Sec. 1941(b)(1), added a sentence at the end of subsec. (e) ... Sec. 1941(b)(2), added "and the rules of section 2056(b)(10) shall apply" before the period at the end of para. (f)(3), effective for gifts made after 10/24/92.

In 1990, P.L. 101-508, Sec. 11702(g)(1), added the last sentence of subsec. (i), effective for gifts on or after 7/14/88.

In 1989, P.L. 101-239, Sec. 7815(d)(1)(A), substituted "which are made by the donor to such spouse and with respect to which a deduction would be allowable under this section but for paragraph (1)" for "made by the donor to such spouse" in para. (i)(2), effective for gifts made after 6/29/89.

—P.L. 101-239, Sec. 7815(d)(2), deleted "who is a citizen or resident" after "Where a donor" in subsec. (a), effective for gifts on or after 7/14/88.

—P.L. 101-239, Sec. 7815(d)(14), provides:

"(14) In the case of the estate of, or gift by, an individual who was not a citizen or resident of the United States but was a resident of a foreign country with which the United States has a tax treaty with respect to estate, inheritance, or gift taxes, the amendments made by section 5033 of the 1988 Act [P. L. 100-647] shall not apply to the extent such amendments would be inconsistent with the provisions of such treaty relating to estate, inheritance, or gift tax marital deductions. In the case of the estate of an individual dying before the date 3 years after the date of the enactment of this Act, or a gift by an individual before the date 3 years after the date of the enactment of this Act, the requirement of the preceding sentence that the individual not be a citizen or resident of the United States shall not apply."

In 1988, P.L. 100-647, Sec. 5033(b), added subsec. (i), effective for gifts on or after 7/14/88.

—P.L. 100-647, Sec. 6152(b), added para. (f)(6), effective as provided in Sec. 6152(c)(1)(B), (2), and (3) which read as follows:

"(c) Effective dates.—

"(1) In general.—Except as otherwise provided in this subsection—

"(B) the amendment made by subsection (b) shall apply to transfers after December 31, 1981.

"(2) Not to apply to extent inconsistent with prior return. — In the case of any estate or gift tax return filed before the date of the enactment of this Act, the amendments made by this section shall not apply to the extent such amendments would be inconsistent with the treatment of the annuity on such return unless the executor or donor (as the case may be) otherwise elects under this paragraph before the day 2 years after the date of the enactment of this Act.

"(3) Extension of time for election out. — The time for making an election under section 2056(b)(7)(C)(ii) or 2523(f)(6)(B) of the 1986 Code (as added by this subsection) shall not expire before the day 2 years after the date of the enactment of this Act (and, if such election is made within the time permitted under this paragraph, the requirement of such section 2056(b)(7)(C)(ii) that it be made on the return shall not apply)."

In 1986, P.L. 99-514, Sec. 1879(n)(1), amended subpara. (f)(4)(A), effective for transfers made after 12/31/85. For special rules, see Sec. 1879(a)(3) of this Act which reads as follows:

"(3) Special rule for certain transfers in October 1984. — An election under section 2523(f) of the Internal Revenue Code of 1954 with respect to an interest in property which—

"(A) was transferred during October 1984, and

"(B) was transferred pursuant to a trust instrument stating that the grantor's intention was that the property of the trust would constitute qualified terminable interest property as to which a Federal gift tax marital deduction would be allowed upon the grantor's election,

shall be made on the return of tax imposed by section 2501 of such Code for the calendar year 1984 which is filed on or before the due date of such return or, if a timely return is not filed, on the first such return filed after the due date of such return and before December 31, 1986."

Prior to amendment, subpara. (f)(4)(A) read as follows:

"(A) Time and manner. An election under this subsection with respect to any property shall be made on or before the first April 15th after the calendar year in which the interest was transferred and shall be made in such manner as the Secretary shall by regulations prescribe."

In 1983, P.L. 97-448, Sec. 104(a)(2)(B), added subsec. (h) . . . Sec. 104(a)(4), amended para. (f)(4) . . . Sec. 104(a)(5), added para. (f)(5) . . . Sec. 104(a)(6), substituted "rules similar to the rules of" for "the rules of" in para. (f)(3), effective for gifts made after 12/31/81.

Prior to amendment, para. (f)(4) read as follows:

"(4) Election. An election under this subsection with respect to any property shall be made on the return of the tax imposed by section 2501 for the calendar year in which the interest was transferred. Such an election, once made, shall be irrevocable."

In 1981, P.L. 97-34, Sec. 403(b)(1), amended subsec. (a) . . . Sec. 403(b)(2), deleted subsec. (f) . . . Sec. 403(d)(2), added subsecs. (f) and (g), effective for gifts made after 12/31/81.

Prior to amendment, subsec. (a) read follows:

"(a) Allowance of deduction.

"(1) In general. Where a donor who is a citizen or resident transfers during the calendar quarter by gift an interest in property to a donee who at the time of the gift is the donor's spouse, there shall be allowed as a deduction in computing taxable gifts for the calendar quarter an amount with respect to such interest equal to its value.

"(2) Limitation. The aggregate of the deductions allowed under paragraph (1) for any calendar quarter shall not exceed the sum of—

"(A) $100,000 reduced (but not below zero) by the aggregate of the deductions allowed under this section for preceding calendar quarters beginning after December 31, 1976; plus

"(B) 50 percent of the lesser of—

"(i) the amount of the deductions allowable under paragraph (1) for such calendar quarter (determined without regard to this paragraph); or

"(ii) the amount (if any) by which the aggregate of amounts determined under clause (i) for the calendar quarter and for each preceding calendar quarter beginning after December 31, 1976, exceeds $200,000."

Prior to amendment, subsec. (f) read as follows:

"(f) Community property.

"(1) A deduction otherwise allowable under this section shall be allowed only to the extent that the transfer can be shown to represent a gift of property which is not, at the time of the gift, held as community property under the law of any State, possession of the United States, or of any foreign country.

"(2) For purposes of paragraph (1), community property (except property which is considered as community property solely by reason of paragraph (3)) shall not be considered as 'held as community property' if the entire value of such property (and not merely one-half thereof) is treated as the amount of the gift.

"(3) If during the calendar year 1942 or in succeeding calendar years, property held as such community property (unless considered by reason of paragraph (2) as not so held) was by the donor and the donee spouse converted, by one transaction or a series of transactions, into separate property of the donor and such spouse (including any form of co-ownership by them), the separate property so acquired by the donor and any property acquired at any time by the donor in exchange therefor (by one exchange or series of exchanges) shall, for purposes of paragraph (1), be considered as 'held as community property.'

"(4) Where the value (at the time of such conversion) of the separate property so acquired by the donor exceeded the value (at such time) of the separate property so acquired by such spouse, paragraph (3) shall apply only with respect to the same portion of such separate property of the donor as the portion which the value (as of such time) of such separate property so acquired by such spouse is of the value (as of such time) of the separate property so acquired by the donor."

In 1976, P.L. 94-455, Sec. 1902(a)(12)(E), deleted "Territory, or" which followed "any State,", in para. (f)(1), for gifts made after 12/31/76.

— P.L. 94-455, Sec. 2002(b), amended subsec. (a), effective for gifts made after 12/31/76.

Prior to amendment, subsec. (a) read as follows:

"(a) In general.

"Where a donor who is a citizen or resident transfers during the calendar quarter by gift an interest in property to a donee who at the time of the gift is the donor's spouse, there shall be allowed as a deduction in computing taxable gifts for the calendar quarter an amount with respect to such interest equal to one-half of its value."

In 1970, P.L. 91-614, Sec. 102(c)(3), substituted "quarter" for "year" each place it appeared in subsec. (a), effective for gifts made after 12/31/70.

Sec. 2524. Extent of deductions.

The deductions provided in sections 2522 and 2523 shall be allowed only to the extent that the gifts therein specified are included in the amount of gifts against which such deductions are applied.

CHAPTER 13. — TAX ON GENERATION-SKIPPING TRANSFERS

• **Caution:** Code Sec. 2664, provides that Chapter 13 of Subchapter B will not apply to generation-skipping transfers after 12/31/2009.

Subchapter

A. Tax imposed.
B. Generation-skipping transfers.
C. Taxable amount.
D. GST exemption.
E. Applicable rate; inclusion ratio.
F. Other definitions and special rules.
G. Administration.

In 1986, P.L. 99-514, Sec. 1431(a), amended Chapter 13.

Prior to amendment, Chapter 13 read as follows:

"CHAPTER 13 — TAX ON CERTAIN GENERATION-SKIPPING TRANSFERS

"Subchapter

"A. Tax imposed.

"B. Definitions and special rules.

"C. Administration."

In 1976, P.L. 94-455, Sec. 2006(a), added Chapter 13.

"Subchapter A — Tax Imposed

"Sec.

"2601. Tax imposed.

"2602. Amount of tax.

"2603. Liability for tax."

In 1976, P.L. 94-455, Sec. 2006(a), added the items for Subchapter A.

"SEC. 2601. TAX IMPOSED.

"A tax is hereby imposed on every generation-skipping transfer in the amount determined under section 2602."

In 1981, P.L. 97-34, Sec. 428, amended Sec. 2006(c)(2)(B) of P. L. 94-455 (as amended by Sec. 702(n)(1) of P. L. 95-600) by substituting "January 1, 1983" for "January 1, 1982" [see below].

In 1978, P.L. 95-600, Sec. 702(n)(1), amended. Sec. 2006(c) of P. L. 94-455, by substituting "June 11, 1976" for "April 30, 1976" each place it appears, [see below].

In 1976, P.L. 94-455, Sec. 2006(a), added Code Sec. 2601. Sec. 2006(c) of the Act, provides as follows:

"(c) Effective dates. —

"(1) In general. — Except as provided in paragraph (2), the amendments made by this section shall apply to any generation-skipping transfer (within the meaning of section 2611(a) of the Internal Revenue Code of 1954) made after June 11, 1976.

Tax on generation-skipping transfers   Chapter 13

"(2) Exceptions.— The amendments made by this section shall not apply to any generation-skipping transfer—

"(A) under a trust which was irrevocable on June 11, 1976, but only to the extent that the transfer is not made out of corpus added to the trust after June 11, 1976, or

"(B) in the case of a decedent dying before January 1, 1983, pursuant to a will (or revocable trust) which was in existence on June 11, 1976, and was not amended at any time after that date in any respect which will result in the creation of, or increasing the amount of, any generation-skipping transfer.

For purposes of subparagraph (B), if the decedent on June 11, 1976, was under a mental disability to change the disposition of his property, the period set forth in such subparagraph shall not expire before the date which is 2 years after the date on which he first regains his competence to dispose of such property.

"(3) Trust equivalents.— For purposes of paragraph (2), in the case of a trust equivalent within the meaning of subsection (d) of section 2611 of the Internal Revenue Code of 1954, the provisions of such subsection (d) shall apply."

"SEC. 2602. AMOUNT OF TAX.

"(a) General rule.

"The amount of the tax imposed by section 2601 with respect to any transfer shall be the excess of—

"(1) a tentative tax computed in accordance with the rate schedule set forth in section 2001(c) (as in effect on the date of transfer) on the sum of—

"(A) the fair market value of the property transferred determined as of the date of transfer (or in the case of an election under subsection (d), as of the applicable valuation date prescribed by section 2032),

"(B) the aggregate fair market value (determined for purposes of this chapter) of all prior transfers of the deemed transferor to which this chapter applied,

"(C) the amount of the adjusted taxable gifts (within the meaning of section 2001(b), as modified by section 2001(e)) made by the deemed transferor before this transfer, and

"(D) if the deemed transferor has died at the same time as, or before, this transfer, the taxable estate of the deemed transferor, over

"(2) a tentative tax (similarly computed) on the sum of the amounts determined under subparagraphs (B), (C), and (D) of paragraph (1).

"(b) Multiple simultaneous transfers.

"If two or more transfers which are taxable under section 2601 and which have the same deemed transferor occur by reason of the same event, the tax imposed by section 2601 on each such transfer shall be the amount which bears the same ratio to—

"(1) the amount of the tax which would be imposed by section 2601 if the aggregate of such transfers were a single transfer, as

"(2) the fair market value of the property transferred in such transfer bears to the aggregate fair market value of all property transferred in such transfers.

"(c) Deductions, credits, etc.

"(1) General rule. Except as otherwise provided in this subsection, no deduction, exclusion, exemption, or credit shall be allowed against the tax imposed by section 2601.

"(2) Charitable deductions allowed. The deduction under section 2055, 2106(a)(2), or 2522, whichever is appropriate, shall be allowed in determining the tax imposed by section 2601.

"(3) Unused portion of unified credit. If the generation-skipping transfer occurs at the same time as, or after, the death of the deemed transferor, then the portion of the credit under section 2010(a) (relating to unified credit) which exceeds the sum of—

"(A) the tax imposed by section 2001, and

"(B) the taxes theretofore imposed by section 2601 with respect to this deemed transferor,

"shall be allowed as a credit against the tax imposed by section 2601. The amount of the credit allowed by the preceding sentence shall not exceed the amount of the tax imposed by section 2601.

"(4) Credit for tax on prior transfers. The credit under section 2013 (relating to credit for tax on prior transfers) shall be allowed against the tax imposed by section 2601. For purposes of the preceding sentence, section 2013 shall be applied as if so much of the property subject to tax under section 2601 as is not taken into account for purposes of determining the credit allowable by section 2013 with respect to the estate of the deemed transferor passed from the transferor (as defined in section 2013) to the deemed transferor.

"(5) Coordination with estate tax.

"(A) Certain expenses attributable to generation-skipping transfer. If the generation-skipping transfer occurs at the same time as, or after, the death of the deemed transferor, for purposes of this section, the amount taken into account with respect to such transfer shall be reduced—

"(i) in the case of a taxable termination, by any item referred to in section 2053 or 2054 to the extent that a deduction would have been allowable under such section for such item if the amount of the trust had been includible in the deemed transferor's gross estate and if the deemed transferor had died immediately before such transfer, or

"(ii) in the case of a taxable distribution, by any expense incurred in connection with the determination, collection, or refund of the tax imposed by section 2601 on such transfer.

"(B) Credit for state inheritance tax. If the generation-skipping transfer occurs at the same time as, or after, the death of the deemed transferor, there shall be allowed as a credit against the tax imposed by section 2601 an amount equal to that portion of the estate, inheritance, legacy, or succession tax actually paid to any State or the District of Columbia in respect of any property included in the generation-skipping transfer, but only to the extent of the lesser of—

"(i) that portion of such taxes which is levied on such transfer, or

"(ii) the excess of the limitation applicable under section 2011(b) if the adjusted taxable estate of the decedent had been increased by the amount of the transfer and all prior generation-skipping transfers to which this subparagraph applied which had the same deemed transferor, over the sum of the amount allowable as a credit under section 2011 with respect to the estate of the decedent plus the aggregate amounts allowable under this subparagraph with respect to such prior generation-skipping transfers.

"(d) Alternate valuation.

"(1) In general. In the case of—

"(A) 1 or more generation-skipping transfers from the same trust which have the same deemed transferor and which are taxable terminations occurring at the same time as the death of such deemed transferor (or at the same time as the death of a beneficiary of the trust assigned to a higher generation than such deemed transferor);

"(B) 1 or more generation-skipping transfers from the same trust with different deemed transferors—

"(i) which are taxable terminations occurring on the same day; and

"(ii) which would, but for section 2613(b)(2), have occurred at the same time as the death of the individuals who are the deemed transferors with respect to the transfers;

"the trustee may elect to value all of the property transferred in such transfers in accordance with section 2032.

"(2) Special rules. If the trustee makes an election under paragraph (1) with respect to any generation-skipping transfer, section 2032 shall be applied by taking into account (in lieu of the date of the decedent's death) the following date:

"(A) in the case of any generation-skipping transfer described in paragraph (1)(A), the date of the death of the deemed transferor (or beneficiary) described in such paragraph, or

"(B) in the case of any generation-skipping transfer described in paragraph (1)(B), the date on which such transfer occurred.

"(e) Transfers within 3 years of death of deemed transferor.

"Under regulations prescribed by the Secretary, the principles of section 2035 shall apply with respect to transfers made during the 3-year period ending on the date of the deemed transferor's death. In the case of any transfer to which this subsection applies, the amount of the tax imposed by this chapter shall be determined as if the transfer occurred after the death of the deemed transferor and appropriate adjustments shall be made with respect to the amount of any prior transfer which is taken into account under subparagraph (B) or (C) of subsection (a)(1)."

In 1981, P.L. 97-34, Sec. 403(a)(2)(B), deleted subpara. (c)(5)(A) and redesignated subparas. (c)(5)(B) and (C) as subparas. (c)(5)(A) and (B), effective for estates of decedents dying after 12/31/81. For an exception to this effective date, see Sec. 403(e)(3) of this Act reproduced in note following Code Sec. 2056. Prior to deletion, subpara. (c)(5)(A) read as follows:

"(A) Adjustments to marital deduction. If the generation-skipping transfer occurs at the same time as, or within 9 months after, the death of the deemed transferor, for purposes of section 2056 (relating to bequests, etc., to surviving spouse), the value of the gross estate of the deemed transferor shall be deemed to be increased by the amount of such transfer."

In 1978, P.L. 95-600, Sec. 702(h)(2), substituted "section 2001(b), as modified by section 2001(e))" for "section 2001(b))" in subpara. (a)(1)(C), effective for estates of decedents dying after '76, except for transfers made before 1/1/77.

—P.L. 95-600, Sec. 702(n)(4), added "(or at the same time as the death of a beneficiary of the trust assigned to a higher generation than such deemed transferor)" following "such deemed transferor" in subpara. (d)(1)(A) . . . added "(or beneficiary)" following "deemed transferor" in subpara. (d)(2)(a), effective as if included in the amendments made by Sec. 2006 of P. L. 94-455 (see note following Code Sec. 2601).

In 1976, P.L. 94-455, Sec. 2006(a), added Code Sec. 2602. For effective date, see Code Sec. 2601.

"SEC. 2603. LIABILITY FOR TAX.

"(a) Personal liability.

"(1) In general. If the tax imposed by section 2601 is not paid, when due then—

"(A) except to the extent provided in paragraph (2), the trustee shall be personally liable for any portion of such tax which is attributable to a taxable termination, and

"(B) the distributee of the property shall be personally liable for such tax to the extent provided in paragraph (3).

"(2) Limitation of personal liability of trustee who relies on certain information furnished by the Secretary.

"(A) Information with respect to rates. The trustee shall not be personally liable for any increase in the tax imposed by section 2601 which is attributable to the application to the transfer of rates of tax which exceeds the rates of tax furnished by the Secretary to the trustee as being the rates at which the transfer may reasonably be expected to be taxed.

"(B) Amount of remaining exclusion. The trustee shall not be personally liable for any increase in the tax imposed by section 2601 which is attributable to the fact that—

"(i) the amount furnished by the Secretary to the trustee as being the amount of exclusion for a transfer to a grandchild of the grantor of the trust which may reasonably be expected to remain with respect to the deemed transferor, is less than

"(ii) the amount of such exclusion remaining with respect to such deemed transferor.

3,041

Chapter 13 — Tax on generation-skipping transfers

"(3) Limitation on personal liability of distributee. The distributee of the property shall be personally liable for the tax imposed by section 2601 only to the extent of an amount equal to the fair market value (determined as of the time of the distribution) of the property received by the distributee in the distribution.
"(b) Lien.
"The tax imposed by section 2601 on any transfer shall be a lien on the property transferred until the tax is paid in full or becomes unenforceable by reason of lapse of time."

In 1976, P.L. 94-455, Sec. 2006(a), added Code Sec. 2603. For effective date, see Code Sec. 2601.

"Subchapter B — Definitions and Special Rules
"Sec.
"2611. Generation-skipping transfer.
"2612. Deemed transferor.
"2613. Other definitions.
"2614. Special rules."

In 1976, P.L. 94-455, Sec. 2006(a), added Subchapter B.

"SEC. 2611. GENERATION-SKIPPING TRANSFER.
"(a) Generation-skipping transfer defined.
"For purposes of this chapter, the terms 'generation-skipping transfer' and 'transfer' mean any taxable distribution or taxable termination with respect to a generation-skipping trust or trust equivalent.
"(b) Generation-skipping trust.
"For purposes of this chapter, the term 'generation-skipping trust' means any trust having younger generation beneficiaries (within the meaning of section 2613(c)(1)) who are assigned to more than one generation.
"(c) Ascertainment of generation.
"For purposes of this chapter, the generation to which any person (other than the grantor) belongs shall be determined in accordance with the following rules:
"(1) an individual who is a lineal descendent of a grandparent of the grantor shall be assigned to that generation which results from comparing the number of generations between the grandparent and such individual with the number of generations between the grandparent and the grantor,
"(2) an individual who has been at any time married to a person described in paragraph (1) shall be assigned to the generation of the person so described and an individual who has been at any time married to the grantor shall be assigned to the grantor's generation,
"(3) a relationship by the half blood shall be treated as a relationship by the whole blood,
"(4) a relationship by legal adoption shall be treated as a relationship by blood,
"(5) an individual who is not assigned to a generation by reason of the foregoing paragraphs shall be assigned to a generation on the basis of the date of such individual's birth, with—
"(A) an individual born not more than 12½ years after the date of the birth of the grantor assigned to the grantor's generation,
"(B) an individual born more than 12½ years but not more than 37½ years after the date of the birth of the grantor assigned to the first generation younger than the grantor, and
"(C) similar rules for a new generation every 25 years,
"(6) an individual who, but for this paragraph, would be assigned to more than one generation shall be assigned to the youngest such generation, and
"(7) if any beneficiary of the trust is an estate or a trust, partnership, corporation, or other entity (other than an organization described in section 511(a)(2) and other than a charitable trust described in section 511(b)(2)), each individual having an indirect interest or power in the trust through such entity shall be treated as a beneficiary of the trust and shall be assigned to a generation under the foregoing provisions of this subsection.
"(d) Generation-skipping trust equivalent.
"(1) In general. For purposes of this chapter, the term 'generation-skipping trust equivalent' means any arrangement which, although not a trust, has substantially the same effect as a generation-skipping trust.
"(2) Examples of arrangements to which subsection relates. Arrangements to be taken into account for purposes of determining whether or not paragraph (1) applies include (but are not limited to) arrangements involving life estates and remainders, estates for years, insurance and annuities, and split interests.
"(3) References to trust include references to trust equivalents. Any reference in this chapter in respect of a generation-skipping trust shall include the appropriate reference in respect of a generation-skipping trust equivalent."

In 1976, P.L. 94-455, Sec. 2006(a), added Code Sec. 2611. For effective date, see Code Sec. 2601.

"SEC. 2612. DEEMED TRANSFEROR.
"(a) General rule.
"For purposes of this chapter, the deemed transferor with respect to a transfer is—
"(1) except as provided in paragraph (2), the parent of the transferee of the property who is more closely related to the grantor of the trust than the other parent of such transferee (or if neither parent is related to such grantor, the parent having a closer affinity to the grantor), or

"(2) if the parent described in paragraph (1) is not a younger generation beneficiary of the trust but 1 or more ancestors of the transferee is a younger generation beneficiary related by blood or adoption to the grantor of the trust, the youngest of such ancestors.
"(b) Determination of relationship.
"For purposes of subsection (a), a parent related to the grantor of the trust by blood or adoption is more closely related than a parent related to such grantor by marriage."

In 1976, P.L. 94-455, Sec. 2006(a), added Code Sec. 2612. For effective date, see Code Sec. 2601.

"SEC. 2613. OTHER DEFINITIONS.
"(a) Taxable distribution.
"For purposes of this chapter—
"(1) In general. The term 'taxable distribution' means any distribution which is not out of the income of the trust (within the meaning of section 643(b)) from a generation-skipping trust to any younger generation beneficiary who is assigned to a generation younger than the generation assignment of any other person who is a younger generation beneficiary. For purposes of the preceding sentence, an individual who at no time has had anything other than a future interest or future power (or both) in the trust shall not be considered as a younger generation beneficiary.
"(2) Source of distribution. If, during the taxable year of the trust, there are distributions out of the income of the trust (within the meaning of section 643(b)) and out of other amounts, for purposes of paragraph (1) the distributions of such income shall be deemed to have been made to the beneficiaries (to the extent of the aggregate distributions made to each such beneficiary during such year) in descending order of generations, beginning with the beneficiaries assigned to the oldest generation.
"(3) Payment of tax. If any portion of the tax imposed by this chapter with respect to any transfer is paid out of the income or corpus of the trust, an amount equal to the portion so paid shall be deemed to be a generation-skipping transfer.
"(4) Certain distributions excluded from tax. The term 'taxable distribution' does not include—
"(A) any transfer to the extent such transfer is to a grandchild of the grantor of the trust and does not exceed the limitation provided by subsection (b)(6), and
"(B) any transfer to the extent such transfer is subject to tax imposed by chapter 11 or 12.
"(b) Taxable termination.
"For purposes of this chapter—
"(1) In general. The term 'taxable termination' means the termination (by death, lapse of time, exercise or nonexercise, or otherwise) of the interest or power in a generation-skipping trust of any younger generation beneficiary who is assigned to any generation older than the generation assignment of any other person who is a younger generation beneficiary of that trust. Such term does not include a termination of the interest or power of any person who at no time has had anything other than a future interest or future power (or both) in the trust.
"(2) Time certain terminations deemed to occur.
"(A) Where 2 or more beneficiaries are assigned to same generation. In any case where 2 or more younger generation beneficiaries of a trust are assigned to the same generation, except to the extent provided in regulations prescribed by the Secretary, the transfer constituting the termination with respect to each such beneficiary shall be treated as occurring at the time when the last such termination occurs.
"(B) Same beneficiary has more than 1 interest or power. In any case where a younger generation beneficiary of a trust has both a present interest and a present power, or more than 1 interest or power, in the trust, except to the extent provided in regulations prescribed by the Secretary, the termination with respect to each such present interest or present power shall be treated as occurring at the time when the last such termination occurs.
"(C) Unusual order of termination.
"(i) In general. If—
"(I) but for this subparagraph, there would have been a termination (determined after the application of subparagraphs (A) and (B)) of an interest or power of a younger generation beneficiary (hereinafter in this subparagraph referred to as the 'younger beneficiary'), and
"(II) at the time such termination would have occurred, a beneficiary (hereinafter in this subparagraph referred to as the 'older beneficiary') of the trust assigned to a higher generation than the generation of the younger beneficiary has a present interest or power in the trust,
then, except to the extent provided in regulations prescribed by the Secretary, the transfer constituting the termination with respect to the younger beneficiary shall be treated as occurring at the time when the termination of the last present interest or power of the older beneficiary occurs.
"(ii) Special rules. If clause (i) applies with respect to any younger beneficiary—
"(I) this chapter shall be applied first to the termination of the interest or power of the older beneficiary as if such termination occurred before the termination of the power or interest of the younger beneficiary; and
"(II) the value of the property taken into account for purposes of determining the tax (if any) imposed by this chapter with respect to the termination of the interest or power of the younger beneficiary shall be reduced by the tax (if any) imposed by this chapter with respect to the termination of the interest or power of the older beneficiary.
"(D) Special rule. Subparagraphs (A) and (C) shall also apply where a person assigned to the same generation as, or a higher generation than, the person whose

Tax on generation-skipping transfers   Chapter 13

power or interest terminates has a present power or interest immediately after the termination and such power or interest arises as a result of such termination.

"(3) Deemed transferees of certain terminations. Where, at the time of any termination, it is not clear who will be the transferee of any portion of the property transferred, except to the extent provided in regulations prescribed by the Secretary, such portion shall be deemed transferred pro rata to all beneficiaries of the trust in accordance with the amount which each of them would receive under a maximum exercise of discretion on their behalf. For purposes of the preceding sentence, where it is not clear whether discretion will be exercised per stirpes or per capita, it shall be presumed that the discretion will be exercised per stirpes.

"(4) Termination of power. In the case of the termination of any power, the property transferred shall be deemed to be the property subject to the power immediately before the termination (determined without the application of paragraph (2)).

"(5) Certain terminations excluded from tax. The term 'taxable termination' does not include—

"(A) any transfer to the extent such transfer is to a grandchild of the grantor of the trust and does not exceed the limitation provided by paragraph (6), and

"(B) any transfer to the extent such transfer is subject to a tax imposed by chapter 11 or 12.

"(6) $250,000 limit on exclusion of transfers to grandchildren. In the case of any deemed transferor, the maximum amount excluded from the terms 'taxable distribution' and 'taxable termination' by reason of provisions exempting from such terms transfers to the grandchildren of the grantor of the trust shall be $250,000. The preceding sentence shall be applied to transfers from one or more trusts in the order in which such transfers are made or deemed made.

"(7) Coordination with subsection (a).

"(A) Termination take precedence over distributions. If—

"(i) the death of an individual or any other occurrence is a taxable termination with respect to any property, and

"(ii) such occurrence also requires the distribution of part or all of such property in a distribution which would (but for this subparagraph) be a taxable distribution,

then a taxable distribution shall be deemed not to have occurred with respect to the portion described in clause (i).

"(B) Certain prior transfers. To the extent that—

"(i) the deemed transferor in any prior transfer of the property of the trust being transferred in this transfer was assigned to the same generation as (or a lower generation than) the generation assignment of the deemed transferor in this transfer,

"(ii) the transferee in such prior transfer was assigned to the same generation as (or a higher generation than) the generation assignment of the transferee in this transfer, and

"(iii) such transfers do not have the effect of avoiding tax under this chapter with respect to any transfer,

the terms 'taxable termination' and 'taxable distribution' do not include this later transfer.

"(c) Younger generation beneficiary; beneficiary.

"For purposes of this chapter—

"(1) Younger generation beneficiary. The term 'younger generation beneficiary' means any beneficiary who is assigned to a generation younger than the grantor's generation.

"(2) Time for ascertaining younger generation beneficiaries. A person is a younger generation beneficiary of a trust with respect to any transfer only if such person was a younger generation beneficiary of the trust immediately before the transfer (or, in the case of a series of related transfers, only if such person was a younger generation beneficiary of the trust immediately before the first of such transfers).

"(3) Beneficiary. The term 'beneficiary' means any person who has a present or future interest or power in the trust.

"(d) Interest or power.

"For purposes of this chapter—

"(1) Interest. A person has an interest in a trust if such person—

"(A) Has a right to receive income or corpus from the trust, or

"(B) is a permissible recipient of such income or corpus.

"(2) Power. The term 'power' means any power to establish or alter beneficial enjoyment of the corpus or income of the trust.

"(e) Certain powers not taken into account.

"(1) Limited power to appoint among lineal descendants of the grantor. For purposes of this chapter, an individual shall be treated as not having any power in a trust if such individual does not have any present or future power in the trust other than a power to dispose of the corpus of the trust or the income therefrom to a beneficiary or a class of beneficiaries who are lineal descendants of the grantor assigned to a generation younger than the generation assignment of such individual.

"(2) Powers of independent trustees.

"(A) In general. For purposes of this chapter, an individual shall be treated as not having any power in a trust if such individual—

"(i) is a trustee who has no interest in the trust, (other than as a potential appointee under a power of appointment held by another)

"(ii) is not a related or subordinate trustee, and

"(iii) does not have any present or future power in the trust other than a power to dispose of the corpus of the trust or the income therefrom to a beneficiary or a class of beneficiaries designated in the trust instrument.

"(B) Related or subordinate trustee defined. For purposes of subparagraph (A), the term 'related or subordinate trustee' means any trustee who is assigned to a younger generation than the grantor's generation and who is—

"(i) the spouse of the grantor or of any beneficiary,

"(ii) the father, mother, lineal descendant, brother, or sister of the grantor or of any beneficiary,

"(iii) an employee of the grantor or of any beneficiary,

"(iv) an employee of a corporation in which the stockholdings of the grantor, the trust, and the beneficiaries of the trust are significant from the viewpoint of voting control,

"(v) an employee of a corporation in which the grantor or any beneficiary of the trust is an executive,

"(vi) a partner of a partnership in which the interest of the grantor, the trust, and the beneficiaries of the trust are significant from the viewpoint of operating control or distributive share of partnership income, or

"(vii) an employee of a partnership in which the grantor or any beneficiary of the trust is a partner.

"(f) Effect of adoption.

"For purposes of this chapter, a relationship by legal adoption shall be treated as a relationship by blood."

In 1980, P.L. 96-222, Sec. 107(a)(2)(B)(i), added "(other than as a potential appointee under a power of appointment held by another)" after "the trust" in clause (e)(2)(A)(i) . . . Sec. 107(a)(2)(B)(ii)(I), added new clause (e)(2)(B)(iii) . . . Sec. 107(a)(2)(B)(ii)(II), deleted clause (vi) and redesignated clauses (iii), (iv), and (v) as (iv), (v), and (vi) . . . Sec. 107(a)(2)(B)(ii)(III), added "or" at the end of clause (e)(2)(B)(vi) (as so redesignated), effective as if included in the amendments made by Sec. 2006 of P. L. 94-455 (see note following Code Sec. 2601) Prior to deletion, clause (e)(2)(B)(vi) read as follows:

"(vi) an employee of a corporation in which the grantor or any beneficiary of the trust is an executive, or"

In 1978, P.L. 95-600, Sec. 702(n)(2), amended subsec. (e) . . . Sec. 702(n)(3), substituted "a present interest and a present power" for "an interest and a power" . . . substituted "present interest or present power" for "interest or power in subpara. (b)(2)(B), effective as if included in the amendments made by Sec. 2006 of P. L. 94-455 (see note following Code Sec. 2601).

Prior to amendment, subsec. (e) read as follows:

"(e) Limited power to appoint among lineal descendants of grantor not taken into account in certain cases.

"For purposes of this chapter, if any individual does not have any present or future power in the trust other than a power to dispose of the corpus of the trust or the income therefrom to a beneficiary or a class of beneficiaries who are lineal descendants of the grantor assigned to a generation younger than the generation assignment of such individual, then such individual shall be treated as not having any power in the trust."

In 1976, P.L. 94-455, Sec. 2006(a), added Code Sec. 2613. For effective date, see Code Sec. 2601.

"SEC. 2614. SPECIAL RULES.

"(a) Basis adjustment.

"If property is transferred to any person pursuant to a generation-skipping transfer which occurs before the death of the deemed transferor, the basis of such property in the hands of the transferee shall be increased (but not above the fair market value of such property) by an amount equal to that portion of the tax imposed by section 2601 with respect to the transfer which is attributable to the excess of the fair market value of such property over its adjusted basis immediately before the transfer. If property is transferred in a generation-skipping transfer subject to tax under this chapter which occurs at the same time as, or after, the death of the deemed transferor, the basis of such property shall be adjusted in a manner similar to the manner provided under section 1014(a).

"(b) Nonresidents not citizens of the United States.

"If the deemed transferor of any transfer is, at the time of the transfer, a nonresident not a citizen of the United States and—

"(1) if the deemed transferor is alive at the time of the transfer, there shall be taken into account only property which would be taken into account for purposes of chapter 12, or

"(2) if the deemed transferor has died at the same time as, or before, the transfer, there shall be taken into account only property which would be taken into account for purposes of chapter 11.

"(c) Disclaimers.

"For provisions relating to the effect of a qualified disclaimer for purposes of this chapter, see section 2518."

In 1980, P.L. 96-223, Sec. 401(c)(3), amended subsec. (a), in respect of decedents dying after 12/31/76.

Prior to amendment, subsec. (a) read as follows:

"(a) Basis adjustment.

"If property is transferred to any person pursuant to a generation-skipping transfer which occurs before the death of the deemed transferor, the basis of such property in the hands of the transferee shall be increased (but not above the fair market value of such property) by an amount equal to that portion of the tax imposed by section 2601 with respect to the transfer which is attributable to the excess of the fair market value of such property over its adjusted basis immediately before the transfer. If property is transferred in a generation-skipping transfer subject to tax under this chapter which occurs at the same time as, or after, the death of the deemed transferor, the basis of such property shall be adjusted—

"(1) in the case of such a transfer occurring after June 11, 1976, and before January 1, 1980, in a manner similar to the manner provided under section 1014(a), and

Chapter 13   Tax on generation-skipping transfers

"(2) in the case of such a transfer occurring after December 31, 1979, in a manner similar to the manner provided by section 1023 without regard to subsection (d) thereof (relating to basis of property passing from a decedent dying after December 31, 1979)."

In 1978, P.L. 95-600, Sec. 702(c)(1)(B), amended the second sentence of subsec. (a), effective as if included in the amendments made by Sec. 2006 of P. L. 94-455 (see note following Code Sec. 2601).

Prior to amendment, the second sentence of subsec. (a) read as follows: "If property is transferred in a generation-skipping transfer subject to tax under this chapter which occurs at the same time as, or after, the death of the deemed transferor, the basis of such property shall be adjusted in a manner similar to the manner provided by section 1023 without regard to subsection (d) thereof (relating to basis of property passing from a decedent dying after December 31, 1976)."

In 1976, P.L. 94-455, Sec. 2006(a), added Code Sec. 2614. For effective date, see Code Sec. 2601.

"Subchapter C — Administration
"Sec.
"2621. Administration.
"2622. Regulations."

In 1976, P.L. 94-455, Sec. 2006(a), added Subchapter C.

"Sec. 2621. Administration.
"(a) General rule.
"Insofar as applicable and not inconsistent with the provisions of this chapter—
"(1) if the deemed transferor is not alive at the time of the transfer, all provisions of subtitle F (including penalties) applicable to chapter 11 or section 2001 are hereby made applicable in respect of this chapter or section 2601, as the case may be, and
"(2) if the deemed transferor is alive at the time of the transfer, all provisions of subtitle F (including penalties) applicable to chapter 12 or section 2501 are hereby made applicable in respect of this chapter or section 2601, as the case may be.
"(b) Section 6166 not applicable.
"For purposes of this chapter, section 6166 (relating to extension of time for payment of estate tax where estate consists largely of interest in closely held business) shall not apply.
"(c) Return requirements.
"(1) In general. The Secretary shall prescribe by regulations the person who is required to make the return with respect to the tax imposed by this chapter and the time by which any such return must be filed. To the extent practicable, such regulations shall provide that—
"(A) the person who is required to make such return shall be—
"(i) in the case of a taxable distribution, the distributee, or
"(ii) in the case of a taxable termination, the trustee; and
"(B) the return shall be filed—
"(i) in the case of a generation-skipping transfer occurring before the death of the deemed transferor, on or before the 90th day after the close of the taxable year of the trust in which such transfer occurred, or
"(ii) in the case of a generation-skipping transfer occurring at the same time as, or after, the death of the deemed transferor, on or before the 90th day ater the last day prescribed by law (including extensions) for filing the return of tax under chapter 11 with respect to the estate of the deemed transferor (or if later, the day which is 9 months after the day on which such generation-skipping transfer occurred).
"(2) Information returns. The Secretary may by regulations require the trustee to furnish the Secretary with such information as he determines to be necessary for purposes of this chapter."

In 1981, P.L. 97-34, Sec. 422(e)(4), substituted "section 6166 (relating to extension" for "sections 6166 and 6166A (relating to extensions" in subsec. (b) and substituted "Section 6166" for "Sections 6166 and 6166A" in the heading of subsec. (b), effective for estates of decedents dying after 12/31/81.

In 1976, P.L. 94-455, Sec. 2006(a), added Code Sec. 2621. For effective date, see Code Sec. 2601.

"Sec. 2622. Regulations.
"The Secretary shall prescribe such regulations as may be necessary or appropriate to carry out the purposes of this chapter, including regulations providing the extent to which substantially separate and independent shares of different beneficiaries in the trust shall be treated as separate trusts."

In 1976, P.L. 94-455, Sec. 2006(a), added Code Sec. 2622. For effective date, see Code Sec. 2601.

Subchapter A. — Tax Imposed
Sec.
2601. Tax imposed.
2602. Amount of tax.
2603. Liability for tax.

2604. Credit for certain State taxes.

In 2004, P.L. 108-311, Sec. 408(a)(21), added item 2604.
In 2001, P.L. 107-16, Sec. 532(c)(15), [Caution] deleted item 2604. Sec. 532(c)(10) of this Act provides that Code Sec. 2604 shall not apply to generation-skipping transfers after 12/31/2004. Item 2604 was reinstated by Sec. 408(a)(21) of P. L. 108-311, see above.

⌐   ⌐
• **Caution:** Code Sec. 2664, provides that Chapter 13 of Subchapter B will not apply to generation-skipping transfers after 12/31/2009.
⌐   ⌐

Sec. 2601. Tax imposed.

A tax is hereby imposed on every generation-skipping transfer (within the meaning of subchapter B).

In 1990, P.L. 101-508, Sec. 11703(c)(3), [with respect to Sec. 1433(b)(2)(C) of P. L. 99-514, see below] provides:

"(3) Subparagraph (C) of section 1433(b)(2) of the Tax Reform Act of 1986 shall not exempt any generation-skipping transfer from the amendments made by subtitle D of title XVI of such Act to the extent such transfer is attributable to property transferred by gift or by reason of the death of another person to the decedent (or trust) referred to in such subparagraph after August 3, 1990."

In 1988, P.L. 100-647, Sec. 1014(h)(2)(A), substituted "this subtitle" for "this part", in Sec. 1433(b)(2) of P. L. 99-514 [reproduced below]... Sec. 1014(h)(2)(B), added "(or out of income attributable to corpus so added)", before the comma at the end of Sec. 1433(b)(2)(A) of P. L. 99-514... Sec. 1014(h)(2)(C), added "or revocable trust" after "a will" in Sec. 1433(b)(2)(B) of P. L. 99-514... Sec. 1014(h)(3)(A), deleted Sec. 1433(b)(3) of P. L. 99-514 and added new Secs. 1433(b)(3) and (4) of P. L. 99-514 [see below].

Prior to deletion, Sec. 1433(b)(3) of P. L. 99-514 read as follows:
"(3) Treatment of certain transfers to grandchildren — For purposes of chapter 13 of the Internal Revenue Code of 1986, the term 'direct skip' shall not include any transfer before January 1, 1990, from a transferor to a grandchild of the transferor to the extent that the aggregate transfers from such transferor to such grandchild do not exceed $2,000,000."
—P.L. 100-647, Sec. 1014(h)(3)(B), of this Act provides:
"(B) Clause (iii) of section 1443(b)(3)(B) of the Reform Act [P. L. 99-514] (as amended by subparagraph (A)) shall apply only to transfers after June 10, 1987."
—P.L. 100-647, Sec. 1014(h)(4)(A), substituted "shall be treated as a direct skip to a grandchild" for "shall be treated as a direct skip" in Sec. 1433(d) of P. L. 99-514... Sec. 1014(h)(4)(B), substituted "would be a direct skip to a grandchild" for "would be a direct skip" in Sec. 1433(d)(1)(B) of P. L. 99-514 ... Sec. 1014(h)(4)(C), added the last sentence to Sec. 1433(d) of P. L. 99-514
—P.L. 100-647, Sec. 1014(h)(5), of this Act provides:
"(5) Subparagraph (C) of section 1433(b)(2) of the Reform Act shall not exempt any direct skip from the amendments made by subtitle D of title XIV of the Reform Act if—
"(A) such direct skip results from the application of section 2044 of the 1986 Code, and
"(B) such direct skip is attributable to property transferred to the trust after October 21, 1988."

In 1986, P.L. 99-514, Sec. 1431(a), added Code Sec. 2601 as part of the amendments to Chapter 13, effective for any generation-skipping transfer (within the meaning of Code Sec. 2611) made after 10/22/86, except as provided in Sec. 1433(b)-(d) of this Act [as amended by Sec. 1014(h)(2)-(4) of P. L. 100-647, see above], which reads as follows:

"(b) Special rules. —
"(1) Treatment of certain inter vivos transfers made after September 25, 1985. — For purposes of subsection (a) (and chapter 13 of the Internal Revenue Code of 1986 as amended by this part), any inter vivos transfer after September 25, 1985, and on or before the date of the enactment of this Act shall be treated as if it were made on the 1st day after the date of enactment of this Act.
"(2) Exceptions. — The amendments made by this subtitle shall not apply to—
"(A) any generation-skipping transfer under a trust which was irrevocable on September 25, 1985, but only to the extent that such transfer is not made out of corpus added to the trust after September 25, 1985 (or out of income attributable to corpus so added),
"(B) any generation-skipping transfer under a will or revocable trust executed before the date of the enactment of this Act if the decedent dies before January 1, 1987, and
"(C) any generation-skipping transfer—
"(i) under a trust to the extent such trust consists of property included in the gross estate of a decedent (other than property transferred by the decedent during his life after the date of the enactment of this Act), or reinvestments thereof, or
"(ii) which is a direct skip which occurs by reason of the death of any decedent;

Tax on generation-skipping transfers

Code Sec. 2604(c)

but only if such decedent was, on the date of the enactment of this Act, under a mental disability to change the disposition of his property and did not regain his competence to dispose of such property before the date of his death.

"(3) Treatment of certain transfers to grandchildren.

"(A) In general. For purposes of chapter 13 of the Internal Revenue Code of 1986, the term 'direct skip' shall not include any transfer before January 1, 1990, from a transferor to a grandchild of the transferor to the extent the aggregate transfers from such transferor to such grandchild do not exceed $2,000,000.

"(B) Treatment of transfers in trust. For purposes of subparagraph (A), a transfer in trust for the benefit of a grandchild shall be treated as a transfer to such grandchild if (and only if)—

"(i) during the life of the grandchild, no portion of the corpus or income of the trust may be distributed to (or for the benefit of) any person other than such grandchild,

"(ii) the assets of the trust will be includible in the gross estate of the grandchild if the grandchild dies before the trust is terminated, and

"(iii) all of the income of the trust for periods after the grandchild has attained age 21 will be distributed to (or for the benefit of) such grandchild not less frequently than annually.

"(C) Coordination with section 2653(a) of the 1986 Code. In the case of any transfer which would be a generation-skipping transfer but for subparagraph (A), the rules of section 2653(a) of the Internal Revenue Code of 1986 shall apply as if such transfer were a generation-skipping transfer.

"(D) Coordination with taxable terminations and taxable distributions. For purposes of chapter 13 of the Internal Revenue Code of 1986, the terms 'taxable termination' and 'taxable distribution' shall not include any transfer which would be a direct skip but for subparagraph (A).

"(4) Definitions. Terms used in this section shall have the same respective meanings as when used in chapter 13 of the Internal Revenue Code of 1986; except that section 2612(c)(2) of such Code shall not apply in determining whether an individual is a grandchild of the transferor.

"(c) Repeal of existing tax on generation-skipping transfers.—

"(1) In general.—In the case of any tax imposed by chapter 13 of the Internal Revenue Code of 1954 (as in effect on the day before the date of the enactment of this Act), such tax (including interest, additions to tax, and additional amounts) shall not be assessed and if assessed, the assessment shall be abated, and if collected, shall be credited or refunded (with interest) as an overpayment.

"(2) Waiver of statute of limitations.—If on the date of the enactment of this Act (or at any time within 1 year after such date of enactment) refund or credit of any overpayment of tax resulting from the application of paragraph (1) is barred by any law or rule of law, refund or credit of such overpayment shall, nevertheless, be made or allowed if claim therefore is filed before the date 1 year after the date of the enactment of this Act.

"(d) Election for certain transfers benefiting grandchild.—

"(1) In general.— For purposes of chapter 13 of the Internal Revenue Code of 1986 (as amended by this Act) and subsection (b) of this section, any transfer in trust for the benefit of a grandchild of a transferor shall be treated as a direct skip to such grandchild if—

"(A) the transfer occurs before the date of enactment of this Act,

"(B) the transfer would be a direct skip to a grandchild except for the fact that the trust instrument provides that, if the grandchild dies before vesting of the interest transferred, the interest is transferred to the grandchild's heir (rather than the grandchild's estate), and

"(C) an election under this subsection applies to such transfer.

Any transfer treated as a direct skip by reason of the preceding sentence shall be subject to Federal estate tax on the grandchild's death in the same manner as if the contingent gift would have been to the grandchild's estate.

"(2) Election.— An election under paragraph (1) shall be made at such time and in such manner as the Secretary of the Treasury or his delegate may prescribe.

"Unless the grandchild otherwise directs by will, the estate of such grandchild shall be entitled to recover from the person receiving the property on the death of the grandchild any increase in Federal estate tax on the estate of the grandchild by reason of the preceding sentence."

• **Caution:** Code Sec. 2664, provides that Chapter 13 of Subchapter B will not apply to generation-skipping transfers after 12/31/2009.

Sec. 2602. Amount of tax.

The amount of the tax imposed by section 2601 is—

(1) the taxable amount (determined under subchapter C), multiplied by

(2) the applicable rate (determined under subchapter E).

In 1986, P.L. 99-514, Sec. 1431(a), added Code Sec. 2602 as part of the amendments to Chapter 13, effective for any generation-skipping transfer (within the meaning of Code Sec. 2611) made after 10/22/86, except as provided in Sec. 1433(b)-(d) of this Act, reproduced in the note following Code Sec. 2601.

• **Caution:** Code Sec. 2664, provides that Chapter 13 of Subchapter B will not apply to generation-skipping transfers after 12/31/2009.

Sec. 2603. Liability for tax.
(a) Personal liability.

(1) Taxable distributions. In the case of a taxable distribution, the tax imposed by section 2601 shall be paid by the transferee.

(2) Taxable termination. In the case of a taxable termination or a direct skip from a trust, the tax shall be paid by the trustee.

(3) Direct skip. In the case of a direct skip (other than a direct skip from a trust), the tax shall be paid by the transferor.

(b) Source of tax.

Unless otherwise directed pursuant to the governing instrument by specific reference to the tax imposed by this chapter, the tax imposed by this chapter on a generation-skipping transfer shall be charged to the property constituting such transfer.

(c) Cross reference.

For provisions making estate and gift tax provisions with respect to transferee liability, liens, and related matters applicable to the tax imposed by section 2601, see section 2661.

In 1986, P.L. 99-514, Sec. 1431(a), added Code Sec. 2603 as part of the amendments to Chapter 13, effective for any generation-skipping transfer (within the meaning of Code Sec. 2611) made after 10/22/86, except as provided in Sec. 1433(b)-(d) of this Act, reproduced in the note following Code Sec. 2601.

• **Caution:** Code Sec. 2604, provides that Chapter 13 of Subchapter B will not apply to generation-skipping transfers after 12/31/2009.

Sec. 2604. Credit for certain State taxes.
(a) General rule.

If a generation-skipping transfer (other than a direct skip) occurs at the same time as and as a result of the death of an individual, a credit against the tax imposed by section 2601 shall be allowed in an amount equal to the generation-skipping transfer tax actually paid to any State in respect to any property included in the generation-skipping transfer.

(b) Limitation.

The aggregate amount allowed as a credit under this section with respect to any transfer shall not exceed 5 percent of the amount of the tax imposed by section 2601 on such transfer.

• **Caution:** Code Sec. 2604(c), following, was added by Sec. 532(c)(10), P.L. 107-16, the Economic Growth and Tax Relief Reconciliation Act of 2001 (EGTRRA). These provisions generally sunset for tax years beginning after 12/31/2012. For specific sunset provisions, see Sec. 901, P.L. 107-16 (as amended) reproduced in history notes for this Code Sec.

(c) Termination.

This section shall not apply to the generation-skipping transfers after December 31, 2004.

Code Sec. 2604 — Tax on generation-skipping transfers

In 2010, P.L. 111-312, Sec. 101(a)(1), substituted "December 31, 2012" for "December 31, 2010" both places it appears in Sec. 901, P.L. 107-16, see below, effective as if included in the enactment of P.L. 107-16, EGTRRA, 6/7/2001.

In 2002, P.L. 107-358, Sec. 2, added subsec. (c) in Sec. 901 of P. L. 107-16 [see below], effective 12/17/2002.

In 2001, P.L. 107-16, Sec. 532(c)(10), added subsec. (c), effective for estates of decedents dying, and generation-skipping transfers, after 12/31/2004.

—P.L. 107-16, Sec. 901, of this Act [as amended by Sec. 2, P. L. 107-358, and Sec. 101(a)(1), P.L. 111-312, see above], reads as follows:

"SEC. 901. SUNSET OF PROVISIONS OF ACT.

"(a) In general. All provisions of, and amendments made by, this Act shall not apply—

"(1) to taxable, plan, or limitation years beginning after December 31, 2012, or

"(2) in the case of title V, to estates of decedents dying, gifts made, or generation skipping transfers, after December 31, 2012.

"(b) Application of certain laws. The Internal Revenue Code of 1986 and the Employee Retirement Income Security Act of 1974 shall be applied and administered to years, estates, gifts, and transfers described in subsection (a) as if the provisions and amendments described in subsection (a) had never been enacted.

"(c) Exception. Subsection (a) shall not apply to section 803 (relating to no federal income tax on restitution received by victims of the Nazi regime or their heirs or estates)."

In 1986, P.L. 99-514, Sec. 1431(a), added Code Sec. 2604 as part of the amendments to Chapter 13, effective for any generation-skipping transfer (within the meaning of Code Sec. 2611) made after 10/22/86, except as provided in Sec. 1433(b)-(d) of this Act, reproduced in the note following Code Sec. 2601.

Subchapter B.—Generation-Skipping Transfers

Sec.
2611. Generation-skipping transfer defined.
2612. Taxable termination; taxable distribution; direct skip.
2613. Skip person and non-skip person defined.

⌐ • **Caution:** Code Sec. 2664, provides that Chapter 13 of Subchapter B will not apply to generation-skipping transfers after 12/31/2009. ⌐

Sec. 2611. Generation-skipping transfer defined.
(a) In general.

For purposes of this chapter, the term "generation-skipping transfer" means—

(1) a taxable distribution,

(2) a taxable termination, and

(3) a direct skip.

(b) Certain transfers excluded.

The term "generation-skipping transfer" does not include—

(1) any transfer which, if made inter vivos by an individual, would not be treated as a taxable gift by reason of section 2503(e) (relating to exclusion of certain transfers for educational or medical expenses), and

(2) any transfer to the extent—

(A) the property transferred was subject to a prior tax imposed under this chapter,

(B) the transferee in the prior transfer was assigned to the same generation as (or a lower generation than) the generation assignment of the transferee in this transfer, and

(C) such transfers do not have the effect of avoiding tax under this chapter with respect to any transfer.

In 1988, P.L. 100-647, Sec. 1014(g)(1), substituted "generation-skipping transfer" for "generation-skipping transfers" in subsec. (a)... Sec. 1014(g)(2), deleted para. (b)(1) and redesignated paras. (b)(2) and (b)(3) as paras. (b)(1) and (b)(2) ... Sec. 1018(u)(43), substituted "means" for "mean" in subsec. (a), effective for any generation-skipping transfer (within the meaning of Code Sec. 2611) made after 10/22/86, except as provided in Sec. 1433(b)-(d) of P. L. 99-514, reproduced in the note following Code Sec. 2601.

Prior to deletion, para. (b)(1) read as follows:

"(1) any transfer (other than a direct skip) from a trust, to the extent such transfer is subject to a tax imposed by chapter 11 or 12 with respect to a person in the 1st generation below that of the grantor, and".

In 1986, P.L. 99-514, Sec. 1431(a), added Code Sec. 2611 as part of the amendments to Chapter 13, effective for any generation-skipping transfer (within the meaning of '86 Code Sec. 2611) made after 10/22/86, except as provided in Sec. 1433(b)-(d) of this Act, reproduced in the note following Code Sec. 2601.

⌐ • **Caution:** Code Sec. 2664, provides that Chapter 13 of Subchapter B will not apply to generation-skipping transfers after 12/31/2009. ⌐

Sec. 2612. Taxable termination; taxable distribution; direct skip.
(a) Taxable termination.

(1) **General rule.** For purposes of this chapter, the term "taxable termination" means the termination (by death, lapse of time, release of power, or otherwise) of an interest in property held in a trust unless—

(A) immediately after such termination, a non-skip person has an interest in such property, or

(B) at no time after such termination may a distribution (including distributions on termination) be made from such trust to a skip person.

(2) **Certain partial terminations treated as taxable.** If, upon the termination of an interest in property held in trust by reason of the death of a lineal descendant of the transferor, a specified portion of the trust's assets are distributed to 1 or more skip persons (or 1 or more trusts for the exclusive benefit of such persons), such termination shall constitute a taxable termination with respect to such portion of the trust property.

(b) Taxable distribution.

For purposes of this chapter, the term "taxable distribution" means any distribution from a trust to a skip person (other than a taxable termination or a direct skip).

(c) Direct skip.

For purposes of this chapter—

(1) **In general.** The term "direct skip" means a transfer subject to a tax imposed by chapter 11 or 12 of an interest in property to a skip person.

(2) **Look-thru rules not to apply.** Solely for purposes of determining whether any transfer to a trust is a direct skip, the rules of section 2651(f)(2) shall not apply.

In 1997, P.L. 105-34, Sec. 511(b)(1), deleted para. (c)(2) and redesignated para. (c)(3) as para. (c)(2)... Sec. 511(b)(2), substituted "section 2651(f)(2)" for "section 2651(e)(2)" in para. (c)(2) [as redesignated, see above], effective for terminations, distributions, and transfers occurring after 12/31/97.

Prior to deletion, para. (c)(2) read as follows:

"(2) Special rule for transfers to grandchildren. For purposes of determining whether any transfer is a direct skip, if—

"(A) an individual is a grandchild of the transferor (or the transferor's spouse or former spouse), and

"(B) as of the time of the transfer, the parent of such individual who is a lineal descendant of the transferor (or the transferor's spouse or former spouse) is dead, such individual shall be treated as if such individual were a child of the transferor and all of that grandchild's children shall be treated as if they were grandchildren of the transferor. In the case of lineal descendants below a grandchild, the preceding sentence may be reapplied. If any transfer of property to a trust would be a direct skip but for this paragraph, any generation assignment under this paragraph shall apply also for purposes of applying this chapter to transfers from the portion of the trust attributable to such property."

In 1988, P.L. 100-647, Sec. 1014(g)(5)(B), added para. (c)(3)... Sec. 1014(g)(7), added the last sentence to para. (c)(2)... Sec. 1014(g)(15), amended para. (a)(2), effective for any generation-skipping transfer (within the meaning of Code Sec. 2611) made after 10/22/86, except as provided in Sec. 1433(b)-(d) of P. L. 99-514, reproduced in the note following Code Sec. 2601.

Prior to amendment, para. (a)(2) read as follows:

"(2) Certain partial terminations treated as taxable. If, upon the termination of an interest in property held in a trust, a specified portion of the trust assets are

Tax on generation-skipping transfers   Code Sec. 2624

distributed to skip persons who are lineal descendants of the holder of such interest (or to 1 or more trusts for the exclusive benefit of such persons) such termination shall constitute a taxable termination with respect to such portion of the trust property."

In 1986, P.L. 99-514, Sec. 1431(a), added Code Sec. 2612 as part of the amendments to Chapter 13, effective for any generation-skipping transfer (within the meaning of Code Sec. 2611) made after 10/22/86, except as provided in Sec. 1433(b)-(d) of this Act, reproduced in the note following Code Sec. 2601.

> • **Caution:** Code Sec. 2664, provides that Chapter 13 of Subchapter B will not apply to generation-skipping transfers after 12/31/2009.

Sec. 2613. Skip person and non-skip person defined.
(a) Skip person.

For purposes of this chapter, the term "skip person" means—

(1) a natural person assigned to a generation which is 2 or more generations below the generation assignment of the transferor, or

(2) a trust—

(A) if all interests in such trust are held by skip persons, or

(B) if—

(i) there is no person holding an interest in such trust, and

(ii) at no time after such transfer may a distribution (including distributions on termination) be made from such trust to a non-skip person.

(b) Non-skip person.

For purposes of this chapter, the term "non-skip person" means any person who is not a skip person.

In 1988, P.L. 100-647, Sec. 1014(g)(5)(A), substituted "a natural person assigned" for "a person assigned" in para. (a)(1), effective for any generation-skipping transfer (within the meaning of Code Sec. 2611) made after 10/22/86, except as provided in Sec. 1433(b)-(d), of P. L. 99-514, reproduced in note following Code Sec. 2601.

In 1986, P.L. 99-514, Sec. 1431(a), added Code Sec. 2613 as part of the amendments to Chapter 13, effective for any generation-skipping transfer (within the meaning of Code Sec. 2611) made after 10/22/86, except as provided in Sec. 1433(b)-(d) of this Act, which is reproduced in the note following Code Sec. 2601.

Subchapter C.—Taxable Amount
Sec.
2621. Taxable amount in case of taxable distribution.
2622. Taxable amount in case of taxable termination.
2623. Taxable amount in case of direct skip.
2624. Valuation.

> • **Caution:** Code Sec. 2664, provides that Chapter 13 of Subchapter B will not apply to generation-skipping transfers after 12/31/2009.

Sec. 2621. Taxable amount in case of taxable distribution.
(a) In general.

For purposes of this chapter, the taxable amount in the case of any taxable distribution shall be—

(1) the value of the property received by the transferee, reduced by

(2) any expense incurred by the transferee in connection with the determination, collection, or refund of the tax imposed by this chapter with respect to such distribution.

(b) Payment of GST tax treated as taxable distribution.

For purposes of this chapter, if any of the tax imposed by this chapter with respect to any taxable distribution is paid out of the trust, an amount equal to the portion so paid shall be treated as a taxable distribution.

In 1986, P.L. 99-514, Sec. 1431(a), added Code Sec. 2621 as part of the amendments to Chapter 13, effective for any generation-skipping transfer (within the meaning of Code Sec. 2611) made after 10/22/86, except as provided in Sec. 1433(b)-(d) of this Act, reproduced in the note following Code Sec. 2601.

> • **Caution:** Code Sec. 2664, provides that Chapter 13 of Subchapter B will not apply to generation-skipping transfers after 12/31/2009.

Sec. 2622. Taxable amount in case of taxable termination.
(a) In general.

For purposes of this chapter, the taxable amount in the case of a taxable termination shall be—

(1) the value of all property with respect to which the taxable termination has occurred, reduced by

(2) any deduction allowed under subsection (b).

(b) Deduction for certain expenses.

For purposes of subsection (a), there shall be allowed a deduction similar to the deduction allowed by section 2053 (relating to expenses, indebtedness, and taxes) for amounts attributable to the property with respect to which the taxable termination has occurred.

In 1986, P.L. 99-514, Sec. 1431(a), added Code Sec. 2622 as part of the amendments to Chapter 13, effective for any generation-skipping transfer (within the meaning of Code Sec. 2611) made after 10/22/86, except as provided in Sec. 1433(b)-(d) of this Act, reproduced in the note following Code Sec. 2601.

> • **Caution:** Code Sec. 2664, provides that Chapter 13 of Subchapter B will not apply to generation-skipping transfers after 12/31/2009.

Sec. 2623. Taxable amount in case of direct skip.

For purposes of this chapter, the taxable amount in the case of a direct skip shall be the value of the property received by the transferee.

In 1986, P.L. 99-514, Sec. 1431(a), added Code Sec. 2623 as part of the amendments to Chapter 13, effective for any generation-skipping transfer (within the meaning of Code Sec. 2611) made after 10/22/86, except as provided in Sec. 1433(b)-(d) of this Act, reproduced in the note following Code Sec. 2601.

> • **Caution:** Code Sec. 2664, provides that Chapter 13 of Subchapter B will not apply to generation-skipping transfers after 12/31/2009.

Code Sec. 2624 — Tax on generation-skipping transfers

Sec. 2624. Valuation.
(a) General rule.
Except as otherwise provided in this chapter, property shall be valued as of the time of the generation-skipping transfer.
(b) Alternate valuation and special use valuation elections apply to certain direct skips.
In the case of any direct skip of property which is included in the transferor's gross estate, the value of such property for purposes of this chapter shall be the same as its value for purposes of chapter 11 (determined with regard to sections 2032 and 2032A).
(c) Alternate valuation election permitted in the case of taxable terminations occurring at death.
If 1 or more taxable terminations with respect to the same trust occur at the same time as and as a result of the death of an individual, an election may be made to value all of the property included in such terminations in accordance with section 2032.
(d) Reduction for consideration provided by transferee.
For purposes of this chapter, the value of the property transferred shall be reduced by the amount of any consideration provided by the transferee.

In **1986**, P.L. 99-514, Sec. 1431(a), added Code Sec. 2624 as part of the amendments to Chapter 13, effective for any generation-skipping transfer (within the meaning of Code Sec. 2611) made after 10/22/86, except as provided in Sec. 1433(b)-(d) of this Act, reproduced in the note following Code Sec. 2601.

Subchapter D.—GST Exemption

Sec.
2631. GST exemption.
2632. Special rules for allocation of GST exemption.

Sec. 2631. GST exemption.

> • *Caution:* Code Sec. 2631(a), following, was amended by P.L. 107-16, EGTRRA. These provisions generally sunset for tax years beginning after 12/31/2012. For specific sunset provisions, see Sec. 901, P.L. 107-16 (as amended) reproduced in history notes for this Code Sec.

(a) General rule.
For purposes of determining the inclusion ratio, every individual shall be allowed a GST exemption amount which may be allocated by such individual (or his executor) to any property with respect to which such individual is the transferor.
(b) Allocations irrevocable.
Any allocation under subsection (a), once made, shall be irrevocable.

> • *Caution:* Code Sec. 2631(c), following, was amended by P.L. 107-16, EGTRRA, and subsequently amended by Sec. 303(b)(2) of P.L. 111-312. These provisions generally sunset for tax years beginning after 12/31/2012. For specific sunset provisions, see Sec. 901, P.L. 107-16 (as amended) reproduced in history notes for this Code Sec.

(c) GST exemption amount.
For purposes of subsection (a), the GST exemption amount for any calendar year shall be equal to the basic exclusion amount under section 2010(c) for such calendar year.

In **2010**, P.L. 111-312, Sec. 101(a)(1), substituted "December 31, 2012" for "December 31, 2010" both places it appeared in Sec. 901, P.L. 107-16 [see below], effective as if included in the enactment of P.L. 107-16, EGTRRA, 6/7/2001.
—P.L. 111-312, Sec. 303(b)(2), substituted "the basic exclusion amount" for "the applicable exclusion amount" in subsec. (c), effective for generation-skipping transfers after 12/31/2010.
—P.L. 111-312, Sec. 304, of this Act, provides
"SEC. 304. APPLICATION OF EGTRRA SUNSET TO THIS TITLE.
" Section 901 of the Economic Growth and Tax Relief Reconciliation Act of 2001 shall apply to the amendments made by this title."
In **2002**, P.L. 107-358, Sec. 2, added subsec. (c) in Sec. 901 of P. L. 107-16 [see below], effective 12/17/2002.
In **2001**, P.L. 107-16, Sec. 521(c)(1), substituted "amount" for "of $1,000,000" in subsec. (a) . . . Sec. 521(c)(2), amended subsec. (c), effective for estates of decedents dying, and generation-skipping transfers, after 12/31/2003.
Prior to amendment, subsec. (c) read as follows:
"(c) Inflation adjustment.
"(1) In general. In the case of any calendar year after 1998, the $1,000,000 amount contained in subsection (a) shall be increased by an amount equal to—
"(A) $1,000,000, multiplied by
"(B) the cost-of-living adjustment determined under section 1(f)(3) for such calendar year by substituting 'calendar year 1997' for 'calendar year 1992' in subparagraph (B) thereof.
If any amount as adjusted under the preceding sentence is not a multiple of $10,000, such amount shall be rounded to the next lowest multiple of $10,000.
"(2) Allocation of increase. Any increase under paragraph (1) for any calendar year shall apply only to generation-skipping transfers made during or after such calendar year; except that no such increase for calendar years after the calendar year in which the transferor dies shall apply to transfers by such transferor."
—P.L. 107-16, Sec. 901, of this Act [as amended by Sec. 2, P. L. 107-358, and Sec. 101(a)(1), P.L. 111-312, see above], reads as follows:
"Sec. 901. Sunset of provisions of Act.
"(a) In general. All provisions of, and amendments made by, this Act shall not apply—
"(1) to taxable, plan, or limitation years beginning after December 31, 2012, or
"(2) in the case of title V, to estates of decedents dying, gifts made, or generation skipping transfers, after December 31, 2012.
"(b) Application of certain laws. The Internal Revenue Code of 1986 and the Employee Retirement Income Security Act of 1974 shall be applied and administered to years, estates, gifts, and transfers described in subsection (a) as if the provisions and amendments described in subsection (a) had never been enacted.
"(c) Exception. Subsection (a) shall not apply to section 803 (relating to no federal income tax on restitution received by victims of the Nazi regime or their heirs or estates)."
In **1998**, P.L. 105-206, Sec. 6007(a)(1), amended subsec. (c), effective 8/5/97.
Prior to amendment, subsec. (c) read as follows:
"(c) Inflation adjustment. In the case of an individual who dies in any calendar year after 1998, the $1,000,000 amount contained in subsection (a) shall be increased by an amount equal to—
"(1) $1,000,000, multiplied by
"(2) the cost-of-living adjustment determined under section 1(f)(3) for such calendar year by substituting 'calendar year 1997' for 'calendar year 1992' in subparagraph (B) thereof.
If any amount as adjusted under the preceding sentence is not a multiple of $10,000, such amount shall be rounded to the next lowest multiple of $10,000."
—P.L. 105-206, Sec. 6007(a)(2), added "(other than the amendment made by subsection (d))" after "this section" in Sec. 501(f) of P. L. 105-34, the effective date for amendments made by Sec. 501, [see below].
In **1997**, P.L. 105-34, Sec. 501(d), added subsec. (c), effective [as amended by Sec. 6007(a)(3), 105-206, see above] 8/5/97.
In **1986**, P.L. 99-514, Sec. 1431(a), added Code Sec. 2631 as part of the amendments to Chapter 13, effective for any generation-skipping transfer (within the meaning of Code Sec. 2611) made after 10/22/86, except as provided in Sec. 1433(b)-(d) of this Act, reproduced in the note following Code Sec. 2601.

> • *Caution:* Code Sec. 2664, provides that Chapter 13 of Subchapter B will not apply to generation-skipping transfers after 12/31/2009.

> • *Caution:* Code Sec. 2632, following, was amended by P.L. 107-16, the Economic Growth and Tax Relief Reconciliation Act of 2001 (EGTRRA). These provisions generally sunset for tax years beginning after 12/31/2012. For

specific sunset provisions, see Sec. 901, P.L. 107-16 (as amended) reproduced in history notes for this Code Sec.

Sec. 2632. Special rules for allocation of GST exemption.

(a) Time and manner of allocation.

(1) Time. Any allocation by an individual of his GST exemption under section 2631(a) may be made at any time on or before the date prescribed for filing the estate tax return for such individual's estate (determined with regard to extensions), regardless of whether such a return is required to be filed.

(2) Manner. The Secretary shall prescribe by forms or regulations the manner in which any allocation referred to in paragraph (1) is to be made.

(b) Deemed allocation to certain lifetime direct skips.

(1) In general. If any individual makes a direct skip during his lifetime, any unused portion of such individual's GST exemption shall be allocated to the property transferred to the extent necessary to make the inclusion ratio for such property zero. If the amount of the direct skip exceeds such unused portion, the entire unused portion shall be allocated to the property transferred.

(2) Unused portion. For purposes of paragraph (1), the unused portion of an individual's GST exemption is that portion of such exemption which has not previously been allocated by such individual (or treated as allocated under paragraph (1) or subsection (c)(1)).

(3) Subsection not to apply in certain cases. An individual may elect to have this subsection not apply to a transfer.

(c) Deemed allocation to certain lifetime transfers to GST trusts.

(1) In general. If any individual makes an indirect skip during such individual's lifetime, any unused portion of such individual's GST exemption shall be allocated to the property transferred to the extent necessary to make the inclusion ratio for such property zero. If the amount of the indirect skip exceeds such unused portion, the entire unused portion shall be allocated to the property transferred.

(2) Unused portion. For purposes of paragraph (1), the unused portion of an individual's GST exemption is that portion of such exemption which has not previously been—

(A) allocated by such individual,

(B) treated as allocated under subsection (b) with respect to a direct skip occurring during or before the calendar year in which the indirect skip is made, or

(C) treated as allocated under paragraph (1) with respect to a prior indirect skip.

(3) Definitions.

(A) Indirect skip. For purposes of this subsection, the term "indirect skip" means any transfer of property (other than a direct skip) subject to the tax imposed by chapter 12 made to a GST trust.

(B) GST trust. The term "GST trust" means a trust that could have a generation-skipping transfer with respect to the transferor unless—

(i) the trust instrument provides that more than 25 percent of the trust corpus must be distributed to or may be withdrawn by one or more individuals who are non-skip persons—

(I) before the date that the individual attains age 46,

(II) on or before one or more dates specified in the trust instrument that will occur before the date that such individual attains age 46, or

(III) upon the occurrence of an event that, in accordance with regulations prescribed by the Secretary, may reasonably be expected to occur before the date that such individual attains age 46,

(ii) the trust instrument provides that more than 25 percent of the trust corpus must be distributed to or may be withdrawn by one or more individuals who are non-skip persons and who are living on the date of death of another person identified in the instrument (by name or by class) who is more than 10 years older than such individuals,

(iii) the trust instrument provides that, if one or more individuals who are non-skip persons die on or before a date or event described in clause (i) or (ii), more than 25 percent of the trust corpus either must be distributed to the estate or estates of one or more of such individuals or is subject to a general power of appointment exercisable by one or more of such individuals,

(iv) the trust is a trust any portion of which would be included in the gross estate of a non-skip person (other than the transferor) if such person died immediately after the transfer,

(v) the trust is a charitable lead annuity trust (within the meaning of section 2642(e)(3)(A)) or a charitable remainder annuity trust or a charitable remainder unitrust (within the meaning of section 664(d)), or

(vi) the trust is a trust with respect to which a deduction was allowed under section 2522 for the amount of an interest in the form of the right to receive annual payments of a fixed percentage of the net fair market value of the trust property (determined yearly) and which is required to pay principal to a non-skip person if such person is alive when the yearly payments for which the deduction was allowed terminate.

For purposes of this subparagraph, the value of transferred property shall not be considered to be includible in the gross estate of a non-skip person or subject to a right of withdrawal by reason of such person holding a right to withdraw so much of such property as does not exceed the amount referred to in section 2503(b) with respect to any transferor, and it shall be assumed that powers of appointment held by non-skip persons will not be exercised.

(4) Automatic allocations to certain GST trusts. For purposes of this subsection, an indirect skip to which section 2642(f) applies shall be deemed to have been made only at the close of the estate tax inclusion period. The fair market value of such transfer shall be the fair market value of the trust property at the close of the estate tax inclusion period.

(5) Applicability and effect.

(A) In general. An individual—

(i) may elect to have this subsection not apply to—

(I) an indirect skip, or

(II) any or all transfers made by such individual to a particular trust, and

(ii) may elect to treat any trust as a GST trust for purposes of this subsection with respect to any or all transfers made by such individual to such trust.

(B) Elections.

(i) Elections with respect to indirect skips. An election under subparagraph (A)(i)(I) shall be deemed to be timely if filed on a timely filed gift tax return for the calendar year in which the transfer was made or deemed to have been made pursuant to paragraph (4) or on such later date or dates as may be prescribed by the Secretary.

(ii) Other elections. An election under clause (i)(II) or (ii) of subparagraph (A) may be made on a timely filed gift tax return for the calendar year for which the election is to become effective.

(d) Retroactive allocations.

(1) In general. If—

(A) a non-skip person has an interest or a future interest in a trust to which any transfer has been made,

(B) such person—

(i) is a lineal descendant of a grandparent of the transferor or of a grandparent of the transferor's spouse or former spouse, and

(ii) is assigned to a generation below the generation assignment of the transferor, and

(C) such person predeceases the transferor,

then the transferor may make an allocation of any of such transferor's unused GST exemption to any previous transfer or transfers to the trust on a chronological basis.

(2) Special rules. If the allocation under paragraph (1) by the transferor is made on a gift tax return filed on or before the date prescribed by section 6075(b) for gifts made within the calendar year within which the non-skip person's death occurred—

(A) the value of such transfer or transfers for purposes of section 2642(a) shall be determined as if such allocation had been made on a timely filed gift tax return for each calendar year within which each transfer was made,

(B) such allocation shall be effective immediately before such death, and

(C) the amount of the transferor's unused GST exemption available to be allocated shall be determined immediately before such death.

(3) Future interest. For purposes of this subsection, a person has a future interest in a trust if the trust may permit income or corpus to be paid to such person on a date or dates in the future.

(e) Allocation of unused GST exemption.

(1) In general. Any portion of an individual's GST exemption which has not been allocated within the time prescribed by subsection (a) shall be deemed to be allocated as follows—

(A) first, to property which is the subject of a direct skip occurring at such individual's death, and

(B) second, to trusts with respect to which such individual is the transferor and from which a taxable distribution or a taxable termination might occur at or after such individual's death.

(2) Allocation within categories.

(A) In general. The allocation under paragraph (1) shall be made among the properties described in subparagraph (A) thereof and the trusts described in subparagraph (B) thereof, as the case may be, in proportion to the respective amounts (at the time of allocation) of the nonexempt portions of such properties or trusts.

(B) Nonexempt portion. For purposes of subparagraph (A), the term "nonexempt portion" means the value (at the time of allocation) of the property or trust, multiplied by the inclusion ratio with respect to such property or trust.

In 2010, P.L. 111-312, Sec. 101(a)(1), substituted "December 31, 2012" for "December 31, 2010" both places it appears in Sec. 901, P.L. 107-16, see below, effective as if included in the enactment of P.L. 107-16, EGTRRA, 6/7/2001.

In 2002, P.L. 107-358, Sec. 2, added subsec. (c) in Sec. 901 of P. L. 107-16 [see below], effective 12/17/2002.

In 2001, P.L. 107-16, Sec. 561(a), redesignated subsec. (c) as (e) and added new subsecs. (c) and (d)... Sec. 561(b), substituted "or subsection (c)(1)" for "with respect to a prior direct skip" in para. (b)(2), effective as provided in Sec. 561(c) of this Act, which reads as follows:

"(c) Effective dates.

"(1) Deemed allocation. Section 2632(c) of the Internal Revenue Code of 1986 (as added by subsection (a)), and the amendment made by subsection (b), shall apply to transfers subject to chapter 11 or 12 made after December 31, 2000, and to estate tax inclusion periods ending after December 31, 2000.

"(2) Retroactive allocations. Section 2632(d) of the Internal Revenue Code of 1986 (as added by subsection (a)) shall apply to deaths of non-skip persons occurring after December 31, 2000."

—P.L. 107-16, Sec. 901, of this Act [as amended by Sec. 2, P. L. 107-358, and Sec. 101(a)(1), P.L. 111-312, see above], reads as follows:

"SEC. 901. SUNSET OF PROVISIONS OF ACT.

"(a) In general. All provisions of, and amendments made by, this Act shall not apply—

"(1) to taxable, plan, or limitation years beginning after December 31, 2012, or

"(2) in the case of title V, to estates of decedents dying, gifts made, or generation skipping transfers, after December 31, 2012.

"(b) Application of certain laws. The Internal Revenue Code of 1986 and the Employee Retirement Income Security Act of 1974 shall be applied and administered to years, estates, gifts, and transfers described in subsection (a) as if the provisions and amendments described in subsection (a) had never been enacted.

"(c) Exception. Subsection (a) shall not apply to section 803 (relating to no federal income tax on restitution received by victims of the Nazi regime or their heirs or estates)."

In 1988, P.L. 100-647, Sec. 1014(g)(16), substituted "paragraph (1) with respect to a prior direct skip" for "paragraph (1)) with a prior direct skip", effective for any generation-skipping transfer (within the meaning of Code Sec. 2611) made after 10/22/86, except as provided in Sec. 1433(b)-(d) of this Act, reproduced in the note following Code Sec. 2601.

In 1986, P.L. 99-514, Sec. 1431(a), added Code Sec. 2632 as part of the amendments to Chapter 13, effective for any generation-skipping transfer (within the meaning of Code Sec. 2611) made after 10/22/86, except as provided in Sec. 1433(b)-(d) of this Act, reproduced in the note following Code Sec. 2601.

Subchapter E.—Applicable Rate; Inclusion Ratio

Sec.
2641. Applicable rate.
2642. Inclusion ratio.

• *Caution:* Code Sec. 2664, provides that Chapter 13 of Subchapter B will not apply to generation-skipping transfers after 12/31/2009.

Sec. 2641. Applicable rate.

(a) General rule.

For purposes of this chapter, the term "applicable rate" means, with respect to any generation-skipping transfer, the product of—

(1) the maximum Federal estate tax rate, and

(2) the inclusion ratio with respect to the transfer.

(b) Maximum Federal estate tax rate.

For purposes of subsection (a), the term "maximum Federal estate tax rate" means the maximum rate imposed by section 2001 on the estates of decedents dying at the time of the taxable distribution, taxable termination, or direct skip, as the case may be.

In 2010, P.L. 111-312, Sec. 302(c), of this Act provides:

"(c) Modification of generation-skipping transfer tax. In the case of any generation-skipping transfer made after December 31, 2009, and before January 1, 2011, the applicable rate determined under section 2641(a) of the Internal Revenue Code of 1986 shall be zero."

In 1986, P.L. 99-514, Sec. 1431(a), added Code Sec. 2641 as part of the amendments to Chapter 13, effective for any generation-skipping transfer (within the

Tax on generation-skipping transfers Code Sec. 2642

(2) **Valuation.** In the case of any property to which paragraph (1) applies, the value of such property shall be—
(A) if such property is includible in the gross estate of the transferor (other than by reason of section 2035), its value for purposes of chapter 11, or
(B) if subparagraph (A) does not apply, its value as of the close of the estate tax inclusion period (or, if any allocation of GST exemption to such property is not made on a timely filed gift tax return for the calendar year in which such period ends, its value as of the time such allocation is filed with the Secretary).

(3) **Estate tax inclusion period.** For purposes of this subsection, the term "estate tax inclusion period" means any period after the transfer described in paragraph (1) during which the value of the property involved in such transfer would be includible in the gross estate of the transferor under chapter 11 if he died. Such period shall in no event extend beyond the earlier of—
(A) the date on which there is a generation-skipping transfer with respect to such property, or
(B) the date of the death of the transferor.

(4) **Treatment of spouse.** Except as provided in regulations, any reference in this subsection to an individual or transferor shall be treated as including a reference to the spouse of such individual or transferor.

(5) **Coordination with subsection (d).** Under regulations, appropriate adjustments shall be made in the application of subsection (d) to take into account the provisions of this subsection.

• *Caution:* Code Sec. 2642(g), following, was amended by Sec. 564(a), P.L. 107-16, the Economic Growth and Tax Relief Reconciliation Act of 2001 (EGTRRA). These provisions generally sunset for tax years beginning after 12/31/2012. For specific sunset provisions, see Sec. 901, P.L. 107-16 (as amended) reproduced in history notes for this Code Sec.

(g) **Relief provisions.**
(1) **Relief from late elections.**
(A) In general. The Secretary shall by regulation prescribe such circumstances and procedures under which extensions of time will be granted to make—
(i) an allocation of GST exemption described in paragraph (1) or (2) of subsection (b), and
(ii) an election under subsection (b)(3) or (c)(5) of section 2632.
Such regulations shall include procedures for requesting comparable relief with respect to transfers made before the date of the enactment of this paragraph.
(B) Basis for determinations. In determining whether to grant relief under this paragraph, the Secretary shall take into account all relevant circumstances, including evidence of intent contained in the trust instrument or instrument of transfer and such other factors as the Secretary deems relevant. For purposes of determining whether to grant relief under this paragraph, the time for making the allocation (or election) shall be treated as if not expressly prescribed by statute.

(2) **Substantial compliance.** An allocation of GST exemption under section 2632 that demonstrates an intent to have the lowest possible inclusion ratio with respect to a transfer or a trust shall be deemed to be an allocation of so much of the transferor's unused GST exemption as produces the lowest possible inclusion ratio. In determining whether there has been substantial compliance, all relevant circumstances shall be taken into account, including evidence of intent contained in the trust instrument or instrument of transfer and such other factors as the Secretary deems relevant.

In 2010, P.L. 111-312, Sec. 101(a)(1), substituted "December 31, 2012" for "December 31, 2010" both places it appears in Sec. 901, P.L. 107-16, see below, effective as if included in the enactment of P.L. 107-16, EGTRRA, 6/7/2001.

In 2002, P.L. 107-358, Sec. 2, added subsec. (c) in Sec. 901 of P. L. 107-16 [see below], effective 12/17/2002.

In 2001, P.L. 107-16, Sec. 562(a), added para. (a)(3), effective for severances after 12/31/2000.

—P.L. 107-16, Sec. 563(a), amended para. (b)(1) . . . Sec. 563(b), amended subpara. (b)(2)(A), effective for transfers subject to chapter 11 or 12 of the Internal Revenue Code of 1986 made after 12/31/2000.

Prior to amendment, para. (b)(1) read as follows:
"(b) Valuation rules, etc. Except as provided in subsection (f)—
"(1) Gifts for which gift tax return filed or deemed allocation made. If the allocation of the GST exemption to any property is made on a gift tax return filed on or before the date prescribed by section 6075(b) or is deemed to be made under section 2632(b)(1)—
"(A) the value of such property for purposes of subsection (a) shall be its value for purposes of chapter 12, and
"(B) such allocation shall be effective on and after the date of such transfer."
Prior to amendment, subpara. (b)(2)(A) read as follows:
"(A) Transfers at death. If property is transferred as a result of the death of the transferor, the value of such property for purposes of subsection (a) shall be its value for purposes of chapter 11; except that, if the requirements prescribed by the Secretary respecting allocation of post-death changes in value are not met, the value of such property shall be determined as of the time of the distribution concerned."

—P.L. 107-16, Sec. 564(a), added subsec. (g), effective as provided in Sec. 564(b) of this Act, which reads as follows:
"(b) Effective dates.
"(1) Relief from late elections. Section 2642(g)(1) of the Internal Revenue Code of 1986 (as added by subsection (a)) shall apply to requests pending on, or filed after, December 31, 2000.
"(2) Substantial compliance. Section 2642(g)(2) of such Code (as so added) shall apply to transfers subject to chapter 11 or 12 of the Internal Revenue Code of 1986 made after December 31, 2000. No implication is intended with respect to the availability of relief from late elections or the application of a rule of substantial compliance on or before such date."

—P.L. 107-16, Sec. 901, of this Act [as amended by Sec. 2, P. L. 107-358, and Sec. 101(a)(1), P.L. 111-312, see above], reads as follows:
"SEC. 901. SUNSET OF PROVISIONS OF ACT.
"(a) In general. All provisions of, and amendments made by, this Act shall not apply—
"(1) to taxable, plan, or limitation years beginning after December 31, 2012, or
"(2) in the case of title V, to estates of decedents dying, gifts made, or generation skipping transfers, after December 31, 2012.
"(b) Application of certain laws. The Internal Revenue Code of 1986 and the Employee Retirement Income Security Act of 1974 shall be applied and administered to years, estates, gifts, and transfers described in subsection (a) as if the provisions and amendments described in subsection (a) had never been enacted.
"(c) Exception. Subsection (a) shall not apply to section 803 (relating to no federal income tax on restitution received by victims of the Nazi regime or their heirs or estates)."

In 1990, P.L. 101-508, Sec. 11703(c)(1), substituted "the trust does not terminate before the individual dies" for "such individual dies before the trust is terminated" in subpara. (c)(2)(B) . . . Sec. 11703(c)(2), added the last sentence of para. (c)(2), effective for transfers after 3/31/88.

—P.L. 101-508, Sec. 11704(a)(17), substituted "State" for "state" in subclause (d)(2)(B)(i)(I), effective 11/5/90.

In 1989, P.L. 101-239, Sec. 7811(j)(4), substituted "a gift tax return filed on or before the date prescribed by section 6075(b)" for "a timely filed gift tax return required by section 6019" in paras. (b)(1) and (b)(3), effective for any generation-skipping transfer (within the meaning of Code Sec. 2611) made after 10/22/86, except as provided in Sec. 1433(b)-(d) of P. L. 99-514, reproduced in the note following Code Sec. 2601.

In 1988, P.L. 100-647, Sec. 1014(g)(3)(A), added subsec. (e), effective for purposes of determining the inclusion ratio for property transferred after 10/31/87.

—P.L. 100-647, Sec. 1014(g)(4)(A), added subsec. (f) . . . Sec. 1014(g)(4)(B), deleted the last sentence of para. (a)(2) . . . Sec. 1014(g)(4)(C), added "; except that, if the requirements prescribed by the Secretary respecting allocation of post-death changes in value are not met, the value of such property shall be determined as of the time of the distribution concerned" before the period at the end of subpara. (b)(2)(A) . . . Sec. 1014(g)(4)(D), added "Except as provided in subsection (f)" immediately after heading of subsec. (b) . . . Sec. 1014(g)(4)(E)(i), substituted "to property transferred as a result of the death of the transferor" for "at or after the death of the transferor" in subpara. (b)(2)(B) . . . Sec. 1014(g)(4)(E)(ii), substituted "to property transferred at death" for "at or after death" in the heading of subpara. (b)(2)(B) . . . Sec. 1014(g)(4)(F)(i), substituted "to any property not transferred as a result of the death of the transferor is" for "to any property is made during the life of the transferor but is" in para. (b)(3) . . . Sec. 1014(g)(4)(F)(ii),

3,053

substituted "Allocations to inter vivos transfers" for "Inter vivos allocations" in the heading of para. (b)(3), effective for any generation-skipping transfer (within the meaning of Code Sec. 2611) made after 10/22/86, except as provided in Sec. 1433(b)-(d) of P. L. 99-514, reproduced in the note following Code Sec. 2601.
Prior to deletion, the last sentence of para. (a)(2) read as follows:

"Except as provided in paragraphs (3) and (4) of subsection (b), the value determined under subparagraph (B)(i) shall be of the property as of the time of the transfer to the trust (or the direct skip)."

—P.L. 100-647, Sec. 1014(g)(17)(A), amended subsec. (c)... Sec. 1014(g)(17)(B), deleted "(other than a nontaxable gift)" after "property" in para. (d)(1), effective for transfers after 3/31/88.
Prior to amendment, subsec. (c) read as follows:

"(c) Treatment of certain nontaxable gifts.

"(1) Direct skips. In the case of any direct skip which is a nontaxable gift, the inclusion ratio shall be zero.

"(2) Treatment of nontaxable gifts made to trusts.

"(A) In general. Except as provided in subparagraph (B), any nontaxable gift which is not a direct skip and which is made to a trust shall not be taken into account under subsection (a)(2)(B).

"(B) Determination of 1st transfer to trust. In the case of any nontaxable gift referred to in subparagraph (A) which is the 1st transfer to the trust, the inclusion ratio for such trust shall be zero.

"(3) Nontaxable gift. For purposes of this section, the term 'nontaxable gift' means any transfer of property to the extent such transfer is not treated as a taxable gift by reason of—

"(A) section 2503(b) (taking into account the application of section 2513), or

"(B) section 2503(e).".

—P.L. 100-647, Sec. 1014(g)(18), amended clause (d)(2)(B)(i), effective for any generation-skipping transfer (within the meaning of Code Sec. 2611) made after 10/22/86, except as provided in Sec. 1433(b)-(d) of P. L. 99-514, reproduced in the note following Code Sec. 2601.

Prior to amendment, clause (d)(2)(B)(i) read as follows:

"(i) the value of the property involved in such transfer, reduced by any charitable deduction allowed under section 2055 or 2522 with respect to such property, and".

In 1986, P.L. 99-514, Sec. 1431(a), added Code Sec. 2642 as part of the amendments to Chapter 13, effective for any generation-skipping transfer (within the meaning of Code Sec. 2611) made after 10/22/86, except as provided in Sec. 1433(b)-(d) of this Act, reproduced in the note following Code Sec. 2601.

Subchapter F.— Other Definitions and Special Rules

Sec.
2651. Generation assignment.
2652. Other definitions.
2653. Taxation of multiple skips.
2654. Special rules.

> • **Caution:** Code Sec. 2664, provides that Chapter 13 of Subchapter B will not apply to generation-skipping transfers after 12/31/2009.

Sec. 2651. Generation assignment.
(a) In general.
For purposes of this chapter, the generation to which any person (other than the transferor) belongs shall be determined in accordance with the rules set forth in this section.
(b) Lineal descendants.
(1) In general. An individual who is a lineal descendant of a grandparent of the transferor shall be assigned to that generation which results from comparing the number of generations between the grandparent and such individual with the number of generations between the grandparent and the transferor.
(2) On spouse's side. An individual who is a lineal descendant of a grandparent of a spouse (or former spouse) of the transferor (other than such spouse) shall be assigned to that generation which results from comparing the number of generations between such grandparent and such individual with the number of generations between such grandparent and such spouse.

(3) Treatment of legal adoptions, etc. For purposes of this subsection—
(A) Legal adoptions. A relationship by legal adoption shall be treated as a relationship by blood.
(B) Relationships by half-blood. A relationship by the half-blood shall be treated as a relationship of the whole-blood.
(c) Marital relationship.
(1) Marriage to transferor. An individual who has been married at any time to the transferor shall be assigned to the transferor's generation.
(2) Marriage to other lineal descendants. An individual who has been married at any time to an individual described in subsection (b) shall be assigned to the generation of the individual so described.
(d) Persons who are not lineal descendants.
An individual who is not assigned to a generation by reason of the foregoing provisions of this section shall be assigned to a generation on the basis of the date of such individual's birth with—
(1) an individual born not more than 12 ½ years after the date of the birth of the transferor assigned to the transferor's generation,
(2) an individual born more than 12 ½ years but not more than 37 ½ years after the date of the birth of the transferor assigned to the first generation younger than the transferor, and
(3) similar rules for a new generation every 25 years.
(e) Special rule for persons with a deceased parent.
(1) In general. For purposes of determining whether any transfer is a generation-skipping transfer, if—
(A) an individual is a descendant of a parent of the transferor (or the transferor's spouse or former spouse), and
(B) such individual's parent who is a lineal descendant of the parent of the transferor (or the transferor's spouse or former spouse) is dead at the time the transfer (from which an interest of such individual is established or derived) is subject to a tax imposed by chapter 11 or 12 upon the transferor (and if there shall be more than 1 such time, then at the earliest such time),
such individual shall be treated as if such individual were a member of the generation which is 1 generation below the lower of the transferor's generation or the generation assignment of the youngest living ancestor of such individual who is also a descendant of the parent of the transferor (or the transferor's spouse or former spouse), and the generation assignment of any descendant of such individual shall be adjusted accordingly.
(2) Limited application of subsection to collateral heirs. This subsection shall not apply with respect to a transfer to any individual who is not a lineal descendant of the transferor (or the transferor's spouse or former spouse) if, at the time of the transfer, such transferor has any living lineal descendant.
(f) Other special rules.
(1) Individuals assigned to more than 1 generation. Except as provided in regulations, an individual who, but for this subsection, would be assigned to more than 1 generation shall be assigned to the youngest such generation.
(2) Interests through entities. Except as provided in paragraph (3), if an estate, trust, partnership, corporation, or other entity has an interest in property, each individual having a beneficial interest in such entity shall be treated as having an interest in such property and shall be assigned to a generation under the foregoing provisions of this subsection.

(3) Treatment of certain charitable organizations and governmental entities. Any—
(A) organization described in section 511(a)(2),
(B) charitable trust described in section 511(b)(2), and
(C) governmental entity,
shall be assigned to the transferor's generation.

In 1997, P.L. 105-34, Sec. 511(a), redesignated subsec. (e) as (f) and added new subsec. (e), effective for terminations, distributions, and transfers, occurring after 12/31/97.

In 1988, P.L. 100-647, Sec. 1014(g)(11), amended para. (e)(3)... Sec. 1014(g)(19), substituted "a spouse (or former spouse) of the transferor" for "a spouse of the transferor", in para. (b)(2) effective for any generation-skipping transfer (within the meaning of Code Sec. 2611) made after 10/22/86, except as provided in Sec. 1433(b)-(d) of this Act, reproduced in the note following Code Sec. 2601.

Prior to amendment, para. (e)(3) read as follows:

"(3) Treatment of certain charitable organizations. Any organization described in section 511(a)(2) and any charitable trust described in section 511(b)(2) shall be assigned to the transferor's generation."

In 1986, P.L. 99-514, Sec. 1431(a), added Code Sec. 2651 as part of the amendments to Chapter 13, effective for any generation-skipping transfer (within the meaning of Code Sec. 2611) made after 10/22/86, except as provided in Sec. 1433(b)-(d) of this Act, reproduced in the note following Code Sec. 2601.

Sec. 2652. Other definitions.
(a) Transferor.
For purposes of this chapter—
(1) In general. Except as provided in this subsection or section 2653(a), the term "transferor" means—
(A) in the case of any property subject to the tax imposed by chapter 11, the decedent, and
(B) in the case of any property subject to the tax imposed by chapter 12, the donor.
An individual shall be treated as transferring any property with respect to which such individual is the transferor.
(2) Gift-splitting by married couples. If, under section 2513, one-half of a gift is treated as made by an individual and one-half of such gift is treated as made by the spouse of such individual, such gift shall be so treated for purposes of this chapter.
(3) Special election for qualified terminable interest property. In the case of—
(A) any trust with respect to which a deduction is allowed to the decedent under section 2056 by reason of subsection (b)(7) thereof, and
(B) any trust with respect to which a deduction to the donor spouse is allowed under section 2523 by reason of subsection (f) thereof,
the estate of the decedent or the donor spouse, as the case may be, may elect to treat all of the property in such trust for purposes of this chapter as if the election to be treated as qualified terminable interest property had not been made.
(b) Trust and trustee.
(1) Trust. The term "trust" includes any arrangement (other than an estate) which, although not a trust, has substantially the same effect as a trust.
(2) Trustee. In the case of an arrangement which is not a trust but which is treated as a trust under this subsection, the term "trustee" shall mean the person in actual or constructive possession of the property subject to such arrangement.
(3) Examples. Arrangements to which this subsection applies include arrangements involving life estates and remainders, estates for years, and insurance and annuity contracts.
(c) Interest.
(1) In general. A person has an interest in property held in trust if (at the time the determination is made) such person—
(A) has a right (other than a future right) to receive income or corpus from the trust,
(B) is a permissible current recipient of income or corpus from the trust and is not described in section 2055(a), or
(C) is described in section 2055(a) and the trust is—
(i) a charitable remainder annuity trust,
(ii) a charitable remainder unitrust within the meaning of section 664, or
(iii) a pooled income fund within the meaning of section 642(c)(5).
(2) Certain interests disregarded. For purposes of paragraph (1), an interest which is used primarily to postpone or avoid any tax imposed by this chapter shall be disregarded.
(3) Certain support obligations disregarded. The fact that income or corpus of the trust may be used to satisfy an obligation of support arising under State law shall be disregarded in determining whether a person has an interest in the trust, if—
(A) such use is discretionary, or
(B) such use is pursuant to the provisions of any State law substantially equivalent to the Uniform Gifts to Minors Act.
(d) Executor.
For purposes of this chapter, the term "executor" has the meaning given such term by section 2203.

In 2010, P.L. 111-312, Sec. 301(c), of this Act, provides:

"(c) Special election with respect to estates of decedents dying in 2010. Notwithstanding subsection (a), in the case of an estate of a decedent dying after December 31, 2009, and before January 1, 2011, the executor (within the meaning of section 2203 of the Internal Revenue Code of 1986) may elect to apply such Code as though the amendments made by subsection (a) do not apply with respect to chapter 11 of such Code and with respect to property acquired or passing from such decedent (within the meaning of section 1014(b) of such Code). Such election shall be made at such time and in such manner as the Secretary of the Treasury or the Secretary's delegate shall provide. Such an election once made shall be revocable only with the consent of the Secretary of the Treasury or the Secretary's delegate. For purposes of section 2652(a)(1) of such Code, the determination of whether any property is subject to the tax imposed by such chapter 11 shall be made without regard to any election made under this subsection."

—P.L. 111-312, Sec. 301(d), of this Act, provides:

"(d) Extension of time for performing certain acts.

"(1) Estate tax. In the case of the estate of a decedent dying after December 31, 2009, and before the date of the enactment of this Act [12/17/2010], the due date for—

"(A) filing any return under section 6018 of the Internal Revenue Code of 1986 (including any election required to be made on such a return) as such section is in effect after the date of the enactment of this Act [12/17/2010] without regard to any election under subsection (c),

"(B) making any payment of tax under chapter 11 of such Code, and

"(C) making any disclaimer described in section 2518(b) of such Code of an interest in property passing by reason of the death of such decedent,

"shall not be earlier than the date which is 9 months after the date of the enactment of this Act [enacted 12/17/2010].

"(2) Generation-skipping tax. In the case of any generation-skipping transfer made after December 31, 2009, and before the date of the enactment of this Act [12/17/2010], the due date for filing any return under section 2662 of the Internal Revenue Code of 1986 (including any election required to be made on such a return) shall not be earlier than the date which is 9 months after the date of the enactment of this Act [enacted 12/17/2010]."

In 1998, P.L. 105-206, Sec. 6013(a)(3), substituted "section 645" for "section 646" in para. (b)(1)... Sec. 6013(a)(4)(A), deleted "Such term shall not include any trust during any period the trust is treated as part of an estate under section 645." in para. (b)(1) [as amended by Sec. 6013(a)(3) of this Act, see above], effective for estates of decedents dying after 8/5/97.

In 1997, P.L. 105-34, Sec. 1305(b), added a sentence at the end of para. (b)(1), effective for estates of decedents dying after 8/5/97.

In 1988, P.L. 100-647, Sec. 1014(g)(6), added para. (c)(3)... Sec. 1014(g)(8)(A), substituted "interests" for "nominal interests" in the heading of para. (c)(2)... Sec. 1014(g)(8)(B), substituted "any tax" for "the tax", in para (c)(2)... Sec. 1014(g)(9)(A), substituted "any property" for "a transfer of a kind" each place it appeared in para. (a)(1)... Sec. 1014(g)(9)(B), added a sentence at the end of para. (a)(1)... Sec. 1014(g)(14)(A), substituted "any trust" for "any property" in subparas (a)(3)(A) and (B)... Sec. 1014(g)(14)(B), substituted "may elect to treat all of the property in such trust" for "may elect to treat such property" in para. (a)(3)... Sec. 1014(g)(20), added new subsec. (d), effective for any generation-skipping transfer (within the meaning of Code Sec. 2611) made after 10/22/86, except as provided in Sec. 1433(b)-(d) of P. l. 99-514, reproduced in the note following Code Sec. 2601.

In 1986, P.L. 99-514, Sec. 1431(a), added Code Sec. 2652 as part of the amendments to Chapter 13, effective for any generation-skipping transfer (within the meaning of Code Sec. 2611) made after 10/22/86, except as provided in Secs. 1433(b)-(d) of this Act, reproduced in the note following Code Sec. 2601.

• **Caution:** Code Sec. 2664, provides that Chapter 13 of Subchapter B will not apply to generation-skipping transfers after 12/31/2009.

Sec. 2653. Taxation of multiple skips.
(a) General rule.

For purposes of this chapter, if—

(1) there is a generation-skipping transfer of any property, and

(2) immediately after such transfer such property is held in trust,

for purposes of applying this chapter (other than section 2651) to subsequent transfers from the portion of such trust attributable to such property, the trust will be treated as if the transferor of such property were assigned to the first generation above the highest generation of any person who has an interest in such trust immediately after the transfer.

(b) Trust retains inclusion ratio.

(1) **In general.** Except as provided in paragraph (2), the provisions of subsection (a) shall not affect the inclusion ratio determined with respect to any trust. Under regulations prescribed by the Secretary, notwithstanding the preceding sentence, proper adjustment shall be made to the inclusion ratio with respect to such trust to take into account any tax under this chapter borne by such trust which is imposed by this chapter on the transfer described in subsection (a).

(2) **Special rule for pour-over trust.**

(A) **In general.** If the generation-skipping transfer referred to in subsection (a) involves the transfer of property from 1 trust to another trust (hereinafter in this paragraph referred to as the "pour-over trust"), the inclusion ratio for the pour-over trust shall be determined by treating the nontax portion of such distribution as if it were a part of a GST exemption allocated to such trust.

(B) **Nontax portion.** For purposes of subparagraph (A), the nontax portion of any distribution is the amount of such distribution multiplied by the applicable fraction which applies to such distribution.

In 1986, P.L. 99-514, Sec. 1431(a), added Code Sec. 2653 as part of the amendments to Chapter 13, effective for any generation-skipping transfer (within the meaning of Code Sec. 2611) made after 10/22/86, except as provided in Sec. 1433(b)-(d) of this Act, reproduced in the note following Code Sec. 2601.

• **Caution:** Code Sec. 2664, provides that Chapter 13 of Subchapter B will not apply to generation-skipping transfers after 12/31/2009.

Sec. 2654. Special rules.
(a) Basis adjustment.

(1) **In general.** Except as provided in paragraph (2), if property is transferred in a generation-skipping transfer, the basis of such property shall be increased (but not above the fair market value of such property) by an amount equal to that portion of the tax imposed by section 2601 (computed without regard to section 2604) with respect to the transfer which is attributable to the excess of the fair market value of such property over its adjusted basis immediately before the transfer. The preceding shall be applied after any basis adjustment under section 1015 with respect to the transfer.

(2) **Certain transfers at death.** If property is transferred in a taxable termination which occurs at the same time as and as a result of the death of an individual, the basis of such property shall be adjusted in a manner similar to the manner provided under section 1014(a); except that, if the inclusion ratio with respect to such property is less than 1, any increase or decrease in basis shall be limited by multiplying such increase or decrease (as the case may be) by the inclusion ratio.

(b) Certain trusts treated as separate trusts.

For purposes of this chapter—

(1) the portions of a trust attributable to transfers from different transferors shall be treated as separate trusts, and

(2) substantially separate and independent shares of different beneficiaries in a trust shall be treated as separate trusts.

Except as provided in the preceding sentence, nothing in this chapter shall be construed as authorizing a single trust to be treated as 2 or more trusts. For purposes of this subsection, a trust shall be treated as part of an estate during any period that the trust is so treated under section 645.

(c) Disclaimers.

For provisions relating to the effect of a qualified disclaimer for purposes of this chapter, see section 2518.

(d) Limitation on personal liability of trustee.

A trustee shall not be personally liable for any increase in the tax imposed by section 2601 which is attributable to the fact that—

(1) section 2642(c) (relating to exemption of certain nontaxable gifts) does not apply to a transfer to the trust which was made during the life of the transferor and for which a gift tax return was not filed, or

(2) the inclusion ratio with respect to the trust is greater than the amount of such ratio as computed on the basis of the return on which was made (or was deemed made) an allocation of the GST exemption to property transferred to such trust.

The preceding sentence shall not apply if the trustee has knowledge of facts sufficient reasonably to conclude that a gift tax return was required to be filed or that the inclusion ratio was erroneous.

In 1998, P.L. 105-206, Sec. 6013(a)(4)(B), added a sentence at the end of subsec. (b), effective for estates of decedents dying after 8/5/97.

In 1989, P.L. 101-239, Sec. 7811(j)(2), added the sentence at the end of para. (a)(1), effective for any generation-skipping transfer (within the meaning of '86 Code Sec. 2611) made after 10/22/86, except as provided in Sec. 1433(b)-(d) of P. L. 99-514, reproduced in the note following Code Sec. 2601.

In 1988, P.L. 100-647, Sec. 1014(g)(12)(A), added "or decrease" after "any increase" in para. (a)(2) ... Sec. 1014(g)(12)(B), added "or decrease (as the case may be)" after "such decrease" in para. (a)(2) ... Sec. 1014(g)(13), amended subsec. (b), effective for any generation-skipping transfer (within the meaning of Code Sec. 2611) made after 10/22/86, except as provided in Sec. 1433(b)-(d) of P. L. 99-514, reproduced in the note following Code Sec. 2601.

Prior to amendment, subsec. (b) read as follows:

"(b) Separate shares treated as separate trusts.

"Substantially separate and independent shares of different beneficiaries in a trust shall be treated as separate trusts."

In 1986, P.L. 99-514, Sec. 1431(a), added Code Sec. 2654 as part of the amendments to Chapter 13, effective for any generation-skipping transfer (within the

Code Sec. 2664   Tax on generation-skipping transfers

Sec. 2664. Termination.

This chapter shall not apply to generation-skipping transfers after December 31, 2009.

In 2010, P.L. 111-312, Sec. 101(a)(1), substituted "December 31, 2012" for "December 31, 2010" both places it appeared in Sec. 901, P.L. 107-16 [see below], effective as if included in the enactment of P.L. 107-16, EGTRRA, 6/7/2001.

—P.L. 111-312, Sec. 301(a), provides that Code Sec. 2664 (as added by Sec. 501(b), P.L. 107-16, will read as if such amendment had never been enacted, effective for estates of decedents dying, and transfers made, after 12/31/2009.

Sec. 301(a) of P.L. 111-312, provides:

"(a) In general. Each provision of law amended by subtitle A or E of title V of the Economic Growth and Tax Relief Reconciliation Act of 2001 [P.L. 107-16, see below] is amended to read as such provision would read if such subtitle had never been enacted."

Prior to the enactment of Sec. 301(a) of P.L. 111-312, Code Sec. 2664 read as follows:

"Sec. 2664. Termination.

"This chapter shall not apply to generation-skipping transfers after December 31, 2009.

In 2002, P.L. 107-358, Sec. 2, added subsec. (c) in Sec. 901 of P. L. 107-16 [see below], effective 12/17/2002.

In 2001, P.L. 107-16, Sec. 501(b), added Code Sec. 2664, effective for the estates of decedents dying, and generation-skipping transfers, after 12/31/2009.

—P.L. 107-16, Sec. 901, of this Act [as amended by Sec. 2 of P.L. 107-358, and Sec. 101(a)(1), P.L. 111-312, see above], reads as follows:

"SEC. 901. SUNSET OF PROVISIONS OF ACT.

"(a) In general. All provisions of, and amendments made by, this Act shall not apply —

"(1) to taxable, plan, or limitation years beginning after December 31, 2012, or

"(2) in the case of title V, to estates of decedents dying, gifts made, or generation skipping transfers, after December 31, 2012.

"(b) Application of certain laws. The Internal Revenue Code of 1986 and the Employee Retirement Income Security Act of 1974 shall be applied and administered to years, estates, gifts, and transfers described in subsection (a) as if the provisions and amendments described in subsection (a) had never been enacted.

"(c) Exception. Subsection (a) shall not apply to section 803 (relating to no federal income tax on restitution received by victims of the Nazi regime or their heirs or estates)."

CHAPTER 14.—SPECIAL VALUATION RULES

Sec.

2701. Special valuation rules in case of transfers of certain interests in corporations or partnerships.

2702. Special valuation rules in case of transfers of interests in trusts.

2703. Certain rights and restrictions disregarded.

2704. Treatment of certain lapsing rights and restrictions.

Sec. 2701. Special valuation rules in case of transfers of certain interests in corporations or partnerships.

(a) Valuation rules.

(1) In general. Solely for purposes of determining whether a transfer of an interest in a corporation or partnership to (or for the benefit of) a member of the transferor's family is a gift (and the value of such transfer), the value of any right—

(A) which is described in subparagraph (A) or (B) of subsection (b)(1), and

(B) which is with respect to any applicable retained interest that is held by the transferor or an applicable family member immediately after the transfer,

shall be determined under paragraph (3). This paragraph shall not apply to the transfer of any interest for which market quotations are readily available (as of the date of transfer) on an established securities market.

(2) Exceptions for marketable retained interests, etc. Paragraph (1) shall not apply to any right with respect to an applicable retained interest if—

(A) market quotations are readily available (as of the date of the transfer) for such interest on an established securities market,

(B) such interest is of the same class as the transferred interest, or

(C) such interest is proportionally the same as the transferred interest, without regard to nonlapsing differences in voting power (or, for a partnership, nonlapsing differences with respect to management and limitations on liability).

Subparagraph (C) shall not apply to any interest in a partnership if the transferor or an applicable family member has the right to alter the liability of the transferee of the transferred property. Except as provided by the Secretary, any difference described in subparagraph (C) which lapses by reason of any Federal or State law shall be treated as a nonlapsing difference for purposes of such subparagraph.

(3) Valuation of rights to which paragraph (1) applies.

(A) In general. The value of any right described in paragraph (1), other than a distribution right which consists of a right to receive a qualified payment, shall be treated as being zero.

(B) Valuation of certain qualified payments. If—

(i) any applicable retained interest confers a distribution right which consists of the right to a qualified payment, and

(ii) there are 1 or more liquidation, put, call, or conversion rights with respect to such interest,

the value of all such rights shall be determined as if each liquidation, put, call, or conversion right were exercised in the manner resulting in the lowest value being determined for all such rights.

(C) Valuation of qualified payments where no liquidation, etc. rights. In the case of an applicable retained interest which is described in subparagraph (B)(i) but not subparagraph (B)(ii), the value of the distribution right shall be determined without regard to this section.

(4) Minimum valuation of junior equity.

(A) In general. In the case of a transfer described in paragraph (1) of a junior equity interest in a corporation or partnership, such interest shall in no event be valued at an amount less than the value which would be determined if the total value of all of the junior equity interests in the entity were equal to 10 percent of the sum of—

(i) the total value of all of the equity interests in such entity, plus

(ii) the total amount of indebtedness of such entity to the transferor (or an applicable family member).

(B) Definitions. For purposes of this paragraph—

(i) Junior equity interest. The term "junior equity interest" means common stock or, in the case of a partnership, any partnership interest under which the rights as to income and capital (or, to the extent provided in regulations, the rights as to either income or capital) are junior to the rights of all other classes of equity interests.

(ii) Equity interest. The term "equity interest" means stock or any interest as a partner, as the case may be.

(b) Applicable retained interests.

For purposes of this section—

(1) In general. The term "applicable retained interest" means any interest in an entity with respect to which there is—

(A) a distribution right, but only if, immediately before the transfer described in subsection (a)(1), the transferor and applicable family members hold (after application of subsection (e)(3)) control of the entity, or

(B) a liquidation, put, call, or conversion right.

3,058

Tax on generation-skipping transfers

Code Sec. 2664

meaning of Code Sec. 2611) made after 10/22/86, except as provided in Sec. 1433(b)-(d) of this Act, reproduced in the note following Code Sec. 2601.

Subchapter G.—Administration

Sec.
2661. Administration.
2662. Return requirements.
2663. Regulations.
2664. Termination.

> • **Caution:** Code Sec. 2664, provides that Chapter 13 of Subchapter B will not apply to generation-skipping transfers after 12/31/2009.

Sec. 2661.   Administration.

Insofar as applicable and not inconsistent with the provisions of this chapter—

(1) except as provided in paragraph (2), all provisions of subtitle F (including penalties) applicable to the gift tax, to chapter 12, or to section 2501, are hereby made applicable in respect of the generation-skipping transfer tax, this chapter, or section 2601, as the case may be, and

(2) in the case of a generation-skipping transfer occurring at the same time as and as a result of the death of an individual, all provisions of subtitle F (including penalties) applicable to the estate tax, to chapter 11, or to section 2001 are hereby made applicable in respect of the generation-skipping transfer tax, this chapter, or section 2601 (as the case may be).

In **1986**, P.L. 99-514, Sec. 1431(a), added Code Sec. 2661 as part of the amendments to Chapter 13, effective for any generation-skipping transfer (within the meaning of Code Sec. 2611) made after 10/22/86, except as provided in Sec. 1433(b)-(d) of this Act, reproduced in the note following Code Sec. 2601.

> • **Caution:** Code Sec. 2664, provides that Chapter 13 of Subchapter B will not apply to generation-skipping transfers after 12/31/2009.

Sec. 2662.   Return requirements.
(a) In general.

The Secretary shall prescribe by regulations the person who is required to make the return with respect to the tax imposed by this chapter and the time by which any such return must be filed. To the extent practicable, such regulations shall provide that—

(1) the person who is required to make such return shall be the person liable under section 2603(a) for payment of such tax, and

(2) the return shall be filed—

(A) in the case of a direct skip (other than from a trust), on or before the date on which an estate or gift tax return is required to be filed with respect to the transfer, and

(B) in all other cases, on or before the 15th day of the 4th month after the close of the taxable year of the person required to make such return in which such transfer occurs.

(b) Information returns.

The Secretary may by regulations require a return to be filed containing such information as he determines to be necessary for purposes of this chapter.

In **2010**, P.L. 111-312, Sec. 301(d), of this Act, provides:
"(d) Extension of time for performing certain acts.
"(1) Estate tax. In the case of the estate of a decedent dying after December 31, 2009, and before the date of the enactment of this Act, the due date for—
"(A) filing any return under section 6018 of the Internal Revenue Code of 1986 (including any election required to be made on such a return) as such section is in effect after the date of the enactment of this Act without regard to any election under subsection (c),
"(B) making any payment of tax under chapter 11 of such Code, and
"(C) making any disclaimer described in section 2518(b) of such Code of an interest in property passing by reason of the death of such decedent,
"shall not be earlier than the date which is 9 months after the date of the enactment of this Act.
"(2) Generation-skipping tax. In the case of any generation-skipping transfer made after December 31, 2009, and before the date of the enactment of this Act, the due date for filing any return under section 2662 of the Internal Revenue Code of 1986 (including any election required to be made on such a return) shall not be earlier than the date which is 9 months after the date of the enactment of this Act."
—P.L. 111-312, Sec. 304, of this Act, provides:
"Sec. 304. Application of EGTRRA sunset to this title.
"Section 901 of the Economic Growth and Tax Relief Reconciliation Act of 2001 shall apply to the amendments made by this section."
In **1986**, P.L. 99-514, Sec. 1431(a), added Code Sec. 2662 as part of the amendments to Chapter 13, effective for any generation-skipping transfer (within the meaning of Code Sec. 2611) made after 10/22/86, except as provided in Sec. 1433(b)-(d) of this Act, reproduced in the note following Code Sec. 2601.

> • **Caution:** Code Sec. 2664, provides that Chapter 13 of Subchapter B will not apply to generation-skipping transfers after 12/31/2009.

Sec. 2663.   Regulations.

The Secretary shall prescribe such regulations as may be necessary or appropriate to carry out the purposes of this chapter, including—

(1) such regulations as may be necessary to coordinate the provisions of this chapter with the recapture tax imposed under section 2032A(c),

(2) regulations (consistent with the principles of chapters 11 and 12) providing for the application of this chapter in the case of transferors who are nonresidents not citizens of the United States, and

(3) regulations providing for such adjustments as may be necessary to the application of this chapter in the case of any arrangement which, although not a trust, is treated as a trust under section 2652(b).

In **1988**, P.L. 100-647, Sec. 1014(g)(10), deleted "and" at the end of para. (1), substituted ", and" for the period at the end of para. (2), and added para. (3), effective for any generation-skipping transfer (within the meaning of Code Sec. 2611) made after 10/22/86, except as provided in Sec. 1433(b)-(d) of P. L. 99-514, reproduced in note following Code Sec. 2601.
In **1986**, P.L. 99-514, Sec. 1431(a), added Code Sec. 2663 as part of the amendments to Chapter 13, effective for any generation-skipping transfer (within the meaning of Code Sec. 2611) made after 10/22/86, except as provided in Sec. 1433(b)-(d) of this Act, reproduced in the note following Code Sec. 2601.

> • **Caution:** Code Sec. 2664, following, was added by Sec. 501(b), P.L. 107-16, EGTRRA. As provided in Sec. 301(a), P.L. 111-312, this amendment will apply as if never enacted, effective for estates of decedents dying, and transfers made, after 12/31/2009.

3,057

(2) **Control.** For purposes of paragraph (1)—
  (A) Corporations. In the case of a corporation, the term "control" means the holding of at least 50 percent (by vote or value) of the stock of the corporation.
  (B) Partnerships. In the case of a partnership, the term "control" means—
    (i) the holding of at least 50 percent of the capital or profits interests in the partnership, or
    (ii) in the case of a limited partnership, the holding of any interest as a general partner.
  (C) Applicable family member. For purposes of this subsection, the term "applicable family member" includes any lineal descendant of any parent of the transferor or the transferor's spouse.

(c) Distribution and other rights; qualified payments.
For purposes of this section—
  (1) Distribution right.
    (A) In general. The term "distribution right" means—
      (i) a right to distributions from a corporation with respect to its stock, and
      (ii) a right to distributions from a partnership with respect to a partner's interest in the partnership.
    (B) Exceptions. The term "distribution right" does not include—
      (i) a right to distributions with respect to any interest which is junior to the rights of the transferred interest,
      (ii) any liquidation, put, call, or conversion right, or
      (iii) any right to receive any guaranteed payment described in section 707(c) of a fixed amount.
  (2) Liquidation, etc. rights.
    (A) In general. The term "liquidation, put, call, or conversion right" means any liquidation, put, call, or conversion right, or any similar right, the exercise or non-exercise of which affects the value of the transferred interest.
    (B) Exception for fixed rights.
      (i) In general. The term "liquidation, put, call, or conversion right" does not include any right which must be exercised at a specific time and at a specific amount.
      (ii) Treatment of certain rights. If a right is assumed to be exercised in a particular manner under subsection (a)(3)(B), such right shall be treated as so exercised for purposes of clause (i).
    (C) Exception for certain rights to convert. The term "liquidation, put, call, or conversion right" does not include any right which—
      (i) is a right to convert into a fixed number (or a fixed percentage) of shares of the same class of stock in a corporation as the transferred stock in such corporation under subsection (a)(1) (or stock which would be of the same class but for nonlapsing differences in voting power),
      (ii) is nonlapsing,
      (iii) is subject to proportionate adjustments for splits, combinations, reclassifications, and similar changes in the capital stock, and
      (iv) is subject to adjustments similar to the adjustments under subsection (d) for accumulated but unpaid distributions.
    A rule similar to the rule of the preceding sentence shall apply for partnerships.
  (3) Qualified payment.
    (A) In general. Except as otherwise provided in this paragraph, the term "qualified payment" means any dividend payable on a periodic basis under any cumulative preferred stock (or a comparable payment under any partnership interest) to the extent that such dividend (or comparable payment) is determined at a fixed rate.
    (B) Treatment of variable rate payments. For purposes of subparagraph (A), a payment shall be treated as fixed as to rate if such payment is determined at a rate which bears a fixed relationship to a specified market interest rate.
    (C) Elections.
      (i) In general. Payments under any interest held by a transferor which (without regard to this subparagraph) are qualified payments shall be treated as qualified payments unless the transferor elects not to treat such payments as qualified payments. Payments described in the preceding sentence which are held by an applicable family member shall be treated as qualified payments only if such member elects to treat such payments as qualified payments.
      (ii) Election to have interest treated as qualified payment. A transferor or applicable family member holding any distribution right which (without regard to this subparagraph) is not a qualified payment may elect to treat such right as a qualified payment, to be paid in the amounts and at the time specified in such election. The preceding sentence shall apply only to the extent that the amounts and times so specified are not inconsistent with the underlying legal instrument giving rise to such right.
      (iii) Elections irrevocable. Any election under this subparagraph with respect to an interest shall, once made, be irrevocable.

(d) Transfer tax treatment of cumulative but unpaid distributions.
  (1) In general. If a taxable event occurs with respect to any distribution right to which subsection (a)(3)(B) or (C) applied, the following shall be increased by the amount determined under paragraph (2):
    (A) The taxable estate of the transferor in the case of a taxable event described in paragraph (3)(A)(i).
    (B) The taxable gifts of the transferor for the calendar year in which the taxable event occurs in the case of a taxable event described in paragraph (3)(A)(ii) or (iii).
  (2) Amount of increase.
    (A) In general. The amount of the increase determined under this paragraph shall be the excess (if any) of—
      (i) the value of the qualified payments payable during the period beginning on the date of the transfer under subsection (a)(1) and ending on the date of the taxable event determined as if—
        (I) all such payments were paid on the date payment was due, and
        (II) all such payments were reinvested by the transferor as of the date of payment at a yield equal to the discount rate used in determining the value of the applicable retained interest described in subsection (a)(1), over
      (ii) the value of such payments paid during such period computed under clause (i) on the basis of the time when such payments were actually paid.
    (B) Limitation on amount of increase.
      (i) In general. The amount of the increase under subparagraph (A) shall not exceed the applicable percentage of the excess (if any) of—
        (I) the value (determined as of the date of the taxable event) of all equity interests in the entity which are junior to the applicable retained interest, over

(II) the value of such interests (determined as of the date of the transfer to which subsection (a)(1) applied).

(ii) Applicable percentage. For purposes of clause (i), the applicable percentage is the percentage determined by dividing—

(I) the number of shares in the corporation held (as of the date of the taxable event) by the transferor which are applicable retained interests of the same class, by

(II) the total number of shares in such corporation (as of such date) which are of the same class as the class described in subclause (I).

A similar percentage shall be determined in the case of interests in a partnership.

(iii) Definition. For purposes of this subparagraph, the term "equity interest" has the meaning given such term by subsection (a)(4)(B).

(C) Grace period. For purposes of subparagraph (A), any payment of any distribution during the 4-year period beginning on its due date shall be treated as having been made on such due date.

(3) Taxable events. For purposes of this subsection—

(A) In general. The term "taxable event" means any of the following:

(i) The death of the transferor if the applicable retained interest conferring the distribution right is includible in the estate of the transferor.

(ii) The transfer of such applicable retained interest.

(iii) At the election of the taxpayer, the payment of any qualified payment after the period described in paragraph (2)(C), but only with respect to such payment.

(B) Exception where spouse is transferee.

(i) Deathtime transfers. Subparagraph (A)(i) shall not apply to any interest includible in the gross estate of the transferor if a deduction with respect to such interest is allowable under section 2056 or 2106(a)(3).

(ii) Lifetime transfers. A transfer to the spouse of the transferor shall not be treated as a taxable event under subparagraph (A)(ii) if such transfer does not result in a taxable gift by reason of—

(I) any deduction allowed under section 2523, or the exclusion under section 2503(b), or

(II) consideration for the transfer provided by the spouse.

(iii) Spouse succeeds to treatment of transferor. If an event is not treated as a taxable event by reason of this subparagraph, the transferee spouse or surviving spouse (as the case may be) shall be treated in the same manner as the transferor in applying this subsection with respect to the interest involved.

(4) Special rules for applicable family members.

(A) Family member treated in same manner as transferor. For purposes of this subsection, an applicable family member shall be treated in the same manner as the transferor with respect to any distribution right retained by such family member to which subsection (a)(3)(B) or (C) applied.

(B) Transfer to applicable family member. In the case of a taxable event described in paragraph (3)(A)(ii) involving the transfer of an applicable retained interest to an applicable family member (other than the spouse of the transferor), the applicable family member shall be treated in the same manner as the transferor in applying

this subsection to distributions accumulating with respect to such interest after such taxable event.

(C) Transfer to transferors. In the case of a taxable event described in paragraph (3)(A)(ii) involving a transfer of an applicable retained interest from an applicable family member to a transferor, this subsection shall continue to apply to the transferor during any period the transferor holds such interest.

(5) Transfer to include termination. For purposes of this subsection, any termination of an interest shall be treated as a transfer.

(e) Other definitions and rules.

For purposes of this section—

(1) Member of the family. The term "member of the family" means, with respect to any transferor—

(A) the transferor's spouse,

(B) a lineal descendant of the transferor or the transferor's spouse, and

(C) the spouse of any such descendant.

(2) Applicable family member. The term "applicable family member" means, with respect to any transferor—

(A) the transferor's spouse,

(B) an ancestor of the transferor or the transferor's spouse, and

(C) the spouse of any such ancestor.

(3) Attribution of indirect holdings and transfers. An individual shall be treated as holding any interest to the extent such interest is held indirectly by such individual through a corporation, partnership, trust, or other entity. If any individual is treated as holding any interest by reason of the preceding sentence, any transfer which results in such interest being treated as no longer held by such individual shall be treated as a transfer of such interest.

(4) Effect of adoption. A relationship by legal adoption shall be treated as a relationship by blood.

(5) Certain changes treated as transfers. Except as provided in regulations, a contribution to capital or a redemption, recapitalization, or other change in the capital structure of a corporation or partnership shall be treated as a transfer of an interest in such entity to which this section applies if the taxpayer or an applicable family member—

(A) receives an applicable retained interest in such entity pursuant to such transaction, or

(B) under regulations, otherwise holds, immediately after such transactions, an applicable retained interest in such entity.

This paragraph shall not apply to any transaction (other than a contribution to capital) if the interests in the entity held by the transferor, applicable family members, and members of the transferor's family before and after the transaction are substantially identical.

(6) Adjustments. Under regulations prescribed by the Secretary, if there is any subsequent transfer, or inclusion in the gross estate, of any applicable retained interest which was valued under the rules of subsection (a), appropriate adjustments shall be made for purposes of chapter 11, 12, or 13 to reflect the increase in the amount of any prior taxable gift made by the transferor or decedent by reason of such valuation or to reflect the application of subsection (d)

(7) Treatment as separate interests. The Secretary may by regulation provide that any applicable retained interest shall be treated as 2 or more separate interests for purposes of this section.

Special valuation rules   Code Sec. 2702

In 1996, P.L. 104-188, Sec. 1702(f)(1)(A), added subpara. (a)(3)(C)... Sec. 1702(f)(1)(B), added "certain" before "qualified" in the heading of subpara. (a)(3)(B)... Sec. 1702(f)(1)(C), substituted "subsection (a)(3)(B) or (C)" for "subsection (a)(3)(B)" in paras. (d)(1) and (d)(4)... Sec. 1702(f)(2), added "(or, to the extent provided in regulations, the rights as to either income or capital)" after "income and capital" in clause (a)(4)(B)(i)... Sec. 1702(f)(3)(A), added subpara. (b)(2)(C)... Sec. 1702(f)(3)(B)(i), deleted subpara. (e)(3)(B)... Sec. 1702(f)(3)(B)(ii), substituted "(3) Attribution of indirect holdings and transfers. An individual" for "(3) Attribution rules. (A) Indirect holdings and transfers. An individual" in para. (e)(3)... Sec. 1702(f)(4), amended clause (c)(1)(B)(i)... Sec. 1702(f)(5)(A), amended clause (c)(3)(C)(i)... Sec. 1702(f)(5)(B), substituted "A transferor or applicable family member holding any distribution right which (without regard to this subparagraph) is not a qualified payment may elect to treat such right as a qualified payment, to be paid in the amounts and at the time specified in such election." for "A transferor or any applicable family member may elect to treat any distribution right as a qualified payment, to be paid in the amounts and at the times specified in such election." in clause (c)(3)(C)(ii), effective for transfers after 10/8/90, except as provided in Sec. 11602(e)(1)(B) of P. L. 101-508, reproduced below.

Prior to deletion, subpara. (e)(3)(B) read as follows:

"(B) Control. For purposes of subsections (b)(1), an individual shall be treated as holding any interest held by the individual's brothers, sisters, or lineal descendants."

Prior to amendment, clause (c)(1)(B)(i) read as follows:

"(i) a right to distributions with respect to any junior equity interest (as defined in subsection (a)(4)(B)(i))."

Prior to amendment, clause (c)(3)(C)(i) read as follows:

"(i) Waiver of qualified payment treatment. A transferor or applicable family member may elect with respect to payments under any interest specified in such election to treat such payments as payments which are not qualified payments."

—P.L. 104-188, Sec. 1702(f)(5)(C), of this Act provides

"(C) The time for making an election under the second sentence of section 2701(c)(3)(C)(i) of the Internal Revenue Code of 1986 (as amended by subparagraph (A)) shall not expire before the due date (including extensions) for filing the transferor's return of the tax imposed by section 2501 of such Code for the first calendar year ending after the date of enactment."

—P.L. 104-188, Sec. 1702(f)(6), deleted "the period ending on the date of" after "with respect to" in clause (d)(3)(A)(iii)... Sec. 1702(f)(7), added "or the exclusion under section 2503(b)," after "section 2523" in subclause (d)(3)(B)(ii)(I)... Sec. 1702(f)(8)(A), substituted "such transaction" for "such contribution to capital or such redemption, recapitalization, or other change" in subpara. (e)(5)(A)... Sec. 1702(f)(8)(B), substituted "such transaction" for "the transfer" in para. (e)(5)... Sec. 1702(f)(9), added subpara. (d)(4)(C)... Sec. 1702(f)(10), added "or to reflect the application of subsection (d)" at the end of para. (e)(6), effective for transfers after 10/8/90, except as provided in Sec. 11602(e)(1)(B) of P. L. 101-508, reproduced below.

In 1990, P.L. 101-508, Sec. 11602(a), added Code Sec. 2701 as part of the amendment to subtitle B which added chap. 14, effective for transfers after 10/8/90, except as provided in Sec. 11602(e)(1)(B) of this Act, which reads as follows:

"(B) Exception. For purposes of subparagraph (A)(i), with respect to property transferred before October 9, 1990—

"(i) any failure to exercise a right of conversion,

"(ii) any failure to pay dividends, and

"(iii) any failure to exercise other rights specified in regulations, shall not be treated as a subsequent transfer."

Sec. 2702. Special valuation rules in case of transfers of interests in trusts.

(a) Valuation rules.

(1) In general. Solely for purposes of determining whether a transfer of an interest in trust to (or for the benefit of) a member of the transferor's family is a gift (and the value of such transfer), the value of any interest in such trust retained by the transferor or any applicable family member (as defined in section 2701(e)(2)) shall be determined as provided in paragraph (2).

(2) Valuation of retained interests.

(A) In general. The value of any retained interest which is not a qualified interest shall be treated as being zero.

(B) Valuation of qualified interest. The value of any retained interest which is a qualified interest shall be determined under section 7520.

(3) Exceptions.

(A) In general. This subsection shall not apply to any transfer—

(i) if such transfer is an incomplete gift,

(ii) if such transfer involves the transfer of an interest in trust all the property in which consists of a residence to be used as a personal residence by persons holding term interests in such trust, or

(iii) to the extent that regulations provide that such transfer is not inconsistent with the purposes of this section.

(B) Incomplete gift. For purposes of subparagraph (A), the term "incomplete gift" means any transfer which would not be treated as a gift whether or not consideration was received for such transfer.

(b) Qualified interest.

For purposes of this section, the term "qualified interest" means—

(1) any interest which consists of the right to receive fixed amounts payable not less frequently than annually,

(2) any interest which consists of the right to receive amounts which are payable not less frequently than annually and are a fixed percentage of the fair market value of the property in the trust (determined annually), and

(3) any noncontingent remainder interest if all of the other interests in the trust consist of interests described in paragraph (1) or (2).

(c) Certain property treated as held in trust.

For purposes of this section—

(1) In general. The transfer of an interest in property with respect to which there is 1 or more term interests shall be treated as a transfer of an interest in a trust.

(2) Joint purchases. If 2 or more members of the same family acquire interests in any property described in paragraph (1) in the same transaction (or a series of related transactions), the person (or persons) acquiring the term interests in such property shall be treated as having acquired the entire property and then transferred to the other persons the interests acquired by such other persons in the transaction (or series of transactions). Such transfer shall be treated as made in exchange for the consideration (if any) provided by such other persons for the acquisition of their interests in such property.

(3) Term interest. The term "term interest" means—

(A) a life interest in property, or

(B) an interest in property for a term of years.

(4) Valuation rule for certain term interests. If the nonexercise of rights under a term interest in tangible property would not have a substantial effect on the valuation of the remainder interest in such property—

(A) subparagraph (A) of subsection (a)(2) shall not apply to such term interest, and

(B) the value of such term interest for purposes of applying subsection (a)(1) shall be the amount which the holder of the term interest establishes as the amount for which such interest could be sold to an unrelated third party.

(d) Treatment of transfers of interests in portion of trust.

In the case of a transfer of an income or remainder interest with respect to a specified portion of the property in a trust, only such portion shall be taken into account in applying this section to such transfer.

(e) Member of the family.

For purposes of this section, the term "member of the family" shall have the meaning given such term by section 2704(c)(2).

In 1996, P.L. 104-188, Sec. 1702(f)(11)(A)(i), substituted "if" for "to the extent" in clause (a)(3)(A)(i)... Sec. 1702(f)(11)(A)(ii), deleted "or" at the end of clause (a)(3)(A)(i)... Sec. 1702(f)(11)(A)(iii), substituted ", or" for the period at the end of clause (a)(3)(A)(ii)... Sec. 1702(f)(11)(A)(iv), added clause (a)(3)(A)(iii)... Sec. 1702(f)(11)(B)(i), substituted "incomplete gift" for "incomplete transfer" each place it appeared in para. (a)(3)... Sec. 1702(f)(11)(B)(ii), substituted "incomplete gift" for "incomplete transfer" in the heading of subpara. (a)(3)(B), ef-

3,061

fective for transfers after 10/8/90, except as provided in Sec. 11602(e)(1)(B) of P. L. 101-508, reproduced below.

In 1990, P.L. 101-508, Sec. 11602(a), added Code Sec. 2702 as part of the amendment to subtitle B which added chap. 14, effective for transfers after 10/8/90, except as provided in Sec. 11602(e)(1)(B) of this Act, which reads as follows:

"(B) Exception. For purposes of subparagraph (A)(i), with respect to property transferred before October 9, 1990—
 "(i) any failure to exercise a right of conversion,
 "(ii) any failure to pay dividends, and
 "(iii) any failure to exercise other rights specified in regulations, shall not be treated as a subsequent transfer."

Sec. 2703. Certain rights and restrictions disregarded.
(a) General rule.

For purposes of this subtitle, the value of any property shall be determined without regard to—

(1) any option, agreement, or other right to acquire or use the property at a price less than the fair market value of the property (without regard to such option, agreement, or right), or

(2) any restriction on the right to sell or use such property.

(b) Exceptions.

Subsection (a) shall not apply to any option, agreement, right, or restriction which meets each of the following requirements:

(1) It is a bona fide business arrangement.

(2) It is not a device to transfer such property to members of the decedent's family for less than full and adequate consideration in money or money's worth.

(3) Its terms are comparable to similar arrangements entered into by persons in an arms' length transaction.

In 1990, P.L. 101-508, Sec. 11602(a), added Code Sec. 2703 as part of the amendment to subtitle B which added chap. 14, effective as provided in Sec. 11602(e)(1)(A)(ii) of this Act, which reads as follows:

"(ii) to the extent such amendment relate to section 2703 of such Code (as so added), shall apply to—
 "(I) agreements, options, rights, or restrictions entered into or granted after October 8, 1990, and
 "(II) agreements, options, rights, or restrictions which are substantially modified after October 8, 1990."

Sec. 2704. Treatment of certain lapsing rights and restrictions.
(a) Treatment of lapsed voting or liquidation rights.

(1) In general. For purposes of this subtitle, if—

(A) there is a lapse of any voting or liquidation right in a corporation or partnership, and

(B) the individual holding such right immediately before the lapse and members of such individual's family hold, both before and after the lapse, control of the entity,

such lapse shall be treated as a transfer by such individual by gift, or a transfer which is includible in the gross estate of the decedent, whichever is applicable, in the amount determined under paragraph (2).

(2) Amount of transfer. For purposes of paragraph (1), the amount determined under this paragraph is the excess (if any) of—

(A) the value of all interests in the entity held by the individual described in paragraph (1) immediately before the lapse (determined as if the voting and liquidation rights were nonlapsing), over

(B) the value of such interests immediately after the lapse.

(3) Similar rights. The Secretary may by regulations apply this subsection to rights similar to voting and liquidation rights.

(b) Certain restrictions on liquidation disregarded.

(1) In general. For purposes of this subtitle, if—

(A) there is a transfer of an interest in a corporation or partnership to (or for the benefit of) a member of the transferor's family, and

(B) the transferor and members of the transferor's family hold, immediately before the transfer, control of the entity,

any applicable restriction shall be disregarded in determining the value of the transferred interest.

(2) Applicable restriction. For purposes of this subsection, the term "applicable restriction" means any restriction—

(A) which effectively limits the ability of the corporation or partnership to liquidate, and

(B) with respect to which either of the following applies:

(i) The restriction lapses, in whole or in part, after the transfer referred to in paragraph (1).

(ii) The transferor or any member of the transferor's family, either alone or collectively, has the right after such transfer to remove, in whole or in part, the restriction.

(3) Exceptions. The term "applicable restriction" shall not include—

(A) any commercially reasonable restriction which arises as part of any financing by the corporation or partnership with a person who is not related to the transferor or transferee, or a member of the family of either, or

(B) any restriction imposed, or required to be imposed, by any Federal or State law.

(4) Other restrictions. The Secretary may by regulations provide that other restrictions shall be disregarded in determining the value of the transfer of any interest in a corporation or partnership to a member of the transferor's family if such restriction has the effect of reducing the value of the transferred interest for purposes of this subtitle but does not ultimately reduce the value of such interest to the transferee.

(c) Definitions and special rules.

For purposes of this section—

(1) Control. The term "control" has the meaning given such term by section 2701(b)(2).

(2) Member of the family. The term "member of the family" means, with respect to any individual—

(A) such individual's spouse,

(B) any ancestor or lineal descendant of such individual or such individual's spouse,

(C) any brother or sister of the individual, and

(D) any spouse of any individual described in subparagraph (B) or (C).

(3) Attribution. The rule of section 2701(e)(3) shall apply for purposes of determining the interests held by any individual.

In 1996, P.L. 104-188, Sec. 1702(f)(3)(C), substituted "section 2701(e)(3)" for "section 2701(e)(3)(A)" in para. (c)(3), effective for restrictions or rights (or limitations on rights) created after 10/8/90.

In 1990, P.L. 101-508, Sec. 11602(a), added Code Sec. 2704 as part of the amendment to subtitle B which added chap. 14, effective for restrictions or rights (or limitations on rights) created after 10/8/90.

Employment taxes

Code Sec. 3101(a)

CHAPTER 15.—GIFTS AND BEQUESTS FROM EXPATRIATES

Sec.
2801. Imposition of tax.

Sec. 2801. Imposition of tax.
(a) In general.

If, during any calendar year, any United States citizen or resident receives any covered gift or bequest, there is hereby imposed a tax equal to the product of—

  (1) the highest rate of tax specified in the table contained in section 2001(c) as in effect on the date of such receipt (or, if greater, the highest rate of tax specified in the table applicable under section 2502(a) as in effect on the date), and

  (2) the value of such covered gift or bequest.

(b) Tax to be paid by recipient.

The tax imposed by subsection (a) on any covered gift or bequest shall be paid by the person receiving such gift or bequest.

(c) Exception for certain gifts.

Subsection (a) shall apply only to the extent that the value of covered gifts and bequests received by any person during the calendar year exceeds the dollar amount in effect under section 2503(b) for such calendar year.

(d) Tax reduced by foreign gift or estate tax.

The tax imposed by subsection (a) on any covered gift or bequest shall be reduced by the amount of any gift or estate tax paid to a foreign country with respect to such covered gift or bequest.

(e) Covered Gift or Bequest

  (1) **In general.** For purposes of this chapter, the term "covered gift or bequest" means—

   (A) any property acquired by gift directly or indirectly from an individual who, at the time of such acquisition, is a covered expatriate, and

   (B) any property acquired directly or indirectly by reason of the death of an individual who, immediately before such death, was a covered expatriate.

  (2) **Exceptions for transfers otherwise subject to estate or gift tax.** Such term shall not include—

   (A) any property shown on a timely filed return of tax imposed by chapter 12 which is a taxable gift by the covered expatriate, and

   (B) any property included in the gross estate of the covered expatriate for purposes of chapter 11 and shown on a timely filed return of tax imposed by chapter 11 of the estate of the covered expatriate.

  (3) **Exceptions for transfers to spouse or charity.** Such term shall not include any property with respect to which a deduction would be allowed under section 2055, 2056, 2522, or 2523, whichever is appropriate, if the decedent or donor were a United States person.

  (4) **Transfers in trust.**

   (A) Domestic trusts. In the case of a covered gift or bequest made to a domestic trust—

    (i) subsection (a) shall apply in the same manner as if such trust were a United States citizen, and

    (ii) the tax imposed by subsection (a) on such gift or bequest shall be paid by such trust.

   (B) Foreign trusts.

    (i) In general. In the case of a covered gift or bequest made to a foreign trust, subsection (a) shall apply to any distribution attributable to such gift or bequest from such trust (whether from income or corpus) to a United States citizen or resident in the same manner as if such distribution were a covered gift or bequest.

    (ii) Deduction for tax paid by recipient. There shall be allowed as a deduction under section 164 the amount of tax imposed by this section which is paid or accrued by a United States citizen or resident by reason of a distribution from a foreign trust, but only to the extent such tax is imposed on the portion of such distribution which is included in the gross income of such citizen or resident.

    (iii) Election to be treated as domestic trust. Solely for purposes of this section, a foreign trust may elect to be treated as a domestic trust. Such an election may be revoked with the consent of the Secretary.

(f) Covered expatriate.

For purposes of this section, the term "covered expatriate" has the meaning given to such term by section 877A(g)(1).

In **2008**, P.L. 110-245, Sec. 301(b)(1), added Code Sec. 2801, effective for any individual whose expatriation date (as so defined) is on or after 6/17/2008. Sec. 301(g)(2) of this Act, provides:

"(2) Gifts and bequests. Chapter 15 of the Internal Revenue Code of 1986 (as added by subsection (b)) shall apply to covered gifts and bequests (as defined in section 2801 of such Code, as so added) received on or after the date of the enactment of this Act from transferors (or from the estates of transferors) whose expatriation date is on or after such date of enactment."

Subtitle C.—Employment Taxes and Collection of Income Tax

Chapter
21. Federal insurance contributions act.
22. Railroad retirement tax act.
23. Federal unemployment tax act.
23A. Railroad unemployment repayment tax.
24. Collection of income tax at source.
25. General provisions relating to employment taxes and collection of income taxes at source.

CHAPTER 21.—FEDERAL INSURANCE CONTRIBUTIONS ACT

Subchapter
A. Tax on employees.
B. Tax on employers.
C. General provisions.

Subchapter A.—Tax on Employees

Sec.
3101. Rate of tax.
3102. Deduction of tax from wages.

Sec. 3101. Rate of tax.
(a) Old-age, survivors, and disability insurance.

In addition to other taxes, there is hereby imposed on the income of every individual a tax equal to the following percentages of the wages (as defined in section 3121(a)) received by him with respect to employment (as defined in section 3121(b))—

In cases of wages received during:	The rate shall be:
1984, 1985, 1986, or 1987	5.7 percent
1988 or 1989	6.06 percent
1990 or thereafter	6.2 percent.

• **Caution:** Code Sec. 3101(b), following, is effective with respect to remuneration received, and tax. yrs. begin., before 1/1/2013. For Code Sec. 3101(b) effective with re-

3,063

Code Sec. 3101(a) — Employment taxes

spect to remuneration received, and tax. yrs. begin., after 12/31/2012 see below.

(b) Hospital insurance.

In addition to the tax imposed by the preceding subsection, there is hereby imposed on the income of every individual a tax equal to the following percentages of the wages (as defined in section 3121(a)) received by him with respect to employment (as defined in section 3121(b))—

(1) with respect to wages received during the calendar years 1974 through 1977, the rate shall be 0.90 percent;

(2) with respect to wages received during the calendar year 1978, the rate shall be 1.00 percent;

(3) with respect to wages received during the calendar years 1979 and 1980, the rate shall be 1.05 percent;

(4) with respect to wages received during the calendar years 1981 through 1984, the rate shall be 1.30 percent;

(5) with respect to wages received during the calendar year 1985, the rate shall be 1.35 percent; and

(6) with respect to wages received after December 31, 1985, the rate shall be 1.45 percent.

- **Caution:** Code Sec. 3101(b), following, is effective with respect to remuneration received, and tax. yrs. begin., after 12/31/2012. For Code Sec. 3101(b) effective with respect to remuneration received, and tax. yrs. begin., before 1/1/2013 see above.

(b) Hospital insurance.

(1) In general. In addition to the tax imposed by the preceding subsection, there is hereby imposed on the income of every individual a tax equal to 1.45 percent of the wages (as defined in section 3121(a)) received by him with respect to employment (as defined in section 3121(b)).

- **Caution:** Code Sec. 3101(b)(2), following, is effective for tax. yrs. begin. before 1/1/2013. For Code Sec. 3101(b)(2) effective for tax. yrs. begin. after 12/31/2012, see below.

(2) Additional tax. In addition to the tax imposed by paragraph (1) and the preceding sub-section, there is hereby imposed on every taxpayer (other than a corporation, estate, or trust) a tax equal to 0.9 percent of wages which are received with respect to employment (as defined in section 3121(b)) during any taxable year beginning after December 31, 2012, and which are in excess of—

(A) in the case of a joint return, $250,000, and

(B) in any other case, $200,000.

- **Caution:** Code Sec. 3101(b)(2), following, is effective for tax. yrs. begin. after 12/31/2012. For Code Sec. 3101(b)(2) effective for tax. yrs. begin. before 1/1/2013, see above.

(2) Additional tax. In addition to the tax imposed by paragraph (1) and the preceding sub-section, there is hereby imposed on every taxpayer (other than a corporation, estate, or trust) a tax equal to 0.9 percent of wages which are received with respect to employment (as defined in section 3121(b)) during any taxable year beginning after December 31, 2012, and which are in excess of—

(A) in the case of a joint return, $250,000,

(B) in the case of a married taxpayer (as defined in section 7703) filing a separate return, ½ of the dollar amount determined under subparagraph (A), and

(C) in any other case, $200,000.

(c) Relief from taxes in cases covered by certain international agreements.

During any period in which there is in effect an agreement entered into pursuant to section 233 of the Social Security Act with any foreign country, wages received by or paid to an individual shall be exempt from the taxes imposed by this section to the extent that such wages are subject under such agreement exclusively to the laws applicable to the social security system of such foreign country.

In 2010, P.L. 111-312, Sec. 601, of this Act, provides:
"SEC. 601. TEMPORARY EMPLOYEE PAYROLL TAX CUT.
"(a) In general. Notwithstanding any other provision of law, —
"(1) with respect to any taxable year which begins in the payroll tax holiday period, the rate of tax under section 1401(a) of the Internal Revenue Code of 1986 shall be 10.40 percent, and
"(2) with respect to remuneration received during the payroll tax holiday period, the rate of tax under 3101(a) of such Code shall be 4.2 percent (including for purposes of determining the applicable percentage under sections 3201(a) and 3211(a)(1) of such Code).
"(b) Coordination with deductions for employment taxes.
"(1) Deduction in computing net earnings from self-employment. For purposes of applying section 1402(a)(12) of the Internal Revenue Code of 1986, the rate of tax imposed by subsection 1401(a) of such Code shall be determined without regard to the reduction in such rate under this section.
"(2) Individual deduction. In the case of the taxes imposed by section 1401 of such Code for any taxable year which begins in the payroll tax holiday period, the deduction under section 164(f) with respect to such taxes shall be equal to the sum of—
"(A) 59.6 percent of the portion of such taxes attributable to the tax imposed by section 1401(a) (determined after the application of this section), plus
"(B) one-half of the portion of such taxes attributable to the tax imposed by section 1401(b).
"(c) Payroll tax holiday period. The term 'payroll tax holiday period' means calendar year 2011.
"(d) Employer notification. The Secretary of the Treasury shall notify employers of the payroll tax holiday period in any manner the Secretary deems appropriate.
"(e) Transfers of funds.
"(1) Transfers to federal old-age and survivors insurance trust fund. There are hereby appropriated to the Federal Old-Age and Survivors Trust Fund and the Federal Disability Insurance Trust Fund established under section 201 of the Social Security Act (42 U.S.C. 401) amounts equal to the reduction in revenues to the Treasury by reason of the application of subsection (a). Amounts appropriated by the preceding sentence shall be transferred from the general fund at such times and in such manner as to replicate to the extent possible the transfers which would have occurred to such Trust Fund had such amendments not been enacted.
"(2) Transfers to social security equivalent benefit account. There are hereby appropriated to the Social Security Equivalent Benefit Account established under section 15A(a) of the Railroad Retirement Act of 1974 (45 U.S.C. 231n-1(a)) amounts equal to the reduction in revenues to the Treasury by reason of the application of subsection (a)(2). Amounts appropriated by the preceding sentence shall be transferred from the general fund at such times and in such manner as to replicate to the extent possible the transfers which would have occurred to such Account had such amendments not been enacted.
"(3) Coordination with other federal laws. For purposes of applying any provision of Federal law other than the provisions of the Internal Revenue Code of 1986, the rate of tax in effect under section 3101(a) of such Code shall be determined without regard to the reduction in such rate under this section."
—P.L. 111-152, Sec. 1402(b)(1)(A), deleted "and" at the end of subpara. (b)(2)(A), added subpara. (b)(2)(B) and redesignated subpara. (b)(2)(B) as (b)(2)(C), effective with respect to remuneration received, and tax. yrs. begin. after, 12/31/2012.
—P.L. 111-148, Sec. 9015(a)(1)(A), substituted "(1) In General. In addition" for "In addition" in subsec. (b) . . . Sec. 9015(a)(1)(B), substituted "1.45 percent of the" for "the following percentages of the" in subsec. (b) . . . Sec. 9015(a)(1)(C), substituted "(as defined in section 3121(b))" for "(as defined in section 3121(b))" and deleted paras. (b)(2)-(6). . . . Sec. 9015(a)(1)(D), added para. (b)(2), effective with respect to remuneration received, and tax. yrs. begin. after 12/31/2012. . . . Sec. 10906(a), substituted "0.9 percent" for "0.5 percent" in para. (b)(2) (as added by Sec. 9015(a)(1) of the Patient Protection and Affordable Care Act), effective with respect to remuneration received, and tax. yrs. begin., after 12/31/2012.

Employment taxes Code Sec. 3101

Prior to amendment paras. (b)(2)-(6) read as follows:

"2. with respect to wages received during the calendar year 1978, the rate shall be 1.00 percent;

"3. with respect to wages received during the calendar years 1979 and 1980, the rate shall be 1.05 percent;

"4. with respect to wages received during the calendar years 1981 through 1984, the rate shall be 1.30 percent

"5. with respect to wages received during the calendar year 1985, the rate shall be 1.35 percent; and

"6. with respect to wages received after December 31, 1985, the rate shall be 1.45 percent."

In 2004, P.L. 108-203, Sec. 415, substituted "exclusively to the laws applicable to" for "to taxes or contributions for similar purposes under" in subsec. (c), effective 3/2/2004.

In 1983, P.L. 98-21, Sec. 123(a)(1), amended subsec. (a), effective for remuneration paid after 12/31/83.

Prior to amendment, subsec. (a) read as follows:

"(a) *Old-age, survivors, and disability insurance.*

"In addition to other taxes, there is hereby imposed on the income of every individual a tax equal to the following percentages of the wages (as defined in section 3121(a)) received by him with respect to employment (as defined in section 3121(b))—

"(1) with respect to wages received during the calendar years 1974 through 1977, the rate shall be 4.95 percent;

"(2) with respect to wages received during the calendar year 1978, the rate shall be 5.05 percent;

"(3) with respect to wages received during the calendar years 1979 and 1980, the rate shall be 5.08 percent;

"(4) with respect to wages received during the calendar year 1981, the rate shall be 5.35 percent;

"(5) with respect to wages received during the calendar years 1982 through 1984, the rate shall be 5.40 percent;

"(6) with respect to wages received during the calendar years 1985 through 1989, the rate shall be 5.70 percent; and

"(7) with respect to wages received after December 31, 1989, the rate shall be 6.20 percent."

In 1977, P.L. 95-216, Sec. 101(a)(1), amended paras. (a)(1) and (2), and added paras. (a)(3)-(7), effective for remunerations paid or received, and tax. yrs. begin. after '77.

Prior to amendment, paras. (a)(1) and (2) read as follows:

"(1) with respect to wages received during the calendar years 1974 through 2010, the rate shall be 4.95 percent; and

"(2) with respect to wages received after December 31, 2010, the rate shall be 5.95 percent."

—P.L. 95-216, Sec. 101(b)(1), amended paras. (b)(1)-(4), and added paras. (a)(5) and (6), effective for remunerations paid or received, and tax. yrs. begin. after '77.

Prior to amendment, paras. (b)(1) through (4) read as follows:

"(1) with respect to wages received during the calendar years 1974 through 1977, the rate shall be 0.90 percent;

"(2) with respect to wages received during the calendar years 1978 through 1980, the rate shall be 1.10 percent;

"(3) with respect to wages received during the calendar years 1981 through 1985, the rate shall be 1.35 percent; and

"(4) with respect to wages received after December 31, 1985, the rate shall be 1.50 percent."

—P.L. 95-216, Sec. 317(b)(2), added subsec. (c), effective 12/20/77 [date of enactment]. Sec. 317(b)(4), effective 12/20/77 [date of enactment], provided as follows:

"(4) Notwithstanding any other provision of law, taxes paid by any individual to any foreign country with respect to any period of employment or self-employment which is covered under the social security system of such foreign country in accordance with the terms of an agreement entered into pursuant to section 233 of the Social Security Act shall not, under the income tax laws of the United States, be deductible by, or creditable against the income tax of, any such individual."

In 1976, P.L. 94-455, Sec. 1903(a)(1)(A), deleted paras. (a)(1) through (a)(4), and redesignated paras. (a)(5) and (a)(6) as paras. (a)(1) and (a)(2) . . . Sec. 1903(a)(1)(B), deleted paras. (b)(1) and (b)(2), and redesignated paras. (b)(3) through (b)(6) as paras. (b)(1) through (b)(4), effective for wages paid after 12/31/76.

Prior to deletion, paras. (a)(1) through (a)(4) read as follows:

"(1) with respect to wages received during the calendar year 1968, the rate shall be 3.8 percent;

"(2) with respect to wages received during the calendar years 1969 and 1970, the rate shall be 4.2 percent;

"(3) with respect to wages received during the calendar years 1971 and 1972, the rate shall be 4.6 percent;

"(4) with respect to wages received during the calendar year 1973, the rate shall be 4.85 percent;"

Prior to deletion paras. (b)(1) and (b)(2) read as follows:

"(1) with respect to wages received during the calendar years 1968, 1969, 1970, 1971, and 1972, the rate shall be 0.60 percent;

"(2) with respect to wages received during the calendar year 1973, the rate shall be 1.0 percent;"

In 1973, P.L. 93-233, Sec. 6(a)(1), amended paras. (a)(4)-(6), effective only for remuneration paid after 12/31/73.

Prior to amendment, paras. (a)(4)-(6) read as follows:

"(4) with respect to wages received during the calendar years 1973, 1974, 1975, 1976, and 1977, the rate shall be 4.85 percent;

"(5) with respect to wages received during the calendar years 1978 through 2010, the rate shall be 4.80 percent; and

"(6) with respect to wages received after December 31, 2010, the rate shall be 5.85 percent."

—P.L. 93-233, Sec. 6(b)(2), amended paras. (b)(2)-(5), and added para. (b)(6), effective for remuneration paid after 12/31/73.

Prior to amendment, paras. (b)(2) through (b)(5) read as follows:

"(2) with respect to wages received during the calendar years 1973, 1974, 1975, 1976, and 1977, the rate shall be 1.0 percent;

"(3) with respect to wages received during the calendar years 1978, 1979, and 1980, the rate shall be 1.25 percent;

"(4) with respect to wages received during the calendar years 1981, 1982, 1983, 1984, and 1985, the rate shall be 1.35 percent; and

"(5) with respect to wages received after December 31, 1985, the rate shall be 1.45 percent."

In 1972, P.L. 92-603, Sec. 135(a)(2), substituted "the calendar years 1971 and 1972" for "any of the calendar years 1971 through 1977" in para. (a)(3), amended paras. (a)(4) and (5), and added para. (a)(6), effective only for remuneration paid after 12/31/72.

Prior to amendment paras. (a)(4) and (a)(5) read as follows:

"(4) with respect to wages received during any of the calendar years 1978 through 2010, the rate shall be 4.5 percent; and

"(5) with respect to wages received after December 31, 2010, the rate shall be 5.35 percent."

—P.L. 92-603, Sec. 135(b)(2), amended paras. (b)(2)—(b)(5), effective only for remuneration paid after 12/31/72.

Prior to amendment paras. (b)(2) through (b)(5) read as follows:

"(2) with respect to wages received during the calendar years 1973, 1974, 1975, 1976, and 1977, the rate shall be 0.9 percent;

"(3) with respect to wages received during the calendar years 1978, 1979, 1980, 1981, 1982, 1983, 1984, and 1985, the rate shall be 1.0 percent;

"(4) with respect to wages received during the calendar years 1986, 1987, 1988, 1989, 1990, 1991, and 1992, the rate shall be 1.1 percent; and

"(5) with respect to wages received after December 31, 1992, the rate shall be 1.2 percent."

—P.L. 92-336, Sec. 204(a)(2), substituted "any of the calendar years 1971 through 1977" for "the calendar years 1971 and 1972" in para. (a)(3), and amended paras. (a)(4) and (a)(5), effective for remuneration paid after 12/31/72.

Prior to amendment, paras. (a)(4) and (a)(5) read as follows:

"(4) with respect to wages received during the calendar years 1973, 1974, and 1975, the rate shall be 5.0 percent; and

"(5) with respect to wages received after December 31, 1975, the rate shall be 5.15 percent."

—P.L. 92-336, Sec. 204(b)(2), amended paras. (b)(2)-(5), effective for remuneration paid after 12/31/72.

In 1971, P.L. 92-5, Sec. 204(a)(1), struck out "and" from the end of para. (a)(3), amended para. (a)(4) and added new para. (a)(5), effective for tax. yrs. begin. after 12/31/71.

Prior to amendment, para. (a)(4) read as follows:

"(4) with respect to wages paid after December 31, 1972, the rate shall be 5.0 percent."

In 1967, P.L. 90-248, Sec. 109(a), amended paras. (a)(1)-(4), effective for remuneration paid after 12/31/67.

Prior to amendment, paras. (a)(1)-(4) read as follows:

"(1) with respect to wages received during the calendar year 1966, the rate shall be 3.85 percent;

"(2) with respect to wages received during the calendar years 1967 and 1968, the rate shall be 3.9 percent;

"(3) with respect to wages received during the calendar years 1969, 1970, 1971, and 1972, the rate shall be 4.4 percent; and

"(4) with respect to wages received after December 31, 1972, the rate shall be 4.85 percent."

—P.L. 90-248, Sec. 109(b), amended paras. (b)(1)-(6), effective for remuneration paid after 12/31/67.

Prior to amendment, paras. (b)(1)-(6) read as follows:

"(1) with respect to wages received during the calendar year 1966, the rate shall be 0.35 percent;

"(2) with respect to wages received during the calendar years 1967, 1968, 1969, 1970, 1971, and 1972, the rate shall be 0.50 percent;

"(3) with respect to wages received during the calendar years 1973, 1974, and 1975, the rate shall be 0.55 percent;

"(4) with respect to wages received during the calendar years 1976, 1977, 1978, and 1979, the rate shall be 0.60 percent;

"(5) with respect to wages received during the calendar years 1980, 1981, 1982, 1983, 1984, 1985, and 1986, the rate shall be 0.70 percent; and

"(6) with respect to wages received after December 31, 1986, the rate shall be 0.80 percent."

In 1965, P.L. 89-97, Sec. 321, amended Code Sec. 3101, effective for remuneration paid after '65. Sec. 111 of that P. L. deleted "but without regard to the provisions of paragraph (9) thereof insofar as it relates to employees" following "section 3121(b)" in subsec. (b).

Prior to amendment, Code Sec. 3101 read as follows:

"SEC. 3101. RATE OF TAX.

"In addition to other taxes, there is hereby imposed on the income of every individual a tax equal to the following percentages of the wages (as defined in section 3121(a)) received by him with respect to employment (as defined in section 3121(b))—

"(1) with respect to wages received during the calendar year 1962, the rate shall be 3⅛ percent;

"(2) with respect to wages received during the calendar years 1963 to 1965, both inclusive, the rate shall be 3⅝ percent;

"(3) with respect to wages received during the calendar years 1966 to 1967, both inclusive, the rate shall be 4⅛ percent; and

"(4) with respect to wages received after December 31, 1967, the rate shall be 4⅝ percent."

In 1961, P.L. 87-64, had increased the rates to the above from the following: calendar '62–3%; '63 thru '65–3½%; '66, '67–4%; '68–4% after '68–4½%, effective for remuneration paid after '61.

In 1958, P.L. 85-840, had increased the rates from the following: calendar '57 thru '59–2¼%; '60 thru '64– 2¾%, '65 thru '69–3¼%; '70 thru '74–3¾%; after '74–4¼%, effective for remuneration paid after '58.

In 1956, ch. 836, Sec. 202(b), had increased the rates from the following: calendar '55 thru '59–2%; '60 thru '64 –2½%; '65 thru '69–3%; '70 thru '74–3½%; after '74–4%, effective for remuneration paid after '56.

In 1954, ch. 1206, Sec. 208(b), had increased the rates from the following: calendar '55 thru '59–2%; '60 thru '64–2½%; '65 thru '69–3%; after '69–3¼%.

Sec. 3102. Deduction of tax from wages.

(a) Requirement.

The tax imposed by section 3101 shall be collected by the employer of the taxpayer, by deducting the amount of the tax from the wages as and when paid. An employer who in any calendar year pays to an employee cash remuneration to which paragraph (7)(B) of section 3121(a) is applicable may deduct an amount equivalent to such tax from any such payment of remuneration, even though at the time of payment the total amount of such remuneration paid to the employee by the employer in the calendar year is less than the applicable dollar threshold (as defined in section 3121(x)) for such year; and an employer who in any calendar year pays to an employee cash remuneration to which paragraph (7)(C) or (10) of section 3121(a) is applicable may deduct an amount equivalent to such tax from any such payments of remuneration, even though at the time of payment the total amount of such remuneration paid to the employee by the employer in the calendar year is less than $100; and an employer who in any calendar year pays to an employee cash remuneration to which paragraph (8)(B) of section 3121(a) is applicable may deduct an amount equivalent to such tax from any such payment of remuneration, even though at the time of payment the total amount of such remuneration paid to the employee by the employer in the calendar year is less than $150; and an employer who is furnished by an employee a written statement of tips (received in a calendar month) pursuant to section 6053(a) to which paragraph (12)(B) of section 3121(a) is applicable may deduct an amount equivalent to such tax with respect to such tips from any wages of the employee (exclusive of tips) under his control, even though at the time such statement is furnished the total amount of the tips included in statements furnished to the employer as having been received by the employee in such calendar month in the course of his employment by such employer is less than $20.

(b) Indemnification of employer.

Every employer required so to deduct the tax shall be liable for the payment of such tax, and shall be indemnified against the claims and demands of any person for the amount of any such payment made by such employer.

(c) Special rule for tips.

(1) In the case of tips which constitute wages, subsection (a) shall be applicable only to such tips as are included in a written statement furnished to the employer pursuant to section 6053(a), and only to the extent that collection can be made by the employer, at or after the time such statement is so furnished and before the close of the 10th day following the calendar month (or, if paragraph (3) applies, the 30th day following the year) in which the tips were deemed paid, by deducting the amount of the tax from such wages of the employee (excluding tips, but including funds turned over by the employee to the employer pursuant to paragraph (2)) as are under control of the employer.

(2) If the tax imposed by section 3101, with respect to tips which are included in written statements furnished in any month to the employer pursuant to section 6053(a), exceeds the wages of the employee (excluding tips) from which the employer is required to collect the tax under paragraph (1), the employee may furnish to the employer on or before the 10th day of the following month (or, if paragraph (3) applies, on or before the 30th day of the following year) an amount of money equal to the amount of the excess.

(3) The Secretary may, under regulations prescribed by him, authorize employers—

(A) to estimate the amount of tips that will be reported by the employee pursuant to section 6053(a) in any calendar year,

(B) to determine the amount to be deducted upon each payment of wages (exclusive of tips) during such year as if the tips so estimated constituted the actual tips so reported, and

(C) to deduct upon any payment of wages (other than tips, but including funds turned over by the employee to the employer pursuant to paragraph (2)) to such employee during such year (and within 30 days thereafter) such amount as may be necessary to adjust the amount actually deducted upon such wages of the employee during the year to the amount required to be deducted in respect of tips included in written statements furnished to the employer during the year.

(4) If the tax imposed by section 3101 with respect to tips which constitute wages exceeds the portion of such tax which can be collected by the employer from the wages of the employee pursuant to paragraph (1) or paragraph (3), such excess shall be paid by the employee.

(d) Special rule for certain taxable group-term life insurance benefits.

(1) In general. In the case of any payment for group-term life insurance to which this subsection applies—

(A) subsection (a) shall not apply,

(B) the employer shall separately include on the statement required under section 6051—

(i) the portion of the wages which consists of payments for group-term life insurance to which this subsection applies, and

(ii) the amount of the tax imposed by section 3101 on such payments, and

(C) the tax imposed by section 3101 on such payments shall be paid by the employee.

(2) Benefits to which subsection applies. This subsection shall apply to any payment for group-term life insurance to the extent—

(A) such payment constitutes wages, and

(B) such payment is for coverage for periods during which an employment relationship no longer exists between the employee and the employer.

(e) Special rule for certain transferred federal employees.

In the case of any payments of wages for service performed in the employ of an international organization pursuant to a transfer to which the provisions of section 3121(y) are applicable—

(1) subsection (a) shall not apply,

Employment taxes   Code Sec. 3111(c)

(2) the head of the Federal agency from which the transfer was made shall separately include on the statement required under section 6051—

(A) the amount determined to be the amount of the wages for such service, and

(B) the amount of the tax imposed by section 3101 on such payments, and

(3) the tax imposed by section 3101 on such payments shall be paid by the employee.

> • *Caution:* Code Sec. 3102(f), following, is effective for remuneration received, and tax. yrs. begin., after 12/31/2012.

(f) **Special rules for additional tax.**

(1) **In general.** In the case of any tax imposed by section 3101(b)(2), subsection (a) shall only apply to the extent to which the taxpayer receives wages from the employer in excess of $200,000, and the employer may disregard the amount of wages received by such taxpayer's spouse.

(2) **Collection of amounts not withheld.** To the extent that the amount of any tax imposed by section 3101(b)(2) is not collected by the employer, such tax shall be paid by the employee.

(3) **Tax paid by recipient.** If an employer, in violation of this chapter, fails to deduct and withhold the tax imposed by section 3101(b)(2) and thereafter the tax is paid by the employee, the tax so required to be deducted and withheld shall not be collected from the employer, but this paragraph shall in no case relieve the employer from liability for any penalties or additions to tax otherwise applicable in respect of such failure to deduct and withhold.

In 2010, P.L. 111-148, Sec. 9015(a)(2), added subsec. (f), effective for remuneration received, and tax. yrs. begin. after 12/31/2012.

In 2004, P.L. 108-203, Sec. 424(b), deleted "and the employee has not performed agricultural labor for the employer on 20 days or more in the calendar year for cash remuneration computed on a time basis" after "is less than $150" in subsec. (a), effective 3/2/2004.

In 1994, P.L. 103-387, Sec. 2(a)(1)(D)(i), substituted "calendar year" for "calendar quarter" each place it appeared in subsec. (a)... Sec. 2(a)(1)(D)(ii), substituted "the applicable dollar threshold (as defined in section 3121(x)) for such year" for "$50" in subsec. (a), effective for remuneration paid after 12/31/93. Sec. 2(a)(4) of this Act provides:

"(4) No loss of social security coverage for 1994; continuation of W-2 filing requirement.— Notwithstanding the amendments made by this subsection, if the wages (as defined in section 3121(a) of the Internal Revenue Code of 1986) paid during 1994 to an employee for domestic service in a private home of the employer are less than $1,000—

"(A) the employer shall file any return or statement required under section 6051 of such Code with respect to such wages (determined without regard to such amendments), and

"(B) the employee shall be entitled to credit under section 209 of the Social Security Act with respect to any such wages required to be included on any such return or statement."

—P.L. 103-296, Sec. 319(a)(3), added subsec. (e), effective for service performed after the calendar quarter following the calendar quarter in which the date of the enactment [8/15/94] of this Act occurs.

In 1990, P.L. 101-508, Sec. 5124(a), added subsec. (d), effective for coverage provided after 12/31/90.

In 1982, P.L. 97-248, Sec. 269(c)(3), of this Act is reproduced in note following Code Sec. 3401.

In 1978, P.L. 95-600, Sec. 530, provides the rules regarding individuals as employees for purposes of the employment taxes. Sec. 530 of P. L. 95-600 is reproduced in the note following Code Sec. 3401.

In 1977, P.L. 95-216, Sec. 355(a), deleted "or (C) or (10)" after "paragraph (7)(B)" in subsec. (a), and added "and an employer who in any calendar year pays to an employee cash remuneration to which paragraph (7)(C) or (1) of section 3121(a) is applicable may deduct an amount equivalent to such tax from any such payment of remuneration, even though at the time of payment the total amount of such remuneration paid to the employee by the employer in the calendar year is less than $100;" after "is less than $50;" in subsec. (a), effective for remuneration paid and tips received after 1977.

—P.L. 95-216, Sec. 355(b)(1), substituted "year" for "quarter" each place it appeared in paras. (c)(1) and (2)... Sec. 355(b)(2)(A), deleted "quarter of the" following "section 6053(a) in any" in subpara. (c)(3)(A)... Sec. 355(b)(2)(B), substituted "year" for "quarter" each place it appeared in subparas. (c)(3)(B) and (C), for remunerations paid and tips received after '77.

In 1976, P.L. 94-455, Sec. 1906(b)(13)(A), substituted "Secretary" for "Secretary or his delegate" in Code Sec. 3102, effective 2/1/77.

In 1965, P.L. 89-97, Sec. 313, added subsec. (c), and added the section beginning "; and an employer who is furnished by an employee a written statement of tips . . ." at the end of subsec. (a), effective for tips received by employees after '65.

In 1956, ch. 836, Sec. 201(h)(3), substituted "$150 and the employee has not performed agricultural labor for the employer on 20 days or more in the calendar year for cash remuneration computed on a time basis" for "$100" in subsec. (a), effective for remuneration paid after 1956.

In 1954, ch. 1206, Sec. 205A, added a new sentence at the end of subsec. (a) permitting in certain instances an employer to deduct employee tax even though payment to the employee is less than $50 for the calendar quarter or $100 for the calendar year.

Subchapter B.—Tax on Employers

Sec.
3111. Rate of tax.
3112. Instrumentalities of the United States.
3113. Repealed.

In 1976, P.L. 94-455, Sec. 1903(b), repealed the item for Code Sec. 3113. Prior to amendment, the item for Code Sec. 3113 read as follows:
"3113. District of Columbia credit unions."
In 1956, added item 3113.

Sec. 3111. Rate of tax.

(a) **Old-age, survivors, and disability insurance.**

In addition to other taxes, there is hereby imposed on every employer an excise tax, with respect to having individuals in his employ, equal to the following percentages of the wages (as defined in section 3121(a)) paid by him with respect to employment (as defined in section 3121(b))—

In cases of wages paid during:	The rate shall be:
1984, 1985, 1986, or 1987	5.7 percent
1988 or 1989	6.06 percent
1990 or thereafter	6.2 percent.

(b) **Hospital insurance.**

In addition to the tax imposed by the preceding subsection, there is hereby imposed on every employer an excise tax, with respect to having individuals in his employ, equal to the following percentages of the wages (as defined in section 3121(a)) paid by him with respect to employment (as defined in section 3121(b))—

(1) with respect to wages paid during the calendar years 1974 through 1977, the rate shall be 0.90 percent;

(2) with respect to wages paid during the calendar year 1978, the rate shall be 1.00 percent;

(3) with respect to wages paid during the calendar years 1979 and 1980, the rate shall be 1.05 percent;

(4) with respect to wages paid during the calendar years 1981 through 1984, the rate shall be 1.30 percent;

(5) with respect to wages paid during the calendar year 1985, the rate shall be 1.35 percent; and

(6) with respect to wages paid after December 31, 1985, the rate shall be 1.45 percent.

(c) **Relief from taxes in cases covered by certain international agreements.**

During any period in which there is in effect an agreement entered into pursuant to section 233 of the Social Security Act with any foreign country, wages received by or paid to an individual shall be exempt from the taxes imposed by this section to the extent that such wages are subject under such agreement exclusively to the laws applicable to the social security system of such foreign country.

(d) Special Exemption for Certain Individuals Hired in 2010.

(1) In general. Subsection (a) shall not apply to wages paid by a qualified employer with respect to employment during the period beginning on the day after the date of the enactment of this subsection and ending on December 31, 2010, of any qualified individual for services performed—

(A) in a trade or business of such qualified employer, or

(B) in the case of a qualified employer exempt from tax under section 501(a), in furtherance of the activities related to the purpose or function constituting the basis of the employer's exemption under section 501.

(2) Qualified employer. For purposes of this subsection—

(A) In general. The term "qualified employer" means any employer other than the United States, any State, or any political subdivision thereof, or any instrumentality of the foregoing.

(B) Treatment of employees of post-secondary educational institutions. Notwithstanding subparagraph (A), the term "qualified employer" includes any employer which is a public institution of higher education (as defined in section 101(b) of the Higher Education Act of 1965).

(3) Qualified individual. For purposes of this subsection, the term "qualified individual" means any individual who—

(A) begins employment with a qualified employer after February 3, 2010, and before January 1, 2011,

(B) certifies by signed affidavit, under penalties of perjury, that such individual has not been employed for more than 40 hours during the 60-day period ending on the date such individual begins such employment,

(C) is not employed by the qualified employer to replace another employee of such employer unless such other employee separated from employment voluntarily or for cause, and

(D) is not an individual described in section 51(i)(1) (applied by substituting "qualified employer" for "taxpayer" each place it appears).

(4) Election. A qualified employer may elect to have this subsection not apply. Such election shall be made in such manner as the Secretary may require.

(5) Special rule for first calendar quarter of 2010.

(A) Nonapplication of exemption during first quarter. Paragraph (1) shall not apply with respect to wages paid during the first calendar quarter of 2010.

(B) Crediting of first quarter exemption during second quarter. The amount by which the tax imposed under subsection (a) would (but for subparagraph (A)) have been reduced with respect to wages paid by a qualified employer during the first calendar quarter of 2010 shall be treated as a payment against the tax imposed under subsection (a) with respect to the qualified employer for the second calendar quarter of 2010 which is made on the date that such tax is due.

In 2010, P.L. 111-147, Sec. 101(a), added subsec. (d), effective for wages paid after 3/18/2010.

—P.L. 111-147, Sec. 102, of this Act, provides:

"SEC. 102. BUSINESS CREDIT FOR RETENTION OF CERTAIN NEWLY HIRED INDIVIDUALS IN 2010.

"(a) In general. In the case of any taxable year ending after the date of the enactment of this Act, the current year business credit determined under section 38(b) of the Internal Revenue Code of 1986 for such taxable year shall be increased, with respect to each retained worker with respect to which subsection (b)(2) is first satisfied during such taxable year, by the lesser of—

"(1) $1,000, and

"(2) 6.2 percent of the wages (as defined in section 3401(a)) paid by the taxpayer to such retained worker during the 52 consecutive week period referred to in subsection (b)(2).

"(b) Retained worker. For purposes of this section, the term 'retained worker' means any qualified individual (as defined in section 3111(d)(3) or section 3221(c)(3) of the Internal Revenue Code of 1986)—

"(1) who was employed by the taxpayer on any date during the taxable year,

"(2) who was so employed by the taxpayer for a period of not less than 52 consecutive weeks, and

"(3) whose wages (as defined in section 3401(a)) for such employment during the last 26 weeks of such period equaled at least 80 percent of such wages for the first 26 weeks of such period.

"(c) Limitation on carrybacks. No portion of the unused business credit under section 38 of the Internal Revenue Code of 1986 for any taxable year which is attributable to the increase in the current year business credit under this section may be carried to a taxable year beginning before the date of the enactment of this section."

In 2004, P.L. 108-203, Sec. 415, substituted "exclusively to the laws applicable to" for "to taxes or contributions for similar purposes under" in subsec. (c), effective 3/2/2004.

In 1987, P.L. 100-203, Sec. 9006(b)(1), deleted "and (t)" after "3121(a)" in subsecs. (a) and (b), effective for tips received (and wages paid) on and after 1/1/88.

In 1983, P.L. 98-21, Sec. 123(a)(2), amended subsec. (a), effective for remuneration paid after 12/31/83.

Prior to amendment, subsec. (a) read as follows:

"(a) Old-age, survivors, and disability insurance.

"In addition to other taxes, there is hereby imposed on every employer an excise tax, with respect to having individuals in his employ, equal to the following percentages of the wages (as defined in section 3121(a) and (t)) paid by him with respect to employment (as defined in section 3121(b))—

"(1) with respect to wages paid during the calendar years 1974 through 1977, the rate shall be 4.95 percent;

"(2) with respect to wages paid during the calendar year 1978, the rate shall be 5.05 percent;

"(3) with respect to wages paid during the calendar years 1979 and 1980, the rate shall be 5.08 percent;

"(4) with respect to wages paid during the calendar year 1981, the rate shall be 5.35 percent;

"(5) with respect to wages paid during the calendar years 1982 through 1984, the rate shall be 5.40 percent;

"(6) with respect to wages paid during the calendar years 1985 through 1989, the rate shall be 5.70 percent; and

"(7) with respect to wages paid after December 31, 1989, the rate shall be 6.20 percent."

In 1977, P.L. 95-216, Sec. 101(a)(2), substituted paras. (a)(1) through (7), for paras. (a)(1) and (2), effective for remunerations paid or received, and tax. yrs. begin. after '77.

Prior to amendment, paras. (a)(1) and (2) read as follows:

"(1) with respect to wages paid during the calendar years 1974 through 2010, the rate shall be 4.95 percent; and

"(2) with respect to wages paid after December 31, 2010, the rate shall be 5.95 percent."

—P.L. 95-216, Sec. 101(b)(2), substituted paras. (b)(1) through (6) for paras. (b)(1) through (4), effective for remunerations paid or received, and for tax. yrs. begin. after '77.

Prior to amendment, paras. (b)(1) through (4) read as follows:

"(1) with respect to wages paid during the calendar years 1974 through 1977, the rate shall be 0.90 percent;

"(2) with respect to wages paid during the calendar years 1978 through 1980, the rate shall be 1.10 percent;

"(3) with respect to wages paid during the calendar years 1981 through 1985, the rate shall be 1.35 percent; and

"(4) with respect to wages paid after December 31, 1985, the rate shall be 1.50 percent."

—P.L. 95-216, Sec. 315(b), added "and (t)" following "3121(a)" in subsecs. (a) and (b), effective for wages paid with respect to employment performed in months after Dec. '77.

—P.L. 95-216, Sec. 317(b)(2), added subsec. (c), effective 12/20/77, [date of enactment]. Sec. 317(b)(4), effective 12/20/77, [date of enactment], provides:

"(4) Notwithstanding any other provision of law, taxes paid by any individual to any foreign country with respect to any period of employment or self-employment which is covered under the social security system of such foreign country in accordance with the terms of an agreement entered into pursuant to section 233 of the Social Security Act shall not, under the income tax laws of the United States, be deductible by, or creditable against the income tax of, any such individual."

In 1976, P.L. 94-455, Sec. 1903(a)(1), deleted paras. (a)(1) through (a)(4), redesignated paras. (a)(5) and (a)(6) as paras. (a)(1) and (a)(2), deleted paras. (b)(1) and (b)(2), redesignated paras. (b)(3) through (b)(6) as paras. (b)(1) through (b)(4), effective for wages paid after 12/31/76.

Prior to amendment, paras. (a)(1) through (a)(4) read as follows:

"(1) with respect to wages paid during the calendar year 1968, the rate shall be 3.8 percent;

"(2) with respect to wages paid during the calendar years 1969 and 1970, the rate shall be 4.2 percent;

"(3) with respect to wages paid during the calendar years 1971 and 1972, the rate shall be 4.6 percent;
"(4) with respect to wages paid during the calendar year 1973, the rate shall be 4.85 percent;"
Prior to amendment, paras. (b)(1) and (b)(2) read as follows:
"(1) with respect to wages paid during the calendar years 1968, 1969, 1970, 1971, and 1972, the rate shall be 0.60 percent;
"(2) with respect to wages paid during the calendar year 1973, the rate shall be 1.0 percent;"
In 1973, P.L. 93-233, Sec. 6(a)(2), amended paras. (a)(4)-(6), effective only for remuneration paid after 12/31/73.
Prior to amendment, paras. (a)(4)-(6) read as follows:
"(4) with respect to wages paid during the calendar years 1973, 1974, 1975, 1976, and 1977, the rate shall be 4.85 percent;
"(5) with respect to wages paid during the calendar years 1978 through 2010, the rate shall be 4.80 percent; and
"(6) with respect to wages paid after December 31, 2010, the rate shall be 5.85 percent."
—P.L. 93-233, Sec. 6(b)(3), amended paras. (b)(2)-(5), effective for remuneration paid after 12/31/73.
Prior to amendment, paras. (b)(2)-(5) read as follows:
"(2) with respect to wages paid during the calendar years 1973, 1974, 1975, 1976, and 1977, the rate shall be 1.0 percent;
"(3) with respect to wages paid during the calendar years 1978, 1979, and 1980, the rate shall be 1.25 percent;
"(4) with respect to wages paid during the calendar years 1981, 1982, 1983, 1984, and 1985, the rate shall be 1.35 percent; and
"(5) with respect to wages paid after December 31, 1985, the rate shall be 1.45 percent."
In 1972, P.L. 92-603, Sec. 135(a)(3), substituted "the calendar years 1971 and 1972" for "any of the calendar years 1971 through 1977" in para. (a)(3) and substituted new paras. (a)(4), (a)(5) and (a)(6) for old paras. (a)(4) and (a)(5), effective only for remuneration paid after 12/31/72.
Prior to amendment, paras. (a)(4) and (a)(5) read as follows:
"(4) with respect to wages paid during any of the calendar years 1978 through 2010, the rate shall be 4.5 percent; and
"(5) with respect to wages paid after December 31, 2010, the rate shall be 5.35 percent."
—P.L. 92-603, Sec. 135(b)(3), amended paras. (b)(2) through (b)(5), effective only for remuneration paid after 12/31/72.
Prior to amendment paras. (b)(2) through (b)(5) read as follows:
"(2) with respect to wages paid during the calendar years 1973, 1974, 1975, 1976, and 1977, the rate shall be 0.9 percent;
"(3) with respect to wages paid during the calendar years 1978, 1979, 1980, 1981, 1982, 1983, 1984, and 1985, the rate shall be 1.0 percent;
"(4) with respect to wages paid during the calendar years 1986, 1987, 1988, 1989, 1990, 1991, and 1992, the rate shall be 1.1 percent; and
"(5) with respect to wages paid after December 31, 1992, the rate shall be 1.2 percent."
—P.L. 92-336, Sec. 204(a)(3), substituted "any of the calendar years 1971 through 1977" for "the calendar years 1971 and 1972", in para. (a)(3), and amended paras. (a)(4) and (a)(5), effective for remuneration paid after 12/31/72.
Prior to amendment, paras. (a)(4) and (a)(5) read as follows:
"(4) with respect to wages paid during the calendar years 1973, 1974, and 1975, the rate shall be 5.0 percent; and
"(5) with respect to wages paid after December 31, 1975, the rate shall be 5.15 percent."
—P.L. 92-336, Sec. 204(b)(3), amended paras. (b)(2) through (b)(5), effective for remuneration paid after 12/31/72.
Prior to amendment, paras. (b)(2)-(5) read as follows:
"(2) with respect to wages received during the calendar years 1973, 1974, and 1975, the rate shall be 0.65 percent;
"(3) with respect to wages received during the calendar years 1976, 1977, 1978, and 1979, the rate shall be 0.70 percent;
"(4) with respect to wages received during the calendar years 1980, 1981, 1982, 1983, 1984, 1985, and 1986, the rate shall be 0.80 percent; and
"(5) with respect to wages received after December 31, 1986, the rate shall be 0.90 percent."
In 1971, P.L. 92-5, Sec. 204(a)(2), deleted "and" from the end of para. (a)(3), amended para. (a)(4), and added para. (a)(5), effective for remuneration paid after 12/31/71.
Prior to amendment, para. (a)(4) read as follows:
"(4) with respect to wages paid after December 31, 1972, the rate shall be 5.0 percent."
In 1967, P.L. 90-248, Sec. 109(a), amended paras (a)(1)-(4), effective for remuneration paid after 12/31/67.
Prior to amendment, paras. (a)(1)-(4) read as follows:
"(1) with respect to wages paid during the calendar year 1966, the rate shall be 3.85 percent;
"(2) with respect to wages paid during the calendar years 1967 and 1968, the rate shall be 3.9 percent;
"(3) with respect to wages paid during the calendar years 1969, 1970, 1971, and 1972, the rate shall be 4.4 percent; and
"(4) with respect to wages paid after December 31, 1972, the rate shall be 4.85 percent."
—P.L. 90-248, Sec. 109(b), amended paras. (b)(1)-(6), effective for renumeration paid after 12/31/67.
Prior to amendment, paras. (b)(1)-(6), read as follows:
"(1) with respect to wages paid during the calendar year 1966, the rate shall be 0.35 percent;
"(2) with respect to wages paid during the calendar years 1967, 1968, 1969, 1970, 1971, and 1972, the rate shall be 0.50 percent;
"(3) with respect to wages paid during the calendar years 1973, 1974, and 1975, the rate shall be 0.55 percent;
"(4) with respect to wages paid during the calendar years 1976, 1977, 1978, and 1979, the rate shall be 0.60 percent;
"(5) with respect to wages paid during the calendar years 1980, 1981, 1982, 1983, 1984, 1985, and 1986, the rate shall be 0.70 percent;
"(6) with respect to wages paid after December 31, 1986, the rate shall be 0.80 percent".
In 1965, P.L. 89-97, Sec. 321, amended Code Sec. 3111, effective for remuneration paid after '65. Sec. 111 of that P.L. deleted "but without regard to the provisions of paragraph (9) thereof insofar as it relates to employees" following "section 3121(b)" in subsec. (b).
Prior to amendment, the section read as follows:
"SEC. 3111. RATE OF TAX.
"In addition to other taxes, there is hereby imposed on every employer an excise tax, with respect to having individuals in his employ, equal to the following percentages of the wages (as defined in section 3121(a)) paid by him with respect to employment (as defined in section 3121(b))—
"(1) with respect to wages paid during the calendar year 1962, the rate shall be 3⅛ percent;
"(2) with respect to wages paid during the calendar years 1963 to 1965, both inclusive, the rates shall be 3⅝ percent;
"(3) with respect to wages paid during the calendar years 1966 to 1967, both inclusive, the rate shall be 4⅛ percent; and
"(4) with respect to wages paid after December 31, 1967, the rate shall be 4⅝ percent."
In 1961, P.L. 87-64, had increased the rates to the above from the following: calendar '62–3%; '63 thru '65–3½%; '66, '67–4%; '68–4% after '68–4½%, effective for remuneration paid after '61.
In 1958, P.L. 85-840, had increased the rates from the following: calendar '57 thru '59–2¼%; '60 thru '64– 2¾%, '65 thru '69–3¼%; '70 thru '74–3¾%; after '74–4¼%, effective for remuneration paid after '58.
In 1956, ch. 836, Sec. 202(c), had increased the rates from the following: calendar '55 thru '59–2%; '60 thru '64 –2½%; '65 thru '69–3%; '70 thru '74–3½%; after '74–4%, effective for remuneration paid after '56.
In 1954, ch. 1206, Sec. 208(c), had increased the rates from the following: calendar '55 thru '59–2%; '60 thru '64–2½%; '65 thru '69–3%; after '69–3¼%.

Sec. 3112. Instrumentalities of the United States.

Notwithstanding any other provision of law (whether enacted before or after the enactment of this section) which grants to any instrumentality of the United States an exemption from taxation, such instrumentality shall not be exempt from the tax imposed by section 3111 unless such other provision of law grants a specific exemption, by reference to section 3111 (or the corresponding section of prior law), from the tax imposed by such section.

Sec. 3113. Repealed.

In 1976, P.L. 94-455, Sec. 1903(a)(2), repealed Code Sec. 3113, effective for wages paid after 12/31/76.
Prior to repeal, Code Sec. 3113 read as follows:
"SEC. 3113. DISTRICT OF COLUMBIA CREDIT UNIONS.
"Notwithstanding the provisions of section 16 of the Act of June 23, 1932 (D.C. Code, sec. 26-516; 47 Stat. 331), or any other provision of law (whether enacted before or after the enactment of this section) which grants to any credit union chartered pursuant to such Act of June 23, 1932, an exemption from taxation, such credit union shall not be exempt from the tax imposed by section 3111."
In 1956, ch. 836, Sec. 201(a)(1), added Code Sec. 3113, effective for remuneration paid after 12/31/56.

Subchapter C.—General Provisions

Sec.
3121. Definitions.
3122. Federal service.
3123. Deductions as constructive payments.
3124. Estimate of revenue reduction.
3125. Returns in the case of governmental employees in States, Guam, American Samoa and District of Columbia.

3126. Return and payment by governmental employer.
3127. Exemption for employers and their employees where both are members of religious faiths opposed to participation in Social Security Act programs.
3128. Short title.

In **1988**, P.L. 100-647, Sec. 8007(a)(2), redesignated item 3127 as item 3128 and added new item 3127.
In **1986**, P.L. 99-509, Sec. 9002(a)(2), redesignated item 3126 as item 3127 and added new item 3126.
In **1986**, P.L. 99-272, Sec. 13205(a)(2)(A)(iii), added "States," before "Guam" in item 3125.
In **1965**, added the "District of Columbia" in item 3125.
In **1960**, added item 3125 and redesignated former item 3125 as 3126.

Sec. 3121. Definitions.
(a) Wages.

For purposes of this chapter, the term "wages" means all remuneration for employment, including the cash value of all remuneration (including benefits) paid in any medium other than cash; except that such term shall not include—

(1) in the case of the taxes imposed by sections 3101(a) and 3111(a) that part of the remuneration which, after remuneration (other than remuneration referred to in the succeeding paragraphs of this subsection) equal to the contribution and benefit base (as determined under section 230 of the Social Security Act) with respect to employment has been paid to an individual by an employer during the calendar year with respect to which such contribution and benefit base is effective, is paid to such individual by such employer during such calendar year. If an employer (hereinafter referred to as successor employer) during any calendar year acquires substantially all the property used in a trade or business of another employer (hereinafter referred to as a predecessor), or used in a separate unit of a trade or business of a predecessor, and immediately after the acquisition employs in his trade or business an individual who immediately prior to the acquisition was employed in the trade or business of such predecessor, then, for the purpose of determining whether the successor employer has paid remuneration (other than remuneration referred to in the succeeding paragraphs of this subsection) with respect to employment equal to the contribution and benefit base (as determined under section 230 of the Social Security Act) to such individual during such calendar year, any remuneration (other than remuneration referred to in the succeeding paragraphs of this subsection) with respect to employment paid (or considered under this paragraph as having been paid) to such individual by such predecessor during such calendar year and prior to such acquisition shall be considered as having been paid by such successor employer;

(2) the amount of any payment (including any amount paid by an employer for insurance or annuities, or into a fund, to provide for any such payment) made to, or on behalf of, an employee or any of his dependents under a plan or system established by an employer which makes provision for his employees generally (or for his employees generally and their dependents) or for a class or classes of his employees (or for a class or classes of his employees and their dependents), on account of—

(A) sickness or accident disability (but, in the case of payments made to an employee or any of his dependents, this subparagraph shall exclude from the term "wages" only payments which are received under a workmen's compensation law), or

(B) medical or hospitalization expenses in connection with sickness or accident disability, or

(C) death, except that this paragraph does not apply to a payment for group-term life insurance to the extent that such payment is includible in the gross income of the employee;

(3) Repealed.

(4) any payment on account of sickness or accident disability, or medical or hospitalization expenses in connection with sickness or accident disability, made by an employer to, or on behalf of, an employee after the expiration of 6 calendar months following the last calendar month in which the employee worked for such employer;

(5) any payment made to, or on behalf of, an employee or his beneficiary—

(A) from or to a trust described in section 401(a) which is exempt from tax under section 501(a) at the time of such payment unless such payment is made to an employee of the trust as remuneration for services rendered as such employee and not as a beneficiary of the trust,

(B) under or to an annuity plan which, at the time of such payment, is a plan described in section 403(a),

(C) under a simplified employee pension (as defined in section 408(k)(1)), other than any contributions described in section 408(k)(6),

(D) under or to an annuity contract described in section 403(b), other than a payment for the purchase of such contract which is made by reason of a salary reduction agreement (whether evidenced by a written instrument or otherwise),

(E) under or to an exempt governmental deferred compensation plan (as defined in subsection (v)(3)),

(F) to supplement pension benefits under a plan or trust described in any of the foregoing provisions of this paragraph to take into account some portion or all of the increase in the cost of living (as determined by the Secretary of Labor) since retirement but only if such supplemental payments are under a plan which is treated as a welfare plan under section 3(2)(B)(ii) of the Employee Retirement Income Security Act of 1974,

(G) under a cafeteria plan (within the meaning of section 125) if such payment would not be treated as wages without regard to such plan and it is reasonable to believe that (if section 125 applied for purposes of this section) section 125 would not treat any wages as constructively received,

(H) under an arrangement to which section 408(p) applies, other than any elective contributions under paragraph (2)(A)(i) thereof, or

(I) under a plan described in section 457(e)(11)(A)(ii) and maintained by an eligible employer (as defined in section 457(e)(1));

(6) the payment by an employer (without deduction from the remuneration of the employee)—

(A) of the tax imposed upon an employee under section 3101, or

(B) of any payment required from an employee under a State unemployment compensation law,

with respect to remuneration paid to an employee for domestic service in a private home of the employer or for agricultural labor;

(7)(A) remuneration paid in any medium other than cash to an employee for service not in the course of the employer's trade or business or for domestic service in a private home of the employer;

(B) cash remuneration paid by an employer in any calendar year to an employee for domestic service in a pri-

Employment taxes   Code Sec. 3121(b)

vate home of the employer (including domestic service on a farm operated for profit), if the cash remuneration paid in such year by the employer to the employee for such service is less than the applicable dollar threshold (as defined in subsection (x)) for such year;

(C) cash remuneration paid by an employer in any calendar year to an employee for service not in the course of the employer's trade or business, if the cash remuneration paid in such year by the employer to the employee for such service is less than $100. As used in this subparagraph, the term "service not in the course of the employer's trade or business" does not include domestic service in a private home of the employer and does not include service described in subsection (g)(5);

(8)(A) remuneration paid in any medium other than cash for agricultural labor;

(B) cash remuneration paid by an employer in any calendar year to an employee for agricultural labor unless—

  (i) the cash remuneration paid in such year by the employer to the employee for such labor is $150 or more, or

  (ii) the employer's expenditures for agricultural labor in such year equal or exceed $2,500,

except that clause (ii) shall not apply in determining whether remuneration paid to an employee constitutes "wages" under this section if such employee (I) is employed as a hand harvest laborer and is paid on a piece rate basis in an operation which has been, and is customarily and generally recognized as having been, paid on a piece rate basis in the region of employment, (II) commutes daily from his permanent residence to the farm on which he is so employed, and (III) has been employed in agriculture less than 13 weeks during the preceding calendar year;

(9) Repealed.

(10) remuneration paid by an employer in any calendar year to an employee for service described in subsection (d)(3)(C) (relating to home workers), if the cash remuneration paid in such year by the employer to the employee for such service is less than $100;

(11) remuneration paid to or on behalf of an employee if (and to the extent that) at the time of the payment of such remuneration it is reasonable to believe that a corresponding deduction is allowable under section 217 (determined without regard to section 274(n));

(12)(A) tips paid in any medium other than cash;

(B) cash tips received by an employee in any calendar month in the course of his employment by an employer unless the amount of such cash tips is $20 or more;

(13) any payment or series of payments by an employer to an employee or any of his dependents which is paid—

  (A) upon or after the termination of an employee's employment relationship because of (i) death, or (ii) retirement for disability, and

  (B) under a plan established by the employer which makes provision for his employees generally or a class or classes of his employees (or for such employees or class or classes of employees and their dependents),

other than any such payment or series of payments which would have been paid if the employee's employment relationship had not been so terminated;

(14) any payment made by an employer to a survivor or the estate of a former employee after the calendar year in which such employee died;

(15) any payment made by an employer to an employee, if at the time such payment is made such employee is entitled to disability insurance benefits under section 223(a) of the Social Security Act and such entitlement commenced prior to the calendar year in which such payment is made, and if such employee did not perform any services for such employer during the period for which such payment is made;

(16) remuneration paid by an organization exempt from income tax under section 501(a) (other than an organization described in section 401(a)) or under section 521 in any calendar year to an employee for service rendered in the employ of such organization, if the remuneration paid in such year by the organization to the employee for such service is less than $100;

(17) any contribution, payment, or service provided by an employer which may be excluded from the gross income of an employee, his spouse, or his dependents, under the provisions of section 120 (relating to amounts received under qualified group legal services plans);

(18) any payment made, or benefit furnished, to or for the benefit of an employee if at the time of such payment or such furnishing it is reasonable to believe that the employee will be able to exclude such payment or benefit from income under section 127, 129, 134(b)(4), or 134(b)(5);

(19) the value of any meals or lodging furnished by or on behalf of the employer if at the time of such furnishing it is reasonable to believe that the employee will be able to exclude such items from income under section 119;

(20) any benefit provided to or on behalf of an employee if at the time such benefit is provided it is reasonable to believe that the employee will be able to exclude such benefit from income under section 74(c), 108(f)(4), 117, or 132;

(21) in the case of a member of an Indian tribe, any remuneration on which no tax is imposed by this chapter by reason of section 7873 (relating to income derived by Indians from exercise of fishing rights);

(22) remuneration on account of—

  (A) a transfer of a share of stock to any individual pursuant to an exercise of an incentive stock option (as defined in section 422(b)) or under an employee stock purchase plan (as defined in section 423(b)), or

  (B) any disposition by the individual of such stock; or

(23) any benefit or payment which is excludable from the gross income of the employee under section 139B(b).

Nothing in the regulations prescribed for purposes of chapter 24 (relating to income tax withholding) which provides an exclusion from "wages" as used in such chapter shall be construed to require a similar exclusion from "wages" in the regulations prescribed for purposes of this chapter.

Except as otherwise provided in regulations prescribed by the Secretary, any third party which makes a payment included in wages solely by reason of the parenthetical matter contained in subparagraph (A) of paragraph (2) shall be treated for purposes of this chapter and chapter 22 as the employer with respect to such wages.

(b) Employment.

For purposes of this chapter, the term "employment" means any service, of whatever nature, performed (A) by an employee for the person employing him, irrespective of the citizenship or residence of either, (i) within the United States, or (ii) on or in connection with an American vessel or American aircraft under a contract of service which is entered into within the United States or during the performance of which and while the employee is employed on the vessel or aircraft it touches at a port in the United States, if the employee is employed on and in connection with such vessel or aircraft when outside the United States, or (B) outside the United States by a citizen or resident of the United States as an employee for an American employer (as defined in subsection (h)), or (C) if it is service, regardless of where or by whom performed, which is designated as employment or recognized as equivalent to employment under an agreement entered into under section 233 of the Social Security Act; except that such term shall not include—

(1) service performed by foreign agricultural workers lawfully admitted to the United States from the Bahamas, Jamaica, and the other British West Indies, or from any other foreign country or possession thereof, on a temporary basis to perform agricultural labor;

(2) domestic service performed in a local college club, or local chapter of a college fraternity or sorority, by a student who is enrolled and is regularly attending classes at a school, college, or university;

(3)(A) service performed by a child under the age of 18 in the employ of his father or mother;

(B) service not in the course of the employer's trade or business, or domestic service in a private home of the employer, performed by an individual under the age of 21 in the employ of his father or mother, or performed by an individual in the employ of his spouse or son or daughter; except that the provisions of this subparagraph shall not be applicable to such domestic service performed by an individual in the employ of his son or daughter if—

(i) the employer is a surviving spouse or a divorced individual and has not remarried, or has a spouse living in the home who has a mental or physical condition which results in such spouse's being incapable of caring for a son, daughter, stepson, or stepdaughter (referred to in clause (ii)) for at least 4 continuous weeks in the calendar quarter in which the service is rendered, and

(ii) a son, daughter, stepson, or stepdaughter of such employer is living in the home, and

(iii) the son, daughter, stepson, or stepdaughter (referred to in clause (ii)) has not attained age 18 or has a mental or physical condition which requires the personal care and supervision of an adult for at least 4 continuous weeks in the calendar quarter in which the service is rendered;

(4) service performed by an individual on or in connection with a vessel not an American vessel, or on or in connection with an aircraft not an American aircraft, if (A) the individual is employed on and in connection with such vessel or aircraft, when outside the United States and (B)(i) such individual is not a citizen of the United States or (ii) the employer is not an American employer;

(5) service performed in the employ of the United States or any instrumentality of the United States, if such service—

(A) would be excluded from the term "employment" for purposes of this title if the provisions of paragraphs (5) and (6) of this subsection as in effect in January 1983 had remained in effect, and

(B) is performed by an individual who—

(i) has been continuously performing service described in subparagraph (A) since December 31, 1983, and for purposes of this clause—

(I) if an individual performing service described in subparagraph (A) returns to the performance of such service after being separated therefrom for a period of less than 366 consecutive days, regardless of whether the period began before, on, or after December 31, 1983, then such service shall be considered continuous,

(II) if an individual performing service described in subparagraph (A) returns to the performance of such service after being detailed or transferred to an international organization as described under section 3343 of subchapter III of chapter 33 of title 5, United States Code, or under section 3581 of chapter 35 of such title, then the service performed for that organization shall be considered service described in subparagraph (A),

(III) if an individual performing service described in subparagraph (A) is reemployed or reinstated after being separated from such service for the purpose of accepting employment with the American Institute in Taiwan as provided under section 3310 of chapter 48 of title 22, United States Code, then the service performed for that Institute shall be considered service described in subparagraph (A),

(IV) if an individual performing service described in subparagraph (A) returns to the performance of such service after performing service as a member of a uniformed service (including, for purposes of this clause, service in the National Guard and temporary service in the Coast Guard Reserve) and after exercising restoration or reemployment rights as provided under chapter 43 of title 38, United States Code, then the service so performed as a member of a uniformed service shall be considered service described in subparagraph (A), and

(V) if an individual performing service described in subparagraph (A) returns to the performance of such service after employment (by a tribal organization) to which section 105(e)(2) of the Indian Self-Determination Act applies, then the service performed for that tribal organization shall be considered service described in subparagraph (A); or

(ii) is receiving an annuity from the Civil Service Retirement and Disability Fund, or benefits (for service as an employee) under another retirement system established by a law of the United States for employees of the Federal Government (other than for members of the uniformed service);

except that this paragraph shall not apply with respect to any such service performed on or after any date on which such individual performs—

(C) service performed as the President or Vice President of the United States,

(D) service performed—

(i) in a position placed in the Executive Schedule under sections 5312 through 5317 of title 5, United States Code,

(ii) as a noncareer appointee in the Senior Executive Service or a noncareer member of the Senior Foreign Service, or

(iii) in a position to which the individual is appointed by the President (or his designee) or the Vice President under section 105(a)(1), 106(a)(1), or 107(a)(1) or (b)(1) of title 3, United States Code, if the maximum rate of basic pay for such position is at or above the rate for level V of the Executive Schedule,

(E) service performed as the Chief Justice of the United States, an Associate Justice of the Supreme Court, a judge of a United States court of appeals, a judge of a United States district court (including the district court of a territory), a judge of the United States Claims Court [United States Court of Federal Claims, see § 902(b), P.L. 102-572], a judge of the United States Court of International Trade, a judge of the United States Tax Court, a United States magistrate, or a referee in bankruptcy or United States bankruptcy judge,

(F) service performed as a Member, Delegate, or Resident Commissioner of or to the Congress,

(G) any other service in the legislative branch of the Federal Government if such service—

(i) is performed by an individual who was not subject to subchapter III of chapter 83 of title 5, United States Code, or to another retirement system established by a law of the United States for employees of the Federal Government (other than for members of the uniformed services), on December 31, 1983, or

(ii) is performed by an individual who has, at any time after December 31, 1983, received a lump-sum payment under section 8342(a) of title 5, United States Code, or under the corresponding provision of the law establishing the other retirement system described in clause (i), or

(iii) is performed by an individual after such individual has otherwise ceased to be subject to subchapter III of chapter 83 of title 5, United States Code (without having an application pending for coverage under such subchapter), while performing service in the legislative branch (determined without regard to the provisions of subparagraph (B) relating to continuity of employment), for any period of time after December 31, 1983,

and for purposes of this subparagraph (G) an individual is subject to such subchapter III or to any such other retirement system at any time only if (a) such individual's pay is subject to deductions, contributions, or similar payments (concurrent with the service being performed at that time) under section 8334(a) of such title 5 or the corresponding provision of the law establishing such other system, or (in a case to which section 8332(k)(1) of such title applies) such individual is making payments of amounts equivalent to such deductions, contributions, or similar payments while on leave without pay, or (b) such individual is receiving an annuity from the Civil Service Retirement and Disability Fund, or is receiving benefits (for service as an employee) under another retirement system established by a law of the United States for employees of the Federal Government (other than for members of the uniformed services), or

(H) service performed by an individual—

(i) on or after the effective date of an election by such individual, under section 301 of the Federal Employees' Retirement System Act of 1986, section 307 of the Central Intelligence Agency Retirement Act (50 U.S.C. 2157), or the Federal Employees' Retirement System Open Enrollment Act of 1997 to become subject to the Federal Employees' Retirement System provided in chapter 84 of title 5, United States Code, or

(ii) on or after the effective date of an election by such individual, under regulations issued under section 860 of the Foreign Service Act of 1980, to become subject to the Foreign Service Pension System provided in subchapter II of chapter 8 of title I of such Act;

(6) service performed in the employ of the United States or any instrumentality of the United States if such service is performed—

(A) in a penal institution of the United States by an inmate thereof;

(B) by any individual as an employee included under section 5351(2) of title 5, United States Code (relating to certain interns, student nurses, and other student employees of hospitals of the Federal Government), other than as a medical or dental intern or a medical or dental resident in training; or

(C) by any individual as an employee serving on a temporary basis in case of fire, storm, earthquake, flood, or other similar emergency;

(7) service performed in the employ of a State, or any political subdivision thereof, or any instrumentality of any one or more of the foregoing which is wholly owned thereby, except that this paragraph shall not apply in the case of—

(A) service which, under subsection (j), constitutes covered transportation service,

(B) service in the employ of the Government of Guam or the Government of American Samoa or any political subdivision thereof, or of any instrumentality of any one or more of the foregoing which is wholly owned thereby, performed by an officer or employee thereof (including a member of the legislature of any such Government or political subdivision), and, for purposes of this title with respect to the taxes imposed by this chapter—

(i) any person whose service as such an officer or employee is not covered by a retirement system established by a law of the United States shall not, with respect to such service, be regarded as an employee of the United States or any agency or instrumentality thereof, and

(ii) the remuneration for service described in clause (i) (including fees paid to a public official) shall be deemed to have been paid by the Government of Guam or the Government of American Samoa or by a political subdivision thereof or an instrumentality of any one or more of the foregoing which is wholly owned thereby, whichever is appropriate,

(C) service performed in the employ of the District of Columbia or any instrumentality which is wholly owned thereby, if such service is not covered by a retirement system established by a law of the United States (other than the Federal Employees Retirement System provided in chapter 84 of title 5, United States Code); except that the provisions of this subparagraph shall not be applicable to service performed—

(i) in a hospital or penal institution by a patient or inmate thereof;

(ii) by any individual as an employee included under section 5351(2) of title 5, United States Code (relating to certain interns, student nurses, and other student employees of hospitals of the District of Columbia Government), other than as a medical or dental intern or as a medical or dental resident in training;

(iii) by any individual as an employee serving on a temporary basis in case of fire, storm, snow, earthquake, flood or other similar emergency; or

(iv) by a member of a board, committee, or council of the District of Columbia, paid on a per diem, meeting, or other fee basis;

(D) service performed in the employ of the Government of Guam (or any instrumentality which is wholly owned by such Government) by an employee properly classified as a temporary or intermittent employee, if such service is not covered by a retirement system established by a law of Guam; except that (i) the provisions of this subparagraph shall not be applicable to services performed by an elected official or a member of the legislature or in a hospital or penal institution by a patient or inmate thereof, and (ii) for purposes of this subparagraph, clauses (i) and (ii) of subparagraph (B) shall apply;

(E) service included under an agreement entered into pursuant to section 218 of the Social Security Act, or

(F) service in the employ of a State (other than the District of Columbia, Guam, or American Samoa), of any political subdivision thereof, or of any instrumentality of any one or more of the foregoing which is wholly owned thereby, by an individual who is not a member of a retirement system of such State, political subdivision, or instrumentality, except that the provisions of this subparagraph shall not be applicable to service performed—

(i) by an individual who is employed to relieve such individual from unemployment;

(ii) in a hospital, home, or other institution by a patient or inmate thereof;

(iii) by any individual as an employee serving on a temporary basis in case of fire, storm, snow, earthquake, flood, or other similar emergency;

(iv) by an election official or election worker if the remuneration paid in a calendar year for such service is less than $1,000 with respect to service performed during any calendar year commencing on or after January 1, 1995, ending on or before December 31, 1999, and the adjusted amount determined under section 218(c)(8)(B) of the Social Security Act for any calendar year commencing on or after January 1, 2000, with respect to service performed during such calendar year; or

(v) by an employee in a position compensated solely on a fee basis which is treated pursuant to section 1402(c)(2)(E) as a trade or business for purposes of inclusion of such fees in net earnings from self-employment;

for purposes of this subparagraph, except as provided in regulations prescribed by the Secretary, the term "retirement system" has the meaning given such term by section 218(b)(4) of the Social Security Act;

(8)(A) service performed by a duly ordained, commissioned, or licensed minister of a church in the exercise of his ministry or by a member of a religious order in the exercise of duties required by such order, except that this subparagraph shall not apply to service performed by a member of such an order in the exercise of such duties, if an election of coverage under subsection (r) is in effect with respect to such order, or with respect to the autonomous subdivision thereof to which such member belongs;

(B) service performed in the employ of a church or qualified church-controlled organization if such church or organization has in effect an election under subsection (w), other than service in an unrelated trade or business (within the meaning of section 513(a));

(9) service performed by an individual as an employee or employee representative as defined in section 3231;

(10) service performed in the employ of—

(A) a school, college, or university, or

(B) an organization described in section 509(a)(3) if the organization is organized, and at all times thereafter is operated, exclusively for the benefit of, to perform the functions of, or to carry out the purposes of a school, college, or university and is operated, supervised, or controlled by or in connection with such school, college, or university, unless it is a school, college, or university of a State or a political subdivision thereof and the services performed in its employ by a student referred to in section 218(c)(5) of the Social Security Act are covered under the agreement between the Commissioner of Social Security and such State entered into pursuant to section 218 of such Act;

if such service is performed by a student who is enrolled and regularly attending classes at such school, college, or university;

(11) service performed in the employ of a foreign government (including service as a consular or other officer or employee or a nondiplomatic representative);

(12) service performed in the employ of an instrumentality wholly owned by a foreign government—

(A) if the service is of a character similar to that performed in foreign countries by employees of the United States Government or of an instrumentality thereof; and

(B) if the Secretary of State shall certify to the Secretary of the Treasury that the foreign government, with respect to whose instrumentality and employees thereof exemption is claimed, grants an equivalent exemption with respect to similar service performed in the foreign country by employees of the United States Government and of instrumentalities thereof;

(13) service performed as a student nurse in the employ of a hospital or a nurses' training school by an individual who is enrolled and is regularly attending classes in a nurses' training school chartered or approved pursuant to State law;

(14)(A) service performed by an individual under the age of 18 in the delivery or distribution of newspapers or shopping news, not including delivery or distribution to any point for subsequent delivery or distribution;

(B) service performed by an individual in, and at the time of, the sale of newspapers or magazines to ultimate consumers, under an arrangement under which the newspapers or magazines are to be sold by him at a fixed price, his compensation being based on the retention of the excess of such price over the amount at which the newspapers or magazines are charged to him, whether or not he is guaranteed a minimum amount of compensation for such service, or is entitled to be credited with the unsold newspapers or magazines turned back;

(15) service performed in the employ of an international organization, except service which constitutes "employment" under subsection (y);

(16) service performed by an individual under an arrangement with the owner or tenant of land pursuant to which—

(A) such individual undertakes to produce agricultural or horticultural commodities (including livestock, bees, poultry, and fur-bearing animals and wildlife) on such land,

Code Sec. 3121(e)(2) **Employment taxes**

An individual who is a citizen of the Commonwealth of Puerto Rico (but not otherwise a citizen of the United States) shall be considered, for purposes of this section, as a citizen of the United States.

(f) American vessel and aircraft.

For purposes of this chapter, the term "American vessel" means any vessel documented or numbered under the laws of the United States; and includes any vessel which is neither documented or numbered under the laws of the United States nor documented under the laws of any foreign country, if its crew is employed solely by one or more citizens or residents of the United States or corporations organized under the laws of the United States or of any State; and the term "American aircraft" means an aircraft registered under the laws of the United States.

(g) Agricultural labor.

For purposes of this chapter, the term "agricultural labor" includes all service performed—

(1) on a farm, in the employ of any person, in connection with cultivating the soil, or in connection with raising or harvesting any agricultural or horticultural commodity, including the raising, shearing, feeding, caring for, training, and management of livestock, bees, poultry, and fur-bearing animals and wildlife;

(2) in the employ of the owner or tenant or other operator of a farm, in connection with the operation, management, conservation, improvement, or maintenance of such farm and its tools and equipment, or in salvaging timber or clearing land of brush and other debris left by a hurricane, if the major part of such service is performed on a farm;

(3) in connection with the production or harvesting of any commodity defined as an agricultural commodity in section 15(g) of the Agricultural Marketing Act, as amended (12 U.S.C. 1141j), or in connection with the ginning of cotton, or in connection with the operation or maintenance of ditches, canals, reservoirs, or waterways, not owned or operated for profit, used exclusively for supplying and storing water for farming purposes;

(4) (A) in the employ of the operator of a farm in handling, planting, drying, packing, packaging, processing, freezing, grading, storing, or delivering to storage or to market or to a carrier for transportation to market, in its unmanufactured state, any agricultural or horticultural commodity; but only if such operator produced more than one-half of the commodity with respect to which such service is performed;

(B) in the employ of a group of operators of farms (other than a cooperative organization) in the performance of service described in subparagraph (A), but only if such operators produced all of the commodity with respect to which such service is performed. For purposes of this subparagraph, any unincorporated group of operators shall be deemed a cooperative organization if the number of operators comprising such group is more than 20 at any time during the calendar year in which such service is performed;

(C) the provisions of subparagraphs (A) and (B) shall not be deemed to be applicable with respect to service performed in connection with commercial canning or commercial freezing or in connection with any agricultural or horticultural commodity after its delivery to a terminal market for distribution for consumption; or

(5) on a farm operated for profit if such service is not in the course of the employer's trade or business .

As used in this subsection, the term "farm" includes stock, dairy, poultry, fruit, fur-bearing animal, and truck farms, plantations, ranches, nurseries, ranges, greenhouses or other similar structures used primarily for the raising of agricultural or horticultural commodities, and orchards.

(h) American employer.

For purposes of this chapter, the term "American employer" means an employer which is—

(1) the United States or any instrumentality thereof,

(2) an individual who is a resident of the United States,

(3) a partnership, if two-thirds or more of the partners are residents of the United States,

(4) a trust, if all of the trustees are residents of the United States, or

(5) a corporation organized under the laws of the United States or of any State.

(i) Computation of wages in certain cases.

(1) Domestic service. For purposes of this chapter, in the case of domestic service described in subsection (a)(7)(B), any payment of cash remuneration for such service which is more or less than a whole-dollar amount shall, under such conditions and to such extent as may be prescribed by regulations made under this chapter, be computed to the nearest dollar. For the purpose of the computation to the nearest dollar, the payment of a fractional part of a dollar shall be disregarded unless it amounts to one-half dollar or more, in which case it shall be increased to $1. The amount of any payment of cash remuneration so computed to the nearest dollar shall, in lieu of the amount actually paid, be deemed to constitute the amount of cash remuneration for purposes of subsection (a)(7)(B).

(2) Service in the uniformed services. For purposes of this chapter, in the case of an individual performing service, as a member of a uniformed service, to which the provisions of subsection (m)(1) are applicable, the term "wages" shall, subject to the provisions of subsection (a)(1) of this section, include as such individual's remuneration for such service only (A) his basic pay as described in chapter 3 and section 1009 of title 37, United States Code, in the case of an individual performing service to which subparagraph (A) of such subsection (m)(1) applies, or (B) his compensation for such service as determined under section 206(a) of title 37, United States Code, in the case of an individual performing service to which subparagraph (B) of such subsection (m)(1) applies.

(3) Peace Corps volunteer service. For purposes of this chapter, in the case of an individual performing service, as a volunteer or volunteer leader within the meaning of the Peace Corps Act, to which the provisions of section 3121(p) are applicable, the term "wages" shall, subject to the provisions of subsection (a)(1) of this section, include as such individual's remuneration for such service only amounts paid pursuant to section 5(c) or 6(1) of the Peace Corps Act.

(4) Service performed by certain members of religious orders. For purposes of this chapter, in any case where an individual is a member of a religious order (as defined in subsection (r)(2)) performing service in the exercise of duties required by such order, and an election of coverage under subsection (r) is in effect with respect to such order or with respect to the autonomous subdivision thereof to which such member belongs, the term "wages" shall, subject to the provisions of subsection (a)(1), include as such individual's remuneration for such service the fair market value of any board, lodging, clothing, and other perquisites furnished to such member by such order or subdivision thereof or by any other person or organization pursuant to an agreement with such order or subdivision, except that the amount included as such individual's remunera-

3,076

| Employment taxes | Code Sec. 3121(e)(2) |

(B) the agricultural or horticultural commodities produced by such individual, or the proceeds therefrom, are to be divided between such individual and such owner or tenant, and

(C) the amount of such individual's share depends on the amount of the agricultural or horticultural commodities produced;

(17) service in the employ of any organization which is performed (A) in any year during any part of which such organization is registered, or there is in effect a final order of the Subversive Activities Control Board requiring such organization to register, under the Internal Security Act of 1950, as amended, as a Communist-action organization, a Communist-front organization, or a Communist-infiltrated organization, and (B) after June 30, 1956;

(18) service performed in Guam by a resident of the Republic of the Philippines while in Guam on a temporary basis as a nonimmigrant alien admitted to Guam pursuant to section 101(a)(15)(H)(ii) of the Immigration and Nationality Act (8 U.S.C. 1101(a)(15)(H)(ii));

(19) service which is performed by a nonresident alien individual for the period he is temporarily present in the United States as a nonimmigrant under subparagraph (F), (J), (M), or (Q) of section 101(a)(15) of the Immigration and Nationality Act, as amended, and which is performed to carry out the purpose specified in subparagraph (F), (J), (M), or (Q), as the case may be;

(20) service (other than service described in paragraph (3)(A)) performed by an individual on a boat engaged in catching fish or other forms of aquatic animal life under an arrangement with the owner or operator of such boat pursuant to which—

(A) such individual does not receive any cash remuneration other than as provided in subparagraph (B) and other than cash remuneration—

(i) which does not exceed $100 per trip;

(ii) which is contingent on a minimum catch; and

(iii) which is paid solely for additional dues (such as mate, engineer, or cook) for which additional cash remuneration is traditional in the industry,

(B) such individual receives a share of the boat's (or the boats' in the case of a fishing operation involving more than one boat) catch of fish or other forms of aquatic animal life or a share of the proceeds from the sale of such catch, and

(C) the amount of such individual's share depends on the amount of the boat's (or the boats' in the case of a fishing operation involving more than one boat) catch of fish or other forms of aquatic animal life,

but only if the operating crew of such boat (or each boat from which the individual receives a share in the case of a fishing operation involving more than one boat) is normally made up of fewer than 10 individuals; or

(21) domestic service in a private home of the employer which—

(A) is performed in any year by an individual under the age of 18 during any portion of such year; and

(B) is not the principal occupation of such employee.

For purposes of paragraph (20), the operating crew of a boat shall be treated as normally made up of fewer than 10 individuals if the average size of the operating crew on trips made during the preceding 4 calendar quarters consisted of fewer than 10 individuals.

(c) **Included and excluded service.**

For purposes of this chapter, if the services performed during one-half or more of any pay period by an employee

for the person employing him constitute employment, all the services of such employee for such period shall be deemed to be employment; but if the services performed during more than one-half of any such pay period by an employee for the person employing him do not constitute employment, then none of the services of such employee for such period shall be deemed to be employment. As used in this subsection, the term "pay period" means a period (of not more than 31 consecutive days) for which a payment of remuneration is ordinarily made to the employee by the person employing him. This subsection shall not be applicable with respect to services performed in a pay period by an employee for the person employing him, where any of such service is excepted by subsection (b)(9).

(d) **Employee.**

For purposes of this chapter, the term "employee" means—

(1) any officer of a corporation; or

(2) any individual who, under the usual common law rules applicable in determining the employer-employee relationship, has the status of an employee; or

(3) any individual (other than an individual who is an employee under paragraph (1) or (2)) who performs services for remuneration for any person—

(A) as an agent-driver or commission-driver engaged in distributing meat products, vegetable products, fruit products, bakery products, beverages (other than milk), or laundry or dry-cleaning services, for his principal;

(B) as a full-time life insurance salesman;

(C) as a home worker performing work, according to specifications furnished by the person for whom the services are performed, on materials or goods furnished by such person which are required to be returned to such person or a person designated by him; or

(D) as a traveling or city salesman, other than as an agent-driver or commission-driver, engaged upon a full-time basis in the solicitation on behalf of, and the transmission to, his principal (except for side-line sales activities on behalf of some other person) of orders from wholesalers, retailers, contractors, or operators of hotels, restaurants, or other similar establishments for merchandise for resale or supplies for use in their business operations;

if the contract of service contemplates that substantially all of such services are to be performed personally by such individual; except that an individual shall not be included in the term "employee" under the provisions of this paragraph if such individual has a substantial investment in facilities used in connection with the performance of such services (other than in facilities for transportation), or if the services are in the nature of a single transaction not part of a continuing relationship with the person for whom the services are performed; or

(4) any individual who performs services that are included under an agreement entered into pursuant to section 218 of the Social Security Act.

(e) **State, United States, and citizen.**

For purposes of this chapter—

(1) **State.** The term "State" includes the District of Columbia, the Commonwealth of Puerto Rico, the Virgin Islands, Guam, and American Samoa.

(2) **United States.** The term "United States" when used in a geographical sense includes the Commonwealth of Puerto Rico, the Virgin Islands, Guam, and American Samoa.

3,075

tion under this paragraph shall not be less than $100 a month.

(5) Service performed by certain retired justices and judges. For purposes of this chapter, in the case of an individual performing service under the provisions of section 294 of title 28, United States Code (relating to assignment of retired justices and judges to active duty), the term "wages" shall not include any payment under section 371(b) of such title 28 which is received during the period of such service.

(j) Covered transportation service.

For purposes of this chapter—

(1) Existing transportation systems—General rule. Except as provided in paragraph (2), all service performed in the employ of a State or political subdivision in connection with its operation of a public transportation system shall constitute covered transportation service if any part of the transportation system was acquired from private ownership after 1936 and prior to 1951.

(2) Existing transportation systems—Cases in which no transportation employees, or only certain employees, are covered. Service performed in the employ of a State or political subdivision in connection with the operation of its public transportation system shall not constitute covered transportation service if—

(A) any part of the transportation system was acquired from private ownership after 1936 and prior to 1951, and substantially all service in connection with the operation of the transportation system was, on December 31, 1950, covered under a general retirement system providing benefits which, by reason of a provision of the State constitution dealing specifically with retirement systems of the State or political subdivisions thereof, cannot be diminished or impaired; or

(B) no part of the transportation system operated by the State or political subdivision on December 31, 1950, was acquired from private ownership after 1936 and prior to 1951;

except that if such State or political subdivision makes an acquisition after 1950 from private ownership of any part of its transportation system, then, in the case of any employee who—

(C) became an employee of such State or political subdivision in connection with and at the time of its acquisition after 1950 of such part, and

(D) prior to such acquisition rendered service in employment (including as employment service covered by an agreement under section 218 of the Social Security Act) in connection with the operation of such part of the transportation system acquired by the State or political subdivision,

the service of such employee in connection with the operation of the transportation system shall constitute covered transportation service, commencing with the first day of the third calendar quarter following the calendar quarter in which the acquisition of such part took place, unless on such first day such service of such employee is covered by a general retirement system which does not, with respect to such employee, contain special provisions applicable only to employees described in subparagraph (C).

(3) Transportation systems acquired after 1950. All service performed in the employ of a State or political subdivision thereof in connection with its operation of a public transportation system shall constitute covered transportation service if the transportation system was not operated by the State or political subdivision prior to 1951 and, at the time of its first acquisition (after 1950) from private ownership of any part of its transportation system, the State or political subdivision did not have a general retirement system covering substantially all service performed in connection with the operation of the transportation system.

(4) Definitions. For purposes of this subsection—

(A) The term "general retirement system" means any pension, annuity, retirement, or similar fund or system established by a State or by a political subdivision thereof for employees of the State, political subdivision, or both; but such term shall not include such a fund or system which covers only service performed in positions connected with the operation of its public transportation system.

(B) A transportation system or a part thereof shall be considered to have been acquired by a State or political subdivision from private ownership if prior to the acquisition service performed by employees in connection with the operation of the system or part thereof acquired constituted employment under this chapter or subchapter A of chapter 9 of the Internal Revenue Code of 1939 or was covered by an agreement made pursuant to section 218 of the Social Security Act and some of such employees became employees of the State or political subdivision in connection with and at the time of such acquisition.

(C) The term "political subdivision" includes an instrumentality of—

(i) a State,

(ii) one or more political subdivisions of a State, or

(iii) a State and one or more of its political subdivisions.

(k) Repealed.

(l) Agreements entered into by American employers with respect to foreign affiliates.

(1) Agreement with respect to certain employees of foreign affiliate. The Secretary shall, at the American employer's request, enter into an agreement (in such manner and form as may be prescribed by the Secretary) with any American employer (as defined in subsection (h)) who desires to have the insurance system established by title II of the Social Security Act extended to service performed outside the United States in the employ of any 1 or more of such employer's foreign affiliates (as defined in paragraph (6)) by all employees who are citizens or residents of the United States, except that the agreement shall not apply to any service performed by, or remuneration paid to, an employee if such service or remuneration would be excluded from the term "employment" or "wages", as defined in this section, had the service been performed in the United States. Such agreement may be amended at any time so as to be made applicable, in the same manner and under the same conditions, with respect to any other foreign affiliate of such American employer. Such agreement shall be applicable with respect to citizens or residents of the United States who, on or after the effective date of the agreement, are employees of and perform services outside the United States for any foreign affiliate specified in the agreement. Such agreement shall provide—

(A) that the American employer shall pay to the Secretary, at such time or times as the Secretary may by regulations prescribe, amounts equivalent to the sum of the taxes which would be imposed by sections 3101 and 3111 (including amounts equivalent to the interest, additions to the taxes, additional amounts, and penalties which would be applicable) with respect to the remuneration which would be wages if the services covered by the agreement constituted employment as defined in this section; and

(B) that the American employer will comply with such regulations relating to payments and reports as the Secretary may prescribe to carry out the purposes of this subsection.

(2) Effective period of agreement. An agreement entered into pursuant to paragraph (1) shall be in effect for the period beginning with the first day of the calendar quarter in which such agreement is entered into or the first day of the succeeding calendar quarter, as may be specified in the agreement; except that in case such agreement is amended to include the services performed for any other affiliate and such amendment is executed after the first month following the first calendar quarter for which the agreement is in effect, the agreement shall be in effect with respect to service performed for such other affiliate only after the calendar quarter in which such amendment is executed. Notwithstanding any other provision of this subsection, the period for which any such agreement is effective with respect to any foreign entity shall terminate at the end of any calendar quarter in which the foreign entity, at any time in such quarter, ceases to be a foreign affiliate as defined in paragraph (6).

(3) No termination of agreement. No agreement under this subsection may be terminated, either in its entirety or with respect to any foreign affiliate, on or after June 15, 1989.

(4) Deposits in trust funds. For purposes of section 201 of the Social Security Act, relating to appropriations to the Federal Old-Age and Survivors Insurance Trust Fund and the Federal Disability Insurance Trust Fund, such remuneration—

(A) paid for services covered by an agreement entered into pursuant to paragraph (1) as would be wages if the services constituted employment, and

(B) as is reported to the Secretary pursuant to the provisions of such agreement or of the regulations issued under this subsection,

shall be considered wages subject to the taxes imposed by this chapter.

(5) Overpayments and underpayments.

(A) If more or less than the correct amount due under an agreement entered into pursuant to this subsection is paid with respect to any payment of remuneration, proper adjustments with respect to the amounts due under such agreement shall be made, without interest, in such manner and at such times as may be required by regulations prescribed by the Secretary.

(B) If an overpayment cannot be adjusted under subparagraph (A), the amount thereof shall be paid by the Secretary, through the Fiscal Service of the Treasury Department, but only if a claim for such overpayment is filed with the Secretary within two years from the time such overpayment was made.

(6) Foreign affiliate defined. For purposes of this subsection and section 210(a) of the Social Security Act—

(A) In general. A foreign affiliate of an American employer is any foreign entity in which such American employer has not less than a 10-percent interest.

(B) Determination of 10-percent interest. For purposes of subparagraph (A), an American employer has a 10-percent interest in any entity if such employer has such an interest directly (or through one or more entities)—

(i) in the case of a corporation, in the voting stock thereof, and

(ii) in the case of any other entity, in the profits thereof.

(7) American employer as separate entity. Each American employer which enters into an agreement pursuant to paragraph (1) of this subsection shall, for purposes of this subsection and section 6413(c)(2)(C), relating to special refunds in the case of employees of certain foreign entities, be considered an employer in its capacity as a party to such agreement separate and distinct from its identity as a person employing individuals on its own account.

(8) Regulations. Regulations of the Secretary to carry out the purposes of this subsection shall be designed to make the requirements imposed on American employers with respect to services covered by an agreement entered into pursuant to this subsection the same, so far as practicable, as those imposed upon employers pursuant to this title with respect to the taxes imposed by this chapter.

(m) Service in the uniformed services.

For purposes of this chapter—

(1) Inclusion of service. The term "employment" shall, notwithstanding the provisions of subsection (b) of this section, include—

(A) service performed by an individual as a member of a uniformed service on active duty, but such term shall not include any such service which is performed while on leave without pay, and

(B) service performed by an individual as a member of a uniformed service on inactive duty training.

(2) Active duty. The term "active duty" means "active duty" as described in paragraph (21) of section 101 of title 38, United States Code, except that it shall also include "active duty for training" as described in paragraph (22) of such section.

(3) Inactive duty training. The term "inactive duty training" means "inactive duty training" as described in paragraph (23) of such section 101.

(n) Member of a uniformed service.

For purposes of this chapter, the term "member of a uniformed service" means any person appointed, enlisted, or inducted in a component of the Army, Navy, Air Force, Marine Corps, or Coast Guard (including a reserve component as defined in section 101(27) of title 38, United States Code), or in one of those services without specification of component, or as a commissioned officer of the Coast and Geodetic Survey, the National Oceanic and Atmospheric Administration Corps, or the Regular or Reserve Corps of the Public Health Service, and any person serving in the Army or Air Force under call or conscription. The term includes—

(1) a retired member of any of those services;

(2) a member of the Fleet Reserve or Fleet Marine Corps Reserve;

(3) a cadet at the United States Military Academy, a midshipman at the United States Naval Academy, and a cadet at the United States Coast Guard Academy or United States Air Force Academy;

(4) a member of the Reserve Officers' Training Corps, the Naval Reserve Officers' Training Corps, or the Air Force Reserve Officers' Training Corps, when ordered to annual training duty for fourteen days or more, and while performing authorized travel to and from that duty; and

(5) any person while en route to or from, or at, a place for final acceptance or for entry upon active duty in the military, naval, or air service—

(A) who has been provisionally accepted for such duty; or

(B) who, under the Military Selective Service Act, has been selected for active military, naval, or air service;

and has been ordered or directed to proceed to such place. The term does not include a temporary member of the Coast Guard Reserve.

(o) Crew leader.

For purposes of this chapter, the term "crew leader" means an individual who furnishes individuals to perform agricultural labor for another person, if such individual pays (either on his own behalf or on behalf of such person) the individuals so furnished by him for the agricultural labor performed by them and if such individual has not entered into a written agreement with such person whereby such individual has been designated as an employee of such person; and such individuals furnished by the crew leader to perform agricultural labor for another person shall be deemed to be the employees of such crew leader. For purposes of this chapter and chapter 2, a crew leader shall, with respect to service performed in furnishing individuals to perform agricultural labor for another person and service performed as a member of the crew, be deemed not to be an employee of such other person.

(p) Peace Corps volunteer service.

For purposes of this chapter, the term "employment" shall, notwithstanding the provisions of subsection (b) of this section, include service performed by an individual as a volunteer or volunteer leader within the meaning of the Peace Corps Act.

(q) Tips included for both employee and employer taxes.

For purposes of this chapter, tips received by an employee in the course of his employment shall be considered remuneration for such employment (and deemed to have been paid by the employer for purposes of subsections (a) and (b) of section 3111). Such remuneration shall be deemed to be paid at the time a written statement including such tips is furnished to the employer pursuant to section 6053(a) or (if no statement including such tips is so furnished) at the time received; except that, in determining the employer's liability in connection with the taxes imposed by section 3111 with respect to such tips in any case where no statement including such tips was so furnished (or to the extent that the statement so furnished was inaccurate or incomplete), such remuneration shall be deemed for purposes of subtitle F to be paid on the date on which notice and demand for such taxes is made to the employer by the Secretary.

(r) Election of coverage by religious orders.

(1) Certificate of election by order. A religious order whose members are required to take a vow of poverty, or any autonomous subdivision of such order, may file a certificate (in such form and manner, and with such official, as may be prescribed by regulations under this chapter) electing to have the insurance system established by title II of the Social Security Act extended to services performed by its members in the exercise of duties required by such order or such subdivision thereof. Such certificate of election shall provide that—

(A) such election of coverage by such order or subdivision shall be irrevocable;

(B) such election shall apply to all current and future members of such order, or in the case of a subdivision thereof to all current and future members of such order who belong to such subdivision;

(C) all services performed by a member of such an order or subdivision in the exercise of duties required by such order or subdivision shall be deemed to have been performed by such member as an employee of such order or subdivision; and

(D) the wages of each member, upon which such order or subdivision shall pay the taxes imposed by sections 3101 and 3111, will be determined as provided in subsection (i)(4).

(2) Definition of member. For purposes of this subsection, a member of a religious order means any individual who is subject to a vow of poverty as a member of such order and who performs tasks usually required (and to the extent usually required) of an active member of such order and who is not considered retired because of old age or total disability.

(3) Effective date for election.

(A) A certificate of election of coverage shall be in effect, for purposes of subsection (b)(8) and for purposes of section 210(a)(8) of the Social Security Act, for the period beginning with whichever of the following may be designated by the order or subdivision thereof:

(i) the first day of the calendar quarter in which the certificate is filed,

(ii) the first day of the calendar quarter succeeding such quarter, or

(iii) the first day of any calendar quarter preceding the calendar quarter in which the certificate is filed, except that such date may not be earlier than the first day of the twentieth calendar quarter preceding the quarter in which such certificate is filed.

Whenever a date is designated under clause (iii), the election shall apply to services performed before the quarter in which the certificate is filed only if the member performing such services was a member at the time such services were performed and is living on the first day of the quarter in which such certificate is filed.

(B) If a certificate of election filed pursuant to this subsection is effective for one or more calendar quarters prior to the quarter in which such certificate is filed, then—

(i) for purposes of computing interest and for purposes of section 6651 (relating to addition to tax for failure to file tax return), the due date for the return and payment of the tax for such prior calendar quarters resulting from the filing of such certificate shall be the last day of the calendar month following the calendar quarter in which the certificate is filed; and

(ii) the statutory period for the assessment of such tax shall not expire before the expiration of 3 years from such due date.

(s) Concurrent employment by two or more employers.

For purposes of sections 3102, 3111, and 3121(a)(1), if two or more related corporations concurrently employ the same individual and compensate such individual through a common paymaster which is one of such corporations, each such corporation shall be considered to have paid as remuneration to such individual only the amounts actually disbursed by it to such individual and shall not be considered to have paid as remuneration to such individual amounts actually disbursed to such individual by another of such corporations.

(t) Repealed.

(u) Application of hospital insurance tax to federal, state, and local employment.

(1) Federal employment. For purposes of the taxes imposed by sections 3101(b) and 3111(b), subsection (b) shall be applied without regard to paragraph (5) thereof.

(2) State and local employment. For purposes of the taxes imposed by sections 3101(b) and 3111(b)—

(A) In general. Except as provided in subparagraphs (B) and (C), subsection (b) shall be applied without regard to paragraph (7) thereof.
(B) Exception for certain services. Service shall not be treated as employment by reason of subparagraph (A) if—
  (i) the service is included under an agreement under section 218 of the Social Security Act, or
  (ii) the service is performed—
    (I) by an individual who is employed by a State or political subdivision thereof to relieve him from unemployment,
    (II) in a hospital, home, or other institution by a patient or inmate thereof as an employee of a State or political subdivision thereof or of the District of Columbia,
    (III) by an individual, as an employee of a State or political subdivision thereof or of the District of Columbia, serving on a temporary basis in case of fire, storm, snow, earthquake, flood or other similar emergency,
    (IV) by any individual as an employee included under section 5351(2) of title 5, United States Code (relating to certain interns, student nurses, and other student employees of hospitals of the District of Columbia Government), other than as a medical or dental intern or a medical or dental resident in training,
    (V) by an election official or election worker if the remuneration paid in a calendar year for such service is less than $1,000 with respect to service performed during any calendar year commencing on or after January 1, 1995, ending on or before December 31, 1999, and the adjusted amount determined under section 218(c)(8)(B) of the Social Security Act for any calendar year commencing on or after January 1, 2000, with respect to service performed during such calendar year, or
    (VI) by an individual in a position described in section 1402(c)(2)(E).
  As used in this subparagraph, the terms "State" and "political subdivision" have the meanings given those terms in section 218(b) of the Social Security Act.
(C) Exception for current employment which continues. Service performed for an employer shall not be treated as employment by reason of subparagraph (A) if—
  (i) such service would be excluded from the term "employment" for purposes of this chapter if subparagraph (A) did not apply;
  (ii) such service is performed by an individual—
    (I) who was performing substantial and regular service for remuneration for that employer before April 1, 1986,
    (II) who is a bona fide employee of that employer on March 31, 1986, and
    (III) whose employment relationship with that employer was not entered into for purposes of meeting the requirements of this subparagraph; and
  (iii) the employment relationship with that employer has not been terminated after March 31, 1986.
(D) Treatment of agencies and instrumentalities. For purposes of subparagraph (C), under regulations—
  (i) All agencies and instrumentalities of a State (as defined in section 218(b) of the Social Security Act) or of the District of Columbia shall be treated as a single employer.
  (ii) All agencies and instrumentalities of a political subdivision of a State (as so defined) shall be treated as a single employer and shall not be treated as described in clause (i).
(3) Medicare qualified government employment. For purposes of this chapter, the term "medicare qualified government employment" means service which—
  (A) is employment (as defined in subsection (b)) with the application of paragraphs (1) and (2), but
  (B) would not be employment (as so defined) without the application of such paragraphs.

(v) Treatment of certain deferred compensation and salary reduction arrangements.
(1) Certain employer contributions treated as wages. Nothing in any paragraph of subsection (a) (other than paragraph (1)) shall exclude from the term "wages" —
  (A) any employer contribution under a qualified cash or deferred arrangement (as defined in section 401(k)) to the extent not included in gross income by reason of section 402(e)(3) or consisting of designated Roth contributions (as defined in section 402A(c)), or
  (B) any amount treated as an employer contribution under section 414(h)(2) where the pickup referred to in such section is pursuant to a salary reduction agreement (whether evidenced by a written instrument or otherwise).

(2) Treatment of certain nonqualified deferred compensation plans.
  (A) In general. Any amount deferred under a nonqualified deferred compensation plan shall be taken into account for purposes of this chapter as of the later of—
    (i) when the services are performed, or
    (ii) when there is no substantial risk of forfeiture of the rights to such amount.
  The preceding sentence shall not apply to any excess parachute payment (as defined in section 280G(b)) or to any specified stock compensation (as defined in section 4985) on which tax is imposed by section 4985.
  (B) Taxed only once. Any amount taken into account as wages by reason of subparagraph (A) (and the income attributable thereto) shall not thereafter be treated as wages for purposes of this chapter.
  (C) Nonqualified deferred compensation plan. For purposes of this paragraph, the term "nonqualified deferred compensation plan" means any plan or other arrangement for deferral of compensation other than a plan described in subsection (a)(5).

(3) Exempt governmental deferred compensation plan. For purposes of subsection (a)(5), the term "exempt governmental deferred compensation plan" means any plan providing for deferral of compensation established and maintained for its employees by the United States, by a State or political subdivision thereof, or by an agency or instrumentality of any of the foregoing. Such term shall not include—
  (A) any plan to which section 83, 402(b), 403(c), 457(a), or 457(f)(1) applies,
  (B) any annuity contract described in section 403(b), and
  (C) the Thrift Savings Fund (within the meaning of subchapter III of chapter 84 of title 5, United States Code).

(w) Exemption of churches and qualified church-controlled organizations.

(1) General rule. Any church or qualified church-controlled organization (as defined in paragraph (3)) may make an election within the time period described in paragraph (2), in accordance with such procedures as the Secretary determines to be appropriate, that services performed in the employ of such church or organization shall be excluded from employment for purposes of title II of the Social Security Act and this chapter. An election may be made under this subsection only if the church or qualified church-controlled organization states that such church or organization is opposed for religious reasons to the payment of the tax imposed under section 3111.

(2) Timing and duration of election. An election under this subsection must be made prior to the first date, more than 90 days after July 18, 1984, on which a quarterly employment tax return for the tax imposed under section 3111 is due, or would be due but for the election, from such church or organization. An election under this subsection shall apply to current and future employees, and shall apply to service performed after December 31, 1983. The election may be revoked by the church or organization under regulations prescribed by the Secretary. The election shall be revoked by the Secretary if such church or organization fails to furnish the information required under section 6051 to the Secretary for a period of 2 years or more with respect to remuneration paid for such services by such church or organization, and, upon request by the Secretary, fails to furnish all such previously unfurnished information for the period covered by the election. Any revocation under the preceding sentence shall apply retroactively to the beginning of the 2-year period for which the information was not furnished.

(3) Definitions.

(A) For purposes of this subsection, the term "church" means a church, a convention or association of churches, or an elementary or secondary school which is controlled, operated, or principally supported by a church or by a convention or association of churches.

(B) For purposes of this subsection, the term "qualified church-controlled organization" means any church-controlled tax-exempt organization described in section 501(c)(3), other than an organization which—

(i) offers goods, services, or facilities for sale, other than on an incidental basis, to the general public, other than goods, services, or facilities which are sold at a nominal charge which is substantially less than the cost of providing such goods, services, or facilities; and

(ii) normally receives more than 25 percent of its support from either (I) governmental sources, or (II) receipts from admissions, sales of merchandise, performance of services, or furnishing of facilities, in activities which are not unrelated trades or businesses, or both.

(x) Applicable dollar threshold.

For purposes of subsection (a)(7)(B), the term "applicable dollar threshold" means $1,000. In the case of calendar years after 1995, the Commissioner of Social Security shall adjust such $1,000 amount at the same time and in the same manner as under section 215(a)(1)(B)(ii) of the Social Security Act with respect to the amounts referred to in section 215(a)(1)(B)(i) of such Act, except that, for purposes of this paragraph, 1993 shall be substituted for the calendar year referred to in section 215(a)(1)(B)(ii)(II) of such Act. If any amount as adjusted under the preceding sentence is not a multiple of $100, such amount shall be rounded to the next lowest multiple of $100.

(y) Service in the employ of international organizations by certain transferred Federal employees.

(1) In general. For purposes of this chapter, service performed in the employ of an international organization by an individual pursuant to a transfer of such individual to such international organization pursuant to section 3582 of title 5, United States Code, shall constitute "employment" if—

(A) immediately before such transfer, such individual performed service with a Federal agency which constituted "employment" under subsection (b) for purposes of the taxes imposed by sections 3101(a) and 3111(a), and

(B) such individual would be entitled, upon separation from such international organization and proper application, to reemployment with such Federal agency under such section 3582.

(2) Definitions. For purposes of this subsection—

(A) Federal agency. The term "Federal agency" means an agency, as defined in section 3581(1) of title 5, United States Code.

(B) International organization. The term "international organization" has the meaning provided such term by section 3581(3) of title 5, United States Code.

(z) Treatment of Certain Foreign Persons as American Employers.

(1) In general. If any employee of a foreign person is performing services in connection with a contract between the United States Government (or any instrumentality thereof) and any member of any domestically controlled group of entities which includes such foreign person, such foreign person shall be treated for purposes of this chapter as an American employer with respect to such services performed by such employee.

(2) Domestically controlled group of entities. For purposes of this subsection—

(A) In general. The term "domestically controlled group of entities" means a controlled group of entities the common parent of which is a domestic corporation.

(B) Controlled group of entities. The term "controlled group of entities" means a controlled group of corporations as defined in section 1563(a)(1), except that—

(i) "more than 50 percent" shall be substituted for "at least 80 percent" each place it appears therein, and

(ii) the determination shall be made without regard to subsections (a)(4) and (b)(2) of section 1563.

A partnership or any other entity (other than a corporation) shall be treated as a member of a controlled group of entities if such entity is controlled (within the meaning of section 954(d)(3)) by members of such group (including any entity treated as a member of such group by reason of this sentence).

(3) Liability of common parent. In the case of a foreign person who is a member of any domestically controlled group of entities, the common parent of such group shall be jointly and severally liable for any tax under this chapter for which such foreign person is liable by reason of this subsection; and for any penalty imposed on such person by this title with respect to any failure to pay such tax or to file any return or statement with respect to such tax or wages subject to such tax. No deduction shall be allowed under this title for any liability imposed by the preceding sentence.

(4) Provisions preventing double taxation.
(A) Agreements. Paragraph (1) shall not apply to any services which are covered by an agreement under subsection (l).
(B) Equivalent foreign taxation. Paragraph (1) shall not apply to any services if the employer establishes to the satisfaction of the Secretary that the remuneration paid by such employer for such services is subject to a tax imposed by a foreign country which is substantially equivalent to the taxes imposed by this chapter.

(5) Cross reference. For relief from taxes in cases covered by certain international agreements, see sections 3101(c) and 3111(c).

In 2008, P.L. 110-458, Sec. 108(k)(1), deleted "or special trial judge" before "of the United States Tax Court" in subpara. (b)(5)(E), effective 8/17/2006, as if included in the provisions of Sec. 854 of the Pension Protection Act of 2006 [P.L. 109-280, see below].
—P.L. 110-245, Sec. 115(a)(1), deleted "or" at the end of para. (a)(21), substituted "; or" for the period at the end of para. (a)(22), and added para. (a)(23), effective for as if included in section 5 of the Mortgage Forgiveness Debt Relief Act of 2007.
—P.L. 110-245, Sec. 302(a), added subsec. (z), effective for services performed in calendar months beginning more than 30 days after the date of the enactment of this Act.
In 2007, P.L. 110-172, Sec. 8(a)(2), added "or consisting of designated Roth contributions (as defined in section 402A(c))" before before the comma at the end of subpara. (v)(1)(A), effective for tax. yrs. begin. after 12/31/2005.
In 2006, P.L. 109-280, Sec. 854(c)(8), added "or special trial judge" before "of the United States Tax Court" in subpara. (b)(5)(E), enacted 8/17/2006.
In 2004, P.L. 108-375, Sec. 585(b)(2)(B), substituted "134(b)(4), or 134(b)(5)" for "or 134(b)(4)" in para. (a)(18), effective for travel benefits provided after 10/28/2004.
—P.L. 108-357, Sec. 251(a)(1)(A), deleted "or" at the end of para. (a)(20), substituted "; or" for the period at the end of para. (a)(21), and added para. (a)(22), effective for stock acquired pursuant to options exercised after 10/22/2004.
—P.L. 108-357, Sec. 320(b)(1), added "108(f)(4)," after "74(c)," in para. (a)(20), effective for amounts received by an individual in tax. yrs. begin. after 12/31/2003.
—P.L. 108-357, Sec. 802(c)(1), added "or to any specified stock compensation (as defined in section 4985) on which tax is imposed by section 4985" before the period at the end of subpara. (v)(2)(A), effective 3/4/2003; except that periods before 3/4/2003 shall not be taken into account in applying the periods in subsections (a) and (e)(1) of Code Sec. 4985, as added by this section.
—P.L. 108-203, Sec. 423(a), substituted "on a farm operated for profit" for "described in subsection (g)(5)" in subpara. (a)(7)(B) . . . Sec. 423(c), deleted "or is domestic service in a private home of the employer" after "trade or business" in para. (g)(5), effective 3/2/2004.
In 2003, P.L. 108-121, Sec. 106(b)(2), substituted ", 129, or 134(b)(4)" for "or 129" in para. (a)(18), effective for tax. yrs. begin. after 12/31/2002. Sec. 106(d) of this Act, provides:
"(d) No inference. No inference may be drawn from the amendments made by this section with respect to the tax treatment of any amounts under the program described in section 134(b)(4) of the Internal Revenue Code of 1986 (as added by this section) for any taxable year beginning before January 1, 2003."
In 2000, P.L. 106-554, Sec. 1(a)(7), [which enacted into law Sec. 319(15) of P.L. 106-554] substituted a comma for the semicolon at the end of subpara. (a)(5)(G), effective 12/21/2000.
In 1998, P.L. 105-277, Sec. 802(a), redesignated Secs. 11246(b)(2) and (3), P.L. 105-33, as Secs. 11246(b)(3) and (4), P.L. 105-33, and added a new Sec. 11246(b)(2), P.L. 105-233 which amends Code Sec. 3121(b)(7)(C). For specifics of amendments, see below.
—P.L. 105-206, Sec. 6023(13)(A), substituted a comma for the semicolon at the end of subparagraph (a)(5)(F) . . . Sec. 6023(13)(B), deleted "or" at the end of subpara. (a)(5)(G) . . . Sec. 6023(13)(C), substituted a semicolon for the period at the end of subpara. (a)(5)(I), effective 7/22/98.
In 1997, P.L. 105-61, Sec. 642(d)(2)(A), substituted a comma for "or" after "1986" in clause (b)(5)(H)(i) . . . Sec. 642(d)(2)(B), added "or the Federal Employees' Retirement System Open Enrollment Act of 1997" after "(50 U.S.C. 2157)," in clause (b)(5)(H)(i), effective 10/10/97.
—P.L. 105-34, Sec. 921(a), provides the following clarification, effective for services performed after 12/31/97:
"SEC. 921 CLARIFICATION OF STANDARD TO BE USED IN DETERMINING EMPLOYMENT TAX STATUS OF SECURITIES BROKERS.
"(a) In General. — In determining for purposes of the Internal Revenue Code of 1986 whether a registered representative of a securities broker-dealer is an employee (as defined in section 3121(d) of the Internal Revenue Code of 1986), no weight shall be given to instructions from the service recipient which are imposed only in compliance with investor protection standards imposed by the Federal Government, any State government, or a governing body pursuant to a delegation by a Federal or State agency."

—P.L. 105-33, Sec. 11246(b)(2),]as added by Sec. 802(a)(2), P.L. 105-277, see above] added "(other than the Federal Employees Retirement System provided in chapter 84 of title 5, United States Code)" after "law of the United States" in para. (b)(7)(C), effective for all months beginning after the date on which the Director of the Office of Personnel Management issues regulations to carry out section 11-1726, District of Columbia Code (as amended by paragraph (1)).
In 1996, P.L. 104-188, Sec. 1116(a)(1)(A), added the sentence to the end of subsec. (b) . . . Sec. 1116(a)(1)(B), amended subpara. (b)(20)(A), effective before for remuneration paid after 12/31/94, and before 12/31/84 and before 1/1/95 unless the payor treated such remuneration (when paid) as being subject to tax under chapter 21 of the Internal Revenue Code of 1986.
Prior to amendment, subpara. (b)(20)(A) read as follows:
"(A) such individual does not receive any cash remuneration (other than as provided in subparagraph (B)),"
—P.L. 104-188, Sec. 1421(b)(8)(A), deleted "or" at the end of subpara. (a)(5)(F), added "or" to the end of subpara. (a)(5)(G), and added subpara. (a)(5)(H), effective for tax. yrs. begin. after 12/31/96.
—P.L. 104-188, Sec. 1458(b)(1), deleted "or" at the end of subpara. (a)(5)(G) [as amended by Sec. 1421(b)(8)(A) of this Act, see above], added "or" to the end of subpara. (a)(5)(H) [as added by Sec. 1421(b)(8)(A) of this Act, see above', and added subpara. (a)(5)(I), effective for remuneration paid after 12/31/96.
—P.L. 104-188, Sec. 1802, of this Act provides:
"Sec. 1802. Treatment of certain university accounts.
"(a) In general. For purposes of subsection (s) of section 3121 of the Internal Revenue Code of 1986 (relating to concurrent employment by 2 or more employers)—
"(1) the following entities shall be deemed to be related corporations that concurrently employ the same individual:
"(A) a State university which employs health professionals as facility members at a medical school, and
"(B) an agency account of a State university which is described in subparagraph (A) and from which there is distributed to such faculty members payments forming a part of the compensation that the State, or such State university, as the case may be, agrees to pay to such faculty members, but only if—
"(i) such agency account is authorized by State law and receives the funds for such payments from a faculty practice plan described in section 501(c)(3) of such Code and exempt from tax under section 501(a) of such Code.
"(ii) such payments are distributed by such agency account to such faculty members who render patient care at such medical school, and
"(iii) such faculty members comprise at least 30 percent of the membership of such faculty practice plan, and
"(2) remuneration which is disbursed by such agency account to any such faculty member of the medical school described in paragraph (1)(A) shall be deemed to have been actually disbursed by the State, or such State university, as the case may be, as a common paymaster and not to have been actually disbursed by such agency account.
"(b) Effective date. The provisions of subsection (a) shall apply to remuneration paid after December 31, 1996."
In 1994, P.L. 103-387, Sec. 2(a)(1)(A), amended subpara. (a)(7)(B) . . . Sec. 2(a)(1)(B), added subsec. (x), effective for remuneration paid after 12/31/93.
Prior to amendment, subpara. (a)(7)(B) read as follows:
"(B) cash remuneration paid by an employer in any calendar quarter to an employee for domestic service in a private home of the employer, if the cash remuneration paid in such quarter by the employer to the employee for such service is less than $50. As used in this subparagraph, the term 'domestic service in a private home of the employer' does not include service described in subsection (g)(5);"
—P.L. 103-387, Sec. 2(a)(1)(C)(i), deleted "; or" at the end of para. (b)(19) . . . Sec. 2(a)(1)(C)(ii), substituted "; or" for the period at the end of para. (b)(20) . . . Sec. 2(a)(1)(C)(iii), added para. (b)(21), effective for services performed after 12/31/94. Sec. 2(a)(4) of this Act provides:
"(4) No loss of social security coverage for 1994; continuation of W-2 filing requirement. — Notwithstanding the amendments made by this subsection, if the wages (as defined in section 3121(a) of the Internal Revenue Code of 1986) paid during 1994 to an employee for domestic service in a private home of the employer are less than $1,000—
"(A) the employer shall file any return or statement required under section 6051 of such Code with respect to such wages (determined without regard to such amendments), and
"(B) the employee shall be entitled to credit under section 209 of the Social Security Act with respect to any such wages required to be included on any such return or statement."
—P.L. 103-296, Sec. 108(h)(2), substituted "Commissioner of Social Security" for "Secretary of Health and Human Services" in subpara. (b)(10)(B), effective 3/31/95.
—P.L. 103-296, Sec. 303(a)(2), substituted "$1,000 with respect to service performed during any calendar year commencing on or after January 1, 1995, ending on or before December 31, 1999, and the adjusted amount determined under section 218(c)(8)(B) of the Social Security Act for any calendar year commencing on or after January 1, 2000, with respect to service performed during such calendar year" for "$100" in clause (b)(7)(F)(iv) . . . Sec. 303(b)(2), substituted "$1,000 with respect to service performed during any calendar year commencing on or after January 1, 1995, ending on or before December 31, 1999, and the adjusted amount determined under section 218(c)(8)(B) of the Social Security Act for any calendar year commencing on or after January 1, 2000, with respect to service performed during such calendar year" for "$100" in subclause (u)(2)(B)(ii)(V), effective for service performed on or after 1/1/95.

—P.L. 103-296, Sec. 319(a)(1), added subsec. (y) . . . Sec. 319(a)(5), added ", except service which constitutes 'employment' under subsection (y)" after "organization", in para. (b)(15), effective for service performed after the calendar quarter following the calendar quarter in which the date of enactment [8/15/94] of this Act occurs.

—P.L. 103-296, Sec. 320(a)(1)(C), substituted "(J), (M), or (Q)" for "(J), or (M)" in para. (b)(19), effective with the calendar quarter following 8/15/94.

In 1993, P.L. 103-178, Sec. 204(c), substituted "section 307 of the Central Intelligence Agency Retirement Act (50 U.S.C. 2157)" for "section 307 of the Central Intelligence Agency Retirement Act of 1964 for Certain Employees" in clause (b)(5)(H)(i), effective 12/3/93.

—P.L. 103-66, Sec. 13207(a)(1)(A), added "in the case of the taxes imposed by section 3101(a) and 3111(a)" after "(1)" in para. (a)(1) . . . Sec. 13207(a)(1)(B), substituted "contribution and benefit base (as determined under section 230 of the Social Security Act)" for "applicable contribution base (as determined under subsection (x))" each place it appeared in para. (a)(1) . . . Sec. 13207(a)(1)(C), substituted "such contribution and benefit base" for "such applicable contribution base" in para. (a)(1) . . . Sec. 13207(a)(2), repealed subsec. (x), effective for 1994 and later calendar yrs.

Prior to repeal, subsec. (x) read as follows:

"(x) Applicable contribution base.

"For purposes of this chapter—

"(1) Old-age, survivors, and disability insurance. For purposes of the taxes imposed by sections 3101(a) and 3111(a), the applicable contribution base for any calendar year is the contribution and benefit base determined under section 230 of the Social Security Act for such calendar year.

"(2) Hospital insurance. For purposes of the taxes imposed by section 3101(b) and 3111(b), the applicable contribution base is—

"(A) $125,000 for calendar year 1991, and

"(B) for any calendar year after 1991, the applicable contribution base for the preceding year adjusted in the same manner as is used in adjusting the contribution and benefit base under section 230(b) of the Social Security Act."

In 1992, P.L. 102-572, Sec. 902(b), effective 10/29/92, relating to Court designation provides as follows:

"(b) Other provisions of law. Reference in any other Federal law or documents to—

"(1) the 'United States Claims Court' shall be deemed to refer to the 'United States Court of Federal Claims'; and

"(2) the 'Claims Court' shall be deemed to refer to the 'Court of Federal Claims'."

—P.L. 102-318, Sec. 521(b)(34), substituted "section 402(e)(3)" for "section 402(a)(8)" in subpara. (v)(1)(A), effective for distributions after 12/31/92. For special rule, see Sec. 521(e)(2) of this Act which reads as follows:

"(2) Special rule for partial distributions. For purposes of section 402(a)(5)(D)(i)(II) of the Internal Revenue Code of 1986 (as in effect before the amendments made by this section), a distribution before January 1, 1993, which is made before or at the same time as a series of periodic payments shall not be treated as one of such series if it is not substantially equal in amount to other payments in such series."

In 1990, P.L. 101-508, Sec. 11331(a)(1)(A), substituted "applicable contribution base (as determined under subsection (x))" for "contribution and benefit base (as determined under section 230 of the Social Security Act)" each place it appeared in para. (a)(1) . . . Sec. 11331(a)(1)(B), substituted "such applicable contribution base" for "such contribution and benefit base" in para. (a)(1) . . . Sec. 11331(a)(2), added subsec. (x), effective for 1991 and later calendar yrs.

—P.L. 101-508, Sec. 11332(b)(1), deleted "or" at the end of subpara. (b)(7)(D) . . . Sec. 11332(b)(2), substituted ", or" for the semicolon at the end of subpara. (b)(7)(E) . . . Sec. 11332(b)(3), added subpara. (b)(7)(F), effective for service performed after 7/1/91.

In 1989, P.L. 101-239, Sec. 10201(a)(1), added the last sentence of para. (1)(2) . . . Sec. 10201(a)(2), deleted paras. (1)(3), (4), and (5) . . . Sec. 10201(a)(3), added new para. (1)(3) . . . Sec. 10201(a)(4), redesignated paras. (1)(6)-(10) as paras. (1)(4)-(8) respectively . . . Sec. 10201(b)(3), substituted "paragraph (6)" for "paragraph (8)" in para. (1)(1), effective for any agreement in effect under 1986 Code Sec. 3121 on or after 6/15/89, for which no notice of termination is in effect on 6/15/89.

Prior to deletion, paras. (1)(3), (4), and (5) read as follows:

"(3) Termination of period by a American employer. The period for which an agreement entered into pursuant to paragraph (1) of this subsection is effective may be terminated with respect to any one or more of its foreign affiliates by the American employer, effective at the end of a calendar quarter, upon giving two years' advance notice in writing, but, only if, at the time of the receipt of such notice the agreement has been in effect for a period of not less than eight years. The notice of termination may be revoked by the American employer by giving, prior to the close of the calendar quarter specified in the notice of termination, a written notice of such revocation. Notice of termination or revocation thereof shall be filed in such form and manner as may be prescribed by regulations. Notwithstanding any other provision of this subsection, the period for which any such agreement is effective with respect to any foreign entity shall terminate at the end of any calendar quarter in which the foreign entity, at any time in such quarter, ceases to be a foreign affiliate as defined in paragraph (8).

"(4) Termination of period by Secretary. If the Secretary finds that any American employer which entered into an agreement pursuant to this subsection has failed to comply substantially with the terms of such agreement, the Secretary shall give such American employer not less than sixty days' advance notice in writing that the period covered by such agreement will terminate at the end of the calendar quarter specified in such notice. Such notice of termination may be revoked by the Secretary by giving, prior to the close of the calendar quarter specified in the notice of termination, written notice of such revocation to the American employer. No notice of termination or of revocation thereof shall be given under this paragraph to an American employer without the prior concurrence of the Secretary of Health, Education, and Welfare.

"(5) No renewal of agreement. If any agreement entered into pursuant to paragraph (1) of this subsection is terminated in its entirety (A) by a notice of termination filed by the American employer to paragraph (3), or (B) by a notice of termination given by the Secretary pursuant to paragraph (4), the American employer may not again enter into an agreement pursuant to paragraph (1). If any such agreement is terminated with respect to any foreign affiliate, such agreement may not thereafter be amended so as again to make it applicable with respect to such affiliate."

—P.L. 101-140, Sec. 203(a)(2), repealed as if not enacted Sec. 1011B(a)(22)(A) of P. L. 100-647 which added subsec. (x).

—P.L. 101-136, Sec. 528, provided that "no monies appropriated by this Act [for the fiscal year ending September 30, '90] may be used to implement or enforce section 1151 of the Tax Reform Act of '86 [P. L. 99-514] or the amendments made by such section." [See below]

In 1988, P.L. 100-647, Sec. 1001(d)(2)(C)(i), substituted "(F), (J), or (M)" for "(F) or (J)" each place it appeared in para. (b)(19), effective for tax. yrs. begin. after 12/31/86 but only in the case of scholarships and fellowships granted after 8/16/86.

—P.L. 100-647, Sec. 1001(g)(4)(B)(i), substituted "section 217 (determined without regard to section 274(n))" for "section 217" in para. (a)(11), effective for tax. yrs. begin. after 12/31/86.

—P.L. 100-647, Sec. 1011(e)(8), substituted "457(f)(1)" for "457(e)(1)" in subpara. (v)(3)(A), effective for tax yrs. begin. after 12/31/88 except as provided by Sec. 1107(c)(2)-(5) of P. L. 99-514, reproduced in note following Code Sec. 457.

—P.L. 100-647, Sec. 1011B(a)(23)(A), added "if such payment would not be treated as wages without regard to such plan and it is reasonable to believe that (if section 125 applied for purposes of this section) section 125 would not treat any wages as constructively received" after "section 125)" in subpara. (a)(5)(G), effective for tax. yrs. begin. after 12/31/83.

—P.L. 100-647, Sec. 1018(r)(2)(A), deleted "or" at the end of subclause (u)(2)(B)(ii)(IV), substituted ", or" for the period at the end of subclause (u)(2)(B)(ii)(V) and added subclause (u)(2)(B)(ii)(VI), effective for services performed after 3/31/86.

—P.L. 100-647, Sec. 1018(u)(35), substituted "Savings" for "Saving" in subpara. (v)(3)(C), effective 10/22/86.

—P.L. 100-647, Sec. 3043(c)(2), deleted "or" at the end of para. (a)(19), substituted "; or" for the period at the end of para. (a)(20) and added para. (a)(21), effective for all periods begin. before, on or after 11/10/88. Sec. 3044(b) of this Act provides:

"(b) No Inference created.

"Nothing in the amendments made by this subtitle shall create any inference as to the existence or nonexistence or scope of any exemption from tax for income derived from fishing rights secured as of March 17, 1988, by any treaty, law, or Executive Order."

—P.L. 100-647, Sec. 8013(a), amended Sec. 9003(b) of P. L. 100-203 [reproduced below], the effective date for changes made by Sec. 9003(a)(2) of P. L. 100-203. Sec. 8013(b) of this Act provides:

"(b) Effective date.

"The amendment made by subsection (a) [Sec. 8013(a)] shall apply as if such amendment had been included or reflected in section 9003(b) of the Omnibus Budget Reconciliation Act of 1987 [P. L. 100-203] at the time of its enactment [12/22/87].

Prior to amendment, Sec. 9003(b) of P. L. 100-203 read as follows:

"(b) Effective date.

"The amendments made by subsection (a) [Sec. 9003(a)] shall apply with respect to group-term life insurance coverage in effect after December 31, 1987."

—P.L. 100-647, Sec. 8015(b)(2), amended subpara. (b)(5)(H), effective as if included or reflected in Sec. 304 of the Federal Employee's Retirement System Act of 1986 [P. L. 99-335] (100 Stat. 606) at the time of its enactment [6/6/86].

Prior to amendment, subpara. (b)(5)(H), read as follows:

"(H) service performed by an individual on or after the effective date of an election by such individual under section 301(a) of the Federal Employees' Retirement System Act of 1986, or under regulations issued under section 860 of the Foreign Service Act of 1980 or section 307 of the Central Intelligence Agency Retirement Act of 1964 for Certain Employees, to become subject to chapter 84 of the title 5, United States Code;"

—P.L. 100-647, Sec. 8015(c)(2), added "any such service performed on or after any date on which such individual performs" after "with respect to" in the matter following clause (b)(5)(B)(ii), effective for any individual only upon the performance by such individual of service described in Sec. 210(a)(5)(C), (D), (E), (F), (G), or (H) of the Social Security Act (42 U.S.C. 410(a)(5)) on or after 11/10/88.

—P.L. 100-647, Sec. 8016(a)(3)(A)(i), redesignated para. (d)(3) as para. (d)(4), and substituted a period for "; or" at the end of para. (d)(4) [as redesignated; see above], moved para. (d)(4) [as redesignated; see above] to the end of subsec. (d) . . . Sec. 8016(a)(3)(A)(ii), redesignated original para. (d)(4) as para. (d)(3) and substituted "; or" for the period at the end of para. (d)(3) [as redesignated], effective as provided in Sec. 9002(d) of P. L. 99-509, reproduced below.

—P.L. 100-647, Sec. 8017(b), amended subpara. (a)(8)(B), effective for remuneration for agricultural labor paid after 12/31/87.

Prior to amendment, subpara. (a)(8)(B) read as follows:

"(B) cash remuneration paid by an employer in any calendar year to an employee for agricultural labor unless (i) the cash remuneration paid in such year by the employer to the employee for such labor is $150 or more, or (ii) the employer's expenditures for agricultural labor in such year equal or exceed $2,500;"

—P.L. 100-647, Sec. 8018, of this Act provides:

"SEC. 8018. CERTAIN EMPLOYER PENSION CONTRIBUTIONS NOT INCLUDED IN FICA WAGE BASE.

"In the case of any State (within the meaning of section 3121(e)(1) of the Internal Revenue Code of 1986) or political subdivision thereof which received a letter ruling of the Internal Revenue Service issued after December 31, 1983, and before the date of the enactment of this Act maintaining that any amount treated as an employer contribution under section 414(h)(2) of the Internal Revenue Code of 1986 is excluded from the definition of 'wages' for purposes of tax liability under section 3121(v)(1)(B) of such Code, such State or political subdivision shall be relieved of any liability for taxes under such section 3121(v)(1)(B) which, in good faith reliance on such letter ruling, were not paid and which would otherwise have been required to be paid (but for this section) on or before the earlier of the date of the enactment of this Act or the date of the receipt of a notice of revocation from the Internal Revenue Service of such letter ruling."

In 1987, P.L. 100-203, Sec. 9001(b)(1), amended para. (m)(1) . . . Sec. 9001(b)(2), amended para. (i)(2), effective for remuneration paid after 12/31/87.

Prior to amendment, para. (m)(1) read as follows:

"(1) Inclusion of service. The term 'employment' shall, notwithstanding the provisions of subsection (b) of this section, include service performed by an individual as a member of a uniformed service on active duty; but such term shall not include any such service which is performed while on leave without pay."

Prior to amendment, para. (i)(2) read as follows:

"(2) Service in the uniformed services. For purposes of this chapter, in the case of an individual performing service, as a member of a uniformed service, to which the provisions of subsection (m)(1) are applicable, the term 'wages' shall, subject to the provisions of subsection (a)(1) of this section, include as such individual's remuneration for such service only his basic pay as described in chapter 3 and section 1009 of title 37, United States Code.".

—P.L. 100-203, Sec. 9002(b), amended clause (a)(8)(B)(ii), effective for remuneration for agricultural labor paid after 12/31/87.

Prior to amendment, clause (a)(8)(B)(ii) read as follows:

"(ii) the employee performs agricultural labor for the employer on 20 days or more during such year for cash remuneration computed on a time basis;".

—P.L. 100-203, Sec. 9003(a)(2), substituted "death, except that this paragraph does not apply to a payment for group-term life insurance to the extent that such payment is includible in the gross income of the employee" for "death" in subpara. (a)(2)(C), effective as provided in Sec. 9003(b) of this Act [as amended by Sec. 8013(a) of P. L. 100-647, see above] which reads as follows:

"(b) Effective date.

"The amendments made by subsection (a) [Sec. 9003(a)] shall apply with respect to group-term life insurance coverage in effect after December 31, 1987, except that such amendments shall not apply with respect to payments by the employer (or a successor of such employer) for group-term life insurance for such employer's former employees who separated from employment with the employer on or before December 31, 1988, to the extent that such payments are not for coverage for any such employee for any period for which such employee is employed by such employer (or a successor of such employer) after the date of such separation."

—P.L. 100-203, Sec. 9004(b)(1), deleted "performed by an individual in the employ of his spouse, and service" before "performed by a child" in subpara. (b)(3)(A) . . . Sec. 9004(b)(2), amended subpara. (b)(3)(B) before clause (i) thereof . . . Sec. 9005(b)(1), substituted "18" for "21" in subpara. (b)(3)(A) . . . Sec. 9005(b)(2), added "under the age of 21 in the employ of his father or mother, or performed by an individual" after the first place "individual" appears in subpara. (b)(3)(B) [as amended by section 9004(b)(2) of this Act, see above], effective for remuneration paid after 12/31/87.

Prior to amendment, subpara. (b)(3)(B), before clause (i) thereof, read as follows:

"(B) service not in the course of the employer's trade or business, or domestic service in a private home of the employer, performed by an individual in the employ of his son or daughter; except that the provisions of this subparagraph shall not be applicable to such domestic service if—"

—P.L. 100-203, Sec. 9006(a)(1), substituted "both employee and employer taxes" for "employee taxes" in the heading of subsec. (q) . . . Sec. 9006(a)(2), deleted "other than for purposes of the taxes imposed by section 3111" after "of this chapter" in subsec. (q) . . . Sec. 9006(a)(3), substituted "remuneration for such employment (and deemed to have been paid by the employer for purposes of subsections (a) and (b) of section 3111)" for "remuneration for employment" in subsec. (q) . . . Sec. 9006(a)(4), added the material after "at the time received" and before the period at the end of subsec. (q) . . . Sec. 9006(b)(2), deleted subsec. (t), effective for tips received (and wages paid) on and after 1/1/88.

Prior to deletion, subsec. (t) read as follows:

"(t) Special rule for determining wages subject to employer tax in case of certain employers whose employees receive income from tips.

"If the wages paid by an employer with respect to the employment during any month of an individual who (for services performed in connection with such employment) receives tips which constitute wages, and to which section 3102(a) applies, are less than the total amount which would be payable (with respect to such employment) at the minimum wage rate applicable to such individual under section 6(a)(1) of the Fair Labor Standards Act of 1938 (determined without regard to section 3(m) of such Act), the wages so paid shall be deemed for purposes of section 3111 to be equal to such total amount.".

—P.L. 100-203, Sec. 9023(d)(1), substituted ", or" for "; or" at the end of subpara. (a)(5)(F) . . . Sec. 9023(d)(2), substituted a semicolon for the comma at the end of subpara. (a)(5)(G), effective 12/22/87.

In 1986, P.L. 99-514, Sec. 122(e)(1), substituted "74(c), 117, or" for "117 or" in para. (a)(20), effective for prizes and awards granted after 12/31/86.

—P.L. 99-514, Sec. 1108(g)(7), amended subpara. (a)(5)(C), effective for yrs. begin. after 12/31/86.

Prior to amendment, subpara. (a)(5)(C) read as follows:

"(C) under a simplified employee pension if, at the time of the payment, it is reasonable to believe that the employee will be entitled to a deduction under section 219(b)(2) for such payment,"

—P.L. 99-514, Sec. 1147(b), deleted "and" from the end of subpara. (v)(3)(A), substituted ", and" for the period at the end of subpara. (v)(3)(B) and added subpara. (v)(3)(C), effective 10/22/86.

—P.L. 99-514, Sec. 1151(d)(2)(A), deleted "or" from the end of subpara. (a)(5)(E), added "or" to the end of subpara. (a)(5)(F) and added subpara. (a)(5)(G), effective for tax. yrs. begin. after 12/31/83.

—P.L. 99-514, Sec. 1882(c), substituted "The election may be revoked by the church or organization under regulations prescribed by the Secretary. The election shall be revoked by the Secretary if such church or organization fails to furnish the information required under section 6051 to the Secretary for a period of 2 years or more with respect to remuneration paid for such services by such church or organization, and, upon request by the Secretary, fails to furnish all such previously unfurnished information for the period covered by the election. Any revocation under the preceding sentence shall apply retroactively to the beginning of the 2-year period for which the information was not furnished." for "The election may not be revoked by the church or organization, but shall be permanently revoked by the Secretary if such church or organization fails to furnish the information required under section 6051 to the Secretary for a period of 2 years or more with respect to remuneration paid for such services by such church or organization, and, upon request by the Secretary, fails to furnish all such previously unfurnished information for the period covered by the election. Such revocation shall apply retroactively to the beginning of the 2-year period for which the information was not furnished." in para. (w)(2), effective for service performed after 12/31/83, and as provided in Sec. 2603(f) of P. L. 98-369, reproduced below.

—P.L. 99-514, Sec. 1883(a)(11)(B), moved subpara. (a)(8)(B) to the left, to align under subpara. (a)(8)(A), effective 10/22/86.

—P.L. 99-514, Sec. 1895(b)(18)(A), deleted "or" from the end of subclause (u)(2)(B)(ii)(III), substituted ", or" for the period at the end of subclause (u)(2)(B)(ii)(IV) and added subclause (u)(2)(B)(ii)(V), effective for services performed after 3/31/86.

—P.L. 99-514, Sec. 1899A(38), substituted "forfeiture" for "forfeiture" in clause (v)(2)(A)(ii) . . . Sec. 1899A(39), substituted "this chapter" for "Chapter 21 of this Code" in the first sentence of para. (w)(1) . . . Sec. 1899A(40), substituted "July 18, 1984" for "the date of enactment of this subsection" in para. (w)(2), effective 10/22/86.

—P.L. 99-509, Sec. 9002(b)(1)(A)(i), substituted a comma for "; or" at the end of subpara. (b)(7)(C) . . . Sec. 9002(b)(1)(A)(ii), substituted ", or" for the semicolon at the end of subpara. (b)(7)(D) . . . Sec. 9002(b)(1)(A)(iii), added subpara. (b)(7)(E) . . . Sec. 9002(b)(2)(A), redesignated para. (d)(3) as para. (d)(4) and added new para. (d)(3), effective as provided in Sec. 9002(d) of this Act which reads as follows:

"(d) Effective date.

"The amendments made by this section [Sec. 9002] are effective with respect to payments due with respect to wages paid after December 31, 1986, including wages paid after such date by a State (or political subdivision thereof) that modified its agreement pursuant to the provisions of section 218(e)(2) of the Social Security Act prior to the date of the enactment of this Act; except that in cases where, in accordance with the currently applicable schedule, deposits of taxes due under an agreement entered into pursuant to section 218 of the Social Security Act would be required within 3 days after the close of an eighth-monthly period, such 3-day requirement shall be changed to a 7-day requirement for wages paid prior to October 1, 1987, and to a 5-day requirement for wages paid after September 30, 1987, and prior to October 1, 1988. For wages paid prior to October 1, 1988, the deposit schedule for taxes imposed under sections 3101 and 3111 shall be determined separately from the deposit schedule for taxes withheld under section 3402 if the taxes imposed under sections 3101 and 3111 are due with respect to service included under an agreement entered into pursuant to section 218 of the Social Security Act."

—P.L. 99-335, Sec. 304(b)(1), deleted "or" at the end of subpara. (b)(5)(F) . . . Sec. 304(b)(2), substituted ", or" for the semicolon at the end of subpara. (b)(5)(G) . . . Sec. 304(b)(3), added subpara. (b)(5)(H), effective 6/6/86.

—P.L. 99-272, Sec. 12112(b), substituted "shall not include" for "shall, subject to the provisions of subsection (a)(1) of this section, include" in para. (i)(5), effective for service performed after 12/31/83.

—P.L. 99-272, Sec. 13205(a)(1), amended subsec. (u), effective for services performed after 3/31/86.

Prior to amendment, subsec. (u) read as follows:

"(u) Application of hospital insurance tax to Federal employment.

"(1) In general. For purposes of the taxes imposed by sections 3101(b) and 3111(b), subsection (b) shall be applied without regard to paragraph (5) thereof.

"(2) Medicare qualified Federal employment. For purposes of this chapter, the term 'medicare qualified Federal employment' means service which—

"(A) is employment (as defined in subsection (b)) with the application of paragraph (1), but

"(B) would not be employment (as so defined) without the application of paragraph (1)."

—P.L. 99-272, Sec. 13303(c)(2), added "(other than service described in paragraph (3)(A))" after "service" in para. (b)(20), effective 4/7/86.

—P.L. 99-221, Sec. 3(b)(1), deleted "and" at the end of subclause (b)(5)(B)(i)(III) . . . Sec. 3(b)(2), substituted ", and" for "; or" at the end of subclause (b)(5)(B)(i)(IV) . . . Sec. 3(b)(3), added subclause (b)(5)(B)(i)(V), effective for any return to the performance of service in the employ of the U.S., or of any instrumentality thereof, after 1983.

In 1984, P.L. 98-369, Sec. 67(c), added the last sentence to subpara. (v)(2)(A), effective for payments under agreements entered into or renewed after 6/14/84 in tax. yrs. end. after 6/14/84, Sec. 67(e)(2) of this Act provides special rules as follows:

"(2) Special rule for contract amendments. Any contract entered into before June 15, 1984, which is amended after June 14, 1984, in any significant relevant aspect shall be treated as a contract entered into after June 14, 1984."

—P.L. 98-369, Sec. 491(d)(36), deleted subpara. (a)(5)(C) and redesignated subparas. (a)(5)(D)-(a)(5)(G) as subparas. (a)(5)(C)-(a)(5)(F), effective for obligations issued after 12/31/83.

Prior to deletion, subpara. (a)(5)(C) read as follows:

"(C) under or to a bond purchase plan which, at the time of such payment, is a qualified bond purchase plan described in section 405(a),"

—P.L. 98-369, Sec. 531(d)(1)(A)(i), substituted "all remuneration (including benefits) paid in any medium" for "all remuneration paid in any medium" in the material preceding para. (a)(1) . . . Sec. 531(d)(1)(A)(ii), deleted "or" at the end of para. (a)(18), substituted "; or" for the period at the end of para. (a)(19), and added para. (a)(20), effective 1/1/85.

—P.L. 98-369, Sec. 2601(b)(1), amended subpara. (b)(5)(B) . . . Sec. 2601(b)(2)(A), substituted "(C)", "(D)", "(E)", "(F)", and "(G)" for "(i)", "(ii)", "(iii)", "(iv)", and "(v)", respectively, in the matter following "except that this paragraph shall not apply with respect to—" in para. (b)(5) . . . Sec. 2601(b)(2)(B), substituted "(i)", "(ii)", and "(iii)" for "(I)", "(II)", and "(III)", respectively, in subpara. (b)(5)(D), [as redesignated by Sec. 2601(b)(2)(A) of the Act, see above] . . . Sec. 2601(b)(2)(C), amended subpara. (b)(5)(G) [as redesignated by Sec. 2601(b)(2)(A) of the Act, see above], effective for service performed after 12/31/83. Sec. 2601(c)-(e)(1) of this Act provides as follows:

"(c) For purposes of section 210(a)(5)(G) of the Social Security Act and section 3121(b)(5)(G) of the Internal Revenue Code of 1954, an individual shall not be considered to be subject to subchapter III of chapter 83 of title 5, United States Code, or to another retirement system established by a law of the United States for employees of the Federal Government (other than for members of the uniformed services), if he is contributing a reduced amount by reason of the Federal Employees' Retirement Contribution Temporary Adjustment Act of 1983.

"(d)(1) Any individual who—

"(A) was subject to subchapter III of chapter 83 of title 5, United States Code, or to another retirement system established by a law of United States for employees of the Federal Government (other than for members of the uniformed services), on December 31, 1983 (as determined for purposes of section 210(a)(5)(G) of the Social Security Act), and

"(B)(i) received a lump-sum payment under section 8342(a) of such title 5, or under the corresponding provision of the law establishing the other retirement system described in subparagraph (A), after December 31, 1983, and prior to June 15, 1984, or received such a payment on or after June 15, 1984, pursuant to an application which was filed in accordance with such section 8342(a) or the corresponding provision of the law establishing such other retirement system prior to that date, or

"(ii) otherwise ceased to be subject to subchapter III of chapter 83 of title 5, United States Code, for a period after December 31, 1983, to which section 210(a)(5)(g)(iii) of the Social Security Act applies,

shall, if such individual again becomes subject to subchapter III of chapter 83 of title 5 (or effectively applies for coverage under such subchapter) after the date on which he last ceased to be subject to such subchapter but prior to, or within 30 days after, the date of the enactment of this Act, requalify for the exemption from social security coverage and taxes under section 210(a)(5) of the Social Security Act and section 3121(b)(5) of the Internal Revenue Code of 1954 as if the cessation of coverage under title 5 had not occurred.

"(2) An individual meeting the requirements of subparagraphs (A) and (B) of paragraph (1) who is not in the employ of the United States or an instrumentality thereof on the date of the enactment of this Act may requalify for such exemptions in the same manner as under paragraph (1) if such individual again becomes subject to subchapter III of chapter 83 of title 5 (or effectively applies for coverage under such subchapter) within 30 days after the date on which he first returns to service in the legislative branch after such date of enactment, if such date (on which he returns to service) is within 365 days after he was last in the employ of the United States or an instrumentality thereof.

"(3) If an individual meeting the requirements of subparagraphs (A) and (B) of paragraph (1) does not again become subject to subchapter III of chapter 83 of title 5 (or effectively apply for coverage under such subchapter) prior to the date of the enactment of this Act or within the relevant 30-day period as provided in paragraph (1) or (2), social security coverage and taxes by reason of section 210(a)(5)(G) of the Social Security Act and section 3121(b)(5)(G) of the Internal Revenue Code of 1954 shall, with respect to such individual's service in the legislative branch of the Federal Government, become effective with the first month beginning after such 30-day period.

"(4) The provisions of paragraphs (1) and (2) shall apply only for purposes of reestablishing an exemption from social security coverage and taxes, and do not affect the amount of service to be credited to an individual for purposes of title 5, United States Code.

"(e)(1) For purposes of section 210(a)(5) of the Social Security Act (as in effect in January 1983 and as in effect on and after January 1, 1984) and section 3121(b)(5) of the Internal Revenue Code of 1954 (as so in effect), service performed in the employ of a nonprofit organization described in section 501(c)(3) of the Internal Revenue Code of 1954 by an employee who is required by law to be subject to subchapter III of chapter 83 of title 5, United States Code, with respect to such service, shall be considered to be service performed in the employ of an instrumentality of the United States."

Prior to amendment, subpara. (b)(5)(B) read as follows:

"(B) is performed by an individual who (i) has been continuously in the employ of the United States or an instrumentality thereof since December 31, 1983 (and for this purpose an individual who returns to the performance of such service after being separated therefrom following a previous period of such service shall nevertheless be considered upon such return as having been continuously in the employ of the United States or an instrumentality thereof, regardless of whether the period of such separation began before, on, or after December 31, 1983, if the period of such separation does not exceed 365 consecutive days), or (ii) is receiving an annuity from the Civil Service Retirement and Disability Fund, or benefits (for service as an employee) under another retirement system established by law of the United States for employees of the Federal Government (other than for members of the uniformed services);"

Prior to amendment, subpara. (b)(5)(G) [as redesignated by Sec. 2601(b)(2)(A) of the Act, see above] read as follows:

"(G) any other service in the legislative branch of the Federal Government if such service is performed by an individual who, on December 31, 1983, is not subject to subchapter III of chapter 83 of title 5, United States Code;"

—P.L. 98-369, Sec. 2603(a)(2), added "(A)" after "(8)" and substituted "this subparagraph" for "this paragraph" in para. (b)(8), and added subpara. (b)(8)(B) . . . Sec. 2603(b), added subsec. (w), effective for service performed after 12/31/83. Sec. 2603(f) of this Act provides as follows:

"(f) In any case where a church or qualified church-controlled organization makes an election under section 3121(w) of the Internal Revenue Code of 1954, the Secretary of the Treasury shall refund (without interest) to such church or organization any taxes paid under sections 3101 and 3111 of such Code with respect to service performed after December 31, 1983, which is covered under such election. The refund shall be conditional upon the church or organization agreeing to pay to each employee (or former employee) the portion of the refund attributable to the tax imposed on such employee (or former employee) under section 3101, and such employee (or former employee) may not receive any other refund payment of such taxes."

—P.L. 98-369, Sec. 2661(o)(3), amended subpara. (v)(1)(B), effective 1/1/84.

Prior to amendment, subpara. (v)(1)(B) read as follows:

"(B) any amount treated as an employer contribution under section 414(h)(2)."

—P.L. 98-369, Sec. 2662(a), amended Sec. 101(d) of P. L. 98-21, the effective date for changes made by Sec. 101(b) and (c) of P. L. 98-21, by substituting "service performed" for "remuneration paid", see below.

—P.L. 98-369, Sec. 2662(f)(2)(A), amended Sec. 324(d)(1) of P. L. 98-21, the effective date for changes made by Sec. 324 of P. L. 98-21, by adding the last sentence (reproduced below) . . . Sec. 2662(f)(2)(C), amended Sec. 324(d)(4) of P. L. 98-21, part of the effective date for changes made by Sec. 324 of P. L. 98-21, by adding the last sentence (reproduced below).

—P.L. 98-369, Sec. 2662(g), amended Sec. 327(d) of P. L. 98-21, the effective date for changes made by Sec. 327 of P. L. 98-21 (reproduced below).

Prior to amendment Sec. 327(d) of P. L. 98-21 read as follows:

"(d)(1) Except as provided in paragraph (2), the amendments made by subsections (a) and (b) [Sec. 327] shall apply to remuneration paid after December 31, 1983.

"(2) The amendments made by subsection (c) [Sec. 327] shall apply to remuneration paid after December 31, 1984."

—P.L. 98-369, Sec. 2663(i)(1), deleted "(A) under contracts entered into in accordance with title V of the Agricultural Act of 1949, as amended (7 U.S.C. 1461–1468), or (B)" from after "agricultural workers" in para. (b)(1) . . . Sec. 2663(i)(2), substituted "chapter 3 and section 1009 of title 37, United States Code" for "section 102(10) of the Servicemen's and Veterans' Survivor Benefits Act" in para. (i)(2) . . . Sec. 2663(i)(3)(A), substituted "paragraph (21) of section 101 of title 38, United States Code" for "section 102 of the Servicemen's and Veterans' Survivor Benefits Act" in para. (m)(2) . . . Sec. 2663(i)(3)(B), substituted "paragraph (22) of such section" for "such section" in para. (m)(2) . . . Sec. 2663(i)(4), substituted "paragraph (23) of such section 101" for "such section 102" in para. (m)(3) . . . Sec. 2663(i)(5)(A), substituted "a reserve component as defined in section 101(27) of title 38, United States Code" for "a reserve component of a uniformed service as defined in section 102(3) of the Servicemen's and Veterans' Survivor Benefits Act" in the first sentence of subsec. (n) . . . Sec. 2663(i)(5)(B), added ", the National Oceanic and Atmospheric Administration Corps," after "Coast and Geodetic Survey" in the first sentence of subsec. (n) . . . Sec. 2663(i)(5)(C), substituted "military, naval, or air" for "military or naval" each place it appeared in para. (n)(5) . . . Sec. 2663(i)(5)(D), substituted "Military Selective Service Act" for "Universal Military Training and Service Act" in subpara. (n)(5)(B) . . . Sec. 2663(j)(5)(C), substituted "Health and Human Services" for "Health, Education, and Welfare" each place it appeared in subpara. (b)(10)(B), effective on 7/18/84 except as provided in Sec. 2664(b) of the Act, which reads as follows:

"(b) Except to the extent otherwise specifically provided in this subtitle, the amendments made by section 2663 shall be effective on the date of the enactment of this Act; but none of such amendments shall be construed as changing or affecting any right, liability, status, or interpretation which existed (under the provisions of law involved) before that date."

In 1983, P.L. 98-118, Sec. 4, provides as follows:

"Sec. 4. Notwithstanding section 101(d) of the Social Security Amendments of 1983, the amendments made by section 101(c) of such Act shall apply only with respect to remuneration paid after December 31, 1985. Remuneration paid prior to January 1, 1986, under section 371(b) of title 28, United States Code, to an individual performing service under section 294 of such title, shall not be included in the term 'wages' for purposes of section 209 of the Social Security Act or section 3121(a) of the Internal Revenue Code of 1954."

—P.L. 98-21, Sec. 101(b)(1), amended paras. (b)(5) and (b)(6) . . . Sec. 101(b)(2), amended para. (u)(1) . . . Sec. 101(c)(2), added para. (i)(5), effective [as amended by Sec. 2662(a) of P. L. 98-369, see above] for services performed after 12/31/83. Prior to amendment, paras. (b)(5) and (b)(6) read as follows:

"(5) service performed in the employ of any instrumentality of the United States, if such instrumentality is exempt from the tax imposed by section 3111 by virtue of any provision of law which specifically refers to such section (or the corresponding section of prior law) in granting such exemption;

"(6)(A) service performed in the employ of the United States or in the employ of any instrumentality of the United States, if such service is covered by a retirement system established by a law of the United States;

"(B) service performed, by an individual in the employ of an instrumentality of the United States if such an instrumentality was exempt from the tax imposed by section 1410 of the Internal Revenue Code of 1939 on December 31, 1950, and if such service is covered by a retirement system established by such instrumentality; except that the provisions of this subparagraph shall not be applicable to—

"(i) service performed in the employ of a corporation which is wholly owned by the United States;

"(ii) service performed in the employ of a Federal land bank, a Federal intermediate credit bank, a bank for cooperatives, a Federal land bank association, a production credit association, a Federal Reserve Bank, a Federal Home Loan Bank, or a Federal Credit Union;

"(iii) service performed in the employ of a State, county, or community committee under the Commodity Stabilization Service;

"(iv) service performed by a civilian employee, not compensated from funds appropriated by the Congress, in the Army and Air Force Exchange Service, Army and Air Force Motion Picture Service, Navy Exchanges, Marine Corps Exchanges, or other activities, conducted by an instrumentality of the United States subject to the jurisdiction of the Secretary of Defense, at installations of the Department of Defense for the comfort, pleasure, contentment, and mental and physical improvement of personnel of such Department or;

"(v) service performed by a civilian employee, not compensated from funds appropriated by the Congress, in the Coast Guard Exchanges or other activities, conducted by an instrumentality of the United States subject to the jurisdiction of the Secretary of Transportation, at installations of the Coast Guard for the comfort, pleasure, contentment, and mental and physical improvement of personnel of the Coast Guard;

"(C) service performed in the employ of the United States or in the employ of any instrumentality of the United States, if such service is performed—

"(i) as the President or Vice President of the United States or as a member, Delegate, or Resident Commissioner of or to the Congress;

"(ii) in the legislative branch;

"(iii) in a penal institution of the United States by an inmate thereof;

"(iv) by any individual as an employee included under section 5351(2) of title 5, United States Code (relating to certain interns, student nurses, and other student employees of hospitals of the Federal Government, other than as a medical or dental intern or a medical or dental resident in training;

"(v) by any individual as an employee serving on a temporary basis in case of fire, storm, earthquake, flood, or other similar emergency; or

"(vi) by any individual to whom subchapter III of Chapter 83 of title 5, United States Code, does not apply because such individual is subject to another retirement system (other than the retirement system of the Tennessee Valley Authority);"

Prior to amendment, para. (u)(1) read as follows:

"(1) In general. For purposes of the taxes imposed by sections 3101(b) and 3111(b)—

"(A) paragraph (6) of subsection (b) shall be applied without regard to subparagraphs (A), (B), and (C)(i), (ii), and (vi) thereof, and

"(B) paragraph (5) of subsection (b) (and the provisions of law referred to therein) shall not apply."

—P.L. 98-21, Sec. 102(b)(1), amended para. (b)(8) . . . Sec. 102(b)(2), repealed subsec. (k) . . . Sec. 102(b)(3), substituted "subsection (b)(8)" for "subsection (b)(8)(A)" and "section 210(a)(8)" for "section 210(a)(8)(A)" in para. (r)(3) . . . Sec. 102(b)(3)(B), deleted para. (r)(4), effective for service performed after 12/31/83 (but the provisions of sections 2 and 3 of P. L. 94-563 and Sec. 312(c) of P. L. 95-216 shall continue in effect, to the extent applicable, as though such amendments had not been made).

Prior to amendment, para. (b)(8) read as follows:

"(8)(A) service performed by a duly ordained, commissioned, or licensed minister of a church in the exercise of his ministry or by a member of a religious order in the exercise of duties required by such order, except that this subparagraph shall not apply to service performed by a member of such an order in the exercise of such duties, if an election of coverage under subsection (r) is in effect with respect to such order, or with respect to the autonomous subdivision thereof to which such member belongs;

"(B) service performed in the employ of a religious, charitable, educational, or other organization described in section 501(c)(3) which is exempt from income tax under section 501(a), but this subparagraph shall not apply to service performed during the period for which a certificate, filed pursuant to subsection (k) (or the corresponding subsection of prior law) or deemed to have been so filed under paragraph (4) or (5) of such subsection, is in effect if such service is performed by an employee—

"(i) whose signature appears on the list filed (or deemed to have been filed) by such organization under subsection (k) (or the corresponding subsection of prior law),

"(ii) who became an employee of such organization after the calendar quarter in which the certificate (other than a certificate referred to in clause (iii)) was filed (or deemed to have been filed) or

"(iii) who, after the calendar quarter in which the certificate was filed (or deemed to have been filed) with respect to a group described in section 3121(k)(1)(E), became a member of such group,

except that this subparagraph shall apply with respect to service performed by an employee as a member of a group described in section 3121(k)(1)(E) with respect to which no certificate is (or is deemed to be) in effect;"

Prior to repeal, subsec. (k) read as follows:

"(k) Exemption of religious, charitable, and certain other organizations.

"(1) Waiver of exemption by organization.

"(A) An organization described in section 501(c)(3) which is exempt from income tax under section 501(a) may file a certificate (in such form and manner, and with such official, as may be prescribed by regulations made under this chapter) certifying that it desires to have the insurance system established by title II of the Social Security Act extended to service performed by its employees. Such certificate may be filed only if it is accompanied by a list containing the signature, address, and social security account number (if any) of each employee (if any) who concurs in the filing of the certificate. Such list may be amended at any time prior to the expiration of the twenty-fourth month following the calendar quarter in which the certificate is filed by filing with the prescribed official a supplemental list or lists containing the signature, address, and social security account number (if any) of each additional employee who concurs in the filing of the certificate. The list and any supplemental list shall be filed in such form and manner as may be prescribed by regulations made under this chapter.

"(B) The certificate shall be in effect (for purposes of subsection (b)(8)(B) and for purposes of section 210(a)(8)(B) of the Social Security Act) for the period beginning with whichever of the following may be designated by the organization:

"(i) the first day of the calendar quarter in which the certificate is filed,

"(ii) the first day of the calendar quarter succeeding such quarter, or

"(iii) the first day of any calendar quarter preceding the calendar quarter in which the certificate is filed, except that, such date may not be earlier than the first day of the twentieth calendar quarter preceding the quarter in which such certificate is filed.

"(C) In the case of service performed by an employee whose name appears on a supplemental list filed after the first month following the calendar quarter in which the certificate is filed, the certificate shall be in effect (for purposes of subsection (b)(8)(B) and for purposes of section 210(a)(8)(B) of the Social Security Act) only with respect to service performed by such individual for the period beginning with the first day of the calendar quarter in which such supplemental list is filed.

"(D) The period for which a certificate filed pursuant to this subsection or the corresponding subsection of prior law is effective may be terminated by the organization, effective at the end of a calendar quarter, upon giving 2 years' advance notice in writing, but only if, at the time of the receipt of such notice, the certificate has been in effect for a period of not less than 8 years. The notice of termination may be revoked by the organization by giving, prior to the close of the calendar quarter specified in the notice of termination, a written notice of such revocation. Notice of termination or revocation. Notice of termination or revocation thereof shall be filed in such form and manner, and with such official, as may be prescribed by regulations made under this chapter.

"(E) If an organization described in subparagraph (A) employs both individuals who are in positions covered by a pension, annuity, retirement, or similar fund or system established by a State or by a political subdivision thereof and individuals who are not in such positions the organization shall divide its employees into two separate groups. One group shall consist of all employees who are in positions covered by such a fund or system and (i) are members of such fund or system, or (ii) are not members of such fund or system but are eligible to become members thereof; and the other group shall consist of all remaining employees. An organization which has so divided its employees into two groups may file a certificate pursuant to subparagraph (A) with respect to the employees in either group, or may file a separate certificate pursuant to such subparagraph with respect to the employees in each group.

"(F) If a certificate filed pursuant to this paragraph is effective for one or more calendar quarters prior to the quarter in which the certificate is filed, then—

"(i) for purposes of computing interest and for purposes of section 6651 (relating to addition to tax for failure to file tax return or pay tax), the due date for the return and payment of the tax for such prior calendar quarters resulting from the filing of such certificate shall be the last day of the calendar month following the calendar quarter in which the certificate is filed; and

"(ii) the statutory period for the assessment of such tax shall not expire before the expiration of 3 years from such due date.

"(2) Termination of waiver period by Secretary. If the Secretary finds that any organization which filed a certificate pursuant to this subsection or the corresponding subsection of prior law has failed to comply substantially with the requirements applicable with respect to the taxes imposed by this chapter or the corresponding provisions of prior law or is no longer able to comply with the requirements applicable with respect to the taxes imposed by this chapter, the Secretary shall give such organization not less than 60 days' advance notice in writing that the period covered by such certificate will terminate at the end of the calendar quarter specified in such notice. Such notice of termination may be revoked by the Secretary by giving, prior to the close of the calendar quarter specified in the notice of termination, written notice of such revocation to the organization. No notice of termination or of revocation thereof shall be given under this paragraph to an organization without the prior concurrence of the Secretary of Health, Education, and Welfare.

Employment taxes Code Sec. 3121

"(3) No renewal of waiver. In the event the period covered by a certificate filed pursuant to this subsection or the corresponding subsection of prior law is terminated by the organization, no certificate may again be filed by such organization pursuant to this subsection.

"(4) Constructive filing of certificate where no refund or credit of taxes has been made.

"(A) In any case where—

"(i) an organization described in section 501(c)(3) which is exempt from income tax under section 501(a) has not filed a valid waiver certificate under paragraph (1) of this subsection (or under the corresponding provision of prior law) as of the date of the enactment of this paragraph or, if later, as of the earliest date on which it satisfies clause (ii) of this subparagraph, but

"(ii) the taxes imposed by sections 3101 and 3111 have been paid with respect to the remuneration paid by such organization to its employees, as though such a certificate had been filed, during any period (subject to subparagraph (B)(i)) of not less than three consecutive calendar quarters,

such organization shall be deemed (except as provided in subparagraph (B) of this paragraph) for purposes of subsection (b)(8)(B) and section 210(a)(8)(B) of the Social Security Act, to have filed a valid waiver certificate under paragraph (1) of this subsection (or under the corresponding provision of prior law) on the first day of the period described in clause (ii) of this subparagraph effective (subject to subparagraph (C)) on the first day of the calendar quarter in which such period began, and to have accompanied such certificate with a list containing the signature, address, and social security number (if any) of each employee with respect to whom the taxes described in such subparagraph were paid (and each such employee shall be deemed for such purposes to have concurred in the filing of the certificate).

"(B) Subparagraph (A) shall not apply with respect to any organization if—

"(i) the period referred to in clause (ii) of such subparagraph (in the case of that organization) terminated before the end of the earliest calendar quarter falling wholly or partly within the time limitation (as defined in section 205(c)(1)(B) of the Social Security Act) immediately preceding the date of the enactment of this paragraph, or

"(ii) a refund or credit of any part of the taxes which were paid as described in clause (ii) of such subparagraph with respect to remuneration for services performed on or after the first day of the earliest calendar quarter falling wholly or partly within the time limitation (as defined in section 205(c)(1)(B) of the Social Security Act) immediately preceding the first day of the calendar quarter of enactment of this paragraph (other than a refund or credit which would have been allowed if a valid waiver certificate filed under paragraph (1) had been in effect) has been obtained by the organization or its employees prior to September 9, 1976; or

"(iii) the organization, prior to the end of the period referred to in clause (ii) of such subparagraph (and, in the case of an organization organized on or before October 9, 1969, prior to October 19, 1976), had applied for a ruling or determination letter acknowledging it to be exempt from income tax under section 501(c)(3), and it subsequently received such ruling or determination letter and did not pay any taxes under sections 3101 and 3111 with respect to any employee with respect to any quarter ending after the twelfth month following the date of mailing of such ruling or determination letter and did not pay any such taxes with respect to any quarter beginning after the later of (I) December 31, 1975 or (II) the date on which such ruling or determination letter was issued.

"(C) In the case of any organization which is deemed under this paragraph to have filed a valid waiver certificate under paragraph (1), if—

"(i) the period with respect to which the taxes imposed by sections 3101 and 3111 were paid by such organization (as described in subparagraph (A)(ii)) terminated prior to October 1, 1976, or

"(ii) the taxes imposed by sections 3101 and 3111 were not paid during the period referred to in clause (i) (whether such period has terminated or not) with respect to remuneration paid by such organization to individuals who became its employees after the close of the calendar quarter in which such period began,

taxes under sections 3101 and 3111—

"(iii) in the case of an organization which meets the requirements of this subparagraph by reason of clause (i), with respect to remuneration paid by such organization after the termination of the period referred to in clause (i) and prior to July 1, 1977; or

"(iv) in the case of an organization which meets the requirements of this subparagraph by reason of clause (ii), with respect to remuneration paid prior to July 1, 1977, to individuals who became its employees after the close of the calendar quarter in which the period referred to in clause (i) began,

which remain unpaid on the date of the enactment of this subparagraph, or which were paid after October 19, 1976, but prior to the date of the enactment of this subparagraph, shall not be due or payable (or, if paid, shall be refunded); and the certificate which such organization is deemed under this paragraph to have filed shall not apply to any service with respect to the remuneration for which the taxes imposed by sections 3101 and 3111 (which remain unpaid on the date of the enactment of this subparagraph, or were paid after October 19, 1976, but prior to the date of the enactment of this subparagraph) are not due and payable (or are refunded) by reason of the preceding provisions of this subparagraph. In applying this subparagraph for purposes of title II of the Social Security Act, the period during which reports of wages subject to the taxes imposed by sections 3101 and 3111 were made by any organization may be conclusively treated as the period (described in subparagraph (A)(ii)) during which the taxes imposed by such sections were paid by such organization.

"(5) Constructive filing of certificate where refund or credit has been made and new certificate is not filed. In any case where—

"(A) an organization described in section 501(c)(3) which is exempt from income tax under section 501(a) would be deemed under paragraph (4) of this subsection to have filed a valid waiver certificate under paragraph (1) if it were not excluded from such paragraph (4) (pursuant to subparagraph (B)(ii) thereof) because a refund or credit of all or a part of the taxes described in paragraph (4)(A)(ii) was obtained prior to September 9, 1976; and

"(B) such organization has not, prior to April 1, 1978, filed a valid waiver certificate under paragraph (1) which is effective for a period beginning on or before the first day of the first calendar quarter with respect to which such refund or credit was made (or, if later, with the first day of the earliest calendar quarter for which such certificate may be in effect under paragraph (1)(B)(iii)) and which is accompanied by the list described in paragraph (1)(A),

such organization shall be deemed, for purposes of subsection (b)(8)(B) and section 210(a)(8)(B) of the Social Security Act, to have filed a valid waiver certificate under paragraph (1) of this subsection on April 1, 1978, effective for the period beginning on the first day of the first calendar quarter with respect to which the refund or credit referred to in subparagraph (A) of this paragraph was made (or, if later, with the first day of the earliest calendar quarter falling wholly or partly within the time limitation (as defined in section 205(c)(1)(B) of the Social Security Act) immediately preceding the date of the enactment of this paragraph), and to have accompanied such certificate with a list containing the signature, address, and social security number (if any) of each employee described in subparagraph (A) of paragraph (4) including any employee with respect to whom taxes were refunded or credited as described in subparagraph (A) of this paragraph (and each such employee shall be deemed for such purposes to have concurred in the filing of the certificate). A certificate which is deemed to have been filed by an organization on April 1, 1978, shall supersede any certificate which may have been actually filed by such organization prior to that day except to the extent prescribed by the Secretary.

"(6) Application of certain provisions to cases of constructive filing. All of the provisions of this subsection (other than subparagraphs (B), (F), and (H) of paragraph (1)), including the provisions requiring payment of taxes under sections 3101 and 3111 with respect to the services involved (except as provided in paragraph 4(C)), shall apply with respect to any certificate which is deemed to have been filed by an organization on any day under paragraph (4) or (5), in the same way they would apply if the certificate had been actually filed on that day under paragraph (1); except that—

"(A) the provisions relating to the filing of supplemental lists of concurring employees in the third sentence of paragraph (1)(A), and in paragraph (1)(C), shall apply to the extent prescribed by the Secretary;

"(B) the provisions of paragraph (1)(E) shall not apply unless the taxes described in paragraph (4)(A)(ii) were paid by the organization as though a separate certificate had been filed with respect to one or both of the groups to which such provisions relate; and

"(C) the action of the organization in obtaining the refund or credit described in paragraph (5)(A) shall not be considered a termination of such organization's coverage period for purposes of paragraph (3). Any organization which is deemed to have filed a waiver certificate under paragraph (4) or (5) shall be considered for purposes of section 3102(b) to have been required to deduct the taxes imposed by section 3101 with respect to the services involved.

"(7) Both employee and employer taxes payable by organization for retroactive period in cases of constructive filing. Notwithstanding any other provision of this chapter, in any case where an organization described in paragraph (5)(A) has not filed a valid waiver certificate under paragraph (1) prior to April 1, 1978, and is accordingly deemed under paragraph (5) to have filed such a certificate on the 181st day after such date, the taxes due under section 3101, with respect to services constituting employment by reason of such certificate for any period prior to that date (along with the taxes due under section 3111 with respect to such services and the amount of any interest paid in connection with the refund or credit described in paragraph (5)(A)) shall be paid by such organization from its own funds and without any deduction from the wages of the individuals who performed such services; and those individuals shall have no liability for the payment of such taxes.

"(8) Extended period for payment of taxes for retroactive coverage. Notwithstanding any other provision of this title, in any case where—

"(A) an organization is deemed under paragraph (4) to have filed a valid waiver certificate under paragraph (1), but the applicable period described in paragraph (4)(A)(ii) has terminated and part or all of the taxes imposed by sections 3101 and 3111 with respect to remuneration paid by such organization to its employees after the close of such period remains payable notwithstanding paragraph (4)(C), or

"(B) an organization described in paragraph (5)(A) files a valid waiver certificate under paragraph (1) by March 31, 1978, as described in paragraph (5)(B), or (not having filed such a certificate by that date) is deemed under paragraph (5) to have filed such a certificate on April 1, 1978, or

"(C) an individual files a request under Sec. 3 of P. L. 94-563, or under section 312(c) of the Social Security Amendments of 1977, to have service treated as constituting remuneration for employment (as defined in section 3121(b) and in section 210(a) of the Social Security Act),

the taxes due under sections 3101 and 3111 with respect to services constituting employment by reason of such certificate for any period prior to the first day of the calendar quarter in which the date of such filing or constructive filing occurs, or with respect to service constituting employment by reason of such request, may be paid in installments over an appropriate period of time, as determined under regulations prescribed by the Secretary, rather than in a lump sum."

Prior to deletion, para. (r)(4) read as follows:

"(4) Coordination with coverage of lay employees. Notwithstanding the preceding provisions of this subsection, no certificate of election shall become effective with respect to an order or subdivision thereof, unless—

"(A) if at the time the certificate of election is filed a certificate of waiver of exemption under subsection (k) is in effect with respect to such order or subdivision, such order or subdivision amends such certificate of waiver of exemption (in such form and manner as may be prescribed by regulations made under this chapter) to provide that it may not be revoked, or

"(B) if at the time the certificate of election is filed a certificate of waiver of exemption under such subsection is not in effect with respect to such order or subdivision, such order or subdivision files such certificate of waiver of exemption under the provisions of such subsection except that such certificate of waiver of exemption cannot become effective at a later date than the certificate of election and such certificate of waiver of exemption must specify that such certificate of waiver of exemption may not be revoked. The certificate of waiver of exemption required under this subparagraph shall be filed notwithstanding the provisions of subsection (k)(3)."

—P.L. 98-21, Sec. 102(d), and (e) provide as follows:

"(d) The period for which a certificate is in effect under section 3121(k) of the Internal Revenue Code of 1954 may not be terminated under paragraph (1)(D) or (2) thereof on or after March 31, 1983; but no such certificate shall be effective with respect to any service to which the amendments made by this section apply.

"(e)(1) If any individual—

"(A) on January 1, 1984, is age 55 or over, and is an employee of an organization described in section 210(a)(8)(B) of the Social Security Act (A) which does not have in effect (on that date) a waiver certificate under section 3121(k) of the Internal Revenue Code of 1954 and (B) to the employees of which social security coverage is extended on January 1, 1984, solely by reason of the enactment of this section, and

"(B) after December 31, 1983, acquires the number of quarters of coverage (within the meaning of section 213 of the Social Security Act) which is required for purposes of this subparagraph under paragraph (2),

then such individual shall be deemed to be a fully insured individual (as defined in section 214 of the Social Security Act) for all of the purposes of title II of such Act.

"(2) The number of quarters of coverage which is required for purposes of subparagraph (B) of paragraph (1) shall be determined as follows:

"In the case of an individual who on January 1, 1984, is—	The number of quarters of— coverage so required shall be—
age 60 or over	6
age 59 or over but less than age 60	8
age 58 or over but less than age 59	12
age 57 or over but less than age 58	16
age 55 or over but less than age 57	20."

—P.L. 98-21, Sec. 125, provides:

"SEC. 125. TREATMENT OF CERTAIN FACULTY PRACTICE PLANS.

"(a) General Rule. For purposes of subsection (s) of section 3121 of the Internal Revenue Code of 1954 (relating to concurrent employment by 2 or more employers)—

"(1) the following entities shall be deemed to be related corporations:

"(A) a State university which employs health professionals as faculty members at a medical school, and

"(B) a faculty practice plan described in section 501(c)(3) of such Code and exempt from tax under section 501(a) of such Code—

"(i) which employs faculty members of such medical school, and

"(ii) 30 percent or more of the employees of which are concurrently employed by such medical school; and

"(2) remuneration which is disbursed by such faculty practice plan to a health professional employed by both such entities shall be deemed to have been actually disbursed by such university as a common paymaster and not to have been actually disbursed by such faculty practice plan.

"(b) Effective date. The provisions of subsection (a) shall apply to remuneration paid after December 31, 1983."

—P.L. 98-21, Sec. 321(a)(1), amended the heading of subsec. (1) and so much of para. (l)(1) that precedes the second sentence . . . Sec. 321(a)(2), amended para. (l)(8) . . . Sec. 321(e)(1), substituted "American employer" for "domestic corporation", "American employers" for "domestic corporations", "affiliate" for "subsidiary", "affiliates" for "subsidiaries", "foreign entity" for "foreign corporation", "foreign entities" for "foreign corporations" "citizens or residents" for "citizens" and "an American employer" for "a domestic corporation" each place it appeared in subsec. (1), effective as provided in Sec. 321(f)(1)(A) and (B) of this Act which reads as follows:

"(f)(1)(A) The amendments made by this section [Sec. 321] (other than subsection (d)) shall apply to agreements entered into after the date of the enactment of this Act [4/20/83].

"(B) At the election of any American employer, the amendments made by this section (other than subsection (d)) shall also apply to any agreement entered into on or before the date of the enactment of this Act [4/20/83]. Any such election shall be made at such time and in such manner as the Secretary may by regulations prescribe."

Prior to amendment, the heading of subsec. (1) and so much of para. (l)(1) that precedes the second sentence read as follows:

"(l) Agreements entered into by domestic corporations with respect to foreign subsidiaries.

"(1) Agreement with respect to certain employees of foreign subsidiaries. The Secretary shall, at the request of any domestic corporation, enter into an agreement (in such form and manner as may be prescribed by the Secretary) with any such corporation which desires to have the insurance system established by title II of the Social Security Act extended to service performed outside the United States in the employ of any one or more of its foreign subsidiaries (as defined in paragraph (8)) by all employees who are citizens of the United States, except that the agreement shall not be applicable to any service performed by, or remuneration paid to, an employee if such service or remuneration would be excluded from the term 'employment' or 'wages', as defined in this section, had the service been performed in the United States."

Prior to amendment, para. (l)(8) read as follows:

"(8) Definition of foreign subsidiary. For purposes of this subsection and section 210(a) of the Social Security Act, a foreign subsidiary of a domestic corporation is—

"(A) a foreign corporation not less than 20 percent of the voting stock of which is owned by such domestic corporation; or

"(B) a foreign corporation more than 50 percent of the voting stock of which is owned by the foreign corporation described in subparagraph (A)."

—P.L. 98-21, Sec. 322(a)(2)(A), deleted "either" before "(A)" . . . Sec. 322(a)(2)(B), added ", or (C) if it is service, regardless of where or by whom performed, which is designated as employment or recognized as equivalent to employment under an agreement entered into under section 233 of the Social Security Act" before "; except" in the matter preceding para. (b)(1), effective for tax. yrs. begin. on or after 4/20/83.

—P.L. 98-21, Sec. 323(a)(1), substituted "a citizen or resident of the United States" for "a citizen of the United States" in the matter preceding para. (b)(1), effective for remuneration paid after 12/31/83.

—P.L. 98-21, Sec. 324(a)(1), added subsec. (v) . . . Sec. 324(a)(2)(A), deleted "or" at the end of subpara. (a)(5)(C) . . . Sec. 324(a)(2)(B), substituted a comma for the semicolon at the end of subpara. (a)(5)(D) . . . Sec. 324(a)(2)(C), added subparas. (a)(5)(E), (F) and (G) . . . Sec. 324(a)(3)(A), deleted subpara. (a)(2)(A) and redesignated subparas. (a)(2)(B), (C), and (D) as subparas. (a)(2)(A), (B), and (C) . . . Sec. 324(a)(3)(B), deleted paras. (a)(3) and (a)(9) . . . Sec. 324(a)(3)(C), added "or" after "death," in subpara. (a)(13)(A) and deleted "or (iii) retirement after attaining an age specified in the plan referred to in subparagraph (B) or in a pension plan of the employer," in subpara. (a)(13)(A) . . . Sec. 324(a)(3)(D), substituted "subparagraph (A)" for "subparagraph (B)" in the last sentence of subsec. (a), effective [as amended by Sec. 2662(f)(2)(A) of P. L. 94-369, see above] as provided in Sec. 324(d)(1), (d)(3), and (d)(4) of this Act, which read as follows:

"(d)(1) Except as otherwise provided in this subsection, the amendments made by this section shall apply to remuneration paid after December 31, 1983. For purposes of applying such amendments to remuneration paid after December 31, 1983, which would have been taken into account before January 1, 1984, if such amendments had applied to periods before January 1, 1984, such remuneration shall be taken into account when paid (or, at the election of the payor, at the time which would be paid appropriate if such amendments had applied).

* * *

"(3) The amendments made by this section shall not apply to employer contributions made during 1984 and attributable to services performed during 1983 under a qualified cash or deferred arrangement (as defined in section 401(k) of the Internal Revenue Code of 1954) if, under the terms of such arrangement as in effect on March 24, 1983—

"(A) the employee makes an election with respect to such contribution before January 1, 1984, and

"(B) the employer identifies the amount of such contribution before January 1, 1984.

In the case of the amendments made by subsection (b), the preceding sentence shall be applied by substituting '1985' for '1984' each place it appears and by substituting 'during 1984' for 'during 1983'.

"(4) In the case of an agreement in existence on March 24, 1983, between a nonqualified deferred compensation plan (as defined in section 3121(v)(2)(C) of the Internal Revenue Code of 1954, as added by this section) and an individual—

"(A) the amendments made by this section (other than subsection (b)) shall apply with respect to services performed by such individual after December 31, 1983, and

"(B) the amendments made by subsection (b) shall apply with respect to services performed by such individual after December 31, 1984.

The preceding sentence shall not apply in the case of a plan to which section 457(a) of such Code applies. For purposes of this paragraph, any plan or agreement to make payments described in paragraph (2), (3), or (13)(A)(iii) of section 3121(a) of such Code (as in effect on the day before the date of the enactment of this Act) shall be treated as a nonqualified deferred compensation plan."

Prior to deletion, subpara. (a)(2)(A) read as follows:

"(A) retirement, or"

Prior to deletion, para. (a)(3) read as follows:

"(3) any payment made to an employee (including any amount paid by an employer for insurance or annuities, or into a fund, to provide for any such payment) on account of retirement;"

Prior to deletion, para. (a)(9) read as follows:

"(9) any payment (other than vacation or sick pay) made to an employee after the month in which he attains age 62, if such employee did not work for the employer in the period for which such payment is made;"

—P.L. 98-21, Sec. 327(a)(1), deleted "or" at the end of para. (a)(17), substituted "; or" for the period at the end of para. (a)(18), and added para. (a)(19), effective [as amended by Sec. 2662(g) of P. L. 98-369, see above] for remuneration paid after 12/31/83.

"(d)(1) The amendment made by subsection (a) [Sec. 327] shall apply to remuneration paid after December 31, 1983."

—P.L. 98-21, Sec. 327(b)(1), added "Nothing in the regulations prescribed for purposes of chapter 24 of the Internal Revenue Code of 1954 (relating to income tax withholding) which provides an exclusion from 'wages' as used in such chapter shall be construed to require a similar exclusion from 'wages' in the regulations prescribed for purposes of this title." after para. (a)(19), effective as provided in Sec. 327(d)(2) [as amended by Sec. 2662(g) of P. L. 98-369, see above] of this Act, which reads as follows:

"(2) The amendments made by subsection (b) and subsection (c)(4) [Sec. 327] shall apply to remuneration (other than amounts excluded under section 119 of the Internal Revenue Code of 1954) paid after March 4, 1983, and to any such remuneration paid on or before such date which the employer treated as wages when paid."

—P.L. 98-21, Sec. 328(a), substituted "section 219(b)(2)" for "section 219" in subpara (a)(5)(D), effective for remuneration paid after 12/31/83.

In 1982, P.L. 97-248, Sec. 278(a)(1), added subsec. (u), effective for remuneration paid after 12/31/82.

In 1981, P.L. 97-123, Sec. 3(b)(1), amended subpara. (a)(2)(B) . . . Sec. 3(b)(2), added the sentence at the end of subsec. (a), effective for remuneration paid after 12/31/81 except as provided in Sec. 3(g)(2) of this Act, which reads as follows:

"(2) This section (and the amendments made by this section) shall not apply with respect to any payment made by a third party to an employee pursuant to a contractual relationship of an employer with such third party entered into before December 14, 1981, if—

"(A) coverage by such third party for the group in which such employee falls ceases before March 1, 1982, and

"(B) no payment by such third party is made to such employee under such relationship after February 28, 1982."

Prior to amendment, subpara. (a)(2)(B) read as follows:

"(B) sickness or accident disability, or"

—P.L. 97-123, Sec. 3(d)(1), and (2) provides:

"(d)(1) The regulations prescribed under the last sentence of section 3121(a) of the Internal Revenue Code of 1954, and the regulations prescribed under subparagraph (D) of section 3231(e)(4) of such Code, shall provide procedures under which, if (with respect to any employee) the third party promptly—

"(A) withholds the employee portion of the taxes involved,

"(B) deposits such portion under section 6302 of such Code, and

"(C) notifies the employer of the amount of the wages or compensation involved,

the employer (and not the third party) shall be liable for the employer portion of the taxes involved and for meeting the requirements of section 6051 of such Code (relating to receipts for employees) with respects to the wages or compensation involved.

"(2) For purposes of paragraph (1)—

"(A) the term 'employer' means the employer for whom services are normally rendered,

"(B) the term 'taxes involved' means, in the case of any employee, the taxes under chapters 21 and 22 which are payable solely by reason of the parenthetical matter contained in subparagraph (B) of section 3121(a)(2) of such Code, or solely by reason of paragraph (4) of section 3231(e) of such Code, and

"(C) the term 'wages or compensation involved' means, in the case of any employee, wages or compensation with respect to which taxes described in subparagraph (B) are imposed."

—P.L. 97-34, Sec. 124(e)(2), substituted "section 127 or 129" for "section 127" in para. (a)(18), effective for remuneration paid after 12/31/81.

In 1980, P.L. 96-605, Sec. 401, provides:

"SEC. 401. TREATMENT OF CERTAIN SOCIAL SECURITY TAX WAIVER EXEMPTIONS.

"(a) Waiver certificate.

"(1) In general. Notwithstanding any other provision of law, any waiver certificate filed by a qualified corporation (hereinafter in this section referred to as the 'corporation') under section 3121(k)(1) of the Internal Revenue Code of 1954 (relating to waiver of exemption from social security taxes by certain organizations) shall be deemed not to be effective, for purposes of the taxes imposed by section 3101 of such Code, with respect to any wages—

"(A) paid by the Corporation to any employee thereof after December 31, 1972, and before April 1, 1975, if the Corporation furnishes to the Secretary of the Treasury or his delegate evidence reasonably satisfactory to him that the corporation as refunded, prior to February 1, 1977, to such employee (or to his survivors or estate) the full amount of the taxes imposed by section 3101 of such Code on such wages, or

"(B) paid after March 31, 1975, and prior to July 1, 1977, by the Corporation to an individual as an employee of the Corporation, if the Corporation furnishes to the Secretary of the Treasury or his delegate evidence reasonably satisfactory to him that (i) such individual was not an employee of the Corporation on June 30, 1978, and (ii) no amount of the taxes imposed by section 3101 of such Code on such wages were withheld by the Corporation from such wages.

"(2) Application of paragraph (1).—

"(A) Evidence to be submitted to secretary. The provisions of paragraph (1) shall not apply to wages described in subparagraph (A) or (B) of such paragraph unless, prior to the close of the one-year period which begins on the date of the enactment of this Act, the Corporation furnishes to the Secretary of the Treasury or his delegate the evidence referred to in either such subparagraph.

"(B) Tax not imposed. If the provisions of paragraph (1) apply with respect to any wages paid by the Corporation to an employee thereof, no taxes imposed on such wages by section 3101 of the Internal Revenue Code of 1954 shall be payable, and no interest or penalty with respect to the imposition of taxes by such section on such wages (or with respect to the imposition of taxes by such section or section 3111 of such Code on any wages paid by the Corporation prior to January 1, 1978) shall be imposed or collected.

"(C) Credit against tax. Under regulations prescribed by the Secretary, there shall be allowed as a one-time credit against the tax imposed on the Corporation under section 3101 or 3111 of the Internal Revenue Code of 1954 (and any interest or penalties imposed thereon) an amount equal to the sum of—

"(i) all amounts of tax imposed by section 3101 of such Code which have been paid by the Corporation with respect to wages to which paragraph (1) applies, and

"(ii) all amounts paid by such Corporation as a penalty on or interest with respect to the tax imposed by section 3101 or 3111 of such Code on such wages.

"(b) Treatment for purposes of Social Security Act.

"In the administration of titles II and XVIII of the Social Security Act, any wages paid to any individual to which the provisions of subsection (a) apply shall be treated as wages (within the meaning of section 209 of such Act) for purposes of determining—

"(1) entitlement to, or amount of, any insurance benefit payable to such individual or any other person on the basis of the wages and self-employment income of such individual, or

"(2) entitlement of such individual to benefits under title XVIII of such Act or entitlement of any other person to such benefits on the basis of the wages and self-employment income of such individual.

"(c) Qualified corporation defined.

"For purposes of this section, the term 'qualified corporation' means any corporation which—

"(1) filed a waiver certificate under section 3121 of the Internal Revenue Code of 1954 during 1968;

"(2) filed a second waiver certificate under such section during 1975 believing that no other waiver certificate had been filed;

"(3) received a refund of the taxes imposed by sections 3101 and 3111 of such Code with respect to certain wages paid to more than 120 but less than 180 employees who did not concur in the filing of the second waiver certificate; and

"(4) was notified during 1977 by the Internal Revenue Service that the certificate had been filed during 1968.

"(d) Liability for taxes.

"Except as provided in subsection (a)(2)(C)(ii), nothing in this section shall be construed to relieve the Corporation of any liability for the payment of the taxes imposed by section 3111 of the Internal Revenue Code of 1954 with respect to any wages paid by it to any individual for any period."

—P.L. 96-499, Sec. 1141(a)(1), amended para. (a)(6), effective for remuneration paid after 12/31/80 except as provided in Sec. 1141(c)(2) of this Act, which provides:

"(2) Exception for state and local governments.

"(A) The amendments made by this section (insofar as they affect the application of section 218 of the Social Security Act) shall not apply to any payment made before January 1, 1984, by any governmental unit for positions of a kind for which all or a substantial portion of the social security employee taxes were paid by such governmental unit (without deduction from the remuneration of the employee) under the practices of such governmental unit in effect on October 1, 1980.

"(B) For purposes of subparagraph (A) the term 'social security employee taxes' means the amount required to be paid under section 218 of the Social Security Act as the equivalent of the taxes imposed by section 3101 of the Internal Revenue Code of 1954.

"(C) For purposes of subparagraph (A), the term 'Governmental unit' means a State or political subdivision thereof within the meaning of section 218 of the Social Security Act."

Prior to amendment, para (a)(6) read as follows:

"(6) the payment by an employer (without deduction from the remuneration of the employee)—

"(A) of the tax imposed upon an employee under section 3101 (or the corresponding section of prior law), or

"(B) of any payment required from an employee under a State unemployment compensation law;"

—P.L. 96-222, Sec. 101(a)(10)(B)(i), deleted "or" at the end of subpara. (a)(5)(B), substituted ", or" for the semicolon at the end of subpara. (a)(5)(C) and added subpara. (a)(5)(D), effective for payments made on or after 1/1/79.

In 1978, P.L. 95-600, Sec. 164(b)(3)(A), deleted "or" at the end of para. (a)(16) . . . Sec. 164(b)(3)(B), substituted "; or" for the period at the end of para. (a)(17) . . . Sec. 164(b)(3)(C), added para. (a)(18), effective for tax. yrs. begin. after 12/31/78.

—P.L. 95-600, Sec. 701(z)(1), substituted "December 31, 1954" for "December 31, 1971" each place it appeared in Sec. 1207(f)(4)(B) of P. L. 94-455, the effective date for amendments made by Sec. 1207(e)(1)(A) [see below], effective 10/4/76.

—P.L. 95-472, Sec. 3(b)(1), deleted "or" at the end of para. (a)(16) . . . Sec. 3(b)(2), substituted "; or" for the period at the end of para. (a)(16) . . . Sec. 3(b)(3), added para. (a)(17), effective for tax. yrs. begin. after 12/31/76.

In 1977, P.L. 95-216, Sec. 312(a)(1)(A), substituted "prior to April 1, 1978," for "prior to the expiration of 180 days after the date of the enactment of this paragraph," in subpara. (k)(5)(8) . . . Sec. 312(a)(1)(B), substituted "April 1, 1978," for "the 181st day after the date of the enactment of this paragraph," and "such 181st day" in the matter following subpara. (k)(5)(B) . . . Sec. 312(a)(2)(A), substituted "prior to April 1, 1978," for "prior to the expiration of 180 days after the date of the enactment of this paragraph" in para. (k)(7) . . . Sec. 312(a)(2)(B), substituted "April 1, 1978," for "the 181st day after such date" in para. (k)(7) . . . Sec. 312(a)(2)(C), substituted "prior to that date" for "prior to the first day of the calendar quarter in which such 181st day occurs" in para. (k)(7) . . . Sec. 312(a)(3)(A), substituted "prior to April 1, 1978," for "by the end of the 180-day period following the date of the enactment of this paragraph" in para. (k)(8) . . . Sec. 312(a)(3)(B), substituted "prior to April 1, 1978" for "within that period" in para. (k)(8) . . . Sec. 312(a)(3)(C), substituted "on that date" for "on the 181st day

3,089

following that date" in para. (k)(8) . . . Sec. 312(b)(1), added subpara. (k)(4)(C) . . . Sec. 312(b)(2), added "(subject to subparagraph (C))" following "effective" in the matter following clause (k)(4)(A)(ii) . . . Sec. 312(b)(3), added "(except as provided in paragraph (4)(C))" following "services involved" in the matter preceding subpara. (k)(6)(A) . . . Sec. 312(b)(4), substituted "first day of the calendar quarter" for "date" following "immediately preceding the" in clause (k)(4)(B)(ii) . . . Sec. 312(d), amended para. (k)(8) [as amended by Sec. 312(a)(3) of this Act, see above], effective as provided in Sec. 312(h), reproduced below.

Prior to amendment, para. (k)(8) read as follows:

"(8) Extended period for payment of taxes for retroactive coverage. Notwithstanding any other provision of this title, in any case where an organization described in paragraph (5)(A) files a valid waiver certificate under paragraph (1) prior to April 1, 1978, as described in paragraph (5)(B), or (not having filed such a certificate prior to April 1, 1978) is deemed under paragraph (5) to have filed such a certificate on that date, the taxes due under sections 3101 and 3111 with respect to services constituting employment by reason of such certificate for any period prior to the first day of the calendar quarter in which the date of such filing or constructive filing occurs may be paid in installments over an appropriate period of time, as determined under regulations prescribed by the Secretary, rather than in a lump sum."

—P.L. 95-216, Sec. 312(e)(1), added "on or before April 15, 1980," after "filed" in the matter following para. (3) of Sec. 3 of P. L. 94-563 . . . Sec. 312(e)(2), added "(or by satisfactory evidence that appropriate arrangements have been made for the repayment of such taxes in installments as provided in section 3121(k)(8) of such Code)" after "so refunded or credited" in the matter following para. (3) of P. L. 94-563, the effective date for amendments made by Sec. 1 of P. L. 94-563, see below.

—P.L. 95-216, Sec. 312(f), substituted "(or, if later, as of the earliest date on which it satisfies clause (ii) of this subparagraph.)" for "or any subsequent date" in clause (k)(4)(A)(i). . . . Sec. 312(g)(1), substituted ", or" for the period at the end of clause (k)(4)(B)(ii) . . . Sec. 312(g)(2), added clause (k)(4)(B)(iii), effective as provided in Sec. 312(h) of this Act, which reads as follows:

"(h) The amendments made by subsections (a), (b), (d), (e), (f), and (g) of this section shall be effective as though they had been included as a part of the amendments made to section 3121(k) of the Internal Revenue Code of 1954 by the first section of P. L. 94-563 (or, in the case of the amendments made by subsection (e), as a part of section 3 of such Public Law)."

—P.L. 95-216, Sec. 312(c), of this Act, provides:

"(c) In any case where—

"(1) an individual performed service, as an employee of an organization which is deemed under section 3121(k)(4) of the Internal Revenue Code of 1954 to have filed a waiver certificate under section 3121(k)(1) of such Code, on or after the first day of the applicable period described in subparagraph (a)(ii) of such section 3121(k)(4) and before July 1, 1977; and

"(2) the service so performed does not constitute employment (as defined in section 210(a) of the Social Security Act and section 3121(b) of such Code) because the waiver certificate which the organization is deemed to have filed is made inapplicable to such service by section 3121(k)(4)(C) of such Code, but would constitute employment (as so defined) in the absence of such section 3121(k)(4)(C).

the remuneration paid for such service shall, upon the request of such individual (filed on or before April 15, 1980, in such manner and form, and with such official, as may be prescribed by regulations made under title II of the Social Security Act) accompanied by full payment of all of the taxes which would have been paid under section 3101 of such Code with respect to such remuneration but for such section 3121(k)(4)(C) (or by satisfactory evidence that appropriate arrangements have been made for the payment of such taxes in installments as provided in section 3121(k)(8) of such Code), be deemed to constitute remuneration for employment as so defined. In any case where remuneration paid by an organization to an individual is deemed under the preceding sentence to constitute remuneration for employment, such organization shall be liable (notwithstanding any other provision of such Code) for payment of the taxes which it would have been required to pay under section 3111 of such Code with respect to such remuneration in the absence of such section 3121(k)(4)(C)."

—P.L. 95-216, Sec. 314(a), added subsec. (s), effective for wages paid after 12/31/78.

—P.L. 95-216, Sec. 315(a), added subsec. (t), effective for wages paid with respect to employment performed in months after 1977.

—P.L. 95-216, Sec. 356(a), substituted "year" for "quarter" and substituted "$100" for "$50" each place they appeared in subpara. (a)(7)(C) and para. (a)(10) . . . Sec. 356(b), deleted "or" at the end of para. (a)(14), substituted "; or" for the period at the end of para. (a)(15) and added para. (a)(16) . . . Sec. 356(c), substituted "(10) service" for "(10)(A)" and all that follows through "(B) service" in para. (b)(10) and redesignated clauses (b)(10)(A)(i) and (b)(10)(A)(ii) as subparas. (b)(10)(A) and (b)(10)(B) . . . Sec. 356(d), substituted "year" for "quarter" in subparas. (b)(17)(A) and (g)(4)(B), effective for remuneration paid and services rendered after 12/31/77.

Prior to amendment, para. (b)(10) up to, but not including clause (i) read as follows:

"(10)(A) service performed in any calendar quarter in the employ of any organization exempt from income tax under section 501(a) (other than an organization described in section 401(a)) or under section 521, if the remuneration for such service is less than $50;

"(B) service performed in the employ of—"

In 1976, P.L. 94-563, Sec. 1(b)(1), added "or deemed to have been so filed under paragraph (4) or (5) of such subsection" after "filed pursuant to subsection (k) (or the corresponding subsection of prior law" in the matter preceding clause (b)(8)(i) . . . Sec. 1(b)(2), added "(or deemed to have been filed)" after "filed" in clauses (b)(8)(i), (ii), and (iii) . . . Sec. 1(b)(3), substituted "is (or is deemed to be) in effect" for "is in effect" in the matter following clause (b)(8)(iii) . . . Sec. 1(c), added paras. (k)(4), (5), (6), (7), and (8), effective for services performed after 1950 to the extent covered by waiver certificates filed or deemed to have been filed under Code Sec. 3121(k)(4) or (5) [as added above], Secs. 2 and 3 [as amended by Sec. 312(e)(1) and (2) of P. L. 95-216, see above] of this Act provide special rules as follows:

"Sec. 2. Notwithstanding any other provision of law, no refund or credit of any tax paid under section 3101 or 3111 of the Internal Revenue Code of 1954 by an organization described in section 501(c)(3) of such Code which is exempt from income tax under section 501(a) of such Code shall be made on or after September 9, 1976, by reason of such organization's failure to file a waiver certificate under section 3121(k)(1) of such Code (or the corresponding provision of prior law), if such organization is deemed to have filed such a certificate under section 3121(k)(4) of such Code (as added by the first section of this Act).

"Sec. 3. In any case where—

"(1) an individual performed service, as an employee of an organization which is deemed under section 3121(k)(5) of the Internal Revenue Code of 1954 to have filed a waiver certificate under section 3121(k)(1) of such Code, at any time prior to the period for which such certificate is effective;

"(2) the taxes imposed by sections 3101 and 3111 of such Code were paid with respect to remuneration paid for such service, but such service (or any part thereof) does not constitute employment (as defined in section 210 (a) of the Social Security Act and section 3121(b) of such Code) because the applicable taxes so paid were refunded or credited (otherwise than through a refund or credit which would have been allowed if a valid waiver certificate filed under section 3121(k)(1) of such Code had been in effect) prior to September 9, 1976; and

"(3) any portion of such service (with respect to which taxes were paid and refunded or credited as described in paragraph (2)) would constitute employment (as so defined) if the organization had actually filed under section 3121(k)(1) of such Code a valid waiver certificate effective as provided in section 3121(k)(5)(B) thereof (with such individual's signature appearing on the accompanying list),

the remuneration paid for the portion of such service described in paragraph (3) shall, upon the request of such individual (filed on or before April 15, 1980, in such manner and form, and with such official, as may be prescribed by regulations made under title II of the Social Security Act) accompanied by full repayment of the taxes which were paid under section 3101 of such Code with respect to such remuneration and so refunded or credited, (or by satisfactory evidence that appropriate arrangements have been made for the repayment of such taxes in installments as provided in section 3121(k)(9) of such Code) be deemed to constitute remuneration for employment as so defined. In any case where remuneration paid by an organization to an individual is deemed under the preceding sentence to constitute remuneration for employment, such organization shall be liable (notwithstanding any other provision of such Code) for repayment of any taxes which it paid under section 3111 of such Code with respect to such remuneration and which were refunded or credited to it."

—P.L. 94-455, Sec. 1207(e)(1)(A), deleted "or" at the end of para. (b)(18), substituted "; or" for the period at the end of para. (b)(19), and added para. (b)(20), effective [as amended by Sec. 701(z)(1) of P. L. 95-600, see above] for services performed after 12/31/54. Sec. 1207(f)(4)(B) of this Act [as amended by Sec. 701(z)(1) of P. L. 95-600, see above] provides as follows:

"(B) Notwithstanding subparagraph (A), if the owner or operator of any boat treated a share of the boat's catch of fish or other aquatic animal life (or a share of the proceeds therefrom) received by an individual after December 31, 1954, and before the date of the enactment of this Act for services performed by such individual after December 31, 1954, on such boat as being subject to the tax under chapter 21 of the Internal Revenue Code of 1954, then the amendments made by paragraphs (1)(A) and (B) and (2) of subsection (e) shall not apply with respect to such services performed by such individual (and the share of the catch, or proceeds therefrom, received by him for such services)."

—P.L. 94-455, Sec. 1903(a)(3)(A), substituted ", of whatever nature, performed" for "performed after 1936 and prior to 1955 which was employment for purposes of subchapter A of chapter 9 of the Internal Revenue Code of 1939 under the law applicable to the period in which such service was performed, and any service, of whatever nature, performed after 1954" following "For purposes of this chapter, the term 'employment' means any service", and deleted "in the case of service performed after 1954," following "(as defined in subsection (h)); except that," in subsec. (b) . . . Sec. 1903(a)(3)(B), deleted "65 Stat. 119;" following the parenthesis in para. (b)(1) . . . Sec. 1903(a)(3)(C), substituted "Secretary of Transportation" for "Secretary of the Treasury" following "subject to the jurisdiction of the" in clause (b)(6)(B)(v) . . . Sec. 1903(a)(3)(D), deleted "46 Stat. 1550, § 3;" following the parenthesis in para. (g)(3) . . . Sec. 1903(a)(3)(E), deleted subparas. (k)(1)(F) and (k)(1)(H), and redesignated subpara. (k)(1)(G) as (k)(1)(F) . . . Sec. 1903(a)(3)(F), deleted ", but in no case prior to January 1, 1955" following "as may be specified in the agreement" in para. (1)(2) . . . Sec. 1903(a)(3)(G), deleted "after December 1956" following "include service performed" in para. (m)(1), effective for wages paid after 12/31/76.

Prior to amendment, subpara. (k)(1)(F) read as follows:

"(F) An organization which filed a certificate under this subsection after 1955 but prior to the enactment of this subparagraph may file a request at any time before 1960 to have such certificate effective, with respect to the service of individuals who concurred in the filing of such certificate (initially or through the filing of a supplemental list) prior to enactment of this subparagraph and who concur in the filing of such new request, for the period beginning with the first day of any calendar quarter preceding the first calendar quarter for which it was effective and following the last calendar quarter of 1955. Such request shall be filed with such official and in such form and manner as may be prescribed by regulations made under this chapter. If a request is filed pursuant to this subparagraph—

"(i) for purposes of computing interest and for purposes of section 6651 (relating to addition to tax for failure to file tax return or pay tax), the due date for the return and payment of the tax for any calendar quarter resulting from the filing of such request shall be the last day of the calendar month following the calendar quarter in which the request is filed; and

"(ii) the statutory period for the assessment of such tax shall not expire before the expiration of 3 years from such due date."

Prior to amendment, subpara. (k)(1)(H) read as follows:

"(H) An organization which files a certificate under subparagraph (A) before 1966 may amend such certificate during 1965 or 1966 to make the certificate effective with the first day of any calendar quarter preceding the quarter for which such certificate originally became effective, except that such date may not be earlier than the first day of the twentieth calendar quarter preceding the quarter in which such certificate is so amended. If an organization amends its certificate pursuant to the preceding sentence, such amendment shall be effective with respect to the service of individuals who concurred in the filing of such certificate (initially or through the filing of a supplemental list) and who concur in the filing of such amendment. An amendment to a certificate filed pursuant to this subparagraph shall be filed with such official and in such form and manner as may be prescribed by regulations made under this chapter. If an amendment is filed pursuant to this subparagraph—

"(i) for purposes of computing interest and for purposes of section 6651 (relating to addition to tax for failure to file tax return or pay tax), the due date for the return and payment of the tax for any calendar quarter resulting from the filing of such an amendment shall be the last day of the calendar month following the calendar quarter in which the amendment is filed; and

"(ii) the statutory period for the assessment of such tax shall not expire before the expiration of three years from such due date."

—P.L. 94-455, Sec. 1906(b)(13)(A), substituted "Secretary" for "Secretary or his delegate" each place it appeared in subsecs. (k) and (l) . . . Sec. 1906(b)(13)(C), substituted "to the Secretary of the Treasury" for "to the Secretary" in subpara. (b)(12)(B), effective 2/1/77.

In 1973, P.L. 93-66, Sec. 203(b)(2), substituted "$12,600" for the dollar amount each place it appeared in para. (a)(1), effective for remuneration paid after 1973.

—P.L. 93-66, Sec. 203(d), amended Sec. 203(b)(2)(C) of P. L. 92-336 [see below] by substituting "$12,600" for "$12,000".

—P.L. 93-233, Sec. 5(b)(2), substituted "$13,200" for the dollar amount each place it appeared in para. (a)(1), effective for remuneration paid after 1973.

—P.L. 93-233, Sec. 5(d), amended Sec. 203(b)(2)(C) of P. L. 92-336 (see below) by substituting "$13,200" for "$12,600".

In 1972, P.L. 92-603, Sec. 104(i), amended para. (a)(9), effective for payments after 1974.

Prior to amendment, para. (a)(9) read as follows:

"(9) any payment (other than vacation or sick pay) made to an employee after the month in which—

"(A) in the case of a man, he attains the age of 65, or

"(B) in the case of a woman, she attains the age of 62,

if such employee did not work for the employer in the period for which such payment is made;".

—P.L. 92-603, Sec. 122(b), struck out "or" at the end of para. (a)(12), substituted "; or" for the period at the end of para. (a)(13) and added para. (a)(14), effective for any payment made after 12/72.

—P.L. 92-603, Sec. 123(a)(2), added ", except that this subparagraph shall not apply to service performed by a member of such an order in the exercise of such duties, if an election of coverage under subsection (r) is in effect with respect to such order, or with respect to the autonomous subdivision thereof to which such member belongs." before the semicolon at the end of subpara. (b)(8)(A) . . . Sec. 123(b), added subsec. (r) . . . Sec. 123(c)(2), added para. (i)(4), effective as provided in Sec. 125 of this Act, which reads as follows:

"Sec.125. (a) The provisions of section 210(a)(6)(B)(ii) of the Social Security Act and section 3121(b)(6)(B)(ii) of the Internal Revenue Code of 1954, insofar as they relate to service performed in the employ of a Federal home loan bank, shall be effective—

"(1) with respect to all service performed in the employ of a Federal home loan bank on and after the first day of the first calendar quarter which begins on or after the date of the enactment of this Act [1/1/73]; and

"(2) in the case of individuals who are in the employ of a Federal home loan bank on such first day, with respect to any service performed in the employ of a Federal home loan bank after the last day of the sixth calendar year preceding the year in which this Act is enacted; but this paragraph shall be effective only if an amount equal to the taxes imposed by sections 3101 and 3111 of such Code with respect to the services of all such individuals performed in the employ of Federal home loan banks after the last day of the sixth calendar year preceding the year in which this Act is enacted are paid under the provisions of section 3122 of such Code by July 1, 1973, or by such later date as may be provided in an agreement entered into before such date with the Secretary of the Treasury or his delegate for purposes of this paragraph."

—P.L. 92-603, Sec. 128(b), struck out "or" at the end of subpara. (b)(7)(B), substituted ", or" for the semicolon at the end of subpara. (b)(7)(C) and added subpara. (b)(7)(D), effective for service performed on and after 1/1/73.

—P.L. 92-602, Sec. 129(a)(2), amended subpara. (b)(10)(B), effective for services performed after 12/31/72.

Prior to amendment, subpara. (b)(10)(B) read as follows:

"(B) service performed in the employ of a school, college, or university if such service is performed by a student who is enrolled and is regularly attending classes at such school, college, or university;"

—P.L. 92-603, Sec. 138(b), struck out "or" at the end of para. (a)(13), substituted "; or" for the period at the end of para. (a)(14) and added para. (a)(15), effective for any payment made after 12/72.

—P.L. 92-336, Sec. 203(b)(2)(A), substituted "$10,800" for "$9,000" each place it appeared in para. (a)(1), effective for remuneration paid after 12/72.

—P.L. 92-336, Sec. 203(b)(2)(B), substituted "$12,000" for "$10,800" each place it appeared in para. (a)(1), effective for remuneration paid after 1973.

—P.L. 92-336, Sec. 203(b)(2)(C)(i), substituted "the contribution and benefit base (as determined under section 230 of the Social Security Act)" for "$12,000" each place it appeared in para. (a)(1) . . . Sec. 203(b)(2)(C)(ii), substituted "by an employer during the calendar year with respect to which such contribution and benefit base is effective" for "by an employer during any calendar year" in para. (a)(1), effective for remuneration paid after 1974.

In 1971, P.L. 92-5, Sec. 203(b)(2), substituted "$9,000" for "$7,800" each place it appeared in para. (a)(1), effective for remuneration paid after 12/31/71.

In 1969, P.L. 91-172, Sec. 943(c)(1), added "or pay tax" after "tax return" in clause (k)(1)(F)(i) . . . Sec. 943(c)(2), added "or pay tax" after "tax return" in clause (k)(1)(G)(i) . . . Sec. 943(c)(3), added "or pay tax" after "tax return" in clause (k)(1)(H)(i), effective for returns the date prescribed by law (without regard to any extension of time) for filing of which is after 12/31/69, and for notices and demands for payment of tax made after 12/31/69.

In 1967, P.L. 90-248, Sec. 108(b), substituted "$7,800" for "$6,600" in para. (a)(1), effective for remuneration paid after 12/31/67.

—P.L. 90-248, Sec. 123(b), added "except that the provisions of this subparagraph shall not be applicable to such domestic service if—" after the semicolon at the end of subpara. (b)(3)(B) and added clauses (b)(3)(B)(i), (ii), and (iii), effective for services performed after 12/31/67.

—P.L. 90-248, Sec. 403(i)(1), substituted "under section 5351(2) of title 5, United States Code" for "under section 2 of the Act of August 4, 1947" and deleted "; 5 U.S.C., Sec. 1052" in clause (b)(6)(C)(iv) . . . Sec. 403(i)(2), substituted "subchapter III of chapter 83 of title 5, United States Code," for "the Civil Service Retirement Act" in clause (b)(6)(C)(vi) . . . Sec. 403(i)(3), substituted "under section 5351(2) of title 5, United States Code" for "under section 2 of the Act of August 4, 1947" and deleted "; 5 U.S.C. 1052" in clause (b)(7)(C)(ii), effective 1/2/68.

—P.L. 90-248, Sec. 504(a), deleted "or" at the end of para. (a)(11), substituted "; or" for the period at the end of para. (a)(12), and added para. (a)(13), effective for remuneration paid after 1/2/68.

In 1965, P.L. 89-97, Sec. 103(o), deleted "or" at the end of para. (b)(16), substituted "; or" for the period at the end of para. (b)(17), and added para. (b)(18) . . . Sec. 104(b), amended para. (b)(3), effective for service performed after 1960.

Prior to amendment, para. (b)(3) read as follows:

"(3) service performed by an individual in the employ of his son, daughter, or spouse, and service performed by a child under the age of 21 in the employ of his father or mother,".

—P.L. 89-97, Sec. 311(b)(4), added ", other than as a medical or dental intern or a medical or dental resident in training" before the semicolon at the end of clause (b)(6)(C)(iv) . . . Sec. 311(b)(5), deleted all that followed the first semicolon in para. (b)(13), effective only for services performed after 1965.

Prior to deletion, all that followed the first semicolon in para. (b)(13) read as follows:

"and thereof, or any instrumentality of any one or more of the foregoing wholly owned thereby, which is performed after 1960 and after the calendar quarter in which the Secretary of the Treasury receives a certification by the Governor of American Samoa that the Government of American Samoa desires to have the insurance system established by such title II extended to the officers and employees of such Government and such political subdivisions and instrumentalities"

—P.L. 89-97, Sec. 313(c)(3), deleted "or" at the end of para. (a)(10), substituted "; or" for the period at the end of para. (a)(11), and added para. (a)(12) . . . Sec. 313(c)(4), added subsec. (q), effective only for tips received by employees after 1965.

—P.L. 89-97, Sec. 316(a)(1), amended clause (k)(1)(B)(iii), effective for any certificate filed under Code Sec. 3121(k)(1)(A) after 7/30/65.

Prior to amendment, clause (k)(1)(B)(iii) read as follows:

"(iii) the first day of any calendar quarter preceding the calendar quarter in which the certificate is filed, except that, in the case of a certificate filed prior to January 1, 1960, such date may not be earlier than January 1, 1956, and in the case of a certificate filed after 1959, such date may not be earlier than the first day of the fourth calendar quarter preceding the quarter in which such certificate is filed."

—P.L. 89-97, Sec. 316(b), added subpara. (k)(1)(H).

—P.L. 89-97, Sec. 317(b)(1), deleted "or" at the end of subpara. (b)(7)(A) . . . Sec. 317(b)(2), substituted "; or" for the period at the end of subpara. (b)(7)(B) . . . Sec. 317(b)(3), added subpara. (b)(7)(C), effective as provided in Sec. 317(g) of this Act, which reads as follows:

"(g) The amendments made by this section shall apply with respect to service performed after the calendar quarter in which this section is enacted and after the calendar quarter in which the Secretary of the Treasury receives a certification from the Commissioners of the District of Columbia expressing their desire to have the insurance system established by title II (and part A of title XVIII) of the Social Security Act extended to the officers and employees coming under the provisions of such amendments."

—P.L. 89-97, Sec. 320(b)(2), substituted "$6,600" for "$4,800" each place it appeared in para. (a)(1), effective for remuneration paid after 12/65.

In 1964, P.L. 88-650, Sec. 4(b)(1), deleted "or" at the end of para. (a)(9) . . . Sec. 4(b)(2), substituted "; or" for the period at the end of para. (a)(10) . . . Sec.

4(b)(3), added para. (a)(11), effective for remuneration paid on or after the first day of the first calendar month which begins more than ten days after 10/13/64.

—P.L. 88-272, Sec. 220(c)(2), deleted "or" at the end of subpara. (a)(5)(A), amended subpara. (a)(5)(B), and added subpara. (a)(5)(C), effective for remuneration paid after 12/31/62.

Prior to amendment, subpara. (a)(5)(B) read as follows:

"(B) under or to an annuity plan which, at the time of such payment, meets the requirements of section 401(a)(3), (4), (5), and (6);"

In 1961, P.L. 87-256, Sec. 110(e)(1), added para. (b)(19), effective for services after 12/31/61.

—P.L. 87-293, Sec. 202(a)(1), added para. (i)(3) . . . Sec. 202(a)(2), added subsec. (p), effective for service performed after 9/22/61.

In 1960, P.L. 86-624, Sec. 18(c), deleted "Hawaii," in para. (e)(1), effective 8/21/59.

—P.L. 86-778, Sec. 103(n), amended para. (b)(7) . . . Sec. 103(o)(1), deleted "or" at the end of para. (b)(16) . . . Sec. 103(o)(2), substituted; "or" for the period at the end of para. (b)(17) . . . Sec. 103(o)(3), added para. (b)(18) . . . Sec. 103(p), amended subsec. (e), effective as provided in Sec. 103(v) of this Act, which reads as follows:

"(v)(1) The amendments made by subsection (a) shall apply only with respect to reinterments after the date of the enactment of this Act. The amendments made by subsections (b), (e), and (f) shall apply only with respect to service performed after 1960; except that insofar as the carrying on of a trade or business (other than performance of service as an employee) is concerned, such amendments shall apply only in the case of taxable years beginning after 1960. The amendments made by subsection (d), (i), (o), and (p) shall apply only with respect to service performed after 1960. The amendments made by subsections (h) and (l) shall apply only in the case of taxable years beginning after 1960. The amendments made by subsections (c), (n), (q), and (r) shall apply only with respect to (1) service in the employ of the Government of Guam or any political subdivision thereof, or any instrumentality of any one or more of the foregoing wholly owned thereby, which is performed after 1960 and after the calendar quarter in which the Secretary of the Treasury receives a certification by the Governor of Guam that legislation has been enacted by the Government of Guam expressing its desire to have the insurance system established by title II of the Social Security Act extended to the officers and employees of such Government and such political subdivisions and instrumentalities, and (2) service in the employ of the Government of American Samoa or any political subdivision thereof or any instrumentality of any one or more of the foregoing wholly owned thereby, which is performed after 1960 and after the calendar quarter in which the Secretary of the Treasury receives a certification by the Governor of American Samoa that the Government of American Samoa desires to have the insurance system established by such title II extended to the officers and employees of such Government and such political subdivisions and instrumentalities. The amendments made by subsections (g) and (k) shall apply only in the case of taxable years beginning after 1960, except that, insofar as they involve the nonapplication of section 932 of the Internal Revenue Code of 1954 to the Virgin Islands for purposes of chapter 2 of such Code and section 211 of the Social Security Act, such amendments shall be effective in the case of all taxable years with respect to which such chapter 2 (and corresponding provisions of prior law) and such section 211 are applicable. The amendments made by subsections (j), (s), and (t) shall take effect on the date of the enactment of this Act; and there are authorized to be appropriated such sums as may be necessary for the performance by any officer or employee of functions delegated to him by the Secretary of the Treasury in accordance with the amendment made by such subsection (t).

"(2) The amendments made by subsections (c) and (n) shall have application only as expressly provided therein, and determinations as to whether an officer or employee of the Government of Guam or the Government of American Samoa or any political subdivision thereof, or of any instrumentality of any one or more of the foregoing which is wholly owned thereby, is an employee of the United States or any agency or instrumentality thereof within the meaning of any provision of law not affected by such amendments, shall be made without any inferences drawn from such amendments.

"(3) The repeal (by subsection (j)(1)) of section 219 of the Social Security Act, and the elimination (by subsections (e), (f), (h), (j)(2), and (j)(3)) of other provisions of such Act making reference to such section 219, shall not be construed as changing or otherwise affecting the effective date specified in such section for the extension to the Commonwealth of Puerto Rico of the insurance system under title II of such Act, the manner or consequences of such extension, or the status of any individual with respect to whom the provisions so eliminated are applicable."

Prior to amendment, subsec. (e) read as follows:

"(e) State, United States, and Citizen. For purposes of this chapter—

"(1) State. — The term 'State' includes Hawaii, the District of Columbia, Puerto Rico, and the Virgin Islands.

"(2) United States. — The term 'United States' when used in a geographical sense includes Puerto Rico and the Virgin Islands. An individual who is a citizen of Puerto Rico (but not otherwise a citizen of the United States) shall be considered, for purposes of this section, as a citizen of the United States."

—P.L. 86-778, Sec. 104(b), amended para. (b)(3), effective only for services performed after 1960.

—P.L. 86-778, Sec. 105(a)(1), deleted "and that at least two-thirds of its employees concur in the filing of the certificate" in the first sentence of subpara. (k)(1)(A) . . . Sec. 105(a)(2), added "(if any)" after "each employee" in the second sentence of subpara. (k)(1)(A) . . . Sec. 105(a)(3), substituted "An organization which has so divided its employees into two groups may file a certificate pursuant to subparagraph (A) with respect to the employees in either group, or may file a separate certificate pursuant to such subparagraph with respect to the employees in each group." for the last two sentences of subpara. (k)(1)(E), effec-

tive only for certificates filed under Code Sec. 3121(k)(1) after 9/13/60. Sec. 105(b)(1) through (b)(5) of this Act provides special rules as follows:

"(b)(1) If—

"(A) an individual performed service in the employ of an organization after 1950 with respect to which remuneration was paid before July 1, 1960, and such service is excepted from employment under section 210(a)(8)(B) of the Social Security Act,

"(B) such service would have constituted employment as defined in section 210 of such Act if the requirements of section 3121 (k)(1) of the Internal Revenue Code of 1954 (or corresponding provisions of prior law) were satisfied,

"(C) such organization paid before August 11, 1960, any amount, as taxes imposed by sections 3101 and 3111 of the Internal Revenue Code of 1954 (or corresponding provisions of prior law), with respect to such remuneration paid by the organization to the individual for such service,

"(D) such individual (or a fiduciary acting for such individual or his estate, or his survivor (within the meaning of section 205 (c)(1)(C) of the Social Security Act)) requests that such remuneration be deemed to constitute remuneration for employment for purposes of title II of the Social Security Act, and

"(E) the request is made in such form and manner, and with such official, as may be prescribed by regulations made by the Secretary of Health, Education, and Welfare,

then, subject to the conditions stated in paragraphs (2), (3), and (4), the remuneration with respect to which the amount has been paid as taxes shall be deemed to constitute remuneration for employment for purposes of title II of the Social Security Act.

"(2) Paragraph (1) shall not apply with respect to an individual unless the organization referred to in paragraph (1)(A)—

"(A) on or before the date on which the request described in paragraph (1) is made, has filed a certificate pursuant to section 3121(k)(1) of the Internal Revenue Code of 1954 (or corresponding provisions of prior law), or

"(B) no longer has any individual in its employ for remuneration at the time such request is made.

"(3) Paragraph (1) shall not apply with respect to an individual who was in the employ of the organization referred to in paragraph (2)(A) at any time during the 24-month period following the calendar quarter in which the certificate was filed, unless the organization paid an amount as taxes under sections 3101 and 3111 of the Internal Revenue Code of 1954 (or corresponding provisions of prior law) with respect to remuneration paid by the organization to the employee during some portion of such 24-month period.

"(4) If credit or refund of any portion of the amount referred to in paragraph (1)(C) (other than a credit or refund which would be allowed if the service constituted employment for purposes of chapter 21 of the Internal Revenue Code of 1954) has been obtained, paragraph (1) shall not apply with respect to the individual unless the amount credited or refunded (including any interest under section 6611) is repaid before January 1, 1963.

"(5) If—

"(A) any remuneration for service performed by an individual is deemed pursuant to paragraph (1) to constitute remuneration for employment for purposes of title II of the Social Security Act,

"(B) such individual performs service, on or after the date on which the request is made, in the employ of the organization referred to in paragraph (1)(A), and

"(C) the certificate filed by such organization pursuant to section 3121(k)(1) of the Internal Revenue Code of 1954 (or corresponding provisions of prior law) is not effective with respect to service performed by such individual before the first day of the calendar quarter following the quarter in which the request is made,

then, for purposes of clauses (ii) and (iii) of section 210(a)(8)(B) of the Social Security Act and of clauses (ii) and (iii) of section 3121(b)(8)(B) of the Internal Revenue Code of 1954, such individual shall be deemed to have become an employee of such organization (or to have become a member of a group described in section 3121(k)(1)(E) of such Code) on the first day of the calendar quarter following the quarter in which the request is made."

Prior to deletion, the last two sentences of (k)(1)(E) read as follows:

"An organization which has so divided its employees into two groups may file a certificate pursuant to subparagraph (A) with respect to the employees in one of the groups if at least two-thirds of the employees in such groups concur in the filing of the certificate. The organization may also file such a certificate with respect to the employees in the other group if at least two-thirds of the employees in such other group concur in the filing of such certificate."

In 1959, P.L. 86-168, Sec. 104(h), substituted "Federal land bank association" for "national farm loan association", in clause (b)(6)(B)(ii) . . . Sec. 202(a), added "a Federal land bank, a Federal intermediate credit bank, a bank for cooperatives," before "a national farm loan association" in clause (b)(6)(B)(ii), effective 1/1/60.

—P.L. 86-70, Sec. 22(a), deleted "Alaska," in para. (e)(1), effective 1/3/59.

In 1958, P.L. 85-840, Sec. 402(b), substituted "$4,800" for "$4,200" each place it appeared in subsec. (a), effective only for remuneration paid after 1958.

—P.L. 85-840, Sec. 404(a), amended para. (b)(1), effective for service performed after 1958.

Prior to amendment, para. (b)(1) read as follows:

"(1)(A) service performed in connection with the production or harvesting of any commodity defined as an agricultural commodity in section 15(g) of the Agricultural Marketing Act, as amended (46 Stat. 1550 § 3; 12 U.S.C. 1141j);

"(B) service performed by foreign agricultural workers (i) under contracts entered into in accordance with title V of the Agricultural Act of 1949, as amended (65 Stat. 119; 7 U.S.C. 1461-1468), or (ii) lawfully admitted to the United States from the Bahamas, Jamaica, and the other British West Indies, or from any other foreign country or possession thereof, on a temporary basis to perform agricultural labor;"

—P.L. 85-840, Sec. 405(a), amended para. (k)(1) . . . Sec. 405(b), amended subpara. (b)(1)(B) [sic (b)(8)(B)], effective for certificates filed under Code Sec. 3121(k)(1) and request filed under Code Sec. 3121(k)(1)(F) after 8/28/58.
Prior to amendment, para. (k)(1) read as follows:

"(1) Waiver of exemption by organization.—An organization described in section 501(c)(3) which is exempt from income tax under section 501(a) may file a certificate (in such form and manner, and with such official, as may be prescribed by regulations made under this chapter) certifying that it desires to have the insurance system established by title II of the Social Security Act extended to service performed by its employees and that at least two-thirds of its employees concur in the filing of the certificate. Such certificate may be filed only if it is accompanied by a list containing the signature, address, and social security account number (if any) of each employee who concurs in the filing of the certificate. Such list may be amended at any time prior to the expiration of the twenty-fourth month following the first calendar quarter for which the certificate is in effect, or at any time prior to January 1, 1959, whichever is the later, by filing with the prescribed official a supplemental list or lists containing the signature, address, and social security number (if any) of each additional employee who concurs in the filing of the certificate. The list and any supplemental list shall be filed in such form and manner as may be prescribed by regulations made under this chapter. The certificate shall be in effect (for purposes of subsection (b)(8)(B) and for purposes of section 210(a)(8)(B) of the Social Security Act) for the period beginning with the first day of the calendar quarter in which such certificate is filed or the first day of the succeeding calendar quarter, as may be specified in the certificate, except that, in the case of service performed by an individual whose name appears on a supplemental list filed after the first month following the first calendar quarter for which the certificate is in effect, the certificate shall be in effect, for purposes of such subsection (b)(8) and for purposes of section 210(a)(8) of the Social Security Act, only with respect to service performed by such individual after the calendar quarter in which such supplemental list is filed. The period for which a certificate filed pursuant to this subsection or the corresponding subsection of prior law is effective may be terminated by the organization, effective at the end of a calendar quarter, upon giving 2 years' advance notice in writing, but only if, at the time of the receipt of such notice, the certificate has been in effect for a period of not less than 8 years. The notice of termination may be revoked by the organization by giving, prior to the close of the calendar quarter specified in the notice of termination a written notice of such revocation. Notice of termination or revocation thereof shall be filed in such form and manner, and with such official, as may be prescribed by regulations made under this chapter."
Prior to amendment, subpara. (b)(1)(B) [sic (b)(8)(B)] read as follows:

"(B) service performed in the employ of a religious, charitable, educational, or other organization described in section 501(c)(3) which is exempt from income tax under section 501(a), but this subparagraph shall not apply to service performed during the period for which a certificate, filed pursuant to subsection (k) (or the corresponding subsection of prior law), is in effect if such service is performed by an employee—

"(i) whose signature appears on the list filed by such organization under subsection (k) (or the corresponding subsection of prior law), or

"(ii) who became an employee of such organization after the calendar quarter in which the certificate was filed;"

—P.L. 85-866, Sec. 69, substituted "by" for "be" in the heading of para. (1)(3), effective 1/1/54.

In 1956, P.L. 881, Sec. 410, amended subsec. (i) . . . Sec. 411(a), added subsecs. (m) and (n), effective 1/1/57.
Prior to amendment, subsec. (i) read as follows:

"(i) Computation of wages in certain cases.

"For purposes of this chapter in the case of domestic service described in subsection (a)(7)(B), any payment of cash remuneration for such service which is more or less than a whole-dollar amount shall, under such conditions and to such extent as may be prescribed by regulations made under this chapter, be computed to the nearest dollar. For the purpose of the computation to the nearest dollar, the payment of a fractional part of a dollar shall be disregarded unless it amounts to one-half dollar or more, in which case it shall be increased to $1. The amount of any payment of cash remuneration so computed to the nearest dollar shall, in lieu of the amount actually paid, be deemed to constitute the amount of cash remuneration for purposes of subsection (a)(7)(B)."

—P.L. 880, Sec. 103(j)(1), substituted "trust funds" for "trust fund" in the heading of para. (l)(6) . . . Sec. 103(j)(2), added "and the Federal Disability Insurance Trust Fund" after "Federal Old-Age and Survivors Insurance Trust Fund" in para. (l)(6), effective 8/1/56.

—P.L. 880, Sec. 121(d), added para. (b)(17).

—P.L. 880, Sec. 201(b), amended para. (a)(9), effective for remuneration paid after 10/56.
Prior to amendment, para. (a)(9) read as follows:

"(9) any payment (other than vacation or sick pay) made to an employee after the month in which he attains the age of 65, if he did not work for the employer in the period for which such payment is made; or".

—P.L. 880, Sec. 201(c), amended subpara. (b)(1)(B), effective for service performed after 1956.
Prior to amendment, subpara. (b)(1)(B) read as follows:

"(B) service performed by foreign agricultural workers (i) under contracts entered into in accordance with title V of the Agricultural Act of 1949, as amended (65 Stat. 119; 7 U.S.C. 1461-1468), or (ii) lawfully admitted to the United States from the Bahamas, Jamaica, and the other British West Indies on a temporary basis to perform agricultural labor;"

—P.L. 880, Sec. 201(d)(1), added "a Federal Home Loan Bank," after "a Federal Reserve Bank," in clause (b)(6)(B)(ii) . . . Sec. 201(d)(2), amended clause (b)(6)(C)(vi), effective as provided in Sec. 104(i)(2) of this Act which reads as follows:

"(2)(A) Except as provided in subparagraphs (B) and (C), the amendments made by subsection (b) shall apply only with respect to service performed after June 30, 1957, and only if—

"(i) in the case of the amendment made by paragraph (1) of such subsection, the conditions prescribed in subparagraph (B) are met; and

"(ii) in the case of the amendment made by paragraph (2) of such subsection, the conditions prescribed in subparagraph (C) are met.

"(B) the amendment made by paragraph (1) of subsection (b) shall be effective only if—

"(i) the Federal Home Loan Bank Board submits to the Secretary of Health, Education, and Welfare, and the Secretary approves, before July 1, 1957, a plan, with respect to employees of Federal Home Loan Banks, for the coordination, on an equitable basis, of the benefits provided by the retirement system applicable to such employees with the benefits provided by title II of the Social Security Act; and

"(ii) such plan specifies, as the effective date of the plan July 1, 1957, or the first day of a prior calendar quarter beginning not earlier than January 1, 1956. If the plan specifies as the effective date of the plan a day before July 1, 1957, the amendment made by paragraph (1) of subsection (b) shall apply with respect to service performed on or after such effective date; except that, if such effective date is prior to the day on which the Secretary approves the plan, such amendment shall not apply with respect to service performed, prior to the day on which the Secretary approves the plan, by an individual who is not an employee of a Federal Home Loan Bank on such day.

"(C) The amendment made by paragraph (2) of subsection (b) shall be effective only if—

"(i) the Board of Directors of the Tennessee Valley Authority submits to the Secretary of Health, Education, and Welfare, and the Secretary approves, before July 1, 1957, a plan, with respect to employees of the Tennessee Valley Authority, for the coordination, on an equitable basis, of the benefits provided by the retirement system applicable to such employees with the benefits provided by title II of the Social Security Act; and

"(ii) such plan specifies as the effective date of the plan July 1, 1957, or the first day of a prior calendar quarter beginning not earlier than January 1, 1956. If the plan specifies as the effective date of the plan a day before July 1, 1957, the amendment made by paragraph (2) of subsection (b) shall apply with respect to service performed on or after such effective date; except that, if such effective date is prior to the day on which the Secretary approves the plan, such amendment shall not apply with respect to service performed, prior to the day on which the Secretary approves the plan, by an individual who is not an employee of the Tennessee Valley Authority on such day.

"(D) The Secretary of Health, Education, and Welfare shall, on or before July 31, 1957, submit a report to the Congress setting forth the details of any plan approved by him under subparagraph (B) or (C)."
Prior to amendment, clause (b)(6)(C)(vi) read as follows:

"(vi) by any individual to whom the Civil Service Retirement Act of 1930 does not apply because such individual is subject to another retirement system;"

—P.L. 880, Sec. 201(e)(1), deleted "or" at the end of para. (b)(14), substituted a semicolon for the period at the end of para. (b)(15), and added para. (b)(16), effective for service performed after 1954.

—P.L. 880, Sec. 201(h)(1), amended subpara. (a)(8)(B), effective for remuneration paid after 1956.
Prior to amendment, subpara. (a)(8)(B) read as follows:

"(B) cash remuneration paid by an employer in any calendar year to an employee for agricultural labor, if the cash remuneration paid in such year by the employer to the employee for such labor is less than $100;".

—P.L. 880, Sec. 201(h)(2), added subsec. (o), effective for service performed after 1956.

—P.L. 880, Sec. 201(j), amended subpara. (1)(8)(A), effective 8/1/56.
Prior to amendment, subpara. (1)(8)(A) read as follows:

"(A) a foreign corporation more than 50 percent of the voting stock of which is owned by such domestic corporation; or"

—P.L. 880, Sec. 201(k), added "or at any time prior to January 1, 1959, whichever is the later," after "the certificate is in effect," in the third sentence of para. (k)(1) . . . Sec. 201(1), substituted "the first day of the calendar quarter in which such certificate is filed or the first day of the succeeding calendar quarter, as may be specified in the certificate," for "the first day following the close of the calendar quarter in which such certificate is filed," in the fifth sentence in para. (k)(1), effective for certificates filed after 1956 under Code Sec. 3121(k).

In 1954, P.L. 761, Sec. 204(a), substituted "$4,200" for "$3,600" each place it appeared in para. (a)(1) . . . Sec. 204(b)(1), amended subpara. (a)(7)(B) . . . Sec. 204(b)(2), added subpara. (a)(7)(C) . . . Sec. 204(b)(3), redesignated text of para. (a)(8) as subpara. (a)(8)(A) and added subpara. (a)(8)(B), effective for remuneration paid after 1954.
Prior to amendment, subpara. (a)(7)(B) read as follows:

"(B) cash remuneration paid by an employer in any calendar quarter to an employee for domestic service in a private home of the employer, if the cash remuneration paid in the quarter for such service is less than $50 or the employee is not regularly employed by the employer in such quarter of payment. For purposes of this subparagraph, an employee shall be deemed to be regularly employed by an employer during a calendar quarter only if—

"(i) on each of some 24 days during the quarter the employee performs for the employer for some portion of the day domestic service in a private home of the employer, or

"(ii) the employee was regularly employed (as determined under clause (i)) by the employer in the performance of such service during the preceding calendar quarter."
—P.L. 761, Sec. 205(a), amended para. (b)(1)... Sec. 205(b), deleted para. (b)(3) and redesignated paras. (b)(4) through (14) as paras. (b)(3) through (13), effective for services (whether performed after 1954 or prior to 1955) for which remuneration is paid after 1954.

Prior to amendment, para. (b)(1) read as follows:

"(1)(A) agricultural labor (as defined in subsection (g)) performed in any calendar quarter by an employee, unless the cash remuneration paid for such labor (other than service described in subparagraph (B)) is $50 or more and such labor is performed for an employer by an individual who is regularly employed by such employer to perform such agricultural labor. For purposes of this subparagraph, an individual shall be deemed to be regularly employed by an employer during a calendar quarter only if—

"(i) such individual performs agricultural labor (other than service described in subparagraph (B)) for such employer on a full time basis on 60 days during such quarter, and

"(ii) the quarter was immediately preceded by a qualifying quarter.

"For purposes of the preceding sentence, the term 'qualifying quarter' means—

"(I) any quarter during all of which such individual was continuously employed by such employer, or

"(II) any subsequent quarter which meets the test of clause (i) if, after the last quarter during all of which such individual was continuously employed by such employer, each intervening quarter met the test of clause (i).

"Notwithstanding the preceding provisions of this subparagraph, an individual shall also be deemed to be regularly employed by an employer during a calendar quarter if such individual was regularly employed (upon application of clauses (i) and (ii)) by such employer during the preceding calendar quarter;

"(B) service performed in connection with the production or harvesting of any commodity defined as an agricultural commodity in section 15(g) of the Agricultural Marketing Act, as amended (46 Stat. 1550 § 3; 12 U.S.C. 1141j), or in connection with the ginning of cotton;

"(C) service performed by foreign agricultural workers under contracts entered into in accordance with title V of the Agricultural Act of 1949, as amended (65 Stat. 119; 7 U.S.C. 1461-1468);"

Prior to deletion, para. (b)(3) read as follows:

"(3) service not in the course of the employer's trade or business performed in any calendar quarter by an employee, unless the cash remuneration paid for such service is $50 or more and such service is performed by an individual who is regularly employed by such employer to perform such service. For purposes of this paragraph, an individual shall be deemed to be regularly employed by an employer during a calendar quarter only if—

"(A) on each of some 24 days during such quarter such individual performs for such employer for some portion of the day service not in the course of the employer's trade or business, or

"(B) such individual was regularly employed (as determined under subparagraph (A)) by such employer in the performance of such service during the preceding calendar quarter.

"As used in this paragraph, the term 'service not in the course of the employer's trade or business' does not include domestic service in a private home of the employer and does not include service described in subsection (g)(5);"

—P.L. 761, Sec. 205(c), substituted "if (A) the individual is employed on and in connection with such vessel or aircraft, when outside the United States and (B)(i) such individual is not a citizen of the United States or (ii) the employer is not an American employer" for "if the individual is employed on and in connection with such vessel or aircraft when outside the United States" in para. (b)(4) [as redesignated]... Sec. 205(d)(1)(A), added "by an individual" after "service performed" and added "and if such service is covered by a retirement system established by such instrumentality;" after "December 31, 1950," in para. (b)(6)(B) [as redesignated]... Sec. 205(d)(1)(B), deleted "or" at the end of clause (b)(6)(B)(iii) [as redesignated], added "or" at the end of clause (b)(6)(B)(iv) [as redesignated] and added clause (b)(6)(B)(v)... Sec. 205(d)(2), amended subpara. (b)(6)(C) [as redesignated]... Sec. 205(e), deleted para. (b)(15) and redesignated paras. (b)(16) and (b)(17) as paras. (b)(14) and (b)(15), effective for services performed after 1954.

Prior to amendment, subpara. (b)(6)(C) [as redesignated] read as follows:

"(C) service performed in the employ of the United States or in the employ of any instrumentality of the United States, if such service is performed—

"(i) as the President or Vice President of the United States or as a Member, Delegate, or Resident Commissioner, of or to the Congress;

"(ii) in the legislative branch;

"(iii) in the field service of the Post Office Department unless performed by any individual as an employee who is excluded by Executive order from the operation of the Civil Service Retirement Act of 1930 (46 Stat. 470; 5 U.S.C. 693) because he is serving under a temporary appointment pending final determination of eligibility for permanent or indefinite appointment;

"(iv) in or under the Bureau of the Census of the Department of Commerce by temporary employees employed for the taking of any census;

"(v) by any individual as an employee who is excluded by Executive order from the operation of the Civil Service Retirement Act of 1930 (46 Stat. 470; 5 U.S.C. 693) because he is paid on a contract or fee basis;

"(vi) by any individual as an employee receiving nominal compensation of $12 or less per annum;

"(vii) in a hospital, home, or other institution of the United States by a patient or inmate thereof;

"(viii) by any individual as a consular agent appointed under authority of section 551 of the Foreign Service Act of 1946 (60 Stat. 1011; 22 U.S.C. 951);

"(ix) by any individual as an employee included under section 2 of the Act of August 4, 1947 (relating to certain interns, student nurses, and other student employees of hospitals of the Federal Government) (61 Stat. 727; 5 U.S.C. 1052);

"(x) by any individual as an employee serving on a temporary basis in case of fire, storm, earthquake, flood, or other similar emergency;

"(xi) by any individual as an employee who is employed under a Federal relief program to relieve him from unemployment;

"(xii) as a member of a State, county, or community committee under the Commodity Stabilization Service or of any other board, council, committee, or other similar body, unless such board, council, committee, or other body is composed exclusively of individuals otherwise in the full-time employ of the United States; or

"(xiii) by an individual to whom the Civil Service Retirement Act of 1930 (46 Stat. 470; 5 U.S.C. 693) does not apply because such individual is subject to another retirement system;"

Prior to deletion, para. (b)(15) read as follows:

"(15) service performed by an individual in (or as an officer or member of the crew of the vessel while it is engaged in) the catching, taking, harvesting, cultivating, or farming of any kind of fish, shellfish, crustacea, sponges, seaweeds, or other aquatic forms of animal and vegetable life (including service performed by any such individual as an ordinary incident to any such activity), except—

"(A) service performed in connection with the catching or taking of salmon or halibut, for commercial purposes, and

"(B) service performed on or in connection with a vessel of more than 10 net tons (determined in the manner provided for determining the register tonnage of merchant vessels under the laws of the United States);"

—P.L. 761, Sec. 206(a), deleted ", if the performance of such services is subject to licensing requirements under the laws of the State in which such services are performed" in subpara. (d)(3)(C), effective for services performed after 1954.

—P.L. 761, Sec. 207(a), substituted "Such list may be amended at any time prior to the expiration of the twenty-fourth month following the first calendar quarter for which the certificate is in effect, by filing with the prescribed official a supplemental list or lists containing the signature, address, and social security number (if any) of each additional employee who concurs in the filing of the certificate." for "Such list may be amended, at any time prior to the expiration of the first month following the first calendar quarter for which the certificate is in effect, by filing with such official a supplemental list or lists containing the signature, address, and social security account number (if any) of each additional employee who concurs in the filing of the certificate." in the third sentence of para. (k)(1) ... Sec. 207(b), deleted the period after "in which such certificate is filed" and added ", except that, in the case of service performed by an individual whose name appears on a supplemental list filed after the first month following the first calendar quarter for which the certificate is in effect, the certificate shall be in effect, for purposes of such subsection (b)(8) and for purposes of section 210(a)(8) of the Social Security Act, only with respect to service performed by such individual after the calendar quarter in which such supplemental list is filed."... Sec. 209, added subsec. (l), effective 9/1/54.

Sec. 3122. Federal service.

In the case of the taxes imposed by this chapter with respect to service performed in the employ of the United States or in the employ of any instrumentality which is wholly owned by the United States, including such service which is medicare qualified government employment (as defined in section 3121(u)(3)), including service, performed as a member of a uniformed service, to which the provisions of section 3121(m)(1) are applicable, and including service, performed as a volunteer or volunteer leader within the meaning of the Peace Corps Act, to which the provisions of section 3121(p) are applicable, the determination of the amount of remuneration for such service, and the return and payment of the taxes imposed by this chapter, shall be made by the head of the Federal agency or instrumentality having the control of such service, or by such agents as such head may designate. In the case of the taxes imposed by this chapter with respect to service performed in the employ of an international organization pursuant to a transfer to which the provisions of section 3121(y) are applicable, the determination of the amount of remuneration for such service, and the return and payment of the taxes imposed by this chapter, shall be made by the head of the Federal agency from which the transfer was made. Nothing in this paragraph shall be construed to affect the Secretary's authority to determine under subsections (a) and (b) of section 3121 whether any such service constitutes employment, the periods of such employment, and whether remuneration paid for any such service constitutes wages. The person making such return may, for convenience of administration, make payments of the tax imposed under section 3111 with respect to such service without regard to the contribution and benefit base limitation in section 3121(a)(1), and he shall not be required to obtain a refund of the tax paid under section 3111 on that part of the remuneration not included in wages by reason of section 3121(a)(1). Payments of the tax imposed under section 3111 with respect to service, performed by an individual as a member of a uniformed service, to which the provisions of section 3121(m)(1) are applicable, shall be made from appropriations available for the pay of members of such uniformed service. The provisions of this section shall be applicable in the case of service performed by a civilian employee, not compensated from funds appropriated by the Congress, in the Army and Air Force Exchange Service, Army and Air Force Motion Picture Service, Navy Exchanges, Marine Corps Exchanges, or other activities, conducted by an instrumentality of the United States subject to the jurisdiction of the Secretary of Defense, at installations of the Department of Defense for the comfort, pleasure, contentment, and mental and physical improvement of personnel of such Department; and for purposes of this section the Secretary of Defense shall be deemed to be the head of such instrumentality. The provisions of this section shall be applicable also in the case of service performed by a civilian employee, not compensated from funds appropriated by the Congress, in the Coast Guard Exchanges or other activities, conducted by an instrumentality of the United States subject to the jurisdiction of the Secretary of the Department in which the Coast Guard is operating, at installations of the Coast Guard for the comfort, pleasure, contentment, and mental and physical improvement of personnel of the Coast Guard; and for purposes of this section the Secretary of the Department in which the Coast Guard is operating shall be deemed to be the head of such instrumentality.

In 2006, P.L. 109-241, Sec. 902(i), substituted "Secretary of the Department in which the Coast Guard is operating" for "Secretary of Transportation" each place it appeared in Code Sec. 3122, enacted 7/12/2006.

In 1994, P.L. 103-296, Sec. 319(a)(2), added a new sentence after the first sentence in Code Sec. 3122, effective for service performed after the calendar quarter following the calendar quarter in which the date of the enactment [8/15/94] of this Act occurs.

In 1993, P.L. 103-66, Sec. 13207(d)(4), substituted "contribution and benefit base limitation" for "applicable contribution base limitation" in Code Sec. 3122, effective for 1994 and later calendar yrs.

In 1990, P.L. 101-508, Sec. 11331(d)(2), substituted "applicable contribution base limitation" for "contribution and benefit base limitation" in Code Sec. 3122, effective for 1991 and later calendar years.

In 1988, P.L. 100-647, Sec. 8015(a)(2)(A), deleted "the determination whether an individual has performed service which constitutes employment as defined in section 3121(b)," after "the provision of section 3121(p) are applicable" in the first sentence of Code Sec. 3122 ... Sec. 8015(a)(2)(B), deleted "which constitutes wages as defined in section 3121(a)" after "remuneration for such service" in the first sentence of Code Sec. 3122 ... Sec. 8015(a)(2)(C), added the second sentence of Code Sec. 3122, effective for determinations relating to service commenced in any position on or after 11/10/88.

In 1986, P.L. 99-272, Sec. 13205(a)(2)(C), substituted "including such service which is medicare qualified government employment (as defined in section 3121(u)(3))" for "including service which is medicare qualified Federal employment (as defined in section 3121(u)(2))" in Code Sec. 3122, effective for services performed after 3/31/86.

In 1982, P.L. 97-248, Sec. 278(a)(3), added "including service which is medicare qualified Federal employment (as defined in section 3121(u)(2))," after "wholly owned by the United States," in Code Sec. 3122, effective for remuneration paid after 12/31/82.

In 1976, P.L. 94-455, Sec. 1903(a)(4), substituted "Secretary of Transportation" for "Secretary" each place it appeared in the last sentence of Code Sec. 3122, effective for wages paid after 12/31/76.

In 1973, P.L. 93-233, Sec. 5(b)(3), substituted "$13,200" for "$12,600" in the second sentence of Sec. 3122, effective for remuneration paid after 1973.
—P.L. 93-233, Sec. 5(d), amended Sec. 203(b)(3)(C) of P. L. 92-336 (see below) by substituting "$13,200" for "$12,600".
—P.L. 93-66, Sec. 203(b)(3), substituted "$12,600" for "$12,000" in the second sentence of Code Sec. 3122, effective for remuneration paid after 1973.
—P.L. 93-66, Sec. 203(d), amended Sec. 203(b)(3)(C) of P. L. 92-336 (see below) by substituting "$12,600" for "$12,000".

In 1972, P.L. 92-336, Sec. 203(b)(3)(A), substituted "$10,800" for "$9,000" in the second sentence of Code Sec. 3122, effective for remuneration paid after 1972.
—P.L. 92-336, Sec. 203(b)(3)(B), substituted "$12,000" [as amended by Sec. 203(d) of P. L. 93-66, see above] for "$10,800" in the second sentence of Code Sec. 3122, effective for remuneration paid after 1973.
—P.L. 92-336, Sec. 203(b)(3)(C), substituted "the contribution and benefit base limitation" for "the $12,000 limitation" [as amended by Sec. 203(d) of P. L. 93-66 and Sec. 5(d) of P. L. 93-66, see above] in the second sentence of Code Sec. 3122, effective for remuneration paid after 1974.

In 1971, P.L. 92-5, Sec. 203(b)(3), substituted "$9,000" for "$7,800" in the second sentence of Code Sec. 3122, effective for remuneration paid after 12/71.

In 1967, P.L. 90-248, Sec. 108(b), substituted "$7,800" for "$6,600" in the second sentence of Code Sec. 3122, effective for remuneration paid after 1967.

In 1965, P.L. 89-97, Sec. 320, substituted "$6,600" for "$4,800" in Code Sec. 3122, effective for remuneration paid after 1965.

In 1961, P.L. 87-293, Sec. 202(a)(3), added "and including service, performed as a volunteer or volunteer leader within the meaning of the Peace Corps Act, to which the provisions of section p) are applicable," after "section 3121(m)(1) are applicable," in Code Sec. 3122, effective for services performed after 9/22/61, but in the case of persons serving under the Peace Corps agency established by executive order applicable with respect to service performed on or after the effective date of enrollment.

In 1958, P.L. 85-866, Sec. 70, substituted "section" for "subsection" each place it appeared in Code Sec. 3122, effective 1/1/54.
—P.L. 85-840, Sec. 402(c), substituted "$4,800" for "$4,200" in Code Sec. 3122, effective for remuneration paid after 1958.

In 1956, P.L. 881, Sec. 411(b) and (c), included taxes with respect to service, performed as a member of a uniformed service, to which the provisions of section 3121(m)(1) of this title are applicable, and authorized payment of the tax imposed under section 3111 of this title from appropriations available for pay of members of the uniformed service.

In 1954, P.L. 761, Sec. 202(c), substituted "$4,200" for "$3,600" in Code Sec. 3122, effective for remuneration paid after 1954.
—P.L. 761, Sec. 203(a), added provisions making the section applicable to services performed by a civilian employee in the Coast Guard Exchanges or certain other activities at Coast Guard installations, effective 1/1/55.

Sec. 3123. Deductions as constructive payments.

Whenever under this chapter or any act of Congress, or under the law of any State, an employer is required or permitted to deduct any amount from the remuneration of an employee and to pay the amount deducted to the United States, a State, or any political subdivision thereof, then for purposes of this chapter the amount so deducted shall be considered to have been paid to the employee at the time of such deduction.

Sec. 3124. Estimate of revenue reduction.

The Secretary at intervals of not longer than 3 years shall estimate the reduction in the amount of taxes collected under this chapter by reason of the operation of section 3121(b)(9) and shall include such estimate in his annual report.

In 1976, P.L. 94-455, Sec. 1906(b)(13)(A), substituted "Secretary" for "Secretary or his delegate" in Code Sec. 3124, effective 2/1/77.

In 1954, ch. 1206, Sec. 205(b), changed reference from "section 3121(b)(10)" to "section 3121(b)(9)".

Sec. 3125. Returns in the case of governmental employees in States, Guam, American Samoa, and the District of Columbia.
(a) States.

Except as otherwise provided in this section, in the case of the taxes imposed by sections 3101(b) and 3111(b) with respect to service performed in the employ of a State or any political subdivision thereof (or any instrumentality of any one or more of the foregoing which is wholly owned thereby), the return and payment of such taxes may be made by the head of the agency or instrumentality having the control of such service, or by such agents as such head may designate. The person making such return may, for convenience of administration, make payments of the tax imposed under section 3111 with respect to the service of such individuals without regard to the contribution and benefit base limitation in section 3121(a)(1).

Code Sec. 3125(b)

(b) Guam.

The return and payment of the taxes imposed by this chapter on the income of individuals who are officers or employees of the Government of Guam or any political subdivision thereof or of any instrumentality of any one or more of the foregoing which is wholly owned thereby, and those imposed on such Government or political subdivision or instrumentality with respect to having such individuals in its employ, may be made by the Governor of Guam or by such agents as he may designate. The person making such return may, for convenience of administration, make payments of the tax imposed under section 3111 with respect to the service of such individuals without regard to the contribution and benefit base limitation in section 3121(a)(1).

(c) American Samoa.

The return and payment of the taxes imposed by this chapter on the income of individuals who are officers or employees of the Government of American Samoa or any political subdivision thereof or of any instrumentality of any one or more of the foregoing which is wholly owned thereby, and those imposed on such Government or political subdivision or instrumentality with respect to having such individuals in its employ, may be made by the Governor of American Samoa or by such agents as he may designate. The person making such return may, for convenience of administration, make payments of the tax imposed under section 3111 with respect to the service of such individuals without regard to the contribution and benefit base limitation in section 3121(a)(1).

(d) District of Columbia.

In the case of the taxes imposed by this chapter with respect to service performed in the employ of the District of Columbia or in the employ of any instrumentality which is wholly owned thereby, the return and payment of the taxes may be made by the Mayor of the District of Columbia or by such agents as he may designate. The person making such return may, for convenience of administration, make payments of the tax imposed by section 3111 with respect to such service without regard to the contribution and benefit base limitation in section 3121(a)(1).

In **1993**, P.L. 103-66, Sec. 13207(d)(4), substituted "contribution and benefit base limitation" for "applicable contribution base limitation" each place it appeared in Code Sec. 3125, effective for 1994 and later calendar yrs.

In **1990**, P.L. 101-508, Sec. 11331(d)(2), substituted "applicable contribution base limitation" for "contribution and benefit base limitation" each place it appeared in Code Sec. 3125, effective for 1991 and later calendar years.

In **1986**, P.L. 99-272, Sec. 13205(a)(2)(A)(i), redesignated subsecs. (a), (b) and (c) as subsecs. (b), (c) and (d) and added new subsec. (a)... Sec. 13205(a)(2)(A)(ii), added "States," before "Guam" in the title of Code Sec. 3125, effective for services performed after 3/31/86.

In **1976**, P.L. 94-455, Sec. 1903(a)(5), substituted "Mayor of the District of Columbia or such agents as he may designate" for "Commissioners of the District of Columbia or such agents as they may designate" in subsec. (c), effective for wages paid after '76.

In **1973**, P.L. 93-66, Sec. 203(b)(4), substituted "$12,600" for "$12,000" each place it appeared in Code Sec. 3125, effective for remuneration paid after 1973.
—P.L. 93-66, Sec. 203(d), amended Sec. 203(b)(4)(C) of P. L. 92-336 (see below) by substituting "$12,600" for "$12,000".
—P.L. 93-233, Sec. 5(b)(4), substituted "$13,200" for "$12,600" each place it appeared in Code Sec. 3125, effective for remuneration paid after 1973.
—P.L. 93-233, Sec. 5(d), amended Sec. 203(b)(4)(C) of P. L. 92-336 (see below) by substituting "$13,200" for "$12,600".

In **1972**, P.L. 92-336, Sec. 203(b)(4)(A), substituted "$10,800" for "$9,000" each place it appeared in Code Sec. 3125, effective for remuneration paid after 12/31/72.
—P.L. 92-336, Sec. 203(b)(4)(B), substituted "$12,000" [as amended by Sec. 203(d) of P. L. 93-66 and Sec. 5(d) of P. L. 93-233, see above] for "$10,800" each place it appeared in Code Sec. 3125, effective for remuneration paid after 1973.
—P.L. 92-336, Sec. 203(b)(4)(C), substituted "the contribution and benefit base limitation" for "the $12,000 limitation" [as amended by Sec. 203(d) of P. L. 93-66, see above] each place it appeared in Code Sec. 3125, effective for remuneration paid after 1974.

In **1971**, P.L. 92-5, Sec. 203(b)(4), substituted "$9,000" for "$7,800" each place it appeared in Code Sec. 3125, effective for remuneration paid after 12/71.

In **1967**, P.L. 90-248, Sec. 108(b), amended Sec. 3125 by substituting "$7,800" for "$6,600" in subsecs. (a), (b) and (c), effective for remuneration paid after 1967.

In **1965**, P.L. 89-97, Sec. 320(b)(4), substituted "$6,600" for "$4,800" in subsec. (a) and (b); ... Sec. 317(c)(1), added subsec. (c), and added reference to District of Columbia in catchline.

In **1960**, P.L. 86-778, Sec. 103(q)(1), added Code Sec. 3125.

Sec. 3126. Return and payment by governmental employer.

If the employer is a State or political subdivision thereof, or an agency or instrumentality of any one or more of the foregoing, the return of the amount deducted and withheld upon any wages under section 3101 and the amount of the tax imposed by section 3111 may be made by any officer or employee of such State or political subdivision or such agency or instrumentality, as the case may be, having control of the payment of such wages, or appropriately designated for that purpose.

In **1986**, P.L. 99-509, Sec. 9002(a)(1), added Code Sec. 3126, effective as provided in Sec. 9002(d) of this Act:

"(d) Effective date.

"The amendments made by this section are effective with respect to payments due with respect to wages paid after December 31, 1986, including wages paid after such date by a State (or political subdivision thereof) that modified its agreement pursuant to the provisions of section 218(e)(2) of the Social Security Act prior to the date of the enactment of this Act; except that in cases where, in accordance with the currently applicable schedule, deposits of taxes due under an agreement entered into pursuant to section 218 of the Social Security Act would be required within 3 days after the close of an eighth-monthly period, such 3-day requirement shall be changed to a 7-day requirement for wages paid prior to October 1, 1987, and to a 5-day requirement for wages paid after September 30, 1987, and prior to October 1, 1988. For wages paid prior to October 1, 1988, the deposit schedule for taxes imposed under section 3101 and 3111 shall be determined separately from the deposit schedule for taxes withheld under section 3402 if the taxes imposed under sections 3101 and 3111 are due with respect to service included under an agreement entered into pursuant to section 218 of the Social Security Act."

Sec. 3127. Exemption for employers and their employees where both are members of religious faiths opposed to participation in Social Security Act programs.

(a) In general.

Notwithstanding any other provision of this chapter (and under regulations prescribed to carry out this section), in any case where—

(1) an employer (or, if the employer is a partnership, each partner therein) is a member of a recognized religious sect or division thereof described in section 1402(g)(1) and an adherent of established tenets or teachings of such sect or division as described in such section, and has filed and had approved under subsection (b) an application (in such form and manner, and with such official, as may be prescribed by such regulations) for an exemption from the taxes imposed by section 3111, and

(2) an employee of such employer who is also a member of such a religious sect or division and an adherent of its established tenets or teachings has filed and had approved under subsection (b) an identical application for exemption from the taxes imposed by section 3101,

such employer shall be exempt from the taxes imposed by section 3111 with respect to wages paid to each of the employees thereof who meets the requirements of paragraph (2) and each such employee shall be exempt from the taxes imposed by section 3101 with respect to such wages paid to him by such employer.

(b) Approval of application.

An application for exemption filed by an employer (or a partner) under subsection (a)(1) or by an employee under subsection (a)(2) shall be approved only if—

(1) such application contains or is accompanied by the evidence described in section 1402(g)(1)(A) and a waiver described in section 1402(g)(1)(B),

(2) the Commissioner of Social Security makes the findings (with respect to such sect or division) described in section 1402(g)(1)(C), (D), and (E), and

(3) no benefit or other payment referred to in section 1402(g)(1)(B) became payable (or, but for section 203 or 222(b) of the Social Security Act, would have become payable) to the individual filing the application at or before the time of such filing.

(c) Effective period of exemption.

An exemption granted under this section to any employer with respect to wages paid to any of the employees thereof, or granted to any such employee, shall apply with respect to wages paid by such employer during the period—

(1) commencing with the first day of the first calendar quarter, after the quarter in which such application is filed, throughout which such employer (or, if the employer is a partnership, each partner therein) or employee meets the applicable requirements specified in subsections (a) and (b), and

(2) ending with the last day of the calendar quarter preceding the first calendar quarter thereafter in which (A) such employer (or, if the employer is a partnership, any partner therein) or the employee involved does not meet the applicable requirements of subsection (a), or (B) the sect or division thereof of which such employer (or, if the employer is a partnership, any partner therein) or employee is a member is found by the Commissioner of Social Security to have ceased to meet the requirements of subsection (b)(2).

In 1994, P.L. 103-296, Sec. 108(h)(3), substituted "Commissioner of Social Security" for "Secretary of Health and Human Services" in paras. (b)(2) and (c)(2), effective 3/31/95.

In 1989, P.L. 101-239, Sec. 10204(b)(1)(A), added "(or, if the employer is a partnership, each partner therein)" after "an employer" in para. (a)(1) . . . Sec. 10204(b)(1)(B), substituted "the employees thereof" for "his employees" in the flush language following para. (a)(2) . . . Sec. 10204(b)(1)(C), added "(or a partner)" after "an employer" in subsec. (b) . . . Sec. 10204(b)(1)(D), substituted "the employees thereof" for "his employees" in subsec. (c) . . . Sec. 10204(b)(1)(E), added "(or, if the employer is a partnership, each partner therein)" after "such employer" in para. (c)(1) . . . Sec. 10204(b)(1)(F), substituted "such employer (or, if the employer is a partnership, any partner therein) or the employee involved does not meet" for "such employer or the employee involved ceases to meet" and added "(or, if the employer is a partnership, any partner therein)" after "such employer" the second place it appeared in para. (c)(2), effective for wages paid after 12/31/88.

In 1988, P.L. 100-647, Sec. 8007(a)(1), added Code Sec. 3127, effective for wages paid after 12/31/88.

Sec. 3128. Short title.

This chapter may be cited as the "Federal Insurance Contributions Act."

In 1988, P.L. 100-647, Sec. 8007(a)(1), redesignated Code Sec. 3127 as Code Sec. 3128, effective for wages paid after 12/31/88.

In 1986, P.L. 99-509, Sec. 9002(a)(1), redesignated Code Sec. 3126 as Code Sec. 3127, effective as provided in Sec. 9002(d) of this Act reproduced in note following Code Sec. 3126.

In 1960, P.L. 86-778, Sec. 103(q), redesignated Code Sec. 3125 as Code Sec. 3126.

CHAPTER 22.—RAILROAD RETIREMENT TAX ACT

Subchapter

A. Tax on employees.

B. Tax on employee representatives.

C. Tax on employers.

D. General provisions.

E. Tier 2 tax rate determination.

Subchapter A.—Tax on Employees

Sec.

3201. Rate of tax.

3202. Deduction of tax from compensation.

Sec. 3201. Rate of tax.

(a) Tier 1 tax.

In addition to other taxes, there is hereby imposed on the income of each employee a tax equal to the applicable percentage of the compensation received during any calendar year by such employee for services rendered by such employee. For purposes of the preceding sentence, the term "applicable percentage" means the percentage equal to the sum of the rates of tax in effect under subsections (a) and (b) of section 3101 for the calendar year.

(b) Tier 2 tax.

(1) In general. In addition to other taxes, there is hereby imposed on the income of each employee a tax equal to the applicable percentage of the compensation received during any calendar year by such employee for services rendered by such employee.

(2) Applicable percentage. For purposes of paragraph (1), the term "applicable percentage" means—

(A) 4.90 percent in the case of compensation received during 2002 or 2003, and

(B) in the case of compensation received during any calendar year after 2003, the percentage determined under section 3241 for such calendar year.

(c) Cross reference.

For application of different contribution bases with respect to the taxes imposed by subsections (a) and (b), see section 3231(e)(2).

In 2001, P.L. 107-90, Sec. 204(c), amended subsec. (b), effective for calendar yrs. begin. after 12/31/2001.

Prior to amendment, subsec. (b) read as follows:

"*(b) Tier 2 tax.* In addition to other taxes, there is hereby imposed on the income of each employee a tax equal to 4.90 percent of the compensation received during any calendar year by such employee for services rendered by such employee."

In 1990, P.L. 101-508, Sec. 5125(a), amended subsec. (a), effective 11/5/90.

Prior to amendment, subsec. (a) read as follows:

"*(a) Tier 1 tax.*

"In addition to other taxes, there is hereby imposed on the income of each employee a tax equal to the following percentage of the compensation received during any calendar year by such employee for services rendered by such employee:

"In the case of compensation received during:	The rate shall be:
1985	7.05
1986 or 1987	7.15
1988 or 1989	7.51
1990 or thereafter	7.65"

In 1987, P.L. 100-203, Sec. 9031(a), amended subsec. (b), effective for compensation received after 12/31/87.

Prior to amendment, subsec. (b) read as follows:

"*(b) Tier 2 tax.*

"In addition to other taxes, there is hereby imposed on the income of each employee a tax equal to the following percentage of the compensation received during any calendar year by such employee for services rendered by such employee:

"In the case of compensation received during:	The rate shall be:
1985	3.50
1986 or thereafter	4.25."

In 1983, P.L. 98-76, Sec. 211(a), substituted "2.75 percent" for "2.0 percent" in subsec. (a), effective for compensation paid for services rendered after 12/31/83 and before 1/1/85.

—P.L. 98-76, Sec. 221, amended Code Sec. 3201, effective for remuneration paid after 12/31/84.

Prior to amendment, Code Sec. 3201 read as follows:

"SEC. 3201. RATE OF TAX.

"*(a)* In addition to other taxes, there is hereby imposed on the income of each employee a tax equal to 2.75 percent of so much of the compensation paid in any calendar month to such employee for services rendered by him as is not in excess of an amount equal to one-twelfth of the current maximum annual taxable 'wages' as defined in section 3121 for any month.

"*(b)* The rate of tax imposed by subsection (a) shall be increased by the rate of the tax imposed with respect to wages by section 3101(a) plus the rate imposed by section 3101(b) of so much of the compensation paid in any calendar month to such employee for services rendered by him not in excess of an amount equal to one-twelfth of the current maximum annual taxable 'wages' as defined in section 3121 for any month."

In 1981, P.L. 97-34, Sec. 741(a), amended Code Sec. 3201, effective for compensation paid for services rendered after 9/30/81.

Prior to amendment, Code Sec. 3201 read as follows:

"SEC. 3201. RATE OF TAX.

"In addition to other taxes, there is hereby imposed on the income of every employee a tax equal to the rate of the tax imposed with respect to wages by section 3101(a) plus the rate imposed by section 3101(b) of so much of the compensation paid in any calendar month to such employee for services rendered by him not in excess of an amount equal to one-twelfth of the current maximum annual taxable 'wages' as defined in section 3121 for any month."

In 1976, P.L. 94-455, Sec. 1903(a)(6), amended Code Sec. 3201, for compensation paid for services rendered after 12/31/76.

Prior to amendment, Code Sec. 3201 read as follows:

"SEC. 3201. RATE OF TAX.

"In addition to other taxes, there is hereby imposed on the income of every employee a tax equal to the rate of the tax imposed with respect to wages by section 3101(a) of the Internal Revenue Code of 1954 plus the rate imposed by section 3101(b) of such Code of so much of the compensation paid in any calendar month to such employee for services rendered by him after September 30, 1973, as is not in excess of an amount equal to one-twelfth of the current maximum annual taxable 'wages' as defined in section 3121 of the Internal Revenue Code of 1954 for any month after September 30, 1973."

In 1975, P.L. 94-93, Sec. 201, substituted "compensation paid in any calendar month to such employee" for "compensation paid to such employee", effective for tax. yrs. end on or after 8/9/75 and for tax. yrs. end before 8/9/75 as to which the period for assessment and collection of tax or the filing of a claim for credit or refund has not expired on 8/9/75.

In 1973, P.L. 93-69, Sec. 102(a), amended Sec. 3201, effective 10/1/73 but only with respect to compensation paid for services rendered on or after 10/1/73: Provided, however, That such amendments shall not be applicable to any dock company, common carrier railroad, or railway labor organization described in section 1(a) of the Railroad Retirement Act of 1937, with respect to those of its employees covered as of October 1, 1973, by a private supplemental pension plan established through collective bargaining, where a moratorium in an agreement made on or before March 8, 1973, is applicable to changes in rates of pay contained in the current collective-bargaining agreement covering such employees, until the earlier of (1) the date as of which such moratorium expires, or (2) the date as of which such dock company, common carrier railroad, or railway labor organization agrees through collective bargaining to make the provisions of such amendments applicable.

Prior to amendment, Code Sec. 3201 read as follows:

"In addition to other taxes, there is hereby imposed on the income of every employee a tax equal to—

"(1) 6¼ percent of so much of the compensation paid to such employee for services rendered by him after September 30, 1965,

"(2) 6½ percent of so much of the compensation paid to such employee for services rendered by him after December 31, 1965,

"(3) 7 percent of so much of the compensation paid to such employee for services rendered by him after December 31, 1965,

"(4) 7¼ percent of so much of the compensation paid to such employee for services rendered by him after December 31, 1967, and

"(5) 7½ percent of so much of the compensation paid to such employee for services rendered by him after December 31, 1968,

as is not in excess of (i) $450, or (ii) an amount equal to one-twelfth of the current maximum annual taxable 'wages' as defined in section 3121 of the Internal Revenue Code of 1954, whichever is greater, for any month after September 30, 1965:*Provided,* That the rate of tax imposed by this section shall be increased, with respect to compensation paid for services rendered after September 30, 1965, by a number of percentage points (including fractional points) equal at any given time to the number of percentage points (including fractional points) by which the rate of the tax imposed with respect to wages by section 3101(a) plus the rate imposed by section 3101(b) at such time exceeds 2¾ percent (the rate provided by paragraph (2) of section 3101 as amended by the Social Security Amendments of 1956)."

In 1966, P.L. 89-699, Sec. 301, increased the rates of tax from 6¾% after '66, 7% after '67 and 7¼% after '68, effective 10/30/66.

—P.L. 89-700, Sec. 301, deleted "$400 for any calendar month before the calendar month next following the month in which this provision was amended in 1963, or $450 for any calendar month after the month in which this provision was so amended and before the calendar month next following the calendar month in which this provision was amended in 1965, or" before "(i) $450", and substituted September 30, 1965 for December 31, 1964 in the proviso, effective 10/30/66.

In 1965, P.L. 89-212, Sec. 5(a), rewrote the first part of Code Sec. 3201 up to the proviso. The change in rates in par. (1–5) applies to compensation paid for services rendered after 9/30/65. The addition of the clause before the proviso applies to calendar months after 9/65.

—P.L. 89-97, Sec. 105 and 111, rewrote the proviso of Code Sec. 3201, effective for compensation paid for services rendered after '65.

Prior to amendment, Code Sec. 3201 read as follows:

"SEC. 3201. RATE OF TAX.

"In addition to other taxes, there is hereby imposed on the income of every employee a tax equal to—

"(1) 6¾ percent of so much of the compensation paid to such employee for services rendered by him after the month in which this provision was amended in 1959, and before January 1, 1962, and

"(2) 7¼ percent of so much of the compensation paid to such employee for services rendered by him after December 31, 1961, as is not in excess of $400 for any calendar month before the calendar month next following the month in which this provision was amended in 1963, or $450 for any calendar month after the month in which this provision was so amended:*Provided,* That the rate of tax imposed by this section shall be increased, with respect to compensation paid for services rendered after December 31, 1964, by a number of percentage points (including fractional points) equal at any given time to the number of percentage points (including fractional points) by which the rate of the tax imposed with respect to wages by section 3101 at such time exceeds the rate provided by paragraph (2) of such section 3101 as amended by the Social Security Amendments of 1956."

In 1963, P.L. 88-133, Sec. 201, limited the existing taxable compensation base of $400 to any calendar month before Nov. 1963 and increased such base to $450 for any calendar month after Oct. 1963.

In 1959, P.L. 86-28, Sec. 201(c), increased the tax from 6¼ percent of the compensation not in excess of $350 for any calendar month to 6¾ percent of the compensation not in excess of $400 for any calendar month for services rendered before Jan. 1, 1962, and to 7¼ percent for services rendered after Dec. 31, 1961, and required an increase in the rate of tax with respect to compensation paid for services rendered after Dec. 31, 1964, by a number of percentage points equal at any given time to the number of percentage points by which the rate of tax imposed by section 3101 of this title at such time exceeds the rate provided by par. (2) of such section 3101 as amended by the Social Security Amendments of 1956 for compensation paid after 5/59 for services after that date.

In 1954, P.L. 746, Sec. 206(a), substituted "$350" for "$300" effective as if originally enacted in the '54 Code.

Sec. 3202. Deduction of tax from compensation.

(a) Requirement.

The taxes imposed by section 3201 shall be collected by the employer of the taxpayer by deducting the amount of the taxes from the compensation of the employee as and when paid. An employer who is furnished by an employee a written statement of tips (received in a calendar month) pursuant to section 6053(a) to which paragraph (3) of section 3231(e) is applicable may deduct an amount equivalent to such taxes with respect to such tips from any compensation of the employee (exclusive of tips) under his control, even though at the time such statement is furnished the total amount of the tips included in statements furnished to the employer as having been received by the employee in such calendar month in the course of his employment by such employer is less than $20.

(b) Indemnification of employer.

Every employer required under subsection (a) to deduct the tax shall be liable for the payment of such tax and shall not be liable to any person for the amount of any such payment.

(c) Special rule for tips.

(1) In the case of tips which constitute compensation, subsection (a) shall be applicable only to such tips as are included in a written statement furnished to the employer pursuant to section 6053(a), and only to the extent that collection can be made by the employer, at or after the time such statement is so furnished and before the close of the 10th day following the calendar month (or, if paragraph (3) applies, the 30th day following the quarter) in which the tips were deemed paid, by deducting the amount of the tax from such compensation of the employee (excluding tips, but including funds turned over by the employee to the employer pursuant to paragraph (2)) as are under control of the employer.

(2) If the taxes imposed by section 3201, with respect to tips which are included in written statements furnished in any month to the employer pursuant to section 6053(a), exceed the compensation of the employee (excluding tips) from which the employer is required to collect the taxes under paragraph (1), the employee may furnish to the employer on or before the 10th day of the following month

Employment taxes   Code Sec. 3211(a)

(or, if paragraph (3) applies, on or before the 30th day of the following quarter) an amount of money equal to the amount of the excess.

(3) The Secretary may, under regulations prescribed by him, authorize employers—

(A) to estimate the amount of tips that will be reported by the employee pursuant to section 6053(a) in any quarter of the calendar year,

(B) to determine the amount to be deducted upon each payment of compensation (exclusive of tips) during such quarter as if the tips so estimated constituted actual tips so reported, and

(C) to deduct upon any payment of compensation (other than tips, but including funds turned over by the employee to the employer pursuant to paragraph (2)) to such employee during such quarter (and within 30 days thereafter) such amount as may be necessary to adjust the amount actually deducted upon such compensation of the employee during the quarter to the amount required to be deducted in respect of tips included in written statements furnished to the employer during the quarter.

(4) If the taxes imposed by section 3201 with respect to tips which constitute compensation exceed the portion of such taxes which can be collected by the employer from the compensation of the employee pursuant to paragraph (1) or paragraph (3), such excess shall be paid by the employee.

(d) Special rule for certain taxable group-term life insurance benefits.

(1) In general. In the case of any payment for group-term life insurance to which this subsection applies—

(A) subsection (a) shall not apply,

(B) the employer shall separately include on the statement required under section 6051—

(i) the portion of the compensation which consists of payments for group-term life insurance to which this subsection applies, and

(ii) the amount of the tax imposed by section 3201 on such payments, and

(C) the tax imposed by section 3201 on such payments shall be paid by the employee.

(2) Benefits to which subsection applies. This subsection shall apply to any payment for group-term life insurance to the extent—

(A) such payment constitutes compensation, and

(B) such payment is for coverage for periods during which an employment relationship no longer exists between the employee and the employer.

In **1990,** P.L. 101-508, Sec. 5124(b), added subsec. (d), effective for coverage provided after 12/31/90.

In **1983,** P.L. 98-76, Sec. 225(a)(2), deleted the second sentence of subsec. (a) . . . Sec. 225(c)(1)(A) & (B), substituted "taxes imposed by section 3201" for "tax imposed by section 3201" in subsec. (a) and in paras. (c)(2) and (c)(4) . . . Sec. 225(c)(2), substituted "the amount of the taxes" for "the amount of the tax" and substituted "such taxes" for "such tax" in subsec. (a) . . . Sec. 225(c)(3), substituted "the taxes under paragraph (1)" for "the tax under paragraph (1)" in para. (c)(2) . . . Sec. 225(c)(4), substituted "such taxes" for "such tax" in para. (c)(4) . . . Sec. 225(c)(5), substituted "exceed" for "exceeds" in paras. (c)(2) and (c)(4), for remuneration paid after 12/31/84.

Prior to deletion, the second sentence of subsec. (a) read as follows:

"If an employee is paid compensation by more than one employer for services rendered during any calendar month and the aggregate of such compensation is in excess of an amount equal to one-twelfth of the current maximum annual taxable 'wages' as defined in section 3121 for any month the tax to be deducted by each employer other than a subordinate unit of a national railway-labor-organization employer from the compensation paid by him to the employee with respect to such month shall be that proportion of the tax with respect to such compensation paid by all such employers which the compensation paid by him to the employee for services rendered during such month bears to the total compensation paid by all such employers to such employee for services rendered during such month;

and in the event that the compensation so paid by such employers to the employee for services rendered during such month is less than an amount equal to one-twelfth of the current maximum annual taxable 'wages' as defined in section 3121 for any month each subordinate unit of a national railway-labor organization employer shall deduct such proportion of any additional tax as the compensation paid by such employer to such employee for services rendered during such month bears to the total compensation paid by all such employers to such employee for services rendered during such month."

In **1976,** P.L. 94-455, Sec. 1903(a)(7)(A)(i), deleted "after September 30, 1973," each place it appeared in subsec. (a) . . . Sec. 1903(a)(7)(A)(ii), substituted "and the aggregate" for "after September 30, 1973 [sic 1965] and the aggregate" in subsec. (a) . . . Sec. 1903(a)(7)(A)(iii), deleted "of the Internal Revenue Code of 1954" each place it appeared in subsec. (a) . . . Sec. 1903(a)(3)(A)(iv), added a comma immediately after "for any month" each place it appeared in the second sentence of subsec. (a), effective for compensation paid for services rendered after 12/31/76.

—P.L. 94-455, Sec. 1903(a)(7)(B), deleted "made" after "deduct the tax shall be" in subsec. (b), effective for compensation paid for services rendered after 12/31/76.

—P.L. 94-455, Sec. 1906(b)(13)(A), substituted "Secretary" for "Secretary or his delegate" in subsec. (c), effective 2/1/77.

In **1973,** P.L. 93-69, Sec. 102(b), amended the second sentence of subsec. (a) effective with respect to compensation paid for services rendered on or after 10/1/73, subject to proviso reproduced in note at Code Sec. 3201.

Prior to amendment, the second sentence of subsec. (a) read as follows:

"If an employee is paid compensation after September 30, 1965, by more than one employer for services rendered during any calendar month after September 30, 1965 and the aggregate of such compensation is in excess of (i) $450, or (ii) an amount equal to one-twelfth of the current maximum annual taxable 'wages' as defined in section 3121 of the Internal Revenue Code of 1954, whichever is greater, for any month after September 30, 1965, the tax to be deducted by each employer other than a subordinate unit of a national railway-labor-organization employer from the compensation paid by him to the employee with respect to such month shall be that proportion of the tax with respect to such compensation paid by all such employers which the compensation paid by him after September 30, 1965, to the employee for services rendered during such month bears to the total compensation paid by all such employers to such employee for services rendered during such month; and in the event that the compensation so paid by such employers to the employee for services rendered during such month is less than (i) $450, or (ii) an amount equal to one-twelfth of the current maximum annual taxable 'wages' as defined in section 3121 of the Internal Revenue Code of 1954, whichever is greater, for any month after September 30, 1965, each subordinate unit of a national railway-labor organization employer shall deduct such proportion of any additional tax as the compensation paid by such employer after September 30, 1965, to such employee for services rendered during such month bears to the total compensation paid by all such employers after September 30, 1965, to such employee for services rendered during such month."

In **1966,** P.L. 89-700, Sec. 301, substituted "after September 30, 1965" for "after the month in which this provision was amended in 1959", and deleted "$400 for any calendar month before the calendar month next following the month in which this provision was amended in 1963, or $450 for any calendar month after the month in which this provision was so amended and before the calendar month next following the calendar month in which this provision was amended in 1965, or" before "(i) $450" in subsec. (a), effective 10/30/66.

In **1965,** P.L. 89-212, Sec. 2(a)(1), added the last sentence of subsec. (a) . . . Sec. 2(a)(2), added subsec. (c), effective for tips received after 1965 . . . Sec. 4, added "and before the calendar month next following the calendar month in which this provision was amended in 1965, or (i) $450, or (ii) an amount equal to one-twelfth of the current maximum annual taxable 'wages' as defined in section 3121 of the Internal Revenue Code of 1954, whichever is greater, for any month after the month in which this provision was so amended" after "$450 for any calendar month after the month in which this provision was so amended" in two places in subsec. (a) for calendar months after 9/65.

In **1963,** P.L. 88-133, Sec. 201, limited the existing taxable compensation base of $400 to any calendar month before Nov. 1963 and increased such base to $450 for any calendar month after Oct. 1963 in subsec. (a).

In **1959,** P.L. 86-28, Sec. 201(c), substituted "after the month in which this provision was amended in 1959" for "after 1954" and for "after December 31, 1954" in five places, and "$400" for "$350" in two places in subsec. (a) for the first day of June '59.

In **1954,** P.L. 746, Sec. 206(a), substituted "$350" for "300" wherever appearing in subsec. (a) as if originally enacted in the '54 Code.

Subchapter B.—Tax on Employee Representatives

Sec.

3211. Rate of tax.

3212. Determination of compensation.

Sec. 3211.   Rate of tax.

(a) Tier 1 tax.

In addition to other taxes, there is hereby imposed on the income of each employee representative a tax equal to the applicable percentage of the compensation received during

3,099

Code Sec. 3211(a) — Employment taxes

any calendar year by such employee representative for services rendered by such employee representative. For purposes of the preceding sentence, the term "applicable percentage" means the percentage equal to the sum of the rates of tax in effect under subsections (a) and (b) of section 3101 and subsections (a) and (b) of section 3111 for the calendar year.

(b) Tier 2 tax.

(1) In general. In addition to other taxes, there is hereby imposed on the income of each employee representative a tax equal to the applicable percentage of the compensation received during any calendar year by such employee representatives for services rendered by such employee representative.

(2) Applicable percentage. For purposes of paragraph (1), the term "applicable percentage" means—

(A) 14.75 percent in the case of compensation received during 2002,

(B) 14.20 percent in the case of compensation received during 2003, and

(C) in the case of compensation received during any calendar year after 2003, the percentage determined under section 3241 for such calendar year.

(c) Cross reference.

For application of different contribution bases with respect to the taxes imposed by subsections (a) and (b), see section 3231(e)(2).

In **2001**, P.L. 107-90, Sec. 203(a), deleted subsec. (b), effective for calendar yrs. begin. after 12/31/2001.

Prior to deletion, subsec. (b) read as follows:

"(b) In addition to other taxes, there is hereby imposed on the income of each employee representative a tax at a rate equal to the rate of excise tax imposed on every employer, provided for in section 3221(c), for each man-hour for which compensation is paid to him for services rendered as an employee representative."

—P.L. 107-90, Sec. 204(b), amended subsec. (a) and added subsecs. (b) and (c), effective for calendar yrs. begin. after 12/31/2001.

Prior to amendment, subsec. (a) read as follows:

"(a) Imposition of taxes.

"(1) Tier 1 tax. In addition to other taxes, there is hereby imposed on the income of each employee representative a tax equal to the applicable percentage of the compensation received during any calendar year by such employee representative for services rendered by such employee representative. For purposes of the preceding sentence, the term 'applicable percentage' means the percentage equal to the sum of the rates of tax in effect under subsections (a) and (b) of section 3101 and subsections (a) and (b) of section 3111 for the calendar year.

"(2) Tier 2 tax. In addition to other taxes, there is hereby imposed on the income of each employee representative a tax equal to the following percentage of the compensation received during any calendar year by such employee representatives for services rendered by such employee representative:

In the case of compensation received during:	The rate shall be:
1985	13.75
1986 or thereafter	14.75.

"(3) Cross reference. For application of different contribution bases with respect to the taxes imposed by paragraphs (1) and (2), see section 3231(e)(2)."

In **1990**, P.L. 101-508, Sec. 5125(b), amended para. (a)(1), effective 11/5/90.

Prior to amendment, para. (a)(1) read as follows:

"(a) Imposition of taxes.

"(1) Tier 1 tax. In addition to other taxes, there is hereby imposed on the income of each employee representative a tax equal to the following percentage of the compensation received during any calendar year by such employee representative for services rendered by such employee representative:

"In the case of compensation received during:	The rate shall be:
1985	14.10
1986 or 1987	14.30
1988 or 1989	15.02
1990 or thereafter	15.30."

In **1983**, P.L. 98-76, Sec. 211(c), substituted "12.75 percent" for "11.75 percent" in subsec. (a), effective for compensation paid for services rendered after 12/31/83 and before 1/1/85.

—P.L. 98-76, Sec. 223, amended subsec. (a), effective for remuneration after 12/31/84.

Prior to amendment, subsec. (a) read as follows:

"(a) In addition to other taxes there is hereby imposed on the income of each employee representative a tax equal to 12.75 percent plus the sum of the rates of tax

imposed with respect to wages by sections 3101(a), 3101(b), 3111(a), and 3111(b) of so much of the compensation paid in any calendar month to such employee representative for services rendered by him as is not in excess of an amount equal to one-twelfth of the current maximum annual taxable 'wages' as defined in section 3121, for any month."

In **1981**, P.L. 97-34, Sec. 741(b), substituted "11.75" for "9.5" in subsec. (a), effective for compensation paid for services rendered after 9/30/81.

In **1976**, P.L. 94-455, Sec. 1903(a)(8), substituted "3111(a), and 3111(b)" for "3111(a), 3111(b)", deleted "of the Internal Revenue Code of 1954" each time it appeared, substituted "rendered by him" for "rendered by him after September 31, 1973," deleted "after September 30, 1973" in subsec. (a) effective for compensation paid for services rendered after 12/31/76.

In **1975**, P.L. 94-93, Sec. 202, substituted "compensation paid in any calendar month to such employee representative" for "compensation paid to such employee representative" in subsec. (a), effective for tax. yrs. end. on or after 8/9/75 and for tax. yrs. end. before 8/9/75 as to which the period for assessment and collection of tax or the filing of a claim for credit or refund has not expired on 8/9/75.

In **1973**, P.L. 93-69, Sec. 102(c), amended subsec. (a) effective for compensation paid for services rendered on or after 10/1/73, subject to proviso reproduced in note at Code Sec. 3201.

Prior to amendment, subsec. (a) read as follows:

"(a) In addition to other taxes, there is hereby imposed on the income of each employee representative a tax equal to—

"(1) 12½ percent of so much of the compensation paid to such employee representative for services rendered by him after September 30, 1965,

"(2) 13 percent of so much of the compensation paid to such employee representative for services rendered by him after December 31, 1965,

"(3) 14 percent of so much of the compensation paid to such employee representative for services rendered by him after December 31, 1966,

"(4) 14½ percent of so much of the compensation paid to such employee representative for services rendered by him after December 31, 1967, and

"(5) 15 percent of so much of the compensation paid to such employee representative for services rendered by him after December 31, 1968,

as is not in excess of (i) $450, or (ii) an amount equal to one-twelfth of the current maximum annual taxable 'wages' as defined in section 3121 of the Internal Revenue Code of 1954, whichever is greater, for any month after September 30, 1965: Provided, That the rate of tax imposed by this section shall be increased, with respect to compensation paid for services rendered after September 30, 1965, by a number of percentage points (including fractional points) equal at any given time to twice the number of percentage points (including fractional points) by which the rate of the tax imposed with respect to wages by section 3101(a) plus the rate imposed by section 3101(b) at such time exceeds 2¼ percent (the rate provided by paragraph (2) of section 3101 as amended by the Social Security Amendments of 1956)."

1. "(a)" placed here in S. Rept. No. 1718, 89th Cong., p. 34, although final law inadvertently placed "a" following "Sec. 3211" in heading.

In **1970**, P.L. 91-215, Sec. 4, amended subsec. (b).

Prior to amendment, subsec. (b) read as follows:

"(b) In addition to other taxes, there is hereby imposed on the income of each employee representative a tax equal to 2 cents per man-hour for which compensation is paid to him for services rendered as an employee representative."

In **1966**, P.L. 89-699, Sec. 301, increased the rates of tax from 13½% after '66, 14% after '67 and 14½% after '68, effective 10/30/66 . . . added the (a) after Sec. 3211 . . . and added subsec. (b), effective for man hours, for 60 months beginning 11/66, for which compensation is paid.

—P.L. 89-700, Sec. 301, deleted "$400 for any calendar month before the calendar month next following the month in which this provision was amended in 1963, or $450 for any calendar month after the month in which this provision was so amended and before the calendar month next following the calendar month in which this provision was amended in 1965, or" before "(i) $450", and substituted September 30, 1965 for December 31, 1964 in the proviso effective. 10/30/66.

In **1965**, P.L. 89-212, Sec. 5(b), amended the first part of Code Sec. 3211 up to the proviso. The change in rates in par. (1–5) applies to compensation paid for services rendered after 9/30/65. The addition of the clause before the proviso applies to calendar months after 9/65.

—P.L. 89-97, Sec. 105 and 111, amended the proviso of Code Sec. 3211 for compensation paid for services rendered after '65.

Prior to these amendments, Code Sec. 3211 read as follows:

"SEC. 3211. RATE OF TAX.

"In addition to other taxes, there is hereby imposed on the income of each employee representative a tax equal to—

"(1) 13½ percent of so much of the compensation paid to such employee representative for services rendered by him after the month in which this provision was amended in 1959, and before January 1, 1962, and

"(2) 14½ percent of so much of the compensation paid to such employee representative for services rendered by him after December 31, 1961,

as is not in excess of $400 for any calendar month before the calendar month next following the month in which this provision was amended in 1963, or $450 for any calendar month after the month in which this provision was so amended: Provided, That the rate of tax imposed by this section shall be increased, with respect to compensation paid for services rendered after December 31, 1964, by a number of percentage points (including fractional points) equal at any given time to twice the number of percentage points (including fractional points) by which the rate of the tax imposed with respect to wages by section 3101 at such time exceeds the rate provided by paragraph (2) of such section 3101 as amended by the Social Security Amendments of 1956."

Employment taxes   Code Sec. 3221

In 1963, P.L. 88-133, Sec. 201, limited the existing taxable compensation base of $400 to any calendar month before Nov. 1963 and increased such base to $450 for any calendar month after Oct. 1963.

In 1959, P.L. 86-28, Sec. 201(c), increased the tax from 12½ percent of the compensation not in excess of $350 for any calendar month to 13½ percent of the compensation not in excess of $400 for any calendar month for services rendered before Jan. 1, 1962, and to 14½ percent for services rendered after Dec. 31, 1961, and required an increase in the rate of tax with respect to compensation paid for services rendered after December 31, 1964, by a number of percentage points equal at any given time to twice the number of percentage points by which the rate of tax imposed by section 3101 of this title at such time exceeds the rate provided by par. (2) of such section 3101 as amended by the Social Security Amendments of 1956.

In 1954, P.L. 746, Sec. 206(a), substituted "$350" for "$300", effective as if originally enacted in the '54 Code.

Sec. 3212. Determination of compensation.

The compensation of an employee representative for the purpose of ascertaining the tax thereon shall be determined in the same manner and with the same effect as if the employee organization by which such employee representative is employed were an employer as defined in section 3231(a).

Subchapter C.—Tax on Employers

Sec.
3221. Rate of tax.

Sec. 3221. Rate of tax.

(a) Tier 1 tax.

In addition to other taxes, there is hereby imposed on every employer an excise tax, with respect to having individuals in his employ, equal to the applicable percentage of compensation paid during any calendar year by such employer for services rendered to such employer. For purposes of the preceding sentence, the term "applicable percentage" means the percentage equal to the sum of the rates of tax in effect under subsections (a) and (b) of section 3111 for the calendar year.

(b) Tier 2 tax.

(1) **In general.** In addition to other taxes, there is hereby imposed on every employer an excise tax, with respect to having individuals in his employ, equal to the applicable percentage of the compensation paid during any calendar year by such employer for services rendered to such employer.

(2) **Applicable percentage.** For purposes of paragraph (1), the term "applicable percentage" means—

(A) 15.6 percent in the case of compensation paid during 2002,

(B) 14.2 percent in the case of compensation paid during 2003, and

(C) in the case of compensation paid during any calendar year after 2003, the percentage determined under section 3241 for such calendar year.

(c) Special rate for certain individuals hired in 2010.

(1) **In general.** In the case of compensation paid by a qualified employer during the period beginning on the day after the date of the enactment of this subsection and ending on December 31, 2010, with respect to having a qualified individual in the employer's employ for services rendered to such qualified employer, the applicable percentage under subsection (a) shall be equal to the rate of tax in effect under section 3111(b) for the calendar year.

(2) **Qualified employer.** The term "qualified employer" means any employer other than the United States, any State, or any political subdivision thereof, or any instrumentality of the foregoing.

(3) **Qualified individual.** For purposes of this subsection, the term "qualified individual" means any individual who—

(A) begins employment with a qualified employer after February 3, 2010, and before January 1, 2011,

(B) certifies by signed affidavit, under penalties of perjury, that such individual has not been employed for more than 40 hours during the 60-day period ending on the date such individual begins such employment,

(C) is not employed by the qualified employer to replace another employee of such employer unless such other employee separated from employment voluntarily or for cause, and

(D) is not an individual described in section 51(i)(1) (applied by substituting "qualified employer" for "taxpayer" each place it appears).

(4) **Election.** A qualified employer may elect to have this subsection not apply. Such election shall be made in such manner as the Secretary may require.

(5) **Special rule for first calendar quarter of 2010.**

(A) Nonapplication of exemption during first quarter. Paragraph (1) shall not apply with respect to compensation paid during the first calendar quarter of 2010.

(B) Crediting of first quarter exemption during second quarter. The amount by which the tax imposed under subsection (a) would (but for subparagraph (A)) have been reduced with respect to compensation paid by a qualified employer during the first calendar quarter of 2010 shall be treated as a payment against the tax imposed under subsection (a) with respect to the qualified employer for the second calendar quarter of 2010 which is made on the date that such tax is due.

(d) Cross reference.

For application of different contribution bases with respect to the taxes imposed by subsections (a) and (b), see section 3231(e)(2).

In 2010, P.L. 111-147, Sec. 101(d)(1), redesignated subsec. (c) as subsec. (d) and added subsec. (c), effective for compensation paid after 3/18/2010.

In 2001, P.L. 107-90, Sec. 203(b), deleted subsecs. (c) and (d) and redesignated subsec. (e) as (c), effective for calendar yrs. begin. after 12/31/2001.

Prior to deletion, subsecs. (c) and (d) read as follows:

"(c) In addition to other taxes, there is hereby imposed on every employer an excise tax, with respect to having individuals in his employ, for each man-hour for which compensation is paid by such employer for services rendered to him during any calendar quarter, an excise tax at such rate as will make available sufficient funds to meet the obligation to pay supplemental annuities at the level provided under section 3(j) of the Railroad Retirement Act of 1937 as in effect on December 31, 1974 and administrative expenses in connection therewith. For the purpose of this subsection, the Railroad Retirement Board is directed to determine what rate is required for each calendar quarter. The Railroad Retirement Board shall make the determinations provided for not later than fifteen days before each calendar quarter. As soon as practicable after each determination of the rate, as provided in this subsection, the Railroad Retirement Board shall publish a notice in the Federal Register, and shall advise all employers, employee representatives, and the Secretary, of the rate so determined. With respect to daily, weekly, or monthly rates of compensation such tax shall apply to the number of hours comprehended in the rate together with the number of overtime hours for which compensation in addition to the daily, weekly, or monthly rate is paid. With respect to compensation paid on a mileage or piecework basis such tax shall apply to the number of hours constituting the hourly equivalent of the compensation paid.

"Each employer of employees whose supplemental annuities are reduced pursuant to section 3(j)(2) of the Railroad Retirement Act of 1937 or section 2(h)(2) of the Railroad Retirement Act of 1974 shall be allowed as a credit against the tax imposed by this subsection an amount equivalent in each month to the aggregate amount of reductions in supplemental annuities accruing in such month to employees of such employer. If the credit so allowed to such an employer for any month exceeds the tax liability of such employer accruing under this subsection in such month, the excess may be carried forward for credit against such taxes accruing in subsequent months but the total credit allowed by this paragraph to an employer shall not exceed the total of the taxes on such employer imposed by this subsection. At the end of each calendar quarter the Railroad Retirement Board shall certify to the Secretary with respect to each such employer the amount of credit accruing to such employer under this paragraph during such quarter and shall notify such employer as to the amount so certified."

"(d) Notwithstanding the provisions of subsection (c) of this section, the tax imposed by such subsection (c) shall not apply to an employer with respect to employees who are covered by a supplemental pension plan which is established pursuant to an agreement reached through collective bargaining between the employer and employees. There is hereby imposed on every such employer an excise tax equal to the amount of the supplemental annuity paid to each such employee under section 2(b) of the Railroad Retirement Act of 1974, plus a percentage thereof determined by the Railroad Retirement Board to be sufficient to cover the administrative costs attributable to such payments under section 2(b) of such Act."

—P.L. 107-90, Sec. 204(a), amended subsec. (b), effective for calendar yrs. begin. after 12/31/2001.

Prior to amendment, subsec. (b) read as follows:

"(b) Tier 2 tax. In addition to other taxes, there is hereby imposed on every employer an excise tax, with respect to having individuals in his employ, equal to 16.10 percent of the compensation paid during any calendar year by such employer for services rendered to such employer."

In 1990, P.L. 101-508, Sec. 5125(c), amended subsec. (a), effective 11/5/90.

Prior to amendment, subsec. (a) read as follows:

"(a) Tier 1 tax.

"In addition to other taxes, there is hereby imposed on every employer an excise tax, with respect to having individuals in his employ, equal to the following percentage of compensation paid during any calendar year by such employer for services rendered to such employer:

"In the case of compensation paid during:	The rate shall be:
1985	7.05
1986 or 1987	7.15
1988 or 1989	7.51
1990 or thereafter	7.65."

In 1987, P.L. 100-203, Sec. 9032(a), amended subsec. (b), effective for compensation paid after 12/31/87.

Prior to amendment, subsec. (b) read as follows:

"(b) Tier 2 tax.

"In addition to other taxes, there is hereby imposed on every employer an excise tax, with respect to having individuals in his employ, equal to the following percentage of compensation paid during any calendar year by such employer for services rendered to such employer:

"In the case of compensation paid during:	The rate shall be:
1985	13.75
1986 or thereafter	14.75."

In 1983, P.L. 98-76, Sec. 211(b), substituted "12.75 percent" for "11.75 percent" in subsec. (a), effective for compensation paid for services rendered after 12/31/83 and before 1/1/85.

—P.L. 98-76, Sec. 222(a), amended subsecs. (a) and (b) . . . Sec. 222(b), added new subsec. (e), effective for remuneration paid after 12/31/84.

Prior to amendment, subsecs. (a) and (b) read as follows:

"(a) In addition to other taxes, there is hereby imposed on every employer an excise tax, with respect to having individuals in his employ, equal to 12.75 percent of so much of the compensation paid in any calendar month by such employer for services rendered to him as is with respect to any employee for any calendar month, not in excess of an amount equal to one-twelfth of the current maximum annual taxable 'wages' as defined in section 3121 for any month except that if any employee is paid compensation after the month in which this provision was amended in 1959, by more than one employer for services rendered during any calendar month the tax imposed by this section shall apply to not more than an amount equal to one-twelfth of the current maximum annual taxable 'wages' as defined in section 3121 for any month of the aggregate compensation paid to such employee by all such employers for services rendered during such month, and each employer other than a subordinate unit of a national railway-labor-organization employer shall be liable for that proportion of the tax with respect to such compensation paid by all such employers which the compensation paid by him to the employee for services rendered during such month bears to the total compensation paid by all such employers to such employee for services rendered during such month; and in the event that the compensation so paid by such employers to the employee for services rendered during such month is less than an amount equal to one-twelfth of the current maximum annual taxable 'wages' as defined in section 3121 for any month after the month in which this provision was so amended, each subordinate unit of a national railway-labor-organization employer shall be liable for such proportion of any additional tax as the compensation paid by such employer to such employee for services rendered during such month bears to the total compensation paid by all such employers to such employee for services rendered during such month. Where compensation for services rendered in a month is paid an employee by two or more employers, one of the employers who has knowledge of such joint employment may, by proper notice to the Secretary, and by agreement with such other employer or employers as to settlement of their respective liabilities under this section and section 3202, elect for the tax imposed by section 3201 and this section to apply to all of the compensation paid by such employer for such month as does not exceed the maximum amount of compensation in respect to which taxes are imposed by such section 3201 and this section; and in such a case the liability of such other employer or employers under this section and section 3202 shall be limited to the difference, if any, between the compensation paid by the electing employer and the maximum amount of compensation to which section 3201 and this section apply.

"(b) The rate of tax imposed by subsection (b) shall be increased by the rate of tax imposed with respect to wages by section 3111(a) plus the rate imposed by section 3111(b)."

In 1981, P.L. 97-34, Sec. 741(c), substituted "11.75" for "9.5" in the first sentence of subsec. (a), effective for compensation paid for services rendered after 9/30/81.

In 1976, P.L. 94-455, Sec. 1903(a)(9)(A), and (B), amended subsecs. (a) and (b), effective for compensation paid for services rendered after 12/31/76.

Prior to amendment, subsecs. (a) and (b) read as follows:

"(a) In addition to other taxes, there is hereby imposed on every employer an excise tax, with respect to having individuals in his employ, equal to 9.5 percent of so much of the compensation paid in any calendar month by such employer for services rendered to him after September 30, 1973, as is with respect to any employee for any calendar month, not in excess of an amount equal to one-twelfth of the current maximum annual taxable 'wages' as defined in section 3121 of the Internal Revenue Code of 1954 for any month after September 30, 1973; except that if any employee is paid compensation after the month in which this provision was amended in 1959, by more than one employer for services rendered during any calendar month after September 30, 1973, the tax imposed by this section shall apply to not more than an amount equal to one-twelfth of the current maximum annual taxable 'wages' as defined in section 3121 of the Internal Revenue Code of 1954, for any month after September 30, 1973 of the aggregate compensation paid to such employee by all such employers after September 30, 1973, for services rendered during such month, and each employer other than a subordinate unit of a national railway-labor-organization employer shall be liable for that proportion of the tax with respect to such compensation paid by all such employers which the compensation paid by him after September 30, 1973, to the employee for services rendered during such month bears to the total compensation paid by all such employers after September 30, 1973, to such employee for services rendered during such month; and in the event that the compensation so paid by such employers to the employee for services rendered during such month is less than an amount equal to one-twelfth of the current maximum annual taxable 'wages' as defined in section 3121 of the Internal Revenue Code of 1954 for any month after the month in which this provision was so amended, each subordinate unit of a national railway-labor-organization employer shall be liable for such proportion of any additional tax as the compensation paid by such employer after September 30, 1973, to such employee for services rendered during such month bears to the total compensation paid by all such employers after September 30, 1973 to such employee for services rendered during such month. Where compensation for services rendered in a month is paid an employee by two or more employers, one of the employers who has knowledge of such joint employment may, by proper notice to the Secretary of the Treasury, and by agreement with such other employer or employers as to settlement of their respective liabilities under this section and section 3202, elect for the tax imposed by section 3201 and this section to apply to all of the compensation paid by such employer for such month as does not exceed the maximum amount of compensation in respect to which taxes are imposed by such section 3201 and this section; and in such a case the liability of such other employer or employers under this section and section 3202 shall be limited to the difference, if any, between the compensation paid by the electing employer and the maximum amount of compensation to which section 3201 and this section apply.

"(b) The rate of tax imposed by subsection (a) shall be increased, with respect to compensation paid for services rendered after September 30, 1973, by the rate of tax imposed with respect to wages by section 3111(a) of the Internal Revenue Code of 1954 plus the rate imposed by section 3111(b) of such Code."

—P.L. 94-455, Sec. 1903(a)(9)(C), deleted "(1) at the rate of 2 cents for the period beginning November 1, 1966, and ending March 31, 1970, and (2) commencing April 1, 1970," after "rendered to him during any calendar quarter,", deleted "commencing with the quarter beginning April 1, 1970" following "rate is required for each calendar quarter" in subsec. (c), effective for compensation for services rendered after 12/31/76.

—P.L. 94-455, Sec. 1906(b)(13)(G), deleted "of the Treasury" each place it appeared in subsecs. (a) and (c), effective 2/1/77.

In 1975, P.L. 94-93, Sec. 203, substituted "compensation paid in any calendar month by such employer" for "compensation paid by such employer" in subsec. (a), effective for tax. yrs. end. on or after 8/9/75 and for tax. yrs. end. before 8/9/75 as to which the period for assessment and collection of tax or the filing of a claim for credit or refund has not expired on 8/9/75.

In 1974, P.L. 93-445, Sec. 501(a)(1), struck out "for appropriation to the Railroad Retirement Supplemental Account provided for in section 15(b) of the Railroad Retirement Act of 1937" immediately after "at such rate as will make available" in subsec. (c), effective 1/1/75 with respect to compensation paid for services rendered on or after that date.

—P.L. 93-445, Sec. 501(a)(2), substituted "at the level provided under section 3(j) of the Railroad Retirement Act of 1937 as in effect on December 31, 1974" for "under section 3(j) of such Act" in subsec. (c), effective 1/1/75 with respect to compensation paid for services rendered on or after that date.

—P.L. 93-445, Sec. 501(a)(3), added "or section 2(h)(2) of the Railroad Retirement Act of 1974" after "section 3(j)(2) of the Railroad Retirement Act of 1937" in subsec. (c), effective 1/1/75 with respect to compensation paid for services rendered on or after that date.

—P.L. 93-445, Sec. 501(b)(1), substituted "section 2(b) of the Railroad Retirement Act of 1974" for "section 3(j) of the Railroad Retirement Act of 1937" in subsec. (d), effective 1/1/75 with respect to compensation paid for services rendered on or after that date.

—P.L. 93-445, Sec. 501(b)(2), substituted "section 2(b) of such Act" for "section 3(j) of such Act" in subsec. (d), effective 1/1/75 with respect to compensation paid for services rendered on or after that date.

In 1973, P.L. 93-69, Sec. 102(d), and (e) amended the first sentence of subsec. (a) effective with respect to compensation paid for services rendered on or after 10/1/73 subject to proviso reproduced in note at Code Sec. 3201.

Prior to amendment, the first sentence of subsec. (a) read as follows:

"(a) In addition to other taxes, there is hereby imposed on every employer an excise tax, with respect to having individuals in his employ, equal to—

"(1) 6¼ percent of so much of the compensation paid by such employer for services rendered to him after September 30, 1965,

"(2) 6½ percent of so much of the compensation paid by such employer for services rendered to him after December 31, 1965,

"(3) 7 percent of so much of the compensation paid by such employer for services rendered to him after December 31, 1966,

"(4) 7¼ percent of so much of the compensation paid by such employer for services rendered to him after December 31, 1967, and

"(5) 7½ percent of so much of the compensation paid by such employer for services rendered to him after December 31, 1968,

as is, with respect to any employee for any calendar month, not in excess of (i) $450, or (ii) an amount equal to one-twelfth of the current maximum annual taxable 'wages' as defined in section 3121 of the Internal Revenue Code of 1954, whichever is greater for any month after September 30, 1965; except that if an employee is paid compensation after the month in which this provision was amended in 1959, by more than one employer for services rendered during any calendar month after September 30, 1965, the tax imposed by this section shall apply to not more than (i) $450, or (ii) an amount equal to one-twelfth of the current maximum annual taxable 'wages' as defined in section 3121 of the Internal Revenue Code of 1954, whichever is greater for any month after September 30, 1965 of the aggregate compensation paid to such employee by all such employers after September 30, 1965, for services rendered during such month, and each employer other than a subordinate unit of a national railway-labor-organization employer shall be liable for that proportion of the tax with respect to such compensation paid by all such employers which the compensation paid by him after September 30, 1965, to the employee for services rendered during such month bears to the total compensation paid by all such employers after September 30, 1965, to such employee for services rendered during such month; and in the event that the compensation so paid by such employers to the employee for services rendered during such month is less than (i) $450, or (ii) an amount equal to one-twelfth of the current maximum annual taxable 'wages' as defined in section 3121 of the Internal Revenue Code of 1954, whichever is greater, for any month after the month in which this provision was so amended, each subordinate unit of a national railway-labor-organization employer shall be liable for such proportion of any additional tax as the compensation paid by such employer after September 30, 1965, to such employee for services rendered during such month bears to the total compensation paid by all such employers after September 30, 1965 to such employee for services rendered during such month."

—P.L. 93-69, Sec. 102(f), amended subsec. (b) effective with respect to compensation paid for services rendered on or after 10/1/73, subject to proviso reproduced in note at Code Sec. 3201.

Prior to amendment, subsec. (b) read as follows:

"The rate of tax imposed by subsection (a) shall be increased, with respect to compensation paid for services rendered after December 31, 1964, by a number of percentage points (including fractional points) equal at any given time to the number of percentage points (including fractional points) by which the rate of the tax imposed with respect to wages by section 3111(a) plus the rate imposed by section 3111(b) at such time exceeds 2¾ percent (the rate provided by paragraph (2) of section 3111 as amended by the Social Security Amendments of 1956)."

In 1970, P.L. 91-215, Sec. 5(a), deleted the first sentence and added the first four sentences in subsec. (c).

Prior to deletion, the first sentence in subsec. (c) read as follows:

"In addition to other taxes, there is hereby imposed on every employer an excise tax, with respect to having individuals in his employ, equal to 2 cents for each man-hour, for which compensation is paid."

—P.L. 91-215, Sec. 5(b), added subsec. (d), applicable to (a) supplemental annuities paid on or after 4/1/70, and (b) man-hours with respect to which compensation is paid for services rendered to such employer on or after such day.

In 1966, P.L. 89-699, Sec. 301, increased the rates of tax from 6¾% after '66, 7% after '67, and 7¼% after '68, effective 10/30/66 . . . added subsec. (c) with respect to man-hours, for 60 months beginning Nov. '66, for which compensation is paid.

—P.L. 89-700, Sec. 301, substituted "after September 30, 1965" for "after the month in which this provision was amended in 1959", deleted "$400 for any calendar month before the calendar month next following the month in which this provision was amended in 1963, or $450 for any calendar month after the month in which this provision was so amended and before the calendar month next following the calendar month in which this provision was amended in 1965, or" before "(i) $450" in subsec. (a), and added last sentence in subsec. (a), effective 10/30/66.

In 1965, P.L. 89-212, Sec. 4, added "and before the calendar month next following the calendar month in which this provision was amended in 1965, or (i) $450, or (ii) an amount equal to one-twelfth of the current maximum annual taxable 'wages' as defined in section 3121 of the Internal Revenue Code of 1954, whichever is greater, for any month after the month in which this provision was so amended" following "or $450 for any calendar month after the month in which the provision was so amended" in 3 places in subsec. (a), for calendar months after 9/65. . . . Sec. 5(c), substituted the new rates in par. (1–5) for "(1) 6¾ percent of so much of the compensation paid by such employer for services rendered to him after the month in which this provision was amended in 1959, and before January 1, 1962, and (2) 7¼ percent of so much of the compensation paid by such employer for services rendered to him after December 31, 1961," for compensation paid for services rendered after 9/30/65

—P.L. 89-97, Sec. 105 and 111, added "(a) plus the rate imposed by section 3111(b)" and "2¾ percent" in subsec. (b) for compensation paid for services rendered after '65.

In 1963, P.L. 88-133, Sec. 201, limited the existing taxable compensation base of $400 to any calendar month before Nov. 1963 and increased such base to $450 for any calendar month after Oct. 1963.

In 1959, P.L. 86-28, Sec. 201(c), designated former provisions of section as subsec. (a) and added subsec. (b), increased the tax from 6¼% of the compensation not in excess of $350 for any calendar month to 6¾% of the compensation not in excess of $400 for any calendar month for services rendered before '62, and to 7¼% for services rendered after '61, and substituted "after the month in which this provision was amended in 1959" for "after 1954" and for "after December 31, 1954" in six instances, "not more than $400" for "not more than $350", and "less than $400" for "less than $350" effective 6/1/59.

In 1954, P.L. 746, Sec. 206(a), substituted "350" for "$300" wherever appearing, effective as if originally enacted in the '54 Code.

Subchapter D.—General Provisions

Sec.
3231. Definitions.
3232. Court jurisdiction.
3233. Short title.

Sec. 3231. Definitions.

(a) Employer.

For purposes of this chapter, the term "employer" means any carrier (as defined in subsection (g)), and any company which is directly or indirectly owned or controlled by one or more such carriers or under common control therewith, and which operates any equipment or facility or performs any service (except trucking service, casual service, and the casual operation of equipment, or facilities) in connection with the transportation of passengers or property by railroad, or the receipt, delivery, elevation, transfer in transit, refrigeration or icing, storage, or handling of property transported by railroad, and any receiver, trustee, or other individual or body, judicial or otherwise, when in the possession of the property or operating all or any part of the business of any such employer; except that the term "employer" shall not include any street, interurban, or suburban electric railway, unless such railway is operating as a part of a general steam-railroad system of transportation, but shall not exclude any part of the general steam-railroad system of transportation now or hereafter operated by any other motive power. The Surface Transportation Board is hereby authorized and directed upon request of the Secretary, or upon complaint of any party interested, to determine after hearing whether any line operated by electric power falls within the terms of this exception. The term "employer" shall also include railroad associations, traffic associations, tariff bureaus, demurrage bureaus, weighing and inspection bureaus, collection agencies and other associations, bureaus, agencies, or organizations controlled and maintained wholly or principally by two or more employers as hereinbefore defined and engaged in the performance of services in connection with or incidental to railroad transportation; and railway labor organizations, national in scope, which have been or may be organized in accordance with the provisions of the Railway Labor Act, as amended (45 U.S.C., chapter 8), and their State and National legislative committees and their general committees and their insurance departments and their local lodges and divisions, established pursuant to the constitutions and bylaws of such organizations. The term "employer" shall not include any company by reason of its being engaged in the mining of coal, the supplying of coal to an employer where delivery is not beyond the mine tipple, and the operation of equipment or facilities therefor, or in any of such activities.

(b) Employee.

For purposes of this chapter, the term "employee" means any individual in the service of one or more employers for compensation; except that the term "employee" shall include an employee of a local lodge or division defined as an employer in subsection (a) only if he was in the service of or in the employment relation to a carrier on or after August 29, 1935. An individual shall be deemed to have been in the employment relation to a carrier on August 29, 1935, if—

(1) he was on that date on leave of absence from his employment, expressly granted to him by the carrier by whom he was employed, or by a duly authorized representative of such carrier, and the grant of such leave of absence was established to the satisfaction of the Railroad Retirement Board before July 1947; or

(2) he was in the service of a carrier after August 29, 1935, and before January 1946 in each of 6 calendar months, whether or not consecutive; or

(3) before August 29, 1935, he did not retire and was not retired or discharged from the service of the last carrier by whom he was employed or its corporate or operating successor, but—

(A) solely by reason of his physical or mental disability he ceased before August 29, 1935, to be in the service of such carrier and thereafter remained continuously disabled until he attained age 65 or until August 1945, or

(B) solely for such last stated reason a carrier by whom he was employed before August 29, 1935, or a carrier who is its successor did not on or after August 29, 1935, and before August 1945 call him to return to service, or

(C) if he was so called he was solely for such reason unable to render service in 6 calendar months as provided in paragraph (2); or

(4) he was on August 29, 1935, absent from the service of a carrier by reason of a discharge which, within 1 year after the effective date thereof, was protested, to an appropriate labor representative or to the carrier, as wrongful, and which was followed within 10 years of the effective date thereof by his reinstatement in good faith to his former service with all his seniority rights;

except that an individual shall not be deemed to have been on August 29, 1935, in the employment relation to a carrier if before that date he was granted a pension or gratuity on the basis of which a pension was awarded to him pursuant to section 6 of the Railroad Retirement Act of 1937 (45 U.S.C. 228f), or if during the last payroll period before August 29, 1935, in which he rendered service to a carrier he was not in the service of an employer, in accordance with subsection (d), with respect to any service in such payroll period, or if he could have been in the employment relation to an employer only by reason of his having been, either before or after August 29, 1935, in the service of a local lodge or division defined as an employer in subsection (a). The term "employee" includes an officer of an employer. The term "employee" shall not include any individual while such individual is engaged in the physical operations consisting of the mining of coal, the preparation of coal, the handling (other than movement by rail with standard railroad locomotives) of coal not beyond the mine tipple, or the loading of coal at the tipple.

(c) **Employee representative.**

For purposes of this chapter, the term "employee representative" means any officer or official representative of a railway labor organization other than a labor organization included in the term "employer" as defined in subsection (a), who before or after June 29, 1937, was in the service of an employer as defined in subsection (a) and who is duly authorized and designated to represent employees in accordance with the Railway Labor Act (45 U.S.C., chapter 8), as amended, and any individual who is regularly assigned to or regularly employed by such officer or official representative in connection with the duties of his office.

(d) **Service.**

For purposes of this chapter, an individual is in the service of an employer whether his service is rendered within or without the United States, if—

(1) he is subject to the continuing authority of the employer to supervise and direct the manner of rendition of his service, or he is rendering professional or technical services and is integrated into the staff of the employer, or he is rendering, on the property used in the employer's operations, other personal services the rendition of which is integrated into the employer's operations, and

(2) he renders such service for compensation;

except that an individual shall be deemed to be in the service of an employer, other than a local lodge or division or a general committee of a railway-labor-organization employer, not conducting the principal part of its business in the United States, only when he is rendering service to it in the United States; and an individual shall be deemed to be in the service of such a local lodge or division only if—

(3) all, or substantially all, the individuals constituting its membership are employees of an employer conducting the principal part of its business in the United States; or

(4) the headquarters of such local lodge or division is located in the United States;

and an individual shall be deemed to be in the service of such a general committee only if—

(5) he is representing a local lodge or division described in paragraph (3) or (4) immediately above; or

(6) all, or substantially all, the individuals represented by it are employees of an employer conducting the principal part of its business in the United States; or

(7) he acts in the capacity of a general chairman or an assistant general chairman of a general committee which represents individuals rendering service in the United States to an employer, but in such case if his office or headquarters is not located in the United States and the individuals represented by such general committee are employees of an employer not conducting the principal part of its business in the United States, only such proportion of the remuneration for such service shall be regarded as compensation as the proportion which the mileage in the United States under the jurisdiction of such general committee bears to the total mileage under its jurisdiction, unless such mileage formula is inapplicable, in which case such other formula as the Railroad Retirement Board may have prescribed pursuant to section 1(c) of the Railroad Retirement Act of 1937 (45 U.S.C 228a) shall be applicable, and if the application of such mileage formula, or such other formula as the Board may prescribe, would result in the compensation of the individual being less than 10 percent of his remuneration for such service, no part of such remuneration shall be regarded as compensation;

Provided however, That an individual not a citizen or resident of the United States shall not be deemed to be in the service of an employer when rendering service outside the United States to an employer who is required under the laws applicable in the place where the service is rendered to employ therein, in whole or in part, citizens or residents thereof; and the laws applicable on August 29, 1935, in the place where the service is rendered shall be deemed to have been applicable there at all times prior to that date.

(e) **Compensation.**

For purposes of this chapter—

(1) The term "compensation" means any form of money remuneration paid to an individual for services rendered

as an employee to one or more employers. Such term does not include (i) the amount of any payment (including any amount paid by an employer for insurance or annuities, or into a fund, to provide for any such payment) made to, or on behalf of, an employee or any of his dependents under a plan or system established by an employer which makes provision for his employees generally (or for his employees generally and their dependents) or for a class or classes of his employees (or for a class or classes of his employees and their dependents), on account of sickness or accident disability or medical or hospitalization expenses in connection with sickness or accident disability or death, except that this clause does not apply to a payment for group-term life insurance to the extent that such payment is includible in the gross income of the employee, (ii) tips (except as is provided under paragraph (3)), (iii) an amount paid specifically—either as an advance, as reimbursement or allowance—for traveling or other bona fide and necessary expenses incurred or reasonably expected to be incurred in the business of the employer provided any such payment is identified by the employer either by a separate payment or by specifically indicating the separate amounts where both wages and expense reimbursement or allowance are combined in a single payment. Such term does not include remuneration for service which is performed by a nonresident alien individual for the period he is temporarily present in the United States as a nonimmigrant under subparagraph (F), (J), (M), or (Q) of section 101(a)(15) of the Immigration and Nationality Act, as amended, and which is performed to carry out the purpose specified in subparagraph (F), (J), (M) or (Q) as the case may be. For the purpose of determining the amount of taxes under sections 3201 and 3221, compensation earned in the service of a local lodge or division of a railway-labor-organization employer shall be disregarded with respect to any calendar month if the amount thereof is less than $25. Compensation for service as a delegate to a national or international convention of a railway labor organization defined as an "employer" in subsection (a) of this section shall be disregarded for purposes of determining the amount of taxes due pursuant to this chapter if the individual rendering such service has not previously rendered service, other than as such a delegate, which may be included in his "years of service" for purposes of the Railroad Retirement Act, or (iv) any remuneration which would not (if chapter 21 applied to such remuneration) be treated as wages (as defined in section 3121(a)) by reason of section 3121(a)(5). Nothing in the regulations prescribed for purposes of chapter 24 (relating to wage withholding) which provides an exclusion from "wages" as used in such chapter shall be construed to require a similar exclusion from "compensation" in regulations prescribed for purposes of this chapter.

(2) Application of contribution bases.

(A) Compensation in excess of applicable base excluded.

(i) In general. The term "compensation" does not include that part of remuneration paid during any calendar year to an individual by an employer after remuneration equal to the applicable base has been paid during such calendar year to such individual by such employer for services rendered as an employee to such employer.

(ii) Remuneration not treated as compensation excluded. There shall not be taken into account under clause (i) remuneration which (without regard to clause (i)) is not treated as compensation under this subsection.

(iii) Hospital insurance taxes. Clause (i) shall not apply to—

(I) so much of the rate applicable under section 3201(a) or 3221(a) as does not exceed the rate of tax in effect under section 3101(b), and

(II) so much of the rate applicable under section 3211(a) as does not exceed the rate of tax in effect under section 1401(b).

(B) Applicable base.

(i) Tier 1 taxes. Except as provided in clause (ii), the term "applicable base" means for any calendar year the contribution and benefit base determined under section 230 of the Social Security Act for such calendar year.

(ii) Tier 2 taxes, etc. For purposes of—

(I) the taxes imposed by sections 3201(b), 3211(b), and 3221(b), and

(II) computing average monthly compensation under section 3(j) of the Railroad Retirement Act of 1974 (except with respect to annuity amounts determined under subsection (a) or (f)(3) of section 3 of such Act),

clause (2) of the first sentence, and the second sentence, of subsection (c) of section 230 of the Social Security Act shall be disregarded.

(C) Successor employers. For purposes of this paragraph, the second sentence of section 3121(a)(1) (relating to successor employers) shall apply, except that—

(i) the term "services" shall be substituted for "employment" each place it appears,

(ii) the term "compensation" shall be substituted for "remuneration (other than remuneration referred to in the succeeding paragraphs of this subsection)" each place it appears, and

(iii) the terms "employer", "services", and "compensation" shall have the meanings given such terms by this section.

(3) Solely for purposes of the taxes imposed by section 3201 and other provisions of this chapter insofar as they relate to such taxes, the term "compensation" also includes cash tips received by an employee in any calendar month in the course of his employment by an employer unless the amount of such cash tips is less than $20.

(4)(A) For purposes of applying sections 3201(a), 3211(a), and 3221(a), in the case of payments made to an employee or any of his dependents on account of sickness or accident disability, clause (i) of the second sentence of paragraph (1) shall exclude from the term "compensation" only—

(i) payments which are received under a workmen's compensation law, and

(ii) benefits received under the Railroad Retirement Act of 1974.

(B) Notwithstanding any other provision of law, for purposes of the sections specified in subparagraph (A), the term "compensation" shall include benefits paid under section 2(a) of the Railroad Unemployment Insurance Act for days of sickness, except to the extent that such sickness (as determined in accordance with standards prescribed by the Railroad Retirement Board) is the result of on-the-job injury.

(C) Under regulations prescribed by the Secretary, subparagraphs (A) and (B) shall not apply to payments made after the expiration of a 6-month period comparable to the 6-month period described in section 3121(a)(4).

(D) Except as otherwise provided in regulations prescribed by the Secretary, any third party which makes a payment included in compensation solely by reason of subparagraph (A) or (B) shall be treated for purposes of this chapter as the employer with respect to such compensation.

(5) The term "compensation" shall not include any benefit provided to or on behalf of an employee if at the time such benefit is provided it is reasonable to believe that the employee will be able to exclude such benefit from income under section 74(c), 108(f)(4), 117, or 132.

(6) The term "compensation" shall not include any payment made, or benefit furnished, to or for the benefit of an employee if at the time of such payment or such furnishing it is reasonable to believe that the employee will be able to exclude such payment or benefit from income under section 127.

(7) The term "compensation" shall not include any contribution, payment, or service provided by an employer which may be excluded from the gross income of an employee, his spouse, or his dependents, under the provisions of section 120 (relating to amounts received under qualified group legal services plans).

(8) **Treatment of certain deferred compensation and salary reduction arrangements.**

(A) Certain employer contributions treated as compensation. Nothing in any paragraph of this subsection (other than paragraph (2)) shall exclude from the term "compensation" any amount described in subparagraph (A) or (B) of section 3121(v)(1).

(B) Treatment of certain nonqualified deferred compensation. The rules of section 3121(v)(2) which apply for purposes of chapter 21 shall also apply for purposes of this chapter.

(9) **Meals and lodging.** The term "compensation" shall not include the value of meals or lodging furnished by or on behalf of the employer if at the time of such furnishing it is reasonable to believe that the employee will be able to exclude such items from income under section 119.

(10) **Archer MSA contributions.** The term "compensation" shall not include any payment made to or for the benefit of an employee if at the time of such payment it is reasonable to believe that the employee will be able to exclude such payment from income under section 106(b).

(11) **Health savings account contributions.** The term "compensation" shall not include any payment made to or for the benefit of an employee if at the time of such payment it is reasonable to believe that the employee will be able to exclude such payment from income under section 106(d).

(12) **Qualified stock options.** The term "compensation" shall not include any remuneration on account of—

(A) a transfer of a share of stock to any individual pursuant to an exercise of an incentive stock option (as defined in section 422(b)) or under an employee stock purchase plan (as defined in section 423(b)), or

(B) any disposition by the individual of such stock.

(f) **Company.**

For purposes of this chapter, the term "company" includes corporations, associations, and joint-stock companies.

(g) **Carrier.**

For purposes of this chapter, the term "carrier" means a rail carrier subject to part A of subtitle IV of title 49.

(h) **Tips constituting compensation, time deemed paid.**

For purposes of this chapter, tips which constitute compensation for purposes of the taxes imposed by section 3201 shall be deemed to be paid at the time a written statement including such tips is furnished to the employer pursuant to section 6053(a) or (if no statement including such tips is so furnished) at the time received.

(i) **Concurrent employment by 2 or more employers.**

For purposes of this chapter, if 2 or more related corporations which are employers concurrently employ the same individual and compensate such individual through a common paymaster which is 1 of such corporations, each such corporation shall be considered to have paid as remuneration to such individual only the amounts actually disbursed by it to such individual and shall not be considered to have paid as remuneration to such individual amounts actually disbursed to such individual by another of such corporations.

In **2004**, P.L. 108-357, Sec. 251(a)(2), added para. (e)(12), effective for stock acquired pursuant to options exercised after 10/22/2004.
—P.L. 108-357, Sec. 320(b)(2), added "108(f)(4)," after "74(c)," in para. (e)(5), effective for amounts received by an individual in tax. yrs. begin. after 12/31/2003.

In **2003**, P.L. 108-173, Sec. 1201(d)(2)(A), added para. (e)(11), effective for tax. yrs. begin. after 12/31/2003.

In **2001**, P.L. 107-90, Sec. 204(e)(3), substituted "3211(a)" for "3211(a)(1)" in subclause (e)(2)(A)(iii)(II) and subpara. (e)(4)(A) . . . Sec. 204(e)(4), substituted "3211(b)" for "3211(a)(2)" in subclause (e)(2)(B)(ii)(I), effective for calendar yrs. begin. after 12/31/2001.

In **2000**, P.L. 106-554, Sec. 1(a)(7), [which enacted into law Sec. 202(b)(5) of P.L. 106-554] substituted "Archer MSA" for "medical savings account" in the heading of para. (e)(10), effective 12/21/2000.

In **1996**, P.L. 104-191, Sec. 301(c)(2)(A), added para. (e)(10), effective for tax. yrs. begin. after 12/31/96.

In **1995**, P.L. 104-88, Sec. 304(d)(1), substituted "Surface Transportation Board" for "Interstate Commerce Commission" in subsec. (a) . . . Sec. 304(d)(2), substituted "a rail carrier subject to part A of subtitle IV" for "an express carrier, sleeping car carrier, or rail carrier providing transportation subject to subchapter I of chapter 105" in subsec. (g), effective 12/29/95.

In **1994**, P.L. 103-296, Sec. 320(a)(1)(D), substituted "(J), (M), or (Q)" for "(J), or (M)" each place it appeared in para. (e)(1), effective with the calendar quarter following 8/15/94.

In **1993**, P.L. 103-66, Sec. 13207(c)(1), added clause (e)(2)(A)(iii) . . . Sec. 13207(c)(2), amended clause (e)(2)(B)(i), effective for 1994 and later calendar yrs. Prior to amendment, clause (e)(2)(B)(i) read as follows:

"(i) Tier 1 taxes.

"(I) In general. Except as provided in subclause (II) of this clause and in clause (ii), the term 'applicable base' means for any calendar year the contribution and benefit base determined under section 230 of the Social Security Act for such calendar year.

"(II) Hospital insurance taxes. For purposes of applying so much of the rate applicable under section 3201(a) or 3221(a) (as the case may be) as does not exceed the rate of tax in effect under section 3101(b), and for purposes of applying so much of the rate of tax applicable under section 3211(a)(1) as does not exceed the rate of tax in effect under section 1401(b), the term 'applicable base' means for any calendar year the applicable contribution base determined under section 3121(x)(2) for such calendar year."

In **1990**, P.L. 101-508, Sec. 11331(c), amended clause (e)(2)(B)(i), effective for 1991 and later calendar years.
Prior to amendment, clause (e)(2)(B)(i) read as follows:

"(i) Tier 1 taxes. Except as provided in clause (I), the term 'applicable base' means for any calendar year the contribution and benefit base determined under section 230 of the Social Security Act for such calendar year."
—P.L. 101-508, Sec. 11704(a)(19), redesignated paras. (e)(9) and (e)(10) as paras. (e)(8) and (e)(9), effective 11/5/90.

In **1989**, P.L. 101-239, Sec. 10205(a), substituted "or death, except that this clause does not apply to a payment for group-term life insurance to the extent that such payment is includible in the gross income of the employee, (ii) tips" for ", (ii) tips" in para. (e)(1), effective for group-term life insurance coverage in effect after 12/31/89 and remuneration paid before 1/1/90, which the employer treated as compensation when paid except as provided in Sec. 10205(b)(2) and (3), which reads as follows:

"(2) Exception. The amendment made by subsection (a) shall not apply with respect to payments by the employer (or a successor of such employer) for groupterm life insurance for such employer's former employees who separated from employment with the employer on or before December 31, 1989, to the extent that such payments are not for coverage for any such employee for any period for which such employee is employed by such employer (or a successor of such employer) after the date of such separation.

"(3) Benefit determinations to take into account remuneration on which tax paid. The term 'compensation' as defined in section 1(h) of the Railroad Retirement Act of 1974 includes any remuneration which is included in the term 'compensation' as defined in section 3231(e)(1) of the Internal Revenue Code of 1986 by reason of the amendment made by subsection (a)."

—P.L. 101-239, Sec. 10206(a), substituted "(iii)" for "or (iii)" and added ", or (iv) any remuneration which would not (if chapter 21 applied to such remuneration) be treated as wages (as defined in section 3121(a)) by reason of section 3121(a)(5)" before the period at the end of the second sentence of para. (e)(1), effective for remuneration paid after 12/31/89.

—P.L. 101-239, Sec. 10206(b), added para. (e)(9) [sic (e)(8)], effective for remuneration paid after 12/31/89, and remuneration paid before 1/1/90, which the employer treated as compensation when paid except as provided in Sec. 10206(c)(2)(B), (c)(3), (4) and (5), which reads as follows:

"(B) Benefit determinations to take into account remuneration on which tax paid.—The term 'compensation' as defined in section 1(h) of the Railroad Retirement Act of 1974 includes any remuneration which is included in the term 'compensation' as defined in section 3231(e)(1) of the Internal Revenue Code of 1986 by reason of the amendment made by subsection (b).

"(3) Special rule for certain payments.—For purposes of applying the amendment made by subsection (b) to remuneration paid after December 31, 1989, which would have been taken into account before January 1, 1990, if such amendments had applied to periods before January 1, 1990, such remuneration shall be taken into account when paid (or, at the election of the payor, at the time which would be appropriate if such amendments had applied).

"(4) Exception for certain 401(k) contributions.—The amendment made by subsection (b) shall not apply to employer contributions made during 1990 and attributable to services performed during 1989 under a qualified cash or deferred arrangement (as defined in section 401(k) of the Internal Revenue Code of 1986) if, under the terms of the arrangement as in effect on June 15, 1989—

"(A) the employee makes an election with respect to such contributions before January 1, 1990, and

"(B) the employer identifies the amount of such contribution before January 1, 1990.

"(5) Special rule with respect to nonqualified deferred compensation plans.—In the case of an agreement in existence on June 15, 1989, between a nonqualified deferred compensation plan (as defined in section 3121(v)(2)(C) of such Code) and an individual, the amendment made by subsection (b) shall apply with respect to services performed by the individual after December 31, 1989. The preceding sentence shall not apply in the case of a plan to which section 457(a) of such Code applies."

—P.L. 101-239, Sec. 10207(a), added para. (e)(10) [sic (e)(9)] . . . Sec. 10207(b), added the last sentence in para. (e)(1), effective for remuneration paid after 12/31/89.

—P.L. 101-140, Sec. 203(a)(2), repealed as if not enacted Sec. 1011B(a)(22)(B) of P. L. 100-647 which added para. (e)(8).

In 1988, P.L. 100-647, Sec. 1001(d)(2)(C)(ii), substituted "(F), (J), or (M)" for "(F) or (J)" each place it appeared in para. (e)(1), effective for compensation received after 12/31/87.

In 1986, P.L. 99-514, Sec. 122(e)(2), substituted "74(c), 117 or" for " 117 or" in para. (e)(5), effective for prizes and awards granted after 12/31/86.

—P.L. 99-514, Sec. 1899A(41), redesignated para. (e)(6) as (e)(7), effective for tax. yrs. begin. after 10/22/86.

In 1984, P.L. 98-612, Sec. 1(c), added para. (e)(7), effective for remuneration paid after 12/31/84.

—P.L. 98-611, Sec. 1(f), added para. (e)(6), effective for remuneration paid after 12/31/84.

—P.L. 98-369, Sec. 531(d)(2), added para. (e)(5), effective on 1/1/85.

In 1983, P.L. 98-76, Sec. 225(a)(1), amended para. (e)(2) . . . Sec. 225(a)(3), deleted the fourth and fifth sentences of para. (e)(1) . . . Sec. 225(b), added subsec. (i) . . . Sec. 225(c)(1)(C), substituted "taxes imposed by section 3201" for "tax imposed by section 3201" in para. (e)(3) . . . Sec. 225(c)(6), substituted "such taxes" for "such tax" in para. (e)(3) . . . Sec. 225(c)(7), substituted "3201(a), 3211(a)(1), and 3221(a)" for "3201(b) and 3221(b) (and so much of section 3211(a) as relates to the rates of the taxes imposed by sections 3101 and 3111)" in subpara. (e)(4)(A) . . . Sec. 225(c)(8)(A), substituted "taxes imposed by section 3201" for "tax imposed under section 3201" in subsec. (h) . . . Sec. 225(c)(8)(B), substituted a period for "and tips so deemed to be paid in any month shall be deemed paid for services rendered in such month" after "received" in subsec. (h), effective for remuneration paid after 12/31/84.

Prior to amendment, para. (e)(2) read as follows:

"(2) A payment made by an employer to an individual through the employer's payroll shall be presumed, in the absence of evidence to the contrary, to be compensation for service rendered by such individual as an employee of the employer in the period with respect to which the payment is made. An employee shall be deemed to be paid compensation in the period during which such compensation is earned only upon a written request by such employee, made within six months following the payment, and a showing that such compensation was earned during a period other than the period in which it was paid. An employee receiving retroactive wage payments shall be deemed to be paid 'for time lost' the amount he is paid by an employer with respect to an identifiable period of absence from the active service of the employer, including absence on account of personal injury, and the amount he is paid by the employer for loss of earnings resulting from his displacement to a less remunerative position or occupation. If a payment is made by an employer with respect to a personal injury and includes pay for time lost, the total payment shall be deemed to be paid for time lost unless, at the time of payment, a part of such payment is specifically apportioned to factors other than time lost, in which event only such part of the payment as is not so apportioned shall be deemed to be paid for time lost."

Prior to deletion, the fourth and fifth sentences of para. (e)(1) read as follows:

"Compensation which is paid in one calendar month but which would be payable in a prior or subsequent taxable month but for the fact that prescribed date of payment would fall on a Saturday, Sunday or legal holiday shall be deemed to have been paid in such prior or subsequent taxable month. Compensation which is earned during the period for which the Secretary shall require a return of taxes under this chapter to be made and which is payable during the calendar month following such period shall be deemed to have been paid during such period only."

In 1981, P.L. 97-123, Sec. 3(c), added para. (e)(4), effective for remuneration paid after 12/31/81, except as provided in Sec. 3(g)(2) of this Act, which reads as follows:

"(2) This section (and the amendments made by this section) shall not apply with respect to any payment made by a third party to an employee pursuant to a contractual relationship of an employer with such third party entered into before December 14, 1981, if—

"(A) coverage by such third party for the group in which such employee falls ceases before March 1, 1982, and

"(B) no payment by such third party is made to such employee under such relationship after February 28, 1982."

For further procedures, see Sec. 3(d)(1) and (2) of P. L. 97-123, reproduced in note following Code Sec. 3121.

—P.L. 97-34, Sec. 741(d)(2), substituted "or (iii)" for "(iii) the voluntary payment by an employer, without deduction from the remuneration of the employee, of the tax imposed on such employee by section 3201, or (iv)" in para. (e)(1), effective for compensation paid for services rendered after 9/30/81.

—P.L. 97-34, Sec. 743(a), added the sentence at the end of para. (e)(1) . . . Sec. 743(b), added the sentence at the beginning of para. (e)(2) . . . Sec. 743(c), substituted "An employee receiving retroactive wage payments" for "An employee" in the second sentence of para. (e)(2) [as amended by Sec. 743(b) of this Act, see above], effective for tax. yrs. begin. after 12/31/81.

In 1978, P.L. 95-473, Sec. 2(a)(2)(G), substituted "express carrier, sleeping car carrier, or rail carrier providing transportation subject to subchapter I of chapter 105 of title 49" for "express company, sleeping-car company, or carrier by railroad, subject to part I of the Interstate Commerce Act (49 U.S.C., chapter 1)" in subsec. (g), effective 10/17/78.

In 1976, P.L. 94-547, Sec. 4(b), amended the second sentence of subsec. (e), effective for tax. yrs. end. after 12/31/53, except as provided by Sec. 4(c)(2) of this Act:

"That any taxes paid under the Railroad Retirement Tax Act prior to the date on which this Act is enacted [10/18/76] shall not be affected or adjusted by reason of the amendments made by such sub section (b) except to the extent that the applicable period of limitation for the assessment of tax and the filing of a claim for credit or refund has not expired prior to the date on which this Act is enacted [10/18/76]. If the applicable period of limitation for the filing of a claim for credit or refund would expire within the six-month period following the date on which this Act is enacted [10/18/76], the applicable period for the filing of such a claim for credit or refund shall be extended to include such six-month period."

Prior to amendment, the second sentence of subsec. (e) read as follows:

"Such term does not include tips (except as is provided under paragraph (3)), or the voluntary payment by an employer, without deduction from the remuneration of the employee, of the tax imposed on such employee by section 3201."

—P.L. 94-455, Sec. 1903(a)(10)(A), deleted "44 Stat. 577;" in subsec. (a) . . . Sec. 1903(a)(10)(B), deleted "50 Stat. 312;" in subsec. (b) . . . Sec. 1903(a)(10)(C), deleted "44 Stat. 577;" in subsec. (c) . . . Sec. 1903(a)(10)(D), deleted "50 Stat. 308;" in para. (d)(7), effective for compensation paid for services rendered after 12/31/76.

—P.L. 94-455, Sec. 1906(b)(13)(A), substituted "Secretary" for " Secretary or his delegate" in subsecs. (a) and (e), effective 2/1/77.

In 1975, P.L. 94-93, Sec. 204, amended the first sentence of para. (e)(1) . . . Sec. 205, deleted the first sentence of para. (e)(2), effective for tax. yrs. end. on or after 8/9/75 and for tax. yrs. end. before 8/9/75 for which the period for assessment and collection of tax or the filing of a claim for credit or refund has not expired on 8/9/75.

Prior to amendment, the first sentence of para. (e)(1) read as follows:

"(1) The term 'compensation' means any form of money remuneration earned by an individual for services rendered as an employee to one or more employers, or as an employee representative, including remuneration paid for time lost as an employee, but remuneration paid for time lost shall be deemed earned in the month in which such time is lost."

Prior to deletion, the first sentence in para. (e)(2) read as follows:

"(2) A payment made by an employer to an individual through the employer's payroll shall be presumed, in the absence of evidence to the contrary, to be compensation for service rendered by such individual as an employee of the employer in the period with respect to which the payment is made."

—P.L. 94-93, Sec. 206, added the sentence at the beginning of para. (e)(2), effective for tax. yrs. begin. on or after 8/9/75, provided that for payment made prior to 8/9/75, the employee may file a written request under Sec. 206 of this Act within six months after 8/9/75.

In 1975, P.L. 94-92, Sec. 203(b), substituted "$25" for "$3" in the fifth sentence of para. (e)(1), effective 1/1/75 with respect to compensation paid for services rendered on or after 1/1/75.

In 1968, P.L. 90-624, Sec. 1, added the third sentence to para. (e)(1), effective for service performed after 12/31/61, Sec. 4(a)(2) and (3) of this Act provide special rules as follows:

"(2) Notwithstanding the expiration before the date of the enactment of this Act or within 6 months after such date of the period for filing claim for credit or refund, claim for credit or refund of any overpayment of any tax imposed by chap-

Code Sec. 3231 — Employment taxes

ter 22 of the Internal Revenue Code of 1954 attributable to the amendment made by the first section of this Act may be filed at any time within one year after such date of enactment.

"(3) Any credit or refund of an overpayment of the tax imposed by section 3201 or 3211 of the Internal Revenue Code of 1954 which is attributable to the amendment made by the first section of this Act shall be appropriately adjusted for any lump-sum payment which has been made under section 5(f)(2) of the Railroad Retirement Act of 1937 before the date of the allowance of such credit or the making of such refund."

In 1965, P.L. 89-212, Sec. 2(b)(1), added "(except as is provided under paragraph (3))" after "tips" in the second sentence of para. (e)(1) . . . Sec. 2(b)(2), added para. (e)(3) . . . Sec. 2(b)(3), added subsec. (h), effective for tips received after 1965.

In 1954, P.L. 746, Sec. 206(b), added a sentence to the end of para. (e)(1), effective for service as a delegate to a national or international convention of a railway labor organization, of any person who has no other previous creditable service as if originally enacted in the '54 Code.

Sec. 3232. Court jurisdiction.

The several district courts of the United States shall have jurisdiction to entertain an application by the Attorney General on behalf of the Secretary to compel an employee or other person residing within the jurisdiction of the court or an employer subject to service of process within its jurisdiction to comply with any obligations imposed on such employee, employer, or other person under the provisions of this chapter. The jurisdiction herein specifically conferred upon such Federal courts shall not be held exclusive of any jurisdiction otherwise possessed by such courts to entertain civil actions, whether legal or equitable in nature, in aid of the enforcement of rights or obligations arising under the provisions of this chapter.

In 1976, P.L. 94-455, Sec. 1906(b)(13)(A), substituted "Secretary" for "Secretary or his delegate" in Code Sec. 3232, effective 2/1/77.

Sec. 3233. Short title.

This chapter may be cited as the "Railroad Retirement Tax Act."

Subchapter E.—Tier 2 Tax Rate Determination

Sec.
3241. Determination of tier 2 tax rate based on average account benefits ratio.

In 2001, P.L. 107-90, Sec. 204(d), added subchapter E.

Sec. 3241. Determination of tier 2 tax rate based on average account benefits ratio.

(a) In general.

For purposes of sections 3201(b), 3211(b), and 3221(b), the applicable percentage for any calendar year is the percentage determined in accordance with the table in subsection (b).

(b) Tax rate schedule.

Average account benefits ratio		Applicable percentage for sections 3211(b) and 3221(b)	Applicable percentage for section 3201(b)
At least	But less than		
	2.5	22.1	4.9
2.5	3.0	18.1	4.9
3.0	3.5	15.1	4.9
3.5	4.0	14.1	4.9
4.0	6.1	13.1	4.9
6.1	6.5	12.6	4.4
6.5	7.0	12.1	3.9
7.0	7.5	11.6	3.4
7.5	8.0	11.1	2.9
8.0	8.5	10.1	1.9
8.5	9.0	9.1	0.9
9.0		8.2	0

(c) Definitions related to determination of rates of tax.

(1) Average account benefits ratio. For purposes of this section, the term "average account benefits ratio" means, with respect to any calendar year, the average determined by the Secretary of the account benefits ratios for the 10 most recent fiscal years ending before such calendar year. If the amount determined under the preceding sentence is not a multiple of 0.1, such amount shall be increased to the next highest multiple of 0.1.

(2) Account benefits ratio. For purposes of this section, the term "account benefits ratio" means, with respect to any fiscal year, the amount determined by the Railroad Retirement Board by dividing the fair market value of the assets in the Railroad Retirement Account and of the National Railroad Retirement Investment Trust (and for years before 2002, the Social Security Equivalent Benefits Account) as of the close of such fiscal year by the total benefits and administrative expenses paid from the Railroad Retirement Account and the National Railroad Retirement Investment Trust during such fiscal year.

(d) Notice.

No later than December 1 of each calendar year, the Secretary shall publish a notice in the Federal Register of the rates of tax determined under this section which are applicable for the following calendar year.

In 2001, P.L. 107-90, Sec. 204(d), added Code Sec. 3241 as part of new subchapter E of Chapter 22 of subtitle C, effective for calendar yrs. begin. after 12/31/2001.

CHAPTER 23.—FEDERAL UNEMPLOYMENT TAX ACT

Sec.
3301. Rate of tax.
3302. Credits against tax.
3303. Conditions of additional credit allowance.
3304. Approval of State laws.
3305. Applicability of State law.
3306. Definitions.
3307. Deductions as constructive payments.
3308. Instrumentalities of the United States.
3309. State law coverage of services performed for nonprofit organizations or governmental entities.
3310. Judicial review.
3311. Short title.

In 1976, P.L. 94-566, Sec. 115(c)(4), amended the item for Code Sec. 3309.
In 1970, added items 3309 and 3310 and redesignated former item 3309 as 3311.
In 1960, added item 3308 and redesignated former item 3308 as 3309.

Sec. 3301. Rate of tax.

There is hereby imposed on every employer (as defined in section 3306(a)) for each calendar year an excise tax, with respect to having individuals in his employ, equal to—

(1) 6.2 percent in the case of calendar years 1988 through 2010 and the first 6 months of calendar year 2011; or

(2) 6.0 percent in the case of the remainder of calendar year 2011 and each calendar year thereafter;

of the total wages (as defined in section 3306(b)) paid by him during the calendar year (or portion of the calendar year) with respect to employment (as defined in section 3306(c)).

In 2009, P.L. 111-92, Sec. 10(a)(1), substituted "through 2010 and the first 6 months of calendar year 2011" for "through 2009" in para. (1) . . . Sec. 10(a)(2), substituted "the remainder of calendar year 2011" for "calendar year 2010" in

Employment taxes

Code Sec. 3302(c)(2)(A)(ii)

para. (2)... Sec. 10(a)(3), added "(or portion of the calendar year)" after "during the calendar year" in the matter following para. (2), effective for wages paid after 12/31/2009.

In 2008, P.L. 110-343, Sec. 404(a)(1)DivB, substituted "through 2009" for "through 2008" in para. (1)... Sec. 404(a)(2)DivB, substituted "calendar year 2010" for "calendar year 2009" in para. (2), effective for wages paid after 12/31/2008.

In 2007, P.L. 110-140, Sec. 1502(a)(1), substituted "2008" for "2007" in para. (1)... Sec. 1502(a)(2), substituted "2009" for "2008" in para. (2), effective for wages paid after 12/31/2007.

In 1997, P.L. 105-34, Sec. 1035(1), substituted "2007" for "1998" in para. (1)... Sec. 1035(2), substituted "2008" for "1999" in para. (2), effective 8/5/97.

In 1993, P.L. 103-66, Sec. 13751(1), substituted "1998" for "1996" in para. (1)... Sec. 13751(2), substituted "1999" for "1997" in para. (2), effective 8/10/93.

In 1991, P.L. 102-164, Sec. 402(1), substituted "1996" for "1995" in para. (1)... Sec. 402(2), substituted "1997" for "1996" in para. (2), effective 11/15/91.

In 1990, P.L. 101-508, Sec. 11333(a)(1), substituted "1988 through 1995" for "1988, 1989, and 1990" in para. (1)... Sec. 11333(a)(2), substituted "1996" for "1991" in para. (2), effective for wages paid after 12/31/90.

In 1987, P.L. 100-203, Sec. 9153(a), amended paras. (a)(1) and (a)(2), effective for wages paid on or after 1/1/88.

Prior to amendment, paras. (a)(1) and (a)(2) read as follows:

"(1) 6.2 percent, in the case of a calendar year beginning before the first calendar year after 1976, as of January 1 of which there is not a balance of repayable advances made to the extended unemployment compensation account (established by section 905(a) of the Social Security Act); or

"(2) 6.0 percent, in the case of such first calendar year and each calendar year thereafter;"

In 1986, P.L. 99-514, Sec. 1899A(42), substituted "unemployment" for "unemployed" in para. (1), effective 10/22/86.

In 1982, P.L. 97-248, Sec. 271(b)(1), substituted "3.5 percent" for "3.4 percent" in para. (1), effective for remuneration paid after 12/31/82.

—P.L. 97-248, Sec. 271(c)(1)(A) & (B), substituted "6.2 percent" for "3.5 percent" and substituted "6.0 percent" for "3.2 percent" in Code Sec. 3301 (as amended by Sec. 271(b)(1) of this Act), for remuneration paid after 12/31/84.

In 1976, P.L. 94-566, Sec. 211(b), amended Code Sec. 3301, effective for remunerations paid after 12/31/76.

—P.L. 94-455, Sec. 1903(a)(11), deleted "the calendar year 1970 and each calendar year thereafter" following "(as defined in section 3306(a)) for" and deleted "In the case of wages paid during the calendar year 1973, the rate of such tax shall be 3.28 percent in lieu of 3.2 percent." at the end of Code Sec. 3301, effective for wages paid after 12/31/76.

Prior to amendment, Code Sec. 3301 read as follows:

"SEC. 3301. RATE OF TAX.

"There is hereby imposed on every employer (as defined in section 3306(a)) for the calendar year 1970 and each calendar year thereafter an excise tax, with respect to having individuals in his employ equal to 3.2 percent of the total wages (as defined in section 3306(a)) for the calendar year with respect to employment (as defined in section 3306(c)). In the case of wages paid during the calendar year 1973, the rate of such tax shall be 3.28 percent in lieu of 3.2 percent."

In 1972, P.L. 92-329, Sec. 2(a), added a new sentence to the end of Code Sec. 3301.

In 1970, P.L. 91-373, Sec. 301, amended Code Sec. 3301, effective for remuneration paid after 12/31/69.

Prior to amendment Sec. 3301 read as follows:

"There is hereby imposed on every employer (as defined in section 3306(a)) for the calendar year 1961 and for each calendar year thereafter an excise tax, with respect to having individuals in his employ, equal to 3.1 percent of the total wages (as defined in section 3306(b)) paid by him during the calendar year with respect to employment (as defined in section 3306(c)) after December 31, 1938. In the case of wages paid during the calendar year 1962, the rate of such tax shall be 3.5 percent in lieu of 3.1 percent. In the case of wages paid during the calendar year 1963, the rate of such tax shall be 3.35 percent in lieu of 3.1 percent."

In 1963, P.L. 88-31, Sec. 2(a), substituted "In the case of wages paid during the calendar year 1962, the rate of such tax shall be 3.5 percent in lieu of 3.1 percent. In the case of wages paid during the calendar year 1963, the rate of such tax shall be 3.35 percent in lieu of 3.1 percent." for the last sentence in Code Sec. 3301.

In 1961, P.L. 87-6, Sec. 14(a), added the last sentence to Code Sec. 3301.

In 1960, P.L. 86-778, Sec. 523(a), substituted "1961" for "1955" and "3.1 percent", effective for "3 percent for calendar '61 and thereafter."

Sec. 3302. Credits against tax.

(a) Contributions to State unemployment funds.

(1) The taxpayer may, to the extent provided in this subsection and subsection (c), credit against the tax imposed by section 3301 the amount of contributions paid by him into an unemployment fund maintained during the taxable year under the unemployment compensation law of a State which is certified as provided in section 3304 for the 12-month period ending on October 31 of such year.

(2) The credit shall be permitted against the tax for the taxable year only for the amount of contributions paid with respect to such taxable year.

(3) The credit against the tax for any taxable year shall be permitted only for contributions paid on or before the last day upon which the taxpayer is required under section 6071 to file a return for such year; except that credit shall be permitted for contributions paid after such last day, but such credit shall not exceed 90 percent of the amount which would have been allowable as credit on account of such contributions had they been paid on or before such last day.

(4) Upon the payment of contributions into the unemployment fund of a State which are required under the unemployment compensation law of that State with respect to remuneration on the basis of which, prior to such payment into the proper fund, the taxpayer erroneously paid an amount as contributions under another unemployment compensation law, the payment into the proper fund shall, for purposes of credit against the tax, be deemed to have been made at the time of the erroneous payment. If, by reason of such other law, the taxpayer was entitled to cease paying contributions with respect to services subject to such other law, the payment into the proper fund shall, for purposes of credit against the tax, be deemed to have been made on the date the return for the taxable year was filed under section 6071.

(5) In the case of wages paid by the trustee of an estate under title 11 of the United States Code, if the failure to pay contributions on time was without fault by the trustee, paragraph (3) shall be applied by substituting "100 percent" for "90 percent".

(b) Additional credit.

In addition to the credit allowed under subsection (a), a taxpayer may credit against the tax imposed by section 3301 for any taxable year an amount, with respect to the unemployment compensation law of each State certified as provided in section 3303 for the 12-month period ending on October 31 of such year, or with respect to any provisions thereof so certified, equal to the amount, if any, by which the contributions required to be paid by him with respect to the taxable year were less than the contributions such taxpayer would have been required to pay if throughout the taxable year he had been subject under such State law to the highest rate applied thereunder in such 12-month period to any person having individuals in his employ, or to a rate of 5.4% whichever rate is lower.

(c) Limit on total credits.

(1) The total credits allowed to a taxpayer under this section shall not exceed 90 percent of the tax against which such credits are allowable.

(2) If an advance or advances have been made to the unemployment account of a State under title XII of the Social Security Act, then the total credits (after applying subsections (a) and (b) and paragraph (1) of this subsection) otherwise allowable under this section for the taxable year in the case of a taxpayer subject to the unemployment compensation law of such State shall be reduced—

(A)(i) in the case of a taxable year beginning with the second consecutive January 1 as of the beginning of which there is a balance of such advances, by 5 percent of the tax imposed by section 3301 with respect to the wages paid by such taxpayer during such taxable year which are attributable to such State; and

(ii) in the case of any succeeding taxable year beginning with a consecutive January 1 as of the beginning of which there is a balance of such advances, by an

3,109

additional 5 percent, for each such succeeding taxable year, of the tax imposed by section 3301 with respect to the wages paid by such taxpayer during such taxable year which are attributable to such State;

(B) in the case of a taxable year beginning with the third or fourth consecutive January 1 as of the beginning of which there is a balance of such advances, by the amount determined by multiplying the wages paid by such taxpayer during such taxable year which are attributable to such State by the percentage (if any), multiplied by a fraction, the numerator of which is the State's average annual wage in covered employment for the calendar year in which the determination is made and the denominator of which is the wage base under this chapter, by which—

(i) 2.7 percent multiplied by a fraction, the numerator of which is the wage base under this chapter and the denominator of which is the estimated United States average annual wage in covered employment for the calendar year in which the determination is to be made, exceeds

(ii) the average employer contribution rate for such State for the calendar year preceding such taxable year; and

(C) in the case of a taxable year beginning with the fifth or any succeeding consecutive January 1 as of the beginning of which there is a balance of such advances, by the amount determined by multiplying the wages paid by such taxpayer during such taxable year which are attributable to such State by the percentage (if any) by which—

(i) the 5-year benefit cost rate applicable to such State for such taxable year or (if higher) 2.7 percent, exceeds

(ii) the average employer contribution rate for such State for the calendar year preceding such taxable year.

The provisions of the preceding sentence shall not be applicable with respect to the taxable year beginning January 1, 1975, or any succeeding taxable year which begins before January 1, 1980; and, for purposes of such sentence, January 1, 1980, shall be deemed to be the first January 1 occurring after January 1, 1974, and consecutive taxable years in the period commencing January 1, 1980, shall be determined as if the taxable year which begins on January 1, 1980, were the taxable year immediately succeeding the taxable year which began on January 1, 1974. Subparagraph (C) shall not apply with respect to any taxable year to which it would otherwise apply (but subparagraph (B) shall apply to such taxable year) if the Secretary of Labor determines (on or before November 10 of such taxable year) that the State meets the requirements of subsection (f)(2)(B) for such taxable year.

> • **Caution:** If the Secretary of Labor determines that a State meets the requirements of Sec. 304(b) of P.L. 102-318, reproduced in note following Code Sec. 3302, then para. (c)(2), below, as amended by Sec. 304(a) of P.L. 102-318, is effective with respect to such State for tax. yrs. after 1991. For special rules, see Sec. 304(c) of P.L. 102-318, reproduced in note following Code Sec. 3302. For para. (c)(2), before amendment by P.L. 102-318, see above.

(2) If an advance or advances have been made to the unemployment account of a State under title XII of the Social Security Act, then the total credits (after applying subsections (a) and (b) and paragraph (1) of this subsection) otherwise allowable under this section for the taxable year in the case of a taxpayer subject to the unemployment compensation law of such State shall be reduced—

(A)(i) in the case of a taxable year beginning with the third consecutive January 1 as of the beginning of which there is a balance of such advances, by 5 percent of the tax imposed by section 3301 with respect to the wages paid by such taxpayer during such taxable year which are attributable to such State; and

(ii) in the case of any succeeding taxable year beginning with a consecutive January 1 as of the beginning of which there is a balance of such advances, by an additional 5 percent, for each such succeeding taxable year, of the tax imposed by section 3301 with respect to the wages paid by such taxpayer during such taxable year which are attributable to such State;

(B) in the case of a taxable year beginning with the fourth or fifth consecutive January 1 as of the beginning of which there is a balance of such advances, by the amount determined by multiplying the wages paid by such taxpayer during such taxable year which are attributable to such State by the percentage (if any), multiplied by a fraction, the numerator of which is the State's average annual wage in covered employment for the calendar year in which the determination is made and the denominator of which is the wage base under this chapter, by which—

(i) 2.7 percent multiplied by a fraction, the numerator of which is the wage base under this chapter and the denominator of which is the estimated United States average annual wage in covered employment for the calendar year in which the determination is to be made, exceeds

(ii) the average employer contribution rate for such State for the calendar year preceding such taxable year; and

(C) in the case of a taxable year beginning with the sixth or any succeeding consecutive January 1 as of the beginning of which there is a balance of such advances, by the amount determined by multiplying the wages paid by such taxpayer during such taxable year which are attributable to such State by the percentage (if any) by which—

(i) the 5-year benefit cost rate applicable to such State for such taxable year or (if higher) 2.7 percent, exceeds

(ii) the average employer contribution rate for such State for the calendar year preceding such taxable year.

The provisions of the preceding sentence shall not be applicable with respect to the taxable year beginning January 1, 1975, or any succeeding taxable year which begins before January 1, 1980; and, for purposes of such sentence, January 1, 1980, shall be deemed to be the first January 1 occurring after January 1, 1974, and consecutive taxable years in the period commencing January 1, 1980, shall be determined as if the taxable year which begins on January 1, 1980, were the taxable year immediately succeeding the taxable year which began on January 1, 1974. Subparagraph (C) shall not apply with respect to any taxable year to which it would otherwise apply (but subparagraph (B) shall apply to such taxable year) if the Secretary of Labor determines

Employment taxes

(on or before November 10 of such taxable year) that the State meets the requirements of subsection (f)(2)(B) for such taxable year.

(3) If the Secretary of Labor determines that a State, or State agency, has not—

(A) entered into the agreement described in section 239 of the Trade Act of 1974, with the Secretary of Labor before July 15, 1975, or

(B) fulfilled its commitments under an agreement with the Secretary of Labor as described in section 239 of the Trade Act of 1974,

then, in the case of a taxpayer subject to the unemployment compensation law of such State, the total credits (after applying subsections (a) and (b) and paragraphs (1) and (2) of this section) otherwise allowable under this section for a year during which such State or agency does not enter into or fulfill such an agreement shall be reduced by 7 ½ percent of the tax imposed with respect to wages paid by such taxpayer during such year which are attributable to such State.

(d) Definitions and special rules relating to subsection (c).

(1) Rate of tax deemed to be 6 percent. In applying subsection (c), the tax imposed by section 3301 shall be computed at the rate of 6 percent in lieu of the rate provided by such section.

(2) Wages attributable to a particular State. For purposes of subsection (c), wages shall be attributable to a particular State if they are subject to the unemployment compensation law of the State, or (if not subject to the unemployment compensation law of any State) if they are determined (under rules or regulations prescribed by the Secretary) to be attributable to such State.

(3) Additional taxes inapplicable where advances are repaid before November 10 of taxable year. Paragraph (2) of subsection (c) shall not apply with respect to any State for the taxable year if (as of the beginning of November 10 of such year) there is no balance of advances referred to in such paragraph.

(4) Average employer contribution rate. For purposes of subparagraphs (B) and (C) of subsection (c)(2), the average employer contribution rate for any State for any calendar year is that percentage obtained by dividing—

(A) the total of the contributions paid into the State unemployment fund with respect to such calendar year, by

(B)(i) for purposes of subparagraph (B) of subsection (c)(2), the total of the wages (as determined without any limitation on amount) attributable to such State subject to contributions under this chapter with respect to such calendar year, and

(ii) for purposes of subparagraph (C) of subsection (c)(2), the total of the remuneration subject to contributions under the State unemployment compensation law with respect to such calendar year.

For purposes of subparagraph (C) of subsection (c)(2), if the average employer contribution rate for any State for any calendar year (determined without regard to this sentence) equals or exceeds 2.7 percent, such rate shall be determined by increasing the amount taken into account under subparagraph (A) of the preceding sentence by the aggregate amount of employee payments (if any) into the unemployment fund of such State with respect to such calendar year which are to be used solely in the payment of unemployment compensation.

(5) 5-year benefit cost rate. For purposes of subparagraph (C) of subsection (c)(2), the 5-year benefit cost rate applicable to any State for any taxable year is that percentage obtained by dividing—

(A) one-fifth of the total of the compensation paid under the State unemployment compensation law during the 5-year period ending at the close of the second calendar year preceding such taxable year, by

(B) the total of the remuneration subject to contributions under the State unemployment compensation law with respect to the first calendar year preceding such taxable year.

(6) Rounding. If any percentage referred to in either subparagraph (B) or (C) of subsection (c)(2) is not a multiple of .1 percent, it shall be rounded to the nearest multiple of .1 percent.

(7) Determination and certification of percentages. The percentage referred to in subsection (c)(2)(B) or (C) for any taxable year for any State having a balance referred to therein shall be determined by the Secretary of Labor, and shall be certified by him to the Secretary of the Treasury before June 1 of such year, on the basis of a report furnished by such State to the Secretary of Labor before May 1 of such year. Any such State report shall be made as of the close of March 31 of the taxable year, and shall be made on such forms, and shall contain such information, as the Secretary of Labor deems necessary to the performance of his duties under this section.

(e) Successor employer.

Subject to the limits provided by subsection (c), if—

(1) an employer acquires during any calendar year substantially all the property used in the trade or business of another person, or used in a separate unit of a trade or business of such other person, and immediately after the acquisition employs in his trade or business one or more individuals who immediately prior to the acquisition were employed in the trade or business of such other person, and

(2) such other person is not an employer for the calendar year in which the acquisition takes place,

then, for the calendar year in which the acquisition takes place, in addition to the credits allowed under subsections (a) and (b), such employer may credit against the tax imposed by section 3301 for such year an amount equal to the credits which (without regard to subsection (c)) would have been allowable to such other person under subsections (a) and (b) and this subsection for such year, if such other person had been an employer, with respect to remuneration subject to contributions under the unemployment compensation law of a State paid by such other person to the individual or individuals described in paragraph (1).

(f) Limitation on credit reduction.

(1) Limitation. In the case of any State which meets the requirements of paragraph (2) with respect to any taxable year the reduction under subsection (c)(2) in credits otherwise applicable to taxpayers subject to the unemployment compensation law of such State shall not exceed the greater of—

(A) the reduction which was in effect with respect to such State under subsection (c)(2) for the preceding taxable year, or

(B) 0.6 percent of the wages paid by the taxpayer during such taxable year which are attributable to such State.

(2) Requirements. The requirements of this paragraph are met by any State with respect to any taxable year if the Secretary of Labor determines (on or before November 10 of such taxable year) that—

(A) no State action was taken during the 12-month period ending on September 30 of such taxable year (excluding any action required under State law as in effect prior to the date of the enactment of this subsection) which has resulted or will result in a reduction in such State's unemployment tax effort (as defined by the Secretary of Labor in regulations),

(B) no State action was taken during the 12-month period ending on September 30 of such taxable year (excluding any action required under State law as in effect prior to the date of the enactment of this subsection) which has resulted or will result in a net decrease in the solvency of the State unemployment compensation system (as defined by the Secretary of Labor in regulations),

(C) the State unemployment tax rate for the taxable year equals or exceeds the average benefit cost ratio for calendar years in the 5-calendar year period ending with the last calendar year before the taxable year, and

(D) the outstanding balance for such State of advances under title XII of the Social Security Act on September 30 of such taxable year was not greater than the outstanding balance for such State of such advances on September 30 of the third preceding taxable year (or, for purposes of applying this subparagraph to taxable year 1983, September 30, 1981).

The requirements of subparagraphs (C) and (D) shall not apply to taxable years 1981 and 1982.

(3) Credit reductions for subsequent years. If the credit reduction under subsection (c)(2) is limited by reason of paragraph (1) of this subsection for any taxable year, for purposes of applying subsection (c)(2) to subsequent taxable years (including years after 1987), the taxable year for which the credit reduction was so limited (and January 1 thereof) shall not be taken into account.

(4) State unemployment tax rate. For purposes of this subsection—

(A) In general. The State unemployment tax rate for any taxable year is the percentage obtained by dividing—

(i) the total amount of contributions paid into the State unemployment fund with respect to such taxable year, by

(ii) the total amount of the remuneration subject to contributions under the State unemployment compensation law with respect to such taxable year (determined without regard to any limitation on the amount of wages subject to contribution under the State law).

(B) Treatment of additional tax under this chapter.

(i) Taxable year 1983. In the case of taxable year 1983, any additional tax imposed under this chapter with respect to any State by reason of subsection (c)(2) shall be treated as contributions paid into the State unemployment fund with respect to such taxable year.

(ii) Taxable year 1984. In the case of taxable year 1984, any additional tax imposed under this chapter with respect to any State by reason of subsection (c)(2) shall (to the extent such additional tax is attributable to a credit reduction in excess of 0.6 of wages attributable to such State) be treated as contributions paid into the State unemployment fund with respect to such taxable year.

(5) Benefit cost ratio. For purposes of this subsection—

(A) In general. The benefit cost ratio for any calendar year is the percentage determined by dividing—

(i) the sum of the total of the compensation paid under the State unemployment compensation law during such calendar year and any interest paid during such calendar year on advances made to the State under title XII of the Social Security Act, by

(ii) the total amount of the remuneration subject to contributions under the State unemployment compensation law with respect to such calendar year (determined without regard to any limitation on the amount of remuneration subject to contribution under the State law).

(B) Reimbursable benefits not taken into account. For purposes of subparagraph (A), compensation shall not be taken into account to the extent—

(i) the State is entitled to reimbursement for such compensation under the provisions of any Federal law, or

(ii) such compensation is attributable to services performed for a reimbursing employer.

(C) Reimbursing employer. The term "reimbursing employer" means any governmental entity or other organization (or group of governmental entities or any other organizations) which makes reimbursements in lieu of contributions to the State unemployment fund.

(D) Special rules for years before 1985.

(i) Taxable year 1983. For purposes of determining whether a State meets the requirements of paragraph (2)(C) for taxable year 1983, only regular compensation (as defined in section 205 of the Federal-State Extended Unemployment Compensation Act of 1970) shall be taken into account for purposes of determining the benefit ratio for any preceding calendar year before 1982.

(ii) Taxable year 1984. For purposes of determining whether a State meets the requirements of paragraph (2)(C) for taxable year 1984, only regular compensation (as so defined) shall be taken into account for purposes of determining the benefit ratio for any preceding calendar year before 1981.

(E) Rounding. If any percentage determined under subparagraph (A) is not a multiple of .1 percent, such percentage shall be reduced to the nearest multiple of .1 percent.

(6) Reports. The Secretary of Labor may, by regulations, require a State to furnish such information at such time and in such manner as may be necessary for purposes of this subsection.

(7) Definitions and special rules. The definitions and special rules set forth in subsection (d) shall apply to this subsection in the same manner as they apply to subsection (c).

(8) Partial limitation.

(A) In the case of a State which would meet the requirements of this subsection for a taxable year prior to 1986 but for its failure to meet one of the requirements contained in subparagraph (C) or (D) of paragraph (2), the reduction under subsection (c)(2) in credits otherwise applicable to taxpayers in such State for such taxable year and each subsequent year (in a period of consecutive years for each of which a credit reduction is in effect for taxpayers in such State) shall be reduced by 0.1 percentage point.

(B) In the case of a State which does not meet the requirements of paragraph (2) but meets the requirements of subparagraphs (A) and (B) of paragraph (2) and which also meets the requirements of section

Employment taxes — Code Sec. 3302

1202(b)(8)(B) of the Social Security Act with respect to such taxable year, the reduction under subsection (c)(2) in credits otherwise applicable to taxpayers in such State for such taxable year and each subsequent year (in a period of consecutive years for each of which a credit reduction is in effect for taxpayers in such State) shall be further reduced by an additional 0.1 percentage point.

(C) In no case shall the application of subparagraphs (A) and (B) reduce the credit reduction otherwise applicable under subsection (c)(2) below the limitation under paragraph (1).

(g) Credit reduction not to apply when state makes certain repayments.

(1) In general. In the case of any State which meets requirements of paragraph (2) with respect to any taxable year, subsection (c)(2) shall not apply to such taxable year; except that such taxable year (and January 1 of such taxable year) shall (except as provided in subsection (f)(3)) be taken into account for purposes of applying subsection (c)(2) to succeeding taxable years.

(2) Requirements. The requirements of this paragraph are met by any State with respect to any taxable year if the Secretary of Labor determines that—

(A) the repayments during the 1-year period ending on November 9 of such taxable year made by such State of advances under title XII of the Social Security Act are not less than the sum of—

(i) the potential additional taxes for such taxable year, and

(ii) any advances made to such State during such 1-year period under such title XII,

(B) there will be sufficient amounts in the State unemployment fund to pay all compensation during the 3-month period beginning on November 1 of such taxable year without receiving any advance under title XII of the Social Security Act, and

(C) there is a net increase in the solvency of the State unemployment compensation system for the taxable year attributable to changes made in the State law after the date on which the first advance taken into account in determining the amount of the potential additional taxes was made (or, if later, after the date of the enactment of this subsection) and such net increase equals or exceeds the potential additional taxes for such taxable year.

(3) Definitions. For purposes of paragraph (2)—

(A) Potential additional taxes. The term "potential additional taxes" means, with respect to any State for any taxable year, the aggregate amount of the additional tax which would be payable under this chapter for such taxable year by all taxpayers subject to the unemployment compensation law of such State for such taxable year if paragraph (2) of subsection (c) had applied to such taxable year and any preceding taxable year without regard to this subsection but with regard to subsection (f).

(B) Treatment of certain reductions. Any reduction in the State's balance under section 901(d)(1) of the Social Security Act shall not be treated as a repayment made by such State.

(4) Reports. The Secretary of Labor may require a State to furnish such information at such time and in such manner as may be necessary for purposes of paragraph (2).

In 1992, P.L. 102-318, Sec. 304, of this Act provides:

"SEC. 304. EXTENSION OF PERIOD FOR REPAYMENT OF FEDERAL LOANS TO STATE UNEMPLOYMENT FUNDS.

"(a) General rule. If the Secretary of Labor determines that a State meets the requirements of subsection (b), paragraph (2) of section 3302(c) of the Internal Revenue Code of 1986 shall be applied with respect to such State for taxable years after 1991—

"(1) by substituting 'third' for 'second' in subparagraph (A)(i),

"(2) by substituting 'fourth or fifth' for 'third or fourth' in subparagraph (B), and

"(3) by substituting 'sixth' for 'fifth' in subparagraph (C).

"(b) Requirements. A State meets the requirements of this subsection if, during calendar year 1992 or 1993, the State amended its unemployment compensation law to increase estimated contributions required under such law by at least 25 percent.

"(c) Special rule. This section shall not apply to any taxable year after 1994 unless—

"(1) such taxable year is in a series of consecutive taxable years as of the beginning of each of which there was a balance referred to in section 3302(c)(2) of such Code, and

(2) such series includes a taxable year beginning in 1992, 1993, or 1994."

—P.L. 102-244, Sec. 4, regarding the extention of time for payment of additional FUTA taxes, is reproduced in note following Code Sec. 6601.

In 1986, P.L. 99-514, Sec. 1884(1)(A), substituted "denominator" for "determination" in the second place it appeared in the material preceding clause (c)(2)(B)(i) ... Sec. 1884(1)(B)(i), deleted "percent" preceding the comma at the end of clause (c)(2)(B)(i) ... Sec. 1884(1)(B)(ii), added "percent" following "2.7" in clause (c)(2)(B)(i) ... Sec. 1884(2), substituted "1986" for "1987" in subpara. (f)(8)(A), effective 10/22/86.

In 1984, P.L. 98-601, Sec. (a), added Sec. 271(d)(4) to P. L. 97-248 (reproduced below), effective for remuneration paid after 12/31/84.

In 1983, P.L. 98-21, Sec. 512(a)(1), added para. (f)(8), effective for tax. yr. 1983 and tax. yrs. thereafter.

—P.L. 98-21, Sec. 512(b), deleted "beginning before January 1, 1988," in para. (f)(1) effective 4/20/83.

—P.L. 98-21, Sec. 513(a), amended subpara. (d)(4)(B) ... Sec. 513(b), substituted "2.7 [sic percent] multiplied by a fraction, the numerator of which is the wage base under this chapter and the denominator of which is the estimated United States average annual wage in covered employment for the calendar year in which the determination is to be made" for "2.7 [sic percent]" in clause (c)(2)(B)(i) ... Sec. 513(c), added ", multiplied by a fraction, the numerator of which is the State's average annual wage in covered employment for the calendar year in which the determination is made and the determination of which is the wage base under this chapter," after "(if any)" in subpara. (c)(2)(B), effective for tax. yr. 1983 and tax. yrs. thereafter.

Prior to amendment, subpara. (d)(4)(B) read as follows:

"(B) the total of the remuneration subject to contributions under the State unemployment compensation law with respect to such calendar year."

In 1982, P.L. 97-248, Sec. 271(c)(2)(A), substituted "5.4%" for "2.7%" in subsec. (b) ... Sec. 271(c)(2)(B), substituted "6 percent" for "3 percent" each place it appeared in para. (d)(1) ... Sec. 271(c)(3)(A), substituted "5 percent" for "10 percent" each place it appeared in para. (d)(1) ... Sec. 271(c)(3)(B), substituted "7½ percent" for "15 percent" in para. (c)(3), effective for remuneration paid after 12/31/84. Sec. 271(d)(3) and (d)(4) [Sec. 271(d)(4) added by Sec. (a) of P. L. 98-601, see above] provides:

"(3) Transitional rule for certain employees.

"(A) In general.—Notwithstanding section 3303 of the Internal Revenue Code of 1954, in the case of taxable years beginning after December 31, 1984, and before January 1, 1989, a taxpayer shall be allowed the additional credit under section 3302(b) of such Code with respect to any employee covered by a qualified specific industry provision if the requirements of subparagraph (B) are met with respect to such employee.

"(B) Requirements.—The requirements of this subparagraph are met for any taxable year with respect to any employee covered by a specific industry provision if the amount of contributions required to be paid for the taxable year to the unemployment fund of the State with respect to such employee are not less than the product of the required rate multiplied by the wages paid by the employer during the taxable year.

"(C) Required rate.—For purposes of subparagraph (B), the required rate for any taxable year is the sum of—

"(i) the rate at which contributions were required to be made under the specific industry provision as in effect on August 10, 1982, and

"(ii) the applicable percentage of the excess of 5.4 percent over the rate described in clause (i).

"(D) Applicable percentage.—For purposes of subparagraph (C), the term 'applicable percentage' means—

"(i) 20 percent in the case of taxable year 1985,

"(ii) 40 percent in the case of taxable year 1986,

"(iii) 60 percent in the case of taxable year 1987, and

"(iv) 80 percent in the case of taxable year 1988.

"(E) Qualified specific industry provision.— For purposes of this paragraph, the term, 'qualified specific industry provision' means a provision contained in a State unemployment compensation law (as in effect on August 10, 1982)—

"(i) which applies to employees in a specific industry or to an otherwise defined type of employees, and

"(ii) under which employers may elect to make contributions at a specified rate (without experience rating) which exceeds 2.7 percent.

"(4) Transitional rule for certain small businesses. —

"(A) In general.—Notwithstanding section 3303 of the Internal Revenue Code of 1954, in the case of taxable years beginning after December 31, 1984, and before January 1, 1989, a taxpayer shall be allowed the additional credit under section 3302(b) of such Code with respect to any employee covered by a qualified small business provision if the requirements of subparagraph (B) are met with respect to such employee.

"(B) Requirements.—The requirements of this subparagraph are met for any taxable year with respect to any employee covered by a qualified small business provision if the amount of contributions required to be paid for the taxable year to the unemployment fund of the State with respect to such employee are not less than the product of the required rate multiplied by the wages paid by the employer during the taxable year.

"(C) Required rate.—For purposes of subparagraph (B), the required rate for any taxable year is the sum of—

"(i) 3.1 percent, plus

"(ii) the applicable percentage (as defined in paragraph (3)(D)) of the excess of 5.4 percent over the rate described in clause (i).

"(D) Qualified small business provision.—For purposes of this paragraph, the term 'qualified small business provision' means a provision contained in a State unemployment compensation law (as in effect on the date of the enactment of this paragraph) which provides a maximum rate at which an employer is subject to contribution for wages paid during a calendar quarter if the total wages paid by such employer during such calendar quarter are less than $50,000.

"(E) Definition.—For purposes of this paragraph, the term 'wages' means the remuneration subject to contributions under the State unemployment compensation law, except that for purposes of subparagraph (D) the amount of total wages paid by an employer shall be determined without regard to any limitation on the amount subject to contribution."

—P.L. 97-248, Sec. 272(a), added subsec. (g) . . . Sec. 273(a), added the last sentence to para. (c)(2), effective for tax. yrs. begin. after 12/31/82.

In 1981, P.L. 97-35, Sec. 2406(a), added subsec. (f), effective for tax. yrs. begin. after 12/31/80.

In 1980, P.L. 96-589, Sec. 6(f), added para. (a)(5), effective 10/1/79, except for any proceeding under the Bankruptcy Act begun before 10/1/79. Sec. 7(g) of this Act provides:

"(g) Definitions.

"For purposes of this section—

"(1) Bankruptcy case. The term 'bankruptcy case' means any case under title 11 of the United States Code (as recodified by P. L. 95-598).

"(2) Similar judicial proceeding. The term 'similar judicial proceeding' means a receivership, foreclosure, or similar proceeding in a Federal or State court (as modified by section 368(a)(3)(D) of the Internal Revenue Code of 1954)."

In 1977, P.L. 95-19, Sec. 201(a), substituted "January 1, 1980" for "January 1, 1978" each place it appeared in the last sentence of para. (c)(2), effective 4/12/77. Sec. 201(b) of the Act provided as follows:

"(b) State requirements.—

"The amendment made by subsection (a) shall not apply in the case of any State unless the Secretary of Labor finds that such State meets the requirements of section 110(b) of the Emergency Compensation and Special Unemployment Assistance Extension Act of 1975 [P. L. 94-45]."

In 1976, P.L. 94-455, Sec. 1903(a)(12)(A), deleted "(10-month period in the case of October 31, 1972)" in subsec. (a) . . . Sec. 1903(a)(12)(B)(i), deleted "(10-month period in the case of October 31, 1972)" in subsec. (b) . . . Sec. 1903(a)(12)(B)(ii), substituted "12-month period" for "12 or 10-month period, as the case may be," in subsec. (b) . . . Sec. 1903(a)(12)(C)(i), deleted para. (c)(2) and the unnumbered paragraph immediately following para. (c)(2), and redesignated paras. (c)(3) and (c)(4) as paras. (c)(2) and (c)(3) . . . Sec. 1903(a)(12)(C)(ii), deleted "on or after the date of the enactment of the Employment Security Act of 1960", and substituted "paragraph (1)" for "paragraphs (1) and (2)" in para. (c)(2) (as redesignated by Sec. 1903(a)(12)(C)(i) of this Act, see above.) . . . Sec. 1903(a)(12)(C)(iii), substituted "paragraphs (1) and (2)" for "paragraphs (1), (2), and (3)" in para. (c)(3) (as redesignated by Sec. 1903(a)(12)(C)(i) of this Act, see above) . . . Sec. 1903(a)(12)(C)(iv), deleted "or (3)" in para. (d)(3) . . . Sec. 1903(a)(12)(C)(v), substituted "subsection (c)(2)" for "subsection (c)(3)" each place it appeared in paras. (d)(4), (d)(5) and (d)(6) . . . Sec. 1903(a)(12)(C)(vi), substituted "subsection (c)(2)(B) or (C)" for "subsection (c)(3)(B) or (C)" in para. (d)(7) . . . Sec. 1903(a)(12)(D), deleted para (d)(8), effective for wages paid after 12/31/76.

Prior to amendment, paras. (c)(2) and the unnumbered paragraph immediately following read as follows:

"(2) If an advance or advances have been made to the unemployment account of a State under title XII of the Social Security Act before the date of the enactment of the Employment Security Act of 1960, then the total credits (after applying subsections (a) and (b) and paragraph (1) of this subsection) otherwise allowable under this section for the taxable year in the case of a taxpayer subject to the unemployment compensation law of such State shall be reduced—

"(A) in the case of a taxable year beginning on January 1, 1963 (and in the case of any succeeding taxable year beginning before January 1, 1968), as of the beginning of which there is a balance of such advances, by 5 percent of the tax imposed by section 3301 with respect to the wages paid by such taxpayer during such taxable year which are attributable to such State; and

"(B) in the case of any succeeding taxable year beginning on or after January 1, 1968, as of the beginning of which there is a balance of such advances, by an additional 5 percent, for each such succeeding taxable year, of the tax imposed by section 3301 with respect to the wages paid by such taxpayer during such taxable year which are attributable to such State.

At the request (made before November 1 of the taxable year) of the Governor of any State, the Secretary of Labor shall, as soon as practicable after June 30 or (if later) the date of the receipt of such request, certify to such Governor and to the Secretary of the Treasury the amount he estimates equals .15 percent (plus an additional .15 percent for each additional 5-percent reduction, provided by subparagraph (B)) of the total of the remuneration which would have been subject to contributions under the State unemployment compensation law with respect to the calendar year preceding such certification if the dollar limit on remuneration subject to contributions under such law were equal to the dollar limit under section 3306(b)(1) for such calendar year. If, after receiving such certification and before November 10 of the taxable year, the State pays into the Federal unemployment account the amount so certified (and designates such payment as being made for purposes of this sentence), the reduction provided by the first sentence of this paragraph shall not apply for such taxable year."

Prior to deletion, para. (d)(8) read as follows:

"(8) Cross reference. For reduction of total credits allowable under subsection (c), see section 104 of the Temporary Unemployment Compensation Act of 1958."

—P.L. 94-455, Sec. 1906(b)(13)(A), substituted "Secretary" for "Secretary or his delegate" each place it appeared in Code Sec. 3302, effective 2/1/77.

In 1975, P.L. 94-45, Sec. 110(a), added the last sentence to para. (c)(3), effective 6/30/75, subject to restrictions imposed by Sec. 110(b)(1) of the Act, reproduced below:

"(b)(1) The amendment made by subsection (a) shall not be applicable in the case of any State unless the Secretary of Labor finds that such State has studied and taken appropriate action with respect to the financing of its unemployment programs so as substantially to accomplish the purpose of restoring the fiscal soundness of the State's unemployment account in the Unemployment Trust Fund and permitting the repayment within a reasonable time of any advances made to such account under title XII of the Social Security Act. For purposes of the preceding sentence, appropriate action with respect to the financing of a State's unemployment programs means an increase in the State's unemployment tax rate, an increase in the State's unemployment tax base, a change in the experience rating formulas, or a combination thereof."

—P.L. 94-45, Sec. 302, substituted "July 15, 1975" for "July 1, 1975" in subpara. (c)(4)(A).

In 1975, P.L. 93-618, Sec. 239(e), added para. (c)(4), effective for the period beginning 4/3/75 and ending on 9/30/82.

In 1970, P.L. 91-373, Sec. 142(a)(1), deleted "for the taxable year" following "certified" in para. (a)(1) . . . Sec. 142(a)(2), added "for the 12-month period ending on October 31 of such year (10-month period in the case of October 31, 1972)" before the period at the end of para. (a)(1) . . . Sec. 142(b)(1), deleted "for the taxable year" after "certified" in subsec. (b) . . . Sec. 142(b)(2), substituted "for the 12-month period ending on October 31 of such year (10-month period in the case of October 31, 1972), or with respect to any provisions thereof so certified)," for "(or with respect to any provisions thereof so certified)," in subsec. (b) . . . Sec. 142(b)(3), substituted "such 12 or 10-month period, as the case may be" for "the taxable year" the last place it appeared in subsec. (b), effective for tax. year. 1972 and tax. yrs. thereafter.

In 1963, P.L. 88-173, Sec. 1(a), amended subpara. (c)(2)(A) . . . Sec. 1(b), substituted "beginning on or after January 1, 1968," for "beginning with a consecutive January 1" in subpara. (b)(2)(C) . . . Sec. 1(c), added "At the request (made before November 1 of the taxable year) of the Governor of any State, the Secretary of Labor shall, as soon as practicable after June 30 or (if later) the date of the receipt of such request, certify to such Governor and to the Secretary of the Treasury the amount he estimates equals .15 percent (plus an additional . 15 percent for each additional 5-percent reduction, provided by subparagraph (B)) of the total of the remuneration which would have been subject to contributions under the State unemployment compensation law with respect to the calendar year preceding such certification if the dollar limit on remuneration subject to contributions under such law were equal to the dollar limit under section 3306(b)(1) for such calendar year. If, after receiving such certification and before November 10 of the taxable year, the State pays into the Federal unemployment account the amount so certified (and designates such payment as being made for purposes of this sentence), the reduction provided by the first sentence of this paragraph shall not apply for such taxable year." after subpara. (c)(2)(B), effective for tax. yrs. begin. on or after 1/1/63.

Prior to amendment, subpara. (c)(2)(A) read as follows:

"(A) in the case of a taxable year beginning with the fourth consecutive January 1 as of the beginning of which there is a balance of such advances, by 5 percent of the tax imposed by section 3301 with respect to the wages paid by such taxpayer during such taxable year which are attributable to such State; and"

—P.L. 88-31, Sec. (2)(b), amended para. (d)(1).

Prior to amendment, para. (d)(1) read as follows:

"(1) Rate of tax deemed to be 3 percent.—In applying subsection (c), the tax imposed by section 3301 shall be computed at the rate of 3 percent in lieu of 3.1 percent (or, in the case of the tax imposed with respect to the calendar years 1962 and 1963, in lieu of 3.5 percent)."

In 1961, P.L. 87-6, Sec. 14(b), amended para. (d)(1).

Prior to amendment, para. (d)(1) read as follows:

"(1) Rate of tax deemed to be 3 percent.—In applying subsection (c), the tax imposed by section 3301 shall be computed at the rate of 3 percent in lieu of 3.1 percent."

—P.L. 87-321, Sec. 1, added subsec. (e), effective for calendar 1961 and calendar yrs. thereafter.

In 1960, P.L. 86-778, Sec. 523(b), amended subsec. (c), and added subsec. (d), effective 9/13/60.

Prior to amendment, subsec. (c) read as follows:

"(c) Limit on total credits.—

"(1) The total credits allowed to a taxpayer under this section shall not exceed 90 percent of the tax against which such credits are allowable.

"(2) If an advance or advances have been made to the unemployment account of a State under title XII of the Social Security Act, and if any balance of such advance or advances has not been returned to the Federal unemployment account as provided in that title before December 1 of the taxable year, then the total credits (after other reductions under this section) otherwise allowable under this section for such taxable year in the case of a taxpayer subject to the unemployment compensation law of such State shall be reduced—

"(A) in the case of a taxable year beginning with the fourth consecutive January 1 on which such a balance of unreturned advances existed, by 5 percent of the tax imposed by section 3301 with respect to the wages paid by such taxpayer during such taxable year which are attributable to such State; and

"(B) in the case of any succeeding taxable year beginning with a consecutive January 1 on which such a balance of unreturned advances existed, by an additional 5 percent, for each such succeeding taxable year, of the tax imposed by section 3301 with respect to the wages paid by such taxpayer during such taxable year which are attributable to such State.

For purposes of this paragraph, wages shall be attributable to a particular State if they are subject to the unemployment compensation law of the State, or (if not subject to the unemployment compensation law of any State) if they are determined (under rules or regulations prescribed by the Secretary or his delegate) to be attributable to such State."

Sec. 3303. Conditions of additional credit allowance.
(a) State standards.

A taxpayer shall be allowed an additional credit under section 3302(b) with respect to any reduced rate of contributions permitted by a State law, only if the Secretary of Labor finds that under such law—

(1) no reduced rate of contributions to a pooled fund or to a partially pooled account is permitted to a person (or group of persons) having individuals in his (or their) employ except on the basis of his (or their) experience with respect to unemployment or other factors bearing a direct relation to unemployment risk during not less than the 3 consecutive years immediately preceding the computation date;

(2) no reduced rate of contributions to a guaranteed employment account is permitted to a person (or a group of persons) having individuals in his (or their) employ unless—

(A) the guaranty of remuneration was fulfilled in the year preceding the computation date; and

(B) the balance of such account amounts to not less than 2 ½ percent of that part of the payroll or payrolls for the 3 years preceding the computation date by which contributions to such account were measured; and

(C) such contributions were payable to such account with respect to 3 years preceding the computation date;

(3) no reduced rate of contributions to a reserve account is permitted to a person (or group of persons) having individuals in his (or their) employ unless—

(A) compensation has been payable from such account throughout the year preceding the computation date, and

(B) the balance of such account amounts to not less than five times the largest amount of compensation paid from such account within any 1 of the 3 years preceding such date, and

(C) the balance of such account amounts to not less than 2 ½ percent of that part of the payroll or payrolls for the 3 years preceding such date by which contributions to such account were measured, and

(D) such contributions were payable to such account with respect to the 3 years preceding the computation date.

For any person (or group of persons) who has (or have) not been subject to the State law for a period of time sufficient to compute the reduced rates permitted by paragraphs (1), (2), and (3) of this subsection on a 3-year basis (i) the period of time required may be reduced to the amount of time the person (or group of persons) has (or have) had experience under or has (or have) been subject to the State law, whichever is appropriate, but in no case less than 1 year immediately preceding the computation date, or (ii) a reduced rate (not less than 1 percent) may be permitted by the State law on a reasonable basis other than as permitted by paragraph (1), (2), or (3).

(b) Certification by the Secretary of Labor with respect to additional credit allowance.

(1) On October 31 of each calendar year, the Secretary of Labor shall certify to the Secretary of the Treasury the law of each State (certified by the Secretary of Labor as provided in section 3304 for the 12-month period ending on such October 31, with respect to which he finds that reduced rates of contributions were allowable with respect to such 12-month period only in accordance with the provisions of subsection (a).

(2) If the Secretary of Labor finds that under the law of a single State (certified by the Secretary of Labor as provided in section 3304) more than one type of fund or account is maintained, and reduced rates of contributions to more than one type of fund or account were allowable with respect to any 12-month period ending on October 31, and one or more of such reduced rates were allowable under conditions not fulfilling the requirements of subsection (a), the Secretary of Labor shall, on October 31, certify to the Secretary of the Treasury only those provisions of the State law pursuant to which reduced rates of contributions were allowable with respect to such 12-month period under conditions fulfilling the requirements of subsection (a), and shall, in connection therewith, designate the kind of fund or account, as defined in subsection (c), established by the provisions so certified. If the Secretary of Labor finds that a part of any reduced rate of contributions payable under such law or under such provisions is required to be paid into one fund or account and a part into another fund or account, the Secretary of Labor shall make such certification pursuant to this paragraph as he finds will assure the allowance of additional credits only with respect to that part of the reduced rate of contributions which is allowed under provisions which do fulfill the requirements of subsection (a).

(3) The Secretary of Labor shall, within 30 days after any State law is submitted to him for such purpose, certify to the State agency his findings with respect to reduced rates of contributions to a type of fund or account, as defined in subsection (c), which are allowable under such State law only in accordance with the provisions of subsection (a). After making such findings, the Secretary of Labor shall not withhold his certification to the Secretary of the Treasury of such State law, or of the provisions thereof with respect to which such findings were made, for any 12-month period ending on October 31 pursuant to paragraph (1) or (2) unless, after reasonable notice and opportunity for hearing to the State agency, the Secretary of Labor finds the State law no longer contains the provisions specified in subsection (a) or the State has, with respect to such 12-month period, failed to comply substantially with any such provision.

(c) Definitions.
As used in this section—

(1) Reserve account. The term "reserve account" means a separate account in an unemployment fund, maintained with respect to a person (or group of persons) having individuals in his (or their) employ, from which account, unless such account is exhausted, is paid all and only compensation payable on the basis of services performed for such person (or for one or more of the persons comprising the group).

(2) Pooled fund. The term "pooled fund" means an unemployment fund or any part thereof (other than a reserve account or a guaranteed employment account) into which the total contributions of persons contributing thereto are payable, in which all contributions are mingled and undivided, and from which compensation is payable to all individuals eligible for compensation from such fund.

(3) Partially pooled account. The term "partially pooled account" means a part of an unemployment fund in which part of the fund all contributions thereto are mingled and undivided, and from which part of the fund compensation is payable only to individuals to whom compensation would be payable from a reserve account or from a guaranteed employment account but for the exhaustion or termination of such reserve account or of such guaranteed employment account. Payments from a reserve account or guaranteed employment account into a partially pooled account shall not be construed to be inconsistent with the provisions of paragraph (1) or (4).

(4) Guaranteed employment account. The term "guaranteed employment account" means a separate account, in an unemployment fund, maintained with respect to a person (or group of persons) having individuals in his (or their) employ who, in accordance with the provisions of the State law or of a plan thereunder approved by the State agency,

(A) guarantees in advance at least 30 hours of work, for which remuneration will be paid at not less than stated rates, for each of 40 weeks (or if more, 1 weekly hour may be deducted for each added week guaranteed) in a year, to all the individuals who are in his (or their) employ in, and who continue to be available for suitable work in, one or more distinct establishments, except that any such individual's guaranty may commence after a probationary period (included within the 11 or less consecutive weeks immediately following the first week in which the individual renders services), and

(B) gives security or assurance, satisfactory to the State agency, for the fulfillment of such guaranties, from which account, unless such account is exhausted or terminated, is paid all and only compensation, payable on the basis of services performed for such person (or for one or more of the persons comprising the group), to any such individual whose guaranteed remuneration has not been paid (either pursuant to the guaranty or from the security or assurance provided for the fulfillment of the guaranty), or whose guaranty is not renewed and who is otherwise eligible for compensation under the State law.

(5) Year. The term "year" means any 12 consecutive calendar months.

(6) Balance. The term "balance", with respect to a reserve account or a guaranteed employment account, means the amount standing to the credit of the account as of the computation date; except that, if subsequent to January 1, 1940, any moneys have been paid into or credited to such account other than payments thereto by persons having individuals in their employ, such term shall mean the amount in such account as of the computation date less the total of such other moneys paid into or credited to such account subsequent to January 1, 1940.

(7) Computation date. The term "computation date" means the date, occurring at least once in each calendar year and within 27 weeks prior to the effective date of new rates of contributions, as of which such rates are computed.

(8) Reduced rate. The term "reduced rate" means a rate of contributions lower than the standard rate applicable under the State law, and the term "standard rate" means the rate on the basis of which variations therefrom are computed.

(d) Voluntary contributions.

A State law may, without being deemed to violate the standards set forth in subsection (a), permit voluntary contributions to be used in the computation of reduced rates if such contributions are paid prior to the expiration of 120 days after the beginning of the year for which such rates are effective.

(e) Payments by certain nonprofit organizations.

A State may, without being deemed to violate the standards set forth in subsection (a), permit an organization (or a group of organizations) described in section 501(c)(3) which is exempt from income tax under section 501(a) to elect (in lieu of paying contributions) to pay into the State unemployment fund amounts equal to the amounts of compensation attributable under the State law to service performed in the employ of such organization (or group).

(f) Transition.

To facilitate the orderly transition to coverage of service to which section 3309(a)(1)(A) applies, a State law may provide that an organization (or group of organizations) which elects before April 1, 1972, to make payments (in lieu of contributions) into the State unemployment fund as provided in section 3309(a)(2), and which had paid contributions into such fund under the State law with respect to such service performed in its employ before January 1, 1969, is not required to make any such payments (in lieu of contributions) on account of compensation paid after its election as heretofore described which is attributable under the State law to service performed in its employ, until the total of such compensation equals the amount—

(1) by which the contributions paid by such organization (or group) with respect to a period before the election provided by section 3309(a)(2), exceed

(2) the unemployment compensation for the same period which was charged to the experience-rating account of such organization (or group) or paid under the State law on the basis of wages paid by it or service performed in its employ, whichever is appropriate.

(g) Transitional rule for Unemployment Compensation Amendments of 1976.

To facilitate the orderly transition to coverage of service to which section 3309(a)(1)(A) applies by reason of the enactment of the Unemployment Compensation Amendments of 1976, a State law may provide that an organization (or group of organizations) which elects, when such election first becomes available under the State law with respect to such service, to make payments (in lieu of contributions) into the State unemployment fund as provided in section 3309(a)(2), and which had paid contributions into such fund under the State law with respect to such service performed in its employ before the date of the enactment of this subsection, is not required to make any such payment (in lieu of contributions) on account of compensation paid after its election as heretofore described which is attributable under the State law to such service performed in its employ, until the total of such compensation equals the amount—

(1) by which the contributions paid by such organization (or group) on the basis of wages for such service with respect to a period before the election provided by section 3309(a)(2), exceed

(2) the unemployment compensation for the same period which was charged to the experience-rating account of such organization (or group) or paid under the State law on the basis of such service performed in its employ or wages paid for such service, whichever is appropriate.

In 1983, P.L. 98-21, Sec. 524, provides as follows:
"SEC. 524. If —
"(1) an organization did not make an election to make payments (in lieu of contributions) as provided in section 3309(a)(2) of the Internal Revenue Code of 1954 before April 1, 1972, because such organization, as of such date, was treated as an organization described in section 501(c)(4) of such Code,
"(2) the Internal Revenue Service subsequently determined that such organization was described in section 501(c)(3) of such Code, and
"(3) such organization made such an election before the earlier of —
"(A) the date 18 months after such election was first available to it under the State law, or
"(B) January 1, 1984,
then section 3303(f) of such Code shall be applied with respect to such organization as if it did not contain the requirement that the election be made before April 1, 1972, and by substituting 'January 1, 1982' for 'January 1, 1969'."

In 1976, P.L. 94-566, Sec. 122(a), added subsec. (g), effective 10/20/76.
—P.L. 94-566, Sec. 122(b), substituted "which elects before April 1, 1972," for "which elects when such election first becomes available under the State law," in subsec. (f), effective 1/1/70.
—P.L. 94-455, Sec. 1903(a)(13), deleted "(10-month period in the case of October 31, 1972)" each place it appeared in subsec. (b), substituted "12-month period" for "12- or 10-month period, as the case may be" each place it appeared in paras. (b)(1) and (2), substituted "12-month period," for "12- or 10-month period, as the case may be," in para. (b)(3), effective for wages paid after 12/31/76.
—P.L. 94-455, Sec. 1906(b)(13)(C), substituted "to the Secretary of the Treasury" for "to the Secretary" each place it appeared in subsec. (b), effective 2/1/77.

In 1970, P.L. 91-373, Sec. 104(c), added subsecs. (e) and (f), effective 1/1/70.
—P.L. 91-373, Sec. 122, effective for tax. yrs. begin. after 12/31/71.
Prior to amendment, the last sentence of subsec. (a) read as follows:
"For any person (or group of persons) who has (or have) not been subject to the State law for a period of time sufficient to compute the reduced rates permitted by paragraphs (1), (2), and (3) of this subsection on a 3-year basis, the period of time required may be reduced to the amount of time the person (or group of persons) has (or have) had experience under or has (or have) been subject to the State law, whichever is appropriate, but in no case less than 1 year immediately preceding the computation date."
—P.L. 91-373, Sec. 142(c), (d), and (e) amended subsec. (b), effective for tax. yr. 1972 and tax. yrs. thereafter.
Prior to amendment, subsec. (b) read as follows:
"(b) *Certification by the Secretary of Labor with respect to additional credit allowance.*
"(1) On December 31 in each taxable year, the Secretary of Labor shall certify to the Secretary the law of each State (certified with respect to such year by the Secretary of Labor as provided in section 3304) with respect to which he finds that reduced rates of contributions were allowable with respect to such taxable year only in accordance with the provisions of subsection (a).
"(2) If the Secretary of Labor finds that under the law of a single State (certified by the Secretary of Labor as provided in section 3304) more than one type of fund or account is maintained, and reduced rates of contributions to more than one type of fund or account were allowable with respect to any taxable year, and one or more of such reduced rates were allowable under conditions not fulfilling the requirements of subsection (a), the Secretary of Labor shall, on December 31 of such taxable year, certify to the Secretary only those provisions of the State law pursuant to which reduced rates of contributions were allowable with respect to such taxable year under conditions fulfilling the requirements of subsection (a), and shall, in connection therewith, designate the kind of fund or account, as defined in subsection (c), established by the provisions so certified. If the Secretary of Labor finds that a part of any reduced rate of contributions payable under such law or under such provisions is required to be paid into one fund or account and a part into another fund or account, the Secretary of Labor shall make such certification pursuant to this paragraph as he finds will assure the allowance of additional credits only with respect to that part of the reduced rate of contributions which is allowed under provisions which do fulfill the requirements of subsection (a).
"(3) The Secretary of Labor shall, within 30 days after any State law is submitted to him for such purpose, certify to the State agency his findings with respect to reduced rates of contributions to a type of fund or account, as defined in subsection (c), which are allowable under such State law only in accordance with the provisions of subsection (a). After making such findings, the Secretary of Labor shall not withhold his certification to the Secretary of such State law, or of the provisions thereof with respect to which such findings were made, for any taxable year pursuant to paragraph (1) or (2) unless, after reasonable notice and opportunity for hearing to the State agency, the Secretary of Labor finds the State law no longer contains the provisions specified in subsection (a) or the State has, with respect to such taxable year, failed to comply substantially with any such provision."

In 1954, ch. 1212, Sec. 2, added para. relating to reduced rates for new employers in subsec. (a), effective after 12/31/54.

Sec. 3304. Approval of State laws.
(a) Requirements.

The Secretary of Labor shall approve any State law submitted to him, within 30 days of such submission, which he finds provides that—

(1) all compensation is to be paid through public employment offices or such other agencies as the Secretary of Labor may approve;

(2) no compensation shall be payable with respect to any day of unemployment occurring within 2 years after the first day of the first period with respect to which contributions are required;

(3) all money received in the unemployment fund shall (except for refunds of sums erroneously paid into such fund and except for refunds paid in accordance with the provisions of section 3305(b)) immediately upon such receipt be paid over to the Secretary of the Treasury to the credit of the Unemployment Trust Fund established by section 904 of the Social Security Act (42 U.S.C. 1104);

(4) all money withdrawn from the unemployment fund of the State shall be used solely in the payment of unemployment compensation, exclusive of expenses of administration, and for refunds of sums erroneously paid into such fund and refunds paid in accordance with the provisions of section 3305(b); except that—

(A) an amount equal to the amount of employee payments into the unemployment fund of a State may be used in the payment of cash benefits to individuals with respect to their disability, exclusive of expenses of administration;

(B) the amounts specified by section 903(c)(2) or 903(d)(4) of the Social Security Act may, subject to the conditions prescribed in such section, be used for expenses incurred by the State for administration of its unemployment compensation law and public employment offices;

(C) nothing in this paragraph shall be construed to prohibit deducting an amount from unemployment compensation otherwise payable to an individual and using the amount so deducted to pay for health insurance, or the withholding of Federal, State, or local individual income tax, if the individual elected to have such deduction made and such deduction was made under a program approved by the Secretary of Labor;

(D) amounts may be deducted from unemployment benefits and used to repay overpayments as provided in section 303(g) of the Social Security Act;

(E) amounts may be withdrawn for the payment of short-time compensation under a plan approved by the Secretary of Labor;

(F) amounts may be withdrawn for the payment of allowances under a self-employment assistance program (as defined in section 3306(t)); and

(G) with respect to amounts of covered unemployment compensation debt (as defined in section 6402(f)(4)) collected under section 6402(f)—

(i) amounts may be deducted to pay any fees authorized under such section; and

(ii) the penalties and interest described in section 6402(f)(4)(B) may be transferred to the appropriate State fund into which the State would have deposited such amounts had the person owing the debt paid such amounts directly to the State;

(5) compensation shall not be denied in such State to any otherwise eligible individual for refusing to accept new work under any of the following conditions:

(A) if the position offered is vacant due directly to a strike, lockout, or other labor dispute;

(B) if the wages, hours, or other conditions of the work offered are substantially less favorable to the individual than those prevailing for similar work in the locality;

(C) if as a condition of being employed the individual would be required to join a company union or to resign from or refrain from joining any bona fide labor organization;

(6)(A) compensation is payable on the basis of service to which section 3309(a)(1) applies, in the same amount, on the same terms, and subject to the same conditions as compensation payable on the basis of other service subject to such law; except that—

(i) with respect to services in an instructional, research, or principal administrative capacity for an educational institution to which section 3309(a)(1) applies, compensation shall not be payable based on such services for any week commencing during the period between two successive academic years or terms (or, when an agreement provides instead for a similar period between two regular but not successive terms, during such period) to any individual if such individual performs such services in the first of such academic years (or terms) and if there is a contract or reasonable assurance that such individual will perform services in any such capacity for any educational institution in the second of such academic years or terms,

(ii) with respect to services in any other capacity for an educational institution to which section 3309(a)(1) applies—

(I) compensation payable on the basis of such services may be denied to any individual for any week which commences during a period between 2 successive academic years or terms if such individual performs such services in the first of such academic years or terms and there is a reasonable assurance that such individual will perform such services in the second of such academic years or terms, except that

(II) if compensation is denied to any individual for any week under subclause (I) and such individual was not offered an opportunity to perform such services for the educational institution for the second of such academic years or terms, such individual shall be entitled to a retroactive payment of the compensation for each week for which the individual filed a timely claim for compensation and for which compensation was denied solely by reason of subclause (I),

(iii) with respect to any services described in clause (i) or (ii), compensation payable on the basis of such services shall be denied to any individual for any week which commences during an established and customary vacation period or holiday recess if such individual performs such services in the period immediately before such vacation period or holiday recess, and there is a reasonable assurance that such individual will perform such services in the period immediately following such vacation period or holiday recess,

(iv) with respect to any services described in clause (i) or (ii), compensation payable on the basis of services in any such capacity shall be denied as specified in clauses (i), (ii), and (iii) to any individual who performed such services in an educational institution while in the employ of an educational service agency, and for this purpose the term "educational service agency" means a governmental agency or governmental entity which is established and operated exclusively for the purpose of providing such services to one or more educational institutions,

(v) with respect to services to which section 3309(a)(1) applies, if such services are provided to or on behalf of an educational institution, compensation may be denied under the same circumstances as described in clauses (i) through (iv), and

(vi) with respect to services described in clause (ii), clauses (iii) and (iv) shall be applied by substituting "may be denied" for "shall be denied", and

(B) payments (in lieu of contributions) with respect to service to which section 3309(a)(1) applies may be made into the State unemployment fund on the basis set forth in section 3309(a)(2);

(7) an individual who has received compensation during his benefit year is required to have had work since the beginning of such year in order to qualify for compensation in his next benefit year;

(8) compensation shall not be denied to an individual for any week because he is in training with the approval of the State agency (or because of the application, to any such week in training, of State law provisions relating to availability for work, active search for work, or refusal to accept work);

(9)(A) compensation shall not be denied or reduced to an individual solely because he files a claim in another State (or a contiguous country with which the United States has an agreement with respect to unemployment compensation) or because he resides in another State (or such a contiguous country) at the time he files a claim for unemployment compensation;

(B) the State shall participate in any arrangements for the payment of compensation on the basis of combining an individual's wages and employment covered under the State law with his wages and employment covered under the unemployment compensation law of other States which are approved by the Secretary of Labor in consultation with the State unemployment compensation agencies as reasonably calculated to assure the prompt and full payment of compensation in such situations. Any such arrangement shall include provisions for (i) applying the base period of a single State law to a claim involving the combining of an individual's wages and employment covered under two or more State laws, and (ii) avoiding duplicate use of wages and employment by reason of such combining;

(10) compensation shall not be denied to any individual by reason of cancellation of wage credits or total reduction of his benefit rights for any cause other than discharge for misconduct connected with his work, fraud in connection with a claim for compensation, or receipt of disqualifying income;

(11) extended compensation shall be payable as provided by the Federal-State Extended Unemployment Compensation Act of 1970;

(12) no person shall be denied compensation under such State law solely on the basis of pregnancy or termination of pregnancy;

(13) compensation shall not be payable to any individual on the basis of any services, substantially all of which

Employment taxes Code Sec. 3304(c)

consist of participating in sports or athletic events or training or preparing to so participate, for any week which commences during the period between two successive sport seasons (or similar periods) if such individual performed such services in the first of such seasons (or similar periods) and there is a reasonable assurance that such individual will perform such services in the later of such seasons (or similar periods);

(14)(A) compensation shall not be payable on the basis of services performed by an alien unless such alien is an individual who was lawfully admitted for permanent residence at the time such services were performed, was lawfully present for purposes of performing such services, or was permanently residing in the United States under color of law at the time such services were performed (including an alien who was lawfully present in the United States as a result of the application of the provisions of section 212(d)(5) of the Immigration and Nationality Act),

(B) any data or information required of individuals applying for compensation to determine whether compensation is not payable to them because of their alien status shall be uniformly required from all applicants for compensation, and

(C) in the case of an individual whose application for compensation would otherwise be approved, no determination by the State agency that compensation to such individual is not payable because of his alien status shall be made except upon a preponderance of the evidence;

(15)(A) subject to subparagraph (B), the amount of compensation payable to an individual for any week which begins after March 31, 1980, and which begins in a period with respect to which such individual is receiving a governmental or other pension, retirement or retired pay, annuity, or any other similar periodic payment which is based on the previous work of such individual shall be reduced (but not below zero) by an amount equal to the amount of such pension, retirement or retired pay, annuity, or other payment, which is reasonably attributable to such week except that—

(i) the requirements of this paragraph shall apply to any pension, retirement or retired pay, annuity, or similar periodic payment only if—

(I) such pension, retirement or retired pay, annuity, or similar payment is under a plan maintained (or contributed to) by a base period employer or chargeable employer (as determined under applicable law), and

(II) in the case of such a payment not made under the Social Security Act or the Railroad Retirement Act of 1974 (or the corresponding provisions of prior law), services performed for such employer by the individual after the beginning of the base period (or remuneration for such services) affect eligibility for, or increase the amount of, such pension, retirement or retired pay, annuity, or similar payment, and

(ii) the State law may provide for limitations on the amount of any such a reduction to take into account contributions made by the individual for the pension, retirement or retired pay, annuity, or other similar periodic payment, and

(B) the amount of compensation shall not be reduced on account of any payments of governmental or other pensions, retirement or retired pay, annuity, or other similar payments which are not includible in the gross income of the individual for the taxable year in which it was paid because it was part of a rollover distribution;

(16)(A) wage information contained in the records of the agency administering the State law which is necessary (as determined by the Secretary of Health and Human Services in regulations) for purposes of determining an individual's eligibility for assistance, or the amount of such assistance, under a State program funded under part A of title IV of the Social Security Act, shall be made available to a State or political subdivision thereof when such information is specifically requested by such State or political subdivision for such purposes,

(B) wage and unemployment compensation information contained in the records of such agency shall be furnished to the Secretary of Health and Human Services (in accordance with regulations promulgated by such Secretary) as necessary for the purposes of the National Directory of New Hires established under section 453(i) of the Social Security Act, and

(C) such safeguards are established as are necessary (as determined by the Secretary of Health and Human Services in regulations) to insure that information furnished under subparagraph (A) or (B) is used only for the purposes authorized under such subparagraph;

(17) any interest required to be paid on advances under title XII of the Social Security Act shall be paid in a timely manner and shall not be paid, directly or indirectly (by an equivalent reduction in State unemployment taxes or otherwise) by such State from amounts in such State's unemployment fund;

(18) Federal individual income tax from unemployment compensation is to be deducted and withheld if an individual receiving such compensation voluntarily requests such deduction and withholding; and

(19) all the rights, privileges, or immunities conferred by such law or by acts done pursuant thereto shall exist subject to the power of the legislature to amend or repeal such law at any time.

(b) Notification.

The Secretary of Labor shall, upon approving such law, notify the governor of the State of his approval.

(c) Certification.

On October 31 of each taxable year the Secretary of Labor shall certify to the Secretary of the Treasury each State whose law he has previously approved, except that he shall not certify any State which, after reasonable notice and opportunity for hearing to the State agency, the Secretary of Labor finds has amended its law so that it no longer contains the provisions specified in subsection (a) or has with respect to the 12-month period ending on such October 31 failed to comply substantially with any such provision in such subsection. No finding of a failure to comply substantially with any provision in paragraph (5) of subsection (a) shall be based on an application or interpretation of State law (1) until all administrative review provided for under the laws of the State has been exhausted, or (2) with respect to which the time for judicial review provided by the laws of the State has not expired, or (3) with respect to which any judicial review is pending. On October 31 of any taxable year, the Secretary of Labor shall not certify any State which, after reasonable notice and opportunity for hearing to the State agency, the Secretary of Labor finds has failed to amend its law so that it contains each of the provisions required by law to be included therein (including provisions relating to the Federal-State Extended Unemployment Compensation Act of 1970 (or any amendments thereto) as required under subsection (a)(11)), or has, with respect to the twelve-month period ending on such October 31, failed to comply substantially with any such provision.

(d) Notice of noncertification.

If at any time the Secretary of Labor has reason to believe that a State whose law he has previously approved may not be certified under subsection (c), he shall promptly so notify the governor of such State.

(e) Change of law during 12-month period.

Whenever—

(1) any provision of this section, section 3302, or section 3303 refers to a 12-month period ending on October 31 of a year, and

(2) the law applicable to one portion of such period differs from the law applicable to another portion of such period, then such provision shall be applied by taking into account for each such portion the law applicable to such portion.

(f) Definition of institution of higher education.

For purposes of subsection (a)(6), the term "institution of higher education" means an educational institution in any State which—

(1) admits as regular students only individuals having a certificate of graduation from a high school, or the recognized equivalent of such a certificate;

(2) is legally authorized within such State to provide a program of education beyond high school;

(3) provides an educational program for it which awards a bachelor's or higher degree, or provides a program which is acceptable for full credit toward such a degree, or offers a program of training to prepare students for gainful employment in a recognized occupation; and

(4) is a public or other nonprofit institution.

In 2010, P.L. 111-312, Sec. 501(a)(1)(A), substituted "January 3, 2012" for "November 30, 2010" each place it appeared in Sec. 4007 of P.L. 110-252 [see below];... Sec. 501(a)(1)(B), substituted "January 3, 2012" for "November 30, 2010" in the heading of Sec. 4007(b)(2) of P.L. 110-252 [see below];... Sec. 501(a)(1)(C), substituted "June 9, 2012" for "April 30, 2011" in Sec. 4007(b)(3) of P.L. 110-252 [see below];... Sec. 501(a)(2)(A), substituted "January 4, 2012" for "December 1, 2010" each place it appeared in Sec. 2005 of P.L. 111-5 [see below];... Sec. 501(a)(2)(B), substituted "June 11, 2012" for "May 1, 2011" in Sec. 2005(c) of P.L. 111-5 [see below];... Sec. 501(a)(3), substituted "June 10, 2012" for "April 30, 2011" in Sec. 5 of P.L. 110-449 [see below];... Sec. 501(b)(1), deleted "and" at the end of Sec. 4004(e)(1)(E) of P.L. 110-252 [see below];... Sec. 501(b)(2), added subpara. (G) to Sec. 4004(e)(1) of P.L. 110-252 [see below]; effective 7/22/2010, as if included in the enactment of the Unemployment Compensation Extension Act of 2010 [P.L. 111-205, see below].

—P.L. 111-312, Sec. 502(a), added the second sentence in the flush paragraph following para. (d)(2) of Sec. 203 of the Federal-State Extended Unemployment Compensation Act of 1970 [P.L. 91-373] see below].... Sec. 502(b)(1), redesignated para. (f)(2) of Sec. 203 of P.L. 91-373 [see below] as para. (f)(3)... Sec. 502(b)(2), added para. (f)(2) to Sec. 203 of P.L. 91-373 [see below].

—P.L. 111-205, Sec. 2(a)(1)(A), substituted "November 30, 2010" for "June 2, 2010" each place it appeared in Sec. 4007 of P.L. 110-252 [see below];... Sec. 2(a)(1)(B), substituted "November 30, 2010" for "June 2, 2010" in the heading of Sec. 4007(b)(2) of P.L. 110-252 [see below];... Sec. 2(a)(1)(C), substituted "April 30, 2011" for "November 6, 2010" in Sec. 4007(b)(3) of P.L. 110-252 [see below];... Sec. 2(a)(2)(A), substituted "December 1, 2010" for "June 2, 2010" each place it appeared in Sec. 2005 of P.L. 111-5 [see below];... Sec. 2(a)(2)(B), substituted "May 1, 2011" for "November 6, 2010" in Sec. 2005(c) of P.L. 111-5 [see below];... Sec. 2(a)(3), substituted "April 30, 2011" for "November 6, 2010" in Sec. 5 of P.L. 110-449 [see below];... Sec. 2(b)(1), deleted "and" at the end of Sec. 4004(e)(1)(D) of P.L. 110-252 [see below];... Sec. 2(b)(2), added subpara. (F) to Sec. 4004(e)(1) of P.L. 110-252 [see below];... Sec. 2(c), added "(including terms and conditions relating to availability for work, active search for work, and refusal to accept work)" before "shall apply" in Sec. 4001(d)(2) of P.L. 110-252 [see below].

—P.L. 111-205, Sec. 2(d), of this Act, reads as follows:

"(d) Effective date. The amendments made by this section shall take effect as if included in the enactment of the Continuing Extension Act of 2010 (Public Law 111-157)."

—P.L. 111-205, Sec. 3(a), added subsec. (g) to Sec. 4002 of P.L. 110-252 [see below].

—P.L. 111-205, Sec. 3(b), of this Act, reads as follows:

"(b) Effective date. The amendment made by this section shall apply to individuals whose benefit years, as described in section 4002(g)(1)(B) the Supplemental Appropriations Act, 2008 (Public Law 110-252; 26 U.S.C. 3304 note), as amended by this section, expire after the date of enactment of this Act."

—P.L. 111-205, Sec. 4, added subsec. (g) to Sec. 4001 of P.L. 110-252 [see below].

—P.L. 111-157, Sec. 2(a)(1)(A), substituted "June 2, 2010" for "April 5, 2010" each place it appeared in Sec. 4007 of P.L. 110-252 [see below];... Sec. 2(a)(1)(B), substituted "June 2, 2010" for "April 5, 2010" in the heading of Sec. 4007(b)(2) of P.L. 110-252 [see below];... Sec. 2(a)(1)(C), substituted "November 6, 2010" for "September 4, 2010" in Sec. 4007(b)(3) of P.L. 110-252 [see below];... Sec. 2(a)(2)(A), substituted "June 2, 2010" for "April 5, 2010" in Sec. 2002(e)(1)(B) of P.L. 111-5 [see below];... Sec. 2(a)(2)(B), substituted "June 2, 2010" for "April 5, 2010" in the heading of Sec. 2002(e)(2) of P.L. 111-5 [see below];... Sec. 2(a)(2)(C), substituted "December 7, 2010" for "October 5, 2010" in Sec. 2002(e)(3) of P.L. 111-5 [see below];... Sec. 2(a)(3)(A), substituted "June 2, 2010" for "April 5, 2010" each place it appeared in Sec. 2005 of P.L. 111-5 [see below];... Sec. 2(a)(3)(B), substituted "November 6, 2010" for "September 4, 2010" in Sec. 2005(c) of P.L. 111-5 [see below];... Sec. 2(a)(4), substituted "November 6, 2010" for "September 4, 2010" in Sec. 5 of P.L. 110-449 [see below];... Sec. 2(b)(1), deleted "and" at the end of Sec. 4004(e)(1)(C) of P.L. 110-252 [see below];... Sec. 2(b)(2), added Subpara. (E) to Sec. 4004(e)(1) of P.L. 110-252 [see below].

—P.L. 111-144, Sec. 2(a)(1)(A), substituted "April 5, 2010" for "February 28, 2010" each place it appeared in Sec. 4007 of P.L. 110-252 [see below];... Sec. 2(a)(1)(B), substituted "April 5, 2010" for "February 28, 2010" in the heading of Sec. 4007(b)(2) of P.L. 110-252 [see below];... Sec. 2(a)(1)(C), substituted "September 4, 2010" for "July 31, 2010" in Sec. 4007(b)(3) of P.L. 110-252 [see below];... Sec. 2(a)(2)(A), substituted "April 5, 2010" for "February 28, 2010" in Sec. 2002(e)(1)(B) of P.L. 111-5 [see below];... Sec. 2(a)(2)(B), substituted "April 5, 2010" for "February 28, 2010" in the heading of Sec. 2002(e)(2) of P.L. 111-5 [see below];... Sec. 2(a)(2)(C), substituted "October 5, 2010" for "August 31, 2010" in Sec. 2002(e)(3) of P.L. 111-5 [see below];... Sec. 2(a)(3)(A), substituted "April 5, 2010" for "February 28, 2010" each place it appeared in Sec. 2005 of P.L. 111-5 [see below];... Sec. 2(a)(3)(B), substituted "September 4, 2010" for "July 31, 2010" in Sec. 2005(c) of P.L. 111-5 [see below];... Sec. 2(a)(4), substituted "September 4, 2010" for "July 31, 2010" in Sec. 5 of P.L. 110-449 [see below];... Sec. 2(b)(1), deleted "and" at the end of Sec. 4004(e)(1)(B) of P.L. 110-252 [see below];... Sec. 2(b)(2), substituted "1009(a)(1)" for "1009" in Sec. 4004(e)(1)(C) of P.L. 110-252 [see below];... Sec. 2(b)(3), added subpara. (D) to Sec. 4004(e)(1) of P.L. 110-252 [see below].

In 2009, P.L. 111-118, Sec. 1009(a)(1)(A)DivB, substituted "February 28, 2010" for "December 31, 2009" each place it appeared in Sec. 4007 of P.L. 110-252 [see below];... Sec. 1009(a)(1)(B)DivB, substituted "February 28, 2010" for "December 31, 2009" in the heading of Sec. 4007(b)(2) of P.L. 110-252 [see below];... Sec. 1009(a)(1)(C)DivB, substituted "July 31, 2010" for "May 31, 2010" in Sec. 4007(b)(3) of P.L. 110-252 [see below];... Sec. 1009(a)(2)(A)DivB, substituted "on or before February 28, 2010" for "before January 1, 2010" in Sec. 2002(e)(1)(B) of P.L. 111-5 [see below];... Sec. 1009(a)(2)(B)DivB, substituted "February 28, 2010" for "January 1, 2010" in the heading of Sec. 2002(e)(2) of P.L. 111-5 [see below];... Sec. 1009(a)(2)(C)DivB, substituted "August 31, 2010" for "June 30, 2010" in Sec. 2002(e)(3) of P.L. 111-5 [see below];... Sec. 1009(a)(3)(A)DivB, substituted "February 28, 2010" for "January 1, 2010" each place it appeared in Sec. 2005 of P.L. 111-5 [see below];... Sec. 1009(a)(3)(B)DivB, substituted "July 31, 2010" for "June 1, 2010" in Sec. 2005(c) of P.L. 111-5 [see below];... Sec. 1009(a)(4)DivB, substituted "July 31, 2010" for "May 30, 2010" in Sec. 5 of P.L. 110-449 [see below].

—P.L. 111-118, Sec. 1009(b)DivB, substituted "by reason of—(A) the amendments made by section 2001(a) of the Assistance for Unemployed Workers and Struggling Families Act; (B) the amendments made by sections 2 through 4 of the Worker, Homeownership, and Business Assistance Act of 2009; and (C) the amendments made by section 1009 of the Department of Defense Appropriations Act, 2010; and" for "by reason of the amendments made by section 2001(a) of the Assistance for Unemployed Workers and Struggling Families Act and sections 2, 3, and 4 of the Worker, Homeownership, and Business Assistance Act of 2009; and" in Sec. 4004(e)(1) of P.L. 110-252 [see below]

—P.L. 111-118, Sec. 1009(c)DivB, provides:

"(c) Amounts in this section are designated as emergency requirements and necessary to meet emergency needs pursuant to sections 403 and 423(b) of S. Con. Res. 13 (111th Congress), the concurrent resolution on the budget for fiscal year 2010."

—P.L. 111-92, Sec. 2(a)(1)(A), substituted "At the time that the amount established in an individual's account under subsection (b)(1) is exhausted" for "If, at the time that the amount established in an individual's account under subsection (b)(1) is exhausted or at any time thereafter, such individual's State is in an extended benefit period (as determined under paragraph (2))" in the opening paragraph of Sec. 4002(c)(1) of P.L. 110-252 [see below];... Sec. 2(a)(1)(B), substituted "54 percent" for "50 percent" in Sec. 4002(c)(1)(A) of P.L. 110-252 [see below];... Sec. 2(a)(1)(C), substituted "14" for "13" in Sec. 4002(c)(1)(B) of P.L. 110-252 [see below];... Sec. 2(a)(2), deleted Sec. 4002(c)(2) of P.L. 110-252 [see below];... Sec. 2(a)(3), redesignated Sec. 4002(c)(3) as 4002(c)(2) of P.L. 110-252 [see below].

Prior to deletion, para. (2) of Sec. 4002(c) of P.L. 110-252 read as follows:

"(2) Extended benefit period. For purposes of paragraph (1), a State shall be considered to be in an extended benefit period, as of any given time, if—

"(A) such a period is then in effect for such State under the Federal-State Extended Unemployment Compensation Act of 1970;

"(B) such a period would then be in effect for such State under such Act if section 203(d) of such Act—

"(i) were applied by substituting '4' for '5' each place it appears; and

"(ii) did not include the requirement under paragraph (1)(A) thereof; or

"(C) such a period would then be in effect for such State under such Act if—

Employment taxes   Code Sec. 3304

"(i) section 203(f) of such Act were applied to such State (regardless of whether the State by law had provided for such application); and

"(ii) such section 203(f)—

"(I) were applied by substituting '6.0' for '6.5' in paragraph (1)(A)(i) thereof; and

"(II) did not include the requirement under paragraph (1)(A)(ii) thereof."

—P.L. 111-92, Sec. 2(b), provides:

"(b) Effective Date. The amendments made by this section [Sec. 2(a)(1)-(2) of PL 111-92, see above] shall apply as if included in the enactment of the Supplemental Appropriations Act, 2008 [P.L. 110-252, enacted 6/30/2008], except that no amount shall be payable by virtue of such amendments with respect to any week of unemployment commencing before the date of the enactment of this Act."

—P.L. 111-92, Sec. 3(a), added subsec. (d) to Sec. 4002 of P.L. 110-252 [see below]; . . . Sec. 3(b)(1), substituted "then subsections (c) and (d) of section 4002" for "then section 4002(c)" in Sec. 4007(b)(2) of P.L. 110-252 [see below]; . . . Sec. 3(b)(2), substituted "paragraph (2) of such subsection (c) or (d) (as the case may be))" for "paragraph (2) of such section)" in Sec. 4007(b)(2) of P.L. 110-252 [see below];

—P.L. 111-92, Sec. 3(c), provides:

"(c) Effective date. The amendments made by this section [Sec. 3(a)-(b) of P.L. 111-92, see above] shall apply as if included in the enactment of the Supplemental Appropriations Act, 2008 [P.L. 110-252, enacted 6/30/2008], except that no amount shall be payable by virtue of such amendments with respect to any week of unemployment commencing before the date of the enactment of this Act."

—P.L. 111-92, Sec. 4(a), added subsec. (e) to Sec. 4002 of P.L. 110-252 [see below]; . . . Sec. 4(b)(1), substituted ", (d), and (e) of section 4002" for "and (d)" in Sec. 4007(b)(2) [as amended by Sec. 3(b)(1)-(2) of this Act] of P.L. 110-252 [see below]; . . . Sec. 4(b)(2), substituted ", (d), or (e) (as the case may be))" for "or (d)" in Sec. 4007(b)(2) [as amended by Sec. 3(b)(1)-(2) of this Act] of P.L. 110-252 [see below];

—P.L. 111-92, Sec. 4(c), provides:

"(c) Effective date. The amendments made by this section [Sec. 4(a)-(b) of P.L. 111-92, see above] shall apply as if included in the enactment of the Supplemental Appropriations Act, 2008 [P.L. 110-252, enacted 6/30/2008], except that no amount shall be payable by virtue of such amendments with respect to any week of unemployment commencing before the date of the enactment of this Act."

—P.L. 111-92, Sec. 5, added subsec. (f) to Sec. 4002 of P.L. 110-252 [see below];

—P.L. 111-92, Sec. 6, substituted "Act and sections 2, 3, and 4 of the Worker, Homeownership, and Business Assistance Act of 2009" for "Act;" in Sec. 4004(e)(1) of P.L. 110-252 [see below];

—P.L. 111-92, Sec. 8, provides:

"Sec. 8. Treatment of Additional Regular Compensation. The monthly equivalent of any additional compensation paid by reason of section 2002 of the Assistance for Unemployed Workers and Struggling Families Act, as contained in Public Law 111-5 (26 U.S.C. 3304 note; 123 Stat. 438) shall be disregarded after the date of the enactment of this Act in considering the amount of income and assets of an individual for purposes of determining such individual's eligibility for, or amount of, benefits under the Supplemental Nutrition Assistance Program (SNAP)."

—P.L. 111-5, Sec. 2001(a)(1), substituted "December 31, 2009" for "March 31, 2009" each place it appeared in Sec. 4007 of P.L. 110-252 [see below]; . . . Sec. 2001(a)(2), substituted "December 31, 2009" for "March 31, 2009" in the heading of Sec. 4007(b)(2) of P.L. 110-252 [see below]; . . . Sec. 2001(a)(3), substituted "May 31, 2010" for "August 27, 2009" in Sec. 4007(b)(3) of P.L. 110-252 [see below]; . . . Sec. 2001(b), added subsec. (e) to Sec. 4004 of P.L. 110-252 [see below]

—P.L. 111-5, Sec. 2002, of this Act [as amended by Sec. 1009(a)(2)(A)-(C) of P.L. 111-118 and Sec. 2(a)(2) of P.L.111-144, see above] provides:

"Sec. 2002. Increase in Unemployment Compensation Benefits.

"(a) Federal-State Agreements. Any State which desires to do so may enter into and participate in an agreement under this section with the Secretary of Labor (hereinafter in this section referred to as the 'Secretary'). Any State which is a party to an agreement under this section may, upon providing 30 days' written notice to the Secretary, terminate such agreement.

"(b) Provisions of Agreement.

"(1) Additional Compensation. Any agreement under this section shall provide that the State agency of the State will make payments of regular compensation to individuals in amounts and to the extent that they would be determined if the State law of the State were applied, with respect to any week for which the individual is (disregarding this section) otherwise entitled under the State law to receive regular compensation, as if such State law had been modified in a manner such that the amount of regular compensation (including dependents' allowances) payable for any week shall be equal to the amount determined under the State law (before the application of this paragraph) plus an additional $25.

"(2) Allowable Methods of Payment. Any additional compensation provided for in accordance with paragraph (1) shall be payable either—

"(A) as an amount which is paid at the same time and in the same manner as any regular compensation otherwise payable for the week involved; or

"(B) at the option of the State, by payments which are made separately from, but on the same weekly basis as, any regular compensation otherwise payable.

"(c) Nonreduction Rule. An agreement under this section shall not apply (or shall cease to apply) with respect to a State upon a determination by the Secretary that the method governing the computation of regular compensation under the State law of that State has been modified in a manner such that—

"(1) the average weekly benefit amount of regular compensation which will be payable during the period of the agreement (determined disregarding any additional amounts attributable to the modification described in subsection (b)(1)) will be less than

"(2) the average weekly benefit amount of regular compensation which would otherwise have been payable during such period under the State law, as in effect on December 31, 2008.

"(d) Payments to States.

"(1) In General.

"(A) Full Reimbursement. There shall be paid to each State which has entered into an agreement under this section an amount equal to 100 percent of—

"(i) the total amount of additional compensation (as described in subsection (b)(1)) paid to individuals by the State pursuant to such agreement; and

"(ii) any additional administrative expenses incurred by the State by reason of such agreement (as determined by the Secretary).

"(B) Terms of Payments. Sums payable to any State by reason of such State's having an agreement under this section shall be payable, either in advance or by way of reimbursement (as determined by the Secretary), in such amounts as the Secretary estimates the State will be entitled to receive under this section for each calendar month, reduced or increased, as the case may be, by any amount by which the Secretary finds that his estimates for any prior calendar month were greater or less than the amounts which should have been paid to the State. Such estimates may be made on the basis of such statistical, sampling, or other method as may be agreed upon by the Secretary and the State agency of the State involved.

"(2) Certifications. The Secretary shall from time to time certify to the Secretary of the Treasury for payment to each State the sums payable to such State under this section.

"(3) Appropriation. There are appropriated from the general fund of the Treasury, without fiscal year limitation, such sums as may be necessary for purposes of this subsection.

"(e) Applicability.

"(1) In General. An agreement entered into under this section shall apply to weeks of unemployment—

"(A) beginning after the date on which such agreement is entered into; and

"(B) ending on or before June 2, 2010.

"(2) Transition Rule for Individuals Remaining Entitled to Regular Compensation as of June 2, 2010. In the case of any individual who, as of the date specified in paragraph (1)(B), has not yet exhausted all rights to regular compensation under the State law of a State with respect to a benefit year that began before such date, additional compensation (as described in subsection (b)(1)) shall continue to be payable to such individual for any week beginning on or after such date for which the individual is otherwise eligible for regular compensation with respect to such benefit year.

"(3) Termination. Notwithstanding any other provision of this subsection, no additional compensation (as described in subsection (b)(1)) shall be payable for any week beginning after December 7, 2010.

"(f) Fraud and Overpayments. The provisions of section 4005 of the Supplemental Appropriations Act, 2008 (Public Law 110-252; 122 Stat. 2356) shall apply with respect to additional compensation (as described in subsection (b)(1)) to the same extent and in the same manner as in the case of emergency unemployment compensation.

"(g) Application to Other Unemployment Benefits.

"(1) In General. Each agreement under this section shall include provisions to provide that the purposes of the preceding provisions of this section shall be applied with respect to unemployment benefits described in subsection (i)(3) to the same extent and in the same manner as if those benefits were regular compensation.

"(2) Eligibility and Termination Rules. Additional compensation (as described in subsection (b)(1))—

"(A) shall not be payable, pursuant to this subsection, with respect to any unemployment benefits described in subsection (i)(3) for any week beginning on or after the date specified in subsection (e)(1)(B), except in the case of any individual who was eligible to receive additional compensation (as so described) in connection with any regular compensation or any unemployment benefits described in subsection (i)(3) for any period of unemployment ending before such date; and

"(B) shall in no event be payable for any week beginning after the date specified in subsection (e)(3).

"(h) Disregard of Additional Compensation for Purposes of MEDICAID and SCHIP. The monthly equivalent of any additional compensation paid under this section shall be disregarded in considering the amount of income of an individual for any purposes under title XIX and title XXI of the Social Security Act.

"(i) Definitions. For purposes of this section—

"(1) the terms 'compensation', 'regular compensation', 'benefit year', 'State', 'State agency', 'State law', and 'week' have the respective meanings given such terms under section 205 of the Federal-State Extended Unemployment Compensation Act of 1970 (26 U.S.C. 3304 note);

"(2) the term 'emergency unemployment compensation' means emergency unemployment compensation under title IV of the Supplemental Appropriations Act, 2008 (Public Law 110-252; 122 Stat. 2353); and

"(3) any reference to unemployment benefits described in this paragraph shall be considered to refer to—

"(A) extended compensation (as defined by section 205 of the Federal-State Extended Unemployment Compensation Act of 1970); and

"(B) unemployment compensation (as defined by section 85(b) of the Internal Revenue Code of 1986) provided under any program administered by a State under an agreement with the Secretary."

—P.L. 111-5, Sec. 2005, of this Act [as amended by Sec. 1009(a)(3)(A)-(B) Div. B, of P.L. 111-118, Sec. 2(a)(3) of P.L. 111-144, Sec. 2(a)(3) of P.L. 111-157, and Sec. 2(a)(2)(A)-(B) of P.L. 111-205, and Sec. 501(a)(2)(A)-(C) of P.L. 111-312, see above] provides:

"SEC. 2005. FULL FEDERAL FUNDING OF EXTENDED UNEMPLOYMENT COMPENSATION FOR A LIMITED PERIOD.

"(a) In general. In the case of sharable extended compensation and sharable regular compensation paid for weeks of unemployment beginning after the date of the enactment of this section and before January 4, 2012, section 204(a)(1) of the Federal-State Extended Unemployment Compensation Act of 1970 (26 U.S.C. 3304 note) shall be applied by substituting '100 percent of' for 'one-half of'.

"(b) Special rule. At the option of a State, for any weeks of unemployment beginning after the date of the enactment of this section and before January 4, 2012, an individual's eligibility period (as described in section 203(c) of the Federal-State Extended Unemployment Compensation Act of 1970) shall, for purposes of any determination of eligibility for extended compensation under the State law of such State, be considered to include any week which begins—

"(1) after the date as of which such individual exhausts all rights to emergency unemployment compensation; and

"(2) during an extended benefit period that began on or before the date described in paragraph (1).

""(c) Limited extension. In the case of an individual who receives extended compensation with respect to 1 or more weeks of unemployment beginning after the date of the enactment of this Act [Feb. 17, 2009] and before January 4, 2012, the provisions of subsections (a) and (b) shall, at the option of a State, be applied by substituting 'ending before June 11, 2012' for 'before January 4, 2012'.

"(d) Extension of temporary federal matching for the first week of extended benefits for states with no waiting week.

"(1) In general. Section 5 of the Unemployment Compensation Extension Act of 2008 (Public Law 110-449) is amended by striking 'December 8, 2009' and inserting 'May 30, 2010'.

"(2) Effective date. The amendment made by paragraph (1) shall take effect as if included in the enactment of the Unemployment Compensation Extension Act of 2008 (Public Law 110-449).

"(e) Definitions. For purposes of this section—

"(1) the terms 'sharable extended compensation' and 'sharable regular compensation' have the respective meanings given such terms under section 204 of the Federal-State Extended Unemployment Compensation Act of 1970;

"(2) the terms 'extended compensation', 'State', 'State law', and 'week' have the respective meanings given such terms under section 205 of the Federal-State Extended Unemployment Compensation Act of 1970;

"(3) the term 'emergency unemployment compensation' means benefits payable to individuals under title IV of the Supplemental Appropriations Act, 2008 with respect to their unemployment; and

"(4) the term 'extended benefit period' means an extended benefit period as determined in accordance with applicable provisions of the Federal-State Extended Unemployment Compensation Act of 1970.

"(f) Regulations. The Secretary of Labor may prescribe any operating instructions or regulations necessary to carry out this section."

In 2008, P.L. 110-458, Sec. 111(b)(1)(A), redesignated clauses (a)(15)(A)(i)-(ii) as subclauses (a)(15)(A)(i)(I)-(II) . . . Sec. 111(b)(1)(B), redesignated subparas. (a)(15)(A)-(B) as clauses (a)(15)(A)(i)-(ii) . . . Sec. 111(b)(1)(C), substituted ", and" for the semicolon at the end of clause (a)(15)(A)(ii) [as redesignated] . . . Sec. 111(b)(1)(D), substituted "(15)(A) subject to subparagraph (B)," for "(15)" in para. (a)(15) . . . Sec. 111(b)(1)(E), added subpara. (a)(15)(B) . . . Sec. 111(b)(2), deleted the last sentence of subsec. (a), effective for weeks beginning on or after 8/17/2006, as if included in the provisions of Sec. 1105 of the Pension Protection Act of 2006, P.L. 109-280 [see below].

Prior to deletion, the last sentence of subsec. (a) read as follows:

"Compensation shall not be reduced under paragraph (15) for any pension, retirement or retired pay, annuity, or similar payment which is not includible in gross income of the individual for the taxable year in which paid because it was part of a rollover distribution."

—P.L. 110-449, Sec. 2(1), substituted "80" for "50" in Sec. 4002(b)(1)(A) of P.L. 110-252 [see below]; . . . Sec. 2(2), substituted "20" for "13" in Sec. 4002(b)(1)(B) of P.L. 110-252 [see below]; . . . Sec. 3, added subsec. (c) to Sec. 4002 of P.L. 110-252 [see below]; . . . Sec. 4(1), substituted "paragraphs (2) and (3)," for "paragraph (2)," in Sec. 4007(b)(1) of P.L. 110-252 [see below]; . . . Sec. 4(2), amended para. (2) and added para. (3) of Sec. 4007(b) of P.L. 110-252 [see below].

—P.L. 110-449, Secs. 5, and (6) [as amended by Sec. 2005(d)(1) of P.L. 111-5, Sec. 1009(a)(4) Div. B, of P.L. 111-118, Sec. 2(a)(4) of P.L.111-144, Sec. 2(a)(4) of P.L. 111-157, Apr. 15, 2010, Sec. 2(a)(3) of P.L. 111-205, and Sec. 501(a)(3) of P.L. 111-312, see above] provides:

"SEC. 5. TEMPORARY FEDERAL MATCHING FOR THE FIRST WEEK OF EXTENDED BENEFITS FOR STATES WITH NO WAITING WEEK. With respect to weeks of unemployment beginning after the date of the enactment of this Act [Nov. 21, 2008] and ending on or before June 10, 2012, subparagraph (B) of section 204(a)(2) of the Federal-State Extended Unemployment Compensation Act of 1970 (26 U.S.C. 3304 note) shall not apply.

"SEC. 6. EFFECTIVE DATE.

"(a) In general. The amendments made by sections 2, 3, and 4 shall apply as if included in the enactment of the Supplemental Appropriations Act, 2008, subject to subsection (b).

"(b) Additional benefits. In applying the amendments made by sections 2 and 3, any additional emergency unemployment compensation made payable by such amendments (which would not otherwise have been payable if such amendments had not been enacted) shall be payable only with respect to any week of unemployment beginning on or after the date of the enactment of this Act."

Prior to amendment, para. (2) of Sec. 4007(b) of P.L. 110-252 read as follows:

"(2) Limit on Compensation. No compensation shall be payable by reason of paragraph (1) for any week beginning after June 30, 2009."

—P.L. 110-328, Sec. 3(c)(1), deleted "and" after the semicolon in subpara. (a)(4)(E) . . . Sec. 3(c)(2), substituted "; and" for "." in subpara. (a)(4)(F) . . . Sec. 3(c)(3), added subpara. (a)(4)(G), effective for refunds payable under section 6402 of the Internal Revenue Code of 1986 on or after 9/30/2008.

—P.L. 110-252, Sec. 4001, through 4007 [as amended by Secs. 2 through 4 of P.L. 110-449, Sec. 2001 of P.L. 111-5, Secs. 2 through 6 of P.L. 111-92, Sec. 1009(a)(1)(A)-(C) and (b) Div. B, of P.L. 111-118, and Sec. 2(a)(1) and (b) of P.L. 111-144, Sec. 2(a)(1), (b) of P.L. 111-157, Apr. 15, 2010, and Sec. 2(a)(1), (b), (c), Sec. 3(a) and Sec. 4 of P.L. 111-205, and Secs. 501(a)(1)(A)-(C), and (b)(1)-(2), of P.L. 111-312, see above] of this Act, provides:

"TITLE IV. EMERGENCY UNEMPLOYMENT COMPENSATION FEDERAL-STATE AGREEMENTS

"SEC. 4001. (a) In general. Any State which desires to do so may enter into and participate in an agreement under this title with the Secretary of Labor (in this title referred to as the 'Secretary'). Any State which is a party to an agreement under this title may, upon providing 30 days' written notice to the Secretary, terminate such agreement.

"(b) Provisions of agreement. Any agreement under subsection (a) shall provide that the State agency of the State will make payments of emergency unemployment compensation to individuals who—

"(1) have exhausted all rights to regular compensation under the State law or under Federal law with respect to a benefit year (excluding any benefit year that ended before May 1, 2007);

"(2) have no rights to regular compensation or extended compensation with respect to a week under such law or any other State unemployment compensation law or to compensation under any other Federal law (except as provided under subsection (e)); and

"(3) are not receiving compensation with respect to such week under the unemployment compensation law of Canada.

"(c) Exhaustion of benefits. For purposes of subsection (b)(1), an individual shall be deemed to have exhausted such individual's rights to regular compensation under a State law when—

"(1) no payments of regular compensation can be made under such law because such individual has received all regular compensation available to such individual based on employment or wages during such individual's base period; or

"(2) such individual's rights to such compensation have been terminated by reason of the expiration of the benefit year with respect to which such rights existed.

"(d) Weekly benefit amount, etc. For purposes of any agreement under this title—

"(1) the amount of emergency unemployment compensation which shall be payable to any individual for any week of total unemployment shall be equal to the amount of the regular compensation (including dependents' allowances) payable to such individual during such individual's benefit year under the State law for a week of total unemployment;

"(2) the terms and conditions of the State law which apply to claims for regular compensation and to the payment thereof (including terms and conditions relating to availability for work, active search for work, and refusal to accept work) shall apply to claims for emergency unemployment compensation and the payment thereof, except—

"(A) that an individual shall not be eligible for emergency unemployment compensation under this title unless, in the base period with respect to which the individual exhausted all rights to regular compensation under the State law, the individual had 20 weeks of full-time insured employment or the equivalent in insured wages, as determined under the provisions of the State law implementing section 202(a)(5) of the Federal-State Extended Unemployment Compensation Act of 1970 (26 U.S.C. 3304 note); and

"(B) where otherwise inconsistent with the provisions of this title or with the regulations or operating instructions of the Secretary promulgated to carry out this title; and

"(3) the maximum amount of emergency unemployment compensation payable to any individual for whom an emergency unemployment compensation account is established under section 4002 shall not exceed the amount established in such account for such individual.

"(e) Election by states. Notwithstanding any other provision of Federal law (and if State law permits), the Governor of a State that is in an extended benefit period may provide for the payment of emergency unemployment compensation prior to extended compensation to individuals who otherwise meet the requirements of this section.

"(f) Unauthorized aliens ineligible. A State shall require as a condition of eligibility for emergency unemployment compensation under this Act that each alien who receives such compensation must be legally authorized to work in the United States, as defined for purposes of the Federal Unemployment Tax Act (26 U.S.C. 3301 et seq.). In determining whether an alien meets the requirements of this subsection, a State must follow the procedures provided in section 1137(d) of the Social Security Act (42 U.S.C. 1320b-7(d)).

"(g) Nonreduction rule. An agreement under this section shall not apply (or shall cease to apply) with respect to a State upon a determination by the Secretary that the method governing the computation of regular compensation under the State law of that State has been modified in a manner such that—

"(1) the average weekly benefit amount of regular compensation which will be payable during the period of the agreement occurring on or after June 2, 2010 (determined disregarding any additional amounts attributable to the modification described in section 2002(b)(1) of the Assistance for Unemployed Workers and Struggling Families Act, as contained in Public Law 111-5 (26 U.S.C. 3304 note; 123 Stat. 438)), will be less than

"(2) the average weekly benefit amount of regular compensation which would otherwise have been payable during such period under the State law, as in effect on June 2, 2010.

""SEC. 4002. (a) In general. Any agreement under this title shall provide that the State will establish, for each eligible individual who files an application for emergency unemployment compensation, an emergency unemployment compensation account with respect to such individual's benefit year.

"(b) Amount in account.

"(1) In general. The amount established in an account under subsection (a) shall be equal to the lesser of—

"(A) 80 percent of the total amount of regular compensation (including dependents' allowances) payable to the individual during the individual's benefit year under such law, or

"(B) 20 times the individual's average weekly benefit amount for the benefit year.

"(2) Weekly benefit amount. For purposes of this subsection, an individual's weekly benefit amount for any week is the amount of regular compensation (including dependents' allowances) under the State law payable to such individual for such week for total unemployment.

"(c) Special rule.

"(1) In general. At the time that the amount established in an individual's account under subsection (b)(1) is exhausted, such account shall be augmented by an amount equal to the lesser of—

"(A) 54 percent of the total amount of regular compensation (including dependents' allowances) payable to the individual during the individual's benefit year under the State law, or

"(B) 14 times the individual's average weekly benefit amount (as determined under subsection (b)(2)) for the benefit year.

"(2) Limitation. The account of an individual may be augmented not more than once under this subsection.

"(d) Third-tier emergency unemployment compensation.

"(1) In general. If, at the time that the amount added to an individual's account under subsection (c)(1) (hereinafter 'second-tier emergency unemployment compensation') is exhausted or at any time thereafter, such individual's State is in an extended benefit period (as determined under paragraph (2)), such account shall be further augmented by an amount (hereinafter 'third-tier emergency unemployment compensation') equal to the lesser of—

"(A) 50 percent of the total amount of regular compensation (including dependents' allowances) payable to the individual during the individual's benefit year under the State law; or

"(B) 13 times the individual's average weekly benefit amount (as determined under subsection (b)(2)) for the benefit year.

"(2) Extended benefit period. For purposes of paragraph (1), a State shall be considered to be in an extended benefit period, as of any given time, if—

"(A) such a period would then be in effect for such State under such Act if section 203(d) of such Act—

"(i) were applied by substituting '4' for '5' each place it appears; and

"(ii) did not include the requirement under paragraph (1)(A) thereof; or

"(B) such a period would then be in effect for such State under such Act if—

"(i) section 203(f) of such Act were applied to such State (regardless of whether the State by law had provided for such application); and

"(ii) such section 203(f)—

"(I) were applied by substituting '6.0' for '6.5' in paragraph (1)(A)(i) thereof; and

"(II) did not include the requirement under paragraph (1)(A)(ii) there of.

"(3) Limitation. The account of an individual may be augmented not more than once under this subsection.

"(e) Fourth-tier emergency unemployment compensation.

"(1) In general. If, at the time that the amount added to an individual's account under subsection (d)(1) (third-tier emergency unemployment compensation) is exhausted or at any time thereafter, such individual's State is in an extended benefit period (as determined under paragraph (2)), such account shall be further augmented by an amount (hereinafter 'fourth-tier emergency unemployment compensation') equal to the lesser of—

"(A) 24 percent of the total amount of regular compensation (including dependents' allowances) payable to the individual during the individual's benefit year under the State law; or

"(B) 6 times the individual's average weekly benefit amount (as determined under subsection (b)(2)) for the benefit year.

"(2) Extended benefit period. For purposes of paragraph (1), a State shall be considered to be in an extended benefit period, as of any given time, if—

"(A) such a period would then be in effect for such State under such Act if section 203(d) of such Act—

"(i) were applied by substituting '6' for '5' each place it appears; and

"(ii) did not include the requirement under paragraph (1)(A) thereof; or

"(B) such a period would then be in effect for such State under such Act if—

"(i) section 203(f) of such Act were applied to such State (regardless of whether the State by law had provided for such application); and

"(ii) such section 203(f)—

"(I) were applied by substituting '8.5' for '6.5' in paragraph (1)(A)(i) thereof; and

"(II) did not include the requirement under paragraph (1)(A)(ii) thereof.

"(3) Limitation. The account of an individual may be augmented not more than once under this subsection.

"(f) Coordination rules.

"(1) Coordination with extended compensation. Notwithstanding an election under section 4001(e) by a State to provide for the payment of emergency unemployment compensation prior to extended compensation, such State may pay extended compensation to an otherwise eligible individual prior to any emergency unemployment compensation under subsection (c), (d), or (e) (by reason of the amendments made by sections 2, 3, and 4 of the Worker, Homeownership, and Business Assistance Act of 2009), if such individual claimed extended compensation for at least 1 week of unemployment after the exhaustion of emergency unemployment compensation under subsection (b) (as such subsection was in effect on the day before the date of the enactment of this subsection).

"(2) Coordination with Tiers II, III, and IV. If a State determines that implementation of the increased entitlement to second-tier emergency unemployment compensation by reason of the amendments made by section 2 of the Worker, Homeownership, and Business Assistance Act of 2009 would unduly delay the prompt payment of emergency unemployment compensation under this title by reason of the amendments made by such Act, such State may elect to pay third-tier emergency unemployment compensation prior to the payment of such increased second tier emergency unemployment compensation until such time as such State determines that such increased second-tier emergency unemployment compensation may be paid without such undue delay. If a State makes the election under the preceding sentence, then, for purposes of determining whether an account may be augmented for fourth-tier emergency unemployment compensation under subsection (e), such State shall treat the date of exhaustion of such increased second-tier emergency unemployment compensation as the date of exhaustion of third-tier emergency unemployment compensation, if such date is later than the date of exhaustion of the third-tier emergency unemployment compensation.

"(g) Coordination of emergency unemployment compensation with regular compensation.

"(1) If—

"(A) an individual has been determined to be entitled to emergency unemployment compensation with respect to a benefit year,

"(B) that benefit year has expired,

"(C) that individual has remaining entitlement to emergency unemployment compensation with respect to that benefit year, and

"(D) that individual would qualify for a new benefit year in which the weekly benefit amount of regular compensation is at least either $100 or 25 percent less than the individual's weekly benefit amount in the benefit year referred to in subparagraph (A), then the State shall determine eligibility for compensation as provided in paragraph (2).

"(2) For individuals described in paragraph (1), the State shall determine whether the individual is to be paid emergency unemployment compensation or regular compensation for a week of unemployment using one of the following methods:

"(A) The State shall, if permitted by State law, establish a new benefit year, but defer the payment of regular compensation with respect to that new benefit year until exhaustion of all emergency unemployment compensation payable with respect to the benefit year referred to in paragraph (1)(A);

"(B) The State shall, if permitted by State law, defer the establishment of a new benefit year (which uses all the wages and employment which would have been used to establish a benefit year but for the application of this paragraph), until exhaustion of all emergency unemployment compensation payable with respect to the benefit year referred to in paragraph(1)(A);

"(C) The State shall pay, if permitted by State law—

"(i) regular compensation equal to the weekly benefit amount established under the new benefit year, and

"(ii) emergency unemployment compensation equal to the difference between that weekly benefit amount and the weekly benefit amount for the expired benefit year; or

"(D) The State shall determine rights to emergency unemployment compensation without regard to any rights to regular compensation if the individual elects to not file a claim for regular compensation under the new benefit year.

"PAYMENTS TO STATES HAVING AGREEMENTS FOR THE PAYMENT OF EMERGENCY UNEMPLOYMENT COMPENSATION

"SEC. 4003. (a) General rule. There shall be paid to each State that has entered into an agreement under this title an amount equal to 100 percent of the emergency unemployment compensation paid to individuals by the State pursuant to such agreement.

"(b) Treatment of reimbursable compensation. No payment shall be made to any State under this section in respect of any compensation to the extent the State is entitled to reimbursement in respect of such compensation under the provisions of any Federal law other than this title or chapter 85 of title 5, United States Code. A State shall not be entitled to any reimbursement under such chapter 85 in respect of any compensation to the extent the State is entitled to reimbursement under this title in respect of such compensation.

"(c) Determination of amount. Sums payable to any State by reason of such State having an agreement under this title shall be payable, either in advance or by way of reimbursement (as may be determined by the Secretary), in such amounts as the Secretary estimates the State will be entitled to receive under this title for each calendar month, reduced or increased, as the case may be, by any amount by which the Secretary finds that the Secretary's estimates for any prior calendar month were greater or less than the amounts which should have been paid to the State. Such estimates may be made on the basis of such statistical, sampling, or other method as may be agreed upon by the Secretary and the State agency of the State involved.

"FINANCING PROVISIONS

"SEC. 4004. (a) In general. Funds in the extended unemployment compensation account (as established by section 905(a) of the Social Security Act (42 U.S.C. 1105(a)) of the Unemployment Trust Fund (as established by section 904(a) of such Act (42 U.S.C. 1104(a)] shall be used for the making of payments to States having agreements entered into under this title.

"(b) Certification. The Secretary shall from time to time certify to the Secretary of the Treasury for payment to each State the sums payable to such State under this title. The Secretary of the Treasury, prior to audit or settlement by the Government Accountability Office, shall make payments to the State in accordance with such certification, by transfers from the extended unemployment compensation account (as so established) to the account of such State in the Unemployment Trust Fund (as so established).

"(c) Assistance to states. There are appropriated out of the employment security administration account (as established by section 901(a) of the Social Security Act (42 U.S.C. 1101(a)) of the Unemployment Trust Fund, without fiscal year limitation, such funds as may be necessary for purposes of assisting States (as provided in title III of the Social Security Act (42 U.S.C. 501 et seq.)) in meeting the costs of administration of agreements under this title.

"(d) Appropriations for certain payments. There are appropriated from the general fund of the Treasury, without fiscal year limitation, to the extended unemployment compensation account (as so established) of the Unemployment Trust Fund (as so established) such sums as the Secretary estimates to be necessary to make the payments under this section in respect of—

"(1) compensation payable under chapter 85 of title 5, United States Code; and

"(2) compensation payable on the basis of services to which section 3309(a)(1) of the Internal Revenue Code of 1986 applies. Amounts appropriated pursuant to the preceding sentence shall not be required to be repaid.

"(e) Transfer of funds. Notwithstanding any other provision of law, the Secretary of the Treasury shall transfer from the general fund of the Treasury (from funds not otherwise appropriated)—

"(1) to the extended unemployment compensation account (as established by section 905 of the Social Security Act) such sums as the Secretary of Labor estimates to be necessary to make payments to States under this title by reason of—

"(A) the amendments made by section 2001(a) of the Assistance for Unemployed Workers and Struggling Families Act;

"(B) the amendments made by sections 2 through 4 of the Worker, Homeownership, and Business Assistance Act of 2009;

"(C) the amendments made by section 1009(a)(1) of the Department of Defense Appropriations Act, 2010;

"(D) the amendments made by section 2(a)(1) of the Temporary Extension Act of 2010;

"(E) the amendments made by section 2(a)(1) of the Continuing Extension Act of 2010;

"(F) the amendments made by section 2(a)(1) of the Unemployment Compensation Extension Act of 2010; and

"(G) the amendments made by section 501(a)(1) of the Tax Relief, Unemployment Insurance Reauthorization, and Job Creation Act of 2010; and

"(2) to the employment security administration account (as established by section 901 of the Social Security Act) such sums as the Secretary of Labor estimates to be necessary for purposes of assisting States in meeting administrative costs by reason of the amendments referred to in paragraph (1).

"There are appropriated from the general fund of the Treasury, without fiscal year limitation, the sums referred to in the preceding sentence and such sums shall not be required to be repaid.

"FRAUD AND OVERPAYMENTS

"SEC. 4005. (a) In general. If an individual knowingly has made, or caused to be made by another, a false statement or representation of a material fact, or knowingly has failed, or caused another to fail, to disclose a material fact, and as a result of such false statement or representation or of such nondisclosure such individual has received an amount of emergency unemployment compensation under this title to which such individual was not entitled, such individual—

"(1) shall be ineligible for further emergency unemployment compensation under this title in accordance with the provisions of the applicable State unemployment compensation law relating to fraud in connection with a claim for unemployment compensation; and

"(2) shall be subject to prosecution under section 1001 of title 18, United States Code.

"(b) Repayment. In the case of individuals who have received amounts of emergency unemployment compensation under this title to which they were not entitled, the State shall require such individuals to repay the amounts of such emergency unemployment compensation to the State agency, except that the State agency may waive such repayment if it determines that—

"(1) the payment of such emergency unemployment compensation was without fault on the part of any such individual; and

"(2) such repayment would be contrary to equity and good conscience.

"(c) Recovery by state agency.

"(1) In general. The State agency may recover the amount to be repaid, or any part thereof, by deductions from any emergency unemployment compensation payable to such individual under this title or from any unemployment compensation payable to such individual under any State or Federal unemployment compensation law administered by the State agency or under any other State or Federal law administered by the State agency which provides for the payment of any assistance or allowance with respect to any week of unemployment, during the 3-year period after the date such individuals received the payment of the emergency unemployment compensation to which they were not entitled, except that no single deduction may exceed 50 percent of the weekly benefit amount from which such deduction is made.

"(2) Opportunity for hearing. No repayment shall be required, and no deduction shall be made, until a determination has been made, notice thereof and an opportunity for a fair hearing has been given to the individual, and the determination has become final.

"(d) Review. Any determination by a State agency under this section shall be subject to review in the same manner and to the same extent as determinations under the State unemployment compensation law, and only in that manner and to that extent.

"SEC. 4006. In this title, the terms 'compensation', 'regular compensation', 'extended compensation', 'benefit year', 'base period', 'State', 'State agency', 'State law', and 'week' have the respective meanings given such terms under section 205 of the Federal-State Extended Unemployment Compensation Act of 1970 (26 U.S.C. 3304 note).

"SEC. 4007. (a) In general. Except as provided in subsection (b), an agreement entered into under this title shall apply to weeks of unemployment—

"(1) beginning after the date on which such agreement is entered into; and

"(2) ending on or before January 3, 2012.

"(b) Transition for amount remaining in account.

"(1) In general. Subject to paragraphs (2) and (3), in the case of an individual who has amounts remaining in an account established under section 4002 as of the last day of the last week (as determined in accordance with the applicable State law) ending on or before January 3, 2012, emergency unemployment compensation shall continue to be payable to such individual from such amounts for any week beginning after such last day for which the individual meets the eligibility requirements of this title.

"(2) No augmentation after January 3, 2012. If the amount established in an individual's account under subsection (b)(1) is exhausted after January 3, 2012, then subsections (c), (d), and (e) of section 4002 of section 4002 [Ed. Note: We believe it was the intent of P.L. 111-92 to eliminate the double text.] shall not apply and such account shall not be augmented under such section, regardless of whether such individual's State is in an extended benefit period (as determined under paragraph (2) of such subsection (c), (d), or (e) as the case may be)) as the case may be)). [Ed. Note: We believe it was the intent of P.L. 111-92 to eliminate the double text.]

"(3) Termination. No compensation under this title shall be payable for any week beginning after June 9, 2012."

In 2006, P.L. 109-280, Sec. 1105(a), added "Compensation shall not be reduced under paragraph (15) for any pension, retirement or retired pay, annuity, or similar payment which is not includible in gross income of the individual for the taxable year in which paid because it was part of a rollover distribution" as a flush sentence at the end of subsec. (a), effective for weeks begin. on or after 8/17/2006.

In 2002, P.L. 107-147, Sec. 209(d)(1), added "or 903(d)(4)" after "section 903(c)(2)" in subpara. (a)(4)(B), effective 3/9/2002.

—P.L. 107-147, Sec. 209(e), of this Act, provides:

"(e) Regulations. The Secretary of Labor may prescribe any operating instructions or regulations necessary to carry out this section and the amendments made by this section."

In 1998, P.L. 105-306, Sec. 3(a), deleted Sec. 507(e)(2) of P. L. 103-182 . . . Sec. 3(b)(1), substituted "Effective date" for "Effective date; sunset" in the heading of Sec. 507(e) of P. L. 103-182 [reproduced below] . . . Sec. 3(b)(2), redesignated Sec. 507(e)(1) of P. L. 103-182 as Sec. 507(e) of P. L. 103-182 [reproduced below], effective 10/28/98.

Prior to deletion, Sec. 507(e)(2) of P. L. 103-182 read as follows:

"(2) Sunset. The authority provided by this section, and the amendments made by this section shall terminate 5 years after the date of the enactment of this Act."

In 1996, P.L. 104-193, Sec. 110(l)(2), substituted "eligibility for assistance, or the amount of such assistance, under a State program funded" for "eligibility for aid or services, or the amount of such aid or services, under a State plan for aid and services to needy families with children approved" in subpara. (a)(16)(A), effective 7/1/97.

—P.L. 104-193, Sec. 316(g)(2)(A), substituted "Secretary of Health and Human Services" for "Secretary of Health, Education, and Welfare" each place it appeared in para. (a)(16) . . . Sec. 316(g)(2)(B), substituted "information furnished under subparagraph (A) or (B) is used only for the purposes authorized under such subparagraph;" for "such information is used only for the purposes authorized under subparagraph (A);" in subpara. (a)(16)(B) [redesignated as subpara. (a)(16)(C) by Sec. 316(g)(2)(D) of this Act, see below] . . . Sec. 316(g)(2)(C), deleted "and" at the end of subpara. (a)(16)(A) . . . Sec. 316(g)(2)(D), redesignated subpara. (a)(16)(B) as subpara. (a)(16)(C) . . . Sec. 316(g)(2)(E), added subpara. (a)(16)(B), effective as provided in Sec. 395(a)-(c) of this Act, which reads as follows:

"(a) In general. Except as otherwise specifically provided (but subject to subsections (b) and (c))—

"(1) the provisions of this title requiring the enactment of State laws under section 466 of the Social Security Act, or revision of State plans under section 454 of such Act, shall be effective with respect to periods beginning on and after October 1, 1996; and

"(2) all other provisions of this title shall become effective upon the date of the enactment of this Act.

"(b) Grace period for State law changes. The provisions of this title shall become effective with respect to a State on the later of —

"(1) the date specified in this title, or

"(2) the effective date of laws enacted by the legislature of such State implementing such provisions,

but in no event later than the 1st day of the 1st calendar quarter beginning after the close of the 1st regular session of the State legislature that begins after the date of the enactment of this Act. For purposes of the previous sentence, in the case of a State that has a 2-year legislative session, each year of such session shall be deemed to be a separate regular session of the State legislature.

Employment taxes Code Sec. 3304

"(c) Grace period for State constitutional amendment. A State shall not be found out of compliance with any requirement enacted by this title if the State is unable to so comply without amending the State constitution until the earlier of—

"(1) 1 year after the effective date of the necessary State constitutional amendment; or

"(2) 5 years after the date of the enactment of this Act."

In 1994, P.L. 103-465, Sec. 702(b), deleted "and" at the end of para. (a)(17), redesignated para. (a)(18) as (a)(19), and added new para. (a)(18) . . . Sec. 702(c)(1), added ", or the withholding of Federal, State, or local individual income tax," after "health insurance" in subpara. (a)(4)(C), effective for payments made after 12/31/96.

In 1993, P.L. 103-182, Sec. 507(b)(1)(A), substituted a semicolon for "; and" in subpara. (a)(4)(D) . . . Sec. 507(b)(1)(B), substituted a "; and" for the semicolon in subpara. (a)(4)(E) . . . Sec. 507(b)(1)(C), added subpara. (a)(4)(F), effective [as amended by Sec. 3 of P. L. 105-306, see above] 12/8/93.

In 1992, P.L. 102-318, Sec. 401(a)(1), deleted "and" at the end of subpara. (a)(4)(C), added "and" at the end of subpara. (a)(4)(D) and added subpara. (a)(4)(E), effective 7/3/92.

In 1991, P.L. 102-164, Sec. 302(a)(1), substituted "may be denied" for "shall be denied" in subclause (a)(6)(A)(ii)(I) . . . Sec. 302(a)(2), deleted "and" at the end of clauses (a)(6)(A)(iii) and (iv), and added clause (a)(6)(A)(vi), effective in the case of compensation paid for weeks begin. on or after 11/15/91 [date of enactment].

In 1990, P.L. 101-649, Sec. 162(e)(4), deleted "section 203(a)(7) or" after "application of the provisions of" in subpara. (a)(14)(A), effective on 10/1/91 and shall apply begin. with fiscal year 1992.

In 1986, P.L. 99-514, Sec. 1899A(43), deleted "and" at the end of clause (a)(6)(A)(iii), effective 10/22/86.

—P.L. 99-272, Sec. 12401(b)(1), deleted "and" at the end of subpara. (a)(4)(B), added "and" at the end of subpara. (a)(4)(C) and added subpara. (a)(4)(D), effective for recoveries made on or after 4/7/86 [date of enactment] and effective for overpayments made before, on, or after 4/7/86.

In 1985, P.L. 99-177, Sec. 256(h)(2)(B), provided that a reduction in weekly benefit payments by a State under certain presidential orders intended to reduce the federal budget deficit are not to be considered as a failure to fulfill the requirements of para. (a)(11).

In 1983, P.L. 98-21, Sec. 515(b), redesignated para. (a)(17) as para. (a)(18) and added a new para. (a)(17).

—P.L. 98-21, Sec. 521(a)(1), added clause (a)(6)(A)(v) . . . Sec. 521(a)(2), substituted "shall be denied" for "may be denied" in clauses (a)(6)(A)(ii), (iii) and (iv), effective for compensation paid for weeks begin. on or after 4/1/84. Sec. 521(b)(2) provides as follows:

"(2) In the case of a State with respect to which the Secretary of Labor has determined that State legislation is required in order to comply with the amendment made by this section, the amendment made by this section shall apply in the case of compensation paid for weeks which begin on or after April 1, 1984, and after the end of the first session of the State legislature which begins after the date of the enactment of this Act, or which began prior to the date of the enactment of this Act and remained in session for at least twenty-five calendar days after such date of enactment. For purposes of the preceding sentence, the term 'session' means a regular, special, budget, or other session of a State legislature."

—P.L. 98-21, Sec. 523(a), deleted "and" at end of subpara. (a)(4)(A), added "and" at the end of subpara. (a)(4)(B), and added subpara. (a)(4)(C), effective 4/20/83.

In 1982, P.L. 97-248, Sec. 193(a), amended clause (a)(6)(A)(ii), effective for weeks of unemployment begin. after 9/3/82. Sec. 193(b)(2) of this Act provides:

"(2) The amendment made by subsection (a), insofar as it requires retroactive payments of compensation to employees of educational institutions other than institutions of higher education (as defined in section 3304(f) of the Internal Revenue Code of 1954), shall not be a requirement for any State law before January 1, 1984."

Prior to amendment, clause (a)(6)(A)(ii) read as follows:

(ii) with respect to services in any other capacity for an educational institution (other than an institution of higher education) to which section 3309(a)(1) applies, compensation payable on the basis of such services shall be denied to any individual for any week which commences during a period between two successive academic years or terms if such individual performs such services in the first of such academic years or terms and there is a reasonable assurance that such individual will perform such services in the second of such academic years or terms,

In 1981, P.L. 97-35, Sec. 2408(a), amended the last two sentences of subsec. (c), effective 8/13/81.

Prior to amendment, the last two sentences of subsec. (c) read as follows:

"On October 31 of any taxable year after 1971, the Secretary of Labor shall not certify any State which, after reasonable notice and opportunity for hearing to the State agency, the Secretary of Labor finds has failed to amend its law so that it contains each of the provisions required by reason of the enactment of the Employment Security Amendments of 1970 to be included therein, or has with respect to the 12-month period ending on such October 31, failed to comply substantially with any such provisions. On October 31 of any taxable year after 1977, the Secretary shall not certify any State which, after reasonable notice and opportunity for a hearing to the State agency, the Secretary of Labor finds has failed to amend its law so that it contains each of the provisions required by reason of the enactment of the Unemployment Compensation Amendments of 1976 to be included therein, or has with respect to the 12-month period ending on such October 31, failed to comply substantially with any such provision."

In 1980, P.L. 96-364, Sec. 414(a), amended para. (a)(15), effective for certifications of States for 1981 and subsequent years.

Prior to amendment, para. (a)(15) read as follows:

"(15) the amount of compensation payable to an individual for any week which begins after March 31, 1980, and which begins in a period with respect to which such individual is receiving a governmental or other pension, retirement or retired pay, annuity, or any other similar periodic payment which is based on the previous work of such individual shall be reduced (but not below zero) by an amount equal to the amount of such pension, retirement or retired pay, annuity, or other payment, which is reasonably attributable to such week;"

In 1977, P.L. 95-216, Sec. 403(b), added para. (a)(16) and redesignated para. (a)(16) as para. (a)(17), effective 12/20/77.

—P.L. 95-171, Sec. 2(a), deleted "and" at the end of clause (a)(6)(A)(ii) and added clause (a)(6)(A)(iv), effective for weeks of unemployment beginning after 12/31/77.

—P.L. 95-19, Sec. 301(a), amended the effective date for amendments made by Sec. 115 of P. L. 94-566 to read as follows, effective 10/20/76:

"(d) Effective date.

"(1) Except as provided in paragraph (2), the amendments made by this section shall apply with respect to certifications of States for 1978 and subsequent years; except that—

"(A) the amendments made by subsections (a) and (b) shall only apply with respect to services performed after December 31, 1977; and

"(B) the amendments made by subsection (c) shall only apply with respect to weeks of unemployment which begin after December 31, 1977.

"(2) In the case of any State the legislature of which does not meet in a regular session which closes during the calendar year 1977, the amendments made by subsection (c) shall only apply with respect to weeks of unemployment which begin after December 31, 1978 (or if earlier, the date provided by State law)."

—P.L. 95-19, Sec. 301(b), amended the effective date for amendments made by Sec. 312 of P. L. 94-566 to read as follows, effective 10/20/76:

"(c) Effective date. —

"(1) Except as provided in paragraph (2), the amendments made by this section shall apply with respect to certifications of States for 1978 and subsequent years.

"(2) In the case of any State the legislature of which does not meet in a regular session which closes during the calendar year 1977, the amendments made by this section shall apply with respect to the certification of such State for 1979 and subsequent years."

—P.L. 95-19, Sec. 301(c), amended the effective date for amendments made by Sec. 506 of P. L. 94-566 to read as follows, effective 10/20/76:

"(c) Effective date. —

"(1) Except as provided in paragraph (2), the amendments made by this section shall apply with respect to certifications of States for 1978 and subsequent years, but only with respect to services performed after December 31, 1977.

"(2) In the case of any State the legislature of which does not meet in a regular session which closes during the calendar year 1977, the amendments made by this section shall apply with respect to the certification of such state for 1979 and subsequent years, but only with respect to services performed after December 31, 1978."

—P.L. 95-19, Sec. 302(a), amended subpara. (a)(14)(A), effective for certifications of States for 1978, and subsequent years, or for 1979, and subsequent years in the case of States the legislatures of which do not meet in a regular session which closes in the calendar year '77. For special provisions, see Sec. 121 or P. L. 94-566, reproduced below.

Prior to amendment, subpara. (a)(14)(A) read as follows:

"(A) compensation shall not be payable on the basis of services performed by an alien unless such alien is an individual who has been lawfully admitted for permanent residence or otherwise is permanently residing in the United States under color of law (including an alien who is lawfully present in the United States as a result of the application of the provisions of section 203(a)(7) or section 212(d)(5) of the Immigration and Nationality Act),"

—P.L. 95-19, Sec. 302(c), substituted "instructional, research" for "instructional research" and "two successive academic years or terms" for "two successive academic years" in clause (a)(6)(A)(i) . . . deleted "and" at the end of clause (a)(6)(A)(i) and added clause (a)(6)(A)(iii), effective for certifications of States for 1978 and subsequent years, but only with respect to services performed after 12/31/77.

—P.L. 95-19, Sec. 302(e), substituted "March 31, 1980" for "September 30, 1979" in para. (a)(15), effective 4/12/77.

In 1976, P.L. 94-566, Sec. 115(c)(1), amended subpara. (a)(6)(A), effective for certifications of states for 1978 and subsequent years, but only for services performed after 12/31/77.

Prior to amendment, subpara. (a)(6)(A) read as follows:

"(6)(A) compensation is payable on the basis of service to which section 3309(a)(1) applies, in the same amount, on the same terms, and subject to the same conditions as compensation payable on the basis of other service subject to such law; except that, with respect to service in an instructional, research, or principal administrative capacity for an institution of higher education to which section 3309(a)(1) applies, compensation shall not be payable based on such service for any week commencing during the period between two successive academic years (or, when the contract provides instead for a similar period between two regular but not successive terms, during such period) to any individual who has a contract to perform services in any such capacity for any institution or institutions of higher education for both of such academic years or both of such term, and"

—P.L. 94-566, Sec. 115(c)(5), added subsec. (f), effective for certifications of states for '78 and subsequent years, but only for services performed after 12/31/77.

—P.L. 94-566, Sec. 116(g), providing the following with respect to Transfers of Funds:

"(g) Transfer of funds.

"The Secretary of Labor shall not approve an unemployment compensation law of the Virgin Islands under section 3304(a) of the Internal Revenue Code of 1954 until the Governor of the Virgin Islands has approved the transfer to the Federal Unemployment Trust Fund established under section 904 of the Social Security Act of an amount equal to the dollar balance credited to the unemployment subfund of the Virgin Islands established under section 310 of title 24 of the Virgin Islands Code."

—P.L. 94-566, Sec. 312(a), amended para. (a)(12), effective for certifications of States for 1978 and subsequent years.

Prior to amendment, para. (a)(12) read as follows:

"(12) each political subdivision of the State shall have the right to elect to have compensation payable to employees thereof (whose services are not otherwise subject to such law) based on service performed by such employees in the hospitals and institutions of higher education (as defined in section 3309(d)) operated by such political subdivision; and, if any such political subdivision does elect to have compensation payable to such employees thereof (A) the political subdivision shall pay into the State unemployment fund, with respect to the service of such employees, payments (in lieu of contributions), and (B) such employees will be entitled to receive, on the basis of such service, compensation payable on the same basis, in the same amount, on the same terms, and subject to the same conditions as compensation which is payable on the basis of similar service for the State which is subject to such law; "

—P.L. 94-566, Sec. 312(b), added the last sentence in subsec. (c), effective for certifications of States for 1978 and subsequent years.

—P.L. 94-566, Sec. 314(a), redesignated para. (a)(13), as para. (a)(16) ... added paras. (a)(13) through (a)(15), effective for certifications of States for 1978, and subsequent years, and for 1979, and subsequent years in the case of States the legislatures of which do not meet in a regular session which closes in the calendar year '77.

—P.L. 94-566, Sec. 121, provided the following transitional provisions:

"SEC. 121. FEDERAL REIMBURSEMENT FOR BENEFITS PAID TO NEWLY COVERED WORKERS DURING TRANSITION PERIOD.

"(a) General rule.

"If any State, the unemployment compensation law of which is approved by the Secretary under section 3304(a) of the Internal Revenue Code of 1954, provides for the payment of compensation for any week of unemployment beginning on or after January 1, 1978, on the basis of previously uncovered services, the Secretary shall pay to the unemployment fund of such State an amount equal to the Federal reimbursement for any compensation paid for a week of unemployment beginning on or after January 1, 1978, to any individual whose base period wages include wages for previously uncovered services.

"(b) Previously uncovered services.

"For purposes of this section, the term 'previously uncovered services' means, with respect to any State, services—

"(1) which were not covered by the State unemployment compensation law, at any time, during the 1-year period ending December 31, 1975; and

"(2) which—

"(A) are agricultural labor (as defined in section 3306(k) of the Internal Revenue Code of 1954) or domestic services referred to in section 3306(c)(2) of such Code (as in effect on the day before the date of the enactment of this Act) and are treated as employment (as defined in section 3306(c) of such Code) by reason of the amendments made by this Act, or

"(B) are services to which section 3309(a)(1) of such Code applies by reason of the amendments made by this Act.

"(c) Federal reimbursement —

"(1) In general. For purposes of this section, the Federal reimbursement for compensation paid to any individual for any week of unemployment shall be an amount which bears the same ratio to the amount of such compensation as the amount of the individual's base period wages which are attributable to previously uncovered services which are reimbursable bears to the total amount of the individual's base period wages.

"(2) Reimbursable services. For purposes of determining the amount of the Federal reimbursement for compensation paid to any individual for any week of unemployment, previously uncovered services shall be treated as being reimbursable—

"(A) if such services were performed—

"(i) before July 1, 1978, in the case of a week of unemployment beginning before July 1, 1978; or

"(ii) before January 1, 1978, in the case of a week of unemployment beginning after July 1, 1978; and

"(B) to the extent that assistance under title II of the Emergency Jobs and Unemployment Assistance Act of 1974 was not paid to such individual on the basis of such services.

"(3) Denial of payment. No payment may be made under subsection (a) to any State in respect of any compensation for which the State is entitled to any reimbursement under the provisions of any Federal law other than this Act or the Federal-State Extended Unemployment Compensation Act of 1970.

"(d) Experience rating of certain employers.

"The unemployment compensation law of any State may, without being deemed to violate the standards set forth in section 3303(a) of the Internal Revenue Code of 1954, provide that the experience-rating account of any employer shall not be charged for the compensation paid to any individual whose base period wages includes wages for previously uncovered services which are reimbursable under subsection (c)(2) to the extent that such individual would not have been eligible to receive such compensation had the State law not provided for the payment of compensation on the basis of such previously uncovered services.

"(e) Certain nonprofit employers.

"The unemployment compensation law of any State may provide that any organization which elects to make payments (in lieu of contributions) into the State unemployment compensation fund as provided in section 3309(a)(2) of the Internal Revenue Code of 1954 shall not be liable to make such payments with respect to the compensation paid to any individual whose base period wages includes wages for previously uncovered services which are reimbursable under subsection (c)(2) to the extent that such individual would not have been eligible to receive such compensation had the State not provided for the payment of compensation on the basis of such previously uncovered services.

"(f) Payments made monthly.

"Payments under subsection (a) shall be made monthly, prior to audit or settlement by the General Accounting Office, on the basis of estimates by the Secretary of the amount payable to such State for such month, reduced or increased, as the case may be, by any amount by which the Secretary finds that his estimates for any prior month were greater or less than the amounts which should have been paid to such State. Such estimates may be made on the basis of such statistical, sampling, or other methods as may be agreed upon by the Secretary and the State.

"(g) Definitions.

"For purposes of this section—

"(1) State. The term 'State' includes the District of Columbia, the Commonwealth of Puerto Rico, and the Virgin Islands.

"(2) Secretary. The term 'Secretary' means the Secretary of Labor.

"(3) Benefit year. The term 'benefit year' means the benefit year as defined in the applicable State unemployment compensation law.

"(4) Base period. The term 'base period' means the base period as defined by the applicable State unemployment compensation law for the benefit year.

"(5) Unemployment fund. The term 'unemployment fund' has the meaning given to such term by section 3306(f) of the Internal Revenue Code of 1954.

"(h) Authorization of appropriations.

"There are authorized to be appropriated from the general fund of the Treasury such sums as may be necessary to carry out the purposes of this section."

—P.L. 94-566, Sec. 506(b), substituted "section 3309 (a)(1)" for "section 3309(a)(1)(A)" following "with respect to service to which" in subpara. (a)(6)(B), effective for certifications of States for 1978 and subsequent years, but only with respect to services performed after 12/31/77.

—P.L. 94-455, Sec. 1903(a)(14)(A), deleted "49 Stat. 640; 52 Stat. 1104; 1105;" after the parenthesis in para. (a)(3) ... Sec. 1903(a)(14)(B), deleted "(10-month period in the case of October 31, 1972)" after "with respect to the 12-month period" in subsec. (c), effective for wages paid after 12/31/76.

—P.L. 94-455, Sec. 1906(b)(13)(C), substituted "to the Secretary of the Treasury" for "to the Secretary" each place it appeared in Code Sec. 3304, effective 2/1/77.

—P.L. 94-455, Sec. 1906(b)(13)(E), substituted "the Secretary of Labor shall" for "the Secretary shall" in the last sentence of subsec. (c), effective 2/1/77.

In 1970, P.L. 91-373, Sec. 104(a), redesignated para. (a)(6) as para. (a)(13) and added new para. (a)(6), effective for certification of State laws for 1972 and subsequent years, but only with respect to service performed after 12/31/71. As provided by Sec. 104(d)(2), para. (a)(6) shall not be a requirement of the State law of any State prior to 7/1/72, if the legislature of such State does not meet in a regular session which closes during the calendar year 1971.

—P.L. 91-373, Sec. 108(a), added para. (a)(12) effective for certification of State laws for '72 and subsequent years; except that para. (a)(12) shall not be a requirement for the State law of any State prior to 7/1/72, if the legislature of such State does not meet in a regular session which closes during the calendar year 1971, or prior to 1/1/75, if compliance with such requirement would necessitate a change in the constitution of such State.

—P.L. 91-373, Sec. 121(a), added paras. (a)(7) through (a)(10), effective 1/1/72 for tax. yr. 1972 and tax. yrs. thereafter. As provided by Sec. 121(b)(2), paras. (a)(7) thru (a)(10) shall not be requirements for the State law of any State prior to 7/1/72, if the legislature of such State does not meet in a regular session which closes during calendar year 1971.

—P.L. 91-373, Sec. 131(b)(2), amended subsec. (c), effective 8/10/70.

Prior to amendment, subsec. (c) read as follows:

"(c) Certification.

"On December 31 of each taxable year the Secretary of Labor shall certify to the Secretary each State whose law he has previously approved, except that he shall not certify any State which, after reasonable notice and opportunity for hearing to the State agency, the Secretary of Labor finds has amended its law so that it no longer contains the provisions specified in subsection (a) or has with respect to such taxable year failed to comply substantially with any such provision and such finding has become effective. Such finding shall become effective on the 90th day after the governor of the State has been notified thereof, unless the State has before such 90th day so amended its law that it will comply substantially with the Secretary of Labor's interpretation of the provision of subsection (a), in which event such finding shall not become effective. No finding of a failure to comply substantially with the provision in State law specified in paragraph (5) of subsection (a) shall be based on an application or interpretation of State law with respect to which further administrative or judicial review is provided for under the laws of the State."

—P.L. 91-373, Sec. 142(f), amended subsec. (c) [as amended by Sec. 131(b)(2) of this Act, see above] ... Sec. 142(g), substituted "If at any time" for "If, at any time during the taxable year," in subsec. (d), effective for tax. yr. 1972 and tax. yrs. thereafter.

Prior to amendment, subsec. (c) read as follows:

Employment taxes   Code Sec. 3304

"(c) Certification.

On December 31 of each taxable year the Secretary of Labor shall certify to the Secretary each State whose law he has previously approved, except that he shall not certify any State which, after reasonable notice and opportunity for hearing to the State agency, the Secretary of Labor finds has amended its law so that it no longer contains the provisions specified in subsection (a) or has with respect to the taxable year failed to comply substantially with any such provision in such subsection. No finding of a failure to comply substantially with any provision in paragraph (5) of subsection (a) shall be based on an application or interpretation of State law (1) until all administrative review provided for under the laws of the State has been exhausted, or (2) with respect to which the time for judicial review provided by the laws of the State has not expired, or (3) with respect to which any judicial review is pending."

—P.L. 91-373, Sec. 142(h), added new subsec. (e), effective for tax. yr. 1972 and tax. yrs. thereafter.

—P.L. 91-373, Sec. 201, through 207 [as amended by P.L. 92-599, Sec. 501; P.L. 93-53, Sec. 5; P.L. 93-233, Sec. 20; P.L. 93-256, Sec. 2; P.L. 93-329, Sec. 2; P.L. 93-368, Sec. 3; P.L. 93-572, Secs. 106, 107, 108; P.L. 94-45, Sec. 102(b); P.L. 94-566, Title I, Sec. 116(d)(1) to (3), Sec. 212(a), Title III, Sec. 311(a), (b); P.L. 96-364, Title IV, Sec. 416(a); P.L. 96-499, Title X, Secs. 1022(a) 1024(a); P.L. 97-35, Title XXIV, Secs. 2401(a), (b), 2402(a), 2403(a), 2404(a), (b), Title XXV, Sec. 2505(b); P.L. 97-248, Title I, Sec. 191(a); P.L. 97-258, Sec. 5(b); P.L. 98-21, Title V, Sec. 522(a); P.L. 99-514, Sec. 2; P.L. 102-318, Title II, Secs. 201, 202(a)(1), (b)(1); P.L. 108-271, Sec. 8(b), and Sec. 502(a), and (b)(1)-(2) of P.L. 111-312] provides:

"Federal-State Extended Unemployment Compensation Act of 1970"

"Sec. 201 [Short title]. This title [this note] may be cited as the 'Federal-State Extended Unemployment Compensation Act of 1970'.

"Sec. 202 [Payment of extended compensation].

"(a) [State law requirements] (1) For purposes of section 3304(a)(11) of the Internal Revenue Code of 1986 [(formerly I.R.C. 1954) subsec. (a)(11) of this section] a State law shall provide that payment of extended compensation shall be made, for any week of unemployment which begins in the individual's eligibility period, to individuals who have exhausted all rights to regular compensation under the State law and who have no rights to regular compensation with respect to such week under such law or any other State unemployment compensation law or to compensation under any other Federal law and are not receiving compensation with respect to such week under the unemployment compensation law of Canada. For purposes of the preceding sentence, an individual shall have exhausted his rights to regular compensation under a State law (A) when no payments of regular compensation can be made under such law because such individual has received all regular compensation available to him based on employment or wages during his base period, or (B) when his rights to such compensation having terminated by reason of the expiration of the benefit year with respect to which such rights existed.

"(2) Except where inconsistent with the provisions of this title [this note], the terms and conditions of the State law which apply to claims for regular compensation and to the payment thereof shall apply to claims for extended compensation and to the payment thereof.

"(3)(A) Notwithstanding the provisions of paragraph (2), payment of extended compensation under this Act [this note] shall not be made to any individual for any week of unemployment in his eligibility period—

"(i) during which he fails to accept any offer of suitable work (as defined in subparagraph (c) [probably means subpar. (C)]) or fails to apply for any suitable work to which he was referred by the State agency; or

"(ii) during which he fails to actively engage in seeking work, unless such individual is not actively engaged in seeking work because such individual is, as determined in accordance with State law—

"(I) before any court of the United States or any State pursuant to a lawfully issued summons to appear for jury duty (as such term may be defined by the Secretary of Labor), or

"(II) hospitalized for treatment of an emergency or a life-threatening condition (as such term may be defined by such Secretary), if such exemptions in clauses (I) and (II) apply to recipients of regular benefits, and the State chooses to apply such exemptions for recipients of extended benefits.

"(B) If any individual is ineligible for extended compensation for any week by reason of a failure described in clause (i) or (ii) of subparagraph (A), the individual shall be ineligible to receive extended compensation for any week which begins during a period which—

"(i) begins with the week following the week in which such failure occurs, and

"(ii) does not end until such individual has been employed during at least 4 weeks which begin after such failure and the total of the remuneration earned by the individual for being so employed is not less than the product of 4 multiplied by the individual's average weekly benefit amount (as determined for purposes of subsection (b)(1)(c) [subsec. (b)(1)(C)]) for his benefit year.

"(C) For purposes of this paragraph, the term 'suitable work' means, with respect to any individual, any work which is within such individual's capabilities; except that, if the individual furnishes evidence satisfactory to the State agency that such individual's prospects for obtaining work in his customary occupation within a reasonably short period are good, the determination of whether any work is suitable work with respect to such individual shall be made in accordance with the applicable State law.

"(D) Extended compensation shall not be denied under clause (i) of subparagraph (A) to any individual for any week by reason of a failure to accept an offer of, or apply for, suitable work—

"(i) if the gross average weekly remuneration payable to such individual for the position does not exceed the sum of—

"(I) the individual's average weekly benefit amount (as determined for purposes of subsection (b)(1)(C)) for his benefit year, plus

"(II) the amount (if any) of supplemental unemployment compensation benefits (as defined in section 501(c)(17)(D) of the Internal Revenue Code of 1986 [26 U.S.C. Sec. 501(c)(17)(D)]) payable to such individual for such week;

"(ii) if the position was not offered to such individual in writing and was not listed with the State employment service;

"(iii) if such failure would not result in a denial of compensation under the provisions of the applicable State law to the extent that such provisions are not inconsistent with the provisions of subparagraphs (C) and (E); or

"(iv) if the position pays wages less than the higher of—

"(I) the minimum wage provided by section 6(a)(1) of the Fair Labor Standards Act of 1938 [29 U.S.C. Sec. 206(a)(1)], without regard to any exemption; or

"(II) any applicable State or local minimum wage.

"(E) For purposes of this paragraph, an individual shall be treated as actively engaged in seeking work during any week if—

"(i) the individual has engaged in a systematic and sustained effort to obtain work during such week, and

"(ii) the individual provides tangible evidence to the State agency that he has engaged in such an effort during such week.

"(F) For purposes of section 3304(a)(11) of the Internal Revenue Code of 1986 [subsec. (a)(11) of this section], a State law shall provide for referring applicants for benefits under this Act [this note] to any suitable work to which clauses (i), (ii), (iii), and (iv) of subparagraph (D) would not apply.

"(4) No provision of State law which terminates a disqualification for voluntarily leaving employment, being discharged for misconduct, or refusing suitable employment shall apply for purposes of determining eligibility for extended compensation unless such termination is based upon employment subsequent to the date of such disqualification.

"(5) Notwithstanding the provisions of paragraph (2), an individual shall not be eligible for extended compensation unless, in the base period with respect to which the individual exhausted all rights to regular compensation under the State law, the individual had 20 weeks of full-time insured employment, or the equivalent in insured wages. For purposes of this paragraph, the equivalent in insured wages shall be earnings covered by the State law for compensation purposes which exceed 40 times the individual's most recent weekly benefit amount or 1 1/2 times the individual's insured wages in that calendar quarter of the base period in which the individual's insured wages were the highest (or one such quarter if his wages were the same for more than one such quarter). The State shall by law provide which one or more of the foregoing methods of measuring employment and earnings shall be used in that State.

"(6) No payment shall be made under this Act [this note] to any State in respect of any extended compensation or sharable regular compensation paid to any individual for any week if, under the rules of paragraphs (3), (4) and (5) extended compensation would not have been payable to such individual for such week.

"(7) Paragraphs (3) and (4) shall not apply to weeks of unemployment beginning after March 6, 1993, and before January 1, 1995, and no provision of State law in conformity with such paragraphs shall apply during such period.

"(b) [Individuals' compensation accounts] (1) The State law shall provide that the State will establish, for each eligible individual who files an application therefor, an extended compensation account with respect to such individual's benefit year. The amount established in such account shall be not less than whichever of the following is the least:

"(A) 50 per centum of the total amount of regular compensation (including dependents' allowances) payable to him during such benefit year under such law,

"(B) thirteen times his average weekly benefit amount, or

"(C) thirty-nine times his average weekly benefit amount, reduced by the regular compensation paid (or deemed paid) to him during such benefit year under such law;

"except that the amount so determined shall (if the State law so provides) be reduced by the aggregate amount of additional compensation paid (or deemed paid) to him under such law for prior weeks of unemployment in such benefit year which did not begin in an extended benefit period.

"(2) For purposes of paragraph (1), an individual's weekly benefit amount for a week is the amount of regular compensation (including dependents' allowances) under the State law payable to such individual for such week for total unemployment.

"(3)(A) Effective with respect to weeks beginning in a high unemployment period, paragraph (1) shall be applied by substituting—

"(i) '80 per centum' for '50 per centum' in subparagraph (A),

"(ii) 'twenty' for 'thirteen' in subparagraph (B), and

"(iii) 'forty-six' for 'thirty-nine' in subparagraph (C).

"(B) For purposes of subparagraph (A), the term 'high unemployment period' means any period during which an extended benefit period would be in effect if section 203(f)(1)(A)(i) were applied by substituting '8 percent' for '6.5 percent'.

"(c) [Cessation of extended benefits when paid under an interstate claim in a state where extended benefit period is not in effect] (1) Except as provided in paragraph (2), payment of extended compensation shall not be made to any individual for any week if--

"(A) extended compensation would (but for this subsection) have been payable for such week pursuant to an interstate claim filed in any State under the interstate benefit payment plan, and

"(B) an extended benefit period is not in effect for such week in such State.

"(2) Paragraph (1) shall not apply with respect to the first 2 weeks for which extended compensation is payable (determined without regard to this subsection) pursuant to an interstate claim filed under the interstate benefit payment plan to the individual from the extended compensation account established for the benefit year.

"(3) Section 3304(a)(9)(A) of the Internal Revenue Code of 1986 [subsec. (a)(9)(A) of this section] shall not apply to any denial of compensation required under this subsection.

"Sec. 203 [Extended benefit period].

"(a) [Beginning and ending] For purposes of this title [this note], in the case of any State, an extended benefit period—

"(1) shall begin with the third week after the first week for which there is a State 'on' indicator; and

"(2) shall end with the third week after the first week for which there is a State 'off' indicator.

"(b) [Special rules] (1) In the case of any State—

"(A) no extended benefit period shall last for a period of less than thirteen consecutive weeks, and

"(B) no extended benefit period may begin before the fourteenth week after the close of a prior extended benefit period with respect to such State.

"(2) When a determination has been made that an extended benefit period is beginning or ending with respect to a State, the Secretary shall cause notice of such determination to be published in the Federal Register.

"(c) [Eligibility period] For purposes of this title [this note], an individual's eligibility period under the State law shall consist of the weeks in his benefit year which begin in an extended benefit period and, if his benefit year ends within such extended benefit period, any weeks thereafter which begin in such extended benefit period.

"(d) [State 'on' and 'off' indicators] For purposes of this section—

"(1) There is a State 'on' indicator for a week if the rate of insured unemployment under the State law for the period consisting of such week and the immediately preceding twelve weeks—

"(A) equaled or exceeded 120 per centum of the average of such rates for the corresponding thirteen-week period ending in each of the preceding two calendar years, and

"(B) equaled or exceeded 5 per centum.

"(2) There is a State 'off' indicator for a week if, for the period consisting of such week and the immediately preceding twelve weeks, either subparagraph (A) or subparagraph (B) of paragraph (1) is not satisfied.

"Effective with respect to compensation for weeks of unemployment beginning after March 30, 1977 (or, if later, the date established pursuant to State law), the State may by law provide that the determination of whether there has been a State 'on' or 'off' indicator beginning or ending any extended benefit period shall be made under this subsection as if (i) paragraph (1) did not contain subparagraph (A) thereof, and (ii) the figure '5' contained in subparagraph (B) thereof were '6'; except that, notwithstanding any such provision of State law, any week for which there would otherwise be a State 'on' indicator shall continue to be such a week and shall not be determined to be a week for which there is a State 'off' indicator. Effective with respect to compensation for weeks of unemployment beginning after the date of enactment of the Tax Relief, Unemployment Insurance Reauthorization, and Job Creation Act of 2010 (or, if later, the date established pursuant to State law), and ending on or before December 31, 2011, the State may by law provide that the determination of whether there has been a State 'on' or 'off' indicator beginning or ending any extended benefit period shall be made under this subsection as if the word 'two' were 'three' in subparagraph (1)(A). For purposes of this subsection, the rate of insured unemployment for any thirteen-week period shall be determined by reference to the average monthly covered employment under the State law for the first four of the most recent six calendar quarters ending before the close of such period.

"(e) [Rate of insured unemployment; covered employment] (1) For purposes of subsections (d), the term 'rate of insured unemployment' means the percentage arrived at by dividing—

"(A) the average weekly number of individuals filing claims for regular compensation for weeks of unemployment with respect to the specified period, as determined on the basis of the reports made by the State agency to the Secretary, by

"(B) the average monthly covered employment for the specified period.

"(2) Determinations under subsection (d) shall be made by the State agency in accordance with regulations prescribed by the Secretary.

"(f) [Alternative trigger] (1) Effective with respect to compensation for weeks of unemployment beginning after March 6, 1993, the State may by law provide that for purposes of beginning or ending any extended benefit period under this section—

"(A) there is a State 'on' indicator for a week if—

"(i) the average rate of total unemployment in such State (seasonally adjusted) for the period consisting of the most recent 3 months for which data for all States are published before the close of such week equals or exceeds 6.5 percent, and

"(ii) the average rate of total unemployment in such State (seasonally adjusted) for the 3-month period referred to in clause (i) equals or exceeds 110 percent of such average rate for either (or both) of the corresponding 3-month periods ending in the 2 preceding calendar years; and

"(B) there is a State 'off' indicator for a week if either the requirements of clause (i) or clause (ii) of subparagraph (A) are not satisfied.

"Notwithstanding the provision of any State law described in this paragraph, any week for which there would otherwise be a State 'on' indicator shall continue to be such a week and shall not be determined to be a week for which there is a State 'off' indicator.

"(2) Effective with respect to compensation for weeks of unemployment beginning after the date of enactment of the Tax Relief, Unemployment Insurance Reauthorization, and Job Creation Act of 2010 (or, if later, the date established pursuant to State law), and ending on or before December 31, 2011, the State may

by law provide that the determination of whether there has been a state 'on' or 'off' indicator beginning or ending any extended benefit period shall be made under this subsection as if the word 'either' were 'any', the word 'both' were 'all', and the figure '2' were '3' in clause (1)(A)(ii).

"(3) For purposes of this subsection, determinations of the rate of total unemployment in any State for any period (and of any seasonal adjustment) shall be made by the Secretary.

"Sec. 204 [Payments to States].

"(a) [Amount payable] (1) There shall be paid to each State an amount equal to one-half of the sum of—

"(A) the sharable extended compensation, and

"(B) the sharable regular compensation,

"paid to individuals under the State law.

"(2) No payment shall be made to any State under this subsection in respect of compensation (A) for which the State is entitled to reimbursement under the provisions of any Federal law other than this Act, (B) paid for the first week in an individual's eligibility period for which extended compensation or sharable regular compensation is paid, if the State law of such State provides for payment (at any time or under any circumstances) of regular compensation to an individual for his first week of otherwise compensable unemployment, (C) paid for any week with respect to which such benefits are not payable by reason of section 233(d) of the Trade Act of 1974 [19 U.S.C.A. 2293(d)], or (D) paid to an individual with respect to a week of unemployment to the extent that such amount exceeds the amount of such compensation which would be paid to such individual if such State had a benefit structure which provided that the amount of compensation otherwise payable to any individual for any week shall be rounded (if not a full dollar amount) to the nearest lower full dollar amount.

"(3) The amount which, but for this paragraph, would be payable under this subsection to any State in respect of any compensation paid to an individual whose base period wages include wages for services to which section 3306(c)(7) of the Internal Revenue Code of 1986 [26 U.S.C.A. Sec. 3306(c)(7)] applies shall be reduced by an amount which bears the same ratio to the amount which, but for this paragraph, would be payable under this subsection to such State in respect of such compensation as the amount of the base period wages attributable to such services bears to the total amount of the base period wages.

"(b) [Sharable extended compensation] For purposes of subsection (a)(1)(A), extended compensation paid to an individual for weeks of unemployment in such individual's eligibility period is sharable extended compensation to the extent that the aggregate extended compensation paid to such individual with respect to any benefit year does not exceed the smallest of the amounts referred to in subparagraphs (A), (B), and (C) of section 202(b)(1).

"(c) [Sharable regular compensation] For purposes of subsection (a)(1)(B), regular compensation paid to an individual for a week of unemployment is sharable regular compensation—

"(1) if such week is in such individual's eligibility period (determined under section 203(c)), and

"(2) to the extent that the sum of such compensation, plus the regular compensation paid (or deemed paid) to him with respect to prior weeks of unemployment in the benefit year, exceeds twenty-six times (and does not exceed thirty-nine, forty-six in any case where section 202(b)(3)(A) applies times [sic]) the average weekly benefit amount (including allowances for dependents) for weeks of total unemployment payable to such individual under the State law in such benefit year.

"(d) [Payment on calendar month basis] There shall be paid to each State either in advance or by way of reimbursement, as may be determined by the Secretary, such sum as the Secretary estimates the State will be entitled to receive under this title [this note] for each calendar month, reduced or increased, as the case may be, by any sum by which the Secretary finds that his estimates for any prior calendar month were greater or less than the amounts which should have been paid to the State. Such estimates may be made upon the basis of such statistical, sampling, or other method as may be agreed upon by the Secretary and the State agency.

"(e) [Certification] The Secretary shall from time to time certify to the Secretary of the Treasury for payment to each State the sums payable to such State under this section. The Secretary of the Treasury, prior to audit or settlement by the General Accounting Office [now Government Accountability Office], shall make payment to the State in accordance with such certification, by transfers from the extended unemployment compensation account to the account of such State in the Unemployment Trust Fund.

"Sec. 205 [Definitions]. For purposes of this title [Title II of Pub.L. 91-373]—

"(1) The term 'compensation' means cash benefits payable to individuals with respect to their unemployment.

"(2) The term 'regular compensation' means compensation payable to an individual under any State unemployment compensation law (including compensation payable pursuant to 5 U.S.C. chapter 85) [5 U.S.C. Sec. 8501 et seq.], other than extended compensation and additional compensation.

"(3) The term 'extended compensation' means compensation (including additional compensation and compensation payable pursuant to 5 U.S.C. chapter 85 [5 U.S.C. Sec. 8501 et seq.]) payable for weeks of unemployment beginning in an extended benefit period to an individual under those provisions of the State law which satisfy the requirements of this title [this note] with respect to the payment of extended compensation.

"(4) The term 'additional compensation' means compensation payable to exhaustees by reason of conditions of high unemployment or by reason of other special factors.

"(5) The term 'benefit year' means the benefit year as defined in the applicable State law.

"(6) The term 'base period' means the base period as determined under applicable State law for the benefit year.

Employment taxes   Code Sec. 3305(f)

"(7) The term 'Secretary' means the Secretary of Labor of the United States.

"(8) The term 'State' includes the District of Columbia, the Commonwealth of Puerto Rico, and the Virgin Islands.

"(9) The term 'State agency' means the agency of the State which administers its State law.

"(10) The term 'State law' means the unemployment compensation law of the State, approved by the Secretary under section 3304 of the Internal Revenue Code of 1986 [this section].

"(11) The term 'week' means a week as defined in the applicable State law.

"Sec. 206 [Approval of State laws]. [Section 206 amended subsec. (a) of this section by adding par. (11) thereof. Such amendment has been executed to the text of subsec. (a) and is therefore not set out here.]

"Sec. 207 [Effective dates]. (a) Except as provided in subsection (b)—

"(1) in applying section 203, no extended benefit period may begin with a week beginning before January 1, 1972; and

"(2) section 204 shall apply only with respect to weeks of unemployment beginning after December 31, 1971.

"(b)(1) In the case of a State law approve under section 3304(a)(11) of the Internal Revenue Code of 1986 [subsec. (a)(11) of this section] such State law may also provide that an extended benefit period may begin with a week established pursuant to such law which begins earlier than January 1, 1972, but not earlier than 60 days after the date of the enactment of this Act [Aug. 10, 1970].

"(2) For purposes of paragraph (1) with respect to weeks beginning before January 1, 1972, the extended benefit period for the State shall be determined under section 203(a) solely by reference to the State 'on' indicator and the State 'off' indicator.

"(3) In the case of a State law containing a provision described in paragraph (1), section 204 shall also apply with respect to weeks of unemployment in extended benefit periods determined pursuant to paragraph (1).

"(c) Section 3304(a)(11) of the Internal Revenue Code of 1954 [subsec. (a)(11) of this section] (as added by section 206) shall not be a requirement for the State law of any State—

"(1) in the case of any State the legislature of which does not meet in a regular session which closes during the calendar year 1971, with respect to any week of unemployment which begins prior to July 1, 1972; or

"(2) in the case of any other State, with respect to any week of unemployment which begins prior to January 1, 1972."

—P.L. 91-373, Sec. 206, added para. (a)(11), effective as provided in Sec. 206(c) which reads as follows:

"(c) Section 3304(a)(11) of the Internal Revenue Code of 1954 (as added by section 206) shall not be a requirement for the State law of any State —

"(1) in the case of any State the legislature of which does not meet in a regular session which closes during the calendar year 1971, with respect to any week of unemployment which begins prior to July 1, 1972; or

"(2) in the case of any other State, with respect to any week of unemployment which begins prior to January 1, 1972. As provided in Sec. 207(b)(1), such State law may also provide that an extended benefit period may begin with a week established pursuant to such law which begins earlier than 1/1/72, but not earlier than 10/9/70."

Sec. 3305. Applicability of State law.
(a) Interstate and foreign commerce.

No person required under a State law to make payments to an unemployment fund shall be relieved from compliance therewith on the ground that he is engaged in interstate or foreign commerce, or that the State law does not distinguish between employees engaged in interstate or foreign commerce and those engaged in intrastate commerce.

(b) Federal instrumentalities in general.

The legislature of any State may require any instrumentality of the United States (other than an instrumentality to which section 3306(c)(6) applies), and the individuals in its employ, to make contributions to an unemployment fund under a State unemployment compensation law approved by the Secretary of Labor under section 3304 and (except as provided in section 5240 of the Revised Statutes, as amended (12 U.S.C., sec. 484), and as modified by subsection (c)), to comply otherwise with such law. The permission granted in this subsection shall apply (A) only to the extent that no discrimination is made against such instrumentality, so that if the rate of contribution is uniform upon all other persons subject to such law on account of having individuals in their employ, and upon all employees of such persons, respectively, the contributions required of such instrumentality or the individuals in its employ shall not be at a greater rate than is required of such other persons and such employees, and if the rates are determined separately for different persons or classes of persons having individuals in their employ or for different classes of employees, the determination shall be based solely upon unemployment experience and other factors bearing a direct relation to unemployment risk; (B) only if such State law makes provision for the refund of any contributions required under such law from an instrumentality of the United States or its employees for any year in the event such State is not certified by the Secretary of Labor under section 3304 with respect to such year; and (C) only if such State law makes provision for the payment of unemployment compensation to any employee of any such instrumentality of the United States in the same amount, on the same terms, and subject to the same conditions as unemployment compensation is payable to employees of other employers under the State unemployment compensation law.

(c) National banks.

Nothing contained in section 5240 of the Revised Statutes, as amended (12 U.S.C. 484), shall prevent any State from requiring any national banking association to render returns and reports relative to the association's employees, their remuneration and services, to the same extent that other persons are required to render like returns and reports under a State law requiring contributions to an unemployment fund. The Comptroller of the Currency shall, upon receipt of a copy of any such return or report of a national banking association from, and upon request of, any duly authorized official, body, or commission of a State, cause an examination of the correctness of such return or report to be made at the time of the next succeeding examination of such association, and shall thereupon transmit to such official, body, or commission a complete statement of his findings respecting the accuracy of such returns or reports.

(d) Federal property.

No person shall be relieved from compliance with a State unemployment compensation law on the ground that services were performed on land or premises owned, held, or possessed by the United States, and any State shall have full jurisdiction and power to enforce the provisions of such law to the same extent and with the same effect as though such place were not owned, held or possessed by the United States.

(e) Repealed.
(f) American vessels.

The legislature of any State in which a person maintains the operating office, from which the operations of an American vessel operating on navigable waters within or within and without the United States are ordinarily and regularly supervised, managed, directed and controlled, may require such person and the officers and members of the crew of such vessel to make contributions to its unemployment fund under its State unemployment compensation law approved by the Secretary of Labor under section 3304 and otherwise to comply with its unemployment compensation law with respect to the service performed by an officer or member of the crew on or in connection with such vessel to the same extent and with the same effect as though such service was performed entirely within such State. Such person and the officers and members of the crew of such vessel shall not be required to make contributions, with respect to such service, to the unemployment fund of any other State. The permission granted by this subsection is subject to the condition that such service shall be treated, for purposes of wage credits given employees, like other service subject to such State unemployment compensation law performed for such person in such State, and also subject to the same limitation, with respect to contributions required from such person and from the officers and members of the crew of such vessel, as is imposed by the second sentence (other than clause (B)

3,129

thereof) of subsection (b) with respect to contributions required from instrumentalities of the United States and from individuals in their employ.

(g) Vessels operated by general agents of United States.

The permission granted by subsection (f) shall apply in the same manner and under the same conditions (including the obligation to comply with all requirements of State unemployment compensation laws) to general agents of the Secretary of Commerce with respect to service performed by officers and members of the crew on or in connection with American vessels—

(1) owned by or bareboat chartered to the United States, and

(2) whose business is conducted by such general agents. As to any such vessel, the State permitted to require contributions on account of such service shall be the State to which the general agent would make contributions if the vessel were operated for his own account. Such general agents are designated, for this purpose, instrumentalities of the United States neither wholly nor partially owned by it and shall not be exempt from the tax imposed by section 3301. The permission granted by this subsection is subject to the same conditions and limitations as are imposed in subsection (f), except that clause (B) of the second sentence of subsection (b) shall apply.

(h) Requirement by State of contributions.

Any State may, as to service performed on account of which contributions are made pursuant to subsection (g)—

(1) require contributions from persons performing such service under its unemployment compensation law or temporary disability insurance law administered in connection therewith, and

(2) require general agents of the Secretary of Commerce to make contributions under such temporary disability insurance law and to make such deductions from wages or remuneration as are required by such unemployment compensation or temporary disability insurance law.

(i) General agent as legal entity.

Each general agent of the Secretary of Commerce making contributions pursuant to subsection (g) or (h) shall, for purposes of such subsections, be considered a legal entity in his capacity as an instrumentality of the United States, separate and distinct from his identity as a person employing individuals on his own account.

(j) Denial of credits in certain cases.

Any person required, pursuant to the permission granted by this section, to make contributions to an unemployment fund under a State unemployment compensation law approved by the Secretary of Labor under section 3304 shall not be entitled to the credits permitted, with respect to the unemployment compensation law of a State, by subsections (a) and (b) of section 3302 against the tax imposed by section 3301 for any taxable year if, on October 31 of such taxable year, the Secretary of Labor certifies to the Secretary of the Treasury his finding, after reasonable notice and opportunity for hearing to the State agency, that the unemployment compensation law of such State is inconsistent with any one or more of the conditions on the basis of which such permission is granted or that, in the application of the State law with respect to the 12-month period ending on such October 31, there has been a substantial failure to comply with any one or more of such conditions. For purposes of section 3310, a finding of the Secretary of Labor under this subsection shall be treated as a finding under section 3304(c).

In **1976,** P.L. 94-455, Sec. 1903(a)(15)(A), deleted "on or after July 1, 1953," following "with respect to service performed" in subsec. (g) . . . Sec. 1903(a)(15)(B), deleted "on or after July 1, 1953, and" after "Any State may, as to service performed" in subsec. (h) . . . Sec. 1903(a)(15)(C), deleted "after December 31, 1971," "by section 3301 for any taxable year" in subsec. (j), effective for wages paid after 12/31/76.
—P.L. 94-455, Sec. 1906(b)(13)(C), substituted "to the Secretary of the Treasury" for "to the Secretary" following "the Secretary of Labor certifies" in subsec. (j), effective 2/1/77.

In **1970,** P.L. 91-373, Sec. 123, added subsec. (j), effective 8/10/70.

In **1960,** P.L. 86-778, Sec. 531(a), substituted "(other than an instrumentality to which section 3306(c)(6) applies)" for "except such as are (1) wholly owned by the United States, or (2) exempt from the tax imposed by section 3301 by virtue of any other provision of law," in subsec. (b) and added cl. (C); . . . Sec. 531(b), substituted "neither wholly nor partially" for "not wholly" in subsec. (g) for remuneration paid after '61 for services after '61.

In **1954,** ch. 1212, Sec. 4(c), repealed subsec. (e), which related to the Bonneville Power Administrator, effective for services performed after 12/31/54.

Sec. 3306. Definitions.

(a) Employer.

For purposes of this chapter—

(1) In general. The term "employer" means, with respect to any calendar year, any person who—

(A) during any calendar quarter in the calendar year or the preceding calendar year paid wages of $1,500 or more, or

(B) on each of some 20 days during the calendar year or during the preceding calendar year, each day being in a different calendar week, employed at least one individual in employment for some portion of the day.

For purposes of this paragraph, there shall not be taken into account any wages paid to, or employment of, an employee performing domestic services referred to in paragraph (3).

(2) Agricultural labor. In the case of agricultural labor, the term "employer" means, with respect to any calendar year, any person who—

(A) during any calendar quarter in the calendar year or the preceding calendar year paid wages of $20,000 or more for agricultural labor, or

(B) on each of some 20 days during the calendar year or during the preceding calendar year, each day being in a different calendar week, employed at least 10 individuals in employment in agricultural labor for some portion of the day.

(3) Domestic service. In the case of domestic service in a private home, local college club, or local chapter of a college fraternity or sorority, the term "employer" means, with respect to any calendar year, any person who during any calendar quarter in the calendar year or the preceding calendar year paid wages in cash of $1,000 or more for such service.

(4) Special rule. A person treated as an employer under paragraph (3) shall not be treated as an employer with respect to wages paid for any service other than domestic service referred to in paragraph (3) unless such person is treated as an employer under paragraph (1) or (2) with respect to such other service.

(b) Wages.

For purposes of this chapter, the term "wages" means all remuneration for employment, including the cash value of all remuneration (including benefits) paid in any medium other than cash; except that such term shall not include—

(1) that part of the remuneration which, after remuneration (other than remuneration referred to in the succeeding paragraphs of this subsection) equal to $7,000 with respect to employment has been paid to an individual by an employer during any calendar year, is paid to such individual by such employer during such calendar year. If an em-

ployer (hereinafter referred to as successor employer) during any calendar year acquires substantially all the property used in a trade or business of another employer (hereinafter referred to as a predecessor), or used in a separate unit of a trade or business of a predecessor, and immediately after the acquisition employs in his trade or business an individual who immediately prior to the acquisition was employed in the trade or business of such predecessor, then, for the purpose of determining whether the successor employer has paid remuneration (other than remuneration referred to in the succeeding paragraphs of this subsection) with respect to employment equal to $7,000 to such individual during such calendar year, any remuneration (other than remuneration referred to in the succeeding paragraphs of this subsection) with respect to employment paid (or considered under this paragraph as having been paid) to such individual by such predecessor during such calendar year and prior to such acquisition shall be considered as having been paid by such successor employer;

(2) the amount of any payment (including any amount paid by an employer for insurance or annuities, or into a fund, to provide for any such payment) made to, or on behalf of, an employee or any of his dependents under a plan or system established by an employer which makes provision for his employees generally (or for his employees generally and their dependents) or for a class or classes of his employees (or for a class or classes of his employees and their dependents), on account of—

(A) sickness or accident disability (but, in the case of payments made to an employee or any of his dependents, this subparagraph shall exclude from the term "wages" only payments which are received under a workmen's compensation law), or

(B) medical or hospitalization expenses in connection with sickness or accident disability, or

(C) death;

(3) Repealed.

(4) any payment on account of sickness or accident disability, or medical or hospitalization expenses in connection with sickness or accident disability, made by an employer to, or on behalf of, an employee after the expiration of 6 calendar months following the last calendar month in which the employee worked for such employer;

(5) any payment made to, or on behalf of, an employee or his beneficiary—

(A) from or to a trust described in section 401(a) which is exempt from tax under section 501(a) at the time of such payment unless such payment is made to an employee of the trust as remuneration for services rendered as such employee and not as a beneficiary of the trust, or

(B) under or to an annuity plan which, at the time of such payment, is a plan described in section 403(a),

(C) under a simplified employee pension (as defined in section 408(k)(l)), other than any contributions described in section 408(k)(6),

(D) under or to an annuity contract described in section 403(b), other than a payment for the purchase of such contract which is made by reason of a salary reduction agreement (whether evidenced by a written instrument or otherwise),

(E) under or to an exempt governmental deferred compensation plan (as defined in section 3121(v)(3)),

(F) to supplement pension benefits under a plan or trust described in any of the foregoing provisions of this paragraph to take into account some portion or all of the increase in the cost of living (as determined by the Secretary of Labor) since retirement but only if such supplemental payments are under a plan which is treated as a welfare plan under section 3(2)(B)(ii) of the Employee Retirement Income Security Act of 1974;

(G) under a cafeteria plan (within the meaning of section 125) if such payment would not be treated as wages without regard to such plan and it is reasonable to believe that (if section 125 applied for purposes of this section) section 125 would not treat any wages as constructively received, or

(H) under an arrangement to which section 408(p) applies, other than any elective contributions under paragraph (2)(A)(i) thereof;

(6) the payment by an employer (without deduction from the remuneration of the employee)—

(A) of the tax imposed upon an employee under section 3101, or

(B) of any payment required from an employee under a State unemployment compensation law,

with respect to remuneration paid to an employee for domestic service in a private home of the employer or for agricultural labor;

(7) remuneration paid in any medium other than cash to an employee for service not in the course of the employer's trade or business;

(8) Repealed.

(9) remuneration paid to or on behalf of an employee if (and to the extent that) at the time of the payment of such remuneration it is reasonable to believe that a corresponding deduction is allowable under section 217 (determined without regard to section 274(n));

(10) any payment or series of payments by an employer to an employee or any of his dependents which is paid—

(A) upon or after the termination of an employee's employment relationship because of (i) death, or (ii) retirement for disability, and

(B) under a plan established by the employer which makes provision for his employees generally or a class or classes of his employees (or for such employees or class or classes of employees and their dependents),

other than any such payment or series of payments which would have been paid if the employee's employment relationship had not been so terminated;

(11) remuneration for agricultural labor paid in any medium other than cash;

(12) any contribution, payment, or service, provided by an employer which may be excluded from the gross income of an employee, his spouse, or his dependents, under the provisions of section 120 (relating to amounts received under qualified group legal services plans);

(13) any payment made, or benefit furnished, to or for the benefit of an employee if at the time of such payment or such furnishing it is reasonable to believe that the employee will be able to exclude such payment or benefit from income under section 127, 129, 134(b)(4), or 134(b)(5);

(14) the value of any meals or lodging furnished by or on behalf of the employer if at the time of such furnishing it is reasonable to believe that the employee will be able to exclude such items from income under section 119;

(15) any payment made by an employer to a survivor or the estate of a former employee after the calendar year in which such employee died;

(16) any benefit provided to or on behalf of an employee if at the time such benefit is provided it is reasonable to believe that the employee will be able to exclude such benefit from income under section 74(c), 108(f)(4), 117, or 132;

(17) any payment made to or for the benefit of an employee if at the time of such payment it is reasonable to believe that the employee will be able to exclude such payment from income under section 106(b);

(18) any payment made to or for the benefit of an employee if at the time of such payment it is reasonable to believe that the employee will be able to exclude such payment from income under section 106(d);

(19) remuneration on account of—
   (A) a transfer of a share of stock to any individual pursuant to an exercise of an incentive stock option (as defined in section 422(b)) or under an employee stock purchase plan (as defined in section 423(b)), or
   (B) any disposition by the individual of such stock; or

(20) any benefit or payment which is excludable from the gross income of the employee under section 139B(b).

Except as otherwise provided in regulations prescribed by the Secretary, any third party which makes a payment included in wages solely by reason of the parenthetical matter contained in subparagraph (A) of paragraph (2) shall be treated for purposes of this chapter and chapter 22 as the employer with respect to such wages. Nothing in the regulations prescribed for purposes of chapter 24 (relating to income tax withholding) which provides an exclusion from "wages" as used in such chapter shall be construed to require a similar exclusion from "wages" in the regulations prescribed for purposes of this chapter.

(c) Employment.

For purposes of this chapter, the term "employment" means any service performed prior to 1955, which was employment for purposes of subchapter C of chapter 9 of the Internal Revenue Code of 1939 under the law applicable to the period in which such service was performed, and (A) any service, of whatever nature, performed after 1954 by an employee for the person employing him, irrespective of the citizenship or residence of either, (i) within the United States, or (ii) on or in connection with an American vessel or American aircraft under a contract of service which is entered into within the United States or during the performance of which and while the employee is employed on the vessel or aircraft it touches at a port in the United States, if the employee is employed on and in connection with such vessel or aircraft when outside the United States, and (B) any service, of whatever nature, performed after 1971 outside the United States (except in a contiguous country with which the United States has an agreement relating to unemployment compensation) by a citizen of the United States as an employee of an American employer (as defined in subsection (j)(3)), except

(1) agricultural labor (as defined in subsection (k)) unless—
   (A) such labor is performed for a person who—
      (i) during any calendar quarter in the calendar year or the preceding calendar year paid remuneration in cash of $20,000 or more to individuals employed in agricultural labor (including labor performed by an alien referred to in subparagraph (B)), or
      (ii) on each of some 20 days during the calendar year or the preceding calendar year, each day being in a different calendar week, employed in agricultural labor (including labor performed by an alien referred to in subparagraph (B)) for some portion of the day (whether or not at the same moment of time) 10 or more individuals; and
   (B) such labor is not agricultural labor performed by an individual who is an alien admitted to the United States to perform agricultural labor pursuant to sections 214(c) and 101(a)(15)(H) of the Immigration and Nationality Act;

(2) domestic service in a private home, local college club, or local chapter of a college fraternity or sorority unless performed for a person who paid cash remuneration of $1,000 or more to individuals employed in such domestic service in any calendar quarter in the calendar year or the preceding calendar year;

(3) service not in the course of the employer's trade or business performed in any calendar quarter by an employee, unless the cash remuneration paid for such service is $50 or more and such service is performed by an individual who is regularly employed by such employer to perform such service. For purposes of this paragraph, an individual shall be deemed to be regularly employed by an employer during a calendar quarter only if—
   (A) on each of some 24 days during such quarter such individual performs for such employer for some portion of the day service not in the course of the employer's trade or business, or
   (B) such individual was regularly employed (as determined under subparagraph (A)) by such employer in the performance of such service during the preceding calendar quarter;

(4) service performed on or in connection with a vessel or aircraft not an American vessel or American aircraft, if the employee is employed on and in connection with such vessel or aircraft when outside the United States;

(5) service performed by an individual in the employ of his son, daughter, or spouse, and service performed by a child under the age of 21 in the employ of his father or mother;

(6) service performed in the employ of the United States Government or of an instrumentality of the United States which is—
   (A) wholly or partially owned by the United States, or
   (B) exempt from the tax imposed by section 3301 by virtue of any provision of law which specifically refers to such section (or the corresponding section of prior law) in granting such exemption;

(7) service performed in the employ of a State, or any political subdivision thereof, or in the employ of an Indian tribe, or any instrumentality of any one or more of the foregoing which is wholly owned by one or more States or political subdivisions or Indian tribes; and any service performed in the employ of any instrumentality of one or more States or political subdivisions to the extent that the instrumentality is, with respect to such service, immune under the Constitution of the United States from the tax imposed by section 3301;

(8) service performed in the employ of a religious, charitable, educational, or other organization described in section 501(c)(3) which is exempt from income tax under section 501(a);

(9) service performed by an individual as an employee or employee representative as defined in section 1 of the Railroad Unemployment Insurance Act (45 U.S.C. 351);

(10)(A) service performed in any calendar quarter in the employ of any organization exempt from income tax under section 501(a) (other than an organization described in section 401(a)) or under section 521, if the remuneration for such service is less than $50, or

(B) service performed in the employ of a school, college, or university, if such service is performed (i) by a student who is enrolled and is regularly attending classes at such school, college, or university, or (ii) by the spouse of such a student, if such spouse is advised, at the time such spouse commences to perform such service, that (I) the employment of such spouse to perform such service is provided under a program to provide financial assistance to such student by such school, college, or university, and (II) such employment will not be covered by any program of unemployment insurance, or

(C) service performed by an individual who is enrolled at a nonprofit or public educational institution which normally maintains a regular faculty and curriculum and normally has a regularly organized body of students in attendance at the place where its educational activities are carried on as a student in a full-time program, taken for credit at such institution, which combines academic instruction with work experience, if such service is an integral part of such program, and such institution has so certified to the employer, except that this subparagraph shall not apply to service performed in a program established for or on behalf of an employer or group of employers, or

(D) service performed in the employ of a hospital, if such service is performed by a patient of such hospital;

(11) service performed in the employ of a foreign government (including service as a consular or other officer or employee or a nondiplomatic representative);

(12) service performed in the employ of an instrumentality wholly owned by a foreign government—

(A) if the service is of a character similar to that performed in foreign countries by employees of the United States Government or of an instrumentality thereof; and

(B) if the Secretary of State shall certify to the Secretary of the Treasury that the foreign government, with respect to whose instrumentality exemption is claimed, grants an equivalent exemption with respect to similar service performed in the foreign country by employees of the United States Government and of instrumentalities thereof;

(13) service performed as a student nurse in the employ of a hospital or a nurses' training school by an individual who is enrolled and is regularly attending classes in a nurses' training school chartered or approved pursuant to State law; and service performed as an intern in the employ of a hospital by an individual who has completed a 4 years' course in a medical school chartered or approved pursuant to State law;

(14) service performed by an individual for a person as an insurance agent or as an insurance solicitor, if all such service performed by such individual for such person is performed for remuneration solely by way of commission;

(15)(A) service performed by an individual under the age of 18 in the delivery or distribution of newspapers or shopping news, not including delivery or distribution to any point for subsequent delivery or distribution;

(B) service performed by an individual in, and at the time of, the sale of newspapers or magazines to ultimate consumers, under an arrangement under which the newspapers or magazines are to be sold by him at a fixed price, his compensation being based on the retention of the excess of such price over the amount at which the newspapers or magazines are charged to him, whether or not he is guaranteed a minimum amount of compensation for such service, or is entitled to be credited with the unsold newspapers or magazines turned back;

(16) service performed in the employ of an international organization;

(17) service performed by an individual in (or as an officer or member of the crew of a vessel while it is engaged in) the catching, taking, harvesting, cultivating, or farming of any kind of fish, shellfish, crustacea, sponges, seaweeds, or other aquatic forms of animal and vegetable life (including service performed by any such individual as an ordinary incident to any such activity), except—

(A) service performed in connection with the catching or taking of salmon or halibut, for commercial purposes, and

(B) service performed on or in connection with a vessel of more than 10 net tons (determined in the manner provided for determining the register tonnage of merchant vessels under the laws of the United States);

(18) service described in section 3121(b)(20);

(19) service which is performed by a nonresident alien individual for the period he is temporarily present in the United States as a nonimmigrant under subparagraph (F), (J), (M), or (Q) of section 101(a)(15) of the Immigration and Nationality Act, as amended (8 U.S.C. 1101(a)(15)(F), (J), (M), or (Q)), and which is performed to carry out the purpose specified in subparagraph (F), (J), (M), or (Q) as the case may be;

(20) service performed by a full time student (as defined in subsection (q)) in the employ of an organized camp

(A) if such camp—

(i) did not operate for more than 7 months in the calendar year and did not operate for more than 7 months in the preceding calendar year, or

(ii) had average gross receipts for any 6 months in the preceding calendar year which were not more than 33⅓ percent of its average gross receipts for the other 6 months in the preceding calendar year; and

(B) if such full time student performed services in the employ of such camp for less than 13 calendar weeks in such calendar year; or

(21) service performed by a person committed to a penal institution.

(d) Included and excluded service.

For purposes of this chapter, if the services performed during one-half or more of any pay period by an employee for the person employing him constitute employment, all the services of such employee for such period shall be deemed to be employment; but if the services performed during more than one-half of any such pay period by an employee for the person employing him do not constitute employment, then none of the services of such employee for such period shall be deemed to be employment. As used in this subsection, the term "pay period" means a period (of not more than 31 consecutive days) for which a payment of remuneration is ordinarily made to the employee by the person employing him. This subsection shall not be applicable with respect to services performed in a pay period by an employee for the person employing him, where any of such service is excepted by subsection (c)(9).

(e) State agency.

For purposes of this chapter, the term "State agency" means any State officer, board, or other authority, designated under a State law to administer the unemployment fund in such State.

(f) Unemployment fund.

For purposes of this chapter, the term "unemployment fund" means a special fund, established under a State law and administered by a State agency, for the payment of compensation. Any sums standing to the account of the State agency in the Unemployment Trust Fund established by section 904 of the Social Security Act, as amended (42 U.S.C. 1104), shall be deemed to be a part of the unemployment fund of the State, and no sums paid out of the Unemployment Trust Fund to such State agency shall cease to be a part of the unemployment fund of the State until expended by such State agency. An unemployment fund shall be deemed to be maintained during a taxable year only if throughout such year, or such portion of the year as the unemployment fund was in existence, no part of the moneys of such fund was expended for any purpose other than the payment of compensation (exclusive of expenses of administration) and for refunds of sums erroneously paid into such fund and refunds paid in accordance with the provisions of section 3305(b); except that—

(1) an amount equal to the amount of employee payments into the unemployment fund of a State may be used in the payments of cash benefits to individuals with respect to their disability, exclusive of expenses of administration;

(2) the amounts specified by section 903(c)(2) or 903(d)(4) of the Social Security Act may, subject to the conditions prescribed in such section, be used for expenses incurred by the State for administration of its unemployment compensation law and public employment offices,

(3) nothing in this subsection shall be construed to prohibit deducting any amount from unemployment compensation otherwise payable to an individual and using the amount so deducted to pay for health insurance, or the withholding of Federal, State, or local individual income tax, if the individual elected to have such deduction made and such deduction was made under a program approved by the Secretary of Labor;

(4) amounts may be deducted from unemployment benefits and used to repay overpayments as provided in section 303(g) of the Social Security Act; and

(5) amounts may be withdrawn for the payment of short-time compensation under a plan approved by the Secretary of Labor.

([6]) amounts may be withdrawn for the payment of allowances under a self-employment assistance program (as defined in subsection (t)).

(g) Contributions.

For purposes of this chapter, the term "contributions" means payments required by a State law to be made into an unemployment fund by any person on account of having individuals in his employ, to the extent that such payments are made by him without being deducted or deductible from the remuneration of individuals in his employ.

(h) Compensation.

For purposes of this chapter, the term "compensation" means cash benefits payable to individuals with respect to their unemployment.

(i) Employee.

For purposes of this chapter, the term "employee" has the meaning assigned to such term by section 3121(d), except that paragraph (4) and subparagraphs (B) and (C) of paragraph (3) shall not apply.

(j) State, United States, and American employer.

For purposes of this chapter—

(1) **State.** The term "State" includes the District of Columbia, the Commonwealth of Puerto Rico, and the Virgin Islands.

(2) **United States.** The term "United States" when used in a geographical sense includes the States, the District of Columbia, the Commonwealth of Puerto Rico, and the Virgin Islands.

(3) **American employer.** The term "American employer" means a person who is—

(A) an individual who is a resident of the United States,

(B) a partnership, if two-thirds or more of the partners are residents of the United States,

(C) a trust, if all of the trustees are residents of the United States, or

(D) a corporation organized under the laws of the United States or of any State.

An individual who is a citizen of the Commonwealth of Puerto Rico or the Virgin Islands (but not otherwise a citizen of the United States) shall be considered, for purposes of this section, as a citizen of the United States.

(k) Agricultural labor.

For purposes of this chapter, the term "agricultural labor" has the meaning assigned to such term by subsection (g) of section 3121, except that for purposes of this chapter subparagraph (B) of paragraph (4) of such subsection (g) shall be treated as reading:

"(B) in the employ of a group of operators of farms (or a cooperative organization of which such operators are members) in the performance of service described in subparagraph (A), but only if such operators produced more than one-half of the commodity with respect to which such service is performed;".

(l) Repealed.

(m) American vessel and aircraft.

For purposes of this chapter, the term "American vessel" means any vessel documented or numbered under the laws of the United States; and includes any vessel which is neither documented or numbered under the laws of the United States nor documented under the laws of any foreign country, if its crew is employed solely by one or more citizens or residents of the United States or corporations organized under the laws of the United States or of any State; and the term "American aircraft" means an aircraft registered under the laws of the United States.

(n) Vessels operated by general agents of United States.

Notwithstanding the provisions of subsection (c)(6), service performed by officers and members of the crew of a vessel which would otherwise be included as employment under subsection (c) shall not be excluded by reason of the fact that it is performed on or in connection with an American vessel—

(1) owned by or bareboat chartered to the United States and

(2) whose business is conducted by a general agent of the Secretary of Commerce.

For purposes of this chapter, each such general agent shall be considered a legal entity in his capacity as such general agent, separate and distinct from his identity as a person employing individuals on his own account, and the officers and members of the crew of such an American vessel whose business is conducted by a general agent of the Secretary of Commerce shall be deemed to be performing services for such general agent rather than the United States. Each such general agent who in his capacity as such is an employer within the meaning of subsection (a) shall be subject to all the requirements imposed upon an employer under this chapter with respect to service which constitutes employment by reason of this subsection.

(o) Special rule in case of certain agricultural workers.

(1) Crew leaders who are registered or provide specialized agricultural labor. For purposes of this chapter, any individual who is a member of a crew furnished by a crew leader to perform agricultural labor for any other person shall be treated as an employee of such crew leader—
  (A) if—
    (i) such crew leader holds a valid certificate of registration under the Migrant and Seasonal Agricultural Worker Protection Act; or
    (ii) substantially all the members of such crew operate or maintain tractors, mechanized harvesting or crop-dusting equipment, or any other mechanized equipment, which is provided by such crew leader; and
  (B) if such individual is not an employee of such other person within the meaning of subsection (a).

(2) Other crew leaders. For purposes of this chapter, in the case of any individual who is furnished by a crew leader to perform agricultural labor for any other person and who is not treated as an employee of such crew leader under paragraph (1)—
  (A) such other person and not the crew leader shall be treated as the employer of such individual; and
  (B) such other person shall be treated as having paid cash remuneration to such individual in an amount equal to the amount of cash remuneration paid to such individual by the crew leader (either on his behalf or on behalf of such other person) for the agricultural labor performed for such other person.

(3) Crew leader. For purposes of this subsection, the term "crew leader" means an individual who—
  (A) furnishes individuals to perform agricultural labor for any other person,
  (B) pays (either on his behalf or on behalf of such other person) the individuals so furnished by him for the agricultural labor performed by them, and
  (C) has not entered into a written agreement with such other person under which such individual is designated as an employee of such other person.

(p) Concurrent employment by two or more employers.

For purposes of sections 3301, 3302, and 3306(b)(1), if two or more related corporations concurrently employ the same individual and compensate such individual through a common paymaster which is one of such corporations, each such corporation shall be considered to have paid as remuneration to such individual only the amounts actually disbursed by it to such individual and shall not be considered to have paid as remuneration to such individual amounts actually disbursed to such individual by another of such corporations.

(q) Full time student.

For purposes of subsection (c)(20), an individual shall be treated as a full time student for any period
  (1) during which the individual is enrolled as a full time student at an educational institution, or
  (2) which is between academic years or terms if—
    (A) the individual was enrolled as a full time student at an educational institution for the immediately preceding academic year or term, and
    (B) there is a reasonable assurance that the individual will be so enrolled for the immediately succeeding academic year or term after the period described in subparagraph (A).

(r) Treatment of certain deferred compensation and salary reduction arrangements.

(1) Certain employer contributions treated as wages. Nothing in any paragraph of subsection (b) (other than paragraph (1)) shall exclude from the term "wages"—
  (A) any employer contribution under a qualified cash or deferred arrangement (as defined in section 401(k)) to the extent not included in gross income by reason of section 402(e)(3), or
  (B) any amount treated as an employer contribution under section 414(h)(2) where the pickup referred to in such section is pursuant to a salary reduction agreement (whether evidenced by a written instrument or otherwise).

(2) Treatment of certain nonqualified deferred compensation plans.
  (A) In general. Any amount deferred under a nonqualified deferred compensation plan shall be taken into account for purposes of this chapter as of the later of—
    (i) when the services are performed, or
    (ii) when there is no substantial risk of forfeiture of the rights to such amount.
  (B) Taxed only once. Any amount taken into account as wages by reason of subparagraph (A) (and the income attributable thereto) shall not thereafter be treated as wages for purposes of this chapter.
  (C) Nonqualified deferred compensation plan. For purposes of this paragraph, the term "nonqualified deferred compensation plan" means any plan or other arrangement for deferral of compensation other than a plan described in subsection (b)(5).

(s) Tips treated as wages.

For purposes of this chapter, the term "wages" includes tips which are—
  (1) received while performing services which constitute employment, and
  (2) included in a written statement furnished to the employer pursuant to section 6053(a).

(t) Self-employment assistance program.

For the purposes of this chapter, the term "self-employment assistance program" means a program under which—
  (1) individuals who meet the requirements described in paragraph (3) are eligible to receive an allowance in lieu of regular unemployment compensation under the State law for the purpose of assisting such individuals in establishing a business and becoming self-employed;
  (2) the allowance payable to individuals pursuant to paragraph (1) is payable in the same amount, at the same interval, on the same terms, and subject to the same conditions, as regular unemployment compensation under the State law, except that—
    (A) State requirements relating to availability for work, active search for work, and refusal to accept work are not applicable to such individuals;
    (B) State requirements relating to disqualifying income are not applicable to income earned from self-employment by such individuals; and
    (C) such individuals are considered to be unemployed for the purposes of Federal and State laws applicable to unemployment compensation,
as long as such individuals meet the requirements applicable under this subsection;
  (3) individuals may receive the allowance described in paragraph (1) if such individuals—

(A) are eligible to receive regular unemployment compensation under the State law, or would be eligible to receive such compensation except for the requirements described in subparagraph (A) or (B) of paragraph (2);
(B) are identified pursuant to a State worker profiling system as individuals likely to exhaust regular unemployment compensation; and
(C) are participating in self-employment assistance activities which—
 (i) include entrepreneurial training, business counseling, and technical assistance; and
 (ii) are approved by the State agency; and
(D) are actively engaged on a full-time basis in activities (which may include training) relating to the establishment of a business and becoming self-employed;
(4) the aggregate number of individuals receiving the allowance under the program does not at any time exceed 5 percent of the number of individuals receiving regular unemployment compensation under the State law at such time;
(5) the program does not result in any cost to the Unemployment Trust Fund (established by section 904(a) of the Social Security Act) in excess of the cost that would be incurred by such State and charged to such Fund if the State had not participated in such program; and
(6) the program meets such other requirements as the Secretary of Labor determines to be appropriate.

(u) Indian tribe.

For purposes of this chapter, the term "Indian tribe" has the meaning given to such term by section 4(e) of the Indian Self-Determination and Education Assistance Act (25 U.S.C. 450b(e)), and includes any subdivision, subsidiary, or business enterprise wholly owned by such an Indian tribe.

In 2008, P.L. 110-245, Sec. 115(b), deleted "or" at the end of para. (b)(18), substituted "; or" for the period at the end of para. (b)(19), and added para. (b)(20), effective for tax. yrs. begin. after 12/31/2007 [as if included in section 5 of the Mortgage Forgiveness Debt Relief Act of 2007 P.L. 110-142].

In 2004, P.L. 108-375, Sec. 585(b)(2)(C), substituted "134(b)(4), or 134(b)(5)" for "or 134(b)(4)" in para. (b)(13), effective for travel benefits provided after 10/28/2004.

—P.L. 108-357, Sec. 251(a)(3), deleted "or" at the end of para. (b)(17), substituted "; or" for the period at the end of para. (b)(18), and added para. (b)(19), effective for stock acquired pursuant to options exercised after 10/22/2004.

—P.L. 108-357, Sec. 320(b)(3), added "108(f)(4)," after "74(c)," in para. (b)(16), effective for amounts received by an individual in tax. yrs. begin. after 12/31/2003.

In 2003, P.L. 108-173, Sec. 1201(d)(2)(B), deleted "or" at the end of para. (b)(16), substituted "; or" for the period at the end of para. (b)(17), and added para. (b)(18), effective for tax. yrs. begin. after 12/31/2003.

—P.L. 108-121, Sec. 106(b)(3), substituted ", 129, or 134(b)(4)" for "or 129" in para. (b)(13), effective for tax. yrs. begin. after 12/31/2002. Sec. 106(d) of this Act, provides:

"(d) No inference. No inference may be drawn from the amendments made by this section with respect to the tax treatment of any amounts under the program described in section 134(b)(4) of the Internal Revenue Code of 1986 (as added by this section) for any taxable year beginning before January 1, 2003."

In 2002, P.L. 107-147, Sec. 209(d)(1), added "or 903(d)(4)" after "section 903(c)(2)" in para. (f)(2), effective 3/9/2002.

—P.L. 107-147, Sec. 209(e), of this Act, provides:

"(e) Regulations. The Secretary of Labor may prescribe any operating instructions or regulations necessary to carry out this section and the amendments made by this section."

In 2000, P.L. 106-554, Sec. 1(a)(7), [which enacted into law Sec. 166(a)(1) of P.L. 106-554] added "or in the employ of an Indian tribe," after "subdivision thereof," in para. (b)(7) . . . Sec. 1(a)(7), [which enacted into law Sec. 166(a)(2) of P.L. 106-554] added "or Indian tribes" after "political subdivisions" in para. (c)(7) . . . Sec. 1(a)(7), [which enacted into law Sec. 166(d) of P.L. 106-554] added subsec. (u), effective for service performed on or after 12/21/2000. Sec. 166(e)(2) of this Act provides:

"(2) Transition rule. For purposes of the Federal Unemployment Tax Act, service performed in the employ of an Indian tribe (as defined in section 3306(u) of the Internal Revenue Code of 1986 (as added by this section)) shall not be treated as employment (within the meaning of section 3306 of such Code) if—

"(A) it is service which is performed before the date of the enactment of this Act and with respect to which the tax imposed under the Federal Unemployment Tax Act has not been paid, and

"(B) such Indian tribe reimburses a State unemployment fund for unemployment benefits paid for service attributable to such tribe for such period."

In 1997, P.L. 105-306, Sec. 3(a), deleted Sec. 507(e)(2) of P. L. 103-182 . . . Sec. 3(b)(1), substituted "Effective date" for "Effective date; sunset" in the heading of Sec. 507(e) of P. L. 103-182 [reproduced below] . . . Sec. 3(b)(2), redesignated Sec. 507(e)(1) of P. L. 103-182 as Sec. 507(e) of P. L. 103-182 [reproduced below], effective 10/28/98.

Prior to deletion, Sec. 507(e)(2) of P. L. 103-182 read as follows:

"(2) Sunset. The authority provided by this section, and the amendments made by this section shall terminate 5 years after the date of the enactment of this Act."

—P.L. 105-33, Sec. 5406(a)(1), deleted "or" at the end of para. (c)(19) . . . Sec. 5406(a)(2), substituted "; or" for the period at the end of para. (c)(20) . . . Sec. 5406(a)(3), added para. (c)(21), effective for service performed after 1/1/94.

In 1996, P.L. 104-188, Sec. 1203(a), deleted "before January 1, 1995," after "labor performed" in subpara. (c)(1)(B), effective for services performed after 12/31/94.

—P.L. 104-188, Sec. 1421(b)(8)(C), deleted "or" at the end of subpara. (b)(5)(F), added "or" to the end of subpara. (b)(5)(G), and added subpara. (b)(5)(H), effective for tax. yrs. begin. after 12/31/96.

—P.L. 104-188, Sec. 1704(t)(10), added a period to the end of subsec. (k), effective 8/20/96.

—P.L. 104-191, Sec. 301(c)(2)(B), deleted "or" at the end of para. (b)(15), substituted "; or" for the period at the end of para. (b)(16), and added para. (b)(17), effective for tax. yrs. begin. after 12/31/96.

In 1994, P.L. 103-465, Sec. 702(c)(2), redesignated paras. (f)(3) and (4) as paras. (f)(4) and (5), and added new para. (f)(3), effective for payments made after 12/31/96.

—P.L. 103-296, Sec. 320(a)(1)(E), substituted "(J), (M), or (Q)" for "(J), or (M)" each place it appeared in para. (c)(19), effective with the calendar quarter following 8/15/94.

In 1993, P.L. 103-182, Sec. 507(a), added subsec. (t) . . . Sec. 507(b)(2)(A), substituted a semicolon for "; and" in para. (f)(3) . . . Sec. 507(b)(2)(B), substituted "; and" for the period in para. (f)(4) . . . Sec. 507(b)(2)(C), added para. (f)(5), effective [as amended by Sec. 3 of P. L. 105-306, see above] 12/8/93.

In 1992, P.L. 102-318, Sec. 303(a), substituted "January 1, 1995" for "January 1, 1993" in subpara. (c)(1)(B) . . . Sec. 401(a)(2), deleted "and" at the end of para. (f)(2), substituted "; and" for the period at the end of para. (f)(3) and added para. (f)(4), effective 7/3/92.

—P.L. 102-318, Sec. 521(b)(35), substituted "section 402(e)(3)" for "section 402(a)(8)" in subpara. (r)(1)(A), effective for distributions after 12/31/92. For special rule, see Sec. 521(e)(2) of this Act which reads as follows:

"(2) Special rule for partial distributions. For purposes of section 402(a)(5)(D)(i)(II) of the Internal Revenue Code of 1986 (as in effect before the amendments made by this section), a distribution before January 1, 1993, which is made before or at the same time as a series of periodic payments shall not be treated as one of such series if it is not substantially equal in amount to other payments in such series."

In 1989, P.L. 101-140, Sec. 203(a)(2), repealed as if not enacted Sec. 1011B(a)(22)(C) of P. L. 100-647 which added subsec. (t).

—P.L. 101-136, Sec. 528, provided that "no monies appropriated by this Act [for the fiscal year ending September 30, '90] may be used to implement or enforce section 1151 of the Tax Reform Act of '86 [P. L. 99-514] or the amendments made by such section." [See below]

In 1988, P.L. 100-647, Sec. 1001(d)(2)(C)(iii), substituted "(F), (J) or (M)" for "(F) or (J)" each place it appeared in para. (c)(19), effective for tax. yrs. begin. after 12/31/86, but only in the case of scholarships and fellowships granted after 8/16/86.

—P.L. 100-647, Sec. 1001(g)(4)(B)(ii), substituted "section 217 (determined without regard to section 274(n))" for "section 217" in para. (b)(9), effective for tax. yrs. begin. after 12/31/86.

—P.L. 100-647, Sec. 1011B(a)(23)(A), added "if such payment would not be treated as wages without regard to such plan and it is reasonable to believe that (if section 125 applied for purposes of this section) section 125 would not treat any wages as constructively received" after "section 125)" in subpara. (b)(5)(G), effective as provided in Sec. 1151(k)(1) of P. L. 99-514 [reproduced below].

—P.L. 100-647, Sec. 1018(u)(50), added a comma after "1988" in Sec. 13303(a) of P. L. 99-272, [reproduced below] part of the effective date for changes made by Sec. 13303(a) of P. L. 99-272.

—P.L. 100-647, Sec. 8016(a)(3)(B), substituted "paragraph (4) and subparagraphs (B) and (C) of paragraph (3)" for "paragraph (3) and subparagraphs (B) and (C) of paragraph (4)" in subsec. (i), effective 11/10/88. Sec. 8016(b)(2) of this Act provides

"(2) Any amendment made by this section to a provision of a particular Public Law which is referred to by its number, or to a provision of the Social Security Act or the Internal Revenue Code of 1986 as added or amended by a provision of a particular Public Law which is so referred to, shall be effective as though it had been included or reflected in the relevant provisions of that Public Law at the time of its enactment."

In 1986, P.L. 99-595, substituted "before January 1, 1993," for "before January 1, 1988," in subpara. (c)(1)(B), effective 10/31/86.

—P.L. 99-514, Sec. 122(e)(3), substituted "74(c), 117, or" for "117 or" in para. (b)(16), effective for prizes and awards granted after 12/31/86.

—P.L. 99-514, Sec. 1108(g)(8), amended subpara. (b)(5)(C), effective for yrs. begin. after 12/31/86.

Employment taxes   Code Sec. 3306

Prior to amendment, subpara. (b)(5)(C) read as follows:

"(C) under a simplified employee pension if, at the time of the payment, it is reasonable to believe that the employee will be entitled to a deduction under section 219(b)(2) for such payment,"

— P.L. 99-514, Sec. 1151(d)(2)(B), deleted "or" at the end of subpara. (b)(5)(E), added "or" at the end of subpara. (b)(5)(F), and added subpara. (b)(5)(G), effective for tax yrs. begin. after 12/31/83.

— P.L. 99-514, Sec. 1705, provides:

"Sec. 1705. Applicability of unemployment compensation tax to certain services performed for certain Indian tribal governments.

"(a) In general.

"For purposes of the Federal Unemployment Tax Act, service performed in the employ of a qualified Indian tribal government shall not be treated as employment (within the meaning of section 3306 of such Act) if it is service —

"(1) which is performed —

"(A) before, on, or after the date of the enactment of this Act, but before January 1, 1988, and

"(B) during a period in which the Indian tribal government is not covered by a State unemployment compensation program, and

"(2) with respect to which the tax imposed under the Federal Unemployment Tax Act has not been paid.

"(b) Definition.

"For purposes of this section, the term 'qualified Indian tribal government' means an Indian tribal government the service for which is not covered by a State unemployment compensation program on June 11, 1986."

— P.L. 99-514, Sec. 1884(3), substituted "Migrant and Seasonal Agricultural Worker Protection Act" for "Farm Labor Contractor Registration Act of 1963" in clause (o)(1)(A)(i) . . . Sec. 1899A(44), substituted "workmen's compensation" for "workman's compensation" in subpara. (b)(2)(A) . . . Sec. 1899A(45), substituted a semicolon for the comma at the end of para. (b)(13), effective 10/22/86.

— P.L. 99-509, Sec. 9002(b)(2)(B), substituted "paragraph (3) and subparagraphs (B) and (C) of paragraph (4)" for "subparagraphs (B) and (C) of paragraph (3)", effective as provided in Sec. 9002(d) of this Act reproduced in note following Code Sec. 3126.

— P.L. 99-272, Sec. 12401(b)(2)(A), deleted "and" at the end of para. (f)(1) . . . Sec. 12401(b)(2)(B), substituted ", and" for the period at the end of para. (f)(2) . . . Sec. 12401(b)(2)(C), added para. (f)(3), effective for recoveries made on or after 4/7/86 and for overpayments made before, on, or after 4/7/86.

— P.L. 99-272, Sec. 13303(a), [as amended by Sec. 1018(u)(50) of P. L. 100-647, see above]. substituted "January 1, 1988," for "January 1, 1986" in subpara. (c)(1)(B), effective 4/7/86.

— P.L. 99-272, Sec. 13303(b), amended the effective date for amendments made by Sec. 276(b)(1) and (2) of P. L. 97-248 to also apply to remuneration paid after 9/19/85 [see below].

— P.L. 99-272, Sec. 13303(c), amended Sec. 822(b) of P. L. 97-34, [as amended by Sec. 203 of P. L. 97-362 and Sec. 1074 of P. L. 98-369, above] the effective date for changes made by Sec. 822(a) of P. L. 97-34, to read "[t]he amendments made by subsection (a) [Sec. 822(a)] shall apply to remuneration paid after December 31, 1980" for "[t]he amendments made by subsection (a) [Sec. 822(a)] shall apply to remuneration paid after December 31, 1980 and before January 1, 1985" (see below).

In 1984, P.L. 98-369, Sec. 491(d)(37), deleted subpara. (b)(5)(C) and redesignated subparas. (b)(5)(D) through (b)(5)(G) as (b)(5)(C) through (b)(5)(F), effective for obligations issued after 12/31/83.

Prior to deletion, subpara. (b)(5)(C) read as follows:

"(C) under or to a bond purchase plan which, at the time of such payment, is a qualified bond purchase plan described in section 405(a),"

— P.L. 98-369, Sec. 531(d)(3)(A), substituted "all remuneration (including benefits) paid in any medium" for "all remuneration paid in any medium" in subsec. (b) . . . Sec. 531(d)(3)(B), deleted "or" at the end of para. (b)(14), substituted "; or" for the period at the end of (b)(15) and added para. (b)(16), effective 1/1/85.

— P.L. 98-369, Sec. 1073(a), added subsec. (s), effective 1/1/86, except as provided in Sec. 1073(b)(2) of the Act which reads as follows:

"(2) Exception for certain states. — In the case of any State the legislature of which —

"(A) did not meet in a regular session which begins during 1984 and after the date of the enactment of this Act, and

"(B) did not meet in a session which began before the date of the enactment of this Act and remained in session for at least 25 calendar days after such date of enactment,

the amendment made by subsection (a) shall take effect on January 1, 1987."

— P.L. 98-369, Sec. 1074, amended Sec. 822(b) of P. L. 97-34, the effective date for changes made by Sec. 822(a) of P. L. 97-34 (see below), by substituting "and before January 1, 1985" for "and before January 1, 1983".

— P.L. 98-369, Sec. 2661(o)(4), amended subpara. (r)(1)(B), effective 1/1/85.

Prior to amendment, subpara. (r)(1)(B) read as follows:

"(B) any amount treated as an employer contribution under section 414(h)(2)."

— P.L. 98-369, Sec. 2662(f)(2)(B), amended Sec. 324(d)(2) of P. L.98-21, the effective date for changes made by Sec. 324(b) of P. L. 98-21 by adding the last sentence (reproduced below).

— P.L. 98-369, Sec. 2662(f)(2)(C), amended Sec. 324(d)(4) of P. L. 98-21, part of the effective date for changes made by Sec. 324 of P. L. 98-21, by adding the last sentence (reproduced below).

— P.L. 98-369, Sec. 2662(g), amended Sec. 327(d) of P. L. 98-21, the effective date for changes made by Sec. 327 of P. L. 98-21 (reproduced below).

Prior to amendment Sec. 327(d) of P. L. 98-21read as follows:

"(d)(1) Except as provided in paragraph (2), the amendments made by subsections (a) and (b) [Sec. 327] shall apply to remuneration paid after December 31, 1983.

"(2) The amendments made by subsection (c) [Sec. 327] shall apply to remuneration paid after December 31, 1984."

In 1983, P.L. 98-135, Sec. 201(a), deleted the period at the end of para. (b)(13), substituted "; or" for the period at the end of para. (b)(14), and added para. (b)(15), effective for remuneration paid after 10/24/83.

— P.L. 98-135, Sec. 202, substituted "January 1, 1986" for "January 1, 1984" in subpara. (c)(1)(B), effective 10/24/83.

— P.L. 98-21, Sec. 324(b)(1), added subsec. (r) . . . Sec. 324(b)(2)(A), deleted "or" from the end of subpara. (b)(5)(C) . . . Sec. 324(b)(2)(B), substituted a comma for the semicolon at the end of subpara. (b)(5)(D) . . . Sec. 324(b)(2)(C), added subparas. (b)(5)(E), (b)(5)(F) and (b)(5)(G) . . . Sec. 324(b)(3)(A), deleted subpara. (b)(2)(A) and redesignated subparas. (b)(2)(B), (b)(2)(C) and (b)(2)(D) as subparas. (b)(2)(A), (b)(2)(B) and (b)(2)(C) . . . Sec. 324(b)(3)(B), deleted paras. (b)(3) and (b)(8) . . . Sec. 324(b)(3)(C)(i), added "or" after "death," in subpara. (b)(10)(A) . . . Sec. 324(b)(3)(C)(ii), deleted "or (iii) retirement after attaining an age specified in the plan referred to in subparagraph (B) or in a pension plan of the employer," in subpara. (b)(10)(A) . . . Sec. 324(b)(4)(A), amended subpara. (b)(2)(A) [as redesignated by Sec. 324(b)(3)(A), see above] . . . Sec. 324(b)(4)(B), added the last sentence to subsec. (b), effective as provided in Sec. 324(d)(2), (d)(3) and (d)(4) of this Act which read as follows:

"(2) Except as otherwise provided in this subsection, the amendments made by subsection (b) [Sec. 324(b)] shall apply to remuneration paid after December 31, 1984. For purposes of applying such amendments to remuneration paid after December 31, 1984, which would have been taken into account before January 1, 1985, if such amendments had applied to periods before January 1, 1985, such remuneration shall be taken into account when paid (or, at the election of the payor, at the time which would be appropriate if such amendments had applied).

"(3) The amendments made by this section shall not apply to employer contributions made during 1984 and attributable to services performed during 1983 under a qualified cash or deferred arrangement (as defined in section 401(k) of the Internal Revenue Code of 1954) if, under the terms of such arrangement as in effect on March 24, 1983 —

"(A) the employee makes an election with respect to such contribution before January 1, 1984, and

"(B) the employer identifies the amount of such contribution before January 1, 1984.

In the case of the amendments made by subsection (b), the preceding sentence shall be applied by substituting '1985' for '1984' each place it appears and by substituting 'during 1984' for 'during 1983'.

"(4) In the case of an agreement in existence on March 24, 1983, between a nonqualified deferred compensation plan (as defined in section 3121(v)(2)(C) of the Internal Revenue Code of 1954, as added by this section) and an individual —

"(A) the amendments made by this section (other than subsection (b)) shall apply with respect to services performed by such individual after December 31, 1983, and

"(B) the amendments made by subsection (b) shall apply with respect to services performed by such individual after December 31, 1984.

The preceding sentence shall not apply in the case of a plan to which section 457(a) of such Code applies. For purposes of this paragraph, any plan or agreement to make payments described in paragraph (2), (3), or (13)(A)(iii) of section 3121(a) of such Code (as in effect on the day before the date of the enactment of this Act) shall be treated as a nonqualified deferred compensation plan."

Prior to deletion, subpara. (b)(2)(A) read as follows:

"(A) retirement, or"

Prior to deletion, para. (b)(3) read as follows:

"(3) any payment made to an employee (including any amount paid by an employer for insurance or annuities, or into a fund, to provide for any such payment) on account of retirement;"

Prior to deletion, para. (b)(8) read as follows:

"(8) any payment (other than vacation or sick pay) made to an employee after the month in which he attains the age of 65, if he did not work for the employer in the period for which such payment is made;"

Prior to amendment, subpara. (b)(2)(A) [as redesignated by Sec. 324(b)(3)(A), see above] read as follows:

"(A) sickness or accident disability, or"

— P.L. 98-21, Sec. 324(b)(4)(C), provides:

"(C) Rules similar to the rules of subsections (d) and (e) of section 3 of the Act entitled 'An Act to amend the Omnibus Reconciliation Act of 1981 to restore minimum benefits under the Social Security Act' (P. L. 97-123), approved December 29, 1981, shall apply in the administration of section 3306(b)(2)(A) of such Code (as amended by subparagraph (A))."

— P.L. 98-21, Sec. 327(c)(1), deleted "or" at the end of para. (b)(12) . . . Sec. 327(c)(2), substituted ", or" for the period at the end of para. (b)(13) . . . Sec. 327(c)(3), added para. (b)(14), effective for remuneration paid after 12/31/84.

— P.L. 98-21, Sec. 327(c)(4), added the last sentence to subsec. (b), effective as provided in Sec. 327(d)(2) of this Act of this Act which reads as follows:

"(2) The amendments made by subsection (b) and subsection (c)(4) [Sec. 327] shall apply to remuneration (other than amounts excluded under section 119 of the Internal Revenue Code of 1954) paid after March 4, 1983, and to any such remuneration paid on or before such date which the employer treated as wages when paid."

— P.L. 98-21, Sec. 328(c), substituted "section 219(b)(2)" for "section 219" in subpara. (b)(5)(D), effective for remuneration paid after 12/31/84.

3,137

In 1982, P.L. 97-362, Sec. 203, amended Sec. 822(b) of P. L. 97-34, the effective date for changes made by Sec. 822(a) of P. L. 97-34 (see below), by substituting "after December 31, 1980, and before January 1, 1983" for "during 1981".

—P.L. 97-248, Sec. 271(a), substituted "$7,000" for "$6,000" each place it appeared in para. (b)(1), effective for remuneration paid after 12/31/82.

—P.L. 97-248, Sec. 276(a)(1), deleted "under the age of 22" after "by an individual" in subpara. (c)(10)(C), effective for services rendered after 9/3/82.

—P.L. 97-248, Sec. 276(b)(1)(A), deleted "or" at the end of para. (c)(18) ... Sec. 276(b)(1)(B), substituted "; or" for the period at the end of para. (c)(19) ... Sec. 276(b)(1)(C), added para. (c)(20) ... Sec. 276(b)(2), added subsec. (q), effective for remuneration paid after 12/31/82 and before 1/1/84 and for remuneration paid after 9/19/85 [see Sec. 13303(b) of P. L. 99-272, above].

—P.L. 97-248, Sec. 277, substituted "January 1, 1984" for "January 1, 1982" in subpara. (c)(1)(B), effective 9/3/82.

In 1981, P.L. 97-34, Sec. 124(e)(2), substituted "section 127 or 129" for "section 127" in para. (b)(13), effective for remuneration paid after 12/31/81.

—P.L. 97-34, Sec. 822(a)(1), (2), and (3), [as amended by Sec. 203 of P. L. 97-362, and Sec. 1074 of P. L. 98-369 and Sec. 13303(c) of P. L. 99-272, see above] deleted "or" at the end of para. (c)(17), redesignated para. (c)(18) as (c)(19), and added new para. (c)(18), effective for remuneration paid after 12/31/80.

In 1980, P.L. 96-499, Sec. 1141(b), amended para. (b)(6), effective with respect to remuneration paid after 12/31/80. Sec. 1141(c)(2) provides:

"(2) Exception for state and local governments.—

"(A) The amendments made by this section (insofar as they affect the application of section 218 of the Social Security Act) shall not apply to any payment made before January 1, 1984, by any governmental unit for positions of any kind for which all or a substantial portion of the social security employee taxes were paid by such governmental unit (without deduction from the remuneration of the employee) under the practices of such governmental unit in effect on October 1, 1980.

"(B) For purposes of subparagraph (A), the term 'social security employee taxes' means the amount required to be paid under section 218 of the Social Security Act as the equivalent of the taxes imposed by section 3101 of the Internal Revenue Code of 1954.

"(C) For purposes of subparagraph (A), the term 'Governmental unit' means a State or political subdivision thereof within the meaning of section 218 of the Social Security Act."

Prior to amendment, para. (b)(6) read as follows:

"(6) the payment by an employer (without deduction from the remuneration of the employee)—

"(A) of the tax imposed upon an employee under section 3101 (or the corresponding section of prior law), or

"(B) of any payment required from an employee under a State unemployment compensation law;"

—P.L. 96-222, Sec. 101(a)(10)(B)(ii), deleted "or" at the end of subpara. (b)(5)(B) and substituted "; or" for the semicolon at the end of subpara. (b)(5)(C) and added subpara. (b)(5)(D) effective for payments made on or after 1/1/79.

In 1979, P.L. 96-84, Sec. 4(a), substituted "January 1, 1982" for "January 1, 1980" in subpara. (c)(1)(B) and substituted "including labor performed by" for "not taking into account labor performed before January 1, 1980, by" each place it appeared in subpara. (c)(1)(A), effective for remuneration paid, and for services rendered after 12/31/79.

In 1978, P.L. 95-600, Sec. 164(b)(2)(A), deleted "or" at the end of para. (b)(11) ... Sec. 164(b)(2)(B), substituted "; or" for the period at the end of para. (b)(12) ... Sec. 164(b)(2)(C), added para. (b)(13), effective for tax. yrs. begin. after 12/31/78.

—P.L. 95-472, Sec. 3(a)(1), deleted "or" at the end of para. (b)(10) ... Sec. 3(a)(2), substituted ";or" for the period at the end of para. (b)(11) ... Sec. 3(a)(3), added para. (b)(12), effective for tax. yrs. begin. after 12/31/76.

In 1977, P.L. 95-216, Sec. 314(b), added subsec. (p), effective for wages paid after 12/31/78.

In 1976, P.L. 94-566, Sec. 111(a), deleted "or" at the end of para. (b)(9), substituted ";or" for the period at the end of para. (b)(10), and added para. (b)(11) ... Sec. 111(b), amended para. (c)(1) ... Sec. 112(a), added subsec. (o) ... Sec. 113(a), amended para. (c)(2) ... Sec. 114(a), amended subsec. (a), effective for remuneration paid, and for services rendered after 12/31/77.

Prior to amendment, para. (c)(1) read as follows:

"(1) agricultural labor (as defined in subsection (k));"

Prior to amendment, para. (c)(2) read as follows:

"(2) domestic service in a private home, local college club, or local chapter of a college fraternity or sorority;"

Prior to amendment, subsec. (a) read as follows:

"(a) Employer.

"For purposes of this chapter, the term 'employer' means, with respect to any calendar year, any person who—

"(1) during any calendar quarter in the calendar year or the preceding calendar year paid wages of $1,500 or more, or

"(2) on each of some 20 days during the calendar year or during the preceding calendar year, each day being in a different calendar week, employed at least one individual in employment for some portion of the day."

—P.L. 94-566, Sec. 116(b)(1), deleted "or in the Virgin Islands", following "to unemployment compensation" in subsec. (c). ... Sec. 116(b)(2), amended subsec. (j), effective for remuneration paid after December 31 of the year in which the Secretary of Labor approves for the first time an unemployment compensation law submitted to him from the Virgin Islands for approval, for services performed for services after such December 31.

Prior to amendment, subsec. (j) read as follows:

"(j) State, United States, and citizen.

"For purposes of this chapter—

"(1) State. The term 'State' includes the District of Columbia and the Commonwealth of Puerto Rico.

"(2) United States. The term 'United States' when used in a geographical sense includes the States, the District of Columbia, and the Commonwealth of Puerto Rico."

An individual who is a citizen of the Commonwealth of Puerto Rico (but not otherwise a citizen of the United States) shall be considered for purposes of this section, as a citizen of the United States.

"(3) American employer. The term 'American employer' means a person who is—

"(A) an individual who is a resident of the United States,

"(B) a partnership, if two-thirds or more of the partners are residents of the United States,

"(C) a trust, if all of the trustees are residents of the United States, or

"(D) a corporation organized under the laws of the United States or of any State."

—P.L. 94-566, Sec. 211(a), substituted "$6,000" for "$4,200" each place it appeared in para. (b)(1), effective for remuneration paid after 12/31/77.

—P.L. 94-455, Sec. 1903(a)(16)(A), deleted "52 Stat. 1094, 1095;" after the parenthesis in para. (c)(9) ... Sec. 1903(a)(16)(B), added "(8 U.S.C. 1101(a)(15)(F) or (J))" following "the Immigration and Nationality Act, as amended" in para. (c)(18) ... Sec. 1903(a)(16)(C), deleted "49 Stat. 1104, 1105;" after the parenthesis in subsec. (f) ... Sec. 1903(a)(16)(D), deleted "on or after July 1, 1953," after "service performed" in subsec. (n), effective for wages paid after 12/31/76.

—P.L. 94-455, Sec. 1903(b)(13)(C), substituted "to the Secretary of the Treasury" for "to the Secretary" in subpara. (c)(12)(B), effective 2/1/77.

In 1970, P.L. 91-373, Sec. 101(a), amended subsec. (a), effective for calendar years begin. after 12/31/71.

Prior to amendment, subsec. (a) read as follows:

"For purposes of this chapter, the term 'employer' does not include any person unless on each of some 20 days during the taxable year or during the preceding taxable year, each day being in a different calendar week, the total number of individuals who were employed by him in employment for some portion of the day (whether or not at the same moment of time) was 4 or more."

—P.L. 91-373, Sec. 102(a), amended subsec. (i) ... Sec. 103(a), amended subsec. (k), effective. for remuneration paid, and services rendered after 12/31/71.

Prior to amendment, subsec. (i) read as follows:

"(i) Employee.

"For purposes of this chapter, the term 'employee' includes an officer of a corporation, but such term does not include—

"(1) any individual who, under the usual common law rules applicable in determining the employer-employee relationship, has the status of an independent contractor, or

"(2) any individual (except an officer of a corporation) who is not an employee under such common law rules."

Prior to amendment, subsec. (k) read as follows:

"(k) Agricultural labor.

"For purposes of this chapter, the term 'agricultural labor' includes all service performed—

"(1) on a farm, in the employ of any person, in connection with cultivating the soil, or in connection with raising or harvesting any agricultural or horticultural commodity, including the raising, shearing, feeding, caring for, training and management of livestock, bees, poultry, and fur-bearing animals and wildlife;

"(2) in the employ of the owner or tenant or other operator of a farm, in connection with the operation, management, conservation, improvement, or maintenance of such farm and its tools and equipment or in salvaging timber or clearing land of brush and other debris left by a hurricane, if the major part of such service is performed on a farm;

"(3) in connection with the production of harvesting of maple syrup or maple sugar or any commodity defined as an agricultural commodity in section 15(g) of the Agricultural Marketing Act, as amended (46 Stat. 1550, § 3; 12 U.S.C. 1141j), or in connection with the raising or harvesting of mushrooms, or in connection with the hatching of poultry, or in connection with the ginning of cotton, or in connection with the operation or maintenance of ditches, canals, reservoirs, or waterways used exclusively for supplying and storing water for farming purposes; or

"(4) in handling, planting, drying, packing, packaging, processing, freezing, grading, storing, or delivering to storage or to market or to a carrier for transportation to market, any agricultural or horticultural commodity; but only if such service is performed as an incident to ordinary farming operations or, in the case of fruits and vegetables, as an incident to the preparation of such fruits or vegetables for market. The provisions of this paragraph shall not be deemed to be applicable with respect to service performed in connection with commercial canning or commercial freezing or in connection with any agricultural or horticultural commodity after its delivery to a terminal market for distribution for consumption.

"As used in this subsection, the term 'farm' includes stock, dairy, poultry, fruit, fur-bearing animal and truck farms, plantations, ranches, nurseries, ranges, greenhouses or other similar structures used primarily for the raising of agricultural or horticultural commodities, and orchards."

—P.L. 91-373, Sec. 105(a), amended the material preceding para. (c)(1) ... Sec. 105(b), added para. (j)(3), effective for services rendered after 12/31/71.

Prior to amendment, the material preceding para. (c)(1) read as follows:

"(c) Employment.

"For purposes of this chapter, the term 'employment' means any service performed prior to 1955, which was employment for purposes of subchapter C of chapter 9 of the Internal Revenue Code of 1939 under the law applicable to the

Employment taxes
Code Sec. 3309(a)(1)

period in which such service was performed, and any service, of whatever nature, performed after 1954 by an employee for the person employing him, irrespective of the citizenship or residence of either, (A) within the United States, or (B) on or in connection with an American vessel or American aircraft under a contract of service which is entered into within the United States or during the performance of which and while the employee is employed on the vessel or aircraft it touches at a port in the United States, if the employee is employed on and in connection with such vessel or aircraft when outside the United States, except—"

—P.L. 91-373, Sec. 106(a), amended subpara. (c)(10)(B) and added subparas. (c)(10)(C) and (c)(10)(D), effective for remuneration paid after 12/31/69.

Prior to amendment, subpara. (c)(10)(B) read as follows:

"(B) service performed in the employ of a school, college, or university, if such service is performed by a student who is enrolled in and is regularly attending classes at such school, college, or university;"

—P.L. 91-373, Sec. 302, substituted "$4,200" for "$3,000" each place it appeared in para. (b)(1), effective for remuneration paid after 12/31/71.

In 1969, P.L. 91-53, Sec. 1, amended subsec. (a), effective for calendar years begin. after 12/31/69.

Prior to amendment, subsec. (a) read as follows:

"(a) Employer. For purposes of this chapter, the term 'employer' does not include any person unless on each of some 20 days during the taxable year, each day being in a different calendar week, the total number of individuals who were employed by him in employment for some portion of the day (whether or not at the same moment of time) was 4 or more."

In 1967, P.L. 90-248, Sec. 504(b), deleted "or" at the end of para. (b)(8), substituted ";or" for the period at the end of para. (b)(9), and added para. (b)(10), effective for remuneration paid after 1/2/68.

In 1964, P.L. 88-650, Sec. 4(c)(1), substituted ";or" for the period at the end of para. (b)(8) ... Sec. 4(c)(2), added para. (b)(9), effective for remuneration paid on or after the first day of the first calendar month which begins more than ten days after 10/13/64.

In 1962, P.L. 87-792, Sec. 7(k), amended subpara. (b)(5)(B) and added subpara. (b)(5)(C), effective for tax. yrs. begin. after 12/31/62.

Prior to amendment, subpara. (b)(5)(B) read as follows:

"(B) under or to an annuity plan which, at the time of such payment, meets the requirements of section 401(a)(3), (4), (5), and (6);".

In 1961, P.L. 87-256, Sec. 110(f)(1), deleted "or" at the end of para. (c)(16) ... Sec. 110(f)(2), substituted ";or" for the period at the end of para. (c)(17) ... Sec. 110(f)(3), added para. (c)(18), effective for services rendered after 12/31/61.

In 1960, P.L. 86-778, Sec. 531(c), amended para. (c)(6) ... Sec. 532(a), substituted "or (B) on or in connection with an American vessel or American aircraft under a contract of service which is entered into within the United States or during the performance of which and while the employee is employed on the vessel or aircraft it touches at a port in the United States, if the employee is employed on and in connection with such vessel or aircraft when outside the United States," for "or (B) on or in connection with an American vessel under a contract of service which is entered into within the United States or during the performance of which the vessel touches at a port in the United States, if the employee is employed on and in connection with such vessel when outside the United States," in the material preceding para. (c)(1) in subsec. (c). . . Sec. 532(b), amended para. (c)(4) ... Sec. 532(c)(1), amended the heading of subsec. (m) ... Sec. 532(c)(2), substituted "; and the term 'American aircraft' means an aircraft registered under the laws of the United States." for the period at the end of subsec. (m) ... Sec. 533, amended para. (c)(8) ... Sec. 534, amended para. (c)(10), effective for remuneration paid, and services performed after 1961.

Prior to amendment, para. (c)(6) read as follows:

"(6) service performed in the employ of the United States Government or of an instrumentality of the United States which is—

"(A) wholly owned by the United States, or

"(B) exempt from the tax imposed by section 3301 by virtue of any other provision of law;"

Prior to amendment, para. (c)(4) read as follows:

"(4) service performed on or in connection with a vessel not an American vessel by an employee, if the employee is employed on and in connection with such vessel when outside the United States;".

Prior to amendment, the heading of subsec. (m) read as follows:

"(m) American vessel."

Prior to amendment, para. (c)(8) read as follows:

"(8) service performed in the employ of a corporation, community chest, fund, or foundation, organized and operated exclusively for religious, charitable, scientific, testing for public safety, literary, or educational purposes, or for the prevention of cruelty to children or animals, no part of the net earnings of which inures to the benefit of any private shareholder or individual, and no substantial part of the activities of which is carrying on propaganda, or otherwise attempting, to influence legislation;"

Prior to amendment, para. (c)(10) read as follows:

"(10)(A) service performed in any calendar quarter in the employ of any organization exempt from income tax under section 501(a) (other than an organization described in section 401(a)) or under section 521, if—

"(i) the remuneration for such service is less than $50, or

"(ii) such service is in connection with the collection of dues or premiums for a fraternal beneficiary society, order, or association, and is performed away from the home office, or is ritualistic service in connection with any such society, order or association, or

"(iii) such service is performed by a student who is enrolled and is regularly attending classes at a school, college, or university;

"(B) service performed in the employ of an agricultural or horticultural organization described in section 501(c)(5) which is exempt from tax under section 501(a);

"(C) service performed in the employ of a voluntary employees' beneficiary association providing for the payment of life, sick, accident, or other benefits to the members of such association or their dependents, if—

"(i) no part of its net earnings inures (other than through such payments) to the benefit of any private shareholder or individual, and

"(ii) 85 percent or more of the income consists of amounts collected from members for the sole purpose of making such payments and meeting expenses;

"(D) service performed in the employ of a voluntary employees' beneficiary association providing for the payment of life, sick, accident, or other benefits to the members of such association or their dependents or their designated beneficiaries, if—

"(i) admission to membership in such association is limited to individuals who are officers or employees of the United States Government, and

"(ii) no part of the net earnings of such association inures (other than through such payments) to the benefit of any private shareholder or individual;

"(E) service performed in the employ of a school, college, or university, not exempt from income tax under section 501(a), if such service is performed by a student who is enrolled and is regularly attending classes at such school, college, or university;".

—P.L. 86-778, Sec. 543(a), amended subsec. (j), effective for remuneration paid, and services rendered after 12/31/60.

Prior to amendment, subsec. (j) read as follows:

"(j) State. For purposes of this chapter, the term 'state' includes the District of Columbia."

—P.L. 86-624, Sec. 18(d), deleted "Hawaii, and" preceding "the District of Columbia" in subsec. (j), effective 8/21/59.

In 1959, P.L. 86-70, Sec. 22(a), deleted "Alaska," before "Hawaii" in subsec. (j), effective 1/3/59.

In 1954, P.L. 767, Sec. 1, substituted "4 or more" for "eight or more" in subsec. (a), effective for services rendered after 12/31/55.

—P.L. 767, Sec. 4(c), repealed subsec. (l), effective for services rendered after 12/31/54.

Prior to repeal, subsec. (l) read as follows:

"(l) Certain employees of Bonneville Power Administrator. For purposes of this chapter—

"(1) The term 'employment' shall include such service as is determined by the Bonneville Power Administrator to be performed after December 31, 1945, by a laborer, mechanic, or workman, in connection with construction work or the operation and maintenance of electrical facilities, as an employee performing service for the Administrator.

"(2) The term 'wages' means, with respect to service which constitutes employment by reason of this subsection, such amount of remuneration as is determined (subject to the provisions of this section) by the Administrator to be paid for such service.

The Administrator is authorized and directed to comply with the provisions of the internal revenue laws on behalf of the United States as the employer of individuals whose service constitutes employment by reason of this subsection."

Sec. 3307. Deductions as constructive payments.

Whenever under this chapter or any act of Congress, or under the law of any State, an employer is required or permitted to deduct any amount from the remuneration of an employee and to pay the amount deducted to the United States, a State, or any political subdivision thereof, then for purposes of this chapter the amount so deducted shall be considered to have been paid to the employee at the time of such deduction.

Sec. 3308. Instrumentalities of the United States.

Notwithstanding any other provision of law (whether enacted before or after the enactment of this section) which grants to any instrumentality of the United States an exemption from taxation, such instrumentality shall not be exempt from the tax imposed by section 3301 unless such other provision of law grants a specific exemption, by reference to section 3301 (or the corresponding section of prior law), from the tax imposed by such section.

In 1960, P.L. 86-778, Sec. 531(d), added Code Sec. 3308, effective for remuneration paid after 12/31/61 for services after 12/31/61.

Sec. 3309. State law coverage of services performed for nonprofit organizations or governmental entities.

(a) State law requirements.

For purposes of section 3304(a)(6)—

(1) except as otherwise provided in subsections (b) and (c), the services to which this paragraph applies are—

(A) service excluded from the term "employment" solely by reason of paragraph (8) of section 3306(c), and

(B) service excluded from the term "employment" solely by reason of paragraph (7) of section 3306(c); and

(2) the State law shall provide that a governmental entity, including an Indian tribe, or any other organization (or group of governmental entities or other organizations) which, but for the requirements of this paragraph, would be liable for contributions with respect to service to which paragraph (1) applies may elect, for such minimum period and at such time as may be provided by State law, to pay (in lieu of such contributions) into the State unemployment fund amounts equal to the amounts of compensation attributable under the State law to such service. The State law may provide safeguards to ensure that governmental entities or other organizations so electing will make the payments required under such elections.

(b) Section not to apply to certain service.

This section shall not apply to service performed—

(1) in the employ of (A) a church or convention or association of churches, (B) an organization which is operated primarily for religious purposes and which is operated, supervised, controlled, or principally supported by a church or convention or association of churches, or (C) an elementary or secondary school which is operated primarily for religious purposes, which is described in section 501(c)(3), and which is exempt from tax under section 501(a);

(2) by a duly ordained, commissioned, or licensed minister of a church in the exercise of his ministry or by a member of a religious order in the exercise of duties required by such order;

(3) in the employ of a governmental entity referred to in paragraph (7) of section 3306(c), if such service is performed by an individual in the exercise of his duties—

(A) as an elected official;

(B) as a member of a legislative body, or a member of the judiciary, of a State or political subdivision thereof, or of an Indian tribe;

(C) as a member of the State National Guard or Air National Guard;

(D) as an employee serving on a temporary basis in case of fire, storm, snow, earthquake, flood, or similar emergency;

(E) in a position which, under or pursuant to the State or tribal law, is designated as (i) a major nontenured policymaking or advisory position, or (ii) a policymaking or advisory position the performance of the duties of which ordinarily does not require more than 8 hours per week; or

(F) as an election official or election worker if the amount of remuneration received by the individual during the calendar year for services as an election official or election worker is less than $1,000;

(4) in a facility conducted for the purpose of carrying out a program of—

(A) rehabilitation for individuals whose earning capacity is impaired by age or physical or mental deficiency or injury, or

(B) providing remunerative work for individuals who because of their impaired physical or mental capacity cannot be readily absorbed in the competitive labor market, by an individual receiving such rehabilitation or remunerative work;

(5) as part of an unemployment work-relief or work-training program assisted or financed in whole or in part by any Federal agency or an agency of a State or political subdivision thereof or of an Indian tribe, by an individual receiving such work relief or work training; and

(6) by an inmate of a custodial or penal institution.

(c) Nonprofit organizations must employ 4 or more.

This section shall not apply to service performed during any calendar year in the employ of any organization unless on each of some 20 days during such calendar year or the preceding calendar year, each day being in a different calendar week, the total number of individuals who were employed by such organization in employment (determined without regard to section 3306(c)(8) and by excluding service to which this section does not apply by reason of subsection (b)) for some portion of the day (whether or not at the same moment of time) was 4 or more.

(d) Election by Indian tribe.

The State law shall provide that an Indian tribe may make contributions for employment as if the employment is within the meaning of section 3306 or make payments in lieu of contributions under this section, and shall provide that an Indian tribe may make separate elections for itself and each subdivision, subsidiary, or business enterprise wholly owned by such Indian tribe. State law may require a tribe to post a payment bond or take other reasonable measures to assure the making of payments in lieu of contributions under this section. Notwithstanding the requirements of section 3306(a)(6), if, within 90 days of having received a notice of delinquency, a tribe fails to make contributions, payments in lieu of contributions, or payment of penalties or interest (at amounts or rates comparable to those applied to all other employers covered under the State law) assessed with respect to such failure, or if the tribe fails to post a required payment bond, then service for the tribe shall not be excepted from employment under section 3306(c)(7) until any such failure is corrected. This subsection shall apply to an Indian tribe within the meaning of section 4(e) of the Indian Self-Determination and Education Assistance Act (25 U.S.C. 450b(e)).

In 2000, P.L. 106-554, Sec. 1(a)(7), [which enacted into law Sec. 166(b)(1) of P.L. 106-554] added ", including an Indian tribe," after "governmental entity" in para. (a)(2) . . . Sec. 1(a)(7), [which enacted into law Sec. 166(b)(2) of P.L. 106-554] added ", or of an Indian tribe" after "subdivision thereof" in subpara. (b)(3)(B) . . . Sec. 1(a)(7), [which enacted into law Sec. 166(b)(3) of P.L. 106-554] added "or tribal" after "the State" in subpara. (b)(3)(E) . . . Sec. 1(a)(7), [which enacted into law Sec. 166(b)(4) of P.L. 106-554] added "or of an Indian tribe" after "political subdivision thereof" in para. (b)(5) . . . Sec. 1(a)(7), [which enacted into law Sec. 166(c) of P.L. 106-554] added subsec. (d), effective for service performed on or after 12/21/2000. Sec. 166(e)(2) of this Act provides:

"(2) Transition rule. For purposes of the Federal Unemployment Tax Act, service performed in the employ of an Indian tribe (as defined in section 3306(u) of the Internal Revenue Code of 1986 (as added by this section)) shall not be treated as employment (within the meaning of section 3306 of such Code) if—

"(A) it is service which is performed before the date of the enactment of this Act and with respect to which the tax imposed under the Federal Unemployment Tax Act has not been paid, and

"(B) such Indian tribe reimburses a State unemployment fund for unemployment benefits paid for service attributable to such tribe for such period."

In 1997, P.L. 105-33, Sec. 5405(a)(1), deleted "or" at the end of subpara. (b)(3)(D) . . . Sec. 5405(a)(2), added "or" at the end of subpara. (b)(3)(E) . . . Sec. 5405(a)(3), added subpara. (b)(3)(F), effective for service performed after 8/5/97.

—P.L. 105-33, Sec. 5407(a)(1), deleted "or" after "churches," in para. (b)(1) . . . Sec. 5407(a)(2), added ", or (C) an elementary or secondary school which is operated primarily for religious purposes, which is described in section 501(c)(3), and which is exempt from tax under section 501(a)" before the semicolon at the end of para. (b)(1), effective for service performed after 8/5/97.

In 1983, P.L. 98-21, Sec. 524, provides as follows:

"Sec. 524.

"If—

"(1) an organization did not make an election to make payments (in lieu of contributions) as provided in section 3309(a)(2) of the Internal Revenue Code of 1954 before April 1, 1972, because such organization, as of such date, was treated as an organization described in section 501(c)(4) of such Code,

Employment taxes — Code Sec. 3311

"(2) the Internal Revenue Service subsequently determined that such organization was described in section 501(c)(3) of such Code, and

"(3) such organization made such an election before the earlier of—

"(A) the date 18 months after such election was first available to it under the State law, or

"(B) January 1, 1984,

then section 3303(f) of such Code shall be applied with respect to such organization as if it did not contain the requirement that the election be made before April 1, 1972, and by substituting 'January 1, 1982' for 'January 1, 1969'."

In **1977**, P.L. 95-19, Sec. 301(a), amended the effective date for amendments made by Sec. 115 of P. L. 94-566 to read as follows, effective 10/20/76:

"(d) Effective date.—

"(1) Except as provided in paragraph (2), the amendments made by this section shall apply with respect to certifications of States for 1978 and subsequent years; except that

"(A) the amendments made by subsections (a) and (b) shall only apply with respect to services performed after December 31, 1977; and

"(B) the amendments made by subsection (c) shall only apply with respect to weeks of unemployment which begin after December 31, 1977.

"(2) In the case of any State the legislature of which does not meet in a regular session which closes during the calendar year 1977, the amendments made by subsection (c) shall only apply with respect to weeks of unemployment which begin after December 31, 1978 (or if earlier, the date provided by State law)."

—P.L. 95-19, Sec. 301(c), amended the effective date for amendments made by Sec. 506 of P. L. 94-566 to read as follows, effective 10/20/76:

"(c) Effective date.—

"(1) Except as provided in paragraph (2), the amendments made by this section shall apply with respect to certifications of States for 1978 and subsequent years, but only with respect to services performed after December 31, 1977.

"(2) In the case of any State the legislature of which does not meet in a regular session which closes during the calendar year 1977, the amendments made by this section shall apply with respect to the certification of such State for 1979 and subsequent years, but only with respect to services performed after December 31, 1978."

—P.L. 95-19, Sec. 302(b), substituted "or group of governmental entities or other organizations" for "or group of organizations" in para. (a)(2), effective for certifications of States for 1978, and subsequent yrs. for services performed after 1977.

In **1976**, P.L. 94-566, Sec. 115(a), amended subpara. (a)(1)(B), effective for certifications of States for '78 and subsequent years, but only for services rendered after '77.

Prior to amendment, subpara. (a)(1)(B) read as follows:

"(B) service preformed in the employ of the State, or any instrumentality of the State or of the State and one or more other States, for a hospital or institution of higher education located in the State, if such service is excluded from the term 'employment' solely by reason of paragraph (7) of section 3306(c); and"

—P.L. 94-566, Sec. 115(b)(1), amended para. (b)(3), effective for certifications of States for '78 and subsequent years, but only for services rendered after '77.

Prior to amendment, para. (b)(3) read as follows:

"(3) in the employ of a school which is not an institution of higher education;"

—P.L. 94-566, Sec. 115(b)(2), amended para. (b)(6), effective for certifications of States for '78 and subsequent years, but only for services rendered after '77.

Prior to amendment, para. (b)(6) read as follows:

"(6) for a hospital in a State prison or other State correctional institution by an inmate of the prison or correctional institution."

—P.L. 94-566, Sec. 115(c)(2), deleted subsec. (d), effective for certifications of States for 1978 and subsequent years, but only for services rendered after '77.

Prior to deletion, subsec. (d) read as follows:

"(d) Definition of institution of higher education. For purposes of this section, the term 'institution of higher education' means an educational institution in any State which—

"(1) admits as regular students only individuals having a certificate of graduation from a high school, or the recognized equivalent of such a certificate;

"(2) is legally authorized within such State to provide a program of education beyond high school;

"(3) provides an educational program for which it awards a bachelor's or higher degree, or provides a program which is acceptable for full credit toward such a degree, or offers a program of training to prepare students for gainful employment in a recognized occupation; and

"(4) is a public or other nonprofit institution."

—P.L. 94-566, Sec. 115(c)(3), amended the heading for Code Sec. 3309, effective for certifications of States for 1978 and subsequent years, but only for services performed after '77.

Prior to amendment, the heading of Code Sec. 3309 read as follows:

"SEC. 3309. STATE LAW COVERAGE OF CERTAIN SERVICES PERFORMED FOR NONPROFIT ORGANIZATIONS AND FOR STATE HOSPITALS AND INSTITUTIONS OF HIGHER EDUCATION."

—P.L. 94-566, Sec. 506(a), substituted "a governmental entity or any other organization" for "an organization", substituted "paragraph (1)" for "paragraph (1)(A)", substituted "that governmental entities or other organizations" for "that organizations" in para. (a)(2), effective for certifications of States for '78, and subsequent years, with respect to services performed after '77.

In **1970**, P.L. 91-373, Sec. 104(b), substituted new Code Sec. 3309, effective for certification of State laws for 1972 and subsequent years, but only with respect to services performed after 12/31/71.

Prior to amendment, Code Sec. 3309 read as follows:

"SEC. 3309. SHORT TITLE.

"This chapter may be cited as the 'Federal Unemployment Tax Act.'"

Sec. 3310. Judicial review.

(a) In general.

Whenever under section 3303(b) or section 3304(c) the Secretary of Labor makes a finding pursuant to which he is required to withhold a certification with respect to a State under such section, such State may, within 60 days after the Governor of the State has been notified of such action, file with the United States court of appeals for the circuit in which such State is located or with the United States Court of Appeals for the District of Columbia, a petition for review of such action. A copy of the petition shall be forthwith transmitted by the clerk of the court to the Secretary of Labor. The Secretary of Labor thereupon shall file in the court the record of the proceedings on which he based his action as provided in section 2112 of title 28 of the United States Code.

(b) Findings of fact.

The findings of fact by the Secretary of Labor, if supported by substantial evidence, shall be conclusive; but the court, for good cause shown, may remand the case to the Secretary of Labor to take further evidence, and the Secretary of Labor may thereupon make new or modified findings of fact and may modify his previous action, and shall certify to the court the record of the further proceedings. Such new or modified findings of fact shall likewise be conclusive if supported by substantial evidence.

(c) Jurisdiction of court; review.

The court shall have jurisdiction to affirm the action of the Secretary of Labor or to set it aside, in whole or in part. The judgment of the court shall be subject to review by the Supreme Court of the United States upon certiorari or certification as provided in section 1254 of title 28 of the United States Code.

(d) Stay of Secretary of Labor's action.

(1) The Secretary of Labor shall not withhold any certification under section 3303(b) or section 3304(c) until the expiration of 60 days after the Governor of the State has been notified of the action referred to in subsection (a) or until the State has filed a petition for review of such action, whichever is earlier.

(2) The commencement of judicial proceedings under this section shall stay the Secretary of Labor's action for a period of 30 days, and the court may thereafter grant interim relief if warranted, including a further stay of the Secretary of Labor's action and including such other relief as may be necessary to preserve status or rights.

In **1984**, P.L. 98-620, Sec. 402(28)(A), deleted subsec. (e), effective 11/8/84, except for cases pending on 11/8/84.

Prior to deletion, subsec. (e) read as follows:

"(e) Preference. Any judicial proceedings under this section shall be entitled to, and, upon request of the Secretary of Labor or the State, shall receive a preference and shall be heard and determined as expeditiously as possible."

In **1976**, P.L. 94-455, Sec. 1906(b)(13)(F), substituted "the Secretary of Labor's action" for "the Secretary's action" each place it appeared in para. (d)(2), effective 2/1/77.

—P.L. 94-455, Sec. 1906(b)(13)(H), substituted "of the Secretary of Labor" for "of the Secretary" following "upon request" in subsec. (e), effective 2/1/77.

In **1970**, P.L. 91-373, Sec. 131(b)(1), added Code Sec. 3310, effective 8/10/70.

Sec. 3311. Short title.

This chapter may be cited as the "Federal Unemployment Tax Act."

In **1970**, P.L. 91-373, Sec. 104(b)(1), redesignated Code Sec. 3309 as Code Sec. 3311, effective for certifications of State laws for 1972 and subsequent years, but only with respect to service performed after 12/31/71.

3,141

CHAPTER 23A.—RAILROAD UNEMPLOYMENT REPAYMENT TAX

Sec.
3321. Imposition of tax.
3322. Definitions.

In 1988, P.L. 100-647, Sec. 7106(a), amended Chapter 23A of the '86 Code, effective for remuneration paid after 12/31/88.
Prior to amendment, Chapter 23A read as follows:
"CHAPTER 23A.—RAILROAD UNEMPLOYMENT REPAYMENT TAX
"Sec.
"3321. Imposition of tax.
"3322. Taxable period.
"3323. Other definitions.

In 1983, P.L. 98-76, Sec. 231(c), added the item for Chapter 23A.

"SEC. 3321. IMPOSITION OF TAX.
"(a) General rule.
There is hereby imposed on every rail employer for each taxable period an excise tax, with respect to having individuals in his employ, equal to the applicable percentage of the total rail wages paid by him during the taxable period.
"(b) Tax on employee representatives.
"(1) In general. There is hereby imposed on the income of each employee representative a tax equal to the applicable percentage of the rail wages paid to him during the taxable period.
"(2) Determination of wages. The rail wages of an employee representative for purposes of paragraph (1) shall be determined in the same manner and with the same effect as if the employee organization by which such employee representative is employed were a rail employer.
"(c) Rate of tax.
For purposes of this section—
"(1) In general. The applicable percentage for any taxable period shall be the sum of —
"(A) the basic rate for such period, and
"(B) the surtax rate (if any) for such period.
"(2) Basic rate. For purposes of paragraph (1)—
"(A) For periods before 1989. The basic rate shall be—
"(i) 4.3 percent for the taxable period beginning on July 1, 1986, and ending on December 31, 1986,
"(ii) 4.7 percent for the 1987 taxable period, and
"(iii) 6 percent for the 1988 taxable period.
"(B) For periods after 1988. For any taxable period beginning after December 31, 1988, the basic rate shall be the sum of —
"(i) 2.9 percent, plus
"(ii) 0.3 percent for each preceding taxable period after 1988.
In no event shall the basic rate under this subparagraph exceed 5 percent.
"(3) Surtax rate. For purposes of paragraph (1), the surtax rate shall be—
"(A) 3.5 percent for any taxable period if, as of September 30 of the preceding calendar year, there was a balance of transfers (or unpaid interest thereon) made after September 30, 1985, to the railroad unemployment insurance account under section 10(d) of the Railroad Unemployment Insurance Act, and
"(B) zero for any other taxable period.
"(4) Basic rate not to apply to rail wages paid after September 30, 1990. The basic rate under paragraph (1)(A) shall not apply to rail wages paid after September 30, 1990.

In 1988, P.L. 100-647, Sec. 1018(u)(17), added the period at the end of para. (c)(4), effective for remuneration paid after 6/30/86.
In 1986, P.L. 99-272, Sec. 13301(a), amended subsec. (c). Prior to amendment, subsec. (c) read as follows:
"(c) Rate of tax.
"For purposes of this section
"(1) For taxable period July 1 through December 31, 1986. The applicable percentage for the taxable period beginning on July 1, 1986, and ending on December 31, 1986, shall be 2 percent.
"(2) Subsequent taxable periods. The applicable percentage for any taxable period beginning after 1986 shall be the sum of —
"(A) 2 percent, plus
"(B) 0.3 percent for each preceding taxable period. In no event shall the applicable percentage exceed 5 percent."
In 1983, P.L. 98-76, Sec. 231(a), added Code Sec. 3321, for remuneration paid after 6/30/86.

"SEC. 3322. TAXABLE PERIOD.
"(a) General rule.
For purposes of this chapter, except as provided in subsection (b), the term 'taxable period' means—
"(1) the period beginning on July 1, 1986, and ending on December 31, 1986, and
"(2) each calendar year after 1986.
"(b) Earlier termination if loans to rail unemployment fund repaid.

The basic rate under section 3321(c)(1)(A) of the tax imposed by section 3321 shall not apply to any rail wages paid on or after the first January 1 after 1986 as of which there is—
"(1) no balance of transfers made before October 1, 1985, to the railroad unemployment insurance account under section 10(d) of the Railroad Unemployment Insurance Act, and
"(2) no unpaid interest on such transfers."

In 1986, P.L. 99-272, Sec. 13301(d)(1), added "and" at the end of para. (a)(1), deleted paras. (a)(2) and (a)(3) and added new para. (a)(2) ... Sec. 13301(d)(2), substituted "The basic rate under section 3321(c)(1)(A) of the tax imposed by section 3321 shall not apply" for "The tax imposed by this chapter shall not apply" in subsec. (b) and added "made before October 1, 1985," after "no balance of transfers" in para. (b)(1).
Prior to deletion, paras. (a)(2) and (a)(3) read as follows:
"(2) each calendar year after 1986 and before 1990, and
"(3) the period beginning on January 1, 1990, and ending on September 30, 1990."
In 1983, P.L. 98-76, Sec. 231(a), added Code Sec. 3322, for remuneration paid after 6/30/86.

"SEC. 3323. OTHER DEFINITIONS.
"(a) Rail employer.
For purposes of this chapter, the term 'rail employer' means any person who is an employer as defined in section 1 of the Railroad Unemployment Insurance Act.
"(b) Rail wages.
"(1) In general. For purposes of this chapter, the term 'rail wages' means compensation (as defined in section 3231(e) for purposes of the tax imposed by section 3201(a)) with the modifications specified in paragraph (2).
"(2) Modifications. In applying subsection (e) of section 3231 for purposes of paragraph (1)—
"(A) Only employment covered by Railroad Unemployment Insurance Act taken into account. Such subsection (e) shall be applied—
"(i) by substituting 'rail employment' for 'services' each place it appears,
"(ii) by substituting 'rail employer' for 'employer' each place it appears, and
"(iii) by substituting 'rail employee' for 'employee' each place it appears.
"(B) $7,000 wage base. Such subsection (e) shall be applied by substituting for 'the applicable base' in paragraph (2)(A)(i) thereof—
"(i) except as provided in clauses (ii) and (iii), '$7,000',
"(ii) '$3,500' for the taxable period beginning on July 1, 1986, and ending on December 31, 1986, and
"(iii) for purposes of applying the basic rate under section 3321(c)(1)(A), '$5,250' for the taxable period beginning on January 1, 1990.
"(C) Successor employers. For purposes of this subsection, rules similar to the rules applicable under section 3231(e)(2)(C) shall apply.
"(c) Rail employment.
For purposes of this chapter, the term 'rail employment' means services performed by an individual as a rail employee or employee representative.
"(d) Rail employee and employee representative.
For purposes of this chapter
"(1) Rail employee. The term 'rail employee' means any person who is an employee as defined in section 1 of the Railroad Unemployment Insurance Act.
"(2) Employee representative. The term 'employee representative' has the meaning given such term by section 1 of the Railroad Unemployment Insurance Act.
"(e) Concurrent employment by 2 or more rail employers.
For purposes of this chapter, if 2 or more related corporations which are rail employers concurrently employ the same individual and compensate such individual through a common paymaster which is 1 of such corporations, each such corporation shall be considered to have paid as remuneration to such individual only the amounts actually disbursed by it to such individual and shall not be considered to have paid as remuneration to such individual amounts actually disbursed to such individual by another of such corporations.
"(f) Certain rules made applicable.
For purposes of this chapter, rules similar to the rules of sections 3307 and 3308 shall apply.

In 1986, P.L. 99-272, Sec. 13301(b), amended subsec. (b).
Prior to amendment, subsec. (b) read as follows:
"(b) Rail wages.
"(1) In general. For purposes of this chapter, the term 'rail wages' means wages as defined in section 3306(b) with the modifications specified in paragraph (2).
"(2) Modifications. In applying subsection (b) of section 3306 for purposes of paragraph (1)—
"(A) Only railroad employment taken into account. Such subsection (b) shall be applied—
"(i) by substituting 'rail employment' for 'employment' each place it appears, and
"(ii) by substituting 'rail employer' for 'employer' each place it appears.
"(B) Wage base for first taxable period. In the case of the taxable period beginning on July 1, 1986, and ending on December 31, 1986, such subsection (b) shall be applied by substituting '$3,500' for '$7,000' each place it appears in paragraph (1) thereof.
"(C) Wage base for last taxable period. In the case of the taxable period beginning on January 1, 1990, and ending on September 30, 1990, such subsection (b)

Wage withholding   Code Sec. 3401(a)(8)(A)

shall be applied by substituting '$5,250' for '$7,000' each place it appears in paragraph (1) thereof."

In 1983, P.L. 98-76, Sec. 231(a), added Code Sec. 3323, for remuneration paid after 6/30/86.

In 1983, P.L. 98-76, Sec. 231(c), added the item for Chapter 23A.

Sec. 3321. Imposition of tax.
(a) General rule.

There is hereby imposed on every rail employer for each calendar month an excise tax, with respect to having individuals in his employ, equal to 4 percent of the total rail wages paid by him during such month.

(b) Tax on employee representatives.

(1) **In general.** There is hereby imposed on the income of each employee representative a tax equal to 4 percent of the rail wages paid to him during the calendar month.

(2) **Determination of wages.** The rail wages of an employee representative for purposes of paragraph (1) shall be determined in the same manner and with the same effect as if the employee organization by which such employee representative is employed were a rail employer.

(c) Termination if loans to railroad unemployment fund repaid.

The tax imposed by this section shall not apply to rail wages paid on or after the 1st day of any calendar month if, as of such 1st day, there is—

(1) no balance of transfers made before October 1, 1985, to the railroad unemployment insurance account under section 10(d) of the Railroad Unemployment Insurance Act, and

(2) no unpaid interest on such transfers.

In 1988, P.L. 100-647, Sec. 7106(a), added Code Sec. 3321, effective for remuneration paid after 12/31/88.

—P.L. 100-647, Sec. 7106(b)(1), and (2) of this Act provide:

"(b) Continuation of surtax rate through 1990.

"(1) In general. In the case of any calendar month beginning before January 1, 1991—

"(A) there shall be substituted for '4 percent' in subsections (a) and (b) of section 3321 of the 1986 Code the percentage equal to the sum of —

"(i) 4 percent, plus

"(ii) the surtax rate (if any) for such calendar month, and

"(B) subsection (c) of such section shall not apply to so much of the tax imposed by such section as is attributable to the surtax rate.

"(2) Surtax rate. For purposes of paragraph (1), the surtax rate shall be—

"(A) 3.5 percent for each month during a calendar year if, as of September 30, of the preceding calendar year, there was a balance of transfers (or unpaid interest thereon) made after September 30, 1985, to the railroad unemployment insurance account under section 10(d) of the Railroad Unemployment Insurance Act, and

"(B) zero for any other calendar month."

Sec. 3322. Definitions.
(a) Rail employer.

For purposes of this chapter, the term "rail employer" means any person who is an employer as defined in section 1 of the Railroad Unemployment Insurance Act.

(b) Rail wages.

For purposes of this chapter, the term "rail wages" means, with respect to any calendar month, so much of the remuneration paid during such month which is subject to contributions under section 8(a) of the Railroad Unemployment Insurance Act.

(c) Employee representative.

For purposes of this chapter, the term "employee representative" has the meaning given such term by section 1 of the Railroad Unemployment Insurance Act.

(d) Certain rules made applicable.

For purposes of this chapter, rules similar to the rules of section 3307 and 3308 shall apply.

In 1988, P.L. 100-647, Sec. 7106(a), added new Code Sec. 3322, effective for remuneration paid after 12/31/88.

CHAPTER 24.—COLLECTION OF INCOME TAX AT SOURCE

Subchapter

A. Withholding from wages.

B. Withholding from interest and dividends.

Subchapter A.—Withholding From Wages

Sec.

3401. Definitions.

3402. Income tax collected at source.

3403. Liability for tax.

3404. Return and payment by governmental employer.

3405. Special rules for pensions, annuities, and certain other deferred income.

3406. Backup withholding.

In 1983, P.L. 98-67, Sec. 104(d)(4), added item 3406.

In 1982, P.L. 97-248, Sec. 307(b)(4), amended the chapter heading.

Prior to amendment, the chapter heading read as follows:

"CHAPTER 24.—COLLECTION OF INCOME TAX AT SOURCE ON WAGES"

Sec. 3401. Definitions.
(a) Wages.

For purposes of this chapter, the term "wages" means all remuneration (other than fees paid to a public official) for services performed by an employee for his employer, including the cash value of all remuneration (including benefits) paid in any medium other than cash; except that such term shall not include remuneration paid—

(1) for active service performed in a month for which such employee is entitled to the benefits of section 112 (relating to certain combat zone compensation of members of the Armed Forces of the United States) to the extent remuneration for such service is excludable from gross income under such section; or

(2) for agricultural labor (as defined in section 3121(g)) unless the remuneration paid for such labor is wages (as defined in section 3121(a)); or

(3) for domestic service in a private home, local college club, or local chapter of a college fraternity or sorority; or

(4) for service not in the course of the employer's trade or business performed in any calendar quarter by an employee, unless the cash remuneration paid for such service is $50 or more and such service is performed by an individual who is regularly employed by such employer to perform such service. For purposes of this paragraph, an individual shall be deemed to be regularly employed by an employer during a calendar quarter only if—

(A) on each of some 24 days during such quarter such individual performs for such employer for some portion of the day service not in the course of the employer's trade or business; or

(B) such individual was regularly employed (as determined under subparagraph (A)) by such employer in the performance of such service during the preceding calendar quarter; or

(5) for services by a citizen or resident of the United States for a foreign government or an international organization; or

(6) for such services, performed by a nonresident alien individual, as may be designated by regulations prescribed by the Secretary; or

(7) Repealed.

(8)(A) for services for an employer (other than the United States or any agency thereof)—

3,143

(i) performed by a citizen of the United States if, at the time of the payment of such remuneration, it is reasonable to believe that such remuneration will be excluded from gross income under section 911; or

(ii) performed in a foreign country or in a possession of the United States by such a citizen if, at the time of the payment of such remuneration, the employer is required by the law of any foreign country or possession of the United States to withhold income tax upon such remuneration; or

(B) for services for an employer (other than the United States or any agency thereof) performed by a citizen of the United States within a possession of the United States (other than Puerto Rico), if it is reasonable to believe that at least 80 percent of the remuneration to be paid to the employee by such employer during the calendar year will be for such services; or

(C) for services for an employer (other than the United States or any agency thereof) performed by a citizen of the United States within Puerto Rico, if it is reasonable to believe that during the entire calendar year the employee will be a bona fide resident of Puerto Rico; or

(D) for services for the United States (or any agency thereof) performed by a citizen of the United States within a possession of the United States to the extent the United States (or such agency) withholds taxes on such remuneration pursuant to an agreement with such possession; or

(9) for services performed by a duly ordained, commissioned, or licensed minister of a church in the exercise of his ministry or by a member of a religious order in the exercise of duties required by such order; or

(10)(A) for services performed by an individual under the age of 18 in the delivery or distribution of newspapers or shopping news, not including delivery or distribution to any point for subsequent delivery or distribution; or

(B) for services performed by an individual in, and at the time of, the sale of newspapers or magazines to ultimate consumers, under an arrangement under which the newspapers or magazines are to be sold by him at a fixed price, his compensation being based on the retention of the excess of such price over the amount at which the newspapers or magazines are charged to him, whether or not he is guaranteed a minimum amount of compensation for such services, or is entitled to be credited with the unsold newspapers or magazines turned back; or

(11) for services not in the course of the employer's trade or business, to the extent paid in any medium other than cash; or

(12) to, or on behalf of, an employee or his beneficiary—
(A) from or to a trust described in section 401(a) which is exempt from tax under section 501(a) at the time of such payment unless such payment is made to an employee of the trust as remuneration for services rendered as such employee and not as a beneficiary of the trust; or
(B) under or to an annuity plan which, at the time of such payment, is a plan described in section 403(a); or
(C) for a payment described in section 402(h)(1) and (2) if, at the time of such payment, it is reasonable to believe that the employee will be entitled to an exclusion under such section for payment; or
(D) under an arrangement to which section 408(p) applies; or

(E) under or to an eligible deferred compensation plan which, at the time of such payment, is a plan described in section 457(b) which is maintained by an eligible employer described in section 457(e)(1)(A), or

(13) pursuant to any provision of law other than section 5(c) or 6(1) of the Peace Corps Act, for service performed as a volunteer or volunteer leader within the meaning of such Act; or

(14) in the form of group-term life insurance on the life of an employee; or

(15) to or on behalf of an employee if (and to the extent that) at the time of the payment of such remuneration it is reasonable to believe that a corresponding deduction is allowable under section 217 (determined without regard to section 274(n)); or

(16)(A) as tips in any medium other than cash;
(B) as cash tips to an employee in any calendar month in the course of his employment by an employer unless the amount of such cash tips is $20 or more;

(17) for service described in section 3121(b)(20);

(18) for any payment made, or benefit furnished, to or for the benefit of an employee if at the time of such payment or such furnishing it is reasonable to believe that the employee will be able to exclude such payment or benefit from income under section 127, 129, 134(b)(4), or 134(b)(5);

(19) for any benefit provided to or on behalf of an employee if at the time such benefit is provided it is reasonable to believe that the employee will be able to exclude such benefit from income under section 74(c), 108(f)(4), 117, or 132;

(20) for any medical care reimbursement made to or for the benefit of an employee under a self-insured medical reimbursement plan (within the meaning of section 105(h)(6));

(21) for any payment made to or for the benefit of an employee if at the time of such payment it is reasonable to believe that the employee will be able to exclude such payment from income under section 106(b);

(22) any payment made to or for the benefit of an employee if at the time of such payment it is reasonable to believe that the employee will be able to exclude such payment from income under section 106(d); or

The term "wages" includes any amount includible in gross income of an employee under section 409A and payment of such amount shall be treated as having been made in the taxable year in which the amount is so includible.

(23) for any benefit or payment which is excludable from the gross income of the employee under section 139B(b).

(b) Payroll period.

For purposes of this chapter, the term "payroll period" means a period for which a payment of wages is ordinarily made to the employee by his employer, and the term "miscellaneous payroll period" means a payroll period other than a daily, weekly, biweekly, semimonthly, monthly, quarterly, semiannual, or annual payroll period.

(c) Employee.

For purposes of this chapter, the term "employee" includes an officer, employee, or elected official of the United States, a State, or any political subdivision thereof, or the District of Columbia, or any agency or instrumentality of any one or more of the foregoing. The term "employee" also includes an officer of a corporation.

(d) Employer.

For purposes of this chapter, the term "employer" means the person for whom an individual performs or performed

Wage withholding — Code Sec. 3401

any service, of whatever nature, as the employee of such person, except that—

(1) if the person for whom the individual performs or performed the services does not have control of the payment of the wages for such services, the term "employer" (except for purposes of subsection (a)) means the person having control of the payment of such wages, and

(2) in the case of a person paying wages on behalf of a nonresident alien individual, foreign partnership, or foreign corporation, not engaged in trade or business within the United States, the term "employer" (except for purposes of subsection (a)) means such person.

(e) **Number of withholding exemptions claimed.**

For purposes of this chapter, the term "number of withholding exemptions claimed" means the number of withholding exemptions claimed in a withholding exemption certificate in effect under section 3402(f), or in effect under the corresponding section of prior law, except that if no such certificate is in effect, the number of withholding exemptions claimed shall be considered to be zero.

(f) **Tips.**

For purposes of subsection (a), the term "wages" includes tips received by an employee in the course of his employment. Such wages shall be deemed to be paid at the time a written statement including such tips is furnished to the employer pursuant to section 6053(a) or (if no statement including such tips is so furnished) at the time received.

(g) **Crew leader rules to apply.**

Rules similar to the rules of section 3121(o) shall apply for purposes of this chapter.

(h)

Differential Wage Payments to Active Duty Members of the Uniformed Services.

(1) **In general.** For purposes of subsection (a), any differential wage payment shall be treated as a payment of wages by the employer to the employee.

(2) **Differential wage payment.** For purposes of paragraph (1), the term 'differential wage payment' means any payment which—

(A) is made by an employer to an individual with respect to any period during which the individual is performing service in the uniformed services (as defined in chapter 43 of title 38, United States Code) while on active duty for a period of more than 30 days, and

(B) represents all or a portion of the wages the individual would have received from the employer if the individual were performing service for the employer.

In 2010, P.L. 111-312, Sec. 101(a)(1), substituted "December 31, 2012" for "December 31, 2010" both places it appeared in Sec. 901 of P.L. 107-16, [see below] effective as if included in the enactment of P.L. 107-16, EGTRRA, 6/7/2001.

In 2008, P.L. 110-458, Sec. 108(m), of this Act [relating to Sec. 864(a) of P.L. 109-280], provides:

"(m) Amendment related to section 864. Section 864(a) of the 2006 Act is amended by striking 'Reconciliation'.

—P.L. 110-245, Sec. 105(a)(1), added subsec. (h), effective for remuneration paid after 12/31/2008.

—P.L. 110-245, Sec. 115(c), deleted 'or' at the end of para. (a)(21), substituted '; or' for the period at the end of para. (a)(22), and added para. (a)(23), effective as if included in section 5 of the Mortgage Forgiveness Debt Relief Act of 2007.

In 2006, P.L. 109-280, Sec. 811, of this Act [relating to Sec. 901 of P. L. 107-16, see below], provides:

"SEC. 811. PENSIONS AND INDIVIDUAL RETIREMENT ARRANGEMENT PROVISIONS OF ECONOMIC GROWTH AND TAX RELIEF RECONCILIATION ACT OF 2001 MADE PERMANENT.

"Title IX of the Economic Growth and Tax Relief Reconciliation Act of 2001 shall not apply to the provisions of, and amendments made by, subtitles A through F of title VI of such Act (relating to pension and individual retirement arrangement provisions)."

—P.L. 109-280, Sec. 864(a), added subsec. (f) in Sec. 530 of P. L. 95-600 [see below], effective for remuneration for services performed after 12/31/2006.

In 2005, P.L. 109-135, Sec. 412(tt), redesignated subsec. (h) as subsec. (g), effective 12/21/2005.

In 2004, P.L. 108-375, Sec. 585(b)(2)(D), substituted "134(b)(4), or 134(b)(5)" for "or 134(b)(4)" in para. (a)(18), effective for travel benefits provided after 10/28/2004.

—P.L. 108-357, Sec. 320(b)(4), added "108(f)(4)," after "74(c)," in para. (a)(19), effective for amounts received by an individual in tax. yrs. begin. after 12/31/2003.

—P.L. 108-357, Sec. 885(b)(2), added a flush sentence at the end of subsec. (a), effective for amounts deferred after 12/31/2004. Sec. 885(d)(2) and (3) of this Act, provides:

"(2) Special rules.

"(A) Earnings. The amendments made by this section shall apply to earnings on deferred compensation only to the extent that such amendments apply to such compensation.

"(B) Material modifications. For purposes of this subsection, amounts deferred in taxable years beginning before January 1, 2005, shall be treated as amounts deferred in a taxable year beginning on or after such date if the plan under which the deferral is made is materially modified after October 3, 2004, unless such modification is pursuant to the guidance issued under subsection (f).

"(3) Exception for nonelective deferred compensation. The amendments made by this section shall not apply to any nonelective deferred compensation to which section 457 of the Internal Revenue Code of 1986 does not apply by reason of section 457(e)(12) of such Code, but only if such compensation is provided under a nonqualified deferred compensation plan—

"(A) which was in existence on May 1, 2004,

"(B) which was providing nonelective deferred compensation described in such section 457(e)(12) on such date, and

"(C) which is established or maintained by an organization incorporated on July 2, 1974.

"If, after May 1, 2004, a plan described in the preceding sentence adopts a plan amendment which provides a material change in the classes of individuals eligible to participate in the plan, this paragraph shall not apply to any nonelective deferred compensation provided under the plan on or after the date of the adoption of the amendment."

In 2003, P.L. 108-173, Sec. 1201(d)(2)(C), deleted "or" at the end of para. (a)(20), substituted "; or" for the period at the end of para. (a)(21), and added para. (a)(22), effective for tax. yrs. begin. after 12/31/2003.

—P.L. 108-121, Sec. 106(b)(4), substituted ", 129, or 134(b)(4)" for "or 129" in para. (a)(18), effective for tax. yrs. begin. after 12/31/2002. Sec. 106(d) of this Act, provides:

"(d) No inference. No inference may be drawn from the amendments made by this section with respect to the tax treatment of any amounts under the program described in section 134(b)(4) of the Internal Revenue Code of 1986 (as added by this section) for any taxable year beginning before January 1, 2003."

In 2002, P.L. 107-358, Sec. 2, added subsec. (c) in Sec. 901 of P. L. 107-16 [see below], effective 12/17/2002.

In 2001, P.L. 107-16, Sec. 641(a)(1)(D)(i), added subpara. (a)(12)(E), effective for distributions after 12/31/2001. Sec. 641(f)(2) and (3) of this Act, provides:

"(2) Reasonable notice. No penalty shall be imposed on a plan for the failure to provide the information required by the amendment made by subsection (c) with respect to any distribution made before the date that is 90 days after the date on which the Secretary of the Treasury issues a safe harbor rollover notice after the date of the enactment of this Act, if the administrator of such plan makes a reasonable attempt to comply with such requirement.

"(3) Special rule. Notwithstanding any other provision of law, subsections (h)(3) and (h)(5) of section 1122 of the Tax Reform Act of 1986 shall not apply to any distribution from an eligible retirement plan (as defined in clause (iii) or (iv) of section 402(c)(8)(B) of the Internal Revenue Code of 1986) on behalf of an individual if there was a rollover to such plan on behalf of such individual which is permitted solely by reason of any amendment made by this section."

—P.L. 107-16, Sec. 901, of this Act [as amended by Sec. 2 of P.L. 107-358, and Sec. 101(a)(1) of P.L. 111-312, see above], reads as follows:

"SEC. 901. SUNSET OF PROVISIONS OF ACT.

"(a) In general. All provisions of, and amendments made by, this Act shall not apply—

"(1) to taxable, plan, or limitation years beginning after December 31, 2012, or

"(2) in the case of title V, to estates of decedents dying, gifts made, or generation skipping transfers, after December 31, 2012.

"(b) Application of certain laws. The Internal Revenue Code of 1986 and the Employee Retirement Income Security Act of 1974 shall be applied and administered to years, estates, gifts, and transfers described in subsection (a) as if the provisions and amendments described in subsection (a) had never been enacted.

"(c) Exception. Subsection (a) shall not apply to section 803 (relating to no federal income tax on restitution received by victims of the Nazi regime or their heirs or estates)."

In 1998, P.L. 105-206, Sec. 6023(14), added "for" before "any benefit provided to" in para. (a)(19) . . . Sec. 6023(15), added "for" before "any payment made" in para. (a)(21), effective 7/22/98.

In 1996, P.L. 104-188, Sec. 1122(a), amended Sec. 530 of P. L. 95-600 by adding subsec. (e), see below, effective as provided in Sec. 1122(b), of this Act, which reads as follows:

"(b) Effective dates.

"(1) In general. The amendment made by this section shall apply to periods after December 31, 1996.

3,145

Code Sec. 3401 — Wage withholding

"(2) Notice by Internal Revenue Service. Section 530(e)(1) of the Revenue Act of 1978 (as added by subsection (a)) shall apply to audits which commence after December 31, 1996.

"(3) Burden of proof.

"(A) In general. Section 530(e)(4) of the Revenue Act of 1978 (as added by subsection (a)) shall apply to disputes involving periods after December 31, 1996.

"(B) No inference. Nothing in the amendments made by this section shall be construed to infer the proper treatment of the burden of proof with respect to disputes involving periods before January 1, 1997."

—P.L. 104-188, Sec. 1421(b)(8)(D), added subpara. (a)(12)(D), effective for tax. yrs. begin. after 12/31/96.

—P.L. 104-188, Sec. 1704(t)(4)(C), substituted "combat zone compensation" for "combat pay" in para. (a)(1), effective 8/20/96.

—P.L. 104-191, Sec. 301(c)(2)(C), deleted "or" at the end of para. (a)(19), substituted "; or" for the period at the end of para. (a)(20), and added para. (a)(21), effective for tax. yrs. begin. after 12/31/96.

—P.L. 104-117, Sec. 1(a)(5), of this Act, regarding treatment of certain individuals performing services in certain hazardous duty areas, effective for remuneration paid after 3/20/96, provides:

"(a) General rule. For purposes of the following provisions of the Internal Revenue Code of 1986, a qualified hazardous duty area shall be treated in the same manner as if it were a combat zone (as determined under section 112 of such Code):

* * *

"(5) Section 3401(a)(1) (defining wages relating to combat pay for members of the Armed Forces)."

—P.L. 104-117, Sec. 1(b), of this Act, regarding treatment of certain individuals performing services in certain hazardous duty areas, effective 11/21/95, provides:

"(b) Qualified hazardous duty area. For purposes of this section, the term 'qualified hazardous duty area' means Bosnia and Herzegovina, Croatia, or Macedonia, if as of the date of the enactment of this section any member of the Armed Forces of the United States is entitled to special pay under section 310 of title 37, United States Code (relating to special pay; duty subject to hostile fire or imminent danger) for services performed in such country. Such term includes any such country only during the period such entitlement is in effect. Solely for purposes of applying section 7508 of the Internal Revenue Code of 1986, in the case of an individual who is performing services as part of Operation Joint Endeavor outside the United States while deployed away from such individual's permanent duty station, the term 'qualified hazardous duty area' includes, during the period for which such entitlement is in effect, any area in which such services are performed."

—P.L. 104-117, Sec. 1(c), added "to the extent remuneration for such service is excludable from gross income under such section" after "the United States)" in para. (a)(1), effective for remuneration paid after 3/20/96.

In 1990, P.L. 101-508, Sec. 11703(f)(1), deleted "or" at the end of para. (a)(18), substituted "; or" for the period at the end of para. (a)(19), and added para. (a)(20), effective as provided in Sec. 1151(k)(1) of P. L. 99-514 [reproduced in note following Code Sec. 414] but shall not apply for any amount paid before the date of enactment of this Act [11/5/90] which the employee treated as wages for purposes of Chapter 24 of the Internal Revenue Code of 1986 when paid.

In 1989, P.L. 101-239, Sec. 7631(a), amended para. (a)(2) . . . Sec. 7631(b), added subsec. (h) [sic (g)], effective for remunerations paid after 12/31/89.

Prior to amendment, para. (a)(2) read as follows:

"(2) for agricultural labor (as defined in section 3121(g)); or "

—P.L. 101-140, Sec. 203(a)(2), repealed as if not enacted Sec. 1011B(a)(22)(D) of P. L. 100-647 which added subsec. (g).

In 1988, P.L. 100-647, Sec. 1001(g)(4)(B)(iii), substituted "section 217 (determined without regard to section 274(n))" for "section 217" in para. (a)(15), . . . Sec. 1011(f)(9)(A), substituted "section 402(h)(1) and (2)" for "section 219" in subpara. (a)(12)(C) . . . Sec. 1011(f)(9)(B), substituted "an exclusion" for "a deduction" in subpara. (a)(12)(C), effective for yrs. begin. after 12/31/86.

—P.L. 100-647, Sec. 1011B(a)(33), added "or" at end of para. (a)(18), deleted para. (a)(19) and redesignated para. (a)(20) as para. (a)(19), effective as provided in Sec. 1151(k)(1) of P. L. 99-514 reproduced in note following Code Sec. 414.

Prior to deletion, para. (a)(19) read as follows:

"(19) for any medical care reimbursement made to or for the benefit of an employee under a self-insured medical reimbursement plan (within the meaning of section 105(h)(6)); or"

—P.L. 100-647, Sec. 6305, of this Act provides:

"Sec. 6305. Treatment of certain family services providers.

"(a) In general.

"A State may treat a person who renders dependent care or similar services as other than an employee employment tax purposes for the applicable period if all of the following conditions are satisfied with respect to such person for such applicable period:

"(i) The person does not provide any dependent care or similar services in any facility owned or operated by the State;

"(ii) The person is compensated by the State for such services, directly or indirectly, out of funds provided pursuant to chapter 7 of title 42 of the United States Code, or the provisions and amendments made by the Family Security Act of 1988.

"(iii) The State does not treat the person, with respect to the provision of dependent care or similar services, as an employee for employment tax purposes;

"(iv) The State files all Federal income tax returns (including information returns) required to be filed with respect to such person on a basis consistent with the State's treatment of such person as other than an employee beginning on the date of the enactment of this section; and

"(v) No more than ten percent of the State's employees are provided with insurance under title II of the Social Security Act pursuant to voluntary agreements with the Secretary of Health and Human Services under section 218 of such title.

"(b) State.

"For purposes of this section, the term 'State' shall mean the government of the United States, District of Columbia, any State or political subdivision thereof, and any agency or instrumentality of any of the foregoing.

"(c) Employment tax.

"For purposes of this section, the term 'employment tax' means any tax imposed by subtitle C of the Internal Revenue Code of 1986.

"(d) Applicable period.

"For purposes of this section, the term 'applicable period' means the period beginning on January 1, 1984 and ending on December 31, 1990.

"(e) Report.

"The Secretary of Treasury shall report to the Senate Committee on Finance and the House Committee on Ways and Means on the text status of day care providers compensated pursuant to the program described in the section no later than December 31, 1989."

In 1986, P.L. 99-514, Sec. 122(e)(4), substituted "74(c), 117, or" for "117 or" in para. (a)(20), effective for prizes and awards granted after 12/31/86.

—P.L. 99-514, Sec. 1272(c), added subpara. (a)(8)(D), effective for tax. yrs. begin. after 12/31/86.

—P.L. 99-514, Sec. 1706(a), added subsec. (d) to Sec. 530 of P. L. 95-600 [reproduced below], effective for remuneration paid and services rendered after 12/31/86.

In 1984, P.L. 98-369, Sec. 491(d)(38), deleted subpara. (a)(12)(C) and redesignated subpara. (a)(12)(D) as subpara. (a)(12)(C), effective for obligations issued after 12/31/83.

Prior to deletion, subpara. (a)(12)(C) read as follows:

"(C) under or to a bond purchase plan which, at the time of such payment, is a qualified bond purchase plan described in section 405(a); or"

—P.L. 98-369, Sec. 531(d)(4), substituted "all remuneration (including benefits) paid in any medium" for "all remuneration paid in any medium" in the material preceding para. (a)(1), deleted "or" at the end of para. (a)(18), substituted "; or" for the period at the end of para. (a)(19), and added new para. (a)(20), effective 1/1/85.

In 1983, P.L. 97-448, Sec. 103(c)(12)(B), substituted "section 219" for "section 219(a)" in subpara. (a)(12)(D), effective for tax. yrs. begin. after 12/31/81.

In 1982, P.L. 97-248, Sec. 269(c)(1), and (2) amended Sec. 530 of P. L. 95-600 (reproduced below) by deleting "ending before July 1, 1982" after "for any period" in subpara. (a)(1)(A) . . . by deleting "and before July 1, 1982," after "after December 31, 1978." in para. (a)(3) . . . by deleting "for periods before July 1, 1982" after "Termination of certain employment tax liability" in the heading of subsec. (a) . . . be deleting "July 1, 1982 (or, if earlier," after "and before" in subsec. (b) . . . by substituting "taxes" for "taxes)" in subsec. (b).

Sec. 269(c)(3) of this Act provides:

"(3) Certain regulations, etc. permitted. Nothing in section 530 of the Revenue Act of 1978 shall be construed to prohibit the implementation of the amendments made by this section [Sec. 269 of this Act]."

In 1981, P.L. 97-34, Sec. 112(b)(5), deleted para. (a)(18) and redesignated paras. (a)(19) and (a)(20) as paras. (a)(18) and (a)(19), effective for tax. yrs. begin. after 12/31/81.

Prior to deletion, para. (a)(18) read as follows:

"(18) to or on behalf of an employee if (and to the extent that) at the time of the payment of such remuneration it is reasonable to believe that a corresponding deduction is allowable under section 913 (relating to deduction for certain expenses of living abroad);"

—P.L. 97-34, Sec. 124(e)(2)(A), substituted "section 127 or 129" for "section 127" in para. (a)(19) [prior to redesignation as (a)(18) by Sec. 112(b)(5) of this Act], for remuneration paid after 12/31/81.

—P.L. 97-34, Sec. 311(h)(6), substituted "section 219(a)" for "section 219(a) or 220(a)" in subpara. (a)(12)(D), effective for tax. yrs. begin. after 12/31/81. For transitional rule, see Sec. 311(i)(2) of this Act reproduced in note following Code Sec. 219.

In 1980, P.L. 96-541, Sec. 1(a), amended Sec. 530 of P. L. 95-600 (reproduced below) by substituting "July 1, 1982" for "January 1, 1981" in subpara. (a)(1)(A) and para. (a)(3) . . . substituting "July 1, 1982" for "1981" in the heading for subsec. (a) . . . substituted "prior" for "1979 and 1980" in the heading of para. (a)(3).

—P.L. 96-541, Sec. 1(b), amended Sec. 530 of P. L. 95-600 (reproduced below) by substituting "July 1, 1982" for "January 1, 1981" in subsec. (b).

—P.L. 96-222, Sec. 103(a)(13)(A)(i), deleted "or" at the end of para. (a)(17) . . . Sec. 103(a)(13)(A)(ii), substituted a semicolon for the period at the end of para. (a)(18) (as added by Sec. 207(a) of P. L. 95-615) . . . Sec. 103(a)(13)(A)(iii), redesignated para. (a)(18) (as added by Sec. 164(b)(1) of P. L. 95-600) as para. (a)(19) . . . Sec. 103(a)(13)(A)(iv), substituted "section 127; or" for "section 124." in para. (a)(19) [as redesignated by Sec. 103(a)(13)(A)(iii) of this Act, see above] . . . Sec. 103(a)(13)(A)(v), added para. (a)(20), effective for tax. yrs. begin. after 12/31/79.

In 1979, P.L. 96-167, Sec. 9(d)(1), amended Sec. 530 of P. L. 95-600 (reproduced below) by substituting "January 1, 1981" for "January 1, 1980" in paras. (a)(1)(A) and (3) . . . substituted "1981" for "1980" in the heading of subsec. (a) . . . substituted "1979 and 1980" for "1979" in the heading of para. (a)(3).

—P.L. 96-167, Sec. 9(d)(2), amended Sec. 530 of P. L. 95-600 (reproduced below) by substituting "January 1, 1981" for "January 1, 1980" in subsec. (b).

Wage withholding — Code Sec. 3401

In 1978, P.L. 95-615, Sec. 207(a), substituted "; or" for the period at the end of para. (a)(17) and added para. (a)(18), effective for remuneration paid after 11/8/78.

—P.L. 95-600, Sec. 164(b)(1)(A), deleted "or" at the end of para. (a)(16) . . . Sec. 164(b)(1)(B), deleted the period at the end of para. (a)(17) . . . Sec. 164(b)(1)(C), added para. (a)(18) effective for tax. yrs. begin. after 12/31/78.

—P.L. 95-600, Sec. 530, [as amended by Sec. 9(d)(1) of P. L. 96-167, (2), Sec. 1(a) of P. L. 96-541, (b), Sec. 269(c)(1) of P. L. 97-248, (c)(2), Sec. 1706(a) of P. L. 99-514, Sec. 1122(a) of P. L. 104-188, and Sec. 864(a) of P. L. 109-280], provides the following rules regarding individuals as employees for purposes of employment taxes:

"Sec. 530. Controversies involving whether individuals are employees for purposes of the employment taxes.

"(a) Termination of certain employment tax liability.

"(1) In general. If—

"(A) for purposes of employment taxes, the taxpayer did not treat an individual as an employee for any period, and

"(B) in the case of periods after December 31, 1978, all Federal tax returns (including information returns) required to be filed by the taxpayer with respect to such individual for such period are filed on a basis consistent with the taxpayer's treatment of such individual as not being an employee,

then, for purposes of applying such taxes for such period with respect to the taxpayer, the individual shall be deemed not to be an employee unless the taxpayer had no reasonable basis for not treating such individual as an employee.

"(2) Statutory standards providing one method of satisfying the requirements of paragraph (1). For purposes of paragraph (1), a taxpayer shall in any case be treated as having a reasonable basis for not treating an individual as an employee for a period if the taxpayer's treatment of such individual for such period was in reasonable reliance on any of the following:

"(A) judicial precedent, published rulings, technical advice with respect to the taxpayer, or a letter ruling to the taxpayer;

"(B) a past Internal Revenue Service audit of the taxpayer in which there was no assessment attributable to the treatment (for employment tax purposes) of the individuals holding positions substantially similar to the position held by this individual; or

"(C) long-standing recognized practice of a significant segment of the industry in which such individual was engaged.

"(3) Consistency required in the case of prior tax treatment. Paragraph (1) shall not apply with respect to the treatment of any individual for employment tax purposes for any period ending after December 31, 1978, if the taxpayer (or a predecessor) has treated any individual holding a substantially similar position as an employee for purposes of the employment taxes for any period beginning after December 31, 1977.

"(4) Refund or credit of overpayment. If refund or credit of any overpayment of an employment tax resulting from the application of paragraph (1) is not barred on the date of the enactment of this Act by any law or rule of law, the period for filing a claim for refund or credit of such overpayment (to the extent attributable to the application of paragraph (1) shall not expire before the date 1 year after the date of the enactment of this Act.

"(b) Prohibition against regulations and rulings on employment status. No regulation or Revenue Ruling shall be published on or after the date of the enactment of this Act and before the effective date of any law hereafter enacted clarifying the employment status of individuals for purposes of the employment taxes by the Department of the Treasury (including the Internal Revenue Service) with respect to the employment status of any individual for purposes of the employment taxes.

"(c) Definitions. For purposes of this section—

"(1) Employment tax. The term 'employment tax' means any tax imposed by subtitle C of the Internal Revenue Code of 1954.

"(2) Employment status. The term 'employment status' means the status of an individual, under the usual common law rules applicable in determining the employer-employee relationship, as an employee or as an independent contractor (or other individual who is not an employee).

"(d) Exception.

"This section shall not apply in the case of an individual who, pursuant to an arrangement between the taxpayer and another person, provides services for such other person as an engineer, designer, drafter, computer programmer, systems analyst, or other similarly skilled worker engaged in a similar line of work.

"(e) Special rules for application of section.

"(1) Notice of availability of section. An officer or employee of the Internal Revenue Service shall, before or at the commencement of any audit inquiry relating to the employment status of one or more individuals who perform services for the taxpayer, provide the taxpayer with a written notice of the provisions of this section.

"(2) Rules relating to statutory standards. For purposes of subsection (a)(2)—

"(A) a taxpayer may not rely on an audit commenced after December 31, 1996, for purposes of subparagraph (B) thereof unless such audit included an examination for employment tax purposes of whether the individual involved (or any individual holding a position substantially similar to the position held by the individual involved) should be treated as an employee of the taxpayer,

"(B) in no event shall the significant segment requirement of subparagraph (C) thereof be construed to require a reasonable showing of the practice of more than 25 percent of the industry (determined by not taking into account the taxpayer), and

"(C) in applying the long-standing recognized practice requirement of subparagraph (C) thereof—

"(i) such requirement shall not be construed as requiring the practice to have continued for more than 10 years, and

"(ii) a practice shall not fail to be treated as long-standing merely because such practice began after 1978.

"(3) Availability of safe harbors. Nothing in this section shall be construed to provide that subsection (a) only applies where the individual involved is otherwise an employee of the taxpayer.

"(4) Burden of proof.

"(A) In general. If—

"(i) a taxpayer establishes a prima facie case that it was reasonable not to treat an individual as an employee for purposes of this section, and

"(ii) the taxpayer has fully cooperated with reasonable requests from the Secretary of the Treasury or his delegate,

then the burden of proof with respect to such treatment shall be on the Secretary.

"(B) Exception for other reasonable basis. In the case of any issue involving whether the taxpayer had a reasonable basis not to treat an individual as an employee for purposes of this section, subparagraph (A) shall only apply for purposes of determining whether the taxpayer meets the requirements of subparagraph (A), (B), or (C) of subsection (a)(2).

"(5) Preservation of prior period safe harbor. If—

"(A) an individual would (but for the treatment referred to in subparagraph (B)) be deemed not to be an employee of the taxpayer under subsection (a) for any prior period, and

"(B) such individual is treated by the taxpayer as an employee for employment tax purposes for any subsequent period,

then, for purposes of applying such taxes for such prior period with respect to the taxpayer, the individual shall be deemed not to be an employee.

"(6) Substantially similar position. For purposes of this section, the determination as to whether an individual holds a position substantially similar to a position held by another individual shall include consideration of the relationship between the taxpayer and such individuals.

"(f) Treatment of Test Room Supervisors and Proctors Who Assist in the Administration of College Entrance and Placement Exams.

"(1) In general. In the case of an individual described in paragraph (2) who is providing services as a test proctor or room supervisor by assisting in the administration of college entrance or placement examinations, this section shall be applied to such services performed after December 31, 2006 (and remuneration paid for such services) without regard to subsection (a)(3) thereof.

"(2) Applicability. An individual is described in this paragraph if the individual—

"(A) is providing the services described in subsection (a) to an organization described in section 501(c), and exempt from tax under section 501(a), of the Internal Revenue Code of 1986, and

"(B) is not otherwise treated as an employee of such organization for purposes of subtitle C of such Code (relating to employment taxes)."

—P.L. 95-600, Sec. 701(z)(1), amended the effective date for changes made by Sec. 1207(e)(1)(C) of P. L. 94-455 [see below] by substituting "December 31, 1954" for "December 31, 1971" each place it appeared in Sec. 1207(f)(4) of P. L. 94-455, effective 10/4/76.

In 1976, P.L. 94-455, Sec. 1207(e)(1)(C), substituted "; or" for the period at the end of para. (a)(16) and added para. (a)(17), effective [as amended by Sec. 701(z)(1) of P. L. 95-600, see above] for tax. yrs. end. after 12/31/54.

—P.L. 94-455, Sec. 1501(b)(7), added "or 220(a)" after "219(a)" in subpara. (a)(12)(D), effective for tax. yrs. begin. after 12/31/76.

—P.L. 94-455, Sec. 1903(c), deleted "Territory," after "a State," in subsec. (c), effective for wages paid after 12/31/76.

—P.L. 94-455, Sec. 1906(b)(13)(A), substituted "Secretary" for "Secretary or his delegate" in para. (a)(6), effective 2/1/77.

In 1974, P.L. 93-406, Sec. 2002(g)(7), added subpara. (a)(12)(D), effective 1/1/75.

In 1972, P.L. 92-279, Sec. 2, amended para. (a)(1), effective for wages paid on or after 6/1/72.

Prior to amendment, para. (a)(1) read as follows:

"(1) for active service as a member of the Armed Forces of the United States performed in a month for which such member is entitled to the benefits of section 112; or"

In 1966, P.L. 89-809, Sec. 103(k), amended para. (a)(6) and deleted para. (a)(7), effective for remuneration paid after 12/31/66.

Prior to amendment, para. (a)(6) read as follows:

"(6) for services performed by a nonresident alien individual, other than—

"(A) a resident of a contiguous country who enters and leaves the United States at frequent intervals; or

"(B) a resident of Puerto Rico if such services are performed as an employee of the United States or any agency thereof; or

"(C) an individual who is temporarily present in the United States as a nonimmigrant under subparagraph (F) or (J) of section 101(a)(15) of the Immigration and Nationality Act, as amended, if such remuneration is exempt, under section 1441(c)(4)(B), from deduction and withholding under section 1441(a), and is not exempt from taxation under section 872(b)(3); or"

Prior to deletion, para. (a)(7) read as follows:

"(7) for such services, performed by a nonresident alien individual who is a resident of a contiguous country and who enters and leaves the United States at frequent intervals, as may be designated by regulations prescribed by the Secretary or his delegate; or"

In 1965, P.L. 89-97, Sec. 313(d)(1), added subsec. (f) . . . Sec. 313(d)(2), substituted "; or" for ", or" at the end of para. (a)(6), substituted "; or" for the period at the end of para. (a)(12), substituted "; or" for the period at the end of para. (a)(15) and added para. (a)(16), effective only for tips received by employees after 1965.

3,147

Code Sec. 3401

In **1964,** P.L. 88-272, Sec. 204(b), substituted "; or" for the period at the end of para. (a)(13) and added para. (a)(14), effective for remuneration paid after 12/31/63 in the form of group term life insurance provided after 12/31/63.
—P.L. 88-272, Sec. 213(c), added para. (a)(15) after para. (a)(14) [as added by Sec. 204(b) of this Act, see above], effective for remuneration paid after the seventh day following 2/26/64.

In **1962,** P.L. 87-792, Sec. 7(1), amended subpara. (a)(12)(B) and added subpara. (a)(12)(C), effective for tax. yrs. begin. after 12/31/62.

Prior to amendment, subpara. (a)(12)(B) read as follows:

"(B) under or to an annuity plan which, at the time of such payment, meets the requirements of section 401(a)(3), (4), (5), and (6); or".

In **1961,** P.L. 87-256, Sec. 110(g)(1), added subpara. (a)(6)(C), effective for wages paid after 12/31/61.
—P.L. 87-293, Sec. 201(c), added para. (a)(13), effective for remuneration paid after 9/22/61.

In **1955,** P.L. 321, Sec. [1](a), amended subsec. (a), effective 8/9/55.

Prior to amendment, subsec. (a) read as follows:

"(a) Wages. For purposes of this chapter, the term 'wages' means all remuneration (other than fees paid to a public official) for services performed by an employee for his employer, including the cash value of all remuneration paid in any medium other than cash; except that such term shall not include remuneration paid—

"(1) for active service as a member of the Armed Forces of the United States performed in a month for which such member is entitled to the benefits of section 112; or

"(2) for agricultural labor (as defined in section 3121(g); or

"(3) for domestic service in a private home, local college club, or local chapter of a college fraternity or sorority; or

"(4) for service not in the course of the employer's trade or business performed in any calendar quarter by an employee, unless the cash remuneration paid for such service is $50 or more and such service is performed by an individual who is regularly employed by such employer to perform such service. For purposes of this paragraph, an individual shall be deemed to be regularly employed by an employer during a calendar quarter only if—

"(A) on each of some 24 days during such quarter such individual performs for such employer for some portion of the day service not in the course of the employer's trade or business; or

"(B) such individual was regularly employed (as determined under subparagraph (A)) by such employer in the performance of such service during the preceding calendar quarter; or

"(5) for services by a citizen or resident of the United States for a foreign government or an international organization; or

"(6) for services performed by a nonresident alien individual, other than—

"(A) a resident of a contiguous country who enters and leaves the United States at frequent intervals; or

"(B) a resident of Puerto Rico if such services are performed as an employee of the United States or any agency thereof; or

"(7) for such services, performed by a nonresident alien individual who is a resident of a contiguous country and who enters and leaves the United States at frequent intervals, as may be designated by regulations prescribed by the Secretary or his delegate; or

"(8)(A) for services for an employer (other than the United States or any agency thereof)—

"(i) performed by a citizen of the United States if, at the time of the payment of such remuneration, it is reasonable to believe that such remuneration will be excluded from gross income under section 911; or

"(ii) performed in a foreign country by such a citizen if, at the time of the payment of such remuneration, the employer is required by the law of any foreign country to withhold income tax upon such remuneration; or

"(B) for services for an employer (other than the United States or any agency thereof) performed by a citizen of the United States within a possession of the United States (other than Puerto Rico), if it is reasonable to believe that at least 80 percent of the remuneration to be paid to the employee by such employer during the calendar year will be for such services; or

"(C) for services for an employer (other than the United States or any agency thereof) performed by a citizen of the United States within Puerto Rico, if it is reasonable to believe that during the entire calendar year the employee will be a bona fide resident of Puerto Rico; or

"(9) for services performed by a duly ordained, commissioned, or licensed minister of a church in the exercise of his ministry or by a member of a religious order in the exercise of duties required by such order; or

"(10)(A) for services performed by an individual under the age of 18 in the delivery or distribution of newspapers or shopping news, not including delivery or distribution to any point for subsequent delivery or distribution; or

"(B) for services performed by an individual in, and at the time of, the sale of newspapers or magazines to ultimate consumers, under an arrangement under which the newspapers or magazines are to be sold by him at a fixed price, his compensation being based on the retention of the excess of such price over the amount at which the newspapers or magazines are charged to him, whether or not he is guaranteed a minimum amount of compensation for such service, or is entitled to be credited with the unsold newspapers or magazines turned back; or

"(11) for services not in the course of the employer's trade or business, to the extent paid in any medium other than cash; or

"(12) to, or on behalf of, an employee or his beneficiary—

"(A) from or to a trust described in section 401(a) which is exempt from tax under section 501(a) at the time of such payment unless such payment is made to

an employee of the trust as remuneration for services rendered as such employee and not as a beneficiary of the trust; or

"(B) under or to an annuity plan which, at the time of such payment, meets the requirements of section 401(a)(3), (4), (5), and (6)."

Sec. 3402. Income tax collected at source.

(a) Requirement of withholding.

(1) In general. Except as otherwise provided in this section, every employer making payment of wages shall deduct and withhold upon such wages a tax determined in accordance with tables or computational procedures prescribed by the Secretary. Any tables or procedures prescribed under this paragraph shall—

(A) apply with respect to the amount of wages paid during such periods as the Secretary may prescribe, and (B) be in such form, and provide for such amounts to be deducted and withheld, as the Secretary determines to be most appropriate to carry out the purposes of this chapter and to reflect the provisions of chapter 1 applicable to such periods.

(2) Amount of wages. For purposes of applying tables or procedures prescribed under paragraph (1), the term "the amount of wages" means the amount by which the wages exceed the number of withholding exemptions claimed multiplied by the amount of one such exemption. The amount of each withholding exemption shall be equal to the amount of one personal exemption provided in section 151(b), prorated to the payroll period. The maximum number of withholding exemptions permitted shall be calculated in accordance with regulations prescribed by the Secretary under this section, taking into account any reduction in withholding to which an employee is entitled under this section.

(b) Percentage method of withholding.

(1) If wages are paid with respect to a period which is not a payroll period, the withholding exemption allowable with respect to each payment of such wages shall be the exemption allowed for a miscellaneous payroll period containing a number of days (including Sundays and holidays) equal to the number of days in the period with respect to which such wages are paid.

(2) In any case in which wages are paid by an employer without regard to any payroll period or other period, the withholding exemption allowable with respect to each payment of such wages shall be the exemption allowed for a miscellaneous payroll period containing a number of days equal to the number of days (including Sundays and holidays) which have elapsed since the date of the last payment of such wages by such employer during the calendar year, or the date of commencement of employment with such employer during such year, or January 1 of such year, whichever is the later.

(3) In any case in which the period, or the time described in paragraph (2), in respect of any wages is less than one week, the Secretary, under regulations prescribed by him, may authorize an employer to compute the tax to be deducted and withheld as if the aggregate of the wages paid to the employee during the calendar week were paid for a weekly payroll period.

(4) In determining the amount to be deducted and withheld under this subsection, the wages may, at the election of the employer, be computed to the nearest dollar.

(c) Wage bracket withholding.

(1) At the election of the employer with respect to any employee, the employer shall deduct and withhold upon the wages paid to such employee a tax (in lieu of the tax required to be deducted and withheld under subsection

Wage withholding

Code Sec. 3402(f)(3)(A)

(a)) determined in accordance with tables prescribed by the Secretary in accordance with paragraph (6).

(2) If wages are paid with respect to a period which is not a payroll period, the amount to be deducted and withheld shall be that applicable in the case of a miscellaneous payroll period containing a number of days (including Sundays and holidays) equal to the number of days in the period with respect to which such wages are paid.

(3) In any case in which wages are paid by an employer without regard to any payroll period or other period, the amount to be deducted and withheld shall be that applicable in the case of a miscellaneous payroll period containing a number of days equal to the number of days (including Sundays and holidays) which have elapsed since the date of the last payment of such wages by such employer during the calendar year, or the date of commencement of employment with such employer during such year, or January 1 of such year, whichever is the later.

(4) In any case in which the period, or the time described in paragraph (3), in respect of any wages is less than one week, the Secretary, under regulations prescribed by him, may authorize an employer to determine the amount to be deducted and withheld under the tables applicable in the case of a weekly payroll period, in which case the aggregate of the wages paid to the employee during the calendar week shall be considered the weekly wages.

(5) If the wages exceed the highest wage bracket, in determining the amount to be deducted and withheld under this subsection, the wages may, at the election of the employer, be computed to the nearest dollar.

(6) In the case of wages paid after December 31, 1969, the amount deducted and withheld under paragraph (1) shall be determined in accordance with tables prescribed by the Secretary. In the tables so prescribed, the amounts set forth as amounts of wages and amounts of income tax to be deducted and withheld shall be computed on the basis of table for an annual payroll period prescribed pursuant to subsection (a).

(d) Tax paid by recipient.

If the employer, in violation of the provisions of this chapter, fails to deduct and withhold the tax under this chapter, and thereafter the tax against which such tax may be credited is paid, the tax so required to be deducted and withheld shall not be collected from the employer; but this subsection shall in no case relieve the employer from liability for any penalties or additions to the tax otherwise applicable in respect of such failure to deduct and withhold.

(e) Included and excluded wages.

If the remuneration paid by an employer to an employee for services performed during one-half or more of any payroll period of not more than 31 consecutive days constitutes wages, all the remuneration paid by such employer to such employee for such period shall be deemed to be wages; but if the remuneration paid by an employer to an employee for services performed during more than one-half of any such payroll period does not constitute wages, then none of the remuneration paid by such employer to such employee for such period shall be deemed to be wages.

(f) Withholding exemptions.

(1) **In general.** An employee receiving wages shall on any day be entitled to the following withholding exemptions:

(A) an exemption for himself unless he is an individual described in section 151(d)(2);

(B) if the employee is married, any exemption to which his spouse is entitled, or would be entitled if such spouse were an employee receiving wages, under subparagraph (A) or (D), but only if such spouse does not have in effect a withholding exemption certificate claiming such exemption;

(C) an exemption for each individual with respect to whom, on the basis of facts existing at the beginning of such day, there may reasonably be expected to be allowable an exemption under section 151(c) for the taxable year under subtitle A in respect of which amounts deducted and withheld under this chapter in the calendar year in which such day falls are allowed as a credit;

(D) any allowance to which he is entitled under subsection (m), but only if his spouse does not have in effect a withholding exemption certificate claiming such allowance; and

(E) a standard deduction allowance which shall be an amount equal to one exemption (or more than one exemption if so prescribed by the Secretary) unless (i) he is married (as determined under section 7703) and his spouse is an employee receiving wages subject to withholding or (ii) he has withholding exemption certificates in effect with respect to more than one employer.

For purposes of this title, any standard deduction allowance under subparagraph (E) shall be treated as if it were denominated a withholding exemption.

(2) **Exemption certificates.**

(A) On commencement of employment. On or before the date of the commencement of employment with an employer, the employee shall furnish the employer with a signed withholding exemption certificate relating to the number of withholding exemptions which he claims, which shall in no event exceed the number to which he is entitled.

(B) Change of status. If, on any day during the calendar year, the number of withholding exemptions to which the employee is entitled is less than the number of withholding exemptions claimed by the employee on the withholding exemption certificate then in effect with respect to him, the employee shall within 10 days thereafter furnish the employer with a new withholding exemption certificate relating to the number of withholding exemptions which the employee then claims, which shall in no event exceed the number to which he is entitled on such day. If, on any day during the calendar year, the number of withholding exemptions to which the employee is entitled is greater than the number of withholding exemptions claimed, the employee may furnish the employer with a new withholding exemption certificate relating to the number of withholding exemptions which the employee then claims, which shall in no event exceed the number to which he is entitled on such day.

(C) Change of status which affects next calendar year. If on any day during the calendar year the number of withholding exemptions to which the employee will be, or may reasonably be expected to be, entitled at the beginning of his next taxable year under subtitle A is different from the number to which the employee is entitled on such day, the employee shall, in such cases and at such times as the Secretary may by regulations prescribe, furnish the employer with a withholding exemption certificate relating to the number of withholding exemptions which he claims with respect to such next taxable year, which shall in no event exceed the number to which he will be, or may reasonably be expected to be, so entitled.

(3) **When certificate takes effect.**

(A) First certificate furnished. A withholding exemption certificate furnished the employer in cases in which no previous such certificate is in effect shall take effect as of the beginning of the first payroll period ending, or the first payment of wages made without regard to a payroll period, on or after the date on which such certificate is so furnished.

(B) Furnished to take place of existing certificate.

(i) In general. Except as provided in clauses (ii) and (iii), a withholding exemption certificate furnished to the employer in cases in which a previous such certificate is in effect shall take effect as of the beginning of the 1st payroll period ending (or the 1st payment of wages made without regard to a payroll period) on or after the 30th day after the day on which such certificate is so furnished.

(ii) Employer may elect earlier effective date. At the election of the employer, a certificate described in clause (i) may be made effective beginning with any payment of wages made on or after the day on which the certificate is so furnished and before the 30th day referred to in clause (i).

(iii) Change of status which affects next year. Any certificate furnished pursuant to paragraph (2)(C) shall not take effect, and may not be made effective, with respect to any payment of wages made in the calendar year in which the certificate is furnished.

(4) **Period during which certificate remains in effect.** A withholding exemption certificate which takes effect under this subsection, or which on December 31, 1954, was in effect under the corresponding subsection of prior law, shall continue in effect with respect to the employer until another such certificate takes effect under this subsection.

(5) **Form and contents of certificate.** Withholding exemption certificates shall be in such form and contain such information as the Secretary may by regulations prescribe.

(6) **Exemption of certain nonresident aliens.** Notwithstanding the provisions of paragraph (1), a nonresident alien individual (other than an individual described in section 3401(a)(6)(A) or (B)) shall be entitled to only one withholding exemption.

(7) **Exemption where certificate with another employer is in effect.** If a withholding exemption certificate is in effect with respect to one employer, an employee shall not be entitled under a certificate in effect with any other employer to any withholding exemption which he has claimed under such first certificate.

(g) **Overlapping pay periods, and payment by agent or fiduciary.**

If a payment of wages is made to an employee by an employer—

(1) with respect to a payroll period or other period, any part of which is included in a payroll period or other period with respect to which wages are also paid to such employee by such employer, or

(2) without regard to any payroll period or other period, but on or prior to the expiration of a payroll period or other period with respect to which wages are also paid to such employee by such employer, or

(3) with respect to a period beginning in one and ending in another calendar year, or

(4) through an agent, fiduciary, or other person who also has the control, receipt, custody, or disposal of, or pays, the wages payable by another employer to such employee, the manner of withholding and the amount to be deducted and withheld under this chapter shall be determined in accordance with regulations prescribed by the Secretary under which the withholding exemption allowed to the employee in any calendar year shall approximate the withholding exemption allowable with respect to an annual payroll period.

(h) **Alternative methods of computing amount to be withheld.**

The Secretary may, under regulations prescribed by him, authorize—

(1) **Withholding on basis of average wages.** An employer—

(A) to estimate the wages which will be paid to any employee in any quarter of the calendar year,

(B) to determine the amount to be deducted and withheld upon each payment of wages to such employee during such quarter as if the appropriate average of the wages so estimated constituted the actual wages paid, and

(C) to deduct and withhold upon any payment of wages to such employee during such quarter (and, in the case of tips referred to in subsection (k), within 30 days thereafter) such amount as may be necessary to adjust the amount actually deducted and withheld upon the wages of such employee during such quarter to the amount required to be deducted and withheld during such quarter without regard to this subsection.

(2) **Withholding on basis of annualized wages.** An employer to determine the amount of tax to be deducted and withheld upon a payment of wages to an employee for a payroll period by—

(A) multiplying the amount of an employee's wages for a payroll period by the number of such payroll periods in the calendar year,

(B) determining the amount of tax which would be required to be deducted and withheld upon the amount determined under subparagraph (A) if such amount constituted the actual wages for the calendar year and the payroll period of the employee were an annual payroll period, and

(C) dividing the amount of tax determined under subparagraph (B) by the number of payroll periods (described in subparagraph (A)) in the calendar year.

(3) **Withholding on basis of cumulative wages.** An employer, in the case of any employee who requests to have the amount of tax to be withheld from his wages computed on the basis of his cumulative wages, to—

(A) add the amount of the wages to be paid to the employee for the payroll period to the total amount of wages paid by the employer to the employee during the calendar year,

(B) divide the aggregate amount of wages computed under subparagraph (A) by the number of payroll periods to which such aggregate amount of wages relates,

(C) compute the total amount of tax that would have been required to be deducted and withheld under subsection (a) if the average amount of wages (as computed under subparagraph (B)) had been paid to the employee for the number of payroll periods to which the aggregate amount of wages (computed under subparagraph (A)) relates,

(D) determine the excess, if any, of the amount of tax computed under subparagraph (C) over the total amount of tax deducted and withheld by the employer from wages paid to the employee during the calendar year, and

(E) deduct and withhold upon the payment of wages (referred to in subparagraph (A)) to the employee an

Wage withholding Code Sec. 3402(o)(1)(B)

amount equal to the excess (if any) computed under subparagraph (D).

(4) Other methods. An employer to determine the amount of tax to be deducted and withheld upon the wages paid to an employee by any other method which will require the employer to deduct and withhold upon such wages substantially the same amount as would be required to be deducted and withheld by applying subsection (a) or (c), either with respect to a payroll period or with respect to the entire taxable year.

(i) Changes in withholding.

(1) In general. The Secretary may by regulations provide for increases in the amount of withholding otherwise required under this section in cases where the employee requests such changes.

(2) Treatment as tax. Any increased withholding under paragraph (1) shall for all purposes be considered tax required to be deducted and withheld under this chapter.

(j) Noncash remuneration to retail commission salesman.

In the case of remuneration paid in any medium other than cash for services performed by an individual as a retail salesman for a person, where the service performed by such individual for such person is ordinarily performed for remuneration solely by way of cash commission an employer shall not be required to deduct or withhold any tax under this subchapter with respect to such remuneration, provided that such employer files with the Secretary such information with respect to such remuneration as the Secretary may by regulation prescribe.

(k) Tips.

In the case of tips which constitute wages, subsection (a) shall be applicable only to such tips as are included in a written statement furnished to the employer pursuant to section 6053(a), and only to the extent that the tax can be deducted and withheld by the employer, at or after the time such statement is so furnished and before the close of the calendar year in which such statement is furnished, from such wages of the employee (excluding tips, but including funds turned over by the employee to the employer for the purpose of such deduction and withholding) as are under the control of the employer; and an employer who is furnished by an employee a written statement of tips (received in a calendar month) pursuant to section 6053(a) to which paragraph (16)(B) of section 3401(a) is applicable may deduct and withhold the tax with respect to such tips from any wages of the employee (excluding tips) under his control, even though at the time such statement is furnished the total amount of the tips included in statements furnished to the employer as having been received by the employee in such calendar month in the course of his employment by such employer is less than $20. Such tax shall not at any time be deducted and withheld in an amount which exceeds the aggregate of such wages and funds (including funds turned over under section 3102(c)(2) or section 3202(c)(2)) minus any tax required by section 3102(a) or section 3202(a) to be collected from such wages and funds.

(l) Determination and disclosure of marital status.

(1) Determination of status by employer. For purposes of applying the tables in subsections (a) and (c) to a payment of wages, the employer shall treat the employee as a single person unless there is in effect with respect to such payment of wages a withholding exemption certificate furnished to the employer by the employee after the date of the enactment of this subsection indicating that the employee is married.

(2) Disclosure of status by employee. An employee shall be entitled to furnish the employer with a withholding exemption certificate indicating he is married only if, on the day of such furnishing, he is married (determined with the application of the rules in paragraph (3)). An employee whose marital status changes from married to single shall, at such time as the Secretary may by regulations prescribe, furnish the employer with a new withholding exemption certificate.

(3) Determination of marital status. For purposes of paragraph (2), an employee shall on any day be considered—

(A) as not married, if (i) he is legally separated from his spouse under a decree of divorce or separate maintenance, or (ii) either he or his spouse is, or on any preceding day within the calendar year was, a nonresident alien; or

(B) as married, if (i) his spouse (other than a spouse referred to in subparagraph (A)) died within the portion of his taxable year which precedes such day, or (ii) his spouse died during one of the two taxable years immediately preceding the current taxable year and, on the basis of facts existing at the beginning of such day, the employee reasonably expects, at the close of his taxable year, to be a surviving spouse (as defined in section 2(a)).

(m) Withholding allowances.

Under regulations prescribed by the Secretary, an employee shall be entitled to additional withholding allowances or additional reductions in withholding under this subsection. In determining the number of additional withholding allowances or the amount of additional reductions in withholding under this subsection, the employee may take into account (to the extent and in the manner provided by such regulations)—

(1) estimated itemized deductions allowable under chapter 1 (other than the deductions referred to in section 151 and other than the deductions required to be taken into account in determining adjusted gross income under section 62(a) (other than paragraph (10) thereof)),

(2) estimated tax credits allowable under chapter 1, and

(3) such additional deductions (including the additional standard deduction under section 63(c)(3) for the aged and blind) and other items as may be specified by the Secretary in regulations.

(n) Employees incurring no income tax liability.

Notwithstanding any other provision of this section, an employer shall not be required to deduct and withhold any tax under this chapter upon a payment of wages to an employee if there is in effect with respect to such payment a withholding exemption certificate (in such form and containing such other information as the Secretary may prescribe) furnished to the employer by the employee certifying that the employee—

(1) incurred no liability for income tax imposed under subtitle A for his preceding taxable year, and

(2) anticipates that he will incur no liability for income tax imposed under subtitle A for his current taxable year.

The Secretary shall by regulations provide for the coordination of the provisions of this subsection with the provisions of subsection (f).

(o) Extension of withholding to certain payments other than wages.

(1) General rule. For purposes of this chapter (and so much of subtitle F as relates to this chapter)—

(A) any supplemental unemployment compensation benefit paid to an individual,

(B) any payment of an annuity to an individual, if at the time the payment is made a request that such annuity be subject to withholding under this chapter is in effect, and

(C) any payment to an individual of sick pay which does not constitute wages (determined without regard to this subsection), if at the time the payment is made a request that such sick pay be subject to withholding under this chapter is in effect,

shall be treated as if it were a payment of wages by an employer to an employee for a payroll period.

(2) Definitions.

(A) Supplemental unemployment compensation benefits. For purposes of paragraph (1), the term "supplemental unemployment compensation benefits" means amounts which are paid to an employee, pursuant to a plan to which the employer is a party, because of an employee's involuntary separation from employment (whether or not such separation is temporary), resulting directly from a reduction in force, the discontinuance of a plant or operation, or other similar conditions, but only to the extent such benefits are includible in the employee's gross income.

(B) Annuity. For purposes of this subsection, the term "annuity" means any amount paid to an individual as a pension or annuity.

(C) Sick pay. For purposes of this subsection, the term "sick pay" means any amount which—

(i) is paid to an employee pursuant to a plan to which the employer is a party, and

(ii) constitutes remuneration or a payment in lieu of remuneration for any period during which the employee is temporarily absent from work on account of sickness or personal injuries.

(3) Amount withheld from annuity payments or sick pay. If a payee makes a request that an annuity or any sick pay be subject to withholding under this chapter, the amount to be deducted and withheld under this chapter from any payment to which such request applies shall be an amount (not less than a minimum amount determined under regulations prescribed by the Secretary) specified by the payee in such request. The amount deducted and withheld with respect to a payment which is greater or less than a full payment shall bear the same relation to the specified amount as such payment bears to a full payment.

(4) Request for withholding. A request that an annuity or any sick pay be subject to withholding under this chapter—

(A) shall be made by the payee in writing to the person making the payments and shall contain the social security number of the payee,

(B) shall specify the amount to be deducted and withheld from each full payment, and

(C) shall take effect—

(i) in the case of sick pay, with respect to payments made more than 7 days after the date on which such request is furnished to the payor, or

(ii) in the case of an annuity, at such time (after the date on which such request is furnished to the payor) as the Secretary shall by regulations prescribe.

Such a request may be changed or terminated by furnishing to the person making the payments a written statement of change or termination which shall take effect in the same manner as provided in subparagraph (C). At the election of the payor, any such request (or statement of change or revocation) may take effect earlier than as provided in subparagraph (C).

(5) Special rule for sick pay paid pursuant to certain collective-bargaining agreements. In the case of any sick pay paid pursuant to a collective-bargaining agreement between employee representatives and one or more employers which contains a provision specifying that this paragraph is to apply to sick pay paid pursuant to such agreement and contains a provision for determining the amount to be deducted and withheld from each payment of such sick pay—

(A) the requirement of paragraph (1)(C) that a request for withholding be in effect shall not apply, and

(B) except as provided in subsection (n), the amounts to be deducted and withheld under this chapter shall be determined in accordance with such agreement.

The preceding sentence shall not apply with respect to sick pay paid pursuant to any agreement to any individual unless the social security number of such individual is furnished to the payor and the payor is furnished with such information as is necessary to determine whether the payment is pursuant to the agreement and to determine the amount to be deducted and withheld.

(6) Coordination with withholding on designated distributions under section 3405. This subsection shall not apply to any amount which is a designated distribution (within the meaning of section 3405(e)(1)).

(p) Voluntary withholding agreements.

(1) Certain federal payments.

(A) In general. If, at the time a specified Federal payment is made to any person, a request by such person is in effect that such payment be subject to withholding under this chapter, then for purposes of this chapter and so much of subtitle F as relates to this chapter, such payment shall be treated as if it were a payment of wages by an employer to an employee.

• *Caution:* Code Sec. 3402(p)(1)(B), following, was amended by Sec. 101(c)(6), P.L. 107-16, the Economic Growth and Tax Relief Reconciliation Act of 2001 (EGTRRA). These provisions generally sunset for tax years beginning after 12/31/2012. For specific sunset provisions, see Sec. 901, P.L. 107-16 (as amended) reproduced in history notes for this Code Sec.

(B) Amount withheld. The amount to be deducted and withheld under this chapter from any payment to which any request under subparagraph (A) applies shall be an amount equal to the percentage of such payment specified in such request. Such a request shall apply to any payment only if the percentage specified is 7 percent, any percentage applicable to any of the 3 lowest income brackets in the table under section 1(c), or such other percentage as is permitted under regulations prescribed by the Secretary.

(C) Specified federal payments. For purposes of this paragraph, the term "specified Federal payment" means—

(i) any payment of a social security benefit (as defined in section 86(d)),

(ii) any payment referred to in the second sentence of section 451(d) which is treated as insurance proceeds,

(iii) any amount which is includible in gross income under section 77(a), and

(iv) any other payment made pursuant to Federal law which is specified by the Secretary for purposes of this paragraph.

(D) Requests for withholding. Rules similar to the rules that apply to annuities under subsection (o)(4) shall apply to requests under this paragraph and paragraph (2).

• *Caution:* Code Sec. 3402(p)(2), following, was amended by Sec. 101(c)(7), P.L. 107-16, the Economic Growth and Tax Relief Reconciliation Act of 2001 (EGTRRA). These provisions generally sunset for tax years beginning after 12/31/2012. For specific sunset provisions see Sec. 901, P.L. 107-16 (as amended) reproduced in history notes for this Code Sec.

---

(2) **Voluntary withholding on unemployment benefits.** If, at the time a payment of unemployment compensation (as defined in section 85(b)) is made to any person, a request by such person is in effect that such payment be subject to withholding under this chapter, then for purposes of this chapter and so much of subtitle F as relates to this chapter, such payment shall be treated as if it were a payment of wages by an employer to an employee. The amount to be deducted and withheld under this chapter from any payment to which any request under this paragraph applies shall be an amount equal to 10 percent of such payment.

(3) **Authority for other voluntary withholding.** The Secretary is authorized by regulations to provide for withholding—

(A) from remuneration for services performed by an employee for the employee's employer which (without regard to this paragraph) does not constitute wages, and

(B) from any other type of payment with respect to which the Secretary finds that withholding would be appropriate under the provisions of this chapter,

if the employer and employee, or the person making and the person receiving such other type of payment, agree to such withholding. Such agreement shall be in such form and manner as the Secretary may by regulations prescribe. For purposes of this chapter (and so much of subtitle F as relates to this chapter), remuneration or other payments with respect to which such agreement is made shall be treated as if they were wages paid by an employer to an employee to the extent that such remuneration is paid or other payments are made during the period for which the agreement is in effect.

(q) **Extension of withholding to certain gambling winnings.**

• *Caution:* Code Sec. 3402(q)(1), following, was amended by Sec. 101(c)(8), P.L. 107-16, the Economic Growth and Tax Relief Reconciliation Act of 2001 (EGTRRA). These provisions generally sunset for tax years beginning after 12/31/2012. For specific sunset provisions see Sec. 901, P.L. 107-16 (as amended) reproduced in history notes for this Code Sec.

---

(1) **General rule.** Every person, including the Government of the United States, a State, or a political subdivision thereof, or any instrumentalities of the foregoing, making any payment of winnings which are subject to withholding shall deduct and withhold from such payment a tax in an amount equal to the product of the third lowest rate of tax applicable under section 1(c) and such payment.

(2) **Exemption where tax otherwise withheld.** In the case of any payment of winnings which are subject to withholding made to a nonresident alien individual or a foreign corporation, the tax imposed under paragraph (1) shall not apply to any such payment subject to tax under section 1441(a) (relating to withholding on nonresident aliens) or tax under section 1442(a) (relating to withholding on foreign corporations).

(3) **Winnings which are subject to withholding.** For purposes of this subsection, the term "winnings which are subject to withholding" means proceeds from a wager determined in accordance with the following:

(A) In general. Except as provided in subparagraphs (B) and (C), proceeds of more than $5,000 from a wagering transaction, if the amount of such proceeds is at least 300 times as large as the amount wagered.

(B) State-conducted lotteries. Proceeds of more than $5,000 from a wager placed in a lottery conducted by an agency of a State acting under authority of State law, but only if such wager is placed with the State agency conducting such lottery, or with its authorized employees or agents.

(C) Sweepstakes, wagering pools, certain pari-mutuel pools, jai alai, and lotteries. Proceeds of more than $5,000 from—

(i) a wager placed in a sweepstakes, wagering pool, or lottery (other than a wager described in subparagraph (B)), or

(ii) a wagering transaction in a pari-mutuel pool with respect to horse races, dog races, or jai alai if the amount of such proceeds is at least 300 times as large as the amount wagered.

(4) **Rules for determining proceeds from a wager.** For purposes of this subsection—

(A) proceeds from a wager shall be determined by reducing the amount received by the amount of the wager, and

(B) proceeds which are not money shall be taken into account at their fair market value.

(5) **Exemption for bingo, keno, and slot machines.** The tax imposed under paragraph (1) shall not apply to winnings from a slot machine, keno, and bingo.

(6) **Statement by recipient.** Every person who is to receive a payment of winnings which are subject to withholding shall furnish the person making such payment a statement, made under the penalties of perjury, containing the name, address, and taxpayer identification number of the person receiving the payment and of each person entitled to any portion of such payment.

(7) **Coordination with other sections.** For purposes of sections 3403 and 3404 and for purposes of so much of subtitle F (except section 7205) as relates to this chapter, payments to any person of winnings which are subject to withholding shall be treated as if they were wages paid by an employer to an employee.

(r) **Extension of withholding to certain taxable payments of Indian casino profits.**

(1) **In general.** Every person, including an Indian tribe, making a payment to a member of an Indian tribe from the net revenues of any class II or class III gaming activ-

ity conducted or licensed by such tribe shall deduct and withhold from such payment a tax in an amount equal to such payment's proportionate share of the annualized tax.

(2) Exception. The tax imposed by paragraph (1) shall not apply to any payment to the extent that the payment, when annualized, does not exceed an amount equal to the sum of—

(A) the basic standard deduction (as defined in section 63(c)) for an individual to whom section 63(c)(2)(C) applies, and

(B) the exemption amount (as defined in section 151(d)).

⌐ • *Caution:* Code Sec. 3402(r)(3), following, was amended by Sec. 101(c)(9), P.L. 107-16, the Economic Growth and Tax Relief Reconciliation Act of 2001 (EGTRRA). These provisions generally sunset for tax years beginning after 12/31/2012. For specific sunset provisions see Sec. 901, P.L. 107-16 (as amended) reproduced in history notes for this Code Sec. ⌐

(3) Annualized tax. For purposes of paragraph (1), the term "annualized tax" means, with respect to any payment, the amount of tax which would be imposed by section 1(c) (determined without regard to any rate of tax in excess of the fourth lowest rate of tax applicable under section 1(c)) on an amount of taxable income equal to the excess of—

(A) the annualized amount of such payment, over

(B) the amount determined under paragraph (2).

(4) Classes of gaming activities, etc. For purposes of this subsection, terms used in paragraph (1) which are defined in section 4 of the Indian Gaming Regulatory Act (25 U.S.C. 2701 et seq.), as in effect on the date of the enactment of this subsection, shall have the respective meanings given such terms by such section.

(5) Annualization. Payments shall be placed on an annualized basis under regulations prescribed by the Secretary.

(6) Alternate withholding procedures. At the election of an Indian tribe, the tax imposed by this subsection on any payment made by such tribe shall be determined in accordance with such tables or computational procedures as may be specified in regulations prescribed by the Secretary (in lieu of in accordance with paragraphs (2) and (3)).

(7) Coordination with other sections. For purposes of this chapter and so much of subtitle F as relates to this chapter, payments to any person which are subject to withholding under this subsection shall be treated as if they were wages paid by an employer to an employee.

(s) Exemption from withholding for any vehicle fringe benefit.

(1) Employer election not to withhold. The employer may elect not to deduct and withhold any tax under this chapter with respect to any vehicle fringe benefit provided to any employee if such employee is notified by the employer of such election (at such time and in such manner as the Secretary shall by regulations prescribe). The preceding sentence shall not apply to any vehicle fringe benefit unless the amount of such benefit is included by the employer on a statement timely furnished under section 6051.

(2) Employer must furnish W-2. Any vehicle fringe benefit shall be treated as wages from which amounts are required to be deducted and withheld under this chapter for purposes of section 6051.

(3) Vehicle fringe benefit. For purposes of this subsection, the term "vehicle fringe benefit" means any fringe benefit—

(A) which constitutes wages (as defined in section 3401), and

(B) which consists of providing a highway motor vehicle for the use of the employee.

(t) Extension of withholding to certain payments made by government entities.

(1) General rule. The Government of the United States, every State, every political subdivision thereof, and every instrumentality of the foregoing (including multi-State agencies) making any payment to any person providing any property or services (including any payment made in connection with a government voucher or certificate program which functions as a payment for property or services) shall deduct and withhold from such payment a tax in an amount equal to 3 percent of such payment.

(2) Property and services subject to withholding. Paragraph (1) shall not apply to any payment—

(A) except as provided in subparagraph (B), which is subject to withholding under any other provision of this chapter or chapter 3,

(B) which is subject to withholding under section 3406 and from which amounts are being withheld under such section,

(C) of interest,

(D) for real property,

(E) to any governmental entity subject to the requirements of paragraph (1), any tax-exempt entity, or any foreign government,

(F) made pursuant to a classified or confidential contract described in section 6050M(e)(3),

(G) made by a political subdivision of a State (or any instrumentality thereof) which makes less than $100,000,000 of such payments annually,

(H) which is in connection with a public assistance or public welfare program for which eligibility is determined by a needs or income test, and

(I) to any government employee not otherwise excludable with respect to their services as an employee.

(3) Coordination with other sections. For purposes of sections 3403 and 3404 and for purposes of so much of subtitle F (except section 7205) as relates to this chapter, payments to any person for property or services which are subject to withholding shall be treated as if such payments were wages paid by an employer to an employee.

In 2010, P.L. 111-312, Sec. 101(a)(1), substituted "December 31, 2012" for "December 31, 2010" both places it appears in Sec. 901, P.L. 107-16, see below, effective as if included in the enactment of P.L. 107-16, EGTRRA, 6/7/2001.

In 2009, P.L. 111-5, Sec. 1511, substituted "December 31, 2011" for "December 31, 2010" in Sec. 511(b) [the effective date provision of Sec. 511(a) of the Tax Increase Prevention and Reconciliation Act of 2005 [P.L. 109-222, see below]".

In 2006, P.L. 109-222, Sec. 511(a), added subsec. (t), effective for payments made after 12/31/2011 [as amended by Sec. 1511 of the American Recovery and Reinvestment Act of 2009, P.L. 111-5, see above].

In 2004, P.L. 108-357, Sec. 904(a)-(b), of this Act, provides:

"SEC. 904. INCREASE IN WITHHOLDING FROM SUPPLEMENTAL WAGE PAYMENTS IN EXCESS OF $1,000,000.

"(a) In general. If an employer elects under Treasury Regulation 31.3402(g)-1 to determine the amount to be deducted and withheld from any supplemental wage payment by using a flat percentage rate, the rate to be used in determining the amount to be so deducted and withheld shall not be less than 28 percent (or the corresponding rate in effect under section 1(i)(2) of the Internal Revenue Code of 1986 for taxable years beginning in the calendar year in which the payment is made).

"(b) Special rule for large payments.

Wage withholding Code Sec. 3402

"(1) In general. Notwithstanding subsection (a), if the supplemental wage payment, when added to all such payments previously made by the employer to the employee during the calendar year, exceeds $1,000,000, the rate used with respect to such excess shall be equal to the maximum rate of tax in effect under section 1 of such Code for taxable years beginning in such calendar year.

"(2) Aggregation. All persons treated as a single employer under subsection (a) or (b) of section 52 of the Internal Revenue Code of 1986 shall be treated as a single employer for purposes of this subsection."

—P.L. 108-357, Sec. 904(c), repealed Sec. 13273 of P. L. 103-66, see below.

—P.L. 108-357, Sec. 904(d), of this Act, provides:

"(d) Effective date. The provisions of, and the amendment made by, this section shall apply to payments made after December 31, 2004."

In 2002, P.L. 107-358, Sec. 2, added subsec. (c) in Sec. 901 of P. L. 107-16 [see below], effective 12/17/2002.

In 2001, P.L. 107-16, Sec. 101(c)(6), substituted "7 percent, any percentage applicable to any of the 3 lowest income brackets in the table under section 1(c)," for "7, 15, 28, or 31 percent" in subpara. (p)(1)(B) . . . Sec. 101(c)(7), substituted "10 percent" for "15 percent" in para. (p)(2) . . . Sec. 101(c)(8), substituted "equal to the product of the third lowest rate of tax applicable under section 1(c) and such payment" for "equal to 28 percent of such payment" in para. (q)(1) . . . Sec. 101(c)(9), substituted "the fourth lowest rate of tax applicable under section 1(c)" for "31 percent" in para. (r)(3), effective for amounts paid after the 60th day after 6/7/2001. References to income brackets and rates of tax in Sec. 101(c)(6)-(11) of this Act shall be applied without regard to section 1(i)(1)(D) of the Internal Revenue Code of 1986.

—P.L. 107-16, Sec. 101(c)(11), substituted "the third lowest rate of tax applicable under section 1(c) of the Internal Revenue Code of 1986" for "28 percent" in Sec. 13273 of P. L. 103-66, see below.

—P.L. 107-16, Sec. 901, of this Act [as amended by Sec. 2, P. L. 107-358, and Sec. 101(a)(1), P.L. 111-312, see above], reads as follows:

"SEC. 901. SUNSET OF PROVISIONS OF ACT.

"(a) In general. All provisions of, and amendments made by, this Act shall not apply—

"(1) to taxable, plan, or limitation years beginning after December 31, 2012, or

"(2) in the case of title V, to estates of decedents dying, gifts made, or generation skipping transfers, after December 31, 2012.

"(b) Application of certain laws. The Internal Revenue Code of 1986 and the Employee Retirement Income Security Act of 1974 shall be applied and administered to years, estates, gifts, and transfers described in subsection (a) as if the provisions and amendments described in subsection (a) had never been enacted.

"(c) Exception. Subsection (a) shall not apply to section 803 (relating to no federal income tax on restitution received by victims of the Nazi regime or their heirs or estates)."

In 1994, P.L. 103-465, Sec. 701(a), added subsec. (r), effective for payments made after 12/31/94.

—P.L. 103-465, Sec. 702(a), amended subsec. (p), effective for payments made after 12/31/96.

Prior to amendment, subsec. (p) read as follows:

"(p) Voluntary withholding agreements.

"The Secretary is authorized by regulations to provide for withholding—

"(1) from remuneration for services performed by an employee for his employer which (without regard to this subsection) does not constitute wages, and

"(2) from any other type of payment with respect to which the Secretary finds that withholding would be appropriate under the provisions of this chapter,

if the employer and the employee, or in the case of any other type of payment the person making and the person receiving the payment, agree to such withholding. Such agreement shall be made in such form and manner as the Secretary may by regulations provide. For purposes of this chapter (and so much of subtitle F as relates to this chapter) remuneration or other payments with respect to which such agreement is made shall be treated as if they were wages paid by an employer to an employee to the extent that such remuneration is paid or other payments are made during the period for which the agreement is in effect."

In 1993, P.L. 103-66, Sec. 13273, of this Act [as amended by Sec. 101(c)(11) of P. L. 107-16 and prior to repeal by Sec. 904(c) of P. L. 108-357, see above] provides:

"SEC. 13273. INCREASE IN WITHHOLDING FROM SUPPLEMENTAL WAGE PAYMENTS.

"If an employer elects under Treasury Regulation 31.3402(g)-1 to determine the amount to be deducted and withheld from any supplemental wage payment by using a flat percentage rate, the rate to be used in determining the amount to be so deducted and withheld shall not be less than the third lowest rate of tax applicable under section 1(c) of the Internal Revenue Code of 1986. The preceding sentence shall apply to payments made after December 31, 1993."

In 1992, P.L. 102-486, Sec. 1934(a), substituted "28 percent" for "20 percent" in para. (q)(1), effective for payments received after 12/31/92.

—P.L. 102-486, Sec. 1942(a), substituted "$5,000" for "$1,000" in subpara. (q)(3)(A) . . . Sec. 1942(a), substituted "$5,000" for "$1,000" in subpara. (q)(3)(C), effective for payments of winnings after 12/31/92.

—P.L. 102-318, Sec. 522(b)(2)(D), substituted "section 3405(e)(1)" for "section 3405(d)(1)" in para. (o)(6), effective for distributions after 12/31/92, except as provided in Sec. 522(d)(2) of this Act which reads as follows:

"(2) Transition rule for certain annuity contracts. If, as of July 1, 1992, a State law prohibits a direct trustee-to-trustee transfer from an annuity contract described in section 403(b) of the Internal Revenue Code of 1986 which was purchased for an employee by an employer which is a State or a political subdivision thereof (or an agency or instrumentality of any 1 or more of either), the amendments made by this section shall not apply to distributions before the earlier of—

"(A) 90 days after the first day after July 1, 1992, on which such transfer is allowed under State law, or

"(B) January 1, 1994."

In 1990, P.L. 101-508, Sec. 11801(a)(41), deleted para. (a)(3), effective 11/5/90, except as provided in Sec. 11821(b) of this Act, which reads as follows:

"(b) Savings provision. If—

"(1) any provision amended or repealed by this part applied to—

"(A) any transaction occurring before the date of the enactment of this Act [11/5/90],

"(B) any property acquired before such date of enactment [11/5/90], or

"(C) any item of income, loss, deduction, or credit taken into account before such date of enactment [11/5/90], and

"(2) the treatment of such transaction, property, or item under such provision would (without regard to the amendments made by this part) affect liability for tax for periods ending after such date of enactment [11/5/90],

nothing in the amendments made by this part shall be construed to affect the treatment of such transaction, property, or item for purposes of determining liability for tax for periods ending after such date of enactment [11/5/90]."

Prior to deletion, para. (a)(3) read as follows:

"(3) Changes made by section 101 of the economic recovery tax act of 1981. Notwithstanding the provisions of this subsection, the Secretary shall modify the tables and procedures under paragraph (1) to reflect—

"(A) the amendments made by section 101(b) of the Economic Recovery Tax Act of 1981, and such modification shall take effect on October 1, 1981, as if such amendments made a 5-percent reduction effective on such date, and

"(B) the amendments made by section 101(a) of such Act, and such modifications shall take effect—

"(i) on July 1, 1982, as if the reductions in the rate of tax under section 1 (as amended by such section) were attributable to a 10-percent reduction effective on such date, and

"(ii) on July 1, 1983, as if such reductions were attributable to a 10-percent reduction effective on such date."

In 1988, P.L. 100-647, Sec. 1003(a)(2), substituted "section 62(a) (other than paragraph (10) thereof)" for "section 62) (other than paragraph (13) thereof", in para. (m)(1), effective for tax. yrs. begin. after 12/31/86.

—P.L. 100-647, Sec. 1015(p), amended Sec. 1581(c) of P. L. 99-514 [part of special rules for changes made by Sec. 1581(b) of P. L. 99-514] by adding the last sentence, see below.

In 1987, P.L. 100-203, Sec. 10302(a), amended subpara. (f)(3)(B), effective for certificates furnished after 1/12/87.

Prior to amendment, subpara. (f)(3)(B) read as follows:

"(B) Furnished to take place of existing certificate. A withholding exemption certificate furnished the employer in cases in which a previous such certificate is in effect shall take effect with respect to the first payment of wages made on or after the first status determination date which occurs at least 30 days from the date on which such certificate is so furnished, except that at the election of the employer such certificate may be made effective with respect to any payment of wages made on or after the date on which such certificate is so furnished; but a certificate furnished pursuant to paragraph (2)(C) shall not take effect, and may not be made effective, with respect to any payment of wages made in the calendar year in which the certificate is furnished. For purposes of this subparagraph the term 'status determination date' means January 1, May 1, July 1 and October 1 of each year."

In 1986, P.L. 99-514, Sec. 104(b)(15)(A), deleted subparas. (f)(1)(B) and (C) and redesignated subparas. (f)(1)(D) through (G) as subparas. (f)(1)(B) through (E) . . . Sec. 104(b)(15)(B), added "unless he is an individual described in section 151(d)(2)" after "himself" in subpara. (f)(1)(A) . . . Sec. 104(b)(15)(C), substituted "subparagraph (A) or (D)" for "subparagraph (A), (B), (C), or (F)" [sic "subparagraph (A), (B), or (C)"] in subpara. (f)(1)(B) [as redesignated] . . . Sec. 104(b)(15)(D), substituted "section 151(c)" for "section 151(e)" in subpara. (f)(1)(C) [as redesignated] . . . Sec. 104(b)(15)(E), substituted "standard deduction" for "zero bracket" in subpara. (f)(1)(E) [as redesignated] . . . Sec. 104(b)(15)(F), substituted "subparagraph (E)" for "subparagraph (G)" and substituted "standard deduction" for "zero bracket" in the last sentence of para. (f)(1) . . . Sec. 104(b)(15)(G), added "(including the additional standard deduction under section 63(c)(3) for the aged and blind)" after "deductions" in para. (m)(3), effective for tax. yrs. begin. after 12/31/86.

Prior to deletion, subparas. (f)(1)(B) and (C) read as follows:

"(B) one additional exemption for himself if, on the basis of facts existing at the beginning of such day, there may reasonably be expected to be allowable an exemption under section 151(c)(1) (relating to old age) for the taxable year under subtitle A in respect of which amounts deducted and withheld under this chapter in the calendar year in which such day falls are allowed as a credit;

"(C) one additional exemption for himself if, on the basis of facts existing at the beginning of such day, there may reasonably be expected to be allowable an exemption under section 151(d)(1) (relating to the blind) for the taxable year subtitle A in respect of which amounts deducted and withheld under this chapter in the calendar year in which such day falls are allowed as a credit;"

—P.L. 99-514, Sec. 1301(j)(8), substituted "section 7703" for "section 143" in subpara. (f)(1)(E), effective for bonds issued after 8/15/86.

—P.L. 99-514, Sec. 1303(b)(4), deleted subsec. (r), effective 10/22/86.

Prior to deletion, subsec. (r) read as follows:

"(r) Extension of withholding to GSOC distributions.

"(1) General rule. An electing GSOC making any distribution to its shareholders shall deduct and withhold from such payment a tax in an amount equal to 25 percent of such payment.

Code Sec. 3402 — Wage withholding

"(2) Coordination with other sections. For purposes of sections 3403 and 3404 and for purposes of so much of subtitle F (except section 7205) as relates to this chapter, distributions of an electing GSOC to any shareholder which are subject to withholding shall be treated as if they were wages paid by an employer to an employee."

—P.L. 99-514, Sec. 1581(b), deleted "or decreases" after "increases" in subsec. (i), effective 10/22/86. Sec. 1581(a) and (c) of this Act provide:

"(a) In general.

"The Secretary of the Treasury or his delegate shall modify the withholding schedules and withholding exemption certificates under section 3402 of the Internal Revenue Code of 1954 to better approximate actual tax liability under the amendments made by this Act."

* * *

"(c) Employer's responsibility.

"If an employee has not filed a revised withholding allowance certificate before October 1, 1987, the employer shall withhold income taxes from the employee's wages—

"(1) as if the employee claimed 1 withholding allowance, if the employee checked the 'single' box on the employee's previous withholding allowance certificate, or

"(2) as if the employee claimed 2 withholding allowances, if the employee checked the 'married' box on the employee's previous withholding allowance certificate.

The preceding sentence shall not apply if its application would result in an increase in the number of withholding allowances for the employee."

In 1985, P.L. 99-44, Sec. 3, added subsec. (s), effective 1/1/85.

In 1983, P.L. 98-67, Sec. 104(d)(3), deleted subsec. (s), effective for payments made after 12/31/83.

Prior to deletion, subsec. (s) read as follows:

"(s) Extension of withholding to certain payments where identifying number not furnished or inaccurate.

"(1) In general. In the case of any backup withholding payment

"(A) the payee fails to furnish his taxpayer identification number to the payor, or

"(B) the Secretary notifies the payor that the number furnished by the payee is incorrect, then the payor shall deduct and withhold from such payment a tax equal to 15 percent of such payment.

"(2) Period for which withholding is in effect.

"(A) Failure to furnish number. In the case of any failure described in subparagraph (A) of paragraph (1), paragraph (1) shall apply to any backup withholding payment made during the period during which the taxpayer identification number has not been furnished.

"(B) Notification of incorrect number. In any case where there is a notification described in subparagraph (B) of paragraph (1), paragraph (1) shall apply to any backup withholding payment made

"(i) after the close of the 15th day after the day on which the payor was so notified, and

"(ii) before the payee furnishes another taxpayer identification number.

"(C) 15-day grace periods.

"(i) After correction. Unless the payor otherwise elects, paragraph (1) shall also apply to any backup withholding payment made after the close of the period described in subparagraph (A) or (B) (as the case may be) and before the 16th day after the close of such period.

"(ii) After notification. If the payor so elects, paragraph (1) shall also apply to any backup withholding payment made during the 15-day period described in clause (i) of subparagraph (B).

"(3) Backup withholding payments.

"(A) In general. For purposes of this subsection, the term 'backup withholding payment' means any payment of a kind, and to a payee, required to be shown on a return required under

"(i) section 6041(a) or (b) (relating to certain information at source),

"(ii) section 6041A(a) (relating to returns regarding payments to nonemployees),

"(iii) section 6042(a) (relating to payments of dividends),

"(iv) section 6044 (relating to returns regarding patronage dividends) but only to the extent of payments of money,

"(v) section 6045 (relating to returns of brokers),

"(vi) section 6049(a) (relating to payments of interest), or

"(vii) section 6050A (relating to reporting requirements of certain fishing boat operators), but only to the extent of payments of the proceeds of the catch.

"(B) Special rule. For purposes of this subsection, the determination of whether any payment is of a kind required to be shown on a return described in subparagraph (A) shall be made without regard to any minimum amount which must be paid before a return is required.

"(4) Payments must aggregate $600 before withholding required from payments described in section 6041(a) or 6041A. In the case of any payment which is of a kind required to be shown on a return required under section 6041(a) or 6041A(a) and which is made during any calendar year, no amount shall be deducted and withheld with respect to such payment unless—

"(A) the aggregate amount of such payment and all previous such payments to the payee involved during such calendar year equals or exceeds $600, or

"(B) the payor was required under section 6041(a) or 6041A(a) to file a return for the preceding calendar year with respect to payments to the payee involved, or

"(C) during the preceding calendar year the payor made backup withholding payments to the payee with respect to which amounts were required to be deducted and withheld under paragraph (1).

"(5) Definitions and special rules. For purposes of this subsection—

"(A) Obviously incorrect number. A payee shall be treated as failing to furnish his taxpayer identification number if the number furnished does not contain the proper number of digits.

"(B) Payee furnishes 2 incorrect numbers. If the payee furnishes a payor 2 incorrect numbers, the payor shall, after receiving notice of the second incorrect number, treat the payee as not having furnished another taxpayer identification number under paragraph (2)(B)(ii) until the day on which the payor receives notification from the Secretary that a correct taxpayer identification number has been furnished.

"(C) Exception for payments to certain payees. Paragraph (1) shall not apply to any payment made to—

"(i) the United States (as defined in section 3455(a)(3)),

"(ii) any State (as defined in section 3455(a)(2)),

"(iii) an organization which is exempt from taxation under section 501(a),

"(iv) any foreign government (as defined in section 3455(a)(4)) or international organization (as defined in section 3455(a)(5)), or

"(v) any other person specified in regulations.

"(D) Taxpayer identification number. The term 'taxpayer identification number' means the identifying number assigned to a person under section 6109.

"(E) Amounts for which withholding otherwise required. No tax shall be deducted or withheld under this subsection with respect to any amount for which withholding is otherwise required by this title.

"(F) Exemption while waiting for number. The Secretary shall prescribe regulations for exemptions from the tax imposed by paragraph (1) during periods during which a person is waiting for receipt of a taxpayer identification number.

"(G) Nominees. In the case of a backup withholding payment described in clause (i) or (v) of paragraph (3)(A) to a nominee, in the manner provided in regulations, both the nominee and the ultimate payee shall be treated as the payee.

"(H) Requirement of notice to payee. Whenever the Secretary notifies a payor under paragraph (1)(B) that the taxpayer identification number furnished by any payee is incorrect, the Secretary shall at the same time furnish a copy of such notice to the payor, and the payor shall promptly furnish such copy to the payee.

"(I) Requirement of notice to secretary. If the Secretary notifies a payor under paragraph (1)(B) that the taxpayer identification number furnished by any payee is incorrect and such payee subsequently furnishes another taxpayer identification number to the payor, the payor shall promptly notify the Secretary of the other taxpayer identification number so furnished.

"(J) Coordination with other sections. For purposes of section 31, this chapter (other than subsection (n) of this section), and so much of subtitle F (other than section 7205) as relates to this chapter, payments which are subject to withholding under this subsection shall be treated as if they were wages paid by an employer to an employee."

In 1982, P.L. 97-248, Sec. 317(a), added subsec. (s), effective for payments made after 12/31/83.

—P.L. 97-248, Sec. 334(d), added para. (o)(6), effective for payments or other distributions made after 12/31/82.

In 1981, P.L. 97-34, Sec. 101(e)(1), amended subsec. (a) . . . Sec. 101(e)(2), deleted para. (b)(1) and redesignated paras. (b)(2), (3), (4) and (5) as paras. (b)(1), (2), (3), and (4) and amended para. (b)(3) [as redesignated] . . . Sec. 101(e)(3), added "(or more than one exemption is so prescribed by the Secretary)" after "one exemption" in subpara. (f)(1)(G) . . . Sec. 101(e)(4), amended subsec. (i), effective for remuneration paid after 9/30/81.

Prior to amendment, subsec. (a) read as follows:

"(a) Requirement of withholding.

"Except as otherwise provided in this section, every employer making payment of wages shall deduct and withhold upon such wages a tax determined in accordance with tables prescribed by the Secretary. With respect to wages paid after December 31, 1978, the tables so prescribed shall be the same as the tables prescribed under this subsection which were in effect on January 1, 1975, except that such tables shall be modified to the extent necessary to reflect the amendments made by sections 101 and 102 of the Tax Reduction and Simplification Act of 1977 and the amendments made by section 101 of the Revenue Act of 1978. For purposes of applying such tables, the term 'the amount of wages' means the amount by which the wages exceed the number of withholding exemptions claimed, multiplied by the amount of one such exemption as shown in the table prescribed under subsection (b)(1)."

Prior to deletion, para. (b)(1) read as follows

"(b) Percentage method of withholding.

"(1) The table referred to in subsection (a) is as follows:

"**Percentage Method Withholding Table**

Payroll period	Amount of one withholding exemption
Weekly	$19.23
Biweekly	38.46
Semimonthly	41.66
Monthly	83.33
Quarterly	250.00
Semiannual	500.00
Annual	1,000.00
Daily or miscellaneous (per day of such period)	2.74"

Prior to amendment, para. (b)(3) [as redesignated by Sec. 101(e)(2) of this Act] read as follows:

"(3) In any case in which wages are paid by an employer without regard to any payroll period or other period, the withholding exemption allowable with respect

Wage withholding — Code Sec. 3402

to each payment of such wages shall be the exemption allowed for a miscellaneous payroll period containing a number of days equal to the number of days (including Sundays and holidays) which have elapsed since the date of the last payment of such wages by such employer during the calendar year, or the date of commencement of employment with such employer during such year, or January 1 of such year, whichever is the later."

Prior to amendment, subsec. (i) read as follows:

"(i) Additional withholding.

"The Secretary is authorized by regulations to provide, under such conditions and to such extent as he deems proper, for withholding in addition to that otherwise required under this section in cases in which the employer and the employee agree (in such form as the Secretary may by regulations prescribe) to such additional withholding. Such additional withholding shall for all purposes be considered tax required to be deducted and withheld under this chapter."

— P.L. 97-34, Sec. 101(e)(5), amended subsec. (m), effective for remuneration paid after 12/31/81.

Prior to amendment, subsec. (m) read as follows:

"(m) Withholding allowances based on itemized deductions.

"(1) General rule. An employee shall be entitled to withholding allowances under this subsection with respect to a payment of wages in a number equal to the number determined by dividing by $1,000 the excess of—

"(A) his estimated itemized deductions, over

"(B) an amount equal to $3,400 ($2,300 in the case of an individual who is not married (within the meaning of section 143) and who is not a surviving spouse (as defined in section 2(a))).

For purposes of this subsection, a fractional number shall not be taken into account unless it amounts to one-half or more, in which case it shall be increased to 1.

"(2) Definitions. For purposes of this subsection—

"(A) Estimated itemized deductions. The term 'estimated itemized deductions' means the aggregate amount which he reasonably expects will be allowable as deductions under chapter 1 (other than the deductions referred to in section 151 and other than the deductions required to be taken into account in determining adjusted gross income under section 62 (other than paragraph (13) thereof)) for the estimation year. In no case shall such aggregate amount be greater than the sum of (i) the amount of such deductions (or the zero bracket amount (within the meaning of section 63(d))) reflected in his return of tax under subtitle A for the taxable year preceding the estimation year of (if such a return has not been filed for such preceding taxable year at the time the withholding exemption certificate is furnished the employer) the second taxable year preceding the estimation year and (ii) the amount of his determinable additional deductions for the estimation year.

"(B) Estimated wages. The term 'estimated wages' means the aggregate amount which he reasonably expects will constitute wages for the estimation year.

"(C) Determinable additional deductions. The term 'determinable additional deductions' means those estimated itemized deductions which (i) are in excess of the deductions referred to in subparagraph (A) (or the zero bracket amount) reflected on his return of tax under subtitle A for the taxable year preceding the estimation year, and (ii) are demonstrably attributable to an identifiable event during the estimation year or the preceding taxable year which can reasonably be expected to cause an increase in the amount of such deductions on the return of tax under subtitle A for the estimation year.

"(D) Estimation year. In the case of an employee who files his return on the basis of a calendar year, the term 'estimation year' means the calendar year in which the wages are paid.

In the case of an employee who files his return on a basis other than the calendar year, his estimation year, and the amounts deducted and withheld to be governed by such estimation year, shall be determined under regulations prescribed by the Secretary.

"(3) Special rules.

"(A) Married individuals. The number of withholding allowances to which a husband and wife are entitled under this subsection shall be determined on the basis of their combined wages and deductions. This subparagraph shall not apply to a husband and wife who filed separate returns for the taxable year preceding the estimation year and who reasonably expect to file separate returns for the estimation year.

"(B) Limitation. In the case of employees whose estimated wages are at levels at which the amounts deducted and withheld under this chapter generally are insufficient (taking into account a reasonable allowance for deductions and exemptions) to offset the liability for tax under chapter 1 with respect to the wages from which such amounts are deducted and withheld, the Secretary may by regulation reduce the withholding allowances to which such employees would, but for this subparagraph, be entitled under this subsection.

"(C) Treatment of allowances. For purposes of this title, any withholding allowance under this subsection shall be treated as if it were denominated a withholding exemption.

"(4) Authority to prescribe tables. The Secretary may prescribe tables pursuant to which employees shall determine the number of withholding allowances to which they are entitled under this subsection (in lieu of making such determination under paragraphs (1) and (3)). Such tables shall be consistent with the provisions of paragraphs (1) and (3), except that such tables—

"(A) shall provide for entitlement to withholding allowances based on reasonable wage and itemized deduction brackets,

"(B) may increase or decrease the number of withholding allowances to which employees in the various wage and itemized deduction brackets would, but for this subparagraph, be entitled to the end that, to the extent practicable, amounts deducted and withheld under this chapter (i) generally do not exceed the liability for tax under chapter 1 with respect to the wages from which such amounts are

deducted and withheld, and (ii) generally are sufficient to offset such liability for tax, and

"(C) may take into account tax credits to which employees are entitled."

In 1980, P.L. 96-601, Sec. 4(a), deleted "and" at the end of subpara. (o)(1)(A), added "and" at the end of subpara. (o)(1)(B) and added subpara. (o)(1)(C) . . . Sec. 4(b), amended para. (o)(3) and added paras. (o)(4) and (o)(5) . . . Sec. 4(c), added new subpara. (o)(2)(C) . . . Sec. 4(d), deleted ", but only to the extent that the amount is includible in the gross income of such individual" at the end of subpara. (o)(2)(B), for payments made on or after 5/1/81 [the first day of the first calendar month begin. more than 120 days after 12/24/80.

Prior to amendment, subpara. (o)(2)(B) read as follows:

"(3) Request for withholding. A request that an annuity be subject to withholding under this chapter shall be made by the payee in writing to the person making the annuity payments, shall be accompanied by a withholding exemption certificate, executed in accordance with the provisions of subsection (f)(2), and shall take effect as provided in subsection (f)(3). Such a request may, notwithstanding the provisions of subsection (f)(4), be terminated by furnishing to the person making the payments a written statement of termination which shall be treated as a withholding exemption certificate for purposes of subsection (f)(3)(B)."

In 1978, P.L. 95-600, Sec. 101(e)(1), deleted the second and third sentences of subsec. (a) . . . added a new second sentence . . . Sec. 101(e)(2), substituted "$3,400" for "$3,200" and "$2,300" for "$2,200" in subpara. (m)(1)(B), effective for remuneration paid after '78.

Prior to amendment, the second and third sentences of subsec. (a) read as follows:

"With respect to wages paid after May 31, 1977, and before January 1, 1979, the tables so prescribed shall be the same as the tables prescribed under this section which were in effect on January 1, 1976; except that such tables shall be modified to the extent necessary so that, had they been in effect for all of 1977, they would reflect the full year effect of the amendments made by sections 101 and 102 of the Tax Reduction and Simplification Act of 1977. With respect to wages paid after December 31, 1978, the tables so prescribed shall be the same as the tables prescribed under this subsection which were in effect on January 1, 1975, except that such tables shall be modified to the extent necessary to reflect the amendments made by sections 101 and 102 of the Tax Reduction and Simplification Act of 1977."

— P.L. 95-600, Sec. 102(c)(1), amended the table in para. (b)(1) . . . Sec. 102(c)(2), substituted "$1,000" for "$750" in para. (m)(1), for remuneration paid after '78.

Prior to amendment, the table in para. (b)(1) read as follows:

"Percentage Method Withholding Table

"Payroll period	Amount of one withholding exemption:
Weekly	$14.40
Biweekly	28.80
Semimonthly	31.30
Monthly	62.50
Quarterly	187.50
Semiannual	375.00
Annual	750.00
Daily or miscellaneous (per day of such period)	2.10"

— P.L. 95-600, Sec. 601(b)(2), added subsec. (r), effective for corporations chartered after '78 and before '84.

In 1977, P.L. 95-30, Sec. 105, amended subsec. (a) . . . substituted "a zero bracket" for "a standard deduction" in subpara. (f)(1)(G) . . . substituted "zero bracket" for "standard deduction" in the sentence following subpara. (f)(1)(G) . . . amended subpara. (m)(1)(B) . . . substituted "section" for "sections 141 and" in subpara. (m)(2)(A) . . . substituted "(or the zero bracket amount (within the meaning of section 63(d)))" for "(or the amount of the standard deduction)" in subpara. (m)(2)(A) . . . substituted "(or the zero bracket amount)" for "(or the standard deduction)" in subpara. (m)(2)(C), effective for wages paid after 4/30/77.

Prior to amendment, subsec. (a) read as follows:

"(a) Requirement of withholding.

"Except as otherwise provided in this section, every employer making payment of wages shall deduct and withhold upon such wages a tax determined in accordance with tables prescribed by the Secretary. With respect to wages paid prior to January 1, 1978, the tables so prescribed shall be the same as the tables prescribed under this section which were in effect on January 1, 1976. With respect to wages paid after December 31, 1977, the Secretary shall prescribe new tables which shall be the same as the tables prescribed under this subsection which were in effect on January 1, 1975, except that such tables shall be modified to the extent necessary to reflect the amendments made to subsections (b) and (c) of section 141 by the Tax Reform Act of 1976. For purposes of applying such tables, the term 'the amount of wages' means the amount by which the wages exceed the number of withholding exemptions claimed, multiplied by the amount of one such exemption as shown in the table in subsection (b)(1)."

Prior to amendment, subpara. (m)(1)(B) read as follows:

"(B) an amount equal to the lesser of (i) 16 percent of his estimated wages, or (ii) $2,800 ($2,400 in the case of an individual who is not married (within the meaning of section 143) and who is not a surviving spouse (as defined in section 2(a)))."

— P.L. 95-30, Sec. 304, provided as follows:

"SEC. 304. UNDERWITHHOLDING.

"No person shall be liable in respect of any failure to deduct and withhold under section 3402 of the Internal Revenue Code of 1954 (relating to income tax collected at source) on remuneration paid before January 1, 1977, to the extent

Code Sec. 3402 — Wage withholding

that the duty to deduct and withhold was created or increased by any provision of the Tax Reform Act of 1976."

— P.L. 95-30, Sec. 405, amended subpara. (q)(3)(C), effective for payments made after 4/30/77.

Prior to amendment, subpara. (q)(3)(C) read as follows:

"(C) Sweepstakes, wagering pools, and other lotteries. Proceeds of more than $1,000 from a wager placed in a sweepstakes, wagering pool, or lottery (other than a wager described in subparagraph (B))."

In 1976, P.L. 94-455, Sec. 401(d)(1), amended subsec. (a), effective for wages paid after 9/14/76 [sic]. For wages paid after 4/30/75 and before 10/1/76, subsec. (a) read as follows:

"(a) Requirement of withholding.

"Except as otherwise provided in this section, every employer making payment of wages shall deduct and withhold upon such wages a tax determined in accordance with tables prescribed by the Secretary or his delegate. The tables so prescribed shall be the same as the tables contained in this subsection as in effect on January 1, 1975, except that the amounts set forth as amounts of income tax to be withheld with respect to wages paid after April 30, 1975, and before January 1, 1976, shall reflect the full calendar year effect for 1975 of the amendments made by sections 201, 202, 203, and 204 of the Tax Reduction Act of 1975. The tables so prescribed with respect to wages paid after December 31, 1975, and before July 1, 1976, shall be the same as the tables prescribed under this subsection which were in effect on December 10, 1975. For purposes of applying such tables, the term 'the amount of wages' means the amount by which the wages exceed the number of withholding exemptions claimed, multiplied by the amount of one such exemption as shown in the table in subsection (b)(1)."

For wages paid before 5/1/75, subsec. (a) read as follows:

"(a) Requirement of withholding.

"Every employer making payment of wages shall deduct and withhold upon such wages (except as otherwise provided in this section) a tax determined in accordance with the following tables. For purposes of applying such tables, the term 'the amount of wages' means the amount by which the wages exceed the number of withholding exemptions claimed, multiplied by the amount of one such exemption as shown in the table in subsection (b)(1):

"**TABLE 1** — If the payroll period with respect to an employee is WEEKLY

"(a) Single Person — Including Head of Household:

"If the amount of wages is	The amount of income tax to be withheld shall be:
Not over $11	0.
Over $11 but not over $35	14% of excess over $11.
Over $35 but not over $73	$3.36 plus 18% of excess over $35.
Over $73 but not over $202	$10.20 plus 21% of excess over $73.
Over $202 but not over $231	$37.29 plus 23% of excess over $202.
Over $231 but not over $269	$43.96 plus 27% of excess over $231.
Over $269 but not over $333	$54.22 plus 31% of excess over $269.
Over $333	$74.06 plus 35% of excess over $333.

"(b) Married Person:

"If the amount of wages is:	The amount of income tax to be withheld shall be:
Not over $11	0.
Over $11 but not over $39	14% of excess over $11.
Over $39 but not over $167	$3.92 plus 16% of excess over $39.
Over $167 but not over $207	$24.40 plus 20% of excess over $167.
Over $207 but not over $324	$32.40 plus 24% of excess over $207.
Over $324 but not over $409	$60.48 plus 28% of excess over $324.
Over $409 but not over $486	$84.28 plus 32% of excess over $409.
Over $486	$108.92 plus 36% of excess over $486.

"**TABLE 2** — If the payroll period with respect to an employee is BI-WEEKLY

"(a) Single Person — Including Head of Household:

"If the amount of wages is:	The amount of income tax to be withheld shall be:
Not over $21	0.
Over $21 but not over $69	14% of excess over $21.
Over $69 but not over $146	$6.72 plus 18% of excess over $69.
Over $146 but not over $404	$20.58 plus 21% of excess over $146.
Over $404 but not over $462	$74.76 plus 23% of excess over $404.
Over $462 but not over $538	$88.10 plus 27% of excess over $462.
Over $538 but not over $665	$108.62 plus 31% of excess over $538.
Over $665	$147.99 plus 35% of excess over $665.

"(b) Married Person:

"If the amount of wages is:	The amount of income tax to be withheld shall be:
Not over $21	0.
Over $21 but not over $79	14% of excess over $21.
Over $79 but not over $335	$8.12 plus 16% of excess over $79.
Over $335 but not over $413	$49.08 plus 20% of excess over $335.
Over $413 but not over $648	$64.68 plus 24% of excess over $413.
Over $648 but not over $817	$121.08 plus 28% of excess over $648.
Over $817 but not over $971	$168.40 plus 32% of excess over $817.
Over $971	$217.68 plus 36% of excess over $971.

"**TABLE 3** — If the payroll period with respect to an employee is SEMI-MONTHLY

"(a) Single Person — Including Head of Household:

"If the amount of wages is:	The amount of income tax to be withheld shall be:
Not over $23	0.
Over $23 but not over $75	14% of excess over $23.
Over $75 but not over $158	$7.28 plus 18% of excess over $75.
Over $158 but not over $438	$22.22 plus 21% of excess over $158.
Over $438 but not over $500	$81.02 plus 23% of excess over $438.
Over $500 but not over $583	$95.28 plus 27% of excess over $500.
Over $583 but not over $721	$117.69 plus 31% of excess over $583.
Over $721	$160.47 plus 35% of excess over $721.

"(b) Married Person:

"If the amount of wages is:	The amount of income tax to be withheld shall be:
Not over $23	0.
Over $23 but not over $85	14% of excess over $23.
Over $85 but not over $363	$8.68 plus 16% of excess over $85.
Over $363 but not over $448	$53.16 plus 20% of excess over $363.
Over $448 but not over $702	$70.16 plus 24% of excess over $448.
Over $702 but not over $885	$131.12 plus 28% of excess over $702.
Over $885 but not over $1,052	$182.36 plus 32% of excess over $885.
Over $1,052	$235.60 plus 36% of excess over $1,052.

"**TABLE 4** — If the payroll period with respect to an employee is MONTHLY

"(a) Single Person — Including Head of Household:

"If the amount of wages is:	The amount of income tax to be withheld shall be:
Not over $46	0.
Over $46 but not over $150	14% of excess over $46.
Over $150 but not over $317	$14.56 plus 18% of excess over $150.
Over $317 but not over $875	$44.62 plus 21% of excess over $317.
Over $875 but not over $1,000	$161.80 plus 23% of excess over $875.
Over $1,000 but not over $1,167	$190.55 plus 27% of excess over $1,000.
Over $1,167 but not over $1,442	235.64 plus 31% of excess over $1,167.
Over $1,442	$320.89 plus 35% of excess over $1,442.

Wage withholding   Code Sec. 3402

"(b) Married Person:

"If the amount of wages is:	The amount of income tax to be withheld shall be:
Not over $46	0.
Over $46 but not over $171	14% of excess over $46.
Over $171 but not over $725	$17.50 plus 16% of excess over $171.
Over $725 but not over $896	$106.14 plus 20% of excess over $725.
Over $896 but not over $1,404	$140.34 plus 24% of excess over $896.
Over $1,404 but not over $1,771	$262.26 plus 28% of excess over $1,404.
Over $1,771 but not over $2,104	$365.02 plus 32% of excess over $1,771.
Over $2,104	$471.58 plus 36% of excess over $2,104.

"**TABLE 5** — If the payroll period with respect to an employee is QUARTERLY:
"(a) Single Person — Including Head of Household:

"If the amount of wages is:	The amount of income tax to be withheld shall be:
Not over $138	0.
Over $138 but not over $450	14% of excess over $138.
Over $450 but not over $950	$43.68 plus 18% of excess over $450.
Over $950 but not over $2,625	$133.68 plus 21% of excess over $950.
Over $2,625 but not over $3,000	$485.43 plus 23% of excess over $2,625.
Over $3,000 but not over $3,500	$571.68 plus 27% of excess over $3,000.
Over $3,500 but not over $4,325	$706.68 plus 31% of excess over $3,500.
Over $4,325	$962.43 plus 35% of excess over $4,325.

"(b) Married Person:

"If the amount of wages is:	The amount of income tax to be withheld shall be:
Not over $138	0.
Over $138 but not over $513	14% of excess over $138.
Over $513 but not over $2,175	$52.50 plus 16% of excess over $513.
Over $2,175 but not over $2,688	$318.42 plus 20% of excess over $2,175.
Over $2,688 but not over $4,213	$421.02 plus 24% of excess over $2,688.
Over $4,213 but not over $5,313	$787.02 plus 28% of excess over $4,213.
Over $5,313 but not over $6,313	$1,095.02 plus 32% of excess over $5,313.
Over $6,313	$1,415.02 plus 36% of excess over $6,313.

"**TABLE 6** — If the payroll period with respect to an employee is SEMIANNUAL:
"(a) Single Person — Including Head of Household:

"If the amount of wages is:	The amount of income tax to be withheld shall be:
Not over $275	0.
Over $275 but not over $900	14% of excess over $275.
Over $900 but not over $1,900	$87.50 plus 18% of excess over $900.
Over $1,900 but not over $5,250	$267.50 plus 21% of excess over $1,900.
Over $5,250 but not over $6,000	$971.00 plus 23% of excess over $5,250.
Over $6,000 but not over $7,000	$1,143.50 plus 27% of excess over $6,000.
Over $7,000 but not over $8,650	$1,413.50 plus 31% of excess over $7,000.
Over $8,650	$1,925.00 plus 35% of excess over $8,650.

"(b) Married Person:

"If the amount of wages is:	The amount of income tax to be withheld shall be:
Not over $275	0.
Over $275 but not over $1,025	14% of excess over $275.
Over $1,025 but not over $4,350	$105.00 plus 16% of excess over $1,025.
Over $4,350 but not over $5,375	$637.00 plus 20% of excess over $4,350.
Over $5,375 but not over $8,425	$842.00 plus 24% of excess over $5,375.
Over $8,425 but not over $10,625	$1,574.00 plus 28% of excess over $8,425.
Over $10,625 but not over $12,625	$2,190.00 plus 32% of excess over $10,625.
Over $12,625	$2,830.00 plus 36% of excess over $12,625.

"**TABLE 7** — If the payroll period with respect to an employee is ANNUAL:
"(a) Single Person — Including Head of Household:

"If the amount of wages is:	The amount of income tax to be withheld shall be:
Not over $550	0.
Over $550 but not over $1,800	14% of excess over $550.
Over $1,800 but not over $3,800	$175.00 plus 18% of excess over $1,800.
Over $3,800 but not over $10,500	$535.00 plus 21% of excess over $3,800.
Over $10,500 but not over $12,000	$1,942.00 plus 23% of excess over $10,500.
Over $12,000 but not over $14,000	$2,287.00 plus 27% of excess over $12,000.
Over $14,000 but not over $17,300	$2,827.00 plus 31% of excess over $14,000.
Over $17,300	$3,850.00 plus 35% of excess over $17,300.

"(b) Married Person:

"If the amount of wages is:	The amount of income tax to be withheld shall be:
Not over $550	0.
Over $550 but not over $2,050	14% of excess over $550.
Over $2,050 but not over $8,700	$210.00 plus 16% of excess over $2,050.
Over $8,700 but not over $10,750	$1,274.00 plus 20% of excess over $8,700.
Over $10,750 but not over $16,850	$1,684.00 plus 24% of excess over $10,750.
Over $16,850 but not over $21,250	$3,148.00 plus 28% of excess over $16,850.
Over $21,250 but not over $25,250	$4,380.00 plus 32% of excess over $21,250.
Over $25,250	$5,660.00 plus 36% of excess over $25,250.

"**TABLE 8** — If the payroll period with respect to an employee is a DAILY payroll period or a miscellaneous payroll period:
"(a) Single Person — Including Head of Household:

"If the amount of wages divided by the number of days in the payroll period is:	The amount of income tax to be withheld shall be:
Not over $1.50	0.
Over $1.50 but not over $4.90	14% of excess over $1.50.
Over $4.90 but not over $10.40	$0.48 plus 18% of excess over $4.90.
Over $10.40 but not over $28.80	$1.47 plus 21% of excess over $10.40.
Over $28.80 but not over $32.90	$5.33 plus 23% of excess over $28.80.
Over $32.90 but not over $38.40	$6.27 plus 27% of excess over $32.90.
Over $38.40 but not over $47.40	$7.76 plus 31% of excess over $38.40.
Over $47.40	$10.55 plus 35% of excess over $47.40.

"(b) Married Person:

"If the amount of wages divided by the number of days in the payroll period is:	The amount of income tax to be withheld shall be:
Not over $1.50	0.
Over $1.50 but not over $5.60	14% of excess over $1.50.
Over $5.60 but not over $23.80	$0.57 plus 16% of excess over $5.60.
Over $23.80 but not over $29.50	$3.48 plus 20% of excess over $23.80.
Over $29.50 but not over $46.20	$4.62 plus 24% of excess over $29.50.

Code Sec. 3402 — Wage withholding

Over $46.20 but not over $58.20	$8.63 plus 28% of excess over $46.20.
Over $58.20 but not over $69.20	$11.99 plus 32% of excess over $58.20.
Over $69.20	$15.51 plus 36% of excess over $69.20."

—P.L. 94-455, Sec. 401(d)(2), substituted "the table for an annual payroll period prescribed pursuant to subsection (a)" for "table 7 contained in subsection (a)" in para. (c)(6), for wages paid after 9/14/76 [sic]. For wages paid after 4/30/75 and before 10/1/76, para. (c)(6) read as follows:

"(6) in the case of wages paid after December 31, 1969, the amount deducted and withheld under paragraph (1) shall be determined in accordance with tables prescribed by the Secretary or his delegate. In the tables so prescribed, the amounts set forth as amounts of wages and amounts of income tax to be deducted and withheld shall be computed on the basis of the table for an annual payroll period prescribed pursuant to subsection (a)."

For wages paid before 5/1/75, para. (c)(6) read as follows:

"(6) In the case of wages paid after December 31, 1969, the amount deducted and withheld under paragraph (1) shall be determined in accordance with tables prescribed by the Secretary or his delegate. In the tables so prescribed, the amounts set forth as amounts of wages and amounts of income tax to be deducted and withheld shall be computed on the basis of table 7 contained in subsection (a)."

—P.L. 94-455, Sec. 401(d)(3), amended subpara. (m)(1)(B), effective for wages paid after 9/14/76 [sic]. For wages paid after 4/30/75 and before 10/1/76, subpara. (m)(1)(B) read as follows:

"(B) an amount equal to the lesser of (i) 16 percent of his estimated wages, or (ii) $2,600 ($2,300 in the case of an individual who is not married (within the meaning of section 143) and who is not a surviving spouse (as defined in section 2(a)))."

For wages paid before 5/1/75, subpara. (m)(1)(B) read as follows:

"(B) an amount equal to the lesser of (i) $2,000 or (ii) 15 percent of his estimated wages."

—P.L. 94-455, Sec. 502(b), substituted "under section 62 (other than paragraph (13) thereof)" for "under section 62" in subpara. (m)(2)(A), for tax. yrs. begin. after '76.

—P.L. 94-455, Sec. 504(c)(3), deleted "and" at the end of subpara. (m)(4)(A) ... substituted ", and" for the period at the end of subpara. (m)(4)(B) ... added subpara. (m)(4)(C), for tax. yrs. begin. after '75.

—P.L. 94-455, Sec. 1207(d), added subsec. (q), effective for payments of winnings made after Jan. 2, '77.

—P.L. 94-455, Sec. 1903(a)(17), substituted "section 2(a)" for "section 2(b)", for wages paid after '76.

—P.L. 94-455, Sec. 1906(b)(13)(A), substituted "Secretary" for "Secretary or his delegate" each place it appeared in Code Sec. 3402, effective 2/1/77.

—P.L. 94-414, Sec. 3(a)(1), substituted "October 1, 1976" for "September 15, 1976" in subsec. (a), effective 9/17/76.

—P.L. 94-414, Sec. 3(a)(2), extended the effective date for amendments made by P. L. 94-12, Secs. 202(b), 205(a) and 205(b), to include wages paid after 4/30/75 and before 10/1/76.

—P.L. 94-396, Sec. 2(a)(1), substituted "September 15, 1976" for "September 1, 1976" in subsec. (a), effective 9/3/76.

—P.L. 94-396, Sec. 2(b), extended the effective date for amendments made by P. L. 94-12, Secs. 202(b), 205(a) and 205(b), to include wages paid after 4/30/75 and before 9/15/76.

—P.L. 94-331, Sec. 3(a)(1), substituted "September 1, 1976" for "July 1, 1976" in subsec. (a), effective 6/30/76.

—P.L. 94-331, Sec. 3(a)(2), extended the effective date for amendments made by P. L. 94-12, Secs. 202(b), 205(a) and 205(b), to include wages paid after 4/30/75 and before 9/1/76.

In 1975, P.L. 94-164, Sec. 5(a)(1), added the third sentence in subsec. (a), effective date of enactment [12/23/75].

—P.L. 94-164, Sec. 2(b)(2), substituted "$2,800" for "$2,600" and "$2,400" for "$2,300" in subpara. (m)(1)(B), effective for tax. yrs. end. after 12/31/75 and before 1/1/77.

—P.L. 94-164, Sec. 5(a)(2), extended the effective date for amendments made by P. L. 94-12, Secs. 202(b), 205(a), and 205(b), to include wages paid after 4/30/75 and before 7/1/76.

—P.L. 94-12, Sec. 205(a), amended subsec. (a) ... Sec. 205(b), substituted "the table for an annual payroll period prescribed pursuant to subsection (a)" for "table 7 contained in subsection (a)" in para. (c)(6) ... Sec. 202(b), amended subpara. (m)(1)(B), effective with respect to wages paid after 4/30/75 and before 1/1/76.

In 1971, P.L. 92-178, Sec. 208(a), substituted new tables 1 through 8 for paras. (a)(1) through (5), for wages paid after 1/15/72 and extended the table in para. (3) from 1/1/72 to 1/16/72.

Prior to amendment paras. (a)(1) through (5) read as follows:

"(1) In the case of wages paid after December 31, 1969, and before July 1, 1970:

[Tables not reproduced]

—P.L. 92-178, Sec. 208(b)(1), substituted new para. (b)(1), for wages paid after 1/15/72.

Prior to amendment, para. (b)(1) read as follows:

"Percentage Method Withholding Table [for wages paid after '69 before July 1, '70]

"Payroll period	Amount of one withholding exemption:
Weekly	$ 11.50
Biweekly	23.00
Semimonthly	25.00
Monthly	50.00
Quarterly	150.00
Semiannual	300.00
Annual	600.00
Daily or miscellaneous (per day of such period)	1.60

[for wages paid after June 30, '70 and before '72]

"Payroll period	Amount of one withholding exemption:
Weekly	$ 12.50
Biweekly	25.00
Semimonthly	27.10
Monthly	54.20
Quarterly	162.50
Semiannual	325.00
Annual	650.00
Daily or miscellaneous (per day of such period)	1.80

[for wages paid during '72]

"Payroll period	Amount of one withholding exemption:
Weekly	$ 13.50
Biweekly	26.90
Semimonthly	29.20
Monthly	58.30
Quarterly	175.00
Semiannual	350.00
Annual	700.00
Daily or miscellaneous (per day of such period)	1.90

[for wages paid during '72]

"Payroll period	Amount of one withholding exemption:
Weekly	$ 14.40
Biweekly	28.80
Semimonthly	31.30
Monthly	62.50
Quarterly	187.50
Semiannual	375.00
Annual	750.00
Daily or miscellaneous (per day of such period)	2.10"

—P.L. 92-178, Sec. 208(c), deleted "and" at the end of subpara. (f)(1)(E), substituted "; and" in place of the period in subpara. (f)(1)(F), and added subpara. (f)(1)(G) ... Sec. 208(d), added para. (f)(7) ... Sec. 208(e), amended subpara. (m)(1)(B), effective for wages paid after 1/15/72.

Prior to amendment, subpara. (m)(1)(B) read as follows:

"(B) an amount equal to 15 percent of his estimated wages."

—P.L. 92-178, Sec. 208(f), substituted in the second sentence of para. (m)(2)(A) "for the taxable year preceding the estimation year or (if such a return has not been filed for such preceding taxable year at the time the withholding exemption certificate is furnished the employer) the second taxable year preceding the estimation year" for "for the taxable year preceding the estimation year", in the second sentence of subpara. (m)(2)(A), amended the first sentence of subpara. (m)(2)(D), deleted subparas. (m)(3)(B) and (C), and redesignated subparas. (m)(3)(D) and (E) as subparas. (m)(3)(B) and (C), effective for wages paid after 1/15/72.

Prior to amendment, the first sentence of subpara. (m)(2)(D) read as follows:

"(D) Estimation year. In the case of an employee who files his return on the basis of a calendar year, the term 'estimation year' means —

(i) with respect to payments of wages after April 30 and on or before December 31 of any calendar year, such calendar year, and (ii) with respect to payments of wages on or after January 1 and before May 1, of any calendar year, the preceding calendar year (except that with respect to an exemption certificate furnished by an employee after he has filed his return for the preceding calendar year, such term means the current calendar year)."

Prior to deletion, former subparas. (m)(3)(B) and (C) read as follows:

"(B) Only one certificate to be in effect. — In the case of any employee, withholding allowances under this subsection may not be claimed with more than one employer at any one time.

"(C) Termination of effectiveness. — In the case of an employee who files his return on the basis of a calendar year, that portion of a withholding exemption certificate which relates to allowances under this subsection shall not be effective with respect to payments of wages after the first April 30 following the close of the estimation year on which it is based."

Wage withholding Code Sec. 3403

—P.L. 92-178, Sec. 208(g), deleted "paragraph (1), (2), (3), (4), or (5) (whichever is applicable) of" in para. (c)(6), for wages paid after 1/15/72 . . . Sec. 208(h), substituted "January 16, 1972" for "January 1, 1972", in para. (a)(3), effective for wages paid after 12/31/71, and before 1/16/72.

In **1969**, P.L. 91-172, Sec. 805(a), amended paras. (a)(1) and (2) and added paras. (a)(3), (4), and (5), effective for remuneration paid after 12/31/69.

Prior to amendment, paras. (a)(1) and (2) read as follows:

"(1) In the case of wages paid on or before the 15th day after the date of the enactment of the Revenue and Expenditure Control Act of 1968 or after July 31, 1969:

[Tables not reproduced]

—P.L. 91-172, Sec. 805(b), amended the percentage method withholding table in para. (b)(1), effective for wages paid after 12/31/69, and before 7/1/70; for wages paid after 6/30/70, and before 1/1/72; for wages paid during '72; and for wages paid after '72, see above, effective with respect to remuneration paid after 12/31/69.

Prior to amendment the table read as follows:

"Percentage Method Withholding Table

Payroll period	Amount of one withholding exemption:
Weekly	$ 13.50
Biweekly	26.90
Semimonthly	29.20
Monthly	58.30
Quarterly	175.00
Semiannual	350.00
Annual	700.00
Daily or miscellaneous (per day of such period)	1.90

. . . Sec. 805(c)(1), amended para. (c)(1), effective for remuneration paid after 12/31/69.

Prior to amendment, para. (c)(1) read as follows:

"(1) At the election of the employer with respect to any employee, the employer shall deduct and withhold upon the wages paid to such employee a tax determined in accordance with the following tables, which shall be in lieu of the tax required to be deducted and withheld under subsection (a):"

(The previous tables appear below)

—P.L. 91-172, Sec. 805(c)(2), amended para. (c)(6), effective for remuneration paid after 12/31/69.

Prior to amendment, para. (c)(6) read as follows:

"(6) In the case of wages paid after the 15th day of the enactment of the Revenue and Expenditure Control Act of 1968, and before August 1, 1969, the amount deducted and withheld under paragraph (1) shall be determined in accordance with tables prescribed by the Secretary or his delegate in lieu of the tables contained in paragraph (1). The tables so prescribed shall be the same as the tables contained in paragraph (1), except that amounts and rates set forth as amounts and rates of tax to be deducted and withheld shall be computed on the basis of table 7 contained in subsection (a)(2)."

—P.L. 91-172, Sec. 805(d), amended subsec. (h), effective for remuneration paid after 12/31/69.

Prior to amendment, subsec. (h) read as follows:

"(h) Withholding on basis of average wages.

"The Secretary or his delegate may, under regulations prescribed by him, authorize employers—

"(1) to estimate the wages which will be paid to any employee in any quarter of the calendar year.

"(2) to determine the amount to be deducted and withheld upon each payment of wages to such employee during such quarter as if the appropriate average of the wages so estimated constituted the actual wages paid, and

"(3) to deduct and withhold upon any payment of wages to such employee during such quarter (and, in the case of tips referred to in subsection (k), within 30 days thereafter) such amount as may be necessary to adjust the amount actually deducted and withheld upon the wages of such employee during such quarter to the amount required to be deducted and withheld during such quarter without regard to this subsection."

—P.L. 91-172, Sec. 805(e), redesignated former par. (2)(C) as par. (2)(D) in subsec. (m) and amended that portion of subsec. (m) as preceded subpara. (m)(2)(D) (as redesignated), effective for remuneration paid after 12/31/69.

Prior to amendment, the portion of subsec. (m) preceding subpara. (m)(2)(D) read as follows:

"(m) Withholding allowances based on itemized deductions.

"(1) General rule. An employee shall be entitled to withholding allowances under this subsection with respect to a payment of wages in a number equal to the number determined by dividing by $700 the excess of—

"(A) his estimated itemized deductions, over

"(B) an amount equal to the sum of 10 percent of the first $7,500 of his estimated wages and 17 percent of the remainder of his estimated wages.

For purposes of this subsection, fractional numbers shall not be taken into account.

"(2) Definitions. For purposes of this subsection—

"(A) Estimated itemized deductions. The term 'estimated itemized deductions' means the aggregate amount which he reasonably expects will be allowable as deductions under chapter 1 (other than the deductions referred to in sections 141 and 151 and other than the deductions required to be taken into account in determining adjusted gross income under section 62) for the estimation year. In no case shall such aggregate amount be greater than (i) the amount of such deductions shown on his return of tax under subtitle A for the taxable year preceding the estimation year, or (ii) in the case of an employee who did not show such deductions on his return for such preceding taxable year, an amount equal to the lesser of $1,000 or 10 percent of the wages shown on his return for such preceding taxable year.

"(B) Estimated wages. The term 'estimated wages' means the aggregate amount which he reasonably expects will constitute wages for the estimation year. In no case shall such aggregate amount be less than the amount of wages shown on his return for the taxable year preceding the estimation year."

—P.L. 91-172, Sec. 805(f)(1), added subsec. (n), effective for wages paid after 4/30/70. . . . Sec. 805(g), added subsec. (o), effective for payments made after 1/31/70 and subsec. (p), effective for payments made after 6/30/70.

—P.L. 91-53, Sec. 6(a)(1), substituted "December 31, 1969" for "July 31, 1969" in para. (a)(1) . . . Sec. 6(a)(2), substituted "January 1, 1970" for "August 1, 1969" in para. (a)(2) . . . Sec. 6(a)(3), substituted "January 1, 1970" for "August 1, 1969" in para. (c)(6), effective for wages paid after 7/31/69 and before 1/1/70.

—P.L. 91-36, Sec. 2(a)(1), substituted "July 31, 1969" for "June 30, 1969" in para. (a)(1) . . . Sec. 2(a)(2), substituted "August 1, 1969" for "July 1, 1969" in para. (a)(2) . . . Sec. 2(a)(3), substituted "August 1, 1969" for "July 1, 1969" in para. (c)(6), effective for wages paid after 6/30/69.

In **1968**, P.L. 90-364, Sec. 102(c)(1)(A), added para. (a)(1) . . . Sec. 102(c)(1)(B), added para. (a)(2) . . . Sec. 102(c)(2), added para. (a)(6).

In **1966**, P.L. 89-368, Sec. 101(a), amended subsec. (a) . . . Sec. 101(b), amended table in para. (b)(1) . . . Sec. 101(c), amended tables in para. (c)(1) . . . Sec. 101(d), added subsec. (l), effective for remuneration paid after 4/30/66.

—P.L. 89-368, Sec. 101(e)(1)(A), deleted "and" at the end of subpara. (f)(1)(D) . . . Sec. 101(e)(1)(B), substituted "; and" for the period at the end of subpara. (f)(1)(E) . . . Sec. 101(e)(1)(C), added subpara. (f)(1)(F) . . . Sec. 101(e)(2), added subsec. (m) . . . Sec. 101(e)(3), amended last sentence of subpara. (f)(3)(B). Sec. 101(f) of this Act provides:

"(f) Transitional determination status date. Notwithstanding section 3402(f)(3)(B) of the Internal Revenue Code of 1954, a withholding exemption certificate furnished the employer after the date of the enactment [3/15/66] of this Act and before May 1, 1966, shall take effect with respect to the first payment of wages made on or after May 1, 1966, or the 10th day after the date on which such certificate is furnished to the employer, whichever is later, and at the election of the employer such certificate may be made effective with respect to any payment of wages made on or after the date on which such certificate is furnished."

Prior to amendment, subsecs. (a) and (b)(1) and the withholding tables read as follows:

"(a) Requirement of withholding.

"Every employer making payment of wages shall deduct and withhold upon such wages (except as provided in subsection (j) and (k) a tax equal to 14 percent of the amount by which the wages exceed the number of withholding exemptions claimed, multiplied by the amount of one such exemption as shown in subsection (b)(1).

"(b) Percentage method of withholding.

"(1) The table referred to in subsection (a) is as follows:

"Percentage Method Withholding Table

Payroll period	Amount of one withholding exemption
Weekly	$ 13.00
Biweekly	26.00
Semimonthly	28.00
Monthly	56.00
Quarterly	167.00
Semiannual	333.00
Annual	667.00
Daily or miscellaneous (per day of such period)	1.80

[The previous tables are not reproduced]

In **1965**, P.L. 89-212, Sec. 2(c), added "or section 3202(c)(2)" and "or section 3202(a)" in subsec. (k), effective for tips received after 1965.

—P.L. 89-97, Sec. 313(d)(3), substituted "subsections (j) and (k)" for "subsection (j)" in subsec. (a) . . . Sec. 313(d)(4), added "(and in the case of tips referred to in subsection (k), within 30 days thereafter" after "quarter" the first place it appeared in par. (h)(3) . . . Sec. 313(d)(5), added subsec. (k), effective for tips received by employees after 1965.

In **1964**, P.L. 88-272, Sec. 302(a), substituted "14 percent" for "18 percent" in subsec. (a) . . . Sec. 302(b), amended para. (c)(1), effective for remuneration paid after 3/4/64.

In **1961**, P.L. 87-256, Sec. 110(g)(2), added para. (f)(6), effective for wages paid after 1961.

In **1955**, P.L. 306, Sec. 2(a), added "(except as provided in subsection (j))" after "upon such wages" in subsec. (a) . . . Sec. 2(b), added subsec. (j), effective for remuneration paid after 8/9/55.

Sec. 3403. Liability for tax.

The employer shall be liable for the payment of the tax required to be deducted and withheld under this chapter, and shall not be liable to any person for the amount of any such payment.

In 1983, P.L. 98-67, Sec. 102(a), deleted the amendment made by Sec. 307(a)(2) of P. L. 97-248 [see below] as if it had never been enacted, effective 6/30/83.
In 1982, P.L. 97-248, Sec. 307(a)(2), substituted "this subchapter" for "this chapter" in Code Sec. 3403, effective 7/1/83.

Sec. 3404. Return and payment by governmental employer.

If the employer is the United States, or a State, or political subdivision thereof, or the District of Columbia, or any agency or instrumentality of any one or more of the foregoing, the return of the amount deducted and withheld upon any wages may be made by any officer or employee of the United States, or of such State, or political subdivision, or of the District of Columbia, or of such agency or instrumentality, as the case may be, having control of the payment of such wages, or appropriately designated for that purpose.

In 1976, P.L. 94-455, Sec. 1903(c), deleted "Territory," each place it appeared in Code Sec. 3404, effective for wages paid after 12/31/76.

Sec. 3405. Special rules for pensions, annuities, and certain other deferred income.

(a) Periodic payments.
(1) Withholding as if payment were wages. The payor of any periodic payment (as defined in subsection (e)(2)) shall withhold from such payment the amount which would be required to be withheld from such payment if such payment were a payment of wages by an employer to an employee for the appropriate payroll period.
(2) Election of no withholding. An individual may elect to have paragraph (1) not apply with respect to periodic payments made to such individual. Such an election shall remain in effect until revoked by such individual.
(3) When election takes effect. Any election under this subsection (and any revocation of such an election) shall take effect as provided by subsection (f)(3) of section 3402 for withholding exemption certificates.
(4) Amount withheld where no withholding exemption certificate in effect. In the case of any payment with respect to which a withholding exemption certificate is not in effect, the amount withheld under paragraph (1) shall be determined by treating the payee as a married individual claiming 3 withholding exemptions.
(b) Nonperiodic distribution.
(1) Withholding. The payor of any nonperiodic distribution (as defined in subsection (e)(3)) shall withhold from such distribution an amount equal to 10 percent of such distribution.
(2) Election of no withholding.
  (A) In general. An individual may elect not to have paragraph (1) apply with respect to any nonperiodic distribution.
  (B) Scope of election. An election under subparagraph (A)—
    (i) except as provided in clause (ii), shall be on a distribution-by-distribution basis, or
    (ii) to the extent provided in regulations, may apply to subsequent nonperiodic distributions made by the payor to the payee under the same arrangement.
(c) Eligible rollover distributions.
(1) In general. In the case of any designated distribution which is an eligible rollover distribution—
  (A) subsections (a) and (b) shall not apply, and
  (B) the payor of such distribution shall withhold from such distribution an amount equal to 20 percent of such distribution.

(2) Exception. Paragraph (1)(B) shall not apply to any distribution if the distributee elects under section 401(a)(31)(A) to have such distribution paid directly to an eligible retirement plan.
(3) Eligible rollover distribution. For purposes of this subsection, the term "eligible rollover distribution" has the meaning given such term by section 402(f)(2)(A).
(d) Liability for withholding.
(1) In general. Except as provided in paragraph (2), the payor of a designated distribution (as defined in subsection (e)(1)) shall withhold, and be liable for, payment of the tax required to be withheld under this section.
(2) Plan administrator liable in certain cases.
  (A) In general. In the case of any plan to which this paragraph applies, paragraph (1) shall not apply and the plan administrator shall withhold, and be liable for, payment of the tax unless the plan administrator
    (i) directs the payor to withhold such tax, and
    (ii) provides the payor with such information as the Secretary may require by regulations.
  (B) Plans to which paragraph applies. This paragraph applies to any plan described in, or which at any time has been determined to be described in
    (i) section 401(a),
    (ii) section 403(a),
    (iii) section 301(d) of the Tax Reduction Act of 1975, or
    (iv) section 457(b) and which is maintained by an eligible employer described in section 457(e)(1)(A).
(e) Definitions and special rules.
For purposes of this section
(1) Designated distribution.
  (A) In general. Except as provided in subparagraph (B), the term "designated distribution" means any distribution or payment from or under—
    (i) an employer deferred compensation plan,
    (ii) an individual retirement plan (as defined in section 7701(a)(37)), or
    (iii) a commercial annuity.
  (B) Exceptions. The term "designated distribution" shall not include—
    (i) any amount which is wages without regard to this section,
    (ii) the portion of a distribution or payment which it is reasonable to believe is not includible in gross income,
    (iii) any amount which is subject to withholding under subchapter A of chapter 3 (relating to withholding of tax on nonresident aliens and foreign corporations) by the person paying such amount or which would be so subject but for a tax treaty, or
    (iv) any distribution described in section 404(k)(2).
For purposes of clause (ii), any distribution or payment from or under an individual retirement plan (other than a Roth IRA) shall be treated as includible in gross income.
(2) Periodic payment. The term "periodic payment" means a designated distribution which is an annuity or similar periodic payment.
(3) Nonperiodic distribution. The term "nonperiodic distribution" means any designated distribution which is not a periodic payment.
(4) Repealed.
(5) Employer deferred compensation plan. The term "employer deferred compensation plan" means any pen-

Wage withholding — Code Sec. 3405

sion, annuity, profit-sharing, or stock bonus plan or other plan deferring the receipt of compensation.

(6) Commercial annuity. The term "commercial annuity" means an annuity, endowment, or life insurance contract issued by an insurance company licensed to do business under the laws of any State.

(7) Plan administrator. The term "plan administrator" has the meaning given such term by section 414(g).

(8) Maximum amount withheld. The maximum amount to be withheld under this section on any designated distribution shall not exceed the sum of the amount of money and the fair market value of other property (other than securities of the employer corporation) received in the distribution. No amount shall be required to be withheld under this section in the case of any designated distribution which consists only of securities of the employer corporation and cash (not in excess of $200) in lieu of financial shares. For purposes of this paragraph, the term "securities of the employer corporation" has the meaning given such term by section 402(e)(4)(E).

(9) Separate arrangements to be treated separately. If the payor has more than 1 arrangement under which designated distributions may be made to any individual, each such arrangement shall be treated separately.

(10) Time and manner of election.

(A) In general. Any election and any revocation under this section shall be made at such time and in such manner as the Secretary shall prescribe.

(B) Payor required to notify payee of rights to elect.

(i) Periodic payments. The payor of any periodic payment—

(I) shall transmit to the payee notice of the right to make an election under subsection (a) not earlier than 6 months before the first of such payments and not later than when making the first of such payments,

(II) if such a notice is not transmitted under subclause (I) when making such first payment, shall transmit such a notice when making such first payment, and

(III) shall transmit to payees, not less frequently than once each calendar year, notice of their rights to make elections under subsection (a) and to revoke such elections.

(ii) Nonperiodic distributions. The payor of any nonperiodic distribution shall transmit to the payee notice of the right to make any election provided in subsection (b) at the time of the distribution (or at such earlier time as may be provided in regulations).

(iii) Notice. Any notice transmitted pursuant to this subparagraph shall be in such form and contain such information as the Secretary shall prescribe.

(11) Withholding includes deduction. The terms "withholding", "withhold", and "withheld" include "deducting", "deduct", and "deducted".

(12) Failure to provide correct TIN. If—

(A) a payee fails to furnish his TIN to the payor in the manner required by the Secretary, or

(B) the Secretary notifies the payor before any payment or distribution that the TIN furnished by the payee is incorrect,

no election under subsection (a)(2) or (b)(2) shall be treated as in effect and subsection (a)(4) shall not apply to such payee.

(13) Election may not be made with respect to certain payments outside the United States or its possessions.

(A) In general. Except as provided in subparagraph (B), in the case of any periodic payment or nonperiodic distribution which is to be delivered outside of the United States and any possession of the United States, no election may be made under subsection (a)(2) or (b)(2) with respect to such payment.

(B) Exception. Subparagraph (A) shall not apply if the recipient certifies to the payor, in such manner as the Secretary may prescribe, that such person is not—

(i) a United States citizen or a resident alien of the United States, or

(ii) an individual to whom section 877 applies.

(f) Withholding to be treated as wage withholding under section 3402 for other purposes.

For purposes of this chapter (and so much of subtitle F as relates to this chapter)

(1) any designated distribution (whether or not an election under this section applies to such distribution) shall be treated as if it were wages paid by an employer to an employee with respect to which there has been withholding under section 3402, and

(2) in the case of any designated distribution not subject to withholding under this section by reason of an election under this section, the amount withheld shall be treated as zero.

In 2010, P.L. 111-312, Sec. 101(a)(1), substituted "December 31, 2012" for "December 31, 2010" both places it appeared in Sec. 901 of P.L. 107-16, [see below] effective as if included in the enactment of P.L. 107-16, EGTRRA, 6/7/2001.

In 2006, P.L. 109-280, Sec. 811, of this Act [relating to Sec. 901 of P. L. 107-16, see below], provides:

"SEC. 811. PENSIONS AND INDIVIDUAL RETIREMENT ARRANGEMENT PROVISIONS OF ECONOMIC GROWTH AND TAX RELIEF RECONCILIATION ACT OF 2001 MADE PERMANENT.

"Title IX of the Economic Growth and Tax Relief Reconciliation Act of 2001 shall not apply to the provisions of, and amendments made by, subtitles A through F of title VI of such Act (relating to pension and individual retirement arrangement provisions)."

In 2005, P.L. 109-135, Sec. 201(b)(4)(A), repealed Sec. 101 of P. L. 109-73. Prior to repeal, Sec. 101 of P. L. 109-73 read as follows:

"SEC. 101. TAX-FAVORED WITHDRAWALS FROM RETIREMENT PLANS FOR RELIEF RELATING TO HURRICANE KATRINA.

"(a) In general. Section 72(t) of the Internal Revenue Code of 1986 shall not apply to any qualified Hurricane Katrina distribution.

"(b) Aggregate dollar limitation.

"(1) In general. For purposes of this section, the aggregate amount of distributions received by an individual which may be treated as qualified Hurricane Katrina distributions for any taxable year shall not exceed the excess (if any) of—

"(A) $100,000, over

"(B) the aggregate amounts treated as qualified Hurricane Katrina distributions received by such individual for all prior taxable years.

"(2) Treatment of plan distributions. If a distribution to an individual would (without regard to paragraph (1)) be a qualified Hurricane Katrina distribution, a plan shall not be treated as violating any requirement of the Internal Revenue Code of 1986 merely because the plan treats such distribution as a qualified Hurricane Katrina distribution, unless the aggregate amount of such distributions from all plans maintained by the employer (and any member of any controlled group which includes the employer) to such individual exceeds $100,000.

"(3) Controlled group. For purposes of paragraph (2), the term 'controlled group' means any group treated as a single employer under subsection (b), (c), (m), or (o) of section 414 of such Code.

"(c) Amount distributed may be repaid.

"(1) In general. Any individual who receives a qualified Hurricane Katrina distribution may, at any time during the 3-year period beginning on the day after the date on which such distribution was received, make one or more contributions in an aggregate amount not to exceed the amount of such distribution to an eligible retirement plan of which such individual is a beneficiary and to which a rollover contribution of such distribution could be made under section 402(c), 403(a)(4), 403(b)(8), 408(d)(3), or 457(e)(16) of such Code, as the case may be.

"(2) Treatment of repayments of distributions from eligible retirement plans other than IRAs. For purposes of such Code, if a contribution is made pursuant to paragraph (1) with respect to a qualified Hurricane Katrina distribution from an eligible retirement plan other than an individual retirement plan, then the taxpayer shall, to the extent of the amount of the contribution, be treated as having received the qualified Hurricane Katrina distribution in an eligible rollover distribution (as defined in section 402(c)(4) of such Code) and as having transferred the amount to the eligible retirement plan in a direct trustee to trustee transfer within 60 days of the distribution.

"(3) Treatment of repayments for distributions from IRAs. For purposes of such Code, if a contribution is made pursuant to paragraph (1) with respect to a qualified Hurricane Katrina distribution from an individual retirement plan (as defined by section 7701(a)(37) of such Code), then, to the extent of the amount of the contribution, the qualified Hurricane Katrina distribution shall be treated as a distribution described in section 408(d)(3) of such Code and as having been transferred to the eligible retirement plan in a direct trustee to trustee transfer within 60 days of the distribution.

"(d) Definitions. For purposes of this section—

"(1) Qualified Hurricane Katrina distribution. Except as provided in subsection (b), the term 'qualified Hurricane Katrina distribution' means any distribution from an eligible retirement plan made on or after August 25, 2005, and before January 1, 2007, to an individual whose principal place of abode on August 28, 2005, is located in the Hurricane Katrina disaster area and who has sustained an economic loss by reason of Hurricane Katrina.

"(2) Eligible retirement plan. The term 'eligible retirement plan' shall have the meaning given such term by section 402(c)(8)(B) of such Code.

"(e) Income inclusion spread over 3 year period for qualified Hurricane Katrina distributions.

"(1) In general. In the case of any qualified Hurricane Katrina distribution, unless the taxpayer elects not to have this subsection apply for any taxable year, any amount required to be included in gross income for such taxable year shall be so included ratably over the 3-taxable year period beginning with such taxable year.

"(2) Special rule. For purposes of paragraph (1), rules similar to the rules of subparagraph (E) of section 408A(d)(3) of such Code shall apply.

"(f) Special rules.

"(1) Exemption of distributions from trustee to trustee transfer and withholding rules. For purposes of sections 401(a)(31), 402(f), and 3405 of such Code, qualified Hurricane Katrina distributions shall not be treated as eligible rollover distributions.

"(2) Qualified Hurricane Katrina distributions treated as meeting plan distribution requirements. For purposes of such Code, a qualified Hurricane Katrina distribution shall be treated as meeting the requirements of sections 401(k)(2)(B)(i), 403(b)(7)(A)(ii), 403(b)(11), and 457(d)(1)(A) of such Code."

In 2002, P.L. 107-358, Sec. 2, added subsec. (c) in Sec. 901 of P. L. 107-16 [see below], effective 12/17/2002.

In 2001, P.L. 107-16, Sec. 641(a)(1)(D)(ii), amended para. (c)(3) . . . Sec. 641(a)(1)(D)(iii), deleted "or" at the end of clause (d)(2)(B)(ii), substituted ", or" for the period at the end of clause (d)(2)(B)(iii), and added clause (d)(2)(B)(iv), effective for distributions after 12/31/2001. Sec. 641(f)(2) and (3) of this Act, provides:

"(2) Reasonable notice. No penalty shall be imposed on a plan for the failure to provide the information required by the amendment made by subsection (c) with respect to any distribution made before the date that is 90 days after the date on which the Secretary of the Treasury issues a safe harbor rollover notice after the date of the enactment of this Act, if the administrator of such plan makes a reasonable attempt to comply with such requirement.

"(3) Special rule. Notwithstanding any other provision of law, subsections (h)(3) and (h)(5) of section 1122 of the Tax Reform Act of 1986 shall not apply to any distribution from an eligible retirement plan (as defined in clause (iii) or (iv) of section 402(c)(8)(B) of the Internal Revenue Code of 1986) on behalf of an individual if there was a rollover to such plan on behalf of such individual which is permitted solely by reason of any amendment made by this section."

Prior to amendment, para. (c)(3) read as follows:

"(3) Eligible rollover distribution. For purposes of this subsection, the term 'eligible rollover distribution' has the meaning given such term by section 402(f)(2)(A) (or in the case of an annuity contract under section 403(b), a distribution from such contract described in section 402(f)(2)(A))."

—P.L. 107-16, Sec. 901, of this Act [as amended by Sec. 2 of P.L. 107-358, and Sec. 101(a)(1) of P.L. 111-312, see above], reads as follows:

"SEC. 901. SUNSET OF PROVISIONS OF ACT.

"(a) In general. All provisions of, and amendments made by, this Act shall not apply—

"(1) to taxable, plan, or limitation years beginning after December 31, 2012, or

"(2) in the case of title V, to estates of decedents dying, gifts made, or generation skipping transfers, after December 31, 2012.

"(b) Application of certain laws. The Internal Revenue Code of 1986 and the Employee Retirement Income Security Act of 1974 shall be applied and administered to years, estates, gifts, and transfers described in subsection (a) as if the provisions and amendments described in subsection (a) had never been enacted.

"(c) Exception. Subsection (a) shall not apply to section 803 (relating to no federal income tax on restitution received by victims of the Nazi regime or their heirs or estates)."

In 2000, P.L. 106-554, Sec. 1(a)(7), [which enacted into law Sec. 314(b) of P.L. 106-554] added "(other than a Roth IRA)" after "individual retirement plan" in subpara. (e)(1)(B), effective for tax. yrs. begin. after 12/31/97.

In 1996, P.L. 104-188, Sec. 1704(t)(71), substituted "(b)(2)" for "(b)(3)" in para. (e)(12), effective 8/20/96.

In 1992, P.L. 102-318, Sec. 521(b)(36), substituted "Periodic payments." for "Pensions, annuities, etc." in the heading of subsec. (a) . . . Sec. 521(b)(37)(A), substituted "an amount equal to 10 percent of such distribution" for "the amount determined under paragraph (2)" in para. (b)(1) . . . Sec. 521(b)(37)(B), deleted para. (b)(2) and redesignated para. (b)(3) as para. (b)(2) . . . Sec. 521(b)(38), deleted para. (d)(4) . . . Sec. 521(b)(39), amended para. (d)(8) . . . Sec. 521(b)(40), substituted "(b)(2)" for "(b)(3)" in subpara. (d)(13)(A), effective for distributions after 12/31/92. For special rule, see Sec. 521(e)(2) of this Act which reads as follows:

"(2) Special rule for partial distributions. For purposes of section 402(a)(5)(D)(i)(II) of the Internal Revenue Code of 1986 (as in effect before the amendments made by this section), a distribution before January 1, 1993, which is made before or at the same time as a series of periodic payments shall not be treated as one of such series if it is not substantially equal in amount to other payments in such series."

Prior to deletion, para. (b)(2) read as follows:

"(2) Amount of withholding.

"(A) Distributions which are not qualified total distributions. In the case of any nonperiodic distribution which is not a qualified total distribution, the amount withheld under paragraph (1) shall be the amount determined by multiplying such distribution by 10 percent.

"(B) Qualified total distributions. In the case of any nonperiodic distribution which is a qualified total distribution, the amount withheld under paragraph (1) shall be determined under tables (or other computational procedures) prescribed by the Secretary which are based on the amount of tax which would be imposed on such distribution under section 402(e) if the recipient elected to treat such distribution as a lump-sum distribution (within the meaning of section 402(e)(4)(A)).

"(C) Special rule for distributions by reason of death. In the case of any nonperiodic distribution from or under any plan or contract described in section 401(a), 403(a), or 403(b)—

"(i) which is made by reason of a participant's death, and

"(ii) with respect to which the requirements of clauses (ii) and (iv) of subsection (d)(4)(A) are met,

subparagraph (A) or (B) (as the case may be) shall be applied by taking into account the exclusion from gross income provided by section 101(b) (whether or not allowable)."

Prior to deletion, para. (d)(4) read as follows:

"(4) Qualified total distribution.

"(A) In general. The term 'qualified total distribution' means any distribution which—

"(i) is a designated distribution,

"(ii) it is reasonable to believe is made within 1 taxable year of the recipient,

"(iii) is made under a plan described in section 401(a), or 403(a), and

"(iv) consists of the balance to the credit of the employee under such plan.

"(B) Special rule for accumulated deductible employee contributions. For purposes of subparagraph (A), accumulated deductible employee contributions (within the meaning of section 72(o)(5)(B)) shall be treated separately in determining if there has been a qualified total distribution."

Prior to amendment, para. (d)(8) read as follows:

"(8) Maximum amount withheld. The maximum amount to be withheld under this section on any designated distribution shall not exceed the sum of the amount of money and the fair market value of other property (other than employer securities of the employer corporation (within the meaning of section 402(a)(3))) received in the distribution. No amount shall be required to be withheld under this section in the case of any designated distribution which consists only of employer securities of the employer corporation (within the meaning of section 402(a)(3)) and cash (not in excess of $200) in lieu of fractional shares."

—P.L. 102-318, Sec. 522(b)(1), redesignated subsecs. (c), (d) and (e) as subsecs. (d), (e) and (f) and added new subsec. (c) . . . Sec. 522(b)(2)(A), substituted "subsection (e)(2)" for "subsection (d)(2)" in para. (a)(1) . . . Sec. 522(b)(2)(B), substituted "subsection (e)(3)" for "subsection (d)(3)" in para. (b)(1) . . . Sec. 522(b)(2)(C), substituted "subsection (e)(1)" for "subsection (d)(1)" in para. (d)(1) [as redesignated by Sec. 522(b)(1), see above], effective for distributions after 12/31/92, except as provided in Sec. 522(d)(2) of this Act which reads as follows:

"(2) Transition rule for certain annuity contracts. If, as of July 1, 1992, a State law prohibits a direct trustee-to-trustee transfer from an annuity contract described in section 403(b) of the Internal Revenue Code of 1986 which was purchased for an employee by an employer which is a State or a political subdivision thereof (or an agency or instrumentality of any 1 or more of either), the amendments made by this section shall not apply to distributions before the earlier of—

"(A) 90 days after the first day after July 1, 1992, on which such transfer is allowed under State law, or

(B) January 1, 1994."

In 1988, P.L. 100-647, Sec. 1012(bb)(2)(A), substituted "the United States and any possession of the United States" for "the United States" in subpara. (d)(13)(A) . . . Sec. 1012(bb)(2)(B), amended clause (d)(13)(B)(i) . . . Sec. 1012(bb)(2)(C), substituted "United States or its possessions" for "United States" in the heading of para. (d)(13), effective for distributions made after 11/10/88.

Prior to amendment, clause (d)(13)(B)(i) read as follows:

"(i) a United States citizen who is a bona fide resident of a foreign country, or".

In 1986, P.L. 99-514, Sec. 1102(e)(1), added the sentence at the end of subpara. (d)(1)(B), effective for contributions and distributions for tax. yrs. begin. after 12/31/86.

—P.L. 99-514, Sec. 1234(b)(1), added para. (d)(13), effective for payments after 12/31/86.

—P.L. 99-514, Sec. 1875(c)(10), deleted "or" at the end of clause (d)(1)(B)(ii), redesignated clause (d)(1)(B)(iii) as clause (d)(1)(B)(iv), and added new clause (d)(1)(B)(iii), effective for tax. yrs. begin. after 7/18/84.

In 1984, P.L. 98-369, Sec. 542(c), deleted "and" at the end of clause (d)(1)(B)(i), substituted ", or" for the period at the end of clause (d)(1)(B)(ii), and added clause (d)(1)(B)(iii), effective for tax. yrs. begin. after 7/18/84.

—P.L. 98-369, Sec. 714(j)(1), amended subpara. (b)(2)(C) . . . Sec. 714(j)(4), deleted "and" at the end of clause (d)(1)(B)(i), substituted ", and" for the period at the end of clause (d)(1)(B)(ii), and added clause (d)(1)(B)(iii) . . . Sec. 714(j)(5),

Wage withholding   Code Sec. 3406(b)(6)

added the sentence at the end of para. (d)(8), effective for payments or other distributions made after 12/31/82, except as provided by Secs. 334(e)(4) and (5) of P. L. 97-248 [reproduced below].

Prior to amendment, subpara. (b)(2)(C) read as follows:

"(C) Special rule for distributions by reasons of death. In the case of any distribution described in subparagraph (B) from or under any plan or contract described in section 401(a), 403(a), or 403(b) which is made by reason of a participant's death, the Secretary, in prescribing tables or procedures under paragraph (1), shall take into account the exclusion from gross income provided by section 101(b) (whether or not allowable)."

— P.L. 98-369, Sec. 722(h)(4)(A), added para. (d)(12), effective for payments or distributions after 12/31/84, unless the payor elects to have such para. effective for payments or distributions before 1/1/85.

In 1982, P.L. 97-248, Sec. 334(a), added Code Sec. 3405, effective for payments or other distributions made after 12/31/82. Secs. 334(e)(4) and (5) of this Act provide exceptions as follows:

"(4) Periodic payments beginning before January 1, 1983. — For purposes of section 3405(a) of the Internal Revenue Code of 1954, in the case of periodic payments beginning before January 1, 1983, the first periodic payment after December 31, 1982, shall be treated as the first such periodic payment.

"(5) Delay in application. — The Secretary of the Treasury shall prescribe such regulations which delay (but not beyond June 30, 1983) the application of some or all of the amendments made by this section with respect to any payor until such time as such payor is able to comply without undue hardship with the requirements of such provisions."

Sec. 3406. Backup withholding.
(a) Requirement to deduct and withhold.

> • **Caution:** Code Sec. 3406(a)(1), following, was amended by Sec. 101(c)(10), P.L. 107-16, the Economic Growth and Tax Relief Reconciliation Act of 2001 (EGTRRA). These provisions generally sunset for tax years beginning after 12/31/2012. For specific sunset provisions, see Sec. 901, P.L. 107-16 (as amended) reproduced in history notes for this Code Sec.

(1) **In general.** In the case of any reportable payment, if—

(A) the payee fails to furnish his TIN to the payor in the manner required,

(B) the Secretary notifies the payor that the TIN furnished by the payee is incorrect,

(C) there has been a notified payee under-reporting described in subsection (c), or

(D) there has been a payee certification failure described in subsection (d), then the payor shall deduct and withhold from such payment a tax equal to the product of the fourth lowest rate of tax applicable under section 1(c) and such payment.

(2) **Subparagraphs (C) and (D) of paragraph (1) apply only to interest and dividend payments.** Subparagraphs (C) and (D) of paragraph (1) shall apply only to reportable interest or dividend payments.

(b) Reportable payment, etc.

For purposes of this section—

(1) **Reportable payment.** The term "reportable payment" means—

(A) any reportable interest or dividend payment, and

(B) any other reportable payment.

(2) **Reportable interest or dividend payment.**

(A) In general. The term "reportable interest or dividend payment" means any payment of a kind, and to a payee, required to be shown on a return required under—

(i) section 6049 (relating to payments of interest),

(ii) section 6042 (relating to payments of dividends), or

(iii) section 6044 (relating to payments of patronage dividends) but only to the extent such payment is in money.

(B) Special rule for patronage dividends. For purposes of subparagraphs (C) and (D) of subsection (a)(1), the term "reportable interest or dividend payment" shall not include any payment to which section 6044 (relating to patronage dividends) applies unless 50 percent or more of such payment is in money.

(3) **Other reportable payment.** The term "other reportable payment" means any payment of a kind, and to a payee, required to be shown on a return required under—

(A) section 6041 (relating to certain information at source),

(B) section 6041A(a) (relating to payments of remuneration for services),

(C) section 6045 (relating to returns of brokers),

> • **Caution:** Code Sec. 3406(b)(3)(D), (E), following, are effective for amounts paid before 1/1/2012. For Code Sec. 3406(b)(3)(D)-(F), effective for amounts paid after 12/31/2011, see below.

(D) section 6050A (relating to reporting requirements of certain fishing boat operators), but only to the extent such payment is in money and represents a share of the proceeds of the catch, or

(E) section 6050N (relating to payments of royalties).

> • **Caution:** Code Sec. 3406(b)(3)(D)-(F), following, are effective for amounts paid after 12/31/2011. For Code Sec. 3406(b)(3)(D), (E), effective for amounts paid before 1/1/2012, see above.

(D) section 6050A (relating to reporting requirements of certain fishing boat operators), but only to the extent such payment is in money and represents a share of the proceeds of the catch,

(E) section 6050N (relating to payments of royalties), or

(F) section 6050W (relating to returns relating to payments made in settlement of payment card transactions).

(4) **Whether payment is of reportable kind determined without regard to minimum amount.** The determination of whether any payment is of a kind required to be shown on a return described in paragraph (2) or (3) shall be made without regard to any minimum amount which must be paid before a return is required.

(5) **Exception for certain small payments.** To the extent provided in regulations, the term "reportable payment" shall not include any payment which—

(A) does not exceed $10, and

(B) if determined for a 1-year period, would not exceed $10.

(6) **Other reportable payments include payments described in section 6041(a) or 6041A(a) only where aggregate for calendar year is $600 or more.** Any payment of a kind required to be shown on a return required under section 6041(a) or 6041A(a) which is made during any calendar year shall be treated as a reportable payment only if—

3,165

(A) the aggregate amount of such payment and all previous payments described in such sections by the payor to the payee during such calendar year equals or exceeds $600,
(B) the payor was required under section 6041(a) or 6041A(a) to file a return for the preceding calendar year with respect to payments to the payee, or
(C) during the preceding calendar year, the payor made reportable payments to the payee with respect to which amounts were required to be deducted and withheld under subsection (a).

(7) Exception for certain window payments of interest, etc. For purposes of subparagraphs (C) and (D) of subsection (a)(1), the term "reportable interest or dividend payment" shall not include any payment—
(A) in redemption of a coupon on a bearer instrument or in redemption of a United States savings bond, or
(B) to the extent provided in regulations, of interest on instruments similar to those described in subparagraph (A).

The preceding sentence shall not apply for purposes of determining whether there is payee underreporting described in subsection (c).

(c) Notified payee underreporting with respect to interest and dividends.

(1) Notified payee underreporting. If—
(A) the Secretary determines with respect to any payee that there has been payee underreporting,
(B) at least 4 notices have been mailed by the Secretary to the payee (over a period of at least 120 days) with respect to the underreporting, and
(C) in the case of any payee who has filed a return for the taxable year, any deficiency of tax attributable to such failure has been assessed,

the Secretary may notify payors of reportable interest or dividend payments with respect to such payee of the requirement to deduct and withhold under subsection (a)(1)(C) (but not the reasons for the withholding under subsection (a)(1)(C)).

(2) Payee underreporting defined. For purposes of this section, there has been payee underreporting if for any taxable year the Secretary determines that—
(A) the payee failed to include in his return of tax under chapter 1 for such year any portion of a reportable interest or dividend payment required to be shown on such return, or
(B) the payee may be required to file a return for such year and to include a reportable interest or dividend payment in such return, but failed to file such return.

(3) Determination by secretary to stop (or not to start) withholding.
(A) In general. If the Secretary determines that—
(i) there was no payee underreporting,
(ii) any payee underreporting has been corrected (and any tax, penalty, or interest with respect to the payee underreporting has been paid),
(iii) withholding under subsection (a)(1)(C) has caused (or would cause) undue hardship to the payee and it is unlikely that any payee underreporting by such payee will occur again, or
(iv) there is a bona fide dispute as to whether there has been any payee underreporting,

then the Secretary shall take the action described in subparagraph (B).
(B) Secretary to take action to stop (or not to start) withholding. For purposes of subparagraph (A), if at the time of the Secretary's determination under subparagraph (A)—
(i) no notice has been given under paragraph (1) to any payor with respect to the underreporting, the Secretary shall not give any such notice, or
(ii) if such notice has been given, the Secretary shall—
(I) provide the payee with a written certification that withholding under subsection (a)(1)(C) is to stop, and
(II) notify the applicable payors (and brokers) that such withholding is to stop.
(C) Time for taking action where notice to payor has been given. In any case where notice has been given under paragraph (1) to any payor with respect to any underreporting, if the Secretary makes a determination under subparagraph (A) during the 12-month period ending on October 15 of any calendar year—
(i) except as provided in clause (ii), the Secretary shall take the action described in subparagraph (B)(ii) to bring about the stopping of withholding no later than December 1 of such calendar year, or
(ii) in the case of—
(I) a no payee underreporting determination under clause (i) of subparagraph (A), or
(II) a hardship determination under clause (iii) of subparagraph (A),

such action shall be taken no later than the 45th day after the day on which the Secretary made the determination.
(D) Opportunity to request determination. The Secretary shall prescribe procedures under which—
(i) a payee may request a determination under subparagraph (A), and
(ii) the payee may provide information with respect to such request.

(4) Payor notifies payee of withholding because of payee underreporting. Any payor required to withhold any tax under subsection (a)(1)(C) shall, at the time such withholding begins, notify the payee of such withholding.

(5) Payee may be required to notify secretary who his payors and brokers are. For purposes of this section, the Secretary may require any payee of reportable interest or dividend payments who is subject to withholding under subsection (a)(1)(C) to notify the Secretary of—
(A) all payors from whom the payee receives reportable interest or dividend payments, and
(B) all brokers with whom the payee has accounts which may involve reportable interest or dividend payments.

The Secretary may notify any such broker that such payee is subject to withholding under subsection (a)(1)(C).

(d) Interest and dividend backup withholding applies to new accounts and instruments unless payee certifies that he is not subject to such withholding.

(1) In general. There is a payee certification failure unless the payee has certified to the payor, under penalty of perjury, that such payee is not subject to withholding under subsection (a)(1)(C).

(2) Special rules for readily tradable instruments.
(A) In general. Subsection (a)(1)(D) shall apply to any reportable interest or dividend payment to any payee on any readily tradable instrument if (and only if) the payor was notified by a broker under subparagraph (B) or no certification was provided to the payor by the payee under paragraph (1) and—

Wage withholding   Code Sec. 3406(e)(5)(A)

(i) such instrument was acquired directly by the payee from the payor, or

(ii) such instrument is held by the payor as nominee for the payee.

(B) Broker notifies payor. If—

(i) a payee acquires any readily tradable instrument through a broker, and

(ii) with respect to such acquisition

(I) the payee fails to furnish his TIN to the broker in the manner required under subsection (a)(1)(A),

(II) the Secretary notifies such broker before such acquisition that the TIN furnished by the payee is incorrect,

(III) the Secretary notifies such broker before such acquisition that such payee is subject to withholding under subsection (a)(1)(C), or

(IV) the payee does not provide a certification to such broker under subparagraph (C),

such broker shall, within such period as the Secretary may prescribe by regulations (but not later than 15 days after such acquisition), notify the payor that such payee is subject to withholding under subparagraph (A), (B), (C), or (D) of subsection (a)(1), respectively.

(C) Time for payee to provide certification to broker. In the case of any readily tradable instrument acquired by a payee through a broker, the certification described in paragraph (1) may be provided by the payee to such broker—

(i) at any time after the payee's account with the broker was established and before the acquisition of such instrument, or

(ii) in connection with the acquisition of such instrument.

(3) **Exception for existing accounts, etc.** This subsection and subsection (a)(1)(D) shall not apply to any reportable interest or dividend payment which is paid or credited—

(A) in the case of interest or any other amount of a kind reportable under section 6049, with respect to any account (whatever called) established before January 1, 1984, or with respect to any instrument acquired before January 1, 1984,

(B) in the case of dividends or any other amount reportable under section 6042, on any stock or other instrument acquired before January 1, 1984, or

(C) in the case of patronage dividends or other amounts of a kind reportable under section 6044, with respect to any membership acquired, or contract entered into, before January 1, 1984.

(4) **Exception for readily tradable instruments acquired through existing brokerage accounts.** Subparagraph (B) of paragraph (2) shall not apply with respect to a readily tradable instrument which was acquired through an account with a broker if—

(A) such account was established before January 1, 1984, and

(B) during 1983, such broker bought or sold instruments for the payee (or acted as a nominee for the payee) through such account.

The preceding sentence shall not apply with respect to any readily tradable instrument acquired through such account after the broker was notified by the Secretary that the payee is subject to withholding under subsection (a)(1)(C).

(e) **Period for which withholding is in effect.**

(1) **Failure to furnish TIN.** In the case of any failure by a payee to furnish his TIN to a payor in the manner required, subsection (a) shall apply to any reportable payment made by such payor during the period during which the TIN has not been furnished in the manner required. The Secretary may require that a TIN required to be furnished under subsection (a)(1)(A) be provided under penalties of perjury only with respect to interest, dividends, patronage dividends, and amounts subject to broker reporting.

(2) **Notification of incorrect number.** In any case in which the Secretary notifies the payor that the TIN furnished by the payee is incorrect, subsection (a) shall apply to any reportable payment made by such payor—

(A) after the close of the 30th day after the day on which the payor received such notification, and

(B) before the payee furnishes another TIN in the manner required.

(3) **Notified payee underreporting described in subsection (c).**

(A) In general. In the case of any notified payee underreporting described in subsection (c), subsection (a) shall apply to any reportable interest or dividend payment made—

(i) after the close of the 30th day after the day on which the payor received notification from the Secretary of such underreporting, and

(ii) before the stop date.

(B) Stop date. For purposes of this subsection, the term "stop date" means the determination effective date or, if later, the earlier of—

(i) the day on which the payor received notification from the Secretary under subsection (c)(3)(B) to stop withholding, or

(ii) the day on which the payor receives from the payee a certification provided by the Secretary under subsection (c)(3)(B).

(C) Determination effective date. For purposes of this subsection—

(i) In general. Except as provided in clause (ii), the determination effective date of any determination under subsection (c)(3)(A) which is made during the 12-month period ending on October 15 of any calendar year shall be the first January 1 following such October 15.

(ii) Determination that there was no underreporting; hardship. In the case of any determination under clause (i) or (iii) of subsection (c)(3)(A), the determination effective date shall be the date on which the Secretary's determination is made.

(4) **Failure to provide certification that payee is not subject to withholding.**

(A) In general. In the case of any payee certification failure described in subsection (d)(1), subsection (a) shall apply to any reportable interest or dividend payment made during the period during which the certification described in subsection (d)(1) has not been furnished to the payor.

(B) Special rule for readily tradable instruments acquired through broker where notification. In the case of any readily tradable instrument acquired by the payee through a broker, the period described in subparagraph (A) shall start with payments to the payee made after the close of the 30th day after the payor receives notification from a broker under subsection (d)(2)(B).

(5) **30-day grace periods.**

(A) Start-up. If the payor elects the application of this subparagraph with respect to the payee, subsection (a) shall also apply to any reportable payment made during the 30-day period described in paragraph (2)(A), (3)(A), or (4)(B).

(B) **Stopping.** Unless the payor elects not to have this subparagraph apply with respect to the payee, subsection (a) shall also apply to any reportable payment made after the close of the period described in paragraph (1), (2), or (4) (as the case may be) and before the 30th day after the close of such period. A similar rule shall also apply with respect to the period described in paragraph (3)(A) where the stop date is determined under clause (i) or (ii) of paragraph (3)(B).

(C) **Election of shorter grace period.** The payor may elect a period shorter than the grace period set forth in subparagraph (A) or (B), as the case may be.

(f) Confidentiality of information.

(1) **In general.** No person may use any information obtained under this section (including any failure to certify under subsection (d)) except for purposes of meeting any requirement under this section or (subject to the safeguards set forth in section 6103) for purposes permitted under section 6103.

(2) **Cross reference.** For provision providing for civil damages for violation of paragraph (1), see section 7431.

(g) Exceptions.

(1) **Payments to certain payees.** Subsection (a) shall not apply to any payment made to—

(A) any organization or governmental unit described in subparagraph (B), (C), (D), (E), or (F) of section 6049(b)(4), or

(B) any other person specified in regulations.

(2) **Amounts for which withholding otherwise required.** Subsection (a) shall not apply to any amount for which withholding is otherwise required by this title.

(3) **Exemption while waiting for TIN.** The Secretary shall prescribe regulations for exemptions from the tax imposed by subsection (a) during the period during which a person is waiting for receipt of a TIN.

(h) Other definitions and special rules.

For purposes of this section—

(1) **Obviously incorrect number.** A person shall be treated as failing to furnish his TIN if the TIN furnished does not contain the proper number of digits.

(2) **Payee furnishes 2 incorrect TINs.** If the payee furnishes the payor 2 incorrect TINs in any 3-year period, the payor shall, after receiving notice of the second incorrect TIN, treat the payee as not having furnished another TIN under subsection (e)(2)(B) until the day on which the payor receives notification from the Secretary that a correct TIN has been furnished.

(3) **Joint payees.** Except to the extent otherwise provided in regulations, any payment to joint payees shall be treated as if all the payment were made to the first person listed in the payment.

(4) **Payor defined.** The term "payor" means, with respect to any reportable payment, a person required to file a return described in paragraph (2) or (3) of subsection (b) with respect to such payment.

(5) **Broker.**

(A) **In general.** The term "broker" has the meaning given to such term by section 6045(c)(1).

(B) Only 1 broker per acquisition. If, but for this subparagraph, there would be more than 1 broker with respect to any acquisition, only the broker having the closest contact with the payee shall be treated as the broker.

(C) **Payor not treated as broker.** In the case of any instrument, such term shall not include any person who is the payor with respect to such instrument.

(D) **Real estate broker not treated as a broker.** Except as provided by regulations, such term shall not include any real estate broker (as defined in section 6045(e)(2)).

(6) **Readily tradable instrument.** The term "readily tradable instrument" means—

(A) any instrument which is part of an issue any portion of which is traded on an established securities market (within the meaning of section 453(f)(5)), and

(B) except as otherwise provided in regulations prescribed by the Secretary, any instrument which is regularly quoted by brokers or dealers making a market.

(7) **Original issue discount.** To the extent provided in regulations, rules similar to the rules of paragraph (6) of section 6049(d) shall apply.

(8) **Requirement of notice to payee.** Whenever the Secretary notifies a payor under paragraph (1)(B) of subsection (a) that the TIN furnished by any payee is incorrect, the Secretary shall at the same time furnish a copy of such notice to the payor, and the payor shall promptly furnish such copy to the payee.

(9) **Requirement of notice to Secretary.** If the Secretary notifies a payor under paragraph (1)(B) of subsection (a) that the TIN furnished by any payee is incorrect and such payee subsequently furnishes another TIN to the payor, the payor shall promptly notify the Secretary of the other TIN so furnished.

(10) **Coordination with other sections.** For purposes of section 31, this chapter (other than section 3402(n)), and so much of subtitle F (other than section 7205) as relates to this chapter, payments which are subject to withholding under this section shall be treated as if they were wages paid by an employer to an employee (and amounts deducted and withheld under this section shall be treated as if deducted and withheld under section 3402).

(i) Regulations.

The Secretary shall prescribe such regulations as may be necessary or appropriate to carry out the purposes of this section.

In 2010, P.L. 111-312, Sec. 101(a)(1), substituted "December 31, 2012" for "December 31, 2010" both places it appears in Sec. 901, P.L. 107-16, see below, effective as if included in the enactment of P.L. 107-16, EGTRRA, 6/7/2001.

In 2008, P.L. 110-289, Sec. 3091(c), deleted "or" at the end of subpara. (b)(3)(D), substituted ", or" for the period at the end of subpara. (b)(3)(E), and added subpara. (b)(3)(F), effective for amounts paid after 12/31/2011. Sec. 3091(e)(2)(B) of this Act provides:

"(B) Eligibility for tin matching program. Solely for purposes of carrying out any TIN matching program established by the Secretary under section 3406(i) of the Internal Revenue Code of 1986

"(i) the amendments made this section shall be treated as taking effect on the date of the enactment of this Act, and

"(ii) each person responsible for setting the standards and mechanisms referred to in section 6050W(d)(2)(C) of such Code, as added by this section, for settling transactions involving payment cards shall be treated in the same manner as a payment settlement entity."

In 2002, P.L. 107-358, Sec. 2, added subsec. (c) in Sec. 901 of P. L. 107-16 [see below], effective 12/17/2002.

In 2001, P.L. 107-16, Sec. 101(c)(10), substituted "equal to the product of the fourth lowest rate of tax applicable under section 1(c) and such payment" for "equal to 31 percent of such payment" in subpara. (a)(1)(D), effective for amounts paid after the 60th day after 6/7/2001. References to income brackets and rates of tax in Sec. 101(c)(6)-(11) of this Act shall be applied without regard to section 1(i)(1)(D) of the Internal Revenue Code of 1986.

—P.L. 107-16, Sec. 901, of this Act [as amended by Sec. 2, P. L. 107-358, and Sec. 101(a)(1), P.L. 111-312, see above], reads as follows:

"SEC. 901. SUNSET OF PROVISIONS OF ACT.

"(a) In general. All provisions of, and amendments made by, this Act shall not apply—

"(1) to taxable, plan, or limitation years beginning after December 31, 2012, or

"(2) in the case of title V, to estates of decedents dying, gifts made, or generation skipping transfers, after December 31, 2012.

Wage withholding   Code Sec. B

"(b) Application of certain laws. The Internal Revenue Code of 1986 and the Employee Retirement Income Security Act of 1974 shall be applied and administered to years, estates, gifts, and transfers described in subsection (a) as if the provisions and amendments described in subsection (a) had never been enacted.

"(c) Exception. Subsection (a) shall not apply to section 803 (relating to no federal income tax on restitution received by victims of the Nazi regime or their heirs or estates)."

In 1992, P.L. 102-486, Sec. 1935(a), substituted "31 percent" for "20 percent" in para. (a)(1), effective for amounts paid after 12/31/92.

In 1988, P.L. 100-647, Sec. 1018(u)(44), added a period at the end of subpara. (h)(5)(D), effective for real estate transactions closing after 12/31/86.

In 1986, P.L. 99-514, Sec. 1521(b), added subpara. (h)(5)(D), effective for real estate transactions closing after 12/31/86.

—P.L. 99-514, Sec. 1523(b)(1)(A)-(C), deleted "or" at the end of subpara. (b)(3)(C) or" for the period at the end of subpara. (b)(3)(D), and added subpara. (b)(3)(E), effective for payments made after 12/31/86.

—P.L. 99-514, Sec. 1899A(46), substituted "6041A(a)" for "6041(A)(a)" in the heading of para. (b)(6), effective 10/22/86.

In 1984, P.L. 98-369, Sec. 152(a), added the last sentence of para. (e)(1), effective on 7/18/84.

—P.L. 98-369, Sec. 722(h)(1)(A)(i), added "the payor was notified by a broker under subparagraph (B) or" after "if (and only if)" in subpara. (d)(2)(A)... Sec. 722(h)(1)(A)(ii), deleted clause (d)(2)(A)(i) and redesignated clauses (d)(2)(A)(ii) and (iii) as clauses (d)(2)(A)(i) and (ii)... Sec. 722(h)(1)(B), amended subpara. (d)(2)(B)... Sec. 722(h)(2), substituted "(but not the reasons for the withholding under subsection (a)(1)(C))" for "(but not the reasons therefor)" in para. (c)(1), effective for payments made after 12/31/83.

Prior to deletion, clause (d)(2)(A)(i) read as follows:

"(i) the payor was notified by a broker under subparagraph (B),"

Prior to amendment, subpara. (d)(2)(B) read as follows:

"(B) Broker notifies payor. If—

"(i) a payee acquires any readily tradable instrument through a broker, and

"(ii)(I) the payee does not provide a certification to such broker under subparagraph (C), or (II) such broker is notified by the Secretary before such acquisition that such payee is subject to withholding under subsection (a)(1)(C),

such broker shall, within 15 days after the date of the acquisition, notify the payor that such payee is subject to withholding under subsection (a)(1)(D) (or subsection (a)(1)(C) in the case of a notification described in clause (ii)(II))."

In 1983, P.L. 98-67, Sec. 104(a), added Code Sec. 3406, effective for payments made after 12/31/83.

Subchapter B. Repealed [Withholding From Interest and Dividends]

Sec.

3451. Repealed [Income tax collected at source on interest, dividends, and patronage dividends.]

3452. Repealed [Exemptions from withholding.]

3453. Repealed [Payor defined.]

3454. Repealed [Definitions of interest, dividend, and patronage dividend.]

3455. Repealed [Other definitions and special rules.]

3456. Repealed [Administrative provisions.]

In 1983, P.L. 98-67, Sec. 102(a), repealed Subtitle A of Title III of P. L. 97-248 (which added Subchapter B of Chapter 24), effective 6/30/83. Sec. 102(b)-(d) of this Act provides:

"(b) Conforming amendment. Except as provided in this section, the Internal revenue Code of 1954 shall be applied and administered as if such subtitle A (and the amendments made by such subtitle A) had not been enacted.

"(c) Repeal not to apply to amounts deducted and withheld before September 2, 1983.

"(1) In general. If, notwithstanding the repeal made by subsection (a) (and the provisions of subsection (b)), an amount is deducted and withheld before September 2, 1983, under subchapter B of chapter 24 of the Internal Revenue Code of 1954 (as in effect before its repeal by subsection (a)), the repeal made by subsection (a) (and the provisions of subsection (b)) shall not apply to the amount so deducted and withheld.

"(2) Election to have paragraph (1) not apply. Paragraph (1) shall not apply with respect to any payor who elects (at the time and in the manner prescribed by the Secretary of the Treasury or his delegate) to have paragraph (1) not apply.

"(d) Estimated tax payments. For purposes of determining the amount of any addition to tax under section 6654 of the Internal Revenue Code of 1954 with respect to any installment required to be paid before July 1, 1983, the amount of the credit allowed by section 31 of such Code for any taxable year which includes any portion of the period beginning July 1, 1983, and ending December 31, 1983, shall be increased by an amount equal to 10 percent of the aggregate amount of payments—

"(1) which are received during the portion of such taxable year after June 30, 1983, and before January 1, 1984, and

"(2) which (but for the repeal made by subsection (a)) would have been subject to withholding under subchapter B of chapter 24 of such Code (determined without regard to any exemption described in section 3452 of such subchapter B).

Prior to repeal, Subchapter B of Chapter 24 read as follows:

"Subchapter B. Withholding From Interest and Dividends.

"Sec.

"3451 Income tax collected at source on interest, dividends, and patronage dividends.

"3452 Exemptions from withholding.

"3453 Payor defined.

"3454 Definitions of interest, dividend, and patronage dividend.

"3455 Other definitions and special rules.

"3456 Administrative provisions."

In 1982, P.L. 97-248, Sec. 301, added Subchapter B of Chapter 24, effective as provided in Sec. 308 of this Act, which reads as follows:

"Sec. 308. Effective dates; special rules.

"(a) In general. Except as provided in this section, the amendments made by this part shall apply to payments of interest, dividends, and patronage dividends paid or credited after June 30, 1983.

"(b) Delay in application to certain payors. The Secretary of the Treasury shall prescribe such regulations which delay (but not beyond December 31, 1983) the application of some or all of the provisions of subchapter B of chapter 24 of the Internal Revenue Code of 1954 to any payor until such time as such payor is able to comply without undue hardship with the requirements of such provisions.

"(c) Temporary rule for certain withholding exemptions. Until regulations are prescribed by the Secretary of the Treasury or his delegate under section 3452(c)(1)(B) of the Internal Revenue Code of 1954 (as added by this part), the payor may treat any person whose name reasonable indicates that such parson is described in paragraph (2) of section 3452(c) of such Cod e(other than subparagraph (J) or (K) thereof) as an exempt recipient.

"(d) Delay in making deposits. The time for making deposits under section 6302 of the Internal Revenue Code of 1954 of the tax imposed by section 3451 of such Code which is withheld by any person shall, to the extent provided in regulations, take into account the cost to such person of instituting a withholding system in order to comply with subchapter B of chapter 24 of such Code."

"SEC. 3451. INCOME TAX COLLECTED AT SOURCE ON INTEREST, DIVIDENDS, AND PATRONAGE DIVIDENDS.

"(a) Requirement of withholding.

"Except as otherwise provided in this subchapter, the payor of any interest, dividend, or patronage dividend shall withhold a tax equal to 10 percent of the amount of the payment.

"(b) Special rules.

"(1) Time of withholding. Except as otherwise provided in this subchapter, for purposes of this subchapter—

"(A) any payment of interest, dividend, or patronage dividend shall be treated as made, and

"(B) the tax imposed by this section shall be withheld,

at the time such interest, dividend, or patronage dividend is paid or credited.

"(2) Payee unknown. If a payor is unable to determine the person to whom any interest, dividend, or patronage dividend is payable or creditable, the tax under this section shall be withheld at the time withholding would be required under paragraph (1) if the payee were known and were an individual.

"(3) Amount of dividend, etc., unknown.

"(A) In general. If the payor is unable to determine the portion of a distribution which is a dividend, the tax under this section shall be computed on the gross amount of the distribution. To the extent provided in regulations, a similar rule shall apply in the case of interest and patronage dividends.

"(B) Distributions which are not dividends. To the extent provided in regulations, this section shall not apply to the extent that the portion of a distribution which is not a dividend may reasonably be estimated.

"(4) Withholding from alternative source. The Secretary shall prescribe regulations setting forth the circumstances under which the tax imposed by this section may be paid from an account or source other than the payment which gives rise to the liability for tax.

"(c) Liability for payment.

"(1) Payor liable. Except as otherwise provided in this subchapter, the payor—

"(A) shall be liable for the payment of the tax imposed by this section which such payor is required to withhold under this section, and

"(B) shall not be liable to any person (other than the United States) for the amount of any such payment.

"(2) Reliance on exemption certificates. The payor shall not be liable for the payment of tax imposed by this section which such payor is required to withhold under this section if—

"(A) such payor fails to withhold such tax, and

"(B) such failure is due to reasonable reliance on an exemption certificate delivered to such payor under section 3452(f) which is in effect with respect to the payee at the time such tax is required to be withheld under this section."

In 1983, P.L. 98-67, Sec. 102(a), repealed Code Sec. 3451 as part of the repeal of Subtitle A of Title III of P. L. 97-248 (which added Subchapter B of Chapter 24), effective 6/30/83. See Sec. 102(b)-(d) of this Act, reproduced in note after Table of Code Sections for Subchapter B of Chapter 24.

3,169

Code Sec. B

In 1982, P.L. 97-248, Sec. 301, added Subchapter B of Chapter 24, effective as provided in Sec. 308 of this Act reproduced in note following Table of Code Sections for Subchapter B of Chapter 24.

"SEC. 3452. EXEMPTIONS FROM WITHHOLDING.
"(a) In general.
"Section 3451 shall not apply with respect to—
"(1) any payment to an exempt individual,
"(2) any payment to an exempt recipient,
"(3) any minimal interest payment, or
"(4) any qualified consumer cooperative payment.
"(b) Exempt individuals.
"(1) In general. For purposes of this section, the term 'exempt individual' means any individual—
"(A) who is described in paragraph (2), and
"(B) with respect to whom an exemption certificate is in effect.
"(2) Individuals described in this paragraph. An individual is described in this paragraph if—
"(A) such individual's income tax liability for the preceding taxable year did not exceed $600 ($1,000 in the case of a joint return under section 6013), or
"(B)(i) such individual is 65 or older, and
"(ii) such individual's income tax liability for the preceding taxable year did not exceed $1,500 ($2,500 in the case of a joint return under section 6013).
"(3) Special rule for married persons. A husband and wife shall each be treated as satisfying the requirements of paragraph (2)(B)(i) if—
"(A) either spouse is 65 or older, and
"(B) such husband and wife made a joint return under section 6013 for the preceding taxable year.
"(4) Special rule for certain trusts distributing currently. Under regulations, a trust—
"(A) the terms of which provide that all of its income is required to be distributed currently, and
"(B) all the beneficiaries of which are individuals described in paragraph (2) or organizations described in sub-section (c)(2)(B),
shall be treated as an individual described in paragraph (2).
"(5) Income tax liability. For purposes of this subsection, the term 'income tax liability' means the amount of the tax imposed by subtitle A for the taxable year, reduced by the sum of the credits allowable against such tax (other than credits allowable by sections 31, 39, and 43).
"(c) Exempt recipients.
"(1) In general. For purposes of this section, the term 'exempt recipient' means any person described in paragraph (2)—
"(A) with respect to whom an exemption certificate is in effect, or
"(B) who is described in regulations prescribed by the Secretary which permit exemption from withholding without certification.
"(2) Persons described in this paragraph. A person is described in this paragraph if such person is—
"(A) a corporation,
"(B) an organization exempt from taxation under section 501(a) or an individual retirement plan,
"(C) the United States or a State,
"(D) a foreign government or international organization,
"(E) a foreign central bank of issue,
"(F) a dealer in securities or commodities required to register as such under the laws of the United States or a State,
"(G) a real estate investment trust (as defined in section 856),
"(H) an entity registered at all times during the taxable year under the Investment Company Act of 1940,
"(I) a common trust fund (as defined in section 584(a)),
"(J) a nominee or custodian (except as otherwise provided in regulations),
"(K) to the extent provided in regulations—
"(i) a financial institution,
"(ii) a broker, or
"(iii) any other person specified in such regulations, who collects any interest, dividend, or patronage dividend for the payee or otherwise acts as a middleman between the payor and the payee, or
"(L) any trust which—
"(i) is exempt from tax under section 664(c), or
"(ii) is described in section 4947(a)(1).
"(3) Payor may require certification. A person described in paragraph (1)(B) shall not be treated as an exempt recipient for purposes of this section with respect to any payment of such payor if—
"(A) an exemption certificate is not in effect with respect to such person, and
"(B) the payor does not treat such person as an exempt recipient.
"(d) Minimal interest payments.
"(1) In general. For purposes of this section, the term 'minimal interest payment' means any payment of interest—
"(A) with respect to which an election by the payor made under paragraph (3) is in effect, and
"(B) which—
"(i) does not exceed $150, and
"(ii) if determined for a 1-year period would not exceed $150.
"(2) Aggregation of payments to same payee. To the extent provided in regulations prescribed by the Secretary, payments of interest by a payor to the same payee shall be aggregated for purposes of applying paragraph (1)(B).
"(3) Election.

Wage withholding

"(A) In general. Any payor may make an election under this paragraph with respect to any type of interest payments.
"(B) Effective until revoked. Except as provided in regulations prescribed by the Secretary, an election made by any person under this paragraph shall remain in effect until revoked by such person.
"(C) Time and manner. Any election or revocation of an election made under this paragraph shall be made at such time and in such manner as the Secretary shall prescribe by regulations.
"(e) Qualified consumer cooperative payment. For purposes of this section, the term 'qualified consumer cooperative payment' means any payment by a cooperative which is exempt from reporting requirements under section 6044(a) by reason of section 6044(c).
"(f) Exemption certificates.
"(1) In general.
"(A) Delivery. An exempt individual or exempt recipient may deliver an exemption certificate to a payor at any time. Such certificate shall be in such form and contain such information as the Secretary shall prescribe.
"(B) Change of status. Any person who ceases to be an exempt individual or exempt recipient shall, not later than the close of the 10th day after the date of such cessation, notify each payor with whom such person has an exemption certificate of such change in status. No notice shall be required under the preceding sentence with respect to any payor if it reasonably appears that the person will not thereafter receive a payment of interest, dividends, or patronage dividends from such payor.
"(2) Effectiveness of certificates.
"(A) General rule. Except as otherwise provided in regulations prescribed by the Secretary, an exemption certificate shall be effective until—
"(i) revoked, or
"(ii) notice of change in status is provided pursuant to paragraph (1)(B).
"(B) When certificate takes effect. The Secretary shall prescribe regulations setting forth—
"(i) the day on which a filed exemption certificate shall be considered effective, and
"(ii) the circumstances under which a payor shall treat an exemption certificate as having ceased to be effective where the Secretary has determined that the person described therein is not an exempt individual or exempt recipient."

In 1983, P.L. 98-67, Sec. 102(a), repealed Code Sec. 3452 as part of the repeal of Subtitle A of Title III of P. L. 97-248 (which added Subchapter B of Chapter 24), effective 6/30/83. See Sec. 102(b)-(d) of this Act, reproduced in note after Table of Code Sections for Subchapter B of Chapter 24.

In 1982, P.L. 97-248, Sec. 301, added Subchapter B of Chapter 24, effective as provided in Sec. 308 of this Act reproduced in note following Table of Code Sections for Subchapter B of Chapter 24.

"SEC. 3453. PAYOR DEFINED.
"(a) General rule.
"Except as otherwise provided in this subchapter, for purposes of this subchapter, the term 'payor' means the person paying or crediting the interest, dividend, or patronage dividend.
"(b) Certain middlemen treated as payors.
"For purposes of this subchapter—
"(1) In general. To the extent provided in regulations—
"(A) any custodian for, or nominee of, the payee,
"(B) any corporate trustee of a trust which is the payee,
"(C) any person which collects the payment for the payee or otherwise acts as a middleman between the payor and the payee, or
"(D) any S corporation which receives any payment,
shall be treated as a payor with respect to the payment.
"(2) Receipt treated as payment. To the extent provided in regulations, any person treated as a payor under paragraph (1) shall be treated as having paid the interest, dividend, or patronage dividend when such person received such amount.
"(c) Agents, etc.
"In the case of—
"(1) a fiduciary or agent with respect to the payment or crediting of any interest, dividend, or patronage dividend, or
"(2) any other person who has the control, receipt, custody, or disposal of, or pays or credits any interest, dividend, or patronage dividend for any payor,
the Secretary, under regulations prescribed by him, may designate such fiduciary, agent, or other person as a payor with respect to such payment or crediting for purposes of this subchapter.
"(d) Treatment of persons to whom subsection (b) or (c) applies.
"Any person treated as a payor under subsection (b) or (c)—
"(1) shall perform such acts as are required of a payor (within the meaning of subsection (a)) and as may be specified by the Secretary, and
"(2) shall be treated as a payor for all provisions of law (including penalties) applicable in respect to a payor (within the meaning of subsection (a)).
"(e) Relief From double withholding.
"The Secretary may by regulations provide that where any person is treated as a payor under subsection (b) or (c) with respect to any payment, any other person who (but for this subsection) would be treated as a payor with respect to such payment shall be relieved from the requirements of this subchapter to the extent provided in such regulations.
"(f) Liability of third parties paying or providing interest, dividends, or patronage dividends.

Wage withholding   Code Sec. B

"To the extent provided in regulations prescribed by the Secretary, rules similar to the rules of section 3505 (relating to liability of third parties paying or providing for wages) shall apply for purposes of this subchapter. For purposes of the preceding sentence, the last sentence of subsection (b) of section 3505 shall be applied by substituting '10 percent' for '25 percent'."

In 1983, P.L. 98-67, Sec. 102(a), repealed Code Sec. 3453 as part of the repeal of Subtitle A of Title III of P. L. 97-248 (which added Subchapter B of Chapter 24), effective 6/30/83. See Sec. 102(b)-(d) of this Act, reproduced in note after Table of Code Sections for Subchapter B of Chapter 24.

In 1982, P.L. 97-248, Sec. 301, added Subchapter B of Chapter 24, effective as provided in Sec. 308 of this Act reproduced in note following Table of Code Sections for Subchapter B of Chapter 24.

"SEC. 3454. DEFINITIONS OF INTEREST, DIVIDEND, AND PATRONAGE DIVIDEND.

"(a) Interest defined.

"For purposes of this subchapter—

"(1) General rule. The term 'interest' means—

"(A) interest on any obligation in registered form or of a type offered to the public,

"(B) interest on deposits with persons carrying on the banking business,

"(C) amounts (whether or not designated as interest) paid by a mutual savings bank, savings and loan association, building and loan association, cooperative bank, homestead association, credit union, industrial loan association or bank, or similar organization, in respect of deposits, investment certificates, or withdrawable or repurchasable shares,

"(D) interest on amounts held by an insurance company under an agreement to pay interest thereon,

"(E) interest on deposits with brokers (as defined in section 6045(c)), and

"(F) interest paid on amounts held by investment companies (as defined in section 3 of the Investment Company Act of 1940 (15 U.S.C. 80a-3)) and on amounts invested in other pooled funds or trusts.

"(2) Exceptions. The term 'interest' does not include—

"(A) interest on any obligation issued by a natural person,

"(B) interest on any obligation if such interest is exempt from taxation under section 103(a) or if such interest is exempt from tax (without regard to the identity of the holder) under any other provision of this title,

"(C) any amount paid on a depository institution tax-exempt certificate (as defined in section 128(c)(1) (as in effect for taxable years beginning before January 1, 1985)),

"(D) any amount which is subject to withholding under subchapter A of chapter 3 (relating to withholding of tax on nonresident aliens and foreign corporations) by the person paying such amount,

"(E) any amount which would be subject to withholding under subchapter A of chapter 3 by the person paying such amount but for the fact that—

"(i) such amount is income from sources outside the United States,

"(ii) the payor thereof is excepted from the application of section 1441(a) by reason of section 1441(c) or a tax treaty, or

"(iii) such amount is original issue discount (within the meaning of section 1232(b)(1)),

"(F) any amount which is exempt from tax under—

"(i) section 892 (relating to income of foreign governments and of international organizations), or

"(ii) section 895 (relating to income derived by a foreign central bank of issue from obligations of the United States or from bank deposits),

"(G) except to the extent otherwise provided in regulations, any amount paid by—

"(i) a foreign government or international organization or any agency or instrumentality thereof,

"(ii) a foreign central bank of issue,

"(iii) a foreign corporation not engaged in trade or business in the United States,

"(iv) a foreign corporation, the interest payments of which would be exempt from withholding under subchapter A of chapter 3 if paid to a person who is not a United States person, or

"(v) a partnership not engaged in a trade or business in the United States and composed in whole of nonresident aliens, individuals and persons described in clause (i), (ii), or (iii),

"(H) any amount on which the person making payment is required to withhold a tax under section 1451 (relating to tax-free covenant bonds), or would be so required but for section 1451(d) (relating to benefit of personal exemptions), and

"(I) except to the extent otherwise provided in regulations, any amount not described in the foregoing provisions of this paragraph which is paid outside the United States and is income from sources outside the United States.

"(3) Adjustment for penalty because of premature withdrawal of funds from time savings accounts or deposits. To the extent provided in regulations, the amount of any interest on a time savings account, certificate of deposit, or similar class of deposits shall be appropriately reduced for purposes of this subchapter by the amount of any penalty imposed for the premature withdrawal of funds.

"(b) Dividend defined.

"For purposes of this subchapter—

"(1) General rule. The term 'dividend' means—

"(A) any distribution by a corporation which is a dividend (as defined in section 316), and

"(B) any payment made by a stockbroker to any person as a substitute for a dividend (as so defined).

"(2) Exceptions. The term 'dividend' shall not include—

"(A) any amount paid as a distribution of stock described in section 305(e)(2)(A) (relating to reinvestment of dividends in stock of public utilities),

"(B) any amount which is treated as a taxable dividend by reason of section 302 (relating to redemptions of stock), 306 (relating to disposition of certain stock), 356 (relating to receipt of additional consideration in connection with certain reorganizations), or 1081(e)(2) (relating to certain distributions pursuant to order of the Securities and Exchange Commission),

"(C) any amount described in subparagraph (D), (E), or (F) of subsection (a)(2),

"(D) to the extent provided in regulations, any amount paid by a foreign corporation not engaged in a trade or business in the United States,

"(E) any amount which is a capital gain dividend distributed by—

"(i) a regulated investment company (as defined in section 852(b)(3)(C)), or

"(ii) a real estate investment trust (as defined in section 857(b)(3)(C)),

"(F) any amount which is an exempt-interest dividend of a regulated investment company (as defined in section 852(b)(5)(A)), and

"(G) any amount paid or treated as paid by a regulated investment company during a year if, under regulations prescribed by the Secretary, it is anticipated that at least 95 percent of the dividends paid or treated as paid during such year (not including capital gain distributions) will be exempt-interest dividends.

"(c) Patronage dividend.

"For purposes of this subchapter—

"(1) In general. The term 'patronage dividend' means—

"(A) the amount of any patronage dividend (as defined in section 1388(a)) which is paid in money, qualified written notice of allocation, or other property (except a nonqualified written notice of allocation),

"(B) any amount, described in section 1382(c)(2)(A) (relating to certain nonpatronage distributions), which is paid in money, qualified written notice of allocation, or other property (except nonqualified written notice of allocation) by an organization exempt from tax under section 521 (relating to exemption of farmers' cooperatives from tax), and

"(C) any amount paid in money or other property (except written notice of allocation) in redemption of a nonqualified written notice of allocation attributable to any source described in subparagraph (A) or (B).

"(2) Exceptions. The term 'patronage dividend' shall not include any amount described in subparagraph (D), (E), or (F) of subsection (a)(2).

"(3) Special rules. In determining the amount of any patronage dividend—

"(A) property (other than a written notice of allocation) shall be taken into account at its fair market value,

"(B) a qualified written notice of allocation described in section 1388(c)(1)(A) shall be taken into account at its stated dollar amount, and

"(C) a patronage dividend part of which is a qualified written notice of allocation described in section 1388(c)(1)(B) (and not in section 1388(c)(1)(A)) shall be taken into account only if 50 percent or more of such dividend is paid in money or by a qualified check, and any such qualified written notice of allocation which is taken into account after the application of this subparagraph shall be taken into account at its stated dollar amount.

"(4) Definitions. For purposes of this subsection—

"(A) Qualified written notice of allocation. The term 'qualified written notice of allocation' has the meaning given to such term by section 1388(c).

"(B) Nonqualified written notice of allocation. The term nonqualified written notice of allocation has the meaning given to such term by section 1388(d).

"(C) Qualified check. The term 'qualified check' has the meaning given to such term by section 1388(c)(4)."

In 1983, P.L. 98-67, Sec. 102(a), repealed Code Sec. 3454 as part of the repeal of Subtitle A of Title III of P. L. 97-248 (which added Subchapter B of Chapter 24), effective 6/30/83. See Sec. 102(b)-(d) of this Act, reproduced in note after Table of Code Sections for Subchapter B of Chapter 24.

In 1982, P.L. 97-248, Sec. 301, added Subchapter B of Chapter 24, effective as provided in Sec. 308 of this Act reproduced in note following Table of Code Sections for Subchapter B of Chapter 24.

"SEC. 3455. OTHER DEFINITIONS AND SPECIAL RULES.

"(a) Definitions.

"For purposes of this subchapter—

"(1) Person. The term 'person' includes any governmental unit and any agency or instrumentality thereof and any international organization.

"(2) State. The term 'State' means a State, the District of Columbia, a possession of the United States, any political subdivision of any of the foregoing, and any wholly owned agency or instrumentality of any one or more of the foregoing.

"(3) United States. The term 'United States' means the United States and any wholly owned agency or instrumentality thereof.

"(4) Foreign government. The term 'foreign government' means a foreign government, a political subdivision of a foreign government, and any wholly owned agency or instrumentality of any one or more of the foregoing.

"(5) International organization. The term 'international organization' means an international organization and any wholly owned agency or instrumentality thereof.

"(6) Nonresident alien. The term 'nonresident alien individual' includes an alien resident of Puerto Rico.

"(7) Withhold, etc., include deduct. The terms 'withhold', 'withholding', and 'withheld' include deduct, deducting, and deducted.

"(b) Treatment of original issue discount.

"(1) In general. Except as provided in paragraphs (2) and (3) the tax imposed by section 3451 shall apply to the amount of original issue discount on any obligation which is includible in the gross income of the holder during the calendar year. Any such amount shall be treated as a payment for purposes of this subchapter.

"(2) Transferred obligations.

"(A) In general. In the case of original issue discount on any obligation which has been transferred from the original holder, the tax imposed by section 3451 shall apply to such original issue discount as if the subsequent holder were the original holder.

"(B) Special rule for short-term obligations. In the case of any obligation with a fixed maturity date not exceeding 1 year from the date of issue which has been transferred from the original holder, if any subsequent purchaser establishes the date on which, and the purchase price at which, he acquired such obligation, the amount of original issue discount on such obligation shall be determined (subject to such regulations as the Secretary may prescribe) as if it were issued on the date such subsequent purchaser acquired such obligation for an issue price equal to the purchase price at which such subsequent purchaser acquired such obligation.

"(3) Limitation on amount withheld.

"(A) In general. The amount of tax imposed by section 3451 on the original issue discount on any obligation which is required to be withheld under section 3451(a) in any calendar year shall not exceed the amount of cash paid with respect to such obligation during such calendar year.

"(B) Authority secretary to eliminate limitation in certain cases. If the Secretary determines by regulations that a type of obligation is frequently used to avoid the purposes of this subchapter, subparagraph (A) shall not apply with respect to original issue discount on any obligation of such type which is issued more than 30 days after the first date on which such regulations are published in the Federal Register.

"(C) Payments from which withholding is to be made. Except to the extent otherwise provided in regulations, the tax imposed by section 3451 with respect to original issue discount for any calendar year shall be withheld from each cash payment made with respect to such obligation during such calendar year in the proportion which the amount of such payment bears to the aggregate of such payments.

"(4) Original issue discount defined. For purposes of this subsection, the term 'original issue discount' has the meaning given such term by section 1232(b)(1)."

In 1983, P.L. 98-67, Sec. 102(a), repealed Code Sec. 3455 as part of the repeal of Subtitle A of Title III of P. L. 97-248 (which added Subchapter B of Chapter 24), effective 6/30/83. See Sec. 102(b)-(d) of this Act, reproduced in note after Table of Code Sections for Subchapter B of Chapter 24.

In 1982, P.L. 97-248, Sec. 301, added Subchapter B of Chapter 24, effective as provided in Sec. 308 of this Act reproduced in note following Table of Code Sections for Subchapter B of Chapter 24.

"Sec. 3456. ADMINISTRATIVE PROVISIONS.
"(a) Return and payment by governmental units.

"If the payor of any payment subject to withholding under section 3451 is the United States or a State, or an agency or instrumentality thereof, the return of the tax withheld under this subchapter shall be made by the officer or employee having control of the payment of the amount subject to withholding or by any officer or employee appropriately designated to make such withholding.

"(b) Annual withholding by financial institutions.

"(1) In general. Under regulations prescribed by the Secretary, a financial institution described in subparagraph (B) or (C) of section 3454(a)(1) may elect to defer withholding of the tax imposed by section 3451 during any calendar year on interest paid on savings accounts, interest-bearing checking accounts, and similar accounts until a date which is not later than the last day of such year.

"(2) Condition for election. The regulations prescribed under paragraph (1) shall provide that an election under such paragraph is conditional on agreement by the person making the election—

"(A) that the balance in any account subject to such election shall at no time be less than an amount equal to the tax under section 3451 which would have been withheld as of such time if such election were not in effect, and

"(B) that if an account subject to such election is closed before the date on which the tax under section 3451 would (but for this subparagraph) be withheld as a result of such an election, the tax shall be withheld before the time of closing such account.

"(c) Tax paid by recipient.

"If a payor, in violation of the provisions of this subchapter, fails to withhold the tax imposed under section 3451, and thereafter the tax against which such tax may be credited is paid, the tax so required to be withheld shall not be collected from the payor; but this subsection shall in no case relieve the payor from liability for any penalties or additions to the tax otherwise applicable in respect of such failure to withhold.

"(d) Regulations.

"The Secretary shall prescribe such regulations as may be necessary or appropriate to carry out the purposes of this subchapter."

In 1983, P.L. 98-67, Sec. 102(a), repealed Code Sec. 3456 as part of the repeal of Subtitle A of Title III of P. L. 97-248 (which added Subchapter B of Chapter 24), effective 6/30/83. See Sec. 102(b)-(d) of this Act, reproduced in note after Table of Code Sections for Subchapter B of Chapter 24.

In 1982, P.L. 97-248, Sec. 301, added Subchapter B of Chapter 24, effective as provided in Sec. 308 of this Act reproduced in note following Table of Code Sections for Subchapter B of Chapter 24.

CHAPTER 25.—GENERAL PROVISIONS RELATING TO EMPLOYMENT TAXES AND COLLECTION OF INCOME TAXES AT SOURCE

Sec.
3501. Collection and payment of taxes.
3502. Nondeductibility of taxes in computing taxable income.
3503. Erroneous payments.
3504. Acts to be performed by agents.
3505. Liability of third parties paying or providing for wages.
3506. Individuals providing companion sitting placement services.
3507. Advance payment of earned income credit.
3508. Treatment of real estate agents and direct sellers.
3509. Determination of employer's liability for certain employment taxes.
3510. Coordination of collection of domestic service employment taxes with collection of income taxes.

In 1994, P.L. 103-387, Sec. 2(b)(2), added item 3510.
In 1990, P.L. 101-508, Sec. 11801(b)(16), deleted item 3510.
Prior to deletion, item 3510 read as follows:
"3510. Credit for increased social security employee taxes and railroad retirement tier 1 employee taxes imposed during 1984."
In 1983, P.L. 98-21, Sec. 123(b)(2), added item 3510.
In 1982, P.L. 97-248, Sec. 307(b)(5), amended the chapter heading.
Prior to amendment, the chapter heading read as follows:
"CHAPTER 25.—GENERAL PROVISIONS RELATING TO EMPLOYMENT TAXES"
—97-248, Sec. 269(d), added item 3508.
—97-248, Sec. 270(b), added item 3509.
In 1978, P.L. 95-600, Sec. 105(b)(2), added item 3507.
In 1977, P.L. 95-171, Sec. 10(b), added item 3506.

Sec. 3501. Collection and payment of taxes.
(a) General rule.

The taxes imposed by this subtitle shall be collected by the Secretary and shall be paid into the Treasury of the United States as internal-revenue collections.

(b) Taxes with respect to non-cash fringe benefits.

The taxes imposed by this subtitle with respect to non-cash fringe benefits shall be collected (or paid) by the employer at the time and in the manner prescribed by the Secretary by regulations.

In 1984, P.L. 98-369, Sec. 531(d)(5), amended Code Sec. 3501, effective 1/1/85.
Prior to amendment, Code Sec. 3501 read as follows:
"SEC. 3501. COLLECTION AND PAYMENT OF TAXES.

The taxes imposed by this subtitle shall be collected by the Secretary and shall be paid into the Treasury of the United States as internal-revenue collections."
In 1976, P.L. 94-455, Sec. 1906(b)(13)(A), substituted "Secretary" for "Secretary or his delegate" in Code Sec. 3501, effective 2/1/77.

Sec. 3502. Nondeductibility of taxes in computing taxable income.
(a)

The taxes imposed by section 3101 of chapter 21, and by sections 3201 and 3211 of chapter 22 shall not be allowed as a deduction to the taxpayer in computing taxable income under subtitle A.
(b)

The tax deducted and withheld under chapter 24 shall not be allowed as a deduction either to the employer or to the recipient of the income in computing taxable income under subtitle A.

In 1983, P.L. 98-67, Sec. 102(a), deleted the amendments made by Secs. 305(b)(1) and (2) of P. L. 97-248[see below] as if they had never been enacted, effective 6/30/83.
Prior to deletion, subsec. (c) read as follows:

Employment taxes

"(c) The tax withheld under subchapter B of chapter 24 shall not be allowed as a deduction in computing taxable income under subtitle A either to the person withholding the tax or to the recipient of the amounts subject to withholding."

In 1982, P.L. 97-248, Sec. 305(b)(1), substituted "under subchapter A of chapter 24" for "under chapter 24" in subsec. (b) . . . Sec. 305(b)(2), added subsec. (c) [prior to deletion by Sec. 102(a) of P. L. 98-67, see above], effective 7/1/83.

Sec. 3503. Erroneous payments.

Any tax paid under chapter 21 or 22 by a taxpayer with respect to any period with respect to which he is not liable to tax under such chapter shall be credited against the tax, if any, imposed by such other chapter upon the taxpayer, and the balance, if any, shall be refunded.

Sec. 3504. Acts to be performed by agents.

In case a fiduciary, agent, or other person has the control, receipt, custody, or disposal of, or pays the wages of an employee or group of employees, employed by one or more employers, the Secretary, under regulations prescribed by him, is authorized to designate such fiduciary, agent, or other person to perform such acts as are required of employers under this title and as the Secretary may specify. Except as may be otherwise prescribed by the Secretary, all provisions of law (including penalties) applicable in respect of an employer shall be applicable to a fiduciary, agent, or other person so designated but, except as so provided, the employer for whom such fiduciary, agent, or other person acts shall remain subject to the provisions of law (including penalties) applicable in respect of employers.

In 1976, P.L. 94-455, Sec. 1906(b)(13)(A), substituted "Secretary" for "Secretary or his delegate" each place it appeared in Code Sec. 3504, effective 2/1/77.

In 1958, P.L. 85-866, Sec. 71, substituted "title" for "subtitle" in the first sentence of Code Sec. 3504.

Sec. 3505. Liability of third parties paying or providing for wages.
(a) Direct payment by third parties.

For purposes of sections 3102, 3202, 3402, and 3403, if a lender, surety, or other person, who is not an employer under such sections with respect to an employee or group of employees, pays wages directly to such an employee or group of employees, employed by one or more employers, or to an agent on behalf of such employee or employees, such lender, surety, or other person shall be liable in his own person and estate to the United States in a sum equal to the taxes (together with interest) required to be deducted and withheld from such wages by such employer.

(b) Personal liability where funds are supplied.

If a lender, surety, or other person supplies funds to or for the account of an employer for the specific purpose of paying wages of the employees of such employer, with actual notice or knowledge (within the meaning of section 6323(i)(1)) that such employer does not intend to or will not be able to make timely payment or deposit of the amounts of tax required by this subtitle to be deducted and withheld by such employer from such wages, such lender, surety, or other person shall be liable in his own person and estate to the United States in a sum equal to the taxes (together with interest) which are not paid over to the United States by such employer with respect to such wages. However, the liability of such lender, surety, or other person shall be limited to an amount equal to 25 percent of the amount so supplied to or for the account of such employer for such purpose.

(c) Effect of payment.

Any amounts paid to the United States pursuant to this section shall be credited against the liability of the employer.

In 1966, P.L. 89-719, Sec. 105, added Code Sec. 3505, effective for wages paid on or after 1/1/67.

Sec. 3506. Individuals providing companion sitting placement services.
(a) In general.

For purposes of this subtitle, a person engaged in the trade or business of putting sitters in touch with individuals who wish to employ them shall not be treated as the employer of such sitters (and such sitters shall not be treated as employees of such person) if such person does not pay or receive the salary or wages of the sitters and is compensated by the sitters or the persons who employ them on a fee basis.

(b) Definition.

For purposes of this section, the term "sitters" means individuals who furnish personal attendance, companionship, or household care services to children or to individuals who are elderly or disabled.

(c) Regulations.

The Secretary shall prescribe such regulations as may be necessary to carry out the purpose of this section.

In 1977, P.L. 95-171, Sec. 10(a), added Code Sec. 3506, effective for remuneration received after 12/31/74. Sec. 10(d) of this Act provides:

"(d) The amendments made by this section shall not be construed as affecting (1) any individual's right to receive unemployment compensation based on services performed before the date of the enactment of this Act, or (2) any individual's eligibility for social security benefits to the extent based on services performed before that date."

Sec. 3507.

> • **Caution:** Code Sec. 3507, following, was repealed by Sec. 219(a)(1) of the Education Jobs and Medicaid Assistance Act, P.L. 111-226, 8/10/2010, effective for tax. yrs. begin. after 12/31/2010.

Advance payment of earned income credit.
(a) General rule.

Except as otherwise provided in this section, every employer making payment of wages to an employee with respect to whom an earned income eligibility certificate is in effect shall, at the time of paying such wages, make an additional payment to such employee equal to such employee's earned income advance amount.

(b) Earned income eligibility certificate.

For purposes of this title, an earned income eligibility certificate is a statement furnished by an employee to the employer which—

(1) certifies that the employee will be eligible to receive the credit provided by section 32 for the taxable year,

(2) certifies that the employee has 1 or more qualifying children (within the meaning of section 32(c)(3)) for such taxable year,

(3) certifies that the employee does not have an earned income eligibility certificate in effect for the calendar year with respect to the payment of wages by another employer, and

(4) states whether or not the employee's spouse has an earned income eligibility certificate in effect.

For purposes of this section, a certificate shall be treated as being in effect with respect to a spouse if such a certificate will be in effect on the first status determination date following the date on which the employee furnishes the statement in question.

(c) Earned income advance amount.

(1) **In general.** For purposes of this title, the term "earned income advance amount" means, with respect to any payroll period, the amount determined—

(A) on the basis of the employee's wages from the employer for such period, and
(B) in accordance with tables prescribed by the Secretary.

In the case of an employee who is a member of the Armed Forces of the United States, the earned income advance amount shall be determined by taking into account such employee's earned income as determined for purposes of section 32.

(2) Advance amount tables. The tables referred to in paragraph (1)(B)—

(A) shall be similar in form to the tables prescribed under section 3402 and, to the maximum extent feasible, shall be coordinated with such tables, and

(B) if the employee is not married, or if no earned income eligibility certificate is in effect with respect to the spouse of the employee, shall treat the credit provided by section 32 as if it were a credit—

(i) of not more than 60 percent of the credit percentage in effect under section 32(b)(1) for an eligible individual with 1 qualifying child and with earned income not in excess of the earned income amount in effect under section 32(b)(2) for such an eligible individual, which

(ii) phases out at 60 percent of the phaseout percentage in effect under section 32(b)(1) for such an eligible individual between the phaseout amount in effect under section 32(b)(2) for such an eligible individual and the amount of earned income at which the credit under section 32(a) phases out for such an eligible individual, or

(C) if an earned income eligibility certificate is in effect with respect to the spouse of the employee, shall treat the credit as if it were a credit determined under subparagraph (B) by substituting ½ of the amounts of earned income described in such subparagraph for such amounts.

(d) Payments to be treated as payments of withholding and FICA taxes.

(1) In general. For purposes of this title, payments made by an employer under subsection (a) to his employees for any payroll period—

(A) shall not be treated as the payment of compensation, and

(B) shall be treated as made out of—

(i) amounts required to be deducted and withheld for the payroll period under section 3401 (relating to wage withholding), and

(ii) amounts required to be deducted for the payroll period under section 3102 (relating to FICA employee taxes), and

(iii) amounts of the taxes imposed for the payroll period under section 3111 (relating to FICA employer taxes),

as if the employer had paid to the Secretary, on the day on which the wages are paid to the employees, an amount equal to such payments.

(2) Advance payments exceed taxes due. In the case of any employer, if for any payroll period the aggregate amount of earned income advance payments exceeds the sum of the amounts referred to in paragraph (1)(B), each such advance payment shall be reduced by an amount which bears the same ratio to such excess as such advance payment bears to the aggregate amount of all such advance payments.

(3) Employer may make full advance payments. The Secretary shall prescribe regulations under which an employer may elect (in lieu of any application of paragraph (2))—

(A) to pay in full all earned income advance amounts, and

(B) to have additional amounts paid by reason of this paragraph treated as the advance payment of taxes imposed by this title.

(4) Failure to make advance payments. For purposes of this title (including penalties), failure to make any advance payment under this section at the time provided therefor shall be treated as the failure at such time to deduct and withhold under chapter 24 an amount equal to the amount of such advance payment.

(e) Furnishing and taking effect of certificates.

For purposes of this section—

(1) When certificate takes effect.

(A) First certificate furnished. An earned income eligibility certificate furnished the employer in cases in which no previous such certificate had been in effect for the calendar year shall take effect as of the beginning of the first payroll period ending, or the first payment of wages made without regard to a payroll period, on or after the date on which such certificate is so furnished (or if later, the first day of the calendar year for which furnished).

(B) Later certificate. An earned income eligibility certificate furnished the employer in cases in which a previous such certificate had been in effect for the calendar year shall take effect with respect to the first payment of wages made on or after the first status determination date which occurs at least 30 days after the date on which such certificate is so furnished, except that at the election of the employer such certificate may be made effective with respect to any payment of wages made on or after the date on which such certificate is so furnished. For purposes of this section, the term "status determination date" means January 1, May 1, July 1, and October 1 of each year.

(2) Period during which certificate remains in effect. An earned income eligibility certificate which takes effect under this section for any calendar year shall continue in effect with respect to the employee during such calendar year until revoked by the employee or until another such certificate takes effect under this section.

(3) Change of status.

(A) Requirement to revoke or furnish new certificate. If, after an employee has furnished an earned income eligibility certificate under this section, there has been a change of circumstances which has the effect of—

(i) making the employee ineligible for the credit provided by section 32 for the taxable year, or

(ii) causing an earned income eligibility certificate to be in effect with respect to the spouse of the employee,

the employee shall, within 10 days after such change in circumstances, furnish the employer with a revocation of such certificate or with a new certificate (as the case may be). Such a revocation (or such a new certificate) shall take effect under the rules provided by paragraph (1)(B) for a later certificate and shall be made in such form as the Secretary shall by regulations prescribe.

(B) Certificate no longer in effect. If, after an employee has furnished an earned income eligibility certificate under this section which certifies that such a certificate is in effect with respect to the spouse of the employee, such a certificate is no longer in effect with respect to

Employment taxes

such spouse, then the employee may furnish the employer with a new earned income eligibility certificate.

(4) Form and contents of certificate. Earned income eligibility certificates shall be in such form and contain such other information as the Secretary may by regulations prescribe.

(5) Taxable year defined. The term "taxable year" means the last taxable year of the employee under subtitle A beginning in the calendar year in which the wages are paid.

(f) Internal Revenue Service notification.

The Internal Revenue Service shall take such steps as may be appropriate to ensure that taxpayers who have 1 or more qualifying children and who receive a refund of the credit under section 32 are aware of the availability of earned income advance amounts under this section.

In 2010, P.L. 111-226, Sec. 219(a)(1), repealed Code Sec. 3507, effective for tax. yrs. after 12/31/2010.

Prior to repeal, Code Sec. 3507 read as follows:

"Sec. 3507. Advance payment of earned income credit.

"(a) General rule. Except as otherwise provided in this section, every employer making payment of wages to an employee with respect to whom an earned income eligibility certificate is in effect shall, at the time of paying such wages, make an additional payment to such employee equal to such employee's earned income advance amount.

"(b) Earned income eligibility certificate. For purposes of this title, an earned income eligibility certificate is a statement furnished by an employee to the employer which—

"(1) certifies that the employee will be eligible to receive the credit provided by section 32 for the taxable year,

"(2) certifies that the employee has 1 or more qualifying children (within the meaning of section 32(c)(3)) for such taxable year,

"(3) certifies that the employee does not have an earned income eligibility certificate in effect for the calendar year with respect to the payment of wages by another employer, and

"(4) states whether or not the employee's spouse has an earned income eligibility certificate in effect.

"For purposes of this section, a certificate shall be treated as being in effect with respect to a spouse if such a certificate will be in effect on the first status determination date following the date on which the employee furnishes the statement in question.

"(c) Earned income advance amount.

"(1) In general. For purposes of this title, the term 'earned income advance amount' means, with respect to any payroll period, the amount determined—

"(A) on the basis of the employee's wages from the employer for such period, and

"(B) in accordance with tables prescribed by the Secretary.

"In the case of an employee who is a member of the Armed Forces of the United States, the earned income advance amount shall be determined by taking into account such employee's earned income as determined for purposes of section 32.

"(2) Advance amount tables. The tables referred to in paragraph (1)(B)—

"(A) shall be similar in form to the tables prescribed under section 3402 and, to the maximum extent feasible, shall be coordinated with such tables, and

"(B) if the employee is not married, or if no earned income eligibility certificate is in effect with respect to the spouse of the employee, shall treat the credit provided by section 32 as if it were a credit—

"(i) of not more than 60 percent of the credit percentage in effect under section 32(b)(1) for an eligible individual with 1 qualifying child and with earned income not in excess of the earned income amount in effect under section 32(b)(2) for such an eligible individual, which

"(ii) phases out at 60 percent of the phaseout percentage in effect under section 32(b)(1) for such an eligible individual between the phaseout amount in effect under section 32(b)(2) for such an eligible individual and the amount of earned income at which the credit under section 32(a) phases out for such an eligible individual, or

"(C) if an earned income eligibility certificate is in effect with respect to the spouse of the employee, shall treat the credit as if it were a credit determined under subparagraph (B) by substituting ½ of the amounts of earned income described in such subparagraph for such amounts.

"(d) Payments to be treated as payments of withholding and FICA taxes.

"(1) In general. For purposes of this title, payments made by an employer under subsection (a) to his employees for any payroll period—

'(A) shall not be treated as the payment of compensation, and

"(B) shall be treated as made out of—

"(i) amounts required to be deducted and withheld for the payroll period under section 3401 (relating to wage withholding), and

"(ii) amounts required to be deducted for the payroll period under section 3102 (relating to FICA employee taxes), and

"(iii) amounts of the taxes imposed for the payroll period under section 3111 (relating to FICA employer taxes),

"as if the employer had paid to the Secretary, on the day on which the wages are paid to the employees, an amount equal to such payments.

"(2) Advance payments exceed taxes due. In the case of any employer, if for any payroll period the aggregate amount of earned income advance payments exceeds the sum of the amounts referred to in paragraph (1)(B), each such advance payment shall be reduced by an amount which bears the same ratio to such excess as such advance payment bears to the aggregate amount of all such advance payments.

"(3) Employer may make full advance payments. The Secretary shall prescribe regulations under which an employer may elect (in lieu of any application of paragraph (2))—

"(A) to pay in full all earned income advance amounts, and

"(B) to have additional amounts paid by reason of this paragraph treated as the advance payment of taxes imposed by this title.

" (4) Failure to make advance payments. For purposes of this title (including penalties), failure to make any advance payment under this section at the time provided therefor shall be treated as the failure at such time to deduct and withhold under chapter 24 an amount equal to the amount of such advance payment.

"(e) Furnishing and taking effect of certificates. For purposes of this section—

"(1) When certificate takes effect.

"(A) First certificate furnished. An earned income eligibility certificate furnished the employer in cases in which no previous such certificate had been in effect for the calendar year shall take effect as of the beginning of the first payroll period ending, or the first payment of wages made without regard to a payroll period, on or after the date on which such certificate is so furnished (or if later, the first day of the calendar year for which furnished).

"(B) Later certificate. An earned income eligibility certificate furnished the employer in cases in which a previous such certificate had been in effect for the calendar year shall take effect with respect to the first payment of wages made on or after the first status determination date which occurs at least 30 days after the date on which such certificate is so furnished, except that at the election of the employer such certificate may be made effective with respect to any payment of wages made on or after the date on which such certificate is so furnished. For purposes of this section, the term 'status determination date' means January 1, May 1, July 1, and October 1 of each year.

"(2) Period during which certificate remains in effect. An earned income eligibility certificate which takes effect under this section for any calendar year shall continue in effect with respect to the employee during such calendar year until revoked by the employee or until another such certificate takes effect under this section.

"(3) Change of status.

"(A) Requirement to revoke or furnish new certificate. If, after an employee has furnished an earned income eligibility certificate under this section, there has been a change of circumstances which has the effect of—

"(i) making the employee ineligible for the credit provided by section 32 for the taxable year, or

"(ii) causing an earned income eligibility certificate to be in effect with respect to the spouse of the employee,

"the employee shall, within 10 days after such change in circumstances, furnish the employer with a revocation of such certificate or with a new certificate (as the case may be). Such a revocation (or such a new certificate) shall take effect under the rules provided by paragraph (1)(B) for a later certificate and shall be made in such form as the Secretary shall by regulations prescribe.

"(B) Certificate no longer in effect. If, after an employee has furnished an earned income eligibility certificate under this section which certifies that such a certificate is in effect with respect to the spouse of the employee, such a certificate is no longer in effect with respect to such spouse, then the employee may furnish the employer with a new earned income eligibility certificate.

"(4) Form and contents of certificate. Earned income eligibility certificates shall be in such form and contain such other information as the Secretary may by regulations prescribe.

"(5) Taxable year defined. The term 'taxable year' means the last taxable year of the employee under subtitle A beginning in the calendar year in which the wages are paid.

"(f) Internal Revenue Service notification. The Internal Revenue Service shall take such steps as may be appropriate to ensure that taxpayers who have 1 or more qualifying children and who receive a refund of the credit under section 32 are aware of the availability of earned income advance amounts under this section."

In 1994, P.L. 103-465, Sec. 721(c), added the last sentence at the end of para. (c)(1), effective for remuneration paid after 12/31/94.

In 1993, P.L. 103-66, Sec. 13131(d)(4), redesignated paras. (b)(2) and (3) as paras. (b)(3) and (4) and added new para. (b)(2)... Sec. 13131(d)(5), amended clauses (c)(2)(B)(i) and (ii)... Sec. 13131(d)(6), added subsec. (f), effective for tax. yrs. begin. after 12/31/93.

Prior to amendment, clauses (c)(2)(B)(i) and (ii) read as follows:

"(i) of not more than the credit percentage under section 32(b)(1) (without regard to subparagraph (D) thereof) for an eligible individual with 1 qualifying child and with earned income not in excess of the amount of earned income taken into account under section 32(a)(1), which

"(ii) phases out between the amount of earned income at which the phaseout begins under section 32(b)(1)(B)(ii) and the amount of income at which the credit under section 32(a)(1) phases out for an eligible individual with 1 qualifying child, or"

In 1990, P.L. 101-508, Sec. 11111(c), amended subparas. (c)(2)(B) and (c)(2)(C), effective for tax. yrs. begin. after 12/31/90.

Prior to amendment, subparas. (c)(2)(B) and (c)(2)(C) read as follows:

3,175

Code Sec. 3507   **Employment taxes**

"(B) if the employee is not married, or if no earned income eligibility certificate is in effect with respect to the spouse of the employee, shall treat the credit provided by section 32 as if it were a credit—

"(i) of not more than 14 percent of earned income not in excess of the amount of earned income taken into account under section 32(a), which

"(ii) phases out between the amount of earned income at which the phaseout begins under subsection (b) of section 32 and the amount of earned income at which the credit under section 32 is phased out under such subsection, or

"(C) if an earned income eligibility certificate is in effect with respect to the spouse of the employee, shall treat the credit provided by section 32 as if it were a credit—

"(i) of not more than 14 percent of earned income not in excess of ½ of the amount of earned income taken into account under section 32(a), which

"(ii) phases out between amounts of earned income which are ½ of the amounts of earned income described in subparagraph (B)(ii)."

In 1986, P.L. 99-514, Sec. 111(d)(2), amended clauses (c)(2)(B)(i) and (c)(2)(B)(ii)... Sec. 111(d)(3), amended clauses (c)(2)(C)(i) and (c)(2)(C)(ii), effective for tax. yrs. begin. after 12/31/86.

Prior to amendment, clauses (c)(2)(B)(i) and (c)(2)(B)(ii) read as follows:

"(i) of note more than 11 percent of the first $5,000 of earned income, which

"(ii) phases out between $6,500 and $11,000 of earned income, or"

Prior to amendment, clauses (c)(2)(C)(i) and (c)(2)(C)(ii) read as follows:

"(i) of note more than 11 percent of the first $2,500 of earned income, which

"(ii) phases out between $3,250 and $5,500 of earned income."

—P.L. 99-514, Sec. 111(e), provides as follows:

"(e) Employee notification.—

"The Secretary of the Treasury is directed to require, under regulations, employers to notify any employee who has not had any tax withheld from wages (other than an employee whose wages are exempt from withholding pursuant to section 3402(n) of the Internal Revenue Code of 1986) that such employee may be eligible for a refund because of the earned income credit."

In 1984, P.L. 98-369, Sec. 474(r)(30), substituted "section 32" for "section 43" each place it appeared in subsections (b), (c) and (e), effective for tax. yrs. begin. after 12/31/83, and to carrybacks from such years.

—P.L. 98-369, Sec. 1042(d)(3), amended clauses (c)(2)(B)(i) and (ii)... Sec. 1042(d)(4), amended clauses (c)(2)(C)(i) and (ii), effective for tax. yrs. begin. after 12/31/84.

Prior to amendment, clauses (c)(2)(B)(i) and (ii) read as follows:

"(i) of not more than 10 percent of the first $5,000 of earned income, which

"(ii) phases out between $6,000 and $10,000 of earned income, or"

Prior to amendment, clauses (c)(2)(C)(i) and (ii) read as follows:

"(i) of note more than 10 percent of the first $2,500 or earned income, which

"(ii) phases out between $3,000 and $5,000 of earned income."

In 1980, P.L. 96-222, Sec. 101(a)(2)(D), changed the effective date for amendments made by Sec. 105(b)(1) of P. L. 95-600, from remuneration paid after 6/30/78, to remuneration paid after 6/30/79, see below.

In 1978, P.L. 95-600, Sec. 105(b)(1), added Code Sec. 3507, effective [as amended by Sec. 101(a)(2)(D) of P. L. 96-222, see above] for remuneration paid after 6/30/79.

Sec. 3508. Treatment of real estate agents and direct sellers.

(a) General rule.

For purposes of this title, in the case of services performed as a qualified real estate agent or as a direct seller—

(1) the individual performing such services shall not be treated as an employee, and

(2) the person for whom such services are performed shall not be treated as an employer.

(b) Definitions.

For purposes of this section—

(1) Qualified real estate agent. The term "qualified real estate agent" means any individual who is a sales person if—

(A) such individual is a licensed real estate agent,

(B) substantially all of the remuneration (whether or not paid in cash) for the services performed by such individual as a real estate agent is directly related to sales or other output (including the performance of services) rather than to the number of hours worked, and

(C) the services performed by the individual are performed pursuant to a written contract between such individual and the person for whom the services are performed and such contract provides that the individual will not be treated as an employee with respect to such services for Federal tax purposes.

(2) Direct seller. The term "direct seller" means any person if—

(A) such person—

(i) is engaged in the trade or business of selling (or soliciting the sale of) consumer products to any buyer on a buy-sell basis, a deposit-commission basis, or any similar basis which the Secretary prescribes by regulations, for resale (by the buyer or any other person) in the home or otherwise than in a permanent retail establishment,

(ii) is engaged in the trade or business of selling (or soliciting the sale of) consumer products in the home or otherwise than in a permanent retail establishment, or

(iii) is engaged in the trade or business of the delivering or distribution of newspapers or shopping news (including any services directly related to such trade or business),

(B) substantially all the remuneration (whether or not paid in cash) for the performance of the services described in subparagraph (A) is directly related to sales or other output (including the performance of services) rather than to the number of hours worked, and

(C) the services performed by the person are performed pursuant to a written contract between such person and the person for whom the services are performed and such contract provides that the person will not be treated as an employee with respect to such services for Federal tax purposes.

(3) Coordination with retirement plans for self-employed. This section shall not apply for purposes of subtitle A to the extent that the individual is treated as an employee under section 401(c)(1) (relating to self-employed individuals).

In 1996, P.L. 104-188, Sec. 1118(a), deleted "or" at the end of clause (b)(2)(A)(i), added "or" to the end of clause (b)(2)(A)(ii), and added clause (b)(2)(A)(iii), effective for services performed after 12/31/95.

In 1982, P.L. 97-248, Sec. 269(a), added Code Sec. 3508, effective for services performed after 12/31/82.

Sec. 3509. Determination of employer's liability for certain employment taxes.

(a) In general.

If any employer fails to deduct and withhold any tax under chapter 24 or subchapter A of chapter 21 with respect to any employee by reason of treating such employee as not being an employee for purposes of such chapter or subchapter, the amount of the employer's liability for—

(1) Withholding taxes. Tax under chapter 24 for such year with respect to such employee shall be determined as if the amount required to be deducted and withheld were equal to 1.5 percent of the wages (as defined in section 3401) paid to such employee.

(2) Employee social security tax. Taxes under subchapter A of chapter 21 with respect to such employee shall be determined as if the taxes imposed under such subchapter were 20 percent of the amount imposed under such subchapter without regard to this subparagraph.

(b) Employer's liability increased where employer disregards reporting requirements.

(1) In general. In the case of an employer who fails to meet the applicable requirements of section 6041(a), 6041A, or 6051 with respect to any employee, unless such failure is due to reasonable cause and not willful neglect, subsection (a) shall be applied with respect to such employee

(A) by substituting "3 percent" for "1.5 percent" in paragraph (1); and

3,176

Employment taxes

(B) by substituting "40 percent" for "20 percent" in paragraph (2).

(2) Applicable requirements. For purposes of paragraph (1), the term "applicable requirements" means the requirements described in paragraph (1) which would be applicable consistent with the employer's treatment of the employee as not being an employee for purposes of chapter 24 or subchapter A of chapter 21.

(c) Section not to apply in cases of intentional disregard.

This section shall not apply to the determination of the employer's liability for tax under chapter 24 or subchapter A of chapter 21 if such liability is due to the employer's intentional disregard of the requirement to deduct and withhold such tax.

(d) Special rules.

For purposes of this section—

(1) Determination of liability. If the amount of any liability for tax is determined under this section—

(A) the employee's liability for tax shall not be affected by the assessment or collection of the tax so determined,

(B) the employer shall not be entitled to recover from the employee any tax so determined, and

(C) sections 3402(d) and section 6521 shall not apply.

(2) Section not to apply where employer deducts wage but not social security taxes. This section shall not apply to any employer with respect to any wages if—

(A) the employer deducted and withheld any amount of the tax imposed by chapter 24 on such wages, but

(B) failed to deduct and withhold the amount of the tax imposed by subchapter A of chapter 21 with respect to such wages.

(3) Section not to apply to certain statutory employees. This section shall not apply to any tax under subchapter A of chapter 21 with respect to an individual described in subsection (d)(3) of section 3121 (without regard to whether such individual is described in paragraph (1) or (2) of such subsection).

In 1990, P.L. 101-508, Sec. 5130(a)(4), substituted "subsection (d)(3)" for "subsection (d)(4)" in para. (d)(3), effective for remuneration for agricultural labor paid after 12/31/87.

In 1988, P.L. 100-647, Sec. 2003(d), substituted "subsection (d)(4)" for "subsection (d)(3)" in para. (d)(3), effective for remuneration for agricultural labor paid after 12/31/87.

In 1982, P.L. 97-248, Sec. 270(a), added Code Sec. 3509, effective 9/3/82, except for assessments made before 1/1/83.

Sec. 3510. Coordination of collection of domestic service employment taxes with collection of income taxes.

(a) General rule.

Except as otherwise provided in this section—

(1) returns with respect to domestic service employment taxes shall be made on a calendar year basis,

(2) any such return for any calendar year shall be filed on or before the 15th day of the fourth month following the close of the employer's taxable year which begins in such calendar year, and

(3) no requirement to make deposits (or to pay installments under section 6157) shall apply with respect to such taxes.

(b) Domestic service employment taxes subject to estimated tax provisions.

(1) In general. Solely for purposes of section 6654, domestic service employment taxes imposed with respect to any calendar year shall be treated as a tax imposed by chapter 2 for the taxable year of the employer which begins in such calendar year.

(2) Employers not otherwise required to make estimated payments. Paragraph (1) shall not apply to any employer for any calendar year if—

(A) no credit for wage withholding is allowed under section 31 to such employer for the taxable year of the employer which begins in such calendar year, and

(B) no addition to tax would (but for this section) be imposed under section 6654 for such taxable year by reason of section 6654(e).

(3) Annualization. Under regulations prescribed by the Secretary, appropriate adjustments shall be made in the application of section 6654(d)(2) in respect of the amount treated as tax under paragraph (1).

(4) Transitional rule. In the case of any taxable year beginning before January 1, 1998, no addition to tax shall be made under section 6654 with respect to any underpayment to the extent such underpayment was created or increased by this section.

(c) Domestic service employment taxes.

For purposes of this section, the term "domestic service employment taxes" means—

(1) any taxes imposed by chapter 21 or 23 on remuneration paid for domestic service in a private home of the employer, and

(2) any amount withheld from such remuneration pursuant to an agreement under section 3402(p).

For purposes of this subsection, the term "domestic service in a private home of the employer" includes domestic service described in section 3121(g)(5).

(d) Exception where employer liable for other employment taxes.

To the extent provided in regulations prescribed by the Secretary, this section shall not apply to any employer for any calendar year if such employer is liable for any tax under this subtitle with respect to remuneration for services other than domestic service in a private home of the employer.

(e) General regulatory authority.

The Secretary shall prescribe such regulations as may be necessary or appropriate to carry out the purposes of this section. Such regulations may treat domestic service employment taxes as taxes imposed by chapter 1 for purposes of coordinating the assessment and collection of such employment taxes with the assessment and collection of domestic employers' income taxes.

(f) Authority to enter into agreements to collect State unemployment taxes.

(1) In general. The Secretary is hereby authorized to enter into an agreement with any State to collect, as the agent of such State, such State's unemployment taxes imposed on remuneration paid for domestic service in a private home of the employer. Any taxes to be collected by the Secretary pursuant to such an agreement shall be treated as domestic service employment taxes for purposes of this section.

(2) Transfers to State account. Any amount collected under an agreement referred to in paragraph (1) shall be transferred by the Secretary to the account of the State in the Unemployment Trust Fund.

(3) Subtitle F made applicable. For purposes of subtitle F, any amount required to be collected under an agreement under paragraph (1) shall be treated as a tax imposed by chapter 23.

(4) State. For purposes of this subsection, the term "State" has the meaning given such term by section 3306(j)(1).

In 1994, P.L. 103-387, Sec. 2(b)(1), added Code Sec. 3510, effective for remuneration paid in calendar years beginning after 12/31/94. Sec. 2(b)(4) of this Act provides:

"(4) Expanded information to employers. The Secretary of the Treasury or the Secretary's delegate shall prepare and make available information on the Federal tax obligations of employers with respect to employees performing domestic service in a private home of the employer. Such information shall also include a statement that such employers may have obligations with respect to such employees under State laws relating to unemployment insurance and workers compensation."

Sec. 3510. Repealed.

In 1990, P.L. 101-508, Sec. 11801(a)(42), repealed Code Sec. 3510, effective 11/5/90, except as provided in Sec. 11821(b) of this Act, which reads as follows:
"(b) Savings provision.
"If—
"(1) any provision amended or repealed by this part applied to—
"(A) any transaction occurring before the date of the enactment of this Act [11/5/90],
"(B) any property acquired before such date of enactment [11/5/90], or
"(C) any item of income, loss, deduction, or credit taken into account before such date of enactment [11/5/90], and
"(2) the treatment of such transaction, property, or item under such provision would (without regard to the amendments made by this part) affect liability for tax for periods ending after such date of enactment [11/5/90],
nothing in the amendments made by this part shall be construed to affect the treatment of such transaction, property, or item for purposes of determining liability for tax for periods ending after such date of enactment [11/5/90]."
Prior to repeal, Code Sec. 3510 read as follows:
"SEC. 3510. CREDIT FOR INCREASED SOCIAL SECURITY EMPLOYEE TAXES AND RAILROAD RETIREMENT TIER 1 EMPLOYEE TAXES IMPOSED DURING 1984.
"(a) General rule.
"There shall be allowed as a credit against the tax imposed by section 3101(a) on wages received during 1984 an amount equal to 3/10 of 1 percent of the wages so received.
"(b) Time credit allowed.
"The credit under subsection (a) shall be taken into account in determining the amount of the tax deducted under section 3102(a).
"(c) Wages.
"For purposes of this section, the term 'wages' has the meaning given to such term by section 3121(a).
"(d) Application to agreements under section 218 of the Social Security Act.
"For purposes of determining amounts equivalent to the tax imposed by section 3101(a) with respect to remuneration which—
"(1) is covered by an agreement under section 218 of the Social Security Act, and
"(2) is paid during 1984,
the credit allowed by subsection (a) shall be taken into account. A similar rule shall also apply in the case of an agreement under section 3121(1).
"(e) Credit against railroad retirement employee and employee representative taxes.
"(1) In general. There shall be allowed as a credit against the taxes imposed by sections 3201(a) and 3211(a) on compensation paid during 1984 and subject to such taxes at rates determined by reference to section 3101 an amount equal to 3/10 of 1 percent of such compensation.
"(2) Time credit allowed. The credit under paragraph (1) shall be taken into account in determining the amount of the tax deducted under section 3202(a) (or the amount of the tax under section 3211(a)).
"(3) Compensation. For purposes of this subsection, the term 'compensation' has the meaning given to such term by section 3231(e).
"(f) Coordination with section 6413(c).
"For purposes of subsection (c) of section 6413, in determining the amount of the tax imposed by section 3101 or 3201, any credit allowed by this section shall be taken into account".
In 1983, P.L. 98-21, Sec. 123(b)(1), added Code Sec. 3510, effective for remuneration paid after 12/31/83 and before 1/1/85.
Sec. 123(b)(4) and (5) of the Act provide as follows:
"(4) Deposits in social security trust funds.— For purposes of subsection (h) of section 218 of the Social Security Act (relating to deposits in social security trust funds of amounts received under section 218 agreements), amounts allowed as a credit pursuant to subsection (d) of section 3510 of the Internal Revenue Code of 1954 (relating to credit for remuneration paid during 1984 which is covered under an agreement under section 218 of the Social Security Act) shall be treated as amounts received under such an agreement.
"(5) Deposits in railroad retirement account.— For purposes of subsection (a) of section 15 of the Railroad Retirement Act of 1974, amounts allowed as a credit under subsection (e) of section 3510 of the Internal Revenue Code of 1954 shall be treated as amounts covered into the Treasury under subsection (a) of section 3201 of such Code."

Subtitle D.—Miscellaneous Excise Taxes

Chap.
31. Retail excise taxes.
32. Manufacturers excise taxes.
33. Facilities and services.
34. Policies issued by foreign insurers.
35. Taxes on wagering.
36. Certain other excise taxes.
37. Repealed.
38. Environmental taxes.
39. Registration-required obligations.
40. General provisions relating to occupational taxes.
41. Public charities.
42. Private foundations and certain other tax-exempt organizations.
43. Qualified pension, etc., plans.
44. Qualified investment entities.
45. Provisions relating to expatriated entities.
45. [Repealed] Windfall profit tax on domestic crude oil.
46. Golden parachute payments.
47. Certain group health plans.
48. Maintenance of minimum essential coverage.
49. Cosmetic Services.
50. Foreign Procurement.

In 2010, P.L. 111-347, Sec. 301(a)(2), added the item for Chapter 50.
In 2004, P.L. 108-357, Sec. 802(c)(2), added the item for Chapter 45.
In 1990, P.L. 101-508, Sec. 11801(b)(17), deleted the item for Chapter 37.
Prior to deletion, the item for Chapter 37 read as follows:
"37. Sugar."
In 1989, P.L. 101-239, Sec. 6202(b)(4)(B), deleted "large" which followed "Certain" from the item for Chapter 47.
In 1986, P.L. 99-509, Sec. 9319(d)(2), added the item for Chapter 47.
In 1984, P.L. 98-369, Sec. 67(d)(2), added the item for Chapter 46.
In 1983, P.L. 97-448, Sec. 512(b)(2)(B), amended the item for Chapter 31.
Prior to amendment the the item for Chapter 31 read as follows:
"31. Retailers excise taxes."
In 1982, P.L. 97-248, Sec. 310(b)(4)(B), added the item for Chapter 39.
In 1980, P.L. 96-223, Sec. 101(a)(2), added the item for Chapter 45.
In 1978, P.L. 95-227, Sec. 4(c)(2)(C), amended the item for chapter 42.
Prior to amendment the item for chapter 42 read as follows:
"42. Private Foundations".
In 1976, P.L. 94-455, Sec. 1307(d)(3)(A), added the item for Chapter 41.
—P.L. 94-455, Sec. 1605(c), added the item for Chapter 44.
In 1969, P.L. 91-172, Sec. 101(j)(59), added chapter 42.
In 1964, added the heading of chapter 41.

CHAPTER 31.—RETAIL EXCISE TAXES

Subchapter
A. Luxury passenger automobiles.
B. Special fuels.
C. Heavy trucks and trailers.

In 1993, P.L. 103-66, Sec. 13161(b)(3), amended the item for subchapter A in the table of subchapters for Chapter 31.
Prior to amendment, the item for subchapter A read as follows:
"A. Certain luxury items."
In 1990, P.L. 101-508, Sec. 11221(e), amended the table of subchapters for Chapter 31.
Prior to amendment, the table of subchapters for Chapter 31 read as follows:
"Subchapter
"A. Special fuels.
"B. Heavy trucks and trailers."
In 1983, P.L. 97-424, Sec. 512(b)(2)(A), amended the heading of Chapter 31.
Prior to amendment, the heading of Chapter 31 read as follows:
"CHAPTER 31.—SPECIAL FUELS"
In 1976, P.L. 94-455, Sec. 1904(a)(1)(A), amended the heading of Chapter 31 and deleted the items for subchapters E and F.
Prior to amendment the heading of Chapter 31 and the items for subchapters E and F read as follows:
"CHAPTER 31.—RETAILERS EXCISE TAXES

Employment taxes   Subchapter A

"Subchapter
"E. Special fuels.
"F. Special provisions applicable to retailers tax."

Subchapter A.—Luxury Passenger Automobiles
4001. Imposition of tax.
4002. 1st retail sale; uses, etc. treated as sales; determination of price.
4003. Special rules.

In 1993, P.L. 103-66, Sec. 13161(a), amended the Subchapter A of Chapter 31, effective 1/1/93.
Prior to amendment, Subchapter A of Chapter 31 read as follows:
"Subchapter A.—Certain luxury items
"Part I. Imposition of taxes.
"Part II. Rules of general applicability.
"PART I.— IMPOSITION OF TAXES
"Subpart A. Passenger vehicles, boats, and aircraft.
"Subpart B. Jewelry and furs.
SUBPART A.— PASSENGER VEHICELS, BOATS, AND AIRCRAFT
Sec.
"4001. Passenger vehicles.
"4002. Boats.
"4003. Aircraft.
"4004. Rules applicable to subpart A.
"Sec. 4001. Passenger vehicles.
"(a) Imposition of tax.
"There is hereby imposed on the 1st retail sale of any passenger vehicle a tax equal to 10 percent of the price for which so sold to the extent such price exceeds $30,000.
"(b) Passenger vehicle.
"(1) In general. For purposes of subsection (a), the term 'passenger vehicle' means any 4-wheeled vehicle—
"(A) which is manufactured primarily for use on public streets, roads, and highways, and
"(B) which is rated at 6,000 pounds unloaded gross vehicle weight or less.
"(2) Special rules.
"(A) Trucks and vans. In the case of a truck or van, paragraph (1)(B) shall be applied by substituting 'gross vehicle weight' for 'unloaded gross vehicle weight'.
"(B) Limousines. In the case of a limousine, paragraph (1) shall be applied without regard to subparagraph (B) thereof.
"(c) Exceptions for taxicabs, etc.
"The tax imposed by this section shall not apply to the sale of any passenger vehicle for use by the purchaser exclusively in the active conduct of a trade or business of transporting persons or property for compensation or hire.".

In 1990, P.L. 101-508, Sec. 11221(a), added Code Sec. 4001 as part of the amendment to chap. 31, which redesignated subchaps. A and B as subchaps. B and C and added subchap. A, effective 1/1/91 except as provided in Sec. 11221(f)(2) of this Act, which reads as follows:
"(2) Exception for binding contracts. In determining whether any tax imposed by subchapter A of chapter 31 of the Internal Revenue Code of 1986, as added by this section, applies to any sale after December 31, 1990, there shall not be taken into account the amount paid for any article (or any part or accessory therefor) if the purchaser held on September 30, 1990, a contract (which was binding on such date and at all times thereafter before the purchase) for the purchase of such article (or such part or accessory)."

"Sec. 4002. Boats.
"(a) Imposition of tax.
"There is hereby imposed on the 1st retail sale of any boat a tax equal to 10 percent of the price for which so sold to the extent such price exceeds $100,000.
"(b) Exceptions.
"The tax imposed by this section shall not apply to the sale of any boat for use by the purchaser exclusively in the active conduct of—
"(1) a trade or business of commercial fishing or transporting persons or property for compensation or hire, or
"(2) any other trade or business unless the boat is to be used predominantly in any activity which is of a type generally considered to constitute entertainment, amusement, or recreation.".

In 1990, P.L. 101-508, Sec. 11221(a), added Code Sec. 4002 as part of the amendment to chap. 31, which redesignated subchaps. A and B as subchaps. B and C and added subchap. A, effective 1/1/91 except as provided in Sec. 11221(f)(2) of the Act, reproduced in note following Code Sec. 4001.

"Sec. 4003 Aircraft.
"(a) Imposition of tax.
"There is hereby imposed on the 1st retail sale of any aircraft a tax equal to 10 percent of the price for which so sold to the extent such price exceeds $250,000.
"(b) Aircraft.

"For purposes of this section, the term 'aircraft' means any aircraft—
"(1) which is propelled by a motor, and
"(2) which is capable of carrying 1 or more individuals.
"(c) 80 percent general business use.
"(1) In general. The tax imposed by this section shall not apply to the sale of any aircraft if 80 percent of the use by the purchaser is in any trade or business.
"(2) Proof of business use. On the income tax return for each of the 1st 2 taxable years ending after the date an aircraft on which no tax was imposed by this section by reason of paragraph (1) was placed in service, the taxpayer filing such return shall demonstrate to the satisfaction of the Secretary that the use of such aircraft during each such year met the requirement of paragraph (1).
"(3) Imposition of luxury tax where failure of proof. If the requirement of paragraph (2) is not met for either of the taxable years referred to therein, the taxpayer filing such returns shall pay the tax which would (but for paragraph (1)) have been imposed on such aircraft plus interest determined under subchapter C of chapter 67 during the period beginning on the date such tax would otherwise have been imposed. If such taxpayer fails to pay the tax imposed pursuant to the preceding sentence, no deduction shall be allowed under section 168 for any taxable year with respect to the aircraft involved.
"(d) Other exceptions.
"The tax imposed by this section shall not apply to the sale of any aircraft for use by the purchaser exclusively—
"(1) in the aerial application of fertilizers or other substances,
"(2) in the case of a helicopter, in a use described in paragraph (1) or (2) of section 4261(e),
"(3) in a trade or business of providing flight training, or
"(4) in a trade or business of transporting persons or property for compensation or hire.".

In 1990, P.L. 101-508, Sec. 11221(a), added Code Sec. 4003 as part of the amendment to chap. 31, which redesignated subchaps. A and B as subchaps. B and C and added subchap. A, effective 1/1/91 except as provided in Sec. 11221(f)(2) of this Act, reproduced in note following Code Sec. 4001.

"Sec. 4004 Rules applicable to subpart A.
"(a) Exemption for law enforcement uses, etc.
"No tax shall be imposed under this subpart on the sale of any article—
"(1) to the Federal Government, or a State or local government, for use exclusively in police, firefighting, search and rescue, or other law enforcement or public safety activities, or in public works activities, or
"(2) to any person for use exclusively in providing emergency medical services.
"(b) Separate purchase of article and parts and accessories therefor.
"Under regulations prescribed by the Secretary—
"(1) In general. Except as provided in paragraph (2), if—
"(A) the owner, lessee, or operator of any article taxable under this subpart (determined without regard to price) installs (or causes to be installed) any part or accessory on such article, and
"(B) such installation is not later than the date 6 months after the date the article was 1st placed in service,
then there is hereby imposed on such installation a tax equal to 10 percent of the price of such part or accessory and its installation.
"(2) Limitation. The tax imposed by paragraph (1) on the installation of any part or accessory shall not exceed 10 percent of the excess (if any) of—
"(A) the sum of—
"(i) the price of such part or accessory and its installation,
"(ii) the aggregate price of the parts and accessories (and their installation) installed before such part or accessory, plus
"(iii) the price for which the passenger vehicle, boat, or aircraft was sold, over
"(B) $30,000 in the case of a passenger vehicle, $100,000 in the case of a boat, and $250,000 in the case of an aircraft.
"(3) Exceptions. Paragraph (1) shall not apply if—
"(A) the part or accessory installed is a replacement part or accessory,
"(B) the part or accessory is installed on a passenger vehicle to enable or assist an individual with a disability to operate the vehicle, or to enter or exit the vehicle, by compensating for the effect of such disability, or
"(C) the aggregate price of the parts and accessories (and their installation) described in paragraph (1) with respect to the taxable article does not exceed $200 (or such other amount or amounts as the Secretary may by regulation prescribe).
The price of any part or accessory (and its installation) to which paragraph (1) does not apply by reason of this paragraph shall not be taken into account under paragraph (2)(A).
"(4) Installers secondarily liable for tax. The owners of the trade or business installing the parts or accessories shall be secondarily liable for the tax imposed by this subsection.
"(c) Imposition of tax on sales, etc., within 2 years of articles purchased tax-free.
"(1) In general. If—
"(A) no tax was imposed under this subchapter on the 1st retail sale of any article by reason of its exempt use, and
"(B) within 2 years after the date of such 1st retail sale, such article is resold by the purchaser or such purchaser makes a substantial non-exempt use of such article,
then such sale or use of such article by such purchaser shall be treated as the 1st retail sale of such article for a price equal to its fair market value at the time of such sale or use.

3,179

Subchapter A — Employment taxes

"(2) Exempt use. For purposes of this subsection, the term 'exempt use' means any use of an article if the 1st retail sale of such article is not taxable under this subchapter by reason of such use."

In 1993, P.L. 103-66, Sec. 13162(a)(1), deleted "or" at the end of subpara. (b)(3)(A).... Sec. 13162(a)(2), redesignated subpara. (b)(3)(B) as subpara. (b)(3)(C).... Sec. 13162(a)(3), added subpara. (b)(3)(B).... Sec. 13162(a)(4), added "The price of any part or accessory (and its installation) to which paragraph (1) does not apply by reason of this paragraph shall not be taken into account under paragraph (2)(A)." to the end of para. (b)(3), effective 1/1/91, except as provided in Sec. 11221(f)(2) of P.L. 101-508 reproduced in note following Code Sec. 4001.

—P.L. 103-66, Sec. 13162(c), of this act provides:

"(c) Period for filing claims. If refund or credit of any overpayment of tax resulting from the application of the amendments made by this section is prevented at any time before the close of the 1-year period beginning on the date of the enactment of this Act by the operation of any law or rule of law (including res judicata), refund or credit of such overpayment (to the extent attributable to such amendments) may, nevertheless, be made or allowed if claim therefor is filed before the close of such 1-year period."

In 1990, P.L. 101-508, Sec. 11221(a), added Code Sec. 4004, as part of the amendment to chap. 31, which redesignated subchaps. A and B as subchaps. B and C and added subchap. A, effective 1/1/91, except as provided in Sec. 11221(f)(2) of the Act, reproduced in note following Code Sec. 4001.

SUBPART B.—JEWELRY AND FURS
"Sec.
"4006. Jewelry.
"4007. Furs.
"Sec. 4006 Jewelry.
"(a) Imposition of tax.

"There is hereby imposed on the 1st retail sale of any jewelry a tax equal to 10 percent of the price for which so sold to the extent such price exceeds $10,000.
"(b) Jewelry.

"For purposes of subsection (a), the term 'jewelry' means all articles commonly or commercially known as jewelry, whether real or imitation, including watches.
"(c) Manufacture from customer's material.

"If—
"(1) a person, in the course of a trade or business, produces jewelry from material furnished directly or indirectly by a customer, and
"(2) the jewelry is for the use of, and not for resale by, such customer, the delivery of such jewelry to such customer shall be treated as the 1st retail sale of such jewelry for a price equal to its fair market value at the time of such delivery."

In 1990, P.L. 101-508, Sec. 11221(a), added Code Sec. 4006 as part of the amendment to chap. 31, which redesignated subchaps. A and B as subchaps. B and C and added subchap. A, effective 1/1/91 except as provided in Sec. 11221(f)(2) of this Act, reproduced in note following Code Sec. 4001.

"Sec. 4007 Furs.
"(a) Imposition of tax.

There is hereby imposed on the 1st retail sale of the following articles a tax equal to 10 percent of the price for which so sold to the extent such price exceeds $10,000:
"(1) Articles made of fur on the hide or pelt.
"(2) Articles of which such fur is a major component.
"(b) Manufacture from customer's material.

"If—
"(1) a person, in the course of a trade or business, produces an article of the kind described in subsection (a) from fur on the hide or pelt furnished, directly or indirectly, by a customer, and
"(2) the article is for the use of, and not for resale by, such customer, the delivery of such article to such customer shall be treated as the 1st retail sale of such article for a price equal to its fair market value at the time of such delivery."

In 1990, P.L. 101-508, Sec. 11221(a), added Code Sec. 4007 as part of the amendment to chap. 31, which redesignated subchaps. A and B as subchaps. B and C and added subchap. A, effective 1/1/91 except as provided in Sec. 11221(f)(2) of this Act, reproduced in note following Code Sec. 4001.

"PART II. RULES OF GENERAL APPLICABILITY
"Sec. 4011. Definitions and special rules.
"Sec. 4012. Termination.
"Sec. 4011 Definitions and special rules.
"(a) 1st retail sale.

For purposes of this subchapter, the term '1st retail sale' means the 1st sale, for a purpose other than resale, after manufacture, production, or importation.
"(b) Use treated as sale.

"(1) In general. If any person uses an article taxable under this subchapter (including any use after importation) before the 1st retail sale of such article, then such person shall be liable for tax under this subchapter in the same manner as if such article were sold at retail by him.

"(2) Exemption for further manufacture. Paragraph (1) shall not apply to use of an article as material in the manufacture or production of, or as a component part of, another article taxable under this subchapter to be manufactured or produced by him.

"(3) Exemption for demonstration use of passenger vehicles. Paragraph (1) shall not apply to any use of a passenger vehicle as a demonstrator for a potential customer while the potential customer is in the vehicle.

"(4) Exception for use after importation of certain articles. Paragraph (1) shall not apply to the use of an article after importation if the user or importer establishes to the satisfaction of the Secretary that the 1st use of the article occurred before January 1, 1991, outside the United States.

"(5) Computation of tax. In the case of any person made liable for tax by paragraph (1), the tax shall be computed on the price at which similar articles are sold at retail in the ordinary course of trade, as determined by the Secretary.
"(c) Leases considered as sales.

For purposes of this subchapter—

"(1) In general. Except as otherwise provided in this subsection, the lease of an article (including any renewal or any extension of a lease or any subsequent lease of such article) by any person shall be considered a sale of such article at retail.

"(2) Special rules for certain leases of passenger vehicles, boats, and aircraft.

"(A) Tax not imposed on sale for leasing in a qualified lease. The sale of a passenger vehicle, boat, or aircraft to a person engaged in a leasing or rental trade or business of the article involved for leasing by such person in a qualified lease shall not be treated as the 1st retail sale of such article.

"(B) Qualified lease. For purposes of subparagraph (A), the term 'qualified lease' means—

"(i) any lease in the case of a boat or an aircraft, and

"(ii) any long-term lease (as defined in section 4052) in the case of any passenger vehicle.

"(C) Special rules. In the case of a qualified lease of an article which is treated as the 1st retail sale of such article—

"(i) Determination of price. The tax under this subchapter shall be computed on the lowest price for which the article is sold by retailers in the ordinary course of trade.

"(ii) Payment of tax. Rules similar to the rules of section 4217(e)(2) shall apply.

"(iii) No tax where exempt use by lessee. No tax shall be imposed on any lease payment under a qualified lease if the lessee's use of the article under such lease is an exempt use (as defined in section 4004(c)) of such article.
"(d) Determination of price.

"(1) In general. In determining price for purposes of this subchapter—

"(A) there shall be included any charge incident to placing the article in condition ready for use,

"(B) there shall be excluded—

"(i) the amount of the tax imposed by this subchapter,

"(ii) if stated as a separate charge, the amount of any retail sales tax imposed by any State or political subdivision thereof or the District of Columbia, whether the liability for such tax is imposed on the vendor or vendee, and

"(iii) the value of any component of such article if—

"(I) such component is furnished by the 1st user of such article, and

"(II) such component has been used before such furnishing, and

"(C) the price shall be determined without regard to any trade-in.

Subparagraph (B)(iii) shall not apply for purposes of the taxes imposed by sections 4006 and 4007.

"(2) Other rules. Rules similar to the rules of paragraphs (2) and (4) of section 4052(b) shall apply for purposes of this subchapter.
"(e) Parts and accessories sold with taxable article.

Parts and accessories sold on, in connection with, or with the sale of any article taxable under this subchapter shall be treated as part of the article.
"(f) Partial payments, etc.

In the case of a contract, sale, or arrangement described in paragraph (2), (3), or (4) of section 4216(c), rules similar to the rules of section 4217(e)(2) shall apply for purposes of this subchapter."

In 1990, P.L. 101-508, Sec. 11221(a), added Code Sec. 4011 as part of the amendment to chap. 31, which redesignated subchaps. A and B as subchaps. B and C and added subchap. A, effective 1/1/91 except as provided in Sec. 11221(f)(2) of this Act, reproduced in note following Code Sec. 4001.

"Sec. 4012 Termination. The taxes imposed by this subchapter shall not apply to any sale or use after December 31, 1999."

In 1990, P.L. 101-508, Sec. 11221(a), added Code Sec. 4012 as part of the amendment to chap. 31, which redesignated subchaps. A and B as subchaps. B and C and added subchap. A, effective 1/1/91 except as provided in Sec. 11221(f)(2) of this Act, reproduced in note following Code Sec. 4001.

Sec. 4001. Imposition of tax.
(a) Imposition of tax.

(1) In general. There is hereby imposed on the 1st retail sale of any passenger vehicle a tax equal to 10 percent of the price for which so sold to the extent such price exceeds the applicable amount.

(2) Applicable amount.
  (A) In general. Except as provided in subparagraphs (B) and (C), the applicable amount is $30,000.
  (B) Qualified clean-fuel vehicle property. In the case of a passenger vehicle which is propelled by a fuel which is not a clean-burning fuel and to which is installed qualified clean-fuel vehicle property (as defined in section 179A(c)(1)(A)) for purposes of permitting such vehicle to be propelled by a clean-burning fuel, the applicable amount is equal to the sum of—
    (i) the dollar amount in effect under subparagraph (A), plus
    (ii) the increase in the price for which the passenger vehicle was sold (within the meaning of section 4002) due to the installation of such property.
  (C) Purpose built passenger vehicle.
    (i) In general. In the case of a purpose built passenger vehicle, the applicable amount is equal to 150 percent of the dollar amount in effect under subparagraph (A).
    (ii) Purpose built passenger vehicle. For purposes of clause (i), the term "purpose built passenger vehicle" means a passenger vehicle produced by an original equipment manufacturer and designed so that the vehicle may be propelled primarily by electricity.

(b) Passenger vehicle.
  (1) In general. For purposes of this subchapter, the term "passenger vehicle" means any 4-wheeled vehicle—
    (A) which is manufactured primarily for use on public streets, roads, and highways, and
    (B) which is rated at 6,000 pounds unloaded gross vehicle weight or less.
  (2) Special rules.
    (A) Trucks and vans. In the case of a truck or van, paragraph (1)(B) shall be applied by substituting "gross vehicle weight" for "unloaded gross vehicle weight".
    (B) Limousines. In the case of a limousine, paragraph (1) shall be applied without regard to subparagraph (B) thereof.

(c) Exceptions for taxicabs, etc.
  The tax imposed by this section shall not apply to the sale of any passenger vehicle for use by the purchaser exclusively in the active conduct of a trade or business of transporting persons or property for compensation or hire.

(d) Exemption for law enforcement uses, etc.
  No tax shall be imposed by this section on the sale of any passenger vehicle—
    (1) to the Federal Government, or a State or local government, for use exclusively in police, fire-fighting, search and rescue, or other law enforcement or public safety activities, or in public works activities, or
    (2) to any person for use exclusively in providing emergency medical services.

(e) Inflation adjustment.
  (1) In general. The $30,000 amount in subsection (a) shall be increased by an amount equal to—
    (A) $30,000, multiplied by
    (B) the cost-of-living adjustment under section 1(f)(3) for the calendar year in which the vehicle is sold, determined by substituting "calendar year 1990" for "calendar year 1992" in subparagraph (B) thereof.
  (2) Rounding. If any amount as adjusted under paragraph (1) is not a multiple of $2,000, such amount shall be rounded to the next lowest multiple of $2,000.

(f) Phasedown.
  For sales occurring in calendar years after 1995 and before 2003, subsection (a)(1) and section 4003(a) shall be applied by substituting for "10 percent", each place it appears, the percentage determined in accordance with the following table.

If the calendar year is:	The percentage is:
1996	9 percent
1997	8 percent
1998	7 percent
1999	6 percent
2000	5 percent
2001	4 percent
2002	3 percent

(g) Termination.
  The taxes imposed by this section and section 4003 shall not apply to any sale, use, or installation after December 31, 2002.

In **1997,** P.L. 105-34, Sec. 906(a), amended subsec. (a) . . . Sec. 906(b)(1), deleted "and section 4003(a)" after "subsection (a)" in para. (e)(1) . . . Sec. 906(b)(2), substituted "subsection (a)(1)" for "subsection (a)" in subsec. (f), effective for sales and installations occurring after 8/5/97.
Prior to amendment, subsec. (a) read as follows:
"(a) Imposition of tax. There is hereby imposed on the 1st retail sale of any passenger vehicle a tax equal to 10 percent of the price for which so sold to the extent such price exceeds $30,000."
—P.L. 105-34, Sec. 1601(f)(3)(A)(i), added "and section 4003(a)" after "subsection (a)" in subsec. (f) . . . Sec. 1601(f)(3)(A)(ii), added ", each place it appears," before "the percentage" in subsec. (f) . . . Sec. 1601(f)(3)(B), substituted "taxes imposed by this section and section 4003" for "tax imposed by this section" in subsec. (g), and substituted ", use, or installation" for "or use" in subsec. (g), effective for sales occurring after the date which is 7 days after 8/20/96.
In **1996,** P.L. 104-188, Sec. 1607(a), substituted "2002" for "1999" in subsec. (f) . . . Sec. 1607(b), redesignated subsec. (f) [as amended by Sec. 1607(a) of this Act] as subsec. (g) and added a new subsec. (f), effective for sales occurring after the date which is 7 days after 8/20/96.
—P.L. 104-188, Sec. 1703(c)(1), amended subsec. (e), effective 8/20/96.
Prior to amendment, subsec. (e) read as follows:
"(e) Inflation adjustment.
"(1) In general. If, for any calendar year, the excess (if any) of—
"(A) $30,000, increased by the cost-of-living adjustment for the calendar year, over
"(B) the dollar amount in effect under subsection (a) for the calendar year.
is equal to or greater than $2,000, then the $30,000 amount in subsection (a) and section 4003(a) (as previously adjusted under this subsection) for any subsequent calendar year shall be increased by the amount of such excess rounded to the next lowest multiple of $2,000.
"(2) Cost-of-living adjustment. For purposes of paragraph (1), the cost-of-living adjustment for any calendar year shall be the cost-of-living adjustment under section 1(f)(3) for such calendar year, determined by substituting "calendar year 1990" for "calendar year 1992" in subparagraph (B) thereof."
In **1993,** P.L. 103-66, Sec. 13161(a), added Code Sec. 4001, effective 1/1/93, except that the provisions of section 4001(e) of the Internal Revenue Code of 1986 (as emended by subsection (a)) shall be effective 8/10/93.

Sec. 4002.   1st retail sale; uses, etc. treated as sales; determination of price.
(a) 1st retail sale.
  For purposes of this subchapter, the term "1st retail sale" means the 1st sale, for a purpose other than resale, after manufacture, production, or importation.
(b) Use treated as sale.
  (1) In general. If any person uses a passenger vehicle (including any use after importation) before the 1st retail sale of such vehicle, then such person shall be liable for tax under this subchapter in the same manner as if such vehicle were sold at retail by him.
  (2) Exemption for further manufacture. Paragraph (1) shall not apply to use of a vehicle as material in the manufacture or production of, or as a component part of, another vehicle taxable under this subchapter to be manufactured or produced by him.

(3) Exemption for demonstration use. Paragraph (1) shall not apply to any use of a passenger vehicle as a demonstrator.

(4) Exception for use after importation of certain vehicles. Paragraph (1) shall not apply to the use of a vehicle after importation if the user or importer establishes to the satisfaction of the Secretary that the 1st use of the vehicle occurred before January 1, 1991, outside the United States.

(5) Computation of tax. In the case of any person made liable for tax by paragraph (1), the tax shall be computed on the price at which similar vehicles are sold at retail in the ordinary course of trade, as determined by the Secretary.

(c) Leases considered as sales.
For purposes of this subchapter—
(1) In general. Except as otherwise provided in this subsection, the lease of a vehicle (including any renewal or any extension of a lease or any subsequent lease of such vehicle) by any person shall be considered a sale of such vehicle at retail.
(2) Special rules for long-term leases.
(A) Tax not imposed on sale for leasing in a qualified lease. The sale of a passenger vehicle to a person engaged in a passenger vehicle leasing or rental trade or business for leasing by such person in a long-term lease shall not be treated as the 1st retail sale of such vehicle.
(B) Long-term lease. For purposes of subparagraph (A), the term "long-term lease" means any long-term lease (as defined in section 4052).
(C) Special rules. In the case of a long-term lease of a vehicle which is treated as the 1st retail sale of such vehicle—
  (i) Determination of price. The tax under this subchapter shall be computed on the lowest price for which the vehicle is sold by retailers in the ordinary course of trade.
  (ii) Payment of tax. Rules similar to the rules of section 4217(e)(2) shall apply.
  (iii) No tax where exempt use by lessee. No tax shall be imposed on any lease payment under a long-term lease if the lessee's use of the vehicle under such lease is an exempt use (as defined in section 4003(b)) of such vehicle.

(d) Determination of price.
(1) In general. In determining price for purposes of this subchapter—
(A) there shall be included any charge incident to placing the passenger vehicle in condition ready for use,
(B) there shall be excluded—
  (i) the amount of the tax imposed by this subchapter,
  (ii) if stated as a separate charge, the amount of any retail sales tax imposed by any State or political subdivision thereof or the District of Columbia, whether the liability for such tax is imposed on the vendor or vendee, and
  (iii) the value of any component of such passenger vehicle if—
    (I) such component is furnished by the 1st user of such passenger vehicle, and
    (II) such component has been used before such furnishing, and
(C) the price shall be determined without regard to any trade-in.

(2) Other rules. Rules similar to the rules of paragraphs (2) and (4) of section 4052(b) shall apply for purposes of this subchapter.

In 1993, P.L. 103-66, Sec. 13161(a), added Code Sec. 4002, effective 1/1/93.

Sec. 4003. Special rules.
(a) Separate purchase of vehicle and parts and accessories therefor.
Under regulations prescribed by the Secretary—
(1) In general. Except as provided in paragraph (2), if—
(A) the owner, lessee, or operator of any passenger vehicle installs (or causes to be installed) any part or accessory (other than property described in section 4001(a)(2)(B)) on such vehicle, and
(B) such installation is not later than the date 6 months after the date the vehicle was 1st placed in service,
then there is hereby imposed on such installation a tax equal to 10 percent of the price of such part or accessory and its installation.
(2) Limitation. The tax imposed by paragraph (1) on the installation of any part or accessory shall not exceed 10 percent of the excess (if any) of—
(A) the sum of—
  (i) the price of such part or accessory and its installation,
  (ii) the aggregate price of the parts and accessories (and their installation) installed before such part or accessory, plus
  (iii) the price for which the passenger vehicle was sold, over
(B) the appropriate applicable amount as determined under section 4001(a)(2).
(3) Exceptions. Paragraph (1) shall not apply if—
(A) the part or accessory installed is a replacement part or accessory,
(B) the part or accessory is installed to enable or assist an individual with a disability to operate the vehicle, or to enter or exit the vehicle, by compensating for the effect of such disability, or
(C) the aggregate price of the parts and accessories (and their installation) described in paragraph (1) with respect to the vehicle does not exceed $1,000 (or such other amount or amounts as the Secretary may by regulation prescribe).
The price of any part or accessory (and its installation) to which paragraph (1) does not apply by reason of this paragraph shall not be taken into account under paragraph (2)(A).
(4) Installers secondarily liable for tax. The owners of the trade or business installing the parts or accessories shall be secondarily liable for the tax imposed by this subsection.

(b) Imposition of tax on sales, etc., within 2 years of vehicles purchased tax-free.
(1) In general. If—
(A) no tax was imposed under this subchapter on the 1st retail sale of any passenger vehicle by reason of its exempt use, and
(B) within 2 years after the date of such 1st retail sale, such vehicle is resold by the purchaser or such purchaser makes a substantial nonexempt use of such vehicle,
then such sale or use of such vehicle by such purchaser shall be treated as the 1st retail sale of such vehicle for a price equal to its fair market value at the time of such sale or use.

Excise and miscellaneous taxes Code Sec. 4041(b)(1)(B)

(2) Exempt use. For purposes of this subsection, the term "exempt use" means any use of a vehicle if the 1st retail sale of such vehicle is not taxable under this subchapter by reason of such use.

(c) Parts and accessories sold with taxable passenger vehicle.

Parts and accessories sold on, in connection with, or with the sale of any passenger vehicle shall be treated as part of the vehicle.

(d) Partial payments, etc.

In the case of a contract, sale, or arrangement described in paragraph (2), (3), or (4) of section 4216(c), rules similar to the rules of section 4217(e)(2) shall apply for purposes of this subchapter.

In 1997, P.L. 105-34, Sec. 906(b)(3), added "(other than property described in section 4001(a)(2)(B))" after "part or accessory" in subpara. (a)(1)(A) ... Sec. 906(b)(4), amended subpara. (a)(2)(B), effective for sales and installations occurring after 8/5/97.
Prior to amendment, subpara. (a)(2)(B) read as follows:
"(B) $30,000."
—P.L. 105-34, Sec. 1401(a), substituted "$1,000" for "$200" in subpara. (a)(3)(C), effective for installations on vehicles sold after 8/5/97.
In 1993, P.L. 103-66, Sec. 13161(a), added Code Sec. 4003, effective 1/1/93.

Subchapter B.—Special Fuels

Sec.
4041. Imposition of tax.
4042. Tax on fuel used in commercial transportation on inland waterways.

In 1990, P.L. 101-508, Sec. 11221(a), redesignated Subchapter A as Subchapter B.
In 1978, P.L. 95-502, Sec. 202(c), added item 4042.

Sec. 4041. Imposition of tax.
(a) Diesel fuel and special motor fuels.
(1) Tax on diesel fuel and kerosene in certain cases.
(A) In general. There is hereby imposed a tax on any liquid other than gasoline (as defined in section 4083)—
(i) sold by any person to an owner, lessee, or other operator of a diesel-powered highway vehicle or a diesel-powered train for use as a fuel in such vehicle or train, or
(ii) used by any person as a fuel in a diesel-powered highway vehicle or a diesel-powered train unless there was a taxable sale of such fuel under clause (i).
(B) Exemption for previously taxed fuel. No tax shall be imposed by this paragraph on the sale or use of any liquid if tax was imposed on such liquid under section 4081 (other than such tax at the Leaking Underground Storage Tank Trust Fund financing rate) and the tax thereon was not credited or refunded.
(C) Rate of tax.
(i) In general. Except as otherwise provided in this subparagraph, the rate of tax imposed by this paragraph shall be the rate of tax specified in section 4081(a)(2)(A) on diesel fuel which is in effect at the time of such sale or use.
(ii) Rate of tax on trains. In the case of any sale for use, or use, of diesel fuel in a train, the rate of tax imposed by this paragraph shall be—
(I) 3.3 cents per gallon after December 31, 2004, and before July 1, 2005,
(II) 2.3 cents per gallon after June 30, 2005, and before January 1, 2007, and
(III) 0 after December 31, 2006.

(iii) Rate of tax on certain buses.
(I) In general. Except as provided in subclause (II), in the case of fuel sold for use or used in a use described in section 6427(b)(1) (after the application of section 6427(b)(3)), the rate of tax imposed by this paragraph shall be 7.3 cents per gallon (4.3 cents per gallon after September 30, 2011).
(II) School bus and intracity transportation. No tax shall be imposed by this paragraph on any sale for use, or use, described in subparagraph (B) or (C) of section 6427(b)(2).
(2) Alternative fuels.
(A) In general. There is hereby imposed a tax on any liquid (other than gas oil, fuel oil, or any product taxable under section 4081 (other than such tax at the Leaking Underground Storage Tank Trust Fund financing rate))—
(i) sold by any person to an owner, lessee, or other operator of a motor vehicle or motorboat for use as a fuel in such motor vehicle or motorboat, or
(ii) used by any person as a fuel in a motor vehicle or motorboat unless there was a taxable sale of such liquid under clause (i).
(B) Rate of tax. The rate of the tax imposed by this paragraph shall be—
(i) except as otherwise provided in this subparagraph, the rate of tax specified in section 4081(a)(2)(A)(i) which is in effect at the time of such sale or use, and
(ii) in the case of liquefied natural gas, any liquid fuel (other than ethanol and methanol) derived from coal (including peat), and liquid hydrocarbons derived from biomass (as defined in section 45K(c)(3)), 24.3 cents per gallon.
(3) Compressed natural gas.
(A) In general. There is hereby imposed a tax on compressed natural gas—
(i) sold by any person to an owner, lessee, or other operator of a motor vehicle or motorboat for use as a fuel in such motor vehicle or motorboat, or
(ii) used by any person as a fuel in a motor vehicle or motorboat unless there was a taxable sale of such gas under clause (i).
The rate of the tax imposed by this paragraph shall be 18.3 cents per energy equivalent of a gallon of gasoline.
(B) Bus uses. No tax shall be imposed by this paragraph on any sale for use, or use, described in subparagraph (B) or (C) of section 6427(b)(2) (relating to school bus and intracity transportation).
(C) Administrative provisions. For purposes of applying this title with respect to the taxes imposed by this subsection, references to any liquid subject to tax under this subsection shall be treated as including references to compressed natural gas subject to tax under this paragraph, and references to gallons shall be treated as including references to energy equivalent of a gallon of gasoline with respect to such gas.
(b) Exemption for off-highway business use; reduction in tax for qualified methanol and ethanol fuel.
(1) Exemption for off-highway business use.
(A) In general. No tax shall be imposed by subsection (a) on liquids sold for use or used in an off-highway business use.
(B) Tax where other use. If a liquid on which no tax was imposed by reason of subparagraph (A) is used otherwise than in an off-highway business use, a tax shall be imposed by paragraph (1)(B), (2)(B), or

(3)(A)(ii) of subsection (a) (whichever is appropriate) and by the corresponding provision of subsection (d)(1) (if any).

(C) **Off-highway business use defined.** For purposes of this subsection, the term "off-highway business use" has the meaning given to such term by section 6421(e)(2); except that such term shall not, for purposes of this subsection (a)(1), include use in a diesel-powered train.

(2) **Qualified methanol and ethanol fuel.**

(A) **In general.** In the case of any qualified methanol or ethanol fuel—

(i) the rate applicable under subsection (a)(2) shall be the applicable blender rate per gallon less than the otherwise applicable rate (6 cents per gallon in the case of a mixture none of the alcohol in which consists of ethanol), and

(ii) subsection (d)(1) shall be applied by substituting "0.05 cent" for "0.1 cent" with respect to the sales and uses to which clause (i) applies.

(B) **Qualfied methanol and ethanol fuel produced from coal.** The term "qualified methanol or ethanol fuel" means any liquid at least 85 percent of which consists of methanol, ethanol, or other alcohol produced from coal (including peat).

(C) **Applicable blender rate.** For purposes of subparagraph (A)(i), the applicable blender rate is—

(i) except as provided in clause (ii), 5.4 cents, and

(ii) for sales or uses during calendar years 2001 through 2008, 1/10 of the blender amount applicable under section 40(h)(2) for the calendar year in which the sale or use occurs.

(D) **Termination.** On and after January 1, 2009, subparagraph (A) shall not apply.

(c) **Certain liquids used as a fuel in aviation.**

(1) **In general.** There is hereby imposed a tax upon any liquid for use as a fuel other than aviation gasoline—

(A) sold by any person to an owner, lessee, or other operator of an aircraft for use in such aircraft, or

(B) used by any person in an aircraft unless there was a taxable sale of such fuel under subparagraph (A).

(2) **Exemption for previously taxed fuel.** No tax shall be imposed by this subsection on the sale or use of any liquid for use as a fuel other than aviation gasoline if tax was imposed on such liquid under section 4081 (other than such tax at the Leaking Underground Storage Tank Trust Fund financing rate) and the tax thereon was not credited or refunded.

(3) **Rate of tax.** The rate of tax imposed by this subsection shall be 21.8 cents per gallon (4.3 cents per gallon with respect to any sale or use for commercial aviation).

(d) **Additional taxes to fund Leaking Underground Storage Tank Trust Fund.**

(1) **Tax on sales and uses subject to tax under subsection (a).** In addition to the taxes imposed by subsection (a), there is hereby imposed a tax of 0.1 cent a gallon on the sale or use of any liquid (other than liquefied petroleum gas and other than liquefied natural gas) if tax is imposed by subsection (a)(1) or (2), on such sale or use. No tax shall be imposed under the preceding sentence on the sale or use of any liquid if tax was imposed with respect to such liquid under section 4081 at the Leaking Underground Storage Tank Trust Fund financing rate.

(2) **Liquids used in aviation.** In addition to the taxes imposed by subsection (c), there is hereby imposed a tax of 0.1 cent a gallon on any liquid (other than gasoline (as defined in section 4083))—

(A) sold by any person to an owner, lessee, or other operator of an aircraft for use as a fuel in such aircraft, or

(B) used by any person as a fuel in an aircraft unless there was a taxable sale of such liquid under subparagraph (A).

No tax shall be imposed by this paragraph on the sale or use of any liquid if there was a taxable sale of such liquid under section 4081.

(3) **Diesel fuel used in trains.** In the case of any sale for use or use after December 31, 2006, there is hereby imposed a tax of 0.1 cent per gallon on any liquid other than gasoline (as defined in section 4083)—

(A) sold by any person to an owner, lessee, or other operator of a diesel-powered train for use as a fuel in such train, or

(B) used by any person as a fuel in a diesel-powered train unless there was a taxable sale of such fuel under subparagraph (A).

No tax shall be imposed by this paragraph on the sale or use of any liquid if tax was imposed on such liquid under section 4081.

(4) **Termination.** The taxes imposed by this subsection shall not apply during any period during which the Leaking Underground Storage Tank Trust Fund financing rate under section 4081 does not apply.

(5) **Nonapplication of exemptions other than for exports.** For purposes of this section, the tax imposed under this subsection shall be determined without regard to subsections (b)(1)(A), (f), (g), (h), and (l). The preceding sentence shall not apply with respect to subsection (g)(3) and so much of subsection (g)(1) as relates to vessels (within the meaning of section 4221(d)(3)) employed in foreign trade or trade between the United States and any of its possessions.

(e) **Repealed.**

(f) **Exemption for farm use.**

(1) **Exemption.** Under regulations prescribed by the Secretary, no tax shall be imposed under this section on any liquid sold for use or used on a farm for farming purposes.

(2) **Use on a farm for farming purposes.** For purposes of paragraph (1) of this subsection, use on a farm for farming purposes shall be determined in accordance with paragraphs (1), (2), and (3) of section 6420(c).

(g) **Other exemptions.**

Under regulations prescribed by the Secretary, no tax shall be imposed under this section—

(1) on any liquid sold for use or used as supplies for vessels or aircraft (within the meaning of section 4221(d)(3));

(2) with respect to the sale of any liquid for the exclusive use of any State, any political subdivision of a State, or the District of Columbia, or with respect to the use by any of the foregoing of any liquid as a fuel;

(3) upon the sale of any liquid for export, or for shipment to a possession of the United States, and in due course so exported or shipped;

(4) with respect to the sale of any liquid to a nonprofit educational organization for its exclusive use, or with respect to the use by a nonprofit educational organization of any liquid as a fuel; and

(5) with respect to the sale of any liquid to a qualified blood collector organization (as defined in section 7701(a)(49)) for such organization's exclusive use in the collection, storage, or transportation of blood.

Excise and miscellaneous taxes   Code Sec. 4041

For purposes of paragraph (4), the term "nonprofit educational organization" means an educational organization described in section 170(b)(1)(A)(ii) which is exempt from income tax under section 501(a). The term also includes a school operated as an activity of an organization described in section 501(c)(3) which is exempt from income tax under section 501(a), if such school normally maintains a regular faculty and curriculum and normally has a regularly enrolled body of pupils or students in attendance at the place where its educational activities are regularly carried on.

(h) Exemption for use by certain aircraft museums.

(1) **Exemption.** Under regulations prescribed by the Secretary or his delegate, no tax shall be imposed under this section on any liquid sold for use or used by an aircraft museum in an aircraft or vehicle owned by such museum and used exclusively for purposes set forth in paragraph (2)(C).

(2) **Definition of aircraft museum.** For purposes of this subsection, the term "aircraft museum" means an organization—

(A) described in section 501(c)(3) which is exempt from income tax under section 501(a),

(B) operated as a museum under charter by a State or the District of Columbia, and

(C) operated exclusively for the procurement, care, and exhibition of aircraft of the type used for combat or transport in World War II.

(i) Repealed.

(j) Sales by United States, etc.

The taxes imposed by this section shall apply with respect to liquids sold at retail by the United States, or by any agency or instrumentality of the United States, unless sales by such agency or instrumentality are by statute specifically exempted from such taxes.

(k) Repealed.

(l) Exemption for certain uses.

No tax shall be imposed under this section on any liquid sold for use in, or used in, a helicopter or a fixed-wing aircraft for purposes of providing transportation with respect to which the requirements of subsection (f) or (g) of section 4261 are met.

(m) Certain alcohol fuels.

(1) **In general.** In the case of the sale or use of any partially exempt methanol or ethanol fuel the rate of the tax imposed by subsection (a)(2) shall be—

(A) after September 30, 1997, and before October 1, 2011—

(i) in the case of fuel none of the alcohol in which consists of ethanol, 9.15 cents per gallon, and

(ii) in any other case, 11.3 cents per gallon, and

(B) after September 30, 2011—

(i) in the case of fuel none of the alcohol in which consists of ethanol, 2.15 cents per gallon, and

(ii) in any other case, 4.3 cents per gallon.

(2) **Partially exempt methanol or ethanol fuel.** The term "partially exempt methanol or ethanol fuel" means any liquid at least 85 percent of which consists of methanol, ethanol, or other alcohol produced from natural gas.

In 2007, P.L. 110-172, Sec. 6(d)(1)(A), added a sentence at the end of para. (d)(1), effective for fuel entered, removed, or sold after 9/30/2005.

—P.L. 110-172, Sec. 6(d)(1)(C), of this Act, reads as follows:

"(C) Notwithstanding section 6430 of the Internal Revenue Code of 1986, a refund, credit, or payment may be made under subchapter B of chapter 65 of such Code for taxes imposed with respect to any liquid after September 30, 2005, and before the date of the enactment of this Act under section 4041(d)(1) or 4042 of such Code at the Leaking Underground Storage Tank Trust Fund financing rate to the extent that tax was imposed with respect to such liquid under section 4081 at the Leaking Underground Storage Tank Trust Fund financing rate."

—P.L. 110-172, Sec. 6(d)(2)(A)(i), deleted "(other than with respect to any sale for export under paragraph (3) thereof)" after "without regard to subsections (f), (g)" in para. (d)(5)... Sec. 6(d)(2)(A)(ii), added a sentence at the end of para. (d)(5), effective for fuel entered, removed, or sold after 9/30/2005.

—P.L. 110-172, Sec. 6(d)(3), added "(b)(1)(A)," after "subsections" in para. (d)(5), effective for fuel sold for use or used after 12/29/2007.

In 2006, P.L. 109-432, Sec. 208(a), substituted "January 1, 2009" for "October 1, 2007" in subpara. (b)(2)(D)... Sec. 208(b), substituted "2008" for "2007" in clause (b)(2)(C)(ii)... Sec. 208(c), substituted "Qualified methanol and ethanol fuel produced from coal" for "Qualified methanol or ethanol fuel", in the heading of subpara. (b)(2)(B), enacted 12/20/2006.

—P.L. 109-432, Sec. 420(d), Sec. 420 of this Act relating to modification of refunds for kerosene used in aviation, reads as follows:

"Sec. 420. Modification of refunds for kerosene used in aviation.

"(d) Special rule for kerosene used in aviation on a farm for farming purposes.

"(1) Refunds for purchases after December 31, 2004, and before October 1, 2005. The Secretary of the Treasury shall pay to the ultimate purchaser of any kerosene which is used in aviation on a farm for farming purposes and which was purchased after December 31, 2004, and before October 1, 2005, an amount equal to the aggregate amount of tax imposed on such fuel under section 4041 or 4081 of the Internal Revenue Code of 1986, as the case may be, reduced by any payment to the ultimate vendor under section 6427(l)(5)(C) of such Code (as in effect on the day before the date of the enactment of the Safe, Accountable, Flexible, Efficient Transportation Equity Act: a Legacy for Users).

"(2) Use on a farm for farming purposes. For purposes of paragraph (1), kerosene shall be treated as used on a farm for farming purposes if such kerosene is used for farming purposes (within the meaning of section 6420(c)(3) of the Internal Revenue Code of 1986) in carrying on a trade or business on a farm situated in the United States. For purposes of the preceding sentence, rules similar to the rules of section 6420(c)(4) of such Code shall apply.

"(3) Time for filing claims. No claim shall be allowed under paragraph (1) unless the ultimate purchaser files such claim before the date that is 3 months after the date of the enactment of this Act.

"(4) No double benefit. No amount shall be paid under paragraph (1) or section 6427(l) of the Internal Revenue Code of 1986 with respect to any kerosene described in paragraph (1) to the extent that such amount is in excess of the tax imposed on such kerosene under section 4041 or 4081 of such Code, as the case may be.

"(5) Applicable laws. For purposes of this subsection, rules similar to the rules of section 6427(j) of the Internal Revenue Code of 1986 shall apply."

—P.L. 109-280, Sec. 1207(a), deleted "and" at the end of para. (g)(3), substituted "; and" for the period at the end of para. (g)(4), and added para. (g)(5), effective 1/1/2007.

In 2005, P.L. 109-59, Sec. 11101(a)(1)(A), substituted "2011" for "2005" in subclause (a)(1)(C)(iii)(I)... Sec. 11101(a)(1)(B), substituted "2011" for "2005" in subpara. (a)(2)(B)... Sec. 11101(a)(1)(C), substituted "2011" for "2005" in para. (m)(1), effective 8/10/2005.

—P.L. 109-59, Sec. 11113(a)(1)(A), added "and" at the end of clause (a)(2)(B)(i)... Sec. 11113(a)(1)(B), deleted clauses (a)(2)(B)(ii) and (iii)... Sec. 11113(a)(1)(C), deleted "In the case of any sale or use after September 30, 2011, clause (ii) shall be applied by substituting '3.2 cents' for '13.6 cents', and clause (iii) shall be applied by substituting '2.8 cents' for '11.9 cents'." at the end of subpara. (a)(2)(B)... Sec. 11113(a)(1)(D), added clause (a)(2)(B)(ii)... Sec. 11113(a)(2)(A), substituted "18.3 cents per energy equivalent of a gallon of gasoline" for "48.54 cents per MCF (determined at standard temperature and pressure)" in subpara. (a)(3)(A)... Sec. 11113(a)(2)(B), substituted "energy equivalent of a gallon of gasoline" for "MCF" in subpara. (a)(3)(C)... Sec. 11113(a)(3), substituted "alternative fuels" for "special motor fuels" in the heading of para. (a)(2), effective for any sale or use for any period after 9/30/2006.

Prior to deletion, clauses (a)(2)(B)(ii) and (iii) read as follows:

"(ii) 13.6 cents per gallon in the case of liquefied petroleum gas, and

"(iii) 11.9 cents per gallon in the case of liquefied natural gas."

—P.L. 109-59, Sec. 11151(e)(2), substituted "section 45K(c)(3)" for "section 29(c)(3)" in clause (a)(2)(B)(ii), effective after 12/31/2005 as if included in the Energy Tax Incentives Act of 2005, P. L. 109-58.

—P.L. 109-59, Sec. 11161(b)(1)(A), substituted "any liquid for use as a fuel other than aviation gasoline" for "aviation-grade kerosene" in para. (c)(1)... Sec. 11161(b)(1)(B), substituted "liquid for use as a fuel other than aviation gasoline" for "aviation-grade kerosene" in para. (c)(2)... Sec. 11161(b)(1)(C), amended para. (c)(3)... Sec. 11161(b)(1)(D), substituted "certain liquids used as a fuel in aviation" for "aviation-grade kerosene" in the heading of subsec. (c)... Sec. 11161(b)(3)(A), deleted "This subparagraph shall not apply to aviation-grade kerosene" at the end of subpara. (a)(1)(B), effective for fuels or liquids removed, entered, or sold after 9/30/2005.

Prior to amendment, para. (c)(3) read as follows:

"(3) Rate of tax. The rate of tax imposed by this subsection shall be the rate of tax applicable under section 4081(a)(2)(A)(iv) which is in effect at the time of such sale or use."

—P.L. 109-58, Sec. 1362(b)(2)(A), added "(other than such tax at the Leaking Underground Storage Tank Trust Fund financing rate)" after "section 4081" in subparas. (a)(1)(B) and (a)(2)(A) and para. (c)(2)... Sec. 1362(b)(2)(B), deleted "or (d)(1)" after "subsection (a)" in subpara. (b)(1)(A)... Sec. 1362(b)(2)(C), added para. (d)(5), effective for fuel entered, removed, or sold after 9/30/2005.

In 2004, P.L. 108-357, Sec. 241(a)(1), amended subclauses (a)(1)(C)(ii)(I)-(III). ... Sec. 241(a)(2)(A), redesignated para. (d)(3) as (d)(4) and added para. (d)(3), effective 1/1/2005.

Prior to amendment, subclauses (a)(1)(C)(ii)(I)-(III) read as follows:

3,185

Code Sec. 4041 — Excise and miscellaneous taxes

"(I) 6.8 cents per gallon after September 30, 1993, and before October 1, 1995,
"(II) 5.55 cents per gallon after September 30, 1995, and before November 1, 1998, and
"(III) 4.3 cents per gallon after October 31, 1998."
—P.L. 108-357, Sec. 301(c)(5), substituted "coal (including peat)" for "a substance other than petroleum or natural gas" in subpar. (b)(2)(B) . . . Sec. 301(c)(6), deleted subsec. (k), effective for fuel sold or used after 12/31/2004.
Prior to deletion, subsec. (k) read as follows:
"*(k) Fuels containing alcohol.*
"(1) In general. Under regulations prescribed by the Secretary, in the case of the sale or use of any liquid at least 10 percent of which consists of alcohol (as defined in section 4081(c)(3))—
"(A) the rates under paragraphs (1) and (2) of subsection (a) shall be the comparable rates under section 4081(c), and
"(B) the rate of the tax imposed by subsection (c)(1) shall be the comparable rate under section 4091(c).
"(2) Later separation. If any person separates the liquid fuel from a mixture of the liquid fuel and alcohol to which paragraph (1) applied, such separation shall be treated as a sale of the liquid fuel. Any tax imposed on such sale shall be reduced by the amount (if any) of the tax imposed on the sale of such mixture.
"(3) Termination. Paragraph (1) shall not apply to any sale or use after September 30, 2007."
—P.L. 108-357, Sec. 853(a)(6)(A), added "This subparagraph shall not apply to aviation-grade kerosene." at the end of subpara. (a)(1)(B) . . . Sec. 853(a)(6)(B), added "and kerosene" after "diesel fuel" in the heading of para. (a)(1) . . . Sec. 853(d)(2)(A), amended subsec. (c) . . . Sec. 853(d)(2)(B), substituted "section 4081" for "section 4091" in para. (d)(2) . . . Sec. 853(d)(2)(C), deleted subsec. (e) . . . Sec. 853(d)(2)(D), deleted subsec. (i) . . . Sec. 853(d)(2)(E), amended para. (m)(1), effective for aviation-grade kerosene removed, entered, or sold after 12/31/2004.
Prior to amendment, subsec. (c) read as follows:
"*(c) Noncommercial aviation.*
"(1) Tax on nongasoline fuels where no tax imposed on fuel under section 4091. There is hereby imposed a tax upon kerosene and any other liquid (other than any product taxable under section 4081)—
"(A) sold by any person to an owner, lessee, or other operator of an aircraft, for use as a fuel in such aircraft in noncommercial aviation; or
"(B) used by any person as a fuel in an aircraft in noncommercial aviation, unless there was a taxable sale of such liquid under this section.
"The rate of the tax imposed by this paragraph shall be the rate of tax specified in section 4091(b)(1) which is in effect at the time of such sale or use. No tax shall be imposed by this paragraph on the sale or use of kerosene and any other liquid if there was a taxable sale of such liquid under section 4091.
"(2) Definition of noncommercial aviation. For purposes of this chapter, the term 'noncommercial aviation' means any use of an aircraft, other than use in a business of transporting persons or property for compensation or hire by air. The term also includes any use of an aircraft, in a business described in the preceding sentence, which is properly allocable to any transportation exempt from the taxes imposed by sections 4261 and 4271 by reason of section 4281 or 4282 or by reason of section 4261(h).
"(3) Termination. The rate of the taxes imposed by paragraph (1) shall be 4.3 cents per gallon—
"(A) after December 31, 1996, and before the date which is 7 days after the date of the enactment [2/28/97] of the Airport and Airway Trust Fund Reinstatement Act 1997, and
"(B) after September 30, 2007."
Prior to deletion, subsec. (e) read as follows:
"*(e) Additional tax.* If a liquid on which tax was imposed on the sale thereof is taxable at a higher rate under subsection (c)(1) of this section on the use thereof, there is hereby imposed a tax equal to the difference between the tax so imposed and the tax payable at such higher rate."
Prior to deletion, subsec. (i) read as follows:
"*(i) Registration.* If any liquid is sold by any person for use as a fuel in an aircraft, it shall be presumed for purposes of this section that a tax imposed by this section applies to the sale of such liquid unless the purchaser is registered in such manner (and furnishes such information in respect of the use of the liquid) as the Secretary shall by regulations provide."
Prior to amendment, para. (m)(1) read as follows:
"(1) In general. In the case of the sale or use of any partially exempt methanol or ethanol fuel—
"(A) the rate of the tax imposed by subsection (a)(2) shall be—
"(i) after September 30, 1997, and before October 1, 2005—
"(I) in the case of fuel none of the alcohol in which consists of ethanol, 9.15 cents per gallon, and
"(II) in any other case, 11.3 cents per gallon, and
"(ii) after September 30, 2005,—
"(I) in the case of fuel none of the alcohol in which consists of ethanol, 2.15 cents per gallon, and
"(II) in any other case, 4.3 cents per gallon, and
"(B) the rate of the tax imposed by subsection (c)(1) shall be the comparable rate under section 4091(c)(1)."
In 1998, P.L. 105-206, Sec. 6010(g)(1), substituted "subsection (f) or (g)" for "subsection (e) or (f)" in subsec. (l), effective 10/1/97.
In 1998, P.L. 105-178, Sec. 9002(a)(1)(A), substituted "2005" for "1999" in subclause (a)(1)(C)(iii)(I) . . . Sec. 9002(a)(1)(B), substituted "2005" for "1999" in subpara. (a)(2)(B) . . . Sec. 9002(a)(1)(C), substituted "2005" for "1999" each place it appeared in subpara. (m)(1)(A) . . . Sec. 9003(a)(1)(A), substituted "2007" for "2000" in subpara. (b)(2)(C) . . . Sec. 9003(a)(1)(B), substituted "2007" for "2000" in para. (k)(3), effective 6/9/98.
—P.L. 105-178, Sec. 9003(b)(2)(A)(i), substituted "the applicable blender rate" for "5.4 cents" in clause (b)(2)(A)(i) . . . Sec. 9003(b)(2)(A)(ii), redesignated subpara. (b)(2)(C) [as amended by Sec. 9002(a)(1)(A) of this Act, see above] as (D) and added subpara. (b)(2)(C), effective 1/1/2001.
—P.L. 105-178, Sec. 9006(a)(1), substituted "November 1, 1998" for "October 1, 1999" in subclause (a)(1)(C)(ii)(II) . . . Sec. 9006(a)(2), substituted "October 31, 1998" for "September 30, 1999" in subclause (a)(1)(C)(ii)(III), effective 6/9/98.
In 1997, P.L. 105-34, Sec. 902(b)(1)(A), substituted "or a diesel-powered train" for ", a diesel-powered train, or a diesel-powered boat" each place it appeared in subpara. (a)(1)(A) . . . Sec. 902(b)(1)(B), substituted "vehicle or train" for "vehicle, train, or boat" in subpara. (a)(1)(A) . . . Sec. 902(b)(2), deleted subpara. (a)(1)(D), effective 1/1/98.
Prior to deletion, subpara. (a)(1)(D) read as follows:
"(D) Diesel fuel used in motorboats. In the case of any sale for use, or use, of fuel in a diesel-powered motorboat—
"(i) no tax shall be imposed by subsection (a) or (d)(1) during the period beginning on the date which is 7 days after the date of the enactment of the Small Business Job Protection Act of 1996 and ending on December 31, 1997,
"(ii) effective during the period after September 30, 1999, and before January 1, 2000, the rate of tax imposed by this paragraph is 24.3 cents per gallon, and
"(iii) the termination of the tax under subsection (d) shall not occur before January 1, 2000."
—P.L. 105-34, Sec. 907(a)(1), amended para. (a)(2) . . . Sec. 907(a)(2), added "and other than liquefied natural gas" after "liquefied petroleum gas" in para. (d)(1) . . . Sec. 907(b), amended subpara. (m)(1)(A), effective 10/1/97.
Prior to amendment, para. (a)(2) read as follows:
"(2) Special motor fuels. There is hereby imposed a tax on benzol, benzene, naphtha, liquefied petroleum gas, casing head and natural gasoline, or any other liquid (other than kerosene, gas oil, or fuel oil, or any product taxable under section 4081)—
"(A) sold by any person to an owner, lessee, or other operator of a motor vehicle or motorboat for use as a fuel in such motor vehicle or motorboat, or
"(B) used by any person as a fuel in a motor vehicle or motorboat unless there was a taxable sale of such liquid under subparagraph (A).
The rate of the tax imposed by this paragraph shall be the rate of tax specified in section 4081(a)(2)(A)(i) on gasoline which is in effect at the time of such sale or use."
Prior to amendment, subpara. (m)(1)(A) read as follows:
"(A) the rate of the tax imposed by subsection (a)(2) shall be—
"(i) 11.3 cents per gallon after September 30, 1993, and before October 1, 1999, and
"(ii) 4.3 cents per gallon after September 30, 1999, and"
—P.L. 105-34, Sec. 1031(a)(3), substituted "September 30, 2007" for "September 30, 1997" in subpara. (c)(3)(B), effective 10/1/97.
—P.L. 105-34, Sec. 1032(e)(1), deleted "kerosene," after "other than" in subpara. (a)(2)(A) [as amended by Sec. 907(a)(1) of this Act, see above] . . . Sec. 1032(e)(2), substituted "kerosene and any other liquid" for "any liquid" each place it appeared in para. (c)(1), effective 7/1/98.
—P.L. 105-34, Sec. 1435(b), added "or by reason of section 4261(h)" before the period at the end of para. (c)(2), effective 10/1/97.
—P.L. 105-34, Sec. 1601(f)(4)(A)(i), added "or a fixed-wing aircraft" after "helicopter" in subsec. (l) . . . Sec. 1601(f)(4)(A)(ii), deleted "helicopter" after "for certain" in the heading of subsec. (l) . . . Sec. 1601(f)(4)(B), substituted "section 4081(a)(2)(A)(i)" for "section 4081(a)(2)(A)" in para. (a)(2) [prior to amendment by Sec. 907(a)(1) of this Act, see above], effective on the 7th calendar day after 8/20/96.
—P.L. 105-2, Sec. 2(a)(3), amended para. (c)(3), effective for periods beginning on or after the 7th calendar day after 2/28/97.
Prior to amendment, para. (c)(3) read as follows:
"(3) Termination. The taxes imposed by paragraph (1) shall apply during the period beginning on September 1, 1982, and ending on December 31, 1995, and during the period beginning on the date which is 7 calendar days after the date of the enactment of the Small business Job Protection act of 1996 and ending on December 31, 1996. The termination under the preceding sentence shall not apply to so much of the tax imposed by paragraph (1) as does not exceed 4.3 cents per gallon."
In 1996, P.L. 104-188, Sec. 1208, redesignated clauses (a)(1)(D)(i) and (ii) as clauses (a)(1)(D)(ii) and (iii), and added a new clause (a)(1)(D)(i), effective 8/20/96.
—P.L. 104-188, Sec. 1609(a)(3), added ", and during the period beginning on the date which is 7 calendar days after the date of the enactment of the Small business Job Protection act of 1996 and ending on December 31, 1996" after "December 31, 1995" in para. (c)(5) [redesignated as para. (c)(3) by Sec. 1609(g)(3)(A) of this Act, see below.] . . . Sec. 1609(g)(3)(A), deleted paras. (c)(2) and (3) and redesignated paras. (c)(4) and (5) as paras. (c)(2) and (3) . . . Sec. 1609(g)(3)(B), substituted "paragraph (1)" for "paragraphs (1) and (2)" in para. (c)(3) [as redesignated by Sec. 1609(g)(3)(A) of this Act, see above] . . . Sec. 1609(g)(4)(A), added "and" to the end of subpara. (k)(1)(A), substituted a period for ", and" at the end of subpara. (k)(1)(B), and deleted subpara. (k)(1)(C), effective on the 7th calendar day after 8/20/96.
Prior to deletion, paras. (c)(2) and (3) read as follows:
"(2) Gasoline. There is hereby imposed a tax (at the rate specified in paragraph (3)) upon gasoline (as defined in section 4083)—

3,186

Excise and miscellaneous taxes — Code Sec. 4041

"(A) sold by any person to an owner, lessee, or other operator of an aircraft, for use as a fuel in such aircraft in noncommercial aviation; or

"(B) used by any person as a fuel in an aircraft in noncommercial aviation, unless there was a taxable sale of such product under subparagraph (A).

The tax imposed by this paragraph shall be in addition to any tax imposed under section 4081.

"(3) Rate of tax. The rate of tax imposed by paragraph (2) on any gasoline is 1 cent per gallon."

Prior to deletion, subpara. (k)(1)(C) read as follows:

"(C) no tax shall be imposed by subsection (c)(2)."

In 1993, P.L. 103-66, Sec. 13163(a)(2)(A), substituted "diesel-powered highway vehicle or diesel-powered boat" for "diesel-powered highway vehicle" each place it appeared in para. (a)(1) . . . Sec. 13163(a)(2)(B), substituted "such vehicle or boat" for "such vehicle" in para. (a)(1), effective 1/1/94.
—P.L. 103-66, Sec. 13241(b)(2)(A), amended para. (c)(3) . . . Sec. 13241(b)(2)(B)(iii), deleted "of 17.5 cents a gallon" after "imposed a tax" and added the sentence before the last sentence of para. (c)(1) . . . Sec. 13241(c), amended subpara. (m)(1)(A) . . . Sec. 13241(e)(1), added para. (a)(3) . . . Sec. 13241(e)(2), substituted "subsection (a)(1) or (2)" for "subsection (a)" the second place it appeared in para. (d)(1) . . . Sec. 13241(f)(1), deleted para. (f)(3) . . . Sec. 13242(f)(2), deleted the last sentence of subsec. (g), effective 10/1/93.

Prior to amendment, para. (c)(3) read as follows:

"(3) Rate of tax. The rate of tax imposed by paragraph (2) on any gasoline is the excess of 15 cents a gallon over the sum of the Highway Trust Fund financing rate plus the deficit reduction rate at which tax was imposed on such gasoline under section 4081."

Prior to deletion, para. (f)(3) read as follows:

"(3) Termination. Except with respect to the taxes imposed by subsection (d), paragraph (1) shall not apply on and after October 1, 1999."

Prior to deletion, the last sentence of subsec. (g) read as follows:

"Except with respect to the taxes imposed by subsection (d), paragraphs (2) and (4) shall not apply on and after October 1, 1999."

Prior to amendment, subpara. (m)(1)(A) read as follows:

"(A) under subsection (a)(2) the Highway Trust Fund financing rate shall be 5.75 cents per gallon and the deficit reduction rate shall be 1.25 cents per gallon, and"

—P.L. 103-66, Sec. 13242(d)(3), amended para. (a)(1) (as amended by Sec. 13163(a)(2)(A) and (B) of this Act) . . . Sec. 13242(d)(4)(A), deleted "or paragraph (1) of this subsection" following "under section 4081" in para. (a)(2) . . . Sec. 13242(d)(4)(B), substituted "The rate of the tax imposed by this paragraph shall be the rate of tax specified in section 4081(a)(2)(A) on gasoline which is in effect at the time of such sale or use." for "The rate of the tax imposed by this paragraph shall be the sum of the Highway Trust Fund financing rate and the deficit reduction rate in effect under section 4081 at the time of such sale or use." in para. (a)(2) . . . Sec. 13242(d)(5)(A), substituted "paragraph (1)(B), (2)(B), or (3)(A)(ii)" for "paragraph (1)(B) or (2)(B)" and inserted before the period "(if any)" in subpara. (b)(1)(B) . . . Sec. 13242(d)(5)(B), inserted "; except that such term shall not, for purposes of subsection (a)(1), include use in a diesel-powered train" before the period in subpara. (b)(1)(C) . . . Sec. 13242(d)(5)(C), deleted "Highway Trust Fund financing" before "rate applicable under" in clause (b)(2)(A)(i) . . . Sec. 13242(d)(6), substituted "The rate of the tax imposed by this paragraph shall be the rate of tax specified in section 4091(b)(1) which is in effect at the time of such sale or use." for "The rate of the tax imposed by this paragraph shall be the sum of the Airport and Airway Trust Fund financing rate and the aviation fuel deficit reduction rate in effect under section 4091 at the time of such sale or use." in the next to last sentence of para. (c)(1) (as amended by Sec. 13241(b)(2)(B)(iii) of this Act) . . . Sec. 13242(d)(7), substituted "gasoline (as defined in section 4083)" for "any product taxable under section 4081" in para. (c)(2) . . . Sec. 13242(d)(8), added the last sentence of para. (c)(5) . . . Sec. 13242(d)(9), deleted para. (d)(2) and redesignated paras. (d)(3) and (4) as paras. (d)(2) and (3) . . . Sec. 13242(d)(10), substituted "(other than gasoline (as defined in section 4083))" for "(other than any product taxable under section 4081)" in para. (d)(2) (as redesignated) . . . Sec. 13242(d)(11)(A), deleted "Highway Trust Fund financing" before "rates under paragraphs" in subpara. (k)(1)(A) . . . Sec. 13242(d)(11)(B), substituted "section 4081(c)" for "sections 4081(c) and 4091(c), as the case may be" in subpara. (k)(1)(A) . . . Sec. 13242(d)(12), substituted "4091(c)" for "4091(d)" in subpara. (k)(1)(B) . . . Sec. 13242(d)(13), amended subpara. (m)(1)(A) (as amended by Sec. 13241(c) of this Act) and subpara. (m)(1)(B), effective 1/1/94.

Prior to amendment, para. (a)(1) [as amended by Sec. 13163(a)(2)(A) and (B) of this Act, see above] read as follows:

"(1) Tax on diesel fuel where no tax imposed on fuel under section 4091. There is hereby imposed a tax on any liquid (other than any product taxable under section 4081)—

"(A) sold by any person to an owner, lessee, or other operator of a diesel-powered highway vehicle or diesel-powered boat for use as a fuel in such vehicle or boat, or

"(B) used by any person as a fuel in a diesel-powered highway vehicle or diesel-powered boat unless there was a taxable sale of such liquid under subparagraph (A).

The rate of the tax imposed by this paragraph shall be the sum of the Highway Trust Fund financing rate and the diesel fuel deficit reduction rate in effect under section 4091 at the time of such sale or use.

No tax shall be imposed by this paragraph on the sale or use of any liquid if there was a taxable sale of such liquid under section 4091."

Prior to deletion, para. (d)(2) read as follows:

"(2) Tax on diesel fuel used in trains. There is hereby imposed a tax of 0.1 cent a gallon on any liquid (other than a product taxable under section 4081)—

"(A) sold by any person to an owner, lessee, or other operator of a diesel-powered train for use as a fuel in such train, or

"(B) used by any person as a fuel in a diesel-powered train unless there was a taxable sale of such liquid under subparagraph (A).

No tax shall be imposed by this paragraph on the sale or use of any liquid if there was a taxable sale of such liquid under section 4091."

Prior to amendment, subpara. (m)(1)(A) (as amended by Sec. 13241(c) of this Act) and subpara. (m)(1)(B) read as follows:

"(A) under subsection (a)(2)—

"(i) the Highway Trust Fund financing rate shall be 5.75 cents per gallon, and

"(ii) the deficit reduction rate shall be 5.55 cents per gallon.

"(B) the rate of the tax imposed by subsection (c)(1) shall be the comparable rate under section 4091(d)(1)."

—P.L. 103-66, Sec. 13243, of this Act provides:

"Sec. 13243. Floor stocks tax.

"(a) In general. There is hereby imposed a floor stocks tax on diesel fuel held by any person on January 1, 1994, if—

"(1) no tax was imposed on such fuel under section 4041(a) or 4091 of the Internal Revenue Code of 1986 as in effect on December 31, 1993, and

"(2) tax would have been imposed by section 4081 of such Code, as amended by this Act, on any prior removal, entry, or sale of such fuel had such section 4081 applied to such fuel for periods before January 1, 1994.

"(b) Rate of tax. The rate of the tax imposed by subsection (a) shall be the amount of tax which would be imposed under section 4081 of the Internal Revenue Code of 1986 if there were a taxable sale of such fuel on such date.

"(c) Liability and payment of tax.

"(1) Liability for tax. A person holding the diesel fuel on January 1, 1994, to which the tax imposed by this section applies shall be liable for such tax.

"(2) Method of payment. The tax imposed by this section shall be paid in such manner as the Secretary shall prescribe.

"(3) Time for payment. The tax imposed by this section shall be paid on or before July 31, 1994.

"(d) Definitions. For purposes of this section—

"(1) Diesel fuel. The term 'diesel fuel' has the meaning given such term by section 4083(a) of such Code.

"(2) Secretary. The term 'Secretary' means the Secretary of the Treasury or his delegate.

"(e) Exceptions.

"(1) Persons entitled to credit or refund. The tax imposed by this section shall not apply to fuel held by any person exclusively for any use to the extent a credit or refund of the tax imposed by section 4081 is allowable for such use.

"(2) Compliance with dyeing required. Paragraph (1) shall not apply to the holder of any fuel if the holder of such fuel fails to comply with any requirement imposed by the Secretary with respect to dyeing and marking such fuel.

"(f) Other laws applicable. All provisions of law, including penalties, applicable with respect to the taxes imposed by section 4081 of such Code shall, insofar as applicable and not inconsistent with the provisions of this section, apply with respect to the floor stock taxes imposed by this section to the same extent as if such taxes were imposed by such section 4081."

In 1991, P.L. 102-240, Sec. 8002(b)(1), substituted "1999" for "1995" in para. (f)(3) . . . Sec. 8002(b)(2), substituted "1999" for "1995" in subsec. (g), effective 12/18/91.

In 1990, P.L. 101-508, Sec. 11211(a)(4)(A), substituted "15 cents" for "12 cents" in para. (c)(3) . . . Sec. 11211(a)(4)(B), substituted "the sum of the Highway Trust Fund financing rate plus the deficit reduction rate" for "the Highway Trust Fund financing rate" in para. (c)(3), effective for gasoline removed (as defined in Code Sec. 4082) after 11/30/90.
—P.L. 101-508, Sec. 11211(b)(3), deleted "of 9 cents a gallon" after "There is hereby imposed a tax" and added the last sentence, in para. (a)(2) . . . Sec. 11211(b)(6)(C)(i), deleted "of 15 cents a gallon" after "There is hereby imposed a tax" and added the sentence after subpara. (a)(1)(B) . . . Sec. 11211(b)(6)(C)(ii), deleted para. (a)(3) . . . Sec. 11211(b)(6)(D), amended clause (b)(2)(A)(i) . . . Sec. 11211(b)(6)(E)(i), amended subparas. (k)(1)(A), (k)(1)(B), and (k)(1)(C) . . . Sec. 11211(b)(6)(F), amended subpara. (m)(1)(A), effective 12/1/90.

Prior to deletion, para. (a)(3) read as follows:

"(3) Termination. On and after October 1, 1993, the taxes imposed by this subsection shall not apply."

Prior to amendment, clause (b)(2)(A)(i) read as follows:

"(i) subsection (a)(2) shall be applied by substituting '3 cents' for '9 cents', and"

Prior to amendment, subparas. (k)(1)(A), (k)(1)(B), and (k)(1)(C) read as follows:

"(A) subsection (a)(1) shall be applied by substituting '9 cents' for '15 cents,' and

"(B) subsection (a)(2) shall be applied by substituting '3 cents' for '9 cents,' and

"(C) no tax shall be imposed by subsection (c)."

Prior to amendment, subpara. (m)(1)(A) read as follows:

"(A) subsection (a)(2) shall be applied by substituting '4½ cents' for '9 cents,' and"

—P.L. 101-508, Sec. 11211(d)(1), substituted "1995" for "1993" in para. (f)(3) . . . Sec. 11211(d)(2), substituted "1995" for "1993" in last sentence of subsec. (g) . . . Sec. 11211(e)(1), substituted "2000" for "1993" in subpara. (b)(2)(C) . . . Sec. 11211(e)(2), substituted "2000" for "1993" in para. (k)(3), effective 11/5/90.
—P.L. 101-508, Sec. 11213(b)(2)(A), substituted "17.5 cents" for "14 cents" in para. (c)(1) . . . Sec. 11213(b)(2)(B)(i), amended subpara. (k)(1)(B), [as amended

3,187

by Sec. 11211(b)(6)(A)(i) of this Act] . . . Sec. 11213(b)(2)(B)(ii), amended subpara. (m)(1)(B), effective 12/1/90.

Prior to amendment, subpara. (k)(1)(B) as amended by Sec. 11211(b)(6)(A)(i) of this Act, read as follows:

"(B) no tax shall be imposed by subsection (c)(1), and"

—P.L. 101-508, Sec. 11213(b)(5), relating to floor stocks taxes, is reproduced in note following Code Sec. 4091.

—P.L. 101-508, Sec. 11213(d)(2)(B), substituted "December 31, 1995" for "December 31, 1990" in para. (c)(5) . . . Sec. 11213(e)(3), deleted para. (c)(6), effective 11/5/90.

Prior to amendment, subpara. (m)(1)(B) read as follows:

"(B) no tax shall be imposed by subsection (c)."

Prior to deletion, para. (c)(6) read as follows:

"(6) Reduction in rates of tax in certain circumstances. For reduction of rates of taxes imposed by paragraphs (1) and (2) in certain circumstances, see section 4283."

—P.L. 101-508, Sec. 11218, relating to floor stocks tax treatment of articles in foreign trade zones, is reproduced in note following Code Sec. 5001.

In 1988, P.L. 100-647, Sec. 1017(c)(3), substituted "6421(e)(2)" for "6421(d)(2)" in subpara. (b)(1)(C) . . . Sec. 1017(c)(4), amended para. (f)(3), effective for gasoline removed (as defined in Code Sec. 4082) after 12/31/87.

Prior to amendment, para. (f)(3) read as follows:

"(3) Termination. Except with respect to the taxes imposed by subsection (d), on and after October 1, 1993, paragraph (1) shall not apply."

—P.L. 100-647, Sec. 2001(d)(1)(A), changed the effective date for amendments made by Sec. 10502(b)(3) of P. L. 100-203 from "sales after 3/31/88" to "12/31/86" except that [as provided in this section] the last sentence of paragraphs (2) and (3) of section 4041(d) of the Internal Revenue Code of 1986 (as amended by such subsection (b)(3)) and the reference to section 4091 of such Code in section 9508(c)(2)(A) of such Code (as amended by such subsection (d)(1)) shall not apply to sales before April 1, 1988.

—P.L. 100-647, Sec. 2001(d)(2), added "Highway Trust Fund financing" before "rate at which" in para. (c)(3) . . . Sec. 2001(d)(3)(A), added "or (d)(1)" after "subsection (a)" in subpara. (b)(1)(A) . . . Sec. 2001(d)(3)(B), added "and by the corresponding provision of subsection (d)(1)" before the period at the end of subpara. (b)(1)(B) . . . Sec. 2001(d)(3)(C), deleted para. (b)(3) . . . Sec. 2001(d)(3)(D), amended subpara. (b)(2)(A), effective after 12/31/86.

Prior to deletion, para. (b)(3) read as follows:

"(3) Coordination with taxes imposed by subsection (d).

"(A) Off-highway business use.

"(i) In general. Except as provided in clause (ii), rules similar to the rules of paragraph (1) shall apply with respect to the taxes imposed by subsection (d).

"(ii) Limitation on exemption for off-highway business use. For purposes of subparagraph (A), paragraph (1) shall apply only with respect to off-highway business use in a vessel employed in the fisheries or in the whaling business.

"(B) Qualified methanol and ethanol fuel. In the case of qualified methanol or ethanol fuel, subsection (d) shall be applied by substituting '0.05 cents' for '0.1 cents' in paragraph (1) thereof."

Prior to amendment, subpara. (b)(2)(A) read as follows:

"(2) Qualified methanol and ethanol fuel.

"(A) In general. In the case of any qualified methanol or ethanol fuel, subsection (a)(2) shall be applied by substituting '3 cents' for '9 cents'.".

In 1987, P.L. 100-223, Sec. 402(b), substituted "December 31, 1990" for "December 31, 1987" in para. (c)(5), effective 12/30/87.

—P.L. 100-223, Sec. 404(b), amended subsec. (l), effective 10/1/88.

Prior to amendment, subsec. (l) read as follows:

"(l) Exemption for certain helicopter uses.

"No tax shall be imposed under this section on any liquid sold for use in, or used in, a helicopter for the purpose of—

"transporting individuals, equipment, or supplies in the exploration for, or the development or removal of, hard minerals, oil, or gas, or

"(A) the exploration for, or the development or removal of, hard minerals, or

"(B) the exploration for oil or gas, or

"(2) the planting, cultivation, cutting or transportation of, or caring for, trees (including logging operation),

but only if the helicopter does not take off from, or land at, a facility eligible for assistance under the Airport and Airway Development Act of 1970, or otherwise use services provided pursuant to the Airport and Airway Improvement Act of 1982 during such use."

—P.L. 100-223, Sec. 405(b)(3), added para. (c)(6), effective 12/30/87.

—P.L. 100-203, Sec. 10502(b)(1)(A), amended the heading for para. (a)(1) . . . Sec. 10502(b)(1)(B), added the last sentence to para. (a)(1) . . . Sec. 10502(b)(2)(A), amended the heading for para. (c)(1) . . . Sec. 10502(b)(2)(B), added the last sentence to para. (c)(1) . . . Sec. 10502(b)(4), deleted subsec. (n), effective for sales after 3/31/88.

Prior to amendment, the heading for para. (a)(1) read as follows:

"(1) Diesel fuel."

Prior to amendment, the heading for para. (c)(1) read as follows:

"(1) In general."

Prior to deletion, subsec. (n) read as follows:

"(n) Tax on diesel fuel for highway vehicle use may be imposed on sale to retailer. Under regulations prescribed by the Secretary—

"(1) In general. Upon the written consent of the seller, the tax imposed by subsection (a)(1)

"(A) shall apply to the sale of diesel fuel to a qualified retailer (and such sale shall be treated as described in subsection (a)(1)(A)), and

"(B) shall not apply to the sale of diesel fuel by such retailer or the use of diesel fuel described in subsection (a)(1)(B) if tax was imposed on such fuel under subparagraph (A) of this paragraph.

"(2) Liability for violation of certification. Notwithstanding paragraph (1), a qualified retailer shall be liable for the tax on liquid described in paragraph (3)(C)(ii) if such liquid is used as fuel in a diesel-powered highway vehicle.

"(3) Definitions. For purposes of this subsection—

"(A) Qualified retailer. The term 'qualified retailer' means any retailer—

"(i) who elects (under such terms and conditions as may be prescribed by the Secretary) to have paragraph (1) apply to all sales of diesel fuel to such retailer by any person, and

"(ii) who agrees to provide a written notice to such person that paragraph (1) applies to all sales of diesel fuel by such person to such retailer.

Such election and notice shall be effective for such period or periods as may be prescribed by the Secretary.

"(B) Retailer. The term 'retailer' means any person who sells diesel fuel for use as a fuel in a diesel-powered highway vehicle. Such term does not include any person who sells diesel fuel primarily for resale.

"(C) Diesel fuel.

"(i) In general. The term 'diesel fuel' means any liquid on which tax would be imposed by subsection (a)(1) if sold to a person, and for a use, described in subsection (a)(1)(A).

"(ii) Exceptions. A liquid shall not be treated as diesel fuel for purposes of this subsection if the retailer certifies in writing to the seller of such liquid that such liquid will not be sold for use as a fuel in a diesel-powered highway vehicle.

"(4) Failure to notify seller.

"(A) In general. If a qualified retailer fails to provide the notice described in paragraph (3)(A)(ii) to any seller of diesel fuel to such retailer—

"(i) paragraph (1) shall not apply to sales of diesel fuel by such seller to such retailer during the period for which such failure continues, and

"(ii) any diesel fuel sold by such seller to such retailer during such period shall be treated as sold by such retailer (in a sale described in subsection (a)(1)(A)) on the date such fuel was sold to such retailer.

"(B) Penalty. For penalty for failing to notify seller, see section 6652(j).

"(5) Exemptions not to apply.

"(A) In general. No exemption from the tax imposed by subsection (a)(1) shall apply to a sale to which paragraph (1) or (4)(A) of this subsection applies.

"(B) Cross reference. For provisions allowing a credit or refund for certain sales and uses of fuel, see sections 6416 and 6427."

—P.L. 100-203, Sec. 10502(b)(3), redesignated para. (d)(3) as (d)(4), amended paras. (d)(1) and (d)(2), and added new para. (d)(3), effective [see Sec. 2001(d)(1)(A) of P. L. 100-647, above] 12/31/86 except that the last sentence of paras. (d)(2) and (3) shall not apply to sales before 1/1/88.

Prior to amendment, paras. (d)(1) and (d)(2) read as follows:

"(1) Liquids other than gasoline, etc., used in motor vehicles, motorboats, or trains. In addition to the taxes imposed by subsection (a), there is hereby imposed a tax of 0.1 cents a gallon on benzol, benzene, naphtha, casing head and natural gasoline, or any other liquid (other than kerosene, gas oil, liquefied petroleum gas, or fuel oil, or any product taxable under section 4081)—

"(A) sold by any person to an owner, lessee, or other operator of a motor vehicle, motorboat, or train for use as a fuel in such motor vehicle, motorboat, or train, or

"(B) used by any person as a fuel in a motor vehicle, motorboat, or train unless there was a taxable sale of such liquid under subparagraph (A).

"(2) Liquids used in aviation. In addition to the taxes imposed by subsection (c) and section 4081, there is hereby imposed a tax of 0.1 cents a gallon on any liquid—

"(A) sold by any person to an owner, lessee, or other operator of an aircraft for use as a fuel in such aircraft, or

"(B) used by any person as a fuel in an aircraft unless there was a taxable sale of such liquid under subparagraph (A). The tax imposed by this paragraph shall not apply to any product taxable under section 4081 which is used as a fuel in an aircraft other than an noncommercial aviation."

—P.L. 100-17, Sec. 502(a)(1), substituted "1993" for "1988" in para. (a)(3) . . . Sec. 502(b)(1), substituted "1993" for "1988" in subpara. (b)(2)(C) . . . Sec. 502(b)(2), substituted "1993" for "1988" in para. (f)(3) . . . Sec. 502(b)(3), substituted "1993" for "1988" in subsec. (g) . . . Sec. 502(c)(1), substituted "September 30, 1993" for "December 31, 1992" in para. (k)(3), effective 4/2/87.

In 1986, P.L. 99-514, Sec. 422(a)(1), amended subpara. (b)(2)(A) . . . Sec. 422(a)(2), substituted "reduction in tax" for "exemption" in the heading for subsec. (b), effective 1/1/87.

Prior to amendment, subpara. (b)(2)(A) read as follows:

"(A) In general. No tax shall be imposed by subsection (a) on any qualified methanol or ethanol fuel."

—P.L. 99-514, Sec. 1702(a), added subsec. (n), effective for sales after the first calendar quarter beginning more than 60 days after 10/22/86.

—P.L. 99-514, Sec. 1878(c)(1), amended para. (l)(1), effective 4/1/84.

Prior to amendment, para. (l)(1) read as follows:

"(1) transporting individuals, equipment, or supplies in

"(A) the exploration for, or the development or removal of, hard minerals, or

"(B) the exploration for oil or gas, or"

—P.L. 99-499, Sec. 521(a)(2), redesignated subsec. (d) as subsec. (e) and added new subsec. (d) . . . Sec. 521(d)(1), added para. (b)(3) . . . Sec. 521(d)(2), substituted "Except with respect to the taxes imposed by subsection (d), on or after" for "On or after" in para. (f)(3) . . . Sec. 521(d)(3), substituted "Except with respect to the taxes imposed by subsection (d), paragraphs" for "Paragraphs" in the last sentence of subsec. (g), effective after 12/31/86.

Excise and miscellaneous taxes   **Code Sec. 4041**

In **1984**, P.L. 98-369, Sec. 911(a), substituted "15 cents" for "9 cents" in para. (a)(1), effective 8/1/84.
—P.L. 98-369, Sec. 912(a), amended para. (k)(1), effective on 1/1/85.
Prior to amendment, para. (k)(1) read as follows:
"(1) In general. Under regulations prescribed by the Secretary, in the case of the sale or use of any liquid fuel at least 10 percent of which consists of alcohol (as defined in section 4081(c)(3))—
"(A) subsection (a) shall be applied by substituting '4 cents' for '9 cents' each place it appears, and
"(B) no tax shall be imposed by subsection (c)."
—P.L. 98-369, Sec. 913(a), added subsec. (m), effective on 8/1/84.
—P.L. 98-369, Sec. 1018(a), amended para. (l)(1), effective on 4/1/84.
Prior to amendment, para. (l)(1) read as follows:
"(1) transporting individuals, equipment, or supplies in the exploration for, or the development or removal of, hard minerals, or"
In **1983**, P.L. 97-424, Sec. 511(a)(2), deleted subsecs. (a) and (b) and added new subsec. (a) . . . Sec. 511(b)(1), added para. (b)(2) . . . Sec. 511(c)(2), added subsec. (b) . . . Sec. 511(d)(2), amended subsec. (k) . . . Sec. 511(g)(1), amended para. (c)(3), effective 4/1/83.
Prior to deletion, subsec. (a) read as follows:
"(a) Diesel fuel. There is hereby imposed a tax of 4 cents a gallon upon any liquid (other than any product taxable under section 4081)—
"(1) sold by any person to an owner, lessee, or other operator of a diesel-powered highway vehicle, for use as a fuel in such vehicle; or
"(2) used by any person as a fuel in a diesel-powered highway vehicle unless there was a taxable sale of such liquid under paragraph (1).
In the case of liquid taxable under this subsection sold for use or used as a fuel in a diesel-powered highway vehicle (A) which (at the time of such sale or use) is not registered, and is not required to be registered, for highway use under the laws of any State or foreign country, or (B) which, in the case of a diesel-powered highway vehicle owned by the United States, is not used on the highway, the tax imposed by paragraph (1) or by paragraph (2) shall be 2 cents a gallon. If a liquid on which tax was imposed by paragraph (1) at the rate of 2 cents a gallon by reason of the preceding sentence is used as a fuel in a diesel-powered highway vehicle (A) which (at the time of such use) is registered, or is required to be registered, for highway use under the laws of any State or foreign country, or (B) which, in the case of a diesel-powered highway vehicle owned by the United States, is used on the highway, a tax of 2 cents a gallon shall be imposed under paragraph (2)."
Prior to deletion, subsec. (b) read as follows:
"(b) Special motor fuels. There is hereby imposed a tax of 4 cents a gallon upon benzol, benzene, naphtha, liquefied petroleum gas, casinghead and natural gasoline or any other liquid (other than kerosene, gas oil, or fuel oil, or any product taxable under section 4081 or subsection (a) of this section)—
"(1) sold by any person to an owner, lessee, or other operator of a motor vehicle or motorboat for use as a fuel in a motor vehicle or motorboat; or
"(2) used by any person as a fuel in a motor vehicle or motorboat unless there was a taxable sale of such liquid under paragraph (1).
In the case of a liquid taxable under this subsection sold for use, or used, in a qualified business use, the tax imposed by paragraph (1) or by paragraph (2) shall be 2 cents a gallon. If a liquid on which tax was imposed by paragraph (1) at the rate of 2 cents a gallon by reason of the preceding sentence is used otherwise than in a qualified business use, a tax of 2 cents a gallon shall be imposed under paragraph (2). For purposes of this subsection, the term 'qualified business use' has the meaning given to such term by section 6421(d)(2)."
Prior to amendment, subsec. (k) read as follows:
"(k) Fuels containing alcohol.
"(1) In general. Under regulations prescribed by the Secretary, no tax shall be imposed by this section on the sale or use of any liquid fuel at least 10 percent of which consists of alcohol (as defined by section 4081(c)(3)).
"(2) Later separation. If any person separates the liquid fuel from a mixture of the liquid fuel and alcohol on which tax was not imposed by reason of this subsection, such separation shall be treated as a sale of the liquid fuel.
"(3) Termination. Paragraph (1) shall not apply to any sale or use after December 31, 1992."
Prior to amendment, para. (c)(3) read as follows:
"(3) Rate of tax. The rate of tax imposed by paragraph (2) is 8 cents a gallon (10½ cents a gallon in the case of any gasoline with respect to which a tax is imposed under section 4081 at the rate set forth in subsection (b) thereof)."
—P.L. 97-424, Sec. 516(a)(1)(A), added para. (a)(3) . . . Sec. 516(a)(1)(B), deleted subsec. (e) . . . Sec. 516(b)(1)(A), added para. (f)(3) . . . Sec. 516(b)(1)(B), added the last sentence to subsec. (g), effective 1/6/83.
Prior to deletion, subsec. (e) read as follows:
"(e) Rate reduction. On and after October 1, 1984—
"(1) the taxes imposed by subsections (a) and (b) shall be 1½ cents a gallon, and
"(2) the second and third sentences of subsections (a) and (b) shall not apply."
In **1982**, P.L. 97-248, Sec. 279(a)(1), substituted "8 cents a gallon (10½ cents a gallon in the case of any gasoline with respect to which a tax is imposed under section 4081 at the rate set forth in subsection (b) thereof)" for "3 cents a gallon" in para. (c)(3) . . . Sec. 279(a)(2), substituted "14 cents" for "7 cents" in para. (c)(1) . . . Sec. 279(a)(3), amended para. (c)(5) . . . Sec. 279(b)(1), added subsec. (l), effective 9/1/82.
Prior to amendment, para. (c)(5) read as follows:
"(5) Termination. On and after October 1, 1980, the taxes imposed by paragraphs (1) and (2) shall not apply."

In **1980**, P.L. 96-298, Sec. 1(a), substituted "October 1, 1980" for "July 1, 1980" in para. (c)(5), effective 7/1/80.
—P.L. 96-223, Sec. 232(a)(2), added para. (k)(3).
—P.L. 96-223, Sec. 232(a)(3), extended the effective date of changes made by Sec. 221(b)(1) of P. L. 95-618 to apply to sales or use after 12/31/78 [see below].
Prior to amendment Sec. 221(b)(2) [effective date] of P. L. 95-618 read as follows:
"(2) The amendment made by paragraph (1) shall apply to sales or use after December 31, 1978, and before October 1, 1984."
—P.L. 96-223, Sec. 232(f), provides:
"(f) Study of imported alcohol. Within 180 days after the date of the enactment of this Act, the Secretary of the Treasury shall furnish to the Committee on Finance of the United States Senate and to the Committee on Ways and Means of the United States House of Representatives recommendations as to what methods, if any, may be used to limit the importing of alcohol into the United States for fuel purposes, including, but not limited to—
"(1) denial of the exemption under sections 4081(c) and 4041(k) of the Internal Revenue Code of 1954 or of the credit under section 44E of such Code to fuels produced from imported alcohol,
"(2) import quotas and duties on such alcohol, and
"(3) strict surveillance of such imports to monitor their effect on the domestic fuel alcohol industry."
—P.L. 96-223, Sec. 232(g), amended Sec. 221(c) of P. L. 95-618 [reproduced below].
Prior to amendment, Sec. 221(c) of P. L. 95-618 read as follows:
"(c) Reports.
"(1) Annual report. On April 1 of each year, beginning with April 1, 1980, and ending on April 1, 1984, the Secretary of Energy, in consultation with the Secretary of the Treasury and the Secretary of Transportation, shall submit to the Congress a report on the use of alcohol in fuel. The report shall include—
"(A) a description of the firms engaged in the alcohol fuel industry,
"(B) the amount of alcohol fuels sold in each State, and the amount of gasoline saved in each State by reason of the use of alcohol fuels,
"(C) the revenue loss resulting from the exemptions from tax for alcohol fuels under sections 4041(k) and 4081(c) of the Internal Revenue Code of 1954, and
"(D) the cost of production and the retail cost of alcohol fuels as compared to gasoline and special fuels before the imposition of any Federal excise taxes.
"(2) Report. The report submitted to the Congress on April 1, 1984, shall contain, in addition to the information required under paragraph (1), an analysis of the effect on the alcohol fuel industry of the termination of the exemption from excise taxes provided under sections 4041(k) and 4081(c) of the Internal Revenue Code of 1954."
In **1978**, P.L. 95-618, Sec. 221(b)(1), added subsec. (k), effective for sales or use after 12/31/78. Sec. 221(c) of the Act provides:
"(c) Reports. On April 1 of each year, beginning with April 1, 1981, and ending with April 1, 1992, the Secretary of Energy, in consultation with the Secretary of the Treasury and the Secretary of Transportation, shall submit to the Congress a report on the use of alcohol in fuel. The report shall include—
"(1) a description of the firms engaged in the alcohol fuel industry,
"(2) the amount of alcohol fuel sold in each State, and the amount of gasoline saved in each State by reason of the use of alcohol fuels,
"(3) the revenue loss resulting from the exemptions from tax for alcohol fuels under sections 4041(k) and 4081(c) of the Internal Revenue Code of 1954 and the credit allowable under section 44E of such Code and the impact of such revenue loss on the Highway Trust Fund, and
"(4) the cost of production and the retail cost of alcohol fuels as compared to gasoline and special fuels not mixed with alcohol."
—P.L. 95-618, Sec. 222(a)(2), amended the second and third sentences in para. (b)(2), effective for uses after 12/31/78.
Prior to amendment, the second and third sentences of para. (b)(2) read as follows:
"In the case of a liquid taxable under this subsection sold for use or used otherwise than as a fuel in a highway vehicle (A) which (at the time of such sale or use) is registered, or is required to be registered, for highway use under the laws of any State or foreign country, or (B) which, in the case of a highway vehicle owned by the United States, is used on the highway, the tax imposed by paragraph (1) or by paragraph (2) shall be 2 cents a gallon. If a liquid on which tax was imposed by paragraph (1) at the rate of 2 cents a gallon by reason of the preceding sentence is used as a fuel in a highway vehicle (A) which (at the time of such use) is registered, or is required to be registered, for highway use under the laws of any State or foreign country, or (B) which, in the case of a highway vehicle owned by the United States, is used on the highway, a tax of 2 cents a gallon shall be imposed under paragraph (2)."
—P.L. 95-618, Sec. 233(a)(3)(B), substituted "section 6421(b)(2)" for "section 6421(b)(3)" in the last sentence of subsec. (b), as amended by Sec. 222(a)(2) of this Act, effective the first day of the first calendar month which begins more than 10 days after 11/9/78.
—P.L. 95-600, Sec. 703(l)(1), substituted "term 'aircraft museum' means" for "term 'aircraft' means" in para. (h)(2) . . . Sec. 703(l)(2), redesignated subsec. (i), as added by Sec. 1904(a)(1)(C) of P. L. 94-455, as subsec. (j), effective 10/4/76.
—P.L. 95-599, Sec. 502(a)(1), substituted "1984" for "1979" in subsec. (e) . . . Sec. 502(b), amended para. (c)(3), effective 11/6/78.
Prior to amendment, para. (c)(3) read as follows:
"(3) Rate of tax. The rate of tax imposed by paragraph (2) is as follows:
3 cents a gallon for the period ending September 30, 1979.
5½ cents a gallon for the period after September 30, 1979."

3,189

In 1976, P.L. 94-530, Sec. 1(a), redesignated subsec. (h) as subsec. (i) [sic] and added new subsec. (h), effective 10/1/76.

—P.L. 94-455, Sec. 1904(a)(1)(B), amended subsec. (g)... Sec. 1904(a)(1)(C), added subsec. (i), effective 2/1/77.

Prior to amendment, subsec. (g) read as follows:

"(g) Exemption for use as supplies for vessels. Under regulations prescribed by the Secretary or his delegate, no tax shall be imposed under this section on any liquid sold for use or used as supplies for vessels or aircraft (within the meaning of section 4221(d)(3))."

—P.L. 94-455, Sec. 1906(b)(13)(A), substituted "Secretary" for "Secretary or his delegate" each place it appeared in Code Sec. 4041 effective 2/1/77.

—P.L. 94-280, Sec. 303(a)(1), and (a)(2), substituted "1979" for "1977" each place it appeared in para. (c)(3) and subsec. (e), effective 5/5/76.

In 1970, P.L. 91-605, Sec. 303(a)(1), substituted "1977" for "1972," each place it appeared in para. (c)(3)... Sec. 303(a)(2), substituted "1977" for "1972," each place it appeared in subsec. (e).

—P.L. 91-258, Sec. 202(a), amended subsecs. (c), (d), and (e), and added subsec. (f), (g), and (h)... Sec. 202(b), substituted "motor vehicle or motorboat" for "motor vehicle, motorboat, or airplane" each place it appeared and substituted "in" for "for the propulsion of", each place it appeared in subsec. (b), effective 7/1/70.

Prior to amendment, subsecs. (c), (d), and (e) read as follows:

"(c) Rate reduction. On and after October 1, 1972—

"(1) the taxes imposed by this section shall be 1½ cents a gallon; and

"(2) the second and third sentences of subsections (a) and (b) shall not apply.

"(d) Exemption for farm use.

"(1) Exemption. Under regulations prescribed by the Secretary or his delegate—

"(A) no tax shall be imposed under subsection (a)(1) or (b)(1) on the sale of any liquid sold for use on a farm for farming purposes, and

"(B) no tax shall be imposed under subsection (a)(2) or (b)(2) on the use of any liquid used on a farm for farming purposes.

"(2) use on a farm for farming purposes. For purposes of paragraph (1) of this subsection, use on a farm for farming purposes shall be determined in accordance with paragraphs (1), (2), and (3) of section 6420(c).

"(e) Exemption for use as supplies for vessels. Under regulations prescribed by the Secretary or his delegate, no tax shall be imposed under subsection (b) in the case of any fuel sold for use or used as supplies for vessels or aircraft (within the meaning of section 4221(d)(3))."

In 1965, P.L. 89-44, Sec. 802, added "casinghead and natural gasoline" in the first sentence of subsec. (b) for casinghead and natural gasoline sold or used on or after July 1, '65, except that such amendment shall not apply to a sale or use of casinghead or natural gasoline which was sold by a producer or importer before such date if tax under section 4081 of the Code (as in effect prior to the amendment made by subsection (a)(1)) was imposed with respect to such sale.

In 1961, P.L. 87-61, Sec. 201 (a),(c),(d), substituted "4 cents" for "3 cents", and substituted "a tax of 2 cents a gallon shall be imposed under paragraph (2)" for "a tax of 1 cent a gallon shall be imposed under paragraph (2)" in subsec. (a), substituted "4 cents" for "3 cents", and substituted "a tax of 2 cents a gallon shall be imposed under paragraph (2)" for "a tax of 1 cent a gallon shall be imposed under paragraph (2)" in subsec. (b) substituted "October 1, 1972" for "July 1, 1972" in subsec. (c), repealed subsec. (f), which authorized a temporary increase in the taxes under subsecs. (a) and (b), effective 7/1/61.

In 1959, P.L. 86-342, Sec. 201(b), deleted "in lieu of 3 cents a gallon" after "shall be 2 cents a gallon" in subsecs. (a) and (b) and added subsec. (f).

In 1958, P.L. 85-859, Sec. 119(b)(1), added subsec. (e), effective 1/1/59.

In 1956, P.L. 627, Sec. 202, increased the tax on diesel fuel from 2 cents a gallon to 3 cents a gallon, and added provisions which retained the tax at 2 cents a gallon for diesel fuel used in vehicles not registered, and not required to be registered, for highway use, or vehicles owned by the United States and not used on the highway in subsec. (a) ... in subsec. (b) increased the tax on special motor fuels from 2 cents a gallon to 3 cents a gallon, and added provisions which retained the tax at 2 cents a gallon for special motor fuels sold for use or used otherwise than as a fuel for the propulsion of a highway vehicle which is registered, or is required to be registered, for highway use, or vehicles owned by the United States used on the highway ... in subsec. (c) substituted "July 1, 1972" for "April 1, 1956" and provided for the nonapplication of the second and third sentences of subsec. (a) and (b), effective 7/1/56.

—P.L. 458, Sec. 2, substituted "1957" for "1956" in subsec. (c).

—P.L. 466, Sec. 3, added subsec. (d), effective 4/2/56.

In 1955, P.L. 18, Sec. 3, substituted "1956" for "1955".

Sec. 4042. Tax on fuel used in commercial transportation on inland waterways.

(a) In general.

There is hereby imposed a tax on any liquid used during any calendar quarter by any person as a fuel in a vessel in commercial waterway transportation.

(b) Amount of tax.

(1) In general. The rate of the tax imposed by subsection (a) is the sum of—

(A) the Inland Waterways Trust Fund financing rate,

(B) the Leaking Underground Storage Tank Trust Fund financing rate, and

(C) the deficit reduction rate.

(2) Rates. For purposes of paragraph (1)—

(A) The Inland Waterways Trust Fund financing rate is the rate determined in accordance with the following table:

If the use occurs:	The tax per gallon is:
Before 1990	10 cents
During 1990	11 cents
During 1991	13 cents
During 1992	15 cents
During 1993	17 cents
During 1994	19 cents
After 1994	20 cents

(B) The Leaking Underground Storage Tank Trust Fund financing rate is 0.1 cent per gallon.

(C) The deficit reduction rate is—

(i) 3.3 cents per gallon after December 31, 2004, and before July 1, 2005,

(ii) 2.3 cents per gallon after June 30, 2005, and before January 1, 2007, and

(iii) 0 after December 31, 2006.

(3) Exception for fuel on which leaking underground storage tank trust fund financing rate separately imposed. The Leaking Underground Storage Tank Trust Fund financing rate under paragraph (2)(B) shall not apply to the use of any fuel if tax was imposed with respect to such fuel under section 4041(d) or 4081 at the Leaking Underground Storage Tank Trust Fund financing rate.

(4) Termination of leaking underground storage tank trust fund financing rate. The Leaking Underground Storage Tank Trust Fund financing rate under paragraph (2)(B) shall not apply during any period during which the Leaking Underground Storage Tank Trust Fund financing rate under section 4081 does not apply.

(c) Exemptions.

(1) Deep-draft ocean-going vessels. The tax imposed by subsection (a) shall not apply with respect to any vessel designed primarily for use on the high seas which has a draft of more than 12 feet.

(2) Passenger vessels. The tax imposed by subsection (a) shall not apply with respect to any vessel used primarily for the transportation of persons.

(3) Use by State or local government in transporting property in a State or local business. Subparagraph (B) of subsection (d)(1) shall not apply with respect to use by a State or political subdivision thereof.

(4) Use in moving LASH and SEABEE ocean-going barges. The tax imposed by subsection (a) shall not apply with respect to use for movement by tug of exclusively LASH (Lighter-aboard-ship) and SEABEE ocean-going barges released by their ocean-going carriers solely to pick up or deliver international cargoes.

(d) Definitions.

For purposes of this section—

(1) Commercial waterway transportation. The term "commercial waterway transportation" means any use of a vessel on any inland or intracoastal waterway of the United States—

(A) in the business of transporting property for compensation or hire, or

Excise and miscellaneous taxes — Code Sec. 4051(b)

(B) in transporting property in the business of the owner, lessee, or operator of the vessel (other than fish or other aquatic animal life caught on the voyage).

(2) Inland or intracoastal waterway of the United States. The term "inland or intracoastal waterway of the United States" means any inland or intracoastal waterway of the United States which is described in section 206 of the Inland Waterways Revenue Act of 1978.

(3) Person. The term "person" includes the United States, a State, a political subdivision of a State, or any agency or instrumentality of any of the foregoing.

(e) Date for filing return.

The date for filing the return of the tax imposed by this section for any calendar quarter shall be the last day of the first month following such quarter.

In 2007, P.L. 110-172, Sec. 6(d)(1)(B), amended para. (b)(3), effective for fuel entered, removed, or sold after 9/30/2005. Sec. 6(d)(1)(C) of this Act, provides:

"(C) Notwithstanding section 6430 of the Internal Revenue Code of 1986, a refund, credit, or payment may be made under subchapter B of chapter 65 of such Code for taxes imposed with respect to any liquid after September 30, 2005, and before the date of the enactment of this Act under section 4041(d)(1) or 4042 of such Code at the Leaking Underground Storage Tank Trust Fund financing rate to the extent that tax was imposed with respect to such liquid under section 4081 at the Leaking Underground Storage Tank Trust Fund financing rate."

Prior to amendment, para. (b)(3) read as follows:

"(3) Exception for fuel taxed under section 4041(d). The Leaking Underground Storage Tank Trust Fund financing rate under paragraph (2)(B) shall not apply to the use of any fuel if tax under section 4041(d) was imposed on the sale of such fuel or is imposed on such use."

In 2005, P.L. 109-59, Sec. 11166(a), of this Act, read as follows:

"(a) In general. On and after the date of the enactment of this Act, the Secretary of the Treasury shall require that a vessel described in section 4042(c)(1) of the Internal Revenue Code of 1986 be considered a vessel for purposes of the registration of the operator of such vessel under section 4101 of such Code, unless such operator uses such vessel exclusively for purposes of the entry of taxable fuel."

In 2004, P.L. 108-357, Sec. 241(b), amended subpara. (b)(2)(C), effective 1/1/2005.

Prior to amendment, subpara. (b)(2)(C) read as follows:

"(C) The deficit reduction rate is 4.3 cents per gallon."

In 1993, P.L. 103-66, Sec. 13241(d)(1)(A), deleted "and" at the end of subpara. (b)(1)(A) . . . Sec. 13241(d)(1)(B), substituted ", and" for the period at the end of subpara. (b)(1)(B) . . . Sec. 13241(d)(1)(C), added subpara. (b)(1)(C) . . . Sec. 13241(d)(2), added subpara. (b)(2)(C), effective 10/1/93.

In 1988, P.L. 100-647, Sec. 2002(a)(1), provides:

"(a) Order of enactments.—

"(1) For purposes of section 4042 of the 1986 Code, the amendment made by section 521(a)(3) of the Superfund Revenue Act of 1986 [P. L. 99-499] shall be treated as enacted after the amendment made by section 1404(a) of the Harbor Maintenance Revenue Act of 1986 [P. L. 99-662]."

—P.L. 100-647, Sec. 2002(a)(2), amended para. (b)(2), effective 1/1/87.

Prior to amendment, para. (b)(2), read as follows:

"(2) Rates. For purposes of paragraph (1)—

"(A) the Inland Waterways Trust Fund financing rate is 10 cents a gallon, and

"(B) the Leaking Underground Storage Tank Trust Fund financing rate is 0.1 cents a gallon."

In 1986, P.L. 99-662, Sec. 1404(a), amended subsec. (b), effective 1/1/87.

Prior to amendment, subsec. (b) [see Sec. 2002(a)(1) of P. L. 100-647 above] read as follows:

"(b) Amount of tax.

"The tax imposed by subsection (a) shall be determined from the following table:

"If the use occurs—	The tax is—
After September 30, 1980 and before October 1, 1981	4 cents a gallon
After September 30, 1981 and before October 1, 1983	6 cents a gallon
After September 30, 1983 and before October 1, 1985	8 cents a gallon
After September 30, 1985	10 cents a gallon"

—P.L. 99-499, Sec. 521(a)(3), amended subsec. (b), effective 1/1/87.

Prior to amendment, subsec. (b) [see Sec. 2002(a)(1) of P. L. 100-647 above] read as follows:

"(b) Amount of tax.

"The tax imposed by subsection (a) shall be determined from the following table:

"If the use occurs:	The tax per gallon is:
Before 1990	10 cents
During 1990	11 cents
During 1991	13 cents
During 1992	15 cents
During 1993	17 cents
During 1994	19 cents
After 1994	20 cents."

In 1978, P.L. 95-502, Sec. 202(a), added Code Sec. 4042, effective 10/1/80.

Subchapter C.—Heavy Trucks and Trailers

Sec.

4051. Imposition of tax on heavy trucks and trailers sold at retail.

4052. Definitions and special rules.

4053. Exemptions.

In 1990, P.L. 101-508, Sec. 11221(a), redesignated Subchapter B as Subchapter C.

In 1983, P.L. 97-424, Sec. 512(b)(1), added Subchapter B.

Sec. 4051. Imposition of tax on heavy trucks and trailers sold at retail.

(a) Imposition of tax.

(1) In general. There is hereby imposed on the first retail sale of the following articles (including in each case parts or accessories sold on or in connection therewith or with the sale thereof) a tax of 12 percent of the amount for which the article is so sold:

(A) Automobile truck chassis.

(B) Automobile truck bodies.

(C) Truck trailer and semitrailer chassis.

(D) Truck trailer and semitrailer bodies.

(E) Tractors of the kind chiefly used for highway transportation in combination with a trailer or semitrailer.

(2) Exclusion for trucks weighing 33,000 pounds or less. The tax imposed by paragraph (1) shall not apply to automobile truck chassis and automobile truck bodies, suitable for use with a vehicle which has a gross vehicle weight of 33,000 pounds or less (as determined under regulations prescribed by the Secretary).

(3) Exclusion for trailers weighing 26,000 pounds or less. The tax imposed by paragraph (1) shall not apply to truck trailer and semitrailer chassis and bodies, suitable for use with a trailer or semitrailer which has a gross vehicle weight of 26,000 pounds or less (as determined under regulations prescribed by the Secretary).

(4) Exclusion for tractors weighing 19,500 pounds or less. The tax imposed by paragraph (1) shall not apply to tractors of the kind chiefly used for highway transportation in combination with a trailer or semitrailer if—

(A) such tractor has a gross vehicle weight of 19,500 pounds or less (as determined by the Secretary), and

(B) such tractor, in combination with a trailer or semitrailer, has a gross combined weight of 33,000 pounds or less (as determined by the Secretary).

(5) Sale of trucks, etc., treated as sale of chassis and body. For purposes of this subsection, a sale of an automobile truck or truck trailer or semitrailer shall be considered to be a sale of a chassis and of a body described in paragraph (1).

(b) Separate purchase of truck or trailer and parts and accessories therefor.

Under regulations prescribed by the Secretary—

(1) In general. If—

(A) the owner, lessee, or operator of any vehicle which contains an article taxable under subsection (a) installs (or causes to be installed) any part or accessory on such vehicle, and

(B) such installation is not later than the date 6 months after the date such vehicle (as it contains such article) was first placed in service,

then there is hereby imposed on such installation a tax equal to 12 percent of the price of such part or accessory and its installation.

(2) Exceptions. Paragraph (1) shall not apply if—

(A) the part or accessory installed is a replacement part or accessory, or

(B) the aggregate price of the parts and accessories (and their installation) described in paragraph (1) with respect to any vehicle does not exceed $1,000 (or such other amount or amounts as the Secretary may by regulations prescribe).

(3) Installers secondarily liable for tax. The owners of the trade or business installing the parts or accessories shall be secondarily liable for the tax imposed by paragraph (1).

(c) Termination.

On and after October 1, 2011, the taxes imposed by this section shall not apply.

(d) Credit against tax for tire tax.

If—

(1) tires are sold on or in connection with the sale of any article, and

(2) tax is imposed by this subchapter on the sale of such tires,

there shall be allowed as a credit against the tax imposed by this subchapter an amount equal to the tax (if any) imposed by section 4071 on such tires.

In 2005, P.L. 109-59, Sec. 11101(a)(1)(D), substituted "2011" for "2005" in subsec. (c), effective 8/10/2005.

—P.L. 109-59, Sec. 11112(a), redesignated para. (a)(4) as (5) and added para. (a)(4), effective for sales after 9/30/2005.

In 1998, P.L. 105-178, Sec. 9002(a)(1)(D), substituted "2005" for "1999" in subsec. (c), effective 6/9/98.

In 1997, P.L. 105-34, Sec. 1401(a), substituted "$1,000" for "$200" in subpara. (b)(2)(B), effective for installations on vehicles sold after 8/5/97.

—P.L. 105-34, Sec. 1402(a), amended subsec (e), effective 1/1/98.

Prior to amendment, subsec. (e) read as follows:

"(e) Transitional rule. In the case of any article taxable under subsection (a) on which tax was imposed under section 4061(a), subsection (a) shall be applied by substituting '2 percent' for '12 percent'."

—P.L. 105-34, Sec. 1432(a), deleted subsec. (d) and redesignated subsec. (e) [as amended by Sec. 1402(a) of this Act, see above] as subsec. (d), effective 8/5/97.

Prior to deletion, subsec. (d) read as follows:

"(d) Temporary reduction in tax on certain piggyback trailers.

"(1) In general. In the case of piggyback trailers or semitrailers sold within the 1-year period beginning on July 18, 1984, subsection (a) shall be applied by substituting '6 percent' for '12 percent'.

"(2) Piggyback trailers or semitrailers. For purposes of this subsection, the term 'piggyback trailers or semitrailers' means any trailer or semitrailer—

"(A) which is designed for use principally in connection with trailer-on-flatcar service by rail, and

"(B)(i) both the seller and the purchaser of which are registered in a manner similar to registration under section 4222, and

"(ii) with respect to which the purchaser certifies (at such time and in such form and manner as the Secretary prescribes by regulations) to the seller that such trailer or semitrailer—

"(I) will be used, or resold for use, principally in connection with such service, or

"(II) will be incorporated into an article which will be so used or resold.

"(3) Additional tax where nonqualified use. If any piggyback trailer or semitrailer was subject to tax under subsection (a) at the 6 percent rate and such trailer or semitrailer is used or resold for use other than for a use described in paragraph (2)—

"(A) such use or resale shall be treated as a sale to which subsection (a) applies,

"(B) the amount of the tax imposed under subsection (a) on such sale shall be equal to the amount of the tax which was imposed on the first retail sale, and

"(C) the person so using or reselling such trailer or semitrailer shall be liable for the tax imposed by subsection (a).

No tax shall be imposed by reason of this paragraph on any use or resale which occurs more than 6 years after the date of the first retail sale."

In 1991, P.L. 102-240, Sec. 8002(a)(1), substituted "1999" for "1995" in subsec. (c), effective 12/18/91.

In 1990, P.L. 101-508, Sec. 11211(c)(1), substituted "1995" for "1993" in subsec. (c), effective 11/5/90.

In 1987, P.L. 100-17, Sec. 502(a)(2), substituted "1993" for "1988" in subsec. (c), effective 4/2/87.

In 1986, P.L. 99-514, Sec. 1877(c), added the last sentence to para. (d)(3), effective for sales after the first calendar quarter begin. more than 60 days after 10/22/86.

—P.L. 99-514, Sec. 1899A(47), substituted "July 18, 1984" for "the date of enactment of the Tax Reform Act of 1984," in para. (d)(1), effective 10/22/86.

In 1984, P.L. 98-369, Sec. 734(g), amended para. (b)(3), effective 4/1/83.

Prior to amendment, para. (b)(3) read as follows:

"(3) Installers secondarily liable for tax. In addition to the owner, lessee, or operator of the vehicle, the owner of the trade or business installing the part or accessory shall be liable for the tax imposed by paragraph (1)."

—P.L. 98-369, Sec. 921, redesignated subsec. (d) as subsec. (e) and added new subsec. (d), effective 7/18/84.

In 1983, P.L. 97-424, Sec. 512(b)(1), added Code Sec. 4051, effective 4/1/83.

Sec. 4052. Definitions and special rules.

(a) First retail sale.

For purposes of this subchapter—

(1) In general. The term "first retail sale" means the first sale, for a purpose other than for resale or leasing in a long-term lease, after production, manufacture, or importation.

(2) Leases considered as sales. Rules similar to the rules of section 4217 shall apply.

(3) Use treated as sale.

(A) In general. If any person uses an article taxable under section 4051 before the first retail sale of such article, then such person shall be liable for tax under section 4051 in the same manner as if such article were sold at retail by him.

(B) Exemption for use in further manufacture. Subparagraph (A) shall not apply to use of an article as material in the manufacture or production of, or as a component part of, another article to be manufactured or produced by him.

(C) Computation of tax. In the case of any person made liable for tax by subparagraph (A), the tax shall be computed on the price at which similar articles are sold at retail in the ordinary course of trade, as determined by the Secretary.

(b) Determination of price.

(1) In general. In determining price for purposes of this subchapter—

(A) there shall be included any charge incident to placing the article in condition ready for use,

(B) there shall be excluded—

(i) the amount of the tax imposed by this subchapter,

(ii) if stated as a separate charge, the amount of any retail sales tax imposed by any State or political subdivision thereof or the District of Columbia, whether the liability for such tax is imposed on the vendor or vendee, and

(iii) the value of any component of such article if—

(I) such component is furnished by the first user of such article, and

(II) such component has been used before such furnishing, and

(C) the price shall be determined without regard to any trade-in.

(2) Sales not at arm's length. In the case of any article sold (otherwise than through an arm's-length transaction) at less than the fair market price, the tax under this subchapter shall be computed on the price for which similar

Excise and miscellaneous taxes   Code Sec. 4053(1)

articles are sold at retail in the ordinary course of trade, as determined by the Secretary.

(3) Long-term lease.

(A) In general. In the case of any long-term lease of an article which is treated as the first retail sale of such article, the tax under this subchapter shall be computed on a price equal to—

(i) the sum of—

(I) the price (determined under this subchapter but without regard to paragraph (4)) at which such article was sold to the lessor, and

(II) the cost of any parts and accessories installed by the lessor on such article before the first use by the lessee or leased in connection with such long-term lease, plus

(ii) an amount equal to the presumed markup percentage of the sum described in clause (i).

(B) Presumed markup percentage. For purposes of subparagraph (A), the term "presumed markup percentage" means the average markup percentage of retailers of articles of the type involved, as determined by the Secretary.

(C) Exceptions under regulations. To the extent provided in regulations prescribed by the Secretary, subparagraph (A) shall not apply to specified types of leases where its application is not necessary to carry out the purposes of this subsection.

(4) Special rule where tax paid by manufacturer, producer, or importer.

(A) In general. In any case where the manufacturer, producer, or importer of any article (or a related person) is liable for tax imposed by this subchapter with respect to such article, the tax under this subchapter shall be computed on a price equal to the sum of—

(i) the price which would (but for this paragraph) be determined under this subchapter, plus

(ii) the product of the price referred to in clause (i) and the presumed markup percentage determined under paragraph (3)(B).

(B) Related person. For purposes of this paragraph—

(i) In general. Except as provided in clause (ii), the term "related person" means any person who is a member of the same controlled group (within the meaning of section 5061(e)(3)) as the manufacturer, producer, or importer.

(ii) Exception for retail establishment. To the extent provided in regulations prescribed by the Secretary, a person shall not be treated as a related person with respect to the sale of any article if such article is sold through a permanent retail establishment in the normal course of the trade or business of being a retailer.

(c) Certain combinations not treated as manufacture.

(1) In general. For purposes of this subchapter (other than subsection (a)(3)(B)), a person shall not be treated as engaged in the manufacture of any article by reason of merely combining such article with any item listed in paragraph (2).

(2) Items. The items listed in this paragraph are any coupling device (including any fifth wheel), wrecker crane, loading and unloading equipment (including any crane, hoist, winch, or power liftgate), aerial ladder or tower, snow and ice control equipment, earthmoving, excavation and construction equipment, spreader, sleeper cab, cab shield, or wood or metal floor.

(d) Certain other rules made applicable.

Under regulations prescribed by the Secretary, rules similar to the rules of subsections (c) and (d) of section 4216 (relating to partial payments) shall apply for purposes of this subchapter.

(e) Long-term lease.

For purposes of this section, the term "long-term lease" means any lease with a term of 1 year or more. In determining a lease term for purposes of the preceding sentence, the rules of section 168(i)(3)(A) shall apply.

(f) Certain repairs and modifications not treated as manufacture.

(1) In general. An article described in section 4051(a)(1) shall not be treated as manufactured or produced solely by reason of repairs or modifications to the article (including any modification which changes the transportation function of the article or restores a wrecked article to a functional condition) if the cost of such repairs and modifications does not exceed 75 percent of the retail price of a comparable new article.

(2) Exception. Paragraph (1) shall not apply if the article (as repaired or modified) would, if new, be taxable under section 4051 and the article when new was not taxable under such section or the corresponding provision of prior law.

(g) Regulations.

The Secretary shall prescribe regulations which permit, in lieu of any other certification, persons who are purchasing articles taxable under this subchapter for resale or leasing in a long-term lease to execute a statement (made under penalties of perjury) on the sale invoice that such sale is for resale. The Secretary shall not impose any registration requirement as a condition of using such procedure.

In 1998, P.L. 105-206, Sec. 6014(c), substituted "such section" for "this section" in para. (f)(2), effective 1/1/98.

In 1997, P.L. 105-34, Sec. 1402(b), added "and" at the end of clause (b)(1)(B)(ii), deleted clause (b)(1)(B)(iii), and redesignated clause (b)(1)(B)(iv) as (b)(1)(B)(iii), effective 1/1/98.

Prior to deletion, clause (b)(1)(B)(iii) read as follows:

"(iii) the fair market value (including any tax imposed by section 4071) at retail of any tires (not including any metal rim or rim base), and"

—P.L. 105-34, Sec. 1434(a), redesignated subsec. (f) [sic (e)] as subsec. (e) and added subsec. (f)... Sec. 1434(b)(1), amended subsec. (d)... Sec. 1434(b)(2), added subsec. (g), effective 1/1/98.

Prior to amendment, subsec. (d) read as follows:

"(d) Certain other rules made applicable. Under regulations prescribed by the Secretary, rules similar to the rules of—

"(1) subsections (c) and (d) of section 4216 (relating to partial payments), and

"(2) section 4222 (relating to registration), shall apply for purposes of this subchapter."

In 1988, P.L. 100-647, Sec. 6111(a), substituted "production, manufacture" for "manufacture, production" in para. (a)(1), effective 1/1/88.

In 1987, P.L. 100-17, Sec. 505(a), substituted "other than for resale or leasing in a long-term lease" for "other than for resale" in para. (a)(1)... Sec. 505(b), added para. (b)(3)... Sec. 505(c), added subsec. (f) [sic (e)]... Sec. 506(a), added para. (b)(4), effective for articles sold by the manufacturer, producer, or importer on or after the 1st day of the 1st calendar quarter which begins more than 90 days after 4/2/87.

In 1984, P.L. 98-369, Sec. 731, deleted "and" at the end of clause (b)(1)(B)(ii) and added clause (b)(1)(B)(iv)... Sec. 735(b)(2), amended subsec. (c), effective on 4/1/83.

Prior to amendment, subsec. (c) read as follows:

"(c) Certain combinations not treated as manufacture.

"For purposes of this subchapter (other than subsection (a)(3)(B)), a person shall not be treated as engaged in the manufacture of any article by reason of merely combining such article with any equipment or other item listed in section 4063(d)."

In 1983, P.L. 97-424, Sec. 512(b)(1), added Code Sec. 4052, effective on 4/1/83.

Sec. 4053. Exemptions.

No tax shall be imposed by section 4051 on any of the following articles:

(1) Camper coaches bodies for self-propelled mobile homes. Any article designed—

3,193

(A) to be mounted or placed on automobile trucks, automobile truck chassis, or automobile chassis, and

(B) to be used primarily as living quarters or camping accommodations.

(2) Feed, seed, and fertilizer equipment. Any body primarily designed—

(A) to process or prepare seed, feed, or fertilizer for use on farms,

(B) to haul feed, seed, or fertilizer to and on farms,

(C) to spread feed, seed, or fertilizer on farms,

(D) to load or unload feed, seed, or fertilizer on farms, or

(E) for any combination of the foregoing.

(3) House trailers. Any house trailer.

(4) Ambulances, hearses, etc. Any ambulance, hearse, or combination ambulance-hearse.

(5) Concrete mixers. Any article designed—

(A) to be placed or mounted on an automobile truck chassis or truck trailer or semitrailer chassis, and

(B) to be used to process or prepare concrete.

(6) Trash containers, etc. Any box, container, receptacle, bin or other similar article—

(A) which is designed to be used as a trash container and is not designed for the transportation of freight other than trash, and

(B) which is not designed to be permanently mounted on or permanently affixed to an automobile truck chassis or body.

(7) Rail trailers and rail vans. Any chassis or body of a trailer or semitrailer which is designed for use both as a highway vehicle and a railroad car. For purposes of the preceding sentence, piggy-back trailer or semitrailer shall not be treated as designed for use as a railroad car.

(8) Mobile machinery. Any vehicle which consists of a chassis—

(A) to which there has been permanently mounted (by welding, bolting, riveting, or other means) machinery or equipment to perform a construction, manufacturing, processing, farming, mining, drilling, timbering, or similar operation if the operation of the machinery or equipment is unrelated to transportation on or off the public highways,

(B) which has been specially designed to serve only as a mobile carriage and mount (and a power source, where applicable) for the particular machinery or equipment involved, whether or not such machinery or equipment is in operation, and

(C) which, by reason of such special design, could not, without substantial structural modification, be used as a component of a vehicle designed to perform a function of transporting any load other than that particular machinery or equipment or similar machinery or equipment requiring such a specially designed chassis.

(9) Idling reduction device. Any device or system of devices which—

(A) is designed to provide to a vehicle those services (such as heat, air conditioning, or electricity) that would otherwise require the operation of the main drive engine while the vehicle is temporarily parked or remains stationary using one or more devices affixed to a tractor, and

(B) is determined by the Administrator of the Environmental Protection Agency, in consultation with the Secretary of Energy and the Secretary of Transportation, to reduce idling of such vehicle at a motor vehicle rest stop or other location where such vehicles are temporarily parked or remain stationary.

(10) Advanced insulation. Any insulation that has an R value of not less than R35 per inch.

In **2008,** P.L. 110-343, Sec. 206(a)DivB, added paras. (9) and (10), effective for sales or installations after 10/3/2008.

In **2004,** P.L. 108-357, Sec. 851(a)(1), added para. (8), effective on the day after 10/22/2004.

In **1984,** P.L. 98-369, Sec. 735(b)(1), amended Code Sec. 4053, effective 4/1/83. Prior to amendment, Code Sec. 4053 read as follows:

"Sec. 4053. Exemptions.

"(a) *Exemption of specified articles.*

"No tax shall be imposed under section 4051 on any article specified in subsection (a) of section 4063.

"(b) *Certain exemptions made applicable.*

"The exemptions provided by section 4221(a) are hereby extended to the tax imposed by section 4051."

In **1983,** P.L. 97-424, Sec. 512(b)(1), added Code Sec. 4053, effective 4/1/83.

CHAPTER 32.—MANUFACTURERS EXCISE TAXES

Subchapter

A. Automotive and related items.
B. Coal.
C. Certain vaccines.
D. Recreational equipment.
E. Medical Devices.
F. Special provisions applicable to manufacturers tax.
G. Exemptions, registration, etc.

In **2010,** P.L. 111-152, Sec. 1405(a)(2), added subchapter E.
In **1978,** P.L. 95-227, Sec. 2(c), added subchapter B.
In **1965,** deleted subchapters B, C and E dealing with household type equipment, entertainment equipment and other items.

Subchapter A.—Automotive and Related Items

Part

I. Gas guzzlers.
II. Tires.
III. Petroleum products.

In **1984,** P.L. 98-369, Sec. 735(a)(3), amended the heading of Part I. Prior to amendment, Part I read as follows.
"I. Motor vehicles."
—P.L. 98-369, Sec. 735(c)(5)(B), deleted "and tubes" from the end of the item for Part II.

PART I.—GAS GUZZLERS

Sec.
4061. Repealed [Imposition of tax.]
4062. Repealed [Articles classified as parts.]
4063. Repealed [Exemptions.]
4064. Gas guzzlers tax.

In **1984,** P.L. 98-369, Sec. 735(a)(2), amended the part heading and the items for Code Secs. 4061–4064.
Prior to amendment, Part I read as follows:
"PART I.—MOTOR VEHICLES
"4061. Imposition of tax.
"4062. Articles classified as parts.
"4063. Exemptions.
"4064. Gas guzzler tax."
In **1978,** P.L. 95-618, Sec. 201(f), added item 4064.
In **1971,** P.L. 92-178, Sec. 401(g)(2), substituted new item 4062 which formerly read "Definitions."

Sec. 4061. Repealed.

In **1984,** P.L. 98-369, Sec. 735(a)(1), repealed Code Sec. 4061, effective 1/7/83. Prior to repeal, Code Sec. 4061 read as follows:
"Sec. 4061. Imposition of tax.
"(a) Trucks, buses, tractors, etc.

"(1) Tax imposed. There is hereby imposed upon the following articles (including in each case parts or accessories therefor sold on or in connection therewith or with the sale thereof) sold by the manufacturer, producer, or importer a tax of 10 percent of the price for which so sold, except that on and after October 1, 1984, the rate shall be 5 percent —
"Automobile truck chassis.
"Automobile truck bodies.
"Automobile bus chassis.
"Automobile bus bodies.
"Truck and bus trailer and semitrailer chassis.
"Truck and bus trailer and semitrailer bodies.
Tractors of the kind chiefly used for highway transportation in combination with a trailer or semitrailer.
"A sale of an automobile truck, bus, truck or bus trailer or semitrailer shall, for the purposes of this subsection, be considered to be a sale of a chassis and of a body enumerated in this subsection.
"(2) Exclusion for trucks with gross vehicle weight of 33,000 pounds or less, and certain trailers.
"(A) The tax imposed by paragraph (1) shall not apply to automobile truck chassis and automobile truck bodies, suitable for use with a vehicle which has a gross vehicle weight of 33,000 pounds or less (as determined under regulations prescribed by the Secretary).
"(B) The tax imposed by paragraph (1) shall not apply to truck trailer and semitrailer chassis and bodies, suitable for use with a trailer or semitrailer which has a gross vehicle weight of 26,000 pounds or less (as determined under regulations prescribed by the Secretary).
"(b) Parts and accessories.
"(1) Except as provided in paragraph (2), there is hereby imposed upon parts or accessories (other than tires and inner tubes) for any of the articles enumerated in subsection (a)(1) sold by the manufacturer, producer, or importer a tax equivalent to 8 percent of the price for which so sold, except that on and after October 1, 1984, the rate shall be 5 percent.
"(2) No tax shall be imposed under this subsection upon any part or accessory which is suitable for use (and ordinarily is used) on or in connection with, or as a component part of, any chassis or body for a passenger automobile, any chassis or body for a trailer or semitrailer suitable for use in connection with a passenger automobile, or a house trailer.
"(c) Termination.
"(1) Tax on parts and accessories. On and after the day after the date of the enactment of this subsection, the tax imposed by subsection (b) shall not apply.
"(2) Tax on trucks. On and after April 1, 1983, the tax imposed by subsection (a) shall not apply."
In 1983, P.L. 97-424, Sec. 512(a)(1), amended para. (a)(2) . . . Sec. 512(a)(2), added subsec. (c), effective 1/7/83.
Prior to amendment, para. (a)(2) read as follows:
"(2) Exclusion for light-duty trucks, etc. The tax imposed by paragraph (1) shall not apply to a sale by the manufacturer, producer, or importer of the following articles suitable for use with a vehicle having a gross vehicle weight of 10,000 pounds or less (as determined under regulations prescribed by the Secretary) —
"Automobile truck chassis.
"Automobile truck bodies.
"Automobile bus chassis.
"Automobile bus bodies.
"Truck trailer and semitrailer chassis and bodies, suitable for use with a trailer or semitrailer having a gross vehicle weight of 10,000 pounds or less (as so determined)."
In 1978, P.L. 95-599, Sec. 502(a)(2), and (3), substituted "1984" for "1979" in paras. (a)(1) and (b)(1), effective 11/6/78.
In 1976, P.L. 94-455, Sec. 1906(b)(13)(A), substituted "Secretary" for "Secretary or his delegate" in para (a)(2), effective 2/1/77.
—P.L. 94-280, Sec. 303(a)(3), and (a)(4), substituted "1979" for "1977" in paras. (a)(1) and (b)(1), effective 5/5/76.
In 1971, P.L. 92-178, Sec. 401(a)(1), amended subsec. (a), effective for articles sold on or after 12/10/71, except as provided in Sec. 401(h)(2) and (3) of this Act, which reads:
"(2) For purposes of paragraph (1), an article shall not be considered sold before the day after the date of the enactment of this Act [12/10/71] unless possession or right to possession passes to the purchaser before such day.
"(3) In the case of —
"(A) a lease,
"(B) a contract for the sale of an article where it is provided that the price shall be paid by installments and title to the article sold does not pass until a future date notwithstanding partial payment of installments,
"(C) a conditional sale, or
"(D) a chattel mortgage arrangement wherein it is provided that the sale price shall be paid in installments,
entered into on or before the date of the enactment of this Act [12/10/71], payments made after such date with respect to the article leased or sold shall, for purposes of this subsection, be considered as payments made with respect to an article sold after such date, if the lessor or vendor establishes that the amount of payments payable after such date with respect to such article has been reduced by an amount equal to that portion of the tax applicable with respect to the lease or sale of such article which is due and payable after such date. If the lessor or vendor does not establish that the payments have been so reduced, they shall be treated as payments made in respect of an article sold before the day after the date of the enactment of this Act [12/10/71]."
Prior to amendment, subsec. (a) read as follows:

"(a) Automobiles.
"There is hereby imposed upon the following articles (including in each case parts or accessories therefor sold on or in connection therewith or with the sale thereof) sold by the manufacturer, producer, or importer a tax equivalent to the specified percent of the price for which so sold:
"(1) Articles taxable at 10 percent, except that on and after October 1, 1977, the rate shall be 5 percent —
"Automobile truck chassis.
"Automobile truck bodies.
"Automobile bus chassis.
"Automobile bus bodies.
"Truck and bus trailer and semitrailer chassis.
"Truck and bus trailer and semitrailer bodies.
"Tractors of the kind chiefly used for highway transportation combination with a trailer or semitrailer.
A sale of an automobile truck, bus, truck or bus trailer or semitrailer shall, for the purposes of this paragraph, be considered to be a sale of chassis and of a body enumerated in this paragraph.
"(2)(A) Articles enumerated in subparagraph (B) are taxable at whichever of the following rates is applicable:

"If the article is sold —	The tax rate is —
"Before January 1, 1973	7 percent
"During 1973	6 percent
"During 1974, 1975, 1976, or 1977	5 percent
"During 1978	4 percent
"During 1979	3 percent
"During 1980	2 percent
"During 1981	1 percent

"The tax imposed by this subsection shall not apply with respect to articles enumerated in subparagraph (B) which are sold by the manufacturer, producer, or importer after December 31, 1981.
"(B) The articles to which subparagraph (A) applies are:
Automobile chassis and bodies other than those taxable under paragraph (1).
Chassis and bodies for trailers and semi-trailers (other than house trailers) suitable for use in connection with passenger automobiles.
A sale of an automobile, or of a trailer or semi-trailer suitable for use in connection with a passenger automobile, shall, for the purposes of this paragraph, be considered to be a sale of a chassis and of a body enumerated in this subparagraph."
—P.L. 92-178, Sec. 401(c), provides as follows:
"(c) Refunds with respect to certain consumer purchases.
"(1) In general. — Except as otherwise provided in paragraph (2), where —
"(A) after August 15, 1971, with respect to any article which was subject to the tax imposed by section 4061(a)(2) of the Internal Revenue Code of 1954 (as in effect on the day before the date of the enactment of this Act), or
"(B) after September 22, 1971, with respect to any article which was subject to the tax imposed by section 4061(a)(1) of such Code (as in effect on the day before the date of the enactment of this Act),
and on or before such date of enactment, a tax-repealed article (as defined in subsection (e)) has been sold to an ultimate purchaser, there shall be credited or refunded (without interest) to the manufacturer, producer, or importer of such article an amount equal to the tax paid by such manufacturer, producer, or importer on his sale of the article.
"(2) Limitation on eligibility for credit or refund. — No manufacturer, producer, or importer shall be entitled to a credit or refund under paragraph (1) with respect to an article unless —
"(A) he has in his possession such evidence of the sale of the article to an ultimate purchaser, and of the reimbursement of the tax to such purchaser, as may be required by regulations prescribed by the Secretary of the Treasury or his delegate under this subsection;
"(B) claim for such credit or refund is filed with the Secretary of the Treasury or his delegate before the first day of the 10th calendar month beginning after the day after the date of the enactment of this Act based upon information submitted to the manufacturer, producer, or importer before the first day of the 7th calendar month beginning after the day after the date of the enactment of this Act by the person who sold the article (in respect of which the credit or refund is claimed) to the ultimate purchaser; and
"(C) on or before the first day of such 10th calendar month reimbursement has been made to the ultimate purchaser in an amount equal to the tax paid on the article.
"(3) Other laws applicable. — All provisions of law, including penalties, applicable with respect to the taxes imposed by section 4061(a) of the Internal Revenue Code of 1954 shall, insofar as applicable and not inconsistent with paragraph (1) or (2) of this subsection, apply in respect of the credits and refunds provided for in paragraph (1) to the same extent as if the credits or refunds constituted overpayments of the tax."
—P.L. 92-178, Sec. 401(e), provides as follows:
"(e) Definitions.
"For purposes of this section —
"(1) The term 'dealer' includes a wholesaler jobber, distributor, or retailer.
"(2) An article shall be considered as 'held by a dealer' if title thereto has passed to such dealer (whether or not delivery to him has been made) and if for purposes of consumption title to such article or possession thereof has not at any time been transferred to any person other than a dealer.
"(3) The term 'tax-repealed article' means an article on which a tax was imposed by section 4061(a) of the Internal Revenue Code of 1954 as in effect on the

day before the date of the enactment of this Act [date of enactment is 12/10/71] and is not imposed (without regard to the amendment made by paragraph (2) of subsection (a) of this section) under such section 4061(a) as in effect on the day after the date of the enactment of this Act [date of enactment is 12/10/71]."

—P.L. 92-178, Sec. 401(g)(1), substituted "any chassis or body for a passenger automobile, any chassis or body for a trailer or semitrailer suitable for use in connection with a passenger automobile, or a house trailer" for "any article enumerated in subsection (a)(2) or a house trailer" in para. (b)(2), effective for articles sold on or after 12/10/71.

—P.L. 91-678, Sec. 1, of this Act provides:

"(a) where before January 1, 1970, and after June 30, 1968, any cement mixer subject to the tax imposed by section 4061 of the Internal Revenue Code of 1954 during such period, had been sold by the manufacturer, producer, or importer, and on January 1, 1970, was held by a dealer and had not been used and was intended for sale, there shall be credited or refunded (without interest) to the manufacturer, producer, or importer an amount equal to the tax paid by the manufacturer, producer, or importer on his sale of the cement mixer, if—

"(1) claim for such credit or refund is filed with the Secretary of the Treasury or his delegate on or before the last day of the ninth calendar month beginning after the date of enactment of this Act, based upon a request submitted to the manufacturer, producer, or importer on or before the last day of the sixth calendar month beginning after the date of enactment of this Act, by the dealer who held the cement mixer in respect of which the credit or refund is claimed; and

"(2) on or before the last day of the ninth calendar month beginning after the date of enactment of this Act, reimbursement has been made to the dealer by the manufacturer, producer, or importer for the tax on the cement mixer or written consent has been obtained from the dealer to allowance of the credit or refund.

"(b) For the purposes of this section—

"(1) The term 'cement mixer' means—

"(A) any article designed (i) to be placed or mounted on an automobile truck chassis or truck trailer or semitrailer chassis and (ii) to be used to process or prepare concrete, and

"(B) parts or accessories designed primarily for use on or in connection with an article described in subparagraph (A).

"(2) The term 'dealer' includes a wholesaler, jobber, distributor, or retailer.

"(3) A cement mixer shall be considered as 'held by a dealer' if title thereto has passed to the dealer (whether or not delivery to him has been made), and if for purposes of consumption title to the cement mixer or possession thereof had not at any time prior to January 1, 1970, been transferred to any person other than a dealer. For purposes of subsection (a) and notwithstanding the preceding sentence, a cement mixer shall be considered as 'held by a dealer' and not to have been used, although possession of such cement mixer has been transferred to another person, if such cement mixer is returned to the dealer in a transaction under which any amount paid or deposited by the transferee for such cement mixer is refunded to him (other than amounts retained by the dealer to cover damage to the cement mixer). Moreover, such a cement mixer shall be considered as held by a dealer on January 1, 1970, even though it was in the possession of the transferee on such day, if it was returned to the dealer (in a transaction described in the preceding sentence) before January 31, 1970.

"(c) No manufacturer, producer, or importer shall be entitled to credit or refund under subsection (a) unless he has in his possession such evidence of the inventories with respect to which the credit or refund is claimed as may be required by regulations prescribed by the Secretary of the Treasury or his delegate under this subsection.

"(d) All provisions of law, including penalties, applicable in respect of the taxes imposed by section 4061 of such Code shall, insofar as applicable and not inconsistent with subsections (a), (b), and (c) of this section, apply in respect of the credits and refunds provided for in subsection (a) to the same extent as if the credits or refunds constituted overpayments of the taxes."

In 1970, P.L. 91-605, Sec. 303(a)(3), and (a)(4), substituted "1977" for "1972" in paras. (a)(1) and (b)(1), effective 12/31/70.

—P.L. 91-614, Sec. 201(a)(1), amended the table and substituted "1981" for "1973" in subpara. (a)(2)(A), effective 12/31/70.

Prior to amendment, the table read as follows:

"If the article is sold—	The tax rate is—
Before January 1, 1971	7 percent
During 1971	5 percent
During 1972	3 percent
During 1973	1 percent"

In 1969, P.L. 91-172, Sec. 702(a)(1), amended subsec. (a)(2)(A), effective 12/30/69.

Prior to amendment, subsec. (a)(2)(A) read as follows:

"(2)(A) Articles enumerated in subparagraph (B) are taxable at whichever of the following rates is applicable:

"If the article is sold—	The tax rate is—
Before January 1, 1970	7 percent
During 1970	5 percent
During 1971	3 percent
During 1972	1 percent

The tax imposed by this subsection shall not apply with respect to articles enumerated in subparagraph (B) which are sold by the manufacturer, producer, or importer after December 31, 1972."

In 1968, P.L. 90-364, Sec. 105, amended subpara. (a)(2)(A) by changing the tax rates, effective 4/30/68. Before amendment, articles sold between 3/15/66 and 4/30/68 were taxed at 7%, articles sold between 5/1/68 and 12/31/68 were taxed at 2%, and articles sold after 12/31/68 were taxed at 1%.

—P.L. 90-285, Sec. 1(a)(1), substituted "April 30, 1968" for "March 31, 1968" in subpara. (a)(2)(A), and substituted "May 1, 1968" for "April 1, 1968", effective 3/31/68.

In 1966, P.L. 89-368, Sec. 201, amended subpara. (a)(2)(A), effective for articles sold after 3/15/66.

Prior to amendment, subpara. (a)(2)(A) read as follows:

"(2)(A) Articles enumerated in subparagraph (B) are taxable at whichever of the following rates is applicable:

"10 percent for the period ending on the date of the enactment of the Excise Tax Reduction Act of 1965 [6/21/65].

"7 percent for the period beginning with the day after the date of enactment of the Excise Tax Reduction Act of 1965 [6/22/65] through December 31, 1965.

"6 percent for the period January 1, 1966, through December 31, 1966.

"4 percent for the period January 1, 1967, through December 31, 1967.

"2 percent for the period January 1, 1968, through December 31, 1968.

"1 percent for the period after December 31, 1968.

"(B) The articles to which subparagraph (A) applies are:

"Automobile chassis and bodies other than those taxable under paragraph (1).

"Chassis and bodies for trailers and semitrailers (other than house trailers) suitable for use in connection with passenger automobiles.

A sale of an automobile, or of a trailer or semitrailer suitable for use in connection with a passenger automobile, shall, for the purposes of this paragraph, be considered to be a sale of a chassis and of a body enumerated in this subparagraph."

In 1965, P.L. 89-44, Sec. 201(a), amended subsec. (a), effective 6/21/65.

Prior to amendment, subsec. (a) read as follows:

"(a) Automobiles.

"There is hereby imposed upon the following articles (including in each case parts or accessories therefor sold on or in connection therewith or with the sale thereof) sold by the manufacturer, producer, or importer a tax equivalent to the specified percent of the price for which so sold:

"(1) Articles taxable at 10 percent, except that on and after October 1, 1972, the rate shall be 5 percent—

"Automobile truck chassis.

"Automobile truck bodies.

"Automobile bus chassis.

"Automobile bus bodies.

"Truck and bus trailer and semitrailer chassis.

"Truck and bus trailer and semitrailer bodies.

"Tractors of the kind chiefly used for highway transportation in combination with a trailer or semitrailer.

"A sale of an automobile truck, bus, truck or bus trailer or semitrailer shall, for the purposes of this paragraph, be considered to be a sale of the chassis and of the body.

"(2) Articles taxable at 10 percent except that on and after July 1, 1965, the rate shall be 7 percent—

"Automobile chassis and bodies other than those taxable under paragraph (1).

"Chassis and bodies for trailers and semitrailers (other than house trailers) suitable for use in connection with passenger automobiles.

"A sale of an automobile, trailer, or semitrailer shall, for the purposes of this paragraph, be considered to be a sale of the chassis and of the body."

—P.L. 89-44, Sec. 201(b)(2), amended subsec. (b), effective for articles sold after 12/31/65. Sec. 701(a)(3) of this Act, provides:

"(3) Installment sales, etc. For purposes of paragraphs (1) and (2), an article shall not be considered sold before the date of the enactment of this Act [6/21/65] or before January 1, 1966, as the case may be, unless possession or right to possession passes to the purchaser before such day or date. In the case of—

"(A) a lease,

"(B) a contract for the sale of an article where it is provided that the price shall be paid by installments and title to the article sold does not pass until a future date notwithstanding partial payment by installments,

"(C) a conditional sale, or

"(D) a chattel mortgage arrangement wherein it is provided that the sale price shall be paid in installments,

entered into before such day or date, payments made on or after such day or date with respect to the article leased or sold shall, for purposes of this subsection, be considered as payments made with respect to an article sold on or after such day or such date, if the lessor or vendor establishes that the amount of payments payable on or after such day or such date with respect to such article has been reduced by an amount equal to the tax reduction applicable with respect to the lease or sale of such article."

Prior to amendment, subsec. (b) read as follows:

"(b) Parts and accessories.

"There is hereby imposed upon parts or accessories (other than tires and inner tubes and other than automobile radio and television receiving sets) for any of the articles enumerated in subsection (a) sold by the manufacturer, producer, or importer a tax equivalent to 8 percent of the price for which so sold, except that on and after July 1, 1965, the rate shall be 5 percent."

In 1964, P.L. 88-348, Sec. 2(a)(1), substituted "July 1, 1965" for "July 1, 1964" each place it appeared, effective 7/17/64.

In 1963, P.L. 88-52, Sec. 3(a)(1), substituted "July 1, 1964" for "July 1, 1963" each place it appeared, effective 6/29/63.

Excise and miscellaneous taxes   Code Sec. 4063

In 1962, P.L. 87-508, Sec. 3(a)(1), substituted "July 1, 1963" for "July 1, 1962" each place it appeared, effective 6/28/62.
In 1961, P.L. 87-72, Sec. 3(a)(1), substituted "July 1, 1962" for "July 1, 1961" each place it appeared, effective 6/30/61.
—P.L. 87-61, Sec. 204, substituted "October 1, 1972" for "July 1, 1972" in subsec. (a)(1), effective 6/29/61.
In 1960, P.L. 86-562, Sec. 202(a)(1), substituted "July 1, 1961" for "July 1, 1960" each place it appeared, effective 6/30/60.
In 1959, P.L. 86-75, Sec. 3(a)(1), substituted "July 1, 1960" for "July 1, 1959" each place it appeared, effective 6/30/59.
In 1958, P.L. 85-475, Sec. 3(a)(1), substituted "July 1, 1959" for "July 1, 1958" each place it appeared, effective 6/30/58.
In 1957, P.L. 85-12, Sec. 3(a)(1), substituted "July 1, 1958" for "April 1, 1957" each place it appeared, effective 3/29/57.
In 1956, P.L. 627, Sec. 203, substituted "Articles taxable at 10 percent, except that on and after July 1, 1972, the rate shall be 5 percent" for "Articles taxable at 8 percent except that on and after April 1, 1956, the rate shall be 5 percent." in para. (a)(1), effective 1/1/56.
—P.L. 458, Sec. 3(a)(1), substituted "April 1, 1957" for "April 1, 1956" each place it appeared, effective 3/29/57.
In 1955, P.L. 379, Sec. [1], deleted "Motorcycles" in para. (a)(2), effective for articles sold after 8/31/55.
—P.L. 18, Sec. 3(a)(2), substituted "April 1, 1956" for "April 1, 1955" each place it appeared, effective 3/30/55.

Sec. 4062. Repealed.

In 1984, P.L. 98-369, Sec. 735(a)(1), repealed Code Sec. 4062, effective 1/7/83. Prior to repeal, Code Sec. 4062 read as follows:
"SEC. 4062. ARTICLES CLASSIFIED AS PARTS.
"For the purposes of section 4061, spark plugs, storage batteries, leaf springs, coils, timers, and tire chains, which are suitable for use on or in connection with, or as component parts of, any of the articles enumerated in section 4061(a), shall be considered parts or accessories for such articles, whether or not primarily adapted for such use."
In 1971, P.L. 92-178, Sec. 401(g)(2), amended Code Sec. 4062, effective for articles sold on or after 12/10/71. For special rules, see Sec. 401(h) of this Act reproduced in note following Code Sec. 4061.
Prior to amendment, Code Sec. 4062 read as follows:
"SEC. 4062. DEFINITIONS.
"(a) Certain articles considered as parts.
"For the purposes of section 4061, spark plugs, storage batteries, leaf springs, coils, timers, and tire chains, which are suitable for use on or in connection with, or as component parts of, any of the articles enumerated in section 4061(a), shall be considered parts or accessories for such articles, whether or not primarily adapted for such use.
"(b) Ambulances, hearses, etc.
"For purposes of section 4061(a), a sale of an ambulance, hearse, or combination ambulance-hearse shall be considered to be a sale of an automobile chassis and an automobile body enumerated in subparagraph (B) of section 4061(a)(2)."
In 1966, P.L. 89-809, Sec. 212, added subsec. (b), effective for articles sold after 11/13/66.
In 1964, P.L. 88-653, Sec. 5(b), repealed subsec. (b), effective for articles sold on or after the first day of the first calendar quarter which begins after 10/13/64.
Prior to amendment, subsec. (b) read as follows:
"(b) Sale price of rebuilt parts. In determining the sale price of a rebuilt automobile part or accessory there shall be excluded from the price, in accordance with regulations prescribed by the Secretary or his delegate, the value of a like part or accessory accepted in exchange."

Sec. 4063. Repealed.

In 1984, P.L. 98-369, Sec. 735(a)(1), repealed Code Sec. 4063, effective 1/7/83. Prior to repeal, Code Sec. 4063 read as follows:
"SEC. 4063. EXEMPTIONS.
"(a) Specified articles.
"(1) Camper coaches; bodies for self-propelled mobile homes. The tax imposed under section 4061 shall not apply in the case of articles designed—
"(A) to be mounted or placed on automobile trucks, automobile truck chassis, or automobile chassis, and
"(B) to be used primarily as living quarters or camping accommodations.
"(2) Feed, seed, and fertilizer equipment. The tax imposed under section 4061 shall not apply in the case of any body, part, or accessory primarily designed—
"(A) to process or prepare seed, feed, or fertilizer for use on farms;
"(B) to haul feed, seed, or fertilizer to and on farms;
"(C) to spread feed, seed, or fertilizer on farms;
"(D) to load or unload feed, seed, or fertilizer on farms; or
"(E) for any combination of the foregoing.
"(3) House trailers. The tax imposed under section 4061(a) shall not apply in the case of house trailers.
"(4) Ambulances, hearses, etc. The tax imposed by section 4061(a) shall not apply in the case of an ambulance, hearse, or combination ambulance-hearse.
"(5) Concrete mixers. The tax imposed under section 4061 shall not apply in the case of—

"(A) any article designed (i) to be placed or mounted on an automobile truck chassis or truck trailer or semitrailer chassis and (ii) to be used to process or prepare concrete, and
"(B) parts or accessories designed primarily for use on or in connection with an article described in subparagraph (A).
"(6) Buses. The tax imposed under section 4061(a) shall not apply in the case of any automobile bus chassis or automobile bus body.
"(7) Trash containers, etc. The tax imposed under section 4061(a) shall not apply in the case of any box, container, receptacle, bin, or other similar article which is to be used as a trash container and is not designed for the transportation of freight other than trash, and which is not designed to be permanently mounted on or permanently affixed to an automobile truck chassis or body, or in the case of parts or accessories designed primarily for use on, in connection with, or as a component part of any such article.
"(8) Rail trailers and rail vans. The tax imposed under section 4061 shall not apply in the case of—
"(A) any chassis or body of a trailer or semitrailer which is designed for use both as a highway vehicle and a railroad car, and
"(B) any parts or accessories designed primarily for use on or in connection with an article described in subparagraph (A).
For purposes of this paragraph, a piggy-back trailer or semitrailer shall not be treated as designed for use as a railroad car.
"(b) Sales to manufacturers.
"Under regulations prescribed by the Secretary, the tax under section 4061 shall not apply in the case of sales of bodies by the manufacturer, producer, or importer to a manufacturer or producer of automobile trucks or other automobiles to be sold by such vendee. For the purposes of section 4061, such vendee shall be considered the manufacturer or producer of such bodies.
"(c) Rebuilt parts and accessories.
"Under regulations prescribed by the Secretary, the tax imposed under section 4061(b) shall not apply in the case of rebuilt parts or accessories.
"(d) Resale after certain modifications.
" Under regulations prescribed by the Secretary, the tax imposed by section 4061 shall not apply to the resale of any article described in section 4061(a)(1) if before such resale such article was merely combined with any coupling device (including any fifth wheel), wrecker crane, loading and unloading equipment (including any crane, hoist, winch, or power liftgate), aerial ladder or tower, snow and ice control equipment, earthmoving, excavation and construction equipment, spreader, sleeper cab, cab shield, or wood or metal floor.
"(e) Parts for light-duty trucks.
" The tax imposed by section 4061(b) shall not apply to the sale by the manufacturer, producer, or importer of any article which is to be resold by the purchaser on or in connection with the first retail sale of a light-duty truck, as described in section 4061(a)(2), or which is to be resold by the purchaser to a second purchaser for resale by such second purchaser on or in connection with the first retail sale of a light-duty truck."
In 1983, P.L. 97-424, Sec. 512(a)(3), added para. (a)(8), effective 1/7/83.
In 1982, P.L. 97-248, Sec. 294(a), substituted "December 31, 1982" for "the first day of such 10th calendar month" in subpara. (c)(2)(C) of P.L. 95-618 (see below).
—P.L. 97-248, Sec. 294(b), added ", or, in lieu of evidence of reimbursement, he makes such reimbursement simultaneously with the receipt of such a refund under an arrangement satisfactory to such Secretary which assures such simultaneous reimbursement" before the semi-colon in subpara. (c)(2)(A) of P.L. 95-618 (see below).
In 1978, P.L. 95-618, Sec. 231(a), amended para. (a)(6), effective for articles sold after 11/9/78. Sec. 231(b)-(e) of this Act provides:
"(b) Floor stocks refunds. —
"(1) In general. — Where, before the day after the date of the enactment of this Act, any tax-repealed article (as defined in subsection (e)) has been sold by the manufacturer, producer, or importer and on such day is held by a dealer and has not been used and is intended for sale, there shall be credited or refunded (without interest) to the manufacturer, producer, or importer an amount equal to the tax paid by such manufacturer, producer, or importer on his sale of the article, if—
"(A) a claim for such credit or refund is filed with the Secretary of the Treasury before the first day of the 10th calendar month beginning after the day after the date of the enactment of this Act based upon a request submitted to the manufacturer, producer, or importer before the first day of the 7th calendar month beginning after the day after the date of the enactment of this Act by the dealer who held the article in respect of which the credit or refunds is claimed; and
"(B) on or before the first day of such 10th calendar month reimbursement has been made to the dealer by the manufacturer, producer, or importer in an amount equal to the tax paid on the article or written consent has been obtained from the dealer to allowance of the credit or refunds.
"(2) Limitation on eligibility for credit or refund. — No manufacturer, producer, or importer shall be entitled to credit or refund under paragraph (1) unless he has in his possession such evidence of the reimbursement with respect to which the credit or refund is claimed as may be required by regulations prescribed by the Secretary of the Treasury under this subsection.
"(3) Other laws applicable. — All provisions of law, including penalties, applicable with respect to the taxes imposed by section 4061(a) of the Internal Revenue Code of 1954 shall, insofar as applicable and not inconsistent with paragraphs (1) and (2) of this subsection, apply in respect of the credits and refunds provided for in paragraph (1) to the same extent as if the credits or refunds constituted overpayments of the tax.
"(c) Refunds with respect to certain consumer purchases. —

3,197

"(1) In general.—Except as otherwise provided in paragraph (2), where on or after April 20, 1977, and on or before the date of the enactment of this Act, a tax-repealed article (as defined in subsection (e)) has been sold to an ultimate purchaser, there shall be credited or refunded (without interest) to the manufacturer, producer, or importer of such article an amount equal to the tax paid by such manufacturer, producer, or importer on his sale of the article.

"(2) Limitation on eligibility for credit or refund.—No manufacturer, producer, or importer shall be entitled to a credit or refund under paragraph (1) with respect to an article unless—

"(A) he has in his possession such evidence of the sale of the article to an ultimate purchaser, and of the reimbursement of the tax to such purchaser, as may be required by regulations prescribed by the Secretary of the Treasury under this subsection, or in lieu of evidence of reimbursement, he makes such reimbursement simultaneously with the receipt of such a refund under an arrangement satisfactory to such Secretary which assures such simultaneous reimbursement;

"(B) claim for such credit or refund is filed with the Secretary of the Treasury before the first day of the 10th calendar month beginning after the day after the date of the enactment of this Act based upon information submitted to the manufacturer, producer, or importer before the first day of the 7th calendar month beginning after the day after the date of the enactment of this Act by the person who sold the article (in respect of which the credit or refund is claimed) to the ultimate purchaser; and

"(C) on or before December 31, 1982 reimbursement has been made to the ultimate purchaser in an amount equal to the tax paid on the article.

"(3) Other laws applicable.— All provisions of laws, including penalties, applicable with respect to the taxes imposed by section 4061(a) of such Code shall, insofar as applicable and not inconsistent with paragraph (1) or (2) of this subsection, apply with respect to the credits and refunds provided for in paragraph (1) to the same extent as if the credits or refunds constituted overpayment of the tax.

"(d) Certain uses by manufacturer, etc. Any tax paid by reason of section 4218(a) of such Code (relating to use by manufacturer or importer considered sale) on any tax-repealed article shall be deemed an overpayment of such tax if the tax was imposed on subch article by reason of such subsection 4218(a) on or after April 20, 1977.

"(e) Definitions. For purposes of this section—

"(1) The term 'dealer' includes a wholesaler, jobber, distributor, or retailer.

"(2) An article shall be considered as 'held by a dealer' if title thereto has passed to such dealer (whether or not delivery to him has been made) and if, for purposes of consumption, title to such article or possession thereof has not at any time been transferred to any person other than a dealer.

"(3) The term 'tax-repealed article' means an article on which a tax was imposed by section 4061(a) of such Code (as in effect on the day before the date of the enactment of this Act) and which is exempted from such tax by paragraph (6) of section 4063(a) of such Code (as amended by subsection (a) of this section).

'Sec. 231(g)(2) and (3) of the Act provides:

"(2) For purposes of paragraph (1), an article shall not be considered sold on or before the date of the enactment of this Act unless possession or right to possession passes to the purchaser on or before such date.

"(3) In the case of —

"(A) a lease,

"(B) a contract for the sale of an article providing that the price shall be paid by installments and title to the article sold does not pass until a future date notwithstanding partial payment by installments,

"(C) a conditional sale, or

"(D) a chattel mortgage arrangement providing that the sale price shall be paid in installments,

entered into on or before the date of the enactment of this Act, payments made after such date with respect to the article leased or sold shall, for purposes of this subsection, be considered as payments made with respect to an article sold after such date, if the lessor or vendor establishes that the amount of payments payable after such date with respect to such article has been reduced by an amount equal to that portion of the tax applicable with respect to the lease or sale of such article which is due and payable after such date. If the lessor or vendor does not establish that the payments have been so reduced, they shall be treated as payments made in respect of an article sold on or before the date of the enactment of this Act."

Prior to amendment para. (a)(6) read as follows:

"(6) Local transit buses. The tax imposed under section 4061(a) shall not apply in the case of automobile bus chassis or automobile bus bodies which are to be used predominantly by the purchaser in mass transportation service in urban areas."

—P.L. 95-600, Sec. 701(ff)(1), added subsec. (e), effective 12/1/78 (the first day of the first calendar month beginning more than 20 days after 11/6/78).

In 1976, P.L. 94-455, Sec. 1906(b)(13)(A), substituted "Secretary" for "Secretary or his delegate", each place it appeared in Code Sec. 4063, effective 2/1/77.

—P.L. 94-455, Sec. 2109, added subsec. (d), effective for resale of any article on or after 10/4/76.

In 1971, P.L. 92-178, Sec. 401(a)(2), added paras. (a)(6) and (7)... Sec. 401(g)(3), substituted new para. (a)(4), effective for articles sold on or after 12/10/71, except as provided in Sec. 401(h)(2) and (3) of this Act reproduced in note following Code Sec. 4061.

Prior to amendment para. (a)(4) read as follows:

"(4) Small 3-wheeled trucks.—The tax imposed under section 4061(a) shall not apply in the case of —

"(A) an automobile truck chassis which—

"(i) has only 3 wheels;

"(ii) is powered by a motor which does not exceed 18 brake horsepower (rated at 4,000 revolutions per minute), and

"(iii) does not exceed 1,000 pounds gross weight; or

"(B) a body designed primarily to be mounted on a chassis described in subparagraph (A)."

In 1970, P.L. 91-614, Sec. 303(a), added "or camping accommodations" at the end of subpara. (a)(1)(B), effective for sales made after 12/31/70.

In 1969, P.L. 91-172, Sec. 931, added para. (a)(5), effective for articles sold after 12/31/69.

In 1965, P.L. 89-44, Sec. 801(a), substituted subsec. (a) for a provision exempting house trailers and tractors, effective for articles sold on and after 6/22/65.

In 1964, P.L. 88-653, Sec. 5(a), added subsec. (c), effective for articles sold after '64.

In 1955, P.L. 367, Sec. 1, struck out "or parts or accessories" after "bodies", in the first and second sentences of subsec. (b), effective 9/1/55.

Sec. 4064. Gas guzzler tax.
(a) Imposition of tax.

There is hereby imposed on the sale by the manufacturer of each automobile a tax determined in accordance with the following table:

If the fuel economy of the model type in which the automobile falls is:	The tax is:
At least 22.5	0
At least 21.5 but less than 22.5	$1,000
At least 20.5 but less than 21.5	1,300
At least 19.5 but less than 20.5	1,700
At least 18.5 but less than 19.5	2,100
At least 17.5 but less than 18.5	2,600
At least 16.5 but less than 17.5	3,000
At least 15.5 but less than 16.5	3,700
At least 14.5 but less than 15.5	4,500
At least 13.5 but less than 14.5	5,400
At least 12.5 but less than 13.5	6,400
Less than 12.5	7,700

(b) Definitions.

For purposes of this section—

(1) Automobile.

(A) In general. The term "automobile" means any 4-wheeled vehicle propelled by fuel—

(i) which is manufactured primarily for use on public streets, roads, and highways (except any vehicle operated exclusively on a rail or rails), and

(ii) which is rated at 6,000 pounds unloaded gross vehicle weight or less.

(B) Exception for certain vehicles. The term "automobile" does not include any vehicle which is treated as a nonpassenger automobile under the rules which were prescribed by the Secretary of Transportation for purposes of section 32901 of title 49, United States Code, and which were in effect on the date of the enactment of this section.

(C) Exception for emergency vehicles. The term "automobile" does not include any vehicle sold for use and used—

(i) as an ambulance or combination ambulance-hearse,

(ii) by the United States or by a State or local government for police or other law enforcement purposes, or

(iii) for other emergency uses prescribed by the Secretary by regulations.

(2) Fuel economy. The term "fuel economy" means the average number of miles traveled by an automobile per gallon of gasoline (or equivalent amount of other fuel) consumed, as determined by the EPA Administrator in accordance with procedures established under subsection (c).

Excise and miscellaneous taxes Code Sec. 4064

(3) Model type. The term "model type" means a particular class of automobile as determined by regulation by the EPA Administrator.

(4) Model year. The term "model year", with reference to any specific calendar year, means a manufacturer's annual production period (as determined by the EPA Administrator) which includes January 1 of such calendar year. If a manufacturer has no annual production period, the term "model year" means the calendar year.

(5) Manufacturer.

(A) In general. The term "manufacturer" includes a producer or importer.

(B) Lengthening treated as manufacture. For purposes of this section, subchapter G of this chapter, and section 6416(b)(3), the lengthening of an automobile by any person shall be treated as the manufacture of an automobile by such person.

(6) EPA Administrator. The term "EPA Administrator" means the Administrator of the Environmental Protection Agency.

(7) Fuel. The term "fuel" means gasoline and diesel fuel. The Secretary (after consultation with the Secretary of Transportation) may, by regulation, include any product of petroleum or natural gas within the meaning of such term if he determines that such inclusion is consistent with the need of the Nation to conserve energy.

(c) Determination of fuel economy.

For purposes of this section—

(1) In general. Fuel economy for any model type shall be measured in accordance with testing and calculation procedures established by the EPA Administrator by regulation. Procedures so established shall be the procedures utilized by the EPA Administrator for model year 1975 (weighted 55 percent urban cycle, and 45 percent highway cycle), or procedures which yield comparable results. Procedures under this subsection, to the extent practicable, shall require that fuel economy tests be conducted in conjunction with emissions tests conducted under section 206 of the Clean Air Act. The EPA Administrator shall report any measurements of fuel economy to the Secretary.

(2) Special rule for fuels other than gasoline. The EPA Administrator shall by regulation determine that quantity of any other fuel which is the equivalent of one gallon of gasoline.

(3) Time by which regulations must be issued. Testing and calculation procedures applicable to a model year, and any amendment to such procedures (other than a technical or clerical amendment), shall be promulgated not less than 12 months before the model year to which such procedures apply.

In 2005, P.L. 109-59, Sec. 11111(a), deleted "In the case of a limousine, the preceding sentence shall be applied without regard to clause (ii)." at the end of subpara. (b)(1)(A), effective 10/1/2005.

In 1994, P.L. 103-272, Sec. 5(g)(1), substituted "section 32901 of title 49, United States Code," for "section 501 of the Motor Vehicle Information and Cost Savings Act (15 U.S.C. 2001)" in subpara. (b)(1)(B), effective 7/5/94.

In 1990, P.L. 101-508, Sec. 11216(a), amended subsec. (a) . . . Sec. 11216(b), added the last sentence to subpara. (b)(1)(A), effective for sales after 12/31/90. Prior to amendment, subsec. (a) read as follows:

"(a) Imposition of tax.

"There is hereby imposed on the sale by the manufacturer of each automobile a tax determined in accordance with the following tables:

"(1) In the case of a 1980 model year automobile:

If the fuel economy of the model type in which the automobile falls is:	The tax is:
At least 15	0
At least 14 but less than 15	$200
At 13 but less than 14	300
Less than 13	550

"(2) In the case of a 1981 model year automobile:

If the fuel economy of the model type in which the automobile falls is:	The tax is:
At least 17	0
At least 16 but less than 17	$200
At least 15 but less than 16	350
At least 14 but less than 15	450
At least 13 but less than 14	550
Less than 13	650

"(3) In the case of a 1982 model year automobile:

If the fuel economy of the model type in which the automobile falls is:	The tax is:
At least 18.5	0
At least 17.5 but less than 18.5	$200
At least 16.5 but less than 17.5	350
At least 15.5 but less than 16.5	450
At least 14.5 but less than 15.5	600
At least 13.5 but less than 14.5	750
At least 12.5 but less than 13.5	950
Less than 12.5	1,200

"(4) In the case of a 1983 model year automobile:

If the fuel economy of the model type in which the automobile falls is:	The tax is:
At least 19	0
At least 18 but less than 19	$350
At least 17 but less than 18	500
At least 16 but less than 17	650
At least 15 but less than 16	800
At least 14 but less than 15	1,000
At least 13 but less than 14	1,250
Less than 13	1,550

"(5) In the case of a 1984 model year automobile:

If the fuel economy of the model type in which the automobile falls is:	The tax is:
At least 19.5	0
At least 18.5 but less than 19.5	$450
At least 17.5 but less than 18.5	600
At least 16.5 but less than 17.5	750
At least 15.5 but less than 16.5	950
At least 14.5 but less than 15.5	1,150
At least 13.5 but less than 14.5	1,450
At least 12.5 but less than 13.5	1,750
Less than 12.5	2,150

"(6) In the case of a 1985 model year automobile:

If the fuel economy of the model type in which the automobile falls is:	The tax is:
At least 21	0
At least 20 but less than 21	$500
At least 19 but less than 20	600
At least 18 but less than 19	800
At least 17 but less than 18	1,000
At least 16 but less than 17	1,200
At least 15 but less than 16	1,500
At least 14 but less than 15	1,800
At least 13 but less than 14	2,200
Less than 13	2,650

"(7) In the case of a 1986 or later model year automobile:

If the fuel economy of the model type in which the automobile falls is:	The tax is:
At least 22.5	0
At least 21.5 but less than 22.5	$500
At least 20.5 but less then 21.5	650
At least 19.5 but less than 20.5	850
At least 18.5 but less than 19.5	1,050
At least 17.5 but less than 18.5	1,300
At least 16.5 but less than 17.5	1,500
At least 15.5 but less than 16.5	1,850
At least 14.5 but less than 15.5	2,250
At least 13.5 but less than 14.5	2,700
At least 12.5 but less than 13.5	3,200
Less than 12.5	3,850"

—P.L. 101-508, Sec. 11216(c), amended subpara. (b)(5)(B), effective 1/1/91. Prior to amendment, subpara. (b)(5)(B) read as follows:

"(B) Exception for certain small manufacturers. A person shall not be treated as the manufacturer of any automobile if—

"(i) such person would (but for this subparagraph) be so treated solely by reason of lengthening an existing automobile, and

"(ii) such person is a small manufacturer (as defined in subsection (d)(4)) for the model year in which such lengthening occurs."

—P.L. 101-508, Sec. 11216(d), deleted subsec. (d), effective 11/5/90.
Prior to deletion, subsec. (d) read as follows:

"(d) Special rules for small manufacturers.

"(1) In general. If, on the application of a small manufacturer, the Secretary determines that it is not feasible for such manufacturer to meet the tax-free fuel economy level for the model year with respect to all automobiles produced by such manufacturer or with respect to a model type produced by such manufacturer, the Secretary may by regulation prescribe an alternate rate schedule for such model year for all automobiles produced by such manufacturer for such model type, as the case may be. The alternate rate schedule shall be based on the maximum feasible fuel economy level which such manufacturer can meet for such model year with respect to all automobiles or with respect to such model type, as the case may be.

"(2) Application to include necessary information. An application under this subsection for any model year shall contain such information as the Secretary may by regulations prescribe.

"(3) Determinations to be made only after consultation. Determinations under paragraph (1) shall be made by the Secretary only after consultation with the Secretary of Energy, the Secretary of Transportation, and other appropriate Federal officers.

"(4) Small manufacturer defined.

"(A) In general. For purposes of this subsection, the term 'small manufacturer' means any manufacturer—

"(i) who manufactured (whether or not in the United States) fewer than 10,000 automobiles in the second model year preceding the model year for which the determination under paragraph (1) is being made, and

"(ii) who can reasonably be expected to manufacture (whether or not in the United States) fewer than 10,000 automobiles in the model year for which the determination under paragraph (1) is being made.

"(B) Special rules. For purposes of subparagraph (A)—

"(i) Manufacturer of automobiles produced abroad determined without regard to importation. The meaning of the term 'manufacturer' shall be determined without regard to subsection(b)(5).

"(ii) Controlled groups. Persons who are members of the same controlled group of corporations shall be treated as one manufacturer. For purposes of the preceding sentence, the term 'controlled group of corporations' has the meaning given to such term by section 1563(a); except that 'more than 50 percent' shall be substituted for 'at least 80 percent' each place it appears in section 1563(a)."

In **1986**, P.L. 99-514, Sec. 1812(e)(1)(B)(i), substituted "unloaded gross vehicle weight" for "gross vehicle weight."... Sec. 1812(e)(1)(B)(ii), amended para. (b)(5), effective for 1980 and later model automobiles (as defined in Code Sec. 4064(d)) except that the amendment made by clause (i) [Sec. 1812(e)(1)(B)(ii)] shall not apply to any station wagon if—

(I) such station wagon is originally equipped with more than 6 seat belts,
(II) such station wagon was manufactured before November 1, 1985, and
(III) such station wagon is of the 1985 or 1986 model year.

Prior to amendment, para. (b)(5) read as follows:

"(5) Manufacturer. The term 'manufacturer' includes a producer or importer."

In **1978**, P.L. 95-618, Sec. 201(a), added Code Sec. 4064, effective with respect to 1980 and later model automobiles (as defined in Code Sec. 4064(d)).

PART II.—TIRES

Sec.
4071. Imposition of tax.
4072. Definitions.
4073. Exemptions.

In **2004**, P.L. 108-357, Sec. 869(d)(2) [sic (e)(2)], amended item 4073.
Prior to amendment, item 4073 read as follows:
"4073. Exemption for tires with internal wire fastening."

In **1984**, P.L. 98-369, Sec. 735(c)(5)(A), deleted "and tubes" from the end of the heading for Part II... Sec. 735(c)(5)(C), amended the item for Code Sec. 4073.
Prior to amendment the item for Code Sec. 4073 read as follows
"4073. Exemptions."

In **1956**, P.L. 627, Sec. 204(d), substituted "Definitions" for "Definition of rubber" in item "4072".

Sec. 4071. Imposition of tax.
(a) Imposition and rate of tax.

There is hereby imposed on taxable tires sold by the manufacturer, producer, or importer thereof a tax at the rate of 9.45 cents (4.725 cents in the case of a biasply tire or super single tire) for each 10 pounds so much of the maximum rated load capacity thereof as exceeds 3,500 pounds.

(b) Special rule for manufacturers who sell at retail.

Under regulations prescribed by the Secretary, if the manufacturer, producer, or importer of any tire delivers such tire to a retail store or retail outlet of such manufacturer, producer, or importer, he shall be liable for tax under subsection (a) in respect of such tire in the same manner as if it had been sold at the time it was delivered to such retail store or outlet. This subsection shall not apply to an article in respect to which tax has been imposed by subsection (a). Subsection (a) shall not apply to an article in respect of which tax has been imposed by this subsection.

(c) Tires on imported articles.

For the purposes of subsection (a), if an article imported into the United States is equipped with tires—

(1) the importer of the article shall be treated as the importer of the tires with which such article is equipped, and
(2) the sale of the article by the importer thereof shall be treated as the sale of the tires with which such article is equipped.

This subsection shall not apply with respect to the sale of an automobile bus chassis or an automobile bus body.

(d) Termination.

On and after October 1, 2011, the taxes imposed by subsection (a) shall not apply.

In **2005**, P.L. 109-59, Sec. 11101(a)(1)(E), substituted "2011" for "2005" in subsec. (d), effective 8/10/2005.
—P.L. 109-58, Sec. 1364(c), of this Act, reads as follows:
"(c) Study.
"(1) In general. With respect to the 1-year period beginning on January 1, 2006, the Secretary of the Treasury shall conduct a study to determine—
"(A) the amount of tax collected during such period under section 4071 of the Internal Revenue Code of 1986 with respect to each class of tire, and
"(B) the number of tires in each such class on which tax is imposed under such section during such period.
"(2) Report. Not later than July 1, 2007, the Secretary of the Treasury shall submit to Congress a report on the study conducted under paragraph (1)."

In **2004**, P.L. 108-357, Sec. 869(a), amended subsec. (a)... Sec. 869(d)(1) [sic (e)(1)], deleted subsec. (c) and redesignated subsec. (e) as (c), effective for sales in calendar yrs. begin. more than 30 days after 10/22/2004.
Prior to amendment, subsec. (a) read as follows:
"(a) Imposition and rate of tax. There is hereby imposed on tires of the type used on highway vehicles, if wholly or in part made of rubber, sold by the manufacturer, producer, or importer a tax at the following rates:

If the tire weighs:	The rate of tax is:
Not more than 40 lbs.	No tax.
More than 40 lbs. but not more than 70 lbs.	15 cents per lb. in excess of 40 lbs.
More than 70 lbs. but not more than 90 lbs.	$4.50 plus 30 cents per lb. in excess of 70 lbs.
More than 90 lbs.	$10.50 plus 50 cents per lb. in excess of 90 lbs."

Prior to deletion, subsec. (c) read as follows:
"(c) Determination of weight. For purposes of this section, weight shall be based on total weight exclusive of metal rims or rim bases. Total weight of the articles shall be determined under regulations prescribed by the Secretary."

In **1998**, P.L. 105-178, Sec. 9002(a)(1)(E), substituted "2005" for "1999" in subsec. (d), effective 6/9/98.

In **1991**, P.L. 102-240, Sec. 8002(a)(2), substituted "1999" for "1995" in subsec. (d), effective 12/18/91.

In **1990**, P.L. 101-508, Sec. 11211(c)(2), substituted "1995" for "1993" in subsec. (d), effective 11/5/90.

In **1987**, P.L. 100-17, Sec. 502(a)(3), substituted "1993" for "1988" in subsec. (d), effective 4/2/87.

In **1984**, P.L. 98-369, Sec. 735(c)(2)(A), deleted "or tube" and "or inner tube" each place it appeared in subsec. (b)... Sec. 735(c)(2)(B), substituted "on total weight exclusive of metal rims or rim bases." for "on total weight, except that in the case of tires such total weight shall be exclusive of metal rims or rim bases." in the first sentence of subsec. (c)... Sec. 735(c)(2)(C)(i)–(iii), amended subsec. (e)... Sec. 735(c)(2)(D), deleted subsec. (f), effective for articles sold on or after 1/1/84.
Prior to amendment, subsec. (e) read as follows:
"(e) Tires on imported articles. For the purposes of subsection (a), if an article imported into the United States is equipped with tires or inner tubes (other than bicycle tires and inner tubes)—
"(1) the importer of the article shall be treated as the importer of the tires and inner tubes with which such article is equipped, and
"(2) the sale of the article by the importer thereof shall be treated as the sale of the tires and inner tubes with which such article is equipped.
This subsection shall not apply with respect to the sale of an article if a tax on such sale is imposed under section 4061 or if such article is an automobile bus chassis or an automobile bus body."
Prior to deletion, subsec. (f) read as follows:
"(f) Imported recapped or retreaded United States tires.

"(1) In general. For purposes of subsection (a)(4), in the case of a tire which has been exported from the United States, recapped or retreaded (other than from bead to bead) outside the United States, and imported into the United States—
"(A) the person importing such tire shall be treated as importing the tread rubber used in such recapping or retreading (determined as of the completion of the recapping or retreading), and
"(B) the sale of such tire by the importer thereof shall be treated as the sale of such tread rubber.
"(2) Exception for certain taxable sales. Paragraph (1) shall not apply with respect to the sale of any tire if such tire is sold on or in connection with the sale of an article on which tax is imposed under section 4061."
In **1983**, P.L. 97-424, Sec. 514(a), amended subsec. (a), effective for articles sold on or after 1/1/84.
Prior to amendment, subsec. (a) read as follows:
"*(a) Imposition of rate of tax.* There is hereby imposed upon the following articles, if wholly or in part of rubber, sold by the manufacturer, producer, or importer, a tax at the following rates:
"(1) Tires of the type used on highway vehicles, 9.75 cents a pound.
"(2) Other tires (other than laminated tires to which paragraph (5) applies), 4.875 cents a pound.
"(3) Inner tubes for tires, 10 cents a pound.
"(4) Tread rubber, 5 cents a pound.
"(5) Laminated tires (not of the type used on highway vehicles) which consist wholly of scrap rubber from used tire casings with an internal metal fastening agent, 1 cent a pound."
—P.L. 97-424, Sec. 516(a)(2), amended subsec. (d), effective 1/6/83.
Prior to amendment, subsec. (d) read as follows:
"*(d) Rate reduction.* On and after October 1, 1984—
"(1) the tax imposed by paragraph (1) of subsection (a) shall be 4.875 cents a pound;
"(2) the tax imposed by paragraph (3) of subsection (a) shall be 9 cents a pound; and
"(3) paragraph (4) of subsection (a) shall not apply."
—P.L. 97-424, Sec. 521(a)–(e), provided provisions on floor stocks taxes which are reproduced in note following Code Sec. 4081.
In **1980**, P.L. 96-598, Sec. 1(d), added subsec. (f), effective on the first day of the first calendar month which begins more than 10 days after 12/24/80.
—P.L. 96-596, Sec. 4(a)(1)(A), substituted "9.75 cents" for "10 cents" in para. (a)(1) . . . Sec. 4(a)(1)(B), substituted "4.875 cents" for "5 cents" in para. (a)(2) . . . Sec. 4(a)(1)(C), substituted "4.875 cents" for "5 cents" in para. (d)(1), effective on or after 1/1/81.
—P.L. 96-596, Sec. 4(b), provides:
"*(b) Determination of overpayment.*
"(1) In general. The determination of the extent to which any overpayment of tax imposed by section 4071(a)(1) or (2) or section 4071(b) has arisen by reason of an adjustment of a tire after the original sale pursuant to a warranty or guarantee, and the allowance of a credit or refund of any such overpayment, shall be determined in accordance with the principles set forth in regulations and rulings relating thereto to the extent in effect on March 31, 1978.
"(2) Effective date. This subsection shall apply to the adjustment of any tire after March 31, 1978, and prior to January 1, 1983."
—P.L. 96-222, Sec. 108(c)(2)(C), added "or if such article is an automobile bus chassis or an automobile bus body." following "under section 4061" in subsec. (e), effective 11/6/78.
In **1978**, P.L. 95-599, Sec. 502(a)(4), substituted "1984" for "1979" in subsec. (d), effective 11/6/78.
In **1976**, P.L. 94-455, Sec. 1906(b)(13)(A), substituted "Secretary" for "Secretary or his delegate" each place it appeared in Code Sec. 4071, effective 2/1/77.
—P.L. 94-280, Sec. 303(a)(5), substituted "1979" for "1977" in subsec. (d), effective 5/5/76.
In **1971**, P.L. 92-178, Sec. 401(f), added subsec. (e), for articles sold on or after 12/10/71 (subject to certain limitations—see note following Code Sec. 4061).
In **1970**, P.L. 91-605, Sec. 303(a)(5), substituted "1977" for "1972" in subsec. (d).
In **1966**, P.L. 89-523, Sec. 1(a), redesignated subsecs. (b) and (c) as subsecs. (c) and (d) and added subsec. (b), effective on the first day of the first calendar quarter which begins more than 20 days after 8/1/66.
In **1961**, P.L. 87-61, Sec. 202(a), substituted "10 cents" for "8 cents" in para. (a)(1) . . . Sec. 202(b), substituted "10 cents" for "9 cents" in para. (a)(3) . . . Sec. 202(c), substituted "5 cents" for "3 cents" in para. (a)(4) . . . Sec. 202(d), substituted "October 1, 1972" for "July 1, 1972", in subsec. (c), added para. (c)(2) and redesignated para. (c)(2) as para. (c)(3), effective 7/1/61.
In **1960**, P.L. 86-440, Sec. 1(a), added "(other than laminated tires to which paragraph (5) applies)" after "other tires" in para. (a)(2) and added para. (a)(5), effective for items sold after 5/31/60.
In **1956**, ch. 462, Sec. 204(a), increased the tax on tires of the type used on highway vehicles from 5 cents a pound to 8 cents a pound, provided for a tax of 3 cents a pound on tread rubber, and required on and after July 1, 1972, a reduction in the tax on tires of the type used on highway vehicles from 8 cents a pound to 5 cents a pound, and elimination of the tax on tread rubber, effective 7/1/56.

Sec. 4072. Definitions.
(a) Taxable tire.

For purposes of this chapter, the term "taxable tire" means any tire of the type used on highway vehicles if wholly or in part made of rubber and if marked pursuant to Federal regulations for highway use.
(b) Rubber.
For purposes of this chapter, the term "rubber" includes synthetic and substitute rubber.
(c) Tires of the type used on highway vehicles.
For purposes of this part, the term "tires of the type used on highway vehicles" means tires of the type used on—
(1) motor vehicles which are highway vehicles, or
(2) vehicles of the type used in connection with motor vehicles which are highway vehicles.
Such term shall not include tires of a type used exclusively on vehicles described in section 4053(8).
(d) Biasply.
For purposes of this part, the term "biasply tire" means a pneumatic tire on which the ply cords that extend to the beads are laid at alternate angles substantially less than 90 degrees to the centerline of the tread.
(e) Super single tire.
For purposes of this part, the term "super single tire" means a single tire greater than 13 inches in cross section width designed to replace 2 tires in a dual fitment. Such term shall not include any tire designed for steering.

In **2005**, P.L. 109-58, Sec. 1364(a), added "Such term shall not include any tire designed for steering." at the end of subsec. (e), effective for sales in calendar yrs. begin. more than 30 days after 10/22/2004 as if included in Sec. 869 of P.L. 108-357, the American Jobs Creation Act of 2004.
In **2004**, P.L. 108-357, Sec. 851(c)(1), added "Such term shall not include tires of a type used exclusively on vehicles described in section 4053(8)." flush left at the end of para. (b)(2) [sic subsec. (c), as redesignated by Sec. 869(b) [sic (c)] of this Act, see below], effective the day after 10/22/2004.
—P.L. 108-357, Sec. 869(b), added subsecs. (c) and (d) . . . Sec. 869(b) [sic (c)], redesignated subsecs. (a)-(d) as (b)-(e) [as amended by Sec. 869(b) of this Act, see above] and added subsec. (a), effective for sales in calendar yrs. begin. more than 30 days after 10/22/2004.
In **1984**, P.L. 98-369, Sec. 753(c)(3), deleted subsec. (b) and redesignated subsec. (c) as subsec. (b), effective for articles sold on or after 1/1/84.
Prior to amendment, subsec. (b) read as follows:
"*(b) Tread rubber.*
"For purposes of this chapter, the term 'tread rubber' means any material—
"(1) which is commonly or commercially known as tread rubber or camelback; or
"(2) which is a substitute for a material described in paragraph (1) and is of a type used in recapping or retreading tires."
In **1956**, P.L. 627, Sec. 204(c), substituted "Definitions" for "Definition of rubber" in the heading and designated existing provisions as subsec. (a) and added subsecs. (b) and (c), effective 7/1/56.

Sec. 4073. Exemptions.

The tax imposed by section 4071 shall not apply to tires sold for the exclusive use of the Department of Defense or the Coast Guard.

In **2004**, P.L. 108-357, Sec. 869(c) [sic (d)], amended Code Sec. 4073, effective for sales in calendar yrs. begin. more than 30 days after 10/22/2004.
Prior to amendment, Code Sec. 4073 read as follows:
"SEC. 4073 EXEMPTION FOR TIRES WITH INTERNAL WIRE FASTENING.
"The tax imposed by section 4071 shall not apply to tires of extruded tiring with an internal wire fastening agent."
In **1984**, P.L. 98-369, Sec. 735(c)(4), amended Code Sec. 4073, effective for articles sold on or after 1/1/84.
Prior to amendment, Code Sec. 4073 read as follows:
"SEC. 4073. EXEMPTIONS.
"*(a) Tires of certain sizes.*
"The tax imposed by section 4071 shall not apply to tires which are not more than 20 inches in diameter and not more than 1¾ inches in cross-section, if such tires are of all-rubber construction (whether hollow center or solid) without fabric or metal reinforcement.
"*(b) Tires with internal wire fastening.*
"The tax imposed by section 4071 shall not apply to tires of extruded tiring with an internal wire fastening agent.
"*(c) Exemption from tax on tread rubber in certain cases.*
"Under regulations prescribed by the Secretary, the tax imposed by section 4071(a)(4) shall not apply to tread rubber sold by the manufacturer, producer, or importer, to any person for use by such person otherwise than in the recapping or retreading of tires of the type used on highway vehicles."

In 1976, P.L. 94-455, Sec. 1906(b)(13)(A), substituted "Secretary" for "Secretary or his delegate" in subsec. (c), effective 2/1/77.
In 1956, ch. 462, Sec. 204(c), added subsec. (c), effective 7/1/56.

PART III.—PETROLEUM PRODUCTS
Subpart
A. Motor and aviation fuels.
B. Special provisions applicable to fuels tax.

In 2004, P.L. 108-357, Sec. 853(d)(2)(R), amended the table of subparts for part III of subchapter A of chapter 32.
Prior to amendment, the table of subparts for part III of subchapter A of chapter 32 read as follows:
"A. Gasoline and diesel fuel.
"B. Aviation fuel.
"C. Special provisions applicable to petroleum products."
In 1993, P.L. 103-66, Sec. 13242(d)(43), amended the table of subparts for part III of subchapter A of chapter 32.
Prior to amendment, the table of subparts for part III of subchapter A of chapter 32 read as follows:
"A. Gasoline.
"C. Special provisions applicable to petroleum products.
In 1983, deleted the item for subpart B from the table of subparts for part III of subchapter A of chapter 32.
Prior to deletion the item for subpart B read as follows: "B. Lubricating oil."

SUBPART A.—MOTOR AND AVIATION FUELS
Sec.
4081. Imposition of tax.
4082. Exemptions for diesel fuel and kerosene.
4083. Definitions; special rule; administrative authority.
4084. Cross references.

In 2004, P.L. 108-357, Sec. 853(d)(2)(S), amended the heading for Subpart A.
Prior to amendment, the heading for Subpart A read as follows:
"A. Gasoline and Diesel Fuel"
In 1997, P.L. 105-34, Sec. 1032(e)(3)(B), added "and kerosene" after "diesel fuel" in item 4082.
In 1993, P.L. 103-66, Sec. 13242(a), amended subpart A of Part III of subchapter A of chapter 32.
Prior to amendment, subpart A of Part III of subchapter A of chapter 32 read as follows:
"SUBPART A.—GASOLINE
"Sec.
"4081. Imposition of tax.
"4082. Definitions.
"4083. Cross references.

"Sec. 4081 Imposition of tax.
"(a) Tax imposed.
"(1) Tax on removal, entry, or sale.
"(A) In general. There is hereby imposed a tax at the rate specified in paragraph (2) on—
"(i) the removal of gasoline from any refinery,
"(ii) the removal of gasoline from any terminal,
"(iii) the entry into the United States of gasoline for consumption, use, or warehousing, and
"(iv) the sale of gasoline to any person who is not registered under section 4101 unless there was a prior taxable removal or entry of such gasoline under clause (i), (ii), or (iii).
"(B) Exception for bulk transfers to registered terminals. The tax imposed by this paragraph shall not apply to any removal or entry of gasoline transferred in bulk to a terminal if the person removing or entering the gasoline and the operator of such terminal are registered under section 4101.
"(2) Rates of tax.
"(A) In general. The rate of the tax imposed by this section is the sum of—
"(i) the Highway Trust Fund financing rate,
"(ii) the Leaking Underground Storage Tank Trust Fund financing rate, and
"(iii) the deficit reduction rate.
"(B) Rates. For purposes of subparagraph (A)—
"(i) the Highway Trust Fund financing rate is 11.5 cents a gallon,
"(ii) the Leaking Underground Storage Tank Trust Fund financing rate is 0.1 cent a gallon, and
"(iii) the deficit reduction rate is 6.8 cents per gallon.
"(b) Treatment of removal or subsequent sale by blender or compounder.
"(1) In general. There is hereby imposed a tax at the rate specified in subsection (a) on gasoline removed or sold by the blender or compounder thereof.
"(2) Credit for tax previously paid. If—
"(A) tax is imposed on the removal or sale of gasoline by reason of paragraph (1), and

"(B) the blender or compounder establishes the amount of the tax paid with respect to such gasoline by reason of subsection (a),
the amount of the tax so paid shall be allowed as a credit against the tax imposed by reason of paragraph (1).
"(c) Gasoline mixed with alcohol at refinery, etc.
"(1) In general. Under regulations prescribed by the Secretary, subsection (a) shall be applied by multiplying the otherwise applicable rate by a fraction the numerator of which is 10 and the denominator of which is—
"(A) 9 in the case of 10 percent gasohol,
"(B) 9.23 in the case of 7.7 percent gasohol, and
"(C) 9.43 in the case of 5.7 percent gasohol,
in the case of the removal or entry of any gasoline for use in producing gasohol at the time of such removal or entry. Subject to such terms and conditions as the Secretary may prescribe (including the application of section 4101), the treatment under the preceding sentence also shall apply to use in producing gasohol after the time of such removal or entry.
"(2) Later separation of gasoline from gasohol. If any person separates the gasoline from a mixture of gasoline and alcohol on which tax was imposed under subsection (a) at a Highway Trust Fund financing rate equivalent to an otherwise applicable rate by reason of this subsection (or with respect to which a credit or payment was allowed or made by reason of section 6427(f)(1)), such person shall be treated as the refiner of such gasoline. The amount of tax imposed on any sale of such gasoline by such person shall be reduced by the amount of tax imposed (and not credited or refunded) on any prior removal or sale of such fuel.
"(3) Alcohol defined. For purposes of this subsection, the term 'alcohol' includes methanol and ethanol but does not include alcohol produced from petroleum, natural gas, or coal (including peat). Such term does not include alcohol with a proof of less than 190 (determined without regard to any added denaturants).
"(4) Otherwise applicable rate. For purposes of this subsection—
"(A) In general. In the case of the Highway Trust Fund financing rate, the term 'otherwise applicable rate' means—
"(i) 6.1 cents a gallon for 10 percent gasohol,
"(ii) 7.342 cents a gallon for 7.7 percent gasohol, and
"(iii) 8.422 cents a gallon for 5.7 percent gasohol.
In the case of gasohol none of the alcohol in which consists of ethanol, clauses (i), (ii), and (iii) shall be applied by substituting '5.5 cents' for '6.1 cents', '6.88 cents' for '7.342 cents', and '8.08 cents' for '8.422 cents'.
"(B) 10 percent gasohol. The term '10 percent gasohol' means any mixture of gasoline with alcohol if at least 10 percent of such mixture is alcohol.
"(C) 7.7 percent gasohol. The term '7.7 percent gasohol' means any mixture of gasoline with alcohol if at least 7.7 percent, but not 10 percent or more, of such mixture is alcohol.
"(D) 5.7 percent gasohol. The term '5.7 percent gasohol' means any mixture of gasoline with alcohol if at least 5.7 percent, but not 7.7 percent or more, of such mixture is alcohol.
"(5) Termination. Paragraph (1) shall not apply to any removal or sale after September 30, 2000.
"(d) Termination.
"(1) Highway trust fund financing rate. On and after October 1, 1999, the Highway Trust Fund financing rate under subsection (a)(2) shall not apply.
"(2) Leaking underground storage tank trust fund financing rate. The Leaking Underground Storage Tank Trust Fund financing rate under subsection (a)(2) shall not apply after December 31, 1995.
"(3) Deficit reduction rate. On and after October 1, 1995, the deficit reduction rate under subsection (a)(2) shall not apply.
"(e) Refunds in certain cases.
Under regulations prescribed by the Secretary, if any person who paid the tax imposed by this section with respect to any gasoline establishes to the satisfaction of the Secretary that a prior tax was paid (and not credited or refunded) with respect to such gasoline, then an amount equal to the tax paid by such person shall be allowed as a refund (without interest) to such person in the same manner as if it were an overpayment of tax imposed by this section."

In 1993, P.L. 103-66, Sec. 13241(a), amended clause (a)(2)(B)(iii), effective 10/1/93.
Prior to amendment, clause (a)(2)(B)(iii) read as follows:
"(iii) the deficit reduction rate is 2.5 cents a gallon."
In 1992, P.L. 102-486, Sec. 1920(a), amended para. (c)(1) . . . Sec. 1920(b)(1), substituted "an otherwise applicable rate" for "6.1 cents a gallon" in para. (c)(2) . . . Sec. 1920(b)(2), amended para. (c)(4), effective for gasoline removed (as defined in Code Sec. 4082) or entered after 12/31/92.
Prior to amendment, para. (c)(1) read as follows:
"(1) In general. Under regulations prescribed by the Secretary, subsection (a) shall be applied by substituting rates which are ¹⁰⁄₉th of the otherwise applicable rates in the case of the removal or sale of any gasoline for use in producing gasohol at the time of such removal or sale. Subject to such terms and conditions as the Secretary may prescribe (including the application of section 4101), the treatment under the preceding sentence also shall apply to use in producing gasohol after the time of such removal or sale. For purposes of this paragraph, the term 'gasohol' means any mixture of gasoline if at least 10 percent of such mixture is alcohol. For purposes of this subsection, in the case of the Highway Trust Fund financing rate, the otherwise applicable rate is 6.1 cents a gallon."
Prior to amendment, para. (c)(4) read as follows:
"(4) Lower rate on gasohol made other than from ethanol. In the case of gasohol none of the alcohol in which consists of ethanol, paragraphs (1) and (2) shall be applied by substituting '5.5 cents' for '6.1 cents'."

In 1991, P.L. 102-240, Sec. 8002(a)(3), substituted "1999" for "1995" in para. (d)(1), effective 12/18/91.

In 1990, P.L. 101-508, Sec. 11211(a)(1)(A), deleted "and" at the end of clause (a)(2)(A)(i) . . . Sec. 11211(a)(1)(B), substituted ", and" for the period at the end of clause (a)(2)(A)(ii) . . . Sec. 11211(a)(1)(C), added clause (a)(2)(A)(iii) . . . Sec. 11211(a)(2)(A), substituted "11.5 cents a gallon," for "9 cents a gallon, and" in clause (a)(2)(B)(i) . . . Sec. 11211(a)(2)(B), substituted ", and" for the period at the end of clause (a)(2)(B)(ii) . . . Sec. 11211(a)(2)(C), added clause (a)(2)(B)(iii) . . . Sec. 11211(a)(3), added para. (d)(3) . . . Sec. 11211(a)(5)(A)(i), substituted "applied by substituting rates with are ¹⁰⁄₉th of the otherwise applicable rates in the case" for "applied by substituting '3⅓ cents' for '9 cents' and by substituting '⅑ cent' for '0.1 cent' in the case" in para. (c)(1) . . . Sec. 11211(a)(5)(A)(ii), added the last sentence to para. (c)(1) . . . Sec. 11211(a)(5)(B), substituted "at a Highway Trust Fund financing rate equivalent to 6.1 cents" for "at a [Highway Trust Fund financing] rate equivalent to 3 cents" in para. (c)(2) . . . Sec. 11211(a)(5)(C), redesignated para. (c)(4) as (c)(5), and added new para. (c)(4), effective for gasoline removed (as defined in Code Sec. 4082) after 11/30/90.

—P.L. 101-508, Sec. 11211(c)(3), substituted "1995" for "1993" in para. (d)(1) . . . Sec. 11211(e)(3), substituted "2000" for "1993" in para. (c)(5) (as redesignated by Sec. 11211(a)(5)(C) of this Act), effective 11/5/90.

—P.L. 101-508, Sec. 11211(j), provides:

"(j) Floor stocks taxes.—

"(1) Imposition of tax. In the case of—

"(A) gasoline and diesel fuel on which tax was imposed under section 4081 or 4091 of such Code before December 1, 1990, and which is held on such date by any person, or

"(B) diesel fuel on which no tax was imposed under section 4091 of such Code at the Highway Trust Fund financing rate before December 1, 1990, and which is held on such date by any person for use as a fuel in a train,

there is herby imposed a floor stocks tax on such gasoline and diesel fuel.

"(2) Rate of tax. The rate of the tax imposed by paragraph (1) shall be—

"(A) 5 cents per gallon in the case of fuel described in paragraph (1)(A), and

"(B) 2.5 cents per gallon in the case of fuel described in paragraph (1)(B).

In the case of any fuel held for use in producing a mixture described in section 4081(c)(1) or section 4091(c)(1)(A) of such Code, subparagraph (A) shall be applied by substituting '6.22 cents' for '5 cents'. If no alcohol in such mixture is ethanol, the preceding sentence shall be applied by substituting '5.56 cents' for '6.22 cents'.

"(3) Liability for tax and method of payment.—

"(A) Liability for tax. A person holding gasoline or diesel fuel on December 1, 1990, to which the tax imposed by paragraph (1) applies shall be liable for such tax.

"(B) Method of payment. The tax imposed by paragraph (1) shall be paid in such manner as the Secretary shall prescribe.

"(C) Time for payment. The tax imposed by paragraph (1) shall be paid on or before May 31, 1991.

"(4) Definitions. For purposes of this subsection—

"(A) Held by person. Gasoline and diesel fuel shall be considered as 'held by a person' if title thereto has passed to such person (whether or not delivery to the person has been made).

"(B) Gasoline. The term 'gasoline' has the meaning given such term by section 4082 of such Code.

"(C) Diesel fuel. The term 'diesel fuel' has the meaning given such term by section 4092 of such Code.

"(D) Secretary. The term 'Secretary' means the Secretary of the Treasury or his delegate.

"(5) Exception for exempt uses. The tax imposed by paragraph (1) shall not apply to gasoline or diesel fuel held by any person exclusively for any use to the extent a credit or refund of the tax imposed by section 4081 or 4091 of such Code, as the case may be, is allowable for such use.

"(6) Exception for fuel held in vehicle tank. No tax shall be imposed by paragraph (1) on gasoline or diesel fuel held in the tank of a motor vehicle or motorboat.

"(7) Exception for certain amounts of fuel.—

"(A) In general. No tax shall be imposed by paragraph (1)—

"(i) on gasoline held on December 1, 1990, by any person if the aggregate amount of gasoline held by such person on such date does not exceed 4,000 gallons, and

"(ii) on diesel fuel held on December 1, 1990, by any person if the aggregate amount of diesel fuel held by such person on such date does not exceed 2,000 gallons.

The preceding sentence shall apply only if such person submits to the Secretary (at the time and in the manner required by the Secretary) such information as the Secretary shall require for purposes of this paragraph.

"(B) Exempt fuel. For purposes of subparagraph (A), there shall not be taken into account fuel held by any person which is exempt from the tax imposed by paragraph (1) by reason of paragraph (5) or (6).

"(C) Controlled groups. For purposes of this paragraph, rules similar to the rules of paragraph (6) of section 11201(e) of this Act shall apply.

"(8) Other laws applicable. All provisions of law, including penalties, applicable with respect to the taxes imposed by section 4081 of such Code in the case of gasoline and section 4091 of such Code in the case of diesel fuel shall, insofar as applicable and not inconsistent with the provisions of this subsection, apply with respect to the floor stock taxes imposed by paragraph (1) to the same extent as if such taxes were imposed by such section 4081 or 4091.

"(9) Transfer of portion of floor stocks revenue to highway trust fund. For purposes of determining the amount transferred to the Highway Trust Fund, the tax imposed by paragraph (1) on fuel described in subparagraph (A) thereof shall be treated as imposed at a Highway Trust Fund financing rate to the extent of 2.5 cents per gallon."

—P.L. 101-508, Sec. 11212(a), amended para. (a)(1) . . . Sec. 11212(d)(1), added subsec. (e) . . . Sec. 11212(e)(2), deleted para. (a)(3), effective 7/1/91.

Prior to amendment, para. (a)(1) read as follows:

"(1) In general. There is hereby imposed a tax at the rate specified in paragraph (2) on the earlier of—

"(A) the removal, or

"(B) the sale,

of gasoline by the refiner or importer thereof or the terminal operator."

Prior to deletion, para. (a)(3) read as follows:

"(3) Bulk transfer to terminal operator. For purposes of paragraph (1), the bulk transfer of gasoline to a terminal operator by a refiner or importer shall not be considered a removal or sale of gasoline by such refiner or importer."

—P.L. 101-508, Sec. 11215(a), amended para. (d)(2), effective 12/1/90.

Prior to amendment, para. (d)(2) read as follows:

"(2) Leaking underground storage tank trust fund financing rate.

"(A) In general. The Leaking Underground Storage Tank Trust Fund financing rate under subsection (a)(2) shall not apply after the earlier of—

"(i) December 31, 1991, or

"(ii) the last day of the termination month.

"(B) Termination month. For purposes of subparagraph (A), the termination month is the 1st month as of the close of which the Secretary estimates that the net revenues are at least $500,000,000 from taxes imposed by section 4041(d) and taxes attributable to Leaking Underground Storage Tank Trust Fund financing rate imposed under this section and sections 4042 and 4091.

"(C) Net revenues. For purposes of subparagraph (B), the term 'net revenues' means the excess of gross revenues over amounts payable by reason of section 9508(c)(2) (relating to transfer from Leaking Underground Storage Tank Trust Fund for certain repayments and credits)."

—P.L. 100-508, Sec. 11218, relating to floor stocks tax treatment of articles in foreign trade zones, is reproduced in note following Code Sec. 5001.

In 1988, P.L. 100-647, Sec. 1017(c)(1)(A), redesignated para. (a)(2) as para. (a)(3), amended para. (a)(1), and added para. (a)(2) . . . Sec. 1017(c)(1)(B), substituted "subsection (a)" for "subsection (d)" in subsecs. (b) and (c) . . . Sec. 1017(c)(1)(C), substituted "subsection (a)(2)" for "subsection (d)(2)(A)" in para. (e)(1), and substituted "subsection (a)(2)" for "subsection (d)(2)(B)" each place it appeared in para. (e)(2) . . . Sec. 1017(c)(1)(D), deleted subsec. (d) and redesignated subsec. (e) as subsec. (d) . . . Sec. 1017(c)(14), substituted "3⅓ cents" for "3 cents" in para. (c)(1), effective for gasoline removed (as defined in Code Sec. 4082 as amended by Sec. 1703(a) of P.L. 100-203) after 12/31/87.

Prior to amendment para. (a)(1) read as follows:

"(a) Tax imposed.

"(1) In general. There is hereby imposed a tax at the rate specified in subsection (d) on the earlier of —

"(A) the removal, or

"(B) the sale,

of gasoline by the refiner or importer thereof or the terminal operator."

Prior to deletion subsec. (d) read as follows:

"(d) Rate of tax.

"(1) In general. The rate of the tax imposed by this section is the sum of —

"(A) the Highway Trust Fund financing rate, and

"(B) the Leaking Underground Storage Tank Trust Fund financing rate."

—P.L. 100-647, Sec. 1017(c)(13), amended Sec. 1703(f)(2) of P.L. 99-514 [reproduced below], provisions on floor stock taxes, by adding the last sentence, see below.

—P.L. 100-647, Sec. 2001(d)(4)(A), amended Sec. 1703(f)(1) of P.L. 99-514 [reproduced below], provisions on floor stock taxes, by substituting "9.1 cents" for "9 cents", see below . . . Sec. 2001(d)(4)(B), amended Sec. 1703(f)(4) of P.L. 99-514, reproduced below.

Prior to amendment Sec. 1703(f)(4) of P.L. 99-514 read as follows:

"(4) Transfer of floor stocks taxes to highway trust fund.—For purposes of determining the amount transferred to the Highway Trust Fund for any period, the taxes imposed by this subsection shall be treated as if they were imposed by section 4081 of the Internal Revenue Code of 1986."

—P.L. 100-647, Sec. 2001(d)(5)(A), added "and by substituting '⅑ cent' for '0.1 cent'" before "in the case of the removal" in para. (c)(1) . . . Sec. 2001(d)(5)(B), substituted "reduced by the amount of tax imposed (and not credited or refunded) on any prior removal or sale of such fuel" for "5⅔ cents a gallon" in para. (c)(2), effective 1/1/87.

—P.L. 100-647, Sec. 6104(a), added "Subject to such terms and conditions as the Secretary may prescribe (including the application of section 4101), the treatment under the preceding sentence also shall apply to use in producing gasohol after the time of such removal or sale." after the first sentence in para. (c)(1), effective 10/1/89.

In 1987, P.L. 100-203, Sec. 10502(d)(2), amended subpara. (e)(2)(B), effective for sales after 3/31/88.

Prior to amendment, subpara. (e)(2)(B) read as follows:

"(B) Termination month. For purposes of subparagraph (A), the termination month is the 1st month as of the close of which the Secretary estimates that the net revenues from the taxes imposed by this section (to the extent attributable to the Leaking Underground Storage Tank Trust Fund financing rate under subsection (d)(2)(B)), section 4041(d), and section 4042 (to the extent attributable to the Leaking Underground Storage Tank Trust Fund financing rate under section 4042(b)) are at least $500,000,000."

—P.L. 100-17, Sec. 502(a)(4), substituted "1993" for "1988" in para. (e)(1)... Sec. 502(c)(2), substituted "September 30, 1993" for "December 31, 1992" in para. (c)(4), effective 4/2/87.

In 1986, P.L. 99-514, Sec. 1703(a), amended Code Sec. 4081, as part of the amendments to subpart A of Part III of subchapter A of chapter 32, effective for gasoline removed (as defined in Code Sec 4082 as amended by Sec. 1703(a) of this Act) after 12/31/87. Sec. 1703(f) of this Act [as amended by Sec. 1017(c)(13) of P.L. 100-647 and Sec. 2001(d)(4)(A) and (B), see above] provides:

"(f) Floor stock taxes.—

"(1) In general.—On gasoline subject to tax under section 4081 of the Internal Revenue Code of 1986 which, on January 1, 1988, is held by a dealer for sale, and with respect to which no tax has been imposed under such section, there is hereby imposed a floor stocks tax at the rate of 9.1 cents a gallon.

"(2) Overpayment of floor stocks taxes.— Section 6416 of such Code shall apply in respect of the floor stocks taxes imposed by this section, so as to entitle, subject to all provisions of such section, any person paying such floor stocks taxes to a credit or refund thereof for any reasons specified in such section. All other provisions of law, including penalties, applicable with respect to the taxes imposed by section 4081 of the Internal Revenue Code of 1986 shall apply to the floor stocks taxes imposed by this section.

"(3) Due date of taxes.— The taxes imposed by this subsection shall be paid before February 16, 1988.

"(4) Transfer of floor stock tax revenues to trust funds.— For purposes of determining the amount transferred to any trust fund, the tax imposed by this section shall be treated as imposed by section 4081 of the Internal Revenue Code of 1986—

"(A) at the Highway Trust Fund financing rate under such section to the extent of 9 cents per gallon, and

"(B) at the Leaking Underground Storage Tank Trust Fund financing rate under such section to the extent of 0.1 cent per gallon.

"(5) Definitions and special rule.— For purposes of this subsection—

"(A) Dealer.— The term 'dealer' includes a wholesaler, jobber, distributor, or retailer.

"(B) Held by a dealer.— Gasoline shall be considered as 'held by a dealer' if title thereto has passed to such dealer (whether or not delivery to him has been made) and if for purposes of consumption title to such gasoline or possession thereof has not at any time been transferred to any person other than a dealer.

"(C) Gasoline.— The term 'gasoline' has the same meaning given to such term by section 4082(a) of the Internal Revenue Code of 1986."

—P.L. 99-499, Sec. 521(a)(1)(B)(i), substituted "at the rate specified in subsection (d)" for "of 9 cents a gallon" in subsecs. (a) and (b)... Sec. 521(a)(1)(B)(ii), amended subsec. (d) and added subsec. (e)... Sec. 521(a)(1)(B)(iii), substituted "subsection (a)" for "subsection (a)" in para. (c)(1) and substituted "a Highway Trust Fund financing rate" for "a rate" in para. (c)(2), effective 1/1/87.

Prior to amendment, subsec. (d) read as follows:

"(d) Termination.

"On and after October 1, 1988, the taxes imposed by this section shall not apply."

Sec. 4082 Definitions.

"(a) Gasoline.

For purposes of this subpart, the term 'gasoline' includes, to the extent prescribed in regulations—

"(1) gasoline blend stocks, and

"(2) products commonly used as additives in gasoline.

For purposes of paragraph (1), the term 'gasoline blend stocks' means any petroleum product component of gasoline.

"(b) Certain uses defined as removal.

If a refiner, importer, terminal operator, blender, or compounder uses (other than in the production of gasoline or special fuels referred to in section 4041) gasoline refined, imported, blended, or compounded by him, such use shall for the purposes of this chapter be considered a removal."

In 1986, P.L. 99-514, Sec. 1703(a), amended Code Sec. 4082, as part of the amendments to subpart A of Part III of subchapter A of chapter 32, effective for gasoline removed (as defined in this Code Section) after 12/31/87.

"Sec. 4083 Cross references.

"(1) For provisions to relieve farmers from excise tax in the case of gasoline used on the farm for farming purposes, see section 6420.

"(2) For provisions to relieve purchasers of gasoline from excise tax in the case of gasoline used for certain nonhighway purposes, used by local transit systems, or sold for certain exempt purposes, see section 6421.

"(3) For provisions to relieve purchasers of gasoline from excise tax in the case of gasoline not used for taxable purposes, see section 6427."

In 1986, P.L. 99-514, Sec. 1703(a), amended Code Sec. 4083, as part of the amendments to subpart A of Part III of subchapter A of chapter 32, effective for gasoline removed (as defined in Code Sec. 4082 as amended by Sec. 1703(a) of this Act) after 12/31/87.

In 1986, P.L. 99-514, Sec. 1703(a), amended subpart A of Part III of subchapter A of chapter 32.

Prior to amendment, subpart A of Part III of subchapter A of chapter 32 read as follows:

"SUBPART A. — GASOLINE

"Sec.

"4081. Imposition of tax.

"4082. Definitions.

"4083. Exemption of sales to producer.

"4084. Cross references."

In 1956, inserted item "4084. Relief of farmers from tax in case of gasoline used on the farm" and P.L. 627 amended item "4084" by substituting "Cross references."

"SEC. 4081. IMPOSITION OF TAX.

"(a) In general.

"There is hereby imposed on gasoline sold by the producer or importer thereof, or by any producer of gasoline, a tax at the rate specified in subsection (b).

"(b) Rate of tax.

"(1) In general. The rate of the tax imposed by this section is the sum of—

"(A) the Highway Trust Fund financing rate, and

"(B) the Leaking Underground Storage Tank Trust Fund financing rate.

"(2) Rates. For purposes of paragraph (1)—

"(A) the Highway Trust Fund financing rate is 9 cents a gallon, and

"(B) the Leaking Underground Storage Tank Trust Fund financing rate is 0.1 cents a gallon.

"(c) Gasoline mixed with alcohol.

"(1) In general. Under regulations prescribed by the Secretary, subsection (b) shall be applied

"(A) by substituting '3 cents' for '9 cents' in the case of the sale of any gasohol (the gasoline in which was not taxed under subparagraph (B)), and

"(B) by substituting '3⅓ cents' for '9 cents' in the case of the sale of any gasoline for use in producing gasohol.

For purposes of this paragraph, the term 'gasohol' means any mixture of gasoline if at least 10 percent of such mixture is alcohol.

"(2) Later separation of gasoline. If any person separates the gasoline from a mixture of gasoline and alcohol on which tax was imposed under subsection (a) at a Highway Trust Fund financing rate equivalent to 3 cents a gallon by reason of this subsection (or with respect to which a credit or payment was allowed or made by reason of section 6427(f)(1)), such person shall be treated as the producer of such gasoline. The amount of tax imposed on any sale of such gasoline by such person shall be 5⅓ cents a gallon.

"(3) Alcohol defined. For purposes of this subsection, the term 'alcohol' includes methanol and ethanol but does not include alcohol produced from petroleum, natural gas, or coal (including peat). Such term does not include alcohol with a proof of less than 190 (determined without regard to any added denaturants).

"(4) Termination. Paragraph (1) shall not apply to any sale after December 31, 1992.

"(d) Termination.

"(1) Highway Trust Fund Financing Rate. On and after October 1, 1988, the Highway Trust Fund financing rate under subsection (b)(2)(A) shall not apply.

"(2) Leaking Underground Storage Tank Trust Fund Financing Rate.

"(A) In general. The Leaking Underground Storage Tank Trust Fund financing rate under subsection (b)(2)(B) shall not apply after the earlier of—

"(i) December 31, 1991, or

"(ii) the last day of the termination month.

"(B) Termination month. For purposes of subparagraph (A), the termination month is the 1st month as of the close of which the Secretary estimates that the net revenues from the taxes imposed by this section (to the extent attributable to the Leaking Underground Storage Tank Trust Fund financing rate under subsection (b)(2)(B)), section 4041(d), and section 4042 (to the extent attributable to the Leaking Underground Storage Tank Trust Fund financing rate under section 4042(b)) are at least $500,000,000.

"(C) Net revenues. For purposes of subparagraph (B), the term 'net revenues' means the excess of gross revenues over amounts payable by reason of section 9508(c)(2) (relating to transfer from Leaking Underground Storage Tank Trust Fund for certain repayments and credits)".

In 1986, P.L. 99-499, Sec. 521(a)(1)(A)(i), amended subsecs. (a) and (b)... Sec. 521(a)(1)(A)(ii), added subsec. (d)... Sec. 521(a)(1)(A)(iii), substituted "subsection (b)" for "subsection (a)" in para. (c)(1) and substituted "a Highway Trust Fund financing rate" for "a rate" in para. (c)(2), effective 1/1/87.

Prior to amendment, subsecs. (a) and (b) read as follows:

"(a) In general.

"There is hereby imposed on gasoline sold by the producer or importer thereof, or by any producer of gasoline, a tax of 9 cents a gallon.

"(b) Termination.

"On and after October 1, 1988, the taxes imposed by this section shall not apply."

In 1984, P.L. 98-369, Sec. 732(a)(1), amended para. (c)(1)... Sec. 732(a)(2), substituted "at a rate equivalent to 4 cents a gallon" for "at the rate of 4 cents a gallon" and "4⅚ cents" for "5 cents" in para. (c)(2), effective 4/1/83.

Prior to amendment, para. (c)(1) read as follows:

"(1) In general. Under regulations prescribed by the Secretary, subsection (a) shall be applied by substituting '4 cents' for '9 cents' in the case of the sale of any gasoline—

"(A) in a mixture with alcohol, if at least 10 percent of the mixture is alcohol, or

"(B) for use in producing a mixture at least 10 percent of which is alcohol."

—P.L. 98-369, Sec. 732(b), amended Sec. 521(a) of P.L. 97-424 (reproduced below), by adding "4 cents a gallon in the case of a gallon of gasohol, as defined in section 4081(c))" after "5 cents a gallon".

—P.L. 98-369, Sec. 734(a)(1), amended Sec. 523(b) of P.L.97-424 (reproduced below), by adding "(or will be subject to a lower rate of tax under such section)" after "and which will not be subject to tax under such section" in Sec. 523(b)(1) of P.L. 97-424 . . . Sec. 734(a)(2), amended Sec. 523(b) of P.L. 97-424 (reproduced below), by adding Sec. 523(b)(3) to P.L. 97-424 and by substituting "Except as provided in paragraph (3), in the case of" for "In the case of" in Sec. 523(b)(2) of P.L. 97-424 . . . Sec. 734(d), amended Sec. 523(b)(1) of P.L. 97-424 (reproduced below), by adding the last sentence.

—P.L. 98-369, Sec. 734(e), amended Sec. 521(c) of P.L. 97-424 (reproduced below), by adding the last sentence.

—P.L. 98-369, Sec. 912(b), substituted "3 cents" for "4 cents", "3⅓ cents" for "4⅘ cents" and "5⅔ cents" for "4⅘ cents" in subsec. (c) . . . Sec. 912(f), substituted "coal (including peat)" for "coal" in para. (c)(3), effective on 1/1/85.

In 1983, P.L. 97-424, Sec. 511(a)(1), substituted "9 cents a gallon" for "4 cents a gallon" in subsec. (a) . . . Sec. 511(d)(1)(A), substituted "subsection (a) shall be applied by substituting '4 cents' for '9 cents' in the case of the sale of any gasoline" for "no tax shall be imposed by this section on the sale of any gasoline" in para. (c)(1) . . . Sec. 511(d)(1)(B)(i), and (ii), substituted "tax was imposed under subsection (a) at the rate of 4 cents a gallon by reason of this subsection" for "tax was not imposed by reason of this subsection" in para. (c)(2), and added the last sentence to para. (c)(2), effective 4/1/83.

—P.L. 97-424, Sec. 516(a)(3), amended subsec. (b), effective 1/6/83.

Prior to amendment, subsec. (b) read as follows:

"(b) Rate reduction.

"On and after October 1, 1984, the tax imposed by this section shall be 1½ cents a gallon."

—P.L. 97-424, Sec. 521(a)–(e), [as amended by Sec. 732(b) of P.L. 98-369, see above] provide:

"SEC. 521. FLOOR STOCKS TAXES.

"(a) 1983 Tax on gasoline.—On gasoline subject to tax under section 4081 which, on April 1, 1983, is held by a dealer for sale, there is hereby imposed a floor stocks tax at the rate of 5 cents a gallon. (4 cents a gallon in the case of a gallon of gasohol, as defined in section 4081(c)).

"(b) 1984 Tax on tires.—On any article which would be subject to tax under section 4071(a) if sold by the manufacturer, producer, or importer on or after January 1, 1984, which on January 1, 1984, is held by a dealer and has not been used and is intended for sale, there shall be imposed a floor stocks tax equal to the excess of the amount of tax which would be imposed on such article if it were sold by the manufacturer, producer, or importer after January 1, 1984, over the amount of tax imposed under section 4071(a) on the sale of such article by the manufacturer, producer, or importer.

"(c) Overpayment of floor stocks taxes.—Section 6416 shall apply in respect of the floor stocks taxes imposed by this section, so as to entitle, subject to all provisions of section 6416, any person paying such floor stocks taxes to a credit or refund thereof for any of the reasons specified in section 6416. All other provisions of law, including penalties, applicable with respect to the taxes imposed by section 4081 or 4071(a) (whichever is appropriate) shall apply to the floor stocks taxes imposed by this section.

"(d) Due date of taxes.—The taxes imposed by this section shall be paid at such time after—

"(1) May 15, 1983, in the case of the tax imposed by subsection (a), or

"(2) February 15, 1984, in the case of the tax imposed by subsection (b),

as may be prescribed by the Secretary of the Treasury or his delegate.

"(e) Transfer of floor stocks taxes to highway trust fund.—For purposes of determining the amount transferred to the Highway Trust Fund for any period, the taxes imposed by this section shall be treated as if they were imposed by section 4081 or 4071 of the Internal Revenue Code of 1954, whichever is appropriate."

—P.L. 97-424, Sec. 523(a), and (b) [as amended by Secs. 734(a)(1), (a)(2) and (d) of P.L. 98-369, see above] provide:

"SEC. 523. DEFINITIONS AND SPECIAL RULE.

"(a) In general.—For purposes of this subtitle—

"(1) The term 'dealer' includes a wholesaler, jobber, distributor, or retailer.

"(2) An article shall be considered as 'held by a dealer' if title thereto has passed to such dealer (whether or not delivery to him has been made) and if for purposes of consumption title to such article or possession thereof has not at any time been transferred to any person other than a dealer.

"(3) The term 'tax-repealed article' means any article on which a tax was imposed by section 4061(a), 4061(b), or section 4091 as in effect on the day before the date of the enactment of this Act, and which will not be subject to tax under section 4061(a), 4061(b), or 4091 as in effect on the day after the date of the enactment of this Act.

"(4) Except as otherwise expressly provided herein, any reference in this subtitle to a section or other provision shall be treated as a reference to a section or other provision of the Internal Revenue Code of 1954.

"(b) 1984 Extension of floor stocks refund to tires.—

"(1) In general.—In the case of an article on which a tax was imposed by section 4071(a) as in effect on December 31, 1983, and which will not be subject to tax under such section (or will be subject to a lower rate of tax under such section) as in effect on January 1, 1984, such article shall be treated as a tax-repealed article for purposes of subsection (a) of section 522. Any tread rubber which was subject to tax under section 4071(a)(4) as in effect on December 31, 1983, and which on January 1, 1984, is part of a retread tire which is held by a dealer and has not been used and is intended for sale shall be treated as a tax-repealed article for purposes of subsection (a) of section 522.

"(2) Allowance of refund.—Except as provided in paragraph (3), in the case of a tax-repealed article to which paragraph (1) applies, subsection (a) of section 522 shall be applied—

"(A) by treating January 1, 1984, as the day after the date of the enactment of this Act, and

"(B) by substituting '1984' for '1983' each place it appears in paragraph (1) of such subsection (a).

"(3) Special rules for tires taxed at lower rate after January 1, 1984.—In the case of any tire which is a tax-repealed article solely by reason of the amendment made by subsection (a)(1) or (d) of section 734 of the Tax Reform Act of 1984

"(A) the amount of the credit or refund under subsection (a) shall not exceed the excess of—

"(i) the tax imposed with respect to such tire by section 4071(a) as in effect on December 31, 1983, over

"(ii) the tax which would have been imposed with respect to such tire by section 4071(a) on January 1, 1984, and

"(B) paragraph (1) of section 522(a) shall be applied

"(i) by substituting 'January 1, 1985' for 'July 1, 1983', and

"(ii) by substituting 'April 1, 1985' for 'October 1, 1983' each place it appears."

In 1980, P.L. 96-223, Sec. 232(a)(1), added para. (c)(4).

—P.L. 96-223, Sec. 232(a)(3), extended the effective date of changes made by Sec. 221(a)(1) of P.L. 95-618 to apply to sales after 12/31/78 [see below].

Prior to amendment Sec. 221(a)(2) [effective date] of P.L. 95-618 read as follows:

"(2) The amendment made by paragraph (1) shall apply to sales after December 31, 1978, and before October 1, 1984."

—P.L. 96-223, Sec. 232(b)(3)(A), added the last sentence to the end of para. (c)(3), to apply to sales or uses in tax. yrs. end. after 9/30/80.

—P.L. 96-223, Sec. 232(d)(3), added the phrase beginning "(or with respect" following "after this subsection" in para. (c)(2), effective 1/1/79; Sec. 232(h)(2)(B) of the Act provides:

"(B) Transitional rule.

"Any mixture sold or used on or after January 1, 1979, and before the date of the enactment of this Act which is described in section 6427(f)(1) of the Internal Revenue Code of 1954 (as amended by subsection (d)) shall, for purposes of section 6427 of such Code, be treated as sold or used on the date of the enactment of this Act."

—P.L. 96-223, Sec. 232(e)(2)(E), repealed Sec. 221(d) of P.L. 95-618, effective 7/1/80 [see below].

In 1978, P.L. 95-618, Sec. 221(a)(1), added subsec. (c), effective for sales after 12/31/78. Sec. 221(d), following, was repealed by Sec. 232(e)(2)(E) of P.L. 96-223, effective 7/1/80. Sec. 221(d) of P.L. 95-618 provides:

"(d) Expedition of certain ethanol production applications.

"The Secretary of the Treasury shall expedite, to the maximum extent possible, action on the application of any person with respect to the production of ethanol for use in producing gasoline described in section 4081(c) (or in producing liquid fuel described in section 4041(k)) of the Internal Revenue Code of 1954. Within 6 months after the date of the enactment of this Act, the Secretary shall furnish to the Committee on Finance, United States Senate, and to the Committee on Ways and Means, United States House of Representatives, recommendations for legislation necessary to provide for changes in the provisions of chapter 51 of the Internal Revenue Code of 1954 to provide a simple, expeditious procedure for processing such applications and to simplify the regulation of such persons for purposes of such chapter consistent with adequate safeguards against the use of such applications to avoid or evade compliance with the provisions of such chapter relating to distilled spirits procured, dealt in, or used for other purposes."

—P.L. 95-599, Sec. 502(a)(5), substituted "1984" for "1979" in subsec. (b), effective 11/6/78.

In 1976, P.L. 94-280, Sec. 303(a)(6), substituted "1979" for "1977" in subsec. (b), effective 5/5/76.

In 1970, 12/31/70, Sec. 303(a)(6), substituted "1977" for "1972" in subsec. (b).

In 1961, increased the tax from 3 to 4 cents a gallon in subsec. (a), substituted "October 1, 1972" for "July 1, 1972" in subsec. (b), repealed former subsec. (c), which authorized a temporary increase in tax to 4 cents a gallon for the period Oct. 1, '59 to July 1, '61, effective 7/1/61.

In 1959, added subsec. (c).

In 1956, substituted "April 1, 1957" for "April 1, 1956".

—redesignated first sentence as subsec. (a), and increased the tax from 2 cents a gallon to 3 cents a gallon, redesignated second sentence as subsec. (b), and substituted "July 1, 1972" for "April 1, 1956", effective 7/1/56.

In 1955, substituted "April 1, 1956" for "April 1, 1955".

"SEC. 4082. DEFINITIONS.

"(a) Producer.

"As used in this subpart, the term 'producer' includes a refiner, compounder, blender, or wholesale distributor, and a dealer, selling gasoline exclusively to producers of gasoline, as well as a producer. Any person to whom gasoline is sold tax-free under this subpart shall be considered the producer of such gasoline.

"(b) Gasoline.

"As used in this subpart, the term 'gasoline' means all products commonly or commercially known or sold as gasoline which are suitable as a motor fuel.

"(c) Certain uses defined as sales.

"If a producer or importer uses (otherwise than in the production of gasoline or of special fuels referred to in section 4041) gasoline sold to him free of tax, or produced or imported by him, such use shall for the purposes of this chapter be considered a sale.

"(d) *Wholesale distributor.*
"As used in subsection (a), the term 'wholesale distributor' includes
"(1) any person who—
"(A) sells gasoline to producers, retailers, or to users who purchase in bulk quantities and deliver into bulk storage tanks, or
"(B) purchases gasoline from a producer and distributes such gasoline to 10 or more retail gasoline stations under common management with such person,
"(2) but only if such person elects to register with respect to the tax imposed by section 4081.
Such term does not include any person who (excluding the term 'wholesale distributor' from subsection (a)) is a producer or importer.
"(e) *Certain sellers of gasoline for use in noncommercial aviation treated as producers.*
"For purposes of this subpart, the term 'producer' includes any person who regularly sells gasoline to owners, lessees, or operators of aircraft for use as fuel in such aircraft in noncommercial aviation (as defined in section 4041(c)(4)).

In 1984, P.L. 98-369, Sec. 733(a), amended subsec. (d), effective on the first day of the first calendar quarter begin. after 7/18/84 [10/1/84].
Prior to amendment, subsec. (d) read as follows:
"(d) *Wholesale distributor.*
"As used in subsection (a), the term 'wholesale distributor' includes any person who—
"(1) sells gasoline to producers, to retailers, or to users who purchase in bulk quantities for delivery into bulk storage tanks, and
"(2) elects to register with respect to the tax imposed by section 4081.
Such term does not include any person who (excluding the term 'wholesale distributor' from subsection (a)) is a producer or importer."
—P.L. 98-369, Sec. 734(c)(1), added subsec. (e), effective on the first day of the first calendar quarter begin. after 7/18/84 [10/1/84].
In 1970, P.L. 91-258, Sec. 205(c)(6), substituted "or of special fuels referred to in section 4041" for "or of special motor fuels referred to in section 4041(b)" in subsec. (c), effective 7/1/70.
In 1965, substituted "which are suitable as a motor fuel" for "(including casinghead and natural gasoline)" in subsec. (b) and deleted "and give a bond" after "register" in subsec. (d)(2), for articles sold after 6/30/65.
In 1959, included wholesale distributors in subsec. (a) and added subsec. (d), effective 1/1/60.

"SEC. 4083. EXEMPTION OF SALES TO PRODUCER.
"Under regulations prescribed by the Secretary the tax imposed by section 4081 shall not apply in the case of sales of gasoline to a producer of gasoline."

In 1976, P.L. 94-455, Sec. 1906(b)(13)(A), substituted "Secretary" for "Secretary or his delegate" in Code Sec. 4083, effective 2/1/77.

"SEC. 4084. CROSS REFERENCES.
"(1) For provisions to relieve farmers from excise tax in the case of gasoline used on the farm for farming purposes, see section 6420.
"(2) For provisions to relieve purchasers of gasoline from excise tax in the case of gasoline used for certain nonhighway purposes or by local transit systems, see section 6421."

In 1956, substituted "Cross references" for "Relief of farmers from tax in case of gasoline used on the farm" in the catchline, designated former provisions as par. (1) and added par. (2).
—added Code Sec. 4084.

Sec. 4081. Imposition of tax.
(a) Tax imposed.
   (1) Tax on removal, entry, or sale.
      (A) In general. There is hereby imposed a tax at the rate specified in paragraph (2) on—
         (i) the removal of a taxable fuel from any refinery,
         (ii) the removal of a taxable fuel from any terminal,
         (iii) the entry into the United States of any taxable fuel for consumption, use, or warehousing, and
         (iv) the sale of a taxable fuel to any person who is not registered under section 4101 unless there was a prior taxable removal or entry of such fuel under clause (i), (ii), or (iii).
      (B) Exemption for bulk transfers to registered terminals or refineries.
         (i) In general. The tax imposed by this paragraph shall not apply to any removal or entry of a taxable fuel transferred in bulk by pipeline or vessel to a terminal or refinery if the person removing or entering the taxable fuel, the operator of such pipeline or vessel (except as provided in clause (ii)), and the operator of such terminal or refinery are registered under section 4101.
         (ii) Nonapplication of registration to vessel operators entering by deep-draft vessel. For purposes of clause (i), a vessel operator is not required to be registered with respect to the entry of a taxable fuel transferred in bulk by a vessel described in section 4042(c)(1).
   (2) Rates of tax.
      (A) In general. The rate of the tax imposed by this section is—
         (i) in the case of gasoline other than aviation gasoline, 18.3 cents per gallon
         (ii) in the case of aviation gasoline, 19.3 cents per gallon, and
         (iii) in the case of diesel fuel or kerosene, 24.3 cents per gallon.
      (B) Leaking Underground Storage Tank Trust Fund tax. The rates of tax specified in subparagraph (A) shall each be increased by 0.1 cent per gallon. The increase in tax under this subparagraph shall in this title be referred to as the Leaking Underground Storage Tank Trust Fund financing rate.
      (C) Taxes imposed on fuel used in aviation. In the case of kerosene which is removed from any refinery or terminal directly into the fuel tank of an aircraft for use in aviation, the rate of tax under subparagraph (A)(iii) shall be—
         (i) in the case of use for commercial aviation by a person registered for such use under section 4101, 4.3 cents per gallon, and
         (ii) in the case of use for aviation not described in clause (i), 21.8 cents per gallon.
      (D) Diesel-water fuel emulsion. In the case of diesel-water fuel emulsion at least 14 percent of which is water and with respect to which the emulsion additive is registered by a United States manufacturer with the Environmental Protection Agency pursuant to section 211 of the Clean Air Act (as in effect on March 31, 2003), subparagraph (A)(iii) shall be applied by substituting "19.7 cents" for "24.3 cents". The preceding sentence shall not apply to the removal, sale, or use of diesel-water fuel emulsion unless the person so removing, selling, or using such fuel is registered under section 4101.
   (3) Certain refueler trucks, tankers, and tank wagons treated as terminal.
      (A) In general. For purposes of paragraph (2)(C), a refueler truck, tanker, or tank wagon shall be treated as part of a terminal if—
         (i) such terminal is located within an airport,
         (ii) any kerosene which is loaded in such truck, tanker, or wagon at such terminal is for delivery only into aircraft at the airport in which such terminal is located,
         (iii) such truck, tanker, or wagon meets the requirements of subparagraph (B) with respect to such terminal, and
         (iv) except in the case of exigent circumstances identified by the Secretary in regulations, no vehicle registered for highway use is loaded with kerosene at such terminal.
      (B) Requirements. A refueler truck, tanker, or tank wagon meets the requirements of this subparagraph with respect to a terminal if such truck, tanker, or wagon—

(i) has storage tanks, hose, and coupling equipment designed and used for the purposes of fueling aircraft,

(ii) is not registered for highway use, and

(iii) is operated by—

(I) the terminal operator of such terminal, or

(II) a person that makes a daily accounting to such terminal operator of each delivery of fuel from such truck, tanker, or wagon.

(C) Reporting. The Secretary shall require under section 4101(d) reporting by such terminal operator of—

(i) any information obtained under subparagraph (B)(iii)(II), and

(ii) any similar information maintained by such terminal operator with respect to deliveries of fuel made by trucks, tankers, or wagons operated by such terminal operator.

(D) Applicable rate. For purposes of paragraph (2)(C), in the case of any kerosene treated as removed from a terminal by reason of this paragraph—

(i) the rate of tax specified in paragraph (2)(C)(i) in the case of use described in such paragraph shall apply if such terminal is located within a secured area of an airport, and

(ii) the rate of tax specified in paragraph (2)(C)(ii) shall apply in all other cases.

(4) Liability for tax on kerosene used in commercial aviation. For purposes of paragraph (2)(C)(i), the person who uses the fuel for commercial aviation shall pay the tax imposed under such paragraph. For purposes of the preceding sentence, fuel shall be treated as used when such fuel is removed into the fuel tank.

(b) Treatment of removal or subsequent sale by blender.

(1) In general. There is hereby imposed a tax at the rate determined under subsection (a) on taxable fuel removed or sold by the blender thereof.

(2) Credit for tax previously paid. If—

(A) a tax is imposed on the removal or sale of a taxable fuel by reason of paragraph (1), and

(B) the blender establishes the amount of the tax paid with respect to such fuel by reason of subsection (a),

the amount of the tax so paid shall be allowed as a credit against the tax imposed by reason of paragraph (1).

(c) Later separation of fuel from diesel-water fuel emulsion.

If any person separates the taxable fuel from a diesel-water fuel emulsion on which tax was imposed under subsection (a) at a rate determined under subsection (a)(2)(D) (or with respect to which a credit or payment was allowed or made by reason of section 6427), such person shall be treated as the refiner of such taxable fuel. The amount of tax imposed on any removal of such fuel by such person shall be reduced by the amount of tax imposed (and not credited or refunded) on any prior removal or entry of such fuel.

(d) Termination.

(1) In general. The rates of tax specified in clauses (i) and (iii) of subsection (a)(2)(A) shall be 4.3 cents per gallon after September 30, 2011.

(2) Aviation fuels. The rates of tax specified in subsections (a)(2)(A)(ii) and (a)(2)(C)(ii) shall be 4.3 cents per gallon—

(A) after December 31, 1996, and before the date which is 7 days after the date of the enactment [2/28/97] of the Airport and Airway Trust Fund Tax Reinstatement Act of 1997, and

(B) after July 22, 2011.

(3) Leaking Underground Storage Tank Trust Fund financing rate. The Leaking Underground Storage Tank Trust Fund financing rate under subsection (a)(2) shall apply after September 30, 1997, and before October 1, 2011.

(e) Refunds in certain cases.

Under regulations prescribed by the Secretary, if any person who paid the tax imposed by this section with respect to any taxable fuel establishes to the satisfaction of the Secretary that a prior tax was paid (and not credited or refunded) with respect to such taxable fuel, then an amount equal to the tax paid by such person shall be allowed as a refund (without interest) to such person in the same manner as if it were an overpayment of tax imposed by this section.

In 2011, P.L. 112-21, Sec. 2(a), substituted "July 22, 2011" for "June 30, 2011" in subpara. (d)(2)(B), effective 7/1/2011.

—P.L. 112-16, Sec. 2(a), substituted "June 30, 2011" for "May 31, 2011" in subpara. (d)(2)(B), effective 6/1/2011.

—P.L. 112-7, Sec. 2(a), substituted "May 31, 2011" for "March 31, 2011" in subpara. (d)(2)(B), effective 4/1/2011.

In 2010, P.L. 111-329, Sec. 2(a), substituted "March 31, 2011" for "December 31, 2010" in subpara. (d)(2)(B), effective 1/1/2011.

—P.L. 111-249, Sec. 2(a), substituted "December 31, 2010" for "September 30, 2010" in subpara. (d)(2)(B), effective 10/1/2010.

—P.L. 111-216, Sec. 101(a), substituted "September 30, 2010" for "August 1, 2010" in subpara. (d)(2)(B), effective 8/2/2010.

—P.L. 111-197, Sec. 2(a), substituted "August 1, 2010" for "July 3, 2010" in subpara. (d)(2)(B), effective 7/4/2010.

—P.L. 111-161, Sec. 2(a), substituted "July 3, 2010" for "April 30, 2010" in subpara. (d)(2)(B), effective 5/1/2010.

—P.L. 111-153, Sec. 2(a), substituted "April 30, 2010" for "March 31, 2010" in subpara. (d)(2)(B), effective 4/1/2010.

In 2009, P.L. 111-116, Sec. 2(a), substituted "March 31, 2010" for "December 31, 2009" in subpara. (d)(2)(B), effective 1/1/2010.

—P.L. 111-69, Sec. 2(a), substituted "December 31, 2009" for "September 30, 2009" in subpara. (d)(2)(B), effective 10/1/2009.

—P.L. 111-12, Sec. 2(a), substituted "September 30, 2009" for "March 31, 2009" in subpara. (d)(2)(B), effective 4/1/2009.

In 2008, P.L. 110-330, Sec. 2(a), substituted "March 31, 2009" for "September 30, 2008" in subpara. (d)(2)(B), effective 10/1/2008.

—P.L. 110-253, Sec. 2(a), substituted "October 1, 2008" for "July 1, 2008" in subpara. (d)(2)(B), effective 7/1/2008.

—P.L. 110-190, Sec. 2(a), substituted "June 30, 2008" for "February 29, 2008" in subpara. (d)(2)(B), effective 3/1/2008.

In 2007, P.L. 110-172, Sec. 6(d)(1)(C), of this Act provides:

"(C) Notwithstanding section 6430 of the Internal Revenue Code of 1986, a refund, credit, or payment may be made under subchapter B of chapter 65 of such Code for taxes imposed with respect to any liquid after September 30, 2005, and before the date of the enactment of this Act under section 4041(d)(1) or 4042 of such Code at the Leaking Underground Storage Tank Trust Fund financing rate to the extent that tax was imposed with respect to such liquid under section 4081 at the Leaking Underground Storage Tank Trust Fund financing rate."

—P.L. 110-161, Sec. 116(a), substituted "February 29, 2008" for "September 30, 2007" in subpara. (d)(2)(B), effective 10/1/2007.

In 2006, P.L. 109-432, Sec. 420(d), Sec. 420(d) of this Act, reads as follows:

"(d) Special rule for kerosene used in aviation on a farm for farming purposes.

"(1) Refunds for purchases after December 31, 2004, and before October 1, 2005. The Secretary of the Treasury shall pay to the ultimate purchaser of any kerosene which is used in aviation on a farm for farming purposes and which was purchased after December 31, 2004, and before October 1, 2005, an amount equal to the aggregate amount of tax imposed on such fuel under section 4041 or 4081 of the Internal Revenue Code of 1986, as the case may be, reduced by any payment to the ultimate vendor under section 6427(l)(5)(C) of such Code (as in effect on the day before the date of the enactment of the Safe, Accountable, Flexible, Efficient Transportation Equity Act: a Legacy for Users).

"(2) Use on a farm for farming purposes. For purposes of paragraph (1), kerosene shall be treated as used on a farm for farming pur-poses if such kerosene is used for farming purposes (within the meaning of section 6420(c)(3) of the Internal Revenue Code of 1986) in carrying on a trade or business on a farm situated in the United States. For purposes of the preceding sentence, rules similar to the rules of section 6420(c)(4) of such Code shall apply.

"(3) Time for filing claims. No claim shall be allowed under paragraph (1) unless the ultimate purchaser files such claim before the date that is 3 months after the date of the enactment of this Act.

"(4) No double benefit. No amount shall be paid under paragraph (1) or section 6427(l) of the Internal Revenue Code of 1986 with respect to any kerosene described in paragraph (1) to the extent that such amount is in excess of the tax imposed on such kerosene under section 4041 or 4081 of such Code, as the case may be.

"(5) Applicable laws. For purposes of this subsection, rules similar to the rules of section 6427(j) of the Internal Revenue Code of 1986 shall apply."

In 2005, P.L. 109-59, Sec. 11101(a)(1)(F), substituted "2011" for "2005" in para. (d)(1), effective 8/10/2005.

—P.L. 109-59, Sec. 11151(b)(1), substituted "for use in commercial aviation by a person registered for such use under section 4101" for "for use in commercial aviation" in subpara. (a)(2)(C)... Sec. 11151(b)(2), amended so much of para. (d)(2) as precedes subpara. (d)(2)(A), effective for aviation-grade kerosene removed, entered, or sold after 12/31/2004 as if included in the American Jobs Creation Act of 2004, Sec. 853(e) of P.L. 108-357.

Prior to amendment, so much of para. (d)(2) as precedes subpara. (d)(2)(A) read as follows:

"(2) Aviation gasoline. The rate of tax specified in subsection (a)(2)(A)(ii) shall be 4.3 cents per gallon."

—P.L. 109-59, Sec. 11161(a)(1), added "and" at the end of clause (a)(2)(A)(ii), substituted a period for ", and" at the end of clause (a)(2)(A)(iii), and deleted clause (a)(2)(A)(iv)... Sec. 11161(a)(2), amended subpara. (a)(2)(C)... Sec. 11161(a)(3)(A), deleted "a secured area of" in clause (a)(3)(A)(i)... Sec. 11161(a)(3)(B), added subpara. (a)(3)(D)... Sec. 11161(a)(4)(A), deleted "aviation-grade" each place it appeared in subpara. (a)(3)(A)... Sec. 11161(a)(4)(B), substituted "paragraph (2)(C)(i)" for "paragraph (2)(C)" in para. (a)(4)... Sec. 11161(a)(4)(C), deleted "aviation-grade" in the heading of para. (a)(4)... Sec. 11161(a)(4)(D), amended so much of para. (d)(2) as precedes subpara. (d)(2)(A) [as amended by Sec. 11151(b)(2) of this Act, see above], effective for fuels or liquids removed, entered, or sold after 9/30/2005.

Prior to deletion, clause (a)(2)(A)(iv) read as follows:

"(iv) in the case of aviation-grade kerosene, 21.8 cents per gallon."

Prior to amendment, subpara. (a)(2)(C) read as follows:

"(C) Taxes imposed on fuel used in commercial aviation. In the case of aviation-grade kerosene which is removed from any refinery or terminal directly into the fuel tank of an aircraft for use in commercial aviation by a person registered for such use under section 4101, the rate of tax under subparagraph (A)(iv) shall be 4.3 cents per gallon."

Prior to amendment, so much of para. (d)(2) as precedes subpara. (d)(2)(A) [as amended by Sec. 11151(b)(2) of this Act, see above] read as follows:

"(2) Aviation fuels. The rates of tax specified in clauses (ii) and (iv) of subsection (a)(2)(A) shall be 4.3 cents per gallon—"

—P.L. 109-59, Sec. 11166(b)(1), amended subpara. (a)(1)(B), effective 8/10/2005.

Prior to amendment, subpara. (a)(1)(B) read as follows:

"(B) Exemption for bulk transfers to registered terminals or refineries. The tax imposed by this paragraph shall not apply to any removal or entry of a taxable fuel transferred in bulk by pipeline or vessel to a terminal or refinery if the person removing or entering the taxable fuel, the operator of such pipeline or vessel, and the operator of such terminal or refinery are registered under section 4101."

—P.L. 109-58, Sec. 1343(a), added subpara. (a)(2)(D), effective 1/1/2006.

—P.L. 109-58, Sec. 1343(b)(2), added subsec. (c), effective 1/1/2006.

—P.L. 109-58, Sec. 1362(a), substituted "2011" for "2005" in para. (d)(3), effective 10/1/2005.

—P.L. 109-6, Sec. 1(a), substituted "October 1, 2005" for "April 1, 2005" in para. (d)(3), effective 3/31/2005.

In 2004, P.L. 108-357, Sec. 301(c)(7), deleted subsec. (c), effective for fuel sold or used after 12/31/2004.

Prior to deletion, subsec. (c) read as follows:

"(c) Taxable fuels mixed with alcohol. Under regulations prescribed by the Secretary.

"(1) In general. The rate of tax under subsection (a) shall be the alcohol mixture rate in the case of the removal or entry of any qualified alcohol mixture.

"(2) Tax prior to mixing.

"(A) In general. In the case of the removal or entry of any taxable fuel for use in producing at the time of such removal or entry a qualified alcohol mixture, the rate of tax under subsection (a) shall be the applicable fraction of the alcohol mixture rate. Subject to such terms and conditions as the Secretary may prescribe (including the application of section 4101), the treatment under the preceding sentence also shall apply to use in producing a qualified alcohol mixture after the time of such removal or entry.

"(B) Applicable fraction. For purposes of subparagraph (A), the applicable fraction is—

"(i) in the case of a qualified alcohol mixture which contains gasoline, the fraction the numerator of which is 10 and the denominator of which is—

"(I) 9 in the case of 10 percent gasohol,

"(II) 9.23 in the case of 7.7 percent gasohol, and

"(III) 9.43 in the case of 5.7 percent gasohol, and

"(ii) in the case of a qualified alcohol mixture which does not contain gasoline, 10/9.

"(3) Alcohol; qualified alcohol mixture. For purposes of this subsection—

"(A) Alcohol. The term 'alcohol' includes methanol and ethanol but does not include alcohol produced from petroleum, natural gas, or coal (including peat). Such term does not include alcohol with a proof of less than 190 (determined without regard to any added denaturants).

"(B) Qualified alcohol mixture. The term 'qualified alcohol mixture' means—

"(i) any mixture of gasoline with alcohol if at least 5.7 percent of such mixture is alcohol, and

"(ii) any mixture of diesel fuel with alcohol if at least 10 percent of such mixture is alcohol.

"(4) Alcohol mixture rates for gasoline mixtures. For purposes of this subsection—

"(A) General rules.

"(i) Mixtures containing ethanol. Except as provided in clause (ii), in the case of a qualified alcohol mixture which contains gasoline, the alcohol mixture rate is the excess of the rate which would (but for this paragraph) be determined under subsection (a) over—

"(I) in the case of 10 percent gasohol, the applicable blender rate (as defined in section 4041(b)(2)(C)) per gallon,

"(II) in the case of 7.7 percent gasohol, the number of cents per gallon equal to 77 percent of such applicable blender rate, and

"(III) in the case for 5.7 percent gasohol, the number of cents per gallon equal to 57 percent of such applicable blender rate.

"(ii) Mixtures not containing ethanol. In the case of a qualified alcohol mixture which contains gasoline and none of the alcohol in which consists of ethanol, the alcohol mixture rate is the excess of the rate which would (but for this paragraph) be determined under subsection (a) over—

"(I) in the case of 10 percent gasohol, 6 cents per gallon,

"(II) in the case of 7.7 percent gasohol, 4.62 cents per gallon, and

"(III) in the case of 5.7 percent gasohol, 3.42 cents per gallon.

"(B) 10 percent gasohol. The term '10 percent gasohol' means any mixture of gasoline with alcohol if at least 10 percent of such mixture is alcohol.

"(C) 7.7 percent gasohol. The term '7.7 percent gasohol' means any mixture of gasoline with alcohol if at least 7.7 percent, but not 10 percent or more, of such mixture is alcohol.

"(D) 5.7 percent gasohol. The term '5.7 percent gasohol' means any mixture of gasoline with alcohol if at least 5.7 percent, but not 7.7 percent or more, of such mixture is alcohol.

"(5) Alcohol mixture rate for diesel fuel mixtures. The alcohol mixture rate for a qualified alcohol mixture which does not contain gasoline is the excess of the rate which would (but for this paragraph) be determined under subsection (a) over the applicable blender rate (as defined in section 4041(b)(2)(C)) per gallon (6 cents per gallon in the case of a qualified alcohol mixture none of the alcohol in which consists of ethanol).

"(6) Limitation. In no event shall any alcohol mixture rate determined under this subsection be less than 4.3 cents per gallon.

"(7) Later separation of fuel from qualified alcohol mixture. If any person separates the taxable fuel from a qualified alcohol mixture on which tax was imposed under subsection (a) at a rate determined under paragraph (1) or (2) (or with respect to which a credit or payment was allowed or made by reason of section 6427(f)(1)), such person shall be treated as the refiner of such taxable fuel. The amount of tax imposed on any removal of such fuel by such person shall be reduced by the amount of tax imposed (and not credited or refunded) on any prior removal or entry of such fuel.

"(8) Termination. Paragraphs (1) and (2) shall not apply to any removal, entry, or sale after September 30, 2007."

—P.L. 108-357, Sec. 853(a)(1), deleted "and" at the end of clause (a)(2)(A)(ii), substituted ", and" for the period at the end of clause (a)(2)(A)(iii), and added clause (a)(2)(A)(iv)... Sec. 853(a)(2), added subpara. (a)(2)(C)... Sec. 853(a)(3)(A), added para. (a)(3)... Sec. 853(a)(3)(B), of this Act, provides:

"(B) List of airports with secured terminals. Not later than December 15, 2004, the Secretary of the Treasury shall publish and maintain a list of airports which include a secured area in which a terminal is located (within the meaning of section 4081(a)(3)(A)(i) of the Internal Revenue Code of 1986, as added by this paragraph)."... Sec. 853(a)(4), added para. (a)(4), effective for aviation-grade kerosene removed, entered, or sold after 12/31/2004.... Sec. 853(f), of this Act, provides:

"(f) Floor stocks tax.

"(1) In general. There is hereby imposed on aviation-grade kerosene held on January 1, 2005, by any person a tax equal to—

"(A) the tax which would have been imposed before such date on such kerosene had the amendments made by this section been in effect at all times before such date, reduced by

"(B) the sum of—

"(i) the tax imposed before such date on such kerosene under section 4091 of the Internal Revenue Code of 1986, as in effect on such date, and

"(ii) in the case of kerosene held exclusively for such person's own use, the amount which such person would (but for this clause) reasonably expect (as of such date) to be paid as a refund under section 6427(l) of such Code with respect to such kerosene.

"(2) Exception for fuel held in aircraft fuel tank. Paragraph (1) shall not apply to kerosene held in the fuel tank of an aircraft on January 1, 2005.

"(3) Liability for tax and method of payment.

"(A) Liability for tax. The person holding the kerosene on January 1, 2005, to which the tax imposed by paragraph (1) applies shall be liable for such tax.

"(B) Method and time for payment. The tax imposed by paragraph (1) shall be paid at such time and in such manner as the Secretary of the Treasury (or the Secretary's delegate) shall prescribe, including the nonapplication of such tax on de minimis amounts of kerosene.

"(4) Transfer of floor stock tax revenues to trust funds. For purposes of determining the amount transferred to any trust fund, the tax imposed by this subsection shall be treated as imposed by section 4081 of the Internal Revenue Code of 1986—

"(A) in any case in which tax was not imposed by section 4091 of such Code, at the Leaking Underground Storage Tank Trust Fund financing rate under such section to the extent of 0.1 cents per gallon, and

"(B) at the rate under section 4081(a)(2)(A)(iv) of such Code to the extent of the remainder.

"(5) Held by a person. For purposes of this subsection, kerosene shall be considered as held by a person if title thereto has passed to such person (whether or not delivery to the person has been made).

"(6) Other laws applicable. All provisions of law, including penalties, applicable with respect to the tax imposed by section 4081 of such Code shall, insofar as applicable and not inconsistent with the provisions of this subsection, apply with respect to the floor stock tax imposed by paragraph (1) to the same extent as if such tax were imposed by such section."

—P.L. 108-357, Sec. 860(a)(1), added "by pipeline or vessel" after "transferred in bulk" in subpara. (a)(1)(B)... Sec. 860(a)(2), added ", the operator of such pipeline or vessel," after "the taxable fuel" subpara. (a)(1)(B), effective 3/1/2005.

In 1998, P.L. 105-178, Sec. 9002(a)(1)(F), substituted "2005" for "1999" in para. (d)(1)... Sec. 9003(a)(1)(C), substituted "2007" for "2000" in para. (c)(8), effective 6/9/98.

—P.L. 105-178, Sec. 9003(b)(2)(B), amended subpara. (c)(4)(A)... Sec. 9003(b)(2)(C), substituted "the applicable blender rate (as defined in section 4041(b)(2)(C))" for "5.4 cents" in para. (c)(5), effective 1/1/2001.

Prior to amendment, subpara. (c)(4)(A) read as follows:

"(A) In general. The alcohol mixture rate for a qualified alcohol mixture which contains gasoline is the excess of the rate which would (but for this paragraph) be determined under subsection (a) over—

"(i) 5.4 cents per gallon for 10 percent gasohol,

"(ii) 4.158 cents per gallon for 7.7 percent gasohol, and

"(iii) 3.078 cents per gallon for 5.7 percent gasohol.

In the case of a mixture none of the alcohol in which consists of ethanol, clauses (i), (ii), and (iii) shall be applied by substituting '6 cents' for '5.4 cents', '4.62 cents' for '4.158 cents', and '3.42 cents' for '3.078 cents'".

In 1997, P.L. 105-34, Sec. 1031(a)(2), substituted "September 30, 2007" for "September 30, 1997" in subpara. (d)(2)(B), effective 10/1/97.

—P.L. 105-34, Sec. 1032(b), added "or kerosene" after "diesel fuel" in clause (a)(2)(A)(iii), effective 7/1/98.

—P.L. 105-34, Sec. 1032(g), of this Act, reads as follows:

"(g) Floor stock taxes.

"(1) Imposition of tax. In the case of kerosene which is held on July 1, 1998, by any person, there is hereby imposed a floor stocks tax of 24.4 cents per gallon.

"(2) Liability for tax and method of payment.

"(A) Liability for tax. A person holding kerosene on July 1, 1998, to which the tax imposed by paragraph (1) applies shall be liable for such tax.

"(B) Method of payment. The tax imposed by paragraph (1) shall be paid in such manner as the Secretary shall prescribe.

"(C) Time for payment. The tax imposed by paragraph (1) shall be paid on or before August 31, 1998.

"(3) Definitions. For purposes of this subsection—

"(A) Held by a person. Kerosene shall be considered as 'held by a person' if title thereto has passed to such person (whether or not delivery to the person has been made).

"(B) Secretary. The term 'Secretary' means the Secretary of the Treasury or his delegate.

"(4) Exception for exempt uses. The tax imposed by paragraph (1) shall not apply to kerosene held by any person exclusively for any use to the extent a credit or refund of the tax imposed by section 4081 of the Internal Revenue Code of 1986 is allowable for such use.

"(5) Exception for fuel held in vehicle tank. No tax shall be imposed by paragraph (1) on kerosene held in the tank of a motor vehicle or motorboat.

"(6) Exception for certain amounts of fuel.

"(A) In general. No tax shall be imposed by paragraph (1) on kerosene held on July 1, 1998, by any person if the aggregate amount of kerosene held by such person on such date does not exceed 2,000 gallons. The preceding sentence shall apply only if such person submits to the Secretary (at the time and in the manner required by the Secretary) such information as the Secretary shall require for purposes of this paragraph.

"(B) Exempt fuel. For purposes of subparagraph (A), there shall not be taken into account fuel held by any person which is exempt from the tax imposed by paragraph (1) by reason of paragraph (4) or (5).

"(C) Controlled groups. For purposes of this paragraph—

"(i) Corporations.

"(I) In general. All persons treated as a controlled group shall be treated as 1 person.

"(II) Controlled group. The term 'controlled group' has the meaning given to such term by subsection (a) of section 1563 of such Code; except that for such purposes the phrase 'more than 50 percent' shall be substituted for the phrase 'at least 80 percent' each place it appears in such subsection.

"(ii) Nonincorporated persons under common control. Under regulations prescribed by the Secretary, principles similar to the principles of clause (i) shall apply to a group of persons under common control where 1 or more of such persons is not a corporation.

"(7) Coordination with section 4081. No tax shall be imposed by paragraph (1) on kerosene to the extent that tax has been (or will be) imposed on such kerosene under section 4081 or 4091 of such Code.

"(8) Other laws applicable. All provisions of law, including penalties, applicable with respect to the taxes imposed by section 4081 of such Code shall, insofar as applicable and not inconsistent with the provisions of this subsection, apply with respect to the floor stock taxes imposed by paragraph (1) to the same extent as if such taxes were imposed by such section 4081."

—P.L. 105-34, Sec. 1033, substituted "shall apply after September 30, 1997, and before April 1, 2005" for "shall not apply after December 31, 1995" in para. (d)(3), effective 8/5/97.

—P.L. 105-34, Sec. 1601(f)(4)(E), substituted "paragraph (3)(A)" for "paragraph (3)(A)(i)" in Sec. 1609(h)(1) of P.L. 104-188 [reproduced below]

—P.L. 105-34, Sec. 1601(f)(4)(F), added "or exclusively for the use described in section 4092(b) of such Code" before the period at the end of Sec. 1609(h)(4) of P.L. 104-188 [reproduced below].

—P.L. 105-2, Sec. 2(a)(2), deleted para. (d)(3) as added by Sec. 1609(a) of P.L. 104-88, relating to aviation gasoline, see below, and amended paras. (d)(1) and (2), effective for periods beginning on or after the 7th calendar day after 2/28/97.

Prior to deletion, para. (d)(3) read as follows:

"(3) Aviation gasoline. After December 31, 1996, the rate of tax specified in subsection (a)(2)(A)(i) on aviation gasoline shall be 4.3 cents per gallon."

Prior to amendment, paras. (d)(1) and (2) read as follows:

"(1) In general. On and after October 1, 1999, the rates of tax specified in clauses (i) and (iii) of subsection (a)(2)(A) (other than the tax on aviation gasoline) shall be 4.3 cents per gallon.

"(2) Aviation gasoline. On and after January 1, 1997, the rate specified in subsection (a)(2)(A)(ii) shall be 4.3 cents per gallon.

"(3) Leaking Underground Storage Tank Trust Fund financing rate. The Leaking Underground Storage Tank Trust Fund financing rate under subsection (a)(2) shall not apply after December 31, 1995."

In 1996, P.L. 104-188, Sec. 1609(a)(2)(A), added para. (d)(3)... Sec. 1609(a)(2)(B), added "(other than the tax on aviation gasoline)" after "subsection (a)(2)(A)" in subsec. (d)... Sec. 1609(g)(1), redesignated clause (a)(2)(A)(ii) as clause (a)(2)(A)(iii), deleted clause (a)(2)(A)(i), and added new clauses (a)(2)(A)(i) and (ii)... Sec. 1609(g)(2), redesignated para. (d)(2) as para. (d)(3) and added a new para. (d)(2) [para. (d)(3), as added by Sec. 1609(a)(2)(A), see above, was not redesignated as para. (d)(4)]... Sec. 1609(g)(4)(B), substituted "the rates of tax specified in clauses (i) and (iii) of subsection (a)(2)(A)" for "each rate of tax specified in subsection (a)(2)(A)" in para. (d)(1), effective on the 7th calendar day after 8/20/96.

Prior to deletion, clause (a)(2)(A)(i) read as follows:

"(i) in the case of gasoline, 18.3 cents per gallon, and"

—P.L. 104-188, Sec. 1609(h), of this Act [as amended by Sec. 1601(f)(4)(E) and (F) of P.L. 105-34, see above] provides:

"(h) Floor stocks taxes on aviation fuel.

"(1) Imposition of tax. In the case of aviation fuel on which tax was imposed under section 4091 of the Internal Revenue Code of 1986 before the tax-increase date described in paragraph (3)(A) and which is held on such date by any person, there is hereby imposed a floor stocks tax of 17.5 cents per gallon.

"(2) Liability for tax and method of payment.

"(A) Liability for tax. A person holding aviation fuel on a tax-increase date to which the tax imposed by paragraph (1) applies shall be liable for such tax.

"(B) Method of payment. The tax imposed by paragraph (1) shall be paid in such manner as the Secretary shall prescribe.

"(C) Time for payment. The tax imposed by paragraph (1) with respect to any tax-increase date shall be paid on or before the first day of the 7th month beginning after such tax-increase date.

"(3) Definitions. For purposes of this subsection—

"(A) Tax increase date. The term 'tax-increase date' means the date which is 7 calendar days after the date of the enactment of this Act.

"(B) Aviation fuel. The term 'aviation fuel' has the meaning given such term by section 4093 of such Code.

"(C) Held by a person. Aviation fuel shall be considered as 'held by a person' if title thereto has passed to such person (whether or not delivery to the person has been made).

"(D) Secretary. The term 'Secretary' means the Secretary of the Treasury or his delegate.

"(4) Exception for exempt uses. The tax imposed by paragraph (1) shall not apply to aviation fuel held by any person on any tax-increase date exclusively for any use for which a credit or refund of the entire tax imposed by section 4091 of such Code is allowable for aviation fuel purchased on or after such tax-increase date for such use or exclusively for the use described in section 4092(b) of such Code.

"(5) Exception for certain amounts of fuel.

"(A) In general. No tax shall be imposed by paragraph (1) on aviation fuel held on any tax-increase date by any person if the aggregate amount of aviation fuel held by such person on such date does not exceed 2,000 gallons. The preceding sentence shall apply only if such person submits to the Secretary (at the time and in the manner required by the Secretary) such information as the Secretary shall require for purposes of this paragraph.

"(B) Exempt fuel. For purposes of subparagraph (A), there shall not be taken into account fuel held by any person which is exempt from the tax imposed by paragraph (1) by reason of paragraph (4).

"(C) Controlled groups. For purposes of this paragraph—

"(i) Corporations.

"(I) In general. All persons treated as a controlled group shall be treated as 1 person.

"(II) Controlled group. The term 'controlled group' has the meaning given to such term by subsection (a) of section 1563 of such Code; except that for such purposes the phrase 'more than 50 percent' shall be substituted for the phrase 'at least 80 percent' each place it appears in such subsection.

"(ii) Nonincorporated persons under common control. Under regulations prescribed by the Secretary, principles similar to the principles of clause (i) shall apply to a group of persons under common control where 1 or more of such persons is not a corporation.

"(6) Other law applicable. All provisions of law, including penalties, applicable with respect to the taxes imposed by section 4091 of such Code shall, insofar as applicable and not inconsistent with the provisions of this subsection, apply with

Code Sec. 4081 — Excise and miscellaneous taxes

respect to the floor stock taxes imposed by paragraph (1) to the same extent as if such taxes were imposed by such section 4091."

In 1993, P.L. 103-66, Sec. 13241(a), amended clause (a)(2)(B)(iii), effective 10/1/93.

Prior to amendment, clause (a)(2)(B)(iii) read as follows:

"(iii) the deficit reduction rate is 2.5 cents a gallon."

—P.L. 103-66, Sec. 13241(h), of this Act provides:

"(h) Floor stocks taxes.

"(1) Imposition of tax. In the case of gasoline, diesel fuel, and aviation fuel on which tax was imposed under section 4081 or 4091 of the Internal Revenue Code of 1986 before October 1, 1993, and which is held on such date by any person, there is hereby imposed a floor stocks tax of 4.3 cents per gallon on such gasoline, diesel fuel, and aviation fuel.

"(2) Liability for tax and method of payment.

"(A) Liability for tax. A person holding gasoline, diesel fuel, or aviation fuel on October 1, 1993, to which the tax imposed by paragraph (1) applies shall be liable for such tax.

"(B) Method of payment. The tax imposed by paragraph (1) shall be paid in such manner as the Secretary shall prescribe.

"(C) Time for payment. The tax imposed by paragraph (1) shall be paid on or before November 30, 1993.

"(3) Definitions. For purposes of this subsection—

"(A) Held by a person. Gasoline, diesel fuel, and aviation fuel shall be considered as 'held by a person' if title thereto has passed to such person (whether or not delivery to the person has been made).

"(B) Gasoline. The term 'gasoline' has the meaning given such term by section 4082 of such Code.

"(C) Diesel fuel. The term 'diesel fuel' has the meaning given such term by section 4092 of such Code.

"(D) Aviation fuel. The term 'aviation fuel' has the meaning given such term by section 4092 of such Code.

"(E) Secretary. The term 'Secretary' means the Secretary of the Treasury or his delegate.

"(4) Exception for exempt uses. The tax imposed by paragraph (1) shall not apply to gasoline, diesel fuel, or aviation fuel held by any person exclusively for any use to the extent a credit or refund of the tax imposed by section 4081 or 4091 of such Code, as the case may be, is allowable for such use.

"(5) Exception for fuel held in vehicle tank. No tax shall be imposed by paragraph (1) on gasoline or diesel fuel held in the tax of a motor vehicle or motorboat.

"(6) Exception for certain amounts of fuel.

"(A) In general. No tax shall be imposed by paragraph (1)—

"(i) on gasoline held on October 1, 1993, by any person if the aggregate amount of gasoline held by such person on such date does not exceed 4,000 gallons, and

"(ii) on diesel fuel or aviation fuel held on October 1, 1993, by any person if the aggregate amount of diesel fuel or aviation fuel held by such person on such date does not exceed 2,000 gallons.

"The preceding sentence shall apply only if such person submits to the Secretary (at the time and in the manner required by the Secretary) such information as the Secretary shall require for purposes of this paragraph.

"(B) Exempt fuel. For purposes of subparagraph (A), there shall not be taken into account fuel held by any person which is exempt from the tax imposed by paragraph (1) by reason of paragraph (4) or (5).

"(C) Controlled groups. For purposes of this paragraph—

"(i) Corporations.

"(I) In general. All persons treated as a controlled group shall be treated as 1 person.

"(II) Controlled group. The term 'controlled group' has the meaning given to such term by subsection (a) of section 1563 of such Code; except that for such purposes the phrase 'more than 50 percent' shall be substituted for the phrase 'at least 80 percent' each place it appears in such subsection.

"(ii) Nonincorporated persons under common control. Under regulations prescribed by the Secretary, principles similar to the principles of clause (i) shall apply to a group of persons under common control where 1 or more of such persons is not a corporation.

"(7) Other law applicable. All provisions of law, including penalties, applicable with respect to the taxes imposed by section 4081 of such Code in the case of gasoline and section 4091 of such Code in the case of diesel fuel and aviation fuel shall, insofar as applicable and not inconsistent with the provisions of this subsection, apply with respect to the floor stock taxes imposed by paragraph (1) to the same extent as if such taxes were imposed by such section 4081 or 4091."

—P.L. 103-66, Sec. 13242(a), amended Code Sec. 4081 (as amended by Sec. 13241(a) of this Act) as part of the amendments to subpart A of part III of subchapter 32, effective 1/1/94.

Prior to amendment, Code Sec. 4081 (as amended by Sec. 13241(a) of this Act) read as follows:

"Sec. 4081. Imposition of tax.

"(a) Tax imposed.

"(1) Tax on removal, entry, or sale.

"(A) In general. There is hereby imposed a tax at the rate specified in paragraph (2) on—

"(i) the removal of gasoline from any refinery,

"(ii) the removal of gasoline from any terminal,

"(iii) the entry into the United States of gasoline for consumption, use, or warehousing, and

"(iv) the sale of gasoline to any person who is not registered under section 4101 unless there was a prior taxable removal or entry of such gasoline under clause (i), (ii), or (iii).

"(B) Exception for bulk transfers to registered terminals. The tax imposed by this paragraph shall not apply to any removal or entry of gasoline transferred in bulk to a terminal if the person removing or entering the gasoline and the operator of such terminal are registered under section 4101.

"(2) Rates of tax.

"(A) In general. The rate of the tax imposed by this section is the sum of—

"(i) the Highway Trust Fund financing rate,

"(ii) the Leaking Underground Storage Tank Trust Fund financing rate, and

"(iii) the deficit reduction rate.

"(B) Rates. For purposes of subparagraph (A)—

"(i) the Highway Trust Fund financing rate is 11.5 cents a gallon,

"(ii) the Leaking Underground Storage Tank Trust Fund financing rate is 0.1 cent a gallon, and

"(iii) the deficit reduction rate is 6.8 cents per gallon.

"(b) Treatment of removal or subsequent sale by blender or compounder.

"(1) In general. There is hereby imposed a tax at the rate specified in subsection (a) on gasoline removed or sold by the blender or compounder thereof.

"(2) Credit for tax previously paid. If—

"(A) tax is imposed on the removal or sale of gasoline by reason of paragraph (1), and

"(B) the blender or compounder establishes the amount of the tax paid with respect to such gasoline by reason of subsection (a),

the amount of the tax so paid shall be allowed as a credit against the tax imposed by reason of paragraph (1).

"(c) Gasoline mixed with alcohol at refinery, etc.

"(1) In general. Under regulations prescribed by the Secretary, subsection (a) shall be applied by multiplying the otherwise applicable rate by a fraction the numerator of which is 10 and the denominator of which is—

"(A) 9 in the case of 10 percent gasohol,

"(B) 9.23 in the case of 7.7 percent gasohol, and

"(C) 9.43 in the case of 5.7 percent gasohol,

in the case of the removal or entry of any gasoline for use in producing gasohol at the time of such removal or entry. Subject to such terms and conditions as the Secretary may prescribe (including the application of section 4101), the treatment under the preceding sentence shall also apply to use in producing gasohol after the time of such removal or entry.

"(2) Later separation of gasoline from gasohol. If any person separates the gasoline from a mixture of gasoline and alcohol on which tax was imposed under subsection (a) at a Highway Trust Fund financing rate equivalent to an otherwise applicable rate by reason of this subsection (or with respect to which a credit or payment was allowed or made by reason of section 6427(f)(1)), such person shall be treated as the refiner of such gasoline. The amount of tax imposed on any sale of such gasoline by such person shall be reduced by the amount of tax imposed (and not credited or refunded) on any prior removal or sale of such fuel.

"(3) Alcohol defined. For purposes of this subsection, the term 'alcohol' includes methanol and ethanol but does not include alcohol produced from petroleum, natural gas, or coal (including peat). Such term does not include alcohol with a proof of less than 190 (determined without regard to any added denaturants).

"(4) Otherwise applicable rate. For purposes of this subsection—

"(A) In general. In the case of the Highway Trust Fund financing rate, the term 'otherwise applicable rate' means—

"(i) 6.1 cents a gallon for 10 percent gasohol,

"(ii) 7.342 cents a gallon for 7.7 percent gasohol, and

"(iii) 8.422 cents a gallon for 5.7 percent gasohol.

In the case of gasohol none of the alcohol in which consists of ethanol, clauses (i), (ii), and (iii) shall be applied by substituting '5.5 cents' for '6.1 cents', '6.88 cents' for '7.342 cents', and '8.08 cents' for '8.422 cents'.

"(B) 10 percent gasohol. The term '10 percent gasohol' means any mixture of gasoline with alcohol if at least 10 percent of such mixture is alcohol.

"(C) 7.7 percent gasohol. The term '7.7 percent gasohol' means any mixture of gasoline with alcohol if at least 7.7 percent, but not 10 percent or more, of such mixture is alcohol.

"(D) 5.7 percent gasohol. The term '5.7 percent gasohol' means any mixture of gasoline with alcohol if at least 5.7 percent, but not 7.7 percent or more, of such mixture is alcohol.

"(5) Termination. Paragraph (1) shall not apply to any removal or sale after September 30, 2000.

"(d) Termination.

"(1) Highway trust fund financing rate. On and after October 1, 1999, the Highway Trust Fund financing rate under subsection (a)(2) shall not apply.

"(2) Leaking underground storage tank trust fund financing rate. The Leaking Underground Storage Tank Trust Fund financing rate under subsection (a)(2) shall not apply after December 31, 1995.

"(3) Deficit reduction rate. On and after October 1, 1995, the deficit reduction rate under subsection (a)(2) shall not apply.

"(e) Refunds in certain cases. Under regulations prescribed by the Secretary, if any person who paid the tax imposed by this section with respect to any gasoline establishes to the satisfaction of the Secretary that a prior tax was paid (and not credited or refunded) with respect to such gasoline, then an amount equal to the tax paid by such person shall be allowed as a refund (without interest) to such person in the same manner as if it were an overpayment of tax imposed by this section."

In 1992, P.L. 102-486, Sec. 1920(a), amended para. (c)(1) . . . Sec. 1920(b)(1), substituted "an otherwise applicable rate" for "6.1 cents a gallon" in para. (c)(2) . . . Sec. 1920(b)(2), amended para. (c)(4), effective for gasoline removed (as defined in Code Sec. 4082) or entered after 12/31/92.

Prior to amendment, para. (c)(1) read as follows:

"(1) In general. Under regulations prescribed by the Secretary, subsection (a) shall be applied by substituting rates which are ¹⁰⁄₆₁th of the otherwise applicable rates in the case of the removal or sale of any gasoline for use in producing gasohol at the time of such removal or sale. Subject to such terms and conditions as the Secretary may prescribe (including the application of section 4101), the treatment under the preceding sentence also shall apply to use in producing gasohol after the time of such removal or sale. For purposes of this paragraph, the term 'gasohol' means any mixture of gasoline if at least 10 percent of such mixture is alcohol. For purposes of this subsection, in the case of the Highway Trust Fund financing rate, the otherwise applicable rate is 6.1 cents a gallon."

Prior to amendment, para. (c)(4) read as follows:

"(4) Lower rate on gasohol made other than from ethanol. In the case of gasohol none of the alcohol in which consists of ethanol, paragraphs (1) and (2) shall be applied by substituting '5.5 cents' for '6.1 cents'."

In 1991, P.L. 102-240, Sec. 8002(a)(3), substituted "1999" for "1995" in para. (d)(1), effective 12/18/91.

In 1990, P.L. 101-508, Sec. 11211(a)(1)(A), deleted "and" at the end of clause (a)(2)(A)(i) . . . Sec. 11211(a)(1)(B), substituted ", and" for the period at the end of clause (a)(2)(A)(ii) . . . Sec. 11211(a)(1)(C), added clause (a)(2)(A)(iii) . . . Sec. 11211(a)(2)(A), substituted "11.5 cents a gallon," for "9 cents a gallon, and" in clause (a)(2)(B)(i) . . . Sec. 11211(a)(2)(B), substituted ", and" for the period at the end of clause (a)(2)(B)(ii) . . . Sec. 11211(a)(2)(C), added clause (a)(2)(B)(iii) . . . Sec. 11211(a)(3), added para. (d)(3) . . . Sec. 11211(a)(5)(A)(i), substituted "applied by substituting rates with are ¹⁰⁄₆₁th of the otherwise applicable rates in the case" for "applied by substituting '3⅓ cents' for '9 cents' and by substituting '⅑ cent' for '0.1 cent' in the case" in para. (c)(1) . . . Sec. 11211(a)(5)(A)(ii), added the last sentence to para. (c)(1) . . . Sec. 11211(a)(5)(B), substituted "at a Highway Trust Fund financing rate equivalent to 6.1 cents" for "at a [Highway Trust Fund financing] rate equivalent to 3 cents" in para. (c)(2) . . . Sec. 11211(a)(5)(C), redesignated para. (c)(4) as (c)(5), and added new para. (c)(4), effective for gasoline removed (as defined in Code Sec. 4082) after 11/30/90.

—P.L. 101-508, Sec. 11211(c)(3), substituted "1995" for "1993" in para. (d)(1) . . . Sec. 11211(e)(3), substituted "2000" for "1993" in para. (c)(5) (as redesignated by Sec. 11211(a)(5)(C) of this Act), effective 11/5/90.

—P.L. 101-508, Sec. 11211(j), provides:

"(j) Floor stocks taxes.

"(1) Imposition of tax. In the case of—

"(A) gasoline and diesel fuel on which tax was imposed under section 4081 or 4091 of such Code before December 1, 1990, and which is held on such date by any person, or

"(B) diesel fuel on which no tax was imposed under section 4091 of such Code at the Highway Trust Fund financing rate before December 1, 1990, and which is held on such date by any person for use as a fuel in a train,

there is hereby imposed a floor stocks tax on such gasoline and diesel fuel.

"(2) Rate of tax. The rate of the tax imposed by paragraph (1) shall be—

"(A) 5 cents per gallon in the case of fuel described in paragraph (1)(A), and

"(B) 2.5 cents per gallon in the case of fuel described in paragraph (1)(B).

In the case of any fuel held for use in producing a mixture described in section 4081(c)(1) or section 4091(c)(1)(A) of such Code, subparagraph (A) shall be applied by substituting '6.22 cents' for '5 cents'. If no alcohol in such mixture is ethanol, the preceding sentence shall be applied by substituting '5.56 cents' for '6.22 cents'.

"(3) Liability for tax and method of payment.

"(A) Liability for tax. A person holding gasoline or diesel fuel on December 1, 1990, to which the tax imposed by paragraph (1) applies shall be liable for such tax.

"(B) Method of payment. The tax imposed by paragraph (1) shall be paid in such manner as the Secretary shall prescribe.

"(C) Time for payment. The tax imposed by paragraph (1) shall be paid on or before May 31, 1991.

"(4) Definitions. For purposes of this subsection—

"(A) Held by person. Gasoline and diesel fuel shall be considered as 'held by a person' if title thereto has passed to such person (whether or not delivery to the person has been made).

"(B) Gasoline. The term 'gasoline' has the meaning given such term by section 4082 of such Code.

"(C) Diesel fuel. The term 'diesel fuel' has the meaning given such term by section 4092 of such Code.

"(D) Secretary. The term 'Secretary' means the Secretary of the Treasury or his delegate.

"(5) Exception for exempt uses. The tax imposed by paragraph (1) shall not apply to gasoline or diesel fuel held by any person exclusively for any use to the extent a credit or refund of the tax imposed by section 4081 or 4091 of such Code, as the case may be, is allowable for such use.

"(6) Exception for fuel held in vehicle tank. No tax shall be imposed by paragraph (1) on gasoline or diesel fuel held in the tank of a motor vehicle or motorboat.

"(7) Exception for certain amounts of fuel.

"(A) In general. No tax shall be imposed by paragraph (1)—

"(i) on gasoline held on December 1, 1990, by any person if the aggregate amount of gasoline held by such person on such date does not exceed 4,000 gallons, and

"(ii) on diesel fuel held on December 1, 1990, by any person if the aggregate amount of diesel fuel held by such person on such date does not exceed 2,000 gallons.

The preceding sentence shall apply only if such person submits to the Secretary (at the time and in the manner required by the Secretary) such information as the Secretary shall require for purposes of this paragraph.

"(B) Exempt fuel. For purposes of subparagraph (A), there shall not be taken into account fuel held by any person which is exempt from the tax imposed by paragraph (1) by reason of paragraph (5) or (6).

"(C) Controlled groups. For purposes of this paragraph, rules similar to the rules of paragraph (6) of section 11201(e) of this Act shall apply.

"(8) Other laws applicable. All provisions of law, including penalties, applicable with respect to the taxes imposed by section 4081 of such Code in the case of gasoline and section 4091 of such Code in the case of diesel fuel shall, insofar as applicable and not inconsistent with the provisions of this subsection, apply with respect to the floor stock taxes imposed by paragraph (1) to the same extent as if such taxes were imposed by such section 4081 or 4091.

"(9) Transfer of portion of floor stocks revenue to highway trust fund. For purposes of determining the amount transferred to the Highway Trust Fund, the tax imposed by paragraph (1) on fuel described in subparagraph (A) thereof shall be treated as imposed at a Highway Trust Fund financing rate to the extent of 2.5 cents per gallon."

—P.L. 101-508, Sec. 11212(a), amended para. (a)(1) . . . Sec. 11212(d)(1), added subsec. (e) . . . Sec. 11212(e)(2), deleted para. (a)(3), effective 7/1/91.

Prior to amendment, para. (a)(1) read as follows:

"(1) In general. There is hereby imposed a tax at the rate specified in paragraph (2) on the earlier of—

"(A) the removal, or

"(B) the sale,

of gasoline by the refiner or importer thereof or the terminal operator."

Prior to deletion, para. (a)(3) read as follows:

"(3) Bulk transfer to terminal operator. For purposes of paragraph (1), the bulk transfer of gasoline to a terminal operator by a refiner or importer shall not be considered a removal or sale of gasoline by such refiner or importer."

—P.L. 101-508, Sec. 11215(a), amended para. (d)(2), effective 12/1/90.

Prior to amendment, para. (d)(2) read as follows:

"(2) Leaking underground storage tank trust fund financing rate.

"(A) In general. The Leaking Underground Storage Tank Trust Fund financing rate under subsection (a)(2) shall not apply after the earlier of—

"(i) December 31, 1991, or

"(ii) the last day of the termination month.

"(B) Termination month. For purposes of subparagraph (A), the termination month is the 1st month as of the close of which the Secretary estimates that the net revenues are at least $500,000,000 from taxes imposed by section 4041(d) and taxes attributable to Leaking Underground Storage Tank Trust Fund financing rate imposed under this section and sections 4042 and 4091.

"(C) Net revenues. For purposes of subparagraph (B), the term 'net revenues' means the excess of gross revenues over amounts payable by reason of section 9508(c)(2) (relating to transfer from Leaking Underground Storage Tank Trust Fund for certain repayments and credits)."

—P.L. 101-508, Sec. 11218, relating to floor stocks tax treatment of articles in foreign trade zones, is reproduced in note following Code Sec. 5001.

In 1988, P.L. 100-647, Sec. 1017(c)(1)(A), redesignated para. (a)(2) as para. (a)(3), amended para. (a)(1), and added para. (a)(2) . . . Sec. 1017(c)(1)(B), substituted "subsection (a)" for "subsection (d)" in subsecs. (b) and (c) . . . Sec. 1017(c)(1)(C), substituted "subsection (a)(2)" for "subsection (d)(2)(A)" in para. (e)(1), and substituted "subsection (a)(2)" for "subsection (d)(2)(B)" each place it appeared in para. (e)(2) . . . Sec. 1017(c)(1)(D), deleted subsec. (d) and redesignated subsec. (e) as subsec. (d) . . . Sec. 1017(c)(14), substituted "3⅓ cents" for "3 cents" in para. (c)(1), effective for gasoline removed (as defined in Code Sec. 4082 as amended by Sec. 1703(a) of P.L. 100-203) after 12/31/87.

Prior to amendment para. (a)(1) read as follows:

"(a) Tax imposed.

"(1) In general. There is hereby imposed a tax at the rate specified in subsection (d) on the earlier of —

"(A) the removal, or

"(B) the sale,

of gasoline by the refiner or importer thereof or the terminal operator."

Prior to deletion subsec. (d) read as follows:

"(d) Rate of tax.

"(1) In general. The rate of the tax imposed by this section is the sum of —

"(A) the Highway Trust Fund financing rate, and

"(B) the Leaking Underground Storage Tank Trust Fund financing rate."

—P.L. 100-647, Sec. 1017(c)(13), amended Sec. 1703(f)(2) of P.L. 99-514 [reproduced below], provisions on floor stock taxes, by adding the last sentence, see below.

—P.L. 100-647, Sec. 2001(d)(4)(A), amended Sec. 1703(f)(1) of P.L. 99-514 [reproduced below], provisions on floor stock taxes, by substituting "9.1 cents" for "9 cents", see below . . . Sec. 2001(d)(4)(B), amended Sec. 1703(f)(4) of P.L. 99-514, reproduced below.

Prior to amendment, Sec. 1703(f)(4) of P.L. 99-514 read as follows:

"(4) Transfer of floor stocks taxes to highway trust fund. For purposes of determining the amount transferred to the Highway Trust Fund for any period, the taxes imposed by this subsection shall be treated as if they were imposed by section 4081 of the Internal Revenue Code of 1986."

—P.L. 100-647, Sec. 2001(d)(5)(A), added "and by substituting '⅑ cent' for '0.1 cent'" before "in the case of the removal" in para. (c)(1) . . . Sec. 2001(d)(5)(B),

Code Sec. 4081 — Excise and miscellaneous taxes

substituted "reduced by the amount of tax imposed (and not credited or refunded) on any prior removal or sale of such fuel" for "5⅔ cents a gallon" in para. (c)(2), effective 1/1/87.

—P.L. 100-647, Sec. 6104(a), added "Subject to such terms and conditions as the Secretary may prescribe (including the application of section 4101), the treatment under the preceding sentence also shall apply to use in producing gasohol after the time of such removal or sale." after the first sentence in para. (c)(1), effective 10/1/89.

In 1987, P.L. 100-203, Sec. 10502(d)(2), amended subpara. (e)(2)(B), effective for sales after 3/31/88.

Prior to amendment, subpara. (e)(2)(B) read as follows:

"(B) Termination month. For purposes of subparagraph (A), the termination month is the 1st month as of the close of which the Secretary estimates that the net revenues from the taxes imposed by this section (to the extent attributable to the Leaking Underground Storage Tank Trust Fund financing rate under subsection (d)(2)(B)), section 4041(d), and section 4042 (to the extent attributable to the Leaking Underground Storage Tank Trust Fund financing rate under section 4042(b)) are at least $500,000,000."

—P.L. 100-17, Sec. 502(a)(4), substituted "1993" for "1988" in para. (e)(1) . . . Sec. 502(c)(2), substituted "September 30, 1993" for "December 31, 1992" in para. (c)(4), effective 4/2/87.

In 1986, P.L. 99-514, Sec. 1703(a), amended Code Sec. 4081, as part of the amendments to subpart A of Part III of subchapter A of chapter 32, effective for gasoline removed (as defined in Code Sec. 4082 as amended by Sec. 1703(a) of this Act) after 12/31/87. Sec. 1703(f) of this Act [as amended by Sec. 1017(c)(13) of P.L. 100-647 and Sec. 2001(d)(4)(A) and (B), see above] provides:

"(f) Floor stock taxes.

"(1) In general. On gasoline subject to tax under section 4081 of the Internal Revenue Code of 1986 which, on January 1, 1988, is held by a dealer for sale, and with respect to which no tax has been imposed under such section, there is hereby imposed a floor stocks tax at the rate of 9.1 cents a gallon.

"(2) Overpayment of floor stocks taxes. Section 6416 of such Code shall apply in respect of the floor stocks taxes imposed by this section, so as to entitle, subject to all provisions of such section, any person paying such floor stocks taxes to a credit or refund thereof for any reasons specified in such section. All other provisions of law, including penalties, applicable with respect to the taxes imposed by section 4081 of the Internal Revenue Code of 1986 shall apply to the floor stocks taxes imposed by this section.

"(3) Due date of taxes. The taxes imposed by this subsection shall be paid before February 16, 1988.

"(4) Transfer of floor stock tax revenues to trust funds. For purposes of determining the amount transferred to any trust fund, the taxes imposed by this section shall be treated as imposed by section 4081 of the Internal Revenue Code of 1986—

"(A) at the Highway Trust Fund financing rate under such section to the extent of 9 cents per gallon, and

"(B) at the Leaking Underground Storage Tank Trust Fund financing rate under such section to the extent of 0.1 cent per gallon.

"(5) Definitions and special rule. For purposes of this subsection—

"(A) Dealer.The term 'dealer' includes a wholesaler, jobber, distributor, or retailer.

"(B) Held by a dealer. Gasoline shall be considered as 'held by a dealer' if title thereto has passed to such dealer (whether or not delivery to him has been made) and if for purposes of consumption title to such gasoline or possession thereof has not at any time been transferred to any person other than a dealer.

"(C) Gasoline. The term 'gasoline' has the same meaning given to such term by section 4082(a) of the Internal Revenue Code of 1986."

—P.L. 99-499, Sec. 521(a)(1)(B)(i), substituted "at the rate specified in subsection (d)" for "of 9 cents a gallon" in subsecs. (a) and (b) . . . Sec. 521(a)(1)(B)(ii), amended subsec. (d) and added subsec. (e) . . . Sec. 521(a)(1)(B)(iii), substituted "subsection (d)" for "subsection (a)" in para. (c)(1) and substituted "a Highway Trust Fund financing rate" for "a rate" in para. (c)(2), effective 1/1/87.

Prior to amendment, subsec. (d) read as follows:

"(d) Termination. On and after October 1, 1988, the taxes imposed by this section shall not apply."

Sec. 4082. Exemptions for diesel fuel and kerosene.

(a) In general.

The tax imposed by section 4081 shall not apply to diesel fuel and kerosene—

(1) which the Secretary determines is destined for a nontaxable use,

(2) which is indelibly dyed by mechanical injection in accordance with regulations which the Secretary shall prescribe, and

(3) which meets such marking requirements (if any) as may be prescribed by the Secretary in regulations.

Such regulations shall allow an individual choice of dye color approved by the Secretary or chosen from any list of approved dye colors that the Secretary may publish.

(b) Nontaxable use.

For purposes of this section, the term "nontaxable use" means—

(1) any use which is exempt from the tax imposed by section 4041(a)(1) other than by reason of a prior imposition of tax,

(2) any use in a train, and

(3) any use described in section 4041(a)(1)(C)(iii)(II).

The term "nontaxable use" does not include the use of kerosene in an aircraft and such term shall not include any use described in section 6421(e)(2)(C).

(c) Exception to dyeing requirements.

Paragraph (2) of subsection (a) shall not apply with respect to any diesel fuel and kerosene—

(1) removed, entered, or sold in a State for ultimate sale or use in an area of such State during the period such area is exempted from the fuel dyeing requirements under subsection (i) of section 211 of the Clean Air Act (as in effect on the date of the enactment of this subsection) by the Administrator of the Environmental Protection Agency under paragraph (4) of such subsection (i) (as so in effect), and

(2) the use of which is certified pursuant to regulations issued by the Secretary.

(d) Additional exceptions to dyeing requirements for kerosene.

(1) **Use for non-fuel feedstock purposes.** Subsection (a)(2) shall not apply to kerosene—

(A) received by pipeline or vessel for use by the person receiving the kerosene in the manufacture or production of any substance (other than gasoline, diesel fuel, or special fuels referred to in section 4041), or

(B) to the extent provided in regulations, removed or entered—

(i) for such a use by the person removing or entering the kerosene, or

(ii) for resale by such person for such a use by the purchaser,

but only if the person receiving, removing, or entering the kerosene and such purchaser (if any) are registered under section 4101 with respect to the tax imposed by section 4081.

(2) **Wholesale distributors.** To the extent provided in regulations, subsection (a)(2) shall not apply to kerosene received by a wholesale distributor of kerosene if such distributor—

(A) is registered under section 4101 with respect to the tax imposed by section 4081 on kerosene, and

(B) sells kerosene exclusively to ultimate vendors described in section 6427(l)(5)(B) with respect to kerosene.

(e) Kerosene removed into an aircraft.

In the case of kerosene which is exempt from the tax imposed by section 4041(c) (other than by reason of a prior imposition of tax) and which is removed from any refinery or terminal directly into the fuel tank of an aircraft—

(1) the rate of tax under section 4081(a)(2)(A)(iii) shall be zero, and

(2) if such aircraft is employed in foreign trade or trade between the United States and any of its possessions, the increase in such rate under section 4081(a)(2)(B) shall be zero.

For purposes of this subsection, any removal described in section 4081(a)(3)(A) shall be treated as a removal from a terminal but only if such terminal is located within a secure area of an airport.

Excise and miscellaneous taxes — Code Sec. 4083(a)(2)(B)(ii)

(f) Exception for leaking Underground Storage Tank Trust Fund financing rate.

(1) In general. Subsection (a) shall not apply to the tax imposed under section 4081 at the Leaking Underground Storage Tank Trust Fund financing rate.

(2) Exception for export, etc. Paragraph (1) shall not apply with respect to any fuel if the Secretary determines that such fuel is destined for export or for use by the purchaser as supplies for vessels (within the meaning of section 4221(d)(3)) employed in foreign trade or trade between the United States and any of its possessions.

(g) Regulations.

The Secretary shall prescribe such regulations as may be necessary to carry out this section, including regulations requiring the conspicuous labeling of retail diesel fuel and kerosene pumps and other delivery facilities to assure that persons are aware of which fuel is available only for nontaxable uses.

(h) Cross reference.

For tax on train and certain bus uses of fuel purchased tax-free, see subsections (a)(1) and (d)(3) of section 4041.

In 2007, P.L. 110-172, Sec. 6(d)(2)(B)(i), deleted "(other than such tax at the Leaking Underground Storage Tank Trust Fund financing rate imposed in all cases other than for export)" after "imposed by section 4081" in subsec. (a) . . . Sec. 6(d)(2)(B)(ii), redesignated subsecs. (f)-(g) as (g)-(h) and added subsec. (f) . . . Sec. 6(d)(2)(C)(i), substituted "an aircraft — (1) the rate of tax under section 4081(a)(2)(A)(iii) shall be zero, and (2) if such aircraft is employed in foreign trade or trade between the United States and any of its possessions, the increase in such rate under section 4081(a)(2)(B) shall be zero," for "an aircraft, the rate of tax under section 4081(a)(2)(A)(iii) shall be zero." effective for fuel entered, removed, or sold after 9/30/2005.
— P.L. 110-172, Sec. 6(d)(2)(C)(ii), made the last sentence of subsec. (e) flush, effective for fuels or liquids removed, entered or sold after 9/30/2005.
Prior to amendment, subsec. (e) read as follows:
"*(e) Kerosene removed into an aircraft.* In the case of kerosene which is exempt from the tax imposed by section 4041(c) (other than by reason of a prior imposition of tax) and which is removed from any refinery or terminal directly into the fuel tank of an aircraft, the rate of tax under section 4081(a)(2)(A)(iii) shall be zero. For purposes of this subsection, any removal described in section 4081(a)(3)(A)shall be treated as a removal from a terminal but only if such terminal is located within a secure area of an airport."
— P.L. 110-172, Sec. 11(a)(28), amended subsec. (b), effective 12/29/2007.
Prior to amendment, subsec. (b) read as follows:
"*(b) Nontaxable use.* For purposes of this section, the term 'nontaxable use' means—
"(1) any use which is exempt from the tax imposed by section 4041(a)(1) other than by reason of a prior imposition of tax,
"(2) any use in a train, and
"(3) any use described in section 4041(a)(1)(C)(iii)(II)."
The term 'nontaxable use' does not include the use of kerosene in an aircraft and such term shall not include any use described in section 6421(e)(2)(C).."
In 2006, P.L. 109-432, Sec. 420(b)(2), substituted "section 6427(l)(5)(B)" for "section 6427(l)(6)(B)" in subpara. (d)(2)(B), effective for kerosene sold after 9/30/2005.
In 2005, P.L. 109-59, Sec. 11161(a)(4)(A), deleted "aviation-grade" before "kerosene" in subsec. (b) . . . Sec. 11161(a)(4)(E)(i), deleted "aviation-grade" before "kerosene" in subsec. (e) . . . Sec. 11161(a)(4)(E)(ii), substituted "section 4081(a)(2)(A)(iii)" for "section 4081(a)(2)(A)(iv)" in subsec. (e) . . . Sec. 11161(a)(4)(E)(iii), added "For purposes of this subsection, any removal described in section 4081(a)(3)(A) shall be treated as a removal from a terminal but only if such terminal is located within a secure area of an airport." at the end of subsec. (e) . . . Sec. 11161(a)(4)(E)(iv), substituted "Kerosene removed into an aircraft" for "Aviation-grade kerosene" in the heading of subsec. (e) . . . Sec. 11161(b)(3)(C), substituted "section 6427(l)(6)(B)" for "section 6427(l)(5)(B)" in subpara. (d)(2)(B), effective for fuels or liquids removed, entered, or sold after 9/30/2005.
— P.L. 109-58, Sec. 1362(b)(1), added "(other than such tax at the Leaking Underground Storage Tank Trust Fund financing rate imposed in all cases other than for export)" after "section 4081" in subsec. (a), effective for fuel entered, removed, or sold after 9/30/2005.
In 2004, P.L. 108-357, Sec. 241(a)(2)(B), substituted "subsections (a)(1) and (d)(3) of section 4041" for "section 4041(a)(1)" in subsec. (f) [subsequently redesignated (g) by this Act, see below], effective 1/1/2005
— P.L. 108-357, Sec. 851(d)(2), added "and such term shall not include any use described in section 6421(e)(2)(C)" before the period at the end of subsec. (b), effective for tax. yrs. begin. after 10/22/2004.
— P.L. 108-357, Sec. 853(a)(5)(A), redesignated subsecs. (e) and (f) as (f) and (g) respectively, and added subsec. (e) . . . Sec. 853(a)(5)(B)(i), added "The term 'nontaxable use' does not include the use of aviation-grade kerosene in an aircraft." flush at the end of subsec. (b) . . . Sec. 853(a)(5)(B)(ii), deleted para. (d)(1) and redesignated paras. (d)(2) and (3) as (d)(1) and (2), effective for aviation-grade kerosene removed, entered, or sold after 12/31/2004.
Prior to deletion, para. (d)(1) read as follows:
"(1) Aviation-grade kerosene. Subsection (a)(2) shall not apply to aviation-grade kerosene (as determined under regulations prescribed by the Secretary) which the Secretary determines is destined for use as a fuel in an aircraft."
— P.L. 108-357, Sec. 854(a), added "by mechanical injection" after "indelibly dyed" in para. (a)(2), effective on the 180th day after the date on which the Secretary issues the regulations described in Sec. 854(b) of this Act, which provides:
"(b) Dye injector security. Not later than 180 days after the date of the enactment of this Act, the Secretary of the Treasury shall issue regulations regarding mechanical dye injection systems described in the amendment made by subsection (a), and such regulations shall include standards for making such systems tamper resistant."
— P.L. 108-357, Sec. 857(a), amended para. (b)(3) [as amended by Sec. 851(d)(2) of this Act, see above], effective for fuel sold after 12/31/2004.
Prior to amendment, para. (b)(3) read as follows:
"(3) any use described in section 6427(b)(1) (after the application of section 6427(b)(3)) and such term shall not include any use described in section 6421(e)(2)(C)."
In 1998, P.L. 105-206, Sec. 6010(h)(3), amended para. (d)(1). . . . Sec. 6010(h)(4), substituted "kerosene received by" for "a removal, entry, or sale of kerosene to" in para (d)(3), effective 7/1/98.
Prior to amendment, para. (1) read as follows:
"(1) Aviation-grade kerosene. Subsection (a)(2) shall not apply to a removal, entry, or sale of aviation-grade kerosene (as determined under regulations prescribed by the Secretary) if the person receiving the kerosene is registered under section 4101 with respect to the tax imposed by section 4091." . . . Sec. 6010(h)(4), substituted "a removal, entry, or sale of kerosene to" for "kerosene received by" in para. (3)
In 1997, P.L. 105-34, Sec. 1032(c)(1), substituted "diesel fuel and kerosene" for "diesel fuel" each place it appeared in subsecs. (a), (c) and (d) . . . Sec. 1032(c)(2), redesignated subsecs. (d) and (e) as subsecs. (e) and (f), and added new subsec. (d) . . . Sec. 1032(e)(3)(A), added "and kerosene" after "diesel fuel" in the heading of Code Sec. 4082, effective 7/1/98.
In 1996, P.L. 104-188, Sec. 1801(a), redesignated subsecs. (c) and (d) as subsecs. (d) and (e) and added a new subsec. (c), effective for fuel removed, entered, or sold on or after the first day of the first calendar quarter beginning after 8/20/96.
In 1993, P.L. 103-66, Sec. 13242(a), amended Code Sec. 4082 as part of the amendments to subpart A of part III of subchapter A of chapter 32, effective 1/1/94.
Prior to amendment, Code Sec. 4082 read as follows:
"Sec. 4082 Definitions.
"(a) Gasoline.
For purposes of this subpart, the term 'gasoline' includes, to the extent prescribed in regulations—
"(1) gasoline blend stocks, and
"(2) products commonly used as additives in gasoline.
For purposes of paragraph (1), the term 'gasoline blend stocks' means any petroleum product component of gasoline.
"(b) Certain uses defined as removal.
If a refiner, importer, terminal operator, blender, or compounder uses (other than in the production of gasoline or special fuels referred to in section 4041) gasoline refined, imported, blended, or compounded by him, such use shall for the purposes of this chapter be considered a removal."
In 1986, P.L. 99-514, Sec. 1703(a), amended Code Sec. 4082 as part of the amendments to subpart A of Part III of subchapter A of chapter 32, effective for gasoline removed (as defined in this Code Section) after 12/31/87.

Sec. 4083. Definitions; special rule; administrative authority.

(a) Taxable fuel.

For purposes of this subpart—

(1) In general. The term "taxable fuel" means—
(A) gasoline,
(B) diesel fuel, and
(C) kerosene.

(2) Gasoline. The term "gasoline"—
(A) includes any gasoline blend, other than qualified methanol or ethanol fuel (as defined in section 4041(b)(2)(B)), partially exempt methanol or ethanol fuel (as defined in section 4041(m)(2)), or a denatured alcohol, and
(B) includes, to the extent prescribed in regulations—
(i) any gasoline blend stock, and
(ii) any product commonly used as an additive in gasoline (other than alcohol).

For purposes of subparagraph (B)(i), the term "gasoline blend stock" means any petroleum product component of gasoline.

(3) **Diesel fuel.**
   (A) **In general.** The term "diesel fuel" means—
      (i) any liquid (other than gasoline) which is suitable for use as a fuel in a diesel-powered highway vehicle, or a diesel-powered train,
      (ii) transmix, and
      (iii) diesel fuel blend stocks identified by the Secretary.
   (B) **Transmix.** For purposes of subparagraph (A), the term "transmix" means a byproduct of refined products pipeline operations created by the mixing of different specification products during pipeline transportation.

(b) **Commercial aviation.**
For purposes of this subpart, the term "commercial aviation" means any use of an aircraft in a business of transporting persons or property for compensation or hire by air, unless properly allocable to any transportation exempt from the taxes imposed by sections 4261 and 4271 by reason of section 4281 or 4282 or by reason of subsection (h) or (i) of section 4261.

(c) **Certain uses defined as removal.**
If any person uses taxable fuel (other than in the production of taxable fuels or special fuels referred to in section 4041), such use shall for the purposes of this chapter be considered a removal.

(d) **Administrative authority.**
   (1) **In general.** In addition to the authority otherwise granted by this title, the Secretary may in administering compliance with this subpart, section 4041, and penalties and other administrative provisions related thereto—
      (A) enter any place at which taxable fuel is produced or is stored (or may be stored) for purposes of—
         (i) examining the equipment used to determine the amount or composition of such fuel and the equipment used to store such fuel,
         (ii) taking and removing samples of such fuel, and
         (iii) inspecting any books and records and any shipping papers pertaining to such fuel, and
      (B) detain, for the purposes referred in subparagraph (A), any container which contains or may contain any taxable fuel.
   (2) **Inspection sites.** The Secretary may establish inspection sites for purposes of carrying out the Secretary's authority under paragraph (1)(B).
   (3) **Penalty for refusal of entry.**
      (A) **Forfeiture.** The penalty provided by section 7342 shall apply to any refusal to admit entry or other refusal to permit an action by the Secretary authorized by paragraph (1), except that section 7342 shall be applied by substituting "$1,000" for "$500" for each such refusal.
      (B) **Assessable penalty.** For additional assessable penalty for the refusal to admit entry or other refusal to permit an action by the Secretary authorized by paragraph (1), see section 6717.

In **2005**, P.L. 109-59, Sec. 11123(b), substituted "subsection (h) or (i) of section 4261" for "section 4261(h)" in subsec. (b), effective for transportation begin. after 9/30/2005.

In **2004**, P.L. 108-357, Sec. 301(c)(8), amended para. (a)(2), effective for fuel sold or used after 12/31/2004.
Prior to amendment, para. (a)(2) read as follows:
"(2) Gasoline. The term 'gasoline' includes, to the extent prescribed in regulations—
   "(A) gasoline blend stocks, and
   "(B) products commonly used as additives in gasoline.
For purposes of subparagraph (A), the term 'gasoline blend stock' means any petroleum product component of gasoline."
— P.L. 108-357, Sec. 853(c), redesignated subsecs. (b) and (c) as subsecs. (c) and (d), and added subsec. (b), effective for aviation-grade kerosene removed, entered, or sold after 12/31/2004.

— P.L. 108-357, Sec. 858(a), deleted "and" at the end of clause (d)(1)(A)(i) [as redesignated by Sec. 853(b) of this Act, see above] and added clause (d)(1)(A)(iii) [as redesignated by Sec. 853(b) of this Act, see above], effective 10/22/2004.
— P.L. 108-357, Sec. 859(b)(1)(A), substituted "Entry. (A) Forfeiture. The penalty" for "Entry. The penalty" in para. (d)(3) [as redesignated by Sec. 853(b) of this Act, see above] . . . Sec. 859(b)(1)(B), added subpara. (d)(3)(B) [as redesignated by Sec. 853(b) of this Act, see above], effective 1/1/2005.
— P.L. 108-357, Sec. 870(a), amended para. (a)(3), effective for fuel removed, sold, or used after 12/31/2004.
Prior to amendment, para. (a)(3) read as follows:
"(3) Diesel fuel. The term 'diesel fuel' means any liquid (other than gasoline) which is suitable for use as a fuel in a diesel-powered highway vehicle, or a diesel-powered train."
In **1998**, P.L. 105-206, Sec. 6010(h)(1), substituted "Paragraph (1) of section 4083(a)" for "Subsection (a) of section 4083" in Sec. 1032(a) of P.L. 105-34, see below.
In **1997**, P.L. 105-34, Sec. 902(b)(3), substituted "or a diesel-powered train" for "a diesel-powered train, or a diesel-powered boat" in para. (a)(3), effective 1/1/98.
— P.L. 105-34, Sec. 1032(a), [as amended by Sec. 6010(h)(1), 105-206, see above] deleted "and" from the end of subpara. (a)(1)(A), substituted ", and" for the period at the end of subpara. (a)(1)(B), and added subpara. (a)(1)(C) . . . Sec. 1032(e)(4), substituted "taxable fuels" for "gasoline, diesel fuel," in subsec. (b), effective 7/1/98.
In **1993**, P.L. 103-66, Sec. 13242(a), amended Code Sec. 4083 as part of the amendments to subpart A of part III of subchapter A of chapter 32, effective 1/1/94.
Prior to amendment, Code Sec. 4083 read as follows:
"Sec. 4083 Cross references.
"(1) For provisions to relieve farmers from excise tax in the case of gasoline used on the farm for farming purposes, see section 6420.
"(2) For provisions to relieve purchasers of gasoline from excise tax in the case of gasoline used for certain nonhighway purposes, used by local transit systems, or sold for certain exempt purposes, see section 6421.
"(3) For provisions to relieve purchasers of gasoline from excise tax in the case of gasoline not used for taxable purposes, see section 6427."
In **1986**, P.L. 99-514, Sec. 1703(a), amended Code Sec. 4083, as part of the amendments to subpart A of Part III of subchapter A of chapter 32, effective for gasoline removed (as defined in Code Sec. 4082 as amended by Sec. 1703(a) of this Act) after 12/31/87.

Sec. 4084. Cross references.

(1) For provisions to relieve farmers from excise tax in the case of gasoline used on the farm for farming purposes, see section 6420.

(2) For provisions to relieve purchasers of gasoline from excise tax in the case of gasoline used for certain nonhighway purposes, used by local transit systems, or sold for certain exempt purposes, see section 6421.

(3) For provisions to relieve purchasers from excise tax in the case of taxable fuel not used for taxable purposes, see section 6427.

In **1993**, P.L. 103-66, Sec. 13242(a), amended Code Sec. 4084 as part of the amendments to subpart A of part III of subchapter A of chapter 32, effective 1/1/94.

SUBPART B. REPEALED [AVIATION FUEL]
Sec.
4091. Repealed [Imposition of tax].
4092. Repealed [Exemptions].
4093. Repealed [Definitions].

In **2004**, P.L. 108-357, Sec. 853(d)(1), deleted subpart B of part III of subchapter A of chapter 32 and redesignated subpart C of part III of subchapter A of chapter 32 as subpart B thereof, generally effective as of 12/31/2004.
In **1993**, P.L. 103-66, Sec. 13242(a), amended subpart B of Part III of subchapter A of chapter 32.
Prior to amendment, subpart B of Part III of subchapter A of chapter 32 read as follows:
"Subpart B.—Diesel Fuel and Aviation Fuel
"Sec.
"4091. IMPOSITION OF TAX.
"4092. DEFINITIONS.
"4093. EXEMPTIONS; SPECIAL RULE."

Excise and miscellaneous taxes

"Sec. 4091. Imposition of tax.
"(a) In general.
There is hereby imposed a tax on the sale of any taxable fuel by the producer or the importer thereof or by any producer of a taxable fuel.
"(b) Rate of tax.
"(1) In general. The rate of the tax imposed by subsection (a) shall be the sum of—
"(A)
"(i) the Highway Trust Fund financing rate and the diesel fuel deficit reduction rate in the case of diesel fuel, and
"(ii) the Airport and Airway Trust Fund financing rate and the aviation fuel deficit reduction rate in the case of aviation fuel, and
"(B) the Leaking Underground Storage Tank Trust Fund financing rate in the case of any taxable fuel.
"(2) Highway Trust Fund financing rate. For purposes of paragraph (1), except as provided in subsection (c), the Highway Trust Fund financing rate is 17.5 cents per gallon.
"(3) Airport and Airway Trust Fund financing rate. For purposes of paragraph (1), except as provided in subsection (d), the Airport and Airway Trust Fund financing rate is 17.5 cents per gallon.
"(4) Diesel fuel deficit reduction rate. For purposes of paragraph (1), except as provided in subsection (c), the diesel fuel deficit reduction rate is 6.8 cents per gallon.
"(5) Leaking Underground Storage Tank Trust fund financing rate. For purposes of paragraph (1), except as provided in subsection (c), the Leaking Underground Storage Tank Trust Fund financing rate is 0.1 cent per gallon.
"(6) Aviation fuel deficit reduction rate. For purposes of paragraph (1), the aviation fuel deficit reduction rate is 4.3 cents per gallon.
"(7) Termination of rates.
"(A) The Highway Trust Fund financing rate shall not apply on and after October 1, 1999.
"(B) The Airport and Airway Trust Fund financing rate shall not apply on and after January 1, 1996.
"(C) The Leaking Underground Storage Tank Trust Fund financing rate shall not apply during any period during which the Leaking Underground Storage Tank Trust Fund financing rate under section 4081 does not apply.
"(D) The diesel fuel deficit reduction rate shall not apply on and after October 1, 1995.
"(c) Reduced rate of tax for diesel fuel in alcohol mixture, etc.
Under regulations prescribed by the Secretary—
"(1) In general. The Highway Trust Fund financing rate shall be—
"(A) 12.1 cents per gallon in the case of the sale of any mixture of diesel fuel if—
"(i) at least 10 percent of such mixture consists of alcohol (as defined in section 4081(c)(3)), and
"(ii) the diesel fuel in such mixture was not taxed under subparagraph (B), and
"(B) 13.44 cents per gallon in the case of the sale of diesel fuel for use (at the time of such sale) in producing a mixture described in subparagraph (A).
In the case of a sale described in subparagraph (B), the Leaking Underground Storage Tank Trust Fund financing rate and the diesel fuel deficit reduction rate shall be 10/9th of the otherwise applicable such rates.
"(2) Later separation. If any person separates the diesel fuel from a mixture of the diesel fuel and alcohol on which tax was imposed under subsection (a) at a Highway Trust Fund financing rate equivalent to 12.1 cents a gallon by reason of this subsection (or with respect to which a credit or payment was allowed or made by reason of section 6427(f)(1)), such person shall be treated as the producer of such diesel fuel. The amount of tax imposed on any sale of such diesel fuel by such person shall be reduced by the amount of tax imposed (and not credited or refunded) on any prior sale of such fuel.
"(3) Termination. Paragraph (1) shall not apply to any sale after September 30, 2000.
"(d) Reduced rate of tax for aviation fuel in alcohol mixture, etc.
"(1) In general. The Airport and Airway Trust Fund financing rate shall be—
"(A) 4.1 cents per gallon in the case of the sale of any mixture of aviation fuel if—
"(i) at least 10 percent of such mixture consists of alcohol (as defined in section 4081(c)(3)), and
"(ii) the aviation fuel in such mixture was not taxed under subparagraph (B), and
"(B) 4.56 cents per gallon in the case of the sale of aviation fuel for use (at the time of such sale) in producing a mixture described in subparagraph (A).
In the case of a sale described in subparagraph (B), the Leaking Underground Storage Tank Trust Fund financing rate shall be 1/9 cent per gallon.
"(2) Later separation. If any person separates the aviation fuel from a mixture of the aviation fuel and alcohol on which tax was imposed at the Airport and Airway Trust Fund financing rate equivalent to 4.1 cents per gallon by reason of this subsection (or with respect to which a credit or payment was allowed or made by reason of 6427(f)(1)), such person shall be treated as the producer of such aviation fuel. The amount of tax imposed on any sale of such aviation fuel by such person shall be reduced by the amount of tax imposed (and not credited or refunded) on any prior sale of such fuel.
"(3) Termination. Paragraph (1) shall not apply to any sale after September 30, 2000.
"(e) Lower rates of tax on alcohol mixtures not made from ethanol.
In the case of a mixture described in subsection (c)(1)(A)(i) or (d)(1)(A)(i) none of the alcohol in which is ethanol—

"(1) subsections (c)(1)(A) and (c)(2), and subsections (d)(1)(A) and (d)(2), shall each be applied by substituting rates which are 0.6 cents less than the rates contained therein, and
"(2) subsections (c)(1)(B) and (d)(1)(B) shall be applied by substituting rates which are 10/9 of the rates determined under paragraph (1)."

In 1993, P.L. 103-66, Sec. 13241(b)(1), substituted "6.8 cents" for "2.5 cents" in para. (a)(4) (before amended by Sec. 13242(a) of this Act, see below)... Sec. 13241(b)(2)(B)(i), added "and the aviation fuel deficit reduction rate" after "financing rate" in clause (b)(1)(A)(ii) (before amended by Sec. 13242(a) of this Act, see below)... Sec. 13241(b)(2)(B)(ii), redesignated para. (b)(6) as para. (b)(7) and added new para. (b)(6) (before amended by Sec. 13242(a) of this Act, see below), effective 10/1/93.

In 1991, P.L. 102-240, Sec. 8001(a)(4), substituted "1999" for "1995" in subpara. (b)(6)(A), effective 12/18/91.

In 1990, P.L. 101-508, Sec. 11211(b)(1)(A), inserted "and the diesel fuel deficit reduction rate" after "financing rate" in clause (b)(1)(A)(i)... Sec. 11211(b)(1)(B), redesignated paras. (b)(4) and (b)(5) as paras. (b)(5) and (b)(6) and added new para. (b)(4)... Sec. 11211(b)(1)(C), added subpara. (b)(6)(D)... Sec. 11211(b)(2), substituted "17.5 cents" for "15 cents" in para. (b)(2)... Sec. 11211(b)(6)(A)(i), substituted "12.1 cents" for "9 cents" in subpara. (c)(1)(A) and substituted "13.44 cents" for "10 cents" in subpara. (c)(1)(B)... Sec. 11211(b)(6)(A)(ii), substituted "and the diesel fuel deficit reduction rate shall be 10/9th of the otherwise applicable such rates" for "shall be ⅑ cent per gallon" in the last sentence of para. (c)(1)... Sec. 11211(b)(6)(B), substituted "12.1 cents" for "9 cents" in para. (c)(2), effective 12/1/90.
— P.L. 101-508, Sec. 11211(c)(4), substituted "1995" for "1993" in subpara. (b)(6)(A) [as redesignated by Sec. 11211(b) of this Act]... Sec. 11211(e)(4), substituted "2000" for "1993" in paras. (c)(3) and (d)(3), effective 11/5/90.
— P.L. 101-508, Sec. 11211(j), relating to floor stocks taxes, is reproduced in note following Code Sec. 4081.
— P.L. 101-508, Sec. 11213(b)(1)(A), substituted "17.5 cents" for "14 cents" in para. (b)(3)... Sec. 11213(b)(1)(B), inserted "except as provided in subsection (d)," after "paragraph (1)," in para. (b)(3)... Sec. 11213(b)(2)(C)(i), amended paras. (d)(1) and (d)(2)... Sec. 11213(b)(2)(C)(ii), substituted "Reduced rate of" for "Exemption from" in the heading of subsec. (d)... Sec. 11213(b)(2)(D), added subsec. (e), effective 12/1/90.
Prior to amendment, paras. (d)(1) and (d)(2) read as follows:
"(1) In general. The Airport and Airway Trust Fund financing rate shall not apply to the sale of—
"(A) any mixture of aviation fuel at least 10 percent of which consists of alcohol (as defined in section 4081(c)(3)), or
"(B) any aviation fuel for use (at the time of such sale) in producing a mixture described in subparagraph (A).
"(2) Later separation. If any person separates the aviation fuel from a mixture of the aviation fuel and alcohol on which the Airport and Airway Trust Fund financing rate did not apply by reason of this subsection (or with respect to which a credit or payment was allowed or made by reason of section 6427(f)(2)), such person shall be treated as the producer of such aviation fuel."
— P.L. 101-508, Sec. 11213(d)(2)(A), substituted "January 1, 1996" for "January 1, 1991" in subpara. (b)(6)(B) [as redesignated by Sec. 11211(b)(1)(B) of this Act], effective 11/5/90.
— P.L. 101-508, Sec. 11218, relating to floor stocks tax treatment of articles in foreign trade zones, is reproduced in note following Code Sec. 5001.
— P.L. 101-508, Sec. 11704(a)(38), substituted "5 cents per gallon" for "5 cents a gallon" in Sec. 2001(d)(6)(C) of P.L. 100-647, see below.

In 1988, P.L. 100-647, Sec. 2001(d)(6)(A), added the last sentence in para. (c)(1)... Sec. 2001(d)(6)(B), added "except as provided in subsection (c)," after "paragraph (1)" in para. (b)(4)... Sec. 2001(d)(6)(C), [as amended by Sec. 11704 (a)(38) of P.L. 101-508, see above] substituted "reduced by the amount of tax imposed (and not credited or refunded) on any prior sale of such fuel." for "5 cents per gallon" in the last sentence of para. (c)(2), effective for sales after 3/31/88. For special rules see Sec. 10502(f) of P.L. 100-203, reproduced below.

In 1987, P.L. 100-203, Sec. 10502(a), added Code Sec. 4091, effective for sales after 3/31/88. Sec. 10502(f) of this Act provides:
"(f) Floor stocks tax.—
"(1) Imposition of tax.—On any taxable fuel which on April 1, 1988, is held by a taxable person, there is hereby imposed a floor stocks tax at the rate of tax which would be imposed if such fuel were sold on such date in a sale subject to tax under section 4091 of the Internal Revenue Code of 1986 (as added by this section).
"(2) Overpayment of floor stocks taxes, etc.— Sections 6416 and 6427 of such Code shall apply in respect of the floor stocks taxes imposed by this subsection so as to entitle, subject to all provisions of such sections, any person paying such floor stocks taxes to a credit or refund thereof for any reason specified in such sections. All provisions of law, including penalties, applicable with respect to the taxes imposed by section 4091 of such Code (as so added) shall apply to the floor stocks taxes imposed by this subsection.
"(3) Due date of tax.— The taxes imposed by this subsection shall be paid before June 16, 1988.
"(4) Definitions.— For purposes of this subsection—
"(A) Taxable fuel.—
"(i) In general.— The term 'taxable fuel' means any taxable fuel (as defined in section 4092 of such Code, as added by this section) on which no tax has been imposed under section 4041 of such Code.

"(ii) Exception for fuel held for nontaxable uses.—The term 'taxable fuel' shall not include fuel held exclusively for any use which is a nontaxable use (as defined in section 6427(1) of such Code, as added by this section).

"(B) Taxable person.—The term 'taxable person' means any person other than a producer (as defined in section 4092 of such Code, as so added) or importer of taxable fuel.

"(C) Held by a taxable person.—An article shall be treated as held by a person if title thereto has passed to such person (whether or not delivery to such person has been made).

"(5) Special rule for fuel held for use in trains and commercial aircraft.—Only the Leaking Underground Storage Tank Trust Fund financing rate under section 4091 of such Code shall apply for purposes of this subsection with respect to—

"(A) diesel fuel held exclusively for use as a fuel in a diesel-powered train, and

"(B) aviation fuel held exclusively for use as a fuel in an aircraft not in noncommercial aviation (as defined in section 4041(c)(4) of such Code).

"(6) Transfer of floor stock revenues to trust funds.—For purposes of determining the amount transferred to any trust fund, the tax imposed by this subsection shall be treated as imposed by section 4091 of such Code (as so added)."

—P.L. 100-203, Sec. 10502(g), substituted "January 1, 1991" for "January 1, 1988" in subpara. (b)(5)(B), effective 12/31/87.

"Sec. 4092 Definitions.
"(a) Taxable fuel.
 For purposes of this subpart—
 "(1) In general. The term 'taxable fuel' means—
 "(A) diesel fuel, and
 "(B) aviation fuel.
 "(2) Diesel fuel. The term 'diesel fuel' means any liquid (other than any product taxable under section 4081) which is suitable for use as a fuel in a diesel-powered highway vehicle, a diesel-powered train, or diesel-powered boat.
 "(3) Aviation fuel. The term 'aviation fuel' means any liquid (other than any product taxable under section 4081) which is suitable for use as a fuel in an aircraft.
"(b) Producer.
 For purposes of this subpart—
 "(1) Certain persons treated as producers.
 "(A) In general. The term 'producer' includes any person described in subparagraph (B) who elects to register under section 4101 with respect to the tax imposed by section 4091.
 "(B) Persons described. A person is described in this subparagraph if such person is—
 "(i) a refiner, compounder, blender, or wholesale distributor of a taxable fuel, or
 "(ii) a dealer selling any taxable fuel exclusively to producers of such taxable fuel, or
 "(iii) a retailer selling diesel fuel exclusively to purchasers as supplies for vessels for use in an off-highway business use (as defined in section 6421(e)(2)(B)).
 To the extent provided in regulations, a retailer shall not be treated as not described in clause (iii) by reason of selling de minimis amounts of diesel fuel other than as supplies for vessels for use in an off-highway business use (as defined in section 6421(e)(2)(B)).
 "(C) Tax-free purchasers treated as producers. Any person to whom any taxable fuel is sold tax-free under this subpart shall be treated as the producer of such fuel.
 "(2) Wholesale distributor. For purposes of paragraph (1), the term 'wholesale distributor' includes any person who sells a taxable fuel to producers, retailers, or to users who purchase in bulk quantities and deliver into bulk storage tanks. Such term does not include any person who (excluding the term 'wholesale distributor' from paragraph (1)) is a producer or importer."

In 1993, P.L. 103-66, Sec. 13163(a)(1), substituted ", a diesel-powered train, or a diesel-powered boat" for "or a diesel-powered train" in para. (a)(2) (before amended by Sec. 13242(a) of this Act, see below) ... Sec. 13163(a)(3), substituted "vessels for use in an off-highway business use (as defined in section 6421(e)(2)(B))" for "commercial and noncommercial vessels" each place it appeared in subpara. (b)(1)(B) (before amended by Sec. 13242(a) of this Act, see below), effective 1/1/94.

In 1988, P.L. 100-647, Sec. 3003(a), substituted ", or" for the period at the end of clause (b)(1)(B)(ii), added clause (b)(1)(B)(iii) and the sentence at the end of subpara. (b)(1)(B), effective for sales after 12/31/88.

In 1987, P.L. 100-203, Sec. 10502(a), added Code Sec. 4092, effective for sales after 3/31/88. For provisions on floor stocks tax, see Sec. 10502(f) of this Act reproduced in note following Code Sec. 4091.

"Sec. 4093 Exemptions; special rule.
"(a) Heating oil.
 The tax imposed by section 4091 shall not apply in the case of sales of any taxable fuel which the Secretary determines is destined for use as heating oil.
"(b) Sales to producer.
 Under regulations prescribed by the Secretary, the tax imposed by section 4091 shall not apply in the case of sales of a taxable fuel to a producer of such fuel.
"(c) Exemption for nontaxable uses and bus uses.
 "(1) In general. No tax shall be imposed by section 4091 on fuel sold by a producer or importer for use by the purchaser in a nontaxable use (as defined in section 6427(l)(2)) or a use described in section 6427(b)(1).

"(2) Exceptions.
 "(A) No exemption from certain taxes on fuel used in diesel-powered trains. In the case of fuel sold for use in a diesel-powered train, paragraph (1) shall not apply to so much of the tax imposed by section 4091 as is attributable to the Leaking Underground Storage Tank Trust Fund financing rate and the diesel fuel deficit reduction rate imposed under such section. The preceding sentence shall not apply in the case of fuel sold for exclusive use by a State or any political subdivision thereof.
 "(B) No exemption from Leaking Underground Storage Tank Trust Fund taxes on fuel used in commercial aviation. In the case of fuel sold for use in commercial aviation (other than supplies for vessels or aircraft within the meaning of section 4221(d)(3)), paragraph (1) also shall not apply to so much of the tax imposed by section 4091 as is attributable to the Leaking Underground Storage Tank Trust Fund financing rate imposed by such section. For purposes of the preceding sentence, the term 'commercial aviation,' means any use of an aircraft other than in noncommercial aviation (as defined in section 4041(c)(4)).
 "(C) Certain bus uses. Paragraph (1) shall not apply to so much of the tax imposed by section 4091 as is not refundable by reason of the application of section 6427(b)(2)(A).
 "(3) Registration required. Except to the extent provided by the Secretary, paragraph (1) shall not apply to any sale unless—
 "(A) both the seller and the purchaser are registered under section 4101, and
 "(B) the purchaser's name, address, and registration number under such section are provided to the seller.
 "(4) Information reporting.
 "(A) Returns by producers and importers. Each producer or importer who makes a reduced-tax sale during the calendar year shall make a return (at such time and in such form as the Secretary may by regulations prescribe) showing with respect to each such sale—
 "(i) the name, address, and registration number under section 4101 of the purchaser,
 "(ii) the amount of fuel sold, and
 "(iii) such other information as the Secretary may require.
 "(B) Statements to purchasers. Every person required to make a return under subparagraph (A) shall furnish to each purchaser whose name is required to be set forth on such return a written statement showing the name and address of the person required to make such return, the registration number under section 4101 of such person, and the information required to be shown on the return with respect to such purchaser. The written statement required under the preceding sentence shall be furnished to the purchaser on or before January 31 of the year following the calendar year for which the return under subparagraph (A) is required to be made.
 "(C) Returns by purchasers. Each person who uses during the calendar year fuel purchased in a reduced-tax sale shall make a return (at such time and in such form as the Secretary may by regulations prescribe) showing—
 "(i) whether such use was a nontaxable use (as defined in section 6427(l)(2)) or a use described in section 6427(b)(1) and the amount of fuel so used,
 "(ii) the date of the sale of the fuel so used,
 "(iii) the name, address, and registration number under section 4101 of the seller, and
 "(iv) such other information as the Secretary may require.
 "(D) Reduced-tax sale. For purposes of this paragraph, the term 'reduced-tax sale' means any sale of taxable fuel on which the amount of tax otherwise required to be paid under section 4091 is reduced by reason of paragraph (1) (other than sales described in subsections (a) and (b) of this section).
"(d) Certain aviation fuel sales.
 Under regulations prescribed by the Secretary, the Leaking Underground Storage Tank Trust Fund financing rate and the aviation fuel deficit reduction rate under section 4091 shall not apply to aviation fuel sold for use or used as supplies for vessels or aircraft (within the meaning of section 4221(d)(3)).
"(e) Cross references.
 "(1) For imposition of tax where certain uses of diesel fuel or aviation fuel occur before imposition of tax by section 4091, see subsections (a)(1) and (c)(1) of section 4041.
 "(2) For provisions allowing a credit or refund for fuel not used for certain taxable purposes, see section 6427."

In 1993, P.L. 103-66, Sec. 13241(f)(3), amended subparas. (c)(2)(A) and (B) (before amended by Sec. 13242(a) of this Act, see below) ... Sec. 13241(f)(4), added "and the aviation fuel deficit reduction rate" after "rate" in subsec. (d) (before amended by Sec. 13242(a) of this Act, see below), effective 10/1/93.
Prior to amendment, subparas. (c)(2)(A) and (B) read as follows:
"(A) Certain Leaking Underground Storage Tank Trust Funds taxes. In the case of fuel sold for use in—
"(i) a diesel-powered train, and
"(ii) an aircraft,
paragraph (1) shall not apply to so much of the tax imposed by section 4091 as is attributable to the Leaking Underground Storage Tank Trust Fund financing rate imposed by such section.
"(B) Deficit reduction rate on fuel used in trains. In the case of fuel sold for use in a diesel-powered train, paragraph (1) also shall not apply to so much of the tax imposed by section 4091 as is attributable to the diesel fuel deficit reduction rate imposed by such section."

In 1990, P.L. 101-508, Sec. 11211(b)(4)(A), redesignated subpara. (c)(2)(B) as subpara. (c)(2)(C) and added new subpara. (c)(2)(B) ... Sec. 11212(b)(4), deleted subsec. (e) and redesignated subsec. (f) as subsec. (e), effective 12/1/90.
Prior to deletion, subsec. (e) read as follows:

Excise and miscellaneous taxes Subpart B

"(e) Special administrative rules.
The Secretary may require—
"(1) information reporting by each remitter of the tax imposed by section 4091, and
"(2) information reporting by, and registration of, such other persons as the Secretary deems necessary to carry out this subpart."
— P.L. 101-508, Sec. 11704(a)(20), substituted "reduced-tax sale" for "reduced tax sale" in subpara. (c)(4)(D), effective 11/5/90.

In 1988, P.L. 100-647, Sec. 2004(s)(1), redesignated subsecs. (d) and (e) as subsecs. (e) and (f), and added new subsec. (d), effective for sales after 3/31/88.
— P.L. 100-647, Sec. 3001(a), amended subsec. (c), effective 1/1/89, except as provided in Sec. 3001(c)(2) of this Act which reads as follows:
"(2) Refunds with interest for pre-effective date purchases.
"(A) In general. In the case of fuel—
"(i) which is purchased from a producer or importer during the period beginning on April 1, 1988, and ending on December 31, 1988,
"(ii) which is used (before the claim under this subparagraph is filed) by any person in a nontaxable use (as defined in section 6427(1)(2) of the 1986 Code), and
"(iii) with respect to which a claim is not permitted to be filed for any quarter under section 6427(i) of the 1986 Code,
the Secretary of the Treasury or the Secretary's delegate shall pay (with interest) to such person the amount of tax imposed on such fuel under section 4091 of the 1986 Code (to the extent not attributable to amounts described in section 6427(1)(3) of the 1986 Code) if claim therefor is filed not later than June 30, 1989. Not more than 1 claim may be filed under the preceding sentence and such claim shall not be taken into account under section 6427(i) of the 1986 Code. Any claim for refund filed under this paragraph shall be considered a claim for refund under section 6427(l) of the 1986 Code.
"(B) Interest. The amount of interest payable under subparagraph (A) shall be determined under section 6611 of the 1986 Code except that the date of the overpayment with respect to fuel purchased during any month shall be treated as being the 1st day of the succeeding month. No interest shall be paid under this paragraph with respect to fuel used by any agency of the United States.
"(C) Registration procedures required to be specified. Not later than the 30th day after the date of the enactment of this Act, the Secretary of the Treasury or the Secretary's delegate shall prescribe the procedures for complying with the requirements of section 4093(c)(3) of the 1986 Code (as added by this section)."
Prior to amendment, subsec. (c) read as follows:
"(c) Authority to exempt certain other uses.
"Subject to such terms and conditions as the Secretary may provide (including the application of section 4101), the Secretary may by regulation provide that—
"(1) the Highway Trust Fund financing rate under section 4091 shall not apply to diesel fuel sold for use by any purchaser as a fuel in a diesel-powered train,
"(2) the Airport and Airway Trust Fund financing rate under section 4091 shall not apply to aviation fuel sold for use by any purchaser as a fuel in an aircraft not in noncommercial aviation (as defined in section 4041(c)(4)),
"(3) the tax imposed by section 4091 shall not apply to taxable fuel sold for use by any purchaser other than as a motor fuel, and
"(4) the tax imposed by section 4091 shall not apply to taxable fuel sold for the exclusive use of any State, any political subdivision of a State, or the District of Columbia."

In 1987, P.L. 100-203, Sec. 10502(a), added Code Sec. 4093, effective for sales after 3/31/88. For provisions on floor stocks tax, see Sec. 10502(f) of this Act reproduced in note following Code Sec. 4091.

In 1987, P.L. 100-203, Sec. 10502(a), added new Subpart B to Part III of Subchapter A of Chapter 32.
In 1983, P.L. 97-448, Sec. 515(a), repealed the items for Subpart B and for Code Secs. 4091 through 4094.
Prior to repeal, these items read as follows:
"Subpart B.—Lubricating Oil
"Sec.
"4091. IMPOSITION OF TAX.
"4092. DEFINITIONS.
"4093. EXEMPTIONS.
"4094. CROSS REFERENCE."

In 1978, P.L. 95-618, Sec. 404(c), amended item 4093.
Prior to amendment item 4093 read as follows:
"4093. EXEMPTION OF SALES TO PRODUCERS."
In 1965, added item 4094.
In 1956, substituted "Definitions" for "Definition of certain vendees as a manufacturer".

"SEC. 4091. REPEALED.
In 1983, P.L. 97-424, Sec. 515(a), repealed Code Sec. 4091 effective for articles sold after 1/6/83.
Prior to repeal, Code Sec. 4091 read as follows:
"SEC. 4091. IMPOSITION OF TAX.
"There is hereby imposed on lubricating oil (other than cutting oils) which is sold in the United States by the manufacturer or producer a tax of 6 cents a gallon, to be paid by the manufacturer or producer."
In 1965, rewrote Code Sec. 4091 for articles sold after 12/31/65.
Prior to amendment, it read as follows:

"There is hereby imposed upon the following articles sold in the United States by the manufacturer or producer a tax at the following rates, to be paid by the manufacturer or producer:
"(1) cutting oils, 3 cents a gallon; and
"(2) other lubricating oils, 6 cents a gallon."
In 1955, provided for a tax of 3 cents a gallon on cutting oils instead of 6 cents per gallon and eliminated the provision that the tax should be not more than 10 percent of the manufacturer's price, effective 10/1/55.

"SEC. 4092. REPEALED."
In 1983, P.L. 97-424, Sec. 515(a), repealed Code Sec. 4092, effective for articles sold after 1/6/83.
Prior to repeal, Code Sec. 4092 read as follows:
"SEC. 4092. DEFINITIONS.
"(a) Certain vendees considered as manufacturers.
"For purposes of this subpart, a vendee who has purchased lubricating oils free of tax under section 4093(a) shall be considered the manufacturer or producer of such lubricating oils.
"(b) Cutting oils.
"For purposes of this subpart, the term 'cutting oils' means oils sold for use in cutting and machining operation (including forging, drawing, rolling, shearing, punching, and stamping) on metals."
In 1978, P.L. 95-618, Sec. 404(b), substituted "4093(a)" for "4093" in subsec. (a), effective 12/1/78 (the first day of the first calendar month beginning more than 10 days after 11/9/78).
In 1955, substituted "Definitions" for "Definition of certain vendees as a manufacturer" in the catchline, designated existing provisions thereof as subsec. (a), and added subsec. (b), effective 10/1/55.

"SEC. 4093. REPEALED.
In 1983, P.L. 97-424, Sec. 515(a), repealed Code Sec. 4093, effective for articles sold after 1/6/83.
Prior to repeal, Code Sec. 4093 read as follows:
"SEC. 4093. EXEMPTIONS.
"(a) Sales to manufacturers or producers for resale.
"Under regulations prescribed by the Secretary, no tax shall be imposed by section 4091 on lubricating oils sold to a manufacturer or producer of lubricating oils for resale by him.
"(b) Use in producing rerefined oil.
"(1) Sales to rerefiners. Under regulations prescribed by the Secretary, no tax shall be imposed by section 4091 on lubricating oil sold for use in mixing with used or waste lubricating oil which has been cleaned, renovated, or rerefined. Any person to whom lubricating oil is sold tax-free under this paragraph shall be treated as the producer of such lubricating oil.
"(2) Use in producing rerefined oil. Under regulations prescribed by the Secretary, no tax shall be imposed by section 4091 on lubricating oil used in producing rerefined oil to the extent that the amount of such lubricating oil does not exceed 55 percent of such rerefined oil.
"(3) Rerefined oil defined. For purposes of this subsection, the term 'rerefined oil' means oil 25 percent or more of which is used or waste lubricating oil which has been cleaned, renovated, or rerefined."
In 1978, P.L. 95-618, Sec. 404(a), amended Code Sec. 4093, effective 12/1/78 (the first day of the first calendar month beginning more than 10 days after 11/9/78).
Prior to amendment, Code Sec. 4093 read as follows:
"SEC. 4093. EXEMPTION OF SALES TO PRODUCERS.
"Under regulations prescribed by the Secretary, no tax shall be imposed under this subpart upon lubricating oils sold to a manufacturer or producer of lubricating oils for resale by him."
In 1976, P.L. 94-455, Sec. 1906(b)(13)(A), substituted "Secretary" for "Secretary or his delegate" in Code Sec. 4093, effective 2/1/77.

"SEC. 4094. REPEALED."
In 1983, P.L. 97-424, Sec. 515(a), repealed Code Sec. 4094, effective for articles sold after 1/6/83.
Prior to repeal, Code Sec. 4094 read as follows:
"SEC. 4094. CROSS REFERENCE.
"For provisions to relieve purchasers of lubricating oil from excise tax in the case of lubricating oil used otherwise than in a highway motor vehicle, see sections 39 and 6424."
In 1965, added Code Sec. 4094.

SUBPART B.—SPECIAL PROVISIONS APPLICABLE TO PETROLEUM PRODUCTS

Sec.
4101. Registration and bond.
4102. Inspection of records by local officers.
4103. Certain additional persons liable for tax where willful failure to pay.
4104. Information reporting for persons claiming certain tax benefits.

4105. Two-party exchanges.

In 2004, P.L. 108-357, Sec. 303(b), added item 4104.... Sec. 866(b), added item 4105.
In 1990, P.L. 101-508, Sec. 11212(e)(3), added item 4103.
In 1986, P.L. 99-514, Sec. 1703(b)(2), substituted "Registration and bond" for "Registration" in item 4101.
In 1976, P.L. 94-455, Sec. 2102(c)(2), amended item 4102.
Prior to amendment item 4102 read as follows:
"4102. Inspection of records, returns, etc., by local officers."
In 1965, P.L. 89-44, Sec. 802, struck out "and bond" following "Registration" in item 4101.

Sec. 4091. Repealed.

In 2004, P.L. 108-357, Sec. 853(d)(1), repealed Code Sec. 4091 as part of the repeal of Subpart B of Part III of Subchapter A of Chapter 32, effective for aviation-grade kerosene removed, entered, or sold after 12/31/2004.
Prior to repeal, Code Sec. 4091 read as follows:
"SEC. 4091. IMPOSITION OF TAX.
"(a) Tax on sale.
"(1) In general. There is hereby imposed a tax on the sale of aviation fuel by the producer or the importer thereof or by any producer of aviation fuel.
"(2) Use treated as sale. For purposes of paragraph (1), if any producer uses aviation fuel (other than for a nontaxable use as defined in section 6427(l)(2)(B)) on which no tax has been imposed under such paragraph or on which tax has been credited or refunded, then such use shall be considered a sale.
"(b) Rate of tax.
"(1) In general. The rate of the tax imposed by subsection (a) shall be 21.8 cents per gallon.
"(2) Leaking Underground Storage Tank Trust Fund tax. The rate of tax specified in paragraph (1) shall be increased by 0.1 cent per gallon. The increase in tax under this paragraph shall in this title be referred to as the Leaking Underground Storage Tank Trust Fund financing rate.
"(3) Termination.
"(A) The rate of tax specified in paragraph (1) shall be 4.3 cents per gallon—
"(i) after December 31, 1996, and before the date which is 7 days after the date of the enactment [2/28/97] of the Airport and Airway Trust Fund Tax Reinstatement Act of 1997, and
"(ii) after September 30, 2007.
"(B) The Leaking Underground Storage Tank Trust Fund financing rate shall not apply during any period during which the Leaking Underground Storage Tank Trust Fund financing rate under section 4081 does not apply.
"(c) Reduced rate of tax for aviation fuel in alcohol mixture, etc. Under regulations prescribed by the Secretary.
"(1) In general. The rate of tax under subsection (a) shall be reduced by the applicable blender amount per gallon in the case of the sale of any mixture of aviation fuel if—
"(A) at least 10 percent of such mixture consists of alcohol (as defined in section 4081(c)(3)), and
"(B) the aviation fuel in such mixture was not taxed under paragraph (2).
"In the case of such a mixture none of the alcohol in which is ethanol, the preceding sentence shall be applied by substituting '14 cents' for 'the applicable blender amount'.
"For purposes of this paragraph, the term 'applicable blender amount' means 13.3 cents in the case of any sale or use during 2001 or 2002, 13.2 cents in the case of any sale or use during 2003 or 2004, 13.1 cents in the case of any sale or use during 2005, 2006, or 2007, and 13.4 cents in the case of any sale or use during 2008 or thereafter.
"(2) Tax prior to mixing. In the case of the sale of aviation fuel for use (at the time of such sale) in producing a mixture described in paragraph (1), the rate of tax under subsection (a) shall be ⅑ of the rate which would (but for this paragraph) have been applicable to such mixture had such mixture been created prior to such sale.
"(3) Later separation. If any person separates the aviation fuel from a mixture of the aviation fuel and alcohol on which tax was imposed under subsection (a) at a rate determined under paragraph (1) or (2) (or with respect to which a credit or payment was allowed or made by reason of section 6427(f)(1)), such person shall be treated as the producer of such aviation fuel. The amount of tax imposed on any sale of such aviation fuel by such person shall be reduced by the amount of tax imposed (and not credited or refunded) on any prior sale of such fuel.
"(4) Limitation. In no event shall any rate determined under paragraph (1) be less than 4.3 cents per gallon.
"(5) Termination. Paragraphs (1) and (2) shall not apply to any sale after September 30, 2007.
"(d) Refund of tax-paid aviation fuel to registered producer of fuel. If—
"(1) a producer of aviation fuel is registered under section 4101, and
"(2) such producer establishes to the satisfaction of the Secretary that a prior tax was paid (and not credited or refunded) on aviation fuel held by such producer,
"then an amount equal to the tax so paid shall be allowed as a refund (without interest) to such producer in the same manner as if it were an overpayment of tax imposed by this section."
—P.L. 108-357, Sec. 853(f), of this Act, provides:
"(f) Floor stocks tax.

"(1) In general. There is hereby imposed on aviation-grade kerosene held on January 1, 2005, by any person a tax equal to—
"(A) the tax which would have been imposed before such date on such kerosene had the amendments made by this section been in effect at all times before such date, reduced by
"(B) the sum of—
"(i) the tax imposed before such date on such kerosene under section 4091 of the Internal Revenue Code of 1986, as in effect on such date, and
"(ii) in the case of kerosene held exclusively for such person's own use, the amount which such person would (but for this clause) reasonably expect (as of such date) to be paid as a refund under section 6427(l) of such Code with respect to such kerosene.
"(2) Exception for fuel held in aircraft fuel tank. Paragraph (1) shall not apply to kerosene held in the fuel tank of an aircraft on January 1, 2005.
"(3) Liability for tax and method of payment.
"(A) Liability for tax. The person holding the kerosene on January 1, 2005, to which the tax imposed by paragraph (1) applies shall be liable for such tax.
"(B) Method and time for payment. The tax imposed by paragraph (1) shall be paid at such time and in such manner as the Secretary of the Treasury (or the Secretary's delegate) shall prescribe, including the nonapplication of such tax on de minimis amounts of kerosene.
"(4) Transfer of floor stock tax revenues to trust funds. For purposes of determining the amount transferred to any trust fund, the tax imposed by this subsection shall be treated as imposed by section 4081 of the Internal Revenue Code of 1986—
"(A) in any case in which tax was not imposed by section 4091 of such Code, at the Leaking Underground Storage Tank Trust Fund financing rate under such section to the extent of 0.1 cents per gallon, and
"(B) at the rate under section 4081(a)(2)(A)(iv) of such Code to the extent of the remainder.
"(5) Held by a person. For purposes of this subsection, kerosene shall be considered as held by a person if title thereto has passed to such person (whether or not delivery to the person has been made).
"(6) Other laws applicable. All provisions of law, including penalties, applicable with respect to the tax imposed by section 4081 of such Code shall, insofar as applicable and not inconsistent with the provisions of this subsection, apply with respect to the floor stock tax imposed by paragraph (1) to the same extent as if such tax were imposed by such section."
In 1998, P.L. 105-206, Sec. 6014(d), added "or on which tax has been credited or refunded" after "such paragraph" in para. (a)(2), effective for fuel acquired by the producer after 9/30/97.
—P.L. 105-206, Sec. 6018(e), substituted "paragraph (3)(A)" for "paragraph (e)(A)(i)" in Sec. 1609(h) of P.L. 104-188 [see below].
In 1998, P.L. 105-178, Sec. 9003(a)(1)(D), substituted "2007" for "2000" in para. (c)(5), effective 6/9/98.
—P.L. 105-178, Sec. 9003(b)(2)(D), substituted "the applicable blender amount" for "13.4 cents" each place it appeared in para. (c)(1), and added a sentence at the end of para. (c)(1), effective 1/1/2001.
In 1997, P.L. 105-34, Sec. 1031(a)(1), substituted "September 30, 2007" for "September 30, 1997" in clause (b)(3)(A)(ii), effective 10/1/97.
—P.L. 105-34, Sec. 1436(a), added subsec. (d), effective for fuel acquired by the producer after 9/30/97.
—P.L. 105-34, Sec. 1601(f)(4)(E), substituted "paragraph (3)(A)" for "paragraph (3)(A)(i)" in Sec. 1609(h)(1) of P.L. 104-188 [reproduced below]... Sec. 1601(f)(4)(F), added "or exclusively for the use described in section 4092(b) of such Code" before the period at the end of Sec. 1609(h)(4) of P.L. 104-188 [reproduced below].
—P.L. 105-2, Sec. 2(a)(1), amended subpara. (b)(3)(A), effective for periods beginning on or after the 7th calendar day after 2/28/97.
Prior to amendment, subpara. (b)(3)(A) read as follows:
"(A) The rate of tax specified in paragraph (1) shall be 4.3 cents per gallon—
"(i) after December 31, 1995, and before the date which is 7 calendar days after the date of the enactment of the Small Business Job Protection Act of 1996, and
"(ii) after December 31, 1996."
—P.L. 105-2, Sec. 2(d), of this Act provides:
"(d) Floor stocks taxes on aviation gasoline and aviation fuel.
"(1) Imposition of tax. In the case of any aviation liquid on which tax was imposed under section 4081 or 4091 of the Internal Revenue Code of 1986 before the tax effective date and which is held on such date by any person, there is hereby imposed a floor stocks tax of—
"(A) 15 cents per gallon in the case of aviation gasoline, and
"(B) 17.5 cents per gallon in the case of aviation fuel.
"(2) Liability for tax and method of payment.
"(A) Liability for tax. A person holding, on the tax effective date, any aviation liquid to which the tax imposed by paragraph (1) applies shall be liable for such tax.
"(B) Method of payment. The tax imposed by paragraph (1) shall be paid in such manner as the Secretary shall prescribe.
"(C) Time for payment. The tax imposed by paragraph (1) shall be paid on or before the first day of the 5th month beginning after the tax effective date.
"(3) Definitions. For purposes of this subsection—
"(A) Tax effective date. The term 'tax effective date' means the date which is 7 days after the date of the enactment of this Act.
"(B) Aviation liquid. The term 'aviation liquid' means aviation gasoline and aviation fuel.
"(C) Aviation gasoline. The term 'aviation gasoline' has the meaning given such term in section 4081 of such Code.

Excise and miscellaneous taxes — Code Sec. 4091

"(D) Aviation fuel. The term 'aviation fuel' has the meaning given such term by section 4093 of such Code.

"(E) Held by a person. Aviation liquid shall be considered as 'held by a person' if title thereto has passed to such person (whether or not delivery to the person has been made).

"(F) Secretary. The term 'Secretary' means the Secretary of the Treasury or the Secretary's delegate.

"(4) Exception for exempt uses. The tax imposed by paragraph (1) shall not apply to—

"(A) aviation liquid held by any person on the tax effective date exclusively for any use for which a credit or refund of the entire tax imposed by section 4081 or 4091 of such Code (as the case may be) is allowable for such liquid purchased on or after such tax effective date for such use, or

"(B) aviation fuel held by any person on the tax effective date exclusively for any use described in section 4092(b) of such Code.

"(5) Exception for certain amounts of fuel.

"(A) In general. No tax shall be imposed by paragraph (1) on any aviation liquid held on the tax effective date by any person if the aggregate amount of such liquid (determined separately for aviation gasoline and aviation fuel) held by such person on such date does not exceed 2,000 gallons. The preceding sentence shall apply only if such person submits to the Secretary (at the time and in the manner required by the Secretary) such information as the Secretary shall require for purposes of this paragraph.

"(B) Exempt fuel. Any liquid to which the tax imposed by paragraph (1) does not apply by reason of paragraph (4) shall not be taken into account under subparagraph (A).

"(C) Controlled groups. For purposes of this paragraph—

"(i) Corporations.

"(I) In general. All persons treated as a controlled group shall be treated as 1 person.

"(II) Controlled group. The term 'controlled group' has the meaning given such term by subsection (a) of section 1563 of such Code; except that for such purposes, the phrase 'more than 50 percent' shall be substituted for the phrase 'at least 80 percent' each place it appears in such subsection.

"(ii) Nonincorporated persons under common control. Under regulations prescribed by the Secretary, principles similar to the principles of clause (i) shall apply to a group of persons under common control where 1 or more of such persons is not a corporation.

"(6) Other laws applicable. All provisions of law, including penalties, applicable with respect to the taxes imposed by section 4081 or 4091 of such Code shall, insofar as applicable and not inconsistent with the provisions of this subsection, apply with respect to the floor stocks taxes imposed by paragraph (1) to the same extent as if such taxes were imposed by such section 4081 or 4091, as the case may be."

In 1996, P.L. 104-188, Sec. 1609(a)(1), amended subpara. (b)(3)(A), effective on the 7th calendar day after 8/20/96.

Prior to amendment, subpara. (b)(3)(A) read as follows:

"(A) On and after January 1, 1996, the rate of tax specified in paragraph (1) shall be 4.3 cents per gallon."

—P.L. 104-188, Sec. 1609(h), of this Act [as amended by Sec. 1601(f)(4)(E) and (F) of P.L. 105-34 and Sec. 6018(e) of P.L. 105-206, see above] provides:

"(h) Floor stocks taxes on aviation fuel.

"(1) Imposition of tax. In the case of aviation fuel on which tax was imposition under section 4091 of the Internal Revenue Code of 1986 before the tax-increase date described in paragraph (3)(A) and which is held on such date by any person, there is hereby imposed a floor stocks tax of 17.5 cents per gallon.

"(2) Liability for tax and method of payment.

"(A) Liability for tax. A person holding aviation fuel on a tax-increase date to which the tax imposed by paragraph (1) applies shall be liable for such tax.

"(B) Method of payment. The tax imposed by paragraph (1) shall be paid in such manner as the Secretary shall prescribe.

"(C) Time for payment. The tax imposed by paragraph (1) with respect to any tax-increase date shall be paid on or before the first day of the 7th month beginning after such tax-increase date.

"(3) Definitions. For purposes of this subsection—

"(A) Tax increase date. The term 'tax-increase date' means the date which is 7 calendar days after the date of the enactment of this Act.

"(B) Aviation fuel. The term 'aviation fuel' has the meaning given such term by section 4093 of such Code.

"(C) Held by a person. Aviation fuel shall be considered as 'held by a person' if title thereto has passed to such person (whether or not delivery to the person has been made).

"(D) Secretary. The term 'Secretary' means the Secretary of the Treasury or his delegate.

"(4) Exception for exempt uses. The tax imposed by paragraph (1) shall not apply to aviation fuel held by any person on any tax-increase date exclusively for any use for which a credit or refund of the entire tax imposed by section 4091 of such Code is allowable for aviation fuel purchased on or after such tax-increase date for such use or exclusively for the use described in section 4092(b) of such Code.

"(5) Exception for certain amounts of fuel.

"(A) In general. No tax shall be imposed by paragraph (1) on aviation fuel held on any tax-increase date by any person if the aggregate amount of aviation fuel held by such person on such date does not exceed 2,000 gallons. The preceding sentence shall apply only if such person submits to the Secretary (at the time and in the manner required by the Secretary) such information as the Secretary shall require for purposes of this paragraph.

"(B) Exempt fuel. For purposes of subparagraph (A), there shall not be taken into account fuel held by any person which is exempt from the tax imposed by paragraph (1) by reason of paragraph (4).

"(C) Controlled groups. For purposes of this paragraph—

"(i) Corporations.

"(I) In general. All persons treated as a controlled group shall be treated as 1 person.

"(II) Controlled group. The term 'controlled group' has the meaning given to such term by subsection (a) of section 1563 of such Code; except that for such purposes the phrase 'more than 50 percent' shall be substituted for the phrase 'at least 80 percent' each place it appears in such subsection.

"(ii) Nonincorporated persons under common control. Under regulations prescribed by the Secretary, principles similar to the principles of clause (i) shall apply to a group of persons under common control where 1 or more of such persons is not a corporation.

"(6) Other law applicable. All provisions of law, including penalties, applicable with respect to the taxes imposed by section 4091 of such Code shall, insofar as applicable and not inconsistent with the provisions of this subsection, apply with respect to the floor stock taxes imposed by paragraph (1) to the same extent as if such taxes were imposed by such section 4091."

In 1993, P.L. 103-66, Sec. 13241(b)(1), substituted "6.8 cents" for "2.5 cents" in para. (b)(4) (before amended by Sec. 13242(a) of this Act, see below) . . . Sec. 13241(b)(2)(B)(i), added "and the aviation fuel deficit reduction rate" after "financing rate" in clause (b)(1)(A)(ii) (before amended by Sec. 13242(a) of this Act, see below) . . . Sec. 13241(b)(2)(B)(ii), redesignated para. (b)(6) as para. (b)(7) and added new para. (b)(6) (before amended by Sec. 13242(a) of this Act, see below), effective 10/1/93.

—P.L. 103-66, Sec. 13241(h), of this Act provides:

"(h) Floor stocks taxes.

"(1) Imposition of tax. In the case of gasoline, diesel fuel, and aviation fuel on which tax was imposed under section 4081 or 4091 of the Internal Revenue Code of 1986 before October 1, 1993, and which is held on such date by any person, there is hereby imposed a floor stocks tax of 4.3 cents per gallon on such gasoline, diesel fuel, and aviation fuel.

"(2) Liability for tax and method of payment.

"(A) Liability for tax. A person holding gasoline, diesel fuel, or aviation fuel on October 1, 1993, to which the tax imposed by paragraph (1) applies shall be liable for such tax.

"(B) Method of payment. The tax imposed by paragraph (1) shall be paid in such manner as the Secretary shall prescribe.

"(C) Time for payment. The tax imposed by paragraph (1) shall be paid on or before November 30, 1993.

"(3) Definitions. For purposes of this subsection—

"(A) Held by a person. Gasoline, diesel fuel, and aviation fuel shall be considered as 'held by a person' if title thereto has passed to such person (whether or not delivery to the person has been made).

"(B) Gasoline. The term 'gasoline' has the meaning given such term by section 4082 of such Code.

"(C) Diesel fuel. The term 'diesel fuel' has the meaning given such term by section 4092 of such Code.

"(D) Aviation fuel. The term 'aviation fuel' has the meaning given such term by section 4092 of such Code.

"(E) Secretary. The term 'Secretary' means the Secretary of the Treasury or his delegate.

"(4) Exception for exempt uses. The tax imposed by paragraph (1) shall not apply to gasoline, diesel fuel, or aviation fuel held by any person exclusively for any use to the extent a credit or refund of the tax imposed by section 4081 or 4091 of such Code, as the case may be, is allowable for such use.

"(5) Exception for fuel held in vehicle tank. No tax shall be imposed by paragraph (1) on gasoline or diesel fuel held in the tax of a motor vehicle or motorboat.

"(6) Exception for certain amounts of fuel.

"(A) In general. No tax shall be imposed by paragraph (1)—

"(i) on gasoline held on October 1, 1993, by any person if the aggregate amount of gasoline held by such person on such date does not exceed 4,000 gallons, and

"(ii) on diesel fuel or aviation fuel held on October 1, 1993, by any person if the aggregate amount of diesel fuel or aviation fuel held by such person on such date does not exceed 2,000 gallons.

The preceding sentence shall apply only if such person submits to the Secretary (at the time and in the manner required by the Secretary) such information as the Secretary shall require for purposes of this paragraph.

"(B) Exempt fuel. For purposes of subparagraph (A), there shall not be taken into account fuel held by any person which is exempt from the tax imposed by paragraph (1) by reason of paragraph (4) or (5).

"(C) Controlled groups. For purposes of this paragraph—

"(i) Corporations.

"(I) In general. All persons treated as a controlled group shall be treated as 1 person.

"(II) Controlled group. The term 'controlled group' has the meaning given to such term by subsection (a) of section 1563 of such Code; except that for such purposes the phrase 'more than 50 percent' shall be substituted for the phrase 'at least 80 percent' each place it appeals in such subsection.

"(ii) Nonincorporated persons under common control. Under regulations prescribed by the Secretary, principles similar to the principles of clause (i) shall apply to a group of persons under common control where 1 or more of such persons is not a corporation.

"(7) Other law applicable. All provisions of law, including penalties, applicable with respect to the taxes imposed by section 4081 of such Code in the case of gasoline and section 4091 of such Code in the case of diesel fuel and aviation fuel shall, insofar as applicable and not inconsistent with the provisions of this subsection, apply with respect to the floor stock taxes imposed by paragraph (1) to the same extent as if such taxes were imposed by such section 4081 or 4091."

—P.L. 103-66, Sec. 13242(a), amended Code Sec. 4091 (as amended by Sec. 13241(b) of this Act, see above) as part of the amendments to subpart B of part III of subchapter A of chapter 32, effective 1/1/94.

Prior to amendment, Code Sec. 4091 read as follows:

"SEC. 4091 IMPOSITION OF TAX.

"(a) In general. here is hereby imposed a tax on the sale of any taxable fuel by the producer or the importer thereof or by any producer of a taxable fuel.

"(b) Rate of tax.

"(1) In general. The rate of the tax imposed by subsection (a) shall be the sum of—

"(A)(i) the Highway Trust Fund financing rate and the diesel fuel deficit reduction rate in the case of diesel fuel, and

"(ii) the Airport and Airway Trust Fund financing rate and the aviation fuel deficit reduction rate in the case of aviation fuel, and

"(B) the Leaking Underground Storage Tank Trust Fund financing rate in the case of any taxable fuel.

"(2) Highway Trust Fund financing rate. For purposes of paragraph (1), except as provided in subsection (c), the Highway Trust Fund financing rate is 17.5 cents per gallon.

"(3) Airport and Airway Trust Fund financing rate. For purposes of paragraph (1), except as provided in subsection (d), the Airport and Airway Trust Fund financing rate is 17.5 cents per gallon.

"(4) Diesel fuel deficit reduction rate. For purposes of paragraph (1), except as provided in subsection (c), the diesel fuel deficit reduction rate is 6.8 cents per gallon.

"(5) Leaking Underground Storage Tank Trust fund financing rate. For purposes of paragraph (1), except as provided in subsection (c), the Leaking Underground Storage Tank Trust Fund financing rate is 0.1 cent per gallon.

"(6) Aviation fuel deficit reduction rate. For purposes of paragraph (1), the aviation fuel deficit reduction rate is 4.3 cents per gallon.

"(7) Termination of rates.

"(A) The Highway Trust Fund financing rate shall not apply on and after October 1, 1999.

"(B) The Airport and Airway Trust Fund financing rate shall not apply on and after January 1, 1996.

"(C) The Leaking Underground Storage Tank Trust Fund financing rate shall not apply during any period during which the Leaking Underground Storage Tank Trust Fund financing rate under section 4081 does not apply.

"(D) The diesel fuel deficit reduction rate shall not apply on and after October 1, 1995.

"(c) Reduced rate of tax for diesel fuel in alcohol mixture, etc. Under regulations prescribed by the Secretary—

"(1) In general. The Highway Trust Fund financing rate shall be—

"(A) 12.1 cents per gallon in the case of the sale of any mixture of diesel fuel if—

"(i) at least 10 percent of such mixture consists of alcohol (as defined in section 4081(c)(3)), and

"(ii) the diesel fuel in such mixture was not taxed under subparagraph (B), and

"(B) 13.44 cents per gallon in the case of the sale of diesel fuel for use (at the time of such sale) in producing a mixture described in subparagraph (A).

In the case of a sale described in subparagraph (B), the Leaking Underground Storage Tank Trust Fund financing rate and the diesel fuel deficit reduction rate shall be 10/9th of the otherwise applicable such rates.

"(2) Later separation. If any person separates the diesel fuel from a mixture of the diesel fuel and alcohol on which tax was imposed under subsection (a) at a Highway Trust Fund financing rate equivalent to 12.1 cents a gallon by reason of this subsection (or with respect to which a credit or payment was allowed or made by reason of section 6427(f)(1)), such person shall be treated as the producer of such diesel fuel. The amount of tax imposed on any sale of such diesel fuel by such person shall be reduced by the amount of tax imposed (and not credited or refunded) on any prior sale of such fuel.

"(3) Termination. Paragraph (1) shall not apply to any sale after September 30, 2000.

"(d) Reduced rate of tax for aviation fuel in alcohol mixture, etc.

"(1) In general. The Airport and Airway Trust Fund financing rate shall be—

"(A) 4.1 cents per gallon in the case of the sale of any mixture of aviation fuel if—

"(i) at least 10 percent of such mixture consists of alcohol (as defined in section 4081(c)(3)), and

"(ii) the aviation fuel in such mixture was not taxed under subparagraph (B), and

"(B) 4.56 cents per gallon in the case of the sale of aviation fuel for use (at the time of such sale) in producing a mixture described in subparagraph (A).

In the case of a sale described in subparagraph (B), the Leaking Underground Storage Tank Trust Fund financing rate shall be ⅑ cent per gallon.

"(2) Later separation. If any person separates the aviation fuel from a mixture of the aviation fuel and alcohol on which tax was imposed under subsection (a) at the Airport and Airway Trust Fund financing rate equivalent to 4.1 cents per gallon by reason of this subsection (or with respect to which a credit or payment was allowed or made by reason of section 6427(f)(1)), such person shall be treated as the producer of such aviation fuel. The amount of tax imposed on any sale of such aviation fuel by such person shall be reduced by the amount of tax imposed (and not credited or refunded) on any prior sale of such fuel.

"(3) Termination. Paragraph (1) shall not apply to any sale after September 30, 2000.

"(e) Lower rates of tax on alcohol mixtures not made from ethanol. In the case of a mixture described in subsection (c)(1)(A)(i) or (d)(1)(A)(i) none of the alcohol in which is ethanol—

"(1) subsections (c)(1)(A) and (c)(2), and subsections (d)(1)(A) and (d)(2), shall each be applied by substituting rates which are 0.6 cents less than the rates contained therein, and

"(2) subsections (c)(1)(B) and (d)(1)(B) shall be applied by substituting rates which are 10/9 of the rates determined under paragraph (1)."

—P.L. 103-66, Sec. 13243, of this Act provides:

"SEC. 13243. FLOOR STOCKS TAX.

"(a) In general. here is hereby imposed a floor stocks tax on diesel fuel held by any person on January 1, 1994, if—

"(1) no tax was imposed on such fuel under section 4041(a) or 4091 of the Internal Revenue Code of 1986 as in effect on December 31, 1993, and

"(2) tax would have been imposed by section 4081 of such Code, as amended by this Act, on any prior removal, entry, or sale of such fuel had such section 4081 applied to such fuel for periods before January 1, 1994.

"(b) Rate of tax. The rate of the tax imposed by subsection (a) shall be the amount of tax which would be imposed under section 4081 of the Internal Revenue Code of 1986 if there were a taxable sale of such fuel on such date.

"(c) Liability and payment of tax.

"(1) Liability for tax. A person holding the diesel fuel on January 1, 1994, to which the tax imposed by this section applies shall be liable for such tax.

"(2) Method of payment. The tax imposed by this section shall be paid in such manner as the Secretary shall prescribe.

"(3) Time for payment. The tax imposed by this section shall be paid on or before July 31, 1994.

"(d) Definitions. For purposes of this section—

"(1) Diesel fuel. The term 'diesel fuel' has the meaning given such term by section 4083(a) of such Code.

"(2) Secretary. The term 'Secretary' means the Secretary of the Treasury or his delegate.

"(e) Exceptions.

"(1) Persons entitled to credit or refund. The tax imposed by this section shall not apply to fuel held by any person exclusively for any use to the extent a credit or refund of the tax imposed by section 4081 is allowable for such use.

"(2) Compliance with dyeing required. Paragraph (1) shall not apply to the holder of any fuel if the holder of such fuel fails to comply with any requirement imposed by the Secretary with respect to dyeing and marking such fuel.

"(f) Other laws applicable. All provisions of law, including penalties, applicable with respect to the taxes imposed by section 4081 of such Code shall, insofar as applicable and not inconsistent with the provisions of this section, apply with respect to the floor stock taxes imposed by this section to the same extent as if such taxes were imposed by such section 4081.

—P.L. 103-66, Sec. 13245, of this Act provides:

"SEC. 13245. FLOOR STOCKS TAX ON COMMERCIAL AVIATION FUEL HELD ON OCTOBER 1, 1995.

"(a) Imposition of tax. In the case of commercial aviation fuel on which tax was imposed under section 4091 of the Internal Revenue Code of 1986 before October 1, 1995, and which is held on such date by any person, there is hereby imposed a floor stocks tax of 4.3 cents per gallon.

"(b) Liability for tax and method of payment.

"(1) Liability for tax. A person holding aviation fuel on October 1, 1995, to which the tax imposed by subsection (a) applies shall be liable for such tax.

"(2) Method of payment. The tax imposed by subsection (a) shall be paid in such manner as the Secretary shall prescribe.

"(3) Time for payment. The tax imposed by subsection (a) shall be paid on or before April 30, 1996.

"(c) Definitions. For purposes of this subsection—

"(1) Held by a person. Aviation fuel shall be considered as 'held by a person' if title thereto has passed to such person whether or not delivery to the person has been made).

"(2) Commercial aviation fuel. The term 'commercial aviation fuel' means aviation fuel (as defined in section 4093 of such Code) which is held on October 1, 1995, for sale or use in commercial aviation (as defined in section 4092(b) of such Code).

"(3) Secretary. The term 'Secretary' means the Secretary of the Treasury or his delegate.

"(d) Exception for exempt uses. The tax imposed by subsection (a) shall not apply to aviation fuel held by any person exclusively for any use for which a credit or refund of the entire tax imposed by section 4091 of such Code is allowable for aviation fuel purchased after September 30, 1995, for such use.

"(e) Exception for certain amounts of fuel.

"(1) In general. No tax shall be imposed by subsection (a) on aviation fuel held on October 1, 1995, by any person if the aggregate amount of commercial aviation fuel held by such person on such date does not exceed 2,000 gallons. The preceding sentence shall apply only if such person submits to the Secretary (at the time and in the manner required by the Secretary) such information as the Secretary shall require for purposes of this paragraph.

"(2) Exempt fuel. For purposes of paragraph (1), there shall not be taken into account fuel held by any person which is exempt from the tax imposed by subsection (a) by reason of subsection (d).

"(3) Controlled groups. For purposes of this subsection—

"(A) Corporations.
"(i) In general. All persons treated as a controlled group shall be treated as 1 person.
"(ii) Controlled group. The term 'controlled group' has the meaning given to such term by subsection (a) of section 1563 of such Code; except that for such purposes the phrase 'more than 50 percent' shall be substituted for the phrase 'at least 80 percent' each place it appears in such subsection.
"(B) Nonincorporated persons under common control. Under regulations prescribed by the Secretary, principles similar to the principles of subparagraph (A) shall apply to a group of persons under common control where 1 or more of such persons is not a corporation.
"(f) Other law applicable. All provisions of law, including penalties, applicable with respect to the taxes imposed by section 4091 of such Code shall, insofar as applicable and not inconsistent with the provisions of this section, apply with respect to the floor stock taxes imposed by subsection (a) to the same extent as if such taxes were imposed by such section 4091."

In 1991, P.L. 102-240, Sec. 8001(a)(4), substituted "1999" for "1995" in subpara. (b)(6)(A), effective 12/18/91.

In 1990, P.L. 101-508, Sec. 11211(b)(1)(A), added "and the diesel fuel deficit reduction rate" after "financing rate" in clause (b)(1)(A)(i) ... Sec. 11211(b)(1)(B), redesignated paras. (b)(4) and (b)(5) as paras. (b)(5) and (b)(6) and added new para. (b)(4) ... Sec. 11211(b)(1)(C), added subpara. (b)(6)(D) ... Sec. 11211(b)(2), substituted "17.5 cents" for "15 cents" in para. (b)(2) ... Sec. 11211(b)(6)(A)(i), substituted "12.1 cents" for "9 cents" in subpara. (c)(1)(A) and substituted "13.44 cents" for "10 cents" in subpara. (c)(1)(B) ... Sec. 11211(b)(6)(A)(ii), substituted "and the diesel fuel deficit reduction rate shall be 10/9th of the otherwise applicable such rates" for "shall be ⅛ cent per gallon" in the last sentence of para. (c)(1) ... Sec. 11211(b)(6)(B), substituted "12.1 cents" for "9 cents" in para. (c)(2), effective 12/1/90.
—P.L. 101-508, Sec. 11211(c)(4), substituted "1995" for "1993" in subpara. (b)(6)(A) [as redesignated by Sec. 11211(b) of this Act] ... Sec. 11211(e)(4), substituted "2000" for "1993" in paras. (c)(3) and (d)(3), effective 11/5/90.
—P.L. 101-508, Sec. 11211(j), relating to floor stocks taxes, is reproduced in note following Code Sec. 4081.
—P.L. 101-508, Sec. 11213(b)(1)(A), substituted "17.5 cents" for "14 cents" in para. (b)(3) ... Sec. 11213(b)(1)(B), added "except as provided in subsection (d)," after "paragraph (1)," in para. (b)(3) ... Sec. 11213(b)(2)(C)(i), amended paras. (d)(1) and (d)(2) ... Sec. 11213(b)(2)(C)(ii), substituted "Reduced rate of" for "Exemption from" in the heading of subsec. (d) ... Sec. 11213(b)(2)(D), added subsec. (e), effective 12/1/90.
Prior to amendment, paras. (d)(1) and (d)(2) read as follows:
"(1) In general. The Airport and Airway Trust Fund financing rate shall not apply to the sale of—
"(A) any mixture of aviation fuel at least 10 percent of which consists of alcohol (as defined in section 4081(c)(3)), or
"(B) any aviation fuel for use (at the time of such sale) in producing a mixture described in subparagraph (A).
"(2) Later separation. If any person separates the aviation fuel from a mixture of the aviation fuel and alcohol on which the Airport and Airway Trust Fund financing rate did not apply by reason of this subsection (or with respect to which a credit or payment was allowed or made by reason of section 6427(f)(2)), such person shall be treated as the producer of such aviation fuel."
—P.L. 101-508, Sec. 11213(d)(2)(A), substituted "January 1, 1996" for "January 1, 1991" in subpara. (b)(6)(B) [as redesignated by Sec. 11211(b)(1)(B) of this Act], effective 11/5/90.
—P.L. 101-508, Sec. 11218, relating to floor stocks tax treatment of articles in foreign trade zones, is reproduced in note following Code Sec. 5001.
—P.L. 101-508, Sec. 11704(a)(38), substituted "5 cents per gallon" for "5 cents a gallon" in Sec. 2001(d)(6)(C) of P.L. 100-647, see below.

In 1988, P.L. 100-647, Sec. 2001(d)(6)(A), added the last sentence in para. (c)(1) ... Sec. 2001(d)(6)(B), added "except as provided in subsection (c)," after "paragraph (1)" in para. (b)(4) ... Sec. 2001(d)(6)(C), [as amended by Sec. 11704(a)(38) of P.L. 101-508, see above] substituted "reduced by the amount of tax imposed (and not credited or refunded) on any prior sale of such fuel." for "5 cents per gallon" in the last sentence of para. (c)(2), effective for sales after 3/31/88. For special rules see Sec. 10502(f) of P.L. 100-203, reproduced below.

In 1987, P.L. 100-203, Sec. 10502(a), added Code Sec. 4091, effective for sales after 3/31/88. Sec. 10502(f) of this Act provides:
"(f) Floor stocks tax.
"(1) Imposition of tax. On any taxable fuel which on April 1, 1988, is held by a taxable person, there is hereby imposed a floor stocks tax at the rate of tax which would be imposed if such fuel were sold on such date in a sale subject to tax under section 4091 of the Internal Revenue Code of 1986 (as added by this section).
"(2) Overpayment of floor stocks taxes, etc. Sections 6416 and 6427 of such Code shall apply in respect of the floor stocks taxes imposed by this subsection so as to entitle, subject to all provisions of such sections, any person paying such floor stocks taxes to a credit or refund thereof for any reason specified in such sections. All provisions of law, including penalties, applicable with respect to the taxes imposed by section 4091 of such Code (as so added) shall apply to the floor stocks taxes imposed by this subsection.
"(3) Due date of tax. The taxes imposed by this subsection shall be paid before June 16, 1988.
"(4) Definitions. For purposes of this subsection—
"(A) Taxable fuel.

"(i) In general. The term 'taxable fuel' means any taxable fuel (as defined in section 4092 of such Code, as added by this section) on which no tax has been imposed under section 4041 of such Code.
"(ii) Exception for fuel held for nontaxable uses. The term 'taxable fuel' shall not include fuel held exclusively for any use which is a nontaxable use (as defined in section 6427(1) of such Code, as added by this section).
"(B) Taxable person. The term 'taxable person' means any person other than a producer (as defined in section 4092 of such Code, as so added) or importer of taxable fuel.
"(C) Held by a taxable person. An article shall be treated as held by a person if title thereto has passed to such person (whether or not delivery to such person has been made).
"(5) Special rule for fuel held for use in trains and commercial aircraft. Only the Leaking Underground Storage Tank Trust Fund financing rate under section 4091 of such Code shall apply for purposes of this subsection with respect to—
"(A) diesel fuel held exclusively for use as a fuel in a diesel-powered train, and
"(B) aviation fuel held exclusively for use as a fuel in an aircraft not in noncommercial aviation (as defined in section 4041(c)(4) of such Code).
"(6) Transfer of floor stock revenues to trust funds. For purposes of determining the amount transferred to any trust fund, the tax imposed by this subsection shall be treated as imposed by section 4091 of such Code (as so added)."
—P.L. 100-203, Sec. 10502(g), substituted "January 1, 1991" for "January 1, 1988" in subpara. (b)(5)(B), effective 12/31/87.

Sec. 4092. Repealed.

In 2004, P.L. 108-357, Sec. 853(d)(1), repealed Code Sec. 4092 as part of the repeal of Subpart B of Part III of Subchapter A of Chapter 32, effective for aviation-grade kerosene removed, or sold after 12/31/2004.
Prior to repeal, Code Sec. 4092 read as follows:
"Sec. 4092. Exemptions.
"(a) Nontaxable uses. No tax shall be imposed by section 4091 on aviation fuel sold by a producer or importer for use by the purchaser in a nontaxable use (as defined in section 6427(1)(2)(B)).
"(b) No exemption from certain taxes on fuel used in commercial aviation. In the case of fuel sold for use in commercial aviation (other than supplies for vessels or aircraft within the meaning of section 4221(a)(3)), subsection (a) shall not apply to so much of the tax imposed by section 4091 as is attributable to—
"(1) the Leaking Underground Storage Tank Trust Fund financing rate imposed by such section, and
"(2) in the case of fuel sold after September 30, 1995, 4.3 cents per gallon of the rate specified in section 4091(b)(1).
"For purposes of the preceding sentence, the term 'commercial aviation' means any use of an aircraft other than in noncommercial aviation (as defined in section 4041(c)(2)).
"(c) Sales to producer. Under regulations prescribed by the Secretary, the tax imposed by section 4091 shall not apply to aviation fuel sold to a producer of such fuel."

In 1998, P.L. 105-206, Sec. 6023(16), substituted "section 4041(c)(2)" for "section 4041(c)(4)" in subsec. (b) [this amendment was already made by Sec. 1601(f)(4)(C) of P.L. 105-34, see below], effective 7/22/98.

In 1997, P.L. 105-34, Sec. 1601(f)(4)(C), substituted "section 4041(c)(2)" for "section 4041(c)(4)" in subsec. (b), effective on the 7th calendar day after 8/20/96.

In 1993, P.L. 103-66, Sec. 13163(a)(1), substituted ", a diesel-powered train, or a diesel-powered boat" for "or a diesel-powered train" in para. (a)(2) (before amended by Sec. 13242(a) of this Act, see below) ... Sec. 13163(a)(3), substituted "vessels for use in an off-highway business use (as defined in section 6421(e)(2)(B))" for "commercial and noncommercial vessels" each place it appeared in subpara. (b)(1)(B) (before amended by Sec. 13242(a) of this Act, see below), effective 1/1/94.
—P.L. 103-66, Sec. 13242(a), amended Code Sec. 4092 (as amended by Sec. 13163(a) of this Act, see above) as part of the amendments to subpart B of part III of subchapter A of chapter 32, effective 1/1/94.
Prior to amendment, Code Sec. 4092 read as follows:
"Sec. 4092. Definitions.
"(a) Taxable fuel.
For purposes of this subpart—
"(1) In general. The term 'taxable fuel' means—
"(A) diesel fuel, and
"(B) aviation fuel.
"(2) Diesel fuel. The term 'diesel fuel' means any liquid (other than any product taxable under section 4081) which is suitable for use as a fuel in a diesel-powered highway vehicle, a diesel-powered train, or diesel-powered boat.
"(3) Aviation fuel. The term 'aviation fuel' means any liquid (other than any product taxable under section 4081) which is suitable for use as a fuel in an aircraft.
"(b) Producer.
For purposes of this subpart—
"(1) Certain persons treated as producers.
"(A) In general. The term 'producer' includes any person described in subparagraph (B) who elects to register under section 4101 with respect to the tax imposed by section 4091.

Code Sec. 4092 — Excise and miscellaneous taxes

"(B) Persons described. A person is described in this subparagraph if such person is —

"(i) a refiner, compounder, blender, or wholesale distributor of a taxable fuel, or

"(ii) a dealer selling any taxable fuel exclusively to producers of such taxable fuel, or

"(iii) a retailer selling diesel fuel exclusively to purchasers as supplies for vessels for use in an off-highway business use (as defined in section 6421(e)(2)(B)).

To the extent provided in regulations, a retailer shall not be treated as not described in clause (iii) by reason of selling de minimis amounts of diesel fuel other than as supplies for vessels for use in an off-highway business use (as defined in section 6421(e)(2)(B)).

"(C) Tax-free purchasers treated as producers. Any person to whom any taxable fuel is sold tax-free under this subpart shall be treated as the producer of such fuel.

"(2) Wholesale distributor. **For purposes of paragraph (1), the term 'wholesale distributor' includes any person who sells a taxable fuel to producers, retailers, or to users who purchase in bulk quantities and deliver into bulk storage tanks. Such term does not include any person who (excluding the term 'wholesale distributor' from paragraph (1)) is a producer or importer."**

In 1988, P.L. 100-647, Sec. 3003(a), substituted ", or" for the period at the end of clause (b)(1)(B)(ii), added clause (b)(1)(B)(iii) and the sentence at the end of subpara. (b)(1)(B), effective for sales after 12/31/88.

In 1987, P.L. 100-203, Sec. 10502(a), added Code Sec. 4092, effective for sales after 3/31/88. For provisions on floor stocks tax, see Sec. 10502(f) of this Act reproduced in note following Code Sec. 4091.

Sec. 4093. Repealed.

In 2004, P.L. 108-357, Sec. 853(d)(1), repealed Code Sec. 4093 as part of the repeal of Subpart B of Part III of Subchapter A of Chapter 32, effective for aviation-grade kerosene removed, entered, or sold after 12/31/2004.

Prior to repeal, Code Sec. 4093 read as follows:

"Sec. 4093. Definitions.

"(a) Aviation fuel. For purposes of this subpart, the term 'aviation fuel' means kerosene and any other liquid (other than any product taxable under section 4081) which is suitable for use as a fuel in an aircraft.

"(b) Producer. For purposes of this subpart —

"(1) Certain persons treated as producers.

"(A) In general. The term 'producer' includes any person described in subparagraph (B) and registered under section 4101 with respect to the tax imposed by section 4091.

"(B) Persons described. A person is described in this subparagraph if such person is —

"(i) a refiner, blender, or wholesale distributor of aviation fuel, or

"(ii) a dealer selling aviation fuel exclusively to producers of aviation fuel.

"(C) Reduced rate purchasers treated as producers. Any person to whom aviation fuel is sold at a reduced rate under this subpart shall be treated as the producer of such fuel.

"(2) Wholesale distributor. For purposes of paragraph (1), the term 'wholesale distributor' includes any person who sells aviation fuel to producers, retailers, or to users who purchase in bulk quantities and accept delivery into bulk storage tanks. Such term does not include any person who (excluding the term 'wholesale distributor' from paragraph (1)) is a producer or importer."

In 1997, P.L. 105-34, Sec. 1032(e)(5), substituted "kerosene and any other liquid" for "any liquid" in subsec. (a), effective 7/1/98.

In 1996, P.L. 104-188, Sec. 1702(b)(2)(A), amended subpara. (c)(2)(B), prior to amendment by Secs. 13241(f)(3) and 13242(a) of P.L. 103-66, by adding "unless such fuel is sold for exclusive use by a State or any political subdivision thereof." before the period at the end, effective 12/1/90.

In 1993, P.L. 103-66, Sec. 13241(f)(3), amended subparas. (c)(2)(A) and (B) [as amended by Sec. 1702(b)(2)(A) of P.L. 104-188, see above] (before amended by Sec. 13242(a) of this Act, see below) . . . Sec. 13241(f)(4), added "and the aviation fuel deficit reduction rate" after "rate" in subsec. (d) (before amended by Sec. 13242(a) of this Act, see below), effective 10/1/93.

Prior to amendment, subparas. (c)(2)(A) and (B) [as amended by Sec. 1702(b)(2)(A) of P.L. 104-188, see above] read as follows:

"(A) Certain Leaking Underground Storage Tank Trust Fund taxes. In the case of fuel sold for use in —

"(i) a diesel-powered train, and

"(ii) an aircraft,

paragraph (1) shall not apply to so much of the tax imposed by section 4091 as is attributable to the Leaking Underground Storage Tank Trust Fund financing rate imposed by such section.

"(B) Deficit reduction tax on fuel used in trains. In the case of fuel sold for use in a diesel-powered train, paragraph (1) also shall not apply to so much of the tax imposed by section 4091 as is attributable to the diesel fuel deficit reduction rate imposed by such section unless such fuel is sold for exclusive use by a State or any political subdivision thereof."

—P.L. 103-66, Sec. 13242(a), amended Code Sec. 4093 (as amended by Sec. 13241(f) of this Act, see above) as part of the amendments to subpart B of part III of subchapter A of chapter 32, effective 1/1/94.

Prior to amendment, Code Sec. 4093 read as follows:

"Sec. 4093 Exemptions; special rule.

"(a) Heating oil. The tax imposed by section 4091 shall not apply in the case of sales of any taxable fuel which the Secretary determines is destined for use as heating oil.

"(b) Sales to producer. Under regulations prescribed by the Secretary, the tax imposed by section 4091 shall not apply in the case of sales of a taxable fuel to a producer of such fuel.

"(c) Exemption for nontaxable uses and bus uses.

"(1) In general. No tax shall be imposed by section 4091 on fuel sold by a producer or importer for use by the purchaser in a nontaxable use (as defined in section 6427(l)(2)) or a use described in section 6427(b)(1).

"(2) Exceptions.

"(A) No exemption from certain taxes on fuel used in diesel-powered trains. In the case of fuel sold for use in a diesel-powered train, paragraph (1) shall not apply to so much of the tax imposed by section 4091 as is attributable to the Leaking Underground Storage Tank Trust Fund financing rate and the diesel fuel deficit reduction rate imposed under such section. The preceding sentence shall not apply in the case of fuel sold for exclusive use by a State or any political subdivision thereof.

"(B) No exemption from Leaking Underground Storage Tank Trust Fund taxes on fuel used in commercial aviation. In the case of fuel sold for use in commercial aviation (other than supplies for vessels or aircraft within the meaning of section 4221(d)(3)), paragraph (1) also shall not apply to so much of the tax imposed by section 4091 as is attributable to the Leaking Underground Storage Tank Trust Fund financing rate imposed by such section. For purposes of the preceding sentence, the term 'commercial aviation', means any use of an aircraft other than in noncommercial aviation (as defined in section 4041(c)(4)).

"(C) Certain bus uses. Paragraph (1) shall not apply to so much of the tax imposed by section 4091 as is not refundable by reason of the application of section 6427(b)(2)(A).

"(3) Registration required. Except to the extent provided by the Secretary, paragraph (1) shall not apply to any sale unless —

"(A) both the seller and the purchaser are registered under section 4101, and

"(B) the purchaser's name, address, and registration number under such section are provided to the seller.

"(4) Information reporting.

"(A) Returns by producers and importers. Each producer or importer who makes a reduced-tax sale during the calendar year shall make a return (at such time and in such form as the Secretary may by regulations prescribe) showing with respect to each such sale —

"(i) the name, address, and registration number under section 4101 of the purchaser,

"(ii) the amount of fuel sold, and

"(iii) such other information as the Secretary may require.

"(B) Statements to purchasers. Every person required to make a return under subparagraph (A) shall furnish to each purchaser whose name is required to be set forth on such return a written statement showing the name and address of the person required to make such return, the registration number under section 4101 of such person, and the information required to be shown on the return with respect to such purchaser. The written statement required under the preceding sentence shall be furnished to the purchaser on or before January 31 of the year following the calendar year for which the return under subparagraph (A) is required to be made.

"(C) Returns by purchasers. Each person who uses during the calendar year fuel purchased in a reduced-tax sale shall make a return (at such time and in such form as the Secretary may by regulations prescribe) showing —

"(i) whether such use was a nontaxable use (as defined in section 6427(l)(2)) or a use described in section 6427(b)(1) and the amount of fuel so used,

"(ii) the date of the sale of the fuel so used,

"(iii) the name, address, and registration number under section 4101 of the seller, and

"(iv) such other information as the Secretary may require.

"(D) Reduced-tax sale. For purposes of this paragraph, the term 'reduced-tax sale' means any sale of taxable fuel on which the amount of tax otherwise required to be paid under section 4091 is reduced by reason of paragraph (1) (other than sales described in subsections (a) and (b) of this section).

"(d) Certain aviation fuel sales. Under regulations prescribed by the Secretary, the Leaking Underground Storage Tank Trust Fund financing rate and the aviation fuel deficit reduction rate under section 4091 shall not apply to aviation fuel sold for use or used as supplies for vessels or aircraft (within the meaning of section 4221(d)(3)).

"(e) Cross references.

"(1) For imposition of tax where certain uses of diesel fuel or aviation fuel occur before imposition of tax by section 4091, see subsections (a)(1) and (c)(1) of section 4041.

"(2) For provisions allowing a credit or refund for fuel not used for certain taxable purposes, see section 6427."

—P.L. 103-66, Sec. 13245, of this Act provides:

"SEC. 13245. FLOOR STOCKS TAX ON COMMERCIAL AVIATION FUEL HELD ON OCTOBER 1, 1995.

"(a) Imposition of tax. — In the case of commercial aviation fuel on which was imposed under section 4091 of the Internal Revenue Code of 1986 before October 1, 1995, and which is held on such date by any person, there is hereby imposed a floor stocks tax of 4.3 cents per gallon.

"(b) Liability for tax and method of payment. —

Excise and miscellaneous taxes Code Sec. 4094

"(1) Liability for tax. — A person holding aviation fuel on October 1, 1995, to which the tax imposed by subsection (a) applies shall be liable for such tax.

"(2) Method of payment. — The tax imposed by subsection (a) shall be paid in such manner as the Secretary shall prescribe.

"(3) Time for payment. — The tax imposed by subsection (a) shall be paid on or before April 30, 1996.

"(c) Definitions. — For purposes of this subsection—

"(1) Held by a person. — Aviation fuel shall be considered as 'held by a person' if title thereto has passed to such person whether or not delivery to the person has been made).

"(2) Commercial aviation fuel. — The term 'commercial aviation fuel' means aviation fuel (as defined in section 4093 of such Code) which is held on October 1, 1995, for sale or use in commercial aviation (as defined in section 4092(b) of such Code).

"(3) Secretary. — The term 'Secretary' means the Secretary of the Treasury or his delegate.

"(d) Exception for exempt uses. — The tax imposed by subsection (a) shall not apply to aviation fuel held by any person exclusively for any use for which a credit or refund of the entire tax imposed by section 4091 of such Code is allowable for aviation fuel purchased after September 30, 1995, for such use.

"(e) Exception for certain amounts of fuel. —

"(1) In general. — No tax shall be imposed by subsection (a) on aviation fuel held on October 1, 1995, by any person if the aggregate amount of commercial aviation fuel held by such person on such date does not exceed 2,000 gallons. The preceding sentence shall apply only if such person submits to the Secretary (at the time and in the manner required by the Secretary) such information as the Secretary shall require for purposes of this paragraph.

"(2) Exempt fuel. — For purposes of paragraph (1), there shall not be taken into account fuel held by any person which is exempt from the tax imposed by subsection (a) by reason of subsection (d).

"(3) Controlled groups. — For purposes of this subsection—

"(A) Corporations.—

"(i) In general. — All persons treated as a controlled group shall be treated as 1 person.

"(ii) Controlled group. — The term 'controlled group' has the meaning given to such term by subsection (a) of section 1563 of such Code; except that for such purposes the phrase 'more than 50 percent' shall be substituted for the phrase 'at least 80 percent' each place it appears in such subsection.

"(B) Nonincorporated persons under common control. — Under regulations prescribed by the Secretary, principles similar to the principles of subparagraph (A) shall apply to a group of persons under common control where 1 or more of such persons is not a corporation.

"(f) Other law applicable. — All provisions of law, including penalties, applicable with respect to the taxes imposed by section 4091 of such Code shall, insofar as applicable and not inconsistent with the provisions of this section, apply with respect to the floor stocks taxes imposed by subsection (a) to the same extent as if such taxes were imposed by such section 4091."

In 1990, P.L. 101-508, Sec. 11211(b)(4)(A), redesignated subpara. (c)(2)(B) as subpara. (c)(2)(C) and added new subpara. (c)(2)(B) . . . Sec. 11212(b)(4), deleted subsec. (e) and redesignated subsec. (f) as subsec. (e), effective 12/1/90.

Prior to deletion, subsec. (e) read as follows:

"(e) Special administrative rules.

The Secretary may require —

"(1) information reporting by each remitter of the tax imposed by section 4091, and

"(2) information reporting by, and registration of, such other persons as the Secretary deems necessary to carry out this subpart."

—P.L. 101-508, Sec. 11704(a)(20), substituted "reduced-tax sale" for "reduced tax sale" in subpara. (c)(4)(D), effective 11/5/90.

In 1988, P.L. 100-647, Sec. 2004(s)(1), redesignated subsecs. (d) and (e) as subsecs. (e) and (f), and added new subsec. (d), effective for sales after 3/31/88.

—P.L. 100-647, Sec. 3001(a), amended subsec. (c), effective 1/1/89, except as provided in Sec. 3001(c)(2) of this Act which reads as follows:

"(2) Refunds with interest for pre-effective date purchases.

"(A) In general. In the case of fuel —

"(i) which is purchased from a producer or importer during the period beginning on April 1, 1988, and ending on December 31, 1988,

"(ii) which is used (before the claim under this subparagraph is filed) by any person in a nontaxable use (as defined in section 6427(l)(2) of the 1986 Code), and

"(iii) with respect to which a claim is not permitted to be filed for any quarter under section 6427(i) of the 1986 Code,

the Secretary of the Treasury or the Secretary's delegate shall pay (with interest) to such person the amount of tax imposed on such fuel under section 4091 of the 1986 Code (to the extent not attributable to amounts described in section 6427(l)(3) of the 1986 Code) if claim therefor is filed not later than June 30, 1989. Not more than 1 claim may be filed under the preceding sentence and such claim shall not be taken into account under section 6427(i) of the 1986 Code. Any claim for refund filed under this paragraph shall be considered a claim for refund under section 6427(l) of the 1986 Code.

"(B) Interest. The amount of interest payable under subparagraph (A) shall be determined under section 6611 of the 1986 Code except that the date of the overpayment with respect to fuel purchased during any month shall be treated as being the 1st day of the succeeding month. No interest shall be paid under this paragraph with respect to fuel used by any agency of the United States.

"(C) Registration procedures required to be specified. Not later than the 30th day after the date of the enactment of this Act, the Secretary of the Treasury or the Secretary's delegate shall prescribe the procedures for complying with the requirements of section 4093(c)(3) of the 1986 Code (as added by this section)."

Prior to amendment, subsec. (c) read as follows:

"(c) Authority to exempt certain other uses.

"Subject to such terms and conditions as the Secretary may provide (including the application of section 4101), the Secretary may by regulation provide that—

"(1) the Highway Trust Fund financing rate under section 4091 shall not apply to diesel fuel sold for use by any purchaser as a fuel in a diesel-powered train,

"(2) the Airport and Airway Trust Fund financing rate under section 4091 shall not apply to aviation fuel sold for use by any purchaser as a fuel in an aircraft not in noncommercial aviation (as defined in section 4041(c)(4)),

"(3) the tax imposed by section 4091 shall not apply to taxable fuel sold for use by any purchaser other than as a motor fuel, and

"(4) the tax imposed by section 4091 shall not apply to taxable fuel sold for the exclusive use of any State, any political subdivision of a State, or the District of Columbia."

In 1987, P.L. 100-203, Sec. 10502(a), added Code Sec. 4093, effective for sales after 3/31/88. For provisions on floor stocks tax, see Sec. 10502(f) of this Act reproduced in note following Code Sec. 4091.

Sec. 4094. Repealed.

In 1983, P.L. 97-424, Sec. 515(a), repealed Code Sec. 4094, effective for articles sold after 1/6/83.

Prior to repeal, Code Sec. 4094 read as follows:

"SEC. 4094. CROSS REFERENCE.

"For provisions to relieve purchasers of lubricating oil from excise tax in the case of lubricating oil used otherwise than in a highway motor vehicle, see sections 39 and 6424."

In 1965, P.L. 89-44, Sec. 202(c)(1)(A), added Code Sec. 4094.

SUBPART B.   REPEALED [AVIATION FUEL]

Sec.

4091. Repealed [Imposition of tax].
4092. Repealed [Exemptions].
4093. Repealed [Definitions].

In 2004, P.L. 108-357, Sec. 853(d)(1), deleted subpart B of part III of subchapter A of chapter 32 and redesignated subpart C of part III of subchapter A of chapter 32 as subpart B thereof, generally effective as of 12/31/2004.

In 1993, P.L. 103-66, Sec. 13242(a), amended subpart B of Part III of subchapter A of chapter 32.

Prior to amendment, subpart B of Part III of subchapter A of chapter 32 read as follows:

"Subpart B. — Diesel Fuel and Aviation Fuel

"Sec.

"4091. IMPOSITION OF TAX.

"4092. DEFINITIONS.

"4093. EXEMPTIONS; SPECIAL RULE.

"Sec. 4091. Imposition of tax.

"(a) In general.

There is hereby imposed a tax on the sale of any taxable fuel by the producer or the importer thereof or by any producer of a taxable fuel.

"(b) Rate of tax.

"(1) In general. The rate of the tax imposed by subsection (a) shall be the sum of—

"(A)

"(i) the Highway Trust Fund financing rate and the diesel fuel deficit reduction rate in the case of diesel fuel, and

"(ii) the Airport and Airway Trust Fund financing rate and the aviation fuel deficit reduction rate in the case of aviation fuel, and

"(B) the Leaking Underground Storage Tank Trust Fund financing rate in the case of any taxable fuel.

"(2) Highway Trust Fund financing rate. For purposes of paragraph (1), except as provided in subsection (c), the Highway Trust Fund financing rate is 17.5 cents per gallon.

"(3) Airport and Airway Trust Fund financing rate. For purposes of paragraph (1), except as provided in subsection (d), the Airport and Airway Trust Fund financing rate is 17.5 cents per gallon.

"(4) Diesel fuel deficit reduction rate. For purposes of paragraph (1), except as provided in subsection (c), the diesel fuel deficit reduction rate is 6.8 cents per gallon.

"(5) Leaking Underground Storage Tank Trust fund financing rate. For purposes of paragraph (1), except as provided in subsection (c), the Leaking Underground Storage Tank Trust Fund financing rate is 0.1 cent per gallon.

"(6) Aviation fuel deficit reduction rate. For purposes of paragraph (1), the aviation fuel deficit reduction rate is 4.3 cents per gallon.

"(7) Termination of rates.

"(A) The Highway Trust Fund financing rate shall not apply on and after October 1, 1999.

3,223

"(B) The Airport and Airway Trust Fund financing rate shall not apply on and after January 1, 1996.

"(C) The Leaking Underground Storage Tank Trust Fund financing rate shall not apply during any period during which the Leaking Underground Storage Tank Trust Fund financing rate under section 4081 does not apply.

"(D) The diesel fuel deficit reduction rate shall not apply on and after October 1, 1995.

"(c) Reduced rate of tax for diesel fuel in alcohol mixture, etc.

Under regulations prescribed by the Secretary—

"(1) In general. The Highway Trust Fund financing rate shall be—

"(A) 12.1 cents per gallon in the case of the sale of any mixture of diesel fuel if—

"(i) at least 10 percent of such mixture consists of alcohol (as defined in section 4081(c)(3)), and

"(ii) the diesel fuel in such mixture was not taxed under subparagraph (B), and

"(B) 13.44 cents per gallon in the case of the sale of diesel fuel for use (at the time of such sale) in producing a mixture described in subparagraph (A).

In the case of a sale described in subparagraph (B), the Leaking Underground Storage Tank Trust Fund financing rate and the diesel fuel deficit reduction rate shall be 10/9th of the otherwise applicable such rates.

"(2) Later separation. If any person separates the diesel fuel from a mixture of the aviation fuel and alcohol on which tax was imposed under subsection (a) at a Highway Trust Fund financing rate equivalent to 12.1 cents a gallon by reason of this subsection (or with respect to which a credit or payment was allowed or made by reason of section 6427(f)(1)), such person shall be treated as the producer of such diesel fuel. The amount of tax imposed on any sale of such diesel fuel by such person shall be reduced by the amount of tax imposed (and not credited or refunded) on any prior sale of such fuel.

"(3) Termination. Paragraph (1) shall not apply to any sale after September 30, 2000.

"(d) Reduced rate of tax for aviation fuel in alcohol mixture, etc.

"(1) In general. The Airport and Airway Trust Fund financing rate shall be—

"(A) 4.1 cents per gallon in the case of the sale of any mixture of aviation fuel if—

"(i) at least 10 percent of such mixture consists of alcohol (as defined in section 4081(c)(3)), and

"(ii) the aviation fuel in such mixture was not taxed under subparagraph (B), and

"(B) 4.56 cents per gallon in the case of the sale of aviation fuel for use (at the time of such sale) in producing a mixture described in subparagraph (A).

In the case of a sale described in subparagraph (B), the Leaking Underground Storage Tank Trust Fund financing rate shall be 1/9 cent per gallon.

"(2) Later separation. If any person separates the aviation fuel from a mixture of the aviation fuel and alcohol on which tax was imposed under subsection (a) at the Airport and Airway Trust Fund financing rate equivalent to 4.1 cents per gallon by reason of this subsection (or with respect to which a credit or payment was allowed or made by reason of section 6427(f)(1)), such person shall be treated as the producer of such aviation fuel. The amount of tax imposed on any sale of such aviation fuel by such person shall be reduced by the amount of tax imposed (and not credited or refunded) on any prior sale of such fuel.

"(3) Termination. Paragraph (1) shall not apply to any sale after September 30, 2000.

"(e) Lower rates of tax on alcohol mixtures not made from ethanol.

In the case of a mixture described in subsection (c)(1)(A)(i) or (d)(1)(A)(i) none of the alcohol in which is ethanol—

"(1) subsections (c)(1)(A) and (c)(2), and subsections (d)(1)(A) and (d)(2), shall each be applied by substituting rates which are 0.6 cents less than the rates contained therein, and

"(2) subsections (c)(1)(B) and (d)(1)(B) shall be applied by substituting rates which are 10/9 of the rates determined under paragraph (1)."

In 1993, P.L. 103-66, Sec. 13241(b)(1), substituted "6.8 cents" for "2.5 cents" in para. (a)(4) (before amended by Sec. 13242(a) of this Act, see below)... Sec. 13241(b)(2)(B)(i), added "and the aviation fuel deficit reduction rate" after "financing rate" in clause (b)(1)(A)(ii) (before amended by Sec. 13242(a) of this Act, see below)... Sec. 13241(b)(2)(B)(ii), redesignated para. (b)(6) as para. (b)(7) and added new para. (b)(6) (before amended by Sec. 13242(a) of this Act, see below), effective 10/1/93.

In 1991, P.L. 102-240, Sec. 8001(a)(4), substituted "1999" for "1995" in subpara. (b)(6)(A), effective 12/18/91.

In 1990, P.L. 101-508, Sec. 11211(b)(1)(A), inserted "and the diesel fuel deficit reduction rate" after "financing rate" in clause (b)(1)(A)(i)... Sec. 11211(b)(1)(B), redesignated paras. (b)(4) and (b)(5) as paras. (b)(5) and (b)(6) and added new para. (b)(4)... Sec. 11211(b)(1)(C), added subpara. (b)(6)(D)... Sec. 11211(b)(2), substituted "17.5 cents" for "15 cents" in para. (b)(3)... Sec. 11211(b)(6)(A)(i), substituted "12.1 cents" for "9 cents" in subpara. (c)(1)(A) and substituted "13.44 cents" for "10 cents" in subpara. (c)(1)(B)... Sec. 11211(b)(6)(A)(ii), substituted "and the diesel fuel deficit reduction rate shall be 10/9th of the otherwise applicable such rates" for "shall be 1/9 cent per gallon" in the last sentence of para. (c)(1)... Sec. 11211(b)(6)(B), substituted "12.1 cents" for "9 cents" in para. (c)(2), effective 12/1/90.

—P.L. 101-508, Sec. 11211(c)(4), substituted "1995" for "1993" in subpara. (b)(6)(A) [as redesignated by 11211(b) of this Act]... Sec. 11211(e)(4), substituted "2000" for "1993" in paras. (c)(3) and (d)(3), effective 11/5/90.

—P.L. 101-508, Sec. 11211(j), relating to floor stocks taxes, is reproduced in note following Code Sec. 4081.

—P.L. 101-508, Sec. 11213(b)(1)(A), substituted "17.5 cents" for "14 cents" in para. (b)(3)... Sec. 11213(b)(1)(B), inserted "except as provided in subsection (d)," after "paragraph (1)," in para. (b)(3)... Sec. 11213(b)(2)(C)(i), amended paras. (d)(1) and (d)(2)... Sec. 11213(b)(2)(C)(ii), substituted "Reduced rate of" for "Exemption from" in the heading of subsec. (d)... Sec. 11213(b)(2)(D), added subsec. (e), effective 12/1/90.

Prior to amendment, paras. (d)(1) and (d)(2) read as follows:

"(1) In general. The Airport and Airway Trust Fund financing rate shall not apply to the sale of—

"(A) any mixture of aviation fuel at least 10 percent of which consists of alcohol (as defined in section 4081(c)(3)), or

"(B) any aviation fuel for use (at the time of such sale) in producing a mixture described in subparagraph (A).

"(2) Later separation. If any person separates the aviation fuel from a mixture of the aviation fuel and alcohol on which the Airport and Airway Trust Fund financing rate did not apply by reason of this subsection (or with respect to which a credit or payment was allowed or made by reason of section 6427(f)(2)), such person shall be treated as the producer of such aviation fuel."

—P.L. 101-508, Sec. 11213(d)(2)(A), substituted "January 1, 1996" for "January 1, 1991" in subpara. (b)(6)(B) [as redesignated by Sec. 11211(b)(1)(B) of this Act], effective 11/5/90.

—P.L. 101-508, Sec. 11218, relating to floor stocks tax treatment of articles in foreign trade zones, is reproduced in note following Code Sec. 5001.

—P.L. 101-508, Sec. 11704(a)(38), substituted "5 cents per gallon" for "5 cents a gallon" in Sec. 2001(d)(6)(C) of P.L. 100-647, see below.

In 1988, P.L. 100-647, Sec. 2001(d)(6)(A), added the last sentence in para. (c)(1)... Sec. 2001(d)(6)(B), added "except as provided in subsection (c)," after "paragraph (1)" in para. (b)(4)... Sec. 2001(d)(6)(C), [as amended by Sec. 11704(a)(38) of P.L. 101-508, see above] substituted "reduced by the amount of tax imposed (and not credited or refunded) on any prior sale of such fuel." for "5 cents per gallon" in the last sentence of para. (c)(2), effective for sales after 3/31/88. For special rules see Sec. 10502(f) of P.L. 100-203, reproduced below.

In 1987, P.L. 100-203, Sec. 10502(a), added Code Sec. 4091, effective for sales after 3/31/88. Sec. 10502(f) of this Act provides:

"(f) Floor stocks tax.—

"(1) Imposition of tax.—On any taxable fuel which on April 1, 1988, is held by a taxable person, there is hereby imposed a floor stocks tax at the rate of tax which would be imposed if such fuel were sold on such date in a sale subject to tax under section 4091 of the Internal Revenue Code of 1986 (as added by this section).

"(2) Overpayment of floor stocks taxes, etc.— Sections 6416 and 6427 of such Code shall apply in respect of the floor stocks taxes imposed by this subsection so as to entitle, subject to all provisions of such sections, any person paying such floor stocks taxes to a credit or refund thereof for any reason specified in such sections. All provisions of law, including penalties, applicable with respect to the taxes imposed by section 4091 of such Code (as so added) shall apply to the floor stocks taxes imposed by this subsection.

"(3) Due date of tax.—The taxes imposed by this subsection shall be paid before June 16, 1988.

"(4) Definitions.—For purposes of this subsection—

"(A) Taxable fuel.—

"(i) In general.—The term 'taxable fuel' means any taxable fuel (as defined in section 4092 of such Code, as added by this section) on which no tax has been imposed under section 4041 of such Code.

"(ii) Exception for fuel held for nontaxable uses.—The term 'taxable fuel' shall not include fuel held exclusively for any use which is a nontaxable use (as defined in section 6427(1) of such Code, as added by this section).

"(B) Taxable person.—The term 'taxable person' means any person other than a producer (as defined in section 4092 of such Code, as so added) or importer of taxable fuel.

"(C) Held by a taxable person.—An article shall be treated as held by a person if title thereto has passed to such person (whether or not delivery to such person has been made).

"(5) Special rule for fuel held for use in trains and commercial aircraft.—Only the Leaking Underground Storage Tank Trust Fund financing rate under section 4091 of such Code shall apply for purposes of this subsection with respect to—

"(A) diesel fuel held exclusively for use as a fuel in a diesel-powered train, and

"(B) aviation fuel held exclusively for use as a fuel in an aircraft not in noncommercial aviation (as defined in section 4041(c)(4) of such Code).

"(6) Transfer of floor stock revenues to trust funds.—For purposes of determining the amount transferred to any trust fund, the tax imposed by this subsection shall be treated as imposed by section 4091 of such Code (as so added)."

—P.L. 100-203, Sec. 10502(g), substituted "January 1, 1991" for "January 1, 1988" in subpara. (b)(5)(B), effective 12/31/87.

"Sec. 4092 Definitions.

"(a) Taxable fuel.

For purposes of this subpart—

"(1) In general. The term 'taxable fuel' means—

"(A) diesel fuel, and

"(B) aviation fuel.

"(2) Diesel fuel. The term 'diesel fuel' means any liquid (other than any product taxable under section 4081 which is suitable for use as a fuel in a diesel-powered highway vehicle, a diesel-powered train, or diesel-powered boat.

"(3) Aviation fuel. The term 'aviation fuel' means any liquid (other than any product taxable under section 4081 which is suitable for use as a fuel in an aircraft.

Excise and miscellaneous taxes — Code Sec. 4094

"(b) Producer.

For purposes of this subpart—

"(1) Certain persons treated as producers.

"(A) In general. The term 'producer' includes any person described in subparagraph (B) who elects to register under section 4101 with respect to the tax imposed by section 4091.

"(B) Persons described. A person is described in this subparagraph if such person is—

"(i) a refiner, compounder, blender, or wholesale distributor of a taxable fuel, or

"(ii) a dealer selling any taxable fuel exclusively to producers of such taxable fuel, or

"(iii) a retailer selling diesel fuel exclusively to purchasers as supplies for vessels for use in an off-highway business use (as defined in section 6421(e)(2)(B)).

To the extent provided in regulations, a retailer shall not be treated as not described in clause (iii) by reason of selling de minimis amounts of diesel fuel other than as supplies for vessels for use in an off-highway business use (as defined in section 6421(e)(2)(B)).

"(C) Tax-free purchasers treated as producers. Any person to whom any taxable fuel is sold tax-free under this subpart shall be treated as the producer of such fuel.

"(2) Wholesale distributor. For purposes of paragraph (1), the term 'wholesale distributor' includes any person who sells a taxable fuel to producers, retailers, or to users who purchase in bulk quantities and deliver into bulk storage tanks. Such term does not include any person who (excluding the term 'wholesale distributor' from paragraph (1)) is a producer or importer."

In 1993, P.L. 103-66, Sec. 13163(a)(1), substituted ", a diesel-powered train, or a diesel-powered boat" for "or a diesel-powered train" in para. (a)(2) (before amended by Sec. 13242(a) of this Act, see below)... Sec. 13163(a)(3), substituted "vessels for use in an off-highway business use (as defined in section 6421(e)(2)(B))" for "commercial and noncommercial vessels" each place it appeared in subpara. (b)(1)(B) (before amended by Sec. 13242(a) of this Act, see below), effective 1/1/94.

In 1988, P.L. 100-647, Sec. 3003(a), substituted ", or" for the period at the end of clause (b)(1)(B)(ii), added clause (b)(1)(B)(iii) and the sentence at the end of subpara. (b)(1)(B), effective for sales after 12/31/88.

In 1987, P.L. 100-203, Sec. 10502(a), added Code Sec. 4092, effective for sales after 3/31/88. For provisions on floor stocks tax, see Sec. 10502(f) of this Act reproduced in note following Code Sec. 4091.

"Sec. 4093 Exemptions; special rule.

"(a) Heating oil.

The tax imposed by section 4091 shall not apply in the case of sales of any taxable fuel which the Secretary determines is destined for use as heating oil.

"(b) Sales to producer.

Under regulations prescribed by the Secretary, the tax imposed by section 4091 shall not apply in the case of sales of a taxable fuel to a producer of such fuel.

"(c) Exemption for nontaxable uses and bus uses.

"(1) In general. No tax shall be imposed by section 4091 on fuel sold by a producer or importer for use by the purchaser in a nontaxable use (as defined in section 6427(l)(2)) or a use described in section 6427(b)(1).

"(2) Exceptions.

"(A) No exemption from certain taxes on fuel used in diesel-powered trains. In the case of fuel sold for use in a diesel-powered train, paragraph (1) shall not apply to so much of the tax imposed by section 4091 as is attributable to the Leaking Underground Storage Tank Trust Fund financing rate and the diesel fuel deficit reduction rate imposed under such section. The preceding sentence shall not apply in the case of fuel sold for exclusive use by a State or any political subdivision thereof.

"(B) No exemption from Leaking Underground Storage Tank Trust Fund taxes on fuel used in commercial aviation. In the case of fuel sold for use in commercial aviation (other than supplies for vessels or aircraft within the meaning of section 4221(d)(3)), paragraph (1) also shall not apply to so much of the tax imposed by section 4091 as is attributable to the Leaking Underground Storage Tank Trust Fund financing rate imposed by such section. For purposes of the preceding sentence, the term 'commercial aviation,' means any use of an aircraft other than in noncommercial aviation (as defined in section 4041(c)(4)).

"(C) Certain bus uses. Paragraph (1) shall not apply to so much of the tax imposed by section 4091 as is not refundable by reason of the application of section 6427(b)(2)(A).

"(3) Registration required. Except to the extent provided by the Secretary, paragraph (1) shall not apply to any sale unless—

"(A) both the seller and the purchaser are registered under section 4101, and

"(B) the purchaser's name, address, and registration number under such section are provided to the seller.

"(4) Information reporting.

"(A) Returns by producers and importers. Each producer or importer who makes a reduced-tax sale during the calendar year shall make a return (at such time and in such form as the Secretary may by regulations prescribe) showing with respect to each such sale—

"(i) the name, address, and registration number under section 4101 of the purchaser,

"(ii) the amount of fuel sold, and

"(iii) such other information as the Secretary may require.

"(B) Statements to purchasers. Every person required to make a return under subparagraph (A) shall furnish to each purchaser whose name is required to be set forth on such return a written statement showing the name and address of the person required to make such return, the registration number under section 4101 of such person, and the information required to be shown on the return with respect to such purchaser. The written statement required under the preceding sentence shall be furnished to the purchaser on or before January 31 of the year following the calendar year for which the return under subparagraph (A) is required to be made.

"(C) Returns by purchasers. Each person who uses during the calendar year fuel purchased in a reduced-tax sale shall make a return (at such time and in such form as the Secretary may by regulations prescribe) showing—

"(i) whether such use was a nontaxable use (as defined in section 6427(l)(2)) or a use described in section 6427(b)(1) and the amount of fuel so used,

"(ii) the date of the sale of the fuel so used,

"(iii) the name, address, and registration number under section 4101 of the seller, and

"(iv) such other information as the Secretary may require.

"(D) Reduced-tax sale. For purposes of this paragraph, the term 'reduced-tax sale' means any sale of taxable fuel on which the amount of tax otherwise required to be paid under section 4091 is reduced by reason of paragraph (1) (other than sales described in subsections (a) and (b) of this section).

"(d) Certain aviation fuel sales.

Under regulations prescribed by the Secretary, the Leaking Underground Storage Tank Trust Fund financing rate and the aviation fuel deficit reduction rate under section 4091 shall not apply to aviation fuel sold for use or used as supplies for vessels or aircraft (within the meaning of section 4221(d)(3)).

"(e) Cross references.

"(1) For imposition of tax where certain uses of diesel fuel or aviation fuel occur before imposition of tax by section 4091, see subsections (a)(1) and (c)(1) of section 4041.

"(2) For provisions allowing a credit or refund for fuel not used for certain taxable purposes, see section 6427."

In 1993, P.L. 103-66, Sec. 13241(f)(3), amended subparas. (c)(2)(A) and (B) (before amended by Sec. 13242(a) of this Act, see below)... Sec. 13241(f)(4), added "and the aviation fuel deficit reduction rate" after "rate" in subsec. (d) (before amended by Sec. 13242(a) of this Act, see below), effective 10/1/93.

Prior to amendment, subparas. (c)(2)(A) and (B) read as follows:

"(A) Certain Leaking Underground Storage Tank Trust Fund taxes. In the case of fuel sold for use in—

"(i) a diesel-powered train, and

"(ii) an aircraft,

paragraph (1) shall not apply to so much of the tax imposed by section 4091 as is attributable to the Leaking Underground Storage Tank Trust Fund financing rate imposed by such section.

"(B) Deficit reduction tax on fuel used in trains. In the case of fuel sold for use in a diesel-powered train, paragraph (1) also shall not apply to so much of the tax imposed by section 4091 as is attributable to the diesel fuel deficit reduction rate imposed by such section."

In 1990, P.L. 101-508, Sec. 11211(b)(4)(A), redesignated subpara. (c)(2)(B) as subpara. (c)(2)(C) and added new subpara. (c)(2)(B)... Sec. 11212(b)(4), deleted subsec. (e) and redesignated subsec. (f) as subsec. (e), effective 12/1/90.

Prior to deletion, subsec. (e) read as follows:

"(e) Special administrative rules.

The Secretary may require—

"(1) information reporting by each remitter of the tax imposed by section 4091, and

"(2) information reporting by, and registration of, such other persons as the Secretary deems necessary to carry out this subpart."

—P.L. 101-508, Sec. 11704(a)(20), substituted "reduced-tax sale" for "reduced tax sale" in subpara. (c)(4)(D), effective 11/5/90.

In 1988, P.L. 100-647, Sec. 2004(s)(1), redesignated subsecs. (d) and (e) as subsecs. (e) and (f), and added new subsec. (d), effective for sales after 3/31/88.

—P.L. 100-647, Sec. 3001(a), amended subsec. (c), effective 1/1/89, except as provided in Sec. 3001(c)(2) of this Act which reads as follows:

"(2) Refunds with interest for pre-effective date purchases.

"(A) In general. In the case of fuel—

"(i) which is purchased from a producer or importer during the period beginning on April 1, 1988, and ending on December 31, 1988,

"(ii) which is used (before the claim under this subparagraph is filed) by any person in a nontaxable use (as defined in section 6427(1)(2) of the 1986 Code), and

"(iii) with respect to which a claim is not permitted to be filed for any quarter under section 6427(i) of the 1986 Code,

the Secretary of the Treasury or the Secretary's delegate shall pay (with interest) to such person the amount of tax imposed on such fuel under section 4091 of the 1986 Code (to the extent not attributable to amounts described in section 6427(1)(3) of the 1986 Code) if claim therefor is filed not later than June 30, 1989. Not more than 1 claim may be filed under the preceding sentence and such claim shall not be taken into account under section 6427(i) of the 1986 Code. Any claim for refund filed under this paragraph shall be considered a claim for refund under section 6427(l) of the 1986 Code.

"(B) Interest. The amount of interest payable under subparagraph (A) shall be determined under section 6611 of the 1986 Code except that the date of the overpayment with respect to fuel purchased during any month shall be treated as being the 1st day of the succeeding month. No interest shall be paid under this paragraph with respect to fuel used by any agency of the United States.

Code Sec. 4094 — Excise and miscellaneous taxes

"(C) Registration procedures required to be specified. Not later than the 30th day after the date of the enactment of this Act, the Secretary of the Treasury or the Secretary's delegate shall prescribe the procedures for complying with the requirements of section 4093(c)(3) of the 1986 Code (as added by this section)."

Prior to amendment, subsec. (c) read as follows:

"(c) Authority to exempt certain other uses.

"Subject to such terms and conditions as the Secretary may provide (including the application of section 4101), the Secretary may by regulation provide that—

"(1) the Highway Trust Fund financing rate under section 4091 shall not apply to diesel fuel sold for use by any purchaser as a fuel in a diesel-powered train,

"(2) the Airport and Airway Trust Fund financing rate under section 4091 shall not apply to aviation fuel sold for use by any purchaser as a fuel in an aircraft not in noncommercial aviation (as defined in section 4041(c)(4)),

"(3) the tax imposed by section 4091 shall not apply to taxable fuel sold for use by any purchaser other than as a motor fuel, and

"(4) the tax imposed by section 4091 shall not apply to taxable fuel sold for the exclusive use of any State, any political subdivision of a State, or the District of Columbia."

In 1987, P.L. 100-203, Sec. 10502(a), added Code Sec. 4093, effective for sales after 3/31/88. For provisions on floor stocks tax, see Sec. 10502(f) of this Act reproduced in note following Code Sec. 4091.

In 1987, P.L. 100-203, Sec. 10502(a), added new Subpart B to Part III of Subchapter A of Chapter 32.

In 1983, P.L. 97-448, Sec. 515(a), repealed the items for Subpart B and for Code Secs. 4091 through 4094.

Prior to repeal, these items read as follows:

"Subpart B.—Lubricating Oil

"Sec.

"4091. Imposition of tax.

"4092. Definitions.

"4093. Exemptions.

"4094. Cross reference."

In 1978, P.L. 95-618, Sec. 404(c), amended item 4093.

Prior to amendment item 4093 read as follows:

"4093. Exemption of sales to producers."

In 1965, added item 4094.

In 1956, substituted "Definitions." for "Definition of certain vendees as a manufacturer".

"Sec. 4091. Repealed."

In 1983, P.L. 97-424, Sec. 515(a), repealed Code Sec. 4091 effective for articles sold after 1/6/83.

Prior to repeal, Code Sec. 4091 read as follows:

"Sec. 4091. Imposition of tax.

"There is hereby imposed on lubricating oil (other than cutting oils) which is sold in the United States by the manufacturer or producer a tax of 6 cents a gallon, to be paid by the manufacturer or producer."

In 1965, rewrote Code Sec. 4091 for articles sold after 12/31/65.

Prior to amendment, it read as follows:

"There is hereby imposed upon the following articles sold in the United States by the manufacturer or producer a tax at the following rates, to be paid by the manufacturer or producer:

"(1) cutting oils, 3 cents a gallon; and

"(2) other lubricating oils, 6 cents a gallon."

In 1955, provided for a tax of 3 cents a gallon on cutting oils instead of 6 cents per gallon and eliminated the provision that the tax should be not more than 10 percent of the manufacturer's price, effective 10/1/55.

"Sec. 4092. Repealed."

In 1983, P.L. 97-424, Sec. 515(a), repealed Code Sec. 4092 effective for articles sold after 1/6/83.

Prior to repeal, Code Sec. 4092 read as follows:

"Sec. 4092. Definitions.

"(a) Certain vendees considered as manufacturers.

"For purposes of this subpart, a vendee who has purchased lubricating oils free of tax under section 4093(a) shall be considered the manufacturer or producer of such lubricating oils.

"(b) Cutting oils.

"For purposes of this subpart, the term 'cutting oils' means oils sold for use in cutting and machining operation (including forging, drawing, rolling, shearing, punching, and stamping) on metals."

In 1978, P.L. 95-618, Sec. 404(b), substituted "4093(a)" for "4093" in subsec. (a), effective 12/1/78 (the first day of the first calendar month beginning more than 10 days after 11/9/78).

In 1955, substituted "Definitions." for "Definition of certain vendees as a manufacturer" in the catchline, designated existing provisions thereof as subsec. (a), and added subsec. (b), effective 10/1/55.

"Sec. 4093. Repealed."

In 1983, P.L. 97-424, Sec. 515(a), repealed Code Sec. 4093, effective for articles sold after 1/6/83.

Prior to repeal, Code Sec. 4093 read as follows:

"Sec. 4093. Exemptions.

"(a) Sales to manufacturers or producers for resale.

"Under regulations prescribed by the Secretary, no tax shall be imposed by section 4091 on lubricating oils sold to a manufacturer or producer of lubricating oils for resale by him.

"(b) Use in producing rerefined oil.

"(1) Sales to rerefiners. Under regulations prescribed by the Secretary, no tax shall be imposed by section 4091 on lubricating oil sold for use in mixing with used or waste lubricating oil which has been cleaned, renovated, or rerefined. Any person to whom lubricating oil is sold tax-free under this paragraph shall be treated as the producer of such lubricating oil.

"(2) Use in producing rerefined oil. Under regulations prescribed by the Secretary, no tax shall be imposed by section 4091 on lubricating oil used in producing rerefined oil to the extent that the amount of such lubricating oil does not exceed 55 percent of such rerefined oil.

"(3) Rerefined oil defined. For purposes of this subsection, the term 'rerefined oil' means oil 25 percent or more of which is used or waste lubricating oil which has been cleaned, renovated, or rerefined."

In 1978, P.L. 95-618, Sec. 404(a), amended Code Sec. 4093, effective 12/1/78 (the first day of the first calendar month beginning more than 10 days after 11/9/78).

Prior to amendment, Code Sec. 4093 read as follows:

"Sec. 4093. Exemption of sales to producers.

"Under regulations prescribed by the Secretary, no tax shall be imposed under this subpart upon lubricating oils sold to a manufacturer or producer of lubricating oils for resale by him."

In 1976, P.L. 94-455, Sec. 1906(b)(13)(A), substituted "Secretary" for "Secretary or his delegate" in Code Sec. 4093, effective 2/1/77.

"Sec. 4094. Repealed."

In 1983, P.L. 97-424, Sec. 515(a), repealed Code Sec. 4094, effective for articles sold after 1/6/83.

Prior to repeal, Code Sec. 4094 read as follows:

"Sec. 4094. Cross reference.

"For provisions to relieve purchasers of lubricating oil from excise tax in the case of lubricating oil used otherwise than in a highway motor vehicle, see sections 39 and 6424."

In 1965, added Code Sec. 4094.

Subpart B.—Special Provisions Applicable to Petroleum Products

Sec.

4101. Registration and bond.

4102. Inspection of records by local officers.

4103. Certain additional persons liable for tax where willful failure to pay.

4104. Information reporting for persons claiming certain tax benefits.

4105. Two-party exchanges.

In 2004, P.L. 108-357, Sec. 303(b), added item 4104. ... Sec. 866(b), added item 4105.

In 1990, P.L. 101-508, Sec. 11212(e)(3), added item 4103.

In 1986, P.L. 99-514, Sec. 1703(b)(2), substituted "Registration and bond" for "Registration" in item 4101.

In 1976, P.L. 94-455, Sec. 2102(c)(2), amended item 4102.

Prior to amendment item 4102 read as follows:

"4102. Inspection of records, returns, etc., by local officers."

In 1965, P.L. 89-44, Sec. 802, struck out "and bond" following "Registration" in item 4101.

Sec. 4101. Registration and bond.

(a) Registration.

(1) In general. Every person required by the Secretary to register under this section with respect to the tax imposed by section 4041(a) or 4081, every person producing or importing biodiesel (as defined in section 40A(d)(1)) or alcohol (as defined in section 6426(b)(4)(A)), and every person producing cellulosic biofuel (as defined in section 40(b)(6)(E)) shall register with the Secretary at such time, in such form and manner, and subject to such terms and conditions, as the Secretary may by regulations prescribe. A registration under this section may be used only in accordance with regulations prescribed under this section.

Excise and miscellaneous taxes Code Sec. 4101

(2) Registration of persons within foreign trade zones, etc. The Secretary shall require registration by any person which—

(A) operates a terminal or refinery within a foreign trade zone or within a customs bonded storage facility, or

(B) holds an inventory position with respect to a taxable fuel in such a terminal.

(3) Display of registration. Every operator of a vessel required by the Secretary to register under this section shall display proof of registration through an identification device prescribed by the Secretary on each vessel used by such operator to transport any taxable fuel.

(4) Registration of persons extending credit on certain exempt sales of fuel. The Secretary shall require registration by any person which—

(A) extends credit by credit card to any ultimate purchaser described in subparagraph (C) or (D) of section 6416(b)(2) for the purchase of taxable fuel upon which tax has been imposed under section 4041 or 4081, and

(B) does not collect the amount of such tax from such ultimate purchaser.

(5) Reregistration in event of change in ownership. Under regulations prescribed by the Secretary, a person (other than a corporation the stock of which is regularly traded on an established securities market) shall be required to reregister under this section if after a transaction (or series of related transactions) more than 50 percent of ownership interests in, or assets of, such person are held by persons other than persons (or persons related thereto) who held more than 50 percent of such interests or assets before the transaction (or series of related transactions).

(b) Bonds and liens.

(1) In general. Under regulations prescribed by the Secretary, the Secretary may require, as a condition of permitting any person to be registered under subsection (a), that such person—

(A) give a bond in such sum as the Secretary determines appropriate, and

(B) agree to the imposition of a lien—

(i) on such property (or rights to property) of such person used in the trade or business for which the registration is sought, or

(ii) with the consent of such person, on any other property (or rights to property) of such person as the Secretary determines appropriate.

Rules similar to the rules of section 6323 shall apply to the lien imposed pursuant to this paragraph.

(2) Release or discharge of lien. If a lien is imposed pursuant to paragraph (1), the Secretary shall issue a certificate of discharge or a release of such lien in connection with a transfer of the property if there is furnished to the Secretary (and accepted by him) a bond in such sum as the Secretary determines appropriate or the transferor agrees to the imposition of a substitute lien under paragraph (1)(B) in such sum as the Secretary determines appropriate. The Secretary shall respond to any request to discharge or release a lien imposed pursuant to paragraph (1) in connection with a transfer of property not later than 90 days after the date the request for such a discharge or release is made.

(c) Denial, revocation, or suspension of registration.

Rules similar to the rules of section 4222(c) shall apply to registration under this section.

(d) Information reporting.

The Secretary may require—

(1) information reporting by any person registered under this section, and

(2) information reporting by such other persons as the Secretary deems necessary to carry out this part.

Any person who is required to report under this subsection and who has 25 or more reportable transactions in a month shall file such report in electronic format.

In 2008, P.L. 110-246, Sec. 4, Repeals the duplicative enactment and provides effective date provisions of the Act entitled "An Act to provide for the continuation of agricultural programs through fiscal year 2012, and for other purposes" Sec. 4, P.L. 110-246 reads as follows:

"Sec. 4. Repeal of duplicative enactment.

"(a) In General- The Act entitled 'An Act to provide for the continuation of agricultural programs through fiscal year 2012, and for other purposes' (H.R. 2419 of the 110th Congress), and the amendments made by that Act, are repealed, effective on the date of enactment of that Act.

"(b) Effective Date- Except as otherwise provided in this Act, this Act and the amendments made by this Act shall take effect on the earlier of--

"(1) the date of enactment of this Act; or

"(2) the date of the enactment of the Act entitled 'An Act to provide for the continuation of agricultural programs through fiscal year 2012, and for other purposes' (H.R. 2419 of the 110th Congress)."

—P.L. 110-246, Sec. 15321(b)(3)(A)(i), substituted ", every person" for "and every person" in para. (a)(1) . . . Sec. 15321(b)(3)(A)(ii), inserted ", and every person producing cellulosic biofuel (as defined in section 40(b)(6)(E))" after "section 6426(b)(4)(A))" in para. (a)(1), effective for fuel produced after 12/31/2008. [Ed. Note: May 22, 2008 was the date of enactment for H.R. 2419 (PL 110-234), which was repealed by (2008 Farm Act § 4(a)) (PL 110-246, 6/18/2008), in connection with the reenactment of the farm bill to correct a technical deficiency in its original passage.]

In 2007, P.L. 110-172, Sec. 11(a)(29), redesignated para. (a)(4) as para. (a)(5), enacted 12/29/2009.

In 2005, P.L. 109-59, Sec. 11113(c), substituted "4041(a)" for "4041(a)(1)" in para. (a)(1), effective for any sale or use for any period after 9/30/2006.

—P.L. 109-59, Sec. 11163(a), added para. (a)(4), effective for sales after 12/31/2005.

—P.L. 109-59, Sec. 11164(a), added para. (a)(4) [sic (a)(5)], effective for actions, or failures to act, after 8/10/2005.

—P.L. 109-59, Sec. 11166(a), of this Act, reads as follows:

"(a) In general. On and after the date of the enactment of this Act, the Secretary of the Treasury shall require that a vessel described in section 4042(c)(1) of the Internal Revenue Code of 1986 be considered a vessel for purposes of the registration of the operator of such vessel under section 4101 of such Code, unless such operator uses such vessel exclusively for purposes of the entry of taxable fuel."

In 2004, P.L. 108-357, Sec. 301(b), added "and every person producing or importing biodiesel (as defined in section 40A(d)(1)) or alcohol (as defined in section 6426(b)(4)(A))" before "shall register with the Secretary" in para. (a)(1) [as amended by Sec. 861(a)(1) of this Act, see below], effective 1/1/2005.

—P.L. 108-357, Sec. 853(d)(2)(F), substituted "or 4081" for ", 4081, or 4091" in para. (a)(1) [as amended by Sec. 861(a)(1) of this Act, see below], effective for aviation-grade kerosene removed, entered, or sold after 12/31/2004.

—P.L. 108-357, Sec. 853(f), of this Act, provides:

(f) Floor stocks tax.

"(1) In general. There is hereby imposed on aviation-grade kerosene held on January 1, 2005, by any person a tax equal to—

"(A) the tax which would have been imposed before such date on such kerosene had the amendments made by this section been in effect at all times before such date, reduced by

"(B) the sum of—

"(i) the tax imposed before such date on such kerosene under section 4091 of the Internal Revenue Code of 1986, as in effect on such date, and

"(ii) in the case of kerosene held exclusively for such person's own use, the amount which such person would (but for this clause) reasonably expect (as of such date) to be paid as a refund under section 6427(l) of such Code with respect to such kerosene.

"(2) Exception for fuel held in aircraft fuel tank. Paragraph (1) shall not apply to kerosene held in the fuel tank of an aircraft on January 1, 2005.

"(3) Liability for tax and method of payment.

"(A) Liability for tax. The person holding the kerosene on January 1, 2005, to which the tax imposed by paragraph (1) applies shall be liable for such tax.

"(B) Method and time for payment. The tax imposed by paragraph (1) shall be paid at such time and in such manner as the Secretary of the Treasury (or the Secretary's delegate) shall prescribe, including the nonapplication of such tax on de minimis amounts of kerosene.

"(4) Transfer of floor stock tax revenues to trust funds. For purposes of determining the amount transferred to any trust fund, the tax imposed by this subsection shall be treated as imposed by section 4081 of the Internal Revenue Code of 1986—

"(A) in any case in which tax was not imposed by section 4091 of such Code, at the Leaking Underground Storage Tank Trust Fund financing rate under such section to the extent of 0.1 cents per gallon, and

"(B) at the rate under section 4081(a)(2)(A)(iv) of such Code to the extent of the remainder.

"(5) Held by a person. For purposes of this subsection, kerosene shall be considered as held by a person if title thereto has passed to such person (whether or not delivery to the person has been made).

"(6) Other laws applicable. All provisions of law, including penalties, applicable with respect to the tax imposed by section 4081 of such Code shall, insofar as applicable and not inconsistent with the provisions of this subsection, apply with respect to the floor stock tax imposed by paragraph (1) to the same extent as if such tax were imposed by such section."

—P.L. 108-357, Sec. 860(c), of this Act, reads as follows:

"(c) Publication of registered persons. Beginning on January 1, 2005, the Secretary of the Treasury (or the Secretary's delegate) shall periodically publish under section 6103(k)(7) of the Internal Revenue Code of 1986 a current list of persons registered under section 4101 of such Code who are required to register under such section."

—P.L. 108-357, Sec. 861(a)(1), substituted "(1) In general. Every" for "Every" in subsec. (a) . . . Sec. 861(a)(2), added para. (a)(2), effective 1/1/2005.

—P.L. 108-357, Sec. 862(a), redesignated para. (a)(2) as (a)(3) [as added by Sec. 861(a)(2) of this Act, see above] and added para. (a)(2), effective 1/1/2005.

—P.L. 108-357, Sec. 864(a), added "Any person who is required to report under this subsection and who has 25 or more reportable transactions in a month shall file such report in electronic format." flush left at the end of subsec. (d), effective 1/1/2006.

In 2002, P.L. 107-147, Sec. 615(a), deleted subsec. (e), effective 1/1/2002.

Prior to deletion, subsec. (e) read as follows:

"(e) Certain approved terminals of registered persons required to offer dyed diesel fuel and kerosene for nontaxable purposes.

"(1) In general. A terminal for kerosene or diesel fuel may not be an approved facility for storage of non-tax-paid diesel fuel or kerosene under this section unless the operator of such terminal offers such fuel in a dyed form for removal for nontaxable use in accordance with section 4082(a).

"(2) Exception. Paragraph (1) shall not apply to any terminal exclusively providing aviation grade kerosene by pipeline to an airport."

In 1999, P.L. 106-170, Sec. 524, substituted "January 1, 2002" for "July 1, 2000" in Sec. 1032(f)(2) of P.L. 105-34, see below [as amended by Sec. 9008 of P.L. 105-178, see below], which provides the effective date for amendments made by Sec. 1032(e) of P.L. 105-34, see below.

In 1998, P.L. 105-206, Sec. 6010(h)(5), substituted "such fuel in a dyed form" for "dyed diesel fuel and kerosene" in para. (e)(1), effective 7/1/2000.

—P.L. 105-178, Sec. 9008, amended Sec. 1032(f) of P.L. 105-34, the effective date for amendments made by Sec. 1032 of P.L. 105-34 [see below, prior to amendment by Sec. 524 of P.L. 106-170, see above].

Prior to amendment by Sec. 524 of P.L. 106-170 and Sec. 9008 of P.L. 105-178 Sec. 1032(f) of P.L. 105-34 read as follows:

"(f) Effective date. The amendments made by this section shall take effect on July 1, 1998."

In 1997, P.L. 105-34, Sec. 1032(d), added subsec. (e), effective 1/1/2002, [as amended by Sec. 9008 of P.L. 105-178 and Sec. 524 of P.L. 106-170, see above].

In 1993, P.L. 103-66, Sec. 13242(d)(1), substituted "4041(a)(1), 4081," for "4081" in subsec. (a), effective 1/1/94.

In 1990, P.L. 101-508, Sec. 11212(b)(1), amended Code Sec. 4101, effective 12/1/90.

Prior to amendment, Code Sec. 4101 read as follows:

"SEC. 4101. REGISTRATION AND BOND.

"(a) Registration. Every person subject to tax under section 4081 or 4091 shall, before incurring any liability for tax under such section, register with the Secretary.

"(b) Bond. Under regulations prescribed by the Secretary, every person who registers under subsection (a) may be required to give a bond in such sum as the Secretary determines."

In 1987, P.L. 100-203, Sec. 10502(d)(3), added "or 4091" after "section 4081" in subsec. (a), effective for sales after 3/31/88.

In 1986, P.L. 99-514, Sec. 1703(b)(1), amended Code Sec. 4101, effective for gasoline removed (as defined in Code Sec. 4082, as amended by Sec. 1703(a) of this Act) after 12/31/87.

Prior to amendment, Code Sec. 4101 read as follows:

"SEC. 4101. REGISTRATION. Every person subject to tax under section 4081 shall, before incurring any liability for tax under such sections, register with the Secretary."

In 1983, P.L. 97-424, Sec. 515(b)(8), deleted "or section 4091" after "4081" in Code Sec. 4101, effective for articles sold after 1/6/83.

In 1976, P.L. 94-455, Sec. 1906(b)(13)(A), substituted "Secretary" for "Secretary or his delegate" in Code Sec. 4101, effective 2/1/77.

In 1965, P.L. 89-44, Sec. 802(b)(2), amended Code Sec. 4101, effective for articles sold after 6/30/65.

Prior to amendment, Code Sec. 4101 read as follows:

"SEC. 4101. REGISTRATION AND BOND. Every person subject to tax under section 4081 or section 4091 shall, before incurring any liability for tax under such sections, register with the Secretary or his delegate and shall give a bond, to be approved by the Secretary or his delegate, conditioned that he shall not engage in any attempt, by himself or by collusion with others, to defraud the United States of any tax under such sections; that he shall render truly and completely all returns, statements, and inventories required by law or regulations in pursuance thereof and shall pay all taxes due under such sections; and that he shall comply with all requirements of law and regulations in pursuance thereof with respect to tax under such sections. Such bond shall be in such sum as the Secretary or his delegate may require in accordance with regulations prescribed by him, but not less than $2,000. The Secretary or his delegate may from time to time require a new or additional bond in accordance with this section."

Sec. 4102. Inspection of records by local officers.

Under regulations prescribed by the Secretary, records required to be kept with respect to taxes under this part shall be open to inspection by such officers of a State, or a political subdivision of any such State, as shall be charged with the enforcement or collection of any tax on any taxable fuel (as defined in section 4083).

In 1993, P.L. 103-66, Sec. 13242(d)(2), substituted "any taxable fuel (as defined in section 4083)" for "gasoline" in Code Sec. 4102, effective 1/1/94.

In 1983, P.L. 97-424, Sec. 515(b)(9), deleted "or lubricating oils" after "gasoline" in Code Sec. 4102, effective for articles sold after 1/6/83.

In 1976, P.L. 94-455, Sec. 1202(c)(1), amended Code Sec. 4102, effective 1/1/77. Prior to amendment, Code Sec. 4102 read as follows:

"SEC. 4102. INSPECTION OF RECORDS, RETURNS, ETC., BY LOCAL OFFICERS.

"Under regulations prescribed by the Secretary or his delegate, records required to be kept with respect to taxes under this part, and returns, reports, and statements with respect to such taxes filed with the Secretary or his delegate, shall be open to inspection by such officers of any State or Territory or political subdivision thereof or the district of Columbia as shall be charged with the enforcement or collection of any tax on gasoline or lubricating oils. The Secretary or his delegate shall furnish to any of such officers, upon written request, certified copies of any such statements, reports, or returns filed in his office, upon the payment of a fee of $1 for each 100 words or fraction thereof in the copy or copies requested."

Sec. 4103. Certain additional persons liable for tax where willful failure to pay.

In any case in which there is a willful failure to pay the tax imposed by section 4041(a)(1) or 4081, each person—

(1) who is an officer, employee, or agent of the taxpayer who is under a duty to assure the payment of such tax and who willfully fails to perform such duty, or

(2) who willfully causes the taxpayer to fail to pay such tax,

shall be jointly and severally liable with the taxpayer for the tax to which such failure relates.

In 2004, P.L. 108-357, Sec. 853(d)(1), redesignated subpart C of chapter 32 of subchapter A of part III of subtitle D as subpart B . . . Sec. 853(d)(2)(F), substituted "or 4081" for ", 4081, or 4091" in Code Sec. 4103, effective for aviation-grade kerosene removed, entered, or sold after 12/31/2004.

—P.L. 108-357, Sec. 853(f), of this Act, provides:

(f) Floor stocks tax.

"(1) In general. There is hereby imposed on aviation-grade kerosene held on January 1, 2005, by any person a tax equal to—

"(A) the tax which would have been imposed before such date on such kerosene had the amendments made by this section been in effect at all times before such date, reduced by

"(B) the sum of—

"(i) the tax imposed before such date on such kerosene under section 4091 of the Internal Revenue Code of 1986, as in effect on such date, and

"(ii) in the case of kerosene held exclusively for such person's own use, the amount which such person would (but for this clause) reasonably expect (as of such date) to be paid as a refund under section 6427(l) of such Code with respect to such kerosene.

"(2) Exception for fuel held in aircraft fuel tank. Paragraph (1) shall not apply to kerosene held in the fuel tank of an aircraft on January 1, 2005.

"(3) Liability for tax and method of payment.

"(A) Liability for tax. The person holding the kerosene on January 1, 2005, to which the tax imposed by paragraph (1) applies shall be liable for such tax.

"(B) Method and time for payment. The tax imposed by paragraph (1) shall be paid at such time and in such manner as the Secretary of the Treasury (or the Secretary's delegate) shall prescribe, including the nonapplication of such tax on de minimis amounts of kerosene.

"(4) Transfer of floor stock tax revenues to trust funds. For purposes of determining the amount transferred to any trust fund, the tax imposed by this subsection shall be treated as imposed by section 4081 of the Internal Revenue Code of 1986—

"(A) in any case in which tax was not imposed by section 4091 of such Code, at the Leaking Underground Storage Tank Trust Fund financing rate under such section to the extent of 0.1 cents per gallon, and

"(B) at the rate under section 4081(a)(2)(A)(iv) of such Code to the extent of the remainder.

Excise and miscellaneous taxes   Code Sec. 4121

"(5) Held by a person. For purposes of this subsection, kerosene shall be considered as held by a person if title thereto has passed to such person (whether or not delivery to the person has been made).

"(6) Other laws applicable. All provisions of law, including penalties, applicable with respect to the tax imposed by section 4081 of such Code shall, insofar as applicable and not inconsistent with the provisions of this subsection, apply with respect to the floor stock tax imposed by paragraph (1) to the same extent as if such tax were imposed by such section."

In 1993, P.L. 103-66, Sec. 13242(d)(1), substituted "4041(a)(1), 4081," for "4081" in Code Sec. 4103, effective 1/1/94.

In 1990, P.L. 101-508, Sec. 11212(c), added Code Sec. 4103, effective 12/1/90.

Sec. 4104. Information reporting for persons claiming certain tax benefits.
(a) In general.
The Secretary shall require any person claiming tax benefits—

(1) under the provisions of section 34, 40, and 40A, to file a return at the time such person claims such benefits (in such manner as the Secretary may prescribe), and

(2) under the provisions of section 4041(b)(2), 6426, or 6427(e) to file a quarterly return (in such manner as the Secretary may prescribe).

(b) Contents of return.
Any return filed under this section shall provide such information relating to such benefits and the coordination of such benefits as the Secretary may require to ensure the proper administration and use of such benefits.

(c) Enforcement.
With respect to any person described in subsection (a) and subject to registration requirements under this title, rules similar to rules of section 4222(c) shall apply with respect to any requirement under this section.

In 2004, P.L. 108-357, Sec. 303(a), added Code Sec. 4104, effective 1/1/2005.

Sec. 4105. Two-party exchanges.
(a) In general.
In a two-party exchange, the delivering person shall not be liable for the tax imposed under section 4081(a)(1)(A)(ii).

(b) Two-party exchange.
The term "two-party exchange" means a transaction, other than a sale, in which taxable fuel is transferred from a delivering person registered under section 4101 as a taxable fuel registrant to a receiving person who is so registered where all of the following occur:

(1) The transaction includes a transfer from the delivering person, who holds the inventory position for taxable fuel in the terminal as reflected in the records of the terminal operator.

(2) The exchange transaction occurs before or contemporaneous with completion of removal across the rack from the terminal by the receiving person.

(3) The terminal operator in its books and records treats the receiving person as the person that removes the product across the terminal rack for purposes of reporting the transaction to the Secretary.

(4) The transaction is the subject of a written contract.

In 2004, P.L. 108-357, Sec. 866(a), added Code Sec. 4105, effective 10/22/2004.

Subchapter B.—Coal
Sec.
4121. Imposition of tax.

In 1978, P.L. 95-227, Sec. 2(a), added new subchapter B, to Chapter 32.

Sec. 4121. Imposition of tax.
(a) Tax imposed.
(1) In general. There is hereby imposed on coal from mines located in the United States sold by the producer, a tax equal to the rate per ton determined under subsection (b).

(2) Limitation on tax. The amount of the tax imposed by paragraph (1) with respect to a ton of coal shall not exceed the applicable percentage (determined under subsection (b)) of the price at which such ton of coal is sold by the producer.

(b) Determination of rates and limitation on tax.
For purposes of subsection (a)—

(1) the rate of tax on coal from underground mines shall be $1.10,

(2) the rate of tax on coal from surface mines shall be $.55, and

(3) the applicable percentage shall be 4.4 percent.

(c) Tax not to apply to lignite.
The tax imposed by subsection (a) shall not apply in the case of lignite.

(d) Definitions.
For purposes of this subchapter—

(1) **Coal from surface mines.** Coal shall be treated as produced from a surface mine if all of the geological matter above the coal being mined is removed before the coal is extracted from the earth. Coal extracted by auger shall be treated as coal from a surface mine.

(2) **Coal from underground mines.** Coal shall be treated as produced from an underground mine if it is not produced from a surface mine.

(3) **United States.** The term "United States" has the meaning given to it by paragraph (1) of section 638.

(4) **Ton.** The term "ton" means 2,000 pounds.

(e) Reduction in amount of tax.
(1) In general. Effective with respect to sales after the temporary increase termination date, subsection (b) shall be applied—

(A) by substituting "$.50" for "$1.10",

(B) by substituting "$.25" for "$.55", and

(C) by substituting "2 percent" for "4.4 percent".

(2) Temporary increase termination date. For purposes of paragraph (1), the temporary increase termination date is the earlier of—

(A) December 31, 2018, or

(B) the first December 31 after 2007 as of which there is—

(i) no balance of repayable advances made to the Black Lung Disability Trust Fund, and

(ii) no unpaid interest on such advances.

In 2008, P.L. 110-343, Sec. 113(a)(1)DivB, substituted "December 31, 2018" for "January 1, 2014" in subpara. (e)(2)(A)... Sec. 113(a)(2)DivB, substituted "December 31 after 2007" for "January 1 after 1981" in subpara. (e)(2)(B), enacted 10/3/2008

—P.L. 110-343, Sec. 114DivB, relating to rules for the refund of the coal excise tax, reads as follows:

"Sec. 114. Special rules for refund of the coal excise tax to certain coal producers and exporters.

"(a) Refund.

"(1) Coal producers.

"(A) In general. Notwithstanding subsections (a)(1) and (c) of section 6416 and section 6511 of the Internal Revenue Code of 1986, if—

"(i) a coal producer establishes that such coal producer, or a party related to such coal producer, exported coal produced by such coal producer to a foreign country or shipped coal produced by such coal producer to a possession of the United States, or caused such coal to be exported or shipped, the export or shipment of which was other than through an exporter who meets the requirements of paragraph (2),

"(ii) such coal producer filed an excise tax return on or after October 1, 1990, and on or before the date of the enactment of this Act, and

3,229

"(iii) such coal producer files a claim for refund with the Secretary not later than the close of the 30-day period beginning on the date of the enactment of this Act,
"then the Secretary shall pay to such coal producer an amount equal to the tax paid under section 4121 of such Code on such coal exported or shipped by the coal producer or a party related to such coal producer, or caused by the coal producer or a party related to such coal producer to be exported or shipped.

"(B) Special rules for certain taxpayers. For purposes of this section—

"(i) In general. If a coal producer or a party related to a coal producer has received a judgment described in clause (iii), such coal producer shall be deemed to have established the export of coal to a foreign country or shipment of coal to a possession of the United States under subparagraph (A)(i).

"(ii) Amount of payment. If a taxpayer described in clause (i) is entitled to a payment under subparagraph (A), the amount of such payment shall be reduced by any amount paid pursuant to the judgment described in clause (iii).

"(iii) Judgment described. A judgment is described in this subparagraph if such judgment—
"(I) is made by a court of competent jurisdiction within the United States,
"(II) relates to the constitutionality of any tax paid on exported coal under section 4121 of the Internal Revenue Code of 1986, and
"(III) is in favor of the coal producer or the party related to the coal producer.

"(2) Exporters. Notwithstanding subsections (a)(1) and (c) of section 6416 and section 6511 of the Internal Revenue Code of 1986, and a judgment described in paragraph (1)(B)(iii) of this subsection, if—

"(A) an exporter establishes that such exporter exported coal to a foreign country or shipped coal to a possession of the United States, or caused such coal to be so exported or shipped,

"(B) such exporter filed a tax return on or after October 1, 1990, and on or before the date of the enactment of this Act, and

"(C) such exporter files a claim for refund with the Secretary not later than the close of the 30-day period beginning on the date of the enactment of this Act,
"then the Secretary shall pay to such exporter an amount equal to $0.825 per ton of such coal exported by the exporter or caused to be exported or shipped, or caused to be exported or shipped, by the exporter.

"(b) Limitations. Subsection (a) shall not apply with respect to exported coal if a settlement with the Federal Government has been made with and accepted by, the coal producer, a party related to such coal producer, or the exporter, of such coal, as of the date that the claim is filed under this section with respect to such exported coal. For purposes of this subsection, the term "settlement with the Federal Government" shall not include any settlement or stipulation entered into as of the date of the enactment of this Act, the terms of which contemplate a judgment concerning which any party has reserved the right to file an appeal, or has filed an appeal.

"(c) Subsequent refund prohibited. No refund shall be made under this section to the extent that a credit or refund of such tax on such exported or shipped coal has been paid to any person.

"(d) Definitions. For purposes of this section—

"(1) Coal producer. The term "coal producer" means the person in whom is vested ownership of the coal immediately after the coal is severed from the ground, without regard to the existence of any contractual arrangement for the sale or other disposition of the coal or the payment of any royalties between the producer and third parties. The term includes any person who extracts coal from coal waste refuse piles or from the silt waste product which results from the wet washing (or similar processing) of coal.

"(2) Exporter. The term 'exporter' means a person, other than a coal producer, who does not have a contract, fee arrangement, or any other agreement with a producer or seller of such coal to export or ship such coal to a third party on behalf of the producer or seller of such coal and—

"(A) is indicated in the shipper's export declaration or other documentation as the exporter of record, or

"(B) actually exported such coal to a foreign country or shipped such coal to a possession of the United States, or caused such coal to be so exported or shipped.

"(3) Related party. The term "a party related to such coal producer" means a person who—

"(A) is related to such coal producer through any degree of common management, stock ownership, or voting control,

"(B) is related (within the meaning of section 144(a)(3) of the Internal Revenue Code of 1986) to such coal producer, or

"(C) has a contract, fee arrangement, or any other agreement with such coal producer to sell such coal to a third party on behalf of such coal producer.

"(4) Secretary. The term "Secretary" means the Secretary of Treasury or the Secretary's designee.

"(e) Timing of refund. With respect to any claim for refund filed pursuant to this section, the Secretary shall determine whether the requirements of this section are met not later than 180 days after such claim is filed. If the Secretary determines that the requirements of this section are met, the claim for refund shall be paid not later than 180 days after the Secretary makes such determination.

"(f) Interest. Any refund paid pursuant to this section shall be paid by the Secretary with interest from the date of overpayment determined by using the overpayment rate and method under section 6621 of the Internal Revenue Code of 1986.

"(g) Denial of double benefit. The payment under subsection (a) with respect to any coal shall not exceed—

"(1) in the case of a payment to a coal producer, the amount of tax paid under section 4121 of the Internal Revenue Code of 1986 with respect to such coal by such coal producer or a party related to such coal producer, and

"(2) in the case of a payment to an exporter, an amount equal to $0.825 per ton with respect to such coal exported by the exporter or caused to be exported by the exporter.

"(h) Application of section. This section applies only to claims on coal exported or shipped on or after October 1, 1990, through the date of the enactment of this Act.

"(i) Standing not conferred.

"(1) Exporters. With respect to exporters, this section shall not confer standing upon an exporter to commence, or intervene in, any judicial or administrative proceeding concerning a claim for refund by a coal producer of any Federal or State tax, fee, or royalty paid by the coal producer.

"(2) Coal producers. With respect to coal producers, this section shall not confer standing upon a coal producer to commence, or intervene in, any judicial or administrative proceeding concerning a claim for refund by an exporter of any Federal or State tax, fee, or royalty paid by the producer and alleged to have been passed on to an exporter."

In 1987, P.L. 100-203, Sec. 10503, substituted "January 1, 2014" for "January 1, 1996" in subpara. (e)(2)(A), effective 12/22/87.

In 1986, P.L. 99-514, Sec. 1897(a), deleted ", in the case of sales during any calendar year beginning after December 31, 1985" after "subsection (a)" in subsec. (b), effective for sales after 3/31/86. For special rules see Sec. 13203(b) oc P.L. 99-272, reproduced below.

—P.L. 99-272, Sec. 13203(a), amended subsecs. (a) and (b) . . . Sec. 13203(c), amended the heading of subsec. (e) and para. (e)(1), effective for sales after 3/31/86. Sec. 13203(b) of this Act provides:

"(b) 5-year moratorium on interest accruals with respect to the indebtedness of the Black Lung Disability Trust Fund.—

"No interest shall accrue for the period beginning on October 1, 1985, and ending on September 30, 1990, with respect to any repayable advance to the Black Lung Disability Trust Fund."

Prior to amendment, subsecs. (a) and (b) read as follows:
"(a) Tax imposed.

"There is hereby imposed on coal sold by the producer a tax at the rates of—
"(1) 50 cents per ton in the case of coal from underground mines located in the United States, and
"(2) 25 cents per ton in the case of coal from surface mines located in the United States.
"(b) Limitation on tax.

"The amount of the tax imposed by subsection (a) with respect to a ton of coal shall not exceed 2 percent of the price at which such ton of coal is sold by the producer."

Prior to amendment, the heading of subsec. (e) and para. (e)(1) read as follows:
"(e) Temporary increase in amount of tax.
"(1) In general. Effective with respect to sales after December 31, 1981, and before the temporary increase termination date—
"(A) subsection (a) shall be applied—
"(i) by substituting $1 for 50 cents, and
"(ii) by substituting '50 cents' for '25 cents', and
"(B) subsection (b) shall be applied by substituting '4 percent' for '2 percent'.

In 1981, P.L. 97-119, Sec. 102(a), added subsec. (e), effective for sales after 12/31/81.

In 1978, P.L. 95-227, Sec. 2(a), added Code Sec. 4121, effective for sales after 3/31/78. See note following Code Sec. 192.

Subchapter C.—Certain Vaccines

Sec.
4131. Imposition of tax.
4132. Definitions and special rules.

In 1987, P.L. 100-203, Sec. 9201(a), added Subchapter C.

Sec. 4131. Imposition of tax.
(a) General rule.

There is hereby imposed a tax on any taxable vaccine sold by the manufacturer, producer, or importer thereof.
(b) Amount of tax.

(1) In general. The amount of the tax imposed by subsection (a) shall be 75 cents per dose of any taxable vaccine.

(2) Combinations of vaccines. If any taxable vaccine is described in more than 1 subparagraph of section 4132(a)(1), the amount of the tax imposed by subsection (a) on such vaccine shall be the sum of the amounts for the vaccines which are so included.
(c) Application of section.

The tax imposed by this section shall apply—

(1) after December 31, 1987, and before January 1, 1993, and

Excise and miscellaneous taxes

Code Sec. 4132(c)(1)

(2) during periods after the date of the enactment [8/10/93] of the Revenue Reconciliation Act of 1993.

In 1997, P.L. 105-34, Sec. 904(a), amended subsec. (b), effective on the day after 8/5/97.
Prior to amendment, subsec. (b) read as follows:
"(b) Amount of tax.
"(1) In general. The amount of the tax imposed by subsection (a) shall be determined in accordance with the following table:

If the taxable vaccine is:	The tax per dose is:
DPT vaccine	$4.56
DT vaccine	0.06
MMR vaccine	4.44
Polio vaccine	0.29

"(2) Combinations of vaccines. If any taxable vaccine is included in more than 1 category of vaccines in the table contained in paragraph (1), the amount of the tax imposed by subsection (a) on such vaccine shall be the sum of the amounts determined under such table for each category in which such vaccine is so included."

In 1993, P.L. 103-66, Sec. 13421(a), amended subsec. (c), effective 8/10/93.
Prior to amendment, subsec. (c) read as follows:
"(c) Termination of tax if amounts collected exceed projected fund liability.
"(1) In general. If the Secretary estimates under paragraph (3) that the Vaccine Injury Compensation Trust Fund would not have a negative projected balance were the tax imposed by this section to terminate as of the close of any applicable date, no tax shall be imposed by this section after such date.
"(2) Applicable date. For purposes of paragraph (1), the term 'applicable date' means—
"(A) the close of any calendar quarter ending on or after December 31, 1992, and
"(B) the 1st date on which petitions may not be filed under section 2111 and 2111(a) of the Public Health Service Act by reason of section 2134 of such Act and each date thereafter.
"(3) Estimates by Secretary.
"(A) In general. The Secretary shall estimate the projected balance of the Vaccine Injury Compensation Trust Fund as of—
"(i) the close of each calendar quarter ending on or after December 31, 1992, and
"(ii) such other times as are appropriate in the case of applicable dates described in paragraph (2)(B).
"(B) Determination of projected balance. In determining the projected balance of the Fund as of any date, the Secretary shall assume that—
"(i) the tax imposed by this section will not apply after such date, and
"(ii) there shall be paid from such Trust Fund all claims made or to be made against such Trust Fund—
"(I) with respect to vaccines administered before October 1, 1992, in the case of an applicable date described in paragraph (2)(A), or
"(II) with respect to petitions filed under section 2111 or section 2111(a) of the Public Health Service Act, in the case of an applicable date described in paragraph (2)(B)."
—P.L. 103-66, Sec. 13421(c), of this Act provides:
"(c) Floor stocks tax.
"(1) Imposition of tax. On any taxable vaccine—
"(A) which was sold by the manufacturer, producer, or importer on or before the date of the enactment of this Act,
"(B) on which no tax was imposed by section 4131 of the Internal Revenue Code of 1986 (or, if such tax was imposed, was credited or refunded), and
"(C) which is held on such date by any person for sale or use,
there is hereby imposed a tax in the amount determined under section 4131(b) of such Code.
"(2) Liability for tax and method of payment.
"(A) Liability for tax. The person holding any taxable vaccine to which the tax imposed by paragraph (1) applies shall be liable for such tax.
"(B) Method of payment. The tax imposed by paragraph (1) shall be paid in such manner as the Secretary shall prescribe by regulations.
"(C) Time for payment. The tax imposed by paragraph (1) shall be paid on or before the last day of the 6th month beginning after the date of the enactment of this Act.
"(3) Definitions. For purposes of this subsection, terms used in this subsection which are also used in section 4131 of such Code shall have the respective meanings such terms have in such section.
"(4) Other laws applicable. All provisions of law, including penalties, applicable with respect to the taxes imposed by section 4131 of such Code shall, insofar as applicable and not inconsistent with the provisions of this subsection, apply to the floor stocks taxes imposed by paragraph (1), to the same extent as if such taxes were imposed by such section 4131."

In 1987, P.L. 100-203, Sec. 9201(a), added Code Sec. 4131, effective 1/1/88.

Sec. 4132. Definitions and special rules.
(a) Definitions relating to taxable vaccines.
For purposes of this subchapter—
(1) Taxable vaccine. The term "taxable vaccine" means any of the following vaccines which are manufactured or produced in the United States or entered into the United States for consumption, use, or warehousing:
 (A) Any vaccine containing diphtheria toxoid.
 (B) Any vaccine containing tetanus toxoid.
 (C) Any vaccine containing pertussis bacteria, extracted or partial cell bacteria, or specific pertussis antigens.
 (D) Any vaccine against measles.
 (E) Any vaccine against mumps.
 (F) Any vaccine against rubella.
 (G) Any vaccine containing polio virus.
 (H) Any HIB vaccine.
 (I) Any vaccine against hepatitis A.
 (J) Any vaccine against hepatitis B.
 (K) Any vaccine against chicken pox.
 (L) Any vaccine against rotavirus gastroenteritis.
 (M) Any conjugate vaccine against streptococcus pneumoniae.
 (N) Any trivalent vaccine against influenza.
 (O) Any meningococcal vaccine.
 (P) Any vaccine against the human papillomavirus.
(2) Vaccine. The term "vaccine" means any substance designed to be administered to a human being for the prevention of 1 or more diseases.
(3) United States. The term "United States" has the meaning given such term by section 4612(a)(4).
(4) Importer. The term "importer" means the person entering the vaccine for consumption, use, or warehousing.
(b) Credit or refund where vaccine returned to manufacturer, etc., or destroyed.
(1) In general. Under regulations prescribed by the Secretary, whenever any vaccine on which tax was imposed by section 4131 is—
 (A) returned (other than for resale) to the person who paid such tax, or
 (B) destroyed,
the Secretary shall abate such tax or allow a credit, or pay a refund (without interest), to such person equal to the tax paid under section 4131 with respect to such vaccine.
(2) Claim must be filed within 6 months. Paragraph (1) shall apply to any returned or destroyed vaccine only with respect to claims filed within 6 months after the date the vaccine is returned or destroyed.
(3) Condition of allowance of credit or refund. No credit or refund shall be allowed or made under paragraph (1) with respect to any vaccine unless the person who paid the tax establishes that he—
 (A) has repaid or agreed to repay the amount of the tax to the ultimate purchaser of the vaccine, or
 (B) has obtained the written consent of such purchaser to the allowance of the credit or the making of the refund.
(4) Tax imposed only once. No tax shall be imposed by section 4131 on the sale of any vaccine if tax was imposed by section 4131 on any prior sale of such vaccine and such tax is not abated, credited, or refunded.
(c) Other special rules.
(1) Certain uses treated as sales. Any manufacturer, producer, or importer of a vaccine which uses such vaccine before it is sold shall be liable for the tax imposed by section 4131 in the same manner as if such vaccine were sold by such manufacturer, producer, or importer.

3,231

Code Sec. 4132(c)(2)   **Excise and miscellaneous taxes**

(2) Treatment of vaccines shipped to United States possessions. Section 4221(a)(2) shall not apply to any vaccine shipped to a possession of the United States.

(3) Fractional part of a dose. In the case of a fraction of a dose, the tax imposed by section 4131 shall be the same fraction of the amount of such tax imposed by a whole dose.

(4) Disposition of revenues from Puerto Rico and the Virgin Islands. The provisions of subsections (a)(3) and (b)(3) of section 7652 shall not apply to any tax imposed by section 4131.

In 2006, P.L. 109-432, Sec. 408(a), added subpara. (a)(1)(O) ... Sec. 408(b), added subpara. (a)(1)(P), effective for sales and uses on or after the first day of the first month which begins more than 4 weeks after 12/20/2006, except as provided in Sec. 408(c)(2) of this Act, which reads as follows:

"(2) Deliveries. For purposes of paragraph (1) and section 4131 of the Internal Revenue Code of 1986, in the case of sales on or before the effective date described in such paragraph for which delivery is made after such date, the delivery date shall be considered the sale date."

In 2004, P.L. 108-357, Sec. 889(a), redesignated subparas. (a)(1)(J)-(L) as subparas. (a)(1)(J)-(M), and added subpara. (a)(1)(I), effective as provided in Sec. 889(b) of this Act, which reads as follows:

"(b) Effective date.

"(1) Sales, etc. The amendments made by subsection (a) shall apply to sales and uses on or after the first day of the first month which begins more than 4 weeks after the date of the enactment of this Act.

"(2) Deliveries. For purposes of paragraph (1) and section 4131 of the Internal Revenue Code of 1986, in the case of sales on or before the effective date described in such paragraph for which delivery is made after such date, the delivery date shall be considered the sale date."

—P.L. 108-357, Sec. 890(a), added subpara. (a)(1)(N), effective as provided in Sec. 890(b) of this Act, which reads as follows:

"(b) Effective date.

"(1) Sales, etc. The amendment made by this section shall apply to sales and uses on or after the later of—

"(A) the first day of the first month which begins more than 4 weeks after the date of the enactment of this Act, or

"(B) the date on which the Secretary of Health and Human Services lists any vaccine against influenza for purposes of compensation for any vaccine-related injury or death through the Vaccine Injury Compensation Trust Fund.

"(2) Deliveries. For purposes of paragraph (1) and section 4131 of the Internal Revenue Code of 1986, in the case of sales on or before the effective date described in such paragraph for which delivery is made after such date, the delivery date shall be considered the sale date."

In 1999, P.L. 106-170, Sec. 523(a)(1), added subpara. (a)(1)(L), effective as provided by Sec. 523(a)(2), of this Act, which reads as follows:

"(2) Effective date.

"(A) Sales. The amendment made by this subsection shall apply to vaccine sales after the date of the enactment of this Act, but shall not take effect if subsection (b) does not take effect.

"(B) Deliveries. For purposes of subparagraph (A), in the case of sales on or before the date described in such subparagraph for which delivery is made after such date, the delivery date shall be considered the sale date."

—P.L. 106-170, Sec. 523(b)(1), repealed Sec. 1503 of P.L. 105-277 [see below].

In 1998, P.L. 105-277, Sec. 1503(a), [duplication of Sec. 3002(a), of this Act, see below, and repealed by Sec. 523(b)(1) of P.L. 106-170, see above] added subpara. (a)(1)(K), effective as provided by Sec. 1503(b), of this Act, which reads as follows:

"(b) Effective date.

"(1) Sales. The amendment made by this section shall apply to sales after the date of the enactment of this Act.

"(2) Deliveries. For purposes of paragraph (1), in the case of sales on or before the date of the enactment of this Act for which delivery is made after such date, the delivery date shall be considered the sale date."

—P.L. 105-277, Sec. 3002(a), added subpara. (a)(1)(K), effective as provided by Sec. 3002(b), of this Act, which reads as follows:

"(b) Effective date.

"(1) Sales. The amendment made by this section shall apply to sales after the date of the enactment of this Act.

"(2) Deliveries. For purposes of paragraph (1), in the case of sales on or before the date of the enactment of this Act for which delivery is made after such date, the delivery date shall be considered the sale date."

In 1997, P.L. 105-34, Sec. 904(b), amended para. (a)(1) ... Sec. 904(c), deleted paras. (a)(2)-(5) and redesignated paras. (a)(6)-(8) as paras. (a)(2)-(4), effective on the day after 8/5/97.

Prior to amendment, para. (a)(1) read as follows:

"(1) Taxable vaccine. The term 'taxable vaccine' means any vaccine—

"(A) which is listed in the table contained in section 4131(b)(1), and

"(B) which is manufactured or produced in the United States or entered into the United States for consumption, use, or warehousing."

Prior to deletion, paras. (a)(2)-(5) read as follows:

"(2) DPT vaccine. The term 'DPT vaccine' means any vaccine containing pertussis bacteria, extracted or partial cell bacteria, or specific pertussis antigens.

"(3) DT vaccine. The term 'DT vaccine' means any vaccine (other than a DPT vaccine) containing diphtheria toxoid or tetanus toxoid.

"(4) MMR vaccine. The term 'MMR vaccine' means any vaccine against measles, mumps, or rubella. Not more than 1 tax shall be imposed by section 4131 on any MMR vaccine by reason of being a vaccine against more than 1 of measles, mumps, or rubella.

"(5) Polio vaccine. The term 'polio vaccine' means any vaccine containing polio virus."

—P.L. 105-34, Sec. 904(e), of this Act provides:

"(e) Limitation on certain credits or refunds.

"For purposes of applying section 4131(b) of the Internal Revenue Code of 1986 with respect to any claim for credit or refund file before January 1, 1999, the amount of tax taken into account shall not exceed the tax computed under the rate in effect on the day after the date of the enactment [8/5/97] of this Act."

In 1988, P.L. 100-647, Sec. 2006(a), redesignated paras. (c)(1) and (2), as paras. (c)(3) and (4) and added new paras. (c)(1) and (2), effective 1/1/88.

In 1987, P.L. 100-203, Sec. 9201(a), added Code Sec. 4132, effective 1/1/88.

Subchapter D.—Recreational Equipment

Part

I. Sporting goods.

III. Firearms.

In 1965, deleted Part II. Photographic equipment.

PART I.—SPORTING GOODS

Sec.

4161. Imposition of tax.

4162. Definitions; treatment of certain resales.

In 1984, P.L. 98-369, Sec. 1015(d), added item 4162.

Sec. 4161. Imposition of tax.

(a) Sport fishing equipment.

(1) Imposition of tax.

(A) In general. There is hereby imposed on the sale of any article of sport fishing equipment by the manufacturer, producer, or importer a tax equal to 10 percent of the price for which so sold.

(B) Limitation on tax imposed on fishing rods and poles. The tax imposed by subparagraph (A) on any fishing rod or pole shall not exceed $10.

(2) 3 Percent rate of tax for electric outboard motors. In the case of an electric outboard motor, paragraph (1) shall be applied by substituting "3 percent" for "10 percent".

(3) 3 percent rate of tax for tackle boxes. In the case of fishing tackle boxes, paragraph (1) shall be applied by substituting "3 percent" for "10 percent".

(4) Parts or accessories sold in connection with taxable sale. In the case of any sale by the manufacturer, producer, or importer of any article of sport fishing equipment, such article shall be treated as including any parts or accessories of such article sold on or in connection therewith or with the sale thereof.

(b) Bows and arrows, etc.

(1) Bows.

(A) In general. There is hereby imposed on the sale by the manufacturer, producer, or importer of any bow which has a peak draw weight of 30 pounds or more, a tax equal to 11 percent of the price for which so sold.

(B) Archery equipment. There is hereby imposed on the sale by the manufacturer, producer, or importer—

(i) of any part or accessory suitable for inclusion in or attachment to a bow described in subparagraph (A), and

(ii) of any quiver, broadhead, or point suitable for use with an arrow described in paragraph (2), a tax equal to 11 percent of the price for which so sold.

(2) Arrows.

(A) In general. There is hereby imposed on the first sale by the manufacturer, producer, or importer of any shaft (whether sold separately or incorporated as part of a finished or unfinished product) of a type used in the manufacture of any arrow which after its assembly—

(i) measures 18 inches overall or more in length, or

(ii) measures less than 18 inches overall in length but is suitable for use with a bow described in paragraph (1)(A),

a tax equal to 39 cents per shaft.

(B) Exemption for certain wooden arrow shafts. Subparagraph (A) shall not apply to any shaft consisting of all natural wood with no laminations or artificial means of enhancing the spine of such shaft (whether sold separately or incorporated as part of a finished or unfinished product) of a type used in the manufacture of any arrow which after its assembly—

(i) measures 5/16 of an inch or less in diameter, and

(ii) is not suitable for use with a bow described in paragraph (1)(A).

(C) Adjustment for inflation.

(i) In general. In the case of any calendar year beginning after 2005, the 39-cent amount specified in subparagraph (A) shall be increased by an amount equal to the product of—

(I) such amount, multiplied by

(II) the cost-of-living adjustment determined under section 1(f)(3) for such calendar year, determined by substituting "2004" for "1992" in subparagraph (B) thereof.

(ii) Rounding. If any increase determined under clause (i) is not a multiple of 1 cent, such increase shall be rounded to the nearest multiple of 1 cent.

(3) Coordination with subsection (a). No tax shall be imposed under this subsection with respect to any article taxable under subsection (a).

In **2008**, P.L. 110-343, Sec. 503(a)DivC, redesignated subpara. (b)(2)(B) as subpara. (b)(2)(C) and added new subpara. (b)(2)(B), effective for shafts first sold after 10/3/2008.

In **2005**, P.L. 109-135, Sec. 412(uu), amended para. (a)(2), effective 12/21/2005.
Prior to amendment, para. (a)(2) read as follows:
"(2) 3 percent rate of tax for electric outboard motors and sonar devices suitable for finding fish.
"(A) In general. In the case of an electric outboard motor or a sonar device suitable for finding fish, paragraph shall be applied by substituting '3 percent' for '10 percent'.
"(B) $30 limitation on tax imposed on sonar devices suitable for finding fish. The tax imposed by paragraph (1)(A) on any sonar device suitable for finding fish shall not exceed $30."
— P.L. 109-59, Sec. 11117(a), amended para. (a)(1) . . . Sec. 11117(b), substituted "paragraph (1)(A)" for "paragraph (1)" each place it appeared in para. (a)(2), effective for articles sold by the manufacturer, producer, or importer after 9/30/2005.
Prior to amendment, para. (a)(1) read as follows:
"(1) Imposition of tax. There is hereby imposed on the sale of any article of sport fishing equipment by the manufacturer, producer, or importer a tax equal to 10 percent of the price for which so sold."

In **2004**, P.L. 108-493, Sec. 1(a), deleted para. (b)(3) and redesignated para. (b)(4) as (b)(3) as part of the repeal of subsection (b) of section 332 of the American Jobs Creation Act of 2004, P.L. 108-357, see below, effective 12/23/2004.
Prior to deletion, para. (b)(3) read as follows:
"(3) Arrows.
"(A) In general. There is hereby imposed on the sale by the manufacturer, producer, or importer of any arrow, a tax equal to 12 percent of the price for which so sold.
"(B) Exception. In the case of any arrow of which the shaft or any other component has been previously taxed under paragraph (1) or (2)—
"(i) section 6416(b)(3) shall not apply, and
"(ii) the tax imposed by subparagraph (A) shall be an amount equal to the excess (if any) of—
"(I) the amount of tax imposed by this paragraph (determined without regard to this subparagraph), over

"(II) the amount of tax paid with respect to the tax imposed under paragraph (1) or (2) on such shaft or component.
"(C) Arrow. For purposes of this paragraph, the term 'arrow' means any shaft described in paragraph (2) to which additional components are attached."
— P.L. 108-493, Sec. 1(b), amended para. (b)(2) . . . Sec. 1(c), substituted "quiver, broadhead, or point" for "quiver or broadhead" in clause (b)(1)(B)(ii), effective for articles sold by the manufacturer, producer, or importer after 3/31/2005.
Prior to amendment, para. (b)(2) read as follows:
"(2) Arrow components. There is hereby imposed on the sale by the manufacturer, producer, or importer of any shaft, point (other than broadheads), nock, or vane of a type used in the manufacture of any arrow which after its assembly—
"(A) measures 18 inches overall or more in length, or
"(B) measures less than 18 inches overall in length but is suitable for use with a bow described in paragraph (1)(A),
"a tax equal to 12.4 percent of the price for which so sold."
— P.L. 108-357, Sec. 332(a), amended para. (b)(1) . . . Sec. 332(b), redesignated para. (b)(3) as (b)(4) and added para. (b)(3) [prior to repeal of Sec. 332(b) by Sec. 1(a) of P.L. 108-493, see above] . . . Sec. 332(c)(1), added "(other than broadheads)" after "point" in para. (b)(2) . . . Sec. 332(c)(2), substituted "Arrow components." for "Arrows." in the heading of para. (b)(2), effective for articles sold by the manufacturer, producer, or importer after the date which is 30 days after 10/22/2004.
Prior to amendment, para. (b)(1) read as follows:
"(1) Bows.
"(A) In general. There is hereby imposed on the sale by the manufacturer, producer, or importer of any bow which has a draw weight of 10 pounds or more, a tax equal to 11 percent of the price for which so sold.
"(B) Parts and accessories. There is hereby imposed upon the sale by the manufacturer, producer, or importer—
"(i) of any part of accessory suitable for inclusion in or attachment to a bow described in subparagraph (A), and
"(ii) of any quiver suitable for use with arrows described in paragraph (2), a tax equivalent to 11 percent of the price for which so sold."
— P.L. 108-357, Sec. 333(a), redesignated para. (a)(3) as (a)(4) and added para. (a)(3), effective for articles sold by the manufacturer, producer, or importer after 12/31/2004.

In **1997**, P.L. 105-34, Sec. 1433(a), amended subsec. (b), effective for articles sold by the manufacturer, producer, or importer after 9/30/97.
Prior to amendment, subsec. (b) read as follows:
"(b) Bows and arrows, etc.
"(1) Bows and arrows.
"There is hereby imposed on the sale by the manufacturer, producer, or importer—
"(A) of any bow which has a draw weight of 10 pounds or more, and
"(B) of any arrow which—
"(i) measures 18 inches overall or more in length, or
"(ii) measures less than 18 inches overall in length but is suitable for use with a bow described in subparagraph (A),
a tax equal to 11 percent of the price for which so sold.
"(2) Parts and accessories.
"There is hereby imposed upon the sale by the manufacturer, producer, or importer—
"(A) of any part or accessory suitable for inclusion in or attachment to a bow or arrow described in paragraph (1), and
"(B) of any quiver suitable for use with arrows described in paragraph (1), a tax equivalent to 11 percent of the price for which so sold.
"(3) Coordination with subsection (a).
"No tax shall be imposed under this subsection with respect to any article taxable under subsection (a)."

In **1986**, P.L. 99-514, Sec. 1899A(48), substituted a comma for the period at the end of clause (b)(1)(B)(ii), effective 10/22/86.

In **1984**, P.L. 98-369, Sec. 1015(a), amended subsec. (a) . . . Sec. 1017(a), amended para. (b)(1) . . . Sec. 1017(b)(1), added para. (b)(3) . . . Sec. 1017(b)(2), deleted "(other than a fishing reel)" after "part or accessory" in para. (b)(2), effective for articles sold by the manufacturer, producer, or importer after 9/30/84.
Prior to amendment, subsec. (a) read as follows:
"(a) Rods, creels, etc.
"There is hereby imposed upon the sale of fishing rods, creels, reels, and artificial lures, baits, and flies (including parts or accessories of such articles sold on or in connection therewith, or with the sale thereof) by the manufacturer, producer, or importer a tax equivalent to 10 percent of the price for which so sold."
Prior to amendment, para. (b)(1) read as follows:
"(1) Bows and arrows. There is hereby imposed upon the sale by the manufacturer, producer, or importer—
"(A) of any bow which has a draw weight of 10 pounds or more, and
"(B) of any arrow which measures 18 inches overall or more in length,
a tax equivalent to 11 percent of the price for which so sold."

In **1974**, P.L. 93-313, amended the effective date for changes made by Sec. 201 of P.L. 92-558 (see below) from 7/1/74 to 1/1/75.

In **1972**, P.L. 92-558, Sec. 201(a)(1), added "(a) Rods, creels, etc." after the heading of Code Sec. 4161. . . . Sec. 201(a)(2), added subsec. (b), effective [as amended by P.L. 93-313, see above] for articles sold by the manufacturer, producer, or importer thereof on or after 1/1/75.

In **1965**, P.L. 89-44, Sec. 205(a), amended Code Sec. 4161, effective 6/22/65.
Prior to amendment, Code Sec. 4161 read as follows:

Code Sec. 4161 — Excise and miscellaneous taxes

"There is hereby imposed upon the sale by the manufacturer, producer, or importer of the following articles (including in each case parts or accessories of such articles sold on or in connection therewith, or with the sale thereof) a tax equivalent to 10 percent of the price for which so sold:

"Badminton nets, rackets and racket frames (measuring 22 inches overall or more in length), racket string, shuttlecocks, and standards.

"Billiard and pool tables (measuring 45 inches overall or more in length) and balls and cues for such tables.

"Bowling balls and pins.

"Clay pigeons and traps for throwing clay pigeons.

"Cricket balls and bats.

"Croquet balls and mallets.

"Curling stones.

"Deck tennis rings, nets and posts.

"Fishing rods, creels, reels and artificial lures, baits and flies.

"Golf bags (measuring 26 inches or more in length), balls and clubs (measuring 30 inches or more in length).

"Lacrosse balls and sticks.

"Polo balls and mallets.

"Skis, ski poles, snowshoes, and snow toboggans and sleds (measuring more than 60 inches overall in length).

"Squash balls, rackets and racket frames (measuring 22 inches overall or more in length), and racket string.

"Table tennis tables, balls, nets and paddles.

"Tennis balls, nets, rackets and racket frames (measuring 22 inches overall or more in length) and racket string."

Sec. 4162. Definitions; treatment of certain resales.
(a) Sport fishing equipment defined.

For purposes of this part, the term "sport fishing equipment" means—

(1) fishing rods and poles (and component parts therefor),

(2) fishing reels,

(3) fly fishing lines, and other fishing lines not over 130 pounds test,

(4) fishing spears, spear guns, and spear tips,

(5) items of terminal tackle, including—

  (A) leaders,
  (B) artificial lures,
  (C) artificial baits,
  (D) artificial flies,
  (E) fishing hooks,
  (F) bobbers,
  (G) sinkers,
  (H) snaps,
  (I) drayles, and
  (J) swivels,

but not including natural bait or any item of terminal tackle designed for use and ordinarily used on fishing lines not described in paragraph (3), and

(6) the following items of fishing supplies and accessories—

  (A) fish stringers,
  (B) creels,
  (C) tackle boxes,
  (D) bags, baskets, and other containers designed to hold fish,
  (E) portable bait containers,
  (F) fishing vests,
  (G) landing nets,
  (H) gaff hooks,
  (I) fishing hook disgorgers, and
  (J) dressing for fishing lines and artificial flies,

(7) fishing tip-ups and tilts,

(8) fishing rod belts, fishing rodholders, fishing harnesses, fish fighting chairs, fishing outriggers, and fishing downriggers, and

(9) electric outboard boat motors.

(b) Treatment of certain resales.

(1) In general. If—

  (A) the manufacturer, producer, or importer sells any article taxable under section 4161(a) to any person,

  (B) the constructive sale price rules of section 4216(b) do not apply to such sale, and

  (C) such person (or any other person) sells such article to a related person with respect to the manufacturer, producer, or importer,

then such related person shall be liable for tax under section 4161 in the same manner as if such related person were the manufacturer of the article.

(2) Credit for tax previously paid. If—

  (A) tax is imposed on the sale of any article by reason of paragraph (1), and

  (B) the related person establishes the amount of the tax which was paid on the sale described in paragraph (1)(A),

the amount of the tax so paid shall be allowed as a credit against the tax imposed by reason of paragraph (1).

(3) Related person. For purposes of this subsection, the term "related person" has the meaning given such term by section 465(b)(3)(C).

(4) Regulations. Except to the extent provided in regulations, rules similar to the rules of this subsection shall also apply in cases (not described in paragraph (1)) in which intermediaries or other devices are used for purposes of reducing the amount of the tax imposed by section 4161(a).

In 2004, P.L. 108-357, Sec. 334(a), added "and" at the end of para. (a)(8), substituted a period for ", and" at the end of para. (a)(9), and deleted para. (a)(10) . . . Sec. 334(b), deleted subsec. (b) and redesignated subsec. (c) as (b), effective for articles sold by the manufacturer, producer, or importer after 12/31/2004.

Prior to deletion, para. (a)(10) read as follows:

"(10) sonar devices suitable for finding fish."

Prior to deletion, subsec. (b) read as follows:

"(b) Sonar device suitable for finding fish.

"For purposes of this part, the term 'sonar device suitable for finding fish' shall not include any sonar device which is—

"(1) a graph recorder,
"(2) a digital type,
"(3) a meter readout, or
"(4) a combination graph recorder or combination meter readout."

In 1988, P.L. 100-647, Sec. 1002(c)(3), provides:

"Notwithstanding section 203 of the Reform Act, the amendments made by section 201 of the Reform Act shall apply to any real property which was acquired before January 1, 1987, and was converted on or after such date from personal use to a use for which depreciation is allowable."

In 1986, P.L. 99-514, Sec. 201(d)(7)(C), substituted "section 465(b)(3)(C)" for "section 168(e)(4)(D)" in para. (c)(3). . . . Sec. 201(d)(12), substituted "section 465(b)(3)(C)" for "section 168(e)(4)(D)" in para. (c)(3) [Same amendment as Sec. 201(d)(7)(C), see above.], effective for property placed in service after 12/31/86, in taxable years ending after 12/31/86. [see Sec. 1002(c)(3) of P.L. 100-647, above]. For transitional rules, see Sec. 203(b)-(e) of this Act reproduced in note following Code Sec. 168. Sec. 203(a)(1)(B) of this Act provices as follows:

"(B) Election to have amendments under section 201 apply. A taxpayer may elect (at such time and in such manner as the Secretary of the Treasury or his delegate may prescribe) to have the amendments made by section 201 apply to any property placed in service after July 31, 1986, and before January 1, 1987."

—P.L. 99-514, Sec. 1878(b), substituted "hook" for "hood" in subpara. (a)(6)(I), effective for articles sold by the manufacturer, producer, or importer after 9/30/84.

In 1984, P.L. 98-369, Sec. 1015(b), added Code Sec. 4162, for articles sold by the manufacturer, producer, or importer after 9/30/84. Sec. 1015(e)(2) of this Act provides as follows:

"(2) Treatment of certain resales.—Subsection (c) of section 4162 of the Internal Revenue Code of 1954 (relating to treatment of certain resales), as added by this section, shall apply to sales by related persons (as defined in such subsection) after the date of the enactment of this Act."

PART III.—FIREARMS

Sec.
4181. Imposition of tax.
4182. Exemptions.

Sec. 4181. Imposition of tax.

There is hereby imposed upon the sale by the manufacturer, producer, or importer of the following articles a tax equivalent to the specified percent of the price for which so sold:

Articles taxable at 10 percent—
Pistols.
Revolvers.
Articles taxable at 11 percent—
Firearms (other than pistols and revolvers).
Shells, and cartridges.

Sec. 4182. Exemptions.
(a) Machine guns and short barrelled firearms.
The tax imposed by section 4181 shall not apply to any firearm on which the tax provided by section 5811 has been paid.
(b) Sales to Defense Department.
No firearms, pistols, revolvers, shells, and cartridges purchased with funds appropriated for the military department shall be subject to any tax imposed on the sale or transfer of such articles.
(c) Small manufacturers, etc.
  (1) In general. The tax imposed by section 4181 shall not apply to any pistol, revolver, or firearm described in such section if manufactured, produced, or imported by a person who manufactures, produces, and imports less than an aggregate of 50 of such articles during the calendar year.
  (2) Controlled groups. All persons treated as a single employer for purposes of subsection (a) or (b) of section 52 shall be treated as one person for purposes of paragraph (1).
(d) Records.
Notwithstanding the provisions of sections 922(b)(5) and 923(g) of title 18, United States Code, no person holding a Federal license under chapter 44 of title 18, United States Code, shall be required to record the name, address, or other information about the purchaser of shotgun ammunition, ammunition suitable for use only in rifles generally available in commerce, or component parts for the aforesaid types of ammunition.

In **2005**, P.L. 109-59, Sec. 11131(a), redesignated subsec. (c) as (d), and added subsec. (c), effective for articles sold by the manufacturer, producer, or importer after 9/30/2005. Sec. 11131(b)(2) of this Act, reads as follows:
"(2) No inference. Nothing in the amendments made by this section shall be construed to create any inference with respect to the proper tax treatment of any sales before the effective date of such amendments."
In **1969**, P.L. 91-128, Sec. 5, added subsec. (c), effective 11/26/69.

Subchapter E.—Medical Devices
Sec.
4191. Medical Devices. [effective for sales after 12/31/2012]

In **2010**, P.L. 111-152, Sec. 1405(a)(1), Added Subchapter E.

• **Caution:** Code Sec. 4191, following, is effective for sales after 12/31/2012.

Sec. 4191. Medical devices.
(a) In general.
There is hereby imposed on the sale of any taxable medical device by the manufacturer, producer, or importer a tax equal to 2.3 percent of the price for which so sold.
(b) Taxable medical device.
For purposes of this section—
  (1) In general. The term "taxable medical device" means any device (as defined in section 201(h) of the Federal Food, Drug, and Cosmetic Act) intended for humans.
  (2) Exemptions. Such term shall not include—
    (A) eyeglasses,
    (B) contact lenses,
    (C) hearing aids, and
    (D) any other medical device determined by the Secretary to be of a type which is generally purchased by the general public at retail for individual use.

In **2010**, P.L. 111-152, Sec. 1405(a)(1), added Code Sec. 4191, effective for sales after 12/31/2012.

Subchapter F.—Special Provisions Applicable to Manufacturers Tax
Sec.
4216. Definition of price.
4217. Leases.
4218. Use by manufacturer or importer considered sale.
4219. Application of tax in case of sales by other than manufacturer or importer.

In **1958**, substituted "Leases" for "Lease considered sale" in item 4217, and struck out items 4220–4227 most of which became part of new subchapter G.
In **1956**, redesignated item "4226" as item "4227" and added item "4226. Floor stock taxes."

Sec. 4216. Definition of price.
(a) Containers, packing and transportation charges.
In determining, for the purposes of this chapter, the price for which an article is sold, there shall be included any charge for coverings and containers of whatever nature, and any charge incident to placing the article in condition packed ready for shipment, but there shall be excluded the amount of tax imposed by this chapter, whether or not stated as a separate charge. A transportation, delivery, insurance, installation, or other charge (not required by the foregoing sentence to be included) shall be excluded from the price only if the amount thereof is established to the satisfaction of the Secretary in accordance with the regulations.
(b) Constructive sale price.
  (1) In general. If an article is—
    (A) sold at retail,
    (B) sold on consignment, or
    (C) sold (otherwise than through an arm's length transaction) at less than the fair market price,
  the tax under this chapter shall (if based on the price for which the article is sold) be computed on the price for which such articles are sold, in the ordinary course of trade, by manufacturers or producers thereof, as determined by the Secretary. In the case of an article sold at retail, the computation under the preceding sentence shall be on whichever of the following prices is the lower: (i) the price for which such article is sold, or (ii) the highest price for which such articles are sold to wholesale distributors, in the ordinary course of trade, by manufacturers or producers thereof, as determined by the Secretary. This paragraph shall not apply if paragraph (2) applies.
  (2) Special rule. If an article is sold at retail or to a retailer, and if—
    (A) the manufacturer, producer, or importer of such article regularly sells such articles at retail or to retailers, as the case may be,
    (B) the manufacturer, producer, or importer of such article regularly sells such articles to one or more wholesale distributors in arm's length transactions and he establishes that his prices in such cases are determined

without regard to any tax benefit under this paragraph, and

(C) the transaction is an arm's length transaction, the tax under this chapter shall (if based on the price for which the article is sold) be computed on whichever of the following prices is the lower: (i) the price for which such article is sold, or (ii) the highest price for which such articles are sold by such manufacturer, producer, or importer to wholesale distributors.

(3) Constructive sale price in case of certain articles. Except as provided in paragraph (4), for purposes of paragraph (1), if—

(A) the manufacturer, producer, or importer of an article regularly sells such article to a distributor which is a member of the same affiliated group of corporations (as defined in section 1504(a)) as the manufacturer, producer, or importer, and

(B) such distributor regularly sells such article to one or more independent retailers, but does not regularly sell to wholesale distributors,

the constructive sale price of such article shall be 90 percent of the lowest price for which such distributor regularly sells such article in arm's-length transactions to such independent retailers. The price determined under this paragraph shall not be adjusted for any exclusion (except for the tax imposed on such article) or readjustments under subsections (a) and (e) and under section 6416(b)(1). If both this paragraph and paragraph (4) apply with respect to an article, the constructive sale price for such article shall be the lower of the constructive sale price determined under this paragraph or paragraph (4).

(4) Constructive sale price in case of certain other articles. For purposes of paragraph (1), if—

(A) the manufacturer, producer, or importer of an article regularly sells (except for tax-free sales) only to a distributor which is a member of the same affiliated group of corporations (as defined in section 1504(a)) as the manufacturer, producer, or importer,

(B) the distributor regularly sells (except for tax-free sales) such article only to retailers, and

(C) the normal method of sales for such articles within the industry by manufacturers, producers, or importers is to sell such articles in arm's-length transactions to distributors,

the constructive sale price for such article shall be the price at which such article is sold to retailers by the distributor, reduced by a percentage of such price equal to the percentage which (i) the difference between the price for which comparable articles are sold to wholesale distributors, in the ordinary course of trade, by manufacturers or producers thereof, and the price at which such wholesale distributors in arm's-length transactions sell such comparable articles to retailers, is of (ii) the price at which such wholesale distributors in arm's-length transactions sell such comparable articles to retailers. The price determined under this paragraph shall not be adjusted for any exclusion (except for the tax imposed on such article) or readjustment under subsections (a) and (e) and under section 6416(b)(1).

(5) Definition of lowest price. For purposes of paragraphs (1) and (3) the lowest price shall be determined—

(A) without requiring that any given percentage of sales be made at that price, and

(B) without including any fixed amount to which the purchaser has a right as a result of contractual arrangements existing at the time of the sale.

(c) Partial payments.
In the case of—

(1) a lease (other than a lease to which section 4217(b) applies),

(2) a contract for the sale of an article wherein it is provided that the price shall be paid by installments and title to the article sold does not pass until a future date notwithstanding partial payment by installments,

(3) a conditional sale, or

(4) a chattel mortgage arrangement wherein it is provided that the sales price shall be paid in installments,

there shall be paid upon each payment with respect to the article a percentage of such payment equal to the rate of tax in effect on the date such payment is due.

(d) Sales of installment accounts.
If installment accounts, with respect to payments on which tax is being computed as provided in subsection (c), are sold or otherwise disposed of, then subsection (c) shall not apply with respect to any subsequent payments on such accounts (other than subsequent payments on returned accounts with respect to which credit or refund is allowable by reason of section 6416(b)(5)), but instead—

(1) there shall be paid an amount equal to the difference between (A) the tax previously paid on the payments on such installment accounts, and (B) the total tax which would be payable if such installment accounts had not been sold or otherwise disposed of (computed as provided in subsection (c)); except that

(2) if any such sale is pursuant to the order of, or subject to the approval of, a court of competent jurisdiction in a bankruptcy or insolvency proceeding, the amount computed under paragraph (1) shall not exceed the sum of the amounts computed by multiplying (A) the proportionate share of the amount for which such accounts are sold which is allocable to each unpaid installment payment by (B) the rate of tax under this chapter in effect on the date such unpaid installment payment is or was due.

The sum of the amounts payable under this subsection and subsection (c) in respect of the sale of any article shall not exceed the total tax.

(e) Exclusion of local advertising charge from sale price.

(1) Exclusion. In determining, for purposes of this chapter, the price for which an article is sold, there shall be excluded a charge for local advertising (as defined in paragraph (4)) to the extent that such charge—

(A) does not exceed 5 percent of the price for which the article is sold (as determined under this section by excluding any charge for local advertising),

(B) is a separate charge made when the article is sold, and

(C) is intended to be refunded to the purchaser or any subsequent vendee in reimbursement of costs incurred for local advertising.

In the case of any such charge (or portion thereof) which is not so refunded before the first day of the fifth calendar month following the calendar year during which the article was sold, the exclusion provided by the preceding sentence shall cease to apply as of such first day.

(2) Aggregate amount which may be excluded. In the case of articles upon the sale of which tax was imposed under the same section of this chapter—

(A) The sum of (i) the aggregate of the charges for local advertising excluded under paragraph (1), plus (ii) the aggregate of the readjustments for local advertising under section 6416(b)(1) (relating to credits or refunds for price adjustments), shall not exceed

(B) 5 percent of the aggregate of the prices (determined under this section by excluding all charges for local advertising) at which such articles were sold in sales on which tax was imposed by such section of this chapter. The preceding sentence shall be applied to each manufacturer, producer, and importer as of the close of each calendar quarter, taking into account the items specified in subparagraphs (A) and (B) for such calendar quarter and preceding calendar quarters in the same calendar year.

(3) No adjustment for other advertising charges. Except to the extent provided by paragraphs (1) and (2), no charge or expenditure for advertising shall serve, for purposes of this section or section 6416(b)(1), as the basis for an exclusion from, or as a readjustment of, the price of any article.

(4) Local advertising defined. For purposes of this section and section 6416(b)(1), the term "local advertising" means only advertising which—

(A) is initiated or obtained by the purchaser or any subsequent vendee,

(B) names the article for which the price is determinable under this section and states the location at which such article may be purchased at retail, and

(C) is broadcast over a radio station or television station, appears in a newspaper or magazine, or is displayed by means of an outdoor advertising sign or poster.

In 1984, P.L. 98-369, Sec. 735(c)(6)(A)(i), deleted "(other than an article the sale of which is taxable under section 4061(a))" in the second sentence of para. (b)(1) . . . Sec. 735(c)(6)(A)(ii), deleted the third sentence of para. (b)(1) . . . Sec. 735(c)(6)(B), deleted subpara. (b)(2)(C), added "and" at the end of subpara. (b)(2)(B), and redesignated subpara. (b)(2)(D) as subpara. (b)(2)(C) . . . Sec. 735(c)(6)(C), deleted para. (b)(5) . . . Sec. 735(c)(6)(D), substituted "paragraph (4)" for "paragraphs (4) and (5)" in para. (b)(3) . . . Sec. 735(c)(6)(E), redesignated para. (b)(6) as para. (b)(5) and substituted "(1) and (3)" for "(1), (3), and (5)" in para. (b)(6) [as redesignated by Sec. 735(c)(6)(E) of this Act, see above] . . . Sec. 735(c)(6)(F), repealed subsec. (f), effective 1/7/83.

Prior to deletion, the third sentence of para. (b)(1) read as follows:
"In the case of an article the sale of which is taxable under section 4061(a) and which is sold at retail, the computation under the first sentence of this paragraph shall be a percentage (not greater than 100 percent) of the actual selling price based on the highest price for which such articles are sold by manufacturers and producers in the ordinary course of trade (determined without regard to any individual manufacturer's or producer's cost)."

Prior to deletion, subpara. (b)(2)(C) read as follows:
"(C) in the case of articles upon which tax is imposed under section 4061(a) (relating to trucks, buses, tractors, etc.), the normal method of sales for such articles within the industry is not to sell such articles at retail or to retailers, or combinations thereof, and"

Prior to deletion, para. (b)(5) read as follows:
"(5) Constructive sale price in the case of automobiles, trucks, etc. In the case of articles the sale of which is taxable under section 4061(a) (relating to trucks, buses, tractors, etc.), for purposes of paragraph (1), if—

"(A) the manufacturer, producer, or importer of the article regularly sells such article to a distributor which is a member of the same affiliated group of corporations (as defined in section 1504(a)) as the manufacturer, producer, or importer, and

"(B) such distributor regularly sells such article to one or more independent retailers, the constructive sale price of such article shall be 98½ percent of the lowest price for which such distributor regularly sells such article in arm's-length transactions to such independent retailers. The price determined under this paragraph shall not be adjusted for any exclusion (except for the tax imposed on such article) or readjustments under subsections (a) and (e) and under section 6416(b)(1)."

Prior to repeal, subsec. (f) read as follows:
"(f) Certain trucks incorporating used components.
"For purposes of the tax imposed by section 4061(a)(1) (relating to trucks, buses, etc.), in determining the price for which an article is sold, the value of any component of such article shall be excluded from the price, if—
"(1) such component is furnished by the first user of such article, and
"(2) such component has been used prior to such furnishing."

In 1978, P.L. 95-458, Sec. 1(a), added the third sentence to para. (b)(1) . . . Sec. 1(b), added "(other than an article the sale of which is taxable under section 4061(a))" after "sold at retail" in the second sentence of para. (b)(1), effective for articles sold by the manufacturer or producer on or after the first day of the first calendar quarter beginning 30 days or more after 10/14/78.

In 1976, P.L. 94-455, Sec. 1904(a)(2)(A), redesignated subsecs. (e), (f) and (g) as subsecs. (d), (e) and (f) respectively . . . Sec. 1904(a)(2)(B), substituted "subsections (a) and (e)" for "subsections (a) and (f)" each place it appeared in paras. (b)(3), (b)(4) and (b)(5), effective 2/1/77.

—P.L. 94-455, Sec. 1906(b)(13)(A), substituted "Secretary" for "Secretary or his delegate" in subsec. (a) and each place it appeared in subpara. (b)(1)(C), effective 2/1/77.

In 1971, P.L. 92-178, Sec. 401(g)(4)(A), substituted "(relating to trucks, buses, tractors, etc.)" for "(relating to automobiles, trucks, etc.)" in subpara. (b)(2)(C) and para. (b)(5) . . . Sec. 401(g)(4)(B), added "tractors," after "buses," in subsec. (g), effective for articles sold on or after 12/11/71.

In 1970, P.L. 91-614, Sec. 301(a), added paras. (b)(5) and (b)(6), . . . Sec. 301(b)(1), substituted "paragraphs (4) and (5)" for "paragraph (4)" in the first sentence of para. (b)(3) . . . Sec. 301(b)(2)(A), substituted "Constructive sale price" for "fair market price" in the heading of paras. (b)(3) and (b)(4) . . . Sec. 301(b)(2)(B), substituted "constructive sale price" for "fair market price" each place it appeared in paras. (b)(3) and (b)(4) . . . Sec. 301(b)(2)(C), substituted "paragraph (1)" for "paragraph (1)(C)" in paras. (b)(3) and (b)(4), effective as provided in Sec. 301(c) of this Act, which reads as follows:

"(c) Effective date. The amendments made by this section shall apply with respect to articles sold after December 31, 1970; except that section 4216(b)(6) of the Internal Revenue Code of 1954 (as added by subsection (a)) shall also apply to (1) the application of paragraph (1) of such section 4216(b) to articles sold after June 30, 1962, and before January 1, 1971, and (2) the application of paragraph (3) of such section 4216(b) to articles sold after December 31, 1969, and before January 1, 1971."

In 1969, P.L. 91-172, Sec. 932(a), added paras. (b)(3) and (b)(4), effective for articles sold after 12/31/69.

In 1965, P.L. 89-44, Sec. 207(a), substituted "a percentage of such payment equal to the rate of tax in effect on the date such payment is due" for "that portion of the total tax which is proportionate to the portion of the total amount to be paid represented by such payment." in the material following para. (c)(4) . . . Sec. 207(b)(1), substituted "total tax which would be payable if such installment accounts had not been sold or otherwise disposed of (computed as provided in subsection (c));" for "total tax;" in para. (e)(1) . . . Sec. 207(b)(2), amended para. (e)(2), effective 6/22/65. Sec. 701(a)(3) of this Act provides the following:

"(3) Installment sales, etc.—For purposes of paragraphs (1) and (2), an article shall not be considered sold before the day after the date of the enactment of this Act or before January 1, 1966, as the case may be, unless possession or right to possession passes to the purchaser before such day or such date. In the case of—
"(A) a lease,
"(B) a contract for the sale of an article where it is provided that the price shall be paid by installments and title to the article sold does not pass until a future date notwithstanding partial payment by installments,
"(C) a conditional sale, or
"(D) a chattel mortgage arrangement wherein it is provided that the sale price shall be paid by installments, entered into before such day or such date, payments made on or after such day or such date with respect to the article leased or sold shall, for purposes of this subsection, be considered as payments made with respect to an article sold on or after such day or such date, if the lessor or vendor establishes that the amount of payments payable on or after such day or such date with respect to such article has been reduced by an amount equal to the tax reduction applicable with respect to the lease or sale of such article."

Prior to amendment, para. (e)(2) read as follows:
"(2) if any such sale is pursuant to the order of, or subject to the approval of, a court of competent jurisdiction in a bankruptcy or insolvency proceeding, the amount computed under paragraph (1) shall not exceed the amount computed by multiplying (A) the amount for which such accounts are sold, by (B) the rate of tax under this chapter which applied on the day on which the transaction giving rise to such installment accounts took place."

—P.L. 89-44, Sec. 208(a)(1), amended the material immediately preceding subpara. (b)(2)(A) . . . Sec. 208(a)(2), substituted "or to retailers" for ", to retailers, or to special dealers" in subpara. (b)(2)(A) . . . Sec. 208(a)(3), deleted "(other than special dealers)" each place it appeared in para. (b)(2) . . . Sec. 208(a)(4), deleted "4191 (relating to business machines), or 4211 (relating to matches)", in subpara. (b)(2)(A) . . . Sec. 208(c), deleted para. (b)(3), effective for articles sold on or after 6/21/65. Sec. 701(a)(3) of this Act provides special rules, see above.

Prior to amendment, the material immediately preceding subpara. (b)(2)(A) read as follows:
"If an article is sold at retail, to a retailer, or to a special dealer (as defined in paragraph (3)), then"

Prior to deletion, para. (b)(3) read as follows:
"(3) Special dealer. For purposes of paragraph (2), the term 'special dealer' means a distributor of articles taxable under section 4121 who does not maintain a sales force to resell the article whose constructive price is established under paragraph (2) but relies on salesmen of the manufacturer, producer, or importer of the article for resale of the article to retailers."

—P.L. 89-44, Sec. 801(b), added subsec. (g), effective for articles sold on or after 6/21/65.

In 1962, P.L. 87-858, Sec. 1(a), added "in the case of articles upon which tax is imposed under section 4061(a) (relating to automobiles, trucks, etc.), 4191 (relating to business machines), or 4211 (relating to matches)," before "the normal method" in subpara. (b)(2)(A), effective for articles sold manufacturer, producer, or importer on or after 10/1/62.

—P.L. 87-770, Sec. 2(a), substituted ", appears in a newspaper or magazine, or is displayed by means of an outdoor advertising sign or poster" for "or appears in a newspaper" in clause (f)(4)(C), effective for articles sold on or after the first day of the first calendar quarter beginning more than 20 days after 10/9/62.

Code Sec. 4216   **Excise and miscellaneous taxes**

In **1960**, P.L. 86-781, Sec. 1, added subsec. (f), effective for articles sold on or after the first day of the first calendar quarter more than 20 days after 9/14/60.

In **1958**, P.L. 85-859, Sec. 115, amended subsec. (b)...Sec. 116, added subsec. (e)...Sec. 117(b), deleted subsec. (d), and substituted "section 4217(b)" for "subsection (d)" in subsec. (c), effective on the first day of the first calendar quarter which begins more than 60 days after 9/2/58.

Prior to amendment, subsec. (b) read as follows:

"(b) Constructive Sale Price.—If an article is—
"(1) sold at retail,
"(2) sold on consignment, or
"(3) sold (otherwise than through an arm's length transaction) at less than the fair market price.
the tax under this chapter shall (if based on the price for which the article is sold) be computed on the price for which such articles are sold, in the ordinary course of trade, by manufacturers or producers thereof, as determined by the Secretary or his delegate."

Prior to deletion, subsec. (d) read as follows:

"(d) Leases of Certain Trailers. In the case of any lease of a trailer or semi-trailer taxable under section 4061(a) and suitable for use in connection with passenger automobiles, there shall be paid, at the election of the taxpayer—
"(1) upon the initial lease a tax at the applicable rate specified in section 4061(a) based upon the fair market value on the date of such lease, or
"(2) upon each lease payment with respect to such trailer or semitrailer, a percentage of such payment equal to the rate of tax which would be imposed upon the sale of such trailer or semitrailer, until the total of the tax payments under such lease and any prior lease equals the total tax. In any case where a trailer or semitrailer which has been leased is sold before the total tax has been paid, the tax payable on such sale shall be the difference between the tax paid on the lease payments and the total tax. For purposes of this paragraph, the term 'total tax' means the tax computed, at the rate in effect on the date of the initial lease, on the fair market value on the date of such lease. However, in the case where a trailer or semitrailer which has been leased is sold before the total tax has been paid, the total tax shall not exceed a tax computed, at the rate in effect on the date of the initial lease, on the amount received on such sale (determined without regard to section 4216(b)) plus the total of the payments received by the lessor under any lease of such trailer or a semitrailer."

In **1955**, P.L. 317, Sec. 1, added "(other than a lease to which subsection (d) applies)" after "lease" in para. (c)(1)...Sec. 2, added subsec. (d), effective as provided in Sec. 4 of this Act, which reads as follows:

"Sec. 4. The amendments made by subsection (a) shall take effect on the first day of the first month which begins more than 10 days after the date of the enactment of this Act [8/9/55]. In the application of section 4216(d) of the Internal Revenue Code of 1954 (as added by this Act) to any article which has been leased before the effective date specified in the preceding sentence, under regulations prescribed by the Secretary of the Treasury or his delegate—

"(1) the fair market value of such article shall be the fair market value determined as of such effective date;
"(2) only payments under a lease received on or after such effective date shall be considered in determining when the total tax (as defined in such section 4216(d)) has been paid;
"(3) any lease existing on such effective date, or if there is none, the first lease entered into after such effective date, shall be considered an initial lease (except that fair market value shall be determined as provided in paragraph (1) of this sentence); and
"(4) any lease existing on such effective date shall be considered as having been entered into on such date."

Sec. 4217. Leases.
(a) Lease considered as sale.

For purposes of this chapter, the lease of an article (including any renewal or any extension of a lease or any subsequent lease of such article) by the manufacturer, producer, or importer shall be considered a sale of such article.

(b) Limitation on tax.

In the case of any lease described in subsection (a) of an article taxable under this chapter, if the tax under this chapter is based on the price for which such articles are sold, there shall be paid on each lease payment with respect to such article a percentage of such payment equal to the rate of tax in effect on the date of such payment, until the total of the tax payments under such lease and any prior lease to which this subsection applies equals the total tax.

(c) Definition of total tax.

For purposes of this section, the term "total tax" means—

(1) except as provided in paragraph (2), the tax computed on the constructive sale price for such article which would be determined under section 4216(b) if such article were sold at retail on the date of the first lease to which subsection (b) applies; or

(2) if the first lease to which subsection (b) applies is not the first lease of the article, the tax computed on the fair market value of such article on the date of the first lease to which subsection (b) applies.

Any such computation of tax shall be made at the applicable rate specified in this chapter in effect on the date of the first lease to which subsection (b) applies.

(d) Special rules.

(1) **Lessor must also be engaged in selling.** Subsection (b) shall not apply to any lease of an article unless at the time of making the lease, or any prior lease of such article to which subsection (b) applies, the person making the lease or prior lease was also engaged in the business of selling in arm's length transactions the same type and model of article.

(2) **Sale before total tax becomes payable.** If the taxpayer sells an article before the total tax has become payable, then the tax payable on such sale shall be whichever of the following is the smaller:

(A) the difference between (i) the tax imposed on lease payments under leases of such article to which subsection (b) applies, and (ii) the total tax, or

(B) a tax computed, at the rate in effect on the date of the sale, on the price for which the article is sold.

For purposes of subparagraph (B), if the sale is at arm's length, section 4216(b) shall not apply.

(3) **Sale after total tax has become payable.** If the taxpayer sells an article after the total tax has become payable, no tax shall be imposed under this chapter on such sale.

(e) Leases of automobiles subject to gas guzzler tax.

(1) **In general.** In the case of the lease of an automobile the sale of which by the manufacturer would be taxable under section 4064, the foregoing provisions of this section shall not apply, but, for purposes of this chapter—

(A) the first lease of such automobile by the manufacturer shall be considered to be a sale, and

(B) any lease of such automobile by the manufacturer after the first lease of such automobile shall not be considered to be a sale.

(2) **Payment of tax.** In the case of a lease described in paragraph (1)(A)—

(A) there shall be paid by the manufacturer on each lease payment that portion of the total gas guzzler tax which bears the same ratio to such total gas guzzler tax as such payment bears to the total amount to be paid under such lease,

(B) if such lease is canceled, or the automobile is sold or otherwise disposed of, before the total gas guzzler tax is payable, there shall be paid by the manufacturer on such cancellation, sale, or disposition the difference between the tax imposed under subparagraph (A) on the lease payments and the total gas guzzler tax, and

(C) if the automobile is sold or otherwise disposed of after the total gas guzzler tax is payable, no tax shall be imposed under section 4064 on such sale or disposition.

(3) **Definitions.** For purposes of this subsection—

(A) Manufacturer. The term "manufacturer" includes a producer or importer.

(B) Total gas guzzler tax. The term "total gas guzzler tax" means the tax imposed by section 4064, computed at the rate in effect on the date of the first lease.

In **1978**, P.L. 95-618, Sec. 201(d), added subsec. (e), effective for 1980 and later model year automobiles (as defined in Code Sec. 4064(b)).

In **1976**, P.L. 94-455, Sec. 1904(a)(3), deleted para. (d)(4), effective 2/1/77.

Prior to deletion, para. (d)(4) read as follows:

Excise and miscellaneous taxes   Code Sec. 4218

"(4) Transitional rules. For purposes of this subsection and subsections (b) and (c), in the case of any lease entered into before the effective date of subsection (b) and existing on such date—
"(A) such lease shall be considered as having been entered into on such date;
"(B) the total tax shall be computed on the fair market value of the article on such date; and
"(C) the lease payments under such lease shall include only payments attributable to periods on and after such date."

In **1958**, P.L. 85-859, Sec. 117(a), substituted "Leases" for "Lease considered as sale" in the catchline ... redesignated existing provisions as subsec. (a) and eliminated provisions which made subsection inapplicable to the lease of an article upon which the tax has been paid in the manner provided in section 4216(d)(1) or the total tax has been paid in the manner provided in section 4216(d)(2) of this title ... added subsecs. (b)–(d), effective 1/1/59.
—P.L. 85-859, Sec. 117(a), provided that: "The amendments ... shall not apply to any lease of an article if section 4216(d) of the Internal Revenue Code of 1954 applied to any lease of such article before the effective date specified in section 1(c) of this Act."

In **1955**, ch. 677, Sec. 3, exempted the lease of an article upon which tax has been paid under section 4216(d)(1) or section 4216(d)(2) of this title, effective 9/1/55.

Sec. 4218. Use by manufacturer or importer considered sale.

(a) General rule.

If any person manufactures, produces, or imports an article (other than a tire taxable under section 4071) and uses it (otherwise than as material in the manufacture or production of, or as a component part of, another article taxable under this chapter to be manufactured or produced by him), then he shall be liable for tax under this chapter in the same manner as if such article were sold by him. This subsection shall not apply in the case of gasoline used by any person, for nonfuel purposes, as a material in the manufacture or production of another article to be manufactured or produced by him. For the purpose of applying the first sentence of this subsection to coal taxable under section 4121, the words "(otherwise than as material in the manufacture or production of, or as a component part of, another article taxable under this chapter to be manufactured or produced by him)" shall be disregarded.

(b) Tires.

If any person manufactures, produces, or imports a tire taxable under section 4071, and sells it on or in connection with the sale of any article, or uses it, then he shall be liable for tax under this chapter in the same manner as if such article were sold by him.

(c) Computation of tax.

Except as provided in section 4223(b), in any case in which a person is made liable for tax by the preceding provisions of this section, the tax (if based on the price for which the article is sold) shall be computed on the price at which such or similar articles are sold, in the ordinary course of trade, by manufacturers, producers, or importers, thereof, as determined by the Secretary.

In **1984**, P.L. 98-369, Sec. 735(c)(7)(A), deleted "or inner tube" after "imports a tire" and substituted "If" for "Except as provided in subsection (d), if" in subsec. (b) ... Sec. 735(c)(7)(B), deleted "and tubes" after "Tires" in the heading for subsec. (b) ... Sec. 735(c)(7)(C), deleted subsecs. (c) and (d) and redesignated subsec. (e) as subsec. (c) ... Sec. 735(c)(7)(D), substituted "(other than a tire taxable under section 4071)" for "(other than an article specified in subsection (b), (c), or (d))" in subsec. (a), effective 1/7/83.
Prior to deletion, subsecs. (c) and (d) read as follows:
"(c) Automobile parts and accessories.
"If any person manufactures, produces, or imports a part or accessory taxable under section 4061(b), and uses it (otherwise than as material in the manufacture or production of, or as a component part of, any other article to be manufactured or produced by him), then he shall be liable for tax under this chapter in the same manner as if such article were sold by him.
"(d) Bicycle tires and tubes.
"If any person manufactures, produces, or imports a bicycle tire (as defined in section 4221(e)(4)(B)) or an inner tube for such a tire, and uses it (otherwise than as material in the manufacture or production of, or as a component part of, a bicycle, other than a rebuilt or reconditioned bicycle, to be manufactured or produced by him), then he shall be liable for tax under this chapter in the same manner as if such article were sold by him."

In **1978**, P.L. 95-227, Sec. 2(b)(1), added a sentence at the end of subsec. (a), for sales after 3/31/78. See note following Code Sec. 192.
In **1976**, P.L. 94-455, Sec. 1906(b)(13)(A), substituted "Secretary" for "Secretary or his delegate" in subsec. (e), effective 2/1/77.
In **1971**, P.L. 92-178, Sec. 401(d), provided as follows:
"(d) Certain uses by manufacturer, etc.
"Any tax paid by reason of section 4218(a) of the Internal Revenue Code of 1954 (relating to use by manufacturer or importer considered sale) shall be deemed an overpayment of such tax with respect to—
"(1) any article which was subject to the tax imposed by section 4061(a)(2) of such Code as in effect on the day before the date of the enactment of this Act [date of enactment is 12/10/71] if tax was imposed on such article by reason of such section 4218(a) after August 15, 1971, and
"(2) any article which was subject to the tax imposed by section 4061(a)(1) of such Code as in effect on the day before the date of the enactment of this Act [date of enactment is 12/10/71] and on which such tax is no longer imposed (by reason of subsection (a) of this section) if tax was imposed on such article by reason of such section 4218(a) after September 22, 1971."

In **1965**, P.L. 89-44, Sec. 208(c)(1)-(4), deleted reference to automobile radio and television receiving sets in subsec. (b) and radio or television components and camera lenses in subsec. (c), effective 6/22/65.
In **1961**, P.L. 87-61, added last sentence in subsec. (a), effective for gasoline used after 9/30/61.
In **1960**, P.L. 86-418, Sec. 2(a), substituted "subsection (b), (c), or (d)" for "subsection (b) or (c)" in subsec. (a), substituted "Except as provided in subsection (d), if any" for "If any" in subsec. (b), added subsec. (d), and redesignated former subsec. (d) as (e), effective 5/1/60.
In **1958**, P.L. 85-859, Sec. 118, amended Code Sec. 4218, effective 1/1/59.
Prior to amendment, Code Sec. 4218 read as follows:
"SEC. 4218. USE BY MANUFACTURER OR IMPORTER CONSIDERED SALE.
"(a) General rule.
"If any person manufactures, produces, or imports an article (other than an article specified in subsection (b) or (c)) and uses it (otherwise than as material in the manufacture or production of, or as a component part of, another article taxable under this chapter to be manufactured or produced by him), then he shall be liable for tax under this chapter in the same manner as if such article were sold by him.
"(b) Tires, tubes, and automobile receiving sets.
"If any person manufactures, produces, or imports a tire or inner tube taxable under section 4071, or an automobile radio or television receiving set taxable under section 4141, and sells it on or in connection with the sale of any article, or uses it, then he shall be liable for tax under this chapter in the same manner as if such article were sold by him.
"(c) Automobile parts, radio components, camera lenses, etc.
"If any person manufactures, produces, or imports a part or accessory taxable under section 4061(b), a radio or television component taxable under section 4141, or a camera lens taxable under section 4171, and uses it (otherwise than as material in the manufacture or production of, or as a component part of, any other article to be manufactured or produced by him), then he shall be liable for tax under this chapter in the same manner as if such article were sold by him.
"(d) Computation of tax.
"Except as provided in section 4223(b), in any case in which a person is made liable for tax by the preceding provisions of this section, the tax (if based on the price for which the article is sold) shall be computed on the price at which such or similar articles are sold, in the ordinary course of trade, by manufacturers, producers, or importers, thereof, as determined by the Secretary or his delegate."

In **1955**, ch. 805, Sec. 1(a), (b), amended Code Sec. 4218, effective 9/1/55.
Prior to amendment, Code Sec. 4218 read as follows:
"SEC. 4218. USE BY MANUFACTURER OR IMPORTER CONSIDERED SALE.
"(a) General rule.
"If—
"(1) any person manufactures, produces, or imports an article (other than a tire, inner tube, or automobile radio or television receiving set taxable under section 4141 and other than an automobile part or accessory taxable under section 4061(b), a refrigerator component taxable under section 4111, a radio or television component taxable under section 4141, or a camera lens taxable under section 4171) and uses it (otherwise than as material in the manufacture or production of, or as a component part of, another article to be manufactured or produced by him which will be taxable under this chapter or sold free of tax by virtue of section 4220 or 4224, relating to tax-free sales), or
"(2) any person manufactures, produces, or imports a tire, inner tube, or automobile radio or television receiving set taxable under section 4141 and sells it on or in connection with, or with the sale of, an article taxable under section 4061, relating to the tax on automobiles, or uses it,
he shall be liable for tax under this chapter in the same manner as if such article was sold by him, and the tax (if based on the price for which the article is sold) shall be computed on the price at which such or similar articles are sold, in the ordinary course of trade, by manufacturers, producers, or importers thereof, as determined by the Secretary or his delegate.
"(b) Exception.
"This section shall not apply with respect to the use by the manufacturer, producer, or importer of an automobile part or accessory taxable under section 4061(b), a refrigerator component taxable under section 4111, a radio or television component taxable under section 4141, or a camera lens taxable under section 4171, if such part, accessory, component, or lens is used by him as material in the manufacture or production of, or as a component part of, any article."

3,239

Sec. 4219. Application of tax in case of sales by other than manufacturer or importer.

In case any person acquires from the manufacturer, producer, or importer of an article, by operation of law or as a result of any transaction not taxable under this chapter, the right to sell such article, the sale of such article by such person shall be taxable under this chapter as if made by the manufacturer, producer, or importer, and such person shall be liable for the tax.

Subchapter G.—Exemptions, Registration, Etc.

Sec.
4221. Certain tax-free sales.
4222. Registration.
4223. Special rules relating to further manufacture.
4225. Exemption of articles manufactured or produced by Indians.
4227. Cross references.

In **1986**, P.L. 99-514, Sec. 1899A(74), substituted "reference" for "references" in item 4227.
In **1983**, P.L. 97-473, Sec. 202(b)(9), amended item 4227 [inoperable].
In **1965**, deleted item 4224 dealing with exemption of articles taxable as jewelry.
In **1958**, added subchapter heading and section analysis.

Sec. 4221. Certain tax-free sales.

> • **Caution:** Code Sec. 4221(a), following, is effective for sales before 12/31/2012. For Code Sec. 4221(a), effective for sales after 12/31/2012, see below.

(a) General rule.

Under regulations prescribed by the Secretary, no tax shall be imposed under this chapter (other than under section 4121 or 4081) on the sale by the manufacturer (or under subchapter A or C of chapter 31 on the first retail sale) of an article—

(1) for use by the purchaser for further manufacture, or for resale by the purchaser to a second purchaser for use by such second purchaser in further manufacture,

(2) for export, or for resale by the purchaser to a second purchaser for export,

(3) for use by the purchaser as supplies for vessels or aircraft,

(4) to a State or local government for the exclusive use of a State or local government,

(5) to a nonprofit educational organization for its exclusive use, or

(6) to a qualified blood collector organization (as defined in section 7701(a)(49)) for such organization's exclusive use in the collection, storage, or transportation of blood,

but only if such exportation or use is to occur before any other use. Paragraphs (4), (5), and (6) shall not apply to the tax imposed by section 4064. In the case of taxes imposed by section 4051, or 4071, paragraphs (4) and (5) shall not apply on and after October 1, 2011. In the case of the tax imposed by section 4131, paragraphs (3), (4), and (5) shall not apply and paragraph (2) shall apply only if the use of the exported vaccine meets such requirements as the Secretary may by regulations prescribe. In the case of taxes imposed by subchapter A of chapter 31, paragraphs (1), (3), (4), and (5) shall not apply. In the case of taxes imposed by subchapter C or D, paragraph (6) shall not apply.

> • **Caution:** Code Sec. 4221(a), following, is effective for sales after 12/31/2012. For Code Sec. 4221(a), effective for sales before 12/31/2012, see above.

(a) General rule.

Under regulations prescribed by the Secretary, no tax shall be imposed under this chapter (other than under section 4121 or 4081) on the sale by the manufacturer (or under subchapter A or C of chapter 31 on the first retail sale) of an article—

(1) for use by the purchaser for further manufacture, or for resale by the purchaser to a second purchaser for use by such second purchaser in further manufacture,

(2) for export, or for resale by the purchaser to a second purchaser for export,

(3) for use by the purchaser as supplies for vessels or aircraft,

(4) to a State or local government for the exclusive use of a State or local government,

(5) to a nonprofit educational organization for its exclusive use, or

(6) to a qualified blood collector organization (as defined in section 7701(a)(49)) for such organization's exclusive use in the collection, storage, or transportation of blood,

but only if such exportation or use is to occur before any other use. Paragraphs (4), (5), and (6) shall not apply to the tax imposed by section 4064. In the case of taxes imposed by section 4051, or 4071, paragraphs (4) and (5) shall not apply on and after October 1, 2011. In the case of the tax imposed by section 4131, paragraphs (3), (4), and (5) shall not apply and paragraph (2) shall apply only if the use of the exported vaccine meets such requirements as the Secretary may by regulations prescribe. In the case of taxes imposed by subchapter A of chapter 31, paragraphs (1), (3), (4), and (5) shall not apply. In the case of taxes imposed by subchapter C or D, paragraph (6) shall not apply. In the case of the tax imposed by section 4191, paragraphs (3), (4), (5), and (6) shall not apply.

(b) Proof of resale for further manufacture; proof of export.

Where an article has been sold free of tax under subsection (a)—

(1) for resale by the purchaser to a second purchaser for use by such second purchaser in further manufacture, or

(2) for export, or for resale by the purchaser to a second purchaser for export,

subsection (a) shall cease to apply in respect of such sale of such article unless, within the 6-month period which begins on the date of the sale by the manufacturer (or, if earlier, on the date of shipment by the manufacturer), the manufacturer receives proof that the article has been exported or resold for use in further manufacture.

(c) Manufacturer relieved from liability in certain cases.

In the case of any article sold free of tax under this section (other than a sale to which subsection (b) applies), and in the case of any article sold free of tax under section 4001(c), 4001(d), or 4053(6), if the manufacturer in good faith accepts a certification by the purchaser that the article will be used in accordance with the applicable provisions of law, no tax shall thereafter be imposed under this chapter in respect of such sale by such manufacturer.

(d) Definitions.

For purposes of this section—

(1) Manufacturer. The term "manufacturer" includes a producer or importer of an article, and, in the case of taxes imposed by subchapter A or C of chapter 31, includes the retailer with respect to the first retail sale.

(2) Export. The term "export" includes shipment to a possession of the United States; and the term "exported" includes shipped to a possession of the United States.

(3) Supplies for vessels or aircraft. The term "supplies for vessels or aircraft" means fuel supplies, ships' stores, sea stores, or legitimate equipment on vessels of war of the United States or of any foreign nation, vessels employed in the fisheries or in the whaling business, or vessels actually engaged in foreign trade or trade between the Atlantic and Pacific ports of the United States or between the United States and any of its possessions. For purposes of the preceding sentence, the term "vessels" includes civil aircraft employed in foreign trade or trade between the United States and any of its possessions, and the term "vessels of war of the United States or of any foreign nation" includes aircraft owned by the United States or by any foreign nation and constituting a part of the armed forces thereof.

(4) State or local government. The term "State or local government" means any State, any political subdivision thereof, or the District of Columbia.

(5) Nonprofit educational organization. The term "nonprofit educational organization" means an educational organization described in section 170(b)(1)(A)(ii) which is exempt from income tax under section 501(a). The term also includes a school operated as an activity of an organization described in section 501(c)(3) which is exempt from income tax under section 501(a), if such school normally maintains a regular faculty and curriculum and normally has a regularly enrolled body of pupils or students in attendance at the place where its educational activities are regularly carried on.

(6) Use in further manufacture. An article shall be treated as sold for use in further manufacture if—

(A) such article is sold for use by the purchaser as material in the manufacture or production of, or as a component part of, another article taxable under this chapter to be manufactured or produced by him; or

(B) in the case of gasoline taxable under section 4081, such gasoline is sold for use by the purchaser, for nonfuel purposes, as a material in the manufacture or production of another article to be manufactured or produced by him.

(7) Qualified bus.

(A) In general. The term "qualified bus" means—

(i) an intercity or local bus, and

(ii) a school bus.

(B) Intercity or local bus. The term "intercity or local bus" means any automobile bus which is used predominantly in furnishing (for compensation) passenger land transportation available to the general public if—

(i) such transportation is scheduled and along regular routes, or

(ii) the seating capacity of such bus is at least 20 adults (not including the driver).

(C) School bus. The term "school bus" means any automobile bus substantially all the use of which is in transporting students and employees of schools. For purposes of the preceding sentence, the term "school" means an educational organization which normally maintains a regular faculty and curriculum and normally has a regularly enrolled body of pupils or students in attendance at the place where its educational activities are carried on.

(e) Special rules.

(1) Reciprocity required in case of civil aircraft. In the case of articles sold for use as supplies for aircraft, the privileges granted under subsection (a)(3) in respect of civil aircraft employed in foreign trade or trade between the United States and any of its possessions, in respect of aircraft registered in a foreign country, shall be allowed only if the Secretary of the Treasury has been advised by the Secretary of Commerce that he has found that such foreign country allows, or will allow, substantially reciprocal privileges in respect of aircraft registered in the United States. If the Secretary of the Treasury is advised by the Secretary of Commerce that he has found that a foreign country has discontinued or will discontinue the allowance of such privileges, the privileges granted under subsection (a)(3) shall not apply thereafter in respect of civil aircraft registered in that foreign country and employed in foreign trade or trade between the United States and any of its possessions.

(2) Tires.

(A) Tax-free sales. Under regulations prescribed by the Secretary, no tax shall be imposed under section 4071 on the sale by the manufacturer of a tire if—

(i) such tire is sold for use by the purchaser for sale on or in connection with the sale of another article manufactured or produced by such purchaser; and

(ii) such other article is to be sold by such purchaser in a sale which either will satisfy the requirements of paragraph (2), (3), (4), or (5) of subsection (a) for a tax-free sale, or would satisfy such requirements but for the fact that such other article is not subject to tax under this chapter.

(B) Proof. Where a tire has been sold free of tax under this paragraph, this paragraph shall cease to apply unless, within the 6-month period which begins on the date of the sale by him (or, if earlier, on the date of the shipment by him), the manufacturer of such tire receives proof that the other article referred to in clause (ii) of subparagraph (A) has been sold in a manner which satisfies the requirements of such clause (ii) (including in the case of a sale for export, proof of export of such other article).

(C) Subsection (a)(1) does not apply. Paragraph (1) of subsection (a) shall not apply with respect to the tax imposed under section 4071 on the sale of a tire.

(3) Tires used on intercity, local, and school buses. Under regulations prescribed by the Secretary, the tax imposed by section 4071 shall not apply in the case of tires sold for use by the purchaser on or in connection with a qualified bus.

In **2010**, P.L. 111-152, Sec. 1405(b)(1), added "In the case of the tax imposed by section 4191, paragraphs (3), (4), (5), and (6) shall not apply." at the end of subsec. (a), effective for sales after 12/31/2012.

In **2006**, P.L. 109-280, Sec. 1207(b)(1), deleted "or" at the end of para. (a)(4), added "or" at the end of para. (a)(5), and added para. (a)(6) . . . Sec. 1207(b)(2), added "In the case of taxes imposed by subchapter C or D, paragraph (6) shall not apply." at the end of subsec. (a) . . . Sec. 1207(b)(3)(A), substituted "Paragraphs (4), (5), and (6)" for "Paragraphs (4) and (5)" in subsec. (a), effective 1/1/2007.

In **2005**, P.L. 109-59, Sec. 11101(b)(1), substituted "2011" for "2005" in subsec. (a), effective 8/10/2005.

In **2004**, P.L. 108-357, Sec. 853(d)(2)(F), substituted "or 4081" for ", 4081, or 4091" in subsec. (a), effective for aviation-grade kerosene removed, entered, or sold after 12/31/2004.

—P.L. 108-357, Sec. 853(f), of this Act, provides:

(f) Floor stocks tax.

"(1) In general. There is hereby imposed on aviation-grade kerosene held on January 1, 2005, by any person a tax equal to—

"(A) the tax which would have been imposed before such date on such kerosene had the amendments made by this section been in effect at all times before such date, reduced by

"(B) the sum of—

"(i) the tax imposed before such date on such kerosene under section 4091 of the Internal Revenue Code of 1986, as in effect on such date, and

Code Sec. 4221 Excise and miscellaneous taxes

"(ii) in the case of kerosene held exclusively for such person's own use, the amount which such person would (but for this clause) reasonably expect (as of such date) to be paid as a refund under section 6427(l) of such Code with respect to such kerosene.

"(2) Exception for fuel held in aircraft fuel tank. Paragraph (1) shall not apply to kerosene held in the fuel tank of an aircraft on January 1, 2005.

"(3) Liability for tax and method of payment.

"(A) Liability for tax. The person holding the kerosene on January 1, 2005, to which the tax imposed by paragraph (1) applies shall be liable for such tax.

"(B) Method and time for payment. The tax imposed by paragraph (1) shall be paid at such time and in such manner as the Secretary of the Treasury (or the Secretary's delegate) shall prescribe, including the nonapplication of such tax on de minimis amounts of kerosene.

"(4) Transfer of floor stock tax revenues to trust funds. For purposes of determining the amount transferred to any trust fund, the tax imposed by this subsection shall be treated as imposed by section 4081 of the Internal Revenue Code of 1986—

"(A) in any case in which tax was not imposed by section 4091 of such Code, at the Leaking Underground Storage Tank Trust Fund financing rate under such section to the extent of 0.1 cents per gallon, and

"(B) at the rate under section 4081(a)(2)(A)(iv) of such Code to the extent of the remainder.

"(5) Held by a person. For purposes of this subsection, kerosene shall be considered as held by a person if title thereto has passed to such person (whether or not delivery to the person has been made).

"(6) Other laws applicable. All provisions of law, including penalties, applicable with respect to the tax imposed by section 4081 of such Code shall, insofar as applicable and not inconsistent with the provisions of this subsection, apply with respect to the floor stock tax imposed by paragraph (1) to the same extent as if such tax were imposed by such section."

In 1998, P.L. 105-206, Sec. 6023(17), substituted "4053(6)" for "4053(a)(6)" in subsec. (c), effective 7/22/98.

—P.L. 105-178, Sec. 9002(b)(1), substituted "2005" for "1999" in subsec. (a), effective 6/9/98.

In 1993, P.L. 103-66, Sec. 13161(b)(1), substituted "4001(d)" for "4002(b), 4003(c), 4004(a)" in subsec. (c), effective 1/1/93.

In 1991, P.L. 102-240, Sec. 8002(b)(3), substituted "1999" for "1995" in subsec. (a), effective 12/18/91.

In 1990, P.L. 101-508, Sec. 11211(d)(3), substituted "1995" for "1993" in subsec. (a), effective 11/5/90.

—P.L. 101-508, Sec. 11221(b)(1), substituted "subchapter A or C of chapter 31" for "section 4051" the first place it appeared in subsec. (a) . . . Sec. 11221(b)(2), added sentence to the end of subsec. (a) . . . Sec. 11221(d)(1), substituted "section 4001(c), 4002(b), 4003(c), 4004(a), or 4053(a)(6)" for "section 4053(a)(6)" in subsec. (c) . . . Sec. 11221(d)(2), substituted "taxes imposed by subchapter A or C of chapter 31" for "the tax imposed by section 4051" in para. (d)(1), effective 1/1/91, except as provided in Sec. 11221(f)(2) of this Act which reads as follows:

"(2) Exception for binding contracts. In determining whether any tax imposed by subchapter A of chapter 31 of the Internal Revenue Code of 1986, as added by this section, applies to any sale after December 31, 1990, there shall not be taken into account the amount paid for any article (or any part or accessory therefor) if the purchaser held on September 30, 1990, a contract (which was binding on such date and at all times thereafter before the purchase) for the purchase of such article (or such part or accessory)."

In 1989, P.L. 101-239, Sec. 7841(d)(17), deleted "or 4083" after "4053(a)(6)" in subsec. (c), effective 12/19/89.

In 1988, P.L. 100-647, Sec. 1017(c)(5), changed the effective date for amendments made by Sec. 10502(a)(4) of P.L. 100-203 from "sales after 3/31/88" to "gasoline removed (as defined in Code Sec. 4082 as amended by Sec. 1703 of P.L. 99-514) after 12/31/87 except that [as provided in this section] the reference to Code Sec. 4091 shall not apply to sales before 4/1/88."

In 1987, P.L. 100-203, Sec. 9201(b)(1), added the last sentence of subsec. (a), effective 1/1/88.

—P.L. 100-203, Sec. 10502(d)(4), substituted "(other than under section 4121, 4081, or 4091)" for "(other than under section 4121 or 4081 (at the Highway Trust Fund financing rate))" in subsec. (a), effective [as amended by Sec. 1017(c)(5) of P.L. 100-647, see above] for gasoline removed (as defined in Code Sec. 4082 as amended by Sec. 1703 of P.L. 99-514) after 12/31/87, except that the reference to Code Sec. 4091 in subsec. (a) shall not apply to sales before 4/1/88.

—P.L. 100-17, Sec. 502(b)(4), substituted "1993" for "1988" in subsec. (a), effective 4/2/87.

In 1986, P.L. 99-514, Sec. 1703(c)(2)(C), [as amended by Sec. 521(d)(4)(B) of P.L. 99-499, see below], amended subsec. (a) by adding "or 4081 (at the Highway Trust Fund financing rate)" before "section 4121" in the first sentence, and by substituting "or 4071" for "4071, or 4081 (at the Highway Trust Fund financing rate)" in the last sentence, effective for gasoline removed (as defined in Code Sec. 4082 as amended by Sec. 1703 of this Act) after 12/31/87.

—P.L. 99-499, Sec. 521(d)(4)(A), substituted "4081 (at the Highway Trust Fund financing rate)" for "4081" in the last sentence of subsec. (a), effective 1/1/87.

—P.L. 99-499, Sec. 521(d)(4)(B), amended Sec. 1703(c)(2)(C) of P.L. 99-514 [see above] to reflect the amendments made by Sec. 521(d)(4)(A) of this Act.

In 1984, P.L. 98-369, Sec. 735(c)(8)(A), added "(or under section 4051 on the first retail sale)" after "manufacturer" in subsec. (a) . . . Sec. 735(c)(8)(B), substituted "section 4053(a)(6)" for "section 4063(a)(6) or (7), 4063(b), 4063(e)," in subsec. (c) . . . Sec. 735(c)(8)(C), added ", and, in the case of the tax imposed by section 4051, includes the retailer with respect to the first retail sale" before the period at the end of para. (d)(1), effective 4/1/83.

—P.L. 98-369, Sec. 735(c)(8)(D), deleted subpara. (d)(6)(B) and the sentence "For purposes of subparagraph (B), the rebuilding of a part or accessory which is exempt from tax under section 4063(c) shall not constitute the manufacture or production of such part or accessory." from the end of para. (d)(6), deleted "(other than an article referred to in subparagraph (B))" after "such article" in subpara. (d)(6)(A), redesignated subpara. (d)(6)(C) as subpara. (d)(6)(B), added "or" at the end of subpara. (d)(6)(A), effective 1/7/83.

Prior to deletion, subpara. (d)(6)(B) read as follows:

"(B) in the case of a part or accessory taxable under section 4061(b), such article is sold for use by the purchaser as material in the manufacturer or production of, or as a component part of, another article to be manufacturer or produced by him; or"

—P.L. 98-369, Sec. 735(c)(8)(E), deleted "or inner tube" and "or tube" each place they appeared after "tire" in para. (e)(2) . . . Sec. 735(c)(8)(F), deleted "and tubes" after "Tires" in the heading of subsec. (e) . . . Sec. 735(c)(8)(G), deleted paras. (e)(4), (5), and (6) and added para. (e)(3), effective for articles sold on or after 1/1/84.

Prior to deletion, paras. (e)(4), (5), and (6) read as follows:

"(4) Bicycle tires or tubes sold to bicycle manufacturer.

"(A) In general. Under regulations prescribed by the Secretary, no tax shall be imposed under section 4071 on the sale of a bicycle tire (or an inner tube for such a tire) by the manufacturer thereof if such tire or tube is sold for use by the purchaser as material in the manufacture or production of, or as a component part of, a bicycle (other than a rebuilt or reconditioned bicycle).

"(B) Bicycle tire defined. As used in this paragraph the term 'bicycle tire' means a tire, composed of rubber in combination with fabric or other reinforcing element, which is not more than 28 inches in outer diameter and not more than 2¼ inches in cross section and which is primarily designed or adapted for use on bicycles.

"(C) Proof. Where a bicycle tire or tube has been sold free of tax under this paragraph, this paragraph shall cease to apply unless, within the 6-month period which begins on the date of the sale by him (or, if earlier, on the date of shipment by him), the manufacturer of such bicycle tire or tube receives proof that the tire or tube has been used in the manner described in subparagraph (A).

"(5) Tires, tubes, and tread rubber used on intercity, local, and school buses. Under regulations prescribed by the Secretary.—

"(A) the taxes imposed by paragraphs (1) and (3) of section 4071(a) shall not apply in the case of tires or inner tubes for tires sold for use by the purchaser on or in connection with a qualified bus, and

"(B) the tax imposed by paragraph (4) of section 4071(a) shall not apply in the case of tread rubber sold for use by the purchaser in the recapping or retreading of any tire to be used by the purchaser on or in connection with a qualified bus.

"(6) Bus parts and accessories. Under regulations prescribed by the Secretary, the tax imposed by section 4061(b) shall not apply to any part or accessory which is sold for use by the purchaser on or in connection with an automobile bus, or is to be resold by the purchaser or a second purchaser for such use."

In 1983, P.L. 97-424, Sec. 515(b)(1), substituted "or 4083" for "4083, or 4093" in subsec. (c), effective for articles sold after 1/6/83.

—P.L. 97-424, Sec. 516(b)(2), added the last sentence to subsec. (a), effective 1/6/83.

In 1980, P.L. 96-222, Sec. 108(c)(5), amended para. (e)(6), for sales on or after 12/1/78 [the first day of the first calendar month which begins more than 10 days after 11/9/78, date of enactment].

Prior to amendment, para. (e)(6) read as follows:

"(6) Bus parts and accessories. Under regulations prescribed by the Secretary, the tax imposed by section 4061(b) shall not apply to any part or accessory which is sold for use by the purchaser on or in connection with an automobile bus."

In 1978, P.L. 95-618, Sec. 201(c)(1), added the last sentence in subsec. (a), effective with respect to 1980 and later year model automobiles (as defined in Code Sec. 4064(b)).

—P.L. 95-618, Sec. 232(a), added para. (e)(6), effective for sales on or after 12/1/78 (the first day of the first calendar month beginning more than 10 days after 11/9/78, date of enactment).

—P.L. 95-618, Sec. 233(c)(1), amended para. (e)(5) . . . Sec. 233(c)(2), added para. (d)(7), effective 12/1/78 (the first day of the first calendar month which begins more than 10 days after 11/9/78, date of enactment).

Prior to amendment, para. (e)(5) read as follows:

"(5) School buses. Under regulations prescribed by the Secretary, the tax imposed by section 4061(a) shall not apply to a bus sold to any person for use exclusively in transporting students and employees of schools operated by State or local governments, or by nonprofit educational organizations. For purposes of this paragraph, incidental use of a bus in providing transportation for a State or local government or a nonprofit organization described in section 501(c) which is exempt from tax under section 501(a) shall be disregarded."

—P.L. 95-600, Sec. 701(ff)(2)(A), added "4063(e)," after "4063(b)," in subsec. (c), effective 12/1/78 (the first day of the first calendar month which begins more than 20 days after 11/6/78).

—P.L. 95-227, Sec. 2(b)(2), added "(other than under section 4121)" after "this chapter" in subsec. (a), for sales after 3/31.78. See note following Code Sec. 192.

In 1976, P.L. 94-455, Sec. 1906(b)(13)(A), substituted "Secretary" for "Secretary or his delegate" each place it appeared in Code Sec. 4221, effective 2/1/77.

In 1971, P.L. 92-178, Sec. 401(a)(3)(A), substituted "4063(a)(6) or (7), 4063(b)," for "section 4063(b)," in subsec. (c), effective for articles sold on or after 12/10/71.

Excise and miscellaneous taxes   Code Sec. 4222

In 1969, P.L. 91-172, Sec. 101(j)(26), substituted "170(b)(1)(A)(ii)" for "503(b)(2)" in para. (d)(5), effective 1/1/70.

In 1965, P.L. 89-44, Sec. 208, deleted "a radio or television component taxable under section 4141, or a camera lens taxable under section 4171" after "section 4061(b)" in subpara. (d)(6)(B), deleted "and automobile receiving sets" from the heading of para. (e)(2), and "or 4141" after "4171" in subparas. (e)(2)(A) and (C), substituted "tire or tube" for "tire, tube or receiving set" in clause (e)(2)(A)(i) and subpara. (e)(2)(B), deleted para. (e)(3) and subsec. (f), effective 6/22/65.

Prior to deletion, para. (e)(3) read as follows:

"(3) Musical instruments sold for religious use. Under regulations prescribed by the Secretary or his delegate, the tax imposed by section 4151 shall not apply to musical instruments sold to a religious institution for exclusively religious purposes."

Prior to deletion, subsec. (f) read as follows:

"(f) Sales of mechanical pencils and pens for export. Under regulations prescribed by the Secretary or his delegate, mechanical pencils, fountain pens, and ball point pens subject to the tax imposed by section 4201 may be sold by the manufacturer free of tax for export or for resale for export upon receipt by him of notice of intent to export or to resell for export."

—P.L. 89-44, Sec. 801(c), added the last sentence in para. (d)(6), effective for articles sold after '64

added para. (e)(5), effective for articles sold after 6/21/61

In 1961, P.L. 87-61, Sec. 205(a), added subpara. (d)(6)(C), effective for gasoline sold after 9/61.

In 1960, P.L. 86-624, Sec. 18(e), substituted "any State, any political subdivision thereof, or the District of Columbia" for "any State, Hawaii, the District of Columbia, or any political subdivision of any of the foregoing," in para. (d)(4), effective 8/21/59.

—P.L. 86-418, Sec. 1, added para. (e)(4), effective for sales after 5/1/60.

In 1959, P.L. 86-70, Sec. 22(a), eliminated "Alaska," preceding "Hawaii" in para. (d)(4), effective 1/3/59.

—P.L. 86-344, Sec. 2(b), added the second sentence of para. (d)(5), effective 1/1/59.

In 1958, P.L. 85-859, Sec. 119(a), repealed former Code Sec. 4221 and enacted the present section, effective 1/1/59. The former provision related to exemption of articles taxable as jewelry and was then covered by Code Sec. 4224.

Sec. 4222. Registration.
(a) General rule.

Except as provided in subsection (b), section 4221 shall not apply with respect to the sale of any article unless the manufacturer, the first purchaser, and the second purchaser (if any) are all registered under this section. Registration under this section shall be made at such time, in such manner and form, and subject to such terms and conditions, as the Secretary may by regulations prescribe. A registration under this section may be used only in accordance with regulations prescribed under this section.

(b) Exceptions.

(1) Purchases by State and local governments. Subsection (a) shall not apply to any State or local government in connection with the purchase by it of any article if such State or local government complies with such regulations relating to the use of exemption certificates in lieu of registration as the Secretary shall prescribe to carry out the purpose of this paragraph.

(2) Under regulations. Subject to such regulations as the Secretary may prescribe for the purpose of this paragraph, the Secretary may relieve the purchaser or the second purchaser, or both, from the requirement of registering under this section.

(3) Certain purchases and sales by the United States. Subsection (a) shall apply to purchases and sales by the United States only to the extent provided by regulations prescribed by the Secretary.

(4) Repealed.

(5) Supplies for vessels or aircraft. Subsection (a) shall not apply to a sale of an article for use by the purchaser as supplies for any vessel or aircraft if such purchaser complies with such regulations relating to the use of exemption certificates in lieu of registration as the Secretary shall prescribe to carry out the purpose of this paragraph.

(c) Denial, revocation, or suspension of registration.

Under regulations prescribed by the Secretary, the registration of any person under this section may be denied, revoked, or suspended if the Secretary determines—

(1) that such person has used such registration to avoid the payment of any tax imposed by this chapter, or to postpone or in any manner to interfere with the collection of any such tax, or

(2) that such denial, revocation, or suspension is necessary to protect the revenue.

The denial, revocation, or suspension under this subsection shall be in addition to any penalty provided by law for any act or failure to act.

(d) Registration in the case of certain other exemptions.

The provisions of this section may be extended to, and made applicable with respect to, the exemptions provided by sections 4001(c), 4001(d), 4053(6), 4064(b)(1)(C), 4101, and 4182(b), and the exemptions authorized under section 4293 in respect of the taxes imposed by this chapter, to the extent provided by regulations prescribed by the Secretary.

(e) Definitions.

Terms used in this section which are defined in section 4221(d) shall have the meaning given to them by section 4221(d).

In 1998, P.L. 105-206, Sec. 6023(17), substituted "4053(6)" for "4053(a)(6)" in subsec. (d), effective 7/22/98.

In 1997, P.L. 105-34, Sec. 1431(a)(1), deleted "in the case of any sale or resale for export," after "for the purpose of this paragraph," in para. (b)(2) . . . Sec. 1431(a)(2), substituted "Under regulations" for "Export" in the heading of para. (b)(2), effective 8/5/97.

In 1993, P.L. 103-66, Sec. 13161(b)(2), substituted "4001(d)" for "4002(b), 4003(c), 4004(a)" in subsec. (d), effective 1/1/93.

In 1990, P.L. 101-508, Sec. 11212(b)(2)(A), substituted "denied, revoked, or suspended" for "revoked or suspended", in subsec. (c) . . . Sec. 11212(b)(2)(B), substituted "denial, revocation, or suspension" for "revocation or suspension", each place it appeared in subsec. (c) . . . Sec. 11212(b)(2)(C), substituted "Denial, revocation, or suspension" for "Revocation or suspension", in the heading of subsec. (c), effective 12/1/90.

—P.L. 101-508, Sec. 11221(d)(3), substituted "4001(c), 4002(b), 4003(c), 4004(a), 4053(a)(6)" for "4053(a)(6)", in subsec. (d), effective 1/1/91 except as provided in Sec. 11221(f)(2) of this Act, which reads as follows:

"(2) Exception for binding contracts. In determining whether any tax imposed by subchapter A of chapter 31 of the Internal Revenue Code of 1986, as added by this section, applies to any sale after December 31, 1990, there shall not be taken into account the amount paid for any article (or any part or accessory therefor) if the purchaser establishes that on September 30, 1990, a contract (which was binding on such date and at all times thereafter before the purchase) for the purchase of such article (or such part or accessory)."

In 1988, P.L. 100-647, Sec. 1017(c)(16), substituted "4101" for "4083" in subsec. (d), effective for gasoline removed (as defined in Code Sec. 4082, as amended by Sec. 1703(a) of the Reform Act [P.L. 99-514]) after 12/31/87.

In 1984, P.L. 98-369, Sec. 735(c)(9), substituted "4053(a)(6)," for "4063(a)(7), 4963(b), 4063(e)," in subsec. (d), effective 4/1/83.

In 1983, P.L. 97-424, Sec. 515(b)(2), deleted "4093" after "4083," in subsec. (d), effective for articles sold after 1/6/83.

In 1978, P.L. 95-618, Sec. 201(e), added "4064(b)(1)(C)," after "4063(b)," in subsec. (d), effective for 1980 and later year automobiles (as defined in Code Sec. 4064(b)).

—P.L. 95-618, Sec. 231(f)(2), substituted "4063(a)(7)" for "4063(a)(6) or (7)" in subsec. (d), effective for articles sold after 11/9/78.

—P.L. 95-600, Sec. 701(ff)(2)(B), added "4063(e)," after "4063(b)," in subsec. (d), effective 12/1/78 (the first day of the first calendar month which begins more than 20 days after 11/6/78, date of enactment).

In 1976, P.L. 94-455, Sec. 1906(b)(13)(A), substituted "Secretary" for "Secretary or his delegate" each place it appeared in Code Sec. 4222, effective 2/1/77.

In 1971, P.L. 92-178, Sec. 401(a)(3)(B), substituted "sections 4063(a)(6) and (7), 4063(b)," for "sections 4063(b)," in subsec. (d), effective for articles sold on or after 12/10/71.

In 1965, P.L. 89-44, Sec. 208, deleted para. (b)(4), effective 6/22/65:

Prior to deletion, para. (b)(4) read as follows:

"(4) Mechanical pencils, fountain pens, and ball point pens. Subsection (a) shall not apply in the case of mechanical pencils, fountain pens, and ball point pens subject to the tax imposed by section 4201 sold by the manufacturer for export or for resale for export."

—P.L. 89-44, Sec. 802, added para. (b)(5), effective 7/1/65.

In 1958, P.L. 85-859, Sec. 119(a), repealed Code Sec. 4222 and enacted the present section, effective 1/1/59. The former provision related to exemption from tax

3,243

of certain supplies for vessels and airplanes, and was then covered by Code Sec. 4221.

Sec. 4223. Special rules relating to further Manufacture.
(a) Purchasing manufacturer to be treated as the manufacturer.
For purposes of this chapter, a manufacturer or producer to whom an article is sold or resold free of tax under section 4221(a)(1) for use by him in further manufacture shall be treated as the manufacturer or producer of such article.
(b) Computation of tax.
If the manufacturer or producer referred to in subsection (a) incurs liability for tax under this chapter on his sale or use of an article referred to in subsection (a) and the tax is based on the price for which the article is sold, the article shall be treated as having been sold by him—
(1) at the price for which the article was sold by him (or, where the tax is on his use of the article, at the price referred to in [section] 4218(c)); or
(2) if he so elects and establishes such price to the satisfaction of the Secretary—
(A) at the price for which the article was sold to him; or
(B) at the price for which the article was sold by the person who (without regard to subsection (a)) is the manufacturer, producer, or importer of such article.
For purposes of this subsection, the price for which the article was sold shall be determined as provided in section 4216. For purposes of paragraph (2) no adjustment or readjustment shall be made in such price by reason of any discount, rebate, allowance, return or repossession of a container or covering, or otherwise. An election under paragraph (2) shall be made in the return reporting the tax applicable to the sale or use of the article, and may not be revoked.

In **1984**, P.L. 98-369, Sec. 735(c)(10), substituted "[section] 4218(c)" for "section 4218(e)" in para. (b)(1), effective for articles sold on or after 1/1/84.
In **1976**, P.L. 94-455, Sec. 1906(b)(13)(A), substituted "Secretary" for "Secretary or his delegate" in para. (b)(2), effective 2/1/77.
In **1960**, P.L. 86-418, Sec. 2(b), substituted "section 4218(e)" for "section 4218(d)" para. (b)(1), effective 5/1/60.
In **1958**, P.L. 85-859, Sec. 119(a), repealed Code Sec. 4223 and enacted the present section, effective 1/1/59. The former provision related to exemption of articles manufactured or produced by Indians and was then covered by Code Sec. 4225.

Sec. 4225. Exemption of articles manufactured or produced by Indians.
No tax shall be imposed under this chapter on any article of native Indian handicraft manufactured or produced by Indians on Indian reservations, or in Indian schools, or by Indians under the jurisdiction of the United States Government in Alaska.

In **1958**, P.L. 85-859, Sec. 119(a), repealed Code Sec. 4225 and enacted the present provision, effective 1/1/59. The former provision related to exemption for exports and was then covered by Code Sec. 4221.

Sec. 4227. Cross references.
For exception for a sale to an Indian tribal government (or its subdivision) for the exclusive use of an Indian tribal government (or its subdivision), see section 7871.

In **1986**, P.L. 99-514, Sec. 1899A(49), amended Code Sec. 4227, effective 10/22/86.
Prior to amendment, Code Sec. 4227 read as follows:
"SEC. 4227. CROSS REFERENCES.
"(1) For exemption for a sale to an Indian tribal government (or its subdivision) for the exclusive use of an Indian tribal government (or its subdivision), see section 7871.

"(2) For credit for taxes on tires, see section 6416(c)."
In **1984**, P.L. 98-369, Sec. 735(c)(11), deleted "and tubes" after "taxes on tires" in para. (2), effective for articles sold on or after 1/1/84.
—P.L. 98-369, Sec. 1065(a)(2), amended Sec. 204(5) of P.L. 97-473, the effective date for changes made by Sec. 202(b)(8) of P.L. 97-473 (see below), by deleting ", and shall cease to apply at the close of December 31, 1984".
In **1983**, P.L. 97-473, Sec. 202(b)(8), amended Code Sec. 4227, effective on 1/1/83.
Prior to amendment, Code Sec. 4227 read as follows:
"SEC. 4227. CROSS REFERENCE.
"For credit for taxes on tires and inner tubes, see section 6416(c)."
In **1976**, P.L. 94-455, Sec. 1904(a)(5), amended Code Sec. 4227, effective 2/1/77.
Prior to amendment, Code Sec. 4227 read as follows:
"SEC. 4227. CROSS REFERENCES.
"(1) For exemption from tax in case of certain sales to the United States, see section 4293.
"(2) For credit for taxes on tires and inner tubes, see section 6416(c).
"(3) For administrative provisions of general application to the taxes imposed under this chapter, see subtitle F.".
In **1965**, P.L. 89-44, Sec. 208(f), deleted ", and automobile, radio and television receiving sets," in para. (2), effective 1/1/59.
In **1956**, ch. 462, Sec. 207(a), redesignated Code Sec. 4226 as Code Sec. 4227.

CHAPTER 33.—FACILITIES AND SERVICES
Subchapter
B. Communications.
C. Transportation by air.
E. Special provisions applicable to services and facilities taxes.

In **1970**, substituted "Transportation by air" for "Transportation of persons by air" in Subchapter C.
In **1962**, substituted "Transportation of persons by air" for "Transportation of persons" in Subchapter C.
In **1958**, substituted "Transportation of persons" for "Transportation" in Subchapter C.

Subchapter B.—Communications
Sec.
4251. Imposition of tax.
4252. Definitions.
4253. Exemptions.
4254. Computation of tax.
Sec. 4251. Imposition of tax.
(a) Tax imposed.
(1) **In general.** There is hereby imposed on amounts paid for communications services a tax equal to the applicable percentage of amounts so paid.
(2) **Payment of tax.** The tax imposed by this section shall be paid by the person paying for such services.
(b) Definitions.
For purposes of subsection (a)—
(1) **Communications services.** The term "communications services" means—
(A) local telephone service;
(B) toll telephone service; and
(C) teletypewriter exchange service.
(2) **Applicable percentage.** The term "applicable percentage" means 3 percent.
(c) Special rule.
For purposes of subsections (a) and (b), in the case of communications services rendered before November 1 of a calendar year for which a bill has not been rendered before the close of such year, a bill shall be treated as having been first rendered on December 31 of such year.
(d) Treatment of prepaid telephone cards.
(1) **In general.** For purposes of this subchapter, in the case of communications services acquired by means of a prepaid telephone card—

Excise and miscellaneous taxes Code Sec. 4251

(A) the face amount of such card shall be treated as the amount paid for such communications services, and
(B) that amount shall be treated as paid when the card is transferred by any telecommunications carrier to any person who is not such a carrier.

(2) Determination of face amount in absence of specified dollar amount. In the case of any prepaid telephone card which entitles the user other than to a specified dollar amount of use, the face amount shall be determined under regulations prescribed by the Secretary.

(3) Prepaid telephone card. For purposes of this subsection, the term "prepaid telephone card" means any card or any other similar arrangement which permits its holder to obtain communications services and pay for such services in advance.

In 1998, P.L. 105-206, Sec. 6010(i), substituted "any other similar arrangement" for "other similar arrangement" in para. (d)(3), effective for amounts paid in calendar months begin. more than 60 days after 8/5/97.
In 1997, P.L. 105-34, Sec. 1034(a), added subsec. (d), effective for amounts paid in calendar months begin. more than 60 days after 8/5/97.
In 1990, P.L. 101-508, Sec. 11217(a), substituted "percent." for "percent; except that, with respect to amounts paid pursuant to bills first rendered after 1990, the applicable percentage shall be zero." in para. (b)(2), effective 11/5/90.
In 1987, P.L. 100-203, Sec. 10501, amended para. (b)(2), effective 12/22/87.
Prior to amendment, para. (b)(2) read as follows:
"(2) Applicable percentage. The term 'applicable percentage' means

With respect to amounts paid pursuant to bills first rendered —	The applicable percentage is
During 1983, 1984, 1985, 1986, or 1987	3
During 1988 or thereafter	0."

In 1986, P.L. 99-514, Sec. 1801(b), added "1985," after "1984," in the table in para. (b)(2), effective 7/18/84.
In 1984, P.L. 98-369, Sec. 26, amended para. (b)(2), effective 7/18/84.
Prior to amendment, para. (b)(2) read as follows:
"(2) Applicable percentage. The term 'applicable percentage' means

With respect to amounts paid pursuant to bills first rendered —	The percentage is —
During 1983, 1984, or 1985	3
During 1986 or thereafter	0."

In 1982, P.L. 97-248, Sec. 282(a), amended subsecs. (a) and (b), effective for amounts paid for communications services pursuant to bills first rendered after 12/31/82.
Prior to amendment, subsecs. (a) and (b) read as follows:
"(a) In general.
"(1) Except as provided in subsection (b), there is hereby imposed on amounts paid for the following communication services a tax equal to the percent of the amount so paid specified in paragraph (2):
 Local telephone service.
 Toll telephone service.
 Teletypewriter exchange service.
The taxes imposed by this section shall be paid by the person paying for the services.
"(2) The rate of tax referred to in paragraph (1) is as follows:

Amounts paid pursuant to bills first rendered —	Percent
Before January 1, 1973	10
During 1973	9
During 1974	8
During 1975	7
During 1976	6
During 1977	5
During 1978	4
During 1979	3
During 1980 or 1981	2
During 1982, 1983, or 1984	1

"(b) Termination of tax.
"The tax imposed by subsection (a) shall not apply to amounts paid pursuant to bills first rendered on or after January 1, 1985."
In 1981, P.L. 97-34, Sec. 821(a), substituted "During 1982, 1983, or 1984 . . . . . . 1" for "During 1982 . . . . . 1" in para. (a)(2) . . . Sec. 821(b), substituted "1985" for "1983" in subsec. (b), effective 8/13/81.
In 1980, P.L. 96-499, Sec. 1151(a), amended the last 2 lines of table in para. (a)(2) . . . Sec. 1151(b), substituted "January 1, 1983" for "January 1, 1982" in subsec. (b).
Prior to amendment, the last two lines of the table in para. (a)(2) read as follows:
"During 1980 2

During 1981 . . . . 1"
In 1970, P.L. 91-614, Sec. 201(b)(1), amended the table in para. (a)(2) and substituted "1982" for "1974" in subsec. (b).
Prior to amendment, the table in para. (a)(2) read as follows:

"Amounts paid pursuant to bills first rendered —	Percent
Before January 1, 1971	10
During 1971	5
During 1972	3
During 1973	1"

. . . Sec. 201(b)(3), amended Sec. 105(b)(3), as passed in '68 and further amended in '69 (see below) to read as follows:
"Sec. [105(b)] (3) Repeal of subchapter B of chapter 33.—Effective with respect to amounts paid pursuant to bills first rendered on or after January 1, 1982, subchapter B of chapter 33 (relating to the tax on communications) is repealed. For purposes of the preceding sentence, in the case of communications services rendered before November 1, 1981, for which a bill has not been rendered before January 1, 1982, a bill shall be treated as having been first rendered on December 31, 1981. Effective January 1, 1982, the table of subchapters for chapter 33 is amended by striking out the item relating to such subchapter B."
In 1969, P.L. 91-172, Sec. 702(b)(1), amended the table in para. (a)(2).
Prior to amendment, the table in para. (a)(2) read as follows:

"Amounts paid pursuant to bills first rendered —	Percent
Before January 1, 1970	10
During 1970	5
During 1971	3
During 1972	1"

. . . Sec. 702(b)(2), substituted "January 1, 1974" for "January 1, 1973" in subsec. (b) . . . Sec. 702(b)(3), amended Sec. 105(b)(3) of P.L. 90-285, as passed in '68 (see below) to read as follows:
"Sec. [105(b)] (3) Repeal of subchapter B of chapter 33.—Effective with respect to amounts paid pursuant to bills first rendered on or after January 1, 1974, subchapter B of chapter 33 (relating to the tax on communications) is repealed. For purposes of the preceding sentence, in the case of communications services rendered before November 1, 1973, for which a bill has not been rendered before January 1, 1974, a bill shall be treated as having been first rendered on December 31, 1973. Effective January 1, 1974, the table of subchapters for chapter 33 is amended by striking out the item relating to such subchapter B."
In 1968, P.L. 90-364, Sec. 105, amended Code Sec. 4251 by rewriting the table of tax rates in (a)(2) which were slated for reduction from 10% to 1% for the period ending 1/1/69 . . . changed the termination year in subsec. (b) from 1969 to 1973 . . . amended subsec. (c), effective 4/1/68.
Prior to amendment, subsec. (c) read as follows:
"(c) Special rule.
"For purposes of subsection (a), in the case of communications services rendered before March 1, 1968, for which a bill has not been rendered before May 1, 1968, a bill shall be treated as having been first rendered on April 30, 1968. For purposes of subsections (a) and (b), in the case of communications services rendered after February 29, 1968, and before November 1, 1968, for which a bill has not been rendered before January 1, 1969, a bill shall be treated as having been first rendered on December 31, 1968."
—P.L. 90-285, amended Code Sec. 4251, by extending the periods for imposition of tax from 4/1/68 to 5/1/68 and from 3/31/68 to 4/30/68 in para. (a)(2), and amended subsec. (c), effective 3/31/68.
Prior to amendment, subsec. (c) read as follows:
"(c) Special rule.
"For purposes of subsection (a), in the case of communications services rendered before February 1, 1968, for which a bill has not been rendered before April 1, 1968, a bill shall be treated as having been first rendered on March 31, 1968. For purposes of subsections (a) and (b), in the case of communications services rendered after January 31, 1968, and before November 1, 1968, for which a bill has not been rendered before January 1, 1969, a bill shall be treated as having been first rendered on December 31, 1968."
—P.L. 90-364, Sec. 105(b)(3), provides as follows [But note amendment by Sec. 702(b)(3) of P.L. 91-172 in '69.]:
"Sec. [105(b)] (3) repeal of subchapter B of chapter 33.—Effective with respect to amounts paid pursuant to bills first rendered on or after January 1, 1973, subchapter B of chapter 33 (relating to the tax on communications) is repealed. For purposes of the preceding sentence, in the case of communications services rendered before November 1, 1972, for which a bill has not been rendered before January 1, 1973, a bill shall be treated as having been first rendered on December 31, 1972. Effective January 1, 1973, the table of subchapters for chapter 33 is amended by striking out the item relating to such subchapter B."
In 1966, P.L. 89-368, Sec. 202(a)(1)-(2), amended Code Sec. 4251 by rewriting subsecs. (a)(2) and (c) for amounts paid pursuant to bills first rendered on or after April 1, 1966, for services rendered on or after such date. In the case of amounts paid pursuant to bills rendered on or after such date for services which were rendered before such date and for which no previous bill was rendered, such amendments shall apply except with respect to such services as were rendered more than 2 months before such date. In the case of services rendered more than 2 months before such date, the provisions of subchapter B of chapter 33 of the Code in effect at the time such services were rendered subject to the provision of section 701(b)(2) of the Excise Tax Reduction Act of 1965, shall apply to the amounts paid for such services.
Prior to amendment, para. (a)(2) read as follows:

3,245

Code Sec. 4251 — Excise and miscellaneous taxes

"Amounts paid pursuant to bills first rendered—	Percent—
During 1966	3
During 1967	2
During 1968	1

Prior to amendment, subsec. (c) read as follows:

"(c) Special rule.

"For purposes of subsections (a) and (b), in the case of communication services rendered before November 1 of any calendar year for which a bill has not been rendered before the close of such year, a bill shall be treated as having been first rendered during such year."

In **1965**, P.L. 89-44, Sec. 302, rewrote Code Sec. 4251 for "amount paid pursuant to bills rendered on or after January 1, 1966, for services rendered on or after such date. In the case of amounts paid pursuant to bills rendered on or after January 1, 1966, for services which were rendered before such date and for which no previous bill was rendered, such amendments shall apply except with respect to such services as were rendered more than 2 months before such date. In the case of services rendered more than 2 months before such date, the provisions of subchapter B of chapter 33 of the Code in effect at the time such services were rendered shall apply to the amounts paid for such services."

Prior to amendment, Code Sec. 4251 read as follows:

"Sec. 4251. Imposition of Tax.

"(a) In general.

"There is hereby imposed on amounts paid for the communication services enumerated in the following table a tax equal to the percent of the amount so paid as is specified in such table:

Taxable service	Rate of tax
	Percent
General telephone service	10
Toll telephone service	10
Telegraph service	10
Teletypewriter exchange service	10
Wire mileage service	10
Wire and equipment service	8

The taxes imposed by this section shall be paid by the person paying for the services.

"(b) Termination of tax on general telephone service.

"(1) In general. Effective as provided in paragraph (2), the tax imposed by this section on amounts paid for general telephone service shall cease to apply.

"(2) Effective date.

"(A) Subject to the provisions of subparagraph (B), paragraph (1) shall apply with respect to amounts paid on or after July 1, 1965, for services rendered on or after such date.

"(B) Paragraph (1) shall not apply with respect to amounts paid pursuant to bills rendered before July 1, 1965. In the case of amounts paid pursuant to bills rendered on or after such date for services for which no previous bill was rendered, paragraph (1) shall apply except with respect to such services as were rendered more than 2 months before such date. Paragraph (1) shall not apply with respect to amounts paid for services rendered more than 2 months before such date."

In **1964**, P.L. 88-348, substituted "July 1, 1965" for "July 1, 1964" in two places in para. (b)(2).

In **1963**, P.L. 88-52, substituted "July 1, 1964" for "July 1, 1963" in two places in para. (b)(2).

In **1962**, P.L. 87-508, substituted "July 1, 1963" for "July 1, 1962" in two places in para. (b)(2).

In **1961**, P.L. 87-72, substituted "July 1, 1962" for "July 1, 1961" in two places in para. (b)(2).

In **1960**, P.L. 86-564, substituted "July 1, 1961" for "July 1, 1960" in two places in para. (b)(2).

In **1959**, P.L. 86-75, designated former provisions as subsec. (a) and added subsec. (b).

In **1958**, P.L. 85-859, rewrote Code Sec. 4251, for amounts paid after '58 for service after '58, except that it "shall not apply with respect to amounts paid pursuant to bills rendered before the effective date prescribed in section 1(c) of this Act [1/1/59]. In the case of amounts paid pursuant to bills rendered on or after such date for services for which no previous bill was rendered, such amendments shall apply except with respect to such services as were rendered more than 2 months before such date. In the case of services rendered more than 2 months before such date the provisions of subchapter B of chapter 33 of the Internal Revenue Code of 1954 in effect at the time such services were rendered shall apply to the amounts paid for such services."

Prior to amendment, the section read as follows:

"There is hereby imposed on amounts paid for the communication services or facilities enumerated in the following table a tax equal to the percent of the amount so paid as is specified in such table:

Taxable service	Rate of tax
	Percent
Local telephone service	10
Long distance telephone service	10
Telegraph service	10

Leased wire, teletypewriter or talking circuit special service	10
Wire and equipment service	8

The taxes imposed by this section shall be paid by the person paying for the services or facilities."

Sec. 4252. Definitions.

(a) Local telephone service.

For purposes of this subchapter, the term "local telephone service" means—

(1) the access to a local telephone system, and the privilege of telephonic quality communication with substantially all persons having telephone or radio telephone stations constituting a part of such local telephone system, and

(2) any facility or service provided in connection with a service described in paragraph (1)

The term "local telephone service" does not include any service which is a "toll telephone service" or a "private communication service" as defined in subsections (b) and (d).

(b) Toll telephone service.

For purposes of this subchapter, the term "toll telephone service" means—

(1) a telephonic quality communication for which (A) there is a toll charge which varies in amount with the distance and elapsed transmission time of each individual communication and (B) the charge is paid within the United States, and

(2) a service which entitles the subscriber, upon payment of a periodic charge (determined as a flat amount or upon the basis of total elapsed transmission time), to the privilege of an unlimited number of telephonic communications to or from all or a substantial portion of the persons having telephone or radio telephone stations in a specified area which is outside the local telephone system area in which the station provided with this service is located.

(c) Teletypewriter exchange service.

For purposes of this subchapter, the term "teletypewriter exchange service" means the access from a teletypewriter or other data station to the teletypewriter exchange system of which such station is a part, and the privilege of intercommunication by such station with substantially all persons having teletypewriter or other data stations constituting a part of the same teletypewriter exchange system, to which the subscriber is entitled upon payment of a charge or charges (whether such charge or charges are determined as a flat periodic amount, on the basis of distance and elapsed transmission time, or in some other manner). The term "teletypewriter exchange service" does not include any service which is "local telephone service" as defined in subsection (a).

(d) Private communication service.

For purposes of this subchapter, the term "private communication service" means—

(1) the communication service furnished to a subscriber which entitles the subscriber—

(A) to exclusive or priority use of any communication channel or groups of channels, or

(B) to the use of an intercommunication system for the subscriber's stations,

regardless of whether such channel, groups of channels, or intercommunication system may be connected through switching with a service described in subsection (a), (b), or (c),

(2) switching capacity, extension lines and stations, or other associated services which are provided in connection with, and are necessary or unique to the use of, channels or systems described in paragraph (1), and

Excise and miscellaneous taxes

Code Sec. 4253(i)

(3) the channel mileage which connects a telephone station located outside a local telephone system area with a central office in such local telephone system,

except that such term does not include any communication service unless a separate charge is made for such service.

In 1965, P.L. 89-44, Sec. 302, amended Code Sec. 4252. See note to Code Sec. 4251 for effective date.

Prior to amendment, Code Sec. 4252 read as follows:

"SEC. 4252. DEFINITIONS.

"(a) General telephone service.

"For purposes of this subchapter, the term 'general telephone service' means any telephone or radio telephone service furnished in connection with any fixed or mobile telephone or radio telephone station which may be connected (directly or indirectly) to an exchange operated by a person engaged in the business of furnishing communication service, if by means of such connection communication may be established with any other fixed or mobile telephone or radio telephone station. Without limiting the preceding sentence, any service described therein shall be treated as including the use of—

"(1) any private branch exchange (and any fixed or mobile telephone or radio telephone station connected, directly or indirectly, with such an exchange), and

"(2) any tie line or extension line.

The term 'general telephone service' does not include any service which is toll telephone service or wire and equipment service.

"(b) Toll telephone service.

"For purposes of this subchapter, the term 'toll telephone service' means a telephone or radio telephone message or conversation for which (1) there is a toll charge, and (2) the charge is paid within the United States.

"(c) Telegraph service.

"For purposes of this subchapter, the term 'telegraph service' means a telegram, cable, or radio dispatch or message for which the charge is paid within the United States.

"(d) Teletypewriter exchange service.

"For purposes of this subchapter, the term 'teletypewriter exchange service' means any service where a teletypewriter (or similar device) may be connected (directly or indirectly) to an exchange operated by a person engaged in the business of furnishing communication service, if by means of such connection communication may be established with any other teletypewriter (or similar device).

"(e) Wire mileage service.

"For purposes of this subchapter, the term 'wire mileage service' means—

"(1) any telephone or radiotelephone service not used in the conduct of a trade or business, and

"(2) any other wire or radio circuit service not used in the conduct of a trade or business, not included in any other subsection of this section; except that such term does not include service used exclusively in furnishing wire and equipment service.

"(f) Wire and equipment service.

"For purposes of this subchapter, the term 'wire and equipment service' includes stock quotation and information services, burglar alarm or fire alarm service, and all other similar services (whether or not oral transmission is involved). Such term does not include teletypewriter exchange service."

In 1962, P.L. 87-508, Sec. 4(a), limited wire mileage service in subsecs. (a)(1) and (2) to service not used in the conduct of a trade or business for services after '62.

In 1958, P.L. 85-859, Sec. 133(a), amended Code Sec. 4252. See note to Code Sec. 4251 for effective date.

Prior to amendment, Code Sec. 4252 read as follows:

"SEC. 4252. DEFINITIONS.

"(a) Local telephone service.

"As used in section 4251 the term, 'local telephone service' means any telephone service not taxable as long distance telephone service; leased wire, teletypewriter or talking circuit special service; or wire and equipment service. Amounts paid for the installation of instruments, wires, poles, switchboards, apparatus, and equipment shall not be considered amounts paid for service. This subsection shall not be construed as defining as local telephone service, amounts paid for services and facilities which are exempted from other communication taxes by section 4253(b).

"(b) Long distance telephone service.

"As used in section 4251 the term 'long distance telephone service' means a telephone or radio telephone message or conversation for which the toll charge is more than 24 cents and for which the charge is paid within the United States.

"(c) Telegraph service.

"As used in section 4251 the term 'telegraph service' means a telegraph, cable, or radio dispatch or message for which the charge is paid within the United States.

"(d) Leased wire, teletypewriter or talking circuit special service.

"As used in section 4251 the term 'leased wire, teletypewriter or talking circuit special service' does not include any service used exclusively in rendering a service taxable as wire and equipment service. The tax imposed by section 4251 with respect to a leased wire, teletypewriter or talking circuit special service shall apply whether or not the wires or services are within a local exchange area.

"(e) Wire and equipment service.

"As used in section 4251 the term 'wire and equipment service' shall include stock quotation and information services, burglar alarm or fire alarm service, and all other similar services, but not including service described in subsection (d) of this section. The tax imposed by section 4251 with respect to wire and equipment service shall apply whether or not the wires or services are within a local exchange area."

Sec. 4253. Exemptions.

(a) Certain coin-operated service.

Service paid for by inserting coins in coin-operated telephones available to the public shall not be subject to the tax imposed by section 4251 with respect to local telephone service, or with respect to toll telephone service if the charge for such toll telephone service is less than 25 cents; except that where such coin-operated telephone service is furnished for a guaranteed amount, the amounts paid under such guarantee plus any fixed monthly or other periodic charge shall be subject to the tax.

(b) News services.

No tax shall be imposed under section 4251, except with respect to local telephone service, on any payment received from any person for services used in the collection of news for the public press, or a news ticker service furnishing a general news service similar to that of the public press, or radio broadcasting, or in the dissemination of news through the public press, or a news ticker service furnishing a general news service similar to that of the public press, or by means of radio broadcasting, if the charge for such service is billed in writing to such person.

(c) International, etc., organizations.

No tax shall be imposed under section 4251 on any payment received for services furnished to an international organization, or to the American National Red Cross.

(d) Servicemen in combat zone.

No tax shall be imposed under section 4251 on any payment received for any toll telephone service which originates within a combat zone, as defined in section 112, from a member of the Armed Forces of the United States performing service in such combat zone, as determined under such section, provided a certificate, setting forth such facts as the Secretary may by regulations prescribe, is furnished to the person receiving such payment.

(e) Items otherwise taxed.

Only one payment of tax under section 4251 shall be required with respect to the tax on any service, notwithstanding the lines or stations of one or more persons are used in furnishing such service.

(f) Common carriers and communications companies.

No tax shall be imposed under section 4251 on the amount paid for any toll telephone service described in section 4252(b)(2) to the extent that the amount so paid is for use by a common carrier, telephone or telegraph company, or radio broadcasting station or network in the conduct of its business as such.

(g) Installation charges.

No tax shall be imposed under section 4251 on so much of any amount paid for the installation of any instrument, wire, pole, switchboard, apparatus, or equipment as is properly attributable to such installation.

(h) Nonprofit hospitals.

No tax shall be imposed under section 4251 on any amount paid by a nonprofit hospital for services furnished to such organization. For purposes of this subsection, the term "nonprofit hospital" means a hospital referred to in section 170(b)(1)(A)(iii) which is exempt from income tax under section 501(a).

(i) State and local governmental exemption.

Under regulations prescribed by the Secretary, no tax shall be imposed under section 4251 upon any payment received for services or facilities furnished to the government of any

State, or any political subdivision thereof, or the District of Columbia.

(j) Exemption for nonprofit educational organizations.

Under regulations prescribed by the Secretary, no tax shall be imposed under section 4251 on any amount paid by a nonprofit educational organization for services or facilities furnished to such organization. For purposes of this subsection, the term "nonprofit educational organization" means an educational organization described in section 170(b)(1)(A)(ii) which is exempt from income tax under section 501(a). The term also includes a school operated as an activity of an organization described in section 501(c)(3) which is exempt from income tax under section 501(a), if such school normally maintains a regular faculty and curriculum and normally has a regularly enrolled body of pupils or students in attendance at the place where its educational activities are regularly carried on.

(k) Exemption for qualified blood collector organizations.

Under regulations provided by the Secretary, no tax shall be imposed under section 4251 on any amount paid by a qualified blood collector organization (as defined in section 7701(a)(49)) for services or facilities furnished to such organization.

(l) Filing of exemption certificates.

(1) In general. In order to claim an exemption under subsection (c), (h), (i), (j), or (k), a person shall provide to the provider of communications services a statement (in such form and manner as the Secretary may provide) certifying that such person is entitled to such exemption.

(2) Duration of certificate. Any statement provided under paragraph (1) shall remain in effect until—

(A) the provider of communications services has actual knowledge that the information provided in such statement is false, or

(B) such provider is notified by the Secretary that the provider of the statement is no longer entitled to an exemption described in paragraph (1).

If any information provided in such statement is no longer accurate, the person providing such statement shall inform the provider of communications services within 30 days of any change of information.

In **2006**, P.L. 109-280, Sec. 1207(c)(1), redesignated subsec. (k) as subsec. (l) and added subsec. (k) . . . Sec. 1207(c)(2), substituted "(j), or (k)" for "or (j)" in subsec. (l [as redesignated by Sec. 1207(c)(1) of this Act, see above]), effective 1/1/2007.

In **1996**, P.L. 104-117, Sec. 1(a)(6) and (b), of this Act, regarding treatment of certain individuals performing services in certain hazardous duty areas, effective 11/21/95, provides:

"(a) General rule. For purposes of the following provisions of the Internal Revenue Code of 1986, a qualified hazardous duty area shall be treated in the same manner as if it were a combat zone (as determined under section 112 of such Code):

* * *

"(6) Section 4253(d) (relating to the taxation of phone service originating from a combat zone from members of the Armed Forces."

* * *

"(b) Qualified hazardous duty area. For purposes of this section, the term 'qualified hazardous duty area' means Bosnia and Herzegovina, Croatia, or Macedonia, if as of the date of the enactment [3/20/96] of this section any member of the Armed Forces of the United States is entitled to special pay under section 310 of title 37, United States Code (relating to special pay; duty subject to hostile fire or imminent danger) for services performed in such country. Such term includes any such country only during the period such entitlement is in effect. Solely for purposes of applying section 7508 of the Internal Revenue Code of 1986, in the case of an individual who is performing services as part of Operation Joint Endeavor outside the United States while deployed away from such individual's permanent duty station, the term 'qualified hazardous duty area' includes, during the period for which such entitlement is in effect, any area in which such services are performed."

In **1990**, P.L. 101-508, Sec. 11217(c)(1), added subsec. (k), effective for any claim for exemption made after 11/5/90, except as provided in Sec. 11217(c)(2)(B) of this Act which reads as follows:

"(B) Duration of existing certificates. Any annual certificate of exemption effective on the date of the enactment of this Act shall remain effective until the end of the annual period."

In **1976**, P.L. 94-455, Sec. 1904(a)(6), added subsecs. (i) and (j), effective 2/1/77.
—P.L. 94-455, Sec. 1906(b)(13)(A), substituted "Secretary" for "Secretary or his delegate" in subsec. (d), effective 2/1/77.

In **1969**, P.L. 91-172, Sec. 101(j)(27), substituted "170(b)(1)(A)(iii)" for "503(b)(5)" in subsec. (h), effective 1/1/70.

In **1966**, P.L. 89-368, Sec. 202(b), added subsec. (h). For effective date, see note to Code Sec. 4251.

In **1965**, P.L. 89-44, Sec. 302, amended Code Sec. 4253. For effective date see note to Code Sec. 4251.

Prior to amendment, Code Sec. 4253 read as follows:

"Sec. 4253. Exemptions.

"(a) Certain coin-operated service.

"Services paid for by inserting coins in coin-operated telephones available to the public shall not be subject to the tax imposed by section 4251 with respect to general telephone service, or with respect to toll telephone service or telegraph service if the charge for such toll telephone service or telegraph service is less than 25 cents; except that where such coin-operated telephone service is furnished for a guaranteed amount, the amounts paid under such guarantee plus any fixed monthly or other periodic charge shall be subject to the tax.

"(b) News services.

"No tax shall be imposed under section 4251, except with respect to general telephone service, on any payment received from any person for services used in the collection of news for the public press, or a news ticker service furnishing a general news service similar to that of the public press, or radio broadcasting, or in the dissemination of news through the public press, or a news ticker service furnishing a general news service similar to that of the public press, or by means of radio broadcasting, if the charge for such services is billed in writing to such person.

"(c) Certain organizations.

"No tax shall be imposed under section 4251 on any payment received for services furnished to an international organization, or to the American National Red Cross.

"(d) Servicemen in combat zone.

"No tax shall be imposed under section 4251 on any payment received for any toll telephone service which originates within a combat zone, as defined in section 112, from a member of the Armed Forces of the United States performing service in such combat zone, as determined under such section, provided a certificate, setting forth such facts as the Secretary or his delegate may by regulations prescribe, is furnished to the person receiving such payment.

"(e) For items otherwise taxed.

"Only one payment of tax under section 4251 shall be required with respect to the tax on toll telephone service, telegraph service, or teletypewriter exchange service, notwithstanding the lines or stations of one or more persons are used in furnishing such service.

"(f) Common carriers and communications companies.

"No tax shall be imposed under section 4251 on the amount paid for—

"(1) any wire mileage service or wire and equipment service; or

"(2) the use of any telephone or radio telephone line or channel which constitutes general telephone service (within the meaning of section 4252(a)), but only if such line or channel connects stations between any two of which there would otherwise be a toll charge, to the extent that the amount so paid is for use by a common carrier, telephone or telegraph company or radio broadcasting station or network in the conduct of its business as such.

"(g) Installation charges.

"No tax shall be imposed under section 4251 on so much of any amount paid for the installation of any instrument, wire, pole, switchboard, apparatus, or equipment as is properly attributable to such installation.

"(h) Terminal facilities in case of wire mileage service.

"No tax shall be imposed under section 4251 on so much of any amount paid for wire mileage service as is paid for, and properly attributable to, the use of any sending or receiving set or device which is station terminal equipment.

"(i) Certain interior communication systems.

"No tax shall be imposed under section 4251 on any amount paid for wire mileage service or wire and equipment service, if such service is rendered through the use of an interior communication system. For purposes of the preceding sentence, the term 'interior communication system' means any system—

"(1) no part of which is situated off the premises of the subscriber, and which may not be connected (directly or indirectly) with any communication system any part of which is situated off the premises of the subscriber, or

"(2) which is situated exclusively in a vehicle of the subscriber.

"(j) Certain private communications services.

"No tax shall be imposed under section 4251 on any amount paid for the use of any telephone or radio-telephone line or channel which constitutes general telephone service (within the meaning of section 4252(a)), if—

"(1) such line or channel is furnished between specified locations in different States or between specified locations in different counties, municipalities, or similar political subdivisions of a State, and

"(2) such use is in the conduct of a trade or business."

In **1962**, P.L. 87-508, Sec. 4(b), added subsec. (j), effective for services furnished on or after 1/1/63.

In **1959**, P.L. 86-344, Sec. [1](f), substituted in subsec. (f) "Common carriers and communications companies" for "Special wire service in company business" in the catchline, incorporated existing provisions in the opening and closing statements and par. (1) and added par. (2) for amounts paid after '58 for services after such date, but not to "amounts paid pursuant to bills rendered before January 1, 1959. In the case of amounts paid pursuant to bills rendered on or after such date for services for which no bill was rendered before such date, such amendment shall apply except with respect to such services as were rendered more than 2 months before such date. In the case of services rendered more than 2 months before such date, the provisions of subchapter B of chapter 33 of the Internal Revenue Code of 1954 in effect at the time such services were rendered shall apply to the amounts paid for such services."

In 1958, P.L. 85-859, Sec. 133(a), amended Code Sec. 4253. See note to Code Sec. 4251 for effective date.

Prior to amendment, Code Sec. 4253 read as follows:

"Sec. 4253. Exemptions.

"(a) Certain coin-operated service.

"Services paid for by inserting coins in coin-operated telephones available to the public shall not be subject to the tax imposed by section 4251 with respect to local telephone service, except that where such coin-operated telephone service is furnished for a guaranteed amount, the amounts paid under such guarantee plus any fixed monthly or other periodic charge shall be subject to the tax.

"(b) News services.

"No tax shall be imposed under section 4251, except with respect to local telephone service, upon any payment received from any person for services or facilities utilized in the collection of news for the public press, or a news ticker service furnishing a general news service similar to that of the public press, or radio broadcasting, or in the dissemination of news through the public press, or a news ticker service furnishing a general news service similar to that of the public press, or by means of radio broadcasting, if the charge for such services or facilities is billed in writing to such person.

"(c) Certain organizations.

"No tax shall be imposed under section 4251 upon any payment received for services or facilities furnished to an international organization, or any organization created by act of Congress to act in matters of relief under the treaty of Geneva of August 22, 1864.

"(d) Servicemen in combat zone.

"No tax shall be imposed under section 4251 with respect to long distance telephone service upon any payment received for any telephone or radio telephone message which originates within a combat zone, as defined in section 112, from a member of the Armed Forces of the United States performing service in such combat zone, as determined under such section, provided a certificate, setting forth such facts as the Secretary or his delegate may by regulations prescribe, is furnished to the person receiving such payment.

"(e) For items otherwise taxed.

"Only one payment of tax under section 4251 shall be required with respect to the tax on long distance telephone service or telegraph service notwithstanding the lines or stations of one or more persons are used in the transmission of such dispatch, message or conversation.

"(f) Special wire service in company business.

"No tax shall be imposed under section 4251 on the amount paid for so much of the service described in sections 4252(d) and (e) as is utilized in the conduct, by a common carrier or a telephone or telegraph company or radio broadcasting station or network, of its business as such."

Sec. 4254. Computation of tax.
(a) General rule.

If a bill is rendered the taxpayer for local telephone service or toll telephone service—

(1) the amount on which the tax with respect to such services shall be based shall be the sum of all charges for such services included in the bill; except that

(2) if the person who renders the bill groups individual items for purposes of rendering the bill and computing the tax, then (A) the amount on which the tax with respect to each such group shall be based shall be the sum of all items within that group, and (B) the tax on the remaining items not included in any such group shall be based on the charge for each item separately.

(b) Where payment is made for toll telephone service in coin-operated telephones.

If the tax imposed by section 4251 with respect to toll telephone service is paid by inserting coins in coin-operated telephones, tax shall be computed to the nearest multiple of 5 cents, except that, where the tax is midway between multiples of 5 cents, the next higher multiple shall apply.

(c) Certain State and local taxes not included.

For purposes of this subchapter, in determining the amounts paid for communications services, there shall not be included the amount of any State or local tax imposed on the furnishing or sale of such services, if the amount of such tax is separately stated in the bill.

In 1977, P.L. 95-172, Sec. 2(a), added subsec. (c), effective only with respect to amounts paid pursuant to bill first rendered on or after 1/1/78 [the first day of the first month which begins more than 20 days after 11/12/77, the date of enactment]. In the case of communications services rendered more than 2 months before 1/1/78, no bill shall be treated as having been first rendered on or after 1/1/78.

In 1965, P.L. 89-44, Sec. 302, amended Code Sec. 4254. See Sec. 4251 for effective date.

Prior to amendment, Code Sec. 4254 read as follows:

"SEC. 4254. COMPUTATION OF TAX.

"(a) In general.

"If a bill is rendered the taxpayer for general telephone service, toll telephone service, or telegraph service—

"(1) the amount on which the tax with respect to such services shall be based shall be the sum of all charges for such services included in the bill; except that

"(2) if the person who renders the bill groups individual items for purposes of rendering the bill and computing the tax, then (A) the amount on which the tax with respect to each such group shall be based shall be the sum of all items within that group, and (B) the tax on the remaining items not included in any such group shall be based on the charge for each item separately.

"(b) Where payment is made for toll telephone service or telegraph service in coin-operated telephones.

"If the tax imposed by section 4251 with respect to toll telephone service or telegraph service is paid by inserting coins in coin-operated telephones, tax shall be computed to the nearest multiple of 5 cents, except that where the tax is midway between multiples of 5 cents, the next higher multiple shall apply."

In 1958, P.L. 85-859, Sec. 133(a), amended Code Sec. 4254. See Code Sec. 4251 for effective date.

Prior to amendment, Code Sec. 4254 read as follows:

"SEC 4254. COMPUTATION OF TAX.

"(a) In General.

"If a bill is rendered the taxpayer for telephone services or telegraph services with respect to which a tax is imposed by section 4251, the amount upon which the tax shall be based shall be the sum of all such charges included in the bill, and the tax shall not be based upon the charge for each item, separately, included in the bill.

"(b) Where payment is made for long distance telephone service or telegraph service in coin-operated telephones.

"If the tax imposed by section 4251 with respect to long distance telephone service or telegraph service is paid by inserting coins in coin-operated telephones, tax shall be computed to the nearest multiple of 5 cents, except that where the tax is midway between multiples of 5 cents, the next higher multiple shall apply."

Subchapter C.—Transportation by Air

Part

I. Persons.

II. Property.

III. Special provisions applicable to taxes on transportation by air.

PART I.—PERSONS

Sec.

4261. Imposition of tax.

4262. Definition of taxable transportation.

4263. Special rules.

In 1970, substituted "Transportation by Air" for "Transportation of Persons by Air" in the heading of Subchapter C and added Parts I–III.

In 1970, repealed former Code Sec. 4263 and redesignated former Code Sec. 4264 as Code Sec. 4263.

In 1962, substituted "Transportation of Persons by Air" for "Transportation of Persons" in heading of Subchapter.

In 1958, in the heading of subchapter substituted "Transportation of Persons" for "Transportation", and struck out Parts I–III, which were included in Subchapter C and also related to transportation of property and transportation of oil by pipeline.

In 1956, redesignated item 4262 as 4263, and added items 4262 and 4264.

Sec. 4261. Imposition of tax.
(a) In general.

There is hereby imposed on the amount paid for taxable transportation of any person a tax equal to 7.5 percent of the amount so paid.

(b) Domestic segments of taxable transportation.

(1) In general. There is hereby imposed on the amount paid for each domestic segment of taxable transportation by air a tax in the amount determined in accordance with the following table for the period in which the segment begins:

In the case of segments beginning:	The tax is:
After September 30, 1997, and before October 1, 1998	$ 1.00
After September 30, 1998, and before October 1, 1999	$ 2.00
After September 30, 1999, and before October 1, 2000	$ 2.25
During 2000	$ 2.50
During 2001	$ 2.75
During 2002 or thereafter	$ 3.00

(2) **Domestic segment.** For purposes of this section, the term "domestic segment" means any segment consisting of 1 takeoff and 1 landing and which is taxable transportation described in section 4262(a)(1).

(3) **Changes in segments by reason of rerouting.** If—
  (A) transportation is purchased between 2 locations on specified flights, and
  (B) there is a change in the route taken between such 2 locations which changes the number of domestic segments, but there is no change in the amount charged for such transportation,
the tax imposed by paragraph (1) shall be determined without regard to such change in route.

(c) **Use of international travel facilities.**
  (1) **In general.** There is hereby imposed a tax of $12.00 on any amount paid (whether within or without the United States) for any transportation of any person by air, if such transportation begins or ends in the United States.
  (2) **Exception for transportation entirely taxable under subsection (a).** This subsection shall not apply to any transportation all of which is taxable under subsection (a) (determined without regard to sections 4281 and 4282).
  (3) **Special rule for Alaska and Hawaii.** In any case in which the tax imposed by paragraph (1) applies to a domestic segment beginning or ending in Alaska or Hawaii, such tax shall apply only to departures and shall be at the rate of $6.

(d) **By whom paid.**
Except as provided in section 4263(a), the taxes imposed by this section shall be paid by the person making the payment subject to the tax.

(e) **Special rules.**
  (1) **Segments to and from rural airports.**
    (A) Exception from segment tax. The tax imposed by subsection (b)(1) shall not apply to any domestic segment beginning or ending at an airport which is a rural airport for the calendar year in which such segment begins or ends (as the case may be).
    (B) Rural airport. For purposes of this paragraph, the term "rural airport" means, with respect to any calendar year, any airport if—
      (i) there were fewer than 100,000 commercial passengers departing by air (in the case of any airport described in clause (ii)(III), on flight segments of at least 100 miles) during the second preceding calendar year from such airport, and
      (ii) such airport—
        (I) is not located within 75 miles of another airport which is not described in clause (i),
        (II) is receiving essential air service subsidies as of the date of the enactment of this paragraph, or
        (III) is not connected by paved roads to another airport.

    (C) No phasein of reduced ticket tax. In the case of transportation beginning before October 1, 1999—
      (i) In general. Paragraph (5) shall not apply to any domestic segment beginning or ending at an airport which is a rural airport for the calendar year in which such segment begins or ends (as the case may be).
      (ii) Transportation involving multiple segments. In the case of transportation involving more than 1 domestic segment at least 1 of which does not begin or end at a rural airport, the 7.5 percent rate applicable by reason of clause (i) shall be applied by taking into account only an amount which bears the same ratio to the amount paid for such transportation as the number of specified miles in domestic segments which begin or end at a rural airport bears to the total number of specified miles in such transportation.

  (2) **Amounts paid outside the United States.** In the case of amounts paid outside the United States for taxable transportation, the taxes imposed by subsections (a) and (b) shall apply only if such transportation begins and ends in the United States.

  (3) **Amounts paid for right to award free or reduced rate air transportation.**
    (A) In general. Any amount paid (and the value of any other benefit provided) to an air carrier (or any related person) for the right to provide mileage awards for (or other reductions in the cost of) any transportation of persons by air shall be treated for purposes of subsection (a) as an amount paid for taxable transportation, and such amount shall be taxable under subsection (a) without regard to any other provision of this subchapter.
    (B) Controlled group. For purposes of subparagraph (A), a corporation and all wholly owned subsidiaries of such corporation shall be treated as 1 corporation.
    (C) Regulations. The Secretary shall prescribe rules which reallocate items of income, deduction, credit, exclusion, or other allowance to the extent necessary to prevent the avoidance of tax imposed by reason of this paragraph. The Secretary may prescribe rules which exclude from the tax imposed by subsection (a) amounts attributable to mileage awards which are used other than for transportation of persons by air.

  (4) **Inflation adjustment of dollar rates of tax.**
    (A) In general. In the case of taxable events in a calendar year after the last nonindexed year, the $3.00 amount contained in subsection (b) and each dollar amount contained in subsection (c) shall be increased by an amount equal to—
      (i) such dollar amount, multiplied by
      (ii) the cost-of-living adjustment determined under section 1(f)(3) for such calendar year by substituting the year before the last nonindexed year for "calendar year 1992" in subparagraph (B) thereof.
    If any increase determined under the preceding sentence is not a multiple of 10 cents, such increase shall be rounded to the nearest multiple of 10 cents.
    (B) Last nonindexed year. For purposes of subparagraph (A), the last nonindexed year is—
      (i) 2002 in the case of the $3.00 amount contained in subsection (b), and
      (ii) 1998 in the case of the dollar amounts contained in subsection (c).
    (C) Taxable event. For purposes of subparagraph (A), in the case of the tax imposed by subsection (b), the beginning of the domestic segment shall be treated as the taxable event.

Excise and miscellaneous taxes Code Sec. 4261

(D) Special rule for amounts paid for domestic segments beginning after 2002. If an amount is paid during a calendar year for a domestic segment beginning in a later calendar year, then the rate of tax under subsection (b) on such amount shall be the rate in effect for the calendar year in which such amount is paid.

(5) Rates of ticket tax for transportation beginning before October 1, 1999. Subsection (a) shall be applied by substituting for "7.5 percent" —

(A) "9 percent" in the case of transportation beginning after September 30, 1997, and before October 1, 1998, and

(B) "8 percent" in the case of transportation beginning after September 30, 1998, and before October 1, 1999.

(f) Exemption for certain uses.

No tax shall be imposed under subsection (a) or (b) on air transportation—

(1) by helicopter for the purpose of transporting individuals, equipment, or supplies in the exploration for, or the development or removal of, hard minerals, oil, or gas, or

(2) by helicopter or by fixed-wing aircraft for the purpose of the planting, cultivation, cutting, or transportation of, or caring for, trees (including logging operations),

but only if the helicopter or fixed-wing aircraft does not take off from, or land at, a facility eligible for assistance under the Airport and Airway Development Act of 1970, or otherwise use services provided pursuant to section 44509 or 44913(b) or subchapter I of chapter 471 of title 49, United States Code, during such use. In the case of helicopter transportation described in paragraph (1), this subsection shall be applied by treating each flight segment as a distinct flight.

(g) Exemption for air ambulances providing certain emergency medical transportation.

No tax shall be imposed under this section or section 4271 on any air transportation for the purpose of providing emergency medical services—

(1) by helicopter, or

(2) by a fixed-wing aircraft equipped for and exclusively dedicated on that flight to acute care emergency medical services.

(h) Exemption for skydiving uses.

No tax shall be imposed by this section or section 4721 on any air transportation exclusively for the purposes of skydiving.

(i) Exemption for seaplanes.

No tax shall be imposed by this section or section 4271 on any air transportation by a seaplane with respect to any segment consisting of a takeoff from, and a landing on, water, but only if the places at which such takeoff and landing occur have not received and are not receiving financial assistance from the Airport and Airways Trust Fund.

(j) Application of taxes.

(1) In general. The taxes imposed by this section shall apply to—

(A) transportation beginning during the period—

(i) beginning on the 7th day after the date of the enactment of the Airport and Airway Trust Fund Tax Reinstatement Act of 1997, and

(ii) ending on July 22, 2011, and

(B) amounts paid during such period for transportation beginning after such period.

(2) Refunds. If, as of the date any transportation begins, the taxes imposed by this section would not have applied to such transportation if paid for on such date, any tax paid under paragraph (1)(B) with respect to such transportation shall be treated as overpayment.

In 2011, P.L. 112-21, Sec. 2(b)(1), substituted "July 22, 2011" for "June 30, 2011" in clause (j)(1)(A)(ii), effective 7/1/2011.
—P.L. 112-16, Sec. 2(b)(1), substituted "June 30, 2011" for "May 31, 2011" in clause (j)(1)(A)(ii), effective 6/1/2011.
—P.L. 112-7, Sec. 2(b)(1), substituted "May 31, 2011" for "March 31, 2011" in clause (j)(1)(A)(ii), effective 4/1/2011.
In 2010, P.L. 111-329, Sec. 2(b)(1), substituted "March 31, 2011" for "December 31, 2010" in clause (j)(1)(A)(ii), effective 1/1/2011.
—P.L. 111-249, Sec. 2(b)(1), substituted "December 31, 2010" for "September 30, 2010" in clause (j)(1)(A)(ii), effective 10/1/2010.
—P.L. 111-216, Sec. 101(b)(1), substituted "September 30, 2010" for "August 1, 2010" in clause (j)(1)(A)(ii), effective 8/2/2010.
—P.L. 111-197, Sec. 2(b)(1), substituted "August 1, 2010" for "July 3, 2010" in clause (j)(1)(A)(ii), effective 7/4/2010.
—P.L. 111-161, Sec. 2(b)(1), substituted "July 3, 2010" for "April 30, 2010" in clause (j)(1)(A)(ii), effective 5/1/2010.
—P.L. 111-153, Sec. 2(b)(1), substituted "April 30, 2010" for "March 31, 2010" in clause (j)(1)(A)(ii), effective 4/1/2010.
In 2009, P.L. 111-116, Sec. 2(b)(1), substituted "March 31, 2010" for "December 31, 2009" in clause (j)(1)(A)(ii), effective 1/1/2010.
—P.L. 111-69, Sec. 2(b)(1), substituted "December 31, 2009" for "September 30, 2009" in clause (j)(1)(A)(ii), effective 10/1/2009.
—P.L. 111-12, Sec. 2(b)(1), substituted "September 30, 2009" for "March 31, 2009" in clause (j)(1)(A)(ii), effective 4/1/2009.
In 2008, P.L. 110-330, Sec. 2(b)(1), substituted "March 31, 2009" for "September 30, 2008" in clause (j)(1)(A)(ii), effective 10/1/2008.
—P.L. 110-253, Sec. 2(b)(1), substituted "September 30, 2008" for "June 30, 2008" in clause (j)(1)(A)(ii), effective 7/1/2008.
—P.L. 110-190, Sec. 2(b)(1), substituted "June 30, 2008" for "February 29, 2008" in subpara. (e)(1)(A)(ii), effective 3/1/2008.
In 2007, P.L. 110-161, Sec. 116(b)(1), substituted "February 29, 2008" for "September 30, 2007" in clause (j)(1)(A)(ii), effective 10/1/2007.
In 2005, P.L. 109-135, Sec. 412(vv), substituted "imposed by subsection (b)" for "imposed subsection (b)" in subpara. (e)(4)(C), effective 12/21/2005.
—P.L. 109-59, Sec. 11121(c), amended subsec. (f), effective for fuel use or air transportation after 9/30/2005.
Prior to amendment, subsec. (f) read as follows:
"(f) Exemption for certain helicopter uses. No tax shall be imposed under subsection (a) or (b) on air transportation by helicopter for the purpose of—
"(1) transporting individuals, equipment, or supplies in the exploration for, or the development or removal of, hard minerals, oil, or gas, or
"(2) the planting, cultivation, cutting, or transportation of, or caring for, trees (including logging operations),
but only if the helicopter does not take off from, or land at, a facility eligible for assistance under the Airport and Airway Development Act of 1970, or otherwise use services provided pursuant to section 44509 or 44913(b) or subchapter I of chapter 471 of title 49, United States Code, during such use. In the case of helicopter transportation described in paragraph (1), this subsection shall be applied by treating each flight segment as a distinct flight."
—P.L. 109-59, Sec. 11122(a)(1), added "(in the case of any airport described in clause (ii)(III), on flight segments of at least 100 miles)" after "by air" in clause (e)(1)(B)(i) . . . Sec. 11122(a)(2), deleted "or" at the end of subclause (e)(1)(B)(ii)(I), substituted ", or" for the period at the end of subclause (e)(1)(B)(ii)(II), and added subclause (e)(1)(B)(ii)(III), effective 10/1/2005.
—P.L. 109-59, Sec. 11123(a), redesignated subsec. (i) as (j) and added subsec. (i), effective for transportation begin. after 9/30/2005.
In 2003, P.L. 108-176, Sec. 902(a), added new subpara. (e)(4)(D), effective for transportation begin. on or after 10/1/97.
In 1997, P.L. 105-34, Sec. 1031(b)(1), substituted "September 30, 2007" for "September 30, 1997" in clause (g)(1)(A)(ii), effective for transportation begin. on or after 10/1/97.
—P.L. 105-34, Sec. 1031(c)(1), amended subsecs. (a)-(c), effective for transportation begin. on or after 10/1/97. Sec. 1031(e)(2)(B) of this Act provides:
"(B) Treatment of amounts paid for tickets purchased before October 1, 1997. The amendments made by subsection (c) shall not apply to amounts paid before October 1, 1997; except that—
"(i) the amendment made to section 4261(c) of the Internal Revenue Code of 1986 shall apply to amounts paid more than 7 days after the date of enactment of this Act for transportation beginning on or after October 1, 1997, and
"(ii) the amendment made to section 4263(c) of such Code shall apply to the extent related to taxes imposed under the amendment made to such section 4261(c) on the amounts described in clause (i)."
Prior to amendment, subsecs. (a)-(c) read as follows:
"(a) In general. There is hereby imposed upon the amount paid for taxable transportation (as defined in section 4262) of any person a tax equal to 10 percent of the amount so paid. In the case of amounts paid outside of the United States for taxable transportation, the tax imposed by this subsection shall apply only if such transportation begins and ends in the United States.
"(b) Seats, berths, etc. There is hereby imposed upon the amount paid for seating or sleeping accommodations in connection with transportation and with respect to which a tax is imposed by subsection (a), a tax equal to 10 percent of the amount so paid.
"(c) Use of international travel facilities. There is hereby imposed a tax of $6 upon any amount paid (whether within or without the United States) for any transportation of any person by air, if such transportation begins in the United

3,251

Code Sec. 4261 — Excise and miscellaneous taxes

States. This subsection shall not apply to any transportation all of which is taxable under subsection (a) (determined without regard to sections 4281 and 4282)."

—P.L. 105-34, Sec. 1031(c)(2), redesignated subsecs. (e)-(g) as subsecs. (g)-(h) and added new subsec. (e), effective for transportation begin. on or after 10/1/97. For Sec. 1031(e)(2)(B) of this Act, see above. Sec. 1031(e)(2)(C) of this Act provides:

"(C) Amounts paid for right to award mileage awards.

"(i) In general. Paragraph (3) of section 4261(e) of the Internal Revenue Code of 1986 (as added by the amendment made by subsection (c)) shall apply to amounts paid (and other benefits provided) after September 30, 1997.

"(ii) Payments within controlled group. For purposes of clause (i), any amount paid after June 11, 1997, and before October 1, 1997, by 1 member of a controlled group or a right which is described in such section 4261(e)(3) and is furnished by another member of such group after September 30, 1997, shall be treated as paid after September 30, 1997. For purposes of the preceding sentence, all persons treated as a single employer under subsection (a) or (b) of section 52 of such Code shall be treated as members of a controlled group."

—P.L. 105-34, Sec. 1031(g), of this Act, reads as follows:

"(g) Delayed deposits of Airport Trust Fund Tax Revenues. Notwithstanding section 6302 of the Internal Revenue Code of 1986 —

"(1) in the case of deposits of taxes imposed by section 4261 of such Code, the due date for any such deposit which would (but for this subsection) be required to be made after August 14, 1997, and before October 1, 1997, shall be October 10, 1997,

"(2) in the case of deposits of taxes imposed by section 4261 of such Code, the due date for any such deposit which would (but for this subsection) be required to be made after August 14, 1998, and before October 1, 1998, shall be October 5, 1998, and

"(3) in the case of deposits of taxes imposed by sections 4081(a)(2)(A)(ii), 4091, and 4271 of such Code, the due date for any such deposit which would (but for this subsection) be required to be made after July 31, 1998, and before October 1, 1998, shall be October 5, 1998."

—P.L. 105-34, Sec. 1435(a), redesignated subsec. (h) as subsec. (i) and added new subsec. (h), effective for amounts paid after 9/30/97.

—P.L. 105-34, Sec. 1601(f)(4)(D), added "on that flight" after "dedicated" in para. (g)(2) [as redesignated by Sec. 1031(c)(2) of this Act, see above], effective on the 7th calendar day after 8/20/96.

—P.L. 105-2, Sec. 2(b)(1), amended subsec. (g), effective as provided in Sec. 2(e)(2), of this Act, which reads as follows:

"(2) Ticket taxes.—

"(A) In general.— The amendments made by subsection (b) shall apply to transportation beginning on or after such 7th day.

"(B) Exception for certain payments.— Except as provided in subparagraph (C), the amendments made by subsection (b) shall not apply to any amount paid before such 7th day.

"(C) Payments of property transportation tax within controlled group.— In the case of the tax imposed by section 4271 of the Internal Revenue Code of 1986, subparagraph (B) shall not apply to any amount paid by 1 member of a controlled group for transportation furnished by another member of such group. For purposes of the preceding sentence, all persons treated as a single employer under subsection (a) or (b) of section 52 of the Internal Revenue Code of 1986 shall be treated as members of a controlled group."

Prior to amendment, subsec. (g) read as follows:

"(g) Termination. The taxes imposed by this section shall apply with respect to transportation beginning after August 31, 1982, and before January 1, 1996, and to transportation beginning on or after the date which is 7 calendar days after the date of the enactment of the Small Business Job Protection Act of 1996 and before January 1, 1997."

In 1996, P.L. 104-188, Sec. 1609(b), substituted "January 1, 1996, and to transportation beginning on or after the date which is 7 calendar days after the date of the enactment of the Small Business Job Protection Act of 1996 and before January 1, 1997" for "January 1, 1996" in subsec. (g) . . . Sec. 1609(d), amended subsec. (f) . . . Sec. 1609(e), added the sentence to the end of subsec. (e), effective on the 7th calendar day after 8/20/96, except that amendments made by subsection (b) shall not apply to any amount paid before such date.

Prior to amendment, subsec. (f) read as follows:

"(f) Exemption for certain emergency medical transportation. No tax shall be imposed under this section or section 4271 on any air transportation by helicopter for the purpose of providing emergency medical services if such helicopter—

"(1) does not take off from, or land at, a facility eligible for assistance under the Airport and Airway Development Act of 1970 during such transportation, and

"(2) does not otherwise use services provided pursuant to section 44509 or 44913(b) or subchapter I of chapter 471 of title 49, United States Code, during such transportation."

In 1994, P.L. 103-272, Sec. 5(g)(2), substituted "section 44509 or 44913(b) or subchapter I of chapter 471 of title 49, United States Code," for "the Airport and Airway Improvement Act of 1982" in subsec. (e) and para. (f)(2), effective 7/5/94.

In 1990, P.L. 101-508, Sec. 11213(a)(1), substituted "10 percent" for "8 percent" in subsecs. (a) and (b), effective for transportation begin. after 11/30/90, but not for amounts paid on or before 11/30/90.

—P.L. 101-508, Sec. 11213(d)(1), substituted "January 1, 1996" for "January 1, 1991" in subsec. (g), effective 11/5/90.

In 1989, P.L. 101-239, Sec. 7503(a), substituted "6" for "3", in subsec. (c), effective for transportation begin. after 12/31/89, which was not paid for before 12/31/89.

In 1987, P.L. 100-223, Sec. 402(a)(1), substituted "January 1, 1991" for "January 1, 1988" in subsec. (f), effective 12/30/87.

—P.L. 100-223, Sec. 404(a), redesignated subsec. (f) as subsec. (g) and added new subsec. (f), effective for transportation begin. after 9/30/88, but shall not apply to amounts paid on or before 9/30/88.

—P.L. 100-223, Sec. 404(c), substituted "Improvement Act" for "System Improvement Act" in subsec. (e), effective 12/30/87.

In 1986, P.L. 99-514, Sec. 1878(c)(2), amended para. (e)(1), effective for transportation beginning after 3/31/84, but shall not apply to any amount paid on or before 3/31/84.

Prior to amendment, para. (e)(1) read as follows:

"(1) transporting individuals, equipment, or supplies in—

"(A) the exploration for, or the development or removal of, hard minerals, or

"(B) the exploration for oil or gas, or"

In 1984, P.L. 98-369, Sec. 1018(b), amended para. (e)(1), effective for transportation beginning after 3/31/84, but shall not apply to any amount paid on or before 3/31/84.

Prior to amendment, para. (e)(1) read as follows:

"(1) transporting individuals, equipment, or supplies in the exploration for, or the development or removal of, hard minerals, or"

In 1982, P.L. 97-248, Sec. 280(a), amended subsec. (e) and added subsec. (f), effective for transportation begin. after 8/31/82, except for any amount paid on or before 8/31/82.

Prior to amendment, subsec. (e) read as follows:

"(e) Reduction, etc., of rates.

"Effective with respect to transportation beginning after September 30, 1980 —

"(1) the rate of the taxes imposed by subsection (a) and (b) shall be 5 percent, and

"(2) the tax imposed by subsection (c) shall not apply."

In 1980, P.L. 96-298, Sec. 1(b), substituted "September 30, 1980" for "June 30, 1980" in subsec. (e), effective 7/1/80 [date of enactment].

In 1976, P.L. 94-455, Sec. 1904(a)(7)(A), deleted "which begins after June 30, 1970," after "any person" in subsec. (a) and after "with transportation" in subsec. (b) . . . Sec. 1904(a)(7)(B), deleted "and which begins after June 30, 1970" after "if such transportation begins in the United States" in subsec. (c), effective 2/1/77.

In 1970, P.L. 91-258, Sec. 203(a), amended Code Sec. 4261, effective for transportation begin. after 6/30/70.

Prior to amendment, Code Sec. 4261 read as follows:

"Sec. 4261. Imposition of tax.

"(a) Amounts paid within the United States.

"There is hereby imposed upon the amount paid within the United States for taxable transportation (as defined in section 4642) of any person by air a tax equal to 5 percent of the amount so paid for transportation which begins after November 15, 1962.

"(b) Amounts paid outside the United States.

"There is hereby imposed upon the amount paid without the United States for taxable transportation (as defined in section 4262) of any person by air, but only if such transportation begins and ends in the United States, a tax equal to 5 percent of the amount so paid for transportation which begins after November 15, 1962.

"(c) Seats, berths, etc.

"There is hereby imposed upon the amount paid for seating or sleeping accommodations in connection with transportation with respect to which a tax is imposed by subsection (a) or (b) a tax equivalent to 5 percent of the amount so paid in connection with transportation which begins after November 15, 1962.

"(d) By whom paid.

"Except as provided in section 4264, the taxes imposed by this section shall be paid by the person making the payment subject to the tax."

In 1965, P.L. 89-44, Sec. 303, deleted "and before July 1, 1965" after "November 15, 1962" in subsecs. (a), (b), and (c), effective 7/1/65.

In 1964, P.L. 88-348, Sec. 2(a)(3), substituted "1965" for "1964" each place it appeared, effective 7/17/64.

In 1963, P.L. 88-52, Sec. 3(a)(3), substituted "1964" for "1963" each place it appeared.

In 1962, P.L. 87-508, Sec. 5(a), amended subsecs. (a), (b) and (c), effective 6/28/62.

Prior to amendment, subsecs. (a), (b) and (c) read as follows:

"(a) Amounts paid within the United States.

"There is hereby imposed upon the amount paid within the United States for taxable transportation (as defined in section 4262) of any person by rail, motor vehicle, water, or air a tax equal to—

"(1) 10 percent of the amount so paid before July 1, 1962; or

"(2) 5 percent of the amount so paid on or after July 1, 1962.

"(b) Amounts paid outside the United States.

"There is hereby imposed upon the amount paid without the United States for taxable transportation (as defined in section 4262) of any person by rail, motor vehicle, water, or air, but only if such transportation begins and ends in the United States, a tax equal to—

"(1) 10 percent of the amount so paid before July 1, 1962; or

"(2) 5 percent of the amount so paid on or after July 1, 1962.

"(c) Seats, berths, etc.

"There is hereby imposed upon the amount paid for seating or sleeping accommodations in connection with transportation with respect to which a tax is imposed by subsection (a) or (b) a tax equivalent to—

Excise and miscellaneous taxes Code Sec. 4262(e)(3)

"(1) 10 percent of the amount so paid before July 1, 1962, or
"(2) 5 percent of the amount so paid on or after July 1, 1962."
—P.L. 87-508, Sec. 5(b), amended Code Sec. 4261 [as amended by Sec. 5(a) of this Act], effective for transportation beginning after 11/15/62.
Prior to amendment, Code Sec. 4261 read as follows:
"Sec. 4261. Imposition of Tax.
"(a) Amounts Paid Within the United States.
"There is hereby imposed upon the amount paid within the United States for taxable transportation (as defined in section 4262) of any person by rail, motor vehicle, water, or air a tax equal to 10 percent of the amount so paid for transportation which begins before November 16, 1962.
"(b) Amounts Paid Outside the United States.
"There is hereby imposed upon the amount paid without the United States for taxable transportation (as defined in section 4262) of any person by rail, motor vehicle, water, or air, but only if such transportation begins and ends in the United States, a tax equal to 10 percent of the amount so paid for transportation which begins before November 16, 1962.
"(c) Seats, Berths, etc.
"There is hereby imposed upon the amount paid for seating or sleeping accommodations in connection with transportation with respect to which a tax is imposed by subsection (a) or (b) a tax equivalent to 10 percent of the amount so paid in connection with transportation which begins before November 16, 1962.
"(d) By whom paid.
"Except as provided in section 4264, the taxes imposed by this section shall be paid by the person making the payment subject to the tax."
In 1961, P.L. 87-72, Sec. 3(a)(3), substituted "1962" for "1961" each place it appeared in Code Sec. 4261, effective 6/30/60.
In 1960, P.L. 86-564, Sec. 202(a)(3), substituted "1961" for "1960" each place it appeared in Code Sec. 4261, effective 6/30/60.
In 1959, P.L. 86-75, Sec. 4, reduced tax on transportation of persons from ten to five percent, effective 7/1/60.
In 1956, P.L. 725, Sec. 1, amended subsecs. (a) and (b) . . . Sec. 4(b), substituted "Except as provided in section 4264, the" for "The" in subsec. (d), effective for amounts paid after 9/30/56 for transportation commencing after that date.
Prior to amendment, subsecs. (a) and (b) read as follows:
"(a) Amounts paid within the United States.
"There is hereby imposed upon the amount paid within the United States for the transportation of persons by rail, motor vehicle, water, or air within or without the United States a tax equal to 10 percent of the amount so paid."
"(b) Amounts paid without the United States.
"There is hereby imposed upon the amount paid without the United States for the transportation of persons by rail, motor vehicle, water, or air which begins and ends in the United States a tax equal to 10 percent of the amount so paid."

Sec. 4262. Definition of taxable transportation.
(a) Taxable transportation; in general.
For purposes of this part, except as provided in subsection (b), the term "taxable transportation" means—
(1) transportation by air which begins in the United States or in the 225-mile zone and ends in the United States or in the 225-mile zone; and
(2) in the case of transportation by air other than transportation described in paragraph (1), that portion of such transportation which is directly or indirectly from one port or station in the United States to another port or station in the United States, but only if such portion is not a part of uninterrupted international air transportation (within the meaning of subsection (c)(3)).
(b) Exclusion of certain travel.
For purposes of this part, the term "taxable transportation" does not include that portion of any transportation by air which meets all 4 of the following requirements:
(1) such portion is outside the United States;
(2) neither such portion nor any segment thereof is directly or indirectly—
  (A) between (i) a point where the route of the transportation leaves or enters the continental United States, or (ii) a port or station in the 225-mile zone, and
  (B) a port or station in the 225-mile zone;
(3) such portion—
  (A) begins at either (i) the point where the route of the transportation leaves the United States, or (ii) a port or station in the 225-mile zone, and
  (B) ends at either (i) the point where the route of the transportation enters the United States, or (ii) a port or station in the 225-mile zone; and

(4) a direct line from the point (or the port or station) specified in paragraph (3)(A), to the point (or the port or station) specified in paragraph (3)(B), passes through or over a point which is not within 225 miles of the United States.
(c) Definitions.
For purposes of this section—
(1) Continental United States. The term "continental United States" means the District of Columbia and the States other than Alaska and Hawaii.
(2) 225-mile zone. The term "225-mile zone" means that portion of Canada and Mexico which is not more than 225 miles from the nearest point in the continental United States.
(3) Uninterrupted international air transportation. The term "uninterrupted international air transportation" means any transportation by air which is not transportation described in subsection (a)(1) and in which—
  (A) the scheduled interval between (i) the beginning or end of the portion of such transportation which is directly or indirectly from one port or station in the United States to another port or station in the United States and (ii) the end or beginning of the other portion of such transportation is not more than 12 hours, and
  (B) the scheduled interval between the beginning or end and the end or beginning of any two segments of the portion of such transportation referred to in subparagraph (A)(i) is not more than 12 hours.
For purposes of this paragraph, in the case of personnel of the United States Army, Air Force, Navy, Marine Corps, and Coast Guard traveling in uniform at their own expense when on official leave, furlough, or pass, the scheduled interval described in subparagraph (A) shall be deemed to be not more than 12 hours if a ticket for the subsequent portion of such transportation is purchased within 12 hours after the end of the earlier portion of such transportation and the purchaser accepts and utilizes the first accommodations actually available to him for such subsequent portion.
(d) Transportation.
For purposes of this part, the term "transportation" includes layover or waiting time and movement of the aircraft in deadhead service.
(e) Authority to waive 225-mile zone provisions.
(1) In general. If the Secretary of the Treasury determines that Canada or Mexico has entered into a qualified agreement—
  (A) the Secretary shall publish a notice of such determination in the Federal Register, and
  (B) effective with respect to transportation beginning after the date specified in such notice, to the extent provided in the agreement, the term "225-mile zone" shall not include part or all of the country with respect to which such determination is made.
(2) Termination of waiver. If a determination was made under paragraph (1) with respect to any country and the Secretary of the Treasury subsequently determines that the agreement is no longer in effect or that the agreement is no longer a qualified agreement—
  (A) the Secretary shall publish a notice of such determination in the Federal Register, and
  (B) subparagraph (B) of paragraph (1) shall cease to apply with respect to transportation beginning after the date specified in such notice.
(3) Qualified agreement. For purposes of this subsection, the term "qualified agreement" means an agreement be-

tween the United States and Canada or Mexico (as the case may be)—

(A) setting forth that portion of such country which is not to be treated as within the 225-mile zone, and

(B) providing that the tax imposed by such country on transportation described in subparagraph (A) will be at a level which the Secretary of the Treasury determines to be appropriate.

(4) Requirement that agreement be submitted to Congress. No notice may be published under paragraph (1)(A) with respect to any qualified agreement before the date 90 days after the date on which a copy of such agreement was furnished to the Committee on Ways and Means of the House of Representatives and the Committee on Finance of the Senate.

In **1982**, P.L. 97-248, Sec. 281A(a)(1), substituted "12 hours" for "6 hours" each place it appeared in para. (c)(3) . . . Sec. 281A(a)(2), added subsec. (e), effective for transportation begin. after 8/31/82.

In **1970**, P.L. 91-258, Sec. 203(b), amended subsecs. (a) and (b) and added subsec. (d), effective for transportation beginning after 6/30/70.

Prior to amendment, subsecs. (a) and (b) read as follows:

"(a) Taxable transportation; in general.

"For purposes of this subchapter, except as provided in subsection (b), the term 'taxable transportation' means

"(1) transportation which begins in the United States or in the 225-mile zone and ends in the United States or in the 225-mile zone; and

"(2) in the case of transportation other than transportation described in paragraph (1), that portion of such transportation which is directly or indirectly from one port or station in the United States to another port or station in the United States, but only if such portion is not a part of uninterrupted international air transportation (within the meaning of subsection (c)(3)).

"(b) Exclusion of certain travel.

"For purposes of this subchapter, the term 'taxable transportation' does not include that portion of any transportation which meets all 4 of the following requirements:

"(1) such portion is outside the United States;

"(2) neither such portion nor any segment thereof is directly or indirectly

"(A) between (i) a point where the route of the transportation leaves or enters the continental United States, or (ii) a port or station in the 225-mile zone, and

"(B) a port or station in the 225-mile zone;

"(3) such portion

"(A) begins at either (i) the point where the route of the transportation leaves the United States, or (ii) a port or station in the 225-mile zone, and

"(B) ends at either (i) the point where the route of the transportation enters the United States, or (ii) a port or station in the 225-mile zone; and

"(4) a direct line from the point (or the port or station) specified in paragraph (3)(A), to the point (or the port or station) specified in paragraph (3)(B), passes through or over a point which is not within 225 miles of the United States."

In **1965**, P.L. 89-44, Sec. 803, added the last sentence to subsec. (c)(3), effective for amounts paid for transportation beginning on or after 7/1/65.

In **1962**, P.L. 87-508, Sec. 5(b), substituted in subsecs. (a) and (b) in the introductory phrase "subchapter" for "part", added ", but only if such portion is not a part of uninterrupted international air transportation (within the meaning of subsection (c)(3))" in para. (a)(2), and added subsec. (c)(3), effective for transportation beginning after 11/15/62.

In **1960**, P.L. 86-624, Sec. 18(a), added words "and Hawaii" after "Alaska" in subsec. (c)(1), effective 8/21/59.

In **1959**, P.L. 86-70, Sec. 22(b), substituted "the District of Columbia and the States other than Alaska" for "the existing 48 States and the District of Columbia" in subsec. (c)(1), effective 1/3/59.

In **1956**, ch. 725, Sec. 3, added present Code Sec. 4262 and redesignated former Code Sec. 4262 as 4263, effective for amounts paid on or after 10/1/56 for transportation commencing on or after such day.

Sec. 4263. Special rules.

(a) Payments made outside the United States for prepaid orders.

If the payment upon which tax is imposed by section 4261 is made outside the United States for a prepaid order, exchange order, or similar order, the person furnishing the initial transportation pursuant to such order shall collect the amount of the tax.

(b) Tax deducted upon refunds.

Every person who refunds any amount with respect to a ticket or order which was purchased without payment of the tax imposed by section 4261 shall deduct from the amount refundable, to the extent available, any tax due under such section as a result of the use of a portion of the transportation purchased in connection with such ticket or order, and shall report to the Secretary the amount of any such tax remaining uncollected.

(c) Payment of tax.

Where any tax imposed by section 4261 is not paid at the time payment for transportation is made, then, under regulations prescribed by the Secretary, to the extent that such tax is not collected under any other provision of this subchapter, such tax shall be paid by the carrier providing the initial segment of such transportation which begins or ends in the United States.

(d) Application of tax.

The tax imposed by section 4261 shall apply to any amount paid within the United States for transportation of any person by air unless the taxpayer establishes, pursuant to regulations prescribed by the Secretary, at the time of payment for the transportation, that the transportation is not transportation in respect of which tax is imposed by section 4261.

(e) Round trips.

In applying this subchapter to a round trip, such round trip shall be considered to consist of transportation from the point of departure to the destination, and of separate transportation thereafter.

(f) Transportation outside the northern portion of the Western Hemisphere.

In applying this subchapter to transportation any part of which is outside the northern portion of the Western Hemisphere, if the route of such transportation leaves and reenters the northern portion of the Western Hemisphere, such transportation shall be considered to consist of transportation to a point outside such northern portion, and of separate transportation thereafter. For purposes of this subsection, the term "northern portion of the Western Hemisphere" means the area lying west of the 30th meridian west of Greenwich, east of the international dateline, and north of the Equator, but not including any country of South America.

In **1997**, P.L. 105-34, Sec. 1031(c)(3), substituted "subchapter, such tax shall be paid by the carrier providing the initial segment of such transportation which begins or ends in the United States" for "subchapter—" and paras. (c)(1)-(3), effective for transportation begin. on or after 10/1/97, except as provided in Sec. 1031(e)(2)(B) of this Act, which reads:

"(B) Treatment of amounts paid for tickets purchased before October 1, 1997. The amendments made by subsection (c) shall not apply to amounts paid before October 1, 1997; except that—

"(i) the amendment made to section 4261(c) of the Internal Revenue Code of 1986 shall apply to amounts paid more than 7 days after the date of enactment of this Act for transportation beginning on or after October 1, 1997, and

"(ii) the amendment made to section 4263(c) of such Code shall apply to the extent related to taxes imposed under the amendment made to such section 4261(c) on the amounts described in clause (i)."

Prior to deletion, paras. (c)(1)-(3) read as follows:

"(1) such tax shall be paid by the person paying for the transportation or by the person using the transportation;

"(2) such tax shall be paid within such time as the Secretary shall prescribe by regulations after whichever of the following first occurs:

"(A) the rights to the transportation expire; or

"(B) the time when the transportation becomes subject to tax; and

"(3) payment of such tax shall be made to the Secretary, to the person to whom the payment for transportation was made, or, in the case of transportation other than transportation described in section 4262(a)(1), to any person furnishing any portion of such transportation."

In **1976**, P.L. 94-455, Sec. 1906(b)(13)(A), substituted "Secretary" for "Secretary or his delegate" each place it appeared in Code Sec. 4263, effective 2/1/77.

In **1970**, P.L. 91-258, Sec. 205(c)(2), redesignated former Code Sec. 4264 as Code Sec. 4263, effective 7/1/70.

In **1962**, P.L. 87-508, Sec. 5(b), provided for payment of tax, in the case of transportation other than transportation described in section 4262(a)(1), to any person furnishing any portion of the transportation in subsec. (c)(3); added "by air" after "transportation of any person" in subsec. (d); substituted "subchapter" for "part" in subsec. (e); and amended subsec. (f) effective for transportation beginning after 11/15/62.

Excise and miscellaneous taxes Code Sec. 4271

Prior to amendment, subsec. (f) read as follows:
"(f) Transportation outside the northern portion of the western hemisphere.
"In applying this part to transportation any part of which is outside the northern portion of the Western Hemisphere—
"(1) If the route of such transportation leaves and reenters the northern portion of the Western Hemisphere, such transportation shall be considered to consist of transportation to a point outside such northern portion, and of separate transportation thereafter.
"(2) If such transportation is transportation by water on a vessel which makes one or more intermediate stops at ports within the United States on a voyage which begins or ends in the United States and ends or begins outside the northern portion of the Western Hemisphere, a stop at an intermediate port within the United States at which such vessel is not authorized both to discharge and to take on passengers shall not be considered to be a stop at a port within the United States.
For purposes of this subsection, the term 'northern portion of the Western Hemisphere' means the area lying west of the 30th meridian west of Greenwich, east of the International Date Line, and north of the Equator, but not including any country of South America."
In 1956, P.L. 796, Sec. 0, added Code Sec. 4264 for amounts paid after 9/30/56 for transportation commencing after that date.
Note: Former Code Sec. 4263 repealed.
In 1970, P.L. 91-258, Sec. 205(c)(1), repealed former Code Sec. 4263, effective 7/1/70. Before repeal, Code Sec. 4263 read as follows:
"Sec. 4263. Exemptions.
"(a) Commutation travel, etc.
"The tax imposed by section 4261 shall not apply to amounts paid for transportation which do not exceed 60 cents, to amounts paid for commutation or season tickets for single trips of less than 30 miles, or to amounts paid for commutation tickets for one month or less.
"(b) Certain organizations.
"The tax imposed by section 4261 shall not apply to the payment for transportation or facilities furnished to an international organization, or any corporation created by Act of Congress to act in matters of relief under the treaty of Geneva of August 22, 1864.
"(c) Members of the Armed Forces.
"The tax imposed by section 4261 shall not apply to the payment for transportation or facilities furnished under special tariffs providing for fares of not more than 2.5 cents per mile applicable to roundup tickets sold to personnel of the United States Army, Air Force, Navy, Marine Corps, and Coast Guard traveling in uniform of the United States at their own expense when on official leave, furlough, or pass, including authorized cadets and midshipmen, issued on presentation of properly executed certificate.
"(d) Small aircraft on nonestablished lines.
"The tax imposed by section 4261 shall not apply to transportation by aircraft having—
"(1) a gross takeoff weight (as determined under regulations prescribed by the Secretary or his delegate) of less than 12,500 pounds, and
"(2) a passenger seating capacity of less than ten adult passengers, including the pilot,
except when such aircraft is operated on an established line."
In 1962, P.L. 87-508, Sec. 0, redesignated former subsec. (d) as (b); former subsec. (e) as (c); and former subsec. (f) as (d) for transportation beginning after 11/15/62.
Prior to amendment, subsecs. (b) and (c) read as follows:
"(b) Small vehicles on nonestablished lines.
"The tax imposed by section 4261 shall not apply to transportation by motor vehicles having a passenger seating capacity of less than ten adult passengers, including the driver, except when such vehicle is operated on an established line.
"(c) Fishing trips.
"The tax imposed by section 4261 shall not apply to amounts paid for transportation by boat for the purpose of fishing from such boat."
In 1958, P.L. 85-859, Sec. 0, had added former subsec. (f), effective 1/1/59.
In 1957, P.L. 85-74, Sec. 0, substituted "2.5 cents" for "2.025 cents" in former subsec. (e), for amounts paid after 6/29/57.
In 1956, P.L. 1015, Sec. 0, substituted "60 cents" for "35 cents" in subsec. (a), effective for amounts paid after 8/31/56 for transportation commencing after that date.
—P.L. 796, Sec. 0, renumbered former Code Sec. 4262 to 4263, eliminated former subsec. (a) and redesignated former subsecs. (b) to (f) as (a) to (e) for amounts paid after 9/30/56, for transportation commencing after that date. The former subsec. (a) read as follows:
"(a) Certain foreign travel.
"The tax imposed by section 4261 shall not apply with respect to transportation any part of which is outside the northern portion of the Western Hemisphere, except with respect to any part of such transportation which is from any port or station within the United States, Canada, or Mexico to any other port or station within the United States, Canada, or Mexico. In the case of transportation by water on a vessel which makes one or more intermediate stops at ports within the United States, Canada, or Mexico on a voyage which begins or ends in the United States and ends or begins outside the northern portion of the Western Hemisphere, no part of such transportation shall be considered for the purposes of the preceding sentence to be from any port within the United States, Canada, or Mexico to any other such port if the vessel in stopping at any such intermediate port is not authorized both to discharge and to take on passengers. A port or station within Newfoundland shall not, for the purposes of the preceding two sentences, be considered as a port or station within Canada. For the purposes of this section, the words 'northern portion of the Western Hemisphere' mean the area lying west of the 30th meridian west of Greenwich, east of the International Date Line, and north of the equator, but not including any country of South America."

PART II.—PROPERTY

Sec.
4271. Imposition of tax.
4272. Definition of taxable transportation, etc.

In 1970, added Part II.

Sec. 4271. Imposition of tax.
(a) In general.
There is hereby imposed upon the amount paid within or without the United States for the taxable transportation (as defined in section 4272) of property a tax equal to 6.25 percent of the amount so paid for such transportation. The tax imposed by this subsection shall apply only to amounts paid to a person engaged in the business of transporting property by air for hire.

(b) By whom paid.
(1) In general. Except as provided by paragraph (2), the tax imposed by subsection (a) shall be paid by the person making the payment subject to tax.
(2) Payments made outside the United States. If a payment subject to tax under subsection (a) is made outside the United States and the person making such payment does not pay such tax, such tax—

(A) shall be paid by the person to whom the property is delivered in the United States by the person furnishing the last segment of the taxable transportation in respect of which such tax is imposed, and

(B) shall be collected by the person furnishing the last segment of such taxable transportation.

(c) Determination of amounts paid in certain cases.
For purposes of this section, in any case in which a person engaged in the business of transporting property by air for hire and one or more other persons not so engaged jointly provide services which include taxable transportation of property, and the person so engaged receives, for the furnishing of such taxable transportation, a portion of the receipts from the joint providing of such services, the amount paid for the taxable transportation shall be treated as being the sum of (1) the portion of the receipts so received, and (2) any expenses incurred by any of the persons not so engaged which are properly attributable to such taxable transportation and which are taken into account in determining the portion of the receipts so received.

(d) Application of tax.
(1) In general. The tax imposed by subsection (a) shall apply to—
(A) transportation beginning during the period—
(i) beginning on the 7th day after the date of the enactment [2/28/97] of the Airport and Airway Trust Fund Tax Reinstatement Act of 1997, and
(ii) ending on July 22, 2011, and
(B) amounts paid during such period for transportation beginning after such period.

(2) Refunds. If, as of the date any transportation begins, the taxes imposed by this section would not have applied to such transportation if paid for on such date, any tax paid under paragraph (1)(B) with respect to such transportation shall be treated as an overpayment.

In 2011, P.L. 112-21, Sec. 2(b)(2), substituted "July 22, 2011" for "June 30, 2011" in clause (d)(1)(A)(ii), effective 7/1/2011.
—P.L. 112-16, Sec. 2(b)(2), substituted "June 30, 2011" for "May 31, 2011" in clause (d)(1)(A)(ii), effective 6/1/2011.

Code Sec. 4271 — Excise and miscellaneous taxes

—P.L. 112-7, Sec. 2(b)(2), substituted "May 31, 2011" for "March 31, 2011" in clause (d)(1)(A)(ii), effective 4/1/2011.

In 2010, P.L. 111-329, Sec. 2(b)(2), substituted "March 31, 2011" for "December 31, 2010" in clause (d)(1)(A)(ii), effective 1/1/2011.

—P.L. 111-249, Sec. 2(b)(2), substituted "December 31, 2010" for "September 30, 2010" in clause (d)(1)(A)(ii), effective 10/1/2010.

—P.L. 111-216, Sec. 101(b)(2), substituted "September 30, 2010" for "August 1, 2010" in clause (d)(1)(A)(ii), effective 8/2/2010.

—P.L. 111-197, Sec. 2(b)(2), substituted "August 1, 2010" for "July 3, 2010" in clause (d)(1)(A)(ii), effective 7/4/2010.

—P.L. 111-161, Sec. 2(b)(2), substituted "July 3, 2010" for "April 30, 2010" in clause (d)(1)(A)(ii), effective 5/1/2010.

—P.L. 111-153, Sec. 2(b)(2), substituted "April 30, 2010" for "March 31, 2010" in clause (d)(1)(A)(ii), effective 4/1/2010.

In 2009, P.L. 111-116, Sec. 2(b)(2), substituted "March 31, 2010" for "December 31, 2009" in clause (d)(1)(A)(ii), effective 1/1/2010.

—P.L. 111-69, Sec. 2(b)(2), substituted "December 31, 2009" for "September 30, 2009" in clause (d)(1)(A)(ii), effective 10/1/2009.

—P.L. 111-12, Sec. 2(b)(2), substituted "September 30, 2009" for "March 31, 2009" in clause (d)(1)(A)(ii), effective 4/1/2009.

In 2008, P.L. 110-330, Sec. 2(b)(2), substituted "March 31, 2009" for "September 30, 2008" in clause (d)(1)(A)(ii), effective 10/1/2008.

—P.L. 110-253, Sec. 2(b)(2), substituted "September 30, 2008" for "June 30, 2008" in clause (d)(1)(A)(ii), effective 7/1/2008.

—P.L. 110-190, Sec. 2(b)(2), substituted "June 30, 2008" for "February 29, 2008" in subpara. (d)(1)(A)(ii), effective 3/1/2008.

In 2007, P.L. 110-161, Sec. 116(b)(2), substituted "February 29, 2008" for "September 30, 2007" in clause (d)(1)(A)(ii), effective 10/1/2007.

In 1997, P.L. 105-34, Sec. 1031(b)(2), substituted "September 30, 2007" for "September 30, 1997" in clause (d)(1)(A)(ii), effective for transportation begin. on or after 10/1/97.

—P.L. 105-2, Sec. 2(b)(2), amended subsec. (d), effective as provided in Sec. 2(e)(2), of this Act, which reads as follows:

"(2) Ticket taxes.—

"(A) In general.— The amendments made by subsection (b) shall apply to transportation beginning on or after such 7th day.

"(B) Exception for certain payments.— Except as provided in subparagraph (C), the amendments made by subsection (b) shall not apply to any amount paid before such 7th day.

"(C) Payments of property transportation tax within controlled group.— In the case of the tax imposed by section 4271 of the Internal Revenue Code of 1986, subparagraph (B) shall not apply to any amount paid by 1 member of a controlled group for transportation furnished by another member of such group. For purposes of the preceding sentence, all persons treated as a single employer under subsection (a) or (b) of section 52 of the Internal Revenue Code of 1986 shall be treated as members of a controlled group."

Prior to amendment, subsec. (d) read as follows:

"(d) Termination. The tax imposed by subsection (a) shall apply with respect to transportation beginning after August 31, 1982, and before January 1, 1996, and to transportation beginning on or after the date which is 7 calendar days after the date of the enactment of the Small Business Job Protection Act of 1996 and before January 1, 1997."

In 1996, P.L. 104-188, Sec. 1609(b), substituted "January 1, 1996, and to transportation beginning on or after the date which is 7 calendar days after the date of the enactment of the Small Business Job Protection Act of 1996 and before January 1, 1997" for "January 1, 1996" in subsec. (d), effective on the 7th calendar day after 8/20/96, except that the amendments made by subsection (b) shall not apply to any amount paid before such date.

In 1990, P.L. 101-508, Sec. 11213(a)(2), substituted "6.25 percent" for "5 percent" in subsec. (a), effective for transportation begin. after 11/30/90, but shall not apply for amounts paid before 11/30/90.

—P.L. 101-508, Sec. 11213(b)(1), substituted "January 1, 1996" for "January 1, 1991" in subsec. (d), effective 11/5/90.

In 1987, P.L. 100-223, Sec. 402(a)(2), substituted "January 1, 1991" for "January 1, 1988" in subsec. (d), effective 12/30/87.

In 1982, P.L. 97-248, Sec. 280(b), amended subsec. (d), effective for transportation begin. after 8/31/82, except for any amount paid on or before 8/31/82.

Prior to amendment, subsec. (d) read as follows:

"(d) Termination.

"Effective with respect to transportation beginning after September 30, 1980, the tax imposed by subsection (a) shall not apply."

In 1980, P.L. 96-298, Sec. 1(b), substituted "September 30, 1980" for "June 30, 1980" in subsec. (d), effective 7/1/80 [date of enactment].

In 1976, P.L. 94-455, Sec. 1904(a)(8), deleted "which begins after June 30, 1970," after "of property" in subsec. (a), effective 2/1/77.

In 1970, P.L. 91-258, Sec. 204, added Code Sec. 4271, effective for transportation begin. after 6/30/70.

See note following Sec. 4272 for prior Code Sec. 4271.

Former Secs. 4271–4273. Repealed.

In 1958, P.L. 85-475, Sec. 0, repealed Code Secs. 4271 to 4273 dealing with tax on transportation of property for amounts paid after 7/31/58.

Prior to repeal, Code Secs. 4271, 4272 and 4273 read as follows:

"SEC. 4271. IMPOSITION OF TAX.

"(a) Property other than coal.

"There is hereby imposed upon the amount paid within or without the United States for the transportation of property, except coal, by rail, motor vehicle, water, or air from one point in the United States to another, a tax equal to 3 percent of the amount so paid.

"(b) Coal.

"There is hereby imposed upon the amount paid within or without the United States for the transportation of coal by rail, motor vehicle, water, or air from one point in the United States to another, a tax equal to 4 cents per short ton for the coal so transported.

"(c) Application of tax to transportation partially within the United States.

"In the case of property transported from a point without the United States to a point within the United States, the tax shall apply to the amount paid within the United States for that part of the transportation which takes place within the United States.

"(d) By whom paid.

"The taxes imposed by this section shall be paid by the person making the payment subject to the tax."

"SEC. 4272. EXEMPTIONS.

"(a) Not in business for hire.

"The tax imposed under section 4271 shall apply only to amounts paid to a person engaged in the business of transporting property for hire, including amounts paid to a freight forwarder, express company, or similar person, but not including amounts paid by a freight forwarder, express company, or similar person, for transportation with respect to which a tax has previously been paid under such section.

"(b) Construction projects.

"The tax imposed by section 4271 shall not apply to the transportation of earth, rock, or other material excavated within the boundaries of, and in the course of, a construction project and transported to any place within, or adjacent to, the boundaries of such project.

"(c) Coal previously taxed.

"The tax imposed by section 4271(b) on the transportation of coal shall not apply to the transportation of coal with respect to which there has been a previous taxable transportation.

"(d) Certain organizations.

"The tax imposed by section 4271 shall not apply to amounts paid for the transportation of property to or from an international organization, or any corporation created by act of Congress to act in matters of relief under the treaty of Geneva of August 22, 1864.

"(e) Post Office Department.

"The tax imposed by section 4271 shall not apply to amounts paid to the Post Office Department for the transportation of property."

"SEC. 4273. REGISTRATION.

"Every person engaged in the business of transporting property for hire, including freight forwarders, express companies, and similar persons, shall, within 60 days after first engaging in the business of transportation of property for hire, register his name and his place or places of business with the Secretary or his delegate."

Sec. 4272. Definition of taxable transportation, etc.

(a) In general.

For purposes of this part, except as provided in subsection (b), the term "taxable transportation" means transportation by air which begins and ends in the United States.

(b) Exceptions.

For purposes of this part, the term "taxable transportation" does not include—

(1) that portion of any transportation which meets the requirements of paragraphs (1), (2), (3), and (4) of section 4262(b), or

(2) under regulations prescribed by the Secretary, transportation of property in the course of exportation (including shipment to a possession of the United States) by continuous movement, and in due course so exported.

(c) Excess baggage of passengers.

For purposes of this part, the term "property" does not include excess baggage accompanying a passenger traveling on an aircraft operated on an established line.

(d) Transportation.

For purposes of this part, the term "transportation" includes layover or waiting time and movement of the aircraft in deadhead service.

In 1976, P.L. 94-455, Sec. 1906(b)(13)(A), substituted "Secretary" for "Secretary or his delegate" in para. (b)(2), effective 2/1/77.

In 1970, P.L. 91-258, Sec. 204, added Code Sec. 4272, effective for transportation begin. after 6/30/70.

Excise and miscellaneous taxes — Code Sec. 4283

PART III.—SPECIAL PROVISIONS APPLICABLE TO TAXES ON TRANSPORTATION BY AIR

Sec.
4281. Small aircraft on nonestablished lines.
4282. Transportation by air for other members of affiliated group.

In **1990**, P.L. 101-508, Sec. 11213(e)(2), deleted item 4283. Prior to deletion, item 4283 read as follows:
"4283. Reduction in aviation related taxes in certain cases."
In **1987**, P.L. 100-223, Sec. 405(c), added the item for 4283.
In **1970**, added Part III.

Sec. 4281. Small aircraft on nonestablished lines.

The taxes imposed by sections 4261 and 4271 shall not apply to transportation by an aircraft having a maximum certificated takeoff weight of 6,000 pounds or less, except when such aircraft is operated on an established line. For purposes of the preceding sentence, the term "maximum certificated takeoff weight" means the maximum such weight contained in the type certificate or airworthiness certificate. For purposes of this section, an aircraft shall not be considered as operated on an established line at any time during which such aircraft is being operated on a flight the sole purpose of which is sightseeing.

In **2005**, P.L. 109-59, Sec. 11124(a), added "For purposes of this section, an aircraft shall not be considered as operated on an established line at any time during which such aircraft is being operated on a flight the sole purpose of which is sightseeing." at the end of Code Sec. 4281, effective for transportation begin. after 9/30/2005, but not for any amount paid before 9/30/2005 for such transportation.
In **1982**, P.L. 97-248, Sec. 280(c)(2)(B)(i), deleted "(as defined in section 4492(b))" after "certified takeoff weight" in Code Sec. 4281... Sec. 280(c)(2)(B)(ii), added the last sentence to Code Sec. 4281, effective for transportation begin. after 8/31/82, except for any amount paid on or before 8/31/82.
In **1970**, P.L. 91-258, Sec. 205(a), added Code Sec. 4281, effective 7/1/70.

Sec. 4281. Repealed.

In **1958**, P.L. 85-475, Sec. 4(a), repealed Code Sec. 4281 dealing with tax on transportation of oil by pipeline for amounts paid after 7/31/58 except that in the case of transportation to which the second sentence of Code Sec. 4281 applies, the repeal applies only if the transportation begins after 7/31/58.
Prior to repeal, Code Sec. 4281 read as follows:
"SEC. 4281. IMPOSITION OF TAX.
"There is hereby imposed upon all transportation of crude petroleum and liquid products thereof by pipeline a tax equivalent to 4½ percent of the amount paid for such transportation. If no charge for transportation is made (either by reason of ownership of the commodity transported or for any other reason), or if the payment for transportation is less than the fair charge therefor (other than in the case of an arm's length transaction), such tax shall be imposed on the fair charge for such transportation. The tax imposed by this section is to be paid by the person furnishing such transportation."

Sec. 4282. Transportation by air for other members of affiliated group.

(a) General rule.

Under regulations prescribed by the Secretary, if—

(1) one member of an affiliated group is the owner or lessee of an aircraft, and

(2) such aircraft is not available for hire by persons who are not members of such group,

no tax shall be imposed under section 4261 or 4271 upon any payment received by one member of the affiliated group from another member of such group for services furnished to such other member in connection with the use of such aircraft.

(b) Availability for hire.

For purposes of subsection (a), the determination of whether an aircraft is available for hire by persons who are not members of an affiliated group shall be made on a flight-by-flight basis.

(c) Affiliated group.

For purposes of subsection (a), the term "affiliated group" has the meaning assigned to such term by section 1504(a), except that all corporations shall be treated as includible corporations (without any exclusion under section 1504(b)).

In **1996**, P.L. 104-188, Sec. 1609(f), redesignated subsec. (b) as subsec. (c) and added a new subsec. (b), effective on the 7th calendar day after 8/20/96.
In **1976**, P.L. 94-455, Sec. 1906(b)(13)(A), substituted "Secretary" for "Secretary or his delegate" each place it appeared in Code Sec. 4282, effective 2/1/77.
In **1970**, P.L. 91-258, Sec. 205(a), added Code Sec. 4282, effective 7/1/70.

Sec. 4282. Repealed

In **1958**, P.L. 85-475, Sec. 4(a), repealed Code Sec. 4282 dealing with tax on transportation of oil by pipeline for amounts paid after 7/31/58.
Prior to repeal, section 4282 read as follows:
"Sec. 4282. Definition of fair charge.
"For the purposes of section 4281, the fair charge for transportation shall be computed
"(1) from actual bona fide rates or tariffs; or
"(2) if no such rates or tariffs exist, then on the basis of the actual bona fide rates or tariffs of other pipelines for like services, as determined by the Secretary or his delegate; or
"(3) if no such rates or tariffs exist, then on the basis of a reasonable charge for such transportation, as determined by the Secretary or his delegate."

Sec. 4283. Repealed.

In **1990**, P.L. 101-508, Sec. 11213(e)(1), repealed Code Sec. 4283, effective 11/5/90.
Prior to repeal, Code Sec. 4283 read as follows:
"SEC. 4283. REDUCTION IN AVIATION-RELATED TAXES IN CERTAIN CASES.
"(a) Reduction in rates.
"If the funding percentage is less than 85 percent, with respect to any taxable event occurring during 1991—
"(1) subsections (a) and (b) of section 4261 (relating to tax on transportation of persons by air) shall each be applied by substituting '4 percent' for '8 percent',
"(2) subsection (a) of section 4271 (relating to tax on transportation of property by air) shall be applied by substituting '2.5 percent' for '5 percent',
"(3) paragraph (1) of section 4041(c) (relating to tax on certain fuels used in noncommercial aviation) shall be applied by substituting '7 cents' for '14 cents', and
"(4) paragraph (2) of section 4041(c) (relating to tax on gasoline used in noncommercial aviation) shall not apply.
"(b) Funding percentage.
"(1) In general. For purposes of this section, the funding percentage is the percentage (determined by the Secretary) which—
"(A) the sum of—
"(i) the aggregate amounts obligated under section 505 of the Airport and Airway Improvement Act of 1982 for fiscal years 1989 and 1990, and
"(ii) the aggregate amounts appropriated under subsections (a) and (b) of section 506 of such Act for such fiscal years, is of
"(B) the sum of—
"(i) the aggregate amounts authorized to be obligated under such section 505 for such fiscal years, and
"(ii) the aggregate amounts authorized to be appropriated under subsections (a) and (b) of such section 506 for such fiscal years.
"(2) Rules for applying paragraph (1).
"(A) Treatment of prior year amounts. For purposes of paragraph (1), an amount shall be treated as authorized, obligated, or appropriated only for the 1st fiscal year for which it is authorized, obligated, or appropriated, as the case may be.
"(B) Treatment of sequestered amounts. The determination under paragraph (1)(A) shall be made without regard to the sequestration of any amount described therein pursuant to an order under part C of title II of the Balanced Budget and Emergency Deficit Control Act of 1985 (or any successor law).
"(3) Determination of funding percentage.
"(A) In general. Not later than December 1, 1990, the Secretary shall determine—
"(i) the funding percentage, and
"(ii) whether the rate reductions under this section shall apply to taxable events occurring during 1991.
"(B) Determinations to be published in Federal Register. As soon as practicable after making the determinations under subparagraph (A), the Secretary shall publish such determinations in the Federal Register.
"(c) Taxable event.
"For purposes of this section—
"(1) Taxable transportation by air. In the case of the taxes imposed by section 4261 and 4271, the taxable event shall be treated as occurring when the payment for the taxable transportation is made.
"(2) Sale or use of fuel. In the case of the taxes imposed by section 4041(c), the taxable event shall be the sale or use on which tax is imposed."

In 1989, P.L. 101-239, Sec. 7501(a), substituted "1991" for "1990" in subsec. (a)... Sec. 7501(b)(1), substituted "1989 and 1990" for "1988 and 1989" in clause (b)(1)(A)(i)... Sec. 7501(b)(2)(A), substituted "1991" for "1990" in clause (b)(3)(A)(ii)... Sec. 7501(b)(2)(B), substituted "1990" for "1989" in subpara. (b)(3)(A), effective 12/19/89.

In 1987, P.L. 100-223, Sec. 405(a), added Code Sec. 4283, effective 12/30/87.

Sec. 4283. Repealed

In 1958, P.L. 85-475, repealed Code Sec. 4283 dealing with tax on transportation of oil by pipeline for amounts paid after 7/31/58.
Prior to repeal, Code Sec. 4283 read as follows:
"Sec. 4283. Exemption for Oil Transported Within Premises of a Plant.
"For the purposes of section 4281, the term 'transportation' shall not include any movement through lines of pipe within the premises of a refinery, a bulk plant, a terminal, or a gasoline plant, if such movement is not a continuation of a taxable transportation. The crossing of rights-of-way, streets, highways, railroads, levees, or narrow bodies of water, in connection with such a movement, shall not of itself constitute such movement as being 'transportation.'"

Subchapter E.—Special Provisions Applicable to Services and Facilities Taxes

Sec.
4291. Cases where persons receiving payment must collect tax.
4292. Repealed.
4293. Exemption for United States and possessions.
4294. Repealed.

In 1976, P.L. 94-455, Sec. 1904(b)(4), deleted the items for 4292 and 4294.
Prior to deletion the items for 4292 and 4294 read as follows:
"4292. State and local governmental exemptions.
"4294. Exemption for nonprofit educational organizations."
In 1958, added item 4294 and redesignated former item 4294 as 4295.

Sec. 4291. Cases where persons receiving payment must collect tax.

Except as otherwise provided in section 4263(a), every person receiving any payment for facilities or services on which a tax is imposed upon the payor thereof under this chapter shall collect the amount of the tax from the person making such payment.

In 1970, P.L. 91-258, Sec. 205(c)(3), substituted "section 4263(a)" for "section 4264(a)" in Code Sec. 4291, effective 7/1/70.

In 1965, P.L. 89-44, Sec. 305, amended Code Sec. 4291.
Prior to amendment, Code Sec. 4291 read as follows:
"Except as otherwise provided in sections 4231 and 4264(a), every person receiving any payment for facilities or services on which a tax is imposed upon the payor thereof under this chapter shall collect the amount of the tax from the person making such payment. For the purpose of this section every club or organization having life members shall collect the tax imposed on life memberships by section 4241."

In 1958, P.L. 85-859, Sec. 131(g), substituted "Except as otherwise provided in sections 4231 and 4262(a)" for "Except as provided in section 4264(a)" in Code Sec. 4291, effective 1/1/59.

In 1956, ch. 725, Sec. 4(c), added "Except as provided in section 4264(a)", and eliminated provisions which related to collection of tax where payment specified in section 4261 was made outside the United States for a prepaid order, exchange order, or similar order, effective 10/1/56.

Sec. 4292. Repealed.

In 1976, P.L. 94-455, Sec. 1904(a)(9), repealed Code Sec. 4292, effective 2/1/77.
Prior to repeal, Code Sec. 4292 read as follows:
"Sec. 4292. State and local governmental exemption.
"Under regulations prescribed by the Secretary or his delegate, no tax shall be imposed under section 4251 upon any payment received for services or facilities furnished to the Government of any State, Territory of the United States, or any political subdivision of the foregoing or the District of Columbia."
In 1970, P.L. 91-258, Sec. 205(a)(2), deleted "or 4261" after "4251", effective 7/1/70.
In 1958, P.L. 85-475, Sec. 4(b)(3), eliminated provisions which exempted amounts paid for transportation of property under former Code Sec. 4271.

Sec. 4293. Exemption for United States and possessions.

The Secretary of the Treasury may authorize exemption from the taxes imposed by subchapter A of chapter 31, section 4041, section 4051, chapter 32 (other than the taxes imposed by sections 4064 and 4121) and subchapter B of chapter 33, as to any particular article, or service or class of articles or services, to be purchased for the exclusive use of the United States, if he determines that the imposition of such taxes with respect to such articles or services, or class of articles or services will cause substantial burden or expense which can be avoided by granting tax exemption and that full benefit of such exemption, if granted, will accrue to the United States.

In 1990, P.L. 101-508, Sec. 11221(c), added "subchapter A of chapter 31," before "section 4041" in Code Sec 4293, effective 1/1/91, except as provided in Sec. 11221(f)(2) of this Act, which reads as follows:
"(2) Exception for binding contracts. In determining whether any tax imposed by subchapter A of chapter 31 of the Internal Revenue Code of 1986, as added by this section, applies to any sale after December 31, 1990, there shall not be taken into account the amount paid for any article (or any part or accessory therefor) if the purchaser held on September 30, 1990, a contract (which was binding on such date and at all times thereafter before the purchase) for the purchase of such article (or such part or accessory)."
In 1988, P.L. 100-647, Sec. 6103(a), added "section 4051," after "section 4041," effective 11/10/88.
In 1978, P.L. 95-618, Sec. 201(c)(2), substituted "taxes imposed by sections 4064 and 4121" for "tax imposed by section 4121" in Code Sec. 4293, effective for 1980 and later model year automobiles (as defined in Code Sec. 4064(b)).
—P.L. 95-502, Sec. 202(b), substituted "section 4041, chapter 32" for "chapters 31 and 32" in Code Sec. 4293, effective 10/1/80.
—P.L. 95-227, Sec. 2(b)(3), added "(other than under section 4121)" after "this chapter", effective for sales after 3/31/78. See note following Code Sec. 192.
In 1976, P.L. 94-455, Sec. 1906(b)(13)(B), substituted "Secretary of the Treasury" for "Secretary" in Code Sec. 4293, effective 2/1/77.
In 1970, P.L. 91-258, Sec. 205(a)(3), substituted "subchapter B" for "subchapters B and C", effective 7/1/70.

Sec. 4294. Repealed.

In 1976, P.L. 94-455, Sec. 1904(a)(10), repealed Code Sec. 4294, effective 2/1/77.
Prior to repeal, Code Sec. 4294 read as follows:
"Sec. 4294. Exemption for nonprofit educational organizations.
"(a) Exemption.
"Under regulations prescribed by the Secretary or his delegate, no tax shall be imposed under section 4251 on any amount paid by a nonprofit educational organization for services or facilities furnished to such organization.
"(b) Definition.
"For purposes of subsection (a), the term 'nonprofit educational organization' means an educational organization described in section 170(b)(1)(A)(ii) which is exempt from income tax under section 501(a). The term also includes a school operated as an activity of an organization described in section 501(c)(3) which is exempt from income tax under section 501(a), if such school normally maintains a regular faculty and curriculum and normally has a regularly enrolled body of pupils or students in attendance at the place where its educational activities are regularly carried on."
In 1970, P.L. 91-258, Sec. 205(a)(4), deleted "or 4261" after "4251" in subsec. (a), effective 7/1/70.
In 1969, P.L. 91-172, Sec. 101(j)(28), substituted "170(b)(1)(A)(ii)" for "503(b)(2)" in subsec. (b), effective 1/1/70.
In 1959, P.L. 86-344, Sec. 2(d), added second sentence in subsec. (b), effective 1/1/59.
In 1958, P.L. 85-859, Sec. 135(a), redesignated former Code Sec. 4294 as 4295 and added new Code Sec. 4294, effective 1/1/59.

CHAPTER 34.—Policies issued by foreign insurers

Subchapter
A. Tax on wagers.
B. Insured and Self-Insured Health Plans

Subchapter A.—Tax on Wagers

Sec.
4371. Imposition of tax.
4372. Definitions.
4373. Exemptions.

Excise and miscellaneous taxes — Code Sec. 4372

4374. Liability for tax.

Sec. 4371. Imposition of tax.

There is hereby imposed, on each policy of insurance, indemnity bond, annuity contract, or policy of reinsurance issued by any foreign insurer or reinsurer, a tax at the following rates:

(1) Casualty insurance and indemnity bonds. 4 cents on each dollar, or fractional part thereof, of the premium paid on the policy of casualty insurance or the indemnity bond, if issued to or for, or in the name of, an insured as defined in section 4372(d);

(2) Life insurance, sickness and accident policies, and annuity contracts. 1 cent on each dollar, or fractional part thereof, of the premium paid on the policy of life, sickness, or accident insurance, or annuity contract; and

(3) Reinsurance. 1 cent on each dollar, or fractional part thereof, of the premium paid on the policy of reinsurance covering any of the contracts taxable under paragraph (1) or (2).

In 1989, P.L. 101-239, Sec. 7811(i)(11), deleted ", unless the insurer is subject to tax under section 842(b)" after "or annuity contract" in para. (2), effective for tax. yrs. begin. after 12/31/87.

In 1987, P.L. 100-203, Sec. 10242(c)(3), substituted "section 842(b)" for "section 813" in para. (2), effective for tax. yrs. begin. after 12/31/87.

In 1984, P.L. 98-369, Sec. 211(b)(23), substituted "section 813" for "section 819" in para. (2), effective for tax. yrs. begin. after 12/31/83.

In 1976, P.L. 94-455, Sec. 1904(a)(12), amended Code Sec. 4371, effective 2/1/77.

Prior to amendment, Code Sec. 4371 read as follows:

"Sec. 4371. Imposition of tax.

"There is hereby imposed, on each policy of insurance, indemnity bond, annuity contract, or policy of reinsurance issued by any foreign insurer or reinsurer, a tax at the following rates:

"(1) Casualty insurance and indemnity bonds. Four cents on each dollar, or fractional part thereof, of the premium charged on the policy of casualty insurance or the indemnity bond, if issued to or for, or in the name of, an insured as defined in section 4372(d);

"(2) Life insurance, sickness, and accident policies, and annuity contracts. One cent on each dollar, or fractional part thereof, of the premium charged on the policy of life, sickness, or accident insurance, or annuity contract, unless the insurer is subject to tax under section 819;

"(3) Reinsurance. One cent on each dollar, or fractional part thereof, of the premium charged on the policy of reinsurance covering any of the contracts taxable under paragraph (1) or (2).

If the tax imposed by this section is paid on the basis of a return under regulations prescribed under section 4374, the tax under paragraphs (1), (2), and (3) shall be computed on the premium paid in lieu of the premium charged."

In 1965, P.L. 89-44, Sec. 804, added the last sentence following para (3), effective 7/1/65.

In 1959, P.L. 86-69, Sec. 3(f)(3), substituted "section 819" for "section 816" in para. (2), effective for tax. yrs. begin. after 12/31/57.

In 1958, P.L. 85-859, Sec. 141(a), substituted "is hereby imposed, on each policy of insurance, indemnity bond, annuity contract, or policy of reinsurance issued by any foreign insurer or reinsurer, a tax" for "shall be imposed a tax on each policy of insurance, indemnity bond, annuity contract, or policy of reinsurance issued by any foreign insurer or reinsurer" effective 1/1/59.

In 1956, P.L. 429, Sec. 5(9), substituted "816" for "807" in para. (2), effective for tax. yrs. begin. after 12/31/54.

Sec. 4372. Definitions.

(a) Foreign insurer or reinsurer.

For purposes of section 4371, the term "foreign insurer or reinsurer" means an insurer or reinsurer who is a nonresident alien individual, or a foreign partnership, or a foreign corporation. The term includes a nonresident alien individual, foreign partnership, or foreign corporation which shall become bound by an obligation of the nature of an indemnity bond. The term does not include a foreign government, or municipal or other corporation exercising the taxing power.

(b) Policy of casualty insurance.

For purposes of section 4371(1), the term "policy of casualty insurance" means any policy (other than life) or other instrument by whatever name called whereby a contract of insurance is made, continued, or renewed.

(c) Indemnity bond.

For purposes of this chapter, the term "indemnity bond" means any instrument by whatever name called whereby an obligation of the nature of an indemnity, fidelity, or surety bond is made, continued, or renewed. The term includes any bond for indemnifying any person who shall have become bound or engaged as surety, and any bond for the due execution or performance of any contract, obligation, or requirement, or the duties of any office or position, and to account for money received by virtue thereof, where a premium is charged for the execution of such bond.

(d) Insured.

For purposes of section 4371(1), the term "insured" means—

(1) a domestic corporation or partnership, or an individual resident of the United States, against, or with respect to, hazards, risks, losses, or liabilities wholly or partly within the United States, or

(2) a foreign corporation, foreign partnership, or nonresident individual, engaged in a trade or business within the United States, against, or with respect to, hazards, risks, losses, or liabilities within the United States.

(e) Policy of life, sickness, or accident insurance, or annuity contract.

For purposes of section 4371(2), the term "policy of life, sickness, or accident insurance, or annuity contract" means any policy or other instrument by whatever name called whereby a contract of insurance or an annuity contract is made, continued, or renewed with respect to the life or hazards to the person of a citizen or resident of the United States.

(f) Policy of reinsurance.

For purposes of section 4371(3), the term "policy of reinsurance" means any policy or other instrument by whatever name called whereby a contract of reinsurance is made, continued, or renewed against, or with respect to, any of the hazards, risks, losses, or liabilities covered by contracts taxable under paragraph (1) or (2) of section 4371.

In 1976, P.L. 94-455, Sec. 1904(a)(12), amended Code Sec. 4372, effective 2/1/77.

Prior to amendment, Code Sec. 4372 read as follows:

"Sec. 4372. Definitions.

"(a) Foreign insurer or reinsurer.

"For purposes of this subchapter, the term 'foreign insurer or reinsurer' means an insurer or reinsurer who is a nonresident alien individual, or a foreign partnership, or a foreign corporation. The term includes a nonresident alien individual, foreign partnership, or foreign corporation which shall become bound by an obligation of the nature of an indemnity bond.

"(b) Policy of casualty insurance.

"For purposes of section 4371(1), the term 'policy of casualty insurance' means any policy (other than life) or other instrument by whatever name called whereby a contract of insurance is made, continued, or renewed.

"(c) Indemnity bond.

"For purposes of this subchapter, the term 'indemnity bond' means any instrument by whatever name called whereby an obligation of the nature of an indemnity, fidelity, or surety bond is made, continued, or renewed. The term includes any bond for indemnifying any person who shall have become bound or engaged as surety, and any bond for the due execution or performance of any contract, obligation, or requirement, or the duties of any office or position, and to account for money received by virtue thereof, where a premium is charged for the execution of such bond.

"(d) Insured.

"For purposes of section 4371(1), the term 'insured' means—

"(1) a domestic corporation or partnership, or an individual resident of the United States, against, or with respect to, hazards, risks, losses, or liabilities wholly or partly within the United States, or

"(2) a foreign corporation, foreign partnership, or nonresident individual, engaged in a trade or business within the United States, against, or with respect to, hazards, risks, or liabilities within the United States.

"(e) Policy of life, sickness, or accident insurance, or annuity contract.

"For purposes of section 4371(2), the term 'policy of life, sickness, or accident insurance, or annuity contract' means any policy or other instrument by whatever name called whereby a contract of insurance or an annuity contract is made, continued, or renewed with respect to the life or hazards to the person of a citizen or resident of the United States.

"(f) Policy of reinsurance.

"For purposes of section 4371(3), the term 'policy of reinsurance' means any policy or other instrument by whatever name called whereby a contract of reinsurance is made, continued, or renewed against, or with respect to, any of the hazards, risks, losses, or liabilities covered by contracts taxable under paragraph (1) or (2) of section 4371."

In 1958, P.L. 85-859, Sec. 141(a), substituted "For purposes" for "For the purposes" each place it appeared in Code Sec. 4372, added "against, or" before "with respect to" in para. (d)(2), and subsec. (f), effective 1/1/59.

Sec. 4373. Exemptions.

The tax imposed by section 4371 shall not apply to—

(1) Effectively connected items. Any amount which is effectively connected with the conduct of a trade or business within the United States unless such amount is exempt from the application of section 882(a) pursuant to a treaty obligation of the United States.

(2) Indemnity bond. Any indemnity bond required to be filed by any person to secure payment of any pension, allowance, allotment, relief, or insurance by the United States, or to secure a duplicate for, or the payment of, any bond, note, certificate of indebtedness, war-saving certificate, warrant or check, issued by the United States.

In 1988, P.L. 100-647, Sec. 1012(q)(13)(A), amended para. (1), effective for premiums paid after the date 30 days after 11/10/88.
Prior to amendment, para. (1) read as follows:
"(1) Domestic agent. Any policy, indemnity bond, or annuity contract signed or countersigned by an officer or agent of the insurer in a State, or in the District of Columbia, within which such insurer is authorized to do business; or".
In 1976, P.L. 94-455, Sec. 1904(a)(12), amended Code Sec. 4373, effective 2/1/77.
Prior to amendment Code Sec. 4373 read as follows:
"Sec. 4373. Exemptions.
"The tax imposed by section 4371 shall not apply to—
"(1) Domestic agent. Any policy, indemnity bond, or annuity contract signed or countersigned by an officer or agent of the insurer in a State, Territory, or District of the United States within which such insurer is authorized to do business; or
"(2) Indemnity bond. Any indemnity bond required to be filed by any person to secure payment of any pension, allowance, allotment, relief, or insurance by the United States, or to secure a duplicate for, or the payment of, any bond, note, certificate of indebtedness, war-saving certificate, warrant or check, issued by the United States."

Sec. 4374. Liability for tax.

The tax imposed by this chapter shall be paid, on the basis of a return, by any person who makes, signs, issues, or sells any of the documents and instruments subject to the tax, or for whose use or benefit the same are made, signed, issued, or sold. The United States or any agency or instrumentality thereof shall not be liable for the tax.

In 1976, P.L. 94-455, Sec. 1906(a)(12), amended Code Sec. 4374, effective 2/1/77.
Prior to amendment, Code Sec. 4374 read as follows:
"Sec. 4374. Payment of tax.
"Any person to or for whom or in whose name any policy, indemnity bond, or annuity contract referred to in section 4371 is issued, or any solicitor or broker acting for or on behalf of such person in the procurement of any such instrument, shall affix the proper stamps to such instrument. Notwithstanding the preceding sentence, the Secretary or his delegate may, by regulations, provide that the tax imposed by section 4371 shall be paid on the basis of a return."
In 1965, P.L. 89-44, Sec. 804, substituted "Payment of tax" for "Affixing of stamps" in the heading of Code Sec. 4374, and the last sentence, effective 7/1/65.

Subchapter B.—Insured and Self-Insured Health Plans

4375. Health Insurance
4376. Self-insured health plans.
4377. Definitions and special rules.

In 2010, P.L. 111-148, added items 4375, 4376, and 4377.

Sec. 4375. Health insurance.
(a) Imposition of fee.
There is hereby imposed on each specified health insurance policy for each policy year ending after September 30, 2012, a fee equal to the product of $2 ($1 in the case of policy years ending during fiscal year 2013) multiplied by the average number of lives covered under the policy.
(b) Liability for fee.
The fee imposed by subsection (a) shall be paid by the issuer of the policy.
(c) Specified health insurance policy.
For purposes of this section:
(1) In general. Except as otherwise provided in this section, the term "specified health insurance policy" means any accident or health insurance policy (including a policy under a group health plan) issued with respect to individuals residing in the United States.
(2) Exemption for certain policies. The term "specified health insurance policy" does not include any insurance if substantially all of its coverage is of excepted benefits described in section 9832(c).
(3) Treatment of prepaid health coverage arrangements.

(A) In general. In the case of any arrangement described in subparagraph (B), such arrangement shall be treated as a specified health insurance policy, and the person referred to in such subparagraph shall be treated as the issuer.

(B) Description of arrangements. An arrangement is described in this subparagraph if under such arrangement fixed payments or premiums are received as consideration for any person's agreement to provide or arrange for the provision of accident or health coverage to residents of the United States, regardless of how such coverage is provided or arranged to be provided.

(d) Adjustments for increases in health care spending.
In the case of any policy year ending in any fiscal year beginning after September 30, 2014, the dollar amount in effect under subsection (a) for such policy year shall be equal to the sum of such dollar amount for policy years ending in the previous fiscal year (determined after the application of this subsection), plus an amount equal to the product of.—
(1) such dollar amount for policy years ending in the previous fiscal year, multiplied by
(2) the percentage increase in the projected per capita amount of National Health Expenditures, as most recently published by the Secretary before the beginning of the fiscal year.
(e) Termination.
This section shall not apply to policy years ending after September 30, 2019.

In 2010, P.L. 111-148, Sec. 6301(e)(2)(A), added Code Sec. 4375, enacted 3/23/2010.

Sec. 4376. Self-insured health plans.
(a) Imposition of fee.
In the case of any applicable self-insured health plan for each plan year ending after September 30, 2012, there is hereby imposed a fee equal to $2 ($1 in the case of plan years ending during fiscal year 2013) multiplied by the average number of lives covered under the plan.
(b) Liability for fee.
(1) In general. The fee imposed by subsection (a) shall be paid by the plan sponsor.
(2) Plan sponsor. For purposes of paragraph (1) the term "plan sponsor" means—

(A) the employer in the case of a plan established or maintained by a single employer,
(B) the employee organization in the case of a plan established or maintained by an employee organization,
(C) in the case of—
(i) a plan established or maintained by 2 or more employers or jointly by 1 or more employers and 1 or more employee organizations,
(ii) a multiple employer welfare arrangement, or
(iii) a voluntary employees' beneficiary association described in section 501(c)(9), the association, committee, joint board of trustees, or other similar group of representatives of the parties who establish or maintain the plan, or
(D) the cooperative or association described in subsection (c)(2)(F) in the case of a plan established or maintained by such a cooperative or association.

(c) Applicable self-insured health plan.
For purposes of this section, the term "applicable self-insured health plan" means any plan for providing accident or health coverage if—
(1) any portion of such coverage is provided other than through an insurance policy, and
(2) such plan is established or maintained—
(A) by 1 or more employers for the benefit of their employees or former employees,
(B) by 1 or more employee organizations for the benefit of their members or former members,
(C) jointly by 1 or more employers and 1 or more employee organizations for the benefit of employees or former employees,
(D) by a voluntary employees' beneficiary association described in section 501(c)(9),
(E) by any organization described in section 501(c)(6), or
(F) in the case of a plan not described in the preceding subparagraphs, by a multiple employer welfare arrangement (as defined in section 3(40) of Employee Retirement Income Security Act of 1974), a rural electric cooperative (as defined in section 3(40)(B)(iv) of such Act), or a rural telephone cooperative association (as defined in section 3(40)(B)(v) of such Act).

(d) Adjustments for increases in health care spending.
In the case of any plan year ending in any fiscal year beginning after September 30, 2014, the dollar amount in effect under subsection (a) for such plan year shall be equal to the sum of such dollar amount for plan years ending in the previous fiscal year (determined after the application of this subsection), plus an amount equal to the product of—
(1) such dollar amount for plan years ending in the previous fiscal year, multiplied by
(2) the percentage increase in the projected per capita amount of National Health Expenditures, as most recently published by the Secretary before the beginning of the fiscal year.

(e) Termination.
This section shall not apply to plan years ending after September 30, 2019.

In 2010, P.L. 111-148, Sec. 6301(e)(2)(A), added Code Sec. 4376, effective 3/23/2010.

Sec. 4377. Definitions and special rules.
(a) Definitions.
For purposes of this subchapter—
(1) Accident and health coverage. The term "accident and health coverage" means any coverage which, if provided by an insurance policy, would cause such policy to be a specified health insurance policy (as defined in section 4375(c)).
(2) Insurance policy. The term "insurance policy" means any policy or other instrument whereby a contract of insurance is issued, renewed, or extended.
(3) United States. The term "United States" includes any possession of the United States.

(b) Treatment of governmental entities.
(1) In general. For purposes of this subchapter—
(A) the term "person" includes any governmental entity, and
(B) notwithstanding any other law or rule of law, governmental entities shall not be exempt from the fees imposed by this subchapter except as provided in paragraph (2).
(2) Treatment of exempt governmental programs. In the case of an exempt governmental program, no fee shall be imposed under section 4375 or section 4376 on any covered life under such program.
(3) Exempt governmental program defined. For purposes of this subchapter, the term "exempt governmental program" means—
(A) any insurance program established under title XVIII of the Social Security Act,
(A) the medical assistance program established by title XIX or XXI of the Social Security Act,
(C) any program established by Federal law for providing medical care (other than through insurance policies) to individuals (or the spouses and dependents thereof) by reason of such individuals being members of the Armed Forces of the United States or veterans, and
(D) any program established by Federal law for providing medical care (other than through insurance policies) to members of Indian tribes (as defined in section 4(d) of the Indian Health Care Improvement Act).

(c) Treatment as tax.
For purposes of subtitle F, the fees imposed by this subchapter shall be treated as if they were taxes.

(d) No cover over to possessions.
Notwithstanding any other provision of law, no amount collected under this subchapter shall be covered over to any possession of the United States.

In 2010, P.L. 111-148, Sec. 6301(e)(2)(A), added Code Sec. 4377, effective 3/23/2010.

CHAPTER 35.—TAXES ON WAGERING
Subchapter
A. Tax on wagers.
B. Occupational tax.
C. Miscellaneous provisions.

Subchapter A.—Tax on Wagers
Sec.
4401. Imposition of tax.
4402. Exemptions.
4403. Record requirements.
4404. Territorial extent.
4405. Cross references.

Sec. 4401. Imposition of tax.
(a) Wagers.
(1) State authorized wagers. There shall be imposed on any wager authorized under the law of the State in which

accepted an excise tax equal to 0.25 percent of the amount of such wager.

(2) Unauthorized wagers. There shall be imposed on any wager not described in paragraph (1) an excise tax equal to 2 percent of the amount of such wager.

(b) Amount of wager.

In determining the amount of any wager for the purposes of this subchapter, all charges incident to the placing of such wager shall be included; except that if the taxpayer establishes, in accordance with regulations prescribed by the Secretary, that an amount equal to the tax imposed by this subchapter has been collected as a separate charge from the person placing such wager, the amount so collected shall be excluded.

(c) Persons liable for tax.

Each person who is engaged in the business of accepting wagers shall be liable for and shall pay the tax under this subchapter on all wagers placed with him. Each person who conducts any wagering pool or lottery shall be liable for and shall pay the tax under this subchapter on all wagers placed in such pool or lottery. Any person required to register under section 4412 who receives wagers for or on behalf of another person without having registered under section 4412 the name and place of residence of such other person shall be liable for and shall pay the tax under this subchapter on all such wagers received by him.

In **1982**, P.L. 97-362, Sec. 109(a), amended subsec. (a), effective 1/1/83.
Prior to amendment, subsec. (a) read as follows:
"(a) Wagers.
"There shall be imposed on wagers, as defined in section 4421, an excise tax equal to 2 percent of the amount thereof."
In **1976**, P.L. 94-455, Sec. 1906(b)(13)(A), substituted "Secretary" for "Secretary or his delegate" in subsec. (b), effective 2/1/77.
In **1974**, P.L. 93-499, Sec. 3(a), substituted "2 percent" for "10 percent" in subsec. (a), effective with respect to wagers placed on or after 12/1/74, except as specified in Sec. 3(d)(2) of P.L. 93-499, reproduced below:
"(2) Transitional Rules.—
"(A) Any person who, on December 1, 1974, is engaged in an activity which makes him liable for payment of the tax imposed by section 4411 of the Internal Revenue Code of 1954 (as in effect on such date) shall be treated as commencing such activity on such date for purposes of such section and section 4901 of such Code.
"(B) Any person who, before December 1, 1974.—
"(i) became liable for and paid the tax imposed by section 4411 of the Internal Revenue Code of 1954 (as in effect on July 1, 1974) for the year ending June 30, 1975, shall not be liable for any additional tax under such section for such year, and
"(ii) registered under section 4412 of such Code (as in effect on July 1, 1974) for the year ending June 30, 1975, shall not be required to reregister under such section for such year."
In **1958**, P.L. 85-859, Sec. 151(a), added last sentence of subsec. (c), effective for wagers received after 9/2/58.

Sec. 4402. Exemptions.

No tax shall be imposed by this subchapter—

(1) Parimutuels. On any wager placed with, or on any wager placed in a wagering pool conducted by, a parimutuel wagering enterprise licensed under State law,

(2) Coin-operated devices. On any wager placed in a coin-operated device (as defined in section 4462 as in effect for years beginning before July 1, 1980), or on any amount paid, in lieu of inserting a coin, token, or similar object, to operate a device described in section 4462(a)(2) (as so in effect), or

(3) State-conducted lotteries, etc. On any wager placed in a sweepstakes, wagering pool, or lottery which is conducted by an agency of a State acting under authority of State law, but only if such wager is placed with the State agency conducting such sweepstakes, wagering pool, or lottery, or with its authorized employees or agents.

In **1978**, P.L. 95-600, Sec. 521(c)(1), amended para. (2), effective for yrs. begin. after 6/30/80.
Prior to amendment, para. (2) read as follows:
"(2) Coin-operated devices. On any wager placed in a coin-operated device with respect to which an occupational tax is imposed by section 4461, or on any amount paid, in lieu of inserting a coin, token, or similar object, to operate a device described in section 4462(a)(2), if an occupational tax is imposed with respect to such device by section 4461, or"
In **1976**, P.L. 94-455, Sec. 1208(a), amended para. (3), effective for wagers placed after 3/10/64.
Prior to amendment, para. (3) read as follows:
"(3) State-conducted sweepstakes. On any wager placed in a sweepstakes, wagering pool, or lottery—
"(A) which is conducted by an agency of a State acting under authority of State law, and
"(B) the ultimate winners in which are determined by the results of a horse race,
but only if such wager is placed with the State agency conducting such sweepstakes, wagering pool, or lottery, or with its authorized employees or agents."
In **1965**, P.L. 89-44, Sec. 405, substituted "section 4462(a)(2)" for "section 4462(a)(2)(B)" in para. (2), effective 7/1/65.
—P.L. 89-44, Sec. 813(a), added para. (3), effective for wagers placed after 3/10/64.
In **1958**, P.L. 85-859, Sec. 152(b), added provisions in para. (2) exempting from the tax amounts paid to operate a device described in section 4462(a)(2)(B), if an occupational tax is imposed with respect to such device by section 4461 of this title, effective 1/1/59.

Sec. 4403. Record requirements.

Each person liable for tax under this subchapter shall keep a daily record showing the gross amount of all wagers on which he is so liable, in addition to all other records required pursuant to section 6001(a).

Sec. 4404. Territorial extent.

The tax imposed by this subchapter shall apply only to wagers—

(1) accepted in the United States, or

(2) placed by a person who is in the United States
  (A) with a person who is a citizen or resident of the United States, or
  (B) in a wagering pool or lottery conducted by a person who is a citizen or resident of the United States.

Sec. 4405. Cross references.

For penalties and other administrative provisions applicable to this subchapter, see sections 4421 to 4423, inclusive; and subtitle F.

Subchapter B.—Occupational Tax

Sec.
4411. Imposition of tax.
4412. Registration.
4413. Certain provisions made applicable.
4414. Cross references.

Sec. 4411. Imposition of tax.

(a) In general.

There shall be imposed a special tax of $500 per year to be paid by each person who is liable for the tax imposed under section 4401 or who is engaged in receiving wagers for or on behalf of any person so liable.

(b) Authorized persons.

Subsection (a) shall be applied by substituting "$50" for "$500" in the case of—

(1) any person whose liability for tax under section 4401 is determined only under paragraph (1) of section 4401(a), and

(2) any person who is engaged in receiving wagers only for or on behalf of persons described in paragraph (1).

In **1982**, P.L. 97-362, Sec. 109(b), amended Code Sec. 4411, effective 7/1/83.
Prior to amendment, Code Sec. 4411 read as follows:
"SEC. 4411. IMPOSITION OF TAX.

"There shall be imposed a special tax of $500 per year to be paid by each person who is liable for tax under section 4401 or who is engaged in receiving wagers for or on behalf of any person so liable."

In 1974, P.L. 93-499, Sec. 3(b), substituted "$500" for "$50", effective 12/1/74, and only for wagers placed on or after 12/1/74, except as provided in Sec. 3(d)(2) of this Act, reproduced following Code Sec. 4401.

Sec. 4412. Registration.
(a) Requirement.

Each person required to pay a special tax under this subchapter shall register with the official in charge of the internal revenue district—

(1) his name and place of residence;

(2) if he is liable for tax under subchapter A, each place of business where the activity which makes him so liable is carried on, and the name and place of residence of each person who is engaged in receiving wagers for him or on his behalf; and

(3) if he is engaged in receiving wagers for or on behalf of any person liable for tax under subchapter A, the name and place of residence of each such person.

(b) Firm or company.

Where subsection (a) requires the name and place of residence of a firm or company to be registered, the names and places of residence of the several persons constituting the firm or company shall be registered.

(c) Supplemental information.

In accordance with regulations prescribed by the Secretary, the Secretary may require from time to time such supplemental information from any person required to register under this section as may be needful to the enforcement of this chapter.

In 1976, P.L. 94-455, Sec. 1906(b)(13)(I), substituted "the Secretary" for "he or his delegate" in subsec. (c), effective 2/1/77.

Sec. 4413. Certain provisions made applicable.

Sections 4901, 4902, 4904, 4905, and 4906 shall extend to and apply to the special tax imposed by this subchapter and to the persons upon whom it is imposed, and for that purpose any activity which makes a person liable for special tax under this subchapter shall be considered to be a business or occupation referred to in such sections. No other provision of sections 4901 to 4907, inclusive, shall so extend or apply.

Sec. 4414. Cross references.

For penalties and other general and administrative provisions applicable to this subchapter, see sections 4421 to 4423, inclusive; and subtitle F.

Subchapter C.—Miscellaneous Provisions

Sec.
4421. Definitions.
4422. Applicability of federal and state laws.
4423. Inspection of books.
4424. Disclosure of wagering tax information.

In 1974, P.L. 93-499, Sec. 3(c)(2), added item 4424.

Sec. 4421. Definitions.

For purposes of this chapter—

(1) **Wager.** The term "wager" means—

(A) any wager with respect to a sports event or a contest placed with a person engaged in the business of accepting such wagers,

(B) any wager placed in a wagering pool with respect to a sports event or a contest, if such pool is conducted for profit, and

(C) any wager placed in a lottery conducted for profit.

(2) **Lottery.** The term "lottery" includes the numbers game, policy, and similar types of wagering. The term does not include—

(A) any game of a type in which usually—
  (i) the wagers are placed,
  (ii) the winners are determined, and
  (iii) the distribution of prizes or other property is made, in the presence of all persons placing wagers in such game, and

(B) any drawing conducted by an organization exempt from tax under sections 501 and 521, if no part of the net proceeds derived from such drawing inures to the benefit of any private shareholder or individual.

Sec. 4422. Applicability of Federal and State laws.

The payment of any tax imposed by this chapter with respect to any activity shall not exempt any person from any penalty provided by a law of the United States or of any State for engaging in the same activity, nor shall the payment of any such tax prohibit any State from placing a tax on the same activity for State or other purposes.

Sec. 4423. Inspection of books.

Notwithstanding section 7605(b), the books of account of any person liable for tax under this chapter may be examined and inspected as frequently as may be needful to the enforcement of this chapter.

Sec. 4424. Disclosure of wagering tax information.
(a) General rule.

Except as otherwise provided in this section, neither the Secretary nor any other officer or employee of the Treasury Department may divulge or make known in any manner whatever to any person—

(1) any original, copy, or abstract of any return, payment, or registration made pursuant to this chapter,

(2) any record required for making any such return, payment, or registration, which the Secretary is permitted by the taxpayer to examine or which is produced pursuant to section 7602, or

(3) any information come at by the exploitation of any such return, payment, registration, or record.

(b) Permissible disclosure.

A disclosure otherwise prohibited by subsection (a) may be made in connection with the administration or civil or criminal enforcement of any tax imposed by this title. However, any document or information so disclosed may not be—

(1) divulged or made known in any manner whatever by any officer or employee of the United States to any person except in connection with the administration or civil or criminal enforcement of this title, nor

(2) used, directly or indirectly, in any criminal prosecution for any offense occurring before the date of enactment of this section.

(c) Use of documents possessed by taxpayer.

Except in connection with the administration or civil or criminal enforcement of any tax imposed by this title—

(1) any stamp denoting payment of the special tax under this chapter,

(2) any original, copy, or abstract possessed by a taxpayer of any return, payment, or registration made by such taxpayer pursuant to this chapter, and

(3) any information come at by the exploitation of any such document,

shall not be used against such taxpayer in any criminal proceeding.

Code Sec. 4424(d)

(d) Inspection by Committees of Congress.

Section 6103(f) shall apply with respect to any return, payment, or registration made pursuant to this chapter.

In **1976**, P.L. 94-455, Sec. 1202(h)(6), substituted "6103(f)" for "6103(d)" in subsec. (d), effective 1/1/77.
— P.L. 94-455, Sec. 1906(b)(13)(A), substituted "Secretary" for "Secretary or his delegate" each place it appeared in subsec. (a), effective 2/1/77.
In **1974**, P.L. 93-499, Sec. 3(c), added Code Sec. 4424, effective 12/1/74, and applicable only for wagers placed on or after 12/1/74. For special rules, see Sec. 3(d)(2) of this Act, reproduced in note following Code Sec. 4401.

CHAPTER 36.—CERTAIN OTHER EXCISE TAXES
Subchapter
A. Harbor maintenance tax.
B. Transportation by water.
D. Tax on use of certain vehicles.
F. Repealed.

In **1997**, P.L. 105-34, Sec. 1432(b)(2), deleted item for Subchapter F.
Prior to deletion, the item for Subchapter F read as follows:
"Tax on removal of hard mineral resources from deep seabed."
In **1989**, P.L. 101-239, Sec. 7504(b), added item B.
In **1986**, P.L. 99-662, Sec. 1402(b), added item A.
In **1982**, P.L. 97-248, Sec. 280(c)(2)(A), deleted item E.
Prior to deletion item E read as follows:
"E. Tax on use of civil aircraft."
In **1978**, P.L. 95-600, Sec. 521(b), repealed Subchapter B of Chapter 36.
Prior to repeal Subchapter B of Chapter 36 read as follows:
"Subchapter B.—Occupational Tax on Coin-Operated Devices
"Sec.
"4461. Imposition of tax.
"4462. Definition of coin-operated gaming device.
"4463. Administrative provisions.
"4464. Credit for State-imposed taxes."
In **1971**, P.L. 92-178, Sec. 402(b), added item 4464.
In **1965**, P.L. 89-44, Sec. 402,404, deleted "amusement or" from item 4462.

"Sec. 4461. Repealed.
In **1978**, P.L. 95-600, Sec. 521(b), repealed Code Sec. 4461, effective for yrs. begin. after 6/30/80.
Prior to repeal, Code Sec. 4461 read as follows:
"Sec. 4461. Imposition of tax.
"(a) In general.
"There shall be imposed a special tax to be paid by every person who maintains for use or permits the use of, on any place or premises occupied by him, a coin-operated gaming device (as defined in section 4462) at the following rates:
"(1) $250 a year; and
"(2) $250 a year for each additional device so maintained or the use of which is so permitted. If one such device is replaced by another, such other device shall not be considered an additional device.
"(b) Exception.
"No tax shall be imposed on a device which is commonly known as a claw, crane, or digger machine if—
"(1) the charge for each operation of such device is not more than 10 cents,
"(2) such device never dispenses a prize other than merchandise of a maximum retail value of $1, and with respect to such device there is never a display or offer of any prize or merchandise other than merchandise dispensed by such machine,
"(3) such device is actuated by a crank and operates solely by means of a nonelectrical mechanism, and
"(4) such device is not operated other than in connection with and as part of carnivals or county or State fairs."
In **1965**, P.L. 89-44, Sec. 403, amended the part of Code Sec. 4461 preceding subsec. (b)(1), effective 7/1/65.
Prior to amendment, that part read as follows:
"(a) In general.
"There shall be imposed a special tax to be paid by every person who maintains for use or permits the use of, on any place or premises occupied by him, a coin-operated amusement or gaming device at the following rates:
"(1) $10 a year, in the case of a device defined in paragraph (1) of section 4462(a);
"(2) $250 a year, in the case of a device defined in paragraph (2) of section 4462(a); and
"(3) $10 or $250 a year, as the case may be, for each additional device so maintained or the use of which is so permitted. If one such device is replaced by another, such other device shall not be considered an additional device.
"(b) Reduced rate.
"In the case of a device which is defined in paragraph (2) of section 4462(a) and which is commonly known as a claw, crane, or digger machine, the tax imposed by subsection (a) shall be at the rate of $10 a year (in lieu of $250 a year) if—"
In **1959**, designated former provisions as subsec. (a) and added subsec. (b), effective 6/30/60.

"Sec. 4462. Repealed.
In **1978**, P.L. 95-600, Sec. 521(b), repealed Code Sec. 4462, for yrs. begin. after 6/30/80.
Prior to repeal, Code Sec. 4462 read as follows:
"Sec. 4462. Definition of coin-operated gaming device.
"(a) In general.
"For purposes of this subchapter, the term 'coin-operated gaming device' means any machine which is—
"(1) a so-called 'slot' machine which operates by means of the insertion of a coin, token, or similar object and which, by application of the element of chance, may deliver, or entitle the person playing or operating the machine to receive, cash, premiums, merchandise, or tokens, or
"(2) a machine which is similar to machines described in paragraph (1) and is operated without the insertion of a coin, token, or similar object.
"(b) Exclusions.
"The term 'coin-operated gaming device' does not include—
"(1) a bona fide vending or amusement machine in which gaming features are not incorporated;
"(2) a vending machine operated by means of the insertion of a one cent coin, which, when it dispenses a prize, never dispenses a prize of a retail value of, or entitles a person to receive a prize of a retail value of, more than 5 cents, and if the only prize dispensed is merchandise and not cash or tokens; or
"(3) a vending machine which—
"(A) dispenses tickets on a sweepstakes, wagering pool, or lottery which is conducted by an agency of a State acting under authority of State law, and
"(B) is maintained by the State agency conducting such sweepstakes, wagering pool, or lottery, or by its authorized employees or agents."
In **1976**, P.L. 94-455, Sec. 1208(b), deleted "or" at the end of para. (b)(1) . . . substituted "; or" for the period at the end of para. (b)(2) . . . added para. (b)(3), for periods after 3/10/64.
In **1965**, P.L. 89-44, Sec. 403, rewrote Code Sec. 4462, effective 7/1/65.
Prior to amendment, the section read as follows:

"Sec. 4462. Definition of coin-operated amusement or gaming device.
"(a) In general.
"For purposes of this subchapter, the term 'coin-operated amusement or gaming device' means—
"(1) any machine which is—
"(A) a music machine operated by means of the insertion of a coin, token, or similar object,
"(B) a vending machine operated by means of the insertion of a one cent coin, which, when it dispenses a prize, never dispenses a prize of a retail value of, or entitles a person to receive a prize of a retail value of, more than 5 cents, and if the only prize dispensed is merchandise and not cash or tokens,
"(C) an amusement machine operated by means of the insertion of a coin, token, or similar object, but not including any device defined in paragraph (2) of this subsection, or
"(D) a machine which is similar to machines described in subparagraph (A), (B), or (C), and is operated without the insertion of a coin, token, or similar object; and
"(2) any machine which is—
"(A) a so-called 'slot' machine which operates by means of the insertion of a coin, token, or similar object and which, by application of the element of chance, may deliver, or entitle the person playing or operating the machine to receive cash, premiums, merchandise, or tokens, or
"(B) a machine which is similar to machines described in subparagraph (A) and is operated without the insertion of a coin, token, or similar object.
"(b) Exclusion.
"The term 'coin-operated amusement or gaming device' does not include bona fide vending machines in which are not incorporated gaming or amusement features."
In **1958**, P.L. 85-859, Sec. 152(a), included within the definition of "coin-operated amusement or gaming device" machines and so-called "slot" machines which are operated without the insertion of a coin, token, or similar object, effective 1/1/59.
But in the case of the year beginning July 1, 1958, where the trade or business on which the tax is imposed under section 4461 of the Internal Revenue Code of 1954 was commenced before such effective date, the tax imposed for such year solely by reason of the amendment made by subsection (a)—
"(1) shall be the amount reckoned proportionately from such effective date through June 30, 1959, and
"(2) shall be due on, and payable on or before, the last day of the month the first day of which is such effective date."

"Sec. 4463. Repealed.
In **1978**, P.L. 95-600, Sec. 521(b), repealed Code Sec. 4463, for yrs. begin. after 6/30/80.
Prior to repeal, Code Sec. 4463 read as follows:
"Sec. 4463. Administrative provisions.
"(a) Trade or business.

Excise and miscellaneous taxes

Code Sec. 4462(a)(5)(B)

"An operator of a place or premises who maintains for use or permits the use of any coin-operated device shall be considered, for purposes of chapter 40, to be engaged in a trade or business in respect of each such device.
"(b) Cross reference.
"For penalties and other administrative provisions applicable to this subchapter, see chapter 40 and subtitle F."

"4464. Repealed.
In 1978, P.L. 95-600, Sec. 521(a), substituted '95 percent' for '80 percent' in the heading and text of para. (b)(2), effective for tax. yrs. end. 6/30/79 and 6/30/80.
—P.L. 95-600, Sec. 521(b), repealed Code Sec. 4464, for yrs. begin. after 6/30/80.
Prior to repeal, Code Sec. 4464 read as follows:
"Sec. 4464. Credit for state-imposed taxes.
"(a) In general.
"There shall be allowed as a credit against the tax imposed by section 4461 with respect to any coin-operated gaming device for any year an amount equal to the amount of State tax paid for such year with respect to such device by the person liable for the tax imposed by section 4461, if such State tax (1) is paid under a law of the State in which the place or premises on which such device is maintained or used is located, and (2) is similar to the tax imposed by section 4461 (including a tax, other than a general personal property tax, imposed on such device).
"(b) Limitations.
"(1) Devices must be legal under state law. Credit shall be allowed under subsection (a) for a tax imposed by a State only if the maintenance of the coin-operated gaming device by the person liable for the tax is imposed by section 4461 on the place or premises occupied by him does not violate any law of such State.
"(2) Credit not to exceed 80 percent of tax. The credit under subsection (a) with respect to any coin-operated gaming device shall not exceed 80 percent of the tax imposed by section 4461 with respect to such device.
"(c) Special provisions for payment of tax.
"Under regulations prescribed by the Secretary, a person who believes he will be entitled to a credit under subsection (a) with respect to any coin-operated gaming device for any year shall, for purposes of this subtitle and subtitle F, satisfy his liability for the tax imposed by section 4461 with respect to such device for such year if—
"(1) on or before the date prescribed by law for payment of the tax imposed by section 4461 with respect to such device for such year, he has paid the amount of such tax reduced by the amount of the credit which he estimates will be allowable under subsection (a) with respect to such device for such year, and
"(2) on or before the last day of such year, pays the amount (if any) by which the credit for such year is less than the credit estimated under paragraph (1)."
In 1976, P.L. 94-455, Sec. 1906(b)(13)(A), substituted "Secretary" for "Secretary or his delegate" in subsec. (c), effective 2/1/77.
In 1971, P.L. 92-178, Sec. 402(a), added Code Sec. 4464, effective on or after 7/1/72.

In 1970, added item E.
In 1956, added item D.

Subchapter A.—Harbor Maintenance Tax
Sec.
4461. Imposition of tax.
4462. Definitions and special rules.

Sec. 4461. Imposition of tax.
(a) General rule.
There is hereby imposed a tax on any port use.
(b) Amount of tax.
The amount of the tax imposed by subsection (a) on any port use shall be an amount equal to 0.125 percent of the value of the commercial cargo involved.
(c) Liability and time of imposition of tax.
  (1) Liability. The tax imposed by subsection (a) shall be paid by—
    (A) in the case of cargo entering the United States, the importer, or
    (B) in any other case, the shipper.
  (2) Time of imposition. Except as provided by regulations, the tax imposed by subsection (a) shall be imposed at the time of unloading.

In 2005, P.L. 109-59, Sec. 11116(b)(1), added "or" at the end of subpara. (c)(1)(A), deleted subpara. (c)(1)(B), and redesignated subpara. (c)(1)(C) as (c)(1)(B)... Sec. 11116(b)(2), substituted "imposed" for "imposed—(A) in the case of cargo to be exported from the United States, at the time of loading, and (B) in any other case," in para. (c)(2), effective before, on, and after 8/10/2005.

Prior to deletion, subpara. (c)(1)(B) read as follows:
"(B) in the case of cargo to be exported from the United States, the exporter, or"
In 1990, P.L. 101-508, Sec. 11214(a), substituted "0.125 percent" for "0.04 percent", in subsec (b), effective 1/1/91.
In 1986, P.L. 99-662, Sec. 1402(a), added Code Sec. 4461, as part of subchapter A, chapter 36, effective on 6/1/87.

Sec. 4462. Definitions and special rules.
(a) Definitions.
For purposes of this subchapter—
  (1) Port use. The term "port use" means—
    (A) the loading of commercial cargo on, or
    (B) the unloading of commercial cargo from, a commercial vessel at a port.
  (2) Port.
    (A) In general. The term "port" means any channel or harbor (or component thereof) in the United States, which—
      (i) is not an inland waterway, and
      (ii) is open to public navigation.
    (B) Exception for certain facilities. The term "port" does not include any channel or harbor with respect to which no Federal funds have been used since 1977 for construction, maintenance, or operation, or which was deauthorized by Federal law before 1985.
    (C) Special rule for Columbia River. The term "port" shall include the channels of the Columbia River in the States of Oregon and Washington only up to the downstream side of Bonneville lock and dam.
  (3) Commercial cargo.
    (A) In general. The term "commercial cargo" means any cargo transported on a commercial vessel, including passengers transported for compensation or hire.
    (B) Certain items not included. The term "commercial cargo" does not include—
      (i) bunker fuel, ship's stores, sea stores, or the legitimate equipment necessary to the operation of a vessel, or
      (ii) fish or other aquatic animal life caught and not previously landed on shore.
  (4) Commercial vessel.
    (A) In general. The term "commercial vessel" means any vessel used—
      (i) in transporting cargo by water for compensation or hire, or
      (ii) in transporting cargo by water in the business of the owner, lessee, or operator of the vessel.
    (B) Exclusion of ferries.
      (i) In general. The term "commercial vessel" does not include any ferry engaged primarily in the ferrying of passengers (including their vehicles) between points within the United States, or between the United States and contiguous countries.
      (ii) Ferry. The term "ferry" means any vessel which arrives in the United States on a regular schedule during its operating season at intervals of at least once each business day.
  (5) Value.
    (A) In general. The term "value" means, except as provided in regulations, the value of any commercial cargo as determined by standard commercial documentation.
    (B) Transportation of passengers. In the case of the transportation of passengers for hire, the term "value" means the actual charge paid for such service or the prevailing charge for comparable service if no actual charge is paid.

3,265

(b) Special rule for Alaska, Hawaii, and possessions.
(1) In general. No tax shall be imposed under section 4461(a) with respect to—
(A) cargo loaded on a vessel in a port in the United States mainland for transportation to Alaska, Hawaii, or any possession of the United States for ultimate use or consumption in Alaska, Hawaii, or any possession of the United States,
(B) cargo loaded on a vessel in Alaska, Hawaii, or any possession of the United States for transportation to the United States mainland, Alaska, Hawaii, or such a possession for ultimate use or consumption in the United States mainland, Alaska, Hawaii, or such a possession,
(C) the unloading of cargo described in subparagraph (A) or (B) in Alaska, Hawaii, or any possession of the United States, or in the United States mainland, respectively, or
(D) cargo loaded on a vessel in Alaska, Hawaii, or a possession of the United States and unloaded in the State or possession in which loaded, or passengers transported on United States flag vessels operating solely within the State waters of Alaska or Hawaii and adjacent international waters.
(2) Cargo does not include crude oil with respect to Alaska. For purposes of this subsection, the term "cargo" does not include crude oil with respect to Alaska.
(3) United States mainland. For purposes of this subsection, the term "United States mainland" means the continental United States (not including Alaska).
(c) Coordination of tax where transportation subject to tax imposed by Section 4042.
No tax shall be imposed under this subchapter with respect to the loading or unloading of any cargo on or from a vessel if any fuel of such vessel has been (or will be) subject to the tax imposed by section 4042 (relating to tax on fuel used in commercial transportation on inland waterways).
(d) Nonapplicability of tax to exports.
The tax imposed by section 4461(a) shall not apply to any port use with respect to any commercial cargo to be exported from the United States.
(e) Exemption for United States.
No tax shall be imposed under this subchapter on the United States or any agency or instrumentality thereof.
(f) Extension of provisions of law applicable to customs duty.
(1) In general. Except to the extent otherwise provided in regulations, all administrative and enforcement provisions of customs laws and regulations shall apply in respect of the tax imposed by this subchapter (and in respect of persons liable therefor) as if such tax were a customs duty. For purposes of the preceding sentence, any penalty expressed in terms of a relationship to the amount of the duty shall be treated as not less than the amount which bears a similar relationship to the value of the cargo.
(2) Jurisdiction of courts and agencies. For purposes of determining the jurisdiction of any court of the United States or any agency of the United States, the tax imposed by this subchapter shall be treated as if such tax were a customs duty.
(3) Administrative provisions applicable to tax law not to apply. The tax imposed by this subchapter shall not be treated as a tax for purposes of subtitle F or any other provision of law relating to the administration and enforcement of internal revenue taxes.

(g) Special rules.
Except as provided by regulations—
(1) Tax imposed only once. Only 1 tax shall be imposed under section 4461(a) with respect to the loading on and unloading from, or the unloading from and the loading on, the same vessel of the same cargo.
(2) Exception for intraport movements. Under regulations, no tax shall be imposed under section 4461(a) on the mere movement of cargo within a port.
(3) Relay cargo. Only 1 tax shall be imposed under section 4461(a) on cargo (moving under a single bill of lading) which is unloaded from one vessel and loaded onto another vessel at any port in the United States for relay to or from any port in Alaska, Hawaii, or any possession of the United States. For purposes of this paragraph, the term "cargo" does not include any item not treated as cargo under subsection (b)(2).
(h) Exemption for humanitarian and development assistance cargos.
No tax shall be imposed under this subchapter on any nonprofit organization or cooperative for cargo which is owned or financed by such nonprofit organization or cooperative and which is certified by the United States Customs Service as intended for use in humanitarian or development assistance overseas.
(i) Regulations.
The Secretary may prescribe such additional regulations as may be necessary to carry out the purposes of this subchapter including, but not limited to, regulations—
(1) providing for the manner and method of payment and collection of the tax imposed by this subchapter,
(2) providing for the posting of bonds to secure payment of such tax,
(3) exempting any transaction or class of transactions from such tax where the collection of such tax is not administratively practical, and
(4) providing for the remittance or mitigation of penalties and the settlement or compromise of claims.

In 2005, P.L. 109-59, Sec. 11116(a), amended subsec. (d), effective before, on, and after 8/10/2005.
Prior to amendment, subsec. (d) read as follows:
"(d) Nonapplicability of tax to certain cargo.
"(1) In general. Subject to paragraph (2), the tax imposed by section 4461(a) shall not apply to bonded commercial cargo entering the United States for transportation and direct exportation to a foreign country.
"(2) Imposition of charges. Paragraph (1) shall not apply to any cargo exported to Canada or Mexico—
"(A) during the period—
"(i) after the date on which the Secretary determines that the Government of Canada or Mexico (as the case may be) has imposed a substantially equivalent tax, fee, or charge on commercial vessels or commercial cargo utilizing ports of such country, and
"(ii) subject to subparagraph (B), before the date on which the Secretary determines that such tax, fee, or charge has been discontinued by such country, and
"(B) with respect to a particular United States port (or to any transaction or class of transactions at any such port) to the extent that the study made pursuant to section 1407(a) of the Water Resources Development Act of 1986 (or a review thereof pursuant to section 1407(b) of such Act) finds that—
"(i) the imposition of the tax imposed by this subchapter at such port (or to any transaction or class of transactions at such port) is not likely to divert a significant amount of cargo from such port to a port in a country contiguous to the United States, or that any such diversion is not likely to result in significant economic loss to such port, or
"(ii) the nonapplicability of such tax at such port (or to any transaction or class of transactions at such port) is likely to result in significant economic loss to any other United States port."
In 1996, P.L. 104-188, Sec. 1704(i)(1), added ", or passengers transported on United States flag vessels operating solely within the State waters of Alaska or Hawaii and adjacent international waters" before the period in subpara. (b)(1)(D), effective 4/1/87.
In 1988, P.L. 100-647, Sec. 2002(b), amended subpara. (b)(1)(B), effective 4/1/87.
Prior to amendment, subpara. (b)(1)(B) read as follows:

Excise and miscellaneous taxes   Code Sec. 4481(d)(2)

"(B) cargo loaded on a vessel in Alaska, Hawaii, or any possession of the United States for transportation to the United States mainland for ultimate use or consumption in the United States mainland,".
—P.L. 100-647, Sec. 6109(a), redesignated subsec. (h) as subsec. (i) and added subsec. (g), effective on 4/1/87.
—P.L. 100-647, Sec. 6110(a), added para. (g)(3), effective 11/10/88.
In 1986, P.L. 99-662, Sec. 1402(a), added Code Sec. 4462, as part of subchapter A, chapter 36, effective on 4/1/87.

Subchapter B.—Transportation by Water
Sec.
4471. Imposition of tax.
4472. Definitions.

In 1996, P.L. 104-188, Sec. 1704(t)(11), deleted "and special rules" after "Definitions" in item 4472.
In 1989, added Subchapter B.

Sec. 4471. Imposition of tax.
(a) In general.
There is hereby imposed a tax of $3 per passenger on a covered voyage.
(b) By whom paid.
The tax imposed by this section shall be paid by the person providing the covered voyage.
(c) Time of imposition.
The tax imposed by this section shall be imposed only once for each passenger on a covered voyage, either at the time of first embarkation or disembarkation in the United States.

In 1989, P.L. 101-239, Sec. 7504(a), added Code Sec. 4471 as part of subchapter B of chapter 36, effective for voyages begin. after 12/31/89 which were not paid for before 12/31/89. Sec. 7504(c)(2) of this Act provides:
"(2) No deposits required before April 1, 1990. No deposit of any tax imposed by subchapter B of chapter 36 of the Internal Revenue Code of 1986, as added by this section [Sec. 7504], shall be required to be made before April 1, 1990."

Sec. 4472. Definitions.
For purposes of this subchapter—
(1) Covered voyage.
  (A) In general. The term "covered voyage" means a voyage of—
    (i) a commercial passenger vessel which extends over 1 or more nights, or
    (ii) a commercial vessel transporting passengers engaged in gambling aboard the vessel beyond the territorial waters of the United States,
during which passengers embark or disembark the vessel in the United States. Such term shall not include any voyage on any vessel owned or operated by the United States, a State, or any agency or subdivision thereof.
  (B) Exception for certain voyages on passenger vessels. The term "covered voyage" shall not include a voyage of a passenger vessel of less than 12 hours between 2 ports in the United States.
(2) Passenger vessel. The term "passenger vessel" means any vessel having berth or stateroom accommodations for more than 16 passengers.

In 1989, P.L. 101-239, Sec. 7504(a), added Code Sec. 4472 as part of subchapter B of chapter 36, effective for voyages begin. after 12/31/89 which were not paid for before 12/31/89. Sec. 7504(c)(2) of this Act provides:
"(2) No deposits required before April 1, 1990. No deposit of any tax imposed by subchapter B of chapter 36 of the Internal Revenue Code of 1986, as added by this section, shall be required to be made before April 1, 1990."

Subchapter D.—Tax on Use of Certain Vehicles
Sec.
4481. Imposition of tax.
4482. Definitions.
4483. Exemptions.
4484. Cross references.

In 1983, P.L. 97-473, Sec. 202(b), amended item 4484.
Prior to amendment, item 4484 read as follows:
"4484. CROSS REFERENCE."
In 1956, added Subchapter D.

Sec. 4481. Imposition of tax.
(a) Imposition of tax.
A tax is hereby imposed on the use of any highway motor vehicle which (together with the semitrailers and trailers customarily used in connection with highway motor vehicles of the same type as such highway motor vehicle) has a taxable gross weight of at least 55,000 pounds at the rate specified in the following table:

Taxable gross weight:	Rate of tax:
At least 55,000 pounds, but not over 75,000 pounds ..	$100 per year plus $22 for each 1,000 pounds (or fraction thereof) in excess of 55,000 pounds.
Over 75,000 pounds	$550

(b) By whom paid.
The tax imposed by this section shall be paid by the person in whose name the highway motor vehicle is, or is required to be, registered under the law of the State or contiguous foreign country in which such vehicle is, or is required to be, registered, or, in case the highway motor vehicle is owned by the United States, by the agency or instrumentality of the United States operating such vehicle.
(c) Proration of tax.
  (1) Where first use occurs after first month. If in any taxable period the first use of the highway motor vehicle is after the first month in such period, the tax shall be reckoned proportionately from the first day of the month in which such use occurs to and including the last day in such taxable period.
  (2) Where vehicle sold, destroyed, or stolen.
    (A) In general. If in any taxable period a highway motor vehicle is sold, destroyed, or stolen before the first day of the last month in such period and not subsequently used during such taxable period, the tax shall be reckoned proportionately from the first day of the month in such period in which the first use of such highway motor vehicle occurs to and including the last day of the month in which such highway motor vehicle was sold, destroyed, or stolen.
    (B) Destroyed. For purposes of subparagraph (A), a highway motor vehicle is destroyed if such vehicle is damaged by reason of an accident or other casualty to such an extent that it is not economic to rebuild.
(d) One tax liability per period.
  (1) In general. To the extent that the tax imposed by this section is paid with respect to any highway motor vehicle for any taxable period, no further tax shall be imposed by this section for such taxable period with respect to such vehicle.
  (2) Cross reference. For privilege of paying tax imposed by this section in installments, see section 6156.

(e) Electronic filing.

Any taxpayer who files a return under this section with respect to 25 or more vehicles for any taxable period shall file such return electronically.

(f) Period tax in effect.

The tax imposed by this section shall apply only to use before October 1, 2011.

In 2005, P.L. 109-59, Sec. 11101(a)(2)(A), substituted "2011" for "2006" in subsec. (f), effective 8/10/2005.
—P.L. 109-14, Sec. 9(c)(1), substituted "2006" for "2005" in subsec. (f), effective 5/31/2005.

In 2004, P.L. 108-357, Sec. 867(a)(1), substituted "sold, destroyed, or stolen" for "destroyed or stolen" each place it appeared in subpara. (c)(2)(A)... Sec. 867(a)(2), substituted "sold, destroyed, or stolen" for "destroyed or stolen" in the heading of para. (c)(2)... Sec. 867(c), redesignated subsec. (e) as (f) and added subsec. (e), effective for tax. periods begin. after 10/22/2004.

In 1998, P.L. 105-178, Sec. 9002(a)(1)(G), substituted "2005" for "1999" in subsec. (e), effective 6/9/98.

In 1996, P.L. 104-188, Sec. 1704(t)(57), substituted "4481(e)" for "4481(c)" in Sec. 8802(a)(5) of P.L. 102-240 [see below], effective 8/20/96.

In 1991, P.L. 102-240, Sec. 8002(a)(5), [amended by Sec. 1704(t)(57) of P.L. 104-188, see above] substituted "1999" for "1995" in subsec. (e), effective 12/18/91.

In 1990, P.L. 101-508, Sec. 11211(c)(5), substituted "1995" for "1993" in subsec. (e), effective 11/5/90.

In 1987, P.L. 100-17, Sec. 502(a)(5), substituted "1993" for "1988" in subsec. (e), effective 4/2/87.
—P.L. 100-17, Sec. 507(a), added "or contiguous foreign country" after "State" in subsec. (b), effective 7/1/87. Sec. 507(c) of this Act provides:

"(c) Regulations required within 120 days. The Secretary of the Treasury or the delegate of the Secretary shall within 120 days after the date of the enactment of this section prescribe regulations governing payment of the tax imposed by section 4481 of the Internal Revenue Code of 1986 on any highway motor vehicle operated by a motor carrier domiciled in any contiguous foreign country or owned or controlled by persons of any contiguous foreign country. Such regulations shall include a procedure by which the operator of such motor vehicle shall evidence that such operator has paid such tax at the time such motor vehicle enters the United States. In the event of the failure to provide evidence of payment, such regulations may provide for denial of entry of such motor vehicle into the United States."

In 1984, P.L. 98-369, Sec. 734(f), deleted the sentence "In the case of the taxable period beginning on July 1, 1984, and ending on September 30, 1984, the tax shall be at the rate of 75 cents for such period for each 1,000 pounds of taxable gross weight or fraction thereof." from the end of subsec. (a), as in effect before the amendments made by P.L. 97-424 (see below)... Sec. 901(a), amended subsec. (a) as amended by P.L. 97-424, effective 7/1/84. Sec. 901(b)(1)-(4) of this Act provides the following special rules:

"(b) Special rules in the case of certain owner-operations.

"(1) Special rule for taxable period beginning on July 1, 1984. In the case of a small owner-operator, the amount of the tax imposed by section 4481 of the Internal Revenue Code of 1954 on the use of any highway motor vehicle subject to tax under section 4481 of such Code (as amended by subsection (a)) for the taxable period which begins on July 1, 1984, shall be the lesser of—

"(A) $3 for each 1,000 pounds of taxable gross weight (or fraction thereof), or

"(B) the amount of the tax which would be imposed under such section 4481(a) without regard to this paragraph.

"(2) Exemption for vehicles used for less than 5,000 miles (and certain other amendments) to take effect on July 1, 1984. In the case of a small owner-operator, notwithstanding subsection (f)(2) of section 513 of the Highway Revenue Act of 1982, the amendments made by subsections (b), (c), and (d) of such section shall take effect on July 1, 1984.

"(3) Small owner-operator defined. For purposes of this subsection, the term 'small owner-operator' has the meaning given such term by section 513(f)(2) of the Highway Revenue Act of 1982.

"(4) Taxable gross weight. For purposes of this subsection, the term 'taxable gross weight' has the same meaning as when used in section 4481 of the Internal Revenue Code of 1954.', effective 7/1/84.

Prior to amendment, subsec. (a) read as follows:

"(a) Imposition of tax. A tax is hereby imposed on the use of any highway motor vehicle which (together with the semitrailers and trailers customarily used in connection with highway motor vehicles of the same type as such highway motor vehicle) has a taxable gross weight of at least 33,000 pounds at the rate specified in the following table:

"(1) In general.

"Taxable gross weight		
"At least	But less than	Rate of tax
33,000 pounds	55,000 pounds	$50 a year, plus $25 for each 1,000 pounds or fraction thereof in excess of 33,000 pounds.
55,000 pounds	80,000 pounds	$600 a year, plus the applicable rate for each 1,000 pounds or fraction thereof in excess of 55,000 pounds.
80,000 pounds or more		The maximum tax a year.

"(2) Definitions. For purposes of paragraph (1)—

In the case of the taxable period beginning on July 1 of:	The applicable rate is:	The maximum tax is:
1984	$40	$1,600
1985	40	1,600
1986	44	1,700
1987	48	1,800
1988 or thereafter	52	1,900."

In 1983, P.L. 97-424, Sec. 513(a), amended subsec. (a)... Sec. 513(d), amended subsec. (c), effective 7/1/84 except as provided in Sec. 513(f)(2) of this Act which reads as follows:

"(2) Special rule in the case of certain owner-operators.

"(A) In general. In the case of a small owner-operator, paragraph (1) of this subsection and paragraph (2) of section 4481(a) of the Internal Revenue Code of 1954 (as added by this section) shall be applied by substituting for each date contained in such paragraphs a date which is 1 year after the date so contained.

"(B) Small owner-operator. For purposes of this paragraph, the term 'small owner-operator' means any person who owns and operates at any time during the taxable period no more than 5 highway motor vehicles with respect to which a tax is imposed by section 4481 of such Code for such taxable period.

"(D) Aggregation of vehicle ownerships. For purposes of subparagraph (B), all highway motor vehicles with respect to which a tax is imposed by section 4481 of such Code which are owned by—

"(i) any trade or business (whether or not incorporated) which is under common control with the taxpayer (within the meaning of section 52(b)), or

"(ii) any member of any controlled groups of corporations of which the taxpayer is a member, for any taxable period shall be treated as being owned by the taxpayer during such period. The Secretary shall prescribe regulations which provide attribution rules that take into account, in addition to the persons and entities described in the preceding sentence, taxpayers who own highway motor vehicles through partnerships, joint ventures, and corporations.

"(E) Controlled groups of corporations. For purposes of this paragraph, the term 'controlled group of corporations' has the meaning given to such term by section 1563(a), except that—

"(i) 'more than 50 percent' shall be substituted for 'at least 80 percent' each place it appears in section 1563(a)(1), and

"(ii) the determination shall be made without regard to subsections (a)(4) and (e)(3)(C) of section 1563.

"(F) Highway motor vehicles. For purposes of this paragraph, the term 'highway motor vehicle' has the meaning given to such term by section 4482(a) of such Code."

Sec. 513(g) of this Act provides:

"(g) Study of alternatives to tax on use of heavy trucks.

"(1) In general. The Secretary of Transportation (in consultation with the Secretary of the Treasury) shall conduct a study of—

"(A) alternatives to the tax on heavy vehicles imposed by section 4481(a) of the Internal Revenue Code of 1954, and

"(B) plans for improving the collecting and enforcement of such tax and alternatives to such tax.

"(2) Alternatives included. The alternatives studied under paragraph (1) shall include taxes based either singly or in suitable combinations on vehicle size or configuration; vehicle weight, both registered and actual operating weight; and distance traveled. Plans for improving tax collection and enforcement shall, to the extent practical, provide for Federal and State co-operation in such activities.

"(3) Consultation with State officials and other affected parties. The study required under subsection (a) shall be conducted in consultation with State officials, motor carriers, and other affected parties.

"(4) Report. Not later than January 1, 1985, the Secretary of Transportation shall submit to the Committee on Ways and Means of the House of Representatives and the Committee on Finance of the Senate a report on the study conducted under paragraph (1) together with such recommendations as he may deem advisable."

Prior to amendment, subsec. (a) read as follows:

"(a) Imposition of tax. A tax is hereby imposed on the use of any highway motor vehicle which (together with the semitrailers and trailers customarily used in connection with highway motor vehicles of the same type as such highway motor vehicle) has a taxable gross weight of more than 26,000 pounds, at the rate of $3.00 a year for each 1,000 pounds of taxable gross weight or fraction thereof."

Prior to amendment, subsec. (c) read as follows:

"(c) Proration of tax. If in any taxable period the first use of the highway motor vehicle is after the first month in such period, the tax shall be reckoned proportionately from the first day of the month in which such use occurs to and including the last day in such taxable period."

—P.L. 97-424, Sec. 516(a)(4), substituted "1988" for "1984" in subsec. (e).

In 1978, P.L. 95-599, Sec. 502(a)(6), and (7), substituted "1984" for "1979" each place it appeared in subsecs. (a) and (e), effective 11/6/78.

Excise and miscellaneous taxes

Code Sec. 4483(d)(1)(B)

In 1976, P.L. 94-280, Sec. 303(a)(7), and (a)(8), substituted "1979" for "1977" each place it appeared in subsecs. (a) and (e), effective 5/5/76.
In 1970, P.L. 91-605, Sec. 303(a)(7), and (a)(8), substituted "1977" for "1972" each place it appeared in subsecs. (a) and (e).
In 1961, P.L. 87-61, Sec. 203, increased the rate of tax from $1.50 to $3.00 a year, and provided for a tax at the rate of 75 cents for each 1,000 pounds during the period beginning on 7/1/72 and ending 9/30/72 in subsec. (a), substituted in subsec. (b) "any taxable period" for "any year", "after the first month in such period" for "after July 31", and "the last day in such taxable period" for "the last day of June following", in subsec. (d) made conforming changes to refer to payment of tax for a taxable period instead of payment for a year, and added the cross reference to section 6156 in subsec. (e); substituted "before October 1, 1972" for "after June 30, 1956, and before July 1, 1972", effective 7/1/61.
In 1956, ch. 462, title II, Sec. 206(a), added Code Sec. 4481, effective 6/29/56.

Sec. 4482. Definitions.

(a) Highway motor vehicle.

For purposes of this subchapter, the term "highway motor vehicle" means any motor vehicle which is a highway vehicle.

(b) Taxable gross weight.

For purposes of this subchapter, the term "taxable gross weight" when used with respect to any highway motor vehicle, means the sum of—

(1) the actual unloaded weight of—

(A) such highway motor vehicle fully equipped for service, and

(B) the semitrailers and trailers (fully equipped for service) customarily used in connection with highway motor vehicles of the same type as such highway motor vehicle, and

(2) the weight of the maximum load customarily carried on highway motor vehicles of the same type as such highway motor vehicle and on the semitrailers and trailers referred to in paragraph (1)(B).

Taxable gross weight shall be determined under regulations prescribed by the Secretary (which regulations may include formulas or other methods for determining the taxable gross weight of vehicles by classes, specifications, or otherwise).

(c) Other definitions and special rule.

For purposes of this subchapter—

(1) **State.** The term "State" means a State and the District of Columbia.

(2) **Year.** The term "year" means the one-year period beginning on July 1.

(3) **Use.** The term "use" means use in the United States on the public highways.

(4) **Taxable period.** The term "taxable period" means any year beginning before July 1, 2011, and the period which begins on July 1, 2011, and ends at the close of September 30, 2011.

(5) **Customary use.** A semitrailer or trailer shall be treated as customarily used in connection with a highway motor vehicle if such vehicle is equipped to tow such semitrailer or trailer.

(d) Special rule for taxable period in which termination date occurs.

In the case of the taxable period which ends on September 30, 2011, the amount of the tax imposed by section 4481 with respect to any highway motor vehicle shall be determined by reducing each dollar amount in the table contained in section 4481(a) by 75 percent.

In 2005, P.L. 109-59, Sec. 11101(a)(2)(B), substituted "2011" for "2006" each place it appeared in para. (c)(4)... Sec. 11101(a)(2)(C), substituted "2011" for "2006" in subsec. (d), effective 8/10/2005.
—P.L. 109-14, Sec. 9(c)(2), substituted "2006" for "2005" each place it appeared in para. (c)(4)... Sec. 9(c)(3), substituted "2006" for "2005" in subsec. (d), effective 5/31/2005.
In 1998, P.L. 105-178, Sec. 9002(a)(1)(H), substituted "2005" for "1999" each place it appeared in para. (c)(4)... Sec. 9002(a)(1)(I), substituted "2005" for "1999" in subsec. (d), effective 6/9/98.

In 1991, P.L. 102-240, Sec. 8002(a)(5), substituted "1999" for "1995" each place it appeared in para. (c)(4) and subsec. (d), effective 12/18/91.
In 1990, P.L. 101-508, Sec. 11211(c)(5), substituted "1995" for "1993" each place it appeared in para. (c)(4) and subsec. (d), effective 11/5/90.
In 1987, P.L. 100-17, Sec. 502(a)(5), substituted "1993" for "1988" each place it appeared in para. (c)(4) and subsec. (d), effective 4/2/87.
In 1983, P.L. 97-424, Sec. 513(c)(1), added para. (c)(5)... Sec. 513(c)(2), added "and special rule" after "definitions" in the heading of para. (c)... Sec. 513(e), added subsec. (d), effective 7/1/84. For special rule in the case of certain owner-operators, see Sec. 513(f)(2) of this Act reproduced in note following Code Sec. 4481.
—P.L. 97-424, Sec. 516(a)(4), substituted "1988" for "1984" each place it appeared in para. (c)(4).
In 1978, P.L. 95-599, Sec. 502(a)(8), substituted "1984" for "1979" each place it appeared in para. (c)(4), effective 11/6/78.
In 1976, P.L. 94-455, Sec. 1904(c), deleted ", a Territory of the United States," after "a State" in para. (c)(1), effective 2/1/77.
—P.L. 94-455, Sec. 1906(b)(13)(A), substituted "Secretary" for "Secretary or his delegate", each place it appeared in Code Sec. 4482, effective 2/1/77.
—P.L. 94-280, Sec. 303(a)(9), substituted "1979" for "1977" each place that it appeared in para. (c)(4), effective 5/5/76.
In 1970, P.L. 91-605, Sec. 303(a)(9), substituted "1977" for "1972" each place it appeared in para. (c)(4).
In 1961, P.L. 87-61, Sec. 203(b)(2)(C), added para. (4), effective 7/1/61.
In 1956, ch. 462, Sec. 206(a), added Code Sec. 4482, effective 6/29/56.

Sec. 4483. Exemptions.

(a) State and local governmental exemption.

Under regulations prescribed by the Secretary, no tax shall be imposed by section 4481 on the use of any highway motor vehicle by any State or any political subdivision of a State.

(b) Exemption for United States.

The Secretary of the Treasury may authorize exemption from the tax imposed by section 4481 as to the use by the United States of any particular highway motor vehicle, or class of highway motor vehicles, if he determines that the imposition of such tax with respect to such use will cause substantial burden or expense which can be avoided by granting tax exemption and that full benefit of such exemption, if granted, will accrue to the United States.

(c) Certain transit-type buses.

Under regulations prescribed by the Secretary, no tax shall be imposed by section 4481 on the use of any bus which is of the transit type (rather than of the intercity type) by a person who, for the last 3 months of the preceding year (or for such other period as the Secretary may by regulations prescribe for purposes of this subsection), met the 60-percent passenger fare revenue test set forth in section 6421(b)(2) (as in effect on the day before the date of the enactment [11/9/78] of the Energy Tax Act of 1978) as applied to the period prescribed for purposes of this subsection.

(d) Exemption for trucks used for less than 5,000 miles on public highways.

(1) **Suspension of tax.**

(A) In general. If—

(i) it is reasonable to expect that the use of any highway motor vehicle on public highways during any taxable period will be less than 5,000 miles, and

(ii) the owner of such vehicle furnishes such information as the Secretary may by forms or regulations require with respect to the expected use of such vehicle,

then the collection of the tax imposed by section 4481 with respect to the use of such vehicle shall be suspended during the taxable period.

(B) Suspension ceases to apply where use exceeds 5,000 miles. Subparagraph (A) shall cease to apply with respect to any highway motor vehicle whenever the use of such vehicle on public highways during the taxable period exceeds 5,000 miles.

(2) Exemption. If—
(A) the collection of the tax imposed by section 4481 with respect to any highway motor vehicle is suspended under paragraph (1),
(B) such vehicle is not used during the taxable period on public highways for more than 5,000 miles, and
(C) except as otherwise provided in regulations, the owner of such vehicle furnishes such information as the Secretary may require with respect to the use of such vehicle during the taxable period,

then no tax shall be imposed by section 4481 on the use of such vehicle for the taxable period.

(3) Refund where tax paid and vehicle not used for more than 5,000 miles. If—
(A) the tax imposed by section 4481 is paid with respect to any highway motor vehicle for any taxable period, and
(B) the requirements of subparagraphs (B) and (C) of paragraph (2) are met with respect to such taxable period,

the amount of such tax shall be credited or refunded (without interest) to the person who paid such tax.

(4) Relief from liability for tax under certain circumstances where truck is transferred. Under regulations prescribed by the Secretary, the owner of a highway motor vehicle with respect to which the collection of the tax imposed by section 4481 is suspended under paragraph (1) shall not be liable for the tax imposed by section 4481 (and the new owner shall be liable for such tax) with respect to such vehicle if—
(A) such vehicle is transferred to a new owner,
(B) such suspension is in effect at the time of such transfer, and
(C) the old owner furnishes such information as the Secretary by forms and regulations requires with respect to the transfer of such vehicle.

(5) 7,500-miles exemption for agricultural vehicles.
(A) In general. In the case of an agricultural vehicle, paragraphs (1) and (2) shall be applied by substituting "7,500" for "5,000" each place it appears.
(B) Definitions. For purposes of this paragraph—
(i) Agricultural vehicle. The term "agricultural vehicle" means any highway motor vehicle—
(I) used primarily for farming purposes, and
(II) registered (under the laws of the State in which such vehicle is required to be registered) as a highway motor vehicle used for farming purposes.
(ii) Farming purposes. The term "farming purposes" means the transporting of any farm commodity to or from a farm or the use directly in agricultural production.
(iii) Farm commodity. The term "farm commodity" means any agricultural or horticultural commodity, feed, seed, fertilizer, livestock, bees, poultry, fur-bearing animals, or wildlife.

(6) Owner defined. For purposes of this subsection, the term "owner" means, with respect to any highway motor vehicle, the person described in section 4481(b).

(e) Reduction in tax for trucks used in logging.
The tax imposed by section 4481 shall be reduced by 25 percent with respect to any highway motor vehicle if—
(1) the exclusive use of such vehicle during any taxable period is the transportation, to and from a point located on a forested site, of products harvested from such forested site, and

(2) such vehicle is registered (under the laws of the State in which such vehicle is required to be registered) as a highway motor vehicle used in the transportation of harvested forest products.

(f) Repealed.

(g) Exemption for mobile machinery.
No tax shall be imposed by section 4481 on the use of any vehicle described in section 4053(8).

(h) Exemption for vehicles used in blood collection.
(1) In general. No tax shall be imposed by section 4481 on the use of any qualified blood collector vehicle by a qualified blood collector organization.
(2) Qualified blood collector vehicle. For purposes of this subsection, the term "qualified blood collector vehicle" means a vehicle at least 80 percent of the use of which during the prior taxable period was by a qualified blood collector organization in the collection, storage, or transportation of blood.
(3) Special rule for vehicles first placed in service in a taxable period. In the case of a vehicle first placed in service in a taxable period, a vehicle shall be treated as a qualified blood collector vehicle for such taxable period if such qualified blood collector organization certifies to the Secretary that the organization reasonably expects at least 80 percent of the use of such vehicle by the organization during such taxable period will be in the collection, storage, or transportation of blood.
(4) Qualified blood collector organization. The term "qualified blood collector organization" has the meaning given such term by section 7701(a)(49).

(i) Termination of exemptions.
Subsections (a) and (c) shall not apply on and after October 1, 2011.

In 2006, P.L. 109-280, Sec. 1207(d), redesignated subsec. (h) as subsec. (i) and added subsec. (h), effective for tax. periods begin. on or after 7/1/2007.
In 2005, P.L. 109-59, Sec. 11101(b)(2), substituted "2011" for "2006" in subsec. (h), effective 8/10/2005.
—P.L. 109-14, Sec. 9(c)(4), substituted "2006" for "2005" in subsec. (h), effective 5/31/2005.
In 2004, P.L. 108-357, Sec. 851(b)(1), redesignated subsec. (g) as subsec. (h) and added subsec. (g), effective the day after 10/22/2004.
—P.L. 108-357, Sec. 867(d), deleted subsec. (f), effective for tax. periods begin. after 10/22/2004.
Prior to deletion, subsec. (f) read as follows:
"(f) Reduction in tax for trucks base-plated in a contiguous foreign country. If the base for registration purposes of any highway motor vehicle is in a contiguous foreign country for any taxable period, the tax imposed by section 4481 for such period shall be 75 percent of the tax which would (but for this subsection) be imposed by section 4481 for such period."
In 1998, P.L. 105-178, Sec. 9002(b)(2), substituted "2005" for "1999" in subsec. (g), effective 6/9/98.
In 1991, P.L. 102-240, Sec. 8002(b)(4), substituted "1999" for "1995" in subsec. (g), effective 12/18/91.
In 1990, P.L. 101-508, Sec. 11211(d)(4), substituted "1995" for "1993" each place it appeared in subsec. (g), effective 11/5/90.
In 1987, P.L. 100-17, Sec. 502(b)(5), substituted "1993" for "1988" in subsec. (f), effective 4/2/87.
—P.L. 100-17, Sec. 507(b), redesignated subsec. (f) as subsec. (g) and added new subsec. (f), effective 7/1/87.
In 1984, P.L. 98-369, Sec. 902(a), redesignated subsec. (e) as subsec. (f) and added new subsec. (f) . . . Sec. 903(a), redesignated para. (d)(5) as para. (d)(6) and added new para. (d)(5), effective 7/1/84.
In 1983, P.L. 97-424, Sec. 513(b), added subsec. (d), effective 7/1/84. For special rule in the case of certain owner-operators, see Sec. 513(f)(2) of this Act, reproduced in note following Code Sec. 4481.
—P.L. 97-424, Sec. 516(b)(3), added subsec. (e).
In 1978, P.L. 95-618, Sec. 233(a)(3)(C), added "(as in effect on the day before the date of the enactment of the Energy Tax Act of 1978)" following "section 6421(b)(2)" in subsec. (c), effective the first day of the first calendar month which begins more than 10 days after 11/9/78.
In 1976, P.L. 94-455, Sec. 1906(b)(13)(A), substituted "Secretary" for "Secretary or his delegate" in subsecs. (a) and (c) . . . Sec. 1906(b)(13)(B), substituted "Secretary of the Treasury" for "Secretary" in subsec. (b), effective 2/1/77.
In 1956, ch. 462, Sec. 206(a), added Code Sec. 4483, effective 6/29/56.

Code Sec. 4493

Excise and miscellaneous taxes

Sec. 4484. Cross references.
(1) For penalties and administrative provisions applicable to this subchapter, see subtitle F.
(2) For exemption for uses by Indian tribal governments (or their subdivisions), see section 7871.

In 1984, P.L. 98-369, Sec. 1065(a)(2), changed the effective date for amendments made by Sec. 202(b)(10) of P.L. 97-473 (see below), from effective 1/1/83 and shall cease to apply at the close of 12/31/84, to effective 1/1/83.
In 1983, P.L. 97-473, Sec. 202(b)(10), amended Code Sec. 4484, effective [as amended by Sec. 1065(a)(2) of P.L. 98369, see above] 1/1/83.
Prior to amendment, Code Sec. 4484 read as follows:
"SEC. 4484. CROSS REFERENCE.
"For penalties and administrative provisions applicable to this subchapter, see subtitle F."
In 1956, ch. 462, Sec. 206(a), added Code Sec. 4484, effective 6/29/56.

Subchapter E. Repealed.

Sec.
4491. [Repealed.]
4492. [Repealed.]
4493. [Repealed.]

In 1982, P.L. 97-248, Sec. 280(c)(1), deleted subpart E.
Prior to deletion subpart E read as follows:
"Subchapter E.—Tax on Use of Civil Aircraft
"Sec.
"4491. Imposition of tax.
"4492. Definitions.
"4493. Special rules.
"4494. Cross reference."
In 1970, P.L. 91-258, Sec. 206(a), added Subchapter E.

Sec. 4491. Repealed.

In 1982, P.L. 97-248, Sec. 280(c)(1), repealed Code Sec. 4491, effective for transportation begin. after 8/31/82 except for any amount paid on or before 8/31/82.
Prior to repeal, Code Sec. 4491 read as follows:
"SEC. 4491. IMPOSITION OF TAX.
"(a) Imposition of tax.
"A tax is hereby imposed on the use of any taxable civil aircraft during any year at the rate of—
"(1) $25, plus
"(2)(A) in the case of an aircraft (other than a turbine-engine-powered aircraft), 2 cents a pound for each pound of the maximum certificated takeoff weight in excess of 2,500 pounds, or
"(B) in the case of any turbine engine powered aircraft, 3½ cents a pound for each pound of the maximum certificated takeoff weight.
"(b) By whom paid.
"Except as provided in section 4493(a), the tax imposed by this section shall be paid—
"(1) in the case of a taxable civil aircraft described in section 4492(a)(1), by the person in whose name the aircraft is, or is required to be, registered, or
"(2) in the case of a taxable civil aircraft described in section 4492(a)(2), by the United States person by or for whom the aircraft is owned.
"(c) Proration of tax.
"If in any year the first use of the taxable civil aircraft is after the first month in such year, that portion of the tax which is determined under subsection (a)(2) shall be reckoned proportionately from the first day of the month in which such use occurs to and including the last day in such year.
"(d) One tax liability per year.
"(1) In general. To the extent that the tax imposed by this section is paid with respect to any taxable civil aircraft for any year, no further tax shall be imposed by this section for such year with respect to such aircraft.
"(2) Cross reference. For privilege of paying tax imposed by this section in installments, see section 6156."
"(e) Termination.
"On and after October 1, 1980, the tax imposed by subsection (a) shall not apply."
In 1980, P.L. 96-298, Sec. 1(c), substituted "October 1, 1980" for "July 1, 1980" in subsec. (e), effective 7/1/80 [date of enactment]. Secs. 1(c)(2) and (c)(3) of P.L. 96-298 provides:
"(2) Transitional rule. For the period beginning on July 1, 1980, and ending on October 1, 1980—
"(A) subsection (a) of section 4491 of such Code shall be applied by substituting '$6.25' for '$25', '½ cent' for '2 cents', and '⅞ cent' for '3½ cents', and
"(B) such section 4491 shall be applied by treating such period as a year.

"(3) Postponement of due date for filing return. The due date for filing any return of the tax imposed by section 4491 of the Internal Revenue Code of 1954 with respect to any use after June 30, 1980, shall not be earlier than October 31, 1980."
In 1970, P.L. 91-614, Sec. 305(a), amended subpara. (a)(2)(A), effective 7/1/71.
Prior to amendment, subpara. (a)(2)(A) read as follows:
"(2)(A) in the case of an aircraft (other than a turbine engine powered aircraft) having a maximum certificated takeoff weight of more than 2,500 pounds, 2 cents a pound for each pound of the maximum certificated takeoff weight, or"
P.L. 91-258, Sec. 206(a), added Code Sec. 4491, effective 7/1/70.

Sec. 4492. Repealed.

In 1982, P.L. 97-248, Sec. 280(c)(1), repealed Code Sec. 4492, effective for transportation begin after 8/31/82 except for any amount paid on or before 8/31/82.
Prior to repeal, Code Sec. 4492 read as follows:
"SEC. 4492. DEFINITIONS.
"(a) Taxable civil aircraft.
"For purposes of this subchapter, the term 'taxable civil aircraft' means any engine driven aircraft—
"(1) registered, or required to be registered, under section 501(a) of the Federal Aviation Act of 1958 (49 U.S.C., sec. 1401(a)), or
"(2) which is not described in paragraph (1) but which is owned by or for a United States person.
Such term does not include any aircraft owned by an aircraft museum (as defined in section 4041(h)(2) and used exclusively for purposes set forth in section 4041(h)(2)(C)).
"(b) Weight.
"For purposes of this subchapter, the term 'maximum certificated takeoff weight' means the maximum such weight contained in the type certificate or airworthiness certificate.
"(c) Other definitions.
"For purposes of this subchapter—
"(1) Year. The term 'year' means the one-year period beginning on July 1.
"(2) Use. The term 'use' means use in the navigable airspace of the United States.
"(3) Navigable airspace of the United States. The term 'navigable airspace of the United States' has the definition given to such term by section 101(24) of the Federal Aviation Act of 1958 (49 U.S.C., sec. 1301(24)), except that such term does not include the navigable airspace of the Commonwealth of Puerto Rico or of any possession of the United States."
In 1976, P.L. 94-530, Sec. 2(a), added a sentence at the end of subsec. (a), effective 7/1/76.
In 1970, P.L. 91-258, Sec. 206(a), added Code Sec. 4492, effective 7/1/70.

Sec. 4493. Repealed.

In 1982, P.L. 97-248, Sec. 280(c)(1), repealed Code Sec. 4493, effective for transportation begin after 8/31/82, except for any amount paid on or after 8/31/82.
Prior to repeal, Code Sec. 4493 read as follows:
"SEC. 4493. SPECIAL RULES.
"(a) Payment of tax by lessee.
"(1) In general. Any person who is the lessee of any taxable civil aircraft on the day in any year on which occurs the first use which subjects such aircraft to the tax imposed by section 4491 for such year may, under regulations prescribed by the Secretary, elect to be liable for payment of such tax. Notwithstanding any such election, if such lessee does not pay such tax, the lessor shall also be liable for payment of such tax.
"(2) Exception. No election may be made under paragraph (1) with respect to any taxable civil aircraft which is leased from a person engaged in the business of transporting persons or property for compensation or hire by air.
"(b) Certain persons engaged in foreign air commerce.
"(1) Election to pay tentative tax. Any person who is a significant user of taxable civil aircraft in foreign air commerce may, with respect to that portion of the tax imposed by section 4491 which is determined under section 4491(a)(2) on any taxable civil aircraft for any year, elect to pay the tentative tax determined under paragraph (2). The payment of such tentative tax shall not relieve such person from payment of the net liability for the tax imposed by section 4491 on such taxable civil aircraft (determined as of the close of such year).
"(2) Tentative tax. For purposes of paragraph (1), the tentative tax with respect to any taxable civil aircraft for any year is an amount equal to that portion of the tax imposed by section 4491 on such aircraft for such year which is determined under section 4491(a)(2), reduced by a percentage of such amount equal to the percentage which the aggregate of the payments to which such person was entitled under section 6426 (determined without regard to section 6426(c)(2)) with respect to the preceding year is of the aggregate of the taxes imposed by section 4491 for which such person was liable for payment for the preceding year.
"(3) Significant users of aircraft in foreign air commerce. For purposes of paragraph (1), a person is a significant user of taxable civil aircraft in foreign air commerce for any year only if the aggregate of the payments to which such person was entitled under section 6426 (determined without regard to section 6426(c)(2)) with respect to the preceding year was at least 10 percent of the aggregate of the taxes imposed by section 4491 for which such person was liable for payment for the preceding year.

"(4) Net liability for tax. For purposes of paragraph (1), the net liability for the tax imposed by section 4491 with respect to any taxable civil aircraft for any year is—

"(A) the amount of the tax imposed by such section, reduced by

"(B) the amount payable under section 6426 with respect to such aircraft for the year (determined without regard to section 6426(c)(2))."

In 1976, P.L. 94-455, Sec. 1904(a)(13), deleted "beginning on or after July 1, 1970" after "for any year" in para. (b)(1), and deleted the last sentence of para. (b)(2), effective 2/1/77.

Prior to deletion, the last sentence of para. (b)(2) read as follows:

"In the case of the year beginning on July 1, 1970, this subsection shall apply only if the person electing to pay the tentative tax establishes what the tentative tax would have been for such year if section 4491 had taken effect on July 1, 1969."

—P.L. 94-455, Sec. 1906(b)(13)(A), substituted "Secretary" for "Secretary or his delegate" in subsec. (a), effective 2/1/77.

In 1970, P.L. 91-258, Sec. 206(a), added Code Sec. 4493, effective 7/1/70.

Sec. 4494. Repealed.

In 1982, P.L. 97-248, Sec. 280(c)(1), repealed Code Sec. 4494, effective for transportation begin. after 8/31/82, except for amounts paid on or before 8/31/82.

Prior to repeal, Code Sec. 4494 read as follows:

"SEC. 4494. CROSS REFERENCE.

"For penalties and administrative provisions applicable to this subchapter, see subtitle F."

In 1970, P.L. 91-258, Sec. 206(a), added Code Sec. 4491, effective 7/1/70.

Subchapter F.—Tax on Removal of Hard Mineral Resources From Deep Seabed [Repealed]

Sec.
4495. Repealed [Imposition of tax.]
4496. Repealed [Definitions.]
4497. Repealed [Imputed value.]
4498. Repealed [Termination.]

In 1997, P.L. 105-34, Sec. 1432(b)(1), Repealed Subchapter F

Prior to repeal, Subchapter F read as follows:

"Subchapter F. Tax on Removal of Hard Mineral Resources From Deep Seabed
 "4495. Imposition of tax.
 "4496. Definitions.
 "4497. Imputed value.
 "4498. Termination."

In 1980, P.L. 96-283, Sec. 402(a), added Subchapter F.

Sec. 4495. Repealed.

In 1997, P.L. 105-34, Sec. 1432(b)(1), repealed Code Sec. 4495 as part of the repeal of Subchapter F, of Chapter 36, of Subtitle D, effective 8/5/97.

Prior to repeal, Code Sec. 4495 read as follows:

"SEC. 4495. IMPOSITION OF TAX.

"(a) General rule.

"There is hereby imposed a tax on any removal of a hard mineral resource from the deep seabed pursuant to a deep seabed permit.

"(b) Amount of tax.

"The amount of the tax imposed by subsection (a) on any removal shall be 3.75 percent of the imputed value of the resource so removed.

"(c) Liability for tax.

"The tax imposed by subsection (a) shall be paid by the person to whom the deep seabed permit is issued.

"(d) Time for paying tax.

"The time for paying the tax imposed by subsection (a) shall be the time prescribed by the Secretary by regulations. The time so prescribed with respect to any removal shall be not earlier than the earlier of—

"(1) the commercial use of, or the sale or disposition of, any portion of the resource so removed, or

"(2) the day which is 12 months after the date of the removal of the resource."

In 1980, P.L. 96-283, Sec. 402(a), added Code Sec. 4495, effective 1/1/80.

Sec. 4496. Repealed.

In 1997, P.L. 105-34, Sec. 1432(b)(1), repealed Code Sec. 4496 as part of the repeal of Subchapter F, of Chapter 36, of Subtitle D, effective 8/5/97.

Prior to repeal, Code Sec. 4496 read as follows:

"SEC. 4496. DEFINITIONS.

"(a) Deep seabed permit.

"For purposes of this subchapter, the term 'deep seabed permit' means a permit issued under title I of the Deep Seabed Hard Minerals Resources Act.

"(b) Hard mineral resource.

"For purposes of this subchapter, the term 'hard mineral resource' means any deposit or accretion on, or just below, the surface of the deep seabed of nodules which contain one or more minerals, at least one of which is manganese, nickel, cobalt, or copper.

"(c) Deep seabed.

"For purposes of this subchapter, the term 'deep seabed' means the seabed, and the subsoil thereof to a depth of 10 meters, lying seaward of, and outside—

"(1) the Continental Shelf of any nation; and

"(2) any area of national resource jurisdiction of any foreign nation, if such area extends beyond the Continental Shelf of such nation and such jurisdiction is recognized by the United States.

"(d) Continental Shelf.

"For purposes of this subchapter, the term 'Continental Shelf' means—outside the and subsoil of the submarine areas adjacent to the coast but limit, to wher of the territorial sea, to a depth of 200 meters or, beyond that the natural resour depth to

"(2) the seabed and such as superjacent waters admits of the exploitation of islands." soil of sand

In 1980, P.L. 96-283, Sec. 40 (a), added submarine areas adjacent to the coasts of

Sec. 4497. Repealed.   4496, effective 1/1/80.

In 1997, P.L. 105-34, Sec. 1432(b)(1), repealed Code Se peal of Subchapter F, of Chapter 36, of Subtitle D, effective

Prior to repeal, Code Sec. 4497. read as follows;

"SEC. 4497 IMPUTED VALUE.

"(a) In general.

"For purposes of this subchapter, the term 'imputed value' means, with to any hard mineral resource, 20 percent of the fair market value of the com cially recoverable metals and minerals contained in such resource. Such fair ma ket value shall be determined—

"(1) as of the date of the removal of the hard mineral resource from the deep seabed; and

"(2) as if the metals and minerals contained in such resource were separated from such resource and were in the most basic form for which there is a readily ascertainable market price.

"(b) Commercial recoverability.

"(1) Manganese, nickel, cobalt, and copper. For purposes of subsection (a), manganese, nickel, cobalt, and copper shall be treated as commercially recoverable.

"(2) Minimum quantities and percentages. The Secretary may by regulations prescribe for each metal or mineral quantities or percentages below which the metal or mineral shall be treated as not commercially recoverable.

"(c) Suspension of tax with respect to certain metals and minerals held for later processing.

"(1) Election. The permittee may, in such manner and at such time as may be prescribed by regulations, elect to have the application of the tax suspended with respect to one or more commercially recoverable metals or minerals in the resource which the permittee does not intend to process within one year of the date of extraction. Any metal or mineral affected by such election shall not be taken into account in determining the imputed value of the resource at the time of its removal from the deep seabed. Any suspension under this paragraph with respect to a metal or mineral shall be permanent unless there is a redetermination affecting such metal or mineral under paragraph (2).

"(2) Later computation of tax. If the permittee processes any metal or mineral affected by the election under paragraph (1), or if he sells any portion of the resource containing such a metal or mineral, then the amount of the tax under section 4495 shall be redetermined as if there had been no suspension under paragraph (1) with respect to such metal or mineral. In any such case there shall be added to the increase in tax determined under the preceding sentence an amount equal to the interest (at the underpayment rate established under section 6621) on such increase for the period from the date prescribed for paying the tax on the resources (determined under section 4495(d)) to the date of the processing or sale.

"(d) Determinations of value.

"All determinations of value necessary for the application of this subchapter shall be made by the Secretary (after consultation with other appropriate Federal officials) on the basis of the best available information. Such determinations shall be made under procedures established by the Secretary by regulations."

In 1986, P.L. 99-514, Sec. 1511(c)(7), substituted "at the underpayment rate established under section 6621" for "at rates determined under section 6621" in para. (c)(2), effective for purposes of determining interest for periods after 12/31/86.

In 1980, P.L. 96-283, Sec. 402(a), added Code Sec. 4497, effective 1/1/80.

Sec. 4498. Repealed.

In 1997, P.L. 105-34, Sec. 1432(b)(1), repealed Code Sec. 4498 as part of the repeal of Subchapter F, of Chapter 36, of Subtitle D, effective 8/5/97.

Prior to repeal, Code Sec. 4498 read as follows:

"SEC. 4498. TERMINATION.

"(a) General rule.

"The tax imposed by section 4495 shall not apply to any removal from the deep seabed after the earlier of—

"(1) the date on which an international deep seabed treaty takes effect with respect to the United States, or

Excise and miscellaneous taxes   Chapter 38

"(2) the date 10 years after the date of the enactment of this subchapter. [Note: Date of enactment was June 28, 1980]
"(b) International deep seabed treaty.
"For purposes of subsection (a), the term 'international deep seabed treaty' means any treaty which—
"(1) is adopted by a United Nations Conference on the Law of the Sea, and
"(2) requires contributions to an international fund for the sharing of revenues from deep seabed mining."

In **1980**, P.L. 96-283, Sec. 402(a), added Code Sec. 4498, effective 1/1/80.

CHAPTER 37. REPEALED [SUGAR]

Sec.
4501. Repealed [Imposition of tax].
4502. Repealed [Definitions].
4503. Repealed [Exemptions for sugar manufactured for home consumption.]

In **1990**, P.L. 101-508, Sec. 11801(a)(48), repealed Chapter 37.

Sec. 4501.   Repealed.

In **1990**, P.L. 101-508, Sec. 11801(a)(48), repealed Code Sec. 4501, effective 11/5/90, except as provided in Sec. 11821(b) of this Act which reads as follows:
"(b) Savings provision.
"If—
"(1) any provision amended or repealed by this part applied to—
"(A) any transaction occurring before the date of the enactment of this Act [11/5/90],
"(B) any property acquired before such date of enactment [11/5/90], or
"(C) any item of income, loss, deduction, or credit taken into account before such date of enactment [11/5/90], and
"(2) the treatment of such transaction, property, or item under such provision would (without regard to the amendments made by this part) affect liability for tax for periods ending after such date of enactment [11/5/90],
nothing in the amendments made by this part shall be construed to affect the treatment of such transaction, property, or item for purposes of determining liability for tax for periods ending after such date of enactment [11/5/90]."
Prior to repeal, Code Sec. 4501 read as follows:
"SEC. 4501. IMPOSITION OF TAX.
"(a) General.
"There is hereby imposed upon manufactured sugar manufactured in the United States, a tax, to be paid by the manufacturer at the rate of 0.53 cent per pound of the total sugars therein. The manufacturer shall pay the tax with respect to manufactured sugar (1) which has been sold, or used in the production of other articles, by the manufacturer during the preceding month (if the tax has not already been paid) and (2) which has not been so sold or used within 12 months ending during the preceding calendar month, after it was manufactured (if the tax has not already been paid). For the purpose of determining whether sugar has been sold or used within 12 months after it was manufactured, sugar shall be considered to have been sold or used in the order in which it was manufactured.
"(b) Termination of tax.
"No tax shall be imposed under this subchapter on the manufacture or use of sugar or articles composed in chief value of sugar after June 30, 1975, or June 30 of the first year commencing after the effective date of any law limiting payments under title III of the Sugar Act of 1948, as amended, whichever is the earlier date. Notwithstanding the provisions of subsection (a), no tax shall be imposed under this subchapter with respect to unsold sugar held by a manufacturer on June 30, 1975, or June 30 of the first year commencing after the effective date of any law limiting payments under title III of the Sugar Act of 1948, as amended, whichever is the earlier date, or with respect to sugar or articles composed in chief value of sugar held in customs custody or control on such date."
In **1971**, P.L. 92-138, Sec. 18(b), substituted "June 30, 1975, or June 30 of the first year commencing after the effective date of any law limiting payments under title III of the Sugar Act of 1948, as amended, whichever is the earlier date" for "June 30, 1972" each place it appeared in subsec. (b), effective 1/1/72.
In **1965**, P.L. 89-331, Sec. 13, substituted "1972" for "1967" each place it appeared in subsec. (b), effective 1/1/65.
In **1962**, P.L. 87-456, Sec. 302(a), substituted provisions in subsec. (a) requiring the manufacturer to pay a tax at the rate of 0.53 cent per pound of the total sugars for provisions which required payment of 0.465 cent per pound for all manufactured sugar testing by the polariscope 92 sugar degrees, 0.00875 cent per pound additional for each additional sugar degree shown by the polariscopic test, and fractions of a degree in proportion, and 0.5144 cent per pound of the total sugars on all manufactured sugar testing by the polariscope less than 92 sugar degrees, repealed subsec. (b), and redesignated subsec. (c) as (b), and substituted therein "manufacture or use" for "manufacture, use, or importation" and "subsection (a)" for "subsection (a) or (b)", effective 8/31/63.
Prior to repeal, subsec. (b) read as follows:
"(b) Import Tax.
"In addition to any other tax or duty imposed by law, there is hereby imposed, under such regulations as the Secretary or his delegate shall prescribe, a tax upon articles imported or brought into the United States as follows:

"(1) on all manufactured sugar testing by the polariscope 92 sugar degrees, 0.465 cent per pound, and, for each additional sugar degree shown by the polariscopic test, 0.00875 cent per pound additional, and fractions of a degree in proportion;
"(2) on all manufactured sugar testing by the polariscope less than 92 sugar degrees, 0.5144 cent per pound of the total sugars therein;
"(3) on all articles composed in chief value of manufactured sugar, 0.5144 cent per pound of the total sugars therein."
— P.L. 87-535, Sec. 18(a), substituted "June 30, 1967" for "December 31, 1962", each place it appeared in subsec. (c).
In **1961**, P.L. 87-15, Sec. 2(a), substituted "December 31, 1962" for "September 30, 1961", each place it appeared in subsec. (c).
In **1960**, P.L. 86-592, Sec. 2, substituted "September 30, 1961" for "June 30, 1961", each place it appeared in subsec. (c).
In **1958**, P.L. 85-859, Sec. 162(b), eliminated provisions that authorized refund of an amount equal to the tax paid with respect to any sugar or articles composed in chief value of sugar and which, on June 30, 1961, are held by the importer and intended for sale or other disposition. See section 6412(d) of this title effective 1/1/59.
In **1956**, P.L. 545, Sec. 19, substituted "1961" in lieu of "1957" each place it appeared in subsec. (c), effective 1/1/56.

Sec. 4502.   Repealed.

In **1990**, P.L. 101-508, Sec. 11801(a)(48), repealed Code Sec. 4502, effective 11/5/90 except as provided in Sec. 11821(b) of this Act, reproduced in note following Code Sec. 4501.
Prior to repeal, Code Sec. 4502 read as follows:
"SEC. 4502. DEFINITIONS.
For the purposes of this subchapter—
"(1) Manufacturer. Any person who acquires any sugar which is to be manufactured into manufactured sugar but who, without further refining or otherwise improving it in quality, sells such sugar as manufactured sugar or uses such sugar as manufactured sugar in the production of other articles for sale shall be considered, for the purposes of section 4501(a), the manufacturer of manufactured sugar and, as such, liable for the tax under section 4501(a) with respect thereto.
"(2) Person. The term 'person' means an individual, partnership, corporation, or association.
"(3) Manufactured sugar. The term 'manufactured sugar' means any sugar derived from sugar beets or sugarcane, which is not to be, and which shall not be, further refined or otherwise improved in quality; except sugar in liquid form which contains nonsugar solids (excluding any foreign substance that may have been added or developed in the product) equal to more than 6 per centum of the total soluble solids and except also sirup of cane juice produced from sugarcane grown in continental United States. The grades or types of sugar within the meaning of this definition shall include, but shall not be limited to, granulated sugar, lump sugar, cube sugar, powdered sugar, sugar in the form of blocks, cones, or molded shapes, confectioners' sugar, washed sugar, centrifugal sugar, clarified sugar, turbinado sugar, plantation white sugar, muscovado sugar, refiners' soft sugar, invert sugar mush, raw sugar, sirups, molasses, and sugar mixtures.
"(4) Total sugars. The term 'total sugars' means the total amount of the sucrose and of the reducing or invert sugars.
"(5) United States. The term 'United States' shall be deemed to include the States, the District of Columbia, and Puerto Rico."
In **1960**, P.L. 86-624, Sec. 18(f), deleted "the Territory of Hawaii" after "States" in para. (5), effective 8/21/59.
In **1959**, P.L. 86-70, Sec. 22(c), substituted "the Territory of Hawaii" for "the Territories of Hawaii and Alaska" in para. (5), effective 1/3/59.
In **1956**, P.L. 545, Sec. 20, deleted "(Clerget)" after "sucrose" in para. (4), and deleted provisions relating to the ascertainment of the total sugars contained in any grade or type of manufactured sugar, effective 1/1/56.

Sec. 4503.   Repealed.

In **1990**, P.L. 101-508, Sec. 11801(a)(48), repealed Code Sec. 4503, effective 11/5/90, except as provided in Sec. 11821(b) of this Act, reproduced in note following Code Sec. 4501.
Prior to repeal, Code Sec. 4503 read as follows:
"SEC. 4503. EXEMPTIONS FOR SUGAR MANUFACTURED FOR HOME CONSUMPTION.
"No tax shall be required to be paid under sec. 4501(a) upon the manufacture of manufactured sugar by or for the producer of the sugar beets or sugarcane from which such manufactured sugar was derived, for consumption by the producer's own family, employees, or household."

CHAPTER 38.—ENVIRONMENTAL TAXES

Subchapter
A. Tax on petroleum.
B. Tax on certain chemicals.
C. Tax on certain imported substances.
D. Ozone-depleting chemicals, etc.

In **1989**, P.L. 101-239, Sec. 7506(b), added item D.

3,273

In 1986, P.L. 99-499, Sec. 515(b), added item C.
—P.L. 99-499, Sec. 514(a), repealed Subchapter C.
Prior to repeal Subchapter C read as follows:
"Subchapter C—Tax on Hazardous Wastes
"Sec.
"4681. Imposition of tax.
"4682. Definitions and special rules.
"SEC. 4681. IMPOSITION OF TAX
"(a) General rule.
"There is hereby imposed a tax on the receipt of hazardous waste at a qualified hazardous waste disposal facility
"(b) Amount of tax
"The amount of the tax imposed by subsection (a) shall be equal to $2.13 per dry weight ton of hazardous waste"

In 1986, P.L. 99-499, Sec. 514(a), repealed Code Sec. 4681, as part of the repeal of subchapter C of chapter 38, effective 10/1/83, except as provided in Sec. 514(c)(2) of this Act.
"(2) Waiver of statute of limitations. If on the date of the enactment of this Act (or at any time within 1 year after such date of enactment) refund or credit of any overpayment of tax resulting from the application of this section is barred by any law or rule of law, refund or credit of such overpayment shall, nevertheless be made or allowed if claim therefor is filed before the date 1 year after the date of the enactment of this Act."
Prior to repeal, Sec. 4681 read as follows:
In 1980, P.L. 96-510, Sec. 231(a), added Code Sec. 4681, effective 12/11/80. Sec. 303 of this Act provides:
"Sec. 303 Unless reauthorized by the Congress the authority to collect taxes conferred by this Act shall terminate on September 30, 1985, or when the sum of the amounts received in the Treasury under section 4611 and under 4661 of the Internal Revenue Code of 1954, total $1,380,000,000, whichever occurs first. The Secretary of the Treasury shall estimate when this level of $1,380,000,000 will be reached and shall by regulation, provide procedures for the termination of the tax authorized by this Act and imposed under sections 4611 and 4661 of the Internal Revenue Code of 1954."

"SEC. 4682. DEFINITIONS AND SPECIAL RULES.
"(a) Definitions.
"For purposes of this subchapter
"(1) Hazardous waste. The term 'hazardous waste' means any waste.
"(A) having the characteristics identified under section 3001 of the Solid Waste Disposal Act, as in effect on the date of the enactment of this Act (other than waste the regulation of which under such Act has been suspended by Act of Congress on that date), or
"(B) subject to the reporting or recordkeeping requirements of sections 3002 and 3004 of such Act, as so in effect.
"(2) Qualified hazardous waste disposal facility. The term 'qualified hazardous waste disposal facility' means any facility which has received a permit or is accorded interim status under section 3005 of the Solid Waste Disposal Act.
"(b) Tax imposed on owner or operation
"The tax imposed by section 4681 shall be imposed on the owner or operator of the qualified hazardous waste disposal facility.
"(c) Tax not to apply to certain wastes.
"The tax imposed by section 4681 shall not apply to any hazardous waste which will not remain at the qualified hazardous waste disposal facility after the facility is closed.
"(d) Applicability of section.
"The tax imposed by section 4681 shall apply to the receipt of hazardous waste after September 30, 1983, except that if, as of September 30 of any subsequent calendar year, the unobligated balance of the Post-closure Liability Trust Fund exceeds $200,000,000) no tax shall be imposed under such section during the following calendar year"

In 1986, P.L. 99-499, Sec. 514(a)(1), repealed Code Sec. 4682, as part of the repeal of subchapter C of chapter 38, effective 10/1/83, except as provided in Sec. 514(c)(2) of this Act, reproduced in note following Code Sec. 4681.
In 1980, P.L. 96-510, Sec. 231(a), added Code Sec. 4682, effective 12/11/80.
In 1980, added Chapter 38.

Subchapter A.—Tax on Petroleum
Sec.
4611. Imposition of tax.
4612. Definitions and special rules.
Sec. 4611. Imposition of tax.
(a) General rule.
There is hereby imposed a tax at the rate specified in subsection (c) on—
(1) crude oil received at a United States refinery, and
(2) petroleum products entered into the United States for consumption, use, or warehousing.

(b) Tax on certain uses and exportation.
(1) In general. If—
(A) any domestic crude oil is used in or exported from the United States, and
(B) before such use or exportation, no tax was imposed on such crude oil under subsection (a),
then a tax at the rate specified in subsection (c) is hereby imposed on such crude oil.
(2) Exception for use on premises where produced. Paragraph (1) shall not apply to any use of crude oil for extracting oil or natural gas on the premises where such crude oil was produced.
(c) Rate of tax.
(1) In general. The rate of the taxes imposed by this section is the sum of—
(A) the Hazardous Substance Superfund financing rate, and
(B) the Oil Spill Liability Trust Fund financing rate.
(2) Rates. For purposes of paragraph (1)—
(A) the Hazardous Substance Superfund financing rate is 9.7 cents a barrel, and
(B) the Oil Spill Liability Trust Fund financing rate is—
(i) in the case of crude oil received or petroleum products entered before January 1, 2017, 8 cents a barrel, and
(ii) in the case of crude oil received or petroleum products entered after December 31, 2016, 9 cents a barrel.
(d) Persons liable for tax.
(1) Crude oil received at refinery. The tax imposed by subsection (a)(1) shall be paid by the operator of the United States refinery.
(2) Imported petroleum product. The tax imposed by subsection (a)(2) shall be paid by the person entering the product for consumption, use, or warehousing.
(3) Tax on certain uses or exports. The tax imposed by subsection (b) shall be paid by the person using or exporting the crude oil, as the case may be.
(e) Application of Hazardous Substance Superfund financing rate.
(1) In general. Except as provided in paragraphs (2) and (3), the Hazardous Substance Superfund financing rate under this section shall apply after December 31, 1986, and before January 1, 1996.
(2) No tax if unobligated balance in fund exceeds $3,500,000,000. If on December 31, 1993, or December 31, 1994 —
(A) the unobligated balance in the Hazardous Substance Superfund exceeds $3,500,000,000, and
(B) the Secretary, after consultation with the Administrator of the Environmental Protection Agency, determines that the unobligated balance in the Hazardous Substance Superfund will exceed $3,500,000,000 on December 31 of 1994 or 1995, respectively, if no tax is imposed under section 59A, this section, and sections 4661 and 4671,
then no tax shall be imposed under this section (to the extent attributable to the Hazardous Substance Superfund financing rate) during 1994 or 1995, as the case may be.
(3) No tax if amounts collected exceed $11,970,000,000.
(A) Estimates by Secretary. The Secretary as of the close of each calendar quarter (and at such other times as the Secretary determines appropriate) shall make an estimate of the amount of taxes which will be collected under section 59A, this section (to the extent attributa-

Excise and miscellaneous taxes
Code Sec. 4612(a)(1)

ble to the Hazardous Substance Superfund financing rate), and sections 4661 and 4671 and credited to the Hazardous Substance Superfund during the period beginning January 1, 1987, and ending December 31, 1995.

(B) Termination if $11,970,000,000 credited before January 1, 1996. If the Secretary estimates under subparagraph (A) that more than $11,970,000,000 will be credited to the Fund before January 1, 1996, the Hazardous Substance Superfund financing rate under this section shall not apply after the date on which (as estimated by the Secretary) $11,970,000,000 will be so credited to the Fund.

(f) Application of Oil Spill Liability Trust Fund financing rate.

(1) In general. Except as provided in paragraph (2), the Oil Spill Liability Trust Fund financing rate under subsection (c) shall apply on and after April 1, 2006, or if later, the date which is 30 days after the last day of any calendar quarter for which the Secretary estimates that, as of the close of that quarter, the unobligated balance in the Oil Spill Liability Trust Fund is less than $2,000,000,000.

(2) Termination. The Oil Spill Liability Trust Fund financing rate shall not apply after December 31, 2017.

In 2008, P.L. 110-343, Sec. 405(a)(1)DivB, substituted "is—
"(i) in the case of crude oil received or petroleum products entered before January 1, 2017, 8 cents a barrel, and
"(ii) in the case of crude oil received or petroleum products entered after December 31, 2016, 9 cents a barrel." for "is 5 cents a barrel.", effective on and after the first day of the first calendar quarter beginning more than 60 days after 10/3/2008.
—P.L. 110-343, Sec. 405(b)(1)DivB, repealed paras. (f)(2) and (f)(3) and added a new para. (f)(2)... Sec. 405(b)(2)DivB, substituted "paragraph (2)" for "paragraphs (2) and (3)" in para. (f)(1), effective 10/3/2008.
Prior to repeal, paras. (f)(2) and (f)(3) read as follows:
"(2) Fund balance. The Oil Spill Liability Trust Fund financing rate shall not apply during a calendar quarter if the Secretary estimates that, as of the close of the preceding calendar quarter, the unobligated balance in the Oil Spill Liability Trust Fund exceeds $2,700,000,000.
"(3) Termination. The Oil Spill Liability Trust Fund financing rate shall not apply after December 31, 2014."

In 2005, P.L. 109-58, Sec. 1361, amended subsec. (f), effective 8/8/2005.
Prior to amendment, subsec. (f) read as follows:
"(f) Application of Oil Spill Liability Trust Fund financing rate.
"(1) In general. Except as provided in paragraph (2), the Oil Spill Liability Trust Fund financing rate under subsection (c) shall apply after December 31, 1989, and before January 1, 1995.
"(2) No tax if unobligated balance in fund exceeds $1,000,000,000. The Oil Spill Liability Trust Fund financing rate shall not apply during any calendar quarter if the Secretary estimates that as of the close of the preceding calendar quarter the unobligated balance in the Oil Spill Liability Trust Fund exceeds $1,000,000,000."

In 1990, P.L. 101-508, Sec. 11231(a)(1)(B), substituted "January 1, 1996" for "January 1, 1992" in paras. (e)(1) and (e)(3)... Sec. 11231(a)(2)(A), substituted "1993" for "1989" in para. (e)(2)... Sec. 11231(a)(2)(B), substituted "1994" for "1990" each place it appeared in para. (e)(2)... Sec. 11231(a)(2)(C), substituted "1995" for "1991" each place it appeared in para. (e)(2)... Sec. 11231(b), substituted "$11,970,000,000" for "6,650,000,000" each place it appeared in para. (e)(3) and substituted "December 31, 1995" for "December 31, 1991" in para. (e)(3), effective 11/5/90.

In 1989, P.L. 101-239, Sec. 7505(a)(1), amended subsec. (f)... Sec. 7505(b), substituted "5 cents" for "1.3 cents" in subpara. (c)(2)(B), effective 12/19/89.
Prior to amendment subsec. (f) read as follows:
"(f) Application of oil spill liability trust fund financing rate.
"(1) In general. Except as provided in paragraph (2), the Oil Spill Liability Trust Fund financing rate under subsection (c) shall apply on and after the commencement date and before January 1, 1992.
"(2) Commencement date.
"(A) In general. For purposes of this subsection, the term 'commencement date' means the later of—
"(i) February 1, 1987, or
"(ii) the 1st day of the 1st calendar month beginning more than 30 days after the date of the enactment of qualified authorizing legislation.
"(B) Qualified authorizing legislation. For purposes of subparagraph (A), the term 'qualified authorizing legislation' means any law enacted before December 31, 1990, which is substantially identical to subtitle E of title VI, or subtitle D of title VIII, of H.R. 5300 of the 99th Congress as passed the House of Representatives.

"(3) No tax if amounts collected exceed $300,000,000.
"(A) Estimates by secretary. The Secretary as of the close of each calendar quarter (and at such other times as the Secretary determines appropriate) shall make an estimate of the amount of taxes which will be collected under this section (to the extent attributable to the Oil Spill Liability Trust Fund financing rate) during the period beginning on the commencement date and ending on December 31, 1991.
"(B) Termination if $300,000,000 credited before January 1, 1992. If the Secretary estimates under subparagraph (A) that more than $300,000,000 will be credited to the Fund before January 1, 1992, the Oil Spill Liability Trust Fund financing rate shall not apply after the date on which (as estimated by the Secretary) $300,000,000 will be so credited to the Fund."
—P.L. 101-239, Sec. 7505(d)(1), of this Act provides:
"(d) Oil Spill Liability Trust Fund to be operating fund.
"(1) In general. For purposes of sections 8032(d) [see below] and 8033(c) of the Omnibus Budget Reconciliation Act of 1986 [P.L. 99-509], the commencement date is January 1, 1990."
—P.L. 101-221, Sec. 8(a), amended subpara. (c)(2)(A), effective 12/12/89.
Prior to amendment, subpara. (c)(2)(A) read as follows:
"(A) the Hazardous Substance Superfund financing rate is—
"(i) except as provided in clause (ii), 8.2 cents a barrel, and
"(ii) 11.7 cents a barrel in the case of the tax imposed by subsection (a)(2), and"

In 1988, P.L. 100-647, Sec. 6108, substituted "December 31, 1990" for "September 1, 1987" in subpara. (f)(2)(B), effective 11/10/88.

In 1986, P.L. 99-509, Sec. 8032(a), amended subsec. (c)... Sec. 8032(c)(1)(A), substituted "Hazardous Substance Superfund financing rate" for "taxes" in the heading of subsec. (e)... Sec. 8032(c)(1)(B), substituted "the Hazardous Substance Superfund financing rate under this section" for "the taxes imposed by this section" in para. (e)(1)... Sec. 8032(c)(1)(C), added "(to the extent attributable to the Hazardous Substance Superfund financing rate)" after "this section" in para. (e)(2) and subpara. (e)(3)(A)'... Sec. 8032(c)(1)(D), substituted 'the Hazardous Substance Superfund financing rate under this section shall not apply' for 'no tax shall be imposed under this section' in subpara. (e)(3)(B)... Sec. 8032(c)(2), added subsec. (f), effective as provided in Sec. 8032(d) of this Act, which reads:
"(d) Effective date.
"(1) In general. Except as provided in paragraph (2), the amendments made by this section shall take effect on the commencement date [1/1/90, see Sec. 7505(d)(1) of P.L. 101-239, above] (as defined in section 4611(f)(2) of the Internal Revenue Code of 1954, as added by this section).
"(2) Coordination with superfund reauthorization.— The amendments made by this section shall take effect only if the Superfund Amendments and Reauthorization Act of 1986 [P.L. 99-499] is enacted."
Prior to amendment, subsec. (c) read as follows:
"(c) Rate of tax.
"(1) In general. Except as provided in paragraph (2), the rate of the taxes imposed by this section is 8.2 cents a barrel.
"(2) Imported petroleum products. The rate of the tax imposed by subsection (a)(2) shall be 11.7 cents a barrel."
—P.L. 99-499, Sec. 511(a), amended subsec. (d), [redesignated subsec. (e) by Sec. 512(b) of this Act], effective 1/1/87.
Prior to amendment, subsec. (d) read as follows:
"(d) Termination.
"The taxes imposed by this section shall not apply after September 30, 1985, except that if on September 30, 1983, or September 30, 1984—
"(1) the unobligated balance in the Hazardous Substance Response Trust Fund as of such date exceeds $900,000,000, and
"(2) the Secretary, after consultation with the Administrator of the Environmental Protection Agency, determines that such unobligated balance will exceed $500,000,000 on September 30 of the following year if no tax is imposed under section 4611 or 4661 during the calendar year following the date referred to above.
the no tax shall be imposed by this section during the first calendar year beginning after the date referred to in paragraph (1)."
—P.L. 99-499, Sec. 512(a), substituted "at the rate specified in subsection (c)" for "of 0.79 cent a barrel" in subsecs. (a) and (b)... Sec. 512(b), redesignated subsecs. (c) and (d) [as amended by Sec. 511(a) of this Act], as subsecs. (d) and (e), and added subsec. (c), effective 1/1/87.

In 1980, P.L. 96-510, Sec. 211(a), added Code Sec. 4611, effective 4/1/81. Sec. 303 of this Act provides:
"Sec. 303. Unless reauthorized by the Congress, the authority to collect taxes conferred by this Act shall terminate on September 30, 1985, or when the sum of the amounts received in the Treasury under section 4611 and under 4661 of the Internal Revenue Code of 1954, total $1,380,000,000, whichever occurs first. The Secretary of the Treasury shall estimate when this level of $1,380,000,000 will be reached and shall by regulation, provide procedures for the termination of the tax authorized by this Act and imposed under sections 4611 and 4661 of the Internal Revenue Code of 1954."

Sec. 4612. Definitions and special rules.
(a) Definitions.

For purposes of this subchapter—

(1) Crude oil. The term "crude oil" includes crude oil condensates and natural gasoline.

3,275

(2) Domestic crude oil. The term "domestic crude oil" means any crude oil produced from a well located in the United States.

(3) Petroleum product. The term "petroleum product" includes crude oil.

(4) United States.

(A) In general. The term "United States" means the 50 States, the District of Columbia, the Commonwealth of Puerto Rico, any possession of the United States, the Commonwealth of the Northern Mariana Islands, and the Trust Territory of the Pacific Islands.

(B) United States includes continental shelf areas. The principles of section 638 shall apply for purposes of the term "United States".

(C) United States includes foreign trade zones. The term "United States" includes any foreign trade zone of the United States.

(5) United States refinery. The term "United States refinery" means any facility in the United States at which crude oil is refined.

(6) Refineries which produce natural gasoline. In the case of any United States refinery which produces natural gasoline from natural gas, the gasoline so produced shall be treated as received at such refinery at the time so produced.

(7) Premises. The term "premises" has the same meaning as when used for purposes of determining gross income from the property under section 613.

(8) Barrel. The term "barrel" means 42 United States gallons.

(9) Fractional part of barrel. In the case of a fraction of a barrel, the tax imposed by section 4611 shall be the same fraction of the amount of such tax imposed on a whole barrel.

(b) Only 1 tax imposed with respect to any product.

No tax shall be imposed by section 4611 with respect to any petroleum product if the person who would be liable for such tax establishes that a prior tax imposed by such section has been imposed with respect to such product.

(c) Credit where crude oil returned to pipeline.

Under regulations prescribed by the Secretary, if an operator of a United States refinery—

(1) removes crude oil from a pipeline, and

(2) returns a portion of such crude oil into a stream of other crude oil in the same pipeline,

there shall be allowed as a credit against the tax imposed by section 4611 to such operator an amount equal to the product of the rate of tax imposed by section 4611 on the crude oil so removed by such operator and the number of barrels of crude oil returned by such operator to such pipeline. Any crude oil so returned shall be treated for purposes of this subchapter as crude oil on which no tax has been imposed by section 4611.

(d) Credit against portion of tax attributable to oil spill rate.

There shall be allowed as a credit against so much of the tax imposed by section 4611 as is attributable to the Oil Spill Liability Trust Fund financing rate for any period an amount equal to the excess of—

(1) the sum of—

(A) the aggregate amounts paid by the taxpayer before January 1, 1987, into the Deepwater Port Liability Trust Fund and the Offshore Oil Pollution Compensation Fund, and

(B) the interest accrued on such amounts before such date, over

(2) the amount of such payments taken into account under this subsection for all prior periods.

The preceding sentence shall also apply to amounts paid by the taxpayer into the Trans-Alaska Pipeline Liability Fund to the extent of amounts transferred from such Fund into the Oil Spill Liability Trust Fund. For purposes of this subsection, all taxpayers which would be members of the same affiliated group (as defined in section 1504(a)) if section 1504(a)(2) were applied by substituting "100 percent" for "80 percent" shall be treated as 1 taxpayer.

(e) Income tax credit for unused payments into Trans-Alaska Pipeline Liability Fund.

(1) In general. For purposes of section 38, the current year business credit shall include the credit determined under this subsection.

(2) Determination of credit.

(A) In general. The credit determined under this subsection for any taxable year is an amount equal to the aggregate credit which would be allowed to the taxpayer under subsection (d) for amounts paid into the Trans-Alaska Pipeline Liability Fund had the Oil Spill Liability Trust Fund financing rate not ceased to apply.

(B) Limitation.

(i) In general. The amount of the credit determined under this subsection for any taxable year with respect to any taxpayer shall not exceed the excess of—

(I) the amount determined under clause (ii), over

(II) the aggregate amount of the credit determined under this subsection for prior taxable years with respect to such taxpayer.

(ii) Overall limitation. The amount determined under this clause with respect to any taxpayer is the excess of—

(I) the aggregate amount of credit which would have been allowed under subsection (d) to the taxpayer for periods before the termination date specified in section 4611(f)(1), if amounts in the Trans-Alaska Pipeline Liability Fund which are actually transferred into the Oil Spill Liability Trust Fund were transferred on January 1, 1990, and the Oil Spill Liability Trust Fund financing rate did not terminate before such termination date, over

(II) the aggregate amount of the credit allowed under subsection (d) to the taxpayer.

(3) Cost of income tax credit borne by trust fund.

(A) In general. The Secretary shall from time to time transfer from the Oil Spill Liability Trust Fund to the general fund of the Treasury amounts equal to the credits allowed by reason of this subsection.

(B) Trust fund balance may not be reduced below $1,000,000,000. Transfers may be made under subparagraph (A) only to the extent that the unobligated balance of the Oil Spill Liability Trust Fund exceeds $1,000,000,000. If any transfer is not made by reason of the preceding sentence, such transfer shall be made as soon as permitted under such sentence.

(4) No carryback. No portion of the unused business credit for any taxable year which is attributable to the credit determined under this subsection may be carried to a taxable year beginning on or before the date of the enactment of this paragraph.

(f) Disposition of revenues from Puerto Rico and the Virgin Islands.

The provisions of subsections (a)(3) and (b)(3) of section 7652 shall not apply to any tax imposed by section 4611.

Excise and miscellaneous taxes — Code Sec. 4661

In 1992, P.L. 102-486, Sec. 1922(a), redesignated subsec. (e) as subsec. (f) and added new subsec. (e), effective for tax. yrs. begin. after 10/24/92.

In 1990, P.L. 101-380, Sec. 9002(a), deleted the last sentence of subsec. (d)... Sec. 9002(b), added the new last sentence to subsec. (d), effective 8/18/90.

Prior to deletion, the last sentence of subsec. (d) read as follows:

"Amounts may be transferred from the Trans-Alaska Pipeline Liability Fund into the Oil Spill Liability Trust Fund only to the extent the administrators of the Trans-Alaska Pipeline Liability Fund determine that such amounts are not needed to satisfy claims against such Fund."

In 1989, P.L. 101-239, Sec. 7505(c), added the sentence at the end of subsec. (d), effective 12/19/89.

— P.L. 101-239, Sec. 7505(d)(1), changed the effective date for changes made by Sec. 8032(c)(3) of P.L. 99-509, from effective on the commencement date as defined in Code Sec. 4611(f) to effective on the commencement date which is 1/1/90, see below.

In 1986, P.L. 99-509, Sec. 8032(c), redesignated subsec. (d) as subsec. (e), and added new subsec. (d), effective on the commencement date, which is 1/1/90 [as amended by Sec. 7505(d)(1) of P.L. 101-239, see above].

— P.L. 99-499, Sec. 512(c), redesignated subsec. (c) as subsec. (d), and added new subsec. (c), effective 1/1/87.

In 1980, P.L. 96-510, Sec. 211(a), added Code Sec. 4612, effective 4/1/81.

Subchapter B.—Tax on Certain Chemicals

Sec.
4661. Imposition of tax.
4662. Definitions and special rules.

Sec. 4661. Imposition of tax.

(a) General rule.

There is hereby imposed a tax on any taxable chemical sold by the manufacturer, producer, or importer thereof.

(b) Amount of tax.

The amount of the tax imposed by subsection (a) shall be determined in accordance with the following table:

In the case of:	The tax is the following amount per ton
Acetylene	$4.87
Benzene	4.87
Butane	4.87
Butylene	4.87
Butadiene	4.87
Ethylene	4.87
Methane	3.44
Naphthalene	4.87
Propylene	4.87
Toluene	4.87
Xylene	4.87
Ammonia	2.64
Antimony	4.45
Antimony trioxide	3.75
Arsenic	4.45
Arsenic trioxide	3.41
Barium sulfide	2.30
Bromine	4.45
Cadmium	4.45
Chlorine	2.70
Chromium	4.45
Chromite	1.52
Potassium dichromate	1.69
Sodium dichromate	1.87
Cobalt	4.45
Cupric sulfate	1.87
Cupric oxide	3.59
Cuprous oxide	3.97
Hydrochloric acid	0.29
Hydrogen fluoride	4.23
Lead oxide	4.14
Mercury	4.45
Nickel	4.45
Phosphorus	4.45
Stannous chloride	2.85
Stannic chloride	2.12
Zinc chloride	2.22
Zinc sulfate	1.90
Potassium hydroxide	0.22
Sodium hydroxide	0.28
Sulfuric acid	0.26
Nitric acid	0.24

For periods before 1992, the item relating to xylene in the preceding table shall be applied by substituting "10.13" for "4.87."

(c) Termination.

No tax shall be imposed under this section during any period during which the Hazardous Substance Superfund financing rate under section 4611 does not apply.

In 1989, P.L. 101-239, Sec. 7505(d)(1), changed the effective date for changes made by Code 8032(c)(3) of P.L. 99-509, from effective on commencement date as defined in Code Sec. 4611(f) to effective on the commencement date which is 1/1/90, see below.

In 1986, P.L. 99-509, Sec. 8032(c)(3), substituted "the Hazardous Substance Superfund financing rate under section 4611 does not apply" for "no tax is imposed under section 4611(a)" in subsec. (c), effective on the commencement date which is 1/1/90 [see Sec. 7505(d)(1) of P.L. 101-239, see above]

— P.L. 99-499, Sec. 513(a), added the last sentence of subsec. (b), effective as provided in Sec. 513(h) of this Act which reads as follows:

"*(h) Effective dates.* —

"(1) In general.—Except as otherwise provided in this subsec-tion, the amendments made by this section shall take effect on January 1, 1987.

"(2) Repeal of tax on xylene for periods before October 1, 1985.—

"(A) Refund of tax previously imposed. —

"(i) In general.—In the case of any tax imposed by section 4661 of the Internal Revenue Code of 1954 on the sale or use of xylene before October 1, 1985, such tax (including interest, additions to tax, and additional amounts) shall not be assessed, and if assessed, the assessment shall be abated, and if collected shall be credited or refunded (with interest) as an overpayment.

"(ii) Condition to allowance.—Clause (i) shall not apply to a sale of xylene unless the person who (but for clause (i)) would be liable for the tax imposed by section 4661 on such sale meets requirements similar to the requirements of paragraph (1) of section 6416(a) of such Code. For purposes of the preceding sentence, subparagraph (A) of section 6416(a)(1) of such Code shall be applied without regard to the material preceding 'has not collected'.

"(B) Waiver of statute of limitations.—If on the date of the enactment of this Act (or at any time within 1 year after such date of enactment) refund or credit of any overpayment of tax resulting from the application of subparagraph (A) is barred by any law or rule of law, refund or credit of such overpayment shall, nevertheless, be made or allowed if claim therefor is filed before the date 1 year after the date of the enactment of this Act.

"(C) Xylene to include isomers.—For purposes of this paragraph, the term 'xylene' shall include any isomer of xylene whether or not separated.

"(3) Inventory exchanges.—

"(A) In general.—Except as otherwise provided in this paragraph, the amendment made by subsection (f) shall apply as if included in the amendments made by section 211 of the Hazardous Substance Response Revenue Act of 1980.

"(B) Recipient must agree to treatment as manufacturer.—In the case of any inventory exchange before January 1, 1987, the amendment made by subsection (f) shall apply only if the person receiving the chemical from the manufacturer, producer, or importer in the exchange agrees to be treated as the manufacturer, producer, or importer of such chemical for purposes of subchapter B of chapter 38 of the Internal Revenue Code of 1954.

"(C) Exception where manufacturer paid tax.—In the case of any inventory exchange before January 1, 1987, the amendment made by subsection (f) shall not apply if the manufacturer, producer, or importer treated such exchange as a sale for purposes of section 4661 of such Code and paid the tax imposed by such section.

"(D) Registration requirements.—Section 4662(c)(2)(B) of such Code (as added by subsection (f)) shall apply to exchanges made after December 31, 1986.

"(4) Exports of taxable substances.—Subclause (II) of section 4662(e)(2)(A)(ii) of such Code (as added by this section) shall not apply to the export of any taxable substance (as defined in section 4672(a) of such Code) before January 1, 1989.

"(5) Sales of intermediate hydrocarbon streams. —

"(A) In general.—Except as otherwise provided in this paragraph, the amendment made by subsection (g) shall apply as if included in the amendments made by section 211 of the Hazardous Substances Response Revenue Act of 1980.

"(B) Purchaser must agree to treatment as manufacturer.—In the case of any sale before January 1, 1987, of any intermediate hydrocarbon stream, the amendment made by subsection (g) shall apply only if the purchaser agrees to be treated as the manufacturer, producer, or importer for purposes of subchapter B of chapter 38 of such Code.

"(C) Exception where manufacturer paid tax.— In the case of any sale before January 1, 1987, of any intermediate hydrocarbon stream, the amendment made by subsection (g) shall not apply if the manufacturer, producer, or importer of such stream paid the tax imposed by section 4661 with respect to such sale on all taxable chemicals contained in such stream.

"(D) Registration requirements.— Section 4662(b)(10(C) of such Code (as added by subsection (g)) shall apply to exchanges made after December 31, 1986."

In 1980, P.L. 96-510, Sec. 211(a), added Code Sec. 4661, effective 4/1/81. Sec. 303 of this Act provides:

"Sec. 303. Unless reauthorized by the Congress, the authority to collect taxes conferred by this Act shall terminate on September 30, 1985, or when the sum of the amounts received in the Treasury under section 4611 and under 4661 of the Internal Revenue Code of 1954, total $1,380,000,000, whichever occurs first. The Secretary of the Treasury shall estimate when this level of $1,380,000,000 will be reached and shall by regulation, provide procedures for the termination of the tax authorized by this Act and imposed under sections 4611 and 4661 of the Internal Revenue Code of 1954."

Sec. 4662. Definitions and special rules.
(a) Definitions.
For purposes of this subchapter—

(1) Taxable chemical. Except as provided in subsection (b), the term "taxable chemical" means any substance—
(A) which is listed in the table under section 4661(b), and
(B) which is manufactured or produced in the United States or entered into the United States for consumption, use, or warehousing.

(2) United States. The term "United States" has the meaning given such term by section 4612(a)(4).

(3) Importer. The term "importer" means the person entering the taxable chemical for consumption, use, or warehousing.

(4) Ton. The term "ton" means 2,000 pounds. In the case of any taxable chemical which is a gas, the term "ton" means the amount of such gas in cubic feet which is the equivalent of 2,000 pounds on a molecular weight basis.

(5) Fractional part of ton. In the case of a fraction of a ton, the tax imposed by section 4661 shall be the same fraction of the amount of such tax imposed on a whole ton.

(b) Exceptions; other special rules.
For purposes of this subchapter—

(1) Methane or butane used as a fuel. Under regulations prescribed by the Secretary, methane or butane shall be treated as a taxable chemical only if it is used otherwise than as a fuel or in the manufacture or production of any motor fuel, diesel fuel, aviation fuel, or jet fuel (and, for purposes of section 4661(a), the person so using it shall be treated as the manufacturer thereof).

(2) Substances used in the production of fertilizer.
(A) In general. In the case of nitric acid, sulfuric acid, ammonia, or methane used to produce ammonia which is a qualified fertilizer substance, no tax shall be imposed under section 4661(a).
(B) Qualified fertilizer substance. For purposes of this section, the term "qualified fertilizer substance" means any substance—
  (i) used in a qualified fertilizer use by the manufacturer, producer, or importer,
  (ii) sold for use by any purchaser in a qualified fertilizer use, or
  (iii) sold for resale by any purchaser for use, or resale for ultimate use, in a qualified fertilizer use.
(C) Qualified fertilizer use. The term "qualified fertilizer use" means any use in the manufacture or production of fertilizer or for direct application as a fertilizer.

(D) Taxation of nonqualified sale or use. For purposes of section 4661(a), if no tax was imposed by such section on the sale or use of any chemical by reason of subparagraph (A), the first person who sells or uses such chemical other than in a sale or use described in subparagraph (A) shall be treated as the manufacturer of such chemical.

(3) Sulfuric acid produced as a byproduct of air pollution control. In the case of sulfuric acid produced solely as a byproduct of and on the same site as air pollution control equipment, no tax shall be imposed under section 4661.

(4) Substances derived from coal. For purposes of this subchapter, the term "taxable chemical" shall not include any substance to the extent derived from coal.

(5) Substances used in the production of motor fuel, etc.
(A) In general. In the case of any chemical described in subparagraph (D) which is a qualified fuel substance, no tax shall be imposed under section 4661(a).
(B) Qualified fuel substance. For purposes of this section, the term "qualified fuel substance" means any substance—
  (i) used in a qualified fuel use by the manufacturer, producer, or importer,
  (ii) sold for use by any purchaser in a qualified fuel use, or
  (iii) sold for resale by any purchaser for use, or resale for ultimate use, in a qualified fuel use.
(C) Qualified fuel use. For purposes of this subsection, the term "qualified fuel use" means—
  (i) any use in the manufacture or production of any motor fuel, diesel fuel, aviation fuel, or jet fuel, or
  (ii) any use as such a fuel.
(D) Chemicals to which paragraph applies. For purposes of this subsection, the chemicals described in this subparagraph are acetylene, benzene, butylene, butadiene, ethylene, naphthalene, propylene, toluene, and xylene.
(E) Taxation of nonqualified sale or use. For purposes of section 4661(a), if no tax was imposed by such section on the sale or use of any chemical by reason of subparagraph (A), the first person who sells or uses such chemical other than in a sale or use described in subparagraph (A) shall be treated as the manufacturer of such chemical.

(6) Substance having transitory presence during refining process, etc.
(A) In general. No tax shall be imposed under section 4661(a) on any taxable chemical described in subparagraph (B) by reason of the transitory presence of such chemical during any process of smelting, refining, or otherwise extracting any substance not subject to tax under section 4661(a).
(B) Chemicals to which subparagraph (A) applies. The chemicals described in this subparagraph are—
  (i) barium sulfide, cupric sulfate, cupric oxide, cuprous oxide, lead oxide, zinc chloride, and zinc sulfate, and
  (ii) any solution or mixture containing any chemical described in clause (i).
(C) Removal treated as use. Nothing in subparagraph (A) shall be construed to apply to any chemical which is removed from or ceases to be part of any smelting, refining, or other extraction process.

(7) Special rule for xylene. Except in the case of any substance imported into the United States or exported

Code Sec. 4662(d)(1)(B)   **Excise and miscellaneous taxes**

(B) such chemical was used by any person in the manufacture or production of any other substance which is a taxable chemical,

then an amount equal to the tax so paid shall be allowed as a credit or refund (without interest) to such person in the same manner as if it were an overpayment of tax imposed by such section. In any case to which this paragraph applies, the amount of any such credit or refund shall not exceed the amount of tax imposed by such section on the other substance manufactured or produced (or which would have been imposed by such section on such other substance but for subsection (b) or (e) of this section).

(2) Use as fertilizer. Under regulations prescribed by the Secretary, if—

(A) a tax under section 4661 was paid with respect to nitric acid, sulfuric acid, ammonia, or methane used to make ammonia without regard to subsection (b)(2), and

(B) any person uses such substance as a qualified fertilizer substance,

then an amount equal to the excess of the tax so paid over the tax determined with regard to subsection (b)(2) shall be allowed as a credit or refund (without interest) to such person in the same manner as if it were an overpayment of tax imposed by this section.

(3) Use as qualified fuel. Under regulations prescribed by the Secretary, if—

(A) a tax under section 4661 was paid with respect to any chemical described in subparagraph (D) of subsection (b)(5) without regard to subsection (b)(5), and

(B) any person uses such chemical as a qualified fuel substance,

then an amount equal to the excess of the tax so paid over the tax determined with regard to subsection (b)(5) shall be allowed as a credit or refund (without interest) to such person in the same manner as if it were an overpayment of tax imposed by this section.

(4) Use in the production of animal feed. Under regulations prescribed by the Secretary if—

(A) a tax under section 4661 was paid with respect to nitric acid, sulfuric acid, ammonia, or methane to produce ammonia, without regard to subsection (b)(9), and

(B) any person uses such substance as a qualified animal feed substance,

then an amount equal to the excess of the tax so paid over the tax determined with regard to subsection (b)(9) shall be allowed as a credit or refund (without interest) to such person in the same manner as if it were an overpayment of tax imposed by this section.

(e) Exemption for exports of taxable chemicals.

(1) Tax-free sales.

(A) In general. No tax shall be imposed under section 4661 on the sale by the manufacturer or producer of any taxable chemical for export, or for resale by the purchaser to a second purchaser for export.

(B) Proof of export required. Rules similar to the rules of section 4221(b) shall apply for purposes of subparagraph (A).

(2) Credit or refund where tax paid.

(A) In general. Except as provided in subparagraph (B), if—

(i) tax under section 4661 was paid with respect to any taxable chemical, and

(ii)(I) such chemical was exported by any person, or

(II) such chemical was used as a material in the manufacture or production of a substance which was exported by any person and which, at the time of export was a taxable substance (as defined in section 4672(a)),

credit or refund (without interest) of such tax shall be allowed or made to the person who paid such tax.

(B) Condition to allowance. No credit or refund shall be allowed or made under subparagraph (A) unless the person who paid the tax establishes that he—

(i) has repaid or agreed to repay the amount of the tax to the person who exported the taxable chemical or taxable substance (as so defined), or

(ii) has obtained the written consent of such exporter to the allowance of the credit or the making of the refund.

(3) Refunds directly to exporter. The Secretary shall provide, in regulations, the circumstances under which a credit or refund (without interest) of the tax under section 4661 shall be allowed or made to the person who exported the taxable chemical or taxable substance where—

(A) the person who paid the tax waives his claim to the amount of such credit or refund, and

(B) the person exporting the taxable chemical or taxable substance provides such information as the Secretary may require in such regulations.

(4) Regulations. The Secretary shall prescribe such regulations as may be necessary to carry out the purposes of this subsection.

(f) Disposition of revenues from Puerto Rico and the Virgin Islands.

The provisions of subsections (a)(3) and (b)(3) of section 7652 shall not apply to any tax imposed by section 4661.

In 1999, P.L. 106-170, Sec. 532(c)(2)(U), substituted "section 1221(a)(1)" for "section 1221(1)" in subpara. (c)(2)(C), effective for any instrument held, acquired, or entered into, any transaction entered into, and supplies held or acquired on or after 12/17/99.

In 1988, P.L. 100-647, Sec. 2001(a)(1), redesignated para. (e)(3) as para. (e)(4) and added new para. (e)(3) . . . Sec. 2001(a)(2), substituted "one or more" for "a mixture of" in subpara. (b)(10)(A), effective 1/1/87 except as provided in Secs. 513(h)(2)-(5) of P.L. 99-499 reproduced in note following Code Sec. 4661.

In 1986, P.L. 99-499, Sec. 513(b)(1), redesignated subsec. (e) as (f), and added new subsec. (e) . . . Sec. 513(b)(2)(A), substituted "which is a taxable chemical" for "the sale of which by such person would be taxable under such section" in para. (d)(1) . . . Sec. 513(b)(2)(B), substituted "imposed by such section on the other substance manufactured or produced (or which would have been imposed by such section on such other substance but for subsection (b) or (e) of this section)" for "imposed by such section on the other substance manufactured or produced" in para. (d)(1) . . . Sec. 513(c), added para. (b)(7) . . . Sec. 513(d), added para. (b)(8) . . . Sec. 513(e)(1), added para. (b)(9) . . . Sec. 513(e)(2), added para. (d)(4) . . . Sec. 513(f), amended subsec. (c) . . . Sec. 513(g), added para. (b)(10), effective 1/1/87 except as provided in Sec. 513(h)(2)-(5) of this Act, reproduced in note following Code Sec. 4661.

Prior to amendment, subsec. (c) read as follows:

"(c) Use by manufacturer, etc., considered sale.

"Except as provided in subsection (b), if any person manufactures, produces, or imports a taxable chemical and uses such chemical, then such person shall be liable for tax under section 4661 in the same manner as if such chemical were sold by such person."

In 1984, P.L. 98-369, Sec. 1019(a)(1), added paras. (b)(5) and (b)(6) . . . Sec. 1019(a)(2), added para. (b)(3) . . . Sec. 1019(a)(3), added "or in the manufacture or production of any motor fuel, diesel fuel, aviation fuel, or jet fuel" after "than as a fuel" in para. (b)(1) . . . Sec. 1019(b)(1), amended subparas. (b)(2)(B) and (C) and added subpara. (D) . . . Sec. 1019(b)(2)(A), substituted "qualified fertilizer substance" for "qualified substance" in subpara. (b)(2)(A) . . . Sec. 1019(b)(2)(B), amended subpara. (d)(2)(B) . . . Sec. 1019(c), substituted "Except as provided in subsection (b), if" for "If" in subsec. (c), effective 4/1/81. Sec. 1019(d)(2) of the Act also provides:

"(2) Waiver of limitation. If refund or credit of any overpayment of tax resulting from the application of the amendments made by this section is prevented at any time before the date which for one year after the date of the enactment of this Act by the operation of any law or rule of law (including res judicata), refund or credit of such overpayment (to the extent attributable to the application of such amendments) may, nevertheless, be made or allowed if claim therefor is filed on or before the date which for one year after the date of the enactment of this Act."

Excise and miscellaneous taxes

Code Sec. 4662(d)(1)(A)

from the United States, the term "xylene" does not include any separated isomer of xylene.

(8) Recycled chromium, cobalt, and nickel.

(A) In general. No tax shall be imposed under section 4661(a) on any chromium, cobalt, or nickel which is diverted or recovered in the United States from any solid waste as part of a recycling process (and not as part of the original manufacturing or production process).

(B) Exemption not to apply while corrective action uncompleted. Subparagraph (A) shall not apply during any period that required corrective action by the taxpayer at the unit at which the recycling occurs is uncompleted.

(C) Required corrective action. For purposes of subparagraph (B), required corrective action shall be treated as uncompleted during the period —

(i) beginning on the date that the corrective action is required by the Administrator or an authorized State pursuant to —

(I) a final permit under section 3005 of the Solid Waste Disposal Act or a final order under section 3004 or 3008 of such Act, or

(II) a final order under section 106 of the Comprehensive Environmental Response, Compensation, and Liability Act of 1980, and

(ii) ending on the date the Administrator or such State (as the case may be) certifies to the Secretary that such corrective action has been completed.

(D) Special rule for groundwater treatment. In the case of corrective action requiring groundwater treatment, such action shall be treated as completed as of the close of the 10-year period beginning on the date such action is required if such treatment complies with the permit or order applicable under subparagraph (C)(i) throughout such period. The preceding sentence shall cease to apply beginning on the date such treatment ceases to comply with such permit or order.

(E) Solid waste. For purposes of this paragraph, the term "solid waste" has the meaning given such term by section 1004 of the Solid Waste Disposal Act, except that such term shall not include any byproduct, coproduct, or other waste from any process of smelting, refining, or otherwise extracting any metal.

(9) Substances used in the production of animal feed.

(A) In general. In the case of—

(i) nitric acid,

(ii) sulfuric acid,

(iii) ammonia, or

(iv) methane used to produce ammonia,

which is a qualified animal feed substance, no tax shall be imposed under section 4661(a).

(B) Qualified animal feed substance. For purposes of this section, the term "qualified animal feed substance" means any substance—

(i) used in a qualified animal feed use by the manufacturer, producer, or importer,

(ii) sold for use by any purchaser in a qualified animal feed use, or

(iii) sold for resale by any purchaser for use, or resale for ultimate use, in a qualified animal feed use.

(C) Qualified animal feed use. The term "qualified animal feed use" means any use in the manufacture or production of animal feed or animal feed supplements, or of ingredients used in animal feed or animal feed supplements.

(D) Taxation of nonqualified sale or use. For purposes of section 4661(a), if no tax was imposed by such sec-

tion on the sale or use of any chemical by reason of subparagraph (A), the 1st person who sells or uses such chemical other than in a sale or use described in subparagraph (A) shall be treated as the manufacturer of such chemical.

(10) Hydrocarbon streams containing mixtures of organic taxable chemicals.

(A) In general. No tax shall be imposed under section 4661(a) on any organic taxable chemical while such chemical is part of an intermediate hydrocarbon stream containing one or more organic taxable chemicals.

(B) Removal, etc., treated as use. For purposes of this part, if any organic taxable chemical on which no tax was imposed by reason of subparagraph (A) is isolated, extracted, or otherwise removed from, or ceases to be part of, an intermediate hydrocarbon stream—

(i) such isolation, extraction, removal, or cessation shall be treated as use by the person causing such event, and

(ii) such person shall be treated as the manufacturer of such chemical.

(C) Registration requirement. Subparagraph (A) shall not apply to any sale of any intermediate hydrocarbon stream unless the registration requirements of clauses (i) and (ii) of subsection (c)(2)(B) are satisfied.

(D) Organic taxable chemical. For purposes of this paragraph, the term "organic taxable chemical" means any taxable chemical which is an organic substance.'

(c) Use and certain exchanges by manufacturer, etc.

(1) Use treated as sale. Except as provided in subsections (b) and (e), if any person manufactures, produces, or imports any taxable chemical and uses such chemical, then such person shall be liable for tax under section 4661 in the same manner as if such chemical were sold by such person.

(2) Special rules for inventory exchanges.

(A) In general. Except as provided in this paragraph, in any case in which a manufacturer, producer, or importer of a taxable chemical exchanges such chemical as part of an inventory exchange with another person—

(i) such exchange shall not be treated as a sale, and

(ii) such other person shall, for purposes of section 4661, be treated as the manufacturer, producer, or importer of such chemical.

(B) Registration requirement. Subparagraph (A) shall not apply to any inventory exchange unless—

(i) both parties are registered with the Secretary as manufacturers, producers, or importers of taxable chemicals, and

(ii) the person receiving the taxable chemical has, at such time as the Secretary may prescribe, notified the manufacturer, producer, or importer of such person's registration number and the internal revenue district in which such person is registered.

(C) Inventory exchange. For purposes of this paragraph, the term "inventory exchange" means any exchange in which 2 persons exchange property which is, in the hands of each person, property described in section 1221(a)(1).

(d) Refund or credit for certain uses.

(1) In general. Under regulations prescribed by the Secretary, if—

(A) a tax under section 4661 was paid with respect to any taxable chemical, and

3,279

Excise and miscellaneous taxes — Code Sec. 4672(a)(3)

Prior to amendment, subparas. (b)(2)(B) and (C) read as follows:
"(B) Qualified substance. For purposes of this section, the term 'qualified substance' means any substance—
"(i) used in a qualified use by the manufacturer, producer, or importer,
"(ii) sold for use by the purchaser in a qualified use, or
"(iii) sold for resale by the purchaser to a second purchaser for use by such second purchaser in a qualified use.
"(C) Qualified use. For purposes of this subsection, the term 'qualified use' means any use in the manufacture or production of a fertilizer."
Prior to amendment, subpara. (d)(2)(B) read as follows:
"(B) any person uses such substance, or sells such substance for use, as a qualified substance,"
In 1980, P.L. 96-510, Sec. 211(a), added Code Sec. 4662, effective 4/1/81.

Subchapter C.—Tax on Certain Imported Substances

Sec.
4671. Imposition of tax.
4672. Definitions and special rules.

In 1986, P.L. 99-499, Sec. 515(a), added subchapter C to chapter 38.

Sec. 4671. Imposition of tax.
(a) General rule.
There is hereby imposed a tax on any taxable substance sold or used by the importer thereof.
(b) Amount of tax.
(1) In general. Except as provided in paragraph (2), the amount of the tax imposed by subsection (a) with respect to any taxable substance shall be the amount of the tax which would have been imposed by section 4611 on the taxable chemicals used as materials in the manufacture or production of such substance if such taxable chemicals had been sold in the United States for use in the manufacture or production of such taxable substance.
(2) Rate where importer does not furnish information to Secretary. If the importer does not furnish to the Secretary (at such time and in such manner as the Secretary shall prescribe) sufficient information to determine under paragraph (1) the amount of the tax imposed by subsection (a) on any taxable substance, the amount of the tax imposed on such taxable substance shall be 5 percent of the appraised value of such substance as of the time such substance was entered into the United States for consumption, use, or warehousing.
(3) Authority to prescribe rate in lieu of paragraph (2) rate. The Secretary may prescribe for each taxable substance a tax which, if prescribed, shall apply in lieu of the tax specified in paragraph (2) with respect to such substance. The tax prescribed by the Secretary shall be equal to the amount of tax which would be imposed by subsection (a) with respect to the taxable substance if such substance were produced using the predominant method of production of such substance.
(c) Exemptions for substances taxed under sections 4611 and 4661.
No tax shall be imposed by this section on the sale or use of any substance if tax is imposed on such sale or use under section 4611 or 4661.
(d) Tax-free sales, etc. for substances used as certain fuels or in the production of fertilizer or animal feed.
Rules similar to the following rules shall apply for purposes of applying this section with respect to taxable substances used or sold for use as described in such rules:
(1) Paragraphs (2), (5), and (9) of section 4662(b) (relating to tax-free sales of chemicals used as fuel or in the production of fertilizer or animal feed).
(2) Paragraphs (2), (3), and (4) of section 4662(d) (relating to refund or credit of tax on certain chemicals used as fuel or in the production of fertilizer or animal feed).

(e) Termination.
No tax shall be imposed under this section during any period during which the Hazardous Substance Superfund financing rate under section 4611 does not apply.

In 1989, P.L. 101-239, Sec. 7505(d)(1), changed the effective date for changes made by Sec. 8032(c)(3) of P.L. 99-509, from effective on the commencement date as defined in Code Sec. 4611(f) to effective on the commencement date which is 1/1/90.
In 1986, P.L. 99-509, Sec. 8032(c)(3), substituted "the Hazardous Substance Superfund financing rate under section 4611 does not apply" for "no tax is imposed under section 4611(a)" in subsec. (e), effective [as provided by Sec. 7505(d)(1) of P. L. 101-239, see above]
—P.L. 99-499, Sec. 515(a), added Code Sec. 4671 as part of subchapter C of chapter 38, effective 1/1/89. Sec. 515(d) of this Act provides:
"(d) Study.—
"(1) In general.— The Secretary of the Treasury or his delegate shall conduct a study of issues relating to the implementation of—
"(A) the tax imposed by the section 4671 of the Internal Revenue Code of 1986 (as added by this section), and
"(B) the credit for exports of taxable substances under section 4661(e)(2)(A)(ii)(II) of such Code.
In conducting such study, the Secretary of the Treasury or his delegate shall consult with the Environmental Protection Agency and the International Trade Commission.
"(2) Report.— The report of the study under paragraph (1) shall be submitted not later than January 1, 1988, to the Committee on Ways and Means of the House of Representatives and the Committee on Finance of the Senate."

Sec. 4672. Definitions and special rules.
(a) Taxable substance.
For purposes of this subchapter—
(1) In general. The term "taxable substance" means any substance which, at the time of sale or use by the importer, is listed as a taxable substance by the Secretary for purposes of this subchapter.
(2) Determination of substances on list. A substance shall be listed under paragraph (1) if—
(A) the substance is contained in the list under paragraph (3), or
(B) the Secretary determines, in consultation with the Administrator of the Environmental Protection Agency and the Commissioner of Customs, that taxable chemicals constitute more than 50 percent of the weight (or more than 50 percent of the value) of the materials used to produce such substance (determined on the basis of the predominant method of production).
If an importer or exporter of any substance requests that the Secretary determine whether such substance be listed as a taxable substance under paragraph (1) or be removed from such listing, the Secretary shall make such determination within 180 days after the date the request was filed.
(3) Initial list of taxable substances.

Cumene	Methylene chloride
Styrene	Polypropylene
Ammonium nitrate	Propylene glycol
Nickel oxide	Formaldehyde
Isopropyl alcohol	Acetone
Ethylene glycol	Acrylonitrile
Vinyl chloride	Methanol
Polyethylene resins, total	Propylene oxide
Polybutadiene	Polypropylene resins
Styrene-butadiene, latex	Ethylene oxide
Styrene-butadiene, snpf	Ethylene dichloride
Synthetic rubber, not containing fillers	Cyclohexane
Urea	Isophthalic acid
Ferronickel	Maleic anhydride
Ferrochromium nov 3 pct	Phthalic anhydride
Ferrochrome ov 3 pct. carbon	Ethyl methyl ketone
Unwrought nickel	Chloroform

3,281

Nickel waste and scrap
Wrought nickel rods and wire
Nickel powders
Phenolic resins
Polyvinylchloride resins
Polystyrene resins and copolymers
Ethyl alcohol for non-beverage use
Ethylbenzene
Carbon tetrachloride
Chromic acid
Hydrogen peroxide
Polystyrene homopolymer resins
Melamine
Acrylic and metha-crylic acid resins
Vinyl resins
Vinyl resins, NSPF.

(4) Modifications to list. The Secretary shall add to the list under paragraph (3) substances which meet either the weight or value tests of paragraph (2)(B) and may remove from such list only substances which meet neither of such tests.

(b) Other definitions.

For purposes of this subchapter—

(1) Importer. The term "importer" means the person entering the taxable substance for consumption, use, or warehousing.

(2) Taxable chemicals; United States. The terms "taxable chemical" and "United States" have the respective meanings given such terms by section 4662(a).

(c) Disposition of revenues from Puerto Rico and the Virgin Islands.

The provisions of subsections (a)(3) and (b)(3) of section 7652 shall not apply to any tax imposed by section 4671.

In **1988**, P.L. 100-647, Sec. 2001(b)(1), added "(or more than 50 percent of the value)" after "more than 50 percent of the weight" in subpara. (a)(2)(B) . . . Sec. 2001(b)(2), added the last sentence to para. (a)(2) . . . Sec. 2001(b)(3), amended para. (a)(4), effective 1/1/89.
Prior to amendment, para. (a)(4) read as follows:
"(4) Modifications to list.
"(A) In general. The Secretary may add substances to or remove substances from the list under paragraph (3) (including items listed by reason of paragraph (2)) as necessary to carry out the purposes of this subchapter.
"(B) Authority to add substances to list based on value. The Secretary may, to the extent necessary to carry out the purposes of this subchapter, add any substance to the list under paragraph (3) if such substance would be described in paragraph (2)(B) if 'value' were substituted for 'weight' therein."
In **1986**, P.L. 99-499, Sec. 515(a), added Code Sec. 4672 as part of subchapter C of chapter 38, effective 1/1/89.

Subchapter C. Repealed [Tax on Hazardous Wastes]
Sec.
4681. Repealed [Imposition of tax.]
4682. Repealed [Definitions and special rules.]

In **1986**, P.L. 99-499, Sec. 514(a)(2), repealed Subchapter C.
Prior to repeal, the table of sections for Subchapter C read as follows:
"Subchapter C—Tax on Hazardous Wastes
"Sec.
"4681. Imposition of tax.
"4682. Definitions and special rules."

Sec. 4681. Repealed.

In **1986**, P.L. 99-499, Sec. 514(a), repealed Code Sec. 4681 as part of the repeal of subchapter C of chapter 38, effective 10/1/93, except as provided in Sec. 514(c)(2) of this Act, which reads as follows:
"(2) Waiver of statute of limitations.—If on the date of the enactment of this Act (or at any time within 1 year after such date of enactment) refund or credit of any overpayment of tax resulting from the of this section is barred by any law or rule of law, refund or credit of such overpayment shall, nevertheless, be made or allowed if claimed therefor is filed before the date 1 year after the date of enactment of this Act."
Prior to repeal Code Sec. 4681 read as follows:
"SEC. 4681. IMPOSITION OF TAX.
"(a) General rule.

"There is hereby imposed a tax on the receipt of hazardous waste at a qualified hazardous waste disposal facility.
"(b) Amount of tax.
"The amount of the tax imposed by subsection (a) shall be equal to $2.13 per dry weight ton of hazardous waste."
In **1980**, P.L. 96-510, Sec. Sec. 231(a), added Code Sec. 4681, effective 12/11/80. Sec. 303 of this Act provides:
"Sec. 303. Unless reauthorized by the Congress, the authority to collect taxes conferred by this Act shall terminate on September 30, 1985, or when the sum of the amounts received in the Treasury under section 4611 and under 4661 of the Internal Revenue Code of 1954, total $1,380,000,000, whichever occurs first. The Secretary of the Treasury shall estimate when this level of $1,380,000,000 will be reached and shall by regulation, provide procedures for the termination of the tax authorized by this Act and imposed under sections 4611 and 4661 of the Internal Revenue Code of 1954."

Sec. 4682. Repealed.

In **1986**, P.L. 99-499, Sec. 514(a)(1), repealed Code Sec. 4682 as part of the repeal of subchapter C of chapter 38, effective 10/1/1983, except as provided in Sec. 514(c)(2) of this Act, reproduced in note following Code Sec. 4681.
Prior to repeal, Code Sec. 4682 read as follows:
"Sec. 4682. Definitions and special rules.
"(a) Definitions.
"For purposes of this subchapter—
"(1) Hazardous waste. The term 'hazardous waste' means any waste—
"(A) having the characteristics identified under section 3001 of the Solid Waste Disposal Act, as in effect on the date of the enactment of this Act (other than waste the regulations of which under such Act has been suspended by Act of Congress on that date), or
"(B) subject to the reporting or recordkeeping requirements of sections 3002 and 3004 of such Act, as so in effect.
"(2) Qualified hazardous waste disposal facility. The term 'qualified hazardous waste disposal facility' means any facility which has received a permit or is accorded interim status under section 3005 of the Solid Waste Disposal Act.
"(b) Tax imposed on owner or operator.
"The tax imposed by section 4681 shall be imposed on the owner or operator of the qualified hazardous waste disposal facility.
"(c) Tax not to apply to certain wastes.
"The tax imposed by section 4681 shall not apply to any hazardous waste which will not remain at the qualified hazardous waste disposal facility after the facility is closed.
"(d) Applicability of section.
"The tax imposed by section 4681 shall apply to the receipt of hazardous waste after September 30, 1983, except that if, as of September 30 of any subsequent calendar year, the unobligated balance of the Post-closure Liability Trust Fund exceeds $200,000,000) no tax shall be imposed under such section during the following calendar year."
In **1980**, P.L. 96-510, Sec. 231(a), added Code Sec. 4681, effective 12/11/80.

Subchapter D.—Ozone-Depleting Chemicals, Etc.

Sec.
4681. Imposition of tax.
4682. Definitions and special rules.

Sec. 4681. Imposition of tax.

(a) General rule.

There is hereby imposed a tax on—

(1) any ozone-depleting chemical sold or used by the manufacturer, producer, or importer thereof, and

(2) any imported taxable product sold or used by the importer thereof.

(b) Amount of tax.

(1) Ozone-depleting chemicals.

(A) In general. The amount of the tax imposed by subsection (a) on each pound of ozone-depleting chemical shall be an amount equal to—

(i) the base tax amount, multiplied by

(ii) the ozone-depletion factor for such chemical.

(B) Base tax amount. The base tax amount for purposes of subparagraph (A) with respect to any sale or use during any calendar year after 1995 shall be $5.35 increased by 45 cents for each year after 1995.

(2) Imported taxable product.

(A) In general. The amount of the tax imposed by subsection (a) on any imported taxable product shall be the amount of tax which would have been imposed by subsection (a) on the ozone-depleting chemicals used as materials in the manufacture or production of such product if such ozone-depleting chemicals had been sold in the United States on the date of the sale of such imported taxable product.

(B) Certain rules to apply. Rules similar to the rules of paragraphs (2) and (3) of section 4671(b) shall apply.

In 1997, P.L. 105-34, Sec. 1432(c)(1), deleted subparas. (b)(1)(B) and (C) and added a new subpara. (b)(1)(B), effective 8/5/97.
Prior to deletion, subparas. (b)(1)(B) and (C) read as follows:
"(B) Base tax amount. The base tax amount for purposes of subparagraph (A) with respect to any sale or use during a calendar year before 1996 with respect to any ozone-depleting chemical is the amount determined under the following table for such calendar year:

Calendar year:	Base tax amount
1993	3.35
1994	4.35
1995	5.35

"(C) Base tax amount for later years. The base tax amount for purposes of subparagraph (A) with respect to any sale or use of an ozone-depleting chemical during a calendar year after the last year specified in the table under subparagraph (B) applicable to such chemical shall be the base tax amount for such last year increased by 45 cents for each year after such last year."

In 1992, P.L. 102-486, Sec. 1931(a), amended subpara. (b)(1)(B), effective for taxable chemicals sold or used on or after 1/1/93.
Prior to amendment, subpara. (b)(1)(B) read as follows:
"(B) Base tax amount.
"(i) Initially listed chemicals. The base tax amount for purposes of subparagraph (A) with respect to any sale or use during a calendar year before 1995 with respect to any ozone-depleting chemical other than a newly listed chemical (as defined in section 4682(d)(3)(C)) is the amount determined under the following table for such calendar year:

Calendar Year	Base Tax Amount
1990 or 1991	$1.37
1992	1.67
1993 or 1994	2.65

"(ii) Newly listed chemicals. The base tax amount for purposes of subparagraph (A) with respect to any sale or use during a calendar year before 1996 with respect to any ozone-depleting chemical which is a newly listed chemical (as so defined) is the amount determined under the following table for such calendar year:

Calendar Year	Base Tax Amount
1991 or 1992	$1.37
1993	1.67
1994	3.00
1995	3.10

In 1990, P.L. 101-508, Sec. 11203(c), amended subparas. (b)(1)(B) and (C), effective 1/1/91.
Prior to amendment, subparas. (b)(1)(B) and (C) read as follows:
"(B) Base tax amount for years before 1995. The base tax amount for purposes of subparagraph (A) with respect to any sale or use during a calendar year before 1995 is the amount determined under the following table for such calendar year:

"Calendar year:	Base tax amount
1990 or 1991	$1.37
1992	1.67
1993 or 1994	2.65

"(C) Base tax amount for years after 1994. The base tax amount for purposes of subparagraph (A) with respect to any sale or use during a calendar year after 1994 shall be the base tax amount for 1994 increased by 45 cents for each year after 1994."

In 1989, P.L. 101-239, Sec. 7506(a), added Code Sec. 4681 as part of subchapter D of chapter 38, effective 1/1/90. Sec. 7506(c)(2)-(3) of this Act provides:
"(2) No deposits required before April 1, 1990.—No deposit of any tax imposed by subchapter D of chapter 38 of the Internal Revenue Code of 1986, as added by this section, shall be required to be made before April 1, 1990.
"(3) Notification of changes in international agreements.— The Secretary of the Treasury or his delegate shall notify the Committee on Ways and Means of the House of Representatives and the Committee on Finance of the Senate of changes in the Montreal Protocol and of other international agreements to which the United States is a signatory relating to ozone-depleting chemicals."

Sec. 4682. Definitions and special rules.
(a) Ozone-depleting chemical.
For purposes of this subchapter—
(1) In general. The term "ozone-depleting chemical" means any substance

(A) which, at the time of the sale or use by the manufacturer, producer, or importer, is listed as an ozone-depleting chemical in the table contained in paragraph (2), and
(B) which is manufactured or produced in the United States or entered into the United States for consumption, use, or warehousing.

(2) Ozone-depleting chemicals.

Common name:	Chemical nomenclature:
CFC-11	trichlorofluoromethane
CFC-12	dichlorodifluoromethane
CFC-113	trichlorotrifluoroethane
CFC-114	1,2-dichloro-1,1,2,2-tetrafluoroethane
CFC-115	chloropentafluoroethane
Halon-1211	bromochlorodifluoromethane
Halon-1301	bromotrifluoromethane
Halon-2402	dibromotetrafluoroethane
Carbon tetrachloride	tetrachloromethane
Methyl chloroform	1,1,1-trichloroethane
CFC-13	CF3C1
CFC-111	C2FC15
CFC-112	C2F2C14
CFC-211	C3FC17
CFC-212	C3F2C16
CFC-213	C3F3C15
CFC-214	C3F4C14
CFC-215	C3F5C13
CFC-216	C3F6C12
CFC-217	C3F7C1.

(b) Ozone-depletion factor.
For purposes of this subchapter, the term "ozone-depletion factor" means, with respect to an ozone-depleting chemical, the factor assigned to such chemical under the following table:

Ozone-depleting chemical:	Ozone-depletion factor:
CFC-11	1.0
CFC-12	1.0
CFC-113	0.8
CFC-114	1.0
CFC-115	0.6
Halon-1211	3.0
Halon-1301	10.0
Halon-2402	6.0
Carbon tetrachloride	1.1
Methyl chloroform	0.1
CFC-13	1.0
CFC-111	1.0
CFC-112	1.0
CFC-211	1.0
CFC-212	1.0
CFC-213	1.0
CFC-214	1.0
CFC-215	1.0
CFC-216	1.0
CFC-217	1.0.

(c) Imported taxable product.
For purposes of this subchapter—
(1) In general. The term "imported taxable product" means any product (other than an ozone-depleting chemical) entered into the United States for consumption, use, or warehousing if any ozone-depleting chemical was used

Code Sec. 4682(c)(1) — Excise and miscellaneous taxes

as material in the manufacture or production of such product.

(2) De minimis exception. The term "imported taxable product" shall not include any product specified in regulations prescribed by the Secretary as using a de minimis amount of ozone-depleting chemicals as materials in the manufacture or production thereof. The preceding sentence shall not apply to any product in which any ozone-depleting chemical (other than methyl chloroform) is used for purposes of refrigeration or air conditioning, creating an aerosol or foam, or manufacturing electronic components.

(d) Exceptions.

> • **Caution:** For special rule regarding Halon-1211, see Sec. 1803(c) of P.L. 104-188 reproduced in the history of this Code Sec.

(1) Recycling. No tax shall be imposed by section 4681 on any ozone-depleting chemical which is diverted or recovered in the United States as part of a recycling process (and not as part of the original manufacturing or production process), or on any recycled Halon-1301 or recycled Halon-2402 imported from any country which is a signatory to the Montreal Protocol on Substances that Deplete the Ozone Layer.

(2) Use in further manufacture.

(A) In general. No tax shall be imposed by section 4681—

(i) on the use of any ozone-depleting chemical in the manufacture or production of any other chemical if the ozone-depleting chemical is entirely consumed in such use,

(ii) on the sale by the manufacturer, producer, or importer of any ozone-depleting chemical—

(I) for a use by the purchaser which meets the requirements of clause (i), or

(II) for resale by the purchaser to a second purchaser for a use by the second purchaser which meets the requirements of clause (i).

Clause (ii) shall apply only if the manufacturer, producer, and importer, and the 1st and 2d purchasers (if any), meet such registration requirements as may be prescribed by the Secretary.

(B) Credit or refund. Under regulations prescribed by the Secretary, if—

(i) a tax under this subchapter was paid with respect to any ozone-depleting chemical, and

(ii) such chemical was used (and entirely consumed) by any person in the manufacture or production of any other chemical,

then an amount equal to the tax so paid shall be allowed as a credit or refund (without interest) to such person in the same manner as if it were an overpayment of tax imposed by section 4681.

(3) Exports.

(A) In general. Except as provided in subparagraph (B), rules similar to the rules of section 4662(e) (other than section 4662(e)(2)(A)(ii)(II)) shall apply for purposes of this subchapter.

(B) Limit on benefit.

(i) In general. The aggregate tax benefit allowable under subparagraph (A) with respect to ozone-depleting chemicals manufactured, produced, or imported by any person during a calendar year shall not exceed the sum of—

(I) the amount equal to the 1986 export percentage of the aggregate tax which would (but for this subsection and subsection (g)) be imposed by this subchapter with respect to the maximum quantity of ozone-depleting chemicals permitted to be manufactured or produced by such person during such calendar year under regulations prescribed by the Environmental Protection Agency (other than chemicals with respect to which subclause (II) applies),

(II) the aggregate tax which would (but for this subsection and subsection (g)) be imposed by this subchapter with respect to any additional production allowance granted to such person with respect to ozone-depleting chemicals manufactured or produced by such person during such calendar year by the Environmental Protection Agency under 40 CFR Part 82 (as in effect on September 14, 1989), and

(III) the aggregate tax which was imposed by this subchapter with respect to ozone-depleting chemicals imported by such person during the calendar year.

(ii) 1986 export percentage. A person's 1986 export percentage is the percentage equal to the ozone-depletion factor adjusted pounds of ozone-depleting chemicals manufactured or produced by such person during 1986 which were exported during 1986, divided by the ozone-depletion factor adjusted pounds of all ozone-depleting chemicals manufactured or produced by such person during 1986. The percentage determined under the preceding sentence shall be computed by taking into account the sum of such person's direct 1986 exports (as determined by the Environmental Protection Agency) and such person's indirect 1986 exports (as allocated to such person by such Agency in determining such person's consumption and production rights for ozone-depleting chemicals).

(C) Separate application of limit for newly listed chemicals.

(i) In general. Subparagraph (B) shall be applied separately with respect to newly listed chemicals and other chemicals.

(ii) Application to newly listed chemicals. In applying subparagraph (B) to newly listed chemicals—

(I) subparagraph (B) shall be applied by substituting "1989" for "1986" each place it appears, and

(II) clause (i)(II) thereof shall be applied by substituting for the regulations referred to therein any regulations (whether or not prescribed by the Secretary) which the Secretary determines are comparable to the regulations referred to in such clause with respect to newly listed chemicals.

(iii) Newly listed chemical. For purposes of this subparagraph, the term "newly listed chemical" means any substance which appears in the table contained in subsection (a)(2) below Halon-2402.

(e) Other definitions.

For purposes of this subchapter

(1) Importer. The term "importer" means the person entering the article for consumption, use, or warehousing.

(2) United States. The term "United States" has the meaning given such term by section 4612(a)(4).

(f) Special rules.
  (1) Fractional parts of a pound. In the case of a fraction of a pound, the tax imposed by this subchapter shall be the same fraction of the amount of such tax imposed on a whole pound.
  (2) Disposition of revenues from Puerto Rico and the Virgin Islands. The provisions of subsections (a)(3) and (b)(3) of section 7652 shall not apply to any tax imposed by this subchapter.

(g) Chemicals used as propellants in metered-dose inhalers.
  (1) Exemption from tax.
    (A) In general. No tax shall be imposed by section 4681 on—
      (i) any use of any substance as a propellant in metered-dose inhalers, or
      (ii) any qualified sale by the manufacturer, producer, or importer of any substance.
    (B) Qualified sale. For purposes of subparagraph (A), the term "qualified sale" means any sale by the manufacturer, producer, or importer of any substance—
      (i) for use by the purchaser as a propellant in metered dose inhalers, or
      (ii) for resale by the purchaser to a 2d purchaser for such use by the 2d purchaser.
    The preceding sentence shall apply only if the manufacturer, producer, and importer, and the 1st and 2d purchasers (if any) meet such registration requirements as may be prescribed by the Secretary.
  (2) Overpayments. If any substance on which tax was paid under this subchapter is used by any person as a propellant in metered-dose inhalers, credit or refund without interest shall be allowed to such person in an amount equal to the tax so paid. Amounts payable under the preceding sentence with respect to uses during the taxable year shall be treated as described in section 34(a) for such year unless claim thereof has been timely filed under this paragraph.

(h) Imposition of floor stocks taxes.
  (1) January 1, 1990, tax. On any ozone-depleting chemical which on January 1, 1990, is held by any person (other than the manufacturer, producer, or importer thereof) for sale or for use in further manufacture, there is hereby imposed a floor stocks tax in an amount equal to the tax which would be imposed by section 4681 on such chemical if the sale of such chemical by the manufacturer, producer, or importer thereof had occurred during 1990.
  (2) Other tax-increase dates.
    (A) In general. If, on any tax-increase date, any ozone-depleting chemical is held by any person (other than the manufacturer, producer, or importer thereof) for sale or for use in further manufacture, there is hereby imposed a floor stocks tax.
    (B) Amount of tax. The amount of the tax imposed by subparagraph (A) shall be the excess (if any) of—
      (i) the tax which would be imposed under section 4681 on such substance if the sale of such chemical by the manufacturer, producer, or importer thereof had occurred on the tax-increase date, over
      (ii) the prior tax (if any) imposed by this subchapter on such substance.
    (C) Tax-increase date. For purposes of this paragraph, the term "tax-increase date" means January 1 of any calendar year after 1991.
  (3) Due date. The taxes imposed by this subsection on January 1 of any calendar year shall be paid on or before June 30 of such year.
  (4) Application of other laws. All other provisions of law, including penalties, applicable with respect to the taxes imposed by section 4681 shall apply to the floor stocks taxes imposed by this subsection.

In **1997,** P.L. 105-34, Sec. 903(a), substituted "recycled Halon-1301 or recycled Halon-2402" for "recycled halon" in para. (d)(1), effective 8/5/97.
— P.L. 105-34, Sec. 1432(c)(2), amended subsec. (g), effective 8/5/97.
Prior to amendment, subsec. (g) read as follows:
  "(g) Phase-in of tax on certain substances.
  "(1) Treatment for 1990.
  "(A) Halons. The term 'ozone-depleting chemical' shall not include halon-1211, halon-1301, or halon-2402 with respect to any sale or use during 1990.
  "(B) Chemicals used in rigid foam insulation. No tax shall be imposed by section 4681—
  "(i) on the use during 1990 of any substance in the manufacture of rigid foam insulation,
  "(ii) on the sale during 1990 by the manufacturer, producer, or importer of any substance—
  "(I) for use by the purchaser in the manufacture of rigid foam insulation, or
  "(II) for resale by the purchaser to a second purchaser for such use by the second purchaser, or
  "(iii) on the sale or use during 1990 by the importer of any rigid foam insulation.
  Clause (ii) shall apply only if the manufacturer, producer, and importer, and the 1st and 2d purchasers (if any) meet such registration requirements as may be prescribed by the Secretary.
  "(2) Treatment for 1991, 1992, and 1993.
  "(A) Halons. The tax imposed by section 4681 during 1991, 1992, or 1993 by reason of the treatment of halon-1211, halon-1301, and halon-2402 as ozone-depleting chemicals shall be the applicable percentage (determined under the following table) of the amount of such tax which would (but for this subparagraph) be imposed.

In the case of	The applicable percentage in the case of sales or use during 1993 is:
Halon-1211	2.49
Halon-1301	0.75
Halon-2402	1.24

  "(B) Chemicals used in rigid foam insulation. In the case of a sale or use during 1991, 1992, or 1993 on which no tax would have been imposed by reason of paragraph (1)(B) had such sale or use occurred during 1990, the tax imposed by section 4681 shall be the applicable percentage (determined in accordance with the following table) of the amount of such tax which would (but for this subparagraph) be imposed.

In the case of sales or use during:	The applicable percentage is:
1991	18
1992	15
1993	7.46

  "(3) Overpayments with respect to chemicals used in rigid foam insulation. If any substance on which tax was paid under this subchapter is used during 1990, 1991, 1992, or 1993 by any person in the manufacture of rigid foam insulation, credit or refund (without interest) shall be allowed to such person an amount equal to the excess of—
  "(A) the tax paid under this subchapter on such substance, over
  "(B) the tax (if any) which would be imposed by section 4681 if such substance were used for such use by the manufacturer, producer, or importer thereof on the date of its use by such person.
  Amounts payable under the preceding sentence with respect to uses during the taxable year shall be treated as described in section 34(a) for such year unless claim therefor has been timely filed under this paragraph.
  "(4) Chemicals used as propellants in metered-dose inhalers.
  "(A) Tax-exempt.
  "(i) In general. No tax shall be imposed by section 4681 on—
  "(I) any use of any substance as a propellant in metered-dose inhalers, or
  "(II) any qualified sale by the manufacturer, producer, or importer of any substance.
  "(ii) Qualified sale. For purposes of clause (i), the term 'qualified sale' means any sale by the manufacturer, producer, of importer of any substance—
  "(I) for use by the purchaser as a propellant in metered dose inhalers, or
  "(II) for resale by the purchaser to a 2d purchaser for such use by the 2d purchaser.
  The preceding sentence shall apply only if the manufacturer, producer and importer, and the 1st and 2d purchasers (if any) meet such registration requirements as may be prescribed by the Secretary.
  "(B) Overpayments. If any substance on which tax was paid under this subchapter is used by any person as a propellant in metered-dose inhalers, credit or refund without interest shall be allowed to such person in an amount equal to the

tax so paid. Amounts payable under the preceding sentence with respect to uses during the taxable year shall be treated as described in section 34(a) for such year unless claim thereof has been timely filed under this subparagraph.

"(5) Treatment of methyl chloroform. The tax imposed by section 4681 during 1993 by reason of the treatment of methyl chloroform as an ozone-depleting chemical shall be 63.02 percent of the amount of such tax which would (but for this paragraph) be imposed."

In 1996, P.L. 104-188, Sec. 1803(a)(1), added ", or on any recycled halon imported from any country which is a signatory to the Montreal Protocol on Substances that Deplete the Ozone Layer" before the period at the end of para. (d)(1), effective as provided in Sec. 1803(c)(1), which read as follows:

"(1) Recycled halon.

"(A) In general. Except as provided in subparagraph (B), the amendment made by subsection (a)(1) shall take effect on January 1, 1997.

"(B) Halon-1211. In the case of Halon-1211, the amendment made by subsection (a)(1) shall take effect on January 1, 1998."

—P.L. 104-188, Sec. 1803(a)(2), of this Act provides:

"(2) Certification system. The Secretary of the Treasury, after consultation with the Administrator of the Environmental Protection Agency, shall develop a certification system to ensure the compliance with the recycling requirement for imported halon under section 4682(d)(1) of the Internal Revenue Code of 1986, as amended by paragraph (1)."

—P.L. 104-188, Sec. 1803(b), amended para. (g)(4), effective on the 7th day after 8/20/96.

Prior to amendment, para. (g)(4) read as follows:

"(4) Chemicals used for sterilizing medical instruments and as propellants in metered-dose inhalers.

"(A) Rate of tax.

"(i) In general. In the case of—

"(I) any use during the applicable period of any substance to sterilize medical instruments or as propellants in metered-dose inhalers, or

"(II) any qualified sale during such period by the manufacturer, producer, or importer of any substance,

the tax imposed by section 4681 shall be equal to $1.67 per pound.

"(ii) Qualified sale. For purposes of clause (i), the term 'qualified sale' means any sale by the manufacturer, producer, or importer of any substance—

"(I) for use by the purchaser to sterilize medical instruments or as propellants in metered-dose inhalers, or

"(II) for resale by the purchaser to a 2d purchase for such use by the 2d purchaser.

The preceding sentence shall apply only if the manufacturer, producer, and importer, and the 1st and 2d purchasers (if any) meet such registration requirements as may be prescribed by the Secretary.

"(B) Overpayments. If any substance on which tax was paid under this subchapter is used during the applicable period by any person to sterilize medical instruments or as propellants in metered-dose inhalers, credit or refund without interest shall be allowed to such person in an amount equal to the excess of—

"(i) the tax paid under this subchapter on such substance, or

"(ii) the tax (if any) which would be imposed by section 4681 if such substance were used for such use by the manufacture, producer, or importer thereof on the date of its use by such person.

Amounts payable under the preceding sentence with respect to uses during the taxable year shall be treated as described in section 34(a) for such year unless claim thereof has been timely filed under this subparagraph.

"(C) Applicable period. For purposes of this paragraph, the term 'applicable period' means—

"(i) 1993 in the case of substances to sterilize medical instruments, and

"(ii) any period after 1992 in the case of propellants in metered-dose inhalers."

In 1992, P.L. 102-486, Sec. 1931(b), substituted "7.46" for "10" in the table in subpara. (g)(2)(B) . . . Sec. 1931(c), substituted "of any calendar year after 1991" for "of 1991, 1992, 1993, and 1994" in subpara. (h)(2)(C), effective for taxable chemicals sold or used on or after 1/1/93.

—P.L. 102-486, Sec. 1932(a), amended the table in subpara. (g)(2)(A) . . . Sec. 1932(b), added para. (g)(4) . . . Sec. 1932(c), added para. (g)(5), effective for sales and uses on or after 1/1/93.

Prior to amendment, the table in subpara. (g)(2)(A) read as follows:

In the case of:	The applicable percentage is:		
	For sales or use during 1991	For sales or use during 1992	For sales or use during 1993
Halon-1211	6.0	5.0	3.3
Halon-1301	1.8	1.5	1.0
Halon-2402	3.0	2.5	1.6

In 1990, P.L. 101-508, Sec. 11203(a)(1), amended para. (2) . . . Sec. 11203(a)(2), amended subsec. (b) . . . Sec. 11203(b), added subpara. (d)(3)(C) . . . Sec. 11203(d)(1), added "(other than methyl chloroform)" after "ozone-depleting chemical" in the last sentence of para. (c)(2) . . . Sec. 11203(d)(2), substituted "June 30" for "April 1" in para. (h)(3), effective 1/1/91.

Prior to amendment, para. (a)(2) read as follows:

"(2) Ozone-depleting chemicals

Common name:	Chemical nomenclature:
CFC-11	trichlorofluoromethane
CFC-12	dichlorodifluoromethane
CFC-113	trichlorotrifluoroethane
CFC-114	1,2-dichloro-1,1,2,2-tetrafluoroethane
CFC-115	chloropentafluoroethane
Halon-1211	bromochlorodifluoromethane
Halon-1301	bromotrifluoromethane
Halon-2402	dibromotetrafluoroethane."

Prior to amendment, subsec. (b) read as follows:

"(b) Ozone-depletion factor.

"For purposes of this subchapter, the term 'ozone-depletion factor' means, with respect to an ozone-depleting chemical, the factor assigned to such chemical under the following table:

Ozone-depleting chemical:	Ozone-depletion factor:
CFC-11	1.0
CFC-12	1.0
CFC-113	0.8
CFC-114	1.0
CFC-115	0.6
Halon-1211	3.0
Halon-1301	10.0
Halon-2402	6.0."

—P.L. 101-508, Sec. 11203(f), relating to deposits for 1st quarter of 1991, is reproduced in note following Code Sec. 4681.

—P.L. 101-508, Sec. 11701(g)(1), substituted "produced, or imported" for "or produced" in clause (d)(3)(B)(i) . . . Sec. 11701(g)(2), amended subclause (d)(3)(B)(i)(I) . . . Sec. 11701(g)(3), substituted "tax which would (but for this subsection and subsection (g) be imposed" for "tax imposed" in subclause (d)(3)(B)(i)(II) . . . Sec. 11701(g)(4), substituted "and" for the period at the end of subclause (d)(3)(B)(i)(II) and added subclause (d)(3)(B)(i)(III) . . . Sec. 11701(g)(5), amended the last sentence of clause (d)(3)(B)(ii), effective 1/1/90. For special provisions, see Sec. 7506(c)(2) and (c)(3) in P.L. 101-239 reproduced below.

Prior to amendment, subclause (d)(3)(B)(i)(I) read as follows:

"(I) the amount equal to the 1986 export percentage of the aggregate tax imposed by this subchapter with respect to ozone-depleting chemicals manufactured or produced by such person during such calendar year (other than chemicals with respect to which subclause (II) applies), and"

Prior to amendment, the last sentence of clause (d)(3)(B)(ii) read as follows:

"The percentage determined under the preceding sentence shall be based on data published by the Environmental Protection Agency."

In 1989, P.L. 101-239, Sec. 7506(a), added Code Sec. 4682 as part of subchapter D of chapter 38, effective 1/1/90. Sec. 7506(c)(2) and (3) of this Act provide:

"(2) No deposits required before April 1, 1990.—No deposit of any tax imposed by subchapter D of chapter 38 of the Internal Revenue Code of 1986, as added by this section, shall be required to be made before April 1, 1990.

"(3) Notification of changes in international agreements.—The Secretary of the Treasury or his delegate shall notify the Committee on Ways and Means of the House of Representatives and the Committee on Finance of the Senate of changes in the Montreal Protocol and of other international agreements to which the United States is a signatory relating to ozone-depleting chemicals."

CHAPTER 39.— REGISTRATION-REQUIRED OBLIGATIONS

Sec.

4701. Tax on issuer of registration-required obligation not in registered form.

Sec. 4701. Tax on issuer of registration-required obligation not in registered form.

(a) Imposition of tax.

In the case of any person who issues a registration-required obligation which is not in registered form, there is hereby imposed on such person on the issuance of such obligation a tax in an amount equal to the product of—

(1) 1 percent of the principal amount of such obligation, multiplied by

(2) the number of calendar years (or portions thereof) during the period beginning on the date of issuance of such obligation and ending on the date of maturity.

(b) Definitions.

For purposes of this section—

• *Caution:* Code Sec. 4701(b)(1), following, is effective before obligations issued before 3/19/2012. For Code Sec.

Excise and miscellaneous taxes   Code Sec. 4905(a)

4701(b)(1) effective for obligations issued after 3/18/2012, see below.

(1) Registration-required obligation. The term "registration-required obligation" has the same meaning as when used in section 163(f), except that such term shall not include any obligation required to be registered under section 149(a).

• **Caution:** Code Sec. 4701(b)(1), following, is effective for obligations issued after 3/18/2012. For Code Sec. 4701(b)(1) effective before obligations issued before 3/19/2012, see above.

(1) Registration-required obligation.

(A) In general. The term "registration-required obligation" has the same meaning as when used in section 163(f), except that such term shall not include any obligation which—

(i) is required to be registered under section 149(a), or

(ii) is described in subparagraph (B).

(B) Certain obligations not included. An obligation is described in this subparagraph if—

(i) there are arrangements reasonably designed to ensure that such obligation will be sold (or resold in connection with the original issue) only to a person who is not a United States person,

(ii) interest on such obligation is payable only outside the United States and its possessions, and

(iii) on the face of such obligation there is a statement that any United States person who holds such obligation will be subject to limitations under the United States income tax laws.

(2) Registered form. The term "registered form" has the same meaning as when used in section 163(f).

In 2010, P.L. 111-147, Sec. 502(e), amended para. (b)(1), effective for obligations issued after the date which is 2 years after 3/18/2010.
Prior to amendment, para. (b)(1) read as follows:
"(1) Registration-required obligation.
'The term 'registration-required obligation' has the same meaning as when used in section 163(f), except that such term shall not include any obligation required to be registered under section 149(a)."
In 1986, P.L. 99-514, Sec. 1301(j)(5), substituted "section 149(a)" for "section 103(j)" in para. (b)(1), effective for bonds issued after 8/15/86.
In 1982, P.L. 97-248, Sec. 310(b)(4)(A), added Code Sec. 4701, effective for obligations issued after 12/31/82. Sec. 310(d)(1)(3) of this Act provides:
"(3) Exception for certain warrants, etc. The amendments made by subsection (b) shall not apply to any obligations issued after December 31, 1982, on the exercise of a warrant or the conversion of a convertible obligation if such warrant or obligation was offered or sold outside the United States without registration under the Securities Act of 1933 and was issued before August 10, 1982. A rule similar to the rule of the preceding sentence shall also apply in the case of any regulations issued under section 163(f)(2)(C) of the Internal Revenue Code of 1954 (as added by this section) except that the date on which such regulations take effect shall be substituted for 'August 10, 1982'."

CHAPTER 40.—GENERAL PROVISIONS RELATING TO OCCUPATIONAL TAXES

Sec.
4901. Payment of tax.
4902. Liability of partners.
4903. Liability in case of business in more than one location.
4904. Liability in case of different businesses of same ownership and location.
4905. Liability in case of death or change of location.
4906. Application of State laws.
4907. Federal agencies or instrumentalities.

Sec. 4901. Payment of tax.

(a) Condition precedent to carrying on certain business.

No person shall be engaged in or carry on any trade or business subject to the tax imposed by section 4411 (wagering) until he has paid the special tax therefor.

(b) Computation.

All special taxes shall be imposed as of on the first day of July in each year, or on commencing any trade or business on which such tax is imposed. In the former case the tax shall be reckoned for 1 year, and in the latter case it shall be reckoned proportionately, from the first day of the month in which the liability to a special tax commenced, to and including the 30th day of June following.

In 1978, P.L. 95-600, Sec. 521(c)(2), deleted "or 4461(a)(1) (coin operated gaming devices)" following "(wagering)" in subsec. (a), effective for yrs. begin. after 6/30/80.
In 1976, P.L. 94-455, Sec. 1904(a)(19), deleted subsec. (c), effective 2/1/77.
Prior to deletion, subsec. (c) read as follows:
"(c) How paid.
"(1) Stamp. All special taxes imposed by law shall be paid by stamps denoting the tax.
"(2) Assessment. For authority of the Secretary or his delegate to make assessments where the special taxes have not been duly paid by stamp at the time and in the manner provided by law, see subtitle F."
In 1970, P.L. 91-513, Sec. 1102(a), substituted "or 4461(a)(1)" for ", 4461(a)(1)" and deleted ", 4721 (narcotic drugs), or 4751 (marihuana)" after "(gaming devices)" in subsec. (a), effective 5/1/71.
In 1965, P.L. 89-44, Sec. 405(b), substituted "4461(a)(1)" for "4461(2)" in subsec. (a), effective 7/1/65.

Sec. 4902. Liability of partners.

Any number of persons doing business in copartnership at any one place shall be liable to pay but one special tax.

Sec. 4903. Liability in case of business in more than one location.

The payment of the special tax imposed, other than the tax imposed by section 4411, shall not exempt from an additional special tax the person carrying on a trade or business in any other place than that stated in the register kept in the office of the official in charge of the internal revenue district; but nothing herein contained shall require a special tax for the storage of goods, wares, or merchandise in other places than the place of business, nor, except as provided in this subtitle, for the sale by manufacturers or producers of their own goods, wares, and merchandise, at the place of production or manufacture, and at their principal office or place of business, provided no goods, wares, or merchandise shall be kept except as samples at said office or place of business.

Sec. 4904. Liability in case of different businesses of same ownership and location.

Whenever more than one of the pursuits or occupations described in this subtitle are carried on in the same place by the same person at the same time, except as otherwise provided in this subtitle, the tax shall be paid for each according to the rates severally prescribed.

Sec. 4905. Liability in case of death or change of location.

(a) Requirements.

When any person who has paid the special tax for any trade or business dies, his spouse or child, or executors or administrators or other legal representatives, may occupy the house or premises, and in like manner carry on, for the residue of the term for which the tax is paid, the same trade or

3,287

business as the deceased before carried on, in the same house and upon the same premises, without the payment of any additional tax. When any person removes from the house or premises for which any trade or business was taxed to any other place, he may carry on the trade or business specified in the register kept in the office of the official in charge of the internal revenue district at the place to which he removes, without the payment of any additional tax: *Provided,* That all cases of death, change, or removal, as aforesaid, with the name of the successor to any person deceased, or of the person making such change or removal, shall be registered with the Secretary, under regulations to be prescribed by the Secretary.

(b) Registration.

For registration in case of wagering, see section 4412.

In 1976, P.L. 94-455, Sec. 1904(a)(20), substituted "spouse" for "wife" in subsec. (a)... Sec. 1904(b)(8)(A), amended subsec. (b), effective 2/1/77.
Prior to amendment, subsec. (b) read as follows:
"*(b) Registration.*
"(1) For registration in case of wagering and white phosphorous matches, see sections 4412 and 4804(d), respectively.
"(2) For other provisions relating to registration, see subtitle F."
—P.L. 94-455, Sec. 1906(b)(13)(A), substituted "Secretary" for "Secretary or his delegate" each place it appeared in Code Sec. 4905, effective 2/1/77.
In 1970, P.L. 91-513, Sec. 1102(b), deleted "narcotics, marihuana," after "wagering" and deleted ", 4722, 4753," after "4412", in para. (b)(1), effective 5/1/71.
In 1965, P.L. 89-44, Sec. 405(c), deleted "playing cards" after "wagering", and deleted "4455" after "4412" in para. (b)(1), effective 6/22/65.

Sec. 4906. Application of State laws.

The payment of any special tax imposed by this subtitle for carrying on any trade or business shall not be held to exempt any person from any penalty or punishment provided by the laws of any State for carrying on the same within such State, or in any manner to authorize the commencement or continuance of such trade or business contrary to the laws of such State or in places prohibited by municipal law; nor shall the payment of any such tax be held to prohibit any State from placing a duty or tax on the same trade or business, for State or other purposes.

Sec. 4907. Federal agencies or instrumentalities.

Any special tax imposed by this subtitle, except the tax imposed by section 4411, shall apply to any agency or instrumentality of the United States unless such agency or instrumentality is granted by statute a specific exemption from such tax.

CHAPTER 41.—PUBLIC CHARITIES

Sec.
4911. Tax on excess expenditures to influence legislation.
4912. Tax on disqualifying lobbying expenditures of certain organizations.

In 1987, P.L. 100-203, Sec. 10714(d), added item 4912.
In 1976, P.L. 94-455, Sec. 1307(b), added chapter 41, for tax. yrs. begin. after '76.

Sec. 4911. Tax on excess expenditures to influence legislation.

(a) Tax imposed.

(1) In general. There is hereby imposed on the excess lobbying expenditures of any organization to which this section applies a tax equal to 25 percent of the amount of the excess lobbying expenditures for the taxable year.

(2) Organizations to which this section applies. This section applies to any organization with respect to which an election under section 501(h) (relating to lobbying expenditures by public charities) is in effect for the taxable year.

(b) Excess lobbying expenditures.

For purposes of this section, the term "excess lobbying expenditures" means, for a taxable year, the greater of—

(1) the amount by which the lobbying expenditures made by the organization during the taxable year exceed the lobbying nontaxable amount for such organization for such taxable year, or

(2) the amount by which the grass roots expenditures made by the organization during the taxable year exceed the grass roots nontaxable amount for such organization for such taxable year.

(c) Definitions.

For purposes of this section—

(1) Lobbying expenditures. The term "lobbying expenditures" means expenditures for the purpose of influencing legislation (as defined in subsection (d)).

(2) Lobbying nontaxable amount. The lobbying nontaxable amount for any organization for any taxable year is the lesser of (A) $1,000,000 or (B) the amount determined under the following table:

If the exempt purpose expenditures are—	The lobbying nontaxable amount is—
Not over $500,000	20 percent of the exempt purpose expenditures.
Over $500,000 but not over $1,000,000	$100,000, plus 15 percent of the excess of the exempt purpose expenditures over $500,000.
Over $1,000,000 but not over $1,500,000	$175,000 plus 10 percent of the excess of the exempt purpose expenditures over $1,000,000.
Over $1,500,000	$225,000 plus 5 percent of the excess of the exempt purpose expenditures over $1,500,000.

(3) Grass roots expenditures. The term "grass roots expenditures" means expenditures for the purpose of influencing legislation (as defined in subsection (d) without regard to paragraph (1)(B) thereof).

(4) Grass roots nontaxable amount. The grass roots nontaxable amount for any organization for any taxable year is 25 percent of the lobbying nontaxable amount (determined under paragraph (2)) for such organization for such taxable year.

(d) Influencing legislation.

(1) General rule. Except as otherwise provided in paragraph (2), for purposes of this section, the term "influencing legislation" means—

(A) any attempt to influence any legislation through an attempt to affect the opinions of the general public or any segment thereof, and

(B) any attempt to influence any legislation through communication with any member or employee of a legislative body, or with any government official or employee who may participate in the formulation of the legislation.

(2) Exceptions. For purposes of this section, the term "influencing legislation", with respect to an organization, does not include—

(A) making available the results of nonpartisan analysis, study, or research;
(B) providing of technical advice or assistance (where such advice would otherwise constitute the influencing of legislation) to a governmental body or to a committee or other subdivision thereof in response to a written request by such body or subdivision, as the case may be;
(C) appearances before, or communications to, any legislative body with respect to a possible decision of such body which might affect the existence of the organization, its powers and duties, tax-exempt status, or the deduction of contributions to the organization;
(D) communications between the organization and its bona fide members with respect to legislation or proposed legislation of direct interest to the organization and such members, other than communications described in paragraph (3); and
(E) any communication with a government official or employee, other than—
  (i) a communication with a member or employee of a legislative body (where such communication would otherwise constitute the influencing of legislation), or
  (ii) a communication the principal purpose of which is to influence legislation.
(3) Communications with members.
(A) A communication between an organization and any bona fide member of such organization to directly encourage such member to communicate as provided in paragraph (1)(B) shall be treated as a communication described in paragraph (1)(B).
(B) A communication between an organization and any bona fide member of such organization to directly encourage such member to urge persons other than members to communicate as provided in either subparagraph (A) or subparagraph (B) of paragraph (1) shall be treated as a communication described in paragraph (1)(A).
(e) Other definitions and special rules.
For purposes of this section—
(1) Exempt purpose expenditures.
(A) In general. The term "exempt purpose expenditures" means, with respect to any organization for any taxable year, the total of the amounts paid or incurred by such organization to accomplish purposes described in section 170(c)(2)(B) (relating to religious, charitable, educational, etc., purposes).
(B) Certain amounts included. The term "exempt purpose expenditures" includes—
  (i) administrative expenses paid or incurred for purposes described in section 170(c)(2)(B), and
  (ii) amounts paid or incurred for the purpose of influencing legislation (whether or not for purposes described in section 170(c)(2)(B)).
(C) Certain amounts excluded. The term "exempt purpose expenditures" does not include amounts paid or incurred to or for—
  (i) a separate fundraising unit of such organization, or
  (ii) one or more other organizations, if such amounts are paid or incurred primarily for fundraising.
(2) Legislation. The term "legislation" includes action with respect to Acts, bills, resolutions, or similar items by the Congress, any State legislature, any local council, or similar governing body, or by the public in a referendum, initiative, constitutional amendment, or similar procedure.

(3) Action. The term "action" is limited to the introduction, amendment, enactment, defeat, or repeal of Acts, bills, resolutions, or similar items.
(4) Depreciation, etc., treated as expenditures. In computing expenditures paid or incurred for the purpose of influencing legislation (within the meaning of subsection (b)(1) or (b)(2)) or exempt purpose expenditures (as defined in paragraph (1)), amounts properly chargeable to capital account shall not be taken into account. There shall be taken into account a reasonable allowance for exhaustion, wear and tear, obsolescence, or amortization. Such allowance shall be computed only on the basis of the straight-line method of depreciation. For purposes of this section, a determination of whether an amount is properly chargeable to capital account shall be made on the basis of the principles that apply under subtitle A to amounts which are paid or incurred in a trade or business.
(f) Affiliated organizations.
(1) In general. Except as otherwise provided in paragraph (4), if for a taxable year two or more organizations described in section 501(c)(3) are members of an affiliated group of organizations as defined in paragraph (2), and an election under section 501(h) is effective for at least one such organization for such year, then—
(A) the determination as to whether excess lobbying expenditures have been made and the determination as to whether the expenditure limits of section 501(h)(1) have been exceeded shall be made as though such affiliated group is one organization,
(B) if such group has excess lobbying expenditures, each such organization as to which an election under section 501(h) is effective for such year shall be treated as an organization which has excess lobbying expenditures in an amount which equals such organization's proportionate share of such group's excess lobbying expenditures,
(C) if the expenditure limits of section 501(h)(1) are exceeded, each such organization as to which an election under section 501(h) is effective for such year shall be treated as an organization which is not described in section 501(c)(3) by reason of the application of 501(h), and
(D) subparagraphs (C) and (D) of subsection (d)(2), paragraph (3) of subsection (d), and clause (i) of subsection (e)(1)(C) shall be applied as if such affiliated group were one organization.
(2) Definition of affiliation. For purposes of paragraph (1), two organizations are members of an affiliated group of organizations but only if—
(A) the governing instrument of one such organization requires it to be bound by decisions of the other organization on legislative issues, or
(B) the governing board of one such organization includes persons who—
  (i) are specifically designated representatives of another such organization or are members of the governing board, officers, or paid executive staff members of such other organization, and
  (ii) by aggregating their votes, have sufficient voting power to cause or prevent action on legislative issues by the first such organization.
(3) Different taxable years. If members of an affiliated group of organizations have different taxable years, their expenditures shall be computed for purposes of this section in a manner to be prescribed by regulations promulgated by the Secretary.

(4) Limited control. If two or more organizations are members of an affiliated group of organizations (as defined in paragraph (2) without regard to subparagraph (B) thereof), no two members of such affiliated group are affiliated (as defined in paragraph (2) without regard to subparagraph (A) thereof), and the governing instrument of no such organization requires it to be bound by decisions of any of the other such organizations on legislative issues other than as to action with respect to Acts, bills, resolutions, or similar items by the Congress, then—

(A) in the case of any organization whose decisions bind one or more members of such affiliated group, directly or indirectly, the determination as to whether such organization has paid or incurred excess lobbying expenditures and the determination as to whether such organization has exceeded the expenditure limits of section 501(h)(1) shall be made as though such organization has paid or incurred those amounts paid or incurred by such members of such affiliated group to influence legislation with respect to Acts, bills, resolutions, or similar items by the Congress, and

(B) in the case of any organization to which subparagraph (A) does not apply, but which is a member of such affiliated group, the determination as to whether such organization has paid or incurred excess lobbying expenditures and the determination as to whether such organization has exceeded the expenditure limits of section 501(h)(1) shall be made as though such organization is not a member of such affiliated group.

In **1978**, P.L. 95-600, Sec. 703(g)(1), substituted "exempt purpose expenditures" for "proposed expenditures" in the heading of the table appearing in para. (c)(2), effective 10/4/76.

In **1976**, P.L. 94-455, Sec. 1307(b), added Code Sec. 4911, effective for tax. yrs. begin. after 12/31/76.

Sec. 4912. Tax on disqualifying lobbying expenditures of certain organizations.
(a) Tax on organization.
If an organization to which this section applies is not described in section 501(c)(3) for any taxable year by reason of making lobbying expenditures, there is hereby imposed a tax on the lobbying expenditures of such organization for such taxable year equal to 5 percent of the amount of such expenditures. The tax imposed by this subsection shall be paid by the organization.
(b) On management.
If tax is imposed under subsection (a) on the lobbying expenditures of any organization, there is hereby imposed on the agreement of any organization manager to the making of any such expenditures, knowing that such expenditures are likely to result in the organization not being described in section 501(c)(3), a tax equal to 5 percent of the amount of such expenditures, unless such agreement is not willful and is due to reasonable cause. The tax imposed by this subsection shall be paid by any manager who agreed to the making of the expenditures.
(c) Organizations to which section applies.
(1) In general. Except as provided in paragraph (2), this section shall apply to any organization which was exempt (or was determined by the Secretary to be exempt) from taxation under section 501(a) by reason of being an organization described in section 501(c)(3).
(2) Exceptions. This section shall not apply to any organization—
(A) to which an election under section 501(h) applies,
(B) which is a disqualified organization (within the meaning of section 501(h)(5)), or

(C) which is a private foundation.
(d) Definitions.
(1) Lobbying expenditures. The term "lobbying expenditure" means any amount paid or incurred by the organization in carrying on propaganda, or otherwise attempting to influence legislation.
(2) Organization manager. The term "organization manager" has the meaning given to such term by section 4955(f)(2).
(3) Joint and several liability. If more than 1 person is liable under subsection (b), all such persons shall be jointly and severally liable under such subsection.

In **1987**, P.L. 100-203, Sec. 10714(a), added Code Sec. 4912, effective for tax. yrs. begin. after 12/22/87.

CHAPTER 42.—PRIVATE FOUNDATIONS AND CERTAIN OTHER TAX-EXEMPT ORGANIZATIONS

Subchapter
A. Private Foundations
B. Black lung Benefit trusts
C. Political expenditures of section 501(c)(3) organizations.
D. Failure by certain charitable organizations to meet certain qualification requirements.
E. Abatement of first and second-tier taxes in certain cases.
F. Tax shelter transactions.
G. Donor Advised funds.

In **2006**, P.L. 109-280, Sec. 1231(b)(2), added Subchapter G.
— P.L. 109-222, Sec. 516(a)(1), added Subchapter F.
In **1996**, P.L. 104-168, Sec. 1311(c)(6), amended item D and added item E.
Prior to amendment, item D read as follows:
"Subchapter D. Abatement of first and second-tier taxes in certain cases."
In **1987**, P.L. 100-203, Sec. 10712(c)(7), amended the heading of Chapter 42... Sec. 10712(c)(9), amended the item for subchapter C and added the item for subchapter D.
Prior to amendment, the heading of Chapter 42 read as follows:
"Chapter 42—Private Foundations: Black Lung Benefit Trusts"
Prior to amendment, the item for subchapter C read as follows:
"C. Abatement of first and second tier taxes in certain cases."
In **1984**, P.L. 98-369, Sec. 305(b)(3), amended the item for subchapter C.
Prior to amendment the item for subchapter C read as follows:
"C. Abatement of second tier taxes where there is correction during correction period."

Subchapter A.—Private Foundations
Sec.
4940. Excise tax based on investment income.
4941. Taxes on self-dealing.
4942. Taxes on failure to distribute income.
4943. Taxes on excess business holdings.
4944. Taxes on investments which jeopardize charitable purpose.
4945. Taxes on taxable expenditures.
4946. Definitions and special rules.
4947. Application of taxes to certain nonexempt trusts.
4948. Application of taxes and denial of exemption with respect to certain foreign organizations.

In **1978**, P.L. 95-227, Sec. 4(c)(2)(A), amended the heading of Chapter 42 and added the items for subchapters A and B.
Prior to amendment, the heading of Chapter 42 read as follows:
"Chapter 42—Private foundations".
In **1969**, P.L. 91-172, Sec. 101(b), added Chapter 42.

Excise and miscellaneous taxes

Sec. 4940. Excise tax based on investment income.
(a) Tax-exempt foundations.
There is hereby imposed on each private foundation which is exempt from taxation under section 501(a) for the taxable year, with respect to the carrying on of its activities, a tax equal to 2 percent of the net investment income of such foundation for the taxable year.
(b) Taxable foundations.
There is hereby imposed on each private foundation which is not exempt from taxation under section 501(a) for the taxable year, with respect to the carrying on of its activities, a tax equal to—
(1) the amount (if any) by which the sum of (A) the tax imposed under subsection (a) (computed as if such subsection applied to such private foundation for the taxable year), plus (B) the amount of the tax which would have been imposed under section 511 for the taxable year if such private foundation had been exempt from taxation under section 501(a), exceeds
(2) the tax imposed under subtitle A on such private foundation for the taxable year.
(c) Net investment income defined.
(1) In general. For purposes of subsection (a), the net investment income is the amount by which (A) the sum of the gross investment income and the capital gain net income exceeds (B) the deductions allowed by paragraph (3). Except to the extent inconsistent with the provisions of this section, net investment income shall be determined under the principles of subtitle A.
(2) Gross investment income. For purposes of paragraph (1), the term "gross investment income" means the gross amount of income from interest, dividends, rents, payments with respect to securities loans (as defined in section 512(a)(5)), and royalties, but not including any such income to the extent included in computing the tax imposed by section 511. Such term shall also include income from sources similar to those in the preceding sentence.
(3) Deductions.
(A) In general. For purposes of paragraph (1), there shall be allowed as a deduction all the ordinary and necessary expenses paid or incurred for the production or collection of gross investment income or for the management, conservation, or maintenance of property held for the production of such income, determined with the modifications set forth in subparagraph (B).
(B) Modifications. For purposes of subparagraph (A)—
(i) The deduction provided by section 167 shall be allowed, but only on the basis of the straight line method of depreciation.
(ii) The deduction for depletion provided by section 611 shall be allowed, but such deduction shall be determined without regard to section 613 (relating to percentage depletion).
(4) Capital gains and losses. For purposes of paragraph (1) in determining capital gain net income—
(A) There shall not be taken into account any gain or loss from the sale or other disposition of property to the extent that such gain or loss is taken into account for purposes of computing the tax imposed by section 511.
(B) The basis for determining gain in the case of property held by the private foundation on December 31, 1969, and continuously thereafter to the date of its disposition shall be deemed to be not less than the fair market value of such property on December 31, 1969.
(C) Losses from sales or other dispositions of property shall be allowed only to the extent of gains from such sales or other dispositions, and there shall be no capital loss carryovers or carrybacks.
(D) Except to the extent provided by regulation, under rules similar to the rules of section 1031 (including the exception under subsection (a)(2) thereof), no gain or loss shall be taken into account with respect to any portion of property used for a period of not less than 1 year for a purpose or function constituting the basis of the private foundation's exemption if the entire property is exchanged immediately following such period solely for property of like kind which is to be used primarily for a purpose or function constituting the basis for such foundation's exemption.
(5) Tax-exempt income. For purposes of this section, net investment income shall be determined by applying section 103 (relating to State and local bonds) and section 265 (relating to expenses and interest relating to tax-exempt income).
(d) Exemption for certain operating foundations.
(1) In general. No tax shall be imposed by this section on any private foundation which is an exempt operating foundation for the taxable year.
(2) Exempt operating foundation. For purposes of this subsection, the term "exempt operating foundation" means, with respect to any taxable year, any private foundation if—
(A) such foundation is an operating foundation (as defined in section 4942(j)(3)),
(B) such foundation has been publicly supported for at least 10 taxable years,
(C) at all times during the taxable year, the governing body of such foundation—
(i) consists of individuals at least 75 percent of whom are not disqualified individuals, and
(ii) is broadly representative of the general public, and
(D) at no time during the taxable year does such foundation have an officer who is a disqualified individual.
(3) Definitions. For purposes of this subsection—
(A) Publicly supported. A private foundation is publicly supported for a taxable year if it meets the requirements of section 170(b)(1)(A)(vi) or 509(a)(2) for such taxable year.
(B) Disqualified individual. The term "disqualified individual" means, with respect to any private foundation, an individual who is—
(i) a substantial contributor to the foundation,
(ii) an owner of more than 20 percent of—
(I) the total combined voting power of a corporation,
(II) the profits interest of a partnership, or
(III) the beneficial interest of a trust or unincorporated enterprise,
which is a substantial contributor to the foundation, or
(iii) a member of the family of any individual described in clause (i) or (ii).
(C) Substantial contributor. The term "substantial contributor" means a person who is described in section 507(d)(2).
(D) Family. The term "family" has the meaning given to such term by section 4946(d).
(E) Constructive ownership. The rules of paragraphs (3) and (4) of section 4946(a) shall apply for purposes of subparagraph (B)(ii).

Code Sec. 4940(e) — Excise and miscellaneous taxes

(e) Reduction in tax where private foundation meets certain distribution requirements.

(1) In general. In the case of any private foundation which meets the requirements of paragraph (2) for any taxable year, subsection (a) shall be applied with respect to such taxable year by substituting "1 percent" for "2 percent".

(2) Requirements. A private foundation meets the requirements of this paragraph for any taxable year if—

(A) the amount of the qualifying distributions made by the private foundation during such taxable year equals or exceeds the sum of—

(i) an amount equal to the assets of such foundation for such taxable year multiplied by the average percentage payout for the base period, plus

(ii) 1 percent of the net investment income of such foundation for such taxable year, and

(B) such private foundation was not liable for tax under section 4942 with respect to any year in the base period.

(3) Average percentage payout for base period. For purposes of this subsection—

(A) In general. The average percentage payout for the base period is the average of the percentage payouts for taxable years in the base period.

(B) Percentage payout. The term "percentage payout" means, with respect to any taxable year, the percentage determined by dividing—

(i) the amount of the qualifying distributions made by the private foundation during the taxable year, by

(ii) the assets of the private foundation for the taxable year.

(C) Special rule where tax reduced under this subsection. For purposes of this paragraph, if the amount of the tax imposed by this section for any taxable year in the base period is reduced by reason of this subsection, the amount of the qualifying distributions made by the private foundation during such year shall be reduced by the amount of such reduction in tax.

(4) Base period. For purposes of this subsection—

(A) In general. The term "base period" means, with respect to any taxable year, the 5 taxable years preceding such taxable year.

(B) New private foundations, etc. If an organization has not been a private foundation throughout the base period referred to in subparagraph (A), the base period shall consist of the taxable years during which such foundation has been in existence.

(5) Other definitions. For purposes of this subsection—

(A) Qualifying distribution. The term "qualifying distribution" has the meaning given such term by section 4942(g).

(B) Assets. The assets of a private foundation for any taxable year shall be treated as equal to the excess determined under section 4942(e)(1).

(6) Treatment of successor organizations, etc. In the case of—

(A) a private foundation which is a successor to another private foundation, this subsection shall be applied with respect to such successor by taking into account the experience of such other foundation, and

(B) a merger, reorganization, or division of a private foundation, this subsection shall be applied under regulations prescribed by the Secretary.

In **2007**, P.L. 110-172, Sec. 3(f), amended subpara. (c)(4)(A), effective for tax. yrs. begin. after 8/17/2006.

Prior to amendment, subpara. (c)(4)(A), read as follows

"(A)There shall be taken into account only gains and losses from the sale or other disposition of property used for the production of gross investment income (as defined in paragraph (2)), and property used for the production of income included in computing the tax imposed by section 511 (except to the extent gain or loss from the sale or other disposition of such property is taken into account for purposes of such tax)."

In **2006**, P.L. 109-280, Sec. 1221(a)(1), added "Such term shall also include income from sources similar to those in the preceding sentence." at the end of para. (c)(2)... Sec. 1221(b)(1), substituted "used for the production of gross investment income (as defined in paragraph (2))" for "used for the production of interest, dividends, rents, and royalties" in subpara. (c)(4)(A)... Sec. 1221(b)(2), added "or carrybacks" after "carryovers" in subpara. (c)(4)(C)... Sec. 1221(b)(3), added subpara. (c)(4)(D), effective for tax. yrs. begin. after 8/17/2006.

In **1988**, P.L. 100-647, Sec. 6204, provides:

"SEC. 6204. DETERMINATION OF OPERATING FOUNDATION STATUS FOR CERTAIN PURPOSES.

For purposes of section 302(c)(3) of the Deficit Reduction Act [Sec. 302(c)(3) of P.L. 98-369, reproduced below] of 1984, a private foundation which constituted an operating foundation (as defined in section 4942(j)(3) of the Internal Revenue Code of 1986) for its last taxable year ending before January 1, 1983, shall be treated as constituting an operating foundation as of January 1, 1983."

In **1986**, P.L. 99-514, Sec. 1301(j)(6), substituted "(relating to State and local bonds)" for "(relating to interest on certain governmental obligations)" in para. (c)(5), effective for bonds issued after 8/15/86.

—P.L. 99-514, Sec. 1832, amended subpara. (e)(2)(B) and the material at the end of para. (e)(2), effective for tax. yrs. begin. after 12/31/84.

Prior to amendment, subpara. (e)(2)(B) and the material at the end of para. (e)(2) read as follows:

"(B) the average percentage payout for the base period equals or exceeds 5 percent.

"In the case of an operating foundation (as defined in section 4942(j)(3)), subparagraph (B) shall be applied by substituting '2½ percent' for '5 percent'."

In **1984**, P.L. 98-369, Sec. 302(a), added subsec. (d), effective for tax. yrs. begin. after 12/31/84. Sec 302(c)(3) of the Act provides:

"(3) Certain existing foundations.—A foundation which was an operating foundation (as defined in section 4942(j)(3) of the Internal Revenue Code of 1954) as of January 1, 1983, shall be treated as meeting the requirements of section 4940(d)(2)(B) of such Code (as added by subsection (a))."

—P.L. 98-369, Sec. 303(a), added subsec. (e), effective for tax. yrs. begin. after 12/31/84.

In **1978**, P.L. 95-600, Sec. 520(a), substituted "2 percent" for "4 percent" in subsec. (a), effective for tax. yrs. begin. after 9/30/77.

—P.L. 95-345, Sec. 2(a)(4), added "payments with respect to securities loans (as defined in section 512(a)(5))," after "rents," in para. (c)(2), effective for amounts received after 12/31/76 as payments with respect to securities loans (as defined in Code Sec. 512(a)(5)) and transfers of securities, under agreements described in Code Sec. 1058.

In **1976**, P.L. 94-455, Sec. 1901(b)(33)(N), substituted "capital gain net income" for "net capital gain" in para. (c)(1) and in para. (c)(4), effective for tax. yrs. begin. after 12/31/76.

In **1969**, P.L. 91-172, Sec. 101(b), added Code Sec. 4940, effective for tax. yrs. begin. after 12/31/69, Sec. 101(l)(8) provides as follows:

"(8) Certain redemptions—For purposes of applying section 302(b)(1) to the determination of the amount of gross investment income under sections 4940 and 4948(a) any distribution made to a private foundation in redemption of stock held by such foundation in a business enterprise shall be treated as not essentially equivalent to a dividend, if such redemption is described in paragraph (2)(B) of this subsection" [see note following Code Sec. 4941].

Sec. 4941. Taxes on self-dealing.

(a) Initial taxes.

(1) On self-dealer. There is hereby imposed a tax on each act of self-dealing between a disqualified person and a private foundation. The rate of tax shall be equal to 10 percent of the amount involved with respect to the act of self-dealing for each year (or part thereof) in the taxable period. The tax imposed by this paragraph shall be paid by any disqualified person (other than a foundation manager acting only as such) who participates in the act of self-dealing. In the case of a government official (as defined in section 4946(c)), a tax shall be imposed by this paragraph only if such disqualified person participates in the act of self-dealing knowing that it is such an act.

(2) On foundation manager. In any case in which a tax is imposed by paragraph (1), there is hereby imposed on the participation of any foundation manager in an act of self-dealing between a disqualified person and a private foundation, knowing that it is such an act, a tax equal to 5 percent of the amount involved with respect to the act of self-dealing for each year (or part thereof) in the taxable period, unless such participation is not willful and is due to reasonable cause. The tax imposed by this paragraph shall be paid by any foundation manager who participated in the act of self-dealing.

(b) Additional taxes.

(1) On self-dealer. In any case in which an initial tax is imposed by subsection (a)(1) on an act of self-dealing by a disqualified person with a private foundation and the act is not corrected within the taxable period, there is hereby imposed a tax equal to 200 percent of the amount involved. The tax imposed by this paragraph shall be paid by any disqualified person (other than a foundation manager acting only as such) who participated in the act of self-dealing.

(2) On foundation manager. In any case in which an additional tax is imposed by paragraph (1), if a foundation manager refused to agree to part or all of the correction, there is hereby imposed a tax equal to 50 percent of the amount involved. The tax imposed by this paragraph shall be paid by any foundation manager who refused to agree to part or all of the correction.

(c) Special rules.

For purposes of subsections (a) and (b)—

(1) Joint and several liability. If more than one person is liable under any paragraph of subsection (a) or (b) with respect to any one act of self-dealing, all such persons shall be jointly and severally liable under such paragraph with respect to such act.

(2) $20,000 limit for management. With respect to any one act of self-dealing, the maximum amount of the tax imposed by subsection (a)(2) shall not exceed $20,000, and the maximum amount of the tax imposed by subsection (b)(2) shall not exceed $20,000.

(d) Self-dealing.

(1) In general. For purposes of this section, the term "self-dealing" means any direct or indirect—

(A) sale or exchange, or leasing, of property between a private foundation and a disqualified person;

(B) lending of money or other extension of credit between a private foundation and a disqualified person;

(C) furnishing of goods, services, or facilities between a private foundation and a disqualified person;

(D) payment of compensation (or payment or reimbursement of expenses) by a private foundation to a disqualified person;

(E) transfer to, or use by or for the benefit of, a disqualified person of the income or assets of a private foundation; and

(F) agreement by a private foundation to make any payment of money or other property to a government official (as defined in section 4946(c)), other than an agreement to employ such individual for any period after the termination of his government service if such individual is terminating his government service within a 90-day period.

(2) Special rules. For purposes of paragraph (1)—

(A) the transfer of real or personal property by a disqualified person to a private foundation shall be treated as a sale or exchange if the property is subject to a mortgage or similar lien which the foundation assumes or if it is subject to a mortgage or similar lien which a disqualified person placed on the property within the 10-year period ending on the date of the transfer;

(B) the lending of money by a disqualified person to a private foundation shall not be an act of self-dealing if the loan is without interest or other charge (determined without regard to section 7872) and if the proceeds of the loan are used exclusively for purposes specified in section 501(c)(3);

(C) the furnishing of goods, services, or facilities by a disqualified person to a private foundation shall not be an act of self-dealing if the furnishing is without charge and if the goods, services, or facilities so furnished are used exclusively for purposes specified in section 501(c)(3);

(D) the furnishing of goods, services, or facilities by a private foundation to a disqualified person shall not be an act of self-dealing if such furnishing is made on a basis no more favorable than that on which such goods, services, or facilities are made available to the general public;

(E) except in the case of a government official (as defined in section 4946(c)), the payment of compensation (and the payment or reimbursement of expenses) by a private foundation to a disqualified person for personal services which are reasonable and necessary to carrying out the exempt purpose of the private foundation shall not be an act of self-dealing if the compensation (or payment or reimbursement) is not excessive;

(F) any transaction between a private foundation and a corporation which is a disqualified person (as defined in section 4946(a)), pursuant to any liquidation, merger, redemption, recapitalization, or other corporate adjustment, organization, or reorganization, shall not be an act of self-dealing if all of the securities of the same class as that held by the foundation are subject to the same terms and such terms provide for receipt by the foundation of no less than fair market value;

(G) in the case of a government official (as defined in section 4946(c)), paragraph (1) shall in addition not apply to—

(i) prizes and awards which are subject to the provisions of section 74(b) (without regard to paragraph (3) thereof), if the recipients of such prizes and awards are selected from the general public,

(ii) scholarships and fellowship grants which would be subject to the provisions of section 117(a) (as in effect on the day before the date of the enactment [10/22/86] of the Tax Reform Act of 1986) and are to be used for study at an educational organization described in section 170(b)(1)(A)(ii),

(iii) any annuity or other payment (forming part of a stock-bonus, pension, or profit-sharing plan) by a trust which is a qualified trust under section 401,

(iv) any annuity or other payment under a plan which meets the requirements of section 404(a)(2),

(v) any contribution or gift (other than a contribution or gift of money) to, or services or facilities made available to, any such individual, if the aggregate value of such contributions, gifts, services, and facilities to, or made available to, such individual during any calendar year does not exceed $25,

(vi) any payment made under chapter 41 of title 5, United States Code, or

(vii) any payment or reimbursement of traveling expenses for travel solely from one point in the United States to another point in the United States, but only if such payment or reimbursement does not exceed the actual cost of the transportation involved plus an amount for all other traveling expenses not in excess of 125 percent of the maximum amount payable under section 5702 of title 5, United States Code, for like travel by employees of the United States; and

(H) the leasing by a disqualified person to a private foundation of office space for use by the foundation in a building with other tenants who are not disqualified persons shall not be treated as an act of self-dealing if—

(i) such leasing of office space is pursuant to a binding lease which was in effect on October 9, 1969, or pursuant to renewals of such a lease;

(ii) the execution of such lease was not a prohibited transaction (within the meaning of section 503(b) or any corresponding provision of prior law) at the time of such execution; and

(iii) the terms of the lease (or any renewal) reflect an arm's-length transaction.

(e) Other definitions.

For purposes of this section—

(1) Taxable period. The term "taxable period" means, with respect to any act of self-dealing, the period beginning with the date on which the act of self-dealing occurs and ending on the earliest of—

(A) the date of mailing a notice of deficiency with respect to the tax imposed by subsection (a)(1) under section 6212,

(B) the date on which the tax imposed by subsection (a)(1) is assessed, or

(C) the date on which correction of the act of self-dealing is completed.

(2) Amount involved. The term "amount involved" means, with respect to any act of self-dealing, the greater of the amount of money and the fair market value of the other property given or the amount of money and the fair market value of the other property received; except that, in the case of services described in subsection (d)(2)(E), the amount involved shall be only the excess compensation. For purposes of the preceding sentence, the fair market value—

(A) in the case of the taxes imposed by subsection (a), shall be determined as of the date on which the act of self-dealing occurs; and

(B) in the case of the taxes imposed by subsection (b), shall be the highest fair market value during the taxable period.

(3) Correction. The terms "correction" and "correct" mean, with respect to any act of self-dealing, undoing the transaction to the extent possible, but in any case placing the private foundation in a financial position not worse than that in which it would be if the disqualified person were dealing under the highest fiduciary standards.

In 2006, P.L. 109-280, Sec. 1212(a)(1)(A), substituted "10 percent" for "5 percent" in para. (a)(1) . . . Sec. 1212(a)(1)(B), substituted "5 percent" for "2½ percent" in para. (a)(2) . . . Sec. 1212(a)(2), substituted "$20,000" for "$10,000" each place it appeared in para. (c)(2), effective for tax. yrs. begin. after 8/17/2006.

In 1988, P.L. 100-647, Sec. 1001(d)(1)(A), amended clause (d)(2)(G)(ii), effective for tax. yrs. begin. after 12/31/86, but only in the case of scholarship and fellowships granted after 8/16/86.

Prior to amendment clause (d)(2)(G)(ii) read as follows:

"(ii) scholarships and fellowship grants which are subject to the provisions of section 117(a) and are to be used for study at an educational organization described in section 170(b)(1)(A)(ii),"

In 1986, P.L. 99-514, Sec. 122(a)(2)(A), substituted "section 74(b) (without regard to paragraph (3) thereof)" for "section 74(b)" in clause (d)(2)(G)(i), effective for prizes and awards granted after 12/31/86.

—P.L. 99-514, Sec. 1812(b)(1), substituted "without interest or other charge (determined without regard to section 7872)" for "without interest or other charge" in subpara. (d)(2)(B), effective as provided in Sec. 172(c) of P.L. 98-369, reproduced in note following Code Sec. 7872.

—P.L. 99-234, Sec. 107(c), substituted "5702" for "5702(a)" in clause (d)(2)(G)(vii), effective on the effective date of regulations passed by the Administrator of General Services [150 days after 1/2/86] or effective 180 days after 1/2/86 [date of enactment], whichever occurs first.

In 1984, P.L. 98-369, Sec. 312, provides:

"SEC. 312. TAX ON SELF-DEALING NOT TO APPLY TO CERTAIN STOCK PURCHASES.

"(a) General rule.—Section 4941 of the Internal Revenue Code of 1954 (relating to taxes on self-dealing) shall not apply to the purchase during 1978 of stock from a private foundation (and to any note issued in connection with such purchase) if—

"(1) consideration for such purchase equaled or exceeded the fair market value of such stock,

"(2) the purchaser of such stock did not make any contribution to such foundation at any time during the 5-year period ending on the date of such purchase,

"(3) the aggregate contributions to such foundation by the purchaser before such date were less than $10,000 and less than 2 percent of the total contributions received by the foundation as of such date, and

"(4) such purchase was pursuant to the settlement of litigation involving the purchaser.

"(b) Statute of limitations.—If credit or refund of any overpayment of tax resulting from subsection (a) is prevented at any time before the close of the 1-year period beginning on the date of the enactment of this Act by the operation of any law or rule of law, refund or credit of such overpayment may, nevertheless, be made or allowed if claim therefor is filed before the close of such 1-year period."

In 1980, P.L. 96-608, Sec. 5, deleted "and" at the end of subpara. (d)(2)(F), substituted "; and" for the period at the end of subpara. (d)(2)(G), and added subpara. (d)(2)(H), effective 12/28/80.

—P.L. 96-596, Sec. 2(a)(1)(A), and (B), substituted "taxable period" for "correction period" in para. (b)(1) and clause (e)(2)(B) . . . Sec. 2(a)(2)(A), amended para. (e)(1) . . . Sec. 2(a)(3)(A), deleted para. (e)(4), effective as provided in Sec. 2(d) of this Act which reads as follows:

"(d) Effective dates.

"(1) First tier taxes.—The amendments made by this section with respect to any first tier tax shall take effect as if included in the Internal Revenue Code of 1954 when such tax was first imposed.

"(2) Second tier taxes.—The amendments made by this section with respect to any second tier tax shall apply only with respect to taxes assessed after the date of the enactment of this Act. [12/24/80] Nothing in the preceding sentence shall be construed to permit the assessment of a tax in a case to which, on the date of the enactment of this Act [12/24/80] the doctrine of res judicata applies.

"(3) First and second tier tax.—For purposes of this subsection, the terms 'first tier tax' and 'second tier tax' have the respective meanings given to such terms by section 4962 of the Internal Revenue Code of 1954."

—P.L. 96-597, Sec. 2(a)(2)(A), amended para. (e)(1), effective 1/1/70. Prior to amendment para. (e)(1) read as follows:

"(1) Taxable period. The term 'taxable period' means, with respect to any act of self-dealing, the period beginning with the date on which the act of self-dealing occurs and ending on whichever of the following is the earlier: (A) the date of mailing of a notice of deficiency with respect to the tax imposed by subsection (a)(1) under section 6212, or (B) the date on which correction of the act of self-dealing is completed."

Prior to amendment para. (e)(4) read as follows:

"(4) Correction period. The term 'correction period' means, with respect to any act of self-dealing, the period beginning with the date on which the act of self-dealing occurs and ending 90 days after the date of mailing of a notice of deficiency with respect to the tax imposed by subsection (b)(1) under section 6212, extended by—

"(A) any period in which a deficiency cannot be assessed under section 6213(a), and

"(B) any other period which the Secretary determines is reasonable and necessary to bring about correction of the act of self-dealing."

Prior to amendment para. (e)(1) read as follows:

In 1976, P.L. 94-455, Sec. 1301(a), amended Sec. 101(l)(2) [see below] of P.L. 91-172 by deleting "and" at the end of Sec. 101(l)(2)(D) of P.L. 91-172, by substituting "; and" for the period at the end of Sec. 101(l)(2)(E) of P.L. 91-172 and by adding Sec. 101(l)(2)(F) of P.L. 91-172, effective for dispositions after 10/4/76 in tax. yrs. end. after 10/4/76.

—P.L. 99-455, Sec. 1309(a), amended Sec. 101(l)(2)(B) of P.L. 91-172 [see below] by substituting "January 1, 1977" for "January 1, 1975", effective for dispositions after 10/4/76.

—P.L. 94-455, Sec. 1901(b)(8)(H), substituted "educational organization described in section 170(b)(1)(A)(ii)" for "educational institution described in section 151(e)(4)" in clause (d)(2)(G)(ii), effective for tax. yrs. begin. after 12/31/76.

—P.L. 94-455, Sec. 1906(b)(13)(A), substituted "Secretary" for "Secretary or his delegate" in subpara. (e)(4)(B), effective 2/1/77.

In 1969, P.L. 91-172, Sec. 101(b), added Code Sec. 4941, effective 1/1/70 except as provided in Sec. 101(1)(2) [as amended by Sec. 1301(a) and Sec. 1309(a) of P.L. 94-455, see above] of this Act which reads as follows:

Section 4941 shall not apply to—

"(A) any transaction between a private foundation and a corporation which is a disqualified person (as defined in section 4946), pursuant to the terms of securities of such corporation in existence at the time acquired by the foundation, if such securities were acquired by the foundation before May 27, 1969;

"(B) the sale, exchange, or other disposition of property which is owned by a private foundation on May 26, 1969 (or which is acquired by a private foundation under the terms of a trust which was irrevocable on May 26, 1969, or under the terms of a will executed on or before such date, which are in effect on such date and at all times thereafter), to a disqualified person, if such foundation is required to dispose of such property in order not to be liable for tax under section 4943 (relating to taxes on excess business holdings) applied, in the case of a disposition before January 1, 1977, without taking section 4943(c)(4) into account and it receives in return an amount which equals or exceeds the fair market value of such property at the time of such disposition or at the time a contract for such disposition was previously executed in a transaction which would not constitute a prohibited transaction (within the meaning of section 503(b) or the corresponding provision of prior law);

"(C) the leasing of property or the lending of money or other extension of credit between a disqualified person and a private foundation pursuant to a binding contract in effect on October 9, 1969 (or pursuant to renewals of such a contract), until taxable years beginning after December 31, 1979, if such leasing or lending (or other extension of credit) remains at least as favorable as an arm's-length transaction with an unrelated party and if the execution of such contract was not at the time of such execution a prohibited transaction (within the meaning of section 503(b) or the corresponding provision of prior law);

"(D) the use of goods, services, or facilities which are shared by a private foundation and a disqualified person until taxable years beginning after December 31, 1979, if such use is pursuant to an arrangement in effect before October 9, 1969, and such arrangement was not a prohibited transaction (within the meaning of section 503(b) or the corresponding provisions of prior law) at the time it was made and would not be a prohibited transaction if such section continued to apply;

"(E) the use of property in which a private foundation and a disqualified person have a joint or common interest, if the interests of both in such property were acquired before October 9, 1969; and

"(F) the sale, exchange, or other disposition (other than by lease) of property which is owned by a private foundation to a disqualified person if—

"(i) such foundation is leasing substantially all of such property under a lease to which subparagraph (C) applies.

"(ii) the disposition to such disqualified person occurs before January 1, 1978, and

"(iii) such foundation receives in return for the disposition to such disqualified person an amount which equals or exceeds the fair market value of such property at the time of the disposition or at the time (after June 30, 1976) a contract for the disposition was previously executed in a transaction which would not constitute a prohibited transaction (within the meaning of section 503(b) or any corresponding provision of prior law)."

Sec. 4942. Taxes on failure to distribute income.
(a) Initial tax.

There is hereby imposed on the undistributed income of a private foundation for any taxable year, which has not been distributed before the first day of the second (or any succeeding) taxable year following such taxable year (if such first day falls within the taxable period), a tax equal to 30 percent of the amount of such income remaining undistributed at the beginning of such second (or succeeding) taxable year. The tax imposed by this subsection shall not apply to the undistributed income of a private foundation—

(1) for any taxable year for which it is an operating foundation (as defined in subsection (j)(3)), or

(2) to the extent that the foundation failed to distribute any amount solely because of an incorrect valuation of assets under subsection (e), if—

(A) the failure to value the assets properly was not willful and was due to reasonable cause,

(B) such amount is distributed as qualifying distributions (within the meaning of subsection (g)) by the foundation during the allowable distribution period (as defined in subsection (j)(2)),

(C) the foundation notifies the Secretary that such amount has been distributed (within the meaning of subparagraph (B)) to correct such failure, and

(D) such distribution is treated under subsection (h)(2) as made out of the undistributed income for the taxable year for which a tax would (except for this paragraph) have been imposed under this subsection.

(b) Additional tax.

In any case in which an initial tax is imposed under subsection (a) on the undistributed income of a private foundation for any taxable year, if any portion of such income remains undistributed at the close of the taxable period, there is hereby imposed a tax equal to 100 percent of the amount remaining undistributed at such time.

(c) Undistributed income.

For purposes of this section, the term "undistributed income" means, with respect to any private foundation for any taxable year as of any time, the amount by which—

(1) the distributable amount for such taxable year, exceeds

(2) the qualifying distributions made before such time out of such distributable amount.

(d) Distributable amount.

For purposes of this section, the term "distributable amount" means, with respect to any foundation for any taxable year, an amount equal to—

(1) the sum of the minimum investment return plus the amounts described in subsection (f)(2)(C), reduced by

(2) the sum of the taxes imposed on such private foundation for the taxable year under subtitle A and section 4940.

(e) Minimum investment return.

(1) In general. For purposes of subsection (d), the minimum investment return for any private foundation for any taxable year is 5 percent of the excess of—

(A) the aggregate fair market value of all assets of the foundation other than those which are used (or held for use) directly in carrying out the foundation's exempt purpose, over

(B) the acquisition indebtedness with respect to such assets (determined under section 514(c)(1) without regard to the taxable year in which the indebtedness was incurred).

(2) Valuation.

(A) In general. For purposes of paragraph (1)(A), the fair market value of securities for which market quotations are readily available shall be determined on a monthly basis. For all other assets, the fair market value shall be determined at such times and in such manner as the Secretary shall by regulations prescribe.

(B) Reductions in value for blockage or similar factors. In determining the value of any securities under this paragraph, the fair market value of such securities (determined without regard to any reduction in value) shall not be reduced unless, and only to the extent that, the private foundation establishes that as a result of—

(i) the size of the block of such securities,

(ii) the fact that the securities held are securities in a closely held corporation, or

(iii) the fact that the sale of such securities would result in a forced or distress sale,

the securities could not be liquidated within a reasonable period of time except at a price less than such fair market value. Any reduction in value allowable under this subparagraph shall not exceed 10 percent of such fair market value.

(f) Adjusted net income.

(1) Defined. For purposes of subsection (j), the term "adjusted net income" means the excess (if any) of—

(A) the gross income for the taxable year (determined with the income modifications provided by paragraph (2)), over

(B) the sum of the deductions (determined with the deduction modifications provided by paragraph (3)) which would be allowed to a corporation subject to the tax imposed by section 11 for the taxable year.

(2) Income modifications. The income modifications referred to in paragraph (1)(A) are as follows:

(A) section 103 (relating to State and local bonds) shall not apply,

(B) capital gains and losses from the sale or other disposition of property shall be taken into account only in an amount equal to any net short-term capital gain for the taxable year;

(C) there shall be taken into account—

(i) amounts received or accrued as repayments of amounts which were taken into account as a qualifying distribution within the meaning of subsection (g)(1)(A) for any taxable year;

(ii) notwithstanding subparagraph (B), amounts received or accrued from the sale or other disposition of property to the extent that the acquisition of such property was taken into account as a qualifying distribution (within the meaning of subsection (g)(1)(B)) for any taxable year; and

(iii) any amount set aside under subsection (g)(2) to the extent it is determined that such amount is not necessary for the purposes for which it was set aside; and

(D) section 483 (relating to imputed interest) shall not apply in the case of a binding contract made in a taxable year beginning before January 1, 1970.

(3) Deduction modifications. The deduction modifications referred to in paragraph (1)(B) are as follows:

(A) no deduction shall be allowed other than all the ordinary and necessary expenses paid or incurred for the production or collection of gross income or for the management, conservation, or maintenance of property held for the production of such income and the allowances for depreciation and depletion determined under section 4940(c)(3)(B), and

(B) section 265 (relating to expenses and interest relating to tax-exempt interest) shall not apply.

(4) Transitional rule. For purposes of paragraph (2)(B), the basis (for purposes of determining gain) of property held by a private foundation on December 31, 1969, and continuously thereafter to the date of its disposition, shall be deemed to be not less than the fair market value of such property on December 31, 1969.

(g) Qualifying distributions defined.

(1) In general. For purposes of this section, the term "qualifying distribution" means—

(A) any amount (including that portion of reasonable and necessary administrative expenses) paid to accomplish one or more purposes described in section 170(c)(2)(B), other than any contribution to (i) an organization controlled (directly or indirectly) by the foundation or one or more disqualified persons (as defined in section 4946) with respect to the foundation, except as provided in paragraph (3), or (ii) a private foundation which is not an operating foundation (as defined in subsection (j)(3)), except as provided in paragraph (3), or

(B) any amount paid to acquire an asset used (or held for use) directly in carrying out one or more purposes described in section 170(c)(2)(B).

(2) Certain set-asides.

(A) In general. For all taxable years beginning on or after January 1, 1975, subject to such terms and conditions as may be prescribed by the Secretary, an amount set aside for a specific project which comes within one or more purposes described in section 170(c)(2)(B) may be treated as a qualifying distribution if it meets the requirements of subparagraph (B).

(B) Requirements. An amount set aside for a specific project shall meet the requirements of this subparagraph if at the time of the set-aside the foundation establishes to the satisfaction of the Secretary that the amount will be paid for the specific project within 5 years, and either—

(i) at the time of the set-aside the private foundation establishes to the satisfaction of the Secretary that the project is one which can better be accomplished by such set-aside than by immediate payment of funds, or

(ii)(I) the project will not be completed before the end of the taxable year of the foundation in which the set-aside is made,

(II) the private foundation in each taxable year beginning after December 31, 1975 (or after the end of the fourth taxable year following the year of its creation, whichever is later), distributes amounts, in cash or its equivalent, equal to not less than the distributable amount determined under subsection (d) (without regard to subsection (i)) for purposes described in section 170(c)(2)(B) (including but not limited to payments with respect to set-asides which were treated as qualifying distributions in one or more prior years), and

(III) the private foundation has distributed (including but not limited to payments with respect to set-asides which were treated as qualifying distributions in one or more prior years) during the four taxable years immediately preceding its first taxable year beginning after December 31, 1975, or the fifth taxable year following the year of its creation, whichever is later, an aggregate amount, in cash or its equivalent, of not less than the sum of the following: 80 percent of the first preceding taxable year's distributable amount; 60 percent of the second preceding taxable year's distributable amount; 40 percent of the third preceding taxable year's distributable amount; and 20 percent of the fourth preceding taxable year's distributable amount.

(C) Certain failures to distribute. If, for any taxable year to which clause (ii)(II) of subparagraph (B) applies, the private foundation fails to distribute in cash or its equivalent amounts not less than those required by such clause and—

(i) the failure to distribute such amounts was not willful and was due to reasonable cause, and

(ii) the foundation distributes an amount in cash or its equivalent which is not less than the difference between the amounts required to be distributed under clause (ii)(II) of subparagraph (B) and the amounts actually distributed in cash or its equivalent during that taxable year within the correction period (as defined in section 4963(e)),

such distribution in cash or its equivalent shall be treated for the purposes of this subparagraph as made during such year.

(D) Reduction in distribution amount. If, during the taxable years in the adjustment period for which the organization is a private foundation, the foundation distributes amounts in cash or its equivalent which exceed the amount required to be distributed under clause (ii)(II) of subparagraph (B) (including but not limited to payments with respect to set-asides which were treated as qualifying distributions in prior years), then for purposes of this subsection the distribution required under clause (ii)(II) of subparagraph (B) for the taxable year shall be reduced by an amount equal to such excess.

(E) Adjustment period. For purposes of subparagraph (D), with respect to any taxable year of a private foundation, the taxable years in the adjustment period are the taxable years (not exceeding 5) beginning after December 31, 1975, and immediately preceding the taxable year.

In the case of a set-aside which satisfies the requirements of clause (i) of subparagraph (B), for good cause shown, the period for paying the amount set aside may be extended by the Secretary.

(3) Certain contributions to section 501(c)(3) organizations. For purposes of this section, the term "qualifying distribution" includes a contribution to a section 501(c)(3) organization described in paragraph (1)(A)(i) or (ii) if—

(A) not later than the close of the first taxable year after its taxable year in which such contribution is received, such organization makes a distribution equal to the amount of such contribution and such distribution is a qualifying distribution (within the meaning of paragraph (1) or (2), without regard to this paragraph) which is treated under subsection (h) as a distribution out of corpus (or would be so treated if such section 501(c)(3) organization were a private foundation which is not an operating foundation), and

(B) the private foundation making the contribution obtains adequate records or other sufficient evidence from such organization showing that the qualifying distribution described in subparagraph (A) has been made by such organization.

(4) Limitation on distributions by nonoperating private foundations to supporting organizations.

(A) In general. For purposes of this section, the term "qualifying distribution" shall not include any amount paid by a private foundation which is not an operating foundation to—

(i) any type III supporting organization (as defined in section 4943(f)(5)(A)) which is not a functionally integrated type III supporting organization (as defined in section 4943(f)(5)(B)), and

(ii) any organization which is described in subparagraph (B) or (C) if—

(I) a disqualified person of the private foundation directly or indirectly controls such organization or a supported organization (as defined in section 509(f)(3)) of such organization, or

(II) the Secretary determines by regulations that a distribution to such organization otherwise is inappropriate.

(B) Type I and type II supporting organizations. An organization is described in this subparagraph if the organization meets the requirements of subparagraphs (A) and (C) of section 509(a)(3) and is—

(i) operated, supervised, or controlled by one or more organizations described in paragraph (1) or (2) of section 509(a), or

(ii) supervised or controlled in connection with one or more such organizations.

(C) Functionally integrated type III supporting organizations. An organization is described in this subparagraph if the organization is a functionally integrated type III supporting organization (as defined under section 4943(f)(5)(B)).

(h) Treatment of qualifying distributions.

(1) In general. Except as provided in paragraph (2), any qualifying distribution made during a taxable year shall be treated as made—

(A) first out of the undistributed income of the immediately preceding taxable year (if the private foundation was subject to the tax imposed by this section for such preceding taxable year) to the extent thereof,

(B) second out of the undistributed income for the taxable year to the extent thereof, and

(C) then out of corpus.

For purposes of this paragraph, distributions shall be taken into account in the order of time in which made.

(2) Correction of deficient distributions for prior taxable years, etc. In the case of any qualifying distribution which (under paragraph (1)) is not treated as made out of the undistributed income of the immediately preceding taxable year, the foundation may elect to treat any portion of such distribution as made out of the undistributed income of a designated prior taxable year or out of corpus. The election shall be made by the foundation at such time and in such manner as the Secretary shall by regulations prescribe.

(i) Adjustment of distributable amount where distributions during prior years have exceeded income.

(1) In general. If, for the taxable years in the adjustment period for which an organization is a private foundation—

(A) the aggregate qualifying distributions treated (under subsection (h)) as made out of the undistributed income for such taxable year or as made out of corpus (except to the extent subsection (g)(3) with respect to the recipient private foundation or section 170(b)(1)(F)(ii) [sic . 170(b)(1)(D)(ii)] applies) during such taxable years, exceed

(B) the distributable amounts for such taxable years (determined without regard to this subsection),

then, for purposes of this section (other than subsection (h)), the distributable amount for the taxable year shall be reduced by an amount equal to such excess.

(2) Taxable years in adjustment period. For purposes of paragraph (1), with respect to any taxable year of a private foundation the taxable years in the adjustment period are the taxable years (not exceeding 5) beginning after December 31, 1969, and immediately preceding the taxable year.

(j) Other definitions.

For purposes of this section—

(1) Taxable period. The term "taxable period" means, with respect to the undistributed income for any taxable year, the period beginning with the first day of the taxable year and ending on the earlier of—

(A) the date of mailing of a notice of deficiency with respect to the tax imposed by subsection (a) under section 6212, or

(B) the date on which the tax imposed by subsection (a) is assessed.

(2) Allowable distribution period. The term "allowable distribution period" means, with respect to any private foundation, the period beginning with the first day of the first taxable year following the taxable year in which the incorrect valuation (described in subsection (a)(2)) occurred and ending 90 days after the date of mailing of a notice of deficiency (with respect to the tax imposed by subsection (a)) under section 6212 extended by—

(A) any period in which a deficiency cannot be assessed under section 6213(a), and

(B) any other period which the Secretary determines is reasonable and necessary to permit a distribution of undistributed income under this section.

(3) Operating foundation. For purposes of this section, the term "operating foundation" means any organization—

(A) which makes qualifying distributions (within the meaning of paragraph (1) or (2) of subsection (g)) directly for the active conduct of the activities constituting the purpose or function for which it is organized and operated equal to substantially all of the lesser of—

(i) its adjusted net income (as defined in subsection (f)), or

(ii) its minimum investment return; and

(B)(i) substantially more than half of the assets of which are devoted directly to such activities or to functionally related businesses (as defined in paragraph (4)), or to both, or are stock of a corporation which is controlled by the foundation and substantially all of the assets of which are so devoted,

(ii) which normally makes qualifying distributions (within the meaning of paragraph (1) or (2) of subsection (g)) directly for the active conduct of the activities constituting the purpose or function for which it is organized and operated in an amount not less than two-thirds of its minimum investment return (as defined in subsection (e)), or

(iii) substantially all of the support (other than gross investment income as defined in section 509(e)) of which is normally received from the general public and from 5 or more exempt organizations which are not described in section 4946(a)(1)(H) with respect to each other or the recipient foundation; not more than 25 percent of the support (other than gross investment income) of which is normally received from any one such exempt organization; and not more than half of the support of which is normally received from gross investment income.

Notwithstanding the provisions of subparagraph (A), if the qualifying distributions (within the meaning of paragraph (1) or (2) of subsection (g)) of an organization for the taxable year exceed the minimum investment return for the taxable year, clause (ii) of subparagraph (A) shall not apply unless substantially all of such qualifying distributions are made directly for the active conduct of the activities constituting the purpose or function for which it is organized and operated.

(4) Functionally related business. The term "functionally related business" means—

(A) a trade or business which is not an unrelated trade or business (as defined in section 513), or

(B) an activity which is carried on within a larger aggregate of similar activities or within a larger complex of other endeavors which is related (aside from the need of the organization for income or funds or the use it makes of the profits derived) to the exempt purposes of the organization.

(5) Certain elderly care facilities. For purposes of this section (but no other provisions of this title), the term "operating foundation" includes any organization which, on May 26, 1969, and at all times thereafter before the close of the taxable year, operated and maintained as its principal functional purpose facilities for the long-term care, comfort, maintenance, or education of permanently and totally disabled persons, elderly persons, needy widows, or children but only if such organization meets the requirements of paragraph (3)(B)(ii).

In **2007**, P.L. 110-172, Sec. 11(a)(14)(D), substituted "section 170(b)(1)(F)(ii)" for "section 170(b)(1)(E)(ii)" in subpara. (i)(1)(A), enacted 12/29/2007.

In **2006**, P.L. 109-280, Sec. 1212(b), substituted "30 percent" for "15 percent" in subsec. (a), effective for tax. yrs. begin. after 8/17/2006.

—P.L. 109-280, Sec. 1244(a), amended para. (g)(4), effective for distributions and expenditures after 8/17/2006.

Prior to amendment, para. (g)(4) read as follows:

"(4) Limitation on administrative expenses allocable to making of contributions, gifts, and grants.

"(A) In general. The amount of the grant administrative expenses paid during any taxable year which may be taken into account as qualifying distributions shall not exceed the excess (if any) of—

"(i) .65 percent of the sum of the net assets of the private foundation for such taxable year and the immediately preceding 2 taxable years, over

"(ii) the aggregate amount of grant administrative expenses paid during the 2 preceding taxable years which were taken into account as qualifying distributions.

"(B) Grant administrative expenses. For purposes of this paragraph, the term 'grant administrative expenses' means any administrative expenses which are allocable to the making of qualified grants.

"(C) Qualified grants. For purposes of this paragraph, the term 'qualified grant' means any contribution, gift, or grant which is a qualifying distribution.

"(D) Net asset. For purposes of this paragraph, the term 'net assets' means, with respect to any taxable year, the excess determined under subsection (e)(1) for such taxable year.

"(E) Transitional rule. In the case of any preceding taxable year which begins before January 1, 1985, the amount of the grant administrative expenses taken into account under subparagraph (A)(ii) shall not exceed .65 percent of the net assets of the private foundation for such taxable year.

"(F) Termination. This paragraph shall not apply to taxable years beginning after December 31, 1990."

In **1986**, P.L. 99-514, Sec. 1301(j)(6), substituted "(relating to State and local bonds)" for "(relating to interest on certain governmental obligations)" in subpara. (f)(2)(A), effective for bonds issued after 8/15/86.

In **1984**, P.L. 98-369, Sec. 304(a)(1), added para. (g)(4) . . . Sec. 304(a)(2), substituted "including that portion of reasonable and necessary administrative expenses" for "including administrative expenses" in subpara. (g)(1)(A) . . . Sec. 304(b), amended para. (d)(1), effective for tax. yrs. begin. after 12/31/84.

Prior to amendment, para. (d)(1) read as follows:

"(1) the minimum investment return, reduced by".

—P.L. 98-369, Sec. 305(b)(4), substituted "section 4963(e)" for "section 4962(e)" in subpara. (g)(2)(C), effective for tax. events occurring after 12/31/84.

—P.L. 98-369, Sec. 314(a)(1), substituted "subsection (j)(2)" for "subsection (j)(4)" in subpara. (a)(2)(B) . . . Sec. 314(a)(2), substituted "subsection (j)" for "subsection (d)" in para. (f)(1), effective 7/18/84.

In **1983**, P.L. 97-448, Sec. 108(b), substituted "or" for "and" at the end of clause (j)(3)(A)(i), effective for tax. yrs. begin. after 12/31/81.

In **1981**, P.L. 97-34, Sec. 823(a)(1), deleted "or the adjusted net income (whichever is higher)" in para. (d)(1) . . . Sec. 823(a)(2), amended subpara. (j)(3)(A) . . . Sec. 823(a)(3), added the sentence to the end of para. (j)(3), effective for tax. yrs. begin. after 12/31/81.

Prior to amendment subpara. (j)(3)(A) read as follows:

"(A) which makes qualifying distributions (within the meaning of paragraph (1) or (2) of subsection (g)) directly for the active conduct of the activities constituting the purpose or function for which it is organized and operated equal to substantially all of its adjusted net income (as defined in subsection (f)); and"

In **1980**, P.L. 96-596, Sec. 2(a)(1)(C), substituted "taxable period" for "correction period" in subsec. (b) . . . Sec. 2(a)(2)(B), amended para. (j)(1) . . . Sec. 2(a)(3)(B)(i), deleted para. (j)(2) . . . Sec. 2(a)(3)(B)(ii), substituted "paragraph (4)" for "paragraph (5)" in clause (j)(3)(B)(i) . . . Sec. 2(a)(3)(B)(iii), redesignated para. (j)(4) as para. (j)(2) . . . Sec. 2(a)(3)(B)(iv), redesignated paras. (j)(5) and (j)(6) as paras. (j)(4) and (j)(5) respectively . . . Sec. 2(a)(4)(A), substituted "the correction period (as defined in section 4962(e))" for "the initial correction period provided in subsection (j)(2)" in clause (g)(2)(C)(ii), effective as provided in Sec. 2(d) of this Act which reads as follows:

"(d) Effective dates.—

"(1) First tier taxes. The amendments made by this section with respect to any first tier tax shall take effect as if included in the Internal Revenue Code of 1954 when such tax was first imposed.

"(2) Second tier taxes.—The amendments made by this section with respect to any second tier tax shall apply only with respect to taxes assessed after the date of the enactment of this Act. Nothing in the preceding sentence shall be construed to permit the assessment of a tax in a case to which, on the date of the enactment of this Act, the doctrine of res judicata applies.

"(3) First and second tier taxes.— For purposes of this subsection, the terms 'first tier tax' and 'second tier tax' have the respective meanings given to such terms by section 4962 of the Internal Revenue Code of 1954."

Prior to amendment para. (j)(1) read as follows:

"(1) Taxable period. The term 'taxable period' means, with respect to the undistributed income for any taxable year, the period beginning with the first day of the taxable year and ending on the date of mailing of a notice of deficiency with respect to the tax imposed by subsection (a) under section 6212."

Prior to deletion, para. (j)(2) read as follows:

"(2) Correction period. The term 'correction period' means, with respect to any private foundation for any taxable year, the period beginning with the first day of the taxable year and ending 90 days after the date of mailing of a notice of deficiency (with respect to the tax imposed by subsection (b)) under section 6212, extended by—

"(A) any period in which a deficiency cannot be assessed under section 6213(a), and

"(B) any other period which the Secretary determines is reasonable and necessary to permit a distribution of undistributed income under this section."

In 1978, P.L. 95-600, Sec. 522(a), added para. (j)(6), effective for tax. yrs. begin. after 12/31/69.

In 1976, P.L. 94-455, Sec. 1302(a), amended para. (g)(2), for tax. yrs. begin. after 12/31/74.

Prior to amendment, para. (g)(2) read as follows:

"(2) Certain set-asides. Subject to such terms and conditions as may be prescribed by the Secretary or his delegate, an amount set aside for a specific project which comes within one or more purposes described in section 170(c)(2)(B) may be treated as a qualifying distribution, but only if, at the time of the set-aside, the private foundation establishes to the satisfaction of the Secretary or his delegate that—

"(A) the amount will be paid for the specific project within 5 years, and

"(B) the project is one which can be better accomplished by such set-aside than by immediate payment of funds.

For good cause shown, the period for paying the amount set aside may be extended by the Secretary or his delegate."

—P.L. 94-455, Sec. 1303(a), amended subsec. (e), effective for tax. yrs. begin. after 12/31/75.

Prior to amendment, subsec. (e) read as follows:

"(e) Minimum investment return.

"(1) In general. For purposes of subsection (d), the minimum investment return for any private foundation for any taxable year is the amount determined by multiplying—

"(A) the excess of (i) the aggregate fair market value of all assets of the foundation other than those being used (or held for use) directly in carrying out the foundation's exempt purpose over (ii) the acquisition indebtedness with respect to such assets (determined under section 514(c)(1), but without regard to the taxable year in which the indebtedness was incurred), by

"(B) the applicable percentage for such year, determined under paragraph (3).

"(2) Valuation. For purposes of paragraph (1)(A), the fair market value of securities for which market quotations are readily available shall be determined on a monthly basis. For all other assets, the fair market value shall be determined at such times and in such manner as the Secretary or his delegate shall by regulations prescribe.

"(3) Applicable percentage. For purposes of paragraph (1)(B), the applicable percentage for taxable years beginning in 1970 is 6 percent. The applicable percentage for any taxable year beginning after 1970 shall be determined and published by the Secretary or his delegate and shall bear a relationship to 6 percent which the Secretary or his delegate determines to be comparable to the relationship which the money rates and investment yields for the calendar year immediately preceding the beginning of the taxable year bear to the money rates and investment yields for the calendar year 1969.

"(4) Transitional rules. For special rules applicable to organizations created before May 27, 1969, see section 101(1)(3) of the Tax Reform Act of 1969."

—P.L. 94-455, Sec. 1310(a)(1), deleted "and" at the end of subpara. (f)(2)(B) . . . Sec. 1310(a)(2), substituted "; and" for the period at the end of subpara. (f)(2)(C) . . . Sec. 1310(a)(3), added subpara. (f)(2)(D), effective for tax. yrs. end. after 10/4/76.

—P.L. 94-455, Sec. 1906(b)(13)(A), substituted "Secretary" for "Secretary or his delegate" in paras. (a)(2), (h)(2), (j)(2) and (j)(4), effective 2/1/77.

In 1974, P.L. 93-490, Sec. 4(a), amended Sec. 101(1)(3) of P.L. 91-172, the effective date for amendments made by Sec. 101(b) of P.L. 91-172, by deleting "and" at the end of subpara. (l)(3)(D), and substituted "; and" for the period at the end of subpara. (l)(3)(E), and added subpara. (l)(3)(F) (see below), effective for tax. yrs. begin. after 12/31/71.

In 1969, P.L. 91-172, Sec. 101(b), added Code Sec. 4942, effective for tax. yrs. begin. after 12/31/69. Sec. 101(1)(3) [as amended by Sec. 4(a) of P.L. 93-490, see above] provides as follows:

"In the case of organizations organized before May 27, 1969, section 4942 shall—

"(A) for all purposes other than the determination of the minimum investment return under section 4942(j)(3)(B)(ii), for taxable years beginning before January 1, 1972, apply without regard to section 4942(e) (relating to minimum investment return), and for taxable years beginning in 1972, 1973, and 1974, apply with an applicable percentage (as prescribed in section 4942(e)(3)) which does not exceed 4½ percent, 5 percent, and 5½ percent, respectively;

"(B) not apply to an organization to the extent its income is required to be accumulated pursuant to the mandatory terms (as in effect on May 26, 1969, and at all times thereafter) of an instrument executed before May 27, 1969, which required the transfer of income producing property to such organization, except that section 4942 shall apply to such organization if the organization would have been denied exemption if section 504(a) had not been repealed by this Act, or would have had its deductions under section 642(c) limited if section 681(c) had not been repealed by this Act. In applying the preceding sentence, in addition to the limitations contained in section 504(a) or 681(c) before its repeal, section 504(a)(1) or 681(c)(1) shall be treated as not applying to an organization to the extent its income is required to be accumulated pursuant to the mandatory terms (as in effect on January 1, 1951, and at all times thereafter) of an instrument executed before January 1, 1951, with respect to the transfer of income producing property to such organization before such date, if such transfer was irrevocable on such date;

"(C) apply to a grant to a private foundation described in section 4942(g)(1)(A)(ii) which is not described in section 4942(g)(1)(A)(i), pursuant to a written commitment which was binding on May 26, 1969, and at all times thereafter, as if such grant is a grant to an operating foundation (as defined in section 4942(j)(3)), if such grant is made for one or more of the purposes described in section 170(c)(2)(B) and is to be paid out to such private foundation on or before December 31, 1974;

"(D) apply, for purposes of section 4942(f), in such a manner as to treat any distribution made to a private foundation in redemption of stock held by such private foundation in a business enterprise as not essentially equivalent to a dividend under section 302(b)(1) if such redemption is described in paragraph (2)(B) of this subsection;

"(E) not apply to an organization which is prohibited by its governing instrument or other instrument from distributing capital or corpus to the extent the requirements of section 4942 are inconsistent with such prohibition; and

"(F) apply, in the case of an organization described in paragraph (4)(A) of this subsection,

"(i) by applying section 4942(e) without regard to the stock to which paragraph (4)(A)(ii) of this subsection applies,

"(ii) by applying section 4942(f) without regard to dividend income for [from] such stock, and

"(iii) by defining the distributable amount as the sum of the amount determined under section 4942(d) (after the application of clauses (i) and (ii)), and the amount of the dividend income from such stock.

With respect to taxable years beginning after December 31, 1971, subparagraphs (B) and (E) shall apply only during the pendency of any judicial proceeding by the private foundation which is necessary to reform, or to excuse such foundation from compliance with, its governing instrument or any other instrument (as in effect on May 26, 1969) in order to comply with the provisions of section 4942, and in the case of subparagraph (B) for all periods after the termination of such judicial proceeding during which the governing instrument or any other instrument does not permit compliance with such provisions."

Sec. 4943. Taxes on excess business holdings.
(a) Initial tax.

(1) Imposition. There is hereby imposed on the excess business holdings of any private foundation in a business enterprise during any taxable year which ends during the taxable period a tax equal to 10 percent of the value of such holdings.

(2) Special rules. The tax imposed by paragraph (1)—

(A) shall be imposed on the last day of the taxable year, but

(B) with respect to the private foundation's holdings in any business enterprise, shall be determined as of that day during the taxable year when the foundation's excess holdings in such enterprise were the greatest.

(b) Additional tax.

In any case in which an initial tax is imposed under subsection (a) with respect to the holdings of a private foundation in any business enterprise, if, at the close of the taxable period with respect to such holdings, the foundation still has excess business holdings in such enterprise, there is hereby imposed a tax equal to 200 percent of such excess business holdings.

(c) Excess business holdings.

For purposes of this section—

(1) In general. The term "excess business holdings" means, with respect to the holdings of any private foundation in any business enterprise, the amount of stock or other interest in the enterprise which the foundation would have to dispose of to a person other than a disqualified person in order for the remaining holdings of the foundation in such enterprise to be permitted holdings.

(2) Permitted holdings in a corporation.

(A) In general. The permitted holdings of any private foundation in an incorporated business enterprise are—

(i) 20 percent of the voting stock, reduced by

(ii) the percentage of the voting stock owned by all disqualified persons.

In any case in which all disqualified persons together do not own more than 20 percent of the voting stock of an incorporated business enterprise, nonvoting stock held by the private foundation shall also be treated as permitted holdings.

(B) 35 percent rule where third person has effective control of enterprise. If—

(i) the private foundation and all disqualified persons together do not own more than 35 percent of the voting stock of an incorporated business enterprise, and

(ii) it is established to the satisfaction of the Secretary that effective control of the corporation is in one or more persons who are not disqualified persons with respect to the foundation,

then subparagraph (A) shall be applied by substituting 35 percent for 20 percent.

(C) 2 percent de minimis rule. A private foundation shall not be treated as having excess business holdings in any corporation in which it (together with all other private foundations which are described in section 4946(a)(1)(H)) owns not more than 2 percent of the voting stock and not more than 2 percent in value of all outstanding shares of all classes of stock.

(3) **Permitted holdings in partnerships, etc.** The permitted holdings of a private foundation in any business enterprise which is not incorporated shall be determined under regulations prescribed by the Secretary. Such regulations shall be consistent in principle with paragraphs (2) and (4), except that—

(A) in the case of a partnership or joint venture, "profits interest" shall be substituted for "voting stock", and "capital interest" shall be substituted for "nonvoting stock",

(B) in the case of a proprietorship, there shall be no permitted holdings, and

(C) in any other case, "beneficial interest" shall be substituted for "voting stock".

(4) **Present holdings.**

(A)(i) In applying this section with respect to the holdings of any private foundation in a business enterprise, if such foundation and all disqualified persons together have holdings in such enterprise in excess of 20 percent of the voting stock on May 26, 1969, the percentage of such holdings shall be substituted for "20 percent," and for "35 percent" (if the percentage of such holdings is greater than 35 percent), wherever it appears in paragraph (2), but in no event shall the percentage so substituted be more than 50 percent.

(ii) If the percentage of the holdings of any private foundation and all disqualified persons together in a business enterprise (or if the percentage of the holdings of the private foundation in such enterprise) decreases for any reason, clause (i) and subparagraph (D) shall, except as provided in the next sentence, be applied for all periods after such decrease by substituting such decreased percentage for the percentage held on May 26, 1969, but in no event shall the percentage substituted be less than 20 percent. For purposes of the preceding sentence, any decrease in percentage holdings attributable to issuances of stock (or to issuances of stock coupled with redemptions of stock) shall be disregarded so long as—

(I) the net percentage decrease disregarded under this sentence does not exceed 2 percent, and

(II) the number of shares held by the foundation is not affected by any such issuance or redemption.

(iii) The percentage substituted under clause (i), and any percentage substituted under subparagraph (D), shall be applied both with respect to the voting stock and, separately, with respect to the value of all outstanding shares of all classes of stock.

(iv) In the case of any merger, recapitalization, or other reorganization involving one or more business enterprises, the application of clauses (i), (ii), and (iii) shall be determined under regulations prescribed by the Secretary.

(B) Any interest in a business enterprise which a private foundation holds on May 26, 1969, if the private foundation on such date has excess business holding, shall (while held by the foundation) be treated as held by a disqualified person (rather than by the private foundation)—

(i) during the 20-year period beginning on such date, if the private foundation and all disqualified persons have more than a 95 percent voting stock interest on such date,

(ii) except as provided in clause (i), during the 15-year period beginning on such date, if the foundation and all disqualified persons have more than a 75 percent voting stock interest (or more than a 75 percent profits or beneficial interest in the case of any unincorporated enterprise) on such date or more than a 75 percent interest in the value of all outstanding shares of all classes of stock (or more than a 75 percent capital interest in the case of a partnership or joint venture) on such date, or

(iii) during the 10-year period beginning on such date, in any other case.

(C) The 20-year, 15-year, and 10-year periods described in subparagraph (B) for the disposition of excess business holdings shall be suspended during the pendency of any judicial proceeding by the private foundation which is necessary to reform, or to excuse such foundation from compliance with, its governing instrument or any other instrument (as in effect on May 26, 1969) in order to allow disposition of such holdings.

(D)(i) If, at any time during the second phase, all disqualified persons together have holdings in a business enterprise in excess of 2 percent of the voting stock of such enterprise, then subparagraph (A)(i) shall be applied by substituting for "50 percent" the following: "50 percent, of which not more than 25 percent shall be voting stock held by the private foundation".

(ii) If, immediately before the close of the second phase, clause (i) of this subparagraph did not apply with respect to a business enterprise, then for all periods after the close of the second phase subparagraph (A)(i) shall be applied by substituting for "50 percent" the following: "35 percent, or if at any time after the close of the second phase all disqualified persons together have had holdings in such enterprise which exceed 2 percent of the voting stock, 35 percent, of which not more than 25 percent shall be voting stock held by the private foundation".

(iii) For purposes of this subparagraph, the term "second phase" means the 15-year period immediately following the 20-year, 15-year, or 10-year period described in subparagraph (B), whichever applies, as modified by subparagraph (C).

(E) Clause (ii) of subparagraph (B) shall not apply with respect to any business enterprise if before January 1, 1971, one or more individuals who are substantial contributors (or members of the family (within the meaning of section 4946(d)) of one or more substantial contributors) to the private foundation and who on May 26, 1969, held more than 15 percent of the voting stock of the enterprise elect, in such manner as the Secretary may by regulations prescribe, not to have such clause (ii) apply with respect to such enterprise.

(5) Holdings acquired by trust or will. Paragraph (4) (other than subparagraph (B)(i)) shall apply to any interest in a business enterprise which a private foundation acquires under the terms of a trust which was irrevocable on May 26, 1969, or under the terms of a will executed on or before such date, which are in effect on such date and at all times thereafter, as if such interest were held on May 26, 1969, except that the 15-year and 10-year periods prescribed in clauses (ii) and (iii) of paragraph (4)(B) shall commence with respect to such interest on the date of distribution under the trust or will in lieu of May 26, 1969.

(6) 5-year period to dispose of gifts, bequests, etc. Except as provided in paragraph (5), if, after May 26, 1969, there is a change in the holdings in a business enterprise (other than by purchase by the private foundation or by a disqualified person) which causes the private foundation to have—

(A) excess business holdings in such enterprise, the interest of the foundation in such enterprise (immediately after such change) shall (while held by the foundation) be treated as held by a disqualified person (rather than by the foundation) during the 5-year period beginning on the date of such change in holdings; or

(B) an increase in excess business holdings in such enterprise (determined without regard to subparagraph (A)), subparagraph (A) shall apply, except that the excess holdings immediately preceding the increase therein shall not be treated, solely because of such increase, as held by a disqualified person (rather than by the foundation).

In any case where an acquisition by a disqualified person would result in a substitution under clause (i) or (ii) of subparagraph (D) of paragraph (4), the preceding sentence shall be applied with respect to such acquisition as if it did not contain the phrase "or by a disqualified person" in the material preceding subparagraph (A).

(7) 5-year extension of period to dispose of certain large gifts and bequests. The Secretary may extend for an additional 5-year period the period under paragraph (6) for disposing of excess business holdings in the case of an unusually large gift or bequest of diverse business holdings or holdings with complex corporate structures if—

(A) the foundation establishes that—
  (i) diligent efforts to dispose of such holdings have been made within the initial 5-year period, and
  (ii) disposition within the initial 5-year period has not been possible (except at a price substantially below fair market value) by reason of such size and complexity or diversity of such holdings,

(B) before the close of the initial 5-year period—
  (i) the private foundation submits to the Secretary a plan for disposing of all of the excess business holdings involved in the extension, and
  (ii) the private foundation submits the plan described in clause (i) to the Attorney General (or other appropriate State official) having administrative or supervisory authority or responsibility with respect to the foundation's disposition of the excess business holdings involved and submits to the Secretary any response received by the private foundation from the Attorney General (or other appropriate State official) to such plan during such 5-year period, and

(C) the Secretary determines that such plan can reasonably be expected to be carried out before the close of the extension period.

(d) Definitions; special rules.
For purposes of this section—

(1) Business holdings. In computing the holdings of a private foundation, or a disqualified person (as defined in section 4946) with respect thereto, in any business enterprise, any stock or other interest owned, directly or indirectly, by or for a corporation, partnership, estate, or trust shall be considered as being owned proportionately by or for its shareholders, partners, or beneficiaries. The preceding sentence shall not apply with respect to an income or remainder interest of a private foundation in a trust described in section 4947(a)(2), but only if, in the case of property transferred in trust after May 26, 1969, such foundation holds only an income interest or only a remainder interest in such trust.

(2) Taxable period. The term "taxable period" means, with respect to any excess business holdings of a private foundation in a business enterprise, the period beginning on the first day on which there are excess holdings and ending on the earlier of—

(A) the date of mailing of a notice of deficiency with respect to the tax imposed by subsection (a) under section 6212 in respect of such holdings, or

(B) the date on which the tax imposed by subsection (a) in respect of such holdings is assessed.

(3) Business enterprise. The term "business enterprise" does not include—

(A) a functionally related business (as defined in section 4942(j)(4)), or

(B) a trade or business at least 95 percent of the gross income of which is derived from passive sources.

For purposes of subparagraph (B), gross income from passive sources includes the items excluded by section 512(b)(1), (2), (3), and (5), and income from the sale of goods (including charges or costs passed on at cost to purchasers of such goods or income received in settlement of a dispute concerning or in lieu of the exercise of the right to sell such goods) if the seller does not manufacture, produce, physically receive or deliver, negotiate sales of, or maintain inventories in such goods.

(4) Disqualified person. The term "disqualified person" (as defined in section 4946(a)) does not include a plan described in section 4975(e)(7) with respect to the holdings of a private foundation described in paragraphs (4) and (5) of subsection (c).

(e) Application of tax to donor advised funds.

(1) In general. For purposes of this section, a donor advised fund (as defined in section 4966(d)(2)) shall be treated as a private foundation.

(2) Disqualified person. In applying this section to any donor advised fund (as so defined), the term "disqualified person" means, with respect to the donor advised fund, any person who is—

(A) described in section 4966(d)(2)(A)(iii),

(B) a member of the family of an individual described in subparagraph (A), or

(C) a 35-percent controlled entity (as defined in section 4958(f)(3) by substituting "persons described in subparagraph (A) or (B) of section 4943(e)(2)" for "persons described in subparagraph (A) or (B) of paragraph (1)" in subparagraph (A)(i) thereof).

(3) Present holdings. For purposes of this subsection, rules similar to the rules of paragraphs (4), (5), and (6) of

subsection (c) shall apply to donor advised funds (as so defined), except that—
(A) "the date of the enactment of this subsection" shall be substituted for "May 26, 1969" each place it appears in paragraphs (4), (5), and (6), and
(B) "January 1, 2007" shall be substituted for "January 1, 1970" in paragraph (4)(E).

(f) Application of tax to supporting organizations.
(1) In general. For purposes of this section, an organization which is described in paragraph (3) shall be treated as a private foundation.
(2) Exception. The Secretary may exempt the excess business holdings of any organization from the application of this subsection if the Secretary determines that such holdings are consistent with the purpose or function constituting the basis for its exemption under section 501.
(3) Organizations described. An organization is described in this paragraph if such organization is—
(A) a type III supporting organization (other than a functionally integrated type III supporting organization), or
(B) an organization which meets the requirements of subparagraphs (A) and (C) of section 509(a)(3) and which is supervised or controlled in connection with or one or more organizations described in paragraph (1) or (2) of section 509(a), but only if such organization accepts any gift or contribution from any person described in section 509(f)(2)(B).
(4) Disqualified person.
(A) In general. In applying this section to any organization described in paragraph (3), the term "disqualified person" means, with respect to the organization—
(i) any person who was, at any time during the 5-year period ending on the date described in subsection (a)(2)(A), in a position to exercise substantial influence over the affairs of the organization,
(ii) any member of the family (determined under section 4958(f)(4)) of an individual described in clause (i),
(iii) any 35-percent controlled entity (as defined in section 4958(f)(3) by substituting "persons described in clause (i) or (ii) of section 4943(f)(4)(A)" for "persons described in subparagraph (A) or (B) of paragraph (1)" in subparagraph (A)(i) thereof),
(iv) any person described in section 4958(c)(3)(B), and
(v) any organization—
(I) which is effectively controlled (directly or indirectly) by the same person or persons who control the organization in question, or
(II) substantially all of the contributions to which were made (directly or indirectly) by the same person or persons described in subparagraph (B) or a member of the family (within the meaning of section 4946(d)) of such a person.
(B) Persons described. A person is described in this subparagraph if such person is—
(i) a substantial contributor to the organization (as defined in section 4958(c)(3)(C)),
(ii) an officer, director, or trustee of the organization (or an individual having powers or responsibilities similar to those of the officers, directors, or trustees of the organization), or
(iii) an owner of more than 20 percent of—
(I) the total combined voting power of a corporation,
(II) the profits interest of a partnership, or
(III) the beneficial interest of a trust or unincorporated enterprise,
which is a substantial contributor (as so defined) to the organization.
(5) Type III supporting organization; functionally integrated type III supporting organization. For purposes of this subsection—
(A) Type III supporting organization. The term "type III supporting organization" means an organization which meets the requirements of subparagraphs (A) and (C) of section 509(a)(3) and which is operated in connection with one or more organizations described in paragraph (1) or (2) of section 509(a).
(B) Functionally integrated type III supporting organization. The term "functionally integrated type III supporting organization" means a type III supporting organization which is not required under regulations established by the Secretary to make payments to supported organizations (as defined under section 509(f)(3)) due to the activities of the organization related to performing the functions of, or carrying out the purposes of, such supported organizations.
(6) Special rule for certain holdings of type III supporting organizations. For purposes of this subsection, the term "excess business holdings" shall not include any holdings of a type III supporting organization in any business enterprise if, as of November 18, 2005, the holdings were held (and at all times thereafter, are held) for the benefit of the community pursuant to the direction of a State attorney general or a State official with jurisdiction over such organization.
(7) Present holdings. For purposes of this subsection, rules similar to the rules of paragraphs (4), (5), and (6) of subsection (c) shall apply to organizations described in section 509(a)(3), except that—
(A) "the date of the enactment of this subsection" shall be substituted for "May 26, 1969" each place it appears in paragraphs (4), (5), and (6) and
(B) "January 1, 2007" shall be substituted for "January 1, 1970" in paragraph (4)(E).

In 2006, P.L. 109-280, Sec. 1212(c), substituted "10 percent" for "5 percent" in para. (a)(1), effective for tax. yrs. begin. after 8/17/2006
—P.L. 109-280, Sec. 1233(a), added subsec. (e), effective for tax. yrs. begin. after 8/17/2006
—P.L. 109-280, Sec. 1243(a), added subsec. (f), effective for tax. yrs. begin. after 8/17/2006
In 1984, P.L. 98-369, Sec. 307(a), added para. (c)(7), effective for business holdings for which the 5-year period described in Code Sec. 4943(c)(6) ends on or after 11/1/83. Sec. 307(b)(2) of this Act provides:
"(2) Transitional rule.— Any plan submitted to the Secretary of the Treasury or his delegate on or before the 60th day after the date of the enactment of this Act shall be treated as submitted before the close of the initial 5-year period referred to in section 4943(c)(7)(B) of the Internal Revenue Code of 1954 (as added by subsection (a))."
—P.L. 98-369, Sec. 308(a), amended the second sentence of clause (c)(4)(A)(ii), effective for increases and decreases occurring after 7/18/84.
Prior to amendment, the second sentence of clause (c)(4)(A)(ii) read as follows: "For purposes of this clause, any decrease in percentage holdings attributable to issuances of stock (or to issuances of stock coupled with redemptions of stock) shall be determined only as of the close of each taxable year of the private foundation unless the aggregate of the percentage decreases attributable to the issuances of stock (or such issuances and redemptions) during such taxable year equals or exceeds 1 percent."
—P.L. 98-369, Sec. 309(a), substituted "the private foundation and all disqualified persons have" for "the private foundation has" in clause (c)(4)(B)(i), effective for tax. yrs. begin. after 12/31/69.
—P.L. 98-369, Sec. 310(a), added the last sentence to para. (c)(6), effective for acquisitions after 7/18/84.
—P.L. 98-369, Sec. 314(b)(1), amended Sec. 101(1)(A) of P.L. 91-172, part of the effective date for changes made by Sec. 101 of P.L. 91-172 (reproduced below), by substituting "as if it did not contain the phrase ', but in no event shall

Excise and miscellaneous taxes

Code Sec. 4944(e)(2)

the percentage so substituted be more than 50 percent'" for "by substituting '51 percent' for '50 percent' ".
—P.L. 98-369, Sec. 314(c)(1), added para. (d)(4), effective for tax. yrs. begin. after 7/18/84.

In 1980, P.L. 96-596, Sec. 2(a)(1)(D), substituted "taxable period" for "correction period" in subsec. (b) . . . Sec. 2(a)(2)(C), amended para. (d)(2) . . . Sec. 2(a)(3)(C), deleted para. (d)(3) and redesignated para. (d)(4) as para. (d)(3) . . . Sec. 2(a)(4)(B), substituted "4942(j)(4)" for "4942(j)(5)" in para. (d)(3) as redesignated by Sec. 2(a)(3)(C) of this Act, effective as provided in Sec. 2(d) of this Act which reads as follows:

"(d) Effective dates.

"(1) First tier taxes.

The amendments made by this section with respect to any first tier tax shall take effect as if included in the Internal Revenue Code of 1954 when such tax was first imposed.

"(2) Second tier taxes.

The amendments made by this section with respect to any second tier tax shall apply only with respect to taxes assessed after the date of the enactment of this Act. Nothing in the preceding sentence shall be construed to permit the assessment of a tax in a case to which, on the date of the enactment of this Act, the doctrine of res judicata applies.

"(3) First and second tier tax.

For purposes of this subsection, the terms 'first tier tax' and 'second tier tax' have the respective meanings given to such terms by section 4962 of the Internal Revenue Code of 1954."

Prior to amendment para. (d)(3) read as follows:

"(3) Correction period. The term 'correction period' means, with respect to excess business holdings of a private foundation in a business enterprise, the period ending 90 days after the date of mailing of a notice of deficiency (with respect to the tax imposed by subsection (b)) under section 6212, extended by—

"(A) any period in which a deficiency cannot be assessed under section 6213(a), and

"(B) any other period which the Secretary determines is reasonable and necessary to permit orderly disposition of such excess business holdings."

Prior to amendment para. (d)(2) read as follows:

"(2) Taxable period. The term 'taxable period' means, with respect to any excess business holdings of a private foundation in a business enterprise, the period beginning on the first day on which there are such excess holdings and ending on the date of mailing of a notice of deficiency with respect to the tax imposed by subsection (a) under section 6212 in respect of such holdings."

In 1976, P.L. 94-455, Sec. 1906(b)(13)(A), substituted "Secretary" for "Secretary or his delegate" in paras. (c)(2), (c)(3), (c)(4) and (d)(2), effective 2/1/77.

In 1969, P.L. 91-172, Sec. 101(b), added Code Sec. 4943, for tax. yrs. begin. after 12/31/69. Sec. 101(1)(4) [as amended by Sec. 314(b)(1) of P.L. 98-369]

"(A) In the case of a private foundation—

"(i) which was incorporated before January 1, 1951;

"(ii) substantially all of the assets of which on May 26, 1969, consist of more than 90 percent of the stock of an incorporated business enterprise which is licensed and regulated, the sales or contracts of which are regulated, and the professional representatives of which are licensed, by State regulatory agencies in at least 10 States; and

"(iii) which acquired such stock solely by gift, devise, or bequest, section 4943(c)(4)(A)(i) shall be applied with respect to the holdings of such foundation in such incorporated business enterprise as if it did not contain the phrase ', but in no event shall the percentage so substituted be more than 50 percent', and section 4943(c)(4)(D) shall not apply with respect to such holdings. For purposes of the preceding sentence, stock of such enterprise in a trust created before May 27, 1969, of which the foundation is the remainder beneficiary shall be deemed to be held by such foundation on May 26, 1969, if such foundation held (without regard to such trust) more than 20 percent of the stock of such enterprise on May 26, 1969.

"(B) Subparagraph (A) shall apply to a private foundation only if—

"(i) the foundation does not purchase any stock or other interest in the enterprise described in subparagraph (A) after May 26, 1969, and does not acquire any stock or other interest in any other business enterprise which constitutes excess business holdings under section 4943; and

"(ii) in the last 5 taxable years ending on or before December 31, 1970, the foundation expends substantially all of its adjusted net income (as defined in section 4942(f)) for the purpose or function for which it is organized and operated.

"(C) For purposes of section 4943(c)(6), the term 'purchase' does not include an exchange which is described in paragraph (2)(B) of this subsection and which is pursuant to a plan for disposition of excess business holdings."

Sec. 4944. Taxes on investments which jeopardize charitable purpose.

(a) Initial taxes.

(1) On the private foundation. If a private foundation invests any amount in such a manner as to jeopardize the carrying out of any of its exempt purposes, there is hereby imposed on the making of such investment a tax equal to 10 percent of the amount so invested for each year (or part thereof) in the taxable period. The tax imposed by this paragraph shall be paid by the private foundation.

(2) On the management. In any case in which a tax is imposed by paragraph (1), there is hereby imposed on the participation of any foundation manager in the making of the investment, knowing that it is jeopardizing the carrying out of any of the foundation's exempt purposes, a tax equal to 10 percent of the amount so invested for each year (or part thereof) in the taxable period, unless such participation is not willful and is due to reasonable cause. The tax imposed by this paragraph shall be paid by any foundation manager who participated in the making of the investment.

(b) Additional taxes.

(1) On the foundation. In any case in which an initial tax is imposed by subsection (a)(1) on the making of an investment and such investment is not removed from jeopardy within the taxable period, there is hereby imposed a tax equal to 25 percent of the amount of the investment. The tax imposed by this paragraph shall be paid by the private foundation.

(2) On the management. In any case in which an additional tax is imposed by paragraph (1), if a foundation manager refused to agree to part or all of the removal from jeopardy, there is hereby imposed a tax equal to 5 percent of the amount of the investment. The tax imposed by this paragraph shall be paid by any foundation manager who refused to agree to part or all of the removal from jeopardy.

(c) Exception for program-related investments.

For purposes of this section, investments, the primary purpose of which is to accomplish one or more of the purposes described in section 170(c)(2)(B), and no significant purpose of which is the production of income or the appreciation of property, shall not be considered as investments which jeopardize the carrying out of exempt purposes.

(d) Special rules.

For purposes of subsections (a) and (b)—

(1) Joint and several liability. If more than one person is liable under subsection (a)(2) or (b)(2) with respect to any one investment, all such persons shall be jointly and severally liable under such paragraph with respect to such investment.

(2) Limit for management. With respect to any one investment, the maximum amount of the tax imposed by subsection (a)(2) shall not exceed $10,000, and the maximum amount of the tax imposed by subsection (b)(2) shall not exceed $20,000.

(e) Definitions.

For purposes of this section—

(1) Taxable period. The term "taxable period" means, with respect to any investment which jeopardizes the carrying out of exempt purposes, the period beginning with the date on which the amount is so invested and ending on the earliest of—

(A) the date of mailing of a notice of deficiency with respect to the tax imposed by subsection (a)(1) under section 6212,

(B) the date on which the tax imposed by subsection (a)(1) is assessed, or

(C) the date on which the amount so invested is removed from jeopardy.

(2) Removal from jeopardy. An investment which jeopardizes the carrying out of exempt purposes shall be considered to be removed from jeopardy when such investment is sold or otherwise disposed of, and the proceeds of such sale or other disposition are not investments which jeopardize the carrying out of exempt purposes.

3,303

Code Sec. 4944   **Excise and miscellaneous taxes**

In 2006, P.L. 109-280, Sec. 1212(d)(1), substituted "10 percent" for "5 percent" in paras. (a)(1) and (2)... Sec. 1212(d)(2)(A), substituted "$10,000," for "$5,000," in para. (d)(2)... Sec. 1212(d)(2)(B), substituted "$20,000." for "$10,000." in para. (d)(2), effective for tax. yrs. begin. after 8/17/2006.

In 1980, P.L. 96-596, Sec. 2(a)(1)(E), substituted "taxable period" for "correction period" in para. (b)(1)... Sec. 2(a)(2)(D), amended para. (e)(1)... Sec. 2(a)(3)(D), deleted para. (e)(3), effective as provided in Sec. 2(d) of this Act, which reads as follows:

"(d) *Effective dates.*—

"(1) First tier taxes.—The amendments made by this section with respect to any first tier tax shall take effect as if included in the Internal Revenue Code of 1954 when such tax was first imposed.

"(2) Second tier taxes.—The amendments made by this section with respect to any second tier tax shall apply only with respect to taxes assessed after the date of the enactment of this Act. Nothing in the preceding sentence shall be construed to permit the assessment of a tax in a case to which, on the date of the enactment of this Act, the doctrine of res judicata applies.

"(3) First and second tier tax.—For purposes of this subsection, the terms 'first tier tax' and 'second tier tax' have the respective meanings given to such terms by section 4962 of the Internal Revenue Code of 1954."

Prior to deletion, para. (e)(3) read as follows:

"(3) Correction period. The term 'correction period' means, with respect to any investment which jeopardizes the carrying out of exempt purposes, the period beginning with the date on which such investment is entered into and ending 90 days after the date of mailing of a notice of deficiency with respect to the tax imposed by subsection (b)(1) under section 6212 extended by—

"(A) any period in which a deficiency cannot be assessed under section 6213(a), and

"(B) any other period which the Secretary determines is reasonable and necessary to bring about removal from jeopardy."

Prior to amendment, para. (e)(1) read as follows:

"(1) Taxable period. The term 'taxable period' means, with respect to any investment which jeopardizes the carrying out of exempt purposes, the period beginning with the date on which the amount is so invested and ending on whichever of the following is the earlier: (A) the date of mailing of a notice of deficiency with respect to the tax imposed by subsection (a)(1) under section 6212, or (B) the date on which the amount so invested is removed from jeopardy."

In 1976, P.L. 94-455, Sec. 1906(b)(13)(A), substituted "Secretary" for "Secretary or his delegate" in Code Sec. 4944, effective 2/1/77.

In 1969, P.L. 91-172, Sec. 101(b), added Code Sec. 4944, effective 1/1/70.

Sec. 4945. Taxes on taxable expenditures.

(a) Initial taxes.

(1) On the foundation. There is hereby imposed on each taxable expenditure (as defined in subsection (d)) a tax equal to 20 percent of the amount thereof. The tax imposed by this paragraph shall be paid by the private foundation.

(2) On the management. There is hereby imposed on the agreement of any foundation manager to the making of an expenditure, knowing that it is a taxable expenditure, a tax equal to 5 percent of the amount thereof, unless such agreement is not willful and is due to reasonable cause. The tax imposed by this paragraph shall be paid by any foundation manager who agreed to the making of the expenditure.

(b) Additional taxes.

(1) On the foundation. In any case in which an initial tax is imposed by subsection (a)(1) on a taxable expenditure and such expenditure is not corrected within the taxable period, there is hereby imposed a tax equal to 100 percent of the amount of the expenditure. The tax imposed by this paragraph shall be paid by the private foundation.

(2) On the management. In any case in which an additional tax is imposed by paragraph (1), if a foundation manager refused to agree to part or all of the correction, there is hereby imposed a tax equal to 50 percent of the amount of the taxable expenditure. The tax imposed by this paragraph shall be paid by any foundation manager who refused to agree to part or all of the correction.

(c) Special rules.

For purposes of subsections (a) and (b)—

(1) Joint and several liability. If more than one person is liable under subsection (a)(2) or (b)(2) with respect to the making of a taxable expenditure, all such persons shall be jointly and severally liable under such paragraph with respect to such expenditure.

(2) Limit for management. With respect to any one taxable expenditure, the maximum amount of the tax imposed by subsection (a)(2) shall not exceed $10,000, and the maximum amount of the tax imposed by subsection (b)(2) shall not exceed $20,000.

(d) Taxable expenditure.

For purposes of this section, the term "taxable expenditure" means any amount paid or incurred by a private foundation—

(1) to carry on propaganda, or otherwise to attempt, to influence legislation, within the meaning of subsection (e),

(2) except as provided in subsection (f), to influence the outcome of any specific public election, or to carry on, directly or indirectly, any voter registration drive,

(3) as a grant to an individual for travel, study, or other similar purposes by such individual, unless such grant satisfies the requirements of subsection (g),

(4) as a grant to an organization unless—

  (A) such organization—

    (i) is described in paragraph (1) or (2) of section 509(a),

    (ii) is an organization described in section 509(a)(3) (other than an organization described in clause (i) or (ii) of section 4942(g)(4)(A)), or

    (iii) is an exempt operating foundation (as defined in section 4940(d)(2)), or

  (B) the private foundation exercises expenditure responsibility with respect to such grant in accordance with subsection (h), or

(5) for any purpose other than one specified in section 170(c)(2)(B).

(e) Activities within subsection (d)(1).

For purposes of subsection (d)(1), the term "taxable expenditure" means any amount paid or incurred by a private foundation for—

(1) any attempt to influence any legislation through an attempt to affect the opinion of the general public or any segment thereof, and

(2) any attempt to influence legislation through communication with any member or employee of a legislative body, or with any other government official or employee who may participate in the formulation of the legislation (except technical advice or assistance provided to a governmental body or to a committee or other subdivision thereof in response to a written request by such body or subdivision, as the case may be),

other than through making available the results of nonpartisan analysis, study, or research. Paragraph (2) of this subsection shall not apply to any amount paid or incurred in connection with an appearance before, or communication to, any legislative body with respect to a possible decision of such body which might affect the existence of the private foundation, its powers and duties, its tax-exempt status, or the deduction of contributions to such foundation.

(f) Nonpartisan activities carried on by certain organizations.

Subsection (d)(2) shall not apply to any amount paid or incurred by any organization—

(1) which is described in section 501(c)(3) and exempt from taxation under section 501(a),

(2) the activities of which are nonpartisan, are not confined to one specific election period, and are carried on in 5 or more States,

3,304

(3) substantially all of the income of which is expended directly for the active conduct of the activities constituting the purpose or function for which it is organized and operated,

(4) substantially all of the support (other than gross investment income as defined in section 509(e)) of which is received from exempt organizations, the general public, governmental units described in section 170(c)(1), or any combination of the foregoing; not more than 25 percent of such support is received from any one exempt organization (for this purpose treating private foundations which are described in section 4946(a)(1)(H) with respect to each other as one exempt organization); and not more than half of the support of which is received from gross investment income, and

(5) contributions to which for voter registration drives are not subject to conditions that they may be used only in specified States, possessions of the United States, or political subdivisions or other areas of any of the foregoing, or the District of Columbia, or that they may be used in only one specific election period.

In determining whether the organization meets the requirements of paragraph (4) for any taxable year of such organization, there shall be taken into account the support received by such organization during such taxable year and during the immediately preceding 4 taxable years of such organization (excluding therefrom any preceding taxable year which begins before January 1, 1970). Subsection (d)(4) shall not apply to any grant to an organization which meets the requirements of this subsection.

(g) **Individual grants.**

Subsection (d)(3) shall not apply to an individual grant awarded on an objective and nondiscriminatory basis pursuant to a procedure approved in advance by the Secretary, if it is demonstrated to the satisfaction of the Secretary that—

(1) the grant constitutes a scholarship or fellowship grant which would be subject to the provisions of section 117(a) (as in effect on the day before the date of the enactment [10/22/86] of the Tax Reform Act of 1986) and is to be used for study at an educational organization described in section 170(b)(1)(A)(ii),

(2) the grant constitutes a prize or award which is subject to the provisions of section 74(b) (without regard to paragraph (3) thereof), if the recipient of such prize or award is selected from the general public, or

(3) the purpose of the grant is to achieve a specific objective, produce a report or other similar product, or improve or enhance a literary, artistic, musical, scientific, teaching, or other similar capacity, skill, or talent of the grantee.

(h) **Expenditure responsibility.**

The expenditure responsibility referred to in subsection (d)(4) means that the private foundation is responsible to exert all reasonable efforts and to establish adequate procedures—

(1) to see that the grant is spent solely for the purpose for which made,

(2) to obtain full and complete reports from the grantee on how the funds are spent, and

(3) to make full and detailed reports with respect to such expenditures to the Secretary.

(i) **Other definitions.**

For purposes of this section—

(1) **Correction.** The terms "correction" and "correct" mean, with respect to any taxable expenditure, (A) recovering part or all of the expenditure to the extent recovery is possible, and where full recovery is not possible such additional corrective action as is prescribed by the Secretary by regulations, or (B) in the case of a failure to comply with subsection (h)(2) or (h)(3), obtaining or making the report in question.

(2) **Taxable period.** The term "taxable period" means, with respect to any taxable expenditure, the period beginning with the date on which the taxable expenditure occurs and ending on the earlier of—

(A) the date of mailing a notice of deficiency with respect to the tax imposed by subsection (a)(1) under section 6212, or

(B) the date on which the tax imposed by subsection (a)(1) is assessed.

In 2006, P.L. 109-280, Sec. 1212(e)(1)(A), substituted "20 percent" for "10 percent" in para. (a)(1) . . . Sec. 1212(e)(1)(B), substituted "5 percent" for "2½ percent" in para. (a)(2) . . . Sec. 1212(e)(2)(A), substituted "$10,000," for "$5,000," in para. (c)(2) . . . Sec. 1212(e)(2)(B), substituted "$20,000." for "$10,000." in para. (c)(2), effective for tax. yrs. begin. after 8/17/2006.

—P.L. 109-280, Sec. 1244(b), amended subpara. (d)(4)(A), effective for distributions and expenditures after 8/17/2006.

Prior to amendment, subpara. (d)(4)(A) read as follows:

"(A) such organization is described in paragraph (1), (2), or (3) of section 509(a) or is an exempt operating foundation (as defined in section 4940(d)(2)), or"

In 1988, P.L. 100-647, Sec. 1001(d)(1)(B), amended para. (g)(1), effective for tax. yrs. begin. after 12/31/86, but only in the case of scholarships and fellowships granted after 8/16/86.

Prior to amendment, para. (g)(1) read as follows:

"(1) the grant constitutes a scholarship or fellowship grant which is subject to the provisions of section 117(a) and is to be used for study at an educational organization described in section 170(b)(1)(A)(ii),"

In 1986, P.L. 99-514, Sec. 122(a)(2)(B), substituted "section 74(b) (without regard to paragraph (3) thereof)" for "section 74(b)" in para. (g)(2), effective for prizes and awards granted after 12/31/86.

In 1984, P.L. 98-369, Sec. 302(b), amended para. (d)(4), effective for grants made after 12/31/84, in tax. yrs. end. after 12/31/84.

Prior to amendment, para. (d)(4) read as follows:

"(4) as a grant to an organization (other than an organization described in paragraph (1), (2), or (3) of section 509(a)), unless the private foundation exercises expenditure responsibility with respect to such grant in accordance with subsection (h), or".

In 1980, P.L. 96-596, Sec. 2(a)(1)(F), substituted "taxable period" for "correction period" in para. (b)(1) . . . Sec. 2(a)(2)(E), amended para. (i)(2), effective as provided in Sec. 2(d) of this Act which reads as follows:

(d) Effective dates.—

"(1) First tier taxes.—The amendments made by this section with respect to any first tier tax shall take effect as if included in the Internal Revenue Code of 1954 when such tax was first imposed.

"(2) Second tier taxes.—The amendments made by this section with respect to any second tier tax shall apply only with respect to taxes assessed after the date of the enactment of this Act [12/24/80]. Nothing in the preceding sentence shall be construed to permit the assessment of a tax in a case to which, on the date of the enactment of this Act [12/24/80], the doctrine of res judicata applies.

"(3) First and second tier tax.—For purposes of this subsection, the terms 'first tier tax' and 'second tier tax' have the respective meanings given to such terms by section 4962 of the Internal Revenue Code of 1954."

Prior to amendment, para. (i)(2) read as follows:

"(2) Correction period. The term 'correction period' means, with respect to any taxable expenditure, the period beginning with the date on which the taxable expenditure occurs and ending 90 days after the date of mailing of a notice of deficiency with respect to the tax imposed by subsection (b)(1) under section 6212, extended by—

"(A) any period in which a deficiency cannot be assessed under section 6213(a), and

"(B) any other period which the Secretary determines is reasonable and necessary to bring about correction of the taxable expenditure (except that such determination shall not be made with respect to any taxable expenditure within the meaning of paragraph (1), (2), (3), or (4) of subsection (d) because of any action by an appropriate State officer as defined in section 6104(c)(2))."

In 1976, P.L. 94-455, Sec. 1901(b)(8)(H), substituted "educational organization described in section 170(b)(1)(A)(ii)" for "educational institution described in section 151(e)(4)" in para. (g)(1), effective for tax. yrs. begin. after 12/31/76.

—P.L. 94-455, Sec. 1906(b)(13)(A), substituted "Secretary" for "Secretary or his delegate" each place it appeared in Code Sec. 4945, effective 2/1/77.

In 1969, P.L. 91-172, Sec. 101(b), added Code Sec. 4945, effective 1/1/70; subsecs. (d)(4) and (h) shall not apply to a grant which is described in para. (C) of the note following Code Sec. 4942.

Sec. 4946. Definitions and special rules.
(a) Disqualified person.
(1) In general. For purposes of this subchapter, the term "disqualified person" means, with respect to a private foundation, a person who is—
(A) a substantial contributor to the foundation,
(B) a foundation manager (within the meaning of subsection (b)(1)),
(C) an owner of more than 20 percent of—
(i) the total combined voting power of a corporation,
(ii) the profits interest of a partnership, or
(iii) the beneficial interest of a trust or unincorporated enterprise,
which is a substantial contributor to the foundation,
(D) a member of the family (as defined in subsection (d)) of any individual described in subparagraph (A), (B), or (C),
(E) a corporation of which persons described in subparagraph (A), (B), (C), or (D) own more than 35 percent of the total combined voting power,
(F) a partnership in which persons described in subparagraph (A), (B), (C), or (D) own more than 35 percent of the profits interest,
(G) a trust or estate in which persons described in subparagraph (A), (B), (C), or (D) hold more than 35 percent of the beneficial interest,
(H) only for purposes of section 4943, a private foundation—
(i) which is effectively controlled (directly or indirectly) by the same person or persons who control the private foundation in question, or
(ii) substantially all of the contributions to which were made (directly or indirectly) by the same person or persons described in subparagraph (A), (B), or (C), or members of their families (within the meaning of subsection (d)), who made (directly or indirectly) substantially all of the contributions to the private foundation in question, and
(I) only for purposes of section 4941, a government official (as defined in subsection (c)).
(2) Substantial contributors. For purposes of paragraph (1), the term "substantial contributor" means a person who is described in section 507(d)(2).
(3) Stockholdings. For purposes of paragraphs (1)(C)(i) and (1)(E), there shall be taken into account indirect stockholdings which would be taken into account under section 267(c), except that, for purposes of this paragraph, section 267(c)(4) shall be treated as providing that the members of the family of an individual are the members within the meaning of subsection (d).
(4) Partnerships; trusts. For purposes of paragraphs (1)(C)(ii) and (iii), (1)(F), and (1)(G), the ownership of profits or beneficial interests shall be determined in accordance with the rules for constructive ownership of stock provided in section 267(c) (other than paragraph (3) thereof), except that section 267(c)(4) shall be treated as providing that the members of the family of an individual are the members within the meaning of subsection (d).
(b) Foundation manager.
For purposes of this subchapter, the term "foundation manager" means, with respect to any private foundation—
(1) an officer, director, or trustee of a foundation (or an individual having powers or responsibilities similar to those of officers, directors, or trustees of the foundation), and

(2) with respect to any act (or failure to act), the employees of the foundation having authority or responsibility with respect to such act (or failure to act).
(c) Government official.
For purposes of subsection (a)(1)(I) and section 4941, the term "government official" means, with respect to an act of self-dealing described in section 4941, an individual who, at the time of such act, holds any of the following offices or positions (other than as a "special Government employee", as defined in section 202(a) of title 18, United States Code):
(1) an elective public office in the executive or legislative branch of the Government of the United States,
(2) an office in the executive or judicial branch of the Government of the United States, appointment to which was made by the President,
(3) a position in the executive, legislative, or judicial branch of the Government of the United States—
(A) which is listed in schedule C of rule VI of the Civil Service Rules, or
(B) the compensation for which is equal to or greater than the lowest rate of basic pay for the Senior Executive Service under section 5382 of title 5, United States Code,
(4) a position under the House of Representatives or the Senate of the United States held by an individual receiving gross compensation at an annual rate of $15,000 or more,
(5) an elective or appointive public office in the executive, legislative, or judicial branch of the government of a State, possession of the United States, or political subdivision or other area of any of the foregoing, or of the District of Columbia, held by an individual receiving gross compensation at an annual rate of $20,000 or more,
(6) a position as personal or executive assistant or secretary to any of the foregoing, or
(7) a member of the Internal Revenue Service Oversight Board.
(d) Members of family.
For purposes of subsection (a)(1), the family of any individual shall include only his spouse, ancestors, children, grandchildren, great grandchildren, and the spouses of children, grandchildren, and great grandchildren.

In 2000, P.L. 106-554, Sec. 1(a)(7), [which enacted into law Sec. 319(16) of P.L. 106-554] substituted "the lowest rate of basic pay for the Senior Executive Service under section 5382" for "the lowest rate of compensation prescribed for GS-16 of the General Schedule under section 5332" in subpara. (c)(3)(B), effective 12/21/2000.
In 1998, P.L. 105-206, Sec. 1101(c)(1), deleted "or" at the end of para. (c)(5), substituted ", or" for the period at the end of para. (c)(6) and added para. (c)(7), effective 7/22/98.
In 1986, P.L. 99-514, Sec. 1606(a), substituted "$20,000" for "$15,000" in para. (c)(5), effective for compensation received after 12/31/85.
In 1984, P.L. 98-369, Sec. 306(a), amended subsec. (d), effective 1/1/85.
Prior to amendment, subsec. (d) read as follows:
"(d) Members of family.
"For purposes of subsection (a)(1), the family of any individual shall include only his spouse, ancestors, lineal descendants, and spouses of lineal descendants."
In 1978, P.L. 95-227, Sec. 4(c)(2)(B), substituted "For purposes of this subchapter" for "For purposes of this chapter" effective for contributions, acts, and expenditures made after 12/31/77, in and for tax. yrs. begin. after 12/31/77.
In 1969, P.L. 91-172, Sec. 101(b), added Code Sec. 4946, effective 1/1/70.

Sec. 4947. Application of taxes to certain nonexempt trusts.
(a) Application of tax.
(1) Charitable trusts. For purposes of part II of subchapter F of chapter 1 (other than section 508(a), (b), and (c)) and for purposes of this chapter, a trust which is not exempt from taxation under section 501(a), all of the unexpired interests in which are devoted to one or more of

Excise and miscellaneous taxes Code Sec. 4947

the purposes described in section 170(c)(2)(B), and for which a deduction was allowed under section 170, 545(b)(2), 642(c), 2055, 2106(a)(2), or 2522 (or the corresponding provisions of prior law), shall be treated as an organization described in section 501(c)(3). For purposes of section 509(a)(3)(A), such a trust shall be treated as if organized on the day on which it first becomes subject to this paragraph.

(2) Split-interest trusts. In the case of a trust which is not exempt from tax under section 501(a), not all of the unexpired interests in which are devoted to one or more of the purposes described in section 170(c)(2)(B), and which has amounts in trust for which a deduction was allowed under section 170, 545(b)(2), 642(c), 2055, 2106(a)(2), or 2522, section 507 (relating to termination of private foundation status), section 508(e) (relating to governing instruments) to the extent applicable to a trust described in this paragraph, section 4941 (relating to taxes on self-dealing), section 4943 (relating to taxes on excess business holdings) except as provided in subsection (b)(3), section 4944 (relating to investments which jeopardize charitable purpose) except as provided in subsection (b)(3), and section 4945 (relating to taxes on taxable expenditures) shall apply as if such trust were a private foundation. This paragraph shall not apply with respect to—

> • **Caution:** Sec. 301(a), P.L. 111-312, (reproduced in the history notes following this Code Sec.) provides that the amendments made by Sec. 542(e)(4), P.L. 107-16, EGTRRA, will apply as if never enacted. Code Sec. 4947(a)(2)(A), following, reflects the removal of these amendments, effective for estates of decedents dying, and transfers made, after 12/31/2009.

(A) any amounts payable under the terms of such trust to income beneficiaries, unless a deduction was allowed under section 170(f)(2)(B), 2055(e)(2)(B), or 2522(c)(2)(B),

> • **Caution:** Code Sec. 4947(a)(2)(A), following, was amended by Sec. 542(e)(4), P.L. 107-16, EGTRRA. As provided in Sec. 301(a), P.L. 111-312, this amendment will apply as if never enacted, effective for estates of decedents dying, and transfers made, after 12/31/2009.

(A) any amounts payable under the terms of such trust to income beneficiaries, unless a deduction was allowed under section 170(f)(2)(B), 642(c), 2055(e)(2)(B), or 2522(c)(2)(B),
(B) any amounts in trust other than amounts for which a deduction was allowed under section 170, 545(b)(2), 642(c), 2055, 2106(a)(2), or 2522, if such other amounts are segregated from amounts for which no deduction was allowable, or
(C) any amounts transferred in trust before May 27, 1969.

(3) Segregated amounts. For purposes of paragraph (2)(B), a trust with respect to which amounts are segregated shall separately account for the various income, deduction, and other items properly attributable to each of such segregated amounts.

(b) Special rules.
(1) Regulations. The Secretary shall prescribe such regulations as may be necessary to carry out the purposes of this section.
(2) Limit to segregated amounts. If any amounts in the trust are segregated within the meaning of subsection (a)(2)(B) of this section, the value of the net assets for purposes of subsections (c)(2) and (g) of section 507 shall be limited to such segregated amounts.
(3) Sections 4943 and 4944. Sections 4943 and 4944 shall not apply to a trust which is described in subsection (a)(2) if—

(A) all the income interest (and none of the remainder interest) of such trust is devoted solely to one or more of the purposes described in section 170(c)(2)(B), and all amounts in such trust for which a deduction was allowed under section 170, 545(b)(2), 642(c), 2055, 2106(a)(2), or 2522 have an aggregate value not more than 60 percent of the aggregate fair market value of all amounts in such trusts, or
(B) a deduction was allowed under section 170, 545(b)(2), 642(c), 2055, 2106(a)(2), or 2522 for amounts payable under the terms of such trust to every remainder beneficiary but not to any income beneficiary.

(4) Section 507. The provisions of section 507(a) shall not apply to a trust which is described in subsection (a)(2) by reason of a distribution of qualified employer securities (as defined in section 664(g)(4)) to an employee stock ownership plan (as defined in section 4975(e)(7)) in a qualified gratuitous transfer (as defined by section 664(g)).

In 2010, P.L. 111-312, Sec. 101(a)(1), substituted "December 31, 2012" for "December 31, 2010" both places it appeared in Sec. 901 of P.L. 107-16 [see below], effective as if included in the enactment of P.L. 107-16, EGTRRA, 6/7/2001.
—P.L. 111-312, Sec. 301(a), provides that Code Sec. 4947, as amended by Sec. 542(e)(4), P.L. 107-16 EGTRRA, 6/7/2001 (amended subpara. (a)(2)(A), see below) will read as if such provision had never been enacted, effective for estates of decedents dying, and transfers made, after 12/31/2009.
Sec. 301(a) of P.L. 111-312, provides:
"(a) In general. Each provision of law amended by subtitle A or E of title V of the Economic Growth and Tax Relief Reconciliation Act of 2001 is amended to read as such provision would read if such subtitle had never been enacted."
Prior to the enactment of Sec. 301(a) of P.L. 111-312, subpara. (a)(2)(A) read as follows:
"(A) any amounts payable under the terms of such trust to income beneficiaries, unless a deduction was allowed under section 170(f)(2)(B), 642(c), 2055(e)(2)(B), or 2522(c)(2)(B),
—P.L. 111-312, Sec. 301(c), of this Act, provides:
"(c) Special election with respect to estates of decedents dying in 2010. Notwithstanding subsection (a), in the case of an estate of a decedent dying after December 31, 2009, and before January 1, 2011, the executor (within the meaning of section 2203 of the Internal Revenue Code of 1986) may elect to apply such Code as though the amendments made by subsection (a) do not apply with respect to chapter 11 of such Code and with respect to property acquired or passing from such decedent (within the meaning of section 1014(b) of such Code). Such election shall be made at such time and in such manner as the Secretary of the Treasury or the Secretary's delegate shall provide. Such an election once made shall be revocable only with the consent of the Secretary of the Treasury or the Secretary's delegate. For purposes of section 2652(a)(1) of such Code, the determination of whether any property is subject to the tax imposed by such chapter 11 shall be made without regard to any election made under this subsection."
—P.L. 111-312, Sec. 301(d), of this Act, provides:
"(d) Extension of time for performing certain acts.
"(1) Estate tax. In the case of the estate of a decedent dying after December 31, 2009, and before the date of the enactment of this Act, the due date for—
"(A) filing any return under section 6018 of the Internal Revenue Code of 1986 (including any election required to be made on such a return) as such section is in effect after the date of the enactment of this Act without regard to any election under subsection (c),
"(B) making any payment of tax under chapter 11 of such Code, and
"(C) making any disclaimer described in section 2518(b) of such Code of an interest in property passing by reason of the death of such decedent, shall not be earlier than the date which is 9 months after the date of the enactment of this Act.
"(2) Generation-skipping tax. In the case of any generation-skipping transfer made after December 31, 2009, and before the date of the enactment of this Act, the due date for filing any return under section 2662 of the Internal Revenue Code

of 1986 (including any election required to be made on such a return) shall not be earlier than the date which is 9 months after the date of the enactment of this Act.

In 2004, P.L. 108-357, Sec. 413(c)(30), deleted '556(b)(2),' each place it appeared in Code Sec. 4947, effective for tax. yrs. of foreign corporations begin. after 12/31/2004, and for tax. yrs. of United States shareholders with or within which such tax. yrs. of foreign corporations end.

In 2002, P.L. 107-358, Sec. 2, added subsec. (c) in Sec. 901 of P.L. 107-16 [see below], effective 12/17/2002.

In 2001, P.L. 107-16, Sec. 542(e)(4), added '642(c),' after 'section 170(f)(2)(B),' in subpara. (a)(2)(A), effective for deductions for tax. yrs. begin. after 12/31/2009.
—P.L. 107-16, Sec. 901, of this Act [as amended by Sec. 2 of P.L. 107-358, and Sec. 101(a)(1) of P.L. 111-312, 12/17/2010, see above], reads as follows:
"SEC. 901. SUNSET OF PROVISIONS OF ACT.
"(a) In general. All provisions of, and amendments made by, this Act shall not apply—
"(1) to taxable, plan, or limitation years beginning after December 31, 2012, or
"(2) in the case of title V, to estates of decedents dying, gifts made, or generation skipping transfers, after December 31, 2012.
"(b) Application of certain laws. The Internal Revenue Code of 1986 and the Employee Retirement Income Security Act of 1974 shall be applied and administered to years, estates, gifts, and transfers described in subsection (a) as if the provisions and amendments described in subsection (a) had never been enacted.
"(c) Exception. Subsection (a) shall not apply to section 803 (relating to no federal income tax on restitution received by victims of the Nazi regime or their heirs or estates)."

In 1997, P.L. 105-34, Sec. 1530(c)(9), added para. (b)(4), effective for transfers made by trusts to, or for the use of, an employee stock ownership plan after 8/5/97.

In 1976, P.L. 94-455, Sec. 1906(b)(13)(A), substituted "Secretary" for "Secretary or his delegate" in para. (b)(1), effective 2/1/77.

In 1969, P.L. 91-172, Sec. 101(b), added Code Sec. 4947, effective 1/1/70.

Sec. 4948. Application of taxes and denial of exemption with respect to certain foreign organizations.

(a) Tax on income of certain foreign organizations.

In lieu of the tax imposed by section 4940, there is hereby imposed for each taxable year on the gross investment income (within the meaning of section 4940(c)(2)) derived from sources within the United States (within the meaning of section 861) by every foreign organization which is a private foundation for the taxable year a tax equal to 4 percent of such income.

(b) Certain sections inapplicable.

Section 507 (relating to termination of private foundation status), section 508 (relating to special rules with respect to section 501(c)(3) organizations), and this chapter (other than this section) shall not apply to any foreign organization which has received substantially all of its support (other than gross investment income) from sources outside the United States.

(c) Denial of exemption to foreign organizations engaged in prohibited transactions.

(1) General rule. A foreign organization described in subsection (b) shall not be exempt from taxation under section 501(a) if it has engaged in a prohibited transaction after December 31, 1969.

(2) Prohibited transactions. For purposes of this subsection, the term "prohibited transaction" means any act or failure to act (other than with respect to section 4942(e)) which would subject a foreign organization described in subsection (b), or a disqualified person (as defined in section 4946) with respect thereto, to liability for a penalty under section 6684 or a tax under section 507 if such foreign organization were a domestic organization.

(3) Taxable years affected.

(A) Except as provided in subparagraph (B), a foreign organization described in subsection (b) shall be denied exemption from taxation under section 501(a) by reason of paragraph (1) for all taxable years beginning with the taxable year during which it is notified by the Secretary that it has engaged in a prohibited transaction. The Secretary shall publish such notice in the Federal Register on the day on which he so notifies such foreign organization.

(B) Under regulations prescribed by the Secretary, any foreign organization described in subsection (b) which is denied exemption from taxation under section 501(a) by reason of paragraph (1) may, with respect to the second taxable year following the taxable year in which notice is given under subparagraph (A) (or any taxable year thereafter), file claim for exemption from taxation under section 501(a). If the Secretary is satisfied that such organization will not knowingly again engage in a prohibited transaction, such organization shall not, with respect to taxable years beginning with the taxable year with respect to which such claim is filed, be denied exemption from taxation under section 501(a) by reason of any prohibited transaction which was engaged in before the date on which such notice was given under subparagraph (A).

(4) Disallowance of certain charitable deductions. No gift or bequest shall be allowed as a deduction under section 170, 545(b)(2), 642(c), 2055, 2106(a)(2), or 2522, if made—

(A) to a foreign organization described in subsection (b) after the date on which the Secretary publishes notice under paragraph (3)(A) that he has notified such organization that it has engaged in a prohibited transaction, and

(B) in a taxable year of such organization for which it is not exempt from taxation under section 501(a) by reason of paragraph (1).

In 2004, P.L. 108-357, Sec. 413(c)(30), deleted "556(b)(2)," after "545(b)(2)," in para. (c)(4), effective for tax. yrs. of foreign corporations begin. after 12/31/2004, and for tax. yrs. of United States shareholders with or within which such tax. yrs. of foreign corporations end.

In 1976, P.L. 94-455, Sec. 1906(b)(13)(A), substituted "Secretary" for "Secretary or his delegate" each time it appeared, in para. (c)(3) and (c)(4), effective 2/1/77.

In 1969, P.L. 91-172, Sec. 101(b), added Code Sec. 4948, effective for tax. yrs. begin. after 12/31/69. Sec. 101(1)(8) provides as follows:
"(8) Certain redemptions.—For purposes of applying section 302(b)(1) to the determination of the amount of gross investment income under sections 4940 and 4948(a), any distribution made to a private foundation in redemption of stock held by such private foundation in a business enterprise shall be treated as not essentially equivalent to a dividend, if such redemption is described in paragraph (2)(B) of this subsection [see note following Sec. 4941]."

Subchapter B.—Black Lung Benefit Trusts

Sec.
4951. Taxes on self-dealing.
4952. Taxes on taxable expenditures.
4953. Tax on excess contributions to black lung benefit trusts.

In 1978, P.L. 95-227, Sec. 4(c)(1), added subchapter B.

Sec. 4951. Taxes on self-dealing.

(a) Initial taxes.

(1) On self-dealer. There is hereby imposed a tax on each act of self-dealing between a disqualified person and a trust described in section 501(c)(21). The rate of tax shall be equal to 10 percent of the amount involved with respect to the act of self-dealing for each year (or part thereof) in the taxable period. The tax imposed by this paragraph shall be paid by any disqualified person (other than a trustee acting only as a trustee of the trust) who participates in the act of self-dealing.

(2) On trustee. In any case in which a tax is imposed by paragraph (1), there is hereby imposed on the participation of any trustee of such a trust in an act of self-dealing between a disqualified person and the trust, knowing that it is such an act, a tax equal to 2½ percent of the amount involved with respect to the act of self-dealing for each year (or part thereof) in the taxable period, unless such participation is not willful and is due to reasonable cause. The tax imposed by this paragraph shall be paid by any such trustee who participated in the act of self-dealing.

(b) Additional taxes.

(1) On self-dealer. In any case in which an initial tax is imposed by subsection (a)(1) on an act of self-dealing by a disqualified person with a trust described in section 501(c)(21) and in which the act is not corrected within the taxable period, there is hereby imposed a tax equal to 100 percent of the amount involved. The tax imposed by this paragraph shall be paid by any disqualified person (other than a trustee acting only as a trustee of such a trust) who participated in the act of self-dealing.

(2) On trustee. In any case in which an additional tax is imposed by paragraph (1), if a trustee of such a trust refused to agree to part or all of the correction, there is hereby imposed a tax equal to 50 percent of the amount involved. The tax imposed by this paragraph shall be paid by any such trustee who refused to agree to part or all of the correction.

(c) Joint and several liability.

If more than one person is liable under any paragraph of subsection (a) or (b) with respect to any one act of self-dealing, all such persons shall be jointly and severally liable under such paragraph with respect to such act.

(d) Self-dealing.

(1) In general. For purposes of this section, the term "self-dealing" means any direct or indirect—

(A) sale, exchange, or leasing of real or personal property between a trust described in section 501(c)(21) and a disqualified person;

(B) lending of money or other extension of credit between such a trust and a disqualified person;

(C) furnishing of goods, services, or facilities between such a trust and a disqualified person;

(D) payment of compensation (or payment or reimbursement of expenses) by such a trust to a disqualified person; and

(E) transfer to, or use by or for the benefit of, a disqualified person of the income or assets of such a trust.

(2) Special rules. For purposes of paragraph (1)—

(A) the transfer of personal property by a disqualified person to such a trust shall be treated as a sale or exchange if the property is subject to a mortgage or similar lien;

(B) the furnishing of goods, services, or facilities by a disqualified person to such a trust shall not be an act of self-dealing if the furnishing is without charge and if the goods, services, or facilities so furnished are used exclusively for the purposes specified in section 501(c)(21)(A); and

(C) the payment of compensation (and the payment or reimbursement of expenses) by such a trust to a disqualified person for personal services which are reasonable and necessary to carrying out the exempt purpose of the trust shall not be an act of self-dealing if the compensation (or payment or reimbursement) is not excessive.

(e) Definitions.

For purposes of this section—

(1) Taxable period. The term "taxable period" means, with respect to any act of self-dealing, the period beginning with the date on which the act of self-dealing occurs and ending on the earliest of—

(A) the date of mailing a notice of deficiency with respect to the tax imposed by subsection (a)(1) under section 6212,

(B) the date on which the tax imposed by subsection (a)(1) is assessed, or

(C) the date on which correction of the act of self-dealing is completed.

(2) Amount involved. The term "amount involved" means, with respect to any act of self-dealing, the greater of the amount of money and the fair market value of the other property given or the amount of money and the fair market value of the other property received; except that in the case of services described in subsection (d)(2)(C), the amount involved shall be only the excess compensation. For purposes of the preceding sentence, the fair market value—

(A) in the case of the taxes imposed by subsection (a), shall be determined as of the date on which the act of self-dealing occurs; and

(B) in the case of taxes imposed by subsection (b), shall be the highest fair market value during the taxable period.

(3) Correction. The terms "correction" and "correct" mean, with respect to any act of self-dealing, undoing the transaction to the extent possible, but in any case placing the trust in a financial position not worse than that in which it would be if the disqualified person were dealing under the highest fiduciary standards.

(4) Disqualified person. The term "disqualified person" means, with respect to a trust described in section 501(c)(21), a person who is—

(A) a contributor to the trust,

(B) a trustee of the trust,

(C) an owner of more than 10 percent of—

(i) the total combined voting power of a corporation,

(ii) the profits interest of a partnership, or

(iii) the beneficial interest of a trust or unincorporated enterprise,

which is a contributor to the trust,

(D) an officer, director, or employee of a person who is a contributor to the trust,

(E) the spouse, ancestor, lineal descendant, or spouse of a lineal descendant of an individual described in subparagraph (A), (B), (C), or (D),

(F) a corporation of which persons described in subparagraph (A), (B), (C), (D), or (E) own more than 35 percent of the total combined voting power,

(G) a partnership in which persons described in subparagraph (A), (B), (C), (D), or (E), own more than 35 percent of the profits interest, or

(H) a trust or estate in which persons described in subparagraph (A), (B), (C), (D), or (E), hold more than 35 percent of the beneficial interest.

For purposes of subparagraphs (C)(i) and (F), there shall be taken into account indirect stockholdings which would be taken into account under section 267(c), except that, for purposes of this paragraph, section 267(c)(4) shall be treated as providing that the members of the family of an individual are only those individuals described in subparagraph (E) of this paragraph. For purposes of subparagraphs (C)(ii) and (iii), (G), and (H), the ownership of profits or beneficial interests shall be determined in accordance with the rules for constructive ownership of stock provided in section 267(c) (other than paragraph (3) thereof), except that section 267(c)(4) shall be treated as providing that the members of the family of an individual

Code Sec. 4951(e)(4)(H)   **Excise and miscellaneous taxes**

are only those individuals described in subparagraph (E) of this paragraph.

(f) Payments of benefits.

For purposes of this section, a payment, out of assets or income of a trust described in section 501(c)(21), for the purposes described in subclause (I) or (IV) of section 501(c)(21)(A)(i) shall not be considered an act of self-dealing.

In **1992**, P.L. 102-486, Sec. 1940(b), substituted "subclause (I) or (IV) of section 501(c)(21)(A)(i)" for "clause (i) of section 501(c)(21)(A)" in subsec. (f), effective for tax. yrs. begin. after 12/31/91.

In **1980**, P.L. 96-596, Sec. 2(a)(1)(G), and (H), substituted "taxable period" for "correction period" in para. (b)(1) and subpara. (e)(2)(B) . . . Sec. 2(a)(3)(E), deleted para. (e)(4) and redesignated para. (e)(5) as para. (e)(4), effective as provided in Sec. 2(d)(2) of this Act which reads as follows:

"(4) Second tier taxes. The amendments made by this section with respect to any second tier tax shall apply only with respect to taxes assessed after the date of the enactment of this Act [12/24/80]. Nothing in the preceding sentence shall be construed to permit the assessment of a tax in a case to which, on the date of the enactment of this Act [12/24/80], the doctrine of res judicata applies."

Prior to amendment para. (e)(4) read as follows:

"(4) Correction period. The term 'correction period' means, with respect to any act of self-dealing, the period beginning with the date on which the act of self-dealing occurs and ending 90 days after the date of mailing of a notice of deficiency under section 6212 with respect to the tax imposed by subsection (b)(1), extended by—

"(A) any period in which a deficiency cannot be assessed under section 6213(a), and

"(B) any other period which the Secretary determines is reasonable and necessary to bring about correction of the act of self-dealing."

—P.L. 96-596, Sec. 2(a)(2)(F), amended para. (e)(1), effective as provided in Sec. 2(d) which reads as follows:

"(d) Effective Dates.—

"(1) First tier taxes.

The amendments made by this section with respect to any first tier tax shall take effect as if included in the Internal Revenue Code of 1954 when such tax was first imposed.

"(2) Second tier taxes.

The amendments made by this section with respect to any second tier tax shall apply only with respect to taxes assessed after the date of the enactment of this Act. Nothing in the preceding sentence shall be construed to permit the assessment of a tax in a case to which, on the date of the enactment of this Act, the doctrine of res judicata applies.

"(3) First and second tier tax.

For purposes of this subsection, the terms 'first tier tax' and 'second tier tax' have the respective meanings given to such terms by section 4962 of the Internal Revenue Code of 1954."

Prior to amendment para. (e)(1) read as follows:

"(1) Taxable period. The term 'taxable period' means, with respect to any act of self-dealing, the period beginning with the date on which the act of self-dealing occurs and ending on the earlier of—

"(A) the date of mailing of a notice of deficiency with respect to the tax imposed by subsection (a)(1) under section 6212, or

"(B) the date on which correction of the act of self-dealing is completed."

In **1978**, P.L. 95-227, Sec. 4(c)(1), added Code Sec. 4951, effective for contributions, acts, and expenditures made after 12/31/77, in and for tax. yrs. begin. after 12/31/77. See Sec. 20(c) of P.L. 95-239, note following Code Sec. 192.

Sec. 4952. Taxes on taxable expenditures.

(a) Tax imposed.

(1) On the fund. There is hereby imposed on each taxable expenditure (as defined in subsection (d)) from the assets or income of a trust described in section 501(c)(21) a tax equal to 10 percent of the amount thereof. The tax imposed by this paragraph shall be paid by the trustee out of the assets of the trust.

(2) On the trustee. There is hereby imposed on the agreement of any trustee of such a trust to the making of an expenditure, knowing that it is a taxable expenditure, a tax equal to 2½ percent of the amount thereof, unless such agreement is not willful and is due to reasonable cause. The tax imposed by this paragraph shall be paid by the trustee who agreed to the making of the expenditure.

(b) Additional taxes.

(1) On the fund. In any case in which an initial tax is imposed by subsection (a)(1) on a taxable expenditure and such expenditure is not corrected within the taxable period, there is hereby imposed a tax equal to 100 percent of the amount of the expenditure. The tax imposed by this paragraph shall be paid by the trustee out of the assets of the trust.

(2) On the trustee. In any case in which an additional tax is imposed by paragraph (1), if a trustee refused to agree to a part or all of the correction, there is hereby imposed a tax equal to 50 percent of the amount of the taxable expenditure. The tax imposed by this paragraph shall be paid by any trustee who refused to agree to part or all of the correction.

(c) Joint and several liability.

For purposes of subsections (a) and (b), if more than one person is liable under subsection (a)(2) or (b)(2) with respect to the making of a taxable expenditure, all such persons shall be jointly and severally liable under such paragraph with respect to such expenditure.

(d) Taxable expenditure.

For purposes of this section, the term "taxable expenditure" means any amount paid or incurred by a trust described in section 501(c)(21) other than for a purpose specified in such section.

(e) Definitions.

(1) Correction. The terms "correction" and "correct" mean, with respect to any taxable expenditure, recovering part or all of the expenditure to the extent recovery is possible, and where full recovery is not possible, contributions by the person or persons whose liabilities for black lung benefit claims (as defined in section 192(e)) are to be paid out of the trust to the extent necessary to place the trust in a financial position not worse than that in which it would be if the taxable expenditure had not been made.

(2) Taxable period. The term "taxable period" means, with respect to any taxable expenditure, the period beginning with the date on which the taxable expenditure occurs and ending on the earlier of—

(A) the date of mailing a notice of deficiency with respect to the tax imposed by subsection (a)(1) under section 6212, or

(B) the date on which the tax imposed by subsection (a)(1) is assessed.

In **1980**, P.L. 96-596, Sec. 2(a)(1)(I), substituted "taxable period" for "correction period" in para. (b)(1) . . . Sec. 2(a)(2)(G), amended para. (e)(2), effective as provided in Sec. 2(d) of this Act which reads as follows:

"(d) Effective dates.—

"(1) First tier taxes.—The amendments made by this section with respect to any first tier tax shall take effect as if included in the Internal Revenue Code of 1954 when such tax was first imposed.

"(2) Second tier taxes.—The amendments made by this section with respect to any second tier tax shall apply only with respect to taxes assessed after the date of the enactment of this Act [12/24/80]. Nothing in the preceding sentence shall be construed to permit the assessment of a tax in a case to which, on the date of the enactment of this Act [12/24/80] the doctrine of res judicata applies.

"(3) First and second tier tax.—For purposes of this subsection, the terms 'first tier tax' and 'second tier tax' have the respective meanings given to such terms by section 4962 of the Internal Revenue Code of 1954.

Prior to amendment, para. (e)(2) read as follows:

"(2) Correction period. The term 'correction period' means, with respect to any taxable expenditure, the period beginning with the date on which the taxable expenditure occurs and ending 90 days after the date of mailing of a notice of deficiency under section 6212 with respect to the tax imposed by subsection (b)(1), extended by—

"(A) any period in which a deficiency cannot be assessed under section 6213(a), and

"(B) any other period which the Secretary determines is reasonable and necessary to bring about correction of the taxable expenditure."

In **1978**, P.L. 95-227, Sec. 4(c)(1), added Code Sec. 4952, effective for contributions, acts, and expenditures made after 12/31/77, in and for tax. yrs. begin. after 12/31/77. See note following Code Sec. 192.

Excise and miscellaneous taxes

Sec. 4953. Tax on excess contributions to Black Lung Benefit Trusts.
(a) Tax imposed.
There is hereby imposed for each taxable year a tax in an amount equal to 5 percent of the amount of the excess contributions made by a person to or under a trust or trusts described in section 501(c)(21). The tax imposed by this subsection shall be paid by the person making the excess contribution.
(b) Excess contribution.
For purposes of this section, the term "excess contribution" means the sum of—
(1) the amount by which the amount contributed for the taxable year to a trust or trusts described in section 501(c)(21) exceeds the amount of the deduction allowable to such person for such contributions for the taxable year under section 192, and
(2) the amount determined under this subsection for the preceding taxable year, reduced by the sum of—
  (A) the excess of the maximum amount allowable as a deduction under section 192 for the taxable year over the amount contributed to the trust or trusts for the taxable year, and
  (B) amounts distributed from the trust to the contributor which were excess contributions for the preceding taxable year.
(c) Treatment of withdrawal of excess contributions.
Amounts distributed during the taxable year from a trust described in section 501(c)(21) to the contributor thereof the sum of which does not exceed the amount of the excess contribution made by the contributor shall not be treated as
(1) an act of self-dealing (within the meaning of section 4951),
(2) a taxable expenditure (within the meaning of section 4952), or
(3) an act contrary to the purposes for which the trust is exempt from taxation under section 501(a).

In 1978, P.L. 95-227, Sec. 4(c)(1), added Code Sec. 4953, effective for contributions, acts, and expenditures made after 12/31/77, in and for tax. yrs. begin. after 12/31/77. See note following Code Sec. 192.

Subchapter C.—Political Expenditures of Section 501(c)(3) Organizations
Sec.
4955. Taxes on political expenditures of section 501(c)(3) organizations.

In 1987, P.L. 100-203, Sec. 10712(a), established Subchapter C including in its table of sections, item 4955.

Sec. 4955. Taxes on political expenditures of section 501(c)(3) organizations.
(a) Initial taxes.
(1) **On the organization.** There is hereby imposed on each political expenditure by a section 501(c)(3) organization a tax equal to 10 percent of the amount thereof. The tax imposed by this paragraph shall be paid by the organization.
(2) **On the management.** There is hereby imposed on the agreement of any organization manager to the making of any expenditure, knowing that it is a political expenditure, a tax equal to 2½ percent of the amount thereof, unless such agreement is not willful and is due to reasonable cause. The tax imposed by this paragraph shall be paid by any organization manager who agreed to the making of the expenditure.
(b) Additional taxes.
(1) **On the organization.** In any case in which an initial tax is imposed by subsection (a)(1) on a political expenditure and such expenditure is not corrected within the taxable period, there is hereby imposed a tax equal to 100 percent of the amount of the expenditure. The tax imposed by this paragraph shall be paid by the organization.
(2) **On the management.** In any case in which an additional tax is imposed by paragraph (1), if an organization manager refused to agree to part or all of the correction, there is hereby imposed a tax equal to 50 percent of the amount of the political expenditure. The tax imposed by this paragraph shall be paid by any organization manager who refused to agree to part or all of the correction.
(c) Special rules.
For purposes of subsections (a) and (b)—
(1) **Joint and several liability.** If more than 1 person is liable under subsection (a)(2) or (b)(2) with respect to the making of a political expenditure, all such persons shall be jointly and severally liable under such subsection with respect to such expenditure.
(2) **Limit for management.** With respect to any 1 political expenditure, the maximum amount of the tax imposed by subsection (a)(2) shall not exceed $5,000, and the maximum amount of the tax imposed by subsection (b)(2) shall not exceed $10,000.
(d) Political expenditure.
For purposes of this section—
(1) **In general.** The term "political expenditure" means any amount paid or incurred by a section 501(c)(3) organization in any participation in, or intervention in (including the publication or distribution of statements), any political campaign on behalf of (or in opposition to) any candidate for public office.
(2) **Certain other expenditures included.** In the case of an organization which is formed primarily for purposes of promoting the candidacy (or prospective candidacy) of an individual for public office (or which is effectively controlled by a candidate or prospective candidate and which is availed of primarily for such purposes), the term "political expenditure" includes any of the following amounts paid or incurred by the organization:
  (A) Amounts paid or incurred to such individual for speeches or other services.
  (B) Travel expenses of such individual.
  (C) Expenses of conducting polls, surveys, or other studies, or preparing papers or other materials, for use by such individual.
  (D) Expenses of advertising, publicity, and fundraising for such individual.
  (E) Any other expense which has the primary effect of promoting public recognition, or otherwise primarily accruing to the benefit, of such individual.
(e) Coordination with sections 4945 and 4958.
If tax is imposed under this section with respect to any political expenditure, such expenditure shall not be treated as a taxable expenditure for purposes of section 4945 or an excess benefit for purposes of section 4958.
(f) Other definitions.
For purposes of this section—
(1) **Section 501(c)(3) organization.** The term "section 501(c)(3) organization" means any organization which (without regard to any political expenditure) would be de-

scribed in section 501(c)(3) and exempt from taxation under section 501(a).

(2) Organization manager. The term "organization manager" means—

(A) any officer, director, or trustee of the organization (or individual having powers or responsibilities similar to those of officers, directors, or trustees of the organization), and

(B) with respect to any expenditure, any employee of the organization having authority or responsibility with respect to such expenditure.

(3) Correction. The terms "correction" and "correct" mean, with respect to any political expenditure, recovering part or all of the expenditure to the extent recovery is possible, establishment of safeguards to prevent future political expenditures, and where full recovery is not possible, such additional corrective action as is prescribed by the Secretary by regulations.

(4) Taxable period. The term "taxable period" means, with respect to any political expenditure, the period beginning with the date on which the political expenditure occurs and ending on the earlier of—

(A) the date of mailing of a notice of deficiency under section 6212 with respect to the tax imposed by subsection (a)(1), or

(B) the date on which tax imposed by subsection (a)(1) is assessed.

In 1996, P.L. 104-168, Sec. 1311(c)(1)(A), substituted "sections 4945 and 4958" for "section 4945" in the heading of subsec. (e) . . . Sec. 1311(c)(1)(B), added "or an excess benefit for purposes of section 4958" before the period at the end of subsec. (e), effective for excess benefit transactions occurring on or after 9/14/95. Sec. 1311(d)(2), of this Act, provides:

"(2) Binding contracts. The amendments referred to in paragraph (1) shall not apply to any benefit arising from a transaction pursuant to any written contract which was binding on September 13, 1995, and at all times thereafter before such transaction occurred."

In 1987, P.L. 100-203, Sec. 10712(a), added Code Sec. 4955, effective for tax. yrs. begin. after 12/22/87.

Subchapter D.—Failure by Certain Charitable Organizations to Meet Certain Qualification Requirements

Sec.
4958. Taxes on excess benefit transactions.
4959. Taxes on failures by hospital organizations.

In 2010, P.L. 111-148, Sec. 9007(b)(2), added item 4959.
In 1996, P.L. 104-168, Sec. 1311(a), added Subchapter D.

Sec. 4958. Taxes on excess benefit transactions.
(a) Initial taxes.

(1) On the disqualified person. There is hereby imposed on each excess benefit transaction a tax equal to 25 percent of the excess benefit. The tax imposed by this paragraph shall be paid by any disqualified person referred to in subsection (f)(1) with respect to such transaction.

(2) On the management. In any case in which a tax is imposed by paragraph (1), there is hereby imposed on the participation of any organization manager in the excess benefit transaction, knowing that it is such a transaction, a tax equal to 10 percent of the excess benefit, unless such participation is not willful and is due to reasonable cause. The tax imposed by this paragraph shall be paid by any organization manager who participated in the excess benefit transaction.

(b) Additional tax on the disqualified person.
In any case in which an initial tax is imposed by subsection (a)(1) on an excess benefit transaction and the excess benefit involved in such transaction is not corrected within the taxable period, there is hereby imposed a tax equal to 200 percent of the excess benefit involved. The tax imposed by this subsection shall be paid by any disqualified person referred to in subsection (f)(1) with respect to such transaction.

(c) Excess benefit transaction; excess benefit.
For purposes of this section—

(1) Excess benefit transaction.

(A) In general. The term "excess benefit transaction" means any transaction in which an economic benefit is provided by an applicable tax-exempt organization directly or indirectly to or for the use of any disqualified person if the value of the economic benefit provided exceeds the value of the consideration (including the performance of services) received for providing such benefit. For purposes of the preceding sentence, an economic benefit shall not be treated as consideration for the performance of services unless such organization clearly indicated its intent to so treat such benefit.

(B) Excess benefit. The term "excess benefit" means the excess referred to in subparagraph (A).

(2) Special rules for donor advised funds. In the case of any donor advised fund (as defined in section 4966(d)(2))—

(A) the term "excess benefit transaction" includes any grant, loan, compensation, or other similar payment from such fund to a person described in subsection (f)(7) with respect to such fund, and

(B) the term "excess benefit" includes, with respect to any transaction described in subparagraph (A), the amount of any such grant, loan, compensation, or other similar payment.

(3) Special rules for supporting organizations.

(A) In general. In the case of any organization described in section 509(a)(3)—

(i) the term "excess benefit transaction" includes—

(I) any grant, loan, compensation, or other similar payment provided by such organization to a person described in subparagraph (B), and

(II) any loan provided by such organization to a disqualified person (other than an organization described in subparagraph (C)(ii), and

(ii) the term "excess benefit" includes, with respect to any transaction described in clause (i), the amount of any such grant, loan, compensation, or other similar payment.

(B) Person described. A person is described in this subparagraph if such person is—

(i) a substantial contributor to such organization,

(ii) a member of the family (determined under section 4958(f)(4)) of an individual described in clause (i), or

(iii) a 35-percent controlled entity (as defined in section 4958(f)(3) by substituting "persons described in clause (i) or (ii) of section 4958(c)(3)(B)" for "persons described in subparagraph (A) or (B) of paragraph (1)" in subparagraph (A)(i) thereof).

(C) Substantial contributor. For purposes of this paragraph—

(i) In general. The term "substantial contributor" means any person who contributed or bequeathed an aggregate amount of more than $5,000 to the organization, if such amount is more than 2 percent of the total contributions and bequests received by the organization before the close of the taxable year of the organization in which the contribution or bequest is received by the organization from such person. In the case of a trust, such term also means the creator of the trust. Rules similar to the rules of subparagraphs (B) and (C) of section 507(d)(2) shall apply for purposes of this subparagraph.

(ii) Exception. Such term shall not include

(I) any organization described in paragraph (1), (2), or (4) of section 509(a), and

(II) any organization which is treated as described in such paragraph (2) by reason of the last sentence of section 509(a) and which is a supported organization (as defined in section 509(f)(3)) of the organization to which subparagraph (A) applies.

(4) Authority to include certain other private inurement. To the extent provided in regulations prescribed by the Secretary, the term "excess benefit transaction" includes any transaction in which the amount of any economic benefit provided to or for the use of a disqualified person is determined in whole, or in part by the revenues of 1 or more activities of the organization but only if such transaction results in inurement not permitted under paragraph (3) or (4) of section 501(c), as the case may be. In the case of any such transaction, the excess benefit shall be the amount of the inurement not so permitted.

(d) Special rules.

For purposes of this section—

(1) Joint and several liability. If more than 1 person is liable for any tax imposed by subsection (a) or subsection (b), all such persons shall be jointly and severally liable for such tax.

(2) Limit for management. With respect to any 1 excess benefit transaction, the maximum amount of the tax imposed by subsection (a)(2) shall not exceed $20,000.

(e) Applicable tax-exempt organization.

For purposes of this subchapter, the term "applicable tax-exempt organization" means—

(1) any organization which (without regard to any excess benefit) would be described in paragraph (3), (4), or (29) of section 501(c) and exempt from tax under section 501(a), and

(2) any organization which was described in paragraph (1) at any time during the 5-year period ending on the date of the transaction.

Such term shall not include a private foundation (as defined in section 509(a)).

(f) Other definitions.

For purposes of this section—.

(1) Disqualified person. The term "disqualified person" means, with respect to any transaction—

(A) any person who was, at any time during the 5-year period ending on the date of such transaction, in a position to exercise substantial influence over the affairs of the organization,

(B) a member of the family of an individual described in subparagraph (A),

(C) a 35-percent controlled entity,

(D) any person who is described in subparagraph (A), (B), or (C) with respect to an organization described in section 509(a)(3) and organized and operated exclusively for the benefit of, to perform the functions of, or to carry out the purposes of the applicable tax-exempt organization.

(E) which involves a donor advised fund (as defined in section 4966(d)(2)), any person who is described in paragraph (7) with respect to such donor advised fund (as so defined), and

(F) which involves a sponsoring organization (as defined in section 4966(d)(1)), any person who is described in paragraph (8) with respect to such sponsoring organization (as so defined).

(2) Organization manager. The term "organization manager" means, with respect to any applicable tax-exempt organization, any officer, director, or trustee of such organization (or any individual having powers or responsibilities similar to those of officers, directors, or trustees of the organization).

(3) 35-percent controlled entity.

(A) In general. The term "35-percent controlled entity" means—

(i) a corporation in which persons described in subparagraph (A) or (B) of paragraph (1) own more than 35 percent of the total combined voting power,

(ii) a partnership in which such persons own more than 35 percent of the profits interest, and

(iii) a trust or estate in which such persons own more than 35 percent of the beneficial interest.

(B) Constructive ownership rules. Rules similar to the rules of paragraphs (3) and (4) of section 4946(a) shall apply for purposes of this paragraph.

(4) Family members. The members of an individual's family shall be determined under section 4946(d); except that such members also shall include the brothers and sisters (whether by the whole or half blood) of the individual and their spouses.

(5) Taxable period. The term "taxable period" means, with respect to any excess benefit transaction, the period beginning with the date on which the transaction occurs and ending on the earliest of—

(A) the date of mailing a notice of deficiency under section 6212 with respect to the tax imposed by subsection (a)(1), or

(B) the date on which the tax imposed by subsection (a)(1) is assessed.

(6) Correction. The terms "correction" and "correct" mean, with respect to any excess benefit transaction, undoing the excess benefit to the extent possible, and taking any additional measures necessary to place the organization in a financial position not worse than that in which it would be if the disqualified person were dealing under the highest fiduciary standards, except that in the case of any correction of an excess benefit transaction described in subsection (c)(2), no amount repaid in a manner prescribed by the Secretary may be held in any donor advised fund.

(7) Donors and donor advisors. For purposes of paragraph (1)(E), a person is described in this paragraph if such person—

(A) is described in section 4966(d)(2)(A)(iii),

(B) is a member of the family of an individual described in subparagraph (A), or

(C) is a 35-percent controlled entity (as defined in paragraph (3) by substituting "persons described in subparagraph (A) or (B) of paragraph (7)" for "persons described in subparagraph (A) or (B) of paragraph (1)" in subparagraph (A)(i) thereof).

(8) Investment advisors. For purposes of paragraph (1)(F)—

(A) In general. A person is described in this paragraph if such person—

(i) is an investment advisor,

(ii) is a member of the family of an individual described in clause (i), or

(iii) is a 35-percent controlled entity (as defined in paragraph (3) by substituting "persons described in clause (i) or (ii) of paragraph (8)(A)" for "persons described in subparagraph (A) or (B) of paragraph (1)" in subparagraph (A)(i) thereof).

(B) Investment advisor defined. For purposes of subparagraph (A), the term "investment advisor" means, with respect to any sponsoring organization (as defined in section 4966(d)(1)), any person (other than an employee of such organization) compensated by such organization for managing the investment of, or providing investment advice with respect to, assets maintained in donor advised funds (as defined in section 4966(d)(2)) owned by such organization.

In 2010, P.L. 111-148, Sec. 1322(h)(3), substituted "paragraph (3), (4), or (29)" for "paragraph (3) or (4)" in para. (e)(1), effective 3/23/2010.

In 2007, P.L. 110-172, Sec. 3(i)(1), substituted "subparagraph (C)(ii)" for "paragraph (1), (2), or (4) of section 509(a)" in subclause (c)(3)(A)(i)(II).... Sec. 3(i)(2), amended clause (c)(3)(C)(ii), effective for transactions occurring after 7/25/2006.

Prior to amendment clause (c)(3)(C)(ii) read as follows

"(ii)Exception. Such term shall not include any organization described in paragraph (1), (2), or (4) of section 509(a)."

In 2006, P.L. 109-280, Sec. 1212(a)(3), substituted "$20,000" for "$10,000" in para. (d)(2), effective for tax. yrs. begin. after 8/17/2006.

—P.L. 109-280, Sec. 1232(a)(1), deleted "and" at the end of subpara. (f)(1)(B), substituted a comma for the period at the end of subpara. (f)(1)(C), and added subparas. (f)(1)(D) and (E) ... Sec. 1232(a)(2), added paras. (f)(7) and (8)... Sec. 1232(b)(1), redesignated para. (c)(2) as (3) and added para. (c)(2)... Sec. 1232(b)(2), added ", except that in the case of any correction of an excess benefit transaction described in subsection (c)(2), no amount repaid in a manner prescribed by the Secretary may be held in any donor advised fund" after "standards" in para. (f)(6), effective for transactions occurring after 8/17/2006.

—P.L. 109-280, Sec. 1242(a), redesignated subparas. (f)(1)(D) and (E) [as added by Sec. 1232(a)(1) of this Act, see above] as (f)(1)(E) and (F), and added subpara. (f)(1)(D), effective for transactions occurring after 8/17/2006.

—P.L. 109-280, Sec. 1242(b), redesignated para. (c)(3) [as redesignated by Sec. 1232(b)(1) of this Act, see above] as (c)(4), and added para. (c)(3), effective for transactions occurring after 7/25/2006.

In 1996, P.L. 104-168, Sec. 1311(a), added Code Sec. 4958, effective for excess benefit transactions occurring on or after 9/14/95. Sec. 1311(d)(2), of this Act, provides:

"(2) Binding contracts. The amendments referred to in paragraph (1) shall not apply to any benefit arising from a transaction pursuant to any written contract which was binding on September 13, 1995, and at all times thereafter before such transaction occurred."

Sec. 4959. Taxes on failures by hospital organizations.

If a hospital organization to which section 501(r) applies fails to meet the requirement of section 501(r)(3) for any taxable year, there is imposed on the organization a tax equal to $50,000.

In 2010, P.L. 111-148, Sec. 9007(b)(1), added Sec. 4959, effective for failures occurring after 3/23/2010.

Subchapter E.—Abatement of First and Second Tier Taxes in Certain Cases

Sec.
4961. Abatement of second tier taxes where there is correction.
4962. Abatement of first tier taxes in certain cases.
4963. Definitions.

In 1996, P.L. 104-168, Sec. 1311(a), redesignated Subchapter D as Subchapter E.
In 1987, P.L. 100-203, Sec. 10712(a), redesignated Subchapter C as Subchapter D ... Sec. 10712(b)(5), deleted "privated foundation" from item 4962.

Prior to deletion, item 4962 read as follows:

"4962. Abatement of private foundation first tier taxes in certain cases."

In 1984, P.L. 98-369, Sec. 305(b)(1), amended the subchapter heading ... Sec. 305(b)(2), redesignated item 4962 as 4963 and added new item 4962.

Prior to amendment the subchapter heading read as follows:

"Subchapter C—Abatement of Second Tier Taxes Where There is Correction During Correction Period".

Sec. 4961. Abatement of second tier taxes where there is correction.

(a) General rule.

If any taxable event is corrected during the correction period for such event, then any second tier tax imposed with respect to such event (including interest, additions to the tax, and additional amounts) shall not be assessed, and if assessed the assessment shall be abated, and if collected shall be credited or refunded as an overpayment.

(b) Supplemental proceeding.

If the determination by a court that the taxpayer is liable for a second tier tax has become final, such court shall have jurisdiction to conduct any necessary supplemental proceeding to determine whether the taxable event was corrected during the correction period. Such a supplemental proceeding may be begun only during the period which ends on the 90th day after the last day of the correction period. Where such a supplemental proceeding has begun, the reference in the second sentence of section 6213(a) to a final decision of the Tax Court shall be treated as including a final decision in such supplemental proceeding.

(c) Suspension of period of collection for second tier tax.

(1) Proceeding in district court or United States claims court [United States Court of Federal Claims, see § 902(b), P.L. 102-572]. If, not later than 90 days after the day on which the second tier tax is assessed, the first tier tax is paid in full and a claim for refund of the amount so paid is filed, no levy or proceeding in court for the collection of the second tier tax shall be made, begun, or prosecuted until a final resolution of a proceeding begun as provided in paragraph (2) (and of any supplemental proceeding with respect thereto under subsection (b)). Notwithstanding section 7421(a), the collection by levy or proceeding may be enjoined during the time such prohibition is in force by a proceeding in the proper court.

(2) Suit must be brought to determine liability. If, within 90 days after the day on which his claim for refund is denied, the person against whom the second tier tax was assessed fails to begin a proceeding described in section 7422 for the determination of his liability for such tax, paragraph (1) shall cease to apply with respect to such tax, effective on the day following the close of the 90-day period referred to in this paragraph.

(3) Suspension of running of period of limitations on collection. The running of the period of limitations provided in section 6502 on the collection by levy or by a proceeding in court with respect to any second tier tax described in paragraph (1) shall be suspended for the period during which the Secretary is prohibited from collecting by levy or a proceeding in court.

(4) Jeopardy collection. If the Secretary makes a finding that the collection of the second tier tax is in jeopardy, nothing in this subsection shall prevent the immediate collection of such tax.

In 1992, P.L. 102-572, Sec. 902(b), effective 10/29/92, relating to Court designation provides as follows:

"(b) Other provisions of law. Reference in any other Federal law or documents to —

"(1) the 'United States Claims Court' shall be deemed to refer to the 'United States Court of Federal Claims'; and

"(2) the 'Claims Court' shall be deemed to refer to the 'Court of Federal Claims.'"

In 1986, P.L. 99-514, Sec. 1899A(50), substituted "United States claims court" for "court of claims" in the heading of para. (c)(1), effective 10/22/86.

In 1980, P.L. 96-596, Sec. 2(c)(1), added Code Sec. 4961, effective as provided in Sec. 2(d)(2) of this Act which reads as follows:

"(2) Second tier taxes. The amendments made by this section with respect to any second tier tax shall apply only with respect to taxes assessed after the date of the enactment of this Act [12/24/80]. Nothing in the preceding sentence shall be construed to permit the assessment of a tax in a case to which, on the date of the enactment of this Act [12/24/80], the doctrine of res judicata applies."

Sec. 4962. Abatement of first tier taxes in certain cases.
(a) General rule.

If it is established to the satisfaction of the Secretary that—

(1) a taxable event was due to reasonable cause and not to willful neglect, and

(2) such event was corrected within the correction period for such event,

then any qualified first tier tax imposed with respect to such event (including interest) shall not be assessed and, if assessed, the assessment shall be abated and, if collected, shall be credited or refunded as an overpayment.

(b) Qualified first tier tax.

For purposes of this section, the term "qualified first tier tax" means any first tier tax imposed by subchapter A, C, D, or G of this chapter, except that such term shall not include the tax imposed by section 4941(a) (relating to initial tax on self-dealing).

(c) Special rule for tax on political expenditures of section 501(c)(3) organizations.

In the case of the tax imposed by section 4955(a), subsection (a)(1) shall be applied by substituting "not willful and flagrant" for "due to reasonable cause and not to willful neglect".

In 2007, P.L. 110-172, Sec. 3(h), substituted "D, or G" for "or D" in subsec. (b), effective for tax. yrs. begin. after 8/17/2006.

In 1997, P.L. 105-34, Sec. 1603(a), substituted "subchapter A, C, or D" for "subchapter A or C" in subsec. (b), effective for excess benefit transactions occurring on or after 9/14/95, except as provided in Sec. 1311(d)(2) of P.L. 104-168, which reads as follows:

"(2) Binding contracts. The amendments referred to in paragraph (1) shall not apply to any benefit arising from a transactions pursuant to any written contract which was binding on September, 13, 1995, and at all times thereafter before such transaction occurred."

In 1987, P.L. 100-203, Sec. 10712(b)(1), amended subsec. (b) and added subsec. (c)... Sec. 10712(b)(2), substituted "any qualified first tier tax" for "any private foundation first tier tax" in subsec. (a)... Sec. 10712(b)(4), deleted "private foundation" before "first tier taxes" in the heading of Code Sec. 4962, effective for tax. yrs. begin. after 12/22/87.

Prior to amendment, subsec. (b) read as follows:

"(b) Private foundation first tier tax.

"For purposes of this section, the term 'private foundation first tier tax' means any first tier tax imposed by subchapter A of chapter 42, except that such term shall not include the tax imposed by section 4941(a) (relating to initial tax on self-dealing)."

In 1984, P.L. 98-369, Sec. 305(a), added Code Sec. 4962, effective for tax. events occurring after 12/31/84.

Sec. 4963. Definitions.
(a) First tier tax.

For purposes of this subchapter, the term "first tier tax" means any tax imposed by subsection (a) of section 4941, 4942, 4943, 4944, 4945, 4951, 4952, 4955, 4958, 4966, 4967, 4971, or 4975.

(b) Second tier tax.

For purposes of this subchapter, the term "second tier tax" means any tax imposed by subsection (b) of section 4941, 4942, 4943, 4944, 4945, 4951, 4952, 4955, 4958, 4971, or 4975.

(c) Taxable event.

For purposes of this subchapter, the term "taxable event" means any act (or failure to act) giving rise to liability for tax under section 4941, 4942, 4943, 4944, 4945, 4951, 4952, 4955, 4958, 4966, 4967, 4971, or 4975.

(d) Correct.

For purposes of this subchapter—

(1) In general. Except as provided in paragraph (2), the term "correct" has the same meaning as when used in the section which imposes the second tier tax.

(2) Special rules. The term "correct" means—

(A) in the case of the second tier tax imposed by section 4942(b), reducing the amount of the undistributed income to zero,

(B) in the case of the second tier tax imposed by section 4943(b), reducing the amount of the excess business holdings to zero, and

(C) in the case of the second tier tax imposed by section 4944, removing the investment from jeopardy.

(e) Correction period.

For purposes of this subchapter—

(1) In general. The term "correction period" means, with respect to any taxable event, the period beginning on the date on which such event occurs and ending 90 days after the date of mailing under section 6212 of a notice of deficiency with respect to the second tier tax imposed on such taxable event, extended by—

(A) any period in which a deficiency cannot be assessed under section 6213(a) (determined without regard to the last sentence of section 4961(b)), and

(B) any other period which the Secretary determines is reasonable and necessary to bring about correction of the taxable event.

(2) Special rules for when taxable event occurs. For purposes of paragraph (1), the taxable event shall be treated as occurring—

(A) in the case of section 4942, on the first day of the taxable year for which there was a failure to distribute income,

(B) in the case of section 4943, on the first day on which there are excess business holdings,

(C) in the case of section 4971, on the last day of the plan year in which there is an accumulated funding deficiency, and

(D) in any other case, the date on which such event occurred.

In 2006, P.L. 109-280, Sec. 1231(b)(1), added "4966, 4967," after "4958," each place it appeared in subsecs. (a) and (c), effective for tax. yrs. begin. after 8/17/2006.

In 1996, P.L. 104-168, Sec. 1311(c)(2), added "4958," after "4955," in subsecs. (a), (b), and (c), effective for excess benefit transactions occurring on or after 9/14/95. Sec. 1311(d)(2), of this Act, provides:

"(2) Binding contracts. The amendments referred to in paragraph (1) shall not apply to any benefit arising from a transaction pursuant to any written contract which was binding on September 13, 1995, and at all times thereafter before such transaction occurred."

In 1987, P.L. 100-203, Sec. 10712(b)(3), substituted "4952, 4955" for "4952," in subsecs. (a), (b), and (c), effective for tax. yrs. begin. after 12/22/87.

In 1984, P.L. 98-369, Sec. 305(a), redesignated Code Sec. 4962 as Code Sec. 4963, effective for tax. events occurring after 12/31/84.

In 1980, P.L. 96-596, Sec. 2(c)(1), added Code Sec. 4962, effective as provided in Sec. 2(d) of this Act which reads as follows:

"(d) Effective dates.—

"(1) First tier taxes.—The amendments made by this section with respect to any first tier tax shall take effect as if included in the Internal Revenue Code of 1954 when such tax was first imposed.

"(2) Second tier taxes.—The amendments made by this section with respect to any second tier tax shall apply only with respect to taxes assessed after the date of the enactment of this Act. [12/24/80] Nothing in the preceding sentence shall be construed to permit the assessment of a tax in the case to which, on the date of the enactment of this Act [12/24/80] the doctrine of res judicata applies.

"(3) First and second tier tax.—For purposes of this subsection, the terms 'first tier tax' and 'second tier tax' have the respective meanings given to such terms by section 4962 of the Internal Revenue Code of 1954."

Subchapter F.—Tax Shelter Transactions

Sec.
4965. Excise tax on certain tax-exempt entities entering into prohibited tax shelter transactions.

In 2006, P.L. 109-222, Sec. 516(a)(1), added Subchapter F.

Sec. 4965. Excise tax on certain tax-exempt entities entering into prohibited tax shelter transactions.

(a) Being a party to and approval of prohibited transactions.

   (1) Tax-exempt entity.

      (A) In general. If a transaction is a prohibited tax shelter transaction at the time any tax-exempt entity described in paragraph (1), (2), or (3) of subsection (c) becomes a party to the transaction, such entity shall pay a tax for the taxable year in which the entity becomes such a party and any subsequent taxable year in the amount determined under subsection (b)(1).

      (B) Post-transaction determination. If any tax-exempt entity described in paragraph (1), (2), or (3) of subsection (c) is a party to a subsequently listed transaction at any time during a taxable year, such entity shall pay a tax for such taxable year in the amount determined under subsection (b)(1).

   (2) Entity manager. If any entity manager of a tax-exempt entity approves such entity as (or otherwise causes such entity to be) a party to a prohibited tax shelter transaction at any time during the taxable year and knows or has reason to know that the transaction is a prohibited tax shelter transaction, such manager shall pay a tax for such taxable year in the amount determined under subsection (b)(2).

(b) Amount of tax.

   (1) Entity. In the case of a tax-exempt entity—

      (A) In general. Except as provided in subparagraph (B), the amount of the tax imposed under subsection (a)(1) with respect to any transaction for a taxable year shall be an amount equal to the product of the highest rate of tax under section 11, and the greater of—

         (i) the entity's net income (after taking into account any tax imposed by this subtitle (other than by this section) with respect to such transaction) for such taxable year which—

            (I) in the case of a prohibited tax shelter transaction (other than a subsequently listed transaction), is attributable to such transaction, or

            (II) in the case of a subsequently listed transaction, is attributable to such transaction and which is properly allocable to the period beginning on the later of the date such transaction is identified by guidance as a listed transaction by the Secretary or the first day of the taxable year, or

         (ii) 75 percent of the proceeds received by the entity for the taxable year which—

            (I) in the case of a prohibited tax shelter transaction (other than a subsequently listed transaction), are attributable to such transaction, or

            (II) in the case of a subsequently listed transaction, are attributable to such transaction and which are properly allocable to the period beginning on the later of the date such transaction is identified by guidance as a listed transaction by the Secretary or the first day of the taxable year.

      (B) Increase in tax for certain knowing transactions. In the case of a tax-exempt entity which knew, or had reason to know, a transaction was a prohibited tax shelter transaction at the time the entity became a party to the transaction, the amount of the tax imposed under subsection (a)(1)(A) with respect to any transaction for a taxable year shall be the greater of—

         (i) 100 percent of the entity's net income (after taking into account any tax imposed by this subtitle (other than by this section) with respect to the prohibited tax shelter transaction) for such taxable year which is attributable to the prohibited tax shelter transaction, or

         (ii) 75 percent of the proceeds received by the entity for the taxable year which are attributable to the prohibited tax shelter transaction.

      This subparagraph shall not apply to any prohibited tax shelter transaction to which a tax exempt entity became a party on or before the date of the enactment of this section.

   (2) Entity manager. In the case of each entity manager, the amount of the tax imposed under subsection (a)(2) shall be $20,000 for each approval (or other act causing participation) described in subsection (a)(2).

(c) Tax-exempt entity.

   For purposes of this section, the term "tax-exempt entity" means an entity which is—

   (1) described in section 501(c) or 501(d),

   (2) described in section 170(c) (other than the United States),

   (3) an Indian tribal government (within the meaning of section 7701(a)(40)),

   (4) described in paragraph (1), (2), or (3) of section 4979(e),

   (5) a program described in section 529,

   (6) an eligible deferred compensation plan described in section 457(b) which is maintained by an employer described in section 457(e)(1)(A), or

   (7) an arrangement described in section 4973(a).

(d) Entity manager.

   For purposes of this section, the term "entity manager" means—

   (1) in the case of an entity described in paragraph (1), (2), or (3) of subsection (c)—

      (A) the person with authority or responsibility similar to that exercised by an officer, director, or trustee of an organization, and

      (B) with respect to any act, the person having authority or responsibility with respect to such act, and

   (2) in the case of an entity described in paragraph (4), (5), (6), or (7) of subsection (c), the person who approves or otherwise causes the entity to be a party to the prohibited tax shelter transaction.

(e) Prohibited tax shelter transaction; subsequently listed transaction.

   For purposes of this section—

   (1) Prohibited tax shelter transaction.

      (A) In general. The term "prohibited tax shelter transaction" means—

         (i) any listed transaction, and

         (ii) any prohibited reportable transaction.

      (B) Listed transaction. The term "listed transaction" has the meaning given such term by section 6707A(c)(2).

      (C) Prohibited reportable transaction. The term "prohibited reportable transaction" means any confidential transaction or any transaction with contractual protection (as defined under regulations prescribed by the

Excise and miscellaneous taxes

Secretary) which is a reportable transaction (as defined in section 6707A(c)(1)).

(2) Subsequently listed transaction. The term "subsequently listed transaction" means any transaction to which a tax-exempt entity is a party and which is determined by the Secretary to be a listed transaction at any time after the entity has become a party to the transaction. Such term shall not include a transaction which is a prohibited reportable transaction at the time the entity became a party to the transaction.

(f) Regulatory authority.

The Secretary is authorized to promulgate regulations which provide guidance regarding the determination of the allocation of net income or proceeds of a tax-exempt entity attributable to a transaction to various periods, including before and after the listing of the transaction or the date which is 90 days after the date of the enactment of this section.

(g) Coordination with other taxes and penalties.

The tax imposed by this section is in addition to any other tax, addition to tax, or penalty imposed under this title.

In 2007, P.L. 110-172, Sec. 11(a)(30), substituted "section 457(e)(1)(A)" for "section 4457(e)(1)(A)" in para. (c)(6), enacted 12/29/2007.

In 2006, P.L. 109-222, Sec. 516(a)(1), added Code Sec. 4965, effective for tax. yrs. end. after 5/17/2006, with respect to transactions before, on, or after 5/17/2006, except that no tax under Code Sec. 4965(a) (as added by Sec. 516(a)(1) of P.L. 109-222) shall apply with respect to income or proceeds that are properly allocable to any period end. on or before the date which is 90 days after 5/17/2006.

Subchapter G.—Donor Advised funds

Sec.
4966. Taxes on taxable distributions.
4967. Taxes on prohibited benefits.

In 2006, P.L. 109-280, Sec. 1231(a), added Subchapter G.

Sec. 4966. Taxes on taxable distributions.
(a) Imposition of taxes.

(1) On the sponsoring organization. There is hereby imposed on each taxable distribution a tax equal to 20 percent of the amount thereof. The tax imposed by this paragraph shall be paid by the sponsoring organization with respect to the donor advised fund.

(2) On the fund management. There is hereby imposed on the agreement of any fund manager to the making of a distribution, knowing that it is a taxable distribution, a tax equal to 5 percent of the amount thereof. The tax imposed by this paragraph shall be paid by any fund manager who agreed to the making of the distribution.

(b) Special rules.

For purposes of subsection (a)—

(1) Joint and several liability. If more than one person is liable under subsection (a)(2) with respect to the making of a taxable distribution, all such persons shall be jointly and severally liable under such paragraph with respect to such distribution.

(2) Limit for management. With respect to any one taxable distribution, the maximum amount of the tax imposed by subsection (a)(2) shall not exceed $10,000.

(c) Taxable distribution.

For purposes of this section—

(1) In general. The term "taxable distribution" means any distribution from a donor advised fund—

(A) to any natural person, or
(B) to any other person if—

(i) such distribution is for any purpose other than one specified in section 170(c)(2)(B), or
(ii) the sponsoring organization does not exercise expenditure responsibility with respect to such distribution in accordance with section 4945(h).

(2) Exceptions. Such term shall not include any distribution from a donor advised fund—

(A) to any organization described in section 170(b)(1)(A) (other than a disqualified supporting organization),
(B) to the sponsoring organization of such donor advised fund, or
(C) to any other donor advised fund.

(d) Definitions.

For purposes of this subchapter—

(1) Sponsoring organization. The term "sponsoring organization" means any organization which—

(A) is described in section 170(c) (other than in paragraph (1) thereof, and without regard to paragraph (2)(A) thereof),
(B) is not a private foundation (as defined in section 509(a)), and
(C) maintains 1 or more donor advised funds.

(2) Donor advised fund.

(A) In general. Except as provided in subparagraph (B) or (C), the term "donor advised fund" means a fund or account—

(i) which is separately identified by reference to contributions of a donor or donors,
(ii) which is owned and controlled by a sponsoring organization, and
(iii) with respect to which a donor (or any person appointed or designated by such donor) has, or reasonably expects to have, advisory privileges with respect to the distribution or investment of amounts held in such fund or account by reason of the donor's status as a donor.

(B) Exceptions. The term "donor advised fund" shall not include any fund or account—

(i) which makes distributions only to a single identified organization or governmental entity, or
(ii) with respect to which a person described in subparagraph (A)(iii) advises as to which individuals receive grants for travel, study, or other similar purposes, if—

(I) such person's advisory privileges are performed exclusively by such person in the person's capacity as a member of a committee all of the members of which are appointed by the sponsoring organization,
(II) no combination of persons described in subparagraph (A)(iii) (or persons related to such persons) control, directly or indirectly, such committee, and
(III) all grants from such fund or account are awarded on an objective and nondiscriminatory basis pursuant to a procedure approved in advance by the board of directors of the sponsoring organization, and such procedure is designed to ensure that all such grants meet the requirements of paragraphs (1), (2), or (3) of section 4945(g).

(C) Secretarial authority. The Secretary may exempt a fund or account not described in subparagraph (B) from treatment as a donor advised fund—

(i) if such fund or account is advised by a committee not directly or indirectly controlled by the donor or any person appointed or designated by the donor for the purpose of advising with respect to distributions from such fund (and any related parties), or

(ii) if such fund benefits a single identified charitable purpose.

(3) Fund manager. The term "fund manager" means, with respect to any sponsoring organization—

(A) an officer, director, or trustee of such sponsoring organization (or an individual having powers or responsibilities similar to those of officers, directors, or trustees of the sponsoring organization), and

(B) with respect to any act (or failure to act), the employees of the sponsoring organization having authority or responsibility with respect to such act (or failure to act).

(4) Disqualified supporting organization.

(A) In general. The term "disqualified supporting organization" means, with respect to any distribution—

(i) any type III supporting organization (as defined in section 4943(f)(5)(A)) which is not a functionally integrated type III supporting organization (as defined in section 4943(f)(5)(B)), and

(ii) any organization which is described in subparagraph (B) or (C) if—

(I) the donor or any person designated by the donor for the purpose of advising with respect to distributions from a donor advised fund (and any related parties) directly or indirectly controls a supported organization (as defined in section 509(f)(3)) of such organization, or

(II) the Secretary determines by regulations that a distribution to such organization otherwise is inappropriate.

(B) Type I and type II supporting organizations. An organization is described in this subparagraph if the organization meets the requirements of subparagraphs (A) and (C) of section 509(a)(3) and is—

(i) operated, supervised, or controlled by one or more organizations described in paragraph (1) or (2) of section 509(a), or

(ii) supervised or controlled in connection with one or more such organizations.

(C) Functionally integrated type III supporting organizations. An organization is described in this subparagraph if the organization is a functionally integrated type III supporting organization (as defined under section 4943(f)(5)(B)).

In 2006, P.L. 109-280, Sec. 1226, of this Act, relating to a Study on donor advised funds and supporting organizations, provides:

Sec. 1226. Study on donor advised funds and supporting organizations.

"(a) Study. The Secretary of the Treasury shall undertake a study on the organization and operation of donor advised funds (as defined in section 4966(d)(2) of the Internal Revenue Code of 1986, as added by this Act) and of organizations described in section 509(a)(3) of such Code. The study shall specifically consider—

"(1) whether the deductions allowed for the income, gift, or estate taxes for charitable contributions to sponsoring organizations (as defined in section 4966(d)(1) of such Code, as added by this Act) of donor advised funds or to organizations described in section 509(a)(3) of such Code are appropriate in consideration of—

"(A) the use of contributed assets (including the type, extent, and timing of such use), or

"(B) the use of the assets of such organizations for the benefit of the person making the charitable contribution (or a person related to such person),

"(2) whether donor advised funds should be required to distribute for charitable purposes a specified amount (whether based on the income or assets of the fund) in order to ensure that the sponsoring organization with respect to such donor advised fund is operating consistent with the purposes or functions constituting the basis for its exemption under section 501, or its status as an organization described in section 509(a), of such Code,

"(3) whether the retention by donors to organizations described in paragraph (1) of rights or privileges with respect to amounts transferred to such organizations (including advisory rights or privileges with respect to the making of grants or the investment of assets) is consistent with the treatment of such transfers as completed gifts that qualify for a deduction for income, gift, or estate taxes, and

"(4) whether the issues raised by paragraphs (1), (2), and (3) are also issues with respect to other forms of charities or charitable donations.

"(b) Report. Not later than 1 year after the date of the enactment of this Act, the Secretary of the Treasury shall submit to the Committee on Finance of the Senate and the Committee on Ways and Means of the House of Representatives a report on the study conducted under subsection (a) and make such recommendations as the Secretary of the Treasury considers appropriate."

—P.L. 109-280, Sec. 1231(a), added Code Sec. 4966, effective or the tax. yrs. begin. after 8/17/2006.

Sec. 4967. Taxes on prohibited benefits.
(a) Imposition of taxes.

(1) On the donor, donor advisor, or related person. There is hereby imposed on the advice of any person described in subsection (d) to have a sponsoring organization make a distribution from a donor advised fund which results in such person or any other person described in subsection (d) receiving, directly or indirectly, a more than incidental benefit as a result of such distribution, a tax equal to 125 percent of such benefit. The tax imposed by this paragraph shall be paid by any person described in subsection (d) who advises as to the distribution or who receives such a benefit as a result of the distribution.

(2) On the fund management. There is hereby imposed on the agreement of any fund manager to the making of a distribution, knowing that such distribution would confer a benefit described in paragraph (1), a tax equal to 10 percent of the amount of such benefit. The tax imposed by this paragraph shall be paid by any fund manager who agreed to the making of the distribution.

(b) Exception

No tax shall be imposed under this section with respect to any distribution if a tax has been imposed with respect to such distribution under section 4958.

(c) Special rules

For purposes of subsection (a)—

(1) Joint and several liability. If more than one person is liable under paragraph (1) or (2) of subsection (a) with respect to a distribution described in subsection (a), all such persons shall be jointly and severally liable under such paragraph with respect to such distribution.

(2) Limit for management. With respect to any one distribution described in subsection (a), the maximum amount of the tax imposed by subsection (a)(2) shall not exceed $10,000.

(d) Person described.

A person is described in this subsection if such person is described in section 4958(f)(7) with respect to a donor advised fund.

In 2006, P.L. 109-280, Sec. 1231(a), added Code Sec. 4967, effective for tax. yrs. begin. after 8/17/2006.

CHAPTER 43.—QUALIFIED PENSION, ETC., PLANS

Sec.
4971. Taxes on failure to meet minimum funding standards.
4972. Tax on nondeductible contributions to qualified employer plans.
4973. Tax on excess contributions to certain tax-favored accounts and annuities.
4974. Excise tax on certain accumulations in qualified retirement plans.
4975. Tax on prohibited transactions.
4976. Taxes with respect to funded welfare benefit plans.
4977. Tax on certain fringe benefits provided by an employer.

Excise and miscellaneous taxes — Code Sec. 4971(d)

4978. Tax on certain dispositions by employee stock ownership plans and certain cooperatives.
4978A. Repealed.
4978B. Repealed. [Tax on disposition of employer securities to which section 133 applied.]
4979. Tax on certain excess contributions.
4979A. Tax on certain prohibited allocations of qualified securities.
4980. Tax on reversion of qualified plan assets to employer.
4980A. Tax on excess distributions from qualified retirement plans.
4980B. Failure to satisfy continuation coverage requirements of group health plans.
4980C. Requirements for issuers of qualified long-term care insurance contracts.
4980D. Failure to meet certain group health plan requirements.
4980E. Failure of employer to make comparable Archer MSA contributions.
4980F. Failure of applicable plans reducing benefit accruals to satisfy notice requirements.
4980G. Failure of employer to make comparable health savings account contributions.
4980H. Shared responsibility for employers regarding health coverage. [effective for months begin. after 12/31/2013]
4980I. Excise tax on high cost employer-sponsored health coverage. [effective for tax. yrs. begin. after 12/31/2017]

In 2003, P.L. 111-148, Sec. 1513(b), added item 4980H.... Sec. 9001(b), added item 4980I.
In 2003, P.L. 108-173, Sec. 1201(d)(4)(A), added item 4980G.
In 2002, P.L. 107-147, Sec. 417(17)(B), amended item 4980E.
Prior to amendment, item 4980E read as follows:
"Sec. 4980E. Failure of employer to make comparable medical savings account contributions."
In 2001, P.L. 107-16, Sec. 659(a)(2), added item 4980F.
In 1998, P.L. 105-206, Sec. 6023(18)(B), amended item 4973.
Prior to amendment, item 4973 read as follows:
"4973. Tax on excess contributions to individual retirement accounts, certain section 403(b) contracts, and certain individual retirement annuities."
In 1996, P.L. 104-188, Sec. 1602(b)(5)(B), deleted item 4978B.
Prior to deletion, item 4978B read as follows:
"Sec. 4978B. Tax on disposition of employer securities to which section 133 applied."
—P.L. 104-191, Sec. 301(c)(4)(B), added item 4980E... Sec. 326(b), added item 4980C... Sec. 402(b), added item 4980D.
In 1989, P.L. 101-239, Sec. 7301(d)(2), added item 4978B... Sec. 7304(a)(2)(C)(iii), deleted item 4978A.
Prior to amendment, item 4978A read as follows:
"4978A. Tax on certain dispositions of employer securities to which section 2057 applied."
In 1988, P.L. 100-647, Sec. 1011A(g)(1)(B), redesignated item 4981A as 4980A ... Sec. 3011(c), added item 4980B.
In 1987, P.L. 100-203, Sec. 10413(b)(2), added item 4978A.
In 1986, P.L. 99-514, Sec. 1117(b)(2), added item 4979... Sec. 1121(a)(2), amended item 4974... Sec. 1131(c)(2), added item 4972... Sec. 1132(a), added item 4980... Sec. 1133(b), added item 4981A... Sec. 1854(a)(9)(C), added item 4979A... Sec. 1899A(75)(A), added "section" before "403(b)" in the item for 4973... Sec. 1899A(75)(B), deleted "and allocations" following "dispositions" in item 4978.
Prior to amendment, item 4974 read as follows:
"4974. Excise tax on certain accumulation in individual retirement accounts or annuities."
In 1984, P.L. 98-369, Sec. 491(d)(56), substituted "and certain individual retirement annuities" for "certain individual retirement annuities, and certain retirement bonds" in the item for Code Sec. 4973... Sec. 511(c)(2), added item 4976... Sec. 531(e)(2), added item 4977... Sec. 545(b), added item 4978.
In 1982, P.L. 97-248, Sec. 237(c)(2), deleted item 4972.
Prior to deletion item 4972 read as follows:
"4972. Tax on excess contributions from self-employed individuals."

In 1974, P.L. 93-406, Sec. 1013(b), 2001(f)(2), and 2002(h)(3) established Chapter 43, its table of sections to include 4971 through 4975.

Sec. 4971. Taxes on failure to meet minimum funding standards.

(a) Initial tax.
If at any time during any taxable year an employer maintains a plan to which section 412 applies, there is hereby imposed for the taxable year a tax equal to—
(1) in the case of a single-employer plan, 10 percent of the aggregate unpaid minimum required contributions for all plan years remaining unpaid as of the end of any plan year ending with or within the taxable year, and
(2) in the case of a multiemployer plan, 5 percent of the accumulated funding deficiency determined under section 431 as of the end of any plan year ending with or within the taxable year.

(b) Additional tax.
If—
(1) a tax is imposed under subsection (a)(1) on any unpaid minimum required contribution and such amount remains unpaid as of the close of the taxable period, or
(2) a tax is imposed under subsection (a)(2) on any accumulated funding deficiency and the accumulated funding deficiency is not corrected within the taxable period,
there is hereby imposed a tax equal to 100 percent of the unpaid minimum required contribution or accumulated funding deficiency, whichever is applicable, to the extent not so paid or corrected.

(c) Definitions.
For purposes of this section—
(1) Accumulated funding deficiency. The term "accumulated funding deficiency" has the meaning given to such term by section 431.
(2) Correct. The term "correct" means, with respect to an accumulated funding deficiency, the contribution, to or under the plan, of the amount necessary to reduce such accumulated funding deficiency as of the end of a plan year in which such deficiency arose to zero.
(3) Taxable period. The term "taxable period" means, with respect to an accumulated funding deficiency or unpaid minimum required contribution, whichever is applicable, the period beginning with the end of the plan year in which there is an accumulated funding deficiency or unpaid minimum required contribution, whichever is applicable and ending on the earlier of—
(A) the date of mailing of a notice of deficiency with respect to the tax imposed by subsection (a), or
(B) the date on which the tax imposed by subsection (a) is assessed.
(4) Unpaid minimum required contribution.
(A) In general. The term "unpaid minimum required contribution" means, with respect to any plan year, any minimum required contribution under section 430 for the plan year which is not paid on or before the due date (as determined under section 430(j)(1)) for the plan year.
(B) Ordering rule. Any payment to or under a plan for any plan year shall be allocated first to unpaid minimum required contributions for all preceding plan years on a first-in, first-out basis and then to the minimum required contribution under section 430 for the plan year.

(d) Notification of the Secretary of Labor.
Before issuing a notice of deficiency with respect to the tax imposed by subsection (a) or (b), the Secretary shall notify the Secretary of Labor and provide him a reasonable opportunity (but not more than 60 days)—

(1) to require the employer responsible for contributing to or under the plan to eliminate the accumulated funding deficiency or unpaid minimum required contribution, whichever is applicable, or

(2) to comment on the imposition of such tax.

In the case of a multiemployer plan which is in reorganization under section 418, the same notice and opportunity shall be provided to the Pension Benefit Guaranty Corporation.

(e) **Liability for tax.**

(1) **In general.** Except as provided in paragraph (2), the tax imposed by subsection (a), (b), or (f) shall be paid by the employer responsible for contributing to or under the plan the amount described in section 412(a)(2).

(2) **Joint and several liability where employer member of controlled group.**

(A) In general. If an employer referred to in paragraph (1) is a member of a controlled group, each member of such group shall be jointly and severally liable for the tax imposed by subsection (a), (b), (f), or (g).

(B) Controlled group. For purposes of subparagraph (A), the term "controlled group" means any group treated as a single employer under subsection (b), (c), (m), or (o) of section 414.

(f) **Failure to pay liquidity shortfall.**

(1) **In general.** In the case of a plan to which section 430(j)(4) applies, there is hereby imposed a tax of 10 percent of the excess (if any) of—

(A) the amount of the liquidity shortfall for any quarter, over

(B) the amount of such shortfall which is paid by the required installment under section 430(j) for such quarter (but only if such installment is paid on or before the due date for such installment).

(2) **Additional tax.** If the plan has a liquidity shortfall as of the close of any quarter and as of the close of each of the following 4 quarters, there is hereby imposed a tax equal to 100 percent of the amount on which tax was imposed by paragraph (1) for such first quarter.

(3) **Definitions and special rule.**

(A) Liquidity shortfall; quarter. For purposes of this subsection, the terms "liquidity shortfall" and "quarter" have the respective meanings given such terms by section 412(m)(5).

(B) Special rule. If the tax imposed by paragraph (2) is paid with respect to any liquidity shortfall for any quarter, no further tax shall be imposed by this subsection on such shortfall for such quarter.

(4) **Waiver by Secretary.** If the taxpayer establishes to the satisfaction of the Secretary that—

(A) the liquidity shortfall described in paragraph (1) was due to reasonable cause and not willful neglect, and

(B) reasonable steps have been taken to remedy such liquidity shortfall,

the Secretary may waive all or part of the tax imposed by this subsection.

(g) **Multiemployer plans in endangered or critical status.**

(1) **In general.** Except as provided in this subsection—

(A) no tax shall be imposed under this section for a taxable year with respect to a multiemployer plan if, for the plan years ending with or within the taxable year, the plan is in critical status pursuant to section 432, and

(B) any tax imposed under this subsection for a taxable year with respect to a multiemployer plan if, for the plan years ending with or within the taxable year, the plan is in endangered status pursuant to section 432

shall be in addition to any other tax imposed by this section.

(2) **Failure to comply with funding improvement or rehabilitation plan.**

(A) In general. If any funding improvement plan or rehabilitation plan in effect under section 432 with respect to a multiemployer plan requires an employer to make a contribution to the plan, there is hereby imposed a tax on each failure of the employer to make the required contribution within the time required under such plan.

(B) Amount of tax. The amount of the tax imposed by subparagraph (A) shall be equal to the amount of the required contribution the employer failed to make in a timely manner.

(C) Liability for tax. The tax imposed by subparagraph (A) shall be paid by the employer responsible for contributing to or under the rehabilitation plan which fails to make the contribution.

(3) **Failure to meet requirements for plans in endangered or critical status.** If—

(A) a plan which is in seriously endangered status fails to meet the applicable benchmarks by the end of the funding improvement period, or

(B) a plan which is in critical status either—

(i) fails to meet the requirements of section 432(e) by the end of the rehabilitation period, or

(ii) has received a certification under section 432(b)(3)(A)(ii) for 3 consecutive plan years that the plan is not making the scheduled progress in meeting its requirements under the rehabilitation plan,

the plan shall be treated as having an accumulated funding deficiency for purposes of this section for the last plan year in such funding improvement, rehabilitation, or 3-consecutive year period (and each succeeding plan year until such benchmarks or requirements are met) in an amount equal to the greater of the amount of the contributions necessary to meet such benchmarks or requirements or the amount of such accumulated funding deficiency without regard to this paragraph.

(4) **Failure to adopt rehabilitation plan.**

(A) In general. In the case of a multiemployer plan which is in critical status, there is hereby imposed a tax on the failure of such plan to adopt a rehabilitation plan within the time prescribed under section 432.

(B) Amount of tax. The amount of the tax imposed under subparagraph (A) with respect to any plan sponsor for any taxable year shall be the greater of—

(i) the amount of tax imposed under subsection (a) for the taxable year (determined without regard to this subsection), or

(ii) the amount equal to $1,100 multiplied by the number of days during the taxable year which are included in the period beginning on the day following the close of the 240-day period described in section 432(e)(1)(A) and ending on the day on which the rehabilitation plan is adopted.

(C) Liability for tax.

(i) In general. The tax imposed by subparagraph (A) shall be paid by each plan sponsor.

(ii) Plan sponsor. For purposes of clause (i), the term "plan sponsor" has the meaning given such term by section 432(i)(9).

(5) **Waiver.** In the case of a failure described in paragraph (2) or (3) which is due to reasonable cause and not to willful neglect, the Secretary may waive part or all of the

Excise and miscellaneous taxes   Code Sec. 4971

tax imposed by this subsection. For purposes of this paragraph, reasonable cause includes unanticipated and material market fluctuations, the loss of a significant contributing employer, or other factors to the extent that the payment of tax under this subsection with respect to the failure would be excessive or otherwise inequitable relative to the failure involved.

(6) Terms used in section 432. For purposes of this subsection, any term used in this subsection which is also used in section 432 shall have the meaning given such term by section 432.

(h) Cross references.

For disallowance of deduction for taxes paid under this section, see section 275.

For liability for tax in case of an employer party to collective bargaining agreement, see section 413(b)(6).

For provisions concerning notification of Secretary of Labor of imposition of tax under this section, waiver of the tax imposed by subsection (b), and other coordination between Secretary of the Treasury and Secretary of Labor with respect to compliance with this section, see section 3002(b) of title III of the Employee Retirement Income Security Act of 1974.

In **2008**, P.L. 110-458, Sec. 101(d)(2)(F)(i), substituted "minimum required" for "required minimum" in subsec. (b)(1) . . . Sec. 101(d)(2)(F)(ii), added "or unpaid minimum required contribution, whichever is applicable" after "accumulated funding deficiency" each place it appears in paras. (c)(3) and (d)(1) . . . Sec. 101(d)(2)(F)(iii), substituted "section 412(a)(2)" for "section 412(a)(1)(A)" in para. (e)(1), as if included in Sec. 114, P.L. 109-280 and as provided by Sec. 114(g), P.L. 109-280, [added by Sec. 101(d)(3), P.L. 110-458] reproduced below.
—P.L. 110-458, Sec. 101(d)(3), added Sec. 114(g) of the Pension Protection Act of 2006 [P.L. 109-280, see below]
—P.L. 110-458, Sec. 102(b)(2)(I)(i), substituted "day following the close of" for "first day of" in clause (g)(4)(B)(ii) . . . Sec. 102(b)(2)(I)(ii), amended clause (g)(4)(C)(ii), effective for plan yrs. begin. after 2007 but only for plan yrs. begin. after 2007 which end with or within any such tax. year, as if included in the provisions of Sec. 212, P.L. 109-280. For special rules see Sec. 212(e)(2)-(3) of P.L. 109-280, as amended by Sec. 102(b)(3)(C) of this Act, reproduced below.
Prior to amendment, clause (g)(4)(C)(ii) read as follows:
"(ii) Plan sponsor. For purposes of clause (i) , the term 'plan sponsor' in the case of a multiemployer plan means the association, committee, joint board of trustees, or other similar group of representatives of the parties who establish or maintain the plan."
—P.L. 110-458, Sec. 102(b)(3)(A), substituted "Section 4971(e)(2) of such Code" for "Section 4971(c)(2) of such Code" in Sec. 212(b)(2) of the Pension Protection Act of 2006 [P.L. 109-280, see below]
—P.L. 110-458, Sec. 102(b)(3)(B), added ", except that the amendments made by subsection (b) shall apply to taxable years beginning after 2007 which end with or within any such taxable year" before the period at the end of Sec. 212(e)(1), P.L. 109-280, the effective date provision for amendments made by Sec. 112, P.L. 109-280, see below.
—P.L. 110-458, Sec. 102(b)(3)(C), substituted "section 432(b)(3) of the Internal Revenue Code of 1986" for "section 305(b)(3) of the Employee Retirement Income Security Act of 1974" in Sec. 212(e)(2) of the Pension Protection Act of 2006 [P.L. 109-280, see below]
—P.L. 110-458, Sec. 104(b), substituted "commercial" for "commercial airline" in Sec. 402(c)(1)(A) of the Pension Protection Act of 2006 [P.L. 109-280, see below]
—P.L. 110-458, Sec. 126(a), amended Sec. 402(e)(4)(C) of the Pension Protection Act of 2006 [P.L. 109-280, see below] effective for plan yrs. begin. after 12/31/2007.
Prior to amendment, Sec. 402(e)(4)(C) of P.L. 109-280 read as follows:
"(C) The value of plan assets shall be equal to their fair market value."

In **2006**, P.L. 109-280, Sec. 114(e)(1), amended subsecs. (a) and (b) . . . Sec. 114(e)(2)(A), substituted "section 431" for "the last two sentences of section 412(a)" in para. (c)(1) . . . Sec. 114(e)(2)(B), added para. (c)(4) . . . Sec. 114(e)(3), substituted "section 412(a)(1)(A)" for "section 412(b)(3)(A)" in para. (e)(1) . . . Sec. 114(e)(4)(A), substituted "section 430(j)(4)" for "section 412(m)(5)" in para. (f)(1) . . . Sec. 114(e)(4)(B), substituted "section 430(j)" for "section 412(m)" in para. (f)(1). Sec. 114(g) of this Act, as added by Sec. 101(d)(3) of P.L. 110-458 [see above] reads as follows:
"(g) Effective dates.
"(1) In general. The amendments made by this section shall apply to plan years beginning after 2007.
"(2) Excise tax. The amendments made by subsection (e) shall apply to taxable years beginning after 2007, but only with respect to plan years described in paragraph (1) which end with or within any such taxable year."
Prior to amendment, subsecs. (a) and (b) read as follows:

"(a) Initial tax. For each taxable year of an employer who maintains a plan to which section 412 applies, there is hereby imposed a tax of 10 percent (5 percent in the case of a multiemployer plan) on the amount of the accumulated funding deficiency under the plan, determined as of the end of the plan year ending with or within such taxable year.
"(b) Additional tax. In any case in which an initial tax is imposed by subsection (a) on an accumulated funding deficiency and such accumulated funding deficiency is not corrected within the taxable period, there is hereby imposed a tax equal to 100 percent of such accumulated funding deficiency to the extent not corrected."
—P.L. 109-280, Sec. 206, of this Act, reads as follows:
"Sec. 206. Special rule for certain benefits funded under an agreement approved by the Pension Benefit Guaranty Corporation.
"In the case of a multiemployer plan that is a party to an agreement that was approved by the Pension Benefit Guaranty Corporation prior to June 30, 2005, and that—
"(1) increases benefits, and
"(2) provides for special withdrawal liability rules under section 4203(f) of the Employee Retirement Income Security Act of 1974 (29 U.S.C. 1383),
the amendments made by sections 201, 202, 211, and 212 of this Act shall not apply to the benefit increases under any plan amendment adopted prior to June 30, 2005, that are funded pursuant to such agreement if the plan is funded in compliance with such agreement (and any amendments thereto)."
—P.L. 109-280, Sec. 212(b)(1), redesignated subsec. (g) as (h) and added subsec. (g) . . . Sec. 212(b)(2)(A), substituted "If an" for "In the case of a plan other than a multiemployer plan, if the" in para. (e)(2) [as corrected by Sec. 102(b)(3)(A), P.L. 110-458, see above] . . . Sec. 212(b)(2)(B), substituted "(f), or (g)" for "(f)" in para. (e)(2), effective [as amended by Sec. 102(b)(3)(B), P.L. 110-458, see above] for plan yrs. begin. after 2007, but only for plan yrs. begin. after 2007 which end with or within any such taxable year. Sec. 212(e)(2)-(3), of this Act [as amended by Sec. 102(b)(3)(C) of P.L. 110-458, see above], reads as follows:
"(2) Special rule for certain notices. In any case in which a plan's actuary certifies that it is reasonably expected that a multiemployer plan will be in critical status under section 432(b)(3) of the Internal Revenue Code of 1986, as added by this section, with respect to the first plan year beginning after 2007, the notice required under subparagraph (D) of such section may be provided at any time after the date of enactment, so long as it is provided on or before the last date for providing the notice under such subparagraph.
"(3) Special rule for certain restored benefits. In the case of a multiemployer plan—
"(A) with respect to which benefits were reduced pursuant to a plan amendment adopted on or after January 1, 2002, and before June 30, 2005, and
"(B) which, pursuant to the plan document, the trust agreement, or a formal written communication from the plan sponsor to participants provided before June 30, 2005, provided for the restoration of such benefits,
the amendments made by this section shall not apply to such benefit restorations to the extent that any restriction on the providing or accrual of such benefits would otherwise apply by reason of such amendments."
—P.L. 109-280, Sec. 214, of this Act, reads as follows:
"Sec. 214. Exemption from excise taxes for certain multiemployer pension plans.
"(a) In general. Notwithstanding any other provision of law, no tax shall be imposed under subsection (a) or (b) of section 4971 of the Internal Revenue Code of 1986 with respect to any accumulated funding deficiency of a plan described in subsection (b) of this section for any taxable year beginning before the earlier of—
"(1) the taxable year in which the plan sponsor adopts a rehabilitation plan under section 305(e) of the Employee Retirement Income Security Act of 1974 and section 432(e) of such Code (as added by this Act); or
"(2) the taxable year that contains January 1, 2009.
"(b) Plan described. A plan described under this subsection is a multiemployer pension plan—
"(1) with less than 100 participants;
"(2) with respect to which the contributing employers participated in a Federal fishery capacity reduction program;
"(3) with respect to which employers under the plan participated in the Northeast Fisheries Assistance Program; and
"(4) with respect to which the annual normal cost is less than $100,000 and the plan is experiencing a funding deficiency on the date of enactment of this Act."
—P.L. 109-280, Sec. 221, of this Act, reads as follows:
"Sec. 221. Sunset of additional funding rules.
"(a) Report. Not later than December 31, 2011, the Secretary of Labor, the Secretary of the Treasury, and the Executive Director of the Pension Benefit Guaranty Corporation shall conduct a study of the effect of the amendments made by this subtitle on the operation and funding status of multiemployer plans and shall report the results of such study, including any recommendations for legislation, to the Congress.
"(b) Matters included in study. The study required under subsection (a) shall include—
"(1) the effect of funding difficulties, funding rules in effect before the date of the enactment of this Act, and the amendments made by this subtitle on small businesses participating in multiemployer plans,
"(2) the effect on the financial status of small employers of—
"(A) funding targets set in funding improvement and rehabilitation p lans and associated contribution increases,
"(B) funding deficiencies,
"(C) excise taxes,

"(D) withdrawal liability,

"(E) the possibility of alternatives schedules and procedures for financially-troubled employers, and

"(F) other aspects of the multiemployer system, and

"(3) the role of the multiemployer pension plan system in helping small employers to offer pension benefits.

"*(c) Sunset.*

"(1) In general. Except as provided in this subsection, notwithstanding any other provision of this Act, the provisions of, and the amendments made by, sections 201(b), 202, and 212 shall not apply to plan years beginning after December 31, 2014.

"(2) Funding improvement and rehabilitation plans. If a plan is operating under a funding improvement or rehabilitation plan under section 305 of such Act or 432 of such Code for its last year beginning before January 1, 2015, such plan shall continue to operate under such funding improvement or rehabilitation plan during any period after December 31, 2014, such funding improvement or rehabilitation plan is in effect and all provisions of such Act or Code relating to the operation of such funding improvement or rehabilitation plan shall continue in effect during such period."

—P.L. 109-280, Sec. 402(a)-(g)(1), of this Act [as amended by Sec. 104(b) and Sec. 126(a) of P.L. 110-458, see above], reads as follows:

"*(a) In general.* The plan sponsor of an eligible plan may elect to either—

"(1) have the rules of subsection (b) apply, or

"(2) have section 303 of the Employee Retirement Income Security Act of 1974 and section 430 of the Internal Revenue Code of 1986 applied to its first taxable year beginning in 2008 by amortizing the shortfall amortization base for such taxable year over a period of 10 plan years (rather than 7 plan years) beginning with such plan year.

"*(b) Alternative funding schedule.*

"In general. If an election is made under subsection (a)(1) to have this subsection apply to an eligible plan and the requirements of paragraphs (2) and (3) are met with respect to the plan—

"(A) in the case of any applicable plan year beginning before January 1, 2008, the plan shall not have an accumulated funding deficiency for purposes of section 302 of the Employee Retirement Income Security Act of 1974 and sections 412 and 4971 of the Internal Revenue Code of 1986 if contributions to the plan for the plan year are not less than the minimum required contribution determined under subsection (e) for the plan for the plan year, and

"(B) in the case of any applicable plan year beginning on or after January 1, 2008, the minimum required contribution determined under sections 303 of such Act and 430 of such Code shall, for purposes of sections 302 and 303 of such Act and sections 412, 430, and 4971 of such Code, be equal to the minimum required contribution determined under subsection (e) for the plan for the plan year.

"(2) Accrual restrictions.

"(A) In general. The requirements of this paragraph are met if, effective as of the first day of the first applicable plan year and at all times thereafter while an election under this section is in effect, the plan provides that—

"(i) the accrued benefit, any death or disability benefit, and any social security supplement described in the last sentence of section 411(a)(9) of such Code and section 204(b)(1)(G) of such Act, of each participant are frozen at the amount of such benefit or supplement immediately before such first day, and

"(ii) all other benefits under the plan are eliminated, but only to the extent the freezing or elimination of such benefits would have been permitted under section 411(d)(6) of such Code and section 204(g) of such Act if they had been implemented by a plan amendment adopted immediately before such first day.

"(B) Increases in section 415 limits. If a plan provides that an accrued benefit of a participant which has been subject to any limitation under section 415 of such Code will be increased if such limitation is increased, the plan shall not be treated as meeting the requirements of this section unless, effective as of the first day of the first applicable plan year (or, if later, the date of the enactment of this Act) and at all times thereafter while an election under this section is in effect, the plan provides that any such increase shall not take effect. A plan shall not fail to meet the requirements of section 411(d)(6) of such Code and section 204(g) of such Act solely because the plan is amended to meet the requirements of this subparagraph.

"(3) Restriction on applicable benefit increases.

"(A) In general. The requirements of this paragraph are met if no applicable benefit increase takes effect at any time during the period beginning on July 26, 2005, and ending on the day before the first day of the first applicable plan year.

"(B) Applicable benefit increase. For purposes of this paragraph, the term 'applicable benefit increase' means, with respect to any plan year, any increase in liabilities of the plan by plan amendment (or otherwise provided in regulations provided by the Secretary) which, but for this paragraph, would occur during the plan year by reason of —

"(i) any increase in benefits,

"(ii) any change in the accrual of benefits, or

"(iii) any change in the rate at which benefits become nonforfeitable under the plan.

"(4) Exception for imputed disability service. Paragraphs (2) and (3) shall not apply to any accrual or increase with respect to imputed service provided to a participant during any period of the participant's disability occurring on or after the effective date of the plan amendment providing the restrictions under paragraph (2) (or on or after July 26, 2005, in the case of the restrictions under paragraph (3)) if the participant—

"(A) was receiving disability benefits as of such date, or

"(B) was receiving sick pay and subsequently determined to be eligible for disability benefits as of such date.

"*(c) Definitions.* For purposes of this section—

"(1) Eligible plan. The term 'eligible plan' means a defined benefit plan (other than a multiemployer plan) to which sections 302 of such Act and 412 of such Code applies which is sponsored by an employer—

"(A) which is a commercial passenger airline, or

"(B) the principal business of which is providing catering services to a commercial passenger airline.

"(2) Applicable plan year. The term 'applicable plan year' means each plan year to which the election under subsection (a)(1) applies under subsection (d)(1)(A).

"*(d) Elections and related terms.*

"(1) Years for which election made.

"(A) Alternative funding schedule. If an election under subsection (a)(1) was made with respect to an eligible plan, the plan sponsor may select either a plan year beginning in 2006 or a plan year beginning in 2007 as the first plan year to which such election applies. The election shall apply to such plan year and all subsequent years. The election shall be made—

"(i) not later than December 31, 2006, in the case of an election for a plan year beginning in 2006, or

"(ii) not later than December 31, 2007, in the case of an election for a plan year beginning in 2007.

"(B) 10 year amortization. An election under subsection (a)(2) shall be made not later than December 31, 2007.

"(C) Election of new plan year for alternative funding schedule. In the case of an election under subsection (a)(1), the plan sponsor may specify a new plan year in such election and the plan year of the plan may be changed to such new plan year without the approval of the Secretary of the Treasury.

"(2) Manner of election. A plan sponsor shall make any election under subsection (a) in such manner as the Secretary of the Treasury may prescribe. Such election, once made, may be revoked only with the consent of such Secretary.

"*(e) Minimum required contribution.* In the case of an eligible plan with respect to which an election is made under subsection (a)(1)—

"(1) In general. In the case of any applicable plan year during the amortization period, the minimum required contribution shall be the amount necessary to amortize the unfunded liability of the plan, determined as of the first day of the plan year, in equal annual installments (until fully amortized) over the remainder of the amortization period. Such amount shall be separately determined for each applicable plan year.

"(2) Years after amortization period. In the case of any plan year beginning after the end of the amortization period, section 302(a)(2)(A) of such Act and section 412(a)(2)(A) of such Code shall apply to such plan, but the prefunding balance and funding standard carryover balance as of the first day of the first of such years under section 303(f) of such Act and section 430(f) of such Code shall be zero.

"(3) Definitions. For purposes of this section—

"(A) Unfunded liability. The term 'unfunded liability' means the unfunded accrued liability under the plan, determined under the unit credit funding method.

"Amortization period. The term 'amortization period' means the 17-plan year period beginning with the first applicable plan year.

"(4) Other rules. In determining the minimum required contribution and amortization amount under this subsection—

"(A) the provisions of section 302(c)(3) of such Act and section 412(c)(3) of such Code, as in effect before the date of enactment of this section, shall apply,

"(B) a rate of interest of 8.85 percent shall be used for all calculations requiring an interest rate, and

"(C) the value of plan assets shall be determined under sections 303(g)(3) of such Act and 430(g)(3) of such Code.

"(5) Special rule for certain plan spin-offs. For purposes of subsection (b), if, with respect to any eligible plan to which this subsection applies—

"(A) any applicable plan year includes the date of the enactment of this Act,

"(B) a plan was spun off from the eligible plan during the plan year but before such date of enactment, the minimum required contribution under paragraph (1) for the eligible plan for such applicable plan year shall be an aggregate amount determined as if the plans were a single plan for that plan year (based on the full 12-month plan year in effect prior to the spin-off). The employer shall designate the allocation of such aggregate amount between such plans for the applicable plan year.

"*(f) Special rules for certain balances and waivers.* In the case of an eligible plan with respect to which an election is made under subsection (a)(1)—

"(1) Funding standard account and credit balances. Any charge or credit in the funding standard account under section 302 of such Act or section 412 of such Code, and any prefunding balance or funding standard carryover balance under section 303 of such Act or section 430 of such Code, as of the day before the first day of the first applicable plan year, shall be reduced to zero.

"(2) Waived funding deficiencies. Any waived funding deficiency under sections 302 and 303 of such Act or section 412 of such Code, as in effect before the date of enactment of this section, shall be deemed satisfied as of the first day of the first applicable plan year and the amount of such waived funding deficiency shall be taken into account in determining the plan's unfunded liability under subsection (e)(3)(A). In the case of a plan amendment adopted to satisfy the requirements of subsection (b)(2), the plan shall not be deemed to violate section 304(b) of such Act or section 412(f) of such Code, as so in effect, by reason of such amendment or any increase in benefits provided to such plan's participants under a separate plan that is a defined contribution plan or a multiemployer plan.

"*(g) Other rules for plans making election under this section.*

"(1) Successor plans to certain plans. If—

"(A) an election under paragraph (1) or (2) of subsection (a) is in effect with respect to any eligible plan, and
"(B) the eligible plan is maintained by an employer that establishes or maintains 1 or more other defined benefit plans (other than any multiemployer plan), and such other plans in combination provide benefit accruals to any substantial number of successor employees, the Secretary of the Treasury may, in the Secretary's discretion, determine that any trust of which any other such plan is a part does not constitute a qualified trust under section 401(a) of the Internal Revenue Code of 1986 unless all benefit obligations of the eligible plan have been satisfied. For purposes of this paragraph, the term 'successor employee' means any employee who is or was covered by the eligible plan and any employees who perform substantially the same type of work with respect to the same business operations as an employee covered by such eligible plan."

In 1996, P.L. 104-188, Sec. 1464(a), added para. (f)(4), effective for plan yrs. begin. after 12/31/94.

In 1994, P.L. 103-465, Sec. 751(a)(9)(B)(i), substituted "(a), (b), or (f)" for "(a) or (b)" each place it appeared in subsec. (e) . . . Sec. 751(a)(9)(B)(ii), redesignated subsec. (f) as (g) and added new subsec (f), effective for plan yrs. begin. after 12/31/94.

In 1987, P.L. 100-203, Sec. 9304(c)(1), substituted "10 percent (5 percent in the case of a multiemployer plan)" for "5 percent" in subsec. (a), effective for plan years beginning after 1988.

—P.L. 100-203, Sec. 9305(a)(1), redesignated subsec. (e) as subsec. (f) and added new subsec. (e) . . . Sec. 9305(a)(2)(A), deleted the last sentence of subsec. (a) . . . Sec. 9305(a)(2)(B), deleted the last sentence of subsec. (b), effective for plan years begin. after 12/31/87.

Prior to amendment, the last sentence of subsec. (a) read as follows:
"The tax imposed by this subsection shall be paid by the employer responsible for contributing to or under the plan the amount described in section 412(b)(3)(A)."
Prior to amendment, the last sentence of subsec. (b) read as follows:
"The tax imposed by this subsection shall be paid by the employer described in subsection (a)."

In 1980, P.L. 96-596, Sec. 2(a)(1)(J), substituted "taxable period" for "correction period" in subsec. (b) . . . Sec. 2(a)(2)(H), amended para. (c)(3), effective as provided in Sec. 2(d) of this Act which reads as follows:
"(d) Effective dates.
"(1) First tier taxes.—The amendments made by this section with respect to any first tier tax shall take effect as if included in the Internal Revenue Code of 1954 when such tax was first imposed.
"(2) Second tier taxes.—The amendments made by this section with respect to any second tier tax shall apply only with respect to taxes assessed after the date or the enactment of this Act. [12/24/80] Nothing in the preceding sentence shall be construed to permit the assessment of a tax in a case to which, on the date of the enactment of this Act [12/24/80] the doctrine of res judicata applies.
"(3) First and second tier tax.—For purposes of this subsection, the terms 'first tier tax' and 'second tier tax' have the respective meanings given to such terms by section 4962 of the Internal Revenue Code of 1954."
Prior to amendment, para. (c)(3) read as follows:
"(3) Correction period. The term 'correction period' means, with respect to an accumulated funding deficiency, the period beginning with the end of a plan year in which there is an accumulated funding deficiency and ending 90 days after the date of mailing of a notice of deficiency under section 6212 with respect to the tax imposed by subsection (b), extended—
"(A) by any period in which a deficiency cannot be assessed under section 6213(a), and
"(B) by any other period which the Secretary determines is reasonable and necessary to permit a reduction of the accumulated funding deficiency to zero under this section."
—P.L. 96-364, Sec. 204, substituted "last two sentences" for "last sentence" in subsec. (c), added the last sentence to subsec. (d), effective 9/26/80.

In 1976, P.L. 94-455, Sec. 1906(b)(13)(A), substituted "Secretary" for "Secretary or his delegate" each place it appeared in Code Sec. 4971, effective 2/1/77.

In 1974, P.L. 93-406, Sec. 1013(b), added Code Sec. 4971, effective 9/2/74 or other date as specified in Sec. 1017 of the Act (reproduced following Code Sec. 401.)

Sec. 4972. Tax on nondeductible contributions to qualified employer plans.

(a) Tax imposed.
In the case of any qualified employer plan, there is hereby imposed a tax equal to 10 percent of the nondeductible contributions under the plan (determined as of the close of the taxable year of the employer).

(b) Employer liable for tax.
The tax imposed by this section shall be paid by the employer making the contributions.

(c) Nondeductible contributions.
For purposes of this section—
(1) In general. The term "nondeductible contributions" means, with respect to any qualified employer plan, the sum of—
(A) the excess (if any) of—
(i) the amount contributed for the taxable year by the employer to or under such plan, over
(ii) the amount allowable as a deduction under section 404 for such contributions (determined without regard to subsection (e) thereof), and
(B) the amount determined under this subsection for the preceding taxable year reduced by the sum of—
(i) the portion of the amount so determined returned to the employer during the taxable year, and
(ii) the portion of the amount so determined deductible under section 404 for the taxable year (determined without regard to subsection (e) thereof).

(2) Ordering rule for section 404. For purposes of paragraph (1), the amount allowable as a deduction under section 404 for any taxable year shall be treated as—
(A) first from carryforwards to such taxable year from preceding taxable years (in order of time), and
(B) then from contributions made during such taxable year.

(3) Contributions which may be returned to employer. In determining the amount of nondeductible contributions for any taxable year, there shall not be taken into account any contribution for such taxable year which is distributed to the employer in a distribution described in section 4980(c)(2)(B)(ii) if such distribution is made on or before the last day on which a contribution may be made for such taxable year under section 404(a)(6).

(4) Special rule for self-employed individuals. For purposes of paragraph (1), if—
(A) the amount which is required to be contributed to a plan under section 412 on behalf of an individual who is an employee (within the meaning of section 401(c)(1)), exceeds
(B) the earned income (within the meaning of section 404(a)(8)) of such individual derived from the trade or business with respect to which such plan is established, such excess shall be treated as an amount allowable as a deduction under section 404.

(5) Pre-1987 contributions. The term "nondeductible contribution" shall not include any contribution made for a taxable year beginning before January 1, 1987.

(6) Exceptions. In determining the amount of nondeductible contributions for any taxable year, there shall not be taken into account—
(A) so much of the contributions to 1 or more defined contribution plans which are not deductible when contributed solely because of section 404(a)(7) as does not exceed the amount of contributions described in section 401(m)(4)(A), or
(B) so much of the contributions to a simple retirement account (within the meaning of section 408(p)) or a simple plan (within the meaning of section 401(k)(11)) which are not deductible when contributed solely because such contributions are not made in connection with a trade or business of the employer.
For purposes of subparagraph (A), the deductible limits under section 404(a)(7) shall first be applied to amounts contributed to a defined benefit plan and then to amounts described in subparagraph (A). Subparagraph (B) shall not apply to contributions made on behalf of the employer or a member of the employer's family (as defined in section 447(e)(1)).

(7) Defined benefit plan exception. In determining the amount of nondeductible contributions for any taxable year, an employer may elect for such year not to take into account any contributions to a defined benefit plan except,

Code Sec. 4972(c)(7) — Excise and miscellaneous taxes

in the case of a multiemployer plan, to the extent that such contributions exceed the full-funding limitation (as defined in section 431(c)(6)). For purposes of this paragraph, the deductible limits under section 404(a)(7) shall first be applied to amounts contributed to defined contribution plans and then to amounts described in this paragraph. If an employer makes an election under this paragraph for a taxable year, paragraph (6) shall not apply to such employer for such taxable year.

(d) Definitions.

For purposes of this section—

(1) Qualified employer plan.

(A) In general. The term "qualified employer plan" means—

(i) any plan meeting the requirements of section 401(a) which includes a trust exempt from tax under section 501(a),

(ii) an annuity plan described in section 403(a),

(iii) any simplified employee pension (within the meaning of section 408(k)), and

(iv) any simple retirement account (within the meaning of section 408(p)).

(B) Exemption for governmental and tax exempt plans. The term "qualified employer plan" does not include a plan described in subparagraph (A) or (B) of section 4980(c)(1).

(2) Employer. In the case of a plan which provides contributions or benefits for employees some or all of whom are self-employed individuals within the meaning of section 401(c)(1), the term "employer" means the person treated as the employer under section 401(c)(4).

In 2010, P.L. 111-312, Sec. 101(a)(1), substituted "December 31, 2012" for "December 31, 2010" both places it appeared in Sec. 901 of P.L. 107-16, [see below] effective as if included in the enactment of P.L. 107-16, EGTRRA, 6/7/2001.

In 2008, P.L. 110-458, Sec. 101(d)(3), added subsec. (g) in Sec. 114 of P.L. 109-280, which reads as follows:

"(g) Effective date.

"(1) In general. The amendments made by this section shall apply to plan years beginning after 2007.

"(2) Excise tax. The amendments made by subsection (e) shall apply to taxable years beginning after 2007, but only with respect to plan years described in paragraph (1) which end with or within any such taxable year."

In 2006, P.L. 109-280, Sec. 114(e)(5), substituted "except, in the case of a multiemployer plan, to the extent that such contributions exceed the full-funding limitation (as defined in section 431(c)(6))" for "except to the extent that such contributions exceed the full-funding limitation (as defined in section 412(c)(7), determined without regard to subparagraph (A)(i)(I) thereof)" in para. (c)(7), enacted 8/17/2006

—P.L. 109-280, Sec. 803(c), amended subpara. (c)(6)(A), effective for contributions for tax. yrs. begin. after 12/31/2005.

Prior to amendment, (c)(6)(A) read as follows:

"(A) so much of the contributions to 1 or more defined contribution plans which are not deductible when contributed solely because of section 404(a)(7) as does not exceed the greater of—

"(i) the amount of contributions not in excess of 6 percent of compensation (within the meaning of section 404(a) and as adjusted under section 404(a)(12)) paid or accrued (during the taxable year for which the contributions were made) to beneficiaries under the plans, or

"(ii) the amount of contributions described in section 401(m)(4)(A), or

—P.L. 109-280, Sec. 811, of this Act [relating to Sec. 901 of P.L. 107-16, see below], provides:

"SEC. 811. PENSIONS AND INDIVIDUAL RETIREMENT ARRANGEMENT PROVISIONS OF ECONOMIC GROWTH AND TAX RELIEF RECONCILIATION ACT OF 2001 MADE PERMANENT.

"Title IX of the Economic Growth and Tax Relief Reconciliation Act of 2001 shall not apply to the provisions of, and amendments made by, subtitles A through F of title VI of such Act (relating to pension and individual retirement arrangement provisions)."

In 2004, P.L. 108-311, Sec. 404(c), amended clause (c)(6)(A)(ii), effective for yrs. begin. after 12/31/2001 as if included in Sec. 614 of the Economic Growth and Tax Relief Reconciliation Act of 2001, P.L. 107-16.

Prior to amendment, clause (c)(6)(A)(ii) read as follows:

"(ii) the sum of—

"(I) the amount of contributions described in section 401(m)(4)(A), plus

"(II) the amount of contributions described in section 402(g)(3)(A), or".

—P.L. 108-311, Sec. 408(b)(9), added "each place it appears" before "in the next to last sentence" in Sec. 652(b)(3) of P.L. 107-16, see below.

In 2002, P.L. 107-358, Sec. 2, added subsec. (c) in Sec. 901 of P.L. 107-16 [see below], effective 12/17/2002.

In 2001, P.L. 107-16, Sec. 616(b)(2)(B), substituted "(within the meaning of section 404(a) and as adjusted under section 404(a)(12))" for "(within the meaning of section 404(a))" in clause (c)(6)(A)(i) [as redesignated by Sec. 652(b)(1) of this Act, see below], effective for yrs. begin. after 12/31/2001.

—P.L. 107-16, Sec. 637(a), deleted "and" at the end of subpara. (c)(6)(A) [prior to deletion by Sec. 652(b)(1) of this Act, see below], substituted ", or" for the period at the end of subpara. (c)(6)(A) [as redesignated by Sec. 652(b)(1) of this Act, see below], and added subpara. (c)(6)(C) [prior to redesignation by Sec. 652(b)(1) of this Act, see below]... Sec. 637(b), added a sentence at the end of para. (c)(6) [prior to amendment by Sec. 652(b)(4) of this Act, see below], effective for tax. yrs. begin. after 12/31/2001. Sec. 637(c) of this Act provides:

"(c) No inference. Nothing in the amendments made by this section shall be construed to infer the proper treatment of nondeductible contributions under the laws in effect before such amendments."

—P.L. 107-16, Sec. 652(b)(1), deleted subpara. (c)(6)(A) [as amended by Sec. 637(a) of this Act, see above] and redesignated subparas. (c)(6)(B) [as amended by Secs. 616(b)(2)(B) and 637(a) of this Act, see above] and (C) [as added by Sec. 637(a) of this Act, see above] as subparas. (c)(6)(A) and (B) respectively... Sec. 652(b)(2), deleted "If 1 or more defined benefit plans were taken into account in determining the amount allowable as a deduction under section 404 for contributions to any defined contribution plan, subparagraph (B) shall apply only if such defined benefit plans are described in section 404(a)(1)(D)." before "For purposes" in para. (c)(6)... Sec. 652(b)(3), substituted "subparagraph (A)" for "subparagraph (B)" each place it appeared in the second sentence following subpara. (c)(6)(B) [as clarified by Sec. 408(b)(9) of P.L. 108-311, see above]... Sec. 652(b)(4), substituted "Subparagraph (B)" for "Subparagraph (C)" in para. (c)(6), effective for plan yrs. begin. after 12/31/2001.

Prior to deletion, subpara. (c)(6)(A) [as amended by Sec. 637(a) of this Act, see above] read as follows:

"(A) contributions that would be deductible under section 404(a)(1)(D) if the plan had more than 100 participants if—

"(i) the plan is covered under section 4021 of the Employee Retirement Income Security Act of 1974, and

"(ii) the plan is terminated under section 4041(b) of such Act on or before the last day of the taxable year, and"

—P.L. 107-16, Sec. 653(a), added para. (c)(7), effective for yrs. begin. after 12/31/2001.

—P.L. 107-16, Sec. 901, of this Act [as amended by Sec. 2 of P.L. 107-358, and Sec. 101(a)(1) of P.L. 111-312, see above], reads as follows:

"SEC. 901. SUNSET OF PROVISIONS OF ACT.

"(a) In general. All provisions of, and amendments made by, this Act shall not apply—

"(1) to taxable, plan, or limitation years beginning after December 31, 2012, or

"(2) in the case of title V, to estates of decedents dying, gifts made, or generation skipping transfers, after December 31, 2012.

"(b) Application of certain laws. The Internal Revenue Code of 1986 and the Employee Retirement Income Security Act of 1974 shall be applied and administered to years, estates, gifts, and transfers described in subsection (a) as if the provisions and amendments described in subsection (a) had never been enacted.

"(c) Exception. Subsection (a) shall not apply to section 803 (relating to no federal income tax on restitution received by victims of the Nazi regime or their heirs or estates)."

In 1997, P.L. 105-34, Sec. 1507(a), amended subpara. (c)(6)(B), effective for tax. yrs. begin. after 12/31/97.

Prior to amendment, subpara. (c)(6)(B) read as follows:

"(B) contributions to 1 or more defined contribution plans which are not deductible when contributed solely because of section 404(a)(7), but only to the extent such contributions do not exceed 6 percent of compensation (within the meaning of section 404(a)) paid or accrued (during the taxable year for which the contributions were made) to beneficiaries under the plans."

In 1996, P.L. 104-188, Sec. 1421(b)(9)(D), deleted "and" at the end of clause (d)(1)(A)(ii), substituted ", and" for the period at the end of clause (d)(1)(A)(iii) and added clause (d)(1)(A)(iv), effective for tax. yrs. begin. after 12/31/96.

In 1994, P.L. 103-465, Sec. 755(a), added para. (c)(6), effective as provided in Sec. 755(b) of this Act, which reads as follows:

"(b) Effective dates.

"(1) Section 4972(c)(6)(A).— Section 4972(c)(6)(A) of the Internal Revenue Code of 1986 (as added by this section) shall apply to taxable years ending on or after the date of enactment of this Act.

"(2) Section 4972(c)(6)(B).— Section 4972(c)(6)(B) of such Code (as added by this section) shall apply to taxable years ending on or after December 31, 1992."

In 1989, P.L. 101-239, Sec. 7812(d), changed the effective date for changes made by Sec. 2005(a)(1) of P.L. 100-647, see below, from, effective for plan yrs. begin. after 12/31/88, to effective for tax. yrs. begin. after 12/31/86.

In 1988, P.L. 100-647, Sec. 1011A(e)(1), amended subsec. (c)... Sec. 1011A(e)(2), amended para. (d)(1), effective for tax. yrs. begin. after 12/31/86. For special rules for collective bargaining agreements, see Sec. 1131(d)(2) of P.L. 99-514, reproduced below

Prior to amendment, subsec. (c) read as follows:

"(c) Nondeductible contributions.

For purposes of this section, the term 'nondeductible contributions' means, with respect to any qualified employer plan, the sum of—

"(1) the excess (if any) of—

"(A) the amount contributed for the taxable year by the employer to or under such plan, over

"(B) the amount allowable as a deduction under section 404 for such contributions, and

"(2) the amount determined under this subsection for the preceding taxable year reduced by the sum of—

"(A) the portion of the amount so determined returned to the employer during the taxable year, and

"(B) the portion of the amount so determined deductible under section 404 for the taxable year."

Prior to amendment, para. (d)(1) read as follows

"(1) Qualified employer plan. The term 'qualified employer plan' means—

"(A) any plan meeting the requirements of section 401(a) which includes a trust exempt from the tax under section 501(a),

"(B) an annuity plan described in section 403(a), and

"(C) any simplified employee pension (within the meaning of section 408(k))."

—P.L. 100-647, Sec. 1011A(e)(3), added Sec. 1131(d)(2) of P.L. 99-514, [reproduced below] part of the effective date for Code Sec. 4972 as added by Sec. 1131(c)(1) of P.L. 99-514, see below.

—P.L. 100-647, Sec. 1011(e)(5), of this Act provides:

"(5) In the case of any taxable year beginning in 1987, the amount under section 4972(c)(1)(A)(ii) of the 1986 Code for a plan to which title IV of the Employee Retirement Income Security Act of 1974 applies shall be increased by the amount (if any) by which, as of the close of the plan year with or within which such taxable year begins—

"(A) the liabilities of such plan (determined as if the plan had terminated as of such time), exceed

"(B) the assets of such plan."

—P.L. 100-647, Sec. 2005(a)(1), redesignated para. (c)(4) [as added by Sec. 1011A(e)(1) of this Act] as para. (c)(5) and added para. (c)(4), effective [as amended by Sec. 7812(d) of P.L. 101-239, see above] for tax yrs. begin. after 12/31/86.

In 1986, P.L. 99-514, Sec. 1131(c)(1), added Code Sec. 4972, effective for tax. yrs. begin. after 12/31/86. [see Sec. 1011A(e)(5) of P.L. 100-647, reproduced above].

Sec. 1131(d)(2) [as added by Sec. 1011A(e)(3) of P.L. 100-647] of this Act provides:

"(2) Special rules for collective bargaining agreements.—In the case of a plan maintained pursuant to 1 or more collective bargaining agreements between employee representatives and 1 or more employers ratified before March 1, 1986, the amendments made by this section shall not apply to contributions pursuant to any such agreement for taxable years beginning before the earlier of—

"(A) January 1, 1989, or

"(B) the date on which the last of such collective bargaining agreements terminates (determined without regard to any extension thereof after February 28, 1986)".

Sec. 4972. Repealed.

In 1984, P.L. 98-369, Sec. 491(d)(40), amended the last sentence of subsec. (a), effective for obligations issued after 12/31/83.

Prior to amendment, the last sentence of subsec. (a) read as follows:

"This section applies only to plans which include a trust described in section 401(a), which are described in section 403(a), or which are described in section 405(a)."

In 1983, P.L. 97-448, Sec. 103(c)(10)(B), added the last sentence to para. (b)(2), effective for tax. yrs. begin. after 12/31/81.

—P.L. 97-448, Sec. 103(d)(3), changed Sec. 312(f)(1) of P.L. 97-34, the effective date for changes made by Sec. 312(e)(3) of P.L. 97-34 to "taxable years beginning after December 31, 1981" from "to plans which include employees within the meaning of section 401(c)(1) with respect to taxable years beginning after 12/31/81" [see below].

In 1982, P.L. 97-248, Sec. 237(c)(1), repealed Code Sec. 4972, effective for yrs. begin. after 12/31/83.

Prior to repeal, Code Sec. 4972 read as follows:

"SEC. 4972. TAX ON EXCESS CONTRIBUTIONS FOR SELF-EMPLOYED INDIVIDUALS.

"(a) Tax imposed.

"In the case of a plan which provides contributions or benefits for employees some or all of whom are employees within the meaning of section 401(c)(1), there is imposed, for each taxable year of the employer who maintains such plan, a tax in an amount equal to 6 percent of the amount of the excess contributions under the plan (determined as of the close of the taxable year). The tax imposed by this subsection shall be paid by the employer who maintains the plan. This section applies only to plans which include a trust described in section 401(a) or which are described in section 403(a).

"(b) Excess contributions.

"(1) In general. For purposes of this section, the term 'excess contributions' means the sum of the amounts (if any) determined under paragraphs (2), (3), and (4), reduced by the sum of the correcting distributions (as defined in paragraph (5)) made in all prior taxable years beginning after December 31, 1975. For purposes of this subsection the amount of any contribution which is allocable (determined under regulations prescribed by the Secretary) to the purchase of life, accident, health, or other insurance shall not be taken into account.

"(2) Contributions by owner-employees. The amount determined under this paragraph, in the case of a plan which provides contributions or benefits for employees some or all of whom are owner-employees (within the meaning of section 401(c)(3)), is the sum of—

"(A) the excess (if any) of—

"(i) the amount contributed under the plan by each owner-employee (as an employee) for the taxable year, over

"(ii) the amount permitted to be contributed by each owner-employee (as an employee) for such year, and

"(B) the amount determined under this paragraph for the preceding taxable year of the employer,

reduced by the excess (if any) of the amount described in subparagraph (A)(ii) over the amount described in subparagraph (A)(i). No contribution by an owner-employee which is a deductible employee contribution (as defined in section 72(o)(5)) shall be taken into account under this paragraph.

"(3) Defined benefit plans. The amount determined under this paragraph, in the case of a defined benefit plan, is the amount contributed under the plan by the employer during the taxable year or any prior taxable year beginning after December 31, 1975, if—

"(A) as of the close of the taxable year, the full funding limitation of the plan (determined under section 412(c)(7)) is zero, and

"(B) such amount has not been deductible for the taxable year or any prior taxable year.

"(4) Defined contribution plans. The amount determined under this paragraph, in the case of a plan other than a defined benefit plan, is the portion of the amounts contributed under the plan by the employer during the taxable year and each prior taxable year beginning after December 31, 1975, which has not been deductible for the taxable year or any prior taxable year.

"(5) Correcting distribution. For purposes of this subsection the term 'correcting distribution' means—

"(A) in the case of a contribution made by an owner-employee as an employee, regardless of the type of plan, the amount determined under paragraph (2) distributed to the owner-employee who contributed such amount,

"(B) in the case of a defined benefit plan, the amount determined under paragraph (3) which is distributed from the plan to the employer, and

"(C) in the case of a defined contribution plan, the amount determined under paragraph (4) which is distributed from the plan to the employer or to the employee to the account of whom the amount described was contributed.

"(6) Excess contributions returned before due date. For purposes of this subsection, any contribution which is distributed in a distribution to which section 72(m)(9) applies shall be treated as an amount not contributed

"(c) Amount permitted to be contributed by owner-employee.

"For purposes of subsection (b)(2), the amount permitted to be contributed under a plan by an owner-employee (as an employee) for any taxable year is the smallest of the following:

"(1) $2,500,

"(2) 10 percent of the earned income (as defined in section 401(c)(2)) for such taxable year derived by such owner-employee from the trade or business with respect to which the plan is established, or

"(3) the amount of the contribution which would be contributed by the owner-employee (as an employee) if such contribution were made at the rate of contributions permitted to be made by employees other than owner-employees.

In any case in which there are no employees other than owner-employees, the amount determined under the preceding sentence shall be zero.

"(d) Cross reference.

"For disallowance of deduction for taxes paid under this section, see section 275."

In 1981, P.L. 97-34, Sec. 312(e)(3), added para. (b)(6), effective [as amended by Sec. 103(d)(3) of P.L. 97-448, see above] for tax. yrs. begin. after 12/31/81.

In 1976, P.L. 94-455, Sec. 1906(b)(13)(A), substituted "Secretary" for "Secretary or his delegate" in para. (b)(1), effective 2/1/77.

In 1974, P.L. 93-406, Sec. 2001(f)(1), added Code Sec. 4972, effective for contributions made in tax. yrs. begin. after 12/31/75.

Sec. 4973. Tax on excess contributions to certain tax-favored accounts and annuities.

(a) Tax imposed.

In the case of—

(1) an individual retirement account (within the meaning of section 408(a)),

(2) an Archer MSA (within the meaning of section 220(d)),

(3) an individual retirement annuity (within the meaning of section 408(b)), a custodial account treated as an annuity contract under section 403(b)(7)(A) (relating to custodial accounts for regulated investment company stock),

(4) a Coverdell education savings account (as defined in section 530), or

(5) a health savings account (within the meaning of section 223(d)),

there is imposed for each taxable year a tax in an amount equal to 6 percent of the amount of the excess contributions to such individual's accounts or annuities (determined as of the close of the taxable year). The amount of such tax for any taxable year shall not exceed 6 percent of the value of the account or annuity (determined as of the close of the taxable year). In the case of an endowment contract described in section 408(b), the tax imposed by this section does not apply to any amount allocable to life, health, accident, or other insurance under such contract. The tax imposed by this subsection shall be paid by such individual.

(b) Excess contributions.

For purposes of this section, in the case of individual retirement accounts, or individual retirement annuities, the term "excess contributions" means the sum of—

(1) the excess (if any) of—

(A) the amount contributed for the taxable year to the accounts or for the annuities (other than a contribution to a Roth IRA or a rollover contribution described in section 402(c), 403(a)(4), 403(b)(8), 408(d)(3), or 457(e)(16)), over

(B) the amount allowable as a deduction under section 219 for such contributions, and

(2) the amount determined under this subsection for the preceding taxable year, reduced by the sum of—

(A) the distributions out of the account for the taxable year which were included in the gross income of the payee under section 408(d)(1),

(B) the distributions out of the account for the taxable year to which section 408(d)(5) applies, and

(C) the excess (if any) of the maximum amount allowable as a deduction under section 219 for the taxable year over the amount contributed (determined without regard to section 219(f)(6)) to the accounts or for the annuities (including the amount contributed to a Roth IRA) for the taxable year.

For purposes of this subsection, any contribution which is distributed from the individual retirement account or the individual retirement annuity in a distribution to which section 408(d)(4) applies shall be treated as an amount not contributed. For purposes of paragraphs (1)(B) and (2)(C), the amount allowable as a deduction under section 219 shall be computed without regard to section 219(g).

(c) Section 403(b) contracts.

For purposes of this section, in the case of a custodial account referred to in subsection (a)(3), the term "excess contributions" means the sum of—

(1) the excess (if any) of the amount contributed for the taxable year to such account (other than a rollover contribution described in section 403(b)(8) or 408(d)(3)(A)(iii)), over the lesser of the amount excludable from gross income under section 403(b) or the amount permitted to be contributed under the limitations contained in section 415 (or under whichever such section is applicable, if only one is applicable), and

(2) the amount determined under this subsection for the preceding taxable year, reduced by—

(A) the excess (if any) of the lesser of (i) the amount excludable from gross income under section 403(b) or (ii) the amount permitted to be contributed under the limitations contained in section 415 over the amount contributed to the account for the taxable year (or under whichever such section is applicable, if only one is applicable), and

(B) the sum of the distributions out of the account (for all prior taxable years) which are included in gross income under section 72(e).

(d) Excess contributions to Archer MSAs.

For purposes of this section, in the case of Archer MSAs (within the meaning of section 220(d)), the term "excess contributions" means the sum of—

(1) the aggregate amount contributed for the taxable year to the accounts (other than rollover contributions described in section 220(f)(5)) which is neither excludable from gross income under section 106(b) nor allowable as a deduction under section 220 for such year, and

(2) the amount determined under this subsection for the preceding taxable year, reduced by the sum of—

(A) the distributions out of the accounts which were included in gross income under section 220(f)(2), and

(B) the excess (if any) of—

(i) the maximum amount allowable as a deduction under section 220(b)(1) (determined without regard to section 106(b)) for the taxable year, over

(ii) the amount contributed to the accounts for the taxable year.

For purposes of this subsection, any contribution which is distributed out of the Archer MSA in a distribution to which section 220(f)(3) or section 138(c)(3) applies shall be treated as an amount not contributed.

(e) Excess contributions to Coverdell education savings accounts.

For purposes of this section—

(1) In general. In the case of Coverdell education savings accounts maintained for the benefit of any one beneficiary, the term "excess contributions" means the sum of—

> • *Caution:* Code Sec. 4973(e)(1)(A)-(B), following, was amended by P.L. 107-16, the Economic Growth and Tax Relief Reconciliation Act of 2001 (EGTRRA). These provisions generally sunset for tax years beginning after 12/31/2012. For specific sunset provisions see Sec. 901, P.L. 107-16 (as amended) reproduced in history notes for this Code Sec.

(A) the amount by which the amount contributed for the taxable year to such accounts exceeds $2,000 (or, if less, the sum of the maximum amounts permitted to be contributed under section 530(c) by the contributors to such accounts for such year); and

(B) the amount determined under this subsection for the preceding taxable year, reduced by the sum of—

(i) the distributions out of the accounts for the taxable year (other than rollover distributions); and

(ii) the excess (if any) of the maximum amount which may be contributed to the accounts for the taxable year over the amount contributed to the accounts for the taxable year.

(2) Special rules. For purposes of paragraph (1), the following contributions shall not be taken into account:

(A) Any contribution which is distributed out of the Coverdell education savings account in a distribution to which section 530(d)(4)(C) applies.

(B) Any rollover contribution.

(f) Excess contributions to Roth IRAs.

For purposes of this section, in the case of contributions to a Roth IRA (within the meaning of section 408A(b)), the term "excess contributions" means the sum of—

(1) the excess (if any) of—

Excise and miscellaneous taxes   Code Sec. 4973

(A) the amount contributed for the taxable year to Roth IRAs (other than a qualified rollover contribution described in section 408A(e)), over

(B) the amount allowable as a contribution under sections 408A(c)(2) and (c)(3), and

(2) the amount determined under this subsection for the preceding taxable year, reduced by the sum of—

(A) the distributions out of the accounts for the taxable year, and

(B) the excess (if any) of the maximum amount allowable as a contribution under sections 408A(c)(2) and (c)(3) for the taxable year over the amount contributed by the individual to all individual retirement plans for the taxable year.

For purposes of this subsection, any contribution which is distributed from a Roth IRA in a distribution described in section 408(d)(4) shall be treated as an amount not contributed.

(g) Excess contributions to health savings accounts.

For purposes of this section, in the case of health savings accounts (within the meaning of section 223(d)), the term "excess contributions" means the sum of—

(1) the aggregate amount contributed for the taxable year to the accounts (other than a rollover contribution described in section 220(f)(5) or 223(f)(5)) which is neither excludable from gross income under section 106(d) nor allowable as a deduction under section 223 for such year, and

(2) the amount determined under this subsection for the preceding taxable year, reduced by the sum of—

(A) the distributions out of the accounts which were included in gross income under section 223(f)(2), and

(B) the excess (if any) of—

(i) the maximum amount allowable as a deduction under section 223(b) (determined without regard to section 106(d)) for the taxable year, over

(ii) the amount contributed to the accounts for the taxable year.

For purposes of this subsection, any contribution which is distributed out of the health savings account in a distribution to which section 223(f)(3) applies shall be treated as an amount not contributed.

In 2010, P.L. 111-312, Sec. 101(a)(1), substituted "December 31, 2012" for "December 31, 2010" both places it appeared in Sec. 901 of P.L. 107-16, [see below] effective as if included in the enactment of P.L. 107-16, EGTRRA, 6/7/2001.

In 2006, P.L. 109-280, Sec. 811, of this Act [relating to Sec. 901 of P.L. 107-16, see below], provides:

"SEC. 811. PENSIONS AND INDIVIDUAL RETIREMENT ARRANGEMENT PROVISIONS OF ECONOMIC GROWTH AND TAX RELIEF RECONCILIATION ACT OF 2001 MADE PERMANENT.

"Title IX of the Economic Growth and Tax Relief Reconciliation Act of 2001 shall not apply to the provisions of, and amendments made by, subtitles A through F of title VI of such Act (relating to pension and individual retirement arrangement provisions)."

—P.L. 109-280, Sec. 1304(a), of this Act [relating to Sec. 901 of P.L. 107-16], provides:

"(a) Permanent Extension of Modifications. Section 901 of the Economic Growth and Tax Relief Reconciliation Act of 2001 (relating to sunset provisions) shall not apply to section 402 of such Act (relating to modifications to qualified tuition programs)."

In 2004, P.L. 108-311, Sec. 408(a)(22), substituted "subsection (a)(3)" for "subsection (a)(2)" in subsec. (c), enacted 10/4/2004.

In 2003, P.L. 108-173, Sec. 1201(e)(1), deleted "or" at the end of para. (a)(3), added "or" at the end of para. (a)(4), and added para. (a)(5) . . . Sec. 1201(e)(2), added subsec. (g), effective for tax. yrs. begin. after 12/31/2003.

In 2002, P.L. 107-358, Sec. 2, added subsec. (c) in Sec. 901 of P.L. 107-16 [see below], effective 12/17/2002.

In 2001, P.L. 107-22, Sec. 1(b)(1)(C), substituted "a Coverdell education savings" for "an education individual retirement" in subsec. (a) . . . Sec. 1(b)(2)(B), substituted "Coverdell education savings" for "education individual retirement" in subsec. (e) . . . Sec. 1(b)(4), substituted "Coverdell education savings" for "education individual retirement" in the heading of subsec. (e), effective 7/26/2001.

—P.L. 107-16, Sec. 401(a)(2), substituted "$2,000" for "$500" in subpara. (e)(1)(A) . . . Sec. 401(g)(2)(D), added "and" at the end of subpara. (e)(1)(A), deleted subpara. (e)(1)(B) and redesignated subpara. (e)(1)(C) as (e)(1)(B), effective for tax. yrs. begin. after 12/31/2001.

Prior to deletion, subpara. (e)(1)(B) read as follows:

"(B) if any amount is contributed (other than a contribution described in section 530(b)(2)(B)) during such year to a qualified State tuition program for the benefit of such beneficiary, any amount contributed to such accounts for such taxable year; and"

—P.L. 107-16, Sec. 402(a)(4)(A), substituted "qualified tuition" for "qualified State tuition" in subpara. (e)(1)(B) [as deleted by Sec. 401(g)(2)(D) of this Act, see above], effective for tax. yrs. begin. after 12/31/2001.

—P.L. 107-16, Sec. 641(e)(11), substituted "408(d)(3), or 457(e)(16)" for "or 408(d)(3)" in subpara. (b)(1)(A), effective for distributions after 12/31/2001. Sec. 641(f)(2)-(3) of this Act, provides:

"(2) Reasonable notice. No penalty shall be imposed on a plan for the failure to provide the information required by the amendment made by subsection (c) with respect to any distribution made before the date that is 90 days after the date on which the Secretary of the Treasury issues a safe harbor rollover notice after the date of the enactment of this Act, if the administrator of such plan makes a reasonable attempt to comply with such requirement.

"(3) Special rule. Notwithstanding any other provision of law, subsections (h)(3) and (h)(5) of section 1122 of the Tax Reform Act of 1986 shall not apply to any distribution from an eligible retirement plan (as defined in clause (iii) or (iv) of section 402(c)(8)(B) of the Internal Revenue Code of 1986) on behalf of an individual if there was a rollover to such plan on behalf of such individual which is permitted solely by reason of any amendment made by this section."

—P.L. 107-16, Sec. 901, of this Act [as amended by Sec. 2 of P.L. 107-358, and Sec. 101(a)(1) of P.L. 111-312, see above], reads as follows:

"SEC. 901. SUNSET OF PROVISIONS OF ACT.

"(a) In general. All provisions of, and amendments made by, this Act shall not apply—

"(1) to taxable, plan, or limitation years beginning after December 31, 2012, or

"(2) in the case of title V, to estates of decedents dying, gifts made, or generation skipping transfers, after December 31, 2012.

"(b) Application of certain laws. The Internal Revenue Code of 1986 and the Employee Retirement Income Security Act of 1974 shall be applied and administered to years, estates, gifts, and transfers described in subsection (a) as if the provisions and amendments described in subsection (a) had never been enacted.

"(c) Exception. Subsection (a) shall not apply to section 803 (relating to no federal income tax on restitution received by victims of the Nazi regime or their heirs or estates)."

In 2000, P.L. 106-554, Sec. 1(a)(7), [which enacted into law Sec. 202(a)(6) of P.L. 106-554] substituted "Archer MSA" for "medical savings account" in para. (a)(2) and subsec. (d) . . . Sec. 1(a)(7), [which enacted into law Sec. 202(b)(2)(C) of P.L. 106-554] substituted "Archer MSAs" for "medical savings accounts" in subsec. (d) . . . Sec. 1(a)(7), [which enacted into law Sec. 202(b)(6) of P.L. 106-554] substituted "Archer MSAs" for "medical savings accounts" in the heading of subsec. (d) . . . Sec. 1(a)(7), [which enacted into law Sec. 202(b)(10) of P.L. 106-554] substituted "an Archer" for "a Archer" in para. (a)(2), effective 12/21/2000.

In 1998, P.L. 105-206, Sec. 6004(d)(10)(A), amended para. (e)(1) . . . Sec. 6004(d)(10)(B), deleted subpara. (e)(2)(B) and redesignated subpara. (e)(2)(C) as (B), effective for tax. yrs. begin. after 12/31/97.

Prior to amendment, para. (e)(1) read as follows: In general. In the case of education individual retirement accounts maintained for the benefit of any 1 beneficiary, the term "excess contributions" means—

"(A) the amount by which the amount contributed for the taxable year to such accounts exceeds $500, and

"(B) any amount contributed to such accounts for any taxable year if any amount is contributed during such year to a qualified State tuition program for the benefit of such beneficiary."

Prior to deletion, subpara. (e)(2)(B) read as follows:

"(B) Any contribution described in section 530(b)(2)(B) to a qualified State tuition program."

—P.L. 105-206, Sec. 6005(b)(8)(A)(i), substituted "Roth IRAs" for "such accounts" in subpara. (f)(1)(A) . . . Sec. 6005(b)(8)(A)(ii), substituted "by the individual to all individual retirement plans" for "to the accounts" in subpara. (f)(2)(B) . . . Sec. 6005(b)(8)(B)(i), added "a contribution to a Roth IRA or" after "other than" in subpara. (b)(1)(A) . . . Sec. 6005(b)(8)(B)(ii), added "(including the amount contributed to a Roth IRA)" after "annuities" in subpara. (b)(2)(C), effective for tax. yrs. begin. after 12/31/98.

—P.L. 105-206, Sec. 6023(18)(A), amended the heading of Code Sec. 4973, effective 7/22/98.

Prior to amendment, the heading of Code Sec. 4973 read as follows:

"Sec. 4973. Tax on excess contributions to individual retirement accounts, medical savings accounts, certain section 403(b) contracts, and certain individual retirement annuities."

In 1997, P.L. 105-34, Sec. 213(d)(1), deleted "or" at the end of para. (a)(2), added "or" to the end of para. (a)(3) and added para. (a)(4) . . . Sec. 213(d)(2), added subsec. (e), effective for tax. yrs. begin. after 12/31/97.

—P.L. 105-34, Sec. 302(b), added subsec. (f), effective for tax. yrs. begin. after 12/31/97.

—P.L. 105-34, Sec. 4006(b)(1), added "or section 138(c)(3)" after "section 220(f)(3)" in subsec. (d), effective for tax. yrs. begin. after 12/31/98.

In 1996, P.L. 104-191, Sec. 301(e)(1), added "medical savings accounts" after "accounts" in the heading of Code Sec. 4973 . . . Sec. 301(e)(2), deleted "or" at

Code Sec. 4973 — Excise and miscellaneous taxes

the end of para. (a)(1)... Sec. 301(e)(3), redesignated para. (a)(2) as para. (a)(3) and added new para. (a)(2)... Sec. 301(e)(4), added subsec. (d), effective for tax. yrs. begin. after 12/31/96.

—P.L. 104-188, Sec. 1704(t)(70), substituted "section 402(c)" for "sections 402(c)" in subpara. (b)(1)(A)... Sec. 1704(t)(72), substituted "section" for "sections" in Sec. 521(b)(41) of P.L. 102-318, see below, effective date of enactment.

In 1992, P.L. 102-318, Sec. 521(b)(41), [as amended by Sec. 1704(t)(72) of P.L. 104-188, see above] substituted "section [sic sections] 402(c)" for "section 402(a)(5), 402(a)(7)" in subpara. (b)(1)(A), effective for distributions after 12/31/92. For special rule, see Sec. 521(e)(2) of this Act which reads as follows:

"(2) Special rule for partial distributions. For purposes of section 402(a)(5)(D)(i)(II) of the Internal Revenue Code of 1986 (as in effect before the amendments made by this section), a distribution before January 1, 1993, which is made before or at the same time as a series of periodic payments shall not be treated as one of such series if it is not substantially equal in amount to other payments in such series."

In 1988, P.L. 100-647, Sec. 1011(b)(3), substituted "shall be computed without regard to section 219(g)" for "after application of section 408(o)(2)(B)(ii) shall be increased by the nondeductible limit under section 408(o)(2)(B)" in subsec. (b), effective for tax. yrs begin. after 12/31/86.

In 1986, P.L. 99-514, Sec. 1102(b)(1), added the last sentence of subsec. (b), effective for tax. yrs. begin. after 12/31/86.

—P.L. 99-514, Sec. 1848(f)(1), substituted "or individual retirement annuities" for ", individual retirement annuities, or bonds", in the material preceding para. (b)(1)... Sec. 1848(f)(2), amended subpara. (b)(1)(A)... Sec. 1848(f)(3), deleted "or bonds" in subpara. (b)(2)(C), effective for obligations issued after 12/31/83.

Prior to amendment, subpara. (b)(1)(A) read as follows:

"(A) the amount contributed for the taxable year to the accounts or for the annuities or bonds (other than a rollover contribution described in section 402(a)(5), 402(a)(7), 403(a)(4), 403(b)(8), 405(d)(3), 408(d)(3), over"

In 1984, P.L. 98-369, Sec. 491(d)(41)(A), deleted para. (a)(3)... Sec. 491(d)(41)(B), deleted "or" at the end of para. (a)(2)... Sec. 491(d)(41)(C), added "or" at the end of para. (a)(1)... Sec. 491(d)(41)(D), substituted "or annuities" for ", annuities, or bonds" in subsec. (a)... Sec. 491(d)(41)(E), substituted "or annuity" for "annuity, or bond" in subsec. (a)... Sec. 491(d)(42), substituted "408(d)(3)" for "408(d)(3)), and 409(b)(3)(C)" [sic] "408(d)(3), or 409(b)(3)(C)" in subpara. (b)(1)(A)... Sec. 491(d)(43), substituted "or the individual retirement annuity" for ", individual retirement annuity, or bond" in the last sentence of subsec. (b)... Sec. 491(d)(44), substituted "or 408(d)(3)(A)(iii)" for ", 408(d)(3)(A)(iii), or 409(b)(3)(C)" in para. (c)(1)... Sec. 491(d)(55), substituted "and certain individual retirement annuities" for "certain individual retirement annuities, and certain retirement bonds" in the heading of Code Sec. 4973, effective for obligations issued after 12/31/83.

Prior to deletion, para. (a)(3) read as follows:

"(3) a retirement bond (within the meaning of section 409) established for the benefit of any individual,"

In 1981, P.L. 97-34, Sec. 311(h)(7), substituted "section 219" for "section 219 or 220" each place it appeared in subsec. (b)... Sec. 311(h)(9), substituted "The tax imposed by this subsection shall be paid by such individual." for "The tax imposed by this subsection shall be paid by the individual to whom a deduction is allowed for the taxable year under section 219 (determined without regard to subsection (b)(1) thereof) or section 220 (determined without regard to subsection (b)(1) thereof), whichever is appropriate." in subsec. (a)... Sec. 311(h)(10), substituted "section 219(f)(6)" for "sections 219(c)(5) and 220(c)(6)", in subpara. (b)(2)(C), for tax. yrs. begin. after 12/31/81. For transitional rule see Sec. 311(i)(2) of this Act reproduced in note following Code Sec. 219.

—P.L. 97-34, Sec. 313(b)(2), added "405(d)(3)" after "403(b)(8)" in subpara. (b)(1)(A), effective for redemptions after 8/13/81, in tax. yrs. end. after 8/13/81.

In 1980, P.L. 96-222, Sec. 101(a)(13)(A), amended the effective date for changes made by Sec. 156(c)(3) of P.L. 95-600 for distributions or transfers made after '77, in tax. yrs. begin. after 12/31/77 [see below].

—P.L. 96-222, Sec. 101(a)(13)(C), substituted "409(b)(3)(C)" for "409(b)(3)(C)" in para. (c)(1), effective for distributions or transfers made after '77, in tax. yrs. begin. after 12/31/77.

—P.L. 96-222, Sec. 101(a)(14)(B), added "402(a)(7)" after "section 402(a)(5)," in subpara. (b)(1)(A), effective for distributions or transfers made after '77, in tax. yrs. begin. after 12/31/77.

In 1978, P.L. 95-600, Sec. 156(c)(3), added "403(b)(8)," after "403(a)(4)," in subpara. (b)(1)(A)... Sec. 156(c)(5), added "(other than a rollover contribution described in section 403(b)(8), 408(d)(3)(A)(iii), or 409(b)(3)(C))" following "account" in para. (c)(1), for distributions or transfers made after '77, in tax. yrs. begin. after 12/31/77.

—P.L. 95-600, Sec. 157(b)(3), amended para. (b)(2), effective for determination of deductions for tax. yrs. begin. after '75. Sec. 157(b)(4)(B) of the Act provides:

"(B) Transitional rule—If, but for this subparagraph, an amount would be allowable as a deduction by reason of section 219(c)(5) or 220(c)(6) of the Internal Revenue Code of 1954 for a taxable year beginning before January 1, 1978, such amount shall be allowable only for the taxpayer's first taxable year beginning in 1978."

Prior to amendment, para. (b)(2) read as follows:

"(2) the amount determined under this subsection for the preceding taxable year, reduced by the excess (if any) of the maximum amount allowable as a deduction under section 219 or 220 for the taxable year over the amount contributed to the accounts or for the annuities or bonds for the taxable year and reduced by the sum of the distributions out of the account (for the taxable year and all prior taxable years) which were included in the gross income of the payee under section 408(d)(1)."

—P.L. 95-600, Sec. 157(j)(1), amended the last sentence of subsec. (b), for contributions made for tax. yrs. begin. after '77.

Prior to amendment, the last sentence of subsec. (b) read as follows:

"For purposes of this subsection, any contribution which is distributed from the individual retirement account, individual retirement annuity, or bond in a distribution to which section 408(d)(4) applies shall be treated as an amount not contributed if such distribution consists of an excess contribution solely because of ineligibility and section 219(b)(2) or section 220(b)(3) or by reason of the application of section 219(b)(1) (without regard to the $1,500 limitation) or section 220(b)(1) (without regard to the $1,750 limitation) and only if such distribution does not exceed the excess of $1,500 or $1,750 if applicable, over the amount described in paragraph (1)(B)."

—P.L. 95-600, Sec. 701(aa)(1), substituted "solely because of ineligibility under section 219(b)(2) or section 220(b)(3)" for "solely because of employer contributions to a plan or contract described in section 219(b)(2)" in the last sentence of subsec. (b) [which was amended by Sec. 157(j)(1) of this Act, see above] for tax. yrs. begin. after '76.

—P.L. 95-600, Sec. 703(j)(13), changed the effective date of amendments made by Sec. 1904(a)(22)(A) of P.L. 94-455 to 10/4/76. (See below).

In 1976, P.L. 94-455, Sec. 1501(b)(8), substituted "the individual to whom a deduction is allowed for the taxable year under section 219 (determined without regard to subsection (b)(1) thereof) or section 220 (determined without regard to subsection (b)(1) thereof), whichever is appropriate" for "such individual" in the last sentence of subsec. (a)... added "or 220" after "219" in subpara. (b)(1)(B)... amended para. (b)(2), effective for tax. yrs. begin. after '76.

Prior to amendment, para. (b)(2) read as follows:

"(2) the amount determined under this subsection for the preceding taxable year, reduced by the excess (if any) of the maximum amount allowable as a deduction under section 219 for the taxable year over the amount contributed to the accounts or for the annuities or bonds for the taxable year and reduced by the sum of the distributions out of the account (for all prior taxable years) which were included in the gross income of the payee under section 408(d)(1). For purposes of this paragraph, any contribution which is distributed out of the individual retirement account, individual retirement annuity, or bond in a distribution to which section 408(d)(4) applies shall be treated as an amount not contributed."

—P.L. 94-455, Sec. 1904(a)(22)(A), amended para. (a)(3), effective 2/1/77, to read as follows:

"(3) a retirement bond (within the meaning of section 409), established for the benefit of any individual, there is imposed for each taxable year a tax in an amount equal to 6 percent of the amount of the excess contributions to such individual's accounts, annuities, or bonds (determined as of the close of the taxable year). The amount of such tax for any taxable year shall not exceed 6 percent of the value of the account, annuity, or bond (determined as of the close of the taxable year). In the case of an endowment contract described in section 408(b), the tax imposed by this section does not apply to any amount allocable to life, health, accident, or other insurance under such contract. The tax imposed by this subsection shall be paid by such individual."

—P.L. 94-455, Sec. 1904(a)(22)(B), substituted "subsection (a)(2)" for "subsection (a)(3)" in subsec. (c), effective 2/1/77.

In 1974, P.L. 93-406, Sec. 2002(d), added Code Sec. 4973, effective 1/1/75.

Sec. 4974. Excise tax on certain accumulations in qualified retirement plans.

(a) General rule.

If the amount distributed during the taxable year of the payee under any qualified retirement plan or any eligible deferred compensation plan (as defined in section 457(b)) is less than the minimum required distribution for such taxable year, there is hereby imposed a tax equal to 50 percent of the amount by which such minimum required distribution exceeds the actual amount distributed during the taxable year. The tax imposed by this section shall be paid by the payee.

(b) Minimum required distribution.

For purposes of this section, the term "minimum required distribution" means the minimum amount required to be distributed during a taxable year under section 401(a)(9), 403(b)(10), 408(a)(6), 408(b)(3), or 457(d)(2), as the case may be, as determined under regulations prescribed by the Secretary.

(c) Qualified retirement plan.

For purposes of this section, the term "qualified retirement plan" means—

(1) a plan described in section 401(a) which includes a trust exempt from tax under section 501(a),

(2) an annuity plan described in section 403(a),

(3) an annuity contract described in section 403(b),

(4) an individual retirement account described in section 408(a), or

Excise and miscellaneous taxes Code Sec. 4975(c)(2)(C)

(5) an individual retirement annuity described in section 408(b).

Such term includes any plan, contract, account, or annuity which, at any time, has been determined by the Secretary to be such a plan, contract, account, or annuity.

(d) Waiver of tax in certain cases.

If the taxpayer establishes to the satisfaction of the Secretary that—

(1) the shortfall described in subsection (a) in the amount distributed during any taxable year was due to reasonable error, and

(2) reasonable steps are being taken to remedy the shortfall,

the Secretary may waive the tax imposed by subsection (a) for the taxable year.

In 1988, P.L. 100-647, Sec. 1011A(a)(3), added Sec. 1121(d)(5) of P.L. 99-514, part of the effective date for changes made by Sec. 1121(b) of P.L. 99-514 ... Sec. 1011A(a)(4), substituted "years" for "plan years" in Sec. 1121(d)(2) of P.L. 99-514, part of the effective date for changes made by Sec. 1121(b) of P.L. 514, see below.

In 1986, P.L. 99-514, Sec. 1121(a)(1), amended Code Sec. 4974, effective for yrs. begin. after 12/31/88, except as provided in Sec. 1121(d)(3) [as amended by Sec. 1011A(a)(4) of 100-647], 1121(d)(4) and 1121(d)(5) [as added by Sec. 1011A(a)(3) of P.L. 100-647 of this Act which reads as follows:

"(3) Collective bargaining agreements.—In the case of a plan maintained pursuant to 1 or more collective bargaining agreements between employee representatives and 1 or more employers ratified before March 1, 1986, the amendments made by this section shall not apply to distributions to individuals covered by such agreements in years beginning before the earlier of—

"(A) the later of—

"(i) the date on which the last of such collective bargaining agreements terminates (determined without regard to any extension thereof after February 28, 1986), or

"(ii) January 1, 1989, or

"(B) January 1, 1991.

"(4) Transition rules.—

"(A) The amendments made by subsections (a) and (b) shall not apply with respect to any benefits with respect to which a designation is in effect under section 242(b)(2) of the Tax Equity and Fiscal Responsibility Act of 1982.

"(B)(i) Except as provided in clause (ii), the amendment made by subsection (b) shall not apply in the case of any individual who has attained age 70½ before January 1, 1988.

"(ii) Clause (i) shall not apply to any individual who is a 5-percent owner (as defined in section 416(i) of the Internal Revenue Code of 1986), at any time during—

"(I) the plan year ending with or within the calendar year in which such owner attains age 66½, and

"(II) any subsequent plan year.

"(5) Plans may incorporate section 401(a)(9) requirements by reference.—Notwithstanding any other provision of law, except as provided in regulations prescribed by the Secretary of the Treasury or his delegate, a plan may incorporate by reference the requirements of section 401(a)(9) of the Internal Revenue Code of 1986."

Prior to amendment, Code Sec. 4974 read as follows:

"SEC. 4974. EXCISE TAX ON CERTAIN ACCUMULATIONS IN INDIVIDUAL RETIREMENT ACCOUNTS OR ANNUITIES.

"(a) Imposition of tax.

"If, in the case of an individual retirement account or individual retirement annuity, the amount distributed during the taxable year of the payee is less than the minimum amount required to be distributed under section 408(a)(6) or 408(b)(3) during such year, there is imposed a tax equal to 50 percent of the amount by which the minimum amount required to be distributed during such year exceeds the amount actually distributed during the year. The tax imposed by this section shall be paid by such payee.

"(b) Regulations.

"For purposes of this section, the minimum amount required to be distributed during a taxable year under section 408(a)(6) or 408(b)(3) shall be determined under regulations prescribed by the Secretary.

"(c) Waiver of tax in certain cases.

"If the taxpayer establishes to the satisfaction of the Secretary that—

"(1) the shortfall described in subsection (a) in the amount distributed during any taxable year was due to reasonable error, and

"(2) reasonable steps are being taken to remedy the shortfall, the Secretary may waiver the tax imposed by subsection (a) for the taxable year."

—P.L. 99-514, Sec. 1852(a)(7)(B), substituted "section 408(a)(6) or 408(b)(3)" for "section 408(a)(6) or (7) or, 408(b)(3) or (4)" in subsec. (a) ... Sec. 1852(a)(7)(C), substituted "section 408(a)(6) or 408(b)(3)" for "section 408(a)(6) or (7) or 408(b)(3) or (4)" in subsec. (b), effective for tax. yrs. begin. after 12/31/84. For transitional rules see Sec. 521(e)(3)(5) of P.L. 98-369 reproduced in note following Code Sec. 408.

In 1978, P.L. 95-600, Sec. 157(i)(1), added subsec. (c), effective for tax. yrs. begin. after 12/31/75.

In 1976, P.L. 94-455, Sec. 1906(b)(13)(A), substituted "Secretary" for "Secretary or his delegate" in subsec. (b), effective 2/1/77.

In 1974, P.L. 93-406, Sec. 2002(e), added Code Sec. 4974, effective 1/1/75.

Sec. 4975. Tax on prohibited transactions.

(a) Initial taxes on disqualified person.

There is hereby imposed a tax on each prohibited transaction. The rate of tax shall be equal to 15 percent of the amount involved with respect to the prohibited transaction for each year (or part thereof) in the taxable period. The tax imposed by this subsection shall be paid by any disqualified person who participates in the prohibited transaction (other than a fiduciary acting only as such).

(b) Additional taxes on disqualified person.

In any case in which an initial tax is imposed by subsection (a) on a prohibited transaction and the transaction is not corrected within the taxable period, there is hereby imposed a tax equal to 100 percent of the amount involved. The tax imposed by this subsection shall be paid by any disqualified person who participated in the prohibited transaction (other than a fiduciary acting only as such).

(c) Prohibited transaction.

(1) **General rule.** For purposes of this section, the term "prohibited transaction" means any direct or indirect—

(A) sale or exchange, or leasing, of any property between a plan and a disqualified person;

(B) lending of money or other extension of credit between a plan and a disqualified person;

(C) furnishing of goods, services, or facilities between a plan and a disqualified person;

(D) transfer to, or use by or for the benefit of, a disqualified person of the income or assets of a plan;

(E) act by a disqualified person who is a fiduciary whereby he deals with the income or assets of a plan in his own interest or for his own account; or

(F) receipt of any consideration for his own personal account by any disqualified person who is a fiduciary from any party dealing with the plan in connection with a transaction involving the income or assets of the plan.

(2) **Special exemption.** The Secretary shall establish an exemption procedure for purposes of this subsection. Pursuant to such procedure, he may grant a conditional or unconditional exemption of any disqualified person or transaction, orders of disqualified persons or transactions, from all or part of the restrictions imposed by paragraph (1) of this subsection. Action under this subparagraph may be taken only after consultation and coordination with the Secretary of Labor. The Secretary may not grant an exemption under this paragraph unless he finds that such exemption is—

(A) administratively feasible,

(B) in the interests of the plan and of its participants and beneficiaries, and

(C) protective of the rights of participants and beneficiaries of the plan.

Before granting an exemption under this paragraph, the Secretary shall require adequate notice to be given to interested persons and shall publish notice in the Federal Register of the pendency of such exemption and shall afford interested persons an opportunity to present views. No exemption may be granted under this paragraph with respect to a transaction described in subparagraph (E) or (F) of paragraph (1) unless the Secretary affords an opportunity for a hearing and makes a determination on the record with respect to the findings required under subparagraphs (A), (B), and (C) of this paragraph, except that in lieu of such hearing the Secretary may accept any record made by the Secretary of Labor with respect to an application for exemption under section 408(a) of title I of the Employee Retirement Income Security Act of 1974.

(3) Special rule for individual retirement accounts. An individual for whose benefit an individual retirement account is established and his beneficiaries shall be exempt from the tax imposed by this section with respect to any transaction concerning such account (which would otherwise be taxable under this section) if, with respect to such transaction, the account ceases to be an individual retirement account by reason of the application of section 408(e)(2)(A) or if section 408(e)(4) applies to such account.

(4) Special rule for Archer MSAs. An individual for whose benefit an Archer MSA (within the meaning of section 220(d)) is established shall be exempt from the tax imposed by this section with respect to any transaction concerning such account (which would otherwise be taxable under this section) if section 220(e)(2) applies to such transaction.

(5) Special rule for Coverdell education savings accounts. An individual for whose benefit a Coverdell education savings account is established and any contributor to such account shall be exempt from the tax imposed by this section with respect to any transaction concerning such account (which would otherwise be taxable under this section) if section 530(d) applies with respect to such transaction.

(6) Special rule for health savings accounts. An individual for whose benefit a health savings account (within the meaning of section 223(d)) is established shall be exempt from the tax imposed by this section with respect to any transaction concerning such account (which would otherwise be taxable under this section) if, with respect to such transaction, the account ceases to be a health savings account by reason of the application of section 223(e)(2) to such account.

(d) Exemptions.

Except as provided in subsection (f)(6), the prohibitions provided in subsection (c) shall not apply to—

(1) any loan made by the plan to a disqualified person who is a participant or beneficiary of the plan if such loan—

(A) is available to all such participants or beneficiaries on a reasonably equivalent basis,

(B) is not made available to highly compensated employees (within the meaning of section 414(q)) in an amount greater than the amount made available to other employees,

(C) is made in accordance with specific provisions regarding such loans set forth in the plan,

(D) bears a reasonable rate of interest, and

(E) is adequately secured;

(2) any contract, or reasonable arrangement, made with a disqualified person for office space, or legal, accounting, or other services necessary for the establishment or operation of the plan, if no more than reasonable compensation is paid therefor;

(3) any loan to a leveraged employee stock ownership plan (as defined in subsection (e)(7)), if—

(A) such loan is primarily for the benefit of participants and beneficiaries of the plan, and

(B) such loan is at a reasonable rate of interest, and any collateral which is given to a disqualified person by the plan consists only of qualifying employer securities (as defined in subsection (e)(8));

(4) the investment of all or part of a plan's assets in deposits which bear a reasonable interest rate in a bank or similar financial institution supervised by the United States or a State, if such bank or other institution is a fiduciary of such plan and if—

(A) the plan covers only employees of such bank or other institution and employees of affiliates of such bank or other institution, or

(B) such investment is expressly authorized by a provision of the plan or by a fiduciary (other than such bank or institution or affiliates thereof) who is expressly empowered by the plan to so instruct the trustee with respect to such investment;

(5) any contract for life insurance, health insurance, or annuities with one or more insurers which are qualified to do business in a State if the plan pays no more than adequate consideration, and if each such insurer or insurers is—

(A) the employer maintaining the plan, or

(B) a disqualified person which is wholly owned (directly or indirectly) by the employer establishing the plan, or by any person which is a disqualified person with respect to the plan, but only if the total premiums and annuity considerations written by such insurers for life insurance, health insurance, or annuities for all plans (and their employers) with respect to which such insurers are disqualified persons (not including premiums or annuity considerations written by the employer maintaining the plan) do not exceed 5 percent of the total premiums and annuity considerations written for all lines of insurance in that year by such insurers (not including premiums or annuity considerations written by the employer maintaining the plan);

(6) the provision of any ancillary service by a bank or similar financial institution supervised by the United States or a State, if such service is provided at not more than reasonable compensation, if such bank or other institution is a fiduciary of such plan, and if—

(A) such bank or similar financial institution has adopted adequate internal safeguards which assure that the provision of such ancillary service is consistent with sound banking and financial practice, as determined by Federal or State supervisory authority, and

(B) the extent to which such ancillary service is provided is subject to specific guidelines issued by such bank or similar financial institution (as determined by the Secretary after consultation with Federal and State supervisory authority), and under such guidelines the bank or similar financial institution does not provide such ancillary service—

(i) in an excessive or unreasonable manner, and

(ii) in a manner that would be inconsistent with the best interests of participants and beneficiaries of employee benefit plans;

(7) the exercise of a privilege to convert securities, to the extent provided in regulations of the Secretary, but only if the plan receives no less than adequate consideration pursuant to such conversion;

(8) any transaction between a plan and a common or collective trust fund or pooled investment fund maintained by a disqualified person which is a bank or trust company supervised by a State or Federal agency or between a plan and a pooled investment fund of an insurance company qualified to do business in a State if—

(A) the transaction is a sale or purchase of an interest in the fund,
(B) the bank, trust company, or insurance company receives not more than reasonable compensation, and
(C) such transaction is expressly permitted by the instrument under which the plan is maintained, or by a fiduciary (other than the bank, trust company, or insurance company, or an affiliate thereof) who has authority to manage and control the assets of the plan;

(9) receipt by a disqualified person of any benefit to which he may be entitled as a participant or beneficiary in the plan, so long as the benefit is computed and paid on a basis which is consistent with the terms of the plan as applied to all other participants and beneficiaries;

(10) receipt by a disqualified person of any reasonable compensation for services rendered, or for the reimbursement of expenses properly and actually incurred, in the performance of his duties with the plan, but no person so serving who already receives full-time pay from an employer or an association of employers, whose employees are participants in the plan or from an employee organization whose members are participants in such plan shall receive compensation from such fund, except for reimbursement of expenses properly and actually incurred;

(11) service by a disqualified person as a fiduciary in addition to being an officer, employee, agent, or other representative of a disqualified person;

(12) the making by a fiduciary of a distribution of the assets of the trust in accordance with the terms of the plan if such assets are distributed in the same manner as provided under section 4044 of title IV of the Employee Retirement Income Security Act of 1974 (relating to allocation of assets);

(13) any transaction which is exempt from section 406 of such Act by reason of section 408(e) of such Act (or which would be so exempt if such section 406 applied to such transaction) or which is exempt from section 406 of such Act by reason of section 408(b)(12) of such Act;

(14) any transaction required or permitted under part 1 of subtitle E of title IV or section 4223 of the Employee Retirement Income Security Act of 1974, but this paragraph shall not apply with respect to the application of subsection (c)(1)(E) or (F);

(15) a merger of multiemployer plans, or the transfer of assets or liabilities between multiemployer plans, determined by the Pension Benefit Guaranty Corporation to meet the requirements of section 4231 of such Act, but this paragraph shall not apply with respect to the application of subsection (c)(1)(E) or (F);

(16) a sale of stock held by a trust which constitutes an individual retirement account under section 408(a) to the individual for whose benefit such account is established if—
(A) such stock is in a bank (as defined in section 581) or a depository institution holding company (as defined in section 3(w)(1) of the Federal Deposit Insurance Act (12 U.S.C. 1813(w)(1)),
(B) such stock is held by such trust as of the date of the enactment of this paragraph,
(C) such sale is pursuant to an election under section 1362(a) by such bank or company,
(D) such sale is for fair market value at the time of sale (as established by an independent appraiser) and the terms of the sale are otherwise at least as favorable to such trust as the terms that would apply on a sale to an unrelated party,
(E) such trust does not pay any commissions, costs, or other expenses in connection with the sale, and
(F) the stock is sold in a single transaction for cash not later than 120 days after the S corporation election is made;

(17) Any transaction in connection with the provision of investment advice described in subsection (e)(3)(B) to a participant or beneficiary in a plan that permits such participant or beneficiary to direct the investment of plan assets in an individual account, if—
(A) the transaction is—
(i) the provision of the investment advice to the participant or beneficiary of the plan with respect to a security or other property available as an investment under the plan,
(ii) the acquisition, holding, or sale of a security or other property available as an investment under the plan pursuant to the investment advice, or
(iii) the direct or indirect receipt of fees or other compensation by the fiduciary adviser or an affiliate thereof (or any employee, agent, or registered representative of the fiduciary adviser or affiliate) in connection with the provision of the advice or in connection with an acquisition, holding, or sale of a security or other property available as an investment under the plan pursuant to the investment advice; and
(B) the requirements of subsection (f)(8) are met,

(18) any transaction involving the purchase or sale of securities, or other property (as determined by the Secretary of Labor), between a plan and disqualified person (other than a fiduciary described in subsection (e)(3)) with respect to a plan if—
(A) the transaction involves a block trade,
(B) at the time of the transaction, the interest of the plan (together with the interests of any other plans maintained by the same plan sponsor), does not exceed 10 percent of the aggregate size of the block trade,
(C) the terms of the transaction, including the price, are at least as favorable to the plan as an arm's length transaction, and
(D) the compensation associated with the purchase and sale is not greater than the compensation associated with an arm's length transaction with an unrelated party,

(19) any transaction involving the purchase or sale of securities, or other property (as determined by the Secretary of Labor), between a plan and a disqualified person if—
(A) the transaction is executed through an electronic communication network, alternative trading system, or similar execution system or trading venue subject to regulation and oversight by—
(i) the applicable Federal regulating entity, or
(ii) such foreign regulatory entity as the Secretary of Labor may determine by regulation,
(B) either—
(i) the transaction is effected pursuant to rules designed to match purchases and sales at the best price available through the execution system in accordance with applicable rules of the Securities and Exchange Commission or other relevant governmental authority, or
(ii) neither the execution system nor the parties to the transaction take into account the identity of the parties in the execution of trades,
(C) the price and compensation associated with the purchase and sale are not greater than the price and

compensation associated with an arm's length transaction with an unrelated party,

(D) if the disqualified person has an ownership interest in the system or venue described in subparagraph (A), the system or venue has been authorized by the plan sponsor or other independent fiduciary for transactions described in this paragraph, and

(E) not less than 30 days prior to the initial transaction described in this paragraph executed through any system or venue described in subparagraph (A), a plan fiduciary is provided written or electronic notice of the execution of such transaction through such system or venue,

(20) transactions described in subparagraphs (A), (B), and (D) of subsection (c)(1) between a plan and a person that is a disqualified person other than a fiduciary (or an affiliate) who has or exercises any discretionary authority or control with respect to the investment of the plan assets involved in the transaction or renders investment advice (within the meaning of subsection (e)(3)(B)) with respect to those assets, solely by reason of providing services to the plan or solely by reason of a relationship to such a service provider described in subparagraph (F), (G), (H), or (I) of subsection (e)(2), or both, but only if in connection with such transaction the plan receives no less, nor pays no more, than adequate consideration,

(21) any foreign exchange transactions, between a bank or broker-dealer (or any affiliate of either) and a plan (as defined in this section) with respect to which such bank or broker-dealer (or affiliate) is a trustee, custodian, fiduciary, or other disqualified person person, if—

(A) the transaction is in connection with the purchase, holding, or sale of securities or other investment assets (other than a foreign exchange transaction unrelated to any other investment in securities or other investment assets),

(B) at the time the foreign exchange transaction is entered into, the terms of the transaction are not less favorable to the plan than the terms generally available in comparable arm's length foreign exchange transactions between unrelated parties, or the terms afforded by the bank or broker-dealer (or any affiliate of either) in comparable arm's-length foreign exchange transactions involving unrelated parties,

(C) the exchange rate used by such bank or broker-dealer (or affiliate) for a particular foreign exchange transaction does not deviate by more than 3 percent from the interbank bid and asked rates for transactions of comparable size and maturity at the time of the transaction as displayed on an independent service that reports rates of exchange in the foreign currency market for such currency, and

(D) the bank or broker-dealer (or any affiliate of either) does not have investment discretion, or provide investment advice, with respect to the transaction,

(22) any transaction described in subsection (c)(1)(A) involving the purchase and sale of a security between a plan and any other account managed by the same investment manager, if—

(A) the transaction is a purchase or sale, for no consideration other than cash payment against prompt delivery of a security for which market quotations are readily available,

(B) the transaction is effected at the independent current market price of the security (within the meaning of section 270.17a-7(b) of title 17, Code of Federal Regulations),

(C) no brokerage commission, fee (except for customary transfer fees, the fact of which is disclosed pursuant to subparagraph (D)), or other remuneration is paid in connection with the transaction,

(D) a fiduciary (other than the investment manager engaging in the cross-trades or any affiliate) for each plan participating in the transaction authorizes in advance of any cross-trades (in a document that is separate from any other written agreement of the parties) the investment manager to engage in cross trades at the investment manager's discretion, after such fiduciary has received disclosure regarding the conditions under which cross trades may take place (but only if such disclosure is separate from any other agreement or disclosure involving the asset management relationship), including the written policies and procedures of the investment manager described in subparagraph (H),

(E) each plan participating in the transaction has assets of at least $100,000,000, except that if the assets of a plan are invested in a master trust containing the assets of plans maintained by employers in the same controlled group (as defined in section 407(d)(7) of the Employee Retirement Income Security Act of 1974), the master trust has assets of at least $100,000,000,

(F) the investment manager provides to the plan fiduciary who authorized cross trading under subparagraph (D) a quarterly report detailing all cross trades executed by the investment manager in which the plan participated during such quarter, including the following information, as applicable: (i) the identity of each security bought or sold; (ii) the number of shares or units traded, (iii) the parties involved in the cross-trade; and (iv) trade price and the method used to establish the trade price,

(G) the investment manager does not base its fee schedule on the plan's consent to cross trading, and no other service (other than the investment opportunities and cost savings available through a cross trade) is conditioned on the plan's consent to cross trading,

(H) the investment manager has adopted, and cross-trades are effected in accordance with, written cross-trading policies and procedures that are fair and equitable to all accounts participating in the cross-trading program, and that include a description of the manager's pricing policies and procedures, and the manager's policies and procedures for allocating cross trades in an objective manner among accounts participating in the cross-trading program, and

(I) the investment manager has designated an individual responsible for periodically reviewing such purchases and sales to ensure compliance with the written policies and procedures described in subparagraph (H), and following such review, the individual shall issue an annual written report no later than 90 days following the period to which it relates signed under penalty of perjury to the plan fiduciary who authorized cross trading under subparagraph (D) describing the steps performed during the course of the review, the level of compliance, and any specific instances of non-compliance.

The written report shall also notify the plan fiduciary of the plan's right to terminate participation in the investment manager's cross-trading program at any time, or

(23) except as provided in subsection (f)(11), a transaction described in subparagraph (A), (B), (C), or (D) of subsection (c)(1) in connection with the acquisition, holding, or disposition of any security or commodity, if the transaction is corrected before the end of the correction period.

(e) Definitions.

(1) **Plan.** For purposes of this section, the term "plan" means—

(A) a trust described in section 401(a) which forms a part of a plan, or a plan described in section 403(a), which trust or plan is exempt from tax under section 501(a),

(B) an individual retirement account described in section 408(a),

(C) an individual retirement annuity described in section 408(b),

(D) an Archer MSA described in section 220(d),

(E) a health savings account described in section 223(d),

(F) a Coverdell education savings account described in section 530, or

(G) a trust, plan, account, or annuity which, at any time, has been determined by the Secretary to be described in any preceding subparagraph of this paragraph.

(2) **Disqualified person.** For purposes of this section, the term "disqualified person" means a person who is—

(A) a fiduciary;

(B) a person providing services to the plan;

(C) an employer any of whose employees are covered by the plan;

(D) an employee organization any of whose members are covered by the plan;

(E) an owner, direct or indirect, of 50 percent or more of—

(i) the combined voting power of all classes of stock entitled to vote or the total value of shares of all classes of stock of a corporation,

(ii) the capital interest or the profits interest of a partnership, or

(iii) the beneficial interest of a trust or unincorporated enterprise,

which is an employer or an employee organization described in subparagraph (C) or (D);

(F) a member of the family (as defined in paragraph (6)) of any individual described in subparagraph (A), (B), (C), or (E);

(G) a corporation, partnership, or trust or estate of which (or in which) 50 percent or more of—

(i) the combined voting power of all classes of stock entitled to vote or the total value of shares of all classes of stock of such corporation,

(ii) the capital interest or profits interest of such partnership, or

(iii) the beneficial interest of such trust or estate,

is owned directly or indirectly, or held by persons described in subparagraph (A), (B), (C), (D), or (E);

(H) an officer, director (or an individual having powers or responsibilities similar to those of officers or directors), a 10 percent or more shareholder, or a highly compensated employee (earning 10 percent or more of the yearly wages of an employer) of a person described in subparagraph (C), (D), (E), or (G); or

(I) a 10 percent or more (in capital or profits) partner or joint venturer of a person described in subparagraph (C), (D), (E), or (G).

The Secretary, after consultation and coordination with the Secretary of Labor or his delegate, may by regulation prescribe a percentage lower than 50 percent for subparagraphs (E) and (G) and lower than 10 percent for subparagraphs (H) and (I).

(3) **Fiduciary.** For purposes of this section, the term "fiduciary" means any person who—

(A) exercises any discretionary authority or discretionary control respecting management of such plan or exercises any authority or control respecting management or disposition of its assets,

(B) renders investment advice for a fee or other compensation, direct or indirect, with respect to any moneys or other property of such plan, or has any authority or responsibility to do so, or

(C) has any discretionary authority or discretionary responsibility in the administration of such plan.

Such term includes any person designated under section 405(c)(1)(B) of the Employee Retirement Income Security Act of 1974.

(4) **Stockholdings.** For purposes of paragraphs (2)(E)(i) and (G)(i) there shall be taken into account indirect stockholdings which would be taken into account under section 267(c), except that, for purposes of this paragraph, section 267(c)(4) shall be treated as providing that the members of the family of an individual are the members within the meaning of paragraph (6).

(5) **Partnerships; trusts.** For purposes of paragraphs (2)(E)(ii) and (iii), (G)(ii) and (iii), and (I) the ownership of profits or beneficial interests shall be determined in accordance with the rules for constructive ownership of stock provided in section 267(c) (other than paragraph (3) thereof), except that section 267(c)(4) shall be treated as providing that the members of the family of an individual are the members within the meaning of paragraph (6).

(6) **Member of family.** For purposes of paragraph (2)(F), the family of any individual shall include his spouse, ancestor, lineal descendant, and any spouse of a lineal descendant.

(7) **Employee stock ownership plan.** The term "employee stock ownership plan" means a defined contribution plan—

(A) which is a stock bonus plan which is qualified, or a stock bonus and a money purchase plan both of which are qualified under section 401(a), and which are designed to invest primarily in qualifying employer securities; and

(B) which is otherwise defined in regulations prescribed by the Secretary.

A plan shall not be treated as an employee stock ownership plan unless it meets the requirements of section 409(h), section 409(o), and, if applicable, section 409(n), section 409(p), and section 664(g) and, if the employer has a registration-type class of securities (as defined in section 409(e)(4)), it meets the requirements of section 409(e).

(8) **Qualifying employer security.** The term "qualifying employer security" means any employer security within the meaning of section 409(l). If any moneys or other property of a plan are invested in shares of an investment company registered under the Investment Company Act of 1940, the investment shall not cause that investment company or that investment company's investment adviser or principal underwriter to be treated as a fiduciary or a disqualified person for purposes of this section, except when an investment company or its investment adviser or principal underwriter acts in connection with a plan covering employees of the investment company, its investment adviser, or its principal underwriter.

(9) **Section made applicable to withdrawal liability payment funds.** For purposes of this section—

(A) In general. The term "plan" includes a trust described in section 501(c)(22).

(B) Disqualified person. In the case of any trust to which this section applies by reason of subparagraph (A), the term "disqualified person" includes any person who is a disqualified person with respect to any plan to which such trust is permitted to make payments under section 4223 of the Employee Retirement Income Security Act of 1974.

(f) Other definitions and special rules.
For purposes of this section—

(1) Joint and several liability. If more than one person is liable under subsection (a) or (b) with respect to any one prohibited transaction, all such persons shall be jointly and severally liable under such subsection with respect to such transaction.

(2) Taxable period. The term "taxable period" means, with respect to any prohibited transaction, the period beginning with the date on which the prohibited transaction occurs and ending on the earliest of—

(A) the date of mailing a notice of deficiency with respect to the tax imposed by subsection (a) under section 6212,

(B) the date on which the tax imposed by subsection (a) is assessed, or

(C) the date on which correction of the prohibited transaction is completed.

(3) Sale or exchange; encumbered property. A transfer of real or personal property by a disqualified person to a plan shall be treated as a sale or exchange if the property is subject to a mortgage or similar lien which the plan assumes or if it is subject to a mortgage or similar lien which a disqualified person placed on the property within the 10-year period ending on the date of the transfer.

(4) Amount involved. The term "amount involved" means, with respect to a prohibited transaction, the greater of the amount of money and the fair market value of the other property given or the amount of money and the fair market value of the other property received; except that, in the case of services described in paragraphs (2) and (10) of subsection (d) the amount involved shall be only the excess compensation. For purposes of the preceding sentence, the fair market value—

(A) in the case of the tax imposed by subsection (a), shall be determined as of the date on which the prohibited transaction occurs; and

(B) in the case of the tax imposed by subsection (b), shall be the highest fair market value during the taxable period.

(5) Correction. The terms "correction" and "correct" mean, with respect to a prohibited transaction, undoing the transaction to the extent possible, but in any case placing the plan in a financial position not worse than that in which it would be if the disqualified person were acting under the highest fiduciary standards.

(6) Exemptions not to apply to certain transactions.

(A) In general. In the case of a trust described in section 401(a) which is part of a plan providing contributions or benefits for employees some or all of whom are owner-employees (as defined in section 401(c)(3)), the exemptions provided by subsection (d) (other than paragraphs (9) and (12)) shall not apply to a transaction in which the plan directly or indirectly—

(i) lends any part of the corpus or income of the plan to,

(ii) pays any compensation for personal services rendered to the plan to, or

(iii) acquires for the plan any property from, or sells any property to,

any such owner-employee, a member of the family (as defined in section 267(c)(4)) of any such owner-employee, or any corporation in which any such owner-employee owns, directly or indirectly, 50 percent or more of the total combined voting power of all classes of stock entitled to vote or 50 percent or more of the total value of shares of all classes of stock of the corporation.

(B) Special rules for shareholder-employees, etc.

(i) In general. For purposes of subparagraph (A), the following shall be treated as owner-employees:

(I) A shareholder-employee.

(II) A participant or beneficiary of an individual retirement plan (as defined in section 7701(a)(37)).

(III) An employer or association of employees which establishes such an individual retirement plan under section 408(c).

(ii) Exception for certain transactions involving shareholder-employees. Subparagraph (A)(iii) shall not apply to a transaction which consists of a sale of employer securities to an employee stock ownership plan (as defined in subsection (e)(7)) by a shareholder-employee, a member of the family (as defined in section 267(c)(4)) of such shareholder-employee, or a corporation in which such a shareholder-employee owns stock representing a 50 percent or greater interest described in subparagraph (A).

(iii) Loan exception. For purposes of subparagraph (A)(i), the term "owner-employee" shall only include a person described in subclause (II) or (III) of clause (i).

(C) Shareholder-employee. For purposes of subparagraph (B), the term "shareholder-employee" means an employee or officer of an S corporation who owns (or is considered as owning within the meaning of section 318(a)(1)) more than 5 percent of the outstanding stock of the corporation on any day during the taxable year of such corporation.

(7) S corporation repayment of loans for qualifying employer securities. A plan shall not be treated as violating the requirements of section 401 or 409 or subsection (e)(7), or as engaging in a prohibited transaction for purposes of subsection (d)(3), merely by reason of any distribution (as described in section 1368(a)) with respect to S corporation stock that constitutes qualifying employer securities, which in accordance with the plan provisions is used to make payments on a loan described in subsection (d)(3) the proceeds of which were used to acquire such qualifying employer securities (whether or not allocated to participants). The preceding sentence shall not apply in the case of a distribution which is paid with respect to any employer security which is allocated to a participant unless the plan provides that employer securities with a fair market value of not less than the amount of such distribution are allocated to such participant for the year which (but for the preceding sentence) such distribution would have been allocated to such participant.

(8) Provision of investment advice to participant and beneficiaries.

(A) In general. The prohibitions provided in subsection (c) shall not apply to transactions described in subsection (d)(17) if the investment advice provided by a fiduciary adviser is provided under an eligible investment advice arrangement.

(B) Eligible investment advice arrangement. For purposes of this paragraph, the term "eligible investment advice arrangement" means an arrangement—

(i) which either—

(I) provides that any fees (including any commission or other compensation) received by the fiduciary adviser for investment advice or with respect to the sale, holding, or acquisition of any security or other property for purposes of investment of plan assets do not vary depending on the basis of any investment option selected, or

(II) uses a computer model under an investment advice program meeting the requirements of subparagraph (C) in connection with the provision of investment advice by a fiduciary adviser to a participant or beneficiary, and

(ii) with respect to which the requirements of subparagraphs (D), (E), (F), (G), (H), and (I) are met.

(C) Investment advice program using computer model.

(i) In general. An investment advice program meets the requirements of this subparagraph if the requirements of clauses (ii), (iii), and (iv) are met.

(ii) Computer model. The requirements of this clause are met if the investment advice provided under the investment advice program is provided pursuant to a computer model that—

(I) applies generally accepted investment theories that take into account the historic returns of different asset classes over defined periods of time,

(II) utilizes relevant information about the participant, which may include age, life expectancy, retirement age, risk tolerance, other assets or sources of income, and preferences as to certain types of investments,

(III) utilizes prescribed objective criteria to provide asset allocation portfolios comprised of investment options available under the plan,

(IV) operates in a manner that is not biased in favor of investments offered by the fiduciary adviser or a person with a material affiliation or contractual relationship with the fiduciary adviser, and

(V) takes into account all investment options under the plan in specifying how a participant's account balance should be invested and is not inappropriately weighted with respect to any investment option.

(iii) Certification.

(I) In general. The requirements of this clause are met with respect to any investment advice program if an eligible investment expert certifies, prior to the utilization of the computer model and in accordance with rules prescribed by the Secretary of Labor, that the computer model meets the requirements of clause (ii).

(II) Renewal of certifications. If, as determined under regulations prescribed by the Secretary of Labor, there are material modifications to a computer model, the requirements of this clause are met only if a certification described in subclause (I) is obtained with respect to the computer model as so modified.

(III) Eligible investment expert. The term "eligible investment expert" means any person which meets such requirements as the Secretary of Labor may

provide and which does not bear any material affiliation or contractual relationship with any investment adviser or a related person thereof (or any employee, agent, or registered representative of the investment adviser or related person).

(iv) Exclusivity of recommendation. The requirements of this clause are met with respect to any investment advice program if—

(I) the only investment advice provided under the program is the advice generated by the computer model described in clause (ii), and

(II) any transaction described in (d)(17)(A)(ii) occurs solely at the direction of the participant or beneficiary.

Nothing in the preceding sentence shall preclude the participant or beneficiary from requesting investment advice other than that described in clause (i), but only if such request has not been solicited by any person connected with carrying out the arrangement.

(D) Express authorization by separate fiduciary. The requirements of this subparagraph are met with respect to an arrangement if the arrangement is expressly authorized by a plan fiduciary other than the person offering the investment advice program, any person providing investment options under the plan, or any affiliate of either.

(E) Audits.

(i) In general. The requirements of this subparagraph are met if an independent auditor, who has appropriate technical training or experience and proficiency and so represents in writing—

(I) conducts an annual audit of the arrangement for compliance with the requirements of this paragraph, and

(II) following completion of the annual audit, issues a written report to the fiduciary who authorized use of the arrangement which presents its specific findings regarding compliance of the arrangement with the requirements of this paragraph.

(ii) Special rule for individual retirement and similar plans. In the case of a plan described in subparagraphs (B) through (F) (and so much of subparagraph (G) as relates to such subparagraphs) of subsection (e)(1), in lieu of the requirements of clause (i), audits of the arrangement shall be conducted at such times and in such manner as the Secretary of Labor may prescribe.

(iii) Independent auditor. For purposes of this subparagraph, an auditor is considered independent if it is not related to the person offering the arrangement to the plan and is not related to any person providing investment options under the plan.

(F) Disclosure. The requirements of this subparagraph are met if—

(i) the fiduciary adviser provides to a participant or a beneficiary before the initial provision of the investment advice with regard to any security or other property offered as an investment option, a written notification (which may consist of notification by means of electronic communication)—

(I) of the role of any party that has a material affiliation or contractual relationship with the fiduciary adviser, in the development of the investment advice program and in the selection of investment options available under the plan,

(II) of the past performance and historical rates of return of the investment options available under the plan,

(III) of all fees or other compensation relating to the advice that the fiduciary adviser or any affiliate thereof is to receive (including compensation provided by any third party) in connection with the provision of the advice or in connection with the sale, acquisition, or holding of the security or other property,

(IV) of any material affiliation or contractual relationship of the fiduciary adviser or affiliates thereof in the security or other property,

(V) the manner, and under what circumstances, any participant or beneficiary information provided under the arrangement will be used or disclosed,

(VI) of the types of services provided by the fiduciary adviser in connection with the provision of investment advice by the fiduciary adviser,

(VII) that the adviser is acting as a fiduciary of the plan in connection with the provision of the advice, and

(VIII) that a recipient of the advice may separately arrange for the provision of advice by another adviser, that could have no material affiliation with and receive no fees or other compensation in connection with the security or other property, and

(ii) at all times during the provision of advisory services to the participant or beneficiary, the fiduciary adviser—

(I) maintains the information described in clause (i) in accurate form and in the manner described in subparagraph (H),

(II) provides, without charge, accurate information to the recipient of the advice no less frequently than annually,

(III) provides, without charge, accurate information to the recipient of the advice upon request of the recipient, and

(IV) provides, without charge, accurate information to the recipient of the advice concerning any material change to the information required to be provided to the recipient of the advice at a time reasonably contemporaneous to the change in information.

(G) Other conditions. The requirements of this subparagraph are met if—

(i) the fiduciary adviser provides appropriate disclosure, in connection with the sale, acquisition, or holding of the security or other property, in accordance with all applicable securities laws,

(ii) the sale, acquisition, or holding occurs solely at the direction of the recipient of the advice,

(iii) the compensation received by the fiduciary adviser and affiliates thereof in connection with the sale, acquisition, or holding of the security or other property is reasonable, and

(iv) the terms of the sale, acquisition, or holding of the security or other property are at least as favorable to the plan as an arm's length transaction would be.

(H) Standards for presentation of information.

(i) In general. The requirements of this subparagraph are met if the notification required to be provided to participants and beneficiaries under subparagraph (F)(i) is written in a clear and conspicuous manner and in a manner calculated to be understood by the average plan participant and is sufficiently accurate and comprehensive to reasonably apprise such participants and beneficiaries of the information required to be provided in the notification.

(ii) Model form for disclosure of fees and other compensation. The Secretary of Labor shall issue a model form for the disclosure of fees and other compensation required in subparagraph (F)(i)(III) which meets the requirements of clause (i).

(I) Maintenance for 6 years of evidence of compliance. The requirements of this subparagraph are met if a fiduciary adviser who has provided advice referred to in subparagraph (A) maintains, for a period of not less than 6 years after the provision of the advice, any records necessary for determining whether the requirements of the preceding provisions of this paragraph and of subsection (d)(17) have been met. A transaction prohibited under subsection (c) shall not be considered to have occurred solely because the records are lost or destroyed prior to the end of the 6-year period due to circumstances beyond the control of the fiduciary adviser.

(J) Definitions. For purposes of this paragraph and subsection (d)(17)—

(i) Fiduciary adviser. The term "fiduciary adviser" means, with respect to a plan, a person who is a fiduciary of the plan by reason of the provision of investment advice referred to in subsection (e)(3)(B) by the person to a participant or beneficiary of the plan and who is—

(I) registered as an investment adviser under the Investment Advisers Act of 1940 (15 U.S.C. 80b-1 et seq.) or under the laws of the State in which the fiduciary maintains its principal office and place of business,

(II) a bank or similar financial institution referred to in subsection (d)(4) or a savings association (as defined in section 3(b)(1) of the Federal Deposit Insurance Act (12 U.S.C. 1813(b)(1)), but only if the advice is provided through a trust department of the bank or similar financial institution or savings association which is subject to periodic examination and review by Federal or State banking authorities,

(III) an insurance company qualified to do business under the laws of a State,

(IV) a person registered as a broker or dealer under the Securities Exchange Act of 1934 (15 U.S.C. 78 et seq.),

(V) an affiliate of a person described in any of subclauses (I) through (IV), or

(VI) an employee, agent, or registered representative of a person described in subclauses (I) through (V) who satisfies the requirements of applicable insurance, banking, and securities laws relating to the provision of the advice.

For purposes of this title, a person who develops the computer model described in subparagraph (C)(ii) or markets the investment advice program or computer model shall be treated as a person who is a fiduciary of the plan by reason of the provision of investment advice referred to in subsection (e)(3)(B) to a participant or beneficiary and shall be treated as a fiduciary adviser for purposes of this paragraph and subsection (d)(17), except that the Secretary of Labor may prescribe rules under which only 1 fiduciary adviser may elect to be treated as a fiduciary with respect to the plan.

(ii) *Affiliate.* The term "affiliate" of another entity means an affiliated person of the entity (as defined in section 2(a)(3) of the Investment Company Act of 1940 (15 U.S.C. 80a-2(a)(3))).

(iii) *Registered representative.* The term "registered representative" of another entity means a person described in section 3(a)(18) of the Securities Exchange Act of 1934 (15 U.S.C. 78c(a)(18)) (substituting the entity for the broker or dealer referred to in such section) or a person described in section 202(a)(17) of the Investment Advisers Act of 1940 (15 U.S.C. 80b-2(a)(17)) (substituting the entity for the investment adviser referred to in such section).

(9) Block trade. The term "block trade" means any trade of at least 10,000 shares or with a market value of at least $200,000 which will be allocated across two or more unrelated client accounts of a fiduciary.

(10) Adequate consideration. The term "adequate consideration" means—

(A) in the case of a security for which there is a generally recognized market—

(i) the price of the security prevailing on a national securities exchange which is registered under section 6 of the Securities Exchange Act of 1934, taking into account factors such as the size of the transaction and marketability of the security, or

(ii) if the security is not traded on such a national securities exchange, a price not less favorable to the plan than the offering price for the security as established by the current bid and asked prices quoted by persons independent of the issuer and of the party in interest, taking into account factors such as the size of the transaction and marketability of the security, and

(B) in the case of an asset other than a security for which there is a generally recognized market, the fair market value of the asset as determined in good faith by a fiduciary or fiduciaries in accordance with regulations prescribed by the Secretary of Labor.

(11) Correction period.

(A) *In general.* For purposes of subsection (d)(23), the term "correction period" means the 14-day period beginning on the date on which the disqualified person discovers, or reasonably should have discovered, that the transaction would (without regard to this paragraph and subsection (d)(23)) constitute a prohibited transaction.

(B) *Exceptions.*

(i) *Employer securities.* Subsection (d)(23) does not apply to any transaction between a plan and a plan sponsor or its affiliates that involves the acquisition or sale of an employer security (as defined in section 407(d)(1) of the Employee Retirement Income Security Act of 1974) or the acquisition, sale, or lease of employer real property (as defined in section 407(d)(2) of such Act).

(ii) *Knowing prohibited transaction.* In the case of any disqualified person, subsection (d)(23) does not apply to a transaction if, at the time the transaction is entered into, the disqualified person knew (or reasonably should have known) that the transaction would (without regard to this paragraph) constitute a prohibited transaction.

(C) *Abatement of tax where there is a correction.* If a transaction is not treated as a prohibited transaction by reason of subsection (d)(23), then no tax under subsection (a) and (b) shall be assessed with respect to such transaction, and if assessed the assessment shall be abated, and if collected shall be credited or refunded as an overpayment.

(D) *Definitions.* For purposes of this paragraph and subsection (d)(23)—

(i) *Security.* The term "security" has the meaning given such term by section 475(c)(2) (without regard to subparagraph (F)(iii) and the last sentence thereof).

(ii) *Commodity.* The term "commodity" has the meaning given such term by section 475(e)(2) (without regard to subparagraph (D)(iii) thereof).

(iii) *Correct.* The term "correct" means, with respect to a transaction—

(I) to undo the transaction to the extent possible and in any case to make good to the plan or affected account any losses resulting from the transaction, and

(II) to restore to the plan or affected account any profits made through the use of assets of the plan.

(g) Application of section.

This section shall not apply—

(1) in the case of a plan to which a guaranteed benefit policy (as defined in section 401(b)(2)(B) of the Employee Retirement Income Security Act of 1974) is issued, to any assets of the insurance company, insurance service, or insurance organization merely because of its issuance of such policy;

(2) to a governmental plan (within the meaning of section 414(d)); or

(3) to a church plan (within the meaning of section 414(e)) with respect to which the election provided by section 410(d) has not been made.

In the case of a plan which invests in any security issued by an investment company registered under the Investment Company Act of 1940, the assets of such plan shall be deemed to include such security but shall not, by reason of such investment, be deemed to include any assets of such company.

(h) Notification of Secretary of Labor.

Before sending a notice of deficiency with respect to the tax imposed by subsection (a) or (b), the Secretary shall notify the Secretary of Labor and provide him a reasonable opportunity to obtain a correction of the prohibited transaction or to comment on the imposition of such tax.

(i) Cross reference.

For provisions concerning coordination procedures between Secretary of Labor and Secretary of the Treasury with respect to application of tax imposed by this section and for authority to waive imposition of the tax imposed by subsection (b), see section 3003 of the Employee Retirement Income Security Act of 1974.

In 2010, P.L. 111-312, Sec. 101(a)(1), substituted "December 31, 2012" for "December 31, 2010" both places it appeared in Sec. 901 of P.L. 107-16, [see below] effective as if included in the enactment of P.L. 107-16, EGTRRA, 6/7/2001.

In 2008, P.L. 110-458, Sec. 106(a)(2)(A), substituted "that permits" for "and that permits" in para. (d)(17) . . . Sec. 106(a)(2)(B)(i), substituted "subsection (d)(17)" for "subsection (b)(14)" in subpara. (f)(8)(A) . . . Sec. 106(a)(2)(B)(ii), substituted "(d)(17)(A)(ii)" for "subsection (b)(14)(B)(ii)" in subclause (f)(8)(C)(iv)(II) . . . Sec. 106(a)(2)(B)(iii), substituted "fiduciary adviser," for "financial adviser" in subclause (f)(8)(F)(i)(I) . . . Sec. 106(a)(2)(B)(iv), substituted "subsection (c)" for "section 406" in subpara. (f)(8)(I) . . . Sec. 106(a)(2)(B)(v)(I), substituted "a participant" for "the participant" each place it appears in clause (f)(8)(J)(i) . . . Sec. 106(a)(2)(B)(v)(II), added "referred to in subsection (e)(3)(B)" after "investment advice" in the matter preceding subclause (f)(8)(J)(i)(I) . . . Sec. 106(a)(2)(B)(v)(III), substituted "subsection (d)(4)" for "section 408(b)(4)" in subclause (f)(8)(J)(i)(II), effective [as if included in the provisions of Sec. 601, P.L. 109-280, as amended by Sec. 106(a)(3), P.L. 110-458' for advice referred to in Code Sec. 4975(e)(3)(B) provided after 12/31/2006.

—P.L. 110-458, Sec. 106(a)(3), subsituted '4975(e)(3)(B)' for '4975(c)(3)(B)' in Sec. 601(b)(4), P.L. 109-280, the effective date provision for amendments made by Sec. 601(b), P.L. 109-280, see below.

—P.L. 110-458, Sec. 106(b)(2)(A)(i), substituted 'disqualified person' for 'party in interest' in the matter preceding subpara. (d)(18)(A) . . . Sec. 106(b)(2)(A)(ii), substituted 'subsection (e)(3)' for 'subsection (e)(3)(B)' in the matter preceding subpara. (d)(18)(A) . . . Sec. 106(b)(2)(B), substituted 'disqualified person' for 'party in interest' each place if appears in para. (d)(19)-(21) . . . Sec. 106(b)(2)(C), deleted 'or less' in subpara. (d)(21)(C), effective for transactions occurring after 8/17/2006 (as if included in the amendments made by Sec. 611, P.L. 109-280, see below).

—P.L. 110-458, Sec. 106(c)(1), added 'of the Employee Retirement Income Security Act of 1974' after 'section 407(d)(1)' in clause (f)(11)(B)(i) . . . Sec. 106(c)(2), added 'of such Act' after 'section 407(d)(2)' in clause (f)(11)(B)(i), effective for any transaction which the fiduciary or disqualified person discovers, or reasonably should have discovered, after 8/17/2006 constitutes a prohibited transaction (as if included in the provisions of Sec. 612, P.L. 109-280, see below.

In 2006, P.L. 109-280, Sec. 601(b)(1)(A), deleted 'or' at the end of para. (d)(15) . . . Sec. 601(b)(1)(B), substituted ';or' for the period at the end of para. (d)(16) . . . Sec. 601(b)(1)(C), added para. (d)(17) . . . Sec. 601(b)(2), added para. (f)(8), effective [as amended by Sec. 106(a)(3), P.L. 110-458, see above" for advice referred to in Code Sec. 4975(e)(3)(B) provided after 12/31/2006.

—P.L. 109-280, Sec. 601(b)(3), of this Act, provides:

"(3) Determination of feasibility of application of computer model investment advice programs for individual retirement and similar plans.

"(A) Solicitation of information. As soon as practicable after the date of the enactment of this Act, the Secretary of Labor, in consultation with the Secretary of the Treasury, shall—

"(i) solicit information as to the feasibility of the application of computer model investment advice programs for plans described in subparagraphs (B) through (F) (and so much of subparagraph (G) as relates to such subparagraphs) of section 4975(e)(1) of the Internal Revenue Code of 1986, including soliciting information from—

"(I) at least the top 50 trustees of such plans, determined on the basis of assets held by such trustees, and

"(II) other persons offering computer model investment advice programs based on nonproprietary products, and

"(ii) shall on the basis of such information make the determination under subparagraph (B).

The information solicited by the Secretary of Labor under clause (i) from persons described in subclauses (I) and (II) of clause (i) shall include information on computer modeling capabilities of such persons with respect to the current year and preceding year, including such capabilities for investment accounts maintained by such persons.

"(B) Determination of feasibility. The Secretary of Labor, in consultation with the Secretary of the Treasury, shall, on the basis of information received under subparagraph (A), determine whether there is any computer model investment advice program which may be utilized by a plan described in subparagraph (A)(i) to provide investment advice to the account beneficiary of the plan which—

"(i) utilizes relevant information about the account beneficiary, which may include age, life expectancy, retirement age, risk tolerance, other assets or sources of income, and preferences as to certain types of investments,

"(ii) takes into account the full range of investments, including equities and bonds, in determining the options for the investment portfolio of the account beneficiary, and

"(iii) allows the account beneficiary, in directing the investment of assets, sufficient flexibility in obtaining advice to evaluate and select investment options.

The Secretary of Labor shall report the results of such determination to the committees of Congress referred to in subparagraph (D)(ii) not later than December 31, 2007.

"(C) Application of computer model investment advice program.

"(i) Certification required for use of computer model.

"(I) Restriction on use. Subclause (II) of section 4975(f)(8)(B)(i) of the Internal Revenue Code of 1986 shall not apply to a plan described in subparagraph (A)(i).

"(II) Restriction lifted if model certified. If the Secretary of Labor determines under subparagraph (B) or (D) that there is a computer model investment advice program described in subparagraph (B), subclause (I) shall cease to apply as of the date of such determination.

"(ii) class exemption if no initial certification by Secretary. If the Secretary of Labor determines under subparagraph (B) that there is no computer model investment advice program described in subparagraph (B), the Secretary of Labor shall grant a class exemption from treatment as a prohibited transaction under section 4975(c) of the Internal Revenue Code of 1986 to any transaction described in section 4975(d)(17)(A) of such Code with respect to plans described in subparagraph (A)(i), subject to such conditions as set forth in such exemption as are in the interests of the plan and its account beneficiary and protective of the rights of the account beneficiary and as are necessary to—

"(I) ensure the requirements of sections 4975(d)(17) and 4975(f)(8) (other than subparagraph (C) thereof) of the Internal Revenue Code of 1986 are met, and

"(II) ensure the investment advice provided under the investment advice program utilizes prescribed objective criteria to provide asset allocation portfolios comprised of securities or other property available as investments under the plan.

If the Secretary of Labor solicits any information under subparagraph (A) from a person and such person does not provide such information within 60 days after the solicitation, then, unless such failure was due to reasonable cause and not wilful neglect, such person shall not be entitled to utilize the class exemption under this clause.

"(D) Subsequent determination.

"(i) In general. If the Secretary of Labor initially makes a determination described in subparagraph (C)(ii), the Secretary may subsequently determine that there is a computer model investment advice program described in subparagraph (B). If the Secretary makes such subsequent determination, then the class exemption described in subparagraph (C)(ii) shall cease to apply after the later of—

"(I) the date which is 2 years after such subsequent determination, or

"(II) the date which is 3 years after the first date on which such exemption took effect.

"(ii) Requests for determination. Any person may request the Secretary of Labor to make a determination under this subparagraph with respect to any computer model investment advice program, and the Secretary of Labor shall make a determination with respect to such request within 90 days. If the Secretary of Labor makes a determination that such program is not described in subparagraph (B), the Secretary shall, within 10 days of such determination, notify the Committee on Ways and Means and the Committee on Education and the Workforce of the House of Representatives and the Committee on Finance and the Committee on Health, Education, Labor, and Pensions of the Senate of such determination and the reasons for such determination.

"(E) Effective date. The provisions of this paragraph shall take effect on the date of the enactment of this Act."

—P.L. 110-458, Sec. 106(a)(3), of this Act provides [as added by Sec. 601(b)(4) of P.L. 109-280 of this Act, see below]:

"(4) Effective date. Except as provided in this subsection, the amendments made by this subsection shall apply with respect to advice referred to in section 4975(c)(3)(B) of the Internal Revenue Code of 1986 provided after December 31, 2006"

—P.L. 109-280, Sec. 601(c), of this Act, provides:

"*(c) Coordination with existing exemptions.* Any exemption under section 408(b) of the Employee Retirement Income Security Act of 1974 and section 4975(d) of the Internal Revenue Code of 1986 provided by the amendments made by this section shall not in any manner alter existing individual or class exemptions, provided by statute or administrative action."

—P.L. 109-280, Sec. 611(a)(2)(A), deleted "or" at the end of para. (d)(16) [as amended by Sec. 601(b)(1)(B) of this Act, see above], substituted ", or" for the period at the end of para. (d)(17) [as added by Sec. 601(b)(1)(C) of this Act, see above], and added para. (d)(18) . . . Sec. 611(a)(2)(B), added para. (f)(9) . . . Sec. 611(c)(2), deleted "or" at the end of para. (d)(17) [as amended by Sec. 611(a)(2)(A) of this Act, see above], substituted ", or" for the period at the end of para. (d)(18) [as added by Sec. 611(a)(2)(A) of this Act, see above], and added para. (d)(19) . . . Sec. 611(d)(2)(A), deleted "or" at the end of para. (d)(18) [as amended by Sec. 611(c)(2) of this Act, see above], substituted ", or" for the period at the end of para. (d)(19) [as added by Sec. 611(c)(2) of this Act, see above], and added para. (d)(20) . . . Sec. 611(d)(2)(B), added para. (f)(10) . . . Sec. 611(e)(2), deleted "or" at the end of para. (d)(19) [as amended by Sec. 611(d)(2)(A) of this Act, see above], substituted ", or" for the period at the end of para. (d)(20) [as added by Sec. 611(d)(2)(A) of this Act, see above], and added para. (d)(21) . . . Sec. 611(g)(2), deleted "or" at the end of para. (d)(20) [as amended by Sec. 611(e)(2) of this Act, see above], substituted ", or" for the period at the end of para. (d)(21) [as added by Sec. 611(e)(2) of this Act, see above], and added para. (d)(22), effective for transactions occurring after 8/17/2006.

—P.L. 109-280, Sec. 612(b)(1), deleted "or" at the end of para. (d)(21) [as amended by Sec. 611(g)(2) of this Act, see above], substituted ", or" for the period at the end of para. (d)(22) [as added by Sec. 611(g)(2) of this Act, see above], and added para. (d)(23) . . . Sec. 612(b)(2), added para. (f)(11), effective for any transaction which the fiduciary or disqualified person discovers, or reasonably should have discovered, after 8/17/2006 constitutes a prohibited transaction.

—P.L. 109-280, Sec. 811, of this Act [relating to Sec. 901 of P.L. 107-16, see below], provides:

"SEC. 811. PENSIONS AND INDIVIDUAL RETIREMENT ARRANGEMENT PROVISIONS OF ECONOMIC GROWTH AND TAX RELIEF RECONCILIATION ACT OF 2001 MADE PERMANENT.

"Title IX of the Economic Growth and Tax Relief Reconciliation Act of 2001 shall not apply to the provisions of, and amendments made by, subtitles A through F of title VI of such Act (relating to pension and individual retirement arrangement provisions)."

In 2005, P.L. 109-135, Sec. 413(a)(2)(A), added "or a depository institution holding company (as defined in section 3(w)(1) of the Federal Deposit Insurance Act (12 U.S.C. 1813(w)(1))" after "a bank (as defined in section 581)" in subpara. (d)(16)(A) . . . Sec. 413(a)(2)(B), added "or company" after "such bank" in subpara. (d)(16)(C), effective 10/22/2004 as if included in Sec. 233 of the American Jobs Creation Act of 2004, P.L. 108-357.

In 2004, P.L. 108-357, Sec. 233(c), deleted "or" at the end of para. (d)(14), substituted "; or" for the period at the end of para. (d)(15), and added para. (d)(16), effective 10/22/2004.

—P.L. 108-357, Sec. 240(a), added para. (f)(7), effective for distributions with respect to S corporation stock made after 12/31/97.

In 2003, P.L. 108-173, Sec. 1201(f)(1), added para. (c)(6) . . . Sec. 1201(f)(2), redesignated subparas. (e)(1)(E) and (F) as (e)(1)(F) and (G), and added subpara. (e)(1)(E), effective for tax. yrs. begin. after 12/31/2003.

In 2002, P.L. 107-358, Sec. 2, added subsec. (c) in Sec. 901 of P.L. 107-16 [see below], effective 12/17/2002.

In 2001, P.L. 107-22, Sec. 1(b)(1)(D), substituted "a Coverdell education savings" for "an education individual retirement" in subsecs. (c) and (e) . . . Sec. 1(b)(3)(D), substituted "Coverdell education savings" for "education individual retirement" in the heading of para. (c)(5), effective 7/26/2001.

—P.L. 107-16, Sec. 612(a), added clause (f)(6)(B)(iii), effective for yrs. begin. after 12/31/2001.

—P.L. 107-16, Sec. 656(b), added ", section 409(p)," after "409(n)" in the last sentence of para. (e)(7), effective for plan yrs. begin. after 12/31/2004. Sec. 656(d)(2) of this Act, provides:

"(2) Exception for certain plans. In the case of any—

"(A) employee stock ownership plan established after March 14, 2001, or

"(B) employee stock ownership plan established on or before such date if employer securities held by the plan consist of stock in a corporation with respect to which an election under section 1362(a) of the Internal Revenue Code of 1986 is not in effect on such date,

the amendments made by this section shall apply to plan years ending after March 14, 2001."

—P.L. 107-16, Sec. 901, of this Act [as amended by Sec. 2 of P.L. 107-358, and Sec. 101(a)(1) of P.L. 111-312, see above], reads as follows:

"SEC. 901. SUNSET OF PROVISIONS OF ACT.

"(a) In general. All provisions of, and amendments made by, this Act shall not apply—

"(1) to taxable, plan, or limitation years beginning after December 31, 2012, or

"(2) in the case of title V, to estates of decedents dying, gifts made, or generation skipping transfers, after December 31, 2012.

"(b) Application of certain laws. The Internal Revenue Code of 1986 and the Employee Retirement Income Security Act of 1974 shall be applied and administered to years, estates, gifts, and transfers described in subsection (a) as if the provisions and amendments described in subsection (a) had never been enacted.

"(c) Exception. Subsection (a) shall not apply to section 803 (relating to no federal income tax on restitution received by victims of the Nazi regime or their heirs or estates)."

In 2000, P.L. 106-554, Sec. 1(a)(7), [which enacted into law Sec. 202(a)(7) of P.L. 106-554] substituted "Archer MSA" for "medical savings account" in para. (c)(4) and subpara. (e)(1)(D) . . . Sec. 1(a)(7), [which enacted into law Sec. 202(b)(7) of P.L. 106-554] substituted "Archer MSAs" for "medical savings accounts" in the heading of para. (c)(4) . . . Sec. 1(a)(7), [which enacted into law Sec. 202(b)(10) of P.L. 106-554] substituted "an Archer" for "a Archer" in para. (c)(4), effective 12/21/2000.

In 1998, P.L. 105-206, Sec. 6023(19)(A), substituted "exempt from the tax" for "exempt for the tax" in para. (c)(3) . . . Sec. 6023(19)(B), substituted "Secretary of the Treasury" for "Secretary of Treasury" in subsec. (i), effective 7/22/98.

In 1997, P.L. 105-34, Sec. 213(b)(1), deleted "or" at the end of subpara. (e)(1)(D), redesignated subpara. (e)(1)(E) as subpara. (e)(1)(F), and added new subpara. (e)(1)(E) . . . Sec. 213(b)(2), added para. (c)(5), effective for tax. yrs. begin. after 12/31/97.

—P.L. 105-34, Sec. 1074(a), substituted "15 percent" for "10 percent" in subsec. (a), effective for prohibited transactions occurring after 8/5/97. enactment.

—P.L. 105-34, Sec. 1506(b)(1)(A), added para. (f)(6) . . . Sec. 1506(b)(1)(B)(i), substituted "Except as provided in subsection (f)(6), the prohibitions" for "The prohibitions" in subsec. (d) . . . Sec. 1506(b)(1)(B)(ii), deleted "The exemptions provided by this subsection (other than paragraphs (9) and (12)) shall not apply to any transaction with respect to a trust described in section 401(a) which is part of a plan providing contributions or benefits for employees some or all of whom are owner-employees (as defined in section 401(c)(3)) in which a plan directly or indirectly lends any part of the corpus or income of the plan to, pays any compensation for personal services rendered to the plan to, or acquires for the plan any property from or sells any property to, any such owner-employee, a member of the family (as defined in section 267(c)(4)) of any such owner-employee, or a corporation controlled by any such owner-employee through the ownership, directly or indirectly, of 50 percent or more of the total combined voting power of all classes of stock entitled to vote or 50 percent or more of the total value of shares of all classes of stock of the corporation. For purposes of the preceding sentence, a shareholder-employee (as defined in section 1379, as in effect on the day before the date of the enactment of the Subchapter S Revision Act of 1982), a participant or beneficiary of an individual retirement account or an individual retirement annuity (as defined in section 408), and an employer or association of employees which establishes such an account or annuity under section 408(c) shall be deemed to be an owner-employee." in subsec. (d), effective for tax. yrs. begin. after 12/31/97.

—P.L. 105-34, Sec. 1530(c)(10), added "and section 664(g)" after "section 409(n)" in para. (e)(7), effective for transfers made by trusts to, or for the use of, an employee stock ownership plan after 8/5/97.

—P.L. 105-34, Sec. 1602(a)(5), substituted "if section 220(e)(2) applies to such transaction" for "if, with respect to such transaction, the account ceases to be a medical savings account by reason of the application of section 220(e)(2) to such account" in para. (c)(4), effective for tax. yrs. begin. after 12/31/96.

In 1996, P.L. 104-191, Sec. 301(f)(1), added para. (c)(4) . . . Sec. 301(f)(2), amended para. (e)(1), effective for tax. yrs. begin. after 12/31/96.

Prior to amendment, para. (e)(1) read as follows:

"(1) Plan. For purposes of this section, the term 'plan' means a trust described in section 401(a) which forms a part of a plan, or a plan described in section 403(a), which trust or plan is exempt from tax under section 501(a), an individual retirement account described in section 408(a) or an individual retirement annuity described in section 408(b) (or a trust, plan, account, or annuity, which, at any time, has been determined by the Secretary to be such a trust, plan, or account)."

—P.L. 104-188, Sec. 1453(a), substituted "10 percent" for "5 percent" in subsec. (a), effective for prohibited transactions occurring after 8/20/96.

—P.L. 104-188, Sec. 1702(g)(3), substituted "section 408(b)(12)" for "section 408(b)" in para. (d)(13), effective for plan yrs. begin. after 12/31/88.

In 1990, P.L. 101-508, Sec. 11701(m), added "or which is exempt from section 406 of such Act by reason of section 408(b) of such Act" before the semicolon at the end of para. (d)(13), effective for plan yrs. begin. after 12/31/88.

In 1986, P.L. 99-514, Sec. 1114(b)(15)(A), substituted "highly compensated employees (within the meaning of section 414(q))" for "highly compensated employees, officers, or shareholders" in subpara. (d)(1)(B), effective for yrs. begin. after 12/31/88.

—P.L. 99-514, Sec. 1854(f)(3)(A), added, ", section 409(o), and, if applicable, section 409(n)" after "section 409(h)" in para. (e)(7), effective for tax. yrs. begin. after 10/22/86.

—P.L. 99-514, Sec. 1899A(51), substituted "and (12)) shall not" for "and (12) shall not" in the second sentence of subsec. (d), effective for tax. yrs begin. after 10/22/86.

In 1984, P.L. 98-369, Sec. 491(d)(45), substituted "or an individual retirement annuity (as defined in section 408)" for ", individual retirement annuity, or an individual retirement bond (as defined in section 408 or 409)" in the last sentence of subsec. (d) . . . Sec. 491(d)(46)(A), deleted "or 405(a)" after "section 403(a)" in para. (e)(1) . . . Sec. 491(d)(46)(B), deleted "or a retirement bond, described in section 409" after "section 408(b)" in para. (e)(1) . . . Sec. 491(d)(46)(C), substituted "or annuity" for "annuity, or bond" in para. (e)(1) . . . Sec. 491(d)(46)(D), substituted "or account" for "account, or bond" in para. (e)(1), effective for obligations issued after 12/31/83.

—P.L. 98-369, Sec. 491(e)(7)(A), substituted "section 409(h)" for "section 409A(h)" in para. (e)(7) . . . Sec. 491(e)(7)(B), substituted "section 409(e)(4)" for "section 409A(e)(4)" in para. (e)(7) . . . Sec. 491(e)(7)(C), substituted "section 409(e)" for "section 409A(e)" in para. (e)(7) . . . Sec. 491(e)(8), substituted "section 409(1)" for "section 409A(1)" in para. (e)(8), effective 1/1/84.

In 1983, P.L. 97-448, Sec. 305(d)(5), substituted "section 1379, as in effect on the day before the date of the enactment of the Subchapter S Revision Act of 1982" for "section 1379" in subsec. (d), effective 10/19/82.

In 1980, P.L. 96-596, Sec. 2(a)(1)(K), substituted "taxable period" for "correction period" in subsec. (b) . . . Sec. 2(a)(1)(L), substituted "taxable period" for "correction period" in subpara. (f)(4)(B) . . . Sec. 2(a)(3)(F), deleted para. (f)(6), effective as provided in Sec. 2(d)(2) of this Act, which reads as follows:

"(2) Second tier taxes. The amendments made by this section with respect to any second tier tax shall apply only with respect to taxes assessed after the date of the enactment of this Act [12/24/80]. Nothing in the preceding sentence shall be construed to permit the assessment of a tax in a case to which, on the date of the enactment of this Act [12/24/80], the doctrine of res judicata applies."

Prior to amendment para. (f)(6) read as follows:

"(6) Correction period. The term 'correction period' means, with respect to a prohibited transaction, the period beginning with the date on which the prohibited transaction occurs and ending 90 days after the date of mailing of a notice of deficiency with respect to the tax imposed by subsection (b) under section 6212, extended by—

"(A) any period in which a deficiency cannot be assessed under section 6213(a), and

"(B) any other period which the Secretary determines is reasonable and necessary to bring about the correction of the prohibited transaction."

—P.L. 96-596, Sec. 2(a)(2)(I), amended para. (f)(2), effective 1/1/75.

Prior to amendment para. (f)(2) read as follows:

"(2) Taxable period. The term 'taxable period' means, with respect to any prohibited transaction, the period beginning with the date on which the prohibited transaction occurs and ending on the earlier of—

"(A) the date of mailing of a notice of deficiency pursuant to section 6212, with respect to the tax imposed by subsection (a), or

"(B) the date on which correction of the prohibited transaction is completed."

—P.L. 96-364, Sec. 208(b)(1), deleted "or" at the end of para. (d)(12) . . . Sec. 208(b)(2), substituted a semicolon for the period at the end of para. (d)(13) . . . Sec. 208(b)(3), added new paras. (d)(14) and (d)(15), effective 9/26/80.

—P.L. 96-364, Sec. 209(b), added para. (e)(9), effective for tax. yrs. ending after 9/26/80.

—P.L. 96-222, Sec. 101(a)(7)(B), amended subsec. (g) and added subsec. (h) to Sec. 141 of P.L. 95-600, the effective date for changes made by Sec. 141(f) of P.L. 95-600 [see below].

Prior to amendment, Sec. 141(g) of P.L. 95-600 read as follows:

"(g) Effective dates.

"(1) In general. The amendments made by this section (other than by subsection (f)(3)) shall apply with respect to qualified investment for taxable years beginning after December 31, 1978."

—P.L. 96-222, Sec. 101(a)(7)(C), amended the first sentence of para. (e)(8) . . . Sec. 101(a)(7)(K), amended the last sentence of para. (e)(7) . . . Sec. 101(a)(7)(L)(iv)(III), substituted "employee" for "leveraged employee" each place it appeared in para. (e)(7), other than in the paragraph heading . . . Sec. 101(a)(7)(L)(v)(XI), substituted "Employee" for "Leveraged employee" in the paragraph heading for para. (e)(7), presumably intended by Congress to be effective for stock acquired after 12/31/79 [Sec 101(b)(1)(C)] although technically effective with respect to the estates of decedents dying after 4/1/80 [Sec. 101(b)(1)(D)].

Prior to amendment, the first sentence of para. (e)(8) read as follows:

"The term 'qualifying employer security' means an employer security which is—

"(A) stock or otherwise an equity security, or

"(B) a bond, debenture, note, or certificate or other evidence of indebtedness which is described in paragraphs (1), (2), and (3) of section 503(e)."

Prior to amendment, the last sentence of para. (e)(7) read as follows:

"A plan shall not be treated as a leveraged employee stock ownership plan unless it meets the requirements of subsections (e) and (h) of section 409A."

In 1978, P.L. 95-600, Sec. 141(f)(5)(A), substituted "Leveraged employee" for "Employee" in the heading of para. (e)(7)...Sec. 141(f)(5)(B), substituted "leveraged employee" for "employee" in para. (e)(7)...Sec. 141(f)(5)(C), added the last sentence to para (e)(7)...Sec. 141(f)(6), substituted "leveraged employee" for "employee" in para. (d)(3), effective as provided in Sec. 141(h) of this Act [as added by Sec. 101(a)(7)(B) of P.L. 96-222, see above], which read as follows:

"(h) Effective dates for section 4975 employee stock ownership plans.

Paragraphs (5) and (6) of subsection (f) shall apply—

"(1) insofar as they make the requirements of subsections (e) and (h)(1)(B) of section 409A of the Internal Revenue Code of 1954 applicable to section 4975 of such Code, to stock acquired after December 31, 1979, and

"(2) insofar as they make paragraphs (1)(A) and (2) of section 409A(h) of such Code applicable to such section 4975, to distributions after December 31, 1978."

In 1976, P.L. 94-455, Sec. 1906(b)(13)(A), substituted "Secretary" for "Secretary or his delegate" each place it appeared in subsecs. (c), (e), (f) and (h), effective 2/1/77.

In 1974, P.L. 93-406, Sec. 2003(a), added Code Sec. 4975, effective 1/1/75. Sec. 2003(c) of the Employee Retirement Income Security Act of 1974 provides that:

"(c) Effective date and savings provisions.

"(1)(A) The amendments made by this section shall take effect on January 1, 1975.

"(B) If, before the amendments made by this section take effect, an organization described in section 401(a) of the Internal Revenue Code of 1954 is denied exemption under section 501(a) of such Code by reason of section 503 of such Code, the denial of such exemption shall not apply if the organization properly elects (in such manner and at such time as the Secretary or his delegate shall by regulations prescribe) to pay, with respect to the prohibited transaction (within the meaning of section 503(b) or (g)) which resulted in such denial of exemption, a tax in the amount and in the manner provided with respect to the tax imposed under section 4975 of such Code. An election made under this subparagraph, once made, shall be irrevocable. The Secretary of the Treasury or his delegate shall prescribe such regulations as may be necessary to carry out the purposes of this subparagraph.

"(2) Section 4975 of the Internal Revenue Code of 1954 (relating to tax on prohibited transactions) shall not apply to—

"(A) a loan of money or other extension of credit between a plan and a disqualified person under a binding contract in effect on July 1, 1974 (or pursuant to renewals of such a contract), until June 30, 1984, if such loan or other extension of credit remains at least as favorable to the plan as an arm's-length transaction with an unrelated party would be, and if the execution of the contract, the making of the loan, or the extension of credit was not, at the time of such execution, making, or extension, a prohibited transaction (within the meaning of section 503(b) of such Code or the corresponding provisions of prior law);

"(B) a lease or joint use of property involving the plan and a disqualified person pursuant to a binding contract in effect on July 1, 1974 (or pursuant to renewals of such a contract), until June 30, 1984, if such lease or joint use remains at least as favorable to the plan as an arm's-length transaction with an unrelated party would be and if the execution of the contract was not, at the time of such execution, a prohibited transaction (within the meaning of section 503(b) of such Code) or the corresponding provisions of prior law;

"(C) the sale, exchange, or other disposition of property described in subparagraph (B) between a plan and a disqualified person before June 30, 1984, if—

"(i) in the case of a sale, exchange, or other disposition of the property by the plan to the disqualified person, the plan receives an amount which is not less than the fair market value of the property at the time of such disposition; and

"(ii) in the case of the acquisition of the property by the plan, the plan pays an amount which is not in excess of the fair market value of the property at the time of such acquisition;

"(D) Until June 30, 1977, the provision of services to which subparagraphs (A), (B), and (C) do not apply between a plan and a disqualified person (i) under a binding contract in effect on July 1, 1974 (or pursuant to renewals of such contract), or (ii) if the disqualified person ordinarily and customarily furnished such services on June 30, 1974, if such provision of services remains at least as favorable to the plan as an arm's-length transaction with an unrelated party would be and if the provision of services was not, at the time of such provision, a prohibited transaction (within the meaning of section 503(b) of such Code) or the corresponding provisions of prior law; or

"(E) the sale, exchange, or other disposition of property which is owned by a plan on June 30, 1974, and all times thereafter, to a disqualified person, if such plan is required to dispose of such property in order to comply with the provisions of section 407(a)(2)(A) (relating to the prohibition against holding excess employer securities and employer real property) of the Employee Retirement Income Security Act of 1974, and if the plan receives not less than adequate consideration.

"For the purposes of this paragraph, the term 'disqualified person' has the meaning provided by section 4975(e)(2) of the Internal Revenue Code of 1954."

Sec. 4976. Taxes with respect to funded welfare benefit plans.

(a) General rule.

If—

(1) an employer maintains a welfare benefit fund, and

(2) there is a disqualified benefit provided during any taxable year,

there is hereby imposed on such employer a tax equal to 100 percent of such disqualified benefit.

(b) Disqualified benefit.

For purposes of subsection (a)

(1) In general. The term "disqualified benefit" means—

(A) any post-retirement medical benefit or life insurance benefit provided with respect to a key employee if a separate account is required to be established for such employee under section 419A(d) and such payment is not from such account,

(B) any post-retirement medical benefit or life insurance benefit provided with respect to an individual in whose favor discrimination is prohibited unless the plan meets the requirements of section 505(b) with respect to such benefit (whether or not such requirements apply to such plan), and

(C) any portion of a welfare benefit fund reverting to the benefit of the employer.

(2) Exception for collective bargaining plans. Paragraph (1)(B) shall not apply to any plan maintained pursuant to an agreement between employee representatives and 1 or more employers if the Secretary finds that such agreement is a collective bargaining agreement and that the benefits referred to in paragraph (1)(B) were the subject of good faith bargaining between such employee representatives and such employer or employers.

(3) Exception for nondeductible contributions. Paragraph (1)(C) shall not apply to any amount attributable to a contribution to the fund which is not allowable as a deduction under section 419 for the taxable year or any prior taxable year (and such contribution shall not be included in any carryover under section 419(d)).

(4) Exception for certain amounts charged against existing reserve. Subparagraphs (A) and (B) of paragraph (1) shall not apply to post-retirement benefits charged against an existing reserve for post-retirement medical or life insurance benefits (as defined in section 512(a)(3)(E)) or charged against the income on such reserve.

(c) Definitions.

For purposes of this section, the terms used in this section shall have the same respective meanings as when used in subpart D of part I of subchapter D of chapter 1.

In 1989, P.L. 101-140, Sec. 203(a)(2), repealed as if not enacted Sec. 1011B(a)(27)(A) of P.L. 100-647, which redesignated subsec. (c) as subsec. (d) and added new subsec. (c)...Sec. 203(a)(2), repealed as if not enacted 1011B(a)(27)(B) of P.L. 100-647, which added para. (b)(5).

In 1988, P.L. 100-647, Sec. 3021(a)(1)(C)(i), substituted "any testing year (as defined in section 89(j)(13))" for "any plan year" in para. (c)(1) [as added by Sec. 1011B(a)(27)(A) of P.L. 100-647, see above]...Sec. 3021(a)(1)(C)(ii), substituted "such testing year" for "such plan year" each place it appeared in subpara. (c)(2)(A), effective as provided in Sec. 1151(k)(1)-(3) of P.L. 99-514 reproduced in the notes following Code Sec. 89.

In 1986, P.L. 99-514, Sec. 1851(a)(11), amended subsec. (b), effective for benefits provided after 12/31/85, except as provided by Sec. 511(e)(2)-(5) of P.L. 98-369, reproduced in the note following Code Sec. 419.

Prior to amendment, subsec. (b) read as follows:

"(b) Disqualified benefit.

"For purposes of subsection (a), the term 'disqualified benefit' means—

"(1) any medical benefit or life insurance benefit provided with respect to a key employee other than from a separate account established for such owner under section 419A(d), and

"(2) any post-retirement medical or life insurance benefit unless the plan meets the requirements of section 505(b)(1) with respect to such benefit, and

"(3) any portion of such fund reverting to the benefit of the employer."

—P.L. 99-514, Sec. 1851(a)(12), added Sec. 511(e)(7) to P.L. 98-369, the effective date for changes made by Sec. 511(c) of P.L. 98-369, see below.

In 1984, P.L. 98-369, Sec. 511(c)(1), added Code Sec. 4976, effective for benefits provided after 12/31/85 [amended by Sec. 1851(a)(12) of P.L. 99-514, see above]. For special rules, see Sec. 511(e)(2)-(5) of this Act, reproduced in the note following Code Sec. 419.

Sec. 4977. Tax on certain fringe benefits provided by an employer.

(a) Imposition of tax.

In the case of an employer to whom an election under this section applies for any calendar year, there is hereby imposed a tax for such calendar year equal to 30 percent of the excess fringe benefits.

(b) Excess fringe benefits.

For purposes of subsection (a), the term "excess fringe benefits" means, with respect to any calendar year—

(1) the aggregate value of the fringe benefits provided by the employer during the calendar year which were not includible in gross income under paragraphs (1) and (2) of section 132(a), over

(2) 1 percent of the aggregate amount of compensation—

(A) which was paid by the employer during such calendar year to employees, and

(B) was includible in gross income for purposes of chapter 1.

(c) Effect of election on section 132(a).

If—

(1) an election under this section is in effect with respect to an employer for any calendar year, and

(2) at all times on or after January 1, 1984, and before the close of the calendar year involved, substantially all of the employees of the employer were entitled to employee discounts on goods or services provided by the employer in 1 line of business,

for purposes of paragraphs (1) and (2) of section 132(a) (but not for purposes of section 132(h)), all employees of any line of business of the employer which was in existence on January 1, 1984, shall be treated as employees of the line of business referred to in paragraph (2).

(d) Period of election.

An election under this section shall apply to the calendar year for which made and all subsequent calendar years unless revoked by the employer.

(e) Treatment of controlled groups.

All employees treated as employed by a single employer under subsection (b), (c), or (m) of section 414 shall be treated as employed by a single employer for purposes of this section.

(f) Section to apply only to employment within the United States.

Except as otherwise provided in regulations, this section shall apply only with respect to employment within the United States.

In **1996**, P.L. 104-188, Sec. 1704(t)(66), substituted "section 132(h)" for "section 132(i)(2)" in subsec. (c), effective 8/20/96.

In **1993**, P.L. 103-66, Sec. 13213(d)(3)(D), substituted "section 132(i)(2)" for "section 132(g)(2)" in subsec. (c), effective for reimbursements or other payments in respect of expenses incurred after 12/31/93.

In **1986**, P.L. 99-514, Sec. 1853(c)(1), amended para. (c)(2) . . . Sec. 1853(c)(2), added subsec. (f), effective after 12/31/84. Sec. 1853(c)(3) of this Act, provides as follows:

"(3) For purposes of determining whether the requirements of section 4977(c) of the Internal Revenue Code of 1954 are met in the case of an agricultural cooperative incorporated in 1964, there shall not be taken into account employees of a member of the same controlled group as such cooperative which became a member during July 1980."

Prior to amendment, para. (c)(2) read as follows:

"(2) as of January 1, 1984, substantially all of the employees of the employer were entitled to employee discounts or services provided by the employer in 1 line of business,"

In **1984**, P.L. 98-369, Sec. 531(e)(1), added Code Sec. 4977, effective after 12/31/84.

Sec. 4978. Tax on certain dispositions by employee stock ownership plans and certain cooperatives.

(a) Tax on dispositions of securities to which section 1042 applies before close of minimum holding period.

If, during the 3-year period after the date on which the employee stock ownership plan or eligible worker-owned cooperative acquired any qualified securities in a sale to which section 1042 applied or acquired any qualified employer securities in a qualified gratuitous transfer to which section 664(g) applied, such plan or cooperative disposes of any qualified securities and—

(1) the total number of shares held by such plan or cooperative after such disposition is less than the total number of employer securities held immediately after such sale, or

(2) except to the extent provided in regulations, the value of qualified securities held by such plan or cooperative after such disposition is less than 30 percent of the total value of all employer securities as of such disposition (60 percent of the total value of all employer securities as of such disposition in the case of any qualified employer securities acquired in a qualified gratuitous transfer to which section 664(g) applied),

there is hereby imposed a tax on the disposition equal to the amount determined under subsection (b).

(b) Amount of tax.

(1) **In general.** The amount of the tax imposed by subsection (a) shall be equal to 10 percent of the amount realized on the disposition.

(2) **Limitation.** The amount realized taken into account under paragraph (1) shall not exceed that portion allocable to qualified securities acquired in the sale to which section 1042 applied or acquired in the qualified gratuitous transfer to which section 664(g) applied determined as if such securities were disposed of—

(A) first from qualified securities to which section 1042 applied or to which section 664(g) applied acquired during the 3-year period ending on the date of the disposition, beginning with the securities first so acquired, and

(B) then from any other employer securities.

If subsection (d) applies to a disposition, the disposition shall be treated as made from employer securities in the opposite order of the preceding sentence.

(3) **Distributions to employees.** The amount realized on any distribution to an employee for less than fair market value shall be determined as if the qualified security had been sold to the employee at fair market value.

(c) Liability for payment of taxes.

The tax imposed by this subsection shall be paid by—

(1) the employer, or

(2) the eligible worker-owned cooperative,

that made the written statement described in section 664(g)(1)(E) or in section 1042(b)(3) (as the case may be).

(d) Section not to apply to certain dispositions.

(1) **Certain distributions to employees.** This section shall not apply with respect to any distribution of qualified securities (or sale of such securities) which is made by reason of—

(A) the death of the employee,

(B) the retirement of the employee after the employee has attained 59½ years of age,

(C) the disability of the employee (within the meaning of section 72(m)(7)), or

(D) the separation of the employee from service for any period which results in a 1-year break in service (within the meaning of section 411(a)(6)(A)).

Code Sec. 4978(d)(2) — Excise and miscellaneous taxes

(2) Certain reorganizations. In the case of any exchange of qualified securities in any reorganization described in section 368(a)(1) for stock of another corporation, such exchange shall not be treated as a disposition for purposes of this section.

(3) Liquidation of corporation into cooperative. In the case of any exchange of qualified securities pursuant to the liquidation of the corporation issuing qualified securities into the eligible worker-owned cooperative in a transaction which meets the requirements of section 332 (determined by substituting "100 percent" for "80 percent" each place it appears in section 332(b)(1)), such exchange shall not be treated as a disposition for purposes of this section.

(4) Dispositions to meet diversification requirements. This section shall not apply to any disposition of qualified securities which is required under section 401(a)(28).

(e) Definitions and special rules.

For purposes of this section—

(1) Employee stock ownership plan. The term "employee stock ownership plan" has the meaning given to such term by section 4975(e)(7).

(2) Qualified securities. The term "qualified securities" has the meaning given to such term by section 1042(c)(1); except that such section shall be applied without regard to subparagraph (B) thereof for purposes of applying this section and section 4979A with respect to securities acquired in a qualified gratuitous transfer (as defined in section 664(g)(1)).

(3) Eligible worker-owned cooperative. The term "eligible worker-owned cooperative" has the meaning given to such term by section 1042(c)(2).

(4) Disposition. The term "disposition" includes any distribution.

(5) Employer securities. The term "employer securities" has the meaning given to such term by section 409(l).

In 2004, P.L. 108-311, Sec. 408(a)(23), substituted "(60 percent" for "60 percent" in para. (a)(2), enacted 10/4/2004.

In 1997, P.L. 105-34, Sec. 1530(c)(11)(A), added "or acquired any qualified employer securities in a qualified gratuitous transfer to which section 664(g) applied" after "section 1042 applied" in subsec. (a)...Sec. 1530(c)(11)(B), added "60 percent of the total value of all employer securities as of such disposition in the case of any qualified employer securities acquired in a qualified gratuitous transfer to which section 664(g) applied" before the comma at the end of para. (a)(2)...Sec. 1530(c)(12)(A), added "or acquired in the qualified gratuitous transfer to which section 664(g) applied" after "section 1042 applied" in para. (b)(2)...Sec. 1530(c)(12)(B), added "or to which section 664(g) applied" after "section 1042 applied" in subpara. (b)(2)(A)...Sec. 1530(c)(13), substituted "written statement described in section 664(g)(1)(E) or in section 1042(b)(3) (as the case may be)," for "written statement described in section 1042(b)(3)." in subsec. (c)...Sec. 1530(c)(14), substituted "; except that such section shall be applied without regard to subparagraph (B) thereof for purposes of applying this section and section 4979A with respect to securities acquired in a qualified gratuitous transfer (as defined in section 664(g)(1))." for the period at the end of para. (e)(2), effective for transfers made by trusts to, or for the use of, an employee stock ownership plan after 8/5/97.

In 1996, P.L. 104-188, Sec. 1602(b)(4), deleted subpara. (b)(2)(A) and all that follows and replaced it with subparas. (b)(2)(A) and (B) and the flush sentence at the end of para. (b)(2), effective for loans made after 8/20/96. Secs. 1602(c)(2) and (3) of this Act provide:

"(2) Refinancings. The amendments made by this section shall not apply to loans made after the date of the enactment of this Act to refinance securities acquisition loans (determined without regard to section 133(b)(1)(B) of the Internal Revenue Code of 1986, as in effect on the day before the date of the enactment of this Act) made on or before such date or to refinance loans described in this paragraph if—

"(A) the refinancing loans meet the requirements of section 133 of such Code (as so in effect),

"(B) immediately after the refinancing the principal amount of the loan resulting from the refinancing does not exceed the principal amount of the refinanced loan (immediately before the refinancing), and

"(C) the term of such refinancing loan does not extend beyond the last day of the term of the original securities acquisition loan.

For purposes of this paragraph, the term 'securities acquisition loan' includes a loan from a corporation to an employee stock ownership plan described in section 133(b)(3) of such Code (as so in effect).

"(3) Exception. Any loan made pursuant to a binding written contract in effect before June 10, 1996, and at all times thereafter before such loan is made, shall be treated for purposes of paragraphs (1) and (2) as a loan made on or before the date of the enactment of this Act."

Prior to amendment, subpara. (b)(2)(A) and all that followed read as follows:

"(A) first, from section 133 securities (as defined in section 4978B(e)(2)) acquired during the 3-year period ending on the date of such disposition, beginning with the securities first so acquired.

"second, from section 133 securities (as so defined) acquired before such 3-year period unless such securities (or proceeds from the disposition) have been allocated to accounts of participants or beneficiaries,

"third, from qualified securities to which section 1042 applied acquired during the 3-year period ending on the date of the disposition, beginning with the securities first so acquired, and

"then from any other employer securities.

If subsection (d) or section 4978B(d) applies to a disposition, the disposition shall be treated as made from employer securities in the opposite order of the preceding sentence."

In 1989, P.L. 101-239, Sec. 7304(a)(2)(C)(ii), amended para. (b)(2), effective for the estates of decedents dying after 12/19/89.

Prior to amendment, para. (b)(2) read as follows:

"(2) Limitation. The amount realized taken into account under paragraph (1) shall not exceed that portion allocable to qualified securities acquired in the sale to which section 1042 applied (determined as if such securities were disposed of in the order described in section 4978A(e))."

In 1988, P.L. 100-647, Sec. 1011B(j)(4), added para. (d)(4), effective for stock acquired after 12/31/86.

In 1987, P.L. 100-203, Sec. 10413(b)(1), substituted "(determined as if such securities were disposed of in the order described in section 4978A(e))" for "(determined as if such securities were disposed of before any other securities)" in para. (b)(2), effective for taxable events (within the meaning of [subsec. (c)]) occurring after 2/26/87.

In 1986, P.L. 99-514, Sec. 1854(e)(1), substituted "than" for "then" in para. (a)(1)...Sec. 1854(e)(2), substituted "subsection (a)" for "paragraph (1)" in para. (b)(1)...Sec. 1854(e)(3), substituted "section 1042(b)(3)" for "section 1042(a)(2)(B)" in subsec. (c)...Sec. 1854(e)(4), substituted "section 72(m)(7)" for "section 72(m)(5)" in subpara. (d)(1)(C)...Sec. 1854(e)(5), substituted "section 1042(c)(1)" for "section '1042(b)(1)" in para. (e)(2)...Sec. 1854(e)(6), substituted 'section 1042(c)(2)' for 'section 1042(b)(1)' in para. (e)(3)...Sec. 1854(e)(7), added para. (d)(3), effective for tax. yrs. begin. after 7/18/84.

In 1984, P.L. 98-369, Sec. 545(a), added Code Sec. 4978, effective for tax. yrs. begin. after 7/18/84.

Sec. 4978A. Repealed.

In 1989, P.L. 101-239, Sec. 7304(a)(2)(C)(i), repealed Code Sec. 4978A, effective for estates of decedents dying after 12/19/89.

Prior to repeal, Code Sec. 4978A read as follows:

"SEC. 4978A. TAX ON CERTAIN DISPOSITIONS OF EMPLOYER SECURITIES TO WHICH SECTION 2057 APPLIED.

"(a) Imposition of tax.

"In the case of a taxable event involving qualified employer securities held by an employee stock ownership plan or eligible worker-owned cooperative, there is hereby imposed a tax equal to the amount determined under subsection (b).

"(b) Amount of tax.

"(1) In general. The amount of the tax imposed by subsection (a) shall be equal to 30 percent of—

"(A) the amount realized on the disposition in the case of a taxable event described in paragraph (1) or (2) of subsection (c), or

"(B) the amount repaid on the loan in the case of a taxable event described in paragraph (3) of subsection (c).

"(2) Dispositions other than sales or exchanges. For purposes of paragraph (1), in the case of a disposition of employer securities which is not a sale or exchange, the amount realized on such disposition shall be the fair market value of such employer securities at the time of disposition.

"(c) Taxable event.

"For purposes of this section, the term 'taxable event' means the following:

"(1) Disposition within 3 years of acquisition. Any disposition of employer securities by an employee stock ownership plan or eligible worker-owned cooperative within 3 years after such plan or cooperative acquired qualified employer securities.

"(2) Stocks disposed of before allocation. Any disposition of qualified employer securities to which paragraph (1) does not apply if—

"(A) such disposition occurs before such securities are allocated to accounts of participants or their beneficiaries, and

"(B) the proceeds from such disposition are not so allocated.

"(3) Use of assets to repay acquisition loans. The payment by an employee stock ownership plan of any portion of any loan used to acquire employer securities from transferred assets (within the meaning of section 2057(c)(2)(B)).

"(d) Ordering rules.

"For purposes of this section and section 4978, any disposition of employer securities shall be treated as having been made in the following order:

"(1) First, from qualified employer securities acquired during the 3-year period ending on the date of such disposition, beginning with the securities first so acquired.

"(2) Second, from qualified employer securities acquired before such 3-year period unless such securities (or the proceeds from such disposition) have been allocated to accounts of participants or their beneficiaries.

"(3) Third, from qualified securities (within the meaning of section 4978(e)(2)) to which section 1042 applied acquired during the 3-year period ending on the date of such disposition, beginning with the securities first so acquired.

"(4) Finally, from any other employer securities. In the case of a disposition to which section 4978(d) or subsection (e) applies, the disposition of employer securities shall be treated as having been made in the opposite order of the preceding sentence.

"(e) Section not to apply to certain dispositions.

"(1) In general. This section shall not apply to any disposition described in paragraph (1) or (3) of section 4978(d).

"(2) Certain reorganizations. For purposes of this section, any exchange of qualified employer securities for employer securities of another corporation in any reorganization described in section 368(a)(1) shall not be treated as a disposition, but the employer securities which were received shall be treated—

"(A) as qualified employer securities of the plan or cooperative, and

"(B) as having been held by the plan or cooperative during the period the qualified employer securities were held.

"(3) Disposition to meet diversification requirements. Any disposition which is made to meet the requirements of section 401(a)(28) shall not be treated as a disposition.

"(4) Forced disposition occurring by operation of a state law. Any forced disposition of qualified employer securities by the employee stock ownership plan of a corporation occurring by operation of a State law shall not be treated as a disposition. This paragraph shall only apply to securities which, at the time such securities were purchased by the employee stock ownership plan, were regularly traded on an established securities market.

"(f) Definitions and special rules.

"For purposes of this section—

"(1) Terms used in section 2057. Any term used in this section which is used in section 2057 shall have the meaning given such term by section 2057.

"(2) Qualified employer securities. The term 'qualified employer securities' has the meaning given such term by section 2057, except that such term shall include employer securities sold before February 27, 1987, for which a deduction was allowed under section 2057.

"(3) Disposition. The term 'disposition' includes any distribution.

"(4) Liability for payment of taxes. The tax imposed by this section shall be paid by—

"(A) the employer, or

"(B) the eligible worker-owned cooperative,

which made the written statement described in section 2057(e).''

In 1988, P.L. 100-647, Sec. 6060(a), added para. (e)(4), effective for tax. events (within the meaning of Code Sec. 4978A(c)) occurring after 2/26/87.

In 1987, P.L. 100-203, Sec. 10413(a), added new Code Sec. 4978A, effective for taxable events (within the meaning of Code Sec. 4978A(c)) occurring after 2/26/87.

Sec. 4978B.   Repealed.

In 1996, P.L. 104-188, Sec. 1602(b)(5)(A), repealed Code Sec. 4978B, effective for loans made after 8/20/96. Sec. 1609(c)(2) and (3), of this Act, provides:

"(2) Refinancings. The amendments made by this section shall not apply to loans made after the date of the enactment of this Act to refinance securities acquisition loans (determined without regard to section 133(b)(1)(B) of the Internal Revenue Code of 1986, as in effect on the day before the date of the enactment of this Act) made on or before such date or to refinance loans described in this paragraph if—

"(A) the refinancing loans meet the requirements of section 133 of such Code (as so in effect),

"(B) immediately after the refinancing the principal amount of the loan resulting from the refinancing does not exceed the principal amount of the refinanced loan (immediately before the refinancing), and

"(C) the term of such refinancing loan does not extend beyond the last day of the term of the original securities acquisition loan.

For purposes of this paragraph, the term 'securities acquisition loan' includes a loan from a corporation to an employee stock ownership plan described in section 133(b)(3) of such Code (as so in effect).

"(3) Exception. Any loan made pursuant to a binding written contract in effect before June 10, 1996, and at all times thereafter before such loan is made, shall be treated for purposes of paragraphs (1) and (2) as a loan made on or before the date of the enactment of this Act."

Prior to repeal, Code Sec. 4978B read as follows:

"Code Sec. 4978. Tax on disposition of employer securities to which section 133 applied.

"(a) Imposition of tax. In the case of an employee stock ownership plan which has acquired section 133 securities, there is hereby imposed a tax on each taxable event in an amount equal to the amount determined under subsection (b).

"(b) Amount of tax.

"(1) In general. The amount of the tax imposed by subsection (a) shall be equal to 10 percent of the amount realized on the disposition to the extent allocable to section 133 securities under section 4978(b)(2).

"(2) Dispositions other than sales or exchanges. For purposes of paragraph (1), in the case of a disposition of employer securities which is not a sale or exchange, the amount realized on such disposition shall be the fair market value of such securities at the time of disposition.

"(c) Taxable event. For purposes of this section, the term 'taxable event' means any of the following dispositions:

"(1) Dispositions within 3 years. Any disposition of any employer securities by an employee stock ownership plan within 3 years after such plan acquired section 133 securities if—

"(A) the total number of employer securities held by such plan after such disposition is less than the total number of employer securities held after such acquisition, or

"(B) except to the extent provided in regulations, the value of employer securities held by such plan after the disposition is 50 percent or less of the total value of all employer securities as of the time of the disposition.

For purposes of subparagraph (B), the aggregation rule of section 133(b)(6)(D) shall apply.

"(2) Stock disposed of before allocation. Any disposition of section 133 securities to which paragraph (1) does not apply if—

"(A) such disposition occurs before such securities are allocated to accounts of participants or their beneficiaries, and

"(B) the proceeds from such disposition are not so allocated.

"(d) Section not to apply to certain dispositions.

"(1) In general. This section shall not apply to any disposition described in paragraph (1), (3), or (4) of section 4978(d).

"(2) Certain reorganizations. For purposes of this section, any exchange of section 133 securities for employer securities of another corporation in any reorganization described in section 368(a)(1) shall not be treated as a disposition, but the employer securities received shall be treated as section 133 securities and as having been held by the plan during the period the securities which were exchanged were held.

"(3) Forced disposition occurring by operation of state law. Any forced disposition of section 133 securities by an employee stock ownership plan occurring by operation of a State law shall not be treated as a disposition. This paragraph shall only apply to securities which, at the time the securities were acquired by the plan, were regularly traded on an established securities market.

"(4) Coordination with other taxes. This section shall not apply to any disposition which is subject to tax under section 4978 or section 4978A (as in effect on the day before the date of enactment of this section).

"(e) Definitions and special rules. For purposes of this section—

"(1) Liability for payment of taxes. The tax imposed by this section shall be paid by the employer.

"(2) Section 133 securities. The term 'section 133 securities' means employer securities acquired by an employee stock ownership plan in a transaction to which section 133 applied.

"(3) Disposition. The term 'disposition' includes any distribution.

"(4) Ordering rules. For ordering rules for dispositions of employer securities, see section 4978(b)(2).''

In 1990, P.L. 101-508, Sec. 11701(e)(1), amended para. (e)(2) ... Sec. 11701(e)(2), added para. (d)(4), effective for loans made after 7/10/89, except as provided in Sec. 7301(f)(2)-(6) of P.L. 101-239, reproduced below.

Prior to amendment, para. (e)(2) read as follows:

"(2) Section 133 securities. The term 'section 133 securities' means employer securities acquired by an employee stock ownership plan in a transaction to which section 133 applied, except that such term shall not include—

"(A) qualified securities (as defined in section 4978(e)(2)), or

"(B) qualified employer securities (as defined in section 4978A(f)(2), as in effect on the day before the date of the enactment of this section).''

In 1989, P.L. 101-239, Sec. 7301(d)(1), added Code Sec. 4978B, effective for loans made after 7/10/89, except as provided by Sec. 7301(f)(2)-(6) of this Act which reads as follows:

"(2) Binding commitment exceptions.

"(A) The amendments made by this section shall not apply to any loan—

"(i) which is made pursuant to a binding written commitment in effect on June 6, 1989, and at all times thereafter before such loan is made, or

"(ii) to the extent that the proceeds of such loan are used to acquire employer securities pursuant to a written binding contract (or tender offer registered with the Securities and Exchange Commission) in effect on June 6, 1989, and at all times thereafter before such securities are acquired.

"(B) The amendments made by this section shall not apply to any loan to which subparagraph (A) does not apply which is made pursuant to a binding written commitment in effect on July 10, 1989, and at all times thereafter before such loan is made. The preceding sentence shall only apply to the extent that the proceeds of such loan are used to acquire employer securities pursuant to a written binding contract (or tender offer registered with the Securities and Exchange Commission) in effect on July 10, 1989, and at all times thereafter before such securities are acquired.

"(C) The amendments made by this section shall not apply to any loan made on or before July 10, 1992, pursuant to a written agreement entered into on or before July 10, 1989, if such agreement evidences the intent of the borrower on a periodic basis to enter into securities acquisition loans described in section 133(b)(1)(B) of the Internal Revenue Code of 1986 (as in effect on the day before the date of the enactment of this Act). The preceding sentence shall apply only if one or more securities acquisition loans were made to the borrower on or before July 10, 1989.

"(3) Refinancings.—the amendments made by this section shall not apply to loans made after July 10, 1989, to refinance securities acquisition loans (determined without regard to section 133(b)(2) of the Internal Revenue Code of 1986) made on or before such date or to refinance loans described in this paragraph or paragraph (2), (4), or (5) if—

"(A) such refinancing loans meet the requirements of such section 133 of such Code (as in effect before such amendments) applicable to such loans,

"(B) immediately after the refinancing the principal amount of the loan resulting from the refinancing does not exceed the principal amount of the refinanced loan (immediately before the refinancing), and

"(C) the term of such refinancing loan does not extend beyond the later of—

"(i) the last day of the term of the original securities acquisition loan, or

"(ii) the last day of the 7-year period beginning on the date the original securities acquisition loan was made.

For purposes of this paragraph, the term 'securities acquisition loan' shall include a loan from a corporation to an employee stock ownership plan described in section 133(b)(3) of such Code.

"(4) Collective bargaining agreements.— The amendments made by this section shall not apply to any loan for which such loan is used to acquire employer securities for an employee stock ownership plan pursuant to a collective bargaining agreement which sets forth the material terms of such employee stock ownership plan and which was agreed to on or before June 6, 1989, by one or more employers and employee representatives (and ratified on or before such date or within a reasonable period thereafter).

"(5) Filings with United States.— The amendments made by this section shall not apply to any loan the aggregate principal amount of which was specified in a filing with an agency of the United States on or before June 6, 1989, if—

"(A) such filing specifies such loan is to be a securities acquisition loan for purposes of section 133 of the Internal Revenue Code of 1986 and such filing is for the registration required to permit the offering of such loan, or

"(B) such filing is for the approval required in order for the employee stock ownership plan to acquire more than a certain percentage of the stock of the employer.

"(6) 30-percent test substituted for 50-percent test in case of certain loans.— In the case of a loan to which the amendments made by this section apply—

"(A) which is made before November 18, 1989, or

"(B) with respect to which such amendments would not apply if paragraph (2)(A) were applied by substituting 'November 17, 1989' for 'June 6, 1989' each place it appears,

section 133(b)(6)(A) of the Internal Revenue Code of 1986 (as added by subsection (a)) shall be applied by substituting 'at least 30 percent' for 'more than 50 percent' and section 4978B(c)(1)(B) of such Code (as added by subsection (d)) shall be applied by substituting 'less than 30 percent' for '50 percent or less'. The preceding sentence shall apply to any loan which is used to refinance a loan described in such sentence if the requirements of subparagraphs (A), (B), and (C) of paragraph (3) are met with respect to the refinancing loan."

Sec. 4979. Tax on certain excess contributions.
(a) General rule.

In the case of any plan, there is hereby imposed a tax for the taxable year equal to 10 percent of the sum of—

(1) any excess contributions under such plan for the plan year ending in such taxable year, and

(2) any excess aggregate contributions under the plan for the plan year ending in such taxable year.

(b) Liability for tax.

The tax imposed by subsection (a) shall be paid by the employer.

(c) Excess contributions.

For purposes of this section, the term "excess contributions" has the meaning given such term by sections 401(k)(8)(B), 408(k)(6)(C), and 501(c)(18).

(d) Excess aggregate contribution.

For purposes of this section, the term "excess aggregate contribution" has the meaning given to such term by section 401(m)(6)(B). For purposes of determining excess aggregate contributions under an annuity contract described in section 403(b), such contract shall be treated as a plan described in subsection (e)(1).

(e) Plan.

For purposes of this section, the term "plan" means—

(1) a plan described in section 401(a) which includes a trust exempt from tax under section 501(a),

(2) any annuity plan described in section 403(a),

(3) any annuity contract described in section 403(b),

(4) a simplified employee pension of an employer which satisfies the requirements of section 408(k), and

(5) a plan described in section 501(c)(18).

Such term includes any plan which, at any time, has been determined by the Secretary to be such a plan.

(f) No tax where excess distributed within specified period after close of year.

(1) **In general.** No tax shall be imposed under this section on any excess contribution or excess aggregate contribution, as the case may be, to the extent such contribution (together with any income allocable thereto through the end of the plan year for which the contribution was made) is distributed (or, if forfeitable, is forfeited) before the close of the first 2½ months (6 months in the case of an excess contribution or excess aggregate contribution to an eligible automatic contribution arrangement (as defined in section 414(w)(3))) of the following plan year.

(2) **Year of inclusion.** Any amount distributed as provided in paragraph (1) shall be treaed as earned and received by the recipient in the recipient's taxable year in which such distributions were made.

In **2006,** P.L. 109-280, Sec. 902(e)(1)(A), added "(6 months in the case of an excess contribution or excess aggregate contribution to an eligible automatic contribution arrangement (as defined in section 414(w)(3)))" after "2 ½ months" in para. (f)(1) ... Sec. 902(e)(1)(B), substituted "specified period after" for "2 ½ months of" in the heading of subsec. (f) ... Sec. 902(e)(2), amended para. (f)(2) ... Sec. 902(e)(3)(A), added "through the end of the plan year for which the contribution was made" after "thereto" in para. (f)(1), effective for plan yrs. begin. after 12/31/2007.

Prior to amendment, para. (f)(2) read as follows:

"(2) Year of inclusion.

"(A) In general. Except as provided in subparagraph (B), any amount distributed as provided in paragraph (1) shall be treated as received and earned by the recipient in his taxable year for which such contribution was made.

"(B) De minimis distributions. If the total excess contributions and excess aggregate contributions distributed to a recipient under a plan for any plan year are less than $100, such distributions (and any income allocable thereto) shall be treated as earned and received by the recipient in his taxable year in which such distributions were made."

In **1988,** P.L. 100-647, Sec. 1011(1)(8), deleted "a cash or deferred arrangement which is part of" which followed "contributions under" in para. (a)(1) ... Sec. 1011(1)(9)(A), (B), deleted "403(b)" after "401(k)(8)(B)", and substituted "408(k)(6)(C)" for "408(k)(6)(B)" in subsec. (c) ... Sec. 1011(1)(10), added the last sentence to subsec. (d) ... Sec. 1011(1)(11), amended para. (f)(2), effective for tax. yrs. begin. after 12/31/86. For special rules for collective bargaining agreements, see Secs. 1117(d)(2) and (d)(3) of P.L. 99-514 reproduced in the note following Code Sec. 401.

Prior to amendment para. (f)(2) read as follows:

"(2) Included in prior year. Any amount distributed as provided in paragraph (1) shall be treated as received and earned by the recipient in his taxable year for which such contributions was made."

In **1986,** P.L. 99-514, Sec. 1117(b)(1), added Code Sec. 4979, effective for tax. yrs. begin. after 12/31/86. For special rules for collective bargaining agreements, see Sec. 1117(d)(2) and (d)(3) of this Act, reproduced in the note following Code Sec. 401.

Sec. 4979A. Tax on certain prohibited allocations of qualified securities.
(a) Imposition of tax.

If—

(1) there is a prohibited allocation of qualified securities by any employee stock ownership plan or eligible worker-owned cooperative,

(2) there is an allocation described in section 664(g)(5)(A),

(3) there is any allocation of employer securities which violates the provisions of section 409(p), or a nonallocation year described in subsection (e)(2)(C) with respect to an employee stock ownership plan, or

(4) any synthetic equity is owned by a disqualified person in any nonallocation year,

there is hereby imposed a tax on such allocation or ownership equal to 50 percent of the amount involved.

(b) Prohibited allocation.

For purposes of this section, the term "prohibited allocation" means—

Excise and miscellaneous taxes   Code Sec. 4980(b)

(1) any allocation of qualified securities acquired in a sale to which section 1042 applies which violates the provisions of section 409(n), and

(2) any benefit which accrues to any person in violation of the provisions of section 409(n).

(c) Liability for tax.

The tax imposed by this section shall be paid—

(1) in the case of an allocation referred to in paragraph (1) or (2) of subsection (a), by—

(A) the employer sponsoring such plan, or

(B) the eligible worker-owned cooperative,

which made the written statement described in section 664(g)(1)(E) or in section 1042(b)(3)(B) (as the case may be), and

(2) in the case of an allocation or ownership referred to in paragraph (3) or (4) of subsection (a), by the S corporation the stock in which was so allocated or owned.

(d) Special statute of limitations for tax attributable to certain allocations.

The statutory period for the assessment of any tax imposed by this section on an allocation described in subsection (a)(2) of qualified employer securities shall not expire before the date which is 3 years from the later of—

(1) the 1st allocation of such securities in connection with a qualified gratuitous transfer (as defined in section 664(g)(1)), or

(2) the date on which the Secretary is notified of the allocation described in subsection (a)(2).

(e) Definitions and special rules.

For purposes of this section—

(1) **Definitions.** Except as provided in paragraph (2), terms used in this section have the same respective meanings as when used in sections 409 and 4978.

(2) **Special rules relating to tax imposed by reason of paragraph (3) or (4) of subsection (a).**

(A) Prohibited allocations. The amount involved with respect to any tax imposed by reason of subsection (a)(3) is the amount allocated to the account of any person in violation of section 409(p)(1).

(B) Synthetic equity. The amount involved with respect to any tax imposed by reason of subsection (a)(4) is the value of the shares on which the synthetic equity is based.

(C) Special rule during first nonallocation year. For purposes of subparagraph (A), the amount involved for the first nonallocation year of any employee stock ownership plan shall be determined by taking into account the total value of all the deemed-owned shares of all disqualified persons with respect to such plan.

(D) Statute of limitations. The statutory period for the assessment of any tax imposed by this section by reason of paragraph (3) or (4) of subsection (a) shall not expire before the date which is 3 years from the later of—

(i) the allocation or ownership referred to in such paragraph giving rise to such tax, or

(ii) the date on which the Secretary is notified of such allocation or ownership.

In 2010, P.L. 111-312, Sec. 101(a)(1), substituted "December 31, 2012" for "December 31, 2010" both places it appeared in Sec. 901 of P.L. 107-16, [see below] effective as if included in the enactment of P.L. 107-16, EGTRRA, 6/7/2001.

In 2006, P.L. 109-280, Sec. 811, of this Act [relating to Sec. 901 of P.L. 107-16, see below], provides:

"SEC. 811. PENSIONS AND INDIVIDUAL RETIREMENT ARRANGEMENT PROVISIONS OF ECONOMIC GROWTH AND TAX RELIEF RECONCILIATION ACT OF 2001 MADE PERMANENT.

"Title IX of the Economic Growth and Tax Relief Reconciliation Act of 2001 shall not apply to the provisions of, and amendments made by, subtitles A through F of title VI of such Act (relating to pension and individual retirement arrangement provisions)."

In 2002, P.L. 107-358, Sec. 2, added subsec. (c) in Sec. 901 of P.L. 107-16 [see below], effective 12/17/2002.

In 2001, P.L. 107-16, Sec. 656(c)(1)(A), deleted "or" at the end of para. (a)(1) . . . Sec. 656(c)(1)(B), deleted "there is hereby imposed a tax on such allocation equal to 50 percent of the amount involved." at the end of para. (a)(2), and added paras. (a)(3) and (4) . . . Sec. 656(c)(2), amended subsec. (c) . . . Sec. 656(c)(3), amended subsec. (e), effective for plan yrs. begin. after 12/31/2004. Sec. 656(d)(2) of this Act, provides:

"(2) Exception for certain plans. In the case of any—

"(A) employee stock ownership plan established after March 14, 2001, or

"(B) employee stock ownership plan established on or before such date if employer securities held by the plan consist of stock in a corporation with respect to which an election under section 1362(a) of the Internal Revenue Code of 1986 is not in effect on such date,

the amendments made by this section shall apply to plan years ending after March 14, 2001."

Prior to amendment, subsec. (c) read as follows:

"(c) Liability for tax. The tax imposed by this section shall be paid by—

"(1) the employer sponsoring such plan, or

"(2) the eligible worker-owned cooperative,

which made the written statement described in section 664(g)(1)(E) or in section 1042(b)(3)(B) (as the case may be)."

Prior to amendment, subsec. (e) read as follows:

"(e) Definitions. Terms used in this section have the same respective meaning as when used in section 4978."

—P.L. 107-16, Sec. 901, of this Act [as amended by Sec. 2 of P.L. 107-358, and Sec. 101(a)(1) of P.L. 111-312, see above], reads as follows:

"SEC. 901. SUNSET OF PROVISIONS OF ACT.

"(a) In general. All provisions of, and amendments made by, this Act shall not apply—

"(1) to taxable, plan, or limitation years beginning after December 31, 2012, or

"(2) in the case of title V, to estates of decedents dying, gifts made, or generation skipping transfers, after December 31, 2012.

"(b) Application of certain laws. The Internal Revenue Code of 1986 and the Employee Retirement Income Security Act of 1974 shall be applied and administered to years, estates, gifts, and transfers described in subsection (a) as if the provisions and amendments described in subsection (a) had never been enacted.

"(c) Exception. Subsection (a) shall not apply to section 803 (relating to no federal income tax on restitution received by victims of the Nazi regime or their heirs or estates)."

In 1997, P.L. 105-34, Sec. 1530(c)(15), amended subsec. (a) . . . Sec. 1530(c)(16), amended subsec. (c) . . . Sec. 1530(c)(17), redesignated subsec. (d) as (e) and added a new subsec. (d), effective for transfers made by trusts to, or for the use of, an employee stock ownership plan after 8/5/97.

Prior to amendment, subsec. (a) read as follows:

"(a) Imposition of tax.

"If there is a prohibited allocation of qualified securities by any employee stock ownership plan or eligible worker-owned cooperative, there is hereby imposed a tax on such allocation equal to 50 percent of the amount involved."

Prior to amendment, subsec. (c) read as follows:

"(c) Liability for tax.

"The tax imposed by this section shall be paid by—

"(1) the employer sponsoring such plan, or

"(2) the eligible worker-owned cooperative, which made the written statement described in section 1042(b)(3)(B)."

In 1996, P.L. 104-188, Sec. 1704(t)(22), amended Sec. 7304(a)(2)(D)(ii), P.L. 101-239, by substituting "subsection (c)" for "subsection (c)(2)", see below.

In 1989, P.L. 101-239, Sec. 7304(a)(2)(D)(i), deleted "or section 2057" after "section 1042" in para. (b)(1) . . . Sec. 7304(a)(2)(D)(ii), [as amended by Sec. 1704(t)(22) of P.L. 104-188, see above] deleted "or section 2057(d)" after "section 1042(b)(3)(B)" in subsec. (c), effective for the estates of decedents dying after 12/19/89.

In 1986, P.L. 99-514, Sec. 1172(b)(2)(A), added "or section 2057" after "section 1042" in para. (b)(1) [as added by Sec. 1854(a)(9)(A) of this Act, see below], . . . Sec. 1172(b)(2)(B), added "or section 2057(d)" after "section 1042(b)(3)(B)" in para. (c)(2) [as added by Sec. 1854(a)(9)(A) of this Act, see below], effective for sales after 10/22/86 for which an election is made by the executor of an estate who is required to file the return of the tax imposed by the Internal Revenue Code of 1986 on a date after 10/22/86.

—P.L. 99-514, Sec. 1854(a)(9)(A), added Code Sec. 4979A, effective for sales of securities after 10/22/86.

Sec. 4980. Tax on reversion of qualified plan assets to employer.

(a) Imposition of tax.

There is hereby imposed a tax of 20 percent of the amount of any employer reversion from a qualified plan.

(b) Liability for tax.

The tax imposed by subsection (a) shall be paid by the employer maintaining the plan.

3,345

(c) Definitions and special rules.
For purposes of this section—
(1) Qualified plan. The term "qualified plan" means any plan meeting the requirements of section 401(a) or 403(a), other than—
(A) a plan maintained by an employer if such employer has, at all times, been exempt from tax under subtitle A, or
(B) a governmental plan (within the meaning of section 414(d)).

Such term shall include any plan which, at any time, has been determined by the Secretary to be a qualified plan.

(2) Employer reversion.
(A) In general. The term "employer reversion" means the amount of cash and the fair market value of other property received (directly or indirectly) by an employer from the qualified plan.
(B) Exceptions. The term "employer reversion" shall not include—
(i) except as provided in regulations, any amount distributed to or on behalf of any employee (or his beneficiaries) if such amount could have been so distributed before termination of such plan without violating any provision of section 401,
(ii) any distribution to the employer which is allowable under section 401(a)(2)—
(I) in the case of a multiemployer plan, by reason of mistakes of law or fact or the return of any withdrawal liability payment,
(II) in the case of a plan other than a multiemployer plan, by reason of mistake of fact, or
(III) in the case of any plan, by reason of the failure of the plan to initially qualify or the failure of contributions to be deductible, or
(iii) any transfer described in section 420(f)(2)(B)(ii)(II).

(3) Exception for employee stock ownership plans.
(A) In general. If, upon an employer reversion from a qualified plan, any applicable amount is transferred from such plan to an employee stock ownership plan described in section 4975(e)(7) or a tax credit employee stock ownership plan (as described in section 409), such amount shall not be treated as an employer reversion for purposes of this section (or includible in the gross income of the employer) if the requirements of subparagraphs (B), (C), and (D) are met.
(B) Investment in employer securities. The requirements of this subparagraph are met if, within 90 days after the transfer (or such longer period as the Secretary may prescribe), the amount transferred is invested in employer securities (as defined in section 409(l)) or used to repay loans used to purchase such securities.
(C) Allocation requirements. The requirements of this subparagraph are met if the portion of the amount transferred which is not allocated under the plan to accounts of participants in the plan year in which the transfer occurs—
(i) is credited to a suspense account and allocated from such account to accounts of participants no less rapidly than ratably over a period not to exceed 7 years, and
(ii) when allocated to accounts of participants under the plan, is treated as an employer contribution for purposes of section 415(c), except that—
(I) the annual addition (as determined under section 415(c)) attributable to each such allocation shall not exceed the value of such securities as of the time such securities were credited to such suspense account, and
(II) no additional employer contributions shall be permitted to an employee stock ownership plan described in subparagraph (A) of the employer before the allocation of such amount.

The amount allocated in the year of transfer shall not be less than the lesser of the maximum amount allowable under section 415 or ⅛ of the amount attributable to the securities acquired. In the case of dividends on securities held in the suspense account, the requirements of this subparagraph are met only if the dividends are allocated to accounts of participants or paid to participants in proportion to their accounts, or used to repay loans used to purchase employer securities.

(D) Participants. The requirements of this subparagraph are met if at least half of the participants in the qualified plan are participants in the employee stock ownership plan (as of the close of the 1st plan year for which an allocation of the securities is required).
(E) Applicable amount. For purposes of this paragraph, the term "applicable amount" means any amount which—
(i) is transferred after March 31, 1985, and before January 1, 1989, or
(ii) is transferred after December 31, 1988, pursuant to a termination which occurs after March 31, 1985, and before January 1, 1989.
(F) No credit or deduction allowed. No credit or deduction shall be allowed under chapter 1 for any amount transferred to an employee stock ownership plan in a transfer to which this paragraph applies.
(G) Amount transferred to include income thereon, etc. The amount transferred shall not be treated as meeting the requirements of subparagraphs (B) and (C) unless amounts attributable to such amount also meet such requirements.

(4) Time for payment of tax. For purposes of subtitle F, the time for payment of the tax imposed by subsection (a) shall be the last day of the month following the month in which the employer reversion occurs.

(d) Increase in tax for failure to establish replacement plan or increase benefits.
(1) In general. Subsection (a) shall be applied by substituting "50 percent" for "20 percent" with respect to any employer reversion from a qualified plan unless
(A) the employer establishes or maintains a qualified replacement plan, or
(B) the plan provides benefit increases meeting the requirements of paragraph (3).

(2) Qualified replacement plan. For purposes of this subsection, the term "qualified replacement plan" means a qualified plan established or maintained by the employer in connection with a qualified plan termination (hereinafter referred to as the "replacement plan") with respect to which the following requirements are met:
(A) Participation requirement. At least 95 percent of the active participants in the terminated plan who remain as employees of the employer after the termination are active participants in the replacement plan.
(B) Asset transfer requirement.
(i) 25 percent cushion. A direct transfer from the terminated plan to the replacement plan is made before any employer reversion, and the transfer is in an amount equal to the excess (if any) of

Excise and miscellaneous taxes

Code Sec. 4980(d)(5)(A)(iv)

(I) 25 percent of the maximum amount which the employer could receive as an employer reversion without regard to this subsection, over

(II) the amount determined under clause (ii).

(ii) Reduction for increase in benefits. The amount determined under this clause is an amount equal to the present value of the aggregate increases in the accrued benefits under the terminated plan of any participants or beneficiaries pursuant to a plan amendment which

(I) is adopted during the 60-day period ending on the date of termination of the qualified plan, and

(II) takes effect immediately on the termination date.

(iii) Treatment of amount transferred. In the case of the transfer of any amount under clause (i)—

(I) such amount shall not be includible in the gross income of the employer,

(II) no deduction shall be allowable with respect to such transfer, and

(III) such transfer shall not be treated as an employer reversion for purposes of this section.

(C) Allocation requirements.

(i) In general. In the case of any defined contribution plan, the portion of the amount transferred to the replacement plan under subparagraph (B)(i) is—

(I) allocated under the plan to the accounts of participants in the plan year in which the transfer occurs, or

(II) credited to a suspense account and allocated from such account to accounts of participants no less rapidly than ratably over the 7-plan-year period beginning with the year of the transfer.

(ii) Coordination with section 415 limitation. If, by reason of any limitation under section 415, any amount credited to a suspense account under clause (i)(II) may not be allocated to a participant before the close of the 7-year period under such clause—

(I) such amount shall be allocated to the accounts of other participants, and

(II) if any portion of such amount may not be allocated to other participants by reason of any such limitation, shall be allocated to the participant as provided in section 415.

(iii) Treatment of income. Any income on any amount credited to a suspense account under clause (i)(II) shall be allocated to accounts of participants no less rapidly than ratably over the remainder of the period determined under such clause (after application of clause (ii)).

(iv) Unallocated amounts at termination. If any amount credited to a suspense account under clause (i)(II) is not allocated as of the termination date of the replacement plan—

(I) such amount shall be allocated to the accounts of participants as of such date, except that any amount which may not be allocated by reason of any limitation under section 415 shall be allocated to the accounts of other participants, and

(II) if any portion of such amount may not be allocated to other participants under subclause (I) by reason of such limitation, such portion shall be treated as an employer reversion to which this section applies.

(3) Pro rata benefit increases.

(A) In general. The requirements of this paragraph are met if a plan amendment to the terminated plan is adopted in connection with the termination of the plan which provides pro rata increases in the accrued benefits of all qualified participants which—

(i) have an aggregate present value not less than 20 percent of the maximum amount which the employer could receive as an employer reversion without regard to this subsection, and

(ii) take effect immediately on the termination date.

(B) Pro rata increase. For purposes of subparagraph (A), a pro rata increase is an increase in the present value of the accrued benefit of each qualified participant in an amount which bears the same ratio to the aggregate amount determined under subparagraph (A)(i) as—

(i) the present value of such participant's accrued benefit (determined without regard to this subsection), bears to

(ii) the aggregate present value of accrued benefits of the terminated plan (as so determined).

Notwithstanding the preceding sentence, the aggregate increases in the present value of the accrued benefits of qualified participants who are not active participants shall not exceed 40 percent of the aggregate amount determined under subparagraph (A)(i) by substituting "equal to" for "not less than".

(4) Coordination with other provisions.

(A) Limitations. A benefit may not be increased under paragraph (2)(B)(ii) or (3)(A), and an amount may not be allocated to a participant under paragraph (2)(C), if such increase or allocation would result in a failure to meet any requirement under section 401(a)(4) or 415.

(B) Treatment as employer contributions. Any increase in benefits under paragraph (2)(B)(ii) or (3)(A), or any allocation of any amount (or income allocable thereto) to any account under paragraph (2)(C), shall be treated as an annual benefit or annual addition for purposes of section 415.

(C) 10-year participation requirement. Except as provided by the Secretary, section 415(b)(5)(D) shall not apply to any increase in benefits by reason of this subsection to the extent that the application of this subparagraph does not discriminate in favor of highly compensated employees (as defined in section 414(q)).

(5) Definitions and special rules. For purposes of this subsection

(A) Qualified participant. The term "qualified participant" means an individual who

(i) is an active participant,

(ii) is a participant or beneficiary in pay status as of the termination date,

(iii) is a participant not described in clause (i) or (ii)—

(I) who has a nonforfeitable right to an accrued benefit under the terminated plan as of the termination date, and

(II) whose service, which was creditable under the terminated plan, terminated during the period beginning 3 years before the termination date and ending with the date on which the final distribution of assets occurs, or

(iv) is a beneficiary of a participant described in clause (iii)(II) and has a nonforfeitable right to an ac-

3,347

Code Sec. 4980(d)(5)(A)(iv) — Excise and miscellaneous taxes

crued benefit under the terminated plan as of the termination date.

(B) Present value. Present value shall be determined as of the termination date and on the same basis as liabilities of the plan are determined on termination.

(C) Reallocation of increase. Except as provided in paragraph (2)(C), if any benefit increase is reduced by reason of the last sentence of paragraph (3)(A)(ii) or paragraph (4), the amount of such reduction shall be allocated to the remaining participants on the same basis as other increases (and shall be treated as meeting any allocation requirement of this subsection).

(D) Plans taken into account. For purposes of determining whether there is a qualified replacement plan under paragraph (2), the Secretary may provide that—

(i) 2 or more plans may be treated as 1 plan, or

(ii) a plan of a successor employer may be taken into account.

(E) Special rule for participation requirement. For purposes of paragraph (2)(A), all employers treated as 1 employer under section 414(b), (c), (m), or (o) shall be treated as 1 employer.

(6) Subsection not to apply to employer in bankruptcy. This subsection shall not apply to an employer who, as of the termination date of the qualified plan, is in bankruptcy liquidation under chapter 7 of title 11 of the United States Code or in similar proceedings under State law.

In 2008, P.L. 110-458, Sec. 108(i)(3), deleted "or" at the end of clause (c)(2)(B)(i), substituted ", or" for the period in (c)(2)(B)(ii) and added clause (c)(2)(B)(iii), effective for transfers after 8/17/2006.

In 2006, P.L. 109-280, Sec. 901(a)(2)(C), substituted "if the requirements of subparagraphs (B), (C), and (D) are met." for "if— (i) the requirements of subparagraphs (B), (C), and (D) are met, and (ii) under the plan, employer securities to which subparagraph (B) applies must, except to the extent necessary to meet the requirements of section 401(a)(28), remain in the plan until distribution to participants in accordance with the provisions of such plan." in subpara. (c)(3)(A), effective for plan yrs. begin. after 12/31/2006. Sec. 901(c)(2) and (3) of this Act provides:

"(2) Special rule for collectively bargained agreements. In the case of a plan maintained pursuant to 1 or more collective bargaining agreements between employee representatives and 1 or more employers ratified on or before the date of the enactment of this Act, paragraph (1) shall be applied to benefits pursuant to, and individuals covered by, any such agreement by substituting for 'December 31, 2006' the earlier of—

"(A) the later of—

"(i) December 31, 2007, or

"(ii) the date on which the last of such collective bargaining agreements terminates (determined without regard to any extension thereof after such date of enactment), or

"(B) December 31, 2008.

"(3) Special rule for certain employer securities held in an ESOP.

'In general. In the case of employer securities to which this paragraph applies, the amendments made by this section shall apply to plan years beginning after the earlier of—

"(i) December 31, 2007, or

"(ii) the first date on which the fair market value of such securities exceeds the guaranteed minimum value described in subparagraph (B)(ii).

"(B) Applicable securities. This paragraph shall apply to employer securities which are attributable to employer contributions other than elective deferrals, and which, on September 17, 2003—

"(i) consist of preferred stock, and

"(ii) are within an employee stock ownership plan (as defined in section 4975(e)(7) of the Internal Revenue Code of 1986), the terms of which provide that the value of the securities cannot be less than the guaranteed minimum value specified by the plan on such date.

"(C) Coordination with transition rule. In applying section 401(a)(35)(H) of the Internal Revenue Code of 1986 and section 204(j)(7) of the Employee Retirement Income Security Act of 1974 (as added by this section) to employer securities to which this paragraph applies, the applicable percentage shall be determined without regard to this paragraph. "

In 1990, P.L. 101-508, Sec. 12001, substituted "20 percent" for "15 percent" in subsec. (a) . . . Sec. 12002(a), added subsec. (d), effective for reversions occurring after 9/30/90, except as provided in Sec. 12003(b) of this Act, which reads as follows:

"(b) Exception.

"The amendments made by this subtitle shall not apply to any reversion after September 30, 1990, if—

"(1) in the case of plans subject to title IV of the Employee Retirement Income Security Act of 1974, a notice of intent to terminate under such title was provided to participants (or if no participants, to the Pension Benefit Guaranty Corporation) before October 1, 1990,

"(2) in the case of plans subject to title I (and not to title IV) of such Act, a notice of intent to reduce future accruals under section 204(h) of such Act was provided to participants in connection with the termination before October 1, 1990,

"(3) in the case of plans not subject to title I or IV of such Act, a request for a determination letter with respect to the termination was filed with the Secretary of the Treasury or the Secretary's delegate before October 1, 1990, or

"(4) in the case of plans not subject to title I or IV of such Act and having only 1 participant, a resolution terminating the plan was adopted by the employer before October 1, 1990."

In 1989, P.L. 101-239, Sec. 7861(b), provides the following amendment related to Sec. 1132 of P.L. 99-514 [reproduced below]:

"(b) Amendment related to section 1132 of the Act [Sec. 1132(c)(2) of P.L. 99-514, reproduced below]. —

"(1) Notwithstanding any other provision of law, in the case of any qualified pension plan and welfare benefit plan described in paragraph (2), the assets of such pension plan in excess of its liabilities may be transferred to such welfare benefit plan upon the termination of such pension plan if such assets are to be used to provide retiree health benefits.

"(2) For purposes of paragraph (1), a qualified pension plan and welfare benefit plan are described in this paragraph if—

"(A) both such plans are jointly administered pursuant to a collective bargaining agreement between the employer maintaining such plans and one or more employee representatives,

"(B) the welfare benefit plan provides retiree health benefits, and

"(C) the qualified pension plan has assets in excess of liabilities (determined on a termination basis) and the welfare benefit plan has assets which are less than the present value of the benefits to be provided under the plan (determined as of the time of termination of the pension plan).

"(3) For purposes of the Internal Revenue Code of 1986, any transfer of assets to which paragraph (1) applies shall be treated as a reversion of such assets to the employer maintaining the plan which is includible in the gross income of such employer and subject to the tax imposed by section 4980 of such Code."

In 1988, P.L. 100-647, Sec. 1011(h)(6), amended Sec. 1112(e)(3)(A)(iii) of P.L. 99-514 [reproduced below] by substituting "the plan" for "a plan or merger" . . . Sec. 1011(h)(8), deleted Sec. 1112(e)(3)(C) of P.L. 99-514 and added Sec. 1112(e)(4) of P.L. 99-514, reproduced below . . . Sec. 1011(h)(9), amended Sec. 1112(e)(3)(B) of P.L. 99-514, reproduced below.

Prior to deletion Sec. 1112(e)(3)(C) of P.L. 99-514 read as follows:

"(C) Special rule for plans which may not terminate. — To the extent provided in regulations prescribed by the Secretary of the Treasury or his delegate, if a plan is prohibited from terminating under title IV of the Employee Retirement Income Security Act of 1974 before the 1st year to which the amendment made by subsection (b) applies, subparagraph (A) shall be applied by substituting 'the 1st year in which the plan is able to terminate' for 'the 1st year to which the amendment made by subsection (b) applies'."

Prior to amendment, Sec. 1112(e)(3)(B) of P.L. 99-514 read as follows:

"(B) Determination of amount of revision. — For purposes of the Internal Revenue Code of 1986, in determining the present value of the accrued benefit of any highly compensated employee (within the meaning of section 414(q) of such Code) on the termination or merger of any plan to which subparagraph (A) applies, the plan shall use the highest interest rate which may be used for calculating present value under section 411(a)(11)(B) of such Code."

—P.L. 100-647, Sec. 1011A(f)(1), substituted "subtitle A" for "this subtitle" in subpara. (c)(1)(A) . . . Sec. 1011A(f)(2)(A), added "or a tax credit employee stock ownership plan (as described in section 409)" after "section 4975(e)(7)" in subpara. (c)(3)(A) . . . Sec. 1011A(f)(2)(B), added ", except to the extent necessary to meet the requirements of section 401(a)(28)," after "must" in clause (c)(3)(A)(ii) . . . Sec. 1011A(f)(3)(A), deleted "(by reason of the limitations of section 415)" after "which is not allocated" in subpara. (c)(3)(C) . . . Sec. 1011A(f)(3)(B), added the sentence to the end of subpara. (c)(3)(C), effective for reversions occurring after 12/31/85, except as provided in Secs. 1132(c)(2)-(4) [as amended by Secs. 1011A(f)(4) and (5) of P.L. 100-647, see below] of this Act [reproduced below].

—P.L. 100-647, Sec. 1011A(f)(4), amended Sec. 1132(c)(2)(B) of P.L. 99-514 [reproduced below] part of the effective date for Code Sec. 4980 as added by Sec. 1132(a) of P.L. 99-514, by substituting "September 19, 1978" for "November 19, 1978" in subpara. (c)(2)(B) . . . Sec. 1011A(f)(5), added Sec. 1132(c)(5) of P.L. 99-514 [reproduced below], part of the effective date for Code Sec. 4980 as added by Sec. 1132(a) of P.L. 99-514.

—P.L. 100-647, Sec. 1011A(f)(6), added subparas. (c)(3)(F) and (G) . . . Sec. 1011A(f)(7), added the sentence to the end of subpara. (c)(3)(C), effective for reversions occurring after 12/31/85, except as provided by Secs. 1132(c)(2)-(4) of P.L. 99-514 [reproduced below].

—P.L. 100-647, Sec. 5072(a), added para. (c)(4), effective for reversions after 12/31/88.

—P.L. 100-647, Sec. 6069(a), substituted "15 percent" for "10 percent" in subsec. (a), effective for reversions occurring on or after 10/21/88, except as provided by Sec. 6069(b)(2) of this Act, which reads as follows:

"(2) Exception. The amendment made by subsection (a) shall not apply to any reversion on or after October 21, 1988, pursuant to a plan termination if—

"(A) with respect to plans subject to title IV of the Employee Retirement Income Security Act of 1974, a notice of intent to terminate required under such title was provided to participants (or if no participants, to the Pension Benefit Guaranty Corporation) before October 21, 1988,

Excise and miscellaneous taxes

Code Sec. 4980A

"(B) with respect to plans subject to title I of such Act, a notice of intent to reduce future accruals required under section 204(h) of such Act was provided to participants in connection with the termination before October 21, 1988,

"(C) with respect to plans not subject to title I or IV of such Act, the Board of Directors of the employer approved the termination or the employer took other binding action before October 21, 1988, or

"(D) such plan termination was directed by a final order of a court of competent jurisdiction entered before October 21, 1988, and notice of such order was provided to participants before such date."

In 1986, P.L. 99-514, Sec. 1112(e)(3), [as amended by Sec. 1011(h)(6), (8), and (9) of P.L. 100-647, see above] of this Act provides:

"(3) Waiver of excise tax on reversions. —

"(A) In general. — If —

"(i) a plan is in existence on August 16, 1986.

"(ii) such plan would fail to meet the requirements of section 401(a)(26) of the Internal Revenue Code of 1986 (as added by subsection (b)) if such section were in effect for the plan year including August 16, 1986, and

"(iii) there is no transfer of assets to or liabilities from the plan or spinoff or merger involving such plan after August 16, 1986, then no tax shall be imposed under section 4980 of such Code on any employer revision by reason of the termination or merger of such plan before the 1st year to which the amendment made by subsection (b) applies.

"(B) Interest rate for determining accrued benefit of highly compensated employees for certain purposes. — In the case of a termination, transfer, or distribution of assets of a plan described in subparagraph (A)(ii) before the 1st year to which the amendment made by subsection (b) applies —

"(i) Amount eligible for rollover, income averaging, or tax-free transfer. — For purposes of determining any eligible amount, the present value of the accrued benefit of any highly compensated employee shall be determined by using an interest rate not less than the highest of —

"(I) the applicable rate under the plan's method in effect under the plan on August 16, 1986,

"(II) the highest rate (as of the date of the termination, transfer, or distribution) determined under any of the methods applicable under the plan at any time after August 15, 1986, and before the termination, transfer, or distribution in calculating the present value of the accrued benefit of an employee who is not a highly compensated employee under the plan (or any other plan used in determining whether the plan meets the requirements of section 401 of the Internal Revenue Code of 1986), or

"(III) 5 percent.

"(ii) Eligible amount. — For purposes of clause (i), the term 'eligible amount' means any amount with respect to a highly compensated employee which —

"(I) may be rolled over under section 402(a)(5) of such Code,

"(II) is eligible for income averaging under section 402(e)(1) of such Code, or capital gains treatment under section 402(a)(2) or 403(a)(2) of such Code (as in effect before this Act), or

"(III) may be transferred to another plan without inclusion in gross income.

"(iii) Amount subject to early withdrawal or excess distribution tax. — For purposes of sections 72(t) and 4980A of such Code, there shall not be taken into account the excess (if any) of —

"(I) the amount distributed to a highly compensated employee by reason of such termination or distribution, over

"(II) the amount determined by using the interest rate applicable under clause (i).

"(iv) Distributions of annuity contracts. — If an annuity contract purchased after August 16, 1986, is distributed to a highly compensated employee in connection with such termination or distribution, there shall be included in gross income for the taxable year of such distribution an amount equal to the excess of —

"(I) the purchase price of such contract, over

"(II) the present value of the benefits payable under such contract determined by using the interest rate applicable under clause (i).

Such excess shall not be taken into account for purposes of sections 72(t) and 4980A of such Code.

"(v) Highly compensated employee. — For purposes of this subparagraph, the term 'highly compensated employee' has the meaning given such term by section 414(q) of such Code.

"(4) Special rule for plans which may not terminate. — To the extent provided in regulations prescribed by the Secretary of the Treasury or his delegate, if a plan is prohibited from terminating under title IV of the Employee Retirement Income Security Act of 1974 before the 1st year to which the amendment made by subsection (b) would apply, the amendment made by subsection (b) shall only apply to years after the 1st year in which the plan is able to terminate."

—P.L. 99-514, Sec. 1132(a), added Code Sec. 4980, effective for reversions occurring after 12/31/85, except as provided in Secs. 1132(c)(2)-(5) [as amended by Secs. 1011A(f)(4) and (5) of P.L. 100-647, see above] of this Act, which read as follows [see also, Sec. 7861(b) of P.L. 101-239, above]:

"(2) Exception where termination date occurred before January 1, 1986. —

"(A) In general. — Except as provided in subparagraph (B), the amendments made by this section shall not apply to any reversion after December 31, 1985, which occurs pursuant to a plan termination where the termination date is before January 1, 1986.

"(B) Election to have amendments apply. — A corporation may elect to have the amendments made by this section apply to any reversion after 1985 pursuant to a plan termination occurring before 1986 if such corporation was incorporated in the State of Delaware in March, 1978, and became a parent corporation of the consolidated group on September 19, 1978, pursuant to a merger agreement recorded in the State of Nevada on September 19, 1978.

"(3) Termination date. — For purposes of paragraph (2), the term 'termination date' is the date of the termination (within the meaning of section 411(d)(3) of the Internal Revenue Code of 1986) of the plan.

"(4) Transition rule for certain terminations. —

"(A) In general. — In the case of a taxpayer to which this paragraph applies, the amendments made by this section shall not apply to any termination occurring before the date which is 1 year after the date of the enactment of this Act.

"(B) Taxpayers to whom paragraph applies. — This paragraph shall apply to —

"(i) a corporation incorporated on June 13, 1917, which has its principal place of business in Bartlesville, Oklahoma,

"(ii) a corporation incorporated on January 17, 1917, which is located in Coatesville, Pennsylvania,

"(iii) a corporation incorporated on January 23, 1928, which has its principal place of business in New York, New York,

"(iv) a corporation incorporated on April 23, 1956, which has its principal place of business in Dallas, Texas, and

"(v) a corporation incorporated in the State of Nevada, the principal place of business of which is in Denver, Colorado, and which filed for relief from creditors under the United States Bankruptcy Code on August 28, 1986.

"(5) Special rule for employee stock ownership plans. — Section 4980(c)(3) of the Internal Revenue Code of 1986 (as added by subsection (a)) shall apply to reversions occurring after March 31, 1985."

Sec. 4980A. Repealed.

In 1997, P.L. 105-34, Sec. 1073(a), repealed Code Sec. 4980A, effective for excess distributions received after December 31, 1996. Sec. 1073(c)(2) of this Act provides:

"(2) Excess retirement accumulation tax repeal. The repeal made by subsection (a) with respect to Section 4980A(d) of the Internal Revenue Code of 1986 and the amendments made by subsection (b) shall apply to estates of decedents dying after December 31, 1996."

Prior to repeal, Code Sec. 4980A read as follows:

"SEC. 4980A. TAX ON EXCESS DISTRIBUTIONS FROM QUALIFIED RETIREMENT PLANS.

"(a) General rule. There is hereby imposed a tax equal to 15 percent of the excess distributions with respect to any individual during any calendar year.

"(b) Liability for tax. The individual with respect to whom the excess distributions are made shall be liable for the tax imposed by subsection (a). The amount of the tax imposed by subsection (a) shall be reduced by the amount (if any) of the tax imposed by section 72(t) to the extent attributable to such excess distributions.

"(c) Excess distributions. For purposes of this section —

"(1) In general. The term 'excess distributions' means the aggregate amount of the retirement distributions with respect to any individual during any calendar year to the extent such amount exceeds the greater of —

"(A) $150,000, or

"(B) $112,500 (adjusted at the same time and in the same manner as under section 415(d)).

"(2) Exclusion of certain distributions. The following distributions shall not be taken into account under paragraph (1):

"(A) Any retirement distribution with respect to an individual made after the death of such individual.

"(B) Any retirement distribution with respect to an individual payable to an alternate payee pursuant to a qualified domestic relations order (within the meaning of section 414(p)) if includible in income of the alternate payee.

"(C) Any retirement distribution with respect to an individual which is attributable to the individual's investment in the contract (as defined in section 72(f)).

"(D) Any retirement distribution to the extent not included in gross income by reason of a rollover contribution.

"(E) Any retirement distribution with respect to an individual of an annuity contract the value of which is not includible in gross income at the time of the distribution (other than distributions under, or proceeds from the sale or exchange of, such contract).

"(F) Any retirement distribution with respect to an individual of —

"(i) excess deferrals (and income allocable thereto) under section 402(g)(2)(A)(ii), or

"(ii) excess contributions (and income allocable thereto) under section 401(k)(8) or 408(d)(4) or excess aggregate contributions (and income allocable thereto) under section 401(m)(6).

Any distribution described in subparagraph (B) shall be treated as a retirement distribution to the person to whom paid for purposes of this section.

"(3) Aggregation of payments. If retirement distributions with respect to any individual during any calendar year are received by the individual and 1 or more other persons, all such distributions shall be aggregated for purposes of determining the amount of the excess distributions for the calendar year.

[Caution: Para. (c)(4), following, is effective for tax. yrs. begin. before 1/1/2000. For para. (c)(4) effective for tax. yrs. begin. after 12/31/99, see below. For special rules, see Sec. 1401(c)(2) of P.L. 104-188 reproduced in note following Code Sec. 4980A.]

"(4) Special rule where taxpayer elects income averaging.

If the retirement distributions with respect to any individual during any calendar year include a lump sum distribution to which an election under section 402(d)(4)(B) applies —

"(A) paragraph (1) shall be applied separately with respect to such lump sum distribution and other retirement distributions, and

3,349

Code Sec. 4980A   **Excise and miscellaneous taxes**

"(B) the limitation under paragraph (1) with respect to such lump sum distribution shall be equal to 5 times the amount of such limitation determined without regard to this subparagraph.

[Caution: Para. (c)(4), following, is effective for tax. yrs. begin. after 12/31/99. For special rules, see Sec. 1401(c)(2) of P.L. 104-188 reproduced in note following Code Sec. 4980A. For para. (c)(4) effective for tax. yrs. begin. before 1/1/2000, see above.]

"(4) Special one-time election. If the retirement distributions with respect to any individual during any calendar year include a lump sum distribution (as defined in section 402(e)(4)(D)) with respect to which the individual elects to have this paragraph apply—

"(A) paragraph (1) shall be applied separately with respect to such lump sum distribution and other retirement distributions, and

"(B) the limitation under paragraph (1) with respect to such lump sum distribution shall be equal to 5 times the amount of such limitation determined without regard to this subparagraph.

An individual may elect to have this paragraph apply to only one lump-sum distribution.

"(d) Increase in estate tax if individual dies with excess accumulation.

"(1) In general. The tax imposed by chapter 11 with respect to the estate of any individual shall be increased by an amount equal to 15 percent of the individual's excess retirement accumulation.

"(2) No credit allowable. No credit shall be allowable under chapter 11 with respect to any portion of the tax imposed by chapter 11 attributable to the increase under paragraph (1).

"(3) Excess retirement accumulation. For purposes of paragraph (1), the term 'excess retirement accumulation' means the excess (if any) of—

"(A) the value of the individual's interests (other than as a beneficiary, determined after application of paragraph (5)) in qualified employer plans and individual retirement plans as of the date of the decedent's death (or, in the case of an election under section 2032, the applicable valuation date prescribed by such section), over

"(B) the present value (as determined under rules prescribed by the Secretary as of the valuation date prescribed in subparagraph (A)) of a single life annuity with annual payments equal to the limitation of subsection (c) (as in effect for the year in which death occurs and as if the individual had not died).

"(4) Rules for computing excess retirement accumulation. The excess retirement accumulation of an individual shall be computed without regard to—

"(A) any community property law,

"(B) the value of—

"(i) amounts payable to an alternate payee pursuant to a qualified domestic relations order (within the meaning of section 414(p)) if includible in income of the alternate payee, and

"(ii) the individual's investment in the contract (as defined in section 72(f)), and

"(C) the excess (if any) of—

"(i) any interests which are payable immediately after death, over

"(ii) the value of such interests immediately before death.

"(5) Election by spouse to have excess distribution rule apply.

"(A) In general. If the spouse of an individual is the beneficiary of all of the interests described in paragraph (3)(A), the spouse may elect—

"(i) not to have this subsection apply, and

"(ii) to have this section apply to such interests and any retirement distribution attributable to such interests as if such interests were the spouse's.

"(B) De minimis exception. If 1 or more persons other than the spouse are beneficiaries of a de minimis portion of the interests described in paragraph (3)(A)—

"(i) the spouse shall not be treated as failing to meet the requirements of subparagraph (A), and

"(ii) if the spouse makes the election under subparagraph (A), this section shall not apply to such portion or any retirement distribution attributable to such portion.

"(e) Retirement distributions. For purposes of this section—

"(1) In general. The term 'retirement distribution' means, with respect to any individual, the amount distributed during the taxable year under—

"(A) any qualified employer plan with respect to which such individual is or was the employee, and

"(B) any individual retirement plan.

"(2) Qualified employer plan. The term 'qualified employer plan' means—

"(A) any plan described in section 401(a) which includes a trust exempt from tax under section 501(a),

"(B) an annuity plan described in section 403(a), or

"(C) an annuity contract described in section 403(b).

Such term includes any plan or contract which, at any time, has been determined by the Secretary to be such a plan or contract.

"(f) Exemption of accrued benefits in excess of $562,500 on August 1, 1986. For purposes of this section—

"(1) In general. If an election is made with respect to an eligible individual to have this subsection apply, the individual's excess distributions and excess retirement accumulation shall be computed without regard to any distributions or interests attributable to the accrued benefit of the individual as of August 1, 1986.

"(2) Reduction in amounts which may be received without tax. If this subsection applies to any individual—

"(A) Excess distributions. Subsection (c)(1) shall be applied—

"(i) without regard to subparagraph (A), and

"(ii) by reducing (but not below zero) the amount determined under subparagraph (B) thereof by retirement distributions attributable (as determined under

rules prescribed by the Secretary) to the individual's accrued benefit as of August 1, 1986.

"(B) Excess retirement accumulation. The amount determined under subsection (d)(3)(B) (without regard to subsection (c)(1)(A)) with respect to such individual shall be reduced (but not below zero) by the present value of the individual's accrued benefit as of August 1, 1986, which has not been distributed as of the date of death.

"(3) Eligible individual. For purposes of this subsection, the term 'eligible individual' means any individual if, on August 1, 1986, the present value of such individual's interests in qualified employer plans and individual retirement plans exceeded $562,500.

"(4) Certain amounts excluded. In determining an individual's accrued benefit for purposes of this subsection, there shall not be taken into account any portion of the accrued benefit—

"(A) payable to an alternate payee pursuant to a qualified domestic relations order (within the meaning of section 414(p)) if includible in income of the alternate payee, or

"(B) attributable to the individual's investment in the contract (as defined in section 72(f)).

"(5) Election. An election under paragraph (1) shall be made on an individual's return of tax imposed by chapter 1 or 11 for a taxable year beginning before January 1, 1989.

"(g) Limitation on application. This section shall not apply to distributions during years beginning after December 31, 1996, and before January 1, 2000, and such distributions shall be treated as made first from amounts not described in subsection (f)."

In 1996, P.L. 104-188, Sec. 1401(b)(12)(A), substituted "(as defined in section 402(e)(4)(D)) with respect to which the individual elects to have this paragraph apply." for "to which an election under section 402(d)(4)(B) applies" in para. (c)(4) . . . Sec. 1401(b)(12)(B), added the flush sentence at the end of para. (c)(4) . . . Sec. 1401(b)(12)(C), substituted "(4) Special one-time election." for "(4) Special rule where taxpayer elects income averaging." in the heading of para. (c)(4), effective for tax. yrs. begin. after 12/31/99. Sec. 1401(c)(2) of this Act provides:

"(2) Retention of certain transition rules. The amendments made by this section shall not apply to any distribution for which the taxpayer is eligible to elect the benefits of section 1122 or (h)(5) of the Tax Reform Act of 1986. Notwithstanding the preceding sentence, individuals who elect such benefits after December 31, 1999, shall not be eligible for 5-year averaging under section 402(d) of the Internal Revenue Code of 1986 (as in effect immediately before such amendments)."

—P.L. 104-188, Sec. 1452(b), added subsec. (g), effective for limitation yrs. begin. after 12/31/96.

In 1992, P.L. 102-318, Sec. 521(b)(42), substituted "section 402(d)(4)(B)" for "section 402(e)(4)(B)" in para. (c)(4), effective for distributions after 12/31/92. For special rule, see Sec. 521(e)(2) of this Act which reads as follows:

"(2) Special rule for partial distributions. For purposes of section 402(a)(5)(D)(i)(II) of the Internal Revenue Code of 1986 (as in effect before the amendments made by this section), a distribution before January 1, 1993, which is made before or at the same time as a series of periodic payments shall not be treated as one of such series if it is not substantially equal in amount to other payments in such series."

In 1988, P.L. 100-647, Sec. 1011A(g)(1)(A), redesignated Code Sec. 4981A as Code Sec. 4980A . . . Sec. 1011A(g)(2), substituted "the greater of—

"(A) $150,000, or

"(B) $112,500 (adjusted at the same time and in the same manner as under section 415(d))." for '$112,500 (adjusted at the same time and in the same manner as under section 415(d))' in para. (c)(1) . . . Sec. 1011A(g)(3)(A), substituted 'individual's' for 'employee's' in subpara. (c)(2)(C) . . . Sec. 1011A(g)(3)(B), added subparas. (c)(2)(E) and (F) . . . Sec. 1011A(g)(4)(A), added subsec. (f) . . . Sec. 1011A(g)(4)(B), deleted para. (c)(5) . . . Sec. 1011A(g)(5)(A), substituted 'chapter 11' for 'section 2010' in para. (d)(2) . . . Sec. 1011A(g)(5)(B), added paras. (d)(4) and (5) . . . Sec. 1011A(g)(6), amended subpara. (d)(3)(B) . . . Sec. 1011A(g)(9), added '(other than as a beneficiary, determined after application of paragraph (5))' after 'the individual's interests' in subpara. (d)(3)(A), effective as provided in Sec. 1133(c) of P.L. 99-514, reproduced below."

Prior to deletion, para. (c)(5) read as follows:

"(5) Special rule for accrued benefits as of August 1, 1986.

"(A) In general. If the employee elects on a return filed for a taxable year ending before January 1, 1989 to have this paragraph apply, the portion of any retirement distribution which is attributable (as determined under rules prescribed by the Secretary) to the accrued benefit of an employee as of August 1, 1986, shall be taken into account for purposes of paragraph (1), but no tax shall be imposed under this section with respect to such portion of such distribution.

"(B) Limitation. An employee may not make an election under subparagraph (A) unless the accrued benefit of such employee as of August 1, 1986, exceeds $562,500.

"(C) Taxpayer not making election. If an employee does not elect the application of this paragraph, paragraph (1) shall be applied by substituting $150,000 for such dollar limitation unless such dollar limitation is greater than $150,000."

Prior to amendment, subpara. (d)(3)(B) read as follows:

"(B) the present value (as determined under rules prescribed by the Secretary as of the valuation date prescribed in subparagraph (A)) of an annuity for a term certain—

"(i) with annual payments equal to the limitation of subsection (c) (as in effect for the year in which the death occurs), and

"(ii) payable for a period equal to the life expectancy of the individual immediately before his death."

3,350

Code Sec. 4980B(c)(4)(B)(ii)   **Excise and miscellaneous taxes**

paragraph (A) (and not under this subparagraph) and as if such plan were not a multiemployer plan.

(C) Special rule for persons providing benefits. In the case of a person described in subsection (e)(1)(B) (and not subsection (e)(1)(A)), the aggregate amount of tax imposed by subsection (a) for failures during a taxable year with respect to all plans shall not exceed $2,000,000.

(5) Waiver by Secretary. In the case of a failure which is due to reasonable cause and not to willful neglect, the Secretary may waive part or all of the tax imposed by subsection (a) to the extent that the payment of such tax would be excessive relative to the failure involved.

(d) Tax not to apply to certain plans.

This section shall not apply to—

(1) any failure of a group health plan to meet the requirements of subsection (f) with respect to any qualified beneficiary if the qualifying event with respect to such beneficiary occurred during the calendar year immediately following a calendar year during which all employers maintaining such plan normally employed fewer than 20 employees on a typical business day,

(2) any governmental plan (within the meaning of section 414(d)), or

(3) any church plan (within the meaning of section 414(e)).

(e) Liability for tax.

(1) In general. Except as otherwise provided in this subsection, the following shall be liable for the tax imposed by subsection (a) on a failure:

(A)(i) In the case of a plan other than a multiemployer plan, the employer.

(ii) In the case of a multiemployer plan, the plan.

(B) Each person who is responsible (other than in a capacity as an employee) for administering or providing benefits under the plan and whose act or failure to act caused (in whole or in part) the failure.

(2) Special rules for persons described in paragraph (1)(B).

(A) No liability unless written agreement. Except in the case of liability resulting from the application of subparagraph (B) of this paragraph, a person described in subparagraph (B) (and not in subparagraph (A)) of paragraph (1) shall be liable for the tax imposed by subsection (a) on any failure only if such person assumed (under a legally enforceable written agreement) responsibility for the performance of the act to which the failure relates.

(B) Failure to cover qualified beneficiaries where current employees are covered. A person shall be treated as described in paragraph (1)(B) with respect to a qualified beneficiary if—

(i) such person provides coverage under a group health plan for any similarly situated beneficiary under the plan with respect to whom a qualifying event has not occurred, and

(ii) the—

(I) employer or plan administrator, or

(II) in the case of a qualifying event described in subparagraph (C) or (E) of subsection (f)(3) where the person described in clause (i) is the plan administrator, the qualified beneficiary,

submits to such person a written request that such person make available to such qualified beneficiary the same coverage which such person provides to the beneficiary referred to in clause (i).

(f) Continuation coverage requirements of group health plans.

(1) In general. A group health plan meets the requirements of this subsection only if the coverage of the costs of pediatric vaccines (as defined under section 2162 of the Public Health Service Act) is not reduced below the coverage provided by the plan as of May 1, 1993, and only if each qualified beneficiary who would lose coverage under the plan as a result of a qualifying event is entitled to elect, within the election period, continuation coverage under the plan.

(2) Continuation coverage. For purposes of paragraph (1), the term "continuation coverage" means coverage under the plan which meets the following requirements:

(A) Type of benefit coverage. The coverage must consist of coverage which, as of the time the coverage is being provided, is identical to the coverage provided under the plan to similarly situated beneficiaries under the plan with respect to whom a qualifying event has not occurred. If coverage under the plan is modified for any group of similarly situated beneficiaries, the coverage shall also be modified in the same manner for all individuals who are qualified beneficiaries under the plan pursuant to this subsection in connection with such group.

(B) Period of coverage. The coverage must extend for at least the period beginning on the date of the qualifying event and ending not earlier than the earliest of the following:

(i) Maximum required period.

(I) General rule for terminations and reduced hours. In the case of a qualifying event described in paragraph (3)(B), except as provided in subclause (II), the date which is 18 months after the date of the qualifying event.

(II) Special rule for multiple qualifying events. If a qualifying event (other than a qualifying event described in paragraph (3)(F)) occurs during the 18 months after the date of a qualifying event described in paragraph (3)(B), the date which is 36 months after the date of the qualifying event described in paragraph (3)(B).

(III) Special rule for certain bankruptcy proceedings. In the case of a qualifying event described in paragraph (3)(F) (relating to bankruptcy proceedings), the date of the death of the covered employee or qualified beneficiary (described in subsection (g)(1)(D)(iii)), or in the case of the surviving spouse or dependent children of the covered employee, 36 months after the date of the death of the covered employee.

(IV) General rule for other qualifying events. In the case of a qualifying event not described in paragraph (3)(B) or (3)(F), the date which is 36 months after the date of the qualifying event.

(V) Special rule for PBGC recipients. In the case of a qualifying event described in paragraph (3)(B) with respect to a covered employee who (as of such qualifying event) has a nonforfeitable right to a benefit any portion of which is to be paid by the Pension Benefit Guaranty Corporation under title IV of the Employee Retirement Income Security Act of 1974, notwithstanding subclause (I) or (II), the date of the death of the covered employee, or in the case of the surviving spouse or dependent children of the covered employee, 24 months after the date of the death of the covered employee. The

3,352

Excise and miscellaneous taxes

Code Sec. 4980B(c)(4)(B)(ii)

—P.L. 100-647, Sec. 1011A(g)(8), amended Sec. 1133(c)(1) of P.L. 99-514, part of the effective date for changes made by Sec. 1133(a) of P.L. 99-514, by adding, "other than a distribution with respect to a decedent dying before 1/1/87" after "1986", see below.

In 1986, P.L. 99-514, Sec. 1133(a), added Code Sec. 4981A, effective as provided in Sec. 1133(c) of this Act [as amended by Sec. 1011A(g)(8) of P.L. 100-647, see above] which reads as follows:

"(c) Effective Dates.—

"(1) In General.—Except as provided in this subsection, the amendments made by this section shall apply to distributions made after December 31, 1986 other than a distribution with respect to a decedent dying before January 1, 1987.

"(2) Estate tax.—Section 4981A(d) of the Internal Revenue Code of 1986 (as added by subsection (a)) shall apply to the estates of decedents dying after December 31, 1986.

"(3) Plan terminations before 1987.—The amendments made by this section shall not apply to distributions before January 1, 1988, which are made on account of the termination of a qualified employer plan if such termination occurred before January 1, 1987."

Sec. 4980B. Failure to satisfy continuation coverage requirements of group health plans.

(a) General rule.

There is hereby imposed a tax on the failure of a group health plan to meet the requirements of subsection (f) with respect to any qualified beneficiary.

(b) Amount of tax.

(1) In general. The amount of the tax imposed by subsection (a) on any failure with respect to a qualified beneficiary shall be $100 for each day in the noncompliance period with respect to such failure.

(2) Noncompliance period. For purposes of this section, the term "noncompliance period" means, with respect to any failure, the period—

(A) beginning on the date such failure first occurs, and

(B) ending on the earlier of—

(i) the date such failure is corrected, or

(ii) the date which is 6 months after the last day in the period applicable to the qualified beneficiary under subsection (f)(2)(B) (determined without regard to clause (iii) thereof).

If a person is liable for tax under subsection (e)(1)(B) by reason of subsection (e)(2)(B) with respect to any failure, the noncompliance period for such person with respect to such failure shall not begin before the 45th day after the written request described in subsection (e)(2)(B) is provided to such person.

(3) Minimum tax for non-compliance period where failure discovered after notice of examination. Notwithstanding paragraphs (1) and (2) of subsection (c)—

(A) In general. In the case of 1 or more failures with respect to a qualified beneficiary—

(i) which are not corrected before the date a notice of examination of income tax liability is sent to the employer, and

(ii) which occurred or continued during the period under examination,

the amount of tax imposed by subsection (a) by reason of such failures with respect to such beneficiary shall not be less than the lesser of $2,500 or the amount of tax which would be imposed by subsection (a) without regard to such paragraphs.

(B) Higher minimum tax where violations are more than de minimis. To the extent violations by the employer (or the plan in the case of a multiemployer plan) for any year are more than de minimis, subparagraph (A) shall be applied by substituting "$15,000" for "$2,500" with respect to the employer (or such plan).

(c) Limitations on amount of tax.

(1) Tax not to apply where failure not discovered exercising reasonable diligence. No tax shall be imposed by subsection (a) on any failure during any period for which it is established to the satisfaction of the Secretary that none of the persons referred to in subsection (e) knew, or exercising reasonable diligence would have known, that such failure existed.

(2) Tax not to apply to failures corrected within 30 days. No tax shall be imposed by subsection (a) on any failure if—

(A) such failure was due to reasonable cause and not to willful neglect, and

(B) such failure is corrected during the 30-day period beginning on the 1st date any of the persons referred to in subsection (e) knew, or exercising reasonable diligence would have known, that such failure existed.

(3) $100 limit on amount of tax for failures on any day with respect to a qualified beneficiary.

(A) In general. Except as provided in subparagraph (B), the maximum amount of tax imposed by subsection (a) on failures on any day during the noncompliance period with respect to a qualified beneficiary shall be $100.

(B) Special rule where more than 1 qualified beneficiary. If there is more than 1 qualified beneficiary with respect to the same qualifying event, the maximum amount of tax imposed by subsection (a) on all failures on any day during the noncompliance period with respect to such qualified beneficiaries shall be $200.

(4) Overall limitation for unintentional failures. In the case of failures which are due to reasonable cause and not to willful neglect—

(A) Single employer plans.

(i) In general. In the case of failures with respect to plans other than multiemployer plans, the tax imposed by subsection (a) for failures during the taxable year of the employer shall not exceed the amount equal to the lesser of—

(I) 10 percent of the aggregate amount paid or incurred by the employer (or predecessor employer) during the preceding taxable year for group health plans, or

(II) $500,000.

(ii) Taxable years in the case of certain controlled groups. For purposes of this subparagraph, if not all persons who are treated as a single employer for purposes of this section have the same taxable year, the taxable years taken into account shall be determined under principles similar to the principles of section 1561.

(B) Multiemployer plans.

(i) In general. In the case of failures with respect to a multiemployer plan, the tax imposed by subsection (a) for failures during the taxable year of the trust forming part of such plan shall not exceed the amount equal to the lesser of—

(I) 10 percent of the amount paid or incurred by such trust during such taxable year to provide medical care (as defined in section 213(d)) directly or through insurance, reimbursement, or otherwise, or

(II) $500,000.

For purposes of the preceding sentence, all plans of which the same trust forms a part shall be treated as 1 plan.

(ii) Special rule for employers required to pay tax. If an employer is assessed a tax imposed by subsection (a) by reason of a failure with respect to a multi-employer plan, the limit shall be determined under sub-

3,351

preceding sentence shall not require any period of coverage to extend beyond February 12, 2011.

(VI) Special rule for TAA-eligible individuals. In the case of a qualifying event described in paragraph (3)(B) with respect to a covered employee who is (as of the date that the period of coverage would, but for this subclause or subclause (VII), otherwise terminate under subclause (I) or (II)) a TAA-eligible individual (as defined in paragraph (5)(C)(iv)(II)), the period of coverage shall not terminate by reason of subclause (I) or (II), as the case may be, before the later of the date specified in such subclause or the date on which such individual ceases to be such a TAA-eligible individual. The preceding sentence shall not require any period of coverage to extend beyond February 12, 2011.

(VII) Medicare entitlement followed by qualifying event. In the case of a qualifying event described in paragraph (3)(B) that occurs less than 18 months after the date the covered employee became entitled to benefits under title XVIII of the Social Security Act, the period of coverage for qualified beneficiaries other than the covered employee shall not terminate under this clause before the close of the 36-month period beginning on the date the covered employee became so entitled.

(VIII) Special rule for disability. In the case of a qualified beneficiary who is determined, under title II or XVI of the Social Security Act, to have been disabled at any time during the first 60 days of continuation coverage under this section, any reference in subclause (I) or (II) to 18 months is deemed a reference to 29 months (with respect to all qualified beneficiaries), but only if the qualified beneficiary has provided notice of such determination under paragraph (6)(C) before the end of such 18 months.

(ii) End of plan. The date on which the employer ceases to provide any group health plan to any employee.

(iii) Failure to pay premium. The date on which coverage ceases under the plan by reason of a failure to make timely payment of any premium required under the plan with respect to the qualified beneficiary. The payment of any premium (other than any payment referred to in the last sentence of subparagraph (C)) shall be considered to be timely if made within 30 days after the date due or within such longer period as applies to or under the plan.

(iv) Group health plan coverage or Medicare entitlement. The date on which the qualified beneficiary first becomes, after the date of the election—

(I) covered under any other group health plan (as an employee or otherwise), which does not contain any exclusion or limitation with respect to any pre-existing condition of such beneficiary (other than such an exclusion or limitation which does not apply to (or is satisfied by) such beneficiary by reason of chapter 100 of this title, part 7 of subtitle B of title I of the Employee Retirement Income Security Act of 1974, or title XXVII of the Public Health Services Act), or

(II) in the case of a qualified beneficiary other than a qualified beneficiary described in subsection (g)(1)(D) entitled to benefits under title XVIII of the Social Security Act.

(v) Termination of extended coverage for disability. In the case of a qualified beneficiary who is disabled at any time during the first 60 days of continuation coverage under this section, the month that begins more than 30 days after the date of the final determination under title II or XVI of the Social Security Act that the qualified beneficiary is no longer disabled.

(C) Premium requirements. The plan may require payment of a premium for any period of continuation coverage, except that such premium—

(i) shall not exceed 102 percent of the applicable premium for such period, and

(ii) may, at the election of the payor, be made in monthly installments.

In no event may the plan require the payment of any premium before the day which is 45 days after the day on which the qualified beneficiary made the initial election for continuation coverage. In the case of an individual described in the last sentence of subparagraph (B)(i), any reference in clause (i) of this subparagraph to "102 percent" is deemed a reference to "150 percent" for any month after the 18th month of continuation coverage described in subclause (I) or (II) of subparagraph (B)(i).

(D) No requirement of insurability. The coverage may not be conditioned upon, or discriminate on the basis of lack of, evidence of insurability.

(E) Conversion option. In the case of a qualified beneficiary whose period of continuation coverage expires under subparagraph (B)(i), the plan must, during the 180-day period ending on such expiration date, provide to the qualified beneficiary the option of enrollment under a conversion health plan otherwise generally available under the plan.

(3) Qualifying event. For purposes of this subsection, the term "qualifying event" means, with respect to any covered employee, any of the following events which, but for the continuation coverage required under this subsection, would result in the loss of coverage of a qualified beneficiary—

(A) The death of the covered employee.

(B) The termination (other than by reason of such employee's gross misconduct), or reduction of hours, of the covered employee's employment.

(C) The divorce or legal separation of the covered employee from the employee's spouse.

(D) The covered employee becoming entitled to benefits under title XVIII of the Social Security Act.

(E) A dependent child ceasing to be a dependent child under the generally applicable requirements of the plan.

(F) A proceeding in a case under title 11, United States Code, commencing on or after July 1, 1986, with respect to the employer from whose employment the covered employee retired at any time.

In the case of an event described in subparagraph (F), a loss of coverage includes a substantial elimination of coverage with respect to a qualified beneficiary described in subsection (g)(1)(D) within one year before or after the date of commencement of the proceeding.

(4) Applicable premium. For purposes of this subsection—

(A) In general. The term "applicable premium" means, with respect to any period of continuation coverage of qualified beneficiaries, the cost to the plan for such period of the coverage for similarly situated beneficiaries with respect to whom a qualifying event has not occurred (without regard to whether such cost is paid by the employer or employee).

(B) Special rule for self-insured plans. To the extent that a plan is a self-insured plan—

(i) In general. Except as provided in clause (ii), the applicable premium for any period of continuation coverage of qualified beneficiaries shall be equal to a reasonable estimate of the cost of providing coverage for such period for similarly situated beneficiaries which—

(I) is determined on an actuarial basis, and

(II) takes into account such factors as the Secretary may prescribe in regulations.

(ii) Determination on basis of past cost. If a plan administrator elects to have this clause apply, the applicable premium for any period of continuation coverage of qualified beneficiaries shall be equal to—

(I) the cost to the plan for similarly situated beneficiaries for the same period occurring during the preceding determination period under subparagraph (C), adjusted by

(II) the percentage increase or decrease in the implicit price deflator of the gross national product (calculated by the Department of Commerce and published in the Survey of Current Business) for the 12-month period ending on the last day of the sixth month of such preceding determination period.

(iii) Clause (ii) not to apply where significant change. A plan administrator may not elect to have clause (ii) apply in any case in which there is any significant difference between the determination period and the preceding determination period, in coverage under or in employees covered by, the plan. The determination under the preceding sentence for any determination period shall be made at the same time as the determination under subparagraph (C).

(C) Determination period. The determination of any applicable premium shall be made for a period of 12 months and shall be made before the beginning of such period.

(5) Election. For purposes of this subsection

(A) Election period. The term "election period" means the period which—

(i) begins not later than the date on which coverage terminates under the plan by reason of a qualifying event,

(ii) is of at least 60 days' duration, and

(iii) ends not earlier than 60 days after the later of—

(I) the date described in clause (i), or

(II) in the case of any qualified beneficiary who receives notice under paragraph (6)(D), the date of such notice.

(B) Effect of election on other beneficiaries. Except as otherwise specified in an election, any election of continuation coverage by a qualified beneficiary described in subparagraph (A)(i) or (B) of subsection (g)(1) shall be deemed to include an election of continuation coverage on behalf of any other qualified beneficiary who would lose coverage under the plan by reason of the qualifying event. If there is a choice among types of coverage under the plan, each qualified beneficiary is entitled to make a separate selection among such types of coverage.

(C) Temporary extension of COBRA election period for certain individuals.

(i) In general. In the case of a nonelecting TAA-eligible individual and notwithstanding subparagraph (A), such individual may elect continuation coverage under this subsection during the 60-day period that begins on the first day of the month in which the individual becomes a TAA-eligible individual, but only if such election is made not later than 6 months after the date of the TAA-related loss of coverage.

(ii) Commencement of coverage; no reach-back. Any continuation coverage elected by a TAA-eligible individual under clause (i) shall commence at the beginning of the 60-day election period described in such paragraph and shall not include any period prior to such 60-day election period.

(iii) Preexisting conditions. With respect to an individual who elects continuation coverage pursuant to clause (i), the period—

(I) beginning on the date of the TAA-related loss of coverage, and

(II) ending on the first day of the 60-day election period described in clause (i),

shall be disregarded for purposes of determining the 63-day periods referred to in section 9801(c)(2), section 701(c)(2) of the Employee Retirement Income Security Act of 1974, and section 2701(c)(2) of the Public Health Service Act.

(iv) Definitions. For purposes of this subsection:

(I) Nonelecting TAA-eligible individual. The term "nonelecting TAA-eligible individual" means a TAA-eligible individual who has a TAA-related loss of coverage and did not elect continuation coverage under this subsection during the TAA-related election period.

(II) TAA-eligible individual. The term "TAA-eligible individual" means an eligible TAA recipient (as defined in paragraph (2) of section 35(c)) and an eligible alternative TAA recipient (as defined in paragraph (3) of such section).

(III) TAA-related election period. The term "TAA-related election period" means, with respect to a TAA-related loss of coverage, the 60-day election period under this subsection which is a direct consequence of such loss.

(IV) TAA-related loss of coverage. The term "TAA-related loss of coverage" means, with respect to an individual whose separation from employment gives rise to being an TAA-eligible individual, the loss of health benefits coverage associated with such separation.

(6) Notice requirement. In accordance with regulations prescribed by the Secretary—

(A) The group health plan shall provide, at the time of commencement of coverage under the plan, written notice to each covered employee and spouse of the employee (if any) of the rights provided under this subsection.

(B) The employer of an employee under a plan must notify the plan administrator of a qualifying event described in subparagraph (A), (B), (D), or (F) of paragraph (3) with respect to such employee within 30 days (or, in the case of a group health plan which is a multiemployer plan, such longer period of time as may be provided in the terms of the plan) of the date of the qualifying event.

Code Sec. 4980B

Excise and miscellaneous taxes

ing requirements, shall be construed as creating any new mandate on any party regarding health insurance coverage."

In 1996, P.L. 104-188, Sec. 1704(g)(1)(A), amended subclause (f)(2)(B)(i)(V), effective for plan yrs. begin after 12/31/89.

Prior to amendment, subclause (f)(2)(B)(i)(V) read as follows:

"(V) Qualifying event involving medicare entitlement. In the case of an event described in paragraph (3)(D) (without regard to whether such event is a qualifying event), the period of coverage for qualified beneficiaries other than the covered employee for such event or any subsequent qualifying event shall not terminate before the close of the 36-month period beginning on the date the covered employee becomes entitled to benefits under title XVIII of the Social Security Act."

—P.L. 104-188, Sec. 1704(t)(24), amended Sec. 6701(a)(1) of P.L. 101-239 by substituting "subclause (V)" for "subclause (IV)" in amending language of that section, see below, effective 8/20/96.

—P.L. 104-191, Sec. 321(d)(1), added the sentence to the end of para. (g)(2), effective for contracts issued after 12/31/96. For other provisions, see Sec. 321(f)(2) - (5), of this Act, which reads as follows:

"(2) Continuation of existing policies. In the case of any contract issued before January 1, 1997, which met the long-term care insurance requirements of the State in which the contract was sitused at the time the contract was issued—

"(A) such contract shall be treated for purposes of the Internal Revenue Code of 1986 as a qualified long-term care insurance contract (as defined in section 7702B(b) of such Code), and

"(B) services provided under, or reimbursed by, such contract shall be treated for such purposes as qualified long-term care services (as defined in section 7702B(c) of such Code).

In the case of an individual who is covered on December 31, 1996, under a State long-term care plan (as defined in section 7702B(f)(2) of such Code), the terms of such plan on such date shall be treated for purposes of the preceding sentence as a contract issued on such date which met the long-term care insurance requirements of such State.

"(3) Exchanges of existing policies. If, after the date of enactment of this Act and before January 1, 1998, a contract providing for long-term care insurance coverage is exchanged solely for a qualified long-term care insurance contract (as defined in section 7702B(b) of such Code), no gain or loss shall be recognized on the exchange. If, in addition to a qualified long-term care insurance contract, money or other property is received in the exchange, then any gain shall be recognized to the extent of the sum of the money and the fair market value of the other property received. For purposes of this paragraph, the cancellation of a contract providing for long-term care insurance coverage and reinvestment of the cancellation proceeds in a qualified long-term care insurance contract within 60 days thereafter shall be treated as an exchange.

"(4) Issuance of certain riders permitted. For purposes of applying sections 101(f), 7702, and 7702A of the Internal Revenue Code of 1986 to any contract—

"(A) the issuance of a rider which is treated as a qualified long-term care insurance contract under section 7702B, and

"(B) the addition of any provision required to conform any other long-term care rider to be so treated,

shall not be treated as a modification or material change of such contract.

"(5) Application of per diem limitation to existing contracts. The amount of per diem payments made under a contract issued on or before July 31, 1996, with respect to an insured which are excludable from gross income by reason of section 7702B of the Internal Revenue Code of 1986 (as added by this section) shall not be reduced under subsection (d)(2)(B) thereof by reason of reimbursements received under a contract issued on or before such date. The preceding sentence shall cease to apply as of the date (after July 31, 1996) such contract is exchanged or there is any contract modification which results in an increase in the amount of such per diem payments or the amount of such reimbursements."

—P.L. 104-191, Sec. 421(c)(1)(A)(i), substituted "at any time during the first 60 days after continuation of coverage under this section" for "at the time of a qualifying event described in paragraph (3)(B)" in the last sentence of clause (f)(2)(B)(i) . . . Sec. 421(c)(1)(A)(ii), deleted "with respect to such event" in the last sentence of clause (f)(2)(B)(i) . . . Sec. 421(c)(1)(A)(iii), added "(with respect to all qualified beneficiaries)" after "29 months" in the last sentence of clause (f)(2)(B)(i) . . . Sec. 421(c)(1)(B), added "(other than such an exclusion or limitation which does not apply to (or is satisfied by) such beneficiary by reason of chapter 100 of this title, part 7 of subtitle B of title I of the Employee Retirement Income Security Act of 1974, or title XXVII of the Public Health Service Act)" before ", or" in clause (f)(2)(B)(iv)(I) . . . Sec. 421(c)(1)(C), substituted "at any time during the first 60 days of continuation coverage under this section" for "at the time of a qualifying event described in paragraph (3)(B)" in clause (f)(2)(B)(v) . . . Sec. 421(c)(2), substituted "at any time during the first 60 days of continuation coverage under this section" for "at the time of a qualifying event described in paragraph (3)(B)" in subpara. (f)(6)(C) . . . Sec. 421(c)(3), added the sentence to the end of subpara. (g)(1)(A), effective 1/1/97, regardless of whether the qualifying event occurred before, on, or after such date. Sec. 421(e), of this Act, provides:

"(e) Notification of changes. Not later than November 1, 1996, each group health plan (covered under title XXII of the Public Health Service Act, part 6 of subtitle B of title I of the Employee Retirement Income Security Act of 1974, and section 4980B(f) of the Internal Revenue Code of 1986) shall notify each qualified beneficiary who has elected continuation coverage under such title, part or section of the amendments made by this section."

In 1993, P.L. 103-66, Sec. 13422(a), added "the coverage of the costs of pediatric vaccines (as defined under section 2162 of the Public Health Service Act) is not

reduced below the coverage provided by the plan as of May 1, 1993, and only if" after "only if" in para. (f)(1), effective for plan yrs. begin. after 8/10/93.

In 1990, P.L. 101-508, Sec. 11702(f), amended para. (d)(1), effective for tax. yrs. begin. after 12/31/88.

Prior to amendment, para. (d)(1) read as follows:

"(1) any failure of a group health plan to meet the requirements of subsection (f) if all employers maintaining such plan normally employed fewer than 20 employees on a typical business day during the preceding calendar year."

In 1989, P.L. 101-239, Sec. 6202(b)(3)(B), substituted "5000(b)(1)" for "162(i)" in para. (g)(2), effective for items and services furnished after 12/19/89.

—P.L. 101-239, Sec. 6701(a)(1), [as amended by Sec. 1704(t)(21) of P.L. 104-188, see above] added the last sentence to clause (f)(2)(B)(i) . . . Sec. 6701(a)(2), added clause (f)(2)(B)(v) . . . Sec. 6701(b), [as amended by Sec. 7862(c)(4)(B), see below] added the last sentence to subpara. (f)(2)(C) . . . Sec. 6701(c), added "and each qualified beneficiary who is determined, under title II or XVI of the Social Security Act, to have been disabled at the time of a qualifying event described in paragraph (3)(B) is responsible for notifying the plan administrator of such determination within 60 days after the date of the determination and for notifying the plan administrator within 30 days of the date of any final determination under such title or titles that the qualified beneficiary is no longer disabled". before the period at the end of subpara. (f)(6)(C), effective for plan yrs. begin. on or after 12/19/89, regardless of whether the qualifying event occurred before, on, or after 12/19/89.

—P.L. 101-239, Sec. 7862(c)(2)(B), substituted "the performance of services by the individual for 1 or more persons maintaining the plan (including as an employee defined in section 401(c)(1))" for "the individual's employment or previous employment with an employer" in para. (f)(7), effective for plan yrs. begin. after 12/31/89.

—P.L. 101-239, Sec. 7862(c)(3)(C)(i), substituted "entitlement" for "eligibility" in the heading of clause (f)(2)(B)(iv) . . . Sec. 7862(c)(3)(C)(ii), added "which does not contain any exclusion or limitation with respect to any preexisting condition of such beneficiary" after "or otherwise) in subclause (f)(2)(B)(iv)(I), effective for qualifying events occurring after 12/31/89, except as provided in Sec. 7862(c)(3)(D)(ii) of this Act which reads as follows:

"(ii) in the case of qualified beneficiaries who elected continuation coverage after December 31, 1988, the period for which the required premium was paid (or was attempted to be paid but was rejected as such)."

—P.L. 101-239, Sec. 7862(c)(4)(B), substituted "In no event may the plan require the payment of any premium before the day which is 45 days after the day on which the qualified beneficiary made the initial election for continuation coverage." for "If an election is made after the qualifying event, the plan shall permit payment for continuation coverage during the period preceding the election to be made within 45 days of the date of the election." in subpara. (f)(2)(C) . . . Sec. 7862(c)(5)(A), added subclause (f)(2)(b)(i)(V), effective for plan yrs. begin. after 12/31/89.

—P.L. 101-239, Sec. 7891(d)(1)(B)(i)(I), added "(or, in the case of a group health plan which is a multiemployer plan, such longer period of time as may be provided in the terms of the plan)" after "30 days" in subpara. (f)(6)(B) . . . Sec. 7891(d)(1)(B)(i)(II), added "(or, in the case of a group health plan which is a multiemployer plan, such longer period of time as may be provided in the terms of the plan)" after "14 days" in subpara. (f)(6)(D) . . . Sec. 7891(d)(1)(B)(ii), added after and below subpara. (f)(b)(D) a new flush left sentence. . . . Sec. 7891(d)(2)(A), added para. (f)(8), effective for plan yrs. begin. on or after 1/1/90.

In 1988, P.L. 100-647, Sec. 3011(a), added Code Sec. 4980B, effective as provided in Sec. 3011(d) of this Act which reads as follows:

"(d) Effective date.

"The amendments made by this section shall apply to taxable years beginning after December 31, 1988, but shall not apply to any plan for any plan year to which section 162(k) of the Internal Revenue Code of 1986 (as in effect on the day before the date of the enactment of this Act [11/10/88]) did not apply by reason of section 10001(e)(2) of the Consolidated Omnibus Budget Reconciliation Act of 1985."

Sec. 4980C. Requirements for issuers of qualified long-term care insurance contracts.

(a) General rule.

There is hereby imposed on any person failing to meet the requirements of subsection (c) or (d) a tax in the amount determined under subsection (b).

(b) Amount.

(1) In general. The amount of the tax imposed by subsection (a) shall be $100 per insured for each day any requirement of subsection (c) or (d) is not met with respect to each qualified long-term care insurance contract.

(2) Waiver. In the case of a failure which is due to reasonable cause and not to willful neglect, the Secretary may waive part or all of the tax imposed by subsection (a) to the extent that payment of the tax would be excessive relative to the failure involved.

Excise and miscellaneous taxes

Code Sec. 4980B

(C) Each covered employee or qualified beneficiary is responsible for notifying the plan administrator of the occurrence of any qualifying event described in subparagraph (C) or (E) of paragraph (3) within 60 days after the date of the qualifying event and each qualified beneficiary who is determined, under title II or XVI of the Social Security Act, to have been disabled at any time during the first 60 days of continuation coverage under this section is responsible for notifying the plan administrator of such determination within 60 days after the date of the determination and for notifying the plan administrator within 30 days of the date of any final determination under such title or titles that the qualified beneficiary is no longer disabled.

(D) The plan administrator shall notify—

    (i) in the case of a qualifying event described in subparagraph (A), (B), (D), or (F) of paragraph (3), any qualified beneficiary with respect to such event, and

    (ii) in the case of a qualifying event described in subparagraph (C) or (E) of paragraph (3) where the covered employee notifies the plan administrator under subparagraph (C), any qualified beneficiary with respect to such event,

of such beneficiary's rights under this subsection.

The requirements of subparagraph (B) shall be considered satisfied in the case of a multiemployer plan in connection with a qualifying event described in paragraph (3)(B) if the plan provides that the determination of the occurrence of such qualifying event will be made by the plan administrator. For purposes of subparagraph (D), any notification shall be made within 14 days (or, in the case of a group health plan which is a multiemployer plan, such longer period of time as may be provided in the terms of the plan) of the date on which the plan administrator is notified under subparagraph (B) or (C), whichever is applicable, and any such notification to an individual who is a qualified beneficiary as the spouse of the covered employee shall be treated as notification to all other qualified beneficiaries residing with such spouse at the time such notification is made.

(7) Covered employee. For purposes of this subsection, the term "covered employee" means an individual who is (or was) provided coverage under a group health plan by virtue of the performance of services by the individual for 1 or more persons maintaining the plan (including as an employee defined in section 401(c)(1)).

(8) Optional extension of required periods. A group health plan shall not be treated as failing to meet the requirements of this subsection solely because the plan provides both—

    (A) that the period of extended coverage referred to in paragraph (2)(B) commences with the date of the loss of coverage, and

    (B) that the applicable notice period provided under paragraph (6)(B) commences with the date of the loss of coverage.

(g) Definitions.

For purposes of this section—

(1) Qualified beneficiary.

    (A) In general. The term "qualified beneficiary" means, with respect to a covered employee under a group health plan, any other individual who, on the day before the qualifying event for that employee, is a beneficiary under the plan—

        (i) as the spouse of the covered employee, or

        (ii) as the dependent child of the employee.

Such term shall also include a child who is born to or placed for adoption with the covered employee during the period of continuation coverage under this section.

    (B) Special rule for terminations and reduced employment. In the case of a qualifying event described in subsection (f)(3)(B), the term "qualified beneficiary" includes the covered employee.

    (C) Exception for nonresident aliens. Notwithstanding subparagraphs (A) and (B), the term "qualified beneficiary" does not include an individual whose status as a covered employee is attributable to a period in which such individual was a nonresident alien who received no earned income (within the meaning of section 911(d)(2)) from the employer which constituted income from sources within the United States (within the meaning of section 861(a)(3)). If an individual is not a qualified beneficiary pursuant to the previous sentence, a spouse or dependent child of such individual shall not be considered a qualified beneficiary by virtue of the relationship of the individual.

    (D) Special rule for retirees and widows. In the case of a qualifying event described in subsection (f)(3)(F), the term "qualified beneficiary" includes a covered employee who had retired on or before the date of substantial elimination of coverage and any other individual who, on the day before such qualifying event, is a beneficiary under the plan—

        (i) as the spouse of the covered employee,

        (ii) as the dependent child of the covered employee, or

        (iii) as the surviving spouse of the covered employee.

(2) Group health plan. The term "group health plan" has the meaning given such term by section 5000(b)(1). Such term shall not include any plan substantially all of the coverage under which is for qualified long-term care services (as defined in section 7702B(c)).

(3) Plan administrator. The term "plan administrator" has the meaning given the term "administrator" by section 3(16)(A) of the Employee Retirement Income Security Act of 1974.

(4) Correction. A failure of a group health plan to meet the requirements of subsection (f) with respect to any qualified beneficiary shall be treated as corrected if—

    (A) such failure is retroactively undone to the extent possible, and

    (B) the qualified beneficiary is placed in a financial position which is as good as such beneficiary would have been in had such failure not occurred.

For purposes of applying subparagraph (B), the qualified beneficiary shall be treated as if he had elected the most favorable coverage in light of the expenses he incurred since the failure first occurred.

In 2010, P.L. 111-344, Sec. 116(b)(1), substituted "February 12, 2011" for "December 31, 2010" in subclause (f)(2)(B)(i)(V) ... Sec. 116(b)(2), substituted "February 12, 2011" for "December 31, 2010" in subclause (f)(2)(B)(i)(VI), effective for periods of coverage which would (without regard to the amendments made by this section) end on or after 12/31/2010.

In 2009, P.L. 111-5, Sec. 1899F(b)(1), substituted "(VI) SPECIAL RULE FOR DISABILITY. In the case of a qualified beneficiary" for "In the case of a qualified beneficiary" in clause (f)(2)(B)(i) ... Sec. 1899F(b)(2), redesignated subclauses (f)(2)(B)(i)(V) and (VI), as amended, as subclauses (f)(2)(B)(i)(VII) and (VIII), respectively, and by added new subclauses (f)(2)(B)(i)(V) and (VI) in clause (f)(2)(B)(i), effective for periods of coverage which would (without regard to the amendments made by this section) end. on or after 2/17/2009.

In 2002, P.L. 107-210, Sec. 203(e)(3), added subpara. (f)(5)(C), effective 8/6/2002.

—P.L. 107-210, Sec. 203(f), of this Act, provides:

"(f) Rule of construction. Nothing in this title (or the amendments made by this title), other than provisions relating to COBRA continuation coverage and report-

3,355

(c) Responsibilities.
The requirements of this subsection are as follows:
(1) Requirements of model provisions.
   (A) Model regulation. The following requirements of the model regulation must be met:
      (i) Section 13 (relating to application forms and replacement coverage).
      (ii) Section 14 (relating to reporting requirements), except that the issuer shall also report at least annually the number of claims denied during the reporting period for each class of business (expressed as a percentage of claims denied), other than claims denied for failure to meet the waiting period or because of any applicable preexisting condition.
      (iii) Section 20 (relating to filing requirements for marketing).
      (iv) Section 21 (relating to standards for marketing), including inaccurate completion of medical histories, other than sections 21C(1) and 21C(6) thereof, except that—
         (I) in addition to such requirements, no person shall, in selling or offering to sell a qualified long-term care insurance contract, misrepresent a material fact; and
         (II) no such requirements shall include a requirement to inquire or identify whether a prospective applicant or enrollee for long-term care insurance has accident and sickness insurance.
      (v) Section 22 (relating to appropriateness of recommended purchase).
      (vi) Section 24 (relating to standard format outline of coverage).
      (vii) Section 25 (relating to requirement to deliver shopper's guide).
   (B) Model act. The following requirements of the model Act must be met:
      (i) Section 6F (relating to right to return), except that such section shall also apply to denials of applications and any refund shall be made within 30 days of the return or denial.
      (ii) Section 6G (relating to outline of coverage).
      (iii) Section 6H (relating to requirements for certificates under group plans).
      (iv) Section 6I (relating to policy summary).
      (v) Section 6J (relating to monthly reports on accelerated death benefits).
      (vi) Section 7 (relating to incontestability period).
   (C) Definitions. For purposes of this paragraph, the terms "model regulation" and "model Act" have the meanings given such terms by section 7702B(g)(2)(B).
(2) Delivery of policy. If an application for a qualified long-term care insurance contract (or for a certificate under such a contract for a group) is approved, the issuer shall deliver to the applicant (or policyholder or certificateholder) the contract (or certificate) of insurance not later than 30 days after the date of the approval.
(3) Information on denials of claims. If a claim under a qualified long-term care insurance contract is denied, the issuer shall, within 60 days of the date of a written request by the policyholder or certificateholder (or representative)—
   (A) provide a written explanation of the reasons for the denial, and
   (B) make available all information directly relating to such denial.

(d) Disclosure.
The requirements of this subsection are met if the issuer of a long-term care insurance policy discloses in such policy and in the outline of coverage required under subsection (c)(1)(B)(ii) that the policy is intended to be a qualified long-term care insurance contract under section 7702B(b).
(e) Qualified long-term care insurance contract defined.
For purposes of this section, the term "qualified long-term care insurance contract" has the meaning given such term by section 7702B.
(f) Coordination with State requirements.
If a State imposes any requirement which is more stringent than the analogous requirement imposed by this section or section 7702B(g), the requirement imposed by this section or section 7702B(g) shall be treated as met if the more stringent State requirement is met.

In **1996**, P.L. 104-191, Sec. 326(a), added Code Sec. 4980C, effective for actions taken after 12/31/96.

Sec. 4980D. Failure to meet certain group health plan requirements.
(a) General rule.
There is hereby imposed a tax on any failure of a group health plan to meet the requirements of chapter 100 (relating to group health plan requirements).
(b) Amount of tax.
(1) In general. The amount of the tax imposed by subsection (a) on any failure shall be $100 for each day in the noncompliance period with respect to each individual to whom such failure relates.
(2) Noncompliance period. For purposes of this section, the term "noncompliance period" means, with respect to any failure, the period—
   (A) beginning on the date such failure first occurs, and
   (B) ending on the date such failure is corrected.
(3) Minimum tax for noncompliance period where failure discovered after notice of examination. Notwithstanding paragraphs (1) and (2) of subsection (c)—
   (A) In general. In the case of 1 or more failures with respect to an individual—
      (i) which are not corrected before the date a notice of examination of income tax liability is sent to the employer, and
      (ii) which occurred or continued during the period under examination.
   the amount of tax imposed by subsection (a) by reason of such failures with respect to such individual shall not be less than the lesser of $2,500 or the amount of tax which would be imposed by subsection (a) without regard to such paragraphs.
   (B) Higher minimum tax where violations are more than de minimis. To the extent violations for which any person is liable under subsection (e) for any year are more than de minimis, subparagraph (A) shall be applied by substituting "$15,000" for "$2,500" with respect to such person.
   (C) Exception for church plans. This paragraph shall not apply to any failure under a church plan (as defined in section 414(e)).
(c) Limitations on amount of tax.
(1) Tax not to apply where failure not discovered exercising reasonable diligence. No tax shall be imposed by subsection (a) on any failure during any period for which it is established to the satisfaction of the Secretary that the person otherwise liable for such tax did not know, and ex-

ercising reasonable diligence would not have known, that such failure existed.

(2) Tax not to apply to failures corrected within certain periods. No tax shall be imposed by subsection (a) on any failure if—

(A) such failure was due to reasonable cause and not to willful neglect, and

(B)(i) in the case of a plan other than a church plan (as defined in section 414(e)), such failure is corrected during the 30-day period beginning on the 1st date the person otherwise liable for such tax knew, or exercising reasonable diligence would have known, that such failure existed, and

(ii) in the case of a church plan (as so defined), such failure is corrected before the close of the correction period (determined under the rules of section 414(e)(4)(C)).

(3) Overall limitation for unintentional failures. In the case of failures which are due to reasonable cause and not to willful neglect—

(A) Single employer plans.

(i) In general. In the case of failures with respect to plans other than specified multiple employer health plans, the tax impose by subsection (a) for failures during the taxable year of the employer shall not exceed the amount equal to the lesser of—

(I) 10 percent of the aggregate amount paid or incurred by the employer (or predecessor employer) during the preceding taxable year for group health plans, or

(II) $500,000.

(ii) Taxable years in the case of certain controlled groups. For purposes of this subparagraph, if not all persons who are treated as a single employer for purposes of this section have the same taxable year, the taxable years taken into account shall be determined under principles similar to the principles of section 1561.

(B) Specified multiple employer health plans.

(i) In general. In the case of failures with respect to a specified multiple employer health plan, the tax imposed by subsection (a) for failures during the taxable year of the trust forming part of such plan shall not exceed the amount equal to the lesser of—

(I) 10 percent of the amount paid or incurred by such trust during such taxable year to provide medical care (as defined in section 9832(d)(3)) directly or through insurance, reimbursement, or otherwise, or

(II) $500,000.

For purposes of the preceding sentence, all plans of which the same trust forms a part shall be treated as one plan.

(ii) Special rule for employers required to pay tax. If an employer is assessed a tax imposed by subsection (a) by reason of a failure with respect to a specified multiple employer health plan, the limit shall be determined under subparagraph (A) (and not under this subparagraph) and as if such plan were not a specified multiple employer health plan.

(4) Waiver by Secretary. In the case of a failure which is due to reasonable cause and not to willful neglect, the Secretary may waive part or all of the tax imposed by subsection (a) to the extent that the payment of such tax would be excessive relative to the failure involved.

(d) Tax not to apply to certain insured small employer plans.

(1) In general. In the case of a group health plan of a small employer which provides health insurance coverage solely through a contract with a health insurance issuer, no tax shall be imposed by this section on the employer on any failure (other than a failure attributable to section 9811) which is solely because of the health insurance coverage offered by such issuer.

(2) Small employer.

(A) In general. For purposes of paragraph (1), the term "small employer" means, with respect to a calendar year and a plan year, an employer who employed an average of at least 2 but not more than 50 employees on business days during the preceding calendar year and who employs at least 2 employees on the first day of the plan year. For purposes of the preceding sentence, all persons treated as a single employer under subsection (b), (c), (m), or (o) of section 414 shall be treated as one employer.

(B) Employers not in existence in preceding year. In the case of an employer which was not in existence throughout the preceding calendar year, the determination of whether such employer is a small employer shall be based on the average number of employees that it is reasonably expected such employer will employ on business days in the current calendar year.

(C) Predecessors. Any reference in this paragraph to an employer shall include a reference to any predecessor of such employer.

(3) Health insurance coverage; health insurance issuer. For purposes of paragraph (1), the terms "health insurance coverage" and "health insurance issuer" have the respective meanings given such terms by section 9832.

(e) Liability for tax.

The following shall be liable for the tax imposed by subsection (a) on a failure:

(1) Except as otherwise provided in this subsection, the employer,

(2) In the case of a multiemployer plan, the plan,

(3) In the case of a failure under section 9803 (relating to guaranteed renewability) with respect to a plan described in subsection (f)(2)(B), the plan.

(f) Definitions.

For purposes of this section—

(1) Group health plan. The term "group health plan" has the meaning given such term by section 9832(a).

(2) Specified multiple employer health plan. The term "specified multiple employer health plan" means a group health plan which is—

(A) any multiemployer plan, or

(B) any multiple employer welfare arrangement (as defined in section 3(40) of the Employee Retirement Income Security Act of 1974, as in effect on the date of the enactment of this section).

(3) Correction. A failure of a group health plan shall be treated as corrected if—

(A) such failure is retroactively undone to the extent possible, and

(B) the person to whom the failure relates is placed in a financial position which is as good as such person would have been in had such failure not occurred.

In **2005**, P.L. 109-135, Sec. 412(ww), substituted "plan" for "plans" in subsec. (a), effective 12/21/2005.

In **1997**, P.L. 105-34, Sec. 1531(b)(2)(A), substituted "plans" for "plan portability, access, and renewability" in subsec. (a)... Sec. 1531(b)(2)(B), substituted

Excise and miscellaneous taxes

Code Sec. 4980F(c)(3)(A)

"9832(d)(3)" for "9805(d)(3)" in subclause (c)(3)(B)(i)(I) ... Sec. 1531(b)(2)(C), added "(other than a failure attributable to section 9811)" after "on any failure" in para. (d)(1) ... Sec. 1531(b)(2)(D), substituted "9832" for "9805" in para. (d)(3) ... Sec. 1531(b)(2)(E), substituted "9832(a)" for "9805(a)" in para. (f)(1), effective for group health plans for plan yrs. begin. on or after 1/1/98.

In 1996, P.L. 104-191, Sec. 402(a), added Code Sec. 4980D, effective for failures under chapter 100 of the Internal Revenue Code of 1986 (as added by Sec. 401 of this Act) [see note following Code Sec. 9801].

Sec. 4980E. Failure of employer to make comparable Archer MSA contributions.

(a) General rule.

In the case of an employer who makes a contribution to the Archer MSA of any employee with respect to coverage under a high deductible health plan of the employer during a calendar year, there is hereby imposed a tax on the failure of such employer to meet the requirements of subsection (d) for such calendar year.

(b) Amount of tax.

The amount of the tax imposed by subsection (a) on any failure for any calendar year is the amount equal to 35 percent of the aggregate amount contributed by the employer to Archer MSAs of employees for taxable years of such employees ending with or within such calendar year.

(c) Waiver by Secretary.

In the case of a failure which is due to reasonable cause and not to willful neglect, the Secretary may waive part or all of the tax imposed by subsection (a) to the extent that the payment of such tax would be excessive relative to the failure involved.

(d) Employer required to make comparable MSA contributions for all participating employees.

(1) In general. An employer meets the requirements of this subsection for any calendar year if the employer makes available comparable contributions to the Archer MSAs of all comparable participating employees for each coverage period during such calendar year.

(2) Comparable contributions.

(A) In general. For purposes of paragraph (1), the term "comparable contributions" means contributions—

(i) which are the same amount, or

(ii) which are the same percentage of the annual deductible limit under the high deductible health plan covering the employees.

(B) Part-year employees. In the case of an employee who is employed by the employer for only a portion of the calendar year, a contribution to the Archer MSA of such employee shall be treated as comparable if it is an amount which bears the same ratio to the comparable amount (determined without regard to this subparagraph) as such portion bears to the entire calendar year.

(3) Comparable participating employees. For purposes of paragraph (1), the term "comparable participating employees" means all employees—

(A) who are eligible individuals covered under any high deductible health plan of the employer, and

(B) who have the same category of coverage.

For purposes of subparagraph (B), the categories of coverage are self-only and family coverage.

(4) Part-time employees.

(A) In general. Paragraph (3) shall be applied separately with respect to part-time employees and other employees.

(B) Part-time employee. For purposes of subparagraph (A), the term "part-time employee" means any employee who is customarily employed for fewer than 30 hours per week.

(e) Controlled groups.

For purposes of this section, all persons treated as a single employer under subsection (b), (c), (m), or (o) of section 414 shall be treated as 1 employer.

(f) Definitions.

Terms used in this section which are also used in section 220 have the respective meanings given such terms in section 220.

In 2002, P.L. 107-147, Sec. 417(17)(A), amended the heading of Code Sec. 4980E, effective 3/9/2002.

Prior to amendment, the heading of Code Sec. 4980E read as follows:

"SEC. 4980E. FAILURE OF EMPLOYER TO MAKE COMPARABLE MEDICAL SAVINGS ACCOUNT CONTRIBUTIONS."

In 2000, P.L. 106-554, Sec. 1(a)(7), [which enacted into law Sec. 202(a)(8) of P.L. 106-554] substituted "Archer MSA" for "medical savings account" in subsec. (a) and subpara. (d)(2)(B) ... Sec. 1(a)(7), [which enacted into law Sec. 202(b)(2)(D) of P.L. 106-554] substituted "Archer MSAs" for "medical savings accounts" in subsec. (b) and para. (d)(1), effective 12/21/2000.

In 1996, P.L. 104-191, Sec. 301(c)(4)(A), added Code Sec. 4980E, effective for tax. yrs. begin. after 12/31/96.

Sec. 4980F. Failure of applicable plans reducing benefit accruals to satisfy notice requirements.

(a) Imposition of tax.

There is hereby imposed a tax on the failure of any applicable pension plan to meet the requirements of subsection (e) with respect to any applicable individual.

(b) Amount of tax.

(1) In general. The amount of the tax imposed by subsection (a) on any failure with respect to any applicable individual shall be $100 for each day in the noncompliance period with respect to such failure.

(2) Noncompliance period. For purposes of this section, the term "noncompliance period" means, with respect to any failure, the period beginning on the date the failure first occurs and ending on the date the notice to which the failure relates is provided or the failure is otherwise corrected.

(c) Limitations on amount of tax.

(1) Tax not to apply where failure not discovered and reasonable diligence exercised. No tax shall be imposed by subsection (a) on any failure during any period for which it is established to the satisfaction of the Secretary that any person subject to liability for the tax under subsection (d) did not know that the failure existed and exercised reasonable diligence to meet the requirements of subsection (e).

(2) Tax not to apply to failures corrected within 30 days. No tax shall be imposed by subsection (a) on any failure if—

(A) any person subject to liability for the tax under subsection (d) exercised reasonable diligence to meet the requirements of subsection (e), and

(B) such person provides the notice described in subsection (e) during the 30-day period beginning on the first date such person knew, or exercising reasonable diligence would have known, that such failure existed.

(3) Overall limitation for unintentional failures.

(A) In general. If the person subject to liability for tax under subsection (d) exercised reasonable diligence to meet the requirements of subsection (e), the tax imposed by subsection (a) for failures during the taxable year of the employer (or, in the case of a multiemployer plan, the taxable year of the trust forming part of the plan) shall not exceed $500,000. For purposes of the preceding sentence, all multiemployer plans of which the same trust forms a part shall be treated as 1 plan.

3,359

Code Sec. 4980F(c)(3)(B)   **Excise and miscellaneous taxes**

(B) Taxable years in the case of certain controlled groups. For purposes of this paragraph, if all persons who are treated as a single employer for purposes of this section do not have the same taxable year, the taxable years taken into account shall be determined under principles similar to the principles of section 1561.

(4) Waiver by Secretary. In the case of a failure which is due to reasonable cause and not to willful neglect, the Secretary may waive part or all of the tax imposed by subsection (a) to the extent that the payment of such tax would be excessive or otherwise inequitable relative to the failure involved.

(d) Liability for tax.

The following shall be liable for the tax imposed by subsection (a):

(1) In the case of a plan other than a multiemployer plan, the employer.

(2) In the case of a multiemployer plan, the plan.

(e) Notice requirements for plans significantly reducing benefit accruals.

(1) In general. If an applicable pension plan is amended to provide for a significant reduction in the rate of future benefit accrual, the plan administrator shall provide the notice described in paragraph (2) to each applicable individual (and to each employee organization representing applicable individuals) and to each employer who has an obligation to contribute to the plan.

(2) Notice. The notice required by paragraph (1) shall be written in a manner calculated to be understood by the average plan participant and shall provide sufficient information (as determined in accordance with regulations prescribed by the Secretary) to allow applicable individuals to understand the effect of the plan amendment. The Secretary may provide a simplified form of notice for, or exempt from any notice requirement, a plan—

(A) which has fewer than 100 participants who have accrued a benefit under the plan, or

(B) which offers participants the option to choose between the new benefit formula and the old benefit formula.

(3) Timing of notice. Except as provided in regulations, the notice required by paragraph (1) shall be provided within a reasonable time before the effective date of the plan amendment.

(4) Designees. Any notice under paragraph (1) may be provided to a person designated, in writing, by the person to which it would otherwise be provided.

(5) Notice before adoption of amendment. A plan shall not be treated as failing to meet the requirements of paragraph (1) merely because notice is provided before the adoption of the plan amendment if no material modification of the amendment occurs before the amendment is adopted.

(f) Definitions and special rules.

For purposes of this section—

(1) Applicable individual. The term "applicable individual" means, with respect to any plan amendment—

(A) each participant in the plan, and

(B) any beneficiary who is an alternate payee (within the meaning of section 414(p)(8)) under an applicable qualified domestic relations order (within the meaning of section 414(p)(1)(A)),

whose rate of future benefit accrual under the plan may reasonably be expected to be significantly reduced by such plan amendment.

(2) Applicable pension plan. The term "applicable pension plan" means—

(A) any defined benefit plan described in section 401(a) which includes a trust exempt from tax under section 501(a), or

(B) an individual account plan which is subject to the funding standards of section 412.

Such term shall not include a governmental plan (within the meaning of section 414(d)) or a church plan (within the meaning of section 414(e)) with respect to which the election provided by section 410(d) has not been made.

(3) Early retirement. A plan amendment which eliminates or reduces any early retirement benefit or retirement-type subsidy (within the meaning of section 411(d)(6)(B)(i)) shall be treated as having the effect of reducing the rate of future benefit accrual.

(g) New technologies.

The Secretary may by regulations allow any notice under subsection (e) to be provided by using new technologies.

In 2010, P.L. 111-312, Sec. 101(a)(1), substituted "December 31, 2012" for "December 31, 2010" both places it appeared in Sec. 901 of P.L. 107-16, [see below] effective as if included in the enactment of P.L. 107-16, EGTRRA, 6/7/2001.

In 2006, P.L. 109-280, Sec. 402(g)(4), of this Act, provides:

"(4) Notice. In the case of a plan amendment adopted in order to comply with this section, any notice required under section 204(h) of such Act or section 4980F(e) of such Code shall be provided within 15 days of the effective date of such plan amendment. This subsection shall not apply to any plan unless such plan is maintained pursuant to one or more collective bargaining agreements between employee representatives and 1 or more employers."

—P.L. 109-280, Sec. 502(c)(2), added "and to each employer who has an obligation to contribute to the plan" before the period at the end of para. (e)(1), effective for plan yrs. begin. after 12/31/2007.

—P.L. 109-280, Sec. 811, of this Act [relating to Sec. 901 of P.L. 107-16, see below], provides:

"SEC. 811. PENSIONS AND INDIVIDUAL RETIREMENT ARRANGEMENT PROVISIONS OF ECONOMIC GROWTH AND TAX RELIEF RECONCILIATION ACT OF 2001 MADE PERMANENT.

"Title IX of the Economic Growth and Tax Relief Reconciliation Act of 2001 shall not apply to the provisions of, and amendments made by, subtitles A through F of title VI of such Act (relating to pension and individual retirement arrangement provisions)."

In 2002, P.L. 107-358, Sec. 2, added subsec. (c) in Sec.901 of P.L. 107-16 [see below], effective 12/17/2002.

—P.L. 107-147, Sec. 411(u)(1)(A), substituted "the notice described in paragraph (2)" for "written notice" in para. (e)(1) . . . Sec. 411(u)(1)(B), amended subpara. (f)(2)(A) . . . Sec. 411(u)(1)(C), deleted "significantly" after "eliminates or" and after "effect of" in para. (f)(3), effective for plan amendments taking effect on or after 6/7/2001. For transitional rules, see Sec. 659(c)(2) and (3) of P.L. 107-16 reproduced below.

Prior to amendment, subpara. (f)(2)(A) read as follows:

"(A) any defined benefit plan, or"

—P.L. 107-147, Sec. 411(u)(3), substituted "(and)" for "(or)" in Sec. 659(c)(3)(B) of P.L. 107-16 [see below], effective for plan amendments taking effect on or after 6/7/2001.

In 2001, P.L. 107-16, Sec. 659(a)(1), added Code Sec. 4980F, effective for plan amendments taking effect on or after 6/7/2001. Sec. 659(c)(2)-(3) of this Act, provides:

"(2) Transition. Until such time as the Secretary of the Treasury issues regulations under sections 4980F(e)(2) and (3) of the Internal Revenue Code of 1986, and section 204(h) of the Employee Retirement Income Security Act of 1974, as added by the amendments made by this section, a plan shall be treated as meeting the requirements of such sections if it makes a good faith effort to comply with such requirements.

"(3) Special notice rule.

"(A) In general. The period for providing any notice required by the amendments made by this section shall not end before the date which is 3 months after the date of the enactment of this Act.

"(B) Reasonable notice. The amendments made by this section shall not apply to any plan amendment taking effect on or after the date of the enactment of this Act if, before April 25, 2001, notice was provided to participants and beneficiaries adversely affected by the plan amendment (and their representatives) which was reasonably expected to notify them of the nature and effective date of the plan amendment."

—P.L. 107-16, Sec. 901, of this Act [as amended by Sec. 2 of P.L. 107-358, and Sec. 101(a)(1) of P.L. 111-312, see above], reads as follows:

"SEC. 901. SUNSET OF PROVISIONS OF ACT.

"(a) In general. All provisions of, and amendments made by, this Act shall not apply —

"(1) to taxable, plan, or limitation years beginning after December 31, 2012, or

3,360

Excise and miscellaneous taxes

Code Sec. 4980H(c)(2)(C)(ii)

"(2) in the case of title V, to estates of decedents dying, gifts made, or generation skipping transfers, after December 31, 2012.

"(b) Application of certain laws. The Internal Revenue Code of 1986 and the Employee Retirement Income Security Act of 1974 shall be applied and administered to years, estates, gifts, and transfers described in subsection (a) as if the provisions and amendments described in subsection (a) had never been enacted.

"(c) Exception. Subsection (a) shall not apply to section 803 (relating to no federal income tax on restitution received by victims of the Nazi regime or their heirs or estates)."

Sec. 4980G. Failure of employer to make comparable health savings account contributions.

(a) General rule.

In the case of an employer who makes a contribution to the health savings account of any employee during a calendar year, there is hereby imposed a tax on the failure of such employer to meet the requirements of subsection (b) for such calendar year.

(b) Rules and requirements.

Rules and requirements similar to the rules and requirements of section 4980E shall apply for purposes of this section.

(c) Regulations.

The Secretary shall issue regulations to carry out the purposes of this section, including regulations providing special rules for employers who make contributions to Archer MSAs and health savings accounts during the calendar year.

(d) Exception.

For purposes of applying section 4980E to a contribution to a health savings account of an employee who is not a highly compensated employee (as defined in section 414(q)), highly compensated employees shall not be treated as comparable participating employees.

In 2006, P.L. 109-432, Sec. 306(a), added subsec. (d) effective for tax. yrs. begin. after 12/31/2006.

In 2003, P.L. 108-173, Sec. 1201(d)(4)(A), added Code Sec. 4980G, effective for tax. yrs. begin. after 12/31/2003.

• *Caution:* Code Sec. 4980H is effective for months begin. after 12/31/2013.

Sec. 4980H. Shared responsibility for employers regarding health coverage.

(a) Large employers not offering health coverage.

If—

(1) any applicable large employer fails to offer to its full-time employees (and their dependents) the opportunity to enroll in minimum essential coverage under an eligible employer-sponsored plan (as defined in section 5000A(f)(2)) for any month, and

(2) at least one full-time employee of the applicable large employer has been certified to the employer under section 1411 of the Patient Protection and Affordable Care Act as having enrolled for such month in a qualified health plan with respect to which an applicable premium tax credit or cost-sharing reduction is allowed or paid with respect to the employee,

then there is hereby imposed on the employer an assessable payment equal to the product of the applicable payment amount and the number of individuals employed by the employer as full-time employees during such month.

(b) Large employers offering coverage with employees who qualify for premium tax credits or cost-sharing reductions.

(1) In general. If—

(A) an applicable large employer offers to its full-time employees (and their dependents) the opportunity to enroll in minimum essential coverage under an eligible employer-sponsored plan (as defined in section 5000A(f)(2)) for any month, and

(B) 1 or more full-time employees of the applicable large employer has been certified to the employer under section 1411 of the Patient Protection and Affordable Care Act as having enrolled for such month in a qualified health plan with respect to which an applicable premium tax credit or cost-sharing reduction is allowed or paid with respect to the employee,

then there is hereby imposed on the employer an assessable payment equal to the product of the number of full-time employees of the applicable large employer described in subparagraph (B) for such month and an amount equal to $1/12$ of $3,000.

(2) **Overall limitation.** The aggregate amount of tax determined under paragraph (1) with respect to all employees of an applicable large employer for any month shall not exceed the product of the applicable payment amount and the number of individuals employed by the employer as full-time employees during such month.

(3) **Repealed.**

(c) Definitions and special rules.

For purposes of this section—

(1) **Applicable payment amount.** The term "applicable payment amount" means, with respect to any month, $1/12$ of $2,000.

(2) **Applicable large employer.**

(A) In general. The term "applicable large employer" means, with respect to a calendar year, an employer who employed an average of at least 50 full-time employees on business days during the preceding calendar year.

(B) Exemption for certain employers.

(i) In general. An employer shall not be considered to employ more than 50 full-time employees if—

(I) the employer's workforce exceeds 50 full-time employees for 120 days or fewer during the calendar year, and

(II) the employees in excess of 50 employed during such 120-day period were seasonal workers.

(ii) Definition of seasonal workers. The term "seasonal worker" means a worker who performs labor or services on a seasonal basis as defined by the Secretary of Labor, including workers covered by section 500.20(s)(1) of title 29, Code of Federal Regulations and retail workers employed exclusively during holiday seasons.

(C) Rules for determining employer size. For purposes of this paragraph—

(i) Application of aggregation rule for employers. All persons treated as a single employer under subsection (b), (c), (m), or (o) of section 414 of the Internal Revenue Code of 1986 shall be treated as 1 employer.

(ii) Employers not in existence in preceding year. In the case of an employer which was not in existence throughout the preceding calendar year, the determination of whether such employer is an applicable large employer shall be based on the average number of employees that it is reasonably expected such employer will employ on business days in the current calendar year.

3,361

(iii) Predecessors. Any reference in this subsection to an employer shall include a reference to any predecessor of such employer.

(D) Application of employer size to assessable penalties.

(i) In general. The number of individuals employed by an applicable large employer as full-time employees during any month shall be reduced by 30 solely for purposes of calculating—

(I) the assessable payment under subsection (a), or

(II) the overall limitation under subsection (b)(2).

(ii) Aggregation. In the case of persons treated as 1 employer under subparagraph (C)(i), only 1 reduction under subclause (I) or (II) shall be allowed with respect to such persons and such reduction shall be allocated among such persons ratably on the basis of the number of fulltime employees employed by each such person.

(E) Full-time equivalents treated as full-time employees. Solely for purposes of determining whether an employer is an applicable large employer under this paragraph, an employer shall, in addition to the number of full-time employees for any month otherwise determined, include for such month a number of full-time employees determined by dividing the aggregate number of hours of service of employees who are not full-time employees for the month by 120.

(3) Applicable premium tax credit and cost-sharing reduction. The term "applicable premium tax credit and cost-sharing reduction" means—

(A) any premium tax credit allowed under section 36B,

(B) any cost-sharing reduction under section 1402 of the Patient Protection and Affordable Care Act, and

(C) any advance payment of such credit or reduction under section 1412 of such Act.

(4) Full-time employee.

(A) In general. The term "full-time employee" means, with respect to any month, an employee who is employed on average at least 30 hours of service per week.

(B) Hours of service. The Secretary, in consultation with the Secretary of Labor, shall prescribe such regulations, rules, and guidance as may be necessary to determine the hours of service of an employee, including rules for the application of this paragraph to employees who are not compensated on an hourly basis.

(5) Inflation adjustment.

(A) In general. In the case of any calendar year after 2014, each of the dollar amounts in subsection (b) and paragraph (1) shall be increased by an amount equal to the product of—

(i) such dollar amount, and

(ii) the premium adjustment percentage (as defined in section 1302(c)(4) of the Patient Protection and Affordable Care Act) for the calendar year.

(B) Rounding. If the amount of any increase under subparagraph (A) is not a multiple of $10, such increase shall be rounded to the next lowest multiple of $10.

(6) Other definitions. Any term used in this section which is also used in the Patient Protection and Affordable Care Act shall have the same meaning as when used in such Act.

(7) Tax nondeductible. For denial of deduction for the tax imposed by this section, see section 275(a)(6).

(d) Administration and procedure.

(1) In general. Any assessable payment provided by this section shall be paid upon notice and demand by the Secretary, and shall be assessed and collected in the same manner as an assessable penalty under subchapter B of chapter 68.

(2) Time for payment. The Secretary may provide for the payment of any assessable payment provided by this section on an annual, monthly, or other periodic basis as the Secretary may prescribe.

(3) Coordination with credits, etc.. The Secretary shall prescribe rules, regulations, or guidance for the repayment of any assessable payment (including interest) if such payment is based on the allowance or payment of an applicable premium tax credit or cost-sharing reduction with respect to an employee, such allowance or payment is subsequently disallowed, and the assessable payment would not have been required to be made but for such allowance or payment.

In 2011, P.L. 112-10, Sec. 1858(b)(4), deleted para. (b)(3) [as redesignated by Sec. 1003(d) of P.L. 111-152, see below], effective for months begin. after 12/31/2013, as if included in the provisions of Sec. 10108(i)(1)(A) of P.L. 111-148, [see below].

Prior to deletion, para. (b)(3) read as follows:

"(3) Special rules for employers providing free choice vouchers. No assessable payment shall be imposed under paragraph (1) for any month with respect to any employee to whom the employer provides a free choice voucher under section 10108 of the Patient Protection and Affordable Care Act for such month."

In 2010, P.L. 111-152, Sec. 1003(a), amended subsec. (d)(2)(D).

Prior to amendment, subsec. (d)(2)(D) read as follows:

"(D) Application to construction industry employers. In the case of any employer the substantial annual gross receipts of which are attributable to the construction industry—

"(i) subparagraph (A) shall be applied by substituting 'who employed an average of at least 5 full-time employees on business days during the preceding calendar year and whose annual payroll expenses exceed $250,000 for such preceding calendar year' for 'who employed an average of at least 50 full-time employees on business days during the preceding calendar year', and

"(ii) subparagraph (B) shall be applied by substituting '5' for '50'."

—P.L. 111-152, Sec. 1003(b)(1), substituted "an amount equal to $1/12$ of $3,000" for "400 percent of the applicable payment amount" in the flush language following subsec. (c)(1)(B) . . . Sec. 1003(b)(2), substituted "$2,000" for "$750" in subsec. (d)(1) . . . Sec. 1003(b)(3), substituted "subsection (b) and paragraph (1)" for "subsection (b)(2) and (d)(1)" in subsec. (d)(5)(A). . . Sec. 1003(c), added subpara. (d)(2)(E) . . . Sec. 1003(d), deleted subsec. (b), and redesignated subsecs. (c)-(e) as subsecs. (b)-(d), enacted 3/30/2010.

—P.L. 111-148, Sec. 1513(a), added Code Sec. 4980H, effective for months begin. after 12/31/2013.

—P.L. 111-148, Sec. 1513(c), of this Act, reads as follows:

"(c) Study and report of effect of tax on workers' wages.

"(1) In general. The Secretary of Labor shall conduct a study to determine whether employees' wages are reduced by reason of the application of the assessable payments under section 4980H of the Internal Revenue Code of 1986 (as added by the amendments made by this section). The Secretary shall make such determination on the basis of the National Compensation Survey published by the Bureau of Labor Statistics.

"(2) Report. The Secretary shall report the results of the study under paragraph (1) to the Committee on Ways and Means of the House of Representatives and to the Committee on Finance of the Senate."

—P.L. 111-148, Sec. 10106(e), amended subsec. (b) [as previously added by Sec. 1513(a) of this Act, see above] enacted 3/23/2010.

Prior to amendment, subsec. (b) read as follows:

"(b) Large employers with waiting periods exceeding 30 days.

"(1) In general. In the case of any applicable large employer which requires an extended waiting period to enroll in any minimum essential coverage under an employer-sponsored plan (as defined in section 5000A(f)(2)), there is hereby imposed on the employer an assessable payment, in the amount specified in paragraph (2), for each full-time employee of the employer to whom the extended waiting period applies.

"(2) Amount. For purposes of paragraph (1), the amount specified in this paragraph for a full-time employee is—

"(A) in the case of an extended waiting period which exceeds 30 days but does not exceed 60 days, $400, and

"(B) in the case of an extended waiting period which exceeds 60 days, $600.

"(3) Extended waiting period. The term 'extended waiting period' means any waiting period (as defined in section 2701(b)(4) of the Public Health Service Act) which exceeds 30 days."

—P.L. 111-148, Sec. 10106(f)(1), added ", with respect to any month," after "means" in subpara. (d)(4)(A) [as previously added by Sec. 1513(a) of this Act, see above] enacted 3/23/2010.

Excise and miscellaneous taxes

Code Sec. 4980I(c)(2)(A)

—P.L. 111-148, Sec. 10106(f)(2), added subpara. (d)(2)(D), effective for months begin. after 12/31/2013.
—P.L. 111-148, Sec. 10108(i)(1)(A), added para. (c)(3), effective for months begin. after 12/31/2013.

Sec. 4980I. Excise tax on high cost employer-sponsored health coverage.

> • *Caution:* Code Sec. 4980I, following, is effective for tax. yrs. begin. after 12/31/2017.

(a) Imposition of tax.
If—
(1) an employee is covered under any applicable employer-sponsored coverage of an employer at any time during a taxable period, and
(2) there is any excess benefit with respect to the coverage,
there is hereby imposed a tax equal to 40 percent of the excess benefit.

(b) Excess benefit.
For purposes of this section—
(1) In general. The term "excess benefit" means, with respect to any applicable employer-sponsored coverage made available by an employer to an employee during any taxable period, the sum of the excess amounts determined under paragraph (2) for months during the taxable period.
(2) Monthly excess amount. The excess amount determined under this paragraph for any month is the excess (if any) of—
   (A) the aggregate cost of the applicable employer-sponsored coverage of the employee for the month, over
   (B) an amount equal to $1/12$ of the annual limitation under paragraph (3) for the calendar year in which the month occurs.
(3) Annual limitation. For purposes of this subsection—
   (A) In general. The annual limitation under this paragraph for any calendar year is the dollar limit determined under subparagraph (C) for the calendar year.
   (B) Applicable annual limitation.
      (i) In general. Except as provided in clause (ii), the annual limitation which applies for any month shall be determined on the basis of the type of coverage (as determined under subsection (f)(1)) provided to the employee by the employer as of the beginning of the month.
      (ii) Multiemployer plan coverage. Any coverage provided under a multiemployer plan (as defined in section 414(f)) shall be treated as coverage other than self-only coverage.
   (C) Applicable dollar limit.
      (i) 2018. In the case of 2018, the dollar limit under this subparagraph is—
         (I) in the case of an employee with self-only coverage, $10,200 multiplied by the health cost adjustment percentage (determined by only taking into account self-only coverage), and
         (II) in the case of an employee with coverage other than self-only coverage, $27,500 multiplied by the health cost adjustment percentage (determined by only taking into account coverage other than self-only coverage).
      (ii) Health cost adjustment percentage. For purposes of clause (i), the health cost adjustment percentage is equal to 100 percent plus the excess (if any) of—
         (I) the percentage by which the per employee cost for providing coverage under the Blue Cross/Blue Shield standard benefit option under the Federal Employees Health Benefits Plan for plan year 2018 (determined by using the benefit package for such coverage in 2010) exceeds such cost for plan year 2010, over
         (II) 55 percent.
      (iii) Age and gender adjustment.
         (I) In general. The amount determined under subclause (I) or (II) of clause (i), whichever is applicable, for any taxable period shall be increased by the amount determined under subclause (II).
         (II) Amount determined. The amount determined under this subclause is an amount equal to the excess (if any) of—
            (aa) the premium cost of the Blue Cross/Blue Shield standard benefit option under the Federal Employees Health Benefits Plan for the type of coverage provided such individual in such taxable period if priced for the age and gender characteristics of all employees of the individual's employer, over
            (bb) that premium cost for the provision of such coverage under such option in such taxable period if priced for the age and gender characteristics of the national workforce.
      (iv) Exception for certain individuals. In the case of an individual who is a qualified retiree or who participates in a plan sponsored by an employer the majority of whose employees covered by the plan are engaged in a high-risk profession or employed to repair or install electrical or telecommunications lines—
         (I) the dollar amount in clause (i)(I) shall be increased by $1,650, and
         (II) the dollar amount in clause (i)(II) shall be increased by $3,450,
      (v) Subsequent years. In the case of any calendar year after 2018, each of the dollar amounts under clauses (i) (after the application of clause (ii)) and (iv) shall be increased to the amount equal to such amount as in effect for the calendar year preceding such year, increased by an amount equal to the product of—
         (I) such amount as so in effect, multiplied by
         (II) the cost-of-living adjustment determined under section 1(f)(3) for such year (determined by substituting the calendar year that is 2 years before such year for "1992" in subparagraph (B) thereof), increased by 1 percentage point in the case of determinations for calendar years beginning before 2020.
   If any amount determined under this clause is not a multiple of $50, such amount shall be rounded to the nearest multiple of $50.
   (D) Repealed.

(c) Liability to pay tax.
(1) In general. Each coverage provider shall pay the tax imposed by subsection (a) on its applicable share of the excess benefit with respect to an employee for any taxable period.
(2) Coverage provider. For purposes of this subsection, the term "coverage provider" means each of the following:
   (A) Health insurance coverage. If the applicable employer-sponsored coverage consists of coverage under a

group health plan which provides health insurance coverage, the health insurance issuer.

(B) HSA and MSA contributions. If the applicable employer-sponsored coverage consists of coverage under an arrangement under which the employer makes contributions described in subsection (b) or (d) of section 106, the employer.

(C) Other coverage. In the case of any other applicable employer-sponsored coverage, the person that administers the plan benefits.

(3) Applicable share. For purposes of this subsection, a coverage provider's applicable share of an excess benefit for any taxable period is the amount which bears the same ratio to the amount of such excess benefit as—

(A) the cost of the applicable employer sponsored coverage provided by the provider to the employee during such period, bears to

(B) the aggregate cost of all applicable employer-sponsored coverage provided to the employee by all coverage providers during such period.

(4) Responsibility to calculate tax and applicable shares.

(A) In general. Each employer shall—

(i) calculate for each taxable period the amount of the excess benefit subject to the tax imposed by subsection (a) and the applicable share of such excess benefit for each coverage provider, and

(ii) notify, at such time and in such manner as the Secretary may prescribe, the Secretary and each coverage provider of the amount so determined for the provider.

(B) Special rule for multiemployer plans. In the case of applicable employer-sponsored coverage made available to employees through a multiemployer plan (as defined in section 414(f)), the plan sponsor shall make the calculations, and provide the notice, required under subparagraph (A).

(d) Applicable employer-sponsored coverage; cost.
For purposes of this section—

(1) Applicable employer-sponsored coverage.

(A) In general. The term "applicable employer-sponsored coverage" means, with respect to any employee, coverage under any group health plan made available to the employee by an employer which is excludable from the employee's gross income under section 106, or would be so excludable if it were employer-provided coverage (within the meaning of such section 106).

(B) Exceptions. The term "applicable employer-sponsored coverage" shall not include—

(i) any coverage (whether through insurance or otherwise) described in section 9832(c)(1) (other than subparagraph (G) thereof) or for long-term care, or

(ii) any coverage under a separate policy, certificate, or contract of insurance which provides benefits substantially all of which are for treatment of the mouth (including any organ or structure within the mouth) or for treatment of the eye, or

(iii) any coverage described in section 9832(c)(3) the payment for which is not excludable from gross income and for which a deduction under section 162(l) is not allowable.

(C) Coverage includes employee paid portion. Coverage shall be treated as applicable employer-sponsored coverage without regard to whether the employer or employee pays for the coverage.

(D) Self-employed individual. In the case of an individual who is an employee within the meaning of section 401(c)(1), coverage under any group health plan providing health insurance coverage shall be treated as applicable employer-sponsored coverage if a deduction is allowable under section 162(l) with respect to all or any portion of the cost of the coverage.

(E) Governmental plans included. Applicable employer-sponsored coverage shall include coverage under any group health plan established and maintained primarily for its civilian employees by the Government of the United States, by the government of any State or political subdivision thereof, or by any agency or instrumentality of any such government.

(2) Determination of cost.

(A) In general. The cost of applicable employer-sponsored coverage shall be determined under rules similar to the rules of section 4980B(f)(4), except that in determining such cost, any portion of the cost of such coverage which is attributable to the tax imposed under this section shall not be taken into account and the amount of such cost shall be calculated separately for self-only coverage and other coverage. In the case of applicable employer-sponsored coverage which provides coverage to retired employees, the plan may elect to treat a retired employee who has not attained the age of 65 and a retired employee who has attained the age of 65 as similarly situated beneficiaries.

(B) Health FSAS. In the case of applicable employer-sponsored coverage consisting of coverage under a flexible spending arrangement (as defined in section 106(c)(2)), the cost of the coverage shall be equal to the sum of—

(i) the amount of employer contributions under any salary reduction election under the arrangement, plus

(ii) the amount determined under subparagraph (A) with respect to any reimbursement under the arrangement in excess of the contributions described in clause (i).

(C) Archer MSAS and HSAS. In the case of applicable employer-sponsored coverage consisting of coverage under an arrangement under which the employer makes contributions described in subsection (b) or (d) of section 106, the cost of the coverage shall be equal to the amount of employer contributions under the arrangement.

(D) Allocation on a monthly basis.
If cost is determined on other than a monthly basis, the cost shall be allocated to months in a taxable period on such basis as the Secretary may prescribe.

(3) Employee. The term "employee" includes any former employee, surviving spouse, or other primary insured individual.

(e) Penalty for failure to properly calculate excess benefit.

(1) In general. If, for any taxable period, the tax imposed by subsection (a) exceeds the tax determined under such subsection with respect to the total excess benefit calculated by the employer or plan sponsor under subsection (c)(4)—

(A) each coverage provider shall pay the tax on its applicable share (determined in the same manner as under subsection (c)(4)) of the excess, but no penalty shall be imposed on the provider with respect to such amount, and

Excise and miscellaneous taxes Code Sec. 4980I

(B) the employer or plan sponsor shall, in addition to any tax imposed by subsection (a), pay a penalty in an amount equal to such excess, plus interest at the underpayment rate determined under section 6621 for the period beginning on the due date for the payment of tax imposed by subsection (a) to which the excess relates and ending on the date of payment of the penalty.

(2) Limitations on penalty.

(A) Penalty not to apply where failure not discovered exercising reasonable diligence. No penalty shall be imposed by paragraph (1)(B) on any failure to properly calculate the excess benefit during any period for which it is established to the satisfaction of the Secretary that the employer or plan sponsor neither knew, nor exercising reasonable diligence would have known, that such failure existed.

(B) Penalty not to apply to failures corrected within 30 days. No penalty shall be imposed by paragraph (1)(B) on any such failure if—

(i) such failure was due to reasonable cause and not to willful neglect, and

(ii) such failure is corrected during the 30-day period beginning on the 1st date that the employer knew, or exercising reasonable diligence would have known, that such failure existed.

(C) Waiver by secretary. In the case of any such failure which is due to reasonable cause and not to willful neglect, the Secretary may waive part or all of the penalty imposed by paragraph (1), to the extent that the payment of such penalty would be excessive or otherwise inequitable relative to the failure involved.

(f) Other definitions and special rules.

For purposes of this section—

(1) Coverage determinations.

(A) In general. Except as provided in subparagraph (B), an employee shall be treated as having self-only coverage with respect to any applicable employer-sponsored coverage of an employer.

(B) Minimum essential coverage. An employee shall be treated as having coverage other than self-only coverage only if the employee is enrolled in coverage other than self-only coverage in a group health plan which provides minimum essential coverage (as defined in section 5000A(f)) to the employee and at least one other beneficiary, and the benefits provided under such minimum essential coverage do not vary based on whether any individual covered under such coverage is the employee or another beneficiary.

(2) Qualified retiree. The term "qualified retiree" means any individual who—

(A) is receiving coverage by reason of being a retiree,

(B) has attained age 55, and

(C) is not entitled to benefits or eligible for enrollment under the Medicare program under title XVIII of the Social Security Act.

(3) Employees engaged in high-risk profession. The term "employees engaged in a high risk profession" means law enforcement officers (as such term is defined in section 1204 of the Omnibus Crime Control and Safe Streets Act of 1968), employees in fire protection activities (as such term is defined in section 3(y) of the Fair Labor Standards Act of 1938), individuals who provide out-of-hospital emergency medical care (including emergency medical technicians, paramedics, and first-responders), individuals whose primary work is longshore work (as defined in section 258(b) of the Immigration and Nationality Act (8 U.S.C. 1288(b)), determined without regard to paragraph (2) thereof), and individuals engaged in the construction, mining, agriculture (not including food processing), forestry, and fishing industries. Such term includes an employee who is retired from a high-risk profession described in the preceding sentence, if such employee satisfied the requirements of such sentence for a period of not less than 20 years during the employee's employment.

(4) Group health plan. The term "group health plan" has the meaning given such term by section 5000(b)(1).

(5) Health insurance coverage; health insurance issuer.

(A) Health insurance coverage. The term "health insurance coverage" has the meaning given such term by section 9832(b)(1) (applied without regard to subparagraph (B) thereof, except as provided by the Secretary in regulations).

(B) Health insurance issuer. The term "health insurance issuer" has the meaning given such term by section 9832(b)(2).

(6) Person that administers the plan benefits. The term "person that administers the plan benefits" shall include the plan sponsor if the plan sponsor administers benefits under the plan.

(7) Plan sponsor. The term "plan sponsor" has the meaning given such term in section 3(16)(B) of the Employee Retirement Income Security Act of 1974.

(8) Taxable period. The term "taxable period" means the calendar year or such shorter period as the Secretary may prescribe. The Secretary may have different taxable periods for employers of varying sizes.

(9) Aggregation rules. All employers treated as a single employer under subsection (b), (c), (m), or (o) of section 414 shall be treated as a single employer.

(10) Denial of deduction. For denial of a deduction for the tax imposed by this section, see section 275(a)(6).

(g) Regulations.

The Secretary shall prescribe such regulations as may be necessary to carry out this section.

In 2010, P.L. 111-152, Sec. 1401(a)(1)(A), substituted "(i) In general. Except as provided in clause (ii), the annual" for "The annual" in subpara. (b)(3)(B)... Sec. 1401(a)(1)(B), added clause (b)(3)(B)(ii)... Sec. 1401(a)(2)(A), deleted "Except as provided in subparagraph (D)—" after "Applicable dollar limit." in subpara. (b)(3)(C)... Sec. 1401(a)(2)(B)(i), substituted "2018" for "2013" in the heading and text of clause (b)(3)(C)(i)... Sec. 1401(a)(2)(B)(ii), substituted "$10,200 multiplied by the health cost adjustment percentage (determined by only taking into account self-only coverage)" for "$8,500" in subcl. (b)(3)(C)(i)(I)... Sec. 1401(a)(2)(B)(iii), substituted "$27,500 multiplied by the health cost adjustment percentage (determined by only taking into account coverage other than self-only coverage)" for "$23,000" in subcl. (b)(3)(C)(i)(II)... Sec. 1401(a)(2)(C), redesignated clauses (b)(3)(C)(ii)-(iii) as (iv)-(v), respectively, and added clauses (b)(3)(C)(ii)-(iii)... Sec. 1401(a)(2)(D)(i), added "covered by the plan" after "whose employees" in clause (b)(3)(C)(iv) [as redesignated by Sec. 1401(a)(2)(C) of this Act, see above]... Sec. 1401(a)(2)(D)(ii), amended subcls. (b)(3)(C)(iv)(I)-(II) [as redesignated by Sec. 1401(a)(2)(C) of this Act, see above]

Prior to amendment, subcls. (b)(3)(C)(iv)(I)-(II) read as follows:

"(I) the dollar amount in clause (i)(I) (determined after the application of subparagraph (D)) shall be increased by $1,350, and

"(II) the dollar amount in clause (i)(II) (determined after the application of subparagraph (D)) shall be increased by $3,000."... Sec. 1401(a)(2)(E)(i), substituted "2018" for "2013" in clause (b)(3)(C)(v) [as redesignated by Sec. 1401(a)(2)(C) of this Act, see above]... Sec. 1401(a)(2)(E)(ii), substituted "clauses (i) (after the application of clause (ii)) and (iv)" for "clauses (i) and (ii)" in clause (b)(3)(C)(v) [as redesignated by Sec. 1401(a)(2)(C) of this Act, see above]... Sec. 1401(a)(2)(E)(iii), added "in the case of determinations for calendar years beginning before 2020" after "1 percentage point" in subcl. (b)(3)(C)(v)(II) [as redesignated by Sec. 1401(a)(2)(C) of this Act, see above]... Sec. 1401(a)(3), deleted subpara. (b)(3)(D)

Prior to deletion, subpara. (b)(3)(D) read as follows:

"(D) Transition rule for states with highest coverage costs—

"(i) In general. If an employee is a resident of a high cost State on the first day of any month beginning in 2013, 2014, or 2015, the annual limitation under this paragraph for such month with respect to such employee shall be an amount equal to the applicable percentage of the annual limitation (determined without regard to this subparagraph or subparagraph (C)(ii)).

3,365

"(ii) Applicable percentage. The applicable percentage is 120 percent for 2013, 110 percent for 2014, and 105 percent for 2015.

"(iii) High cost state. The term 'high cost State' means each of the 17 States which the Secretary of Health and Human Services, in consultation with the Secretary, estimates had the highest average cost during 2012 for employer-sponsored coverage under health plans. The Secretary's estimate shall be made on the basis of aggregate premiums paid in the State for such health plans, determined using the most recent data available as of August 31, 2012." . . . Sec. 1401(a)(4), redesignated clause (d)(1)(B)(ii) as (iii) and added clause (d)(1)(B)(ii) . . . Sec. 1401(a)(5), added para. (d)(3), effective for tax. yrs. begin. after 12/31/2012, as if included in the provisions of Sec. 9001(c) of P.L. 111-148.

—P.L. 111-152, Sec. 1401(b)(1), substituted "2017" for "2012" in Sec. 9001(c) of P.L. 111-148 [the effective date provided for the enactment of Code Sec. 4980I, by Sec. 9001(a) of P.L. 111-148, see below] . . . Sec. 1401(b), substituted "2017" for "2012" in Sec. 10901(c) of P.L. 111-148 [the effective date provided for the amendment of Code Sec. 4980I, by Sec. 10901 of P.L. 111-148, see below]

—P.L. 111-148, Sec. 9001(a), added Code Sec. 4980I, effective for tax. yrs. begin. after 12/31/2017 [as amended by Sec. 1401(b)(1) of P.L. 111-152, see above].

—P.L. 111-148, Sec. 10901(a), added "individuals whose primary work is longshore work (as defined in section 258(b) of the Immigration and Nationality Act (8 U.S.C. 1288(b)), determined without regard to paragraph (2) thereof)," before "and individuals engaged in the construction, mining" in para. (f)(3), as previously added by Sec. 9001(a) of this Act, see above

—P.L. 111-148, Sec. 10901(b), substituted "section 9832(c)(1) (other than subparagraph (G) thereof)" for "section 9832(c)(1)(A)" in clause (d)(1)(B)(ii), as previously added by Sec. 9001(a) of this Act, see above, effective for tax. yrs. begin. after 12/31/2017 [as amended by Sec. 1401(b)(2) of P.L. 111-152, see above].

CHAPTER 44.—QUALIFIED INVESTMENT ENTITIES

Sec.
4981. Excise tax on undistributed income of real estate investment trusts.
4982. Excise tax on undistributed income of regulated investment companies.

In 1986, P.L. 99-514, Sec. 651(c), amended the chapter heading and table of sections for chapter 44.
Prior to amendment, items read as follows:
"CHAPTER 44—REAL ESTATE INVESTMENT TRUSTS
"Sec.
"4981. Excise tax based on certain real estate investment trust taxable income not distributed during the taxable year."

Sec. 4981. Excise tax on undistributed income of real estate investment trusts.

(a) Imposition of tax.
There is hereby imposed a tax on every real estate investment trust for each calendar year equal to 4 percent of the excess (if any) of—
(1) the required distribution for such calendar year, over
(2) the distributed amount for such calendar year.

(b) Required distribution.
For purposes of this section—
(1) In general. The term "required distribution" means, with respect to any calendar year, the sum of—
    (A) 85 percent of the real estate investment trust's ordinary income for such calendar year, plus
    (B) 95 percent of the real estate investment trust's capital gain net income for such calendar year.
(2) Increase by prior year shortfall. The amount determined under paragraph (1) for any calendar year shall be increased by the excess (if any) of—
    (A) the grossed up required distribution for the preceding calendar year, over
    (B) the distributed amount for such preceding calendar year.
(3) Grossed up required distribution. The grossed up required distribution for any calendar year is the required distribution for such year determined—
    (A) with the application of paragraph (2) to such taxable year, and
    (B) by substituting "100 percent" for each percentage set forth in paragraph (1).

(c) Distributed amount.
For purposes of this section—
(1) In general. The term "distributed amount" means, with respect to any calendar year, the sum of—
    (A) the deduction for dividends paid (as defined in section 561) during such calendar year (but computed without regard to that portion of such deduction which is attributable to the amount excluded under section 857(b)(2)(D)) and
    (B) any amount on which tax is imposed under subsection (b)(1) or (b)(3)(A) of section 857 for any taxable year ending in such calendar year.
(2) Increase by prior year overdistribution. The amount determined under paragraph (1) for any calendar year shall be increased by the excess (if any) of—
    (A) the distributed amount for the preceding calendar year (determined with the application of this paragraph to such preceding calendar year), over
    (B) the grossed up required distribution for such preceding calendar year.
(3) Determination of dividends paid. The amount of the dividends paid during any calendar year shall be determined without regard to the provisions of section 858.

(d) Time for payment of tax.
The tax imposed by this section for any calendar year shall be paid on or before March 15 of the following calendar year.

(e) Definitions and special rules.
For purposes of this section—
(1) Ordinary income. The term "ordinary income" means the real estate investment trust taxable income (as defined in section 857(b)(2)) determined—
    (A) without regard to subparagraph (B) of section 857(b)(2),
    (B) by not taking into account any gain or loss from the sale or exchange of a capital asset, and
    (C) by treating the calendar year as the trust's taxable year.
(2) Capital gain net income.
    (A) In general. The term "capital gain net income" has the meaning given such term by section 1222(9) (determined by treating the calendar year as the trust's taxable year).
    (B) Reduction for net ordinary loss. The amount determined under subparagraph (A) shall be reduced by the amount of the trust's net ordinary loss for the taxable year.
    (C) Net ordinary loss. For purposes of this paragraph, the net ordinary loss for the calendar year is the amount which would be net operating loss of the trust for the calendar year if the amount of such loss were determined in the same manner as ordinary income is determined under paragraph (1).
(3) Treatment of deficiency distributions. In the case of any deficiency dividend (as defined in section 860(f))—
    (A) such dividend shall be taken into account when paid without regard to section 860, and
    (B) any income giving rise to the adjustment shall be treated as arising when the dividend is paid.

In 1988, P.L. 100-647, Sec. 1006(s)(1), amended para. (e)(2) . . . Sec. 1006(s)(3), substituted "such calendar year (but computed without regard to that portion of such deduction which is attributable to the amount excluded under section 857(b)(2)(D))" for "such calendar year" in subpara. (c)(1)(A), effective for calendar yrs. begin. after 12/31/86.
Prior to amendment, para. (e)(2) read as follows:

"(2) Capital gain net income. The term 'capital gain net income' has the meaning given to such term by section 1222(9) (determined by treating the calendar year as the trust's taxable year)."

In 1986, P.L. 99-514, Sec. 668(a), amended Code Sec. 4981, effective for calendar yrs. begin. after 12/31/86.

Prior to amendment, Code Sec. 4981 read as follows:

"SEC. 4981. EXCISE TAX BASED ON CERTAIN REAL ESTATE INVESTMENT TRUST TAXABLE INCOME NOT DISTRIBUTED DURING THE TAXABLE YEAR.

"Effective with respect to taxable years beginning after December 31, 1979, there is hereby imposed on each real estate investment trust for the taxable year a tax equal to 3 percent of the amount (if any) by which 75 percent of the real estate investment trust taxable income (as defined in section 857(b)(2), but determined without regard to section 857(b)(2)(B), and by excluding any net capital gain for the taxable year) exceeds the amount of the dividends paid deduction (as defined in section 561, but computed without regard to capital gains dividends as defined in section 857(b)(3)(C) and without regard to any dividend paid after the close of the taxable year) for the taxable year. For purposes of the preceding sentence, the determination of the real estate investment trust taxable income shall be made by taking into account only the amount and character of the items of income and deduction as reported by such trust in its return for the taxable year."

In 1976, P.L. 94-455, Sec. 1605(a), added Code Sec. 4981, effective for tax. yrs. of real investment trusts begin. after 10/4/76. Sec. 1608(d)(2) and (3) of this Act, provides:

"(2) If, as a result of a determination (as defined in section 859(c) of the Internal Revenue Code of 1954), occurring after the date of enactment of this Act, with respect to the real estate investment trust, such trust does not meet the requirement of section 856(a)(4) of the Internal Revenue Code of 1954 (as in effect before the amendment of such section by this Act) for any taxable year beginning on or before the date of the enactment of this Act, such trust may elect, within 60 days after such determination in the manner provided in regulations prescribed by the Secretary of the Treasury, to have the provisions of section 1603 (other than paragraphs (1), (2), (3), and (4) of section 1604(c)) apply with respect to such taxable year. Where the provisions of section 1603 apply to a real estate investment trust with respect to any taxable year beginning on or before the date of the enactment of this Act—

"(A) credit or refund of any overpayment of tax which results from the application of section 1603 to such taxable year shall be made as if on the date of the determination (as defined in section 859(c) of the Internal Revenue Code of 1954) 2 years remained before the expiration of the period of limitation prescribed by section 6511 of such Code on the filing of claim for refund for the taxable year to which the overpayment relates,

"(B) the running of the statute of limitations provided in section 6501 of such Code on the making of assessments, and the bringing of distraint or a proceeding in court for collection, in respect of any deficiency (as defined in section 6211 of such Code) established by such a determination, and all interest, additions to tax, additional amounts, or assessable penalties in respect thereof, shall be suspended for a period of 2 years after the date of such determination, and

"(C) the collection of any deficiency (as defined in section 6211 of such Code) established by such determination and all interest, additions to tax, additional amounts, and assessable penalties in respect thereof shall, except in cases of jeopardy, be stayed until the expiration of 60 days after the date of such determination.

No distraint or proceeding in court shall be begun for the collection of an amount the collection of which is stayed under subparagraph (C) during the period for which the collection of such amount is stayed.

"(3) Section 856(g)(3) of the Internal Revenue Code of 1954, as added by section 1604 of this Act, shall not apply with respect to a termination of an election, filed by a taxpayer under section 856(c)(1) of such Code on or before the date of the enactment of this Act, unless the provisions of part II of subchapter M of chapter 1 of subtitle A of such Code apply to such taxpayer for a taxable year ending after the date of the enactment of this Act for which such election is in effect."

Sec. 4982. Excise tax on undistributed income of regulated investment companies.

(a) Imposition of tax.

There is hereby imposed a tax on every regulated investment company for each calendar year equal to 4 percent of the excess (if any) of—

(1) the required distribution for such calendar year, over

(2) the distributed amount for such calendar year.

(b) Required distribution.

For purposes of this section—

(1) **In general.** The term "required distribution" means, with respect to any calendar year, the sum of—

(A) 98 percent of the regulated investment company's ordinary income for such calendar year, plus

(B) 98.2 percent of the regulated investment company's capital gain net income for the 1-year period ending on October 31 of such calendar year.

(2) **Increase by prior year shortfall.** The amount determined under paragraph (1) for any calendar year shall be increased by the excess (if any) of—

(A) the grossed up required distribution for the preceding calendar year, over

(B) the distributed amount for such preceding calendar year.

(3) **Grossed up required distribution.** The grossed up required distribution for any calendar year is the required distribution for such year determined—

(A) with the application of paragraph (2) to such taxable year, and

(B) by substituting "100 percent" for each percentage set forth in paragraph (1).

(c) Distributed amount.

For purposes of this section—

(1) **In general.** The term "distributed amount" means, with respect to any calendar year, the sum of—

(A) the deduction for dividends paid (as defined in section 561) during such calendar year, and

(B) any amount on which tax is imposed under subsection (b)(1) or (b)(3)(A) of section 852 for any taxable year ending in such calendar year.

(2) **Increase by prior year overdistribution.** The amount determined under paragraph (1) for any calendar year shall be increased by the excess (if any) of—

(A) the distributed amount for the preceding calendar year (determined with the application of this paragraph to such preceding calendar year), over

(B) the grossed up required distribution for such preceding calendar year.

(3) **Determination of dividends paid.** The amount of the dividends paid during any calendar year shall be determined without regard to—

(A) the provisions of section 855, and

(B) any exempt-interest dividend as defined in section 852(b)(5).

(4) **Special rule for estimated tax payments.**

(A) In general. In the case of a regulated investment company which elects the application of this paragraph for any calendar year—

(i) the distributed amount with respect to such company for such calendar year shall be increased by the amount on which qualified estimated tax payments are made by such company during such calendar year, and

(ii) the distributed amount with respect to such company for the following calendar year shall be reduced by the amount of such increase.

(B) Qualified estimated tax payments. For purposes of this paragraph, the term "qualified estimated tax payments" means, with respect to any calendar year, payments of estimated tax of a tax described in paragraph (1)(B) for any taxable year which begins (but does not end) in such calendar year.

(d) Time for payment of tax.

The tax imposed by this section for any calendar year shall be paid on or before March 15 of the following calendar year.

(e) Definitions and special rules.

For purposes of this section—

(1) **Ordinary income.** The term "ordinary income" means the investment company taxable income (as defined in section 852(b)(2)) determined—

(A) without regard to subparagraphs (A) and (D) of section 852(b)(2),

(B) by not taking into account any gain or loss from the sale or exchange of a capital asset, and

(C) by treating the calendar year as the company's taxable year.

(2) Capital gain net income.

(A) In general. Except as provided in subparagraph (B), the term "capital gain net income" has the meaning given such term by section 1222(9) (determined by treating the 1-year period ending on October 31 of any calendar year as the company's taxable year).

(B) Reduction by net ordinary loss for calendar year. The amount determined under subparagraph (A) shall be reduced (but not below the net capital gain) by the amount of the company's net ordinary loss for the calendar year.

(C) Definitions. For purposes of this paragraph—

(i) Net capital gain. The term "net capital gain" has the meaning given such term by section 1222(11) (determined by treating the 1-year period ending on October 31 of the calendar year as the company's taxable year).

(ii) Net ordinary loss. The net ordinary loss for the calendar year is the amount which would be the net operating loss of the company for the calendar year if the amount of such loss were determined in the same manner as ordinary income is determined under paragraph (1).

(3) Treatment of deficiency distributions. In the case of any deficiency dividend (as defined in section 860(f))—

(A) such dividend shall be taken into account when paid without regard to section 860, and

(B) any income giving rise to the adjustment shall be treated as arising when the dividend is paid.

(4) Election to use taxable year in certain cases.

(A) In general. If—

(i) the taxable year of the regulated investment company ends with the month of November or December, and

(ii) such company makes an election under this paragraph,

subsection (b)(1)(B) and paragraph (2) of this subsection shall be applied by taking into account the company's taxable year in lieu of the 1-year period ending on October 31 of the calendar year.

(B) Election revocable only with consent. An election under this paragraph, once made, may be revoked only with the consent of the Secretary.

(5) Treatment of specified gains and losses after October 31 of calendar year.

(A) In general. Any specified gain or specified loss which (but for this paragraph) would be properly taken into account for the portion of the calendar year after October 31 shall be treated as arising on January 1 of the following calendar year.

(B) Specified gains and losses. For purposes of this paragraph—

(i) Specified gain. The term "specified gain" means ordinary gain from the sale, exchange, or other disposition of property (including the termination of a position with respect to such property). Such term shall include any foreign currency gain attributable to a section 988 transaction (within the meaning of section 988) and any amount includible in gross income under section 1296(a)(1).

(ii) Specified loss. The term "specified loss" means ordinary loss from the sale, exchange, or other disposition of property (including the termination of a position with respect to such property). Such term shall include any foreign currency loss attributable to a section 988 transaction (within the meaning of section 988) and any amount allowable as a deduction under section 1296(a)(2).

(C) Special rule for companies electing to use the taxable year. In the case of any company making an election under paragraph (4), subparagraph (A) shall be applied by substituting the last day of the company's taxable year for October 31.

(6) Treatment of mark to market gain.

(A) In general. For purposes of determining a regulated investment company's ordinary income, notwithstanding paragraph (1)(C), each specified mark to market provision shall be applied as if such company's taxable year ended on October 31. In the case of a company making an election under paragraph (4), the preceding sentence shall be applied by substituting the last day of the company's taxable year for October 31.

(B) Specified mark to market provision. For purposes of this paragraph, the term "specified mark to market provision" means sections 1256 and 1296 and any other provision of this title (or regulations thereunder) which treats property as disposed of on the last day of the taxable year.

(7) Elective deferral of certain ordinary losses. Except as provided in regulations prescribed by the Secretary, in the case of a regulated investment company which has a taxable year other than the calendar year—

(A) such company may elect to determine its ordinary income for the calendar year without regard to any net ordinary loss (determined without regard to specified gains and losses taken into account under paragraph (5)) which is attributable to the portion of such calendar year which is after the beginning of the taxable year which begins in such calendar year, and

(B) any amount of net ordinary loss not taken into account for a calendar year by reason of subparagraph (A) shall be treated as arising on the 1st day of the following calendar year.

(f) Exception for certain regulated investment companies. This section shall not apply to any regulated investment company for any calendar year if at all times during such calendar year each shareholder in such company was—

(1) a trust described in section 401(a) and exempt from tax under section 501(a),

(2) a segregated asset account of a life insurance company held in connection with variable contracts (as defined in section 817(d))

(3) any other tax-exempt entity whose ownership of beneficial interests in the company would not preclude the application of section 817(h)(4), or

(4) another regulated investment company described in this subsection.

For purposes of the preceding sentence, any shares attributable to an investment in the regulated investment company (not exceeding $250,000) made in connection with the organization of such company shall not be taken into account.

In 2010, P.L. 111-325, Sec. 401(a)(1), deleted "either" in the matter preceding para. (f)(1)

—P.L. 111-325, Sec. 401(a)(2), deleted "or" at the end of para. (f)(1)

—P.L. 111-325, Sec. 401(a)(3), deleted the period at the end of para. (f)(2)

—P.L. 111-325, Sec. 401(a)(4), added paras. (f)(3) and (4), effective for calendar yrs. begin. after 12/22/2010.

—P.L. 111-325, Sec. 402(a), deleted paras. (e)(5) and (6) and added paras. (e)(5)-(7), effective for calendar yrs. begin. after 12/22/2010.

Excise and miscellaneous taxes   Chapter 45

Prior to deletion paras. (e)(5) and (6) read as follows:

"(5) Treatment of foreign currency gains and losses after October 31 of calendar year.

"Any foreign currency gain or loss which is attributable to a section 988 transaction and which is properly taken into account for the portion of the calendar year after October 31 shall not be taken into account in determining the amount of the ordinary income of the regulated investment company for such calendar year but shall be taken into account in determining the ordinary income of the investment company for the following calendar year. In the case of any company making an election under paragraph (4), the preceding sentence shall be applied by substituting the last day of the company's taxable year for October 31.

"(6) Treatment of gain recognized under section 1296.

"For purposes of determining a regulated investment company's ordinary income—

"(A) notwithstanding paragraph (1)(C), section 1296 shall be applied as if such company's taxable year ended on October 31, and

"(B) any ordinary gain or loss from an actual disposition of stock in a passive foreign investment company during the portion of the calendar year after October 31 shall be taken into account in determining such regulated investment company's ordinary income for the following calendar year.

"In the case of a company making an election under paragraph (4), the preceding sentence shall be applied by substituting the last day of the company's taxable year for October 31."

—P.L. 111-325, Sec. 403(a), added para. (c)(4), effective for calendar yrs. begin. after 12/22/2010.

—P.L. 111-325, Sec. 404(a), substituted "98.2 percent" for "98 percent" in subpara. (b)(1)(B), effective for calendar yrs. begin. after 12/22/2010.

In **1997**, P.L. 105-34, Sec. 1122(c)(1), added para. (e)(6), effective for tax. yrs. of United States persons begin. after 12/31/97, and tax. yrs. of foreign corporations end. with or within such tax. yrs. of United States persons.

In **1989**, P.L. 101-239, Sec. 7204(a)(1), substituted "98 percent" for "97 percent" in subpara. (b)(1)(A), effective for calendar yrs. end. after 7/10/89.

In **1988**, P.L. 100-647, Sec. 1006(l)(2), amended para. (e)(2) . . . Sec. 1006(l)(5), added para (e)(5) . . . Sec. 1006(l)(6), added subsec. (f), effective for calendar yrs. begin. after 12/31/86.

Prior to amendment, para. (e)(2) read as follows:

"(2) Capital gain net income. The term 'capital gain net income' has the meaning given to such term by section 1222(9) (determined by treating the 1-year period ending on October 31 of any calendar year as the company's taxable year)."

In **1987**, P.L. 100-203, Sec. 10104(b)(1), substituted "98 percent" for "90 percent" in subpara. (b)(1)(B), effective for tax. yrs. begin. after 12/31/86.

In **1986**, P.L. 99-514, Sec. 651(a), added Code Sec. 4982, effective for calendar years begin. after 12/31/86.

CHAPTER 45.—PROVISIONS RELATING TO EXPATRIATED ENTITIES

Sec.
4985. Stock compensation of insiders in expatriated corporations.

In **2004**, P.L. 108-357, Sec. 802(a), added Chapter 45.

CHAPTER 45. REPEALED

In **1988**, P.L. 100-418, Sec. 1941(a), repealed Chapter 45, effective for crude oil removed from the premises on or after 8/23/88.

Prior to repeal chapter 45 read as follows:

"CHAPTER 45—WINDFALL PROFIT TAX ON DOMESTIC CRUDE OIL
"Subchapter
"A. Imposition and amount of tax.
"B. Categories of oil.
"C. Miscellaneous provisions.
  "**Subchapter A—Imposition and Amount of Tax**
"Sec.
"4986. Imposition of tax.
"4987. Amount of tax.
"4988. Windfall profit; removal price.
"4989. Adjusted base price.
"4990. Phaseout of tax.
"Sec. 4986. Imposition of tax.
"(a) Imposition of tax.

"An excise tax is hereby imposed on the windfall profit from taxable crude oil removed from the premises during each taxable period.

"(b) Tax paid by producer.

"The tax imposed by this section shall be paid by the producer of the crude oil."

In **1984**, P.L. 98-369, Sec. 722(a)(7)(A), and (B) provide the following:

"(7)(A) If—

"(i) there is an overpayment of tax imposed by section 4986 of the Internal Revenue Code of 1954 for any period before January 1, 1983, by reason of section 201(h)(1)(E) of the Technical Corrections Act of 1982,

"(ii) refund of such overpayment is payable to the partners of a partnership, and

"(iii) such partners are obligated to pay over any such refund to 1 or more organizations referred to in such section 201(h)(1)(E),

such partnership shall be treated as authorized to act for each person who was a partner at any time in such partnership in claiming and paying over such refund.

"(B) Notwithstanding section 6511 of the Internal Revenue Code of 1954, the time for filing a claim for credit or refund of the overpayment referred to in subparagraph (A)(i) shall not expire before the date 1 year after the date of the enactment of this Act."

In **1980**, P.L. 96-223, Sec. 101(a)(1), added Code Sec. 4986, to apply to periods after 2/29/80. Sec. 101(i)(2) of the Act provides:

"(2) Transitional rules. For the period ending June 30, 1980, the Secretary of the Treasury or his delegate shall prescribe rules relating to the administration of chapter 45 of the Internal Revenue Code of 1954. To the extent provided in such rules, such rules shall supplement or supplant for such period the administrative provisions contained in chapter 45 of such Code (or in so much of subtitle F of such Code as relates to such chapter 45)."

—P.L. 96-223, Sec. 103, provided as follows:

"Sec. 103. Study of effects of decontrol of oil prices and of windfall profit tax.

"(a) General rule.

"The President shall, not later than January 1, 1983, submit to the Congress a report on the effect of decontrol of oil prices and the windfall profit tax on—

"(1) domestic oil production,
"(2) foreign oil imports,
"(3) profits of the oil industry,
"(4) inflation,
"(5) employment,
"(6) economic growth,
"(7) Federal revenues, and
"(8) national security.

"(b) Report to include recommendations.

"The report required under subsection (a) shall include such legislative recommendations as the President determines to be advisable."

"Sec. 4987. Amount of tax.
"(a) In general.

"The amount of tax imposed by section 4986 with respect to any barrel of taxable crude oil shall be the applicable percentage of the windfall profit on such barrel.

"(b) Applicable percentage.

"For purposes of subsection (a)—

"(1) General rule for tiers 1 and 2. The applicable percentage for tier 1 oil and tier 2 oil which is not independent producer oil is—

Tier 1	70
Tier 2	60

"(2) Independent producer oil. The applicable percentage for independent producer oil which is tier 1 oil or tier 2 oil is—

Tier 1	50
Tier 2	30

"(3) Tier 3 oil.

"(A) In general. The applicable percentage for tier 3 oil which is not newly discovered oil is 30 percent.

"(B) Newly discovered oil. The applicable percentage for newly discovered oil shall be determined in accordance with the following table:

For taxable periods beginning in:	The applicable percentage is:
1984, 1985, 1986, or 1987	22½
1988	20
1989 and thereafter	15

"(c) Fractional part of barrel.

"In the case of a fraction of a barrel, the tax imposed by section 4986 shall be the same fraction of the amount of such tax imposed on the whole barrel."

In **1984**, P.L. 98-369, Sec. 25(a), amended the table in subpara. (b)(3)(B), effective for tax. periods begin. after 12/31/83.

Prior to amendment, the table in subpara. (b)(3)(B) read as follows:

"For taxable periods beginning in:	The applicable percentage is:
"1982	27½
"1983	25
"1984	22½
"1985	20
"1986 and thereafter	15."

In **1981**, P.L. 97-34, Sec. 602(a), amended para. (b)(3), for taxable periods beginning after 12/31/81.

Prior to amendment, para. (b)(3) read as follows:

"(3) Tier 3 oil. The applicable percentage for tier 3 oil is 30 percent."

3,369

Chapter 45 — Excise and miscellaneous taxes

In 1980, P.L. 96-223, Sec. 101(a)(1), added Code Sec. 4987, to apply to periods after 2/29/80. For transitional rule, see Sec. 101(i)(2) of this Act reproduced in note following Code Sec. 4986.

"SEC. 4988. WINDFALL PROFIT; REMOVAL PRICE.
"*(a) General rule.*
"For purposes of this chapter, the term 'windfall profit' means the excess of the removal price of the barrel of crude oil over the sum of—
"(1) the adjusted base price of such barrel, and
"(2) the amount of the severance tax adjustment with respect to such barrel provided by section 4996(c).
"*(b) Net income limitation on windfall profit.*
"(1) In general. The windfall profit on any barrel of crude oil shall not exceed 90 percent of the net income attributable to such barrel.
"(2) Determination of net income. For purposes of paragraph (1), the net income attributable to a barrel shall be determined by dividing—
"(A) the taxable income from the property for the taxable year attributable to taxable crude oil, by
"(B) the number of barrels of taxable crude oil from such property taken into account for such taxable year.
"(3) Taxable income from the property. For purposes of this subsection—
"(A) In general. Except as otherwise provided in this paragraph, the taxable income from the property shall be determined under section 613(a).
"(B) Certain deductions not allowed. No deduction shall be allowed for—
"(i) depletion,
"(ii) the tax imposed by section 4986,
"(iii) section 263(c) costs, or
"(iv) qualified tertiary injectant expenses to which an election under subparagraph (E) applies.
"(C) Taxable income reduced by cost depletion. Taxable income shall be reduced by the cost depletion which would have been allowable for the taxable year with respect to the property if—
"(i) all—
"(I) section 263(c) costs, and
"(II) qualified tertiary injectant expenses to which an election under subparagraph (E) applies,
incurred by the taxpayer had been capitalized and taken into account in computing cost depletion, and
"(ii) cost depletion had been used by the taxpayer with respect to such property for all taxable years.
"(D) Section 263(c) costs. For purposes of this paragraph, the term 'section 263(c) costs' means intangible drilling and development costs incurred by the taxpayer which (by reason of an election under section 263(c)) may be deducted as expenses for purposes of this title (other than this paragraph). Such term shall not include costs incurred in drilling a nonproductive well.
"(E) Election to capitalize qualified tertiary injectant expenses.
"(i) In general. Any taxpayer may elect, with respect to any property, to capitalize qualified tertiary injectant expenses for purposes of this paragraph. Any such election shall apply to all qualified tertiary injectant expenses allocable to the property for which the election is made, and may be revoked only with the consent of the Secretary. Any such election shall be made at such time and in such manner as the Secretary shall by regulations prescribe.
"(ii) Qualified tertiary injectant expenses. The term 'qualified tertiary injectant expenses' means any expense allowable as a deduction under section 193.
"(4) Special rule for applying paragraph (3)(c) to certain transfers of proven oil or gas properties.
"(A) In general. In the case of any proven oil or gas property transfer which (but for this subparagraph), would result in an increase in the amount determined under paragraph (3)(C) with respect to the transferee, paragraph (3)(C) shall be applied with respect to the transferee by taking into account only those amounts which would have been allowable with respect to the transferor under paragraph (3)(C) and those costs incurred during periods after such transfer.
"(B) Proven oil or gas property transfer. For purposes of subparagraph (A), the term 'proven oil or gas property transfer' means any transfer (including the subleasing of a lease or the creation of a production payment which gives the transferee an economic interest in the property) after 1978 of an interest (including an interest in a partnership or trust) in any proven oil or gas property (within the meaning of section 613A(c)(9)(A)).
"(5) Special rule where there is production payment. For purposes of paragraph (2), if any portion of the taxable crude oil removed from the property is applied in discharge of a production payment, the gross income from such portion shall be included in the gross income from the property of both the person holding such production payment and the person holding the interest from which such production payment was created.
"(6) Cost recovery oil covered by net profits agreement. For purposes of paragraph (2), if any person is treated under section 4996(a)(1)(B) as the producer of any portion of the cost recovery oil covered by a net profits agreement (within the meaning of section 4996(h)—
"(A) such person (and only such person) shall include in his gross income from the property the gross income from such portion, and
"(B) the qualified costs allocable to such portion shall be treated as paid or incurred by such person (and only such person).
"*(c) Removal price.*
"For purposes of this chapter—
"(1) In general. Except as otherwise provided in this subsection, the term 'removal price' means the amount for which the barrel is sold.

"(2) Sales between related persons. In the case of a sale between related persons (within the meaning of section 144(a)(3)), the removal price shall not be less than the constructive sales price for purposes of determining gross income from the property under section 613.
"(3) Oil removed from premises before sale. If crude oil is removed from the premises before it is sold, the removal price shall be the constructive sales price for purposes of determining gross income from the property under section 613.
"(4) Refining begun on premises. If the manufacture or conversion of crude oil into refined products begins before such oil is removed from the premises—
"(A) such oil shall be treated as removed on the day such manufacture or conversion begins, and
"(B) the removal price shall be the constructive sales price for purposes of determining gross income from the property under section 613.
"(5) Meaning of terms. The terms 'premises' and 'refined product' have the same meaning as when used for purposes of determining gross income from the property under section 613."

In 1986, P.L. 99-514, Sec. 1301(j)(4), substituted "section 144(a)(3)" for "section 103(b)(6)(C)" in para. (c)(2), effective for bonds issued after 8/15/86.
In 1983, P.L. 97-448, Sec. 201(a)(1), substituted "purposes of this subsection" for "purposes of paragraph (2)" in para. (b)(3) . . . Sec. 201(a)(2), substituted "all taxable years" for "all taxable periods" in clause (b)(3)(C)(ii) . . . Sec. 201(h)(1)(D), added para. (b)(6), effective for periods after 2/29/80.
In 1980, P.L. 96-223, Sec. 101(a)(1), added Code Sec. 4988, to apply to periods after 2/29/80. For the transitional rule see Sec. 101(i)(2) of the Act reproduced in the note following Code Sec. 4986.

"SEC. 4989. ADJUSTED BASE PRICE.
"*(a) Adjusted base price defined.*
"For purposes of this chapter, the term 'adjusted base price' means the base price for the barrel of crude oil plus an amount equal to—
"(1) such base price, multiplied by
"(2) the inflation adjustment for the calendar quarter in which the crude oil is removed from the premises.
"The amount determined under the preceding sentence shall be rounded to the nearest cent.
"*(b) Inflation adjustment.*
"(1) In general. For purposes of subsection (a), the inflation adjustment for any calendar quarter is the percentage by which—
"(A) the implicit price deflator for the gross national product for the second preceding calendar quarter, exceeds
"(B) such deflator for the calendar quarter ending June 30, 1979.
"(2) Additional adjustment for tier 3 oil. The adjusted base price for tier 3 oil shall be determined by substituting for the implicit price deflator referred to in paragraph (1)(A) an amount equal to such deflator multiplied by 1.005 to the nth power where 'n' equals the number of calendar quarters beginning after September 1979 and before the calendar quarter in which the oil is removed from the premises.
"(3) First revision of price deflator used. For purposes of paragraphs (1)(A) and (2), the first revision of the price deflator shall be used. For purposes of applying paragraph (1)(B), the revision of the price deflator which is most consistent with the revision used for purposes of paragraph (1)(A) shall be used.
"*(c) Base price for tier 1 oil.*
"For purposes of this chapter, the base price for tier 1 oil is—
"(1) the ceiling price which would have applied to such oil under the March 1979 energy regulations if it had been produced and sold in May 1979 as upper tier oil, reduced by
"(2) 21 cents.
"*(d) Base prices for tier 2 oil and tier 3 oil.*
"For purposes of this chapter—
"(1) General rule. Except as provided in paragraph (2), the base prices for tier 2 oil and tier 3 oil shall be prices determined pursuant to the method prescribed by the Secretary by regulations. Any method so prescribed shall be designed so as to yield, with respect to oil of any grade, quality, and field, a base price which approximates the price at which such oil would have sold in December 1979 if—
"(A) all domestic crude oil were uncontrolled, and
"(B) the average removal price for all domestic crude oil (other than Sadlerochit oil) were—
"(i) $15.20 a barrel for purposes of determining base prices for tier 2 oil, and
"(ii) $16.55 a barrel for purposes of determining base prices for tier 3 oil.
"(2) Interim rule. For months beginning before October 1980 (or such earlier date as may be provided in regulations taking effect before such earlier date), the base prices for tier 2 oil and tier 3 oil, respectively, shall be the product of—
"(A)(i) the highest posted price for December 31, 1979, for uncontrolled crude oil of the same grade, quality, and field, or
"(ii) if there is no posted price described in clause (i), the highest posted price for such date for uncontrolled crude oil at the nearest domestic field for which prices for oil of the same grade and quality were posted for such date, multiplied by
"(B) a fraction the denominator of which is $35, and the numerator of which is—
"(i) $15.20 for purposes of determining base prices for tier 2 oil, and
"(ii) $16.55 for purposes of determining base prices for tier 3 oil.
For purposes of the preceding sentence, no price which was posted after January 14, 1980, shall be taken into account.

Excise and miscellaneous taxes   Chapter 45

"(3) Minimum interim base price. The base price determined under paragraph (2) for tier 2 oil or tier 3 oil shall not be less than the sum of—
"(A) the ceiling price which would have applied to such oil under the March 1979 energy regulations if it had been produced and sold in May 1979 as upper tier oil, plus
"(B)(i) $1 in the case of tier 2 oil, or
"(ii) $2 in the case of tier 3 oil."

In 1983, P.L. 97-448, Sec. 201(b)(1), and (2), substituted "paragraphs (1)(A) and (2)" for "paragraphs (1) and (2)" and added the last sentence to para. (b)(3), for periods after 2/29/80.
In 1980, P.L. 96-223, Sec. 101(a)(1), added Code Sec. 4989, to apply to periods after 2/29/80. For the transitional rule see Sec. 101(i)(2) of the Act reproduced in the note following Code Sec. 4986.

"SEC. 4990. PHASEOUT OF TAX.
"(a) Phaseout.
"Notwithstanding any other provision of this chapter, the tax imposed by this chapter with respect to any crude oil removed from the premises during any month during the phaseout period shall not exceed—
"(1) the amount of tax which would have been imposed by this chapter with respect to such crude oil but for this subsection, multiplied by
"(2) the phaseout percentage for such month.
"(b) Termination of tax.
"Notwithstanding any other provision of this chapter, no tax shall be imposed by this chapter with respect to any crude oil removed from the premises after the phaseout period.
"(c) Definitions.
For purposes of this section—
"(1) Phaseout period. The term 'phaseout period' means the 33-month period beginning with the month following the target month.
"(2) Phaseout percentage. The phaseout percentage for any month is 100 percent reduced by 3 percentage points for each month after the target month and before the month following the month for which the phaseout percentage is being determined.
"(3) Target month. The term 'target month' means the later of—
"(A) December 1987, or
"(B) the first month for which the Secretary publishes an estimate under subsection (d)(2).
"In no event shall the target month be later than December 1990.
"(d) Determination of aggregate net windfall revenue.
"(1) Estimate by the Secretary. For each month after 1986, the Secretary shall make an estimate of the aggregate net windfall revenue as of the close of such month. Any such estimate shall be made during the preceding month and shall be made on the basis of the best available data as of the date of making such estimate.
"(2) Publication. If the Secretary estimates under paragraph (1) that the aggregate net windfall revenue as of the close of any month will exceed $227,300,000,000, the Secretary shall (not later than the last day of the preceding month) publish notice in the Federal Register that he has made such an estimate for such month.
"(3) Aggregate net windfall revenue defined. For purposes of this subsection, the term 'aggregate net windfall revenue' means the amount which the Secretary estimates to be the excess of—
"(A) the gross revenues from the tax imposed by section 4986 during the period beginning on March 1, 1980, and ending on the last day of the month for which the estimate is being made, over
"(B) the sum of—
"(i) the refunds and other adjustments to such tax for such period, plus
"(ii) the decrease in the income taxes imposed by chapter 1 resulting from the tax imposed by section 4986.
For purposes of subparagraph (A), there shall not be taken into account any revenue attributable to an economic interest in crude oil held by the United States."

In 1980, P.L. 96-223, Sec. 101(a)(1), added Code Sec. 4990, to apply to periods after 2/29/80. For the transitional rule see Sec. 101(i)(2) of the Act reproduced in the note following Code Sec. 4986.

"**Subchapter B — Categories of Oil**
"Sec.
"4991. Taxable crude oil; categories of oil.
"4992. Independent producer oil.
"4993. Incremental tertiary oil.
"4994. Definitions and special rules relating to exemptions.
"SEC. 4991. TAXABLE CRUDE OIL; CATEGORIES OF OIL.
"(a) Taxable crude oil.
"For purposes of this chapter, the term 'taxable crude oil' means all domestic crude oil other than exempt oil.
"(b) Exempt oil.
"For purposes of this chapter, the term 'exempt oil' means—
"(1) any crude oil from a qualified governmental interest or a qualified charitable interest,
"(2) any exempt Indian oil,
"(3) any exempt Alaskan oil,
"(4) any exempt front-end oil,

"(5) exempt royalty oil, and
"(6) exempt stripper well oil.
"(c) Tier 1 oil.
"For purposes of this chapter, the term 'tier 1 oil' means any taxable crude oil other than—
"(1) tier 2 oil, and
"(2) tier 3 oil.
"(d) Tier 2 oil.
"For purposes of this chapter—
"(1) In general. Except as provided in paragraph (2), the term 'tier 2 oil' means—
"(A) any oil which is from a stripper well property within the meaning of the June 1979 energy regulations, and
"(B) any oil from an economic interest in a Naval Petroleum Reserve held by the United States.
"(2) Exclusion of certain oil. The term 'tier 2 oil' does not include tier 3 oil.
"(e) Tier 3 oil.
"For purposes of this chapter—
"(1) In general. The term 'tier 3 oil' means—
"(A) newly discovered oil,
"(B) heavy oil, and
"(C) incremental tertiary oil.
"(2) Newly discovered oil. The term 'newly discovered oil' has the meaning given to such term by the June 1979 energy regulations. Such term includes any production from a property which did not produce oil in commercial quantities during calendar year 1978. For purposes of the preceding sentence, a property shall not be treated as producing oil in commercial quantities during calendar year 1978 if, during calendar year 1978 (A) the aggregate amount of oil produced from such property did not exceed 2,200 barrels (whether or not such oil was sold), and (B) no well on such property was in production for a total of more than 72 hours.
"(3) Heavy oil. The term 'heavy oil' means all crude oil which is produced from a property if crude oil produced and sold from such property during—
"(A) the last month before July 1979 in which crude oil was produced and sold from such property, or
"(B) the taxable period,
"had a weighted average gravity of 16 degrees API or less (corrected to 60 degrees Fahrenheit).
"(4) Incremental tertiary oil. For definition of incremental tertiary oil, see section 4993."

In 1990, P.L. 101-508, Sec. 11703(g)(1), substituted "held by the Protestant Episcopal Church Foundation of the Diocese of Oklahoma or held by" for "held by" in Sec. 1879(o)(1) of P.L. 99-514, see below.
In 1986, P.L. 99-514, Sec. 1879(h)(1), added the last two sentences to para. (e)(2), effective for oil removed after 2/29/80. . . . Sec. 1879(o), [as amended by Sec. 11703(g)(1) of P.L. 101-508, see above] of this Act provides:
"(o) Amendments relating to section 4994.—
"(1) For purposes of section 4991(b), a 'qualified charitable interest' shall include an economic interest in crude oil held by the Protestant Episcopal Church Foundation of the Diocese of Oklahoma or held by Episcopal Royalty Company, an entity created in 1961 as a subsidiary of the Protestant Episcopal Church Foundation of the Diocese of Oklahoma.
"(2) The amendment made by this subsection shall apply to oil removed after February 29, 1980."
In 1983, P.L. 97-448, Sec. 201(c), substituted "Naval Petroleum Reserve" for "National Petroleum Reserve", in subpara. (d)(1)(B), for periods after 2/29/80.
In 1981, P.L. 97-34, Sec. 601(b)(1), added para. (b)(5), for oil removed after 12/31/81.
—P.L. 97-34, Sec. 603(a), added para. (b)(6), for oil removed from the premises after 12/31/82.
In 1980, P.L. 96-223, Sec. 101(a)(1), added Code Sec. 4991, to apply to periods after 2/29/80. For the transitional rule see Sec. 101(i)(2) of the Act reproduced in the note following Code Sec. 4986.

"SEC. 4992. INDEPENDENT PRODUCER OIL.
"(a) General rule.
"For purposes of this chapter, the term 'independent producer oil' means that portion of an independent producer's qualified production for the quarter which does not exceed such person's independent producer amount for such quarter.
"(b) Independent producer defined.
"For purposes of this section—
"(1) In general. The term 'independent producer' means, with respect to any quarter in any calendar year, any person other than a person to whom subsection (c) of section 613A does not apply for such calendar year by reason of paragraph (2) (relating to certain retailers) or paragraph (4) (relating to certain refiners) of section 613A(d).
"(2) Rules for applying paragraphs (2) and (4) of section 613A(d). For purposes of paragraph (1), paragraphs (2) and (4) of section 613A(d) shall be applied by substituting 'calendar year' for 'taxable year' each place it appears in such paragraphs.
"(c) Independent producer amount.
"For purposes of this section—
"(1) In general. A person's independent producer amount for any quarter is the product of—
"(A) 1,000 barrels, multiplied by

3,371

"(B) the number of days in such quarter (31 in the case of the first quarter of 1980).

"(2) Production exceeds amount. If a person's qualified production for any quarter exceeds such person's independent producer amount for such quarter, the independent producer amount shall be allocated—

"(A) between tiers 1 and 2 in proportion for such person's qualified production of oil for such quarter in each such tier, and

"(B) within any tier, on the basis of the removal prices for such person's qualified production of oil in such tier removed during such quarter, beginning with the highest of such prices.

"(d) Qualified production of oil defined.

"For purposes of this section—

"(1) In general. An independent producer's qualified production of oil for any quarter is the number of barrels of taxable crude oil—

"(A) of which such person is the producer,

"(B) which is removed during such quarter,

"(C) which is tier 1 oil or tier 2 oil, and

"(D) which is attributable to the independent producer's working interest in a property.

"(2) Working interest defined.

"(A) In general. The term 'working interest' means an operating mineral interest (within the meaning of section 614(d))—

"(i) which was in existence as such an interest on January 1, 1980, or

"(ii) which is attributable to a qualified overriding royalty interest.

"(B) Qualified overriding royalty interest. For purposes of subparagraph (A)(ii) the term 'qualified overriding royalty interest' means an overriding royalty interest in existence as such an interest on January 1, 1980, but only if on February 20, 1980, there was in existence a binding contract under which such interest was to be converted into an operating mineral interest (within the meaning of section 614(d)).

"(3) Production from transferred property.

"(A) In general. Except as otherwise provided in this paragraph, in the case of a transfer on or after January 1, 1980, of an interest in any property, the qualified production of the transferee shall not include any production attributable to such interest.

"(B) Small producer transfer exemption.

"(i) In general. Subparagraph (A) shall not apply to any transfer of an interest in property if the transferee establishes (in such manner as may be prescribed by the Secretary by regulations) that at no time after December 31, 1979, has the interest been held by a person who was a disqualified transferor for any quarter ending after September 30, 1979, and ending before the date such person transferred the interest.

"(ii) Disqualified transferor. The term 'disqualified transferor' means, with respect to any quarter, any person who—

"(I) had qualified production for such quarter which exceeded such person's independent producer amount for such quarter, or

"(II) was not an independent producer for such quarter.

"(iii) Special rules. For purposes of this paragraph—

"(I) Property held by partnerships. Property held by a partnership at any time shall be treated as owned proportionately by the partners of such partnership at such time.

"(II) Property held by trust or estate. Property held by any trust or estate shall be treated as owned both by such trust or estate and proportionately by its beneficiaries.

"(III) Constructive application. This chapter shall be treated as having been in effect for periods after September 30, 1979, for purposes of making any determination under subclause (I) or (II) of clause (ii).

"(C) Other exceptions. Subparagraph (A) shall not apply in the case of—

"(i) a transfer of property at death,

"(ii) a change of beneficiaries of a trust which qualifies under clause (iii) of section 613A(c)(9)(B) (determined without regard to the exception at the end of such clause), and

"(iii) any transfer so long as the transferor and transferee are required by subsection (e) to share the 1,000 barrel amount contained in subsection (c)(1)(A). The preceding sentence shall apply in the case of any property only if the production from the property was qualified production for the transferor.

"(D) Transfers include subleases, etc. For purposes of this paragraph—

"(i) a sublease shall be treated as a transfer, and

"(ii) an interest in a partnership or trust shall be treated as an interest in property held by the partnership or trust.

"(e) Allocation within related group.

"(1) In general. In the case of persons who are members of the same related group at any time during any quarter, the 1,000 barrel amount contained in subsection (c)(1)(A) for such days during such quarter shall be reduced for each such person by allocating such amount among all such persons in proportion to their respective qualified production for such quarter.

"(2) Related group. For purposes of this subsection, persons shall be treated as members of a related group if they are described in any of the following clauses:

"(A) a family,

"(B) a controlled group of corporations,

"(C) a group of entities under common control, or

"(D) if 50 percent or more of the beneficial interest in 1 or more corporations, trusts, or estates is owned by the same family, all such entities and such family.

"(3) Definitions and special rules. For purposes of this subsection—

"(A) Controlled group of corporations. The term 'controlled group of corporations' has the meaning given such term by section 613A(c)(8)(D)(i).

"(B) Group of entities under common control. The term 'group of entities under common control' means any group of corporations, trusts, or estates which (as determined under regulations prescribed by the Secretary) are under common control. Such regulations shall be based on principles similar to the principles which apply under subparagraph (A).

"(C) Family. The term 'family' means an individual and the spouse and minor children of such individual.

"(D) Constructive ownership. For purposes of paragraph (2)(D), an interest owned by or for a corporation, partnership, trust, or estate shall be considered as owned directly by the entity and proportionately by its shareholders, partners, or beneficiaries, as the case may be.

"(E) Members of more than 1 related group. If a person is a member of more than 1 related group during any quarter, the determination of such person's allocation under paragraph (1) shall be made by reference to the related group which results in the smallest allocation for such person.

"(f) S Corporation treated as partnership.

"For purposes of subsections (d) and (e)—

"(1) an S corporation shall be treated as a partnership, and

"(2) the shareholders of the S corporation shall be treated as partners of such partnership."

In **1983**, P.L. 97-448, Sec. 201(d)(1), amended subsec. (b), effective 1/1/83. Prior to amendment, subsec. (b) read as follows:

"(b) Independent producer defined.

"For purposes of this section—

"(1) In general. The term 'independent producer' means, with respect to any quarter, any person other than a person to whom subsection (c) of section 613A does not apply by reason of paragraph (2) (relating to certain retailers) or paragraph (4) (relating to certain refiners) of section 613A(d).

"(2) Rules for applying paragraphs (2) and (4) of section 613A(d). For purposes of paragraph (1), paragraphs (2) and (4) of section 613A(d) shall be applied—

"(A) by substituting 'quarter' for 'taxable year' each place it appears in such paragraphs, and

"(B) by substituting '$1,250,000' for '$5,000,000' in paragraph (2) of section 613A(d)."

— P.L. 97-448, Sec. 201(d)(2)(A), substituted "such person's qualified production of oil for such quarter" for "such person's production for such quarter of domestic crude oil" in subpara. (c)(2)(A) . . . Sec. 201(d)(2)(B), substituted "such person's qualified production of oil" for "such person's domestic crude oil" in subpara. (c)(2)(B) . . . Sec. 201(d)(2)(C), deleted the last sentence in subsec. (c) . . . Sec. 201(d)(3), substituted "has the interest" for "has the property" in clause (d)(3)(B)(i), effective for periods after 2/29/80.

Prior to amendment, the last sentence of subsec. (c) read as follows:

"For purposes of the preceding sentence, tier 1 oil and tier 2 oil shall be treated as not including exempt stripper well oil."

In **1982**, P.L. 97-354, Sec. (3)(b)(2), added subsec. (f), for tax. yrs. begin. after 12/31/82.

In **1981**, P.L. 97-34, Sec. 603(c), added a new sentence to the end of para. (c)(2), for oil removed from the premises after 12/31/80.

In **1980**, P.L. 96-223, Sec. 101(a)(1), added Code Sec. 4992, to apply to periods after 2/29/80. For the transitional rule see Sec. 101(i)(2) of the Act reproduced in the note following Code Sec. 4986.

"SEC. 4993. INCREMENTAL TERTIARY OIL.

"(a) In general.

"For purposes of this chapter, the term 'incremental tertiary oil' means the excess of—

"(1) the amount of crude oil which is removed from a property during any month and which is produced on or after the project beginning date and during the period for which a qualified tertiary recovery project is in effect on the property, over

"(2) the base level for such property for such month.

"(b) Determination of amount.

"For purposes of this section—

"(1) Base level. The base level for any property for any month is the average monthly amount (determined under rules similar to rules used in determining the base production control level under the June 1979 energy regulations) of crude oil removed from such property during the 6-month period ending March 31, 1979, reduced (but not below zero) by the sum of—

"(A) 1 percent of such amount for each month which begins after 1978 and before the first month beginning after the project beginning date, and

"(B) 2½ percent of such amount for each month which begins after the project beginning date (or after 1978 if the project beginning date is before 1979) and before the month for which the base level is being determined.

"(2) Minimum amount in case of projects certified by DOE. In the case of a project described in subsection (c)(1)(A), for the period during which the project is in effect, the amount of the incremental tertiary oil shall not be less than the incremental production determined under the June 1979 energy regulations.

"(3) Allocation rules. The determination of which barrels of crude oil removed during any month are incremental tertiary oil shall be made—

"(A) first by allocating the amount of incremental tertiary oil between—

"(i) oil which (but for this subsection) would be tier 1 oil, and

"(ii) oil which (but for this subsection) would be tier 2 oil,

"in proportion to the respective amounts of each such oil removed from the property during such month, and

"(B) then by taking into account barrels of crude oil so removed in the order of their respective removal prices, beginning with the highest of such prices.
"(c) Qualified tertiary recovery project.
"For purposes of this section—
"(1) In general. The term 'qualified tertiary recovery project' means—
"(A) a qualified tertiary enhanced recovery project with respect to which a certification as such has been approved and is in effect under the June 1979 energy regulations, or
"(B) any project for enhancing recovery of crude oil which meets the requirements of paragraph (2).
"(2) Requirements. A project meets the requirements of this paragraph if—
"(A) the project involves the application (in accordance with sound engineering principles) of 1 or more tertiary recovery methods which can reasonably be expected to result in more than an insignificant increase in the amount of crude oil which will ultimately be recovered,
"(B) the date on which the injection of liquids, gases, or other matter begins is after May 1979,
"(C) the portion of the property to be affected by the project is adequately delineated,
"(D) the operator submits (at such time and in such manner as the Secretary may by regulations prescribe) to the Secretary—
"(i) a certification from a petroleum engineer that the project meets the requirements of subparagraphs (A), (B), and (C), or
"(ii) a certification that a jurisdictional agency (within the meaning of subsection (d)(5)) has approved the project as meeting the requirements of subparagraphs (A), (B), and (C), and that such approval is still in effect, and
"(E) the operator submits (at such time and in such manner as the Secretary may by regulations prescribe) to the Secretary a certification from a petroleum engineer that the project continues to meet the requirements of subparagraphs (A), (B), and (C).
"(d) Definitions and special rules.
"For purposes of this section—
"(1) Tertiary recovery method. The term 'tertiary recovery method' means—
"(A) any method which is described in subparagraphs (1) through (9) of section 212.78(c) of the June 1979 energy regulations, or
"(B) any other method to provide tertiary enhanced recovery which is approved by the Secretary for purposes of this chapter.
"(2) Project beginning date. The term 'project beginning date' means the later of—
"(A) the date on which the injection of liquids, gases, or other matters begins, or
"(B) the date on which—
"(i) in the case of a project described in subsection (c)(1)(A), the project is certified as a qualified tertiary enhanced recovery project under the June 1979 energy regulations, or
"(ii) in the case of a project described in subsection (c)(1)(B), a petroleum engineer certifies, or a jurisdictional agency approves, the project as meeting the requirements of subparagraphs (A), (B), and (C) of subsection (c)(2).
"(3) Project only affects portion of property. If a qualified tertiary recovery project can reasonably be expected to increase the ultimate recovery of crude oil from only a portion of a property, such portion shall be treated as a separate property.
"(4) Significant expansion treated as separate project. A significant expansion of any project shall be treated as a separate project.
"(5) Jurisdictional agency. The term 'jurisdictional agency' means—
"(A) in the case of an application involving a tertiary recovery project on lands not under Federal jurisdiction—
"(i) the appropriate State agency in the State in which such lands are located which is designated by the Governor of such State in a written notification submitted to the Secretary as the agency which will approve projects under this subsection, or
"(ii) if the Governor of such State does not submit such written notification within 180 days after the date of the enactment of the Crude Oil Windfall Profit Tax Act of 1980, the United States Geological Survey (until such time as the Governor submits such notification), or
"(B) in the case of an application involving a tertiary recovery project on lands under Federal jurisdiction, the United States Geological Survey.
"(6) Basis of review of certain qualified tertiary recovery projects. In the case of any project which is approved under subsection (c)(2)(D)(ii) and for which a certification is submitted to the Secretary, the project shall be considered as meeting the requirements of subparagraphs (A), (B), and (C) of subsection (c)(2) unless the Secretary determines that—
"(A) the approval of the jurisdictional agency was not supported by substantial evidence on the record upon which such approval was based, or
"(B) additional evidence not contained in the record upon which such approval was based demonstrates that such project does not meet the requirements of subparagraph (A), (B), or (C) of subsection (c)(2).
If the Secretary makes a determination described in subparagraph (A) or (B) of the preceding sentence, the determination of whether the project meets the requirements of subparagraphs (A), (B), and (C) of subsection (c)(2) shall be made without regard to the preceding sentence.
"(7) Rulings relating to certain qualified tertiary recovery projects. In the case of any tertiary recovery project for which a certification is submitted to the Secretary under subsection (c)(2)(D)(ii), a taxpayer may request a ruling from the Secretary with respect to whether such project is a qualified tertiary recovery project.

The Secretary shall issue such ruling within 180 days of the date after he receives the request and such information as may be necessary to make a determination."

In 1983, P.L. 97-448, Sec. 201(e), amended subpara. (c)(2)(B), for periods after 2/29/80.
Prior to amendment, subpara. (c)(2)(B) read as follows:
"(B) the project beginning date is after May 1979,".
In 1980, P.L. 96-223, Sec. 101(a)(1), added Code Sec. 4993, to apply to periods after 2/29/80. For the transitional rule see Sec. 101(i)(2) of the Act reproduced in the note following Code Sec. 4986.

"SEC. 4994. DEFINITIONS AND SPECIAL RULES RELATING TO EXEMPTIONS.
"(a) Qualified governmental interest.
"For purposes of section 4991(b)—
"(1) In general. The term 'qualified governmental interest' means an economic interest in crude oil if—
"(A) such interest is held by a State or political subdivision thereof or by an agency or instrumentality of a State or political subdivision thereof, and
"(B) under the applicable State or local law, all of the net income received pursuant to such interest is dedicated to a public purpose.
"(2) Net income. For purposes of this paragraph, the term 'net income' means gross income reduced by production costs, and severance taxes of general application, allocable to the interest.
"(3) Amounts placed in certain permanent funds treated as dedicated to public purpose. The requirements of paragraph (1)(B) shall be treated as met with respect to any net income which, under the applicable State or local law, is placed in a permanent fund the earnings on which are dedicated to a public purpose.
"(b) Qualified charitable interest.
"For purposes of section 4991(b)—
"(1) In general. The term 'qualified charitable interest' means an economic interest in crude oil if—
"(A) such interest is—
"(i) held by an organization described in clause (ii), (iii), or (iv) of section 170(b)(1)(A) which is also described in section 170(c)(2),
"(ii) held by an organization described in section 170(c)(2) which is organized and operated primarily for the residential placement, care, or treatment of delinquent, dependent, orphaned, neglected, or handicapped children,
"(iii) held—
"(I) by an organization described in clause (i) of section 170(b)(1)(A) which is also described in section 170(c)(2), and
"(II) for the benefit of an organization described in clause (i) or (ii) of this subparagraph, or
"(iv) held by an organization described in section 509(a)(3) which is operated exclusively for the benefit of an organization described in—
"(I) clause (ii), or
"(II) section 170(b)(1)(A)(ii) which is also described in section 170(c)(2), and
"(B) such interest was held on January 21, 1980, and at all times thereafter before the last day of the taxable period, by the organization described in clause (i), (ii), or (iv) of subparagraph (A), or subclause (I) of subparagraph (A)(iii).
"(2) Special rule. For purposes of clause (i), (iii), or (iv) of paragraph (1)(A), an interest shall be treated as held for the benefit of an organization described in clause (i), (ii), or (iv) of paragraph (1)(A), whichever is applicable, only if all the proceeds from such interest were dedicated on January 21, 1980, and at all times thereafter before the last day of the taxable period, to the organization described in clause (i), (ii), or (iv) of paragraph (1)(A), whichever is applicable,[.]
"(c) Front-end tertiary oil.
"(1) Exemption for tertiary projects of independents. For purposes of this chapter, the term 'exempt front-end oil' means any domestic crude oil—
"(A) which is removed from the premises before October 1, 1981, and
"(B) which is treated as front-end oil by reason of a front-end tertiary project on one or more properties each of which is a qualified property.
"(2) Refunds for tertiary projects of integrated producers.
"(A) In general. In the case of any front-end tertiary project which does not meet the requirements of paragraph (1)(B), the excess of—
"(i) the allowed expenses of the producer with respect to such project, over
"(ii) the tertiary incentive revenue,
shall be treated as a payment by the producer with respect to the tax imposed by this chapter made on September 30, 1981.
"(B) Limitation based on amount of tax. The amount of the payment determined under subparagraph (A) with respect to any producer shall not exceed the aggregate tax imposed by section 4986 with respect to front-end oil of that producer removed after February 1980 and before October 1981.
"(C) Tertiary incentive revenue. For purposes of this paragraph, the term 'tertiary incentive revenue' has the meaning given such term by the front-end tertiary provisions of the energy regulations.
"(3) Definition of allowed expenses; prepaid expenses not taken into account. For purposes of this subsection (including the application of the front-end tertiary provisions for purposes of this subsection)—
"(A) Allowed expenses. Except as provided in subparagraph (B), allowed expenses shall be determined under the front-end tertiary provisions of the energy regulations.
"(B) Prepaid expenses not taken into account. The term 'allowed expenses' shall not include any amount attributable to periods after September 30, 1981.
"(C) Period to which item is attributable. For purposes of subparagraph (B)—

"(i) any injectant and any fuel shall be treated as attributable to periods before October 1, 1981, if the injectant is injected, or the fuel is used, before October 1, 1981, and

"(ii) any other item shall be treated as attributable to periods before October 1, 1981, only to the extent that under chapter 1 deductions for such item (including depreciation in respect of such item) are properly allocable to periods before October 1, 1981.

For purposes of the preceding sentence, an act shall be treated as taken before a date if it would have been taken before such date but for an act of God, a severe mechanical breakdown, or an injunction.

"(4) Definitions and special rules. For purposes of this subsection—

"(A) Front-end tertiary provisions. The term 'front-end tertiary provisions' means—

"(i) the provisions of section 212.78 of the energy regulations which exempt crude oil from ceiling price limitations to provide financing for tertiary projects (as such provisions took effect on October 1, 1979), and

"(ii) any modification of such provisions, but only to the extent that such modification is for purposes of coordinating such provisions with the tax imposed by this chapter.

"(B) Front-end oil. The term 'front-end oil' means any domestic crude oil which is not subject to a first sale ceiling price under the energy regulations solely by reason of the front-end tertiary provisions of such regulations.

"(C) Qualified property. The term 'qualified property' means any property if, on January 1, 1980, 50 percent or more of the operating mineral interest in such property is held by persons who were independent producers (within the meaning of section 4992(b)) for the last quarter of 1979.

"(D) Front-end tertiary project. The term 'front-end tertiary project' means any project which qualifies under the front-end tertiary provisions of the energy regulations.

"(E) Ordering rule. Front-end oil of any taxpayer shall be treated as attributable first to projects which meet the requirements of paragraph (1)(B).

"(d) Exempt Indian oil.

"For purposes of this chapter, the term 'exempt Indian oil' means any domestic crude oil—

"(1) the producer of which is an Indian tribe, an individual member of an Indian tribe, or an Indian tribal organization under an economic interest held by such a tribe, member, or organization on January 21, 1980, and which is produced from mineral interests which are—

"(A) held in trust by the United States for the tribe, member, or organization, or

"(B) held by the tribe, member, or organization subject to a restriction on alienation imposed by the United States because it is held by an Indian tribe, an individual member of an Indian tribe, or an Indian tribal organization,

"(2) the producer of which is a native corporation organized pursuant to the Alaska Native Claims Settlement Act (as in effect on January 21, 1980), and which—

"(A) is produced from mineral interests held by the corporation which were received under that Act, and

"(B) is removed from the premises before 1992, or

"(3) the proceeds from the sale of which are deposited in the Treasury of the United States to the credit of tribal or native trust funds pursuant to a provision of law in effect on January 21, 1980.

"(e) Exempt Alaskan oil.

"For purposes of this chapter, the term 'exempt Alaskan oil' means any crude oil (other than Sadlerochit oil) which is produced—

"(1) from a well located north of the Arctic Circle or from a reservoir from which oil has been produced in commercial quantities through such a well, or

"(2) from a well located on the northerly side of the divides of the Alaska and Aleutian Ranges and at least 75 miles from the nearest point on the Trans-Alaska Pipeline System.

"(f) Exempt royalty oil.

"(1) In general. For purposes of this chapter, the term 'exempt royalty oil' means that portion of the qualified royalty owner's qualified royalty production for the quarter which does not exceed the royalty limit for such quarter.

"(2) Royalty limit. For purposes of this subsection

"(A) In general. Except as provided in subparagraph (C), a qualified royalty owner's royalty limit for any quarter is the product of

"(i) the number of days in such quarter, multiplied by

"(ii) the limitation in barrels determined under the following table:

In the case of qualified royalty production during:	The limitation in barrels is:
1982	2
1983	2
1984	2
1985 and thereafter	3

"(B) Production exceeds limitation. If a qualified royalty owner's qualified royalty production for any quarter exceeds the royalty limitation for such quarter, such royalty owner may allocate such limit to any qualified royalty production which he selects.

"(C) Election to increase section 6430 royalty credit by reducing exemption under this subsection. Any qualified royalty owner who is a qualified beneficiary (within the meaning of section 6430(d)(1)) for any quarter may elect (at such time and in such manner as the Secretary may prescribe by regulations) to reduce by any amount the qualified royalty owner's royalty limit determined under subparagraph (A) for such quarter (after the application of paragraph (3)(B)).

"(3) Definitions.

"(A) In general. The terms 'qualified royalty owner' and 'qualified royalty production' have the meanings given to such terms by section 6429; except that the reference to qualified taxable crude oil in section 6429(d) shall be treated as a reference to oil which would have been taxable crude oil but for this section.

"(B) Allocation. Rules similar to the rules of pararaphs (2), (3), and (4) of section 6429(c) shall apply to the limitation determined under paragraph (2)(A).

"(g) Exempt stripper well oil.

"(1) In general. For purposes of this chapter, the term 'exempt stripper well oil' means any oil

"(A) the producer of which is an independent producer (within the meaning of section 4992(b)(1)),

"(B) which is from a stripper well property within the meaning of the June 1979 energy regulations, and

"(C) which is attributable to the independent producer's working interest in the stripper well property.

"(2) Limitation for certain transferred properties. Exempt stripper well oil does not include production attributable to an interest in any property which at any time after July 22, 1981, was owned by any person (other than the producer) who during the period of ownership after such date was not an independent producer (within the meaning of section 4992(b)(1)). The preceding sentence shall not apply to property so owned by any person if, at the time of transfer of such property by such person, such property was not a proven property (within the meaning of section 613A(c)(9)(A))."

In 1983, P.L. 97-448, Sec. 106(a)(2), substituted "paragraph (2)(A)" for "subsection (b)(1)" in subpara. (f)(3)(B), for oil removed after 12/31/81.
— P.L. 97-448, Sec. 106(a)(4)(B)(i), substituted "Except as provided in subparagraph (C), a qualified" for "A qualified" in subpara. (f)(2)(A) . . . Sec. 106(a)(4)(B)(ii), added subpara. (f)(2)(C), effective for calendar yrs. begin. after 12/31/81.
— P.L. 97-448, Sec. 106(b), substituted "owned by any person (other than the producer) who during the period of ownership after such date was not an independent producer (within the meaning of section 4992(b)(1)). The preceding sentence shall not apply to property so owned by any person if, at the time of transfer of such property by such person, such property was not a proven property (within the meaning of section 613A(c)(9)(A))" for "owned by a person other than an independent producer (within the meaning of section 4992(b)(1))" in para. (g)(2), effective for oil removed from the premises after 12/31/82.
— P.L. 97-448, Sec. 201(f)(1), substituted "producer" for "the taxpayer" each place it appeared in subpara. (c)(2)(A) . . . Sec. 201(f)(2)(A), amended para. (e)(1) . . . Sec. 201(f)(2)(B), substituted "the divides of the Alaska and Aleutian ranges" for "the divide of the Alaska-Aleutian range" in subpara. (f)(2)(A) . . . Sec. 201(f)(3)(A), deleted "or" at the end of clause (b)(1)(A)(ii), substituted "or" for "and" at the end of clause (b)(1)(A)(iii), and added clause (b)(1)(A)(iv) . . . Sec. 201(f)(3)(B), substituted ", (ii), or (iv)" for "or (ii)" in subpara. (b)(1)(B) . . . Sec. 201(f)(3)(C), substituted "clause (ii), (iii), or (iv)" for "clause (i) or (iii)" in para. (b)(2), substituted "clause (i), (ii), or (iv)" for "clause (i) or (ii)" each place it appeared in para. (b)(2), and added ", whichever is applicable," after "paragraph (1)(A)" each place it appeared in para. (b)(2), effective for periods after 2/29/80.
Prior to amendment, para. (e)(1) read as follows:
"(1) from a reservoir from which oil has been produced in commercial quantities through a well located north of the Arctic Circle, or"
In 1982, P.L. 97-248, Sec. 291, substituted "pursuant to" for "under" the first time it appeared in para. (d)(2), effective 9/3/82.
In 1981, P.L. 97-34, Sec. 601(b)(2), added subsec. (f), for oil removed after 12/31/81.
— P.L. 97-34, Sec. 603(b), added subsec. (g), for oil removed from the premises after 12/31/82.
— P.L. 97-34, Sec. 604(a), redesignated clause (b)(1)(A)(ii) as clause (b)(1)(A)(iii) and added new clause (b)(1)(A)(ii) . . . Sec. 604(b)(1), amended subpara. (b)(1)(B) . . . Sec. 604(b)(2), substituted "clause (ii) or (iii) of paragraph (1)(A)" for "paragraph (1)(A)(ii)" and substituted "clause (i) or (ii) of paragraph (1)(A)" for "paragraph (1)(A)(i)" in para. (b)(2) . . . Sec. 604(c)(1), deleted "or" at the end of clause (b)(1)(A)(ii) . . . Sec. 604(c)(2), added "or (ii)" after "clause (i)", in clause (b)(1)(A)(ii)(II), effective for taxable periods ending after 12/31/80.
Prior to amendment, subpara. (b)(1)(B) read as follows:
"(B) such interest was held by the organization described in clause (i) or subclause (I) of clause (ii) of subparagraph (A) on January 21, 1980, and at all times thereafter before the last day of the taxable period."
In 1980, P.L. 96-223, Sec. 101(a)(1), added Code Sec. 4994, to apply to periods after 2/29/80. For the transitional rule see Sec. 101(i)(2) of the Act reproduced in the note following Code Sec. 4986.

"Subchapter C — Miscellaneous Provisions

"Sec.
"4995. Withholding; depositary requirements.
"4996. Other definitions and special rules.
"4997. Records and information; regulations.
"4998. Cross references.
"SEC. 4995. WITHHOLDING; DEPOSITARY REQUIREMENTS.
"(a) Withholding by purchaser.
"(1) Withholding required. Except to the extent provided in regulations prescribed by the Secretary—
"(A) the first purchaser of any domestic crude oil shall withhold a tax equal to the amount of the tax imposed by section 4986 with respect to such oil from amounts payable by such purchaser to the producer of such oil, and

Excise and miscellaneous taxes   Chapter 45

"(B) the first purchaser of such oil shall be liable for the payment of the tax required to be withheld under subparagraph (A) and shall not be liable to any person for the amount of any such payment.

"(2) Determination of amount to be withheld.

"(A) In general. The purchaser shall determine the amount to be withheld under paragraph (1)—

"(i) on the basis of the certification furnished to the purchaser under section 6050C, unless the purchaser has reason to believe that any information contained in such certification is not correct, or

"(ii) if clause (i) does not apply, under regulations prescribed by the Secretary.

"(B) Net income limitation not to be applied. For purposes of determining the amount to be withheld under paragraph (1), subsection (b) of section 4988 shall not apply.

"(3) Adjustments for withholding errors.

"(A) In general. To the extent provided in regulations prescribed by the Secretary, withholding errors made by a purchaser with respect to the crude oil of a producer shall be corrected by that purchaser by making proper adjustments in the amounts withheld from subsequent payments to such producer for crude oil.

"(B) Withholding error. For purposes of subparagraph (A), there is a withholding error if the amount withheld by the purchaser under paragraph (1) with respect to any payment for any crude oil exceeds (or is less than) the tax imposed by section 4986 with respect to such oil (determined without regard to section 4988(b)).

"(C) Voluntary withholding. The Secretary may by regulations provide for withholding under this subsection of additional amounts from payments by any purchaser to any producer if the purchaser and producer agree to such withholding. For purposes of this title, any amount withheld pursuant to such an agreement shall be treated as an amount required to be withheld under paragraph (1).

"(4) Producer treated as having paid withheld amount.

"(A) In general. The producer of any domestic crude oil shall be treated as having paid any amount withheld with respect to such oil under this subsection.

"(B) Time payment deemed made. For purposes of this chapter (and so much of subtitle F as relates to this chapter), the producer shall be treated as having made any payment described in subparagraph (A) on the last day of the first February after the calendar year in which the oil is removed from the premises.

"(5) Producer required to file return only to extent provided in regulations. Except to the extent provided in regulations, the producer of crude oil with respect to which withholding is required under paragraph (1) shall not be required to file a return of the tax imposed by section 4986 with respect to such oil.

"(6) Purchaser's quarterly returns to contain summary. The purchaser's return of tax under this chapter for any calendar quarter of any calendar year shall contain such information (with respect to such quarter and the prior quarters of such calendar year) as may be necessary to facilitate the coordination of the withholding of tax by such purchaser with respect to each producer with the determination of the tax imposed by section 4986 with respect to such producer.

"(7) Election for purchaser and operator to have operator take place of purchaser.

"(A) In general. If the purchaser of domestic crude oil and the operator of the property from which the crude oil was produced make a joint election under this paragraph with respect to such property (or portion thereof)—

"(i) the operator shall be substituted for the purchaser for purposes of applying this subsection and subsection (b) (and so much of subtitle F as relates to such subsections), and

"(ii) if the operator is not an integrated oil company, the operator shall be treated as having the same status as the purchaser for purposes of applying subsection (b) with respect to amounts withheld by the operator by reason of such election.

"(B) Regulations may limit election. The Secretary may by regulations limit the circumstances under which an election under this paragraph may be made to situations where substituting the operator for the purchaser is administratively more practicable.

"(8) No assessments or refunds before close of the year. Except to the extent provided in regulations prescribed by the Secretary, in the case of any oil subject to withholding under this subsection—

"(A) no notice of any deficiency with respect to the tax imposed by section 4986 may be mailed under section 6212, and

"(B) no proceeding in any court for the refund of the tax imposed by section 4986 may be begun, before the last day of the first February after the calendar year in which such oil was removed from the premises.

"(9) Adjustments to take into account royalty exemption. The Secretary shall prescribe such regulations as may be necessary so that the withholding required under this subsection shall be reduced to take into account the exemption provided by section 4991(b)(5) (relating to exempt royalty oil), and he may prescribe such other regulations as may be necessary to administer such exemption.

"(b) Depositary requirements.

"(1) Integrated oil companies. In the case of an integrated oil company, deposit of the estimated amount of—

"(A) withholding under subsection (a) by such company, and

"(B) such company's liability for the tax imposed by section 4986 with respect to oil for which withholding is not required,

"shall be made twice a month.

"(2) Persons who are not integrated oil companies. In the case of a person, other than an integrated oil company—

"(A) Deposits of withheld amounts. Deposit of the amounts required to be withheld under subsection (a) shall be made not later than—

"(i) except as provided in clause (ii), 45 days after the close of the month in which the oil was removed, or

"(ii) in the case of oil purchased under a contract therefor by an independent refiner under which no payment is required to be made before the 46th day after the close of the month in which the oil is purchased, before the first day of the 3rd month which begins after the close of the month in which such oil was removed.

"(B) Estimated section 4986 tax. Deposits of the estimated amount of such person's liability for the tax imposed by section 4986 with respect to oil for which withholding is not required shall be made not later than 45 days after the close of the month in which the oil was removed from the premises.

"(3) Integrated oil company defined. For purposes of this subsection, the term 'integrated oil company' means a taxpayer described in paragraph (2) or (4) of section 613A(d) who is not an independent refiner.

"(4) Independent refiner. For purposes of this subsection, the term 'independent refiner' has the same meaning as in paragraph (3) of section 3 of the Emergency Petroleum Allocation Act of 1973 (as in effect on January 1, 1980), except that 'the preceding calendar quarter' shall be substituted for 'November 27, 1973' in applying such paragraph for purposes of this paragraph.

"(c) Cross reference.

"For provision authorizing the Secretary to establish by regulations the mode and time for collecting the tax imposed by section 4986 (to the extent not otherwise provided in this chapter), see section 6302(a)."

In 1983, P.L. 97-448, Sec. 201(g)(1)(A), and (B), deleted "removed during any calendar year" after "produced" and "removed during the same calendar year" after "for crude oil" in subpara. (a)(3)(A) . . . Sec. 201(g)(2), deleted subpara. (a)(3)(C) and redesignated subpara. (a)(3)(D) as (a)(3)(C) . . . Sec. 201(g)(3), substituted "For purposes of this chapter (and so much of subtitle F as relates to this chapter), the producer" for "The producer" in subpara. (a)(4)(B), effective for periods after 2/29/80.

Prior to amendment, subpara. (a)(3)(C) read as follows:

"(C) Limitation on amount of adjustments. No adjustment shall be required under subparagraph (A) with respect to any payment for any crude oil to the extent that such adjustment would result in amounts withheld from such payment in excess of the windfall profit from such crude oil."

In 1981, P.L. 97-34, Sec. 601(b)(3), added para. (a)(9), for oil removed after 12/31/80.

In 1980, P.L. 96-223, Sec. 101(a)(1), added Code Sec. 4995, to apply to periods after 2/29/80. For the transitional rule see Sec. 101(i)(2) of the Act reproduced in the note following Code Sec. 4986.

"SEC. 4996. OTHER DEFINITIONS AND SPECIAL RULES.

"(a) Producer and operator.

"For purposes of this chapter—

"(1) Producer.

"(A) In general. Except as provided in subparagraphs (B) and (C), the term 'producer' means the holder of the economic interest with respect to the crude oil.

"(B) Net profits interests.

"(i) In general. Except to the extent otherwise provided by regulations, in the case of any property, all cost recovery oil covered by a net profits agreement (within the meaning of subsection (h)) shall be treated as produced by the parties to such agreement in proportion to their respective shares (determined after reduction for such cost recovery oil) of the production of the crude oil covered by such agreement.

"(ii) Clause (i) not to apply before payout. In the case of any property, clause (i) shall only apply for—

"(I) the first taxable period in which, under the agreement with respect to such property, one or more persons receives a share described in subsection (h)(1)(B), and

"(II) all subsequent taxable periods to which such agreement applies.

"(C) Partnerships.

"(i) In general. If (but for this subparagraph) a partnership would be treated as the producer of any crude oil—

"(I) such crude oil shall be allocated among the partners of such partnership, and

"(II) any partner to whom such crude oil is allocated (and not the partnership) shall be treated as the producer of such crude oil.

"(ii) Allocation. Except to the extent otherwise provided in regulations, any allocation under clause (i)(I) shall be determined on the basis of a person's proportionate share of the income of the partnership.

"(C) Subchapter S corporations.

"(i) In general If (but for this subparagraph) an S corporation would be treated as a producer of any crude oil—

"(I) such crude oil shall be allocated among the shareholders of such corporation, and

"(II) any shareholder to whom such crude oil is allocated (and not the S corporation) shall be treated as the producer of such crude oil.

"(ii) Allocation. Except to the extent otherwise provided in regulations, any allocation under clause (i)(I) shall be determined on the basis of the shareholder's pro rata share (as determined under section 1377(a)) of the income of the corporation.

"(2) Operator.

"(A) In general. Except as provided in subparagraph (B), the term 'operator' means the person primarily responsible for the management and operation of crude oil production on a property.

"(B) Designation of other person. Under regulations prescribed by the Secretary, the term 'operator' means the person (or persons) designated with respect to a property (or portion thereof) as the operator for purposes of this chapter by persons holding operating mineral interests in the property.

3,375

"*(b) Other definitions.*

"For purposes of this chapter—

"(1) Crude oil. The term 'crude oil' has the meaning given to such term by the June 1979 energy regulations. In the case of crude oil which is condensate recovered off the premises by mechanical separation, such crude oil shall be treated as removed from the premises on the date on which it is so recovered.

"(2) Barrel. The term 'barrel' means 42 United States gallons.

"(3) Domestic. The term 'domestic', when used with respect to crude oil, means crude oil produced from a well located in the United States or in a possession of the United States.

"(4) United States. The term 'United States' has the meaning given to such term by paragraph (1) of section 638 (relating to Continental Shelf areas).

"(5) Possession of the United States. The term 'possession of the United States' has the meaning given to such term by paragraph (2) of section 638.

"(6) Indian tribe. The term 'Indian tribe' has the meaning given to such term by section 106(b)(2)(C)(ii) of the Natural Gas Policy Act of 1978 (15 U.S.C. 3316(b)(2)(C)(ii)).

"(7) Taxable period. The term 'taxable period' means—

"(A) March 1980, and

"(B) each calendar quarter beginning after March 1980.

"(8) Energy regulations.

"(A) In general. The term 'energy regulations' means regulations prescribed under section 4(a) of the Emergency Petroleum Allocation Act of 1973 (15 U.S.C. 753(a)).

"(B) March 1979 energy regulations. The March 1979 energy regulations shall be the terms of the energy regulations as such terms existed on March 1, 1979.

"(C) June 1979 energy regulations. The June 1979 energy regulations—

"(i) shall be the terms of the energy regulations as such terms existed on June 1, 1979, and

"(ii) shall be treated as including final action taken pursuant thereto before June 1, 1979, and as including action taken before, on, or after such date with respect to incremental production from qualified tertiary enhanced recovery projects.

"(D) Continued application of regulations after decontrol. Energy regulations shall be treated as continuing in effect without regard to decontrol of oil prices or any other termination of the application of such regulations.

"*(c) Severance tax adjustment.*

"For purposes of this chapter—

"(1) In general. The severance tax adjustment with respect to any barrel of crude oil shall be the amount by which—

"(A) any severance tax imposed with respect to such barrel, exceeds

"(B) the severance tax which would have been imposed if the barrel had been valued at its adjusted base price.

"(2) Severance tax defined. For purposes of this subsection, the term 'severance tax' means a tax—

"(A) imposed by a State with respect to the extraction of oil, and

"(B) determined on the basis of the gross value of the extracted oil.

"(3) Limitations.

"(A) 15 percent limitation. A severance tax shall not be taken into account to the extent that the rate thereof exceeds 15 percent.

"(B) Increases after March 31, 1979, must apply equally. The amount of the severance tax taken into account under paragraph (1) shall not exceed the amount which would have been imposed under a State severance tax in effect on March 31, 1979, unless such excess is attributable to an increase in the rate of the severance tax (or to the imposition of a severance tax) which applies equally to all portions of the gross value of each barrel of oil subject to such tax.

"*(d) Alaskan oil from Sadlerochit reservoir.*

"For purposes of this chapter

"(1) Removal price determined on monthly basis. The removal price of Sadlerochit oil removed during any calendar month shall be the average of the producer's removal prices for such month.

"(2) Sadlerochit oil defined. The term 'Sadlerochit oil' means crude oil produced from the Sadlerochit reservoir in the Prudhoe Bay oilfield.

"*(e) Special rules for post-1978 transfers of property.*

"In the case of a transfer after 1978 of any portion of a property, for purposes of this chapter (including the application of the June 1979 energy regulations for purposes of this chapter), after such transfer crude oil produced from any portion of such property shall not constitute oil from a stripper well property, newly discovered oil, or heavy oil, if such oil would not be so classified if the property had not been transferred.

"*(f) Adjustment of removal price.*

"In determining the removal price of oil from a property in the case of any transaction, the Secretary may adjust the removal price to reflect clearly the fair market value of oil removed.

"*(g) No exemptions from tax.*

"No taxable crude oil, and no producer of such oil, shall be exempt from the tax imposed by this chapter except to the extent provided in this chapter or in any provision of law enacted after the date of the enactment of this chapter which grants a specific exemption, by reference to this chapter, from the tax imposed by this chapter.

"*(h) Terms used in subsection (a)(1)(B).*

"For purposes of subsection (a)(1)(B) and this subsection—

"(1) Net profits agreement. The term 'net profits agreement' means an agreement entered into (or renewed) after March 31, 1982, and providing for sharing part or all of the production of crude oil from a property where—

"(A) 1 or more persons are to be reimbursed for qualified costs by the allocation of cost recovery oil, and

"(B) 1 or more persons are to receive a share of any production of crude oil from the property remaining after reduction for the cost recovery oil referred to in subparagraph (A).

"(2) Cost recovery oil defined. The term 'cost recovery oil' means crude oil produced from the property which is allocated to a person as reimbursement for qualified costs paid or incurred with respect to the property. The Secretary shall by regulation prescribe rules for allocating the cost recovery oil to the oil produced from the property.

"(3) Qualified costs. The term 'qualified costs' means any amount paid or incurred for exploring for, or developing or producing, 1 or more oil or gas wells on the property.

"(4) Scope of agreement. A net profits agreement shall be treated as covering only shares of production of crude oil held by persons who hold economic interests in the property (determined without regard to subsection (a)(1)(B)).

"*(i) Cross reference.*

"For the holder of the economic interest in the case of a production payment, see section 636."

———

In **1983**, P.L. 97-448, Sec. 201(h)(1)(A), redesignated subpara. (a)(1)(B) as (a)(1)(C) and added a new subpara. (a)(1)(B)... Sec. 201(h)(1)(B), substituted "subparagraphs (B) and (C)" for "subparagraph (B)" in subpara. (a)(1)(A)... Sec. 201(h)(1)(C), redesignated subsec. (h) as (i), and added a new subsec. (h), for periods after 2/29/80. Sec. 201(h)(1)(E) of this Act provides:

"(E) If 90 percent or more of the remaining production referred to in subparagraph (B) of section 4996(h)(1) of the Internal Revenue Code of 1954 is to be received by governmental entities, and organizations described in clause (i), (ii), or (iii) of section 4994(b)(1)(A) of such Code, which do not share in the costs referred to in subparagraph (A) of such section 4996(h)(1), then the requirement of paragraph (1) of section 4996(h) of such Code that the agreement be entered into (or renewed) after March 31, 1982, shall not apply."

—P.L. 97-448, Sec. 201(h)(2)(A), added the last sentence to para. (b)(1)... Sec. 201(h)(2)(B), substituted "a well" for "an oil well" in para. (b)(3), for periods after 2/29/80.

—P.L. 97-448, Sec. 203(b)(4), provides:

"(4) No withholding by reason of condensate provision.—No withholding of tax shall be required under section 4995 of the Internal Revenue Code of 1954 by reason of the amendment made by section 201(h)(2)(A) of this Act before the date on which regulations with respect to such amendment are published in the Federal Register."

—P.L. 97-448, Sec. 203(c), provides:

"(c) No interest for past periods resulting from amendments relating to cost recovery oil.—No interest shall be paid or credited with respect to the credit or refund of any overpayment of tax imposed by the Internal Revenue Code of 1954, and no interest shall be assessed or collected with respect to any underpayment of tax imposed by such Code, for any period before the date which is 60 days after the date of the enactment of this Act, to the extent that such overpayment or underpayment is attributable to the amendments made by section 201(h)(1)."

In **1982**, P.L. 97-354, Sec. (3)(b)(1), added subpara. (a)(1)(C), for tax. yrs. begin. after 12/31/82.

—P.L. 97-248, Sec. 284(a), amended subsec. (d), effective with respect to oil removed after 12/31/82.

Prior to amendment, subsec. (d) read as follows:

"*(d) Alaskan oil from Sadlerochit Reservoir.*

"For purposes of this chapter—

"(1) In general. In the case of Sadlerochit oil—

"(A) Adjusted base price increased by TAPS adjustment. The adjusted base price for any calendar quarter (determined without regard to this subsection) shall be increased by the TAPS adjustment (if any) for such quarter provided by paragraph (2).

"(B) Removal price determined on monthly basis. The removal price of such oil removed during any calendar month shall be the average of the producer's removal prices for such month.

"(2) TAPS adjustment.

"(A) In general. The TAPS adjustment for any calendar quarter is the excess (if any) of—

"(i) $6.26 over

"(ii) the TAPS tariff for the preceding calendar quarter.

"(B) TAPS tariff. For purposes of subparagraph (A), the TAPS tariff for the preceding calendar quarter is the average per barrel amount paid for all transportation (ending in such quarter) of crude oil through the TAPS.

"(C) TAPS defined. For purposes of this paragraph, the term 'TAPS' means the Trans-Alaska Pipeline System.

"(3) Sadlerochit oil defined. The term 'Sadlerochit oil' means crude oil produced from the Sadlerochit reservoir in the Prudhoe Bay oilfield."

In **1980**, P.L. 96-223, Sec. 101(a)(1), added Code Sec. 4996, to apply to periods after 2/29/80. For the transitional rule see Sec. 101(i)(2) of the Act reproduced in the note following Code Sec. 4986.

———

"SEC. 4997. RECORDS AND INFORMATION; REGULATIONS.

"*(a) Records and information.*

"Each taxpayer liable for tax under section 4986, each partnership, trust, or estate producing domestic crude oil, each purchaser of domestic crude oil, and each operator of a well from which domestic crude oil was produced, shall keep such records, make such returns, and furnish such statements and other information (to the Secretary and to other persons having an interest in the oil) with respect to such oil as the Secretary may by regulations prescribe.

"*(b) Regulations.*

Excise and miscellaneous taxes

"The Secretary shall prescribe such regulations as may be necessary or appropriate to carry out the purposes of this chapter, including such changes in the application of the energy regulations for purposes of this chapter as may be necessary or appropriate to carry out such purposes."

In 1988, P.L. 100-647, Sec. 6254, provides:
"SEC. 6254. AMENDMENTS RELATED TO CRUDE OIL WINDFALL PROFIT TAX ACT OF 1980.
"The reporting requirements of section 4997 of former chapter 45 of subtitle D of the Internal Revenue Code of 1986, and the related regulations thereunder, are repealed: Provided, That this repeal is effective only for crude oil removed after December 31, 1987, for which no tax is due or withheld under former chapter 45 of subtitle D of the Internal Revenue Code of 1986."

In 1983, P.L. 97-448, Sec. 201(i)(1), substituted "such statements and other information" for "such information" in subsec. (a), for returns and statements the due dates for which (without regard to extensions) are after 1/12/83.

In 1980, P.L. 96-223, Sec. 101(a)(1), added Code Sec. 4997, to apply to periods after 2/29/80. For the transitional rule see Sec. 101(i)(2) of the Act reproduced in the note following Code Sec. 4986.

"SEC. 4998. CROSS REFERENCES.
"(1) For additions to the tax and additional amount for failure to file tax return or to pay tax, see section 6651.
"(2) For additions to the tax and additional amounts for failure to file certain information returns, registration statements, etc., see section 6652.
"(3) For additions to the tax and additional amounts for negligence and fraud, see section 6653.
"(4) For additions to the tax and additional amounts for failure to make deposit of taxes, see section 6656.
"(5) For additions to the tax and additional amounts for failure to collect and pay over tax, or attempt to evade or defeat tax, see section 6672.
"(6) For criminal penalties for attempt to evade or defeat tax, willful failure to collect or pay over tax, willful failure to file return, supply information, or pay tax, and for fraud and false statements, see sections 7201, 7202, 7203, and 7206.
"(7) For criminal penalties for failure to furnish certain information regarding windfall profit tax on domestic crude oil, see section 7241."

In 1980, P.L. 96-223, Sec. 101(a)(1), added Code Sec. 4998, to apply to periods after 2/29/80. For the transitional rule see Sec. 101(i)(2) of the Act reproduced in the note following Code Sec. 4986.

Sec. 4985. Stock compensation of insiders in expatriated corporations.

(a) Imposition of tax.

In the case of an individual who is a disqualified individual with respect to any expatriated corporation, there is hereby imposed on such person a tax equal to—

(1) the rate of tax specified in section 1(h)(1)(C), multiplied by

(2) the value (determined under subsection (b)) of the specified stock compensation held (directly or indirectly) by or for the benefit of such individual or a member of such individual's family (as defined in section 267) at any time during the 12-month period beginning on the date which is 6 months before the expatriation date.

(b) Value.

For purposes of subsection (a)—

(1) In general. The value of specified stock compensation shall be—

(A) in the case of a stock option (or other similar right) or a stock appreciation right, the fair value of such option or right, and

(B) in any other case, the fair market value of such compensation.

(2) Date for determining value. The determination of value shall be made—

(A) in the case of specified stock compensation held on the expatriation date, on such date,

(B) in the case of such compensation which is canceled during the 6 months before the expatriation date, on the day before such cancellation, and

(C) in the case of such compensation which is granted after the expatriation date, on the date such compensation is granted.

(c) Tax to apply only if shareholder gain recognized.

Subsection (a) shall apply to any disqualified individual with respect to an expatriated corporation only if gain (if any) on any stock in such corporation is recognized in whole or part by any shareholder by reason of the acquisition referred to in section 7874(a)(2)(B)(i) with respect to such corporation.

(d) Exception where gain recognized on compensation.

Subsection (a) shall not apply to—

(1) any stock option which is exercised on the expatriation date or during the 6-month period before such date and to the stock acquired in such exercise, if income is recognized under section 83 on or before the expatriation date with respect to the stock acquired pursuant to such exercise, and

(2) any other specified stock compensation which is exercised, sold, exchanged, distributed, cashed-out, or otherwise paid during such period in a transaction in which income, gain, or loss is recognized in full.

(e) Definitions.

For purposes of this section—

(1) Disqualified individual. The term "disqualified individual" means, with respect to a corporation, any individual who, at any time during the 12-month period beginning on the date which is 6 months before the expatriation date—

(A) is subject to the requirements of section 16(a) of the Securities Exchange Act of 1934 with respect to such corporation or any member of the expanded affiliated group which includes such corporation, or

(B) would be subject to such requirements if such corporation or member were an issuer of equity securities referred to in such section.

(2) Expatriated corporation; expatriation date.

(A) Expatriated corporation. The term "expatriated corporation" means any corporation which is an expatriated entity (as defined in section 7874(a)(2)). Such term includes any predecessor or successor of such a corporation.

(B) Expatriation date. The term "expatriation date" means, with respect to a corporation, the date on which the corporation first becomes an expatriated corporation.

(3) Specified stock compensation.

(A) In general. The term "specified stock compensation" means payment (or right to payment) granted by the expatriated corporation (or by any member of the expanded affiliated group which includes such corporation) to any person in connection with the performance of services by a disqualified individual for such corporation or member if the value of such payment or right is based on (or determined by reference to) the value (or change in value) of stock in such corporation (or any such member).

(B) Exceptions. Such term shall not include—

(i) any option to which part II of subchapter D of chapter 1 applies, or

(ii) any payment or right to payment from a plan referred to in section 280G(b)(6).

(4) Expanded affiliated group. The term "expanded affiliated group" means an affiliated group (as defined in section 1504(a) without regard to section 1504(b)(3)); except that section 1504(a) shall be applied by substituting "more than 50 percent" for "at least 80 percent" each place it appears.

(f) Special rules.
For purposes of this section—
  (1) Cancellation of restriction. The cancellation of a restriction which by its terms will never lapse shall be treated as a grant.
  (2) Payment or reimbursement of tax by corporation treated as specified stock compensation. Any payment of the tax imposed by this section directly or indirectly by the expatriated corporation or by any member of the expanded affiliated group which includes such corporation—
    (A) shall be treated as specified stock compensation, and
    (B) shall not be allowed as a deduction under any provision of chapter 1.
  (3) Certain restrictions ignored. Whether there is specified stock compensation, and the value thereof, shall be determined without regard to any restriction other than a restriction which by its terms will never lapse.
  (4) Property transfers. Any transfer of property shall be treated as a payment and any right to a transfer of property shall be treated as a right to a payment.
  (5) Other administrative provisions. For purposes of subtitle F, any tax imposed by this section shall be treated as a tax imposed by subtitle A.
(g) Regulations.
The Secretary shall prescribe such regulations as may be necessary or appropriate to carry out the purposes of this section.

In **2004**, P.L. 108-357, Sec. 802(a), added Code Sec. 4985, effective 3/4/2003; except that periods before such date shall not be taken into account in applying the periods in Code Sec. 4985(a) and (e)(1), as added by Sec. 802(a) of P.L. 108-357.

CHAPTER 46.—GOLDEN PARACHUTE PAYMENTS
Sec.
4999. Golden parachute payments.

In **1984**, P.L. 98-369, Sec. 67(b)(1), added the heading for Chapter 46 and the item for Code Sec. 4999.

Sec. 4999. Golden parachute payments.
(a) Imposition of tax.
There is hereby imposed on any person who receives an excess parachute payment a tax equal to 20 percent of the amount of such payment.
(b) Excess parachute payment defined.
For purposes of this section, the term "excess parachute payment" has the meaning given to such term by section 280G(b).
(c) Administrative provisions.
  (1) Withholding. In the case of any excess parachute payment which is wages (within the meaning of section 3401) the amount deducted and withheld under section 3402 shall be increased by the amount of the tax imposed by this section on such payment.
  (2) Other administrative provisions. For purposes of subtitle F, any tax imposed by this section shall be treated as a tax imposed by subtitle A.

In **1984**, P.L. 98-369, Sec. 67(b)(1), added Code Sec. 4999, effective for payments under agreements entered into or renewed after 6/14/84 in tax. yrs. ending after 6/14/84. Sec. 67(e)(2) of this Act provides:
  "(2) Special rule for contract amendments. Any contract entered into before June 15, 1984, which is amended after June 14, 1984, in any significant relevant aspect shall be treated as a contract entered into after June 14, 1984."

CHAPTER 47.—CERTAIN GROUP HEALTH PLANS
Sec.
5000. Certain group health plans.

In **1989**, P.L. 101-239, Sec. 6202(b)(4)(A)(i), deleted "large" which followed "certain" from the heading of Chapter 47 . . . Sec. 6202(b)(4)(A)(ii), deleted "large" which followed "certain" from item 5000.
In **1986**, P.L. 99-509, Sec. 9319(d)(1), added chapter 47.

Sec. 5000. Certain group health plans.
(a) Imposition of tax.
There is hereby imposed on any employer (including a self-employed person) or employee organization that contributes to a nonconforming group health plan a tax equal to 25 percent of the employer's or employee organization's expenses incurred during the calendar year for each group health plan to which the employer (including a self-employed person) or employee organization contributes.
(b) Group health plan and large group health plan.
For purposes of this section—
  (1) Group health plan. The term "group health plan" means a plan (including a self-insured plan) of, or contributed to by, an employer (including a self-employed person) or employee organization to provide health care (directly or otherwise) to the employees, former employees, the employer, others associated or formerly associated with the employer in a business relationship, or their families.
  (2) Large group health plan. The term "large group health plan" means a plan of, or contributed to by, an employer or employee organization (including a self-insured plan) to provide health care (directly or otherwise) to the employees, former employees, the employer, others associated or formerly associated with the employer in a business relationship, or their families, that covers employees of at least one employer that normally employed at least 100 employees on a typical business day during the previous calendar year. For purposes of the preceding sentence—
    (A) all employers treated as a single employer under subsection (a) or (b) of section 52 shall be treated as a single employer,
    (B) all employees of the members of an affiliated service group (as defined in section 414(m)) shall be treated as employed by a single employer, and
    (C) leased employees (as defined in section 414(n)(2)) shall be treated as employees of the person for whom they perform services to the extent they are so treated under section 414(n).
(c) Nonconforming group health plan.
For purposes of this section, the term "nonconforming group health plan" means a group health plan or large group health plan that at any time during a calendar year does not comply with the requirements of subparagraphs (A) and (C) or subparagraph (B), respectively, of paragraph (1), or with the requirements of paragraph (2), of section 1862(b) of the Social Security Act.
(d) Government entities.
For purposes of this section, the term "employer" does not include a Federal or other governmental entity.

In **1993**, P.L. 103-66, Sec. 13561(d)(2), added "For purposes of the preceding sentence—" and subparas. (b)(2)(A), (B) and (C) to the end of para. (b)(2), effective 90 days after 8/10/93.
—P.L. 103-66, Sec. 13561(e)(2)(A)(i), added "(including a self-employed person)" after "employer" each place it appeared in subsec. (a) . . . Sec. 13561(e)(2)(A)(ii), amended para. (b)(1) . . . Sec. 13561(e)(2)(A)(iii), substituted "of paragraph (1), or with the requirements of paragraph (2), of section 1862(b)" for "of section 1862(b)(1)" in subsec. (c), effective 8/10/93.
Prior to amendment, para. (b)(1) read as follows:

"(1) Group health plan. The term 'group health plan' means any plan of, or contributed to by, an employer (including a self-insured plan) to provide health care (directly or otherwise) to the employer's employees, former employees, or the families of such employees or former employees."

In 1989, P.L. 101-239, Sec. 6202(b)(2)(A), deleted "large" after "certain" in the heading of Code Sec. 5000 . . . Sec. 6202(b)(2)(B), deleted "large" before "group health" each place it appeared in subsec. (a) . . . Sec. 6202(b)(2)(C), amended subsecs. (b) and (c), effective for items and services furnished after 12/19/89.
Prior to amendment, subsecs. (b) and (c) read as follows:

"(b) Large group health plan.

"For purposes of this section, the term 'large group health plan' means a plan of, or contributed to by, an employer or employee organization (including a self-insured plan) to provide health care (directly or otherwise) to the employees, former employees, the employer, others associated or formerly associated with the employer in a business relationship, or their families, that covers employees of at least one employer that normally employed at least 100 employees on a typical business day during the previous calendar year.

"(c) Nonconforming large group health plan.

"For purposes of this section, the term 'nonconforming large group health plan' means a large group health plan that at any time during a calendar year does not comply with the requirements of section 1862(b)(4)(A)(i) of the Social Security Act."

In 1986, P.L. 99-509, Sec. 9319(d)(1), added Code Sec. 5000, part of chapter 47, effective for items and services furnished on or after 1/1/87.

CHAPTER 48.—MAINTENANCE OF MINIMUM ESSENTIAL COVERAGE
Sec.
5000A. Requirement to maintain minimum essential coverage. [effective for tax. yrs. end. after 12/31/2013]

In 2010, P.L. 111-148, Sec. 1501(b), added Chapter 48

• **Caution:** Code Sec. 5000A is effective for tax. yrs. end. after 12/31/2013.

Sec. 5000A. Requirement to maintain minimum essential coverage.

(a) Requirement to maintain minimum essential coverage.

An applicable individual shall for each month beginning after 2013 ensure that the individual, and any dependent of the individual who is an applicable individual, is covered under minimum essential coverage for such month.

(b) Shared responsibility payment.

(1) **In general.** If a taxpayer who is an applicable individual, or an applicable individual for whom the taxpayer is liable under paragraph (3), fails to meet the requirement of subsection (a) for 1 or more months, then, except as provided in subsection (e), there is hereby imposed on the taxpayer a penalty with respect to such failures in the amount determined under subsection (c).

(2) **Inclusion with return.** Any penalty imposed by this section with respect to any month shall be included with a taxpayer's return under chapter 1 for the taxable year which includes such month.

(3) **Payment of penalty.** If an individual with respect to whom a penalty is imposed by this section for any month—

(A) is a dependent (as defined in section 152) of another taxpayer for the other taxpayer's taxable year including such month, such other taxpayer shall be liable for such penalty, or

(B) files a joint return for the taxable year including such month, such individual and the spouse of such individual shall be jointly liable for such penalty.

(c) Amount of penalty.

(1) **In general.** The amount of the penalty imposed by this section on any taxpayer for any taxable year with respect to failures described in subsection (b)(1) shall be equal to the lesser of—

(A) the sum of the monthly penalty amounts determined under paragraph (2) for months in the taxable year during which 1 or more such failures occurred, or

(B) an amount equal to the national average premium for qualified health plans which have a bronze level of coverage, provide coverage for the applicable family size involved, and are offered through Exchanges for plan years beginning in the calendar year with or within which the taxable year ends.

(2) **Monthly penalty amounts.** For purposes of paragraph (1)(A), the monthly penalty amount with respect to any taxpayer for any month during which any failure described in subsection (b)(1) occurred is an amount equal to $1/12$ of the greater of the following amounts:

(A) Flat dollar amount. An amount equal to the lesser of—

(i) the sum of the applicable dollar amounts for all individuals with respect to whom such failure occurred during such month, or

(ii) 300 percent of the applicable dollar amount (determined without regard to paragraph (3)(C)) for the calendar year with or within which the taxable year ends.

(B) Percentage of income. An amount equal to the following percentage of the excess of the taxpayer's household income for the taxable year over the amount of gross income specified in section 6012(a)(1) with respect to the taxpayer for the taxable year:

(i) 1.0 percent for taxable years beginning in 2014.

(ii) 2.0 percent for taxable years beginning in 2015.

(iii) 2.5 percent for taxable years beginning after 2015.

(3) **Applicable dollar amount.** For purposes of paragraph (1)—

(A) In general. Except as provided in subparagraphs (B) and (C), the applicable dollar amount is $695.

(B) Phase in. The applicable dollar amount is $95 for 2014 and $325 for 2015.

(C) Special rule for individuals under age 18. If an applicable individual has not attained the age of 18 as of the beginning of a month, the applicable dollar amount with respect to such individual for the month shall be equal to one-half of the applicable dollar amount for the calendar year in which the month occurs.

(D) Indexing of amount. In the case of any calendar year beginning after 2016, the applicable dollar amount shall be equal to $695, increased by an amount equal to—

(i) $695, multiplied by

(ii) the cost-of-living adjustment determined under section 1(f)(3) for the calendar year, determined by substituting "calendar year 2015" for "calendar year 1992" in subparagraph (B) thereof.

If the amount of any increase under clause (i) is not a multiple of $50, such increase shall be rounded to the next lowest multiple of $50.

(4) **Terms relating to income and families.** For purposes of this section—

(A) Family size. The family size involved with respect to any taxpayer shall be equal to the number of individuals for whom the taxpayer is allowed a deduction under section 151 (relating to allowance of deduction for personal exemptions) for the taxable year.

(B) Household income. The term "household income" means, with respect to any taxpayer for any taxable year, an amount equal to the sum of—

(i) the modified adjusted gross income of the taxpayer, plus

(ii) the aggregate modified adjusted gross incomes of all other individuals who—

(I) were taken into account in determining the taxpayer's family size under paragraph (1), and

(II) were required to file a return of tax imposed by section 1 for the taxable year.

(C) Modified adjusted gross income. The term "modified adjusted gross income" means adjusted gross income increased by—

(i) any amount excluded from gross income under section 911, and

(ii) any amount of interest received or accrued by the taxpayer during the taxable year which is exempt from tax.

(D) Repealed.

(d) Applicable individual.

For purposes of this section—

(1) In general. The term "applicable individual" means, with respect to any month, an individual other than an individual described in paragraph (2), (3), or (4).

(2) Religious exemptions.

(A) Religious conscience exemption. Such term shall not include any individual for any month if such individual has in effect an exemption under section 1311(d)(4)(H) of the Patient Protection and Affordable Care Act which certifies that such individual is—

(i) a member of a recognized religious sect or division thereof which is described in section 1402(g)(1), and

(ii) an adherent of established tenets or teachings of such sect or division as described in such section.

(B) Health care sharing ministry.

(i) In general. Such term shall not include any individual for any month if such individual is a member of a health care sharing ministry for the month.

(ii) Health care sharing ministry. The term "health care sharing ministry" means an organization—

(I) which is described in section 501(c)(3) and is exempt from taxation under section 501(a),

(II) members of which share a common set of ethical or religious beliefs and share medical expenses among members in accordance with those beliefs and without regard to the State in which a member resides or is employed,

(III) members of which retain membership even after they develop a medical condition,

(IV) which (or a predecessor of which) has been in existence at all times since December 31, 1999, and medical expenses of its members have been shared continuously and without interruption since at least December 31, 1999, and

(V) which conducts an annual audit which is performed by an independent certified public accounting firm in accordance with generally accepted accounting principles and which is made available to the public upon request.

(3) Individuals not lawfully present. Such term shall not include an individual for any month if for the month the individual is not a citizen or national of the United States or an alien lawfully present in the United States.

(4) Incarcerated individuals. Such term shall not include an individual for any month if for the month the individual is incarcerated, other than incarceration pending the disposition of charges.

(e) Exemptions.

No penalty shall be imposed under subsection (a) with respect to—

(1) Individuals who cannot afford coverage.

(A) In general. Any applicable individual for any month if the applicable individual's required contribution (determined on an annual basis) for coverage for the month exceeds 8 percent of such individual's household income for the taxable year described in section 1412(b)(1)(B) of the Patient Protection and Affordable Care Act. For purposes of applying this subparagraph, the taxpayer's household income shall be increased by any exclusion from gross income for any portion of the required contribution made through a salary reduction arrangement.

(B) Required contribution. For purposes of this paragraph, the term "required contribution" means—

(i) in the case of an individual eligible to purchase minimum essential coverage consisting of coverage through an eligible employer-sponsored plan, the portion of the annual premium which would be paid by the individual (without regard to whether paid through salary reduction or otherwise) for self-only coverage, or

(ii) in the case of an individual eligible only to purchase minimum essential coverage described in subsection (f)(1)(C), the annual premium for the lowest cost bronze plan available in the individual market through the Exchange in the State in the rating area in which the individual resides (without regard to whether the individual purchased a qualified health plan through the Exchange), reduced by the amount of the credit allowable under section 36B for the taxable year (determined as if the individual was covered by a qualified health plan offered through the Exchange for the entire taxable year).

(C) Special rules for individuals related to employees. For purposes of subparagraph (B)(i), if an applicable individual is eligible for minimum essential coverage through an employer by reason of a relationship to an employee, the determination under subparagraph (A) shall be made by reference to required contribution of the employee.

(D) Indexing. In the case of plan years beginning in any calendar year after 2014, subparagraph (A) shall be applied by substituting for "8 percent" the percentage the Secretary of Health and Human Services determines reflects the excess of the rate of premium growth between the preceding calendar year and 2013 over the rate of income growth for such period.

(2) Taxpayers with income below filing threshold. Any applicable individual for any month during a calendar year if the individual's household income for the taxable year described in section 1412(b)(1)(B) of the Patient Protection and Affordable Care Act is less than the amount of gross income specified in section 6012(a)(1) with respect to the taxpayer.

(3) Members of Indian tribes. Any applicable individual for any month during which the individual is a member of an Indian tribe (as defined in section 45A(c)(6)).

Excise and miscellaneous taxes — Code Sec. 5000A

(4) Months during short coverage gaps.

(A) In general. Any month the last day of which occurred during a period in which the applicable individual was not covered by minimum essential coverage for a continuous period of less than 3 months.

(B) Special rules. For purposes of applying this paragraph—

(i) the length of a continuous period shall be determined without regard to the calendar years in which months in such period occur,

(ii) if a continuous period is greater than the period allowed under subparagraph (A), no exception shall be provided under this paragraph for any month in the period, and

(iii) if there is more than 1 continuous period described in subparagraph (A) covering months in a calendar year, the exception provided by this paragraph shall only apply to months in the first of such periods.

The Secretary shall prescribe rules for the collection of the penalty imposed by this section in cases where continuous periods include months in more than 1 taxable year.

(5) Hardships. Any applicable individual who for any month is determined by the Secretary of Health and Human Services under section 1311(d)(4)(H) to have suffered a hardship with respect to the capability to obtain coverage under a qualified health plan.

(f) Minimum essential coverage.

For purposes of this section—

(1) In general. The term "minimum essential coverage" means any of the following:

(A) Government sponsored programs. Coverage under—

(i) the Medicare program under part A of title XVIII of the Social Security Act,

(ii) the Medicaid program under title XIX of the Social Security Act,

(iii) the CHIP program under title XXI of the Social Security Act,

(iv) the TRICARE for Life program,

(v) a health care program under chapter 17 or 18 of title 38, United States Code, as determined by the Secretary of Veterans Affairs, in coordination with the Secretary of Health and Human Services and the Secretary,

(vi) a health plan under section 2504(e) of title 22, United States Code (relating to Peace Corps volunteers).

(B) Employer-sponsored plan. Coverage under an eligible employer-sponsored plan.

(C) Plans in the individual market. Coverage under a health plan offered in the individual market within a State.

(D) Grandfathered health plan. Coverage under a grandfathered health plan.

(E) Other coverage. Such other health benefits coverage, such as a State health benefits risk pool, as the Secretary of Health and Human Services, in coordination with the Secretary, recognizes for purposes of this subsection.

(2) Eligible employer-sponsored plan. The term "eligible employer-sponsored plan" means, with respect to any employee, a group health plan or group health insurance coverage offered by an employer to the employee which is—

(A) a governmental plan (within the meaning of section 2791(d)(8) of the Public Health Service Act), or

(B) any other plan or coverage offered in the small or large group market within a State.

Such term shall include a grandfathered health plan described in paragraph (1)(D) offered in a group market.

(3) Excepted benefits not treated as minimum essential coverage. The term "minimum essential coverage" shall not include health insurance coverage which consists of coverage of excepted benefits—

(A) described in paragraph (1) of subsection (c) of section 2791 of the Public Health Service Act; or

(B) described in paragraph (2), (3), or (4) of such subsection if the benefits are provided under a separate policy, certificate, or contract of insurance.

(4) Individuals residing outside United States or residents of territories. Any applicable individual shall be treated as having minimum essential coverage for any month—

(A) if such month occurs during any period described in subparagraph (A) or (B) of section 911(d)(1) which is applicable to the individual, or

(B) if such individual is a bona fide resident of any possession of the United States (as determined under section 937(a)) for such month.

(5) Insurance-related terms. Any term used in this section which is also used in title I of the Patient Protection and Affordable Care Act shall have the same meaning as when used in such title.

(g) Administration and procedure.

(1) In general. The penalty provided by this section shall be paid upon notice and demand by the Secretary, and except as provided in paragraph (2), shall be assessed and collected in the same manner as an assessable penalty under subchapter B of chapter 68.

(2) Special rules. Notwithstanding any other provision of law—

(A) Waiver of criminal penalties. In the case of any failure by a taxpayer to timely pay any penalty imposed by this section, such taxpayer shall not be subject to any criminal prosecution or penalty with respect to such failure.

(B) Limitations on liens and levies. The Secretary shall not—

(i) file notice of lien with respect to any property of a taxpayer by reason of any failure to pay the penalty imposed by this section, or

(ii) levy on any such property with respect to such failure.

In **2010,** P.L. 111-173, Sec. 1(a), Sec. 1(a) amended clause (f)(1)(A)(v)
Prior to amendment, clause (f)(1)(A)(v) read as follows:

"(v) the veteran's health care program under chapter 17 of title 38, United States Code, or", effective for tax. yrs. end. after 12/31/2013, as if included in the provisions of Sec. 1501(d) of P.L. 111-148.

—P.L. 111-152, Sec. 1002(a)(1)(A)(i), added "the excess of" before "the taxpayer's household income" in subpara. (c)(2)(B) . . . Sec. 1002(a)(1)(A)(ii), added "for the taxable year over the amount of gross income specified in section 6012(a)(1) with respect to the taxpayer" before "for the taxable year" in subpara. (c)(2)(B) . . . Sec. 1002(a)(1)(B), substituted "1.0" for "0.5" in clause (c)(2)(B)(i) . . . Sec. 1002(a)(1)(C), substituted "2.0" for "1.0" in clause (c)(2)(B)(ii) . . . Sec. 1002(a)(1)(D), substituted "2.5" for "2.0" in clause (c)(2)(B)(iii) . . . Sec. 1002(a)(2)(A), substituted "$695" for "$750" in clause (c)(3)(A) . . . Sec. 1002(a)(2)(B), substituted "$325" for "$495" in clause (c)(3)(B) . . . Sec. 1002(a)(2)(C)(i), substituted "$695" for "$750" in subpara. (c)(3)(D) . . . Sec. 1002(a)(2)(C)(ii), substituted "$695" for "$750" in clause (c)(3)(D)(i) . . . Sec. 1002(b)(1), deleted subpara. (c)(4)(D)

Prior to deletion, subpara. (c)(4)(D) read as follows:

"(D) Poverty line.

"(i) In general. The term 'poverty line' has the meaning given that term in section 2110(c)(5) of the Social Security Act (42 U.S.C. 1397jj(c)(5))" "(ii) Poverty line used. In the case of any taxable year ending with or within a calendar year, the poverty line used shall be the most recently published poverty line as of the 1st day of such calendar year." . . . Sec. 1002(b)(2)(A), substituted "below filing threshold" for "under 100 percent of poverty line" in the heading of para. (e)(2) . . . Sec. 1002(b)(2)(B), substituted "the amount of gross income specified in section 6012(a)(1) with respect to the taxpayer." for "100 percent of the poverty line for the size of the family involved (determined in the same manner as under subsection (b)(4))." in para. (e)(2). . . . Sec. 1004(a)(1)(C), substituted "modified adjusted gross" for "modified gross" in clauses (c)(4)(i)-(ii) [sic (c)(4)(B)(i)-(ii)] . . . Sec. 1004(a)(2)(B), amended subpara. (c)(4)(C), effective for tax. yrs. end. after 12/31/2013, as if included in the provisions of Sec. 1501 of P.L. 111-148 [see below].

Prior to amendment, subpara. (c)(4)(C) read as follows:

"(C) Modified gross income. The term 'modified gross income' means gross income—

"(i) decreased by the amount of any deduction allowable under paragraph (1), (3), (4), or (10) of section 62(a),

"(ii) increased by the amount of interest received or accrued during the taxable year which is exempt from tax imposed by this chapter, and

"(iii) determined without regard to sections 911, 931, and 933."

—P.L. 111-148, Sec. 1501(a), of this Act [as amended by Sec. 10106(a) of this Act, see below], reads as follows:

"Findings. Congress makes the following findings:

"(1) In general. The individual responsibility requirement provided for in this section (in this subsection referred to as the 'requirement') is commercial and economic in nature, and substantially affects interstate commerce, as a result of the effects described in paragraph (2).

"(2) Effects on the national economy and interstate commerce. The effects described in this paragraph are the following:

"(A) The requirement regulates activity that is commercial and economic in nature: economic and financial decisions about how and when health care is paid for, and when health insurance is purchased. In the absence of the requirement, some individuals would make an economic and financial decision to forego health insurance coverage and attempt to self-insure, which increases financial risks to households and medical providers.

"(B) Health insurance and health care services are a significant part of the national economy. National health spending is projected to increase from $2,500,000,000,000, or 17.6 percent of the economy, in 2009 to $4,700,000,000,000 in 2019. Private health insurance spending is projected to be $854,000,000,000 in 2009, and pays for medical supplies, drugs, and equipment that are shipped in interstate commerce. Since most health insurance is sold by national or regional health insurance companies, health insurance is sold in interstate commerce and claims payments flow through interstate commerce.

"(C) The requirement, together with the other provisions of this Act, will add millions of new consumers to the health insurance market, increasing the supply of, and demand for, health care services, and will increase the number and share of Americans who are insured.

"(D) The requirement achieves near-universal coverage by building upon and strengthening the private employer-based health insurance system, which covers 176,000,000 Americans nationwide. In Massachusetts, a similar requirement has strengthened private employer-based coverage: despite the economic downturn, the number of workers offered employer-based coverage has actually increased.

"(E) The economy loses up to $207,000,000,000 a year because of the poorer health and shorter lifespan of the uninsured. By significantly reducing the number of the uninsured, the requirement, together with the other provisions of this Act, will significantly reduce this economic cost.

"(F) The cost of providing uncompensated care to the uninsured was $43,000,000,000 in 2008. To pay for this cost, health care providers pass on the cost to private insurers, which pass on the cost to families. This cost-shifting increases family premiums by on average over $1,000 a year. By significantly reducing the number of the uninsured, the requirement, together with the other provisions of this Act, will lower health insurance premiums.

"(G) 62 percent of all personal bankruptcies are caused in part by medical expenses. By significantly increasing health insurance coverage, the requirement, together with the other provisions of this Act, will improve financial security for families.

"(H) Under the Employee Retirement Income Security Act of 1974 (29 U.S.C. 1001 et seq.), the Public Health Service Act (42 U.S.C. 201 et seq.), and this Act, the Federal Government has a significant role in regulating health insurance. The requirement is an essential part of this larger regulation of economic activity, and the absence of the requirement would undercut Federal regulation of the health insurance market.

"(I) Under sections 2704 and 2705 of the Public Health Service Act (as added by section 1201 of this Act), if there were no requirement, many individuals would wait to purchase health insurance until they needed care. By significantly increasing health insurance coverage, the requirement, together with the other provisions of this Act, will minimize this adverse selection and broaden the health insurance risk pool to include healthy individuals, which will lower health insurance premiums. The requirement is essential to creating effective health insurance markets in which improved health insurance products that are guaranteed issue and do not exclude coverage of pre-existing conditions can be sold.

"(J) Administrative costs for private health insurance, which were $90,000,000,000 in 2006, are 26 to 30 percent of premiums in the current individual and small group markets. By significantly increasing health insurance coverage and the size of purchasing pools, which will increase economies of scale, the requirement, together with the other provisions of this Act, will significantly reduce administrative costs and lower health insurance premiums. The requirement is essential to creating effective health insurance markets that do not require underwriting and eliminate its associated administrative costs.

"(3) Supreme court ruling. In United States v. South-Eastern Underwriters Association (322 U.S. 533 (1944)), the Supreme Court of the United States ruled that insurance is interstate commerce subject to Federal regulation."

—P.L. 111-148, Sec. 1501(b), added Code Sec. 5000A, effective for tax. yrs. end. after 12/31/2013.

—P.L. 111-148, Sec. 1502(c), of this Act, reads as follows:

"(c) Notification of nonenrollment. Not later than June 30 of each year, the Secretary of the Treasury, acting through the Internal Revenue Service and in consultation with the Secretary of Health and Human Services, shall send a notification to each individual who files an individual income tax return and who is not enrolled in minimum essential coverage (as defined in section 5000A of the Internal Revenue Code of 1986). Such notification shall contain information on the services available through the Exchange operating in the State in which such individual resides."

—P.L. 111-148, Sec. 10106(a), amended Sec. 1501(a)(2) of this Act [see above]. . . . Sec. 10106(b)(1), amended para. (b)(1) . . . Sec. 10106(b)(2), amended paras. (c)(1) and (2) . . . Sec. 10106(b)(3), substituted "$495" for "$350" in para. (c)(3) . . . Sec. 10106(c), amended subpara. (d)(2)(A) . . . Sec. 10106(d), amended subpara. (e)(1)(C), effective for tax. yrs. end. after 12/31/2013, as if included in the provisions of Sec. 1501 of this Act [see above].

Prior to amendment, Sec. 1501(a)(2) of this Act read as follows:

"(2) Effects on the national economy and interstate commerce. The effects described in this paragraph are the following:

"(A) The requirement regulates activity that is commercial and economic in nature: economic and financial decisions about how and when health care is paid for, and when health insurance is purchased.

"(B) Health insurance and health care services are a significant part of the national economy. National health spending is projected to increase from $2,500,000,000,000, or 17.6 percent of the economy, in 2009 to $4,700,000,000,000 in 2019. Private health insurance spending is projected to be $854,000,000,000 in 2009, and pays for medical supplies, drugs, and equipment that are shipped in interstate commerce. Since most health insurance is sold by national or regional health insurance companies, health insurance is sold in interstate commerce and claims payments flow through interstate commerce.

"(C) The requirement, together with the other provisions of this Act, will add millions of new consumers to the health insurance market, increasing the supply of, and demand for, health care services. According to the Congressional Budget Office, the requirement will increase the number and share of Americans who are insured.

"(D) The requirement achieves near-universal coverage by building upon and strengthening the private employer-based health insurance system, which covers 176,000,000 Americans nationwide. In Massachusetts, a similar requirement has strengthened private employer-based coverage: despite the economic downturn, the number of workers offered employer-based coverage has actually increased.

"(E) Half of all personal bankruptcies are caused in part by medical expenses. By significantly increasing health insurance coverage, the requirement, together with the other provisions of this Act, will improve financial security for families.

"(F) Under the Employee Retirement Income Security Act of 1974 (29 U.S.C. 1001 et seq.), the Public Health Service Act (42 U.S.C. 201 et seq.), and this Act, the Federal Government has a significant role in regulating health insurance which is in interstate commerce.

"(G) Under sections 2704 and 2705 of the Public Health Service Act (as added by section 1201 of this Act), if there were no requirement, many individuals would wait to purchase health insurance until they needed care. By significantly increasing health insurance coverage, the requirement, together with the other provisions of this Act, will minimize this adverse selection and broaden the health insurance risk pool to include healthy individuals, which will lower health insurance premiums. The requirement is essential to creating effective health insurance markets in which improved health insurance products that are guaranteed issue and do not exclude coverage of pre-existing conditions can be sold.

"(H) Administrative costs for private health insurance, which were $90,000,000,000 in 2006, are 26 to 30 percent of premiums in the current individual and small group markets. By significantly increasing health insurance coverage and the size of purchasing pools, which will increase economies of scale, the requirement, together with the other provisions of this Act, will significantly reduce administrative costs and lower health insurance premiums. The requirement is essential to creating effective health insurance markets that do not require underwriting and eliminate its associated administrative costs."

Prior to amendment, para. (b)(1) read as follows:

"(1) In general. If an applicable individual fails to meet the requirement of subsection (a) for 1 or more months during any calendar year beginning after 2013, then, except as provided in subsection (d), there is hereby imposed a penalty with respect to the individual in the amount determined under subsection (c)."

Prior to amendment, paras. (c)(1) and (2) read as follows:

"(1) In general. The penalty determined under this subsection for any month with respect to any individual is an amount equal to $\frac{1}{12}$ of the applicable dollar amount for the calendar year.

"(2) Dollar limitation. The amount of the penalty imposed by this section on any taxpayer for any taxable year with respect to all individuals for whom the taxpayer is liable under subsection (b)(3) shall not exceed an amount equal to 300 percent the applicable dollar amount (determined without regard to paragraph (3)(C)) for the calendar year with or within which the taxable year ends."

Prior to amendment, subpara. (d)(2)(A) read as follows:

"(A) Religious conscience exemption. Such term shall not include any individual for any month if such individual has in effect an exemption under section 1311(d)(4)(H) of the Patient Protection and Affordable Care Act which certifies

Excise and miscellaneous taxes

that such individual is a member of a recognized religious sect or division thereof described in section 1402(g)(1) and an adherent of established tenets or teachings of such sect or division as described in such section."

Prior to amendment, subpara. (e)(1)(C) read as follows:

"(C) Special rules for individuals related to employees. For purposes of subparagraph (B)(i), if an applicable individual is eligible for minimum essential coverage through an employer by reason of a relationship to an employee, the determination shall be made by reference to the affordability of the coverage to the employee."

CHAPTER 49.—COSMETIC SERVICES

Sec.
5000B. Imposition of tax on indoor tanning services.

In 2010, P.L. 111-148, Sec. 10907(b), added Chapter 49

Sec. 5000B. Imposition of tax on indoor tanning services.

(a) In general.
There is hereby imposed on any indoor tanning service a tax equal to 10 percent of the amount paid for such service (determined without regard to this section), whether paid by insurance or otherwise.

(b) Indoor tanning service.
For purposes of this section—

(1) **In general.** The term "indoor tanning service" means a service employing any electronic product designed to incorporate 1 or more ultraviolet lamps and intended for the irradiation of an individual by ultraviolet radiation, with wavelengths in air between 200 and 400 nanometers, to induce skin tanning.

(2) **Exclusion of phototherapy services.** Such term does not include any phototherapy service performed by a licensed medical professional.

(c) Payment of tax.

(1) **In general.** The tax imposed by this section shall be paid by the individual on whom the service is performed.

(2) **Collection.** Every person receiving a payment for services on which a tax is imposed under subsection (a) shall collect the amount of the tax from the individual on whom the service is performed and remit such tax quarterly to the Secretary at such time and in such manner as provided by the Secretary.

(3) **Secondary liability.** Where any tax imposed by subsection (a) is not paid at the time payments for indoor tanning services are made, then to the extent that such tax is not collected, such tax shall be paid by the person who performs the service.

In 2010, P.L. 111-148, Sec. 9017(a), added Chapter 49 and Code Sec. 5000B [as deemed null, void, and of no effect by Sec. 10907(a) of this Act, see below]

—P.L. 111-148, Sec. 10907(a), provides:

"(a) In general. The provisions of, and amendments made by, section 9017 of this Act are hereby deemed null, void, and of no effect."

—P.L. 111-148, Sec. 10907(b), added Code Sec. 5000B, effective for services performed on or after 7/1/2010.

CHAPTER 50.—Foreign procurement

Sec.
5000C. Imposition of tax on certain foreign procurement.

In 2010, P.L. 111-347, Sec. 301(a)(1), added Chapter 50

Sec. 5000C. Imposition of tax on certain foreign procurement.

(a) Imposition of tax.
There is hereby imposed on any foreign person that receives a specified Federal procurement payment a tax equal to 2 percent of the amount of such specified Federal procurement payment.

(b) Specified federal procurement payment.
For purposes of this section, the term "specified Federal procurement payment" means any payment made pursuant to a contract with the Government of the United States for—

(1) the provision of goods, if such goods are manufactured or produced in any country which is not a party to an international procurement agreement with the United States, or

(2) the provision of services, if such services are provided in any country which is not a party to an international procurement agreement with the United States.

(c) Foreign person.
For purposes of this section, the term "foreign person" means any person other than a United States person.

(d) Administrative provisions.

(1) **Withholding.** The amount deducted and withheld under chapter 3 shall be increased by the amount of tax imposed by this section on such payment.

(2) **Other administrative provisions.** For purposes of subtitle F, any tax imposed by this section shall be treated as a tax imposed by subtitle A.

In 2010, P.L. 111-347, Sec. 301(a)(1), added Chapter 50 and Code Sec. 5000C to Subtitle D, effective for payments received pursuant to contracts entered into on and after 1/2/2011.

—P.L. 111-347, Sec. 301(b), and (c) of this Act, provides:

"(b) Prohibition on reimbursement of fees.

"(1) In general. The head of each executive agency shall take any and all measures necessary to ensure that no funds are disbursed to any foreign contractor in order to reimburse the tax imposed under section 5000C of the Internal Revenue Code of 1986.

"(2) Annual review. The Administrator for Federal Procurement Policy shall annually review the contracting activities of each executive agency to monitor compliance with the requirements of paragraph (1).

"(3) Executive agency. For purposes of this subsection, the term 'executive agency' has the meaning given the term in section 4 of the Office of Federal Procurement Policy Act (41 U.S.C. 403).

"(c) Application. This section and the amendments made by this section shall be applied in a manner consistent with United States obligations under international agreements."

Subtitle E.—Alcohol, Tobacco, and Certain Other Excise Taxes

Chapter
51. Distilled spirits, wines, and beer.
52. Tobacco products and cigarette papers and tubes.
53. Machine guns, destructive devices, and certain other firearms.
54. Greenmail.
55. Structured settlement factoring transactions.

In 2002, P.L. 107-134, Sec. 115(a), added item 55 as part of subtitle E.
In 1997, P.L. 105-33, Sec. 9302(g)(3)(D), amended item 52
Prior to amendment, item 52 read as follows:
"Chapter 52—Cigars, Cigarettes, Smokeless Tobacco, and Cigarette Papers and Tubes"

CHAPTER 51.—DISTILLED SPIRITS, WINES, AND BEER

Subchapter
A. Gallonage and occupational taxes.
B. Qualification requirements for distilled spirits plants.
C. Operation of distilled spirits plants.
D. Industrial use of distilled spirits.
E. General provisions relating to distilled spirits.
F. Bonded and taxpaid wine premises.
G. Breweries.
H. Miscellaneous plants and warehouses.
I. Miscellaneous general provisions.
J. Penalties, seizures, and forfeitures relating to liquors.

3,383

Chapter 51

In 1988, P.L. 100-647, Sec. 5061(c)(4), added "smokeless tobacco" to item 52.
In 1958, added Chapter 51 in place of former Chapter 51 as enacted as part of the '54 Code, generally effective 7/1/59.

Subchapter A.—Gallonage and Occupational Taxes
Part
    I. Gallonage taxes.
    II. Occupational tax.

PART I.—GALLONAGE TAXES
Subpart
A. Distilled spirits.
C. Wines.
D. Beer.
E. General provisions.

In 1979, P.L. 96-39, Sec. 807(b)(1), deleted the item for Subpart B.
Prior to deletion the item for Subpart B read as follows:
"B. RECTIFICATION."

SUBPART A.—DISTILLED SPIRITS
Sec.
5001. Imposition, rate, and attachment of tax.
5002. Definitions.
5003. Cross references to exemptions, etc.
5004. Lien for tax.
5005. Persons liable for tax.
5006. Determination of tax.
5007. Collection of tax on distilled spirits.
5008. Abatement, remission, refund, and allowance for loss or destruction of distilled spirits.
5010. Credit for wine content and for flavors content.
5011. Income tax credit for average cost of carrying excise tax.

In 2005, P.L. 109-59, Sec. 11126(c), added item 5011.
In 1980, P.L. 96-598, Sec. 6(b), added item 5010.
In 1979, P.L. 96-39, Sec. 807(b)(2), deleted the item for Code Sec. 5009.
Prior to deletion, the item for Code Sec. 5009 read as follows:
"5009. DRAWBACK."

Sec. 5001. Imposition, rate, and attachment of tax.
(a) Rate of tax.
    (1) In general. There is hereby imposed on all distilled spirits produced in or imported into the United States a tax at the rate of $13.50 on each proof gallon and a proportionate tax at the like rate on all fractional parts of a proof gallon.
    (2) Products containing distilled spirits. All products of distillation, by whatever name known, which contain distilled spirits, on which the tax imposed by law has not been paid, and any alcoholic ingredient added to such products, shall be considered and taxed as distilled spirits.
    (3) Wines containing more than 24 percent alcohol by volume. Wines containing more than 24 percent of alcohol by volume shall be taxed as distilled spirits.
    (4) Distilled spirits withdrawn free of tax. Any person who removes, sells, transports, or uses distilled spirits, withdrawn free of tax under section 5214(a) or section 7510, in violation of laws or regulations now or hereafter in force pertaining thereto, and all such distilled spirits shall be subject to all provisions of law relating to distilled spirits subject to tax, including those requiring payment of the tax thereon; and the person so removing, selling, transporting, or using the distilled spirits shall be required to pay such tax.

    (5) Denatured distilled spirits or articles. Any person who produces, withdraws, sells, transports, or uses denatured distilled spirits or articles in violation of laws or regulations now or hereafter in force pertaining thereto, and all such denatured distilled spirits or articles shall be subject to all provisions of law pertaining to distilled spirits that are not denatured, including those requiring the payment of tax thereon; and the person so producing, withdrawing, selling, transporting, or using the denatured distilled spirits or articles shall be required to pay such tax.
    (6) Fruit-flavor concentrates. If any volatile fruit-flavor concentrate (or any fruit mash or juice from which such concentrate is produced) containing one-half of 1 percent or more of alcohol by volume, which is manufactured free from tax under section 5511, is sold, transported, or used by any person in violation of the provisions of this chapter or regulations promulgated thereunder, such person and such concentrate, mash, or juice shall be subject to all provisions of this chapter pertaining to distilled spirits and wines, including those requiring the payment of tax thereon; and the person so selling, transporting, or using such concentrate, mash, or juice shall be required to pay such tax.
    (7) Imported liqueurs and cordials. Imported liqueurs and cordials, or similar compounds, containing distilled spirits, shall be taxed as distilled spirits.
    (8) Imported distilled spirits withdrawn for beverage purposes. There is hereby imposed on all imported distilled spirits withdrawn from customs custody under section 5232 without payment of the internal revenue tax, and thereafter withdrawn from bonded premises for beverage purposes, an additional tax equal to the duty which would have been paid had such spirits been imported for beverage purposes, less the duty previously paid thereon.
    (9) Alcoholic compounds from Puerto Rico. Except as provided in section 5314, upon bay rum, or any article containing distilled spirits, brought from Puerto Rico into the United States for consumption or sale there is hereby imposed a tax on the spirits contained therein at the rate imposed on distilled spirits produced in the United States.
(b) Time of attachment on distilled spirits.
The tax shall attach to distilled spirits as soon as this substance is in existence as such, whether it be subsequently separated as pure or impure spirits, or be immediately, or at any subsequent time, transferred into any other substance, either in the process of original production or by any subsequent process.
(c) Cross reference.
For provisions relating to the tax on shipments to the United States of taxable articles from Puerto Rico and the Virgin Islands, see section 7652.

In 1997, P.L. 105-34, Sec. 909, of this Act, provides:
"SEC. 909 STUDY OF FEASIBILITY OF MOVING COLLECTION POINT FOR DISTILLED SPIRITS EXCISE TAX.
"(a) In General.—The Secretary of the Treasury or his delegate shall conduct a study of options for changing the event on which the tax imposed by section 5001 of the Internal Revenue Code of 1986 is determined. One such option which shall be studied is determining such tax on removal from registered wholesale warehouses. In studying each such option, such Secretary shall focus on administrative issues including—
"(1) tax compliance,
"(2) the number of taxpayers required to pay the tax,
"(3) the types of financial responsibility requirements that might be required, and
"(4) special requirements regarding segregation of non-tax-paid distilled spirits from other products.
Such study shall review the effects of each such option on the Department of the Treasury (including staffing and other demands on budgetary resources) and the change in the period between the time such tax is currently paid and the time such tax would be paid under each such option.

"(b) Report. — The report of such study shall be submitted to the Committee on Finance of the Senate and the Committee on Ways and Means of the House of Representatives not later than March 31, 1998."

In 1994, P.L. 103-465, Sec. 136(a), deleted para. (a)(3) and redesignated paras. (a)(4)-(a)(10) as paras. (a)(3)-(a)(9), effective 1/1/95.

Prior to deletion, para. (a)(3) read as follows:

"(3) Imported perfumes containing distilled spirits. There is hereby imposed on all perfumes imported into the United States containing distilled spirits a tax of $13.50 per wine gallon, and a proportionate tax at a like rate on all fractional parts of such wine gallon."

In 1990, P.L. 101-508, Sec. 11201(a)(1), substituted "$13.50" for "$12.50" in paras. (a)(1) and (a)(3), effective 1/1/91.

—P.L. 101-508, Sec. 11201(e), regarding floor stocks taxes, provides:

"(e) Floor stocks taxes.

"(1) Imposition of tax.

"(A) In general. In the case of any tax-increased article—

"(i) on which tax was determined under part I of subchapter A of chapter 51 of the Internal Revenue Code of 1986 or section 7652 of such Code before January 1, 1991, and

"(ii) which is held on such date for sale by any person,

there shall be imposed a tax at the applicable rate on each such article.

"(B) Applicable rate. For purposes of subparagraph (A), the applicable rate is—

"(i) $1 per proof gallon in the case of distilled spirits,

"(ii) $0.90 per wine gallon in the case of wine described in paragraph (1), (2), (3), or (5) of section 5041(b) of such Code, and

"(iii) $9 per barrel in the case of beer.

In the case of a fraction of a gallon or barrel, the tax imposed by subparagraph (A) shall be the same fraction as the amount of such tax imposed on a whole gallon or barrel.

"(C) Tax-increased article. For purposes of this subsection, the term 'tax-increased article' means distilled spirits, wine described in paragraph (1), (2), (3), or (5) of section 5041(b) of such Code, and beer.

"(2) Exception for small domestic producers.

"(A) In the case of wine held by the producer thereof on January 1, 1991, if a credit would have been allowable under section 5041(c) of such Code (as added by this section) on such wine had the amendments made by subsection (b) [Sec. 11201(b) of this Act] applied to all wine removed during 1990 and had the wine so held been removed for consumption on December 31, 1990, the tax imposed by paragraph (1) on such wine shall be reduced by the credit which would have been so allowable.

"(B) In the case of beer held by the producer thereof on January 1, 1991, if the rate of the tax imposed by section 5051 of such Code would have been determined under subsection (a)(2) thereof had the beer so held been removed for consumption on December 31, 1990, the tax imposed by paragraph (1) on such beer shall not apply.

"(C) For purposes of this paragraph, an article shall not be treated as held by the producer if title thereto had at any time been transferred to any other person.

"(3) Exception for certain small wholesale or retail dealers. No tax shall be imposed by paragraph (1) on tax-increased articles held on January 1, 1991, by any dealer if—

"(A) the aggregate liquid volume of tax-increased articles held by such dealer on such date does not exceed 500 wine gallons, and

"(B) such dealer submits to the Secretary (at the time and in the manner required by the Secretary) such information as the Secretary shall require for purposes of this paragraph.

"(4) Credit against tax. Each dealer shall be allowed as a credit against the taxes imposed by paragraph (1) an amount equal to—

"(A) $240 to the extent such taxes are attributable to distilled spirits,

"(B) $270 to the extent such taxes are attributable to wine, and

"(C) $87 to the extent such taxes are attributable to beer.

Such credit shall not exceed the amount of taxes imposed by paragraph (1) with respect to distilled spirits, wine, or beer, as the case may be, for which the dealer is liable.

"(5) Liability for tax and method of payment.

"(A) Liability for tax. A person holding any tax-increased article on January 1, 1991, to which the tax imposed by paragraph (1) applies shall be liable for such tax.

"(B) Method of payment. The tax imposed by paragraph (1) shall be paid in such manner as the Secretary shall prescribe by regulations.

"(C) Time for payment. The tax imposed by paragraph (1) shall be paid on or before June 30, 1991.

"(6) Controlled groups.

"(A) Corporations. In the case of a controlled group—

"(i) the 500 wine gallon amount specified in paragraph (3), and

"(ii) the $240, $270, and $87 amounts specified in paragraph (4),

shall be apportioned among the dealers who are component members of such group in such manner as the Secretary shall by regulations prescribe. For purposes of the preceding sentence, the term 'controlled group' has the meaning given to such term by subsection (a) of section 1563 of such Code; except that for such purposes the phrase 'more than 50 percent' shall be substituted for the phrase 'at least 80 percent' each place it appears in such subsection.

"(B) Nonincorporated dealers under common control. Under regulations prescribed by the Secretary, principles similar to the principles of subparagraph (A) shall apply to a group of dealers under common control where 1 or more of such dealers is not a corporation.

"(7) Other laws applicable.

"(A) In general. All provisions of law, including penalties, applicable to the comparable excise tax with respect to any tax-increased article shall, insofar as applicable and not inconsistent with the provisions of this subsection, apply to the floor stocks taxes imposed by paragraph (1) to the same extent as if such taxes were imposed by the comparable excise tax.

"(B) Comparable excise tax. For purposes of subparagraph (A), the term 'comparable excise tax' means—

"(i) the tax imposed by section 5001 of such Code in the case of distilled spirits,

"(ii) the tax imposed by section 5041 of such Code in the case of wine, and

"(iii) the tax imposed by section 5051 of such Code in the case of beer.

"(8) Definitions. For purposes of this subsection—

"(A) In general. Terms used in this subsection which are also used in subchapter A of chapter 51 of such Code shall have the respective meanings such terms have in such part.

"(B) Person. The term 'person' includes any State or political subdivision thereof, or any agency or instrumentality of a State or political subdivision thereof.

"(C) Secretary. The term 'Secretary' means the Secretary of the Treasury or his delegate.

"(9) Treatment of imported perfumes containing distilled spirits. For purposes of this subsection, any article described in section 5001(a)(3) of such Code shall be treated as distilled spirits; except that the tax imposed by paragraph (1) shall be imposed on a wine gallon basis in lieu of a proof gallon basis. To the extent provided by regulations prescribed by the Secretary, the preceding sentence shall not apply to any article held on January 1, 1991, on the premises of a retail establishment."

—P.L. 101-508, Sec. 11218, regarding floor stocks tax treatment of articles in foreign trade zones, provides:

"SEC. 11218. FLOOR STOCKS TAX TREATMENT OF ARTICLES IN FOREIGN TRADE ZONES. Notwithstanding the Act of June 18, 1934 (48 Stat. 998, 19 U.S.C. 81a) or any other provision of law, any article which is located in a foreign trade zone on the effective date of any increase in tax under the amendments made by this part or part I shall be subject to floor stocks taxes imposed by such parts if—

"(1) internal revenue taxes have been determined, or customs duties liquidated, with respect to such article before such date pursuant to a request made under the 1st proviso of section 3(a) of such Act, or

"(2) such article is held on such date under the supervision of a customs officer pursuant to the 2d proviso of such section 3(a)."

In 1986, P.L. 99-514, Sec. 1801(c)(3), added Sec. 27(b)(7)(F) of P.L. 98-369, [reproduced below], part of the effective date for changes made by Sec. 27(a) of P.L. 98-369, see below.

In 1984, P.L. 98-369, Sec. 27(a)(1), substituted "$12.50" for "$10.50" in paras. (a)(1) and (a)(3), effective 10/1/85. Sec. 27(b) [as amended by Sec. 1801(c)(3) of P.L. 99-514, see above] of this Act provides:

"(b) Floor stocks taxes on distilled spirits.—

"(1) Imposition of tax. — On distilled spirits on which tax was imposed under section 5001 or 7652 of the Internal Revenue Code of 1954 before October 1, 1985, and which were held on such date for sale by any person, there shall be imposed a tax at the rate of $2.00 for each proof gallon and a proportionate tax at the like rate on all fractional parts of a proof gallon.

"(2) Exception for certain small wholesale or retail dealers. — No tax shall be imposed by paragraph (1) on distilled spirits held on October 1, 1985, by any dealer if—

"(A) the aggregate liquid volume of distilled spirits held by such dealer on such date does not exceed 500 wine gallons, and

"(B) such dealer submits to the Secretary (at the time and in the manner required by the Secretary) such information as the Secretary shall require for purposes of this paragraph.

"(3) Credit against tax. — Each dealer shall be allowed as a credit against the taxes imposed by paragraph (1) an amount equal to $800. Such credit shall not exceed the amount of taxes imposed by paragraph (1) for which the dealer is liable.

"(4) Liability for tax and method of payment.—

"(A) Liability for tax. — A person holding a distilled spirits on October 1, 1985, to which the tax imposed by paragraph (1) applies shall be liable for such tax.

"(B) Method of payment. — The tax imposed by paragraph (1) shall be paid in such manner as the Secretary shall by regulations prescribe.

"(C) Time for payment.—

"(i) In general. — Except as provided in clause (ii), the tax imposed by paragraph (1) shall be paid on or before April 1, 1986.

"(ii) Installment payment in case of small or middle-sized dealers. — In the case of any small or middle-sized dealer, the tax imposed by paragraph (1) may be paid in 3 equal installments due as follows:

"(I) The first installment shall be paid on or before April 1, 1986.

"(II) The second installment shall be paid on or before July 1, 1986.

"(III) The third installment shall be paid on or before October 1, 1986.

If the taxpayer does not pay any installment under this clause on or before the date prescribed for its payment, the whole of the unpaid tax shall be paid upon notice and demand from the Secretary.

"(iii) Small or middle-sized dealer. — For purposes of clause (ii), the term 'small or middle-sized dealer' means any dealer if the aggregate gross sales receipts of such dealer for its most recent taxable year ending before October 1, 1985, does not exceed $500,000.

"(5) Controlled groups.

"(A) Controlled groups of corporations. — In the case of a controlled group—

"(i) the 500 wine gallon amount specified in paragraph (2),

Code Sec. 5001 — Excise and miscellaneous taxes

"(ii) the $800 amount specified in paragraph (e), and

"(iii) the $500,000 amount specified in paragraph (4)(C)(iii),

shall be apportioned among the dealers who are component members of such group in such manner as the Secretary shall by regulations prescribe. For purposes of the preceding sentence, the term 'controlled group' has the meaning given to such term by subsection (a) of section 1563 of the Internal Revenue Code of 1954; except that for such purposes the phrase 'more than 50 percent' shall be substituted for the phrase 'at least 80 percent' each place it appears in such subsection.

"(B) Nonincorporated dealers under common control.— Under regulations prescribed by the Secretary, principles similar to the principles of subparagraph (A) shall apply to a group of dealers under common control where 1 or more of such dealers is not a corporation.

"(6) Other laws applicable.— All provisions of law, including penalties, applicable with respect to the taxes imposed by section 5001 of the Internal Revenue Code of 1954 shall, insofar as applicable and not inconsistent with the provisions of this subsection, apply in respect of the taxes imposed by paragraph (1) to the same extent as if such taxes were imposed by such section 5001.

"(7) Definitions and special rules.— For purposes of this subsection—

"(A) Dealer.— The term 'dealer' means—

"(i) any wholesale dealer in liquors (as defined in section 5112(b) of the Internal Revenue Code of 1954), and

"(ii) any retail dealer in liquors (as defined in section 5122(a) of such Code).

"(B) Distilled spirits.— The term 'distilled spirits' has the meaning given such term by section 5002(a)(8) of the Internal Revenue Code of 1954.

"(C) Person.— The term 'person' includes any State or political subdivision thereof, or any agency or instrumentality of a State or political subdivision thereof.

"(D) Secretary.— The term 'Secretary' means the Secretary of the Treasury or his delegate.

"(E) Treatment of imported perfumes containing distilled spirits.— Any article described in section 5001(a)(3) of such Code shall be treated as distilled spirits; except that the tax imposed by paragraph (1) shall be imposed on a wine gallon basis in lieu of a proof gallon basis. To the extent provided in regulations prescribed by the Secretary, the preceding sentence shall not apply to any article held on October 1, 1985, on the premises of a retail establishment.

"(F) Treatment of distilled spirits in foreign trade zones. Notwithstanding the Act of June 18, 1934 (48 Stat. 998, 19 U.S.C. 81a) or any other provision of law, distilled spirits which are located in a foreign trade zone on October 1, 1985, shall be subject to the tax imposed by paragraph (1) and shall be treated for purposes of this subsection as held on such date for sale if—

"(i) internal revenue taxes have been determined, or customs duties liquidated, with respect to such distilled spirits before such date pursuant to a request made under the first proviso of section 3(a) of such Act, or

"(ii) such distilled spirits are held on such date under the supervision of customs pursuant to the second proviso of such section 3(a).

Under regulations prescribed by the Secretary, provisions similar to sections 5062 and 5064 of such Code shall apply to distilled spirits with respect to which tax is imposed by paragraph (1) by reason of this subparagraph."

In 1979, P.L. 96-39, Sec. 802, and Sec. 805(d), amended paras. (a)(1) and (a)(2), effective 1/1/80.

Prior to amendment, paras. (a)(1) and (a)(2) read as follows:

"(1) General. There is hereby imposed on all distilled spirits in bond or produced in or imported into the United States an internal revenue tax at the rate of $10.50 on each proof gallon or wine gallon when below proof and a proportionate tax at a like rate on all fractional parts of such proof or wine gallon.

"(2) Products containing distilled spirits. All products of distillation, by whatever name known, which contain distilled spirits, on which the tax imposed by law has not been paid, shall be considered and taxed as distilled spirits."

In 1965, P.L. 89-44, Sec. 501(a), deleted the last sentence of both paras. (a)(1) and (a)(3), effective on and after 7/1/65.

Prior to deletion, the last sentence of both paras. (1) and (3) read as follows: "On and after July 1, 1965, the rate of tax imposed by this paragraph shall be $9 in lieu of $10.50."

In 1964, P.L. 88-348, Sec. 2(a)(4), and (5), substituted "July 1, 1965" for "July 1, 1964" in paras. (a)(1) and (a)(3).

In 1963, P.L. 88-52, Sec. 3(a)(4), and (5), substituted "July 1, 1964" for "July 1, 1963" in paras. (a)(1) and (a)(3).

In 1962, P.L. 87-508, Sec. 3(a)(3), and (4), substituted "July 1, 1963" for "July 1, 1962" in paras. (a)(1) and (a)(3).

In 1961, P.L. 87-72, Sec. 3(a)(4), and (5), substituted "July 1, 1962" for "July 1, 1961" in paras. (a)(1) and (a)(3).

In 1960, P.L. 86-564, Sec. 202(a)(4), substituted "July 1, 1961" for "July 1, 1960" in paras. (a)(1) and (a)(3).

In 1959, P.L. 86-75, Sec. 3(a), substituted "July 1, 1960" for "July 1, 1959" in paras. (a)(1) and (a)(3).

Sec. 5002. Definitions.

(a) In general.

For purposes of this chapter—

(1) Distilled spirits plant. The term "distilled spirits plant" means an establishment which is qualified under subchapter B to perform any distilled spirits operation.

(2) Distilled spirits operation. The term "distilled spirits operation" means any operation for which qualification is required under subchapter B.

(3) Bonded premises. The term "bonded premises", when used with respect to distilled spirits, means the premises of a distilled spirits plant, or part thereof, on which distilled spirits operations are authorized to be conducted.

(4) Distiller. The term "distiller" includes any person who—

(A) produces distilled spirits from any source or substance,

(B) brews or makes mash, wort, or wash fit for distillation or for the production of distilled spirits (other than the making or using of mash, wort, or wash in the authorized production of wine or beer, or the production of vinegar by fermentation),

(C) by any process separates alcoholic spirits from any fermented substance, or

(D) making or keeping mash, wort, or wash, has a still in his possession or use.

(5) Processor.

(A) In general. The term "processor", when used with respect to distilled spirits, means any person who—

(i) manufactures, mixes, or otherwise processes distilled spirits, or

(ii) manufactures any article.

(B) Rectifier, bottler, etc., included. The term "processor" includes (but is not limited to) a rectifier, bottler, and denaturer.

(6) Certain operations not treated as processing. In applying paragraph (5), there shall not be taken into account—

(A) Operations as distiller. Any process which is the operation of a distiller.

(B) Mixing of taxpaid spirits for immediate consumption. Any mixing (after determination of tax) of distilled spirits for immediate consumption.

(C) Use by apothecaries. Any process performed by an apothecary with respect to distilled spirits which such apothecary uses exclusively in the preparation or making up of medicines unfit for use for beverage purposes.

(7) Warehouseman. The term "warehouseman", when used with respect to distilled spirits, means any person who stores bulk distilled spirits.

(8) Distilled spirits. The terms "distilled spirits", "alcoholic spirits", and "spirits" mean that substance known as ethyl alcohol, ethanol, or spirits of wine in any form (including all dilutions and mixtures thereof from whatever source or by whatever process produced).

(9) Bulk distilled spirits. The term "bulk distilled spirits" means distilled spirits in a container having a capacity in excess of 1 wine gallon.

(10) Proof spirits. The term "proof spirits" means that liquid which contains one-half its volume of ethyl alcohol of a specific gravity of 0.7939 at 60 degrees Fahrenheit (referring to water at 60 degrees Fahrenheit as unity).

(11) Proof gallon. The term "proof gallon" means a United States gallon of proof spirits, or the alcoholic equivalent thereof.

(12) Container. The term "container", when used with respect to distilled spirits, means any receptacle, vessel, or form of package, bottle, tank, or pipeline used, or capable of use, for holding, storing, transferring, or conveying distilled spirits.

Excise and miscellaneous taxes Code Sec. 5003(15)

(13) Approved container. The term "approved container", when used with respect to distilled spirits, means a container the use of which is authorized by regulations prescribed by the Secretary.

(14) Article. Unless another meaning is distinctly expressed or manifestly intended, the term "article" means any substance in the manufacture of which denatured distilled spirits are used.

(15) Export. The terms "export", "exported", and "exportation" include shipments to a possession of the United States.

(b) Cross references.

(1) For definition of manufacturer of stills, see section 5102.

(2) For definition of dealer, see section 5121(c)(3).

(3) For definitions of wholesale dealers, see section 5121(c).

(4) For definitions of retail dealers, see section 5122(c).

(5) For definitions of general application to this title, see chapter 79.

In 2005, P.L. 109-59, Sec. 11125(b)(13)(A), substituted "section 5121(c)(3)" for "section 5112(a)" in subsec. (b)... Sec. 11125(b)(13)(B), substituted "section 5121(c)" for "section 5112" in subsec. (b)... Sec. 11125(b)(13)(C), substituted "section 5122(c)" for "section 5122" in subsec. (b), effective 7/1/2008, but not for taxes imposed for periods before 7/1/2008.

In 1994, P.L. 103-465, Sec. 136(c)(1), deleted para. (b)(1) and redesignated paras. (b)(2)-(b)(6) as paras. (b)(1)-(b)(5), effective 1/1/95.

Prior to deletion, para. (b)(1) read as follows:

"(1) For definition of wine gallon, see section 5041(c)."

In 1990, P.L. 101-508, Sec. 11201(e), regarding floor stocks taxes, is reproduced in note following Code Sec. 5001.

—P.L. 101-508, Sec. 11218, regarding floor stocks tax treatment of articles in foreign trade zones, is reproduced in note following Code Sec. 5001.

In 1979, P.L. 96-39, Sec. 805(e), amended Code Sec. 5002, effective 1/1/80.

Prior to amendment, Code Sec. 5002 read as follows:

"Sec. 5002. Definitions.

"(a) Definitions.

"When used in this chapter—

"(1) Distilled spirits plant. The term 'distilled spirits plant' means an establishment which is qualified under subchapter B to perform any operation, or any combination of operations, for which qualification is required under such subchapter.

"(2) Bonded premises. The term 'bonded premises', when used with reference to distilled spirits, means the premises of a distilled spirits plant, or part thereof, as described in the application required by section 5171(a), on which operations relating to production, storage, denaturation, or bottling of distilled spirits, prior to the payment or determination of the distilled spirits tax, are authorized to be conducted.

"(3) Bottling premises. The term 'bottling premises', when used with reference to distilled spirits plants, means the premises of a distilled spirits plant, or part thereof, as described in the application required by section 5171(a), on which operations relating to the rectification or bottling of distilled spirits or wines on which the tax has been paid or determined, are authorized to be conducted.

"(4) Bonded warehouseman. The term 'bonded warehouseman' means the proprietor of a distilled spirits plant who is authorized to store distilled spirits after entry for deposit in storage and prior to payment or determination of the internal revenue tax or withdrawal as provided in section 5214 or 7510.

"(5) Distiller. The term 'distiller' shall include every person—

"(A) who produces distilled spirits from any source or substance; or

"(B) who brews or makes mash, wort, or wash, fit for distillation or for the production of distilled spirits (except a person making or using such material in the authorized production of wine or beer, or the production of vinegar by fermentation); or

"(C) who by any process separates alcoholic spirits from any fermented substance; or

"(D) who, making or keeping mash, wort, or wash, has also in his possession or use a still.

"(6) Distilled spirits.

"(A) General definition. The terms 'distilled spirits', 'alcoholic spirits', and 'spirits' mean that substance known as ethyl alcohol, ethanol, or spirits of wine, including all dilutions and mixtures thereof, from whatever source or by whatever process produced, and shall include whisky, brandy, rum, gin, and vodka.

"(B) Products of rectification. As used in section 5291(a) the term 'distilled spirits' includes products produced in such manner that the person producing them is a rectifier within the meaning of section 5082.

"(7) Proof spirits. The term 'proof spirits' means that liquid which contains one-half its volume of ethyl alcohol of a specific gravity of seven thousand nine hundred and thirty-nine ten-thousands (.7939) at 60 degrees Fahrenheit referred to water at 60 degrees Fahrenheit as unity.

"(8) Proof gallon. The term 'proof gallon' means a United States gallon of proof spirits, or the alcoholic equivalent thereof.

"(9) Container. The term 'container', when used with respect to distilled spirits, means any receptacle, vessel, or form of package, bottle, tank, or pipeline used, or capable of use, for holding, storing, transferring, or conveying distilled spirits.

"(10) Approved container. The term 'approved container', when used with respect to distilled spirits, means a container the use of which is authorized by regulations prescribed by the Secretary.

"(11) Articles. The term 'articles' means any substance or preparation in the manufacture of which denatured distilled spirits are used, unless another meaning is distinctly expressed or manifestly intended.

"(12) Export. The terms 'export,' 'exported,' and 'exportation' shall include shipments to a possession of the United States.

"(b) Cross references.

"(1) For definition of wine gallon, see section 5041(c).

"(2) For definition of rectifier, see section 5082.

"(3) For definition of manufacturer of stills, see section 5102.

"(4) For definition of dealer, see section 5112(a).

"(5) For definitions of wholesale dealers, see section 5112.

"(6) For definitions of retail dealers, see section 5122.

"(7) For definitions of general application to this title, see chapter 79."

In 1976, P.L. 94-455, Sec. 1906(b)(13)(A), substituted "Secretary" for "Secretary or his delegate" in para. (a)(10), effective 2/1/77.

In 1965, P.L. 89-44, Sec. 807(a), added para. (a)(12), effective 7/1/65.

Sec. 5003. Cross references to exemptions, etc.

(1) For provisions authorizing the withdrawal of distilled spirits free of tax for use by Federal or State agencies, see sections 5214(a)(2) and 5313.

(2) For provisions authorizing the withdrawal of distilled spirits free of tax by nonprofit educational organizations, scientific universities or colleges of learning, laboratories, hospitals, blood banks, sanitariums, and charitable clinics, see section 5214(a)(3).

(3) For provisions authorizing the withdrawal of certain imported distilled spirits from customs custody without payment of tax, see section 5232.

(4) For provisions authorizing the withdrawal of denatured distilled spirits free of tax, see section 5214(a)(1).

(5) For provisions exempting from tax distilled spirits for use in production of vinegar by the vaporizing process, see section 5505(j).

(6) For provisions relating to the withdrawal of wine spirits without payment of tax for use in the production of wine, see section 5373.

(7) For provisions exempting from tax volatile fruit-flavor concentrates, see section 5511.

(8) For provisions authorizing the withdrawal of distilled spirits from bonded premises without payment of tax for export, see section 5214(a)(4).

(9) For provisions authorizing withdrawal of distilled spirits without payment of tax to customs bonded warehouses for export, see section 5214(a)(9).

(10) For provisions relating to withdrawal of distilled spirits without payment of tax as supplies for certain vessels and aircraft, see 19 U.S.C. 1309.

(11) For provisions authorizing regulations for withdrawal of distilled spirits for use of United States free of tax, see section 7510.

(12) For provisions relating to withdrawal of distilled spirits without payment of tax to foreign-trade zones, see 19 U.S.C. 81c.

(13) For provisions relating to exemption from tax of taxable articles going into the possessions of the United States, see section 7653(b).

(14) For provisions authorizing the withdrawal of distilled spirits without payment of tax for use in certain research, development, or testing, see section 5214(a)(10).

(15) For provisions authorizing the withdrawal of distilled spirits without payment of tax for transfer to manufacturing bonded warehouses for manufacturing for export, see section 5214(a)(6).

(16) For provisions authorizing the withdrawal of articles from the bonded premises of a distilled spirits plant free of tax when contained in an article, see section 5214(a)(11).

(17) For provisions relating to allowance for certain losses in bond, see section 5008(a).

In **1990**, P.L. 101-508, Sec. 11201(e), regarding floor stocks taxes, is reproduced in note following Code Sec. 5001.
—P.L. 101-508, Sec. 11218, regarding floor stocks tax treatment of articles in foreign trade zones, is reproduced in note following Code Sec. 5001.
In **1979**, P.L. 96-39, Sec. 807(a)(1)(A), deleted "section 5522(a)" after "for export, see" in para. (9)... Sec. 807(a)(1)(B), redesignated para. (15) as para. (17) and added paras. (15) and (16), effective 1/1/80.
In **1977**, P.L. 95-176, Sec. 3(c), deleted "manufacturing" after "customs" and substituted "and section 5214(a)(9)" for the period at the end of para. (9), effective 3/1/78 [the first day of the first calendar month which begins more than 90 days after 11/14/77, the date of enactment].
—P.L. 95-176, Sec. 4(f), amended para. (14), effective 3/1/78 [the first day of the first calendar month which begins more than 90 days after 11/14/77, the date of enactment].
Prior to amendment, para. (14) read as follows:
"(14) For provisions authorizing the removal of samples free of tax for making tests or laboratory analyses, see section 5214(a)(9)."

Sec. 5004. Lien for tax.

(a) Distilled spirits subject to lien.

(1) General. The tax imposed by section 5001(a)(1) shall be a first lien on the distilled spirits from the time the spirits are in existence as such until the tax is paid.

(2) Exceptions. The lien imposed by paragraph (1), or any similar lien imposed on the spirits under prior provisions of internal revenue law, shall terminate in the case of distilled spirits produced on premises qualified under internal revenue law for the production of distilled spirits when such distilled spirits are—

(A) withdrawn from bonded premises on determination of tax; or

(B) withdrawn from bonded premises free of tax under provisions of section 5214(a)(1), (2), (3), (11), or (12), or section 7510; or

(C) exported, deposited in a foreign-trade zone, used in the production of wine, laden as supplies upon, or used in the maintenance or repair of, certain vessels or aircraft, deposited in a customs bonded warehouse, or used in certain research, development, or testing, as provided by law.

(b) Cross reference.

For provisions relating to extinguishing of lien in case of redistillation, see section 5223(e).

In **1990**, P.L. 101-508, Sec. 11201(e), regarding floor stocks taxes, is reproduced in note following Code Sec 5001.
—P.L. 101-508, Sec. 11218, regarding floor stocks tax treatment of articles in foreign trade zones, is reproduced in note following Code Sec. 5001.
In **1980**, P.L. 96-223, Sec. 232(e)(2)(C), substituted "(11), or (12)," for "or (11)," in subpara. (a)(2)(B), effective the first day of the first calendar month beginning more than 60 days after 4/2/80.
In **1979**, P.L. 96-39, Sec. 807(a)(2)(A), deleted subsec. (b)... Sec. 807(a)(2)(B), redesignated subsec. (c) as subsec. (b)... Sec. 807(a)(2)(C), substituted "(3), or (11)" for "or (3)" in subpara (a)(2)(B), effective 1/1/80.
Prior to deletion, subsec. (b) read as follows:
"*(b) Other property subject to lien.*
"(1) General. The tax imposed by section 5001(a)(1) shall be a first lien on the distillery used for producing the distilled spirits, the stills, vessels, and fixtures therein, the lot or tract of land on which such distillery is situated, and on any building thereon, from the time such spirits are in existence as such until the tax is paid, or until the persons liable for the tax under section 5005(a) or (b) have been relieved of liability for such tax by reason of the provisions of sections 5005(c)(2), (c)(3), (d), or (e). In the case of a distilled spirits plant producing distilled spirits, the premises subject to lien shall comprise the bonded premises of such plant, any building containing any part of the bonded premises and the land on which such building is situated, as described in the application for registration of such plant. Any similar lien on the property described in this paragraph arising under prior provisions of internal revenue law shall not be assertable as to the tax on any distilled spirits in respect to which the persons liable for the tax have been relieved of liability therefor by reason of the provisions of section 5005(c)(2), (c)(3), (d), or (e).

"(2) Exception during term of bond. No lien shall attach to any lot or tract of land, distillery, building, or distilling apparatus, under this subsection, by reason of distilling done during any period included within the term of any bond given under section 5173(b)(1)(C).

"(3) Extinguishment of lien. Any lien under paragraph (1), or any similar lien imposed on the property described in paragraph (1) under prior provisions of internal revenue law, shall be held to be extinguished—

"(A) if the property is no longer used for distilling and there is no outstanding liability against any person referred to in section 5005(a) or (b) for taxes or penalties imposed by law on the distilled spirits produced thereon, and no litigation is pending in respect of any such tax or penalty; or

"(B) if an indemnity bond given under the provisions of section 5173(b)(1)(C), further conditioned to stand in lieu of such lien or liens and to indemnify the United States for the payment of all taxes and penalties which otherwise could be asserted against such property by reason of such lien or liens, is accepted and approved by the Secretary. Such bond shall not be accepted or approved if there is any pending litigation or outstanding assessment with respect to such taxes or penalties, or if the Secretary has knowledge of any circumstances indicating that such bond is tendered with intent to evade payment or defeat collection of any tax or penalty.

"(4) Certificate of discharge. Any person claiming any interest in the property subject to lien under paragraph (1) may apply to the Secretary for a duly acknowledged certificate to the effect that such lien is discharged and, if the Secretary or his delegate determines that such lien is extinguished, the Secretary shall issue such certificate, and any such certificate may be recorded."

In **1977**, P.L. 95-176, Sec. 4(c), deleted "or (9)," before "or section 7510" and added "or" between "(2)," and "(3)" in subpara. (a)(2)(B), amended subpara. (a)(2)(C), effective the first day of the first calendar month which begins more than 90 days after 11/14/77.
Prior to amendment, subpara. (a)(2)(C) read as follows:
"(C) exported, deposited in a foreign-trade zone, used in the production of wine, deposited in customs manufacturing bonded warehouses, or laden as supplies upon, or used in the maintenance or repair of, certain vessels or aircraft, as provided by law."

In **1976**, P.L. 94-455, Sec. 1906(b)(13)(A), substituted "Secretary" for "Secretary or his delegate" each place it appeared in Code Sec. 5004, effective 2/1/77.
In **1965**, P.L. 89-44, Sec. 805(f)(1), substituted "section 5223(e)" for "section 5223(d)" in subsec. (c), effective 10/1/65.

Sec. 5005. Persons liable for tax.

(a) General.

The distiller or importer of distilled spirits shall be liable for the taxes imposed thereon by section 5001(a)(1).

(b) Domestic distilled spirits.

(1) Liability of persons interested in distilling. Every proprietor or possessor of, and every person in any manner interested in the use of, any still, distilling apparatus, or distillery, shall be jointly and severally liable for the taxes imposed by law on the distilled spirits produced therefrom.

(2) Exception. A person owning or having the right of control of not more than 10 percent of any class of stock of a corporate proprietor of a distilled spirits plant shall not be deemed to be a person liable for the tax for which such proprietor is liable under the provisions of paragraph (1). This exception shall not apply to an officer or director of such corporate proprietor.

(c) Proprietors of distilled spirits plants.

(1) Bonded storage. Every person operating bonded premises of a distilled spirits plant shall be liable for the internal revenue tax on all distilled spirits while the distilled spirits are stored on such premises, and on all distilled spirits which are in transit to such premises (from the time of removal from the transferor's bonded premises) pursuant to application made by him. Such liability for the tax on distilled spirits shall continue until the distilled spirits are transferred or withdrawn from bonded premises as authorized by law, or until such liability for tax is relieved by reason of the provisions of section 5008(a). Nothing in this paragraph shall relieve any person from any liability imposed by subsection (a) or (b).

(2) Transfers in bond. When distilled spirits are transferred in bond in accordance with the provisions of section 5212, persons liable for the tax on such spirits under

Excise and miscellaneous taxes   Code Sec. 5006(a)(2)

subsection (a) or (b), or under any similar prior provisions of internal revenue law, shall be relieved of such liability, if proprietors of transferring and receiving premises are independent of each other and neither has a proprietary interest, directly or indirectly, in the business of the other, and all persons liable for the tax under subsection (a) or (b), or under any similar prior provisions of internal revenue law, have divested themselves of all interest in the spirits so transferred. Such relief from liability shall be effective from the time of removal from the transferor's bonded premises, or from the time of divestment of interest, whichever is later.

(d) Withdrawals free of tax.

All persons liable for the tax under subsection (a) or (b), or under any similar prior provisions of internal revenue law, shall be relieved of such liability as to distilled spirits withdrawn free of tax under the provisions of section 5214(a)(1), (2), (3), (11), or (12), or under section 7510, at the time such spirits are so withdrawn from bonded premises.

(e) Withdrawals without payment of tax.

(1) Liability for tax. Any person who withdraws distilled spirits from the bonded premises of a distilled spirits plant without payment of tax, as provided in section 5214(a)(4), (5), (6), (7), (8), (9), (10), or (13), shall be liable for the internal revenue tax on such distilled spirits, from the time of such withdrawal; and all persons liable for the tax on such distilled spirits under subsection (a) or (b), or under any similar prior provisions of internal revenue law, shall, at the time of such withdrawal, be relieved of any such liability on the distilled spirits so withdrawn if the person withdrawing such spirits and the person, or persons, liable for the tax under subsection (a) or (b), or under any similar prior provisions of internal revenue law, are independent of each other and neither has a proprietary interest, directly or indirectly, in the business of the other, and all persons liable for the tax under subsection (a) or (b), or under any similar prior provisions of internal revenue law, have divested themselves of all interest in the spirits so withdrawn.

(2) Relief from liability. All persons liable for the tax on distilled spirits under paragraph (1) of this subsection, or under subsection (a) or (b), or under any similar prior provisions of internal revenue law, shall be relieved of any such liability at the time, as the case may be, the distilled spirits are exported, deposited in a foreign-trade zone, used in the production of wine, used in the production of nonbeverage wine or wine products, deposited in customs bonded warehouses, laden as supplies upon, or used in the maintenance or repair of, certain vessels or aircraft, or used in certain research, development, or testing, as provided by law.

(f) Cross references.

(1) For provisions requiring bond covering operations at, and withdrawals from, distilled spirits plants, see section 5173.

(2) For provisions relating to transfer of tax liability to redistiller in case of redistillation, see section 5223.

(3) For liability for tax on denatured distilled spirits, articles, and volatile fruit-flavor concentrates, see section 5001(a)(5) and (6).

(4) For liability for tax on distilled spirits withdrawn free of tax, see section 5001(a)(4).

(5) For liability of wine producer for unlawfully using wine spirits withdrawn for the production of wine, see section 5391.

(6) For provisions relating to transfer of tax liability for wine, see section 5043(a)(1)(A).

In 1994, P.L. 103-465, Sec. 136(c)(2)(A), substituted "section 5001(a)(5) and (6)" for "section 5001(a)(6) and (7)" in para. (f)(3) . . . Sec. 136(c)(2)(B), substituted "section 5001(a)(4)" for "section 5001(a)(5)" in para. (f)(4), effective 1/1/95.

In 1990, P.L. 101-508, Sec. 11201(e), regarding floor stocks taxes, is reproduced in note following Code Sec. 5001.
—P.L. 101-508, Sec. 11218, regarding floor stocks tax treatment of articles in foreign trade zones, is reproduced in note following Code Sec. 5001.

In 1984, P.L. 98-369, Sec. 455(b)(1), substituted "(10), or (13)" for "or (10)" in para. (e)(1) . . . Sec. 455(b)(2), added "used in the production of nonbeverage wine or wine products," after "used in the production of wine," in para. (e)(2), effective 7/18/84.

In 1980, P.L. 96-223, Sec. 232(e)(2)(D), substituted "(11), or (12)," for "or (11)" in subsec. (d), effective 6/1/80 [the first day of the first calendar month beginning more than 60 days after the date of enactment].

In 1979, P.L. 96-39, Sec. 807(a)(3)(A), deleted para. (c)(3) . . . Sec. 807(a)(3)(B), substituted "(3), or (11)" for "or (3)" in subsec. (d) . . . Sec. 807(a)(3)(C), amended para. (f)(1) . . . Sec. 807(a)(3)(D), added para. (f)(6), effective 1/1/80. Prior to deletion, para. (c)(3) read as follows:

"(3) Withdrawals on determination of tax.

"(A) Any person who withdraws distilled spirits from the bonded premises of a distilled spirits plant on determination of tax, upon giving of a withdrawal bond as provided for in section 5174, shall be liable for payment of the internal revenue tax on the distilled spirits so withdrawn, from the time of such withdrawal.

"(B) All persons liable for the tax on distilled spirits under subsection (a) or (b), or under any similar prior provisions of internal revenue law, shall be relieved of liability with respect to the tax on any distilled spirits withdrawn on determination of tax under withdrawal bond (as provided for in section 5174) if the person withdrawing such spirits and the person, or persons, liable for the tax under subsection (a) or (b), or under any similar prior provisions of internal revenue law, are independent of each other and neither has a proprietary interest, directly or indirectly, in the business of the other, and all persons liable for the tax under subsection (a) or (b), or under any similar prior provisions of internal revenue law, have divested themselves of all interest in the spirits so withdrawn."

Prior to amendment, para. (f)(1) read as follows:

"(1) For provisions conditioning warehousing bonds on the payment of the tax, see section 5173(c)."

In 1977, P.L. 95-176, Sec. 4(b), amended para. (e)(2), effective 3/1/78 [the first day of the first calendar month which begins more than 90 days after 11/4/77, the date of enactment].

Prior to amendment, para. (e)(2) read as follows:

"(2) Relief from liability. All persons liable for the tax on distilled spirits under paragraph (1) of this subsection, or under subsection (a) or (b), or under any similar prior provisions of internal revenue law, shall be relieved of any such liability at the time, as the case may be, the distilled spirits are exported, deposited in a foreign-trade zone, used in the production of wine, deposited in customs manufacturing bonded warehouses, or laden as supplies upon, or used in the maintenance or repair of, certain vessels or aircraft, as provided by law."
—P.L. 95-176, Sec. 4(d), substituted "or (3)" for "(3), or (9)" in subsec. (d) . . . substituted "section 5214 (a)(4), (5), (6), (7), (8), (9), or (10)," for "section 5214(a)(4), (5), (6), (7), or (8)," in para. (e)(1), effective 3/1/78 [the first day of the first calendar month which begins more than 90 days after 11/14/77, the date of enactment].

In 1976, P.L. 94-455, Sec. 1905(a)(1), substituted "Such relief from liability shall be effective from the time of removal from the transferor's bonded premises or from the time of divestment of interest, whichever is later." for "Such relief from liability shall be effective from the time of removal from the transferor's bonded premises, from the time of such divestment of interest, or on July 1, 1959, whichever is later. The provisions of this paragraph shall be construed to apply to distilled spirits transferred in bond, whether such transfers occur prior to or on or after July 1, 1959, but shall not apply in any case in which the tax was paid or determined prior to such date." which were the last two sentences of para. (c)(2), effective 2/1/77.

Sec. 5006. Determination of tax.

(a) Requirements.

(1) In general. Except as otherwise provided in this section, the tax on distilled spirits shall be determined when the spirits are withdrawn from bond. Such tax shall be determined by such means as the Secretary shall by regulations prescribe, and with the use of such devices and apparatus (including but not limited to tanks and pipelines) as the Secretary may require. The tax on distilled spirits withdrawn from the bonded premises of a distilled spirits plant shall be determined upon completion of the gauge for determination of tax and before withdrawal from bonded premises, under such regulations as the Secretary shall prescribe.

(2) Distilled spirits not accounted for. If the Secretary finds that the distiller has not accounted for all the distilled spirits produced by him, he shall, from all the evi-

3,389

dence he can obtain, determine what quantity of distilled spirits was actually produced by such distiller, and an assessment shall be made for the difference between the quantity reported and the quantity shown to have been actually produced at the rate of tax imposed by law for every proof gallon.

(b) Taxable loss.

(1) On original quantity. Where there is evidence satisfactory to the Secretary that there has been any loss of distilled spirits from any cask or other package deposited on bonded premises, other than a loss which by reason of section 5008(a) is not taxable, the Secretary may require the withdrawal from bonded premises of such distilled spirits, and direct the officer designated by him to collect the tax accrued on the original quantity of distilled spirits entered for deposit on bonded premises in such cask or package; except that, under regulations prescribed by the Secretary, when the extent of any loss from causes other than theft or unauthorized voluntary destruction can be established by the proprietor to the satisfaction of the Secretary, an allowance of the tax on the loss so established may be credited against the tax on the original quantity. If such tax is not paid on demand it shall be assessed and collected as other taxes are assessed and collected.

(2) Alternative method. Where there is evidence satisfactory to the Secretary that there has been access, other than is authorized by law, to the contents of casks or packages stored on bonded premises, and the extent of such access is such as to evidence a lack of due diligence or a failure to employ necessary and effective controls on the part of the proprietor, the Secretary (in lieu of requiring the casks or packages to which such access has been had to be withdrawn and tax paid on the original quantity of distilled spirits entered for deposit on bonded premises in such casks or packages as provided in paragraph (1)) may assess an amount equal to the tax on 5 proof gallons of distilled spirits at the prevailing rate on each of the total number of such casks or packages as determined by him.

(3) Application of subsection. The provisions of this subsection shall apply to distilled spirits which are filled into casks or packages, as authorized by law, after entry and deposit on bonded premises, whether by recasking, filling from storage tanks, consolidation of packages, or otherwise; and the quantity filled into such casks or packages shall be deemed to be the original quantity for the purpose of this subsection, in the case of loss from such casks or packages.

(c) Distilled spirits not bonded.

(1) General. The tax on any distilled spirits, removed from the place where they were distilled and (except as otherwise provided by law) not deposited in storage on bonded premises of a distilled spirits plant, shall, at any time within the period of limitation provided in section 6501, when knowledge of such fact is obtained by the Secretary, be assessed on the distiller of such distilled spirits (or other person liable for the tax) and payment of such tax immediately demanded and, on the neglect or refusal of payment, the Secretary shall proceed to collect the same by distraint. This paragraph shall not exclude any other remedy or proceeding provided by law.

(2) Production at other than qualified plants. Except as otherwise provided by law, the tax on any distilled spirits produced in the United States at any place other than a qualified distilled spirits plant shall be due and payable immediately upon production.

(d) Unlawfully imported distilled spirits.

Distilled spirits smuggled or brought into the United States unlawfully shall, for purposes of this chapter, be held to be imported into the United States, and the internal revenue tax shall be due and payable at the time of such importation.

(e) Cross reference.

For provisions relating to removal of distilled spirits from bonded premises on determination of tax, see section 5213.

In 1990, P.L. 101-508, Sec. 11201(e), regarding floor stocks taxes, is reproduced in note following Code Sec. 5001.
—P.L. 101-508, Sec. 11218, regarding floor stocks tax treatment of articles in foreign trade zones, is reproduced in note following Code Sec. 5001.
In 1979, P.L. 96-39, Sec. 804(a), amended subsec. (a) . . . Sec. 807(a)(4)(A), substituted "; except" for ", notwithstanding that the time specified in any bond given for the withdrawal of the spirits entered in storage in such cask or package has not expired, except" in para. (b)(1) . . . Sec. 807(a)(4)(B), substituted "on bonded premises" for "in storage in internal revenue bond" each place it appeared in subsec. (b), effective 1/1/80.
Prior to amendment, subsec. (a) read as follows:
"(a) Requirements.
"(1) In general. Except as otherwise provided in this section, the internal revenue tax on distilled spirits shall be determined when the spirits are withdrawn from bond. Such tax shall be determined by such means as the Secretary shall by regulations prescribe, and with the use of such devices and apparatus (including but not limited to storage, gauging, and bottling tanks and pipelines) as the Secretary may require. The tax on distilled spirits withdrawn from the bonded premises of a distilled spirits plant shall be determined upon completion of the gauge for determination of tax and before withdrawal from bonded premises, under such regulations as the Secretary shall prescribe.
"(2) Distilled spirits entered for storage.
"(A) Bonding period limitation. Except as provided in subparagraph (B), the tax on distilled spirits entered for deposit in storage in internal revenue bond shall be determined within 20 years from the date of original entry for deposit in such storage.
"(B) Exceptions. Subparagraph (A) and section 5173(c)(1)(A) shall not apply in the case of—
"(i) distilled spirits of 190 degrees or more of proof;
"(ii) denatured distilled spirits; or
"(iii) distilled spirits which on July 26, 1936, were 8 years of age or older and which were in bonded warehouses on that date.
"(C) Distilled spirits mingled in internal revenue bond. In applying subparagraph (A) and section 5173(c)(1)(A) to distilled spirits entered for deposit in storage on different dates and lawfully mingled in internal revenue bond, the Secretary shall, by regulations, provide for the application of the 20-year period to such spirits in such manner that no more spirits will remain in bond than would have been the case had such mingling not occurred.
"(3) Distilled spirits not accounted for. If the Secretary finds that the distiller has not accounted for all the distilled spirits produced by him, he shall, from all the evidence he can obtain, determine what quality of distilled spirits was actually produced by such distiller, and an assessment shall be made for the difference between the quantity reported and the quantity shown to have been actually produced, at the rate of tax imposed by law for every proof gallon."
In 1976, P.L. 94-455, Sec. 1906(b)(13)(A), substituted "Secretary" for "Secretary or his delegate" each place it appeared in Code Sec. 5006, effective 2/1/77.

Sec. 5007. Collection of tax on distilled spirits.

(a) Tax on distilled spirits removed from bonded premises.

The tax on domestic distilled spirits and on distilled spirits removed from customs custody under section 5232 shall be paid in accordance with section 5061.

(b) Collection of tax on imported distilled spirits.

The internal revenue tax imposed by section 5001(a)(1) and (2) upon imported distilled spirits shall be collected by the Secretary and deposited as internal revenue collections, under such regulations as the Secretary may prescribe. Section 5688 shall be applicable to the disposition of imported spirits.

(c) Cross references.

(1) For authority of the Secretary to make determinations and assessments of internal revenue taxes and penalties, see section 6201(a).

(2) For authority to assess tax on distilled spirits not bonded, see section 5006(c).

(3) For provisions relating to payment of tax, under certain conditions, on distilled spirits withdrawn free of tax, denatured distilled spirits, articles, and volatile fruit-flavor concentrates, see section 5001(a)(4), (5), and (6).

In 1994, P.L. 103-465, Sec. 136(c)(3), amended subsec. (b)... Sec. 136(c)(4), substituted "section 5001(a)(4), (5), and (6)" for "section 5001(a)(5), (6), and (7)" in para. (c)(3), effective 1/1/95.
Prior to amendment, subsec. (b) read as follows:
"(b) Collection of tax on imported distilled spirits and perfumes containing distilled spirits.
"(1) Distilled spirits. The internal revenue tax imposed by section 5001(a)(1) and (2) upon imported distilled spirits shall be collected by the Secretary and deposited as internal revenue collections, under such regulations as the Secretary may prescribe. Section 5688 shall be applicable to the disposition of imported spirits.
"(2) Perfumes containing distilled spirits. The internal revenue tax imposed by section 5001(a)(3) upon imported perfumes containing distilled spirits shall be collected by the Secretary and deposited as internal revenue collections, under such regulations as the Secretary may prescribe."
In 1990, P.L. 101-508, Sec. 11201(e), regarding floor stocks taxes, is reproduced in note following Code Sec. 5001.
—P.L. 101-508, Sec. 11218, regarding floor stocks tax treatment of articles in foreign trade zones, is reproduced in note following Code Sec. 5001.
In 1979, P.L. 96-39, Sec. 807(a)(5), amended subsec. (a), effective 1/1/80.
Prior to amendment, subsec. (a) read as follows:
"(a) Tax on distilled spirits removed from bonded premises.
"(1) General. The tax on domestic distilled spirits and on distilled spirits removed from customs custody under section 5232 shall be paid in accordance with section 5061.
"(2) Distilled spirits withdrawn to bottling premises under withdrawal bond. If distilled spirits are withdrawn from bonded premises under section 5213 and a withdrawal bond is posted under section 5174(a)(2), the Secretary shall, in fixing the time for filing the return and the time for payment of the tax under section 5061(a), make allowance for the period of transportation of the distilled spirits from the bonded premises to the bottling premises, not to exceed such maximum periods as he may by regulations prescribe."
In 1976, P.L. 94-455, Sec. 1905(b)(2)(A), deleted the second sentence of para. (b)(1), effective 2/1/77.
Prior to amendment, the second sentence of para. (b)(1) read as follows:
"Such tax shall be in addition to any customs duty imposed under the Tariff Act of 1930 (46 Stat. 590; 19 U.S.C. chapter 4), or any subsequent act."
—P.L. 94-455, Sec. 1906(b)(13)(A), substituted "Secretary" for "Secretary or his delegate" each place it appeared in Code Sec. 5007, effective 2/1/77.

Sec. 5008. Abatement, remission, refund, and allowance for loss or destruction of distilled spirits.
(a) Distilled spirits lost or destroyed in bond.
  (1) Extent of loss allowance. No tax shall be collected in respect of distilled spirits lost or destroyed while in bond, except that such tax shall be collected—
    (A) Theft. In the case of loss by theft, unless the Secretary finds that the theft occurred without connivance, collusion, fraud, or negligence on the part of the proprietor of the distilled spirits plant, owner, consignor, consignee, bailee, or carrier, or the employees or agents of any of them;
    (B) Voluntary destruction. In the case of voluntary destruction, unless such destruction is carried out as provided in subsection (b); and
    (C) Unexplained shortage. In the case of an unexplained shortage of bottled distilled spirits.
  (2) Proof of loss. In any case in which distilled spirits are lost or destroyed, whether by theft or otherwise, the Secretary may require the proprietor of the distilled spirits plant or other person liable for the tax to file a claim for relief from the tax and submit proof as to the cause of such loss. In every case where it appears that the loss was by theft, the burden shall be upon the proprietor of the distilled spirits plant or other person responsible for the distilled spirits tax to establish to the satisfaction of the Secretary that such loss did not occur as the result of connivance, collusion, fraud, or negligence on the part of the proprietor of the distilled spirits plant, owner, consignor, consignee, bailee, or carrier, or the employees or agents of any of them.

  (3) Refund of tax. In any case where the tax would not be collectible by virtue of paragraph (1), but such tax has been paid, the Secretary shall refund such tax.
  (4) Limitations. Except as provided in paragraph (5), no tax shall be abated, remitted, credited, or refunded under this subsection where the loss occurred after the tax was determined (as provided in section 5006(a)). The abatement, remission, credit, or refund of taxes provided for by paragraphs (1) and (3) in the case of loss of distilled spirits by theft shall only be allowed to the extent that the claimant is not indemnified against or recompensed in respect of the tax for such loss.
  (5) Applicability. The provisions of this subsection shall extend to and apply in respect of distilled spirits lost after the tax was determined and before completion of the physical removal of the distilled spirits from the bonded premises.
(b) Voluntary destruction.
  The proprietor of the distilled spirits plant or other persons liable for the tax imposed by this chapter or by section 7652 with respect to any distilled spirits in bond may voluntarily destroy such spirits, but only if such destruction is under such supervision and under such regulations as the Secretary may prescribe.
(c) Distilled spirits returned to bonded premises.
  (1) In general. Whenever any distilled spirits on which tax has been determined or paid are returned to the bonded premises of a distilled spirits plant under section 5215(a), the Secretary shall abate or (without interest) credit or refund the tax imposed under section 5001(a)(1) (or the tax equal to such tax imposed under section 7652) on the spirits so returned.
  (2) Claim must be filed within 6 months of return of spirits. No allowance under paragraph (1) may be made unless claim therefor is filed within 6 months of the date of the return of the spirits. Such claim may be filed only by the proprietor of the distilled spirits plant to which the spirits were returned, and shall be filed in such form as the Secretary may by regulations prescribe.
(d) Distilled spirits withdrawn without payment of tax.
  The provisions of subsection (a) shall be applicable to loss of distilled spirits occurring during transportation from bonded premises of a distilled spirits plant to—
  (1) the port of export, in case of withdrawal under section 5214(a)(4);
  (2) the customs manufacturing bonded warehouse, in case of withdrawal under section 5214(a)(6);
  (3) the vessel or aircraft, in case of withdrawal under section 5214(a)(7);
  (4) the foreign-trade zone, in case of withdrawal under section 5214(a)(8); and
  (5) the customs bonded warehouse in the case of withdrawal under sections 5066 and 5214(a)(9).
The provisions of subsection (a) shall be applicable to loss of distilled spirits withdrawn from bonded premises without payment of tax under section 5214(a)(10) for certain research, development, or testing, until such distilled spirits are used as provided by law.
(e) Other laws applicable.
  All provisions of law, including penalties, applicable in respect of the internal revenue tax on distilled spirits, shall, insofar as applicable and not inconsistent with subsection (c), be applicable to the credits or refunds provided for under such subsection to the same extent as if such credits or refunds constituted credits or refunds of such tax.

Code Sec. 5008(f) Excise and miscellaneous taxes

(f) Cross reference.

For provisions relating to allowance for loss in case of wine spirits withdrawn for use in wine production, see section 5373(b)(3).

In 1997, P.L. 105-34, Sec. 1411(a), substituted "on which tax had been determined or paid" or "withdrawn from bonded premises on payment or determination of tax" in para. (c)(1), effective on the 1st day of the 1st calendar quarter that begins at least 180 days after 8/5/97.

In 1990, P.L. 101-508, Sec. 11201(e), regarding floor stocks taxes, is reproduced in note following Code Sec. 5001.

—P.L. 101-508, Sec. 11218, regarding floor stocks tax treatment of articles in foreign trade zones, is reproduced in note following Code Sec. 5001.

In 1979, P.L. 96-39, Sec. 807(a)(6), deleted "and" at the end of subpara (a)(1)(A), substituted "subsection (b); and" for "subsection (b)(1)" " at the end of the subpara. (a)(1)(B), added new subpara. (a)(1)(C), amended para. (a)(5), deleted subsecs. (b), (c), (d), (e), added new subsecs. (b) and (c), redesignated subsecs. (f), (g), (h) as subsecs. (d), (e), and (f), substituted 'subsection (c)' for 'subsections (b)(2), (c), and (d),' and substituted 'under such subsection' for 'under such subsections' in subsec. (e), as redesignated, effective 1/1/80.

Prior to amendment, para. (a)(5) read as follows:

"(5) Applicability. The provisions of this subsection shall extend to and apply in respect of distilled spirits lost after the tax was determined and prior to the completion of the physical removal of the distilled spirits from bonded premises, but shall not be applicable where the loss occurred after the time prescribed for the withdrawal of the distilled spirits from bonded premises under section 5006(a)(2) unless the loss occurred in the course of physical removal of the spirits immediately subsequent to such time. This paragraph shall not be applicable to any loss of distilled spirits for which abatement, remission, credit, or refund of tax is allowable under the provisions of subsection (c), or would be allowable except for the limitations established under subsection (c)(3)."

Prior to deletion, subsecs. (b), (c), (d) and (e) read as follows:

"(b) Voluntary destruction.

"(1) Distilled spirits in bond. The proprietor of the distilled spirits plant or other persons liable for the tax imposed by this chapter or by section 7652 with respect to any distilled spirits in bond may voluntarily destroy such spirits, but only if such destruction is under such supervision, and under such regulations, as the Secretary or his delegate may prescribe.

"(2) Distilled spirits withdrawn for rectification or bottling. Any distilled spirits withdrawn from bond on payment or determination of tax for rectification or bottling may, before removal from the bottling premises of the distilled spirits plant to which removed from bond or after return to such bottling premises, on application to the Secretary, be destroyed after such gauge and under such supervision as the Secretary may by regulations prescribe. If a claim is filed within 6 months from the date of such destruction, the Secretary shall, under such regulations as he may prescribe, abate, remit, or, without interest, credit or refund the taxes imposed under section 5001(a)(1) under subpart B of this part or under section 7652 on the spirits so destroyed, to the proprietor of the distilled spirits plant who withdrew the distilled spirits on payment or determination of tax.

"(c) Loss of distilled spirits withdrawn from bond for rectification or bottling.

"(1) General. Whenever any distilled spirits withdrawn from bond on payment or determination of tax for rectification or bottling are lost before removal from the premises of the distilled spirits plant to which removed from bond, the Secretary shall, under such regulations as he may prescribe, abate, remit, or, without interest, credit or refund the tax imposed on such spirits under section 5001(a)(1) or under Section 7652 to the proprietor of the distilled spirits plant who withdrew the distilled spirits on payment or determination of tax for removal to his bottling premises, if it is established to the satisfaction of the Secretary that—

"(A) such loss occurred (i) by reason of accident while being removed from bond to bottling premises, or (ii) by reason of flood, fire, or other disaster, or (iii) by reason of accident while on the distilled spirits plant premises and amounts to 10 proof gallons or more in respect of any one accident; or

"(B) such loss occurred (i) before the completion of the bottling and casing or other packaging of such spirits for removal from the bottling premises and (ii) by reason of, and was incident to, authorized rectifying, packaging, bottling, or casing operations (including losses by leakage or evaporation occurring during removal from bond to the bottling premises and during storage on bottling premises pending rectification or bottling).

"(2) Limitation. No abatement, remission, credit, or refund of taxes shall be made under this subsection—

"(A) in any case where the claimant is indemnified or recompensed for the tax;

"(B) in excess of the amount allowable under paragraph (3), in case of losses referred to in paragraph (1)(B); or

"(C) unless a claim is filed, under such regulations as the Secretary may prescribe, by the proprietor of the distilled spirits plant who withdrew the distilled spirits on payment or determination of tax, (i) within 6 months from the date of the loss in case of losses referred to in paragraph (1)(A), or (ii) within 6 months from the close of the computation year in which the loss occurred in case of losses referred to in paragraph (1)(B).

The quantity of distilled spirits lost within the meaning of subparagraph (B) of paragraph (1) shall be determined at such times and by such means or methods as the Secretary shall by regulations prescribe.

"(3) Maximum loss allowances.

"(A) If all the alcoholic ingredients used in distilled spirits products during the computation year were distilled spirits withdrawn from bond by the proprietor of the bottling premises on payment or determination of tax, for removal to such premises, the loss allowable in such computation year under paragraph (1)(B) shall not be greater than the excess of losses over gains, and shall not exceed the maximum amount of loss allowable as shown in the following schedule:

If total completions during the computation year in proof gallons are:	The maximum allowable loss in proof gallons is:
Not over 24,000	2 percent of completions.
Over 24,000 but not over 120,000	480 proof gallons plus 1% of excess over 24,000.
Over 120,000 but not over 600,000	1,440 proof gallons plus. 6% of excess over 120,000.
Over 600,000 but not over 2,400,000	4,320 proof gallons plus. 3% of excess over 600,000.
Over 2,400,000	9,720 proof gallons plus. 2% of excess over 2,400,000.

The Secretary may, by regulations, reduce the amount of the maximum allowable losses in the preceding schedule when he finds that such adjustment is necessary for protection of the revenue, or increase the amount of such maximum allowable losses if he finds that such may be done without undue jeopardy to the revenue and is necessary to more nearly provide for the actual losses described in paragraph (1)(B). However, in no event shall allowable losses exceed 2 percent of total completions.

"(B) If alcoholic ingredients other than distilled spirits withdrawn from bond by the proprietor of the bottling premises on payment or determination of tax, for removal to such premises, were used in distilled spirits products during the computation year, the loss allowable under paragraph (1)(B) shall be determined by first obtaining the amount that would have been allowable if all of the ingredients had been distilled spirits withdrawn from bond by the proprietor of the bottling premises on payment or determination of tax, for removal to such premises, and thereafter reducing this amount by an amount proportional to the percentage which the total proof gallons of such alcoholic ingredients bears to the total proof gallons of all alcoholic ingredients used in such distilled spirits products.

"(C) As used in this subsection, the term 'completions' means the distilled spirits products bottled and cased or otherwise packaged or placed in approved containers for removal from the bottling premises, and the term 'computation year' means the period from July 1 of a calendar year through June 30 of the following year.

"(D) The Secretary may, under such regulations and conditions as he may prescribe, make tentative allowances for losses provided for in paragraph (1)(B), for fractional parts of a year, which allowances shall be computed by the procedures prescribed in paragraphs (3)(A) and (3)(B), except that the numerical values for the completions and for the maximum allowable losses in proof gallons in the schedule in paragraph (3)(A) shall be divided by the number of such factional parts within the computation year.

"(E) The loss allowable to any proprietor qualifying for abatement, remission, credit, or refund of taxes under paragraph (1)(B) shall not exceed the quantity which would be allowed by a tentative estimates schedule constructed in accordance with paragraph (3)(D) for the portion of the computation year that such proprietor was qualified to operate the distilled spirits plant.

"(F) Notwithstanding the limitations contained in the schedule in paragraph (3)(A) the Secretary may, under such regulations as he may prescribe, in addition to the losses allowable under paragraph (1)(A) and (1)(B), allow actual determined losses incurred in the manufacture of gin and vodka where produced in closed systems in a manner similar to that authorized on bonded premises.

"(4) Eligible proprietors.

"(A) The term 'proprietor' as used in this subsection and in subsection (b)(2) shall, in the case of a corporation, include all affiliated or subsidiary corporations who are qualified during the computation year for successive operation of the same bottling premises and who make joint application to the Secretary to be treated as one proprietor for the purposes of this subsection and subsection (b)(2) and who comply with such conditions as the Secretary may by regulations prescribe.

"(B) For the purposes of this subsection and subsection (b)(2) a proprietor of bottling premises of a distilled spirits plant who makes application to the Secretary for the withdrawal of distilled spirits from bond on payment of tax for removal to such bottling premises shall be deemed to be the proprietor who withdrew distilled spirits on payment of tax, and the distilled spirits withdrawn pursuant to such application shall be deemed to have been withdrawn by such proprietor on payment of tax, whether or not he was the person who paid the tax.

"(5) Distilled spirits returned to bottling premises. Distilled spirits withdrawn from bond on payment or determination of tax for rectification or bottling which are removed from bottling premises and subsequently returned to the premises from which removed may be dumped and gauged after such return under such regulations as the Secretary may prescribe, and subsequent to such gauge shall be eligible for allowance of loss under this subsection as though they had not been removed from such bottling premises.

"(d) Distilled spirits returned to bonded premises

"(1) General. Whenever any distilled spirits withdrawn from bonded premises on payment or determination of tax are returned to the bonded premises of a distilled spirits plant under section 5215(a), the Secretary shall abate, remit, or (without interest) credit or refund the tax imposed under section 5001(a)(1) (or the tax equal to such tax imposed under section 7652) on the spirits so returned.

"(2) Distilled spirits returned to bonded premises for storage pending exportation. Whenever any distilled spirits are returned under section 5215(b) to the bonded premises of a distilled spirits plant, the Secretary shall (without interest) credit or refund the internal revenue tax found to have been paid or determined with respect to such distilled spirits. Such amount of tax shall be the same amount which would be allowed as a drawback under section 5062(b) on the exportation of such distilled spirits.

"(3) Distilled spirits stamped and labeled as bottled in bond. Whenever any distilled spirits are returned under section 5215(c) to the bonded premises of a distilled spirits plant, the Secretary shall (without interest) credit or refund the tax imposed under section 5001(a)(1) on the spirits so returned.

"(4) Limitation. No allowance under paragraph (1), (2), or (3) shall be made unless a claim is filed under such regulations as the Secretary may prescribe, by the proprietor of the distilled spirits plant to which the distilled spirits are returned within 6 months of the date of return.

"(e) Samples for use by the United States.

"The Secretary shall, under such regulations as he may prescribe, without interest, credit or refund to the proprietor the tax on any samples of distilled spirits removed from the premises of a distilled spirits plant for analysis or testing by the United States."

In 1977, P.L. 95-176, Sec. 2(f), amended subsec. (d), effective the first day of the first calendar month which begins more than 90 days after 11/14/77.

Prior to amendment, subsec. (d) read as follows:

"(d) Distilled spirits returned to bonded premises.

"(1) Allowance of tax. Whenever any distilled spirits withdrawn from bonded premises, on payment or determination of tax are returned under section 5215 to the bonded premises of a distilled spirits plant, the Secretary or his delegate shall abate, remit, or (without interest) credit or refund the tax imposed under section 5001(a)(1) or under section 7652 on the spirits so returned.

"(2) Limitation. No allowance under paragraph (1) shall be made unless a claim is filed, under such regulations as the Secretary may prescribe, by the proprietor of the distilled spirits plant to which the distilled spirits are returned, within 6 months of the date of return."

—P.L. 95-176, Sec. 4(e), deleted "and" at the end of para. (f)(3), substituted ";" and" for the period at the end of para. (f)(4), added new para. (f)(5), effective the first day of the first calendar month which begins more than 90 days after 11/14/77.

In 1976, P.L. 94-455, Sec. 1905(a)(2)(A), added "or by section 7652" after "the tax imposed by this chapter" in para. (b)(1) . . . Sec. 1905(a)(2)(B), substituted "under section 5001(a)(1) under subpart B of this part or under section 7652 on the spirits so destroyed, to the proprietor of the distilled spirits plant who withdrew the distilled spirits on payment or determination of tax." for "under section 5001(a)(1) or under subpart B or [sic] this part on the spirits so destroyed, to the proprietor of the distilled spirits plant who withdrew the distilled spirits on payment of determination of tax." at the end of para. (b)(2) . . . Sec. 1905(a)(2)(C), added "or under section 7652" after "under section 5001(a)(1)" in paras. (c)(1) and (d)(1) . . . Sec. 1905(a)(2)(D), deleted ", on or after July 1, 1959," after "withdrawn from bonded premises" in para. (d)(1), effective 2/1/77.

—P.L. 94-455, Sec. 1906(b)(13)(A), substituted "Secretary" for "Secretary or his delegate" each place it appeared in Code Sec. 5008, effective 2/1/77.

—P.L. 94-273, Sec. 47, substituted "computation year" for "fiscal year" each place it appeared in subsec. (c), effective 4/21/76.

In 1971, P.L. 91-659, Sec. 1, substituted ", or (iii) by reason of accident while on the distilled spirits plant premises and amounts to 10 proof gallons or more in respect of any one accident; or" for "; or", in subpara. (c)(1)(A) . . . Sec. 2(a), amended para. (b)(2), effective 5/1/71.

Prior to amendment, para. (b)(2) read as follows:

"(2) Distilled spirits withdrawn for rectification or bottling. Whenever any distilled spirits withdrawn from bond on or after July 1, 1959, on payment or determination of tax for rectification or bottling are (before the completion of the bottling and casing or other packaging of such spirits for removal from the bottling premises of the distilled spirits plant to which removed from bond) found by the proprietor who withdrew such spirits to be unsuitable for the purpose for which intended to be used, such spirits may, on application to the Secretary or his delegate, be destroyed after such gauge and under such supervision as the Secretary or his delegate may by regulations prescribe. If a claim is filed within 6 months from the date of such destruction, the Secretary or his delegate shall, under such regulations as he may prescribe, abate, remit, or, without interest, credit or refund the tax imposed under section 5001(a)(1) on the spirits so destroyed, to the proprietor of the distilled spirits plant who withdrew the distilled spirits on payment or determination of tax."

—P.L. 91-659, Sec. 2(b), amended para. (c)(5), effective 5/1/71.

Prior to amendment, para. (c)(5) read as follows:

"(5) Applicability. This subsection shall apply in respect of losses of distilled spirits withdrawn from bond on or after July 1, 1959. This subsection shall also apply in respect of losses, occurring on or after July 1, 1959, and after dumping for rectification or bottling, of distilled spirits withdrawn from bond prior to July 1, 1959, and such spirits shall be considered as having been withdrawn from bond on payment or determination of tax by the proprietor of the bottling premises at which the spirits are dumped for rectification or bottling."

In 1968, P.L. 90-630, Sec. 1, substituted "before removal from the premises" for "before the completion of the bottling and casing or other packaging of such spirits for removal from the bottling premises" and added clause (c)(1)(B)(i), effective for losses sustained on or after the first day of the first calendar month (Feb. 1, '69) which begins more than 90 days after the date of the enactment (10/26/68).

In 1965, P.L. 89-44, Sec. 805(a), deleted "; and no claim shall be allowed in respect to any distilled spirits withdrawn from the bonded premises of a distilled

spirits plant more than 6 months prior to the date of such return", from the end of para. (d)(2), effective 7/1/65.

Sec. 5009. Repealed

In 1979, P.L. 96-39, Sec. 807(a)(7), repealed Code Sec. 5009, effective 1/1/80. Prior to repeal, Code Sec. 5009 read as follows:

"SEC. 5009. DRAWBACK.

"(a) Drawback on exportation of distilled spirits in casks or packages.

"On the exportation of distilled spirits in casks or packages containing not less than 20 wine gallons each, filled in internal revenue bond, drawback of the internal revenue tax paid or determined may be allowed, under such regulations, and on the filing of such bonds, reports, returns, and applications, and the keeping of such records, as the Secretary may prescribe. The drawback shall be paid or credited in an amount equal to such tax on the quantity of distilled spirits exported, as ascertained prior to exportation by such gauge as the Secretary may by regulations prescribe. The drawback shall be paid or credited only after all requirements of law and regulations have been complied with and on the filing, with the Secretary, of a proper claim and evidence satisfactory to the Secretary that the tax on such distilled spirits has been paid or determined and that the distilled spirits have been exported.

"(b) Cross references.

"(1) For provisions relating to drawback on distilled spirits packaged or bottled especially for export, see section 5062(b).

"(2) For provisions relating to drawback on designated nonbeverage products, see sections 5131 through 5134.

"(3) For drawback on distilled spirits used in flavoring extracts or medical or toilet preparations exported, see section 313(d) of the Tariff Act of 1930 (19 U. S. C. 1313).

"(4) For drawback on articles removed to foreign-trade zones, see 19 U.S.C. 81c.

"(5) For drawback on shipments from the United States to Puerto Rico, the Virgin Islands, Guam, or American Samoa, see section 7653(c)."

In 1976, P.L. 94-455, Sec. 1905(a)(3), deleted "46 Stat. 694;" before "19 U.S.C. 1313" in para. (b)(3), effective 2/1/77.

—P.L. 94-455, Sec. 1906(b)(13)(A), substituted "Secretary" for "Secretary or his delegate" each place it appeared Code Sec. 5009, effective 2/1/77.

Sec. 5010. Credit for wine content and for flavors content.

(a) Allowance of credit.

(1) **Wine content.** On each proof gallon of the wine content of distilled spirits, there shall be allowed a credit against the tax imposed by section 5001 (or 7652) equal to the excess of—

(A) $13.50, over

(B) the rate of tax which would be imposed on the wine under section 5041(b) but for its removal to bonded premises.

(2) **Flavors content.** On each proof gallon of the flavors content of distilled spirits, there shall be allowed a credit against the tax imposed by section 5001 (or 7652) equal to $13.50.

(3) **Fractional part of proof gallon.** In the case of any fractional part of a proof gallon of the wine content, or of the flavors content, of distilled spirits, a proportionate credit shall be allowed.

(b) Time for determining and allowing credit.

(1) **In general.** The credit allowable by subsection (a)—

(A) shall be determined at the same time the tax is determined under section 5006 (or 7652) on the distilled spirits containing the wine or flavors, and

(B) shall be allowable at the time the tax imposed by section 5001 (or 7652) on such distilled spirits is payable as if the credit allowable by this section constituted a reduction in the rate of tax.

(2) **Determination of content in the case of imports.** For purposes of this section, the wine content, and the flavors content, of imported distilled spirits shall be established by such chemical analysis, certification, or other methods as may be set, forth in regulations prescribed by the Secretary.

3,393

Code Sec. 5010(c) — Excise and miscellaneous taxes

(c) Definitions.
For purposes of this section—
 (1) Wine content.
  (A) In general. The term "wine content" means alcohol derived from wine.
  (B) Wine. The term "wine"—
   (i) means wine on which tax would be imposed by paragraph (1), (2), or (3) of section 5041(b) but for its removal to bonded premises, and
   (ii) does not include any substance which has been subject to distillation at a distilled spirits plant after receipt in bond.
 (2) Flavors content.
  (A) In general. Except as provided in subparagraph (B), the term "flavors content" means alcohol derived from flavors of a type for which drawback is allowable under section 5114.
  (B) Exceptions. The term "flavors content" does not include—
   (i) alcohol derived from flavors made at a distilled spirits plant,
   (ii) alcohol derived from flavors distilled at a distilled spirits plant, and
   (iii) in the case of any distilled spirits product, alcohol derived from flavors to the extent such alcohol exceeds (on a proof gallon basis) 2½ percent of the finished product.

In **2005**, P.L. 109-59, Sec. 11125(b)(14), substituted "section 5114" for "section 5134" in subpara. (c)(2)(A), effective 7/1/2008, but not for taxes imposed for periods before 7/1/2008.
In **1990**, P.L. 101-508, Sec. 11201(a)(2), substituted "$13.50" for "$12.50" in subpara. (a)(1)(A) and para. (a)(2), effective 1/1/91.
—P.L. 101-508, Sec. 11201(e), regarding floor stocks taxes, is reproduced in note following Code Sec. 5001.
—P.L. 101-508, Sec. 11218, regarding floor stocks tax treatment of articles in foreign trade zones, is reproduced in note following Code Sec. 5001.
In **1988**, P.L. 100-647, Sec. 5063(a), deleted "and" at the end of clause (c)(2)(B)(i), redesignated clause (c)(2)(B)(ii) as clause (c)(2)(B)(iii), and added new clause (c)(2)(B)(ii), effective for distilled spirits withdrawn from bond after 11/10/88.
In **1984**, P.L. 98-369, Sec. 27(a)(2), substituted "$12.50" for "$10.50" in paras. (a)(1) and (a)(2), effective 10/1/85.
In **1980**, P.L. 96-598, Sec. 6(a), added Code Sec. 5010, effective 1/1/80.

Sec. 5011. Income tax credit for average cost of carrying excise tax.
(a) In general.
For purposes of section 38, the amount of the distilled spirits credit for any taxable year is the amount equal to the product of—
 (1) in the case of—
  (A) any eligible wholesaler, the number of cases of bottled distilled spirits—
   (i) which were bottled in the United States, and
   (ii) which are purchased by such wholesaler during the taxable year directly from the bottler of such spirits, or
  (B) any person which is subject to section 5005 and which is not an eligible wholesaler, the number of cases of bottled distilled spirits which are stored in a warehouse operated by, or on behalf of, a State or political subdivision thereof, or an agency of either, on which title has not passed on an unconditional sale basis, and
 (2) the average tax-financing cost per case for the most recent calendar year ending before the beginning of such taxable year.
(b) Eligible wholesaler.
For purposes of this section, the term "eligible wholesaler" means any person which holds a permit under the Federal Alcohol Administration Act as a wholesaler of distilled spirits which is not a State or political subdivision thereof, or an agency of either.
(c) Average tax-financing cost.
 (1) In general. For purposes of this section, the average tax-financing cost per case for any calendar year is the amount of interest which would accrue at the deemed financing rate during a 60-day period on an amount equal to the deemed Federal excise tax per case.
 (2) Deemed financing rate. For purposes of paragraph (1), the deemed financing rate for any calendar year is the average of the corporate overpayment rates under paragraph (1) of section 6621(a) (determined without regard to the last sentence of such paragraph) for calendar quarters of such year.
 (3) Deemed Federal excise tax per case. For purposes of paragraph (1), the deemed Federal excise tax per case is $25.68.
(d) Other definitions and special rules.
For purposes of this section—
 (1) Case. The term "case" means 12 80-proof 750-milliliter bottles.
 (2) Number of cases in lot. The number of cases in any lot of distilled spirits shall be determined by dividing the number of liters in such lot by 9.

In **2005**, P.L. 109-59, Sec. 11126(a), added Code Sec. 5011, effective for tax. yrs. begin. after 9/30/2005.

SUBPART B.— RECTIFICATION [REPEALED]

Sec.
5021. Repealed [Imposition and rate of tax]
5022. Repealed [Tax or cordials and liqueurs containing wine]
5023. Repealed [Tax on blending of beverage rums or brandies]
5024. Repealed [Definitions]
5025. Repealed [Exemption from rectification tax]
5026. Repealed [Determination and collection of rectification tax]

Sec. 5021. Repealed.

In **1979**, P.L. 96-39, Sec. 803(a), repealed Code Sec. 5021, effective 1/1/80.
Prior to repeal, Code Sec. 5021 read as follows:
"SEC. 5021. IMPOSITION AND RATE OF TAX.
"In addition to the tax imposed by this chapter on distilled spirits and wines, there is hereby imposed (except as otherwise provided in this chapter) a tax of 30 cents on each proof gallon and a proportionate tax at a like rate on all fractional parts of such proof gallon on all distilled spirits or wines rectified, purified, or refined in such manner, and on all mixtures produced in such manner, that the person so rectifying, purifying, refining, or mixing the same is a rectifier (as defined in section 5082). Spirits or wines shall not twice be subjected to tax under this section because of separate acts of rectification, pursuant to approved formula, between the time such spirits or wines are received on the bottling premises and the time they are removed therefrom."

Sec. 5022. Repealed.

In **1979**, P.L. 96-39, Sec. 803(a), repealed Code Sec. 5022, effective 1/1/80.
Prior to repeal, Code Sec. 5022 read as follows:
"SEC 5022. TAX ON CORDIALS AND LIQUEURS CONTAINING WINE.
"On all liqueurs, cordials, or similar compounds produced in the United States and not produced for sale as wine, wine specialties, or cocktails, which contain more than 2½ percent by volume of wine of an alcoholic content in excess of 14 percent by volume, there shall be paid, in lieu of the tax imposed by section 5021, a tax at the rate of $1.92 per wine gallon and a proportionate tax at a like rate on all fractional parts of such wine gallon. The last sentence of section 5021 shall not be construed to limit the imposition of tax under this section. All other provisions of law applicable to rectification shall apply to the products subject to tax under this section."
In **1965**, P.L. 89-44, Sec. 501(b), deleted "until July 1, 1965, and on or after July 1, 1965, at the rate of $1.60 per wine gallon and a proportionate tax at a like rate

Excise and miscellaneous taxes   Code Sec. 5025

on all fractional parts of such wine gallon", at the end of Code Sec. 5022, effective on and after 7/1/65.

In 1964, P.L. 88-348, Sec. 2(a)(6), substituted "July 1, 1965" for "July 1, 1964" each place it appeared in Code Sec. 5022.

In 1963, P.L. 88-52, Sec. 3(a)(6), substituted "July 1, 1964" for "July 1, 1963" each place it appeared in Code Sec. 5022.

In 1962, P.L. 87-508, Sec. 3(a)(5), substituted "July 1, 1963" for "July 1, 1962" each place it appeared in Code Sec. 5022.

In 1961, P.L. 87-72, Sec. 3(a)(6), substituted "July 1, 1962" for "July 1, 1961" each place it appeared in Code Sec. 5022.

In 1960, P.L. 86-564, Sec. 202(a)(6), substituted "July 1, 1961" for "July 1, 1960" each place it appeared in Code Sec. 5022.

In 1959, P.L. 86-75, Sec. 3(a)(4), substituted "July 1, 1960" for "July 1, 1959" each place it appeared in Code Sec. 5022.

Sec. 5023. Repealed.

In 1979, P.L. 96-39, Sec. 803(a), repealed Code Sec. 5023, effective 1/1/80.
Prior to repeal, Code Sec. 5023 read as follows:
"SEC. 5023. TAX ON BLENDING OF BEVERAGE RUMS OR BRANDIES.
"In the case of rums or fruit brandies mixed or blended pursuant to section 5234(c), in addition to the tax imposed by this chapter on the production of distilled spirits, there shall, except in the case of such rums or brandies which have been aged in wood at least 2 years at the time of their first blending or mixing, be paid a tax of 30 cents as to each proof gallon (and a proportionate tax at a like rate on all fractional parts of such proof gallon) of rums or brandies so mixed or blended and withdrawn from bonded premises, except when such rums or brandies are withdrawn under section 5214 or section 7510."

Sec. 5024. Repealed.

In 1979, P.L. 96-39, Sec. 803(a), repealed Code Sec. 5024, effective 1/1/80.
Prior to repeal, Code Sec. 5024 read as follows:
"SEC. 5024. DEFINITIONS.
"(1) For definition of 'rectifier', see section 5082.
"(2) For definition of 'products of rectification' as 'distilled spirits' for certain purposes, see section 5002(a)(6)(B).
"(3) For other definitions relating to distilled spirits, see section 5002.
"(4) For definitions of general application to this title, see chapter 79."

Sec. 5025. Repealed.

In 1979, P.L. 96-39, Sec. 803(a), repealed Code Sec. 5025, effective 1/1/80.
Prior to repeal, Code Sec. 5025 read as follows:
"SEC. 5025. EXEMPTION FROM RECTIFICATION TAX.
"(a) Absolute alcohol.
"The process of extraction of water from highproof distilled spirits for the production of absolute alcohol shall not be deemed to be rectification within the meaning of sections 5081 and 5082, and absolute alcohol shall not be subject to the tax imposed by section 5021, but the production of such absolute alcohol shall be under such regulations as the Secretary may prescribe.
"(b) Production of gin and vodka.
"The tax imposed by section 5021 shall not apply to gin produced on bottling premises of distilled spirits plants by the redistillation of a pure spirit over juniper berries and other natural aromatics, or the extracted oils of such, or to vodka produced on bottling premises of distilled spirits plants from pure spirits in the manner authorized on bonded premises of distilled spirits plants.
"(c) Refining spirits in course of original distillation.
"The purifying or refining of distilled spirits, in the course of original and continuous distillation or other original and continuous processing, through any material which will not remain incorporated with such spirits when the production thereof is complete shall not be held to be rectification within the meaning of sections 5021, 5081, or 5082, nor shall these sections be held to prohibit such purifying or refining.
"(d) Redistillation of distilled spirits on bonded premises.
"Sections 5021, 5081, and 5082 shall not apply to the redistillation of distilled spirits under section 5223.
"(e) Mingling of distilled spirits.
"Sections 5021, 5081, and 5082 shall not apply to—
"(1) the mingling on bonded premises of spirits distilled at 190 degrees or more of proof; or
"(2) the mingling of distilled spirits on bonded premises, or in the course of removal therefrom, for redistillation, storage, or any other purpose, incident to the requirements of the national defense; or
"(3) the mingling in bulk gauging tanks on bonded premises of heterogeneous distilled spirits for immediate removal to bottling premises, exclusively for use in taxable rectification, or for blending under subsection (f), or for other mingling or treatment under subsection (k); or
"(4) the blending on bonded premises of beverage brandies or rums, under the provisions of section 5234(c); or
"(5) the mingling of homogeneous distilled spirits; or
"(6) the mingling on bonded premises of distilled spirits for immediate redistillation, immediate denaturation, or immediate removal from such premises free of tax under section 5214(a)(2), (3), or section 7510; or

"(7) the mingling on bonded premises of distilled spirits authorized by section 5234(a)(2).
"(f) Blending straight whiskies, rums, fruit brandies, or wines.
"The taxes imposed by this subpart shall not attach—
"(1) to blends made exclusively of two or more pure straight whiskies, differing as to types, aged in wood for a period not less than 4 years and without the addition of coloring or flavoring matter or any other substance than pure water and if not reduced below 80 proof; or
"(2) to blends made exclusively of two or more pure fruit brandies, differing as to types, distilled from the same kind of fruit, aged in wood for a period not less than 2 years and without the addition of coloring or flavoring matter (other than caramel) or any other substance than pure water and if not reduced below 80 proof; or
"(3) to the mixing and blending of wines, where such blending is for the sole purpose of perfecting such wines according to commercial standards; or
"(4) to blends made exclusively of two or more rums, differing as to types, aged in wood for a period not less than 2 years and without the addition of coloring or flavoring matter (other than caramel) or any other substance than pure water and if not reduced below 80 proof.
Such blended whiskies, blended rums, and blended fruit brandies shall be exempt from tax under this subpart only when blended in such tanks and under such conditions and supervision as the Secretary may by regulations prescribe.
"(g) Addition of caramel to brandy or rum.
"The addition of caramel to commercial brandy or rum on the bonded premises of a distilled spirits plant, pursuant to regulations prescribed by the Secretary, shall not be deemed to be rectification within the meaning of sections 5021, 5081, and 5082.
"(h) Apothecaries.
"The taxes imposed by this subpart and by part II of this subchapter shall not be imposed on apothecaries as to wines or distilled spirits which they use exclusively in the preparation or making up of medicines unfit for use for beverage purposes.
"(i) Manufacturer recovering distilled spirits for reuse in products unfit for beverage purposes.
"The taxes imposed by this subpart and by part II of this subchapter shall not be imposed on any manufacturer for recovering distilled spirits, on which the tax has been paid or determined, from dregs or marc of percolation or extraction, or from medicines, medicinal preparations, food products, flavors, or flavoring extracts, which do not meet the manufacturer's standards, if such recovered distilled spirits are used by such manufacturer in the manufacture of medicines, medicinal preparations, food products, flavors, or flavoring extracts, which are unfit for use for beverage purposes.
"(j) Stabilization of distilled spirits.
"The removal, on the premises of a distilled spirits plant, of extraneous insoluble materials from distilled spirits, and minor changes in the soluble color or soluble solids of distilled spirits, which occur solely as a result of such filtrations or other physical treatments (which do not involve the addition of any substance which will remain incorporated in the completed product) at the time of, or preparatory to, the bottling of distilled spirits, or preparatory to exportation, as may be necessary or desirable to produce a stable product, shall not be deemed to be rectification within the meaning of sections 5021, 5081, and 5082, if such changes do not exceed maximum limitations which the Secretary may by regulations provide.
"(k) Other mingling or treatment of distilled spirits.
"The tax imposed by section 5021 shall not apply to the mingling of distilled spirits of the same class and type, or to the treatment of distilled spirits in such a manner as not to change the class and type of the distilled spirits, on bottling premises of a distilled spirits plant under such regulations as the Secretary may prescribe.
"(l) Addition of tracer elements.
"The authorized addition of tracer elements to distilled spirits under provisions of section 5201(d) shall not be deemed to be rectification within the meaning of sections 5021, 5081, and 5082.
"(m) Cross references.
"(1) For provisions exempting distilled spirits and wines rectified in customs manufacturing bonded warehouses, see section 5523.
"(2) For provisions exempting winemakers in the use or treatment of wines or wine spirits, see section 5391.
"(3) For provisions exempting the manufacturer of volatile fruit-flavor concentrates, see section 5511."

In 1977, P.L. 95-176, Sec. 5(b), deleted "for further storage in bond" after "distilled spirits" in para. (e)(7), effective 3/1/78 [the first day of the first calendar month which begins more than 90 days after 11/14/77, the date of enactment].
—P.L. 95-176, Sec. 6, added ", or the extracted oils of such," after "other natural aromatics" in subsec. (b), effective 3/1/78 [the first day of the first calendar month which begins more than 90 days after 11/14/77, the date of enactment].

In 1976, P.L. 94-455, Sec. 1905(a)(4), substituted "the bottling of distilled spirits, or preparatory to exportation" for "the bottling of distilled spirits," following "or preparatory to," in subsec. (j), effective 2/1/77.
—P.L. 94-455, Sec. 1906(b)(13)(A), substituted "Secretary" for "Secretary or his delegate" in subsecs. (a), (f), (g), (j), and (k), effective 2/1/77.

In 1965, P.L. 89-44, Sec. 805, inserted in subsec. (e)(3); "or for blending under subsection (f), or for other mingling or treatment under subsection (k); or" in place of "in rectification under subsection (f); or", effective 10/1/65 . . . inserted in subsec. (f)(1), (2) and (4) ", differing as to types," effective 10/1/65.

3,395

—P.L. 89-44, Sec. 805, added subsec. (k) and redesignated subsecs. (k) and (l) as subsecs. (l) and (m), effective 10/1/65.

Sec. 5026. Repealed.

In 1979, P.L. 96-39, Sec. 803(a), repealed Code Sec. 5026, effective 1/1/80. Prior to repeal, Code Sec. 5026 read as follows:

"SEC. 5026. DETERMINATION AND COLLECTION OF RECTIFICATION TAX.

"(a) *Determination of tax.*

"(1) General. The taxes imposed by sections 5021 and 5022 shall be determined upon the completion of the process of rectification by such means as the Secretary shall by regulations prescribe and with the use of such devices and apparatus (including but not limited to storage, gauging, and bottling tanks, and pipelines) as the Secretary may by regulations prescribe.

"(2) Unauthorized rectification. In the case of taxable rectification on premises other than premises on which rectification is authorized, the tax imposed by section 5021 or 5022 shall be due and payable at the time of such rectification.

"*(b) Payment of tax.*

The taxes imposed by sections 5021, 5022, and 5023, shall be paid in accordance with section 5061."

In 1976, P.L. 94-455, Sec. 1905(b)(2), substituted "The taxes" for "Except as provided in subsection (a)(2), the taxes" at the beginning of subsec. (b), effective 2/1/77.

—P.L. 94-455, Sec. 1906(b)(13)(A), substituted "Secretary" for "Secretary or his delegate" each place it appeared in subsec. (a), effective 2/1/77.

SUBPART C.—WINES

Sec.
5041. Imposition and rate of tax.
5042. Exemption from tax.
5043. Collection of taxes on wines.
5044. Refund of tax on wine.
5045. Cross references.

In 1997, P.L. 105-34, Sec. 1032(e)(3)(B), deleted "unmerchantable" after "tax on" in item 5044.

Sec. 5041. Imposition and rate of tax.
(a) Imposition.

There is hereby imposed on all wines (including imitation, substandard, or artificial wine, and compounds sold as wine) having not in excess of 24 percent of alcohol by volume, in bond in, produced in, or imported into, the United States, taxes at the rates shown in subsection (b), such taxes to be determined as of the time of removal for consumption or sale. All wines containing more than 24 percent of alcohol by volume shall be classed as distilled spirits and taxed accordingly. Still wines shall include those wines containing not more than 0.392 gram of carbon dioxide per hundred milliliters of wine; except that the Secretary may by regulations prescribe such tolerances to this maximum limitation as may be reasonably necessary in good commercial practice.

(b) Rates of tax.

(1) On still wines containing not more than 14 percent of alcohol by volume, $1.07 per wine gallon;

(2) On still wines containing more than 14 percent and not exceeding 21 percent of alcohol by volume, $1.57 per wine gallon;

(3) On still wines containing more than 21 percent and not exceeding 24 percent of alcohol by volume, $3.15 per wine gallon;

(4) On champagne and other sparkling wines, $3.40 per wine gallon;

(5) On artificially carbonated wines, $3.30 per wine gallon; and

(6) On hard cider which is a still wine derived primarily from apples or apple concentrate and water, containing no other fruit product, and containing at least one-half of 1 percent and less than 7 percent alcohol by volume, 22.6 cents per wine gallon.

(c) Credit for small domestic producers.

(1) **Allowance of credit.** Except as provided in paragraph (2), in the case of a person who produces not more than 250,000 wine gallons of wine during the calendar year, there shall be allowed as a credit against any tax imposed by this title (other than chapters 2, 21, and 22) of 90 cents per wine gallon on the 1st 100,000 wine gallons of wine (other than wine described in subsection (b)(4)) which are removed during such year for consumption or sale and which have been produced at qualified facilities in the United States.In the case of wine described in subsection (b)(6), the preceding sentence shall be applied by substituting "5.6 cents" for "90 cents".

(2) **Reduction in credit.** The credit allowable by paragraph (1) shall be reduced (but not below zero) by 1 percent for each 1,000 wine gallons of wine produced in excess of 150,000 wine gallons of wine during the calendar year.

(3) **Time for determining and allowing credit.** The credit allowable by paragraph (1)—

(A) shall be determined at the same time the tax is determined under subsection (a) of this section, and

(B) shall be allowable at the time any tax described in paragraph (1) is payable as if the credit allowable by this subsection constituted a reduction in the rate of such tax.

(4) **Controlled groups.** Rules similar to rules of section 5051(a)(2)(B) shall apply for purposes of this subsection.

(5) **Denial of deduction.** Any deduction under subtitle A with respect to any tax against which a credit is allowed under this subsection shall only be for the amount of such tax as reduced by such credit.

(6) **Credit for transferee in bond.** If—

(A) wine produced by any person would be eligible for any credit under paragraph (1) if removed by such person during the calendar year,

(B) wine produced by such person is removed during such calendar year by any other person (hereafter in this paragraph referred to as the "transferee") to whom such wine was transferred in bond and who is liable for the tax imposed by this section with respect to such wine, and

(C) such producer holds title to such wine at the time of its removal and provides to the transferee such information as is necessary to properly determine the transferee's credit under this paragraph,

then, the transferee (and not the producer) shall be allowed the credit under paragraph (1) which would be allowed to the producer if the wine removed by the transferee had been removed by the producer on that date.

(7) **Regulations.** The Secretary may prescribe such regulations as may be necessary to carry out the purposes of this subsection, including regulations—

(A) to prevent the credit provided in this subsection from benefiting any person who produces more than 250,000 wine gallons of wine during a calendar year, and

(B) to assure proper reduction of such credit for persons producing more than 150,000 wine gallons of wine during a calendar year.

(d) Wine gallon.

For the purpose of this chapter, the term "wine gallon" means a United States gallon of liquid measure equivalent to the volume of 231 cubic inches. On lesser quantities the tax shall be paid proportionately (fractions of less than one-tenth gallon being converted to the nearest one-tenth gallon, and

Excise and miscellaneous taxes

Code Sec. 5043(a)(1)(A)

five-hundredths gallon being converted to the next full one-tenth gallon).

(e) Tolerances.

Where the Secretary finds that the revenue will not be endangered thereby, he may by regulation prescribe tolerances (but not greater than ½ of 1 percent) for bottles and other containers, and, if such tolerances are prescribed, no assessment shall be made and no tax shall be collected for any excess in any case where the contents of a bottle or other container are within the limit of the applicable tolerance prescribed.

(f) Illegally produced wine.

Notwithstanding subsection (a), any wine produced in the United States at any place other than the bonded premises provided for in this chapter shall (except as provided in section 5042 in the case of tax-free production) be subject to tax at the rate prescribed in subsection (b) at the time of production and whether or not removed for consumption or sale.

In **1998**, P.L. 105-206, Sec. 6009(a), added "which is a still wine" after "hard cider" in para. (b)(6), effective 10/1/97.

In **1997**, P.L. 105-34, Sec. 908(a), deleted "and" at the end of para. (b)(4), substituted "; and" for the period at the end of para. (b)(5), and added para. (b)(6) . . . Sec. 908(b), added the sentence at the end of (c)(1), effective 10/1/97.

In **1996**, P.L. 104-188, Sec. 1702(b)(5), deleted para. (c)(6) and added new paras. (c)(6) and (7), effective 1/1/91.

Prior to deletion, para. (c)(6) read as follows:

"(6) Regulations. The Secretary may prescribe such regulations as may be necessary to prevent the credit provided in this subsection from benefiting any person who produces more than 250,000 wine gallons of wine during a calendar year and to assure proper reduction of such credit for persons producing more than 150,000 wine gallons of wine during a calendar year."

In **1990**, P.L. 101-508, Sec. 11201(b)(1)(A), substituted "$1.07" for "17 cents" in para. (b)(1) . . . Sec. 11201(b)(1)(B), substituted "$1.57" for "67 cents" in para. (b)(2) . . . Sec. 11201(b)(1)(C), substituted "$3.15" for "$2.25" in para. (b)(3) . . . Sec. 11201(b)(1)(D), substituted "$3.30" for "$2.40" in para. (b)(5) . . . Sec. 11201(b)(2), redesignated subsecs. (c), (d), and (e) as subsecs. (d), (e), and (f) and added new subsec. (c), effective 1/1/91.

—P.L. 101-508, Sec. 11201(e), regarding floor stocks taxes, is reproduced in note following Code Sec. 5001.

—P.L. 101-508, Sec. 11218, regarding floor stocks tax treatment of articles in foreign trade zones, is reproduced in note following Code Sec. 5001.

In **1988**, P.L. 100-647, Sec. 6101(a), redesignated subsec. (d) as subsec. (e) and added new subsec. (d), effective for wine removed after 12/31/88.

In **1976**, P.L. 94-455, Sec. 1906(b)(13)(A), substituted "Secretary" for "Secretary or his delegate" in subsec. (a), effective 2/1/77.

In **1974**, P.L. 93-490, Sec. 6(a), substituted "0.392" for "0.277" in subsec. (a), effective 2/1/75.

In **1965**, P.L. 89-44, Sec. 806(a), substituted "0.277" for "0.256" in subsec. (a), effective 7/1/65.

—P.L. 89-44, Sec. 501(c), amended subsec. (b), effective 7/1/65.

Prior to amendment, subsec. (b) read as follows:

"(b) Rates of tax.

"(1) On still wines containing not more than 14 percent of alcohol by volume, 17 cents per wine gallon, except that on and after July 1, 1965, the rate shall be 15 cents per wine gallon.

"(2) On still wines containing more than 14 percent and not exceeding 21 percent of alcohol by volume, 67 cents per wine gallon, except that on and after July 1, 1965, the rate shall be 60 cents a wine gallon;

"(3) On still wines containing more than 21 percent and not exceeding 24 percent of alcohol by volume, $2.25 per wine gallon, except that on and after July 1, 1965, the rate shall be $2.00 per wine gallon;

"(4) On champagne and other sparkling wines, $3.40 per wine gallon, except that on and after July 1, 1965, the rate shall be $3.00 per wine gallon; and

"(5) On artificially carbonated wines, $2.40 per wine gallon, except that on and after July 1, 1965, the rate shall be $2.00 per wine gallon."

In **1964**, P.L. 88-348, Sec. 2(a)(7), substituted "July 1, 1965" for "July 1, 1964" each place it appeared in subsec. (b).

In **1963**, P.L. 88-52, Sec. 3(a)(7), substituted "July 1, 1964" for "July 1, 1963" each place it appeared in subsec. (b).

In **1962**, P.L. 87-508, Sec. 3(a)(6), substituted "July 1, 1963" for "July 1, 1962" each place it appeared in subsec. (b).

In **1961**, P.L. 87-72, Sec. 3(a)(7), substituted "July 1, 1962" for "July 1, 1961" each place it appeared in subsec. (b).

In **1960**, P.L. 86-564, Sec. 202(a), substituted "July 1, 1961" for "July 1, 1960" each place it appeared in subsec. (b).

In **1959**, P.L. 86-75, Sec. 3(a), substituted "July 1, 1960" for "July 1, 1959" each place it appeared in subsec. (b).

Sec. 5042. Exemption from tax.

(a) Tax-free production.

(1) Cider. Subject to regulations prescribed by the Secretary, the noneffervescent product of the normal alcoholic fermentation of apple juice only, which is produced at a place other than a bonded wine cellar and without the use of preservative methods or materials, and which is sold or offered for sale as cider and not as wine or as a substitute for wine, shall not be subject to tax as wine nor to the provisions of subchapter F.

(2) Wine for personal or family use. Subject to regulations prescribed by the Secretary—

(A) Exemption. Any adult may, without payment of tax, produce wine for personal or family use and not for sale.

(B) Limitation. The aggregate amount of wine exempt from tax under this paragraph with respect to any household shall not exceed—

(i) 200 gallons per calendar year if there are 2 or more adults in such household, or

(ii) 100 gallons per calendar year if there is only 1 adult in such household.

(C) Adults. For purposes of this paragraph, the term "adult" means an individual who has attained 18 years of age, or the minimum age (if any) established by law applicable in the locality in which the household is situated at which wine may be sold to individuals, whichever is greater.

(3) Experimental wine. Subject to regulations prescribed by the Secretary, any scientific university, college of learning, or institution of scientific research may produce, receive, blend, treat, and store wine, without payment of tax, for experimental or research use but not for consumption (other than organoleptical tests) or sale, and may receive such wine spirits without payment of tax as may be necessary for such production.

(b) Cross references.

(1) For provisions relating to exemption of tax on losses of wine (including losses by theft or authorized destruction), see section 5370.

(2) For provisions exempting from tax samples of wine, see section 5372.

(3) For provisions authorizing withdrawals of wine free of tax or without payment of tax, see section 5362.

In **1990**, P.L. 101-508, Sec. 11201(e), regarding floor stocks taxes, is reproduced in note following Code Sec. 5001.

—P.L. 101-508, Sec. 11218, regarding floor stocks tax treatment of articles in foreign trade zones, is reproduced in note following Code Sec. 5001.

In **1978**, P.L. 95-458, Sec. 2(a), amended para. (a)(2), effective the first day of the first calendar month which begins more than 90 days after 10/14/78.

Prior to amendment, para. (a)(2) read as follows:

"(2) Family wine. Subject to regulations prescribed by the Secretary, the duly registered head of any family may, without payment of tax, produce for family use and not for sale an amount of wine not exceeding 200 gallons per annum."

In **1976**, P.L. 94-455, Sec. 1906(b)(13)(A), substituted "Secretary" for "Secretary or his delegate" each place it appeared in Code Sec. 5042, effective 2/1/77.

Sec. 5043. Collection of taxes on wines.

(a) Persons liable for payment.

The taxes on wine provided for in this subpart shall be paid—

(1) Bonded wine cellars. In the case of wines removed from any bonded wine cellar, by the proprietor of such bonded wine cellar; except that—

(A) in the case of any transfer of wine in bond as authorized under the provisions of section 5362(b), the liability for payment of the tax shall become the liability of the transferee from the time of removal of the wine

3,397

from the transferor's premises, and the transferor shall thereupon be relieved of such liability; and

(B) in the case of any wine withdrawn by a person other than such proprietor without payment of tax as authorized under the provisions of section 5362(c), the liability for payment of the tax shall become the liability of such person from the time of the removal of the wine from the bonded wine cellar, and such proprietor shall thereupon be relieved of such liability.

(2) **Foreign wine.** In the case of foreign wines, which are not transferred to a bonded wine cellar free of tax under section 5364 by the importer thereof.

(3) **Other wines.** Immediately, in the case of any wine produced, imported, received, removed, or possessed otherwise than as authorized by law, by any person producing, importing, receiving, removing, or possessing such wine; and all such persons shall be jointly and severally liable for such tax with each other as well as with any proprietor, transferee, or importer who may be liable for the tax under this subsection.

(b) Payment of tax.

The taxes on wines shall be paid in accordance with section 5061.

In **1998**, P.L. 105-206, Sec. 6014(b)(1), added "which are not transferred to a bonded wine cellar free of tax under section 5364" after "foreign wines" in para. (a)(2), effective on the 1st day of the 1st calendar quarter that begins at least 180 days after 8/5/97.

In **1990**, P.L. 101-508, Sec. 11201(e), regarding floor stocks taxes, is reproduced in note following Code Sec. 5001.

—P.L. 101-508, Sec. 11218, regarding floor stocks tax treatment of articles in foreign trade zones, is reproduced in note following Code Sec. 5001.

In **1979**, P.L. 96-39, Sec. 807(a)(8), deleted "between bonded wine cellars" after "wine in bond", in subpara. (a)(1)(A), effective 1/1/80.

In **1976**, P.L. 94-455, Sec. 1905(b)(2)(C), substituted "The taxes" for "Except as provided in subsection (a)(3), the taxes" in subsec. (b), effective 2/1/77.

Sec. 5044. Refund of tax on wine.
(a) General.

In the case of any wine removed from a bonded wine cellar and returned to bond under section 5361—

(1) any tax imposed by section 5041 shall, if paid, be refunded or credited, without interest, to the proprietor of the bonded wine cellar to which such wine is delivered; or

(2) if any tax so imposed has not been paid, the person liable for the tax may be relieved of liability therefor, under such regulations as the Secretary may prescribe. Such regulations may provide that claim for refund or credit under paragraph (1), or relief from liability under paragraph (2), may be made only with respect to minimum quantities specified in such regulations. The burden of proof in all such cases shall be on the applicant.

(b) Date of filing.

No claim under subsection (a) shall be allowed unless filed within 6 months after the date of the return of the wine to bond.

(c) Status of wine returned to bond.

All provisions of this chapter applicable to wine in bond on the premises of a bonded wine cellar and to removals thereof shall be applicable to wine returned to bond under the provisions of this section.

In **1998**, P.L. 105-206, Sec. 6014(b)(2), substituted "removed from a bonded wine cellar" for "produced in the United States" in subsec. (a), effective on the last day of the first calendar quarter that begins at least 180 days after 8/5/97.

In **1997**, P.L. 105-34, Sec. 1416(a), deleted "as unmerchantable" after "returned to bond" from subsec. (a) . . . Sec. 1416(b)(2), deleted "unmerchantable" after "of tax on" from the heading for Code Sec. 5044, effective on the 1st day of the 1st calendar quarter that begins at least 180 days after 8/5/97.

In **1990**, P.L. 101-508, Sec. 11201(e), regarding floor stocks taxes, is reproduced in note following Code Sec. 5001.

—P.L. 101-508, Sec. 11218, regarding floor stocks tax treatment of articles in foreign trade zones, is reproduced in note following Code Sec. 5001.

In **1976**, P.L. 94-455, Sec. 1906(b)(13)(A), substituted "Secretary" for "Secretary or his delegate" in subsec. (a), effective 2/1/77.

Sec. 5045. Cross references.

For provisions relating to the establishment and operation of wineries, see subchapter F, and for penalties pertaining to wine, see subchapter J.

In **1990**, P.L. 101-508, Sec. 11201(e), regarding floor stocks taxes, is reproduced in note following Code Sec. 5001.

—P.L. 101-508, Sec. 11218, regarding floor stocks tax treatment of articles in foreign trade zones, is reproduced in note following Code Sec. 5001.

SUBPART D.—BEER

Sec.
5051. Imposition and rate of tax.
5052. Definitions.
5053. Exemptions.
5054. Determination and collection of tax on beer.
5055. Drawback of tax.
5056. Refund and credit of tax, or relief from liability.

Sec. 5051. Imposition and rate of tax.
(a) Rate of tax.

(1) In general. A tax is hereby imposed on all beer brewed or produced, and removed for consumption or sale, within the United States, or imported into the United States. Except as provided in paragraph (2), the rate of such tax shall be $18 for every barrel containing not more than 31 gallons and at a like rate for any other quantity or for fractional parts of a barrel.

(2) Reduced rate for certain domestic production.

(A) $7 a barrel rate. In the case of a brewer who produces not more than 2,000,000 barrels of beer during the calendar year, the per barrel rate of the tax imposed by this section shall be $7 on the first 60,000 barrels of beer which are removed in such year for consumption or sale and which have been brewed or produced by such brewer at qualified breweries in the United States.

(B) Controlled groups. In the case of a controlled group, the 2,000,000 barrel quantity specified in subparagraph (A) shall be applied to the controlled group, and the 60,000 barrel quantity specified in subparagraph (A) shall be apportioned among the brewers who are component members of such group in such manner as the Secretary shall by regulations prescribed. For purposes of the preceding sentence, the term "controlled group" has the meaning assigned to it by subsection (a) of section 1563, except that for such purposes the phrase "more than 50 percent" shall be substituted for the phrase "at least 80 percent" in each place it appears in such subsection. Under regulations prescribed by the Secretary, principles similar to the principles of the preceding two sentences shall be applied to a group of brewers under common control where one or more of the brewers is not a corporation.

(C) Regulations. The Secretary may prescribe such regulations as may be necessary to prevent the reduced rates provided in this paragraph from benefiting any person who produces more than 2,000,000 barrels of beer during a calendar year.

(3) Tolerances. Where the Secretary finds that the revenue will not be endangered thereby, he may by regulations prescribe tolerances for barrels and fractional parts of barrels, and, if such tolerances are prescribed, no assessment shall be made and no tax shall be collected for any excess in any case where the contents of a barrel or a fractional part of a barrel are within the limit of the applicable tolerance prescribed.

(b) Assessment on materials used in production in case of fraud.

Nothing contained in this subpart or subchapter G shall be construed to authorize an assessment on the quantity of materials used in producing or purchased for the purpose of producing beer, nor shall the quantity of materials so used or purchased be evidence, for the purpose of taxation, of the quantity of beer produced; but the tax on all beer shall be paid as provided in section 5054, and not otherwise; except that this subsection shall not apply to cases of fraud, and nothing in this subsection shall have the effect to change the rules of law respecting evidence in any prosecution or suit.

(c) Illegally produced beer.

The production of any beer at any place in the United States shall be subject to tax at the rate prescribed in subsection (a) and such tax shall be due and payable as provided in section 5054(a)(3) unless—

(1) such beer is produced in a brewery qualified under the provisions of subchapter G, or

(2) such production is exempt from tax under section 5053(e) (relating to beer for personal or family use).

In 1990, P.L. 101-508, Sec. 11201(c)(1), substituted "$18" for "$9" in para. (a)(1) . . . Sec. 11201(c)(2), added subpara. (a)(2)(C), effective 1/1/91.
—P.L. 101-508, Sec. 11201(e), regarding floor stocks taxes, is reproduced in note following Code Sec. 5001.
—P.L. 101-508, Sec. 11218, regarding floor stocks tax treatment of articles in foreign trade zones, is reproduced in note following Code Sec. 5001.
In 1978, P.L. 95-458, Sec. 2(b)(2)(A), added subsec. (c), effective 2/1/79 (the first day of the first calendar month which begins more than 90 days after 10/14/78, the date of enactment).
In 1976, P.L. 94-529, Sec. 1, amended subsec. (a), effective on the first day of the first calendar year begin. after 10/17/76.
Prior to amendment, subsec. (a) read as follows:
"(a) Rate of tax.

"There is hereby imposed on all beer, brewed or produced, and removed for consumption or sale, within the United States, or imported into the United States, a tax of $9 for every barrel containing not more than 31 gallons and at a like rate for any other quantity or for fractional parts of a barrel. Where the Secretary or his delegate finds that the revenue will not be endangered thereby, he may by regulations prescribe tolerances for barrels and fractional parts of barrels, and, if such tolerances are prescribed, no assessment shall be made and no tax shall be collected for any excess in any case where the contents of a barrel or a fractional part of a barrel are within the limit of the applicable tolerance prescribed."
—P.L. 94-455, Sec. 1906(b)(13)(A), substituted "Secretary" for "Secretary or his delegate" in subsec. (a), effective 2/1/77.
In 1965, P.L. 89-44, Sec. 501(d), deleted the second sentence of subsec. (b).
Prior to amendment, the second sentence of subsec. (b) read as follows:
"On and after July 1, 1965, the tax imposed by this subsection shall be at the rate of $8 in lieu of $9."
In 1964, P.L. 88-348, Sec. 2(a)(8), substituted "July 1, 1965" for "July 1, 1964" in subsec. (a).
In 1963, P.L. 88-52, Sec. 3(a)(8), substituted "July 1, 1964" for "July 1, 1963" in subsec. (a).
In 1962, P.L. 87-508, Sec. 3(a)(7), substituted "July 1, 1963" for "July 1, 1962" in subsec. (a).
In 1961, P.L. 87-72, Sec. 3(a)(8), substituted "July 1, 1962" for "July 1, 1961" in subsec. (a).
In 1960, P.L. 86-564, Sec. 202(a), substituted "July 1, 1961" for "July 1, 1960" in subsec. (a).
In 1959, P.L. 86-75, Sec. 3(a), substituted "July 1, 1960" for "July 1, 1959" in subsec. (a).

Sec. 5052. Definitions.
(a) Beer.

For purposes of this chapter (except when used with reference to distilling or distilling material) the term beer means beer, ale, porter, stout, and other similar fermented beverages (including saké or similar products) of any name or description containing one-half of 1 percent or more of alcohol by volume, brewed or produced from malt, wholly or in part, or from any substitute therefor.

(b) Gallon.

For purposes of this subpart, the term gallon means the liquid measure containing 231 cubic inches.

(c) Removed for consumption or sale.

Except as provided for in the case of removal of beer without payment of tax, the term "removed for consumption or sale", for the purposes of this subpart means—

(1) **Sale of beer.** The sale and transfer of possession of beer for consumption at the brewery; or

(2) **Removals.** Any removal of beer from the brewery.

(d) Brewer.

For purposes of this chapter, the term "brewer" means any person who brews beer or produces beer for sale. Such term shall not include any person who produces only beer exempt from tax under section 5053(e).

In 2005, P.L. 109-59, Sec. 11125(b)(15), amended subsec. (d), effective 7/1/2008, but not for taxes imposed for periods before 7/1/2008.
Prior to amendment, subsec. (d) read as follows:
"(d) Brewer. For definition of brewer, see section 5092."
In 1990, P.L. 101-508, Sec. 11201(e), regarding floor stocks taxes, is reproduced in note following Code Sec. 5001.
—P.L. 101-508, Sec. 11218, regarding floor stocks tax treatment of articles in foreign trade zones, is reproduced in note following Code Sec. 5001.
In 1971, P.L. 91-673, Sec. 1(b), amended para. (c)(2), effective 5/1/71.
Prior to amendment, para. (c)(2) read as follows:
"(2) Removals. Any removal of beer from the brewery, except that such removal shall not include any beer returned to the brewery on the same day such beer is removed from the brewery."

Sec. 5053. Exemptions.
(a) Removals for export.

Beer may be removed from the brewery, without payment of tax, for export, in such containers and under such regulations, and on the giving of such notices, entries, and bonds and other security, as the Secretary may by regulations prescribe.

(b) Removals when unfit for beverage use.

When beer has become sour or damaged, so as to be incapable of use as such, a brewer may remove the same from his brewery without payment of tax, for manufacturing purposes, under such regulations as the Secretary may prescribe.

(c) Removals for laboratory analysis.

Beer may be removed from the brewery, without payment of tax, for laboratory analysis, subject to such limitations and under such regulations as the Secretary may prescribe.

(d) Removals for research, development, or testing.

Under such conditions and regulations as the Secretary may prescribe, beer may be removed from the brewery without payment of tax for use in research, development, or testing (other than consumer testing or other market analysis) of processes, systems, materials, or equipment relating to beer or brewery operations.

(e) Beer for personal or family use.

Subject to regulation prescribed by the Secretary, any adult may, without payment of tax, produce beer for personal or family use and not for sale. The aggregate amount of beer exempt from tax under this subsection with respect to any household shall not exceed—

(1) 200 gallons per calendar year if there are 2 or more adults in such household, or

(2) 100 gallons per calendar year if there is only 1 adult in such household.

For purposes of this subsection, the term "adult" means an individual who has attained 18 years of age, or the minimum age (if any) established by law applicable in the locality in which the household is situated at which beer may be sold to individuals, whichever is greater.

(f) Removal for use as distilling material.
Subject to such regulations as the Secretary may prescribe, beer may be removed from a brewery without payment of tax to any distilled spirits plant for use as distilling material.

(g) Removals for use of foreign embassies, legations, etc.
(1) **In general.** Subject to such regulations as the Secretary may prescribe—
(A) beer may be withdrawn from the brewery without payment of tax for transfer to any customs bonded warehouse for entry pending withdrawal therefrom as provided in subparagraph (B), and
(B) beer entered into any customs bonded warehouse under subparagraph (A) may be withdrawn for consumption in the United States by, and for the official and family use of, such foreign governments, organizations, and individuals as are entitled to withdraw imported beer from such warehouses free of tax.

Beer transferred to any customs bonded warehouse under subparagraph (A) shall be entered, stored, and accounted for in such warehouse under such regulations and bonds as the Secretary may prescribe, and may be withdrawn therefrom by such governments, organizations, and individuals free of tax under the same conditions and procedures as imported beer.

(2) **Other rules to apply.** Rules similar to the rules of paragraphs (2) and (3) of section 5362(e) shall apply for purposes of this subsection.

(h) Removals for destruction.
Subject to such regulations as the Secretary may prescribe, beer may be removed from the brewery without payment of tax for destruction.

(i) Removal as supplies for certain vessels and aircraft.
For exemption as to supplies for certain vessels and aircraft, see section 309 of the Tariff Act of 1930, as amended (19 U.S.C. 1309).

In **1997**, P.L. 105-34, Sec. 1414(b), redesignated subsec. (f) as subsec. (i) and added new subsec. (f), effective the 1st day of the 1st calendar quarter that begins at least 180 days after 8/5/97.
—P.L. 105-34, Sec. 1418(a), added susbsec. (g), effective the 1st day of the 1st calendar quarter that begins at least 180 days after 8/5/97.
—P.L. 105-34, Sec. 1419(a), added subsec. (h), effective the 1st day of the 1st calendar quarter that begins at least 180 days after 8/5/97.
In **1990**, P.L. 101-508, Sec. 11201(e), regarding floor stocks taxes, is reproduced in note following Code Sec. 5001.
—P.L. 101-508, Sec. 11218, regarding floor stocks tax treatment of articles in foreign trade zones, is reproduced in note following Code Sec. 5001.
In **1978**, P.L. 95-458, Sec. 2(b)(1), redesignated subsec. (e) as subsec. (f), added new subsec. (e), effective 2/1/79 (the first day of the first calendar month which begins more than 90 days after 10/14/78, the date of enactment).
In **1976**, P.L. 94-455, Sec. 1906(b)(13)(A), substituted "Secretary" for "Secretary or his delegate" each place it appeared in Code Sec. 5053, effective 2/1/77.
In **1971**, P.L. 91-673, Sec. 2, redesignated subsec. (d) as (e), and added new subsec. (d), effective 5/1/71.
In **1965**, P.L. 89-44, Sec. 807(b), deleted "to a foreign country" after "export", in subsec. (a), effective 7/1/65.

Sec. 5054. Determination and collection of tax on beer.
(a) Time of determination.

(1) **Beer produced in the United States ; certain imported beer.** Except as provided in paragraph (3), the tax imposed by section 5051 on beer produced in the United States, or imported into the United States and transferred to a brewery free of tax under section 5418, shall be determined at the time it is removed for consumption or sale, and shall be paid by the brewer thereof in accordance with section 5061.

(2) **Beer imported into the United States.** Except as provided in paragraph (4), the tax imposed by section 5051 on beer imported into the United States and not transferred to a brewery free of tax under section 5418 shall be determined at the time of the importation thereof, or, if entered for warehousing, at the time of removal from the 1st such warehouse.

(3) **Illegally produced beer.** The tax on any beer produced in the United States shall be due and payable immediately upon production unless—
(A) such beer is produced in a brewery qualified under the provisions of subchapter G, or
(B) such production is exempt from tax under sections 5053(e) (relating to beer for personal or family use).

(4) **Unlawfully imported beer.** Beer smuggled or brought into the United States unlawfully shall, for purposes of this chapter, be held to be imported into the United States, and the internal revenue tax shall be due and payable at the time of such importation.

(b) Tax on returned beer.
Beer which has been removed for consumption or sale and is thereafter returned to the brewery shall be subject to all provisions of this chapter relating to beer prior to removal for consumption or sale, including the tax imposed by section 5051. The tax on any such returned beer which is again removed for consumption or sale shall be determined and paid without respect to the tax which was determined at the time of prior removal of the beer for consumption or sale.

(c) Applicability of other provisions of law.
All administrative and penal provisions of this title, insofar as applicable, shall apply to any tax imposed by section 5051.

In **1998**, P.L. 105-206, Sec. 6014(a)(1)(A), added ", or imported into the United States and transferred to a brewery free of tax under section 5418," after "produced in the United States" in para. (a)(1) . . . Sec. 6014(a)(1)(B), added "; certain imported beer" after "produced in the United States" in the heading of para. (a)(1) . . . Sec. 6014(a)(2), added "and not transferred to a brewery free of tax under section 5418" after "United States" in para. (a)(2), effective on the first day of the first calendar quarter that begins at least 180 days after 8/5/97.
In **1990**, P.L. 101-508, Sec. 11201(e), regarding floor stocks taxes, is reproduced in note following Code Sec. 5001.
—P.L. 101-508, Sec. 11218, regarding floor stocks tax treatment of articles in foreign trade zones, is reproduced in note following Code Sec. 5001.
In **1988**, P.L. 100-647, Sec. 1018(u)(19), added a period at the end of para. (a)(2), effective for removals during semimonthly periods ending on or after 12/31/86. For special rules, see Sec. 8011(c)(2) of P.L. 99-509, reproduced below.
In **1986**, P.L. 99-509, Sec. 8011(b)(2), substituted "if entered for warehousing, at the time of removal from the 1st such warehouse" for "if entered into customs custody, at the time of removal from such custody, and shall be paid under such regulations as the Secretary shall prescribe" in para. (a)(2), effective for removals during semimonthly periods end. on or after 12/31/86. Sec. 8011(c)(2) of this Act provides:
"(2) Imported articles, etc. Subparagraphs (B) and (C) of section 5703(b)(2) of the Internal Revenue Code of 1954 (as added by this section), paragraphs (2) and (3) of section 5061(d) of such Code (as amended by this section), and the amendments made by subsections (a)(2) and (b)(2) [Sec. 8011] shall apply to articles imported, entered for warehousing, or brought into the United States or a foreign trade zone after December 15, 1986."
In **1978**, P.L. 95-458, Sec. 2(b)(2)(B), amended para. (a)(3), effective 2/1/79 (the first day of the first calendar month which begins more than 90 days after 10/14/78, the date of enactment).
Prior to amendment, para. (a)(3) read as follows:
"(3) Illegally produced beer. The tax on any beer produced in the United States at any place other than a qualified brewery shall be due and payable immediately upon production."
In **1976**, P.L. 94-455, Sec. 1905(a)(5), deleted subsec. (c), and redesignated subsec. (d) as subsec. (c), effective 2/1/77.
Prior to deletion, subsec. (c) read as follows:
"(c) Stamps or other devices as evidence of payment of tax.
"When the Secretary or his delegate finds it necessary for the protection of the revenue, he may require stamps, or other devices, evidencing the tax or indicating a compliance with the provisions of this chapter, to be affixed to hogsheads, barrels, or kegs of beer at the time of removal. The Secretary or his delegate shall by regulations prescribe the manner by which such stamps or other devices shall be supplied, affixed, and accounted for."
—P.L. 94-455, Sec. 1906(b)(13)(A), substituted "Secretary" for "Secretary or his delegate" in subsec. (a), effective 2/1/77.

Excise and miscellaneous taxes Code Sec. 5061(b)(2)

Sec. 5055. Drawback of tax.

On the exportation of beer, brewed or produced in the United States, the brewer thereof shall be allowed a drawback equal in amount to the tax paid on such beer if there is such proof of exportation as the Secretary may by regulations require. For the purpose of this section, exportation shall include delivery for use as supplies on the vessels and aircraft described in section 309 of the Tariff Act of 1930, as amended (19 U.S.C. 1309).

In 1997, P.L. 105-34, Sec. 1420(a), substituted "paid on such beer if there is such proof of exportation as the Secretary may by regulations require." for "found to have been paid on such beer, to be paid on submission of such evidence, records and certificates indicating exportation, as the Secretary may by regulations prescribe." in the first sentence of Code Sec. 5055, effective on the 1st day of the 1st calendar quarter that begins at least 180 days after 8/5/97.

In 1990, P.L. 101-508, Sec. 11201(e), regarding floor stocks taxes, is reproduced in note following Code Sec. 5001.

—P.L. 101-508, Sec. 11218, regarding floor stocks tax treatment of articles in foreign trade zones, is reproduced in note following Code Sec. 5001.

In 1976, P.L. 94-455, Sec. 1906(b)(13)(A), substituted "Secretary" for "Secretary or his delegate" in Code Sec. 5055, effective 2/1/77.

Sec. 5056. Refund and credit of tax, or relief from liability.

(a) Beer returned or voluntarily destroyed.

Any tax paid by any brewer on beer removed for consumption or sale may be refunded or credited to the brewer, without interest, or if the tax has not been paid, the brewer may be relieved of liability therefor, under such regulations as the Secretary may prescribe, if such beer is returned to any brewery of the brewer or is destroyed under the supervision required by such regulations. In determining the amount of tax due on beer removed on any day, the quantity of beer returned to the same brewery from which removed shall be allowed, under such regulations as the Secretary may prescribe, as an offset against or deduction from the total quantity of beer removed from that brewery on the day of such return.

(b) Beer lost by fire, theft, casualty, or act of God.

Subject to regulations prescribed by the Secretary, the tax paid by any brewer on beer removed for consumption or sale may be refunded or credited to the brewer, without interest, or if the tax has not been paid, the brewer may be relieved of liability therefor, if such beer is lost, whether by theft or otherwise, or is destroyed or otherwise rendered unmerchantable by fire, casualty, or act of God before the transfer of title thereto to any other person. In any case in which beer is lost or destroyed, whether by theft or otherwise, the Secretary may require the brewer to file a claim for relief from the tax and submit proof as to the cause of such loss. In every case where it appears that the loss was by theft, the first sentence shall not apply unless the brewer establishes to the satisfaction of the Secretary that such theft occurred before removal from the brewery and occurred without connivance, collusion, fraud, or negligence on the part of the brewer, consignor, consignee, bailee, or carrier, or the employees or agents of any of them.

(c) Beer received at a distilled spirits plant.

Any tax paid by any brewer on beer removed for consumption or sale may be refunded or credited to the brewer, without interest, or if the tax has not been paid, the brewer may be relieved of liability therefor, under regulations as the Secretary may prescribe, if such beer is received on the bonded premises of a distilled spirits plant pursuant to the provisions of section 5222(b)(2), for use in the production of distilled spirits.

(d) Limitations.

No claim under this section shall be allowed (1) unless filed within 6 months after the date of the return, loss, destruction, rendering unmerchantable, or receipt on the bonded premises of a distilled spirits plant or (2) if the claimant was indemnified by insurance or otherwise in respect of the tax.

In 1998, P.L. 105-206, Sec. 6014(a)(3), substituted "removed for consumption or sale" for "produced in the United States" each place it appeared in Code Sec. 5056, effective on the first day of the first calendar quarter that begins at least 180 days after 8/5/97.

In 1997, P.L. 105-34, Sec. 1414(c)(1), redesignated subsec. (c) as (d) and added new subsec. (c) . . . Sec. 1414(c)(2), substituted "rendering unmerchantable, or receipt on the bonded premises of a distilled spirits plant" for "or rendering unmerchantable" in subsec. (d) [as redesignated by Sec. 1414(c)(1) of this Act, see above], effective the 1st day of the 1st calendar quarter that begins at least 180 days after 8/5/97.

In 1990, P.L. 101-508, Sec. 11201(e), regarding floor stocks taxes, is reproduced in note following Code Sec. 5001.

—P.L. 101-508, Sec. 11218, regarding floor stocks tax treatment of articles in foreign trade zones, is reproduced in note following Code Sec. 5001.

In 1976, P.L. 94-455, Sec. 1906(b)(13)(A), substituted "Secretary" for "Secretary or his delegate" each place it appeared in Code Sec. 5056, effective 2/1/77.

In 1971, P.L. 91-673, Sec. 1(a), amended Sec. 5056, effective 5/1/71.

Prior to amendment, Code Sec. 5056 read as follows:

"SEC. 5056. REFUND AND CREDIT OF TAX, OR RELIEF FROM LIABILITY.

"(a) Beer removed from market.

"Any tax paid by any brewer on beer produced in the United States may be refunded or credited to the brewer, without interest, or if the tax has not been paid, the brewer may be relieved of liability therefor, under such regulations as the Secretary or his delegate may prescribe, if such beer is removed from the market and is returned to the brewery or is destroyed under the supervision required by such regulations.

"(b) Beer lost by fire, casualty, or act of God.

"Subject to regulations prescribed by the Secretary or his delegate, the tax paid by any brewer on beer produced in the United States may be refunded or credited to the brewer, without interest, or if the tax has not been paid, the brewer may be relieved of liability therefor, if such beer is lost other than by theft, or is destroyed by fire, casualty, or act of God, before the transfer of title thereto to any other person.

"(c) Date of filing.

"No claims under this section shall be allowed unless filed within 6 months after the date of such removal from the market, loss, or destruction, or if the claimant was indemnified by insurance or otherwise in respect of the tax."

SUBPART E.—GENERAL PROVISIONS

Sec.
5061. Method of collecting tax.
5062. Refund and drawback in case of exportation.
5064. Losses resulting from disaster, vandalism, or malicious mischief.
5065. Territorial extent of law.
5066. Distilled spirits for use of foreign embassies, legations, etc.
5067. Cross reference.

In 1978, amended item 5064.
Prior to amendment item 5064 read as follows:
"5064. Losses caused by disaster."

In 1971, P.L. 91-659, Sec. 3(b), redesig. item 5066 as 5067 and added new item 5066.

In 1965, P.L. 89-44, Sec. 501(e), repealed item "5063. Floor stocks tax refunds on distilled spirits, wines, cordials, and beer", effective 7/1/65.

Sec. 5061. Method of collecting tax.

(a) Collection by return.

The taxes on distilled spirits, wines, and beer shall be collected on the basis of a return. The Secretary shall, by regulation, prescribe the period or event for which such return shall be filed, the time for filing such return, the information to be shown in such return, and the time for payment of such tax.

(b) Exceptions.

Notwithstanding the provisions of subsection (a), any taxes imposed on, or amounts to be paid or collected in respect of, distilled spirits, wines, and beer under—

(1) section 5001(a)(4), (5), or (6),
(2) section 5006(c) or (d),

3,401

Code Sec. 5061(b)(3) — Excise and miscellaneous taxes

(3) section 5041(f),
(4) section 5043(a)(3),
(5) section 5054(a)(3) or (4), or
(6) section 5505(a),

shall be immediately due and payable at the time provided by such provisions (or if no specific time for payment is provided, at the time the event referred to in such provision occurs). Such taxes and amounts shall be assessed and collected by the Secretary on the basis of the information available to him in the same manner as taxes payable by return but with respect to which no return has been filed.

(c) Import duties.

The internal revenue taxes imposed by this part shall be in addition to any import duties unless such duties are specifically designated as being in lieu of internal revenue tax.

(d) Time for collecting tax on distilled spirits, wines, and beer.

(1) In general. Except as otherwise provided in this subsection, in the case of distilled spirits, wines, and beer to which this part applies (other than subsection (b) of this section) which are withdrawn under bond for deferred payment of tax, the last day for payment of such tax shall be the 14th day after the last day of the semimonthly period during which the withdrawal occurs.

(2) Imported articles. In the case of distilled spirits, wines, and beer which are imported into the United States (other than in bulk containers)—

(A) In general. The last day for payment of tax shall be the 14th day after the last day of the semimonthly period during which the article is entered into the customs territory of the United States.

(B) Special rule for entry for warehousing. Except as provided in subparagraph (D), in the case of an entry for warehousing, the last day for payment of tax shall not be later than the 14th day after the last day of the semimonthly period during which the article is removed from the 1st such warehouse.

(C) Foreign trade zones. Except as provided in subparagraph (D) and in regulations prescribed by the Secretary, articles brought into a foreign trade zone shall, notwithstanding any other provision of law, be treated for purposes of this subsection as if such zone were a single customs warehouse.

(D) Exception for articles destined for export. Subparagraphs (B) and (C) shall not apply to any article which is shown to the satisfaction of the Secretary to be destined for export.

(3) Distilled spirits, wines, and beer brought into the United States from Puerto Rico. In the case of distilled spirits, wines, and beer which are brought into the United States (other than in bulk containers) from Puerto Rico, the last day for payment of tax shall be the 14th day after the last day of the semimonthly period during which the article is brought into the United States.

(4) Taxpayers liable for taxes of not more than $50,000.

(A) In general. In the case of any taxpayer who reasonably expects to be liable for not more than $50,000 in taxes imposed with respect to distilled spirits, wines, and beer under subparts A, C, and D and section 7652 for the calendar year and who was liable for not more than $50,000 in such taxes in the preceding calendar year, the last day for the payment of tax on withdrawals, removals, and entries (and articles brought into the United States from Puerto Rico) under bond for deferred payment shall be the 14th day after the last day of the calendar quarter during which the action giving rise to the imposition of such tax occurs.

(B) No application after limit exceeded. Subparagraph (A) shall not apply to any taxpayer for any portion of the calendar year following the first date on which the aggregate amount of tax due under subparts A, C, and D and section 7652 from such taxpayer during such calendar year exceeds $50,000, and any tax under such subparts which has not been paid on such date shall be due on the 14th day after the last day of the semimonthly period in which such date occurs.

(C) Calendar quarter. For purposes of this paragraph, the term "calendar quarter" means the three-month period ending on March 31, June 30, September 30, or December 31.

(5) Special rule for tax due in September.

(A) In general. Notwithstanding the preceding provisions of this subsection, the taxes on distilled spirits, wines, and beer for the period beginning on September 16 and ending on September 26 shall be paid not later than September 29.

(B) Safe harbor. The requirement of subparagraph (A) shall be treated as met if the amount paid not later than September 29 is not less than 11/15 of the taxes on distilled spirits, wines, and beer for the period beginning on September 1 and ending on September 15.

(C) Taxpayers not required to use electronic funds transfer. In the case of payments not required to be made by electronic funds transfer, subparagraphs (A) and (B) shall be applied by substituting "September 25" for "September 26", "September 28" for "September 29", and "2/3" for "11/15".

(6) Special rule where due date falls on Saturday, Sunday, or holiday. Notwithstanding section 7503, if, but for this paragraph, the due date under this subsection for payment of tax would fall on a Saturday, Sunday, or a legal holiday (within the meaning of section 7503), such due date shall be the immediately preceding day which is not a Saturday, Sunday, or such a holiday (or the immediately following day where the due date described in paragraph (5) falls on a Sunday).

(e) Payment by electronic fund transfer.

(1) In general. Any person who in any 12-month period ending December 31, was liable for a gross amount equal to or exceeding $5,000,000 in taxes imposed on distilled spirits, wines, or beer by sections 5001, 5041, and 5051 (or 7652), respectively, shall pay such taxes during the succeeding calendar year by electronic fund transfer to a Federal Reserve Bank.

(2) Electronic fund transfer. The term "electronic fund transfer" means any transfer of funds, other than a transaction originated by check, draft, or similar paper instrument, which is initiated through an electronic terminal, telephonic instrument, or computer or magnetic tape so as to order, instruct, or authorize a financial institution to debit or credit an account.

(3) Controlled groups.

(A) In general. In the case of a controlled group of corporations, all corporations which are component members of such group shall be treated as 1 taxpayer. For purposes of the preceding sentence, the term "controlled group of corporations" has the meaning given to such term by subsection (a) of section 1563, except that "more than 50 percent" shall be substituted for "at least 80 percent" each place it appears in such subsection.

"(B) Controlled groups which include nonincorporated persons. Under regulations prescribed by the Secretary, principles similar to the principles of subparagraph (A) shall apply to a group of persons under common control where 1 or more of such persons is not a corporation.

In 2005, P.L. 109-59, Sec. 11127(a), redesignated paras. (d)(4) and (5) as paras. (d)(5) and (6), and added para. (d)(4)... Sec. 11127(b), substituted "paragraph (5)" for "paragraph (4)" in para. (d)(6) [as redesignated by Sec. 11127(a) of this Act, see above], effective for quarterly periods begin. on and after 1/1/2006.
In 1996, P.L. 104-188, Sec. 1702(b)(6), amended para. (b)(3), effective 1/1/91.
Prior to amendment, para. (b)(3) read as follows:
"(3) section 5041(e),".
In 1994, P.L. 103-465, Sec. 136(c)(5), amended para. (b)(1), effective 1/1/95.
Prior to amendment, para. (b)(1) read as follows:
"(1) section 5001(a)(5), (6), or (7),"
—P.L. 103-465, Sec. 712(b)(1), redesignated para. (d)(4) as para. (d)(5) and added new para. (d)(4)... Sec. 712(b)(2)(A), added "(or the immediately following day where the due date described in paragraph (4) falls on a Sunday)" before the period in para. (d)(5) [as redesignated by Sec. 712(b)(1) of this Act, see above]... Sec. 712(b)(2)(B), substituted "due date" for "14th day" in heading of para. (d)(5) [as redesignated by Sec. 712(b)(1) of this Act, see above], effective 1/1/95.
In 1990, P.L. 101-508, Sec. 11201(b)(3), amended para. (b)(3) [same amendment as made by Sec. 11704(a)(21) of this Act, see below], effective 1/1/91.
Prior to amendment, para. (b)(3) read as follows:
"(3) section 5041(d)."
—P.L. 101-508, Sec. 11704(a)(21), amended para. (b)(3), [same amendment as made by Sec. 11201(b)(3) of this Act, see above] effective 11/5/90.
Prior to amendment, para. (b)(3) read as follows:
"(3) section 5041(d)."
—P.L. 101-508, Sec. 11201(e), regarding floor stocks taxes, is reproduced in note following Code Sec. 5001.
—P.L. 101-508, Sec. 11218, regarding floor stocks tax treatment of articles in foreign trade zones, is reproduced in note following Code Sec. 5001.
In 1988, P.L. 100-647, Sec. 2003(b)(1)(A), and (B), substituted "the 14th day after the last day of the semimonthly period during which" for "the 14th day after the date on which" in subparas. (d)(2)(A) and (d)(2)(B) and para. (d)(3), effective for removals during semimonthly periods end. on or after 12/31/86.
In 1986, P.L. 99-514, Sec. 1801(c)(1), added para. (e)(3), effective for taxes required to be paid on or after 9/30/84.
—P.L. 99-509, Sec. 8011(b)(1), amended subsec. (d), effective for removals during semimonthly periods end. on or after 12/31/86. Sec. 8011(c)(2) of this Act provides:
"(2) Imported articles, etc. Subparagraphs (B) and (C) of section 5703(b)(2) of the Internal Revenue Code of 1954 (as added by this section), paragraphs (2) and (3) of section 5061(d) of such Code (as amended by this section), and the amendments made by subsections (a)(2) and (b)(2) [Sec. 8011] shall apply to articles imported, entered for warehousing, or brought into the United States or a foreign trade zone after December 15, 1986."
Prior to amendment, subsec. (d) read as follows:
"(d) Extension of time for collecting tax on distilled spirits.
"In the case of distilled spirits to which subsection (a) applies which are withdrawn from the bonded premises of a distilled spirits plant under bond for deferred payment of tax, the last day for filing a return (with remittances) for each semimonthly return period shall be determined under the following table:

"If the return period is in—	Such last day shall be—
1980	The last day of the first succeeding return period plus 5 days.
1981	The last day of the first succeeding return period plus 10 days.
1982 or any year thereafter	The last day of the second succeeding return period."

In 1984, P.L. 98-369, Sec. 27(c)(1), added subsec. (e), effective for taxes required to be paid on or after 9/30/84.
In 1979, P.L. 96-39, Sec. 804(b), added subsec. (d), effective 1/1/80.
—P.L. 96-39, Sec. 807(a)(9)(A), deleted "rectified distilled spirits and wines," in subsecs. (a) and (b)... Sec. 807(a)(9)(B), deleted para. (b)(3) and redesignated paras. (b)(4)—(b)(7) as paras. (b)(3)—(b)(6), effective 1/1/80.
Sec. 808 of the Act provides as follows:
"Sec. 808. Transitional rules relating to determination and payment of tax.
"(a) Liability for payment of tax.
"Except as otherwise provided in this section, the tax on distilled spirits which have been withdrawn from bond on determination of tax and on which tax has not been paid by the close of December 31, 1979, shall become due on January 1, 1980, and shall be payable in accordance with section 5061 of the Internal Revenue Code of 1954.
"(b) Treatment of controlled stock and bulk wine.
"(1) Election with respect to controlled stock. The proprietor of a distilled spirits plant may elect to convert any distilled spirits or wine which on January 1, 1980, is controlled stock.

"(2) Election with respect to wine. The proprietor of a distilled spirits plant may elect to convert any bulk wine which on January 1, 1980, is on the premises of a distilled spirits plant.
"(3) Effect of election. If an election under paragraph (1) or (2) is in effect with respect to any controlled stock or wine—
"(A) any distilled spirits, wine, or rectification tax previously paid or determined on such controlled stock or wine shall be abated or (without interest) credited or refunded under such regulations as the Secretary shall prescribe, and
"(B) such controlled stock or wine shall be treated as distilled spirits or wine on which tax has not been paid or determined.
"(4) Making of elections. The elections under this subsection shall be made at such time in such manner as the Secretary by regulations prescribe.
"(c) Taxpaid stock.
"(1) Taxpaid stock may remain on bonded premises during 1980. Section 5612(a) of the Internal Revenue Code of 1954 (relating to forfeiture of taxpaid distilled spirits remaining on bonded premises) shall not apply during 1980.
"(2) Separation of taxpaid stock. All distilled spirits and wine on which tax has been paid and which are on the bonded premises of a distilled spirits plant shall be physically separated from other distilled spirits and wine. Such separation shall be by the use of separate tanks, rooms, or buildings, or by partitioning, or by such other methods as the Secretary finds will distinguish such distilled spirits and wine from other distilled spirits and wine on the bonded premises of the distilled spirits plant.
"(d) Return of distilled spirits products containing taxpaid wine.
"With respect to distilled spirits returned to the bonded premises of distilled spirits plants during 1980, section 5008(c)(1) of the Internal Revenue Code of 1954 (relating to refunds for distilled spirits returned to bonded premises) shall be treated as including a reference to section 5041 of such Code.
"(e) Return of distilled spirits products containing other alcoholic ingredients.
"With respect to distilled spirits to which alcoholic ingredients other than distilled spirits have been added and which have been withdrawn from a distilled spirits plant before January 1, 1980, section 5215(a) of the Internal Revenue Code of 1951 shall apply only if such spirits are returned to the distilled spirits plant from which withdrawn.
"(f) Secretary defined.
"For purposes of this section, the term 'Secretary' means the Secretary of the Treasury or his delegate."
Prior to deletion, para. (b)(3) read as follows:
"(3) section 5026(a)(2),".
In 1976, P.L. 94-455, Sec. 1905(a)(6)(A), deleted the last sentence in subsec. (a)... Sec. 1905(a)(6)(B), amended subsec. (b)... Sec. 1905(a)(6)(C), amended subsec. (c), effective 2/1/77.
Prior to deletion, the last sentence in subsec. (a) read as follows:
"Notwithstanding the preceding sentences of this subsection, the taxes shall continue to be paid by stamp until the Secretary or his delegate shall by regulations provide for the collection of the taxes on the basis of a return."
Prior to amendment, subsecs. (b) and (c) read as follows:
"(b) Discretion method of collection.
"Whether or not the method of collecting any tax imposed by this part is specifically provided in this part, any such tax may, under regulations prescribed by the Secretary or his delegate, be collected by stamp, coupon, serially-numbered ticket, or the use of tax-stamp machines, or by such other reasonable device or method as may be necessary or helpful in securing collection of the tax."
"(c) Applicability of other provisions of law.
"All administrative and penalty provisions of this title, insofar as applicable, shall apply to the collection of any tax which the Secretary or his delegate determines or prescribes shall be collected in any manner provided in this section."
—P.L. 94-455, Sec. 1905(b)(2)(E)(iii), deleted subsec. (d), effective 2/1/77.
Prior to amendment, subsec. (d) read as follows:
"(d) Cross reference.
"For penalty and forfeiture for tampering with a stamp machine, see section 5689."
—P.L. 94-455, Sec. 1906(b)(13)(A), substituted "Secretary" for "Secretary or his delegate" in subsec (a), effective 2/1/77.

Sec. 5062. Refund and drawback in case of exportation.
(a) Refund.
Under such regulations as the Secretary may prescribe, the amount of any internal revenue tax erroneously or illegally collected in respect to exported articles may be refunded to the exporter of the article, instead of to the manufacturer, if the manufacturer waives any claim for the amount so to be refunded.

(b) Drawback.
On the exportation of distilled spirits or wines manufactured, produced, bottled, or packaged in casks or other bulk containers in the United States on which an internal revenue tax has been paid or determined, and which are contained in any cask or other bulk container, or in bottles packed in cases or other containers, there shall be allowed, under regulations prescribed by the Secretary, a drawback equal in amount to the tax found to have been paid or determined on

such distilled spirits or wines. In the case of distilled spirits, the preceding sentence shall not apply unless the claim for drawback is filed by the bottler or packager of the spirits and unless such spirits have been marked, especially for export, under regulations prescribed by the Secretary. The Secretary is authorized to prescribe regulations governing the determination and payment or crediting of drawback of internal revenue tax on spirits and wines eligible for drawback under this subsection, including the requirements of such notices, bonds, bills of lading, and other evidence indicating payment or determination of tax and exportation as shall be deemed necessary.

(c) Exportation of imported liquors.

(1) Allowance of tax. Upon the exportation of imported distilled spirits, wines, and beer upon which the duties and internal revenue taxes have been paid or determined incident to their importation into the United States, and which have been found after entry to be unmerchantable or not to conform to sample or specifications, and which have been returned to customs custody, the Secretary shall, under such regulations as he shall prescribe, refund, remit, abate, or credit, without interest, to the importer thereof, the full amount of the internal revenue taxes paid or determined with respect to such distilled spirits, wines, or beer.

(2) Destruction in lieu of exportation. At the option of the importer, such imported distilled spirits, wines, and beer, after return to customs custody, may be destroyed under customs supervision and the importer thereof granted relief in the same manner and to the same extent as provided in this subsection upon exportation.

In 1990, P.L. 101-508, Sec. 11201(e), regarding floor stocks taxes, is reproduced in note following Code Sec. 5001.

—P.L. 101-508, Sec. 11218, regarding floor stocks tax treatment of articles in foreign trade zones, is reproduced in note following Code Sec. 5001.

In 1984, P.L. 98-369, Sec. 454(c)(1), deleted "stamped or restamped, and" after "such spirits have been" in the second sentence of subsec. (b), effective 7/1/85.

In 1977, P.L. 95-176, Sec. 1, amended subsec. (b), effective the first day of the first calendar month which begins more than 90 days after 11/14/77.

Prior to amendment, subsec. (b) read as follows:

"(b) Drawback.

"On the exportation of distilled spirits or wines manufactured or produced in the United States on which an internal revenue tax has been paid or determined, and which are contained in any cask or package, or in bottles packed in cases or other containers, there shall be allowed, under regulations prescribed by the Secretary, a drawback equal in amount to the tax found to have been paid or determined on such distilled spirits or wines. In the case of distilled spirits, the preceding sentence shall not apply unless the claim for drawback is filed by the bottler or packager of the spirits and unless such spirits have been stamped or restamped, and marked, especially for export, under regulations prescribed by the Secretary. The Secretary is authorized to prescribe regulations governing the determination and payment or crediting of drawback of internal revenue tax on domestic distilled spirits and wines, including the requirement of such notices, bonds, bills of lading, and other evidence indicating payment or determination of tax and exportation as shall be deemed necessary."

In 1976, P.L. 94-455, Sec. 1906(b)(13)(A), substituted "Secretary" for "Secretary or his delegate" each place it appeared in Code Sec. 5062, effective 2/1/77.

In 1968, P.L. 90-630, Sec. 2(a), amended the second sentence of subsec. (b), effective for articles exported on or after the first day of the first calendar month which begins more than 90 days after 10/26/68.

Prior to amendment, the second sentence of subsec. (b) read as follows:

"The preceding sentence shall not apply unless such distilled spirits have been packaged or bottled especially for export, or, in the case of distilled spirits originally bottled for domestic use, have been restamped and marked especially for export at the distilled spirits plant where originally bottled and before removal therefrom, under regulations prescribed by the Secretary or his delegate."

In 1965, P.L. 89-44, Sec. 805(f)(6), deleted "within six months of their release therefrom" after "customs custody", in para. (c)(1), effective 7/1/65.

In 1964, P.L. 88-539, added subsec. (c), effective for articles exported or destroyed after 8/31/64.

Sec. 5063. Repealed.

In 1965, P.L. 89-44, Sec. 501(e), repealed Code Sec. 5063, effective 7/1/65.
Prior to repeal, Code Sec. 5063, read as follows:
"SEC. 5063. FLOOR STOCKS TAX REFUNDS ON DISTILLED SPIRITS, WINES, CORDIALS AND BEER.

"(a) General.

"With respect to any article upon which tax is imposed under this part, upon which internal revenue tax (including floor stocks tax) at the applicable rate prescribed has been paid or determined, and which, on July 1, 1965, is held by any person and intended for sale or for use in the manufacture or production of any article intended for sale, there shall be credited or refunded to such person (without interest), subject to such regulations as may be prescribed by the Secretary or his delegate, an amount equal to the difference between the tax so paid or determined and the rate made applicable to such articles on and after July 1, 1965, if claim for such credit or refund is filed with the Secretary or his delegate prior to October 1, 1965, or within 30 days from the promulgation of such regulations, whichever is later.

"(b) Limitations on eligibility for credit or refund.

"No person shall be entitled to credit or refund under subsection (a), unless such person, for such period or periods both before and after July 1, 1965 (but not extending beyond 1 year thereafter), as the Secretary or his delegate shall by regulations prescribe, makes and keeps, and files with the Secretary or his delegate, such records of inventories, sales, and purchases as may be prescribed in such regulations.

"(c) Other laws applicable.

"All provisions of law, including penalties, applicable in respect of internal revenue taxes on distilled spirits, wines, liqueurs and cordials, imported perfumes containing distilled spirits, and beer shall, insofar as applicable and not inconsistent with this section, be applicable in respect of the credits and refunds provided for in this section to the same extent as if such credits or refunds constituted credits or refunds of such taxes."

In 1964, P.L. 88-348, Sec. 2(b)(1)(A), substituted "July 1, 1965" for "July 1, 1964" in three instances and "October 1, 1965" for "October 1, 1964".

In 1963, P.L. 88-52, Sec. 3(b)(1)(A), substituted "July 1, 1964" for "July 1, 1963" in three instances and "October 1, 1964" for "October 1, 1963".

In 1962, P.L. 87-508, Sec. 3(b)(1), substituted "July 1, 1963" for "July 1, 1962" in three instances and "October 1, 1963" for "October 1, 1962".

In 1961, P.L. 87-72, Sec. 3(b)(1), substituted "July 1, 1962" for "July 1, 1961" in three instances and "October 1, 1962" for "October 1, 1961".

In 1960, P.L. 86-564, Sec. 202(b)(1), substituted "July 1, 1961" for "July 1, 1960" in three instances, and "October 1, 1961" for "October 1, 1960".

In 1959, P.L. 86-75, Sec. 3(b)(1), substituted "July 1, 1960" for "July 1, 1959" in three places and "October 1, 1960" for "October 1, 1959".

Sec. 5064. Losses resulting from disaster, vandalism, or malicious mischief.

(a) Payments.

The Secretary, under such regulations as he may prescribe, shall pay (without interest) an amount equal to the amount of the internal revenue taxes paid or determined and customs duties paid on distilled spirits, wines, and beer previously withdrawn, which were lost, rendered unmarketable, or condemned by a duly authorized official by reason of—

(1) fire, flood, casualty, or other disaster, or

(2) breakage, destruction, or other damage (but not including theft) resulting from vandalism or malicious mischief,

if such disaster or damage occurred in the United States and if such distilled spirits, wines, or beer were held and intended for sale at the time of such disaster or other damage. The payments provided for in this section shall be made to the person holding such distilled spirits, wines, or beer for sale at the time of such disaster or other damage.

(b) Claims.

(1) Period for making claim; proof. No claim shall be allowed under this section unless—

(A) filed within 6 months after the date on which such distilled spirits, wines, or beer were lost, rendered unmarketable, or condemned by a duly authorized official, and

(B) the claimant furnishes proof satisfactory to the Secretary that the claimant—

(i) was not indemnified by any valid claim of insurance or otherwise in respect of the tax, or tax and duty, on the distilled spirits, wines, or beer covered by the claim; and

(ii) is entitled to payment under this section.

(2) Minimum claim. Except as provided in paragraph (3)(A), no claim of less than $250 shall be allowed under this section with respect to any disaster or other damage (as the case may be).

Excise and miscellaneous taxes — Code Sec. 5066(c)

(3) Special rules for major disasters. If the President has determined under the Robert T. Stafford Disaster Relief and Emergency Assistance Act that a "major disaster" (as defined in such Act) has occurred in any part of the United States, and if the disaster referred to in subsection (a)(1) occurs in such part of the United States by reason of such major disaster, then—

(A) paragraph (2) shall not apply, and

(B) the filing period set forth in paragraph (1)(A) shall not expire before the day which is 6 months after the date on which the President makes the determination that such major disaster has occurred.

(4) Regulations. Claims under this section shall be filed under such regulations as the Secretary shall prescribe.

(c) Destruction of distilled spirits, wines, or beer.

When the Secretary has made payment under this section in respect of the tax, or tax and duty, on the distilled spirits, wines, or beer condemned by a duly authorized official or rendered unmarketable, such distilled spirits, wines, or beer shall be destroyed under such supervision as the Secretary may prescribe, unless such distilled spirits, wines, or beer were previously destroyed under supervision satisfactory to the Secretary.

(d) Products of Puerto Rico.

The provisions of this section shall not be applicable in respect of distilled spirits, wines, and beer of Puerto Rican manufacture brought into the United States and so lost or rendered unmarketable or condemned.

(e) Other laws applicable.

All provisions of law, including penalties, applicable in respect of internal revenue taxes on distilled spirits, wines, and beer shall, insofar as applicable and not inconsistent with this section, be applied in respect of the payments provided for in this section to the same extent as if such payments constituted refunds of such taxes.

In **2004**, P.L. 108-311, Sec. 408(a)(7)(D), added "Robert T. Stafford" before "Disaster Relief and Emergency Assistance Act" in para. (b)(3), enacted 10/4/2004.

In **1990**, P.L. 101-508, Sec. 11201(e), regarding floor stocks taxes, is reproduced in note following Code Sec. 5001.

—P.L. 101-508, Sec. 11218, regarding floor stocks tax treatment of articles in foreign trade zones, is reproduced in note following Code Sec. 5001.

In **1988**, P.L. 100-707, Sec. 109(1), substituted "and Emergency Assistance Act" for "Act of 1974" in para. (b)(3), effective 11/23/88.

In **1979**, P.L. 96-39, Sec. 807(a)(10), deleted "rectified products," each place it appeared in Code Sec. 5064, effective 1/1/80.

In **1978**, P.L. 95-423, Sec. 1(a), amended the heading and subsecs. (a) and (b), effective for disasters occurring on or after 2/1/79 (the first day of the first calendar month which begins more than 90 days after 10/6/78, date of enactment. Prior to amendment the heading and subsecs. (a) and (b) read as follows:

"SEC. 5064. LOSSES CAUSED BY DISASTER.

"(a) Authorization.

"Where the President has determined under the Disaster Relief Act of 1974, that a 'major disaster' as defined in such Act has occurred in any part of the United States, the Secretary shall pay (without interest) an amount equal to the amount of the internal revenue taxes paid or determined and customs duties paid on distilled spirits, wines, rectified products, and beer previously withdrawn, which were lost, rendered unmarketable, or condemned by a duly authorized official by reason of such disaster occurring in such part of the United Stats after June 30, 1959, if such distilled spirits, wines, rectified products, or beer were held and intended for sale at the time of such disaster. The payments authorized by this section shall be made to the person holding such distilled spirits, wines, rectified products, or beer for sale at the time of such disaster.

"(b) Claims.

"No claim shall be allowed under this section unless—

"(1) filed within 6 months after the date on which the President makes the determination that the disaster referred to in subsection (a) has occurred; and

"(2) the claimant furnishes proof to the satisfaction of the Secretary or his delegate that—

"(A) he was not indemnified by any valid claim of insurance or otherwise in respect of the tax, or tax and duty, on the distilled spirits, wines, rectified products, or beer covered by the claim; and

"(B) he is entitled to payment under this section.

"Claims under this section shall be filed under such regulations as the Secretary shall prescribe."

In **1976**, P.L. 94-455, Sec. 1906(b)(13)(A), substituted "Secretary" for "Secretary or his delegate" in subsecs. (a), (b) and (c), effective 2/1/77.

In **1974**, P.L. 93-288, Sec. 602(i), substituted "Disaster Relief Act of 1974" for "Disaster Relief Act of 1970" in subsec. (a), effective 4/1/74.

In **1970**, P.L. 91-606, Sec. 301(i), substituted "Disaster Relief Act of 1970" for "Act of September 30, 1950 (42 U.S.C., sec. 1855)" in subsec. (a), effective 12/31/70.

Sec. 5065. Territorial extent of law.

The provisions of this part imposing taxes on distilled spirits, wines, and beer shall be held to extend to such articles produced anywhere within the exterior boundaries of the United States, whether the same be within an internal revenue district or not.

In **1990**, P.L. 101-508, Sec. 11201(e), regarding floor stocks taxes, is reproduced in note following Code Sec. 5001.

—P.L. 101-508, Sec. 11218, regarding floor stocks tax treatment of articles in foreign trade zones, is reproduced in note following Code Sec. 5001.

Sec. 5066. Distilled spirits for use of foreign embassies, legations, etc.

(a) Entry into customs bonded warehouses.

(1) Bottled distilled spirits withdrawn from bonded premises. Under such regulations as the Secretary may prescribe, bottled distilled spirits may be withdrawn from bonded premises as provided in section 5214(a)(4) for transfer to customs bonded warehouses in which imported distilled spirits are permitted to be stored in bond for entry therein pending withdrawal therefrom as provided in subsection (b). For the purposes of this chapter, the withdrawal of distilled spirits from bonded premises under the provisions of this paragraph shall be treated as a withdrawal for exportation and all provisions of law applicable to distilled spirits withdrawn for exportation under the provisions of section 5214(a)(4) shall apply with respect to spirits withdrawn under this paragraph.

(2) Bottled distilled spirits eligible for export with benefit of drawback. Under such regulations as the Secretary may prescribe, distilled spirits marked especially for export under the provisions of section 5062(b) may be shipped to a customs bonded warehouse in which imported distilled spirits are permitted to be stored, and entered in such warehouses pending withdrawal therefrom as provided in subsection (b), and the provisions of this chapter shall apply in respect of such distilled spirits as if such spirits were for exportation.

(3) Time deemed exported. For the purposes of this chapter, distilled spirits entered into a customs bonded warehouse as provided in this subsection shall be deemed exported at the time so entered.

(b) Withdrawal from customs bonded warehouses.

Notwithstanding any other provisions of law, distilled spirits entered into customs bonded warehouses under the provisions of subsection (a) may, under such regulations as the Secretary may prescribe, be withdrawn from such warehouses for consumption in the United States by and for the official or family use of such foreign governments, organizations, and individuals who are entitled to withdraw imported distilled spirits from such warehouses free of tax. Distilled spirits transferred to customs bonded warehouses under the provisions of this section shall be entered, stored, and accounted for in such warehouses under such regulations and bonds as the Secretary may prescribe, and may be withdrawn therefrom by such governments, organizations, and individuals free of tax under the same conditions and procedures as imported distilled spirits.

(c) Withdrawal for domestic use.

Distilled spirits entered into customs bonded warehouses as authorized by this section may be withdrawn therefrom for domestic use, in which event they shall be treated as American goods exported and returned.

(d) Sale or unauthorized use prohibited.

No distilled spirits withdrawn from customs bonded warehouses or otherwise brought into the United States free of tax for the official or family use of such foreign governments, organizations, or individuals as are authorized to obtain distilled spirits free of tax shall be sold, or shall be disposed of or possessed for any use other than an authorized use. The provisions of section 5001(a)(5) are hereby extended and made applicable to any person selling, disposing of, or possessing any distilled spirits in violation of the preceding sentence, and to the distilled spirits involved in any such violation.

In **1990**, P.L. 101-508, Sec. 11201(e), regarding floor stocks taxes, is reproduced in note following Code Sec. 5001.
— P.L. 101-508, Sec. 11218, regarding floor stocks tax treatment of articles in foreign trade zones, is reproduced in note following Code Sec. 5001.
In **1984**, P.L. 98-369, Sec. 454(c)(2), substituted "marked" for "stamped or restamped, and marked," in para. (a)(2), effective 7/1/85.
In **1979**, P.L. 96-39, Sec. 807(a)(11)(A), substituted "bottled distilled spirits" for "distilled spirits bottled in bond for export under the provisions of section 5233, or bottled distilled spirits returned to bonded premises under section 5215(b)," in para. (a)(1) . . . Sec. 807(a)(11)(B), substituted "under the provisions of subsection (a), may" for "under the provisions of subsection (a) or domestic distilled spirits transferred to customs bonded warehouses under section 5521(d) may" in subsec. (b), effective 1/1/80.
In **1977**, P.L. 95-176, Sec. 2(d), amended the heading and the first sentence of para. (a)(1), effective 3/1/78 [the first day of the first calendar month which begins more than 90 days after 11/14/77, the date of enactment].
Prior to amendment, the heading and first sentence of para. (a)(1) read as follows:
"(1) Distilled spirits bottled in bond for export. Under such regulations as the Secretary may prescribe, distilled spirits bottled in bond for export under the provisions of section 5233 may be withdrawn from bonded premises as provided in section 5214(a)(4) for transfer to customs bonded warehouses in which imported distilled spirits are permitted to be stored in bond for entry therein pending withdrawal therefrom as provided in subsection (b)."
In **1976**, P.L. 94-455, Sec. 1906(b)(13)(A), substituted "Secretary" for "Secretary or his delegate" each place it appeared in subsecs. (a) and (b), effective 2/1/77.
In **1971**, P.L. 91-659, Sec. 3(a), added Code Sec. 5066, effective 5/1/71.

Sec. 5067. Cross reference.

For general administrative provisions applicable to the assessment, collection, refund, etc., of taxes, see subtitle F.

In **1990**, P.L. 101-508, Sec. 11201(e), regarding floor stocks taxes, is reproduced in note following Code Sec. 5001.
— P.L. 101-508, Sec. 11218, regarding floor stocks tax treatment of articles in foreign trade zones, is reproduced in note following Code Sec. 5001.
In **1971**, P.L. 91-659, Sec. 3(a), redesignated Code Sec. 5066 as Code Sec. 5067, effective 5/1/71.

PART II.— MISCELLANEOUS PROVISIONS

Subpart
A. Repealed. [Proprietors of distilled spirits plants, bonded wine cellars, etc.]
B. Repealed. [Brewer.]
A. Manufacturer of stills.
B. Nonbeverage domestic drawback claimants.
C. Recordkeeping and registration by dealers.
D. Repealed. [Wholesale dealers.]
D. Other provisions.
E. Repealed. [Retail dealers.]
G. Repealed. [General provisions.]

In **2005**, P.L. 109-59, Sec. 11125(a)(1)(A), repealed subpart A. . . . Sec. 11125(a)(1)(B), repealed subpart B. . . . Sec. 11125(a)(1)(C), repealed subpart D. . . . Sec. 11125(a)(1)(D), repealed subpart E. . . . Sec. 11125(a)(1)(E), repealed subpart G (other than sections 5142, 5143, 5145, and 5156). . . . Sec. 11125(b)(1)(A), amended the heading and table of subparts for part II. . . . Sec. 11125(b)(1)(C), Subpart C is redesignated as subpart A. . . . Sec. 11125(b)(3)(A), Subpart F is redesignated as subpart B. . . . Sec. 11125(c)(4), added new subpart C, as redesignated. . . . Sec. 11125(c)(10), added new subpart D.
In **1979**, P.L. 96-39, Sec. 807(b)(3), deleted the item for Subpart A.

Prior to deletion the item for Subpart A read as follows:
"A. Rectifier."

SUBPART A. REPEALED. [PROPRIETORS OF DISTILLED SPIRITS PLANTS, BONDED WINE CELLARS, ETC.]

Sec. 5081. Repealed. [Imposition and rate of tax.]

In **2005**, P.L. 109-59, Sec. 11125(a)(1)(A), repealed subpart A.
In **1987**, P.L. 100-203, Sec. 10512(a)(1)(A), added new subpart A to Part II of Subchapter A of Chapter 51.
In **1979**, P.L. 96-39, Sec. 803(b), repealed Code Secs. 5081, 5082, 5083 and 5084, effective 1/1/80.
Prior to repeal, Code Secs. 5081, 5082, 5083 and 5084 read as follows:
"SEC. 5081. IMPOSITION AND RATE OF TAX.
"Every rectifier of distilled spirits or wines (as defined in section 5082) shall pay a special tax of $220 a year, except that any rectifier of less than 20,000 proof gallons a year shall pay $110 a year."
"SEC. 5082. DEFINITION OF RECTIFIER.
"Every person who rectifies, purifies, or refines distilled spirits or wines by any process (other than by original and continuous distillation, or original and continuous processing, from mash, wort, wash, or any other substance, through continuous closed vessels and pipes, until the production thereof is complete), and every person who, without rectifying, purifying, or refining distilled spirits, shall by mixing such spirits, wine, or other liquor with any material, manufacture any spurious, imitation, or compound liquors for sale, under the name of whisky, brandy, rum, gin, wine, spirits, cordials, or wine bitters, or any other name, shall be regarded as a rectifier, and as being engaged in the business of rectifying."
"SEC. 5083. EXEMPTIONS.
"For exemptions from tax under section 5021 or 5081 in case of —
"(1) Absolute alcohol, see section 5025(a).
"(2) Production of gin and vodka, see section 5025(b).
"(3) Refining spirits in course of original distillation, see section 5025(c).
"(4) Redistillation of spirits on bonded premises of a distilled spirits plant, see section 5025(d).
"(5) Mingling of distilled spirits on bonded premises of a distilled spirits plant, see section 5025(e).
"(6) Apothecaries, see section 5025(h).
"(7) Manufacturers of chemicals and flavoring extracts, see section 5025(i).
"(8) Distilled spirits wines rectified in customs manufacturing bonded warehouses, see section 5523.
"(9) Blending beverage brandies or rums on bonded premises of a distilled spirits plant, see section 5025(c)(4).
"(10) Blending of straight whiskies, fruit brandies, rums or wines, see section 5025(f).
"(11) Addition of caramel to brandy or rum, see section 5025(g).
"(12) Winemakers' use or treatment of wines or wine spirits, see section 5391.
"(13) Stabilization of distilled spirits, see section 5025(j).
"(14) Other mingling or treatment of distilled spirits, see section 5025(k).
"(15) Authorized addition of tracer elements, see section 5025(l)."
In **1965**, amended subsec. (14) and added subsec. (15), effective 10/1/65.
Before amendment subsec. (14) read as follows:
"(14) Authorized addition of tracer elements, see section 5025(k)."
"SEC. 5084. CROSS REFERENCES.
"(1) For provisions relating to gallonage tax on rectification, see subpart B of part 1 of this subchapter.
"(2) For provisions relating to qualification of distilled spirits plants to engage in rectification, see subchapter B.
"(3) For provisions relating to rectifying operations on the premises of distilled spirits plants, see subchapter C.
"(4) For penalties, seizures, and forfeitures relating to rectifying and rectified products, see subchapter J and subtitle F."

Sec. 5081. Repealed.

In **2005**, P.L. 109-59, Sec. 11125(a)(1)(A), repealed Code Sec. 5081, effective 7/1/2008, but not for taxes imposed for periods before 7/1/2008.
Prior to repeal, Code Sec. 5081 read as follows:
"SEC. 5081. IMPOSITION AND RATE OF TAX.
"(a) General rule. Every proprietor of —
"(1) a distilled spirits plant,
"(2) a bonded wine cellar,
"(3) a bonded wine warehouse, or
"(4) a taxpaid wine bottling house,
"shall pay a tax of $1,000 per year in respect of each such premises.
"(b) Reduced rates for small proprietors.
"(1) In general. Subsection (a) shall be applied by substituting "$500" for "$1,000" with respect to any taxpayer not described in subsection (c) the gross receipts of which (for the most recent taxable year ending before the 1st day of the taxable period to which the tax imposed by subsection (a) relates) are less than $500,000.

Exercise and miscellaneous taxes — Code Sec. 5103

"(2) Controlled group rules. All persons treated as 1 taxpayer under section 5061(e)(3) shall be treated as 1 taxpayer for purposes of paragraph (1).

"(3) Certain rules to apply. For purposes of paragraph (1), rules similar to the rules of subparagraphs (B) and (C) of section 448(c)(3) shall apply.

"(c) Exemption for small producers. Subsection (a) shall not apply with respect to any taxpayer who is a proprietor of an eligible distilled spirits plant (as defined in section 5181(c)(4))."

In **1988**, P.L. 100-647, Sec. 6106(a), added subsec. (c)... Sec. 6106(b), added "not described in subsection (c)" after "taxpayer" in para. (b)(1), effective 7/1/89.

In **1987**, P.L. 100-203, Sec. 10512(a)(1)(A), added Code Sec. 5081, effective 1/1/88. Sec. 10512(h)(2) of this Act provides:

"All taxpayers treated as commencing in business on January 1, 1988.—

"(A) In general.— Any person engaged on January 1, 1988, in any trade or business which is subject to an occupational tax shall be treated for purposes of such tax as having 1st engaged in such trade or business on such date.

"(B) Limitation on amount of tax.— In the case of a taxpayer who paid an occupational tax in respect of any premises for any taxable period which began before January 1, 1988, and includes such date, the amount of the occupational tax imposed by reason of subparagraph (A) in respect of such premises shall not exceed an amount equal to ½ the excess (if any) of—

"(i) the rate of such tax as in effect on January 1, 1988, over

"(ii) the rate of such tax as in effect on December 31, 1987.

"(C) Occupational tax.— For purposes of this paragraph, the term 'occupational tax' means any tax imposed under part II of subchapter A of chapter 51, section 5276, section 5731, or section 5801 of the Internal Revenue Code of 1986 (as amended by this section).

"(D) Due date of tax.— The amount of any tax required to be paid by reason of this paragraph shall be due on April 1, 1988."

SUBPART B.— REPEALED. [BREWER]

Sec.

5091. Repealed. [Imposition and rate of tax.]
5092. Repealed. [Definition of brewer.]
5093. Repealed. [Cross references.]

In **2005**, P.L. 109-59, Sec. 11125(a)(1)(B), repealed subpart B.

Sec. 5091. Repealed.

In **2005**, P.L. 109-59, Sec. 11125(a)(1)(B), repealed Code Sec. 5091, effective 7/1/2008, but not for taxes imposed for periods before 7/1/2008.
Prior to repeal, Code Sec. 5091 read as follows:
"SEC. 5091. IMPOSITION AND RATE OF TAX.

"(a) General rule. Every brewer shall pay a tax of $1,000 per year in respect of each brewery.

"(b) Reduced rates for small brewers. Rules similar to the rules of section 5081(b) shall apply for purposes of subsection (a)."

In **1987**, P.L. 100-203, Sec. 10512(a)(2), amended Code Sec. 5091, effective 1/1/88. For special rule, see Sec. 10512(h)(2) of this Act, reproduced in note following Code Sec. 5081.
Prior to amendment, Code Sec. 5091 read as follows:
"SEC. 5091. IMPOSITION AND RATE OF TAX.

Every brewer shall pay $110 a year in respect of each brewery; except that any brewer of less than 500 barrels a year shall pay the sum of $55 a year. Any beer procured by a brewer in his own hogsheads, barrels, or kegs under the provisions of section 5413 shall be included in calculating the liability to brewers' special tax of both the brewer who produces the same and the brewer who procures the same."

Sec. 5092. Repealed.

In **2005**, P.L. 109-59, Sec. 11125(a)(1)(B), repealed Code Sec. 5092, effective 7/1/2008, but not for taxes imposed for periods before 7/1/2008.
Prior to repeal, Code Sec. 5092 read as follows:
"SEC. 5092. DEFINITION OF BREWER.

"Every person who brews beer (except a person who produces only beer exempt from tax under section 5053(e)) and every person who produces beer for sale shall be deemed to be a brewer."

In **1978**, P.L. 95-458, Sec. 2(b)(3), amended Code Sec. 5092, effective on the first day of the first calendar month which begins more than 90 days after 10/14/78.
Prior to amendment, Code Sec. 5092 read as follows:
"Sec. 5092. Definition of brewer.

"Every person who brews or produces beer for sale shall be deemed a brewer."

Sec. 5093. Repealed.

In **2005**, P.L. 109-59, Sec. 11125(a)(1)(B), repealed Code Sec. 5093, effective 7/1/2008, but not for taxes imposed for periods before 7/1/2008.
Prior to repeal, Code Sec. 5093 read as follows:

"SEC. 5093. CROSS REFERENCES.

"(1) For exemption of brewer from special tax as wholesale and retail dealer, see section 5113(a).

"(2) For provisions relating to liability for special tax for carrying on business in more than one location, see section 5143(c).

"(3) For exemption from special tax in case of sales made on purchaser dealers' premises, see section 5113(d)."

SUBPART A.— MANUFACTURERS OF STILLS

Sec.

5101. Notice of manufacture of still; notice of set up of still.
5102. Definition of manufacturer of stills.
5103. Repealed. [Exemptions.]
5105. Repealed. [Notice of manufacture of and permit to set up still.]
5106. Repealed. [Export.]

In **2005**, P.L. 109-59, Sec. 11125(b)(1)(C), Subpart C is redesignated as subpart A.
In **1984**, P.L. 98-369, Sec. 451(a), amended items 5101–5106.
Prior to amendment, items 5101–5106 read as follows:
"5101. Imposition and rate of tax.
"5102. Definition of manufacturer of stills.
"5103. Exemptions.
"5105. Notice of manufacture of and permit to set up still.
"5106. Export."

Sec. 5101. Notice of manufacture of still; notice of set up of still.

(a) Notice requirements.

(1) Notice of manufacture of still. The Secretary may, pursuant to regulations, require any person who manufactures any still, boiler, or other vessel to be used for the purpose of distilling, to give written notice, before the still, boiler, or other vessel is removed from the place of manufacture, setting forth by whom it is to be used, its capacity, and the time of removal from the place of manufacture.

(2) Notice of set up of still. The Secretary may, pursuant to regulations, require that no still, boiler, or other vessel be set up without the manufacturer of the still, boiler, or other vessel first giving written notice to the Secretary of that purpose.

(b) Penalties, etc.

(1) For penalty and forfeiture for failure to give notice of manufacture, or for setting up a still without first giving notice, when required by the Secretary, see sections 5615(2) and 5687.

(2) For penalty and forfeiture for failure to register still or distilling apparatus when set up, see section 5601(a)(1) and 5615(1).

In **1984**, P.L. 98-369, Sec. 451(a), amended Code Sec. 5101, effective on the first day of the first calendar month which begins more than 90 days after 7/18/84.
Prior to amendment, Code Sec. 5101 read as follows:
"SEC. 5101. IMPOSITION AND RATE OF TAX.

"Every manufacturer of stills shall pay a special tax of $55 a year, and $22 for each still or condenser for distilling made by him."

Sec. 5102. Definition of manufacturer of stills.

Any person who manufactures any still or condenser to be used in distilling shall be deemed a manufacturer of stills.

In **1984**, P.L. 98-369, Sec. 451(a), amended Subpart C of part II of subchapter A of chapter 51 which included Code Sec. 5102 [unchanged by Sec. 451(a) amendment], effective 11/1/84.

Sec. 5103. Repealed.

In **1984**, P.L. 98-369, Sec. 451(a), repealed Code Sec. 5103, effective on the first day of the first calendar month which begins more than 90 days after 7/18/84.
Prior to repeal, Code Sec. 5103 read as follows:
"SEC. 5103. EXEMPTIONS.

3,407

"The taxes imposed by section 5101 shall not apply in respect of stills or condensers manufactured by a proprietor of distilled spirits plant exclusively for use in his plant or plants."

Sec. 5105.   Repealed.

In 1984, P.L. 98-369, Sec. 451(a), repealed Code Sec. 5105, effective on the first day of the first calendar month which begins 90 days after 7/18/84.
Prior to repeal, Code Sec. 5105 read as follows:
"Sec. 5105. Notice of manufacture of and permit to set up still.
"(a) Requirement.
"Any person who manufactures any still, boiler, or other vessel to be used for the purpose of distilling shall, before the same is removed from the place of manufacture, notify the Secretary, setting forth in writing by whom it is to be used, its capacity, and the time when the same is to be removed from the place of manufacture; and no such still, boiler, or other vessel shall be set up without the permit in writing to the Secretary for that purpose. The notice required by this section shall be submitted in such form and manner as the Secretary may by regulations prescribe.
"(b) Penalty.
"(1) For penalty and forfeiture for failure to give notice of manufacture, or for setting up still without permit, see sections 5615(2) and 5687.
"(2) For penalty and forfeiture for failure to register still or distilling apparatus when set up, see sections 5601(a)(1) and 5615(1)."
In 1976, P.L. 94-455, Sec. 1905(b)(6)(A), deleted ", 5601(b)(1)," following "sections 5601(a)(1)" in para. (b)(2), effective 2/1/77.
— P.L. 94-455, Sec. 1906(b)(13)(A), substituted "Secretary" for "Secretary or his delegate" each place it appeared in subsec. (a), effective 2/1/77.

Sec. 5106.   Repealed.

In 1984, P.L. 98-369, Sec. 451(a), repealed Code Sec. 5106, effective on the first day of the first calendar month which begins 90 days after 7/18/84.
Prior to repeal, Code Sec. 5106 read as follows:
"Sec. 5106. Export.
"(a) Without payment of tax.
"Under regulations prescribed by the Secretary, stills or condensers for distilling may be removed from the place of manufacture for export without payment of the tax imposed thereon by section 5101.
"(b) Drawback.
"Stills and condensers on which the tax has been paid, and which have not been used, may be exported with the privilege of drawback, under such regulations as the Secretary may prescribe."
In 1976, P.L. 94-455, Sec. 1906(b)(13)(A), substituted "Secretary" for "Secretary or his delegate" in subsecs. (a) and (b), effective 2/1/77.

SUBPART B.—NONBEVERAGE DOMESTIC DRAWBACK CLAIMANTS
Sec.
5111. Eligibility.
5111. Repealed. [Imposition and rate of tax.]
5112. Registration and regulation.
5112. Repealed. [Definitions.]
5113. Investigation of claims.
5114. Drawback.
5115. Repealed. [Sign required on premises.]
5117. Repealed. [Prohibited purchases by dealers.]

In 2005, P.L. 109-59, Sec. 11125(b)(3)(A), Subpart F is redesignated as subpart B.
In 1997, P.L. 105-34, Sec. 1415(b)(3), deleted item 5115.
Prior to deletion, item 5115 read as follows:
"5115. Sign required on premises."

Sec. 5111.   Eligibility.

Any person using distilled spirits on which the tax has been determined, in the manufacture or production of medicines, medicinal preparations, food products, flavors, flavoring extracts, or perfume, which are unfit for beverage purposes shall be eligible for drawback at the time when such distilled spirits are used in the manufacture of such products as provided for in this subpart.

In 2005, P.L. 109-59, Sec. 11125(a)(2), deleted ", on payment of a special tax per annum," after "for beverage purposes" in subsec. (a) . . . Sec. 11125(b)(3)(A), redesignated Code Sec. 5131 as Code Sec. 5111 . . . Sec. 11125(b)(3)(C)(i), deleted "and rate of tax" after "Eligibility" in the heading of Code Sec. 5111(as redesignated) . . . Sec. 11125(b)(3)(C)(ii), deleted "(a) Eligibility for drawback.",

the heading for subsec. (a) . . . Sec. 11125(b)(3)(C)(iii), deleted subsec. (b), effective 7/1/2008, but shall not apply to taxes imposed for periods before 7/1/2008.
Prior to amendment, subsec. (b) read as follows:
"(b) Rate of tax.
"The special tax imposed by subsection (a) shall be $500 per year."
In 1994, P.L. 103-465, Sec. 136(b), substituted "flavoring extracts, or perfume" for "or flavoring extracts" in subsec. (a), effective 1/1/95.
In 1987, P.L. 100-203, Sec. 10512(d), amended subsec. (b), effective 1/1/88. For special rules, see Sec. 10512(h)(2) of this Act, reproduced in note following Code Sec. 5081.
Prior to amendment, subsec. (b) read as follows:
"(b) Rate of tax.
"The special tax imposed by subsection (a) shall be graduated in amount as follows: (1) for total annual use not exceeding 25 proof gallons, $25 a year; (2) for total annual use not exceeding 50 proof gallons, $50 a year; (3) for total annual use of more than 50 proof gallons, $100 a year.
In 1976, P.L. 94-455, Sec. 1905(a)(11), deleted 'produced in a domestic registered distillery or industrial alcohol plant and withdrawn from bond, or using distilled spirits withdrawn from the bonded premises of a distilled spirits plant,' after 'Any person using distilled spirits' in subsec. (a), effective 2/1/77.

Sec. 5111.   Repealed.

In 2005, P.L. 109-59, Sec. 11125(a)(1)(C), repealed Code Sec. 5111, effective 7/1/2008, but shall not apply to taxes imposed for periods before 7/1/2008.
Prior to repeal, Code Sec. 5111 read as follows:
"Sec. 5111. Imposition and rate of tax.
"(a) Wholesale dealers in liquors. Every wholesale dealer in liquors shall pay a special tax of $500 a year.
"(b) Wholesale dealers in beer. Every wholesale dealer in beer shall pay a special tax of $500 a year."
In 1987, P.L. 100-203, Sec. 10512(b)(1), substituted "$500" for "$255" in subsec. (a) . . . Sec. 10512(b)(2), substituted "$500" for "$123" in subsec. (b), effective 1/1/88. For special rules, see Sec. 10512(h)(2) of this Act, reproduced in note following Code Sec. 5081.
In 1976, P.L. 94-455, Sec. 1905(b)(3)(B), deleted the second sentence of subsec. (a), effective 2/1/77.
Prior to amendment, the second sentence of subsec. (a) read as follows:
"The Secretary or his delegate may by regulations provide for the issuance of a stamp denoting payment of such special tax as a 'wholesale dealer in wines' or a 'wholesale dealer in wines and beer' if, as the case may be, wines only, or wines and beer only, are sold by a wholesale dealer in liquors."

Sec. 5112.   Repealed.

In 2005, P.L. 109-59, Sec. 11125(a)(1)(C), repealed Code Sec. 5112, effective 7/1/2008, but shall not apply to taxes imposed for periods before 7/1/2008.
Prior to repeal, Code Sec. 5112 read as follows:
"Sec. 5112 Definitions.
"(a) Dealer. When used in this subpart, subpart E, or subpart G, the term 'dealer' means any person who sells, or offers for sale, any distilled spirits, wines, or beer.
"(b) Wholesale dealer in liquors. When used in this chapter, the term 'wholesale dealer in liquors' means any dealer, other than a wholesale dealer in beer, who sells, or offers for sale, distilled spirits, wines, or beer, to another dealer.
"(c) Wholesale dealer in beer. When used in this chapter, the term 'wholesale dealer in beer' means a dealer who sells, or offers for sale, beer, but not distilled spirits or wines, to another dealer. "

Sec. 5112.   Registration and regulation.

Every person claiming drawback under this subpart shall register annually with the Secretary; keep such books and records as may be necessary to establish the fact that distilled spirits received by him and on which the tax has been determined were used in the manufacture or production of medicines, medicinal preparations, food products, flavors, flavoring extracts, or perfume, which were unfit for use for beverage purposes; and be subject to such rules and regulations in relation thereto as the Secretary shall prescribe to secure the Treasury against frauds.

In 2005, P.L. 109-59, Sec. 11125(b)(3)(A), redesignated Code Sec. 5132 as Code Sec. 5112 as part of the redesignation of subpart F of part II of subchapter A of chapter 51, effective 7/1/2008, but not for taxes imposed for periods before 7/1/2008.
In 1994, P.L. 103-465, Sec. 136(b), substituted "flavoring extracts, or perfume" for "or flavoring extracts" in Code Sec. 5132, effective 1/1/95.
In 1976, P.L. 94-455, Sec. 1906(b)(13)(A), substituted "Secretary" for "Secretary or his delegate" each place it appeared in Code Sec. 5132, effective 2/1/77.

Sec. 5113. Repealed.

In 2005, P.L. 109-59, Sec. 11125(a)(1)(C), repealed Code Sec. 5113, effective 7/1/2008, but shall not apply to taxes imposed for periods before 7/1/2008.
Prior to repeal, Code Sec. 5113 read as follows:
"Sec. 5113. Exemptions.

"(a) Sales by proprietors of controlled premises. No proprietor of a distilled spirits plant, bonded wine cellar, taxpaid wine bottling house, or brewery, shall be required to pay special tax under section 5111 or section 5121 on account of the sale at his principal business office as designated in writing to the Secretary, or at his distilled spirits plant, bonded wine cellar, taxpaid wine bottling house, or brewery, as the case may be, of distilled spirits, wines, or beer, which, at the time of sale, are stored at his distilled spirits plant, bonded wine cellar, taxpaid wine bottling house, or brewery, as the case may be, or had been removed from such premises to a taxpaid storeroom operated in connection therewith and are stored therein. However, no such proprietor shall have more than one place of sale, as to each distilled spirits plant, bonded wine cellar, taxpaid wine bottling house, or brewery, that shall be exempt from special taxes by reason of the sale of distilled spirits, wines, or beer stored at such premises (or removed therefrom and stored as provided in this section), by reason of this subsection.

"(b) Sales by liquor stores operated by states, political subdivisions, etc. No liquor store engaged in the business of selling to persons other than dealers, which is operated by a State, by a political subdivision of a State or by the District of Columbia, shall be required to pay any special tax imposed under section 5111, by reason of selling distilled spirits, wines, or beer to dealers qualified to do business as such in such State, subdivision, or District, if such State, political subdivision, or District has paid the applicable special tax imposed under section 5121, and if such State, political subdivision, or District has paid special tax under section 5111 at its principal place of business.

"(c) Casual sales.

"(1) Sales by creditors, fiduciaries, and officers of court. No person shall be deemed to be a dealer by reason of the sale of distilled spirits, wines, or beer which have been received by him as security for or in payment of a debt, or as an executor, administrator, or other fiduciary, or which have been levied on by any officer under order or process of any court or magistrate, if such distilled spirits, wines, or beer are sold by such person in one parcel only or at public auction in parcels of not less than 20 wine gallons.

"(2) Sales by retiring partners or representatives of deceased partners to incoming or remaining partners. No person shall be deemed to be a dealer by reason of a sale of distilled spirits, wines, or beer made by such person as a retiring partner or the representative of a deceased partner to the incoming, remaining, or surviving partner or partners of a firm.

"(3) Return of liquors for credit, refund, or exchange. No person shall be deemed to be a dealer by reason of the bona fide return of distilled spirits, wines, or beer to the dealer from whom purchased (or to the successor of the vendor's business or line of merchandise) for credit, refund, or exchange, and the giving of such credit, refund, or exchange shall not be deemed to be a purchase within the meaning of section 5117.

"(d) Dealers making sales on purchaser dealer's premises.

"(1) Wholesale dealers in liquors. No wholesale dealer in liquors who has paid the special tax as such dealer shall again be required to pay special tax as such dealer on account of sales of wines or beer to wholesale or retail dealers in liquors, or to limited retail dealers, or of beer to wholesale or retail dealers in beer, consummated at the purchaser's place of business.

"(2) Wholesale dealers in beer. No wholesale dealer in beer who has paid the special tax as such a dealer shall again be required to pay special tax as such dealer on account of sales of beer to wholesale or retail dealers in liquors or beer, or to limited retail dealers, consummated at the purchaser's place of business.

"(e) Sales by retail dealers in liquidation. No retail dealer in liquors or retail dealer in beer, selling in liquidation his entire stock of liquors in one parcel or in parcels embracing not less than his entire stock of distilled spirits, of wines, or of beer to any other dealer, shall be deemed to be a wholesale dealer in liquors or a wholesale dealer in beer, as the case may be, by reason of such sale or sales.

"(f) Sales to limited retail dealers.

"(1) Retail dealers in liquors. No retail dealer in liquors who has paid special tax as such dealer under section 5121(a) shall be required to pay special tax under section 5111 on account of the sale at his place of business of distilled spirits, wines, or beer to limited retail dealers as defined in section 5122(c).

"(2) Retail dealers in beer. No retail dealer in beer who has paid special tax as such dealer under section 5121(b) shall be required to pay special tax under section 5111 on account of the sale at his place of business of beer to limited retail dealers as defined in section 5122(c).

"(g) Coordination of taxes under section 5111. No tax shall be imposed by section 5111(a) with respect to a person's activities at any place during a year if such person has paid the tax imposed by section 5111(b) with respect to such place for such year."

In 1988, P.L. 100-647, Sec. 2004(t)(2)(A), added "taxpaid wine bottling house," after "bonded wine cellar," each place it appeared in subsec. (a)... Sec. 2004(t)(2)(B), substituted "Controlled Premises" for "Distilled Spirits Plants, Bonded Wine Cellars, or Breweries" in the heading of subsec. (a)... Sec. 2004(t)(4), added subsec. (g), effective 1/1/88. For special rules, see Sec. 10512(h)(2) of P.L. 100-203, reproduced in note following Code Sec. 5081.

In 1976, P.L. 94-455, Sec. 1905(a)(7), substituted "distilled spirits, wines, or beer" for "wines or beer" in para. (c)(1), effective 2/1/77.
—P.L. 94-455, Sec. 1906(b)(13)(A), substituted "Secretary" for "Secretary or his delegate" in subsec. (a), effective 2/1/77.

In 1962, P.L. 87-863, Sec. 4(b), substituted in subsec. (b) "if such State, political subdivision, or District" for "if such liquor store" preceding "has paid the", and eliminated references to Territories wherever appearing, effective 7/1/62.

Sec. 5113. Investigation of claims.

For the purpose of ascertaining the correctness of any claim filed under this subpart, the Secretary is authorized to examine any books, papers, records, or memoranda bearing upon the matters required to be alleged in the claim, to require the attendance of the person filing the claim or of any officer or employee of such person or the attendance of any other person having knowledge in the premises, to take testimony with reference to any matter covered by the claim, and to administer oaths to any person giving such testimony.

In 2005, P.L. 109-59, Sec. 11125(b)(3)(A), redesignated Code Sec. 5133 as Code Sec. 5113, effective on 7/1/2008, but shall not apply to taxes imposed for periods before 7/1/2008. For Code Sec. 5113 effective before 7/1/2008, but not for taxes imposed for periods after 7/1/2008, see above.
In 1976, P.L. 94-455, Sec. 1906(b)(13)(A), substituted "Secretary" for "Secretary or his delegate" in Code Sec. 5133, effective 2/1/77.

Sec. 5114. Drawback.
(a) Rate of drawback.

In the case of distilled spirits on which the tax has been paid or determined, and which have been used as provided in this subpart, a drawback shall be allowed on each proof gallon at a rate of $1 less than the rate at which the distilled spirits tax has been paid or determined.

(b) Claims.

Such drawback shall be due and payable quarterly upon filing of a proper claim with the Secretary; except that, where any person entitled to such drawback shall elect in writing to file monthly claims therefor, such drawback shall be due and payable monthly upon filing of a proper claim with the Secretary. The Secretary may require persons electing to file monthly drawback claims to file with him a bond or other security in such amount and with such conditions as he shall by regulations prescribe. Any such election may be revoked on filing of notice thereof with the Secretary. No claim under this subpart shall be allowed unless filed with the Secretary within the 6 months next succeeding the quarter in which the distilled spirits covered by the claim were used as provided in this subpart.

(c) Allowance of drawback even where certain requirements not met.

(1) In general. No claim for drawback under this section shall be denied in the case of a failure to comply with any requirement imposed under this subpart or any rule or regulation issued thereunder upon the claimant's establishing to the satisfaction of the Secretary that distilled spirits on which the tax has been paid or determined were in fact used in the manufacture or production of medicines, medicinal preparations, food products, flavors, flavoring extracts, or perfume, which were unfit for beverage purposes.

(2) Penalty.

(A) In general. In the case of a failure to comply with any requirement imposed under this subpart or any rule or regulation issued thereunder, the claimant shall be liable for a penalty of $1,000 for each failure to comply unless it is shown that the failure to comply was due to reasonable cause.

(B) Penalty may not exceed amount of claim. The aggregate amount of the penalties imposed under subparagraph (A) for failures described in paragraph (1) in respect of any claim shall not exceed the amount of such claim (determined without regard to subparagraph (A)).

(3) Penalty treated as tax. The penalty imposed by paragraph (2) shall be assessed, collected, and paid in the same manner as taxes, as provided in section 6665(a).

In 2005, P.L. 109-59, Sec. 11125(b)(3)(A), redesignated Code Sec. 5134 as Code Sec. 5114, effective on 7/1/2008, but not for taxes imposed for periods before 7/1/2008.
In 1996, P.L. 104-188, Sec. 1704(t)(12), substituted "section 6665(a)" for "section 6662(a)" in para. (c)(3), effective 8/20/96.
In 1994, P.L. 103-465, Sec. 136(b), substituted "flavoring extracts, or perfume" for "or flavoring extracts" in para. (c)(1), effective 1/1/95.
In 1986, P.L. 99-514, Sec. 1845, added Sec. 456(d) to P.L. 98-369, the effective date for changes made by Sec. 452 of P.L. 98-369, (see below) which changed the effective date of subsec. (c) from 11/1/84 to products manufactured or produced after 10/31/84.
In 1984, P.L. 98-369, Sec. 452, added subsec. (c), effective for products manufactured or produced after 10/31/84.
In 1976, P.L. 94-455, Sec. 1906(b)(13)(A), substituted "Secretary" for "Secretary or his delegate" each place it appeared in subsec. (b), effective 2/1/77.
In 1968, P.L. 90-615, Sec. 2, substituted "6 months" for "3 months" in the last sentence of subsec. (b), effective for claims filed on or after 10/21/68.

Sec. 5115. Repealed.

In 1997, P.L. 105-34, Sec. 1415(a), repealed Code Sec. 5115, effective 8/5/97.
Prior to repeal, Code Sec. 5115 read as follows:
"SEC. 5115. SIGN REQUIRED ON PREMISES.
"(a) Requirements.
"Every wholesale dealer in liquors who is required to pay special tax as such dealer shall, in the manner and form prescribed by regulations issued by the Secretary, place and keep conspicuously on the outside of the place of such business a sign, exhibiting, in plain and legible letters, the name or firm of the wholesale dealer, with the words: 'wholesale liquor dealer.' The requirements of this subsection will be met by the posting of a sign of the character prescribed herein, but with words conforming to the designation on the dealer's special tax stamp.
"(b) Penalty.
"For penalty for failure to post sign, or for posting sign without paying the special tax, see section 5681."
In 1976, P.L. 94-455, Sec. 1906(b)(13)(A), substituted "Secretary" for "Secretary or his delegate" in subsec. (a), effective 2/1/77.

Sec. 5117. Repealed.

In 2005, P.L. 109-59, Sec. 11125(a)(1)(C), repealed Code Sec. 5117, effective 7/1/2008, but not for taxes imposed for periods before 7/1/2008.
Prior to repeal, Code Sec. 5117 read as follows:
"SEC. 5117. PROHIBITED PURCHASES BY DEALERS.
"(a) General. It shall be unlawful for any dealer to purchase distilled spirits for resale from any person other than—
"(1) a wholesale dealer in liquors who has paid the special tax as such dealer to cover the place where such purchase is made; or
"(2) a wholesale dealer in liquors who is exempt, at the place where such purchase is made, from payment of such tax under any provision of this chapter; or
"(3) a person who is not required to pay special tax as a wholesale dealer in liquors.
"(b) Limited retail dealers. A limited retail dealer may lawfully purchase distilled spirits for resale from a retail dealer in liquors.
"(c) Penalty and forfeiture. For penalty and forfeiture provisions applicable to violation of subsection (a), see sections 5687 and 7302.
"(d) Special rule during suspension period. Except as provided in subsection (b) or by the Secretary, during the suspension period (as defined in section 5148) it shall be unlawful for any dealer to purchase distilled spirits for resale from any person other than a wholesale dealer in liquors who is required to keep records under section 5114."
In 2004, P.L. 108-357, Sec. 246(b), added subsec. (d), effective 10/22/2004.
In 1976, P.L. 94-455, Sec. 1905(a)(8), redesignated subsec. (b) as subsec. (c), and added new subsec. (b), effective 2/1/77.

SUBPART C.—RECORDKEEPING AND REGISTRATION BY DEALERS
Sec.
5121. Repealed. [Imposition and rate of tax.]
5121. Recordkeeping by wholesale dealers.
5122. Repealed. [Definitions.]
5122. Recordkeeping by retail dealers.
5123. Repealed. [Exemptions.]
5123. Preservation and inspection of records, and entry of premises for inspection.
5124. Repealed. [Records.]
5124. Registration by dealers.
5125. Repealed. [Cross references.]

In 2005, P.L. 109-59, Sec. 11125(c)(4), added new subpart C.

Sec. 5121. Repealed.

In 2005, P.L. 109-59, Sec. 11125(a)(1)(D), repealed Code Sec. 5121, effective 7/1/2008, but not for taxes imposed for periods before 7/1/2008.
Prior to deletion, Code Sec. 5121 read as follows:
"Sec. 5121. Imposition and rate of tax.
"(a) Retail dealers in liquors. Every retail dealer in liquors shall pay a special tax of $250 a year.
"(b) Retail dealers in beer. Every retail dealer in beer shall pay a special tax of $250 a year."
In 1987, P.L. 100-203, Sec. 10512(c)(1), substituted "$250" for "$54" in subsec. (a)... Sec. 10512(c)(2), substituted "$250" for "$24" in subsec. (b)... Sec. 10512(c)(3), deleted subsec. (c), effective 1/1/88. For special rules, see Sec. 10512(h)(2) of this Act, reproduced in note following Code Sec. 5081.
"(C) Occupational tax.—For purposes of this paragraph, the term 'occupational tax' means any tax imposed under part II of subchapter A of chapter 51, section 5276, section 5731, or section 5801 of the Internal Revenue Code of 1986 (as amended by this section).
"(D) Due date of tax.—The amount of any tax required to be paid by reason of this paragraph shall be due on April 1, 1988."
Prior to deletion, subsec. (c) read as follows:
"(c) Limited retail dealers. Every limited retail dealer shall pay a special tax of $4.50 for each calendar month in which sales are made as such dealer; except that the special tax shall be $2.20 for each calendar month in which only sales of beer or wine are made."
In 1976, P.L. 94-455, Sec. 1905(a)(9), amended subsec. (c), effective 2/1/77.
Prior to amendment, subsec. (c) read as follows:
"(c) Limited retail dealers.
"Every limited retail dealer shall pay a special tax of $2.20 for each calendar month in which sales are made as such dealer."
— P.L. 94-455, Sec. 1905(b)(3)(C), deleted the second sentence of subsec. (a), effective 2/1/77.
Prior to deletion, the second sentence of subsec. (a) read as follows:
"The Secretary or his delegate may by regulations provide for the issuance of a stamp denoting payment of such special tax as—
"(1) a 'retail dealer in wines' or a 'retail dealer in wines and beer' if wines only, or wines and beer only, as the case may be, are sold by a retail dealer in liquors, or
"(2) a 'medicinal spirits dealer', in the case of a retail drug store or pharmacy making sales of liquors through a duly licensed pharmacist."

Sec. 5121. Recordkeeping by wholesale dealers.
(a) Requirements.
(1) Distilled spirits. Every wholesale dealer in liquors who sells distilled spirits to other dealers shall keep daily a record of distilled spirits received and disposed of by him, in such form and at such place and containing such information, and shall submit correct summaries of such records to the Secretary at such time and in such form and manner, as the Secretary shall by regulations prescribe. Such dealer shall also submit correct extracts from or copies of such records, at such time and in such form and manner as the Secretary may by regulations prescribe; however, the Secretary may on application by such dealer, in accordance with such regulations, relieve him from this requirement until further notice, whenever the Secretary deems that the submission of such extracts or copies serves no useful purpose in law enforcement or in protection of the revenue.
(2) Wines and beer. Every wholesale dealer in liquors and every wholesale dealer in beer shall provide and keep, at such place as the Secretary shall by regulations prescribe, a record in book form of all wines and beer received, showing the quantities thereof and from whom and the dates received, or shall keep all invoices of, and bills for, all wines and beer received.
(b) Exemption of States, political subdivisions, etc.
The provision of subsection (a) shall not apply to a State, to a political subdivision of a State, to the District of Columbia, or to liquor stores operated by any of them, if they maintain and make available for inspection by internal reve-

Excise and miscellaneous taxes — Code Sec. 5123

nue officers such records as will enable such officers to trace all distilled spirits, wines, and beer received, and all distilled spirits disposed of by them. Such States, subdivisions, District, or liquor stores shall, upon the request of the Secretary, furnish him such transcripts, summaries and copies of their records with respect to distilled spirits as he shall require.

(c) Wholesale dealers.

For purposes of this part—

(1) Wholesale dealer in liquors. The term "wholesale dealer in liquors" means any dealer (other than a wholesale dealer in beer) who sells, or offers for sale, distilled spirits, wines, or beer, to another dealer.

(2) Wholesale dealer in beer. The term "wholesale dealer in beer" means any dealer who sells, or offers for sale, beer, but not distilled spirits or wines, to another dealer.

(3) Dealer. The term "dealer" means any person who sells, or offers for sale, any distilled spirits, wines, or beer.

(4) Presumption in case of sale of 20 wine gallons or more. The sale, or offer for sale, of distilled spirits, wines, or beer, in quantities of 20 wine gallons or more to the same person at the same time, shall be presumptive evidence that the person making such sale, or offer for sale, is engaged in or carrying on the business of a wholesale dealer in liquors or a wholesale dealer in beer, as the case may be. Such presumption may be overcome by evidence satisfactorily showing that such sale, or offer for sale, was made to a person other than a dealer.

(d) Cross references.

(1) For provisions requiring proprietors of distilled spirits plants to keep records and submit reports of receipts and dispositions of distilled spirits, see section 5207.

(2) For penalty for violation of subsection (a), see section 5603.

(3) For provisions relating to the preservation and inspection of records, and entry of premises for inspection, see section 5123.

In 2007, P.L. 110-172, Sec. 11(a)(31), redesignated Code Sec. 5432 [as mistakenly designated by P.L. 109-59, Sec. 11125(b)(5)(B)(i)], relating to recordkeeping by wholesale dealers, as Code Sec. 5121, enacted 12/29/2007.

In 2005, P.L. 109-59, Sec. 11125(b)(5)(A), moved Code Sec. 5114 to subpart C of Subtitle E, Chapter 51, part II as the first Code Sec. of that subpart.... Sec. 11125(b)(5)(B)(i), substituted "Sec. 5432 [5121]. Recordkeeping by wholesale dealers." for "Sec. 5432 [5121]. Records." as the heading of Code Sec. 5432 [5121] [as redesignated by 11125(b)(5)(A) of this Act, see above]... Sec. 11125(b)(5)(B)(ii), redesignated subsec. (c) as subsec. (d) and added subsec. (c) [as redesignated by 1125(b)(5)(A) of this Act, see above]... Sec. 11125(b)(5)(C), substituted "section 5123" for "section 5146" in para. (d)(3), effective on 7/1/2008, but shall not apply to taxes imposed for periods before 7/1/2008.

In 1976, P.L. 94-455, Sec. 1905(a)(9), deleted "or Territory," after "State" each place it appeared in subsec. (b), and deleted "Territories" after "Such States," in the last sentence of subsec. (b), effective 2/1/77.

—P.L. 94-455, Sec. 1906(b)(13)(A), substituted "Secretary" for "Secretary or his delegate" each place it appeared in Code Sec. 5114, effective 2/1/77.

Sec. 5122. Repealed.

In 2005, P.L. 109-59, Sec. 11125(a)(1)(D), repealed Code Sec. 5122, effective 7/1/2008, but shall not apply for taxes imposed for periods before 7/1/2008
Prior to amendment, Code Sec. 5122 read as follows:
"Sec. 5122. Definitions.

"(a) Retail dealers in liquors. When used in this chapter, the term 'retail dealer in liquors' means any dealer, other than a retail dealer in beer or a limited retail dealer, who sells, or offers for sale, any distilled spirits, wines, or beer, to any person other than a dealer.

"(b) Retail dealer in beer. When used in this chapter, the term 'retail dealer in beer' means any dealer, other than a limited retail dealer, who sells, or offers for sale, beer, but not distilled spirits or wines, to any person other than a dealer.

"(c) Limited retail dealer. When used in this chapter, the term 'limited retail dealer' means any fraternal, civic, church, labor, charitable, benevolent, or ex-servicemen's organization making sales of distilled spirits, wine, or beer on the occasion of any kind of entertainment, dance, picnic, bazaar, or festival held by it, or any person making sales of distilled spirits, wine, or beer to the members, guests, or patrons of bona fide fairs, reunions, picnics, carnivals, or other similar outings, if such organization or person is not otherwise engaged in business as a dealer."

In 1976, P.L. 94-455, Sec. 1905(a)(10), substituted "distilled spirits, wine, or beer" for "beer or wine" each place it appeared in subsec. (c), effective 2/1/77.

Sec. 5122. Recordkeeping by retail dealers.

(a) Receipts.

Every retail dealer in liquors and every retail dealer in beer shall provide and keep in his place of business a record in book form of all distilled spirits, wines, and beer received, showing the quantity thereof and from whom and the dates received, or shall keep all invoices of, and bills for, all distilled spirits, wines, and beer received.

(b) Dispositions.

When he deems it necessary for law enforcement purposes or the protection of the revenue, the Secretary may by regulations require retail dealers in liquors and retail dealers in beer to keep records of the disposition of distilled spirits, wines, or beer, in such form or manner and of such quantities as the Secretary may prescribe.

(c) Retail dealers.

For purposes of this section

(1) Retail dealer in liquors. The term "retail dealer in liquors" means any dealer (other than a retail dealer in beer or a limited retail dealer) who sells, or offers for sale, distilled spirits, wines, or beer, to any person other than a dealer.

(2) Retail dealer in beer. The term "retail dealer in beer" means any dealer (other than a limited retail dealer) who sells, or offers for sale, beer, but not distilled spirits or wines, to any person other than a dealer.

(3) Limited retail dealer. The term "limited retail dealer" means any fraternal, civic, church, labor, charitable, benevolent, or ex-servicemen's organization making sales of distilled spirits, wine or beer on the occasion of any kind of entertainment, dance, picnic, bazaar, or festival held by it, or any person making sales of distilled spirits, wine or beer to the members, guests, or patrons of bona fide fairs, reunions, picnics, carnivals, or other similar outings, if such organization or person is not otherwise engaged in business as a dealer.

(4) Dealer The term "dealer" has the meaning given such term by section 5121(c)(3).

(d) Cross references.

For provisions relating to the preservation and inspection of records, and entry of premises for inspection, see section 5123.

In 2005, P.L. 109-59, Sec. 11125(b)(6)(A), redesignated Code Sec. 5124 as Code Sec. 5122... Sec. 11125(b)(6)(B)(i), substituted "Sec. 5122. Recordkeeping by retail address." for "Sec. 5124. Records."... Sec. 11125(b)(6)(B)(ii), substituted "section 5123" for "section 5146" in subsec. (c)... Sec. 11125(b)(6)(B)(iii), redesignated subsec. (c) as subsec. (d) and added new subsec. (c), effective 7/1/2008, but not for taxes imposed for periods before 7/1/2008.

In 1996, P.L. 94-455, Sec. 1906(b)(13)(A), substituted "Secretary" for "Secretary or his delegate" each please it appeared in subsec. (b), effective 2/1/77.

Sec. 5123. Repealed.

In 2005, P.L. 109-59, Sec. 11125(a)(1)(D), repealed Code Sec. 5123, effective 7/1/2008, but not for taxes imposed for periods before 7/1/2008.
Prior to repeal, Code Sec. 5123 read as follows:
1. "SEC. 5123. EXEMPTIONS.
"(a) Wholesale dealers.

"(1) Wholesale dealers in liquors. No special tax shall be imposed under section 5121(a) or (b) on any dealer by reason of the selling, or selling, or offering for sale, of distilled spirits, wines, or beer at any location where such dealer is required to pay special tax under section 5111(a).

"(2) Wholesale dealers in beer. No special tax shall be imposed under section 5121(b) on any dealer by reason of the selling, or offering for sale, of beer at any location where such dealer is required to pay special tax under section 5111(b).

"(b) Business conducted in more than one location.

"(1) Retail dealers at large. Any retail dealer in liquors or retail dealer in beer whose business is such as to require him to travel from place to place in different States of the United States may, under regulations prescribed by the Secretary, procure a special tax stamp "At Large" covering his activities throughout the United States with the payment of but one special tax as a retail dealer in liquors or as a retail dealer in beer, as the case may be.

"(2) Dealers on trains, aircraft, and boats. Nothing contained in this chapter shall prevent the issue, under such regulations as the Secretary may prescribe, of special tax stamps to—

"(A) persons carrying on the business of retail dealers in liquors, or retail dealers in beer, on trains, aircraft, boats, or other vessels, engaged in the business of carrying passengers; or

"(B) persons carrying on the business of retail dealers in liquors, or retail dealers in beer on boats or other vessels operated by them, when such persons operate from a fixed address in a port or harbor and supply exclusively boats or other vessels, or persons thereon, at such port or harbor.

"(3) Liquor stores operated by states, political subdivisions, etc. A State, a political subdivision of a State, or the District of Columbia shall not be required to pay more than one special tax as a retail dealer in liquors under section 5121(a) regardless of the number of locations at which such State, political subdivision, or District carries on business as a retail dealer in liquors.

"(c) Coordination of taxes under section 5121. No tax shall be imposed by section 5121(a) with respect to a person's activities at any place during a year if such person has paid the tax imposed by section 5121(b) with respect to such place for such year.

"(d) Cross references.

"(1) For exemption of proprietors of distilled spirits plants, bonded wine cellars, and breweries from special tax as dealers, see section 5113(a).

"(2) For provisions relating to sales by creditors, fiduciaries, and officers of courts, see section 5113(c)(1).

"(3) For provisions relating to sales by retiring partners or representatives of deceased partners to incoming or remaining partners, see section 5113(c)(2).

"(4) For provisions relating to return of liquors for credit, refund, or exchange, see section 5113(c)(3).

"(5) For provisions relating to sales by retail dealers in liquidation, see section 5113(e)."

In 1988, P.L. 100-647, Sec. 2004(t)(3), redesignated subsec. (c) as subsec. (d) and added new subsec. (c), effective 1/1/88. For special rules, see Sec. 10512(h)(2) of P.L. 100-203, reproduced in note following Code Sec. 5081.

In 1976, P.L. 94-455, Sec. 1906(b)(13)(A), substituted "Secretary" for "Secretary or his delegate" each place it appeared in subsecs. (b), effective 2/1/77.

In 1962, P.L. 87-863, Sec. 4(a), added para. (b)(3), effective 7/1/62.

Sec. 5123. Preservation and inspection of records, and entry of premises for inspection.
(a) Preservation and inspection of records.

Any records or other documents required to be kept under this part or regulations issued pursuant thereto shall be preserved by the person required to keep such records or documents, as the Secretary may by regulations prescribe, and shall be kept available for inspection by any internal revenue officer during business hours.

(b) Entry of premises for inspection.

The Secretary may enter during business hours the premises (including places of storage) of any dealer for the purpose of inspecting or examining any records or other documents required to be kept by such dealer under this chapter or regulations issued pursuant thereto and any distilled spirits, wines, or beer kept or stored by such dealer on such premises.

In 2005, P.L. 109-59, Sec. 11125(b)(7), redesignated Code Sec. 5146 as Code Sec. 5123, effective 7/1/2008, but not for taxes imposed for periods before 7/1/2008.

In 1976, P.L. 94-455, Sec. 1906(b)(13)(A), substituted "Secretary" for "Secretary or his delegate" in subsecs. (a) and (b), effective 2/1/77.

Sec. 5124. Repealed.

In 2005, P.L. 109-59, Sec. 11125(b)(6), redesignated Code Sec. 5124 as Code Sec. 5122, effective 7/1/2008, but not for taxes imposed for periods before 7/1/2008.

In 1996, P.L. 94-455, Sec. 1906(b)(13)(A), substituted "Secretary" for "Secretary or his delegate" each place it appeared in subsec. (b), effective 2/1/77.

Sec. 5124. Registration by dealers.

Every dealer who is subject to the recordkeeping requirements under section 5121 or 5122 shall register with the Secretary such dealer's name or style, place of residence, trade or business, and the place where such trade or business is to be carried on. In the case of a firm or company, the names of the several persons constituting the same, and the places of residence, shall be so registered.

In 2005, P.L. 109-59, Sec. 11125(b)(8), added Code Sec. 5124, effective effective on and after 7/1/2008, but shall not apply for taxes imposed for periods before 7/1/2008.

Sec. 5125. Repealed.

In 2005, P.L. 109-59, Sec. 11125(a)(1)(D), repealed Code Sec. 5125, effective 7/1/2008, but shall not apply for taxes imposed for periods before 7/1/2008.
Prior to repeal, Code Sec. 5125 read as follows:
"SEC. 5125. CROSS REFERENCES.

"(1) For provisions relating to prohibited purchases by dealers, see section 5117.

"(2) For provisions relating to presumptions of liability as wholesale dealer in case of sale of 20 wine gallons or more, see section 5691(b)."

SUBPART D.—OTHER PROVISIONS

Sec.
5131. Packaging distilled spirits for industrial uses.
5132. Prohibited purchases by dealers.

In 2005, P.L. 109-59, Sec. 11125(c)(10), added new subpart D.

Sec. 5131. Packaging distilled spirits for industrial uses.
(a) General.

The Secretary may, at his discretion and under such regulations as he may prescribe, authorize a dealer (as defined in section 5121(c)) engaging in the business of supplying distilled spirits for industrial uses to package distilled spirits, on which the tax has been paid or determined, for such uses in containers of a capacity in excess of 1 wine gallon and not more than 5 wine gallons.

(b) Cross reference.

For provisions relating to containers of distilled spirits, see section 5206.

In 2005, P.L. 109-59, Sec. 11125(b)(11), redesignated Code Sec. 5116 as Code Sec. 5131 and added "(as defined in section 5121(c))" after "dealer" in subsec. (a), effective 7/1/2008, but shall not apply to taxes imposed for periods before 7/1/2008.

In 1984, P.L. 98-369, Sec. 454(c)(3), amended subsec. (b), effective 7/1/85.
Prior to amendment, subsec. (b) read as follows:
"(b) Cross references.

"(1) For provisions relating to stamps for immediate containers, see section 5205(a)(1).

"(2) For provisions relating to containers of distilled spirits, see section 5206."

In 1979, P.L. 96-39, Sec. 807(a)(12), substituted "section 5205(a)(1)" for "section 5205(a)(2)" in para. (b)(1), effective 1/1/80.

In 1976, P.L. 94-455, Sec. 1906(b)(13)(A), substituted "Secretary" for "Secretary or his delegate" in subsec. (a), effective 2/1/77.

Sec. 5132. Prohibited purchases by dealers.
(a) In general.

Except as provided in regulations prescribed by the Secretary, it shall be unlawful for a dealer to purchase distilled spirits for resale from any person other than a wholesale dealer in liquors who is required to keep the records prescribed by section 5121.

(b) Limited retail dealers.

A limited retail dealer may lawfully purchase distilled spirits for resale from a retail dealer in liquors.

(c) Penalty and forfeiture.

For penalty and forfeiture provisions applicable to violations of subsection (a), see sections 5687 and 7302.

In 2005, P.L. 109-59, Sec. 11125(b)(12), added Code Sec. 5132, effective 7/1/2008, but not for taxes imposed for periods before 7/1/2008.

Excise and miscellaneous taxes Code Sec. 5171(d)(2)

SUBPART G. REPEALED. [GENERAL PROVISIONS.]
Sec.
5141. Repealed. [Registration.]
5147. Repealed. [Application of subpart.]
5148. Repealed. [Suspension of occupational tax.]
5149. Repealed. [Cross references.]

In 2005, P.L. 109-59, Sec. 1125(a)(1)(E), repealed Subpart G.
In 2004, P.L. 108-357, Sec. 246(c), deleted item 5148 and added items 5148 and 5149.
Prior to deletion, item 5148 read as follows:
"5148. Cross references."

Sec. 5141. Repealed.

In 2005, P.L. 109-59, Sec. 1125(a)(1)(E), repealed Code Sec. 5141, effective 7/1/2008, but shall not apply to taxes imposed for periods before 7/1/2008.
Prior to repeal, Code Sec. 5141 read as follows:
"SEC. 5141. REGISTRATION.
"For provisions relating to registration in the case of persons engaged in any trade or business on which a special tax is imposed, see section 7011(a)."

Sec. 5147. Repealed.

In 2005, P.L. 109-59, Sec. 11125(a)(1)(E), repealed Code Sec. 5147, effective 7/1/2008, but not for taxes imposed for periods before 7/1/2008.
Prior to repeal, Code Sec. 5147 read as follows:
"SEC. 5147. APPLICATION OF SUBPART.
"The provisions of this subpart shall extend to and apply to the special taxes imposed by the other subparts of this part and to the persons on whom such taxes are imposed."

Sec. 5148. Repealed.

In 2005, P.L. 109-59, Sec. 11125(a)(1)(E), repealed Code Sec. 5148, effective 7/1/2008, but not for taxes imposed for periods before 7/1/2008.
Prior to repeal, Code Sec. 5148 read as follows:
"SEC. 5148. SUSPENSION OF OCCUPATIONAL TAX.
"(a) In general. Notwithstanding sections 5081, 5091, 5111, 5121, and 5131, the rate of tax imposed under such sections for the suspension period shall be zero. During such period, persons engaged in or carrying on a trade or business covered by such sections shall register under section 5141 and shall comply with the recordkeeping requirements under this part.
"(b) Suspension period. For purposes of subsection (a), the suspension period is the period beginning on July 1, 2005, and ending on June 30, 2008."
In 2004, P.L. 108-357, Sec. 246(a), added Code Sec. 5148, effective 10/22/2004.

Sec. 5149. Repealed.

In 2005, P.L. 109-59, Sec. 11125(a)(1)(E), repealed Code Sec. 5149, effective 7/1/2008, but not for taxes imposed for periods before 7/1/2008.
Prior to repeal, Code Sec. 5149 read as follows:
"SEC. 5149. CROSS REFERENCES.
"(1) For penalties for willful nonpayment of special taxes, see section 5691.
"(2) For penalties applicable to this part generally, see subchapter J.
"(3) For penalties, authority for assessments and other general and administrative provisions applicable to this part, see subtitle F."
In 2004, P.L. 108-357, Sec. 246(a), redesignated Code Sec. 5148 as Code Sec. 5149, effective 10/22/2004.
In 1976, P.L. 94-455, Sec. 1905(b)(3)(E), substituted "penalties, authority for assessment" for "penalties" in para. (3), effective 2/1/77.

Subchapter B.—Qualification Requirements for Distilled Spirits Plants

Sec.
5171. Establishment.
5172. Application.
5173. Bonds.
5175. Export bonds.
5176. New or renewed bonds.
5177. Other provisions relating to bonds.
5178. Distilled spirits plants.
5179. Registration of stills.
5180. Signs.
5181. Distilled spirits for fuel use.
5182. Cross references.

In 1980, P.L. 96-223, Sec. 232(e)(2)(F), amended the item for 5181 and added 5182, effective 6/1/80 [the first day of the first calendar month beginning more than 60 days after the date of enactment].
Prior to amendment, the item for 5181 read as follows:
"5181. CROSS REFERENCES."
In 1979, P.L. 96-39, Sec. 807(b)(4), amended the item for 5173 and 5178 and deleted the item for 5174.
Prior to amendment the items for 5173, 5174 and 5178 read as follows:
"5173. Qualification bonds."
"5174. Withdrawal bonds."
"5178. Premises of distilled spirits plants."

Sec. 5171. Establishment.

(a) Certain operations may be conducted only on bonded premises.
Except as otherwise provided by law, operations as a distiller, warehouseman, or processor may be conducted only on the bonded premises of a distilled spirits plant by a person who is qualified under this subchapter.

(b) Establishment of distilled spirits plant.
A distilled spirits plant may be established only by a person who intends to conduct at such plant operations as a distiller, as a warehouseman, or as both.

(c) Registration.

(1) In general. Each person shall, before commencing operations at a distilled spirits plant (and at such other times as the Secretary may by regulations prescribe), make application to the Secretary for, and receive notice of, the registration of such plant.

(2) Application required where new operations are added. No operation in addition to those set forth in the application made pursuant to paragraph (1) may be conducted at a distilled spirits plant until the person has made application to the Secretary for, and received notice of, the registration of such additional operation.

(3) Secretary may establish minimum capacity and level of activity requirements. The Secretary may by regulations prescribe for each type of operation minimum capacity and level of activity requirements for qualifying premises as a distilled spirits plant.

(4) Applicant must comply with law and regulations. No plant (or additional operation) shall be registered under this section until the applicant has complied with the requirements of law and regulations in relation to the qualification of such plant (or additional operation).

(d) Permits.

(1) Requirements. Each person required to file an application for registration under subsection (c) whose distilled spirits operations (or any part thereof) are not required to be covered by a basic permit under the Federal Alcohol Administration Act (27 U.S.C. secs. 203 and 204) shall, before commencing the operations (or part thereof) not so covered, apply for and obtain a permit under this subsection from the Secretary to engage in such operations (or part thereof). Subsections (b), (c), (d), (e), (f), (g), and (h) of section 5271 are hereby made applicable to persons filing applications and permits required by or issued under this subsection.

(2) Exceptions for agencies of a state or political subdivisions. Paragraph (1) shall not apply to any agency of a State or political subdivision thereof or to any officer or employee of any such agency, and no such agency, officer, or employee shall be required to obtain a permit thereunder.

3,413

(e) Cross references.

(1) For penalty for failure of a distiller or processor to file application for registration as required by this section, see section 5601(a)(2).

(2) For penalty for the filing of a false application by a distiller, warehouseman, or processor of distilled spirits, see section 5601(a)(3).

In **1979**, P.L. 96-39, Sec. 805(a), amended Code Sec. 5171, effective 1/1/80. Sec. 809 of the Act provides as follows:

"SEC. 809. TRANSITIONAL RULES RELATING TO ALL-IN-BOND METHOD.

"(a) New application required.

"(1) In general. For purposes of section 5171 of the Internal Revenue Code of 1954 (relating to establishment of distilled spirits plants), each person who intends to continue any distilled spirits operation at a premises after December 31, 1979, shall be treated as intending to establish a distilled spirits plant on such premises on January 1, 1980.

"(2) Current registration to remain in effect. Notwithstanding paragraph (1), the registration of any person under section 5171 of the Internal Revenue Code of 1954 which is in effect on December 31, 1979, shall remain in effect until final action on the application required by paragraph (1).

"(b) Continuing operations at existing premises.

"With respect to any operation which was permitted to be conducted on May 1, 1979, at premises which were registered on such date under section 5171 of the Internal Revenue Code of 1954, the determination of whether such premises qualify for registration under such section as a distilled spirits plant shall be made without regard to whether or not—

"(1) the person engaged in operations at such premises is registered under such section with respect to such premises as a distiller or warehouseman, and

"(2) such premises meet the minimum capacity and level of activity requirements for that type of operation.

"(c) New bond required.

"For purposes of section 5173 of the Internal Revenue Code of 1954 (relating to bonds), each person who intends to continue operation at a premises after December 31, 1979, shall be treated as intending to establish a distilled spirits plant on such premises on January 1, 1980."

Prior to amendment, Code Sec. 5171 read as follows:

"Sec. 5171. Establishment

"(a) General requirements.

"Every person shall, before commencing or continuing the business of a distiller, bonded warehouseman, rectifier, or bottler of distilled spirits, and at such other times as the Secretary may by regulations prescribe, make application to the Secretary for and receive notice of the registration of his plant. No plant shall be registered under this section until the applicant has complied with the requirements of law and regulations in relation to the qualification of such business (or businesses).

"(b) Permits.

"(1) Requirements. Every person required to file application for registration under subsection (a) whose distilling, warehousing, or bottling operations (or any part thereof) are not required to be covered by a basic permit under the Federal Alcohol Administration Act (27 U.S.C. 203, 204) shall, before commencing any such operations, apply for and obtain a permit under this subsection from the Secretary or his delegate to engage in such operations. Section 5271(b), (c), (d), (e), (f), (g), and (h), and section 5274 are hereby made applicable to applications, to persons filing applications, and to permits required by or issued under this subsection.

"(2) Exceptions for agency of a State or political subdivision. Paragraph (1) shall not apply to any agency of a State or political subdivision thereof or to any officer or employee of any such agency, and no such agency or officer or employee shall be required to obtain a permit thereunder.

"(c) Cross references.

"For penalty for failure of a distiller or rectifier to file application for registration as required by this section, see section 5601(a)(2), and for penalty for the filing of a false application by a distiller, bonded warehouseman, rectifier, or bottler of distilled spirits, see section 5601(a)(3)."

In **1976**, P.L. 94-455, Sec. 1905(a)(13), deleted "49 Stat. 978;" after the parenthesis in para. (b)(1), deleted para. (b)(3), effective 2/1/77.

Prior to deletion, para. (b)(3) read as follows:

"(3) Continuance of business. Every person required by paragraph (1) to obtain a permit (covering operations not required to be covered by a basic permit under the Federal Alcohol Administration Act) who, on June 30, 1959, is qualified to perform such operations under the internal revenue laws, and who complies with the provisions of this chapter (other than this subsection) relating to qualification of such business or businesses, shall be entitled to continue such operations for permit, and final action thereon."

—P.L. 94-455, Sec. 1906(b)(13)(A), substituted "Secretary" for "Secretary or his delegate" each place it appeared in Code Sec. 5171, effective 2/1/77.

Sec. 5172. Application.

The application for registration required by section 5171(c) shall, in such manner and form as the Secretary may by regulations prescribe, identify the applicant and persons interested in the business (or businesses) covered by the application, show the nature, location and extent of the premises, show the specific type or types of operations to be conducted on such premises, and show any other information which the Secretary may by regulations require for the purpose of carrying out the provisions of this chapter.

In **1979**, P.L. 96-39, Sec. 807(a)(13), substituted "section 5171(c)" for "section 5171(a)" in Code Sec. 5172, effective 1/1/80.

In **1976**, P.L. 94-455, Sec. 1906(b)(13)(A), substituted "Secretary" for "Secretary or his delegate" in Code Sec. 5172, effective 2/1/77.

Sec. 5173. Bonds.

(a) Operations at, and withdrawals from, distilled spirits plant must be covered by bond.

(1) **Operations.** No person intending to establish a distilled spirits plant may commence operations at such plant unless such person has furnished bond covering operations at such plant.

(2) **Withdrawals.** No distilled spirits (other than distilled spirits withdrawn under section 5214 or 7510) may be withdrawn from bonded premises except on payment of tax unless the proprietor of the bonded premises has furnished bond covering such withdrawal.

(b) Operations bonds.

The bond required by paragraph (1) of subsection (a) shall meet the requirements of paragraph (1), (2), or (3) of this subsection:

(1) One plant bond. The bond covers operations at a single distilled spirits plant.

(2) Adjacent wine cellar bond. The bond covers operations at a distilled spirits plant and at an adjacent bonded wine cellar.

(3) Area bond. The bond covers operations at 2 or more distilled spirits plants (and adjacent bonded wine cellars) which—

(A) are located in the same geographical area (as designated in regulations prescribed by the Secretary), and

(B) are operated by the same person (or, in the case of a corporation, by such corporation and its controlled subsidiaries).

(c) Withdrawal bonds.

The bond required by paragraph (2) of subsection (a) shall cover withdrawals from 1 or more bonded premises the operations at which could be covered by the same operations bond under subsection (b).

(d) Unit bonds.

Under regulations prescribed by the Secretary, the requirements of paragraphs (1) and (2) of subsection (a) shall be treated as met by a unit bond which covers both operations at, and withdrawals from, 1 or more bonded premises which could be covered by the same operations bond under subsection (b).

(e) Terms and conditions.

(1) In general. Any bond furnished under this section shall be conditioned that the person furnishing the bond—

(A) will faithfully comply with all provisions of law and regulations relating to the activities covered by such bond, and

(B) will pay—

(i) all taxes imposed by this chapter, and

(ii) all penalties incurred by, or fines imposed on, such person for violation of any such provision.

(2) Other terms and conditions. Any bond furnished under this section shall contain such other terms and conditions as may be required by regulations prescribed by the Secretary.

Excise and miscellaneous taxes Code Sec. 5173

(f) Amount.
(1) In general. The penal sum of any bond shall be the amount determined under regulations prescribed by the Secretary.
(2) Maximum and minimum amount. The Secretary shall by regulations prescribe a minimum amount and a maximum amount for each type of bond which may be furnished under this section.
(g) Total amount available.
The total amount of any bond furnished under this section shall be available for the satisfaction of any liability incurred under the terms and conditions of such bond.
(h) Special rules.
For purposes of this section—
(1) Withdrawal bonds. In the case of any bond furnished under this section which covers withdrawals but not operations—
(A) such bond shall be in addition to the operations bond, and
(B) if distilled spirits are withdrawn under such bond, the operations bond shall no longer cover liability for payment of the tax on the spirits withdrawn.
(2) Adjacent wine cellars.
(A) Requirements. No wine cellar shall be treated as being adjacent to a distilled spirits plant unless—
(i) such distilled spirits plant is qualified under this subchapter for the production of distilled spirits, and
(ii) such wine cellar and the distilled spirits plant are operated by the same person (or, in the case of a corporation, by such corporation and its controlled subsidiaries).
(B) Bond in lieu of wine cellar bond. In the case of any adjacent wine cellar, a bond furnished under this section which covers operations at such wine cellar shall be in lieu of any bond which would otherwise be required under section 5354 with respect to such wine cellar (other than supplemental bonds required under the second sentence of section 5354).

In 1979, P.L. 96-39, Sec. 805(c), amended Code Sec. 5173, effective 1/1/80. Prior to amendment, Code Sec. 5173 read as follows:
"SEC. 5173. QUALIFICATION BONDS.
"(a) General provisions.
"Every person intending to commence or to continue the business of a distiller, bonded warehouseman, or rectifier, on filing with the Secretary an application for registration of his plant, and before commencing or continuing such business, shall file bond in the form prescribed by the Secretary, conditioned that he shall faithfully comply with all the provisions of law and regulations relating to the duties and business of a distiller, bonded warehouseman, or rectifier, as the case may be (including the payment of taxes imposed by this chapter), and shall pay all penalties incurred or fines imposed on him for violation of any of the said provisions.
"(b) Distiller's bond.
"Every person intending to commence or continue the business of a distiller shall give bond in a penal sum not less than the amount of tax on spirits that will be produced in his distillery during a period of 15 days, except that such bond shall be in a sum of not less than $5,000 nor more than $100,000.
"(1) Conditions of approval. In addition to the requirements of subsection (a), the distiller's bond shall be conditioned that he shall not suffer the property, or any part thereof, subject to lien under section 5004(b)(1) to be encumbered by mortgage, judgment, or other lien during the time in which he shall carry on such business (except that this condition shall not apply during the term of any bond given under subparagraph (C)), or to any judgments or other lien covered by a bond given under paragraph (4) and no bond of a distiller shall be approved unless the Secretary is satisfied that the situation of the land and buildings which will constitute his bonded premises (as described in his application for registration) is not such as would enable the distiller to defraud the United States, and unless—
"(A) the distiller is the owner in fee, unencumbered, by any mortgage, judgment, or other liens of the lot or tract of land subject to lien under section 5004(b)(1); or
"(B) the distiller files with the officer designated for the purpose by the Secretary, in connection with his application for registration, the written consent of the owner of the fee, and of any mortgage, judgment creditor, or other person having a lien thereon, duly acknowledged, that such premises may be used for the purpose of distilling spirits, subject to the provisions of law, and expressly stipulating that the lien of the United States, for taxes on distilled spirits produced thereon and penalties relating thereto, shall have priority of such mortgage, judgment, or other encumbrance, and that in the case of the forfeiture of such premises, or any part thereof, the title to the same shall vest in the United States, discharged from such mortgage, judgment, or other encumbrance; or
"(C) the distiller files a bond, approved by the Secretary in the penal sum equal to the appraised value of the property subject to lien under section 5004(b)(1), except that such bond shall not exceed the sum of $300,000. Such value shall be determined, and such bond shall be executed in such form and with such sureties and filed with the officer designated by the Secretary, under such regulations as the Secretary shall prescribe.
"(2) Cancellation of indemnity bond. When the liability for which an indemnity bond given under paragraph (1)(C) or (4) ceases to exist, such bond may be cancelled upon application to the Secretary.
"(3) Judicial sale. In the case of any distillery sold at judicial or other sale in favor of the United States, a bond in lieu of consent under paragraph (1)(B) may be taken at the discretion of the Secretary, and the person giving such bond may be allowed to operate such distillery during the existence of the right of redemption from such sale, on complying with all the other provisions of law.
"(4) Involuntary lien. In the case of a judgment, or other lien imposed on the property subject to lien under section 5004(b)(1) without the consent of the distiller, the distiller may file bond, approved by the Secretary, in the amount of such judgment or other lien to indemnify the United States for any loss resulting from such encumbrance.
"(c) Bonded warehouseman's bonds.
"(1) General requirements. Every person intending to commence or continue the business of a bonded warehouseman shall give bond in a penal sum not less than the amount of tax on distilled spirits stored on such premises and in transit thereto, except that such bond shall not exceed the sum of $200,000. In addition to the requirements in subsection (a), such bond shall be conditioned—
"(A) on the withdrawal of the spirits from storage on bonded premises within the time prescribed for the determination of tax under section 5006(a)(2), and
"(B) on payment of the tax, except as otherwise provided by law, on all spirits withdrawn from storage on the bonded premises.
"(2) Exception. The Secretary may by regulations specify bonded warehousing operations, other than the storage of more than 500 casks or packages of distilled spirits in wooden containers, for which a bond in a maximum sum of less than $200,000 will be approved, and in such cases the Secretary or his delegate shall by regulations prescribe the maximum penal sum of such bonds.
"(d) Rectifier's bond.
"Every person intending to commence or continue the business of a rectifier shall give bond in a penal sum not less than the amount of tax the rectifier will be liable to pay in a period of 30 days under sections 5021 and 5022, except that such bond shall not exceed the sum of $100,000, and shall not be less than $1,000.
"(e) Combined operations.
"(1) Distilled spirits plants. Except as provided in paragraph (2), any person intending to commence or continue business as proprietor of a distilled spirits plant who would otherwise be required to give more than one bond under the provisions of subsections (b) (other than indemnity bonds), (c), and (d), shall, in lieu thereof, give bond in a penal sum equal to the combined penal sums which would have been required under such subsections; but in no case shall the combined operations bond be in a penal sum in excess of $200,000 if all operations are to be conducted on bonded premises, or in excess of $250,000 for the distilled spirits plant. Bonds given under this paragraph shall contain the terms and conditions of the bonds in lieu of which they are given.
"(2) Distilled spirits plants and adjacent bonded wine cellars. Any person intending to commence or continue business as proprietor of a bonded wine cellar and an adjacent distilled spirits plant qualified for the production of distilled spirits shall, in lieu of the bonds which would otherwise be required under the provisions of subsection (b) (other than indemnity bonds), (c), and (d), and section 5354 (other than supplemental bonds to cover additional liability arising as a result of deferral of payment of tax), give bond in a penal sum equal to the combined penal sums which would have been required under such provisions; but in no case shall the combined operations bond be in a penal sum in excess of $150,000 if the distilled spirits plant is qualified solely for the production of distilled spirits, in excess of $250,000 if the distilled spirits plant is qualified only for production and bonded warehousing or for production and rectification and bottling, or in excess of $300,000 for the distilled spirits plant and bonded wine cellar. Bonds given under this paragraph shall contain the terms and conditions of the bonds in lieu of which they are given.
"(f) Blanket bonds.
"The Secretary may by regulations authorize any person (including, in the case of a corporation, controlled or wholly owned subsidiaries) operating more than one distilled spirits plant in a geographical area designated in regulations prescribed by the Secretary to give a blanket bond covering the operation of any two or more of such plants and any bonded wine cellars which are adjacent to such plants and which otherwise could be covered under a combined operations bond as provided for in subsection (e)(2). The penal sum of such blanket bond shall be calculated in accordance with the following table:

3,415

Total penal sums as determined under subsections (b), (c), (d), and (e)	Requirement for penal sum of blanket bond
First $300,000 or any part thereof	100%
Next $300,000 or any part thereof	70%
Next $400,000 or any part thereof	50%
Next $1,000,000 or any part thereof	35%
All over $2,000,000	25%

Bonds given under this subsection shall be in lieu of the bonds required under subsections (b) (other than indemnity bonds), (c), (d), and (e), as the case may be, and shall contain the terms and conditions of such bonds.

"(g) *Liability under combined operations and blanket bonds.*

"The total amount of any bond given under subsection (e) or (f) shall be available for the satisfaction of any liability incurred under the terms or conditions of such bond."

In 1976, P.L. 94-455, Sec. 1906(b)(13)(A), substituted "Secretary" for "Secretary or his delegate" each place it appeared in Code Sec. 5173, effective 2/1/77.

In 1971, P.L. 91-659, Sec. 4(a), added para. (b)(4) . . . Sec. 4(b), added "or to any judgment or other lien covered by a bond given under paragraph (4)" after "bond given under subparagraph (C)" in para. (b)(1) . . . Sec. 4(c), added "or 4" after "paragraph (1)(C)" in para. (b)(2), effective 5/1/71.

Sec. 5174. Repealed.

In 1979, P.L. 96-39, Sec. 807(a)(14), repealed Code Sec. 5174, effective 1/1/80. Prior to repeal, Code Sec. 5174 read as follows:

"Sec. 5174. Withdrawal bonds.

"(a) *Requirements.*

"No distilled spirits, other than distilled spirits withdrawn under section 5214 or section 7510, shall be withdrawn from bonded premises except on payment of tax unless—

"(1) the proprietor of the bonded premises has furnished such bond (in addition to that required in section 5173) to secure payment of the tax on such spirits, under such regulations and conditions, and in such form and penal sum, as the Secretary may prescribe; or

"(2) the proprietor of a distilled spirits plant authorized to rectify or bottle distilled spirits has—

"(A) made application to the Secretary to withdraw distilled spirits from bond and has assumed liability at the receiving plant for payment of the tax thereon;

"(B) furnished bond (in addition to any bond required by section 5173) to secure payment of the tax on such spirits, under such regulations and conditions, and in such form and penal sum, as the Secretary may prescribe; and

"(C) complied with such other requirements as the Secretary may by regulations prescribe.

"(b) *Release of other bonds.*

"When a bond has been filed under subsection (a) and distilled spirits have been withdrawn from bonded premises thereunder, bonds of proprietors covering operations on bonded premises, and bonds given under prior provisions of internal revenue law to cover similar operations, shall no longer cover liability for payment of the tax on such spirits."

In 1976, P.L. 94-455, Sec. 1905(a)(14), substituted "distilled spirits from bond" for "such spirits" in subpara. (a)(2)(A), effective 2/1/77.

—P.L. 94-455, Sec. 1906(b)(13)(A), substituted "Secretary" for "Secretary or his delegate" each place it appeared in subsec. (a), effective 2/1/77.

Sec. 5175. Export bonds.
(a) Requirements.

No distilled spirits shall be withdrawn from bonded premises for exportation, or for transfer to a customs bonded warehouse, without payment of tax unless the exporter has furnished bond to cover such withdrawal under such regulations and conditions, and in such form and penal sum, as the Secretary may prescribe.

(b) Exception where proprietor withdraws spirits for exportation.

In the case of distilled spirits withdrawn from bonded premises by the proprietor for exportation without payment of tax, the bond of such proprietor required to be furnished under paragraph (1) of section 5173(a) covering such premises shall cover such exportation, and subsection (a) shall not apply.

(c) Cancellation or credit of export bonds.

The bonds given under subsection (a) shall be cancelled or credited and the bonds liable under subsection (b) credited if there is such proof of exportation as the Secretary may by regulations require.

In 1997, P.L. 105-34, Sec. 1412(a), substituted "if there is such proof of exportation as the Secretary may by regulations require." for "on the submission of such evidence, records, and certification indicating exportation as the Secretary may by regulations prescribe." in subsec. (c), effective on the 1st day of the 1st calendar quarter that begins at least 180 days after 8/5/97.

In 1979, P.L. 96-39, Sec. 807(a)(15)(A), deleted "for storage therein pending exportation" in subsec (a) . . . Sec. 807(a)(15)(B), amended subsec. (b), effective 1/1/80.

Prior to amendment, subsec. (b) read as follows:

"(b) Exception.

"In case of distilled spirits withdrawn for exportation without payment of tax on application of the proprietor of bonded premises, the bond of such proprietor covering such bonded premises shall cover such exportation and subsection (a) shall not be applicable."

In 1977, P.L. 95-176, Sec. 3(b), amended subsec. (a), effective the first day of the first calendar month which begins more than 90 days after 11/14/76.

Prior to amendment subsec. (a) read as follows:

"(a) Requirements.

"No distilled spirits shall be withdrawn from bonded premises for exportation without payment of tax unless the exporter has furnished bond to cover such withdrawal, under such regulations and conditions, and in such form and penal sum, as the Secretary may prescribe."

In 1976, P.L. 94-455, Sec. 1906(b)(13)(A), substituted "Secretary" for "Secretary or his delegate" in subsecs. (a) and (c), effective 2/1/77.

Sec. 5176. New or renewed bonds.
(a) General.

New bonds shall be required under sections 5173 and 5175 in case of insolvency or removal of any surety, and may, at the discretion of the Secretary, be required in any other contingency affecting the validity or impairing the efficiency of such bond.

(b) Bonds.

If the proprietor of a distilled spirits plant fails or refuses to furnish a bond required under paragraph (1) of section 5173(a) or to renew the same, and neglects to immediately withdraw the spirits and pay the tax thereon, the Secretary shall proceed to collect the tax.

In 1979, P.L. 96-39, Sec. 807(a)(16)(A), substituted "sections 5173, and 5175" for "sections 5173, 5174, and 5175" in subsec. (a) . . . Sec. 807(a)(16)(B), amended subsec. (b), effective 1/1/80.

Prior to amendment, subsec. (b) read as follows:

"(b) Bonded warehouseman's bonds.

"In case the proprietor of a distilled spirits plant fails or refuses—

"(1) to give a warehouseman's bond required under section 5173(c) or to renew the same, and neglects to immediately withdraw the spirits and pay the tax thereon; or

"(2) to withdraw any spirits from storage on bonded premises before the expiration of the time limited in the bond and, except as otherwise provided by law, pay the tax thereon;

the Secretary shall proceed to collect the tax"

In 1976, P.L. 94-455, Sec. 1906(b)(13)(A), substituted "Secretary" for "Secretary or his delegate" in subsecs. (a) and (c), effective 2/1/77.

Sec. 5177. Other provisions relating to bonds.
(a) General provisions relating to bonds.

The provisions of section 5551 shall be applicable to the bonds required by or given under sections 5173 and 5175.

(b) Cross references.

(1) For deposit of United States bonds or notes in lieu of sureties, see section 9303 of title 31, United States Code.

(2) For penalty and forfeiture for failure or refusal to give bond, or for giving false, forged, or fraudulent bond, or for carrying on the business of a distiller without giving bond, see sections 5601(a)(4), 5601(a)(5), 5601(b), and 5615(3).

In 1982, P.L. 97-258, Sec. 3(f)(3), substituted "section 9303 of title 31, United States Code" for "6 U.S.C. 15" in para. (b)(1), effective 9/13/82.

In 1979, P.L. 96-39, Sec. 807(a)(17), substituted "sections 5173, and 5175" for "sections 5173, 5174, and 5175" in subsec. (a), effective 1/1/80.

In 1976, P.L. 94-455, Sec. 1905(b)(6)(B), substituted "5601(b)," for "5601(b)(2)," in para. (b)(2), effective 2/1/77.

Excise and miscellaneous taxes   Code Sec. 5178

Sec. 5178. Premises of distilled spirits plants.
(a) Location, construction, and arrangement.
(1) General.

(A) The premises of a distilled spirits plant shall be as described in the application required by section 5171(c). The Secretary shall prescribe such regulations relating to the location, construction, arrangement, and protection of distilled spirits plants as he deems necessary to facilitate inspection and afford adequate security to the revenue.

(B) No distilled spirits plant for the production of distilled spirits shall be located in any dwelling house, in any shed, yard, or inclosure connected with any dwelling house, or on board any vessel or boat, or on premises where beer or wine is made or produced, or liquors of any description are retailed, or on premises where any other business is carried on (except when authorized under subsection (b)).

(C) Notwithstanding any other provision of this chapter relating to distilled spirits plants the Secretary may approve the location, construction, arrangement, and method of operation of any establishment which was qualified to operate on the date preceding the effective date of this section if he deems that such location, construction, arrangement, and method of operation will afford adequate security to the revenue.

(2) Production operations.

(A) Any person establishing a distilled spirits plant may, as described in his application for registration, produce distilled spirits from any source or substance.

(B) The distilling system shall be continuous and shall be so designed and constructed and so connected as to prevent the unauthorized removal of distilled spirits before their production gauge.

(C) The Secretary is authorized to order and require—

(i) such identification of, changes of, and additions to, distilling apparatus, connecting pipes, pumps, tanks, and any machinery connected with or used in or on the premises, and

(ii) such fastenings, locks, and seals to be part of any of the stills, tubs, pipes, tanks, and other equipment,

as he may deem necessary to facilitate inspection and afford adequate security to the revenue.

(3) Warehousing operations.

(A) Any person establishing a distilled spirits plant for the production of distilled spirits may, as described in the application for registration, warehouse bulk distilled spirits on the bonded premises of such plant.

(B) Distilled spirits plants for the bonded warehousing of bulk distilled spirits elsewhere than as described in subparagraph (A) may be established at the discretion of the Secretary by proprietors referred to in subparagraph (A) or by other persons under such regulations as the Secretary shall prescribe.

(4) Processing operations. Any person establishing a distilled spirits plant may, as described in the application for registration, process distilled spirits on the bonded premises of such plant.

(b) Use of premises for other businesses.

The Secretary may authorize the carrying on of such other businesses (not specifically prohibited by section 5601(a)(6)) on premises of distilled spirits plants, as he finds will not jeopardize the revenue. Such other businesses shall not be carried on until an application to carry on such business has been made to and approved by the Secretary.

(c) Cross references.

(1) For provisions authorizing the Secretary to require installation of meters, tanks, and other apparatus, see section 5552.

(2) For penalty for distilling on prohibited premises, see section 5601(a)(6).

(3) For provisions relating to the bottling of distilled spirits labeled as alcohol, see section 5235.

(4) For provisions relating to the unauthorized use of distilled spirits in any manufacturing process, see section 5601(a)(9).

In **1979**, P.L. 96-39, Sec. 805(b)(1), amended paras. (a)(2), (a)(3), (a)(4) and (a)(5), effective 1/1/80.
Prior to amendment, paras. (a)(2), (a)(3), (a)(4) and (a)(5) read as follows:
"(2) Production facilities.

"(A) Any person establishing a distilled spirits plant may, as described in his application for registration, provide facilities which may be used for the production of distilled spirits from any source or substance.

"(B) The distilling system shall be continuous and closed at all points where potable or readily recoverable spirits are present and the distilling apparatus shall be so designed and constructed and so connected as to prevent the unauthorized removal of such spirits prior to their production gauge.

"(C) The Secretary is authorized to order and require such identification of, changes of, or additions to, distilling apparatus, connecting pipes, pumps, tanks, or any machinery connected with or used in or on the bonded premises, or require to be put on any of the stills, tubs, pipes, tanks, or other equipment, such fastenings, locks or seals as he may deem necessary to facilitate inspection and afford adequate security to the revenue.

"(3) Bonded warehousing facilities.

"(A) Any person establishing a distilled spirits plant for the production of distilled spirits may, as described in his application for registration, establish warehousing facilities on the bonded premises of such plant.

"(B) Distilled spirits plants for the bonded warehousing of distilled spirits elsewhere than as described in subparagraph (A) may be established at the discretion of the Secretary, by proprietors referred to in subparagraph (A) or by other persons, under such regulations as the Secretary shall prescribe.

"(C) Facilities for the storage on bonded premises of distilled spirits in casks, packages, cases, or similar portable approved containers shall be established in a room or building used exclusively for the storage, bottling, or packaging of distilled spirits, and activities related thereto.

"(D) A proprietor who has established facilities for the storage on bonded premises of distilled spirits under subparagraph (C) may establish a portion of such premises as an export storage facility for the storage of distilled spirits returned to bonded premises under section 5215(b).

"(4) Bottling facilities.

"(A) The proprietor of a distilled spirits plant authorized to store distilled spirits in casks, packages, cases, or similar portable approved containers on bonded premises—

"(i) may establish a separate portion of such premises for the bottling in bond of distilled spirits under section 5233 prior to payment or determination of tax, or

"(ii) may elect to use facilities on his bottling premises established under subparagraph (B) or (C) for bottling in accordance with the conditions and requirements of section 5233 and under the supervision provided for in section 5202(g), but after determination of tax.

"Distilled spirits bottled after determination of the internal revenue tax under clause (ii) shall be stamped and labeled in the same manner as distilled spirits bottled before determination of tax under clause (i).

"(B) Facilities for rectification of distilled spirits or wines upon which the tax has been paid or determined, may be established as a separate distilled spirits plant or as a part of a distilled spirits plant qualified for the production or bonded warehousing of distilled spirits. Such facilities, when qualified, may be used for the rectification of distilled spirits or wines, or the bottling or packaging of rectified or unrectified distilled spirits or wines on which the tax has been paid or determined.

"(C) Facilities for bottling or packaging any distilled spirits upon which the tax has been paid or determined (other than bottling facilities established under subparagraph (B)), may be established and maintained only by a State or political subdivision thereof, or by the proprietor of a distilled spirits plant qualified for the production or bonded warehousing of distilled spirits, as a part of such plant or as a separate distilled spirits plant. Such facilities, when qualified, may be used for the bottling or packaging of rectified or unrectified distilled spirits or wines but may not be used for the rectification of distilled spirits or wines.

"(D) Bottling premises established under subparagraphs (B) or (C) may not be located on bonded premises, and if the distilled spirits plant contains both bonded premises and bottling premises they shall be separated by such means or in such manner as the Secretary may by regulations prescribe.

"(5) Denaturing facilities. The Secretary may by regulations require such arrangement and segregation of denaturing facilities as he deems necessary."
—P.L. 96-39, Sec. 807(a)(18), substituted "section 5171(c)" for "section 5171(a)" in subpara. (a)(1)(A), effective 1/1/80.

In **1977**, P.L. 95-176, Sec. 2(b), added subpara. (a)(3)(D), effective the first day of the first calendar month which begins after 11/14/77.

3,417

In 1976, P.L. 94-455, Sec. 1906(b)(13)(A), substituted "Secretary" for "Secretary or his delegate" each place it appeared in Code Sec. 5178, effective 2/1/77.
In 1971, P.L. 91-659, Sec. 5, amended subpara. (a)(4)(A), effective 5/1/71.
Prior to amendment, subpara. (a)(4)(A) read as follows:
"(A) The proprietor of a distilled spirits plant authorized to store distilled spirits in casks, packages, cases, or similar portable approved containers on bonded premises may establish a separate portion of such premises for the bottling in bond of distilled spirits under section 5233 prior to payment or determination of the internal revenue tax."

Sec. 5179. Registration of stills.
(a) Requirements.

Every person having in his possession or custody, or under his control, any still or distilling apparatus set up, shall register such still or apparatus with the Secretary immediately on its being set up, by subscribing and filing with the Secretary a statement, in writing, setting forth the particular place where such still or distilling apparatus is set up, the kind of still and its capacity, the owner thereof, his place of residence, and the purpose for which said still or distilling apparatus has been or is intended to be used (except that stills or distilling apparatus not used or intended to be used for the distillation, redistillation, or recovery of distilled spirits are not required to be registered under this section).

(b) Cross references.

(1) For penalty and forfeiture provisions relating to unregistered stills, see sections 5601(a)(1) and 5615(1).

(2) For provisions requiring notification to set up a still, boiler, or other vessel for distilling, see section 5101(a)(2).

In 1984, P.L. 98-369, Sec. 451(b)(1), amended para. (b)(2), effective on the first day of the first calendar month which begins more than 90 days after 7/18/84.
Prior to amendment, para. (b)(2) read as follows:
"(2) For provisions requiring permit to set up still, boiler or other vessel for distilling, see section 5105."
In 1976, P.L. 94-455, Sec. 1905(b)(6)(C), deleted ", 5601(b)(1)," after "5601(a)(1)" in para. (b)(1), effective 2/1/77.
—P.L. 94-455, Sec. 1906(b)(13)(A), substituted "Secretary" for "Secretary or his delegate" each place it appeared in subsec. (a) and subsec. (b), effective 2/1/77.

Sec. 5180. Signs.
(a) Requirements.

Every person engaged in distilled spirits operations shall place and keep conspicuously on the outside of his place of business a sign showing the name of such person and denoting the business, or businesses, in which engaged. The sign required by this subsection shall be in such form and contain such information as the Secretary shall by regulations prescribe.

(b) Penalty.

For penalty and forfeiture relating to failure to post sign or improperly posting such sign, see section 5681.

In 1979, P.L. 96-39, Sec. 807(a)(19), amended the first sentence of subsec. (a), effective 1/1/80.
Prior to amendment, the first sentence of subsec. (a) read as follows:
"Every person engaged in distilling, bonded warehousing, rectifying, or bottling of distilled spirits shall place and keep conspicuously on the outside of his place of business a sign showing the name of such person and denoting the business, or businesses, in which engaged."
In 1976, P.L. 94-455, Sec. 1906(b)(13)(A), substituted "Secretary" for "Secretary or his delegate" each place it appeared in Code Sec. 5180, effective 2/1/77.

Sec. 5181. Distilled spirits for fuel use.
(a) In general.

(1) **Purposes for which plant may be established.** On such application and bond and in such manner as the Secretary may prescribe by regulation, a person may establish a distilled spirits plant solely for the purpose of—

(A) producing, processing, and storing, and

(B) using or distributing,

distilled spirits to be used exclusively for fuel use.

(2) **Regulations.** In prescribing regulations under paragraph (1) and in carrying out the provisions of this section, the Secretary shall, to the greatest extent possible, take steps to—

(A) expedite all applications;

(B) establish a minimum bond; and

(C) generally encourage and promote (through regulation or otherwise) the production of alcohol for fuel purposes.

(b) Authority to exempt.

The Secretary may by regulation provide for the waiver of any provision of this chapter (other than this section or any provision requiring the payment of tax) for any distilled spirits plant described in subsection (a) if the Secretary finds it necessary to carry out the provisions of this section.

(c) Special rules for small plant production.

(1) **Applications.**

(A) In general. An application for an operating permit for an eligible distilled spirits plant shall be in such a form and manner, and contain such information, as the Secretary may by regulations prescribe; except that the Secretary shall, to the greatest extent possible, take steps to simplify the application so as to expedite the issuance of such permits.

(B) Receipt of application. Within 15 days of receipt of an application under subparagraph (A), the Secretary shall send a written notice of receipt to the applicant, together with a statement as to whether the application meets the requirements of subparagraph (A). If such a notice is not sent and the applicant has a receipt indicating that the Secretary has received an application, paragraph (2) shall apply as if a written notice required by the preceding sentence, together with a statement that the application meets the requirements of subparagraph (A), had been sent on the 15th day after the date the Secretary received the application.

(C) Multiple applications. If more than one application is submitted with respect to any eligible distilled spirits plant in any calendar quarter, the provisions of this section shall apply only to the first application submitted with respect to such plant during such quarter. For purposes of the preceding sentence, if a corrected or amended first application is filed, such application shall not be considered as a separate application, and the 15-day period referred to in subparagraph (A) shall commence with receipt of the corrected or amended application.

(2) **Determination.**

(A) In general. In any case in which the Secretary under paragraph (1)(B) has notified an applicant of receipt of an application which meets the requirements of paragraph (1)(A), the Secretary shall make a determination as to whether such operating permit is to be issued, and shall notify the applicant of such determination, within 45 days of the date on which notice was sent under paragraph (1)(B).

(B) Failure to make determination. If the Secretary has not notified an applicant within the time prescribed under subparagraph (A), the application shall be treated as approved.

(C) Rejection of application. If the Secretary determines under subparagraph (A) that a permit should not be issued—

(i) the Secretary shall include in the notice to the applicant of such determination under subparagraph (A) detailed reasons for such determination, and

Excise and miscellaneous taxes — Code Sec. 5202

(ii) such determination shall not prejudice any further application for such operating permit.

(3) Bond. No bond shall be required for an eligible distilled spirits plant. For purposes of section 5212 and subsection (e)(2) of this section, the premises of an eligible distilled spirits plant shall be treated as bonded premises.

(4) Eligible distilled spirits plant. The term "eligible distilled spirits plant" means a plant which is used to produce distilled spirits exclusively for fuel use and the production from which does not exceed 10,000 proof gallons per year.

(d) Withdrawal free of tax.

Distilled spirits produced under this section may be withdrawn free of tax from the bonded premises (and any premises which are not bonded by reason of subsection (c)(3)) of a distilled spirits plant exclusively for fuel use as provided in section 5214(a)(12).

(e) Prohibited withdrawal, use, sale, or disposition.

(1) In general. Distilled spirits produced under this section shall not be withdrawn, used, sold, or disposed of for other than fuel use.

(2) Rendering unfit for use. For protection of the revenue and under such regulations as the Secretary may prescribe, distilled spirits produced under this section shall, before withdrawal from the bonded premises of a distilled spirits plant, be rendered unfit for beverage use by the addition of substances which will not impair the quality of the spirits for fuel use.

(f) Definition of distilled spirits.

For purposes of this section, the term "distilled spirits" does not include distilled spirits produced from petroleum, natural gas, or coal.

In 1980, P.L. 96-223, Sec. 232(e)(1), redesignated Sec. 5181, "Cross references", as Sec. 5182 and added new Sec. 5181, effective the first day of the first calendar month beginning more than 60 days after 4/2/80.

Sec. 5182. Cross references.

For provisions requiring recordkeeping by wholesale liquor dealers, see section 5112, and by retail liquor dealers, see section 5122.

In 2005, P.L. 109-59, Sec. 11125(b)(16), amended Code Sec. 5182, effective 7/1/2008, but not for taxes imposed for periods before 7/1/2008.
Prior to amendment, Code Sec. 5182 read as follows:
"SEC. 5182. CROSS REFERENCES.
"For provisions requiring payment of special (occupational) tax as wholesale liquor dealer, see section 5111, or as retail liquor dealer, see section 5121."
In 1980, P.L. 96-223, Sec. 232(e)(1), redesignated Code Sec. 5181 as Code Sec. 5182, effective the first day of the first calendar month beginning more than 60 days after 4/2/80.
In 1979, P.L. 96-39, Sec. 807(a)(20), substituted "tax as wholesale liquor dealer" for "tax as rectifier, see section 5081, or as wholesale liquor dealer", effective 1/1/80.

Subchapter C.—Operation of Distilled Spirits Plants

Part
I. General provisions.
II. Operations on bonded premises.

In 1979, P.L. 96-39, Sec. 807(b)(5), deleted the item for part III.
Prior to deletion, the items for part III read as follows: "III. Operations on bottling premises."

PART I.—GENERAL PROVISIONS

Sec.
5201. Regulation of operations.
5202. Supervision of operations.
5203. Entry and examination of premises.
5204. Gauging.
5206. Containers.
5207. Records and reports.

In 1984, P.L. 98-369, Sec. 454(c)(14), deleted item 5205.
Prior to deletion, item 5205 read as follows:
"5205. Stamps."

Sec. 5201. Regulation of operations.
(a) In general.

Proprietors of distilled spirits plants shall conduct all operations authorized to be conducted on the premises of such plants under such regulations as the Secretary shall prescribe.

(b) Distilled spirits for industrial uses.

The regulations of the Secretary under this chapter respecting the production, warehousing, denaturing, distribution, sale, export, and use of distilled spirits for industrial purposes shall be such as he deems necessary, advisable, or proper to secure the revenue, to prevent diversion to illegal uses, and to place the distilled spirits industry and other industries using such distilled spirits as a chemical raw material or for other lawful industrial purposes on the highest possible plane of scientific and commercial efficiency and development consistent with the provisions of this chapter. Where nonpotable chemical mixtures containing distilled spirits are produced for transfer to the bonded premises of a distilled spirits plant for completion of processing, the Secretary may waive any provision of this chapter with respect to the production of such mixtures, and the processing of such mixtures on the bonded premises shall be deemed to be production of distilled spirits for purposes of this chapter.

(c) Hours of operations.

The Secretary may prescribe regulations relating to hours for distillery operations and to hours for removal of distilled spirits from distilled spirits plants; however, such regulations shall not be more restrictive, as to any operation or function, that the provisions of internal revenue law and regulations relating to such operation or function in effect on the day preceding the effective date of this section.

(d) Identification of distilled spirits.

The Secretary may provide by regulations for the addition of tracer elements to distilled spirits to facilitate the enforcement of this chapter. Tracer elements to be added to distilled spirits at any distilled spirits plant under provisions of this subsection shall be of such character and in such quantity as the Secretary may authorize or require, and such as will not impair the quality of the distilled spirits for their intended use.

In 1979, P.L. 96-39, Sec. 807(a)(21), amended subsec. (a), effective 1/1/80.
Prior to amendment, subsec. (a), read as follows:
"(a) General. Proprietors of distilled spirits plants shall conduct their operations relating to the production, storage, denaturing, rectification, and bottling of distilled spirits, and all other operations authorized to be conducted on the premises of such plants, under such regulations as the Secretary shall prescribe."
In 1976, P.L. 94-455, Sec. 1906(b)(13)(A), substituted "Secretary" for "Secretary or his delegate" each place it appeared in Code Sec. 5201, effective 2/1/77.

Sec. 5202. Supervision of operations.

All operations on the premises of a distilled spirits plant shall be conducted under such supervision and controls (including the use of Government locks and seals) as the Secretary shall by regulations prescribe.

In 1979, P.L. 96-39, Sec. 806(a), amended Code Sec. 5202, effective 1/1/80.
Prior to amendment, Code Sec. 5202 read as follows:
"(a) General.
"The operations on the premises of distilled spirits plants shall be conducted under such supervision as the Secretary shall by regulation prescribe. The Secretary shall assign such number of internal revenue officers to distilled spirits plants

3,419

as he deems necessary to maintain supervision of the operations conducted on such premises.

"(b) *Removal of distilled spirits from distilling system.*

"The removal of distilled spirits from the closed distilling system shall be controlled by Government locks or seals, or by meters or other devices or methods as the Secretary may prescribe.

"(c) *Storage tanks.*

"Approved containers for the storage of distilled spirits on bonded premises (other than containers required by subsection (d) to be in a locked room or building or those containing distilled spirits denatured as authorized by law) shall be kept securely closed, and the flow of distilled spirits into and out of such containers shall be controlled by Government locks or seals, or by meters or other devices or methods as the Secretary may prescribe.

"(d) *Storage rooms or buildings.*

"Distilled spirits (other than denatured distilled spirits) on bonded premises in casks, packages, cases, or similar portable approved containers must be stored in a room or building provided as required by section 5178(a)(3)(C), which room or building shall be in the joint custody of the internal revenue officer assigned to such premises and the proprietor thereof, and shall be kept securely locked with Government locks and at no time be unlocked or opened, or remain open, except when such officer or person who may be designated to act for him is on the premises. Deposits of distilled spirits in, or removals of distilled spirits from, such room or building shall be under such supervision by internal revenue officers as the Secretary shall by regulations prescribe.

"(e) *Denaturation of distilled spirits.*

"The denaturation of distilled spirits on bonded premises shall be conducted under such supervision and controlled by such meters or other devices or methods as the Secretary shall prescribe.

"(f) *Gauging.*

"The gauge of production of distilled spirits, gauge for determination of the tax imposed under section 5001(a)(1), and gauge for tax-free removal of other than denatured distilled spirits from bonded premises, shall be made or supervised by internal revenue officers, under such regulations as the Secretary shall prescribe.

"(g) *Bottling in bond.*

"The bottling of distilled spirits in bond shall be supervised by the internal revenue officer assigned to the premises in such manner as the Secretary shall by regulations prescribe."

In 1976, P.L. 94-455, Sec. 1906(b)(13)(A), substituted "Secretary" for "Secretary or his delegate" each place it appeared in Code Sec. 5202, effective 2/1/77.

Sec. 5203. Entry and examination of premises.
(a) Keeping premises accessible.

Every proprietor of a distilled spirits plant shall furnish the Secretary such keys as may be required for internal revenue officers to gain access to the premises and any structures thereon, and such premises shall always be kept accessible to any officer having such keys.

(b) Right of entry and examination.

It shall be lawful for any internal revenue officer at all times, as well by night as by day, to enter any distilled spirits plant, or any other premises where distilled spirits operations are carried on, or structure or place used in connection therewith for storage or other purposes; to make examination of the materials, equipment, and facilities thereon; and make such gauges and inventories as he deems necessary. Whenever any officer, having demanded admittance, and having declared his name and office, is not admitted into such premises by the proprietor or other person having charge thereof, it shall be lawful for such officer, at all times, as well by night as by day, to use such force as is necessary for him to gain entry to such premises.

(c) Furnishing facilities and assistance.

On the demand of any internal revenue officer or agent, every proprietor of a distilled spirits plant shall furnish the necessary facilities and assistance to enable the officer or agent to gauge the spirits in any container or to examine any apparatus, equipment, containers, or materials on such premises. Such proprietor shall also, on demand of such officer or agent, open all doors, and open for examination all boxes, packages, and all casks, barrels, and other vessels on such premises.

(d) Authority to break up grounds or walls.

It shall be lawful for any internal revenue officer, and any person acting in his aid, to break up the ground on any part of a distilled spirits plant or any other premises where distilled spirits operations are carried on, or any ground adjoining or near to such plant or premises, or any wall or partition thereof, or belonging thereto, or other place, to search for any pipe, cock, private conveyance, or utensil; and, upon finding any such pipe or conveyance leading therefrom or thereto, to break up any ground, house, wall, or other place through or into which such pipe or other conveyance leads, and to break or cut away such pipe or other conveyance, and turn any cock, or to examine whether such pipe or other conveyance conveys or conceals any distilled spirits, mash, wort, or beer, or other liquor, from the sight or view of the officer, so as to prevent or hinder him from taking a true account thereof.

(e) Penalty.

For penalty for violation of this section, see section 5687.

In 1979, P.L. 96-39, Sec. 807(a)(22), substituted "where distilled spirits operations are carried on" for "where distilled spirits are produced or rectified" in the first sentences of subsecs. (b) and (d), and substituted "on such premises" for "not under the control of the internal revenue officer in charge" in the last sentence of subsec. (c), effective 1/1/80.

In 1976, P.L. 94-455, Sec. 1906(b)(13)(A), substituted "Secretary" for "Secretary or his delegate" in subsec. (a), effective 2/1/77.

Sec. 5204. Gauging.
(a) General.

The Secretary may by regulations require the gauging of distilled spirits for such purposes as he may deem necessary, and all required gauges shall be made at such times and under such conditions as he may by regulations prescribe.

(b) Gauging instruments.

For the determination of tax and the prevention and detection of frauds, the Secretary may prescribe for use such hydrometers, saccharometers, weighing and gauging instruments, or other means or methods for ascertaining the quantity, gravity, and producing capacity of any mash, wort, or beer used, or to be used, in the production of distilled spirits, and the strength and quantity of spirits subject to tax, as he may deem necessary; and he may prescribe regulations to secure a uniform and correct system of inspection, weighing, marking, and gauging of spirits.

(c) Gauging, marking, and branding by proprietors.

The Secretary may by regulations require the proprietor of a distilled spirits plant, at the proprietor's expense and under such supervision as the Secretary may require, to do such gauging, marking, and branding and such mechanical labor pertaining thereto as the Secretary deems proper and determines may be done without danger to the revenue.

In 1984, P.L. 98-369, Sec. 454(c)(4)(A), deleted "stamping" after "Gauging" in the heading of subsec. (c)... Sec. 454(c)(4)(B), deleted "stamping" after "gauging" in the text of subsec. (c), effective 7/1/85.

In 1979, P.L. 96-39, Sec. 807(a)(23), deleted ", in addition to those specified in section 5202(f)," after "for such purposes" in subsec. (a), effective 1/1/80.

In 1976, P.L. 94-455, Sec. 1906(b)(13)(A), substituted "Secretary" for "Secretary or his delegate" each place it appeared in Code Sec. 5204, effective 2/1/77.

Sec. 5205. Repealed.

In 1984, P.L. 98-369, Sec. 454(a), repealed Code Sec. 5205, effective 7/1/85. Prior to repeal, Code Sec. 5205 read as follows:

"SEC. 5205. STAMPS.

"(a) *Stamps for containers of distilled spirits.*

"(1) Containers of distilled spirits. No person shall transport, possess, buy, sell, or transfer any distilled spirits, unless the immediate container thereof is stamped by a stamp evidencing the determination of the tax or indicating compliance with the provisions of this chapter. The provisions of this paragraph shall not apply to—

"(A) distilled spirits, lawfully withdrawn from bond, placed in containers for immediate consumption on the premises or for preparation for such consumption;

"(B) distilled spirits in bond or in customs custody;

"(C) distilled spirits, lawfully withdrawn from bond, in immediate containers stamped under other provisions of internal revenue or customs law or regulations issued pursuant thereto;

"(D) distilled spirits on which no internal revenue tax is required to be paid;

"(E) distilled spirits lawfully withdrawn from bond and not intended for sale or for use in the manufacture or production of any article intended for sale; or

"(F) any regularly established common carrier receiving, transporting, delivering, or holding for transportation or delivery distilled spirits in the ordinary course of its business as a common carrier.

"(2) Stamp regulations. The Secretary shall prescribe regulations with respect to the supplying or procuring of stamps required under this subsection or section 5235, the time and manner of applying for, issuing, affixing, and destroying such stamps, the form of such stamps and the information to be shown thereon, applications for the stamps, proof that applicants are entitled to such stamps, and the method of accounting for such stamps, and such other regulations as he may deem necessary for the enforcement of this subsection. In the case of a container of a capacity of 5 wine gallons or less, the stamp shall be affixed in such a manner as to be broken when the container is opened, unless the container is one that cannot again be used after opening.

"(b) *Stamps for containers of distilled spirits withdrawn from bonded premises on determination of tax.*

Containers of all distilled spirits withdrawn from bonded premises on determination of tax under section 5006(a) shall be stamped by a stamp under such regulations as the Secretary shall prescribe. This subsection shall not be construed to require stamps on cases of bottled distilled spirits filed and stamped on bonded premises.

"(c) *Stamps for containers of distilled spirits withdrawn for exportation.*

"(1) Exportation without payment of tax. Every container of distilled spirits withdrawn for exportation under section 5214(a)(4) shall be stamped by a stamp under such regulations as the Secretary shall prescribe. This paragraph shall not be construed to require stamps on cases of bottled distilled spirits filled and stamped on bonded premises.

"(2) Exportation with benefit of drawback. The Secretary may require any container of distilled spirits bottled or packaged especially for export with benefit of drawback to be stamped by a stamp under such regulations as he may prescribe.

"(d) *Issue for restamping.*

"The Secretary, under regulations prescribed by him, may authorize restamping of containers of distilled spirits which have been duly stamped but from which the stamps have been lost or destroyed by unavoidable accident.

"(e) *Accountability.*

"All stamps relating to distilled spirits shall be used and accounted for under such regulations as the Secretary may prescribe.

"(f) *Effacement of stamps, marks, and brands on emptied containers.*

"Every person who empties, or causes to be emptied, any immediate container of distilled spirits bearing any stamp, mark, or brand required by law or regulations prescribed pursuant thereto (other than containers stamped under subsection (a) or section 5235) shall at the time of emptying such container efface and obliterate such stamp, mark, or brand, except that the Secretary may, by regulations, waive any requirement of this subsection as to the effacement or obliteration of marks or brands or (portions thereof) where he determines that no jeopardy to the revenue will be involved.

"(g) *Form of stamp.*

"Any stamp required by or prescribed pursuant to the provisions of this section or section 5235 may consist of such coupon, serially-numbered ticket, imprint, design, other form of stamp, or other device as the Secretary shall by regulations prescribe.

"(h) *Cross references.*

"(1) For general provisions relating to stamps, see chapter 69.

"(2) For provisions relating to the stamping, marking, and branding of containers of distilled spirits by proprietors, see section 5204(c).

"(3) For provisions relating to the stamping of bottled alcohol, see section 5235.

"(4) For penalties and forfeitures relating to stamps, marks, and brands, see sections 5604, 5613, 7208, and 7209."

In 1979, P.L. 96-39, Sec. 807(a)(24), deleted para. (a)(1), redesignated paras. (a)(2) and (3) as paras. (a)(1) and (2), amended para. (a)(1) by deleting "OTHER" from the title, deleted subpara. (a)(2)(D), redesignated subparas. (a)(1)(E), (F), and (G) as (a)(1)(D), (E), and (F), amended para. (c)(2) by deleting the last sentence deleted subsec. (d), redesignated subsecs. (e), (f), (g), (h), and (i) as subsecs. (d), (e), (f), (g), and (h), deleted para. (h)(4) and redesignated para. (h)(5) as para (h)(4), effective 1/1/80.

Prior to amendment, para. (a)(1) read as follows:

"(a) *Stamps for containers of distilled spirits.*

"(1) Containers of distilled spirits bottled in bond. Every container of distilled spirits bottled in bond, under section 5233, when filled shall be stamped by a stamp evidencing the bottling of such spirits in bond under the provisions of this paragraph and section 5233."

Prior to amendment, subpara. (a)(1)(D) read as follows:

"(D) distilled spirits, lawfully withdrawn from bond, in actual process of rectification, blending, or bottling, or in actual use in processes of manufacture;"

Prior to amendment, subsec. (d) read as follows:

"(d) *Stamps for containers of 5 wine gallons or more of distilled spirits filled on bottling premises.*

"All containers of distilled spirits containing 5 wine gallons or more, which are filled on bottling premises of a distilled spirits plant for removal therefrom, shall be stamped by a stamp under such regulations as the Secretary shall prescribe."

Prior to amendment, para. (h)(4) read as follows:

"(4) For authority of the Secretary to prescribe regulations regarding stamps for distilled spirits withdrawn to manufacturing bonded warehouses, see section 5522(a)."

In 1977, P.L. 95-176, Sec. 2(c), added a new sentence at the end of para. (c)(2), effective the first day of the first calendar month which begins more than 90 days after 11/14/77.

In 1976, P.L. 94-569, Sec. 1, substituted "other form of stamp, or other device" for "or other form of stamp" in subsec. (h), effective 10/20/76.

—P.L. 94-455, Sec. 1906(b)(13)(A), substituted "Secretary" for "Secretary or his delegate" each place it appeared in Code Sec. 5205, effective 2/1/77.

Sec. 5206. Containers.
(a) Authority to prescribe.

The Secretary shall by regulations prescribe the types or kinds of containers which may be used to contain, store, transfer, convey, remove, or withdraw distilled spirits.

(b) Standards of fill.

The Secretary may by regulations prescribe the standards of fill for approved containers.

(c) Marking, branding, or identification.

Containers of distilled spirits (and cases containing bottles or other containers of such spirits) shall be marked, branded, or identified in such manner as the Secretary shall by regulations prescribe.

(d) Effacement of marks and brands on emptied containers.

Every person who empties, or causes to be emptied, any container of distilled spirits bearing any mark or brand required by law (or regulations pursuant thereto) shall at the time of emptying such container efface and obliterate such mark or brand; except that the Secretary may, by regulations, waive any requirement of this subsection where he determines that no jeopardy to the revenue will be involved.

(e) Applicability.

This section shall be applicable exclusively with respect to containers of distilled spirits for industrial use, with respect to containers of distilled spirits of a capacity of more than one gallon for other than industrial use, and with respect to cases containing bottles or other containers of distilled spirits.

(f) Cross references.

(1) For other provisions relating to regulation of containers of distilled spirits, see section 5301.

(2) For provisions relating to labeling containers of distilled spirits of one gallon or less for nonindustrial uses, see section 105(e) of the Federal Alcohol Administration Act (27 U.S.C. 205(e)).

(3) For provisions relating to the marking and branding of containers of distilled spirits by proprietors, see section 5204(c).

(4) For penalties and forfeitures relating to marks and brands, see sections 5604 and 5613.

In 1996, P.L. 104-188, Sec. 1704(t)(13), substituted "section 105(e)" for "section 5(e)" in para. (f)(2), effective 8/20/96.

In 1984, P.L. 98-369, Sec. 454(c)(5)(A), redesignated subsecs. (d) and (e) as subsecs. (e) and (f), respectively, and added new subsec. (d) . . . Sec. 454(c)(5)(B), added paras. (f)(3) and (4), as redesignated by Sec. 454(c)(5)(A) of the Act, effective 7/1/85.

In 1976, P.L. 94-455, Sec. 1906(b)(13)(A), substituted "Secretary" for "Secretary or his delegate" in subsecs. (a) and (b), effective 2/1/77.

Sec. 5207. Records and reports.
(a) Records of distilled spirits plant proprietors.

Every distilled spirits plant proprietor shall keep records in such form and manner as the Secretary shall by regulations prescribe of:

(1) The following production activities.

(A) the receipt of materials intended for use in the production of distilled spirits, and the use thereof,

(B) the receipt and use of distilled spirits received for redistillation, and

(C) the kind and quantity of distilled spirits produced.

(2) The following storage activities.
(A) the kind and quantity of distilled spirits, wines, and alcoholic ingredients entered into storage,
(B) the kind and quantity of distilled spirits, wines, and alcoholic ingredients removed, and the purpose for which removed, and
(C) the kind and quantity of distilled spirits returned to storage.

(3) The following denaturation activities.
(A) the kind and quantity of denaturants received and used or otherwise disposed of,
(B) the kind and quantity of distilled spirits denatured, and
(C) the kind and quantity of denatured distilled spirits removed.

(4) The following processing activities.
(A) all distilled spirits, wines, and alcoholic ingredients received or transferred,
(B) the kind and quantity of distilled spirits packaged or bottled, and
(C) the kind and quantity of distilled spirits removed from his premises.

(5) Such additional information with respect to activities described in paragraphs (1), (2), (3), and (4), and with respect to other activities, as may by regulations be required.

(b) Reports.
Every person required to keep records under subsection (a) shall render such reports covering his operations, at such times and in such form and manner and containing such information, as the Secretary shall by regulations prescribe.

(c) Preservation and inspection.
The records required by subsection (a) and a copy of each report required by subsection (b) shall be available for inspection by any internal revenue officer during business hours, and shall be preserved by the person required to keep such records and reports for such period as the Secretary shall by regulations prescribe.

(d) Penalty.
For penalty and forfeiture for refusal or neglect to keep records required under this section, or for false entries therein, see sections 5603 and 5615(5).

In **1997**, P.L. 105-34, Sec. 1413(a), deleted "shall be kept on the premises where the operations covered by the record are carried on and" after "required in subsection (b)" in subsec. (c), effective on the 1st day of the 1st calendar quarter that begins at least 180 days after 8/5/97.
In **1984**, P.L. 98-369, Sec. 454(c)(6), deleted subpara. (a)(4)(D), added "and" at the end of subpara. (a)(4)(B), and substituted a period for ", and" at the end of subpara. (a)(4)(C), effective 7/1/85.
Prior to deletion, subpara. (a)(4)(D) read as follows:
"(D) the receipt, use, and balance on hand of all stamps required by law or regulations to be used by him."
In **1979**, P.L. 96-39, Sec. 807(a)(25), amended Code Sec. 5207, effective 1/1/80.
Prior to amendment, Code Sec. 5207 read as follows:
"(a) Records of distillers and bonded warehousemen.
"Every distiller and every bonded warehouseman shall keep records in such form and manner as the Secretary shall by regulations prescribe of—
"(1) the receipt of materials intended for use in the production of distilled spirits, and the use thereof,
"(2) the receipt and use of distilled spirits received for redistillation,
"(3) the kind and quantity of distilled spirits produced,
"(4) the kind and quantity of distilled spirits entered into storage,
"(5) the bottling of distilled spirits in bond,
"(6) the kind and quality of distilled spirits removed from bonded premises, and from any taxpaid storeroom operated in connection therewith, and the purpose for which removed,
"(7) the kind and quantity of denaturants received and used or otherwise disposed of,
"(8) the kind and quantity of distilled spirits denatured,
"(9) the kind and quantity of denatured distilled spirits removed,
"(10) the kind and quantity of distilled spirits returned to bonded premises, and
"(11) such additional information as may by regulations be required.

"(b) Records of rectifiers and bottlers.
"Every rectifier and every bottler of distilled spirits shall keep records in such form and manner as the Secretary shall by regulations prescribe of—
"(1) all distilled spirits and wines received,
"(2) the kind and quantity of distilled spirits and wines rectified and packaged or bottled, or packaged or bottled without rectification,
"(3) the kind and quantity of distilled spirits and wines removed from his premises,
"(4) the receipt, use, and balance on hand of all stamps required by law or regulations to be used by him, and
"(5) such additional information as may by regulations be required.
"(c) Reports.
"Every person required to keep records under subsection (a) or (b) shall render such reports covering his operations, at such times and in such form and manner and containing such information, as the Secretary shall by regulation prescribe.
"(d) Preservation and inspection.
"The records required by subsection (a) and (b), and a copy of each report required by subsection (c) shall be kept on the premises where the operations covered by the record are carried on and shall be available for inspection by any internal revenue officer during business hours, and shall be preserved by the person required to keep such records and reports for such period as the Secretary shall by regulations prescribe.
"(e) Penalty.
"For penalty and forfeiture for refusal or neglect to keep records required under this section, or for false entries therein, see sections 5603 and 5615(5)."
In **1977**, P.L. 95-176, Sec. 2(e), deleted "and" at the end of para. (a)(9), redesignated para. (a)(10) as para. (a)(11), and added new para. (a)(10), effective the first day of the first calendar month which begins more than 90 days after 11/14/77.
In **1976**, P.L. 94-455, Sec. 1906(b)(13)(A), substituted "Secretary" for "Secretary or his delegate" each place it appeared in Code Sec. 5207, effective 2/1/77.

PART II.—OPERATIONS ON BONDED PREMISES

Subpart
A. General.
B. Production.
C. Storage.
D. Denaturation.

SUBPART A.—GENERAL

Sec.
5211. Production and entry of distilled spirits.
5212. Transfer of distilled spirits between bonded premises.
5213. Withdrawal of distilled spirits from bonded premises on determination of tax.
5214. Withdrawal of distilled spirits from bonded premises free of tax or without payment of tax.
5215. Return of tax determined distilled spirits to bonded premises.
5216. Regulation of operations.

Sec. 5211. Production and entry of distilled spirits.

Distilled spirits in the process of production in a distilled spirits plant may be held prior to the production gauge only for so long as is reasonably necessary to complete the process of production. Under such regulations as the Secretary shall prescribe, all distilled spirits produced in a distilled spirits plant shall be gauged and a record made of such gauge within a reasonable time after the production thereof has been completed. The proprietor shall, pursuant to such production gauge and in accordance with such regulations as the Secretary shall prescribe, make appropriate entry for—

(1) deposit of such spirits on bonded premises for storage or processing;

(2) withdrawal upon determination of tax as authorized by law;

(3) withdrawal under the provisions of section 5214; and

(4) transfer for redistillation under the provisions of section 5223.

In **1979**, P.L. 96-39, Sec. 807(a)(26), amended para. (1), added "and" at the end of para. (3), substituted a period for "; or" at the end of para. (4), deleted para. (5), effective 1/1/80.
Prior to amendment, para. (1) read as follows:
"(1) deposit of such spirits in storage on bonded premises;"

Excise and miscellaneous taxes   Code Sec. 5214(b)(6)

Prior to deletion, para. (5) read as follows:
"(5) immediate denaturation."
In **1976**, P.L. 94-455, Sec. 1906(b)(13)(A), substituted "Secretary" for "Secretary or his delegate" each place it appeared in Code Sec. 5211, effective 2/1/77.

Sec. 5212. Transfer of distilled spirits between bonded premises.

Bulk distilled spirits on which the internal revenue tax has not been paid or determined as authorized by law may, under such regulations as the Secretary shall prescribe, be transferred in bond between bonded premises in any approved container. For the purposes of this chapter, the removal of bulk distilled spirits for transfer in bond between bonded premises shall not be construed to be a withdrawal from bonded premises. The provisions of this section restricting transfers to bulk distilled spirits shall not apply to alcohol bottled under the provisions of section 5235 which is to be withdrawn for industrial purposes.

In **1980**, P.L. 96-598, Sec. 6(d), added the last sentence to Code Sec. 5212, effective 12/24/80.
In **1979**, P.L. 96-39, Sec. 805(b)(2), substituted "Bulk distilled spirits" for "Distilled spirits" and substituted "bulk distilled spirits" for "distilled spirits" in Code Sec. 5212, effective 1/1/80.
In **1976**, P.L. 94-455, Sec. 1906(b)(13)(A), substituted "Secretary" for "Secretary or his delegate" in Code Sec. 5212, effective 2/1/77.

Sec. 5213. Withdrawal of distilled spirits from bonded premises on determination of tax.

Subject to the provisions of section 5173, distilled spirits may be withdrawn from the bonded premises of a distilled spirits plant on payment or determination of tax thereon, in approved containers, under such regulations as the Secretary shall prescribe.

In **1979**, P.L. 96-39, Sec. 807(a)(27), amended Code Sec. 5213, effective 1/1/80. Prior to amendment, Code Sec. 5213 read as follows:
"On application to the Secretary and subject to the provisions of section 5174(a), distilled spirits may be withdrawn from the bonded premises of a distilled spirits plant on payment or determination of tax thereon, in approved containers, under such regulations as the Secretary shall prescribe."
In **1976**, P.L. 94-455, Sec. 1906(b)(13)(A), substituted "Secretary" for "Secretary or his delegate" each place it appeared in Code Sec. 5213, effective 2/1/77.

Sec. 5214. Withdrawal of distilled spirits from bonded premises free of tax or without payment of tax.

(a) Purposes.

Distilled spirits on which the internal revenue tax has not been paid or determined may, subject to such regulations as the Secretary shall prescribe, be withdrawn from the bonded premises of any distilled spirits plant in approved containers—

(1) free of tax after denaturation of such spirits in the manner prescribed by law for—

(A) exportation;

(B) use in the manufacture of ether, chloroform, or other definite chemical substance where such distilled spirits are changed into some other chemical substance and do not appear in the finished product; or

(C) any other use in the arts and industries (except for uses prohibited by section 5273(b) or (d)) and for fuel, light, and power; or

(2) free of tax by, and for the use of, the United States or any governmental agency thereof, any State, any political subdivision of a State, or the District of Columbia, for nonbeverage purposes; or

(3) free of tax for nonbeverage purposes and not for resale or use in the manufacture of any product for sale—

(A) for the use of any educational organization described in section 170(b)(1)(A)(ii) which is exempt from income tax under section 501(a), or for the use of any scientific university or college of learning;

(B) for any laboratory for use exclusively in scientific research;

(C) for use at any hospital, blood bank, or sanitarium (including use in making any analysis or test at such hospital, blood bank, or sanitarium), or at any pathological laboratory exclusively engaged in making analyses, or tests, for hospitals or sanitariums; or

(D) for the use of any clinic operated for charity and not for profit (including use in the compounding of bona fide medicines for treatment outside of such clinics of patients thereof); or

(4) without payment of tax for exportation, after making such application and entries, filing such bonds as are required by section 5175, and complying with such other requirements as may by regulations be prescribed; or

(5) without payment of tax for use in wine production, as authorized by section 5373; or

(6) without payment of tax for transfer to manufacturing bonded warehouses for manufacturing in such warehouses for export, as authorized by law; or

(7) without payment of tax for use of certain vessels and aircraft, as authorized by law; or

(8) without payment of tax for transfer to foreign-trade zones, as authorized by law; or

(9) without payment of tax, for transfer (for the purpose of storage pending exportation) to any customs bonded warehouse from which distilled spirits may be exported, and distilled spirits transferred to a customs bonded warehouse under this paragraph shall be entered, stored, and accounted for under such regulations and bonds as the Secretary may prescribe; or

(10) without payment of tax by a proprietor of bonded premises for use in research, development, or testing (other than consumer testing or other market analysis) of processes, systems, materials, or equipment, relating to distilled spirits or distilled spirits operations, under such limitations and conditions as to quantities, use, and accountability as the Secretary may by regulations require for the protection of the revenue; or

(11) free of tax when contained in an article (within the meaning of section 5002(a)(14)); or

(12) free of tax in the case of distilled spirits produced under section 5181; or

(13) without payment of tax for use on bonded wine cellar premises in the production of wine or wine products which will be rendered unfit for beverage use and removed pursuant to section 5362(d).

(b) Cross references.

(1) For provisions relating to denaturation, see sections 5241 and 5242.

(2) For provisions requiring permit for users of distilled spirits withdrawn free of tax and for users of specially denatured distilled spirits, see section 5271.

(3) For provisions relating to withdrawal of distilled spirits without payment of tax for use of certain vessels and aircraft, as authorized by law, see 19 U.S.C. 1309.

(4) For provisions relating to withdrawal of distilled spirits without payment of tax for manufacture in manufacturing bonded warehouse, see 19 U.S.C. 1311.

(5) For provisions relating to foreign-trade zones, see 19 U.S.C. 81c.

(6) For provisions authorizing regulations for withdrawal of distilled spirits free of tax for use of the United States, see section 7510.

Code Sec. 5214(b)(7)   Excise and miscellaneous taxes

(7) For provisions authorizing removal of distillates to bonded wine cellars for use in the production of distilling material, see section 5373(c).

(8) For provisions relating to distilled spirits for use of foreign embassies, legations, etc., see section 5066.

In **1984**, P.L. 98-369, Sec. 455(a), substituted "; or" for the period at the end of para. (a)(12) and added para. (a)(13), effective 7/18/84.
In **1980**, P.L. 96-223, Sec. 232(e)(2)(B), substituted a semicolon and "or" for the period at the end of para. (a)(11) and added para. (a)(12), effective the first day of the first calendar month beginning more than 60 days after 4/2/80.
In **1979**, P.L. 96-39, Sec. 807(a)(28), amended para. (a)(6) ... deleted "in the case of distilled spirits bottled in bond for export under section 5233 or distilled spirits returned to bonded premises under section 5215(b)," after "without payment of tax," in para. (a)(9) ... substituted "distilled spirits operations" for "distillery operations" in para. (a)(10) ... substituted "; or" for the period at the end of para. (a)(10) ... added new para. (a)(11) ... redesignated paras. (b)(4), (b)(5), (b)(6) and (b)(7) as paras. (b)(5), (b)(6), (b)(7) and (b)(8) ... added new para. (b)(4), effective 1/1/80.
Prior to amendment, para. (a)(6) read as follows:
"(6) without payment of tax for transfer to manufacturing bonded warehouses, as authorized by section 5522(a); or"
In **1977**, P.L. 95-176, Sec. 3(a), amended para. (a)(9) ... Sec. 3(d), added para. (b)(7) ... Sec. 4(a), added para. (a)(10), effective the first day of the first calendar month which begins more than 90 days after 11/14/77.
Prior to amendment, para. (a)(9) read as follows:
"(9) free of tax for use as samples in making tests or laboratory analyses."
In **1976**, P.L. 94-455, Sec. 1905(c)(2), deleted "or Territory" each place it appeared in para. (a)(2), effective 2/1/77.
—P.L. 94-455, Sec. 1906(b)(13)(A), substituted "Secretary" for "Secretary or his delegate" in subsec. (a), effective 2/1/77.
In **1969**, P.L. 91-172, Sec. 101(j)(29), substituted "170(b)(1)(A)(ii)" for "503(b)(2)" in subpara. (a)(3)(A), effective 1/1/70.

Sec. 5215. Return of tax determined distilled spirits to bonded premises.
(a) General rule.
Under such regulations as the Secretary may prescribe, distilled spirits on which tax has been determined or paid may be returned to the bonded premises of a distilled spirits plant but only for destruction, denaturation, redistillation, reconditioning, or rebottling.
(b) Applicability of chapter to distilled spirits returned to a distilled spirits plant.
All provisions of this chapter applicable to distilled spirits in bond shall be applicable to distilled spirits returned to bonded premises under the provisions of this section on such return.
(c) Return of bottled distilled spirits for relabeling and reclosing.
Under such regulations as the Secretary shall prescribe, bottled distilled spirits withdrawn from bonded premises may be returned to bonded premises for relabeling or reclosing, and the tax under section 5001 shall not again be collected on such spirits.
(d) Cross reference.
For provisions relating to the abatement, credit, or refund of tax on distilled spirits returned to a distilled spirits plant under this section, see section 5008(c).

In **1984**, P.L. 98-369, Sec. 454(c)(7)(A), substituted "reclosing" for "restamping" in the heading of subsec. (c) ... Sec. 454(c)(7)(B), substituted "reclosing" for "restamping" in the text of subsec. (c), effective 7/1/85.
In **1979**, P.L. 96-39, Sec. 807(a)(29), amended Code Sec. 5215, effective 1/1/80.
Prior to amendment, Code Sec. 5215 read as follows:
"Sec. 5215. Return of tax determined distilled spirits to bonded premises.
"(a) General.
"On such application and under such regulations as the Secretary may prescribe, distilled spirits withdrawn from bonded premises on payment or determination of tax (other than products to which any alcoholic ingredients other than such distilled spirits have been added) may be returned to the bonded premises of a distilled spirits plant. Such returned distilled spirits shall be destroyed, denatured, or redistilled, or shall be mingled as authorized in section 5234(a)(1) (other than subparagraph (C) thereof).
"(b) Distilled spirits returned to bonded premises for storage pending exportation.
"On such application and under such conditions as the Secretary may by regulations prescribe, distilled spirits which would be eligible for allowance of drawback under section 5062(b) on exportation, may be returned by the bottler or packager of such distilled spirits to an export storage facility on the bonded premises of the distilled spirits plant where bottled or packaged, solely for the purpose of storage pending withdrawal without payment of tax under section 5214(a)(4), (7), (8), or (9), or free of tax under section 7510.
"(c) Distilled spirits stamped and labeled as bottled in bond.
"On such application and under such regulations as the Secretary may prescribe, a proprietor of bonded premises who has bottled distilled spirits under section 5178(a)(4)(A)(ii), which are stamped and labeled as bottled in bond for domestic consumption, may return cases of such bottled distilled spirits to appropriate storage facilities on the bonded premises of the distilled spirits plant where bottled for storage pending withdrawal for any purpose for which distilled spirits bottled under section 5178(a)(4)(A)(i) may be withdrawn from bonded premises.
"(d) Applicability of chapter to distilled spirits returned to bonded premises.
"Except as otherwise provided in this section, all provisions of this chapter applicable to distilled spirits in bond shall be applicable to distilled spirits returned to bonded premises under the provisions of this section on such return.
"(e) Cross references.
"(1) For provisions relating to the remission, abatement, credit, or refund of tax on distilled spirits returned to bonded premises under this section, see section 5008(d).
"(2) For provisions relating to the establishment of an export storage facility on the bonded premises of a distilled spirits plant, see section 5178(a)(3)(D)."
In **1977**, P.L. 95-176, Sec. 2(a), amended Code Sec. 5215, effective the first day of the first calendar month which begins more than 90 days after 11/14/77.
Prior to amendment, Code Sec. 5215 read as follows:
"Sec. 5215. Return of tax determined distilled spirits to bonded premises.
"(a) General.
"On such application and under such regulations as the Secretary may prescribe, distilled spirits withdrawn from bonded premises on payment or determination of tax (other than products to which any alcoholic ingredients other than such distilled spirits have been added) may be returned to the bonded premises of a distilled spirits plant. Such returned distilled spirits shall be destroyed, denatured, or redistilled, or shall be mingled as authorized in section 5234(a)(1) (other than subparagraph (C) thereof). All provisions of this chapter applicable to distilled spirits in bond shall be applicable to distilled spirits returned to bonded premises under the provisions of this section on such return.
"(b) Cross reference.
For provisions relating to the remission, abatement, credit, or refund of tax on distilled spirits returned to bonded premises under provisions of this section, see section 5008(d)."
In **1976**, P.L. 94-455, Sec. 1906(b)(13)(A), substituted "Secretary" for "Secretary or his delegate" in subsec. (a), effective 2/1/77.
In **1971**, P.L. 91-659, Sec. 2(c), amended subsec. (a), repealed subsec. (b), and redesignated subsec. (c) as (b), effective 5/1/71.
Prior to amendment, subsecs. (a) and (b) read as follows:
"(a) General.
"On such application and under such regulations as the Secretary or his delegate may prescribe, distilled spirits withdrawn from bonded premises in bulk containers on or after July 1, 1959, on payment or determination of tax may be returned to the bonded premises of a distilled spirits plant, if such spirits have been found to be unsuitable for the purpose for which intended to be used before any processing thereof and before removal from the original container in which such distilled spirits were withdrawn from bonded premises. Such returned distilled spirits shall immediately be destroyed, redistilled or denatured, or may, in lieu of destruction, redistillation, or denaturation, be mingled on bonded premises as authorized in section 5234(a)(1)(A), (a)(1)(D), or (a)(1)(E). All provisions of this chapter applicable to distilled spirits in bond shall be applicable to distilled spirits returned to bonded premises under the provisions of this section on such return.
"(b) Distilled spirits withdrawn by pipeline.
"In the case of distilled spirits removed by pipeline, 'original container in which such distilled spirits were withdrawn from bonded premises' as used in this section shall mean the bulk tank into which the distilled spirits were originally deposited from pipeline, and the permitted return of the spirits to bonded premises may be made by pipeline or by other approved containers."
In **1965**, P.L. 89-44, Sec. 805(c), added "destroyed" and "destruction" in the second sentence of subsec. (a), effective 7/1/65.

Sec. 5216. Regulation of operations.
For general provisions relating to operations on bonded premises see part I of this subchapter.

SUBPART B.—PRODUCTION

Sec.
5221. Commencement, suspension, and resumption of operations.
5222. Production, receipt, removal, and use of distilling materials.
5223. Redistillation of spirits, articles, and residues.

In **1965**, added ", articles and residues" to item 5223, effective 10/1/65.

Excise and miscellaneous taxes — Code Sec. 5223(e)

Sec. 5221. Commencement, suspension, and resumption of operations.
(a) Commencement, suspension, and resumption.

The proprietor of a distilled spirits plant authorized to produce distilled spirits shall not commence production operations until written notice has been given to the Secretary stating when operations will begin. Any proprietor of a distilled spirits plant desiring to suspend production of distilled spirits shall give notice in writing to the Secretary, stating when he will suspend such operations. Pursuant to such notice, an internal revenue officer shall take such action as the Secretary shall prescribe to prevent the production of distilled spirits. No proprietor, after having given such notice, shall, after the time stated therein, produce distilled spirits on such premises until he again gives notice in writing to the Secretary stating the time when he will resume operations. At the time stated in the notice of resuming such operations an internal revenue officer shall take such action as is necessary to permit operations to be resumed. The notices submitted under this section shall be in such form and submitted in such manner as the Secretary may by regulations require. Nothing in this section shall apply to suspensions caused by unavoidable accidents; and the Secretary shall prescribe regulations to govern such cases of involuntary suspension.

(b) Penalty.

For penalty and forfeiture for carrying on the business of distiller after having given notice of suspension, see sections 5601(a)(14) and 5615(3).

In 1979, P.L. 96-39, Sec. 806(b), substituted "until written notice has been given to the Secretary stating when operations will begin" for "until an internal revenue officer has been assigned to the premises" in the first sentence of subsec. (a), effective 1/1/80.

In 1976, P.L. 94-455, Sec. 1906(b)(13)(A), substituted "Secretary" for "Secretary or his delegate" each place it appeared in Code Sec. 5221, effective 2/1/77.

Sec. 5222. Production, receipt, removal, and use of distilling materials.
(a) Production, removal, and use.

(1) No mash, wort, or wash fit for distillation or for the production of distilled spirits shall be made or fermented in any building or on any premises other than on the bonded premises of a distilled spirits plant duly authorized to produce distilled spirits according to law; and no mash, wort, or wash so made or fermented shall be removed from any such premises before being distilled, except as authorized by the Secretary; and no person other than an authorized distiller shall, by distillation or any other process, produce distilled spirits from any mash, wort, wash, or other material.

(2) Nothing in this subsection shall be construed to apply to—

(A) authorized operations performed on the premises of vinegar plants established under part I of subchapter H;
(B) authorized production and removal of fermented materials produced on authorized brewery or bonded wine cellar premises as provided by law;
(C) products exempt from tax under the provisions of section 5042 or 5053(e); or
(D) fermented materials used in the manufacture of vinegar by fermentation.

(b) Receipt.

Under such regulations as the Secretary may prescribe, fermented materials to be used in the production of distilled spirits may be received on the bonded premises of a distilled spirits plant authorized to produce distilled spirits as follows—

(1) from the premises of a bonded wine cellar authorized to remove such material by section 5362(c)(6);
(2) beer conveyed without payment of tax from brewery premises, beer which has been lawfully removed from brewery premises upon determination of tax, or
(3) cider exempt from tax under the provisions of section 5042(a)(1).

(c) Processing of distilled spirits containing extraneous substances.

The Secretary may by regulations provide for the removal from the distilling system, and the addition to the fermented or unfermented distilling material, of distilled spirits containing substantial quantities of fusel oil or aldehydes, or other extraneous substances.

(d) Penalty.

For penalty and forfeiture for unlawful production, removal, or use of material fit for distillation or for the production of distilled spirits, and for penalty and forfeiture for unlawful production of distilled spirits, see sections 5601(a)(7), 5601(a)(8), and 5615(4).

In 1997, P.L. 105-34, Sec. 1414(a), amended para. (b)(2), effective on the 1st day of the 1st calendar quarter that begins at least 180 days after 8/5/97.
Prior to amendment, para. (b)(2) read as follows:
"(2) conveyed without payment of tax from contiguous brewery premises where produced; or"

In 1979, P.L. 96-39, Sec. 807(a)(30), deleted ", in the production facilities of a distilled spirits plant" after "unfermented distilling material" in subsec. (c), effective 1/1/80.

In 1978, P.L. 95-458, Sec. 2(b)(4), substituted "; or" and added "or 5053(e); or" for ", or" in subpara. (a)(2)(C), effective the first day of the first calendar month which begins more than 90 days after 10/14/78.

In 1976, P.L. 94-455, Sec. 1905(b)(6)(D), deleted "5601(b)(3), 5601(b)(4)," after "5601(a)(8)," in subsec. (d), effective 2/1/77.

—P.L. 94-455, Sec. 1906(b)(13)(A), substituted "Secretary" for "Secretary or his delegate" each place it appeared in Code Sec. 5222, effective 2/1/77.

Sec. 5223. Redistillation of spirits, articles, and residues.
(a) Spirits on bonded premises.

The proprietor of a distilled spirits plant authorized to produce distilled spirits may, under such regulations as the Secretary shall prescribe, redistill any distilled spirits which have not been withdrawn from bonded premises.

(b) Distilled spirits returned for redistillation.

Distilled spirits which have been lawfully removed from bonded premises free of tax or without payment of tax may, under such regulations as the Secretary may prescribe, be returned for redistillation to the bonded premises of a distilled spirits plant authorized to produce distilled spirits.

(c) Redistillation of articles and residues.

Articles, containing denatured distilled spirits, which were manufactured under the provisions of subchapter D or on the bonded premises of a distilled spirits plant, and the spirits residues of manufacturing processes related thereto, may be received, and the distilled spirits therein recovered by redistillation, on the bonded premises of a distilled spirits plant authorized to produce distilled spirits, under such regulations as the Secretary may prescribe.

(d) Denatured distilled spirits, articles, and residues.

Distilled spirits recovered by the redistillation of denatured distilled spirits, or by the redistillation of the articles or residues described in subsection (c), may not be withdrawn from bonded premises except for industrial use or after denaturation thereof in the manner prescribed by law.

(e) Products of redistillation.

All distilled spirits redistilled on bonded premises subsequent to production gauge shall be treated the same as if such spirits had been originally produced by the redistiller and all provisions of this chapter applicable to the original production of distilled spirits shall be applicable thereto. Any

Code Sec. 5223(e)

prior obligation as to taxes, liens, and bonds with respect to such distilled spirits shall be extinguished on redistillation. Nothing in this subsection shall be construed as affecting any provision of law relating to the labeling of distilled spirits or as limiting the authority of the Secretary to regulate the marking, branding, or identification of distilled spirits redistilled under this section.

In 1979, P.L. 96-39, Sec. 807(a)(31), added "or on the bonded premises of a distilled spirits plant" after "subchapter D" in subsec. (c) and deleted the last sentence of subsec. (e), effective 1/1/80.
Prior to deletion, the last sentence of subsec. (e) read as follows:
"The processing of distilled spirits, subsequent to production gauge, in the manufacture of vodka in the production facilities of a distilled spirits plant shall be treated for the purposes of this subsection, subsection (a), and sections 5025(d) and 5215 as redistillation of the spirits."
In 1976, P.L. 94-455, Sec. 1906(b)(13)(A), substituted "Secretary" for "Secretary or his delegate" each place it appeared in Code Sec. 5223, effective 2/1/77.
In 1965, P.L. 89-44, Sec. 805(f)(8), added subsec. (c) and redesignated former subsecs. (c) and (d) as (d) and (e), added ", articles and residues" to the catchlines of section 5223 and redesignated subsec. (d), and added in redesignated subsec. (d) ", or by the redistillation of the articles or residues described in subsection (c)," after "denatured distilled spirits" effective 10/1/65.

SUBPART C.—STORAGE

Sec.
5231. Entry for deposit.
5232. Imported distilled spirits.
5233. Repealed. [Bottling of distilled spirits in bond.]
5234. Repealed. [Mingling and blending of distilled spirits.]
5235. Bottling of alcohol for industrial purposes.
5236. Discontinuance of storage facilities and transfer of distilled spirits.

In 1979, P.L. 96-39, Sec. 807(b)(6), amended item 5231 and deleted items 5233 and 5234.
Prior to amendment, items 5231, 5233 and 5234 read as follows:
"5231. Entry for deposit in storage."
"5233. Bottling of distilled spirits in bond."
"5234. Mingling and blending of distilled spirits."

Sec. 5231. Entry for deposit.

All distilled spirits entered for deposit on the bonded premises of a distilled spirits plant under section 5211 shall, under such regulations as the Secretary shall prescribe, be deposited in the facilities on the bonded premises designated in the entry for deposit.

In 1979, P.L. 96-39, Sec. 807(a)(32), amended Code Sec. 5231, effective 1/1/80.
Prior to amendment, Code Sec. 5231 read as follows:
"SEC. 5231. ENTRY FOR DEPOSIT.
"(a) General.
"All distilled spirits entered for deposit in storage under section 5211 shall, under such regulations as the Secretary shall prescribe, be deposited in storage facilities on the bonded premises designated in the entry for deposit.
"(b) Cross reference.
"For provisions requiring that all distilled spirits entered for deposit be withdrawn within 20 years from date of original entry for deposit, see section 5006(a)(2)."
In 1976, P.L. 94-455, Sec. 1906(b)(13)(A), substituted "Secretary" for "Secretary or his delegate" in subsec. (a), effective 2/1/77.

Sec. 5232. Imported distilled spirits.
(a) Transfer to distilled spirits plant without payment of tax.

Distilled spirits imported or brought into the United States in bulk containers may, under such regulations as the Secretary shall prescribe, be withdrawn from customs custody and transferred in such bulk containers or by pipeline to the bonded premises of a distilled spirits plant without payment of the internal revenue tax imposed on such distilled spirits. The person operating the bonded premises of the distilled spirits plant to which such spirits are transferred shall become liable for the tax on distilled spirits withdrawn from customs custody under this section upon release of the spirits from customs custody, and the importer, or the person bringing such distilled spirits into the United States shall thereupon be relieved of his liability for such tax.

(b) Withdrawals, etc.

Distilled spirits transferred pursuant to subsection (a)—
(1) may be redistilled or denatured only if of 185 degrees or more of proof, and
(2) may be withdrawn for any purpose authorized by this chapter, in the same manner as domestic distilled spirits.

In 1979, P.L. 96-39, Sec. 807(a)(33), deleted para. (b)(1) and redesignated paras. (b)(2) and (b)(3) as paras. (b)(1) and (b)(2), effective 1/1/80.
Prior to deletion, para. (b)(1) read as follows:
"(1) may not be bottled in bond under section 5233,"
In 1976, P.L. 94-455, Sec. 1905(a)(15), substituted "and the importer, or the person bringing such distilled spirits into the United States" for "and the importer" in subsec. (a), effective 2/1/77.
—P.L. 94-455, Sec. 1906(b)(13)(A), substituted "Secretary" for "Secretary or his delegate" each place it appeared in Code Sec. 5232, effective 2/1/77.
In 1971, P.L. 91-659, Sec. 7(a), amended the first sentence of subsec. (a), effective 1/8/71.
Prior to amendment, the first sentence of subsec. (a) read as follows:
"Imported distilled spirits in bulk containers may, under such regulations as the Secretary or his delegate shall prescribe, be withdrawn from customs custody and transferred in such bulk containers or by pipeline to the bonded premises of a distilled spirits plant without payment of the internal revenue tax imposed on imported distilled spirits by section 5001."
—P.L. 91-659, Sec. 7(b), amended subsec. (b) by striking out "Imported distilled spirits" and inserting in lieu thereof "Distilled spirits", effective 1/8/71.
In 1968, P.L. 90-630, Sec. 3(a), amended Code Sec. 5232, effective for withdrawals from customs custody on or after the first day of the first calendar month which begins more than 90 days after 10/26/68.
Prior to amendment, Code Sec. 5232 read as follows:
"SEC. 5232. IMPORTED DISTILLED SPIRITS.
"Imported distilled spirits of 185 degrees or more of proof (or spirits of any proof imported for any purpose incident to the requirements of the national defense) may, under such regulations as the Secretary or his delegate shall prescribe, be withdrawn from customs custody, and transferred to the bonded premises of a distilled spirits plant, for nonbeverage use, without payment of the internal revenue tax imposed on imported distilled spirits by section 5001. Such spirits may be redistilled or denatured and may, without redistillation or denaturation, be withdrawn for any purpose authorized by this chapter, in the same manner as domestic distilled spirits."

Sec. 5233. Repealed.

In 1979, P.L. 96-39, Sec. 807(a)(34), repealed Code Sec. 5233, effective 1/1/80.
Prior to repeal, Code Sec. 5233 read as follows:
"SEC. 5233. BOTTLING OF DISTILLED SPIRITS IN BOND.
"(a) General.
"Distilled spirits stored on bonded premises which have been duly entered for bottling in bond before determination of tax or for bottling in bond for export, shall be dumped, gauged, bottled, packed, and cased in the manner which the Secretary shall by regulations prescribe. Such bottling, packing, and casing shall be conducted in the separate facilities provided therefor under section 5178(a)(4)(A).
"(b) Bottling requirements.
"(1) The proprietor of a distilled spirits plant who has made entry for withdrawal of distilled spirits for bottling in bond may, under such regulations as the Secretary shall prescribe,
"(A) remove extraneous insoluble materials, and effect minor changes in the soluble color or soluble solids solely by filtrations or other physical treatments (which do not involve the addition of any substance which will remain incorporated in the completed product), as may be necessary or desirable to produce a stable product, provided such changes shall not exceed maximum limitations prescribed under regulations issued by the Secretary, and
"(B) reduce the proof of such spirits by the addition of pure water only to 100 proof for spirits for domestic use, or to not less than 80 proof for spirits for export purposes, and
"(C) mingle, when dumped for bottling, distilled spirits of the same kind, differing only in proof, produced in the same distilling season by the same distiller at the same distillery.
"(2) Nothing in this section shall authorize or permit any mingling of different products, or of the same products of different distilling seasons, or the addition or subtraction of any substance or material or the application of any method or process to alter or change in any way the original condition or character of the product except as authorized in this section.
"(3) Distilled spirits (except gin and vodka for export) shall not be bottled in bond until they have remained in bond in wooden containers for at least 4 years.
"(4) Nothing in this section shall authorize the labeling of spirits in bottles contrary to regulations issued pursuant to the Federal Alcohol Administration Act (27 U.S.C., chapter 8), or any amendment thereof.
"(c) Trademarks on bottles.

Excise and miscellaneous taxes   Code Sec. 5241

"No trademarks shall be put on any bottle unless the real name of the actual bona fide distiller, or the name of the individual, firm, partnership, corporation, or association in whose name the spirits were produced and warehoused, shall also be placed conspicuously on such bottle.

"(d) Return of bottled distilled spirits for rebottling, relabeling, or restamping.

"Under such regulations as the Secretary shall prescribe, distilled spirits which have been bottled under this section and removed from bonded premises may, on application to the Secretary, be returned to bonded premises for rebottling, relabeling, or restamping, and tax under section 5001(a)(1) shall not again be collected on such spirits.

"(e) Cross references.

"(1) For provisions relating to stamps and stamping of distilled spirits bottled in bond, see section 5205.

"(2) For provisions relating to marking or branding of cases of distilled spirits bottled in bond, see section 5206."

In 1976, P.L. 94-455, Sec. 1905(a)(16), deleted "49 Stat. 977;" following the parenthesis in para. (b)(4), effective 2/1/77.

—P.L. 94-455, Sec. 1906(b)(13)(A), substituted "Secretary" for "Secretary or his delegate" each place it appeared in Code Sec. 5233, effective 2/1/77.

Sec. 5234. Repealed.

In 1979, P.L. 96-39, Sec. 807(a)(35), repealed Code Sec. 5234, effective 1/1/80. Prior to repeal, Code Sec. 5234 read as follows:

"SEC. 5234. MINGLING AND BLENDING OF DISTILLED SPIRITS.

"(a) Mingling of distilled spirits on bonded premises.

"(1) In general. Under such regulations as the Secretary shall prescribe, distilled spirits may be mingled on bonded premises if such spirits—

"(A) were distilled at 190 degrees or more of proof;

"(B) are heterogeneous and are being dumped for gauging in bulk gauging tanks for immediate removal to bottling premises for use exclusively in taxable rectification, or for blending under section 5025(f), or for other mingling or treatment under section 5025(k);

"(C) are homogeneous;

"(D) are for immediate denaturation or immediate removal for an authorized tax-free purpose; or

"(E) are for immediate redistillation.

"(2) Consolidation of packages. Unless such regulations as the Secretary shall prescribe, distilled spirits—

"(A) of the same kind,

"(B) distilled at the same distillery,

"(C) distilled by the same proprietor (under his own or any trade name), and

"(D) which have been stored in internal revenue bond in the same kind of cooperage for not less than 4 years (or 2 years in the case of rum or brandy), may, within 20 years of the date of original entry for deposit of the spirits, be mingled on bonded premises. Where distilled spirits produced in different distilling seasons are mingled under this paragraph, the mingled spirits shall consist of not less than 10 percent of spirits of each such season. No spirits mingled under the provisions of this paragraph shall be again mingled under the provisions thereof until at least one year has elapsed since the last prior mingling. For purposes of this chapter, the date of original entry for deposit of the spirits mingled under the provisions of this paragraph shall be the date of original entry for deposit of the youngest spirits contained in the mingled spirits and the distilling season of such mingled spirits shall be the distilling season of the youngest spirits contained therein. Notwithstanding any other provisions of law, distilled spirits mingled under this paragraph may be bottled and labeled the same as if such spirits had not been so mingled. No statement claiming or implying age in excess of that of the youngest spirits contained in the mingled spirits shall be made on any stamp or label or in any advertisement.

"(b) Mingling of distilled spirits for national defense.

"Under such regulations as the Secretary shall prescribe, distilled spirits may be mingled on bonded premises or in the course of removal therefrom, for any purpose incident to the national defense.

"(c) Blending of beverage rums or brandies.

"Fruit brandies distilled from the same kind of fruit at not more than 170 degrees of proof may, for the sole purpose of perfecting such brandies according to commercial standards, be mixed or blended with each other, or with any such mixture or blend, on bonded premises. Rums may, for the sole purpose of perfecting them according to commercial standards, be mixed or blended with each other, or with any such mixture or blend, on bonded premises. Such rums or brandies so mixed or blended may be packaged, stored, transported, transferred in bond, withdrawn free of tax, withdrawn upon payment or determination of tax, or be otherwise disposed of, in the same manner as rums or brandies not so mixed or blended. The Secretary may make such rules or regulations as he may deem necessary to carry this subsection into effect.

"(d) Cross references.

"For provisions imposing a tax on the blending of beverage rums or brandies under subsection (c), see section 5023."

In 1977, P.L. 95-176, Sec. 5, deleted "for further storage in bond." after "packages" from the heading of para. (a)(2) and second part of the first sentence following subpara. (a)(2)(C), effective the first day of the first calendar month which begins more than 90 days after 11/14/77.

Prior to amendment, that part of the first sentence following subpara. (a)(2)(C) read as follows:

"(D) which have been stored in internal revenue bond in the same kind of cooperage for not less than 4 years (or 2 years in the case of rum or brandy), may, within 20 years of the date of original entry for deposit of the spirits, be mingled on bonded premises for further storage in bond in as many as necessary of the same packages in which the spirits were stored before consolidation."

In 1976, P.L. 94-455, Sec. 1905(a)(17), substituted "20 years" for "8 years" in subsec. (a), effective 2/1/77.

—P.L. 94-455, Sec. 1906(b)(13)(A), substituted "Secretary" for "Secretary or his delegate" each place it appeared in Code Sec. 5234, effective 2/1/77.

In 1965, P.L. 89-44, Sec. 805(f)(11), amended subpara. (a)(1)(B), effective 10/1/65.

Prior to amendment, subpara. (a)(1)(B) read as follows:

"(B) are heterogeneous and are being dumped for gauging in bulk gauging tanks for immediate removal to bottling premises for use exclusively in taxable rectification or rectification under section 5025(f);"

Sec. 5235. Bottling of alcohol for industrial purposes.

Alcohol for industrial purposes may be bottled, labeled, and cased on bonded premises of a distilled spirits plant prior to payment or determination of tax, under such regulations as the Secretary may prescribe.

In 1984, P.L. 98-369, Sec. 454(c)(8), deleted "stamped," in the first sentence of Code Sec. 5235 and deleted the second sentence, effective 7/1/85.

Prior to deletion, the second sentence read as follows:

"The provisions of section 5205(a)(1) shall not apply to alcohol bottled, stamped, and labeled as such under this section."

In 1979, P.L. 96-39, Sec. 807(a)(36), amended the second sentence of Code Sec. 5235, effective 1/1/80.

Prior to amendment, the second sentence of Code Sec. 5235 read as follows: "The provisions of sections 5178(a)(4)(A), 5205(a)(1), and 5233 (relating to the bottling of distilled spirits in bond) shall not be applicable to alcohol bottled, stamped, and labeled as such under this section."

In 1976, P.L. 94-455, Sec. 1906(b)(13)(A), substituted "Secretary" for "Secretary or his delegate" in Code Sec. 5235, effective 2/1/77.

Sec. 5236. Discontinuance of storage facilities and transfer of distilled spirits.

When the Secretary finds any facilities for the storage of distilled spirits on bonded premises to be unsafe or unfit for use, or the spirits contained therein subject to great loss or wastage he may require the discontinuance of the use of such facilities and require the spirits contained therein to be transferred to such other storage facilities as he may designate. Such transfer shall be made at such time and under such supervision as the Secretary may require and the expense of the transfer shall be paid by the owner or the warehouseman of the distilled spirits. Whenever the owner of such distilled spirits or the warehouseman fails to make such transfer within the time prescribed, or to pay the just and proper expense of such transfer, as ascertained and determined by the Secretary, such distilled spirits may be seized and sold by the Secretary in the same manner as goods are sold on distraint for taxes, and the proceeds of such sale shall be applied to the payment of the taxes due thereon and the cost and expenses of such sale and removal, and the balance paid over to the owner of such distilled spirits.

In 1976, P.L. 94-455, Sec. 1906(b)(13)(A), substituted "Secretary" for "Secretary or his delegate" each place it appeared in Code Sec. 5236, effective 2/1/77.

SUBPART D.—DENATURATION

Sec.

5241. Authority to denature.

5242. Denaturing materials.

5243. Sale of abandoned spirits for denaturation without collection of tax.

5244. Cross references.

Sec. 5241. Authority to denature.

Under such regulations as the Secretary shall prescribe, distilled spirits may be denatured on the bonded premises of a distilled spirits plant qualified for the processing of distilled spirits. Distilled spirits to be denatured under this section shall be of such kind and such degree of proof as the Secretary shall by regulations prescribe. Distilled spirits denatured under this section may be used on the bonded prem-

3,427

ises of a distilled spirits plant in the manufacture of any article.

In 1979, P.L. 96-39, Sec. 807(a)(37), amended Code Sec. 5241, effective 1/1/80. Prior to amendment, Code Sec. 5241 read as follows:

"SEC. 5241. AUTHORITY TO DENATURE. Under such regulations as the Secretary shall prescribe, distilled spirits may be denatured on the bonded premises of any distilled spirits plant operated by a proprietor who is authorized to produce distilled spirits at such plant or on other bonded premises. Any other person operating bonded premises may, at the discretion of the Secretary and under such regulations as he may prescribe, be authorized to denature distilled spirits on such bonded premises. Distilled spirits to be denatured under this section shall be of such kind and of such degree of proof as the Secretary shall by regulations prescribe."

In 1976, P.L. 94-455, Sec. 1906(b)(13)(A), substituted "Secretary" for "Secretary or his delegate" each place it appeared in Code Sec. 5241, effective 2/1/77.

Sec. 5242. Denaturing materials.

Methanol or other denaturing materials suitable to the use for which the denatured distilled spirits are intended to be withdrawn shall be used for the denaturation of distilled spirits. Denaturing materials shall be such as to render the spirits with which they are admixed unfit for beverage or internal human medicinal use. The character and the quantity of denaturing materials used shall be as prescribed by the Secretary by regulations.

Sec. 5243. Sale of abandoned spirits for denaturation without collection of tax.

Notwithstanding any other provision of law, any distilled spirits abandoned to the United States may be sold, in such cases as the Secretary may by regulation provide, to the proprietor of any distilled spirits plant for denaturation, or redistillation and denaturation, without the payment of the internal revenue tax thereon.

In 1976, P.L. 94-455, Sec. 1906(b)(13)(A), substituted "Secretary" for "Secretary or his delegate" in Code Sec. 5242, effective 2/1/77.

Sec. 5244. Cross references.

(1) For provisions authorizing the withdrawal from the bonded premises of a distilled spirits plant of denatured distilled spirits, see section 5214(a)(1).

(2) For provisions requiring a permit to procure specially denatured distilled spirits, see section 5271.

Subchapter D.—Industrial Use of Distilled Spirits

Sec.
5271. Permits.
5272. Bonds.
5273. Sale, use, and recovery of denatured distilled spirits.
5274. Applicability of other laws.
5275. Records and reports.
5276. Repealed. [Occupational tax.]

In 2005, P.L. 109-59, Sec. 11125(a)(3), repealed Code Sec. 5276, effective 7/1/2008, but not for taxes imposed for periods before 7/1/2008.

In 1987, P.L. 100-203, Sec. 10512(e)(2), added item 5276.

Sec. 5271. Permits.

(a) Requirements.

No person shall—

(1) procure or use distilled spirits free of tax under the provisions of section 5214(a)(2) or (3); or

(2) procure, deal in, or use specially denatured distilled spirits; or

(3) recover specially or completely denatured distilled spirits, until he has filed an application with and received a permit to do so from the Secretary.

(b) Form of application and permit.

(1) The application required by subsection (a) shall be in such form, shall be submitted at such times, and shall contain such information, as the Secretary shall by regulations prescribe.

(2) Permits under this section shall, under such regulations as the Secretary shall prescribe, designate and limit the acts which are permitted, and the place where and time when such acts may be performed. Such permits shall be issued in such form and under such conditions as the Secretary may by regulations prescribe.

(c) Disapproval of application.

Any application submitted under this section may be disapproved and the permit denied if the Secretary, after notice and opportunity for hearing, finds that—

(1) in case of an application to withdraw and use distilled spirits free of tax, the applicant is not authorized by law or regulations issued pursuant thereto to withdraw or use such distilled spirits; or

(2) the applicant (including, in the case of a corporation, any officer, director, or principal stockholder, and, in the case of a partnership, a partner) is, by reason of his business experience, financial standing, or trade connections, not likely to maintain operations in compliance with this chapter; or

(3) the applicant has failed to disclose any material information required, or made any false statement as to any material fact, in connection with his application; or

(4) the premises on which it is proposed to conduct the business are not adequate to protect the revenue.

(d) Changes after issuance of permit.

With respect to any change relating to the information contained in the application for a permit issued under this section, the Secretary may by regulations require the filing of written notice of such change and, where the change affects the terms of the permit, require the filing of an amended application.

(e) Suspension or revocation.

If, after notice and hearing, the Secretary finds that any person holding a permit issued under this section—

(1) has not in good faith complied with the provisions of this chapter or regulations issued thereunder; or

(2) has violated the conditions of such permit; or

(3) has made any false statement as to any material fact in his application therefor; or

(4) has failed to disclose any material information required to be furnished; or

(5) has violated or conspired to violate any law of the United States relating to intoxicating liquor, or has been convicted of any offense under this title punishable as a felony or of any conspiracy to commit such offense; or

(6) is, in the case of any person who has a permit under subsection (a)(1) or (a)(2), by reason of his operations, no longer warranted in procuring or using the distilled spirits or specially denatured distilled spirits authorized by his permit; or

(7) has, in the case of any person who has a permit under subsection (a)(2), manufactured articles which do not correspond to the descriptions and limitations prescribed by law and regulations; or

(8) has not engaged in any of the operations authorized by the permit for a period of more than 2 years;

such permit may, in whole or in part, be revoked or be suspended for such period as the Secretary deems proper.

(f) Duration of permits.

Permits issued under this section, unless terminated by the terms of the permit, shall continue in effect until suspended or revoked as provided in this section, or until voluntarily surrendered.

(g) Posting of permits.

Permits issued under this section, to use distilled spirits free of tax, to deal in or use specially denatured distilled spirits, or to recover specially or completely denatured distilled spirits, shall be kept posted available for inspection on the premises covered by the permit.

(h) Regulations.

The Secretary shall prescribe all necessary regulations relating to issuance, denial, suspension, or revocation, of permits under this section, and for the disposition of distilled spirits (including specially denatured distilled spirits) procured under permit pursuant to this section which remain unused when such permit is no longer in effect.

In 1976, P.L. 94-455, Sec. 1906(b)(13)(A), substituted "Secretary" for "Secretary or his delegate" each place it appeared in Code Sec. 5271, effective 2/1/77.

Sec. 5272. Bonds.
(a) Requirements.

Before any permit required by section 5271(a) is granted, the Secretary may require a bond, in such form and amount as he may prescribe, to insure compliance with the terms of the permit and the provisions of this chapter.

(b) Exceptions.

No bond shall be required in the case of permits issued to the United States or any governmental agency thereof, or to the several States or any political subdivision thereof, or to the District of Columbia.

In 1976, P.L. 94-455, Sec. 1905(c)(3), deleted "and Territories" after "several States" in subsec. (b), effective 2/1/77.
—P.L. 94-455, Sec. 1906(b)(13)(A), substituted "Secretary" for "Secretary or his delegate" in subsec. (a), effective 2/1/77.

Sec. 5273. Sale, use, and recovery of denatured distilled spirits.
(a) Use of specially denatured distilled spirits.

Any person using specially denatured distilled spirits in the manufacture of articles shall file such formulas and statements of process, submit such samples, and comply with such other requirements, as the Secretary shall by regulations prescribe, and no person shall use specially denatured distilled spirits in the manufacture or production of any article until approval of the article, formula, and process has been obtained from the Secretary.

(b) Internal medicinal preparations and flavoring extracts.

(1) Manufacture. No person shall use denatured distilled spirits in the manufacture of medicinal preparations or flavoring extracts for internal human use where any of the spirits remains in the finished product.

(2) Sale. No person shall sell or offer for sale for internal human use any medicinal preparations or flavoring extracts manufactured from denatured distilled spirits where any of the spirits remains in the finished product.

(c) Recovery of spirits for reuse in manufacturing.

Manufacturers employing processes in which denatured distilled spirits withdrawn under section 5214(a)(1) are expressed, evaporated, or otherwise removed, from the articles manufactured shall be permitted to recover such distilled spirits and to have such distilled spirits restored to a condition suitable solely for reuse in manufacturing processes under such regulations as the Secretary may prescribe.

(d) Prohibited withdrawal or sale.

No person shall withdraw or sell denatured distilled spirits, or sell any article containing denatured distilled spirits for beverage purposes.

(e) Cross references.

(1) For penalty and forfeiture for unlawful use or concealment of denatured distilled spirits, see section 5607.

(2) For applicability of all provisions of law relating to distilled spirits that are not denatured, including those requiring payment of tax, to denatured distilled spirits or articles produced, withdrawn, sold, transported, or used in violation of law or regulations, see section 5001(a)(6).

(3) For definition of "articles", see section 5002(a)(14).

In 1979, P.L. 96-39, Sec. 807(a)(39), substituted "section 5002(a)(14)" for "section '5002(a)(11)' in para. (e)(3), effective 1/1/80.
In 1976, P.L. 94-455, Sec. 1906(b)(13)(A), substituted 'Secretary' for 'Secretary or his delegate' each place it appeared in Code Sec. 5273, effective 2/1/77.

Sec. 5274. Applicability of other laws.

The provisions, including penalties, of sections 9 and 10 of the Federal Trade Commission Act (15 U.S.C., secs. 49, 50), as now or hereafter amended, shall apply to the jurisdiction, powers, and duties of the Secretary under this subtitle, and to any person (whether or not a corporation) subject to the provisions of this subtitle.

In 1976, P.L. 94-455, Sec. 1906(b)(13)(A), substituted "Secretary" for "Secretary or his delegate" in Code Sec. 5274, effective 2/1/77.

Sec. 5275. Records and reports.

Every person procuring or using distilled spirits withdrawn under section 5214(a)(2) or (3), or procuring, dealing in, or using specially denatured distilled spirits, or recovering specially denatured or completely denatured distilled spirits, shall keep such records and file such reports of the receipt and use of distilled spirits withdrawn free of tax, of the receipt, disposition, use, and recovery of denatured distilled spirits, the manufacture and disposition of articles, and such other information as the Secretary may by regulations require. The Secretary may require any person reprocessing, bottling or repackaging articles, or dealing in completely denatured distilled spirits or articles, to keep such records, submit such reports, and comply with such other requirements as he may by regulations prescribe. Records required to be kept under this section and a copy of all reports required to be filed shall be preserved as regulations shall prescribe and shall be kept available for inspection by any internal revenue officer during business hours. Such officer may also inspect and take samples of distilled spirits, denatured distilled spirits, or articles (including any substances for use in the manufacture thereof), to which such records or reports relate.

In 1976, P.L. 94-455, Sec. 1906(b)(13)(A), substituted "Secretary" for "Secretary or his delegate" each place it appeared in Code Sec. 5275, effective 2/1/77.

Sec. 5276. Repealed.

In 2005, P.L. 109-59, Sec. 11125(a)(3), repealed Code Sec. 5276, effective 7/1/2008, but not for taxes imposed for periods before 7/1/2008.
Prior to repeal, Code Sec. 5276 read as follows:
"Sec. 5276. Occupational tax.

"(a) General rule. Except as otherwise provided in this section, a permit issued under section 5271 shall not be valid with respect to acts conducted at any place unless the person holding such permit pays a special tax of $250 with respect to such place.

"(b) Certain occupational tax rules to apply. Rules similar to the rules of subpart G of part II of subchapter A shall apply for purposes of this section.

"(c) Exception for United States. Subsection (a) shall not apply to any permit issued to an agency or instrumentality of the United States.

"(d) Exception for certain educational institutions. Subsection (a) shall not apply with respect to any scientific university, college of learning, or institution of scientific research which—

"(1) is issued a permit under section 5271, and

"(2) with respect to any calendar year during which such permit is in effect, procures less than 25 gallons on distilled spirits free of tax for experimental or research use but not for consumption (other than organoleptic tests) or sale."

In 1989, P.L. 101-239, Sec. 7816(o)(1)(A), substituted "(d) Exception" for "(c) Exemption" in the heading of subsec. (c) [sic (d)] . . . Sec. 7816(o)(1)(B), substituted "section 5271" for "section 5271(a)(2)" in para. (c)(1) . . . Sec. 7816(o)(1)(C), substituted "distilled spirits free of tax" for "specially denatured distilled spirits" in para. (c)(2) . . . Sec. 7816(o)(2), substituted "Except as otherwise provided in this section," for "Except as provided in subsection (c)," in subsec. (a), effective 7/1/89.

In 1988, P.L. 100-647, Sec. 2004(t)(1), added subsec. (c), effective 1/1/88, except as provided in Sec. 10512(h)(2) of P.L. 100-203, reproduced below.

—P.L. 100-647, Sec. 6105(a), added new subsec. (c) [sic (d)] . . . Sec. 6105(b), substituted "Except as provided in subsection (c) [sic (d)], a permit" for "A permit" in subsec. (a), effective 7/1/89.

In 1987, P.L. 100-203, Sec. 10512(e)(1), added Code Sec. 5276, effective 1/1/88. Sec. 10512(h)(2) of the Act also provides:

"(2) All taxpayers treated as commencing in business on January 1, 1988.—

"(A) In general.— Any person engaged on January 1, 1988, in any trade or business which is subject to an occupational tax shall be treated for purposes of such tax as having 1st engaged in such trade or business on such date.

"(B) Limitation on amount of tax.— In the case of a taxpayer who paid an occupational tax in respect of any premises for any taxable period which began before January 1, 1988, and includes such date, the amount of the occupational tax imposed by reason of subparagraph (A) in respect of such premises shall not exceed an amount equal to ½ the excess (if any) of—

"(i) the rate of such tax as in effect on January 1, 1988, over

"(ii) the rate of such tax as in effect on December 31, 1987.

"(C) Occupational tax.— For purposes of this subparagraph, the term 'occupational tax' means any tax imposed under part II of subchapter A of chapter 51, section 5276, section 5731, or section 5801 of the Internal Revenue Code of 1986 (as amended by this section).

"(D) Due date of tax.— The amount of any tax required to be paid by reason of this paragraph shall be due on April 1, 1988."

Subchapter E.— General Provisions Relating to Distilled Spirits

Part
  I. Return of materials used in the manufacture or recovery of distilled spirits.
  II. Regulation of traffic in containers of distilled spirits.
  III. Miscellaneous provisions.

PART I.— RETURN OF MATERIALS USED IN THE MANUFACTURE OR RECOVERY OF DISTILLED SPIRITS

Sec.
5291. General.

Sec. 5291.   General.
(a) Requirement.

Every person disposing of any substance of the character used in the manufacture of distilled spirits, or disposing of denatured distilled spirits or articles from which distilled spirits may be recovered, shall, when required by the Secretary, render a correct return, in such form and manner as the Secretary may by regulations prescribe, showing the name and address of the person to whom each disposition was made, with such details, as to the quantity so disposed of or other information which the Secretary may require as to each such disposition, as will enable the Secretary to determine whether all taxes due with respect to any distilled spirits manufactured or recovered from any such substance, denatured, distilled spirits, or articles, have been paid. Every person required to render a return under this section shall keep such records as will enable such person to render a correct return. Such records shall be preserved for such period as the Secretary shall by regulations prescribe, and shall be kept available for inspection by any internal revenue officer during business hours.

(b) Cross references.

(1) For the definition of distilled spirits, see section 5002(a)(8).

(2) For the definition of articles, see section 5002(a)(14).

(3) For penalty for violation of subsection (a), see section 5605.

In 1979, P.L. 96-39, Sec. 807(a)(40), substituted "section 5002(a)(8)" for "section 5002(a)(6)" in para. (b)(1) and substituted "section 5002(a)(14)" for "section 5002(a)(11)" in para. (b)(2), effective 1/1/80.

In 1976, P.L. 94-455, Sec. 1906(b)(13)(A), substituted "Secretary" for "Secretary or his delegate" each place it appeared in Code Sec. 5291, effective 2/1/77.

PART II.— REGULATION OF TRAFFIC IN CONTAINERS OF DISTILLED SPIRITS

Sec.
5301. General.

Sec. 5301.   General.
(a) Requirements.

Whenever in his judgment such action is necessary to protect the revenue, the Secretary is authorized, by the regulations prescribed by him and permits issued thereunder if required by him—

(1) to regulate the kind, size, branding, marking, sale, resale, possession, use, and reuse of containers (of a capacity of not more than 5 wine gallons) designed or intended for use for the sale of distilled spirits (within the meaning of such term as it is used in section 5002(a)(8)) for other than industrial use; and

(2) to require, of persons manufacturing, dealing in, or using any such containers, the submission to such inspection, the keeping of such records, and the filing of such reports as may be deemed by him reasonably necessary in connection therewith.

Any requirements imposed under this section shall be in addition to any other requirements imposed by, or pursuant to, law and shall apply as well to persons not liable for tax under the internal revenue laws as to persons so liable.

(b) Disposition.

Every person disposing of containers of the character used for the packaging of distilled spirits shall, when required by the Secretary, for protection of the revenue, render a correct return, in such form and manner as the Secretary may by regulations prescribe, showing the name and address of the person to whom each disposition was made, with such details as to the quantities so disposed of or other information which the Secretary may require as to each such disposition. Every person required to render a return under this section shall keep such records as will enable such person to render a correct return. Such records shall be preserved for such period as the Secretary shall by regulations prescribe, and shall be kept available for inspection by any internal revenue officer during business hours.

(c) Refilling of liquor bottles.

No person who sells, or offers for sale, distilled spirits, or agent or employee of such person, shall—

(1) place in any liquor bottle any distilled spirits whatsoever other than those contained in such bottle at the time of tax determination under the provisions of this chapter; or

(2) possess any liquor bottle in which any distilled spirits have been placed in violation of the provisions of paragraph (1); or

(3) by the addition of any substance whatsoever to any liquor bottle, in any manner alter or increase any portion of the original contents contained in such bottle at the time of tax determination under the provisions of this chapter; or

(4) possess any liquor bottle, any portion of the contents of which has been altered or increased in violation of the provisions of paragraph (3);

except that the Secretary may by regulations authorize the reuse of liquor bottles, under such conditions as he may by regulations prescribe. When used in this subsection the term "liquor bottle" shall mean a liquor bottle or other container which has been used for the bottling or packaging of distilled spirits under regulations issued pursuant to subsection (a).

(d) Closures.

The immediate container of distilled spirits withdrawn from bonded premises, or from customs custody, on determination of tax shall bear a closure or other device which is designed so as to require breaking in order to gain access to the contents of such container. The preceding sentence shall not apply to containers of bulk distilled spirits.

(e) Penalty.

For penalty for violation of this section, see section 5606.

In 1984, P.L. 98-369, Sec. 454(b), redesignated subsec. (d) as subsec. (e) and added new subsec. (d) . . . Sec. 454(c)(9)(A), substituted "tax determination" for "stamping" in paras. (c)(1) and (c)(3) . . . Sec. 454(c)(9)(B), deleted ", if the liquor bottles are to be again stamped under the provisions of this chapter" at the end of the next to last sentence in subsec. (c), effective 7/1/85.

In 1979, P.L. 96-39, Sec. 807(a)(41), substituted "section 5002(a)(8)" for "section 5002(a)(6)" in para. (a)(1), effective 1/1/80.

In 1976, P.L. 94-455, Sec. 1906(b)(13)(A), substituted "Secretary" for "Secretary or his delegate" each place it appeared in Code Sec. 5301, effective 2/1/77.

PART III.—MISCELLANEOUS PROVISIONS

Sec.
5311. Detention of containers.
5312. Production and use of distilled spirits for experimental research.
5313. Withdrawal of distilled spirits from customs custody free of tax for use of the United States.
5314. Special applicability of certain provisions.

Sec. 5311. Detention of containers.

It shall be lawful for any internal revenue officer to detain any container, containing or supposed to contain, distilled spirits, wines, or beer, when he has reason to believe that the tax imposed by law on such distilled spirits, wines, or beer has not been paid or determined as required by law, or that such container is being removed in violation of law; and every such container may be held by him at a safe place until it shall be determined whether the property so detained is liable by law to be proceeded against for forfeiture; but such summary detention shall not continue in any case longer than 72 hours without process of law or intervention of the officer to whom such detention is to be reported.

Sec. 5312. Production and use of distilled spirits for experimental research.

(a) Scientific institutions and colleges of learning.

Under such regulations as the Secretary may prescribe and on the filing of such bonds and applications as he may require, any scientific university, college of learning, or institution of scientific research may produce, receive, blend, treat, test, and store distilled spirits, without payment of tax, for experimental or research use but not for consumption (other than organoleptic tests) or sale, in such quantities as may be reasonably necessary for such purposes.

(b) Experimental distilled spirits plants.

Under such regulations as the Secretary may prescribe and on the filing of such bonds and applications as he may require, experimental distilled spirits plants may, at the discretion of the Secretary, be established and operated for specific and limited periods of time solely for experimentation in, or development of—

(1) sources of materials from which distilled spirits may be produced;

(2) processes by which distilled spirits may be produced or refined; or

(3) industrial uses of distilled spirits.

(c) Authority to exempt.

The Secretary may by regulations provide for the waiver of any provision of this chapter (other than this section) to the extent he deems necessary to effectuate the purposes of this section, except that he may not waive the payment of any tax on distilled spirits removed from any such university, college, institution, or plant.

In 1976, P.L. 94-455, Sec. 1906(b)(13)(A), substituted "Secretary" for "Secretary or his delegate" each place it appeared in Code Sec. 5312, effective 2/1/77.

Sec. 5313. Withdrawal of distilled spirits from customs custody free of tax for use of the United States.

Distilled spirits may be withdrawn free of tax from customs custody by the United States or any governmental agency thereof for its own use for nonbeverage purposes, under such regulations as may be prescribed by the Secretary.

In 1976, P.L. 94-455, Sec. 1906(b)(13)(A), substituted "Secretary" for "Secretary or his delegate" in Code Sec. 5313, effective 2/1/77.

Sec. 5314. Special applicability of certain provisions.
(a) Puerto Rico.

(1) Applicability. The provisions of this subsection shall not apply to the Commonwealth of Puerto Rico unless the Legislative Assembly of the Commonwealth of Puerto Rico expressly consents thereto in the manner prescribed in the constitution of the Commonwealth of Puerto Rico, for the enactment of a law.

(2) In general. Distilled spirits for the purposes authorized in section 5214(a)(2) and (3), denatured distilled spirits, and articles, as described in this paragraph, produced or manufactured in Puerto Rico, may be brought into the United States free of any tax imposed by section 5001(a)(10) or 7652(a)(1) for disposal under the same conditions as like spirits, denatured spirits, and articles, produced or manufactured in the United States; and the provisions of this chapter and regulations promulgated thereunder (and all other provisions of the internal revenue laws applicable to the enforcement thereof, including the penalties of special application thereto) relating to the production, bonded warehousing, and denaturation of distilled spirits, to the withdrawal of distilled spirits or denatured distilled spirits, and to the manufacture of articles from denatured distilled spirits, shall, insofar as applicable, extend to and apply in Puerto Rico in respect of—

(A) distilled spirits for shipment to the United States for the purposes authorized in section 5214(a)(2) and (3);

(B) distilled spirits for denaturation;

(C) denatured distilled spirits for shipment to the United States;

(D) denatured distilled spirits for use in the manufacture of articles for shipment to the United States; and

(E) articles, manufactured from denatured distilled spirits, for shipment to the United States.

(3) Withdrawals authorized by Puerto Rico. Distilled spirits (including denatured distilled spirits) may be withdrawn from the bonded premises of a distilled spirits plant in Puerto Rico pursuant to authorization issued under the laws of the Commonwealth of Puerto Rico; such spirits so withdrawn, and products containing such spirits so withdrawn, may not be brought into the United States free of tax.

(4) Costs of administration. Any expenses incurred by the Treasury Department in connection with the enforcement in Puerto Rico of the provisions of this subtitle and section 7652(a), and regulations promulgated thereunder, shall be charged against and retained out of taxes collected under this title in respect of commodities of Puerto Rican manufacture brought into the United States. The funds so retained shall be deposited as a reimbursement to the appropriation to which such expenses were originally charged.

(b) Virgin Islands.

(1) In general. Distilled spirits for the purposes authorized in section 5214(a)(2) and (3), denatured distilled spirits, and articles, as described in this paragraph, produced or manufactured in the Virgin Islands, may be brought into the United States free of any tax imposed by section 7652(b)(1) for disposal under the same conditions as like spirits, denatured spirits, and articles, produced or manufactured in the United States; and the provisions of this chapter and regulations promulgated thereunder (and all other provisions of the internal revenue laws applicable to the enforcement thereof, including the penalties of special application thereto) relating to the production, bonded warehousing, and denaturation of distilled spirits, to the withdrawal of distilled spirits or denatured distilled spirits, and to the manufacture of articles from denatured distilled spirits, shall, insofar as applicable, extend to and apply in the Virgin Islands in respect of—

(A) distilled spirits for shipment to the United States for the purposes authorized in section 5214(a)(2) and (3);

(B) distilled spirits for denaturation;

(C) denatured distilled spirits for shipment to the United States;

(D) denatured distilled spirits for use in the manufacture of articles for shipment to the United States; and

(E) articles, manufactured from denatured distilled spirits, for shipment to the United States.

(2) Advance of funds. The insular government of the Virgin Islands shall advance to the Treasury of the United States such funds as may be required from time to time by the Secretary for the purpose of defraying all expenses incurred by the Treasury Department in connection with the enforcement in the Virgin Islands of paragraph (1) and regulations promulgated thereunder. The funds so advanced shall be deposited in a separate trust fund in the Treasury of the United States and shall be available to the Treasury Department for the purposes of this subsection.

(3) Regulations issued by Virgin Islands. The Secretary may authorize the Governor of the Virgin Islands, or his duly authorized agents, to issue or adopt such regulations, to approve such bonds, and to issue, suspend, or revoke such permits, as are necessary to carry out the provisions of this subsection. When regulations have been issued or adopted under this paragraph with concurrence of the Secretary he may exempt the Virgin Islands from any provisions of law and regulations otherwise made applicable by the provisions of paragraph (1), except that denatured distilled spirits, articles, and distilled spirits for tax-free purposes which are brought into the United States from the Virgin Islands under the provisions of this subsection shall in all respects conform to the requirements of law and regulations imposed on like products of domestic manufacture.

In **1976**, P.L. 94-455, Sec. 1905(a)(18), substituted "section 5001(a)(10)" for "section 5001(a)(4)" in para. (a)(2), effective 2/1/77.

—P.L. 94-455, Sec. 1906(b)(13)(A), substituted "Secretary" for "Secretary or his delegate" each place it appeared in Code Sec. 5314, effective 2/1/77.

Subchapter F.—Bonded and Taxpaid Wine Premises

Part

I. Establishment.
II. Operations.
III. Cellar treatment and classification of wine.
IV. General.

PART I.—ESTABLISHMENT

Sec.
5351. Bonded wine cellar.
5352. Taxpaid wine bottling house.
5353. Bonded wine warehouse.
5354. Bond.
5355. General provisions relating to bonds.
5356. Application.
5357. Premises.

Sec. 5351. Bonded wine cellar.

Any person establishing premises for the production, blending, cellar treatment, storage, bottling, packaging, or repackaging of untaxpaid wine (other than wine produced exempt from tax under section 5042), including the use of wine spirits in wine production, shall, before commencing operations, make application to the Secretary and file bond and receive permission to operate. Such premises shall be known as "bonded wine cellars"; except that any such premises engaging in production operations may, in the discretion of the Secretary, be designated as a "bonded winery".

In **1976**, P.L. 94-455, Sec. 1906(b)(13)(A), substituted "Secretary" for "Secretary or his delegate" each place it appeared in Code Sec. 5351, effective 2/1/77.

Sec. 5352. Taxpaid wine bottling house.

Any person bottling, packaging, or repackaging taxpaid wines shall, before commencing such operations, make application to the Secretary and receive permission to operate. Such premises shall be known as "taxpaid wine bottling houses".

In **1979**, P.L. 96-39, Sec. 807(a)(42), deleted "at premises other than the bottling premises of a distilled spirits plant" after "repackaging tax-paid wines" in the first sentence of Code Sec. 5352, effective 1/1/80.

In **1976**, P.L. 94-455, Sec. 1906(b)(13)(A), substituted "Secretary" for "Secretary or his delegate" in Code Sec. 5352, effective 2/1/77.

Sec. 5353. Bonded wine warehouse.

Any responsible warehouse company or other responsible person may, upon filing application with the Secretary and consent of the proprietor and the surety on the bond of any bonded wine cellar, under regulations prescribed by the Secretary, establish on such premises facilities for the storage of wines and allied products for credit purposes, to be known as a "bonded wine warehouse". The proprietor of the bonded wine cellar shall remain responsible in all respects for operations in the warehouse and the tax on the wine or wine spirit stored therein.

In **1976**, P.L. 94-455, Sec. 1906(b)(13)(A), substituted "Secretary" for "Secretary or his delegate" each place it appeared in Code Sec. 5353, effective 2/1/77.

Sec. 5354. Bond.

The bond for a bonded wine cellar shall be in such form, on such conditions, and with such adequate surety, as regulations issued by the Secretary shall prescribe, and shall be in a penal sum not less than the tax on any wine or distilled spirits possessed or in transit at any one time (taking into account the appropriate amount of credit with respect to such wine under section 5041(c)), but not less than $1,000 nor more than $50,000; except that where the tax on such wine and on such distilled spirits exceeds $250,000, the penal sum of the bond shall be not more than $100,000. Where additional liability arises as a result of deferral of payment of tax payable on any return, the Secretary may require the proprietor to file a supplemental bond in such amount as may be necessary to protect the revenue. The liability of any person on any such bond shall apply whether the transaction or operation on which the liability of the proprietor is based occurred on or off the proprietor's premises.

In 1996, P.L. 104-188, Sec. 1702(b)(7), added "(taking into account the appropriate amount of credit with respect to such wine under section 5041(c))" after "any one time", effective 1/1/91.
In 1984, P.L. 98-369, Sec. 455(c), substituted "distilled spirits" for "wine spirits" each place it appeared in Code Sec. 5354, effective 7/18/84.
In 1976, P.L. 94-455, Sec. 1906(b)(13)(A), substituted "Secretary" for "Secretary or his delegate" each place it appeared in Code Sec. 5354, effective 2/1/77.

Sec. 5355. General provisions relating to bonds.
The provisions of section 5551 (relating to bonds) shall be applicable to the bonds required under section 5354.

Sec. 5356. Application.
The application required by this part shall disclose, as regulations issued by the Secretary shall provide, such information as may be necessary to enable the Secretary to determine the location and extent of the premises, the type of operations to be conducted on such premises, and whether the operations will be in conformity with law and regulations.

In 1976, P.L. 94-455, Sec. 1906(b)(13)(A), substituted "Secretary" for "Secretary or his delegate" each place it appeared in Code Sec. 5356, effective 2/1/77.

Sec. 5357. Premises.
Bonded wine cellar premises, including noncontiguous portions thereof, shall be so located, constructed, and equipped, as to afford adequate protection to the revenue, as regulations prescribed by the Secretary may provide.

In 1976, P.L. 94-455, Sec. 1906(b)(13)(A), substituted "Secretary" for "Secretary or his delegate" in Code Sec. 5357, effective 2/1/77.

PART II.—OPERATIONS
Sec.
5361. Bonded wine cellar operations.
5362. Removals of wine from bonded wine cellars.
5363. Taxpaid wine bottling house operations.
5364. Wine imported in bulk.
5365. Segregation of operations.
5366. Supervision.
5367. Records.
5368. Gauging and marking.
5369. Inventories.
5370. Losses.
5371. Insurance coverage, etc.
5372. Sampling.
5373. Wine spirits.

In 1997, P.L. 105-34, Sec. 1422(b), added item 5364.
In 1979, P.L. 96-39, Sec. 807(b)(7), deleted item 5364.
Prior to deletion, item 5364 read as follows:
"5364. Standard wine premises."
In 1976, P.L. 94-455, Sec. 1905(b)(5), amended item 5368.
Prior to amendment, item 5368 read as follows:
"5368. Gauging, marking, and stamping."

Sec. 5361. Bonded wine cellar operations.
In addition to the operations described in section 5351, the proprietor of a bonded wine cellar may, subject to regulations prescribed by the Secretary, on such premises receive taxpaid wine for return to bond, reconditioning, or destruction; prepare for market and store commercial fruit products and by-products not taxable as wines; produce or receive distilling material or vinegar stock; produce (with or without added wine spirits, and without added sugar) or receive on wine premises, subject to tax as wine but not for sale or consumption as beverage wine, (1) heavy bodied blending wines and Spanish-type blending sherries, and (2) other wine products made from natural wine for nonbeverage purposes; and such other operations as may be conducted in a manner that will not jeopardize the revenue or conflict with wine operations.

In 1997, P.L. 105-34, Sec. 1416(b)(1), deleted "unmerchantable" after "such premises receive" in Code Sec. 5361, effective on the 1st day of the 1st calendar quarter that begins at least 180 days after 8/5/97.
In 1979, P.L. 96-39, Sec. 807(a)(43), substituted "or receive on wine premises" for "or receive on standard wine premises only" in Code Sec. 5361, effective 1/1/80.
In 1976, P.L. 94-455, Sec. 1906(b)(13)(A), substituted "Secretary" for "Secretary or his delegate" in Code Sec. 5361, effective 2/1/77.

Sec. 5362. Removals of wine from bonded wine cellars.
(a) Withdrawals on determination of tax.
Wine may be withdrawn from bonded wine cellars on payment or determination of the tax thereon, under such regulations as the Secretary shall prescribe.

(b) Transfers of wine between bonded premises.
(1) **In general.** Wine on which the tax has not been paid or determined may, under such regulations as the Secretary shall prescribe, be transferred in bond between bonded premises.

(2) **Wine transferred to a distilled spirits plant may not be removed for consumption or sale as wine.** Any wine transferred to the bonded premises of a distilled spirits plant—

(A) may be used in the manufacture of a distilled spirits product, and

(B) may not be removed from such bonded premises for consumption or sale as wine.

(3) **Continued liability for tax.** The liability for tax on wine transferred to the bonded premises of a distilled spirits plant pursuant to paragraph (1) shall (except as otherwise provided by law) continue until the wine is used in a distilled spirits product.

(4) **Transfer in bond not treated as removal for consumption or sale.** For purposes of this chapter, the removal of wine for transfer in bond between bonded premises shall not be treated as a removal for consumption or sale.

(5) **Bonded premises.** For purposes of this subsection, the term "bonded premises" means a bonded wine cellar or the bonded premises of a distilled spirits plant.

(c) Withdrawals of wine free of tax or without payment of tax.
Wine on which the tax has not been paid or determined may, under such regulations and bonds as the Secretary may deem necessary to protect the revenue, be withdrawn from bonded wine cellars—

(1) without payment of tax for export by the proprietor or by any authorized exporter;

(2) without payment of tax for transfer to any foreign-trade zone;

(3) without payment of tax for use of certain vessels and aircraft as authorized by law;

(4) without payment of tax for transfer to any customs bonded warehouse;

(5) without payment of tax for use in the production of vinegar;

(6) without payment of tax for use in distillation in any distilled spirits plant authorized to produce distilled spirits;

(7) free of tax for experimental or research purposes by any scientific university, college of learning, or institution of scientific research;

(8) free of tax for use by or for the account of the proprietor or his agents for analysis or testing, organoleptic or otherwise; and

(9) free of tax for use by the United States or any agency thereof, and for use for analysis, testing, research, or experimentation by the governments of the several States and the District of Columbia or of any political subdivision thereof or by any agency of such governments. No bond shall be required of any such government or agency under this paragraph.

(d) Withdrawal free of tax of wine and wine products unfit for beverage use.

Under such regulations as the Secretary may deem necessary to protect the revenue, wine, or wine products made from wine, when rendered unfit for beverage use, on which the tax has not been paid or determined, may be withdrawn from bonded wine cellars free of tax. The wine or wine products to be so withdrawn may be treated with methods or materials which render such wine or wine products suitable for their intended use. No wine or wine products so withdrawn shall contain more than 21 percent of alcohol by volume, or be used in the compounding of distilled spirits or wine for beverage use or in the manufacture of any product intended to be used in such compounding.

(e) Withdrawal from customs bonded warehouses for use of foreign embassies, legations, etc.

(1) In general. Notwithstanding any other provision of law, wine entered into customs bonded warehouses under subsection (c)(4) may, under such regulations as the Secretary may prescribe, be withdrawn from such warehouses for consumption in the United States by and for the official or family use of such foreign governments, organizations, and individuals who are entitled to withdraw imported wines from such warehouses free of tax. Wines transferred to customs bonded warehouses under subsection (c)(4) shall be entered, stored, and accounted for in such warehouses under such regulations and bonds as the Secretary may prescribe, and may be withdrawn therefrom by such governments, organizations, and individuals free of tax under the same conditions and procedures as imported wines.

(2) Withdrawal for domestic use. Wine entered into customs bonded warehouses under subsection (c)(4) for purposes of removal under paragraph (1) may be withdrawn therefrom for domestic use. Wines so withdrawn shall be treated as American goods exported and returned.

(3) Sale or unauthorized use prohibited. Wine withdrawn from customs bonded warehouses or otherwise brought into the United States free of tax for the official or family use of foreign governments, organizations, or individuals authorized to obtain wine free of tax shall not be sold and shall not be disposed of or possessed for any use other than an authorized use. The provisions of paragraphs (1)(B) and (3) of section 5043(a) are hereby extended and made applicable to any person selling, disposing of, or possessing any wine in violation of the preceding sentence, and to the wine involved in any such violation.

In **1980**, P.L. 96-601, Sec. 2(a), amended para. (c)(4); ... Sec. 2(b), added new subsec. (e), effective the first day of the first calendar month begin. more than 90 days after 12/24/80.

Prior to amendment, para. (c)(4) read as follows:

"(4) without payment of tax for transfer to any class 6 customs manufacturing warehouse;"

In **1979**, P.L. 96-39, Sec. 807(a)(44), amended subsec. (b), effective 1/1/80.

Prior to amendment, subsec. (b) read as follows:

"*(b) Transfers of wine between bonded wine cellars.*

"Wine on which the internal revenue tax has not been paid or determined may, under such regulations as the Secretary shall prescribe, be transferred in bond between bonded wine cellars. For the purposes of this chapter, the removal of wine for transfer in bond between bonded wine cellars shall not be construed to be a removal for consumption or sale."

In **1976**, P.L. 94-455, Sec. 1905(c)(4), deleted "and Territories", after "the several States", in para. c)(9), effective 2/1/77.

— P.L. 94-455, Sec. 1906(b)(13)(A), substituted "Secretary" for "Secretary or his delegate" each place it appeared in Code Sec. 5362, effective 2/1/77.

In **1967**, P.L. 90-73, Sec. 1(a), added subsec. (d), effective 12/1/67.

Sec. 5363. Taxpaid wine bottling house operations.

In addition to the operations described in section 5352, the proprietor of a taxpaid wine bottling house may, subject to regulations issued by the Secretary, on such premises mix wine of the same kind and taxable grade to facilitate handling; preserve, filter, or clarify wine; and conduct operations not involving wine where such operations will not jeopardize the revenue or conflict with wine operations.

In **1979**, P.L. 96-39, Sec. 807(a)(45), deleted the last two sentences of Code Sec. 5363, effective 1/1/80.

Prior to deletion, the last two sentences of Code Sec. 5363 read as follows:

"This subchapter shall apply to any wine received on the bottling premises of any distilled spirits plant for bottling, packaging, or repackaging, and to all operations relative thereto. Sections 5021, 5081, and 5082 shall not apply to the mixing or treatment of taxpaid wine under this section."

In **1976**, P.L. 94-455, Sec. 1906(b)(13)(A), substituted "Secretary" for "Secretary or his delegate" in Code Sec. 5363, effective 2/1/77.

Sec. 5364. Wine imported in bulk.

Natural wine (as defined in section 5381) imported or brought into the United States in bulk containers may, under such regulations as the Secretary may prescribe, be withdrawn from customs custody and transferred in such bulk containers to the premises of a bonded wine cellar without payment of the internal revenue tax imposed on such wine. The proprietor of a bonded wine cellar to which such wine is transferred shall become liable for the tax on the wine withdrawn from customs custody under this section upon release of the wine from customs custody, and the importer, or the person bringing such wine into the United States, shall thereupon be relieved of the liability for such tax.

In **1998**, P.L. 105-206, Sec. 6014(b)(3), substituted "Natural wine (as defined in section 5381) imported or brought into" for "Wine imported or brought into" in Code Sec. 5364, effective on the first day of the first calendar quarter begin. at least 180 days after 8/5/97.

In **1997**, P.L. 105-34, Sec. 1422(a), added Code Sec. 5364, effective on the first day of the first calendar quarter begin. at least 180 days after 8/5/97.

Sec. 5364. Repealed.

In **1979**, P.L. 96-39, Sec. 807(a)(46), repealed Code Sec. 5364, effective 1/1/80.

Prior to repeal, Code Sec. 5364 read as follows:

"SEC. 5364. STANDARD WINE PREMISES.

"Except as otherwise specifically provided in this subchapter, no proprietor of a bonded wine cellar or taxpaid wine bottling house engaged in producing, receiving, storing or using any standard wine, shall produce, receive, store, or use any wine other than standard wine. The limitation contained in the preceding sentence shall not prohibit the production or receipt of high fermentation wines, distilling material, or vinegar stock in any bonded wine cellar."

Sec. 5365. Segregation of operations.

The Secretary may require by regulations such segregation of operations within the premises, by partitions or otherwise, as may be necessary to prevent jeopardy to the revenue, to prevent confusion between untaxpaid wine operations and such other operations as are authorized in this subchapter, to prevent substitution with respect to the several methods of producing effervescent wines, and to prevent the commingling of standard wines with other than standard wines.

In 1979, P.L. 96-39, Sec. 807(a)(47), amended Code Sec. 5365, effective 1/1/80. Prior to amendment, Code Sec. 5365 read as follows:
"SEC. 5365. SEGREGATION OF OPERATION.
"The Secretary may require by regulations such segregation of operations within the premises, by partitions or otherwise, as may be necessary to prevent jeopardy to the revenue, to prevent confusion between untaxpaid wine operations and such other operations as are authorized in this subchapter, or to prevent substitution with respect to the several methods of producing effervescent wines."
In 1976, P.L. 94-455, Sec. 1906(b)(13)(A), substituted "Secretary" for "Secretary or his delegate" in Code Sec. 5365, effective 2/1/77.

Sec. 5366. Supervision.

The Secretary may by regulations require that operations at a bonded wine cellar or taxpaid wine bottling house be supervised by an internal revenue officer where necessary for the protection of the revenue or for the proper enforcement of this subchapter.

In 1976, P.L. 94-455, Sec. 1906(b)(13)(A), substituted "Secretary" for "Secretary or his delegate" in Code Sec. 5366, effective 2/1/77.

Sec. 5367. Records.

The proprietor of a bonded wine cellar or a taxpaid wine bottling house shall keep such records and file such returns, in such form and containing such information, as the Secretary may by regulations provide.

In 1976, P.L. 94-455, Sec. 1906(b)(13)(A), substituted "Secretary" for "Secretary or his delegate" in Code Sec. 5367, effective 2/1/77.

Sec. 5368. Gauging and marking.
(a) Gauging and marking.

All wine or wine spirits shall be locked, sealed, and gauged, and shall be marked, branded, labeled, or otherwise identified, in such manner as the Secretary may by regulations prescribe.

(b) Marking.

Wines shall be removed in such containers (including vessels, vehicles, and pipelines) bearing such marks and labels, evidencing compliance with this chapter, as the Secretary may by regulations prescribe.

In 1976, P.L. 94-455, Sec. 1905(a)(20)(A), amended the heading of Code Sec. 5368 ... Sec. 1905(a)(20)(B), amended subsec. (b), effective 2/1/77.
Prior to amendment, the heading of Code Sec. 5368 read as follows:
"SEC. 5368. GAUGING, MARKING, AND STAMPING."
Prior to amendment, subsec. (b) read as follows:
"(b) Stamping.
"Wines shall be removed in such containers (including vessels, vehicles, and pipelines) bearing such marks, labels, and stamps, evidencing compliance with this chapter, as the Secretary or his delegate may by regulations prescribe."
—P.L. 94-455, Sec. 1906(b)(13)(A), substituted "Secretary" for "Secretary or his delegate" in subsec. (a), effective 2/1/77.

Sec. 5369. Inventories.

Each proprietor of premises subject to the provisions of this subchapter shall take and report such inventories as the Secretary may by regulations prescribe.

In 1976, P.L. 94-455, Sec. 1906(b)(13)(A), substituted "Secretary" for "Secretary or his delegate" in Code Sec. 5369, effective 2/1/77.

Sec. 5370. Losses.
(a) General.

No tax shall be collected in respect of any wines lost or destroyed while in bond, except that tax shall be collected—

(1) Theft. In the case of loss by theft, unless the Secretary shall find that the theft occurred without connivance, collusion, fraud, or negligence on the part of the proprietor or other person responsible for the tax, or the owner, consignor, consignee, bailee, or carrier, or the agents or employees of any of them; and

(2) Voluntary destruction. In the case of voluntary destruction, unless the wine was destroyed under Government supervision, or on such adequate notice to, and approval by, the Secretary as regulations shall provide.

(b) Proof of loss.

In any case in which the wine is lost or destroyed, whether by theft or otherwise, the Secretary may require by regulations the proprietor of the bonded wine cellar or other person liable for the tax to file a claim for relief from the tax and submit proof as to the cause of such loss. In every case where it appears that the loss was by theft, the burden shall be on the proprietor or other person liable for the tax to establish to the satisfaction of the Secretary, that such loss did not occur as the result of connivance, collusion, fraud, or negligence on the part of the proprietor, owner, consignor, consignee, bailee, or carrier, or the agents or employees of any of them.

In 1976, P.L. 94-455, Sec. 1906(b)(13)(A), substituted "Secretary" for "Secretary or his delegate" each place it appeared in Code Sec. 5370, effective 2/1/77.

Sec. 5371. Insurance coverage, etc.

Any remission, abatement, refund, or credit of, or other relief from, taxes on wines or wine spirits authorized by law shall be allowed only to the extent that the claimant is not indemnified or recompensed for the tax.

Sec. 5372. Sampling.

Under regulations prescribed by the Secretary, wine may be utilized in any bonded wine cellar for testing, tasting, or sampling, free of tax.

In 1976, P.L. 94-455, Sec. 1906(b)(13)(A), substituted "Secretary" for "Secretary or his delegate" in Code Sec. 5372, effective 2/1/77.

Sec. 5373. Wine spirits.
(a) In general.

The wine spirits authorized to be used in wine production shall be brandy or wine spirits produced in a distilled spirits plant (with or without the use of water to facilitate extraction and distillation) exclusively from—

(1) fresh or dried fruit, or their residues,

(2) the wine or wine residues therefrom, or

(3) special natural wine under such conditions as the Secretary may by regulations prescribe;

except that where, in the production of natural wine or special natural wine, sugar has been used, the wine or the residuum thereof may not be used if the unfermented sugars therein have been refermented. Such wine spirits shall not be reduced with water from distillation proof, nor be distilled, unless regulations otherwise provide, at less than 140 degrees of proof (except that commercial brandy aged in wood for a period of not less than 2 years, and barreled at not less than 100 degrees of proof, shall be deemed wine spirits for the purpose of this subsection).

(b) Withdrawal of wine spirits.

(1) The proprietor of any bonded wine cellar may withdraw and receive wine spirits without payment of tax from the bonded premises of any distilled spirits plant, or from any bonded wine cellar as provided in paragraph (2), for use in the production of natural wine, for addition to concentrated or unconcentrated juice for use in wine production, or for such other uses as may be authorized in this subchapter.

(2) Wine spirits so withdrawn, and not used in wine production or as otherwise authorized in this subchapter, may, as provided by regulations prescribed by the Secre-

tary, be transferred to the bonded premises of any distilled spirits plant or bonded wine cellar, or may be taxpaid and removed as provided by law.

(3) On such use, transfer, or taxpayment, the Secretary shall credit the proprietor with the amount of wine spirits so used or transferred or taxpaid and, in addition, with such portion of wine spirits so withdrawn as may have been lost either in transit or on the bonded wine cellar premises, to the extent allowable under section 5008(a). Where the proprietor has used wine spirits in actual wine production but in violation of the requirements of this subchapter, the Secretary shall also extend such credit to the wine spirits so used if the proprietor satisfactorily shows that such wine spirits were not knowingly used in violation of law.

(4) Suitable samples of brandy or wine spirits may, under regulations prescribed by the Secretary, be withdrawn free of tax from the bonded premises of any distilled spirits plant, bonded wine cellar, or authorized experimental premises, for analysis or testing.

(c) Distillates containing aldehydes.

When the Secretary deems such removal and use will not jeopardize the revenue nor unduly increase administrative supervision, distillates containing aldehydes may, under such regulations as the Secretary may prescribe, be removed without payment of tax from the bonded premises of a distilled spirits plant to an adjacent bonded wine cellar and used therein in fermentation of wine to be used as distilling material at the distilled spirits plant from which such unfinished distilled spirits were removed.

In 1976, P.L. 94-455, Sec. 1906(b)(13)(A), substituted "Secretary" for "Secretary or his delegate" each place it appeared in Code Sec. 5373, effective 2/1/77.

In 1968, P.L. 90-619, Sec. 1, amended the first sentence of subsec. (a), effective the first day of the first month which begins 90 days or more after 10/25/68. Prior to amendment, the sentence reads as follows:

"The wine spirits authorized to be used in wine production shall be brandy or wine spirits produced in a distilled spirits plant (with or without the use of water to facilitate extraction and distillation) exclusively from fresh or dried fruit, or their residues, or the wine or wine residue therefrom (except that where, in the production of natural wine, sugar has been used, the wine or the residuum thereof may not be used, if the unfermented sugars therein have been refermented)."

PART III.—CELLAR TREATMENT AND CLASSIFICATION OF WINE

Sec.
5381. Natural wine.
5382. Cellar treatment of natural wine.
5383. Amelioration and sweetening limitations for natural grape wines.
5384. Amelioration and sweetening limitations for natural fruit and berry wines.
5385. Specially sweetened natural wines.
5386. Special natural wines.
5387. Agricultural wines.
5388. Designation of wines.

Sec. 5381. Natural wine.

Natural wine is the product of the juice or must of sound, ripe grapes or other sound, ripe fruit, made with such cellar treatment as may be authorized under section 5382 and containing not more than 21 percent by weight of total solids. Any wine conforming to such definition except for having become substandard by reason of its condition shall be deemed not to be natural wine, unless the condition is corrected.

In 1979, P.L. 96-39, Sec. 807(a)(48), amended the last sentence of Code Sec. 5381, effective 1/1/80.

Prior to amendment, the last sentence of Code Sec. 5381 read as follows:

"Any wine conforming to such definition except for having become substandard by reason of its condition shall be deemed not to be natural wine and shall, unless the condition is corrected, be removed in due course for distillation, destroyed under Government supervision, or transferred to premises in which wines other than natural wine may be stored or used."

Sec. 5382. Cellar treatment of natural wine.
(a) Proper cellar treatment.

(1) **In general.** Proper cellar treatment of natural wine constitutes—

(A) subject to paragraph (2), those practices and procedures in the United States, whether historical or newly developed, of using various methods and materials to correct or stabilize the wine, or the fruit juice from which it is made, so as to produce a finished product acceptable in good commercial practice in accordance with regulations prescribed by the Secretary; and

(B) subject to paragraph (3), in the case of wine produced and imported subject to an international agreement or treaty, those practices and procedures acceptable to the United States under such agreement or treaty.

(2) **Recognition of continuing treatment.** For purposes of paragraph (1)(A), where a particular treatment has been used in customary commercial practice in the United States, it shall continue to be recognized as a proper cellar treatment in the absence of regulations prescribed by the Secretary finding such treatment not to be proper cellar treatment within the meaning of this subsection.

(3) **Certification of practices and procedures for imported wine.**

(A) In general. In the case of imported wine produced after December 31, 2004, the Secretary shall accept the practices and procedures used to produce such wine, if, at the time of importation—

(i) the Secretary has on file or is provided with a certification from the government of the producing country, accompanied by an affirmed laboratory analysis, that the practices and procedures used to produce the wine constitute proper cellar treatment under paragraph (1)(A),

(ii) the Secretary has on file or is provided with such certification, if any, as may be required by an international agreement or treaty under paragraph (1)(B), or

(iii) in the case of an importer that owns or controls or that has an affiliate that owns or controls a winery operating under a basic permit issued by the Secretary, the importer certifies that the practices and procedures used to produce the wine constitute proper cellar treatment under paragraph (1)(A).

(B) Affiliate defined. For purposes of this paragraph, the term "affiliate" has the meaning given such term by section 117(a)(4) of the Federal Alcohol Administration Act (27 U.S.C. 211(a)(4)) and includes a winery's parent or subsidiary or any other entity in which the winery's parent or subsidiary has an ownership interest.

(b) Specifically authorized treatments.

The practices and procedures specifically enumerated in this subsection shall be deemed proper cellar treatment for natural wine:

(1) The preparation and use of pure concentrated or unconcentrated juice or must. Concentrated juice or must reduced with water to its original density or to not less than 22 degrees Brix or unconcentrated juice or must reduced with water to not less than 22 degrees Brix shall be deemed to be juice or must, and shall include such

Excise and miscellaneous taxes Code Sec. 5383(b)(2)

amounts of water to clear crushing equipment as regulations prescribed by the Secretary may provide.

(2) The addition to natural wine, or to concentrated or unconcentrated juice or must, from one kind of fruit, of wine spirits (whether or not taxpaid) distilled in the United States from the same kind of fruit; except that (A) the wine, juice, or concentrate shall not have an alcoholic content in excess of 24 percent by volume after the addition of wine spirits, and (B) in the case of still wines, wine spirits may be added in any State only to natural wines, produced by fermentation in bonded wine cellars located within the same State.

(3) Amelioration and sweetening of natural grape wines in accordance with section 5383.

(4) Amelioration and sweetening of natural wines from fruits other than grapes in accordance with section 5384.

(5) In the case of effervescent wines, such preparations for refermentation and for dosage as may be acceptable in good commercial practice, but only if the alcoholic content of the finished product does not exceed 14 percent by volume.

(6) The natural darkening of the sugars or other elements in juice, must, or wine due to storage, concentration, heating processes, or natural oxidation.

(7) The blending of natural wines with each other or with heavy-bodied blending wine or with concentrated or unconcentrated juice, whether or not such juice contains wine spirits, if the wines, juice, or wine spirits are from the same kind of fruit.

(8) Such use of acids to correct natural deficiencies and stabilize the wine as may be acceptable in good commercial practice.

(9) The addition—

(A) to natural grape or berry wine of the winemaker's own production, of volatile fruit-flavor concentrate produced from the same kind and variety of grape or berry at a plant qualified under section 5511, or

(B) to natural fruit wine (other than grape or berry) of the winemaker's own production, of volatile fruit-flavor concentrate produced from the same kind of fruit at such a plant,

so long as the proportion of the volatile fruit-flavor concentrate to the wine does not exceed the proportion of the volatile fruit-flavor concentrate to the original juice or must from which it was produced. The transfer of volatile fruit-flavor concentrate from a plant qualified under section 5511 to a bonded wine cellar and its storage and use in such cellar shall be under such applications and bonds, and under such other requirements, as may be provided in regulations prescribed by the Secretary.

(c) Other authorized treatment.

The Secretary may by regulations prescribe limitations on the preparation and use of clarifying, stabilizing, preserving, fermenting, and corrective methods or materials, to the extent that such preparation or use is not acceptable in good commercial practice.

(d) Use of juice or must from which volatile fruit flavor has been removed.

For purposes of this part, juice, concentrated juice, or must processed at a plant qualified under section 5511 may be deemed to be pure juice, concentrated juice, or must even though volatile fruit flavor has been removed if, at a plant qualified under section 5511 or at the bonded wine cellar, there is added to such juice, concentrated juice, or must, or (in the case of a bonded wine cellar) to wine of the winemaker's own production made therefrom, either the identical volatile flavor removed or—

(1) in the case of natural grape or berry wine of the winemaker's own production, an equivalent quantity of volatile fruit-flavor concentrate produced at such a plant and derived from the same kind and variety of grape or berry, or

(2) in the case of natural fruit wine (other than grape or berry wine) of the winemaker's own production, an equivalent quantity of volatile fruit-flavor concentrate produced at such a plant and derived from the same kind of fruit.

In **2006**, P.L. 109-432, Sec. 3007, substituted "correct or stabilize" for "stabilize" enacted 12/20/06.

In **2004**, P.L. 108-429, Sec. 2002(a), amended subsec. (a), effective 1/1/2005. Prior to amendment, subsec. (a) read as follows:

"(a) General. Proper cellar treatment of natural wine constitutes those practices and procedures in the United States and elsewhere, whether historical or newly developed, of using various methods and materials to correct or stabilize the wine, or the fruit juice from which it is made, so as to produce a finished product acceptable in good commercial practice. Where a particular treatment has been used in customary commercial practice, it shall continue to be recognized as a proper cellar treatment in the absence of regulations prescribed by the Secretary finding such treatment not to be a proper cellar treatment within the meaning of this subsection."

In **1976**, P.L. 94-455, Sec. 1906(b)(13)(A), substituted "Secretary" for "Secretary or his delegate" each place it appeared in Code Sec. 5382, effective 2/1/77.

In **1968**, P.L. 90-619, Sec. 2, amended subpara. (b)(2)(B), effective the first day of the first month which begins 90 days or more after 10/25/68.
Prior to amendment, subpara. (b)(2)(B) read as follows:
"(B) in the case of still wines, wine spirits may be added only to natural wines of the winemaker's own production."

In **1965**, P.L. 89-44, Sec. 806(c)(1), deleted "made without added sugar or reserved as provided in sections 5383(b) and 5384(b))", from para. (b)(2), effective 1/1/66.

In **1964**, P.L. 88-653, Sec. 1, 2, added para. (b)(9) and subsec. (d), effective on the first day of the second month which begins more than 10 days after 10/13/64.

Sec. 5383. Amelioration and sweetening limitations for natural grape wines.

(a) Sweetening of grape wines.

Any natural grape wine may be sweetened after fermentation and before tax payment with pure dry sugar or liquid sugar if the total solids content of the finished wine does not exceed 12 percent of the weight of the wine and the alcoholic content of the finished wine after sweetening is not more than 14 percent by volume; except that the use under this subsection of liquid sugar shall be limited so that the resultant volume will not exceed the volume which could result from the maximum authorized use of pure dry sugar only.

(b) High acid wines.

(1) Amelioration. Before, during, and after fermentation, ameliorating materials consisting of pure dry sugar or liquid sugar, water, or a combination of sugar and water, may be added to natural grape wines of a winemaker's own production when such wines are made from juice having a natural fixed acid content of more than five parts per thousand (calculated before fermentation and as tartaric acid). Ameliorating material so added shall not reduce the natural fixed acid content of the juice to less than five parts per thousand, nor exceed 35 percent of the volume of juice (calculated exclusive of pulp) and ameliorating material combined.

(2) Sweetening. Any wine produced under this subsection may be sweetened by the producer thereof, after amelioration and fermentation, with pure dry sugar or liquid sugar if the total solids content of the finished wine does not exceed (A) 17 percent by weight if the alcoholic content is more than 14 percent by volume, or (B) 21 percent by weight if the alcoholic content is not more than 14 percent by volume. The use under this paragraph of liquid sugar shall be limited to cases where the resultant volume does not exceed the volume which could result from the maximum authorized use of pure dry sugar only.

(3) Wine spirits. Wine spirits may be added (whether or not wine spirits were previously added) to wine produced under this subsection only if the wine contains not more than 14 percent of alcohol by volume derived from fermentation.

In **1968**, P.L. 90-619, Sec. 3(b), substituted "not more than 14 percent" for "less than 14 percent", in subsec. (a) . . . Sec. 3(a), amended subsec. (b), effective '69 the first day of the first month which begins 90 days or more after the date of enactment 10/22/68.
Prior to amendment, subsec. (b) read as follows:
"(b) High acid wines.
"(1) In general. Before, during, and after fermentation, ameliorating material consisting of pure dry sugar or liquid sugar, water, or combination of sugar and water, may be added to natural grape wines of the winemaker's own production when such wines are made from juice having a natural fixed acid content of more than five parts per thousand (calculated before fermentation and as tartaric acid).
"(2) Limitations. (A) Ameliorating material shall not reduce the natural fixed acid content of the juice to less than five parts per thousand.
"(B) The volume of authorized ameliorating material shall not exceed 35 percent of the volume of juice (calculated exclusive of pulp) and ameliorating material combined.
"(C) Sweetening material, consisting of pure dry sugar or liquid sugar, may be added to ameliorated wine in an amount which shall not increase its volume by more than 0.0675 gallon per gallon of juice and ameliorating material combined.
"(D) Wine spirits may be added only if the juice or wine contains less than 14 percent of alcohol by volume.
"(E) The total solids content of the finished wine shall not exceed 17 percent by weight if the alcoholic content is 14 percent or more by volume, nor more than 21 percent by weight if the alcoholic content is less than 14 percent by volume."
In **1965**, P.L. 89-44, Sec. 806(b)(1), amended Code Sec. 5383, effective 1/1/66.
Prior to amendment, Code Sec. 5383 read as follows:
"SEC. 5383. AMELIORATION AND SWEETENING LIMITATIONS FOR NATURAL GRAPE WINES.
"(a) Sweetening of grape wines.
"Any natural grape wine made under this section may, if not in reserve inventory as hereinafter provided, be sweetened after fermentation and before taxpayment with pure dry sugar if the sugar solids content of the finished wine does not exceed 10 percent of the weight of the wine and the alcoholic content of the finished wine after sweetening is less than 14 percent by volume.
"(b) High acid wines.
"(1) Any natural grape wine of a winemaker's own production may, under this subsection, be ameliorated to correct high acid content, and, whether or not ameliorated, may be reserved as herein provided.
"(2) To wines produced under this subsection, there may be added to the juice or to the wine, or both, before or during fermentation (including wines held pursuant to regulation in intermediate storage for completion of amelioration), ameliorating material consisting of either water, or pure dry sugar, or a combination of water and pure dry sugar, in such total volume as may be necessary to reduce the natural fixed acid content of the mixture of juice and such ameliorating material to a minimum of 5 parts per thousand (calculated before fermentation and as tartaric acid), but in no event shall the volume of such ameliorating material exceed 35 percent of the total volume of such ameliorated juice (calculated exclusive of pulp). The wine so made shall be transferred to a reserve inventory established as regulation issued by the Secretary or his delegate shall require; except that such wine containing less than 14 percent alcohol by volume after complete fermentation, or after complete fermentation and sweetening, need not be transferred into reserve inventory if all claim to further amelioration is waived.
"(3) The wines in the reserve inventory may be sweetened with dry sugar in an amount not exceeding, for the aggregate of the inventory—
"(A) the dry sugar equivalent of any volume of authorized ameliorating material not used for wine so transferred, plus
"(B) nine-tenths pound of dry sugar for each gallon of wine so transferred and such unused ameliorating material combined.
"(4) Wines so reserved may be blended together and sweetened with pure dry sugar to the extent provided in paragraph (3) or with concentrated or unconcentrated grape juice, and may have wine spirits added if such wine contains less than 14 percent of alcohol by volume at the time of such addition (unless wine spirits were previously added). Any wines withdrawn from reserve inventory shall have an alcoholic content of less than 14 percent by volume and a total solids content not exceeding 21 percent by weight, except that, if wine spirits have been added and the alcoholic content is 14 percent by volume or more, the sugar solids content shall not exceed 15 percent by weight.
"(5) The winemaker shall maintain and balance for his reserve inventory such accounts as regulations issued by the Secretary or his delegate shall prescribe."

Sec. 5384. Amelioration and sweetening limitations for natural fruit and berry wines.

(a) In general.
To natural wine made from berries or fruit other than grapes, pure dry sugar or liquid sugar may be added to the juice in the fermenter, or to the wine after fermentation; but only if such wine has not more than 14 percent alcohol by volume after complete fermentation, or after complete fermentation and sweetening, and a total solids content not in excess of 21 percent by weight; and except that the use under this subsection of liquid sugar shall be limited so that the resultant volume will not exceed the volume which could result from the maximum authorized use of pure dry sugar only.

(b) Ameliorated fruit and berry wines.
(1) Any natural fruit or berry wine (other than grape wine) of a winemaker's own production may, if not made under subsection (a) of this section, be ameliorated to correct high acid content. Ameliorating material calculations and accounting shall be separate for wines made from each different kind of fruit.

(2) Pure dry sugar or liquid sugar may be used in the production of wines under this subsection for the purpose of correcting natural deficiencies, but not to such an extent as would reduce the natural fixed acid in the corrected juice or wine to five parts per thousand. The quantity of sugar so used shall not exceed the quantity which would have been required to adjust the juice, prior to fermentation, to a total solids content of 25 degrees (Brix). Such sugar shall be added prior to the completion of fermentation of the wine. After such addition of the sugar, the wine or juice shall be treated and accounted for as provided in section 5383(b), covering the production of high acid grape wines, except that—

(A) Natural fixed acid shall be calculated as malic acid for apple wine and as citric acid for other fruit and berry wines, instead of tartaric acid;

(B) Juice adjusted with pure dry sugar or liquid sugar as provided in this paragraph shall be treated in the same manner as original natural juice under the provisions of section 5383(b); except that if liquid sugar is used, the volume of water contained therein must be deducted from the volume of ameliorating material authorized;

(C) Wines made under this subsection shall have a total solids content of not more than 21 percent by weight, whether or not wine spirits have been added; and

(D) Wines made exclusively from any fruit or berry with a natural fixed acid of 20 parts per thousand or more (before any correction of such fruit or berry) shall be entitled to a volume of ameliorating material not in excess of 60 percent (in lieu of 35 percent).

In **1997**, P.L. 105-34, Sec. 1417(a), substituted "any fruit or berry with a natural fixed acid of 20 parts per thousand or more (before any correction of such fruit or berry)" for "loganberries, currants, or gooseberries," in subpara. (b)(2)(D), effective on the 1st day of the 1st calendar quarter that begins at least 180 days after 8/5/97.
In **1968**, P.L. 90-619, Sec. 3(b), substituted "not more than 14 percent" for "less than 14 percent" effective the first day of the first month which begins 90 days or more after 10/22/68.
In **1965**, P.L. 89-44, Sec. 806, amended Code Sec. 5384, effective 1/1/66.
Prior to amendment, Code Sec. 5384 read as follows:
"SEC. 5384. AMELIORATION AND SWEETENING LIMITATIONS FOR NATURAL FRUIT AND BERRY WINES.
"(a) In General.
"To natural wine made from berries or fruit other than grapes, pure dry sugar may be added to the juice in the fermenter, or to the wine after fermentation; but only if such wine has less than 14 percent alcohol by volume after complete fermentation, or after complete fermentation and sweetening, and a total solids content not in excess of 21 percent by weight.
"(b) Reserve Fruit and Berry Wines.
"(1) Any natural fruit or berry wine (other than grape wine) of a winemaker's own production may, if not made under subsection (a) of this section, be ameliorated to correct high acid content, and, whether or not ameliorated, may be reserved as herein provided. Separate reserve inventories shall be established for wines made from each different kind of fruit.

"(2) Pure dry sugar may be used in the production of wines under this subsection for the purpose of correcting natural deficiencies. The quantity of sugar so used shall not exceed the quantity which would have been required to adjust the juice, prior to fermentation, to a total solids content of 25 degrees (Brix). Such sugar shall be added prior to the completion of fermentation of the wine. After such addition of the sugar, the wine or juice shall be treated and accounted for as provided in section 5383(b), covering the production of reserved high acid grape wines, except that—

"(A) Natural fixed acid shall be calculated as malic acid for apple wine and as citric acid for other fruit and berry wines, instead of tartaric acid;

"(B) Juice adjusted with pure dry sugar as provided in this paragraph shall be treated in the same manner as original natural juice under the provisions of section 5383(b);

"(C) Wines made under this subsection may be withdrawn from reserve inventory with a total solids content of not more than 21 percent by weight, whether or not wine spirits have been added; and

"(D) Wines made exclusively from loganberries, currants, or gooseberries, shall be entitled to a volume of ameliorating material not in excess of 60 percent (in lieu of 35 percent)."

Sec. 5385. Specially sweetened natural wines.
(a) Definition.
Specially sweetened natural wine is the product made by adding to natural wine of the winemaker's own production a sufficient quantity of pure dry sugar, or juice or concentrated juice from the same kind of fruit, separately or in combination, to produce a finished product having a total solids content in excess of 17 percent by weight and an alcoholic content of not more than 14 percent by volume, and shall include extra sweet kosher wine and similarly heavily sweetened wines.

(b) Cellar treatment.
Specially sweetened natural wines may be blended with each other, or with natural wine or heavy bodied blending wine in the further production of specially sweetened natural wine only, if the wines so blended are made from the same kind of fruit. Wines produced under this section may be cellar treated under the provisions of section 5382(a) and (c). Wine spirits may not be added to specially sweetened natural wine.

In **1968**, P.L. 90-619, Sec. 3(b), substituted "not more than 14 percent" for "less than 14 percent," in subsec. (a) . . . Sec. 4, amended subsec. (b), effective the first day of the first month which begins 90 days or more after the date of enactment 10/22/68.
Prior to amendment, subsec. (b) read as follows:
"(b) Blending, etc.
"The winemaker may blend specially sweetened natural wine from the same kind of fruit either before or after the special sweeting, or with additional natural wine or heavy-bodied blending wine from the same kind of fruit in the further production of specially sweetened natural wine only, and may cellar treat any such wines as provided in section 5382(c). Wine spirits may not be added to specially sweetened natural wine, nor may such wine be blended except to produce a specially sweetened natural wine."
In **1965**, P.L. 89-44, Sec. 806(c)(4), substituted "a total solids content in excess of 17 percent" for "a sugar solids content in excess of 15 percent", effective 1/1/66.

Sec. 5386. Special natural wines.
(a) In general.
Special natural wines are the products made, pursuant to a formula approved under this section, from a base of natural wine (including heavy-bodied blending wine) exclusively, with the addition, before, during or after fermentation, of natural herbs, spices, fruit juices, aromatics, essences, and other natural flavorings in such quantities or proportions as to enable such products to be distinguished from any natural wine not so treated, and with or without carbon dioxide naturally or artificially added, and with or without the addition, separately or in combination, of pure dry sugar or a solution of pure dry sugar and water, or caramel. No added wine spirits or alcohol or other spirits shall be used in any wine under this section except as may be contained in the natural wine (including heavy-bodied blending wine) used as a base or except as may be necessary in the production of approved essences or similar approved flavorings. The Brix degree of any solution of pure dry sugar and water used may be limited by regulations prescribed by the Secretary in accordance with good commercial practice.

(b) Cellar treatment.
Special natural wines may be cellar treated under the provisions of section 5382(a) and (c).

In **1976**, P.L. 94-455, Sec. 1906(b)(13)(A), substituted "Secretary" for "Secretary or his delegate" in subsec. (a), effective 2/1/77.
In **1968**, P.L. 90-619, Sec. 5, amended subsec. (b) effective 2/1/69.
Prior to amendment, subsec. (b) read as follows:
"Special natural wines may be cellar treated as provided in section 5382(c)."

Sec. 5387. Agricultural wines.
(a) In general.
Wines made from agricultural products other than the juice of fruit shall be made in accordance with good commercial practice as may be prescribed by the Secretary by regulations. Wines made in accordance with such regulations shall be classed as "standard agricultural wines". Wines made under this section may be cellar treated under the provisions of section 5382(a) and (c).

(b) Limitations.
No wine spirits may be added to wines produced under this section, nor shall any coloring material or herbs or other flavoring material (except hops in the case of honey wine) be used in their production.

(c) Restriction on blending.
Wines from different agricultural commodities shall not be blended together.

In **1976**, P.L. 94-455, Sec. 1906(b)(13)(A), substituted "Secretary" for "Secretary or his delegate" in subsec. (a), effective 2/1/77.
In **1968**, P.L. 90-619, Sec. 5, substituted "under the provisions of section 5382(a) and (c)" for "as provided in section 5382(c)" in subsec. (a), effective 2/1/69.

Sec. 5388. Designation of wines.
(a) Standard wines.
Standard wines may be removed from premises subject to the provisions of this subchapter and be marked, transported, and sold under their proper designation as to kind and origin, or, if there is no such designation known to the trade or consumers, then under a truthful and adequate statement of composition.

(b) Other wines.
Wines other than standard wines may be removed for consumption or sale and be marked, transported, or sold only under such designation as to kind and origin as adequately describes the true composition of such products and as adequately distinguish them from standard wines, as regulations prescribed by the Secretary shall provide.

(c) Use of semi-generic designations.
(1) **In general.** Semi-generic designations may be used to designate wines of an origin other than that indicated by such name only if—
   (A) there appears in direct conjunction therewith an appropriate appellation of origin disclosing the true place of origin of the wine, and
   (B) the wine so designated conforms to the standard of identity, if any, for such wine contained in the regulations under this section or, if there is no such standard, to the trade understanding of such class or type.
(2) **Determination of whether name is semi-generic.**
   (A) **In general.** Except as provided in subparagraph (B), a name of geographic significance, which is also the designation of a class or type of wine, shall be deemed to have become semi-generic only if so found by the Secretary.

(B) Certain names treated as semi-generic. The following names shall be treated as semi-generic: Angelica, Burgundy, Claret, Chablis, Champagne, Chianti, Malaga, Marsala, Madeira, Moselle, Port, Rhine Wine or Hock, Sauterne, Haut Sauterne, Sherry, Tokay.

(3) Special rule for use of certain semi-generic designations.

(A) In general. In the case of any wine to which this paragraph applies—
   (i) paragraph (1) shall not apply,
   (ii) in the case of wine of the European Community, designations referred to in subparagraph (C)(i) may be used for such wine only if the requirement of subparagraph (B)(ii) is met, and
   (iii) in the case any other wine bearing a brand name, or brand name and fanciful name, semi-generic designations may be used for such wine only if the requirements of clauses (i), (ii), and (iii) of subparagraph (B) are met.

(B) Requirements.
   (i) The requirement of this clause is met if there appears in direct conjunction with the semi-generic designation an appropriate appellation of origin disclosing the origin of the wine.
   (ii) The requirement of this clause is met if the wine conforms to the standard of identity, if any, for such wine contained in the regulations under this section or, if there is no such standard, to the trade understanding of such class or type.
   (iii) The requirement of this clause is met if the person, or its successor in interest, using the semi-generic designation held a Certificate of Label Approval or Certificate of Exemption from Label Approval issued by the Secretary for a wine label bearing such brand name, or brand name and fanciful name, before March 10, 2006, on which such semi-generic designation appeared.

(C) Wines to which paragraph applies.
   (i) In general. Except as provided in clause (ii), this paragraph shall apply to any grape wine which is designated as Burgundy, Claret, Chablis, Champagne, Chianti, Malaga, Marsala, Madeira, Moselle, Port, Retsina, Rhine Wine or Hock, Sauterne, Haut Sauterne, Sherry, or Tokay.
   (ii) Exception. This paragraph shall not apply to wine which—
      (I) contains less than 7 percent or more than 24 percent alcohol by volume,
      (II) is intended for sale outside the United States, or
      (III) does not bear a brand name.

In 2006, P.L. 109-432, Sec. 422(a), added para. (c)(3) effective for wine imported or bottled in the U.S. on or after 12/20/2006.

In 1997, P.L. 105-34, Sec. 910(a), added subsec. (c), effective 8/5/97.

In 1976, P.L. 94-455, Sec. 1906(b)(13)(A), substituted "Secretary" for "Secretary or his delegate" in subsec. (b), effective 2/1/77.

PART IV.—GENERAL

Sec.
5391. Exemption from distilled spirits taxes.
5392. Definitions.

In 1979, P.L. 96-39, Sec. 807(b)(8), amended item 5391. Prior to amendment, item 5391 read as follows:
"5391. Exemption from rectifying and spirits taxes."

Sec. 5391. Exemption from distilled spirits taxes.

Notwithstanding any other provision of law, the tax imposed by section 5001 on distilled spirits shall not, except as provided in this subchapter, be assessed, levied, or collected from the proprietor of any bonded wine cellar with respect to his use of wine spirits in wine production, in such premises; except that, whenever wine or wine spirits are used in violation of this subchapter, the applicable tax imposed by section 5001 shall be collected unless the proprietor satisfactorily shows that such wine or wine spirits were not knowingly used in violation of law.

In 1979, P.L. 96-39, Sec. 807(a)(49), amended Code Sec. 5391, effective 1/1/80. Prior to amendment, Code Sec. 5391 read as follows:
"SEC. 5391. EXEMPTION FROM RECTIFYING AND SPIRITS TAXES.
"Notwithstanding any other provision of law, the taxes imposed by sections 5001 and 5021 on distilled spirits generally and on rectified spirits and wines shall not, except as provided in this subchapter, be assessed, levied, or collected from the proprietor of any bonded wine cellar with respect to his use or treatment of wine, or use of wine spirits in wine production, in such premises, nor shall such proprietor, by reason of such treatment or use, be deemed to be a rectifier within the meaning of section 5082; except that, whenever wine or wine spirits are used in violation of this subchapter, the applicable tax imposed by sections 5001 and 5021 shall be collected unless the proprietor satisfactorily shows that such wine or wine spirits were not knowingly used in violation of law."

Sec. 5392. Definitions.

(a) Standard wine.

For purposes of this subchapter the term "standard wine" means natural wine, specially sweetened natural wine, special natural wine, and standard agricultural wine, produced in accordance with the provisions of sections 5381, 5385, 5386, and 5387, respectively.

(b) Heavy bodied blending wine.

For purposes of this subchapter the term "heavy bodied blending wine" means wine made from fruit without added sugar, and with or without added wine spirits, and conforming to the definition of natural wine in all respects except as to maximum total solids content.

(c) Pure sugar.

For purposes of this subchapter the term "pure sugar" means pure refined sugar, suitable for human consumption, having a dextrose equivalent of not less than 95 percent on a dry basis, and produced from cane, beets, or fruit, or from grain or other sources of starch. Invert sugar syrup produced from such pure sugar by recognized methods of inversion may be used to prepare any sugar syrup, or solution of water and pure sugar, authorized in this subchapter.

(d) Total solids.

For purposes of this subchapter the term "total solids", in the case of wine, means the degrees Brix of the dealcoholized wine.

(e) Same kind of fruit.

For purposes of this subchapter the term "same kind of fruit" includes, in the case of grapes, all of the several species and varieties of grapes. In the case of fruits other than grapes, this term includes all of the several species and varieties of any given kind; except that this shall not preclude a more precise identification of the composition of the product for the purpose of its designation.

(f) Own production.

For purposes of this subchapter the term "own production", when used with reference to wine in a bonded wine cellar, means wine produced by fermentation in the same bonded wine cellar, whether or not produced by a predecessor in interest at such bonded wine cellar. This term may also include, under regulations, wine produced by fermentation in bonded wine cellars owned or controlled by the same or affiliated persons or firms when located within the same State; the term "affiliated" shall be deemed to include any

Excise and miscellaneous taxes — Part II

one or more bonded wine cellar proprietors associated as members of any farm cooperative, or any one or more bonded wine cellar proprietors affiliated within the meaning of section 17(a)(5) of the Federal Alcohol Administration Act, as amended (27 U.S.C. 211).

(g) Liquid sugar.

For purposes of this subchapter the term "liquid sugar" means a substantially colorless pure sugar and water solution containing not less than 60 percent pure sugar by weight (60 degrees Brix).

In 1976, P.L. 94-455, Sec. 1905(a)(21), deleted "49 Stat. 990", before "27 U.S.C. 211", in subsec. (f), effective 2/1/77.
In 1965, P.L. 89-44, Sec. 806(b)(3)(A), amended the first sentence of subsec. (c) ... Sec. 806(b)(3)(B), added subsec. (g), effective 1/1/66.
Prior to amendment, the first sentence of subsec. (c) read as follows:
"For purposes of this subchapter the term 'pure sugar' means pure refined cane or beet sugar, or pure refined anhydrous or monohydrate dextrose sugar, of not less than 95 percent purity calculated on a dry basis."

Subchapter G. — Breweries

Part
  I. Establishment.
  II. Operations.

PART I. — ESTABLISHMENT

Sec.
5401. Qualifying documents.
5402. Definitions.
5403. Cross references.

Sec. 5401. Qualifying documents.
(a) Notice.

Every brewer shall, before commencing or continuing business, file with the officer designated for that purpose by the Secretary a notice in writing, in such form and containing such information as the Secretary shall by regulations prescribe as necessary to protect and insure collection of the revenue.

(b) Bonds.

Every brewer, on filing notice as provided by subsection (a) of his intention to commence business, shall execute a bond to the United States in such reasonable penal sum as the Secretary shall by regulation prescribe as necessary to protect and insure collection of the revenue. The bond shall be conditioned (1) that the brewer shall pay, or cause to be paid, as herein provided, the tax required by law on all beer, including all beer removed for transfer to the brewery from other breweries owned by him as provided in section 5414; (2) that he shall pay or cause to be paid the tax on all beer removed free of tax for export as provided in section 5053(a), which beer is not exported or returned to the brewery; and (3) that he shall in all respects faithfully comply, without fraud or evasion, with all requirements of law relating to the production and sale of any beer aforesaid. Once in every 4 years, or whenever required so to do by the Secretary, the brewer shall execute a new bond or a continuation certificate, in the penal sum prescribed in pursuance of this section, and conditioned as above provided, which bond or continuation certificate shall be in lieu of any former bond or bonds, or former continuation certificate or certificates, of such brewer in respect to all liabilities accruing after its approval. If the contract of surety between the brewer and the surety on an expiring bond or continuation certificate is continued in force between the parties for a succeeding period of not less than 4 years, the brewer may submit, in lieu of a new bond, a certificate executed, under penalties of perjury, by the brewer and the surety attesting to continuation of the bond, which certificate shall constitute a bond subject to all provisions of law applicable to bonds given pursuant to this section.

In 1976, P.L. 94-455, Sec. 1906(b)(13)(A), substituted "Secretary" for "Secretary or his delegate" each place it appeared in Code Sec. 5401, effective 2/1/77.
In 1971, P.L. 91-673, Sec. 3(a), amended subsec. (b), effective 5/1/71.
Prior to amendment, subsec. (b) read as follows:
"(b) Bonds.
"Every brewer, on filing notice as provided by subsection (a) of his intention to commence business, shall execute a bond to the United States in such reasonable penal sum as the Secretary or his delegate shall by regulations prescribe as necessary to protect and insure collection of the revenue. The bond shall be conditioned (1) that the brewer shall pay, or cause to be paid, as herein provided, the tax required by law on all beer, including all beer removed for transfer to the brewery from other breweries owned by him as provided in section 5414; (2) that he shall pay or cause to be paid the tax on all beer removed free of tax for export as provided in section 5053(a), which beer is not exported or returned to the brewery; and (3) that he shall in all respects, faithfully comply, without fraud or evasion, with all requirements of law relating to the production and sale of any beer aforesaid. Once in every 4 years, or whenever required so to do by the Secretary or his delegate, the brewer shall execute a new bond in the penal sum prescribed in pursuance of this section, and conditioned as above provided, which bond shall be in lieu of any former bond or bonds of such brewer in respect to all liabilities accruing after its approval."

Sec. 5402. Definitions.
(a) Brewery.

The brewery shall consist of the land and buildings described in the brewer's notice. The continuity of the brewery must be unbroken except where separated by public passageways, streets, highways, waterways, or carrier rights-of-way, or partitions; and if parts of the brewery are so separated they must abut on the dividing medium and be adjacent to each other. Notwithstanding the preceding sentence, facilities under the control of the brewer for case packing, loading, or storing which are located within reasonable proximity to the brewery packaging facilities may be approved by the Secretary as a part of the brewery if the revenue will not be jeopardized thereby.

(b) Brewer.

For definition of brewer, see section 5052(d).

In 2005, P.L. 109-59, Sec. 11125(b)(17), substituted "section 5052(d)" for "section 5092" in subsec. (b), effective 7/1/2008, but not for taxes imposed for periods before 7/1/2008.
In 1976, P.L. 94-455, Sec. 1906(b)(13)(A), substituted "Secretary" for "Secretary or his delegate" in subsec. (a), effective 2/1/77.
In 1971, P.L. 91-673, Sec. 3(b), amended subsec. (a), effective 5/1/71.
Prior to amendment, subsec. (a) read as follows:
"(a) Brewery.
"This shall consist of the land and buildings described in the brewer's notice."

Sec. 5403. Cross references.

(1) For authority of Secretary to disapprove brewers' bonds, see section 5551.
(2) For authority of Secretary to require the installation and use of meters, tanks, and other apparatus, see section 5552.
(3) For deposit of United States bonds or notes in lieu of sureties, see section 9303 of title 31, United States Code.

In 1982, P.L. 97-258, Sec. 3(f)(3), substituted "section 9303 of title 31, United States Code" for "6 U.S.C. 15" in para. (3), effective 9/13/82.
In 1976, P.L. 94-455, Sec. 1906(b)(13)(A), substituted "Secretary" for "Secretary or his delegate" in Code Sec. 5403, effective 2/1/77.

PART II. — OPERATIONS

Sec.
5411. Use of brewery.
5412. Removal of beer in containers or by pipeline.
5413. Brewers procuring beer from other brewers.
5414. Removals from one brewery to another belonging to the same brewer.
5415. Records and returns.

5416. Definitions of package and packaging.
5417. Pilot brewing plants.
5418. Beer imported in bulk.

In **1997**, P.L. 105-34, Sec. 1421(b), added item 5418.
In **1971**, P.L. 91-673, Sec. 4(b), substituted "packaging" for "bottle and bottling" in item 5416, and added item 5417.

Sec. 5411. Use of brewery.

The brewery shall be used under regulations prescribed by the Secretary only for the purpose of producing, packaging, and storing beer, cereal beverages containing less than one-half of 1 percent of alcohol by volume, vitamins, ice, malt, malt sirup, and other byproducts and of soft drinks; for the purpose of processing spent grain, carbon dioxide, and yeast; and for such other purposes as the Secretary by regulation may find will not jeopardize the revenue.

In **1976**, P.L. 94-455, Sec. 1906(b)(13)(A), substituted "Secretary" for "Secretary or his delegate" each place it appeared in Code Sec. 5411, effective 2/1/77.
In **1971**, P.L. 91-673, Sec. 3(c), amended Code Sec. 5411, effective 5/1/71.
Prior to amendment, Code Sec. 5411 read as follows:
"Sec. 5411. Use of brewery.
"The brewery shall be used under regulations prescribed by the Secretary or his delegate only for the purpose of producing beer, cereal beverages containing less than one-half of one percent of alcohol by volume, vitamins, ice, malt, malt sirup, and other byproducts; of bottling beer and cereal beverages; of drying spent grain from the brewery; of recovering carbon dioxide and yeast; and of producing and bottling soft drinks; and for such other purposes as the Secretary or his delegate by regulation may find will not jeopardize the revenue. The bottling of beer and cereal beverages shall be conducted only in the brewery bottle house which shall consist of a separate portion of the brewery designated for that purpose."

Sec. 5412. Removal of beer in containers or by pipeline.

Beer may be removed from the brewery for consumption or sale only in hogsheads, packages, and similar containers, marked, branded, or labeled in such manner as the Secretary may by regulation require, except that beer may be removed from the brewery by pipeline to contiguous distilled spirits plants under section 5222.

In **1976**, P.L. 94-455, Sec. 1906(b)(13)(A), substituted "Secretary" for "Secretary or his delegate" in Code Sec. 5412, effective 2/1/77.
In **1971**, P.L. 91-673, Sec. 3(d), substituted "packages," for "barrels, kegs, bottles," in Code Sec. 5412, effective 5/1/71.

Sec. 5413. Brewers procuring beer from other brewers.

A brewer, under such regulations as the Secretary shall prescribe, may obtain beer in his own hogsheads, barrels, and kegs, marked with his name and address, from another brewer, with taxpayment thereof to be by the producer in the manner prescribed by section 5054.

In **1976**, P.L. 94-455, Sec. 1906(b)(13)(A), substituted "Secretary" for "Secretary or his delegate" in Code Sec. 5413, effective 2/1/77.

Sec. 5414. Removals from one brewery to another belonging to the same brewer.

Beer may be removed from one brewery to another brewery belonging to the same brewer, without payment of tax, and may be mingled with beer at the receiving brewery, subject to such conditions, including payment of the tax, and in such containers, as the Secretary by regulations shall prescribe. The removal from one brewery to another brewery belonging to the same brewer shall be deemed to include any removal from a brewery owned by one corporation to a brewery owned by another corporation when (1) one such corporation owns the controlling interest in the other such corporation, or (2) the controlling interest in each such corporation is owned by the same person or persons.

In **1976**, P.L. 94-455, Sec. 1906(b)(13)(A), substituted "Secretary" for "Secretary or his delegate" in Code Sec. 5414, effective 2/1/77.

Sec. 5415. Records and returns.
(a) Records.

Every brewer shall keep records, in such form and containing such information as the Secretary shall prescribe by regulations as necessary for protection of the revenue. These records shall be preserved by the person required to keep such records for such period as the Secretary shall by regulations prescribe, and shall be available during business hours for examination and taking of abstracts therefrom by any internal revenue officer.

(b) Returns.

Every brewer shall make true and accurate returns of his operations and transactions in the form, at the times, and for such periods as the Secretary shall by regulation prescribe.

In **1976**, P.L. 94-455, Sec. 1906(b)(13)(A), substituted "Secretary" for "Secretary or his delegate" each place it appeared in Code Sec. 5415, effective 2/1/77.

Sec. 5416. Definitions of package and packaging.

For purposes of this subchapter, the term "package" means a bottle, can, keg, barrel, or other original consumer container, and the term "packaging" means the filling of any package.

In **1971**, P.L. 91-673, Sec. 3(e), amended Code Sec. 5416, effective 5/1/71.
Prior to amendment, Code Sec. 5416 read as follows:
"Sec. 5416. Definitions of bottle and bottling.
"For purposes of this subchapter, the word 'bottle' means a bottle, can, or similar container, and the word 'bottling' means the filling of bottles, cans, and similar containers."

Sec. 5417. Pilot brewing plants.

Under such regulations as the Secretary may prescribe, and on the filing of such bonds and applications as he may require, pilot brewing plants may, at the discretion of the Secretary, be established and operated off the brewery premises for research, analytical, experimental, or development purposes with regard to beer or brewery operations. Nothing in this section shall be construed as authority to waive the filing of any bond or the payment of any tax provided for in this chapter.

In **1976**, P.L. 94-455, Sec. 1906(b)(13)(A), substituted "Secretary" for "Secretary or his delegate" each place it appeared in Code Sec. 5417, effective 2/1/77.
In **1971**, P.L. 91-673, Sec. 4(a), added Code Sec. 5417, effective 5/1/71.

Sec. 5418. Beer imported in bulk.

Beer imported or brought into the United States in bulk containers may, under such regulations as the Secretary may prescribe, be withdrawn from customs custody and transferred in such bulk containers to the premises of a brewery without payment of the internal revenue tax imposed on such beer. The proprietor of a brewery to which such beer is transferred shall become liable for the tax on the beer withdrawn from customs custody under this section upon release of the beer from customs custody, and the importer, or the person bringing such beer into the United States, shall thereupon be relieved of the liability for such tax.

In **1997**, P.L. 105-34, Sec. 1421(c), added Code Sec. 5418, effective on the first day of the first calendar quarter begin. at least 180 days after 8/5/97.

Subchapter H. — Miscellaneous Plants and Warehouses

Part
    I. Vinegar plants.
    II. Volatile fruit-flavor concentrate plants.

III. Repealed [Manufacturing Bonded Warehouses]

In 1979, P.L. 96-39, Sec. 807(b)(9), deleted the item for part III. Prior to deletion, the item for part III read as follows: "III. Manufacturing bonded warehouses."

PART I.—VINEGAR PLANTS
Sec.
5501. Establishment.
5502. Qualification.
5503. Construction and equipment.
5504. Operation.
5505. Applicability of provisions of this chapter.

Sec. 5501. Establishment.
Plants for the production of vinegar by the vaporizing process, where distilled spirits of not more than 15 percent of alcohol by volume are to be produced exclusively for use in the manufacture of vinegar on the premises, may be established under this part.

Sec. 5502. Qualification.
(a) Requirements.
Every person, before commencing the business of manufacturing vinegar by the vaporizing process, and at such other times as the Secretary may by regulations prescribe, shall make application to the Secretary for the registration of his plant and receive permission to operate. No application required under this section shall be approved until the applicant has complied with all requirements of law, and regulations prescribed by the Secretary, in relation to such business. With respect to any change in such business after approval of an application, the Secretary may by regulations authorize the filing of written notice of such change or require the filing of an application to make such change.

(b) Form of application.
The application required by subsection (a) shall be in such form and contain such information as the Secretary shall by regulations prescribe to enable him to determine the identity of the applicant, the location and extent of the premises, the type of operations to be conducted on such premises, and whether the operations will be in conformity with law and regulations.

In 1976, P.L. 94-455, Sec. 1906(b)(13)(A), substituted "Secretary" for "Secretary or his delegate" each place it appeared in Code Sec. 5502, effective 2/1/77.

Sec. 5503. Construction and equipment.
Plants established under this part for the manufacture of vinegar by the vaporizing process shall be constructed and equipped in accordance with such regulations as the Secretary shall prescribe.

In 1976, P.L. 94-455, Sec. 1906(b)(13)(A), substituted "Secretary" for "Secretary or his delegate" in Code Sec. 5503, effective 2/1/77.

Sec. 5504. Operation.
(a) General.
Any manufacturer of vinegar qualified under this part may, under such regulations as the Secretary shall prescribe, separate by a vaporizing process the distilled spirits from the mash produced by him, and condense the vapor by introducing it into the water or other liquid used in making vinegar in his plant.
(b) Removals.
No person shall remove, or cause to be removed, from any plant established under this part any vinegar or other fluid or material containing a greater proportion than 2 percent of proof spirits.

(c) Records.
Every person manufacturing vinegar by the vaporizing process shall keep such records and file such reports as the Secretary shall by regulations prescribe of the kind and quantity of materials received on his premises and fermented or mashed, the quantity of low wines produced, the quantity of such low wines used in the manufacture of vinegar, the quantity of vinegar produced, the quantity of vinegar removed from the premises, and such other information as may by regulations be required. Such records, and a copy of such reports, shall be preserved as regulations shall prescribe, and shall be kept available for inspection by any internal revenue officer during business hours.

In 1976, P.L. 94-455, Sec. 1906(b)(13)(A), substituted "Secretary" for "Secretary or his delegate" each place it appeared in Code Sec. 5504, effective 2/1/77.

Sec. 5505. Applicability of provisions of this chapter.
(a) Tax.
The taxes imposed by subchapter A shall be applicable to any distilled spirits produced in violation of section 5501 or removed in violation of section 5504(b).
(b) Prohibited premises.
Plants established under this part shall not be located on any premises where distilling is prohibited under section 5601(a)(6).
(c) Entry and examination of premises.
The provisions of section 5203(b), (c), and (d), relating to right of entry and examination, furnishing facilities and assistance, and authority to break up grounds or walls, shall be applicable to all premises established under this part, and to all proprietors thereof, and their workmen or other persons employed by them.
(d) Registration of stills.
Stills on the premises of plants established under this part shall be registered as provided in section 5179.
(e) Installation of meters, tanks, and other apparatus.
The provisions of section 5552 relating to the installation of meters, tanks, and other apparatus shall be applicable to plants established under this part.
(f) Assignment of internal revenue officers.
The provisions of section 5553(a) relating to the assignment of internal revenue officers shall be applicable to plants established under this part.
(g) Authority to waive records, statements, and returns.
The provisions of section 5555(b) relating to the authority of the Secretary to waive records, statements, and returns shall be applicable to records, statements, or returns required by this part.
(h) Regulations.
The provisions of section 5556 relating to the prescribing of regulations shall be applicable to this part.
(i) Penalties.
The penalties and forfeitures provided in sections 5601(a)(1), (6), and (12), 5603, 5615(1) and (4), 5686, and 5687 shall be applicable to this part.
(j) Other provisions.
This chapter (other than this part and the provisions referred to in subsection (a), (b), (c), (d), (e), (f), (g), (h), (i) shall not be applicable with respect to plants established or operations conducted under this part.

In 1976, P.L. 94-455, Sec. 1905(b)(6)(E), deleted "5601(b)(1)", after "and (12),", in subsec. (i), effective 2/1/77.

Part II — Excise and miscellaneous taxes

PART II.—VOLATILE FRUIT-FLAVOR CONCENTRATE PLANTS

Sec.
5511. Establishment and operation.
5512. Control of products after manufacture.

Sec. 5511. Establishment and operation.

This chapter (other than sections 5178(a)(2)(C), 5179, 5203(b), (c), and (d), and 5552) shall not be applicable with respect to the manufacture, by any process which includes evaporations from the mash or juice of any fruit, of any volatile fruit-flavor concentrate if—

(1) such concentrate, and the mash or juice from which it is produced, contains no more alcohol than is reasonably unavoidable in the manufacture of such concentrate; and

(2) such concentrate is rendered unfit for use as a beverage before removal from the place of manufacture, or (in the case of a concentrate which does not exceed 24 percent alcohol by volume) such concentrate is transferred to a bonded wine cellar for use in production of natural wine as provided in section 5382; and

(3) the manufacturer thereof makes such application, keeps such records, renders such reports, files such bonds, and complies with such other requirements with respect to the production, removal, sale, transportation, and use of such concentrate and of the mash or juice from which such concentrate is produced, as the Secretary may by regulations prescribe as necessary for the protection of the revenue.

In 1976, P.L. 94-455, Sec. 1906(b)(13)(A), substituted "Secretary" for "Secretary or his delegate" in para. (3), effective 2/1/77.

In 1964, P.L. 88-653, Sec. 3, added "or (in the case of a concentrate which does not exceed 24 percent alcohol by volume) such concentrate is transferred to a bonded wine cellar for use in production of natural wine as provided in section 5382" after "manufacture" in para. (2), effective on the first day of the second month which begins more than 10 days after 10/13/64.

Sec. 5512. Control of products after manufacture.

For applicability of all provisions of this chapter pertaining to distilled spirits and wines, including those requiring payment of tax, to volatile fruit-flavor concentrates sold, transported, or used in violation of law or regulations, see section 5001(a)(7).

PART III.—Manufacturing Bonded Warehouses [Repealed]

Sec.
5521. Repealed [Establishment and operation]
5522. Repealed [Withdrawal of distilled spirits to manufacturing bonded warehouses]
5523. Repealed [Special provisions relating to distilled spirits and wines rectified in manufacturing bonded warehouses]

Sec. 5521. Repealed.

In 1979, P.L. 96-39, Sec. 807(a)(50), repealed Code Sec. 5521.
Prior to repeal, Code Sec. 5521 read as follows:
"SEC. 5521. ESTABLISHMENT AND OPERATION.
"(a) Establishment.
"All medicines, preparations, compositions, perfumery, cosmetics, cordials, and other liquors manufactured wholly or in part of domestic spirits, intended for exportation, as provided by law, in order to be manufactured and sold or removed, without being charged with duty and without having a stamp affixed thereto, shall, under such regulations as the Secretary may prescribe, be made and manufactured in warehouses similarly constructed to those known and designated in Treasury regulations as bonded warehouses, class six. The manufacturer shall first give satisfactory bonds to the Secretary for the faithful observance of all the provisions of law and the regulations as aforesaid, in amount not less than half of that required by the regulations of the Secretary from persons allowed bonded warehouses.
"(b) Supervision.
"All labor performed and services rendered under this section shall be under the supervision of an officer of the customs, and at the expense of the manufacturer.

"(c) Materials for manufacture.
"(1) Exportable free of tax. Any manufacturer of the articles specified in subsection (a), or of any of them, having such bonded warehouse, shall be at liberty, under such regulations as the Secretary may prescribe, to convey therein any materials to be used in such manufacture which are allowed by the provisions of law to be exported free from tax or duty, as well as the necessary materials, implements, packages, vessels, brands, and labels for the preparation, putting up, and export of such manufactured articles; and every article so used shall be exempt from the payment of stamp and excise duty by such manufacturer. Articles and materials so to be used may be transferred from any bonded warehouse under such regulations as the Secretary may prescribe, into any bonded warehouse in which such manufacture may be conducted, and may be used in such manufacture, and when so used shall be exempt from stamp and excise duty; and the receipt of the officer in charge shall be received as a voucher for the manufacture of such articles.
"(2) Imported materials. Any materials imported into the United States may, under such regulations as the Secretary may prescribe, and under the direction of the proper officer, be removed in original packages from on shipboard, or from the bonded warehouse in which the same may be, into the bonded warehouse in which such manufacture may be carried on, for the purpose of being used in such manufacture, without payment of duties thereon, and may there be used in such manufacture. No article so removed, nor any article manufactured in said bonded warehouse, shall be taken therefrom except for exportation, under the direction of the proper officer having charge thereof, whose certificate, describing the articles by their mark or otherwise, the quantity, the date of importation, and name of vessel, with such additional particulars as may from time to time be required, shall be received by the collector of customs in cancellation of the bond, or return of the amount of foreign import duties.
"(d) Removals.
"(1) General. Such goods, when manufactured in such warehouses, may be removed for exportation under the direction of the proper officer having charge thereof, who shall be designated by the Secretary, without being charged with duty and without having a stamp affixed thereto.
"(2) Transportation for export. Any article manufactured in a bonded warehouse established under subsection (a) may be removed therefrom for transportation to a customs bonded warehouse at any port, for the purpose only of being exported therefrom, under such regulations and on the execution of such bonds or other security as the Secretary may prescribe."
In 1976, P.L. 94-455, Sec. 1906(b)(13)(A), substituted "Secretary" for "Secretary or his delegate" each place it appeared in Code Sec. 5521, effective 2/1/77.

Sec. 5522. Repealed.

In 1979, P.L. 96-39, Sec. 807(a)(50), repealed Code Sec. 5522.
Prior to repeal, Code Sec. 5522 read as follows:
"SEC. 5522. WITHDRAWAL OF DISTILLED SPIRITS TO MANUFACTURING BONDED WAREHOUSES.
"(a) Authorization.
"Under such regulations and requirement as to stamps, bonds, and other security as shall be prescribed by the Secretary, any manufacturer of medicines, preparations, compositions, perfumery, cosmetics, cordials, and other liquors, for export, manufacturing the same in a duly constituted manufacturing bonded warehouse, shall be authorized to withdraw, from the bonded premises of any distilled spirits plant, so much distilled spirits as he may require for such purpose, without the payment of the internal revenue tax thereon.
"(b) Allowance for loss or leakage.
"For provisions relating to allowance for loss of distilled spirits withdrawn under subsection (a), see section 5008(f)."
In 1976, P.L. 94-455, Sec. 1906(b)(13)(A), substituted "Secretary" for "Secretary or his delegate" in Code Sec. 5522, effective 2/1/77.

Sec. 5523. Repealed.

In 1979, P.L. 96-39, Sec. 807(a)(50), repealed Code Sec. 5523.
Prior to repeal, Code Sec. 5523 read as follows:
"SEC. 5523. SPECIAL PROVISIONS RELATING TO DISTILLED SPIRITS AND WINES RECTIFIED IN MANUFACTURING BONDED WAREHOUSES.
"Distilled spirits and wines which are rectified in manufacturing bonded warehouses, class six, and distilled spirits which are reduced in proof and bottled or packaged in such warehouses, shall be deemed to have been manufactured within the meaning of section 311 of the Tariff Act of 1930 (19 U. S. C. 1311), and may be withdrawn as provided in such section, and likewise for shipment in bond to Puerto Rico, subject to the provisions of such section, and under such regulations as the Secretary may prescribe, there to be withdrawn for consumption or be rewarehoused and subsequently withdrawn for consumption. No internal revenue tax shall be imposed on distilled spirits and wines rectified in class six warehouses if such distilled spirits and wines are exported or shipped in accordance with such section 311. No person rectifying distilled spirits or wines in such warehouses shall be subject by reason of such rectification to the payment of special tax as a rectifier."
In 1976, P.L. 94-455, Sec. 1906(b)(13)(A), substituted "Secretary" for "Secretary or his delegate" in Code Sec. 5523, effective 2/1/77.

Subchapter I.—Miscellaneous General Provisions

Sec.
5551. General provisions relating to bonds.
5552. Installation of meters, tanks, and other apparatus.
5553. Supervision of premises and operations.
5554. Pilot operations.
5555. Records, statements, and returns.
5556. Regulations.
5557. Officers and agents authorized to investigate, issue search warrants, and prosecute for violations.
5558. Authority of enforcement officers.
5559. Determinations.
5560. Other provisions applicable.
5561. Exemptions to meet the requirements of the national defense.
5562. Exemptions from certain requirements in cases of disaster.

Sec. 5551. General provisions relating to bonds.
(a) Approval as condition to commencing business.

No individual, firm, partnership, corporation, or association, intending to commence or to continue the business of a distiller, warehouseman, processor, brewer, or winemaker, shall commence or continue the business of a distiller, warehouseman, processor, brewer, or winemaker until all bonds in respect of such a business, required by any provision of law, have been approved by the Secretary of the Treasury or the officer designated by him.

(b) Disapproval.

The Secretary of the Treasury or any officer designated by him may disapprove any such bond or bonds if the individual, firm, partnership, or corporation, or association giving such bond or bonds, or owning, controlling, or actively participating in the management of the business of the individual, firm, partnership, corporation, or association giving such bond or bonds, shall have been previously convicted, in a court of competent jurisdiction, of—

(1) any fraudulent noncompliance with any provision of any law of the United States, if such provision related to internal revenue or customs taxation of distilled spirits, wines, or beer, or if such an offense shall have been compromised with the individual, firm, partnership, corporation, or association on payment of penalties or otherwise, or

(2) any felony under a law of any State, the District of Columbia, or the United States, prohibiting the manufacture, sale, importation, or transportation of distilled spirits, wine, beer, or other intoxicating liquor.

(c) Appeal from disapproval.

In case the disapproval is by an officer designated by the Secretary of the Treasury to approve or disapprove such bonds, the individual, firm, partnership, corporation, or association giving the bond may appeal from such disapproval to the Secretary of the Treasury or an officer designated by him to hear such appeals, and the disapproval of the bond by the Secretary of the Treasury or officer designated to hear such appeals shall be final.

In **1979**, P.L. 96-39, Sec. 807(a)(51), substituted "warehouseman, processor," for "bonded warehouseman, rectifier," each place it appeared in subsec. (a), effective 1/1/80.

In **1976**, P.L. 94-455, Sec. 1905(c)(5), deleted "Territory, or" after "of any State,", in para. (b)(2), effective 2/1/77.

—P.L. 94-455, Sec. 1906(b)(13)(B), substituted "Secretary of the Treasury" for "Secretary" each place it appeared in Code Sec. 5551, effective 2/1/77.

Sec. 5552. Installation of meters, tanks, and other apparatus.

The Secretary is authorized to require at distilled spirits plants, breweries, and at any other premises established pursuant to this chapter as in his judgment may be deemed advisable, the installation of meters, tanks, pipes, or any other apparatus for the purpose of protecting the revenue, and such meters, tanks, and pipes and all necessary labor incident thereto shall be at the expense of the person on whose premises the installation is required. Any such person refusing or neglecting to install such apparatus when so required by the Secretary shall not be permitted to conduct business on such premises.

In **1976**, P.L. 94-455, Sec. 1906(b)(13)(A), substituted "Secretary" for "Secretary or his delegate" each place it appeared in Code Sec. 5552, effective 2/1/77.

Sec. 5553. Supervision of premises and operations.
(a) Assignment of internal revenue officers.

The Secretary is authorized to assign to any premises established under the provisions of this chapter such number of internal revenue officers as may be deemed necessary.

(b) Functions of internal revenue officer.

When used in this chapter, the term "internal revenue officer assigned to the premises" means the internal revenue officer assigned by the Secretary to duties at premises established and operated under the provisions of this chapter.

In **1976**, P.L. 94-455, Sec. 1906(b)(13)(A), substituted "Secretary" for "Secretary or his delegate" each place it appeared in Code Sec. 5553, effective 2/1/77.

Sec. 5554. Pilot operations.

For the purpose of facilitating the development and testing of improved methods of governmental supervision (necessary for the protection of the revenue) over distilled spirits plants established under this chapter, the Secretary is authorized to waive any regulatory provisions of this chapter for temporary pilot or experimental operations. Nothing in this section shall be construed as authority to waive the filing of any bond or the payment of any tax provided for in this chapter.

In **1976**, P.L. 94-455, Sec. 1906(b)(13)(A), substituted "Secretary" for "Secretary or his delegate" in Code Sec. 5554, effective 2/1/77.

Sec. 5555. Records, statements, and returns.
(a) General.

Every person liable to any tax imposed by this chapter, or for the collection thereof, shall keep such records, render such statements, make such returns, and comply with such rules and regulations as the Secretary may prescribe.

(b) Authority to waive.

Whenever in this chapter any record is required to be made or kept, or statement or return is required to be made by any person, the Secretary may by regulation waive, in whole or in part, such requirement when he deems such requirement to no longer serve a necessary purpose. This subsection shall not be construed as authorizing the waiver of the payment of any tax.

(c) Photographic copies.

Whenever in this chapter any record is required to be made and preserved by any person, the Secretary may by regulations authorize such person to record, copy, or reproduce by any photographic, photostatic, microfilm, microcard, miniature photographic, or other process, which accurately reproduces or forms a durable medium for so reproducing the original of such record and to retain such reproduction in lieu of the original. Every person who is authorized to retain such reproduction in lieu of the original shall, under such regulations as the Secretary may prescribe, preserve such reproduction in conveniently accessible files and make provision for examining, viewing, and using such reproduction the same as if it were the original. Such reproduction shall be treated and considered for all purposes as though it were the original record and all provisions of law applicable to the original shall be applicable to such reproduction. Such reproduction, or enlargement or facsimile thereof, shall be admissible in evidence in the same manner and under the same conditions as provided for the admission of reproductions, enlargements, or facsimiles of records made in the regular course of business under section 1732(b) of title 28 of the United States Code.

In 1984, P.L. 98-369, Sec. 454(c)(10), deleted "or for the affixing of any stamp required to be affixed by this chapter," after "the collection thereof," in subsec. (a), effective 7/1/85.

In 1976, P.L. 94-455, Sec. 1906(b)(13)(A), substituted "Secretary" for "Secretary or his delegate" each place it appeared in Code Sec. 5555, effective 2/1/77.

Sec. 5556. Regulations.

The regulations prescribed by the Secretary for enforcement of this chapter may make such distinctions in requirements relating to construction, equipment, or methods of operation as he deems necessary or desirable due to differences in materials or variations in methods used in production, processing, or storage of distilled spirits.

In 1976, P.L. 94-455, Sec. 1906(b)(13)(A), substituted "Secretary" for "Secretary or his delegate" in Code Sec. 5556, effective 2/1/77.

Sec. 5557. Officers and agents authorized to investigate, issue search warrants, and prosecute for violations.

(a) General.

The Secretary shall investigate violations of this subtitle and in any case in which prosecution appears warranted the Secretary shall report the violation to the United States Attorney for the district in which such violation was committed, who is hereby charged with the duty of prosecuting the offenders, subject to the direction of the Attorney General, as in the case of other offenses against the laws of the United States; and the Secretary may swear out warrants before United States commissioners or other officers or courts authorized to issue warrants for the apprehension of such offenders, and may, subject to the control of such United States Attorney, conduct the prosecution at the committing trial for the purpose of having the offenders held for the action of a grand jury. Section 3041 of title 18 of the United States Code is hereby made applicable in the enforcement of this subtitle.

(b) Cross reference.

For provisions relating to the issuance of search warrants, see the Federal Rules of Criminal Procedure.

In 1976, P.L. 94-455, Sec. 1906(b)(13)(A), substituted "Secretary" for "Secretary or his delegate" each place it appeared in Code Sec. 5557, effective 2/1/77.

Sec. 5558. Authority of enforcement officers.

For provisions relating to the authority of internal revenue enforcement officers, see section 7608.

Sec. 5559. Determinations.

Whenever the Secretary is required or authorized, in this chapter, to make or verify any quantitative determination, such determination or verification may be made by actual count, weight, or measurement, or by the application of statistical methods, or by other means, under such regulations as the Secretary may prescribe.

In 1976, P.L. 94-455, Sec. 1906(b)(13)(A), substituted "Secretary" for "Secretary or his delegate" each place it appeared in Code Sec. 5559, effective 2/1/77.

Sec. 5560. Other provisions applicable.

All provision of subtitle F, insofar as applicable and not inconsistent with the provisions of this subtitle, are hereby extended to and made a part of this subtitle.

Sec. 5561. Exemptions to meet the requirements of the national defense.

The Secretary may temporarily exempt proprietors of distilled spirits plants from any provision of the internal revenue laws relating to distilled spirits, except those requiring payment of the tax thereon, whenever in his judgment it may seem expedient to do so to meet the requirements of the national defense. Whenever the Secretary shall exercise the authority conferred by this section he may prescribe such regulations as may be necessary to accomplish the purpose which caused him to grant the exemption.

In 1976, P.L. 94-455, Sec. 1906(b)(13)(A), substituted "Secretary" for "Secretary or his delegate" each place it appeared in Code Sec. 5561, effective 2/1/77.

Sec. 5562. Exemptions from certain requirements in cases of disaster.

Whenever the Secretary finds that it is necessary or desirable, by reason of disaster, to waive provisions of internal revenue law with regard to distilled spirits, he may temporarily exempt proprietors of distilled spirits plants from any provision of the internal revenue laws relating to distilled spirits, except those requiring payment of the tax thereon, to the extent he may deem necessary or desirable.

In 1976, P.L. 94-455, Sec. 1906(b)(13)(A), substituted "Secretary" for "Secretary or his delegate" in Code Sec. 5562, effective 2/1/77.

Subchapter J.— Penalties, Seizures, and Forfeitures Relating to Liquors

Part
- I. Penalty, seizure, and forfeiture provisions applicable to distilling, rectifying, and distilled and rectified products.
- II. Penalty and forfeiture provisions applicable to wine and wine production.
- III. Penalty, seizure, and forfeiture provisions applicable to beer and brewing.
- IV. Penalty, seizure, and forfeiture provisions common to liquors.
- V. Penalties applicable to occupational taxes.

PART I.—PENALTY, SEIZURE, AND FORFEITURE PROVISIONS APPLICABLE TO DISTILLING, RECTIFYING, AND DISTILLED AND RECTIFIED PRODUCTS

Sec.
5601. Criminal penalties.
5602. Penalty for tax fraud by distiller.
5603. Penalty relating to records, returns, and reports.
5604. Penalties relating to marks, brands, and containers.
5605. Penalty relating to return of materials used in the manufacture of distilled spirits, or from which distilled spirits may be recovered.
5606. Penalty relating to containers of distilled spirits.
5607. Penalty and forfeiture for unlawful use, recovery, or concealment of denatured distilled spirits, or articles.

Excise and miscellaneous taxes Code Sec. 5601

5608. Penalty and forfeiture for fraudulent claims for export drawback or unlawful relanding.
5609. Destruction of unregistered stills, distilling apparatus, equipment, and materials.
5610. Disposal of forfeited equipment and material for distilling.
5611. Release of distillery before judgment.
5612. Forfeiture of taxpaid distilled spirits remaining on bonded premises.
5613. Forfeiture of distilled spirits not closed, marked, or branded as required by law.
5614. Burden of proof in cases of seizure of spirits.
5615. Property subject to forfeiture.

In **1984**, P.L. 98-369, Sec. 454(c)(11)(B), deleted "stamps," after "relating to" in item 5604 ... Sec. 454(c)(12)(C), substituted "closed" for "stamped" in item 5613.

Sec. 5601. Criminal penalties.
(a) Offenses.

Any person who—

(1) Unregistered stills. Has in his possession or custody, or under his control, any still or distilling apparatus set up which is not registered, as required by section 5179(a); or

(2) Failure to file application. Engages in the business of a distiller or processor without having filed application for and received notice of registration, as required by section 5171(c); or

(3) False or fraudulent application. Engages, or intends to engage, in the business of distiller, warehouseman, or processor of distilled spirits, and files a false or fraudulent application under section 5171; or

(4) Failure or refusal of distiller, warehouseman, or processor to give bond. Carries on the business of a distiller, warehouseman, or processor without having given bond as required by law; or

(5) False, forged, or fraudulent bond. Engages, or intends to engage, in the business of distiller, warehouseman, or processor of distilled spirits, and gives any false, forged, or fraudulent bond, under subchapter B; or

(6) Distilling on prohibited premises. Uses, or possesses with intent to use, any still, boiler, or other utensil for the purpose of producing distilled spirits, or aids or assists therein, or causes or procures the same to be done, in any dwelling house, or in any shed, yard, or inclosure connected with such dwelling house (except as authorized under section 5178(a)(1)(C)), or on board any vessel or boat, or on any premises where beer or wine is made or produced, or where liquors of any description are retailed, or on premises where any other business is carried on (except when authorized under section 5178(b)); or

(7) Unlawful production, removal, or use of material fit for production of distilled spirits. Except as otherwise provided in this chapter, makes or ferments mash, wort, or wash, fit for distillation or for the production of distilled spirits, in any building or on any premises other than the designated premises of a distilled spirits plant lawfully qualified to produce distilled spirits, or removes, without authorization by the Secretary, any mash, wort, or wash, so made or fermented, from the designated premises of such lawfully qualified plant before being distilled; or

(8) Unlawful production of distilled spirits. Not being a distiller authorized by law to produce distilled spirits, produces distilled spirits by distillation or any other process from any mash, wort, wash, or other material; or

(9) Unauthorized use of distilled spirits in manufacturing processes. Except as otherwise provided in this chapter, uses distilled spirits in any process of manufacture unless such spirits—

(A) have been produced in the United States by a distiller authorized by law to produce distilled spirits and withdrawn in compliance with law; or

(B) have been imported (or otherwise brought into the United States) and withdrawn in compliance with law; or

(10) Unlawful processing. Engages in or carries on the business of a processor—

(A) with intent to defraud the United States of any tax on the distilled spirits processed by him; or

(B) with intent to aid, abet, or assist any person or persons in defrauding the United States of the tax on any distilled spirits; or

(11) Unlawful purchase, receipt, or processing of distilled spirits. Purchases, receives, or processes any distilled spirits, knowing or having reasonable grounds to believe that any tax due on such spirits has not been paid or determined as required by law; or

(12) Unlawful removal or concealment of distilled spirits. Removes, other than as authorized by law, any distilled spirits on which the tax has not been paid or determined, from the place of manufacture or storage, or from any instrument of transportation, or conceals spirits so removed; or

(13) Creation of fictitious proof. Adds, or causes to be added, any ingredient or substance (other than ingredients or substances authorized by law to be added) to any distilled spirits before the tax is paid thereon, or determined as provided by law, for the purpose of creating fictitious proof; or

(14) Distilling after notice of suspension. After the time fixed in the notice given under section 5221(a) to suspend operations as a distiller, carries on the business of a distiller on the premises covered by the notice of suspension, or has mash, wort, or beer on such premises, or on any premises connected therewith, or has in his possession or under his control any mash, wort, or beer, with intent to distill the same on such premises; or

(15) Unauthorized withdrawal, use, sale, or distribution of distilled spirits for fuel use. Withdraws, uses, sells, or otherwise disposes of distilled spirits produced under section 5181 for other than fuel use;

shall be fined not more than $10,000, or imprisoned not more than 5 years, or both, for each such offense.

(b) Presumption.

Whenever on trial for violation of subsection (a)(4) the defendant is shown to have been at the site or place where, and at the time when, the business of a distiller or processor was so engaged in or carried on, such presence of the defendant shall be deemed sufficient evidence to authorize conviction, unless the defendant explains such presence to the satisfaction of the jury (or of the court when tried without jury).

In **1980**, P.L. 96-223, Sec. 232(e)(2)(A), added "or" to the end of para. (a)(14), and added para. (a)(15), effective the first day of the first calendar month beginning more than 60 days after 4/2/80.
In **1979**, P.L. 96-39, Sec. 807(a)(52), amended paras. (a)(2), (a)(4), (a)(10) and (a)(11), and substituted "warehouseman, or processor" for "bonded warehouseman, rectifier, or bottler" in paras. (a)(3) and (a)(5), and substituted "processor" for "rectifier" in subsec. (b), effective 1/1/80.
Prior to amendment, para. (a)(2) read as follows:
"(2) Failure of distiller or rectifier to file application. Engages, in the business of a distiller or rectifier without having filed application for and received notice of registration, as required by section 5171(a); or"
Prior to amendment, para. (a)(4) read as follows:
"(4) Failure or refusal of distiller or rectifier to give bond. Carries on the business of a distiller or rectifier without having given bond as required by law; or"

3,447

Prior to amendment, paras. (a)(10) and (a)(11) read as follows:
"(10) Unlawful rectifying or bottling. Engages in or carries on the business of a rectifier, or a bottler of distilled spirits—
"(A) with intent to defraud the United States of any tax on the distilled spirits rectified or bottled by him; or
"(B) with intent to aid, abet, or assist any person or persons in defrauding the United States of the tax on any distilled spirits; or
"(11) Unlawful purchase, receipt, rectification, or bottling of distilled spirits. Purchases, receives, rectifies, or bottles any distilled spirits, knowing or having reasonable grounds to believe that any tax due on such spirits has not been paid or determined as required by law; or"

In 1976, P.L. 94-455, Sec. 1905(a)(22), amended subsec. (b), effective 2/1/77.
Prior to amendment, subsec. (b) read as follows:
"*(b) Presumptions.*
"(1) Unregistered stills. Whenever on trial for violation of subsection (a)(1) the defendant is shown to have been at the site or place where, and at the time when, a still or distilling apparatus was set up without having been registered, such presence of the defendant shall be deemed sufficient evidence to authorize conviction, unless the defendant explains such presence to the satisfaction of the jury (or of the court when tried without jury).
"(2) Failure or refusal of distiller or rectifier to give bond. Whenever on trial for violation of subsection (a)(4) the defendant is shown to have been at the site or place where, and at the time when, the business of a distiller or rectifier was so engaged in or carried on, such presence of the defendant shall be deemed sufficient evidence to authorize conviction, unless the defendant explains such presence to the satisfaction of the jury (or of the court when tried without jury).
"(3) Unlawful production, removal, or use of material fit for production of distilled spirits. Whenever on trial for violation of subsection (a)(7) the defendant is shown to have been at the place in the building or on the premises where such mash, wort, or wash fit for distillation or the production of distilled spirits, was made or fermented, and at the time such mash, wort, or wash was there possessed, such presence of the defendant shall be deemed sufficient evidence to authorize conviction, unless the defendant explains such presence to the satisfaction of the jury (or of the court when tried without jury).
"(4) Unlawful production of distilled spirits. Whenever on trial for violation of subsection (a)(8) the defendant is shown to have been at the site or place where, and at the time when, such distilled spirits were produced by distillation or any other process from mash, wort, wash, or other material, such presence of the defendant shall be deemed sufficient evidence to authorize conviction, unless the defendant explains such presence to the satisfaction of the jury (or of the court when tried without jury)."
—P.L. 94-455, Sec. 1906(b)(13)(A), substituted "Secretary" for "Secretary or his delegate" in Code Sec. 5601, effective 2/1/77.

Sec. 5602. Penalty for tax fraud by distiller.

Whenever any person engaged in or carrying on the business of a distiller defrauds, attempts to defraud, or engages in such business with intent to defraud the United States of the tax on the spirits distilled by him, or of any part thereof, he shall be fined not more than $10,000, or imprisoned not more than 5 years, or both. No discontinuance or nolle prosequi of any prosecution under this section shall be allowed without the permission in writing of the Attorney General.

Sec. 5603. Penalty relating to records, returns and reports.

(a) Fraudulent noncompliance.

Any person required by this chapter (other than subchapters F and G) or regulations issued pursuant thereto to keep or file any record, return, report, summary, transcript, or other document, who, with intent to defraud the United States, shall—

(1) fail to keep any such document or to make required entries therein; or

(2) make any false entry in such document; or

(3) cancel, alter, or obliterate any part of such document or any entry therein, or destroy any part of such document or any entry therein; or

(4) hinder or obstruct any internal revenue officer from inspecting any such document or taking any abstracts therefrom; or

(5) fail or refuse to preserve or produce any such document, as required by this chapter or regulations issued pursuant thereto;

or who shall, with intent to defraud the United States, cause or procure the same to be done, shall be fined not more than $10,000, or imprisoned not more than 5 years, or both, for each such offense.

(b) Failure to comply.

Any person required by this chapter (other than subchapters F and G) or regulations issued pursuant thereto to keep or file any record, return, report, summary, transcript, or other document, who, otherwise than with intent to defraud the United States, shall—

(1) fail to keep any such document or to make required entries therein; or

(2) make any false entry in such document; or

(3) cancel, alter, or obliterate any part of such document or any entry therein, or destroy any part of such document, or any entry therein, except as provided by this title or regulations issued pursuant thereto; or

(4) hinder or obstruct any internal revenue officer from inspecting any such document or taking any abstracts therefrom; or

(5) fail to refuse to preserve or produce any such document, as required by this chapter or regulations issued pursuant thereto;

or who shall, otherwise than with intent to defraud the United States, cause or procure the same to be done, shall be fined not more than $1,000, or imprisoned not more than 1 year, or both, for each such offense.

Sec. 5604. Penalties relating to marks, brands, and containers.

(a) In general.

Any person who shall—

(1) transport, possess, buy, sell, or transfer any distilled spirits unless the immediate container bears the type of closure or other device required by section 5301(d),

(2) with intent to defraud the United States, empty a container bearing the closure or other device required by section 5301(d) without breaking such closure or other device,

(3) empty, or cause to be emptied, any distilled spirits from an immediate container bearing any mark or brand required by law without effacing and obliterating such mark or brand as required by section 5206(d),

(4) place any distilled spirits in any bottle, or reuse any bottle for the purpose of containing distilled spirits, which has once been filled and fitted with a closure or other device under the provisions of this chapter, without removing and destroying such closure or other device,

(5) willfully and unlawfully remove, change, or deface any mark, brand, label, or seal affixed to any case of distilled spirits, or to any bottle contained therein,

(6) with intent to defraud the United States, purchase, sell, receive with intent to transport, or transport any empty cask or package having thereon any mark or brand required by law to be affixed to any cask or package containing distilled spirits, or

(7) change or alter any mark or brand on any cask or package containing distilled spirits, or put into any cask or package spirits of greater strength than is indicated by the inspection mark thereon, or fraudulently use any cask or package having any inspection mark thereon, for the purpose of selling other spirits, or spirits of quantity or quality different from the spirits previously inspected,

shall be fined not more than $10,000 or imprisoned not more than 5 years, or both, for each such offense.

(b) Cross references.

For provisions relating to the authority of internal revenue officers to enforce provisions of this section, see sections 5203, 5557, and 7608.

Excise and miscellaneous taxes   Code Sec. 5608(a)

In 1984, P.L. 98-369, Sec. 454(c)(11)(A), amended Code Sec. 5604, effective 7/1/85.
Prior to amendment, Code Sec. 5604 read as follows:
"Sec. 5604. Penalties relating to stamps, marks, brands and containers.
"(a) General.
"Any person who shall—
"(1) transport, possess, buy, sell, or transfer any distilled spirits, required to be stamped under the provisions of section 5205(a)(1), unless the immediate container thereof has affixed thereto a stamp as required by such section; or
"(2) with intent to defraud the United States, empty a container stamped under the provisions of section 5205(a)(1) or section 5235 without destroying the stamp thereon as required by section 5205(a)(2) or regulations prescribed pursuant thereto; or
"(3) empty, or cause to be emptied, any distilled spirits from any immediate container (other than a container stamped under section 5205(a) or section 5235) bearing any stamp, mark, or brand required by law without effacing and obliterating such stamp, mark, or brand as required by section 5205(f); or
"(4) with intent to defraud the United States, falsely make, forge, alter, or counterfeit any stamp required under section 5205 or section 5235; or
"(5) use, sell, or have in his possession any forged or fraudulently altered stamp, or counterfeit of any stamp, required under section 5205 or section 5235, or any plate or die used or which may be used in the manufacture thereof; or
"(6) with intent to defraud the United States, use, reuse, sell, or have in his possession any stamp required to be destroyed by section 5205(a)(2) or regulations prescribed pursuant thereto; or
"(7) remove any stamp required by law or regulations from any cask or package containing, or which had contained, distilled spirits, without defacing or destroying such stamp at the time of such removal; or
"(8) have in his possession any undestroyed or undefaced stamp removed from any cask or package containing, or which had contained, distilled spirits; or
"(9) have in his possession any cancelled stamp or any stamp which has been used, or which purports to have been used, upon any cask or package of distilled spirits; or
"(10) make, use, sell, or have in his possession any paper in imitation of the paper used in the manufacture of any stamp required under section 5205 or section 5235; or
"(11) reuse any stamp required under section 5205(a) or section 5235, after the same shall have once been affixed to a container as provided in such sections or regulations issued pursuant thereto; or
"(12) place any distilled spirits in any bottle, or reuse any bottle for the purpose of containing distilled spirits, which has once been filled and stamped under the provisions of this chapter, without removing and destroying the stamp so previously affixed to such bottle; or
"(13) affix any stamp required pursuant to section 5205(a) to any container containing distilled spirits on which any tax due is unpaid or undetermined; or
"(14) make any false statement in any application for stamps under section 5205; or
"(15) possess any stamp prescribed under section 5205 or section 5235 obtained by him otherwise than as provided by such sections or regulations issued pursuant thereto; or
"(16) willfully and unlawfully remove, change, or deface any stamp, mark, brand, label, or seal affixed to any case of distilled spirits, or to any bottle contained therein; or
"(17) with intent to defraud the United States, purchase, sell, receive with intent to transport, or transport any empty cask or package having thereon any stamp, mark, or brand required by law to be affixed to any cask or package containing distilled spirits; or
"(18) change or alter any stamp, mark, or brand on any cask or package containing distilled spirits, or put into any cask or package spirits of greater strength than is indicated by the inspection-mark thereon, or fraudulently use any cask or package having any inspection-mark or stamp thereon, for the purpose of selling other spirits, or spirits of quantity or quality different from the spirits previously inspected therein; or
"(19) affix, or cause to be affixed, to or on any cask or package containing, or intended to contain, distilled spirits, any imitation stamp or other engraved, printed, stamped, or photographed label, device, or token, whether the same be designed as a trade mark, caution notice, caution, or otherwise, and which shall be in the similitude or likeness of, or shall have the resemblance or general appearance of, any internal revenue stamp required by law to be affixed to or upon any cask or package containing distilled spirits;
shall be fined not more than $10,000, or imprisoned not more than 5 years, or both, for each such offense.
"(b) Officers authorized to enforce this section.
"Any officer authorized to enforce any provision of law relating to internal revenue stamps is authorized to enforce this section."
In 1979, P.L. 96-39, Sec. 807(a)(53), substituted "section 5205(a)(1)" for "section 5205(a)(2)" in para. (a)(1), substituted "section 5105(a)(2)" for "section 5205(a)(1) or (2)" and substituted "section 5205(a)(2)" for "section 5205(a)(3)" in para. (a)(2), substituted "section 5205(f)" for "section 5205(g)" in para. (a)(3), substituted "section 5205(a)(2)" for "section 5205(a)(3)" in para. (a)(6), substituted "section 5205(a)" for "section 5205(a)(2) and (3)" in para. (a)(13), effective 1/1/80.

Sec. 5605. Penalty relating to return of materials used in the manufacture of distilled spirits, or from which distilled spirits may be recovered.

Any person who willfully violates any provision of section 5291(a), or of any regulation issued pursuant thereto, and any officer, director, or agent of any such person who knowingly participates in such violation, shall be fined not more than $1,000, or imprisoned not more than 2 years, or both.

Sec. 5606. Penalty relating to containers of distilled spirits.

Whoever violates any provision of section 5301, or of any regulation issued pursuant thereto, or the terms or conditions of any permit issued pursuant to the authorization contained in such section, and any officer, director, or agent of any corporation who knowingly participates in such violation, shall, upon conviction, be fined not more than $1,000, or imprisoned not more than 1 year, or both, for each such offense.

Sec. 5607. Penalty and forfeiture for unlawful use, recovery, or concealment of denatured distilled spirits, or articles.

Any person who—

(1) uses denatured distilled spirits withdrawn free of tax under section 5214(a)(1) in the manufacture of any medicinal preparation or flavoring extract in violation of the provisions of section 5273(b)(1) or knowingly sells, or offers for sale, any such medicinal preparation or flavoring extract in violation of section 5273(b)(2); or

(2) knowingly withdraws any denatured distilled spirits free of tax under section 5214(a)(1) for beverage purposes; or

(3) knowingly sells any denatured distilled spirits withdrawn free of tax under section 5214(a)(1), or any articles containing such denatured distilled spirits, for beverage purposes; or

(4) recovers or attempts to recover by redistillation or by any other process or means (except as authorized in section 5223 or in section 5273(c)) any distilled spirits from any denatured distilled spirits withdrawn free of tax under section 5214(a)(1), or from any articles manufactured therefrom, or knowingly uses, sells, conceals, or otherwise disposes of distilled spirits so recovered or redistilled;

shall be fined not more than $10,000, or imprisoned not more than 5 years, or both, for each such offense; and all personal property used in connection with his business, together with the buildings and ground constituting the premises on which such unlawful acts are performed or permitted to be performed shall be forfeited to the United States.

Sec. 5608. Penalty and forfeiture for fraudulent claims for export drawback or unlawful relanding.

(a) Fraudulent claim for drawback.

Every person who fraudulently claims, or seeks, or obtains an allowance of drawback on any distilled spirits, or fraudulently claims any greater allowance or drawback than the tax actually paid or determined thereon, shall forfeit and pay to the Government of the United States triple the amount wrongfully and fraudulently sought to be obtained, and shall be imprisoned not more than 5 years; and every owner, agent, or master of any vessel or other person who knowingly aids or abets in the fraudulent collection or fraudulent attempts to collect any drawback upon, or knowingly aids or permits any fraudulent change in the spirits so shipped, shall be fined not more than $5,000, or imprisoned not more than 3 years, or both, and the ship or vessel on board of which such shipment was made or pretended to be made shall be forfeited to the United States, whether a conviction of the

Code Sec. 5608(a)   **Excise and miscellaneous taxes**

master or owner be had or otherwise, and proceedings may be had in admiralty by libel for such forfeiture.

(b) Unlawful relanding.

Every person who, with intent to defraud the United States, relands within the jurisdiction of the United States any distilled spirits which have been shipped for exportation under the provisions of this chapter, or who receives such relanded distilled spirits, and every person who aids or abets in such relanding or receiving of such spirits, shall be fined not more than $5,000, or imprisoned not more than 3 years, or both; and all distilled spirits so relanded, together with the vessel from which the same were relanded within the jurisdiction of the United States, and all vessels, vehicles, or aircraft used in relanding and removing such distilled spirits, shall be forfeited to the United States.

In **1965**, P.L. 89-44, Sec. 805(e), substituted ", with intent to defraud the United States," for "intentionally" in subsec. (b), effective 7/1/65.

Sec. 5609. Destruction of unregistered stills, distilling apparatus, equipment, and materials.
(a) General.

In the case of seizure elsewhere than on premises qualified under this chapter of any unregistered still, distilling or fermenting equipment or apparatus, or distilling or fermenting material, for any offense involving forfeiture of the same, where it shall be impracticable to remove the same to a place of safe storage from the place where seized, the seizing officer is authorized to destroy the same. In the case of seizure, other than on premises qualified under this chapter or in transit thereto or therefrom, of any distilled spirits on which the tax has not been paid or determined, for any offense involving forfeiture of the same, the seizing officer is authorized to destroy the distilled spirits forthwith. Any destruction under this subsection shall be in the presence of at least one credible witness. The seizing officer shall make such report of said seizure and destruction and take such samples as the Secretary may require.

(b) Claims.

Within 1 year after destruction made pursuant to subsection (a) the owner of, including any person having an interest in, the property so destroyed may make application to the Secretary for reimbursement of the value of such property. If the claimant establishes to the satisfaction of the Secretary that—

(1) such property had not been used in violation of law; or

(2) any unlawful use of such property had been without his consent or knowledge,

the Secretary shall make an allowance to such claimant not exceeding the value of the property destroyed.

In **1976**, P.L. 94-455, Sec. 1906(b)(13)(A), substituted "Secretary" for "Secretary or his delegate" each place it appeared in Code Sec. 5609, effective 2/1/77.

Sec. 5610. Disposal of forfeited equipment and material for distilling.

All boilers, stills, or other vessels, tools and implements, used in distilling or processing, and forfeited under any of the provisions of this chapter, and all condemned material, together with any engine or other machinery connected therewith, and all empty barrels, and all grain or other material suitable for fermentation or distillation, shall be sold at public auction or otherwise disposed of as the court in which forfeiture was recovered shall in its discretion direct.

In **1979**, P.L. 96-39, Sec. 807(a)(54), substituted "or processing" for "or rectifying" in Code Sec. 5610, effective 1/1/80.

Sec. 5611. Release of distillery before judgment.

Any distillery or distilling apparatus seized on any premises qualified under this chapter, for any violation of law, may, in the discretion of the court, be released before final judgment to a receiver appointed by the court to operate such distillery or apparatus. Such receiver shall give bond, which shall be approved in open court, with corporate surety, for the full appraised value of all the property seized, to be ascertained by three competent appraisers designated and appointed by the court. Funds obtained from such operation shall be impounded as the court shall direct pending such final judgment.

Sec. 5612. Forfeiture of taxpaid distilled spirits remaining on bonded premises.
(a) General.

No distilled spirits on which tax has been paid or determined shall be stored or allowed to remain on the bonded premises of any distilled spirits plant, under the penalty of forfeiture of all spirits so found.

(b) Exceptions.

Subsection (a) shall not apply in the case of—

(1) distilled spirits in the process of prompt removal from bonded premises on payment or determination of the tax; or

(2) distilled spirits returned to bonded premises in accordance with the provisions of section 5215.

In **1979**, P.L. 96-39, Sec. 807(a)(55), amended subsec. (b), effective 1/1/80. Prior to amendment, subsec. (b) read as follows:

"(b) Exceptions.

"Subsection (a) shall not apply in the case of—

"(1) distilled spirits which have been bottled in bond under section 5233, and which are returned to bonded premises for rebottling, relabeling, or restamping in accordance with the provisions of section 5233(d); or

"(2) distilled spirits in the process of prompt removal from bonded premises on payment or determination of the tax; or

"(3) distilled spirits returned to bonded premises in accordance with the provisions of section 5215; or

"(4) distilled spirits, held on bonded premises, on which the tax has become payable by operation of law, but on which the tax has not been paid."

Sec. 5613. Forfeiture of distilled spirits not closed, marked, or branded as required by law.
(a) Unmarked or unbranded casks or packages.

All distilled spirits found in any cask or package required by this chapter or any regulation issued pursuant thereto to bear a mark, brand, or identification, which cask or package is not marked, branded, or identified in compliance with this chapter and regulations issued pursuant thereto, shall be forfeited to the United States.

(b) Containers without closures.

All distilled spirits found in any container which is required by this chapter to bear a closure or other device and which does not bear a closure or other device in compliance with this chapter shall be forfeited to the United States.

In **1984**, P.L. 98-369, Sec. 454(c)(12)(A), amended subsec. (b)... Sec. 454(c)(12)(B), substituted "closed" for "stamped" in the heading of Code Sec. 5613, effective 7/1/85.

Prior to amendment, subsec. (b) read as follows:

"(b) Unstamped containers.

"All distilled spirits found in any container required by this chapter or any regulations issued pursuant thereto to bear a stamp, which container is not stamped in compliance with this chapter and regulations issued pursuant thereto, shall be forfeited to the United States."

Sec. 5614. Burden of proof in cases of seizure of spirits.

Whenever seizure is made of any distilled spirits found elsewhere than on the premises of a distilled spirits plant, or than in any warehouse authorized by law, or than in the store or place of business of a wholesale liquor dealer, or than in transit from any one of said places; or of any dis-

Excise and miscellaneous taxes — Part II

tilled spirits found in any one of the places aforesaid, or in transit therefrom, which have not been received into or sent out therefrom in conformity to law, or in regard to which any of the entries required by law, or regulations issued pursuant thereto, to be made in respect of such spirits, have not been made at the time or in the manner required, or in respect to which any owner or person having possession, control, or charge of said spirits, has omitted to do any act required to be done, or has done or committed any act prohibited in regard to said spirits, the burden of proof shall be upon the claimant of said spirits to show that no fraud has been committed, and that all the requirements of the law in relation to the payment of the tax have been complied with.

Sec. 5615. Property subject to forfeiture.

The following property shall be forfeited to the United States:

(1) Unregistered still or distilling apparatus. Every still or distilling apparatus not registered as required by section 5179, together with all personal property in the possession or custody or under the control of the person required by section 5179 to register the still or distilling apparatus, and found in the building or in any yard or inclosure connected with the building in which such still or distilling apparatus is set up; and

(2) Distilling apparatus removed without notice or set up without notice. Any still, boiler, or other vessel to be used for the purpose of distilling—

(A) which is removed without notice having been given when required by section 5101(a)(1), or

(B) which is set up without notice having been given when required by section 5101(a)(2), or

(3) Distilling without giving bond or with intent to defraud. Whenever any person carries on the business of a distiller without having given bond as required by law or gives any false, forged, or fraudulent bond; or engages in or carries on the business of a distiller with intent to defraud the United States of the tax on the distilled spirits distilled by him, or any part thereof; or after the time fixed in the notice declaring his intention to suspend work, filed under section 5221(a), carries on the business of a distiller on the premises covered by such notice, or has mash, wort, or beer on such premises, or on any premises connected therewith, or has in his possession or under his control any mash, wort, or beer, with intent to distill the same on such premises—

(A) all distilled spirits or wines, and all stills or other apparatus fit or intended to be used for the distillation or rectification of spirits, or for the compounding of liquors, owned by such person, wherever found; and

(B) all distilled spirits, wines, raw materials for the production of distilled spirits, and personal property found in the distillery or in any building, room, yard, or inclosure connected therewith and used with or constituting a part of the premises; and

(C) all the right, title, and interest of such person in the lot or tract of land on which the distillery is situated; and

(D) all the right, title, and interest in the lot or tract of land on which the distillery is located of every person who knowingly has suffered or permitted the business of a distiller to be there carried on, or has connived at the same; and

(E) all personal property owned by or in possession of any person who has permitted or suffered any building, yard, or inclosure, or any part thereof, to be used for purposes of ingress or egress to or from the distillery, which shall be found in any such building, yard, or inclosure; and

(F) all the right, title, and interest of every person in any premises used for ingress or egress to or from the distillery who knowingly has suffered or permitted such premises to be used for such ingress or egress; and

(4) Unlawful production and removals from vinegar plants.

(A) all distilled spirits in excess of 15 percent of alcohol by volume produced on the premises of a vinegar plant; and

(B) all vinegar or other fluid or other material containing a greater proportion than 2 percent of proof spirits removed from any vinegar plant; and

(5) False or omitted entries in records, returns, and reports. Whenever any person required by section 5207 to keep or file any record, return, report, summary, transcript, or other document, shall, with intent to defraud the United States—

(A) fail to keep any such document or to make required entries therein; or

(B) make any false entry in such document; or

(C) cancel, alter, or obliterate any part of such document, or any entry therein, or destroy any part of such document, or entry therein; or

(D) hinder or obstruct any internal revenue officer from inspecting any such document or taking any abstracts therefrom; or

(E) fail or refuse to preserve or produce any such document, as required by this chapter or regulations issued pursuant thereto; or

(F) permit any of the acts described in the preceding subparagraphs to be performed;

all interest of such person in the distilled spirits plant where such acts or omissions occur, and in the equipment thereon, and in the lot or tract of land on which such distilled spirits plant stands, and in all personal property on the premises of the distilled spirits plants where such acts or omissions occur, used in the business there carried on; and

(6) Unlawful removal of distilled spirits. All distilled spirits on which the tax has not been paid or determined which have been removed, other than as authorized by law, from the place of manufacture, storage, or instrument of transportation; and

(7) Creation of fictitious proof. All distilled spirits on which the tax has not been paid or determined as provided by law to which any ingredient or substance has been added for the purpose of creating fictitious proof.

In 1984, P.L. 98-369, Sec. 451(b)(2), amended para. (2), effective the first day of the first calendar month which begins more than 90 days after 7/18/84.
Prior to amendment, para. (2) read as follows:
"(2) Distilling apparatus removed without notice or set up without permit. Any still, boiler, or other vessel to be used for the purpose of distilling which is removed without notice having been given as required by section 5105(a) or which is set up without permit first having been obtained as required by such section; and"

In 1979, P.L. 96-39, Sec. 807(a)(56), substituted "distilled spirits plant" for "distillery, bonded warehouse, or rectifying or bottling establishment" each place it appeared in para. (5), effective 1/1/80.

PART II.—PENALTY AND FORFEITURE PROVISIONS APPLICABLE TO WINE AND WINE PRODUCTION

Sec.

5661. Penalty and forfeiture for violation of laws and regulations relating to wine.

5662. Penalty for alteration of wine labels.

3,451

Part II

5663. Cross reference.

Sec. 5661. Penalty and forfeiture for violation of laws and regulations relating to wine.

(a) Fraudulent offenses.

Whoever, with intent to defraud the United States, fails to pay any tax imposed upon wine or violates, or fails to comply with, any provision of subchapter F or subpart C of part I of subchapter A, or regulations issued pursuant thereto, or recovers or attempts to recover any spirits from wine, shall be fined not more than $5,000, or imprisoned not more than 5 years, or both, for each such offense, and all products and materials used in any such violation shall be forfeited to the United States.

(b) Other offenses.

Any proprietor of premises subject to the provisions of subchapter F, or any employee or agent of such proprietor, or any other person, who otherwise than with intent to defraud the United States violates or fails to comply with any provision of subchapter F or subpart C of part I of subchapter A, or regulations issued pursuant thereto, or who aids or abets in any such violation, shall be fined not more than $1,000, or imprisoned not more than 1 year, or both, for each such offense.

Sec. 5662. Penalty for alteration of wine labels.

Any person who, without the permission of the Secretary, so alters as to materially change the meaning of any mark, brand, or label required to appear upon any wine upon its removal from premises subject to the provisions of subchapter F, or from customs custody, or who, after such removal, represents any wine, whether in its original containers or otherwise, to be of an identity or origin other than its proper identity or origin as shown by such mark, brand, or label, or who, directly or indirectly, and whether by manner of packaging or advertising or any other form of representation, represents any still wine to be an effervescent wine or a substitute for an effervescent wine, shall be fined not more than $1,000, or imprisoned not more than 1 year, or both, for each such offense.

In 1976, P.L. 94-455, Sec. 1905(b)(2)(D), deleted "stamp," before "mark," each place it appeared in Code Sec. 5662, effective 2/1/77.
—P.L. 94-455, Sec. 1906(b)(13)(A), substituted "Secretary" for "Secretary or his delegate" in Code Sec. 5662, effective 2/1/77.

Sec. 5663. Cross reference.

For penalties of common application pertaining to liquors, including wines, see part IV.

In 1979, P.L. 96-39, Sec. 807(a)(57), deleted ", and for penalties for rectified products, see part I" after "see part IV" in Code Sec. 5663, effective 1/1/80.

PART III.—PENALTY, SEIZURE, AND FORFEITURE PROVISIONS APPLICABLE TO BEER AND BREWING

Sec.
5671. Penalty and forfeiture for evasion of beer tax and fraudulent noncompliance with requirements.
5672. Penalty for failure of brewer to comply with requirements and to keep records and file returns.
5673. Forfeiture for flagrant and willful removal of beer without taxpayment.
5674. Penalty for unlawful production or removal of beer.
5675. Penalty for intentional removal or defacement of brewer's marks and brands.

In 1978, P.L. 95-458, Sec. 2(b)(5)(B), amended item 5674. Prior to amendment item 5674 read as follows:
"5674. Penalty for unlawful removal of beer."

Excise and miscellaneous taxes

Sec. 5671. Penalty and forfeiture for evasion of beer tax and fraudulent noncompliance with requirements.

Whoever evades or attempts to evade any tax imposed by section 5051, or with intent to defraud the United States fails or refuses to keep and file true and accurate records and returns as required by section 5415 and regulations issued pursuant thereto, shall be fined not more than $5,000, or imprisoned not more than 5 years, or both, for each such offense, and shall forfeit all beer made by him or for him, and all the vessels, utensils, and apparatus used in making the same.

In 2005, P.L. 109-59, Sec. 11125(b)(18), deleted "or 5091" after "section 5051" in Code Sec. 5671, effective 7/1/2008, but not for taxes imposed for periods before 7/1/2008.
Prior to amendment, Code Sec. 5671 read as follows:
"SEC. 5671. PENALTY AND FORFEITURE FOR EVASION OF BEER TAX AND FRAUDULENT NONCOMPLIANCE WITH REQUIREMENTS.
"Whoever evades or attempts to evade any tax imposed by section 5051 or 5091, or with intent to defraud the United States fails or refuses to keep file true and accurate records and returns as required by section 5415 and regulations issued pursuant thereto, shall be fined not more than $5,000, or imprisoned not more than 5 years, or both, for each such offense, and shall forfeit all beer made by him or for him, and all the vessels, utensils, and apparatus used in making the same."

Sec. 5672. Penalty for failure of brewer to comply with requirements and to keep records and file returns.

Every brewer who, otherwise than with intent to defraud the United States, fails or refuses to keep the records and file the returns required by section 5415 and regulations issued pursuant thereto, or refuses to permit any internal revenue officer to inspect his records in the manner provided, or violates any of the provisions of subchapter G or regulations issued pursuant thereto shall be fined not more than $1,000, or imprisoned not more than 1 year, or both, for each such offense.

Sec. 5673. Forfeiture for flagrant and willful removal of beer without taxpayment.

For flagrant and willful removal of taxable beer for consumption or sale, with intent to defraud the United States of the tax thereon, all the right, title, and interest of each person who knowingly has suffered or permitted such removal, or has connived at the same, in the lands and buildings constituting the brewery shall be forfeited by a proceeding in rem in the District Court of the United States having jurisdiction thereof.

Sec. 5674. Penalty for unlawful production or removal of beer.

(a) Unlawful production.

Any person who brews beer or produces beer shall be fined not more than $1,000, or imprisoned not more than 1 year, or both, unless such beer is brewed or produced in a brewery qualified under subchapter G or such production is exempt from tax under section 5053(e) (relating to beer for personal or family use).

(b) Unlawful removal.

Any brewer or other person who removes or in any way aids in the removal from any brewery of beer without complying with the provisions of this chapter or regulations issued pursuant thereto shall be fined not more than $1,000, or imprisoned not more than 1 year, or both.

In 1978, P.L. 95-458, Sec. 2(b)(5)(A), amended Code Sec. 5674, effective the first day of the first calendar month which begins more than 90 days after 10/14/78.
Prior to amendment, Code Sec. 5674 read as follows:
"SEC. 5674. PENALTY FOR UNLAWFUL REMOVAL OF BEER.
Any brewer or other person who removes or in any way aids in the removal from any brewery of beer without complying with the provisions of this chapter or regulations issued pursuant thereto shall be fined not more than $1,000, or imprisoned not more than 1 year, or both."

Excise and miscellaneous taxes   Code Sec. 5684(c)(2)

Sec. 5675. Penalty for intentional removal or defacement of brewer's marks and brands.

Every person other than the owner, or his agent authorized so to do, who intentionally removes or defaces any mark, brand, or label required by section 5412 and regulations issued pursuant thereto shall be liable to a penalty of $50 for each barrel or other container from which such mark, brand, or label is so removed or defaced.

PART IV.—PENALTY, SEIZURE, AND FORFEITURE PROVISIONS COMMON TO LIQUORS

Sec.
5681. Penalty relating to signs.
5682. Penalty for breaking locks or gaining access.
5683. Penalty and forfeiture for removal of liquors under improper brands.
5684. Penalties relating to the payment and collection of liquor taxes.
5685. Penalty and forfeiture relating to possession of devices for emitting gas, smoke, etc., explosives and firearms, when violating liquor laws.
5686. Penalty for having, possessing, or using liquor or property intended to be used in violating provisions of this chapter.
5687. Penalty for offenses not specifically covered.
5688. Disposition and release of seized property.
5690. Definition of the term "person".

Sec. 5681. Penalty relating to signs.
(a) Failure to post required sign.

Every person engaged in distilled spirits operations who fails to post the sign required by section 5180(a) shall be fined not more than $1,000, or imprisoned not more than 1 year, or both.

(b) Posting or displaying false sign.

Every person, other than a distiller, warehouseman, or processor of distilled spirits who has received notice of registration of his plant under the provisions of section 5171(c), or other than a wholesale dealer in liquors who has paid the special tax (or who is exempt from payment of such special tax by reason of the provisions of section 5113(a)), who puts up or keeps up any sign indicating that he may lawfully carry on the business of a distiller, warehouseman, or processor of distilled spirits, or wholesale dealer in liquors, as the case may be, shall be fined not more than $1,000, or imprisoned not more than 1 year, or both.

(c) Premises where no sign is placed or kept.

Every person who works in any distilled spirits plant on which no sign required by section 5180(a) is placed or kept, and every person who knowingly receives at, or carries or conveys any distilled spirits to or from any such distilled spirits plant or who knowingly carries or delivers any grain, molasses, or other raw material to any distilled spirits plant on which such a sign is not placed and kept, shall forfeit all vehicles, aircraft, or vessels used in carrying or conveying such property and shall be fined not more than $1,000, or imprisoned not more than 1 year, or both.

(d) Presumption.

Whenever on trial for violation of subsection (c) by working in a distilled spirits plant on which no sign required by section 5180(a) is placed or kept, the defendant is shown to have been present at such premises, such presence of the defendant shall be deemed sufficient evidence to authorize conviction, unless the defendant explains such presence to the satisfaction of the jury (or of the court when tried without jury).

In 1997, P.L. 105-34, Sec. 1415(b)(1), deleted ", and every wholesale dealer in liquors," after "distilled spirits operations" in subsec. (a) and deleted "section 5115(a) or" after "required by" in subsec. (a)... Sec. 1415(b)(2)(A), substituted "on which no sign required by" for "or wholesale liquor establishment, on which no sign required by section 5115(a) or" in subsec. (c)... Sec. 1415(b)(2)(B), substituted "or who" for "or wholesale liquor establishment, or who" in subsec. (c), effective 8/5/97.

In 1979, P.L. 96-39, Sec. 807(a)(58)(A), substituted "distilled spirits operations" for "distilling, warehousing of distilled spirits, rectifying, or bottling of distilled spirits" in subsec. (a)... Sec. 807(a)(58)(B), substituted "distiller, warehouseman, or processor of distilled spirits" for "distiller, warehouseman of distilled spirits, rectifier, or bottler of distilled spirits" in subsec. (b), substituted "section 5171(c)" for "section 5171(a)" in subsec. (b), substituted "distiller, warehouseman, or processor of distilled spirits" for "distiller, bonded warehouseman, rectifier, bottler of distilled spirits" in subsec. (b)... Sec. 807(a)(58)(C), amended subsec. (c)... Sec. 807(a)(58)(D), substituted "distilled spirits plant" for "distillery or rectifying establishment" in subsec. (d), effective 1/1/80.

Prior to amendment, subsec. (c) read as follows:

"(c) Premises where no sign is placed or kept.

"Every person who works in any distillery, or in any rectifying, distilled spirits bottling, or wholesale liquor establishment, on which no sign required by section 5115(a) or section 5180(a) is placed or kept, and every person who knowingly receives at, or carries or conveys any distilled spirits to or from any such distillery, or to or from any such rectifying, distilled spirits bottling, or wholesale liquor establishment, or who knowingly carries or delivers any grain, molasses, or other raw material to any distillery on which said sign is not placed and kept, shall forfeit all vehicles, aircraft, or vessels used in carrying or conveying such property and shall be fined not more than $1,000, or imprisoned not more than 1 year, or both."

Sec. 5682. Penalty for breaking locks or gaining access.

Every person, who destroys, breaks, injures, or tampers with any lock or seal which may be placed on any room, building, tank, vessel, or apparatus, by any authorized internal revenue officer or any approved lock or seal placed thereon by a distilled spirits plant proprietor, or who opens said lock, seal, room, building, tank, vessel, or apparatus, or in any manner gains access to the contents therein, in the absence of the proper officer, or otherwise than as authorized by law, shall be fined not more than $5,000, or imprisoned not more than 3 years, or both.

In 1979, P.L. 96-39, Sec. 807(a)(59), substituted "authorized internal revenue officer or any approved lock or seal placed thereon by a distilled spirits plant proprietor, or who" for "duly authorized internal revenue officer, or" in Code Sec. 5682, effective 1/1/80.

Sec. 5683. Penalty and forfeiture for removal of liquors under improper brands.

Whenever any person ships, transports, or removes any distilled spirits, wines, or beer, under any other than the proper name or brand known to the trade as designating the kind and quality of the contents of the casks or packages containing the same, or causes such act to be done, he shall be fined not more than $1,000, or imprisoned not more than 1 year, or both, and shall forfeit such distilled spirits, wines, or beer, and casks or packages.

Sec. 5684. Penalties relating to the payment and collection of liquor taxes.
(a) Failure to pay tax.

Whoever fails to pay any tax imposed by part I of subchapter A at the time prescribed shall, in addition to any other penalty provided in this title, be liable to a penalty of 5 percent of the tax due but unpaid.

(b) Applicability of section 6665.

The penalties imposed by subsection (a) shall be assessed, collected, and paid in the same manner as taxes, as provided in section 6665(a).

(c) Cross references.

(1) For provisions relating to interest in the case of taxes not paid when due, see section 6601.

(2) For penalty for failure to file tax return or pay tax, see section 6651.

3,453

(3) For additional penalties for failure to pay tax, see section 6653.

(4) For penalty for failure to make deposits or for overstatement of deposits, see section 6656.

(5) For penalty for attempt to evade or defeat any tax imposed by this title, see section 7201.

(6) For penalty for willful failure to file return, supply information, or pay tax, see section 7203.

In 1989, P.L. 101-239, Sec. 7721(c)(3)(A), substituted "6665(a)" for "6662(a)" in subsec. (b)... Sec. 7721(c)(3)(B), substituted "6665" for "6662" in the heading of subsec. (b), effective for returns the due date for which (determined without regard to extensions) is after 12/31/89.

In 1984, P.L. 98-369, Sec. 714(h)(1)(A), substituted "section 6662" for "section 6660" in the heading of subsec. (b)... Sec. 714(h)(1)(B), substituted "section 6662(a)" for "section 6660(a)" in subsec. (b), effective for returns whose filing due date (determined without regard to extensions) is after 12/31/82.

—P.L. 98-369, Sec. 722(a)(5), substituted "subsection (a)" for "subsections (a) and (b)" in subsec. (b), effective for returns filed after 8/13/81.

In 1981, P.L. 97-34, Sec. 722(a)(3), substituted "6660" for "6659" in the heading and text of subsec. (c) [redesignated subsec. (b) by Sec. 724(b)(4)(A) of this Act], effective for returns filed after 12/31/81.

—P.L. 97-34, Sec. 724(b)(4)(A), deleted subsec. (b), and redesignated subsecs. (c) and (d) as subsecs. (b) and (c)... Sec. 724(b)(4)(B), redesignated paras. (c)(4) and (5) (as redesignated by Sec. 724(b)(4)(A) of this Act) as paras. (c)(5) and (6), and added new para. (c)(4), effective for returns filed after 8/13/81.

Prior to deletion, subsec. (b) read as follows:

"(b) Failure to make deposit of taxes.

"Section 6656 relating to failure to make deposit of taxes shall apply to the failure to make any deposit of taxes imposed under part I of subchapter A on the date prescribed therefor, except that the penalty for such failure shall be 5 percent of the amount of the underpayment in lieu of the penalty provided by such section."

In 1969, P.L. 91-172, Sec. 943(c)(4), added "or pay tax" after "tax return" in para. (d)(2), effective for returns the date prescribed by law (without regard to any extension of time) for filing of which is after 12/31/69, and with respect to notices and demands for payment of tax made after 12/31/69.

Sec. 5685. Penalty and forfeiture relating to possession of devices for emitting gas, smoke, etc., explosives and firearms, when violating liquor laws.

(a) Penalty for possession of devices for emitting gas, smoke, etc.

Whoever, when violating any law of the United States, or of any possession of the United States, or of the District of Columbia, in regard to the manufacture, taxation, or transportation of or traffic in distilled spirits, wines, or beer, or when aiding in any such violation, has in his possession or in his control any device capable of causing emission of gas, smoke, or fumes, and which may be used for the purpose of hindering, delaying, or preventing pursuit or capture, any explosive, or any firearm (as defined in section 5845), except a machine gun, or a shotgun having a barrel or barrels less than 18 inches in length, or a rifle having a barrel or barrels less than 16 inches in length, shall be fined not more than $5,000, or imprisoned not more than 10 years, or both, and all persons engaged in any such violation or in aiding in any such violation shall be held to be in possession or control of such device, firearm, or explosive.

(b) Penalty for possession of machine gun, etc.

Whoever, when violating any such law, has in his possession or in his control a machine gun, or any shotgun having a barrel or barrels less than 18 inches in length, or a rifle having a barrel or barrels less than 16 inches in length, shall be imprisoned not more than 20 years; and all persons engaged in any such violation or in aiding in any such violation shall be held to be in possession and control of such machine gun, shotgun, or rifle.

(c) Forfeiture of firearms, devices, etc.

Every such firearm or device for emitting gas, smoke, or fumes, and every such explosive, machine gun, shotgun, or rifle, in the possession or control of any person when violating any such law, shall be seized and shall be forfeited and disposed of in the manner provided by section 5872.

(d) Definition of machine gun.

As used in this section, the term "machine gun" means a machine gun as defined in section 5845(b).

In 1976, P.L. 94-455, Sec. 1905(a)(23)(A), substituted "section 5845" for "section 5848" in subsec. (a)... Sec. 1905(a)(23)(B), substituted "section 5872" for "section 5862" in subsec. (c)... Sec. 1905(a)(23)(c), amended subsec. (d), effective 2/1/77.

Prior to amendment, subsec. (d) read as follows:

"(d) Definition of machine gun.

"As used in this section the term 'machine gun' means any weapon which shoots, or is designed to shoot, automatically or semiautomatically, more than one shot, without manual reloading, by a single function of the trigger."

—P.L. 94-455, Sec. 1905(c)(6), deleted "Territory or", before "possession of the United States," in subsec. (a), effective 2/1/77.

In 1960, P.L. 86-478, Sec. 4, substituted "shotgun having a barrel or barrels less than 18 inches in length, or a rifle having a barrel or barrels less than 16 inches in length" for "shotgun or rifle having a barrel or barrels less than 18 inches in length" in subsecs. (a) and (b), effective 7/1/60 and, for purposes of the rate of the special tax imposed by section 5801, applicable with respect to periods beginning after 6/30/60.

Sec. 5686. Penalty for having, possessing, or using liquor or property intended to be used in violating provisions of this chapter.

(a) General.

It shall be unlawful to have or possess any liquor or property intended for use in violating any provision of this chapter or regulations issued pursuant thereto, or which has been so used, and every person so having or possessing or using such liquor or property, shall be fined not more than $5,000, or imprisoned not more than 1 year, or both.

(b) Cross reference.

For seizure and forfeiture of liquor and property had, possessed, or used in violation of subsection (a), see section 7302.

Sec. 5687. Penalty for offenses not specifically covered.

Whoever violates any provision of this chapter or regulations issued pursuant thereto, for which a specific criminal penalty is not prescribed by this chapter, shall be fined not more than $1,000, or imprisoned not more than 1 year, or both, for each such offense.

Sec. 5688. Disposition and release of seized property.

(a) Forfeiture.

(1) Delivery. All distilled spirits, wines, and beer forfeited, summarily or by order of court, under any law of the United States, shall be delivered to the Administrator of General Services to be disposed of as hereinafter provided.

(2) Disposal. The Administrator of General Services shall dispose of all distilled spirits, wines, and beer which have been delivered to him pursuant to paragraph (1)—

(A) by delivery to such Government agencies as, in his opinion, have a need for such distilled spirits, wines, or beer for medicinal, scientific, or mechanical purposes, or for any other official purpose for which appropriated funds may be expended by a Government agency; or

(B) by gifts to such eleemosynary institutions as, in his opinion, have a need for such distilled spirits, wines, or beer for medicinal purposes; or

(C) by destruction.

(3) Limitation on disposal. Except as otherwise provided by law, no distilled spirits, wines, or beer which have been seized under any law of the United States may be disposed of in any manner whatsoever except after forfeiture and as provided in this subsection.

(4) Regulations. The Administrator of General Services is authorized to make all rules and regulations necessary to carry out the provisions of this subsection.

Excise and miscellaneous taxes

(5) Remission or mitigation of forfeitures. Nothing in this section shall affect the authority of the Secretary, under the customs or internal revenue laws, to remit or mitigate the forfeiture, or alleged forfeiture, of such distilled spirits, wines, or beer, or the authority of the Secretary, to compromise any civil or criminal case in respect of such distilled spirits, wines, or beer prior to commencement of suit thereon, or the authority of the Secretary to compromise any claim under the customs laws in respect to such distilled spirits, wines, or beer.

(b) Distraint or judicial process.

Except as provided in section 5243, all distilled spirits sold by order of court, or under process of distraint, shall be sold subject to tax; and the purchaser shall immediately, and before he takes possession of said spirits, pay the tax thereon, pursuant to the applicable provisions of this chapter and in accordance with regulations to be prescribed by the Secretary.

(c) Release of seized vessels or vehicles by courts.

Notwithstanding any provisions of law relating to the return on bond of any vessel or vehicle seized for the violation of any law of the United States, the court having jurisdiction of the subject matter may, in its discretion and upon good cause shown by the United States, refuse to order such return of any such vessel or vehicle to the claimant thereof. As used in this subsection, the word "vessel" includes every description of watercraft used, or capable of being used, as a means of transportation in water or in water and air; and the word "vehicle" includes every animal and description of carriage or other contrivance used, or capable of being used, as a means of transportation on land or through the air.

In **1976**, P.L. 94-455, Sec. 1906(b)(13)(A), substituted "Secretary" for "Secretary or his delegate" each place it appeared in Code Sec. 5688, effective 2/1/77.

Sec. 5690. Definition of the term "person".

The term "person", as used in this subchapter, includes an officer or employee of a corporation or a member or employee of a partnership, who as such officer, employee, or member is under a duty to perform the act in respect of which the violation occurs.

PART V.—PENALTIES APPLICABLE TO OCCUPATIONAL TAXES

Sec.

5691. Repealed. [Penalties for nonpayment of special taxes.]

5692. Repealed. [Penalties relating to posting of special tax stamps]

In **1987**, P.L. 100-203, Sec. 10512(a)(1)(B)(iii), deleted "relating to liquors" from item 5691.
Prior to deletion, item 5691 read as follows:
"5691. Penalties for nonpayment of special taxes relating to liquors.".
In **1968**, deleted item 5692.
Prior to deletion, item 5692 read as follows:
"Sec. 5692. Penalties relating to posting of special tax stamps"

Sec. 5691. Repealed.

In **2005**, P.L. 109-59, Sec. 11125(b)(19)(A), repealed Code Sec. 5691, effective 7/1/2008, but not for taxes imposed for periods before 7/1/2008.
Prior to repeal, Code Sec. 5691 read as follows:
"SEC. 5691. PENALTIES FOR NONPAYMENT OF SPECIAL TAXES.

"(a) General. Any person who shall carry on a business subject to a special tax imposed by part II of subchapter A or section 5276 (relating to occupational taxes) and willfully fail to pay the special tax as required by law, shall be fined not more than $5,000, or imprisoned not more than 2 years, or both, for each such offense.

"(b) Presumption in case of the sale of 20 wine gallons or more. For the purposes of this chapter, the sale, or offer for sale, of distilled spirits, wines, or beer, in quantities of 20 wine gallons or more to the same person at the same time, shall be presumptive evidence that the person making such sale, or offer for sale, is engaged in or carrying on the business of a wholesale dealer in liquors or a wholesale dealer in beer, as the case may be. Such presumption may be overcome by evidence satisfactorily showing that such sale, or offer for sale, was made to a person other than a dealer, as defined in section 5112(a)."
In **1987**, P.L. 100-203, Sec. 10512(a)(1)(B)(i), substituted "a business subject to a special tax imposed by part II of subchapter A or section 5276 (relating to occupational taxes)" for "the business of a brewer, wholesale dealer in liquors, retail dealer in liquors, wholesale dealer in beer, retail dealer in beer, or limited retail dealer," in subsec (a) ... Sec. 10512(a)(1)(B)(ii), deleted "relating to liquors" after "taxes" in the heading of Code Sec. 5691, effective 1/1/88. For special rules, see Sec. 10512(h)(2) of this Act, reproduced in note following Code Sec. 5081.
In **1984**, P.L. 98-369, Sec. 451(b)(3), substituted "or limited retail dealer" for "limited retail dealer, or manufacturer of stills" in subsec. (a), effective the first day of the first calendar month which begins more than 90 days after 7/18/84.
In **1979**, P.L. 96-39, Sec. 807(a)(60), deleted "rectifier," after "brewer," in subsec. (a), effective 1/1/80.

Sec. 5692. Repealed.

In **1968**, P.L. 90-618, Sec. 201, repealed Code Sec. 5692, effective 8/1/68.
Prior to repeal, Code Sec. 5692 read as follows:
"SEC. 5692. PENALTIES RELATING TO POSTING OF SPECIAL TAX STAMPS.
"For penalty for failure to post Special tax stamps, see Section 7273(a)."

CHAPTER 52.—TOBACCO PRODUCTS AND CIGARETTE PAPERS AND TUBES

Subchapter

A. Definitions; rate and payment of tax; exemption from tax; and refund and drawback of tax.

B. Qualification requirements for manufacturers and importers of tobacco products and cigarette papers and tubes, and export warehouse proprietors.

C. Operations by manufacturers and importers of tobacco products and cigarette papers and tubes and export warehouse proprietors.

D. Occupational tax.

E. Records of manufacturers and importers of tobacco products and cigarette papers and tubes, and export warehouse proprietors.

F. General provisions.

G. Penalties and forfeitures.

In **1997**, P.L. 105-33, Sec. 9302(g)(3)(C), amended the heading for Chapter 52 ... Sec. 9302(h)(2)(D), added "and importers" after "Manufacturers" in the item for Subchapter B
Prior to amendment, the heading for Chapter 52 read as follows:
"Chapter 52—Cigars, Cigarettes, Smokeless Tobacco, and Cigarette Papers and Tubes"
In **1986**, P.L. 99-272, Sec. 13202(b)(1), added "SMOKELESS TOBACCO," after "CIGARETTES," in the title of chapter 52.
In **1976**, P.L. 94-455, Sec. 2128(d)(2), amended the title for subchapter D.
Prior to amendment, the title read as follows:
"D. Records of manufacturers of tobacco products and cigarette papers and tubes, and export warehouse proprietors."
In **1965**, P.L. 89-44, Sec. 502(b)(1), deleted "Tobacco," from Chapter heading, deleted from Subchapters B and D "dealers in tobacco materials", deleted Subchapter "D. Operations by dealers in tobacco materials", and redesignated Subchapters E, F and G as D, E and F, respectively, effective 1/1/66.
In **1958**, P.L. 85-859, Sec. 202, substituted "manufacturers of tobacco products and cigarette papers and tubes, export warehouse proprietors, and" for "manufacturers of articles and" in the heading of Subchapters B and E, "manufacturers and importers of tobacco products and cigarette papers and tubes and export warehouse proprietors" for "manufacturers of articles" in the heading of Subchapter C, and "Penalties and forfeitures" for "Fines, penalties and forfeitures" in the heading of Subchapter G.

Subchapter A.—Definitions; Rate and Payment of Tax; Exemption From Tax; and Refund and Drawback of Tax

Sec.

5701. Rate of tax.

5702. Definitions.

5703. Liability for tax and method of payment.

5704. Exemption from tax.

5705. Credit, refund or allowance of tax.

5706. Drawback of tax.
5708. Losses caused by disaster.

In 1965, P.L. 89-44, Sec. 501(g), deleted item 5707 "Floor stocks refund on cigarettes" and inserted in item 5705 "Credit," before "refund."
In 1958, added item 5708.

Sec. 5701. Rate of tax.
(a) Cigars

On cigars, manufactured in or imported into the United States, there shall be imposed the following taxes:

(1) Small cigars. On cigars, weighing not more than 3 pounds per thousand, $50.33 per thousand;

(2) Large cigars. On cigars weighing more than 3 pounds per thousand, a tax equal to 52.75 percent of the price for which sold but not more than 40.26 cents per cigar.

Cigars not exempt from tax under this chapter which are removed but not intended for sale shall be taxed at the same rate as similar cigars removed for sale.

(b) Cigarettes.

On cigarettes, manufactured in or imported into the United States, there shall be imposed the following taxes:

(1) Small cigarettes. On cigarettes, weighing not more than 3 pounds per thousand, $50.33 per thousand.

(2) Large cigarettes. On cigarettes, weighing more than 3 pounds per thousand, $105.69 per thousand; except that, if more than 6½ inches in length, they shall be taxable at the rate prescribed for cigarettes weighing not more than 3 pounds per thousand, counting each 2¾ inches, or fraction thereof, of the length of each as one cigarette.

(c) Cigarette papers.

On cigarette papers, manufactured in or imported into the United States, there shall be imposed a tax of 3.15 cents for each 50 papers or fractional part thereof; except that, if cigarette papers measure more than 6½ inches in length, they shall be taxable at the rate prescribed, counting each 2¾ inches, or fraction thereof, of the length of each as one cigarette paper.

(d) Cigarette tubes.

On cigarette tubes, manufactured in or imported into the United States, there shall be imposed a tax of 6.30 cents for each 50 tubes or fractional part thereof, except that if cigarette tubes measure more than 6½ inches in length, they shall be taxable at the rate prescribed, counting each 2¾ inches, or fraction thereof, of the length of each as one cigarette tube.

(e) Smokeless tobacco.

On smokeless tobacco, manufactured in or imported into the United States, there shall be imposed the following taxes:

(1) Snuff. On snuff, $1.51 per pound and a proportionate tax at the like rate on all fractional parts of a pound.

(2) Chewing tobacco. On chewing tobacco, 50.33 cents per pound and a proportionate tax at the like rate on all fractional parts of a pound.

(f) Pipe tobacco.

On pipe tobacco, manufactured in or imported into the United States, there shall be imposed a tax of $2.8311 cents per pound (and a proportionate tax at the like rate on all fractional parts of a pound).

(g) Roll-your-own tobacco.

On roll-your-own tobacco, manufactured in or imported into the United States, there shall be imposed a tax of $24.78 per pound (and a proportionate tax at the like rate on all fractional parts of a pound).

(h) Imported tobacco products and cigarette papers and tubes.

The taxes imposed by this section on tobacco products and cigarette papers and tubes imported into the United States shall be in addition to any import duties imposed on such articles, unless such import duties are imposed in lieu of internal revenue tax.

In 2009, P.L. 111-3, Sec. 701(a)(1), substituted "$50.33 per thousand" for "$1.828 cents per thousand ($1.594 cents per thousand on cigars removed during 2000 or 2001)" in para. (a)(1) . . . Sec. 701(a)(2), substituted "52.75 percent" for "20.719 percent (18.063 percent on cigars removed during 2000 or 2001)" in para. (a)(2) . . . Sec. 701(a)(3), substituted "40.26 cents per cigar" for "$48.75 per thousand ($42.50 per thousand on cigars removed during 2000 or 2001)" in para. (a)(2) . . . Sec. 701(b)(1), substituted "$50.33 per thousand" for "$19.50 per thousand ($17 per thousand on cigarettes removed during 2000 or 2001)" in para. (b)(1) . . . Sec. 701(b)(2), substituted "$105.69 per thousand" for "$40.95 per thousand ($35.70 per thousand on cigarettes removed during 2000 or 2001)" in para. (b)(2) . . . Sec. 701(c), substituted "3.15 cents" for "1.22 cents (1.06 cents on cigarette papers removed during 2000 or 2001)" in subsec. (c) . . . Sec. 701(d), substituted "6.30 cents" for "2.44 cents (2.13 cents on cigarette tubes removed during 2000 or 2001)" in subsec. (d) . . . Sec. 701(e)(1), substituted "$1.51" for "58.5 cents (51 cents on snuff removed during 2000 or 2001)" in para. (e)(1) . . . Sec. 701(e)(2), substituted "50.33 cents" for "19.5 cents (17 cents on chewing tobacco removed during 2000 or 2001)" in para. (e)(2) . . . Sec. 701(f), substituted "$2.8311 cents" for "$1.0969 cents (95.67 cents on pipe tobacco removed during 2000 or 2001)" in subsec. (f) . . . Sec. 701(g), substituted "$24.78" for "$1.0969 cents (95.67 cents on roll-your-own tobacco removed during 2000 or 2001)" in subsec. (g), effective for articles removed (as defined in Code Sec. 5702(j)) after 3/31/2009.

—P.L. 111-3, Sec. 701(h), of this Act, reads as follows:
"*(h) Floor stocks taxes.*

"(1) Imposition of tax. On tobacco products (other than cigars described in section 5701(a)(2) of the Internal Revenue Code of 1986) and cigarette papers and tubes manufactured in or imported into the United States which are removed before April 1, 2009, and held on such date for sale by any person, there is hereby imposed a tax in an amount equal to the excess of—

"(A) the tax which would be imposed under section 5701 of such Code on the article if the article had been removed on such date, over

"(B) the prior tax (if any) imposed under section 5701 of such Code on such article.

"(2) Credit against tax. Each person shall be allowed as a credit against the taxes imposed by paragraph (1) an amount equal to $500. Such credit shall not exceed the amount of taxes imposed by paragraph (1) on April 1, 2009, for which such person is liable.

"(3) Liability for tax and method of payment.

"(A) Liability for tax. A person holding tobacco products, cigarette papers, or cigarette tubes on April 1, 2009, to which any tax imposed by paragraph (1) applies shall be liable for such tax.

"(B) Method of payment. The tax imposed by paragraph (1) shall be paid in such manner as the Secretary shall prescribe by regulations.

"(C) Time for payment. The tax imposed by paragraph (1) shall be paid on or before August 1, 2009.

"(4) Articles in foreign trade zones. Notwithstanding the Act of June 18, 1934 (commonly known as the Foreign Trade Zone Act, 48 Stat. 998, 19 U.S.C. 81a et seq.) or any other provision of law, any article which is located in a foreign trade zone on April 1, 2009, shall be subject to the tax imposed by paragraph (1) if—

"(A) internal revenue taxes have been determined, or customs duties liquidated, with respect to such article before such date pursuant to a request made under the 1st proviso of section 3(a) of such Act, or

"(B) such article is held on such date under the supervision of an officer of the United States Customs and Border Protection of the Department of Homeland Security pursuant to the 2d proviso of such section 3(a).

"(5) Definitions. For purposes of this subsection—

"(A) In general. Any term used in this subsection which is also used in section 5702 of the Internal Revenue Code of 1986 shall have the same meaning as such term has in such section.

"(B) Secretary. The term 'Secretary' means the Secretary of the Treasury or the Secretary's delegate.

"(6) Controlled groups. Rules similar to the rules of section 5061(e)(3) of such Code shall apply for purposes of this subsection.

"(7) Other laws applicable. All provisions of law, including penalties, applicable with respect to the taxes imposed by section 5701 of such Code shall, insofar as applicable and not inconsistent with the provisions of this subsection, apply to the floor stocks taxes imposed by paragraph (1), to the same extent as if such taxes were imposed by such section 5701. The Secretary may treat any person who bore the ultimate burden of the tax imposed by paragraph (1) as the person to whom a credit or refund under such provisions may be allowed or made."

In 2000, P.L. 106-554, Sec. 1(a)(7), [which enacted into law Sec. 315(a)(1) of P.L. 106-554] substituted "cigarettes" for "tobacco products and cigarette papers and tubes" in Sec. 9302(j)(1) of P.L. 105-33, see below.

In 1997, P.L. 105-78, Sec. 519, deleted subsec. (k) of Sec. 9302 of P.L. 105-33, as added by Sec. 1604(f)(3) of P.L. 105-34, see below.

Prior to deletion, subsec. (k) read as follows:

Excise and miscellaneous taxes Code Sec. 5701

"(k) Coordination with tobacco industry settlement agreement. The increase in excise taxes collected as a result of the amendments made by subsections (a), (e), and (g) of this section shall be credited against the total payments made by parties pursuant to Federal legislation implementing the tobacco industry settlement agreement of June 20, 1997."

—P.L. 105-34, Sec. 1604(f)(3), added Sec. 9302(k) of P.L. 105-33, see below. This subsection (k) was repealed by Sec. 519 of P.L. 105-78, see above.

—P.L. 105-33, Sec. 9302(a)(1), substituted "$19.50 per thousand ($17 per thousand on cigarettes removed during 2000 or 2001)" for "$12 per thousand ($10 per thousand on cigarettes removed during 1991 or 1992)" in para. (b)(1) . . . Sec. 9302(a)(2), substituted "$40.95 per thousand ($35.70 per thousand on cigarettes removed during 2000 or 2001)" for "$25.20 per thousand ($21 per thousand on cigarettes removed during 1991 or 1992)" in para. (b)(2) . . . Sec. 9302(b)(1), substituted "$1.828 cents per thousand ($1.594 cents per thousand on cigars removed during 2000 or 2001)" for "$1.25 cents per thousand (93.75 per thousand on cigars removed during 1991 or 1992)" in para. (a)(1) . . . Sec. 9302(b)(2), substituted "equal to 20.719 percent ($18.063 percent on cigars removed during 2000 or 2001) of the price for which sold but not more than $48.75 per thousand ($42.50 per thousand on cigars removed during 2000 or 2001)." for "equal to

"(A) 10.625 percent of the price for which sold but not more than $25 per thousand on cigars removed during 1991 or 1992, and

"12.75 percent of the price for which sold but not more than $30 per thousand on cigars removed after 1992."

in para. (a)(2) . . . Sec. 9302(c), substituted "1.22 cents (1.06 cents on cigarette papers removed during 2000 or 2001)" for "0.75 cent (0.625 cent on cigarette papers removed during 1991 or 1992)" in subsec. (c) . . . Sec. 9302(d), substituted "2.44 cents (2.13 cents on cigarette tubes removed during 2000 or 2001)" for "1.5 cents (1.25 cents on cigarette tubes removed during 1991 or 1992)" in subsec. (d) . . . Sec. 9302(e)(1), substituted "58.5 cents (51 cents on snuff removed during 2000 or 2001)" for "36 cents (30 cents on snuff removed during 1991 or 1992)" in para. (e)(1) . . . Sec. 9302(e)(2), substituted "19.5 cents (17 cents on chewing tobacco removed during 2000 or 2001)" for "12 cents (10 cents on chewing tobacco removed during 1991 or 1992)" in para. (e)(2) . . . Sec. 9302(f), substituted "$1.0969 cents (95.67 cents on pipe tobacco removed during 2000 or 2001)" for "67.5 cents (56.25 cents on pipe tobacco removed during 1991 or 1992)" in subsec. (f) . . . Sec. 9302(g)(1), redesignated subsec. (g) as subsec. (h) and added new subsec. (g) . . . Sec. 9302(h)(3), substituted "On cigarette papers," for "On each book or set of cigarette papers containing more than 25 papers," in subsec. (c), effective for articles removed (as defined in Code Sec. 5702(k), as amended [see above]) after 12/31/99. Sec. 9302(i)(2) of this Act provides:

"(2) Transitional rule. Any person who—

"(A) on the date of the enactment of this Act is engaged in business as a manufacturer of roll-your-own tobacco or as an importer of tobacco products or cigarette papers and tubes, and

"(B) before January 1, 2000, submits an application under subchapter B of chapter 52 of such Code to engage in such business, may, notwithstanding such subchapter B, continue to engage in such business pending final action on such application. Pending such final action, all provisions of such chapter 52 shall apply to such applicant in the same manner and to the same extent as if such applicant were a holder of a permit under such chapter 52 to engage in such business."

—P.L. 105-33, Sec. 9302(j), of this Act provides:

"(j) Floor Stocks Taxes.—

"(1) Imposition of tax.—On cigarettes manufactured in or imported into the United States which are removed before any tax increase date, and held on such date for sale by any person, there is hereby imposed a tax in an amount equal to the excess of—

"(A) the tax which would be imposed under section 5701 of the Internal Revenue Code of 1986 on the article if the article had been removed on such date, over

"(B) the prior tax (if any) imposed under section 5701 of such Code on such article.

"(2) Authority to exempt cigarettes held in vending machines.— To the extent provided in regulations prescribed by the Secretary, no tax shall be imposed by paragraph (1) on cigarettes held for retail sale on any tax increase date, by any person in any vending machine. If the Secretary provides such a benefit with respect to any person, the Secretary may reduce the $500 amount in paragraph (3) with respect to such person.

"(3) Credit against tax.—Each person shall be allowed as a credit against the taxes imposed by paragraph (1) an amount equal to $500. Such credit shall not exceed the amount of taxes imposed by paragraph (1) on any tax increase date, for which such person is liable.

"(4) Liability for tax and method of payment.—

"(A) Liability for tax.—A person holding cigarettes on any tax increase date, to which any tax imposed by paragraph (1) applies shall be liable for such tax.

"(B) Method of payment.—The tax imposed by paragraph (1) shall be paid in such manner as the Secretary shall prescribe by regulations.

"(C) Time for payment.—The tax imposed by paragraph (1) shall be paid on or before April 1 following any tax increase date.

"(5) Articles in foreign trade zones.—Notwithstanding the Act of June 18, 1934 (48 Stat. 998, 19 U.S.C. 81a) and any other provision of law, any article which is located in a foreign trade zone on any tax increase date, shall be subject to the tax imposed by paragraph (1) if—

"(A) internal revenue taxes have been determined, or customs duties liquidated, with respect to such article before such date pursuant to a request made under the 1st proviso of section 3(a) of such Act, or

"(B) such article is held on such date under the supervision of a customs officer pursuant to the 2d proviso of such section 3(a).

"(6) Definitions.—For purposes of this subsection—

"(A) In general.—Terms used in this subsection which are also used in section 5702 of the Internal Revenue Code of 1986 shall have the respective meanings such terms have in such section, as amended by this Act.

"(B) Tax increase date.—The term 'tax increase date' means January 1, 2000, and January 1, 2002.

"(C) Secretary.—The term 'Secretary' means the Secretary of the Treasury or the Secretary's delegate.

"(7) Controlled groups.—Rules similar to the rules of section 5061(e)(3) of such Code shall apply for purposes of this subsection.

"(8) Other laws applicable.—All provisions of law, including penalties, applicable with respect to the taxes imposed by section 5701 of such Code shall, insofar as applicable and not inconsistent with the provisions of this subsection, apply to the floor stocks taxes imposed by paragraph (1), to the same extent as if such taxes were imposed by such section 5701. The Secretary may treat any person who bore the ultimate burden of the tax imposed by paragraph (1) as the person to whom a credit or refund under such provisions may be allowed or made."

—P.L. 105-33, Sec. 9302(k), of this Act was added by Sec. 1604(f)(3) of P.L. 105-34. This subsection (k) was repealed by Sec. 519 of P.L. 105-78, see above.

In 1990, P.L. 101-508, Sec. 11202(a)(1), substituted "$1.125 cents per thousand (93.75 cents per thousand on cigars removed during 1991 or 1992)" for "75 cents per thousand" in para. (a)(1) . . . Sec. 11202(a)(2), amended para. (a)(2) . . . Sec. 11202(b)(1), substituted "$12 per thousand ($10 per thousand on cigarettes removed during 1991 or 1992)" for "$8 per thousand" in para. (b)(1) . . . Sec. 11202(b)(2), substituted "$25.20 per thousand ($21 per thousand on cigarettes removed during 1991 or 1992)" for "$16.80 per thousand" in para. (b)(2) . . . Sec. 11202(c), substituted "0.75 cent (0.625 cent on cigarette papers removed during 1991 or 1992)" for "½ cent" in subsec. (c) . . . Sec. 11202(d), substituted "1.5 cents (1.25 cents on cigarette tubes removed during 1991 or 1992)" for "1 cent" in subsec. (d) . . . Sec. 11202(e)(1), substituted "36 cents (30 cents on snuff removed during 1991 or 1992)" for "24 cents" in para. (e)(1) . . . Sec. 11202(e)(2), substituted "12 cents (10 cents on chewing tobacco removed during 1991 or 1992)" for "8 cents" in para. (e)(2) . . . Sec. 11202(f), substituted "67.5 cents (56.25 cents on pipe tobacco removed during 1991 or 1992)" for "45 cents" in subsec. (f), effective for articles removed after 12/31/90.

Prior to amendment, para. (a)(2) read as follows:

"(2) Large cigars. On cigars weighing more than 3 pounds per thousand, a tax equal to 8½ percent of the wholesale price, but not more than $20 per thousand."

—P.L. 101-508, Sec. 11202(i), relating to floor stocks taxes on cigarettes, provides:

"(i) Floor stocks taxes on cigarettes.—

"(1) Imposition of tax. On cigarettes manufactured in or imported into the United States which are removed before any tax-increase date and held on such date for sale by any person, there shall be imposed the following taxes:

"(A) Small cigarettes. On cigarettes, weighing not more than 3 pounds per thousand, $2 per thousand.

"(B) Large cigarettes. On cigarettes weighing more than 3 pounds per thousand, $4.20 per thousand; except that, if more than 6½ inches in length, they shall be taxable at the rate prescribed for cigarettes weighing not more than 3 pounds per thousand, counting each 2¾ inches, or fraction thereof, of the length of each as one cigarette.

"(2) Exception for certain amounts of cigarettes.—

"(A) In general. No tax shall be imposed by paragraph (1) on cigarettes held on any tax-increase date by any person if—

"(i) the aggregate number of cigarettes held by such person on such date does not exceed 30,000, and

"(ii) such person submits to the Secretary (at the time and in the manner required by the Secretary) such information as the Secretary shall require for purposes of this subparagraph.

For purposes of this subparagraph, in the case of cigarettes measuring more than 6½ inches in length, each 2¾ inches (or fraction thereof) of the length of each shall be counted as one cigarette.

"(B) Authority to exempt cigarettes held in vending machines. To the extent provided in regulations prescribed by the Secretary, no tax shall be imposed by paragraph (1) on cigarettes held for retail sale on any tax-increase date by any person in any vending machine. If the Secretary provides such a benefit with respect to any person, the Secretary may reduce the 30,000 amount in subparagraph (A) and the $60 amount in paragraph (3) with respect to such person.

"(3) Credit against tax. Each person shall be allowed as a credit against the taxes imposed by paragraph (2) an amount equal to $60. Such credit shall not exceed the amount of taxes imposed by paragraph (1) for which such person is liable.

"(4) Liability for tax and method of payment.—

"(A) Liability for tax. A person holding cigarettes on any tax-increase date to which any tax imposed by paragraph (1) applies shall be liable for such tax.

"(B) Method of payment. The tax imposed by paragraph (1) shall be paid in such manner as the Secretary shall prescribe by regulations.

"(C) Time for payment. The tax imposed by paragraph (1) shall be paid on or before the 1st June 30 following the tax-increase date.

"(5) Definitions. For purposes of this subsection—

"(A) Tax-increase date. The term 'tax-increase date' means January 1, 1991, and January 1, 1993.

"(B) Other definitions. Terms used in this subsection which are also used in section 5702 of the Internal Revenue Code of 1986 shall have the respective meanings such terms have in such section.

"(C) Secretary. The term 'Secretary' means the Secretary of the Treasury or his delegate.

"(6) Controlled groups. Rules similar to the rules of section 11201(e)(6) shall apply for purposes of this subsection.

"(7) Other laws applicable. All provisions of law, including penalties, applicable with respect to the taxes imposed by section 5701 of such Code shall, insofar as applicable and not inconsistent with the provisions of this subsection, apply to the floor stocks taxes imposed by paragraph (1), to the same extent as if such taxes were imposed by such section 5701."

— P.L. 101-508, Sec. 11218, regarding floor stocks tax treatment of articles in foreign trade zones, is reproduced in note following Code Sec. 5001.

In 1988, P.L. 100-647, Sec. 5061(a), added new subsec. (f) and redesignated subsec. (f) as (g), effective for pipe tobacco removed (within the meaning of Code Sec 5702(k)) after 12/31/88. Sec. 5061(d)(2) of this Act provides

"(2) Transitional rule.— Any person who—

"(A) on the date of the enactment of this Act, is engaged in business as a manufacturer of pipe tobacco, and

"(B) before January 1, 1989, submits an application under subchapter B of chapter 52 of the 1986 Code to engage in such business,

may, notwithstanding such subchapter B, continue to engage in such business pending final action on such application. Pending such final action, all provisions of chapter 52 of the 1986 Code shall apply to such applicant in the same manner and to the same extent as if such applicant were a holder of a permit to manufacturer pipe tobacco under such chapter 52."

— P.L. 100-647, Sec. 5061(e), of this Act provides:

"(1) Imposition of tax.— On pipe tobacco manufactured in or imported into the United States which is removed before January 1, 1989, and held on such date for sale by any person, there is hereby imposed a tax of 45 cents per pound (and a proportionate tax at the like rate on all fractional parts of a pound).

"(2) Liability for tax and method of payment.—

"(A) Liability for tax.— A person holding pipe tobacco on January 1, 1989, to which the tax imposed by paragraph (1) applies shall be liable for such tax.

"(B) Method of payment.— The tax imposed by paragraph (1) shall be treated as a tax imposed by section 5701 of the 1986 Code and shall be due and payable on February 14, 1989, in the same manner as the tax imposed by such section is payable with respect to pipe tobacco removed on or after January 1, 1989.

"(C) Treatment of pipe tobacco in foreign trade zones.— Notwithstanding the Act of June 18, 1934 (48 Stat. 998, 19 U.S.C. 81a) or any other provision of law, pipe tobacco which is located in a foreign trade zone on January 1, 1989, shall be subject to the tax imposed by paragraph (1) and shall be treated for purposes of this subsection as held on such date for sale if—

"(i) internal revenue taxes have been determined, or customs duties liquidated, with respect to such pipe tobacco before such date pursuant to a request made under the first proviso of section 3(a) of such Act, or

"(ii) such pipe tobacco is held on such date under the supervision of a customs officer pursuant to the second proviso of such section 3(a).

"Under regulations prescribed by the Secretary of the Treasury or his delegate, provisions similar to sections 5706 and 5708 of the 1986 Code shall apply to pipe tobacco with respect to which tax is imposed by paragraph (1) by reason of this subparagraph.

"(3) Pipe tobacco. For purposes of this subsection, the term 'pipe tobacco' shall have the meaning given to such term by subsection (o) of section 5702 of the 1986 Code.

"(4) Exception where liability does not exceed $1,000. No tax shall be imposed by paragraph (1) on any person if the tax which would but for this paragraph be imposed on such person does not exceed $1,000. For purposes of the preceding sentence, all persons who are treated as a single taxpayer under section 5061(e)(3) of the 1986 Code shall be treated as 1 person."

In 1986, P.L. 99-272, Sec. 13201(a), amended Sec. 283(c) of P.L. 97-248 [as amended by P.L. 99-201, 99-189, 99-181, 99-155 and 99-107, below], the effective date for changes made by Sec. 283(a) of P.L. 97-248 by substituting a period for "and before March 15, 1986", effective 3/14/86.

— P.L. 99-272, Sec. 13202(a), redesignated subsec. (e) as subsec. (f), and added new subsec. (e), effective for smokeless tobacco removed after 6/30/86. Sec. 13202(c)(2) of this Act provides:

"(2) Transitional rule.— Any person who—

"(A) on the date of the enactment on this Act, is engaged in business as a manufacturer of smokeless tobacco, and

"(B) before July 1, 1986, submits an application under subchapter B of chapter 52 of the Internal Revenue Code of 1954 to engage in such business,

may, notwithstanding such subchapter B, continue to engage in such business pending final action on such application. Pending such final action, all provisions of chapter 52 of such Code shall apply to such applicant in the same manner and to the same extent as if such applicant were a holder of a permit to manufacture smokeless tobacco under such chapter 52."

In 1985, P.L. 99-201, Sec. 1, amended Sec. 283(c) of P.L. 97-248, the effective date for changes made by Sec. 283(a) of P.L. 97-248, (as amended by Sec. 1 of P.L. 99-189, see below) by substituting "March 15, 1986" for "December 20, 1985", see below.

— P.L. 99-189, Sec. 1, amended Sec. 283(c) of P.L. 97-248, the effective date for changes made by Sec. 283(a) of P.L. 97-248, (as amended by Sec. 1 of P.L. 99-181, see below) by substituting "December 20, 1985" for "December 19, 1985", see below.

— P.L. 99-181, Sec. 1, amended Sec. 283(c) of P.L. 97-248, the effective date for changes made by Sec. 283(a) of P.L. 97-248, (as amended by Sec. 2 of P.L. 99-155, see below) by substituting "December 19, 1985" for "December 15, 1985", see below.

— P.L. 99-155, Sec. 2, amended Sec. 283(c) of P.L. 97-248, the effective date for changes made by Sec. 283(a) of P.L. 97-248, (as amended by Sec. 2 of P.L. 99-107, see below) by substituting "December 15, 1985" for "November 15, 1985", see below.

— P.L. 99-107, Sec. 2, amended Sec. 283(c) of P.L. 97-248, the effective date for changes made by Sec. 283(a) of P.L. 97-248, by substituting "November 15, 1985" for "October 1, 1985", see below.

In 1983, P.L. 97-448, Sec. 306(a)(14), substituted "February 17" for "January 18" in Sec. 283(b)(2)(B) of P.L. 97-248, reproduced below.

In 1982, P.L. 97-248, Sec. 283(a)(1), substituted "$8" for "$4" in para. (b)(1) . . . Sec. 283(a)(2), substituted "$16.80" for "$8.40" in para. (b)(2), effective for cigarettes removed after 12/31/82. (See P.L. 99-272 and for temporary extension dates see P.L. 99-201, 99-189, 99-181, 99-155 and 99-107, above). Sec. 283(b) of this Act provides:

"(b) Floor stocks.

"(1) Imposition of tax. On cigarettes manufactured in or imported into the United States which are removed before January 1, 1983, and held on such date for sale by any person, there shall be imposed the following taxes:

"(A) Small cigarettes. On cigarettes, weighing not more than 3 pounds per thousand, $4 per thousand;

"(B) Large cigarettes. On cigarettes, weighing more than 3 pounds per thousand, $8.40 per thousand; except that, if more than 6½ inches in length, they shall be taxable at the rate prescribed for cigarettes weighing not more than 3 pounds per thousand, counting each 2¾ inches, or fraction thereof, of the length of each as one cigarette.

"(2) Liability for tax and method of payment.

"(A) Liability for tax. A person holding cigarettes on January 1, 1983, to which any tax imposed by paragraph (1) applies shall be liable for such tax.

"(B) Method of payment. The tax imposed by paragraph

"(1) shall be treated as a tax imposed under section 5701 and shall be due and payable on February 17, 1983 in the same manner as the tax imposed under such section is payable with respect to cigarettes removed on January 1, 1983.

"(3) Cigarette. For purposes of this subsection, the term 'cigarette' shall have the meaning given to such term by subsection (b) of section 5702 of the Internal Revenue Code of 1954.

"(4) Exception for retailers. The taxes imposed by paragraph (1) shall not apply to cigarettes in retail stocks held on January 1, 1983, at the place where intended to be sold at retail."

In 1976, P.L. 94-455, Sec. 1905(a)(24), substituted "such articles, unless such import duties are imposed in lieu of internal revenue tax" for "such articles" in subsec. (e), effective 2/1/77.

— P.L. 94-455, Sec. 2128(a), amended so much of subsec. (a) as follows para. (a)(1), effective 2/1/77.

Prior to amendment, so much of subsec. (a) as follows para. (a)(1) read as follows:

"(2) Large cigars. On cigars, weighing more than 3 pounds per thousand;

"(A) If removed to retail at not more than 2½ cents each, $2.50 per thousand;

"(B) If removed to retail at more than 2½ cents each and not more than 4 cents each, $3 per thousand;

"(C) If removed to retail at more than 4 cents each and not more than 6 cents each, $4 per thousand;

"(D) If removed to retail at more than 6 cents each and not more than 8 cents each, $7 per thousand;

"(E) If removed to retail at more than 8 cents each and not more than 15 cents each, $10 per thousand;

"(F) If removed to retail at more than 15 cents each and not more than 20 cents each, $15 per thousand;

"(G) If removed to retail at more than 20 cents each, $20 per thousand.

In determining the retail price, for tax purposes, regard shall be had to the ordinary retail price of a single cigar in its principal market, exclusive of any State or local taxes imposed on cigars as a commodity. For purposes of the preceding sentence, the amount of State or local tax excluded from the retail price shall be the actual tax imposed; except that, if the combined taxes result in a numerical figure ending in a fraction of a cent, the amount so excluded shall be rounded to the next highest full cent unless such rounding would result in a tax lower than the tax which would be imposed in the absence of State or local tax. Cigars not exempt from tax under this chapter which are removed but not intended for sale shall be taxed at the same rate as similar cigars removed for sale."

In 1968, P.L. 90-240, Sec. 4(a), added the next to the last sentence of Code Sec. 5701(a), effective the removal of cigars on or after the first day of the first calendar quarter which begins more than 30 days after 1/2/68 [date of enactment of P.L. 90-240].

In 1965, P.L. 89-44, Sec. 502(a), deleted subsec. (a) and redesignated subsecs. (b), (c), (d), (e) and (f) as subsecs. (a), (b), (c), (d), and (e), effective 1/1/66. Prior to deletion, subsec. (a) read as follows:

"(a) Tobacco. On tobacco, manufactured in or imported into the United States, there shall be imposed a tax of 10 cents per pound."

— P.L. 89-44, Sec. 501(f), deleted from the end of para. (c)(1) "until July 1, 1965 and $3.50 per thousand on and after July 1, 1965", effective 7/1/65.

In 1964, P.L. 88-348, Sec. 2(a)(9), substituted "July 1, 1965" for "July 1, 1964" each place it appeared in para. (c)(1).

In 1963, P.L. 88-52, Sec. 3(a)(9), substituted "July 1, 1964" for "July 1, 1963" each place it appeared in para. (c)(1).

In 1962, P.L. 87-508, Sec. 3(a)(8), substituted "July 1, 1963" for "July 1, 1962" each place it appeared in para. (c)(1).

In 1961, P.L. 87-72, Sec. 3(a)(9), substituted "July 1, 1962" for "July 1, 1961" each place it appeared in para. (c)(1).

In 1960, P.L. 86-779, Sec. 1, substituted "imposed on cigars as a commodity" for "imposed on the retail sales of cigars" in subsec. (b), effective for cigars removed after 10/8/60.

—P.L. 86-564, Sec. 202(a)(9), substituted "July 1, 1961" for "July 1, 1960" each place it appeared in para. (c)(1).
In 1959, P.L. 86-75, Sec. 3(a)(7), substituted "July 1, 1960" for "July 1, 1959" each place it appeared in para. (c)(1).
In 1958, P.L. 85-859, Sec. 202, provided in subsec. (b) that in determining the retail price, for tax purposes, regard shall be had to the ordinary retail price of a single cigar in its principal market, exclusive of any State or local taxes imposed on the retail sale of cigars, and required cigars not exempt from tax under this chapter which are removed but not intended for sale to be taxed at the same rate as similar cigars removed for sale, effective 9/3/58.
—P.L. 85-859, Sec. 202, substituted "On each book or set of cigarette papers containing more than 25 papers, manufactured in or imported into the United States, there shall be imposed" for "On cigarette papers, manufactured in or imported into the United States, there shall be imposed, on each package, book, or set containing more than 25 papers" in subsec. (d), effective 9/3/58.
—P.L. 85-859, Sec. 202, substituted "imposed by this section on tobacco products and cigarette papers and tubes imported into the United States" for "imposed on articles by this section" in subsec. (f), effective 9/3/58.
—P.L. 85-475, Sec. 3(a)(7), substituted "July 1, 1959" for "July 1, 1958" each place it appeared in para. (c)(1).
In 1957, P.L. 85-12, Sec. 3(a)(7), substituted "July 1, 1958" for "April 1, 1957" each place it appeared in para. (c)(1).
In 1956, P.L. 458, Sec. 3, substituted "April 1, 1957" for "April 1, 1956" each place it appeared in para. (c)(1).
In 1955, P.L. 18, Sec. 3(a)(9), substituted "April 1, 1956" for "April 1, 1955" each place it appeared in para. (c)(1).

Sec. 5702. Definitions.

When used in this chapter—

(a) Cigar.

"Cigar" means any roll of tobacco wrapped in leaf tobacco or in any substance containing tobacco (other than any roll of tobacco which is a cigarette within the meaning of subsection (b)(2)).

(b) Cigarette.

"Cigarette" means—

(1) any roll of tobacco wrapped in paper or in any substance not containing tobacco, and

(2) any roll of tobacco wrapped in any substance containing tobacco which, because of its appearance, the type of tobacco used in the filler, or its packaging and labeling, is likely to be offered to, or purchased by, consumers as a cigarette described in paragraph (1).

(c) Tobacco products.

"Tobacco products" means cigars, cigarettes, smokeless tobacco, pipe tobacco, and roll-your-own tobacco.

(d) Manufacturer of tobacco products.

"Manufacturer of tobacco products" means any person who manufactures cigars, cigarettes, smokeless tobacco pipe tobacco, or roll-your-own tobacco except that such term shall not include—

(1) a person who produces cigars, cigarettes, smokeless tobacco, pipe tobacco, or roll-your-own tobacco solely for the person's own personal consumption or use, and

(2) a proprietor of a customs bonded manufacturing warehouse with respect to the operation of such warehouse.

(e) Cigarette paper.

"Cigarette paper" means paper, or any other material except tobacco, prepared for use as a cigarette wrapper.

(f) Cigarette tube.

"Cigarette tube" means cigarette paper made into a hollow cylinder for use in making cigarettes.

(g) Manufacturer of cigarette papers and tubes.

"Manufacturer of cigarette papers and tubes" means any person who manufactures cigarette paper, or makes up cigarette paper into tubes, except for his own personal use or consumption.

(h) Export warehouse.

"Export warehouse" means a bonded internal revenue warehouse for the storage of tobacco products or cigarette papers or tubes or any processed tobacco, upon which the internal revenue tax has not been paid, for subsequent shipment to a foreign country, Puerto Rico, the Virgin Islands, or a possession of the United States, or for consumption beyond the jurisdiction of the internal revenue laws of the United States.

(i) Export warehouse proprietor.

"Export warehouse proprietor" means any person who operates an export warehouse.

(j) Removal or remove.

"Removal" or "remove" means the removal of tobacco products or cigarette papers or tubes, or any processed tobacco, from the factory or from internal revenue bond under section 5704, as the Secretary shall by regulation prescribe, or release from customs custody, and shall also include the smuggling or other unlawful importation of such articles into the United States.

(k) Importer.

"Importer" means any person in the United States to whom nontaxpaid tobacco products or cigarette papers or tubes, or any processed tobacco, manufactured in a foreign country, Puerto Rico, the Virgin Islands, or a possession of the United States are shipped or consigned; any person who removes cigars or cigarettes for sale or consumption in the United States from a customs bonded manufacturing warehouse; and any person who smuggles or otherwise unlawfully brings tobacco products or cigarette papers or tubes into the United States.

(l) Determination of price on cigars.

In determining price for purposes of section 5701(a)(2)—

(1) there shall be included any charge incident to placing the article in condition ready for use,

(2) there shall be excluded—

(A) the amount of the tax imposed by this chapter or section 7652, and

(B) if stated as a separate charge, the amount of any retail sales tax imposed by any State or political subdivision thereof or the District of Columbia, whether the liability for such tax is imposed on the vendor or vendee, and

(3) rules similar to the rules of section 4216(b) shall apply.

(m) Definitions relating to smokeless tobacco.

(1) **Smokeless tobacco.** The term "smokeless tobacco" means any snuff or chewing tobacco.

(2) **Snuff.** The term "snuff" means any finely cut, ground, or powdered tobacco that is not intended to be smoked.

(3) **Chewing tobacco.** The term "chewing tobacco" means any leaf tobacco that is not intended to be smoked.

(n) Pipe tobacco.

The term "pipe tobacco" means any tobacco which, because of its appearance, type, packaging, or labeling, is suitable for use and likely to be offered to, or purchased by, consumers as tobacco to be smoked in a pipe.

(o) Roll-your-own tobacco.

The term "roll-your-own tobacco" means any tobacco which, because of its appearance, type, packaging, or labeling, is suitable for use and likely to be offered to, or purchased by, consumers as tobacco for making cigarettes or cigars, or for use as wrappers thereof.

(p) Manufacturer of processed tobacco.

(1) **In general.** The term "manufacturer of processed tobacco" means any person who processes any tobacco other than tobacco products.

(2) **Processed tobacco.** The processing of tobacco shall not include the farming or growing of tobacco or the handling of tobacco solely for sale, shipment, or delivery to a manufacturer of tobacco products or processed tobacco.

In 2009, P.L. 111-3, Sec. 702(a)(4), added subsec. (p)... Sec. 702(a)(5)(A), substituted "tobacco products or cigarette papers or tubes or any processed tobacco" for "tobacco products and cigarette papers and tubes" in subsec. (h)... Sec. 702(a)(5)(B), added ", or any processed tobacco," after "tobacco products or cigarette papers or tubes" in subsec. (j) and after "nontaxpaid tobacco products or cigarette papers or tubes" in subsec. (k), effective 4/1/2009.

—P.L. 111-3, Sec. 702(d)(1), added "or cigars, or for use as wrappers thereof" before the period at the end of subsec. (o), effective for articles removed (as defined in Code Sec. 5702(j)) after 3/31/2009.

In 2000, P.L. 106-554, Sec. 1(a)(7), [which enacted into law Sec. 315(a)(2)(A) of P.L. 106-554] amended subsec. (h)... Sec. 1(a)(7), [which enacted into law Sec. 315(a)(2)(B) of P.L. 106-554] deleted subsec. (f) and redesignated subsec. (g)–(p) [as amended by Sec. 315(a)(2)(A) of this Act, see above] as subsec. (f)–(o), effective 8/5/97.

Prior to deletion, subsec. (f) read as follows:

"(f) Cigarette papers. 'Cigarette papers' means taxable books or sets of cigarette papers."

Prior to amendment, subsec. (h) read as follows:

"(h) Manufacturer of cigarette papers and tubes. 'Manufacturer of cigarette papers and tubes' means any person who makes up cigarette paper into books or sets containing more than 25 papers each, or into tubes, except for his own personal use or consumption."

In 1997, P.L. 105-33, Sec. 9302(g)(2), added subsec. (p)... Sec. 9302(g)(3)(A), substituted "pipe tobacco, and roll-your-own tobacco" for "and pipe tobacco" in subsec. (c)... Sec. 9302(g)(3)(B)(i), substituted "pipe tobacco, or roll-your-own tobacco" for "or pipe tobacco" in subsec. (d)... Sec. 9302(g)(3)(B)(ii), amended para. (d)(1)... Sec. 9302(h)(4), added "under section 5704" after "internal revenue bond" in subsec. (k), effective for articles removed (as defined in Code Sec. 5702(k), as amended [see above]) after 12/31/99. Sec. 9302(i)(2) of this Act reads as follows:

"(2) Transitional rule. Any person who—

"(A) on the date of the enactment of this Act is engaged in business as a manufacturer of roll-your-own tobacco or as an importer of tobacco products or cigarette papers and tubes, and

"(B) before January 1, 2000, submits an application under subchapter B of chapter 52 of such Code to engage in such business,

may, notwithstanding such subchapter B, continue to engage in such business pending final action on such application. Pending such final action, all provisions of such chapter 52 shall apply to such applicant in the same manner and to the same extent as if such applicant were a holder of a permit under such chapter 52 to engage in such business."

Prior to amendment, para. (d)(1) read as follows:

"(1) a person who produces cigars, cigarettes, smokeless tobacco, or pipe tobacco solely for his own personal consumption or use; or"

In 1990, P.L. 101-508, Sec. 11202(g), amended subsec. (m), effective for articles removed after 12/31/90.

Prior to amendment, subsec. (m) read as follows:

"(m) Wholesale price.

"'Wholesale price' means the manufacturer's, or importer's, suggested delivered price at which the cigars are to be sold to retailers, inclusive of the tax imposed by this chapter or section 7652, but exclusive of any State or local taxes imposed on cigars as a commodity, and before any trade, cash, or other discounts, or any promotion, advertising, display, or similar allowances. Where the manufacturer's or importer's suggested delivered price to retailers is not adequately supported by bona fide arm's length sales, or where the manufacturer or importer has no suggested delivered price to retailers, the wholesale price shall be the price for which cigars of comparable retail price are sold to retailers in the ordinary course of trade as determined by the Secretary."

In 1988, P.L. 100-647, Sec. 5061(b), added subsec. (o)... Sec. 5061(c)(1), substituted "smokeless tobacco, and pipe tobacco" for "and smokeless tobacco" in subsec. (c)... Sec. 5061(c)(2), substituted "smokeless tobacco, or pipe tobacco" for "or smokeless tobacco" in subsec. (d), effective for pipe tobacco (within the meaning of '86 Code Sec. 5702(k)) after 12/31/88. Sec. 5061(d)(2) of this Act provides:

"(2) Transitional rule. Any person who—

"(A) on the date of the enactment of this Act, is engaged in business as a manufacturer of pipe tobacco, and

"(B) before January 1, 1989, submits an application under subchapter B of chapter 52 of the 1986 Code to engage in such business,

may, notwithstanding such subchapter B, continue to engage in such business pending final action on such application. Pending such final action, all provisions of chapter 52 of the 1986 Code shall apply to such applicant in the same manner and to the same extent as if such applicant were a holder of a permit to manufacture pipe tobacco under such chapter 52."

Sec. 5061(e) of P.L. 100-647, for special rules relating to Floor Stocks Tax, see Sec. 5061(e) of this Act, reproduced in the note following Code Sec. 5701.

In 1986, P.L. 99-272, Sec. 13202(b)(2), substituted ", cigarettes, and smokeless tobacco" for "and cigarettes" in subsec. (c)... Sec. 13202(b)(3), substituted "cigars, cigarettes, or smokeless tobacco" for "cigars or cigarettes" each place it appeared in subsec. (d)... Sec. 13202(b)(4), added subsec. (n), effective for smokeless tobacco removed after 6/30/86. Sec. 13302(c) of this Act provides:

"(2) Transitional rule.— Any person who—

"(A) on the date of the enactment of this Act, is engaged in business as a manufacturer of smokeless tobacco, and

"(B) before July 1, 1986, submits an application under subchapter B of chapter 52 of the Internal Revenue Code of 1954 to engage in such business,

may, notwithstanding such subchapter B, continue to engage in such business pending final action on such application. Pending such final action, all provisions of chapter 52 of such Code shall apply to such applicant in the same manner and to the same extent as if such applicant were a holder of a permit to manufacture smokeless tobacco under such chapter 52."

In 1976, P.L. 94-455, Sec. 1906(b)(13)(A), substituted "Secretary" for "Secretary or his delegate" in subsec. (k),... Sec. 2128(b), added subsec. (m), effective 2/1/77.

In 1965, P.L. 89-44, Sec. 502(b)(3)(A), deleted subsecs. (a), (l) and (m), and redesignated subsecs. (b), (c), (d), (e), (f), (g), (h), (i), (j), (k), (n) and (o) as subsecs. (a), (b), (c), (d), (e), (f), (g), (h), (i), (j), (k), and (l) respectively... Sec. 502(b)(3)(B), substituted "cigars and" for "manufactured tobacco, cigars, and" in subsec. (c) (as redesignated, see above)... Sec. 502(b)(3)(C), amended subsec. (d) (as redesignated, see above), effective on and after 1/1/66.

Prior to deletion, subsec. (a) read as follows:

"(a) Manufactured tobacco—

"'Manufactured tobacco' means tobacco (other than cigars and cigarettes) prepared, processed, manipulated, or packaged, for removal, or merely removed, for consumption by smoking or for use in the mouth or nose, and any tobacco (other than cigars and cigarettes), not exempt from tax under this chapter, sold or delivered to any person contrary to this chapter or regulations prescribed thereunder."

Prior to deletion, subsecs. (l) and (m) read as follows:

"(l) Tobacco materials.

" 'Tobacco materials' means tobacco other than manufactured tobacco, cigars, and cigarettes.

"(m) Dealer in tobacco materials.

" 'Dealer in tobacco materials' means any person who receives and handles tobacco materials for sale, shipment, or delivery to another dealer in such materials, to a manufacturer of tobacco products, or to a foreign country. Puerto Rico, the Virgin Islands, or a possession of the United States, or who receives tobacco materials, other than stems and waste, for use by him in the production of fertilizer, insecticide, or nicotine. The term 'dealer in tobacco materials' shall not include

"(1) an operator of a warehouse who stores tobacco materials solely for a qualified dealer in tobacco materials, for a qualified manufacturer of tobacco products, for a farmer or grower of tobacco, or for a bona fide association of farmers or growers of tobacco; or

"(2) a farmer or grower of tobacco with respect to the sale of leaf tobacco of his own growth or raising, or a bona fide association of farmers or growers of tobacco with respect to sales of leaf tobacco grown by farmer or grower members, if the tobacco so sold is in the condition as cured on the farm: Provided, That such association maintains records of all leaf tobacco acquired or received and sold or otherwise disposed of by the association, in such manner as the Secretary or his delegate shall by regulation prescribe; or

"(3) a person who buys leaf tobacco on the floor of an auction warehouse, or who buys leaf tobacco from a farmer or grower, and places the tobacco on the floor of such a warehouse, or who purchases and sells warehouse receipts without taking physical possession of the tobacco covered thereby; or

"(4) a qualified manufacturer of tobacco products with respect to tobacco materials received by him under his bond as such a manufacturer."

Prior to amendment, subsec. (d) (as redesignated, see above) read as follows:

"(d) Manufacturer of tobacco products—

"'Manufacturer of tobacco products' means any person who manufactures cigars or cigarettes, or who prepares, processes, manipulates, or packages, for removal, or merely removes, tobacco (other than cigars and cigarettes) for consumption by smoking or for use in the mouth or nose, or who sells or delivers any tobacco (other than cigars and cigarettes) contrary to this chapter or regulations prescribed thereunder. The term 'manufacturer of tobacco products' shall not include—

"(1) a person who in any manner prepares tobacco, or produces cigars or cigarettes, solely for his own personal consumption or use; or

"(2) a proprietor of a customs bonded manufacturing warehouse with respect to the operation of such warehouse; or

"(3) a farmer or grower of tobacco with respect to the sale of leaf tobacco of his own growth or raising, if it is in the condition as cured on the farm; or

"(4) a bona fide association of farmers or growers of tobacco with respect to sales of leaf tobacco grown by farmer or grower members, if the tobacco so sold is in the condition as cured on the farm, and if the association maintains records of all leaf tobacco, acquired or received and sold or otherwise disposed of, in such manner as the Secretary or his delegate shall by regulations prescribe."

—P.L. 89-44, Sec. 808(a), amended subsecs. (a) and (b) [as redesignated by Sec. 502(b)(3)(A) of this Act, see above], effective 7/1/65.

Prior to amendment, subsecs. (a) and (b) (as redesignated, see above) read as follows:

"(a) Cigar

" 'Cigar' means any roll of tobacco wrapped in tobacco.

"(b) Cigarette— 'Cigarette' means any roll of tobacco, wrapped in paper or any substance other than tobacco."

In 1958, P.L. 85-859, Sec. 202(a), amended Code Sec. 5702, effective 9/3/58.

Prior to amendment, Code Sec. 5702 read as follows:

"SEC. 5702. DEFINITIONS.

"(a) Manufactured tobacco.

"'Manufactured tobacco' means all tobacco, other than cigars and cigarettes, prepared, processed, manipulated, or packaged for consumption by smoking or for use in the mouth or nose. Any other tobacco not exempt from tax under this chapter, which is sold or delivered to any person contrary to this chapter and regulations prescribed thereunder, shall be regarded as manufactured tobacco.

"(b) Manufacturer of tobacco.—

"'Manufacturer of tobacco' means any person who manufactures tobacco by any method of preparing, processing, or manipulating, except for his own personal consumption or use; or who packages any tobacco for consumption by smoking or for use in the mouth or nose; or who sells or delivers any tobacco, not exempt from tax under this chapter, to any person, contrary to the provisions of this chapter and regulations prescribed thereunder. The term 'manufacturer of tobacco' shall not include—

"(1) a farmer or grower of tobacco who sells leaf tobacco of his own growth or raising, or a bona fide association of farmers or growers of tobacco which sells only leaf tobacco grown by farmer or grower members, if the tobacco so sold is in the condition as cured on the farm; or

"(2) a dealer in tobacco materials who handles tobacco solely for sale, shipment, or delivery, in bulk, to another dealer in such materials or to a manufacturer of tobacco products, or to a foreign country, Puerto Rico, the Virgin Islands, or a possession of the United States.

"(c) Cigar.

"'Cigar' means any roll of tobacco wrapped in tobacco.

"(d) Cigarette.

"'Cigarette' means any roll of tobacco, wrapped in paper or any substance other than tobacco.

"(e) Manufacturer of cigars and cigarettes.

"'Manufacturer of cigars and cigarettes' means every person who produces cigars or cigarettes, except for his own personal consumption.

"(f) Tobacco products

"'Tobacco products' means manufactured tobacco, cigars, and cigarettes.

"(g) Cigarette paper.

"'Cigarette paper' means paper, or any other material except tobacco, prepared for use as a cigarette wrapper.

"(h) Cigarette tube.

"'Cigarette tube' means cigarette paper made into a hollow cylinder for use in making cigarettes.

"(i) Manufacturer of cigarette papers and tubes.

"'Manufacturer of cigarette papers and tubes' means any person who makes up cigarette paper into packages, books, sets, or tubes, except for his own personal use or consumption.

"(j) Articles.

"'Articles' means manufactured tobacco, cigars, cigarettes, and cigarette papers and tubes.

"(k) Tobacco materials.

"'Tobacco materials' means tobacco in process, leaf tobacco, and tobacco scraps, cuttings, clippings, siftings, dust, stems, and waste.

"(l) Dealer in tobacco materials.

"'Dealer in tobacco materials' means any person who handles tobacco materials for sale, shipment, or delivery solely to another dealer in such materials, to a manufacturer of tobacco products, or to a foreign country, Puerto Rico, the Virgin Islands, or a possession of the United States, but shall not include—

"(1) an operator of a warehouse who stores tobacco materials solely for a dealer in tobacco materials, for a manufacturer of tobacco products, for a farmer or grower of tobacco, or for a bona fide association of farmers or growers of tobacco; or

"(2) a farmer or grower of tobacco who sells leaf tobacco of his own growth or raising, or a bona fide association of farmers or growers of tobacco which sells only leaf tobacco grown by a farmer or grower members, if the tobacco so sold is in the condition as cured on the farm.

"(m) Removal or remove.

"'Removal' or 'remove' means removal of articles from the factory or from internal revenue bond, as the Secretary or his delegate shall, by regulation, prescribe, or from customs custody, and shall also include the smuggling or other unlawful importation of articles into the United States.

"(n) Importer.

"'Importer' means any person in the United States to whom nontaxpaid articles manufactured in a foreign country, Puerto Rico, the Virgin Islands, or a possession of the United States are shipped or consigned, and any person who smuggles or otherwise unlawfully brings such nontaxpaid articles into the United States."

Sec. 5703. Liability for tax and method of payment.

(a) Liability for tax.

(1) Original liability. The manufacturer or importer of tobacco products and cigarette papers and tubes shall be liable for the taxes imposed thereon by section 5701.

(2) Transfer of liability. When tobacco products and cigarette papers and tubes are transferred, without payment of tax, pursuant to section 5704, the liability or tax shall be transferred in accordance with the provisions of this paragraph. When tobacco products and cigarette papers and tubes are transferred between the bonded premises of manufacturers and export warehouse proprietors, the transferee shall become liable for the tax upon receipt by him of such articles, and the transferor shall thereupon be relieved of his liability for such tax. When tobacco products and cigarette papers and tubes are released in bond from customs custody for transfer to the bonded premises of a manufacturer of tobacco products or cigarette papers and tubes, the transferee shall become liable for the tax on such articles upon release from customs custody, and the importer shall thereupon be relieved of his liability for such tax. All provisions of this chapter applicable to tobacco products and cigarette papers and tubes in bond shall be applicable to such articles returned to bond upon withdrawal from the market or returned to bond after previous removal for a tax-exempt purpose.

(b) Method of payment of tax.

(1) In general. The taxes imposed by section 5701 shall be determined at the time of removal of the tobacco products and cigarette papers and tubes. Such taxes shall be paid on the basis of return. The Secretary shall, by regulations, prescribe the period or the event for which such return shall be made and the information to be furnished on such return. Any postponement under this subsection of the payment of taxes determined at the time of removal shall be conditioned upon the filing of such additional bonds, and upon compliance with such requirements, as the Secretary may prescribe for the protection of the revenue. The Secretary may, by regulations, require payment of tax on the basis of a return prior to removal of the tobacco products and cigarette papers and tubes where a person defaults in the postponed payment of tax on the basis of a return under this subsection or regulations prescribed thereunder. All administrative and penalty provisions of this title, insofar as applicable, shall apply to any tax imposed by section 5701.

(2) Time for payment of taxes.

(A) In general. Except as otherwise provided in this paragraph, in the case of taxes on tobacco products and cigarette papers and tubes removed during any semimonthly period under bond for deferred payment of tax, the last day for payment of such taxes shall be the 14th day after the last day of such semimonthly period.

(B) Imported articles. In the case of tobacco products and cigarette papers and tubes which are imported into the United States—

(i) In general. The last day for payment of tax shall be the 14th day after the last day of the semimonthly period during which the article is entered into the customs territory of the United States.

(ii) Special rule for entry for warehousing. Except as provided in clause (iv), in the case of an entry for warehousing, the last day for payment of tax shall not be later than the 14th day after the last day of the semimonthly period during which the article is removed from the 1st such warehouse.

(iii) Foreign trade zones. Except as provided in clause (iv) and in regulations prescribed by the Secretary, articles brought into a foreign trade zone shall, notwithstanding any other provision of law, be treated for purposes of this subsection as if such zone were a single customs warehouse.

(iv) Exception for articles destined for export. Clauses (ii) and (iii) shall not apply to any article which is shown to the satisfaction of the Secretary to be destined for export.

(C) Tobacco products and cigarette papers and tubes brought into the United States from Puerto Rico. In the case of tobacco products and cigarette papers and tubes which are brought into the United States from Puerto Rico, the last day for payment of tax shall be the 14th day after the last day of the semimonthly period during which the article is brought into the United States.

(D) Special rule for tax due in September.
(i) In general. Notwithstanding the preceding provisions of this paragraph, the taxes on tobacco products and cigarette papers and tubes for the period beginning on September 16 and ending on September 26 shall be paid not later than September 29.
(ii) Safe harbor. The requirement of clause (i) shall be treated as met if the amount paid not later than September 29 is not less than $^{11}/_{15}$ of the taxes on tobacco products and cigarette papers and tubes for the period beginning on September 1 and ending on September 15.
(iii) Taxpayers not required to use electronic funds transfer. In the case of payments not required to be made by electronic funds transfer, clauses (i) and (ii) shall be applied by substituting "September 25" for "September 26", "September 28" for "September 29", and "$^{2}/_{3}$" for "$^{11}/_{15}$".
(E) Special rule where due date falls on Saturday, Sunday, or holiday. Notwithstanding section 7503, if, but for this subparagraph, the due date under this paragraph would fall on a Saturday, Sunday, or a legal holiday (as defined in section 7503), such due date shall be the immediately preceding day which is not a Saturday, Sunday, or such a holiday (or the immediately following day where the due date described in subparagraph (D) falls on a Sunday).
(F) Special rule for unlawfully manufactured tobacco products. In the case of any tobacco products, cigarette paper, or cigarette tubes manufactured in the United States at any place other than the premises of a manufacturer of tobacco products, cigarette paper, or cigarette tubes that has filed the bond and obtained the permit required under this chapter, tax shall be due and payable immediately upon manufacture.

(3) Payment by electronic fund transfer. Any person who in any 12-month period, ending December 31, was liable for a gross amount equal to or exceeding $5,000,000 in taxes imposed on tobacco products and cigarette papers and tubes by section 5701 (or 7652) shall pay such taxes during the succeeding calendar year by electronic fund transfer (as defined in section 5061(e)(2)) to a Federal Reserve Bank. Rules similar to the rules of section 5061(e)(3) shall apply to the $5,000,000 amount specified in the preceding sentence.

(c) Use of government depositaries.
The Secretary may authorize Federal Reserve banks, and incorporated banks or trust companies which are depositaries or financial agents of the United States, to receive any tax imposed by this chapter, in such manner, at such times, and under such conditions as he may prescribe; and he shall prescribe the manner, time, and condition under which the receipt of such tax by such banks and trust companies is to be treated as payment for tax purposes.

(d) Assessment.
Whenever any tax required to be paid by this chapter is not paid in full at the time required for such payment, it shall be the duty of the Secretary, subject to the limitations prescribed in section 6501, on proof satisfactory to him, to determine the amount of tax which has been omitted to be paid, and to make an assessment therefor against the person liable for the tax. The tax so assessed shall be in addition to the penalties imposed by law for failure to pay such tax when required. Except in cases where delay may jeopardize collection of the tax, or where the amount is nominal or the result of an evident mathematical error, no such assessment shall be made until and after the person liable for the tax has been afforded reasonable notice and opportunity to show cause, in writing, against such assessment.

In **2009**, P.L. 111-3, Sec. 702(e)(1), added subpara. (b)(2)(F), effective 2/4/2009.
In **1994**, P.L. 103-465, Sec. 712(c)(1), redesignated subpara. (b)(2)(D) as subpara. (b)(2)(E), and added new subpara. (b)(2)(D) ... Sec. 712(c)(2)(A), added "(or the immediately following day where the due date described in subparagraph (D) falls on a Sunday)" before the period at the end of subpara. (b)(2)(E) [as redesignated by Sec. 712(c)(1) of this Act, see above] ... Sec. 712(c)(2)(B), substituted "due date" for "14th day" in the heading of subpara. (b)(2)(E) [as redesignated by Sec. 712(c)(1) of this Act, see above], effective 1/1/95.
In **1988**, P.L. 100-647, Sec. 2003(b)(1)(C), and (D), substituted "the 14th day after the last day of the semimonthly period during which" for "the 14th day after the date on which" in clauses (b)(2)(B)(i) and (ii) and subpara. (b)(2)(C), effective for removals during semimonthly periods end. on or after 12/31/86, except as provided in Sec. 8011(c)(2)-(4) of P.L. 99-509, reproduced below.
In **1986**, P.L. 99-514, Sec. 1801(c)(2), added the sentence at the end of para. (b)(3), effective for taxes required to be paid on or after 9/30/84.
—P.L. 99-509, Sec. 8011(a)(1), amended para. (b)(2), effective for removals during semimonthly periods end. on or after 12/31/86. Secs. 8011(c)(2)-(4) of this Act provide:
"(2) Imported articles, etc. Subparagraphs (B) and (C) of section 5703(b)(2) of the Internal Revenue Code of 1954 (as added by this section), paragraphs (2) and (3) of section 5061(d) of such Code (as amended by this section), and the amendments made by subsections (a)(2) and (b)(2) shall apply to articles imported, entered for warehousing, or brought into the United States or a foreign trade zone after December 15, 1986.
"(3) Special rule for distilled spirits and tobacco for semimonthly period ending December 15, 1986. With respect to remittances of—
"(A) taxes imposed on distilled spirits by section 5001 or 7652 of such Code, and
"(B) taxes imposed on tobacco products and cigarette papers and tubes by section 5701 or 7652 of such Code,
for the semimonthly period ending December 15, 1986, the last day for payment of such remittances shall be January 14, 1987.
"(4) Treatment of smokeless tobacco in inventory on June 30, 1986. The tax imposed by section 5701(e) of the Internal Revenue Code of 1954 shall not apply to any smokeless tobacco which—
"(A) on June 30, 1986, was in the inventory of the manufacturer or importer, and
"(B) on such date was in a form ready for sale."
Prior to amendment, para. (b)(2) read as follows:
"(2) Time for making of return and payment of taxes. In the case of tobacco products and cigarette papers and tubes removed after December 31, 1982, under bond for deferred payment of tax, the last day for filing a return and paying any tax due for each return period shall be the last day of the first succeeding return period plus 10 days."
In **1984**, P.L. 98-369, Sec. 27(c)(2), added para. (b)(3), effective for taxes required to be paid on or after 9/30/84.
In **1983**, P.L. 97-448, Sec. 308(a), amended subsec. (b), effective for tobacco products and cigarette papers and tubes removed after 12/31/82.
Prior to amendment, subsec. (b) read as follows:
"(b) Method of payment of tax.
"The taxes imposed by section 5701 shall be determined at the time of removal of the tobacco products and cigarette papers and tubes. Such taxes shall be paid on the basis of a return. The Secretary shall, by regulations, prescribe the period or event for which such return shall be made, the information to be furnished on such return, the time for making such return, and the time for payment of such taxes. Any postponement under this subsection of the payment of taxes determined at the time of removal shall be conditional upon the filing of such additional bonds, and upon compliance with such requirements, as the Secretary may, by regulations, prescribe for the protection of the revenue. The Secretary may, by regulations, require payment of tax on the basis of a return prior to removal of the tobacco products and cigarette papers and tubes where a person defaults in the postponed payment of tax on the basis of a return under this subsection or regulations prescribed thereunder. All administrative and penal provisions of this title, insofar as applicable, shall apply to any tax imposed by section 5701."
In **1976**, P.L. 94-455, Sec. 1905(a)(25)(A), added the last sentence in para. (a)(2) ... Sec. 1905(a)(25)(B), deleted ", except that the taxes shall continue to be paid by stamp until the Secretary or his delegate provides, by regulations, for the payment of the taxes on the basis of a return" in the second sentence of subsec. (b) ... Sec. 1905(a)(25)(C), deleted subsec. (c) and redesignated subsecs. (d) and (e) as (c) and (d), effective 2/1/77.
Prior to deletion, subsec. (c) read as follows:
"(c) Stamps to evidence the tax.
"If the Secretary or his delegate shall be regulation provide for the payment of tax by return and require the use of stamps to evidence the tax imposed by this chapter or to indicate compliance therewith, the Secretary or his delegate shall cause to be prepared suitable stamps to be issued to manufacturers and importers of tobacco products, to be used and accounted for, in accordance with such regulations as the Secretary or his delegate shall prescribe."
—P.L. 94-455, Sec. 1906(b)(13)(A), substituted "Secretary" for "Secretary or his delegate" each place it appeared in Code Sec. 5703, effective 2/1/77.
In **1958**, P.L. 85-859, Sec. 202, amended Code Sec. 5703 as part of the amendments to Chapter 52, by designating part of first sentence of subsec. (a) as para. (a)(1) thereof and redesignated the remainder of subsec. (a) as (b), added para.

(a)(2), substituted in redesignated subsec. (b) "tobacco products and cigarette papers and tubes" for "articles", and added provisions relating to postponements, and to payment of the tax on the basis of a return prior to removal of the tobacco products and cigarette papers and tubes where a person defaults in the postponed payment of the tax, redesignated former subsecs. (b) as (c) and substituted "If the Secretary or his delegate shall by regulation provide for the payment of tax by return and require the use of" for "If the Secretary or his delegate shall, by regulation, require the use", and "tobacco products" for "articles", redesignated former subsec. (c) as subsec. (b) and former subsec. (d) as subsec. (e), permitted in redesignated subsec. (e) assessments in cases where delay may jeopardize collection of the tax, or where the amount is nominal or the result of an evident mathematical error, effective 9/3/58.

Sec. 5704. Exemption from tax.

(a) Tobacco products furnished for employee use or experimental purposes.

Tobacco products may be furnished by a manufacturer of such products, without payment of tax, for use or consumption by employees or for experimental purposes, in such quantities, and in such manner as the Secretary shall by regulation prescribe.

(b) Tobacco products and cigarette papers and tubes transferred or removed in bond from domestic factories and export warehouses.

A manufacturer or export warehouse proprietor may transfer tobacco products and cigarette papers and tubes, without payment of tax, to the bonded premises of another manufacturer or export warehouse proprietor, or remove such articles, without payment of tax, for shipment to a foreign country, Puerto Rico, the Virgin Islands, or a possession of the United States, or for consumption beyond the jurisdiction of the internal revenue laws of the United States; and manufacturers may similarly remove such articles for use of the United States; in accordance with such regulations and under such bonds as the Secretary shall prescribe. Tobacco products and cigarette papers and tubes may not be transferred or removed under this subsection unless such products or papers and tubes bear such marks, labels, or notices as the Secretary shall by regulations prescribe.

(c) Tobacco products and cigarette papers and tubes released in bond from customs custody.

Tobacco products and cigarette papers and tubes, imported or brought into the United States, may be released from customs custody, without payment of tax, for delivery to the proprietor of an export warehouse, or to a manufacturer of tobacco products or cigarette papers and tubes if such articles are not put up in packages, in accordance with such regulations and under such bond as the Secretary shall prescribe.

(d) Tobacco products and cigarette papers and tubes exported and returned.

Tobacco products and cigarette papers and tubes classifiable under item 804.00 of title I of the Tariff Act of 1930 (relating to duty on certain articles previously exported and returned) may be released from customs custody, without payment of that part of the duty attributable to the internal revenue tax for delivery to the original manufacturer of such tobacco products or cigarette papers and tubes or to the proprietor of an export warehouse authorized by such manufacturer to receive such articles, in accordance with such regulations and under such bond as the Secretary shall prescribe. Upon such release such products, papers, and tubes shall be subject to this chapter as if they had not been exported or otherwise removed from internal-revenue bond.

In **2000**, P.L. 106-476, Sec. 4002(b)(1), substituted "the original manufacturer of such" for "a manufacturer of" in subsec. (d) . . . Sec. 4002(b)(2), added "authorized by such manufacturer to receive such articles" after "proprietor of an export warehouse" in subsec. (d), effective 90 days following 11/9/2000.

—P.L. 106-476, Sec. 4002(e), of this Act, reads as follows:

"(e) Study. The Secretary of the Treasury shall report to Congress on the impact of requiring export warehouses to be authorized by the original manufacturer to receive relanded export-labeled cigarettes."

In **1997**, P.L. 105-33, Sec. 9302(h)(1)(A), added a sentence at the end of subsec. (b), effective for articles removed (as defined in Code Sec. 5702(k), as amended [see above]) after 12/31/99. Sec. 9302(i)(2) of this Act provides:

"(2) Transitional rule. Any person who—

"(A) on the date of the enactment of this Act is engaged in business as a manufacturer of roll-your-own tobacco or as an importer of tobacco products or cigarette papers and tubes, and

"(B) before January 1, 2000, submits an application under subchapter B of chapter 52 of such Code to engage in such business, may, notwithstanding such subchapter B, continue to engage in such business pending final action on such application. Pending such final action, all provisions of such chapter 52 shall apply to such applicant in the same manner and to the same extent as if such applicant were a holder of a permit under such chapter 52 to engage in such business."

In **1989**, P.L. 101-239, Sec. 7508(a), added "or to a manufacturer of tobacco products or cigarette papers and tubes if such articles are not put up in packages," after "export warehouse," in subsec. (c), effective for articles imported or brought to the United States after the 12/19/89.

In **1986**, P.L. 99-509, Sec. 8011(a)(2), deleted "to a manufacturer of tobacco products or cigarette papers and tubes or" after "for delivery", in subsec. (c), effective for removals during semimonthly periods end. or on after 12/31/86. Sec. 8011(c)(2) of this Act provides:

"(2) Imported articles, etc. Subparagraphs (B) and (C) of section 5703(b)(2) of the Internal Revenue Code of 1954 (as added by this section), paragraphs (2) and (3) of section 5061(d) of such Code (as amended by this section), and the amendments made by subsections (a)(2) and (b)(2) [Sec. 8011] shall apply to articles imported, entered for warehousing, or brought into the United States or a foreign trade zone after December 15, 1986."

In **1976**, P.L. 94-455, Sec. 1905(a)(26), added "or to the proprietor of an export warehouse" after "to a manufacturer of tobacco products or cigarette papers and tubes" in subsecs. (c) and (d) . . . Sec. 1906(b)(13)(A), substituted "Secretary" for "Secretary or his delegate" each place it appeared in Code Sec. 5704, effective 2/1/77.

In **1965**, P.L. 89-44, Sec. 502, deleted subsec. (c), redesignated subsecs. (d) and (e) as subsecs. (c) and (d) and amended redesignated subsec. (c), effective 1/1/66. Prior to amendment, subsec. (c) and (d) read as follows:

"(c) Tobacco materials shipped or delivered in bond.

"A dealer in tobacco materials or a manufacturer of tobacco products may ship or deliver tobacco materials, without payment of tax, to another such dealer or manufacturer, or to a foreign country, Puerto Rico, the Virgin Islands, or a possession of the United States; or, in the case of tobacco stems and waste only, to any person for use by him as fertilizer or insecticide or in the production of fertilizer, insecticide, or nicotine; in accordance with such regulations and under such bonds as the Secretary or his delegate shall prescribe.

"(d) Tobacco products, cigarette papers and tubes, and tobacco materials released in bond from customs custody.

"Tobacco products, cigarette papers and tubes, tobacco materials, imported or brought into the United States, may be released from customs custody, without payment of tax, for delivery to a manufacturer of tobacco products or cigarette papers and tubes and such tobacco materials may be similarly released for delivery to a dealer in tobacco materials, in accordance with such regulations and under such bond as the Secretary or his delegate shall prescribe."

In **1964**, P.L. 88-342, Sec. 1(b), added subsec. (e), effective for articles entered, or withdrawn from warehouse, for consumption after 6/30/64.

In **1958**, P.L. 85-859, Sec. 202, included in subsec. (b) transfers by export warehouse proprietors, and substituted "tobacco products and cigarette papers and tubes" for "articles", preceding "without payment of tax", authorized in subsec. (c) shipments without payment of tax of tobacco stems and waste only, to any person for use by him as fertilizer or insecticide or in the production of fertilizer, insecticide, or nicotine, substituted in subsec. (d) "tobacco products, cigarette papers and tubes" for "articles" wherever appearing, and eliminated provisions which related to delivery to bonded premises of manufacturers and dealers, effective 9/3/58.

Sec. 5705. Credit, refund, or allowance of tax.

(a) Credit or refund.

Credit or refund of any tax imposed by this chapter or section 7652 shall be allowed or made (without interest) to the manufacturer, importer, or export warehouse proprietor, on proof satisfactory to the Secretary that the claimant manufacturer, importer, or export warehouse proprietor has paid the tax on tobacco products and cigarette papers and tubes withdrawn by him from the market; or on such articles lost (otherwise than by theft) or destroyed, by fire, casualty, or act of God, while in the possession or ownership of the claimant.

(b) Allowance.

If the tax has not yet been paid on tobacco products and cigarette papers and tubes proved to have been withdrawn from the market or lost or destroyed as aforesaid, relief from the tax on such articles may be extended upon the filing of a claim for allowance therefor in accordance with such regulations as the Secretary shall prescribe.

(c) Limitation.

Any claim for credit refund of tax under this section shall be filed within 6 months after the date of the withdrawal from the market, loss, or destruction of the articles to which the claim relates, and shall be in such form and contain such information as the Secretary shall by regulations prescribe.

In **1976**, P.L. 94-455, Sec. 1906(b)(13)(A), substituted "Secretary" for "Secretary or his delegate" each place it appeared in Code Sec. 5705, effective 2/1/77.

In **1965**, P.L. 89-44, Sec. 808, added to section catchline and to subsec. (a) references to "credit" and "section 7652", and added to subsec. (c) reference to "credit", effective 10/1/65.

In **1958**, P.L. 85-859, Sec. 202, authorized in subsec. (a) refunds to export warehouse proprietors, provided for refunds to be made without interest, and eliminated provisions which authorized refunds where the tax has been paid in error, permitted in subsec. (b) relief where a tax has not yet been paid on tobacco products and cigarette papers and tubes proved to have been withdrawn from the market, substituted in subsec. (c) "under this section shall be filed within 6 months after the date of the withdrawal from the market, loss, or destruction of the articles to which the claim relates" for "imposed by this chapter shall be filed within 3 years of the date of payment of tax", effective 9/3/58.

Sec. 5706. Drawback of tax.

There shall be an allowance of drawback of tax paid on tobacco products and cigarette papers and tubes, when shipped from the United States, in accordance with such regulations and upon the filing of such bond as the Secretary shall prescribe.

In **1976**, P.L. 94-455, Sec. 1906(b)(13)(A), substituted "Secretary" for "Secretary or his delegate" in Code Sec. 5706, effective 2/1/77.

In **1958**, P.L. 85-859, Sec. 202, substituted "tobacco products and cigarette papers and tubes" for "articles", effective 9/3/58.

Sec. 5707. Repealed.

In **1965**, P.L. 89-44, Sec. 501, repealed Code Sec. 5707, effective 7/1/65.
Prior to repeal, Code Sec. 5707 read as follows:
"Sec. 5707. FLOOR STOCKS REFUND ON CIGARETTES.
"(a) In general.

"With respect to cigarettes, weighing not more than 3 pounds per thousand, upon which the tax imposed by subsection (c)(1) of section 5701 has been paid and which, on July 1, 1965, are held by any person and intended for sale, or are in transit from foreign countries or insular possessions of the United States to any person in the United States for sale, there shall be credited or refunded to such person (without interest), subject to such regulations as shall be prescribed by the Secretary or his delegate, an amount equal to the difference between the tax paid on such cigarettes and the tax made applicable to such articles on July 1, 1965, if claim for such credit or refund is filed with the Secretary or his delegate before October 1, 1965.

"(b) Limitations on eligibility for credit or refund.

"No person shall be entitled to credit or refund under subsection (a) unless such person, for such period or periods both before and after July 1, 1965, (but not extending beyond 1 year thereafter), as the Secretary or his delegate shall by regulation prescribe, makes and keeps, and files with the Secretary or his delegate, such records of inventories, sales, and purchases as may be prescribed in such regulations.

"(c) Penalty and administrative procedures.

"All provisions of law, including penalties, applicable in respect of internal revenue taxes on cigarettes shall, insofar as applicable and not inconsistent with this section, be applicable in respect of the credits and refunds provided for in this section to the same extent as if such credits or refunds constituted credits or refunds of such taxes."

In **1964**, P.L. 88-348, Sec. 2(b)(1)(B), substituted in subsecs. (a) and (b) "1965" for "1964" in two instances, and "October 1, 1965" for "October 1, 1964".

In **1963**, P.L. 88-52, Sec. 3(b)(1)(B), substituted in subsecs. (a) and (b), "1964" for "1963".

In **1962**, P.L. 87-508, Sec. 3(b)(2), substituted in subsecs. (a) and (b), "1963" for "1962".

In **1961**, P.L. 87-72, Sec. 3(b)(2), substituted in subsecs. (a) and (b), "1962" for "1961".

In **1960**, P.L. 86-564, Sec. 202(b)(2), substituted in subsecs. (a) and (b), "1961" for "1960".

In **1959**, P.L. 86-75, Sec. 3(b)(2), substituted in subsecs. (a) and (b), "1960" for "1959".

In **1958**, P.L. 85-475, Sec. 3(b)(3), substituted in subsecs. (a) and (b), "1959" for "1958", and substituted in subsec. (b) "shall be prescribed" for "may be prescribed".

In **1957**, P.L. 85-12, Sec. 3(b)(3), substituted in subsec. (a) "July 1, 1958" for "April 1, 1957" in two places, and "October 1, 1958" for "July 1, 1957", and substituted in subsec. (b) "July 1, 1958" for "April 1, 1957".

In **1956**, P.L. 458, Sec. 3(b)(3), substituted in subsecs. (a) and (b), "1957" for "1956".

In **1955**, P.L. 18, Sec. 3(b)(3), substituted in subsecs. (a) and (b), "1956" for "1955".

Sec. 5708. Losses caused by disaster.
(a) Authorization.

Where the President has determined under the Robert T. Stafford Disaster Relief and Emergency Assistance Act, that a "major disaster" as defined in such Act has occurred in any part of the United States, the Secretary shall pay (without interest) an amount equal to the amount of the internal revenue taxes paid or determined and customs duties paid on tobacco products and cigarette papers and tubes removed, which were lost, rendered unmarketable, or condemned by a duly authorized official by reason of such disaster occurring in such part of the United States on and after the effective date of this section, if such tobacco products or cigarette papers or tubes were held and intended for sale at the time of such disaster. The payments authorized by this section shall be made to the person holding such tobacco products or cigarette papers or tubes for sale at the time of such disaster.

(b) Claims.

No claim shall be allowed under this section unless—

(1) filed within 6 months after the date on which the President makes the determination that the disaster referred to in subsection (a) has occurred; and

(2) the claimant furnishes proof to the satisfaction of the Secretary that—

(A) he was not indemnified by any valid claim of insurance or otherwise in respect of the tax, or tax and duty, on the tobacco products or cigarette papers or tubes covered by the claim, and

(B) he is entitled to payment under this section.

Claims under this section shall be filed under such regulations as the Secretary shall prescribe.

(c) Destruction of tobacco products or cigarette papers or tubes.

Before the Secretary makes payment under this section in respect of the tax, or tax and duty, on the tobacco products or cigarette papers or tubes condemned by a duly authorized official or rendered unmarketable, such tobacco products or cigarette papers or tubes shall be destroyed under such supervision as the Secretary may prescribe, unless such tobacco products or cigarette papers or tubes were previously destroyed under supervision satisfactory to the Secretary.

(d) Other laws applicable.

All provisions of law, including penalties, applicable in respect of internal revenue taxes on tobacco products and cigarette papers and tubes shall, insofar as applicable and not inconsistent with this section, be applied in respect of the payments provided for in this section to the same extent as if such payments constituted refunds of such taxes.

In **2004**, P.L. 108-311, Sec. 408(a)(7)(E), added "Robert T. Stafford" before "Disaster Relief and Emergency Assistance Act" in subsec. (a), enacted 10/4/2004.

In **1988**, P.L. 100-707, Sec. 109(1), substituted "and Emergency Assistance Act" for "Act of 1974" in subsec. (a), effective 11/23/88.

In **1976**, P.L. 94-455, Sec. 1906(b)(13)(A), substituted "Secretary" for "Secretary or his delegate" each place it appeared in Code Sec. 5708, effective 2/1/77.

In **1974**, P.L. 93-288, Sec. 602(j), substituted "Disaster Relief Act of 1974" for "Disaster Relief Act of 1970" in subsec. (a), effective 4/1/74.

In **1970**, P.L. 91-606, Sec. 301(j), substituted "Disaster Relief Act of 1970" for "Act of September 30, 1950 (42 U.S.C., sec 1855)" in subsec. (a), effective 12/31/70.

In **1958**, P.L. 85-859, Sec. 202, added Code Sec. 5708, effective 9/3/58.

Excise and miscellaneous taxes — Code Sec. 5713(b)(1)(E)

Subchapter B.—Qualification Requirements for Manufacturers and Importers of Tobacco Products and Cigarette Papers and Tubes, and Export Warehouse Proprietors

Sec.
5711. Bond.
5712. Application for permit.
5713. Permit.

In 1997, P.L. 105-33, Sec. 9302(h)(2)(C), added "and Importers" after "Manufacturers" in the heading of Subchapter B
In 1965, deleted "dealers in tobacco products" from the heading of Subchapter B.

Sec. 5711. Bond.
(a) When required.

Every person, before commencing business as a manufacturer of tobacco products or cigarette papers and tubes, or as an export warehouse proprietor, shall file such bond, conditioned upon compliance with this chapter and regulations issued thereunder, in such form, amount, and manner as the Secretary shall by regulation prescribe. A new or additional bond may be required whenever the Secretary considers such action necessary for the protection of the revenue.

(b) Approval or disapproval.

No person shall engage in such business until he receives notice of approval of such bond. A bond may be disapproved, upon notice to the principal on the bond, if the Secretary determines that the bond is not adequate to protect the revenue.

(c) Cancellation.

Any bond filed hereunder may be canceled, upon notice to the principal on the bond, whenever the Secretary determines that the bond no longer adequately protects the revenue.

In 1976, P.L. 94-455, Sec. 1906(b)(13)(A), substituted "Secretary" for "Secretary or his delegate" each place it appeared in Code Sec. 5711, effective 2/1/77.
In 1965, P.L. 89-44, Sec. 502(b)(6), deleted from subsec. (a) "a dealer in tobacco materials", effective 1/1/66.
In 1958, P.L. 85-859, Sec. 202, included in subsec. (a) export warehouse proprietors, and substituted "manufacturer of tobacco products or cigarette products or cigarette papers and tubes" for "manufacturer of articles", effective 9/3/58.

Sec. 5712. Application for permit.

Every person, before commencing business as a manufacturer or importer of tobacco products or processed tobacco or as an export warehouse proprietor, and at such other time as the Secretary shall by regulation prescribe, shall make application for the permit provided for in section 5713. The application shall be in such form as the Secretary shall prescribe and shall set forth, truthfully and accurately, the information called for on the form. Such application may be rejected and the permit denied if the Secretary, after notice and opportunity for hearing, find that—

(1) the premises on which it is proposed to conduct the business are not adequate to protect the revenue;

(2) the activity proposed to be carried out at such premises does not meet such minimum capacity or activity requirements as the Secretary may prescribe, or

(3) such person (including, in the case of a corporation, any officer, director, or principal stockholder and, in the case of a partnership, a partner)—

(A) is, by reason of his business experience, financial standing, or trade connections or by reason of previous or current legal proceedings involving a felony violation of any other provision of Federal criminal law relating to tobacco products, processed tobacco, cigarette paper, or cigarette tubes, not likely to maintain operations in compliance with this chapter,

(B) has been convicted of a felony violation of any provision of Federal or State criminal law relating to tobacco products, processed tobacco, cigarette paper, or cigarette tubes, or

(C) has failed to disclose any material information required or made any material false statement in the application therefor.

In 2009, P.L. 111-3, Sec. 702(a)(1)(A), added "or processed tobacco" after "tobacco products" in the introductory paragraph of Code Sec. 5712, effective 4/1/2009.
—P.L. 111-3, Sec. 702(b)(1), amended para. (3), effective 2/4/2009.
Prior to amendment, para. (3) read as follows:
"(3) such person (including, in the case of a corporation, any officer, director, or principal stockholder and, in the case of a partnership, a partner) is, by reason of his business experience, financial standing, or trade connections, not likely to maintain operations in compliance with this chapter, or has failed to disclose any material information required or made any material false statement in the application therefor."
In 1997, P.L. 105-33, Sec. 9302(h)(2)(A), added "or importer" after "manufacturer" in Code Sec. 5712 . . . Sec. 9302(h)(5), deleted "or" at the end of para. (1), redesignated para. (2) as para. (3) and added new para. (2), effective for articles removed (as defined in Code Sec. 5702(k), as amended [see above]) after 12/31/99. Sec. 9302(i)(2) of this Act provides:
"(2) Transitional rule. Any person who—
"(A) on the date of the enactment of this Act is engaged in business as a manufacturer of roll-your-own tobacco or as an importer of tobacco products or cigarette papers and tubes, and
"(B) before January 1, 2000, submits an application under subchapter B of chapter 52 of such Code to engage in such business, may, notwithstanding such subchapter B, continue to engage in such business pending final action on such application. Pending such final action, all provisions of such chapter 52 shall apply to such applicant in the same manner and to the same extent as if such applicant were a holder of a permit under such chapter 52 to engage in such business."
In 1976, P.L. 94-455, Sec. 1905(a)(27), deleted the last sentence in Code Sec. 5712, effective 2/1/77.
Prior to amendment, the last sentence in Code Sec. 5712 read as follows:
"No person subject to this section, who is lawfully engaged in business on the date of the enactment of the Excise Tax Technical Changes Act of 1958 [9/2/58], shall be denied the right to carry on such business pending reasonable opportunity to make application for permit and final action thereon."
—P.L. 94-455, Sec. 1906(b)(13)(A), substituted "Secretary" for "Secretary or his delegate" each place it appeared in Code Sec. 5712, effective 2/1/77.
In 1958, P.L. 85-859, Sec. 202, included export warehouse proprietors, and excluded dealers in tobacco materials, effective 9/3/58.

Sec. 5713. Permit.
(a) Issuance.

A person shall not engage in business as a manufacturer or importer of tobacco products or processed tobacco or as an export warehouse proprietor without a permit to engage in such business. Such permit, conditioned upon compliance with this chapter and regulations issued thereunder, shall be issued in such form and in such manner as the Secretary shall by regulation prescribe, to every person properly qualified under sections 5711 and 5712. A new permit may be required at such other time as the Secretary shall by regulation prescribe.

(b) Suspension or revocation.

(1) **Show cause hearing.** If the Secretary has reason to believe that any person holding a permit—

(A) has not in good faith complied with this chapter, or with any other provision of this title involving intent to defraud,

(B) has violated the conditions of such permit,

(C) has failed to disclose any material information required or made any material false statement in the application for such permit,

(D) has failed to maintain his premises in such manner as to protect the revenue,

(E) is, by reason of previous or current legal proceedings involving a felony violation of any other provision of Federal criminal law relating to tobacco products, processed tobacco, cigarette paper, or cigarette tubes, not likely to maintain operations in compliance with this chapter, or

3,465

(F) has been convicted of a felony violation of any provision of Federal or State criminal law relating to tobacco products, processed tobacco, cigarette paper, or cigarette tubes,

the Secretary shall issue an order, stating the facts charged, citing such person to show cause why his permit should not be suspended or revoked.

(2) Action following hearing. If, after hearing, the Secretary finds that such person has not shown cause why his permit should not be suspended or revoked, such permit shall be suspended for such period as the Secretary deems proper or shall be revoked.

In **2009**, P.L. 111-3, Sec. 702(a)(1)(B), added "or processed tobacco" after "tobacco products" in subsec. (a), effective 4/1/2009.
—P.L. 111-3, Sec. 702(b)(2), amended subsec. (b), effective 2/4/2009.
Prior to amendment, subsec. (b) read as follows:
"**(b) Revocation.** If the Secretary has reason to believe that any person holding a permit has not in good faith complied with this chapter, or with any other provision of this title involving intent to defraud, or has violated the conditions of such permit, or has failed to disclose any material information required or made any material false statement in the application for such permit, or has failed to maintain his premises in such manner as to protect the revenue, the Secretary shall issue an order, stating the facts charged, citing such person to show cause why his permit should not be suspended or revoked. If, after hearing, the Secretary finds that such person has not in good faith complied with this chapter or with any other provision of this title involving intent to defraud, has violated the conditions of such permit, has failed to disclose any material information required or made any material false statement in the application therefor, or has failed to maintain his premises in such manner as to protect the revenue, such permit shall be suspended for such period as the Secretary deems proper or shall be revoked."
In **1997**, P.L. 105-33, Sec. 9302(h)(2)(A), added "or importer" after "manufacturer" in subsec. (a), effective for articles removed (as defined in Code Sec. 5702(k), as amended [see above]) after 12/31/99. Sec. 9302(i)(2) of this Act reads as follows:
"(2) Transitional rule. Any person who—
"(A) on the date of the enactment of this Act is engaged in business as a manufacturer of roll-your-own tobacco or as an importer of tobacco products or cigarette papers and tubes, and
"(B) before January 1, 2000, submits an application under subchapter B of chapter 52 of such Code to engage in such business,
may, notwithstanding such subchapter B, continue to engage in such business pending final action on such application. Pending such final action, all provisions of such chapter 52 shall apply to such applicant in the same manner and to the same extent as if such applicant were a holder of a permit under such chapter 52 to engage in such business."
In **1976**, P.L. 94-455, Sec. 1906(b)(13)(A), substituted "Secretary" for "Secretary or his delegate" each place it appeared in Code Sec. 5713, effective 2/1/77.
In **1958**, P.L. 85-859, Sec. 202, substituted "manufacturer of tobacco products" for "manufacturer of articles", in subsec. (a) included export warehouse proprietors, and eliminated provisions which related to dealers in tobacco materials, and redesignated former subsec. (c) as (b) and omitted former subsec. (b) that required permits to be posted, effective 9/3/58.

Subchapter C.—Operations by Manufacturers and Importers of Tobacco Products and Cigarette Papers and Tubes and Export Warehouse Proprietors

Sec.
5721. Inventories.
5722. Reports.
5723. Packages, marks, labels, and notices.

In **1976**, P.L. 94-455, Sec. 1905(b)(7)(D), amended item 5723.
Prior to amendment, item 5723 read as follows:
"5723. Packages, marks, labels, notices, and stamps."
In **1958**, P.L. 85-859, Sec. 202, substituted "Manufacturers and Importers of Tobacco Products and Cigarette Papers and Tubes and Export Warehouse Proprietors" for "Manufacturers of Articles" in heading of subchapter and included marks in item 5723.

Sec. 5721. Inventories.

Every manufacturer or importer of tobacco products, processed tobacco or cigarette papers and tubes, and every export warehouse proprietor, shall make a true and accurate inventory at the time of commencing business, at the time of concluding business, and at such other times, in such manner and form, and to include such items, as the Secretary shall by regulation prescribe. Such inventories shall be subject to verification by any internal revenue officer.

In **2009**, P.L. 111-3, Sec. 702(a)(2)(A), added ", processed tobacco," after "tobacco products" in Code Sec. 5721, effective 4/1/2009.
In **1997**, P.L. 105-33, Sec. 9302(h)(2)(A), added "or importer" after "manufacturer" in Code Sec. 5721, effective for articles removed (as defined in Code Sec. 5702(k), as amended) after 12/31/99. Sec. 9302(i)(2) of this Act reads as follows:
"(2) Transitional rule. Any person who—
"(A) on the date of the enactment of this Act is engaged in business as a manufacturer of roll-your-own tobacco or as an importer of tobacco products or cigarette papers and tubes, and
"(B) before January 1, 2000, submits an application under subchapter B of chapter 52 of such Code to engage in such business,
may, notwithstanding such subchapter B, continue to engage in such business pending final action on such application. Pending such final action, all provisions of such chapter 52 shall apply to such applicant in the same manner and to the same extent as if such applicant were a holder of a permit under such chapter 52 to engage in such business."
In **1976**, P.L. 94-455, Sec. 1906(b)(13)(A), substituted "Secretary" for "Secretary or his delegate" in Code Sec. 5721, effective 2/1/77.
In **1958**, P.L. 85-859, Sec. 202, substituted "manufacturer of tobacco products or cigarette papers and tubes" for "manufacturer of articles" and "internal revenue officer" for "revenue officer", and added provisions to include export warehouse proprietors, effective 9/3/58.

Sec. 5722. Reports.

Every manufacturer or importer of tobacco products, processed tobacco, or cigarette papers and tubes, and every export warehouse proprietor, shall make reports containing such information, in such form, at such times, and for such periods as the Secretary shall by regulation prescribe.

In **2009**, P.L. 111-3, Sec. 702(a)(2)(B), added ", processed tobacco," after "tobacco products" in Code Sec. 5722, effective 4/1/2009.
In **1997**, P.L. 105-33, Sec. 9302(h)(2)(A), added "or importer" after "manufacturer" in Code Sec. 5722, effective for articles removed (as defined in Code Sec. 5702(k), as amended) after 12/31/99. Sec. 9302(i)(2) of this Act reads as follows:
"(2) Transitional rule. Any person who—
"(A) on the date of the enactment of this Act is engaged in business as a manufacturer of roll-your-own tobacco or as an importer of tobacco products or cigarette papers and tubes, and
"(B) before January 1, 2000, submits an application under subchapter B of chapter 52 of such Code to engage in such business,
may, notwithstanding such subchapter B, continue to engage in such business pending final action on such application. Pending such final action, all provisions of such chapter 52 shall apply to such applicant in the same manner and to the same extent as if such applicant were a holder of a permit under such chapter 52 to engage in such business."
In **1976**, P.L. 94-455, Sec. 1906(b)(13)(A), substituted "Secretary" for "Secretary or his delegate" in Code Sec. 5722, effective 2/1/77.
In **1958**, P.L. 85-859, Sec. 202, substituted "manufacturer of tobacco products or cigarette papers and tubes, and every export warehouse proprietor" for "manufacturer of articles", effective 9/3/58.

Sec. 5723. Packages, marks, labels, and notices.
(a) Packages.

All tobacco products, processed tobacco, and cigarette papers and tubes shall, before removal, be put up in such packages as the Secretary shall by regulation prescribe.
(b) Marks, labels, and notices.

Every package of tobacco products, processed tobacco, or cigarette papers or tubes shall, before removal, bear the marks, labels, and notices, if any, that the Secretary by regulation prescribes.
(c) Lottery features.

No certificate, coupon, or other device purporting to be or to represent a ticket, chance, share, or an interest in, or dependent on, the event of a lottery shall be contained in, attached to, or stamped, marked, written, or printed on any package of tobacco products, processed tobacco, or cigarette papers or tubes.
(d) Indecent or immoral material prohibited.

No indecent or immoral picture, print, or representation shall be contained in, attached to, or stamped, marked, writ-

ten, or printed on any package of tobacco products, processed tobacco, or cigarette papers or tubes.
(e) Exceptions.

Tobacco products furnished by manufacturers of such products for use or consumption by their employees, or for experimental purposes, and tobacco products, processed tobacco, and cigarette papers and tubes transferred to the bonded premises of another manufacturer or export warehouse proprietor or released in bond from customs custody for delivery to a manufacturer of tobacco products, processed tobacco, or cigarette papers and tubes, may be exempted from subsection (a) and (b) in accordance with such regulations as the Secretary shall prescribe.

In 2009, P.L. 111-3, Sec. 702(a)(2)(C), added ", processed tobacco," after "tobacco products" each place it appears in Code Sec. 5723, effective 4/1/2009.

In 1976, P.L. 94-455, Sec. 1905(a)(28)(A), substituted "and notices" for "notices, and stamps" in the heading of Code Sec. 5723 . . . Sec. 1905(a)(28)(B), amended subsec. (b), effective 2/1/77.

Prior to amendment, subsec. (b) read as follows:

"*(b) Marks, labels, notices, and stamps.*

"Every package of tobacco products or cigarette papers or tubes shall, before removal, bear the marks, labels, notices, and stamps, if any, that the Secretary or his delegate by regulation prescribes."

—P.L. 94-455, Sec. 1906(b)(13)(A), substituted "Secretary" for "Secretary or his delegate" each place it appeared in Code Sec. 5723, effective 2/1/77.

In 1958, P.L. 85-859, Sec. 202, substituted in subsec. (a) "Packages" for "Packages, labels, notices, and stamps" in the catchline, and "All tobacco products and cigarette papers and tubes shall, before removal, be put up in such packages as" for "All articles shall, before removal, be put up in packages having such labels, notices, and stamps as", in the text of subsec. (a), added subsec. (b), redesignated former subsec. (b) as (c) and substituted "tobacco products or cigarette papers or tubes" for "articles", redesignated former subsec. (c) as (d) and substituted "tobacco products or cigarette papers or tubes" for "articles", redesignated former subsec. (d) as (e) and permitted exemption of tobacco products and cigarette papers and tubes transferred to the bonded premises of another manufacturer or export warehouse proprietor or released in bond from customs custody for delivery to a manufacturer of tobacco products or cigarette papers and tubes, and eliminated provisions which authorized exemption of articles removed for shipment to a foreign country, Puerto Rico, the Virgin Islands, or a possession of the United States, and so shipped, effective 9/3/58.

Subchapter D.   Repealed.

In 1965, repealed Subchapter D, effective 1/1/65.
Prior to repeal, Subchapter D read as follows:
"SUBCHAPTER D.—OPERATIONS BY DEALERS IN TOBACCO MATERIALS
"Sec.
"5731. Shipments and deliveries restricted.
"5732. Inventory, and statement of shipments and deliveries.

Sec. 5731.   Repealed

In 1965, P.L. 89-44, repealed Code Sec. 5731, effective 1/1/65.
Prior to repeal, Code Sec. 5731 read as follows:
"SEC. 5731. SHIPMENTS AND DELIVERIES RESTRICTED.
"Every dealer in tobacco materials shall make all shipments or deliveries of tobacco materials in accordance with such regulations as the Secretary or his delegate shall prescribe. Tobacco materials shipped or delivered in violation of such regulations shall be subject to tax as manufactured tobacco and the dealer shipping or delivering the same shall be subject as a manufacturer of tobacco to the provisions of this chapter."
In 1958, P.L. 85-859, Sec. 202, substituted in section 5731 "subject to tax as manufactured tobacco and the dealer shipping or delivering the same shall be subject as a manufacturer of tobacco to the provisions of this chapter" for "regarded as manufactured tobacco and subject to tax, and the dealer shipping or delivering the same shall be regarded as a manufacturer of tobacco and subject, as such, to this chapter", effective 9/3/58.

Sec. 5732.   Repealed

In 1965, P.L. 89-44, repealed Code Sec. 5732, effective 1/1/65.
Prior to repeal, Code Sec. 5732 read as follows:
"SEC. 5732. INVENTORY, AND STATEMENT OF SHIPMENTS AND DELIVERIES.
"A dealer in tobacco materials shall make, upon demand of any internal revenue officer, a true and accurate inventory of all such materials held by the dealer, and shall, upon similar demand, furnish a true and complete statement of the quantity of such materials shipped or delivered to any person named in such demand."

In 1958, P.L. 85-859, Sec. 202, amended section 5732 to require a dealer to make a true and accurate inventory when demanded by any internal revenue officer, effective 9/3/58.

Subchapter D.—Occupational Tax

Sec.
5731. Imposition and rate of tax.
5732. Payment of tax.
5733. Provisions relating to liability for occupational taxes.
5734. Application of State laws.

In 2005, P.L. 109-59, Sec. 11125(b)(20)(D), added items 5732, 5733, and 5734
In 1987, P.L. 100-203, Sec. 10512(f)(1), added new Subchapter D.

Sec. 5731.   Imposition and rate of tax.
(a) General rule.

Every person engaged in business as—

   (1) a manufacturer of tobacco products,

   (2) a manufacturer of cigarette papers and tubes, or

   (3) an export warehouse proprietor,

shall pay a tax of $1,000 per year in respect of each premises at which such business is carried on.

(b) Reduced rates for small proprietors.

   (1) In general. Subsection (a) shall be applied by substituting "$500" for "$1,000" with respect to any taxpayer the gross receipts of which (for the most recent taxable year ending before the 1st day of the taxable period to which the tax imposed by subsection (a) relates) are less than $500,000.

   (2) Controlled group rules. All persons treated as 1 taxpayer under section 5061(e)(3) shall be treated as 1 taxpayer for purposes of paragraph (1).

   (3) Certain rules to apply. For purposes of paragraph (1), rules similar to the rules of subparagraphs (B) and (C) of section 448(c)(3) shall apply.

(c) Penalty for failure to register.

Any person engaged in a business referred to in subsection (a) who willfully fails to pay the tax imposed by subsection (a) shall be fined not more than $5,000, or imprisoned not more than 2 years, or both, for each such offense.

In 2005, P.L. 109-59, Sec. 11125(b)(20)(E), deleted subsec. (c) and redesignated subsec. (d) as (c), effective 7/1/2008, but not for taxes imposed for periods before 7/1/2008.

Prior to deletion, subsec. (c) read as follows:

"(c) Certain occupational tax rules to apply. Rules similar to the rules of subpart G of part II of subchapter A of chapter 51 shall apply for purposes of this section."

In 1987, P.L. 100-203, Sec. 10512(f)(1), added Code Sec. 5731, effective 1/1/88. For special rules, see Sec. 10512(h)(2) of this Act, reproduced in note following Code Sec. 5081.

Sec. 5732.   Payment of tax.
(a) Condition precedent to carrying on business.

No person shall be engaged in or carry on any trade or business subject to tax under this subchapter until he has paid the special tax therefor.

(b) Computation.

All special taxes under this subchapter shall be imposed as of on the first day of July in each year, or on commencing any trade or business on which such tax is imposed. In the former case the tax shall be reckoned for 1 year, and in the latter case it shall be reckoned proportionately, from the first day of the month in which the liability to a special tax commenced, to and including the 30th day of June following.

(c) How paid.

   (1) Payment by return. The special taxes imposed by this subchapter shall be paid on the basis of a return under such regulations as the Secretary shall prescribe.

(2) Stamp denoting payment of tax. After receiving a properly executed return and remittance of any special tax imposed by this subchapter, the Secretary shall issue to the taxpayer an appropriate stamp as a receipt denoting payment of the tax. This paragraph shall not apply in the case of a return covering liability for a past period.

In 2007, P.L. 110-172, Sec. 11(a)(32), substituted "this subchapter" for "this subpart" in para. (c)(2), enacted 12/29/2007.

In 2005, P.L. 109-59, Sec. 11125(b)(20)(A), redesignated Code Sec. 5142 as Code Sec. 5732 and substituted "this subchapter" for "this part" each place it appeared in newly redesignated Code Sec. 5732 ... Sec. 11125(b)(20)(B), deleted "(except the tax imposed by section 5131)" each place it appeared in newly redesignated Code Sec. 5732, effective 7/1/2008, but not for taxes imposed for periods before 7/1/2008.

In 1976, P.L. 94-455, Sec. 1905(a)(12), amended subsec. (c), effective 2/1/77. Prior to amendment, subsec. (c) read as follows:

"(c) How paid.

"(1) Stamp. All special taxes imposed by this part shall be paid by stamps denoting the tax.

"(2) Assessment. For authority of the Secretary or his delegate to make assessments where the special taxes have not been duly paid by stamp at the time and in the manner provided by law, see subtitle F."

Sec. 5733. Provisions relating to liability for occupational taxes.

(a) Partners.

Any number of persons doing business in partnership at any one place shall be required to pay but one special tax.

(b) Different businesses of same ownership and location.

Whenever more than one of the pursuits or occupations described in this subchapter are carried on in the same place by the same person at the same time, except as otherwise provided in this subchapter, the tax shall be paid for each according to the rates severally prescribed.

(c) Businesses in more than one location.

(1) Liability for tax. The payment of a special tax imposed by this subchapter shall not exempt from an additional special tax the person carrying on a trade or business in any other place than that stated in the register kept in the office of the official in charge of the internal revenue district.

(2) Storage. Nothing contained in paragraph (1) shall require a special tax for the storage of tobacco products and cigarette papers and tubes at a location other than the place where tobacco products and cigarette papers and tubes are sold or offered for sale.

(3) Definition of place. The term "place" as used in this section means the entire office, plant or area of the business in any one location under the same proprietorship; and passageways, streets, highways, rail crossings, waterways, or partitions dividing the premises, shall not be deemed sufficient separation to require additional special tax, if the various divisions are otherwise contiguous.

(d) Death or change of location.

Certain persons, other than the person who has paid the special tax under this subchapter for the carrying on of any business at any place, may secure the right to carry on, without incurring additional special tax, the same business at the same place for the remainder of the taxable period for which the special tax was paid. The persons who may secure such right are:

(1) the surviving spouse or child, or executor or administrator or other legal representative, of a deceased taxpayer;

(2) a husband or wife succeeding to the business of his or her living spouse;

(3) a receiver or trustee in bankruptcy, or an assignee for benefit of creditors; and

(4) the partner or partners remaining after death or withdrawal of a member of a partnership.

When any person moves to any place other than the place for which special tax was paid for the carrying on of any business, he may secure the right to carry on, without incurring additional special tax, the same business at his new location for the remainder of the taxable period for which the special tax was paid. To secure the right to carry on the business without incurring additional special tax, the successor, or the person relocating his business, must register the succession or relocation with the Secretary in accordance with regulations prescribed by the Secretary.

(e) Federal agencies or instrumentalities.

Any tax imposed by this subchapter shall apply to any agency or instrumentality of the United States unless such agency or instrumentality is granted by statute a specific exemption from such tax.

In 2005, P.L. 109-59, Sec. 11125(b)(20)(A), redesignated Code Sec. 5143 as Code Sec. 5733 and substituted "this subchapter" for "this part" each place it appeared in newly redesignated Code Sec. 5733 ... Sec. 11125(b)(20)(C), substituted "tobacco products and cigarette papers and tubes" for "liquors" each place it appeared in para. (c)(2), effective 7/1/2008, but not apply for taxes imposed for periods before 7/1/2008.

In 1976, P.L. 94-455, Sec. 1906(b)(13)(A), substituted "Secretary" for "Secretary or his delegate" each place it appeared in subsec. (d), effective 2/1/77.

Sec. 5734. Application of State laws.

The payment of any tax imposed by this subchapter for carrying on any trade or business shall not be held to exempt any person from any penalty or punishment provided by the laws of any State for carrying on such trade or business within such State, or in any manner to authorize the commencement or continuance of such trade or business contrary to the laws of such State or in places prohibited by municipal law; nor shall the payment of any such tax be held to prohibit any State from placing a duty or tax on the same trade or business, for State or other purposes.

In 2005, P.L. 109-59, Sec. 11125(b)(20)(A), redesignated Code Sec. 5145 as Code Sec. 5734 and substituted "this subchapter" for "this part" each place it appeared in newly redesignated Code Sec. 5734, effective 7/1/2008, but not for taxes imposed for periods before 7/1/2008.

Subchapter E.—Records of Manufacturers and Importers of Tobacco Products and Cigarette Papers and Tubes, and Export Warehouse Proprietors

Sec.

5741. Records to be maintained.

In 1987, P.L. 100-203, Sec. 10512(f)(1), redesignated Subchapter D as Subchapter E.

In 1976, P.L. 94-455, Sec. 2128(d)(1), amended the heading of subchapter D. Prior to amendment, the heading of subchapter D read as follows:

"Subchapter D. Records of Manufacturers of Tobacco Products and Cigarette Papers and Tubes, and Export Warehouse Proprietors."

In 1965, P.L. 89-44, Sec. 502(b)(7), redesignated Subchapter E as Subchapter D and deleted "and Dealers in tobacco materials".

In 1958, P.L. 85-859, Sec. 202, substituted "Manufacturers of Tobacco Products and Cigarette Papers and Tubes, Export Warehouse Proprietors, and" for "Manufacturers of Articles and" in heading of subchapter.

Sec. 5741. Records to be maintained.

Every manufacturer of tobacco products, processed tobacco, or cigarette papers and tubes, every importer, and every export warehouse proprietor shall keep such records in such manner as the Secretary shall by regulation prescribe. The records required under this section shall be available for inspection by any internal revenue officer during business hours.

Excise and miscellaneous taxes   Code Sec. 5753

In 2009, P.L. 111-3, Sec. 702(a)(2)(C), added ", processed tobacco," after "tobacco products" in Code Sec. 5741, effective 4/1/2009.
In 1976, P.L. 94-455, Sec. 2128(c), amended Code Sec. 5741, effective 2/1/77.
Prior to amendment, Code Sec. 5741 read as follows:
"Sec. 5741. Records to be maintained.
"Every manufacturer of tobacco products or cigarette papers and tubes, and every export warehouse proprietor, shall keep such records in such manner as the Secretary or his delegate shall by regulation prescribe."
In 1965, P.L. 89-44, Sec. 502(b)(9), deleted "every dealer in tobacco materials", after ", and" effective 1/1/66.
In 1958, P.L. 85-859, Sec. 202, substituted "tobacco products or cigarette papers and tubes, every export warehouse proprietor, and every dealer" for "articles and dealer", and "such manner" for "such form", effective 9/3/58.

Subchapter F.—General Provisions

Sec.
5751. Purchase, receipt, possession, or sale of tobacco products and cigarette papers and tubes, after removal.
5752. Restrictions relating to marks, labels, notices, and packages.
5753. Disposal of forfeited, condemned, and abandoned tobacco products, and cigarette papers and tubes.
5754. Restriction on importation of previously exported tobacco products.

In 1997, P.L. 105-33, Sec. 9302(h)(1)(E)(ii), added item 5754
In 1987, P.L. 100-203, Sec. 10512(f)(1), redesignated Subchapter E as Subchapter F.
In 1976, P.L. 94-455, Sec. 1905(b)(7)(B)(iii), amended item 5752.
Prior to amendment, item 5752 read as follows:
"5752. Restrictions relating to marks, labels, notices, stamps, and packages."
In 1965, P.L. 89-44, Sec. 502(b)(7), redesignated Subchapter F as Subchapter E, and removed from item 5753 a reference to "tobacco materials".
In 1958, P.L. 85-859, Sec. 202, substituted "sale of tobacco products and cigarette papers and tubes, after removal" for "sale of articles, after removal not exempt from tax" in item 5751, included marks and notices in item 5752, and substituted "tobacco products, cigarette papers and tubes, and" for "articles and" in item 5753.

Sec. 5751. Purchase, receipt, possession, or sale of tobacco products and cigarette papers and tubes, after removal.
(a) Restriction.
No person shall—
(1) with intent to defraud the United States, purchase, receive, possess, offer for sale, or sell or otherwise dispose of, after removal, any tobacco products or cigarette papers or tubes—
(A) upon which the tax has not been paid or determined in the manner and at the time prescribed by this chapter or regulations thereunder; or
(B) which, after removal without payment of tax pursuant to section 5704, have been diverted from the applicable purpose or use specified in that section; or
(2) with intent to defraud the United States, purchase, receive, possess, offer for sale, or sell or otherwise dispose of, after removal, any tobacco products or cigarette papers or tubes, which are not put up in packages as required under section 5723 or which are put up in packages not bearing the marks, labels, and notices, as required under such section; or
(3) otherwise than with intent to defraud the United States, purchase, receive, possess, offer for sale, or sell or otherwise dispose of, after removal, any tobacco products or cigarette papers or tubes, which are not put up in packages as required under section 5723 or which are put up in packages not bearing the marks, labels, and notices, as required under such section. This paragraph shall not prevent the sale or delivery of tobacco products or cigarette papers or tubes directly to consumers from proper packages, nor apply to such articles when so sold or delivered.
(b) Liability to tax.
Any person who possesses tobacco products or cigarette papers or tubes in violation of subsection (a)(1) or (a)(2) shall be liable for a tax equal to the tax on such articles.

In 1976, P.L. 94-455, Sec. 1905(b)(7)(A), substituted "and notices" for "notices, and stamps" in paras. (a)(2) and (3), effective 2/1/77.
In 1958, P.L. 85-859, Sec. 202, substituted "tobacco products and cigarette papers and tubes, after removal" for "articles, after removal, not exempt from tax" in the heading of Code Sec. 5751, effective 9/3/58.
—P.L. 85-859, Sec. 202, amended subsec. (a) to include within the restrictions, purchase, receipt, possession, offer for sale, or sale or other disposition of tobacco products or cigarette papers or tubes, after removal, upon which the tax has not been paid or determined, or which after removal without payment of tax have been diverted from the applicable purpose or use specified in section 5704, and to provide that para. (3) shall not prevent the delivery of tobacco products or cigarette papers or tubes directly to consumers from proper packages, nor apply to such articles when so delivered, effective 9/3/58.
—P.L. 85-859, Sec. 202, substituted "tobacco products or cigarette papers or tubes in violation of subsection (a)(1) or (a)(2) shall be liable for a tax equal to the tax on such articles" for "articles in violation of subsection (a) of this section, shall incur liability to the tax thereon in addition to the penalties prescribed elsewhere in this title" in subsec. (b), effective 9/3/58.

Sec. 5752. Restrictions relating to marks, labels, notices, and packages.
No person shall, with intent to defraud the United States, destroy, obliterate, or detach any mark, label, or notice prescribed or authorized, by this chapter or regulations thereunder, to appear on, or be affixed to, any package of tobacco products or cigarette papers or tubes, before such package is emptied.

In 1976, P.L. 94-455, Sec. 1905(b)(7)(B)(i), amended Code Sec. 5752, effective 2/1/77.
Prior to amendment, Code Sec. 5752 read as follows:
"Sec. 5752. Restrictions relating to marks, labels, notices, stamps, and packages.
"No person shall, with intent to defraud the United States—
"(a) destroy, obliterate, or detach any mark, label, notice, or stamp prescribed or authorized, by this chapter or regulations thereunder, to appear on, or be affixed to, any package of tobacco products or cigarette papers or tubes, before such package is emptied; or
"(b) empty any package of tobacco products or cigarette papers or tubes without destroying any stamp thereon to evidence the tax or indicate compliance with this chapter, prescribed by this chapter or regulations thereunder to be affixed to such package; or
"(c) detach, or cause to be detached, from any package of tobacco products or cigarette papers or tubes any stamp, prescribed by this chapter or regulations thereunder, to evidence the tax or indicate compliance with this chapter, or purchase, receive, possess, sell, or dispose of, by gift or otherwise, any such stamp which has been so detached; or
"(d) purchase, receive, possess, sell, or dispose of, by gift or otherwise, any package which previously contained tobacco products or cigarette papers or tubes which has been emptied, and upon which any stamp prescribed by this chapter or regulations thereunder, to evidence the tax or indicate compliance with this chapter, has not been destroyed."
In 1958, P.L. 85-859, Sec. 202, included marks and notices in the catchline, limited the penalties to cases where there is intent to defraud the United States, and prohibited the destruction, obliteration, or detachment of any mark, label, notice or stamp before a package of tobacco products or cigarette papers or tubes is emptied, effective 9/3/58.

Sec. 5753. Disposal of forfeited, condemned, and abandoned tobacco products, and cigarette papers and tubes.
If it appears that any forfeited, condemned, or abandoned tobacco products, or cigarette papers and tubes, when offered for sale, will not bring a price equal to the tax due and payable thereon, and the expenses incident to the sale thereof, such articles shall not be sold for consumption in the United States but shall be disposed of in accordance with such regulations as the Secretary shall prescribe.

In 1976, P.L. 94-455, Sec. 1906(b)(13)(A), substituted "Secretary" for "Secretary or his delegate" in Code Sec. 5753, effective 2/1/77.
In 1965, P.L. 89-44, Sec. 502(b)(11), amended Code Sec. 5753, effective 1/1/66.
Prior to amendment, Code Sec. 5753 read as follows:

3,469

"Sec. 5753. Disposal of Forfeited, Condemned, and Abandoned Tobacco Products, Cigarette Papers and Tubes, and Tobacco Materials.

"If it appears that any forfeited, condemned, or abandoned tobacco products, cigarette papers and tubes, or tobacco materials, when offered for sale, will not bring a price equal to the tax due and payable thereon, and the expenses incident to the sale thereof, such articles and tobacco materials shall not be sold for consumption in the United Sates but shall be disposed of in accordance with such regulations as the Secretary or his delegate shall prescribe."

In **1958,** P.L. 85-859, Sec. 202, substituted "tobacco products, cigarette papers and tubes" for "articles" each place it appeared, effective 9/3/58.

Sec. 5754. Restriction on importation of previously exported tobacco products.
(a) Export-labeled tobacco products.
(1) In general. Tobacco products and cigarette papers and tubes manufactured in the United States and labeled for exportation under this chapter—

(A) may be transferred to or removed from the premises of a manufacturer or an export warehouse proprietor only if such articles are being transferred or removed without tax in accordance with section 5704;

(B) may be imported or brought into the United States, after their exportation, only if such articles either are eligible to be released from customs custody with the partial duty exemption provided in section 5704(d) or are returned to the original manufacturer of such article as provided in section 5704(c); and

(C) may not be sold or held for sale for domestic consumption in the United States unless such articles are removed from their export packaging and repackaged by the original manufacturer into new packaging that does not contain an export label.

(2) Alterations by persons other than original manufacturer. This section shall apply to articles labeled for export even if the packaging or the appearance of such packaging to the consumer of such articles has been modified or altered by a person other than the original manufacturer so as to remove or conceal or attempt to remove or conceal (including by the placement of a sticker over) any export label.

(3) Exports include shipments to Puerto Rico. For purposes of this section, section 5704(d), section 5761, and such other provisions as the Secretary may specify by regulations, references to exportation shall be treated as including a reference to shipment to the Commonwealth of Puerto Rico.

(b) Export label.
For purposes of this section, an article is labeled for export or contains an export label if it bears the mark, label, or notice required under section 5704(b).

(c) Cross references.
(1) For exception to this section for personal use, see section 5761(d).

(2) For civil penalties related to violations of this section, see section 5761(c).

(3) For a criminal penalty applicable to any violation of this section, see section 5762(b).

(4) For forfeiture provisions related to violations of this section, see section 5761(c).

In **2006,** P.L. 109-432, Sec. 401(f)(2)(B), substituted "section 5761(d)" for "section 5761(c)" in para. (c)(1), effective for goods entered, or withdrawn from warehouse for consumption, on or after the 15th day after 12/20/2006.

In **2000,** P.L. 106-476, Sec. 4002(a), amended Code Sec. 5754, effective 90 days after 11/9/2000.

Prior to amendment, Code Sec. 5754 read as follows:

"Sec. 5754. Restriction on importation of previously exported tobacco products.

"(a) In general. Tobacco products and cigarette papers and tubes previously exported from the United States may be imported or brought into the United States only as provided in section 5704(d). For purposes of this section, section 5704(d), section 5761, and such other provisions as the Secretary may specify by regulations, references to exportation shall be treated as including a reference to shipment to the Commonwealth of Puerto Rico.

"(b) Cross reference. For penalty for the sale of tobacco products and cigarette papers and tubes in the United States which are labeled for export, see section 5761(c)."

In **1997,** P.L. 105-33, Sec. 9302(h)(1)(E)(i), added Code Sec. 5754, effective for articles removed (as defined in Code Sec. 5702(k), as amended [see above]) after 12/31/99. Sec. 9302(i)(2) of this Act reads as follows:

"(2) Transitional rule. Any person who—

"(A) on the date of the enactment of this Act is engaged in business as a manufacturer of roll-your-own tobacco or as an importer of tobacco products or cigarette papers and tubes, and

"(B) before January 1, 2000, submits an application under subchapter B of chapter 52 of such Code to engage in such business,

may, notwithstanding such subchapter B, continue to engage in such business pending final action on such application. Pending such final action, all provisions of such chapter 52 shall apply to such applicant in the same manner and to the same extent as if such applicant were a holder of a permit under such chapter 52 to engage in such business."

Subchapter G.—Penalties and Forfeitures
Sec.
5761. Civil penalties.
5762. Criminal penalties.
5763. Forfeitures.

In **1987,** P.L. 100-203, Sec. 10512(f)(1), redesignated Subchapter F as Subchapter G.

In **1965,** redesignated Subchapter G as Subchapter F.

In **1958,** P.L. 85-859, Sec. 202, substituted "Penalties and Forfeitures" for "Fines, Penalties, and Forfeitures" in subchapter heading.

Sec. 5761. Civil penalties.
(a) Omitting things required or doing things forbidden.
Whoever willfully omits, neglects, or refuses to comply with any duty imposed upon him by this chapter, or to do, or cause to be done, any of the things required by this chapter, or does anything prohibited by this chapter, shall, in addition to any other penalty provided in this title, be liable to a penalty of $1,000, to be recovered, with costs of suit, in a civil action, except where a penalty under subsection (b) or (c) or under section 6651 or 6653 or part II of subchapter A of chapter 68 may be collected from such person by assessment.

(b) Failure to pay tax.
Whoever fails to pay any tax imposed by this chapter at the time prescribed by law or regulations, shall, in addition to any other penalty provided in this title, be liable to a penalty of 5 percent of the tax due but unpaid.

(c) Sale of tobacco products and cigarette papers and tubes for export.
Except as provided in subsections (b) and (d) of section 5704—

(1) every person who sells, relands, or receives within the jurisdiction of the United States any tobacco products or cigarette papers or tubes which have been labeled or shipped for exportation under this chapter,

(2) every person who sells or receives such relanded tobacco products or cigarette papers or tubes, and

(3) every person who aids or abets in such selling, relanding, or receiving,

shall, in addition to the tax and any other penalty provided in this title, be liable for a penalty equal to the greater of $1,000 or 5 times the amount of the tax imposed by this chapter. All tobacco products and cigarette papers and tubes relanded within the jurisdiction of the United States shall be forfeited to the United States and destroyed. All vessels, vehicles, and aircraft used in such relanding or in removing such products, papers, and tubes from the place where relanded, shall be forfeited to the United States. This subsection and section 5754 shall not apply to any person who re-

Excise and miscellaneous taxes
Code Sec. 5762(a)(4)

lands or receives tobacco products in the quantity allowed entry free of tax and duty under subchapter IV of chapter 98 of the Harmonized Tariff Schedule of the United States. No quantity of tobacco products other than the quantity referred to in the preceding sentence may be relanded or received as a personal use quantity.

(d) Personal use quantities.

(1) In general. No quantity of tobacco products other than the quantity referred to in paragraph (2) may be relanded or received as a personal use quantity.

(2) Exception for personal use quantity. Subsection (c) and section 5754 shall not apply to any person who relands or receives tobacco products in the quantity allowed entry free of tax and duty under chapter 98 of the Harmonized Tariff Schedule of the United States, and such person may voluntarily relinquish to the Secretary at the time of entry any excess of such quantity without incurring the penalty under subsection (c).

(3) Special rule for delivery sales.

(A) In general. Paragraph (2) shall not apply to any tobacco product sold in connection with a delivery sale.

(B) Delivery sale. For purposes of subparagraph (A), the term "delivery sale" means any sale of a tobacco product to a consumer if—

(i) the consumer submits the order for such sale by means of a telephone or other method of voice transmission, mail, or the Internet or other online service, or the seller is otherwise not in the physical presence of the buyer when the request for purchase or order is made; or

(ii) the tobacco product is delivered by use of a common carrier, private delivery service, or the mail, or the seller is not in the physical presence of the buyer when the buyer obtains personal possession of the tobacco product.

(e) Applicability of section 6665.

The penalties imposed by subsections (b) and (c) shall be assessed, collected, and paid in the same manner as taxes, as provided in section 6665(a).

(f) Cross references.

For penalty for failure to make deposits or for overstatement of deposits, see section 6656.

In **2006**, P.L. 109-432, Sec. 401(f)(1), redesignated subsecs. (d) and (e) as subsecs. (e) and (f), and added subsec. (d) . . . Sec. 401(f)(2)(A), deleted the last two sentence of subsec. (c), effective for goods entered, or withdrawn from warehouse for consumption, on or after the 15th day after 12/20/2006.
Prior to deletion, the last two sentences of subsec. (c) read as follows:
"This subsection and section 5754 shall not apply to any person who relands or receives tobacco products in the quantity allowed entry free of tax and duty under chapter 98 of the Harmonized Tariff Schedule of the United States, and such person may voluntarily relinquish to the Secretary at the time of entry any excess of such quantity without incurring the penalty under this subsection. No quantity of tobacco products other than the quantity referred to in the preceding sentence may be relanded or received as a personal use quantity."
In **2000**, P.L. 106-554, Sec. 1(a)(7), [which enacted into law Sec. 315(a)(3) of P.L. 106-554] directed the addition of "This subsection and section 5754 shall not apply to any person who relands or receives tobacco products in the quantity allowed entry free of tax and duty under chapter 98 of the Harmonized Tariff Schedule of the United States, and such person may voluntarily relinquish to the Secretary at the time of entry any excess of such quantity without incurring the penalty under this subsection. No quantity of tobacco products other than the quantity referred to in the preceding sentence may be relanded or received as a personal use quantity." at the end of subsec. (c), effective 8/5/97. [Note: This amendment conflicts with Sec. 4003(a) of P.L. 106-476 which added similar, overlapping language].
—P.L. 106-476, Sec. 4002(c), substituted "the jurisdiction of the United States shall be forfeited to the United States and destroyed. All vessels, vehicles, and aircraft used in such relanding or in removing such products, papers, and tubes from the place where relanded, shall be forfeited to the United States." for "the jurisdiction of the United States, and all vessels, vehicles, and aircraft used in such relanding or in removing such products, papers, and tubes from the place where relanded, shall be forfeited to the United States." in the last sentence of subsec. (c), effective 90 days after 11/9/2000. . . . Sec. 4003(a), added "This subsection and section 5754 shall not apply to any person who relands or receives tobacco products in the quantity allowed entry free of tax and duty under subchapter IV of chapter 98 of the Harmonized Tariff Schedule of the United States. No quantity of tobacco products other than the quantity referred to in the preceding sentence may be relanded or received as a personal use quantity." at the end of subsec. (c), effective for articles removed (as defined in Code Sec. 5702(k), as amended) after 12/31/99. For transitional rule, see Sec. 9302(i)(2) of P.L. 105-33, reproduced below.
In **1997**, P.L. 105-33, Sec. 9302(h)(1)(B), redesignated subsecs. (c) and (d) as subsecs. (d) and (e), and added a new subsec. (c) . . . Sec. 9302(h)(1)(C), substituted "subsection (b) or (c)" for "subsection (b)" in subsec. (a) . . . Sec. 9302(h)(1)(D), substituted "The penalties imposed by subsections (b) and (c)" for "The penalty imposed by subsection (b)" in subsec. (d) [as redes. by Sec. 9302(h)(1)(B), see above], effective for articles removed (as defined in Code Sec. 5702(k), as amended) after 12/31/99. Sec. 9302(i)(2) of this Act reads as follows:
"(2) Transitional rule. Any person who—
"(A) on the date of the enactment of this Act is engaged in business as a manufacturer of roll-your-own tobacco or as an importer of tobacco products or cigarette papers and tubes, and
"(B) before January 1, 2000, submits an application under subchapter B of chapter 52 of such Code to engage in such business,
may, notwithstanding such subchapter B, continue to engage in such business pending final action on such application. Pending such final action, all provisions of such chapter 52 shall apply to such applicant in the same manner and to the same extent as if such applicant were a holder of a permit under such chapter 52 to engage in such business."
In **1989**, P.L. 101-239, Sec. 7721(c)(4), substituted "or 6653 or part II of subchapter A of chapter 68" for "or 6653" in subsec. (a) . . . Sec. 7721(c)(5)(A), substituted "6665(a)" for "6662(a)" in subsec. (c) . . . Sec. 7721(c)(5)(B), substituted "6665" for "6662" in the heading of subsec. (c), effective for returns the due date for which (determined without regard to extensions) is after 12/31/89.
In **1984**, P.L. 98-369, Sec. 714(h)(2)(A), substituted "section 6662" for "section 6660" in the heading of subsec. (c) . . . Sec. 714(h)(2)(B), substituted "section 6662(a)" for "section 6660(a)" in subsec. (c), effective for returns whose filing due date (determined without regard to extensions) is after 12/31/82.
In **1983**, P.L. 97-448, Sec. 107(b), substituted "section 6660(a)" for "section 6659(a)" in subsec. (c), and substituted "Section 6660" for "Section 6659" in the heading of subsec. (c), effective for returns filed after 12/31/81.
In **1981**, P.L. 97-34, Sec. 722(a)(3), substituted "6660" for "6659" in subsec. (d), effective for returns filed after 12/31/81.
—P.L. 97-34, Sec. 724(b)(5), amended subsecs. (c) and (d), effective for returns filed after 8/13/81.
Prior to amendment, subsecs. (c) and (d) read as follows:
"(c) Failure to make deposit of taxes.
"Section 6656 relating to failure to make deposit of taxes shall apply to the failure to make any deposit of taxes imposed under subchapter A on the date prescribed therefor, except that the penalty for such failure shall be 5 percent of the amount of the underpayment in lieu of the penalty provided by such section.
"(d) Applicability of section 6660.
"The penalties imposed by subsections (b) and (c) shall be assessed, collected, and paid in the same manner as taxes, as provided in section 6660(a)."
In **1958**, P.L. 85-859, Sec. 202, eliminated from subsec. (a) a reference to section 6652, substituted in subsec. (c) provisions relating to failure to make deposit of taxes for provisions which authorized a penalty of 5 percent of the tax due but unpaid where a person failed to pay tax at the time prescribed, and required the penalties to be added to the tax and assessed and collected at the same time, in the same manner, and as a part of the tax, and added subsec. (d), effective 9/3/58.

Sec. 5762. Criminal penalties.

(a) Fraudulent offenses.

Whoever, with intent to defraud the United States—

(1) Engaging in business unlawfully. Engages in business as a manufacturer or importer of tobacco products or cigarette papers and tubes, or as an export warehouse proprietor, without filing the bond and obtaining the permit where required by this chapter or regulations thereunder; or

(2) Failing to furnish information or furnishing false information. Fails to keep or make any record, return, report, or inventory, or keeps or makes any false or fraudulent record, return, report, or inventory, required by this chapter or regulations thereunder; or

(3) Refusing to pay or evading tax. Refuses to pay any tax imposed by this chapter, or attempts in any manner to evade or defeat the tax or the payment thereof; or

(4) Removing tobacco products or cigarette papers or tubes unlawfully. Removes, contrary to this chapter or regulations thereunder, any tobacco products or cigarette papers or tubes subject to tax under this chapter; or

(5) Purchasing, receiving, possessing, or selling tobacco products or cigarette papers or tubes unlawfully. Violates any provision of section 5751(a)(1) or (a)(2); or

(6) Destroying, obliterating, or detaching marks, labels, or notices before packages are emptied. Violates any provision of section 5752;

shall, for each such offense, be fined not more than $10,000, or imprisoned not more than 5 years, or both.

(b) Other offenses.

Whoever, otherwise than as provided in subsection (a), violates any provision of this chapter, or of regulations prescribed thereunder, shall, for each such offense, be fined not more than $1,000, or imprisoned not more than 1 year, or both.

In **1997**, P.L. 105-33, Sec. 9302(h)(2)(A), added "or importer" after "manufacturer" in para. (a)(1), effective for articles removed (as defined in Code Sec. 5702(k), as amended) after 12/31/99. Sec. 9302(i)(2) of this Act reads as follows:

"(2) Transitional rule. Any person who—

"(A) on the date of the enactment of this Act is engaged in business as a manufacturer of roll-your-own tobacco or as an importer of tobacco products or cigarette papers and tubes, and

"(B) before January 1, 2000, submits an application under subchapter B of chapter 52 of such Code to engage in such business,

may, notwithstanding such subchapter B, continue to engage in such business pending final action on such application. Pending such final action, all provisions of such chapter 52 shall apply to such applicant in the same manner and to the same extent as if such applicant were a holder of a permit under such chapter 52 to engage in such business."

In **1976**, P.L. 94-455, Sec. 1905(b)(7)(B)(ii), deleted paras. (a)(6), (7), (8), (9), (10) and (11), and added new para. (a)(6), effective 2/1/77.

Prior to amendment, paras. (a)(6) through (a)(11) read as follows:

"(6) Affixing improper stamps. Affixes to any package containing tobacco products or cigarette papers or tubes any improper or counterfeit stamp, or a stamp prescribed by this chapter or regulations thereunder which has been previously used on a package of such articles; or

"(7) Destroying, obliterating, or detaching marks, labels, notices, or stamps before packages are emptied. Violates any provision of section 5752(a); or

"(8) Emptying packages without destroying stamps. Violates any provision of section 5752(b); or

"(9) Possessing emptied packages bearing stamps. Violates any provision of section 5752(d); or

"(10) Refilling packages bearing stamps. Puts tobacco products or cigarette papers or tubes into any package which previously contained such articles and which bears a stamp prescribed by this chapter or regulations thereunder without destroying such stamp; or

"(11) Detaching stamps or possessing used stamps. Violates any provision of section 5752(c);"

In **1965**, P.L. 89-44, Sec. 502(b)(12), deleted from para. (a)(1) reference to "a dealer in tobacco materials", and deleted from para. (a)(2) reference to "statement", effective 1/1/66.

In **1958**, P.L. 85-859, Sec. 202, included export warehouse proprietors in para. (a)(1), eliminated provisions in paras. (a)(6) and (9)–(11) which related to labels and notices, and added paras. (a)(7) and (8), effective 9/3/58.

Sec. 5763. Forfeitures.

(a) Tobacco products and cigarette papers and tubes unlawfully possessed.

(1) Tobacco products and cigarette papers and tubes possessed with intent to defraud. All tobacco products and cigarette papers and tubes which, after removal, are possessed with intent to defraud the United States shall be forfeited to the United States.

(2) Tobacco products and cigarette papers and tubes not properly packaged. All tobacco products and cigarette papers and tubes not in packages as required under section 5723 or which are in packages not bearing the marks, labels, and notices, as required under such section, which, after removal, are possessed otherwise than with intent to defraud the United States, shall be forfeited to the United States. This paragraph shall not apply to tobacco products or cigarette papers or tubes sold or delivered directly to consumers from proper packages.

(b) Personal property of qualified manufacturers, qualified importers, and export warehouse proprietors, acting with intent to defraud.

All tobacco products and cigarette papers and tubes, packages, machinery, fixtures, equipment, and all other materials and personal property on the premises of any qualified manufacturer or importer of tobacco products or cigarette papers and tubes, or export warehouse proprietor, who, with intent to defraud the United States, fails to keep or make any record, return, report, or inventory, or keeps or makes any false or fraudulent record, return, report, or inventory, required by this chapter; or refuses to pay any tax imposed by this chapter, or attempts in any manner to evade or defeat the tax or the payment thereof; or removes, contrary to any provision of this chapter, any article subject to tax under this chapter, shall be forfeited to the United States.

(c) Real and personal property of illicit operators.

All tobacco products, cigarette papers and tubes, machinery, fixtures, equipment, and other materials and personal property on the premises of any person engaged in business as a manufacturer or importer of tobacco products or cigarette papers and tubes, or export warehouse proprietor, without filing the bond or obtaining the permit, as required by this chapter, together with all his right, title, and interest in the building in which such business is conducted, and the lot or tract of ground on which the building is located, shall be forfeited to the United States.

(d) General.

All property intended for use in violating the provisions of this chapter, or regulations thereunder, or which has been so used, shall be forfeited to the United States as provided in section 7302.

In **1997**, P.L. 105-33, Sec. 9302(h)(2)(A), added "or importer" after "manufacturer" in subsecs. (b) and (c) . . . Sec. 9302(h)(2)(B), added "qualified importers," after "manufacturers," in the heading of subsec. (b), effective for articles removed (as defined in Code Sec. 5702(k), as amended) after 12/31/99. Sec. 9302(i)(2) of this Act reads as follows:

"(2) Transitional rule. Any person who—

"(A) on the date of the enactment of this Act is engaged in business as a manufacturer of roll-your-own tobacco or as an importer of tobacco products or cigarette papers and tubes, and

"(B) before January 1, 2000, submits an application under subchapter B of chapter 52 of such Code to engage in such business,

may, notwithstanding such subchapter B, continue to engage in such business pending final action on such application. Pending such final action, all provisions of such chapter 52 shall apply to such applicant in the same manner and to the same extent as if such applicant were a holder of a permit under such chapter 52 to engage in such business."

In **1976**, P.L. 94-455, Sec. 1905(b)(7)(C)(i), substituted "and notices" for "notices, and stamps" in para. (a)(2) . . . Sec. 1905(b)(7)(C)(ii), deleted "internal revenue stamps," after "packages," in subsec. (b), effective 2/1/77.

In **1965**, P.L. 89-44, Sec. 502(b)(13), amended subsecs. (b) and (c), effective 1/1/66.

Prior to amendment, subsecs. (b) and (c) read as follows:

"(b) Personal property of qualified manufacturers, export warehouse proprietors, and dealers acting with intent to defraud.

"All tobacco products and cigarette papers and tubes, tobacco materials, packages, internal revenue stamps, machinery, fixtures, equipment, and all other materials and personal property on the premises of any qualified manufacturer of tobacco products or cigarette papers and tubes, export warehouse proprietor, or dealer in tobacco materials who, with intent to defraud the United States, fails to keep or make any record, return, report, inventory, or statement, or keeps or makes any false or fraudulent record, return, report, inventory, or statement, required by this chapter, or attempts in any manner to evade or defeat the tax or the payment thereof; or removes, contrary to any provision of this chapter, any article subject to tax under this chapter, shall be forfeited to the United States.

"(c) Real and personal property of illicit operators.

"All tobacco products, cigarette papers and tubes, tobacco materials, machinery, fixtures, equipment, and other materials and personal property on the premises of any person engaged in business as a manufacturer of tobacco products or cigarette papers and tubes, export warehouse proprietor, or dealer in tobacco materials, without filing the bond or obtaining the permit, as required by this chapter, together with all his right, title, and interest in the building in which such business is conducted, and the lot or tract of ground on which the building is located, shall be forfeited to the United States."

In **1958**, P.L. 85-859, Sec. 202, substituted in subsec. (a) "tobacco products and cigarette papers and tubes" for "articles" wherever appearing and added provisions in subsec. (a)(2) making it inapplicable to tobacco products or cigarette papers or tubes delivered directly to consumers from proper packages, included in subsecs. (b) and (c) property of export warehouse proprietors, included in subsec.

Excise and miscellaneous taxes — Code Sec. 5812(a)

(d) property intended for use, or used, in violating regulations under this chapter, effective 9/3/58.

CHAPTER 53.—MACHINE GUNS, DESTRUCTIVE DEVICES, AND CERTAIN OTHER FIREARMS

Subchapter
A. Taxes.
B. General provisions and exemptions.
C. Prohibited acts.
D. Penalties and forfeitures.

In 1968, P.L. 90-618, Sec. 201, rewrote Chapter 53 of the Internal Revenue Code of 1954. See note following Code Sec. 5872.

Subchapter A.—Taxes

Part
I. Special (occupational) taxes.
II. Tax on transferring firearms.
III. Tax on making firearms.

PART I.—SPECIAL (OCCUPATIONAL) TAXES
Sec.
5801. Imposition of tax.
5802. Registration of importers, manufacturers, and dealers.

In 1987, P.L. 100-203, Sec. 10512(g)(2), amended item 5801.
Prior to amendment, item 5801 read as follows:
"5801. Tax."

Sec. 5801. Imposition of tax.
(a) General rule.
On 1st engaging in business and thereafter on or before July 1 of each year, every importer, manufacturer, and dealer in firearms shall pay a special (occupational) tax for each place of business at the following rates:

(1) Importers and manufacturers: $1,000 a year or fraction thereof.

(2) Dealers: $500 a year or fraction thereof.

(b) Reduced rates of tax for small importers and manufacturers.

(1) In general. Paragraph (1) of subsection (a) shall be applied by substituting "$500" for "$1,000" with respect to any taxpayer the gross receipts of which (for the most recent taxable year ending before the 1st day of the taxable period to which the tax imposed by subsection (a) relates) are less than $500,000.

(2) Controlled group rules. All persons treated as 1 taxpayer under section 5061(e)(3) shall be treated as 1 taxpayer for purposes of paragraph (1).

(3) Certain rules to apply. For purposes of paragraph (1), rules similar to the rules of subparagraphs (B) and (C) of section 448(c)(2) shall apply.

In 1987, P.L. 100-203, Sec. 10512(g)(1), amended Code Sec. 5801, effective 1/1/88. Sec. 10512(h)(2) also provides:
"(2) All taxpayers treated as commencing in business on January 1, 1988.
"(A) In general.—Any person engaged on January 1, 1988, in any trade or business which is subject to an occupational tax shall be treated for purposes of such tax as having 1st engaged in such trade or business on such date.
"(B) Limitation on amount of tax.—In the case of a taxpayer who paid an occupational tax in respect of any premises for any taxable period which began before January 1, 1988, and includes such date, the amount of the occupational tax imposed by reason of subparagraph (A) in respect of such premises shall not exceed an amount equal to ½ the excess (if any) of—
"(i) the rate of such tax as in effect on January 1, 1988, over
"(ii) the rate of such tax as in effect on December 31, 1987.
"(C) Occupational tax.—For purposes of this paragraph, the term 'occupational tax' means any tax imposed under part II of subchapter A of chapter 51, section 5276, section 5731, or section 5801 of the Internal Revenue Code of 1986 (as amended by this section)."

"(D) Due date of tax.—The amount of any tax required to be paid by reason of this paragraph shall be due on April 1, 1988."
Prior to amendment, Sec. 5801 read as follows:
"Sec. 5801. Tax.
"On first engaging in business and thereafter on or before the first day of July of each year, every importer, manufacturer, and dealer in firearms shall pay a special (occupational) tax for each place of business at the following rates:
"(1) Importers.—$500 a year or fraction thereof;
"(2) Manufacturers.—$500 a year or fraction thereof;
"(3) Dealers.—$200 a year or fraction thereof. Except an importer, manufacturer, or dealer who imports, manufactures, or deals in only weapons classified as 'any other weapon' under section 5845(e), shall pay a special (occupational) tax for each place of business at the following rates: Importers, $25 a year or fraction thereof; manufacturers, $25 a year or fraction thereof; dealers, $10 a year or fraction thereof."
In 1968, P.L. 90-618, Sec. 201, added Code Sec. 5801, effective 11/1/68.

Sec. 5802. Registration of importers, manufacturers, and dealers.

On first engaging in business and thereafter on or before the first day of July of each year, each importer, manufacturer, and dealer in firearms shall register with the Secretary in each internal revenue district in which such business is to be carried on, his name, including any trade name, and the address of each location in the district where he will conduct such business. An individual required to register under this section shall include a photograph and fingerprints of the individual with the initial application. Where there is a change during the taxable year in the location of, or the trade name used in, such business, the importer, manufacturer, or dealer shall file an application with the Secretary to amend his registration. Firearms operations of an importer, manufacturer, or dealer may not be commenced at the new location or under a new trade name prior to approval by the Secretary of the application.

In 1994, P.L. 103-322, Sec. 110301(b), added a new sentence after the first sentence of Code Sec. 5802, effective 9/13/94.
In 1976, P.L. 94-455, Sec. 1906(b)(13)(A), substituted "Secretary" for "Secretary or his delegate" each place it appeared in Code Sec. 5802, effective 2/1/77.
In 1968, P.L. 90-618, Sec. 201, added Code Sec. 5802, effective 11/1/68.

PART II.—TAX ON TRANSFERRING FIREARMS
Sec.
5811. Transfer tax.
5812. Transfers.

In 1968, P.L. 90-618, Sec. 201, rewrote Chapter 53 of the Internal Revenue Code of 1954.

Sec. 5811. Transfer tax.
(a) Rate.
There shall be levied, collected, and paid on firearms transferred a tax at the rate of $200 for each firearm transferred, except, the transfer tax on any firearm classified as any other weapon under section 5845(e) shall be at the rate of $5 for each such firearm transferred.
(b) By whom paid.
The tax imposed by subsection (a) of this section shall be paid by the transferor.
(c) Payment.
The tax imposed by subsection (a) of this section shall be payable by the appropriate stamps prescribed for payment by the Secretary.

In 1976, P.L. 94-455, Sec. 1906(b)(13)(A), substituted "Secretary" for "Secretary or his delegate" in subsec. (c), effective 2/1/77.
In 1968, P.L. 90-618, Sec. 201, added Code Sec. 5811, effective 11/1/68.

Sec. 5812. Transfers.
(a) Application.
A firearm shall not be transferred unless (1) the transferor of the firearm has filed with the Secretary a written applica-

3,473

tion, in duplicate, for the transfer and registration of the firearm to the transferee on the application form prescribed by the Secretary; (2) any tax payable on the transfer is paid as evidenced by the proper stamp affixed to the original application form; (3) the transferee is identified in the application form in such manner as the Secretary may by regulations prescribe, except that, if such person is an individual, the identification must include his fingerprints and his photograph; (4) the transferor of the firearm is identified in the application form in such manner as the Secretary may by regulations prescribe; (5) the firearm is identified in the application form in such manner as the Secretary may by regulations prescribe; and (6) the application form shows that the Secretary has approved the transfer and the registration of the firearm to the transferee. Applications shall be denied if the transfer, receipt, or possession of the firearm would place the transferee in violation of law.

(b) Transfer of possession.

The transferee of a firearm shall not take possession of the firearm unless the Secretary has approved the transfer and registration of the firearm to the transferee as required by subsection (a) of this section.

In **1976**, P.L. 94-455, Sec. 1906(b)(13)(A), substituted "Secretary" for "Secretary or his delegate" each place it appeared in Code Sec. 5812, effective 2/1/77.
In **1968**, P.L. 90-618, Sec. 201, added Code Sec. 5812, effective 11/1/68.

PART III.—TAX ON MAKING FIREARMS

Sec.
5821. Making tax.
5822. Making.

In **1968**, P.L. 90-618, Sec. 201, rewrote Chapter 53 of the Internal Revenue Code of 1954.

Sec. 5821. Making tax.
(a) Rate.

There shall be levied, collected, and paid upon the making of a firearm a tax at the rate of $200 for each firearm made.

(b) By whom paid.

The tax imposed by subsection (a) of this section shall be paid by the person making the firearm.

(c) Payment.

The tax imposed by subsection (a) of this section shall be payable by the stamp prescribed for payment by the Secretary.

In **1976**, P.L. 94-455, Sec. 1906(b)(13)(A), substituted "Secretary" for "Secretary or his delegate" in subsec. (c) effective 2/1/77.
In **1968**, P.L. 90-618, Sec. 201, added Code Sec. 5821, effective 11/1/68.

Sec. 5822. Making.

No person shall make a firearm unless he has (a) filed with the Secretary a written application, in duplicate, to make and register the firearm on the form prescribed by the Secretary; (b) paid any tax payable on the making and such payment is evidenced by the proper stamp affixed to the original application form; (c) identified the firearm to be made in the application form in such manner as the Secretary may by regulations prescribe; (d) identified himself in the application form in such manner as the Secretary may by regulations prescribe, except that, if such person is an individual, the identification must include his fingerprints and his photograph; and (e) obtained the approval of the Secretary to make and register the firearm and the application form shows such approval. Applications shall be denied if the making or possession of the firearm would place the person making the firearm in violation of law.

In **1976**, P.L. 94-455, Sec. 1906(b)(13)(A), substituted "Secretary" for "Secretary or his delegate" each place it appeared in Code Sec. 5822, effective 2/1/77.
In **1968**, P.L. 90-618, Sec. 201, added Code Sec. 5822, effective 11/1/68.

Subchapter B.—General Provisions and Exemptions

Part
  I. General provisions.
  II. Exemptions.

PART I.—GENERAL PROVISIONS

Sec.
5841. Registration of firearms.
5842. Identification of firearms.
5843. Records and returns.
5844. Importation.
5845. Definitions.
5846. Other laws applicable.
5847. Effect on other law.
5848. Restrictive use of information.
5849. Citation of chapter.

In **1968**, P.L. 90-618, Sec. 201, rewrote Chapter 53 of the Internal Revenue Code of the Internal Revenue Code of 1954.

Sec. 5841. Registration of firearms.
(a) Central registry.

The Secretary shall maintain a central registry of all firearms in the United States which are not in the possession or under the control of the United States. This registry shall be known as the National Firearms Registration and Transfer Record. The registry shall include—
  (1) identification of the firearm;
  (2) date of registration; and
  (3) identification and address of person entitled to possession of the firearm.

(b) By whom registered.

Each manufacturer, importer, and maker shall register each firearm he manufactures, imports, or makes. Each firearm transferred shall be registered to the transferee by the transferor.

(c) How registered.

Each manufacturer shall notify the Secretary of the manufacture of a firearm in such manner as may by regulations be prescribed and such notification shall effect the registration of the firearm required by this section. Each importer, maker, and transferor of a firearm shall, prior to importing, making, or transferring a firearm, obtain authorization in such manner as required by this chapter or regulations issued thereunder to import, make, or transfer the firearm, and such authorization shall effect the registration of the firearm required by this section.

(d) Firearms registered on effective date of this act.

A person shown as possessing a firearm by the records maintained by the Secretary pursuant to the National Firearms Act in force on the day immediately prior to the effective date of the National Firearms Act of 1968 shall be considered to have registered under this section the firearms in his possession which are disclosed by that record as being in his possession.

(e) Proof of registration.

A person possessing a firearm registered as required by this section shall retain proof of registration which shall be made available to the Secretary upon request.

In 1976, P.L. 94-455, Sec. 1906(b)(13)(A), substituted "Secretary" for "Secretary or his delegate" each place it appeared in Code Sec. 5841, effective 2/1/77.
In 1968, P.L. 90-618, Sec. 201, added Code Sec. 5841, effective 11/1/68.

Sec. 5842. Identification of firearms.
(a) Identification of firearms other than destructive devices.

Each manufacturer and importer and anyone making a firearm shall identify each firearm, other than a destructive device, manufactured, imported, or made by a serial number which may not be readily removed, obliterated, or altered, the name of the manufacturer, importer, or maker, and such other identification as the Secretary may by regulations prescribe.

(b) Firearms without serial number.

Any person who possesses a firearm, other than a destructive device, which does not bear the serial number and other information required by subsection (a) of this section shall identify the firearm with a serial number assigned by the Secretary and any other information the Secretary may by regulations prescribe.

(c) Identification of destructive device.

Any firearm classified as a destructive device shall be identified in such manner as the Secretary may by regulations prescribe.

In 1976, P.L. 94-455, Sec. 1906(b)(13)(A), substituted "Secretary" for "Secretary or his delegate" each place it appeared in Code Sec. 5842, effective 2/1/77.
In 1968, P.L. 90-618, Sec. 201, added Code Sec. 5842, effective 11/1/68.

Sec. 5843. Records and returns.

Importers, manufacturers, and dealers shall keep such records of, and render such returns in relation to, the importation, manufacture, making, receipt, and sale, or other disposition, of firearms as the Secretary may by regulations prescribe.

In 1976, P.L. 94-455, Sec. 1906(b)(13)(A), substituted "Secretary" for "Secretary or his delegate" in Code Sec. 5843, effective 2/1/77.
In 1968, P.L. 90-618, Sec. 201, added Code Sec. 5843, effective 11/1/68.

Sec. 5844. Importation.

No firearm shall be imported or brought into the United States or any territory under its control or jurisdiction unless the importer establishes, under regulations as may be prescribed by the Secretary, that the firearm to be imported or brought in is—

(1) being imported or brought in for the use of the United States or any department, independent establishment, or agency thereof or any State or possession or any political subdivision thereof; or

(2) being imported or brought in for scientific or research purposes; or

(3) being imported or brought in solely for testing or use as a model by a registered manufacturer or solely for use as a sample by a registered importer or registered dealer;
except that, the Secretary may permit the conditional importation or bringing in of a firearm for examination and testing in connection with classifying the firearm.

In 1976, P.L. 94-455, Sec. 1906(b)(13)(A), substituted "Secretary" for "Secretary or his delegate" each place it appeared in Code Sec. 5844, effective 2/1/77.
In 1968, P.L. 90-618, Sec. 201, added Code Sec. 5844, effective 11/1/68.

Sec. 5845. Definitions.

For the purpose of this chapter—
(a) Firearm.

The term "firearm" means (1) a shotgun having a barrel or barrels of less than 18 inches in length; (2) a weapon made from a shotgun if such weapon as modified has an overall length of less than 26 inches or a barrel or barrels of less than 18 inches in length; (3) a rifle having a barrel or barrels of less than 16 inches in length; (4) a weapon made from a rifle if such weapon as modified has an overall length of less than 26 inches or a barrel or barrels of less than 16 inches in length; (5) any other weapon, as defined in subsection (e); (6) a machinegun; (7) any silencer (as defined in section 921 of title 18, United States Code); and (8) a destructive device. The term "firearm" shall not include an antique firearm or any device (other than a machinegun or destructive device) which, although designed as a weapon, the Secretary finds by reason of the date of its manufacture, value, design, and other characteristics is primarily a collector's item and is not likely to be used as a weapon.

(b) Machinegun.

The term "machinegun" means any weapon which shoots, is designed to shoot, or can be readily restored to shoot, automatically more than one shot, without manual reloading, by a single function of the trigger. The term shall also include the frame or receiver of any such weapon, any part designed and intended solely and exclusively, or combination of parts designed and intended, for use in converting a weapon into a machinegun, and any combination of parts from which a machinegun can be assembled if such parts are in the possession or under the control of a person.

(c) Rifle.

The term "rifle" means a weapon designed or redesigned, made or remade, and intended to be fired from the shoulder and designed or redesigned and made or remade to use the energy of the explosive in a fixed cartridge to fire only a single projectile through a rifled bore for each single pull of the trigger, and shall include any such weapon which may be readily restored to fire a fixed cartridge.

(d) Shotgun.

The term "shotgun" means a weapon designed or redesigned, made or remade, and intended to be fired from the shoulder and designed or redesigned and made or remade to use the energy of the explosive in a fixed shotgun shell to fire through a smooth bore either a number of projectiles (ball shot) or a single projectile for each pull of the trigger, and shall include any such weapon which may be readily restored to fire a fixed shotgun shell.

(e) Any other weapon.

The term "any other weapon" means any weapon or device capable of being concealed on the person from which a shot can be discharged through the energy of an explosive, a pistol or revolver having a barrel with a smooth bore designed or redesigned to fire a fixed shotgun shell, weapons with combination shotgun and rifle barrels 12 inches or more, less than 18 inches in length, from which only a single discharge can be made from either barrel without manual reloading, and shall include any such weapon which may be readily restored to fire. Such term shall not include a pistol or a revolver having a rifled bore, or rifled bores, or weapons designed, made, or intended to be fired from the shoulder and not capable of firing fixed ammunition.

(f) Destructive device.

The term "destructive device" means (1) any explosive, incendiary, or poison gas (A) bomb, (B) grenade, (C) rocket having a propellant charge of more than four ounces, (D) missile having an explosive or incendiary charge of more than one-quarter ounce, (E) mine, or (F) similar device; (2) any type of weapon by whatever name known which will, or which may be readily converted to, expel a projectile by the action of an explosive or other propellant, the barrel or barrels of which have a bore of more than one-half inch in diameter, except a shotgun or shotgun shell which the Secretary finds is generally recognized as particularly suitable for sporting purposes; and (3) any combination of parts either designed or intended for use in converting any device into a destructive device as defined in subparagraphs (1) and (2) and from which a destructive device may be readily assembled. The term "destructive device" shall not include any device which is neither designed nor redesigned for use as a weapon; any device, although originally designed for use as a weapon, which is redesigned for use as a signaling, pyrotechnic, line throwing, safety, or similar device; surplus ordnance sold, loaned, or given by the Secretary of the Army pursuant to the provisions of section 4684(2), 4685, or 4686 of title 10 of the United States Code; or any other device which the Secretary finds is not likely to be used as a weapon, or is an antique or is a rifle which the owner intends to use solely for sporting purposes.

(g) Antique firearm.
The term "antique firearm" means any firearm not designed or redesigned for using rim fire or conventional center fire ignition with fixed ammunition and manufactured in or before 1898 (including any matchlock, flintlock, percussion cap, or similar type of ignition system or replica thereof, whether actually manufactured before or after the year 1898) and also any firearm using fixed ammunition manufactured in or before 1898, for which ammunition is no longer manufactured in the United States and is not readily available in the ordinary channels of commercial trade.

(h) Unserviceable firearm.
The term "unserviceable firearm" means a firearm which is incapable of discharging a shot by means of an explosive and incapable of being readily restored to a firing condition.

(i) Make.
The term "make", and the various derivatives of such word, shall include manufacturing (other than by one qualified to engage in such business under this chapter), putting together, altering, any combination of these, or otherwise producing a firearm.

(j) Transfer.
The term "transfer" and the various derivatives of such word, shall include selling, assigning, pledging, leasing, loaning, giving away, or otherwise disposing of.

(k) Dealer.
The term "dealer" means any person, not a manufacturer or importer, engaged in the business of selling, renting, leasing, or loaning firearms and shall include pawnbrokers who accept firearms as collateral for loans.

(l) Importer.
The term "importer" means any person who is engaged in the business of importing or bringing firearms into the United States.

(m) Manufacturer.
The term "manufacturer" means any person who is engaged in the business of manufacturing firearms.

In **1986,** P.L. 99-308, Sec. 109(a), substituted "any part designed and intended solely and exclusively, or combination of parts designed and intended, for use in converting a weapon into a machinegun," for "any combination of parts designed and intended for use in converting a weapon into a machinegun," in subsec. (b) ... Sec. 109(b), amended para. (a)(7), effective 180 days after 5/19/86.
Prior to amendment, para. (a)(7) read as follows:
"(7) a muffler of a silencer for any firearm whether or not such firearm is included within this definition;"

In **1976,** P.L. 94-455, Sec. 1906(b)(13)(A), substituted "Secretary" for "Secretary or his delegate" each place it appeared in Subsec. 5845, effective 2/1/77.
—P.L. 94-455, Sec. 1906(b)(13)(J), deleted "of the Treasury or his delegate", after "device which the Secretary", in the last sentence of subsec. (f), effective 2/1/77.

In **1968,** P.L. 90-618, Sec. 201, added Code Sec. 5845, effective 11/1/68.

Sec. 5846. Other laws applicable.
All provisions of law relating to special taxes imposed by chapter 51 and to engraving, issuance, sale, accountability, cancellation, and distribution of stamps for tax payment shall, insofar as not inconsistent with the provisions of this chapter, be applicable with respect to the taxes imposed by sections 5801, 5811, and 5821.

In **1968,** P.L. 90-618, Sec. 201, added Code Sec. 5846, effective 11/1/68.

Sec. 5847. Effect on other laws.
Nothing in this chapter shall be construed as modifying or affecting the requirements of section 414 of the Mutual Security Act of 1954, as amended, with respect to the manufacture, exportation, and importation of arms, ammunition, and implements of war.

In **1968,** P.L. 90-618, Sec. 201, added Code Sec. 5847, effective 11/1/68.

Sec. 5848. Restrictive use of information.
(a) General rule.
No information or evidence obtained from an application, registration, or records required to be submitted or retained by a natural person in order to comply with any provision of this chapter or regulations issued thereunder, shall, except as provided in subsection (b) of this section, be used, directly or indirectly, as evidence against that person in a criminal proceeding with respect to a violation of law occurring prior to or concurrently with the filing of the application or registration, or the compiling of the records containing the information or evidence.

(b) Furnishing false information.
Subsection (a) of this section shall not preclude the use of any such information or evidence in a prosecution or other action under any applicable provision of law with respect to the furnishing of false information.

In **1968,** P.L. 90-618, Sec. 201, added Code Sec. 5848, effective 11/1/68.

Sec. 5849. Citation of chapter.
This chapter may be cited as the "National Firearms Act" and any reference in any other provision of law to the "National Firearms Act" shall be held to refer to the provisions of this chapter.

In **1968,** P.L. 90-618, Sec. 201, added Code Sec. 5849, effective 11/1/68.

PART II.—EXEMPTIONS
Sec.
5851. Special (occupational) tax exemption.
5852. General transfer and making tax exemption.
5853. Transfer and making tax exemption available to certain governmental entities.
5854. Exportation of firearms exempt from transfer tax.

In **1968,** P.L. 90-618, Sec. 201, rewrote Chapter 53 of the Internal Revenue Code of 1954.

Sec. 5851. Special (occupational) tax exemption.
(a) Business with United States.
Any person required to pay special (occupational) tax under section 5801 shall be relieved from payment of that tax if he establishes to the satisfaction of the Secretary that his business is conducted exclusively with, or on behalf of, the United States or any department, independent establishment, or agency thereof. The Secretary may relieve any person manufacturing firearms for, or on behalf of, the United

Excise and miscellaneous taxes — Subchapter D

States from compliance with any provision of this chapter in the conduct of such business.

(b) Application.

The exemption provided for in subsection (a) of this section may be obtained by filing with the Secretary an application on such form and containing such information as may by regulations be prescribed. The exemptions must thereafter be renewed on or before July 1 of each year. Approval of the application by the Secretary shall entitle the applicant to the exemptions stated on the approved application.

In 1976, P.L. 94-455, Sec. 1906(b)(13)(A), substituted "Secretary" for "Secretary or his delegate" each place it appeared in Code Sec. 5851, effective 2/1/77.
In 1968, P.L. 90-618, Sec. 201, added Code Sec. 5851, effective 11/1/68.

Sec. 5852. General transfer and making tax exemption.

(a) Transfer.

Any firearm may be transferred to the United States or any department, independent establishment, or agency thereof, without payment of the transfer tax imposed by section 5811.

(b) Making by a person other than a qualified manufacturer.

Any firearm may be made by, or on behalf of, the United States, or any department, independent establishment, or agency thereof, without payment of the making tax imposed by section 5821.

(c) Making by a qualified manufacturer.

A manufacturer qualified under this chapter to engage in such business may make the type of firearm which he is qualified to manufacture without payment of the making tax imposed by section 5821.

(d) Transfers between special (occupational) taxpayers.

A firearm registered to a person qualified under this chapter to engage in business as an importer, manufacturer, or dealer may be transferred by that person without payment of the transfer tax imposed by section 5811 to any other person qualified under this chapter to manufacture, import, or deal in that type of firearm.

(e) Unserviceable firearm.

An unserviceable firearm may be transferred as a curio or ornament without payment of the transfer tax imposed by section 5811, under such requirements as the Secretary may by regulations prescribe.

(f) Right to exemption.

No firearm may be transferred or made exempt from tax under the provisions of this section unless the transfer or making is performed pursuant to an application in such form and manner as the Secretary may by regulations prescribe.

In 1976, P.L. 94-455, Sec. 1906(b)(13)(A), substituted "Secretary" for "Secretary or his delegate" in Code Sec. 5852, effective 2/1/77.
In 1968, P.L. 90-618, Sec. 201, added Code Sec. 5852, effective 11/1/68.

Sec. 5853. Transfer and making tax exemption available to certain governmental entities.

(a) Transfer.

A firearm may be transferred without the payment of the transfer tax imposed by section 5811 to any State, possession of the United States, any political subdivision thereof, or any official police organization of such a government entity engaged in criminal investigations.

(b) Making.

A firearm may be made without payment of the making tax imposed by section 5821 by, or on behalf of, any State, or possession of the United States, any political subdivision thereof, or any official police organization of such a government entity engaged in criminal investigations.

(c) Right to exemption.

No firearm may be transferred or made exempt from tax under this section unless the transfer or making is performed pursuant to an application in such form and manner as the Secretary may by regulations prescribe.

In 1976, P.L. 94-455, Sec. 1906(b)(13)(A), substituted "Secretary" for "Secretary or his delegate" in subsec. (c), effective 2/1/77.
In 1968, P.L. 90-618, Sec. 201, added Code Sec. 5853, effective 11/1/68.

Sec. 5854. Exportation of firearms exempt from transfer tax.

A firearm may be exported without payment of the transfer tax imposed under section 5811 provided that proof of the exportation is furnished in such form and manner as the Secretary may by regulations prescribe.

In 1976, P.L. 94-455, Sec. 1906(b)(13)(A), substituted "Secretary" for "Secretary or his delegate" in Code Sec. 5854, effective 2/1/77.
In 1968, P.L. 90-618, Sec. 201, added Code Sec. 5854, effective 11/1/68.

Subchapter C.—Prohibited Acts

Sec.
5861. Prohibited acts.

Sec. 5861. Prohibited acts.

It shall be unlawful for any person—

(a) to engage in business as a manufacturer or importer of, or dealer in, firearms without having paid the special (occupational) tax required by section 5801 for his business or having registered as required by section 5802; or

(b) to receive or possess a firearm transferred to him in violation of the provisions of this chapter; or

(c) to receive or possess a firearm made in violation of the provisions of this chapter; or

(d) to receive or possess a firearm which is not registered to him in the National Firearms Registration and Transfer Record; or

(e) to transfer a firearm in violation of the provisions of this chapter; or

(f) to make a firearm in violation of the provisions of this chapter; or

(g) to obliterate, remove, change, or alter the serial number or other identification of a firearm required by this chapter; or

(h) to receive or possess a firearm having the serial number or other identification required by this chapter obliterated, removed, changed, or altered; or

(i) to receive or possess a firearm which is not identified by a serial number as required by this chapter; or

(j) to transport, deliver, or receive any firearm in interstate commerce which has not been registered as required by this chapter; or

(k) to receive or possess a firearm which has been imported or brought into the United States in violation of section 5844; or

(l) to make, or cause the making of, a false entry on any application, return, or record required by this chapter, knowing such entry to be false.

In 1968, P.L. 90-618, Sec. 201, added Code Sec. 5861, effective 11/1/68.

Subchapter D.—Penalties and Forfeitures

Sec.
5871. Penalties.
5872. Forfeitures.

Sec. 5871. Penalties.

Any person who violates or fails to comply with any provision of this chapter shall, upon conviction, be fined not more than $10,000, or be imprisoned not more than ten years, or both.

In 1984, P.L. 98-473, Sec. 227, deleted ", and shall become eligible for parole as the Board of Parole shall determine" after "or both" in Code Sec. 5871, effective 10/12/84.

In 1968, P.L. 90-618, Sec. 201, added Code Sec. 5871, effective 11/1/68.

Sec. 5872. Forfeitures.
(a) Laws applicable.

Any firearm involved in any violation of the provisions of this chapter shall be subject to seizure and forfeiture, and (except as provided in subsection (b)) all the provisions of internal revenue laws relating to searches, seizures, and forfeitures of unstamped articles are extended to and made to apply to the articles taxed under this chapter, and the persons to whom this chapter applies.

(b) Disposal.

In the case of the forfeiture of any firearm by reason of a violation of this chapter, no notice of public sale shall be required; no such firearm shall be sold at public sale; if such firearm is forfeited for a violation of this chapter and there is no remission or mitigation of forfeiture thereof, it shall be delivered by the Secretary to the Administrator of General Services, General Services Administration, who may order such firearm destroyed or may sell it to any State, or possession, or political subdivision thereof, or at the request of the Secretary, may authorize its retention for official use of the Treasury Department, or may transfer it without charge to any executive department or independent establishment of the Government for use by it.

In 1976, P.L. 94-455, Sec. 1906(b)(13)(A), substituted "Secretary" for "Secretary or his delegate" each place it appeared in subsec. (b), effective 2/1/77.
In 1968, P.L. 90-618, Sec. 201, added Code Sec. 5872, effective 11/1/68.

CHAPTER 54.—GREENMAIL

5881. Greenmail.

In 1987, P.L. 100-203, Sec. 10228(c), established Chapter 54, its table of sections to include item 5881.

Sec. 5881. Greenmail.
(a) Imposition of tax.

There is hereby imposed on any person who receives greenmail a tax equal to 50 percent of gain or other income of such person by reason of such receipt.

(b) Greenmail.

For purposes of this section, the term "greenmail" means any consideration transferred by a corporation (or any person acting in concert with such corporation) to directly or indirectly acquire stock of such corporation from any shareholder if—

(1) such shareholder held such stock (as determined under section 1223) for less than 2 years before entering into the agreement to make the transfer,

(2) at some time during the 2-year period ending on the date of such acquisition—

(A) such shareholder,

(B) any person acting in concert with such shareholder, or

(C) any person who is related to such shareholder or person described in subparagraph (B),

made or threatened to make a public tender offer for stock of such corporation, and

(3) such acquisition is pursuant to an offer which was not made on the same terms to all shareholders.

For purposes of the preceding sentence, payments made in connection with, or in transactions related to, an acquisition shall be treated as paid in such acquisition.

(c) Other definitions.

For purposes of this section—

(1) Public tender offer. The term "public tender offer" means any offer to purchase or otherwise acquire stock or assets in a corporation if such offer was or would be required to be filed or registered with any Federal or State agency regulating securities.

(2) Related person. A person is related to another person if the relationship between such persons would result in the disallowance of losses under section 267 or 707(b).

(d) Tax applies whether or not amount recognized.

The tax imposed by this section shall apply whether or not the gain or other income referred to in subsection (a) is recognized.

(e) Administrative provisions.

For purposes of the deficiency procedures of subtitle F, any tax imposed by this section shall be treated as a tax imposed by subtitle A.

In 1988, P.L. 100-647, Sec. 2004(o)(1)(A), substituted "gain or other income of such person by reason of such receipt" for "gain realized by such person on such receipt" in subsec. (a) . . . Sec. 2004(o)(1)(C)(i), substituted "the gain or other income" for "the gain" in subsec. (d) . . . Sec. 2004(o)(1)(C)(ii), substituted "amount recognized" for "gain recognized" in the heading of subsec. (d) . . . Sec. 2004(o)(2), added subsec. (e), effective for consideration received after 12/22/87 in tax. yrs. end. after 12/22/87, except not applicable for any acquisition pursuant to a written binding contract in effect on 12/15/87, and at all times thereafter before the acquisition.
— P.L. 100-647, Sec. 2004(o)(1)(B)(i), substituted "a corporation (or any person acting in concert with such corporation) to directly or indirectly acquire stock of such corporation" for "a corporation to directly or indirectly acquire its stock" in subsec. (b), effective for transactions occurring on or after 3/31/88.
In 1987, P.L. 100-203, Sec. 10228(a), added Code Sec. 5881, effective for consideration received after 12/22/87 in tax. yrs. end. after 12/22/87, except not applicable for any acquisition pursuant to a written binding contract in effect on 12/15/87, and at all times thereafter before the acquisition.

CHAPTER 55.—STRUCTURED SETTLEMENT FACTORING TRANSACTIONS

5891. Structured settlement factoring transactions.

In 2002, P.L. 107-134, Sec. 115(b), added Chapter 55.

Sec. 5891. Structured settlement factoring transactions.
(a) Imposition of tax.

There is hereby imposed on any person who acquires directly or indirectly structured settlement payment rights in a structured settlement factoring transaction a tax equal to 40 percent of the factoring discount as determined under subsection (c)(4) with respect to such factoring transaction.

(b) Exception for certain approved transactions.

(1) In general. The tax under subsection (a) shall not apply in the case of a structured settlement factoring transaction in which the transfer of structured settlement payment rights is approved in advance in a qualified order.

(2) Qualified order. For purposes of this section, the term "qualified order" means a final order, judgment, or decree which—

(A) finds that the transfer described in paragraph (1)—

(i) does not contravene any Federal or State statute or the order of any court or responsible administrative authority, and

(ii) is in the best interest of the payee, taking into account the welfare and support of the payee's dependents, and

(B) is issued—

(i) under the authority of an applicable State statute by an applicable State court, or

(ii) by the responsible administrative authority (if any) which has exclusive jurisdiction over the underlying action or proceeding which was resolved by means of the structured settlement.

(3) Applicable State statute. For purposes of this section, the term "applicable State statute" means a statute providing for the entry of an order, judgment, or decree described in paragraph (2)(A) which is enacted by—

(A) the State in which the payee of the structured settlement is domiciled, or

(B) if there is no statute described in subparagraph (A), the State in which either the party to the structured settlement (including an assignee under a qualified assignment under section 130) or the person issuing the funding asset for the structured settlement is domiciled or has its principal place of business.

(4) Applicable State court. For purposes of this section—

(A) In general. The term "applicable State court" means, with respect to any applicable State statute, a court of the State which enacted such statute.

(B) Special rule. In the case of an applicable State statute described in paragraph (3)(B), such term also includes a court of the State in which the payee of the structured settlement is domiciled.

(5) Qualified order dispositive. A qualified order shall be treated as dispositive for purposes of the exception under this subsection.

(c) Definitions.

For purposes of this section—

(1) Structured settlement. The term "structured settlement" means an arrangement—

(A) which is established by—

(i) suit or agreement for the periodic payment of damages excludable from the gross income of the recipient under section 104(a)(2), or

(ii) agreement for the periodic payment of compensation under any workers' compensation law excludable from the gross income of the recipient under section 104(a)(1), and

(B) under which the periodic payments are—

(i) of the character described in subparagraphs (A) and (B) of section 130(c)(2), and

(ii) payable by a person who is a party to the suit or agreement or to the workers' compensation claim or by a person who has assumed the liability for such periodic payments under a qualified assignment in accordance with section 130.

(2) Structured settlement payment rights. The term "structured settlement payment rights" means rights to receive payments under a structured settlement.

(3) Structured settlement factoring transaction.

(A) In general. The term "structured settlement factoring transaction" means a transfer of structured settlement payment rights (including portions of structured settlement payments) made for consideration by means of sale, assignment, pledge, or other form of encumbrance or alienation for consideration.

(B) Exception. Such term shall not include—

(i) the creation or perfection of a security interest in structured settlement payment rights under a blanket security agreement entered into with an insured depository institution in the absence of any action to re-direct the structured settlement payments to such institution (or agent or successor thereof) or otherwise to enforce such blanket security interest as against the structured settlement payment rights, or

(ii) a subsequent transfer of structured settlement payment rights acquired in a structured settlement factoring transaction.

(4) Factoring discount. The term "factoring discount" means an amount equal to the excess of—

(A) the aggregate undiscounted amount of structured settlement payments being acquired in the structured settlement factoring transaction, over

(B) the total amount actually paid by the acquirer to the person from whom such structured settlement payments are acquired.

(5) Responsible administrative authority. The term "responsible administrative authority" means the administrative authority which had jurisdiction over the underlying action or proceeding which was resolved by means of the structured settlement.

(6) State. The term "State" includes the Commonwealth of Puerto Rico and any possession of the United States.

(d) Coordination with other provisions.

(1) In general. If the applicable requirements of sections 72, 104(a)(1), 104(a)(2), 130, and 461(h) were satisfied at the time the structured settlement involving structured settlement payment rights was entered into, the subsequent occurrence of a structured settlement factoring transaction shall not affect the application of the provisions of such sections to the parties to the structured settlement (including an assignee under a qualified assignment under section 130) in any taxable year.

(2) No withholding of tax. The provisions of section 3405 regarding withholding of tax shall not apply to the person making the payments in the event of a structured settlement factoring transaction.

In 2002, P.L. 107-134, Sec. 115(a), added Code Sec. 5891, effective as provided in Sec. 115(c) of this Act, which reads as follows:

"(c) Effective dates.—

"(1) In general. The amendments made by this section (other than the provisions of section 5891(d) of the Internal Revenue Code of 1986, as added by this section) shall apply to structured settlement factoring transactions (as defined in section 5891(c) of such Code (as so added)) entered into on or after the 30th day following the date of the enactment of this Act.

"(2) Clarification of existing law. Section 5891(d) of such Code (as so added) shall apply to structured settlement factoring transactions (as defined in section 5891(c) of such Code (as so added)) entered into before, on, or after such 30th day.

"(3) Transition rule. In the case of a structured settlement factoring transaction entered into during the period beginning on the 30th day following the date of the enactment of this Act and ending on July 1, 2002, no tax shall be imposed under section 5891(a) of such Code if—

"(A) the structured settlement payee is domiciled in a State (or possession of the United States) which has not enacted a statute providing that the structured settlement factoring transaction is ineffective unless the transaction has been approved by an order, judgment, or decree of a court (or where applicable, a responsible administrative authority) which finds that such transaction—

"(i) does not contravene any Federal or State statute or the order of any court (or responsible administrative authority); and

"(ii) is in the best interest of the structured settlement payee or is appropriate in light of a hardship faced by the payee; and

"(B) the person acquiring the structured settlement payment rights discloses to the structured settlement payee in advance of the structured settlement factoring transaction the amounts and due dates of the payments to be transferred, the aggregate amount to be transferred, the consideration to be received by the structured settlement payee for the transferred payments, the discounted present value of the transferred payments (including the present value as determined in the manner described in section 7520 of such Code), and the expenses required under the terms of the structured settlement factoring transaction to be paid by the structured settlement payee or deducted from the proceeds of such transaction."

Subtitle F — Excise and miscellaneous taxes

Subtitle F. — Procedure and Administration

Chapter
61. Information and returns.
62. Time and place for paying tax.
63. Assessment.
64. Collection.
65. Abatements, credits, and refunds.
66. Limitations.
67. Interest.
68. Additions to the tax, additional amounts, and assessable penalties.
69. General provisions relating to stamps.
70. Jeopardy, receiverships, etc.
71. Transferees and fiduciaries.
72. Licensing and registration.
73. Bonds.
74. Closing agreements and compromises.
75. Crimes, other offenses, and forfeitures.
76. Judicial proceedings.
77. Miscellaneous provisions.
78. Discovery of liability and enforcement of title.
79. Definitions.
80. General rules.

In **1980**, P.L. 96-589, Sec. 6(g)(3)(E), amended item for chapter 70. Prior to amendment, item 70 read as follows:
"70. Jeopardy, bankruptcy, and receiverships."

CHAPTER 61. — INFORMATION AND RETURNS

Subchapter
A. Returns and records.
B. Miscellaneous provisions.

Subchapter A. — Returns and Records

Part
I. Records, statements, and special returns.
II. Tax returns or statements.
III. Information returns.
IV. Signing and verifying of returns and other documents.
V. Time for filing returns and other documents.
VI. Extension of time for filing returns.
VII. Place for filing returns or other documents.
VIII. Designation of income tax payments to Presidential Election Campaign Fund.

PART I. — RECORDS, STATEMENTS, AND SPECIAL RETURNS

Sec.
6001. Notice or regulations requiring records, statements, and special returns.

Sec. 6001. Notice or regulations requiring records, statements, and special returns.

Every person liable for any tax imposed by this title, or for the collection thereof, shall keep such records, render such statements, make such returns, and comply with such rules and regulations as the Secretary may from time to time prescribe. Whenever in the judgment of the Secretary it is necessary, he may require any person, by notice served upon such person or by regulations, to make such returns, render such statements, or keep such records, as the Secretary deems sufficient to show whether or not such person is liable for tax under this title. The only records which an employer shall be required to keep under this section in connection with charged tips shall be charge receipts, records necessary to comply with section 6053(c), and copies of statements furnished by employees under section 6053(a).

In **1984**, P.L. 98-369, Sec. 219, provides:
"SEC. 219. CLARIFICATION OF AUTHORITY TO REQUIRE CERTAIN INFORMATION.
"Nothing in any provision of law shall be construed to prevent the Secretary of the Treasury or his delegate from requiring (from time to time) life insurance companies to provide such data with respect to taxable years beginning before January 1, 1984, as may be necessary to carry out the provisions of section 809 of such Code (as added by this title)."
In **1982**, P.L. 97-248, Sec. 314(d), added ", records necessary to comply with section 6053(c)," after "charge receipts" in Code Sec. 6001, effective for calendar yrs. begin. after 12/31/82.
In **1978**, P.L. 95-600, Sec. 501(a), added a new sentence to the end of Code Sec. 6001, effective for payments made after 12/31/78.
In **1976**, P.L. 94-455, Sec. 1906(b)(13)(A), substituted "Secretary" for "Secretary or his delegate" each place it appeared in Code Sec. 6001, effective 2/1/77.

PART II. — TAX RETURNS OR STATEMENTS

Subpart
A. General requirement.
B. Income tax returns.
C. Returns relating to transfers during life or at death.
D. Miscellaneous provisions.

SUBPART A. — GENERAL REQUIREMENT

Sec.
6011. General requirement of return, statement, or list.

Sec. 6011. General requirement of return, statement, or list.

(a) General rule.
When required by regulations prescribed by the Secretary any person made liable for any tax imposed by this title, or with respect to the collection thereof, shall make a return or statement according to the forms and regulations prescribed by the Secretary. Every person required to make a return or statement shall include therein the information required by such forms or regulations.

(b) Identification of taxpayer.
The Secretary is authorized to require such information with respect to persons subject to the taxes imposed by chapter 21 or chapter 24 as is necessary or helpful in securing proper identification of such persons.

(c) Returns, etc., of DISCs and former DISCs and former FSC's.
(1) **Records and information.** A DISC, former DISC, or former FSC (as defined in section 922 as in effect before its repeal by the FSC Repeal and Extraterritorial Income Exclusion Act of 200) all for the taxable year—
  (A) furnish such information to persons who were shareholders at any time during such taxable year, and to the Secretary, and
  (B) keep such records, as may be required by regulations prescribed by the Secretary.
(2) **Returns.** A DISC shall file for the taxable year such returns as may be prescribed by the Secretary by forms or regulations.

(d) Authority to require information concerning section 912 allowances.
The Secretary may by regulations require any individual who receives allowances which are excluded from gross income under section 912 for any taxable year to include on his return of the taxes imposed by subtitle A for such taxable year such information with respect to the amount and type of such allowances as the Secretary determines to be appropriate.

(e) Regulations requiring returns on magnetic media, etc.
(1) **In general.** The Secretary shall prescribe regulations providing standards for determining which returns must be filed on magnetic media or in other machine-readable

Information and returns Code Sec. 6011

form. Except as provided in paragraph (3), the Secretary may not require returns of any tax imposed by subtitle A on individuals, estates, and trusts to be other than on paper forms supplied by the Secretary.

(2) Requirements of regulations. In prescribing regulations under paragraph (1), the Secretary—

(A) shall not require any person to file returns on magnetic media unless such person is required to file at least 250 returns during the calendar year, and

(B) shall take into account (among other relevant factors) the ability of the taxpayer to comply at reasonable cost with the requirements of such regulations.

Notwithstanding the preceding sentence, the Secretary shall require partnerships having more than 100 partners to file returns on magnetic media.

(3) Special rule for tax return preparers.

(A) In general. The Secretary shall require than any individual income tax return prepared by a tax return preparer be filed on magnetic media if—

(i) such return is filed by such tax return preparer, and

(ii) such tax return preparer is a specified tax return preparer for the calendar year during which such return is filed.

(B) Specified tax return preparer. For purposes of this paragraph, the term "specified tax return preparer" means, with respect to any calendar year, any tax return preparer unless such preparer reasonably expects to file 10 or fewer individual income tax returns during such calendar year.

(C) Individual income tax return. For purposes of this paragraph, the term "individual income tax return" means any return of the tax imposed by subtitle A on individuals, estates, or trusts.

(4) Special rule for returns filed by financial institutions with respect to withholding on foreign transfers. The numerical limitation under paragraph (2)(A) shall not apply to any return filed by a financial institution (as defined in section 1471(d)(5)) with respect to tax for which such institution is made liable under section 1461 or 1474(a).

(f) Promotion of electronic filing.

(1) In general. The Secretary is authorized to promote the benefits of and encourage the use of electronic tax administration programs, as they become available, through the use of mass communications and other means.

(2) Incentives. The Secretary may implement procedures to provide for the payment of appropriate incentives for electronically filed returns.

(g) Disclosure of reportable transaction to tax-exempt entity.

Any taxable party to a prohibited tax shelter transaction (as defined in section 4965(e)(1)) shall by statement disclose to any tax-exempt entity (as defined in section 4965(c)) which is a party to such transaction that such transaction is such a prohibited tax shelter transaction.

(h) Income, estate, and gift taxes.

For requirement that returns of income, estate, and gift taxes be made whether or not there is tax liability, see subparts B and C.

In **2010**, P.L. 111-147, Sec. 522(a), added para. (e)(4), effective for returns the due date for which (determined without regard to extensions) is after 3/18/2010.

In **2009**, P.L. 111-92, Sec. 17(a), added para. (e)(3) ... Sec. 17(b), substituted "Except as provided in paragraph (3), the Secretary may not" for "The Secretary may not" in para. (e)(1), effective for returns filed after 12/31/2010.

In **2007**, P.L. 110-172, Sec. 11(g)(19)(A), substituted ", former DISC, or former FSC (as defined in section 922 as in effect before its repeal by the FSC Repeal and Extraterritorial Income Exclusion Act of 2000)" for "or former DISC or a FSC or former FSC" in para. (c)(1). . . . Sec. 11(g)(19)(B), deleted "AND FSC'S" in the heading of subsec. (c), enacted 12/29/2007.

In **2006**, P.L. 109-222, Sec. 516(b)(2), redesignated subsec. (g) as (h) and added subsec. (g), effective for disclosures the due date for which are after 5/17/2006.

In **1998**, P.L. 105-206, Sec. 2001(c), redesignated subsec. (f) as (g) and added new subsec. (f), effective 7/22/98.

—P.L. 105-206, Sec. 6012(e), substituted "beginning" for "ending on or" in Sec. 1226 of P.L. 105-34, see below.

In **1997**, P.L. 105-34, Sec. 1224, added the sentence to the end of para. (e)(2), effective [as amended by Sec. 6012(d) of 105-206, see above] for partnership tax. yrs. begin. after 12/31/97.

In **1989**, P.L. 101-239, Sec. 7713(a), amended subsec. (e), effective for returns the due date for which (determined without regard to extensions) is after 12/31/89. Prior to amendment, subsec. (e) read as follows:

"(e) Regulations requiring returns on magnetic tape, etc.

"(1) In general. The Secretary shall prescribe regulations providing standards for determining which returns must be filed on magnetic media or in other machine-readable form. The Secretary may not require returns of any tax imposed by subtitle A on individuals, estates, and trusts to be other than on paper forms supplied by the Secretary. In prescribing such regulations, the Secretary shall take into account (among other relevant factors) the ability of the taxpayer to comply at reasonable cost with such a filing requirement.

"(2) Certain returns must be filed on magnetic media.

"(A) In general. In the case of any person who is required to file returns under sections 6042(a), 6044(a), and 6049(a) with respect to more than 50 payees for any calendar year, all returns under such sections shall be on magnetic media.

"(B) Hardship exception. Subparagraph (A) shall not apply to any person for any period if such person establishes to the satisfaction of the Secretary that its application to such person for such period would result in undue hardship."

In **1988**, P.L. 100-647, Sec. 1015(q)(1), substituted "with respect to the collection thereof" for "for the collection thereof" in subsec. (a), effective on 11/10/88.

In **1986**, P.L. 99-514, Sec. 1899A(52), substituted "subparts B and C" for "sections 6012 to 6019, inclusive" in subsec. (f), effective 10/22/86.

In **1984**, P.L. 98-369, Sec. 801(d)(12)(A), added "or a FSC or former FSC" after "former DISC" in para. (c)(1) . . . Sec. 801(d)(12)(B), added "and FSC's and former FSC's" after "Former DISC's" in the heading of subsec. (c), effective for transactions after 12/31/84, in tax. yrs. end. after 12/31/84.

In **1983**, P.L. 98-67, Sec. 109(a), amended subsec. (e), effective for payments made after 12/31/83. Sec. 109(b) of this Act provides:

"(b) Study of wage returns on magnetic tape.—

"(1) Study.—The Secretary of the Treasury, in consultation with the Secretary of Health and Human Services, shall conduct a study of the feasibility of requiring persons to file, on magnetic media, returns under section 6011 of the Internal Revenue Code of 1954 containing information described in section 6051(a) of such Code (relating to W-2s).

"(2) Report to Congress.—Not later than July 1, 1984, the Secretary of the Treasury shall submit to the Committee on Ways and Means of the House of Representatives and the Committee on Finance of the Senate the results of the study conducted under paragraph (1)."

Prior to amendment, subsec. (e) read as follows:

"(e) Regulations requiring returns on magnetic tape, etc.

"The Secretary shall prescribe regulations providing standards for determining which returns must be filed on magnetic media or in other machine-readable form. The Secretary may not require returns of any tax imposed by subtitle A on individuals, estates, and trusts to be other than on paper forms supplied by the Secretary. In prescribing such regulations, the Secretary shall take into account (among other relevant factors) the ability of the taxpayer to comply at a reasonable cost with such a filing requirement."

In **1982**, P.L. 97-248, Sec. 319, redesignated subsec. (e) as subsec. (f) and added new subsec. (e), effective 9/3/82.

In **1978**, P.L. 95-615, Sec. 207(c), redesignated subsec. (d) as subsec. (e) and added new subsec. (d), effective for tax. yrs. begin. after 12/31/77.

In **1976**, P.L. 94-455, Sec. 1904(b)(10)(A)(ii), deleted subsec. (d) and redesignated subsecs. (e) and (f) as subsecs. (c) and (d), respectively . . . Sec. 1906(b)(13)(A), substituted "Secretary" for "Secretary or his delegate" each place it appeared in Code Sec. 6011, effective 2/1/77.

Prior to deletion subsec. (d) read as follows:

"(d) Interest equalization tax returns, etc.

"(1) In general.

"(A) Every person shall make a return for each calendar quarter during which he incurs liability for the tax imposed by section 4911, or would so incur liability but for the provisions of section 4918. The return shall, in addition to such other information as the Secretary or his delegate may by regulations require, include a list of all acquisitions made by such person during the calendar quarter for which exemption is claimed under section 4918 accompanied by a copy of any return made during such quarter under subparagraph (B). No return or accompanying evidence shall be required under this paragraph, in connection with any acquisition with respect to which—

"(i) an IET clean confirmation is obtained in accordance with the provisions of section 4918(b),

"(ii) a validation certificate described in section 4918(b) issued to the person from whom such acquisition was made is obtained, and such certificate was filed in accordance with the requirements prescribed by the Secretary or his delegate, or

3,481

Code Sec. 6011 — Information and returns

"(iii) a validation certificate was obtained by the acquiring person after such acquisition and before the date prescribed by section 6076(a) for the filing of the return,

nor shall any such acquisition be required to be listed in any return made under this paragraph.

"(B) Every person who incurs liability for tax imposed by section 4911 shall, if he disposes of the stock or debt obligation with respect to which such liability was incurred prior to the filing of the return required by subparagraph (A) (unless such disposition is made under circumstances which entitle such person to a credit under the provisions of section 4919), make a return of such tax.

"(2) Information returns of commercial banks. Every United States person (as defined in section 4920(a)(4)) which is a commercial bank shall file a return with respect to loans and commitments to foreign obligors at such times, in such manner, and setting forth such information as the Secretary or his delegate shall by forms and regulations prescribe.

"(3) Reporting requirements for certain members of exchanges and associations. Every member or member organization of a national securities exchange or of a national securities association registered with the Securities and Exchange Commission, which is not subject to the provisions of section 4918(c), shall keep such records and file such information as the Secretary or his delegate may by forms or regulations prescribe in connection with acquisitions and sales effected by such member or member organization, as a broker or for his own account, of stock of a foreign issuer or debt obligations of a foreign obligor—

"(A) with respect to which a validation certificate described in section 4918(b)(1)(A) has been received by such member or member organization; or

"(B) with respect to which an acquiring United States person is subject to the tax imposed by section 4911."

In 1971, P.L. 92-178, Sec. 504(a), redesignated subsec. (e) as subsec. (f) and added new subsec. (e), effective for tax. yrs. end. after 12/31/71, except that a corporation may not be a DISC for any tax. yr. begin. before 1/1/72.

In 1969, P.L. 91-128, Sec. 4(f), (added "[sic C] unless such disposition is made under circumstances which entitle such person to a credit under the provisions of section 4919)" after "subparagraph (A)" in subpara. (d)(1)(B) ... Sec. 4(g), amended para. (d)(3), effective 11/26/69.

Prior to amendment, para. (d)(3) read as follows:

"(3) Reporting requirements for members of exchanges and associations. Every member or member organization of a national securities exchange or of a national securities association registered with the Securities and Exchange Commission shall keep such records and file such information as the Secretary or his delegate may by regulations prescribe in connection with acquisitions and sales effected by such member or member organization as a broker, and acquisitions made for the account of such member or member organization, of stock or debt obligations—

"(A) as to which a certificate of American ownership or blanket certificate of American ownership is executed and filed with such member organization as prescribed under section 4918(e); and

"(B) as to which a written confirmation is furnished to a United States person stating that the acquisition—

"(i) in the case of a transaction on a national securities exchange, was made subject to a special contract, or

"(ii) in the case of a transaction not on a national securities exchange, was from a person who had not filed a certificate of American ownership with respect to such stock or debt obligation or a blanket certificate of American ownership with respect to the account from which such stock or debt obligation was made."

In 1967, P.L. 90-59, Sec. 4(b), amended para. (d)(1), effective for acquisitions of stock and debt obligations made after 7/14/67.

Prior to amendment, para (d)(1) read as follows:

"(1) In general. Every person shall make a return for each calendar quarter during which he incurs liability for the tax imposed by section 4911, or would so incur liability but for the provisions of section 4918. The return shall, in addition to such other information as the Secretary or his delegate may by regulations require, include a list of all acquisitions made by such person during the calendar quarter which are exempt under the provisions of section 4918, and shall, with respect to each such acquisitions, be accompanied either (A) by a certificate of American ownership which complies with the provisions of section 4918(e), or (B) in the case of an acquisition for which other proof of exemption is permitted under section 4918(f), by a statement setting forth a summary of the evidence establishing such exemption and the reasons for the person's inability to establish prior American ownership under subsection (b), (c), or (d) of section 4918. No return or accompanying evidence shall be required under this paragraph in connection with any acquisition with respect to which a written confirmation, furnished in accordance with the requirements described in section 4918(c) or (d), is treated as conclusive proof of prior American ownership; nor shall any such acquisition be required to be listed in any return made under this paragraph."

In 1965, P.L. 89-44, Sec. 101(b)(6), deleted subsec. (c), effective 6/22/65.

Prior to deletion, subsec. (c) read as follows:

"(c) Return of retailers excise taxes by suppliers.

"(1) General rule. Under regulations prescribed by the Secretary or his delegate, the Secretary or his delegate may enter into an agreement with any supplier with respect to any retailers excise tax imposed by chapter 31 (not including the taxes imposed by section 4041), whereby such supplier will be liable to return and pay such tax (for the period for which such agreement is in effect) for the person who (without regard to this subsection) is required to return and pay such tax. Except as provided in the regulations prescribed under this subsection—

"(A) all provisions of law (including penalties) applicable in respect of the person who (without regard to this subsection) is required to return and pay the tax shall apply to the supplier entering into the agreement, and

"(B) the person who (without regard to this subsection) is required to return and pay such tax remain subject to all provisions of law (including penalties) applicable in respect of such person.

"(2) Limitations on agreement authority in the case of house-to-house salesmen. In the case of sales, by house-to-house salesmen, of articles subject to tax under chapter 31 (other than section 4041) which are supplied by a manufacturer or distributor, if the manufacturer or distributor establishes the retail list price at which such articles are to be sold, the Secretary or his delegate shall not, as a condition to entering into an agreement under paragraph (1), require—

"(A) that such house-to-house salesmen execute powers of attorney making such manufacturer or distributor an agent for the return and payment of such tax,

"(B) that the manufacturer or distributor make separate returns with respect to each such house-to-house salesman, or

"(C) that the manufacturer or distributor assume any liability for tax on articles supplied by any person other than such manufacturer or distributor."

In 1964, P.L. 88-563, Sec. (3)(a), redesignated subsec. (d) as subsec. (e), and added new subsec. (d). Sec. 3(e) of this Act provides as follows:

"(e) First return period.—Notwithstanding any provision of section 6011(d)(1) of the Internal Revenue Code of 1954, the first period for which returns shall be made under such section 6011(d)(1) shall be the period commencing July 19, 1963, and ending at the close of the calendar quarter in which the enactment of this Act [9/2/64] occurs.

In 1958, P.L. 85-859, Sec. 161, redesignated subsec. (c) as subsec. (d), and added new subsec. (c), effective on the first day of the first calendar quarter which begins more than 60 days after 9/2/58.

SUBPART B.—INCOME TAX RETURNS

Sec.
6012. Persons required to make returns of income.
6013. Joint returns of income tax by husband and wife.
6014. Income tax return—tax not computed by taxpayer.
6015. Relief from joint and several liability on joint return.
6015. Repealed [Declaration of estimated income tax by individuals.]
6016. Repealed [Declarations of estimated income tax by corporations.]
6017. Self-employment tax returns.
6017A. Repealed [Place of residence.]

In 1998, P.L. 105-206, Sec. 3201(f), added item 6015.
In 1989, P.L. 101-239, Sec. 7711(b)(3), deleted item 6017A.
Prior to deletion item 6017A read as follows:
"6017A. Place of residence."
In 1984, P.L. 98-369, Sec. 412(c)(1), deleted item 6015.
Prior to deletion, item 6015 read as follows:
"6015. Declaration of estimated income tax by individuals."
In 1972, added item 6017A.
In 1968, P.L. 90-364, Sec. 103, deleted item 6016.
Prior to deletion, item 6016 read as follows:
"6016. Declarations of estimated income tax by corporations."

Sec. 6012. Persons required to make returns of income.
(a) General rule.

Returns with respect to income taxes under subtitle A shall be made by the following:

(1)(A) Every individual having for the taxable year gross income which equals or exceeds the exemption amount, except that a return shall not be required of an individual—

(i) who is not married (determined by applying section 7703), is not a surviving spouse (as defined in section 2(a)), is not a head of a household (as defined in section 2(b)), and for the taxable year has gross income of less than the sum of the exemption amount plus the basic standard deduction applicable to such an individual,

(ii) who is a head of a household (as so defined) and for the taxable year has gross income of less than the sum of the exemption amount plus the basic standard deduction applicable to such an individual,

(iii) who is a surviving spouse (as so defined) and for the taxable year has gross income of less than the sum of the exemption amount plus the basic standard deduction applicable to such an individual, or

Information and returns

(iv) who is entitled to make a joint return and whose gross income, when combined with the gross income of his spouse, is, for the taxable year, less than the sum of twice the exemption amount plus the basic standard deduction applicable to a joint return, but only if such individual and his spouse, at the close of the taxable year, had the same household as their home.

Clause (iv) shall not apply if for the taxable year such spouse makes a separate return or any other taxpayer is entitled to an exemption for such spouse under section 151(c).

(B) The amount specified in clause (i), (ii), or (iii) of subparagraph (A) shall be increased by the amount of 1 additional standard deduction (within the meaning of section 63(c)(3)) in the case of an individual entitled to such deduction by reason of section 63(f)(1)(A) (relating to individuals age 65 or more), and the amount specified in clause (iv) of subparagraph (A) shall be increased by the amount of the additional standard deduction for each additional standard deduction to which the individual or his spouse is entitled by reason of section 63(f)(1).

(C) The exception under subparagraph (A) shall not apply to any individual—

(i) who is described in section 63(c)(5) and who has—

(I) income (other than earned income) in excess of the sum of the amount in effect under section 63(c)(5)(A) plus the additional standard deduction (if any) to which the individual is entitled, or

(II) total gross income in excess of the standard deduction, or

(ii) for whom the standard deduction is zero under section 63(c)(6).

(D) For purposes of this subsection—

(i) The terms "standard deduction", "basic standard deduction" and "additional standard deduction" have the respective meanings given such terms by section 63(c).

(ii) The term "exemption amount" has the meaning given such term by section 151(d). In the case of an individual described in section 151(d)(2), the exemption amount shall be zero.

(2) Every corporation subject to taxation under subtitle A;

(3) Every estate the gross income of which for the taxable year is $600 or more;

(4) Every trust having for the taxable year any taxable income, or having gross income of $600 or over, regardless of the amount of taxable income;

(5) Every estate or trust of which any beneficiary is a nonresident alien;

(6) Every political organization (within the meaning of section 527(e)(1)), and every fund treated under section 527(g) as if it constituted a political organization, which has political organization taxable income (within the meaning of section 527(c)(1)) for the taxable year; and

(7) Every homeowners association (within the meaning of section 528(c)(1)) which has homeowners association taxable income (within the meaning of section 528(d)) for the taxable year[;]

(8) Every estate of an individual under chapter 7 or 11 of title 11 of the United States Code (relating to bankruptcy) the gross income of which for the taxable year is not less than the sum of the exemption amount plus the basic standard deduction under section 63(c)(2)(D).

except that subject to such conditions, limitations, and exceptions and under such regulations as may be prescribed by the Secretary, nonresident alien individuals subject to the tax imposed by section 871 and foreign corporations subject to the tax imposed by section 881 may be exempted from the requirement of making returns under this section.

(b) Returns made by fiduciaries and receivers.

(1) Returns of decedents. If an individual is deceased, the return of such individual required under subsection (a) shall be made by his executor, administrator, or other person charged with the property of such decedent.

(2) Persons under a disability. If an individual is unable to make a return required under subsection (a), the return of such individual shall be made by a duly authorized agent, his committee, guardian, fiduciary or other person charged with the care of the person or property of such individual. The preceding sentence shall not apply in the case of a receiver appointed by authority of law in possession of only a part of the property of an individual.

(3) Receivers, trustees and assignees for corporations. In a case where a receiver, trustee in a case under title 11 of the United States Code, or assignee, by order of a court of competent jurisdiction, by operation of law or otherwise, has possession of or holds title to all or substantially all the property or business of a corporation, whether or not such property or business is being operated, such receiver, trustee, or assignee shall make the return of income for such corporation in the same manner and form as corporations are required to make such returns.

(4) Returns of estates and trusts. Returns of an estate, a trust, or an estate of an individual under chapter 7 or 11 of title 11 of the United States Code shall be made by the fiduciary thereof.

(5) Joint fiduciaries. Under such regulations as the Secretary may prescribe, a return made by one of two or more joint fiduciaries shall be sufficient compliance with the requirements of this section. A return made pursuant to this paragraph shall contain a statement that the fiduciary has sufficient knowledge of the affairs of the person for whom the return is made to enable him to make the return, and that the return is, to the best of his knowledge and belief, true and correct.

(6) IRA share of partnership income. In the case of a trust which is exempt from taxation under section 408(e), for purposes of this section, the trust's distributive share of items of gross income and gain of any partnership to which subchapter C or D of chapter 63 applies shall be treated as equal to the trust's distributive share of the taxable income of such partnership.

(c) Certain income earned abroad or from sale of residence.

For purposes of this section, gross income shall be computed without regard to the exclusion provided for in section 121 (relating to gain from sale of principal residence) and without regard to the exclusion provided for in section 911 (relating to citizens or residents of the United States living abroad).

(d) Tax-exempt interest required to be shown on return.

Every person required to file a return under this section for the taxable year shall include on such return the amount of interest received or accrued during the taxable year which is exempt from the tax imposed by chapter 1.

(e) Consolidated returns.

For provisions relating to consolidated returns by affiliated corporations, see chapter 6.

Code Sec. 6012   **Information and returns**

In 2010, P.L. 111-226, Sec. 219(b)(1), deleted para. (a)(8) and redesignated para. (a)(9) as para. (a)(8), effective for tax. yrs. begin. after 12/31/2010.

Prior to deletion, para. (a)(8) read as follows:

"(8) Every individual who receives payments during the calendar year in which the taxable year begins under section 3507 (relating to advance payment of earned income credit)[; and]"

In 2002, P.L. 107-276, Sec. 3(a), deleted "or which has gross receipts of $25,000 or more for the taxable year (other than an organization to which section 527 applies solely by reason of subsection (f)(1) of such section)" after "taxable year" in para. (a)(6), effective for tax. yrs. begin. after 6/30/2000.

In 2000, P.L. 106-230, Sec. 3(a)(1), added "or which has gross receipts of $25,000 or more for the taxable year (other than an organization to which section 527 applies solely by reason of subsection (f)(1) of such section)" after "taxable year" in subsec. (a)(6), effective for tax. yrs. begin. after 6/30/2000.

In 1998, P.L. 105-206, Sec. 2004, of this Act, reads as follows:

"SEC. 2004. RETURN-FREE TAX SYSTEM.

"(a) In general. The Secretary of the Treasury or the Secretary's delegate shall develop procedures for the implementation of a return-free tax system under which appropriate individuals would be permitted to comply with the Internal Revenue Code of 1986 without making the return required under section 6012 of such Code for taxable years beginning after 2007.

"(b) Report. Not later than June 30 of each calendar year after 1999, the Secretary shall report to the Committee on Ways and Means of the House of Representatives and the Committee on Finance of the Senate on —

"(1) what additional resources the Internal Revenue Service would need to implement such a system;

"(2) the changes to the Internal Revenue Code of 1986 that could enhance the use of such a system;

"(3) the procedures developed pursuant to subsection (a); and

"(4) the number and classes of taxpayers that would be permitted to use the procedures developed pursuant to subsection (a)."

—P.L. 105-206, Sec. 6005(e)(3), added "on or" before "before" each place it appeared in Sec. 312(d)(2) [sic (e)(2)] of P.L. 105-34, see below.

—P.L. 105-206, Sec. 6012(e), substituted "beginning" for "ending on or" in Sec. 1226 of P.L. 105-34, see below.

In 1997, P.L. 105-34, Sec. 312(d)(11), substituted "(relating to gain from sale of principal residence)" for "(relating to one-time exclusion of gain from sale of principal residence by individual who has attained age 55)" in subsec. (c), effective for sales and exchanges after 5/6/97, except as provided by Sec. 312(d)(2)-(4) [(e)(2)-(4)] of this Act [as amended by Sec. 6005(e)(3) of 105-206, see above], which reads as follows:

"(2) Sales on or before date of enactment. At the election of the taxpayer, the amendments made by this section shall not apply to any sale or exchange on or before the date of the enactment of this Act.

"(3) Certain sales within 2 years after date of enactment. Section 121 of the Internal Revenue Code of 1986 (as amended by this section) shall be applied without regard to subsection (c)(2)(B) thereof in the case of any sale or exchange of property during the 2-year period beginning on the date of the enactment of this Act if the taxpayer held such property on the date of the enactment of this Act and fails to meet the ownership and use requirements of subsection (a) thereof with respect to such property.

"(4) Binding contracts. At the election of the taxpayer, the amendments made by this section shall not apply to a sale or exchange after the date of the enactment of this Act, if —

"(A) such sale or exchange is pursuant to a contract which was binding on such date, or

"(B) without regard to such amendments, gain would not be recognized under section 1034 of the Internal Revenue Code of 1986 (as in effect on the day before the date of the enactment of this Act) on such sale or exchange by reason of a new residence acquired on or before such date or with respect to the acquisition of which by the taxpayer a binding contract was in effect on such date.

This paragraph shall not apply to any sale or exchange by an individual if the treatment provided by section 877(a)(1) of the Internal Revenue Code of 1986 applies to such individual."

—P.L. 105-34, Sec. 1225, added para. (b)(6), effective [as amended by Sec. 6012(d), 105-206, see above] for partnership tax. yrs. begin. after 12/31/97.

In 1988, P.L. 100-647, Sec. 1001(b)(2), amended subclause (a)(1)(C)(i)(I), effective for tax. yrs. begin. after 12/31/86.

Prior to amendment, clause (a)(1)(C)(i)(I) read as follows:

"(I) income (other than earned income) in excess of the amount in effect under section 63(c)(5)(A) (relating to limitation on standard deduction in the case of certain dependents), or"

In 1986, P.L. 99-514, Sec. 104(a)(1)(A), amended para. (a)(1) . . . Sec. 104(a)(1)(B), substituted "not less than the sum of the exemption amount plus the basic standard deduction under section 63(c)(2)(D)" for "$2,700 or more" in para. (a)(9), effective for tax. yrs. begin. after 12/31/86.

Prior to amendment, para. (a)(1) read as follows:

"(1)(A) Every individual having for the taxable year a gross income of the exemption amount or more, except that a return shall not be required of an individual (other than an individual described in subparagraph (c))—

"(i) who is not married (determined by applying section 143), is not a surviving spouse (as defined in section 2(a)), and for the taxable year has a gross income of less than the sum of the exemption amount plus the zero bracket amount applicable to such an individual,

"(ii) who is a surviving spouse (as so defined) and for the taxable year has a gross income of less than the sum of the exemption amount plus the zero bracket amount applicable to such an individual, or

"(iii) who is entitled to make a joint return under section 6013 and whose gross income, when combined with the gross income of his spouse, is, for the taxable year, less than the sum of twice the exemption amount plus the zero bracket amount applicable to a joint return, but only if such individual and his spouse, at the close of the taxable year, had the same household as their home.

Clause (iii) shall not apply if for the taxable year such spouse makes a separate return or any other taxpayer is entitled to an exemption for such spouse under section 151(e).

"(B) The amount specified in clause (i) or (ii) of subparagraph (A) shall be increased by the exemption amount in the case of an individual entitled to an additional personal exemption under section 151(c)(1), and the amount specified in clause (iii) of subparagraph (A) shall be increased by the exemption amount for each additional personal exemption to which the individual or his spouse is entitled under section 151(c);

"(C) The exception under subparagraph (A) shall not apply to —

"(i) a nonresident alien individual;

"(ii) a citizen of the United States entitled to the benefits of section 931;

"(iii) an individual making a return under section 443(a)(1) for a period of less than 12 months on account of a change in his annual accounting period;

"(iv) an individual who has income (other than earned income) of the exemption amount or more and who is described in section 63(e)(1)(D)); or

"(v) an estate or trust.

"(D) For purposes of this paragraph —

"(i) The term 'zero bracket amount' has the meaning given to such term by section 63(d).

"(ii) The term 'exemption amount' has the meaning given to such term by section 151(f)."

—P.L. 99-514, Sec. 1525(a), redesignated subsec. (d) as (e) and added new subsec. (d), effective for tax. yrs. begin. after 12/31/86.

In 1984, P.L. 98-369, Sec. 412(b)(3), deleted "or section 6015(a)" after "subsection (a)" in para. (b)(2), effective for tax. yrs. begin. after 12/31/84.

In 1983, P.L. 97-424, Sec. 542(a), and (b) provide:

"SEC. 542. NO RETURN REQUIRED OF INDIVIDUAL WHOSE ONLY GROSS INCOME IS GRANT OF $1,000 FROM STATE.

"(a) In General. — Nothing in section 6012(a) of the Internal Revenue Code of 1954 shall be construed to require the filing of a return with respect to income taxes under subtitle A of such code by an individual whose only gross income for the taxable year is a grant of $1,000 received from a State which made such grants generally to residents of such State.

"(b) Effective Date. — Subsection (a) shall apply to taxable years beginning after December 31, 1981."

In 1982, P.L. 97-248, Sec. 353, of this Act provides:

"SEC. 353. REPORT ON FORMS.

"Not later than June 30, 1983, the Secretary of the Treasury or his delegate shall study and report to the Congress methods of modifying the design of the forms used by the Internal Revenue Service to achieve greater accuracy in the reporting of income and the matching of information reports and returns with the returns of tax imposed by chapter 1 of the Internal Revenue Code of 1954"

In 1981, P.L. 97-34, Sec. 104(d)(1)(A), substituted "the sum of the exemption amount plus the zero bracket amount applicable to such an individual" for "$3,300" in clause (a)(1)(A)(i) . . . Sec. 104(d)(1)(B), substituted "the sum of the exemption amount plus the zero bracket amount applicable to such an individual" for "$4,400" in clause (a)(1)(A)(ii) . . . Sec. 104(d)(1)(C), substituted "the sum of twice the exemption amount plus the zero bracket amount applicable to a joint return" for "$5,400" in clause (a)(1)(A)(iii) . . . Sec. 104(d)(1)(D), substituted "the exemption amount" for "$1,000" each place it appeared in para. (a)(1) . . . Sec. 104(d)(1)(E), added new subpara. (a)(1)(D), effective for tax. yrs. begin. after 12/31/84.

—P.L. 97-34, Sec. 111(b)(3), substituted "relating to citizens or residents of the United States living abroad" for "relating to income earned by employees in certain camps", effective for tax. yrs. begin. after 12/13/81.

In 1980, P.L. 96-589, Sec. 3(b)(1), added new para. (a)(9) . . . Sec. 3(b)(2), substituted "an estate, a trust, or an estate of an individual under chapter 7 or 11 of title 11 of the United States Code" for "an estate or a trust" in para. (b)(4), effective for any bankruptcy case begin. after 3/25/81 [more than 90 days after the date of enactment (12/24/80)]. Sec. 7(g) of this Act provides:

"(g) Definitions.

"For purposes of this section —

"(1) Bankruptcy case. The term 'bankruptcy case' means any case under title 11 of the United States Code (as recodified by P.L. 95-598).

"(2) Similar judicial proceeding. The term 'similar judicial proceeding' means a receivership, foreclosure, or similar proceeding in a Federal or State court (as modified by section 368(a)(3)(D) of the Internal Revenue Code of 1954)."

—P.L. 96-589, Sec. 6(i)(5), substituted "trustee in a case under title 11 of the United States Code" for "trustee in bankruptcy" in para. (b)(3), effective 10/1/79, except for any proceeding under the Bankruptcy Act begun before 10/1/79. See Sec. 7(g) of this Act, reproduced above.

—P.L. 96-222, Sec. 108(a)(1)(A), redesignated Sec. 202(f) of P.L. 95-600 as Sec. 202(g) [see below].

In 1978, P.L. 95-615, Sec. 202(f)(5), substituted "income earned by employees in certain camps" for "earned income from sources without the United States" in subsec. (c), for tax. yrs. begin. after '77.

—P.L. 95-600, Sec. 101(c), substituted "$3,050" for "$2,950", substituted "$4,150" for "$3,950" and substituted "$4,900" for "$4,700" in para. (a)(1), effective for tax. yrs. begin. after 12/31/78.
—P.L. 95-600, Sec. 102(b)(1), substituted "$1,000", "$3,300", "$4,400", and "$5,400" for "$750", "$3,050", "$4,150", and "$4,900" respectively each place it appeared in para. (a)(1), as amended by Sec. 101(c) of this Act, effective for tax. yrs. begin. after 12/31/78.
—P.L. 95-600, Sec. 105(d), added para. (a)(8), effective for tax. yrs. begin. after 12/31/76.
—P.L. 95-600, Sec. 404(c)(8), substituted "relating to one-time exclusion of gain from sale of principal residence by individual who has attained age 55" for "relating to sale of residence by individual who has attained age 65" in subsec. (c), effective for sales or exchanges after 7/26/78, in tax. yrs. ending after 7/26/78. Sec. 404(d)(2), of the Act, provides as follows:
"In the case of a sale or exchange of a residence before July 26, 1981, a taxpayer who has attained age 65 on the date of such sale or exchange may elect to have section 121 of the Internal Revenue Code of 1954 applied by substituting '8-year period' for '5-year period' and '5 years' for '3 years' in subsections (a), (d)(2), and (d)(5) of such section."
In 1977, P.L. 95-30, Sec. 104, amended para. (a)(1), effective for tax. yrs. begin. after 12/31/76.
Prior to amendment, para. (a)(1) read as follows:
"(1)(A) Every individual having for the taxable year a gross income of $750 or more, except that a return shall not be required of an individual (other than an individual referred to in section 142(b))—
"(i) who is not married (determined by applying section 143), is not a surviving spouse (as defined in section 2(a)), and for the taxable year has a gross income of less than $2,450,
"(ii) who is a surviving spouse (as so defined) and for the taxable year has a gross income of less than $2,850, or
"(iii) who is entitled to make a joint return under section 6013 and whose gross income, when combined with the gross income of his spouse, is, for the taxable year, less than $3,600 but only if such individual and his spouse, at the close of the taxable year, had the same household as their home.
"Clause (iii) shall not apply if for the taxable year such spouse makes a separate return or any other taxpayer is entitled to an exemption for such spouse under section 151(e).
"(B) The amount specified in clause (i) or (ii) of subparagraph (A) shall be increased by $750 in the case of an individual entitled to an additional personal exemption under section 151(c)(1), and the amount specified in clause (iii) of subparagraph (A) shall be increased by $750 for each additional personal exemption to which the individual or his spouse is entitled under section 151(c);
"(C) Every individual having for the taxable year a gross income of $750 or more and to whom section 141(e) (relating to limitations in case of certain dependent taxpayers) applies;"
In 1976, P.L. 94-455, Sec. 401(b)(3), amended so much of para. (a)(1) as preceded subpara. (C), effective for tax. yrs. end. after 12/31/75.
Prior to amendment so much of para. (a)(1) that preceded subpara. (C) read as follows:
"(1)(A) Every individual having for the taxable year a gross income of $750 or more, except that a return shall not be required of an individual (other than an individual referred to in section 142(b))—
"(i) who is not married (determined by applying section 143(a)) and for the taxable year has a gross income of less than $2,050, or
"(ii) who is entitled to make a joint return under section 6013 and whose gross income, when combined with the gross income of his spouse, is, for the taxable year, less than $2,800 but only if such individual and his spouse, at the close of the taxable year, had the same household as their home.
Clause (ii) shall not apply if for the taxable year such spouse makes a separate return or any other taxpayer is entitled to an exemption for such spouse under section 151(e).
"(B) The $2,050 amount specified in subparagraph (A)(i) shall be increased to $2,800 in the case of an individual entitled to an additional personal exemption under section 151(c)(1), and the $2,800 amount specified in subparagraph (A)(ii) shall be increased by $750 for each additional personal exemption to which the individual or his spouse is entitled under section 151(c)."
—P.L. 94-455, Sec. 1906(b)(13)(A), substituted "Secretary" for "Secretary or his delegate" in subsec. (a), and para. (b)(5), effective 2/1/77.
—P.L. 94-455, Sec. 2101(c), deleted "and" at the end of para. (a)(5), added "and" at the end of para. (a)(6) and added para. (a)(7), effective for tax. yrs. begin. after 12/31/73.
In 1975, P.L. 94-164, Sec. 2(a)(2), substituted "$2,450" for "$2,350" in clause (a)(1)(A)(i), substituted "$2,650" for "$2,450" in clause (a)(1)(A)(ii), and substituted "$3,600" for "$3,400" in clause (a)(1)(A)(iii), effective for taxable years ending after 12/31/75 and before 1/1/77.
—P.L. 94-164, Sec. 2(e), extended the effective date for amendments made by Sec. 201(b) of P.L. 94-12, to include tax. yrs. end. after 12/31/74 and before 1/1/77.
—P.L. 94-12, Sec. 201(b), amended subparas. (a)(1)(A) and (B), effective for tax. yrs. end. after 12/31/74 and before 1/1/76.
Prior to amendment, subparas. (a)(1)(A) and (B), read as follows:
"(1)(A) Every individual having for the taxable year a gross income of $750 or more, except that a return shall not be required of an individual (other than an individual referred to in section 142(b))—
"(i) who is not married (determined by applying section 143), is not a surviving spouse (as defined in section 2(a)), and for the taxable year has a gross income of less than $2,350,

"(ii) who is a surviving spouse (as so defined) and for the taxable year has a gross income of less than $2,650, or
"(iii) who is entitled to make a joint return under section 6013 and whose gross income, when combined with the gross income of his spouse, is, for the taxable year, less than $3,400 but only if such individual and his spouse, at the close of the taxable year, had the same household as their home.
Clause (iii) shall not apply if for the taxable year such spouse makes a separate return or any other taxpayer is entitled to an exemption for such spouse under section 151(e).
"(B) The amount specified in clause (i) or (ii) of subparagraph (A) shall be increased by $750 in the case of an individual entitled to an additional personal exemption under section 151(c)(1), and the amount specified in clause (iii) of subparagraph (A) shall be increased by $750 for each additional personal exemption to which the individual or his spouse is entitled under section 151(c);"
—P.L. 93-625, Sec. 10(b), deleted "and" at the end of para. (a)(4), inserted "and" at the end of para. (a)(5), added new para. (a)(6), and deleted the final sentence in subsec. (a), effective for tax. yrs. begin. after 12/31/74.
Prior to deletion, the final sentence in subsec. (a) read as follows:
"The Secretary or his delegate shall, by regulation, exempt from the requirement of making returns under this section any political committee (as defined in section 301(d) of the Federal Election Campaign Act of 1971) having no gross income for the taxable year."
—Sec.10(f) of P.L. 93-625 provides as follows:
"(f) Exemption from filing requirement for prior years where income of political party was $100 or less.
"In the case of a taxable year beginning after December 31, 1971, and before January 1, 1975, nothing in the Internal Revenue Code of 1954 shall be deemed to require any organization described in section 527(e)(1) of such Code to file a return for the taxable year under such Code if such organization would be exempt from so filing under section 6012(a)(6) of such Code if such section applied to such taxable year."
In 1974, P.L. 93-443, Sec. 407, added the final sentence to subsec. (a), effective for tax. yrs. begin. after 12/31/71.
In 1971, P.L. 92-178, Sec. 204(a), substituted "$750" for "$600" each place it appeared; substituted "$2,050" for "$1,700" each place it appeared; substituted "$2,800" for "$2,300" each place it appeared; and added subpara. (a)(1)(C), effective for tax. yrs. begin. after 12/31/71.
In 1969, P.L. 91-172, Sec. 941(a), amended para. (a)(1), effective for tax. yrs. begin. after 12/31/69.
Prior to amendment para. (a)(1) read as follows:
"(1) Every individual having for the taxable year a gross income of $600 or more (except that any individual who has attained the age of 65 before the close of his taxable year shall be required to make a return only if he has for the taxable year a gross income of $1,200 or more);"
—P.L. 91-172, Sec. 941(d), amended para. (a)(1) for tax. yrs. begin. after 12/31/72.
In 1964, P.L. 88-272, Sec. 206(b)(1), amended subsec. (c), effective for dispositions after 12/31/63, in tax. yrs. end. after 12/31/62.
Prior to amendment, subsec. (c) read as follows:
"(c) Certain income earned abroad. For purposes of this section, gross income shall be computed without regard to the exclusion provided for in section 911 (relating to earned income from sources without the United States)."
In 1958, P.L. 85-866, Sec. 72(a), added subsec. (c) and redesignated former subsec. (c) as (d), effective for to tax. yrs. begin. after 12/31/57.

Sec. 6013. Joint returns of income tax by husband and wife.

(a) Joint returns.

A husband and wife may make a single return jointly of income taxes under subtitle A, even though one of the spouses has neither gross income nor deductions, except as provided below:

(1) no joint return shall be made if either the husband or wife at any time during the taxable year is a nonresident alien;

(2) no joint return shall be made if the husband and wife have different taxable years; except that if such taxable years begin on the same day and end on different days because of the death of either or both, then the joint return may be made with respect to the taxable year of each. The above exception shall not apply if the surviving spouse remarries before the close of his taxable year, nor if the taxable year of either spouse is a fractional part of a year under section 443(a)(1);

(3) in the case of death of one spouse or both spouses the joint return with respect to the decedent may be made only by his executor or administrator; except that in the case of the death of one spouse the joint return may be made by the surviving spouse with respect to both himself and the decedent if no return for the taxable year has been made by the decedent, no executor or administrator has been appointed, and no executor or administrator is appointed before the last day prescribed by law for filing the return of the surviving spouse. If an executor or administrator of the decedent is appointed after the making of the joint return by the surviving spouse, the executor or administrator may disaffirm such joint return by making, within 1 year after the last day prescribed by law for filing the return of the surviving spouse, a separate return for the taxable year of the decedent with respect to which the joint return was made, in which case the return made by the survivor shall constitute his separate return.

(b) Joint return after filing separate return.

(1) **In general.** Except as provided in paragraph (2), if an individual has filed a separate return for a taxable year for which a joint return could have been made by him and his spouse under subsection (a) and the time prescribed by law for filing the return for such taxable year has expired, such individual and his spouse may nevertheless make a joint return for such taxable year. A joint return filed by the husband and wife under this subsection shall constitute the return of the husband and wife for such taxable year, and all payments, credits, refunds, or other repayments made or allowed with respect to the separate return of either spouse for such taxable year shall be taken into account in determining the extent to which the tax based upon the joint return has been paid. If a joint return is made under this subsection, any election (other than the election to file a separate return) made by either spouse in his separate return for such taxable year with respect to the treatment of any income, deduction, or credit of such spouse shall not be changed in the making of the joint return where such election would have been irrevocable if the joint return had not been made. If a joint return is made under this subsection after the death of either spouse, such return with respect to the decedent can be made only by his executor or administrator.

(2) **Limitations for making of election.** The election provided for in paragraph (1) may not be made—

(A) after the expiration of 3 years from the last date prescribed by law for filing the return for such taxable year (determined without regard to any extension of time granted to either spouse); or

(B) after there has been mailed to either spouse, with respect to such taxable year, a notice of deficiency under section 6212, if the spouse, as to such notice, files a petition with the Tax Court within the time prescribed in section 6213; or

(C) after either spouse has commenced a suit in any court for the recovery of any part of the tax for such taxable year; or

(D) after either spouse has entered into a closing agreement under section 7121 with respect to such taxable year, or after any civil or criminal case arising against either spouse with respect to such taxable year has been compromised under section 7122.

(3) **When return deemed filed.**

(A) Assessment and collection. For purposes of section 6501 (relating to periods of limitations on assessment and collection), and for purposes of section 6651 (relating to delinquent returns), a joint return made under this subsection shall be deemed to have been filed—

(i) Where both spouses filed separate returns prior to making the joint return—on the date the last separate return was filed (but not earlier than the last date prescribed by law for filing the return of either spouse);

(ii) Where only one spouse filed a separate return prior to the making of the joint return, and the other spouse had less than the exemption amount of gross income for such taxable year—on the date of the filing of such separate return (but not earlier than the last date prescribed by law for the filing of such separate return); or

(iii) Where only one spouse filed a separate return prior to the making of the joint return, and the other spouse had gross income of the exemption amount or more for such taxable year—on the date of the filing of such joint return.

For purposes of this subparagraph, the term "exemption amount" has the meaning given to such term by section 151(d). For purposes of clauses (ii) and (iii), if the spouse whose gross income is being compared to the exemption amount is 65 or over, such clauses shall be applied by substituting "the sum of the exemption amount and the additional standard deduction under section 63(c)(2) by reason of section 63(f)(1)(A)" for "the exemption amount".

(B) Credit or refund. For purposes of section 6511, a joint return made under this subsection shall be deemed to have been filed on the last date prescribed by law for filing the return for such taxable year (determined without regard to any extension of time granted to either spouse).

(4) **Additional time for assessment.** If a joint return is made under this subsection, the periods of limitations provided in sections 6501 and 6502 on the making of assessments and the beginning of levy or a proceeding in court for collection shall with respect to such return include one year immediately after the date of the filing of such joint return (computed without regard to the provisions of paragraph (3)).

(5) **Additions to the tax and penalties.**

(A) Coordination with part II of subchapter A of chapter 68. For purposes of part II of subchapter A of chapter 68, where the sum of the amounts shown as tax on the separate returns of each spouse is less than the amount shown as tax on the joint return made under this subsection—

(i) such sum shall be treated as the amount shown on the joint return,

(ii) any negligence (or disregard of rules or regulations) on either separate return shall be treated as negligence (or such disregard) on the joint return, and

(iii) any fraud on either separate return shall be treated as fraud on the joint return.

(B) Criminal penalty. For purposes of section 7206(1) and (2) and section 7207 (relating to criminal penalties in the case of fraudulent returns) the term "return" includes a separate return filed by a spouse with respect to a taxable year for which a joint return is made under this subsection after the filing of such separate return.

(c) Treatment of joint return after death of either spouse.

For purposes of sections 15, 443, and 7851(a)(1)(A), where the husband and wife have different taxable years because of the death of either spouse, the joint return shall be treated as if the taxable years of both spouses ended on the date of the closing of the surviving spouse's taxable year.

(d) Special rules.

For purposes of this section—

(1) the status as husband and wife of two individuals having taxable years beginning on the same day shall be determined—

(A) if both have the same taxable year—as of the close of such year; or

(B) if one dies before the close of the taxable year of the other—as of the time of such death;

(2) an individual who is legally separated from his spouse under a decree of divorce or of separate maintenance shall not be considered as married; and

(3) if a joint return is made, the tax shall be computed on the aggregate income and the liability with respect to the tax shall be joint and several.

(e) Repealed.

(f) Joint return where individual is in missing status. For purposes of this section and subtitle A—

(1) Election by spouse. If—

(A) an individual is in a missing status (within the meaning of paragraph (3)) as a result of service in a combat zone (as determined for purposes of section 112), and

(B) the spouse of such individual is otherwise entitled to file a joint return for any taxable year which begins on or before the day which is 2 years after the date designated under section 112 as the date of termination of combatant activities in such zone,

then such spouse may elect under subsection (a) to file a joint return for such taxable year. With respect to service in the combat zone designated for purposes of the Vietnam conflict, such election may be made for any taxable year while an individual is in missing status.

(2) Effect of election. If the spouse of an individual described in paragraph (1)(A) elects to file a joint return under subsection (a) for a taxable year, then, until such election is revoked—

(A) such election shall be valid even if such individual died before the beginning of such year, and

(B) except for purposes of section 692 (relating to income taxes of members of the Armed Forces, astronauts, and victims of certain terrorist attacks on death), the income tax liability of such individual, his spouse, and his estate shall be determined as if he were alive throughout the taxable year.

(3) Missing status. For purposes of this subsection—

(A) Uniformed services. A member of a uniformed service (within the meaning of section 101(3) of title 37 of the United States Code) is in a missing status for any period for which he is entitled to pay and allowances under section 552 of such title 37.

(B) Civilian employees. An employee (within the meaning of section 5561(2) of title 5 of the United States Code) is in a missing status for any period for which he is entitled to pay and allowances under section 5562 of such title 5.

(4) Making of election; revocation. An election described in this subsection with respect to any taxable year may be made by filing a joint return in accordance with subsection (a) and under such regulations as may be prescribed by the Secretary. Such an election may be revoked by either spouse on or before the due date (including extensions) for such taxable year, and, in the case of an executor or administrator, may be revoked by disaffirming as provided in the last sentence of subsection (a)(3).

(g) Election to treat nonresident alien individual as resident of the United States.

(1) In general. A nonresident alien individual with respect to whom this subsection is in effect for the taxable year shall be treated as a resident of the United States—

(A) for purposes of chapter 1 for all of such taxable year, and

(B) for purposes of chapter 24 (relating to wage withholding) for payments of wages made during such taxable year.

(2) Individuals with respect to whom this subsection is in effect. This subsection shall be in effect with respect to any individual who, at the close of the taxable year for which an election under this subsection was made, was a nonresident alien individual married to a citizen or resident of the United States, if both of them made such election to have the benefits of this subsection apply to them.

(3) Duration of election. An election under this subsection shall apply to the taxable year for which made and to all subsequent taxable years until terminated under paragraph (4) or (5); except that any such election shall not apply for any taxable year if neither spouse is a citizen or resident of the United States at any time during such year.

(4) Termination of election. An election under this subsection shall terminate at the earliest of the following times:

(A) Revocation by taxpayers. If either taxpayer revokes the election, as of the first taxable year for which the last day prescribed by law for filing the return of tax under chapter 1 has not yet occurred.

(B) Death. In the case of the death of either spouse, as of the beginning of the first taxable year of the spouse who survives following the taxable year in which such death occurred; except that if the spouse who survives is a citizen or resident of the United States who is a surviving spouse entitled to the benefits of section 2, the time provided by this subparagraph shall be as of the close of the last taxable year for which such individual is entitled to the benefits of section 2.

(C) Legal separation. In the case of the legal separation of the couple under a decree of divorce or of separate maintenance, as of the beginning of the taxable year in which such legal separation occurs.

(D) Termination by Secretary. At the time provided in paragraph (5).

(5) Termination by Secretary. The Secretary may terminate any election under this subsection for any taxable year if he determines that either spouse has failed—

(A) to keep such books and records,

(B) to grant such access to such books and records, or

(C) to supply such other information,

as may be reasonably necessary to ascertain the amount of liability for taxes under chapter 1 of either spouse for such taxable year.

(6) Only one election. If any election under this subsection for any two individuals is terminated under paragraph (4) or (5) for any taxable year, such two individuals shall be ineligible to make an election under this subsection for any subsequent taxable year.

(h) Joint return, etc., for year in which nonresident alien becomes resident of United States.

(1) In general. If—

(A) any individual is a nonresident alien individual at the beginning of any taxable year but is a resident of the United States at the close of such taxable year,

(B) at the close of such taxable year, such individual is married to a citizen or resident of the United States, and

(C) both individuals elect the benefits of this subsection at the time and in the manner prescribed by the Secretary by regulation,

then the individual referred to in subparagraph (A) shall be treated as a resident of the United States for purposes of chapter 1 for all of such taxable year, and for purposes of chapter 24 (relating to wage withholding) for payments of wages made during such taxable year.

(2) Only one election. If any election under this subsection applies for any 2 individuals for any taxable year, such 2 individuals shall be ineligible to make an election under this subsection for any subsequent taxable year.

In 2003, P.L. 108-121, Sec. 110(a)(2)(B), added ", astronauts," after "Forces" in subpara. (f)(2)(B), effective for any astronaut whose death occurs after 12/31/2002.

In 2002, P.L. 107-134, Sec. 101(b)(2), added "and victims of certain terrorist attacks" after "Armed Forces" in subpara. (f)(2)(B), effective for tax. yrs. end. before, on, or after 9/11/2001. Sec. 101(d)(2) of this Act provides:

"(2) Waiver of limitations. If refund or credit of any overpayment of tax resulting from the amendments made by this section is prevented at any time before the close of the 1-year period beginning on the date of the enactment of this Act by the operation of any law or rule of law (including res judicata), such refund or credit may nevertheless be made or allowed if claim therefor is filed before the close of such period."

In 1998, P.L. 105-206, Sec. 3201(d), of this Act provides:
"(d) Separate notice to each filer. The Secretary of the Treasury shall, wherever practicable, send any notice relating to a joint return under section 6013 of the Internal Revenue Code of 1986 separately to each individual filing the joint return."
— P.L. 105-206, Sec. 3201(e)(1), deleted subsec. (e), effective for any liability for tax arising after 7/22/98 and any liability for tax arising on or before 7/22/98 but remaining unpaid as of 7/22/98.
Sec. 3201(g)(2) of this Act provides:

"(2) 2-year period. The 2-year period under subsection (b)(1)(E) or (c)(3)(B) of section 6015 of the Internal Revenue Code of 1986 shall not expire before the date which is 2 years after the date of the first collection activity after the date of the enactment of this Act."
Prior to deletion, subsec. (e) read as follows:
"(e) Spouse relieved of liability in certain cases.
"(1) In general. Under regulations prescribed by the Secretary, if—
"(A) a joint return has been made under this section for a taxable year,
"(B) on such return there is a substantial understatement of tax attributable to grossly erroneous items of one spouse,
"(C) the other spouse establishes that in signing the return he or she did not know, and had no reason to know, that there was such substantial understatement, and
"(D) taking into account all the facts and circumstances, it is inequitable to hold the other spouse liable for the deficiency in tax for such taxable year attributable to such substantial understatement,
then the other spouse shall be relieved of liability for tax (including interest, penalties, and other amounts) for such taxable year to the extent such liability is attributable to such substantial understatement.

"(2) Grossly erroneous items. For purposes of this subsection, the term 'grossly erroneous items' means, with respect to any spouse—
"(A) any item of gross income attributable to such spouse which is omitted from gross income, and
"(B) any claim of a deduction, credit, or basis by such spouse in an amount for which there is no basis in fact or law.
"(3) Substantial understatement. For purposes of this subsection, the term 'substantial understatement' means any understatement (as defined in section 6662(d)(2)(A)) which exceeds $500.
"(4) Understatement must exceed specified percentage of spouse's income.
"(A) Adjusted gross income of $20,000 or less. If the spouse's adjusted gross income for the preadjustment year is $20,000 or less, this subsection shall apply only if the liability described in paragraph (1) is greater than 10 percent of such adjusted gross income.
"(B) Adjusted gross income of more than $20,000. If the spouse's adjusted gross income for the preadjustment year is more than $20,000, subparagraph (A) shall be applied by substituting '25 percent' for '10 percent'.
"(C) Preadjustment year. For purposes of this paragraph, the term 'preadjustment year' means the most recent taxable year of the spouse ending before the date the deficiency notice is mailed.
"(D) Computation of spouse's adjusted gross income. If the spouse is married to another spouse at the close of the preadjustment year, the spouse's adjusted gross income shall include the income of the new spouse (whether or not they file a joint return).
"(E) Exception for omissions from gross income. This paragraph shall not apply to any liability attributable to the omission of an item from gross income.
"(5) Special rule for community property income. For purposes of this subsection, the determination of the spouse to whom items of gross income (other than gross income from property) are attributable shall be made without regard to community property laws."
— P.L. 105-206, Sec. 6011(e)(2), substituted "chapter 1" for "chapters 1 and 5" each place it appeared in subpara. (g)(1)(A), para. (g)(5) and para. (h)(1), effective 8/5/97.

In 1996, P.L. 104-168, Sec. 402(a), deleted subpara. (b)(2)(A) and redesignated subparas. (b)(2)(B) - (E) as (b)(2)(A) - (D), effective for tax. yrs. begin. after 7/30/96.
Prior to amendment, subpara. (b)(2)(A) read as follows:
"(A) unless there is paid in full at or before the time of the filing of the joint return the amount shown as tax upon such joint return; or"

— P.L. 104-117, Sec. 1(a)(7) and (b), of this Act, regarding treatment of certain individuals performing services in certain hazardous duty areas, effective 11/21/95, provides:
"(a) General rule. For purposes of the following provisions of the Internal Revenue Code of 1986, a qualified hazardous duty area shall be treated in the same manner as if it were a combat zone (as determined under section 112 of such Code):
* * *
"(7) Section 6013(f)(1) (relating to joint return where individual is in missing status).
* * *
"(b) Qualified hazardous duty area. For purposes of this section, the term 'qualified hazardous duty area' means Bosnia and Herzegovina, Croatia, or Macedonia, if as of the date of the enactment [3/20/96] of this section any member of the Armed Forces of the United States is entitled to special pay under section 310 of title 37, United States Code (relating to special pay; duty subject to hostile fire or imminent danger) for services performed in such country. Such term includes any such country only during the period such entitlement is in effect. Solely for purposes of applying section 7508 of the Internal Revenue Code of 1986, in the case of an individual who is performing services as part of Operation Joint Endeavor outside the United States while deployed away from such individual's permanent duty station, the term 'qualified hazardous duty area' includes, during the period for which such entitlement is in effect, any area in which such services are performed."

In 1990, P.L. 101-508, Sec. 11704(a)(22), substituted "section 6662(d)(2)(A)" for "section 6661(b)(2)(A)" in para. (e)(3), effective 11/5/90.

In 1989, P.L. 101-239, Sec. 7721(c)(6)(A), substituted "part II of subchapter A of chapter 68" for "section 6653" in subpara. (b)(5)(A) . . . Sec. 7721(c)(6)(B), substituted "part II of subchapter A of chapter 68" for "section 6653" in the heading of subpara. (b)(5)(A), effective for returns the due date for which (determined without regard to extensions) is after 12/31/89.

In 1988, P.L. 100-647, Sec. 1015(b)(1), amended subpara. (b)(5)(A), effective for returns the due date for which (determined without regard to extensions) is after 12/31/88.
Prior to amendment, subpara. (b)(5)(A) read as follows:
"(A) Additions to the tax. Where the amount shown as the tax by the husband and wife on a joint return made under this subsection exceeds the aggregate of the amounts shown as the tax upon the separate return of each spouse—
"(i) Negligence. If any part of such excess is attributable to negligence or intentional disregard of rules and regulations (but without intent to defraud) at the time of the making of such separate return, then 5 percent of the total amount of such excess shall be added to the tax;
"(ii) Fraud. If any part of such excess is attributable to fraud with intent to evade tax at the time of the making of such separate return, then 50 percent of the total amount of such excess shall be added to the tax."
— P.L. 100-647, Sec. 6004, added Sec. 424(c)(3) of P.L. 98-369, transitional rules for changes made by Sec. 424(a) of P.L. 98-369, see below.

In 1986, P.L. 99-514, Sec. 104(a)(2)(A), deleted "(twice the exemption amount in case such spouse was 65 or over)" each place it appeared in subpara. (b)(3)(A) . . . Sec. 104(a)(2)(B), substituted "section 151(d)" for "section 151(f)" in subpara. (b)(3)(A) . . . Sec. 104(a)(2)(C), added the last sentence to subpara. (b)(3)(A), effective for tax. yrs. begin. after 12/31/86.
— P.L. 99-514, Sec. 1708(a)(3), substituted "such election may be made for any taxable year while an individual is in missing status" for "no such election may be made for any taxable year beginning after December 31, 1982" in the last sentence of para. (f)(1), effective for tax. yrs. begin. after 12/31/82.

In 1984, P.L. 98-369, Sec. 424(a), amended subsec. (e), effective as provided in Sec. 424(c)(1) of this Act, which reads as follows:
"(1) In general.—Except as provided in paragraph (2), [not applicable to Code Sec. 6013] the amendments made by subsections (a) and (b) shall apply to all taxable years to which the Internal Revenue Code of 1954 applies. Corresponding provisions shall be deemed to be included in the Internal Revenue Code of 1939 and shall apply to all taxable years to which such Code applies."
— P.L. 98-369, Sec. 424(c)(3), of this Act, [as added by Sec. 6004 of P.L. 100-647] provides:
"(3) Transitional rule.—If—
"(A) a joint return under section 6013 of the Internal Revenue Code of 1954 was filed before January 1, 1985.
"(B) on such return there is an understatement (as defined in section 6661(b)(2)(A) of such Code) which is attributable to disallowed deductions attributable to activities of one spouse,
"(C) the amount of such disallowed deductions exceeds the taxable income shown on such return,
"(D) without regard to any determination before October 21, 1988, the other spouse establishes that in signing the return he or she did not know, and had no reason to know, that there was such an understatement, and
"(E) the marriage between such spouses terminated and immediately after such termination the net worth of the other spouse was less than $10,000
notwithstanding any law or rule of law (including res judicata), the other spouse shall be relieved of liability for tax (including interest, penalties, and other amounts) for such taxable year to the extent such liability is attributable to such understatement, and, to the extent the liability so attributable has been collected from such other spouse, it shall be refunded or credited to such other spouse. No credit or refund shall be made under the preceding sentence unless claim therefor has been submitted to the Secretary of the Treasury or his delegate before the date 1 year after the date of the enactment of this paragraph, and no interest on such credit or refund shall be allowed for any period before such [7/22/98]"

Information and returns   Code Sec. 6014(a)

Prior to amendment, subsec. (e) read as follows:
"(e) Spouse relieved of liability in certain cases.
"(1) In general. Under regulations prescribed by the Secretary or his delegate, if—
"(A) a joint return has been made under this section for a taxable year and on such return there was omitted from gross income an amount properly includable therein which is attributable to one spouse and which is in excess of 25 percent of the amount of gross income stated in the return.
"(B) the other spouse establishes that in signing the return he or she did not know of, and had no reason to know of, such omission, and
"(C) taking into account whether or not the other spouse significantly benefited directly or indirectly from the items omitted from gross income and taking into account all other facts and circumstances, it is inequitable to hold the other spouse liable for the deficiency in tax for such taxable year attributable to such omission, then the other spouse shall be relieved of liability for tax (including interest, penalties, and other amounts) for such taxable year to the extent that such liability is attributable to such omission from gross income.
"(2) Special rules. For purposes of paragraph (1)—
"(A) the determination of spouse to whom item of gross income (other than gross income from property) are attributable shall be made without regard to community property laws, and
"(B) the amount omitted from gross income shall be determined in the manner provided by section 6501(e)(1)(A)."
—P.L. 98-369, Sec. 474(b)(2), substituted "15" for "21" in subsec. (c), effective for tax. yrs. begin. after 12/31/83, and to carrybacks from 12/31/83.
In 1983, P.L. 98-67, Sec. 102(a), repealed as if not enacted amendments made by Sec. 307(a)(4) and 307(a)(5) of P.L. 97-248 [see below].
—P.L. 97-448, Sec. 307(c), substituted "December 31, 1982" for "January 2, 1978" in the last sentence of para. (f)(1).
In 1982, P.L. 97-248, Sec. 307(a)(4), substituted "[sic]relating to withholding on wages, interest, dividends, and patronage dividends)" for "(relating to wage withholding)", and deleted "of wages" in subpara. (g)(1)(B) . . . Sec. 307(a)(5), substituted "(relating to withholding on wages, interest, dividends, and patronage dividends)" for "(relating to wage withholding)", and deleted "of wages" in para. (h)(1), effective 7/1/83. [These amendments were repealed as if not enacted by Sec. 102(a) of P.L. 98-67, see above.]
In 1981, P.L. 97-34, Sec. 104(d)(2)(A), substituted "the exemption amount" for "$1,000" each place it appeared in subpara. (b)(3)(A) . . . Sec. 104(d)(2)(B), substituted "twice the exemption amount" for "$2,000" each place it appeared in subpara. (b)(3)(A) . . . Sec. 104(d)(2)(C), added the last sentence to subpara. (b)(3)(A), effective for tax. yrs. begin. after 12/31/84.
In 1980, P.L. 96-449, Sec. 203, provides:
"Sec. 203. Spouse may file joint return.
"(a) General rule. If an individual is an American hostage who is in captive status, such individual's spouse may elect to file a joint return under section 6013(a) of the Internal Revenue Code of 1954 for any taxable year—
"(1) which begins on or before the day which is 2 years after the date of which the hostage period ends, and
"(2) for which such spouse is otherwise entitled to file such a joint return.
"(b) Certain rules made applicable. For purposes of subsection (a), paragraphs (2) and (4) of section 6013(f) of such Code (relating to joint return where individual is in missing status) shall apply as if the election described in subsection (a) of this section were an election described in paragraph (1) of such section 6013(f)."
For definitions and special rules see Sec. 205 of P.L. 96-449 reproduced in note following Code Sec. 1.
In 1978, P.L. 95-600, Sec. 102(b)(2), substituted "$1,000" for "$750", and substituted "$2,000" for "$1,500" each place it appeared in subpara. (b)(3)(A), effective for tax. yrs. begin. after 12/31/78.
—P.L. 95-600, Sec. 701(u)(15)(A), amended para. (g)(1) . . . Sec. 701(u)(15)(B), substituted "chapters 1 and 5" for "chapter 1" in para. (g)(5) . . . Sec. 701(u)(15)(C), substituted "chapters 1 and 5" for "chapter 1" in para. (h)(1), and added ", and for purposes of chapter 24 (relating to wage withholding) for payments of wages made during such taxable year." after "taxable year" at the end of para. (h)(1), effective as provided in Sec. 701(u)(15)(E), of this Act, which reads as follows:
"(E) Effective dates. The amendments made by this paragraph—
"(i) to the extent that they relate to chapter 1 or 5 of the Internal Revenue Code of 1954, shall apply to taxable years ending on or after December 31, 1975, and
"(ii) to the extent that they relate to wage withholding under chapter 24 of such Code, shall apply to remuneration paid on or after the first day of the first month which begins more than 90 days after the date of the enactment of this Act."
Prior to amendment, para. (g)(1) read as follows:
"(1) In general. A nonresident alien individual with respect to whom this subsection is in effect for the taxable year shall be treated as a resident of the United States for purposes of chapter 1 for all of such taxable year."
—P.L. 95-600, Sec. 701(u)(16)(A), substituted "who, at the close of the taxable year for which an election under this subsection was made," for "who, at the time an election was made under this subsection," in para. (g)(2), effective for tax. yrs. begin. after 12/31/78.
In 1976, P.L. 94-569, Sec. 3(d), substituted "after January 2, 1978" for "more than 2 years after the date of the enactment of this sentence" in the last sentence of para. (f)(1), effective 10/20/76.
—P.L. 94-455, Sec. 1012(a), added subsecs. (g) and (h), effective for tax. yrs. end. on or after 12/31/75.
—P.L. 94-455, Sec. 1906(a)(1)(A), deleted "of the United States" after "Tax Court" in subpara. (b)(2)(C) . . . Sec. 1906(a)(1)(B), amended the heading of subsec. (d) . . . Sec. 1906(a)(1)(C), substituted "or" for "and" at the end subpara.

(d)(1)(A), and deleted "and" at the end of subpara. (d)(1)(B), effective on the first day of the first month that begins more than 90 days after 10/4/76.
Prior to amendment the heading of subsec. (d) read as follows:
"(d) Definitions."
—P.L. 94-455, Sec. 1906(a)(13)(A), substituted "Secretary" for "Secretary or his delegate" in para. (f)(4), effective 2/1/77.
—P.L. 94-455, Sec. 2114(a), amended Sec. 3 of P.L. 91-679 [effective date for changes made by Sec. 1 of P.L. 91-679, see below] by adding the following to the end thereof:
"Upon application by a taxpayer, the Secretary of the Treasury shall redetermine the liability for tax (including interest, penalties, and other amounts) of such taxpayer for taxable years beginning after December 31, 1961, and ending before January 13, 1971. The preceding sentence shall apply solely to a taxpayer to whom the application of the provisions of section 6013(e) of the Internal Revenue Code of 1954, as added by this Act, for such taxable years is prevented by the operation of res judicata, and such redetermination shall be made without regard to such rule of law. Any overpayment of tax by such taxpayer for such taxable years resulting from the redetermination made under this Act shall be refunded to such taxpayer."
Effective as provided in Sec. 2114(b) of this Act, which reads as follows:
"(b) Effective date. The application permitted under the amendment made by subsection (a) of this section must be filed with the Secretary of the Treasury during the first calendar year beginning after the date of the enactment of this Act [10/4/76]."
In 1975, P.L. 93-597, Sec. 3(a), added subsec. (f), effective for tax. yrs. end. on or after 2/28/61.
In 1971, P.L. 92-178, Sec. 201(a)(2), substituted "$675" for "$650", and substituted "$1,350" for "$1,300" each place they appeared in subpara. (b)(3)(A), effective for tax. yrs. begin. after 12/31/70 and before 1/1/72.
—P.L. 92-178, Sec. 201(b)(2), substituted "$750" for "$675", and substituted "$1,500" for "$1,350" each place they appear in subpara. (b)(3)(A) [as amended by Sec. 201(a)(2) of this Act, see above], effective for tax. yrs. begin. after 12/31/71.
—P.L. 92-178, Sec. 201(c), repealed subsecs. 801(c) and 801(d) of P.L. 91-172 which made amendments to subpara. (b)(3)(A), see below.
—P.L. 91-679, Sec. 1, added subsec. (e), effective as provided in Sec. 3 of this Act [as amended by Sec. 2114(a) of P.L. 94-455, see above], which provides:
"Sec. 3. The amendments made by the first two sections of this Act shall apply to all taxable years to which the Internal Revenue Code of 1954 applies. Corresponding provisions shall be deemed to be included in the Internal Revenue Code of 1939 and shall apply to all taxable years to which such Code applies. Upon application by a taxpayer, the Secretary of the Treasury shall redetermine the liability for tax (including interest, penalties, and other amounts) of such taxpayer for taxable years beginning after December 31, 1961, and ending before January 13, 1971. The preceding sentence shall apply solely to a taxpayer to whom the application of the provisions of section 6013(e) of the Internal Revenue Code of 1954, as added by this Act, for such taxable years is prevented by the operation of res judicata, and such redetermination shall be made without regard to such rule of law. Any overpayment of tax by such taxpayer for such taxable years resulting from the redetermination made under this Act shall be refunded to such taxpayer."
In 1969, P.L. 91-172, Sec. 801(a)(2), substituted "$625" for "$600", and substituted "$1,250" for "$1,200" each place they appeared in subpara. (b)(3)(A), effective for tax. yrs. begin. after 12/31/69.
—P.L. 91-172, Sec. 801(b)(2), substituted "$650" for "$625", and substituted "$1,300" for "$1,250" each place they appeared in subpara. (b)(3)(A), effective for tax. yrs. begin. after 12/31/70.
—P.L. 91-172, Sec. 801(c)(2), substituted "$700" for "$650", and substituted "$1,400" for "$1,300" each place they appeared in subpara. (b)(3)(A) [amendment repealed by Sec. 201(c) of P.L. 92-178, see above], effective for tax. yrs. begin. after 12/31/71.
—P.L. 91-172, Sec. 801(d)(2), substituted "$750" for "$700", and substituted "$1,500" for "$1,400" each place they appeared in subpara. (b)(3)(A) [amendment repealed by Sec. 201(c) of P.L. 92-178, see above], effective for tax. yrs. begin. after 12/31/72.
In 1958, P.L. 85-866, Sec. 73, substituted "section 6213" for "such section" in subpara. (b)(2)(C), effective 8/17/54 (as provided in Code Sec. 7851).

Sec. 6014. Income tax return—tax not computed by taxpayer.

(a) Election by taxpayer.

An individual who does not itemize his deductions and who is not described in section 6012(a)(1)(C)(i), whose gross income is less than $10,000 and includes no income other than remuneration for services performed by him as an employee, dividends or interest, and whose gross income other than wages, as defined in section 3401(a), does not exceed $100, shall at his election not be required to show on the return the tax imposed by section 1. Such election shall be made by using the form prescribed for purposes of this section. In such case the tax shall be computed by the Secretary who shall mail to the taxpayer a notice stating the amount determined as payable.

3,489

Code Sec. 6014(b)

(b) Regulations.

The Secretary shall prescribe regulations for carrying out this section, and such regulations may provide for the application of the rules of this section—

(1) to cases where the gross income includes items other than those enumerated by subsection (a),

(2) to cases where the gross income from sources other than wages on which the tax has been withheld at the source is more than $100,

(3) to cases where the gross income is $10,000 or more, or

(4) to cases where the taxpayer itemizes his deductions or where the taxpayer claims a reduced standard deduction by reason of section 63(c)(5).

Such regulations shall provide for the application of this section in the case of husband and wife, including provisions determining when a joint return under this section may be permitted or required, whether the liability shall be joint and several, and whether one spouse may make return under this section and the other without regard to this section.

In **1986**, P.L. 99-514, Sec. 104(b)(16)(A), substituted "who is not described in section 6012(a)(1)(C)(i)" for "who does not have an unused zero bracket amount (determined under section 63(e))" in subsec. (a)... Sec. 104(b)(16)(B), amended para. (b)(4), effective for tax. yrs. begin. after 12/31/86.
Prior to amendment, para (b)(4) read as follows:
"(4) to cases where the taxpayer itemizes his deductions or has an unused zero bracket amount."

In **1977**, P.L. 95-30, Sec. 101(d)(13), substituted "who does not itemize his deductions and who does not have an unused zero bracket amount (determined under section 63(e))," for "entitled to take the standard deduction provided by section 141 (other than an individual described in section 141(e))" in the first sentence of subsec. (a), and deleted "and shall constitute an election to take the standard deduction", after "of this section", in the second sentence of subsec. (a), effective for tax. yrs. begin. after 12/31/76.
—P.L. 95-30, Sec. 101(d)(14), amended para. (b)(4), effective for tax. yrs. begin. after 12/31/76.
Prior to amendment, para. (b)(4) read as follows:
"(4) to cases where the taxpayer does not elect the standard deduction or where the taxpayer elects the standard deduction but is subject to the provisions of section 141(e) (relating to limitations in case of certain dependent taxpayers)."

In **1976**, P.L. 94-455, Sec. 501(b)(8), substituted "entitled to take the standard deduction provided by section 141 (other than an individual described in section 141(e))" for "entitled to elect to pay the tax imposed by section 3" in the first sentence of subsec. (a), substituted "take the standard deduction" for "pay the tax imposed by section 3" in the second sentence of subsec. (a), effective for tax. yrs. begin. after 12/31/75.
—P.L. 94-455, Sec. 501(b)(9), amended para. (b)(5), effective for tax. yrs. begin. after 12/31/75.
Prior to amendment, para. (b)(5) read as follows:
"(5) to cases where the taxpayer does not elect the standard deduction."
—P.L. 94-455, Sec. 503(b)(2), deleted the last sentence of subsec. (a), effective for tax. yrs. begin. after 12/31/75.
Prior to deletion, the last sentence of subsec. (a) read as follows:
"In determining the amount payable, the credit against such tax provided for by section 37 shall not be allowed."
—P.L. 94-455, Sec. 503(b)(3), deleted para. (b)(4), redesignated para. (b)(5) [as amended by Sec. 501(b)(9) of the Act] as para. (b)(4), and added "or" at the end of para. (b)(3), effective for tax. yrs. begin. after 12/31/75.
Prior to deletion para. (b)(4) read as follows:
"(4) to cases where the taxpayer is entitled to the credit provided by section 37 (relating to retirement income credit), or".
—P.L. 94-455, Sec. 1906(b)(13)(A), substituted "Secretary" for "Secretary or his delegate" each place it appeared in Code Sec. 6014, effective 2/1/77.

In **1969**, P.L. 91-172, Sec. 803(d)(1), substituted "$10,000" for "$5,000" in the first sentence and deleted the last two sentences of subsec. (a), effective for tax. yrs. begin. after 12/31/69.
Prior to amendment, the last two sentences of subsec. (a) read as follows:
"In the case of a head of a household (as defined in section 1(b)) or a surviving spouse (as defined in section 2(b)) electing the benefits of this subsection, the tax shall be computed by the Secretary or his delegate without regard to the taxpayer's status as a head of household or as a surviving spouse. In the case of a married individual filing a separate return and electing the benefits of this subsection, neither Table V in section 3(a) nor Table V in section 3(b) shall apply."
—P.L. 91-172, Sec. 942, amended the first sentence of subsec. (b), effective for tax. yrs. begin. after 12/31/69.
Prior to amendment, the first sentence of subsec. (b) read as follows:
"The Secretary or his delegate shall prescribe regulations for carrying out this section, and such regulations may provide for the application of the rules of this section to cases where the gross income includes items other than those enumer-

Information and returns

ated by subsection (a), to cases where the gross income from sources other than wages on which the tax has been withheld at the source is more than $100 but not more than $200, and to cases where the gross income is $5,000 or more but not more than $5,200."

In **1964**, P.L. 88-272, Sec. 201(d)(14), deleted "34 or" before "37 shall not be allowed", in subsec. (a), effective for dividends received after 12/31/64 in tax. yrs. end. after 12/31/64 ... added last sentence in subsec. (a) for tax. yrs. begin. after '63.

Sec. 6015. Relief from joint and several liability on joint return.

(a) In general.

Notwithstanding section 6013(d)(3)—

(1) an individual who has made a joint return may elect to seek relief under the procedures prescribed under subsection(b), and

(2) if such individual is eligible to elect the application of subsection (c), such individual may, in addition to any election under paragraph (1), elect to limit such individual's liability for any deficiency with respect to such joint return in the manner prescribed under subsection (c).

Any determination under this section shall be made without regard to community property laws.

(b) Procedures for relief from liability applicable to all joint filers.

(1) In general. Under procedures prescribed by the Secretary, if—

(A) a joint return has been made for a taxable year;

(B) on such return there is an understatement of tax attributable to erroneous items of one individual filing the joint return;

(C) the other individual filing the joint return establishes that in signing the return he or she did not know, and had no reason to know, that there was such understatement,

(D) taking into account all the facts and circumstances, it is inequitable to hold the other individual liable for the deficiency in tax for such taxable year attributable to such understatement, and

(E) the other individual elects (in such form as the Secretary may prescribe) the benefits of this subsection not later than the date which is 2 years after the date the Secretary has begun collection activities with respect to the individual making the election,

then the other individual shall be relieved of liability for tax (including interest, penalties, and other amounts) for such taxable year to the extent such liability is attributable to such understatement.

(2) Apportionment of relief. If an individual who, but for paragraph (1)(C), would be relieved of liability under paragraph (1), establishes that in signing the return such individual did not know, and had no reason to know, the extent of such understatement, then such individual shall be relieved of liability for tax (including interest, penalties, and other amounts) for such taxable year to the extent that such liability is attributable to the portion of such understatement of which such individual did not know and had no reason to know.

(3) Understatement. For purposes of this subsection, the term "understatement" has the meaning given to such term by section 6662(d)(2)(A).

(c) Procedures to limit liability for taxpayers no longer married or taxpayers legally separated or not living together.

(1) In general. Except as provided in this subsection, if an individual who has made a joint return for any taxable year elects the application of this subsection, the individual's liability for any deficiency which is assessed with respect to the return shall not exceed the portion of such deficiency properly allocable to the individual under subsection (d).

(2) Burden of proof. Except as provided in subparagraph (A)(ii) or (C) of paragraph (3), each individual who elects the application of this subsection shall have the burden of proof with respect to establishing the portion of any deficiency allocable to such individual.

(3) Election.

(A) Individuals eligible to make election.

(i) In general. An individual shall only be eligible to elect the application of this subsection if—

(I) at the time such election is filed, such individual is no longer married to, or is legally separated from, the individual with whom such individual filed the joint return to which the election relates; or

(II) such individual was not a member of the same household as the individual with whom such joint return was filed at any time during the 12-month period ending on the date such election is filed.

(ii) Certain taxpayers ineligible to elect. If the Secretary demonstrates that assets were transferred between individuals filing a joint return as part of a fraudulent scheme by such individuals, an election under this subsection by either individual shall be invalid (and section 6013(d)(3) shall apply to the joint return).

(B) Time for election. An election under this subsection for any taxable year may be made at any time after a deficiency for such year is asserted but not later than 2 years after the date on which the Secretary has begun collection activities with respect to the individual making the election.

(C) Election not valid with respect to certain deficiencies. If the Secretary demonstrates that an individual making an election under this subsection had actual knowledge, at the time such individual signed the return, of any item giving rise to a deficiency (or portion thereof) which is not allocable to such individual under subsection (d), such election shall not apply to such deficiency (or portion). This subparagraph shall not apply where the individual with actual knowledge establishes that individual signed the return under duress.

(4) Liability increased by reason of transfers of property to avoid tax.

(A) In general. Notwithstanding any other provision of this subsection, the portion of the deficiency for which the individual electing the application of this subsection is liable (without regard to this paragraph) shall be increased by the value of any disqualified asset transferred to the individual.

(B) Disqualified asset. For purposes of this paragraph—

(i) In general. The term "disqualified asset" means any property or right to property transferred to an individual making the election under this subsection with respect to a joint return by the other individual filing such joint return if the principal purpose of the transfer was the avoidance of tax or payment of tax.

(ii) Presumption.

(I) In general. For purposes of clause (i), except as provided in subclause (II), any transfer which is made after the date which is 1 year before the date on which the first letter of proposed deficiency which allows the taxpayer an opportunity for administrative review in the Internal Revenue Service Office of Appeals is sent shall be presumed to

have as its principal purpose the avoidance of tax or payment of tax.

(II) Exceptions. Subclause (I) shall not apply to any transfer pursuant to a decree of divorce or separate maintenance or a written instrument incident to such a decree or to any transfer which an individual establishes did not have as its principal purpose the avoidance of tax or payment of tax.

(d) Allocation of deficiency.

For purposes of subsection (c)—

(1) In general. The portion of any deficiency on a joint return allocated to an individual shall be the amount which bears the same ratio to such deficiency as the net amount of items taken into account in computing the deficiency and allocable to the individual under paragraph (3) bears to the net amount of all items taken into account in computing the deficiency.

(2) Separate treatment of certain items. If a deficiency (or portion thereof) is attributable to—

(A) the disallowance of a credit; or

(B) any tax (other than tax imposed by section 1 or 55) required to be included with the joint return,

and such item is allocated to one individual under paragraph (3), such deficiency (or portion) shall be allocated to such individual. Any such item shall not be taken into account under paragraph (1).

(3) Allocation of items giving rise to the deficiency. For purposes of this subsection—

(A) In general. Except as provided in paragraphs (4) and (5), any item giving rise to a deficiency on a joint return shall be allocated to individuals filing the return in the same manner as it would have been allocated if the individuals had filed separate returns for the taxable year.

(B) Exception where other spouse benefits. Under rules prescribed by the Secretary, an item otherwise allocable to an individual under subparagraph (A) shall be allocated to the other individual filing the joint return to the extent the item gave rise to a tax benefit on the joint return to the other individual.

(C) Exception for fraud. The Secretary may provide for an allocation of any item in a manner not prescribed by subparagraph (A) if the Secretary establishes that such allocation is appropriate due to fraud of one or both individuals.

(4) Limitations on separate returns disregarded. If an item of deduction or credit is disallowed in its entirety solely because a separate return is filed, such disallowance shall be disregarded and the item shall be computed as if a joint return had been filed and then allocated between the spouses appropriately. A similar rule shall apply for purposes of section 86.

(5) Child's liability. If the liability of a child of a taxpayer is included on a joint return, such liability shall be disregarded in computing the separate liability of either spouse and such liability shall be allocated appropriately between the spouses.

(e) Petition for review by tax court.

(1) In general. In the case of an individual against whom a deficiency has been asserted and who elects to have subsection (b) or (c) apply , or in the case of an individual who requests equitable relief under subsection (f)—

(A) In general. In addition to any other remedy provided by law, the individual may petition the Tax Court (and the Tax Court shall have jurisdiction) to determine the appropriate relief available to the individual under this section if such petition is filed—

(i) at any time after the earlier of—
(I) the date the Secretary mails, by certified or registered mail to the taxpayer's last known address, notice of the Secretary's final determination of relief available to the individual, or
(II) the date which is 6 months after the date such election is filed or request is made with the Secretary, and
(ii) not later than the close of the 90th day after the date described in clause (i)(I).
(B) Restrictions applicable to collection of assessment.
(i) In general. Except as otherwise provided in section 6851 or 6861, no levy or proceeding in court shall be made, begun, or prosecuted against the individual making an election under subsection (b) or (c) or requesting equitable relief under subsection (f) for collection of any assessment to which such election or request relates until the close of the 90th day referred to in subparagraph (A)(ii), or, if a petition has been filed with the Tax Court under subparagraph (A), until the decision of the Tax Court has become final. Rules similar to the rules of section 7485 shall apply with respect to the collection of such assessment.
(ii) Authority to enjoin collection actions. Notwithstanding the provisions of section 7421(a), the beginning of such levy or proceeding during the time the prohibition under clause (i) is in force may be enjoined by a proceeding in the proper court, including the Tax Court. The Tax Court shall have no jurisdiction under this subparagraph to enjoin any action or proceeding unless a timely petition has been filed under subparagraph (A) and then only in respect of the amount of the assessment to which the election under subsection (b) or (c) relates or to which the request under subsection (f) relates.
(2) **Suspension of running of period of limitations.** The running of the period of limitations in section 6502 on the collection of the assessment to which the petition under paragraph (1)(A) relates shall be suspended—
(A) for the period during which the Secretary is prohibited by paragraph (1)(B) from collecting by levy or a proceeding in court and for 60 days thereafter, and
(B) if a waiver under paragraph (5) is made, from the date the claim for relief was filed until 60 days after the waiver is filed with the Secretary.
(3) **Limitation on Tax Court jurisdiction.** If a suit for refund is begun by either individual filing the joint return pursuant to section 6532—
(A) The Tax Court shall lose jurisdiction of the individual's action under this section to whatever extent jurisdiction is acquired by the district court or the United States Court of Federal Claims over the taxable years that are the subject of the suit for refund, and
(B) the court acquiring jurisdiction shall have jurisdiction over the petition filed under this subsection.
(4) **Notice to other spouse.** The Tax Court shall establish rules which provide the individual filing a joint return but not making the election under subsection (b) or (c) or the request for equitable relief under subsection (f) with adequate notice and an opportunity to become a party to a proceeding under either such subsection.
(5) **Waiver.** An individual who elects the application of subsection (b) or (c) or who requests equitable relief under subsection (f) (and who agrees with the Secretary's determination of relief) may waive in writing at any time the restrictions in paragraph (1)(B) with respect to collection of the outstanding assessment (whether or not a notice of the Secretary's final determination of relief has been mailed).
(f) **Equitable relief.**
Under procedures prescribed by the Secretary, if—
(1) taking into account all the facts and circumstances, it is inequitable to hold the individual liable for any unpaid tax or any deficiency (or any portion of either); and
(2) relief is not available to such individual under subsection (b) or (c),
the Secretary may relieve such individual of such liability.
(g) **Credits and refunds.**
(1) **In general.** Except as provided in paragraphs (2) and (3), notwithstanding any other law or rule of law (other than section 6511, 6512(b), 7121, or 7122), credit or refund shall be allowed or made to the extent attributable to the application of this section.
(2) **Res judicata.** In the case of any election under subsection (b) or (c) or of any request for equitable relief under subsection (f), if a decision of a court in any prior proceeding for the same taxable year has become final, such decision shall be conclusive except with respect to the qualification of the individual for relief which was not an issue in such proceeding. The exception contained in the preceding sentence shall not apply if the court determines that the individual participated meaningfully in such prior proceeding.
(3) **Credit and refund not allowed under subsection (c).** No credit or refund shall be allowed as a result of an election under subsection (c).
(h) **Regulations.**
The Secretary shall prescribe such regulations as are necessary to carry out the provisions of this section, including—
(1) regulations providing methods for allocation of items other than the methods under subsection (d)(3); and
(2) regulations providing the opportunity for an individual to have notice of, and an opportunity to participate in, any administrative proceeding with respect to an election made under subsection (b) or (c) or a request for equitable relief made under subsection (f) by the other individual filing the joint return.

In 2006, P.L. 109-432, Sec. 408(a), added ", or in the case of an individual who requests equitable relief under subsection (f)" after "who elects to have subsection (b) or (c) apply" in para. (e)(1)... Sec. 408(b)(1), added "or request is made' after "election is filed" in subclause (e)(1)(A)(i)(II)... Sec. 408(b)(2)(A), added "or requesting equitable relief under subsection (f)" after "making an election under subsection (b) or (c)" in clause (e)(1)(B)(i)... Sec. 408(b)(2)(B), added "or request" after "to which such election" in clause (e)(1)(B)(i)... Sec. 408(b)(3), added "or to which the request under subsection (f) relates" after "to which the election under subsection (b) or (c) relates" in clause (e)(1)(B)(ii)... Sec. 408(b)(4), added "or the request for equitable relief under subsection (f)" after "the election under subsection (b) or (c)" in para. (e)(4)... Sec. 408(b)(5), added "or who requests equitable relief under subsection (f)" after "who elects the application of subsection (b) or (c)" in para (e)(5)... Sec. 408(b)(6), added "or of any request for equitable relief under subsection (f)" after "any election under subsection (b) or (c)' in para. (g)(2)... Sec. 408(b)(7), added "or a request for equitable relief made under subsection (f)" after "with respect to an election made under subsection (b) or (c)" in para. (h)(2), effective for liability for taxes arising or remaining unpaid on or after 12/20/2006.
In 2000, P.L. 106-554, Sec. 1(a)(7), [which enacted into law Sec. 313(a)(1) of P.L. 106-554] substituted "may be made at any time after a deficiency for such year is asserted but" for "shall be made" in subpara. (c)(3)(B)... Sec. 1(a)(7), [which enacted into law Sec. 313(a)(2)(A) of P.L. 106-554] redesignated subsec. (g) as (h) and added subsec. (g)... Sec. 1(a)(7), [which enacted into law Sec. 313(a)(2)(B) of P.L. 106-554] amended para. (e)(3)... Sec. 1(a)(7), [which enacted into law Sec. 313(a)(3)(A) of P.L. 106-554] added "against whom a deficiency has been asserted and" after "an individual" in para. (e)(1)... Sec. 1(a)(7), [which enacted into law Sec. 313(a)(3)(B) of P.L. 106-554] amended subpara. (e)(1)(A)... Sec. 1(a)(7), [which enacted into law Sec. 313(a)(3)(C)(i) of P.L. 106-554] substituted "until the close of the 90th day referred to in subparagraph (A)(ii)" for "until the expiration of the 90-day period described in subparagraph (A)" in clause (e)(1)(B)(i)... Sec. 1(a)(7), [which enacted into law Sec.

Information and returns Code Sec. 6015

313(a)(3)(C)(ii) of P.L. 106-554] added "under subparagraph (A)" after "filed with the Tax Court" in clause (e)(1)(B)(i)... Sec. 1(a)(7), [which enacted into law Sec. 313(a)(3)(D)(i) of P.L. 106-554] added para. (e)(5)... Sec. 1(a)(7), [which enacted into law Sec. 313(a)(3)(D)(ii) of P.L. 106-554] amended para. (e)(2), effective 12/21/2000.

Prior to amendment, para. (e)(3) read as follows:

"(3) Applicable rules.

"(A) Allowance of credit or refund. Except as provided in subparagraph (B), notwithstanding any other law or rule of law (other than section 6512(b), 7121, or 7122), credit or refund shall be allowed or made to the extent attributable to the application of subsection (b) or (f).

"(B) Res judicata. In the case of any election under subsection (b) or (c), if a decision of the Tax Court in any prior proceeding for the same taxable year has become final, such decision shall be conclusive except with respect to the qualification of the individual for relief which was not an issue in such proceeding. The exception contained in the preceding sentence shall not apply if the Tax Court determines that the individual participated meaningfully in such prior proceeding.

"(C) Limitation on tax court jurisdiction. If a suit for refund is begun by either individual filing the joint return pursuant to section 6532—

"(i) the Tax Court shall lose jurisdiction of the individual's action under this section to whatever extent jurisdiction is acquired by the district court or the United States Court of Federal Claims over the taxable years that are the subject of the suit for refund, and

"(ii) the court acquiring jurisdiction shall have jurisdiction over the petition filed under this subsection."

Prior to amendment, subpara. (e)(1)(A) read as follows:

"(A) In general. The individual may petition the Tax Court (and the Tax Court shall have jurisdiction) to determine the appropriate relief available to the individual under this section if such petition is filed during the 90-day period beginning on the date on which the Secretary mails by certified or registered mail a notice to such individual of the Secretary's determination of relief available to the individual. Notwithstanding the preceding sentence, an individual may file such petition at any time after the date which is 6 months after the date such election is filed with the Secretary and before the close of such 90-day period."

Prior to amendment, para. (e)(2) read as follows:

"(2) Suspension of running of period of limitations. The running of the period of limitations in section 6502 on the collection of the assessment to which the petition under paragraph (1)(A) relates shall be suspended for the period during which the Secretary is prohibited by paragraph (1)(B) from collecting by levy or a proceeding in court and for 60 days thereafter."

In 1998, P.L. 105-277, Sec. 4002(c)(2), substituted "of subsection (b) or (f)" for "of this section" in subpara. (e)(3)(A), effective for any liability for tax arising after 7/22/98 and any liability for tax arising on or before 7/22/98 but remaining unpaid as of 7/22/98 [For Sec. 3201(g)(2) of P.L. 105-206, see below]

— P.L. 105-206, Sec. 3201(a), added Code Sec. 6015, effective for any liability for tax arising after 7/22/98 and any liability for tax arising on or before 7/22/98 but remaining unpaid as of 7/22/98.

Sec. 3201(g)(2) of this Act provides:

"(2) 2-year period. The 2-year period under subsection (b)(1)(E) or (c)(3)(B) of section 6015 of the Internal Revenue Code of 1986 shall not expire before the date which is 2 years after the date of the first collection activity after the date of the enactment of this Act."

— P.L. 105-206, Sec. 3201(c), of this Act, reads as follows:

"(c) Separate form for applying for spousal relief. Not later than 180 days after the date of the enactment of this Act, the Secretary of the Treasury shall develop a separate form with instructions for use by taxpayers in applying for relief under section 6015(a) of the Internal Revenue Code of 1986, as added by this section."

— P.L. 105-206, Sec. 3501, of this Act, reads as follows:

"SEC. 3501. EXPLANATION OF JOINT AND SEVERAL LIABILITY.

"(a) In general. The Secretary of the Treasury or the Secretary's delegate shall, as soon as practicable, but not later than 180 days after the date of the enactment of this Act, establish procedures to clearly alert married taxpayers of their joint and several liabilities on all appropriate publications and instructions.

"(b) Right to limit liability. The procedures under subsection (a) shall include requirements that notice of an individual's right to relief under section 6015 of the Internal Revenue Code of 1986 shall be included in the statement required by section 6227 of the Omnibus Taxpayer Bill of Rights (Internal Revenue Service Publication No. 1) and in any collection-related notices."

Sec. 6015. Repealed.

In 1984, P.L. 98-369, Sec. 412(a)(1), repealed Code Sec. 6015, effective for tax. yrs. begin. after 12/31/84.

Prior to repeal, Code Sec. 6015 read as follows:

"SEC. 6015. DECLARATION OF ESTIMATED INCOME TAX BY INDIVIDUALS.

"(a) Requirement of declaration.

"Except as otherwise provided in this section, every individual shall make a declaration of his estimated tax for the taxable year if—

"(1) the gross income for the taxable year can reasonably be expected to exceed—

"(A) $20,000, in case of—

"(i) a single individual, including a head of a household (as defined in section 2(b)) or a surviving spouse (as defined in section 2(a)); or

"(ii) a married individual entitled under subsection (c) to file a joint declaration with his spouse, but only if his spouse has not received wages (as defined in section 3401(a)) for the taxable year; or

"(B) $10,000, in the case of a married individual entitled under subsection (c) to file a joint declaration with his spouse, but only if both he and his spouse have received wages (as defined in section 3401(a)) for the taxable year; or

"(C) $5,000, in the case of a married individual not entitled under subsection (c) to file a joint declaration with his spouse; or

"(2) the gross income can reasonably be expected to include more than $500 from sources other than wages (as defined in section 3401(a)).

"(b) Declaration not required in certain cases.

"No declaration shall be required under subsection (a) if the estimated tax (as defined in subsection (d)) is less than the amount determined in accordance with the following table:

"In the case of taxable years beginning in:	The amount is:
1981	$ 100
1982	200
1983	300
1984	400
1985 and thereafter	500.

"(c) Joint declaration by husband and wife.

"In the case of a husband and wife, a single declaration under this section may be made by them jointly, in which case the liability with respect to the estimated tax shall be joint and several. No joint declaration may be made if either the husband or the wife is a nonresident alien, if they are separated under a decree of divorce or of separate maintenance, or if they have different taxable years. If a joint declaration is made but a joint return is not made for the taxable year, the estimated tax for such year may be treated as the estimated tax of either the husband or the wife, or may be divided between them.

"(d) Estimated tax.

"For purposes of this title, in the case of an individual, the term 'estimated tax' means—

"(1) the amount which the individual estimates as the amount of the income tax imposed by chapter 1 for the taxable year (other than the tax imposed by section 55), plus

"(2) the amount which the individual estimates as the amount of the self-employment tax imposed by chapter 2 of the taxable year, minus

"(3) the amount which the individual estimates as the sum of—

"(A) any credits against tax provided by part IV of subchapter A of chapter 1, and

"(B) to the extent allowed under regulations prescribed by the Secretary, any overpayment of the tax imposed by section 4986.

"(e) Contents of declaration.

"The declaration shall contain such pertinent information as the Secretary may by forms or regulations prescribe.

"(f) Amendment of declaration.

"An individual may make amendments of a declaration filed during the taxable year under regulations prescribed by the Secretary.

"(g) Return as declaration or amendment.

"If on or before January 31, (or March 1, in the case of an individual referred to in section 6073(b), relating to income from farming or fishing) of the succeeding taxable year the taxpayer files a return, for the taxable year for which the declaration is required, and pays in full the amount computed on the return as payable, then, under regulations prescribed by the Secretary—

"(1) if the declaration is not required to be filed during the taxable year, but is required to be filed on or before January 15, such return shall be considered as such declaration; and

"(2) if the tax shown on the return (reduced by the sum of the credits against tax provided on part IV of subchapter A of chapter 1) is greater than the estimated tax shown in a declaration previously made, or in the last amendment thereof, such return shall be considered as the amendment of the declaration permitted by subsection (e) to be filed on or before January 15.

In the application of this subsection in the case of a taxable year beginning on any date other than January 1, there shall be substituted, for the 15th or last day of the months specified in this subsection, the 15th or last day of the months which correspond thereto.

"(h) Short taxable years.

"An individual with a taxable year of less than 12 months shall make a declaration in accordance with regulations prescribed by the Secretary.

"(i) Estates and trusts.

"The provisions of this section shall not apply to an estate or trust.

"(j) Nonresident alien individuals.

"No declaration shall be required to be made under this section by a nonresident alien individual unless—

"(1) withholding under chapter 24 is made applicable to the wages, as defined in section 3401(a), of such individual,

"(2) such individual has income (other than compensation for personal services subject to deduction and withholding under section 1441) which is effectively connected with the conduct of a trade or business within the United States, or

"(3) such individual is a resident of Puerto Rico during the entire taxable year.

"(k) Termination.

"No declaration shall be required under this section for any taxable year beginning after December 31, 1982."

In 1983, P.L. 97-448, Sec. 107(c)(2), substituted "entitled under subsection (c)" for "entitled under subsection (b)" each place it appeared in subsec. (a), for estimated tax. yrs. begin. after 12/31/80.

— P.L. 97-448, Sec. 201(j)(1), amended para. (d)(3), effective for periods after 2/29/80.

Prior to amendment, para. (d)(3) read as follows:

"(3) the amount which the individual estimates as the sum of any credits against tax provided by part IV of subchapter A of chapter I."

—P.L. 97-448, Sec. 306(a)(1)(A)(i), redesignated the second Sec. 201(c) of P.L. 97-248 as Sec. 201(d) of P.L. 97-248, see below.

In **1982**, P.L. 97-248, Sec. 201(d)(7), deleted "or 56" after "section 55" in para. (d)(1), effective for tax. yrs. begin. after 12/31/82.

—P.L. 97-248, Sec. 328(b)(1), added subsec. (k), effective for tax. yrs. begin. after 12/31/82.

In **1981**, P.L. 97-34, Sec. 725(a), redesignated subsecs. (b) through (i) as subsecs. (c) through (j) and added new subsec. (b) . . . Sec. 725(c)(2), deleted the last sentence of subsec. (a), effective for estimated tax for tax. yrs. begin. after 12/31/80.
Prior to deletion, the last sentence of subsec. (a) read as follows:
"Notwithstanding the provisions of this subsection, no declaration is required if the estimated tax (as defined in subsection (c)) can reasonably be expected to be less than $100."

In **1978**, P.L. 95-600, Sec. 421(e)(7), substituted "section 55 or 56" for "section 56" in para. (c)(1), effective for tax. yrs. begin. after 12/31/78.

In **1976**, P.L. 94-455, Sec. 1906(a)(2), deleted subsec. (j), effective 2/1/77.
Prior to deletion subsec. (j) read as follows:
"(j) Applicability.
"This section shall be applicable only with respect to taxable years beginning after December 31, 1954; and sections 58, 59, and 60 of the Internal Revenue Code of 1939 shall continue in force with respect to taxable years beginning before January 1, 1955."

—P.L. 94-455, Sec. 1906(b)(13)(A), substituted "Secretary" for "Secretary or his delegate" each place it appeared in Code Sec. 6015, effective 2/1/77.

In **1971**, P.L. 92-178, Sec. 209, amended subsec. (a), effective for estimated tax for tax. yrs. begin. after 12/31/71.
Prior to amendment subsec. (a) read as follows:
"(a) Requirement of declaration.
"Except as otherwise provided in subsection (i), every individual shall make a declaration of his estimated tax for the taxable year, if—
"(1) the gross income for the taxable year can reasonably be expected to exceed—
"(A) $5,000, in the case of—
"(i) a single individual other than a head of a household (as defined in section 2(b)) or a surviving spouse (as defined in section 2(a));
"(ii) a married individual not entitled under subsection (b) to file a joint declaration with his spouse; or
"(iii) a married individual entitled under subsection (b) to file a joint declaration with his spouse, but only if the aggregate gross income of such individual and his spouse for the taxable year can reasonably be expected to exceed $10,000; or
"(B) $10,000, in the case of—
"(i) a head of a household (as defined in section 2(b)); or
"(ii) a surviving spouse (as defined in section 2(a)); or
"(2) the gross income can reasonably be expected to include more than $200 from sources other than wages (as defined in section 3401(a)). Notwithstanding the provisions of this subsection, no declaration is required if the estimated tax (as defined in subsection (c)) can reasonably be expected to be less than $40."

In **1969**, P.L. 91-172, Sec. 301(b)(12), inserted "(other than the tax imposed by section 56)" after "taxable year" in subsec. (c)(1), effective for tax. yrs. end. after 12/31/69.

—P.L. 91-172, Sec. 803(d)(7), substituted "section 2(b)" for "section 1(b)(2)" and substituted "section 2(a)" for "section 2(b)" each place they appeared in subsec. (a)(1), effective for tax yrs. begin. after 12/31/70.

—P.L. 91-172, Sec. 944, substituted "March 1" for "February 15" in subsec. (f), for tax yrs. begin. after 12/31/68.

In **1966**, P.L. 89-809, Sec. 103, amended the portion of subsec. (a) preceding para. (a)(1), added subsec. (i), and redesignated former subsec. (i) as subsec. (j), effective for tax. yrs. begin. after '66.
Prior to amendment, the portion of subsec. (a) preceding para. (a)(1) read as follows:
"(a) Requirement of declaration.
"Every individual (other than a nonresident alien with respect to whose wages, as defined in section 3401(a), withholding under chapter 24 is not made applicable, but including every alien individual who is a resident of Puerto Rico during the entire taxable year) shall make a declaration of his estimated tax for the taxable year if—"

—P.L. 89-368, Sec. 102, amended subsec. (c), effective for tax yrs. begin. after '66.
Prior to amendment, subsec. (c) read as follows:
"(c) Estimated tax.
"For purposes of this title, in the case of an individual, the term 'estimated tax' means the amount which the individual estimates as the amount of the income tax imposed by chapter 1 for the taxable year, minus the amount which the individual estimates as the sum of any credits against tax provided by part IV of subchapter A of chapter 1."

In **1962**, P.L. 87-682, Sec. 1(a)(1), inserted "or fishing" following "from farming" in subsec. (f) for tax. yrs. begin. after '62.

In **1960**, P.L. 86-779, Sec. 5(a), amended subsec. (a), effective for tax. yrs. begin. after 12/31/60.
Prior to amendment, subsec. (a) read as follows:
"(a) Requirement of declaration.
"Every individual (other than a nonresident alien with respect to whose wages, as defined in section 3401(a), withholding under chapter 24 is not made applicable, but including every alien individual who is a resident of Puerto Rico during the entire taxable year) shall make a declaration of his estimated tax for the taxable year if—
"(1) the gross income for the taxable year can reasonably be expected to consist of wages (as defined in section 3401(a)) and of not more than $100 from sources other than such wages, and can reasonably be expected to exceed—
"(A) $5,000, in the case of a single individual other than a head of a household (as defined in section 1(b)(2)) or a surviving spouse (as defined in section 2(b)) or in the case of a married individual not entitled to file a joint declaration with his spouse;
"(B) $10,000, in the case of a head of a household (as defined in section 1(b)(2)) or a surviving spouse (as defined in section 2(b)); or
"(C) $5,000 in the case of a married individual entitled under subsection (b) to file a joint declaration with his spouse, and the aggregate gross income of such individual and his spouse for the taxable year can reasonably be expected to exceed $10,000; or
"(2) the gross income can reasonably be expected to include more than $100 from sources other than wages (as defined in section 3401(a)) and can reasonably be expected to exceed the sum of—
"(A) the amount obtained by multiplying $600 by the number of exemptions to which he is entitled under section 151 plus
"(B) $400."

In **1958**, P.L. 85-866, Sec. 74, added last sentence of subsec. (f), effective 8/17/54.

Sec. 6017. Self-employment tax returns.

Every individual (other than a nonresident alien individual) having net earnings from self-employment of $400 or more for the taxable year shall make a return with respect to the self-employment tax imposed by chapter 2. In the case of a husband and wife filing a joint return under section 6013, the tax imposed by chapter 2 shall not be computed on the aggregate income but shall be the sum of the taxes computed under such chapter on the separate self-employment income of each spouse.

Sec. 6017A. Repealed.

In **1989**, P.L. 101-239, Sec. 7711(b)(1), repealed Code Sec. 6017A, effective for returns and statements the due date for which (determined without regard to extensions) is after 12/31/89.
Prior to repeal, Code Sec. 6017A read as follows:
"Sec. 6017A. Place of residence.
"In the case of an individual, the information required on any return with respect to the taxes imposed by chapter 1 for any period shall include information as to the State, county, municipality, and any other unit of local government in which the taxpayer (and any other individual with respect to whom an exemption is claimed on such return) resided on one or more dates (determined in the manner provided by regulations prescribed by the Secretary) during such period."

In **1976**, P.L. 94-455, Sec. 1906(b)(13)(A), substituted "Secretary" for "Secretary or his delegate" in Code Sec. 6017A, effective 2/1/77.

In **1972**, P.L. 92-512, Sec. 144(a), added Sec. 6017A, effective 10/20/72.

SUBPART C.—RETURNS RELATING TO TRANSFERS DURING LIFE OR AT DEATH

Sec.
6018. Returns relating to large transfers at death.
6019. Gift tax returns.

> • **Caution:** Sec. 301(a), P.L. 111-312, (reproduced in the history notes following this Code Sec.) provides that the amendments made by Sec. 542(b)(1), P.L. 107-16, EGTRRA, will apply as if never enacted. Code Sec. 6018, following, reflects the removal of these amendments, effective for estates of decedents dying, and transfers made, after 12/31/2009.

Sec. 6018. Returns relating to large transfers at death.
(a) In general.

If this section applies to property acquired from a decedent, the executor of the estate of such decedent shall make a return containing the information specified in subsection (c) with respect to such property.

Information and returns

Code Sec. 6018

(b) Property to which section applies.
(1) Large transfers. This section shall apply to all property (other than cash) acquired from a decedent if the fair market value of such property acquired from the decedent exceeds the dollar amount applicable under section 1022(b)(2)(B) (without regard to section 1022(b)(2)(C)).
(2) Transfers of certain gifts received by decedent within 3 years of death. This section shall apply to any appreciated property acquired from the decedent if—
   (A) subsections (b) and (c) of section 1022 do not apply to such property by reason of section 1022(d)(1)(C), and
   (B) such property was required to be included on a return required to be filed under section 6019.
(3) Nonresidents not citizens of the United States. In the case of a decedent who is a nonresident not a citizen of the United States, paragraphs (1) and (2) shall be applied—
   (A) by taking into account only—
      (i) tangible property situated in the United States, and
      (ii) other property acquired from the decedent by a United States person, and
   (B) by substituting the dollar amount applicable under section 1022(b)(3) for the dollar amount referred to in paragraph (1).
(4) Returns by trustees or beneficiaries. If the executor is unable to make a complete return as to any property acquired from or passing from the decedent, the executor shall include in the return a description of such property and the name of every person holding a legal or beneficial interest therein. Upon notice from the Secretary, such person shall in like manner make a return as to such property.

(c) Information required to be furnished.
The information specified in this subsection with respect to any property acquired from the decedent is—
(1) the name and TIN of the recipient of such property,
(2) an accurate description of such property,
(3) the adjusted basis of such property in the hands of the decedent and its fair market value at the time of death,
(4) the decedent's holding period for such property,
(5) sufficient information to determine whether any gain on the sale of the property would be treated as ordinary income,
(6) the amount of basis increase allocated to the property under subsection (b) or (c) of section 1022, and
(7) such other information as the Secretary may by regulations prescribe.

(d) Property acquired from decedent.
For purposes of this section, section 1022 shall apply for purposes of determining the property acquired from a decedent.

(e) Statements to be furnished to certain persons.
Every person required to make a return under subsection (a) shall furnish to each person whose name is required to be set forth in such return (other than the person required to make such return) a written statement showing—
(1) the name, address, and phone number of the person required to make such return, and
(2) the information specified in subsection (c) with respect to property acquired from, or passing from, the decedent to the person required to receive such statement.
The written statement required under the preceding sentence shall be furnished not later than 30 days after the date that the return required by subsection (a) is filed.

> • **Caution:** Code Sec. 6018, following, reflects amendments made by Sec. 542(b)(1), P.L. 107-16, EGTRRA. As provided in Sec. 301(a), P.L. 111-312, these amendments will apply as if never enacted, effective for estates of decedents dying, and transfers made, after 12/31/2009.

Sec. 6018. Estate tax returns.
(a) Returns by executor.
(1) Citizens or residents. In all cases where the gross estate at the death of a citizen or resident exceeds the basic exclusion amount in effect under section 2010(c) for the calendar year which includes the date of death, the executor shall make a return with respect to the estate tax imposed by subtitle B.
(2) Nonresidents not citizens of the United States. In the case of the estate of every nonresident not a citizen of the United States if that part of the gross estate which is situated in the United States exceeds $60,000, the executor shall make a return with respect to the estate tax imposed by subtitle B.
(3) Adjustment for certain gifts. The amount applicable under paragraph (1) and the amount set forth in paragraph (2) shall each be reduced (but not below zero) by the sum of—
   (A) the amount of the adjusted taxable gifts (within the meaning of section 2001(b)) made by the decedent after December 31, 1976, plus
   (B) the aggregate amount allowed as a specific exemption under section 2521 (as in effect before its repeal by the Tax Reform Act of 1976) with respect to gifts made by the decedent after September 8, 1976.

(b) Returns by beneficiaries.
If the executor is unable to make a complete return as to any part of the gross estate of the decedent, he shall include in his return a description of such part and the name of every person holding a legal or beneficial interest therein. Upon notice from the Secretary such person shall in like manner make a return as to such part of the gross estate.

In 2010, P.L. 111-312, Sec. 101(a)(1), substituted "December 31, 2012" for "December 31, 2010" both places it appeared in Sec. 901, P.L. 107-16 [see below], effective as if included in the enactment of P.L. 107-16, EGTRRA, 6/7/2001.
—P.L. 111-312, Sec. 301(a), provides that Code Sec. 6018, as amended by Sec. 542(b)(1), P.L. 107-16, EGTRRA, 6/7/2001 (see below), will read as if such provision had never been enacted, effective for estates of decedents dying, and transfers made, after 12/31/2009.
Sec. 301(a), P.L. 111-312, 12/17/2010, provides:
"(a) In general. Each provision of law amended by subtitle A or E of title V of the Economic Growth and Tax Relief Reconciliation Act of 2001 [P.L. 107-16, see below] is amended to read as such provision would read if such subtitle had never been enacted."
Prior to the enactment of Sec. 301(a) of P.L. 111-312, Code Sec. 6018 read as follows:
"Sec. 6018. Returns relating to large transfers at death.
"(a) In general. If this section applies to property acquired from a decedent, the executor of the estate of such decedent shall make a return containing the information specified in subsection (c) with respect to such property.
"(b) Property to which section applies.
"(1) Large transfers. This section shall apply to all property (other than cash) acquired from a decedent if the fair market value of such property acquired from the decedent exceeds the dollar amount applicable under section 1022(b)(2)(B) (without regard to section 1022(b)(2)(C)).
"(2) Transfers of certain gifts received by decedent within 3 years of death. This section shall apply to any appreciated property acquired from the decedent if—
"(A) subsections (b) and (c) of section 1022 do not apply to such property by reason of section 1022(d)(1)(C), and
"(B) such property was required to be included on a return required to be filed under section 6019.
"(3) Nonresidents not citizens of the United States. In the case of a decedent who is a nonresident not a citizen of the United States, paragraphs (1) and (2) shall be applied—
"(A) by taking into account only—
"(i) tangible property situated in the United States, and

Code Sec. 6018   Information and returns

"(ii) other property acquired from the decedent by a United States person, and

"(B) by substituting the dollar amount applicable under section 1022(b)(3) for the dollar amount referred to in paragraph (1).

"(4) Returns by trustees or beneficiaries. If the executor is unable to make a complete return as to any property acquired from or passing from the decedent, the executor shall include in the return a description of such property and the name of every person holding a legal or beneficial interest therein. Upon notice from the Secretary, such person shall in like manner make a return as to such property.

"(c) Information required to be furnished. The information specified in this subsection with respect to any property acquired from the decedent is—

"(1) the name and TIN of the recipient of such property,

"(2) an accurate description of such property,

"(3) the adjusted basis of such property in the hands of the decedent and its fair market value at the time of death,

"(4) the decedent's holding period for such property,

"(5) sufficient information to determine whether any gain on the sale of the property would be treated as ordinary income,

"(6) the amount of basis increase allocated to the property under subsection (b) or (c) of section 1022 , and

"(7) such other information as the Secretary may by regulations prescribe.

"(d) Property acquired from decedent. For purposes of this section, section 1022 shall apply for purposes of determining the property acquired from a decedent.

"(e) Statements to be furnished to certain persons. Every person required to make a return under subsection (a) shall furnish to each person whose name is required to be set forth in such return (other than the person required to make such return) a written statement showing—

"(1) the name, address, and phone number of the person required to make such return, and

"(2) the information specified in subsection (c) with respect to property acquired from, or passing from, the decedent to the person required to receive such statement.

"The written statement required under the preceding sentence shall be furnished not later than 30 days after the date that the return required by subsection (a) is filed."

—P.L. 111-312, Sec. 303(b)(3), substituted "basic exclusion amount" for "applicable exclusion amount" in para. (a)(1), effective for estates of decedents dying and gifts made after 12/31/2010.

In 2002, P.L. 107-358, Sec. 2, added subsec. (c) in Sec. 901 of P.L. 107-16 [see below], effective 12/17/2002.

In 2001, P.L. 107-16, Sec. 542(b)(1), amended Code Sec. 6018, effective for estates of decedents dying after 12/31/2009. Sec. 301(a), P.L. 111-312 (reproduced above) provides that these amendments shall be treated as never enacted.

Prior to amendment, Code Sec. 6018 read as follows:

"Sec. 6018. Estate tax returns.

"(a) Returns by executor.

"(1) Citizens or residents. In all cases where the gross estate at the death of a citizen or resident exceeds the applicable exclusion amount in effect under section 2010(c) for the calendar year which includes the date of death, the executor shall make a return with respect to the estate tax imposed by subtitle B.

"(2) Nonresidents not citizens of the United States. In the case of the estate of every nonresident not a citizen of the United States if that part of the gross estate which is situated in the United States exceeds $60,000, the executor shall make a return with respect to the estate tax imposed by subtitle B.

"(3) Adjustment for certain gifts. The amount applicable under paragraph (1) and the amount set forth in paragraph (2) shall each be reduced (but not below zero) by the sum of—

"(A) the amount of the adjusted taxable gifts (within the meaning of section 2001(b)) made by the decedent after December 31, 1976, plus

"(B) the aggregate amount allowed as a specific exemption under section 2521 (as in effect before its repeal by the Tax Reform Act of 1976) with respect to gifts made by the decedent after September 8, 1976.

"(b) Returns by beneficiaries. If the executor is unable to make a complete return as to any part of the gross estate of the decedent, he shall include in his return a description of such part and the name of every person holding a legal or beneficial interest therein. Upon notice from the Secretary such person shall in like manner make a return as to such part of the gross estate."

—P.L. 107-16, Sec. 901, of this Act [as amended by Sec. 2, P.L. 107-358 and Sec. 101(a)(1), P.L. 111-312, see above], reads as follows:

"Sec. 901. Sunset of provisions of Act.

"(a) In general. All provisions of, and amendments made by, this Act shall not apply—

"(1) to taxable, plan, or limitation years beginning after December 31, 2012, or

"(2) in the case of title V, to estates of decedents dying, gifts made, or generation skipping transfers, after December 31, 2012.

"(b) Application of certain laws. The Internal Revenue Code of 1986 and the Employee Retirement Income Security Act of 1974 shall be applied and administered to years, estates, gifts, and transfers described in subsection (a) as if the provisions and amendments described in subsection (a) had never been enacted.

"(c) Exception. Subsection (a) shall not apply to section 803 (relating to no federal income tax on restitution received by victims of the Nazi regime or their heirs or estates)."

In 1997, P.L. 105-34, Sec. 501(a)(1)(C), substituted "the applicable exclusion amount in effect under section 2010(c) for the calendar year which includes the date of death" for "$600,000" in para. (a)(1), effective for estates of decedents dying, and gifts made, after 12/31/97.

—P.L. 105-34, Sec. 1073(b)(4), deleted para. (a)(4), effective for estates of decedents dying after 12/31/96.

Prior to deletion, para. (a)(4) read as follows:

"(4) Return required if excess retirement accumulation tax. The executor shall make a return with respect to the estate tax imposed by subtitle B in any case where such tax is increased by reason of section 4980A(d)."

In 1990, P.L. 101-508, Sec. 11801(a)(43), deleted para. (a)(3) . . . Sec. 11801(c)(19)(C), redesignated paras. (a)(4) and (a)(5) as paras. (a)(3) and (a)(4), effective 11/5/90 except as provided in Sec. 11821(b) of this Act, which reads as follows:

"(b) Savings provision. If—

"(1) any provision amended or repealed by this part applied to

"(A) any transaction occurring before such date of enactment of this Act [11/5/90],

"(B) any property acquired before such date of enactment [11/5/90],

"(C) any item of income, loss, deduction, or credit taken into account before such date of the enactment [11/5/90] and

"(2) the treatment of such transaction, property, or item under such provision would (without regard to the amendments made by this part) affect liability for tax for periods ending after such date of enactment [11/5/90], nothing in the amendments made by this part shall be construed to affect the treatment of such transaction, property, or item for purposes of determining liability for tax for periods ending after such date of enactment [11/5/90]."

Prior to deletion, para. (a)(3) read as follows:

"(3) Phase-in of filing requirement amount.

In the case of decedents dying in:	Paragraph (1) shall be applied by substituting for '$600,000' the following amount:
1982	$ 225,000
1983	275,000
1984	325,000
1985	400,000
1986	500,000."

In 1989, P.L. 101-239, Sec. 7304(b)(2)(B), repealed subsec. (c), effective for estates of decedents dying after 7/12/89.

Prior to amendment, subsec. (c) read as follows:

"(c) Election under section 2210.

"In all cases in which subsection (a) requires the filing of a return, if an executor elects the applications of section 2210—

"(1) Return by executor. The return which the executor is required to file under the provisions of subsection (a) shall be made with respect to that portion of the estate tax imposed by subtitle B which the executor is required to pay.

"(2) Return by plan administrator. The plan administrator of an employee stock ownership plan or the eligible worker-owned cooperative, as the case may be, shall make a return with respect to that portion of the tax imposed by section 2001 which such plan or cooperative is required to pay under section 2210(b)."

In 1988, P.L. 100-647, Sec. 1011A(g)(12), added para. (a)(5), effective for distributions made after 12/31/86, except as provided in Secs. 1133(c)(2) and (c)(3) of P.L. 99-514 reproduced in note following Code Sec. 4980A.

In 1984, P.L. 98-369, Sec. 544(b)(3), added subsec. (c), effective for those estates of decedents which are required to file returns on a date (including any extensions) after 7/18/84.

In 1981, P.L. 97-34, Sec. 401(a)(2)(B)(i), substituted "$600,000" for "$175,000" in para. (a)(1) . . . Sec. 401(a)(2)(B)(ii), amended para. (a)(3), effective for estates of decedents dying after 12/31/81.

Prior to amendment, para. (a)(3) read as follows:

"(3) Phase-in of filing requirement amount. In the case of a decedent dying before 1981, paragraph (1) shall be applied—

"(A) in the case of decedent dying during 1977, by substituting '$120,000' for '$175,000',

"(B) in the case of a decedent dying during 1978, by substituting '$134,000' for '$175,000',

"(C) in the case of a decedent dying during 1979, by substituting '$147,000' for '$175,000', and

"(D) in the case of a decedent dying during 1980, by substituting '$161,000' for '$175,000.'"

In 1976, P.L. 94-455, Sec. 2001(c)(1)(J), substituted "$175,000" for "$60,000" in para. (a)(1), substituted "$60,000" for "$30,000" in para. (a)(2), and added paras. (a)(3) and (a)(4), effective for estates of decedents dying after 12/31/76.

—P.L. 94-455, Sec. 1906(b)(13)(A), substituted "Secretary" for "Secretary or his delegate" in Code Sec. 6018, effective 2/1/77.

In 1966, P.L. 89-809, Sec. 108, amended para. (a)(2), effective for estates of decedents dying after 11/13/66.

Prior to amendment a return was required if the gross U.S. estate exceeded $2,000.

Sec. 6019.   Gift tax returns.

• **Caution:** Sec. 301(a), P.L. 111-312, (reproduced in the history notes following this Code Sec.) provides that the

3,496

Information and returns Code Sec. 6019

amendments made by 542(b)(2)(A)-(B), P.L. 107-16, EGTRRA, will apply as if never enacted. Code Sec. 6019, following, reflects the removal of these amendments, effective for estates of decedents dying, and transfers made, after 12/31/2009.

(a) In general.
Any individual who in any calendar year makes any transfer by gift other than—
(1) a transfer which under subsection (b) or (e) of section 2503 is not to be included in the total amount of gifts for such year,
(2) a transfer of an interest with respect to which a deduction is allowed under section 2523, or
(3) a transfer with respect to which a deduction is allowed under section 2522 but only if—
  (A)(i) such transfer is of the donor's entire interest in the property transferred, and
  (ii) no other interest in such property is or has been transferred (for less than adequate and full consideration in money or money's worth) from the donor to a person, or to a use, not described in subsection (a) or (b) of section 2522, or
  (B) such transfer is described in section 2522(d),
shall make a return for such year with respect to the gift tax imposed by subtitle B.

(b) Statements to be furnished to certain persons.
Every person required to make a return under subsection (a) shall furnish to each person whose name is required to be set forth in such return (other than the person required to make such return) a written statement showing—
(1) the name, address, and phone number of the person required to make such return, and
(2) the information specified in such return with respect to property received by the person required to receive such statement.

The written statement required under the preceding sentence shall be furnished not later than 30 days after the date that the return required by subsection (a) is filed.

• **Caution:** Code Sec. 6019, was amended by Sec. 542(b)(2)(A)-(B), P.L. 107-16, EGTRRA. As provided in Sec. 301(a), P.L. 111-312, this amendment will apply as if never enacted, effective for estates of decedents dying, and transfers made, after 12/31/2009.

Any individual who in any calendar year makes any transfer by gift other than—
(1) a transfer which under subsection (b) or (e) of section 2503 is not to be included in the total amount of gifts for such year,
(2) a transfer of an interest with respect to which a deduction is allowed under section 2523, or
(3) a transfer with respect to which a deduction is allowed under section 2522 but only if—
  (A)(i) such transfer is of the donor's entire interest in the property transferred, and
  (ii) no other interest in such property is or has been transferred (for less than adequate and full consideration in money or money's worth) from the donor to a person, or to a use, not described in subsection (a) or (b) of section 2522, or
  (B) such transfer is described in section 2522(d),
shall make a return for such year with respect to the gift tax imposed by subtitle B.

In 2010, P.L. 111-312, Sec. 101(a)(1), substituted "December 31, 2012" for "December 31, 2010" both places it appeared in Sec. 901, P.L. 107-16 [see below], effective as if included in the enactment of P.L. 107-16, EGTRRA, 6/7/2001.
—P.L. 111-312, Sec. 301(a), provides that Code Sec. 6019, as amended by Sec. 542(b)(2)(A)-(B), P.L. 107-16, EGTRRA, 6/7/2001 [see below], will read as if such provision had never been enacted, effective as provided in Sec. 301(e) of this Act, which reads as follows:
"(e) Effective date. Except as otherwise provided in this section, the amendments made by this section shall apply to estates of decedents dying, and transfers made, after December 31, 2009."
Sec. 301(a), P.L. 111-312, 12/17/2010, provides:
"(a) In general. Each provision of law amended by subtitle A or E of title V of the Economic Growth and Tax Relief Reconciliation Act of 2001 is amended to read as such provision would read if such subtitle had never been enacted."
Prior to the enactment of Sec. 301(a) of P.L. 111-312, Code Sec. 6019 read as follows:
"Sec. 6019. Gift tax returns.
"(a) In general. Any individual who in any calendar year makes any transfer by gift other than—
"(1) a transfer which under subsection (b) or (e) of section 2503 is not to be included in the total amount of gifts for such year,
"(2) a transfer of an interest with respect to which a deduction is allowed under section 2523 , or
"(3) a transfer with respect to which a deduction is allowed under section 2522 but only if—
"(A)(i) such transfer is of the donor's entire interest in the property transferred, and
"(ii) no other interest in such property is or has been transferred (for less than adequate and full consideration in money or money's worth) from the donor to a person, or to a use, not described in subsection (a) or (b) of section 2522 , or
"(B) such transfer is described in section 2522(d),
"shall make a return for such year with respect to the gift tax imposed by subtitle B.
"(b) Statements to be furnished to certain persons. Every person required to make a return under subsection (a) shall furnish to each person whose name is required to be set forth in such return (other than the person required to make such return) a written statement showing—
"(1) the name, address, and phone number of the person required to make such return, and
"(2) the information specified in such return with respect to property received by the person required to receive such statement.
"The written statement required under the preceding sentence shall be furnished not later than 30 days after the date that the return required by subsection (a) is filed."

In 2002, P.L. 107-358, Sec. 2, added subsec. (c) in Sec. 901 of P.L. 107-16 [see below], effective 12/17/2002.

In 2001, P.L. 107-16, Sec. 542(b)(2)(A), substituted "(a) In general. Any individual" for "Any individual" in Code Sec. 6019 . . . Sec. 542(b)(2)(B), added subsec. (b), effective for estates of decedents dying after 12/31/2009.
—P.L. 107-16, Sec. 901, of this Act [as amended by Sec. 2 of P.L. 107-358 and 101(a)(1), P.L. 111-312, see above], reads as follows:
"Sec. 901. Sunset of provisions of Act.
"(a) In general. All provisions of, and amendments made by, this Act shall not apply—
"(1) to taxable, plan, or limitation years beginning after December 31, 2012, or
"(2) in the case of title V, to estates of decedents dying, gifts made, or generation skipping transfers, after December 31, 2012.
"(b) Application of certain laws. The Internal Revenue Code of 1986 and the Employee Retirement Income Security Act of 1974 shall be applied and administered to years, estates, gifts, and transfers described in subsection (a) as if the provisions and amendments described in subsection (a) had never been enacted.
"(c) Exception. Subsection (a) shall not apply to section 803 (relating to no federal income tax on restitution received by victims of the Nazi regime or their heirs or estates)."

In 1997, P.L. 105-34, Sec. 1301(a), deleted "or" at the end of para. (1), added "or" at the end of para. (2), and added para. (3), effective for gifts made after 8/5/97.

In 1981, P.L. 97-34, Sec. 403(b)(3)(A), amended so much of Code Sec. 6019 as follows the heading and precedes subsec. (b) [as repealed by Sec. 442(d)(2) of this Act, see below] . . . Sec. 403(c)(3)(B), deleted subsec. (c), effective for gifts made after 12/31/81.
Prior to amendment, so much of Code Sec. 6019 as follows the heading and precedes subsec. (b) read as follows:
"(a) In general. Any individual who in any calendar quarter makes any transfers by gift (other than transfers which under section 2503(b) are not to be included in the total amount of gifts for such quarter and other than qualified charitable transfers) shall make a return for such quarter with respect to the gift tax imposed by subtitle B."
Prior to deletion, subsec. (c) read as follows:
"(c) Tenancy by the entirety. For provisions relating to requirement of return in the case of election as to the treatment of gift by creation of tenancy by the entirety, see section 2515(c)."

3,497

—P.L. 97-34, Sec. 442(d)(2), deleted subsec. (b), effective for gifts made after 12/31/81.
Prior to deletion, subsec. (b) read as follows:
"(b) *Qualified charitable transfers.*
"(1) Return requirement. A return shall be made of any qualified charitable transfer—
"(A) for the first calendar quarter, in the calendar year in which the transfer is made, for which a return is required to be filed under subsection (a), or
"(B) if no return is required to be filed under subparagraph (A), for the fourth calendar quarter in the calendar year in which such transfer is made.
A return made pursuant to the provisions of this paragraph shall be deemed to be a return with respect to any transfer reported as a qualified charitable transfer for the calendar quarter in which such transfer was made.
"(2) Definition of qualified charitable transfer. For purposes of this section, the term 'qualified charitable transfer' means a transfer by gift with respect to which a deduction is allowable under section 2522 in an amount equal to the amount transferred."
In **1970,** P.L. 91-614, Sec. 102(d)(3), amended Code Sec. 6019, effective for gifts made after 12/31/70.
Prior to amendment, Code Sec. 6019 read as follows:
"SEC. 6019. GIFT TAX RETURNS.
"(a) *In general.*
"Any individual who in any calendar year makes any transfers by gift (except those which under section 2503(b) are not to be included in the total amount of gifts for such year) shall make a return with respect to the gift tax imposed by subtitle B.
"(b) *Tenancy by the entirety.*
"For provisions relating to requirement of return in the case of election as to the treatment of gift by creation of tenancy by the entirety, see section 2515(c)."

SUBPART D. — MISCELLANEOUS PROVISIONS
Sec.
6020. Returns prepared for or executed by Secretary.
6021. Listing by Secretary of taxable objects owned by nonresidents of internal revenue districts.

Sec. 6020. Returns prepared for or executed by Secretary.

(a) Preparation of return by Secretary.

If any person shall fail to make a return required by this title or by regulations prescribed thereunder, but shall consent to disclose all information necessary for the preparation thereof, then, and in that case, the Secretary may prepare such return, which, being signed by such person, may be received by the Secretary as the return of such person.

(b) Execution of return by Secretary.

(1) Authority of Secretary to execute return. If any person fails to make any return required by any internal revenue law or regulation made thereunder at the time prescribed therefor, or makes, willfully or otherwise, a false or fraudulent return, the Secretary shall make such return from his own knowledge and from such information as he can obtain through testimony or otherwise.

(2) Status of returns. Any return so made and subscribed by the Secretary shall be prima facie good and sufficient for all legal purposes.

In **1984,** P.L. 98-369, Sec. 412(b)(4), deleted "(other than a declaration of estimated tax required under section 6015)" after "any return" in para. (b)(1), effective for tax. yrs. begin. after 12/31/84.
In **1976,** P.L. 94-455, Sec. 1906(b)(13)(A), substituted "Secretary" for "Secretary or his delegate" each place it appeared in Code Sec. 6020, effective 2/1/77.
In **1968,** P.L. 90-364, Sec. 103, deleted "or 6016" at end of parenthetical phrase, in para. (b)(1), effective for tax. yrs. begin. after 12/31/67. For special provision on effective date see Sec. 104 of the P.L. 90-364, reproduced in note following Code Sec. 6425.

Sec. 6021. Listing by Secretary of taxable objects owned by nonresidents of internal revenue districts.

Whenever there are in any internal revenue district any articles subject to tax, which are not owned or possessed by or under the care or control of any person within such district, and of which no list has been transmitted to the Secretary, as required by law or by regulations prescribed pursuant to law, the Secretary shall enter the premises where such articles are situated, shall make such inspection of the articles as may be necessary and make lists of the same, according to the forms prescribed. Such lists, being subscribed by the Secretary, shall be sufficient lists of such articles for all purposes.

In **1976,** P.L. 94-455, Sec. 1906(b)(13)(A), substituted "Secretary" for "Secretary or his delegate" each place it appeared in Code Sec. 6021, effective 2/1/77.

PART III. — INFORMATION RETURNS

Subpart
A. Information concerning persons subject to special provisions.
B. Information concerning transactions with other persons.
C. Information regarding wages paid employees.
D. Information regarding health insurance coverage.
E. Registration of and information concerning pension, etc., plans.
F. Information concerning tax return preparers.

In **2010,** P.L. 111-148, Sec. 1502(d), added item D.
In **1998,** P.L. 105-206, Sec. 2002(b), of this Act, reads as follows:
"(b) Study relating to time for providing notice to recipients.
"(1) In general. The Secretary of the Treasury shall conduct a study evaluating the effect of extending the deadline for providing statements to persons with respect to whom information is required to be furnished under subparts B and C of part III of subchapter A of chapter 61 of the Internal Revenue Code of 1986 (other than section 6051 of such Code) from January 31 to February 15 of the year in which the return to which the statement relates is required to be filed.
"(2) Report. Not later than June 30, 1999, the Secretary of the Treasury shall submit a report on the study under paragraph (1) to the Committee on Ways and Means of the House of Representatives and the Committee on Finance of the Senate."
In **1976,** P.L. 94-455, Sec. 1203(i)(1), added item F.
In **1974,** P.L. 93-406, Sec. 1031(c)(1), added item E.
In **1969,** P.L. 91-172, Sec. 101(j)(64), added item D.

SUBPART A. — INFORMATION CONCERNING PERSONS SUBJECT TO SPECIAL PROVISIONS
Sec.
6031. Return of partnership income.
6032. Returns of banks with respect to common trust funds.
6033. Returns by exempt organizations.
6034. Returns by certain trusts.
6034A. Information to beneficiaries of estates and trusts.
6035. Repealed [Returns of officers, directors, and shareholders of foreign personal holding companies].
6036. Notice of qualification as executor or receiver.
6037. Return of S corporation.
6038. Information reporting with respect to certain foreign corporations and partnerships.
6038A. Information with respect to certain foreign-owned corporations.
6038B. Notice of certain transfers to foreign persons.
6038C. Information with respect to foreign corporations engaged in U.S. business.
6038D. Information with respect to foreign financial assets.
6039. Information required in connection with certain options.
6039C. Returns with respect to foreign person's holding direct investments in United States real property interests.
6039D. Returns and records with respect to certain fringe benefit plans.
6039E. Information concerning resident status.
6039F. Notice of large gifts received from foreign persons.
6039G. Information on individuals losing United States citizenship.

Information and returns — Code Sec. 6031

6039H. Information with respect to Alaska Native Settlement Trusts and sponsoring Native Corporations.
6039I. Returns and records with respect to employer-owned life insurance contracts.
6039J. Information reporting with respect to Commodity Credit Corporation transactions.
6040. Cross references.

In 2010, P.L. 111-147, Sec. 511(a), added item 6038D.
In 2008, P.L. 110-234, Sec. 15353(b), added item 6039J.
In 2006, P.L. 109-280, Sec. 863(c)(2), added item 6039I.
—P.L. 109-280, Sec. 1201(b)(4), amended item 6034.
In 2004, P.L. 108-357, Sec. 413(c)(33), deleted item 6035.
Prior to deletion, item 6035 read as follows:
"6035. Returns of officers, directors, and shareholders of foreign personal holding companies."
In 2001, P.L. 107-16, Sec. 671(c)(2), added item 6039H.
In 1997, P.L. 105-34, Sec. 1142(e)(5), amended item 6038.
Prior to amendment, item 6038 read as follows:
"6038. Information with respect to certain foreign corporations."
—P.L. 105-34, Sec. 1602(h)(2), deleted item 6039F [sic G] and added item 6039G.
Prior to deletion, item 6039F [sic G] read as follows:
"6039F [sic G]. Information on individuals losing United States citizenship.
In 1996, P.L. 104-188, Sec. 1905(b), added item 6039F.
—P.L. 104-191, Sec. 512(b), added item for 6039F [sic G] regarding individuals losing United States citizenship.
In 1990, P.L. 101-508, Sec. 11315(b)(2), added item 6038C.
In 1986, P.L. 99-514, Sec. 1234(a)(2), added item 6039E . . . Sec. 1303(c)(2), repealed item 6039B . . . Sec. 1879(d)(2), repealed item 6039D [inoperative as added by Sec. 1(b)(1) of P.L. 98-612, see below].
Prior to repeal, item 6039B read as follows:
"6039B. Return of general stock ownership corporation."
In 1984, P.L. 98-612, Sec. 1(b)(4), added item 6039D. [Inoperative, same amendment made by Sec. 4(d)(4) of P.L. 98-611, below.]
—P.L. 98-611, Sec. 4(d)(4), added item 6039D.
—P.L. 98-369, Sec. 129(b)(2), added "foreign persons holding direct investments in" after "with respect to" in item 6039C . . . Sec. 131(d)(3), added item 6038B . . . Sec. 714(q)(4), added item 6034A.
In 1982, P.L. 97-354, Sec. 5(a)(39)(B), substituted "S corporation" for "electing small business corporation" in item 6037.
—P.L. 97-248, Sec. 339(b), added item 6038A.
In 1980, P.L. 96-603, Sec. 1(e)(1), substituted "4947(a)(2)" for "4947(a)" in item 6034.
—P.L. 96-499, Sec. 1123(c), added item 6039C.
—P.L. 96-223, Sec. 401(a), repealed Sec. 2005(e)(3) of P.L. 94-455 and the amendment made by Sec. 2005(e)(3) [see below].
In 1978, P.L. 95-600, Sec. 601(c)(2), added item 6039B.
In 1976, P.L. 94-455, Sec. 2005(e)(3), added item 6039A, but Sec. 2005(e)(3) was repealed by Sec. 401(a) of P.L. 96-223 [see above]. The item for 6039A added by Sec. 2005(e)(3) read as follows:
"6039A. INFORMATION REGARDING CARRYOVER BASIS PROPERTY ACQUIRED FROM A DECEDENT."
In 1964, redesignated item 6039 as 6040, and added item 6039.
In 1960, added item 6038, and redesignated former item 6038 as 6039.
In 1968, added item 6037, and redesignated former item 6037 as 6038.

Sec. 6031. Return of partnership income.
(a) General rule.

Every partnership (as defined in section 761(a)) shall make a return for each taxable year, stating specifically the items of its gross income and the deductions allowable by subtitle A, and such other information for the purpose of carrying out the provisions of subtitle A as the Secretary may by forms and regulations prescribe, and shall include in the return the names and addresses of the individuals who would be entitled to share in the taxable income if distributed and the amount of the distributive share of each individual.

(b) Copies to partners.

Each partnership required to file a return under subsection (a) for any partnership taxable year shall (on or before the day on which the return for such taxable year was required to be filed) furnish to each person who is a partner or who holds an interest in such partnership as a nominee for another person at any time during such taxable year a copy of such information required to be shown on such return as may be required by regulations. In the case of an electing large partnership (as defined in section 775), such information shall be furnished on or before the first March 15 following the close of such taxable year.

(c) Nominee reporting.

Any person who holds an interest in a partnership as a nominee for another person—

(1) shall furnish to the partnership, in the manner prescribed by the Secretary, the name and address of such other person, and any other information for such taxable year as the Secretary may by form and regulation prescribe, and

(2) shall furnish in the manner prescribed by the Secretary such other person the information provided by such partnership under subsection (b).

(d) Separate statement of items of unrelated business taxable income.

In the case of any partnership regularly carrying on a trade or business (within the meaning of section 512(c)(1)), the information required under subsection (b) to be furnished to its partners shall include such information as is necessary to enable each partner to compute its distributive share of partnership income or loss from such trade or business in accordance with section 512(a)(1), but without regard to the modifications described in paragraphs (8) through (15) of section 512(b).

(e) Foreign partnerships.

(1) **Exception for foreign partnership.** Except as provided in paragraph (2), the preceding provisions of this section shall not apply to a foreign partnership.

(2) **Certain foreign partnerships required to file return.** Except as provided in regulations prescribed by the Secretary, this section shall apply to a foreign partnership for any taxable year if for such year, such partnership has—

(A) gross income derived from sources within the United States, or

(B) gross income which is effectively connected with the conduct of a trade or business within the United States.

The Secretary may provide simplified filing procedures for foreign partnerships to which this section applies.

(f) Electing investment partnerships.

In the case of any electing investment partnership (as defined in section 743(e)(6)), the information required under subsection (b) to be furnished to any partner to whom section 743(e)(2) applies shall include such information as is necessary to enable the partner to compute the amount of losses disallowed under section 743(e).

In 2007, P.L. 110-141, Sec. 2, of this Act, reads as follows:
"Sec. 2. Modification of penalty for failure to file partnership returns. For any return of a partnership required to be filed under section 6031 of the Internal Revenue Code of 1986 for a taxable year beginning in 2008, the dollar amount in effect under section 6698(b)(1) of such Code shall be increased by $1."
In 2004, P.L. 108-357, Sec. 833(b)(4)(B), added subsec. (f), effective for transfers after 10/22/2004. Sec. 833(d)(2)(B) of this Act, provides:
"(B) Transition rule. In the case of an electing investment partnership which is in existence on June 4, 2004, section 743(e)(6)(H) of the Internal Revenue Code of 1986, as added by this section, shall not apply to such partnership and section 743(e)(6)(I) of such Code, as so added, shall be applied by substituting '20 years' for '15 years'."
In 1998, P.L. 105-206, Sec. 6012(e), substituted "beginning" for "ending on or" in Sec. 1226 of P.L. 105-34, the effective date for amendments made by Sec. 1223 of P.L. 105-34, see below.
In 1997, P.L. 105-34, Sec. 1141(a), added subsec. (e), effective for tax. yrs. begin. after 8/5/97.
—P.L. 105-34, Sec. 1223(a), added the sentence at the end of subsec. (b), effective for partnership tax. yrs. begin. after 12/31/97.

3,499

Code Sec. 6031   **Information and returns**

In **1988**, P.L. 100-647, Sec. 5074(a), added subsec. (d), effective for tax. yrs. begin. after 12/31/88.

In **1986**, P.L. 99-514, Sec. 1501(c)(16)(A), substituted "was required to be filed" for "was filed" in subsec. (b) . . . Sec. 1501(c)(16)(B), substituted "required to be shown on such return" for "shown on such return", in subsec. (b), effective for returns the due date for which (determined without regard to extensions) is after 12/31/86.

—P.L. 99-514, Sec. 1811(b)(1)(A)(i), added "or who holds an interest in such partnership as a nominee for another person" after "who is a partner" in subsec. (b) . . . Sec. 1811(b)(1)(A)(ii), added subsec. (c), effective for partnership tax. yrs. begin. after 10/22/86.

In **1982**, P.L. 97-248, Sec. 403(a), added subsec. (b) . . . Sec. 403(b), substituted "(a) General Rule. Every partnership" for "Every partnership" in Code Sec. 6031, effective for partnership tax. yrs. begin. after 9/3/82.

—P.L. 97-248, Sec. 407(a)(3), of this Act provides:

"(3) The amendments made by sections 402, 403, and 404 shall apply to any partnership taxable year (or in the case of section 6232 of such Code, to any period) ending after the date of the enactment of this Act if the partnership, each partner, and each indirect partner requests such application and the Secretary of the Treasury or his delegate consents to such application."

—P.L. 97-248, Sec. 404, of this Act provides:

"SEC. 404. RETURNS REQUIRED FROM ALL PARTNERSHIPS WITH UNITED STATES PARTNERS.

"Except as hereafter provided in regulations prescribed by the Secretary of the Treasury or his delegate, nothing in section 6031 of the Internal Revenue Code of 1954 shall be treated as excluding any partnership from the filing requirements of such section for any taxable year if the income tax liability under subtitle A of such code of any United States person is determined in whole or in part by taking into account (directly or indirectly) partnership items of such partnership for such taxable year."

—P.L. 97-248, Sec. 406, of this Act provides:

"SEC. 406. SPECIAL RULE FOR CERTAIN INTERNATIONAL SATELLITE PARTNERSHIP.

"Subchapter C of chapter 63 of the Internal Revenue Code of 1954 (relating to tax treatment of partnership items), section 6031 of such Code (relating to returns of partnership income), and section 6046A of such Code (relating to returns as to interest in foreign partnerships) shall not apply to the International Telecommunications Satellite Organization, the International Maritime Satellite Organization, and any organization which is a successor of either of such organizations."

In **1976**, P.L. 94-455, Sec. 1906(b)(13)(A), substituted "Secretary" for "Secretary or his delegate" in Code Sec. 6031, effective 2/1/77.

Sec. 6032. Returns of banks with respect to common trust funds.

Every bank (as defined in section 581) maintaining a common trust fund shall make a return for each taxable year, stating specifically, with respect to such fund, the items of gross income and the deductions allowed by subtitle A, and shall include in the return the names and addresses of the participants who would be entitled to share in the taxable income if distributed and the amount of the proportionate share of each participant. The return shall be executed in the same manner as a return made by a corporation pursuant to the requirements of sections 6012 and 6062.

Sec. 6033. Returns by exempt organizations.

(a) Organizations required to file.

(1) In general. Except as provided in paragraph (3), every organization exempt from taxation under section 501(a) shall file an annual return, stating specifically the items of gross income, receipts, and disbursements, and such other information for the purpose of carrying out the internal revenue laws as the Secretary may by forms or regulations prescribe, and shall keep such records, render under oath such statements, make such other returns, and comply with such rules and regulations as the Secretary may from time to time prescribe; except that, in the discretion of the Secretary, any organization described in section 401(a) may be relieved from stating in its return any information which is reported in returns filed by the employer which established such organization.

(2) Being a party to certain reportable transactions. Every tax-exempt entity described in section 4965(c) shall file (in such form and manner and at such time as determined by the Secretary) a disclosure of—

(A) such entity's being a party to any prohibited tax shelter transaction (as defined in section 4965(e)), and

(B) the identity of any other party to such transaction which is known by such tax-exempt entity.

(3) Exceptions from filing.

(A) Mandatory exceptions. Paragraph (1) shall not apply to—

(i) churches, their integrated auxiliaries, and conventions or associations of churches,

(ii) any organization (other than a private foundation, as defined in section 509(a)) described in subparagraph (C), the gross receipts of which in each taxable year are normally not more than $5,000, or

(iii) the exclusively religious activities of any religious order.

(B) Discretionary exceptions. The Secretary may relieve any organization required under paragraph (1) (other than an organization described in section 509(a)(3)) to file an information return from filing such a return where he determines that such filing is not necessary to the efficient administration of the internal revenue laws.

(C) Certain organizations. The organizations referred to in subparagraph (A)(ii) are—

(i) a religious organization described in section 501(c)(3);

(ii) an educational organization described in section 170(b)(1)(A)(ii);

(iii) a charitable organization, or an organization for the prevention of cruelty to children or animals, described in section 501(c)(3), if such organization is supported, in whole or in part, by funds contributed by the United States or any State or political subdivision thereof, or is primarily supported by contributions of the general public;

(iv) an organization described in section 501(c)(3), if such organization is operated, supervised, or controlled by or in connection with a religious organization described in clause (i);

(v) an organization described in section 501(c)(8); and

(vi) an organization described in section 501(c)(1), if such organization is a corporation wholly owned by the United States or any agency or instrumentality thereof, or a wholly-owned subsidiary of such a corporation.

(b) Certain organizations described in section 501(c)(3).

Every organization described in section 501(c)(3) which is subject to the requirements of subsection (a) shall furnish annually information, at such time and in such manner as the Secretary may by forms or regulations prescribe, setting forth—

(1) its gross income for the year,

(2) its expenses attributable to such income and incurred within the year,

(3) its disbursements within the year for the purposes for which it is exempt,

(4) a balance sheet showing its assets, liabilities, and net worth as of the beginning of such such year,

(5) the total of the contributions and gifts received by it during the year, and the names and addresses of all substantial contributors,

(6) the names and addresses of its foundation managers (within the meaning of section 4946(b)(1)) and highly compensated employees,

(7) the compensation and other payments made during the year to each individual described in paragraph (6),

(8) in the case of an organization with respect to which an election under section 501(h) is effective for the taxable

Information and returns

year, the following amounts for such organization for such taxable year:

(A) the lobbying expenditures (as defined in section 4911(c)(1)),

(B) the lobbying nontaxable amount (as defined in section 4911(c)(2)),

(C) the grass roots expenditures (as defined in section 4911(c)(3)), and

(D) the grass roots nontaxable amount (as defined in section 4911(c)(4)),

(9) such other information with respect to direct or indirect transfers to, and other direct or indirect transactions and relationships with, other organizations described in section 501(c) (other than paragraph (3) thereof) or section 527 as the Secretary may require to prevent—

(A) diversion of funds from the organization's exempt purpose, or

(B) misallocation of revenues or expenses,

(10) the respective amounts (if any) of the taxes imposed on the organization, or any organization manager of the organization, during the taxable year under any of the following provisions (and the respective amounts (if any) of reimbursements paid by the organization during the taxable year with respect to taxes imposed on any such organization manager under any of such provisions):

(A) section 4911 (relating to tax on excess expenditures to influence legislation),

(B) section 4912 (relating to tax on disqualifying lobbying expenditures of certain organizations),

(C) section 4955 (relating to taxes on political expenditures of section 501(c)(3) organizations), except to the extent that, by reason of section 4962, the taxes imposed under such section are not required to be paid or are credited or refunded, and

(D) section 4959 (relating to taxes on failures by hospital organizations),

(11) the respective amounts (if any) of—

(A) the taxes imposed with respect to the organization on any organization manager, or any disqualified person, during the taxable year under section 4958 (relating to taxes on private excess benefit from certain charitable organizations), and

(B) reimbursements paid by the organization during the taxable year with respect to taxes imposed under such section,

except to the extent that, by reason of section 4962, the taxes imposed under such section are not required to be paid or are credited or refunded,

(12) such information as the Secretary may require with respect to any excess benefit transaction (as defined in section 4958),

(13) such information with respect to disqualified persons as the Secretary may prescribe,

(14) such information as the Secretary may require with respect to disaster relief activities, including the amount and use of qualified contributions to which section 1400S(a) applies,

(15) in the case of an organization to which the requirements of section 501(r) apply for the taxable year—

(A) a description of how the organization is addressing the needs identified in each community health needs assessment conducted under section 501(r)(3) and a description of any such needs that are not being addressed together with the reasons why such needs are not being addressed, and

(B) the audited financial statements of such organization (or, in the case of an organization the financial statements of which are included in a consolidated financial statement with other organizations, such consolidated financial statement).

(16) such other information for purposes of carrying out the internal revenue laws as the Secretary may require.

For purposes of paragraph (8), if section 4911(f) applies to the organization for the taxable year, such organization shall furnish the amounts with respect to the affiliated group as well as with respect to such organization,

(c) **Additional provisions relating to private foundations.** In the case of an organization which is a private foundation (within the meaning of section 509(a))—

(1) the Secretary shall by regulations provide that the private foundation shall include in its annual return under this section such information (not required to be furnished by subsection (b) or the forms or regulations prescribed thereunder) as would have been required to be furnished under section 6056 (relating to annual reports by private foundations) as such section 6056 was in effect on January 1, 1979, and

(2) the foundation managers shall furnish copies of the annual return under this section to such State officials, at such times, and under such conditions, as the Secretary may by regulations prescribe.

Nothing in paragraph (1) shall require the inclusion of the name and address of any recipient (other than a disqualified person within the meaning of section 4946) of 1 or more charitable gifts or grants made by the foundation to such recipient as an indigent or needy person if the aggregate of such gifts or grants made by the foundation to such recipient during the year does not exceed $1,000.

(d) **Section to apply to nonexempt charitable trusts and nonexempt private foundations.**

The following organizations shall comply with the requirements of this section in the same manner as organizations described in section 501(c)(3) which are exempt from tax under section 501(a):

(1) **Nonexempt charitable trusts.** A trust described in section 4947(a)(1) (relating to nonexempt charitable trusts).

(2) **Nonexempt private foundations.** A private foundation which is not exempt from tax under section 501(a).

(e) **Special rules relating to lobbying activities.**

(1) **Reporting requirements.**

(A) In general. If this subsection applies to an organization for any taxable year, such organization—

(i) shall include on any return required to be filed under subsection (a) for such year information setting forth the total expenditures of the organization to which section 162(e)(1) applies and the total amount of the dues or other similar amounts paid to the organization to which such expenditures are allocable, and

(ii) except as provided in paragraphs (2)(A)(i) and (3), shall, at the time of assessment or payment of such dues or other similar amounts, provide notice to each person making such payment which contains a reasonable estimate of the portion of such dues or other similar amounts to which such expenditures are so allocable.

(B) Organizations to which subsection applies.

(i) In general. This subsection shall apply to any organization which is exempt from taxation under section 501 other than an organization described in section 501(c)(3).

3,501

(ii) Special rule for in-house expenditures. This subsection shall not apply to the in-house expenditures (within the meaning of section 162(e)(5)(B)(ii)) of an organization for a taxable year if such expenditures do not exceed $2,000. In determining whether a taxpayer exceeds the $2,000 limit under this clause, there shall not be taken into account overhead costs otherwise allocable to activities described in subparagraphs (A) and (D) of section 162(e)(1).
(iii) Coordination with section 527(f). This subsection shall not apply to any amount on which tax is imposed by reason of section 527(f).
(C) Allocation. For purposes of this paragraph—
(i) In general. Expenditures to which section 162(e)(1) applies shall be treated as paid out of dues or other similar amounts to the extent thereof.
(ii) Carryover of lobbying expenditures in excess of dues. If expenditures to which section 162(e)(1) applies exceed the dues or other similar amounts for any taxable year, such excess shall be treated as expenditures to which section 162(e)(1) applies which are paid or incurred by the organization during the following taxable year.

(2) **Tax imposed where organization does not notify.**
(A) In general. If an organization—
(i) elects not to provide the notices described in paragraph (1)(A) for any taxable year, or
(ii) fails to include in such notices the amount allocable to expenditures to which section 162(e)(1) applies (determined on the basis of actual amounts rather than the reasonable estimates under paragraph (1)(A)(ii)),
then there is hereby imposed on such organization for such taxable year a tax in an amount equal to the product of the highest rate of tax imposed by section 11 for the taxable year and the aggregate amount not included in such notices by reason of such election or failure.
(B) Waiver where future adjustments made. The Secretary may waive the tax imposed by subparagraph (A)(ii) for any taxable year if the organization agrees to adjust its estimates under paragraph (1)(A)(ii) for the following taxable year to correct any failures.
(C) Tax treated as income tax. For purposes of this title, the tax imposed by subparagraph (A) shall be treated in the same manner as a tax imposed by chapter 1 (relating to income taxes).

(3) **Exception where dues generally nondeductible.** Paragraph (1)(A) shall not apply to an organization which establishes to the satisfaction of the Secretary that substantially all of the dues or other similar amounts paid by persons to such organization are not deductible without regard to section 162(e).

(f) **Certain organizations described in section 501(c)(4).**
Every organization described in section 501(c)(4) which is subject to the requirements of subsection (a) shall include on the return required under subsection (a) the information referred to in paragraphs (11), (12) and (13) of subsection (b) with respect to such organization.

(g) **Returns required by political organizations.**
(1) **In general.** This section shall apply to a political organization (as defined by section 527(e)(1)) which has gross receipts of $25,000 or more for the taxable year. In the case of a political organization which is a qualified State or local political organization (as defined in section 527(e)(5)), the preceding sentence shall be applied by substituting "$100,000" for "$25,000".

(2) **Annual returns.** Political organizations described in paragraph (1) shall file an annual return—
(A) containing the information required, and complying with the other requirements, under subsection (a)(1) for organizations exempt from taxation under section 501(a), with such modifications as the Secretary considers appropriate to require only information which is necessary for the purposes of carrying out section 527, and
(B) containing such other information as the Secretary deems necessary to carry out the provisions of this subsection.

(3) **Mandatory exceptions from filing.** Paragraph (2) shall not apply to an organization—
(A) which is a State or local committee of a political party, or political committee of a State or local candidate,
(B) which is a caucus or association of State or local officials,
(C) which is an authorized committee (as defined in section 301(6) of the Federal Election Campaign Act of 1971) of a candidate for Federal office,
(D) which is a national committee (as defined in section 301(14) of the Federal Election Campaign Act of 1971) of a political party,
(E) which is a United States House of Representatives or United States Senate campaign committee of a political party committee,
(F) which is required to report under the Federal Election Campaign Act of 1971 as a political committee (as defined in section 301(4) of such Act), or
(G) to which section 527 applies for the taxable year solely by reason of subsection (f)(1) of such section.

(4) **Discretionary exception.** The Secretary may relieve any organization required under paragraph (2) to file an information return from filing such a return if the Secretary determines that such filing is not necessary to the efficient administration of the internal revenue laws.

(h) **Controlling organizations.**
Each controlling organization (within the meaning of section 512(b)(13)) which is subject to the requirements of subsection (a) shall include on the return required under subsection (a)—
(1) any interest, annuities, royalties, or rents received from each controlled entity (within the meaning of section 512(b)(13)),
(2) any loans made to each such controlled entity, and
(3) any transfers of funds between such controlling organization and each such controlled entity.

(i) **Additional notification requirements.**
Any organization the gross receipts of which in any taxable year result in such organization being referred to in subsection (a)(3)(A)(ii) or (a)(3)(B)—
(1) shall furnish annually, in electronic form, and at such time and in such manner as the Secretary may by regulations prescribe, information setting forth—
(A) the legal name of the organization,
(B) any name under which such organization operates or does business,
(C) the organization's mailing address and Internet web site address (if any),
(D) the organization's taxpayer identification number,
(E) the name and address of a principal officer, and
(F) evidence of the continuing basis for the organization's exemption from the filing requirements under subsection (a)(1), and

Information and returns — Code Sec. 6033

(2) upon the termination of the existence of the organization, shall furnish notice of such termination.

(j) Loss of exempt status for failure to file return or notice.

(1) In general. If an organization described in subsection (a)(1) or (i) fails to file an annual return or notice required under either subsection for 3 consecutive years, such organization's status as an organization exempt from tax under section 501(a) shall be considered revoked on and after the date set by the Secretary for the filing of the third annual return or notice. The Secretary shall publish and maintain a list of any organization the status of which is so revoked.

(2) Application necessary for reinstatement. Any organization the tax-exempt status of which is revoked under paragraph (1) must apply in order to obtain reinstatement of such status regardless of whether such organization was originally required to make such an application.

(3) Retroactive reinstatement if reasonable cause shown for failure. If, upon application for reinstatement of status as an organization exempt from tax under section 501(a), an organization described in paragraph (1) can show to the satisfaction of the Secretary evidence of reasonable cause for the failure described in such paragraph, the organization's exempt status may, in the discretion of the Secretary, be reinstated effective from the date of the revocation under such paragraph.

(k) Additional provisions relating to sponsoring organizations.

Every organization described in section 4966(d)(1) shall, on the return required under subsection (a) for the taxable year—

(1) list the total number of donor advised funds (as defined in section 4966(d)(2)) it owns at the end of such taxable year,

(2) indicate the aggregate value of assets held in such funds at the end of such taxable year, and

(3) indicate the aggregate contributions to and grants made from such funds during such taxable year.

(l) Additional provisions relating to supporting organizations.

Every organization described in section 509(a)(3) shall, on the return required under subsection (a)—

(1) list the supported organizations (as defined in section 509(f)(3)) with respect to which such organization provides support,

(2) indicate whether the organization meets the requirements of clause (i), (ii), or (iii) of section 509(a)(3)(B), and

(3) certify that the organization meets the requirements of section 509(a)(3)(C).

(m) Additional information required from CO-OP insurers.

An organization described in section 501(c)(29) shall include on the return required under subsection (a) the following information:

(1) The amount of the reserves required by each State in which the organization is licensed to issue qualified health plans.

(2) The amount of reserves on hand.

(n) Cross reference.

For provisions relating to statements, etc., regarding exempt status of organizations, see section 6001.

For reporting requirements as to certain liquidations, dissolutions, terminations, and contractions, see section 6043(b). For provisions relating to penalties for failure to file a return required by this section, see section 6652(c).

For provisions relating to information required in connection with certain plans of deferred compensation, see section 6058.

In 2010, P.L. 111-148, Sec. 1322(h)(2), redesignated subsec. (m) as subsec. (n) and added subsec. (m), enacted 3/23/2010.
—P.L. 111-148, Sec. 9007(d)(1), deleted "and" at the end of para. (b)(14), redesignated para. (b)(15) as para. (b)(16), and added para. (b)(15)
—P.L. 111-148, Sec. 9007(d)(2), deleted "and" at the end of subpara. (b)(10)(B), added "and" at the end of subpara. (b)(10)(C), and added subpara. (b)(10)(D), effective for tax. yrs. begin. after 3/23/2010.

In 2008, P.L. 110-343, Sec. 703(a)DivC, deleted "and" at the end of para. (b)(13), redesignated para. (b)(14) as para. (b)(15), and added a new para. (b)(14), effective for returns the due date for which (determined without regard to any extension) occurs after 12/31/2008.

In 2006, P.L. 109-280, Sec. 1205(b)(1), redesignated subsec. (h) as subsec. (i) and added subsec. (h), effective for returns the due date (determined without regard to extensions) of which is after 8/17/2006.
—P.L. 109-280, Sec. 1223(a), redesignated subsec. (i) [as redesignated by Sec. 1205(b)(1) of this Act] as subsec. (j) and added new subsec. (i) . . . Sec. 1223(b), redesignated subsec. (j) [as redesignated by Sec. 1223(a) of this Act] as subsec. (k) and added subsec. (j), effective for notices and returns with respect to annual periods begin. after 2006.
—P.L. 109-280, Sec. 1223(e), of this Act, provides
"(e) Secretarial outreach requirements.
"(1) Notice requirement. The Secretary of the Treasury shall notify in a timely manner every organization described in section 6033(i) of the Internal Revenue Code of 1986 (as added by this section) of the requirement under such section 6033(i) and of the penalty established under section 6033(j) of such Code—
"(A) by mail, in the case of any organization the identity and address of which is included in the list of exempt organizations maintained by the Secretary, and
"(B) by Internet or other means of outreach, in the case of any other organization.
"(2) Loss of status penalty for failure to file return. The Secretary of the Treasury shall publicize, in a timely manner in appropriate forms and instructions and through other appropriate means, the penalty established under section 6033(j) of such Code for the failure to file a return under subsection (a)(1) or (i) of section 6033 of such Code."
—P.L. 109-280, Sec. 1235(a)(1), redesignated subsec. (k) [as redesignated by Sec. 1223(b) of this Act, see above] as subsec. (l) and added subsec. (k), effective for returns filed for tax. yrs. end. after 8/17/2006.
—P.L. 109-280, Sec. 1245(a), added "(other than an organization described in section 509(a)(3))" after "paragraph (1)" in subpara. (a)(3)(B) . . . Sec. 1245(b), redesignated subsec. (l) [as redesignated by Sec. 1235(a)(1) of this Act, see above] as subsec. (m) and added subsec. (l), effective for returns filed for tax. yrs. end. after 8/17/2006.
—P.L. 109-222, Sec. 516(b)(1)(A), redesignated para. (a)(2) as (a)(3) and added para. (a)(2) . . . Sec. 516(b)(1)(B), substituted "paragraph (3)" for "paragraph (2)" in para. (a)(1), effective for disclosures the due date for which are after 5/17/2006.

In 2002, P.L. 107-276, Sec. 3(c), amended subsec. (g), effective for tax. yrs. begin. after 6/30/2000.
Prior to amendment, subsec. (g) read as follows:
"(g) Returns required by political organizations. In the case of a political organization required to file a return under section 6012(a)(6)—
"(1) such organization shall file a return—
"(A) containing the information required, and complying with the other requirements, under subsection (a)(1) for organizations exempt from taxation under section 501(a), and
"(B) containing such other information as the Secretary deems necessary to carry out the provisions of this subsection, and
"(2) subsection (a)(2)(B) (relating to discretionary exceptions) shall apply with respect to such return."

In 2000, P.L. 106-230, Sec. 3(a)(2), redesignated subsec. (g) as subsec. (h) and added new subsec. (g), effective for tax. yrs. begin. after 6/30/2000.

In 1998, P.L. 105-277, Sec. 1004(b)(2)(A), added "and" at the end of para. (c)(1), deleted para. (c)(2), and redesignated para. (c)(3) as (c)(2), effective as provided in Sec. 1004(b)(3), of this Act, which reads as follows:
"(3) Effective date.
"(A) In general. Except as provided in subparagraph (B), the amendments made by this subsection shall apply to requests made after the later of December 31, 1998, or the 60th day after the Secretary of the Treasury first issues the regulations referred to in section 6104(d)(4) of the Internal Revenue Code of 1986, as amended by this section.
"(B) Publication of annual returns. Section 6104(d) of such Code, as in effect before the amendments made by this subsection, shall not apply to any return the due date for which is after the date such amendments take effect under subparagraph (A)."
Prior to deletion, para. (c)(2) read as follows:
"(2) a copy of the notice required by section 6104(d) (relating to public inspection of private foundations' annual returns), together with proof of publication thereof, shall be filed by the foundation together with the annual return under this section, and"

In 1997, P.L. 105-34, Sec. 1603(b)(1)(A), substituted "the respective amounts (if any) of the taxes imposed on the organization, or any organization manager of the organization, during the taxable year under any of the following provisions (and the respective amounts (if any) of reimbursements paid by the organization during

3,503

the taxable year with respect to taxes imposed on any such organization manager under any of such provisions):" for "the respective amounts (if any) of the taxes paid by the organization during the taxable year under the following provisions:" in para. (b)(10) . . . Sec. 1603(b)(1)(B), added "except to the extent that, by reason of section 4962, the taxes imposed under such section are not required to be paid or are credited or refunded," at the end of subpara. (b)(10)(C) . . . Sec. 1603(b)(2), amended para. (b)(11), effective for returns for tax. yrs. begin. after 7/30/96.

Prior to amendment, para. (b)(11) read as follows:

"(11) the respective amounts (if any) of the taxes paid by the organization, or any disqualified person with respect to such organization, during the taxable year under section 4958 (relating to taxes on private excess benefit from certain charitable organizations),"

In 1996, P.L. 104-188, Sec. 1703(g)(1), added clause (e)(1)(B)(iii) . . . Sec. 1703(g)(2), substituted "section 501" for "this subtitle" in clause (e)(1)(B)(i), effective for amounts paid or incurred after 12/31/93.

—P.L. 104-168, Sec. 1312(a), deleted "and" at the end of para. (b)(9), redesignated para. (b)(10) as para. (b)(14), and added paras. (b)(10)-(13) . . . Sec. 1312(b), redesignated subsec. (f) as subsec. (g) and added new subsec. (f), effective for returns for tax yrs. begin. after 7/30/96.

In 1993, P.L. 103-66, Sec. 13222(c), redesignated subsec. (e) as subsec. (f) and added new subsec. (e), effective for amounts paid or incurred after 12/31/93.

In 1987, P.L. 100-203, Sec. 10703(a), deleted "and" at the end of para. (b)(7), substituted a comma for the period at the end of para (b)(8), and added new paras. (b)(9) and (b)(10), effective for yrs. begin. after 12/31/87.

In 1986, P.L. 99-514, Sec. 1501(d)(1)(C), substituted "section 6652(c)" for "section 6652(d)" in subsec. (e), effective for returns the due date for which (determined without regard to extensions) is after 12/31/86.

In 1980, P.L. 96-603, Sec. 1(a), redesignated subsec. (c) as subsec. (e) and added new subsecs. (c) and (d), effective for tax. yrs. begin. after 12/31/80.

In 1976, P.L. 94-455, Sec. 1307(a)(4), deleted "and" at the end of para. (b)(6), substituted ", and" for the period at the end of para. (b)(7) and added new para. (b)(8) and the flush sentence to subsec. (b), effective on or after 10/4/76.

—P.L. 94-455, Sec. 1906(b)(13)(A), substituted "Secretary" for "Secretary or his delegate" each place it appeared in subsecs. (a) and (b), effective 2/1/77.

In 1974, P.L. 93-406, Sec. 1031(c)(2), added a new paragraph at the end of subsec. (c), effective 9/2/74.

In 1969, P.L. 91-172, Sec. 101(d)(1), amended subsec. (a) . . . Sec. 101(d)(2), amended subsec. (c) . . . Sec. 101(j)(30), deleted "and" from the end of para. (b)(4) [as amended by Sec. 101(d)(2) of this Act] . . . Sec. 101(j)(31), added new para. to the end of subsec. (c), effective for tax. yrs. begin. after 12/31/69.

Prior to amendment, subsecs. (a) and (b) read as follows:

"(a) General.

"Every organization, except as hereinafter provided, exempt from taxation under section 501(a) shall file an annual return, stating specifically the items of gross income, receipts, and disbursements, and such other information for the purpose of carrying out the provisions of subtitle A as the Secretary or his delegate may by forms or regulations prescribe, and shall keep such records, render under oath such statements, make such other returns, and comply with such rules and regulations, as the Secretary or his delegate may from time to time prescribe, except that, in the discretion of the Secretary or his delegate, an organization described in section 401(a) may be relieved from stating in its return any information which is reported in returns filed by the employer which established such organization. No such annual return need be filed under this subsection by any organization exempt from taxation under the provisions of section 501(a)—

"(1) which is a religious organization described in section 501(c)(3); or

"(2) which is an educational organization described in section 501(c)(3), if such organization normally maintains a regular faculty and curriculum and normally has a regularly organized body of pupils or students in attendance at the place where its educational activities are regularly carried on; or

"(3) which is a charitable organization, or an organization for the prevention of cruelty to children or animals, described in section 501(c)(3), if such organization is supported, in whole or in part, by funds contributed by the United States or any State or political subdivision thereof, or is primarily supported by contributions of the general public; or

"(4) which is an organization described in section 501(c)(3), if such organization is operated, supervised, or controlled by or in connection with a religious organization described in paragraph (1); or

"(5) which is an organization described in section 501(c)(8); or

"(6) which is an organization described in section 501(c)(1), if such organization is a corporation wholly-owned by the United States or any agency or instrumentality thereof, or a wholly-owned subsidiary of such a corporation.

"(b) Certain organizations described in section 501(c)(3).

"Every organization described in section 501(c)(3) which is subject to the requirements of subsection (a) shall furnish annually information, at such time and in such manner as the Secretary or his delegate may by forms or regulations prescribe, setting forth—

"(1) its gross income for the year,

"(2) its expenses attributable to such income and incurred within the year,

"(3) its disbursements out of income within the year for the purposes for which it is exempt,

"(4) its accumulation of income within the year,

"(5) its aggregate accumulations of income at the beginning of the year,

"(6) its disbursements out of principal in the current and prior years for the purposes for which it is exempt,

"(7) a balance sheet showing its assets, liabilities, and net worth as of the beginning of such year, and

"(8) the total of the contributions and gifts received by it during the year."

In 1958, P.L. 85-866, Sec. 75(b), deleted "and" at the end of para. (b)(6), substituted ", and" for the period at the end of para. (b)(7), and added para. (b)(8), effective for tax. yrs. end. on or after 12/31/58.

Sec. 6034. Returns by certain trusts.

(a) Split-interest trusts.

Every trust described in section 4947(a)(2) shall furnish such information with respect to the taxable year as the Secretary may by forms or regulations require.

(b) Trusts claiming certain charitable deductions.

(1) In general. Every trust not required to file a return under subsection (a) but claiming a deduction under section 642(c) for the taxable year shall furnish such information with respect to such taxable year as the Secretary may by forms or regulations prescribe, including—

(A) the amount of the deduction taken under section 642(c) within such year,

(B) the amount paid out within such year which represents amounts for which deductions under section 642(c) have been taken in prior years,

(C) the amount for which such deductions have been taken in prior years but which has not been paid out at the beginning of such year,

(D) the amount paid out of principal in the current and prior years for the purposes described in section 642(c),

(E) the total income of the trust within such year and the expenses attributable thereto, and

(F) a balance sheet showing the assets, liabilities, and net worth of the trust as of the beginning of such year.

(2) Exceptions. Paragraph (1) shall not apply to a trust for any taxable year if—

(A) all the net income for such year, determined under the applicable principles of the law of trusts, is required to be distributed currently to the beneficiaries, or

(B) the trust is described in section 4947(a)(1).

In 2006, P.L. 109-280, Sec. 1201(b)(1), amended Code Sec. 6034, effective for returns for tax. yrs. begin. after 12/31/2006.

Prior to amendment, Code Sec. 6034 read as follows:

"SEC. 6034. RETURNS BY TRUSTS DESCRIBED IN SECTION 4947(A)(2) OR CLAIMING CHARITABLE DEDUCTIONS UNDER SECTION 642(C).

"(a) General rule. Every trust described in section 4947(a)(2) or claiming a charitable, etc., deduction under section 642(c) for the taxable year shall furnish such information with respect to such taxable year as the Secretary may by forms or regulations prescribe, including—

"(1) the amount of the charitable, etc., deduction taken under section 642(c) within such year,

"(2) the amount paid out within such year which represents amounts for which charitable, etc., deductions under section 642(c) have been taken in prior years,

"(3) the amount for which charitable, etc., deductions have been taken in prior years but which has not been paid out at the beginning of such year,

"(4) the amount paid out of principal in the current and prior years for charitable, etc., purposes,

"(5) the total income of the trust within such year and the expenses attributable thereto, and

"(6) a balance sheet showing the assets, liabilities, and net worth of the trust as of the beginning of such year.

"(b) Exceptions. This section shall not apply in the case of a taxable year if all the net income for such year, determined under the applicable principles of the law of trusts, is required to be distributed currently to the beneficiaries. This section shall not apply in the case of a trust described in section 4947(a)(1).

"(c) Cross reference. For provisions relating to penalties for failure to file a return required by this section, see section 6652(c)."

In 1986, P.L. 99-514, Sec. 1501(d)(1)(C), substituted "section 6652(c)" for "section 6652(d)", in subsec. (c), effective for returns the due date for which (determined without regard to extensions) is after 12/31/86.

In 1980, P.L. 96-603, Sec. 1(d)(1)(A), substituted "section 4947(a)(2)" for "section 4947(a)" in subsec. (a) . . . Sec. 1(d)(1)(B), added the last sentence of subsec. (b) . . . Sec. 1(d)(1)(C), substituted "exceptions" for "exception" in the heading of subsec. (b) . . . Sec. 1(d)(1)(D), substituted "section 4947(a)(2)" for "section 4947(a)" in the heading of Code Sec. 6034, effective for tax. yrs. begin after 12/31/80.

In 1976, P.L. 94-455, Sec. 1906(b)(13)(A), substituted "Secretary" for "Secretary or his delegate" in Code Sec. 6034, effective 2/1/77.

In 1969, P.L. 91-172, Sec. 101(j)(32), and (33), so much of Code Sec. 6034 as preceded para. (a)(2) . . . Sec. 101(j)(34), added subsec. (c), for tax. yrs. begin. after 12/31/69.

Information and returns   Code Sec. 6035

Prior to amendment, the material preceding para. (a)(2) of Code Sec. 6034 read as follows:

"Sec. 6034. Returns by trusts claiming charitable deductions under section 642(c).

"(a) General rule.

"Every trust claiming a charitable, etc., deduction under section 642(c) for the taxable year shall furnish such information with respect to such taxable year as the Secretary or his delegate may by forms or regulations prescribe, setting forth—

"(1) the amount of the charitable, etc., deduction taken under section 642(c) within such year (showing separately the amount of such deduction which was paid out and the amount which was permanently set aside for charitable, etc., purposes during such year),"

Sec. 6034A. Information to beneficiaries of estates and trusts.

(a) General rule.

The fiduciary of any estate or trust required to file a return under section 6012(a) for any taxable year shall, on or before the date on which such return was required to be filed, furnish to each beneficiary (or nominee thereof)—

(1) who receives a distribution from such estate or trust with respect to such taxable year, or

(2) to whom any item with respect to such taxable year is allocated,

a statement containing such information required to be shown on such return as the Secretary may prescribe.

(b) Nominee reporting.

Any person who holds an interest in an estate or trust as a nominee for another person—

(1) shall furnish to the estate or trust, in the manner prescribed by the Secretary, the name and address of such other person, and any other information for the taxable year as the Secretary may by form and regulations prescribe, and

(2) shall furnish in the manner prescribed by the Secretary to such other person the information provided by the estate or trust under subsection (a).

(c) Beneficiary's return must be consistent with estate or trust return or Secretary notified of inconsistency.

(1) In general. A beneficiary of any estate or trust to which subsection (a) applies shall, on such beneficiary's return, treat any reported item in a manner which is consistent with the treatment of such item on the applicable entity's return.

(2) Notification of inconsistent treatment.

(A) In general. In the case of any reported item, if—

(i)(I) the applicable entity has filed a return but the beneficiary's treatment on such beneficiary's return is (or may be) inconsistent with the treatment of the item on the applicable entity's return, or

(II) the applicable entity has not filed a return, and

(ii) the beneficiary files with the Secretary a statement identifying the inconsistency,

paragraph (1) shall not apply to such item.

(B) Beneficiary receiving incorrect information. A beneficiary shall be treated as having complied with clause (i) of subparagraph (A) with respect to a reported item if the beneficiary—

(i) demonstrates to the satisfaction of the Secretary that the treatment of the reported item on the beneficiary's return is consistent with the treatment of the item on the statement furnished under subsection (a) to the beneficiary by the applicable entity, and

(ii) elects to have this paragraph apply with respect to that item.

(3) Effect of failure to notify. In any case—

(A) described in subparagraph (A)(i)(I) of paragraph (2), and

(B) in which the beneficiary does not comply with subparagraph (A)(ii) of paragraph (2),

any adjustment required to make the treatment of the items by such beneficiary consistent with the treatment of the items on the applicable entity's return shall be treated as arising out of mathematical or clerical errors and assessed according to section 6213(b)(1). Paragraph (2) of section 6213(b) shall not apply to any assessment referred to in the preceding sentence.

(4) Definitions. For purposes of this subsection—

(A) Reported item. The term "reported item" means any item for which information is required to be furnished under subsection (a).

(B) Applicable entity. The term "applicable entity" means the estate or trust of which the taxpayer is the beneficiary.

(5) Addition to tax for failure to comply with section. For addition to tax in the case of a beneficiary's negligence in connection with, or disregard of, the requirements of this section, see part II of subchapter A of chapter 68.

In 1997, P.L. 105-34, Sec. 1027(a), added subsec. (c), effective for returns of beneficiaries and owners filed after 8/597.

In 1986, P.L. 99-514, Sec. 1501(c)(15)(A), substituted "required to file a return" for "making the return required to be filed" in subsec. (a)... Sec. 1501(c)(15)(B), substituted "was required to be filed" for "was filed" in subsec. (a)... Sec. 1501(c)(15)(C), substituted "required to be shown on such return" for "shown on such return" in subsec. (a), effective for returns the due date for which (determined without regard to extensions) is after 12/31/86.

—P.L. 99-514, Sec. 1875(d)(3)(A)(i), substituted "(a) General rule. The fiduciary" for "The fiduciary" in subsec. (a)... Sec. 1875(d)(3)(A)(ii), substituted "each beneficiary (or nominee thereof)" for "each beneficiary" in subsec. (a)... Sec. 1875(d)(3)(A)(iii), added subsec. (b), effective for tax. yrs. of estates and trusts beginning after 10/22/86.

In 1984, P.L. 98-369, Sec. 714(q)(1), added Code Sec. 6034A, effective for tax. yrs. begin. after 12/31/84.

Sec. 6035. Repealed.

In 2004, P.L. 108-357, Sec. 413(c)(26), repealed Code Sec. 6035, effective for tax. yrs. of foreign corporations begin. after 12/31/2004, and for tax. yrs. of United States shareholders with or within which such tax. yrs. of foreign corporations end.

Prior to repeal, Code Sec. 6035 read as follows:

"Sec. 6035. Returns of officers, directors, and shareholders of foreign personal holding companies.

"(a) General rule. Each United States citizen or resident who is an officer, director, or 10-percent shareholder of a corporation which was a foreign personal holding company (as defined in section 552) for any taxable year shall file a return with respect to such taxable year setting forth—

"(1) the shareholder information required by subsection (b),

"(2) the income information required by subsection (c), and

"(3) such other information with respect to such corporation as the Secretary shall by forms or regulations prescribe as necessary for carrying out the purposes of this title.

"(b) Shareholder information. The shareholder information required by this subsection with respect to any taxable year shall be—

"(1) the name and address of each person who at any time during such taxable year held any share in the corporation,

"(2) a description of each class of shares and the total number of shares of such class outstanding at the close of the taxable year,

"(3) the number of shares of each class held by each person, and

"(4) any changes in the holdings of shares during the taxable year.

"For purposes of paragraphs (1), (3), and (4), the term 'share' includes any security convertible into a share in the corporation and any option granted by the corporation with respect to any share in the corporation.

"(c) Income information. The income information required by this subsection for any taxable year shall be the gross income, deductions, credits, taxable income, and undistributed foreign personal holding company income of the corporation for the taxable year.

"(d) Time and manner for furnishing information. The information required under subsection (a) shall be furnished at such time and in such manner as the Secretary shall by forms and regulations prescribe.

"(e) Definition and special rules.

"(1) 10-percent shareholder. For purposes of this section, the term '10-percent shareholder' means any individual who owns directly or indirectly (within the meaning of section 554) 10 percent or more in value of the outstanding stock of a foreign corporation.

"(2) Time for making determinations.

3,505

"(A) In general. Except as provided in subparagraph (B), the determination of whether any person is an officer, director, or 10-percent shareholder with respect to any foreign corporation shall be made as of the date on which the return is required to be filed.

"(B) Special rule. If after the application of subparagraph (A) no person is required to file a return under subsection (a) with respect to any foreign corporation for any taxable year, the determination of whether any person is an officer, director, or 10-percent shareholder with respect to such foreign corporation shall be made on the last day of such taxable year on which there was such a person who was a United States citizen or resident.

"(3) 2 or more persons required to furnish information with respect to same foreign corporation. If, but for this paragraph, 2 or more persons would be required to furnish information under subsection (a) with respect to the same foreign corporation for the same taxable year, the Secretary may by regulations provide that such information shall be furnished only from 1 person."

In 1982, P.L. 97-248, Sec. 340(a), amended Code Sec. 6035, effective for tax. yrs. of foreign corporations begin after 9/3/82.

Prior to amendment, Code Sec. 6035 read as follows:

"SEC. 6035. RETURNS OF OFFICERS, DIRECTORS, AND SHAREHOLDERS OF FOREIGN PERSONAL HOLDING COMPANIES.

"(a) Officers and directors.

"(1) Monthly returns. On the 15th day of each month each individual who on such day is an officer or a director of a foreign corporation which, with respect to its taxable year preceding the taxable year in which such month occurs, was a foreign personal holding company (as defined in section 552), shall make a return setting forth with respect to the preceding calendar month the name and address of each shareholder, the class and number of shares held by each, together with any changes in stockholdings during such period, the name and address of any holder of securities convertible into stock of such corporation, and such other information with respect to the stock and securities of the corporation as the Secretary shall by forms or regulations prescribe as necessary for carrying out the provisions of this title. The Secretary may by regulations prescribe, as the period with respect to which returns shall be made, a longer period than a month. In such case the return shall be due on the 15th day of the succeeding period, and shall be made by the individuals who on such day are officers or directors of the corporation.

"(2) Annual returns. On the 60th day after the close of the taxable year of a foreign personal holding company (as defined in section 552), each individual who on such 60th day is an officer or director of the corporation shall make a return setting forth—

"(A) in complete detail the gross income, deductions and credits, taxable income, and undistributed foreign personal holding company income of such foreign personal holding company for such taxable year; and

"(B) the same information with respect to such taxable year as is required in paragraph (1), except that if all the required returns with respect to such year have been filed under paragraph (1), no information under this subparagraph need be set forth in the return filed under this paragraph.

"(b) Shareholders.

"(1) Monthly returns. On the 15th day of each month each United States shareholder, by or for whom 50 percent or more in value of the outstanding stock of a foreign corporation is owned directly or indirectly (including, in the case of an individual, stock owned by the members of his family as defined in section 544(a)(2)), if such foreign corporation with respect to its taxable year preceding the taxable year in which such month occurs was a foreign personal holding company (as defined in section 552), shall make a return setting forth with respect to the preceding calendar month the name and address of each shareholder, the class and number of shares held by each, together with any changes in stockholdings during such period, the name and address of any holder of securities convertible into stock of such corporation, and such other information with respect to the stock and securities of the corporation as the Secretary shall by forms or regulations prescribe as necessary for carrying out the provisions of this title. The Secretary may by regulations prescribe, as the period with respect to which returns shall be made, a longer period than a month. In such case the return shall be due on the 15th day of the succeeding period, and shall be made by the persons who on such day are United States shareholders.

"(2) Annual returns. On the 60th day after the close of the taxable year of a foreign personal holding company (as defined in section 552) each United States shareholder by or for whom on such 60th day 50 percent or more in value of the outstanding stock of such company is owned directly or indirectly (including, in the case of an individual, stock owned by members of his family as defined in section 544(a)(2)) shall make a return setting forth the same information with respect to such taxable year as is required in paragraph (1), except that, if all the required returns with respect to such year have been made under paragraph (1), no return shall be required under this paragraph."

In 1976, P.L. 94-455, Sec. 1906(b)(13)(A), substituted "Secretary" for "Secretary or his delegate" each place it appeared in Code Sec. 6035, effective 2/1/77.

Sec. 6036. Notice of qualification as executor or receiver.

Every receiver, trustee in a case under title 11 of the United States Code, assignee for benefit of creditors, or other like fiduciary, and every executor (as defined in section 2203), shall give notice of his qualification as such to the Secretary in such manner and at such time as may be required by regulations of the Secretary. The Secretary may by regulation provide such exemptions from the requirements of this section as the Secretary deems proper.

In 1980, P.L. 96-589, Sec. 6(i)(6), substituted "trustee in a case under title 11 of the United States Code" for "trustee in bankruptcy" in Code Sec. 6036, effective 10/1/79, except for any proceeding under the Bankruptcy Act begun before 10/1/79.

In 1976, P.L. 94-455, Sec. 1906(b)(13)(A), substituted "Secretary" for "Secretary or his delegate" each place it appeared in Code Sec. 6036, effective 2/1/77.

Sec. 6037. Return of S corporation.

(a) In general.

Every S corporation shall make a return for each taxable year, stating specifically the items of its gross income and the deductions allowable by subtitle A, the names and addresses of all persons owning stock in the corporation at any time during the taxable year, the number of shares of stock owned by each shareholder at all times during the taxable year, the amount of money and other property distributed by the corporation during the taxable year to each shareholder, the date of each such distribution, each shareholder's pro rata share of each item of the corporation for the taxable year, and such other information, for the purpose of carrying out the provisions of subchapter S of chapter 1, as the Secretary may by forms and regulations prescribe. Any return filed pursuant to this section shall, for purposes of chapter 66 (relating to limitations), be treated as a return filed by the corporation under section 6012.

(b) Copies to shareholders.

Each S corporation required to file a return under subsection (a) for any taxable year shall (on or before the day on which the return for such taxable year was filed) furnish to each person who is a shareholder at any time during such taxable year a copy of such information shown on such return as may be required by regulations.

(c) Shareholder's return must be consistent with corporate return or secretary notified of inconsistency.

(1) In general. A shareholder of an S corporation shall, on such shareholder's return, treat a subchapter S item in a manner which is consistent with the treatment of such item on the corporate return.

(2) Notification of inconsistent treatment.

(A) In general. In the case of any subchapter S item, if—

(i)(I) the corporation has filed a return but the shareholder's treatment on his return is (or may be) inconsistent with the treatment of the item on the corporate return, or

(II) the corporation has not filed a return, and

(ii) the shareholder files with the Secretary a statement identifying the inconsistency,

paragraph (1) shall not apply to such item.

(B) Shareholder receiving incorrect information. A shareholder shall be treated as having complied with clause (ii) of subparagraph (A) with respect to a subchapter S item if the shareholder—

(i) demonstrates to the satisfaction of the Secretary that the treatment of the subchapter S item on the shareholder's return is consistent with the treatment of the item on the schedule furnished to the shareholder by the corporation, and

(ii) elects to have this paragraph apply with respect to that item.

(3) Effect of failure to notify. In any case—

(A) described in subparagraph (A)(i)(I) of paragraph (2), and

(B) in which the shareholder does not comply with subparagraph (A)(ii) of paragraph (2), any adjustment required to make the treatment of the items by such shareholder consistent with the treatment of the items on the corporate return shall be treated as arising out of mathematical or clerical errors and assessed according to section 6213(b)(1). Paragraph (2) of section 6213(b) shall not apply to any assessment referred to in the preceding sentence.

(4) Subchapter S item. For purposes of this subsection, the term "subchapter S item" means any item of an S corporation to the extent that regulations prescribed by the Secretary provide that, for purposes of this subtitle, such item is more appropriately determined at the corporation level than at the shareholder level.

(5) Addition to tax for failure to comply with section. For addition to tax in the case of a shareholder's negligence in connection with, or disregard of, the requirements of this section, see part II of subchapter A of chapter 68.

In **1996,** P.L. 104-188, Sec. 1307(c)(2), added subsec. (c), effective for tax. yrs. begin. after 12/31/96.

In **1984,** P.L. 98-369, Sec. 714(q)(2)(A), added "(a) In general.—Every" for "Every" ... Sec. 714(q)(2)(B), added subsec. (b), effective for tax. yrs. begin. after 12/31/84.

In **1982,** P.L. 97-354, Sec. 5(a)(39)(A), substituted "Every S corporation" for "Every electing small business corporation (as defined in section 1371(b))", substituted "each shareholder's pro rata share of each item of the corporation for the taxable year, and such other information" for "and such information" in Code Sec. 6037, and substituted "S corporation" for "electing small business corporation" in the heading of Code Sec. 6037, effective for tax. yrs. begin. after 12/31/82.

In **1976,** P.L. 94-455, Sec. 1906(a)(3), substituted "section 1371(b)" for "section 1371(a)(2)," in Code Sec. 6037, ... Sec. 1906(b)(13)(A), substituted "Secretary" for "Secretary or his delegate" in Code Sec. 6037, effective 2/1/77.

In **1958,** P.L. 85-866, Sec. 64(c), redesignated Code Sec. 6037 as Code Sec. 6038 and added Code Sec. 6037, effective for tax. yrs. begin. after 12/31/57.

Sec. 6038. Information reporting with respect to certain foreign corporations and partnerships.

(a) Requirement.

(1) In general. Every United States person shall furnish, with respect to any foreign business entity which such person controls, such information as the Secretary may prescribe relating to—

(A) the name, the principal place of business, and the nature of business of such entity, and the country under whose laws such entity is incorporated (or organized in the case of a partnership);

(B) in the case of a foreign corporation, its post-1986 undistributed earnings (as defined in section 902(c));

(C) a balance sheet for such entity listing assets, liabilities, and capital;

(D) transactions between such entity and—
 (i) such person,
 (ii) any corporation or partnership which such person controls, and
 (iii) any United States person owning, at the time the transaction takes place—
  (I) in the case of a foreign corporation, 10 percent or more of the value of any class of stock outstanding of such corporation, and
  (II) in the case of a foreign partnership, at least a 10-percent interest in such partnership; and

(E)(i) in the case of a foreign corporation, a description of the various classes of stock outstanding, and a list showing the name and address of, and number of shares held by, each United States person who is a shareholder of record owning at any time during the annual accounting period 5 percent or more in value of any class of stock outstanding of such foreign corporation, and

(ii) information comparable to the information described in clause (i) in the case of a foreign partnership.

The Secretary may also require the furnishing of any other information which is similar or related in nature to that specified in the preceding sentence or which the Secretary determines to be appropriate to carry out the provisions of this title.

(2) Period for which information is to be furnished, etc. The information required under paragraph (1) shall be furnished for the annual accounting period of the foreign business entity ending with or within the United States person's taxable year. The information so required shall be furnished at such time and in such manner as the Secretary shall prescribe.

(3) Limitation. No information shall be required to be furnished under this subsection with respect to any foreign business entity for any annual accounting period unless the Secretary has prescribed the furnishing of such information on or before the first day of such annual accounting period.

(4) Information required from certain shareholders in certain cases. If any foreign corporation is treated as a controlled foreign corporation for any purpose under subpart F of part III of subchapter N of chapter 1, the Secretary may require any United States person treated as a United States shareholder of such corporation for any purpose under subpart F to furnish the information required under paragraph (1).

(5) Information required from 10-percent partner of controlled foreign partnership. In the case of a foreign partnership which is controlled by United States persons holding at least 10-percent interests (but not by any one United States person), the Secretary may require each United States person who holds a 10-percent interest in such partnership to furnish information relating to such partnership, including information relating to such partner's ownership interests in the partnership and allocations to such partner of partnership items.

(b) Dollar penalty for failure to furnish information.

(1) In general. If any person fails to furnish, within the time prescribed under paragraph (2) of subsection (a), any information with respect to any foreign business entity required under paragraph (1) of subsection (a), such person shall pay a penalty of $10,000 for each annual accounting period with respect to which such failure exists.

(2) Increase in penalty where failure continues after notification. If any failure described in paragraph (1) continues for more than 90 days after the day on which the Secretary mails notice of such failure to the United States person, such person shall pay a penalty (in addition to the amount required under paragraph (1)) of $10,000 for each 30-day period (or fraction thereof) during which such failure continues with respect to any annual accounting period after the expiration of such 90-day period. The increase in any penalty under this paragraph shall not exceed $50,000.

(c) Penalty of reducing foreign tax credit.

(1) In general. If a United States person fails to furnish, within the time prescribed under paragraph (2) of subsection (a), any information with respect to any foreign business entity required under paragraph (1) of subsection (a), then—

(A) in applying section 901 (relating to taxes of foreign countries and possessions of the United States) to such United States person for the taxable year, the amount of taxes (other than taxes reduced under subparagraph (B)) paid or deemed paid (other than those deemed paid under section 904(c)) to any foreign country or possession of the United States for the taxable year shall be reduced by 10 percent, and

(B) in the case of a foreign business entity which is a foreign corporation, in applying sections 902 (relating to foreign tax credit for corporate stockholder in foreign corporation) and 960 (relating to special rules for foreign tax credit) to any such United States person which is a corporation (or to any person who acquires from any other person any portion of the interest of such other person in any such foreign corporation, but only to the extent of such portion) for any taxable year, the amount of taxes paid or deemed paid by each foreign corporation with respect to which such person is required to furnish information during the annual accounting period or periods with respect to which such information is required under paragraph (2) of subsection (a) shall be reduced by 10 percent.

If such failure continues 90 days or more after notice of such failure by the Secretary to the United States person, then the amount of the reduction under this paragraph shall be 10 percent plus an additional 5 percent for each 3-month period, or fraction thereof, during which such failure to furnish information continues after the expiration of such 90-day period.

(2) Limitation. The amount of the reduction under paragraph (1) for each failure to furnish information with respect to a foreign business entity required under subsection (a)(1) shall not exceed whichever of the following amounts is the greater:

(A) $10,000, or

(B) the income of the foreign business entity for its annual accounting period with respect to which the failure occurs.

(3) Coordination with subsection (b). The amount of the reduction which (but for this paragraph) would be made under paragraph (1) with respect to any annual accounting period shall be reduced by the amount of the penalty imposed by subsection (b) with respect to such period.

(4) Special rules.

(A) No taxes shall be reduced under this subsection more than once for the same failure.

(B) For purposes of this subsection and subsection (b), the time prescribed under paragraph (2) of subsection (a) to furnish information (and the beginning of the 90-day period after notice by the Secretary) shall be treated as being not earlier than the last day on which (as shown to the satisfaction of the Secretary) reasonable cause existed for failure to furnish such information.

(C) In applying subsections (a) and (b) of section 902, and in applying subsection (a) of section 960, the reduction provided by this subsection shall not apply for purposes of determining the amount of post-1986 undistributed earnings.

(d) Two or more persons required to furnish information with respect to same foreign business entity.

Where, but for this subsection, two or more United States persons would be required to furnish information under subsection (a) with respect to the same foreign business entity for the same period, the Secretary may by regulations provide that such information shall be required only from one person. To the extent practicable, the determination of which person shall furnish the information shall be made on the basis of actual ownership of stock.

(e) Definitions.

For purposes of this section—

(1) Foreign business entity. The term "foreign business entity" means a foreign corporation and a foreign partnership.

(2) Control of corporation. A person is in control of a corporation if such person owns stock possessing more than 50 percent of the total combined voting power of all classes of stock entitled to vote, or more than 50 percent of the total value of shares of all classes of stock, of a corporation. If a person is in control (within the meaning of the preceding sentence) of a corporation which in turn owns more than 50 percent of the total combined voting power of all classes of stock entitled to vote of another corporation, or owns more than 50 percent of the total value of the shares of all classes of stock of another corporation, then such person shall be treated as in control of such other corporation. For purposes of this paragraph, the rules prescribed by section 318(a) for determining ownership of stock shall apply; except that—

(A) subparagraphs (A), (B), and (C) of section 318(a)(3) shall not be applied so as to consider a United States person as owning stock which is owned by a person who is not a United States person, and

(B) in applying subparagraph (C) of section 318(a)(2), the phrase "10 percent" shall be substituted for the phrase "50 percent" used in subparagraph (C).

(3) Partnership-related definitions.

(A) Control. A person is in control of a partnership if such person owns directly or indirectly more than a 50 percent interest in such partnership.

(B) 50-percent interest. For purposes of subparagraph (A), a 50-percent interest in a partnership is—

(i) an interest equal to 50 percent of the capital interest, or 50 percent of the profits interest, in such partnership, or

(ii) to the extent provided in regulations, an interest to which 50 percent of the deductions or losses of such partnership are allocated.

For purposes of the preceding sentence, rules similar to the rules of section 267(c) (other than paragraph (3)) shall apply,

(C) 10-percent interest. A 10-percent interest in a partnership is an interest which would be described in subparagraph (B) if "10 percent" were substituted for "50 percent" each place it appears.

(4) Annual accounting period. The annual accounting period of a foreign business entity is the annual period on the basis of which such foreign business entity regularly computes its income in keeping its books. In the case of a specified foreign business entity (as defined in section 898), the taxable year of such foreign business entity shall be treated as its annual accounting period.

(f) Cross references.

(1) For provisions relating to penalties for violations of this section, see section 7203.

(2) For definition of the term "United States person", see section 7701(a)(30).

In 1998, P.L. 105-206, Sec. 6011(f)(1), deleted "by regulations" after "in such manner as the Secretary shall" in para. (a)(2) . . . Sec. 6011(f)(2), substituted "the Secretary has prescribed the furnishing of such information on or before the first day of such annual accounting period." for "such information was required to be furnished under regulations in effect on the first day of such annual accounting period." in para. (a)(3) . . . Sec. 6011(f)(3), substituted "foreign business entity" for "corporation" each place it appeared in para. (e)(4), effective for annual accountability periods begin. after 8/5/97.

In 1997, P.L. 105-34, Sec. 1142(a), amended all that precedes para. (a)(2) . . . Sec. 1142(b)(1)(A), redesignated paras. (e)(1) and (2) as paras. (e)(2) and (4) . . . Sec.

1142(b)(1)(B), added para. (e)(1) . . . Sec. 1142(b)(1)(C), added para. (e)(3) . . . Sec. 1142(b)(2), added "of corporation" after "Control" in the heading of para. (e)(2) [as redesignated by Sec. 1142(b)(1)(A) of this Act, see above] . . . Sec. 1142(c)(1)(A), substituted "$10,000" for "$1,000" each place it appeared in subsec. (b) . . . Sec. 1142(c)(1)(B), substituted "$50,000" for "$24,000" in para. (b)(2) . . . Sec. 1142(d), added para. (a)(5) . . . Sec. 1142(e)(1)(A), substituted "foreign business entity" for "foreign corporation" in paras. (a)(2) and (3) . . . Sec. 1142(e)(1)(B), substituted "foreign business entity" for "foreign corporation" in para. (b)(1) . . . Sec. 1142(e)(1)(C), substituted "foreign business entity" for "foreign corporation" each place it appeared in subsec. (c), except for subpara. (c)(1)(B) . . . Sec. 1142(e)(1)(D), substituted "foreign business entity" for "foreign corporation" each place it appeared in subsec. (d) . . . Sec. 1142(e)(1)(E), substituted "foreign business entity" for "foreign corporation" each place it appeared in para. (e)(4) [as redesignated by Sec. 1142(b)(1)(B) of this Act, see above] . . . Sec. 1142(e)(2), added "in the case of a foreign business entity which is a foreign corporation," before "in applying sections 902" in subpara. (c)(1)(B), effective for annual accounting periods begin. after 8/5/97.

Prior to amendment, all that precedes para. (a)(2) read as follows:

"SEC. 6038. INFORMATION WITH RESPECT TO CERTAIN FOREIGN CORPORATIONS.

"(a) Requirement.

"(1) In general. Every United States person shall furnish, with respect to any foreign corporation which such person controls (within the meaning of subsection (e)(1)), such information as the Secretary may prescribe by regulations relating to—

"(A) the name, the principal place of business, and the nature of business of such foreign corporation, and the country under whose laws incorporated;

"(B) the post-1986 undistributed earnings (as defined in section 902(c)) of such foreign corporation,

"(C) a balance sheet for such foreign corporation listing assets, liabilities, and capital;

"(D) transactions between such foreign corporation and—

"(i) such person,

"(ii) any other corporation which such person controls, and

"(iii) any United States person owning, at the time the transaction takes place, 10 percent or more of the value of any class of stock outstanding of such foreign corporation;

"(E) a description of the various classes of stock outstanding, and a list showing the name and address of, and number of shares held by, each United States person who is a shareholder of record owning at any time during the annual accounting period 5 percent or more in value of any class of stock outstanding of such foreign corporation.

The Secretary may also require the furnishing of any other information which is similar or related in nature to that specified in the preceding sentence or which the Secretary determines to be appropriate to carry out the provisions of this title."

In 1996, P.L. 104-188, Sec. 1704(f)(5)(A), deleted ", and" at the end of subpara. (a)(1)(E) and deleted subpara. (a)(1)(F) . . . Sec. 1704(t)(40), redesignated subsec. (e) relating to cross references as subsec. (f), effective 8/20/96.

Prior to deletion, subpara. (a)(1)(F) read as follows:

"(F) such information as the Secretary may require for purposes of carrying out the provisions of section 453C."

—P.L. 104-188, Sec. 1704(t)(46), added "(relating to definitions)" after "section 6038(e)" in Sec. 11701(f) of P.L. 101-508, see below.

In 1990, P.L. 101-508, Sec. 11701(f), added the last sentence to para. (e)(2) [amended by Sec. 1704(t)(46) of P.L. 104-188, see above], effective for tax. yrs. begin. after 7/10/89, except as provided in Sec. 7401(d)(2) of P.L. 101-239, reproduced in note following Code Sec. 898.

In 1989, P.L. 101-239, Sec. 7712(a)(1), added para. (a)(4) . . . Sec. 7712(a)(2), added "or which the Secretary determines to be appropriate to carry out the provisions of this title" before the period of the last sentence in para. (a)(1), effective for returns and statements the due date for which (determined without regard to extensions) is after 12/31/89.

In 1986, P.L. 99-514, Sec. 1202(c)(1), amended subpara. (a)(1)(B) . . . Sec. 1202(c)(2), substituted "post-1986 undistributed earnings" for "accumulated profits in excess of income, war profits, and excess profits taxes" in subpara. (c)(4)(C), effective for distributions by foreign corporations out of, and inclusions under attributable to, earnings and profits for tax. yrs. begin. after 12/31/86.

Prior to amendment, subpara. (a)(1)(B) read as follows:

"(B) the accumulated profits (as defined in section 902(c)) of such foreign corporation, including the items of income (whether or not included in gross income under chapter 1), deductions (whether or not allowed in computing taxable income under chapter 1), and any other times taken into account in computing such accumulated profits;"

—P.L. 99-514, Sec. 1245(b)(5), deleted "and" at the end of subpara. (a)(1)(D), substituted ", and" for the period at the end of subpara. (a)(1)(E), and added subpara. (a)(1)(F), effective for tax. yrs. begin. after 12/31/86.

In 1982, P.L. 97-248, Sec. 338(a), redesignated subsecs. (b), (c) and (d) as subsecs. (c), (d) and (e) and added new subsec. (b) . . . Sec. 338(b)(1), added "and subsection (b)" after "subsection" in subpara. (c)(3)(B) (as redesignated by Sec. 338(a) of this Act) . . . Sec. 338(b)(2), redesignated para. (c)(3) (as redesignated by Sec. 338(a) of this Act) as para. (c)(4) and added new para. (c)(3) . . . Sec. 338(c)(1), amended the heading of subsec. (c) (as redesignated by Sec. 338(a) of this Act) . . . Sec. 338(c)(2), substituted "within the meaning of subsection (e)(1)" for "within the meaning of subsection (d)(1)" in para. (a)(1) . . . Sec. 338(c)(3), added "of such failure" after "notice" in para. (c)(1) (as redesignated by Sec. 338(a) of this Act), effective for information for annual accounting periods ending after 9/3/82.

Prior to amendment, the heading of subsec. (c) read as follows:

"(c) Effect of failure to furnish information."

In 1976, P.L. 94-455, Sec. 1031(b)(5), substituted "section 904(c)" for "section 904(d)" in subpara. (b)(1)(A), effective for tax. yrs. begin. after 12/31/75.

—P.L. 94-455, Sec. 1906(b)(13)(A), substituted "Secretary" for "Secretary or his delegate" each place it appeared in Code Sec. 6038, effective 2/1/77.

In 1964, P.L. 88-554, Sec. 4(b)(6), substituted "subparagraphs (A), (B), and (C) of section 318(a)(3)" for "the second sentence of subparagraphs (A) and (B), and clause (ii) of subparagraph (C), of section 318(a)(2)" in subpara. (d)(1)(A), and deleted "clause (i) of" after "in applying" in subpara. (d)(1)(B), effective 8/31/64, except that for purposes of sections 302 and 304 of this title, such amendments shall not apply to distributions in payment for stock acquisitions or redemptions, if such acquisitions or redemptions occurred on 8/31/64.

In 1962, P.L. 87-834, Sec. 20, amended Code Sec. 6038, effective for annual accounting periods of foreign corporations beginning after 12/31/62.

Prior to amendment, Code Sec. 6038 read as follows:

"(a) Requirement.

"(1) In general. A domestic corporation shall furnish, with respect to any foreign corporation which it controls (within the meaning of subsection (c)(1)) and with respect to any foreign subsidiary of any such foreign corporation (within the meaning of subsection (c)(2)), such information as the Secretary or his delegate may prescribe by regulations relating to—

"(A) the name, the principal place of business, and the nature of business of such foreign corporation or foreign subsidiary, and the country under whose laws incorporated;

"(B) the accumulated profits (as defined in section 902(c)) of such foreign corporation or foreign subsidiary, including the items of income (whether or not included in gross income under chapter 1), deductions (whether or not allowed in computing taxable income under chapter 1), and any other items taken into account in computing such accumulated profits;

"(C) a balance sheet for such foreign corporation or foreign subsidiary, listing assets, liabilities, and capital;

"(D) transactions between such foreign corporation or foreign subsidiary and—

"(i) any foreign corporation controlled by the domestic corporation,

"(ii) any foreign subsidiary of a foreign corporation controlled by the domestic corporation, and

"(iii) the domestic corporation or any shareholder of the domestic corporation owning at the time the transaction takes place the 10 percent or more of the value of any class of stock outstanding of the domestic corporation; and

"(E) a description of the various classes of stock outstanding, and a list showing the name and address of, and number of shares held by, each citizen or resident of the United States and each domestic corporation who is a shareholder of record owning at any time during the annual accounting period 5 percent or more in value of any class of stock outstanding of such foreign corporation or foreign subsidiary.

"(2) Period for which information is to be furnished, etc. The information required under paragraph (1) shall be furnished—

"(A) in the case of a foreign corporation, for its annual accounting period ending with or within the domestic corporation's taxable year, and

"(B) in the case of any foreign subsidiary of such foreign corporation, for such subsidiary's annual accounting period ending with or within such foreign corporation's annual accounting period described in subparagraph (A).

The information required under this subsection shall be furnished at such time and in such manner as the Secretary or his delegate shall by regulations prescribe.

"(3) Limitation. No information shall be required to be furnished under this subsection with respect to any foreign corporation or foreign subsidiary for any annual accounting period unless such information was required to be furnished under regulations in effect on the first day of such annual accounting period.

"(b) Effect of failure to furnish information.

"If a domestic corporation fails to furnish, within the time prescribed under paragraph (2) of subsection (a), any information with respect to any foreign corporation or foreign subsidiary required under paragraph (1) of subsection (a), then, in applying section 902 (relating to foreign tax credit for corporate stockholder in foreign corporation) to such domestic corporation (or to any person who acquires from any person any portion of the interest of such domestic corporation in any such foreign corporation or foreign subsidiary, but only to the extent of such portion) for any taxable year, the amount of taxes paid or deemed paid by each foreign corporation and foreign subsidiary with respect to which the domestic corporation is required to furnish information during the annual accounting period or periods with respect to which such information is required under such paragraph (2) of subsection (a) shall be reduced by 10 percent. If such failure continues 90 days or more after notice by the Secretary or his delegate to the domestic corporation, then the amount of the reduction under this subsection shall be 10 percent plus an additional 5 percent for each 3-month period, or fraction thereof, during which such failure to furnish information continues after the expiration of such 90-day period. No taxes shall be reduced under this subsection more than once for the same failure. For purposes of this subsection, the time prescribed under paragraph (2) of subsection (a) to furnish information (and the beginning of the 90-day period after notice by the Secretary) shall be treated as being not earlier than the last day on which (as shown to the satisfaction of the Secretary or his delegate) reasonable cause existed for failure to furnish such information.

"(c) Control, Etc.

"For purposes of this section—

"(1) If at any time during its taxable year a domestic corporation owns more than 50 percent of the voting stock of a foreign corporation, it shall be deemed to be in control of such foreign corporation.

"(2) If at any time during its annual accounting period a foreign corporation owns more than 50 percent of the voting stock of another foreign corporation, such other corporation shall be considered a foreign subsidiary of the corporation owning such stock.

"(d) Annual Accounting Period.

"For purposes of this section, the annual accounting period of a foreign corporation or of a foreign subsidiary is the annual period on the basis of which such foreign corporation or such foreign subsidiary regularly computes its income in keeping its books.

"(e) Cross references.

"For provisions relating to penalties for violations of this section, see section 7203."

In 1960, P.L. 86-780, Sec. 6(a), redesignated Code Sec. 6038 as 6039 and added Code Sec. 6038, effective for tax. yrs. of domestic corporations begin. after '60 with respect to information relating to a foreign corporation or a foreign subsidiary described in section 6038(a) of the Internal Revenue Code of 1954 (as added by subsection (a)) for its annual accounting periods beginning after December 31, 1960.

Sec. 6038A. Information with respect to certain foreign-owned corporations.

(a) Requirement.

If, at any time during a taxable year, a corporation (hereinafter in this section referred to as the "reporting corporation")—

(1) is a domestic corporation, and

(2) is 25-percent foreign-owned,

such corporation shall furnish, at such time and in such manner as the Secretary shall by regulations prescribe, the information described in subsection (b) and such corporation shall maintain (in the location, in the manner, and to the extent prescribed in regulations) such records as may be appropriate to determine the correct treatment of transactions with related parties as the Secretary shall by regulations prescribe (or shall cause another person to so maintain such records).

(b) Required information.

For purposes of subsection (a), the information described in this subsection is such information as the Secretary may prescribe by regulations relating to—

(1) the name, principal place of business, nature of business, and country or countries in which organized or resident, of each person which—

(A) is a related party to the reporting corporation, and

(B) had any transaction with the reporting corporation during its taxable year,

(2) the manner in which the reporting corporation is related to each person referred to in paragraph (1), and

(3) transactions between the reporting corporation and each foreign person which is a related party to the reporting. corporation

(c) Definitions.

For purposes of this section—

(1) **25-percent foreign-owned.** A corporation is 25-percent foreign-owned if at least 25 percent of—

(A) the total voting power of all classes of stock of such corporation entitled to vote, or

(B) the total value of all classes of stock of such corporation,

is owned at any time during the taxable year by 1 foreign person (hereinafter in this section referred to as a "25-percent foreign shareholder").

(2) **Related party.** The term "related party" means—

(A) any 25-percent foreign shareholder of the reporting corporation,

(B) any person who is related (within the meaning of section 267(b) or 707(b)(1)) to the reporting corporation or to a 25-percent foreign shareholder of the reporting corporation, and

(C) any other person who is related (within the meaning of section 482) to the reporting corporation.

(3) **Foreign person.** The term "foreign person" means any person who is not a United States person. For purposes of the preceding sentence, the term "United States person" has the meaning given to such term by section 7701(a)(30), except that any individual who is a citizen of any possession of the United States (but not otherwise a citizen of the United States) and who is not a resident of the United States shall not be treated as a United States person.

(4) **Records.** The term "records" includes any books, papers, or other data.

(5) **Section 318 to apply.** Section 318 shall apply for purposes of paragraphs (1) and (2), except that—

(A) "10 percent" shall be substituted for "50 percent" in section 318(a)(2)(C), and

(B) subparagraphs (A), (B), and (C) of section 318(a)(3) shall not be applied so as to consider a United States person as owning stock which is owned by a person who is not a United States person.

(d) Penalty for failure to furnish information or maintain records.

(1) **In general.** If a reporting corporation—

(A) fails to furnish (within the time prescribed by regulations) any information described in subsection (b), or

(B) fails to maintain (or cause another to maintain) records as required by subsection (a),

such corporation shall pay a penalty of $10,000 for each taxable year with respect to which such failure occurs.

(2) **Increase in penalty where failure continues after notification.** If any failure described in paragraph (1) continues for more than 90 days after the day on which the Secretary mails notice of such failure to the reporting corporation, such corporation shall pay a penalty (in addition to the amount required under paragraph (1)) of $10,000 for each 30-day period (or fraction thereof) during which such failure continues after the expiration of such 90-day period.

(3) **Reasonable cause.** For purposes of this subsection, the time prescribed by regulations to furnish information or maintain records (and the beginning of the 90-day period after notice by the Secretary) shall be treated as not earlier than the last day on which (as shown to the satisfaction of the Secretary) reasonable cause existed for failure to furnish the information or maintain the records.

(e) Enforcement of requests for certain records.

(1) **Agreement to treat corporation as agent.** The rules of paragraph (3) shall apply to any transaction between the reporting corporation and any related party who is a foreign person unless such related party agrees (in such manner and at such time as the Secretary shall prescribe) to authorize the reporting corporation to act as such related party's limited agent solely for purposes of applying sections 7602, 7603, and 7604 with respect to any request by the Secretary to examine records or produce testimony related to any such transaction or with respect to any summons by the Secretary for such records or testimony. The appearance of persons or production of records by reason of the reporting corporation being such an agent shall not subject such persons or records to legal process for any purpose other than determining the correct treatment under this title of any transaction between the reporting corporation and such related party.

(2) **Rules where information not furnished.** If—

(A) for purposes of determining the correct treatment under this title of any transaction between the reporting corporation and a related party who is a foreign person, the Secretary issues a summons to such corporation to produce (either directly or as agent for such related party) any records or testimony,

Information and returns Code Sec. 6038A

(B) such summons is not quashed in a proceeding begun under paragraph (4) and is not determined to be invalid in a proceeding begun under section 7604(b) to enforce such summons, and

(C) the reporting corporation does not substantially comply in a timely manner with such summons and the Secretary has sent by certified or registered mail a notice to such reporting corporation that such reporting corporation has not so substantially complied,

the Secretary may apply the rules of paragraph (3) with respect to such transaction (whether or not the Secretary begins a proceeding to enforce such summons). If the reporting corporation fails to maintain (or cause another to maintain) records as required by subsection (a), and by reason of that failure, the summons is quashed in a proceeding described in subparagraph (B) or the reporting corporation is not able to provide the records requested in the summons, the Secretary may apply the rules of paragraph (3) with respect to any transaction to which the records relate.

(3) Applicable rules in cases of noncompliance. If the rules of this paragraph apply to any transaction—

(A) the amount of the deduction allowed under subtitle A for any amount paid or incurred by the reporting corporation to the related party in connection with such transaction, and

(B) the cost to the reporting corporation of any property acquired in such transaction from the related party (or transferred by such corporation in such transaction to the related party),

shall be the amount determined by the Secretary in the Secretary's sole discretion from the Secretary's own knowledge or from such information as the Secretary may obtain through testimony or otherwise.

(4) Judicial proceedings.

(A) Proceedings to quash. Notwithstanding any law or rule of law, any reporting corporation to which the Secretary issues a summons referred to in paragraph (2)(A) shall have the right to begin a proceeding to quash such summons not later than the 90th day after such summons was issued. In any such proceeding, the Secretary may seek to compel compliance with such summons.

(B) Review of secretarial determination of noncompliance. Notwithstanding any law or rule of law, any reporting corporation which has been notified by the Secretary that the Secretary has determined that such corporation has not substantially complied with a summons referred to in paragraph (2) shall have the right to begin a proceeding to review such determination not later than the 90th day after the day on which the notice referred to in paragraph (2)(C) was mailed. If such a proceeding is not begun on or before such 90th day, such determination by the Secretary shall be binding and shall not be reviewed by any court.

(C) Jurisdiction. The United States district court for the district in which the person (to whom the summons is issued) resides or is found shall have jurisdiction to hear any proceeding brought under subparagraph (A) or (B). Any order or other determination in such a proceeding shall be treated as a final order which may be appealed.

(D) Suspension of statute of limitations. If the reporting corporation brings an action under subparagraph (A) or (B), the running of any period of limitations under section 6501 (relating to assessment and collection of tax) or under section 6531 (relating to criminal prosecutions) with respect to any affected taxable year shall be suspended for the period during which such proceeding, and appeals therein, are pending. In no event shall any such period expire before the 90th day after the day on which there is a final determination in such proceeding. For purposes of this subparagraph, the term "affected taxable year" means any taxable year if the determination of the amount of tax imposed for such taxable year is affected by the treatment of the transaction to which the summons relates.

(f) Cross reference.

For provisions relating to criminal penalties for violation of this section, see section 7203.

In 1996, P.L. 104-188, Sec. 1702(c)(5)(A), substituted "any affected taxable year" for "any transaction to which the summons relates" in subpara. (e)(4)(D) ... Sec. 1702(c)(5)(B), added a sentence at the end of subpara. (e)(4)(D), effective for tax. yrs. begin. after 7/10/89.

—P.L. 104-188, Sec. 1704(f)(5)(B), added "and" at the end of para. (b)(2), substituted a period for ", and" at the end of para. (b)(3), and deleted para. (b)(4), effective 8/20/96.

Prior to deleted, para. (b)(4) read as follows:

"(4) such information as the Secretary may require for purposes of carrying out the provisions of section 453C."

In 1990, P.L. 101-508, Sec. 11314, provided the following provisions on application of amendments made by Sec. 7403 of P.L. 101-239 [see below]:

"SEC. 11314. APPLICATION OF AMENDMENTS MADE BY SECTION 7403 OF REVENUE RECONCILIATION ACT OF 1989 TO TAXABLE YEARS BEGINNING ON OR BEFORE JULY 10, 1989.

"(a) General rule.

"The amendments made by section 7403 of the Revenue Reconciliation Act of 1989 shall apply to—

"(1) any requirement to furnish information under section 6038A(a) of the Internal Revenue Code of 1986 (as amended by such section 7403) if the time for furnishing such information under such section is after the date of the enactment of this Act [11/5/90],

"(2) any requirement under such section 6038A(a) to maintain records which were in existence on or after March 20, 1990,

"(3) any requirement to authorize a corporation to act as a limited agent under section 6038A(e)(1) of such Code (as so amended) if the time for authorizing such action is after the date of the enactment of this Act [11/5/90], and

"(4) any summons issued after such date of enactment, [11/5/90]

without regard to when the taxable year (to which the information, records, authorization, or summons relates) began. Such amendments shall also apply in any case to which they would apply without regard to this section.

"(b) Continuation of old failures.

"In the case of any failure with respect to a taxable year beginning on or before July 10, 1989, which first occurs on or before the date of the enactment of this Act [11/5/90] but which continues after such date of enactment, section 6038A(d)(2) of the Internal Revenue Code of 1986 (as amended by subsection (c) of such section 7403) shall apply for purposes of determining the amount of the penalty imposed for such 30-day periods referred to in such section 6038A(d)(2) which begin after the date of the enactment of this Act [11/5/90]."

—P.L. 101-508, Sec. 11315(b)(1), deleted "or is a foreign corporation engaged in trade or business within the United States" after "domestic corporation" in para. (a)(1), effective as provided in Sec. 11315(c) of this Act, which reads as follows:

"(c) Effective date.—

"The amendments made by this section [Sec. 11315] shall apply to—

"(1) any requirement to furnish information under section 6038C(a) of the Internal Revenue Code of 1986 (as added by this section [Sec. 11315]) if the time for furnishing such information under such section is after the date of the enactment of this Act [11/5/90],

"(2) any requirement under such section 6038C(a) to maintain records which were in existence on or after March 20, 1990,

"(3) any requirement to authorize a corporation to act as a limited agent under section 6038C(d)(1) of such Code (as so added) if the time for authorizing such action is after the date of the enactment of this Act, and

"(4) any summons issued after such date of enactment [11/5/90], without regard to when the taxable year (to which the information, records, authorization, or summons relates) began."

—P.L. 101-508, Sec. 11704(a)(23), redesignated paras. (c)(4), (c)(5) and (c)(6) as paras. (c)(3), (c)(4) and (c)(5), respectively, effective 11/5/90.

In 1989, P.L. 101-239, Sec. 7403(a)(1), amended para. (a)(2) ... Sec. 7403(a)(2), amended subsec. (c) ... Sec. 7403(b), added "and such corporation shall maintain (in the location, in the manner, and to the extent prescribed in regulations) such records as may be appropriate to determine the correct treatment of transactions with related parties as the Secretary shall by regulations prescribe (or shall cause another person to so maintain such records)" before the period at the end of subsec. (a) ... Sec. 7403(c), amended subsec. (d) ... Sec. 7403(d), redesignated subsec. (e) as subsec. (f) and added new subsec. (e), effective for tax. yrs. begin. after 7/10/89. For application of amendments made by Sec. 7403 of this Act, see Sec. 11314 of P.L. 101-508, reproduced above.

Prior to amendment, para. (a)(2) read as follows:

"(2) is controlled by a foreign person".

Code Sec. 6038A

Prior to amendment, subsec. (c) read as follows:
"(c) Definitions.
"For purposes of this section—
"(1) Control. The term 'control' has the meaning given to such term by section 6038(e)(1); except that 'at least 50 percent' shall be substituted for 'more than 50 percent' each place it appears in such section.
"(2) Related party. The term 'related party' means—
"(A) any person who is related to the reporting corporation within the meaning of section 267(b) or 707(b)(1), and
"(B) any other person who is related (within the meaning of section 482) to the reporting corporation.
"(3) Foreign person. The term 'foreign person' means any person who is not a United States person. For purposes of the preceding sentence, the term 'United States person' has the meaning given to such term by section 7701(a)(30); except that any individual who is a citizen of any possession of the United States (but not otherwise a citizen of the United States) and who is not a resident of the United States shall not be treated as a United States person."
Prior to amendment, subsec. (d) read as follows:
"(d) Penalty for failure to furnish information.
"(1) In general. If a reporting corporation fails to furnish (within the time prescribed by regulations) any information described in subsection (a), such corporation shall pay a penalty of $1,000 for each taxable year with respect to which such failure occurs.
"(2) Increase in penalty where failure continues after notification. If any failure described in paragraph (1) continues for more than 90 days after the day on which the Secretary mails notice of such failure to the reporting corporation, such corporation shall pay a penalty (in addition to the amount required under paragraph (1)) of $1,000 for each 30-day period (or fraction thereof) during which such failure continues after the expiration of such 90-day period. The increase in any penalty under this paragraph shall not exceed $24,000.
"(3) Reasonable cause. For purposes of this subsection, the time prescribed by regulations to furnish information (and the beginning of the 90-day period after notice by the Secretary) shall be treated as not earlier than the last day on which (as shown to the satisfaction of the Secretary) reasonable cause existed for failure to furnish the information."
In 1986, P.L. 99-514, Sec. 1245(a)(1), substituted "each person" for "each corporation" in para. (b)(1), ... Sec. 1245(a)(2), amended subpara. (b)(1)(A) ... Sec. 1245(b)(1), substituted "each person" for "each corporation" in para. (b)(2) ... Sec. 1245(b)(2), amended para. (b)(3) ... Sec. 1245(b)(3), deleted "and" from the end of para. (b)(2), substituted ", and" for the period at the end of para. (b)(3), and added para. (b)(4) ... Sec. 1245(b)(4), amended para. (c)(2), effective for tax. yrs. begin. after 12/31/86.
Prior to amendment, subpara. (b)(1)(A) read as follows:
"(A) is a member of the same controlled group as the reporting corporation, and"
Prior to amendment, para. (b)(3) read as follows:
"(3) transactions between the reporting corporation and each foreign corporation which is a member of the same controlled as the reporting corporation."
Prior to amendment, para. (c)(2) read as follows:
"(2) Controlled group. The term 'controlled group' means any controlled group of corporations within the meaning of section 1563(a); except that—
"(A) 'at least 50 percent' shall be substituted for—
"(i) for 'at least 80 percent' each place it appears in section 1563(a)(1), and
"(ii) for 'more than 50 percent' each place it appears in section 1563(a)(2)(B), and
"(B) the determination shall be made without regard to subsections (a)(4), (b)(2)(C), and (e)(3)(C) of section 1563."
In 1984, P.L. 98-369, Sec. 714(I), substituted "section 6038(e)(1)" for "section 6038(d)(1)" in para. (c)(1), effective for tax. yrs. begin. after 12/31/82.
In 1983, P.L. 97-448, Sec. 306(b)(4), added ", b)(2)(C)," after "(a)(4)" in subpara. (c)(2)(B), effective for tax. yrs. begin. after 12/31/82.
In 1982, P.L. 97-248, Sec. 339(a), added Code Sec. 6038A, effective for tax. yrs. begin. after 12/31/82.

Sec. 6038B. Notice of certain transfers to foreign persons.
(a) In general.
Each United States person who—
(1) transfers property to—
(A) a foreign corporation in an exchange described in section 332, 351, 354, 355, 356, or 361, or
(B) a foreign partnership in a contribution described in section 721 or in any other contribution described in regulations described by the Secretary, or
(2) makes a distribution described in section 336 to a person who is not a United States person,
shall furnish to the Secretary, at such time and in such manner as the Secretary shall by regulations prescribe, such information with respect to such exchange or distribution as the Secretary may require in such regulations.

Information and returns

(b) Exceptions for certain transfers to foreign partnerships; special rule.
(1) Exceptions. Subsection (a)(1)(B) shall apply to a transfer by a United States person to a foreign partnership only if—
(A) the United States person holds (immediately after the transfer) directly or indirectly at least a 10-percent interest (as defined in section 6046A(d)) in the partnership, or
(B) the value of the property transferred (when added to the value of the property transferred by such person or any related person to such partnership or a related partnership during the 12-month period ending on the date of the transfer) exceeds $100,000.
For purposes of the preceding sentence, the value of any transferred property is its fair market value at the time of its transfer.
(2) Special rule. If by reason of an adjustment under section 482 or otherwise, a contribution described in subsection (a)(1) is deemed to have been made, such contribution shall be treated for purposes of this section as having been made not earlier than the date specified by the Secretary.
(c) Penalty for failure to furnish information.
(1) In general. If any United States person fails to furnish the information described in subsection (a) at the time and in the manner required by regulations, such person shall pay a penalty equal to 10 percent of the fair market value of the property at the time of the exchange (and, in the case of a contribution described in subsection (a)(1)(B), such person shall recognize gain as if the contributed property had been sold for such value at the time of such contribution).
(2) Reasonable cause exception. Paragraph (1) shall not apply to any failure if the United States person shows such failure is due to reasonable cause and not to willful neglect.
(3) Limit on penalty. The penalty under paragraph (1) with respect to any exchange shall not exceed $100,000 unless the failure with respect to such exchange was due to intentional disregard.

In 2005, P.L. 109-135, Sec. 409(c), added "or" at the end of subpara. (a)(1)(B), effective for transfers made after 8/5/97 as if included in Sec. 1144 of the Taxpayer Relief Act of 1997, P.L. 105-34. For special rule, see Sec. 1144(d)(2) of P.L. 105-34, reproduced below.
In 1998, P.L. 105-206, Sec. 6011(g), substituted "6038B(c) (as redesignated by subsection (b))" for "6038B(b)" each place it appeared in Sec. 1144(c)(1) and (2) of P.L. 105-34 [see below], effective as if included in the provisions of P.L. 105-34 of 8/5/97.
In 1997, P.L. 105-34, Sec. 1144(a), amended para. (a)(1) ... Sec. 1144(b), redesignated subsec. (b) as subsec. (c) and added new subsec. (b) ... Sec. 1144(c)(1), substituted "equal to 10 percent of the fair market value of the property at the time of the exchange (and, in the case of a contribution described in subsection (a)(1)(B), such person shall recognize gain as if the contributed property had been sold for such value at the time of such contribution)." for "equal to 25 percent of the amount of the gain realized on the exchange." in para. (c)(1) [as redesignated by Sec. 1144(b), see above] [as clarified by Sec. 6011(g) of P.L. 105-206, see above] ... Sec. 1144(c)(2), added para. (c)(3) [as redesignated by Sec. 1144(b), see above] [as clarified by Sec. 6011(g) of P.L. 105-206, see above], effective for transfers made after 8/5/97. Sec. 1144(d)(2) of this Act reads as follows:
"(2) Election of retroactive effect. Section 1494(c) of the Internal Revenue Code of 1986 shall not apply to any transfer after August 20, 1996, if all applicable reporting requirements under section 6038B of such Code (as amended by this section) are satisfied. The Secretary of the Treasury or his delegate may prescribe simplified reporting under the preceding sentence."
Prior to amendment, para. (a)(1) read as follows:
"(1) transfers property to a foreign corporation in an exchange described in section 332, 351, 354, 355, 356, or 361, or"
In 1984, P.L. 98-369, Sec. 131(d)(1), added Code Sec. 6038B, effective for transfers or exchanges after 12/31/84, in tax. yrs. ending after 12/31/84. Sec. 131(g)(1) and (3) of the Act provides the following special rules:
"(2) Special rule for certain transfers of intangibles.—

Information and returns

"(A) In general.—If, after June 6, 1984, and before January 1, 1985, a United States person transfers any intangible property (within the meaning of section 936(h)(3)(B) of the Internal Revenue Code of 1954) to a foreign corporation or in a transfer described in section 1491, such transfer shall be treated for purposes of sections 367(a), 1492(2), and 1494(b) of such Code as pursuant to a plan having as 1 of its principal purposes the avoidance of Federal income tax.

"(B) Waiver.—Subject to such terms and conditions as the Secretary of the Treasury or his delegate may prescribe, the Secretary may waive the application of subparagraph (A) with respect to any transfer.

"(3) Ruling request before March 1, 1984.—The amendments made by this section (and the provisions of paragraph (2) of this subsection) shall not apply to any transfer or exchange of property described in a request filed before March 1, 1984, under section 367(a), 1492(2), or 1494(b) of the Internal Revenue Code of 1954 (as in effect before such amendments)."

Sec. 6038C. Information with respect to foreign corporations engaged in U.S. business.

(a) Requirement.

If a foreign corporation (hereinafter in this section referred to as the "reporting corporation") is engaged in a trade or business within the United States at any time during a taxable year—

(1) such corporation shall furnish (at such time and in such manner as the Secretary shall by regulations prescribe) the information described in subsection (b), and

(2) such corporation shall maintain (at the location, in the manner, and to the extent prescribed in regulations) such records as may be appropriate to determine the liability of such corporation for tax under this title as the Secretary shall by regulations prescribe (or shall cause another person to so maintain such records).

(b) Required information.

For purposes of subsection (a), the information described in this subsection is—

(1) the information described in section 6038A(b), and

(2) such other information as the Secretary may prescribe by regulations relating to any item not directly connected with a transaction for which information is required under paragraph (1).

(c) Penalty for failure to furnish information or maintain records.

The provisions of subsection (d) of section 6038A shall apply to—

(1) any failure to furnish (within the time prescribed by regulations) any information described in subsection (b), and

(2) any failure to maintain (or cause another to maintain) records as required by subsection (a),

in the same manner as if such failure were a failure to comply with the provisions of section 6038A.

(d) Enforcement of requests for certain records.

(1) **Agreement to treat corporation as agent.** The rules of paragraph (3) shall apply to any transaction between the reporting corporation and any related party who is a foreign person unless such related party agrees (in such manner and at such time as the Secretary shall prescribe) to authorize the reporting corporation to act as such related party's limited agent solely for purposes of applying sections 7602, 7603, and 7604 with respect to any request by the Secretary to examine records or produce testimony related to any such transaction or with respect to any summons by the Secretary for such records or testimony. The appearance of persons or production of records by reason of the reporting corporation being such an agent shall not subject such persons or records to legal process for any purpose other than determining the correct treatment under this title of any transaction between the reporting corporation and such related party.

(2) **Rules where information not furnished.** If—

(A) for purposes of determining the amount of the reporting corporation's liability for tax under this title, the Secretary issues a summons to such corporation to produce (either directly or as an agent for a related party who is a foreign person) any records or testimony,

(B) such summons is not quashed in a proceeding begun under paragraph (4) of section 6038A(e) (as made applicable by paragraph (4) of this subsection) and is not determined to be invalid in a proceeding begun under section 7604(b) to enforce such summons, and

(C) the reporting corporation does not substantially comply in a timely manner with such summons and the Secretary has sent by certified or registered mail a notice to such reporting corporation that such reporting corporation has not so substantially complied,

the Secretary may apply the rules of paragraph (3) with respect to any transaction or item to which such summons relates (whether or not the Secretary begins a proceeding to enforce such summons). If the reporting corporation fails to maintain (or cause another to maintain) records as required by subsection (a), and by reason of that failure, the summons is quashed in a proceeding described in subparagraph (B) or the reporting corporation is not able to provide the records requested in the summons, the Secretary may apply the rules of paragraph (3) with respect to any transaction or item to which the records relate.

(3) **Applicable rules.** If the rules of this paragraph apply to any transaction or item, the treatment of such transaction (or the amount and treatment of any such item) shall be determined by the Secretary in the Secretary's sole discretion from the Secretary's own knowledge or from such information as the Secretary may obtain through testimony or otherwise.

(4) **Judicial proceedings.** The provisions of section 6038A(e)(4) shall apply with respect to any summons referred to in paragraph (2)(A); except that subparagraph (D) of such section shall be applied by substituting "transaction or item" for "transaction".

(e) Definitions.

For purposes of this section, the terms "related party", "foreign person", and "records" have the respective meanings given to such terms by section 6038A(c).

In 1990, P.L. 101-508, Sec. 11315(a), added Code Sec. 6038C, effective as provided in Sec. 11315(c) of this Act, which reads as follows:

"(c) Effective date.

"The amendments made by this section shall apply to—

"(1) any requirement to furnish information under section 6038C(a) of the Internal Revenue Code of 1986 (as added by this section [Sec. 11315(a)]) if the time for furnishing such information under such section is after the date of the enactment of this Act [11/5/90],

"(2) any requirement under such section 6038C(a) to maintain records which were in existence on or after March 20, 1990,

"(3) any requirement to authorize a corporation to act as a limited agent under section 6038C(d)(1) of such Code (as so added) if the time for authorizing such action is after the date of the enactment of this Act [11/5/90], and

"(4) any summons issued after such date of enactment [11/5/90], without regard to when the taxable year (to which the information, records, authorization, or summons relates) began."

Sec. 6038D. Information with respect to foreign financial assets.

(a) In general.

Any individual who, during any taxable year, holds any interest in a specified foreign financial asset shall attach to such person's return of tax imposed by subtitle A for such taxable year the information described in subsection (c) with respect to each such asset if the aggregate value of all such assets exceeds $50,000 (or such higher dollar amount as the Secretary may prescribe).

(b) Specified foreign financial assets.
For purposes of this section, the term "specified foreign financial asset" means—
  (1) any financial account (as defined in section 1471(d)(2)) maintained by a foreign financial institution (as defined in section 1471(d)(4)), and
  (2) any of the following assets which are not held in an account maintained by a financial institution (as defined in section 1471(d)(5))—
    (A) any stock or security issued by a person other than a United States person,
    (B) any financial instrument or contract held for investment that has an issuer or counterparty which is other than a United States person, and
    (C) any interest in a foreign entity (as defined in section 1473).

(c) Required information.
The information described in this subsection with respect to any asset is:
  (1) In the case of any account, the name and address of the financial institution in which such account is maintained and the number of such account.
  (2) In the case of any stock or security, the name and address of the issuer and such information as is necessary to identify the class or issue of which such stock or security is a part.
  (3) In the case of any other instrument, contract, or interest—
    (A) such information as is necessary to identify such instrument, contract, or interest, and
    (B) the names and addresses of all issuers and counterparties with respect to such instrument, contract, or interest.
  (4) The maximum value of the asset during the taxable year.

(d) Penalty for failure to disclose.
  (1) In general. If any individual fails to furnish the information described in subsection (c) with respect to any taxable year at the time and in the manner described in subsection (a), such person shall pay a penalty of $10,000.
  (2) Increase in penalty where failure continues after notification. If any failure described in paragraph (1) continues for more than 90 days after the day on which the Secretary mails notice of such failure to the individual, such individual shall pay a penalty (in addition to the penalties under paragraph (1)) of $10,000 for each 30-day period (or fraction thereof) during which such failure continues after the expiration of such 90-day period. The penalty imposed under this paragraph with respect to any failure shall not exceed $50,000.

(e) Presumption that value of specified foreign financial assets exceeds dollar threshold.
If—
  (1) the Secretary determines that an individual has an interest in one or more specified foreign financial assets, and
  (2) such individual does not provide sufficient information to demonstrate the aggregate value of such assets,
then the aggregate value of such assets shall be treated as being in excess of $50,000 (or such higher dollar amount as the Secretary prescribes for purposes of subsection (a)) for purposes of assessing the penalties imposed under this section.

(f) Application to certain entities.
To the extent provided by the Secretary in regulations or other guidance, the provisions of this section shall apply to any domestic entity which is formed or availed of for purposes of holding, directly or indirectly, specified foreign financial assets, in the same manner as if such entity were an individual.

(g) Reasonable cause exception.
No penalty shall be imposed by this section on any failure which is shown to be due to reasonable cause and not due to willful neglect. The fact that a foreign jurisdiction would impose a civil or criminal penalty on the taxpayer (or any other person) for disclosing the required information is not reasonable cause.

(h) Regulations.
The Secretary shall prescribe such regulations or other guidance as may be necessary or appropriate to carry out the purposes of this section, including regulations or other guidance which provide appropriate exceptions from the application of this section in the case of—
  (1) classes of assets identified by the Secretary, including any assets with respect to which the Secretary determines that disclosure under this section would be duplicative of other disclosures,
  (2) nonresident aliens, and
  (3) bona fide residents of any possession of the United States.

In **2010**, P.L. 111-147, Sec. 511(a), added Code Sec. 6038D, effective for tax. yrs. begin. after 3/18/2010.

Sec. 6039. Returns required in connection with certain options.
(a) Requirement of reporting.
Every corporation—
  (1) which in any calendar year transfers to any person a share of stock pursuant to such person's exercise of an incentive stock option, or
  (2) which in any calendar year records (or has by its agent recorded) a transfer of the legal title of a share of stock acquired by the transferor pursuant to his exercise of an option described in section 423(c) (relating to special rule where option price is between 85 percent and 100 percent of value of stock),
shall, for such calendar year, make a return at such time and in such manner, and setting forth such information, as the Secretary may by regulations prescribe.

(b) Statements to be furnished to persons with respect to whom information is reported.
Every corporation making a return under subsection (a) shall furnish to each person whose name is set forth in such return a written statement setting forth such information as the Secretary may by regulations prescribe. The written statement required under the preceding sentence shall be furnished to such person on or before January 31 of the year following the calendar year for which the return under subsection (a) was made.

(c) Special rules.
For purposes of this section—
  (1) Treatment by employer to be determinative. Any option which the corporation treats as an incentive stock option or an option granted under an employee stock purchase plan shall be deemed to be such an option.
  (2) Subsection (a)(2) applies only to first transfer described therein. A statement is required by reason of a transfer described in subsection (a)(2) of a share only with respect to the first transfer of such share by the person who exercised the option.
  (3) Identification of stock. Any corporation which transfers any share of stock pursuant to the exercise of any op-

tion described in subsection (a)(2) shall identify such stock in a manner adequate to carry out the purposes of this section.

(d) Cross references.

For definition of—

(1) the term "incentive stock option" see section 422(b), and

(2) the term "employee stock purchase plan" see section 423(b).

In 2006, P.L. 109-432, Sec. 403(a), substituted "shall, for such calendar year, make a return at such time and in such manner, and setting forth such information, as the Secretary may by regulations prescribe" for "shall (on or before January 31 of the following calendar year) furnish to such person a written statement in such manner and setting forth such information as the Secretary may by regulations prescribe." in subsec. (a) . . . Sec. 403(b), redesignated subsecs. (b) and (c) as subsecs. (c) and (d) and added new subsec. (b) . . . Sec. 403(c)(3), substituted "Returns" for "Information" in the heading of Code Sec. 6039 . . . Sec. 403(c)(4), substituted "Requirement of reporting" for "Furnishing of information" in the heading of subsec. (a), effective for calendar yrs. begin. after 12/20/2006.

In 1998, P.L. 105-206, Sec. 6023(20), added "to any person" after "transfers" in para. (a)(1), effective 7/22/98.

In 1990, P.L. 101-508, Sec. 11801(c)(9)(J)(i), amended paras. (a)(1) and (a)(2) . . . Sec. 11801(c)(9)(j)(ii), substituted "an incentive stock option or an" for "a qualified stock option, incentive stock option, a restricted stock option, or an" in para. (b)(1) . . . Sec. 11801(c)(9)(J)(iii), amended subsec. (c), effective 11/5/90 except as provided in Sec. 11821(b) of this Act, reproduced in note following Code Sec. 422.

Prior to amendment, paras. (a)(1) and (a)(2) read as follows:

"(1) which in any calendar year transfers a share of stock to any person pursuant to such person's exercise of a qualified stock option, an incentive stock option, or a restricted stock option, or

"(2) which in any calendar year records (or has by its agent recorded) a transfer of the legal title of a share of stock—

"(A) acquired by the transferor pursuant to his exercise of an option described in section 423(c) (relating to special rule where option price is between 85 percent and 100 percent of value of stock), or

"(B) acquired by the transferor pursuant to his exercise of a restricted stock option described in section 424(c)(1) (relating to options under which option price is between 85 percent and 95 percent of value of stock),"

Prior to amendment, subsec. (c) read as follows:

"(c) Cross references.

"For definition of—

"(1) The term 'qualified stock option', see section 422(b).

"(2) The term 'employee stock purchase plan', see section 423(b).

"(3) The term 'restricted stock option', see section 424(b).

"(4) The term 'incentive stock option', see section 422A(b)."

In 1981, P.L. 97-34, Sec. 251(b)(5)(A), added ", an incentive stock option," after "qualified stock option" in para. (a)(1) . . . Sec. 251(b)(5)(B), added "[an] incentive stock option," after "qualified stock option," in para. (b)(1) . . . Sec. 251(b)(5)(C), added para. (c)(4), effective for options granted on or after 1/1/76, and exercised on or after 1/1/81, or outstanding on 1/1/81. For election and designation of options and changes in terms of options, see Sec. 251(c)(1)(B) and (c)(2) of this Act reproduced in note following Code Sec. 422A.

In 1979, P.L. 96-167, Sec. 7(a), amended Code Sec. 6039, effective for calendar yrs. begin. after 12/31/79.

Prior to amendment, Code Sec. 6039 read as follows:

"SEC. 6039. INFORMATION REQUIRED IN CONNECTION WITH CERTAIN OPTIONS.

"(a) Requirement of reporting.

"Every corporation—

"(1) which in any calendar year transfers a share of stock to any person pursuant to such person's exercise of a qualified stock option or a restricted stock option, or

"(2) which in any calendar year records (or has by its agent recorded) a transfer of the legal title of a share of stock—

"(A) acquired by the transferor pursuant to his exercise of an option described in section 423(c) (relating to special rule where option price is between 85 percent and 100 percent of value of stock), or

"(B) acquired by the transferor pursuant to his exercise of a restricted stock option described in section 424(c)(1) (relating to options under which option price is between 85 percent and 95 percent of value of stock),

"shall, for such calendar year, make a return at such time and in such manner, and setting forth such information, as the Secretary may by regulations prescribe. For purposes of the preceding sentence, any option which a corporation treats as a qualified stock option, a restricted stock option, or an option granted under an employee stock purchase plan, shall be deemed to be such an option. A return is required by reason of a transfer described in paragraph (2) of a share only with respect to the first transfer of such share by the person who exercised the option.

"(b) Statements to be furnished to persons with respect to whom information is furnished.

"Every corporation making a return under subsection (a) shall furnish to each person whose name is set forth in such return a written statement setting forth such information as the Secretary may by regulations prescribe. The written statement required under the preceding sentence shall be furnished to the person on or before January 31 of the year following the calendar year for which the return under subsection (a) was made."

In 1976, P.L. 94-455, Sec. 1906(b)(13)(A), substituted "Secretary" for "Secretary or his delegate" each place it appeared in Code Sec. 6039, effective 2/1/77.

In 1964, P.L. 88-272, Sec. 221(b)(1), added Code Sec. 6039 and redesignated former Code Sec. 6039 as 6040, effective for stock transferred pursuant to options exercised on or after 1/1/64.

Sec. 6039A. Repealed.

In 1980, P.L. 96-223, Sec. 401(a), repealed Sec. 2005(d)(1) and the amendment made by Sec. 2005(d)(1), effective for decedents dying after '76 [see below]. Sec. 401(b) of P.L. 96-223 provides as follows:

"(b) Revival of prior law. Except to the extent necessary to carry out subsection (d), the Internal Revenue Code of 1954 shall be applied and administered as if the provisions repealed by subsection (a), and the amendments made by those provisions, had not been enacted."

In 1978, P.L. 95-600, Sec. 515(6), amended the effective date for changes made by Sec. 2005(d)(1) of P.L. 94-455, by substituting '79 for '76, see below [inoperative].

In 1976, P.L. 94-455, Sec. 2005(d)(1), added Code Sec. 6039A, for decedents dying after '79, but Sec. 2005(d)(1) was repealed by Sec. 401(a) of P.L. 96-223 [see above]. For Code Sec. 6039A added by Sec. 2005(d)(1) see note for Sec. 401(d) of P.L. 96-223 following Code Sec. 1014.

Sec. 6039B. Repealed.

In 1986, P.L. 99-514, Sec. 1303(b)(5), repealed Code Sec. 6039B, effective 10/22/86.

Prior to repeal, Code Sec. 6039B read as follows:

"SEC. 6039B. RETURN OF GENERAL STOCK OWNERSHIP CORPORATION.

"Every general stock ownership corporation (as defined in section 1391) which makes the election provided by section 1392 shall make a return for each taxable year, stating specifically the items of its gross income and the deductions allowable by subtitle A, the amount of investment credit or additional tax, as the case may be, the names and addresses of all persons owning stock in the corporation at any time during the taxable year, the number of shares of stock owned by each shareholder at all times during the taxable year, the amount of money and other property distributed by the corporation during the taxable year to each shareholder, the date of each such distribution, and such other information, for the purpose of carrying out the provisions of subchapter U of chapter 1, as the Secretary may by regulation prescribe. Any return filed pursuant to this section shall, for purposes of chapter 66 (relating to limitations), be treated as a return filed by the corporation under section 6012. Every electing GSOC shall file an annual report with the Secretary summarizing its operations for such year."

In 1980, P.L. 96-595, Sec. 3(b), added "electing" after "Every" in the last sentence of Code Sec. 6039B, effective with respect to corporations chartered after 12/31/78 and before 1/1/84.

In 1978, P.L. 95-600, Sec. 601(b)(4), added Code Sec. 6039B, effective for corporations chartered after 12/31/78, and before 1/1/84.

Sec. 6039C. Returns with respect to foreign persons holding direct investments in United States real property interests.

(a) General rule.

To the extent provided in regulations, any foreign person holding direct investments in United States real property interests for the calendar year shall make a return setting forth—

(1) the name and address of such person,

(2) a description of all United States real property interests held by such person at any time during the calendar year, and

(3) such other information as the Secretary may by regulations prescribe.

(b) Definition of foreign persons holding direct investments in United States real property interests.

For purposes of this section, a foreign person shall be treated as holding direct investments in United States real property interests during any calendar year if—

(1) such person did not engage in a trade or business in the United States at any time during such calendar year, and

(2) the fair market value of the United States real property interests held directly by such person at any time during such year equals or exceeds $50,000.

Code Sec. 6039C(c) — Information and returns

(c) Definitions and special rules.
For purposes of this section—

(1) United States real property interest. The term "United States real property interest" has the meaning given to such term by section 897(c).

(2) Foreign person. The term "foreign person" means any person who is not a United States person.

(3) Attribution of ownership. For purposes of subsection (b)(2)—

(A) Interests held by partnerships, etc. United States real property interests held by a partnership, trust, or estate shall be treated as owned proportionately by its partners or beneficiaries.

(B) Interests held by family members. United States real property interests held by the spouse or any minor child of an individual shall be treated as owned by such individual.

(4) Time and manner of filing return All returns required to be made under this section shall be made at such time and in such manner as the Secretary shall by regulations prescribe.

(d) Special rule for United States interest and Virgin Islands interest.

A nonresident alien individual or foreign corporation subject to tax under section 897(a) (and any person required to withhold tax under section 1445) shall pay any tax and file any return required by this title—

(1) to the United States, in the case of any interest in real property located in the United States and an interest (other than an interest solely as a creditor) in a domestic corporation (with respect to the United States) described in section 897(c)(1)(A)(ii), and

(2) to the Virgin Islands, in the case of any interest in real property located in the Virgin Islands and an interest (other than an interest solely as a creditor) in a domestic corporation (with respect to the Virgin Islands) described in section 897(c)(1)(A)(ii).

In **1986,** P.L. 99-514, Sec. 1810(f)(7), substituted "897(a) (and any person required to withhold tax under section 1445)" for "897(a)" in subsec. (d), effective for calendar yr. 1980 and subsequent calendar yrs.

In **1984,** P.L. 98-369, Sec. 129(b)(1), amended Code Sec. 6039C, effective for calendar yr. 1980 and subsequent calendar yrs.

Prior to amendment, Code Sec. 6039C read as follows:

"Sec. 6039C. Returns with respect to United States real property interests.
"(a) Return of certain domestic corporations having foreign shareholders.

"(1) General rule.

"(A) Return requirement. If this subsection applies to a domestic corporation for the calendar year, such corporation shall make a return for the calendar year setting forth—

"(i) the name and address (if known by the corporation) of each person who was a shareholder at any time during the calendar year and who is known by the corporation to be a foreign person,

"(ii) such information with respect to transfers of stock in such corporation to or from foreign persons during the calendar year as the Secretary may by regulations prescribe, and

"(iii) such other information as the Secretary may by regulations prescribe.

"(B) Corporations to which subsection applies. This subsection applies to any domestic corporation for the calendar year if—

"(i) at any time during the calendar year 1 or more of the shareholders of such corporation is a foreign person, and

"(ii) at any time during the calendar year or during any of the 4 immediately preceding calendar years, such corporation was a United States real property holding corporation (as defined in section 897(c)(2)).

"(2) Subsection does not apply to publicly traded corporations. This subsection shall not apply to a corporation the stock of which is regularly traded on an established securities market at all times during the calendar year.
Stock held by nominees. If—

"(A) a nominee holds stock in a domestic corporation for a foreign person, and

"(B) such foreign person does not furnish the information required to be furnished pursuant to paragraph (1)(A) with respect to such stock,

the nominee shall file a return under this subsection with respect to such stock.
"(b) Return of certain persons holding United States real property interests.

"(1) Return requirement. If any entity to which this subsection applies has at any time during the calendar year a substantial investor in United States real property, such entity shall make a return for the calendar year setting forth—

"(A) the name and address of each such substantial investor,

"(B) such information with respect to the assets of the entity during the calendar year as the Secretary may by regulations prescribe, and

"(C) such other information as the Secretary may by regulations prescribe.

"(2) Exception where security furnished. This subsection shall not apply to any entity for the calendar year if such entity furnishes to the Secretary such security as the Secretary determines to be necessary to ensure that any tax imposed by chapter 1 with respect to United States real property interests held by such entity will be paid.

"(3) Statements to be furnished to substantial investor in United States real property. Every entity making a return under paragraph (1) shall furnish to each substantial investor in United States real property a statement showing—

"(A) the name and address of the entity making such return,

"(B) such substantial investor's pro rata share of the United States real property interests held by such entity, and

"(C) such other information as the Secretary shall by regulations prescribe.

"(4) Definitions. For purpose of this subsection—

"(A) Entities to which this subsection applies. This subsection shall apply to any foreign corporation and to any partnership, trust, or estate (whether foreign or domestic).

"(B) Substantial investor in United States real property.

"(i) In general. The term 'substantial investor in United States real property' means any foreign person who at any time during the calendar year held an interest in the entity but only if the fair market value of such person's pro rata share of the United States real property interests held by such entity exceeded $50,000.

"(ii) Special rule for corporations. In the case of any foreign corporation, clause (i) shall be applied by substituting 'person (whether foreign or domestic)' for 'foreign person'.

"(C) Indirect holdings. For purposes of determining whether an entity to which this subsection applies has a substantial investor in United States real property, the assets of any person shall include the person's pro rata share of the United States real property interest held by any corporation (whether domestic or foreign) if the person's pro rata share of the United States real property interests exceeded $50,000.
"(c) Return of certain foreign persons holding direct investments in United States real property interests.

"(1) Return requirement. If this subsection applies to any foreign person for the calendar year, such person shall make a return for the calendar year setting forth—

"(A) the name and address of such person,

"(B) a description of all United States real property interests held by such person at any time during the calendar year, and

"(C) such other information as the Secretary may by regulations prescribe.

"(2) Persons to whom this subsection applies. This subsection applies to any foreign person for the calendar year if—

"(A) such person did not engage in a trade or business in the United States at any time during the calendar year,

"(B) the fair market value of the United States real property interests held by such person at any time during such year equals or exceeds $50,000, and

"(C) such person is not required to file a return under subsection (b) of such year.
"(d) Definitions.

"For purposes of this section—

"(1) United States real property interest. The term 'United States real property interest' has the meaning given to such term by section 897(c).

"(2) Foreign person. The term 'foreign person' means any person who is not a United States person."
"(e) Special rules.

"(1) Attribution of ownership. For purposes of subsections (b)(4) and (c)(2)(B)—

"(A) Interests held by partnerships, etc. United States real property interests held by a partnership, trust, or estate shall be treated as owned proportionately by its partners or beneficiaries.

"(B) Interests held by family members. United States real property interests held by the spouse or any minor child of an individual shall be treated as owned by such individual.

"(2) Returns, etc. All returns, statements, and information required to be made or furnished under this section shall be made or furnished at such time and in such manner as the Secretary shall by regulations prescribe.
"(f) Special rule for United States interest and Virgin Islands interest.

"A nonresident alien individual or foreign corporation subject to tax under section 897(a) shall pay any tax and file any return required by this title—

"(1) to the United States, in the case of any interest in real property located in the United States and an interest (other than an interest solely as a creditor) in a domestic corporation (with respect to the United States) described in section 897(c)(1)(A)(ii), and

"(2) to the Virgin Islands, in the case of an interest in real property located in the Virgin Islands and an interest (other than an interest solely as a creditor) in a domestic corporation (with respect to the Virgin Islands) described in section 897(c)(1)(A)(ii)."

In **1981,** P.L. 97-34, Sec. 831(a)(3), added subsec. (f)... Sec. 831(e), amended subpara. (b)(4)(C), effective for dispositions after 6/18/80, in tax. yrs. end. after 6/18/80.

Prior to amendment, subpara. (b)(4)(C) read as follows:

Information and returns
Code Sec. 6039D

"(C) Indirect holdings. The assets of any entity to which this subsection applies shall include its pro rata share of the United States real property interests held by any corporation in which the entity is a substantial investor in United States real property."

In **1980**, P.L. 96-499, Sec. 1123(a), added Code Sec. 6039C, effective for calendar year 1980 and subsequent calendar years. Calendar year 1980 is treated as beginning on 6/19/80, and ending on 12/31/80.

Sec. 6039D. Returns and records with respect to certain fringe benefit plans.

(a) In general.

Every employer maintaining a specified fringe benefit plan during any year beginning after December 31, 1984, for any portion of which the applicable exclusion applies, shall file a return (at such time and in such manner as the Secretary shall by regulations prescribe) with respect to such plan showing for such year—

(1) the number of employees of the employer,

(2) the number of employees of the employer eligible to participate under the plan,

(3) the number of employees participating under the plan,

(4) the total cost of the plan during the year,

(5) the name, address, and taxpayer identification number of the employer and the type of business in which the employer is engaged, and

(6) the number of highly compensated employees among the employees described in paragraphs (1), (2), and (3).

(b) Recordkeeping requirement.

Each employer maintaining a specified fringe benefit plan during any year shall keep such records as may be necessary for purposes of determining whether the requirements of the applicable exclusion are met.

(c) Additional information when required by the Secretary.

Any employer—

(1) who maintains a specified fringe benefit plan during any year for which a return is required under subsection (a), and

(2) who is required by the Secretary to file an additional return for such year, shall file such additional return. Such additional return shall be filed at such time and in such manner as the Secretary shall prescribe and shall contain such information as the Secretary shall prescribe. The Secretary may require returns under this subsection only from a representative group of employers.

(d) Definitions and special rules.

For purposes of this section—

(1) **Specified fringe benefit plan.** The term "specified fringe benefit plan" means any plan under section 79, 105, 106, 120, 125, 127, 129, or 137.

(2) **Applicable exclusion.** The term "applicable exclusion" means, with respect to any specified fringe benefit plan, the section specified under paragraph (1) under which benefits under such plan are excludable from gross income.

(3) **Special rule for multiemployer plans.** In the case of a multiemployer plan, the plan shall be required to provide any information required by this section which the Secretary determines, on the basis of the agreement between the plan and employer, is held by the plan (and not the employer).

In **1997**, P.L. 105-34, Sec. 1601(h)(2)(D)(iii), substituted "129, or 137" for "or 129" in para. (d)(1), effective for tax. yrs. begin. after 12/31/96.

In **1990**, P.L. 101-508, Sec. 11704(a)(24), substituted "the employer)." for "the employer)" in para. (d)(3), effective 11/5/90.

In **1989**, P.L. 101-136, Sec. 528, provided that "no monies appropriated by this Act [for the fiscal year ending September 30, '90] may be used to implement or enforce section 1151 of the Tax Reform Act of '86 [P.L. 99-514] or the amendments made by such section." [See below]

In **1988**, P.L. 100-647, Sec. 1011B(a)(24), amended Sec. 1151(h)(3) of P.L. 99-514 so that it added the last sentence to subsec. (c) of Code Sec. 6039D instead of 6039B, see below Sec. 1011B(a)(25), amended Sec. 1151(k)(1) of P.L. 99-514 [reproduced below], part of the effective date for changes made by Sec. 1151(h)(1), (2), and (3) of P.L. 99-514, by adding the last sentence, see below.
— P.L. 100-647, Sec. 3021(a)(15)(A)(i), added para. (d)(3) . . . Sec. 3021(a)(15)(A)(ii), added "and special rules" after "Definitions" in the heading of subsec. (d), effective yrs. begin. after 1984.

In **1986**, P.L. 99-514, Sec. 1151(h)(1), amended subsec. (d) . . . Sec. 1151(h)(2), deleted "and" from the end of para. (a)(4), substituted ", and" for the period at the end of para. (a)(5), and added para. (a)(6) . . . Sec. 1151(h)(3), [amended by Sec. 1011B(a)(24) of P.L. 100-647, see above] added the last sentence to subsec. (c) [Sec. 1151(h)(3) erroneously adds the last sentence to Code Sec. 6039B(c)] effective as provided in Sec. 1151(k)(1) of this Act:
"(k) Effective dates.—
"(1) In general.—The amendments made by this section shall apply to years beginning after the later of—
"(A) December 31, 1987, or
"(B) the earlier of—
"(i) the date which is 3 months after the date on which the Secretary of the Treasury or his delegate issues such regulations as are necessary to carry out the provisions of section 89 of the Internal Revenue Code of 1986 (as added by this section), or
"(ii) December 31, 1988.
"Notwithstanding the preceding sentence, the amendments made by subsections (e)(1) and (i)(3)(C) shall, to the extent they relate to sections 106, 162(i)(2), and 162(k) of the Internal Revenue Code of 1986, apply to years beginning after 1986."
Prior to amendment, subsec. (d) [as amended by Sec. 1879(d)(1) of this Act, see below] read as follows:
"(d) Definitions.—
"For purposes of this section—
"(1) Specified fringe benefit plan.—The term 'specified fringe benefit plan' means—
"(A) any qualified group legal services plan (as defined in section 120),
"(B) any cafeteria plan (as defined in section 125), and
"(C) any educational assistance plan (as defined in section 127).
"(2) Applicable exclusion.—The term 'applicable exclusion' means—
"(A) section 120 in the case of a qualified group legal services plan,
"(B) section 125 in the case of a cafeteria plan, and
"(C) section 127 in the case of an educational assistance plan."
—P.L. 99-514, Sec. 1879(d)(1), amended subsec. (d) [before amendment by Sec. 1151(h)(1) of this Act, see above], effective 1/1/85.
Prior to amendment, subsec. (d) read as follows:
"(d) Definitions.
"For purposes of this section—
"(1) Specified fringe benefit plan. The term 'specified fringe benefit plan' means—
"(A) any cafeteria plan (as defined in section 125), and
"(B) any educational assistance program (as defined in section 127).
"(2) Applicable exclusion. The term 'applicable exclusion' means—
"(A) section 125, in the case of a cafeteria plan, and
"(B) section 127, in the case of an educational assistance program."

In **1984**, P.L. 98-611, Sec. 1(d)(1), added Code Sec. 6039D, effective 1/1/85.

Sec. 6039D. Repealed.

In **1986**, P.L. 99-514, Sec. 1879(d)(2), repealed Code Sec. 6039D (as added by Sec. 1(b)(1) of P.L. 98-612), effective 1/1/85.
Prior to repeal, Code Sec. 6039D (added by Sec. 1(b)(1) of P.L. 98-612) read:
"Sec. 6039D. Returns and records with respect to certain fringe benefits plans.
"(a) In general.
"Every employer maintaining a specified fringe benefit plan during any year beginning after December 31, 1984, for any portion of which the applicable exclusion applies, shall file a return (at such time and in such manner as the Secretary shall by regulations prescribe) with respect to such plan showing for such year—
"(1) the number of employees of the employer,
"(2) the number of employees of the employer eligible to participate under the plan,
"(3) the number of employees participating under the plan,
"(4) the total cost of the plan during the year, and
"(5) the name, address, and taxpayer identification number of the employer and the type of business in which the employer is engaged.
"(b) Recordkeeping requirement.
"Each employer maintaining a specified fringe benefit plan during any year shall keep such records as may be necessary for purposes of determining whether the requirements of the applicable exclusion are met.
"(c) Additional information when required by the Secretary.
"Any employer—
"(1) who maintains a specified fringe benefit plan during any year for which a return is required under subsection (a), and
"(2) who is required by the Secretary to file an additional return for such year, shall file such additional return. Such additional return shall be filed at such time and in such manner as the Secretary shall prescribe and shall contain such information as the Secretary shall prescribe.

"(d) Definitions.
"For purposes of this section—
"(1) Specified fringe benefit plan. The term 'specified fringe benefit plan' means—
"(A) any qualified group legal services plan (as defined in section 120), and
"(B) any cafeteria plan (as defined in section 125).
"(2) Applicable exclusion. The term 'applicable exclusion' means—
"(A) section 120, in the case of a qualified group legal services plan, and
"(B) section 125, in the case of a cafeteria plan."

In 1984, P.L. 98-612, Sec. 1(b)(1), added Code Sec. 6039D, effective 1/1/85.

Sec. 6039E. Information concerning resident status.
(a) General rule.

Notwithstanding any other provision of law, any individual who—

(1) applies for a United States passport (or a renewal thereof), or

(2) applies to be lawfully accorded the privilege of residing permanently in the United States as an immigrant in accordance with the immigration laws,

shall include with any such application a statement which includes the information described in subsection (b).

(b) Information to be provided.

Information required under subsection (a) shall include—

(1) the taxpayer's TIN (if any),

(2) in the case of a passport applicant, any foreign country in which such individual is residing,

(3) in the case of an individual seeking permanent residence, information with respect to whether such individual is required to file a return of the tax imposed by chapter 1 for such individual's most recent 3 taxable years, and

(4) such other information as the Secretary may prescribe.

(c) Penalty.

Any individual failing to provide a statement required under subsection (a) shall be subject to a penalty equal to $500 for each such failure, unless it is shown that such failure is due to reasonable cause and not to willful neglect.

(d) Information to be provided to secretary.

Notwithstanding any other provision of law, any agency of the United States which collects (or is required to collect) the statement under subsection (a) shall—

(1) provide any such statement to the Secretary, and

(2) provide to the Secretary the name (and any other identifying information) of any individual refusing to comply with the provisions of subsection (a).

Nothing in the preceding sentence shall be construed to require the disclosure of information which is subject to section 245A of the Immigration and Nationality Act (as in effect on the date of the enactment of this sentence).

(e) Exemption.

The Secretary may by regulations exempt any class of individuals from the requirements of this section if he determines that applying this section to such individuals is not necessary to carry out the purposes of this section.

In 1988, P.L. 100-647, Sec. 1012(o), added the last sentence of subsec. (d), effective for applications submitted after 12/31/87 (or, if earlier, the effective date (which shall not be earlier than 1/1/87) of the initial regulations issued under this Code Sec.).

In 1986, P.L. 99-514, Sec. 1234(a)(1), added Code Sec. 6039E, effective for applications submitted after 12/31/87 (or, if earlier, the effective date (which shall not be earlier than 1/1/87) of the initial regulations issued under this Code Sec.).

Sec. 6039F. Notice of large gifts received from foreign persons.
(a) In general.

If the value of the aggregate foreign gifts received by a United States person (other than an organization described in section 501(c) and exempt from tax under section 501(a)) during any taxable year exceeds $10,000, such United States person shall furnish (at such time and in such manner as the Secretary shall prescribe) such information as the Secretary may prescribe regarding each foreign gift received during such year.

(b) Foreign gift.

For purposes of this section, the term "foreign gift" means any amount received from a person other than a United States person which the recipient treats as a gift or bequest. Such term shall not include any qualified transfer (within the meaning of section 2503(e)(2)) or any distribution properly disclosed in a return under section 6048(c).

(c) Penalty for failure to file information.

(1) **In general.** If a United States person fails to furnish the information required by subsection (a) with respect to any foreign gift within the time prescribed therefor (including extensions)—

(A) the tax consequences of the receipt of such gift shall be determined by the Secretary, and

(B) such United States person shall pay (upon notice and demand by the Secretary and in the same manner as tax) an amount equal to 5 percent of the amount of such foreign gift for each month for which the failure continues (not to exceed 25 percent of such amount in the aggregate).

(2) **Reasonable cause exception.** Paragraph (1) shall not apply to any failure to report a foreign gift if the United States person shows that the failure is due to reasonable cause and not due to willful neglect.

(d) Cost-of-living adjustment.

In the case of any taxable year beginning after December 31, 1996, the $10,000 amount under subsection (a) shall be increased by an amount equal to the product of such amount and the cost-of-living adjustment for such taxable year under section 1(f)(3), except that subparagraph (B) thereof shall be applied by substituting "1995" for "1992".

(e) Regulations.

The Secretary shall prescribe such regulations as may be necessary or appropriate to carry out the purposes of this section.

In 1996, P.L. 104-188, Sec. 1905(a), added Code Sec. 6039F, effective for amounts received after 8/20/96 in tax. yrs. end. after such date.

Sec. 6039G. Information on individuals losing United States citizenship.
(a) In general.

Notwithstanding any other provision of law, any individual to whom section 877(b) or 877A applies for any taxable year shall provide a statement for such taxable year which includes the information described in subsection (b).

(b) Information to be provided.

Information required under subsection (a) shall include—

(1) the taxpayer's TIN,

(2) the mailing address of such individual's principal foreign residence,

(3) the foreign country in which such individual is residing,

(4) the foreign country of which such individual is a citizen,

(5) information detailing the income, assets, and liabilities of such individual,

(6) the number of days during any portion of which that the individual was physically present in the United States during the taxable year, and

(7) such other information as the Secretary may prescribe.

Information and returns Code Sec. 6039H(c)(2)

(c) Penalty.

If—

(1) an individual is required to file a statement under subsection (a) for any taxable year, and

(2) fails to file such a statement with the Secretary on or before the date such statement is required to be filed or fails to include all the information required to be shown on the statement or includes incorrect information,

such individual shall pay a penalty of $10,000 unless it is shown that such failure is due to reasonable cause and not to willful neglect.

(d) Information to be provided to Secretary.

Notwithstanding any other provision of law—

(1) any Federal agency or court which collects (or is required to collect) the statement under subsection (a) shall provide to the Secretary—

  (A) a copy of any such statement, and

  (B) the name (and any other identifying information) of any individual refusing to comply with the provisions of subsection (a),

(2) the Secretary of State shall provide to the Secretary a copy of each certificate as to the loss of American nationality under section 358 of the Immigration and Nationality Act which is approved by the Secretary of State, and

(3) the Federal agency primarily responsible for administering the immigration laws shall provide to the Secretary the name of each lawful permanent resident of the United States (within the meaning of section 7701(b)(6)) whose status as such has been revoked or has been administratively or judicially determined to have been abandoned.

Notwithstanding any other provision of law, not later than 30 days after the close of each calendar quarter, the Secretary shall publish in the Federal Register the name of each individual losing United States citizenship (within the meaning of section 877(a) or 877A) with respect to whom the Secretary receives information under the preceding sentence during such quarter.

In 2008, P.L. 110-245, Sec. 301(e)(1), added "or 877A" after "section 877(b)" in subsec. (a)

— P.L. 110-245, Sec. 301(e)(2), added "or 877A" after "section 877(a)" in subsec. (d), effective on or after 6/17/2008.

In 2004, P.L. 108-357, Sec. 804(e)(1), amended subsec. (a)... Sec. 804(e)(2), amended subsec. (b)... Sec. 804(e)(3), amended subsec. (d) [prior to redesignation as subsec. (c) by Sec. 804(e)(4) of this Act, see below]... Sec. 804(e)(4), deleted subsecs. (c), (f) and (g), and redesignated subsecs. (d) [as amended by Sec. 804(e)(3) of this Act, see above] and (e) as subsecs. (c) and (d), effective for individuals who expatriate after 6/3/2004.

Prior to amendment, subsec. (a) read as follows:

"(a) In general. Notwithstanding any other provision of law, any individual who loses United States citizenship (within the meaning of section 877(a)) shall provide a statement which includes the information described in subsection (b). Such statement shall be—

"(1) provided not later than the earliest date of any act referred to in subsection (c), and

"(2) provided to the person or court referred to in subsection (c) with respect to such act."

Prior to amendment, subsec. (b) read as follows:

"(b) Information to be provided. Information required under subsection (a) shall include—

"(1) the taxpayer's TIN,

"(2) the mailing address of such individual's principal foreign residence,

"(3) the foreign country in which such individual is residing,

"(4) the foreign country of which such individual is a citizen,

"(5) in the case of an individual having a net worth of at least the dollar amount applicable under section 877(a)(2)(B), information detailing the assets and liabilities of such individual, and

"(6) such other information as the Secretary may prescribe."

Prior to deletion, subsec. (c) read as follows:

"(c) Acts described. For purposes of this section, the acts referred to in this subsection are—

"(1) the individual's renunciation of his United States nationality before a diplomatic or consular officer of the United States pursuant to paragraph (5) of section 349(a) of the Immigration and Nationality Act (8 U.S.C. 1481(a)(5)),

"(2) the individual's furnishing to the United States Department of State a signed statement of voluntary relinquishment of United States nationality confirming the performance of an act of expatriation specified in paragraph (1), (2), (3), or (4) of section 349(a) of the Immigration and Nationality Act (8 U.S.C. 1481(a)(1)-(4)),

"(3) the issuance by the United States Department of State of a certificate of loss of nationality to the individual, or

"(4) the cancellation by a court of the United States of a naturalized citizen's certificate of naturalization."

Prior to amendment, subsec. (d) read as follows:

"(d) Penalty. Any individual failing to provide a statement required under subsection (a) shall be subject to a penalty for each year (of the 10-year period beginning on the date of loss of United States citizenship) during any portion of which such failure continues in an amount equal to the greater of—

"(1) 5 percent of the tax required to be paid under section 877 for the taxable year ending during such year, or

"(2) $1,000,

"unless it is shown that such failure is due to reasonable cause and not to willful neglect."

Prior to deletion, subsec. (f) read as follows:

"(f) Reporting by long-term lawful permanent residents who cease to be taxed as residents. In lieu of applying the last sentence of subsection (a), any individual who is required to provide a statement under this section by reason of section 877(e)(1) shall provide such statement with the return of tax imposed by chapter 1 for the taxable year during which the event described in such section occurs."

Prior to deletion, subsec. (g) read as follows:

"(g) Exemption. The Secretary may by regulations exempt any class of individuals from the requirements of this section if he determines that applying this section to such individuals is not necessary to carry out the purposes of this section."

In 1997, P.L. 105-34, Sec. 1602(h)(1), redesignated Code Sec. 6039F added by Sec. 512 of P.L. 104-191, as Code Sec. 6030G, effective as provided in Sec. 512(c) of P.L. 104-191, reproduced below.

In 1996, P.L. 104-191, Sec. 512(a), added Code Sec. 6039F[sic G], effective as provided in Sec. 512(c) of this Act, which reads as follows:

"(c) Effective date. The amendments made by this section shall apply to—

"(1) individuals losing United States citizenship (within the meaning of section 877 of the Internal Revenue Code of 1986) on or after February 6, 1995, and

"(2) long-term residents of the United States with respect to whom an event described in subparagraph (A) or (B) of section 877(e)(1) of such Code occurs on or after such date.

In no event shall any statement required by such amendments be due before the 90th day after the date of the enactment of this Act."

> • **Caution:** P.L. 107-16, the Economic Growth and Tax Relief Reconciliation Act of 2001 (EGTRRA) added Code Sec. 6039H. These provisions generally sunset for tax years beginning after 12/31/2012. For specific sunset provisions, see Sec. 901, P.L. 107-16 (as amended) reproduced in history notes for this Code Sec.

Sec. 6039H. Information with respect to Alaska Native Settlement Trusts and sponsoring Native Corporations.

(a) Requirement.

The fiduciary of an electing Settlement Trust (as defined in section 646(h)(1)) shall include with the return of income of the trust a statement containing the information required under subsection (c).

(b) Application with other requirements.

The filing of any statement under this section shall be in lieu of the reporting requirements under section 6034A to furnish any statement to a beneficiary regarding amounts distributed to such beneficiary (and such other reporting rules as the Secretary deems appropriate).

(c) Required information.

The information required under this subsection shall include—

(1) the amount of distributions made during the taxable year to each beneficiary,

(2) the treatment of such distribution under the applicable provision of section 646, including the amount that is excludable from the recipient beneficiary's gross income under section 646, and

(3) the amount (if any) of any distribution during such year that is deemed to have been made by the sponsoring Native Corporation (as defined in section 646(h)(5)).
(d) Sponsoring Native Corporation.
(1) In general. The electing Settlement Trust shall, on or before the date on which the statement under subsection (a) is required to be filed, furnish such statement to the sponsoring Native Corporation (as so defined).
(2) Distributees. The sponsoring Native Corporation shall furnish each recipient of a distribution described in section 646(e)(3) a statement containing the amount deemed to have been distributed to such recipient by such corporation for the taxable year.

In 2010, P.L. 111-312, Sec. 101(a)(1), substituted "December 31, 2012" for "December 31, 2010" both places it appears in Sec. 901, P.L. 107-16, see below, effective as if included in the enactment of P.L. 107-16, EGTRRA, 6/7/2001.

In 2002, P.L. 107-358, Sec. 2, added subsec. (c) in Sec. 901 of P.L. 107-16 [see below], effective 12/17/2002.

In 2001, P.L. 107-16, Sec. 671(b), added Code Sec. 6039H, effective for tax. yrs. end. after 6/7/2001 and for contributions made to electing Settlement Trusts for such year or any subsequent year.

—P.L. 107-16, Sec. 901, of this Act [as amended by Sec. 2, P.L. 107-358, and Sec. 101(a)(1), P.L. 111-312, see above], reads as follows:

"SEC. 901. SUNSET OF PROVISIONS OF ACT.

"(a) In general. All provisions of, and amendments made by, this Act shall not apply—

"(1) to taxable, plan, or limitation years beginning after December 31, 2012, or

"(2) in the case of title V, to estates of decedents dying, gifts made, or generation skipping transfers, after December 31, 2012.

"(b) Application of certain laws. The Internal Revenue Code of 1986 and the Employee Retirement Income Security Act of 1974 shall be applied and administered to years, estates, gifts, and transfers described in subsection (a) as if the provisions and amendments described in subsection (a) had never been enacted.

"(c) Exception. Subsection (a) shall not apply to section 803 (relating to no federal income tax on restitution received by victims of the Nazi regime or their heirs or estates)."

Sec. 6039I. Returns and records with respect to employer-owned life insurance contracts.

(a) In general.
Every applicable policyholder owning 1 or more employer-owned life insurance contracts issued after the date of the enactment of this section shall file a return (at such time and in such manner as the Secretary shall by regulations prescribe) showing for each year such contracts are owned—
(1) the number of employees of the applicable policyholder at the end of the year,
(2) the number of such employees insured under such contracts at the end of the year,
(3) the total amount of insurance in force at the end of the year under such contracts,
(4) the name, address, and taxpayer identification number of the applicable policyholder and the type of business in which the policyholder is engaged, and
(5) that the applicable policyholder has a valid consent for each insured employee (or, if all such consents are not obtained, the number of insured employees for whom such consent was not obtained).
(b) Recordkeeping requirement.
Each applicable policyholder owning 1 or more employer-owned life insurance contracts during any year shall keep such records as may be necessary for purposes of determining whether the requirements of this section and section 101(j) are met.
(c) Definitions.
Any term used in this section which is used in section 101(j) shall have the same meaning given such term by section 101(j).

In 2006, P.L. 109-280, Sec. 863(b), added Code Sec. 6039I, effective as provided in Sec. 863(d) of this Act, which reads as follows:

"(d) Effective date.

"The amendments made by this section shall apply to life insurance contracts issued after the date of the enactment of this Act, except for a contract issued after such date pursuant to an exchange described in section 1035 of the Internal Revenue Code of 1986 for a contract issued on or prior to that date. For purposes of the preceding sentence, any material increase in the death benefit or other material change shall cause the contract to be treated as a new contract except that, in the case of a master contract (within the meaning of section 264(f)(4)(E) of such Code), the addition of covered lives shall be treated as a new contract only with respect to such additional covered lives."

Sec. 6039J. Information reporting with respect to commodity credit corporation transactions.

(a) Requirement of reporting.
The Commodity Credit Corporation, through the Secretary of Agriculture, shall make a return, according to the forms and regulations prescribed by the Secretary of the Treasury, setting forth any market gain realized by a taxpayer during the taxable year in relation to the repayment of a loan issued by the Commodity Credit Corporation, without regard to the manner in which such loan was repaid.
(b) Statements to be furnished to persons with respect to whom information is required.
The Secretary of Agriculture shall furnish to each person whose name is required to be set forth in a return required under subsection (a) a written statement showing the amount of market gain reported in such return.

In 2008, P.L. 110-246, Sec. 4, Repeals the duplicative enactment and provides effective date provisions of the Act entitled "An Act to provide for the continuation of agricultural programs through fiscal year 2012, and for other purposes" Sec. 4, P.L. 110-246 reads as follows:

"Sec. 4. Repeal of duplicative enactment.

"(a) In General- The Act entitled 'An Act to provide for the continuation of agricultural programs through fiscal year 2012, and for other purposes' (H.R. 2419 of the 110th Congress), and the amendments made by that Act, are repealed, effective on the date of enactment of that Act.

"(b) Effective Date- Except as otherwise provided in this Act, this Act and the amendments made by this Act shall take effect on the earlier of--

"(1) the date of enactment of this Act; or

"(2) the date of the enactment of the Act entitled 'An Act to provide for the continuation of agricultural programs through fiscal year 2012, and for other purposes' (H.R. 2419 of the 110th Congress)."

—P.L. 110-246, Sec. 15353(a), added new Code. Sec. 6039J, effective for loans repaid on or after 1/1/2007. [Ed. Note: May 22, 2008 was the date of enactment for H.R. 2419 (PL 110-234), which was repealed by (2008 Farm Bill § 4(a)) (PL 110-246, 6/18/2008), in connection with the reenactment of the farm bill to correct a technical deficiency in its original passage.]

Sec. 6040. Cross references.

(1) For the notice required of persons acting in a fiduciary capacity for taxpayers or for transferees, see sections 6212, 6901(g), and 6903.
(2) For application by fiduciary for determination of tax and discharge from personal liability therefor, see section 2204.
(3) For the notice required of taxpayers for redetermination of taxes claimed as credits, see sections 905(c) and 2016.
(4) For exemption certificates required to be furnished to employers by employees, see section 3402(f)(2), (3), (4), and (5).
(5) For receipts, constituting information returns, required to be furnished to employees, see section 6051.
(6) Repealed.
(7) For information required with respect to the redemption of stamps, see section 6805.
(8) For the statement required to be filed by a corporation expecting a net operating loss carryback or unused excess profits credit carryback, see section 6164.
(9) For the application, which a taxpayer may file for a tentative carryback adjustment of income taxes, see section 6411.

Information and returns Subpart B

In 1970, P.L. 91-614, Sec. 101(d)(2), substituted "fiduciary" for "executor" in para. (2), effective for decedents dying after 12/31/70.
In 1965, P.L. 89-44, Sec. 305, repealed para. (6), effective for admissions, services, and uses after noon 12/31/65.
In '58, '60 and '64 present Code Sec. 6040 had been renumbered from 6037 to 6038 to 6039 to 6040 by P. L.s 85-866, 86-780 and 88-272, respectively.

SUBPART B.— INFORMATION CONCERNING TRANSACTIONS WITH OTHER PERSONS

Sec.
6041. Information at source.
6041A. [Returns regarding payments of remuneration for services and direct sales.]
6042. Returns regarding payments of dividends, and corporate earnings and profits.
6043. Liquidating, etc., transactions.
6043A. Returns relating to taxable mergers and acquisitions.
6044. Returns regarding payments of patronage dividends.
6045. Returns of brokers.
6045A. Information required in connection with transfers of covered securities to brokers.
6045B. Returns relating to actions affecting basis of specified securities.
6046. Returns as to organization or reorganization of foreign corporations, and as to acquisitions of their stock.
6046A. Returns as to interests in foreign partnerships.
6047. Information relating to certain trusts and annuity plans.
6048. Information with respect to certain foreign trusts.
6049. Returns regarding payments of interest.
6050A. Reporting requirements of certain fishing boat operators.
6050B. Returns relating to unemployment compensation.
6050D. Returns relating to energy grants and financing.
6050E. State and local income tax refunds.
6050F. Returns relating to social security benefits.
6050G. Returns relating to certain railroad retirement benefits.
6050H. Returns relating to mortgage interest received in trade or business from individuals.
6050I. Returns relating to cash received in trade or business, etc.
6050J. Returns relating to foreclosures and abandonments of security.
6050K. Returns relating to exchanges of certain partnership interests.
6050L. Returns relating to certain donated property.
6050M. Returns relating to persons receiving contracts from Federal executive agencies.
6050N. Returns regarding payments of royalties.
6050P. Returns relating to the cancellation of indebtedness by certain entities.
6050Q. Certain long-term care benefits.
6050R. Returns relating to certain purchases of fish.
6050S. Returns relating to higher education tuition and related expenses.
6050T. Returns relating to credit for health insurance costs of eligible individuals.
6050U. Charges or payments for qualified long-term care insurance contracts under combined arrangements.
6050V. Returns relating to applicable insurance contracts in which certain exempt organizations hold interests.
6050W. Returns relating to payments made in settlement of payment card transactions.

In 2008, P.L. 110-343, Sec. 6045A, added Code Sec. 6045A, effective on January 1, 2011.
—P.L. 110-343, Sec. 6045B, added Code Sec. 6045B, effective on January 1, 2011.
—P.L. 110-298, Sec. 3091(d), added item 6050W
In 2006, P.L. 109-280, Sec. 844(d)(3), added item 6050U.
—P.L. 109-280, Sec. 1211(a)(2), added item 6050V.
In 2004, P.L. 108-357, Sec. 805(c), added item 6043A. . . . Sec. 882(c)(2), deleted item 6050L and added item 6050L.
Prior to deletion, item 6050L read as follows:
"6050L. Returns relating to certain dispositions of donated property."
In 2002, P.L. 107-210, Sec. 202(d)(2), added item 6050T.
In 1998, P.L. 105-206, Sec. 6018(a), substituted "chapter 61" for "chapter 68" in Sec. 1116(b)(2)(C) of P.L. 104-188 [see below].
In 1997, P.L. 105-34, Sec. 201(c)(3), added item 6050S.
In 1996, P.L. 104-188, Sec. 1116(b)(2)(C), added item 6050R. . . . Sec. 1704(t)(18), substituted a comma for the semicolon after "Liquidating". . . Sec. 1901(c)(2), amended item 6048.
Prior to amendment, item 6048 read as follows:
"Sec. 6048. Returns as to certain foreign trusts."
—P.L. 104-191, Sec. 323(c), added item 6050Q.
—P.L. 104-134, Sec. 31001(m)(2)(D)(ii), amended item 6050P.
Prior to amendment, item 6050P read as follows:
"Sec. 6050P. Returns relating to the cancellation if indebtedness by certain financial securities."
In 1994, P.L. 103-322, Sec. 20415(b)(4), substituted "business, etc." for "business" in item 6050I.
In 1993, P.L. 103-66, Sec. 13252(c), added item 6050P.
In 1989, P.L. 101-239, Sec. 7208(b)(3)(C), amended item 6043.
Prior to amendment item 6043 read as follows:
"6043. Return regarding corporate dissolution or liquidation." [sic]
In 1988, P.L. 100-418, Sec. 1941(b)(3)(B), deleted item 6050C.
Prior to deletion, item 6050C read as follows:
"6050C. Information regarding windfall profit tax on domestic crude oil."
In 1986, P.L. 99-514, Sec. 1522(b), added item 6050M . . . Sec. 1523(c), added item 6050N.
In 1984, P.L. 98-369, Sec. 145(c), added item 6050H . . . Sec. 146(c), added item 6050I . . . Sec. 148(c), added item 6050J . . . Sec. 149(c), added item 6050K . . . Sec. 155(b)(3), added item 6050L . . . Sec. 491(d)(58), deleted "and bond purchase" after "annuity" in item 6047.
In 1983, P.L. 98-76, Sec. 224(b)(2), added item 6050G.
—P.L. 98-21, Sec. 124(f)(4), added item 6050F.
In 1982, P.L. 97-248, Sec. 312(a), added Code Sec. 6041A without adding item 6041A. . . . Sec. 313(b), added item 6050E . . . Sec. 405(c)(1), added item 6046A.
In 1980, P.L. 96-223, Sec. 101(d)(2)(B), added item 6050C.
—P.L. 96-223, Sec. 203(b)(2), added item 6050D.
In 1979, P.L. 96-167, Sec. 5(b), deleted item 6050.
Prior to deletion, item 6050 read as follows:
"6050. Returns relating to certain transfers to exempt organizations."
In 1978, P.L. 95-600, Sec. 112(c)(2), added item 6050B.
In 1976, P.L. 94-455, Sec. 1013(e)(5), amended item 6048.
Prior to amendment, item 6048 read as follows:
"6048. Returns as to creation of or transfers to certain foreign trusts."
In 1969, P.L. 91-172, Sec. 121(e)(2), added item 6050.
In 1962, P.L. 87-834, Sec. 7(i)(2), added item 6048 . . . Sec. 19(g)(1)(A), amended items 6042 . . . Sec. 19(g)(1)(B), added "payments of" to item 6044 . . . Sec. 19(g)(1)(C), added item 6049 . . . Sec. 20(d)(2), amended item 6046.
Prior to amendment, item 6042 read as follows:
"Sec. 6042. Returns regarding corporate dividends, earnings and profits"
Prior to amendment, item 6046 read as follows:
"Sec. 6046. Returns as to creation or organization, or reorganization of foreign corporations"
— added item 6047.
In 1960, amended item 6046
Prior to amendment, item 6046 read as follows:
"Sec. 6046. Returns as to formation or reorganization of foreign corporations."
Related Statute: Foreign Transactions
— 10/26/70, enacted the following as part of its Title II:
"SEC. 241. RECORDS AND REPORTS REQUIRED.
"(a) The Secretary of the Treasury, having due regard for the need to avoid impeding or controlling the export or import of currency or other monetary instruments and having due regard also for the need to avoid burdening unreasonably persons who legitimately engage in transactions with foreign financial agencies, shall by regulation require any resident or citizen of the United States, or person in the United States and doing business therein, who engages in any transaction or maintains any relationship, directly or indirectly, on behalf of himself or another,

3,521

with a foreign financial agency to maintain records or to file reports, or both, setting forth such of the following information, in such form and in such detail, as the Secretary may require:

"(1) The identities and addresses of the parties to the transaction or relationship.

"(2) The legal capacities in which the parties to the transaction or relationship are acting, and the identities of the real parties in interest if one or more of the parties are not acting solely as principals.

"(3) A description of the transaction or relationship including the amounts of money, credit, or other property involved.

"(b) No person required to maintain records under this section shall be required to produce or otherwise disclose the contents of the records except in compliance with a subpena or summons duly authorized and issued as may otherwise be required by law."

"Sec. 242. Classifications and requirements.

The Secretary may prescribe:

"(1) Any reasonable classification of persons subject to or exempt from any requirement imposed under section 241.

"(2) The foreign country or countries as to which any requirement imposed under section 241 applies or does not apply if, in the judgment of the Secretary, uniform applicability of any such requirement to all foreign countries is unnecessary or undesirable.

"(3) The magnitude of transactions subject to any requirement imposed under section 241.

"(4) Types of transactions subject to or exempt from any requirement imposed under section 241.

"(5) Such other matters as he may deem necessary to the application of this chapter."

In Title IV it provided:

"SEC. 401. EFFECTIVE DATES.

"(a) Except as otherwise provided in this section, titles I, II, and III of this Act and the amendments made thereby take effect on the first day of the seventh calendar month which begins after the date of enactment.

"(b) The Secretary of the Treasury may by regulation provide that any provision of title I or II or any amendment made thereby shall be effective on any date not earlier than the publication of the regulation in the Federal Register and not later than the first day of the thirteenth calendar month which begins after the date of enactment.

"(c) . . ."

Sec. 6041. Information at source.
(a) Payments of $600 or more.

All persons engaged in a trade or business and making payment in the course of such trade or business to another person, of rent, salaries, wages, premiums, annuities, compensations, remunerations, emoluments, or other fixed or determinable gains, profits, and income (other than payments to which section 6042(a)(1), 6044(a)(1), 6047(e), 6049(a), or 6050N(a) applies, and other than payments with respect to which a statement is required under the authority of section 6042(a)(2), 6044(a)(2), or 6045), of $600 or more in any taxable year, or, in the case of such payments made by the United States, the officers or employees of the United States having information as to such payments and required to make returns in regard thereto by the regulations hereinafter provided for, shall render a true and accurate return to the Secretary, under such regulations and in such form and manner and to such extent as may be prescribed by the Secretary, setting forth the amount of such gains, profits, and income, and the name and address of the recipient of such payment.

(b) Collection of foreign items.

In the case of collections of items (not payable in the United States) of interest upon the bonds of foreign countries and interest upon the bonds of and dividends from foreign corporations by any person undertaking as a matter of business or for profit the collection of foreign payments of such interest or dividends by means of coupons, checks, or bills of exchange, such person shall make a return according to the forms or regulations prescribed by the Secretary, setting forth the amount paid and the name and address of the recipient of each such payment.

(c) Recipient to furnish name and address.

When necessary to make effective the provisions of this section, the name and address of the recipient of income shall be furnished upon demand of the person paying the income.

(d) Statements to be furnished to persons with respect to whom information is required.

Every person required to make a return under subsection (a) shall furnish to each person with respect to whom such a return is required a written statement showing—

(1) the name, address, and phone number of the information contact of the person required to make such return, and

(2) the aggregate amount of payments to the person required to be shown on the return.

The written statement required under the preceding sentence shall be furnished to the person on or before January 31 of the year following the calendar year for which the return under subsection (a) was required to be made. To the extent provided in regulations prescribed by the Secretary, this subsection shall also apply to persons required to make returns under subsection (b).

(e) Section does not apply to certain tips.

This section shall not apply to tips with respect to which section 6053(a) (relating to reporting of tips) applies.

(f) Section does not apply to certain health arrangements.

This section shall not apply to any payment for medical care (as defined in section 213(d)) made under—

(1) a flexible spending arrangement (as defined in section 106(c)(2)), or

(2) a health reimbursement arrangement which is treated as employer-provided coverage under an accident or health plan for purposes of section 106.

(g) Nonqualified deferred compensation.

Subsection (a) shall apply to—

(1) any deferrals for the year under a nonqualified deferred compensation plan (within the meaning of section 409A(d)), whether or not paid, except that this paragraph shall not apply to deferrals which are required to be reported under section 6051(a)(13) (without regard to any de minimis exception), and

(2) any amount includible under section 409A and which is not treated as wages under section 3401(a).

(h) Repealed.
(i) Repealed.
(j) Repealed.

In 2011, P.L. 112-9, Sec. 2(a),
deleted subsecs. (i)-(j) [as originally added by Sec. 9006(a) of P.L. 111-148 and redesignated by Sec. 2101(a) of P.L. 111-240, see below], effective for payments made after 12/31/2011.
Prior to deletion, subsecs. (i)-(j) read as follows:
"(i) Application to corporations.
"Notwithstanding any regulation prescribed by the Secretary before the date of the enactment of this subsection, for purposes of this section the term "person" includes any corporation that is not an organization exempt from tax under section 501(a)."
"(j) Regulations.
"The Secretary may prescribe such regulations and other guidance as may be appropriate or necessary to carry out the purposes of this section, including rules to prevent duplicative reporting of transactions."
—P.L. 112-9, Sec. 2(b)(1), deleted "amounts in consideration for property," after "of rent, salaries, wages," in subsec. (a) [as amended by Sec. 9006(b)(1) of P.L. 111-148, see below] . . . Sec. 2(b)(2), deleted "gross proceeds," after "emoluments, or other" in subsec. (a) [as amended by Sec. 9006(b)(2) of P.L. 111-148, see below] . . . Sec. 2(b)(2), deleted "gross proceeds," after "setting forth the amount of such" in subsec. (a) [as amended by Sec. 9006(b)(3) of P.L. 111-148, see below], effective for payments made after December 31, 2011.
—P.L. 112-9, Sec. 3(a), deleted subsec. (h) [as added by Sec. 2101(a) of P.L. 111-240, see below], effective for payments made after 12/31/2010.
Prior to deletion, subsec. (h) read as follows:
"(h) Treatment of rental property expense payments.
"(1) In general. Solely for purposes of subsection (a) and except as provided in paragraph (2), a person receiving rental income from real estate shall be considered to be engaged in a trade or business of renting property.
"(2) Exceptions. Paragraph (1) shall not apply to—
"(A) any individual, including any individual who is an active member of the uniformed services or an employee of the intelligence community (as defined in section 121(d)(9)(C)(iv), if substantially all rental income is derived from renting

Information and returns
Code Sec. 6041A(b)(2)(A)

the principal residence (within the meaning of section 121) of such individual on a temporary basis,

"(B) any individual who receives rental income of not more than the minimal amount, as determined under regulations prescribed by the Secretary, and

"(C) any other individual for whom the requirements of this section would cause hardship, as determined under regulations prescribed by the Secretary."

In 2010, P.L. 111-240, Sec. 2101(a), redesignated subsecs. (h) and (i) [as added by Sec. 9006(a) of PL 111-148, see below] as subsecs. (i) and (j), respectively, and added subsec. (h), effective for payments made after 12/31/2010.

—P.L. 111-148, Sec. 9006(a), added subsecs. (h) and (i)... Sec. 9006(b)(1), added "amounts in consideration for property" after "wages" in subsec. (a)... Sec. 9006(b)(2), added "gross proceeds" after "emoluments, or other" in subsec. (a)... Sec. 9006(b)(3), added "gross proceeds" after "setting forth the amount of such" in subsec. (a), effective for payments made after 12/31/2011.

In 2004, P.L. 108-357, Sec. 885(b)(3), added subsec. (g), effective for amounts deferred after 12/31/2004, except as provided in Sec. 885(d)(2) and (3) of this Act, which reads as follows:

"(2) Special rules.

"(A) Earnings. The amendments made by this section shall apply to earnings on deferred compensation only to the extent that such amendments apply to such compensation.

"(B) Material modifications. For purposes of this subsection, amounts deferred in taxable years beginning before January 1, 2005, shall be treated as amounts deferred in a taxable year beginning on or after such date if the plan under which the deferral is made is materially modified after October 3, 2004, unless such modification is pursuant to the guidance issued under subsection (f).

"(3) Exception for nonelective deferred compensation. The amendments made by this section shall not apply to any nonelective deferred compensation to which section 457 of the Internal Revenue Code of 1986 does not apply by reason of section 457(e)(12) of such Code, but only if such compensation is provided under a nonqualified deferred compensation plan—

"(A) which was in existence on May 1, 2004,

"(B) which was providing nonelective deferred compensation described in such section 457(e)(12) on such date, and

"(C) which is established or maintained by an organization incorporated on July 2, 1974.

"If, after May 1, 2004, a plan described in the preceding sentence adopts a plan amendment which provides a material change in the classes of individuals eligible to participate in the plan, this paragraph shall not apply to any nonelective deferred compensation provided under the plan on or after the date of the adoption of the amendment."

In 2003, P.L. 108-173, Sec. 1203(a), added subsec. (f), effective for payments made after 12/31/2002.

In 2002, P.L. 107-147, Sec. 401, of this Act, provides:

"SEC. 401. ALLOWANCE OF ELECTRONIC 1099'S.

"Any person required to furnish a statement under any section of subpart B of part III of subchapter A of chapter 61 of the Internal Revenue Code of 1986 for any taxable year ending after the date of the enactment of this Act, may electronically furnish such statement (without regard to any first class mailing requirement) to any recipient who has consented to the electronic provision of the statement in a manner similar to the one permitted under regulations issued under section 6051 of such Code or in such other manner as provided by the Secretary."

In 1997, P.L. 105-34, Sec. 1021(b), of this Act, provides:

"(b) Reporting of attorneys' fees payable to corporations. The regulations providing an exception under section 6041 of the Internal Revenue Code of 1986 for payments made to corporations shall not apply to payments of attorney's fees."

In 1996, P.L. 104-168, Sec. 1201(a)(1), substituted "name, address, and phone number of the information contact" for "name and address" in para. (d)(1), effective for statements required to be furnished after 12/31/96 (determined without regard to any extension).

In 1986, P.L. 99-514, Sec. 1501(c)(1), amended subsec. (d), effective for returns having due dates (determined without regard to extensions) after 12/31/86.

Prior to amendment, subsec. (d) read as follows:

"(d) Statements to be furnished to persons with respect to whom information is furnished.

"Every person making a return under subsection (a) shall furnish to each person whose name is set forth in such return a written statement showing—

"(1) the name, address, and identification number of the person making such return, and

"(2) the aggregate amount of payments to the person shown on the return.

The written statement required under the preceding sentence shall be furnished to the person on or before January 31 of the year following the calendar year for which the return under subsection (a) was made. To the extent provided in regulations prescribed by the Secretary, this subsection shall also apply to persons making returns under subsection (b)."

—P.L. 99-514, Sec. 1523(b)(2), substituted "6049(a), or 6050N(a)" for "or 6049(a)" in subsec. (a), effective for payments made after 12/31/86.

In 1984, P.L. 98-369, Sec. 722(h)(4)(B), added "6047(e)," after "6044(a)(1)," in subsec. (a), effective for payments or distributions made after 12/31/84, unless the payor elects to have such amendment apply to payments or distributions before 1/1/85.

In 1982, P.L. 97-248, Sec. 309(b)(1)(A), substituted "6049(a)" for "6049(a)(1)" in subsec. (a)... Sec. 309(b)(1)(B), substituted "or 6045" for "6045, 6049(a)(2), or 6049(a)(3)", in subsec. (a), effective for amounts paid (or treated as paid) after 12/31/82.

In 1981, P.L. 97-34, Sec. 723(b)(1), redesignated subsec. (d) as subsec. (e) and added a new subsec. (d), effective for returns and statements required to be furnished after 12/31/81.

In 1978, P.L. 95-600, Sec. 501(b), redesignated subsec. (d) as subsec. (c), and added new subsec. (d), effective for payments made after 12/31/78.

In 1976, P.L. 94-455, Sec. 1906(b)(13)(A), substituted "Secretary" for "Secretary or his delegate" each place it appeared in Code Sec. 6041, effective 2/1/77. Sec. 2111 of the Act provides as follows:

"SEC. 2111. EMPLOYER'S DUTIES IN CONNECTION WITH THE RECORDING AND REPORTING OF TIPS.

"(a) Suspension of rulings.

"Until January 1, 1979, the law with respect to the duty of an employer under section 6041(a) of the Internal Revenue Code of 1954 to report charge account tips of employees to the Internal Revenue Service (other than charge account tips included in statements furnished to the employer under section 6053(a) of such Code) shall be administered—

"(1) without regard to Revenue Rulings 75-400 and 76-231, and

"(2) in accordance with the manner in which such law was administered before the issuance of such rulings.

"(b) Effective date.

"This section shall take effect on January 1, 1976."

In 1962, P.L. 87-834, Sec. 19, substituted "(other than payments to which section 6042(a)(1), 6044(a)(1), or 6049(a)(1) applies, and other than payments with respect to which a statement is required under the authority of section 6042(a)(2), 6044(a)(2), 6045, 6049(a)(2), or 6049(a)(3))" for "(other than payments described in section 6042(1) or section 6045)" in subsec. (a), and deleted subsec. (c), effective for payments of dividends and interest made on or after 1/1/63, and to payments of amounts described in Code Sec. 6044(b) made on or after 1/1/63, for patronage occurring on or after the first day of the first tax. yr. of the cooperative begin. on or after 1/1/63.

Prior to deletion, subsec. (c) read as follows:

"(c) Payments of interest by corporations. Every corporation making payments of interest, regardless of amounts, shall, when required by regulations of the Secretary or his delegate, make a return according to the forms or regulations prescribed by the Secretary or his delegate, setting forth the amount paid and the name and address of the recipient of each such payment."

Sec. 6041A. Returns regarding payments of remuneration for services and direct sales.

(a) Returns regarding remuneration for services.

If—

(1) any service-recipient engaged in a trade or business pays in the course of such trade or business during any calendar year remuneration to any person for services performed by such person, and

(2) the aggregate of such remuneration paid to such person during such calendar year is $600 or more,

then the service-recipient shall make a return, according to the forms or regulations prescribed by the Secretary, setting forth the aggregate amount of such payments and the name and address of the recipient of such payments. For purposes of the preceding sentence, the term "service-recipient" means the person for whom the service is performed.

(b) Direct sales of $5,000 or more.

(1) In general. If—

(A) any person engaged in a trade or business in the course of such trade or business during any calendar year sells consumer products to any buyer on a buy-sell basis, a deposit-commission basis, or any similar basis which the Secretary prescribes by regulations, for resale (by the buyer or any other person) in the home or otherwise than in a permanent retail establishment, and

(B) the aggregate amount of the sales to such buyer during such calendar year is $5,000 or more,

then such person shall make a return, according to the forms or regulations prescribed by the Secretary, setting forth the name and address of the buyer to whom such sales are made.

(2) Definitions. For purposes of paragraph (1)—

(A) Buy-sell basis. A transaction is on a buy-sell basis if the buyer performing the services is entitled to retain part or all of the difference between the price at which the buyer purchases the product and the price at which the buyer sells the product as part or all of the buyer's remuneration for the services, and

3,523

(B) **Deposit-commission basis.** A transaction is on a deposit-commission basis if the buyer performing the services is entitled to retain part or all of a purchase deposit paid by the consumer in connection with the transaction as part or all of the buyer's remuneration for the services.

(c) Certain services not included.

No return shall be required under subsection (a) or (b) if a statement with respect to the services is required to be furnished under section 6051, 6052, or 6053.

(d) Applications to governmental units.

(1) **Treated as persons.** The term "person" includes any governmental unit (and any agency or instrumentality thereof).

(2) **Special rules.** In the case of any payment by a governmental entity or any agency or instrumentality thereof—

(A) subsection (a) shall be applied without regard to the trade or business requirement contained therein, and

(B) any return under this section shall be made by the officer or employee having control of the payment or appropriately designated for the purpose of making such return.

(3) **Payments to corporations by federal executive agencies.**

(A) In general. Notwithstanding any regulation prescribed by the Secretary before the date of the enactment of this paragraph, subsection (a) shall apply to remuneration paid to a corporation by any Federal executive agency (as defined in section 6050M(b)).

(B) Exception. Subparagraph (A) shall not apply to—

(i) services under contracts described in section 6050M(e)(3) with respect to which the requirements of section 6050M(e)(2) are met, and

(ii) such other services as the Secretary may specify in regulations prescribed after the date of the enactment of this paragraph.

(e) Statements to be furnished to persons with respect to whom information is required to be furnished.

Every person required to make a return under subsection (a) or (b) shall furnish to each person whose name is required to be set forth in such return a written statement showing—

(1) the name, address, and phone number of the information contact of the person required to make such return, and

(2) in the case of subsection (a), the aggregate amount of payments to the person required to be shown on such return.

The written statement required under the preceding sentence shall be furnished to the person on or before January 31 of the year following the calendar year for which the return under subsection (a) was made.

(f) Recipient to furnish name, address, and identification number; inclusion on return.

(1) **Furnishing of information.** Any person with respect to whom a return or statement is required under this section to be made by another person shall furnish to such other person his name, address, and identification number at such time and in such manner as the Secretary may prescribe by regulations.

(2) **Inclusion on return.** The person to whom an identification number is furnished under paragraph (1) shall include such number on any return which such person is required to file under this section and to which such identification number relates.

In 1997, P.L. 105-34, Sec. 1022(a), added para. (d)(3), effective for returns the due date for which (determined without regard to any extension) is more than 90 days after 8/5/97.

In 1996, P.L. 104-168, Sec. 1201(a)(2), substituted "name, address, and phone number of the information contact" for "name and address" in para. (e)(1), effective for statements required to be furnished after 12/31/96 (determined without regard to any extension).

In 1982, P.L. 97-248, Sec. 312(a), added Code Sec. 6041A, effective for payments and sales made after 12/31/82.

Sec. 6042. Returns regarding payments of dividends and corporate earnings and profits.

(a) Requirement of reporting.

(1) **In general.** Every person—

(A) who makes payments of dividends aggregating $10 or more to any other person during any calendar year, or

(B) who receives payments of dividends as a nominee and who makes payments aggregating $10 or more during any calendar year to any other person with respect to the dividends so received,

shall make a return according to the forms or regulations prescribed by the Secretary, setting forth the aggregate amount of such payments and the name and address of the person to whom paid.

(2) **Returns required by the Secretary.** Every person who makes payments of dividends aggregating less than $10 to any other person during any calendar year shall, when required by the Secretary, make a return setting forth the aggregate amount of such payments, and the name and address of the person to whom paid.

(b) Dividend defined.

(1) **General rule.** For purposes of this section, the term "dividend" means—

(A) any distribution by a corporation which is a dividend (as defined in section 316); and

(B) any payment made by a stockbroker to any person as a substitute for a dividend (as so defined).

(2) **Exceptions.** For purposes of this section, the term "dividend" does not include any distribution or payment—

(A) to the extent provided in regulations prescribed by the Secretary—

(i) by a foreign corporation, or

(ii) to a foreign corporation, a nonresident alien, or a partnership not engaged in a trade or business in the United States and composed in whole or in part of nonresident aliens, or

(B) except to the extent otherwise provided in regulations prescribed by the Secretary, to any person described in section 6049(b)(4).

(3) **Special rule.** If the person making any payment described in subsection (a)(1)(A) or (B) is unable to determine the portion of such payment which is a dividend or is paid with respect to a dividend, he shall, for purposes of subsection (a)(1), treat the entire amount of such payment as a dividend or as an amount paid with respect to a dividend.

(c) Statements to be furnished to persons with respect to whom information is required.

Every person required to make a return under subsection (a) shall furnish to each person whose name is required to be set forth in such return a written statement showing—

(1) the name, address, and phone number of information contact of the person required to make such return, and

(2) the aggregate amount of payments to the person required to be shown on the return.

The written statement required under the preceding sentence shall be furnished (either in person or in a statement mailing by first-class mail which includes adequate notice that the statement is enclosed) to the person on or before January 31 of the year following the calendar year for which the return under subsection (a) was required to be made and shall be in such form as the Secretary may prescribe by regulations.

(d) Statements to be furnished by corporations to Secretary.

Every corporation shall, when required by the Secretary—
(1) furnish to the Secretary a statement stating the name and address of each shareholder, and the number of shares owned by each shareholder;
(2) furnish to the Secretary a statement of such facts as will enable him to determine the portion of the earnings and profits of the corporation (including gains, profits, and income not taxed) accumulated during such periods as the Secretary may specify, which have been distributed or ordered to be distributed, respectively, to its shareholders during such taxable years as the Secretary may specify; and
(3) furnish to the Secretary a statement of its accumulated earnings and profits and the names and addresses of the individuals or shareholders who would be entitled to such accumulated earnings and profits if divided or distributed, and of the amounts that would be payable to each.

In 1996, P.L. 104-168, Sec. 1201(a)(3), substituted "name, address, and phone number of the information contact" for "name and address" in para. (c)(1), effective for statements required to be furnished after 12/31/96 (determined without regard to any extension).

In 1986, P.L. 99-514, Sec. 1501(c)(2), amended subsec. (c), effective for returns having due dates (determined without regard to extensions) after 10/22/86.
Prior to amendment, subsec. (c) read as follows:
"(c) Statements to be furnished to persons with respect to whom information is furnished.
"Every person making a return under subsection (a)(1) shall furnish to each person whose name is set forth in such return a written statement showing—
"(1) the name and address of the person making such return, and
"(2) the aggregate amount of payments to the person as shown on such return.
The written statement required under the preceding sentence shall be furnished (either in person or in a separate mailing by first-class mail) to the person on or before January 31 of the year following the calendar year for which the return under subsection (a) was made, and shall be in such form as the Secretary may prescribe by regulations. No statement shall be required to be furnished to any person under this subsection if the aggregate amount of payments to such person as shown on the return made under subsection (a)(1) is less than $10."

In 1984, P.L. 98-369, Sec. 714(d), amended para. (b)(2), effective for amounts paid (or treated as paid) after 12/31/82.
Prior to amendment, para. (b)(2) read as follows:
"(2) Exceptions. For purposes of this section, to the extent provided in regulations prescribed by the Secretary, the term 'dividend' does not include any distribution or payment—
"(A) by a foreign corporation, or
"(B) to a foreign corporation, a nonresident alien, or a partnership not engaged in a trade or business in the United States and composed in whole or in part of nonresident aliens."

In 1983, P.L. 98-67, Sec. 108(b), amended the second sentence of subsec. (c), effective for payments made after 12/31/83.
Prior to amendment, the second sentence of subsec. (c) read as follows:
"The written statement required under the preceding sentence shall be furnished to the person on or before January 31 of the year following the calendar year for which the return under subsection (a)(1) was made."

In 1982, P.L. 97-354, Sec. 5(a)(40), amended para. (b)(2), effective for tax. yrs. begin. after 12/31/82.
Prior to amendment, para. (b)(2) read as follows:
"(2) Exceptions. For purposes of this section, the term 'dividend' does not include—
"(A) to the extent provided in regulations prescribed by the Secretary, any distribution or payment—
"(i) by a foreign corporation, or
"(ii) to a foreign corporation, a nonresident alien, or a partnership not engaged in trade or business in the United States and composed in whole or in part of nonresident aliens; and
"(B) any amount described in section 1373 (relating to undistributed taxable income of electing small business corporations)."

In 1976, P.L. 94-455, Sec. 1906(b)(13)(A), substituted "Secretary" for "Secretary or his delegate" each place it appeared in Code Sec. 6042, effective 2/1/77.

In 1962, P.L. 87-834, Sec. 19(a), amended Code Sec. 6042, effective for payments made on or after 1/1/63.
Prior to amendment, Code Sec. 6042 read as follows:
"Sec. 6042. Returns regarding corporate dividends, earnings, and profits.
"Every corporation shall, when required by the Secretary or his delegate—
"(1) Make a return of its payments of dividends, stating the name and address of, the number of shares owned by, and the amount of dividends paid to, each shareholder;
"(2) Furnish to the Secretary or his delegate a statement of such facts as will enable him to determine the portion of the earnings or profits of the corporation (including gains, profits, and income not taxed) accumulated during such periods as the Secretary or his delegate may specify, which have been distributed or ordered to be distributed, respectively, to its shareholders during such taxable years as the Secretary or his delegate may specify; and
"(3) Furnish to the Secretary or his delegate a statement of its accumulated earnings and profits and the names and addresses of the individuals or shareholders who would be entitled to such accumulated earnings and profits if divided or distributed, and of the amounts that would be payable to each."

Sec. 6043. Liquidating, etc., transactions.

(a) Corporate liquidating, etc., transactions.

Every corporation shall—
(1) Within 30 days after the adoption by the corporation of a resolution or plan for the dissolution of the corporation or for the liquidation of the whole or any part of its capital stock, make a return setting forth the terms of such resolution or plan and such other information as the Secretary shall by forms or regulations prescribe; and
(2) When required by the Secretary, make a return regarding its distributions in liquidation, stating the name and address of, the number and class of shares owned by, and the amount paid to, each shareholder, or, if the distribution is in property other than money, the fair market value (as of the date the distribution is made) of the property distributed to each shareholder.

(b) Exempt organizations.

Every organization which for any of its last 5 taxable years preceding its liquidation, dissolution, termination, or substantial contraction was exempt from taxation under section 501(a) shall file such return and other information with respect to such liquidation, dissolution, termination, or substantial contraction as the Secretary, shall by forms or regulations prescribe; except that—
(1) no return shall be required under this subsection from churches, their integrated auxiliaries, conventions or associations of churches, or any organization which is not a private foundation (as defined in section 509(a)) and the gross receipts of which in each taxable year are normally not more than $5,000, and
(2) the Secretary may relieve any organization from such filing where he determines that such filing is not necessary to the efficient administration of the internal revenue laws or, with respect to an organization described in section 401(a), where the employer who established such organization files such a return.

(c) Changes in control and recapitalizations.

If—
(1) control (as defined in section 304(c)(1)) of a corporation is acquired by any person (or group of persons) in a transaction (or series of related transactions), or
(2) there is a recapitalization of a corporation or other substantial change in the capital structure of a corporation, when required by the Secretary, such corporation shall make a return (at such time and in such manner as the Secretary may prescribe) setting forth the identity of the parties to the transaction, the fees involved, the changes in the capital structure involved, and such other information as the Secretary may require with respect to such transaction.

(d) Cross references.

For provisions relating to penalties for failure to file—
(1) a return under subsection (b), see section 6652(c), or

(2) a return under subsection (c), see section 6652(l).

In 1996, P.L. 104-188, Sec. 1704(t)(17), substituted a comma for the semicolon in the heading of Code Sec. 6043, effective 8/20/96.

In 1989, P.L. 101-239, Sec. 7208(b)(1), deleted subsec. (c) and added new subsecs. (c) and (d) . . . Sec. 7208(b)(3)(A), substituted "Corporate liquidating, etc., transactions." for "Corporations." in the heading of subsec. (a) . . . Sec. 7208(b)(3)(B), amended the heading of Code Sec. 6043, effective for transactions after 3/31/90.

Prior to amendment, the heading of Code Sec. 6043 read as follows:

"Sec. 6043. Returns regarding liquidation, dissolution, termination, or contraction."

Prior to deletion, subsec. (c) read as follows:

"(c) Cross references.

"For provisions relating to penalties for failure to file a return required by subsection (b), see section 6652(c)."

In 1986, P.L. 99-514, Sec. 1501(d)(1)(C), substituted "6652(c)" for "6652(d)" in subsec. (c), effective for returns the due date for which (determined without regard to extensions) is after 12/31/86.

In 1976, P.L. 94-455, Sec. 1906(b)(13)(A), substituted "Secretary" for "Secretary or his delegate" each place it appeared in Code Sec. 6043, effective 2/1/77.

In 1969, P.L. 91-172, Sec. 101(j)(35), amended the heading which formerly read "Return regarding corporate dissolution or liquidation" and added "(a) Corporations.", added subsecs. (b) and (c), effective for tax. yrs. begin. after 12/21/69.

Sec. 6043A. Returns relating to taxable mergers and acquisitions.

(a) In general.

According to the forms or regulations prescribed by the Secretary, the acquiring corporation in any taxable acquisition shall make a return setting forth—

(1) a description of the acquisition,

(2) the name and address of each shareholder of the acquired corporation who is required to recognize gain (if any) as a result of the acquisition,

(3) the amount of money and the fair market value of other property transferred to each such shareholder as part of such acquisition, and

(4) such other information as the Secretary may prescribe.

To the extent provided by the Secretary, the requirements of this section applicable to the acquiring corporation shall be applicable to the acquired corporation and not to the acquiring corporation.

(b) Nominees.

According to the forms or regulations prescribed by the Secretary—

(1) **Reporting.** Any person who holds stock as a nominee for another person shall furnish in the manner prescribed by the Secretary to such other person the information provided by the corporation under subsection (d).

(2) **Reporting to nominees.** In the case of stock held by any person as a nominee, references in this section (other than in subsection (c)) to a shareholder shall be treated as a reference to the nominee.

(c) Taxable acquisition.

For purposes of this section, the term "taxable acquisition" means any acquisition by a corporation of stock in or property of another corporation if any shareholder of the acquired corporation is required to recognize gain (if any) as a result of such acquisition.

(d) Statements to be furnished to shareholders.

According to the forms or regulations prescribed by the Secretary, every person required to make a return under subsection (a) shall furnish to each shareholder whose name is required to be set forth in such return a written statement showing—

(1) the name, address, and phone number of the information contact of the person required to make such return,

(2) the information required to be shown on such return with respect to such shareholder, and

(3) such other information as the Secretary may prescribe.

The written statement required under the preceding sentence shall be furnished to the shareholder on or before January 31 of the year following the calendar year during which the taxable acquisition occurred.

In 2004, P.L. 108-357, Sec. 805(a), added Code Sec. 6043A, effective for acquisitions after 10/22/2004.

Sec. 6044. Returns regarding payments of patronage dividends.

(a) Requirement of reporting.

(1) **In general.** Except as otherwise provided in this section, every cooperative to which part I of subchapter T of chapter 1 applies, which makes payments of amounts described in subsection (b) aggregating $10 or more to any person during any calendar year, shall make a return according to the forms of regulations prescribed by the Secretary, setting forth the aggregate amount of such payments and the name and address of the person to whom paid.

(2) **Returns required by the Secretary.** Every such cooperative which makes payments of amounts described in subsection (b) aggregating less than $10 to any person during any calendar year shall, when required by the Secretary, make a return setting forth the aggregate amount of such payments and the name and address of the person to whom paid.

(b) Amounts subject to reporting.

(1) **General rule.** Except as otherwise provided in this section, the amounts subject to reporting under subsection (a) are—

(A) the amount of any patronage dividend (as defined in section 1388(a)) which is paid in money, qualified written notices of allocation (as defined in section 1388(c)), or other property (except nonqualified written notices of allocation as defined in section 1388(d)),

(B) any amount described in section 1382(c)(2)(A) (relating to certain nonpatronage distributions) which is paid in money, qualified written notices of allocation, or other property (except nonqualified written notices of allocation) by an organization exempt from tax under section 521 (relating to exemption of farmers' cooperatives from tax),

(C) any amount described in section 1382(b)(2) (relating to redemption of nonqualified written notices of allocation) and, in the case of an organization described in section 1381(a)(1), any amount described in section 1382(c)(2)(B) (relating to redemption of nonqualified written notices of allocation paid with respect to earnings derived from sources other than patronage), and

(D) the amount of any per-unit retain allocation (as defined in section 1388(f)) which is paid in qualified per-unit retain certificates (as defined in section 1388(h)), and

(E) any amount described in section 1382(b)(4) (relating to redemption of nonqualified per-unit retain certificates).

(2) **Exceptions.** The provisions of subsection (a) shall not apply, to the extent provided in regulations prescribed by the Secretary, to any payment—

(A) by a foreign corporation, or

(B) to a foreign corporation, a nonresident alien, or a partnership not engaged in trade or business in the United States and composed in whole or in part of nonresident aliens.

Information and returns

(c) Exemption for certain consumer cooperatives.

A cooperative which the Secretary determines is primarily engaged in selling at retail goods or services of a type that are generally for personal, living, or family use shall, upon application to the Secretary, be granted exemption from the reporting requirements imposed by subsection (a). Application for exemption under this subsection shall be made in accordance with regulations prescribed by the Secretary.

(d) Determination of amount paid.

For purposes of this section, in determining the amount of any payment—

(1) property (other than a qualified written notice of allocation or a qualified per-unit retain certificate) shall be taken into account at its fair market value, and

(2) a qualified written notice of allocation or a qualified per-unit retain certificate shall be taken into account at its stated dollar amount.

(e) Statements to be furnished to persons with respect to whom information is required.

Every cooperative required to make a return under subsection (a) shall furnish to each person whose name is required to be set forth in such return a written statement showing—

(1) the name, address, and phone number of the information contact of the cooperative required to make such return, and

(2) the aggregate amount of payments to the person required to be shown on the return.

The written statement required under the preceding sentence shall be furnished (either in person or in a statement mailing by first-class mail which includes adequate notice that the statement is enclosed) to the person on or before January 31 of the year following the calendar year for which the return under subsection (a) was required to be made and shall be in such form as the Secretary may prescribe by regulations.

In **1996**, P.L. 104-168, Sec. 1201(a)(4), substituted "name, address, and phone number of the information contact" for "name and address" in para. (e)(1), effective for statements required to be furnished after 12/31/96 (determined without regard to any extension).

In **1986**, P.L. 99-514, Sec. 1501(c)(3), amended subsec. (e), effective for returns having due dates (determined without regard to extensions) after 10/22/86. Prior to amendment, subsec. (e) read as follows:

"(e) Statements to be furnished to persons with respect to whom information is furnished.

"Every cooperative making a return under subsection (a)(1) shall furnish to each person whose name is set forth in such return a written statement showing—

"(1) the name and address of the cooperative making such return, and

"(2) the aggregate amount of payments to the person as shown on such return.

The written statement required under the preceding sentence shall be furnished (either in person or in a separate mailing by first-class mail) to the person on or before January 31 of the year following the calendar year for which the return under subsection (a) was made, and shall be in such form as the Secretary may prescribe by regulations. No statement shall be required to be furnished to any person under this subsection if the aggregate amount of payments to such person as shown on the return made under subsection (a)(1) is less than $10."

In **1983**, P.L. 98-67, Sec. 108(c), amended the second sentence of subsec. (e), effective for payments made after 12/31/83.

Prior to amendment, the second sentence of subsec. (e) read as follows:

"The written statement required under the preceding sentence shall be furnished to the person on or before January 31 of the year following the calendar year for which the return under subsection (a)(1) was made."

In **1976**, P.L. 94-455, Sec. 1906(b)(13)(A), substituted "Secretary" for "Secretary or his delegate" each place it appears in subsecs. (a), (b), and (c), effective 2/1/77.

In **1966**, P.L. 89-809, Sec. 211(d), added subpars. (D) and (E) and included per-unit retain certificates in subsecs. (d)(1) and (2) for calendar years after '66.

In **1962**, P.L. 87-834, Sec. 19(b), amended Code Sec. 6044, effective for payments after 12/31/62 with respect to patronage on or after the first day of the first taxable year of the cooperative beginning after 12/31/62.

Prior to amendment, Code Sec. 6044 read as follows:

"(a) Payments of $100 or more.

"Any corporation allocating amounts as patronage dividends, rebates, or refunds (whether in cash, merchandise, capital stock, revolving fund certificates, retain certificates, certificates of indebtedness, letters of advice, or in some other manner that discloses to each patron the amount of such dividend, refund, or rebate) shall make a return showing—

"(1) The name and address of each patron to whom it has made such allocations amounting to $100 or more during the calendar year; and

"(2) The amount of such allocations to each patron.

"(b) Payments regardless of amount.

"If required by the Secretary or his delegate, any such corporation shall make a return of all patronage dividends, rebates, or refunds made during the calendar year to its patrons.

"(c) Exceptions.

"This section shall not apply in the case of any corporation (including any cooperative or nonprofit corporation engaged in rural electrification) described in section 501(c)(12) or (15) which is exempt from tax under section 501(a), or in the case of any corporation subject to a tax imposed by subchapter L of chapter 1."

Sec. 6045. Returns of brokers.

(a) General rule.

Every person doing business as a broker shall, when required by the Secretary, make a return, in accordance with such regulations as the Secretary may prescribe, showing the name and address of each customer, with such details regarding gross proceeds and such other information as the Secretary may by forms or regulations require with respect to such business.

(b) Statements to be furnished to customers.

Every person required to make a return under subsection (a) shall furnish to each customer whose name is required to be set forth in such return a written statement showing—

(1) the name, address, and phone number of the information contact of the person required to make such return, and

(2) the information required to be shown on such return with respect to such customer.

The written statement required under the preceding sentence shall be furnished to the customer on or before February 15 of the year following the calendar year for which the return under subsection (a) was required to be made. In the case of a consolidated reporting statement (as defined in regulations) with respect to any customer, any statement which would otherwise be required to be furnished on or before January 31 of a calendar year with respect to any item reportable to the taxpayer shall instead be required to be furnished on or before February 15 of such calendar year if furnished with such consolidated reporting statement.

(c) Definitions.

For purposes of this section—

(1) Broker. The term "broker" includes—

(A) a dealer,

(B) a barter exchange, and

(C) any other person who (for a consideration) regularly acts as a middleman with respect to property or services.

A person shall not be treated as a broker with respect to activities consisting of managing a farm on behalf of another person.

(2) Customer. The term "customer" means any person for whom the broker has transacted any business.

(3) Barter exchange. The term "barter exchange" means any organization of members providing property or services who jointly contract to trade or barter such property or services.

(4) Person. The term "person" includes any governmental unit and any agency or instrumentality thereof.

(d) Statements required in case of certain substitute payments.

If any broker—

(1) transfers securities of a customer for use in a short sale or similar transaction, and

(2) receives (on behalf of the customer) a payment in lieu of—

(A) a dividend,

(B) tax-exempt interest, or
(C) such other items as the Secretary may prescribe by regulations,

during the period such short sale or similar transaction is open, the broker shall furnish such customer a written statement (in the manner as the Secretary shall prescribe by regulations) identifying such payment as being in lieu of the dividend, tax-exempt interest, or such other item. The written statement required under the preceding sentence shall be furnished on or before February 15 of the year following the calendar year in which the payment was made. The Secretary may prescribe regulations which require the broker to make a return which includes the information contained in such written statement.

(e) Return required in the case of real estate transactions.

(1) In general. In the case of a real estate transaction, the real estate reporting person shall file a return under subsection (a) and a statement under subsection (b) with respect to such transaction.

(2) Real estate reporting person. For purposes of this subsection, the term "real estate reporting person" means any of the following persons involved in a real estate transaction in the following order:

(A) the person (including any attorney or title company) responsible for closing the transaction,
(B) the mortgage lender,
(C) the seller's broker,
(D) the buyer's broker, or
(E) such other person designated in regulations prescribed by the Secretary.

Any person treated as a real estate reporting person under the preceding sentence shall be treated as a broker for purposes of subsection (c)(1).

(3) Prohibition of separate charge for filing return. It shall be unlawful for any real estate reporting person to separately charge any customer for complying with any requirement of paragraph (1). Nothing in this paragraph shall be construed to prohibit the real estate reporting person from taking into account its cost of complying with such requirement in establishing its charge (other than a separate charge for complying with such requirement) to any customer for performing services in the case of a real estate transaction.

(4) Additional information required. In the case of a real estate transaction involving a residence, the real estate reporting person shall include the following information on the return under subsection (a) and on the statement under subsection (b):

(A) The portion of any real property tax which is treated as a tax imposed on the purchaser by reason of section 164(d)(1)(B).
(B) Whether or not the financing (if any) of the seller was federally-subsidized indebtedness (as defined in section 143(m)(3)).

(5) Exception for sales or exchanges of certain principal residences.

(A) In general. Paragraph (1) shall not apply to any sale or exchange of a residence for $250,000 or less if the person referred to in paragraph (2) receives written assurance in a form acceptable to the Secretary from the seller that—

(i) such residence is the principal residence (within the meaning of section 121) of the seller,
(ii) if the Secretary requires the inclusion on the return under subsection (a) of information as to whether there is federally subsidized mortgage financing assistance with respect to the mortgage on residences, that there is no such assistance with respect to the mortgage on such residence, and
(iii) the full amount of the gain on such sale or exchange is excludable from gross income under section 121.

If such assurance includes an assurance that the seller is married, the preceding sentence shall be applied by substituting "$500,000" for "$250,000". The Secretary may by regulation increase the dollar amounts under this subparagraph if the Secretary determines that such an increase will not materially reduce revenues to the Treasury.

(B) Seller. For purposes of this paragraph, the term "seller" includes the person relinquishing the residence in an exchange.

(f) Return required in the case of payments to attorneys.

(1) In general. Any person engaged in a trade or business and making a payment (in the course of such trade or business) to which this subsection applies shall file a return under subsection (a) and a statement under subsection (b) with respect to such payment.

(2) Application of subsection.

(A) In general. This subsection shall apply to any payment to an attorney in connection with legal services (whether or not such services are performed for the payor).
(B) Exception. This subsection shall not apply to the portion of any payment which is required to be reported under section 6041(a) (or would be so required but for the dollar limitation contained therein) or section 6051.

(g) Additional information required in the case of securities transactions, etc.

(1) In general. If a broker is otherwise required to make a return under subsection (a) with respect to the gross proceeds of the sale of a covered security, the broker shall include in such return the information described in paragraph (2).

(2) Additional information required.

(A) In general. The information required under paragraph (1) to be shown on a return with respect to a covered security of a customer shall include the customer's adjusted basis in such security and whether any gain or loss with respect to such security is long-term or short-term (within the meaning of section 1222).
(B) Determination of adjusted basis. For purposes of subparagraph (A)—

(i) In general. The customer's adjusted basis shall be determined—

(I) in the case of any security (other than any stock for which an average basis method is permissible under section 1012), in accordance with the first-in first-out method unless the customer notifies the broker by means of making an adequate identification of the stock sold or transferred, and
(II) in the case of any stock for which an average basis method is permissible under section 1012, in accordance with the broker's default method unless the customer notifies the broker that he elects another acceptable method under section 1012 with respect to the account in which such stock is held.

(ii) Exception for wash sales. Except as otherwise provided by the Secretary, the customer's adjusted basis shall be determined without regard to section 1091 (relating to loss from wash sales of stock or securities) unless the transactions occur in the same account with respect to identical securities.

(3) Covered security. For purposes of this subsection—
   (A) In general. The term "covered security" means any specified security acquired on or after the applicable date if such security—
      (i) was acquired through a transaction in the account in which such security is held, or
      (ii) was transferred to such account from an account in which such security was a covered security, but only if the broker received a statement under section 6045A with respect to the transfer.
   (B) Specified security. The term "specified security" means—
      (i) any share of stock in a corporation,
      (ii) any note, bond, debenture, or other evidence of indebtedness,
      (iii) any commodity, or contract or derivative with respect to such commodity, if the Secretary determines that adjusted basis reporting is appropriate for purposes of this subsection, and
      (iv) any other financial instrument with respect to which the Secretary determines that adjusted basis reporting is appropriate for purposes of this subsection.
   (C) Applicable date. The term "applicable date" means—
      (i) January 1, 2011, in the case of any specified security which is stock in a corporation (other than any stock described in clause (ii)),
      (ii) January 1, 2012, in the case of any stock for which an average basis method is permissible under section 1012, and
      (iii) January 1, 2013, or such later date determined by the Secretary in the case of any other specified security.
(4) Treatment of S corporations. In the case of the sale of a covered security acquired by an S corporation (other than a financial institution) after December 31, 2011, such S corporation shall be treated in the same manner as a partnership for purposes of this section.
(5) Special rules for short sales. In the case of a short sale, reporting under this section shall be made for the year in which such sale is closed.

(h) Application to options on securities.
   (1) Exercise of option. For purposes of this section, if a covered security is acquired or disposed of pursuant to the exercise of an option that was granted or acquired in the same account as the covered security, the amount received with respect to the grant or paid with respect to the acquisition of such option shall be treated as an adjustment to gross proceeds or as an adjustment to basis, as the case may be.
   (2) Lapse or closing transaction. In the case of the lapse (or closing transaction (as defined in section 1234(b)(2)(A))) of an option on a specified security or the exercise of a cash-settled option on a specified security, reporting under subsections (a) and (g) with respect to such option shall be made for the calendar year which includes the date of such lapse, closing transaction, or exercise.
   (3) Prospective application. Paragraphs (1) and (2) shall not apply to any option which is granted or acquired before January 1, 2013.
   (4) Definitions. For purposes of this subsection, the terms "covered security" and "specified security" shall have the meanings given such terms in subsection (g)(5).

In 2008, P.L. 110-343, Sec. 403(a)(1)DivB, added subsec. (g)... Sec. 403(a)(2)DivB, added subsec. (h), effective 1/1/2011.
—P.L. 110-343, Sec. 403(a)(3)(A)DivB, substituted "February 15" for "January 31" in subsec. (b)... Sec. 403(a)(3)(B)(i)DivB, deleted "at such time and" in subsec. (d)... Sec. 403(a)(3)(B)(ii)DivB, added "The written statement required under the preceding sentence shall be furnished on or before February 15 of the year following the calendar year in which the payment was made." after "other item." in subsec. (d)... Sec. 403(a)(3)(C)DivB, added "In the case of a consolidated reporting statement (as defined in regulations) with respect to any customer, any statement which would otherwise be required to be furnished on or before January 31 of a calendar year with respect to any item reportable to the taxpayer shall instead be required to be furnished on or before February 15 of such calendar year if furnished with such consolidated reporting statement." at the end of subsec. (b), effective for statements required to be furnished after 12/31/2008.
In 2005, P.L. 109-135, Sec. 412(xx), substituted "for '$250,000'. The Secretary may by regulation increase the dollar amounts under this subparagraph if the Secretary determines that such an increase will not materially reduce revenues to the Treasury." for "for '$250,000'. The Secretary may by regulation increase the dollar amounts under this subparagraph if the Secretary determines that such an increase will not materially reduce revenues to the Treasury." in the matter following clause (e)(5)(A)(iii), effective 12/21/2005.
In 1998, P.L. 105-206, Sec. 6005(e)(3), added "on or" before "before" each place it appeared in the heading and text of Sec. 312(d)(2)[sic (e)] of P.L. 105-34, see below.
In 1997, P.L. 105-34, Sec. 312(c), added para. (e)(5), effective for sales and exchanges after 5/6/97, except as provided in Secs. 312(d)(2)-(4) [sic (e)(2)-(4)] of this Act [as amended by Sec. 6005(e)(3) of P.L. 105-206, see above], which reads as follows:
"(2) Sales on or before date of enactment.—At the election of the taxpayer, the amendments made by this section shall not apply to any sale or exchange on or before the date of the enactment of this Act.
"(3) Certain sales within 2 years after date of enactment. Section 121 of the Internal Revenue Code of 1986 (as amended by this section) shall be applied without regard to subsection (c)(2)(B) thereof in the case of any sale or exchange of property during the 2-year period beginning on the date of the enactment of this Act if the taxpayer held such property on the date of the enactment of this Act and fails to meet the ownership and use requirements of subsection (a) thereof with respect to such property.
"(4) Binding contracts.—At the election of the taxpayer, the amendments made by this section shall not apply to a sale or exchange after the date of the enactment of this Act, if—
"(A) such sale or exchange is pursuant to a contract which was binding on such date, or
"(B) without regard to such amendments, gain would not be recognized under section 1034 of the Internal Revenue Code of 1986 (as in effect on the day before the date of the enactment of this Act) on such sale or exchange by reason of a new residence acquired on or before such date or with respect to the acquisition of which by the taxpayer a binding contract was in effect on such date.
This paragraph shall not apply to any sale or exchange by an individual if the treatment provided by section 877(a)(1) of the Internal Revenue Code of 1986 applies to such individual."
—P.L. 105-34, Sec. 1021(a), added subsec (f), effective for payments made after 12/31/97.
In 1996, P.L. 104-188, Sec. 1704(o)(1), added the sentence at the end of para. (e)(3), effective 11/10/88.
—P.L. 104-168, Sec. 1201(a)(5), substituted "name, address, and phone number of the information contact" for "name and address" in para. (b)(1), effective for statements required to be furnished after 12/31/96 (determined without regard to any extension).
In 1992, P.L. 102-486, Sec. 1939(a), amended para. (e)(4), effective for transactions after 12/31/92.
Prior to amendment, para. (e)(4) read as follows:
"(4) Whether seller's financing was federally-subsidized. In the case of a real estate transaction involving a residence, the real estate reporting person shall specify on the return under subsection (a) and the statement under subsection (b) whether or not the financing (if any) of the seller was federally-subsidized indebtedness (as defined in section 143(m)(3))."
In 1990, P.L. 101-508, Sec. 11704(a)(25), substituted "reporting person" for "broker" in para. (e)(4), effective 11/5/90.
In 1989, P.L. 101-239, Sec. 7814(c)(1), redesignated para. (e)(3) [as added by Sec. 4005(g)(3) of P.L. 100-647] as para. (e)(4), effective for financing provided and mortgage credit certificates issued after 12/31/90, except as provided in Sec. 4005(h)(3)(B) of P.L. 100-647, reproduced in the note following Code Sec. 143.
In 1988, P.L. 100-647, Sec. 1015(e)(1)(A), added the last sentence to para. (c)(1), effective 9/3/82, except as provided in Secs. 311(c)(1)(A) and (B) of P.L. 97-248, reproduced below.
—P.L. 100-647, Sec. 1015(e)(2)(A), added para. (e)(3), effective 11/10/88.
—P.L. 100-647, Sec. 1015(e)(3)(A), substituted "real estate reporting person" for "real estate broker" each time it appeared in subsec. (e)... Sec. 1015(e)(3)(B), substituted "Real estate reporting person" for "Real estate broker" in the heading of para. (e)(2), effective for real estate transactions closing after 12/31/86.
—P.L. 100-647, Sec. 4005(g)(3), added para. (e)(3)[(4)], effective for financing provided and mortgage credit certificates issued after 12/31/90, except as provided in Sec. 4005(h)(3)(B) of this Act, reproduced in note following Code Sec. 143.

Code Sec. 6045

In **1986**, P.L. 99-514, Sec. 1501(c)(4), amended subsec. (b), effective for returns having due dates (determined without regard to extensions) after 12/31/86.
Prior to amendment, subsec. (b) read as follows:
"(b) Statements to be furnished to customers. Every person making a return under subsection (a) shall furnish to each customer whose name is set forth in such return a written statement showing—
"(1) the name and address of the person making such return, and
"(2) the information shown on such return with respect to such customer.
The written statement required under the preceding sentence shall be furnished to the customer on or before January 31 of the year following the calendar year for which the return under subsection (a) was made."
—P.L. 99-514, Sec. 1521(a), added subsec. (e), effective for real estate transactions closing after 12/31/86.
In **1984**, P.L. 98-369, Sec. 150(a), added subsec. (d), effective for payments received after 12/31/84.
—P.L. 98-369, Sec. 714(e)(1), added para. (c)(4), effective 9/3/82, except as provided in Sec. 311(c)(1)(A) and (B) of P.L. 97-248, reproduced below, and as provided in Sec. 714(e)(2) of this Act which reads as follows:
"(2) No penalty for payments before January 1, 1985.—No penalty shall be imposed under the Internal Revenue Code of 1954 with respect to any person required (by reason of the amendment made by paragraph (1)) to file a return under section 6045 of such Code with respect to any payment before January 1, 1985."
In **1982**, P.L. 97-248, Sec. 311(a)(1), amended Code Sec. 6045, effective 9/3/82, except as provided in Secs. 311(c)(1)(A) and (B) of this Act which reads as follows:
"(A) regulations relating to reporting by commodities and securities brokers shall be issued under section 6045 of the Internal Revenue Code of 1954 (as amended by this Act) within 6 months after the date of the enactment of this Act [9/3/82], and
"(B) such regulations shall not apply to transactions occurring before January 1, 1983."
Prior to amendment, Code Sec. 6045 read as follows:
"SEC. 6045. RETURNS OF BROKERS.
"Every person doing business as a broker shall, when required by the Secretary, make a return, in accordance with such regulations as the Secretary may prescribe, showing the names of customers for whom such person has transacted any business, with such details regarding the profits and losses and such other information as the Secretary may by forms or regulations require with respect to each customer as will enable the Secretary to determine the amount of such profits or losses."
In **1976**, P.L. 94-455, Sec. 1906(b)(13)(A), substituted "Secretary" for "Secretary or his delegate" each place it appeared in Code Sec. 6045, effective 2/1/77.

Sec. 6045A. Information required in connection with transfers of covered securities to brokers.

(a) Furnishing of information.

Every applicable person which transfers to a broker (as defined in section 6045(c)(1)) a security which is a covered security (as defined in section 6045(g)(3)) in the hands of such applicable person shall furnish to such broker a written statement in such manner and setting forth such information as the Secretary may by regulations prescribe for purposes of enabling such broker to meet the requirements of section 6045(g).

(b) Applicable person.

For purposes of subsection (a), the term "applicable person" means—
(1) any broker (as defined in section 6045(c)(1)), and
(2) any other person as provided by the Secretary in regulations.

(c) Time for furnishing statement.

Except as otherwise provided by the Secretary, any statement required by subsection (a) shall be furnished not later than 15 days after the date of the transfer described in such subsection.

In **2008**, P.L. 110-343, Sec. 6045ADivB, added Code Sec. 6045A, effective 1/1/2011.

Sec. 6045B. Returns relating to actions affecting basis of specified securities.

(a) In general.

According to the forms or regulations prescribed by the Secretary, any issuer of a specified security shall make a return setting forth—
(1) a description of any organizational action which affects the basis of such specified security of such issuer,

(2) the quantitative effect on the basis of such specified security resulting from such action, and
(3) such other information as the Secretary may prescribe.

(b) Time for filing return.

Any return required by subsection (a) shall be filed not later than the earlier of—
(1) 45 days after the date of the action described in subsection (a), or
(2) January 15 of the year following the calendar year during which such action occurred.

(c) Statements to be furnished to holders of specified securities or their nominees.

According to the forms or regulations prescribed by the Secretary, every person required to make a return under subsection (a) with respect to a specified security shall furnish to the nominee with respect to the specified security (or certificate holder if there is no nominee) a written statement showing—
(1) the name, address, and phone number of the information contact of the person required to make such return,
(2) the information required to be shown on such return with respect to such security, and
(3) such other information as the Secretary may prescribe.
The written statement required under the preceding sentence shall be furnished to the holder on or before January 15 of the year following the calendar year during which the action described in subsection (a) occurred.

(d) Specified security.

For purposes of this section, the term "specified security" has the meaning given such term by section 6045(g)(3)(B). No return shall be required under this section with respect to actions described in subsection (a) with respect to a specified security which occur before the applicable date (as defined in section 6045(g)(3)(C)) with respect to such security.

(e) Public reporting in lieu of return

The Secretary may waive the requirements under subsections (a) and (c) with respect to a specified security, if the person required to make the return under subsection (a) makes publicly available, in such form and manner as the Secretary determines necessary to carry out the purposes of this section—
(1) the name, address, phone number, and email address of the information contact of such person, and
(2) the information described in paragraphs (1), (2), and (3) of subsection (a).

In **2008**, P.L. 110-343, Sec. 6045BDiv B, added Code Sec. 6045B, effective 1/1/2011.

Sec. 6046. Returns as to organization or reorganization of foreign corporations and as to acquisitions of their stock.

(a) Requirement of return.

(1) In general. A return complying with the requirements of subsection (b) shall be made by—
(A) each United States citizen or resident who becomes an officer or director of a foreign corporation if a United States person (as defined in section 7701(a)(30)) meets the stock ownership requirements of paragraph (2) with respect to such corporation,
(B) each United States person—
(i) who acquires stock which, when added to any stock owned on the date of such acquisition, meets the stock ownership requirements of paragraph (2) with respect to a foreign corporation, or
(ii) who acquires stock which, without regard to stock owned on the date of such acquisition, meets

the stock ownership requirements of paragraph (2) with respect to a foreign corporation,

(C) each person (not described in subparagraph (B)) who is treated as a United States shareholder under section 953(c) with respect to a foreign corporation, and

(D) each person who becomes a United States person while meeting the stock ownership requirements of paragraph (2) with respect to stock of a foreign corporation.

In the case of a foreign corporation with respect to which any person is treated as a United States shareholder under section 953(c), subparagraph (A) shall be treated as including a reference to each United States person who is an officer or director of such corporation.

(2) Stock ownership requirements. A person meets the stock ownership requirements of this paragraph with respect to any corporation if such person owns 10 percent or more of—

(A) the total combined voting power of all classes of stock of such corporation entitled to vote, or

(B) the total value of the stock of such corporation.

(b) Form and contents of returns.

The returns required by subsection (a) shall be in such form and shall set forth, in respect of the foreign corporation, such information as the Secretary prescribes by forms or regulations as necessary for carrying out the provisions of the income tax laws, except that in the case of persons described only in subsection (a)(1)(A) the information required shall be limited to the names and addresses of persons described in subparagraph (B) or (C) of subsection (a)(1).

(c) Ownership of stock.

For purposes of subsection (a), stock owned directly or indirectly by a person (including, in the case of an individual, stock owned by members of his family) shall be taken into account. For purposes of the preceding sentence, the family of an individual shall be considered as including only his brothers and sisters (whether by the whole or half blood), spouse, ancestors, and lineal descendants.

(d) Time for filing.

Any return required by subsection (a) shall be filed on or before the 90th day after the day on which, under any provision of subsection (a), the United States citizen, resident, or person becomes liable to file such return (or on or before such later day as the Secretary may by forms or regulations prescribe).

(e) Limitation.

No information shall be required to be furnished under this section with respect to any foreign corporation unless such information was required to be furnished under regulations which have been in effect for at least 90 days before the date on which the United States citizen, resident, or person becomes liable to file a return required under subsection (a).

(f) Cross reference.

For provisions relating to penalties for violations of this section, see sections 6679 and 7203.

In 2007, P.L. 110-172, Sec. 11(a)(33)(A), substituted "subsection (a)(1)(A)" for "subsection (a)(1)" in subsec. (b) . . . Sec. 11(a)(33)(B), substituted "subparagraph (B) or (C) of subsection (a)(1)" for "paragraph (2) or (3) of subsection (a)" in subsec. (b), enacted 12/29/2007.

In 1997, P.L. 105-34, Sec. 1146(a), amended subsec. (a), effective 1/1/98.
Prior to amendment, subsec. (a) read as follows:
"(a) Requirement of return. A return complying with the requirements of subsection (b) shall be made by—
"(1) each United States citizen or resident who is on January 1, 1963, an officer or director of a foreign corporation, 5 percent or more in value of the stock of which is owned by a United States person (as defined in section 7701(a)(30)), or who becomes such an officer or director at any time after such date,

"(2) each United States person who on January 1, 1963, owns 5 percent or more in value of the stock of a foreign corporation, or who, at any time after such date—
"(A) acquires stock which, when added to any stock owned on January 1, 1963, has a value equal to 5 percent or more of the value of the stock of a foreign corporation, or
"(B) acquires an additional 5 percent or more in value of the stock of a foreign corporation,
"(3) each person (not described in paragraph (2)) who, at any time after January 1, 1987, is treated as a United States shareholder under section 953(c) with respect to a foreign corporation, and
"(4) each person who at any time after January 1, 1963, becomes a United States person while owning 5 percent or more in value of the stock of a foreign corporation.
In the case of a foreign corporation with respect to which any person is treated as a United States shareholder under section 953(c), paragraph (1) shall be treated as including a reference to each United States person who is an officer or director of such corporation."

In 1988, P.L. 100-647, Sec. 1012(i)(19)(A), deleted "and" at the end of subpara. (a)(2)(B), redesignated para. (a)(3) as (a)(4), and added new para. (a)(3) . . . Sec. 1012(i)(19)(B), substituted "paragraph (2) or (3) of subsection (a)" for "subsection (a)(2)" in subsec. (b) . . . Sec. 1012(i)(19)(C), added the last sentence to subsec. (a), effective for tax. yrs. of foreign corporations begin. after 12/31/86, except as provided by Sec. 1221(g)(3) of P.L. 99-514 [reproduced in the notes following Code Sec. 953].

In 1982, P.L. 97-248, Sec. 341(a), added "(or on or before such later day as the Secretary may by forms or regulations prescribe)" before the period at the end of subsec. (d), effective for returns filed after 9/3/82.

In 1976, P.L. 94-455, Sec. 1906(a)(4), amended subsec. (e), effective 2/1/77.
Prior to amendment, subsec. (e) read as follows:
"(e) Limitation.
"(1) General rule. Except as provided in paragraph (2), no information shall be required to be furnished under this section with respect to any foreign corporation unless such information was required to be furnished under regulations which have been in effect for at least 90 days before the date on which the United States citizen, resident, or person becomes liable to file a return required under subsection (a).
"(2) Exception. In the case of liability to file a return under subsection (a) arising on or after January 1, 1963, and before June 1, 1963—
"(A) no information shall be required to be furnished under this section with respect to any foreign corporation unless such information was required to be furnished under regulations in effect on or before March 1, 1963, and
"(B) if the date on which regulations become effective is later than the day on which such liability arose, any return required by subsection (a) shall (in lieu of the time prescribed by subsection (d)) be filed on or before the 90th day after such date."
—P.L. 94-455, Sec. 1906(b)(13)(A), substituted "Secretary" for "Secretary or his delegate" in Code Sec. 6046, effective 2/1/77.

In 1962, P.L. 87-834, Sec. 20(b), amended the heading of Code Sec. 6046, amended subsecs. (a), (b) and (c), added subsecs. (d) and (e) and redesignated subsec. (d) as subsec. (f), effective 1/1/63.
Prior to amendment, the heading of Code Sec. 6046 read as follows:
"SEC. 6046. RETURNS AS TO CREATION OR ORGANIZATION, OR REORGANIZATION, OF FOREIGN CORPORATIONS
Prior to amendment, subsecs. (a), (b) and (c) read as follows:
"(a) General rule.
"On or before the 90th day after the creation or organization. or reorganization, of any foreign corporation—
"(1) Each United States citizen or resident who was an officer or director of the corporation at any time within 60 days after the creation or organization, or reorganization thereof, and
"(2) Each United States shareholder of the corporation by or for whom, at any time within 60 days after the creation or organization or reorganization of the corporation, 5 percent or more in value of the stock of the corporation outstanding was owned directly or indirectly (including, in the case of an individual, stock owned by members of his family), shall make a return in compliance with the provisions of subsection (b).
"(b) Form and contents of returns.
"The returns required by subsection (a) shall be in such form and shall set forth, in respect of the foreign corporation, such information as the Secretary or his delegate prescribes by forms or regulations as necessary for carrying out the provisions of the income tax laws.
"(c) Meaning of terms.
"For the purpose of this section—
"(1) United States shareholder. The term 'United States shareholder' includes a citizen or resident of the United States, a domestic corporation, a domestic partnership or an estate or trust (other than an estate or trust the gross income of which under subtitle A includes only income from sources within the United States).
"(2) Members of family. The family of an individual shall be considered as including only his brothers and sisters (whether by the whole or half blood), spouse, ancestors, and lineal descendants."

In 1960, P.L. 86-780, Sec. 7(a), amended Code Sec. 6046, effective for foreign corporations created, organized or reorganized after 9/14/60.
Prior to amendment, Code Sec. 6046 read as follows:
"SEC. 6046. RETURNS AS TO FORMATION OR REORGANIZATION OF FOREIGN CORPORATIONS.

Code Sec. 6046 — Information and returns

"(a) Requirement.

"Every attorney, accountant, fiduciary, bank, trust company, financial institution, or other person, who aids, assists, counsels, or advises in, or with respect to, the formation, organization, or reorganization of any foreign corporation, shall, within 30 days thereafter, make a return in accordance with regulations prescribed by the Secretary or his delegate.

"(b) Form and contents of return.

"Such return shall be in such form, and shall set forth, in respect of each such corporation, to the full extent of the information within the possession or knowledge or under the control of the person required to make the return, such information as the Secretary or his delegate prescribes by forms or regulations as necessary for carrying out the provisions of the income tax laws.

"(c) Privileged communications.

"Nothing in this section shall be construed to require the making of a return by an attorney-at-law with respect to any advice given or information obtained through the relationship of attorney and client."

Sec. 6046A. Returns as to interests in foreign partnerships.

(a) Requirement of return.

Any United States person, except to the extent otherwise provided by regulations—

(1) who acquires any interest in a foreign partnership,

(2) who disposes of any portion of his interest in a foreign partnership, or

(3) whose proportional interest in a foreign partnership changes substantially, shall file a return.

Paragraphs (1) and (2) shall apply to any acquisition or disposition only if the United States person directly or indirectly holds at least a 10-percent interest in such partnership either before or after such acquisition or disposition, and paragraph (3) shall apply to any change only if the change is equivalent to at least a 10-interest in such partnership.

(b) Form and contents of return.

Any return required by subsection (a) shall be in such form and set forth such information as the Secretary shall by regulations prescribe.

(c) Time for filing return.

Any return required by subsection (a) shall be filed on or before the 90th day (or on or before such later day as the Secretary may by regulations prescribe) after the day on which the United States person becomes liable to file such return.

(d) 10-percent interest.

For purposes of subsection (a), a 10-percent interest in a partnership is an interest described in section 6038(e)(3)(C).

(e) Cross reference.

For provisions relating to penalties for violations of this section, see sections 6679 and 7203.

In **1997**, P.L. 105-34, Sec. 1143(a)(1), added a sentence at the end of subsec. (a) ... Sec. 1143(a)(2), redesignated subsec. (d) as subsec. (e) and added a new subsec. (d), effective for transfers and changes after 8/5/97.

In **1982**, P.L. 97-248, Sec. 405(a), added Code Sec. 6046A, effective for acquisitions or dispositions of, or substantial changes in, interests in foreign partnerships occurring after 9/3/82.

—P.L. 97-248, Sec. 406, provides as follows:

"SEC. 406. SPECIAL RULE FOR CERTAIN INTERNATIONAL SATELLITE PARTNERSHIPS.

"Subchapter C of chapter 63 of the Internal Revenue Code of 1954 (relating to tax treatment of partnership items), section 6031 of such Code (relating to returns of partnership income), and section 6046A of such Code (relating to returns as to interest in foreign partnerships) shall not apply to the International Telecommunications Satellite Organization, the International Maritime Satellite Organization, and any organization which is a successor of either of such organizations."

Sec. 6047. Information relating to certain trusts and annuity plans.

(a) Trustees and insurance companies.

The trustee of a trust described in section 401(a) which is exempt from tax under section 501(a) to which contributions have been paid under a plan on behalf of any owner-employee (as defined in section 401(c)(3)), and each insurance company or other person which is the issuer of a contract purchased by such a trust, or purchased under a plan described in section 403(a), contributions for which have been paid on behalf of any owner-employee, shall file such returns (in such form and at such times), keep such records, make such identification of contracts and funds (and accounts within such funds), and supply such information, as the Secretary shall by forms or regulations prescribe.

(b) Owner-employees.

Every individual on whose behalf contributions have been paid as an owner-employee (as defined in section 401(c)(3))—

(1) to a trust described in section 401(a) which is exempt from tax under section 501(a), or

(2) to an insurance company or other person under a plan described in section 403(a),

shall furnish the trustee, insurance company, or other person, as the case may be, such information at such times and in such form and manner as the Secretary shall prescribe by forms or regulations.

(c) Other programs.

To the extent provided by regulations prescribed by the Secretary, the provisions of this section apply with respect to any payment described in section 219 and to transactions of any trust described in section 408(a) or under an individual retirement annuity described in section 408(b).

(d) Reports by employers, plan administrators, etc.

(1) **In general.** The Secretary shall by forms or regulations require that—

(A) the employer maintaining, or the plan administrator (within the meaning of section 414(g)) of, a plan from which designated distributions (as defined in section 3405(e)(1)) may be made, and

(B) any person issuing any contract under which designated distributions (as so defined) may be made,

make returns and reports regarding such plan (or contract) to the Secretary, to the participants and beneficiaries of such plan (or contract), and to such other persons as the Secretary may by regulations prescribe. No return or report may be required under the preceding sentence with respect to distributions to any person during any year unless such distributions aggregate $10 or more.

(2) **Form, etc., of reports.** Such reports shall be in such form, made at such time, and contain such information as the Secretary may prescribe by forms or regulations.

(e) Employee stock ownership plans.

The Secretary shall require—

(1) any employer maintaining, or the plan administrator (within the meaning of section 414(g)) of, an employee stock ownership plan which holds stock with respect to which section 404(k) applies to dividends paid on such stock, or

(2) both such employer or plan administrator,

to make returns and reports regarding such plan, transaction, or loan to the Secretary and to such other persons as the Secretary may prescribe. Such returns and reports shall be made in such form, shall be made at such time, and shall contain such information as the Secretary may prescribe.

(f) Designated Roth contributions.

The Secretary shall require the plan administrator of each applicable retirement plan (as defined in section 402A) to make such returns and reports regarding designated Roth contributions (as defined in section 402A) to the Secretary, participants and beneficiaires of the plan, and such other persons as the Secretary may prescribe.

(g) Cross references.

(1) For provisions relating to penalties for failure to file returns and reports required under this section, see sections 6652(e), 6721, and 6722.

Information and returns   Code Sec. 6048(a)(3)(A)(ii)

(2) For criminal penalty for furnishing fraudulent information, see section 7207.

(3) For provisions relating to penalty for failure to comply with the provisions of subsection (d), see section 6704.

In 2010, P.L. 111-312, Sec. 101(a)(1), substituted "December 31, 2012" for "December 31, 2010" both places it appeared in Sec. 901 of P.L. 107-16, [see below] effective as if included in the enactment of P.L. 107-16, EGTRRA, 6/7/2001.

In 2006, P.L. 109-280, Sec. 811, of this Act [relating to Sec. 901 of P.L. 107-16, see below], provides:

"SEC. 811. PENSIONS AND INDIVIDUAL RETIREMENT ARRANGEMENT PROVISIONS OF ECONOMIC GROWTH AND TAX RELIEF RECONCILIATION ACT OF 2001 MADE PERMANENT.

"Title IX of the Economic Growth and Tax Relief Reconciliation Act of 2001 shall not apply to the provisions of, and amendments made by, subtitles A through F of title VI of such Act (relating to pension and individual retirement arrangement provisions)."

In 2002, P.L. 107-358, Sec. 2, added subsec. (c) in Sec. 901 of P.L. 107-16 [see below], effective 12/17/2002.

In 2001, P.L. 107-16, Sec. 617(d)(2), redesignated subsec. (f) as (g) and added subsec. (f), effective for tax. yrs. begin. after 12/31/2005.

—P.L. 107-16, Sec. 901, of this Act [as amended by Sec. 2 of P.L. 107-358, and Sec. 101(a)(1) of P.L. 111-312, see above], reads as follows:

"SEC. 901. SUNSET OF PROVISIONS OF ACT.

"(a) In general. All provisions of, and amendments made by, this Act shall not apply—

"(1) to taxable, plan, or limitation years beginning after December 31, 2012, or

"(2) in the case of title V, to estates of decedents dying, gifts made, or generation skipping transfers, after December 31, 2012.

"(b) Application of certain laws. The Internal Revenue Code of 1986 and the Employee Retirement Income Security Act of 1974 shall be applied and administered to years, estates, gifts, and transfers described in subsection (a) as if the provisions and amendments described in subsection (a) had never been enacted.

"(c) Exception. Subsection (a) shall not apply to section 803 (relating to no federal income tax on restitution received by victims of the Nazi regime or their heirs or estates)."

In 1996, P.L. 104-188, Sec. 1455(b)(2), added a sentence at the end of para. (d)(1)...Sec. 1455(d)(1), amended para. (f)(1), effective for returns, reports, and other statements the due date for which (determined without regard to extension) is after 12/31/96.

Prior to amendment, para. (f)(1) read as follows:

"(1) For provisions relating to penalties for failure to file a return required by this section, see section 6652(e)."

—P.L. 104-188, Sec. 1602(b)(6), deleted paras. (e)(1)-(3) and added paras. (e)(1) and (2), effective for loans made after 8/20/96. Sec. 1602(c)(2) and (3) of this Act provides:

"(2) Refinancings. The amendments made by this section shall not apply to loans made after the date of the enactment of this Act to refinance securities acquisition loans (determined without regard to section 133(b)(1)(B) of the Internal Revenue Code of 1986, as in effect on the day before the date of the enactment of this Act) made on or before such date or to refinance loans described in this paragraph if—

"(A) the refinancing loans meet the requirements of section 133 of such Code (as so in effect),

"(B) immediately after the refinancing the principal amount of the loan resulting from the refinancing does not exceed the principal amount of the refinanced loan (immediately before the refinancing), and

"(C) the term of such refinancing loan does not extend beyond the last day of the term of the original securities acquisition loan.

For purposes of this paragraph, the term 'securities acquisition loan' includes a loan from a corporation to an employee stock ownership plan described in section 133(b)(3) of such Code (as so in effect).

"(3) Exception. Any loan made pursuant to a binding written contract in effect before June 10, 1996, and at all times thereafter before such loan is made, shall be treated for purposes of paragraphs (1) and (2) as a loan made on or before the date of the enactment of this Act."

Prior to deletion, paras. (e)(1)-(3) read as follows:

"(1) any employer maintaining, or the plan administrator (within the meaning of section 414(g)) of, an employee stock ownership plan—

"(A) which acquired stock in a transaction to which section 133 applies, or

"(B) which holds stock with respect to which section 404(k) applies to dividends paid on such stock,

"(2) any person making or holding a loan to which section 133 applies, or

"(3) both such employer or plan administrator and such person,"

In 1992, P.L. 102-318, Sec. 522(b)(2)(D), substituted "section 3405(e)(1)" for "section 3405(d)(1)" in subpara. (d)(1)(A)...Sec. 522(b)(2)(E), substituted "section 3405(d)(3) [sic section 3405(e)(1)]" for "section 3405(d)(1)" in subpara. (d)(1)(A)...Sec. 522(b)(2)(E), is an inoperable amendment, see Sec. 522(b)(2)(E) above, effective for distributions after 12/31/92, except as provided in Sec. 522(d)(2) of this Act which reads as follows:

"(2) Transition rule for certain annuity contracts. If, as of July 1, 1992, a State law prohibits a direct trustee-to-trustee transfer from an annuity contract described in section 403(b) of the Internal Revenue Code of 1986 which was purchased for an employee by an employer which is a State or a political subdivision thereof (or an agency or instrumentality of any 1 or more of either), the amendments made by this section shall not apply to distributions before the earlier of—

"(A) 90 days after the first day after July 1, 1992, on which such transfer is allowed under State law, or

"(B) January 1, 1994."

In 1989, P.L. 101-239, Sec. 7301(e), redesignated subsec. (e) as subsec. (f) and added subsec. (e), effective for loans made after 7/10/89, except as provided in Sec. 7301(f)(2) of this Act, reproduced in note following Code Sec. 4978B.

In 1986, P.L. 99-514, Sec. 1501(d)(1)(D), substituted "6652(e)" for "6652(f)" in para. (e)(1), effective for returns the due date for which (determined without regard to extensions) is after 12/31/86.

—P.L. 99-514, Sec. 1848(e)(2), added para. (e)(3), effective for obligations issued after 12/31/83.

In 1984, P.L. 98-369, Sec. 491(d)(47), deleted subsec. (c) and redesignated subsecs. (d), (e), and (f) as subsecs. (c), (d), and (e)...Sec. 491(d)(57), deleted "and bond purchase" after "annuity" in the heading for Code Sec. 6047, effective for obligations issued after 12/31/83.

Prior to deletion, subsec. (c) read as follows:

"(c) Employees under qualified bond purchase plans.

"Every individual in whose name a bond described in section 405(b)(1) is purchased by his employer under a qualified bond purchase plan described in section 401(a), or by a trust described in section 401(a) which is exempt from tax under section 501(a), shall furnish—

"(1) to his employer or to such trust, and

"(2) to the Secretary (or to such person as the Secretary may by regulations prescribe),

such information as the Secretary shall by forms or regulations prescribe."

In 1983, P.L. 97-448, Sec. 103(c)(12)(C), substituted "section 219" for "section 219(a)" in subsec. (d), effective for tax. yrs. begin. after 12/31/81.

In 1982, P.L. 97-248, Sec. 334(b), redesignated subsec. (e) as subsec. (f) and added new subsec. (e), effective 1/1/83, except as provided in Sec. 334(e)(4) of this Act which reads as follows:

"(4) Periodic payments beginning before January 1, 1983.—For purposes of section 3405(a) of the Internal Revenue Code of 1954, in the case of periodic payments beginning before January 1, 1983, the first periodic payment after December 31, 1982, shall be treated as the first such periodic payment."

In 1981, P.L. 97-34, Sec. 311(h)(8), substituted "section 219(a)" for "section 219(a) or 220(a)" in subsec. (d), effective for tax. yrs. begin. after 12/31/81. For transitional rule see Sec. 311(i)(2) of this Act reproduced in note following Code Sec. 219.

In 1976, P.L. 94-455, Sec. 1501(b)(9), added "or 220(a)" after "219(a)" in subsec. (d), effective for tax. yrs. begin. after 12/31/76.

—P.L. 94-455, Sec. 1906(b)(13)(A), substituted "Secretary" for "Secretary or his delegate" each place it appeared in Code Sec. 6047, effective for tax yrs. begin. after 12/31/76.

In 1974, P.L. 93-406, Sec. 2002(g)(8), redesignated subsec. (d) as subsec. (e) and added new subsec. (d), effective 1/1/75.

—P.L. 93-406, Sec. 1031(c)(3), amended subsec. (e) (as redesignated), effective 9/2/74.

Prior to amendment, subsec. (e) read as follows:

"(d) Cross reference.

"For criminal penalty for furnishing fraudulent information, see section 7207."

In 1962, P.L. 87-792, Sec. 7, added Code Sec. 6047, effective for tax. yrs. begin. after '62.

Sec. 6048. Information with respect to certain foreign trusts.

(a) Notice of certain events.

(1) General rule. On or before the 90th day (or such later day as the Secretary may prescribe) after any reportable event, the responsible party shall provide written notice of such event to the Secretary in accordance with paragraph (2).

(2) Contents of notice. The notice required by paragraph (1) shall contain such information as the Secretary may prescribe, including—

(A) the amount of money or other property (if any) transferred to the trust in connection with the reportable event, and

(B) the identity of the trust and of each trustee and beneficiary (or class of beneficiaries) of the trust.

(3) Reportable event. For purposes of this subsection—

(A) In general. The term "reportable event" means—

(i) the creation of any foreign trust by a United States person,

(ii) the transfer of any money or property (directly or indirectly) to a foreign trust by a United States person, including a transfer by reason of death, and

3,533

(iii) the death of a citizen or resident of the United States if—

(I) the decedent was treated as the owner of any portion of a foreign trust under the rules of subpart E of part I of subchapter J of chapter 1, or

(II) any portion of a foreign trust was included in the gross estate of the decedent.

(B) Exceptions.

(i) Fair market value sales. Subparagraph (A)(ii) shall not apply to any transfer of property to a trust in exchange for consideration of at least the fair market value of the transferred property. For purposes of the preceding sentence, consideration other than cash shall be taken into account at its fair market value and the rules of section 679(a)(3) shall apply.

(ii) Deferred compensation and charitable trusts. Subparagraph (A) shall not apply with respect to a trust which is—

(I) described in section 402(b), 404(a)(4), or 404A, or

(II) determined by the Secretary to be described in section 501(c)(3).

(4) Responsible party. For purposes of this subsection, the term "responsible party" means—

(A) the grantor in the case of the creation of an inter vivos trust,

(B) the transferor in the case of a reportable event described in paragraph (3)(A)(ii) other than a transfer by reason of death, and

(C) the executor of the decedent's estate in any other case.

(b) United States owner of foreign trust.

(1) In general. If, at any time during any taxable year of a United States person, such person is treated as the owner of any portion of a foreign trust under the rules of subpart E of part I of subchapter J of chapter 1, such person shall submit such information as the Secretary may prescribe with respect to such trust for such year and shall be responsible to ensure that—

(A) such trust makes a return for such year which sets forth a full and complete accounting of all trust activities and operations for the year, the name of the United States agent for such trust, and such other information as the Secretary may prescribe, and

(B) such trust furnishes such information as the Secretary may prescribe to each United States person (i) who is treated as the owner of any portion of such trust or (ii) who receives (directly or indirectly) any distribution from the trust.

(2) Trusts not having United States agent.

(A) In general. If the rules of this paragraph apply to any foreign trust, the determination of amounts required to be taken into account with respect to such trust by a United States person under the rules of subpart E of part I of subchapter J of chapter 1 shall be determined by the Secretary.

(B) United States agent required. The rules of this paragraph shall apply to any foreign trust to which paragraph (1) applies unless such trust agrees (in such manner, subject to such conditions, and at such time as the Secretary shall prescribe) to authorize a United States person to act as such trust's limited agent solely for purposes of applying sections 7602, 7603, and 7604 with respect to—

(i) any request by the Secretary to examine records or produce testimony related to the proper treatment of amounts required to be taken into account under the rules referred to in subparagraph (A), or

(ii) any summons by the Secretary for such records or testimony.

The appearance of persons or production of records by reason of a United States person being such an agent shall not subject such persons or records to legal process for any purpose other than determining the correct treatment under this title of the amounts required to be taken into account under the rules referred to in subparagraph (A). A foreign trust which appoints an agent described in this subparagraph shall not be considered to have an office or a permanent establishment in the United States, or to be engaged in a trade or business in the United States, solely because of the activities of such agent pursuant to this subsection.

(C) Other rules to apply. Rules similar to the rules of paragraphs (2) and (4) of section 6038A(e) shall apply for purposes of this paragraph.

(c) Reporting by United States beneficiaries of foreign trusts.

(1) In general. If any United States person receives (directly or indirectly) during any taxable year of such person any distribution from a foreign trust, such person shall make a return with respect to such trust for such year which includes—

(A) the name of such trust,

(B) the aggregate amount of the distributions so received from such trust during such taxable year, and

(C) such other information as the Secretary may prescribe.

(2) Inclusion in income if records not provided.

(A) In general. If adequate records are not provided to the Secretary to determine the proper treatment of any distribution from a foreign trust, such distribution shall be treated as an accumulation distribution includible in the gross income of the distributee under chapter 1. To the extent provided in regulations, the preceding sentence shall not apply if the foreign trust elects to be subject to rules similar to the rules of subsection (b)(2)(B).

(B) Application of accumulation distribution rules. For purposes of applying section 668 in a case to which subparagraph (A) applies, the applicable number of years for purposes of section 668(a) shall be ½ of the number of years the trust has been in existence.

(d) Special rules.

(1) Determination of whether United States person makes transfer or receives distribution. For purposes of this section, in determining whether a United States person makes a transfer to, or receives a distribution from, a foreign trust, the fact that a portion of such trust is treated as owned by another person under the rules of subpart E of part I of subchapter J of chapter 1 shall be disregarded.

(2) Domestic trusts with foreign activities. To the extent provided in regulations, a trust which is a United States person shall be treated as a foreign trust for purposes of this section and section 6677 if such trust has substantial activities, or holds substantial property, outside the United States.

(3) Time and manner of filing information. Any notice or return required under this section shall be made at such time and in such manner as the Secretary shall prescribe.

(4) Modification of return requirements. The Secretary is authorized to suspend or modify any requirement of this section if the Secretary determines that the United States

Information and returns Code Sec. 6049(b)(3)(A)

has no significant tax interest in obtaining the required information.

(5) United States person's return must be consistent with trust return or Secretary notified of inconsistency. Rules similar to the rules of section 6034A(c) shall apply to items reported by a trust under subsection (b)(1)(B) and to United States persons referred to in such subsection.

In 2010, P.L. 111-147, Sec. 534(a), added "shall submit such information as the Secretary may prescribe with respect to such trust for such year and" before "shall be responsible to ensure" in para. (b)(1), effective for tax. yrs. begin. after 3/18/2010.

In 1997, P.L. 105-34, Sec. 1027(b), added para. (d)(5), effective for returns of beneficiaries and owners filed after 8/5/97.

—P.L. 105-34, Sec. 1601(i)(1), substituted "owner" for "grantor" in the heading of subsec. (b), effective as provided in Sec. 1901(d) of P.L. 104-188 [see below]

In 1996, P.L. 104-188, Sec. 1901(a), amended Code Sec. 6048, effective as provided in Sec. 1901(d) of this Act, which reads as follows:

"(d) Effective dates.—

"(1) Reportable events.— To the extent related to subsection (a) of section 6048 of the Internal Revenue Code of 1986, as amended by this section, the amendments made by this section shall apply to reportable events (as defined in such section 6048) occurring after the date of the enactment of this Act.

"(2) Grantor trust reporting.— To the extent related to subsection (b) of such section 6048, the amendments made by this section shall apply to taxable years of United States persons beginning after December 31, 1995.

"(3) Reporting by United States — To the extent related to subsection (c) of such section 6048, the amendments made by this section shall apply to distributions received after the date of the enactment of this Act."

Prior to amendment, Code Sec. 6048 read as follows:

"Sec. 6048. Returns as to certain foreign trusts.

"(a) General rule.

"On or before the 90th day (or on or before such later day as the Secretary may by regulations prescribe) after—

"(1) the creation of any foreign trust by a United States person, or

"(2) the transfer of any money or property to a foreign trust by a United States person,

the grantor in the case of an inter vivos trust, the fiduciary of an estate in the case of a testamentary trust, or the transferor, as the case may be, shall make a return in compliance with the provisions of subsection (b).

"(b) Form and contents of returns.

"The returns required by subsection (a) shall be in such form and shall set forth, in respect of the foreign trust, such information as the Secretary prescribes by regulation as necessary for carrying out the provisions of the income tax laws.

"(c) Annual returns for foreign trusts having one or more United States beneficiaries.

"Each taxpayer subject to tax under section 679 (relating to foreign trusts having one or more United States beneficiaries) for his taxable year with respect to any trust shall make a return with respect to such trust for such year at such time and in such manner, and setting forth such information, as the Secretary may by regulations prescribe.

"(d) Cross reference.

"For provisions relating to penalties for violation of this section, see sections 6677 and 7203."

In 1982, P.L. 97-248, Sec. 341(b), added "(or on or before such later day as the Secretary may by regulations prescribe)" after "the 90th day" in subsec. (a), effective for returns filed after 9/3/82.

In 1976, P.L. 94-455, Sec. 1013(d)(1), redesignated subsec. (c) as subsec. (d) and added new subsec. (c) ... Sec. 1013(e)(3), and (4), amended subsec. (d), as redesignated by Sec. 1013(d)(1) of the Act and amended the heading of Code Sec. 6048, effective for tax. yrs. end. after 12/31/75, but only for foreign trusts created after 5/21/74 and transfers of property to foreign trusts after 5/21/74.

Prior to amendment, subsec. (d) read as follows:

"(d) Cross references.

"(1) For provisions relating to penalties for violations of this section, see sections 6677 and 7203.

"(2) For definition of the term 'foreign trust created by a United States person', see section 643(d)."

Prior to amendment, the heading of Code Sec. 6048 read as follows:

"6048. Returns as to creation of or transfers to certain foreign trusts."

—P.L. 94-455, Sec. 1906(b)(13)(A), substituted "Secretary" for "Secretary or his delegate", in Code Sec. 6048, effective 2/1/77.

In 1962, P.L. 87-834, Sec. 7, added Code Sec. 6048, effective 10/1/62.

Sec. 6049. Returns regarding payments of interest.
(a) Requirement of reporting.

Every person—

(1) who makes payments of interest (as defined in subsection (b)) aggregating $10 or more to any other person during any calendar year, or

(2) who receives payments of interest (as so defined) as a nominee and who makes payments aggregating $10 or more during any calendar year to any other person with respect to the interest so received,

shall make a return according to the forms or regulations prescribed by the Secretary, setting forth the aggregate amount of such payments and the name and address of the person to whom paid.

(b) Interest defined.

(1) General rule. For purposes of subsection (a), the term "interest" means—

(A) interest on any obligation—

(i) issued in registered form, or

(ii) of a type offered to the public,

other than any obligation with a maturity (at issue) of not more than 1 year which is held by a corporation,

(B) interest on deposits with persons carrying on the banking business,

(C) amounts (whether or not designated as interest) paid by a mutual savings bank, savings and loan association, building and loan association, cooperative bank, homestead association, credit union, industrial loan association or bank, or similar organization, in respect of deposits, investment certificates, or withdrawable or repurchasable shares,

(D) interest on amounts held by an insurance company under an agreement to pay interest thereon,

(E) interest on deposits with brokers (as defined in section 6045(c)),

(F) interest paid on amounts held by investment companies (as defined in section 3 of the Investment Company Act of 1940 (15 U.S.C. 80a-3)) and on amounts invested in other pooled funds or trusts, and

(G) to the extent provided in regulations prescribed by the Secretary, any other interest (which is not described in paragraph (2)).

(2) Exceptions. For purposes of subsection (a), the term "interest" does not include—

(A) interest on any obligation issued by a natural person,

(B) except to the extent otherwise provided in regulations—

(i) any amount paid to any person described in paragraph (4), or

(ii) any amount described in paragraph (5), and

(C) except to the extent otherwise provided in regulations, any amount not described in subparagraph (B) of this paragraph which is income from sources outside the United States or which is paid by—

(i) a foreign government or international organization or any agency or instrumentality thereof,

(ii) a foreign central bank of issue,

(iii) a foreign corporation not engaged in a trade or business in the United States,

(iv) a foreign corporation, the interest payments of which would be exempt from withholding under subchapter A of chapter 3 if paid to a person who is not a United States person, or

(v) a partnership not engaged in a trade or business in the United States and composed in whole of nonresident alien individuals and persons described in clause (i), (ii), or (iii).

(3) Payments by United States nominees, etc., of United States person. If, within the United States, a United States person—

(A) collects interest (or otherwise acts as a middleman between the payor and payee) from a foreign person described in paragraph (2)(D) or collects interest from a

United States person which is income from sources outside the United States for a second person who is a United States person, or

(B) makes payments of such interest to such second United States person,

notwithstanding paragraph (2)(D), such payment shall be subject to the requirements of subsection (a) with respect to such second United States person.

(4) Persons described in this paragraph. A person is described in this paragraph if such person is—

(A) a corporation,

(B) an organization exempt from taxation under section 501(a) or an individual retirement plan,

(C) the United States or any wholly owned agency or instrumentality thereof,

(D) a State, the District of Columbia, a possession of the United States, any political subdivision of any of the foregoing, or any wholly owned agency or instrumentality of any one or more of the foregoing,

(E) a foreign government, a political subdivision of a foreign government, or any wholly owned agency or instrumentality of any one or more of the foregoing,

(F) an international organization or any wholly owned agency or instrumentality thereof,

(G) a foreign central bank of issue,

(H) a dealer in securities or commodities required to register as such under the laws of the United States or a State, the District of Columbia, or a possession of the United States,

(I) a real estate investment trust (as defined in section 856),

(J) an entity registered at all times during the taxable year under the Investment Company Act of 1940,

(K) a common trust fund (as defined in section 584(a)), or

(L) any trust which—

(i) is exempt from tax under section 664(c), or

(ii) is described in section 4947(a)(1).

(5) Amounts described in this paragraph. An amount is described in this paragraph if such amount—

(A) is subject to withholding under subchapter A of chapter 3 (relating to withholding of tax on nonresident aliens and foreign corporations) by the person paying such amount, or

(B) would be subject to withholding under subchapter A of chapter 3 by the person paying such amount but for the fact that—

(i) such amount is income from sources outside the United States,

(ii) the payor thereof is exempt from the application of section 1441(a) by reason of section 1441(c) or a tax treaty,

(iii) such amount is original issue discount (within the meaning of section 1273(a)), or

(iv) such amount is described in section 871(i)(2).

(c) Statements to be furnished to persons with respect to whom information is required.

(1) In general. Every person required to make a return under subsection (a) shall furnish to each person whose name is required to be set forth in such return a written statement showing—

(A) the name, address, and phone number of the information contact of the person required to make such return, and

(B) the aggregate amount of payments to, or the aggregate amount includible in the gross income of, the person required to be shown on the return.

(2) Time and form of statement. The written statement under paragraph (1)—

(A) shall be furnished (either in person or in a statement mailing by first-class mail which includes adequate notice that the statement is enclosed) to the person on or before January 31 of the year following the calendar year for which the return under subsection (a) was required to be made, and

(B) shall be in such form as the Secretary may prescribe by regulations.

(d) Definitions and special rules.

For purposes of this section—

(1) Person. The term "person" includes any governmental unit and any agency or instrumentality thereof and any international organization and any agency or instrumentality thereof.

(2) Obligation. The term "obligation" includes bonds, debentures, notes, certificates, and other evidences of indebtedness.

(3) Payments by governmental units. In the case of payments made by any governmental unit or any agency or instrumentality thereof, the officer or employee having control of the payment of interest (or the person appropriately designated for purposes of this section) shall make the returns and statements required by this section.

(4) Financial institutions, brokers, etc., collecting interest may be substituted for payor. To the extent and in the manner provided by regulations, in the case of any obligation—

(A) a financial institution, broker, or other person specified in such regulations which collects interest on such obligation for the payee (or otherwise acts as a middleman between the payor and the payee) shall comply with the requirements of subsections (a) and (c), and

(B) no other person shall be required to comply with the requirements of subsections (a) and (c) with respect to any interest on such obligation for which reporting is required pursuant to subparagraph (A).

(5) Interest on certain obligations may be treated on a transactional basis.

(A) In general. To the extent and in the manner provided in regulations, this section shall apply with respect to—

(i) any person described in paragraph (4)(A), and

(ii) in the case of any United States savings bonds, any Federal agency making payments thereon,

on any transactional basis rather than on an annual aggregation basis.

(B) Separate returns and statements. If subparagraph (A) applies to interest on any obligation, the return under subsection (a) and the statement furnished under subsection (c) with respect to such transaction may be made separately, but any such statement shall be furnished to the payee at such time as the Secretary may prescribe by regulations but not later than January 31 of the next calendar year.

(C) Statement to payee required in case of transactions involving $10 or more. In the case of any transaction to which this paragraph applies which involves the payment of $10 or more of interest, a statement of the transaction may be provided to the payee of such interest in lieu of the statement required under subsection (c). Such statement shall be provided during January of

Information and returns Code Sec. 6049

the year following the year in which such payment is made.

(6) Treatment of original issue discount.

(A) In general. Original issue discount on any obligation shall be reported—

(i) as if paid at the time it is includible in gross income under section 1272 (except that for such purpose the amount reportable with respect to any subsequent holder shall be determined as if he were the original holder), and

(ii) if section 1272 does not apply to the obligation, at maturity (or, if earlier, on redemption).

In the case of any obligation not in registered form issued before January 1, 1983, clause (ii) and not clause (i) shall apply.

(B) Original issue discount. For purposes of this paragraph, the term "original issue discount" has the meaning given to such term by section 1273(a).

(7) Interests in REMIC's and certain other debt instruments.

(A) In general. For purposes of subsection (a), the term "interest" includes amounts includible in gross income with respect to regular interests in REMIC's (and such amounts shall be treated as paid when includible in gross income under section 860B(b)).

(B) Reporting to corporations, etc. Except as otherwise provided in regulations, in the case of any interest described in subparagraph (A) of this paragraph and any other debt instrument to which section 1272(a)(6) applies, subsection (b)(4) of this section shall be applied without regard to subparagraphs (A), (H), (I), (J), (K), and (L)(i).

(C) Additional information. Except as otherwise provided in regulations, any return or statement required to be filed or furnished under this section with respect to interest income described in subparagraph (A) and interest on any other debt instrument to which section 1272(a)(6) applies shall also provide information setting forth the adjusted issue price of the interest to which the return or statement relates at the beginning of each accrual period with respect to which interest income is required to be reported on such return or statement and information necessary to compute accrual of market discount.

(D) Regulatory authority. The Secretary may prescribe such regulations as are necessary or appropriate to carry out the purposes of this paragraph, including regulations which require more frequent or more detailed reporting.

(8) Reporting of credit on clean renewable energy bonds.

(A) In general. For purposes of subsection (a), the term "interest" includes amounts includible in gross income under section 54(g) or 1400N(l)(6) and such amounts shall be treated as paid on the credit allowance date (as defined in section 54(b)(4) or 1400N(l)(2)(D), as the case may be).

(B) Reporting to corporations, etc. Except as otherwise provided in regulations, in the case of any interest described in subparagraph (A), subsection (b)(4) shall be applied without regard to subparagraphs (A), (H), (I), (J), (K), and (L)(i) of such subsection.

(C) Regulatory authority. The Secretary may prescribe such regulations as are necessary or appropriate to carry out the purposes of this paragraph, including regulations which require more frequent or more detailed reporting.

(9) Reporting of credit on qualified tax credit bonds.

(A) In general. For purposes of subsection (a), the term "interest" includes amounts includible in gross income under section 54A and such amounts shall be treated as paid on the credit allowance date (as defined in section 54A(e)(1)).

(B) Reporting to corporations, etc. Except as otherwise provided in regulations, in the case of any interest described in subparagraph (A) of this paragraph, subsection (b)(4) of this section shall be applied without regard to subparagraphs (A), (H), (I), (J), (K), and (L)(i).

(C) Regulatory authority. The Secretary may prescribe such regulations as are necessary or appropriate to carry out the purposes of this paragraph, including regulations which require more frequent or more detailed reporting.

In 2008, P.L. 110-246, Sec. 4, Repeals the duplicative enactment and provides effective date provisions of the Act entitled "An Act to provide for the continuation of agricultural programs through fiscal year 2012, and for other purposes" Sec. 4, P.L. 110-246 reads as follows:

"Sec. 4. Repeal of duplicative enactment.

"(a) In General- The Act entitled 'An Act to provide for the continuation of agricultural programs through fiscal year 2012, and for other purposes' (H.R. 2419 of the 110th Congress), and the amendments made by that Act, are repealed, effective on the date of enactment of that Act.

"(b) Effective Date- Except as otherwise provided in this Act, this Act and the amendments made by this Act shall take effect on the earlier of--

"(1) the date of enactment of this Act; or

"(2) the date of the enactment of the Act entitled 'An Act to provide for the continuation of agricultural programs through fiscal year 2012, and for other purposes' (H.R. 2419 of the 110th Congress)."

—P.L. 110-246, Sec. 15316(b), added para. (d)(9), effective for obligations issued after 5/22/2008. [Ed. Note: May 22, 2008 was the date of enactment for H.R. 2419 (PL 110-234), which was repealed by (2008 Farm Act § 4(a)) (PL 110-246, 6/18/2008), in connection with the reenactment of the farm bill to correct a technical deficiency in its original passage.]

In 2006, P.L. 109-222, Sec. 502(a), deleted subpara. (b)(2)(B) and redesignated subparas. (b)(2)(C) and (D) as subparas. (b)(2)(B) and (C) . . . Sec. 502(b), substituted "subparagraph (B)" for "subparagraph (C)" in subpara. (b)(2)(C) [as redesignated by Sec. 502(a) of this Act, see above], effective for interest paid after 12/31/2005.

Prior to deletion, subpara. (b)(2)(B) read as follows:

"(B) interest on any obligation if such interest is exempt from tax under section 103(a) or if such interest is exempt from tax (without regard to the identity of the holder) under any other provision of this title,"

In 2005, P.L. 109-135, Sec. 101(b)(2)(A), added "or 1400N(l)(6)" after "section 54(g)" in subpara. (d)(8)(A) . . . Sec. 101(b)(2)(B), added "or 1400N(l)(2)(D), as the case may be" after "section 54(b)(4)" in subpara. (d)(8)(A), effective for tax. yrs. end. on or after 8/28/2005.

—P.L. 109-58, Sec. 1303(b), added para. (d)(8), effective for bonds issued after 12/31/2005.

In 1996, P.L. 104-168, Sec. 1201(a)(6), substituted "name, address, and phone number of the information contact" for "name and address" in subpara. (c)(1)(A), effective for statements required to be furnished after 12/31/96 (determined without regard to any extension).

In 1988, P.L. 100-647, Sec. 1006(t)(24), substituted "the adjusted issue price" for "the issue price" in subpara. (d)(7)(C) . . . Sec. 1006(v), added "(and such amounts shall be treated as paid when includible in gross income under section 860(b))" before the period at the end of subpara. (d)(7)(A), effective for tax. yrs. begin. after 12/31/87.

—P.L. 100-647, Sec. 1006(w)(1), changed the effective date for changes made by Secs. 671 and 674 of P.L. 99-514 from, effective for tax. yrs. begin. after 12/31/86, to effective for tax. yrs. begin. after 12/31/87, see below.

—P.L. 100-647, Sec. 1012(g)(1)(A), changed the effective date for changes made by Sec. 1214(c) of P.L. 99-514 from, effective for payments after 12/31/86, to, effective for payments made in a tax. yr. of the payor begin. after 12/31/86, see below.

—P.L. 100-647, Sec. 1012(aa)(3)(D) and (4), provides:

"(3) Certain amendments not to apply to the extent inconsistent with treaties. The following amendments made by the Reform Act shall not apply to the extent the application of such amendments would be contrary to any treaty obligation of the United States in effect on the date of the enactment of the Reform Act:

* * *

"(D) The amendments made by section 1214 of the Reform Act; except for purposes of determining the amount of the foreign tax credit."

* * *

"(4) Treatment of technical corrections. For purposes of paragraphs (2) and (3), any amendment made by this title shall be treated as if it had been included in the provison of the Reform Act to which such amendment relates."

In 1986, P.L. 99-514, Sec. 674, added para. (d)(7), effective [as amended by Sec. 1006(w)(1) of P.L. 100-647, see above] for tax. yrs. begin. after 12/31/87.

3,537

Code Sec. 6049

—P.L. 99-514, Sec. 1214(c), deleted "or" at the end of clause (b)(5)(B)(ii), substituted ", or" for the period at the end of clause (b)(5)(B)(iii), and added new clause (b)(5)(B)(iv), effective [as amended by Sec. 1012(g)(1)(A) of P.L. 100-647, see above] for payments made in a tax yr. of the payor begin. after 12/31/86 [see Sec. 1012 of P.L. 100-647(aa)(3)(D) and (4) above]. For special and transitional rules see Secs. 1214(d)(2) and (4) of this Act reproduced in note following Code Sec. 861.

—P.L. 99-514, Sec. 1501(c)(5), amended subsec. (c), effective for returns the due date for which (determined without regard to extensions) is after 10/22/86.

Prior to amendment, subsec. (c) read as follows:

"(c) Statements to be furnished to persons with respect to whom information is furnished.

"(1) In general. Every person making a return under subsection (a) shall furnish to each person whose name is set forth in such return a written statement showing—

"(A) the name and address of the person making such return, and

"(B) the aggregate amount of payments to, or the aggregate amount includible in the gross income of, the person as shown on such return

"(2) Time and form of statement. The written statement under paragraph (1)—

"(A) shall be furnished (either in person or in a separate mailing by first-class mail) to the person on or before January 31 of the year following the calendar year for which the return under subsection (a) was made, and

"(B) shall be in such form as the Secretary may prescribe by regulations.

"(3) No statement required where interest is less than $10. No statement with respect to payments of interest to any person shall be required to be furnished to any person under this subsection if the aggregate amount of payments to such person shown on the return made with respect to paragraph (1) or (2), as the case may be, of subsection (a) is less than $10."

—P.L. 99-514, Sec. 1803(a)(14)(C), substituted "section 1273(a)" for "section 1232(b)(1)" in clause (b)(5)(B)(iii), effective for tax. yrs. end. after 7/18/84.

In 1984, P.L. 98-369, Sec. 42(a)(14)(A), substituted "section 1272" for "section 1232A" each place it appeared in subpara. (d)(6)(A) . . . Sec. 42(a)(14)(B), substituted "section 1273(a)" for "section 1232(b)(1)" in para. (d)(6), effective for tax. yrs. end. after 7/18/84.

—P.L. 98-369, Sec. 474(r)(29)(J)(i), added "and" at the end of subpara. (b)(2)(C), . . . Sec. 474(r)(29)(J)(ii), substituted a period for ", and" at the end of subpara. (b)(2)(D) . . . Sec. 474(r)(29)(J)(iii), deleted subpara. (b)(2)(E), effective as provided in Sec. 475(b) of this Act which reads as follows:

"(b) Tax-free covenant bonds. The amendments made by subsections (j) and (r)(29) of section 474 shall not apply with respect to obligations issued before January 1, 1984."

Prior to deletion, subpara. (b)(2)(E) read as follows:

"(E) any amount on which the person making payment is required to deduct and withhold a tax under section 1451 (relating to tax-free covenant bonds), or would be so required but for section 1451(d) (relating to benefit of personal exemptions)."

In 1983, P.L. 98-67, Sec. 102(a), deleted [as if never enacted] subsec. (e) . . . Sec. 102(e)(1)(A), added "or" at the end of para. (a)(1) . . . Sec. 102(e)(1)(B), deleted "or" at the end of para. (a)(2), . . . Sec. 102(e)(1)(C), deleted para. (a)(3) . . . Sec. 102(e)(1)(D), substituted "and the name and address of the person to whom paid" for ", tax deducted and withheld, and the name and address of the person to whom paid or from whom withheld" in subsec. (a) . . . Sec. 102(e)(2)(A), amended subpara. (b)(2)(C) . . . Sec. 102(e)(2)(B), added paras. (b)(4) and (b)(5) . . . Sec. 102(e)(3)(A), added "and" at the end of subpara. (c)(1)(A) . . . Sec. 102(e)(3)(B), substituted a period for ", and" at the end of subpara. (c)(1)(B), Sec. 102(e)(3)(C), deleted subpara. (c)(1)(C), effective as of the close of 6/30/83.

Prior to deletion, subsec. (e) read as follows:

"(e) Duplicate of subsection (c) statement may be required to be filed with Secretary. A duplicate of any statement made pursuant to subsection (c) which is required to set forth an amount withheld under section 3451 shall, when required by regulations prescribed by the Secretary, be filed with the Secretary."

Prior to deletion, para. (a)(3) read as follows:

"(3) who is required under subchapter B of chapter 24 to withhold tax on the payment of any interest,"

Prior to amendment, subpara. (b)(2)(C) read as follows:

"(C) except to the extent otherwise provided in regulations—

"(i) any amount paid to any person referred to in paragraph (2) of section 3452(c) (other than subparagraphs (J) and (K) thereof), or

"(ii) any amount described in section 3454(a)(2)(D) or (E),"

Prior to deletion, subpara. (c)(1)(C) read as follows:

"(C) the aggregate amount of tax deducted and withheld with respect to such person under subchapter B of chapter 24."

—P.L. 98-67, Sec. 108(a), amended para. (c)(2), effective for payments made after 12/31/83.

Prior to amendment, para. (c)(2) read as follows:

"(2) Statement must be furnished on or before January 31. The written statement required under the preceding sentence shall be furnished to the person on or before January 31 of the year following the calendar year for which the return under subsection (a) was made."

—P.L. 97-424, Sec. 547(b)(4), substituted "this title" for "law" in subpara. (b)(2)(B), effective 1/6/83.

In 1982, P.L. 97-248, Sec. 303(b), added subsec. (e), effective for payments of interest, dividends, and patronage dividends paid or credited after 6/30/83.

—P.L. 97-248, Sec. 309(a), amended Code Sec. 6049, effective for amounts paid (or treated as paid) after 12/31/82.

Prior to amendment, Code Sec. 6049 read as follows:

"SEC. 6049. RETURNS REGARDING PAYMENTS OF INTEREST.

"(a) Requirement of reporting.

"(1) In general. Every person—

"(A) who makes payments of interest (as defined in subsection (b)) aggregating $10 or more to any other person during any calendar year,

"(B) who receives payments of interest as a nominee and who makes payments aggregating $10 or more during any calendar year to any other person with respect to the interest so received, or

"(C) which is a corporation that has outstanding any bond, debenture, note, or certificate or other evidence of indebtedness in registered form as to which there is during any calendar year an amount of original issue discount aggregating $10 or more includible in the gross income of any holder under section 1232(a)(3) without regard to subparagraph (B) thereof,

shall make a return according to the forms or regulations prescribed by the Secretary, setting forth the aggregate amount of such payments and such aggregate amount includible in the gross income of any holder and the name and address of the person to whom paid or such holder.

"(2) Returns required by the Secretary. Every person who makes payments of interest (as defined in subsection (b)) aggregating less than $10 to any other person during any calendar year shall, when required by the Secretary, make a return setting forth the aggregate amount of such payments and the name and address of the person to whom paid.

"(3) Other returns required by Secretary. Every corporation making payments, regardless of amounts, of interest other than interest as defined in subsection (b) shall, when required by regulations prescribed by the Secretary, make a return according to the forms or regulations prescribed by the Secretary, setting forth the amount paid and the name and address of the recipient of each such payment.

"(b) Interest defined.

"(1) General rule. For purposes of subsections (a)(1) and (2), the term 'interest' means—

"(A) interest on evidences of indebtedness (including bonds, debentures, notes, and certificates) issued by a corporation in registered form, and, to the extent provided in regulations prescribed by the Secretary, interest or other evidences of indebtedness issued by a corporation of a type offered by corporations to the public;

"(B) interest on deposits with persons carrying on the banking business;

"(C) amounts (whether or not designated as interest) paid by a mutual savings bank, savings and loan association, building and loan association, cooperative bank, homestead association, credit union, or similar organization, in respect of deposits, investment certificates, or withdrawable or repurchasable shares;

"(D) interest on amounts held by an insurance company under an agreement to pay interest thereon; and

"(E) interest on deposits with stockholders and dealers in securities.

"(2) Exceptions. For purposes of subsections (a)(1) and (2), the term 'interest' does not include—

"(A) interest on obligations described in section 103(a) (relating to interest on certain governmental obligations);

"(B) to the extent provided in regulations prescribed by the Secretary, any amount paid by or to a foreign corporation, a nonresident alien, or a partnership not engaged in trade or business in the United States and composed in whole or in part of nonresident aliens; and

"(C) any amount on which the person making payment is required to deduct and withhold a tax under section 1451 (relating to tax-free covenant bonds), or would be so required but for section 1451(d) (relating to benefit of personal exemptions).

"(c) Statements to be furnished to persons with respect to whom information is furnished.

"Every person making a return under subsection (a)(1) shall furnish to each person whose name is set forth in such return a written statement showing—

"(1) the name and address of the person making such return, and

"(2) the aggregate amount of payments to, or the aggregate amount includible in the gross income of, the person as shown on such return.

The written statement required under the preceding sentence shall be furnished to the person on or before January 31 of the year following the calendar year for which the return under subsection (a)(1) was made. No statement shall be required to be furnished to any person under this subsection if the aggregate amount of payments to, or the aggregate amount includible in the gross income of, such person shown on the return made with respect to subparagraph (A), (B), or (C), as the case may be, of subsection (a)(1) is less than $10."

In 1976, P.L. 94-455, Sec. 1901(b)(6)(A), substituted "section 103(a)" for "section 103(a)(1) or (3)" in subpara. (b)(2)(A), effective for tax. yrs. end. after 12/31/76.

—P.L. 94-455, Sec. 1906(b)(13)(A), substituted "Secretary" for "Secretary or his delegate" each place it appeared in subsecs. (a) and (b), effective 2/1/77.

In 1969, P.L. 91-172, Sec. 413(c), amended para. (a)(1) . . . Sec. 413(d), amended subsec. (c), effective for bonds and other evidences of indebtedness issued after 5/27/69 (other than evidences of indebtedness issued pursuant to a written commitment which was binding on 5/27/69, and at all times thereafter).

Prior to amendment, para. (a)(1) read as follows:

"(1) In general. Every person—

"(A) who makes payments of interest (as defined in subsection (b)) aggregating $10 or more to any other person during any calendar year, or

"(B) who receives payments of interest as a nominee and who makes payments aggregating $10 or more during any calendar year to any other person with respect to the interest so received,

shall make a return according to the forms or regulations prescribed by the Secretary or his delegate, setting forth the aggregate amount of such payments and the name and address of the person to whom paid.

"(2) Returns required by the Secretary. Every person who makes payments of interest (as defined in subsection (b)) aggregating less than $10 to any other person during any calendar year shall, when required by the Secretary or his delegate, make a return setting forth the aggregate amount of such payments and the name and address of the person to whom paid.

"(3) Other returns required by Secretary. Every corporation making payments, regardless of amounts, of interest other than interest as defined in subsection (b) shall, when required by regulations prescribed by the Secretary or his delegate, make a return according to the forms or regulations prescribed by the Secretary or his delegate, setting forth the amount paid and the name and address of the recipient of each such payment."

Prior to amendment, subsec. (c) read as follows:

"(c) Every person making a return under subsection (a)(1) shall furnish to each person whose name is set forth in such return a written statement showing—
"(1) the name and address of the person making such return, and
"(2) the aggregate amount of payments to the person as shown on such return.
"The written statement required under the preceding sentence shall be furnished to the person on or before January 31 of the year following the calendar year for which the return under subsection (a)(1) was made. No statement shall be required to be furnished to any person under this subsection if the aggregate amount of payments to such person as shown on the return made under subsection (a)(1) is less than $10."

In **1962,** P.L. 87-834, Sec. 19, added Code Sec. 6049, effective for payments of dividends and interest made on or after 1/1/63.

Sec. 6050. Repealed.

In **1979,** P.L. 96-167, Sec. 5(a), repealed Code Sec. 6050, effective for transfers made after 12/29/79.

Prior to repeal, Code Sec. 6050 read as follows:

"SEC. 6050. RETURNS RELATING TO CERTAIN TRANSFERS TO EXEMPT ORGANIZATIONS.

"(a) General rule.
"On or before the 90th day after the transfer of income producing property, the transferor shall make a return in compliance with the provisions of subsection (b) if the transferee is known by the transferor to be an organization referred to in section 511(a) or (b) and the property (without regard to any lien) has a fair market value in excess of $50,000.

"(b) Form and contents of returns.
"The return required by subsection (a) shall be in such form and shall set forth, in respect of the transfer, such information as the Secretary prescribes by regulations as necessary for carrying out the provisions of the income tax laws."

In **1976,** P.L. 94-455, Sec. 1906(b)(13)(A), substituted "Secretary" for "Secretary or his delegate" each place it appeared in Code Sec. 6050, effective 2/1/77.

In **1969,** P.L. 91-172, Sec. 121(e)(1), added Code Sec. 6050, effective for transfers of property after 12/31/69.

Sec. 6050A. Reporting requirements of certain fishing boat operators.
(a) Reports.

The operator of a boat on which one or more individuals, during a calendar year, perform services described in section 3121(b)(20) shall submit to the Secretary (at such time, and in such manner and form, as the Secretary shall by regulations prescribe) information respecting—

(1) the identity of each individual performing such services;

(2) the percentage of each such individual's share of the catches of fish or other forms of aquatic animal life, and the percentage of the operator's share of such catches;

(3) if such individual receives his share in kind, the type and weight of such share, together with such other information as the Secretary may prescribe by regulations reasonably necessary to determine the value of such share;

(4) if such individual receives a share of the proceeds of such catches, the amount so received ; and

(5) any cash remuneration described in section 3121(b)(20)(A).

(b) Written statement.

Every person required to make a return under subsection (a) shall furnish to each person whose name is required to be set forth in such return a written statement showing the information relating to such person required to be contained in such return. The written statement required under the preceding sentence shall be furnished to the person on or before January 31 of the year following the calendar year for which the return under subsection (a) was required to be made.

In **1996,** P.L. 104-188, Sec. 1116(a)(1)(C), deleted "and" at the end of para. (a)(3), substituted "; and" for the period at the end of para. (a)(4), and added para. (a)(5), effective for remuneration paid after 12/31/96.

In **1986,** P.L. 99-514, Sec. 1501(c)(6), amended subsec. (b), effective for returns the due date for which (determined without regard to extensions) is after 12/31/86. Prior to amendment, subsec. (b) read as follows:

"(b) Written statement.
"Every person making a return under subsection (a) shall furnish to each person whose name is set forth in such return a written statement showing the information relating to such person contained in such return. The written statement required under the preceding sentence shall be furnished to the person on or before January 31 of the year following the calendar year for which the return under subsection (a) was made."

In **1976,** P.L. 94-455, Sec. 1207(e)(3)(A), added Code Sec. 6050A, effective for calendar yrs. begin. after 10/4/76.

Sec. 6050B. Returns relating to unemployment compensation.
(a) Requirement of reporting.

Every person who makes payments of unemployment compensation aggregating $10 or more to any individual during any calendar year shall make a return according to the forms or regulations prescribed by the Secretary, setting forth the aggregate amounts of such payments and the name and address of the individual to whom paid.

(b) Statements to be furnished to individuals with respect to whom information is required.

Every person required to make a return under subsection (a) shall furnish to each individual whose name is required to be set forth in such return a written statement showing—

(1) the name, address, and phone number of the information contact of the person required to make such return, and

(2) the aggregate amount of payments to the individual required to be shown on such return.

The written statement required under the preceding sentence shall be furnished to the individual on or before January 31 of the year following the calendar year for which the return under subsection (a) was required to be made.

(c) Definitions.

For purposes of this section—

(1) Unemployment compensation. The term "unemployment compensation" has the meaning given to such term by section 85(b).

(2) Person. The term "person" means the officer or employee having control of the payment of the unemployment compensation, or the person appropriately designated for purposes of this section.

In **1996,** P.L. 104-188, Sec. 1704(t)(14), substituted "section 85(b)" for "section 85(c)" in para. (c)(1), effective 8/20/96.

—P.L. 104-168, Sec. 1201(a)(7), substituted "name, address, and phone number of the information contact" for "name and address" in para. (b)(1), effective for statements required to be furnished after 12/31/96 (determined without regard to any extension).

In **1986,** P.L. 99-514, Sec. 1501(c)(7), amended subsec. (b), effective for returns the due date for which (determined without regard to extensions) is after 12/31/86. Prior to amendment, subsec. (b) read as follows:

"(b) Statements to be furnished to individuals with respect to whom information is furnished.

"Every person making a return under subsection (a) shall furnish to each individual whose name is set forth in such return a written statement showing—

"(1) the name and address of the person making such return, and
"(2) the aggregate amount of payments to the individual as shown on such return.

The written statement required under the preceding sentence shall be furnished to the individual on or before January 31 of the year following the calendar year for which the return under subsection (a) was made. No statement shall be required to be furnished to any individual under this subsection if the aggregate amount of payments to such individual shown on the return made under subsection (a) is less than $10."

In **1984,** P.L. 98-369, Sec. 1075(a), amended Sec. 112(d) of P.L. 95-600, the effective date for changes made by Sec. 112(b) of P.L. 95-600. Sec. 1075(b) of this Act provides:

"(b) Waiver of statute of limitations. —If credit or refund of any overpayment of tax resulting from the amendment made by subsection (a) is barred on the date of the enactment of this Act or at any time during the 1-year period beginning on the date of the enactment of this Act by the operation of any law or rule of law (including res judicata) refund or credit of such overpayment (to the extent attributable to the amendment made by subsection (a)) may, nevertheless, be made or allowed if claim therefor is filed before the close of such 1-year period."

Prior to amendment, Sec. 112(d) of P.L. 95-600 read as follows:

"(d) Effective date. The amendments made by this section shall apply to payments of unemployment compensation made after December 31, 1978, in taxable years ending after such date."

In **1978**, P.L. 95-600, Sec. 112(b), added Code Sec. 6050B, effective as provided in Sec. 112(d) of this Act [as amended by Sec. 1075(a) of P.L. 98-369, see above] which reads as follows:

"(d) Effective date. The amendments made by this section shall apply to payments of unemployment compensation made after December 31, 1978, in taxable years ending after such date; except that such amendments shall not apply to payments made for weeks of unemployment ending before December 1, 1978."

Sec. 6050C. Repealed.

In **1988**, P.L. 100-418, Sec. 1941(b)(1), repealed Code Sec. 6050C, effective for crude oil removed from the premises on or after 8/23/88.

Prior to repeal, Code Sec. 6050C read as follows:

"SEC. 6050C. INFORMATION REGARDING WINDFALL PROFIT TAX ON DOMESTIC CRUDE OIL.

"(a) Certification furnished by operator.

"Under regulations prescribed by the Secretary, the operator of a property from which domestic crude oil was produced shall certify (at such time and in such manner as the Secretary shall by regulations prescribe) to the purchaser—

"(1) the adjusted base price (within the meaning of section 4989) with respect to such crude oil,

"(2) the tier and category of such crude oil for purposes of the tax imposed by section 4986,

"(3) if any certification is furnished to the operator by the producer with respect to whether such oil is exempt oil or independent producer oil, a copy of such certification,

"(4) the amount of such crude oil, and

"(5) such other information as the Secretary by regulations may require.

"(b) Agreement between operator and purchaser.

"The Secretary may by regulations provide that, if the operator and purchaser agree thereto, the operator shall be relieved of the duty of furnishing some or all of the information required under subsection (a).

"(c) Special rule for oil not subject to withholding.

"If the tax imposed by section 4986 with respect to any oil for which withholding is not required under section 4995(a)—

"(1) subsections (a) and (b) shall be applied by substituting 'producer' for 'purchaser', and

"(2) paragraph (3) of subsection (a) shall not apply.

"(d) Cross references.

"(1) For additions to tax for failure to furnish information required under this section, see section 6722.

"(2) For penalty for willful failure to supply information required under this section, see section 7241".

In **1986**, P.L. 99-514, Sec. 1501(d)(1)(E), substituted "section 6722" for "section 6652(b)" in para. (d)(1), effective for returns the due date for which (determined without regard to extensions) is after 12/31/86.

In **1980**, P.L. 96-223, Sec. 101(d)(1), added Code Sec. 6050C, effective for periods after 2/29/80.

Sec. 6050D. Returns relating to energy grants and financing.
(a) In general.

Every person who administers a Federal, State, or local program a principal purpose of which is to provide subsidized financing or grants for projects to conserve or produce energy shall, to the extent required under regulations prescribed by the Secretary, make a return setting forth the name and address of each taxpayer receiving financing or a grant under such program and the aggregate amount so received by such individual.

(b) Definition of person.

For purposes of this section, the term "person" means the officer or employee having control of the program, or the person appropriately designated for purposes of this section.

In **1980**, P.L. 96-223, Sec. 203(b)(1), added Code Sec. 6050D, effective for tax. yrs. begin. after 12/31/80, but only with respect to financing or grants made after such date.

Sec. 6050E. State and local income tax refunds.
(a) Requirement of reporting.

Every person who, with respect to any individual, during any calendar year makes payments of refunds of State or local income taxes (or allows credits or offsets with respect to such taxes) aggregating $10 or more shall make a return according to forms or regulations prescribed by the Secretary setting forth the aggregate amount of such payments, credits, or offsets, and the name and address of the individual with respect to whom such payment, credit, or offset was made.

(b) Statements to be furnished to individuals with respect to whom information is required.

Every person required to make a return under subsection (a) shall furnish to each individual whose name is required to be set forth in such return a written statement showing—

(1) the name of the State or political subdivision thereof, and

(2) the information required to be shown on the return with respect to refunds, credits, and offsets to the individual.

The written statement required under the preceding sentence shall be furnished to the individual during January of the calendar year following the calendar year for which the return under subsection (a) was required to be made. No statement shall be required under this subsection with respect to any individual if it is determined (in the manner provided by regulations) that such individual did not claim itemized deductions under chapter 1 for the taxable year giving rise to the refund, credit, or offset.

(c) Person defined.

For purposes of this section, the term "person" means the officer or employee having control of the payment of the refunds (or the allowance of the credits or offsets) or the person appropriately designated for purposes of this section.

In **1986**, P.L. 99-514, Sec. 1501(c)(8), amended subsec. (b), effective for returns the due date for which (determined without regard to extensions) is after 12/31/86. Prior to amendment, subsec. (b) read as follows:

"(b) Statements to be furnished to individuals with respect to whom information is furnished.

"Every person making a return under subsection (a) shall furnish to each individual whose name is set forth in such return a written statement showing—

"(1) the name of the State or political subdivision thereof, and

"(2) the aggregate amount shown on the return of refunds, credits, and offsets to the individual.

The written statement required under the preceding sentence shall be furnished to the individual during January of the calendar year following the calendar year for which the return under subsection (a) was made. No statement shall be required under this subsection with respect to any individual if it is determined (in the manner provided by regulations) that such individual did not claim itemized deductions under chapter 1 for the taxable year giving rise to the refund, credit, or offset."

In **1984**, P.L. 98-369, Sec. 151(a), added the last sentence of subsec. (b), effective for payments of refunds, and credits and offsets made, after 12/31/82.

In **1982**, P.L. 97-248, Sec. 313(a), added Code Sec. 6050E, effective for payments of refunds, and credits and offsets made, after 12/31/82.

Sec. 6050F. Returns relating to social security benefits.
(a) Requirement of reporting.

The appropriate Federal official shall make a return, according to the forms and regulations prescribed by the Secretary, setting forth—

(1) the—

(A) aggregate amount of social security benefits paid with respect to any individual during any calendar year,

(B) aggregate amount of social security benefits repaid by such individual during such calendar year, and

(C) aggregate reductions under section 224 of the Social Security Act (or under section 3(a)(1) of the Railroad Retirement Act of 1974) in benefits which would otherwise have been paid to such individual during the

Information and returns

calendar year on account of amounts received under a workmen's compensation act, and

(2) the name and address of such individual.

(b) Statements to be furnished to persons with respect to whom information is required.

Every person required to make a return under subsection (a) shall furnish to each individual whose name is required to be set forth in such return a written statement showing—

(1) the name of the agency making the payments, and

(2) the aggregate amount of payments, of repayments, and of reductions, with respect to the individual required to be shown on such return.

The written statement required under the preceding sentence shall be furnished to the individual on or before January 31 of the year following the calendar year for which the return under subsection (a) was required to be made.

(c) Definitions.

For purposes of this section—

(1) Appropriate Federal official. The term "appropriate Federal official" means—

(A) the Commissioner of Social Security in the case of social security benefits described in section 86(d)(1)(A), and

(B) the Railroad Retirement Board in the case of social security benefits described in section 86(d)(1)(B).

(2) Social security benefit. The term "social security benefit" has the meaning given to such term by section 86(d)(1).

In **1994,** P.L. 103-296, Sec. 108(h)(4), substituted "Commissioner of Social Security" for "Secretary of Health and Human Services" in subpara. (c)(1)(A), effective 3/31/95.

In **1989,** P.L. 101-234, Sec. 102(a), repealed as if not enacted Sec. 111(b) of P.L. 100-360, which amended subsecs. (a), (b) and (c), effective 12/31/88.

In **1986,** P.L. 99-514, Sec. 1501(c)(9), amended subsec. (b), effective for returns the due date for which (determined without regard to extensions) is after 12/31/86. Prior to amendment, subsec. (b) read as follows:

"*(b) Statements to be furnished to individuals with respect to whom information is furnished.*

"Every person making a return under subsection (a) shall furnish to each individual whose name is set forth in such return a written statement showing—

"(1) the name of the agency making the payments, and

"(2) the aggregate amount of payments, of repayments, and of reductions, with respect to the individual as shown on such return.

The written statement required under the preceding sentence shall be furnished to the individual on or before January 31 of the year following the calendar year for which the return under subsection (a) was made."

In **1983,** P.L. 98-21, Sec. 121(b), added Code Sec. 6050F, effective for benefits received after 12/31/83, in tax. yrs. end. after 12/31/83. Sec. 121(g)(2) of the Act provides as follows:

"(2) Treatment of certain lump-sum payments received after December 31, 1983.—The amendments made by this section shall not apply to any portion of a lump-sum payment of social security benefits (as defined in section 86(d) of the Internal Revenue Code of 1954) received after December 31, 1983, if the generally applicable payment date for such portion was before January 1, 1984."

Sec. 6050G. Returns relating to certain railroad retirement benefits.

(a) In general.

The Railroad Retirement Board shall make a return, according to the forms and regulations prescribed by the Secretary, setting forth—

(1) the aggregate amount of benefits paid under the Railroad Retirement Act of 1974 (other than tier 1 railroad retirement benefits, as defined in section 86(d)(4)) to any individual during any calendar year,

(2) the employee contributions (to the extent not previously taken into account under section 72(d)(1)) which are treated as having been paid for purposes of section 72(r),

(3) the name and address of such individual, and

(4) such other information as the Secretary may require.

(b) Statements to be furnished to persons with respect to whom information is required.

The Railroad Retirement Board shall furnish to each individual whose name is required to be set forth in the return under subsection (a) a written statement showing—

(1) the aggregate amount of payments to such individual, and of employee contributions with respect thereto, required to be shown on the return, and

(2) such other information as the Secretary may require.

The written statement required under the preceding sentence shall be furnished to the individual on or before January 31 of the year following the calendar year for which the return under subsection (a) was required to be made.

In **1986,** P.L. 99-514, Sec. 1501(c)(10), amended subsec. (b), effective for returns the due date for which (determined without regard to extensions) is after 12/31/86. Prior to amendment, subsec. (b) read as follows:

"*(b) Statements to be furnished to individuals with respect to whom information is furnished.*

"The Railroad Retirement Board shall furnish to each individual whose name is set forth in the return under subsection (a) a written statement showing—

"(1) the aggregate amount of payments to such individual, and of employee contributions with respect thereto, as shown on such return, and

"(2) such other information as the Secretary may require. The written statement required under the preceding sentence shall be furnished to the individual on or before January 31 of the year following the calendar year for which the return under subsection (a) was made."

In **1983,** P.L. 98-76, Sec. 224(b)(1), added Code Sec. 6050G, effective for benefits received after 12/31/83, in tax. yrs. end. after 12/31/83, except as provided in Sec. 227(b)(2) and (3) of this Act, reproduced in note following Code Sec. 72.

Sec. 6050H. Returns relating to mortgage interest received in trade or business from individuals.

(a) Mortgage interest of $600 or more.

Any person—

(1) who is engaged in a trade or business, and

(2) who, in the course of such trade or business, receives from any individual interest aggregating $600 or more for any calendar year on any mortgage,

shall make the return described in subsection (b) with respect to each individual from whom such interest was received at such time as the Secretary may by regulations prescribe.

(b) Form and manner of returns.

A return is described in this subsection if such return—

(1) is in such form as the Secretary may prescribe,

(2) contains—

(A) the name and address of the individual from whom the interest described in subsection (a)(2) was received,

(B) the amount of such interest (other than points) received for the calendar year,

(C) the amount of points on the mortgage received during the calendar year and whether such points were paid directly by the borrower, and

(D) such other information as the Secretary may prescribe.

(c) Application to governmental units.

For purposes of subsection (a)—

(1) Treated as persons. The term "person" includes any governmental unit (and any agency or instrumentality thereof).

(2) Special rules. In the case of a governmental unit or any agency or instrumentality thereof—

(A) subsection (a) shall be applied without regard to the trade or business requirement contained therein, and

(B) any return required under subsection (a) shall be made by the officer or employee appropriately designated for the purpose of making such return.

Code Sec. 6050H(d) — Information and returns

(d) Statements to be furnished to individuals with respect to whom information is required.

Every person required to make a return under subsection (a) shall furnish to each individual whose name is required to be set forth in such return a written statement showing—

(1) the name, address, and phone number of information contact of the person required to make such return, and

(2) the aggregate amount of interest described in subsection (a)(2) (other than points) received by the person required to make such return from the individual to whom the statement is required to be furnished (and the information required under subsection (b)(2)(C)).

The written statement required under the preceding sentence shall be furnished on or before January 31 of the year following the calendar year for which the return under subsection (a) was required to be made.

(e) Mortgage defined.

For purposes of this section, except as provided in regulations prescribed by the Secretary, the term "mortgage" means any obligation secured by real property.

(f) Returns which would be required to be made by 2 or more persons.

Except to the extent provided in regulations prescribed by the Secretary, in the case of interest received by any person on behalf of another person, only the person first receiving such interest shall be required to make the return under subsection (a).

(g) Special rules for cooperative housing corporations.

For purposes of subsection (a), an amount received by a cooperative housing corporation from a tenant-stockholder shall be deemed to be interest received on a mortgage in the course of a trade or business engaged in by such corporation, to the extent of the tenant-stockholder's proportionate share of interest described in section 216(a)(2). Terms used in the preceding sentence shall have the same meanings as when used in section 216.

(h) Returns relating to mortgage insurance premiums.

(1) In general. The Secretary may prescribe, by regulations, that any person who, in the course of a trade or business, receives from any individual premiums for mortgage insurance aggregating $600 or more for any calendar year, shall make a return with respect to each such individual. Such return shall be in such form, shall be made at such time, and shall contain such information as the Secretary may prescribe.

(2) Statement to be furnished to individuals with respect to whom information is required. Every person required to make a return under paragraph (1) shall furnish to each individual with respect to whom a return is made a written statement showing such information as the Secretary may prescribe. Such written statement shall be furnished on or before January 31 of the year following the calendar year for which the return under paragraph (1) was required to be made.

(3) Special rules. For purposes of this subsection—

(A) rules similar to the rules of subsection (c) shall apply, and

(B) the term "mortgage insurance" means—

(i) mortgage insurance provided by the Veterans Administration, the Federal Housing Administration, or the Rural Housing Administration, and

(ii) private mortgage insurance (as defined by section 2 of the Homeowners Protection Act of 1998 (12 U.S.C. 4901), as in effect on the date of the enactment of this subsection).

In **2006**, P.L. 109-432, Sec. 419(c), added subsec. (h) effective for amounts paid or accrued after 12/31/2006.

In **1996**, P.L. 104-188, Sec. 1704(t)(23), amended Sec. 7646(b)(1) of P.L. 101-239, by substituting "6050H(b)(2)" for "6050H(b)(1)", see below.

—P.L. 104-168, Sec. 1201(a)(8), substituted "name, address, and phone number of the information contact" for "name and address" in para. (d)(1), effective for statements required to be furnished after 12/31/96 (determined without regard to any extension).

In **1989**, P.L. 101-239, Sec. 7646(a), deleted "and" at the end of subpara. (b)(2)(B), redesignated subpara. (b)(2)(C) as subpara. (b)(2)(D), and added new subpara. (b)(2)(C)... Sec. 7646(b)(1), [as amended by Sec. 1704(t)(23) of P.L. 104-188, see above] added "(other than points)" after "such interest" in subpara. (b)(2)(B)... Sec. 7646(b)(2)(A), added "(other than points)" after "subsection (a)(2)" in para. (d)(2)... Sec. 7646(b)(2)(B), added "(and the information required under subsection (b)(2)(C)" before the period at the end of para. (d)(2), effective for returns and statements the due date for which (determined without regard to extensions) is after 12/31/91.

In **1986**, P.L. 99-514, Sec. 1501(c)(11), amended subsec. (d), effective for returns the due date for which (determined without regard to extensions) is after 12/31/86. Prior to amendment, subsec. (d) read as follows:

"(d) Statements to be furnished to individuals with respect to whom information is furnished.

"Every person making a return under subsection (a) shall furnish to each individual whose name is set forth in such return a written statement showing—

"(1) the name and address of the person making such return, and

"(2) the aggregate amount of interest described in subsection (a)(2) received by the person making such return from the individual to whom the statement is furnished.

The written statement required under the preceding sentence shall be furnished on or before January 31 of the year following the calendar year for which the return under subsection (a) was made."

—P.L. 99-514, Sec. 1811(a)(1), added subsec. (g), effective for amounts received after 12/31/84. For special rules see Sec. 145(d)(2) of P.L. 98-369, reproduced below.

—P.L. 99-514, Sec. 1811(a)(2), amended Sec. 145(d)(2) of P.L. 98-369 [reproduced below], part of the effective date for changes made by Sec. 145(a) of P.L. 98-369, by substituting "section 6676" for "section 6652", see below.

In **1984**, P.L. 98-369, Sec. 145(a), added Code Sec. 6050H, effective for amounts received after 12/31/84. Sec. 145(d)(2) [as amended by Sec. 1811(a)(2) of P.L. 99-514, above] of this Act provides:

"(2) Special rule for obligations in existence on December 31, 1984.—In the case of any obligation in existence on December 31, 1984, no penalty shall be imposed under section 6676 of the Internal Revenue Code of 1954 by reason of the amendments made by this section on any failure to supply a taxpayer identification number with respect to amounts received before January 1, 1986."

Sec. 6050I. Returns relating to cash received in trade or business, etc.

(a) Cash receipts of more than $10,000.

Any person—

(1) who is engaged in a trade or business, and

(2) who, in the course of such trade or business, receives more than $10,000 in cash in 1 transaction (or 2 or more related transactions),

shall make the return described in subsection (b) with respect to such transaction (or related transactions) at such time as the Secretary may by regulations prescribe.

(b) Form and manner of returns.

A return is described in this subsection if such return—

(1) is in such form as the Secretary may prescribe,

(2) contains—

(A) the name, address, and TIN of the person from whom the cash was received,

(B) the amount of cash received,

(C) the date and nature of the transaction, and

(D) such other information as the Secretary may prescribe.

(c) Exceptions.

(1) Cash received by financial institutions. Subsection (a) shall not apply to—

(A) cash received in a transaction reported under title 31, United States Code, if the Secretary determines that reporting under this section would duplicate the reporting to the Treasury under title 31, United States Code, or

Information and returns   Code Sec. 6050I

(B) cash received by any financial institution (as defined in subparagraphs (A), (B), (C), (D), (E), (F), (G), (J), (K), (R), and (S) of section 5312(a)(2) of title 31, United States Code).

(2) Transactions occurring outside the United States. Except to the extent provided in regulations prescribed by the Secretary, subsection (a) shall not apply to any transaction if the entire transaction occurs outside the United States.

(d) Cash includes foreign currency and certain monetary instruments.

For purposes of this section, the term "cash" includes—

(1) foreign currency, and

(2) to the extent provided in regulations prescribed by the Secretary, any monetary instrument (whether or not in bearer form) with a face amount of not more than $10,000.

Paragraph (2) shall not apply to any check drawn on the account of the writer in a financial institution referred to in subsection (c)(1)(B).

(e) Statements to be furnished to persons with respect to whom information is required.

Every person required to make a return under subsection (a) shall furnish to each person whose name is required to be set forth in such return a written statement showing—

(1) the name, address, and phone number of the information contact of the person required to make such return, and

(2) the aggregate amount of cash described in subsection (a) received by the person required to make such return.

The written statement required under the preceding sentence shall be furnished to the person on or before January 31 of the year following the calendar year for which the return under subsection (a) was required to be made.

(f) Structuring transactions to evade reporting requirements prohibited.

(1) In general. No person shall for the purpose of evading the return requirements of this section—

(A) cause or attempt to cause a trade or business to fail to file a return required under this section,

(B) cause or attempt to cause a trade or business to file a return required under this section that contains a material omission or misstatement of fact, or

(C) structure or assist in structuring, or attempt to structure or assist in structuring, any transaction with one or more trades or businesses.

(2) Penalties. A person violating paragraph (1) of this subsection shall be subject to the same civil and criminal sanctions applicable to a person which fails to file or completes a false or incorrect return under this section.

(g) Cash received by criminal court clerks.

(1) In general. Every clerk of a Federal or State criminal court who receives more than $10,000 in cash as bail for any individual charged with a specified criminal offense shall make a return described in paragraph (2) (at such time as the Secretary may by regulations prescribe) with respect to the receipt of such bail.

(2) Return. A return is described in this paragraph if such return—

(A) is in such form as the Secretary may prescribe, and

(B) contains—

(i) the name, address, and TIN of—

(I) the individual charged with the specified criminal offense, and

(II) each person posting the bail (other than a person licensed as a bail bondsman),

(ii) the amount of cash received,

(iii) the date the cash was received, and

(iv) such other information as the Secretary may prescribe.

(3) Specified criminal offense. For purposes of this subsection, the term "specified criminal offense" means—

(A) any Federal criminal offense involving a controlled substance,

(B) racketeering (as defined in section 1951, 1952, or 1955 of title 18, United States Code),

(C) money laundering (as defined in section 1956 or 1957 of such title), and

(D) any State criminal offense substantially similar to an offense described in subparagraph (A), (B), or (C).

(4) Information to federal prosecutors. Each clerk required to include on a return under paragraph (1) the information described in paragraph (2)(B) with respect to an individual described in paragraph (2)(B)(i)(I) shall furnish (at such time as the Secretary may by regulations prescribe) a written statement showing such information to the United States Attorney for the jurisdiction in which such individual resides and the jurisdiction in which the specified criminal offense occurred.

(5) Information to payors of bail. Each clerk required to make a return under paragraph (1) shall furnish (at such time as the Secretary may by regulations prescribe) to each person whose name is required to be set forth in such return by reason of paragraph (2)(B)(i)(II) a written statement showing—

(A) the name and address of the clerk's office required to make the return, and

(B) the aggregate amount of cash described in paragraph (1) received by such clerk.

In 1996, P.L. 104-168, Sec. 1201(a)(9), substituted "name, address, and phone number of the information contact" for "name and address" in para. (e)(1), effective for statements required to be furnished after 12/31/96 (determined without regard to any extension).

In 1994, P.L. 103-322, Sec. 20415(a), added subsec. (g)... Sec. 20415(b)(3), substituted "business, etc." for "business" in the heading of Code Sec. 6050I, effective on the 60th day after the date on which the temporary regulations are prescribed [effective 2/13/95, see T.D. 8572, 12/12/94] under subsection (c) [Sec. 20415(c) of this Act]. Sec. 20415(c) of this Act regarding regulations, reads as follows:

"(c) Regulations. The Secretary of the Treasury or the Secretary's delegate shall prescribe temporary regulations under the amendments made by this section [Sec. 20415 of this Act] within 90 days after the date of enactment of this Act [9/13/94]."

In 1990, P.L. 101-508, Sec. 11318(a), amended subsec. (d) effective for amounts received after 11/5/90. Sec. 11318(e)(3) of this Act provides:

"(3) Not later than June 1, 1991, the Secretary of the Treasury or his delegate shall prescribe regulations under section 6050I(d)(2) of the Internal Revenue Code of 1986 (as amended by this section)."

Prior to amendment, subsec. (d) read as follows:

"(d) Cash includes foreign currency.

"For purposes of this section, the term 'cash' includes foreign currency."

—P.L. 101-508, Sec. 11318(c), substituted "(f) Structuring transactions to evade reporting requirements prohibited." for "(f) Actions by payors." in the heading of subsec. (f), effective 11/5/90.

In 1988, P.L. 100-690, Sec. 7601(a)(1), added subsec. (f), effective for actions after 11/18/88. Sec. 7601(a)(4) of this Act provides:

"(4) No inference.—No inference shall be drawn from the amendment made by paragraph (1) on the application of the Internal Revenue Code of 1986 without regard to such amendment."

In 1986, P.L. 99-514, Sec. 1501(c)(12), amended subsec. (e), effective for returns the due date for which (determined without regard to extensions) is after 12/31/86. Prior to amendment, subsec. (e) read as follows:

"(e) Statements to be furnished to persons with respect to whom information is furnished.

"Every person making a return under subsection (a) shall furnish to each person whose name is set forth in such return a written statement showing

"(1) the name and address of the person making such return, and

"(2) the aggregate amount of cash described in subsection (a) received by the person making such return.

The written statement required under the preceding sentence shall be furnished to the person on or before January 31 of the year following the calendar year for which the return under subsection (a) was made."

In **1984**, P.L. 98-369, Sec. 146(a), added Code Sec. 6050I, effective for amounts received after 12/31/84.

Sec. 6050J. Returns relating to foreclosures and abandonments of security.

(a) In general.

Any person who, in connection with a trade or business conducted by such person, lends money secured by property and who—

(1) in full or partial satisfaction of any indebtedness, acquires an interest in any property which is security for such indebtedness, or

(2) has reason to know that the property in which such person has a security interest has been abandoned,

shall make a return described in subsection (c) with respect to each of such acquisitions or abandonments, at such time as the Secretary may by regulations prescribe.

(b) Exception.

Subsection (a) shall not apply to any loan to an individual secured by an interest in tangible personal property which is not held for investment and which is not used in a trade or business.

(c) Form and manner of return.

The return required under subsection (a) with respect to any acquisition or abandonment of property—

(1) shall be in such form as the Secretary may prescribe,

(2) shall contain—

(A) the name and address of each person who is a borrower with respect to the indebtedness which is secured,

(B) a general description of the nature of such property and such indebtedness,

(C) in the case of a return required under subsection (a)(1)—

(i) the amount of such indebtedness at the time of such acquisition, and

(ii) the amount of indebtedness satisfied in such acquisition,

(D) in the case of a return required under subsection (a)(2), the amount of such indebtedness at the time of such abandonment, and

(E) such other information as the Secretary may prescribe.

(d) Applications to governmental units.

For purposes of this section—

(1) **Treated as persons.** The term "person" includes any governmental unit (and any agency or instrumentality thereof).

(2) **Special rules.** In the case of a governmental unit or any agency or instrumentality thereof—

(A) subsection (a) shall be applied without regard to the trade or business requirement contained therein, and

(B) any return under this section shall be made by the officer or employee appropriately designated for the purpose of making such return.

(e) Statements to be furnished to persons with respect to whom information is required to be furnished.

Every person required to make a return under subsection (a) shall furnish to each person whose name is required to be set forth in such return a written statement showing the name, address, and phone number of the information contact of the person required to make such return. The written statement required under the preceding sentence shall be furnished to the person on or before January 31 of the year following the calendar year for which the return under subsection (a) was made.

(f) Treatment of other dispositions.

To the extent provided by regulations prescribed by the Secretary, any transfer of the property which secures the indebtedness to a person other than the lender shall be treated as an abandonment of such property.

In **1996**, P.L. 104-168, Sec. 1201(a)(10), substituted "name, address, and phone number of the information contact" for "name and address" in subsec. (e), effective for statements required to be furnished after 12/31/96 (determined without regard to any extension).

In **1984**, P.L. 98-369, Sec. 148(a), added Code Sec. 6050J, effective for acquisitions of property and abandonments of property after 12/31/84.

Sec. 6050K. Returns relating to exchanges of certain partnership interests.

(a) In general.

Except as provided in regulations prescribed by the Secretary, if there is an exchange described in section 751(a) of any interest in a partnership during any calendar year, such partnership shall make a return for such calendar year stating—

(1) the name and address of the transferee and transferor in such exchange, and

(2) such other information as the Secretary may by regulations prescribe.

Such return shall be made at such time and in such manner as the Secretary may require by regulations.

(b) Statements to be furnished to transferor and transferee.

Every partnership required to make a return under subsection (a) shall furnish to each person whose name is required to be set forth in such return a written statement showing—

(1) the name, address, and phone number of information contact of the partnership required to make such return, and

(2) the information required to be shown on the return with respect to such person.

The written statement required under the preceding sentence shall be furnished to the person on or before January 31 of the year following the calendar year for which the return under subsection (a) was required to be made.

(c) Requirement that transferor notify partnership.

(1) **In general.** In the case of any exchange described in subsection (a), the transferor of the partnership interest shall promptly notify the partnership of such exchange.

(2) **Partnership not required to make return until notice.** A partnership shall not be required to make a return under this section with respect to any exchange until the partnership is notified of such exchange.

In **1996**, P.L. 104-168, Sec. 1201(a)(11), substituted "name, address, and phone number of the information contact" for "name and address" in para. (b)(1), effective for statements required to be furnished after 12/31/96 (determined without regard to any extension).

In **1986**, P.L. 99-514, Sec. 1501(c)(13), amended subsec. (b), effective for returns the due date for which (determined without regard to extensions) is after 12/31/86. Prior to amendment, subsec. (b) read as follows:

"(b) Statement to be furnished to transferor and transferee.

"Every partnership making a return under subsection (a) shall furnish to each person whose name is set forth in such return a written statement showing

"(1) the name and address of the partnership making the return, and

"(2) the information shown on the return with respect to such person.

The statement required under the preceding sentence shall be furnished to the person on or before January 31 following the calendar year for which the return under subsection (a) was made."

—P.L. 99-514, Sec. 1811(b)(2), substituted "this section" for "this subsection" in para. (c)(2), effective for exchanges after 12/31/84.

In **1984**, P.L. 98-369, Sec. 149(a), added Code Sec. 6050K, effective for exchanges after 12/31/84.

Information and returns Code Sec. 6050M(e)(2)

Sec. 6050L. Returns relating to certain donated property.

(a) Dispositions of donated property.

(1) **In general.** If the donee of any charitable deduction property sells, exchanges, or otherwise disposes of such property within 3 years after its receipt, the donee shall make a return (in accordance with forms and regulations prescribed by the Secretary) showing—

(A) the name, address, and TIN of the donor,
(B) a description of the property,
(C) the date of the contribution,
(D) the amount received on the disposition,
(E) the date of such disposition,
(F) a description of the donee's use of the property, and
(G) a statement indicating whether the use of the property was related to the purpose or function constituting the basis for the donee's exemption under section 501.

In any case in which the donee indicates that the use of applicable property (as defined in section 170(e)(7)(C)) was related to the purpose or function constituting the basis for the exemption of the donee under section 501 under subparagraph (G), the donee shall include with the return the certification described in section 170(e)(7)(D) if such certification is made under section 170(e)(7).

(2) **Definitions.** For purposes of this subsection—

(A) Charitable deduction property. The term "charitable deduction property" means any property (other than publicly traded securities) contributed in a contribution for which a deduction was claimed under section 170 if the claimed value of such property (plus the claimed value of all similar items of property donated by the donor to 1 or more donees) exceeds $5,000.

(B) Publicly traded securities. The term "publicly traded securities" means securities for which (as of the date of the contribution) market quotations are readily available on an established securities market.

(b) Qualified intellectual property contributions.

(1) **In general.** Each donee with respect to a qualified intellectual property contribution shall make a return (at such time and in such form and manner as the Secretary may by regulations prescribe) with respect to each specified taxable year of the donee showing—

(A) the name, address, and TIN of the donor,
(B) a description of the qualified intellectual property contributed,
(C) the date of the contribution, and
(D) the amount of net income of the donee for the taxable year which is properly allocable to the qualified intellectual property (determined without regard to paragraph (10)(B) of section 170(m) and with the modifications described in paragraphs (5) and (6) of such section).

(2) **Definitions.** For purposes of this subsection—

(A) In general. Terms used in this subsection which are also used in section 170(m) have the respective meanings given such terms in such section.

(B) Specified taxable year. The term "specified taxable year" means, with respect to any qualified intellectual property contribution, any taxable year of the donee any portion of which is part of the 10-year period beginning on the date of such contribution.

(c) Statement to be furnished to donors.

Every person making a return under subsection (a) or (b) shall furnish a copy of such return to the donor at such time and in such manner as the Secretary may by regulations prescribe.

In 2006, P.L. 109-280, Sec. 1215(b)(1), substituted "3 years" for "2 years" in para. (a)(1)... Sec. 1215(b)(2), deleted "and" at the end of subpara. (a)(1)(D), substituted a comma for the period at the end of subpara. (a)(1)(E), added subpara. (a)(1)(F) and (G), effective for returns filed after 9/1/2006.

In 2004, P.L. 108-357, Sec. 882(c)(1), amended Code Sec. 6050L, effective for contributions made after 6/3/2004.

Prior to amendment, Code Sec. 6050L read as follows:

"SEC. 6050L RETURNS RELATING TO CERTAIN DISPOSITIONS OF DONATED PROPERTY.
"(a) General rule. If the donee of any charitable deduction property sells, exchanges, or otherwise disposes of such property within 2 years after its receipt, the donee shall make a return (in accordance with forms and regulations prescribed by the Secretary) showing—
"(1) the name, address, and TIN of the donor,
"(2) a description of the property,
"(3) the date of the contribution,
"(4) the amount received on the disposition, and
"(5) the date of such disposition.
"(b) Charitable deduction property. For purposes of this section, the term 'charitable deduction property' means any property (other than publicly traded securities) contributed in a contribution for which a deduction was claimed under section 170 if the claimed value of such property (plus the claimed value of all similar items of property donated by the donor to 1 or more donees) exceeds $5,000.
"(c) Statement to be furnished to donors. Every person making a return under subsection (a) shall furnish a copy of such return to the donor at such time and in such manner as the Secretary may by regulations prescribe.
"(d) Definition of publicly traded securities. The term 'publicly traded securities' means securities for which (as of the date of the contribution) market quotations are readily available on an established securities market."

In 1984, P.L. 98-369, Sec. 155(b)(1), added Code Sec. 6050L, effective for contributions made after 12/31/84 in tax. yrs. end. after 12/31/84.

Sec. 6050M. Returns relating to persons receiving contracts from Federal executive agencies.

(a) Requirement of reporting.

The head of every Federal executive agency which enters into any contract shall make a return (at such time and in such form as the Secretary may by regulations prescribe) setting forth—

(1) The name, address, and TIN of each person with which such agency entered into a contract during the calendar year, and

(2) such other information as the Secretary may require.

(b) Federal executive agency.

For purposes of this section, the term "Federal executive agency" means—

(1) any Executive agency (as defined in section 105 of title 5, United States Code) other than the Government Accountability Office,

(2) any military department (as defined in section 102 of such title), and

(3) the United States Postal Service and the Postal Rate Commission.

(c) Authority to extend reporting to licenses and subcontracts.

To the extent provided in regulations, this section also shall apply to—

(1) licenses granted by Federal executive agencies, and
(2) subcontracts under contracts to which subsection (a) applies.

(d) Authority to prescribe minimum amounts.

This section shall not apply to contracts or licenses in any class which are below a minimum amount or value which may be prescribed by the Secretary by regulations for such class.

(e) Exception for certain classified or confidential contracts.

(1) **In general.** Except as provided in paragraph (2), this section shall not apply in the case of a contract described in paragraph (3).

(2) **Reporting requirement.** Each Federal executive agency which has entered into a contract described in paragraph (3) shall, upon a request of the Secretary which

identifies a particular person, acknowledge whether such person has entered into such a contract with such agency and, if so, provide to the Secretary—
   (A) the information required under this section with respect to such person, and
   (B) such other information with respect to such person which the Secretary and the head of such Federal executive agency agree is appropriate.
(3) **Description of contract.** For purposes of this subsection, a contract between a Federal executive agency and another person is described in this paragraph if—
   (A) the fact of the existence of such contract or the subject matter of such contract has been designated and clearly marked or clearly represented, pursuant to the provisions of Federal law or an Executive order, as requiring a specific degree of protection against unauthorized disclosure for reasons of national security, or
   (B) the head of such Federal executive agency (or his designee) pursuant to regulations issued by such agency determines, in writing, that filing the required return under this section would interfere with the effective conduct of a confidential law enforcement or foreign counterintelligence activity.

In 2005, P.L. 109-135, Sec. 412(rr)(2), substituted "Government Accountability Office" for "General Accounting Office" in para. (b)(1), effective 12/21/2005.
In 2004, P.L. 108-271, Sec. 8, of this Act, provides:
   "SEC. 8. REDESIGNATION.
   "(a) In general. The General Accounting Office is hereby redesignated the Government Accountability Office.
   "(b) References. Any reference to the General Accounting Office in any law, rule, regulation, certificate, directive, instruction, or other official paper in force on the date of enactment of this Act [7/7/2004] shall be considered to refer and apply to the Government Accountability Office."
In 1988, P.L. 100-647, Sec. 1015(f), added subsec. (e), effective for contracts (and subcontracts) entered into, and licenses granted, before, on, or after 1/1/87.
In 1986, P.L. 99-514, Sec. 1522(a), added Code Sec. 6050M, effective for contracts (and subcontracts) entered into, and licenses granted, before, on, or after 1/1/87.

Sec. 6050N. Returns regarding payments of royalties.
(a) Requirement of reporting.
   Every person—
   (1) who makes payments of royalties (or similar amounts) aggregating $10 or more to any other person during any calendar year, or
   (2) who receives payments of royalties (or similar amounts) as a nominee and who makes payments aggregating $10 or more during any calendar year to any other person with respect to the royalties (or similar amounts) so received,
shall make a return according to the forms or regulations prescribed by the Secretary, setting forth the aggregate amount of such payments and the name and address of the person to whom paid.
(b) Statements to be furnished to persons with respect to whom information is furnished.
   Every person required to make a return under subsection (a) shall furnish to each person whose name is required to be set forth in such return a written statement showing—
   (1) the name, address, and phone number of information contact of the person required to make such return, and
   (2) the aggregate amount of payments to the person required to be shown on such return.
The written statement required under the preceding sentence shall be furnished (either in person or in a statement mailing by first-class mail which includes adequate notice that the statement is enclosed) to the person on or before January 31 of the year following the calendar year for which the return

under subsection (a) was made and shall be in such form as the Secretary may prescribe by regulations.
(c) Exception for payments to certain persons.
   Except to the extent otherwise provided in regulations, this section shall not apply to any amount paid to a person described in subparagraph (A), (B), (C), (D), (E), or (F) of section 6049(b)(4).

In 1996, P.L. 104-168, Sec. 1201(a)(12), substituted "name, address, and phone number of the information contact" for "name and address" in para. (b)(1), effective for statements required to be furnished after 12/31/96 (determined without regard to any extension).
In 1986, P.L. 99-514, Sec. 1523(a), added Code Sec. 6050N, effective for payments made after 12/31/86.

Sec. 6050P. Returns relating to the cancellation of indebtedness by certain entities.
(a) In general.
   Any applicable entity which discharges (in whole or in part) the indebtedness of any person during any calendar year shall make a return (at such time and in such form as the Secretary may by regulations prescribe) setting forth—
   (1) the name, address, and TIN of each person whose indebtedness was discharged during such calendar year,
   (2) the date of the discharge and the amount of the indebtedness discharged, and
   (3) such other information as the Secretary may prescribe.
(b) Exception.
   Subsection (a) shall not apply to any discharge of less than $600.
(c) Definitions and special rules.
   For purposes of this section—
   (1) Applicable entity. The term "applicable entity" means—
      (A) an executive, judicial, or legislative agency (as defined in section 3701(a)(4) of title 31, United States Code), and
      (B) an applicable financial entity.
   (2) Applicable financial entity. The term "applicable financial entity" means—
      (A) any financial institution described in section 581 or 591(a) and any credit union,
      (B) the Federal Deposit Insurance Corporation, the Resolution Trust Corporation, the National Credit Union Administration, and any other Federal executive agency (as defined in section 6050M), and any successor or subunit of any of the foregoing,
      (C) any other corporation which is a direct or indirect subsidiary of an entity referred to in subparagraph (A) but only if, by virtue of being affiliated with such entity, such other corporation is subject to supervision and examination by a Federal or State agency which regulates entities referred to in subparagraph (A), and
      (D) any organization a significant trade or business of which is the lending of money.
   (3) Governmental units. In the case of an entity described in paragraph (1)(A) or (2)(B), any return under this section shall be made by the officer or employee appropriately designated for the purpose of making such return.
(d) Statements to be furnished to persons with respect to whom information is required to be furnished.
   Every applicable entity required to make a return under subsection (a) shall furnish to each person whose name is required to be set forth in such return a written statement showing—
   (1) the name and address of the entity required to make such return, and

Code Sec. 6050S   Information and returns

Sec. 6050S. Returns relating to higher education tuition and related expenses.

(a) In general.

Any person—

(1) which is an eligible educational institution which enrolls any individual for any academic period;

(2) which is engaged in a trade or business of making payments to any individual under an insurance arrangement as reimbursements or refunds (or similar amounts) of qualified tuition and related expenses; or

(3) except as provided in regulations, which is engaged in a trade or business and, in the course of which, receives from any individual interest aggregating $600 or more for any calendar year on one or more qualified education loans,

shall make the return described in subsection (b) with respect to the individual at such time as the Secretary may by regulations prescribe.

(b) Form and manner of returns.

A return is described in this subsection if such return—

(1) is in such form as the Secretary may prescribe, and

(2) contains—

(A) the name, address, and TIN of any individual—

(i) who is or has been enrolled at the institution and with respect to whom transactions described in subparagraph (B) are made during the calendar year, or

(ii) with respect to whom payments described in subsection (a)(2) or (a)(3) were made or received,

(B) the—

(i) aggregate amount of payments received or the aggregate amount billed for qualified tuition and related expenses with respect to the individual described in subparagraph (A) during the calendar year,

(ii) aggregate amount of grants received by such individual for payment of costs of attendance that are administered and processed by the institution during such calendar year,

(iii) amount of any adjustments to the aggregate amounts reported by the institution pursuant to clause (i) or (ii) with respect to such individual for a prior calendar year,

(iv) aggregate amount of reimbursements or refunds (or similar amounts) paid to such individual during the calendar year by a person engaged in a trade or business described in subsection (a)(2), and

(v) aggregate amount of interest received for the calendar year from such individual, and

(C) such other information as the Secretary may prescribe.

(c) Application to governmental units.

For purposes of this section—

(1) a governmental unit or any agency or instrumentality thereof shall be treated as a person, and

(2) any return required under subsection (a) by such governmental entity shall be made by the officer or employee appropriately designated for the purpose of making such return.

(d) Statements to be furnished to individuals with respect to whom information is required.

Every person required to make a return under subsection (a) shall furnish to each individual whose name is required to be set forth in such return under subparagraph (A) of subsection (b)(2) a written statement showing—

(1) the name, address, and phone number of the information contact of the person required to make such return, and

(2) the amounts described in subparagraph (B) of subsection (b)(2).

The written statement required under the preceding sentence shall be furnished on or before January 31 of the year following the calendar year for which the return under subsection (a) was required to be made.

• *Caution:* Code Sec. 6050S(e), following, was amended by Sec. 412(a)(2), P.L. 107-16, the Economic Growth and Tax Relief Reconciliation Act of 2001 (EGTRRA). These provisions generally sunset for tax years beginning after 12/31/2012. For specific sunset provisions, see Sec. 901, P.L. 107-16 (as amended) reproduced in history notes for this Code Sec.

(e) Definitions.

For purposes of this section, the terms "eligible educational institution" and "qualified tuition and related expenses" have the meanings given such terms by section 25A (without regard to subsection (g)(2) thereof), and except as provided in regulations, the term "qualified education loan" has the meaning given such term by section 221(d)(1).

(f) Returns which would be required to be made by 2 or more persons.

Except to the extent provided in regulations prescribed by the Secretary, in the case of any amount received by any person on behalf of another person, only the person first receiving such amount shall be required to make the return under subsection (a).

(g) Regulations.

The Secretary shall prescribe such regulations as may be necessary to carry out the provisions of this section. No penalties shall be imposed under part II of subchapter B of chapter 68 with respect to any return or statement required under this section until such time as such regulations are issued.

In 2010, P.L. 111-312, Sec. 101(a)(1), substituted "December 31, 2012" for "December 31, 2010" both places it appears in Sec. 901, P.L. 107-16, see below, effective as if included in the enactment of P.L. 107-16, EGTRRA, 6/7/2001.

In 2002, P.L. 107-358, Sec. 2, added subsec. (c) in Sec. 901 of P.L. 107-16 [see below], effective 12/17/2002.

—P.L. 107-131, Sec. 1(a), amended para. (a)(1) . . . Sec. 1(b)(1), added "and" after the comma at the end of para. (b)(1) . . . Sec. 1(b)(2), amended subpara. (b)(2)(A) . . . Sec. 1(b)(3), deleted subpara. (b)(2)(B) and redesignated subparas. (b)(2)(C) and (D) as (b)(2)(B) and (C) . . . Sec. 1(b)(4), amended subpara. (b)(2)(B) [as redesignated by Sec. 1(b)(3) of this Act, see above] . . . Sec. 1(c)(1), deleted "or (B)" after "subparagraph (A)" in subsec. (d) . . . Sec. 1(c)(2), substituted "subparagraph (B)" for "subparagraph (C)" in para. (d)(2), effective for expenses paid or assessed after 12/31/2002 (in tax. yrs. end. after 12/31/2002), for education furnished in academic periods begin. after 12/31/2002.

Prior to amendment, para. (a)(1) read as follows:

"(1) which is an eligible educational institution—

"(A) which receives payments for qualified tuition and related expenses with respect to any individual for any calendar year; or

"(B) which makes reimbursements or refunds (or similar amounts) to any individual of qualified tuition and related expenses;"

Prior to amendment, subpara. (b)(2)(A) read as follows:

"(A) the name, address, and TIN of the individual with respect to whom payments or interest described in subsection (a) were received from (or were paid to),"

Prior to deletion, subpara. (b)(2)(B) read as follows:

"(B) the name, address, and TIN of any individual certified by the individual described in subparagraph (A) as the taxpayer who will claim the individual as a dependent for purposes of the deduction allowable under section 151 for any taxable year ending with or within the calendar year, and"

Prior to amendment, subpara. (b)(2)(C) [prior to redesignation by Sec. 1(b)(3) of this Act, see above] read as follows:

"(C) the—

"(i) aggregate amount of payments for qualified tuition and related expenses received with respect to the individual described in subparagraph (A) during the calendar year,

3,548

Information and returns

Code Sec. 6050R

(2) the information required to be shown on the return with respect to such person.

The written statement required under the preceding sentence shall be furnished to the person on or before January 31 of the year following the calendar year for which the return under subsection (a) was made.

(e) Alternative procedure.

In lieu of making a return required under subsection (a), an agency described in subsection (c)(1)(A) may submit to the Secretary (at such time and in such form as the Secretary may by regulations prescribe) information sufficient for the Secretary to complete such a return on behalf of such agency. Upon receipt of such information, the Secretary shall complete such return and provide a copy of such return to such agency.

In 1999, P.L. 106-170, Sec. 533(a), deleted "and" at the end of subpara. (c)(2)(B), substituted ", and" for the period at the end of subpara. (c)(2)(C) and added subpara. (c)(2)(D), effective for discharges of indebtedness after 12/31/99.
In 1996, P.L. 104-134, Sec. 31001(m)(2)(A), substituted "applicable entity" for "applicable financial entity" in subsec. (a)...Sec. 31001(m)(2)(B)(i), redesignated paras. (c)(1) and (2) as paras. (c)(2) and (3), and added new para. (c)(1)...Sec. 31001(m)(2)(B)(ii), substituted "(1)(A) or (2)(B)" for "(1)(B)" in para. (c)(3) [as redesignated]...Sec. 31001(m)(2)(C), added subsec. (e)...Sec. 31001(m)(2)(D)(i), substituted "applicable entity" for "applicable financial entity" in subsec. (d)...Sec. 31001(m)(2)(D)(ii), amended the heading of Code Sec. 6050P, effective 4/26/96.
Prior to amendment, the heading of Code Sec. 6050P read as follows:
"Returns relating to the cancellation of indebtedness by certain financial entities."
In 1993, P.L. 103-66, Sec. 13252(a), added Code Sec. 6050P, effective for discharges of indebtedness after 12/31/93, except as provided in Sec. 13252(d)(2) of this Act, which reads as follows:
"(2) Governmental entities. In the case of an entity referred to in section 6050P(c)(1)(B) of the Internal Revenue Code of 1986 (as added by this section), the amendments made by this section shall apply to discharges of indebtedness after the date of the enactment of this Act."

Sec. 6050Q. Certain long-term care benefits.

(a) Requirement of reporting.

Any person who pays long-term care benefits shall make a return, according to the forms or regulations prescribed by the Secretary, setting forth—

(1) the aggregate amount of such benefits paid by such person to any individual during any calendar year,

(2) whether or not such benefits are paid in whole or in part on a per diem or other periodic basis without regard to the expenses incurred during the period to which the payments relate,

(3) the name, address, and TIN of such individual, and

(4) the name, address, and TIN of the chronically ill or terminally ill individual on account of whose condition such benefits are paid.

(b) Statements to be furnished to persons with respect to whom information is required.

Every person required to make a return under subsection (a) shall furnish to each individual whose name is required to be set forth in such return a written statement showing—

(1) the name, address, and phone number of the information contact of the person making the payments, and

(2) the aggregate amount of long-term care benefits paid to the individual which are required to be shown on such return.

The written statement required under the preceding sentence shall be furnished to the individual on or before January 31 of the year following the calendar year for which the return under subsection (a) was required to be made.

(c) Long-term care benefits.

For purposes of this section, the term "long-term care benefit" means—

(1) any payment under a product which is advertised, marketed, or offered as long-term care insurance, and

(2) any payment which is excludable from gross income by reason of section 101(g).

In 1997, P.L. 105-34, Sec. 1602(d)(1), added ", address, and phone number of the information contact" after "name" in para. (b)(1), effective for benefits paid after 12/31/96.
In 1996, P.L. 104-191, Sec. 323(a), added Code Sec. 6050Q, effective for benefits paid after 12/31/96.

Sec. 6050R. Returns relating to certain purchases of fish.

(a) Requirement of reporting.

Every person—

(1) who is engaged in the trade or business of purchasing fish for resale from any person engaged in the trade or business of catching fish; and

(2) who makes payments in cash in the course of such trade or business to such a person of $600 or more during any calendar year for the purchase of fish,

shall make a return (at such times as the Secretary may prescribe) described in subsection (b) with respect to each person to whom such a payment was made during such calendar year.

(b) Return.

A return is described in this subsection if such return—

(1) is in such form as the Secretary may prescribe, and

(2) contains—

(A) the name, address, and TIN of each person to whom a payment described in subsection (a)(2) was made during the calendar year,

(B) the aggregate amount of such payments made to such person during such calendar year and the date and amount of each such payment, and

(C) such other information as the Secretary may require.

(c) Statement to be furnished with respect to whom information is required.

Every person required to make a return under subsection (a) shall furnish to each person whose name is required to be set forth in such return a written statement showing—

(1) the name, address, and phone number of the information contact of the person required to make such a return, and

(2) the aggregate amount of payments to the person required to be shown on the return.

The written statement required under the preceding sentence shall be furnished to the person on or before January 31 of the year following the calendar year for which the return under subsection (a) is required to be made.

(d) Definitions.

For purposes of this section:

(1) **Cash.** The term "cash" has the meaning given such term by section 6050I(d).

(2) **Fish.** The term "fish" includes other forms of aquatic life.

In 1998, P.L. 105-206, Sec. 6023(21), substituted a comma for the semicolon at the end of subpara. (b)(2)(A), effective 7/22/98.
In 1997, P.L. 105-34, Sec. 1601(a)(1), substituted "name, address, and phone number of the information contact" for "name and address" in para. (c)(1), effective for payments made after 12/31/97.
In 1996, P.L. 104-188, Sec. 1116(b)(1), added Code Sec. 6050R, effective for payments made after 12/31/97.

Information and returns

Code Sec. 6050U

"(ii) the amount of any grant received by such individual for payment of costs of attendance and processed by the person making such return during such calendar year,

"(iii) aggregate amount of reimbursements or refunds (or similar amounts) paid to such individual during the calendar year by the person making such return, and

"(iv) aggregate amount of interest received for the calendar year from such individual and"

In **2001**, P.L. 107-16, Sec. 412(a)(2), substituted "section 221(d)(1)" for "section 221(e)(1)" in subsec. (e), effective for loan interest paid after 12/31/2001, in tax. yrs. ending after 12/31/2001.

—P.L. 107-16, Sec. 901, of this Act [as amended by Sec. 2, P.L. 107-358, and Sec. 101(a)(1), P.L. 111-312, see above], reads as follows:

"Sec. 901. Sunset of provisions of Act.

"(a) In general. All provisions of, and amendments made by, this Act shall not apply—

"(1) to taxable, plan, or limitation years beginning after December 31, 2012, or

"(2) in the case of title V, to estates of decedents dying, gifts made, or generation skipping transfers, after December 31, 2012.

"(b) Application of certain laws. The Internal Revenue Code of 1986 and the Employee Retirement Income Security Act of 1974 shall be applied and administered to years, estates, gifts, and transfers described in subsection (a) as if the provisions and amendments described in subsection (a) had never been enacted.

"(c) Exception. Subsection (a) shall not apply to section 803 (relating to no federal income tax on restitution received by victims of the Nazi regime or their heirs or estates)."

In **1998**, P.L. 105-206, Sec. 3712(a)(1), redesignated clauses (b)(2)(C)(ii) and (iii) as clauses (b)(2)(C)(iii) and (iv) and added new clause (b)(2)(C)(ii)... Sec. 3712(a)(2), added "by the person making such return" after "year" in clause (b)(2)(C)(iii) [as redesignated by Sec. 3712(a)(1) of this Act]... Sec. 3712(a)(3), added "and" at the end of clause (b)(2)(C)(iv) [as redesignated by Sec. 3712(a)(1) of this Act]... Sec. 3712(b)(1), deleted "aggregate" before "amounts described" in para. (d)(2)... Sec. 3712(b)(2), added "(without regard to subsection (g)(2) thereof)" after "section 25A" in subsec. (e), effective for returns required to be filed for tax. yrs. begin. after 12/31/98.

—P.L. 105-206, Sec. 6004(a)(2), amended subsec. (a), effective for expenses paid after 12/31/97 (in tax. yrs. end. after such date), for education furnished in academic periods begin. after 12/31/97.

Prior to amendment, subsec. (a) read as follows:

"(a) In general. Any person—

"(1) which is an eligible educational institution which receives payments for qualified tuition and related expenses with respect to any individual for any calendar year, or

"(2) which is engaged in a trade or business and which, in the course of such trade or business—

"(A) makes payments during any calendar year to any individual which constitutes reimbursements or refunds (or similar amounts) of qualified tuition and related expenses of such individual, or

"(B) except as provided in regulations, receives from any individual interest aggregating $600 or more for any calendar year on 1 or more qualified educations loans,

shall make the return described in subsection (b) with respect to the individual at such time as the Secretary may by regulations prescribe."

In **1997**, P.L. 105-34, Sec. 201(c)(1), added Code Sec. 6050S, effective for expenses paid after 12/31/97 (in tax. yrs. end. after such date), for education furnished in academic periods begin. after 12/31/97.

—P.L. 105-34, Sec. 202(c)(1), amended para. (a)(2)... Sec. 202(c)(2)(A), added "or interest" after "payments" in subpara. (b)(2)(A)... Sec. 202(c)(2)(B), deleted "and" at the end of clause (b)(2)(C)(i), added "and" at the end of clause (b)(2)(C)(ii), [already included in clause (b)(2)(C)(ii)] and added clause (b)(2)(C)(iii)... Sec. 202(c)(3), added ", and except as provided in regulations, the term 'qualified education loan' has the meaning given such term by section 221(e)(1)" after "section 25A" in subsec. (e), effective as provided in Sec. 202(e) of this Act which reads as follows:

"(e) Effective date. The amendments made by this section shall apply to any qualified education loan (as defined in section 221(e)(1) of the Internal Revenue Code of 1986, as added by this section) incurred on, before, or after the date of the enactment of this Act, but only with respect to—

"(1) any loan interest payment due and paid after December 31, 1997, and

"(2) the portion of the 60-month period referred to in section 221(d) of the Internal Revenue Code of 1986 (as added by this section) after December 31, 1997."

Prior to amendment, para. (a)(2) read as follows:

"(2) which is engaged in a trade or business and which, in the course of such trade or business, makes payments during any calendar year to any individual which constitute reimbursements or refunds (or similar amounts) of qualified tuition and related expenses of such individual,"

Sec. 6050T. Returns relating to credit for health insurance costs of eligible individuals.

(a) Requirement of reporting.

Every person who is entitled to receive payments for any month of any calendar year under section 7527 (relating to advance payment of credit for health insurance costs of eligible individuals) with respect to any certified individual (as defined in section 7527(c)) shall, at such time as the Secretary may prescribe, make the return described in subsection (b) with respect to each such individual.

(b) Form and manner of returns.

A return is described in this subsection if such return—

(1) is in such form as the Secretary may prescribe, and

(2) contains—

(A) the name, address, and TIN of each individual referred to in subsection (a),

(B) the number of months for which amounts were entitled to be received with respect to such individual under section 7527 (relating to advance payment of credit for health insurance costs of eligible individuals),

(C) the amount entitled to be received for each such month, and

(D) such other information as the Secretary may prescribe.

(c) Statements to be furnished to individuals with respect to whom information is required.

Every person required to make a return under subsection (a) shall furnish to each individual whose name is required to be set forth in such return a written statement showing—

(1) the name and address of the person required to make such return and the phone number of the information contact for such person, and

(2) the information required to be shown on the return with respect to such individual.

The written statement required under the preceding sentence shall be furnished on or before January 31 of the year following the calendar year for which the return under subsection (a) is required to be made.

In **2002**, P.L. 107-210, Sec. 202(c)(1), added Code Sec. 6050T, effective 8/6/2002.

Sec. 6050U. Charges or payments for qualified long-term care insurance contracts under combined arrangements.

(a) Requirement of reporting.

Any person who makes a charge against the cash value of an annuity contract, or the cash surrender value of a life insurance contract, which is excludible from gross income under section 72(e)(11) shall make a return, according to the forms or regulations prescribed by the Secretary, setting forth—

(1) the amount of the aggregate of such charges against each such contract for the calendar year,

(2) the amount of the reduction in the investment in each such contract by reason of such charges, and

(3) the name, address, and TIN of the individual who is the holder of each such contract.

(b) Statements to be furnished to persons with respect to whom information is required.

Every person required to make a return under subsection (a) shall furnish to each individual whose name is required to be set forth in such return a written statement showing—

(1) the name, address, and phone number of the information contact of the person making the payments, and

(2) the information required to be shown on the return with respect to such individual.

The written statement required under the preceding sentence shall be furnished to the individual on or before January 31 of the year following the calendar year for which the return under subsection (a) was required to be made.

In **2006**, P.L. 109-280, Sec. 844(d)(1), added Code Sec. 6050U, effective for charges made after 12/31/2009.

3,549

Sec. 6050V. Returns relating to applicable insurance contracts in which certain exempt organizations hold interests.

(a) In general.

Each applicable exempt organization which makes a reportable acquisition shall make the return described in subsection (c).

(b) Time for making return.

Any applicable exempt organization required to make a return under subsection (a) shall file such return at such time as may be established by the Secretary.

(c) Form and manner of returns.

A return is described in this subsection if such return—

(1) is in such form as the Secretary prescribes,

(2) contains the name, address, and taxpayer identification number of the applicable exempt organization and the issuer of the applicable insurance contract, and

(3) contains such other information as the Secretary may prescribe.

(d) Definitions.

For purposes of this section—

(1) Reportable acquisition. The term "reportable acquisition" means the acquisition by an applicable exempt organization of a direct or indirect interest in any applicable insurance contract in any case in which such acquisition is a part of a structured transaction involving a pool of such contracts.

(2) Applicable insurance contract.

(A) In general. The term "applicable insurance contract" means any life insurance, annuity, or endowment contract with respect to which both an applicable exempt organization and a person other than an applicable exempt organization have directly or indirectly held an interest in the contract (whether or not at the same time).

(B) Exceptions. Such term shall not include a life insurance, annuity, or endowment contract if—

(i) all persons directly or indirectly holding any interest in the contract (other than applicable exempt organizations) have an insurable interest in the insured under the contract independent of any interest of an applicable exempt organization in the contract,

(ii) the sole interest in the contract of an applicable exempt organization or each person other than an applicable exempt organization is as a named beneficiary, or

(iii) the sole interest in the contract of each person other than an applicable exempt organization is—

(I) as a beneficiary of a trust holding an interest in the contract, but only if the person's designation as such beneficiary was made without consideration and solely on a purely gratuitous basis, or

(II) as a trustee who holds an interest in the contract in a fiduciary capacity solely for the benefit of applicable exempt organizations or persons otherwise described in subclause (I) or clause (i) or (ii).

(3) Applicable exempt organization. The term "applicable exempt organization" means—

(A) an organization described in section 170(c),

(B) an organization described in section 168(h)(2)(A)(iv), or

(C) an organization not described in paragraph (1) or (2) which is described in section 2055(a) or section 2522(a).

(e) Termination.

This section shall not apply to reportable acquisitions occurring after the date which is 2 years after the date of the enactment of this section.

In **2006**, P.L. 109-280, Sec. 1211(a)(1), added Code Sec. 6050V, effective for acquisitions of contracts after 8/17/2006.

—P.L. 109-280, Sec. 1211(c), of this Act provides:

"(c) Study.

"(1) In general. The Secretary of the Treasury shall undertake a study on.

"(A) the use by tax exempt organizations of applicable insurance contracts (as defined under section 6050V(d)(2) of the Internal Revenue Code of 1986, as added by subsection (a)) for the purpose of sharing the benefits of the organization's insurable interest in individuals insured under such contracts with investors, and

"(B) whether such activities are consistent with the tax exempt status of such organizations.

"(2) Report. Not later than 30 months after the date of the enactment of this Act, the Secretary of the Treasury shall report on the study conducted under paragraph (1) to the Committee on Finance of the Senate and the Committee on Ways and Means of the House of Representatives."

Sec. 6050W. Returns relating to payments made in settlement of payment card and third party network transactions.

(a) In general.

Each payment settlement entity shall make a return for each calendar year setting forth—

(1) the name, address, and TIN of each participating payee to whom one or more payments in settlement of reportable payment transactions are made, and

(2) the gross amount of the reportable payment transactions with respect to each such participating payee.

Such return shall be made at such time and in such form and manner as the Secretary may require by regulations.

(b) Payment settlement entity.

For purposes of this section—

(1) In general. The term "payment settlement entity" means—

(A) in the case of a payment card transaction, the merchant acquiring entity, and

(B) in the case of a third party network transaction, the third party settlement organization.

(2) Merchant acquiring entity. The term "merchant acquiring entity" means the bank or other organization which has the contractual obligation to make payment to participating payees in settlement of payment card transactions.

(3) Third party settlement organization. The term "third party settlement organization" means the central organization which has the contractual obligation to make payment to participating payees of third party network transactions.

(4) Special rules related to intermediaries. For purposes of this section—

(A) Aggregated payees. In any case where reportable payment transactions of more than one participating payee are settled through an intermediary—

(i) such intermediary shall be treated as the participating payee for purposes of determining the reporting obligations of the payment settlement entity with respect to such transactions, and

(ii) such intermediary shall be treated as the payment settlement entity with respect to the settlement of such transactions with the participating payees.

(B) Electronic payment facilitators. In any case where an electronic payment facilitator or other third party makes payments in settlement of reportable payment transactions on behalf of the payment settlement entity, the return under subsection (a) shall be made by such

Information and returns

Code Sec. 6051(a)

electronic payment facilitator or other third party in lieu of the payment settlement entity.

(c) Reportable payment transaction.

For purposes of this section—

(1) In general. The term "reportable payment transaction" means any payment card transaction and any third party network transaction.

(2) Payment card transaction. The term "payment card transaction" means any transaction in which a payment card is accepted as payment.

(3) Third party network transaction. The term "third party network transaction" means any transaction which is settled through a third party payment network.

(d) Other definitions.

For purposes of this section—

(1) Participating payee.

(A) In general. The term "participating payee" means—

(i) in the case of a payment card transaction, any person who accepts a payment card as payment, and

(ii) in the case of a third party network transaction, any person who accepts payment from a third party settlement organization in settlement of such transaction.

(B) Exclusion of foreign persons. Except as provided by the Secretary in regulations or other guidance, such term shall not include any person with a foreign address.

(C) Inclusion of governmental units. The term "person" includes any governmental unit (and any agency or instrumentality thereof).

(2) Payment card. The term "payment card" means any card which is issued pursuant to an agreement or arrangement which provides for—

(A) one or more issuers of such cards,

(B) a network of persons unrelated to each other, and to the issuer, who agree to accept such cards as payment, and

(C) standards and mechanisms for settling the transactions between the merchant acquiring entities and the persons who agree to accept such cards as payment.

The acceptance as payment of any account number or other indicia associated with a payment card shall be treated for purposes of this section in the same manner as accepting such payment card as payment.

(3) Third party payment network. The term "third party payment network" means any agreement or arrangement—

(A) which involves the establishment of accounts with a central organization by a substantial number of persons who—

(i) are unrelated to such organization,

(ii) provide goods or services, and

(iii) have agreed to settle transactions for the provision of such goods or services pursuant to such agreement or arrangement,

(B) which provides for standards and mechanisms for settling such transactions, and

(C) which guarantees persons providing goods or services pursuant to such agreement or arrangement that such persons will be paid for providing such goods or services.

Such term shall not include any agreement or arrangement which provides for the issuance of payment cards.

(e) Exception for de minimis payments by third party settlement organizations.

A third party settlement organization shall be required to report any information under subsection (a) with respect to third party network transactions of any participating payee only if—

(1) the amount which would otherwise be reported under subsection (a)(2) with respect to such transactions exceeds $20,000, and

(2) the aggregate number of such transactions exceeds 200.

(f) Statements to be furnished to persons with respect to whom information is required.

Every person required to make a return under subsection (a) shall furnish to each person with respect to whom such a return is required a written statement showing—

(1) the name, address, and phone number of the information contact of the person required to make such return, and

(2) the gross amount of the reportable payment transactions with respect to the person required to be shown on the return.

The written statement required under the preceding sentence shall be furnished to the person on or before January 31 of the year following the calendar year for which the return under subsection (a) was required to be made. Such statement may be furnished electronically, and if so, the email address of the person required to make such return may be shown in lieu of the phone number.

(g) Regulations.

The Secretary may prescribe such regulations or other guidance as may be necessary or appropriate to carry out this section, including rules to prevent the reporting of the same transaction more than once.

In 2008, P.L. 110-289, Sec. 3091(a), added Code Sec. 6050W, effective for returns for calendar yrs. begin. after 12/31/2010. Sec. 3091(e)(2)(B) of this Act, reads as follows:

"(B) Eligibility for TIN matching program. Solely for purposes of carrying out any TIN matching program established by the Secretary under section 3406(i) of the Internal Revenue Code of 1986—

"(i) the amendments made this section shall be treated as taking effect on the date of the enactment of this Act, and

"(ii) each person responsible for setting the standards and mechanisms referred to in section 6050W(d)(2)(C) of such Code, as added by this section, for settling transactions involving payment cards shall be treated in the same manner as a payment settlement entity."

SUBPART C.—INFORMATION REGARDING WAGES PAID EMPLOYEES

Sec.

6051. Receipts for employees.

6052. Returns regarding payment of wages in the form of group-term life insurance.

6053. Reporting of tips.

In 1965, added item 6053.
In 1964, added item 6052.

Sec. 6051.   Receipts for employees.

(a) Requirement.

Every person required to deduct and withhold from an employee a tax under section 3101 or 3402, or who would have been required to deduct and withhold a tax under section 3402 (determined without regard to subsection (n)) if the employee had claimed no more than one withholding exemption, or every employer engaged in a trade or business who pays remuneration for services performed by an employee, including the cash value of such remuneration paid in any medium other than cash, shall furnish to each such employee in respect of the remuneration paid by such person

3,551

Code Sec. 6051(a)

Information and returns

to such employee during the calendar year, on or before January 31 of the succeeding year, or, if his employment is terminated before the close of such calendar year, within 30 days after the date of receipt of a written request from the employee if such 30-day period ends before January 31, a written statement showing the following:

(1) the name of such person,

(2) the name of the employee (and his social security account number if wages as defined in section 3121(a) have been paid),

(3) the total amount of wages as defined in section 3401(a),

(4) the total amount deducted and withheld as tax under section 3402,

(5) the total amount of wages as defined in section 3121(a),

(6) the total amount deducted and withheld as tax under section 3101,

(7) **Repealed.**

(8) the total amount of elective deferrals (within the meaning of section 402(g)(3)) and compensation deferred under section 457, including the amount of designated Roth contributions (as defined in section 402A),

(9) the total amount incurred for dependent care assistance with respect to such employee under a dependent care assistance program described in section 129(d),

(10) in the case of an employee who is a member of the Armed Forces of the United States, such employee's earned income as determined for purposes of section 32 (relating to earned income credit),

(11) the amount contributed to any Archer MSA (as defined in section 220(d)) of such employee or such employee's spouse,

(12) the amount contributed to any health savings account (as defined in section 223(d)) of such employee or such employee's spouse,

(13) the total amount of deferrals for the year under a nonqualified deferred compensation plan (within the meaning of section 409A(d)).

In the case of compensation paid for service as a member of a uniformed service, the statement shall show, in lieu of the amount required to be shown by paragraph (5), the total amount of wages as defined in section 3121(a), computed in accordance with such section and section 3121(i)(2). In the case of compensation paid for service as a volunteer or volunteer leader within the meaning of the Peace Corps Act, the statement shall show, in lieu of the amount required to be shown by paragraph (5), the total amount of wages as defined in section 3121(a), computed in accordance with such section and section 3121(i)(3). In the case of tips received by an employee in the course of his employment, the amounts required to be shown by paragraphs (3) and (5) shall include only such tips as are included in statements furnished to the employer pursuant to section 6053(a). The amounts required to be shown by paragraph (5) shall not include wages which are exempted pursuant to sections 3101(c) and 3111(c) from the taxes imposed by sections 3101 and 3111. In the case of the amounts required to be shown by paragraph (13), the Secretary may (by regulation) establish a minimum amount of deferrals below which paragraph (13) does not apply, and

(14) the aggregate cost (determined under rules similar to the rules of section 4980B(f)(4)) of applicable employer-sponsored coverage (as defined in section 4980I(d)(1)), except that this paragraph shall not apply to—

(A) coverage to which paragraphs (11) and (12) apply, or

(B) the amount of any salary reduction contributions to a flexible spending arrangement (within the meaning of section 125).

(b) Special rule as to compensation of members of Armed Forces.

In the case of compensation paid for service as a member of the Armed Forces, the statement required by subsection (a) shall be furnished if any tax was withheld during the calendar year under section 3402, or if any of the compensation paid during such year is includible in gross income under chapter 1, or if during the calendar year any amount was required to be withheld as tax under section 3101. In lieu of the amount required to be shown by paragraph (3) of subsection (a), such statement shall show as wages paid during the calendar year the amount of such compensation paid during the calendar year which is not excluded from gross income under chapter 1 (whether or not such compensation constituted wages as defined in section 3401(a)).

(c) Additional requirements.

The statements required to be furnished pursuant to this section in respect of any remuneration shall be furnished at such other times, shall contain such other information, and shall be in such form as the Secretary may by regulations prescribe. The statements required under this section shall also show the proportion of the total amount withheld as tax under section 3101 which is for financing the cost of hospital insurance benefits under part A of title XVIII of the Social Security Act.

(d) Statements to constitute information returns.

A duplicate of any statement made pursuant to this section and in accordance with regulations prescribed by the Secretary shall, when required by such regulations, be filed with the Secretary.

(e) Railroad employees.

(1) **Additional requirement.** Every person required to deduct and withhold tax under section 3201 from an employee shall include on or with the statement required to be furnished such employee under subsection (a) a notice concerning the provisions of this title with respect to the allowance of a credit or refund of the tax on wages imposed by section 3101(b) and the tax on compensation imposed by section 3201 or 3211 which is treated as a tax on wages imposed by section 3101(b).

(2) **Information to be supplied to employees.** Each person required to deduct and withhold tax under section 3201 during any year from an employee who has also received wages during such year subject to the tax imposed by section 3101(b) shall, upon request of such employee, furnish to him a written statement showing—

(A) the total amount of compensation with respect to which the tax imposed by section 3201 was deducted,

(B) the total amount deducted as tax under section 3201, and

(C) the portion of the total amount deducted as tax under section 3201 which is for financing the cost of hospital insurance under part A of title XVIII of the Social Security Act.

(f) Statements required in case of sick pay paid by third parties.

(1) **Statements required from payor.**

(A) In general. If, during any calendar year, any person makes a payment of third-party sick pay to an employee, such person shall, on or before January 15 of the succeeding year, furnish a written statement to the employer in respect of whom such payment was made showing—

Information and returns   Code Sec. 6051

(i) the name and, if there is withholding under section 3402(o), the social security number of such employee,

(ii) the total amount of the third-party sick pay paid to such employee during the calendar year, and

(iii) the total amount (if any) deducted and withheld from such sick pay under section 3402.

For purposes of the preceding sentence, the term "third-party sick pay" means any sick pay (as defined in section 3402(o)(2)(C)) which does not constitute wages for purposes of chapter 24 (determined without regard to section 3402(o)(1)).

(B) Special rules.

(i) Statements are in lieu of other reporting requirements. The reporting requirements of subparagraph (A) with respect to any payments shall, with respect to such payments, be in lieu of the requirements of subsection (a) and of section 6041.

(ii) Penalties made applicable. For purposes of sections 6674 and 7204, the statements required to be furnished by subparagraph (A) shall be treated as statements required under this section to be furnished to employees.

(2) Information required to be furnished by employer. Every employer who receives a statement under paragraph (1)(A) with respect to sick pay paid to any employee during any calendar year shall, on or before January 31 of the succeeding year, furnish a written statement to such employee showing—

(A) the information shown on the statement furnished under paragraph (1)(A), and

(B) if any portion of the sick pay is excludable from gross income under section 104(a)(3), the portion which is not so excludable and the portion which is so excludable.

To the extent practicable, the information required under the preceding sentence shall be furnished on or with the statement (if any) required under subsection (a).

In 2010, P.L. 111-312, Sec. 101(a)(1), substituted "December 31, 2012" for "December 31, 2010" both places it appeared in Sec. 901 of P.L. 107-16, [see below] effective as if included in the enactment of P.L. 107-16, EGTRRA, 6/7/2001.

—P.L. 111-226, Sec. 219(a)(3), deleted para. (a)(7), effective for tax. yrs. begin. after 12/31/2010.

Prior to deletion, para. (a)(7) read as follows:

"(7) the total amount paid to the employee under section 3507 (relating to advance payment of earned income credit),"

—P.L. 111-148, Sec. 9002(a), deleted "and" at the end of para. (a)(12), substituted ", and" for the period at the end of para. (a)(13), and added para. (a)(14), effective for tax. yrs. begin. after 12/31/2010.

In 2006, P.L. 109-280, Sec. 811, of this Act [relating to Sec. 901 of P.L. 107-16, see below], provides:

"SEC. 811. PENSIONS AND INDIVIDUAL RETIREMENT ARRANGEMENT PROVISIONS OF ECONOMIC GROWTH AND TAX RELIEF RECONCILIATION ACT OF 2001 MADE PERMANENT.

"Title IX of the Economic Growth and Tax Relief Reconciliation Act of 2001 shall not apply to the provisions of, and amendments made by, subtitles A through F of title VI of such Act (relating to pension and individual retirement arrangement provisions)."

In 2004, P.L. 108-357, Sec. 885(b)(1)(A), deleted "and" at the end of para. (a)(11), substituted ", and" for the period at the end of para. (a)(12), and added para. (a)(13) . . . Sec. 885(b)(1)(B), added "In the case of the amounts required to be shown by paragraph (13), the Secretary may (by regulation) establish a minimum amount of deferrals below which paragraph (13) does not apply." at the end of subsec. (a), effective for amounts deferred after 12/31/2004, except as provided in Sec. 885(d)(2) and (3) of this Act, which reads as follows:

"(2) Special rules.

"(A) Earnings. The amendments made by this section shall apply to earnings on deferred compensation only to the extent that such amendments apply to such compensation.

"(B) Material modifications. For purposes of this subsection, amounts deferred in taxable years beginning before January 1, 2005, shall be treated as amounts deferred in a taxable year beginning on or after such date if the plan under which the deferral is made is materially modified after October 3, 2004, unless such modification is pursuant to the guidance issued under subsection (f).

"(3) Exception for nonelective deferred compensation. The amendments made by this section shall not apply to any nonelective deferred compensation to which section 457 of the Internal Revenue Code of 1986 does not apply by reason of section 457(e)(12) of such Code, but only if such compensation is provided under a nonqualified deferred compensation plan—

"(A) which was in existence on May 1, 2004,

"(B) which was providing nonelective deferred compensation described in such section 457(e)(12) on such date, and

"(C) which is established or maintained by an organization incorporated on July 2, 1974.

"If, after May 1, 2004, a plan described in the preceding sentence adopts a plan amendment which provides a material change in the classes of individuals eligible to participate in the plan, this paragraph shall not apply to any nonelective deferred compensation provided under the plan on or after the date of the adoption of the amendment."

In 2003, P.L. 108-173, Sec. 1201(d)(3), deleted "and" at the end of para. (a)(10), substituted ", and" for the period at the end of para. (a)(11), and added para. (a)(12), effective for tax. yrs. begin. after 12/31/2003.

In 2002, P.L. 107-358, Sec. 2, added subsec. (c) in Sec. 901 of P.L. 107-16 [see below], effective 12/17/2002.

In 2001, P.L. 107-16, Sec. 617(d)(1), added ", including the amount of designated Roth contributions (as defined in section 402A)" before comma at the end of para. (a)(8), effective for tax. yrs. begin. after 12/31/2005.

—P.L. 107-16, Sec. 901, of this Act [as amended by Sec. 2 of P.L. 107-358, and Sec. 101(a)(1) of P.L. 111-312, see above], reads as follows:

"SEC. 901. SUNSET OF PROVISIONS OF ACT.

"(a) In general. All provisions of, and amendments made by, this Act shall not apply—

"(1) to taxable, plan, or limitation years beginning after December 31, 2012, or

"(2) in the case of title V, to estates of decedents dying, gifts made, or generation skipping transfers, after December 31, 2012.

"(b) Application of certain laws. The Internal Revenue Code of 1986 and the Employee Retirement Income Security Act of 1974 shall be applied and administered to years, estates, gifts, and transfers described in subsection (a) as if the provisions and amendments described in subsection (a) had never been enacted.

"(c) Exception. Subsection (a) shall not apply to section 803 (relating to no federal income tax on restitution received by victims of the Nazi regime or their heirs or estates)."

In 2000, P.L. 106-554, Sec. 1(a)(7), [which enacted into law Sec. 202(a)(9) of P.L. 106-554] substituted "Archer MSA" for "medical savings account" in para. (a)(11), effective 12/21/2000.

In 1996, P.L. 104-191, Sec. 301(c)(3), deleted "and" at the end of para. (a)(9), substituted ", and" for the period at the end of para. (a)(10), and added para. (a)(11), effective for tax. yrs. begin. after 12/31/96.

In 1994, P.L. 103-465, Sec. 721(b), deleted "and" at the end of para. (a)(8), substituted "and" for the period at the end of para. (a)(9), and added para. (a)(10), effective for remuneration paid after 12/31/94.

In 1988, P.L. 100-647, Sec. 1011(c)(9), added Sec. 1105(c)(6) of P.L. 99-514, which provides the effective date for changes made by Sec. 1105(b) of P.L. 99-514, see below.

—P.L. 100-647, Sec. 1011B(c)(2)(B), substituted ", and" for the period at the end of para. (a)(8) and added para. (a)(9), effective for tax. yrs. begin. after 12/31/87, except as provided in Sec. 1011B(c)(2)(C)(ii) and (iii) which reads:

"(ii) A taxpayer may elect to have the amendment made by subparagraph (A) apply to taxable years beginning in 1987."

—P.L. 100-647, Sec. 1018(u)(33), added a comma at the end of para. (a)(7), effective for calendar yrs. begin. after 12/31/86.

In 1986, P.L. 99-514, Sec. 1105(b), deleted "and" at the end of para. (a)(6), deleted the period at the end of para. (a)(7), and added para (a)(8), effective for calendar yrs. begin. after 12/31/86. For special rules, see Sec. 1105(c)(2)-(5) reproduced in note following Code Sec. 402.

In 1982, P.L. 97-362, Sec. 107(a), substituted "within 30 days after the date of receipt of a written request from the employee if such 30-day period ends before January 31" for "on the day on which the last payment of remuneration is made" in subsec. (a), effective for employees whose employment is terminated after 10/25/82.

In 1980, P.L. 96-601, Sec. 4(e), added subsec. (f), effective for payments made on or after 5/1/80 [the first day of the first calendar month begin. more than 120 days after the date of enactment (12/24/80)]

—P.L. 96-222, Sec. 101(a)(2)(D), changed the effective date for amendments made by Sec. 105(c) of P.L. 95-600 so that the amendments are effective to remuneration paid after 6/30/79 rather than effective to remuneration paid after 6/30/78.

In 1978, P.L. 95-600, Sec. 105(c), deleted "and" at the end of para. (a)(5), substituted ", and" for the period at the end of para. (a)(6), and added new para. (a)(7), effective [as amended by Sec. 101(a)(2)(D) of P.L. 96-222, see above] for remuneration paid after 6/30/79.

In 1977, P.L. 95-216, Sec. 317(b)(3), added the last sentence of subsec. (a), effective 12/20/77 [date of enactment]. Sec. 317(b)(4) of this Act provides:

"(4) Notwithstanding any other provision of law, taxes paid by any individual to any foreign country with respect to any period of employment or self-employment which is covered under the social security system of such foreign country in accordance with the terms of an agreement entered into pursuant to section 233 of the Social Security Act shall not, under the income tax laws of the United States, be deductible by, or creditable against the income tax of, any such individual."

In 1976, P.L. 94-455, Sec. 1906(a)(5), deleted "and" at the end of para. (a)(6), effective 2/1/77.
— P.L. 94-455, Sec. 1906(b)(13)(A), substituted "Secretary" for "Secretary or his delegate" in subsecs. (b), (c) and (d), effective 2/1/77.
In 1974, P.L. 93-406, Sec. 1022(k), added "or every employer engaged in a trade or business who pays remuneration for services performed by an employee, including the cash value of such remuneration paid in any medium other than cash," before "shall furnish to each such employee" in subsec. (a), effective 9/2/74 or other date as specified in Sec. 1017 of the Act (reproduced following Code Sec. 401).
In 1972, P.L. 92-603, Sec. 293(a)(1), substituted "section 3101 or 3402" for "section 3101, 3201, or 3402" in subsec. (a)... Sec. 293(a)(2), added "and" at the end of para. (a)(5), substituted a period for the comma at the end of para. (a)(6) and deleted paras. (a)(7) and (a)(8), effective for remuneration paid after 12/31/71.
Prior to deletion, paras. (a)(7) and (a)(8) read as follows:
"(7) the total amount of compensation with respect to which the tax imposed by section 3201 was deducted, and
"(8) the total amount deducted as tax under section 3201."
— P.L. 92-603, Sec. 293(b), substituted "section 3101" for "sections 3101 and 3201" in subsec. (c)... Sec. 293(c), added subsec. (e), effective for remuneration paid after 12/31/71.
In 1969, P.L. 91-172, Sec. 805(f)(2), substituted "under section 3402 (determined without regard to subsection (n)) if" for "under section 3402 if" in the first sentence of Code Sec. 6051, effective for wages paid after 4/30/70.
In 1967, P.L. 90-248, Sec. 502(c)(1)(A), substituted "section 3101, 3201, or 3402" for "section 3101 or 3402" in matter preceding para. (a)(1)... Sec. 502(c)(1)(B), deleted "and" at the end of para. (a)(5), substituted "and" for the period at the end of para. (a)(6)... Sec. 502(c)(1)(C), added paras. (a)(7) and (8) ... Sec. 502(c)(2), substituted "sections 3101 and 3201" for "section 3101" in the second sentence of subsec. (c), effective for remuneration paid after 12/31/67.
In 1965, P.L. 89-97, Sec. 107, added a sentence at the end of subsec. (c), effective 7/30/65.
— P.L. 89-97, Sec. 313(e)(1), added a sentence at the end of subsec. (a), effective for tips received by employees after 1965.
In 1961, P.L. 87-293, Sec. 202(a)(4), added a sentence at the end of subsec. (a), effective for services performed after 9/22/61, but in the case of persons serving under the Peace Corps agency established by executive order applicable with respect to service performed on or after the effective date of enrollment.
In 1956, P.L. 881, Sec. 412(a), added a sentence at the end of subsec. (a)... Sec. 412(b), amended subsec. (b), effective 1/1/57.

Sec. 6052. Returns regarding payment of wages in the form of group-term life insurance.
(a) Requirement of reporting.
Every employer who during any calendar year provides group-term life insurance on the life of an employee during part or all of such calendar year under a policy (or policies) carried directly or indirectly by such employer shall make a return according to the forms or regulations prescribed by the Secretary, setting forth the cost of such insurance and the name and address of the employee on whose life such insurance is provided, but only to the extent that the cost of such insurance is includible in the employee's gross income under section 79(a). For purposes of this section, the extent to which the cost of group-term life insurance is includible in the employee's gross income under section 79(a) shall be determined as if the employer were the only employer paying such employee remuneration in the form of such insurance.
(b) Statements to be furnished to employees with respect to whom information is required.
Every employer required to make a return under subsection (a) shall furnish to each employee whose name is required to be set forth in such return a written statement showing the cost of the group-term life insurance shown on such return. The written statement required under the preceding sentence shall be furnished to the employee on or before January 31 of the year following the calendar year for which the return under subsection (a) was required to be made.

In 1986, P.L. 99-514, Sec. 1501(c)(14), amended subsec. (b), effective for returns the due date for which (determined without regard to extensions) is after 12/31/86.
Prior to amendment, subsec. (b) read as follows:
"(b) Statements to be furnished to employees with respect to whom information is furnished.
"Every employer making a return under subsection (a) shall furnish to each employee whose name is set forth in such return a written statement showing the cost of the group-term life insurance shown on such return. The written statement required under the preceding sentence shall be furnished to the employee on or before January 31 of the year following the calendar year for which the return under subsection (a) was made."
In 1976, P.L. 94-455, Sec. 1906(b)(13)(A), substituted "Secretary" for "Secretary or his delegate" each place it appeared in Code Sec. 6052, effective 2/1/77.
In 1964, P.L. 88-272, Sec. 204(c)(1), added Code Sec. 6052, effective for group-term life insurance provided after 12/31/63, in tax. yrs. end. after 12/31/63.

Sec. 6053. Reporting of tips.
(a) Reports by employees.
Every employee who, in the course of his employment by an employer, receives in any calendar month tips which are wages (as defined in section 3121(a) or section 3401(a)) or which are compensation (as defined in section 3231(e)) shall report all such tips in one or more written statements furnished to his employer on or before the 10th day following such month. Such statements shall be furnished by the employee under such regulations, at such other times before such 10th day, and in such form and manner, as may be prescribed by the Secretary.
(b) Statements furnished by employers.
If the tax imposed by section 3101 or section 3201 (as the case may be) with respect to tips reported by an employee pursuant to subsection (a) exceeds the tax which can be collected by the employer pursuant to section 3102 or section 3202 (as the case may be), the employer shall furnish to the employee a written statement showing the amount of such excess. The statement required to be furnished pursuant to this subsection shall be furnished at such time, shall contain such other information, and shall be in such form as the Secretary may by regulations prescribe. When required by such regulations, a duplicate of any such statement shall be filed with the Secretary.
(c) Reporting requirements relating to certain large food or beverage establishments.
(1) **Report to secretary.** In the case of a large food or beverage establishment, each employer shall report to the Secretary, at such time and manner as the Secretary may prescribe by regulation, the following information with respect to each calendar year:
 (A) The gross receipts of such establishment from the provision of food and beverages (other than nonallocable receipts).
 (B) The aggregate amount of charge receipts (other than nonallocable receipts).
 (C) The aggregate amount of charged tips shown on such charge receipts.
 (D) The sum of—
  (i) the aggregate amount reported by employees to the employer under subsection (a), plus
  (ii) the amount the employer is required to report under section 6051 with respect to service charges of less than 10 percent.
 (E) With respect to each employee, the amount allocated to such employee under paragraph (3).
(2) **Furnishing of statement to employees.** Each employer described in paragraph (1) shall furnish, in such manner as the Secretary may prescribe by regulations, to each employee of the large food or beverage establishment a written statement for each calendar year showing the following information:
 (A) The name and address of such employer.
 (B) The name of the employee.
 (C) The amount allocated to the employee under paragraph (3) for all payroll periods ending within the calendar year.

Information and returns

Code Sec. 6055(b)(1)(B)

Any statement under this paragraph shall be furnished to the employee during January of the calendar year following the calendar year for which such statement is made.

(3) Employee allocation of 8 percent of gross receipts.

(A) In general. For purposes of paragraphs (1)(E) and (2)(C), the employer of a large food or beverage establishment shall allocate (as tips for purposes of the requirements of this subsection) among employees performing services during any payroll period who customarily receive tip income an amount equal to the excess of—

(i) 8 percent of the gross receipts (other than nonallocable receipts) of such establishment for the payroll period, over

(ii) the aggregate amount reported by such employees to the employer under subsection (a) for such period.

(B) Method of allocation. The employer shall allocate the amount under subparagraph (A)—

(i) on the basis of a good faith agreement by the employer and the employees, or

(ii) in the absence of an agreement under clause (i), in the manner determined under regulations prescribed by the Secretary.

(C) The secretary may lower the percentage required to be allocated. Upon the petition of the employer or the majority of employees of such employer, the Secretary may reduce (but not below 2 percent) the percentage of gross receipts required to be allocated under subparagraph (A) where he determines that the percentage of gross receipts constituting tips is less than 8 percent.

(4) Large food or beverage establishment. For purposes of this subsection, the term "large food or beverage establishment" means any trade or business (or portion thereof)—

(A) which provides food or beverages,

(B) with respect to which the tipping of employees serving food or beverages by customers is customary, and

(C) which normally employed more than 10 employees on a typical business day during the preceding calendar year.

For purposes of subparagraph (C), rules similar to the rules of subsections (a) and (b) of section 52 shall apply under regulations prescribed by the Secretary, and an individual who owns 50 percent or more in value of the stock of the corporation operating the establishment shall not be treated as an employee.

(5) Employer not to be liable for wrong allocations. The employer shall not be liable to any person if any amount is improperly allocated under paragraph (3)(B) if such allocation is done in accordance with the regulations prescribed under paragraph (3)(B).

(6) Nonallocable receipts defined. For purposes of this subsection, the term "nonallocable receipts" means receipts which are allocable to—

(A) carryout sales, or

(B) services with respect to which a service charge of 10 percent or more is added.

(7) Application to new businesses. The Secretary shall prescribe regulations for the application of this subsection to new businesses.

In 1986, P.L. 99-514, Sec. 1571, provided:
"SEC. 1571. MODIFICATION OF TIPS ALLOCATION METHOD.
"Effective for any payroll period beginning after December 31, 1986, an establishment may utilize the optional method of tips allocation described in the last sentence of section 31.6053-3(f)(1)(iv) of the Internal Revenue Regulations only if such establishment employs less than the equivalent of 25 full-time employees during such payroll period."

In 1984, P.L. 98-369, Sec. 1072(a)(1), substituted "Upon the petition of the employer or the majority of employees of such employer, the Secretary" for "The Secretary" in subpara. (c)(3)(C) . . . Sec. 1072(a)(2), substituted "2 percent" for "5 percent" in subpara. (c)(3)(C), effective 7/18/84.

—P.L. 98-369, Sec. 1072(b), provides:
"(b) *Recordkeeping by tipped employees.*—The Secretary of the Treasury shall prescribe by regulations within 1 year after the date of the enactment of this Act the applicable recordkeeping requirements for tipped employees."

—P.L. 98-369, Sec. 1072(c)(1), added ", and an individual who owns 50 percent or more in value of the stock of the corporation operating the establishment shall not be treated as an employee" after "the Secretary" at the end of para. (c)(4), effective for calendar yrs. begin. after 12/31/82.

In 1982, P.L. 97-248, Sec. 314(a), added subsec. (c), effective for calendar yrs. begin. after 12/31/82. Sec. 314(e)(2) of this Act provides:
"(2) Special rule for 1983. For purposes of section 6053(c) of the Internal Revenue Code of 1954, in the case of payroll periods ending before April 1, 1983, an employer must only report with respect to such periods—
"(A) amounts described in subparagraphs (A), (B), (C), and (D) of section 6053(c)(1) of such Code, and
"(B) the name, and identification number, wages paid to, and tips reported by, each tipped employee."

—P.L. 97-248, Sec. 314(c), provides:
"(c) *Study of tip compliance.*
"The Secretary of the Treasury or his delegate shall submit before January 1, 1987, to the Committee on Ways and Means of the House of Representatives and to the Committee on Finance of the Senate a report with respect to tip compliance in the food and beverage service industry. Such study shall include, but not be limited to, an analysis of tipping patterns, tip-sharing arrangements, and tip compliance patterns."

In 1980, P.L. 96-603, Sec. 1(c), repealed Subpart D.
Prior to repeal, Subpart D read as follows:
"SUBPART D.—INFORMATION CONCERNING PRIVATE FOUNDATIONS
"Sec.
"6056. Annual reports by private foundations."

In 1976, P.L. 94-455, Sec. 1906(b)(13)(A), substituted "Secretary" for "Secretary or his delegate" each place it appeared in Code Sec. 6053, effective 2/1/77.

In 1969, P.L. 91-172, Sec. 101(d)(3), added Subpart D.

In 1965, P.L. 89-212, Sec. 2(d), added "or which are compensation (as defined in section 3231(e))" after "or section 3401(a))" in subsec. (a), added "or section 3201 (as the case may be)" after "section 3101" and "or section 3202 (as the case may be)" after "section 3202" in subsec. (b), effective for tips received after '65.

—P.L. 89-97, Sec. 313, added Code Sec. 6053, effective for tips received by employees after 1965.

SUBPART D.—INFORMATION REGARDING HEALTH INSURANCE COVERAGE

Sec.

6055. Reporting of health insurance coverage. [effective for calendar yrs. begin. after 2013]

6056. Certain employers required to report on health insurance coverage. [effective for calendar yrs. begin. after 2013]

In 2010, P.L. 111-148, Sec. 1502(a), added Subpart D.

⎡
• *Caution:* Code Sec. 6055, following, is effective for calendar yrs. begin. after 2013.
⎦

Sec. 6055. Reporting of health insurance coverage.
(a) In general.

Every person who provides minimum essential coverage to an individual during a calendar year shall, at such time as the Secretary may prescribe, make a return described in subsection (b).

(b) Form and manner of return.

(1) In general. A return is described in this subsection if such return—

(A) is in such form as the Secretary may prescribe, and

(B) contains—

3,555

(i) the name, address and TIN of the primary insured and the name and TIN of each other individual obtaining coverage under the policy,

(ii) the dates during which such individual was covered under minimum essential coverage during the calendar year,

(iii) in the case of minimum essential coverage which consists of health insurance coverage, information concerning—

(I) whether or not the coverage is a qualified health plan offered through an Exchange established under section 1311 of the Patient Protection and Affordable Care Act, and

(II) in the case of a qualified health plan, the amount (if any) of any advance payment under section 1412 of the Patient Protection and Affordable Care Act of any cost-sharing reduction under section 1402 of such Act or of any premium tax credit under section 36B with respect to such coverage, and

(iv) such other information as the Secretary may require.

(2) Information relating to employer-provided coverage. If minimum essential coverage provided to an individual under subsection (a) consists of health insurance coverage of a health insurance issuer provided through a group health plan of an employer, a return described in this subsection shall include—

(A) the name, address, and employer identification number of the employer maintaining the plan,

(B) the portion of the premium (if any) required to be paid by the employer, and

(C) if the health insurance coverage is a qualified health plan in the small group market offered through an Exchange, such other information as the Secretary may require for administration of the credit under section 45R (relating to credit for employee health insurance expenses of small employers).

(c) Statements to be furnished to individuals with respect to whom information is reported.

(1) In general. Every person required to make a return under subsection (a) shall furnish to each individual whose name is required to be set forth in such return a written statement showing—

(A) the name and address of the person required to make such return and the phone number of the information contact for such person, and

(B) the information required to be shown on the return with respect to such individual.

(2) Time for furnishing statements. The written statement required under paragraph (1) shall be furnished on or before January 31 of the year following the calendar year for which the return under subsection (a) was required to be made.

(d) Coverage provided by governmental units.

In the case of coverage provided by any governmental unit or any agency or instrumentality thereof, the officer or employee who enters into the agreement to provide such coverage (or the person appropriately designated for purposes of this section) shall make the returns and statements required by this section.

(e) Minimum essential coverage.

For purposes of this section, the term "minimum essential coverage" has the meaning given such term by section 5000A(f).

In 2010, P.L. 111-148, Sec. 1502(a), added Code Sec. 6055, effective for calendar years begin. after 2013.

> • *Caution:* Code Sec. 6056, following, is effective for periods begin. after 12/31/2013.

Sec. 6056. Certain employers required to report on health insurance coverage.

(a) In general.

Every applicable large employer required to meet the requirements of section 4980H with respect to its full-time employees during a calendar year shall, at such time as the Secretary may prescribe, make a return described in subsection (b).

(b) Form and manner of return.

A return is described in this subsection if such return—

(1) is in such form as the Secretary may prescribe, and

(2) contains—

(A) the name, date, and employer identification number of the employer,

(B) a certification as to whether the employer offers to its full-time employees (and their dependents) the opportunity to enroll in minimum essential coverage under an eligible employer-sponsored plan (as defined in section 5000A(f)(2)),

(C) if the employer certifies that the employer did offer to its full-time employees (and their dependents) the opportunity to so enroll—

(i) the length of any waiting period (as defined in section 2701(b)(4) of the Public Health Service Act) with respect to such coverage,

(ii) the months during the calendar year for which coverage under the plan was available,

(iii) the monthly premium for the lowest cost option in each of the enrollment categories under the plan, and

(iv) the employer's share of the total allowed costs of benefits provided under the plan,

(v) Repealed.

(D) the number of full-time employees for each month during the calendar year,

(E) the name, address, and TIN of each full-time employee during the calendar year and the months (if any) during which such employee (and any dependents) were covered under any such health benefits plans, and

(F) such other information as the Secretary may require. The Secretary shall have the authority to review the accuracy of the information provided under this subsection, including the applicable large employer's share under paragraph (2)(C)(iv).

(c) Statements to be furnished to individuals with respect to whom information is reported.

(1) In general. Every person required to make a return under subsection (a) shall furnish to each full-time employee whose name is required to be set forth in such return under subsection (b)(2)(E) a written statement showing—

(A) the name and address of the person required to make such return and the phone number of the information contact for such person, and

(B) the information required to be shown on the return with respect to such individual.

Information and returns   Code Sec. 6057(a)(1)

(2) Time for furnishing statements. The written statement required under paragraph (1) shall be furnished on or before January 31 of the year following the calendar year for which the return under subsection (a) was required to be made.

(d) Coordination with other requirements.

To the maximum extent feasible, the Secretary may provide that—

(1) any return or statement required to be provided under this section may be provided as part of any return or statement required under section 6051 or 6055, and

(2) in the case of an applicable large employer offering health insurance coverage of a health insurance issuer, the employer may enter into an agreement with the issuer to include information required under this section with the return and statement required to be provided by the issuer under section 6055.

(e) Coverage provided by governmental units.

In the case of any applicable large employer which is a governmental unit or any agency or instrumentality thereof, the person appropriately designated for purposes of this section shall make the returns and statements required by this section.

(f) Definitions.

For purposes of this section, any term used in this section which is also used in section 4980H shall have the meaning given such term by section 4980H.

In **2011**, P.L. 112-10, Sec. 1858(b)(5)(A), deleted "and every offering employer" after "during a calendar year" in subsec. (a) . . . Sec. 1858(b)(5)(B)(i), deleted "in the case of an applicable large employer," before "the length of any waiting period" in clause (b)(2)(C)(i) . . . Sec. 1858(b)(5)(B)(ii), added "and" at the end of clause (b)(2)(C)(iii) . . . Sec. 1858(b)(5)(B)(iii), deleted "and" at the end of clause (b)(2)(C)(iv) . . . Sec. 1858(b)(5)(B)(iv), deleted clause (b)(2)(C)(v) . . . Sec. 1858(b)(5)(C), deleted "or offering employer" after "applicable large employer" in para. (d)(2) and subsec. (e) . . . Sec. 1858(b)(5)(D), amended subsec. (f), effective for periods begin. after 12/31/2013, as if included in the provisions of Sec. 10108(j) of P.L. 111-148 [see below].

Prior to deletion, clause (b)(2)(C)(v) read as follows:

"(v) in the case of an offering employer, the option for which the employer pays the largest portion of the cost of the plan and the portion of the cost paid by the employer in each of the enrollment categories under such option,"

Prior to amendment, subsec. (f) read as follows:

"(f) Definitions. For purposes of this section—

"(1) Offering employer.

"(A) In general. The term 'offering employer' means any offering employer (as defined in section 10108(b) of the Patient Protection and Affordable Care Act) if the required contribution (within the meaning of section 5000A(e)(1)(B)(i)) of any employee exceeds 8 percent of the wages (as defined in section 3121(a)) paid to such employee by such employer.

"(B) Indexing. In the case of any calendar year beginning after 2014, the 8 percent under subparagraph (A) shall be adjusted for the calendar year to reflect the rate of premium growth between the preceding calendar year and 2013 over the rate of income growth for such period.

"(2) Other definitions. Any term used in this section which is also used in section 4980H shall have the meaning given such term by section 4980H."

In **2010**, P.L. 111-148, Sec. 1514(a), added Code Sec. 6056, effective for periods begin. after 12/31/2013.

—P.L. 111-148, Sec. 10106(g), added a flush sentence at the end of subsec. (b), enacted 3/23/2010.

—P.L. 111-148, Sec. 10108(j)(1), added "and every offering employer" before "shall" in subsec. (a) . . . Sec. 10108(j)(2), amended subsec. (f)

Prior to amendment, subsec. (f) read as follows:

"(f) Definitions. For purposes of this section, any term used in this section which is also used in section 4980H shall have the meaning given such term by section 4980H."

—P.L. 111-148, Sec. 10108(j)(3)(A), substituted "Certain" for "Large" in the heading of Code Sec. 6056 . . . Sec. 10108(j)(3)(B)(i), added "in the case of an applicable large employer," before "the length" in clause (b)(2)(C)(i) . . . Sec. 10108(j)(3)(B)(ii), deleted "and" at the end of clause (b)(2)(C)(iii) . . . Sec. 10108(j)(3)(B)(iii), substituted "employer" for "applicable large employer" in clause (b)(2)(C)(iv) . . . Sec. 10108(j)(3)(B)(iv), added "and" at the end of clause (b)(2)(C)(iv) . . . Sec. 10108(j)(3)(B)(v), added clause (b)(2)(C)(v) . . . Sec. 10108(j)(3)(C), added "or offering employer" after "applicable large employer" in para. (d)(2) . . . Sec. 10108(j)(3)(D), added "or offering employer" after "applicable large employer" in subsec. (e), effective for periods begin. after 12/31/2013.

SUBPART D.—REPEALED. [INFORMATION CONCERNING PRIVATE FOUNDATIONS]

Sec.

6056. Repealed [Annual registration, etc.]

In **1980**, P.L. 96-603, Sec. 1(c), repealed Subpart D.

Sec. 6056. Repealed.

In **1980**, P.L. 96-603, Sec. 1(c), repealed Code Sec. 6056, effective for tax. yrs. begin. after 12/31/80.

Prior to repeal, Code Sec. 6056 read as follows:

"SEC. 6056. ANNUAL REPORTS BY PRIVATE FOUNDATIONS.

"(a) General.

"The foundation managers (within the meaning of section 4946(b)) of every organization which is a private foundation (within the meaning of section 509(a)) having at least $5,000 of assets at any time during a taxable year shall file an annual report as of the close of the taxable year at such time and in such manner as the Secretary may by regulations prescribe.

"(b) Contents.

"The foundation managers of the private foundation shall set forth in the annual report required under subsection (a) the following information:

"(1) its gross income for the year,

"(2) its expenses attributable to such income and incurred within the year,

"(3) its disbursements (including administrative expenses) within the year,

"(4) a balance sheet showing its assets, liabilities, and net worth as of the beginning of the year,

"(5) an itemized statement of its securities and all other assets at the close of the year, showing both book and market value,

"(6) the total of the contributions and gifts received by it during the year,

"(7) an itemized list of all grants and contributions made or approved for future payment during the year, showing the amount of each such grant or contribution, the name and address of the recipient, any relationship between any individual recipient and the foundation's managers or substantial contributors, and a concise statement of the purpose of each such grant or contribution,

"(8) the address of the principal office of the foundation and (if different) of the place where its books and records are maintained,

"(9) the names and addresses of its foundation managers (within the meaning of section 4946(b)), and

"(10) a list of all persons described in paragraph (9) that are substantial contributors (within the meaning of section 507(d)(2)) or that own 10 percent or more of the stock of any corporation of which the foundation owns 10 percent or more of the stock, or corresponding interests in partnerships or other entities, in which the foundation has a 10 percent or greater interest.

"(c) Form.

"The annual report may be prepared in printed, typewritten, or any other legible form the foundation chooses. The Secretary shall provide forms which may be used by a private foundation for purposes of the annual report.

"(d) Special rules.

"(1) The annual report required to be filed under this section is in addition to and not in lieu of the information required to be filed under section 6033 (relating to returns by exempt organizations) and shall be filed at the same time as such information.

"(2) A copy of the notice required by section 6104(d) (relating to public inspection of private foundations' annual reports), together with proof of publication thereof, shall be filed by the foundation managers together with the annual report.

"(3) The foundation managers shall furnish copies of the annual report required by this section to such State officials and other persons, at such times and under such conditions, as the Secretary may by regulations prescribe."

In **1976**, P.L. 94-455, Sec. 1906(b)(13)(A), substituted "Secretary" for "Secretary or his delegate" each place it appeared in Code Sec. 6056, effective 2/1/77.

In **1969**, P.L. 91-172, Sec. 101(d)(3), added Code Sec. 6056, effective for tax. yrs. begin. after 12/31/69.

SUBPART E.—REGISTRATION OF AND INFORMATION CONCERNING PENSION, ETC., PLANS

Sec.

6057. Annual registration, etc.

6058. Information required in connection with certain plans of deferred compensation.

6059. Periodic report of actuary.

In **1974**, P.L. 93-406, Sec. 1031(a), added Subpart E.

Sec. 6057. Annual registration, etc.

(a) Annual registration.

(1) General rule. Within such period after the end of a plan year as the Secretary may by regulations prescribe, the plan administrator (within the meaning of section

3,557

414(g)) of each plan to which the vesting standards of section 203 of part 2 of subtitle B of title I of the Employee Retirement Income Security Act of 1974 applies for such plan year shall file a registration statement with the Secretary.

(2) Contents. The registration statement required by paragraph (1) shall set forth—

(A) the name of the plan,
(B) the name and address of the plan administrator,
(C) the name and taxpayer identifying number of each participant in the plan—
   (i) who, during such plan year, separated from the service covered by the plan,
   (ii) who is entitled to a deferred vested benefit under the plan as of the end of such plan year, and
   (iii) with respect to whom retirement benefits were not paid under the plan during such plan year,
(D) the nature, amount, and form of the deferred vested benefit to which such participant is entitled, and
(E) such other information as the Secretary may require.

At the time he files the registration statement under this subsection, the plan administrator shall furnish evidence satisfactory to the Secretary that he has complied with the requirement contained in subsection (e).

(b) Notification of change in status.

Any plan administrator required to register under subsection (a) shall also notify the Secretary, at such time as may be prescribed by regulations, of—

(1) any change in the name of the plan,
(2) any change in the name or address of the plan administrator,
(3) the termination of the plan, or
(4) the merger or consolidation of the plan with any other plan or its division into two or more plans.

(c) Voluntary reports.

To the extent provided in regulations prescribed by the Secretary, the Secretary may receive from—

(1) any plan to which subsection (a) applies, and
(2) any other plan (including any governmental plan or church plan (within the meaning of section 414)),

such information (including information relating to plan years beginning before January 1, 1974) as the plan administrator may wish to file with respect to the deferred vested benefit rights of any participant separated from the service covered by the plan during any plan year.

(d) Transmission of information to Commissioner of Social Security.

The Secretary shall transmit copies of any statements, notifications, reports, or other information obtained by him under this section to the Commissioner of Social Security.

(e) Individual statement to participant.

Each plan administrator required to file a registration statement under subsection (a) shall, before the expiration of the time prescribed for the filing of such registration statement, also furnish to each participant described in subsection (a)(2)(C) an individual statement setting forth the information with respect to such participant required to be contained in such registration statement. Such statement shall also include a notice to the participant of any benefits which are forfeitable if the participant dies before a certain date.

(f) Regulations.

(1) In general. The Secretary, after consultation with the Commissioner of Social Security, may prescribe such regulations as may be necessary to carry out the provisions of this section.

(2) Plans to which more than one employer contributes. This section shall apply to any plan to which more than one employer is required to contribute only to the extent provided in regulations prescribed under this subsection.

(g) Cross references.

For provisions relating to penalties for failure to register or furnish statements required by this section, see section 6652(d) and section 6690.

For coordination between Department of the Treasury and the Department of Labor with regard to administration of this section, see section 3004 of the Employee Retirement Income Security Act of 1974.

In 1997, P.L. 105-34, Sec. 1510, of this Act, relating to new technologies in retirement plans, provides:
"Sec. 1510. New technologies in retirement plans.
"(a) In General.—Not later than December 31, 1998, the Secretary of the Treasury and the Secretary of Labor shall each issue guidance which is designed to—
"(1) interpret the notice, election, consent, disclosure, and time requirements (and related recordkeeping requirements) under the Internal Revenue Code of 1986 and the Employee Retirement Income Security Act of 1974 relating to retirement plans as applied to the use of new technologies by plan sponsors and administrators while maintaining the protection of the rights of participants and beneficiaries, and
"(2) clarify the extent to which writing requirements under the Internal Revenue Code of 1986 relating to retirement plans shall be interpreted to permit paperless transactions.
"(b) Applicability of Final Regulations.—Final regulations applicable to the guidance regarding new technologies described in subsection (a) shall not be effective until the first plan year beginning at least 6 months after the issuance of such final regulations."

In 1994, P.L. 103-296, Sec. 108(h)(5), substituted "Commissioner of Social Security" for "Secretary of Health and Human Services" in subsec. (d) and para. (f)(1), effective 3/31/95.

In 1986, P.L. 99-514, Sec. 1501(d)(1)(F), substituted "section 6652(d)" for "section 6652(e)" in subsec. (g), effective for returns the due date for which (determined without regard to extensions) is after 12/31/86.

In 1984, P.L. 98-397, Sec. 206, added the last sentence of subsec. (e), effective for plan yrs. begin. after 12/31/84.
—P.L. 98-369, Sec. 2663(j)(5)(D), substituted "Health and Human Services" for "Health, Education, and Welfare" each place it appeared in subsecs. (d) and (f), effective on 7/18/84, except as provided in Sec. 2664(b) of this Act which states "none of such amendments shall be construed as changing or affecting any right, liability, status, or interpretation which existed (under the provisions of law involved) before that date."

In 1976, P.L. 94-455, Sec. 1506(b)(13)(A), substituted "Secretary" for "Secretary or his delegate" each place it appeared in Code Sec. 6057, effective 2/1/77.

In 1974, P.L. 93-406, Sec. 1031(a), added Code Sec. 6057, effective for plan yrs. begin. after 12/31/75.

Sec. 6058. Information required in connection with certain plans of deferred compensation.

(a) In general.

Every employer who maintains a pension, annuity, stock bonus, profit-sharing, or other funded plan of deferred compensation described in part I of subchapter D of chapter 1, or the plan administrator (within the meaning of section 414(g)) of the plan, shall file an annual return stating such information as the Secretary may by regulations prescribe with respect to the qualification, financial condition, and operations of the plan; except that, in the discretion of the Secretary, the employer may be relieved from stating in its return any information which is reported in other returns.

(b) Actuarial statement in case of mergers, etc.

Not less than 30 days before a merger, consolidation, or transfer of assets or liabilities of a plan described in subsection (a) to another plan, the plan administrator (within the meaning of section 414(g)) shall file an actuarial statement of valuation evidencing compliance with the requirements of section 401(a)(12).

(c) Employer.

For purposes of this section, the term "employer" includes a person described in section 401(c)(4) and an individual who establishes an individual retirement plan.

Information and returns   Code Sec. 6060

(d) Coordination with income tax returns, etc.

An individual who establishes an individual retirement plan shall not be required to file a return under this section with respect to such plan for any taxable year for which there is—

(1) no special IRP tax, and

(2) no plan activity other than—

(A) the making of contributions (other than rollover contributions), and

(B) the making of distributions.

(e) Special IRP tax defined.

For purposes of this section, the term "special IRP tax" means a tax imposed by—

(1) section 408(f),

(2) section 4973, or

(3) section 4974.

(f) Cross references.

For provisions relating to penalties for failure to file a return required by this section, see section 6652(e).

For coordination between the Department of the Treasury and the Department of Labor with respect to the information required under this section, see section 3004 of title III of the Employee Retirement Income Security Act of 1974.

In 1986, P.L. 99-514, Sec. 1501(d)(1)(D), substituted "section 6652(e)" for "section 6652(f)" in subsec. (f), effective for returns the due date for which (determined without regard to extensions) is after 12/31/86.

In 1984, P.L. 98-369, Sec. 491(d)(48), deleted para. (e)(2) and redesignated paras. (e)(3) and (4) as paras. (e)(2) and (3), effective for obligations issued after 12/31/83.

Prior to deletion, para. (e)(2) read as follows:

"(2) section 409(c),"

In 1978, P.L. 95-600, Sec. 157(k)(1), redesignated subsec. (d) as subsec. (f), deleted subsec. (c), added new subsecs. (c), (d), and (e), effective for returns for tax. yrs. begin. after 12/31/77.

Prior to amendment, subsec. (c) read as follows:

"(c) Employer.

"For purposes of this section, the term 'employer' includes a person described in section 401(c)(4) and an individual who establishes an individual retirement account or annuity described in section 408."

In 1976, P.L. 94-455, Sec. 1906(b)(13)(A), substituted "Secretary" for "Secretary or his delegate" each place it appeared in Code Sec. 6058, effective 2/1/77.

In 1974, P.L. 93-406, Sec. 1031(a), added Code Sec. 6058, except that the requirements of subsec. (a) are effective for plan yrs. begin. after 9/2/74.

Sec. 6059. Periodic report of actuary.

(a) General rule.

The actuarial report described in subsection (b) shall be filed by the plan administrator (as defined in section 414(g)) of each defined benefit plan to which section 412 applies, for the first plan year for which section 412 applies to the plan and for each third plan year thereafter (or more frequently if the Secretary determines that more frequent reports are necessary).

(b) Actuarial report.

The actuarial report of a plan required by subsection (a) shall be prepared and signed by an enrolled actuary (within the meaning of section 7701(a)(35)) and shall contain—

(1) a description of the funding method and actuarial assumptions used to determine costs under the plan,

(2) a certification of the contribution necessary to reduce the minimum required contribution determined under section 430, or the accumulated funding deficiency determined under section 431, to zero,

(3) a statement—

(A) that to the best of his knowledge the report is complete and accurate, and

(B) the requirements for reasonable actuarial assumptions under section 430(h)(1) or 431(c)(3), whichever are applicable, have been complied with,

(4) such other information as may be necessary to fully and fairly disclose the actuarial position of the plan, and

(5) such other information regarding the plan as the Secretary may by regulations require.

(c) Time and manner of filing.

The actuarial report and statement required by this section shall be filed at the time and in the manner provided by regulations prescribed by the Secretary.

(d) Cross reference.

For coordination between the Department of the Treasury and the Department of Labor with respect to the report required to be filed under this section, see section 3004 of title III of the Employee Retirement Income Security Act of 1974.

In 2008, P.L. 110-458, Sec. 101(d)(3), added Sec. 114(g) of the Pension Protection Act of 2006 [see P.L. 109-280 below].

In 2006, P.L. 109-280, Sec. 114(f)(1), substituted "the minimum required contribution determined under section 430, or the accumulated funding deficiency determined under section 431," for "the accumulated funding deficiency (as defined in section 412(a)" in para. (b)(2) ... Sec. 114(f)(2), amended subpara. (b)(3)(B), enacted 8/17/2006. . . . Sec. 114(g), of this Act [as amended by Sec. 101(d)(3), P.L. 110-458, 12/23/2008, see above], read as follows:

"(g) Effective dates.

"(1) In general. The amendments made by this section shall apply to plan years beginning after 2007.

"(2) Excise tax. The amendments made by subsection (e) shall apply to taxable years beginning after 2007, but only with respect to plan years described in paragraph (1) which end with or within any such taxable year."

Prior to amendment, subpara. (b)(3)(B) read as follows:

"(B) the requirements of section 412(c) (relating to reasonable actuarial assumptions) have been complied with,"

In 1976, P.L. 94-455, Sec. 1906(b)(13)(A), substituted 'Secretary' for 'Secretary or his delegate' each place it appeared in Code Sec. 6059, effective 2/1/77.

In 1974, P.L. 93-406, Sec. 1033(a), added Code Sec. 6059, effective 9/2/74 or other date as specified in Sec. 1017 of this Act, reproduced in note following Code Sec. 401.

SUBPART F.—INFORMATION CONCERNING TAX RETURN PREPARERS

Sec.

6060. Information returns of tax return preparers.

Sec. 6060. Information returns of tax return preparers.

(a) General rule.

Any person who employs a tax return preparer to prepare any return or claim for refund other than for such person at any time during a return period shall make a return setting forth the name, taxpayer identification number, and place of work of each tax return preparer employed by him at any time during such period. For purposes of this section, any individual who in acting as a tax return preparer is not the employee of another tax return preparer shall be treated as his own employer. The return required by this section shall be filed, in such manner as the Secretary may by regulations prescribe, on or before the first July 31 following the end of such return period.

(b) Alternative reporting.

In lieu of the return required by subsection (a), the Secretary may approve an alternative reporting method if he determines that the necessary information is available to him from other sources.

(c) Return period defined.

For purposes of subsection (a), the term 'return period' means the 12-month period beginning on July 1 of each year, except that the first return period shall be the 6-month period beginning on January 1, 1977, and ending on June 30, 1977.

In 2007, P.L. 110-28, Sec. 8246(a)(2)(A)(i), substituted 'tax return preparers' for 'income tax return preparers' in the heading of Code Sec. 6060 . . . Sec. 8246(a)(2)(A)(ii)(I), substituted 'a tax return preparer' for 'an income tax return preparer' each place it appeared in subsec. (a) . . . Sec. 8246(a)(2)(A)(ii)(II), substituted 'each tax return preparer' for 'each income tax return preparer' in subsec. (a) . . . Sec. 8246(a)(2)(A)(ii)(III), substituted 'another tax return preparer' for 'an-

3,559

other income tax return preparer' in subsec. (a), effective for returns prepared after 5/25/2007.
In **1976**, P.L. 94-455, Sec. 1203(e), added Code Sec. 6060 as subpart F, effective for documents prepared after 12/31/76.

PART IV.—SIGNING AND VERIFYING OF RETURNS AND OTHER DOCUMENTS

Sec.
6061. Signing of returns and other documents.
6062. Signing of corporation returns.
6063. Signing of partnership returns.
6064. Signature presumed authentic.
6065. Verification of returns.

Sec. 6061. Signing of returns and other documents.
(a) General rule.
Except as otherwise provided by subsection (b) and sections 6062 and 6063, any return, declaration, statement, or other document required to be made under any provision of the internal revenue laws or regulations shall be signed in accordance with forms or regulations prescribed by the Secretary.
(b) Electronic signatures.
   (1) In general. The Secretary shall develop procedures for the acceptance of signatures in digital or other electronic form. Until such time as such procedures are in place, the Secretary may—
      (A) waive the requirement of a signature for; or
      (B) provide for alternative methods of signing or subscribing,
a particular type or class of return, declaration, statement, or other document required or permitted to be made or written under internal revenue laws and regulations.
   (2) Treatment of alternative methods. Notwithstanding any other provision of law, any return, declaration, statement, or other document filed and verified, signed, or subscribed under any method adopted under paragraph (1)(B) shall be treated for all purposes (both civil and criminal, including penalties for perjury) in the same manner as though signed or subscribed.
   (3) Published guidance. The Secretary shall publish guidance as appropriate to define and implement any waiver of the signature requirements or any method adopted under paragraph (1).

In **1998**, P.L. 105-206, Sec. 2003(a)(1), substituted '(a) General Rule. Except as otherwise provided by subsection (b) and' for 'Except as otherwise provided by' in Code Sec. 6061 . . . Sec. 2003(a)(2), added subsec. (b), effective 7/22/98.
In **1976**, P.L. 94-455, Sec. 1906(b)(13)(A), substituted 'Secretary' for 'Secretary or his delegate' in Code Sec. 6061, effective 2/1/77.

Sec. 6062. Signing of corporation returns.
The return of a corporation with respect to income shall be signed by the president, vice-president, treasurer, assistant treasurer, chief accounting officer or any other officer duly authorized so to act. In the case of a return made for a corporation by a fiduciary pursuant to the provisions of section 6012(b)(3), such fiduciary shall sign the return. The fact that an individual's name is signed on the return shall be prima facie evidence that such individual is authorized to sign the return on behalf of the corporation.

Sec. 6063. Signing of partnership returns.
The return of a partnership made under section 6031 shall be signed by any one of the partners. The fact that a partner's name is signed on the return shall be prima facie evidence that such partner is authorized to sign the return on behalf of the partnership.

Sec. 6064. Signature presumed authentic.
The fact that an individual's name is signed to a return, statement, or other document shall be prima facie evidence

for all purposes that the return, statement, or other document was actually signed by him.

Sec. 6065. Verification of returns.
Except as otherwise provided by the Secretary, any return, declaration, statement, or other document required to be made under any provision of the internal revenue laws or regulations shall contain or be verified by a written declaration that it is made under the penalties of perjury.

In **1976**, P.L. 94-455, Sec. 1906(a)(6), deleted subsec. (b) and deleted the heading of subsec. (a), effective 2/1/77.
Prior to deletion subsec. (b) read as follows:
"(b) Oath.
"The Secretary or his delegate may by regulations require that any return, statement, or other document required to be made under any provision of the internal revenue laws or regulations shall be verified by an oath. This subsection shall not apply to returns and declarations with respect to income taxes made by individuals."
Prior to deletion the heading of subsec. (a) read as follows:
"(a) Penalties of perjury."
—P.L. 94-455, Sec. 1906(b)(13)(A), substituted "Secretary" for "Secretary or his delegate" in Code Sec. 6065, effective 2/1/77.

PART V.—TIME FOR FILING RETURNS AND OTHER DOCUMENTS

Sec.
6071. Time for filing returns and other documents.
6072. Time for filing income tax returns.
6073. Repealed [Time for filing declarations of estimated income tax by individuals.]
6075. Time for filing estate and gift tax returns.
6076. Repealed [Time for filing return of windfall profit tax.]

In **1988**, P.L. 100-418, Sec. 1941(b)(3)(C), deleted item 6076.
Prior to deletion, item 6076 read as follows:
"6076. Time for filing return of windfall profit tax."
In **1984**, P.L. 98-369, Sec. 412(c)(2), deleted item 6073.
Prior to deletion, item 6073 read as follows:
"6073. Time for filing declarations of estimated income tax by individuals."
In **1980**, P.L. 96-223, Sec. 101(c)(1)(B), added item 6076.
In **1964**, added item 6075.

Sec. 6071. Time for filing returns and other documents.
(a) General rule.
When not otherwise provided for by this title, the Secretary shall by regulations prescribe the time for filing any return, statement, or other document required by this title or by regulations.
(b) Electronically filed information returns.
Returns made under subparts B and C of part III of this subchapter which are filed electronically shall be filed on or before March 31 of the year following the calendar year to which such returns relate.
(c) Special taxes.
For payment of special taxes before engaging in certain trades and businesses, see section 4901 and section 5732.

In **2005**, P.L. 109-59, Sec. 11125(b)(21), substituted "section 5732" for "section 5142" in subsec. (c), effective 7/1/2008, but not for taxes imposed for periods before 7/1/2008.
In **1998**, P.L. 105-206, Sec. 2002(a), redesignated subsec. (b) as subsec. (c) and added new subsec. (b), effective for returns required to be filed after 12/31/99.
In **1976**, P.L. 94-455, Sec. 1906(b)(13)(A), substituted "Secretary" for "Secretary or his delegate" in subsec. (a) effective 2/1/77.
In **1958**, P.L. 85-859, Sec. 20<(l), added "and section 5142" after "section 4901" in subsec. (b), effective 9/3/58.

Sec. 6072. Time for filing income tax returns.
(a) General rule.
In the case of returns under section 6012, 6013, 6017, or 6031 (relating to income tax under subtitle A), returns made on the basis of the calendar year shall be filed on or before

Information and returns Code Sec. 6073

the 15th day of April following the close of the calendar year and returns made on the basis of a fiscal year shall be filed on or before the 15th day of the fourth month following the close of the fiscal year, except as otherwise provided in the following subsections of this section.

(b) Returns of corporations.

Returns of corporations under section 6012 made on the basis of the calendar year shall be filed on or before the 15th day of March following the close of the calendar year, and such returns made on the basis of a fiscal year shall be filed on or before the 15th day of the third month following the close of the fiscal year. Returns required for a taxable year by section 6011(e)(2) (relating to returns of a DISC) shall be filed on or before the fifteenth day of the ninth month following the close of the taxable year.

(c) Returns by certain nonresident alien individuals and foreign corporations.

Returns made by nonresident alien individuals (other than those whose wages are subject to withholding under chapter 24) and foreign corporations (other than those having an office or place of business in the United States or a former FSC (as defined in section 922 as in effect before its repeal by the FSC Repeal and Extraterritorial Income Exclusion Act of 2000)) under section 6012 on the basis of a calendar year shall be filed on or before the 15th day of June following the close of the calendar year and such returns made on the basis of a fiscal year shall be filed on or before the 15th day of the 6th month following the close of the fiscal year.

(d) Returns of cooperative associations.

In the case of an income tax return of—

(1) an exempt cooperative association described in section 1381(a)(1), or

(2) an organization described in section 1381(a)(2) which is under an obligation to pay patronage dividends (as defined in section 1388(a)) in an amount equal to at least 50 percent of its net earnings from business done with or for its patrons, or which paid patronage dividends in such an amount out of the net earnings from business done with or for patrons during the most recent taxable year for which it had such net earnings,

a return made on the basis of a calendar year shall be filed on or before the 15th day of September following the close of the calendar year, and a return made on the basis of a fiscal year shall be filed on or before the 15th day of the 9th month following the close of the fiscal year.

(e) Organizations exempt from taxation under section 501(a).

In the case of an income tax return of an organization exempt from taxation under section 501(a) (other than an employees' trust described in section 401(a)), a return shall be filed on or before the 15th day of the 5th month following the close of the taxable year.

In **2007,** P.L. 110-172, Sec. 11(g)(20), substituted "a former FSC (as defined in section 922 as in effect before its repeal by the FSC Repeal and Extraterritorial Income Exclusion Act of 2000)" for "a FSC or former FSC" in subsec. (c), enacted 12/29/2007.

In **1984,** P.L. 98-369, Sec. 801(d)(13), added "or a FSC or former FSC" after "United States" in subsec. (c), effective for transactions after 12/31/84, in tax. yrs. end after 12/31/84.

In **1978,** P.L. 95-628, Sec. 6(a), added subsec. (e), effective for tax. yrs. begin. after 11/10/78.

In **1976,** P.L. 94-455, Sec. 1053(d)(3), repealed subsec. (e), effective for tax. yrs. begin. after 12/31/77.

Prior to repeal, subsec. (e) read as follows:

"*(e) Income tax due dates postponed in case of China Trade Act corporations.*

"In the case of any taxable year beginning after December 31, 1948, and ending before October 1, 1956, no Federal income tax return of any corporation organized under the China Trade Act, 1922 (42 Stat. 849, U. S. C., title 15, chapter 4), as amended, shall become due until December 31, 1956, but only with respect to any such corporation and any such taxable year which the Secretary or his delegate may determine reasonable under the circumstances in China pursuant to such regulations as may be prescribed. Such due date shall be subject to the power of the Secretary or his delegate to extend the time for filing such return, as in other cases."

In **1971,** P.L. 92-178, Sec. 504(b), added the sentence at the end of subsec. (b), effective for tax. yrs. end. after 12/31/71, except that a corporation may not be a DISC for any tax. yr. begin. before 1/1/72.

In **1962,** P.L. 87-834, Sec. 17(b)(3), amended subsec. (d), effective for tax. yrs. begin. after 12/31/62.

Prior to amendment, subsec. (d) read as follows:

"*(d) Returns of exempt cooperative associations.*

"In the case of income tax returns of exempt cooperative associations taxable under the provisions of section 522, returns made on the basis of a calendar year shall be filed on or before the 15th day of September following the close of the calendar year and returns made on the basis of a fiscal year shall be filed on or before the 15th day of the 9th month following the close of the fiscal year."

In **1959,** P.L. 86-69, Sec. 3(i), provided that:

"Every life insurance company subject to the tax imposed by section 802(a) of the Internal Revenue Code of 1954 (as amended by section 2 of this Act) shall, after the date of the enactment of this Act [6/25/59] and on or before September 15, 1959 (in lieu of at the time prescribed by section 6072(b) of such Code, make a return for its taxable year beginning in 1958 with respect to the tax imposed by such section (as amended by section 2 of this Act). The return required by this subsection for such taxable year shall constitute the return for such taxable year for all purposes of the Internal Revenue Code of 1954; and no return for such taxable year, with respect to the tax imposed by part I of subchapter L of chapter 1 of such Code (as in effect prior to the effective date of the amendment made by section 2 of this Act), filed on or before the date of the enactment of this Act shall be considered for any of such purposes as a return for such taxable year. All payments made on or before the date of the enactment of this Act with respect to the tax for such taxable year imposed by part I of subchapter L of chapter 1 of such Code (as in effect prior to the effective date of the amendment made by section 2 of this Act), to the extent that such payments have not been credited or refunded, shall be deemed to be payments made on September 15, 1959, on account of the tax for such taxable year imposed by section 802(a) of such Code (as amended by section 2 of this Act). The provisions of section 6152(a)(1) of such Code shall not apply with respect to the tax for such taxable year imposed by section 802(a) of such Code (as amended by section 2 of this Act)."

Sec. 6073. Repealed.

In **1984,** P.L. 98-369, Sec. 412(a)(2), repealed Code Sec. 6073, effective for tax. yrs. begin. after 12/31/84.

Prior to repeal, Code Sec. 6073 read as follows:

"SEC. 6073. TIME FOR FILING DECLARATIONS OF ESTIMATED INCOME TAX BY INDIVIDUALS.

"*(a) Individuals other than farmers or fisherman.*

"Declarations of estimated tax required by section 6015 from individuals regarded as neither farmers nor fisherman for the purpose of that section shall be filed on or before April 15 of the taxable year, except that if the requirements of section 6015 are first met—

"(1) After April 1 and before June 2 of the taxable year, the declaration shall be filed on or before June 15 of the taxable year, or

"(2) After June 1 and before September 2 of the taxable year, the declaration shall be filed on or before September 15 of the taxable year, or

"(3) After September 1 of the taxable year, the declaration shall be filed on or before January 15 of the succeeding taxable year.

In the case of a nonresident alien described in section 6072(c), the requirements of section 6015 shall be deemed to be first met no earlier than after April 1 and before June 2 of the taxable year.

"*(b) Farmers or fishermen.*

"Declarations of estimated tax required by section 6015 from any individual—

"(1) whose estimated gross income from farming or fishing (including oyster farming) for the taxable year is at least two-thirds of the total estimated gross income from all sources for the taxable year, or

"(2) whose gross income from farming or fishing (including oyster farming) shown on the return of the individual for the preceding taxable year is at least two-thirds of the total gross income from all sources shown on such return.

may, in lieu of the time prescribed in subsection (a), be filed at any time on or before January 15 of the taxable year succeeding the taxable year.

"*(c) Amendment.*

"An amendment of a declaration may be filed in any interval between installment dates prescribed for that taxable year, but only one amendment may be filed in each such interval.

"*(d) Short taxable years.*

"The application of this section to taxable years of less than 12 months shall be in accordance with regulations prescribed by the Secretary.

"*(e) Fiscal years.*

"In the application of this section to the case of a taxable year beginning on any date other than January 1, there shall be substituted, for the months specified in this section, the months which correspond thereto.

"*(f) Termination.*

"This section shall not apply to any taxable year beginning after December 31, 1982."

In **1982,** P.L. 97-248, Sec. 328(b)(2), added subsec. (f), effective for tax. yrs. begin. after 12/31/82.

Code Sec. 6073

In 1978, P.L. 95-628, Sec. 7(a), amended subsec. (b), effective for declarations of estimated tax for tax. yrs. begin. after 11/10/78.
Prior to amendment, subsec. (b) read as follows:
"(b) Farmers or fishermen.
"Declarations of estimated tax required by section 6015 from individuals whose estimated gross income from farming or fishing (including oyster farming) for the taxable year is at least two-thirds of the total estimated gross income from all sources for the taxable year may, in lieu of the time prescribed in subsection (a), be filed at any time on or before January 15 of the succeeding taxable year."
In 1976, P.L. 94-455, Sec. 1012(c), added the sentence at the end of subsec. (a), for tax. yrs. end. on or after '75.
—P.L. 94-455, Sec. 1906(b)(13)(A), substituted "Secretary" for "Secretary or his delegate" in subsec. (d), effective 2/1/77.
In 1962, P.L. 87-682, Sec. 1, substituted "individuals regarded as neither farmers nor fishermen" for "individuals not regarded as farmers" in the text, and inserted "or Fishermen" in the catchline of subsec. (a) . . . inserted "or fishing" following "from farming" in the text, and "or Fishermen" in the catchline of subsec. (b), for tax. yrs. begin. after '62.

Sec. 6075. Time for filing estate and gift tax returns.

> • **Caution:** Sec. 301(a), P.L. 111-312, (reproduced in the history notes following this Code Sec.) provides that the amendments made by Sec. 542(b)(3)(A), P.L. 107-16, EGTRRA, will apply as if never enacted. Code Sec. 6075(a), following, reflects the removal of these amendments, effective for estates of decedents dying, and transfers made, after 12/31/2009.

(a) Estate tax returns.
Returns made under section 6018(a) (relating to estate taxes) shall be filed within 9 months after the date of the decedent's death.

> • **Caution:** Code Sec. 6075(a), was amended by Sec. 542(b)(3)(A), P.L. 107-16, EGTRRA. As provided in Sec. 301(a), P.L. 111-312, this amendment will apply as if never enacted, effective for estates of decedents dying, and transfers made, after 12/31/2009.

(a) Returns relating to large transfers at death.
The return required by section 6018 with respect to a decedent shall be filed with the return of the tax imposed by chapter 1 for the decedent's last taxable year or such later date specified in regulations prescribed by the Secretary.

(b) Gift tax returns.
(1) General rule. Returns made under section 6019 (relating to gift taxes) shall be filed on or before the 15th day of April following the close of the calendar year.
(2) Extension where taxpayer granted extension for filing income tax return. Any extension of time granted the taxpayer for filing the return of income taxes imposed by subtitle A for any taxable year which is a calendar year shall be deemed to be also an extension of time granted the taxpayer for filing the return under section 6019 for such calendar year.

> • **Caution:** Sec. 301(a), P.L. 111-312, (reproduced in the history notes following this Code Sec.) provides that the amendments made by Sec. 542(b)(3)(B)(i)-(ii), P.L. 107-16, EGTRRA, will apply as if never enacted. Code Sec. 6075(b)(3), following, reflects the removal of these amendments, effective for estates of decedents dying, and transfers made, after 12/31/2009.

(3) Coordination with due date for estate tax return. Notwithstanding paragraphs (1) and (2), the time for filing the return made under section 6019 for the calendar year which includes the date of death of the donor shall not be later than the time (including extensions) for filing the return made under section 6018 (relating to estate tax returns) with respect to such donor.

> • **Caution:** Code Sec. 6075(b)(3), was amended by Sec. 542(b)(3)(B)(i)-(ii), P.L. 107-16, EGTRRA. As provided in Sec. 301(a), P.L. 111-312, this amendment will apply as if never enacted, effective for estates of decedents dying, and transfers made, after 12/31/2009.

(3) Coordination with due date for section 6018 return. Notwithstanding paragraphs (1) and (2), the time for filing the return made under section 6019 for the calendar year which includes the date of death of the donor shall not be later than the time (including extensions) for filing the return made under section 6018 (relating to returns relating to large transfers at death) with respect to such donor.

In 2010, P.L. 111-312, Sec 101(a)(1), substituted "December 31, 2012" for "December 31, 2010" both places it appeared in Sec. 901, P.L. 107-16 [see below], effective as if included in the enactment of P.L. 107-16, EGTRRA, 6/7/2001.
—P.L. 111-312, Sec. 301(a), provides that Code Sec. 6075, as amended by Sec. 542(b)(3)(A) and (B)(i)-(ii), P.L. 107-16, EGTRRA, 6/7/2001 [see below] will read as if such provision had never been enacted, effective for estates of decedents dying, and transfers made, after 12/31/2009.
Sec. 301(a), P.L. 111-312, 12/17/2010, provides:
"(a) In general. Each provision of law amended by subtitle A or E of title V of the Economic Growth and Tax Relief Reconciliation Act of 2001 [P.L. 107-16, see below] is amended to read as such provision would read if such subtitle had never been enacted."
Prior to amendment by Sec. 542(b)(3)(A) of P.L. 107-16, subsec. (a) read as follows:
"(a) Returns relating to large transfers at death. The return required by section 6018 with respect to a decedent shall be filed with the return of the tax imposed by chapter 1 for the decedent's last taxable year or such later date specified in regulations prescribed by the Secretary."
Prior to amendment by Sec. 542(b)(3)(B)(i)-(ii) of P.L. 107-16, para. (b)(3) read as follows:
"(3) Coordination with due date for section 6018 return. Notwithstanding paragraphs (1) and (2), the time for filing the return made under section 6019 for the calendar year which includes the date of death of the donor shall not be later than the time (including extensions) for filing the return made under section 6018 (relating to returns relating to large transfers at death) with respect to such donor."
—P.L. 111-312, Sec. 301(c), of this Act, provides
"(c) Special election with respect to estates of decedents dying in 2010. Notwithstanding subsection (a), in the case of an estate of a decedent dying after December 31, 2009, and before January 1, 2011, the executor (within the meaning of section 2203 of the Internal Revenue Code of 1986) may elect to apply such Code as though the amendments made by subsection (a) do not apply with respect to chapter 11 of such Code and with respect to property acquired or passing from such decedent (within the meaning of section 1014(b) of such Code). Such election shall be made at such time and in such manner as the Secretary of the Treasury or the Secretary's delegate shall provide. Such an election once made shall be revocable only with the consent of the Secretary of the Treasury or the Secretary's delegate. For purposes of section 2652(a)(1) of such Code, the determination of whether any property is subject to the tax imposed by such chapter 11 shall be made without regard to any election made under this subsection."
—P.L. 111-312, Sec. 301(d), of this Act, provides
"(d) Extension of time for performing certain acts.
"(1) Estate tax. In the case of the estate of a decedent dying after December 31, 2009, and before the date of the enactment of this Act, the due date for—
"(A) filing any return under section 6018 of the Internal Revenue Code of 1986 (including any election required to be made on such a return) as such section is in effect after the date of the enactment of this Act without regard to any election under subsection (c),
"(B) making any payment of tax under chapter 11 of such Code, and
"(C) making any disclaimer described in section 2518(b) of such Code of an interest in property passing by reason of the death of such decedent, shall not be earlier than the date which is 9 months after the date of the enactment of this Act.
"(2) Generation-skipping tax. In the case of any generation-skipping transfer made after December 31, 2009, and before the date of the enactment of this Act, the due date for filing any return under section 2662 of the Internal Revenue Code of 1986 (including any election required to be made on such a return) shall not be

Information and returns

Code Sec. 6091(b)

earlier than the date which is 9 months after the date of the enactment of this Act."

In 2002, P.L. 107-358, Sec. 2, added subsec. (c) in Sec. 901 of P.L. 107-16 [see below], effective 12/17/2002.

In 2001, P.L. 107-16, Sec. 542(b)(3)(A), amended subsec. (a) . . . Sec. 542(b)(3)(B)(i), substituted "section 6018 return" for "estate tax return" in the heading of para. (b)(3) . . . Sec. 542(b)(3)(B)(ii), substituted "(relating to returns relating to large transfers at death)" for "(relating to estate tax returns)" in para. (b)(3), effective for estates of decedents dying after 12/31/2009.

Prior to amendment, subsec. (a) read as follows:

"(a) Estate tax returns. Returns made under section 6018(a) (relating to estate taxes) shall be filed within 9 months after the date of the decedent's death."

—P.L. 107-16, Sec. 901, of this Act [as amended by Sec. 2, P.L. 107-358, and Sec. 101(a)(1), P.L. 111-312, see above], reads as follows:

"SEC. 901. SUNSET OF PROVISIONS OF ACT.

"(a) In general. All provisions of, and amendments made by, this Act shall not apply—

"(1) to taxable, plan, or limitation years beginning after December 31, 2012, or

"(2) in the case of title V, to estates of decedents dying, gifts made, or generation skipping transfers, after December 31, 2012.

"(b) Application of certain laws. The Internal Revenue Code of 1986 and the Employee Retirement Income Security Act of 1974 shall be applied and administered to years, estates, gifts, and transfers described in subsection (a) as if the provisions and amendments described in subsection (a) had never been enacted.

"(c) Exception. Subsection (a) shall not apply to section 803 (relating to no federal income tax on restitution received by victims of the Nazi regime or their heirs or estates)."

In 1981, P.L. 97-34, Sec. 442(d)(3), amended subsec. (b), effective for gifts made after 12/31/81.

Prior to amendment, subsec. (b), read as follows:

"(b) Gift tax returns.

"(1) General rule. Except as provided in paragraph (2), returns made under section 6019 (relating to gift taxes) shall be filed on or before—

"(A) in the case of a return for the first, second, or third calendar quarter of any calendar year, the 15th day of the second month following the close of the calendar quarter, or

"(B) in the case of a return for the fourth calendar quarter of any calendar year, the 15th day of the fourth month following the close of the calendar quarter.

"(2) Special rule where gifts in a calendar quarter total $25,000 or less. If the total amount of taxable gifts made by a person during a calendar quarter is $25,000 or less, the return under section 6019 for such quarter shall be filed on or before the date prescribed by paragraph (1) for filing the return for—

"(A) the first subsequent calendar quarter in the calendar year in which the sum of—

"(i) the taxable gifts made during such subsequent quarter, plus

"(ii) all other taxable gifts made during the calendar year and for which a return has not yet been required to be filed under this subsection,

exceeds $25,000, or

"(B) if a return is not required to be filed under subparagraph (A), the fourth calendar quarter of the calendar year.

"(3) Extension where taxpayer granted extension for filing income tax return. Any extension of time granted the taxpayer for filing the return of income taxes imposed by subtitle A for any taxable year which is a calendar year shall be deemed to be also an extension of time granted the taxpayer for filing the return under section 6019 for the fourth calendar quarter of such taxable year.

"(4) Nonresidents not citizens of the United States. In the case of a nonresident not a citizen of the United States, paragraph (2) shall be applied by substituting '$12,500' for '$25,000' each place it appears."

In 1979, P.L. 96-167, Sec. 8, amended para. (b)(1), redesignated para. (b)(3) as para. (b)(4), added new para. (b)(3), substituted "the date prescribed by paragraph (1) for filing the return for" for "the 15th day of the second month after" in para. (b)(2), deleted "the close of" following "under subparagraph (A)" in subpara. (b)(2)(A), deleted "the close of" at the beginning of subpara. (b)(2)(B), effective for returns for gifts made in calendar yrs. ending after 12/29/79.

Prior to amendment, para. (b)(1) read as follows:

"(1) General rule. Except as provided in paragraph (2), returns made under section 6019 (relating to gift taxes) shall be filed on or before the 15th day of the second month following the close of the calendar quarter."

In 1976, P.L. 94-455, Sec. 2008(b), amended subsec. (b), effective for gifts made after 12/31/76.

Prior to amendment, subsec. (b) read as follows:

"(b) Gift tax returns.

"Returns made under section 6019 (relating to gift taxes) shall be filed on or before the 15th day of the second month following the close of the calendar quarter."

In 1970, P.L. 91-614, Sec. 101(b), substituted "9 months" for "15 months," in subsec. (a), effective for decedents dying after 12/31/70.

—P.L. 91-614, Sec. 102(d)(4), substituted "the second month following the close of the calendar quarter" for "April following the close of the calendar year," effective for gifts made after 12/31/70.

Sec. 6076. Repealed.

In 1988, P.L. 100-418, Sec. 1941(b)(1), repealed Code Sec. 6076, effective for crude oil removed from the premises on or after 8/23/88.

Prior to repeal Code Sec. 6076 read as follows:

"SEC. 6076. TIME FOR FILING RETURN OF WINDFALL PROFIT TAX.

"(a) General rule.

" Except in the case of a return required by regulations prescribed under section 4995(a)(5), each return—

"(1) of the tax imposed by section 4986 (relating to windfall profit tax) for any taxable period (within the meaning of section 4996(b)(7)), or

"(2) by a person required under section 4995(a) to withhold the windfall profit tax for any taxable period,

"shall be filed not later than the last day of the second month following the close of the taxable period.

"(b) Cross reference.

"For depositary requirements applicable to the tax imposed by section 4986, see section 4995(b)."

In 1980, P.L. 96-223, Sec. 101(c)(1)(A), added Code Sec. 6076, effective for periods after 2/29/80.

PART VI.—EXTENSION OF TIME FOR FILING RETURNS

Sec.

6081. Extension of time for filing returns.

Sec. 6081. Extension of time for filing returns.

(a) General rule.

The Secretary may grant a reasonable extension of time for filing any return, declaration, statement, or other document required by this title or by regulations. Except in the case of taxpayers who are abroad, no such extension shall be for more than 6 months.

(b) Automatic extension for corporation income tax returns.

An extension of 3 months for the filing of the return of income taxes imposed by subtitle A shall be allowed any corporation if, in such manner and at such time as the Secretary may by regulations prescribe, there is filed on behalf of such corporation the form prescribed by the Secretary, and if such corporation pays, on or before the date prescribed for payment of the tax, the amount properly estimated as its tax; but this extension may be terminated at any time by the Secretary by mailing to the taxpayer notice of such termination at least 10 days prior to the date for termination fixed in such notice.

(c) Cross references.

For time for performing certain acts postponed by reason of war, see section 7508, and by reason of Presidentially declared disaster or terroristic or military action, see section 7508A.

In 2002, P.L. 107-134, Sec. 112(d)(2), amended subsec. (c), effective for disasters and terroristic or military actions occurring on or after 9/11/2001, with respect to any action of the Secretary of the Treasury, the Secretary of Labor, or the Pension Benefit Guaranty Corporation occurring on or after 1/23/2002.

Prior to amendment, subsec. (c) read as follows:

"(c) Postponement by reason of war. For time for performing certain acts postponed by reason of war, see section 7508."

In 1982, P.L. 97-248, Sec. 234(b)(2)(B), deleted "or the first installment thereof required under section 6152" after "the amount properly estimated as its tax" in subsec. (b), effective for tax. yrs. begin. after 12/31/82.

In 1976, P.L. 94-455, Sec. 1906(b)(13)(A), substituted "Secretary" for "Secretary or his delegate" each place it appeared in Code Sec. 6081, effective 2/1/77.

PART VII.—PLACE FOR FILING RETURNS OR OTHER DOCUMENTS

Sec.

6091. Place for filing returns or other documents.

Sec. 6091. Place for filing returns or other documents.

(a) General rule.

When not otherwise provided for by this title, the Secretary shall by regulations prescribe the place for the filing of any return, declaration, statement, or other document, or copies thereof, required by this title or by regulations.

(b) Tax returns.

In the case of returns of tax required under authority of part II of this subchapter—

3,563

Code Sec. 6091(b)(1) — Information and returns

(1) Persons other than corporations.

(A) General rule. Except as provided in subparagraph (B), a return (other than a corporation return) shall be made to the Secretary—

(i) in the internal revenue district in which is located the legal residence or principal place of business of the person making the return, or

(ii) at a service center serving the internal revenue district referred to in clause (i), as the Secretary may by regulations designate.

(B) Exception. Returns of—

(i) persons who have no legal residence or principal place of business in any internal revenue district,

(ii) citizens of the United States whose principal place of abode for the period with respect to which the return is filed is outside the United States,

(iii) persons who claim the benefits of section 911 (relating to citizens or residents of the United States living abroad), section 931 (relating to income from sources within Guam, American Samoa, or the Northern Mariana Islands), or section 933 (relating to income from sources within Puerto Rico),

(iv) nonresident alien persons, and

(v) persons with respect to whom an assessment was made under section 6851(a) or 6852(a) (relating to termination assessments) with respect to the taxable year,

shall be made at such place as the Secretary may by regulations designate.

(2) Corporations.

(A) General rule. Except as provided in subparagraph (B), a return of a corporation shall be made to the Secretary—

(i) in the internal revenue district in which is located the principal place of business or principal office or agency of the corporation, or

(ii) at a service center serving the internal revenue district referred to in clause (i), as the Secretary may by regulations designate.

(B) Exception. Returns of—

(i) corporations which have no principal place of business or principal office or agency in any internal revenue district,

(ii) corporations which claim the benefits of section 936 (relating to possession tax credit),

(iii) foreign corporations, and

(iv) corporations with respect to which an assessment was made under section 6851(a) (relating to termination assessments) with respect to the taxable year,

shall be made at such place as the Secretary may by regulations designate.

(3) Estate tax returns.

(A) General rule. Except as provided in subparagraph (B), returns of estate tax required under section 6018 shall be made to the Secretary—

(i) in the internal revenue district in which was the domicile of the decedent at the time of his death, or

(ii) at a service center serving the internal revenue district referred to in clause (i), as the Secretary may by regulations designate.

(B) Exception. If the domicile of the decedent was not in an internal revenue district, or if he had no domicile, the estate tax return required under section 6018 shall be made at such place as the Secretary may by regulations designate.

(4) Hand-carried returns. Notwithstanding paragraph (1), (2), or (3), a return to which paragraph (1)(A), (2)(A), or (3)(A) would apply, but for this paragraph, which is made to the Secretary by hand-carrying shall, under regulations prescribed by the Secretary, be made in the internal revenue district referred to in paragraph (1)(A)(i), (2)(A)(i), or (3)(A)(i), as the case may be.

(5) Exceptional cases. Notwithstanding paragraph (1), (2), (3), or (4) of this subsection, the Secretary may permit a return to be filed in any internal revenue district, and may require the return of any officer or employee of the Treasury Department to be filed in any internal revenue district selected by the Secretary.

(6) Alcohol, tobacco, and firearms returns, etc. In the case of any return of tax imposed by section 4181 or subtitle E (relating to taxes on alcohol, tobacco, and firearms), subsection (a) shall apply (and this subsection shall not apply).

In 1989, P.L. 101-239, Sec. 7841(f), added "section 4181 or" before "subtitle E" in para. (b)(6), effective 12/19/89.

In 1987, P.L. 100-203, Sec. 10713(b)(2)(A), substituted "section 6851(a) or 6852(a)" for "section 6581(a)" in clause (b)(1)(B)(v), effective 12/22/87.

In 1986, P.L. 99-514, Sec. 1272(d)(10), substituted "Guam, American Samoa, or the Northern Mariana Islands" for "possessions of the United States" in clause (b)(1)(B)(iii), effective for tax. yrs. begin. after 12/31/86.

Secs. 1277(b) and (e) of this Act provide special rules as follows:

"(b) Special rule for Guam, American Samoa, and the Northern Mariana Islands.

"The amendments made by this subtitle shall apply with respect to Guam, American Samoa, or the Northern Mariana Islands (and to residents thereof and corporations created or organized therein) only if (and so long as) an implementing agreement under section 1271 is in effect between the United States and such possession."

*　　　*　　　*　　　*　　　*

"(e) Treatment of certain United States persons.

"Except as otherwise provided in regulations prescribed by the Secretary of the Treasury or his delegate, if a United States person becomes a resident of Guam, American Samoa, or the Northern Mariana Islands, the rules of section 877(c) of the Internal Revenue Code of 1954 shall apply to such person during the 10-year period beginning when such person became such a resident. The preceding sentence shall apply to dispositions after December 31, 1985, in taxable years ending after such date."

—P.L. 99-514, Sec. 1879(r)(1), added para. (b)(6), effective on the first day of the first calendar month which begins more than 90 days after 10/22/86.

In 1981, P.L. 97-34, Sec. 111(b)(3), substituted "relating to citizens or residents of the United States living abroad" for "relating to income earned by employees in certain camps" in clause (b)(1)(B)(iii) . . . Sec. 112(b)(6), deleted "section 913 (relating to deduction for certain expenses of living abroad)" before "section 931" in subpara. (b)(1)(B), effective for tax. yrs. begin. after 12/31/81.

In 1980, P.L. 96-222, Sec. 108(a)(1)(A), redesignated Sec. 202(f) of P.L. 95-615 as Sec. 202(g) [see below].

In 1978, P.L. 95-615, Sec. 202(g)(5), [as redesignated by Sec. 108(a)(1)(A) of P.L. 96-222, see above] substituted "relating to income earned by employees in certain camps" for "relating to earned income from sources without the United States" in clause (b)(1)(B)(iii) . . . Sec. 207(b), added "section 913 (relating to deduction for certain expenses of living abroad)", before "section 931" in clause (b)(1)(B)(iii), effective for tax. yrs. begin. after 12/31/77.

In 1976, P.L. 94-455, Sec. 1051(h)(4), substituted "section 936 (relating to possession tax credit)," for "section 931 (relating to income from sources within possessions of the United States)," in clause (b)(2)(B)(ii), effective for tax. yrs. begin. after 12/31/79.

—P.L. 94-455, Sec. 1052(c)(6), amended clause (b)(2)(B)(ii), effective for tax. yrs. begin. after 12/31/79.

Prior to amendment, clause (b)(2)(B)(ii) read as follows:

"(ii) corporations which claim the benefits of section 922 (relating to special deduction for Western Hemisphere trade corporations) or section 936 (relating to possession tax credit)."

—P.L. 94-455, Sec. 1053(d)(4), substituted "or" for the comma following "trade corporations)" and deleted "or section 941 (relating to the special deduction for China Trade Act corporations)," in clause (b)(2)(B)(ii), effective for tax. yrs. begin. after 12/31/77.

—P.L. 94-455, Sec. 1204(c)(3)(A), deleted "and" at the end of clause (b)(1)(B)(iii), amended clause (b)(1)(B)(iv), and added clause (b)(1)(B)(v) . . . Sec. 1204(c)(3)(B), deleted "and" at the end of clause (b)(2)(B)(ii), amended clause (b)(2)(B)(iii), and added clause (b)(2)(B)(iv), effective [as amended by Sec. 2(a) of P.L. 94-528, see below] for action taken under Code Secs. 6851, 6861 or 6862 of the Internal Revenue Code of 1954 where notice and demand takes place after 2/28/77.

Prior to amendment, clause (b)(1)(B)(iv) read as follows:

3,564

Information and returns — Code Sec. 6096

"(iv) nonresident alien persons, shall be made at such place as the Secretary or his delegate may by regulations designate."
Prior to amendment, clause (b)(2)(B)(iii) read as follows:
"(iii) foreign corporations, shall be made at such place as the Secretary or his delegate may by regulations designate."
—P.L. 94-455, Sec. 1906(b)(13)(A), substituted "Secretary" for "Secretary or his delegate" each place it appeared in subsecs. (a) and (b), effective 2/1/77.
—P.L. 94-528, Sec. 2(a), substituted "February 28, 1977" for "December 31, 1976" in Sec. 1204(d) of P.L. 94-455, the effective date for amendments made by Sec. 1204(c) of P.L. 94-455 [see above], effective 10/4/76.
In 1970, P.L. 91-614, Sec. 101(i)(1), amended para. (b)(3) . . . Sec. 101(i)(2), amended para. (b)(4), effective for decedents dying after 12/31/70.
Prior to amendment, paras. (b)(3) and (b)(4) read as follows:
"(3) Estate tax returns. Returns of estate tax required under section 6018 shall be made to the Secretary or his delegate in the internal revenue district in which was the domicile of the decedent at the time of his death or, if there was no such domicile in an internal revenue district, then at such place as the Secretary or his delegate may by regulations prescribe.
"(4) Hand-carried returns. Notwithstanding paragraph (1) or (2), a return to which paragraph (1)(A) or (2)(A) would apply, but for this paragraph, which is made to the Secretary or his delegate by hand carrying shall, under regulations prescribed by the Secretary or his delegate, be made in the internal revenue district referred to in paragraph (1)(A)(i) or (2)(A)(i), as the case may be."
In 1966, P.L. 89-713, Sec. 1(a)(1), amended paras. (b)(1) and (2) . . . Sec. 1(a)(2), redesignated para. (b)(4) as para. (b)(5), and substituted "(3), or (4)" for "or (3)" in para. (b)(5) [as redesignated] . . . Sec. 1(a)(3), added new para. (b)(4), effective 11/2/66.
Prior to amendment, paras. (b)(1) and (2) read as follows:
"(1) Individuals. Returns (other than corporation returns) shall be made to the Secretary or his delegate in the internal revenue district in which is located the legal residence or principal place of business of the person making the return, or, if he has no legal residence or principal place of business in any internal revenue district, then at such place as the Secretary or his delegate may by regulations prescribe.
"(2) Corporations. Returns of corporations shall be made to the Secretary or his delegate in the internal revenue district in which is located the principal place of business or principal office or agency of the corporation or, if it has no principal place of business or principal office or agency in any internal revenue district, then at such place as the Secretary or his delegate may by regulations prescribe."

PART VIII.—DESIGNATION OF INCOME TAX PAYMENTS TO PRESIDENTIAL ELECTION CAMPAIGN FUND

Sec.
6096. Designation by individuals.

In 1966, P.L. 89-809, Sec. 302, added Part VIII and item 6096.

Sec. 6096. Designation by individuals.
(a) In general.
Every individual (other than a nonresident alien) whose income tax liability for the taxable year is $3 or more may designate that $3 shall be paid over to the Presidential Election Campaign Fund in accordance with the provisions of section 9006(a). In the case of a joint return of husband and wife having an income tax liability of $6 or more, each spouse may designate that $3 shall be paid to the fund.
(b) Income tax liability.
For purposes of subsection (a), the income tax liability of an individual for any taxable year is the amount of the tax imposed by chapter 1 on such individual for such taxable year (as shown on his return), reduced by the sum of the credits (as shown in his return) allowable under part IV of subchapter A of chapter 1 (other than subpart C thereof).
(c) Manner and time of designation.
A designation under subsection (a) may be made with respect to any taxable year—
  (1) at the time of filing the return of the tax imposed by chapter 1 for such taxable year, or
  (2) at any other time (after the time of filing the return of the tax imposed by chapter 1 for such taxable year) specified in regulations prescribed by the Secretary.
Such designation shall be made in such manner as the Secretary prescribes by regulations except that, if such designation is made at the time of filing the return of the tax imposed by chapter 1 for such taxable year, such designation shall be made either on the first page of the return or on the page bearing the taxpayer's signature.

In 1993, P.L. 103-66, Sec. 13441(a)(1), substituted "$3" for "$1" each place it appeared in subsec. (a) . . . Sec. 13441(a)(2), substituted "$6" for "$2" in subsec. (a), effective for tax returns required to be filed after 12/31/93.
In 1986, P.L. 99-514, Sec. 231(a)(2)(A), amended Sec. 221(d)(1) of P.L. 97-34, the effective date for changes made by Sec. 221(c)(1) of P.L. 97-34, by substituting "amounts paid or incurred after June 30, 1981" for "amounts paid or incurred after June 30, 1981 and before January 1, 1986" [see below].
In 1984, P.L. 98-369, Sec. 474(r)(31), substituted "allowable under part IV of subchapter A of chapter 1 (other than subpart C thereof)" for "allowable under sections 33, 37, 38, 40, 41, 42, 44, 44A, 44B, 44C, 44D, 44E, 44F, 44G, and 44H" in subsec. (b), effective for tax. yrs. begin. after 12/31/83, and for carrybacks from tax. yrs. begin. after 12/31/83.
In 1983, P.L. 97-414, Sec. 4(c)(2), substituted "44G, and 44H" for "and 44G" in subsec. (b), effective amounts paid or incurred after 12/31/82, in tax. yrs. end. after 12/31/82.
In 1981, P.L. 97-34, Sec. 221(c)(1), substituted "44E, and 44F" for "and 44E" in subsec. (b), effective [as amended by Sec. 231(a)(2)(A) of P.L. 99-514, see above] for amounts paid or incurred after June 30, 1981. For transitional rule, see Sec. 221(d)(2) of this Act reproduced in note following Code Sec. 44F.
—P.L. 97-34, Sec. 331(e)(1), substituted "44F and 44G" for "and 44F" in subsec. (b), effective for tax. yrs. begin. after 12/31/81.
In 1980, P.L. 96-223, Sec. 231(b)(2), substituted "44C, and 44D" for "and 44C" in para. (b), for tax. yrs. end. after 12/31/79.
—P.L. 96-223, Sec. 232(b)(3)(C), substituted "44D, and 44E" for "and 44D" in subsec. (b), effective for sales or uses after 9/30/80, in tax. yrs. end. after 9/30/80.
In 1978, P.L. 95-618, Sec. 101(b)(4), substituted "44B, and 44C" for "and 44B" in subsec. (b), effective for tax. yrs. end. on or after 4/20/77.
In 1977, P.L. 95-30, Sec. 202(d)(6), substituted "44A, and 44B" for "and 44A" in subsec. (b), effective for tax. yrs. begin. after 12/31/76 and to credit carrybacks from such yrs.
In 1976, P.L. 94-455, Sec. 401(a)(2)(C), substituted "41, and 42" for "and 41" in subsec. (b), effective for tax. yrs. end. after 12/31/75 and before 1/1/78.
—P.L. 94-455, Sec. 504(c)(2), substituted "44, and 44A" for "and 44" in subsec. (b), effective for tax. yrs. begin. after 12/31/75.
—P.L. 94-455, Sec. 1906(b)(13)(A), substituted "Secretary" for "Secretary or his delegate" in each place it appeared in Code Sec. 6096, effective 2/1/77.
In 1975, P.L. 94-164, Sec. 2(e), extended the effective date for amendments made by Sec. 203 of P.L. 94-12, to include tax. yrs. end. after 12/31/74 and before 1/1/77.
—P.L. 94-12, Sec. 203(b)(4), substituted "41, and 42" for "and 41" in subsec. (b), effective for tax. yrs. end. after 12/31/74 and before 1/1/76.
—P.L. 94-12, Sec. 208(d)(4), substituted "42, and 44" for "and 42" in subsec. (b), as amended by Sec. 203(b)(4) of this Act, effective 3/29/75.
In 1973, P.L. 93-53, Sec. 6(a), amended Code Sec. 6096 effective for to taxable years beginning after December 31, 1972.
"Any designation made under section 6096 of the Internal Revenue Code of 1954 (as in effect for taxable years beginning before January 1, 1973) for the account of the candidates of any specified political party shall, for purposes of section 9006(a) of such Code (as amended by subsection (b)), be treated solely as a designation to the Presidential Election Campaign Fund."
Prior to amendment, Code Sec. 6096, read as follows:
"(a) In general.
"Every individual (other than a nonresident alien) whose income tax liability for any taxable year is $1 or more may designate that $1 shall be paid over to the Presidential Election Campaign Fund for the account of the candidates of any specified political party for President and Vice President of the United States, or if no specific account is designated by such individual, for a general account for all candidates for election to the offices of President and Vice President of the United States, in accordance with the provisions of section 9006(a)(1). In the case of a joint return of husband and wife having an income tax liability of $2 or more, each spouse may designate that $1 shall be paid to any such account in the fund.
"(b) Income tax liability.
"For purposes of subsection (a), the income tax liability of an individual for any taxable year is the amount of the tax imposed by chapter 1 on such individual for such taxable year (as shown on his return), reduced by the sum of the credits (as shown in his return) allowable under sections 32(2), 33, 35, 37, and 38.
"(c) Manner and time of designation.
"A designation under subsection (a) may be made with respect to any taxable year, in such manner as the Secretary or his delegate may prescribe by regulations—
"(1) at the time of filing the return of the tax imposed by chapter 1 for such taxable year, or
"(2) at any other time (after the time of filing the return of the tax imposed by chapter 1 for such taxable year) specified in regulations prescribed by the Secretary or his delegate."
In 1971, P.L. 92-178, Sec. 802(a), amended subsec. (a), effective for tax. yrs. end. on or after 12/31/72.
Prior to amendment, subsec. (a) read as follows:
"(a) In general.
"Every individual (other than a nonresident alien) whose income tax liability for any taxable year is $1 or more may designate that $1 shall be paid into the

3,565

Presidential Election Campaign Fund established by section 303 of the Presidential Election Campaign Fund Act of 1966."

In 1967, P.L. 90-26, Sec. 5, provided that Code Sec. 6096 shall become applicable only after adoption by law of guidelines governing distribution of the funds and such guidelines should state expressly that they were intended to comply with this section.

In 1966, P.L. 89-809, Sec. 302, added Code Sec. 6096, effective for tax. yrs. beginning after 12/31/66.

Subchapter B.—Miscellaneous Provisions

Sec.
6101. Period covered by returns or other documents.
6102. Computations on returns or other documents.
6103. Confidentiality and disclosure of returns and return information.
6104. Publicity of information required from certain exempt organizations and certain trusts.
6105. Confidentiality of information arising under treaty obligations.
6106. Repealed. [Publicity of unemployment tax returns.]
6107. Income tax return preparer must furnish copy of return to taxpayer and must retain a copy or list.
6108. Statistical publications and studies.
6109. Identifying numbers.
6110. Public inspection of written determinations.
6111. Disclosure of reportable transactions.
6112. Material advisors of reportable transactions must keep lists of advisees, etc.
6113. Disclosure of nondeductibility of contributions.
6114. Treaty-based return positions.
6115. Disclosure related to quid pro quo contributions.
6116. Cross reference.

In 2004, P.L. 108-357, Sec. 815(b)(1), amended item 6111.... Sec. 815(b)(4), amended item 6112.
Prior to amendment, items 6111 and 6112 read as follows:
"6111. Registration of tax shelters.
"6112. Organizers and sellers of potentially abusive tax shelters must keep lists of investors."
In 2000, P.L. 106-554, Sec. 1(a)(7) [which enacted into law Sec. 304(b)(2) of H.R. 5662], added the item for Code Sec. 6105
In 1993, P.L. 103-66, Sec. 13173(c)(1), redesignated item 6115 as item 6116 and added new item 6115.
In 1988, P.L. 100-647, Sec. 1012(aa)(5)(C)(i), redesignated item 6114 as item 6115 and added new item 6114.
In 1987, P.L. 100-203, Sec. 10701(c)(1), redesignated item 6113 as 6114 and added new item 6113.
In 1984, P.L. 98-369, Sec. 141(c)(1), redesignated item 6111 as 6112 and added new item 6111 ... Sec. 142(c)(1), redesignated item 6112 as 6113 and added new item 6112.
In 1976, P.L. 94-455, Sec. 1201(c), redesignated the item for Code Sec. 6110 as the item for Code Sec. 6111 ... added a new item for Code Sec. 6110.
—P.L. 94-455, Sec. 1202(a)(2), amended the item for Code Sec. 6103.
Prior to amendment, the item for Code Sec. 6103 read as follows:
"6103. Publicity of returns and disclosures of information as to persons filing income tax returns."
—P.L. 94-455, Sec. 1202(h)(1), repealed Code Sec. 6106, but Congress did not provide an amendment to delete that item from the above table.
—P.L. 94-455, Sec. 1203(i)(2), added the item for Code Sec. 6107.
—P.L. 94-455, Sec. 1906(b)(2), amended the item for Code Sec. 6111, as previously amended by the Act.
Prior to amendment, the item for Code Sec. 6111 read as follows:
"Sec. 6111. Cross References."
In 1966, P.L. 89-713, Sec. 4(b), substituted "disclosure of information as to persons filing income tax returns" for "lists of taxpayers" in item 6103.
In 1961, added item 6109 and redesignated former item 6109 as 6110.

Sec. 6101. Period covered by returns or other documents.

When not otherwise provided for by this title, the Secretary may by regulations prescribe the period for which, or the date as of which, any return, statement, or other document required by this title or by regulations, shall be made.

In 1976, P.L. 94-455, Sec. 1906(b)(13)(A), substituted "Secretary" for "Secretary or his delegate" in Code Sec. 6101, effective 2/1/77.

Sec. 6102. Computations on returns or other documents.

(a) Amounts shown on Internal Revenue forms.

The Secretary is authorized to provide with respect to any amount required to be shown on a form prescribed for any internal revenue return, statement, or other document, that if such amount of such item is other than a whole-dollar amount, either—

(1) the fractional part of a dollar shall be disregarded; or

(2) the fractional part of a dollar shall be disregarded unless it amounts to one-half dollar or more, in which case the amount (determined without regard to the fractional part of a dollar) shall be increased by $1.

(b) Election not to use whole dollar amounts.

Any person making a return, statement, or other document shall be allowed, under regulations prescribed by the Secretary, to make such return, statement, or other document without regard to subsection (a).

(c) Inapplicability to computation of amount.

The provisions of subsections (a) and (b) shall not be applicable to items which must be taken into account in making the computations necessary to determine the amount required to be shown on a form, but shall be applicable only to such final amount.

In 1976, P.L. 94-455, Sec. 1906(b)(13)(A), substituted "Secretary" for "Secretary or his delegate" each place it appeared in Code Sec. 6102, effective 2/1/77.

Sec. 6103. Confidentiality and disclosure of returns and return information.

(a) General rule.

Returns and return information shall be confidential, and except as authorized by this title—

(1) no officer or employee of the United States,

(2) no officer or employee of any State, any local law enforcement agency receiving information under subsection (i)(7)(A), any local child support enforcement agency, or any local agency administering a program listed in subsection (l)(7)(D) who has or had access to returns or return information under this section or section 6104(c), and

(3) no other person (or officer or employee thereof) who has or had access to returns or return information under subsection (e)(1)(D)(iii), paragraph (6), (10), (12), (16), (19), (20) or (21) of subsection (l), paragraph (2) or (4)(B) of subsection (m), or subsection (n),

shall disclose any return or return information obtained by him in any manner in connection with his service as such an officer or an employee or otherwise or under the provisions of this section. For purposes of this subsection, the term "officer or employee" includes a former officer or employee.

(b) Definitions.

For purposes of this section—

(1) **Return.** The term "return" means any tax or information return, declaration of estimated tax, or claim for refund required by, or provided for or permitted under, the provisions of this title which is filed with the Secretary by, on behalf of, or with respect to any person, and any amendment or supplement thereto, including supporting schedules, attachments, or lists which are supplemental to, or part of, the return so filed.

(2) **Return information.** The term "return information" means—

(A) a taxpayer's identity, the nature, source, or amount of his income, payments, receipts, deductions, exemptions, credits, assets, liabilities, net worth, tax liability, tax withheld, deficiencies, over assessments, or tax payments, whether the taxpayer's return was, is being, or will be examined or subject to other investigation or processing, or any other data, received by, recorded by, prepared by, furnished to, or collected by the Secretary with respect to a return or with respect to the determination of the existence, or possible existence, of liability (or the amount thereof) of any person under this title for any tax, penalty, interest, fine, forfeiture, or other imposition, or offense,

(B) any part of any written determination or any background file document relating to such written determination (as such terms are defined in section 6110(b)) which is not open to public inspection under section 6110,

(C) any advance pricing agreement entered into by a taxpayer and the Secretary and any background information related to such agreement or any application for an advance pricing agreement, and

(D) any agreement under section 7121, and any similar agreement, and any background information related to such an agreement or request for such an agreement,

but such term does not include data in a form which cannot be associated with, or otherwise identify, directly or indirectly, a particular taxpayer. Nothing in the preceding sentence, or in any other provision of law, shall be construed to require the disclosure of standards used or to be used for the selection of returns for examination, or data used or to be used for determining such standards, if the Secretary determines that such disclosure will seriously impair assessment, collection, or enforcement under the internal revenue laws.

(3) **Taxpayer return information.** The term "taxpayer return information" means return information as defined in paragraph (2) which is filed with, or furnished to, the Secretary by or on behalf of the taxpayer to whom such return information relates.

(4) **Tax administration.** The term "tax administration"—
   (A) means—
      (i) the administration, management, conduct, direction, and supervision of the execution and application of the internal revenue laws or related statutes (or equivalent laws and statutes of a State) and tax conventions to which the United States is a party, and
      (ii) the development and formulation of Federal tax policy relating to existing or proposed internal revenue laws, related statutes, and tax conventions, and
   (B) includes assessment, collection, enforcement, litigation, publication, and statistical gathering functions under such laws, statutes, or conventions.

(5) **State.**
   (A) In general. The term "State" means—
      (i) any of the 50 States, the District of Columbia, the Commonwealth of Puerto Rico, the Virgin Islands, Guam, American Samoa, and the Commonwealth of the Northern Mariana Islands,
      (ii) for purposes of subsections (a)(2), (b)(4), (d)(1), (h)(4), and (p), any municipality—
         (I) with a population in excess of 250,000 (as determined under the most recent decennial United States census data available),
         (II) which imposes a tax on income or wages, and
         (III) with which the Secretary (in his sole discretion) has entered into an agreement regarding disclosure, and
      (iii) for purposes of subsections (a)(2), (b)(4), (d)(1), (h)(4), and (p), any governmental entity—
         (I) which is formed and operated by a qualified group of municipalities, and
         (II) with which the Secretary (in his sole discretion) has entered into an agreement regarding disclosure.
   (B) Regional income tax agencies. For purposes of subparagraph (A)(iii)—
      (i) Qualified group of municipalities. The term "qualified group of municipalities" means, with respect to any governmental entity, 2 or more municipalities—
         (I) each of which imposes a tax on income or wages,
         (II) each of which, under the authority of a State statute, administers the laws relating to the imposition of such taxes through such entity, and
         (III) which collectively have a population in excess of 250,000 (as determined under the most recent decennial United States census data available).
      (ii) References to state law, etc. For purposes of applying subparagraph (A)(iii) to the subsections referred to in such subparagraph, any reference in such subsections to State law, proceedings, or tax returns shall be treated as references to the law, proceedings, or tax returns, as the case may be, of the municipalities which form and operate the governmental entity referred to in such subparagraph.
      (iii) Disclosure to contractors and other agents. Notwithstanding any other provision of this section, no return or return information shall be disclosed to any contractor or other agent of a governmental entity referred to in subparagraph (A)(iii) unless such entity, to the satisfaction of the Secretary—
         (I) has requirements in effect which require each such contractor or other agent which would have access to returns or return information to provide safeguards (within the meaning of subsection (p)(4)) to protect the confidentiality of such returns or return information,
         (II) agrees to conduct an on-site review every 3 years (or a mid-point review in the case of contracts or agreements of less than 3 years in duration) of each contractor or other agent to determine compliance with such requirements,
         (III) submits the findings of the most recent review conducted under subclause (II) to the Secretary as part of the report required by subsection (p)(4)(E), and
         (IV) certifies to the Secretary for the most recent annual period that such contractor or other agent is in compliance with all such requirements.
   The certification required by subclause (IV) shall include the name and address of each contractor and other agent, a description of the contract or agreement with such contractor or other agent, and the duration of such contract or agreement. The requirements of this clause shall not apply to disclosures pursuant to subsection (n) for purposes of Federal tax administration and a rule similar to the rule of subsection (p)(8)(B) shall apply for purposes of this clause.

(6) **Taxpayer identity.** The term "taxpayer identity" means the name of a person with respect to whom a return is filed, his mailing address, his taxpayer identifying

number (as described in section 6109), or a combination thereof.

(7) Inspection. The terms "inspected" and "inspection" mean any examination of a return or return information.

(8) Disclosure. The term "disclosure" means the making known to any person in any manner whatever a return or return information.

(9) Federal agency. The term "Federal agency" means an agency within the meaning of section 551(1) of title 5, United States Code.

(10) Chief executive officer. The term "chief executive officer" means, with respect to any municipality, any elected official and the chief official (even if not elected) of such municipality.

(11) Terrorist incident, threat, or activity. The term "terrorist incident, threat, or activity" means an incident, threat, or activity involving an act of domestic terrorism (as defined in section 2331(5) of title 18, United States Code) or international terrorism (as defined in section 2331(1) of such title).

(c) Disclosure of returns and return information to designee of taxpayer.

The Secretary may, subject to such requirements and conditions as he may prescribe by regulations, disclose the return of any taxpayer, or return information with respect to such taxpayer, to such person or persons as the taxpayer may designate in a request for or consent to such disclosure, or to any other person at the taxpayer's request to the extent necessary to comply with a request for information or assistance made by the taxpayer to such other person. However, return information shall not be disclosed to such person or persons if the Secretary determines that such disclosure would seriously impair Federal tax administration.

(d) Disclosure to State tax officials and State and local law enforcement agencies.

(1) In general. Returns and return information with respect to taxes imposed by chapters 1, 2, 6, 11, 12, 21, 23, 24, 31, 32, 44, 51, and 52 and subchapter D of chapter 36 shall be open to inspection by, or disclosure to, any State agency, body, or commission, or its legal representative, which is charged under the laws of such State with responsibility for the administration of State tax laws for the purpose of, and only to the extent necessary in, the administration of such laws, including any procedures with respect to locating any person who may be entitled to a refund. Such inspection shall be permitted, or such disclosure made, only upon written request by the head of such agency, body, or commission, and only to the representatives of such agency, body, or commission designated in such written request as the individuals who are to inspect or to receive the returns or return information on behalf of such agency, body, or commission. Such representatives shall not include any individual who is the chief executive officer of such State or who is neither an employee or legal representative of such agency, body, or commission nor a person described in subsection (n). However, such return information shall not be disclosed to the extent that the Secretary determines that such disclosure would identify a confidential informant or seriously impair any civil or criminal tax investigation.

(2) Disclosure to State audit agencies.

(A) In general. Any returns or return information obtained under paragraph (1) by any State agency, body, or commission may be open to inspection by, or disclosure to, officers and employees of the State audit agency for the purpose of, and only to the extent necessary in, making an audit of the State agency, body, or commission referred to in paragraph (1).

(B) State audit agency. For purposes of subparagraph (A), the term "State audit agency" means any State agency, body, or commission which is charged under the laws of the State with the responsibility of auditing State revenues and programs.

(3) Exception for reimbursement under section 7624. Nothing in this section shall be construed to prevent the Secretary from disclosing to any State or local law enforcement agency which may receive a payment under section 7624 the amount of the recovered taxes with respect to which such a payment may be made.

(4) Availability and use of death information.

(A) In general. No returns or return information may be disclosed under paragraph (1) to any agency, body, or commission of any State (or any legal representative thereof) during any period during which a contract meeting the requirements of subparagraph (B) is not in effect between such State and the Secretary of Health and Human Services.

(B) Contractual requirements. A contract meets the requirements of this subparagraph if—

(i) such contract requires the State to furnish the Secretary of Health and Human Services information concerning individuals with respect to whom death certificates (or equivalent documents maintained by the State or any subdivision thereof) have been officially filed with it, and

(ii) such contract does not include any restriction on the use of information obtained by such Secretary pursuant to such contract, except that such contract may provide that such information is only to be used by the Secretary (or any other Federal agency) for purposes of ensuring that Federal benefits or other payments are not erroneously paid to deceased individuals.

Any information obtained by the Secretary of Health and Human Services under such a contract shall be exempt from disclosure under section 552 of title 5, United States Code, and from the requirements of section 552a of such title 5.

(C) Special exception. The provisions of subparagraph (A) shall not apply to any State which on July 1, 1993, was not, pursuant to a contract, furnishing the Secretary of Health and Human Services information concerning individuals with respect to whom death certificates (or equivalent documents maintained by the State or any subdivision thereof) have been officially filed with it.

(5) Disclosure for combined employment tax reporting.

(A) In general. The Secretary may disclose taxpayer identity information and signatures to any agency, body, or commission of any State for the purpose of carrying out with such agency, body, or commission a combined Federal and State employment tax reporting program approved by the Secretary. Subsections (a)(2) and (p)(4) and sections 7213 and 7213A shall not apply with respect to disclosures or inspections made pursuant to this paragraph.

(B) Termination. The Secretary may not make any disclosure under this paragraph after December 31, 2007.

(6) Limitation on disclosure regarding regional income tax agencies treated as states. For purposes of paragraph (1), inspection by or disclosure to an entity described in subsection (b)(5)(A)(iii) shall be for the purpose of, and only to the extent necessary in, the administration of the laws of the member municipalities in such entity re-

Information and returns Code Sec. 6103(e)(9)

lating to the imposition of a tax on income or wages. Such entity may not redisclose any return or return information received pursuant to paragraph (1) to any such member municipality.

(e) Disclosure to persons having material interest.

(1) **In general.** The return of a person shall, upon written request, be open to inspection by or disclosure to—

  (A) in the case of the return of an individual—

   (i) that individual,

   (ii) the spouse of that individual if the individual and such spouse have signified their consent to consider a gift reported on such return as made one-half by him and one-half by the spouse pursuant to the provisions of section 2513; or

   (iii) the child of that individual (or such child's legal representative) to the extent necessary to comply with the provisions of section 1(g);

  (B) in the case of an income tax return filed jointly, either of the individuals with respect to whom the return is filed;

  (C) in the case of the return of a partnership, any person who was a member of such partnership during any part of the period covered by the return;

  (D) in the case of the return of a corporation or a subsidiary thereof—

   (i) any person designated by resolution of its board of directors or other similar governing body,

   (ii) any officer or employee of such corporation upon written request signed by any principal officer and attested to by the secretary or other officer,

   (iii) any bona fide shareholder of record owning 1 percent or more of the outstanding stock of such corporation,

   (iv) if the corporation was an S corporation, any person who was a shareholder during any part of the period covered by such return during which an election under section 1362(a) was in effect, or

   (v) if the corporation has been dissolved, any person authorized by applicable State law to act for the corporation or any person who the Secretary finds to have a material interest which will be affected by information contained therein;

  (E) in the case of the return of an estate—

   (i) the administrator, executor, or trustee of such estate, and

   (ii) any heir at law, next of kin, or beneficiary under the will, of the decedent, but only if the Secretary finds that such heir at law, next of kin, or beneficiary has a material interest which will be affected by information contained therein; and

  (F) in the case of the return of a trust—

   (i) the trustee or trustees, jointly or separately, and

   (ii) any beneficiary of such trust, but only if the Secretary finds that such beneficiary has a material interest which will be affected by information contained therein.

(2) **Incompetency.** If an individual described in paragraph (1) is legally incompetent, the applicable return shall, upon written request, be open to inspection by or disclosure to the committee, trustee, or guardian of his estate.

(3) **Deceased individuals.** The return of a decedent shall, upon written request, be open to inspection by or disclosure to—

  (A) the administrator, executor, or trustee of his estate, and

  (B) any heir at law, next of kin, or beneficiary under the will, of such decedent, or a donee of property, but only if the Secretary finds that such heir at law, next of kin, beneficiary, or donee has a material interest which will be affected by information contained therein.

(4) **Title 11 cases and receivership proceedings.** If—

  (A) there is a trustee in a title 11 case in which the debtor is the person with respect to whom the return is filed, or

  (B) substantially all of the property of the person with respect to whom the return is filed is in the hands of a receiver,

such return or returns for prior years of such person shall, upon written request, be open to inspection by or disclosure to such trustee or receiver, but only if the Secretary finds that such trustee or receiver, in his fiduciary capacity, has a material interest which will be affected by information contained therein.

(5) **Individual's title 11 case.**

  (A) In general. In any case to which section 1398 applies (determined without regard to section 1398(b)(1)), any return of the debtor for the taxable year in which the case commenced or any preceding taxable year shall, upon written request, be open to inspection by or disclosure to the trustee in such case.

  (B) Return of estate available to debtor. Any return of an estate in a case to which section 1398 applies shall, upon written request, be open to inspection by or disclosure to the debtor in such case.

  (C) Special rule for involuntary cases. In an involuntary case, no disclosure shall be made under subparagraph (A) until the order for relief has been entered by the court having jurisdiction of such case unless such court finds that such disclosure is appropriate for purposes of determining whether an order for relief should be entered.

(6) **Attorney in fact.** Any return to which this subsection applies shall, upon written request, also be open to inspection by or disclosure to the attorney in fact duly authorized in writing by any of the persons described in paragraph (1), (2), (3), (4), (5), (8), or (9) to inspect the return or receive the information on his behalf, subject to the conditions provided in such paragraphs.

(7) **Return information.** Return information with respect to any taxpayer may be open to inspection by or disclosure to any person authorized by this subsection to inspect any return of such taxpayer if the Secretary determines that such disclosure would not seriously impair Federal tax administration.

(8) **Disclosure of collection activities with respect to joint return.** If any deficiency of tax with respect to a joint return is assessed and the individuals filing such return are no longer married or no longer reside in the same household, upon request in writing by either of such individuals, the Secretary shall disclose in writing to the individual making the request whether the Secretary has attempted to collect such deficiency from such other individual, the general nature of such collection activities, and the amount collected. The preceding sentence shall not apply to any deficiency which may not be collected by reason of section 6502.

(9) **Disclosure of certain information where more than 1 person subject to penalty under section 6672.** If the Secretary determines that a person is liable for a penalty under section 6672(a) with respect to any failure, upon request in writing of such person, the Secretary shall disclose in writing to such person—

3,569

(A) the name of any other person whom the Secretary has determined to be liable for such penalty with respect to such failure, and

(B) whether the Secretary has attempted to collect such penalty from such other person, the general nature of such collection activities, and the amount collected.

(10) Limitation on certain disclosures under this subsection. In the case of an inspection or disclosure under this subsection relating to the return of a partnership, S corporation, trust, or an estate, the information inspected or disclosed shall not include any supporting schedule, attachment, or list which includes the taxpayer identity information of a person other than the entity making the return or the person conducting the inspection or to whom the disclosure is made.

(f) Disclosure to committees of Congress.

(1) Committee on Ways and Means, Committee on Finance, and Joint Committee on Taxation. Upon written request from the chairman of the Committee on Ways and Means of the House of Representatives, the chairman of the Committee on Finance of the Senate, or the chairman of the Joint Committee on Taxation, the Secretary shall furnish such committee with any return or return information specified in such request, except that any return or return information which can be associated with, or otherwise identify, directly or indirectly, a particular taxpayer shall be furnished to such committee only when sitting in closed executive session unless such taxpayer otherwise consents in writing to such disclosure.

(2) Chief of Staff of Joint Committee on Taxation. Upon written request by the Chief of Staff of the Joint Committee on Taxation, the Secretary shall furnish him with any return or return information specified in such request. Such Chief of Staff may submit such return or return information to any committee described in paragraph (1), except that any return or return information which can be associated with, or otherwise identify, directly or indirectly, a particular taxpayer shall be furnished to such committee only when sitting in closed executive session unless such taxpayer otherwise consents in writing to such disclosure.

(3) Other committees. Pursuant to an action by, and upon written request by the chairman of, a committee of the Senate or the House of Representatives (other than a committee specified in paragraph (1)) specially authorized to inspect any return or return information by a resolution of the Senate or the House of Representatives or, in the case of a joint committee (other than the joint committee specified in paragraph (1)) by concurrent resolution, the Secretary shall furnish such committee, or a duly authorized and designated subcommittee thereof, sitting in closed executive session, with any return or return information which such resolution authorizes the committee or subcommittee to inspect. Any resolution described in this paragraph shall specify the purpose for which the return or return information is to be furnished and that such information cannot reasonably be obtained from any other source.

(4) Agents of committees and submission of information to Senate or House of Representatives.

(A) Committees described in paragraph (1). Any committee described in paragraph (1) or the Chief of Staff of the Joint Committee on Taxation shall have the authority, acting directly, or by or through such examiners or agents as the chairman of such committee or such chief of staff may designate or appoint, to inspect returns and return information at such time and in such manner as may be determined by such chairman or chief of staff. Any return or return information obtained by or on behalf of such committee pursuant to the provisions of this subsection may be submitted by the committee to the Senate or the House of Representatives, or to both. The Joint Committee on Taxation may also submit such return or return information to any other committee described in paragraph (1), except that any return or return information which can be associated with, or otherwise identify, directly or indirectly, a particular taxpayer shall be furnished to such committee only when sitting in closed executive session unless such taxpayer otherwise consents in writing to such disclosure.

(B) Other committees. Any committee or subcommittee described in paragraph (3) shall have the right, acting directly, or by or through no more than four examiners or agents, designated or appointed in writing in equal numbers by the chairman and ranking minority member of such committee or subcommittee, to inspect returns and return information at such time and in such manner as may be determined by such chairman and ranking minority member. Any return or return information obtained by or on behalf of such committee or subcommittee pursuant to the provisions of this subsection may be submitted by the committee to the Senate or the House of Representatives, or to both, except that any return or return information which can be associated with, or otherwise identify, directly or indirectly, a particular taxpayer, shall be furnished to the Senate or the House of Representatives only when sitting in closed executive session unless such taxpayer otherwise consents in writing to such disclosure.

(5) Disclosure by whistleblower. Any person who otherwise has or had access to any return or return information under this section may disclose such return or return information to a committee referred to in paragraph (1) or any individual authorized to receive or inspect information under paragraph (4)(A) if such person believes such return or return information may relate to possible misconduct, maladministration, or taxpayer abuse.

(g) Disclosure to President and certain other persons.

(1) In general. Upon written request by the President, signed by him personally, the Secretary shall furnish to the President, or to such employee or employees of the White House Office as the President may designate by name in such request, a return or return information with respect to any taxpayer named in such request. Any such request shall state—

(A) the name and address of the taxpayer whose return or return information is to be disclosed,

(B) the kind of return or return information which is to be disclosed,

(C) the taxable period or periods covered by such return or return information, and

(D) the specific reason why the inspection or disclosure is requested.

(2) Disclosure of return information as to Presidential appointees and certain other Federal Government appointees. The Secretary may disclose to a duly authorized representative of the Executive Office of the President or to the head of any Federal agency, upon written request by the President or head of such agency, or to the Federal Bureau of Investigation on behalf of and upon written request by the President or such head, return information with respect to an individual who is designated as being under consideration for appointment to a position in the

Information and returns — Code Sec. 6103(h)(5)

executive or judicial branch of the Federal Government. Such return information shall be limited to whether such individual—

(A) has filed returns with respect to the taxes imposed under chapter 1 for not more than the immediately preceding 3 years;

(B) has failed to pay any tax within 10 days after notice and demand, or has been assessed any penalty under this title for negligence, in the current year or immediately preceding 3 years;

(C) has been or is under investigation for possible criminal offenses under the internal revenue laws and the results of any such investigation; or

(D) has been assessed any civil penalty under this title for fraud.

Within 3 days of the receipt of any request for any return information with respect to any individual under this paragraph, the Secretary shall notify such individual in writing that such information has been requested under the provisions of this paragraph.

(3) Restriction on disclosure. The employees to whom returns and return information are disclosed under this subsection shall not disclose such returns and return information to any other person except the President or the head of such agency without the personal written direction of the President or the head of such agency.

(4) Restriction on disclosure to certain employees. Disclosure of returns and return information under this subsection shall not be made to any employee whose annual rate of basic pay is less than the annual rate of basic pay specified for positions subject to section 5316 of title 5, United States Code.

(5) Reporting requirements. Within 30 days after the close of each calendar quarter, the President and the head of any agency requesting returns and return information under this subsection shall each file a report with the Joint Committee on Taxation setting forth the taxpayers with respect to whom such requests were made during such quarter under this subsection, the returns or return information involved, and the reasons for such requests. The President shall not be required to report on any request for returns and return information pertaining to an individual who was an officer or employee of the executive branch of the Federal Government at the time such request was made. Reports filed pursuant to this paragraph shall not be disclosed unless the Joint Committee on Taxation determines that disclosure thereof (including identifying details) would be in the national interest. Such reports shall be maintained by the Joint Committee on Taxation for a period not exceeding 2 years unless, within such period, the Joint Committee on Taxation determines that a disclosure to the Congress is necessary.

(h) Disclosure to certain Federal officers and employees for purposes of tax administration, etc.

(1) Department of the Treasury. Returns and return information shall, without written request, be open to inspection by or disclosure to officers and employees of the Department of the Treasury whose official duties require such inspection or disclosure for tax administration purposes.

(2) Department of Justice. In a matter involving tax administration, a return or return information shall be open to inspection by or disclosure to officers and employees of the Department of Justice (including United States attorneys) personally and directly engaged in, and solely for their use in, any proceeding before a Federal grand jury or preparation for any proceeding (or investigation which may result in such a proceeding) before a Federal grand jury or any Federal or State court, but only if—

(A) the taxpayer is or may be a party to the proceeding, or the proceeding arose out of, or in connection with, determining the taxpayer's civil or criminal liability, or the collection of such civil liability in respect of any tax imposed under this title;

(B) the treatment of an item reflected on such return is or may be related to the resolution of an issue in the proceeding or investigation; or

(C) such return or return information relates or may relate to a transactional relationship between a person who is or may be a party to the proceeding and the taxpayer which affects, or may affect, the resolution of an issue in such proceeding or investigation.

(3) Form of request. In any case in which the Secretary is authorized to disclose a return or return information to the Department of Justice pursuant to the provisions of this subsection—

(A) if the Secretary has referred the case to the Department of Justice, or if the proceeding is authorized by subchapter B of chapter 76, the Secretary may make such disclosure on his own motion, or

(B) if the Secretary receives a written request from the Attorney General, the Deputy Attorney General, or an Assistant Attorney General for a return of, or return information relating to, a person named in such request and setting forth the need for the disclosure, the Secretary shall disclose return or return the information so requested.

(4) Disclosure in judicial and administrative tax proceedings. A return or return information may be disclosed in a Federal or State judicial or administrative proceeding pertaining to tax administration, but only—

(A) if the taxpayer is a party to the proceeding, or the proceeding arose out of, or in connection with, determining the taxpayer's civil or criminal liability, or the collection of such civil liability, in respect of any tax imposed under this title;

(B) if the treatment of an item reflected on such return is directly related to the resolution of an issue in the proceeding;

(C) if such return or return information directly relates to a transactional relationship between a person who is a party to the proceeding and the taxpayer which directly affects the resolution of an issue in the proceeding; or

(D) to the extent required by order of a court pursuant to section 3500 of title 18, United States Code or rule 16 of the Federal Rules of Criminal Procedure, such court being authorized in the issuance of such order to give due consideration to congressional policy favoring the confidentiality of returns and return information as set forth in this title.

However, such return or return information shall not be disclosed as provided in subparagraph (A), (B), or (C) if the Secretary determines that such disclosure would identify a confidential informant or seriously impair a civil or criminal tax investigation.

(5) Withholding of tax from Social Security benefits. Upon written request of the payor agency, the Secretary may disclose available return information from the master files of the Internal Revenue Service with respect to the address and status of an individual as a nonresident alien or as a citizen or resident of the United States to the Social Security Administration or the Railroad Retirement Board (whichever is appropriate) for purposes of carrying out its responsibilities for withholding tax under section 1441 from social security benefits (as defined in section 86(d)).

(6) Internal Revenue Service Oversight Board.

(A) In general. Notwithstanding paragraph (1), and except as provided in subparagraph (B), no return or return information may be disclosed to any member of the Oversight Board described in subparagraph (A) or (D) of section 7802(b)(1) or to any employee or detailee of such Board by reason of their service with the Board. Any request for information not permitted to be disclosed under the preceding sentence, and any contact relating to a specific taxpayer, made by any such individual to an officer or employee of the Internal Revenue Service shall be reported by such officer or employee to the Secretary, the Treasury Inspector General for Tax Administration, and the Joint Committee on Taxation.

(B) Exception for reports to the board. If—

(i) the Commissioner or the Treasury Inspector General for Tax Administration prepares any report or other matter for the Oversight Board in order to assist the Board in carrying out its duties; and

(ii) the Commissioner or such Inspector General determines it is necessary to include any return or return information in such report or other matter to enable the Board to carry out such duties,

such return or return information (other than information regarding taxpayer identity) may be disclosed to members, employees, or detailees of the Board solely for the purpose of carrying out such duties.

(i) Disclosure to Federal officers or employees for administration of Federal laws not relating to tax administration.

(1) Disclosure of returns and return information for use in criminal investigations.

(A) In general. Except as provided in paragraph (6), any return or return information with respect to any specified taxable period or periods shall, pursuant to and upon the grant of an ex parte order by a Federal district court judge or magistrate under subparagraph (B), be open (but only to the extent necessary as provided in such order) to inspection by, or disclosure to, officers and employees of any Federal agency who are personally and directly engaged in—

(i) preparation for any judicial or administrative proceeding pertaining to the enforcement of a specifically designated Federal criminal statute (not involving tax administration) to which the United States or such agency is or may be a party,

(ii) any investigation which may result in such a proceeding, or

(iii) any Federal grand jury proceeding pertaining to enforcement of such a criminal statute to which the United States or such agency is or may be a party,

solely for the use of such officers and employees in such preparation, investigation, or grand jury proceeding.

(B) Application for order. The Attorney General, the Deputy Attorney General, the Associate Attorney General, any Assistant Attorney General, any United States attorney, any special prosecutor appointed under section 593 of title 28, United States Code, or any attorney in charge of a criminal division organized crime strike force established pursuant to section 510 of title 28, United States Code, may authorize an application to a Federal district court judge or magistrate for the order referred to in subparagraph (A). Upon such application, such judge or magistrate may grant such order if he determines on the basis of the facts submitted by the applicant that—

(i) there is reasonable cause to believe, based upon information believed to be reliable, that a specific criminal act has been committed,

(ii) there is reasonable cause to believe that the return or return information is or may be relevant to a matter relating to the commission of such act, and

(iii) the return or return information is sought exclusively for use in a Federal criminal investigation or proceeding concerning such act, and the information sought to be disclosed cannot reasonably be obtained, under the circumstances, from another source.

(2) Disclosure of return information other than taxpayer return information for use in criminal investigations.

(A) In general. Except as provided in paragraph (6), upon receipt by the Secretary of a request which meets the requirements of subparagraph (B) from the head of any Federal agency or the Inspector General thereof, or, in the case of the Department of Justice, the Attorney General, the Deputy Attorney General, the Associate Attorney General, any Assistant Attorney General, the Director of the Federal Bureau of Investigation, the Administrator of the Drug Enforcement Administration, any United States attorney, any special prosecutor appointed under section 593 of title 28, United States Code, or any attorney in charge of a criminal division organized crime strike force established pursuant to section 510 of title 28, United States Code, the Secretary shall disclose return information (other than taxpayer return information) to officers and employees of such agency who are personally and directly engaged in—

(i) preparation for any judicial or administrative proceeding described in paragraph (1)(A)(i),

(ii) any investigation which may result in such a proceeding, or

(iii) any grand jury proceeding described in paragraph (1)(A)(iii),

solely for the use of such officers and employees in such preparation, investigation, or grand jury proceeding.

(B) Requirements. A request meets the requirements of this subparagraph if the request is in writing and sets forth—

(i) the name and address of the taxpayer with respect to whom the requested return information relates;

(ii) the taxable period or periods to which such return information relates;

(iii) the statutory authority under which the proceeding or investigation described in subparagraph (A) is being conducted; and

(iv) the specific reason or reasons why such disclosure is, or may be, relevant to such proceeding or investigation.

(C) Taxpayer identity. For purposes of this paragraph, a taxpayer's identity shall not be treated as taxpayer return information.

(3) Disclosure of return information to apprise appropriate officials of criminal or terrorist activities or emergency circumstances.

(A) Possible violations of federal criminal law.

(i) In general. Except as provided in paragraph (6), the Secretary may disclose in writing return information (other than taxpayer return information) which may constitute evidence of a violation of any Federal criminal law (not involving tax administration) to the extent necessary to apprise the head of the appropriate Federal agency charged with the responsibility of enforcing such law. The head of such agency may disclose such return information to officers and employees of such agency to the extent necessary to enforce such law.

(ii) Taxpayer identity. If there is return information (other than taxpayer return information) which may constitute evidence of a violation by any taxpayer of any Federal criminal law (not involving tax administration), such taxpayer's identity may also be disclosed under clause (i).

(B) Emergency circumstances.

(i) Danger of death or physical injury. Under circumstances involving an imminent danger of death or physical injury to any individual, the Secretary may disclose return information to the extent necessary to apprise appropriate officers or employees of any Federal or State law enforcement agency of such circumstances.

(ii) Flight from federal prosecution. Under circumstances involving the imminent flight of any individual from Federal prosecution, the Secretary may disclose return information to the extent necessary to apprise appropriate officers or employees of any Federal law enforcement agency of such circumstances.

(C) Terrorist activities, etc.

(i) In general. Except as provided in paragraph (6), the Secretary may disclose in writing return information (other than taxpayer return information) that may be related to a terrorist incident, threat, or activity to the extent necessary to apprise the head of the appropriate Federal law enforcement agency responsible for investigating or responding to such terrorist incident, threat, or activity. The head of the agency may disclose such return information to officers and employees of such agency to the extent necessary to investigate or respond to such terrorist incident, threat, or activity.

(ii) Disclosure to the Department of Justice. Returns and taxpayer return information may also be disclosed to the Attorney General under clause (i) to the extent necessary for, and solely for use in preparing, an application under paragraph (7)(D).

(iii) Taxpayer identity. For purposes of this subparagraph, a taxpayer's identity shall not be treated as taxpayer return information.

(4) Use of certain disclosed returns and return information in judicial or administrative proceedings.

(A) Returns and taxpayer return information. Except as provided in subparagraph (C), any return or taxpayer return information obtained under paragraph (1) or (7)(C) may be disclosed in any judicial or administrative proceeding pertaining to enforcement of a specifically designated Federal criminal statute or related civil forfeiture (not involving tax administration) to which the United States or a Federal agency is a party—

(i) if the court finds that such return or taxpayer return information is probative of a matter in issue relevant in establishing the commission of a crime or the guilt or liability of a party, or

(ii) to the extent required by order of the court pursuant to section 3500 of title 18, United States Code, or rule 16 of the Federal Rules of Criminal Procedure.

(B) Return information (other than taxpayer return information). Except as provided in subparagraph (C), any return information (other than taxpayer return information) obtained under paragraph (1), (2), (3)(A) or (C), or (7) may be disclosed in any judicial or administrative proceeding pertaining to enforcement of a specifically designated Federal criminal statute or related civil forfeiture (not involving tax administration) to which the United States or a Federal agency is a party.

(C) Confidential informant; impairment of investigations. No return or return information shall be admitted into evidence under subparagraph (A)(i) or (B) if the Secretary determines and notifies the Attorney General or his delegate or the head of the Federal agency that such admission would identify a confidential informant or seriously impair a civil or criminal tax investigation.

(D) Consideration of confidentiality policy. In ruling upon the admissibility of returns or return information, and in the issuance of an order under subparagraph (A)(ii), the court shall give due consideration to congressional policy favoring the confidentiality of returns and return information as set forth in this title.

(E) Reversible error. The admission into evidence of any return or return information contrary to the provisions of this paragraph shall not, as such, constitute reversible error upon appeal of a judgment in the proceeding.

(5) Disclosure to locate fugitives from justice.

(A) In general. Except as provided in paragraph (6), the return of an individual or return information with respect to such individual shall, pursuant to and upon the grant of an ex parte order by a Federal district court judge or magistrate under subparagraph (B), be open (but only to the extent necessary as provided in such order) to inspection by, or disclosure to, officers and employees of any Federal agency exclusively for use in locating such individual.

(B) Application for order. Any person described in paragraph (1)(B) may authorize an application to a Federal district court judge or magistrate for an order referred to in subparagraph (A). Such judge or magistrate may grant such order if he determines on the basis of the facts submitted by the applicant that—

(i) a Federal arrest warrant relating to the commission of a Federal felony offense has been issued for an individual who is a fugitive from justice,

(ii) the return of such individual or return information with respect to such individual is sought exclusively for use in locating such individual, and

(iii) there is reasonable cause to believe that such return or return information may be relevant in determining the location of such individual.

(6) Confidential informants; impairment of investigations. The Secretary shall not disclose any return or return information under paragraph (1), (2), (3)(A) or (C), (5), (7), or (8) if the Secretary determines (and, in the case of a request for disclosure pursuant to a court order described in paragraph (1)(B) or (5)(B), certifies to the court) that such disclosure would identify a confidential informant or seriously impair a civil or criminal tax investigation.

(7) Disclosure upon request of information relating to terrorist activities, etc.

(A) Disclosure to law enforcement agencies.

(i) In general. Except as provided in paragraph (6), upon receipt by the Secretary of a written request which meets the requirements of clause (iii), the Secretary may disclose return information (other than taxpayer return information) to officers and employees of any Federal law enforcement agency who are personally and directly engaged in the response to or investigation of any terrorist incident, threat, or activity.

(ii) Disclosure to State and local law enforcement agencies. The head of any Federal law enforcement agency may disclose return information obtained under clause (i) to officers and employees of any State or local law enforcement agency but only if such agency is part of a team with the Federal law enforcement agency in such response or investigation and such information is disclosed only to officers and employees who are personally and directly engaged in such response or investigation.

(iii) Requirements. A request meets the requirements of this clause if—

(I) the request is made by the head of any Federal law enforcement agency (or his delegate) involved in the response to or investigation of any terrorist incident, threat, or activity, and

(II) the request sets forth the specific reason or reasons why such disclosure may be relevant to a terrorist incident, threat, or activity.

(iv) Limitation on use of information. Information disclosed under this subparagraph shall be solely for the use of the officers and employees to whom such information is disclosed in such response or investigation.

(v) Taxpayer identity. For purposes of this subparagraph, a taxpayer's identity shall not be treated as taxpayer return information.

(B) Disclosure to intelligence agencies.

(i) In general. Except as provided in paragraph (6), upon receipt by the Secretary of a written request which meets the requirements of clause (ii), the Secretary may disclose return information (other than taxpayer return information) to those officers and employees of the Department of Justice, the Department of the Treasury, and other Federal intelligence agencies who are personally and directly engaged in the collection or analysis of intelligence and counterintelligence information or investigation concerning any terrorist incident, threat, or activity. For purposes of the preceding sentence, the information disclosed under the preceding sentence shall be solely for the use of such officers and employees in such investigation, collection, or analysis.

(ii) Requirements. A request meets the requirements of this subparagraph if the request—

(I) is made by an individual described in clause (iii), and

(II) sets forth the specific reason or reasons why such disclosure may be relevant to a terrorist incident, threat, or activity.

(iii) Requesting individuals. An individual described in this subparagraph is an individual—

(I) who is an officer or employee of the Department of Justice or the Department of the Treasury who is appointed by the President with the advice and consent of the Senate or who is the Director of the United States Secret Service, and

(II) who is responsible for the collection and analysis of intelligence and counterintelligence information concerning any terrorist incident, threat, or activity.

(iv) Taxpayer identity. For purposes of this subparagraph, a taxpayer's identity shall not be treated as taxpayer return information.

(C) Disclosure under ex parte orders.

(i) In general. Except as provided in paragraph (6), any return or return information with respect to any specified taxable period or periods shall, pursuant to and upon the grant of an ex parte order by a Federal district court judge or magistrate under clause (ii), be open (but only to the extent necessary as provided in such order) to inspection by, or disclosure to, officers and employees of any Federal law enforcement agency or Federal intelligence agency who are personally and directly engaged in any investigation, response to, or analysis of intelligence and counterintelligence information concerning any terrorist incident, threat, or activity. Return or return information opened to inspection or disclosure pursuant to the preceding sentence shall be solely for the use of such officers and employees in the investigation, response, or analysis, and in any judicial, administrative, or grand jury proceedings, pertaining to such terrorist incident, threat, or activity.

(ii) Application for order. The Attorney General, the Deputy Attorney General, the Associate Attorney General, any Assistant Attorney General, or any United States attorney may authorize an application to a Federal district court judge or magistrate for the order referred to in clause (i). Upon such application, such judge or magistrate may grant such order if he determines on the basis of the facts submitted by the applicant that—

(I) there is reasonable cause to believe, based upon information believed to be reliable, that the return or return information may be relevant to a matter relating to such terrorist incident, threat, or activity, and

(II) the return or return information is sought exclusively for use in a Federal investigation, analysis, or proceeding concerning any terrorist incident, threat, or activity.

(D) Special rule for ex parte disclosure by the IRS.

(i) In general. Except as provided in paragraph (6), the Secretary may authorize an application to a Federal district court judge or magistrate for the order referred to in subparagraph (C)(i). Upon such application, such judge or magistrate may grant such order if he determines on the basis of the facts submitted by the applicant that the requirements of subparagraph (C)(ii)(I) are met.

(ii) Limitation on use of information. Information disclosed under clause (i)—

(I) may be disclosed only to the extent necessary to apprise the head of the appropriate Federal law enforcement agency responsible for investigating or responding to a terrorist incident, threat, or activity, and

(II) shall be solely for use in a Federal investigation, analysis, or proceeding concerning any terrorist incident, threat, or activity.

The head of such Federal agency may disclose such information to officers and employees of such agency to the extent necessary to investigate or respond to such terrorist incident, threat, or activity.

(E) Repealed.

(8) Comptroller General.
(A) Returns available for inspection. Except as provided in subparagraph (C), upon written request by the Comptroller General of the United States, returns and return information shall be open to inspection by, or disclosure to, officers and employees of the Government Accountability Office for the purpose of, and to the extent necessary in, making—
(i) an audit of the Internal Revenue Service, the Bureau of Alcohol, Tobacco, Firearms, and Explosives, Department of Justice, or the Tax and Trade Bureau, Department of the Treasury, which may be required by section 713 of title 31, United States Code, or
(ii) any audit authorized by subsection (p)(6),
except that no such officer or employee shall, except to the extent authorized by subsection (f) or (p)(6), disclose to any person, other than another officer or employee of such office whose official duties require such disclosure, any return or return information described in section 4424(a) in a form which can be associated with, or otherwise identify, directly or indirectly, a particular taxpayer, nor shall such officer or employee disclose any other return or return information, except as otherwise expressly provided by law, to any person other than such other officer or employee of such office in a form which can be associated with, or otherwise identify, directly or indirectly, a particular taxpayer.
(B) Audits of other agencies.
(i) In general. Nothing in this section shall prohibit any return or return information obtained under this title by any Federal agency (other than an agency referred to in subparagraph (A)) or by a Trustee as defined in the District of Columbia Retirement Protection Act of 1997, for use in any program or activity from being open to inspection by, or disclosure to, officers and employees of the Government Accountability Office if such inspection or disclosure is—
(I) for purposes of, and to the extent necessary in, making an audit authorized by law of such program or activity, and
(II) pursuant to a written request by the Comptroller General of the United States to the head of such Federal agency.
(ii) Information from secretary. If the Comptroller General of the United States determines that the returns or return information available under clause (i) are not sufficient for purposes of making an audit of any program or activity of a Federal agency (other than an agency referred to in subparagraph (A)), upon written request by the Comptroller General to the Secretary, returns and return information (of the type authorized by subsection (l) or (m) to be made available to the Federal agency for use in such program or activity) shall be open to inspection by, or disclosure to, officers and employees of the Government Accountability Office for the purpose of, and to the extent necessary in, making such audit.
(iii) Requirement of notification upon completion of audit. Within 90 days after the completion of an audit with respect to which returns or return information were opened to inspection or disclosed under clause (i) or (ii), the Comptroller General of the United States shall notify in writing the Joint Committee on Taxation of such completion. Such notice shall include—
(I) a description of the use of the returns and return information by the Federal agency involved,
(II) such recommendations with respect to the use of returns and return information by such Federal agency as the Comptroller General deems appropriate, and
(III) a statement on the impact of any such recommendations on confidentiality of returns and return information and the administration of this title.
(iv) Certain restrictions made applicable. The restrictions contained in subparagraph (A) on the disclosure of any returns or return information open to inspection or disclosed under such subparagraph shall also apply to returns and return information open to inspection or disclosed under this subparagraph.
(C) Disapproval by Joint Committee on Taxation. Returns and return information shall not be open to inspection or disclosed under subparagraph (A) or (B) with respect to an audit—
(i) unless the Comptroller General of the United States notifies in writing the Joint Committee on Taxation of such audit, and
(ii) if the Joint Committee on Taxation disapproves such audit by a vote of at least two-thirds of its members within the 30-day period beginning on the day the Joint Committee on Taxation receives such notice.

(j) Statistical use.
(1) Department of Commerce. Upon request in writing by the Secretary of Commerce, the Secretary shall furnish—
(A) such returns, or return information reflected thereon, to officers and employees of the Bureau of the Census, and
(B) such return information reflected on returns of corporations to officers and employees of the Bureau of Economic Analysis,
as the Secretary may prescribe by regulation for the purpose of, but only to the extent necessary in, the structuring of censuses and national economic accounts and conducting related statistical activities authorized by law.
(2) Federal Trade Commission. Upon request in writing by the Chairman of the Federal Trade Commission, the Secretary shall furnish such return information reflected on any return of a corporation with respect to the tax imposed by chapter 1 to officers and employees of the Division of Financial Statistics of the Bureau of Economics of such commission as the Secretary may prescribe by regulation for the purpose of, but only to the extent necessary in, administration by such division of legally authorized economic surveys of corporations.
(3) Department of Treasury. Returns and return information shall be open to inspection by or disclosure to officers and employees of the Department of the Treasury whose official duties require such inspection or disclosure for the purpose of, but only to the extent necessary in, preparing economic or financial forecasts, projections, analyses, and statistical studies and conducting related activities. Such inspection or disclosure shall be permitted only upon written request which sets forth the specific reason or reasons why such inspection or disclosure is necessary and which is signed by the head of the bureau or office of the Department of the Treasury requesting the inspection or disclosure.
(4) Anonymous form. No person who receives a return or return information under this subsection shall disclose such return or return information to any person other than the taxpayer to whom it relates except in a form which

cannot be associated with, or otherwise identify, directly or indirectly, a particular taxpayer.

(5) Department of Agriculture. Upon request in writing by the Secretary of Agriculture, the Secretary shall furnish such returns, or return information reflected thereon, as the Secretary may prescribe by regulation to officers and employees of the Department of Agriculture whose official duties require access to such returns or information for the purpose of, but only to the extent necessary in, structuring, preparing, and conducting the census of agriculture pursuant to the Census of Agriculture Act of 1997 (Public Law 105-113).

(6) Congressional Budget Office. Upon written request by the Director of the Congressional Budget Office, the Secretary shall furnish to officers and employees of the Congressional Budget Office return information for the purpose of, but only to the extent necessary for, long-term models of the social security and medicare programs.

(k) Disclosure of certain returns and return information for tax administration purposes.

(1) Disclosure of accepted offers-in-compromise. Return information shall be disclosed to members of the general public to the extent necessary to permit inspection of any accepted offer-in-compromise under section 7122 relating to the liability for a tax imposed by this title.

(2) Disclosure of amount of outstanding lien. If a notice of lien has been filed pursuant to section 6323(f), the amount of the outstanding obligation secured by such lien may be disclosed to any person who furnishes satisfactory written evidence that he has a right in the property subject to such lien or intends to obtain a right in such property.

(3) Disclosure of return information to correct misstatements of fact. The Secretary may, but only following approval by the Joint Committee on Taxation, disclose such return information or any other information with respect to any specific taxpayer to the extent necessary for tax administration purposes to correct a misstatement of fact published or disclosed with respect to such taxpayer's return or any transaction of the taxpayer with the Internal Revenue Service.

(4) Disclosure to competent authority under tax convention. A return or return information may be disclosed to a competent authority of a foreign government which has an income tax or gift and estate tax convention, or other convention or bilateral agreement relating to the exchange of tax information, with the United States but only to the extent provided in, and subject to the terms and conditions of, such convention or bilateral agreement.

(5) State agencies regulating tax return preparers. Taxpayer identity information with respect to any tax return preparer, and information as to whether or not any penalty has been assessed against such tax return preparer under section 6694, 6695, or 7216, may be furnished to any agency, body, or commission lawfully charged under any State or local law with the licensing, registration, or regulation of tax return preparers. Such information may be furnished only upon written request by the head of such agency, body, or commission designating the officers or employees to whom such information is to be furnished. Information may be furnished and used under this paragraph only for purposes of the licensing, registration, or regulation of tax return preparers.

(6) Disclosure by certain officers and employees for investigative purposes. An internal revenue officer or employee and an officer or employee of the Office of Treasury Inspector General for Tax Administration may, in connection with his official duties relating to any audit, collection activity, or civil or criminal tax investigation or any other offense under the internal revenue laws, disclose return information to the extent that such disclosure is necessary in obtaining information, which is not otherwise reasonably available, with respect to the correct determination of tax, liability for tax, or the amount to be collected or with respect to the enforcement of any other provision of this title. Such disclosures shall be made only in such situations and under such conditions as the Secretary may prescribe by regulation.

(7) Disclosure of excise tax registration information. To the extent the Secretary determines that disclosure is necessary to permit the effective administration of subtitle D, the Secretary may disclose—

(A) the name, address, and registration number of each person who is registered under any provision of subtitle D (and, in the case of a registered terminal operator, the address of each terminal operated by such operator), and

(B) the registration status of any person.

(8) Levies on certain government payments.

(A) Disclosure of return information in levies on financial management service. In serving a notice of levy, or release of such levy, with respect to any applicable government payment, the Secretary may disclose to officers and employees of the Financial Management Service—

(i) return information, including taxpayer identity information,

(ii) the amount of any unpaid liability under this title (including penalties and interest), and

(iii) the type of tax and tax period to which such unpaid liability relates.

(B) Restriction on use of disclosed information. Return information disclosed under subparagraph (A) may be used by officers and employees of the Financial Management Service only for the purpose of, and to the extent necessary in, transferring levied funds in satisfaction of the levy, maintaining appropriate agency records in regard to such levy or the release thereof, notifying the taxpayer and the agency certifying such payment that the levy has been honored, or in the defense of any litigation ensuing from the honor of such levy.

(C) Applicable government payment. For purposes of this paragraph, the term "applicable government payment" means—

(i) any Federal payment (other than a payment for which eligibility is based on the income or assets (or both) of a payee) certified to the Financial Management Service for disbursement, and

(ii) any other payment which is certified to the Financial Management Service for disbursement and which the Secretary designates by published notice.

(9) Disclosure of information to administer section 6311. The Secretary may disclose returns or return information to financial institutions and others to the extent the Secretary deems necessary for the administration of section 6311. Disclosures of information for purposes other than to accept payments by checks or money orders shall be made only to the extent authorized by written procedures promulgated by the Secretary.

(10) Disclosure of certain return information to certain prison officials.

(A) In general. Under such procedures as the Secretary may prescribe, the Secretary may disclose to the head of the Federal Bureau of Prisons and the head of any State agency charged with the responsibility for administration of prisons any return information with respect to individuals incarcerated in Federal or State prison whom the Secretary has determined may have filed or facilitated the filing of a false return to the extent that the Secretary determines that such disclosure is necessary to permit effective Federal tax administration.

(B) Restriction on redisclosure. Notwithstanding subsection (n), the head of the Federal Bureau of Prisons and the head of any State agency charged with the responsibility for administration of prisons may not disclose any information obtained under subparagraph (A) to any person other than an officer or employee of such Bureau or agency.

(C) Restriction on use of disclosed information. Return information received under this paragraph shall be used only for purposes of and to the extent necessary in taking administrative action to prevent the filing of false and fraudulent returns, including administrative actions to address possible violations of administrative rules and regulations of the prison facility.

(D) Termination. No disclosure may be made under this paragraph after December 31, 2011.

(l) Disclosure of returns and return information for purposes other than tax administration.

(1) Disclosure of certain returns and return information to Social Security Administration and Railroad Retirement Board. The Secretary may, upon written request, disclose returns and return information with respect to—

(A) taxes imposed by chapters 2, 21, and 24, to the Social Security Administration for purposes of its administration of the Social Security Act;

(B) a plan to which part I of subchapter D of chapter 1 applies, to the Social Security Administration for purposes of carrying out its responsibility under section 1131 of the Social Security Act, limited, however to return information described in section 6057(d); and

(C) taxes imposed by chapter 22, to the Railroad Retirement Board for purposes of its administration of the Railroad Retirement Act.

(2) Disclosure of returns and return information to the Department of Labor and Pension Benefit Guaranty Corporation. The Secretary may, upon written request, furnish returns and return information to the proper officers and employees of the Department of Labor and the Pension Benefit Guaranty Corporation for purposes of, but only to the extent necessary in, the administration of titles I and IV of the Employee Retirement Income Security Act of 1974.

(3) Disclosure that applicant for Federal loan has tax delinquent account.

(A) In general. Upon written request, the Secretary may disclose to the head of the Federal agency administering any included Federal loan program whether or not an applicant for a loan under such program has a tax delinquent account.

(B) Restriction on disclosure. Any disclosure under subparagraph (A) shall be made only for the purpose of, and to the extent necessary in, determining the creditworthiness of the applicant for the loan in question.

(C) Included Federal loan program defined. For purposes of this paragraph, the term "included Federal loan program" means any program under which the United States or a Federal agency makes, guarantees, or insures loans.

(4) Disclosure of returns and return information for use in personnel or claimant representative matters. The Secretary may disclose returns and return information—

(A) upon written request—

(i) to an employee or former employee of the Department of the Treasury, or to the duly authorized legal representative of such employee or former employee, who is or may be a party to any administrative action or proceeding affecting the personnel rights of such employee or former employee; or

(ii) to any person, or to the duly authorized legal representative of such person, whose rights are or may be affected by an administrative action or proceeding under section 330 of title 31, United States Code,

solely for use in the action or proceeding, or in preparation for the action or proceeding, but only to the extent that the Secretary determines that such returns or return information is or may be relevant and material to the action or proceeding; or

(B) to officers and employees of the Department of the Treasury for use in any action or proceeding described in subparagraph (A), or in preparation for such action or proceeding, to the extent necessary to advance or protect the interests of the United States.

(5) Social Security Administration. Upon written request by the Commissioner of Social Security, the Secretary may disclose information returns filed pursuant to part III of subchapter A of chapter 61 of this subtitle for the purpose of—

(A) carrying out, in accordance with an agreement entered into pursuant to section 232 of the Social Security Act, an effective return processing program; or

(B) providing information regarding the mortality status of individuals for epidemiological and similar research in accordance with section 1106(d) of the Social Security Act.

(6) Disclosure of return information to Federal, State, and local child support enforcement agencies.

(A) Return information from Internal Revenue Service. The Secretary may, upon written request, disclose to the appropriate Federal, State, or local child support enforcement agency—

(i) available return information from the master files of the Internal Revenue Service relating to the social security account number (or numbers, if the individual involved has more than one such number), address, filing status, amounts and nature of income, and the number of dependents reported on any return filed by, or with respect to, any individual with respect to whom child support obligations are sought to be established or enforced pursuant to the provisions of part D of title IV of the Social Security Act and with respect to any individual to whom such support obligations are owing, and

(ii) available return information reflected on any return filed by, or with respect to, any individual described in clause (i) relating to the amount of such individual's gross income (as defined in section 61) or consisting of the names and addresses of payors of such income and the names of any dependents reported on such return, but only if such return information is not reasonably available from any other source.

(B) Disclosure to certain agents. The following information disclosed to any child support enforcement agency under subparagraph (A) with respect to any individual with respect to whom child support obligations are sought to be established or enforced may be disclosed by such agency to any agent of such agency which is under contract with such agency to carry out the purposes described in subparagraph (C):

(i) The address and social security account number (or numbers) of such individual.

(ii) The amount of any reduction under section 6402(c) (relating to offset of past-due support against overpayments) in any overpayment otherwise payable to such individual.

(C) Restriction on disclosure. Information may be disclosed under this paragraph only for purposes of, and to the extent necessary in, establishing and collecting child support obligations from, and locating, individuals owing such obligations.

(7) Disclosure of return information to Federal, State, and local agencies administering certain programs under the Social Security Act, the Food and Nutrition Act of 2008, or Title 38, United States Code, or certain housing assistance programs.

(A) Return information from Social Security Administration. The Commissioner of Social Security shall, upon written request, disclose return information from returns with respect to net earnings from self-employment (as defined in section 1402), wages (as defined in section 3121(a) or 3401(a)), and payments of retirement income, which have been disclosed to the Social Security Administration as provided by paragraph (1) or (5) of this subsection, to any Federal, State, or local agency administering a program listed in subparagraph (D).

(B) Return information from Internal Revenue Service. The Secretary shall, upon written request, disclose current return information from returns with respect to unearned income from the Internal Revenue Service files to any Federal, State, or local agency administering a program listed in subparagraph (D).

(C) Restriction on disclosure. The Commissioner of Social Security and the Secretary shall disclose return information under subparagraphs (A) and (B) only for purposes of, and to the extent necessary in, determining eligibility for, or the correct amount of, benefits under a program listed in subparagraph (D).

(D) Programs to which rule applies. The programs to which this paragraph applies are:

(i) a State program funded under part A of title IV of the Social Security Act;

(ii) medical assistance provided under a State plan approved under title XIX of the Social Security Act or subsidies provided under section 1860D-14 of such Act;

(iii) supplemental security income benefits provided under title XVI of the Social Security Act, and federally administered supplementary payments of the type described in section 1616(a) of such Act (including payments pursuant to an agreement entered into under section 212(a) of Public Law 93-66);

(iv) any benefits provided under a State plan approved under title I, X, XIV, or XVI of the Social Security Act (as those titles apply to Puerto Rico, Guam, and the Virgin Islands);

(v) unemployment compensation provided under a State law described in section 3304 of this title;

(vi) assistance provided under the Food and Nutrition Act of 2008;

(vii) State-administered supplementary payments of the type described in section 1616(a) of the Social Security Act (including payments pursuant to an agreement entered into under section 212(a) of Public Law 93-66);

(viii)(I) any needs-based pension provided under chapter 15 of title 38, United States Code, or under any other law administered by the Secretary of Veterans Affairs;

(II) parents' dependency and indemnity compensation provided under section 1315 of title 38, United States Code;

(III) health-care services furnished under sections 1710(a)(2)(G), 1710(a)(3), and 1710(b) of such title; and

(IV) compensation paid under chapter 11 of title 38, United States Code, at the 100 percent rate based solely on unemployability and without regard to the fact that the disability or disabilities are not rated as 100 percent disabling under the rating schedule.

(ix) any housing assistance program administered by the Department of Housing and Urban Development that involves initial and periodic review of an applicant's or participant's income, except that return information may be disclosed under this clause only on written request by the Secretary of Housing and Urban Development and only for use by officers and employees of the Department of Housing and Urban Development with respect to applicants for and participants in such programs.

Only return information from returns with respect to net earnings from self-employment and wages may be disclosed under this paragraph for use with respect to any program described in clause (viii)(IV).

(8) Disclosure of certain return information by Social Security Administration to Federal, State, and local child support enforcement agencies.

(A) In general. Upon written request, the Commissioner of Social Security shall disclose directly to officers and employees of a Federal or State or local child support enforcement agency return information from returns with respect to social security account numbers, net earnings from self-employment (as defined in section 1402), wages (as defined in section 3121(a) or 3401(a)), and payments of retirement income which have been disclosed to the Social Security Administration as provided by paragraph (1) or (5) of this subsection.

(B) Restriction on disclosure. The Commissioner of Social Security shall disclose return information under subparagraph (A) only for purposes of, and to the extent necessary in, establishing and collecting child support obligations from, and locating, individuals owing such obligations. For purposes of the preceding sentence, the term "child support obligations" only includes obligations which are being enforced pursuant to a plan described in section 454 of the Social Security Act which has been approved by the Secretary of Health and Human Services under part D of title IV of such Act.

(C) State or local child support enforcement agency. For purposes of this paragraph, the term "State or local child support enforcement agency" means any agency of a State or political subdivision thereof operating pursuant to a plan described in subparagraph (B).

(9) Disclosure of alcohol fuel producers to administrators of State alcohol laws. Notwithstanding any other provision of this section, the Secretary may disclose—

Information and returns

(A) the name and address of any person who is qualified to produce alcohol for fuel use under section 5181, and

(B) the location of any premises to be used by such person in producing alcohol for fuel,

to any State agency, body, or commission, or its legal representative, which is charged under the laws of such State with responsibility for administration of State alcohol laws solely for use in the administration of such laws.

(10) Disclosure of certain information to agencies requesting a reduction under subsection (c), (d), (e), or (f) of section 6402.

(A) Return information from Internal Revenue Service. The Secretary may, upon receiving a written request, disclose to officers and employees of any agency seeking a reduction under subsection (c), (d), (e), or (f) of section 6402, to officers and employees of the Department of Labor for purposes of facilitating the exchange of data in connection with a request made under subsection (f)(5) of section 6402, and to officers and employees of the Department of the Treasury in connection with such reduction—

(i) taxpayer identity information with respect to the taxpayer against whom such a reduction was made or not made and with respect to any other person filing a joint return with such taxpayer,

(ii) the fact that a reduction has been made or has not been made under such subsection with respect to such taxpayer,

(iii) the amount of such reduction,

(iv) whether such taxpayer filed a joint return, and

(v) the fact that a payment was made (and the amount of the payment) to the spouse of the taxpayer on the basis of a joint return.

(B)(i) Restriction on use of disclosed information. Any officers and employees of an agency receiving return information under subparagraph (A) shall use such information only for the purposes of, and to the extent necessary in, establishing appropriate agency records, locating any person with respect to whom a reduction under subsection (c), (d), (e), (f) of section 6402 is sought for purposes of collecting the debt with respect to which the reduction is sought, or in the defense of any litigation or administrative procedure ensuing from a reduction made under subsection (c), (d), (e), or (f) of section 6402.

(ii) Notwithstanding clause (i), return information disclosed to officers and employees of the Department of Labor may be accessed by agents who maintain and provide technological support to the Department of Labor's Interstate Connection Network (ICON) solely for the purpose of providing such maintenance and support.

(11) Disclosure of return information to carry out Federal Employees' Retirement System.

(A) In general. The Commissioner of Social Security shall, on written request, disclose to the Office of Personnel Management return information from returns with respect to net earnings from self-employment (as defined in section 1402), wages (as defined in section 3121(a) or 3401(a)), and payments of retirement income, which have been disclosed to the Social Security Administration as provided by paragraph (1) or (5).

(B) Restriction on disclosure. The Commissioner of Social Security shall disclose return information under subparagraph (A) only for purposes of, and to the extent necessary in, the administration of chapters 83 and 84 of title 5, United States Code.

(12) Disclosure of certain taxpayer identity information for verification of employment status of medicare beneficiary and spouse of medicare beneficiary.

(A) Return information from Internal Revenue Service. The Secretary shall, upon written request from the Commissioner of Social Security, disclose to the Commissioner available filing status and taxpayer identity information from the individual master files of the Internal Revenue Service relating to whether any medicare beneficiary identified by the Commissioner was a married individual (as defined in section 7703) for any specified year after 1986, and, if so, the name of the spouse of such individual and such spouse's TIN.

(B) Return information from Social Security Administration. The Commissioner of Social Security shall, upon written request from the Administrator of the Centers for Medicare & Medicaid Services, disclose to the Administrator the following information:

(i) The name and TIN of each medicare beneficiary who is identified as having received wages (as defined in section 3401(a)), above an amount (if any) specified by the Secretary of Health and Human Services, from a qualified employer in a previous year.

(ii) For each medicare beneficiary who was identified as married under subparagraph (A) and whose spouse is identified as having received wages, above an amount (if any) specified by the Secretary of Health and Human Services, from a qualified employer in a previous year—

(I) the name and TIN of the medicare beneficiary, and

(II) the name and TIN of the spouse.

(iii) With respect to each such qualified employer, the name, address, and TIN of the employer and the number of individuals with respect to whom written statements were furnished under section 6051 by the employer with respect to such previous year.

(C) Disclosure by Centers for Medicare & Medicaid Services. With respect to the information disclosed under subparagraph (B), the Administrator of the Centers for Medicare & Medicaid Services may disclose—

(i) to the qualified employer referred to in such subparagraph the name and TIN of each individual identified under such subparagraph as having received wages from the employer (hereinafter in this subparagraph referred to as the "employee") for purposes of determining during what period such employee or the employee's spouse may be (or have been) covered under a group health plan of the employer and what benefits are or were covered under the plan (including the name, address, and identifying number of the plan),

(ii) to any group health plan which provides or provided coverage to such an employee or spouse, the name of such employee and the employee's spouse (if the spouse is a medicare beneficiary) and the name and address of the employer, and, for the purpose of presenting a claim to the plan—

(I) the TIN of such employee if benefits were paid under title XVIII of the Social Security Act with respect to the employee during a period in which the plan was a primary plan (as defined in section 1862(b)(2)(A) of the Social Security Act), and

(II) the TIN of such spouse if benefits were paid under such title with respect to the spouse during such period, and

(iii) to any agent of such Administrator the information referred to in subparagraph (B) for purposes of carrying out clauses (i) and (ii) on behalf of such Administrator.

(D) Special rules.

(i) Restrictions on disclosure. Information may be disclosed under this paragraph only for purposes of, and to the extent necessary in, determining the extent to which any medicare beneficiary is covered under any group health plan.

(ii) Timely response to requests. Any request made under subparagraph (A) or (B) shall be complied with as soon as possible but in no event later than 120 days after the date the request was made.

(E) Definitions. For purposes of this paragraph—

(i) Medicare beneficiary. The term "medicare beneficiary" means an individual entitled to benefits under part A, or enrolled under part B, of title XVIII of the Social Security Act, but does not include such an individual enrolled in part A under section 1818.

(ii) Group health plan. The term "group health plan" means any group health plan (as defined in section 5000(b)(1)).

(iii) Qualified employer. The term "qualified employer" means, for a calendar year, an employer which has furnished written statements under section 6051 with respect to at least 20 individuals for wages paid in the year.

(13) Disclosure of return information to carry out income contingent repayment of student loans.

(A) In general. The Secretary may, upon written request from the Secretary of Education, disclose to officers and employees of the Department of Education return information with respect to a taxpayer who has received an applicable student loan and whose loan repayment amounts are based in whole or in part on the taxpayer's income. Such return information shall be limited to—

(i) taxpayer identity information with respect to such taxpayer,

(ii) the filing status of such taxpayer, and

(iii) the adjusted gross income of such taxpayer.

(B) Restriction on use of disclosed information. Return information disclosed under subparagraph (A) may be used by officers and employees of the Department of Education only for the purposes of, and to the extent necessary in, establishing the appropriate income contingent repayment amount for an applicable student loan.

(C) Applicable student loan. For purposes of this paragraph, the term "applicable student loan" means—

(i) any loan made under the program authorized under part D of title IV of the Higher Education Act of 1965, and

(ii) any loan made under part B or E of title IV of the Higher Education Act of 1965 which is in default and has been assigned to the Department of Education.

(D) Termination. This paragraph shall not apply to any request made after December 31, 2007.

(14) Disclosure of return information to United States Customs Service. The Secretary may, upon written request from the Commissioner of the United States Customs Service, disclose to officers and employees of the Department of the Treasury such return information with respect to taxes imposed by chapters 1 and 6 as the Secretary may prescribe by regulations, solely for the purpose of, and only to the extent necessary in—

(A) ascertaining the correctness of any entry in audits as provided for in section 509 of the Tariff Act of 1930 (19 U.S.C. 1509), or

(B) other actions to recover any loss of revenue, or to collect duties, taxes, and fees, determined to be due and owing pursuant to such audits.

(15) Disclosure of returns filed under section 6050I. The Secretary may, upon written request, disclose to officers and employees of—

(A) any Federal agency,

(B) any agency of a State or local government, or

(C) any agency of the government of a foreign country, information contained on returns filed under section 6050I. Any such disclosure shall be made on the same basis, and subject to the same conditions, as apply to disclosures of information on reports filed under section 5313 of title 31, United States Code; except that no disclosure under this paragraph shall be made for purposes of the administration of any tax law.

(16) Disclosure of return information for purposes of administering the District of Columbia Retirement Protection Act of 1997.

(A) In general. Upon written request available return information (including such information disclosed to the Social Security Administration under paragraph (1) or (5) of this subsection), relating to the amount of wage income (as defined in section 3121(a) or 3401(a)), the name, address, and identifying number assigned under section 6109, of payors of wage income, taxpayer identity (as defined in subsection 6103(b)(6)), and the occupational status reflected on any return filed by, or with respect to, any individual with respect to whom eligibility for, or the correct amount of, benefits under the District of Columbia Retirement Protection Act of 1997, is sought to be determined, shall be disclosed by the Commissioner of Social Security, or to the extent not available from the Social Security Administration, by the Secretary, to any duly authorized officer or employee of the Department of the Treasury, or a Trustee or any designated officer or employee of a Trustee (as defined in the District of Columbia Retirement Protection Act of 1997), or any actuary engaged by a trustee under the terms of the District of Columbia Retirement Protection Act of 1997, whose official duties require such disclosure, solely for the purpose of, and to the extent necessary in, determining an individual's eligibility for, or the correct amount of, benefits under the District of Columbia Retirement Protection Act of 1997.

(B) Disclosure for use in judicial or administrative proceedings. Return information disclosed to any person under this paragraph may be disclosed in a judicial or administrative proceeding relating to the determination of an individual's eligibility for, or the correct amount of, benefits under the District of Columbia Retirement Protection Act of 1997.

(17) Disclosure to National Archives and Records Administration. The Secretary shall, upon written request from the Archivist of the United States, disclose or authorize the disclosure of returns and return information to officers and employees of the National Archives and Records Administration for purposes of, and only to the extent necessary in, the appraisal of records for destruction or retention. No such officer or employee shall, except to the extent authorized by subsection (f), (i)(8), or (p), disclose any return or return information disclosed under the preceding sentence to any person other than to the Secretary, or to another officer or employee of the National Archives and Records Administration whose official duties require such disclosure for purposes of such appraisal.

(18) Disclosure of return information for purposes of carrying out a program for advance payment of credit for health insurance costs of eligible individuals. The Secretary may disclose to providers of health insurance for any certified individual (as defined in section 7527(c)) return information with respect to such certified individual only to the extent necessary to carry out the program established by section 7527 (relating to advance payment of credit for health insurance costs of eligible individuals).

(19) Disclosure of return information for purposes of providing transitional assistance under Medicare discount card program.

(A) In general. The Secretary, upon written request from the Secretary of Health and Human Services pursuant to carrying out section 1860D—31 of the Social Security Act, shall disclose to officers, employees, and contractors of the Department of Health and Human Services with respect to a taxpayer for the applicable year—

(i) (I) whether the adjusted gross income, as modified in accordance with specifications of the Secretary of Health and Human Services for purposes of carrying out such section, of such taxpayer and, if applicable, such taxpayer's spouse, for the applicable year, exceeds the amounts specified by the Secretary of Health and Human Services in order to apply the 100 and 135 percent of the poverty lines under such section, (II) whether the return was a joint return, and (III) the applicable year, or

(ii) if applicable, the fact that there is no return filed for such taxpayer for the applicable year.

(B) Definition of applicable year. For the purposes of this subsection, the term "applicable year" means the most recent taxable year for which information is available in the Internal Revenue Service's taxpayer data information systems, or, if there is no return filed for such taxpayer for such year, the prior taxable year.

(C) Restriction on use of disclosed information. Return information disclosed under this paragraph may be used only for the purposes of determining eligibility for and administering transitional assistance under section 1860D—31 of the Social Security Act.

(20) Disclosure of return information to carry out Medicare part B premium subsidy adjustment and part D base beneficiary premium increase.

(A) In general. The Secretary shall, upon written request from the Commissioner of Social Security, disclose to officers, employees, and contractors of the Social Security Administration return information of a taxpayer whose premium (according to the records of the Secretary) may be subject to adjustment under section 1839(i) or increase under section 1860D-13(a)(7) of the Social Security Act. Such return information shall be limited to—

(i) taxpayer identity information with respect to such taxpayer,

(ii) the filing status of such taxpayer,

(iii) the adjusted gross income of such taxpayer,

(iv) the amounts excluded from such taxpayer's gross income under sections 135 and 911 to the extent such information is available,

(v) the interest received or accrued during the taxable year which is exempt from the tax imposed by chapter 1 to the extent such information is available,

(vi) the amounts excluded from such taxpayer's gross income by sections 931 and 933 to the extent such information is available,

(vii) such other information relating to the liability of the taxpayer as is prescribed by the Secretary by regulation as might indicate in the case of a taxpayer who is an individual described in subsection (i)(4)(B)(iii) of section 1839 of the Social Security Act that the amount of the premium of the taxpayer under such section may be subject to adjustment under subsection (i) of such section or increase under section 1860D-13(a)(7) of such Act and the amount of such adjustment, and

(viii) the taxable year with respect to which the preceding information relates.

(B) Restriction on use of disclosed information.

(i) In general. Return information disclosed under subparagraph (A) may be used by officers, employees, and contractors of the Social Security Administration only for the purposes of, and to the extent necessary in, establishing the appropriate amount of any premium adjustment under such section 1839(i) or increase under such section 1860D-13(a)(7) or for the purpose of resolving taxpayer appeals with respect to any such premium adjustment or increase.

(ii) Disclosure to other agencies. Officers, employees, and contractors of the Social Security Administration may disclose—

(I) the taxpayer identity information and the amount of the premium subsidy adjustment or premium increase with respect to a taxpayer described in subparagraph (A) to officers, employees, and contractors of the Centers for Medicare and Medicaid Services, to the extent that such disclosure is necessary for the collection of the premium subsidy amount or the increased premium amount,

(II) the taxpayer identity information and the amount of the premium subsidy adjustment or the increased premium amount with respect to a taxpayer described in subparagraph (A) to officers and employees of the Office of Personnel Management and the Railroad Retirement Board, to the extent that such disclosure is necessary for the collection of the premium subsidy amount or the increased premium amount,

(III) return information with respect to a taxpayer described in subparagraph (A) to officers and employees of the Department of Health and Human Services to the extent necessary to resolve administrative appeals of such premium subsidy adjustment or increased premium, and

(IV) return information with respect to a taxpayer described in subparagraph (A) to officers and employees of the Department of Justice for use in judicial proceedings to the extent necessary to carry out the purposes described in clause (i).

(21) Disclosure of return information to carry out eligibility requirements for certain programs.

(A) In general. The Secretary, upon written request from the Secretary of Health and Human Services, shall disclose to officers, employees, and contractors of the Department of Health and Human Services return information of any taxpayer whose income is relevant in determining any premium tax credit under section 36B or any cost-sharing reduction under section 1402 of the Patient Protection and Affordable Care Act or eligibility for participation in a State medicaid program under title XIX of the Social Security Act, a State's children's health insurance program under title XXI of the Social Security Act, or a basic health program under section 1331 of Patient Protection and Affordable Care Act. Such return information shall be limited to—

(i) taxpayer identity information with respect to such taxpayer,

(ii) the filing status of such taxpayer,

(iii) the number of individuals for whom a deduction is allowed under section 151 with respect to the taxpayer (including the taxpayer and the taxpayer's spouse),

(iv) the modified gross income (as defined in section 36B) of such taxpayer and each of the other individuals included under clause (iii) who are required to file a return of tax imposed by chapter 1 for the taxable year,

(v) such other information as is prescribed by the Secretary by regulation as might indicate whether the taxpayer is eligible for such credit or reduction (and the amount thereof), and

(vi) the taxable year with respect to which the preceding information relates or, if applicable, the fact that such information is not available.

(B) Information to exchange and state agencies. The Secretary of Health and Human Services may disclose to an Exchange established under the Patient Protection and Affordable Care Act or its contractors, or to a State agency administering a State program described in subparagraph (A) or its contractors, any inconsistency between the information provided by the Exchange or State agency to the Secretary and the information provided to the Secretary under subparagraph (A).

(C) Restriction on use of disclosed information. Return information disclosed under subparagraph (A) or (B) may be used by officers, employees, and contractors of the Department of Health and Human Services, an Exchange, or a State agency only for the purposes of, and to the extent necessary in—

(i) establishing eligibility for participation in the Exchange, and verifying the appropriate amount of, any credit or reduction described in subparagraph (A),

(ii) determining eligibility for participation in the State programs described in subparagraph (A).

(22) Disclosure of return information to Department of Health and Human Services for purposes of enhancing medicare program integrity.

(A) In general. The Secretary shall, upon written request from the Secretary of Health and Human Services, disclose to officers and employees of the Department of Health and Human Services return information with respect to a taxpayer who has applied to enroll, or reenroll, as a provider of services or supplier under the Medicare program under title XVIII of the Social Security Act. Such return information shall be limited to—

(i) the taxpayer identity information with respect to such taxpayer;

(ii) the amount of the delinquent tax debt owed by that taxpayer; and

(iii) the taxable year to which the delinquent tax debt pertains.

(B) Restriction on disclosure. Return information disclosed under subparagraph (A) may be used by officers and employees of the Department of Health and Human Services for the purposes of, and to the extent necessary in, establishing the taxpayer's eligibility for enrollment or reenrollment in the Medicare program, or in any administrative or judicial proceeding relating to, or arising from, a denial of such enrollment or reenrollment, or in determining the level of enhanced oversight to be applied with respect to such taxpayer pursuant to section 1866(j)(3) of the Social Security Act.

(C) Delinquent tax debt. For purposes of this paragraph, the term 'delinquent tax debt' means an outstanding debt under this title for which a notice of lien has been filed pursuant to section 6323, but the term does not include a debt that is being paid in a timely manner pursuant to an agreement under section 6159 or 7122, or a debt with respect to which a collection due process hearing under section 6330 is requested, pending, or completed and no payment is required.

(m) Disclosure of taxpayer identity information.

(1) Tax refunds. The Secretary may disclose taxpayer identity information to the press and other media for purposes of notifying persons entitled to tax refunds when the Secretary, after reasonable effort and lapse of time, has been unable to locate such persons.

(2) Federal claims.

(A) In general. Except as provided in subparagraph (B), the Secretary may, upon written request, disclose the mailing address of a taxpayer for use by officers, employees, or agents of a Federal agency for purposes of locating such taxpayer to collect or compromise a Federal claim against the taxpayer in accordance with sections 3711, 3717, and 3718 of title 31.

(B) Special rule for consumer reporting agency. In the case of an agent of a Federal agency which is a consumer reporting agency (within the meaning of section 603(f) of the Fair Credit Reporting Act (15 U.S.C. 1681a(f))), the mailing address of a taxpayer may be disclosed to such agent under subparagraph (A) only for the purpose of allowing such agent to prepare a commercial credit report on the taxpayer for use by such Federal agency in accordance with sections 3711, 3717, and 3718 of title 31.

(3) National Institute for Occupational Safety and Health. Upon written request, the Secretary may disclose the mailing address of taxpayers to officers and employees of the National Institute for Occupational Safety and Health solely for the purpose of locating individuals who are, or may have been, exposed to occupational hazards in order to determine the status of their health or to inform them of the possible need for medical care and treatment.

(4) Individuals who owe an overpayment of Federal Pell Grants or who have defaulted on student loans administered by the Department of Education.

(A) In general. Upon written request by the Secretary of Education, the Secretary may disclose the mailing address of any taxpayer—

(i) who owes an overpayment of a grant awarded to such taxpayer under subpart 1 of part A of title IV of the Higher Education Act of 1965, or

(ii) who has defaulted on a loan—

(I) made under part B, D, or E of title IV of the Higher Education Act of 1965, or

(II) made pursuant to section 3(a)(1) of the Migration and Refugee Assistance Act of 1962 to a student at an institution of higher education,

for use only by officers, employees, or agents of the Department of Education for purposes of locating such taxpayer for purposes of collecting such overpayment or loan.

(B) Disclosure to educational institutions, etc. Any mailing address disclosed under subparagraph (A)(i) may be disclosed by the Secretary of Education to—

(i) any lender, or any State or nonprofit guarantee agency, which is participating under part B or D of title IV of the Higher Education Act of 1965, or

(ii) any educational institution with which the Secretary of Education has an agreement under subpart 1 of part A, or part D or E, of title IV of such Act,

for use only by officers, employees, or agents of such lender, guarantee agency, or institution whose duties relate to the collection of student loans for purposes of locating individuals who have defaulted on student loans made under such loan programs for purposes of collecting such loans.

(5) Individuals who have defaulted on student loans administered by the Department of Health and Human Services.

(A) In general. Upon written request by the Secretary of Health and Human Services, the Secretary may disclose the mailing address of any taxpayer who has defaulted on a loan made under part C of title VII of the Public Health Service Act or under subpart II of part B of title VIII of such Act, for use only by officers, employees, or agents of the Department of Health and Human Services for purposes of locating such taxpayer for purposes of collecting such loan.

(B) Disclosure to schools and eligible lenders. Any mailing address disclosed under subparagraph (A) may be disclosed by the Secretary of Health and Human Services to—

(i) any school with which the Secretary of Health and Human Services has an agreement under subpart II of part C of title VII of the Public Health Service Act or subpart II of part B of title VIII of such Act, or

(ii) any eligible lender (within the meaning of section 737(4) of such Act) participating under subpart I of part C of title VII of such Act,

for use only by officers, employees, or agents of such school or eligible lender whose duties relate to the collection of student loans for purposes of locating individuals who have defaulted on student loans made under such subparts for the purposes of collecting such loans.

(6) Blood donor locator service.

(A) In general. Upon written request pursuant to section 1141 of the Social Security Act, the Secretary shall disclose the mailing address of taxpayers to officers and employees of the Blood Donor Locator Service in the Department of Health and Human Services.

(B) Restriction on disclosure. The Secretary shall disclose return information under subparagraph (A) only for purposes of, and to the extent necessary in, assisting under the Blood Donor Locator Service authorized persons (as defined in section 1141(h)(1) of the Social Security Act) in locating blood donors who, as indicated by donated blood or products derived therefrom or by the history of the subsequent use of such blood or blood products, have or may have the virus for acquired immune deficiency syndrome, in order to inform such donors of the possible need for medical care and treatment.

(C) Safeguards. The Secretary shall destroy all related blood donor records (as defined in section 1141(h)(2) of the Social Security Act) in the possession of the Department of the Treasury upon completion of their use in making the disclosure required under subparagraph (A), so as to make such records undisclosable.

(7) Social security account statement furnished by Social Security Administration. Upon written request by the Commissioner of Social Security, the Secretary may disclose the mailing address of any taxpayer who is entitled to receive a social security account statement pursuant to section 1143(c) of the Social Security Act, for use only by officers, employees or agents of the Social Security Administration for purposes of mailing such statement to such taxpayer.

(n) Certain other persons.

Pursuant to regulations prescribed by the Secretary, returns and return information may be disclosed to any person, including any person described in section 7513(a), to the extent necessary in connection with the processing, storage, transmission, and reproduction of such returns and return information, the programming, maintenance, repair, testing, and procurement of equipment, and the providing of other services, for purposes of tax administration.

(o) Disclosure of returns and return information with respect to certain taxes.

(1) Taxes imposed by subtitle E.

(A) In general. Returns and return information with respect to taxes imposed by subtitle E (relating to taxes on alcohol, tobacco, and firearms) shall be open to inspection by or disclosure to officers and employees of a Federal agency whose official duties require such inspection or disclosure.

(B) Use in certain proceedings. Returns and return information disclosed to a Federal agency under subparagraph (A) may be used in an action or proceeding (or in preparation for such action or proceeding) brought under section 625 of the American Jobs Creation Act of 2004 for the collection of any unpaid assessment or penalty arising under such Act.

(2) Taxes imposed by chapter 35. Returns and return information with respect to taxes imposed by chapter 35 (relating to taxes on wagering) shall, notwithstanding any other provision of this section, be open to inspection by or disclosure only to such person or persons and for such purpose or purposes as are prescribed by section 4424.

(p) Procedure and recordkeeping.

(1) Manner, time, and place of inspections. Requests for the inspection or disclosure of a return or return information and such inspection or disclosure shall be made in such manner and at such time and place as shall be prescribed by the Secretary.

(2) Procedure.

(A) Reproduction of returns. A reproduction or certified reproduction of a return shall, upon written request, be furnished to any person to whom disclosure or inspection of such return is authorized under this section. A reasonable fee may be prescribed for furnishing such reproduction or certified reproduction.

(B) Disclosure of return information. Return information disclosed to any person under the provisions of this title may be provided in the form of written documents, reproductions of such documents, films or photoimpressions, or electronically produced tapes, disks, or records, or by any other mode or means which the Secretary determines necessary or appropriate. A reasonable fee may be prescribed for furnishing such return information.

(C) Use of reproductions. Any reproduction of any return, document, or other matter made in accordance with this paragraph shall have the same legal status as the original, and any such reproduction shall, if properly authenticated, be admissible in evidence in any judicial or administrative proceeding as if it were the original, whether or not the original is in existence.

(3) Records of inspection and disclosure.
(A) System of recordkeeping. Except as otherwise provided by this paragraph, the Secretary shall maintain a permanent system of standardized records or accountings of all requests for inspection or disclosure of returns and return information (including the reasons for and dates of such requests) and of returns and return information inspected or disclosed under this section and section 6104(c). Notwithstanding the provisions of section 552a(c) of title 5, United States Code, the Secretary shall not be required to maintain a record or accounting of requests for inspection or disclosure of returns and return information, or of returns and return information inspected or disclosed, under the authority of subsections (c), (e), (f)(5), (h)(1), (3)(A), or (4), (i)(4), or (8)(A)(ii), (k)(1), (2), (6), (8), or (9), (l)(1), (4)(B), (5), (7), (8), (9), (10), (11), (12), (13), (14), (15), (16), (17), or (18), (m), or (n). The records or accountings required to be maintained under this paragraph shall be available for examination by the Joint Committee on Taxation or the Chief of Staff of such joint committee. Such record or accounting shall also be available for examination by such person or persons as may be, but only to the extent, authorized to make such examination under section 552a(c)(3) of title 5, United States Code.

(B) Report by the Secretary. The Secretary shall, within 90 days after the close of each calendar year, furnish to the Joint Committee on Taxation a report with respect to, or summary of, the records or accountings described in subparagraph (A) in such form and containing such information as such joint committee or the Chief of Staff of such joint committee may designate. Such report or summary shall not, however, include a record or accounting of any request by the President under subsection (g) for, or the disclosure in response to such request of, any return or return information with respect to any individual who, at the time of such request, was an officer or employee of the executive branch of the Federal Government. Such report or summary, or any part thereof, may be disclosed by such joint committee to such persons and for such purposes as the joint committee may, by record vote of a majority of the members of the joint committee, determine.

(C) Public report on disclosures. The Secretary shall, within 90 days after the close of each calendar year, furnish to the Joint Committee on Taxation for disclosure to the public a report with respect to the records or accountings described in subparagraph (A) which—
 (i) provides with respect to each Federal agency, each agency, body, or commission described in subsection (d), (i)(3)(B)(i) or (7)(A)(ii), or (l)(6), and the Government Accountability Office the number of—
  (I) requests for disclosure of returns and return information,
  (II) instances in which returns and return information were disclosed pursuant to such requests or otherwise,
  (III) taxpayers whose returns, or return information with respect to whom, were disclosed pursuant to such requests, and
 (ii) describes the general purposes for which such requests were made,

(4) Safeguards. Any Federal agency described in subsection (h)(2), (h)(5), (i)(1), (2), (3), (5), or (7), (j)(1), (2), or (5), (k)(8) or (10), (l)(1), (2), (3), (5), (10), (11), (13), (14), (17), or (22) or (o)(1)(A), the Government Accountability Office, the Congressional Budget Office, or any agency, body, or commission described in subsection (d), (i)(3)(B)(i) or 7(A)(ii), or (k)(10),(l)(6), (7), (8), (9), (12), (15), or (16), any appropriate State officer (as defined in section 6104(c)), or any other person described in subsection (l)(10), (16), (18), (19), or (20) , or any entity described in subsection (l)(21), shall, as a condition for receiving returns or return information—

(A) establish and maintain, to the satisfaction of the Secretary, a permanent system of standardized records with respect to any request, the reason for such request, and the date of such request made by or of it and any disclosure of return or return information made by or to it;

(B) establish and maintain, to the satisfaction of the Secretary, a secure area or place in which such returns or return information shall be stored;

(C) restrict, to the satisfaction of the Secretary, access to the returns or return information only to persons whose duties or responsibilities require access and to whom disclosure may be made under the provisions of this title;

(D) provide such other safeguards which the Secretary determines (and which he prescribes in regulations) to be necessary or appropriate to protect the confidentiality of the returns or return information;

(E) furnish a report to the Secretary, at such time and containing such information as the Secretary may prescribe, which describes the procedures established and utilized by such agency, body, or commission, the Government Accountability Office, or the Congressional Budget Office for ensuring the confidentiality of returns and return information required by this paragraph; and

(F) upon completion of use of such returns or return information—
 (i) in the case of an agency, body, or commission described in subsection (d), (i)(3)(B)(i), or (l)(6), (7), (8), (9), or (16), any appropriate State officer (as defined in section 6104(c)), or any other person described in subsection (l)(10), (16), (18), (19), or (20) return to the Secretary such returns or return information (along with any copies made therefrom) or make such returns or return information undisclosable in any manner and furnish a written report to the Secretary describing such manner,
 (ii) in the case of an agency described in subsections (h)(2), (h)(5), (i)(1), (2), (3), (5) or (7), (j)(1), (2), or (5), (k)(8) or (10), (l)(1), (2), (3), (5), (10), (11), (12), (13), (14), (15), (17), or (22), or (o)(1)(A) or any entity described in subsection (l)(21), the Government Accountability Office, or the Congressional Budget Office, either—
  (I) return to the Secretary such returns or return information (along with any copies made therefrom),
  (II) otherwise make such returns or return information undisclosable, or
  (III) to the extent not so returned or made undisclosable, ensure that the conditions of subparagraphs (A), (B), (C), (D), and (E) of this paragraph continue to be met with respect to such returns or return information, and
 (iii) in the case of the Department of Health and Human Services for purposes of subsection (m)(6),

destroy all such return information upon completion of its use in providing the notification for which the information was obtained, so as to make such information undisclosable;

except that the conditions of subparagraphs (A), (B), (C), (D), and (E) shall cease to apply with respect to any return or return information if, and to the extent that, such return or return information is disclosed in the course of any judicial or administrative proceeding and made a part of the public record thereof. If the Secretary determines that any such agency, body, or commission, including an agency, an appropriate State officer (as defined in section 6104(c)), or any other person described in subsection (l)(10), (16), (18), (19), or (20) or any entity described in subsection (l)(21), or the Government Accountability Office or the Congressional Budget Office, has failed to, or does not, meet the requirements of this paragraph, he may, after any proceedings for review established under paragraph (7), take such actions as are necessary to ensure such requirements are met, including refusing to disclose returns or return information to such agency, body, or commission, including an agency, an appropriate State officer (as defined in section 6104(c)), or any other person described in subsection (l)(10), (16), (18), (19), or (20) or any entity described in subsection (l)(21), or the Government Accountability Office or the Congressional Budget Office, until he determines that such requirements have been or will be met. In the case of any agency which receives any mailing address under paragraph (2), (4), (6), or (7) of subsection (m) and which discloses any such mailing address to any agent, or which receives any information under paragraph (6)(A), (10), (12)(B), or (16) of subsection (l) and which discloses any such information to any agent, or any person including an agent described in subsection (l)(10) or (16), this paragraph shall apply to such agency and each such agent or other person (except that, in the case of an agent, or any person including an agent described in subsection (l)(10) or (16), any report to the Secretary or other action with respect to the Secretary shall be made or taken through such agency). For purposes of applying this paragraph in any case to which subsection (m)(6) applies, the term "return information" includes related blood donor records (as defined in section 1141(h)(2) of the Social Security Act).

(5) Report on procedures and safeguards. After the close of each calendar year, the Secretary shall furnish to each committee described in subsection (f)(1) a report which describes the procedures and safeguards established and utilized by such agencies, bodies, or commissions, the Government Accountability Office, and the Congressional Budget Office for ensuring the confidentiality of returns and return information as required by this subsection. Such report shall also describe instances of deficiencies in, and failure to establish or utilize, such procedures.

(6) Audit of procedures and safeguards.

(A) Audit by Comptroller General. The Comptroller General may audit the procedures and safeguards established by such agencies, bodies, or commissions and the Congressional Budget Office pursuant to this subsection to determine whether such safeguards and procedures meet the requirements of this subsection and ensure the confidentiality of returns and return information. The Comptroller General shall notify the Secretary before any such audit is conducted.

(B) Records of inspection and reports by the Comptroller General. The Comptroller General shall—

(i) maintain a permanent system of standardized records and accountings of returns and return information inspected by officers and employees of the Government Accountability Office under subsection (i)(8)(A)(ii) and shall, within 90 days after the close of each calendar year, furnish to the Secretary a report with respect to, or summary of, such records or accountings in such form and containing such information as the Secretary may prescribe, and

(ii) furnish an annual report to each committee described in subsection (f) and to the Secretary setting forth his findings with respect to any audit conducted pursuant to subparagraph (A).

The Secretary may disclose to the Joint Committee any report furnished to him under clause (i).

(7) Administrative review. The Secretary shall by regulations prescribe procedures which provide for administrative review of any determination under paragraph (4) that any agency, body, or commission described in subsection (d) has failed to meet the requirements of such paragraph.

(8) State law requirements.

(A) Safeguards. Notwithstanding any other provision of this section, no return or return information shall be disclosed after December 31, 1978, to any officer or employee of any State which requires a taxpayer to attach to, or include in, any State tax return a copy of any portion of his Federal return, or information reflected on such Federal return, unless such State adopts provisions of law which protect the confidentiality of the copy of the Federal return (or portion thereof) attached to, or the Federal return information reflected on, such State tax return.

(B) Disclosure of returns or return information in State returns. Nothing in subparagraph (A) shall be construed to prohibit the disclosure by an officer or employee of any State of any copy of any portion of a Federal return or any information on a Federal return which is required to be attached or included in a State return to another officer or employee of such State (or political subdivision of such State) if such disclosure is specifically authorized by State law.

(q) Regulations.

The Secretary is authorized to prescribe such other regulations as are necessary to carry out the provisions of this section.

In 2010, P.L. 111-198, Sec. 4(a)(1), added "and the head of any State agency charged with the responsibility for administration of prisons" after "the head of the Federal Bureau of Prisons" in subpara. (k)(10)(A) . . . Sec. 4(a)(2), substituted "Federal or State prison" for "Federal prison" in subpara. (k)(10)(A) . . . Sec. 4(b)(1), added "and the head of any State agency charged with the responsibility for administration of prisons" after "the head of the Federal Bureau of Prisons" in subpara. (k)(10)(B) . . . Sec. 4(b)(2), added "or agency" after "such Bureau" in subpara. (k)(10)(B) . . . Sec. 4(c), added "(k)(10)," before "(l)(6)," in the matter preceding subpara. (p)(4)(A). . . . Sec. 4(d), substituted "TO CERTAIN PRISON OFFICIALS" for "OF PRISONERS TO FEDERAL BUREAU OF PRISONS" in the heading of para. (k)(10), effective for disclosures made after 7/2/2010.
—P.L. 111-192, Sec. 103(a)(1), added para. (l)(22).
—P.L. 111-192, Sec. 103(a)(2), substituted "(17), or (22)" for "or (17)" each place it appears in the matter preceding subparagraph (p)(4)(A) and in subpara. (p)(4)(F)(ii), enacted 6/25/2010.
—P.L. 111-152, Sec. 1004(a)(1)(B), substituted "modified adjusted gross" for "modified gross" each place it appears in clause (l)(21)(A)(iv), enacted 3/30/2010.
—P.L. 111-148, Sec. 1414(a)(1), added para. (l)(21) . . . Sec. 1414(b), substituted ", or any entity described in subsection (l)(21)," after "or (20)" in para. (p)(4) . . . Sec. 1414(c)(2), added "or any entity described in subsection (l)(21)," after "or (o)(1)(A)" in clause (p)(4)(F)(ii) . . . . Sec. 1414(c)(3), added "or any entity described in subsection (l)(21)," after "or (20)" in both places it appears in para. (p)(4) . . . Sec. 3308(b)(2)(A), added "and part D base beneficiary premium increase" after "part B premium subsidy adjustment" in the heading of para. (l)(20) . . . Sec. 3308(b)(2)(B)(i), added "or increase under section 1860D-13(a)(7)" after "1839(i)" in subpara. (l)(20)(A) . . . Sec. 3308(b)(2)(B)(ii), added "or increase under section 1860D-13(a)(7) of such Act" after "subsection (i) of such section"

in clause (l)(20)(A)(vii) . . . Sec. 3308(b)(2)(C)(i), substituted "(i) In general. Return information" for "Return information" in subpara. (l)(20)(B) . . . Sec. 3308(b)(2)(C)(ii), added "or increase under such section 1860D-13(a)(7)" before the period in clause (l)(20)(B)(i), as amended by Sec. 3308(b)(2)(C)(i), above . . . Sec. 3308(b)(2)(C)(iii), added "or for the purpose of resolving taxpayer appeals with respect to any such premium adjustment or increase" before the period in clause (l)(20)(B)(i), as amended by Sec. 3308(b)(2)(C)(i), above . . . Sec. 3308(b)(2)(C)(iv), added clause (l)(20)(B)(ii), enacted 3/23/2010.

In 2009, P.L. 111-3, Sec. 702(f)(1), redesignated the text of para. (o)(1) as subpara. (o)(1)(A), substituted "(A) In general. Returns" for "Returns" in para. (o)(1) and added subpara. (o)(1)(B) . . . Sec. 702(f)(2), substituted "(o)(1)(A)" for "(o)(1)" both places it appeared in para. (p)(4), effective on or after 2/4/2009.

In 2008, P.L. 110-428, Sec. 2(a), added para (k)(10) . . . Sec. 2(b), substituted "(k)(8) or (10)" for "(k)(8)" in both places it appears in para. (p)(4), effective for disclosures made after 12/31/2008.

—P.L. 110-343, Sec. 402(a)DivC, repealed clause (i)(3)(C)(iv) and subpara. (i)(7)(E), effective for disclosures after 10/3/2008.

Prior to repeal, clause (i)(3)(C)(iv) and subpara. (i)(7)(E) read as follows:

"(iv) Termination. No disclosure may be made under this subparagraph after December 31, 2007. "

"(E) Termination. No disclosure may be made under this paragraph after December 31, 2007."

—P.L. 110-328, Sec. 3(b)(1), added "(10)" after "(6)," in para. (a)(3). . . . Sec. 3(b)(2)(A), substituted "(c), (d), (e), or (f)" for "(c), (d), or (e)" in para. (l)(10). . . . Sec. 3(b)(2)(B), added ", to officers and employees of the Department of Labor for purposes of facilitating the exchange of data in connection with a request made under subsection (f)(5) of section 6402," after "section 6402". . . . Sec. 3(b)(2)(C)(i), added clause (l)(10)(B)(i). . . . Sec. 3(b)(2)(C)(ii), added clause (l)(10)(B)(ii) . . . Sec. 3(b)(3)(A), substituted "(l)(10), (16)," for "(l)(16)" in matter preceding subpara. (p)(4)(A). . . . Sec. 3(b)(3)(B), substituted "(l)(10), (16)," for "(l)(16)" in clause (p)(4)(F)(i). . . . Sec. 3(b)(3)(C)(i), substituted "(l)(10), (16)," for "(l)(16)" the first two places it appeared in the matter following subpara. (p)(4)(F)(iii). . . . Sec. 3(b)(3)(C)(ii), added "(10)," after "paragraph (6)(A)," in the matter following subpara. (p)(4)(F)(iii). . . . Sec. 3(b)(3)(C)(iii), substituted "(l)(10) or (16)" for "(l)(16)" in the matter following subpara. (p)(4)(F)(iii), effective for refunds payable under section 6402 of the Internal Revenue Code of 1986 on or after 9/30/2008.

—P.L. 110-246, Sec. 4002(b)(1)(B), substituted "Food and Nutrition Act of 2008" for "Food Stamp Act of 1977" in para. (l)(7) and clause (l)(7)(D)(vi), enacted 5/22/2008. [Ed. Note: May 22, 2008 was the date of enactment for H.R. 2419 (PL 110-234), which was repealed by (2008 Farm Act § 4(a)) (PL 110-246, 6/18/2008), in connection with the reenactment of the Farm Bill to correct a technical deficiency in its original passage.]

—P.L. 110-245, Sec. 108(a), deleted the last sentence in para. (l)(7), effective for requests made after 9/30/2008.

Prior to deletion, the last sentence in para. (l)(7) read as follows:

"Clause (viii) shall not apply after September 30, 2008."

—P.L. 110-245, Sec. 108(b), substituted "sections 1710(a)(2)(G), 1710(a)(3), and 1710(b)" for "sections 1710(a)(1)(I), 1710(a)(2), 1710(b), and 1712(a)(2)(B)" in sbcl. (l)(7)(D)(viii)(III), enacted 6/17/2008.

In 2007, P.L. 110-172, Sec. 11(a)(34)(A), deleted "the Canal Zone," after "the Virgin Islands," in subpara. (b)(5)(A)(i), enacted 12/29/2007.

—P.L. 110-142, Sec. 8(c)(1), added new para. (e)(10), effective 12/20/2007.

—P.L. 110-28, Sec. 8246(a)(2)(B)(i), substituted "tax return preparer" for "income tax return preparer" each place it appeared in para. (k)(5) . . . Sec. 8246(a)(2)(B)(ii), substituted "tax return preparers" for "income tax return preparers" each place it appeared in para. (k)(5), effective for returns prepared after 5/25/2007.

In 2006, P.L. 109-432, Sec. 122(a)(1), substituted "2007" for "2006" in subpara. (d)(5)(B), effective for disclosures after 12/31/2006.

—P.L. 109-432, Sec. 122(b)(1), substituted "2007" for "2006" in clause (i)(3)(C)(iv) and subpara. (i)(7)(E), effective for disclosures after 12/31/2006.

—P.L. 109-432, Sec. 122(c)(1), substituted "2007" for "2006" in subpara. (l)(13)(D), effective for requests made after 12/31/2006.

—P.L. 109-432, Sec. 421(a), amended para. (b)(5) . . . Sec. 421(b), added para. (d)(6), effective for disclosures made after 12/31/2006.

Prior to amendment, para. (b)(5) read as follows:

1. "(5) State. The term 'State' means—

"(A) any of the 50 States, the District of Columbia, the Commonwealth of Puerto Rico, the Virgin Islands, the Canal Zone, Guam, American Samoa, and the Commonwealth of the Northern Mariana Islands, and

"(B) for purposes of subsections (a)(2), (b)(4), (d)(1), (h)(4), and (p) any municipality—

"(i) with a population in excess of 250,000 (as determined under the most recent decennial United States census data available),

"(ii) which imposes a tax on income or wages, and

"(iii) with which the Secretary (in his sole discretion) has entered into an agreement regarding disclosure."

—P.L. 109-280, Sec. 1224(b)(1), added "or section 6104(c)" after "this section" in para. (a)(2) . . . Sec. 1224(b)(2), added "and section 6104(c)" after "section" in the first sentence of subpara. (p)(3)(A) . . . Sec. 1224(b)(3)(A), added ", any appropriate State officer (as defined in section 6104(c))," before "or any other person" in the matter preceding subpara. (p)(4)(A) . . . Sec. 6103(b)(3)(B), added "any appropriate State officer (as defined in section 6104(c))," before "or any other person" in clause (p)(4)(F)(i) . . . Sec. 6103(p)(3)(C), added ", an appropriate State officer (as defined in section 6104(c))," after "including an agency" each place it appears in the matter following subpara. (p)(4)(F), effective 8/17/2006 but not for requests made before 8/17/2006.

In 2005, P.L. 109-135, Sec. 305(a)(1), substituted "December 31, 2006" for "December 31, 2005" in subpara. (d)(5)(B), effective for disclosures after 12/31/2005.

—P.L. 109-135, Sec. 305(b)(1), substituted "December 31, 2006" for "December 31, 2005" in clause (i)(3)(C)(iv) and subpara. (i)(7)(E), effective for disclosures after 12/31/2005.

—P.L. 109-135, Sec. 305(c)(1), substituted "December 31, 2006" for "December 31, 2005" in subpara. (l)(13)(D), effective for requests made after 12/31/2005.

—P.L. 109-135, Sec. 406(a), substituted "subsection (f), (i)(8), or (p)" for "subsection (f), (i)(7), or (p)" in para. (l)(17), effective for disclosures made on or after 1/23/2002 as if included in Sec. 201 of the Victims of Terrorism Tax Relief Act of 2001, P.L. 107-134.

—P.L. 109-135, Sec. 412(rr)(3), substituted "Government Accountability Office" for "General Accounting Office" each place it appeared in subpara. (i)(8)(A) and clauses (i)(8)(B)(i) and (ii) . . . Sec. 412(rr)(4), substituted "Government Accountability Office" for "General Accounting Office" each place it appeared in clause (p)(3)(C)(i), paras. (p)(4) and (5), and subpara. (p)(6)(B) . . . Sec. 412(yy)(1), amended so much of para. (p)(4) as precedes subpara. (p)(4)(A) . . . Sec. 412(yy)(2), amended clause (p)(4)(F)(i) . . . Sec. 412(yy)(3), substituted "If the Secretary determines that any such agency, body, or commission, including an agency or any other person described in subsection (l)(16), (18), (19), or (20), or the Government Accountability Office or the Congressional Budget Office, has failed to, or does not, meet the requirements of this paragraph, he may, after any proceedings for review established under paragraph (7), take such actions as are necessary to ensure such requirements are met, including refusing to disclose returns or return information to such agency, body, or commission, including an agency or any other person described in subsection (l)(16), (18), (19), or (20), or the Government Accountability Office or the Congressional Budget Office, until he determines that such requirements have been or will be met." for "If the Secretary determines that any such agency, body, or commission, including an agency or any other person described in subsection (l)(16) , (18) , (19) , or (20) , or the General Accounting Office or the Congressional Budget Office has failed to, or does not, meet the requirements of this paragraph , he may, after any proceedings for review established under paragraph (7) , take such actions as are necessary to ensure such requirements are met, including refusing to disclose returns or return information to such agency, body, or commission, including an agency or any other person described in subsection (l)(16) , (18) , (19) , or (20) , or the General Accounting Office or the Congressional Budget Office until he determines that such requirements have been or will be met." in para. (p)(4), effective 12/21/2005.

Prior to amendment, so much of para. (p)(4) as precedes subpara. (p)(4)(A) read as follows:

"(4) Safeguards. Any Federal agency described in subsection (h)(2), (h)(5), (i)(1), (2), (3), (5), or (7), (j)(1), (2), or (5), (k)(8), (l)(1), (2), (3), (5), (10), (11), (13), (14) or (17), or (o)(1), the General Accounting Office, the Congressional Budget Office, or any agency, body, or commission described in subsection (d), (i)(3)(B)(i) or (7)(A)(ii), or (l)(6), (7), (8), (9), (12), (15), or (16) or any other person described in subsection (l)(16), (18), (19), or (20) shall, as a condition for receiving returns or return information—"

Prior to amendment, clause (p)(4)(F)(i) read as follows:

"(i) in the case of an agency, body, or commission described in subsection (d), (i)(3)(B)(i), or (l)(6), (7), (8), (9), or (16), or any other person described in subsection (l)(16), (18), (19), or (20) return to the Secretary such returns or return information (along with any copies made therefrom) or make such returns or return information undisclosable in any manner and furnish a written report to the Secretary describing such manner,"

In 2004, P.L. 108-429, Sec. 2004(a)(22), substituted "or (18)" for "or (17)" after "any other person described in subsection (l)(16)" each place it appeared in para. (p)(4), effective 12/3/2004. For additional amendments to para. (p)(4), see Sec. 408(a)(24) of P.L. 108-311 and Secs. 105(e)(3) and 811(c)(2)(B) of P.L. 108-173 below.

—P.L. 108-357, Sec. 413(c)(27), deleted clause (e)(1)(D)(iv) and redesignated clauses (e)(1)(D)(v) and (vi) as clauses (e)(1)(D)(iv) and (v), effective for disclosures of return or return information with respect to tax. yrs. begin. after 12/31/2004.

Prior to deletion, clause (e)(1)(D)(iv) read as follows:

"(iv) if the corporation was a foreign personal holding company, as defined by section 552, any person who was a shareholder during any part of a period covered by such return if with respect to that period, or any part thereof, such shareholder was required under section 551 to include in his gross income undistributed foreign personal holding company income of such company,"

—P.L. 108-357, Sec. 860(c), of this Act, reads as follows:

"(c) Publication of registered persons. Beginning on January 1, 2005, the Secretary of the Treasury (or the Secretary's delegate) shall periodically publish under section 6103(k)(7) of the Internal Revenue Code of 1986 a current list of persons registered under section 4101 of such Code who are required to register under such section."

—P.L. 108-311, Sec. 311(a), amended para. (d)(5), effective 10/4/2004.

Prior to amendment, para. (d)(5) read as follows:

"(5) Disclosure for certain combined reporting project. The Secretary shall disclose taxpayer identities and signatures for purposes of the demonstration project described in section 976 of the Taxpayer Relief Act of 1997. Subsections (a)(2) and (p)(4) and sections 7213 and 7213A shall not apply with respect to disclosures or inspections made pursuant to this paragraph."

—P.L. 108-311, Sec. 317, substituted "December 31, 2005" for "December 31, 2004" in subpara. (l)(13)(D), effective 10/4/2004.

—P.L. 108-311, Sec. 320(a), substituted "December 31, 2005" for "December 31, 2003" in clause (i)(3)(C)(iv) and subpara. (i)(7)(E), effective for disclosures on or after 10/4/2004.

—P.L. 108-311, Sec. 320(b), added clause (i)(7)(A)(v), effective for disclosures made on or after 1/23/2002 as if included in Sec. 201 of the Victims of Terrorism Tax Relief Act of 2001, P.L. 107-134.

—P.L. 108-311, Sec. 408(a)(24), directed the substitution of "subsection (l)(16) or (18)" for "(l)(16) or (l)(17)" each place it appeared in para. (p)(4). This amendment, however, could not be made as directed. Ed. Note: We believe Congress intended to substitute "subsection (l)(16), (18)" for "subsection (l)(16), (17)" in para. (p)(4), enacted 10/4/2004.

—P.L. 108-271, Sec. 8, of this Act, provides:

"SEC. 8. REDESIGNATION.

"(a) In general. The General Accounting Office is hereby redesignated the Government Accountability Office.

"(b) References. Any reference to the General Accounting Office in any law, rule, regulation, certificate, directive, instruction, or other official paper in force on the date of enactment of this Act [7/7/2004] shall be considered to refer and apply to the Government Accountability Office.

In 2003, P.L. 108-173, Sec. 101(e)(6), added "or subsidies provided under section 1860D-14 of such Act" after "Social Security Act" in clause (l)(7)(D)(vi), effective 12/8/2003.

—P.L. 108-173, Sec. 105(e)(1), added para. (l)(19) . . . Sec. 105(e)(2), substituted "(16), or (19)" for "or (16)" in para. (a)(3) . . . Sec. 105(e)(3), substituted "(l)(16), (17), or (19)" for "(l)(16) or (17)" each place it appeared in para. (p)(4), effective 12/8/2003.

—P.L. 108-173, Sec. 811(c)(1), added para. (l)(20) . . . Sec. 811(c)(2)(A), substituted "(19), or (20)" for "or (19)" in para. (a)(3) [as added by Sec. 105(e)(2) of this Act, see above] . . . Sec. 811(c)(2)(B), substituted "(l)(16), (17), (19), or (20)" for "(l)(16), (17), or (19)" each place it appeared in para. (p)(4) [as amended by Sec. 105(e)(3) of this Act, see above], effective 12/8/2003.

—P.L. 108-173, Sec. 900(e)(3)(A), substituted "Centers for Medicare & Medicaid Services" for "Health Care Financing Administration" in matter preceding clause (l)(12)(B)(i) . . . Sec. 900(e)(3)(B)(i), substituted "Centers for Medicare & Medicaid Services" for "Health Care Financing Administration" in heading of subpara. (l)(12)(C) . . . Sec. 900(e)(3)(B)(ii), substituted "Centers for Medicare & Medicaid Services" for "Health Care Financing Administration" in matter preceding clause (l)(12)(C)(i), effective 12/8/2003.

—P.L. 108-89, Sec. 201(a), substituted "December 31, 2004" for "September 30, 2003" in subpara. (l)(13)(D), effective for requests made after 9/30/2003.

In 2002, P.L. 107-330, Sec. 306, substituted "September 30, 2008" for "September 30, 2003" in subpara. (l)(7)(D), effective 12/6/2002.

—P.L. 107-296, Sec. 1112(j), substituted ", the Bureau of Alcohol, Tobacco, Firearms, and Explosives, Department of Justice, or the Tax and Trade Bureau, Department of the Treasury," for "or the Bureau of Alcohol, Tobacco and Firearms" in clause (i)(8)(A)(i), effective 60 days after 11/25/2002.

—P.L. 107-210, Sec. 202(b)(1), added para. (l)(18) . . . Sec. 202(b)(2)(A), substituted "(17), or (18)" for "or (17)" in subpara. (p)(3)(A) . . . Sec. 202(b)(2)(B), added "or (17)" after "any other person described in subsection (l)(16)" each place it appeared in para. (p)(4), effective 8/6/2002.

—P.L. 107-147, Sec. 416(c)(1)(A), substituted "Federal, State, and local" for "State and local" in the heading of para. (l)(8) . . . Sec. 416(c)(1)(B), added "Federal or" before "State or local" in subpara. (l)(8)(A), effective 3/9/2002.

—P.L. 107-134, Sec. 201(a), added subpara. (i)(3)(C) . . . Sec. 201(b), redesignated para. (i)(7) as (i)(8) and added new para. (i)(7) . . . Sec. 201(c)(1), added "any local law enforcement agency receiving information under subsection (i)(7)(A)," after "State," in para. (a)(2) . . . Sec. 201(c)(2), added para. (b)(11) . . . Sec. 201(c)(3), added "or terrorist" after "criminal" in the heading of para. (i)(3) . . . Sec. 201(c)(4)(A), added "or (7)(C)" after "paragraph (1)" in subpara. (i)(4)(A) . . . Sec. 201(c)(4)(B), substituted "(3)(A) or (C), or (7)" for "or (3)(A)" in subpara (i)(4)(B) . . . Sec. 201(c)(5)(A), substituted "(3)(A) or (C)" for "(3)(A)" in para. (i)(6) . . . Sec. 201(c)(5)(B), substituted "(7), or (8)" for "or (7)" in para. (i)(6) . . . Sec. 201(c)(6)(A), substituted "(8)(A)(ii)" for "(7)(A)(ii)" in subpara. (p)(3)(A) . . . Sec. 201(c)(6)(B), substituted "(i)(3)(B)(i) or (7)(A)(ii)" for "(i)(3)(B)(i)" in subpara. (p)(3)(C) . . . Sec. 201(c)(7)(A)(i), substituted "(5), or (7)," for "or (5)," in the matter preceding subpara. (p)(4)(A) . . . Sec. 201(c)(7)(A)(ii), substituted "(i)(3)(B)(i) or (7)(A)(ii)," for "(i)(3)(B)(i)," in the matter preceding subpara. (p)(4)(A) . . . Sec. 201(c)(7)(B), substituted "(5) or (7)," for "or (5)," the first place it appeared in clause (p)(4)(F)(ii) . . . Sec. 201(c)(8), substituted "(i)(8)(A)(ii)" for "(i)(7)(A)(ii)" in clause (p)(6)(B)(i), effective for disclosures made on or after 1/23/2002.

In 2001, P.L. 107-67, Sec. 103, of this Act, reads as follows:

"Sec. 103. The Internal Revenue Service shall institute and enforce policies and procedures that will safeguard the confidentiality of taxpayer information."

In 2000, P.L. 106-554, Sec. 1(a)(7), [which enacted into law Sec. 301 of P.L. 106-554] of this Act, reads as follows:

"Section 3003(a)(1) of the Federal Reports Elimination and Sunset Act of 1995 (31 U.S.C. 1113 note) shall not apply to any report required to be submitted under any of the following provisions of law:"

* * * * * * *

"15(A) Section 6103(p)(5)"

—P.L. 106-554, Sec. 1(a)(7), [which enacted into law Sec. 304(a) of P.L. 106-554] deleted "and" at the end of subpara. (b)(2)(B), added "and" at the end of subpara. (b)(2)(C), and added subpara. (b)(2)(D), effective 12/21/2000.

—P.L. 106-554, Sec. 1(a)(7), [which enacted into law Sec. 310(a)(1) of P.L. 106-554] added para. (j)(6) . . . Sec. 1(a)(7), [which enacted into law Sec. 310(a)(2)(A)(i) of P.L. 106-554] added "the Congressional Budget Office," after "General Accounting Office," in para. (p)(4) . . . Sec. 1(a)(7), [which enacted into law Sec. 310(a)(2)(A)(ii) of P.L. 106-554] substituted "commission, the General Accounting Office, or the Congressional Budget Office" for 'commission or the General Accounting Office" in subpara. (p)(4)(E) . . . Sec. 1(a)(7), [which enacted into law Sec. 310(a)(2)(A)(iii) of P.L. 106-554] substituted "the General Accounting Office, or the Congressional Budget Office," for "or the General Accounting Office," in clause (p)(4)(F)(ii) . . . Sec. 1(a)(7), [which enacted into law Sec. 310(a)(2)(A)(iv) of P.L. 106-554] added "or the Congressional Budget Office" after "General Accounting Office" each place it appeared in the matter following subpara. (p)(4)(F). . . . Sec. 1(a)(7), [which enacted into law Sec. 310(a)(2)(B) of P.L. 106-554] substituted "commissions, the General Accounting Office, and the Congressional Budget Office" for "commissions and the General Accounting Office" in para. (p)(5) . . . Sec. 1(a)(7), [which enacted into law Sec. 310(a)(2)(C) of P.L. 106-554] added "and the Congressional Budget Office" after "commissions" in subpara. (p)(6)(A), effective 12/21/2000.

—P.L. 106-554, Sec. 1(a)(7), [which enacted into law Sec. 313(c)(1) of P.L. 106-554] added "and an officer or employee of the Office of Treasury Inspector General for Tax Administration" after "officer or employee" in para. (k)(6) . . . Sec. 1(a)(7), [which enacted into law Sec. 313(c)(2) of P.L. 106-554] substituted "certain" for "Internal Revenue" in the heading of para. (k)(6), effective 7/22/98.

—P.L. 106-554, Sec. 1(a)(7), [which enacted into law Sec. 319(8)(B) of P.L. 106-554] amended clause (e)(1)(D)(v) . . . Sec. 1(a)(7), [which enacted into law Sec. 319(17)(A)(i) of P.L. 106-554] deleted the second comma after "(13)" in para. (p)(4) . . . Sec. 1(a)(7), [which enacted into law Sec. 319(17)(A)(ii) of P.L. 106-554] substituted "(7), (8), (9), (12), (15), or (16) or any other person described in subsection (l)(16) shall, as a condition" for "(7), (8), (9), (10), (12), or (16), or any other person described in subsection (l)(16) or (15) shall, as a condition" in para. (p)(4) . . . Sec. 1(a)(7), [which enacted into law Sec. 319(17)(B) of P.L. 106-554] deleted the second comma after "(14)" in clause (p)(4)(F)(ii), effective 12/21/2000.

Prior to amendment, clause (e)(1)(D)(v) read as follows:

"(v) if the corporation was an electing small business corporation under subchapter S of chapter 1, any person who was a shareholder during any part of the period covered by such return during which an election was in effect, or"

In 1999, P.L. 106-170, Sec. 521(a)(1), deleted "and" at the end of subpara. (b)(2)(A), added "and" at the end of subpara. (b)(2)(B) and added subpara. (b)(2)(C), effective 12/17/99.

—P.L. 106-170, Sec. 521(b), and (c), of this Act, provides:

"(b) Annual report regarding advance pricing agreements.

"(1) In general. Not later than 90 days after the end of each calendar year, the Secretary of the Treasury shall prepare and publish a report regarding advance pricing agreements.

"(2) Contents of report. The report shall include the following for the calendar year to which such report relates:

"(A) Information about the structure, composition, and operation of the advance pricing agreement program office.

"(B) A copy of each model advance pricing agreement.

"(C) The number of—

"(i) applications filed during such calendar year for advance pricing agreements;

"(ii) advance pricing agreements executed cumulatively to date and during such calendar year;

"(iii) renewals of advance pricing agreements issued;

"(iv) pending requests for advance pricing agreements;

"(v) pending renewals of advance pricing agreements;

"(vi) for each of the items in clauses (ii) through (v), the number that are unilateral, bilateral, and multilateral, respectively;

"(vii) advance pricing agreements revoked or canceled, and the number of withdrawals from the advance pricing agreement program; and

"(viii) advance pricing agreements finalized or renewed by industry.

"(D) General descriptions of —

"(i) the nature of the relationships between the related organizations, trades, or businesses covered by advance pricing agreements;

"(ii) the covered transactions and the business functions performed and risks assumed by such organizations, trades, or businesses;

"(iii) the related organizations, trades, or businesses whose prices or results are tested to determine compliance with transfer pricing methodologies prescribed in advance pricing agreements;

"(iv) methodologies used to evaluate tested parties and transactions and the circumstances leading to the use of those methodologies;

"(v) critical assumptions made and sources of comparables used;

"(vi) comparable selection criteria and the rationale used in determining such criteria;

"(vii) the nature of adjustments to comparables or tested parties;

"(viii) the nature of any ranges agreed to, including information regarding when no range was used and why, when interquartile ranges were used, and when there was a statistical narrowing of the comparables;

"(ix) adjustment mechanisms provided to rectify results that fall outside of the agreed upon advance pricing agreement range;

"(x) the various term lengths for advance pricing agreements, including rollback years, and the number of advance pricing agreements with each such term length;

"(xi) the nature of documentation required; and

"(xii) approaches for sharing of currency or other risks.

"(E) Statistics regarding the amount of time taken to complete new and renewal advance pricing agreements.

"(F) A detailed description of the Secretary of the Treasury's efforts to ensure compliance with existing advance pricing agreements.

"(3) Confidentiality. The reports required by this subsection shall be treated as authorized by the Internal Revenue Code of 1986 for purposes of section 6103 of such Code, but the reports shall not include information—

"(A) which would not be permitted to be disclosed under section 6110(c) of such Code if such report were a written determination as defined in section 6110 of such Code, or

"(B) which can be associated with, or otherwise identify, directly or indirectly, a particular taxpayer.

"(4) First report. The report for calendar year 1999 shall include prior calendar years after 1990.

"(c) Regulations. The Secretary of the Treasury or the Secretary's delegate shall prescribe such regulations as may be necessary or appropriate to carry out the purposes of section 6103(b)(2)(C), and the last sentence of section 6110(b)(1), of the Internal Revenue Code of 1986, as added by this section."

In 1998, P.L. 105-277, Sec. 1006, substituted "September 30, 2003" for "September 30, 1998" in subpara. (l)(13)(D), effective 10/21/98.

—P.L. 105-277, Sec. 4002(a), redesignated para. (h)(5) [sic (6)] as (6), effective 7/22/98 [For Sec. 1102(d)(2) and (3), of P.L. 105-206, see below].

—P.L. 105-277, Sec. 4002(h), added "(f)(5)," after "(c), (e)," in subpara. (p)(3)(A), effective 7/22/98.

—P.L. 105-277, Sec. 4006(a)(1), added para. (j)(5) . . . Sec. 4006(a)(2), substituted "(j)(1), (2), or (5)" for "(j)(1) and (2)" in the introductory text of para. (p)(4) and clause (p)(4)(F)(ii), effective for requests made on or after 10/21/98.

—P.L. 105-206, Sec. 1101(b), added para. (h)(5) [sic (6)], effective 7/22/98. Sec. 1102(d)(2) and (3), of this Act, provides:

"(2) Initial nominations to Internal Revenue Service Oversight Board. The President shall submit the initial nominations under section 7802 of the Internal Revenue Code of 1986, as added by this section, to the Senate not later than 6 months after the date of the enactment of this Act.

"(3) Effect on actions prior to appointment of Oversight Board. Nothing in this section shall be construed to invalidate the actions and authority of the Internal Revenue Service prior to the appointment of the members of the Internal Revenue Oversight Board."

—P.L. 105-206, Sec. 2003(e), of this Act, provides:

"(e) Procedures for authorizing disclosure electronically. The Secretary shall establish procedures for any taxpayer to authorize, on an electronically filed return, the Secretary to disclose information under section 6103(c) of the Internal Revenue Code of 1986 to the preparer of the return."

—P.L. 105-206, Sec. 2005, of this Act, provides:

"Sec. 2005. access to account information.

"(a) In general. Not later than December 31, 2006, the Secretary of the Treasury or the Secretary's delegate shall develop procedures under which a taxpayer filing returns electronically (and their designees under section 6103(c) of the Internal Revenue Code of 1986) would be able to review the taxpayer's account electronically, but only if all necessary safeguards to ensure the privacy of such account information are in place.

"(b) Report. Not later than December 31, 2003, the Secretary of the Treasury shall report on the progress the Secretary is making on the development of procedures under subsection (a) to the Committee on Ways and Means of the House of Representatives and the Committee on Finance of the Senate."

—P.L. 105-206, Sec. 3702(a), added para. (l)(17) . . . Sec. 3702(b)(1), substituted "(16), or (17)" for "or (16)" in subpara. (p)(3)(A) . . . Sec. 3702(b)(2), substituted ", (14) or (17)" for "or (14)" in para. (p)(4) . . . Sec. 3702(b)(3), substituted ", (15), or (17)" for "or (15)" in clause (p)(4)(F)(ii), effective for requests made by the Archivist of the U.S. after 7/22/98

—P.L. 105-206, Sec. 3708(a), added para. (f)(5), effective 7/22/98.

—P.L. 105-206, Sec. 3711(b)(1), substituted "(c), (d), or (e)" for "(c) or (d)" each place it appeared in para. (l)(10) [Note: this amendment was previously made by Sec. 110(l)(3) of P.L. 104-193, see below] . . . Sec. 3711(b)(2), substituted "subsection (c), (d), or (e) of section 6402" for "section 6402(c) or 6402(d)" in the heading of para. (l)(10), effective for refunds payable under Code Sec. 6402 after 12/31/99.

—P.L. 105-206, Sec. 6007(f)(4), deleted clause (e)(1)(A)(ii) and redesignated clauses (e)(1)(A)(iii) and (iv) as (e)(1)(A)(ii) and (iii), effective for sales or exchanges after 8/5/97.

Prior to deletion, clause (e)(1)(A)(ii) read as follows:

"(ii) if property transferred by that individual to a trust is sold or exchanged in a transaction described in section 644, the trustee or trustees, jointly or separately, of such trust to the extent necessary to ascertain any amount of tax imposed upon the trust by section 644,"

—P.L. 105-206, Sec. 6009(d), substituted "section 976 of the Taxpayer Relief Act of 1997. Subsections (a)(2) and (p)(4) and sections 7213 and 7213A shall not apply with respect to disclosures or inspections made pursuant to this paragraph." for "section 967 of the Taxpayer Relief Act of 1997." in para. (d)(5), effective 8/5/97.

—P.L. 105-206, Sec. 6012(b)(2), redesignated para. (k)(8) [sic (9)] as (9) . . . Sec. 6012(b)(4), corrected Sec. 1205(c)(3) of P.L. 105-34 so that it substituted "(8), or (9)" for "or (8)" instead of substituting "(6), or (8)" for "or (6)"in para. (p)(3)(A), see below, effective on the day 9 months after 8/5/97.

—P.L. 105-206, Sec. 6019(c), substituted "(5), (8), or (9)" for "or (5)" in para. (e)(6), effective 7/22/98.

—P.L. 105-206, Sec. 6023(22), added "if" before "the taxpayer is a party to" in subpara. (h)(4)(A), effective 7/22/98.

In 1997, P.L. 105-65, Sec. 542(b), removed "Clause (ix) shall not apply after September 30, 1998." from the end of subpara. (l)(7)(D), effective 10/27/97.

—P.L. 105-34, Sec. 976(a) and (b), of this Act, read as follows:

"(a) In general. The Secretary of the Treasury shall provide for a demonstration project to assess the feasibility and desirability of expanding combined Federal and State tax reporting.

"(b) Description of demonstration project. The demonstration project under subsection (a) shall be—

"(1) carried out between the Internal Revenue Service and the State of Montana for a period ending with the date which is 5 years after the date of the enactment of this Act,

"(2) limited to the reporting of employment taxes, and

"(3) limited to the disclosure of the taxpayer identity (as defined in section 6103(b)(6) of such Code) and the signature of the taxpayer."

—P.L. 105-34, Sec. 976(c), added para. (d)(5), effective 8/5/97.

—P.L. 105-34, Sec. 1023(a), substituted "2003" for "1998" in clause (l)(7)(D)(viii), effective 8/5/97.

—P.L. 105-34, Sec. 1026(a), added para. (k)(8) . . . Sec. 1026(b)(1)(A), substituted "(2), (6), or (8)" for "(2), or (6)" in subpara. (p)(3)(A) . . . Sec. 1026(b)(1)(B), added "(k)(8)" after "(j)(1) or (2)," each place it appeared in para. (p)(4), effective for levies issued after 8/5/97.

—P.L. 105-34, Sec. 1201(b)(2), deleted "or 59(j)" before the semicolon at the end of clause (e)(1)(A)(iv), effective for tax. yrs. begin. after 12/31/97.

—P.L. 105-34, Sec. 1205(c)(1), added para. (k)(8) [sic (k)(9)] . . . Sec. 1205(c)(3), [as amended by Sec. 6012(b)(4), 105-206, see above] substituted "(8), or (9)" for "or (8)" in subpara. (p)(3)(A), effective on the day 9 months after 8/5/97.

—P.L. 105-34, Sec. 1283(a), deleted para. (h)(5) and redesignated para. (h)(6) as para. (h)(5) . . . Sec. 1283(b), substituted "(h)(5)" for "(h)(6)" each place it appeared in para. (p)(4), effective for judicial proceedings commenced after 8/5/97. Prior to deletion, para. (h)(5) read as follows:

"(5) Prospective jurors. In connection with any judicial proceeding described in paragraph (4) to which the United States is a party, the Secretary shall respond to a written inquiry from an attorney of the Department of Justice (including a United States attorney) involved in such proceeding or any person (or his legal representative) who is a party to such proceeding as to whether an individual who is a prospective juror in such proceeding has or has not been the subject of any audit or other tax investigation by the Internal Revenue Service. The Secretary shall limit such response to an affirmative or negative reply to such inquiry."

—P.L. 105-33, Sec. 4631(c)(2), deleted subpara. (l)(12)(F), effective 8/5/97. Prior to deletion, subpara. (l)(12)(F) read as follows:

"(F) Termination. Subparagraphs (A) and (B) shall not apply to—

"(i) any request made after September 30, 1998, and

"(ii) any request made before such date for information relating to—

"(I) 1997 or thereafter in the case of subparagraph (A), or

"(II) 1998 or thereafter in the case of subparagraph (B)."

—P.L. 105-33, Sec. 11024(a), of this Act, reads as follows:

"(a) In general. Except with respect to taxpayer returns and return information subject to section 6103 of the Internal Revenue Code of 1986, the Secretary may—

"(1) secure directly from any department or agency of the United States information necessary to enable the Secretary to verify or confirm benefit determinations under this subtitle; and

"(2) by regulations authorize the Trustee to review such information for purposes of administering this subtitle and the contract."

—P.L. 105-33, Sec. 11024(b)(1), added para. (l)(16) . . . Sec. 11024(b)(2), substituted "(6), (12), or (16)" for "(6) or (12)" in para. (a)(3) . . . Sec. 11024(b)(3), added "or by a Trustee as defined in the District of Columbia retirement Protection Act of 1997," after "(other than an agency referred to in subparagraph (A))" in clause (i)(7)(B)(i) . . . Sec. 11024(b)(4), substituted "(15), or (16)" for "or (15)' in subpara. (p)(3)(A) . . . Sec. 11024(b)(5), substituted "(12), or (16), or any other person described in subsection (l)(16)" for "or (12)" in para. (p)(4) . . . Sec. 11024(b)(6), substituted "(9), or (16), or any other person described in subsection (l)(16)" for "or (9)" in clause (p)(4)(F)(i) . . . Sec. 11024(b)(7)(A), added ", including an agency or any other person described in subsection (l)(16)," after "body or commission" in subpara. (p)(4)(F) . . . Sec. 11024(b)(7)(B), substituted "to such agency, body, or commission, including any agency or any other person described in subsection (l)(16)" for "to such agency, body, or commission" in subpara. (p)(4)(F) . . . Sec. 11024(b)(7)(C), substituted ", (12)(B), or (16)" for "or (12)(B)" in subpara. (p)(4)(F) . . . Sec. 11024(b)(7)(D), added "or any person including an agent described in subsection (l)(16)," after "any agent," in subpara. (p)(4)(F) . . . Sec. 11024(b)(7)(E), added "or other person" after "such agent" in subpara. (p)(4)(F) . . . Sec. 11024(b)(7)(F), added "or any person including an agent described in subsection (l)(16)," after "an agent," in subpara. (p)(4)(F), effective 8/5/97. Sec. 11024(c) of this Act, relating to Confidentiality, provides:

"(c) Confidentiality. The Secretary may issue regulations governing the confidentiality of the information obtained pursuant to subsection (a) and the provisions of law amended by subsection (b)."

—P.L. 105-33, Sec. 5514(a)(1), deleted Sec. 110(l)(4) and (5) of P.L. 104-193 [see below], effective 7/1/97.

In 1996, P.L. 104-188, Sec. 1704(t)(41), substituted "section 1(g) or 59(j);" for "section 1(g) or 59(j);" in clause (e)(1)(A)(iv), effective 8/20/96.

—P.L. 104-193, Sec. 110(l)(3), substituted "a State program funded" for "aid to families with dependent children provided under a State plan approved" in clause (l)(7)(D)(i) . . . Sec. 110(l)(4)(A), substituted "(c), (d), or (e)" for "(c) or (d)" each place it appeared in para. (l)(10) [prior to deletion by Sec. 5514(a)(1) of P.L. 105-33, see above] . . . Sec. 110(l)(4)(B), added a sentence at the end of subpara. (l)(10)(B) [prior to deletion by Sec. 5514(a)(1) of P.L. 105-33, see above] . . . Sec. 110(l)(5)(A), substituted "(5)" for "(5), (10)" in para. (p)(4) [prior to deletion by Sec. 5514(a)(1) of P.L. 105-33, see above] . . . Sec. 110(l)(5)(B), substituted "(9),

(10), or (12)" [(9), (10), (12) or (15)] for "(9), or (12)" [(9), (12) or (15)] in para. (p)(4) [para. (p)(4) was amended by Sec. 1206(b)(3) of P.L. 104-168, see below. Because of this amendment, it is impossible to make the amend para. (p)(4) as directed by Sec. 110(l)(5)(B) of this Act. The material in square brackets indicates the intent of the Act.], effective 7/1/97.

—P.L. 104-193, Sec. 316(g)(4)(A), redesignated subpara. (l)(6)(B) as (l)(6)(C) and added new subpara. (l)(6)(B) . . . Sec. 316(g)(4)(B)(i), substituted "paragraph (6) or (12) of subsection (l)" for "(l)(12)" in para. (a)(3) . . . Sec. 316(g)(4)(B)(ii), amended subpara. (l)(6)(C) [as redesignated by Sec. 316(g)(4)(A) of this Act, see above] . . . Sec. 316(g)(4)(B)(iii), substituted "paragraph (6)(A) or (12)(B) of subsection (l)" for "subsection (l)(12)(B)" in material following subpara. (p)(4)(F), effective as provided in Sec. 395(a)-(c) of this Act, which reads as follows:

"(a) In general. Except as otherwise specifically provided (but subject to subsections (b) and (c))—

"(1) the provisions of this title requiring the enactment of State laws under section 466 of the Social Security Act, or revision of State plans under section 454 of such Act, shall be effective with respect to periods beginning on and after October 1, 1996; and

"(2) all other provisions of this title shall become effective upon the date of the enactment of this Act.

"(b) Grace period for State law changes. The provisions of this title shall become effective with respect to a State on the later of—

"(1) the date specified in this title, or

"(2) the effective date of laws enacted by the legislature of such State implementing such provisions,

but in no event later than the 1st day of the 1st calendar quarter beginning after the close of the 1st regular session of the State legislature that begins after the date of the enactment of this Act. For purposes of the previous sentence, in the case of a State that has a 2-year legislative session, each year of such session shall be deemed to be a separate regular session of the State legislature.

"(c) Grace period for State constitutional amendment. A State shall not be found out of compliance with any requirement enacted by this title if the State is unable to so comply without amending the State constitution until the earlier of—

"(1) 1 year after the effective date of the necessary State constitutional amendment; or

"(2) 5 years after the date of the enactment of this Act."

Prior to amendment, subpara. (l)(6)(C) [as redesignated by Sec. 316(g)(4)(A) of this Act, see above] read as follows:

"(C) Restriction on disclosure. The Secretary shall disclose return information under subparagraph (A) only for purposes of, and to the extent necessary in, establishing and collecting child support obligations from, and locating, individuals owing such obligations."

—P.L. 104-168, Sec. 403(a), added para. (e)(8), effective for requests made after 7/30/96.

—P.L. 104-168, Sec. 902(a), added para. (e)(9), effective 7/30/96.

—P.L. 104-168, Sec. 1206(a), added para. (l)(15) . . . Sec. 1206(b)(1), deleted para. (i)(8) . . . Sec. 1206(b)(2)(A), substituted "or (7)(A)(ii)" for "(7)(A)(ii), or (8)" in subpara. (p)(3)(A) . . . Sec. 1206(b)(2)(B), substituted "(14), or (15)" for "or (14)" in subpara. (p)(3)(A) . . . Sec. 1206(b)(3)(A), substituted "or (5)" for "(5), or (8)" in para. (p)(4) . . . Sec. 1206(b)(3)(B), substituted "(i)(3)(B)(i)," for "(i)(3)(B)(i), or (8)" in para. (p)(4) . . . Sec. 1206(b)(3)(C), substituted "(12), or (15)" for "or (12)" in para. (p)(4) . . . Sec. 1206(b)(4)(A), substituted "or (5)" for "(5), or (8)" in clause (p)(4)(F)(ii) . . . Sec. 1206(b)(4)(B), substituted "(14), or (15)" for "or (14)" in clause (p)(4)(F)(ii), effective 7/30/96.

Prior to deletion, para. (i)(8) read as follows:

"(8) Disclosure of returns filed under section 6050I.

The Secretary may, upon written request, disclose returns filed under section 6050I to officers and employees of any Federal agency whose official duties require such disclosure for the administration of Federal criminal statutes not related to tax administration."

—P.L. 104-168, Sec. 1207, substituted "request for or consent to such disclosure" for "written request for or consent to such disclosure" in subsec. (c), effective 7/30/96.

—P.L. 104-134, Sec. 31001(g)(2), added "and to officers and employees of the Department of the Treasury in connection with such reduction" after "6402" in subpara. (l)(10)(A) . . . Sec. 31001(i)(2), amended subpara. (l)(3)(C), effective 4/26/96.

Prior to amendment, subpara. (l)(3)(C) read as follows:

"(C) Included Federal loan program defined. For purposes of this paragraph, the term 'included Federal loan program' means any program—

"(i) under which the United States or a Federal agency makes, guarantees, or insures loans, and

"(ii) with respect to which there is in effect a determination by the Director of the Office of Management and Budget (which has been published in the Federal Register) that the application of this paragraph to such program will substantially prevent or reduce future delinquencies under such program."

In **1994**, P.L. 103-296, Sec. 108(h)(6)(A), substituted "Social Security Administration" for "Department of Health and Human Services" in the heading of para. (l)(5) . . . Sec. 108(h)(6)(B), substituted "Commissioner of Social Security" for "Secretary of Health and Human Services" in para. (l)(5), effective 3/31/95.

—P.L. 103-296, Sec. 311(b)(1), substituted "for the purpose of — " for "for the purpose of" in para. (l)(5) . . . Sec. 311(b)(2), substituted "(A) carrying out, in accordance with an agreement" for "carrying out, in accordance with an agreement" in para. (l)(5) . . . Sec. 311(b)(3), substituted "program; or" for "program." in subpara. (l)(5)(A) . . . Sec. 311(b)(4), added subpara. (l)(5)(B), effective for requests for information made after 8/15/94.

In **1993**, P.L. 103-182, Sec. 522(a), added para. (l)(14) . . . Sec. 522(b), substituted "(13), or (14)" for "or (13)" each place it appeared in subpara. (p)(3)(A) and para. (p)(4), effective 12/8/93. Sec. 522(c)(2) of this Act reads as follows:

"(2) Regulations. Not later than 90 days after the date of enactment [12/8/93] of this Act, the Secretary of the Treasury or his delegate shall issue temporary regulations to carry out section 6103(l)(14) of the Internal Revenue Code of 1986, as added by this section."

—P.L. 103-66, Sec. 13401(a), substituted "September 30, 1998" for "September 30, 1997" in clause (l)(7)(D)(viii), effective 8/10/93.

—P.L. 103-66, Sec. 13402(a), added para. (l)(13) . . . Sec. 13402(b)(1), amended so much of para. (m)(4) as preceded subpara. (m)(4)(B) . . . Sec. 13402(b)(2)(A), substituted "under part B or D" for "under part B" in clause (m)(4)(B)(i) . . . Sec. 13402(b)(2)(B), substituted "under subpart 1 of part A, or part D or E," for "under part E" in clause (m)(4)(B)(ii) . . . Sec. 13402(b)(3)(A), substituted "(11), (12), or (13), (m)" for "(11), or (12), (m)" in subpara. (p)(3)(A) . . . Sec. 13402(b)(3)(B)(i), substituted "(10), (11), or (13)," for "(10), or (11)," in para. (p)(4) . . . Sec. 13402(b)(3)(B)(ii), substituted "(11), (12), or (13)," for "(11), or (12)," in clause (p)(4)(F)(ii), effective 8/10/93.

Prior to amendment, so much of para. (m)(4) as preceded subpara. (m)(4)(B) read as follows:

"(4) Individuals who have defaulted on student loans administered by the Department of Education.

"(A) In general. Upon written request by the Secretary of Education, the Secretary may disclose the mailing address of any taxpayer who has defaulted on a loan—

"(i) made under part B or E of title IV of the Higher Education Act of 1965, or

"(ii) made pursuant to section 3(a)(1) of the Migration and Refugee Assistance Act of 1962 to a student at an institution of higher education,

for use only by officers, employees, or agents of the Department of Education for purposes of locating such taxpayer for purposes of collecting such loan."

—P.L. 103-66, Sec. 13403(a)(1), deleted "and" at the end of clause (l)(7)(D)(vii) . . . Sec. 13403(a)(2), substituted "; and" for the period at the end of clause (l)(7)(D)(viii) . . . Sec. 13403(a)(3), added clause (l)(7)(D)(ix) . . . Sec. 13403(a)(4), added the sentence at the end of subpara. (l)(7)(D) . . . Sec. 13403(b), added ", or certain housing assistance programs" after "Code" in the heading of para. (l)(7), effective 8/10/93.

—P.L. 103-66, Sec. 13444(a), added para. (d)(4), effective on the date one year after 8/10/93, except as provided in Sec. 13444(b)(2) of this Act, which reads as follows:

"(2) Special rule. The amendment made by subsection (a) shall take effect on the date 2 years after the date of the enactment of this Act in the case of any State if it is established to the satisfaction of the Secretary of the Treasury that—

"(A) under the law of such State as in effect on the date of the enactment of this Act, it is impossible for such State to enter into an agreement meeting the requirements of section 6103(d)(4)(B) of the Internal Revenue Code of 1986 (as added by subsection (a)), and

"(B) it is likely that such State will enter into such an agreement during the extension period under this paragraph."

—P.L. 103-66, Sec. 13561(a)(2)(A), added ", above an amount (if any) specified by the Secretary of Health and Human Services," after "section 3401(a))" in clause (l)(12)(B)(i) . . . Sec. 13561(a)(2)(B), added ", above an amount (if any) specified by the Secretary of Health and Human Services," after "wages" in clause (l)(12)(B)(ii) . . . Sec. 13561(a)(2)(C)(i), substituted "1998" for "1995" in clause (l)(12)(F)(i) . . . Sec. 13561(a)(2)(C)(ii), substituted "1997" for "1994" in subclause (l)(12)(F)(ii)(I) . . . Sec. 13561(a)(2)(C)(iii), substituted "1998" for "1995" in subclause (l)(12)(F)(ii)(II) . . . Sec. 13561(e)(2)(B), amended clause (l)(12)(E)(ii), effective 8/10/93.

Prior to amendment, clause (l)(12)(E)(ii) read as follows:

"(ii) Group health plan. The term 'group health plan' means—

"(I) any group health plan (as defined in section 5000(b)(1)), and

"(II) any large group health plan (as defined in section 5000(b)(2))."

In **1992**, P.L. 102-568, Sec. 602(b)(1), substituted "September 30, 1997" for "September 30, 1992" in the sentence at the end of subpara. (l)(7)(D) . . . Sec. 602(b)(2)(A), substituted "section 1315" for "section 415" in subclause (l)(7)(D)(viii)(II) . . . Sec. 602(b)(2)(B), substituted "sections 1710(a)(1)(I), 1710(a)(2), 1710(b), and 1712(a)(2)(B)" for "section 610(a)(1)(I), 610(a)(2), 610(b), and 612(a)(2)(B)" in subclause (l)(7)(D)(viii)(III), effective 10/29/92.

In **1991**, P.L. 102-164, Sec. 401(a), amended Sec. 2653(c) of P.L. 98-369, the effective date for amendments made by Sec. 2653(b) of P.L. 98-369, so that the amendments are effective for refunds payable under Code Sec. 6402 after 12/31/85, rather than effective for refunds payable under Code Sec. 6402 after 12/31/85 and on or before 1/10/94.

—P.L. 102-54, Sec. 14(g)(3), substituted "Internal Revenue Code of 1986" for "Internal Revenue Code of 1954" in Sec. 502 of P.L. 96-128, reproduced below.

In **1990**, P.L. 101-647, Sec. 3302, of this Act provides:

"Sec. 3302. Disclosure of returns on certain cash transactions.

"(a) Extension of program.

"Paragraph (3) of section 7601(b) of the Anti-Drug Abuse Act of 1988 (relating to effective date) is amended by striking '2-year period' inserting '4-year period'.

"(b) GAO Study.

"(1) In general. The Comptroller General of the United States shall conduct a study of the disclosure of returns to Federal agencies under paragraph (8) of section 6103(i) of the Internal Revenue Code of 1986. The study shall include an evaluation of—

"(A) the Federal agencies requesting disclosure under such paragraph,

"(B) the use of the information so disclosed, and

3,589

"(C) the effect of the use of such information on the administration of Federal criminal statutes.

"(2) Report. Not later than July 1, 1991, the Comptroller General shall submit to the Committee on Ways and Means of the House of Representatives and the Committee on Finance of the Senate the results of the study required in paragraph (1)."

—P.L. 101-647, Sec. 3304, of this Act provides:
"Sec. 3304. Confidentiality of tax return information.
"(a) In general.
"Notwithstanding any other provision of this Act, no commission established by this Act shall have access to any return or return information, except to the extent authorized by section 6103 of the Internal Revenue Code of 1986."
"(b) Definitions.
"For purposes of this section, the terms 'return' and 'return information' have the respective meanings given such terms by section 6103(b) of the Internal Revenue Code of 1986."

—P.L. 101-508, Sec. 4203(a)(2)(A), substituted "September 30, 1995" for "September 30, 1991" in clause (l)(12)(F)(i) . . . Sec. 4203(a)(2)(C), substituted "1995" for "1991" in subclause (l)(12)(F)(ii)(II), effective 11/5/90.

—P.L. 101-508, Sec. 4203(a)(2)(B), substituted "1994" for "1990" in subclause (l)(12)(F)(ii)(I), effective for requests made on or after 11/5/90.

—P.L. 101-508, Sec. 5111(b)(1), added para. (m)(7) . . . Sec. 5111(b)(2), substituted "paragraph (2), (4), (6), or (7) of subsection (m)" for "subsection (m)(2), (4), or (6)" . . . Sec. 8051(a)(1)(A), deleted "and" at the end of clause (l)(7)(D)(vi) . . . Sec. 8051(a)(1)(B), substituted "; and" for the period at the end of clause (l)(7)(D)(vii) . . . Sec. 8051(a)(1)(C), added clause (l)(7)(D)(viii) . . . Sec. 8051(a)(2), substituted ", the Food Stamp Act of 1977, or Title 38, United States Code" for "or the Food Stamp Act of 1977" in the heading of para. (l)(7), effective 11/5/90.

—P.L. 101-508, Sec. 11101(d)(6), substituted "1(g)" for "1(j)" [sic "1(i)"] in clause (e)(1)(A)(iv), effective for tax. yrs. begin. after 12/31/90.

—P.L. 101-508, Sec. 11212(b)(3), added para. (k)(7), effective 12/1/90.

—P.L. 101-508, Sec. 11313(a)(1), substituted "the programming" for "and the programming" in subsec. (n) . . . Sec. 11313(a)(2), added "and the providing of other services," after "of equipment," in subsec. (n), effective 11/5/90.

In 1989, P.L. 101-239, Sec. 6202(a)(1)(A), added para. (l)(12) . . . Sec. 6202(a)(1)(B)(i), added "(l)(12)," after "(e)(1)(D)(iii)," in para. (a)(3) . . . Sec. 6202(a)(1)(B)(ii), substituted "11), or (12)" for "or (11)" in subpara. (p)(3)(A) . . . Sec. 6202(a)(1)(B)(iii), substituted "(9), or (12) shall" for "or (9) shall" in the material preceding subpara. (p)(4)(A) . . . Sec. 6202(a)(1)(B)(iv), substituted "(11), or (12)" for "or (11)" in clause (p)(4)(F)(ii) . . . Sec. 6202(a)(1)(B)(v), added "or which receives any information under subsection (l)(12)(B) and which discloses any such information to any agent" before ", this paragraph" in the next to last sentence of para. (p)(4), effective 12/19/89.

—P.L. 101-239, Sec. 7841(d)(1), deleted "45," which followed "44," in para. (d)(1), effective 12/19/89.

In 1988, P.L. 100-690, Sec. 7601(b)(1), added para. (i)(8) . . . Sec. 7601(b)(2)(A), substituted ", (7)(A)(iii), or (8)" for "or (7)(A)(ii)" in subpara. (p)(3)(A) . . . Sec. 7601(b)(2)(B), substituted "(5), or (8)" for "or (5)", and substituted "(i)(3)(B)(i) or (8)" for "(i)(3)(B)(i)," in the material preceding subpara. (p)(4)(A) . . . Sec. 7601(b)(2)(C), substituted "(5), or (8)" for "or (5)" in clause (p)(4)(F)(ii), effective for requests made on or after 11/18/88, but disclosures may be made pursuant to such amendments only during the 2-year period begin. on 11/18/88.

—P.L. 100-690, Sec. 7602(c), added para. (d)(3) . . . Sec. 7602(d)(2), added "and state and local law enforcement agencies" before the period at the end of the heading of subsec. (d), effective for information first provided more than 90 days after 11/18/88.

—P.L. 100-647, Sec. 1012(bb)(3)(A), substituted "or other convention or bilateral agreement" for "or other convention", and "such convention or bilateral agreement" for "such convention" in para. (k)(4) . . . Sec. 1012(bb)(3)(B), substituted "and the Commonwealth of the Northern Mariana Islands" for "the Commonwealth of the Northern Mariana Islands, the Republic of the Marshall Islands, the Federated States of Micronesia, and the Republic of Palau" in subpara. (b)(5)(A), effective 10/22/86.

—P.L. 100-647, Sec. 1014(e)(4), substituted "section 1(i) or 59(j)" for "section 1(j)" in clause (e)(1)(A)(iv), effective for tax. yrs. begin. after 12/31/86.

—P.L. 100-647, Sec. 6251, substituted "250,000" for "2,000,000" in clause (b)(5)(B)(i), effective 11/10/88.

—P.L. 100-647, Sec. 8008(c)(1), added para. (m)(6) . . . Sec. 8008(c)(2)(A)(i), substituted "manner," for "manner; and" at end of clause (p)(4)(F)(i), added "and" at end of clause (p)(4)(F)(ii)(III), and added clause (p)(4)(F) . . . Sec. 8008(c)(2)(A)(ii), substituted "subsection (m)(2), (4), or (6)" for "subsection (m)(2) or (4)" in the last sentence of subpara. (p)(4)(F) . . . Sec. 8008(c)(2)(A)(iii), added the last sentence of subpara. (p)(4)(F), effective 11/10/88.

—P.L. 100-485, Sec. 701(a), amended Sec. 2653(c) of P.L. 98-369, the effective date for changes made by Sec. 2653(b)(3) of P.L. 98-369, by substituting "on or before January 10, 1994" for "before July 1, 1988", see below.

—P.L. 100-485, Sec. 701(b)(1), amended para. (l)(10) . . . Sec. 701(b)(2)(A), deleted para. (l)(11) and redesignated para. (l)(12) as para. (l)(11) . . . Sec. 701(b)(2)(B), substituted "(10), or (11)" for "(10), (11), or (12)" each place it appeared in subpara. (p)(3)(A) and para. (p)(4), effective 10/13/88. Sec. 701(b)(3)(B) of this Act provides:

"(B) Special rule. Nothing in section 2653(c) of the Deficit Reduction Act of 1984 shall be construed to limit the application of paragraph (10) of section 6103(l) of the Internal Revenue Code of 1986 (as amended by this subsection)."
Prior to amendment, paras. (l)(10) and (11) read as follows:

"(10) Disclosure of certain information to agencies requesting a reduction under section 6402(c) or 6402(d).

"(A) Return information from Internal Revenue Service. The Secretary may, upon receiving a written request, disclose to officers and employees of an agency seeking a reduction under section 6402(c) or 6402(d)—

"(i) the fact that a reduction has been made or has not been made under such subsection with respect to any person;

"(ii) the amount of such reduction; and

"(iii) taxpayer identifying information of the person against whom a reduction was made or not made.

"(B) Restriction on use of disclosed information. Any officers and employees of an agency receiving return information under subparagraph (A) shall use such information only for the purposes of, and to the extent necessary in, establishing appropriate agency records or in the defense of any litigation or administrative procedure ensuing from reduction made under section 6402(c) or section 6402(d).

"(11) Disclosure of certain information to agencies requesting a reduction under section 6402(c).

"(A) Return information from internal revenue service. The Secretary shall, upon receiving a written request, disclose to officers and employees of a State agency seeking a reduction under section 6402(c)—

"(i) the fact that a reduction has been made or has not been made under such subsection with respect to any taxpayer;

"(ii) the amount of such reduction;

"(iii) whether such taxpayer filed a joint return;

"(iv) taxpayer identity information with respect to the taxpayer against whom a reduction was made or not made and of any other person filing a joint return with such taxpayer; and

"(v) the fact that a payment was made (and the amount of the payment) on the basis of a joint return in accordance with section 464(a)(3) of the Social Security Act.

"(B) Restriction on use of disclosed information. Any officers and employees of an agency receiving return information under subparagraph (A) shall use such information only for the purposes of, and to the extent necessary in, establishing appropriate agency records or in the defense of any litigation or administrative procedure ensuing from a reduction made under section 6402(c)."

In 1987, P.L. 100-203, Sec. 9402(a), amended Sec. 2653(c) of P.L. 98-369, the effective date for changes made by Sec. 2653(b)(3) of P.L. 98-369, by substituting "July 1, 1988" for "January 1, 1988", see below.

In 1986, P.L. 99-514, Sec. 1411(b), deleted "or" at the end of clause (e)(1)(A)(ii), added "or" to the end of clause (e)(1)(A)(iii), and added clause (e)(1)(A)(iv), effective for tax. yrs. begin. after 12/31/86.

—P.L. 99-514, Sec. 1568(a)(1), amended para. (b)(5) . . . Sec. 1568(a)(2), added para. (b)(10), effective on 10/22/86.
Prior to amendment, para. (b)(5) read as follows:
"(5) State. The term 'State' means any of the 50 States, the District of Columbia, the Commonwealth of Puerto Rico, the Virgin Islands, the Canal Zone, Guam, American Samoa, the Commonwealth of the Northern Mariana Islands, and the Trust Territory of the Pacific Islands."

—P.L. 99-514, Sec. 1899A(53), substituted "this title" for "this Code" in clause (l)(7)(D)(v), effective 10/22/86.

—P.L. 99-386, Sec. 206(b), substituted "year" for "quarter" in para. (p)(5), effective 8/22/86.

—P.L. 99-335, Sec. 310(a), added para. (l)(12) . . . Sec. 310(b)(1), and (2), substituted "(10), (11), or (12)" for "(10), or (11)" in subparas. (p)(3)(A) and (p)(4)(F) and para. (p)(4), effective 6/6/86. Sec. 310(c) of this Act provides:
"(c) Reimbursement.
"The Office of Personnel Management shall reimburse the costs (as determined by the Secretary of Health and Human Services) of supplying—
"(1) information under section 6103(l)(12) of the Internal Revenue Code of 1954; and
"(2) such other information agreed upon by the Director of the Office of Personnel Management and the Secretary of Health and Human Services, which is required in the administration of chapters 83 and 84 of title 5, United States Code. Section 1106(b) and (c) of the Social Security Act shall apply to any reimbursement under this subsection."

—P.L. 99-92, Sec. 8(h)(1), added "administered by the department of education" after "loans" in the heading of para. (m)(4) . . . Sec. 8(h)(2), added para. (m)(5), effective 10/1/85.

In 1984, P.L. 98-378, Sec. 19(b)(1), added "social security account number (or numbers, if the individual involved has more than one such number)," before "address" in clause (l)(6)(A)(i) . . . Sec. 19(b)(2), added "social security account numbers," before "net earnings" in clause (l)(8)(A), effective 8/16/84.

—P.L. 98-378, Sec. 21(f)(1), added para. (l)(11) . . . Sec. 21(f)(2), substituted "(10), or (11)" for "or (10)" in subpara. (p)(3)(A) . . . Sec. 21(f)(3), substituted "(10), or (11)" for "or (10)" in the matter preceding subpara. (p)(4)(A) . . . Sec. 21(f)(4), substituted "(10), or (11)" for "or (10)" in clause (p)(4)(F)(ii), effective for refunds payable under Code Sec. 6402 after 12/31/85.

—P.L. 98-369, Sec. 449(a), substituted "44, 45, 51" for "44, 51" in para. (d)(1), effective on 7/18/84.

—P.L. 98-369, Sec. 453(a), added para. (l)(9) . . . Sec. 453(b)(1), substituted "(5), (7), (8), or (9)" for "(5), or (7)" in para. (p)(3)(A) . . . Sec. 453(b)(2), substituted "(7), (8), or (9)" for "or (7)" in the material preceding subpara. (p)(4)(A) . . . Sec. 453(b)(3), substituted "(l)(6), (7), (8), or (9)" for "(l)(6), or (7)" in clause (p)(4)(F)(i), effective the first day of the first calendar month which begins more than 90 days after 7/18/84.

—P.L. 98-369, Sec. 453(b)(5), amended Sec. 127(a)(1) of P.L. 96-249 to add para. (7) to subsec. (l) not (i), effective on the first day of the first calendar month which begins more than 90 days after 7/18/84.

3,590

—P.L. 98-369, Sec. 453(b)(6), redesignated para. (l)(7) as added by Sec. 408(a)(1) of P.L. 96-265, as para. (l)(8), effective the first day of the first calendar month which begins more than 90 days after 7/18/84.
—P.L. 98-369, Sec. 2651(k)(1), amended para. (l)(7) . . . Sec. 2651(k)(2), substituted ", any local child support enforcement agency, or any local agency administering a program listed in subsection (l)(7)(D)" for "or any local child support enforcement agency" in para. (a)(2), effective 7/18/84.
Prior to amendment, para. (l)(7) read as follows:
"(7) Disclosure of certain return information by social security administration to department of agriculture and to state food stamp agencies.
"(A) In general. The Commissioner of Social Security may disclose return information from returns with respect to net earnings from self-employment (as defined in section 1402), wages (as defined in section 3121(a) or 3401(a)), and payments of retirement income which have been disclosed to the Social Security Administration as provided by paragraph (1) or (5) of this subsection—
"(i) upon request, to officers and employees of the Department of Agriculture, and
"(ii) upon written request, to officers and employees of a State food stamp agency.
"(B) Restriction on disclosure. The Commissioner of Social Security shall disclose return information under subparagraph (A) only for purposes of, and to the extent necessary in, determining an individual's eligibility for benefits, or the amounts of benefits, under the food stamp program established under the Food Stamp Act of 1977.
"(C) State food stamp agency. For purposes of this paragraph, the term 'State food stamp agency' means any Agency described in section 3(n)(1) of the Food Stamp Act of 1977 which administers the food stamp program established under such Act."
—P.L. 98-369, Sec. 2653(b)(3)(A), added para. (l)(10) . . . Sec. 2653(b)(3)(B)(i), substituted "(9), or (10)" for "or (9)" in para. (p)(3)(A) (as amended by Sec. 453(b)(1)) . . . Sec. 2653(b)(3)(B)(ii), substituted "(l)(1), (2), (3), (5), or (10)" for "(l)(1), (2), (3), or (5)" in para. (p)(4) . . . Sec. 2653(b)(3)(B)(iii), substituted "(l)(1), (2), (3), (5), or (10)" for "(l)(1), (2), (3), or (5)" in clause (p)(4)(F)(ii), effective for refunds payable under Code Sec. 6402 after 12/31/85 [as amended by Sec. 401(a) of P.L. 102-164, Sec. 701(a) of P.L. 100-485, Sec. 9402(a) of P.L. 100-203, see above].
—P.L. 98-369, Sec. 2663(j)(5)(E), substituted "Health and Human Services" for "Health, Education, and Welfare" each place it appeared in para. (l)(5), effective 7/18/84, but (as provided in Sec. 2664(b)) "none of such amendments shall be construed as changing or affecting any right, liability, status, or interpretation which existed (under the provisions of law involved) before that date [7/18/84]."
In 1983, P.L. 98-21, Sec. 121(c)(3)(A), added para. (h)(6) . . . Sec. 121(c)(3)(B), added "(h)(6)," after "(h)(2)," in para. (p)(4) and clause (p)(4)(F)(ii), effective for benefits received after 12/31/83, in tax. yrs. end. after 12/31/83 except as provided in Sec. 121(g)(2) which reads as follows:
"(2) Treatment of certain lump-sum payments received after December 31, 1983. The amendments made by this section shall not apply to any portion of a lump-sum payment of social security benefits (as defined in section 86(d) of the Internal Revenue Code of 1954) received after December 31, 1983, if the generally applicable payment date for such portion was before January 1, 1984."
—P.L. 97-452, Sec. 2(c)(4), substituted "sections 3711, 3717, and 3718 of title 31" for "section 3 of the Federal Claims Collection Act of 1966 (31 U.S.C. 952)" each place it appeared in para. (m)(2).
—P.L. 97-437, Sec. 2, added para. (c)(2) to Sec. 3111 of title 5, United States Code which reads as follows:
"(2) In addition to being considered a Federal employee for the purposes specified in paragraph (1), any student who provides voluntary service as part of a program established under subsection (b) of this section in the Internal Revenue Service, Department of the Treasury, shall be considered an employee of the Department of the Treasury for purposes of—
"(A) section 552a of this title (relating to disclosure of records);
"(B) subsections (a)(1), (h)(1), (k)(6), and (l)(4) of section 6103 of title 26 (relating to confidentiality and disclosure of returns and return information);
"(C) sections 7213(a)(1) and 7431 of title 26 (relating to unauthorized disclosures of returns and return information by Federal employees and other persons); and
"(D) section 7423 of title 26 (relating to suits against employees of the United States);
except that returns and return information (as defined in section 6103(b) of title 26) shall be made available to students under such program only to the extent that the Secretary of the Treasury or his designee determines that the duties assigned to such students so require."
In 1982, P.L. 97-365, Sec. 7(a), amended para. (l)(3) . . . Sec. 7(b)(1), substituted "(l)(6)" for "(l)(3) or (6)" in clause (p)(3)(C)(i) . . . Sec. 7(b)(2)(A), substituted "(l)(1), (2), (3)," for "(l)(1), (2)," in para. (p)(4) . . . Sec. 7(b)(2)(B), substituted "(l)(6)" for "(l)(3), (6)" in para. (p)(4) . . . Sec. 7(b)(2)(C), substituted "(l)(1), (2), (3), or (5), or (o)(1)," for "(l)(1), (2), or (5), or (o)(1), the commission described in subsection (l)(3)" in subpara. (p)(4)(F)(ii), effective for loan applications made after 9/30/82.
Prior to amendment, para. (l)(3) read as follows:
"(3) Disclosure of returns and return information to Privacy Protection Study Commission. The Secretary may, upon written request, disclose returns and return information to the Privacy Protection Study Commission, or to such members, officers, or employees of such commission as may be named in such written request, to the extent provided under section 5 of the Privacy Act of 1974."
—P.L. 97-365, Sec. 8(a), amended para. (m)(2) . . . Sec. 8(b), added the last sentence to para. (p)(4) . . . Sec. Sec. 8(c)(1), substituted "paragraph (2) or (4)(B) of subsection (m)" for "subsection (m)(4)(B)" in para. (a)(3), effective 10/25/82. Sec. 8(e) of the Act provides:
"(e) Except as otherwise provided in section 4 or 7 or the foregoing provisions of this section, nothing in this Act (or in the amendments made by this Act) shall apply to claims or indebtedness arising under, or amounts payable under, the Internal Revenue Code of 1954, the Social Security Act, or the tariff laws of the United States."
Prior to amendment, para. (m)(2) read as follows:
"(2) Federal claims. Upon written request, the Secretary may disclose the mailing address of a taxpayer to officers and employees of an agency personally and directly engaged in, and solely for their use in, preparation for any administrative or judicial proceeding (or investigation which may result in such a proceeding) pertaining to the collection or compromise of a Federal claim against such taxpayer in accordance with the provisions of section 3711 of title 31, United States Code."
—P.L. 97-258, Sec. 3(f)(4), substituted "section 713 of title 31, United States Code" for "section 117 of the Budget and Accounting Procedures Act of 1950 (31 U.S.C. 67)" in clause (a)(6)(A)(i)[sic , (a)(7)(A)(i)] . . . Sec. 3(f)(5), substituted "section 330 of title 31, United States Code" for "section 3 of the Act of July 7, 1884 (23 Stat. 258; 31 U.S.C. 1026)" in clause (l)(4)(A)(ii) . . . Sec. 3(f)(6), substituted "section 3711 of title 31, United States Code" for "section 3 of the Federal Claims Collection Act of 1966" in para. (m)(2), effective 9/13/82.
—P.L. 97-248, Sec. 356(a), redesignated para. (i)(6) as para. (i)(7) and amended paras. (i)(1), (2), (3), (4), and (5) . . . Sec. 356(b)(1)(A), substituted "(7)(A)(ii)" for "(6)(A)(ii)" in subpara. (p)(3)(A) . . . Sec. 356(b)(1)(B), substituted "(d), (i)(3)(B)(i)," for "(d)" in clause (p)(3)(C)(i) . . . Sec. 356(b)(1)(C), substituted "such requests or otherwise" for "such requests" in clause (p)(3)(C)(i) . . . Sec. 356(b)(1)(D), substituted "(i)(1), (2), (3), or (5)" for "(i)(1), (2), or (5)" each place it appeared in para. (p)(4) . . . Sec. 356(b)(1)(E), substituted "(d), (i)(3)(B)(i)," for "(d)" each place it appeared in para. (p)(4) . . . Sec. 356(b)(1)(F), substituted "subsection (i)(7)(A)(ii)" for "subsection (i)(6)(A)(ii)" in clause (p)(6)(B)(i), effective 9/4/82.
—P.L. 97-248, Sec. 358(a), redesignated subpara. (i)(7)(B) (as redesignated by Sec. 356(a) of this Act) as subpara. (i)(7)(C) and added new subpara. (i)(7)(B) . . . Sec. 358(b), substituted "subparagraph (C)" for "subparagraph (B)" and substituted "subparagraph (A) or (B)" for "subparagraph (A)" in subpara. (i)(7)(C) (as redesignated), effective 9/4/82.
Prior to amendment, paras. (i)(1), (2), (3), (4), and (5) read as follows:
"(1) Nontax criminal investigation.
"(A) Information from taxpayer. A return or taxpayer return information shall, pursuant to, and upon the grant of, an ex parte order by a Federal district court judge as provided by this paragraph, be open, but only to the extent necessary as provided in such order, to officers and employees of a Federal agency personally and directly engaged in and solely for their use in, preparation for any administrative or judicial proceeding (or investigation which may result in such a proceeding) pertaining to the enforcement of a specifically designated Federal criminal statute (not involving tax administration) to which the United States or such agency is or may be a party.
"(B) Application for order. The head of any Federal agency described in subparagraph (A) or, in the case of the Department of Justice, the Attorney General, the Deputy Attorney General, or an Assistant Attorney General, may authorize an application to a Federal district court judge for the order referred to in subparagraph (A). Upon such application, such judge may grant such order if he determines on the basis of the facts submitted by the applicant that—
"(i) there is reasonable cause to believe, based upon information believed to be reliable, that a specific criminal act has been committed;
"(ii) there is reason to believe that such return or return information is probative evidence of a matter in issue related to the commission of such criminal act; and
"(iii) the information sought to be disclosed cannot reasonably be obtained from any other source, unless it is determined that, notwithstanding the reasonable availability of the information from another source, the return or return information sought constitutes the most probative evidence of a matter in issue relating to the commission of such criminal act.
However, the Secretary shall not disclose any return or return information under this paragraph if he determines and certifies to the court that such disclosure would identify a confidential informant or seriously impair a civil or criminal tax investigation.
"(2) Return information other than taxpayer return information. Upon written request from the head of a Federal agency described in paragraph (1)(A), or in the case of the Department of Justice, the Attorney General, the Deputy Attorney General, or an Assistant Attorney General, the Secretary shall disclose return information (other than taxpayer return information) to officers and employees of such agency personally and directly engaged in, and solely for their use in, preparation for any administrative or judicial proceeding (or investigation which may result in such a proceeding) described in paragraph (1)(A). Such request shall set forth—
"(A) the name and address of the taxpayer with respect to whom such return information relates;
"(B) the taxable period or periods to which the return information relates;
"(C) the statutory authority under which the proceeding or investigation is being conducted; and
"(D) the specific reason or reasons why such disclosure is or may be material to the proceeding or investigation.
However, the Secretary shall not disclose any return or return information under this paragraph if he determines that such disclosure would identify a confidential informant or seriously impair a civil or criminal tax investigation.

For purposes of this paragraph, the name and address of the taxpayer shall not be treated as taxpayer return information.

"(3) Disclosure of return information concerning possible criminal activities. The Secretary may disclose in writing return information, other than taxpayer return information, which may constitute evidence of a violation of Federal criminal laws to the extent necessary to apprise the head of the appropriate Federal agency charged with the responsibility for enforcing such laws.

"(4) Use in judicial or administrative proceeding. Any return or return information obtained under paragraph (1), (2), or (3) may be entered into evidence in any administrative or judicial proceeding pertaining to enforcement of a specifically designated Federal criminal statute (not involving tax administration) to which the United States or an agency described in paragraph (1)(A) is a party but, in the case of any return or return information obtained under paragraph (1), only if the court finds that such return or return information is probative of a matter in issue relevant in establishing the commission of a crime or the guilt of a party. However, any return or return information obtained under paragraph (1), (2), or (3) shall not be admitted into evidence in such proceeding if the Secretary determines and notifies the Attorney General or his delegate or the head of such agency that such admission would identify a confidential informant or seriously impair a civil or criminal tax investigation. The admission into evidence of any return or return information contrary to the provisions of this paragraph shall not, as such, constitute reversible error upon appeal of a judgment in such proceeding.

For purposes of the preceding sentence, the name and address of the taxpayer shall not be treated as taxpayer return information if there is return information (other than taxpayer return information) which may constitute evidence of a violation of Federal criminal laws.

"(5) Renegotiation of contracts. A return or return information with respect to the tax imposed by chapter 1 upon a taxpayer subject to the provisions of the Renegotiation Act of 1951 shall, upon request in writing by the Chairman of the Renegotiation Board, be open to officers and employees of such board personally and directly engaged in, and solely for their use in, verifying or analyzing financial information required by such Act to be filed with, or otherwise disclosed to, the board, or to the extent necessary to implement the provisions of section 1481 or 1482. The Chairman of the Renegotiation Board may, upon referral of any matter with respect to such Act to the Department of Justice for further legal action, disclose such return and return information to any employee of such department charged with the responsibility for handling such matters.

"(6) Comptroller general.

"(A) Returns available for inspection. Except as provided in subparagraph (B), upon written request by the Comptroller General of the United States, returns and return information shall be open to inspection by, or disclosure to, officers and employees of the General Accounting Office for the purpose of, and to the extent necessary in, making—

"(i) an audit of the Internal Revenue Service or the Bureau of Alcohol, Tobacco and Firearms which may be required by section 117 of the Budget and Accounting Procedures Act of 1950 (31 U.S.C. 67), or

"(ii) any audit authorized by subsection (p)(6),

except that no such officer or employee shall, except to the extent authorized by subsection (f) or (p)(6), disclose to any person, other than another officer or employee of such office whose official duties require such disclosure, any return or return information described in section 4424(a) in a form which can be associated with, or otherwise identify, directly or indirectly, a particular taxpayer, nor shall such officer or employee disclose any other return or return information, except as otherwise expressly provided by law, to any person other than such other officer or employee of such office in a form which can be associated with, or otherwise identify, directly or indirectly, a particular taxpayer.

"(B) Disapproval by Joint Committee on Taxation. Returns and return information shall not be open to inspection or disclosed under subparagraph (A) with respect to an audit—

"(i) unless the Comptroller General of the United States notifies in writing the Joint Committee on Taxation of such audit, and

"(ii) if the Joint Committee on Taxation disapproves such audit by a vote of at least two-thirds of its members within the 30-day period beginning on the day the Joint Committee on Taxation receives such notice."

In 1981, P.L. 97-34, Sec. 701(a), added the last sentence to para. (b)(2), effective for disclosures after 7/19/81.

In 1980, P.L. 96-611, Sec. 11(a)(1), corrected Sec. 127(a)(1) of P.L. 96-249 to add para. (l)(7) instead of para. (i)(7), see below.

—P.L. 96-611, Sec. 11(a)(2), substituted "(8) Disclosure" for "(7) Disclosure" in subsec. (l), effective 6/9/80.

—P.L. 96-598, Sec. 3(a), amended subsec. (d), effective 12/24/80.

Prior to amendment, subsec. (d) read as follows:

"(d) Disclosure to state tax officials.

"Returns and return information with respect to taxes imposed by chapters 1, 2, 6, 11, 12, 21, 23, 24, 31, 44, 51, and 52 and subchapter D of chapter 36, shall be open to inspection by or disclosure to any State agency, body, or commission, or its legal representative, which is charged under the laws of such State with responsibility for the administration of State tax laws for the purpose of, and only to the extent necessary in, the administration of such laws, including any procedures with respect to locating any person who may be entitled to a refund. Such inspection shall be permitted, or such disclosures made, only upon written request by the head of such agency, body, or commission, and only to the representatives of such agency, body, or commission designated in such written request as the individuals who are to inspect or to receive the return or return information on behalf of such agency, body, or commission. Such representatives shall not include any individual who is the chief executive officer of such State or who is neither an employee or legal representative of such agency, body, or commission nor a person described in subsection (n). However, such return information shall not be disclosed to the extent that the Secretary determines that such disclosure would identify a confidential informant or seriously impair any civil or criminal tax investigation."

—P.L. 96-589, Sec. 3(c)(1), deleted para. (e)(4), redesignated paras. (e)(5) and (e)(6) as paras. (e)(6) and (e)(7), and added new paras. (e)(4) and (e)(5) . . . Sec. 3(c)(2), substituted "(4), or (5)" for "or (4)" in para. (e)(6) (as redesignated by Sec. 3(c)(1) of this Act), effective for any bankruptcy case begin. 3/25/81 [more than 90 days after the date of enactment (12/24/80)]. Sec. 7(g) of this Act provides:

"(g) Definitions.

For purposes of this section—

"(1) Bankruptcy case. The term 'bankruptcy case' means any case under title 11 of the United States Code (as recodified by P.L. 95-598).

"(2) Similar judicial proceeding. The term 'similar judicial proceeding' means a receivership, foreclosure, or similar proceeding in a Federal or State court (as modified by section 368(a)(3)(D) of the Internal Revenue Code of 1954)."

Prior to amendment, para. (e)(4) read as follows:

"(4) Bankruptcy. If substantially all of the property of the person with respect to whom the return is filed is in the hands of a trustee in bankruptcy or receiver, such return or returns for prior years of such person shall, upon written request, be open to inspection by or disclosure to such trustee or receiver, but only if the Secretary finds that such receiver or trustee, in his fiduciary capacity, has a material interest which will be affected by information contained therein."

—P.L. 96-499, Sec. 302(a), amended para. (m)(4), effective 12/5/80.

Prior to amendment, para. (m)(4) read as follows:

"(4) Individuals who have defaulted on student loans.

"(A) In general. Upon written request by the Commissioner of Education, the Secretary may disclose the mailing address of any taxpayer who has defaulted on a loan made from the student loan fund established under part E of title IV of the Higher Education Act of 1965 for use only for purposes of locating such taxpayer for purposes of collecting such loan.

"(B) Disclosure to institutions. Any mailing address disclosed under subparagraph (A) may be disclosed by the Commissioner of Education to any educational institution with which he has an agreement under part E of title IV of the Higher Education Act of 1965 only for use by officers, employees or agents of such institution whose duties relate to the collection of student loans for purposes of locating individuals who have defaulted on student loans made by such institution pursuant to such agreement for purposes of collecting such loans."

—P.L. 96-466, Sec. 702, added the last sentence to Sec. 502 of P.L. 96-128, reproduced below, effective 11/28/79.

—P.L. 96-265, Sec. 408(a)(1), added para. (l)(7) . . . Sec. 408(a)(2)(A), substituted "(l)(1), (4)(B), (5), or (7)" for (l)(1) or (4)(b) or (5)' in subpara. (p)(3)(A) . . . Sec. 408(a)(2)(B), substituted '(l)(3), (6), or (7)' for '(l)(3) or (6)' in para. (p)(4) . . . Sec. 408(a)(2)(C), substituted '(l)(6) or (7)' for '(l)(6)' in clause (p)(4)(F)(i), effective 6/9/80.

—P.L. 96-249, Sec. 127(a)(1), added para. (l)(7) . . . Sec. 127(a)(2)(A), through (C), added references to para. (l)(7) in subpara. (p)(3)(A), para. (p)(4) and clause (p)(4)(F)(i), effective 5/26/80.

—P.L. 96-128, Sec. 502, [as amended by Sec. 702 of P.L. 96-466] of this Act provides:

"Sec. 502. In order to effectuate more fully the policy underlying the enactment of section 6103(m)(3) of the Internal Revenue Code of 1986 regarding the location, for certain purposes, of individuals who are, or may have been, exposed to occupational hazards, the Director of the National Institute of Occupational Safety and Health, upon request by the Administrator of Veterans' Affairs (or the head of any other Federal department, agency, or instrumentality), shall (1) pursuant to such section 6103(m)(3), request the mailing addresses of individuals who such Administrator (or such department, agency, or instrumentality head) certifies may have been exposed to occupational hazards during active military, naval, or air service (as defined in section 101(24) of title 38, United States Code), and (2) provide such addresses to such Administrator (or such department, agency, or instrumentality head) to be used solely for the purpose of locating such individuals as part of an activity being carried out by or on behalf of the Veterans' Administration (or such other department agency, or instrumentality) to determine the status of their health or to inform them of the possible need for medical care and treatment and of benefits to which they may be entitled based on disability resulting from exposure to such occupational hazards. Disclosures of information made under this section shall for all purposes be deemed to be disclosures authorized in the Internal Revenue Code of 1986."

In 1978, P.L. 95-600, Sec. 503(a), substituted "In a matter involving tax administration, a" for "A" in the first sentence of para. (h)(2) and substituted "officers and employees" for "attorneys" after "open to inspection by or disclosure to" in para. (h)(2) and added "any proceeding before a Federal grand jury or" before "preparation for any proceeding" in para. (h)(2) and deleted "in a matter involving tax administration" after "or any Federal or State court" in para. (h)(2) . . . Sec. 503(b), amended subpara. (h)(2)(A) . . . amended subpara. (h)(4)(A), effective 11/6/78.

Prior to amendment, subpara. (h)(2)(A) read as follows:

"(A) the taxpayer is or may be a party to such proceeding:"

Prior to amendment, subpara. (h)(4)(A) read as follows:

"(A) it the taxpayer is a party to such proceeding; "

—P.L. 95-600, Sec. 701(bb)(1)(A), amended subsec. (m) . . . Sec. 701(bb)(1)(B), added ", subsection (m)(4)(B)," after "subsection (e)(1)(D)(iii)" in para. (a)(3) . . . Sec. 701(bb)(2), added "31," after "24," in subsec. (d) . . . Sec. 701(bb)(3), added a new sentence at the end of para. (i)(2) . . . Sec. 701(bb)(4), added a new sentence at the end of para. (i)(3) . . . Sec. 701(bb)(5), deleted "income" following "under" in the heading of para. (k)(4) . . . added "or gift and estate tax" after "income tax" in para. (k)(4) . . . added ", or other convention relating to the ex-

Information and returns   Code Sec. 6104(a)(1)(A)

change of tax information," after "convention" the first place it appears in para. (k)(4), effective 1/1/77.
Prior to amendment, subsec. (m) read as follows:
"(m) Disclosure of taxpayer identity information.

"(1) Tax refunds. The Secretary may disclose taxpayer identity information to the press and other media for purposes of notifying persons entitled to tax refunds when the Secretary, after reasonable effort and lapse of time, has been unable to locate such persons.

"(2) Federal claims. Upon written request, the Secretary may disclose the mailing address of a taxpayer to officers and employees of an agency personally and directly engaged in, and solely for their use in, preparation for any administrative or judicial proceeding (or investigation which may result in such a proceeding) pertaining to the collection or compromise of a Federal claim against such taxpayer in accordance with the provisions of section 3 of the Federal Claims Collection Act of 1966.

"(3) National institute for occupational safety and health. Upon written request, the Secretary may disclose the mailing address of taxpayers to officers and employees of the National Institute for Occupational Safety and Health solely for the purpose of locating individuals who are, or may have been, exposed to occupational hazards in order to determine the status of their health or to inform them of the possible need for medical care and treatment."

In 1977, P.L. 95-210, Sec. 5, amended subsec. (m), effective 12/13/77.
Prior to amendment, subsec. (m) read as follows:
"(m) Disclosure of taxpayer identity information.

"The secretary is authorized—

"(1) to disclose taxpayer identity information to the press and other media for purposes of notifying persons entitled to tax refunds when the Secretary, after reasonable effort and lapse of time, has been unable to locate such persons, and

"(2) upon written request, to disclose the mailing address of a taxpayer to officers and employees of an agency personally and directly engaged in, and solely for their use in, preparation for any administrative or judicial proceeding (or investigation which may result in such a proceeding) pertaining to the collection or compromise of a Federal claim against such taxpayer in accordance with the provisions of Section 3 of the Federal Claims Collection Act of 1966."

In 1976, P.L. 94-455, Sec. 1202(a)(1), amended Code Sec. 6103, effective 1/1/77.
Prior to amendment, Code Sec. 6103 read as follows:
"Sec. 6103. Publicity of returns and disclosure of information as to persons filing income tax returns.
"(a) Public record and inspection.

"(1) Returns made with respect to taxes imposed by chapters 1, 2, 3, and 6 upon which the tax has been determined by the Secretary or his delegate shall constitute public records; but, except as hereinafter provided in this section, they shall be open to inspection only upon order of the President and under rules and regulations prescribed by the Secretary or his delegate and approved by the President.

"(2) All returns made with respect to the taxes imposed by chapters 1, 2, 3, 5, 6, 11, 12, and 32, subchapters B and C of chapter 33, subchapter B of chapter 37, and chapter 41 shall constitute public records and shall be open to public examination and inspection to such extent as shall be authorized in rules and regulations promulgated by the President.

"(3) Whenever a return is open to the inspection of any person, a certified copy thereof shall, upon request, be furnished to such person under rules and regulations prescribed by the Secretary or his delegate. The Secretary or his delegate may prescribe a reasonable fee for furnishing such copy.
"(b) Inspection by States.

"(1) State officers. The proper officers of any State may, upon the request of the governor thereof, have access to the returns of any corporation, or to an abstract thereof showing the name and income of any corporation, at such times and in such manner as the Secretary or his delegate may prescribe.

"(2) State bodies or commissions. All income returns filed with respect to the taxes imposed by chapters 1, 2, 3, and 6 (or copies thereof, if so prescribed by regulations made under this subsection), shall be open to inspection by any official, body, or commission, lawfully charged with the administration of any State tax law, if the inspection is for the purpose of such administration or for the purpose of obtaining information to be furnished to local taxing authorities as provided in this paragraph. The inspection shall be permitted only upon written request of the governor of such State, designating the representative of such official, body, or commission to make the inspection on behalf of such official, body, or commission. The inspection shall be made in such manner, and at such times and places, as shall be prescribed by regulations made by the Secretary or his delegate. Any information thus secured by any official, body, or commission of any State may be used only for the administration of the tax laws of such State, except that upon written request of the governor of such State any such information may be furnished to any official, body, or commission of any political subdivision of such State, lawfully charged with the administration of the tax laws of such political subdivision, but may be furnished only for the purpose of, and may be used only for, the administration of such tax laws.
"(c) Inspection by shareholders.

"All bona fide shareholders of record owning 1 percent or more of the outstanding stock of any corporation shall, upon making request of the Secretary or his delegate, be allowed to examine the annual income returns of such corporation and of its subsidiaries.
"(d) Inspection by committees of Congress.

"(1) Committee on Ways and Means and Finance.

"(A) The Secretary and any officer or employee of the Treasury Department, upon request from the Committee on Ways and Means of the House of Representatives, the Committee on Finance of the Senate, or a select committee of the Senate or House specially authorized to investigate returns by a resolution of the Senate or House, or a joint committee so authorized by concurrent resolution, shall furnish such committee sitting in executive session with any data of any character contained in or shown by any return.

"(B) Any such committee shall have the right, acting directly as a committee, or by or through such examiners or agents as it may designate or appoint, to inspect any or all of the returns at such times and in such manner as it may determine.

"(C) Any relevant or useful information thus obtained may be submitted by the committee obtaining it to the Senate or the House, or to both the Senate and the House, as the case may be.

"(2) Joint Committee on Internal Revenue Taxation. The Joint Committee on Internal Revenue Taxation shall have the same right to obtain data and to inspect returns as the Committee on Ways and Means or the Committee on Finance, and to submit any relevant or useful information thus obtained to the Senate, the House of Representatives, the Committee on Ways and Means, or the Committee on Finance. The Committee on Ways and Means or the Committee on Finance may submit such information to the House or the Senate, or to both the House and the Senate, as the case may be.
"(e) Declarations of estimated tax.

"For purposes of this section, a declaration of estimated tax shall be held and considered a return under this chapter.
"(f) Disclosure of information as to persons filing income tax returns.

"The Secretary or his delegate shall, upon inquiry as to whether any person has filed an income tax return in a designated internal revenue district for a particular taxable year, furnish to the inquirer, in such manner as the Secretary or his delegate may determine, information showing that such person has, or has not, filed an income tax return in such district for such taxable year.

"(g) Disclosure of information with respect to deferred compensation plans.

"The Secretary or his delegate is authorized to furnish—

"(1) returns with respect to any tax imposed by this title or information with respect to such returns to the proper officers and employees of the Department of Labor and the Pension Benefit Guaranty Corporation for purposes of administration of Titles I and IV of the Employee Retirement Income Security Act of 1974, and

"(2) registration statements (as described in section 6057) and information with respect to such statements to the proper officers and employees of the Department of Health, Education, and Welfare for purposes of administration of section 1131 of the Social Security Act.

"(g) [sic (h)] Disclosure of information to Secretary of Health, Education, and Welfare.

"The Secretary or his delegate is authorized to make available to the Secretary of Health, Education, and Welfare information returns filed pursuant to part III of subchapter A of 61 of subtitle F for the purpose of carrying out, in accordance with an agreement entered into pursuant to section 232 of the Social Security Act, an effective information return processing program."

In 1976, P.L. 94-202, Sec. 8(g), added new subsec. (g), effective 1/2/76. In P.L. 93-406, Congress also added new subsec. (g), see below.

In 1974, P.L. 93-406, Sec. 1022(h), added new subsec. (g), effective 9/2/74. In P.L. 94-202, Congress also added new subsec. (g), see above.

In 1966, P.L. 89-713, Sec. 4(a)(1), substituted "Sec. 6103. Publicity of Returns and Disclosure of Information as to Persons Filing Income Tax Returns" for "Sec. 6103. Publicity of Returns and Lists of Taxpayers" in heading of Code Sec. 6103 . . . Sec. 4(a)(2), amended subsec. (f), effective 11/2/66.
Prior to amendment, subsec. (f) read as follows:
"(f) Inspection of list of taxpayers.

"The Secretary or his delegate shall as soon as practicable in each year cause to be prepared and made available to public inspection in such manner as he may determine, in the office of the principal internal revenue officer for the internal revenue district in which the return was filed, and in such other places as he may determine, lists containing the name and the post-office address of each person making an income tax return in such district."

In 1965, P.L. 89-44, Sec. 601(a), substituted "B and C" for "B, C, and D" in para. (a)(2).

In 1964, P.L. 88-563, Sec. 3(c), substituted "subchapter B or chapter 37, and chapter 41" for "and subchapter B of chapter 37" in para. (a)(2).

Sec. 6104. Publicity of information required from certain exempt organizations and certain trusts.

(a) Inspection of applications for tax exemption or notice of status.

(1) Public inspection.

(A) Organizations described in section 501 or 527. If an organization described in section 501(c) or (d) is exempt from taxation under section 501(a) for any taxable year or a political organization is exempt from taxation under section 527 for any taxable year, the application filed by the organization with respect to which the Secretary made his determination that such organization was entitled to exemption under section 501(a) or notice of status filed by the organization under section 527(i), together with any papers submitted in support of such application or notice, and any letter or other docu-

3,593

ment issued by the Internal Revenue Service with respect to such application or notice shall be open to public inspection at the national office of the Internal Revenue Service. In the case of any application or notice filed after the date of the enactment of this subparagraph, a copy of such application or notice and such letter or document shall be open to public inspection at the appropriate field office of the Internal Revenue Service (determined under regulations prescribed by the Secretary). Any inspection under this subparagraph may be made at such times, and in such manner, as the Secretary shall by regulations prescribe. After the application of any organization for exemption from taxation under section 501(a) has been opened to public inspection under this subparagraph, the Secretary shall, on the request of any person with respect to such organization, furnish a statement indicating the subsection and paragraph of section 501 which it has been determined describes such organization.

(B) Pension, etc., plans. The following shall be open to public inspection at such times and in such places as the Secretary may prescribe:

(i) any application filed with respect to the qualification of a pension, profit-sharing, or stock bonus plan under section 401(a) or 403(a), an individual retirement account described in section 408(a), or an individual retirement annuity described in section 408(b),

(ii) any application filed with respect to the exemption from tax under section 501(a) of an organization forming part of a plan or account referred to in clause (i),

(iii) any papers submitted in support of an application referred to in clause (i) or (ii), and

(iv) any letter or other document issued by the Internal Revenue Service and dealing with the qualification referred to in clause (i) or the exemption from tax referred to in clause (ii).

Except in the case of a plan participant, this subparagraph shall not apply to any plan referred to in clause (i) having not more than 25 participants.

(C) Certain names and compensation not to be opened to public inspection. In the case of any application, document, or other papers, referred to in subparagraph (B), information from which the compensation (including deferred compensation) of any individual may be ascertained shall not be open to public inspection under subparagraph (B).

(D) Withholding of certain other information. Upon request of the organization submitting any supporting papers described in subparagraph (A) or (B), the Secretary shall withhold from public inspection any information contained therein which he determines relates to any trade secret, patent, process, style of work, or apparatus, of the organization, if he determines that public disclosure of such information would adversely affect the organization. The Secretary shall withhold from public inspection any information contained in supporting papers described in subparagraph (A) or (B) the public disclosure of which he determines would adversely affect the national defense.

(2) Inspection by committees of Congress. Section 6103(f) shall apply with respect to—

(A) the application for exemption of any organization described in section 501(c) or (d) which is exempt from taxation under section 501(a) for any taxable year or notice of status of any political organization which is exempt from taxation under section 527 for any taxable year, and any application referred to in subparagraph (B) of subsection (a)(1) of this section, and

(B) any other papers which are in the possession of the Secretary and which relate to such application,

as if such papers constituted returns.

(3) Information available on internet and in person.

(A) In general. The Secretary shall make publicly available, on the internet and at the offices of the Internal Revenue Service—

(i) a list of all political organizations which file a notice with the Secretary under section 527(i), and

(ii) the name, address, electronic mailing address, custodian of records, and contact person for such organization.

(B) Time to make information available. The Secretary shall make available the information required under subparagraph A not later than 5 business days after the Secretary receives a notice from a political organization under section 527(i).

(b) Inspection of annual returns.

The information required to be furnished by sections 6033, 6034, and 6058, together with the names and addresses of such organizations and trusts, shall be made available to the public at such times and in such places as the Secretary may prescribe. Nothing in this subsection shall authorize the Secretary to disclose the name or address of any contributor to any organization or trust (other than a private foundation, as defined in section 509(a)) or a political organization exempt from taxation under section 527 which is required to furnish such information. In the case of an organization described in section 501(d), this subsection shall not apply to copies referred to in section 6031(b) with respect to such organization. In the case of a trust which is required to file a return under section 6034(a), this subsection shall not apply to information regarding beneficiaries which are not organizations described in section 170(c). Any annual return which is filed under section 6011 by an organization described in section 501(c)(3) and which relates to any tax imposed by section 511 (relating to imposition of tax on unrelated business income of charitable, etc., organizations) shall be treated for purposes of this subsection in the same manner as if furnished under section 6033.

(c) Publication to State officials.

(1) General rule for charitable organizations. In the case of any organization which is described in section 501(c)(3) and exempt from taxation under section 501(a), or has applied under section 508(a) for recognition as an organization described in section 501(c)(3), the Secretary at such times and in such manner as he may by regulations prescribe shall—

(A) notify the appropriate State officer of a refusal to recognize such organization as an organization described in section 501(c)(3), or of the operation of such organization in a manner which does not meet, or no longer meets, the requirements of its exemption,

(B) notify the appropriate State officer of the mailing of a notice of deficiency of tax imposed under section 507 or chapter 41 or 42, and

(C) at the request of such appropriate State officer, make available for inspection and copying such returns, filed statements, records, reports, and other information, relating to a determination under subparagraph (A) or (B) as are relevant to any determination under State law.

(2) Disclosure of proposed actions related to charitable organizations.

Information and returns   Code Sec. 6104(d)(3)(A)

(A) Specific notifications. In the case of an organization to which paragraph (1) applies, the Secretary may disclose to the appropriate State officer—

(i) a notice of proposed refusal to recognize such organization as an organization described in section 501(c)(3) or a notice of proposed revocation of such organization's recognition as an organization exempt from taxation,

(ii) the issuance of a letter of proposed deficiency of tax imposed under section 507 or chapter 41 or 42, and

(iii) the names, addresses, and taxpayer identification numbers of organizations which have applied for recognition as organizations described in section 501(c)(3).

(B) Additional disclosures. Returns and return information of organizations with respect to which information is disclosed under subparagraph (A) may be made available for inspection by or disclosed to an appropriate State officer.

(C) Procedures for disclosure. Information may be inspected or disclosed under subparagraph (A) or (B) only—

(i) upon written request by an appropriate State officer, and

(ii) for the purpose of, and only to the extent necessary in, the administration of State laws regulating such organizations.

Such information may only be inspected by or disclosed to a person other than the appropriate State officer if such person is an officer or employee of the State and is designated by the appropriate State officer to receive the returns or return information under this paragraph on behalf of the appropriate State officer.

(D) Disclosures other than by request. The Secretary may make available for inspection or disclose returns and return information of an organization to which paragraph (1) applies to an appropriate State officer of any State if the Secretary determines that such returns or return information may constitute evidence of noncompliance under the laws within the jurisdiction of the appropriate State officer.

(3) Disclosure with respect to certain other exempt organizations. Upon written request by an appropriate State officer, the Secretary may make available for inspection or disclosure returns and return information of any organization described in section 501(c) (other than organizations described in paragraph (1) or (3) thereof) for the purpose of, and only to the extent necessary in, the administration of State laws regulating the solicitation or administration of the charitable funds or charitable assets of such organizations. Such information may only be inspected by or disclosed to a person other than the appropriate State officer if such person is an officer or employee of the State and is designated by the appropriate State officer to receive the returns or return information under this paragraph on behalf of the appropriate State officer.

(4) Use in civil judicial and administrative proceedings. Returns and return information disclosed pursuant to this subsection may be disclosed in civil administrative and civil judicial proceedings pertaining to the enforcement of State laws regulating such organizations in a manner prescribed by the Secretary similar to that for tax administration proceedings under section 6103(h)(4).

(5) No disclosure if impairment. Returns and return information shall not be disclosed under this subsection, or in any proceeding described in paragraph (4), to the extent that the Secretary determines that such disclosure would seriously impair Federal tax administration.

(6) Definitions. For purposes of this subsection—

(A) Return and return information. The terms "return" and "return information" have the respective meanings given to such terms by section 6103(b).

(B) Appropriate State officer. The term "appropriate State" officer means—

(i) the State attorney general,

(ii) the State tax officer,

(iii) in the case of an organization to which paragraph (1) applies, any other State official charged with overseeing organizations of the type described in section 501(c)(3), and

(iv) in the case of an organization to which paragraph (3) applies, the head of an agency designated by the State attorney general as having primary responsibility for overseeing the solicitation of funds for charitable purposes.

(d) Public inspection of certain annual returns, reports, applications for exemption, and notices of status.

(1) In general. In the case of an organization described in subsection (c) or (d) of section 501 and exempt from taxation under section 501(a) or an organization exempt from taxation under section 527(a)—

(A) a copy of—

(i) the annual return filed under section 6033 (relating to returns by exempt organizations) by such organization,

(ii) any annual return which is filed under section 6011 by an organization described in section 501(c)(3) and which relates to any tax imposed by section 511 (relating to imposition of tax on unrelated business income of charitable, etc., organizations),

(iii) if the organization filed an application for recognition of exemption under section 501 or notice of status under section 527(i), the exempt status application materials or any notice materials of such organization, and

(iv) the reports filed under section 527(j) (relating to required disclosure of expenditures and contributions) by such organization,

shall be made available by such organization for inspection during regular business hours by any individual at the principal office of such organization and, if such organization regularly maintains 1 or more regional or district offices having 3 or more employees, at each such regional or district office, and

(B) upon request of an individual made at such principal office or such a regional or district office, a copy of such annual return, reports, and exempt status application materials or such notice materials shall be provided to such individual without charge other than a reasonable fee for any reproduction and mailing costs.

The request described in subparagraph (B) must be made in person or in writing. If such request is made in person, such copy shall be provided immediately and, if made in writing, shall be provided within 30 days.

(2) 3-year limitation on inspection of returns. Paragraph (1) shall apply to an annual return filed under section 6011 or 6033 only during the 3-year period beginning on the last day prescribed for filing such return (determined with regard to any extension of time for filing).

(3) Exceptions from disclosure requirement.

(A) Nondisclosure of contributors, etc. In the case of an organization which is not a private foundation (within

3,595

the meaning of section 509(a)) or a political organization exempt from taxation under section 527, paragraph (1) shall not require the disclosure of the name or address of any contributor to the organization. In the case of an organization described in section 501(d), paragraph (1) shall not require the disclosure of the copies referred to in section 6031(b) with respect to such organization.

(B) **Nondisclosure of certain other information.** Paragraph (1) shall not require the disclosure of any information if the Secretary withheld such information from public inspection under subsection (a)(1)(D).

(4) **Limitation on providing copies.** Paragraph (1)(B) shall not apply to any request if, in accordance with regulations promulgated by the Secretary, the organization has made the requested documents widely available, or the Secretary determines, upon application by an organization, that such request is part of a harassment campaign and that compliance with such request is not in the public interest.

(5) **Exempt status application materials.** For purposes of paragraph (1), the term "exempt status applicable materials" means the application for recognition of exemption under section 501 and any papers submitted in support of such application and any letter or other document issued by the Internal Revenue Service with respect to such application.

(6) **Notice materials.** For purposes of paragraph (1), the term "notice materials" means the notice of status filed under section 527(i) and any papers submitted in support of such notice and any letter or other document issued by the Internal Revenue Service with respect to such notice.

(6 [sic (7)]) **Disclosure of reports by Internal Revenue Service.** Any report filed by an organization under section 527(j) (relating to required disclosure of expenditures and contributions) shall be made available to the public at such times and in such places as the Secretary may prescribe.

(6 [sic (8)]) **Application to nonexempt charitable trusts and nonexempt private foundations.** The organizations referred to in paragraphs (1) and (2) of section 6033(d) shall comply with the requirements of this subsection relating to annual returns filed under section 6033 in the same manner as the organizations referred to in paragraph (1).

In 2007, P.L. 110-172, Sec. 3(g)(1)(A), deleted "information" before "returns." in the heading of subsec. (b)... Sec. 3(g)(1)(B), added a sentence at the end of subsec. (b)... Sec. 3(g)(2), amended clause (d)(1)(A)(ii)... Sec. 3(g)(3), substituted "section 6011 or 6033" for "section 6033" in para. (d)(2), effective for returns filed after 8/17/2006.

Prior to amendment, clause (d)(1)(A)(ii) read as follows:

"(ii) any annual return filed under section 6011 which relates to any tax imposed by section 511 (relating to imposition of tax on unrelated business income of charitable, etc., organizations) by such organization, but only if such organization is described in section 501(c)(3)."

In 2006, P.L. 109-280, Sec. 1201(b)(3), added "In the case of a trust which is required to file a return under section 6034(a), this subsection shall not apply to information regarding beneficiaries which are not organizations described in section 170(c)" at the end of subsec. (b), effective for returns for tax. yrs. begin. after 12/31/2006.

—P.L. 109-280, Sec. 1224(a), deleted para. (c)(2) and added paras. (c)(2)-(c)(6) ... Sec. 1224(b)(4), added "for charitable organizations" after "rule" in the heading of para. (c)(1), effective 8/17/2006 but not for requests made before 8/17/2006.

Prior to deletion, para. (c)(2) read as follows:

"(2) Appropriate State officer. For purposes of this subsection, the term 'appropriate State officer' means the State attorney general, State tax officer, or any State official charged with overseeing organizations of the type described in section 501(c)(3)."

—P.L. 109-280, Sec. 1225(a), redesignated clauses (d)(1)(A)(ii) and (iii) as clauses (d)(1)(A)(iii) and (iv) and added clause (d)(1)(A)(ii), effective for returns filed after 8/17/2006.

In 2002, P.L. 107-276, Sec. 3(b)(1), deleted "6012(a)(6)," after "furnished by sections" in subsec. (b)... Sec. 3(b)(2)(A), deleted "or section 6012(a)(6) (relating to returns by political organizations)" after "exempt organizations)" in clause (d)(1)(A)(i)... Sec. 3(b)(2)(B), deleted "or section 6012(a)(6)" after "section 6033" in para. (d)(2), effective for tax. yrs. begin. after 6/30/2000.

—P.L. 107-276, Sec. 7, of this Act, provides:

"(7) Effect of amendments on existing disclosures. Notices, reports, or returns that were required to be filed with the Secretary of the Treasury before the date of the enactment of the amendments made by this Act and that were disclosed by the Secretary of the Treasury consistent with the law in effect at the time of such disclosure shall remain subject on and after such date to the disclosure provisions of section 6104 of the Internal Revenue Code of 1986."

In 2000, P.L. 106-554, Sec. 1(a)(7), [which enacted into law Sec. 312(a) of P.L. 106-554] added para. (d)(6) [sic (8)], effective 10/21/98.

—P.L. 106-230, Sec. 1(b)(1)(A)(i), added "or a political organization is exempt from taxation under section 527 for any taxable year" after "taxable year" in subpara. (a)(1)(A)... Sec. 1(b)(1)(A)(ii), added "or notice of status filed by the organization under section 527(i)" before ", together" in subpara. (a)(1)(A)... Sec. 1(b)(1)(A)(iii), added "or notice" after "such application" each place it appears in subpara. (a)(1)(A)... Sec. 1(b)(1)(A)(iv), added "or notice" after "any application" in subpara. (a)(1)(A)... Sec. 1(b)(1)(A)(v), added "for exemption from taxation under section 501(a)" after "any organization" in the last sentence in subpara. (a)(1)(A)... Sec. 1(b)(1)(A)(vi), added "or 527" after "section 501" in the heading in subpara. (a)(1)(A)... Sec. 1(b)(1)(B), added "or notice of status" before the period in the heading in subsec. (a), effective 7/1/2000.

—P.L. 106-230, Sec. 1(b)(2), added para. (a)(3)... Sec. 1(b)(3), added "or notice of status of any political organization which is exempt from taxation under section 527 for any taxable year" after "taxable year" in para. (a)(2), effective 8/15/2000.

—P.L. 106-230, Sec. 1(b)(4)(A), substituted "applications for exemption, and notice of status" for "and applications for exemption" in the heading in subsec. (d) ... Sec. 1(b)(4)(B), added "or notice of status under section 527(i)" after "section 501" and "or any notice materials" after "materials" in clause (d)(1)(A)(ii)... Sec. 1(b)(4)(C), added "or such notice materials" after "materials" in subpara. (d)(1)(B)... Sec. 1(b)(4)(D), added para. (d)(6), effective 7/1/2000.

—P.L. 106-230, Sec. 2(b)(1)(A), added "reports," after "returns," in the heading in subsec. (d)... Sec. 2(b)(1)(B), deleted "and" at the end of clause (d)(1)(A)(i), added "and" at the end of clause (d)(1)(A)(ii), and added clause (d)(1)(A)(iii)... Sec. 2(b)(1)(C), added ", reports," after "return" in subpara. (d)(1)(B)... Sec. 2(b)(2), added "or a political organization exempt from taxation under section 527" after "509(a))" in subpara. (d)(3)(A)... Sec. 2(b)(3), added para. (d)(6) [sic (7)], effective as provided in Sec. 2(d) of this Act, which reads as follows:

"(d) Effective date. The amendment made by subsection (a) shall apply to expenditures made and contributions received after 7/1/2000, except that such amendment shall not apply to expenditures made, or contributions received, after 7/1/2000 pursuant to a contract entered into on or before 7/1/2000."

—P.L. 106-230, Sec. 3(b)(1)(A), added "6012(a)(6)" before "6033" in subsec. (b)... Sec. 3(b)(1)(B), added "or a political organization exempt from taxation under section 527" after "509(a)" in subsec. (b)... Sec. 3(b)(2)(A), added "or section 6012(a)(6) (relating to returns by political organizations)" after "organizations)" in clause (d)(1)(A)(i)... Sec. 3(b)(2)(B)(i), added "or an organization exempt from taxation under section 527(a)" after "501(a)" in para. (d)(1)... Sec. 3(b)(2)(B)(ii), added "or section 6012(a)(6)" after "section 6033" in para. (d)(2), effective for tax. yrs. begin. after 6/30/2000.

In 1998, P.L. 105-277, Sec. 1004(b)(1), deleted subsecs. (d) and (e) and added new subsec. (d), effective as provided in Sec. 1004(b)(3), of this Act, which reads as follows:

"(3) Effective date.

"(A) In general. Except as provided in subparagraph (B), the amendments made by this subsection shall apply to requests made after the later of December 31, 1998, or the 60th day after the Secretary of the Treasury first issues the regulations referred to in section 6104(d)(4) of the Internal Revenue Code of 1986, as amended by this section.

"(B) Publication of annual returns. Section 6104(d) of such Code, as in effect before the amendments made by this subsection, shall not apply to any return the due date for which is after the date such amendments take effect under subparagraph (A)."

Prior to deletion, subsecs. (d) and (e) read as follows:

"(d) Public inspection of private foundations' annual returns. The annual return required to be filed under section 6033 (relating to returns by exempt organizations) by any organization which is a private foundation within the meaning of section 509(a) shall be made available by the foundation managers for inspection at the principal office of the foundation during regular business hours by any citizen on request made within 180 days after the date of the publication of notice of its availability. Such notice shall be published, not later than the day prescribed for filing such annual return (determined with regard to any extension of time for filing), in a newspaper having general circulation in the county in which the principal office of the private foundation is located. The notice shall state that the annual return of the private foundation is available at its principal office for inspection during regular business hours by any citizen who requests it within 180 days after the date of such publication, and shall state the address and the telephone number of the private foundation's principal office and the name of its principal manager.

"(e) Public inspection of certain annual returns and applications for exemption.

"(1) Annual returns. In general. During the 3-year period beginning on the filing date—

"(i) a copy of the annual return filed under section 6033 (relating to returns by exempt organizations) by any organization to which this paragraph applies shall

Information and returns

Code Sec. 6105(c)(1)

be made available by such organization for inspection during regular business hours by any individual at the principal office of such organization and, if such organization regularly maintains 1 or more regional or district offices having 3 or more employees, at each such regional or district office, and

"(ii) upon request of an individual made at such principal office or such a regional or district office, a copy of such annual return shall be provided to such individual without charge other than a reasonable fee for any reproduction and mailing costs.

The request described in clause (ii) must be made in person or in writing. If the request under clause (ii) is made in person, such copy shall be provided immediately and, if made in writing, shall be provided within 30 days.

"(B) Organizations to which paragraph applies. This paragraph shall apply to any organization which—

"(i) is described in subsection (c) or (d) of section 501 and exempt from taxation under section 501(a), and

"(ii) is not a private foundation (within the meaning of section 509(a)).

"(C) Nondisclosure of contributors. Subparagraph (A) shall not require the disclosure of the name or address of any contributor to the organization. In the case of an organization described in section 501(d), subparagraph (A) shall not require the disclosure of the copies referred to in section 6031(b) with respect to such organization.

"(D) Filing date. For purposes of subparagraph (A), the term 'filing date' means the last day prescribed for filing the return under section 6033 (determined with regard to any extension of time for filing).

"(2) Application for exemption. In general. If—

"(i) an organization described in subsection (c) or (d) of section 501 is exempt from taxation under section 501(a), and

"(ii) such organization filed an application for recognition of exemption under section 501,

a copy of such application (together with a copy of any papers submitted in support of such application and any letter or other document issued by the Internal Revenue Service with respect to such application) shall be made available by the organization for inspection during regular business hours by any individual at the principal office of the organization and, if the organization regularly maintains 1 or more regional or district offices having 3 or more employees, at each such regional or district office (and, upon request of an individual made at such principal office or such a regional or district office, a copy of the material requested to be available for inspection under this subparagraph shall be provided (in accordance with the last sentence of paragraph (1)(A)) to such individual without charge other than reasonable fee for any reproduction and mailing costs).

"(B) Nondisclosure of certain information. Subparagraph (A) shall not require the disclosure of any information if the Secretary withheld such information from public inspection under subsection (a)(1)(D).

"(3) Limitation. Paragraph (1)(A)(ii) (and the corresponding provision of paragraph (2)) shall not apply to any request if, in accordance with regulations promulgated by the Secretary, the organization has made the requested documents widely available, or, the Secretary determines, upon application by an organization, that such request is part of a harassment campaign and that compliance with such request is not in the public interest."

—P.L. 105-206, Sec. 6019(a), added a sentence at the end of subsec. (b) . . . Sec. 6019(b), added a sentence at the end of subpara. (e)(1)(C), effective 7/22/98.

In 1996, P.L. 104-168, Sec. 1313(a)(1), amended subpara. (e)(1)(A) . . . Sec. 1313(a)(2), added the material following "district office" and before the period at the end of subpara. (e)(2)(A) . . . Sec. 1313(a)(3), added para. (e)(3), effective for requests made on or after the 60th day after the Secretary of the Treasury first issues the regulations referred to [in] section 6104(e)(3) of the Internal Revenue Code of 1986 [as added by Sec. 1313(a)(3) of this Act, see above].

Prior to amendment, subpara. (e)(1)(A) read as follows:

"(A) In general. During the 3-year period beginning on the filing date, a copy of the annual return filed under section 6033 (relating to returns by exempt organizations) by any organization to which this paragraph applies shall be made available by such organization for inspection during regular business hours by any individual at the principal office of the organization and, if such organization regularly maintains 1 or more regional or district offices having 3 or more employees, at each such regional or district office."

In 1987, P.L. 100-203, Sec. 10702(a), added subsec. (e), effective as provided in Sec. 10702(b) of this Act, which reads as follows:

"(b) Effective date. The amendment made by subsection (a) shall apply—

"(1) to returns for years beginning after December 31, 1986, and

"(2) on and after the 30th day after the date of the enactment of this Act in the case of applications submitted to the Internal Revenue Service—

"(A) after July 15, 1987, or

"(B) on or before July 15, 1987, if the organization has a copy of the application on July 15, 1987."

In 1984, P.L. 98-369, Sec. 306(b), added "and the telephone number" after "shall state the address" in subsec. (d), effective 1/1/85.

—P.L. 98-369, Sec. 491(d)(49), substituted "or 403(a)" for ", 403(a), or 405(a)" in clause (a)(1)(B)(i), effective for obligations issued after 12/31/83.

In 1980, P.L. 96-603, Sec. 1(b)(1), amended the first sentence of subsec. (d) . . . Sec. 1(b)(2), substituted "annual returns" for "annual reports" in the heading of subsec. (d) and substituted "annual return" for "annual report" in the second and third sentences of subsec. (d) . . . Sec. 1(d)(3), deleted "6056," from "sections 6033, 6034," in the first sentence of subsec. (b), effective for tax. yrs. begin. after 12/31/80.

Prior to amendment, the first sentence of subsec. (d) read as follows:

"The annual report required to be filed under section 6056 (relating to annual reports by private foundations) shall be made available by the foundation manag-

ers for inspection at the principal office of the foundation during regular business hours by any citizen on request made within 180 days after the publication of notice of its availability."

In 1978, P.L. 95-600, Sec. 703(m), substituted "Section 6103(f)" for "Section 6103(d)" in para. (a)(2), effective 10/4/76.

—P.L. 95-488, Sec. 1(d)(1), deleted "(other than in paragraph (21) thereof)" after "501(c)" in the first sentence of subpara. (a)(1)(A) . . . Sec. 1(d)(2), deleted the last sentence of subsec. (b), for tax. yrs. begin. after 12/31/77. Sec. 1(e) of this Act provides:

"(e) Nothing in the amendments made by subsection (d) to section 6104 of the Internal Revenue Code of 1954 shall be construed to permit the disclosure under such section 6104 of confidential business information of contributors to any trust described in section 501(c)(21) of such Code."

Prior to deletion, the last sentence of subsec. (b) read as follows:

"This subsection shall not apply to information required to be furnished by a trust described in section 501(c)(21)."

—P.L. 95-227, Sec. 4(e), added "(other than in paragraph (21) thereof)" after "section 501(c)" in subpara (a)(1)(A) . . . added "This subsection shall not apply to information required to be furnished by a trust described in section 501(c)(21).", at the end of subsec. (b), effective for contributions, acts, and expenditures made after 12/31/77, in and for tax. yrs. begin. after 12/31/77.

In 1976, P.L. 94-455, Sec. 1201(d), added "and any letter or other document issued by the Internal Revenue Service with respect to such application" following "such application," in the first sentence of subpara. (a)(1)(A) . . . added "and such letter or document" following "such application" in the second sentence of subpara. (a)(1)(A), effective for any letter or other document issued with respect to applications filed after 10/31/76.

—P.L. 94-455, Sec. 1307(d)(2)(B), substituted "chapter 41 or 42" for "chapter 42" following "under section 507 or" in subpara. (c)(1)(B), effective on or after 10/4/76.

—P.L. 94-455, Sec. 1906(b)(13)(A), substituted "Secretary" for "Secretary or his delegate" each place it appeared in subsecs. (a), (b) and (c), effective 2/1/77.

In 1974, P.L. 93-406, Sec. 1022(g)(1)(A), redesignated subpara. (a)(1)(B) as subpara. (a)(1)(D) and added new subparas. (a)(1)(B) and (C) . . . Sec. 1022(g)(1)(B), amended the heading of subpara. (a)(1)(A) . . . Sec. 1022(g)(1)(C), amended the heading of subpara. (a)(1)(D), as redesignated by Sec. 1022(g)(1)(A) of this Act, see above . . . Sec. 1022(g)(1)(D), substituted "subparagraph (A) or (B)" for "subparagraph (A)" each place it appeared in subpara. (a)(1)(D) as redesignated . . . Sec. 1022(g)(2), added "any application referred to in subparagraph (B) of subsection (a)(1) of this section, and" at the end of subpara. (a)(2)(A) . . . Sec. 1022(g)(3), substituted "6056, and 6058" for "and 6056" in subsec. (b), effective for applications filed (or documents issued) after 9/2/74.

In 1969, P.L. 91-172, Sec. 101(e), added the sentence at the end of subsec. (b), and added subsecs. (c) and (d) . . . Sec. 101(j)(36), substituted "6033, 6034, and 6056" for "6033(b) and 6034" in subsec. (b), effective 1/1/70.

In 1958, P.L. 85-866, Sec. 75(a), designated existing provisions as subsec. (b), and added subsec. (a), effective 11/1/58.

Sec. 6105. Confidentiality of information arising under treaty obligations.

(a) In general.

Tax convention information shall not be disclosed.

(b) Exceptions.

Subsection (a) shall not apply—

(1) to the disclosure of tax convention information to persons or authorities (including courts and administrative bodies) which are entitled to such disclosure pursuant to a tax convention,

(2) to any generally applicable procedural rules regarding applications for relief under a tax convention,

(3) to the disclosure of tax convention information on the same terms as return information may be disclosed under paragraph (3)(C) or (7) of section 6103(i), except that in the case of tax convention information provided by a foreign government, no disclosure may be made under this paragraph without the written consent of the foreign government, or

(4) in any case not described in paragraph (1), (2), or (3), to the disclosure of any tax convention information not relating to a particular taxpayer if the Secretary determines, after consultation with each other party to the tax convention, that such disclosure would not impair tax administration.

(c) Definitions.

For purposes of this section—

(1) Tax convention information. The term "tax convention information" means any—

3,597

(A) agreement entered into with the competent authority of one or more foreign governments pursuant to a tax convention,
(B) application for relief under a tax convention,
(C) background information related to such agreement or application,
(D) document implementing such agreement, and
(E) other information exchanged pursuant to a tax convention which is treated as confidential or secret under the tax convention.
  (2) **Tax convention.** The term "tax convention" means—
(A) any income tax or gift and estate tax convention, or
(B) any other convention or bilateral agreement (including multilateral conventions and agreements and any agreement with a possession of the United States) providing for the avoidance of double taxation, the prevention of fiscal evasion, nondiscrimination with respect to taxes, the exchange of tax relevant information with the United States, or mutual assistance in tax matters.
(d) Cross references.
For penalties for the unauthorized disclosure of tax convention information, which is return or return information, see sections 7213, 7213A, and 7431.

In **2002**, P.L. 107-147, Sec. 417(18), deleted "any" before "background information" in subpara (c)(1)(C) and "other information" in subpara. (c)(1)(E), effective 3/9/2002.
 —P.L. 107-134, Sec. 201(c)(9)(A), deleted "or" at the end of para. (b)(2) . . . Sec. 201(c)(9)(B), substituted "paragraph (1), (2), or (3)" for "paragraphs (1) or (2)" in para. (b)(3) . . . Sec. 201(c)(9)(C), redesignated para. (b)(3) as para. (b)(4) . . . Sec. 201(c)(9)(D), added new para. (b)(3), effective for disclosures made on or after 1/23/2002.
In **2000**, P.L. 106-554, Sec. 1(a)(7), [which enacted into law Sec. 304(b)(1) of P.L. 106-554] added Code Sec. 6105, effective 12/21/2000.

Sec. 6106. Repealed.

In **1976**, P.L. 94-455, Sec. 1202(h)(1), repealed Code Sec. 6106, effective 1/1/77. Prior to repeal, Code Sec. 6106 read as follows:
"SEC. 6106. PUBLICITY OF UNEMPLOYMENT TAX RETURNS.
"Returns filed with respect to the tax imposed by chapter 23 shall be open to inspection in the same manner, to the same extent, and subject to the same provisions of law, including penalties, as returns described in section 6103, except that paragraph (2) of subsections (a) and (b) of section 6103 and section 7213(a)(2) shall not apply."

Sec. 6107. Tax return preparer must furnish copy of return to taxpayer and must retain a copy or list.
(a) Furnishing copy to taxpayer.
Any person who is a tax return preparer with respect to any return or claim for refund shall furnish a completed copy of such return or claim to the taxpayer not later than the time such return or claim is presented for such taxpayer's signature.
(b) Copy or list to be retained by tax return preparer.
Any person who is a tax return preparer with respect to a return or claim for refund shall, for the period ending 3 years after the close of the return period—
  (1) retain a completed copy of such return or claim, or retain, on a list, the name and taxpayer identification number of the taxpayer for whom such return or claim was prepared, and
  (2) make such copy or list available for inspection upon request by the Secretary.
(c) Regulations.
The Secretary shall prescribe regulations under which, in cases where 2 or more persons are tax return preparers with respect to the same return or claim for refund, compliance with the requirements of subsection (a) or (b), as the case may be, of one such person shall be deemed to be compliance with the requirements of such subsection by the other persons.
(d) Definitions.
For purposes of this section, the terms "return" and "claim for refund" have the respective meanings given to such terms by section 6696(e), and the term "return period" has the meaning given to such term by section 6060(c).

In **2007**, P.L. 110-28, Sec. 8246(a)(2)(C)(i)(I), substituted "Tax return preparer" for "Income tax return preparer" in the heading of Code Sec. 6107 . . . Sec. 8246(a)(2)(C)(i)(II), substituted "a tax return preparer" for "an income tax return preparer" each place it appears in subsecs. (a) and (b) . . . Sec. 8246(a)(2)(C)(i)(III), substituted "tax return preparer" for "income tax return preparer" in the heading of subsec. (b) . . . Sec. 8246(a)(2)(C)(i)(IV), substituted "tax return preparers" for "income tax return preparers" in subsec. (c), effective for returns prepared after 5/25/2007.
In **1976**, P.L. 94-455, Sec. 1203(c), added Code Sec. 6107, effective for documents prepared after 12/31/76.

Sec. 6108. Statistical publications and studies.
(a) Publication or other disclosure of statistics of income.
The Secretary shall prepare and publish not less than annually statistics reasonably available with respect to the operations of the internal revenue laws, including classifications of taxpayers and of income, the amounts claimed or allowed as deductions, exemptions, and credits, and any other facts deemed pertinent and valuable.
(b) Special statistical studies.
The Secretary may, upon written request by any party or parties, make special statistical studies and compilations involving return information (as defined in section 6103(b)(2)) and furnish to such party or parties transcripts of any such special statistical study or compilation. A reasonable fee may be prescribed for the cost of the work or services performed for such party or parties.
(c) Anonymous form.
No publication or other disclosure of statistics or other information required or authorized by subsection (a) or special statistical study authorized by subsection (b) shall in any manner permit the statistics, study, or any information so published, furnished, or otherwise disclosed to be associated with, or otherwise identify, directly or indirectly, a particular taxpayer.

In **1976**, P.L. 94-455, Sec. 1202(b), amended Code Sec. 6108, effective 1/1/77. Prior to amendment, Code Sec. 6108 read as follows:
"SEC. 6108. PUBLICATION OF STATISTICS OF INCOME.
"The Secretary or his delegate shall prepare and publish annually statistics reasonably available with respect to the operation of the income tax laws, including classifications of taxpayers and of income, the amounts allowed as deductions, exemptions, and credits, and any other facts deemed pertinent and valuable."

Sec. 6109. Identifying numbers.
(a) Supplying of identifying numbers.
When required by regulations prescribed by the Secretary:
  (1) Inclusion in returns. Any person required under the authority of this title to make a return, statement, or other document shall include in such return, statement, or other document such identifying number as may be prescribed for securing proper identification of such person.
  (2) Furnishing number to other persons. Any person with respect to whom a return, statement, or other document is required under the authority of this title to be made by another person or whose identifying number is required to be shown on a return of another person shall furnish to such other person such identifying number as may be prescribed for securing his proper identification.
  (3) Furnishing number of another person. Any person required under the authority of this title to make a return, statement, or other document with respect to another person shall request from such other person, and shall include

in any such return, statement, or other document, such identifying number as may be prescribed for securing proper identification of such other person.

(4) Furnishing identifying number of tax return preparer. Any return or claim for refund prepared by a tax return preparer shall bear such identifying number for securing proper identification of such preparer, his employer, or both, as may be prescribed. For purposes of this paragraph, the terms "return" and "claim for refund" have the respective meanings given to such terms by section 6696(e).

For purposes of paragraphs (1), (2), and (3), the identifying number of an individual (or his estate) shall be such individual's social security account number.

(b) Limitation.

(1) Except as provided in paragraph (2), a return of any person with respect to his liability for tax, or any statement or other document in support thereof, shall not be considered for purposes of paragraphs (2) and (3) of subsection (a) as a return, statement, or other document with respect to another person.

(2) For purposes of paragraphs (2) and (3) of subsection (a), a return of an estate or trust with respect to its liability for tax, and any statement or other document in support thereof, shall be considered as a return, statement, or other document with respect to each beneficiary of such estate or trust.

(c) Requirement of information.

For purposes of this section, the Secretary is authorized to require such information as may be necessary to assign an identifying number to any person.

(d) Use of social security account number.

The social security account number issued to an individual for purposes of section 205(c)(2)(A) of the Social Security Act shall, except as shall otherwise be specified under regulations of the Secretary, be used as the identifying number for such individual for purposes of this title.

(e) Repealed.

(f) Access to employer identification numbers by Secretary of Agriculture for purposes of Food and Nutrition Act of 2008.

(1) In general. In the administration of section 9 of the Food and Nutrition Act of 2008 (7 U.S.C. 2018) involving the determination of the qualifications of applicants under such Act, the Secretary of Agriculture may, subject to this subsection, require each applicant retail store or wholesale food concern to furnish to the Secretary of Agriculture the employer identification number assigned to the store or concern pursuant to this section. The Secretary of Agriculture shall not have access to any such number for any purpose other than the establishment and maintenance of a list of the names and employer identification numbers of the stores and concerns for use in determining those applicants who have been previously sanctioned or convicted under section 12 or 15 of such Act (7 U.S.C. 2021 or 2024).

(2) Sharing of information and safeguards.

(A) Sharing of information. The Secretary of Agriculture may share any information contained in any list referred to in paragraph (1) with any other agency or instrumentality of the United States which otherwise has access to employer identification numbers in accordance with this section or other applicable Federal law, except that the Secretary of Agriculture may share such information only to the extent that such Secretary determines such sharing would assist in verifying and matching such information against information maintained by such other agency or instrumentality. Any such information shared pursuant to this subparagraph may be used by such other agency or instrumentality only for the purpose of effective administration and enforcement of the Food and Nutrition Act of 2008 or for the purpose of investigation of violations of other Federal laws or enforcement of such laws.

(B) Safeguards. The Secretary of Agriculture, and the head of any other agency or instrumentality referred to in subparagraph (A), shall restrict, to the satisfaction of the Secretary of the Treasury, access to employer identification numbers obtained pursuant to this subsection only to officers and employees of the United States whose duties or responsibilities require access for the purposes described in subparagraph (A). The Secretary of Agriculture, and the head of any agency or instrumentality with which information is shared pursuant to subparagraph (A), shall provide such other safeguards as the Secretary of the Treasury determines to be necessary or appropriate to protect the confidentiality of the employer identification numbers.

(3) Confidentiality and nondisclosure rules. Employer identification numbers that are obtained or maintained pursuant to this subsection by the Secretary of Agriculture or the head of the instrumentality with which the information is shared pursuant to paragraph (2) shall be confidential, and no officer or employee of the United States who has or had access to the social security account numbers shall disclose any such employer identification number obtained thereby in any manner. For purposes of this paragraph, the term "officer or employee" includes a former officer or employee.

(4) Sanctions. Paragraphs (1), (2), and (3) of section 7213(a) shall apply with respect to the unauthorized willful disclosure to any person of employer identification numbers maintained pursuant to this subsection by the Secretary of Agriculture or any agency or instrumentality with which information is shared pursuant to paragraph (2) in the same manner and to the same extent as such paragraphs apply with respect to unauthorized disclosures of return and return information described in such paragraphs. Paragraph (4) of section 7213(a) shall apply with respect to the willful offer of any item of material value in exchange for any such employer identification number in the same manner and to the same extent as such paragraph applies with respect to offers (in exchange for any return or return information) described in such paragraph.

(g) Access to employer identification numbers by Federal Crop Insurance Corporation for purposes of the Federal Crop Insurance Act.

(1) In general. In the administration of section 506 of the Federal Crop Insurance Act, the Federal Crop Insurance Corporation may require each policyholder and each reinsured company to furnish to the insurer or to the Corporation the employer identification number of such policyholder, subject to the requirements of this paragraph. No officer or employee of the Federal Crop Insurance Corporation, or authorized person shall have access to any such number for any purpose other than the establishment of a system of records necessary to the effective administration of such Act. The Manager of the Corporation may require each policyholder to provide to the Manager or authorized person, at such times and in such manner as prescribed by the Manager, the employer identification number of each entity that holds or acquires a substantial beneficial interest in the policyholder. For purposes of this subclause, the term "substantial beneficial interest" means not less than 5 percent of all beneficial interest in the policyholder. The Secretary of Agriculture shall restrict, to the satisfaction of the Secretary of the Treasury, access to employer identification numbers obtained pursuant to this paragraph only to officers and employees of the United States or authorized persons whose duties or responsibilities require access for the administration of the Federal Crop Insurance Act.

(2) **Confidentiality and nondisclosure rules.** Employer identification numbers maintained by the Secretary of Agriculture or the Federal Crop Insurance Corporation pursuant to this subsection shall be confidential, and except as authorized by this subsection, no officer or employee of the United States or authorized person who has or had access to such employer identification numbers shall disclose any such employer identification number obtained thereby in any manner. For purposes of this paragraph, the term "officer or employee" includes a former officer or employee. For purposes of this subsection, the term "authorized person" means an officer or employee of an insurer whom the Manager of the Corporation designates by rule, subject to appropriate safeguards including a prohibition against the release of such social security account numbers (other than to the Corporations) by such person.

(3) **Sanctions.** Paragraphs (1), (2), and (3) of section 7213(a) shall apply with respect to the unauthorized willful disclosure to any person of employer identification numbers maintained by the Secretary of Agriculture or the Federal Crop Insurance Corporation pursuant to this subsection in the same manner and to the same extent as such paragraphs apply with respect to unauthorized disclosures of return and return information described in such paragraphs. Paragraph (4) of section 7213(a) shall apply with respect to the willful offer of any item of material value in exchange for any such employer identification number in the same manner and to the same extent as such paragraph applies with respect to offers (in exchange for any return or return information) described in such paragraph.

(h) **Identifying information required with respect to certain seller-provided financing.**

(1) **Payor.** If any taxpayer claims a deduction under section 163 for qualified residence interest on any seller-provided financing, such taxpayer shall include on the return claiming such deduction the name, address, and TIN of the person to whom such interest is paid or accrued.

(2) **Recipient.** If any person receives or accrues interest referred to in paragraph (1), such person shall include on the return for the taxable year in which such interest is so received or accrued the name, address, and TIN of the person liable for such interest.

(3) **Furnishing of information between payor and recipient.** If any person is required to include the TIN of another person on a return under paragraph (1) or (2), such other person shall furnish his TIN to such person.

(4) **Seller-provided financing.** For purposes of this subsection, the term "seller-provided financing" means any indebtedness incurred in acquiring any residence if the person to whom such indebtedness is owed is the person from which such residence was acquired.

In 2008, P.L. 110-246, Sec. 4, Repeals the duplicative enactment and provides effective date provisions of the Act entitled "An Act to provide for the continuation of agricultural programs through fiscal year 2012, and for other purposes" Sec. 4, P.L. 110-246 reads as follows:

"Sec. 4. Repeal of duplicative enactment.

"(a) In General- The Act entitled 'An Act to provide for the continuation of agricultural programs through fiscal year 2012, and for other purposes' (H.R. 2419 of the 110th Congress), and the amendments made by that Act, are repealed, effective on the date of enactment of that Act.

"(b) Effective Date- Except as otherwise provided in this Act, this Act and the amendments made by this Act shall take effect on the earlier of--

"(1) the date of enactment of this Act; or

"(2) the date of the enactment of the Act entitled 'An Act to provide for the continuation of agricultural programs through fiscal year 2012, and for other purposes' (H.R. 2419 of the 110th Congress)."

—P.L. 110-246, Sec. 4002(b)(1)(B), substituted "Food and Nutrition Act of 2008" for "Food Stamp Act of 1977" each place it appears in Sec. 6109, effective 5/22/2008. [Ed. Note: May 22, 2008 was the date of enactment for H.R. 2419 (PL 110-234), which was repealed by (2008 Farm Act § 4(a)) (PL 110-246, 6/18/2008), in connection with the reenactment of the farm bill to correct a technical deficiency in its original passage.]

In 2007, P.L. 110-28, Sec. 8246(a)(2)(D)(i), substituted "a tax return preparer" for "an income tax return preparer" in para. (a)(4). . . . Sec. 8246(a)(2)(D)(ii), substituted "tax retrun preparer" for "income return preparer" in the heading of para. (a)(4), effective for returns prepared after 5/25/2007.

In 1998, P.L. 105-206, Sec. 3710(a), substituted "For purposes of paragraphs (1), (2), and (3)" for "For purposes of this subsection" in subsec. (a), effective 7/22/98.

In 1996, P.L. 104-188, Sec. 1615(a)(2)(A), deleted subsec. (e), effective for returns the due date for which (without regard to extensions) is on or after the 30th day after 8/20/96. For special rules, see Sec. 1615(d)(2), of this Act, which reads as follows:

"(2) Special rule for 1995 and 1996. In the case of returns for taxable years beginning in 1995 or 1996, a taxpayer shall not be required by the amendments made by this section to provide a taxpayer identification number for a child who is born after October 31, 1995, in the case of a taxable year beginning in 1995 or November 30, 1996, in the case of a taxable year beginning in 1996."

Prior to amendment, subsec. (e) read as follows:

"(e) Furnishing number for dependents. Any taxpayer who claims an exemption under section 151 for any dependent on a return for any taxable year shall include on such return the identifying number (for purposes of this title) of such dependent."

—P.L. 104-188, Sec. 1704(t)(42), redesignated subsec. (f) as subsec. (g) [as added by Sec. 2201(d) of P.L. 101-624, see below], effective 8/20/96.

In 1994, P.L. 103-465, Sec. 742(b), amended subsec. (e), effective for returns for tax. yrs. begin. after 12/31/94, except as provided in Sec. 742(c)(2) of this Act, which reads as follows:

"(2) Exception. The amendments made by this section shall not apply to—

"(A) returns for taxable years beginning in 1995 with respect to individuals who are born after October 31, 1995, and

"(B) returns for taxable years beginning in 1996 with respect to individuals who are born after November 30, 1996."

Prior to amendment, subsec. (e) read as follows:

"(e) Furnishing number for certain dependents.

"If—

"(1) any taxpayer claims an exemption under section 151 for any dependent on a return for any taxable year, and

"(2) such dependent has attained the age of 1 year before the close of such taxable year,

such taxpayer shall include on such return the identifying number (for purposes of this title) of such dependent."

—P.L. 103-296, Sec. 316(b)(1), amended para. (f)(2) . . . Sec. 316(b)(2), substituted "pursuant to this subsection by the Secretary of Agriculture or the head of the instrumentality with which the information is shared pursuant to paragraph (2)" for "by the Secretary of Agriculture pursuant to this subsection" in para. (f)(3) . . . Sec. 316(b)(3), substituted "pursuant to this subsection by the Secretary of Agriculture or any agency or instrumentality with which information is shared pursuant to paragraph (2)" for "by the Secretary of Agriculture pursuant to this subsection" in para. (f)(4), effective 8/15/94.

Prior to amendment, para. (f)(2) read as follows:

"(2) Safeguards. The Secretary of Agriculture shall restrict, to the satisfaction of the Secretary of the Treasury, access to employer identification numbers obtained pursuant to paragraph (1) only to officers and employees of the United States whose duties or responsibilities require access for the administration or enforcement of the Food Stamp Act of 1977. The Secretary of Agriculture shall provide such other safeguards as the Secretary of the Treasury determines to be necessary or appropriate to protect the confidentiality of the employer identification numbers."

In 1992, P.L. 102-486, Sec. 1933(a), added subsec. (h), effective for tax. yrs. begin. after 12/31/91.

In 1990, P.L. 101-624, Sec. 1735(c), added subsec. (f), effective and implemented the 1st day of the month beginning 120 days after the publication of implementing regulations. Such regulations shall be promulgated not later than 10/1/91.

—P.L. 101-624, Sec. 2201(d), added subsec. (f) [sic (g)], effective 11/28/90.

—P.L. 101-508, Sec. 11112(a), substituted "1 year" for "2 years" in para. (e)(2), effective for returns for tax. yrs. begin. after 12/31/90.

In 1988, P.L. 100-485, Sec. 703(c)(3), substituted "or whose identifying number is required to be shown on a return of another person shall furnish" for "shall furnish" in para. (a)(2), effective for tax. yrs. begin. after 12/31/88.

—P.L. 100-485, Sec. 704(a), substituted "age of 2" for "age of 5" in para. (e)(2), effective for returns for the due date for which (determined without regard to extensions) is after 12/31/89.

In 1986, P.L. 99-514, Sec. 1524(a), added subsec. (e), effective for returns the due date for which (determined without regard to extensions) is after 12/31/87.

Information and returns — Code Sec. 6110(f)(1)

In 1976, P.L. 94-455, Sec. 1203(d), added para. (a)(4) and the last sentence in subsec. (a), effective for documents prepared after 12/31/76.
—P.L. 94-455, Sec. 1211(c), added subsec. (d), effective 10/4/76.
—P.L. 94-455, Sec. 1906(b)(13)(A), substituted "Secretary" for "Secretary or his delegate" each place it appeared in Code Sec. 6109, effective 2/1/77.
In 1961, P.L. 87-397, Sec. a, added Code Sec. 6109 and redesignated former Code Sec. 6109 as 6110. Code Sec. 6109(a)(1) shall apply only in respect of returns, statements, and other documents relating to periods begin. after 12/31/61. Code Sec. 6109(a)(2) and (3) shall apply only in respect of returns, statements, or other documents relating to periods begin. after 12/31/62.

Sec. 6110. Public inspection of written determinations.

(a) General rule.

Except as otherwise provided in this section, the text of any written determination and any background file document relating to such written determination shall be open to public inspection at such place as the Secretary may by regulations prescribe.

(b) Definitions.

For purposes of this section—

(1) Written determination.

(A) In general. The term "written determination" means a ruling, determination letter, technical advice memorandum, or Chief Counsel advice.

(B) Exceptions. Such term shall not include any matter referred to in subparagraph (C) or (D) of section 6103(b)(2).

(2) Background file document. The term "background file document" with respect to a written determination includes the request for that written determination, any written material submitted in support of the request, and any communication (written or otherwise) between the Internal Revenue Service and persons outside the Internal Revenue Service in connection with such written determination (other than any communication between the Department of Justice and the Internal Revenue Service relating to a pending civil or criminal case or investigation) received before issuance of the written determination.

(3) Reference and general written determinations.

(A) Reference written determination. The term "reference written determination" means any written determination which has been determined by the Secretary to have significant reference value.

(B) General written determination. The term "general written determination" means any written determination other than a reference written determination.

(c) Exemptions from disclosure.

Before making any written determination or background file document open or available to public inspection under subsection (a), the Secretary shall delete—

(1) the names, addresses, and other identifying details of the person to whom the written determination pertains and of any other person, other than a person with respect to whom a notation is made under subsection (d)(1), identified in the written determination or any background file document;

(2) information specifically authorized under criteria established by an Executive order to be kept secret in the interest of national defense or foreign policy, and which is in fact properly classified pursuant to such Executive order;

(3) information specifically exempted from disclosure by any statute (other than this title) which is applicable to the Internal Revenue Service;

(4) trade secrets and commercial or financial information obtained from a person and privileged or confidential;

(5) information the disclosure of which would constitute a clearly unwarranted invasion of personal privacy;

(6) information contained in or related to examination, operating, or condition reports prepared by, or on behalf of, or for use of an agency responsible for the regulation or supervision of financial institutions; and

(7) geological and geophysical information and data, including maps, concerning wells.

The Secretary shall determine the appropriate extent of such deletions and, except in the case of intentional or willful disregard of this subsection, shall not be required to make such deletions (nor be liable for failure to make deletions) unless the Secretary has agreed to such deletions or has been ordered by a court (in a proceeding under subsection (f)(3)) to make such deletions.

(d) Procedures with regard to third party contacts.

(1) Notations. If, before the issuance of a written determination, the Internal Revenue Service receives any communication (written or otherwise) concerning such written determination, any request for such determination, or any other matter involving such written determination from a person other than an employee of the Internal Revenue Service or the person to whom such written determination pertains (or his authorized representative with regard to such written determination), the Internal Revenue Service shall indicate, on the written determination open to public inspection, the category of the person making such communication and the date of such communication.

(2) Exception. Paragraph (1) shall not apply to any communication made by the Chief of Staff of the Joint Committee on Taxation.

(3) Disclosure of identity. In the case of any written determination to which paragraph (1) applies, any person may file a petition in the United States Tax Court or file a complaint in the United States District Court for the District of Columbia for an order requiring that the identity of any person to whom the written determination pertains be disclosed. The court shall order disclosure of such identity if there is evidence in the record from which one could reasonably conclude that an impropriety occurred or undue influence was exercised with respect to such written determination by or on behalf of such person. The court may also direct the Secretary to disclose any portion of any other deletions made in accordance with subsection (c) where such disclosure is in the public interest. If a proceeding is commenced under this paragraph, the person whose identity is subject to being disclosed and the person about whom a notation is made under paragraph (1) shall be notified of the proceeding in accordance with the procedures described in subsection (f)(4)(B) and shall have the right to intervene in the proceeding (anonymously, if appropriate).

(4) Period in which to bring action. No proceeding shall be commenced under paragraph (3) unless a petition is filed before the expiration of 36 months after the first day that the written determination is open to public inspection.

(e) Background file documents.

Whenever the Secretary makes a written determination open to public inspection under this section, he shall also make available to any person, but only upon the written request of that person, any background file document relating to the written determination.

(f) Resolution of disputes relating to disclosure.

(1) Notice of intention to disclose. Except as otherwise provided by subsection (i), the Secretary shall upon issuance of any written determination, or upon receipt of a request for a background file document, mail a notice of intention to disclose such determination or document to any person to whom the written determination pertains (or a successor in interest, executor, or other person authorized by law to act for or on behalf of such person).

(2) Administrative remedies. The Secretary shall prescribe regulations establishing administrative remedies with respect to—

(A) requests for additional disclosure of any written determination of any background file document, and

(B) requests to restrain disclosure.

(3) Action to restrain disclosure.

(A) Creation of remedy. Any person—

(i) to whom a written determination pertains (or a successor in interest, executor, or other person authorized by law to act for or on behalf of such person), or who has a direct interest in maintaining the confidentiality of any such written determination or background file document (or portion thereof),

(ii) who disagrees with any failure to make a deletion with respect to that portion of any written determination or any background file document which is to be open or available to public inspection, and

(iii) who has exhausted his administrative remedies as prescribed pursuant to paragraph (2),

may, within 60 days after the mailing by the Secretary of a notice of intention to disclose any written determination or background file document under paragraph (1), together with the proposed deletions, file a petition in the United States Tax Court (anonymously, if appropriate) for a determination with respect to that portion of such written determination or background file document which is to be open to public inspection.

(B) Notice to certain persons. The Secretary shall notify any person to whom a written determination pertains (unless such person is the petitioner) of the filing of a petition under this paragraph with respect to such written determination or related background file document, and any such person may intervene (anonymously, if appropriate) in any proceeding conducted pursuant to this paragraph. The Secretary shall send such notice by registered or certified mail to the last known address of such person within 15 days after such petition is served on the Secretary. No person who has received such a notice may thereafter file any petition under this paragraph with respect to such written determination or background file document with respect to which such notice was received.

(4) Action to obtain additional disclosure.

(A) Creation of remedy. Any person who has exhausted the administrative remedies prescribed pursuant to paragraph (2) with respect to a request for disclosure may file a petition in the United States Tax Court or a complaint in the United States District Court for the District of Columbia for an order requiring that any written determination or background file document (or portion thereof) be made open or available to public inspection. Except where inconsistent with subparagraph (B), the provisions of subparagraphs (C), (D), (E), (F), and (G) of section 552(a)(4) of title 5, United States Code, shall apply to any proceeding under this paragraph. The Court shall examine the matter de novo and without regard to a decision of a court under paragraph (3) with respect to such written determination or background file document, and may examine the entire text of such written determination or background file document in order to determine whether such written determination or background file document or any part thereof shall be open or available to public inspection under this section. The burden of proof with respect to the issue of disclosure of any information shall be on the Secretary and any other person seeking to restrain disclosure.

(B) Intervention. If a proceeding is commenced under this paragraph with respect to any written determination or background file document, the Secretary shall, within 15 days after notice of the petition filed under subparagraph (A) is served on him, send notice of the commencement of such proceeding to all persons who are identified by name and address in such written determination or background file document. The Secretary shall send such notice by registered or certified mail to the last known address of such person. Any person to whom such determination or background file document pertains may intervene in the proceeding (anonymously, if appropriate). If such notice is sent, the Secretary shall not be required to defend the action and shall not be liable for public disclosure of the written determination or background file document (or any portion thereof) in accordance with the final decision of the court.

(5) Expedition of determination. The Tax Court shall make a decision with respect to any petition described in paragraph (3) at the earliest practicable date.

(6) Publicity of Tax Court proceedings. Notwithstanding sections 7458 and 7461, the Tax Court may, in order to preserve the anonymity, privacy, or confidentiality of any person under this section, provide by rules adopted under section 7453 that portions of hearings, testimony, evidence, and reports in connection with proceedings under this section may be closed to the public or to inspection by the public.

(g) Time for disclosure.

(1) In general. Except as otherwise provided in this section, the text of any written determination or any background file document (as modified under subsection (c)) shall be open or available to public inspection—

(A) no earlier than 75 days, and no later than 90 days, after the notice provided in subsection (f)(1) is mailed, or, if later,

(B) within 30 days after the date on which a court decision under subsection (f)(3) becomes final.

(2) Postponement by order of court. The court may extend the period referred to in paragraph (1)(B) for such time as the court finds necessary to allow the Secretary to comply with its decision.

(3) Postponement of disclosure for up to 90 days. At the written request of the person by whom or on whose behalf the request for the written determination was made, the period referred to in paragraph (1)(A) shall be extended (for not to exceed an additional 90 days) until the day which is 15 days after the date of the Secretary's determination that the transaction set forth in the written determination has been completed.

(4) Additional 180 days. If—

(A) the transaction set forth in the written determination is not completed during the period set forth in paragraph (3), and

(B) the person by whom or on whose behalf the request for the written determination was made establishes to the satisfaction of the Secretary that good cause exists for additional delay in opening the written determination to public inspection,

the period referred to in paragraph (3) shall be further extended (for not to exceed an additional 180 days) until the day which is 15 days after the date of the Secretary's determination that the transaction set forth in the written determination has been completed.

Information and returns　　　　　　　　　　　　　　**Code Sec. 6110(i)(4)(A)(ii)**

(5) Special rules for certain written determinations, etc. Notwithstanding the provisions of paragraph (1), the Secretary shall not be required to make available to the public—

(A) any technical advice memorandum, any Chief Counsel advice, and any related background file document involving any matter which is the subject of a civil fraud or criminal investigation or jeopardy or termination assessment until after any action relating to such investigation or assessment is completed, or

(B) any general written determination and any related background file document that relates solely to approval of the Secretary of any adoption or change of—

(i) the funding method or plan year of a plan under section 412,

(ii) a taxpayer's annual accounting period under section 442,

(iii) a taxpayer's method of accounting under section 446(e), or

(iv) a partnership's or partner's taxable year under section 706,

but the Secretary shall make any such written determination and related background file document available upon the written request of any person after the date on which (except for this subparagraph) such determination would be open to public inspection.

(h) Disclosure of prior written determinations and related background file documents.

(1) In general. Except as otherwise provided in this subsection, a written determination issued pursuant to a request made before November 1, 1976, and any background file document relating to such written determination shall be open or available to public inspection in accordance with this section.

(2) Time for disclosure. In the case of any written determination or background file document which is to be made open or available to public inspection under paragraph (1)—

(A) subsection (g) shall not apply, but

(B) such written determination or background file document shall be made open or available to public inspection at the earliest practicable date after funds for that purpose have been appropriated and made available to the Internal Revenue Service.

(3) Order of release. Any written determination or background file document described in paragraph (1) shall be open or available to public inspection in the following order starting with the most recent written determination in each category:

(A) reference written determinations issued under this title;

(B) general written determinations issued after July 4, 1967; and

(C) reference written determinations issued under the Internal Revenue Code of 1939 or corresponding provisions of prior law.

General written determinations not described in subparagraph (B) shall be open to public inspection on written request, but not until after the written determinations referred to in subparagraphs (A), (B), and (C) are open to public inspection.

(4) Notice that prior written determinations are open to public inspection. Notwithstanding the provisions of subsections (f)(1) and (f)(3)(A), not less than 90 days before making any portion of a written determination described in this subsection open to public inspection, the Secretary shall issue public notice in the Federal Register

that such written determination is to be made open to public inspection. The person who received a written determination may, within 75 days after the date of publication of notice under this paragraph, file a petition in the United States Tax Court (anonymously, if appropriate) for a determination with respect to that portion of such written determination which is to be made open to public inspection. The provisions of subsections (f)(3)(B), (5), and (6) shall apply if such a petition is filed. If no petition is filed, the text of any written determination shall be open to public inspection no earlier than 90 days, and no later than 120 days, after notice is published in the Federal Register.

(5) Exclusion. Subsection (d) shall not apply to any written determination described in paragraph (1).

(i) Special rules for disclosure of Chief Counsel advice.

(1) Chief Counsel Advice defined.

(A) In general. For purposes of this section, the term "Chief Counsel advice" means written advice or instruction, under whatever name or designation, prepared by any national office component of the Office of Chief Counsel which—

(i) is issued to field or service center employees of the Service or regional or district employees of the Office of Chief Counsel; and

(ii) conveys—

(I) any legal interpretation of a revenue provision;

(II) any Internal Revenue Service or Office of Chief Counsel position or policy concerning a revenue provision; or

(III) any legal interpretation of State law, foreign law, or other Federal law relating to the assessment or collection of any liability under a revenue provision.

(B) Revenue provision defined. For purposes of subparagraph (A), the term "revenue provision" means any existing or former internal revenue law, regulation, revenue ruling, revenue procedure, other published or unpublished guidance, or tax treaty, either in general or as applied to specific taxpayers or groups of specific taxpayers.

(2) Additional documents treated as Chief Counsel advice. The Secretary may by regulation provide that this section shall apply to any advice or instruction prepared and issued by the Office of Chief Counsel which is not described in paragraph (1).

(3) Deletions for Chief Counsel advice. In the case of Chief Counsel advice and related background file documents open to public inspection pursuant to this section—

(A) paragraphs (2) through (7) of subsection (c) shall not apply, but

(B) the Secretary may make deletions of material in accordance with subsections (b) and (c) of section 552 of title 5, United States Code, except that in applying subsection (b)(3) of such section, no statutory provision of this title shall be taken into account.

(4) Notice of intention to disclose.

(A) No taxpayer specific Chief Counsel advice. In the case of Chief Counsel advice which is written without reference to a specific taxpayer or group of specific taxpayers—

(i) subsection (f)(1) shall not apply; and

(ii) the Secretary shall, within 60 days after the issuance of the Chief Counsel advice, complete any deletions described in subsection (c)(1) or paragraph (3) and make the Chief Counsel advice, as so edited, open for public inspection.

3,603

Code Sec. 6110(i)(4)(B) | **Information and returns**

(B) Taxpayer-specific Chief Counsel advice. In the case of Chief Counsel advice which is written with respect to a specific taxpayer or group of specific taxpayers, the Secretary shall, within 60 days after the issuance of the Chief Counsel advice, mail the notice required by subsection (f)(1) to each such taxpayer. The notice shall include a copy of the Chief Counsel advice on which is indicated the information that the Secretary proposes to delete pursuant to subsection (c)(1). The Secretary may also delete from the copy of the text of the Chief Counsel advice any of the information described in paragraph (3), and shall delete the names, addresses, and other identifying details of taxpayers other than the person to whom the advice pertains, except that the Secretary shall not delete from the copy of the Chief Counsel advice that is furnished to the taxpayer any information of which that taxpayer was the source.

(j) Civil remedies.

(1) Civil action. Whenever the Secretary—

(A) fails to make deletions required in accordance with subsection (c), or

(B) fails to follow the procedures in subsection (g) or (i)(4)(B), the recipient of the written determination or any person identified in the written determination shall have as an exclusive civil remedy an action against the Secretary in the United States Claims Court [United States Court of Federal Claims, see § 902(b), P.L. 102-572], which shall have jurisdiction to hear any action under this paragraph.

(2) Damages. In any suit brought under the provisions of paragraph (1)(A) in which the Court determines that an employee of the Internal Revenue Service intentionally or willfully failed to delete in accordance with subsection (c), or in any suit brought under subparagraph (1)(B) in which the Court determines that an employee intentionally or willfully failed to act in accordance withsubsection (g) or (i)(4)(B), the United States shall be liable to the person in an amount equal to the sum of—

(A) actual damages sustained by the person but in no case shall a person be entitled to receive less than the sum of $1,000, and

(B) the costs of the action together with reasonable attorney's fees as determined by the Court.

(k) Special provisions.

(1) Fees. The Secretary is authorized to assess actual costs—

(A) for duplication of any written determination or background file document made open or available to the public under this section, and

(B) incurred in searching for and making deletions required under subsection (c)(1) or (i)(3) from any written determination or background file document which is available to public inspection only upon written request. The Secretary shall furnish any written determination or background file document without charge or at a reduced charge if he determines that waiver or reduction of the fee is in the public interest because furnishing such determination or background file document can be considered as primarily benefiting the general public.

(2) Records disposal procedures. Nothing in this section shall prevent the Secretary from disposing of any general written determination or background file document described in subsection (b) in accordance with established records disposition procedures, but such disposal shall, except as provided in the following sentence, occur not earlier than 3 years after such written determination is first made open to public inspection. In the case of any general

written determination described in subsection (h), the Secretary may dispose of such determination and any related background file document in accordance with such procedures but such disposal shall not occur earlier than 3 years after such written determination is first made open to public inspection if funds are appropriated for such purpose before January 20, 1979, or not earlier than January 20, 1979, if funds are not appropriated before such date. The Secretary shall not dispose of any reference written determinations and related background file documents.

(3) Precedential status. Unless the Secretary otherwise establishes by regulations, a written determination may not be used or cited as precedent. The preceding sentence shall not apply to change the precedential status (if any) of written determinations with regard to taxes imposed by subtitle D of this title.

(l) Section not to apply.

This section shall not apply to—

(1) any matter to which section 6104 or 6105 applies, or

(2) any—

(A) written determination issued pursuant to a request made before November 1, 1976, with respect to the exempt status under section 501(a) of an organization described in section 501(c) or (d), the status of an organization as a private foundation under section 509(a), or the status of an organization as an operating foundation under section 4942(j)(3),

(B) written determination described in subsection (g)(5)(B) issued pursuant to a request made before November 1, 1976,

(C) determination letter not otherwise described in subparagraph (A), (B), or (E) issued pursuant to a request made before November 1, 1976,

(D) background file document relating to any general written determination issued before July 5, 1967, or

(E) letter or other document described in section 6104(a)(1)(B)(iv) issued before September 2, 1974.

(m) Exclusive remedy.

Except as otherwise provided in this title, or with respect to a discovery order made in connection with a judicial proceeding, the Secretary shall not be required by any Court to make any written determination or background file document open or available to public inspection, or to refrain from disclosure of any such documents.

In 2007, P.L. 110-172, Sec. 10(a), added "and related background file documents" after "Chief Counsel advice" in the matter preceding subpara. (i)(3)(A), effective for any Chief Counsel advice issued more than 90 days after 7/22/98. For special rules, see Sec. 3509(d)(2)-(4) of the Internal Revenue Service Restructuring and Reform Act of 1998, which reads as follows:

"(2) Transition rules. The amendments made by this section shall apply to any Chief Counsel advice issued after December 31, 1985, and before the 91st day after the date of the enactment of this Act by the offices of the associate chief counsel for domestic, employee benefits and exempt organizations, and international, except that any such Chief Counsel advice shall be treated as made available on a timely basis if such advice is made available for public inspection not later than the following dates:

"(A) One year after the date of the enactment of this Act, in the case of all litigation guideline memoranda, service center advice, tax litigation bulletins, criminal tax bulletins, and general litigation bulletins.

"(B) Eighteen months after such date of enactment, in the case of field service advice and technical assistance to the field issued on or after January 1, 1994.

"(C) Three years after such date of enactment, in the case of field service advice and technical assistance to the field issued on or after January 1, 1992, and before January 1, 1994.

"(D) Six years after such date of enactment, in the case of any other Chief Counsel advice issued after December 31, 1985.

"(3) Documents treated as Chief Counsel advice. If the Secretary of the Treasury by regulation provides pursuant to section 6110(i)(2) of the Internal Revenue Code of 1986, as added by this section, that any additional advice or instruction issued by the Office of Chief Counsel shall be treated as Chief Counsel advice, such additional advice or instruction shall be made available for public inspection pursuant to section 6110 of such Code, as amended by this section, only in accordance with the effective date set forth in such regulation.

Information and returns Code Sec. 6111(a)(3)

"(4) Chief Counsel advice to be available electronically. The Internal Revenue Service shall make any Chief Counsel advice issued more than 90 days after the date of the enactment of this Act and made available for public inspection pursuant to section 6110 of such Code, as amended by this section, also available by computer telecommunications within 1 year after issuance."

In 2006, P.L. 109-280, Sec. 811, of this Act [relating to Sec. 901 of P.L. 107-16, see below], provides:

"SEC. 811. PENSIONS AND INDIVIDUAL RETIREMENT ARRANGEMENT PROVISIONS OF ECONOMIC GROWTH AND TAX RELIEF RECONCILIATION ACT OF 2001 MADE PERMANENT.

"Title IX of the Economic Growth and Tax Relief Reconciliation Act of 2001 shall not apply to the provisions of, and amendments made by, subtitles A through F of title VI of such Act (relating to pension and individual retirement arrangement provisions)."

In 2003, P.L. 108-89, Sec. 202(b)(2), repealed Sec. 10511 of P.L. 100-203 [see below], effective for requests made after 10/1/2003.

—P.L. 108-89, Sec. 202(b)(3), repealed Sec. 620 of P.L. 107-16 [see below], effective for requests made after 10/1/2003.

In 2001, P.L. 107-16, Sec. 620, of this Act [prior to repeal by Sec. 202(b)(3) of P.L. 108-89, see above], reads as follows:

"SEC. 620. ELIMINATION OF USER FEE FOR REQUESTS TO IRS REGARDING PENSION PLANS.

"(a) *Elimination of certain user fees.* The Secretary of the Treasury or the Secretary's delegate shall not require payment of user fees under the program established under section 10511 of the Revenue Act of 1987 for requests to the Internal Revenue Service for determination letters with respect to the qualified status of a pension benefit plan maintained solely by one or more eligible employers or any trust which is part of the plan. The preceding sentence shall not apply to any request—

"(1) made after the later of—

"(A) the fifth plan year the pension benefit plan is in existence; or

"(B) the end of any remedial amendment period with respect to the plan beginning within the first 5 plan years; or

"(2) made by the sponsor of any prototype or similar plan which the sponsor intends to market to participating employers.

"(b) *Pension benefit plan.* For purposes of this section, the term 'pension benefit plan' means a pension, profit-sharing, stock bonus, annuity, or employee stock ownership plan.

"(c) *Eligible employer.* For purposes of this section, the term 'eligible employer' means an eligible employer (as defined in section 408(p)(2)(C)(i)(I) of the Internal Revenue Code of 1986) which has at least one employee who is not a highly compensated employee (as defined in section 414(q)) and is participating in the plan. The determination of whether an employer is an eligible employer under this section shall be made as of the date of the request described in subsection (a).

"(d) *Determination of average fees charged.* For purposes of any determination of average fees charged, any request to which subsection (a) applies shall not be taken into account.

"(e) *Effective date.* The provisions of this section shall apply with respect to requests made after December 31, 2001."

In 2000, P.L. 106-554, Sec. 1(a)(7), [which enacted into law Sec. 304(c)(1) of P.L. 106-554] amended para. (b)(1) . . . Sec. 1(a)(7), [which enacted into law Sec. 304(c)(2) of P.L. 106-554] added "or 6105" after "section 6104" in para. (l)(1), effective 12/21/2000.

Prior to amendment, para. (b)(1) read as follows:

"(1) Written determination. The term 'written determination' means a ruling, determination letter, technical advice memorandum, or Chief Counsel advice. Such term shall not include any advance pricing agreement entered into by a taxpayer and the Secretary and any background information related to such agreement or any application for an advance pricing agreement."

—P.L. 106-554, Sec. 1(a)(7), [which enacted into law Sec. 313(e) of P.L. 106-554] added ", any Chief Counsel advice," after "technical advice memorandum" in subpara. (g)(5)(A), effective for any Chief Counsel advice issued more than 90 days after 7/22/98. For special rules, see Sec. 3509(d)(2)-(4) of P.L. 105-206, reproduced below.

In 1999, P.L. 106-170, Sec. 521(a)(2), added a sentence at the end of para. (b)(1), effective 12/17/99. Sec. 521(c) of this Act, provides:

"(c) Regulations. The Secretary of the Treasury or the Secretary's delegate shall prescribe such regulations as may be necessary or appropriate to carry out the purposes of section 6103(b)(2)(C), and the last sentence of section 6110(b)(1), of the Internal Revenue Code of 1986, as added by this section."

In 1998, P.L. 105-206, Sec. 3509(a), substituted "technical advice memorandum, or Chief Counsel advice" for "or technical advice memorandum" in para. (b)(1) . . . Sec. 3509(b), redesignated subsecs. (i), (j), (k) and (l) as subsecs. (j), (k), (l) and (m) and added new subsec. (i) . . . Sec. 3509(c)(1), substituted "Except as otherwise provided by subsection (i), the Secretary" for "The Secretary" in para. (f)(1) . . . Sec. 3509(c)(2), substituted "subsection (g) or (i)(4)(B)" for "subsection (g)" each place it appeared in subpara. (j)(1)(B) and para. (j)(2) . . . Sec. 3509(c)(3), substituted "subsection (c)(1) or (i)(3)" for "subsection (c)" in subpara. (k)(1)(B) [as redesignated by Sec. 3509(b) of this Act], effective for any Chief Counsel advice issued more than 90 days after 7/22/98. For special rules, see Sec. 3509(d)(2)-(4) of this Act, which reads as follows:

"(2) Transition rules. The amendments made by this section shall apply to any Chief Counsel advice issued after December 31, 1985, and before the 91st day after the date of the enactment of this Act by the offices of the associate chief counsel for domestic, employee benefits and exempt organizations, and international, except that any such Chief Counsel advice shall be treated as made available on a timely basis if such advice is made available for public inspection not later than the following dates:

"(A) One year after the date of the enactment of this Act, in the case of all litigation guideline memoranda, service center advice, tax litigation bulletins, criminal tax bulletins, and general litigation bulletins.

"(B) Eighteen months after such date of enactment, in the case of field service advice and technical assistance to the field issued on or after January 1, 1994.

"(C) Three years after such date of enactment, in the case of field service advice and technical assistance to the field issued on or after January 1, 1992, and before January 1, 1994.

"(D) Six years after such date of enactment, in the case of any other Chief Counsel advice issued after December 31, 1985.

"(3) Documents treated as Chief Counsel advice. If the Secretary of the Treasury by regulation provides pursuant to section 6110(i)(2) of the Internal Revenue Code of 1986, as added by this section, that any additional advice or instruction issued by the Office of Chief Counsel shall be treated as Chief Counsel advice, such additional advice or instruction shall be made available for public inspection pursuant to section 6110 of such Code, as amended by this section, only in accordance with the effective date set forth in such regulation.

"(4) Chief Counsel advice to be available electronically. The Internal Revenue Service shall make any Chief Counsel advice issued more than 90 days after the date of the enactment of this Act and made available for public inspection pursuant to section 6110 of such Code, as amended by this section, also available by computer telecommunications within 1 year after issuance."

In 1992, P.L. 102-572, Sec. 902(b), effective 10/29/92, relating to Court designation provides as follows:

"(b) Other provisions of law. Reference in any other Federal law or documents to—

"(1) the 'United States Claims Court' shall be deemed to refer to the 'United States Court of Federal Claims'; and

"(2) the 'Claims Court' shall be deemed to refer to the 'Court of Federal Claims'"

In 1987, P.L. 100-203, Sec. 10511, repealed by Sec. 202(b)(2) of P.L. 108-89 [see above], provides rules for fees for requests for ruling, determination, and similar letters. Sec. 10511 of P.L. 100-203 [repealed by Sec. 202(b)(2) of P.L. 108-89] is reproduced in note following Code Sec. 7805.

In 1984, P.L. 98-620, Sec. 103(28)(B), deleted "and the Court of Appeals shall expedite any review of such decision in every way possible" after "practical date" in para. (f)(5), effective 11/8/84 except for cases pending on 11/8/84.

In 1982, P.L. 97-164, Sec. 160(a)(9), substituted "United States Claims Court" for "Court of Claims" in para. (i)(1), effective 10/1/82.

—P.L. 97-164, Sec. 403, of this Act, reads as follows:

"Sec. 403. (a) Any case pending before the Court of Claims on the effective date of this Act in which a report on the merits has been filed by a commissioner, or in which there is pending a request for review, and upon which the court has not acted, shall be transferred to the United States Court of Appeals for the Federal Circuit.

"(b) Any matter pending before the United States Court of Customs and Patent Appeals on the effective date of this Act shall be transferred to the United States Court of Appeals for the Federal Circuit.

"(c) Any petition for rehearing, reconsideration, alteration, modification, or other change in any decision of the United States Court of Claims or the United States Court of Customs and Patent Appeals rendered prior to the effective date of this Act that has not been determined by either of those courts on that date, or that is filed after that date, shall be determined by the United States Court of Appeals for the Federal Circuit.

"(d) Any matter pending before a commissioner of the United States Court of Claims on the effective date of this Act, or any pending dispositive motion that the United States Court of Claims has not determined on that date, shall be determined by the United States Claims Court.

"(e) Any case in which a notice of appeal has been filed in a district court of the United States prior to the effective date of this Act shall be decided by the court of appeals to which the appeal was taken."

In 1976, P.L. 94-455, Sec. 1201(a), redesignated Code Sec. 6110 as Code Sec. 6111 and added new Code Sec. 6110, effective 11/1/76. Sec. 1201(b) of this Act provides:

"(b) Effect upon pending requests. Any written determination or background file document which is the subject of a judicial proceeding pursuant to section 552 of title 5, United States Code, commenced before January 1, 1976, shall not be treated as a written determination subject to subsection (h)(1), but shall be available to the complainant along with the background file document, if requested, as soon as practicable after July 1, 1976."

Sec. 6111. Disclosure of reportable transactions.

(a) In general.

Each material advisor with respect to any reportable transaction shall make a return (in such form as the Secretary may prescribe) setting forth—

(1) information identifying and describing the transaction,

(2) information describing any potential tax benefits expected to result from the transaction, and

(3) such other information as the Secretary may prescribe. Such return shall be filed not later than the date specified by the Secretary.

Code Sec. 6111(b)

(b) Definitions.
For purposes of this section—
(1) Material advisor.
(A) In general. The term "material advisor" means any person—
(i) who provides any material aid, assistance, or advice with respect to organizing, managing, promoting, selling, implementing, insuring, or carrying out any reportable transaction, and
(ii) who directly or indirectly derives gross income in excess of the threshold amount (or such other amount as may be prescribed by the Secretary) for such aid, assistance, or advice.
(B) Threshold amount. For purposes of subparagraph (A), the threshold amount is—
(i) $50,000 in the case of a reportable transaction substantially all of the tax benefits from which are provided to natural persons, and
(ii) $250,000 in any other case.
(2) Reportable transaction. The term "reportable transaction" has the meaning given to such term by section 6707A(c).

(c) Regulations.
The Secretary may prescribe regulations which provide—
(1) that only 1 person shall be required to meet the requirements of subsection (a) in cases in which 2 or more persons would otherwise be required to meet such requirements,
(2) exemptions from the requirements of this section, and
(3) such rules as may be necessary or appropriate to carry out the purposes of this section.

In 2005, P.L. 109-135, Sec. 412(zz), substituted "aid, assistance, or advice" for "advice or assistance" in clause (b)(1)(A)(ii), effective 12/21/2005.

In 2004, P.L. 108-357, Sec. 815(a), amended Code Sec. 6111, effective for transactions with respect to which material aid, assistance, or advice referred to in Code Sec. 6111(b)(1)(A)(i), as added by this Act, is provided after 10/22/2004. Prior to amendment, Code Sec. 6111 read as follows:

"SEC. 6111. REGISTRATION OF TAX SHELTERS.
"(a) Registration.
"(1) In general. Any tax shelter organizer shall register the tax shelter with the Secretary (in such form and in such manner as the Secretary may prescribe) not later than the day on which the first offering for sale of interests in such tax shelter occurs.
"(2) Information included in registration. Any registration under paragraph (1) shall include—
"(A) information identifying and describing the tax shelter,
"(B) information describing the tax benefits of the tax shelter represented (or to be represented) to investors, and
"(C) such other information as the Secretary may prescribe.
"(b) Furnishing of tax shelter identification number; inclusion on return.
"(1) Sellers, etc. Any person who sells (or otherwise transfers) an interest in a tax shelter shall (at such times and in such manner as the Secretary shall prescribe) furnish to each investor who purchases (or otherwise acquires) an interest in such tax shelter from such person the identification number assigned by the Secretary to such tax shelter.
"(2) Inclusion of number on return. Any person claiming any deduction, credit, or other tax benefit by reason of a tax shelter shall include (in such manner as the Secretary may prescribe) on the return of tax on which such deduction, credit, or other benefit is claimed the identification number assigned by the Secretary to such tax shelter.
"(c) Tax shelter. For purposes of this section—
"(1) In general. The term 'tax shelter' means any investment—
"(A) with respect to which any person could reasonably infer from the representations made, or to be made, in connection with the offering for sale of interests in the investment that the tax shelter ratio for any investor as of the close of any of the first 5 years ending after the date on which such investment is offered for sale may be greater than 2 to 1, and
"(B) which is—
"(i) required to be registered under a Federal or State law regulating securities,
"(ii) sold pursuant to an exemption from registration requiring the filing of a notice with a Federal or State agency regulating the offering or sale of securities, or
"(iii) a substantial investment.
"(2) Tax shelter ratio defined. For purposes of this subsection, the term 'tax shelter ratio' means, with respect to any year, the ratio which—

"(A) the aggregate amount of the deductions and 350 percent of the credits which are represented to be potentially allowable to any investor under subtitle A for all periods up to (and including) the close of such year, bears to
"(B) the investment base as of the close of such year.
"(3) Investment base.
"(A) In general. Except as provided in this paragraph, the term 'investment base' means, with respect to any year, the amount of money and the adjusted basis of other property (reduced by any liability to which such other property is subject) contributed by the investor as of the close of such year.
"(B) Certain borrowed amounts excluded. For purposes of subparagraph (A), there shall not be taken into account any amount borrowed from any person—
"(i) who participated in the organization, sale, or management of the investment, or
"(ii) who is a related person (as defined in section 465(b)(3)(C)) to any person described in clause (i),
"unless such amount is unconditionally required to be repaid by the investor before the close of the year for which the determination is being made.
"(C) Certain other amounts included or excluded.
"(i) Amounts held in cash equivalents, etc. No amount shall be taken into account under subparagraph (A) which is to be held in cash equivalent or marketable securities.
"(ii) Amounts included or excluded by Secretary. The Secretary may by regulation—
"(I) exclude from the investment base any amount described in subparagraph (A), or
"(II) include in the investment base any amount not described in subparagraph (A),
"if the Secretary determines that such exclusion or inclusion is necessary to carry out the purposes of this section.
"(4) Substantial investment. An investment is a substantial investment if—
"(A) the aggregate amount which may be offered for sale exceeds $250,000, and
"(B) there are expected to be 5 or more investors.
"(d) Certain confidential arrangements treated as tax shelters.
"(1) In general. For purposes of this section, the term 'tax shelter' includes any entity, plan, arrangement, or transaction—
"(A) a significant purpose of the structure of which is the avoidance or evasion of Federal income tax for a direct or indirect participant which is a corporation,
"(B) which is offered to any potential participant under conditions of confidentiality, and
"(C) for which the tax shelter promoters may receive fees in excess of $100,000 in the aggregate.
"(2) Conditions of confidentiality. For purposes of paragraph (1)(B), an offer is under conditions of confidentiality if—
"(A) the potential participant to whom the offer is made (or any other person acting on behalf of such participant) has an understanding or agreement with or for the benefit of any promoter of the tax shelter that such participant (or such other person) will limit disclosure of the tax shelter or any significant tax features of the tax shelter, or
"(B) any promoter of the tax shelter—
"(i) knows or has reason to know,
"(ii) knows or has reason to know that any other person (other than the potential participant) claims, or
"(iii) causes another person to claim,
"that the tax shelter (or any aspect thereof) is proprietary to any person other than the potential participant or is otherwise protected from disclosure to or use by others.
"For purposes of this subsection, the term 'promoter' means any person or any related person (within the meaning of section 267 or 707) who participates in the organization, management, or sale of the tax shelter.
"(3) Persons other than promoter required to register in certain cases.
"(A) In general. If—
"(i) the requirements of subsection (a) are not met with respect to any tax shelter (as defined in paragraph (1)) by any tax shelter promoter, and
"(ii) no tax shelter promoter is a United States person,
"then each United States person who discussed participation in such shelter shall register such shelter under subsection (a).
"(B) Exception. Subparagraph (A) shall not apply to a United States person who discussed participation in a tax shelter if—
"(i) such person notified the promoter in writing (not later than the close of the 90th day after the day on which such discussions began) that such person would not participate in such shelter, and
"(ii) such person does not participate in such shelter.
"(4) Offer to participate treated as offer for sale. For purposes of subsections (a) and (b), an offer to participate in a tax shelter (as defined in paragraph (1)) shall be treated as an offer for sale.
"(e) Other definitions. For purposes of this section—
"(1) Tax shelter organizer. The term 'tax shelter organizer' means—
"(A) the person principally responsible for organizing the tax shelter,
"(B) if the requirements of subsection (a) are not met by a person described in subparagraph (A) at the time prescribed therefor, any other person who participated in the organization of the tax shelter, and
"(C) if the requirements of subsection (a) are not met by a person described in subparagraph (A) or (B) at the time prescribed therefor, any person participating in the sale or management of the investment at a time when the tax shelter was not registered under subsection (a).
"(2) Year. The term 'year' means—
"(A) the taxable year of the tax shelter, or

Information and returns
Code Sec. 6113(b)(3)

"(B) if the tax shelter has no taxable year, the calendar year.
"(f) Regulations. The Secretary may prescribe regulations which provide—
"(1) rules for the aggregation of similar investments offered by the same person or persons for purposes of applying subsection (c)(4),
"(2) that only 1 person shall be required to meet the requirements of subsection (a) in cases in which 2 or more persons would otherwise be required to meet such requirements,
"(3) exemptions from the requirements of this section, and
"(4) such rules as may be necessary or appropriate to carry out the purposes of this section in the case of foreign tax shelters."

In 1997, P.L. 105-34, Sec. 1028(a), redesignated subsecs. (d) and (e) as subsecs. (e) and (f) and added new subsec. (d), effective for any tax shelter interests in which are offered to potential participants after the Secretary of the Treasury prescribes guidance with respect to meeting requirements added by such amendments.

In 1988, P.L. 100-647, Sec. 1002(c)(3), provides:
Notwithstanding section 203 of the Reform Act, the amendments made by section 201 of the Reform Act shall apply to any real property which was acquired before January 1, 1987, and was converted on or after such date from personal use to a use for which depreciation is allowable.

In 1986, P.L. 99-514, Sec. 201(d)(13), substituted "section 465(b)(3)(C)" for "section 168(e)(4)(D)" in clause (c)(3)(B)(ii), effective for property placed in service after 12/31/86, in tax. yrs. ending after 12/31/86 [see Sec. 1002(c)(3) of P.L. 100-647, above]. For transitional rules, see Sec. 203(b)-(e) of this Act, reproduced in note following Code Sec. 168. Sec. 203(a)(1)(B) of this Act provides:
"(B) Election to have amendments made by section 201 apply. A taxpayer may elect (at such time and in such manner as the Secretary of the Treasury or his delegate may prescribe) to have the amendments made by section 201 apply to any property placed in service after July 31, 1986, and before January 1, 1987."
—P.L. 99-514, Sec. 1531(a), substituted "350 percent" for "200 percent" in subpara. (c)(2)(A), effective for any tax shelter (within the meaning of Code Sec. 6111) interests in which are first offered for sale after 12/31/86.
—P.L. 99-514, Sec. 1899A(54), substituted "subparagraph" for "subpargraph" in subpara. (d)(1)(B), effective 10/22/86.

In 1984, P.L. 98-369, Sec. 141(a), redesignated Code Sec. 6111 as Code Sec. 6112 and added new Code Sec. 6111, effective for any tax shelter (within the meaning of new Code Sec. 6111) any interest in which is first sold to any investor after 8/31/84. Secs. 141(d)(2)–(3) of the Act provide special rules as follows:
"(2) Substantial investment test.—For purposes of determining whether any investment is a tax shelter by reason of section 6111(c)(1)(B)(iii) of such Code (as added by this section), only offers for sale after August 31, 1984, shall be taken into account.
"(3) Furnishing of shelter identification number for interests sold before September 1, 1984.—With respect to interests sold before September 1, 1984, any liability to act under paragraph (1) of section 6111(b) of such Code (as added by this section) which would (but for this sentence) arise before such date shall be deemed to arise on December 31, 1984."

Sec. 6112. Material advisors of reportable transactions must keep lists of advisees, etc.
(a) In general.
Each material advisor (as defined in section 6111) with respect to any reportable transaction (as defined in section 6707A(c)) shall (whether or not required to file a return under section 6111 with respect to such transaction) maintain (in such manner as the Secretary may by regulations prescribe) a list—
(1) identifying each person with respect to whom such advisor acted as a material advisor with respect to such transaction, and
(2) containing such other information as the Secretary may by regulations require.
(b) Special rules.
(1) Availability for inspection; retention of information on list. Any person who is required to maintain a list under subsection (a) (or was required to maintain a list under subsection (a) as in effect before the enactment of the American Jobs Creation Act of 2004)—
(A) shall make such list available to the Secretary for inspection upon written request by the Secretary, and
(B) except as otherwise provided under regulations prescribed by the Secretary, shall retain any information which is required to be included on such list for 7 years.
(2) Lists which would be required to be maintained by 2 or more persons. The Secretary may prescribe regulations which provide that, in cases in which 2 or more persons are required under subsection (a) to maintain the same list (or portion thereof), only 1 person shall be required to maintain such list (or portion).

In 2005, P.L. 109-135, Sec. 403(z), added "(or was required to maintain a list under subsection (a) as in effect before the enactment of the American Jobs Creation Act of 2004)" after "a list under subsection (a)" in para. (b)(1), effective for transactions with respect to which material aid, assistance, or advice referred to in Code Sec. 6111(b)(1)(A)(i) is provided after 10/22/2004 as if included in Sec. 815 of the American Jobs Creation Act of 2004, P.L. 108-357.

In 2004, P.L. 108-357, Sec. 815(b)(2), amended so much of Code Sec. 6112 as came before subsec. (c) . . . Sec. 815(b)(3)(A), redesignated subsec. (c) as (b) . . . Sec. 815(b)(3)(B), added "written" before "request" in subpara. (b)(1)(A) [as redesignated by Sec. 815(b)(3)(A) of this Act, see above] . . . Sec. 815(b)(3)(C), substituted "may prescribe" for "shall prescribe" in para. (b)(2) [as redesignated by Sec. 815(b)(3)(A) of this Act, see above], effective for transactions with respect to which material aid, assistance, or advice referred to in Code Sec. 6111(b)(1)(A)(i), as added by this Act, is provided after 10/22/2004.
Prior to amendment, so much of Code Sec. 6112 as came before subsec. (c) read as follows:
"SEC. 6112. ORGANIZERS AND SELLERS OF POTENTIALLY ABUSIVE TAX SHELTERS MUST KEEP LISTS OF INVESTORS.
"*(a) In general.* Any person who—
"(1) organizes any potentially abusive tax shelter, or
"(2) sells any interest in such a shelter,
shall maintain (in such manner as the Secretary may by regulations prescribe) a list identifying each person who was sold an interest in such shelter and containing such other information as the Secretary may by regulations require.
"*(b) Potentially abusive tax shelter.* For purposes of this section, the term 'potentially abusive tax shelter' means—
"(1) any tax shelter (as defined in section 6111) with respect to which registration is required under section 6111, and
"(2) any entity, investment plan or arrangement, or other plan or arrangement which is of a type which the Secretary determines by regulations as having a potential for tax avoidance or evasion."

In 1984, P.L. 98-369, Sec. 142(a), added Code Sec. 6112, effective for any interest which is first sold to any investor after 8/31/84.

Sec. 6113. Disclosure of nondeductibility of contributions.
(a) General rule.
Each fundraising solicitation by (or on behalf of) an organization to which this section applies shall contain an express statement (in a conspicuous and easily recognizable format) that contributions or gifts to such organization are not deductible as charitable contributions for Federal income tax purposes.
(b) Organizations to which section applies.
(1) In general. Except as otherwise provided in this subsection, this section shall apply to any organization which is not described in section 170(c) and which—
(A) is described in subsection (c) (other than paragraph (1) thereof) or (d) of section 501 and exempt from taxation under section 501(a),
(B) is a political organization (as defined in section 527(e)), or
(C) was an organization described in subparagraph (A) or (B) at any time during the 5-year period ending on the date of the fundraising solicitation or is a successor to an organization so described at any time during such 5-year period.
(2) Exception for small organizations.
(A) Annual gross receipts do not exceed $100,000. This section shall not apply to any organization the gross receipts of which in each taxable year are normally not more than $100,000.
(B) Multiple organization rule. The Secretary may treat any group of 2 or more organizations as 1 organization for purposes of subparagraph (A) where necessary or appropriate to prevent the avoidance of this section through the use of multiple organizations.
(3) Special rule for certain fraternal organizations. For purposes of paragraph (1), an organization described in section 170(c)(4) shall be treated as described in section 170(c) only with respect to solicitations for contributions

3,607

or gifts which are to be used exclusively for purposes referred to in section 170(c)(4).

(c) Fundraising solicitation.

For purposes of this section—

(1) In general. Except as provided in paragraph (2), the term "fundraising solicitation" means any solicitation of contributions or gifts which is made—

(A) in written or printed form,

(B) by television or radio, or

(C) by telephone.

(2) Exception for certain letters or calls. The term "fundraising solicitation" shall not include any letter or telephone call if such letter or call is not part of a coordinated fundraising campaign soliciting more than 10 persons during the calendar year.

In 1987, P.L. 100-203, Sec. 10701(a), added Code Sec. 6113, effective for solicitations after 1/31/88.

Sec. 6114. Treaty-based return positions.

(a) In general.

Each taxpayer who, with respect to any tax imposed by this title, takes the position that a treaty of the United States overrules (or otherwise modifies) an internal revenue law of the United States shall disclose (in such manner as the Secretary may prescribe) such position—

(1) on the return of tax for such tax (or any statement attached to such return), or

(2) if no return of tax is required to be filed, in such form as the Secretary may prescribe.

(b) Waiver authority.

The Secretary may waive the requirements of subsection (a) with respect to classes of cases for which the Secretary determines that the waiver will not impede the assessment and collection of tax.

In 1990, P.L. 101-508, Sec. 11702(c), deleted "by regulations" after "The Secretary may" in subsec. (b), effective for filing returns in tax. periods for which the due date (without extension) occurs after 12/31/88.

In 1988, P.L. 100-647, Sec. 1012(aa)(5)(A), added Code Sec. 6114, effective for filing returns in tax. periods for which the due date (without extension) occurs after 12/31/88.

Sec. 6115. Disclosure related to quid pro quo contributions.

(a) Disclosure requirement.

If an organization described in section 170(c) (other than paragraph (1) thereof) receives a quid pro quo contribution in excess of $75, the organization shall, in connection with the solicitation or receipt of the contribution, provide a written statement which—

(1) informs the donor that the amount of the contribution that is deductible for Federal income tax purposes is limited to the excess of the amount of any money and the value of any property other than money contributed by the donor over the value of the goods or services provided by the organization, and

(2) provides the donor with a good faith estimate of the value of such goods or services.

(b) Quid pro quo contribution.

For purposes of this section, the term "quid pro quo contribution" means a payment made partly as a contribution and partly in consideration for goods or services provided to the payor by the donee organization. A quid pro quo contribution does not include any payment made to an organization, organized exclusively for religious purposes, in return for which the taxpayer receives solely an intangible religious benefit that generally is not sold in a commercial transaction outside the donative context.

In 1993, P.L. 103-66, Sec. 13173(a), added Code Sec. 6115, effective for quid pro quo contributions made on or after 1/1/94.

Sec. 6116. Cross reference.

For inspection of records, returns, etc., concerning gasoline or lubricating oils, see section 4102.

In 1993, P.L. 103-66, Sec. 13173(a), redesignated Code Sec. 6115 as Code Sec. 6116, effective for quid pro quo contributions made on or after 1/1/94.

In 1988, P.L. 100-647, Sec. 1012(aa)(5)(A), redesignated Code Sec. 6114 as Code Sec. 6115, effective for tax. periods the due date for filing returns for which (without extension) occurs after 12/31/88.

In 1987, P.L. 100-203, Sec. 10701(a), redesignated Code Sec. 6113 as Code Sec. 6114, effective for solicitations after 1/31/88.

In 1984, P.L. 98-369, Sec. 141(a), redesignated Code Sec. 6111 as Code Sec. 6112 . . . Sec. 142(a), redesignated Code Sec. 6112 (as redesignated by Sec. 141(a) of the Act) as Code Sec. 6113, effective for tax shelter interests first sold after 8/31/84.

In 1976, P.L. 94-455, Sec. 1201(a), redesignated Code Sec. 6110 as Code Sec. 6111, effective 11/1/76.

—P.L. 94-455, Sec. 1906(a)(8), amended Code Sec. 6111, as redesignated by this Act, effective 2/1/77.

Prior to amendment, Code Sec. 6111 read as follows:

"SEC. 6111. CROSS REFERENCES.

"(1) For reports of Secretary of Agriculture concerning cotton futures, see section 4876.

"(2) For inspection of returns, order forms, and prescriptions concerning narcotics, see section 4773.

"(3) For inspection of returns, order forms, and prescriptions concerning marihuana, see section 4773.

"(4) For authority of Secretary or his delegate to furnish list of special taxpayers, see section 4775.

"(5) For inspection of records, returns, etc., concerning gasoline or lubricating oils, see section 4102."

In 1961, P.L. 87-397, Sec. [1](a), redesignated Code Sec. 6109 as Code Sec. 6110, effective as provided in Sec. [1](d) of this Act, which provides:

"(d) Effective date. Paragraph (1) of section 6109(a) of the Internal Revenue Code of 1954, as added by subsection (a) of this section, shall apply only in respect of returns, statements, and other documents relating to period commencing after December 31, 1961. Paragraphs (2) and (3) of such section 6109(a) shall apply only in respect of returns, statements, or other documents relating to periods commencing after December 31, 1962.

CHAPTER 62.—TIME AND PLACE FOR PAYING TAX

Subchapter

A. Place and due date for payment of tax.

B. Extensions of time for payment.

Subchapter A.—Place and Due Date for Payment of Tax

Sec.

6151. Time and place for paying tax shown on returns.

6155. Payment on notice and demand.

6156. Repealed [Installment payments of tax on use of highway motor vehicles].

6157. Payment of Federal unemployment tax on quarterly or other time period basis.

6159. Agreements for payment of tax liability in installments.

In 2004, P.L. 108-357, Sec. 867(b)(2), deleted item 6156.

Prior to deletion, item 6156 read as follows:

"6156. Installment payments of tax on use of highway motor vehicles."

In 1990, P.L. 101-508, Sec. 11801(b)(13), deleted item 6158.

Prior to deletion, item 6158 read as follows:

"6158. Installment payment of tax attributable to investment pursuant to Bank Holding Company Act amendments of 1970."

In 1988, P.L. 100-647, Sec. 6234(b)(2), added item 6159.

In 1987, P.L. 100-203, Sec. 10301(b)(7), repealed item 6154.

Prior to repeal, item 6154 read as follows:

"6154. Installment payments of estimated income tax by corporations.".

In 1986, P.L. 99-514, Sec. 1404(c)(4), deleted item 6152.

Prior to deletion, item 6152 read as follows:

"6152. Installment payments."

In 1984, P.L. 98-369, Sec. 412(c)(3), deleted item 6153.

Prior to deletion, item 6153 read as follows:

"6153. Installment payments of estimated income tax by individuals."

Payment of tax Code Sec. 6153

In 1982, P.L. 97-248, Sec. 280(c)(2)(F), deleted the words "and civil aircraft" after "motor vehicles" in item 6156.
In 1976, P.L. 94-452, Sec. 3(c)(1), added the item for Code Sec. 6158.
In 1970, added "and civil aircraft" in item 6156.
In 1969, P.L. 91-53, Sec. 2(f)(1), amended the table of sections for subchapter A rewriting item 6157.
Prior to amendment it read as follows: "6157. Payment of taxes under provisions of the Tariff Act."
In 1961, added item 6156 and redesignated former item 6156 as 6157.

Sec. 6151. Time and place for paying tax shown on returns.

(a) General rule.

Except as otherwise provided in this subchapter, when a return of tax is required under this title or regulations, the person required to make such return shall, without assessment or notice and demand from the Secretary, pay such tax to the internal revenue officer with whom the return is filed, and shall pay such tax at the time and place fixed for filing the return (determined without regard to any extension of time for filing the return).

(b) Exceptions.

(1) Income tax not computed by taxpayer. If the taxpayer elects under section 6014 not to show the tax on the return, the amount determined by the Secretary as payable shall be paid within 30 days after the mailing by the Secretary to the taxpayer of a notice stating such amount and making demand therefor.

(2) Use of Government depositaries. For authority of the Secretary to require payments to Government depositaries, see section 6302(c).

(c) Date fixed for payment of tax.

In any case in which a tax is required to be paid on or before a certain date, or within a certain period, any reference in this title to the date fixed for payment of such tax shall be deemed a reference to the last day fixed for such payment (determined without regard to any extension of time for paying the tax).

In 1983, P.L. 97-424, Sec. 521(a)-(e), provided provisions on floor stocks taxes which are reproduced in note following Code Sec. 4081.
In 1976, P.L. 94-455, Sec. 1906(b)(13)(A), substituted "Secretary" for "Secretary or his delegate" each place it appeared in Code Sec. 6151, effective 2/1/77.
—P.L. 94-452, Sec. 3(c)(2), substituted "subchapter" for "section" in subsec. (a), effective 10/1/77, for sales after 7/7/70, in tax. yrs. end. after 7/7/70, but only in the case of qualified bank holding corporations (within the meaning of section 1103(b) of the Internal Revenue Code of 1954 as amended by section 2(a) of this Act).
In 1966, P.L. 89-713, Sec. 1(b), substituted "to the internal revenue officer with whom the return as filed" for "to the principal internal revenue officer for the internal revenue district in which the return is required to be filed," in subsec. (a) effective 11/2/66.

Sec. 6152. Repealed.

In 1986, P.L. 99-514, Sec. 1404(c)(1), repealed Code Sec. 6152, effective for tax. yrs. begin. after 12/31/86.
Prior to repeal, Code Sec. 6152 read as follows:
"SEC. 6152. INSTALLMENT PAYMENTS.
"(a) Privilege to elect to make four installment payments by decedent's estate.
"A decedent's estate subject to the tax imposed by chapter 1 may elect to pay such tax in four equal installments.
"(b) Dates prescribed for payment of four installments.
"In any case (other than payment of estimated income tax) in which the tax may be paid in four installments, the first installment shall be paid on the date prescribed for the payment of the tax, the second installment shall be paid on or before 3 months, the third installment on or before 6 months, and the fourth installment on or before 9 months, after such date.
"(c) Proration of deficiency to installments.
"If an election has been made to pay the tax imposed by chapter 1 in installments and a deficiency has been assessed, the deficiency shall be prorated to such installments. Except as provided in section 6861 (relating to jeopardy assessments), that part of the deficiency so prorated to any installment the date for payment of which has not arrived shall be collected at the same time as and as part of such installment. That part of the deficiency so prorated to any installment the date for payment of which has arrived shall be paid upon notice and demand from the Secretary."

"(d) Acceleration of payment.
"If any installment (other than an installment of estimated income tax) is not paid on or before the date fixed for its payment, the whole of the unpaid tax shall be paid upon notice and demand from the Secretary."
In 1982, P.L. 97-248, Sec. 234(b)(1), amended subsecs. (a) and (b), effective for tax. yrs. begin. after 12/31/82.
Prior to amendment, subsecs. (a) and (b) read as follows:
"(a) Privilege to elect to make installment payments.
"(1) Corporations. A corporation subject to the taxes imposed by chapter 1 may elect to pay the unpaid amount of such taxes in two equal installments.
"(2) Estates of decedents. A decedent's estate subject to the tax imposed by chapter 1 may elect to pay such tax in four equal installments.
"(b) Dates prescribed for payment of installments.
"(1) Four installments. In any case (other than payment of estimated income tax) in which the tax may be paid in four installments, the first installment shall be paid on the date prescribed for the payment of the tax, the second installment shall be paid on or before 3 months, the third installment on or before 6 months, the fourth installment on or before 9 months, after such date.
"(2) Two installments. In any case (other than payment of estimated income tax) in which the tax may be paid in two installments, the first installment shall be paid on the date prescribed for the payment of the tax, and the second installment shall be paid on or before 3 months after such date."
In 1976, P.L. 94-455, Sec. 1906(a)(9), amended para. (a)(1), effective 2/1/77.
Prior to amendment, para. (a)(1) read as follows:
"(1) Corporations. A corporation subject to the taxes imposed by chapter 1 may elect to pay the unpaid amount of such taxes in installments as follows:
"(A) with respect to taxable years ending before December 31, 1954, four installments, the first two of which shall be 45 percent, respectively for such taxes and the last two of which shall be 5 percent respectively, of such taxes;
"(B) with respect to taxable years ending on or after December 31, 1954, two equal installments."
—P.L. 94-455, Sec. 1906(b)(13)(A), substituted "Secretary" for "Secretary or his delegate" each place it appeared in Code Sec. 6152, effective 2/1/77.
In 1954, P.L. 767, Sec. 3, deleted para. (a)(3), effective for tax. yrs. begin. after '55.
Prior to deletion, para. (a)(3) read as follows:
"(3) Employers subject to unemployment tax.—An employer subject to the tax imposed by section 3301 may elect to pay such tax in four equal installments."

Sec. 6153. Repealed.

In 1984, P.L. 98-369, Sec. 412(a)(3), repealed Code Sec. 6153, effective for tax. yrs. begin. after 12/31/84.
Prior to repeal, Code Sec. 6153 read as follows:
"SEC. 6153. INSTALLMENT PAYMENTS OF ESTIMATED INCOME TAX BY INDIVIDUALS.
"(a) General rule.
"The amount of estimated tax (as defined in section 6015(d)) with respect to which a declaration is required under section 6015 shall be paid as follows:
"(1) If the declaration is filed on or before April 15 of the taxable year, the estimated tax shall be paid in four equal installments. The first installment shall be paid at the time of the filing of the declaration, the second and third on June 15 and September 15, respectively, of the taxable year, and the fourth on January 15 of the succeeding taxable year.
"(2) If the declaration is filed after April 15 and not after June 15 of the taxable year, and is not required by section 6073(a) to be filed on or before April 15 of the taxable year, the estimated tax shall be paid in three equal installments. The first installment shall be paid at the time of the filing of the declaration, the second on September 15 of the taxable year, and the third on January 15 of the succeeding taxable year.
"(3) If the declaration is filed after June 15 and not after September 15 of the taxable year, and is not required by section 6073(a) to be filed on or before June 15 of the taxable year, the estimated tax shall be paid in two equal installments. The first installment shall be paid at the time of the filing of the declaration, and the second on January 15 of the succeeding taxable year.
"(4) If the declaration is filed after September 15 of the taxable year, and is not required by section 6073(a) to be filed on or before September 15 of the taxable year, the estimated tax shall be paid in full at the time of the filing of the declaration.
"(5) If the declaration is filed after the time prescribed in section 6073(a) (including cases in which a extension of time for filing the declaration has been granted under section 6081), paragraph (2), (3), and (4) of this subsection shall not apply, and there shall be paid at the time of such filing all installments of estimated tax which would have been payable on or before such time if the declaration had been filed within the time prescribed in section 6073(a), and the remaining installments shall be paid at the times at which, and in the amounts in which, they would have been payable if the declaration had been so filed.
"(b) Farmers or fishermen.
"If an individual referred to in section 6073(b) (relating to income from farming or fishing) makes a declaration of estimated tax after September 15 of the taxable year and on or before January 15 of the succeeding taxable year, the estimated tax shall be paid in full at the time of the filing of the declaration.
"(c) Amendments of declaration.
"If any amendment of a declaration is filed, the remaining installments, if any, shall be ratably increased or decreased, as the case may be, to reflect the increase or decrease, as the case may be, in the estimated tax by reason of such amendment, and if any amendment is made after September 15 of the taxable year, any

3,609

Code Sec. 6153 — Payment of tax

increase in the estimated tax by reason thereof shall be paid at the time of making such amendment.

"*(d) Application to short taxable years.*

"The application of this section to taxable years of less than 12 months shall be in accordance with regulations prescribed by the Secretary.

"*(e) Fiscal years.*

"In the application of this section to the case of a taxable year beginning on any date other than January 1, there shall be substituted, for the months specified in this section, the months which correspond thereto.

"*(f) Installments paid in advance.*

"At the election of the individual, any installment of the estimated tax may be paid prior to the date prescribed for its payment.

"*(g) Special rules for taxable years beginning after 1982.*

"In the case of taxable years beginning after 1982—

"(1) this section shall be applied as if the requirements of sections 6015 and 6073 remained in effect, and

"(2) the amount of the estimated tax taken into account under this section shall be determined under rules similar to the rules of subsections (b) and (d) of section 6654."

In 1982, P.L. 97-248, Sec. 328(b)(3), amended subsec. (g), effective for tax. yrs. begin. after 12/31/82.

Prior to amendment, subsec. (g) read as follows:

"*(g) Six-month application of revenue adjustment act of 1975 changes.*

"In the case of a taxpayer who has as his taxable year the calendar year 1976, the amount of any installment the payment of which is required to be made after December 31, 1975, and before October 1, 1976, may be computed without regard to section 42(a)(2), 43(a)(2), 43(b)(2), 141(b)(2), or 141(c)(2)."

In 1981, P.L. 97-34, Sec. 725(c)(3), substituted "6015(d)" for "6015(c)" in subsec. (a), for tax. yrs. begin. after 12/31/80.

In 1976, P.L. 94-455, Sec. 1906(b)(13)(A), substituted "Secretary" for "Secretary or his delegate" in subsec. (d), effective 2/1/77.

— P.L. 94-414, Sec. 3(b), substituted "October 1, 1976" for "September 15, 1976" in subsec. (g), effective 9/17/76.

— P.L. 94-414, Sec. 3(b), substituted "October 1, 1976" for "September 15, 1976" in subsec. (g), effective 9/17/76.

— P.L. 94-396, Sec. 2(a)(2), substituted "September 15, 1976" for "September 1, 1976" in subsec. (g), effective 9/3/76.

— P.L. 94-331, Sec. 3(b), substituted "September 1, 1976" for "July 1, 1976" in subsec. (g), effective 6/30/76.

In 1975, P.L. 94-164, Sec. 5(b), added new subsec. (g), effective date of enactment (12/23/75).

In 1962, P.L. 87-682, Sec. 1, added "or fishing" after "from farming" in subsec (b), and added "or fishermen" after "farmers" in the heading of subsec. (b), effective for tax. yrs. begin. after 1962.

Sec. 6154. Repealed.

In 1988, P.L. 100-647, Sec. 1007(g)(10), substituted "11, 55, 59A" for "11, 59A" in subsec. (a) [as in effect before its repeal by the Revenue Act of 1987], effective for buildings placed in service after 12/31/86 in tax. yrs. end. after such date.

— P.L. 100-647, Sec. 1015(h)(1), deleted "subject to the tax imposed by section 4940" after "foundation" in para. (h)(1) [as in effect before its repeal by the Revenue Act of 1987] . . . Sec. 1015(h)(2), amended para. (h)(2) [as in effect before its repeal by the Revenue Act of 1987] . . . Sec. 1015(h)(3), added the last sentence to subsec. (h) [as in effect before its repeal by the Revenue Act of 1987], effective for tax. yrs. begin. after 12/31/86.

Prior to amendment, para. (h)(2) read as follows:

"(2) any tax imposed by section 511 or 4940 shall be treated as a tax imposed by section 11, and"

In 1987, P.L. 100-203, Sec. 10301(b)(1), repealed Code Sec. 6154, effective for tax. yrs. begin. after 12/31/87.

Prior to repeal, Code Sec. 6154 read as follows:

SEC. 6154. INSTALLMENT PAYMENTS OF ESTIMATED INCOME TAX BY CORPORATIONS.

"*(a) Corporations required to pay estimated income tax.*

"Every corporation subject to taxation under section 11, 55, 59A, or 1201(a), or subchapter L of chapter 1 (relating to insurance companies), shall make payments of estimated tax (as defined in subsection (c)) during its taxable year as provided in subsection (b) if its estimated tax for such taxable year can reasonably be expected to be $40 or more.

"*(b) Payment in installments.*

"Any corporation required under subsection (a) to make payments of estimated tax (as defined in subsection (c)) shall make such payments in installments as follows:

If the requirements of subsection (a) are first met	The following percentages of the estimated tax shall be paid on the 15th day of the			
	4th month	6th month	9th month	12th month
Before the 1st day of the 4th month of the taxable year	25	25	25	25
After the last day of the 3d month and before the 1st day of the 6th month of the taxable year		33⅓	33⅓	33⅓
After the last day of the 5th month and before the 1st day of the 9th month of the taxable year			50	50
After the last day of the 8th month and before the 1st day of the 12th month of the taxable year				100

"*(c) Estimated tax defined.*

"For purposes of this title, in the case of a corporation the term 'estimated tax' means the excess of—

"(1) The amount which the corporation estimates as the sum of—

"(A) the income tax imposed by section 11 or 1201(a), or subchapter L of chapter 1, whichever applies,

"(B) the minimum tax imposed by section 55, and

"(C) the environmental tax imposed by Section 59A, over

"(2) the amount which the corporation estimates as the sum of—

"(A) any credits against tax provided by part IV of subchapter A of chapter 1, and

"(B) to the extent allowed under regulations prescribed by the Secretary, any overpayment of the tax imposed by section 4986.

"*(d) Recomputation of estimated tax.*

"If, after paying any installment of estimated tax, the taxpayer makes a new estimate, the amount of each remaining installment (if any) shall be the amount which would have been payable if the new estimate had been made when the first estimate for the taxable year was made, increased or decreased (as the case may be) by the amount computed by dividing—

"(1) the difference between—

"(A) the amount of estimated tax required to be paid before the date on which the new estimate is made, and

"(B) the amount of estimated tax which would have been required to be paid before such date if the new estimate had been made when the first estimate was made, by

"(2) the number of installments remaining to be paid on or after the date on which the new estimate is made.

"*(e) Application to short taxable year.*

"The application of this section to taxable years of less than 12 months shall be in accordance with regulations prescribed by the Secretary.

"*(f) Installments paid in advance.*

"At the election of the corporation, any installment of the estimated tax may be paid before the date prescribed for its payment.

"*(g) Certain foreign corporations.*

"For purposes of this section and section 6655, in the case of a foreign corporation subject to taxation under section 11 or 1201(a), or under subchapter L of chapter 1, the tax imposed by section 881 shall be treated as a tax imposed by section 11.

"*(h) Certain tax-exempt organizations.*

"For purposes of this section and section 6655—

"(1) any organization subject to the tax imposed by section 511, and any private foundation shall be treated as a corporation subject to a tax under section 11,

"(2) any tax imposed by section 511, and any tax imposed by section 1 or 4940 on a private foundation, shall be treated as a tax imposed by section 11, and

"(3) any reference to taxable income shall be treated as including a reference to unrelated business taxable income or net investment income (as the case may be).".

"In the case of an organization described in paragraph (1), subsection (d) of section 6655 shall be applied by substituting '5th month' for 'third month' and subsection (d)(3)(A) of section 6655 shall be applied by substituting '2 months' for '3 months' in clause (i), by substituting '4 months' for '5 months, in clause (ii), by substituting '7 months' for '8 months' in clause (iii), and by substituting '10 months' for '11 months' in clause (iv)."

In 1986, P.L. 99-514, Sec. 701(d)(1), amended para. (c)(1) [as amended by Sec. 516(b)(4)(A)(i) of P.L. 99-499, see below], effective for tax. yrs. begin. after 12/31/86.

Prior to amendment, para. (c)(1) read as follows:

"(1) the amount which the corporation estimates as the amount of the income tax imposed by section 11 or 1201(a), or subchapter L of chapter 1, whichever is applicable, over"

— P.L. 99-514, Sec. 1542(a), added subsec. (h), effective for tax. yrs. begin. after 12/31/86.

— P.L. 99-499, Sec. 516(b)(4)(A)(i), deleted "and" at the end of subpara. (c)(1)(A), substituted "and" for "over" at the end of subpara. (c)(1)(B), and added subpara. (b)(1)(C) . . . Sec. 516(b)(4)(A)(ii), substituted "section 11, 59A," for "section 11" in subsec. (a), effective for tax. yrs. begin. after 12/31/86.

In 1983, P.L. 97-448, Sec. 201(j)(2), amended para. (c)(2), effective for periods after 2/29/80.

Prior to amendment, para. (c)(2) read as follows:

"(2) the amount which the corporation estimates as the sum of the credits against tax provided by part IV of subchapter A of chapter 1."

In 1978, P.L. 95-600, Sec. 301(b)(20)(A), amended subsec. (c), effective for tax. yrs. begin. after 12/31/78.

Prior to amendment, subsec. (c) read as follows:

Payment of tax — Code Sec. 6154

"(c) Estimated tax defined.

"(1) In general. For purposes of this title, in the case of a corporation the term estimated tax means the excess of—

"(A) the amount which the corporation estimates as the amount of the income tax imposed by section 11 or 1201(a), or subchapter L of chapter 1, whichever is applicable, over

"(B) the sum of—

"(i) the amount which the corporation estimates as the sum of the credits against tax provided by part IV of subchapter A of chapter 1, and

"(ii) in the case of a taxable year beginning before January 1, 1977, the amount of the corporation's temporary estimated tax exemption for such year.

"(2) Temporary estimated tax exemption.

"(A) In general. For purposes of clause (ii) of paragraph (1)(B), the amount of a corporation's temporary estimated tax exemption for a taxable year equals the applicable percentage (determined under subparagraph

"(B)) multiplied by the lesser of—

"(i) an amount equal to 22 percent of the amount which the corporation estimates as its surtax exemption (as defined in section 11(d)) for such year, or

"(ii) the excess determined under paragraph (1) without regard to clause (ii) of paragraph (1)(B).

"(B) Applicable percentage. For purposes of subparagraph (A) and section 6655(e)(2), the applicable percentage is—

1975	40 percent
1976	20 percent

In 1976, P.L. 94-455, Sec. 901(c)(3), repealed subsec. (h), effective for tax. yrs. end. after 12/31/75.

Prior to repeal, subsec. (h), read as follows:

"(h) Six-month application of revenue adjustment act of 1975 changes. In the case of a corporation which has as its taxable year the calendar year 1976, the amount of any installment the payment of which is required to be made after December 31, 1975, and before October 1, 1976, may be computed without regard to sections 11(b)(2), 11(c)(2), and 11(d)(2)."

— P.L. 94-455, Sec. 1906(a)(10)(A), added "and" following the comma at the end of clause (c)(1)(B)(i), deleted clauses (c)(1)(B)(ii) and (iii), and added a new clause (c)(1)(B)(ii), effective 2/1/77.

Prior to deletion, clauses (c)(1)(B)(ii) and (iii) read as follows:

"(ii) in the case of a taxable year beginning after December 31, 1967, and before January 1, 1977, the amount of the corporation's temporary estimated tax exemption for such year, and

"(iii) in the case of a taxable year beginning after December 31, 1967, and before January 1, 1972, the amount of the corporation's transitional exemption for such year."

— P.L. 94-455, Sec. 1906(a)(10)(B), substituted "clause (ii)" for "clauses (ii) and (iii)" in clause (c)(2)(A)(ii), effective 2/1/77.

— P.L. 94-455, Sec. 1906(a)(10)(C), deleted the following from the chart in subpara. (c)(2)(B), effective 2/1/77:

1972	100 percent
1973	80 percent
1974	60 percent

— P.L. 94-455, Sec. 1906(a)(10)(D), deleted para. (c)(3), effective 2/1/77.

Prior to deletion, para. (c)(3) read as follows:

"(3) Transitional exemption.

"(A) In general. For purposes of clause (iii) of paragraph (1)(B), the amount of a corporation's transitional exemption for a taxable year equals the exclusion of percentage (determined under subparagraph (b)), multiplied by the lesser of—

"(i) $100,000, reduced by the amount of the corporation's temporary estimated tax exemption for such year, or

"(ii) the excess determined under paragraph (1) without regard to clause (iii) of paragraph (1)(B).

"(B) Exclusion percentage. For purposes of subparagraph (A) and section 6655(e)(3), the exclusion percentage is—

In the case of a taxable year beginning in—	
1968	80 percent
1969	60 percent
1970	40 percent
1971	20 percent

— P.L. 94-455, Sec. 1906(b)(13)(A), substituted "Secretary" for "Secretary or his delegate," in subsec. (e), effective 2/1/77.

— P.L. 94-414, Sec. 3(c), substituted "October 1, 1976" for "September 15, 1976" in subsec. (h), effective 9/17/76.

— P.L. 94-396, Sec. 2(a)(3), substituted "September 15, 1976" for "September 1, 1976" in subsec. (h), effective 9/3/76.

— P.L. 94-331, Sec. 3(c), substituted "September 1, 1976" for "July 1, 1976" in subsec. (h), effective 6/30/76.

In 1975, P.L. 94-164, Sec. 5(c), added subsec. (h), effective 12/23/75.

In 1968, P.L. 90-364, Sec. 103(b), amended Code Sec. 6154, generally applicable with respect to tax. yrs. begin. after 12/31/67. For special provision regarding effective date, see Sec. 104 of this Act, reproduced after Code Sec. 6425.

Prior to amendment Code Sec. 6154 read as follows:

"SEC. 6154. INSTALLMENT PAYMENTS OF ESTIMATED INCOME TAX BY CORPORATIONS.

"(a) Amount and time for payment of each installment. The amount of estimated tax (as defined in section 6016(b)) with respect to which a declaration is required under section 6016 shall be paid as follows:

"(1) Taxable years beginning in 1966. With respect to taxable years beginning after December 31, 1965, and before January 1, 1967, such estimated tax shall be paid in installments in accordance with the following table:

If the declaration is timely filed on or before the 15th day of the—	The following percentages of the estimated tax shall be paid on the 15th day of the—			
	4th month	6th month	9th month	12th month
4th month of the taxable year	12	12	25	25
6th month of the taxable year (but after the 15th day of the 4th month)		16	29	29
9th month of the taxable year (but after the 15th day of the 6th month)			37	37
12th month of the taxable year (but after the 15th day of the 9th month)				74

"(2) Taxable years beginning after 1966. With respect to taxable years beginning after December 31, 1966, such estimated tax shall be paid in installments in accordance with the following table:

If the declaration is timely filed on or before the 15th day of the—	The following percentages of the estimated tax shall be paid on the 15th day of the—			
	4th month	6th month	9th month	12th month
4th month of the taxable year	25	25	25	25
6th month of the taxable year (but after the 15th day of the 4th month)		33⅓	33⅓	33⅓
9th month of the taxable year (but after the 15th day of the 6th month)			50	50
12th month of the taxable year (but after the 15th day of the 9th month)				100

"(3) Timely filing. A declaration is timely filed for the purposes of paragraphs (1) and (2) if it is not required by section 6074(a) to be filed on a date (determined without regard to any extension of time for filing the declaration under section 6081) before the date it is actually filed.

"(4) Late filing. If the declaration is filed after the time prescribed in section 6074(a) (determined without regard to any extension of time for filing the declaration under section 6081), there shall be paid at the time of such filing all installments of estimated tax which would have been payable on or before such time if the declaration had been filed within the time prescribed in section 6074(a), and the remaining installments shall be paid at the times at which, and in the amounts in which, they would have been payable if the declaration had been so filed.

"(b) Amendment of declaration.

"If any amendment of a declaration is filed, the amount of each remaining installment (if any) shall be the amount which would have been payable if the new estimate had been made when the first estimate for the taxable year was made, increased or decreased (as the case may be), by the amount computed by dividing—

"(1) the difference between (A) the amount of estimated tax required to be paid before the date on which the amendment is made, and (B) the amount of estimated tax which would have been required to be paid before such date if the new estimate had been made when the first estimate was made, by

"(2) the number of installments remaining to be paid on or after the date on which the amendment is made.

"(c) Application to short taxable year.

"The application of this section to taxable years of less than 12 months shall be in accordance with regulations prescribed by the Secretary or his delegate.

"(d) Installments paid in advance.

"At the election of the corporation, any installment of the estimated tax may be paid before the date prescribed for its payment."

In 1966, P.L. 89-368, Sec. 104, amended subsec. (a), effective for tax. yrs. begin. after 12/31/65.

Prior to amendment, subsec. (a) read as follows:

"(a) Amount and time for payment of each installment.

"The amount of estimated tax (as defined in section 6016(b) with respect to which a declaration is required under section 6016 shall be paid as follows:

"(1) Payment in 4 installments. If the declaration is filed on or before the 15th day of the 4th month of the taxable year, the estimated tax shall be paid in 4 installments. The amount and time for payment of each installment shall be determined in accordance with the following table:

Code Sec. 6154 — Payment of tax

If the taxable year begins in—	The following percentages of the estimated tax shall be paid on the 15th day of the—			
	4th month	6th month	9th month	12th month
1964	1	1	25	25
1965	4	4	25	25
1966	9	9	25	25
1967	14	14	25	25
1968	19	19	25	25
1969	22	22	25	25
1970 or any subsequent year	25	25	25	25

"(2) Payment in 3 installments. If the declaration is filed after the 15th day of the 4th month and not after the 15th day of the 6th month of the taxable year, and is not required by section 6074(a) to be filed on or before the 15th day of such 4th month, the estimated tax shall be paid in 3 installments. The amount and time for payment of each installment shall be determined in accordance with the following table:

If the taxable year begins in—	The following percentages of the estimated tax shall be paid on the 15th day of the—		
	6th month	9th month	12th month
1964	1⅓	25⅓	25⅓
1965	5⅓	26⅓	26⅓
1966	12	28	28
1967	18⅓	29⅓	29⅓
1968	25⅓	31⅓	31⅓
1969	29⅓	32⅓	32⅓
1970 or any subsequent year	33⅓	33⅓	33⅓

"(3) Payment in 2 installments. If the declaration of estimated tax is filed after the 15th day of the 6th month and not after the 15th day of the 9th month of the taxable year, and is not required by section 6074(a) to be filed on or before the 15th day of such 6th month, the estimated tax shall be paid in 2 installments. The amount and time for payment of each installment shall be determined in accordance with the following table:

If the taxable year begins in—	The following percentages of the estimated tax shall be paid on the 15th day of the—	
	9th month	12th month
1964	26	26
1965	29	29
1966	34	34
1967	39	39
1968	44	44
1969	47	47
1970 or any subsequent year	50	50

"(4) Payment in 1 installment. If the declaration of estimated tax is filed after the 15th day of the 9th month of the taxable year, and is not required by section 6074(a) to be filed on or before the 15th day of such 9th month, the estimated tax shall be paid in 1 installment. The amount and time for payment of the installment shall be determined in accordance with the following table:

If the taxable year begins in—	The following percentages of the estimated tax shall be paid on the 15th day of the 12th month
1964	52
1965	58
1966	68
1967	78
1968	88
1969	94
1970 or any subsequent year	100

"(5) Late filing. If the declaration is filed after the time prescribed in section 6074(a) (determined without regard to any extension of time for filing the declaration under section 6081), paragraphs (2), (3), and (4) of this paid at the time of such filing all installments subsection shall not apply, and there shall be of estimated tax which would have been payable on or before such time if the declaration had been filed within the time prescribed in section 6074(a), and the remaining installments shall be paid at the times at which, and in the amounts in which, they would have been payable if the declaration had been so filed."

In **1964**, P.L. 88-272, Sec. 122(a), amended Code Sec. 6154, effective for tax. yrs. begin. after 12/31/63.

Prior to amendment, Code Sec. 6154 read as follows:

"(a) Amount of estimated income tax required to be paid.

"The amount of estimated tax (as defined in section 6016(b)) with respect to which a declaration is required under section 6016 shall be paid as follows:

If the taxable year ends	The amount required to be paid shall be the following percentage of the estimated tax:
On or after December 31, 1955 and before December 31, 1956	10
On or after December 31, 1956 and before December 31, 1957	20
On or after December 31, 1957 and before December 31, 1958	30
On or after December 31, 1958 and before December 31, 1959	40
On or after December 31, 1959	50

"(b) Time for payment of installment.

"If the declaration is filed on or before the 15th month of the taxable year, the amount determined under subsection (a) shall be paid in two equal installments. The first installment shall be paid on or before the 15th day of the 9th month of the taxable year, and the second installment shall be paid on or before the 15th day of the 12th month of the taxable year. If the declaration is filed after the 15th day of the 9th month of the taxable year, the amount determined under subsection (a) shall be paid in full on or before the 15th day of the 12th month of the taxable year.

"(c) Amendment of declaration.

"If any amendment of a declaration is filed, installments payable on the 15th day of the 12th month, if any, shall be ratably increased or decreased, as the case may be, to reflect the increase or decrease, as the case may be, in the estimated tax by reason of such amendment.

"(d) Application to short taxable year.

"The application of this section to taxable years of less than 12 months shall be in accordance with regulations prescribed by the Secretary or his delegate.

"(e) Installments paid in advance.

"At the election of the corporation, any installment of the estimated tax may be paid prior to the date prescribed for its payment."

Sec. 6155. Payment on notice and demand.

(a) General rule.

Upon receipt of notice and demand from the Secretary, there shall be paid at the place and time stated in such notice the amount of any tax (including any interest, additional amounts, additions to tax, and assessable penalties) stated in such notice and demand.

(b) Cross references.

(1) For restrictions on assessment and collection of deficiency assessments of taxes subject to the jurisdiction of the Tax Court, see sections 6212 and 6213.

(2) For provisions relating to assessment of claims allowed in a receivership proceeding, see section 6873.

(3) For provisions relating to jeopardy assessments, see subchapter A of chapter 70.

In **1980**, P.L. 96-589, Sec. 6(i)(7), deleted "bankruptcy or" before "receivership proceeding" in para. (b)(2), effective 10/1/79, except for any proceeding under the Bankruptcy Act begun before 10/1/79. Sec. 7(g) of this Act provides:

"(g) Definitions.

"For purposes of this section—

"(1) Bankruptcy case. The term 'bankruptcy case' means any case under title 11 of the United States Code (as recodified by P.L. 95-598).

"(2) Similar judicial proceeding. The term 'similar judicial proceeding' means a receivership, foreclosure, or similar proceeding in a Federal or State court (as modified by section 368(a)(3)(D) of the Internal Revenue Code of 1954)."

In **1976**, P.L. 94-455, Sec. 1906(b)(13)(A), substituted "Secretary" for "Secretary or his delegate" in Code Sec. 6155, effective 2/1/77.

Sec. 6156. Repealed.

In **2004**, P.L. 108-357, Sec. 867(b)(1), repealed Code Sec. 6156, effective for tax. periods begin. after 10/22/2004.

Prior to repeal, Code Sec. 6156 read as follows:

"Sec. 6156. Installment payments of tax on use of highway motor vehicles.

"(a) Privilege to pay tax in installments. If the taxpayer files a return of the tax imposed by section 4481 on or before the date prescribed for the filing of such return, he may elect to pay the tax shown on such return in equal installments in accordance with the following table:

If liability is incurred in—	The number of installments shall be—
July, August, or September	4
October, November, or December	3
January, February, or March	2

"(b) Dates for paying installments. In the case of any tax payable in installments by reason of an election under subsection (a)—

"(1) the first installment shall be paid on the date prescribed for payment of the tax,

"(2) the second installment shall be paid on or before the last day of the third month following the calendar quarter in which the liability was incurred,

"(3) the third installment (if any) shall be paid on or before the last day of the sixth month following the calendar quarter in which the liability was incurred, and

"(4) the fourth installment (if any) shall be paid on or before the last day of the ninth month following the calendar quarter in which the liability was incurred.

"(c) Proration of additional tax to installments. If an election has been made under subsection (a) in respect of tax reported on a return filed by the taxpayer and tax required to be shown but not shown on such return is assessed before the date prescribed for payment of the last installment, the additional tax shall be prorated equally to the installments for which the election was made. That part of the additional tax so prorated to any installment the date for payment of which has not arrived shall be collected at the same time as and as part of such installment. That part of the additional tax so prorated to any installment the date for payment of which has arrived shall be paid upon notice and demand from the Secretary.

"(d) Acceleration of payments. If the taxpayer does not pay any installment under this section on or before the date prescribed for its payment, the whole of the unpaid tax shall be paid upon notice and demand from the Secretary.

"(e) Section inapplicable to certain liabilities. This section shall not apply to any liability for tax incurred in—

"(1) April, May, or June of any year, or

"(2) July, August, or September of 2005."

In **1998**, P.L. 105-178, Sec. 9002(a)(2)(B), substituted "2005" for "1999" in para. (e)(2), effective 6/9/98.

In **1991**, P.L. 102-240, Sec. 8002(c)(2), substituted "1999" for "1995" in para. (e)(2), effective 12/18/91.

In **1990**, P.L. 101-508, Sec. 11211(f)(2), substituted "1995" for "1993" in para. (e)(2), effective 11/5/90.

In **1987**, P.L. 100-17, Sec. 502(d)(2), substituted "1993" for "1988" in para. (e)(2), effective 4/2/87.

In **1983**, P.L. 97-424, Sec. 516(a)(6), substituted "1988" for "1984" in para. (e)(2), effective 1/6/83.

In **1982**, P.L. 97-248, Sec. 280(c)(2)(C), deleted "or 4491" following "section 4481" in subsec. (a)... Sec. 280(c)(2)(D), deleted "in the case of the tax imposed by section 4481" following "September of 1984," in para. (e)(2)... Sec. 280(c)(2)(E), deleted "and civil aircraft" following "highway motor vehicles" in the heading of Code Sec. 6156, effective for transportation begin. after 8/31/82, except for any amount paid on or before 8/31/82.

In **1978**, P.L. 95-599, Sec. 502(a)(9), substituted "1984" for "1979" in para. (e)(2), effective 11/6/78.

In **1976**, P.L. 94-455, Sec. 1906(b)(13)(A), substituted "Secretary" for "Secretary or his delegate" in subsecs. (b) and (c), effective 2/1/77.

—P.L. 94-280, Sec. 303(a)(10), substituted "1979" for "1977" in para. (e)(2), effective 5/5/76.

In **1970**, P.L. 91-605, Sec. 303(a)(10), substituted "1977" for "1972" in para. (e)(2).

—P.L. 91-258, Sec. 206, added "or 4491" after "4481" in subsec. (a), added "in the case of the tax imposed by section 4481" at the end of subsec. (e), added "and civil aircraft" after "highway motor vehicles" in the heading of Code Sec. 6156, effective 7/1/70.

In **1961**, P.L. 87-61, Sec. 203(c), added Code Sec. 6156, and renumbered former Code Sec. 6156 as 6157, effective 7/1/61.

Sec. 6157. Payment of Federal unemployment tax on quarterly or other time period basis.

(a) General rule.

Every person who for the calendar year is an employer (as defined in section 3306(a)) shall—

(1) if the person is such an employer for the preceding calendar year (determined by only taking into account wages paid and employment during such preceding calendar year), compute the tax imposed by section 3301 for each of the first 3 calendar quarters in the calendar year on wages paid for services with respect to which the person is such an employer for such preceding calendar year (as so determined), and

(2) if the person is not such an employer for the preceding calendar year with respect to any services (as so determined), compute the tax imposed by section 3301 on wages paid for services with respect to which the person is not such an employer for the preceding calendar year (as so determined)—

(A) for the period beginning with the first day of the calendar year and ending with the last day of the calendar quarter (excluding the last calendar quarter) in which such person becomes such an employer with respect to such services, and

(B) for the third calendar quarter of such year, if the period specified in subparagraph (A) includes only the first two calendar quarters of the calendar year.

The tax for any calendar quarter or other period shall be computed as provided in subsection (b) and the tax as so computed shall, except as otherwise provided in subsection (c), be paid in such manner and at such time as may be provided in regulations prescribed by the Secretary.

(b) Computation of tax.

The tax for any calendar quarter or other period referred to in paragraph (1) or (2) of subsection (a) shall be computed by multiplying the amount of wages (as defined in section 3306(b)) paid in such calendar quarter or other period by 0.6 percent. In the case of wages paid in any calendar quarter or other period during a calendar year to which paragraph (1) of section 3301 applies, the amount of such wages shall be multiplied by 0.8 percent in lieu of 0.6 percent.

(c) Special rule where accumulated amount does not exceed $100.

Nothing in this section shall require the payment of tax with respect to any calendar quarter or other period if the tax under section 3301 for such period, plus any unpaid amounts for prior periods in the calendar year, does not exceed $100.

In **1989**, P.L. 101-239, Sec. 7841(d)(12), substituted "subsection (c)" for "subsections (c) and (d)" in subsec. (a), effective 12/19/89.

In **1988**, P.L. 100-647, Sec. 7106(c)(1), deleted subsec. (d), effective for remuneration paid after 12/31/88.

Prior to deletion, subsec. (d) read as follows:

"(d) Quarterly payment of railroad unemployment repayment tax.

"(1) In general. Every rail employer shall compute the tax imposed by section 3321 for each calendar quarter in any taxable period in the manner provided in paragraph (3). The tax so computed shall, except as otherwise provided in paragraph (3), be paid in such manner and at such time as may be provided in regulations prescribed by the Secretary.

"(2) Computation of tax. The tax for any calendar quarter shall be computed by multiplying the aggregate amount of rail wages paid in such calendar quarter by the applicable percentage determined under section 3321(c).

"(3) Exceptions. No payment shall be required under this subsection—

"(A) for the last calendar quarter in any taxable period, and

"(B) for any calendar quarter if the tax under section 3321 for such quarter, plus any unpaid amounts for prior calendar quarters in the taxable period, does not exceed $100

"(4) Definitions. For purposes of this subsection, the terms 'taxable period', 'rail employer', and 'rail wages' have the same respective meanings as when used in chapter 23A."

In **1983**, P.L. 98-76, Sec. 231(b)(1), added subsec. (d), effective for remuneration paid after 6/30/86.

In **1982**, P.L. 97-248, Sec. 271(b)(2)(C), substituted "0.8 percent" for "0.7 percent" in subsec. (b), effective for remuneration paid after 12/31/82.

—P.L. 97-248, Sec. 271(c)(3)(C), substituted "0.6 percent" for "0.5 percent" each place it appeared in subsec. (b), effective for remuneration paid after 12/31/84.

In **1976**, P.L. 94-566, Sec. 114(b), amended subsec. (a), effective for remunerations paid after 12/31/77, for services rendered after such date.

Prior to amendment subsec. (a) read as follows:

"(a) General rule.

"Every person who for the calendar year is an employer (as defined in section 3306(a)) shall—

"(1) if the person—

"(A) during any calendar quarter in the preceding calendar year paid wages of $1,500 or more, or

"(B) on each of some 20 days during the preceding calendar year, each day being in a different calendar week, employed at least one individual in employment, compute the tax imposed by section 3301 for each of the first three calendar quarters in the calendar year, and

"(1) if the person in the preceding calendar year employed 4 or more employees in employment (within the meaning of section 3306(c) and (d)) on each of some 20 days during such preceding calendar year, each such day being in a different calendar week, compute the tax imposed by section 3301 for each of the first three calendar quarters in the calendar year, and

"(2) if paragraph (1) does not apply, compute the tax imposed by section 3301—

"(A) for the period beginning with the first day of the calendar year and ending with the last day of the calendar quarter (excluding the last calendar quarter) in which such person becomes such an employer, and

"(B) for the third calendar quarter of such year, if the period specified in subparagraph (A) includes only the first two calendar quarters of the calendar year.

"The tax for any calendar quarter or other period shall be computed as provided in subsection (b) and the tax as so computed shall, except as otherwise provided in subsection (c), be paid in such manner and at such time as may be provided in regulations prescribed by the Secretary."

—P.L. 94-566, Sec. 211(c), amended the last sentence in subsec. (b), effective 10/20/76.

Prior to amendment, the last sentence in subsec. (b) read as follows:

"In the case of wages paid in any calendar quarter or other period during 1973, the amount of such wages shall be multiplied by 0.58 percent in lieu of 0.5 percent."

—P.L. 94-455, Sec. 1906(a)(11), substituted "subsection (c)" for "subsections (c) and (d)" in subsec. (a), deleted subsec. (c), and redesignated subsec. (d) as subsec. (c), effective 2/1/77.

Prior to amendment, subsec. (c) read as follows:

"(c) *Special rule for calendar years 1970 and 1971.*

"For purposes of subsection (a) the tax computed as provided in subsection (b) for any calendar quarter or other period shall be reduced (1) by 66⅔ percent if such quarter or period is in 1970, and (2) by 33⅓ percent if such quarter or period is in 1971."

—P.L. 94-455, Sec. 1906(b)(13)(A), substituted "Secretary" for "Secretary or his delegate" in subsec. (a), effective 2/1/77.

In 1972, P.L. 92-329, Sec. 2(b), 6/30/72, added a new sentence to the end of subsec. (b).

In 1970, P.L. 91-373, Sec. 101(b)(1), amended para. (a)(1), effective for calendar years begin. after 12/31/71.

Prior to amendment, para. (a)(1) read as follows:

"(1) if the person in the preceding calendar year employed 4 or more employees in employment (within the meaning of section 3306(c) and (d)) on each of some 20 days during such preceding calendar year, each such day being in a different calendar week, compute the tax imposed by section 3301 for each of the first three calendar quarters in the calendar year, and"

—P.L. 91-373, Sec. 101(b)(2), substituted "0.5 percent" for "the number of percentage points (including fractional points) by which the rate of tax specified in section 3301 exceeds 2.7 percent," in subsec. (b), effective for calendar years beginning after 12/31/69.

—P.L. 91-373, Sec. 301(b), provides that in computing tax as required by subsec. (a)(1) & (2), the percentage contained in subsec. (b) applicable for wages paid in any calendar quarter in 1970 ending before 8/10/70 shall be treated as being 0.4 percent.

In 1969, P.L. 91-53, Sec. 2(a), amended Code Sec. 6157, effective for calendar years beginning after 12/31/69.

Prior to amendment it read as follows:

"SEC. 6157. PAYMENT OF TAXES UNDER PROVISIONS OF THE TARIFF ACT.

"For collection under the provisions of the Tariff Act of 1930 of the taxes imposed by section 4501(b), and subchapters A, B, C, D, and E of chapter 38, see sections 4504 and 4601, respectively."

In 1961, P.L. 87-61, Sec. 203(c)(1), redesignated Code Sec. 6156 as Code Sec. 6157.

Sec. 6158. Repealed.

In 1990, P.L. 101-508, Sec. 11801(a)(44), repealed Code Sec. 6158, effective 11/5/90, except as provided in Sec. 11821(b) of this Act, which reads as follows:

"(b) *Savings provision.*

"If—

"(1) any provision amended or repealed by this part applied to—

"(A) any transaction occurring before the date of the enactment of this Act [11/5/90],

"(B) any property acquired before such date of enactment [11/5/90], or

"(C) any item of income, loss, deduction, or credit taken into account before such date of enactment [11/5/90], and

"(2) the treatment of such transaction, property, or item under such provision would (without regard to the amendments made by this part) affect liability for tax for periods ending after such date of enactment [11/5/90],

nothing in the amendments made by this part shall be construed to affect the treatment of such transaction, property, or item for purposes of determining liability for tax for periods ending after such date of enactment [11/5/90]."

Prior to repeal, Code Sec. 6158 read as follows:

"SEC. 6158. INSTALLMENT PAYMENT OF TAX ATTRIBUTABLE TO DIVESTITURES PURSUANT TO BANK HOLDING COMPANY ACT AMENDMENTS OF 1970.

"(a) *Election of extension.*

"If, after July 7, 1970, a qualified bank holding corporation sells bank property or prohibited property, the divestiture of either of which the Board certifies, before such sale, is necessary or appropriate to effectuate section 4 or the policies of the Bank Holding Company Act, the tax under chapter 1 attributable to such sale shall, at the election of the taxpayer, be payable in equal annual installments beginning with the due date (determined without extension) for the taxpayer's return of tax under chapter 1 for the taxable year in which the sale occurred and ending with the corresponding date in 1985. If the number of installments determined under the preceding sentence is less than 10, such number shall be increased to 10 equal annual installments which begin as provided in the preceding sentence and which end on the corresponding date 10 years later. An election under this subsection shall be made at such time and in such manner as the Secretary or his delegate may by regulations prescribe.

"(b) *Limitations.*

"(1) Treatment not available to taxpayer for both bank property and prohibited property. This section shall not apply to any sale of prohibited property if the taxpayer (or a corporation having control of the taxpayer or a subsidiary of the taxpayer) has made an election under subsection (a) with respect to bank property or has made any distribution pursuant to section 1101(b). This section shall not apply to bank property if the taxpayer (or a corporation having control of the taxpayer or a subsidiary of the taxpayer) has made an election under subsection (a) with respect to prohibited property or has made any distribution pursuant to section 1101(a).

"(2) Treatment not available for certain installment sales. No election may be made under subsection (a) with respect to a sale if the income from such sale is being returned at the time and in the manner provided in section 453 (relating to installment method).

"(c) *Acceleration of payments.*

"If an election is made under subsection (a) and before the tax attributable to such sale is paid in full—

"(1) any installment under this section is not paid on or before the date fixed by this section for its payment, or

"(2) the Board fails to make a certification similar to the applicable certification provided in section 1101(e) within the time prescribed therein (for this purpose treating the last such sale as constituting the last distribution),

then the extension of time for payment of tax provided in this section shall cease to apply, and any portion of the tax payable in installments shall be paid on notice and demand from the Secretary or his delegate.

"(d) *Proration of deficiency to installments.*

"If an election is made under subsection (a) and a deficiency attributable to the sale has been assessed, the deficiency shall be prorated to such installments. The part of the deficiency so prorated to any installment the date for payment of which has not arrived shall be collected at the same time as, and as part of, such installment. The part of the deficiency so prorated to any installment the date for payment of which has arrived shall be paid on notice and demand from the Secretary or his delegate. This subsection shall not apply if the deficiency is due to negligence, to intentional disregard of rules and regulations, or to fraud with intent to evade tax.

"(e) *Bond may be required.*

"If an election is made under this section, section 6165 shall apply as though the Secretary were extending the time for payment of the tax.

"(f) *Definitions.*

"For purposes of this section—

"(1) Terms have meanings given to them by section 1103. The terms 'qualified bank holding corporation', 'Bank Holding Company Act', 'Board'; 'control', and 'subsidiary' have the respective meanings given to such terms by section 1103.

"(2) Prohibited property. The term 'prohibited property' means property held by a qualified bank holding corporation which could be distributed without recognition of gain under section 1101(a)(1).

"(3) Bank property. The term 'bank property' means property held by a qualified bank holding corporation which could be distributed without recognition of gain under section 1101(b)(1).

"(g) *Cross references.*

"(1) Security. For authority of the Secretary or his delegate to require security in the case of an extension under this section, see section 6165.

"(2) Period of limitation. For extension of the period of limitation in the case of an extension under this section, see section 6503(i)."

In 1976, P.L. 94-452, Sec. 3(a), added Code Sec. 6158. Sec. 3(d) of the Act provided information with respect to the applicability to certain successor corporations (see the note for Code Sec. 1103). Sec. 3(e) provided the following effective date:

"(1) In general.—The amendments made by this section shall take effect on October 1, 1977, with respect to sales after July 7, 1970, in taxable years ending after July 7, 1970, but only in the case of qualified bank holding corporations (within the meaning of section 1103(b) of the Internal Revenue Code of 1954, as amended by section 2(a) of this Act).

"(2) Special rule for certifying sales which have already taken place.—For purposes of section 6158(a) of the Internal Revenue Code of 1954 (as added by subsection (a) of this section) in the case of any sale which takes place on or before the 90th day after the date of the enactment of this Act, a certification by the Federal Reserve Board described in section 6158(a) shall be treated as made before the sale if application for such certification is made before the close of the 90th day after the date of the enactment of this Act.

"(3) Refund of tax.—

"(A) In general.—If any tax attributable to a sale which occurred before October 1, 1977, is payable in annual installments by reason of an election under section 6158(a) of the Internal Revenue Code of 1954, any portion of such tax for which the due date of the installment does not occur before October 1, 1977, shall, on application of the taxpayer, be treated as an overpayment of tax.

"(B) Interest on overpayments.—For purposes of section 6611(b), in the case of any overpayment attributable to subparagraph (A), the date of the overpayment shall be the day which is 6 months after the latest of the following:

"(i) the date on which application for refund or credit of such overpayment is filed,

Payment of tax   Code Sec. 6159

"(ii) the due date prescribed by law (determined without extensions) for filing the return of tax under chapter 1 of the Internal Revenue Code of 1954 for the taxable year the tax of which is being refunded or credited, or

"(iii) the date of the enactment of this Act.

"(C) Extension of period of limitations.— If any refund or credit of tax attributable to the application of subparagraph (A) is prevented at any time before October 1, 1978, by the operation of any law or rule of law, refund or credit of such overpayment may, nevertheless, be made or allowed if claim therefor is filed before October 1, 1978."

Sec. 6159. Agreements for payment of tax liability in installments.

(a) Authorization of agreements.

The Secretary is authorized to enter into written agreements with any taxpayer under which such taxpayer is allowed to make payment on any tax in installment payments if the Secretary determines that such agreement will facilitate full or partial collection of such liability.

(b) Extent to which agreements remain in effect.

(1) In general. Except as otherwise provided in this subsection, any agreement entered into by the Secretary under subsection (a) shall remain in effect for the term of the agreement.

(2) Inadequate information or jeopardy. The Secretary may terminate any agreement entered into by the Secretary under subsection (a) if—

(A) information which the taxpayer provided to the Secretary prior to the date such agreement was entered into was inaccurate or incomplete, or

(B) the Secretary believes that collection of any tax to which an agreement under this section relates is in jeopardy.

(3) Subsequent change in financial conditions. If the Secretary makes a determination that the financial condition of a taxpayer with whom the Secretary has entered into an agreement under subsection (a) has significantly changed, the Secretary may alter, modify, or terminate such agreement.

(4) Failure to pay an installment or any other tax liability when due or to provide requested financial information. The Secretary may alter, modify, or terminate an agreement entered into by the Secretary under subsection (a) in the case of the failure of the taxpayer—

(A) to pay any installment at the time such installment payment is due under such agreement,

(B) to pay any other tax liability at the time such liability is due, or

(C) to provide a financial condition update as requested by the Secretary.

(5) Notice requirements. The Secretary may not take any action under paragraph (2), (3), or (4) unless—

(A) a notice of such action is provided to the taxpayer not later than the day 30 days before the date of such action, and

(B) such notice includes an explanation why the Secretary intends to take such action.

The preceding sentence shall not apply in any case in which the Secretary believes that collection of any tax to which an agreement under this section relates is in jeopardy.

(c) Secretary required to enter into installment agreements in certain cases.

In the case of a liability for tax of an individual under subtitle A, the Secretary shall enter into an agreement to accept the full payment of such tax in installments if, as of the date the individual offers to enter into the agreement—

(1) the aggregate amount of such liability (determined without regard to interest, penalties, additions to the tax, and additional amounts) does not exceed $10,000;

(2) the taxpayer (and, if such liability relates to a joint return, the taxpayer's spouse) has not, during any of the preceding 5 taxable years—

(A) failed to file any return of tax imposed by subtitle A;

(B) failed to pay any tax required to be shown on any such return; or

(C) entered into an installment agreement under this section for payment of any tax imposed by subtitle A,

(3) the Secretary determines that the taxpayer is financially unable to pay such liability in full when due (and the taxpayer submits such information as the Secretary may require to make such determination);

(4) the agreement requires full payment of such liability within 3 years; and

(5) the taxpayer agrees to comply with the provisions of this title for the period such agreement is in effect.

(d) Secretary required to review installment agreements for partial collection every two years.

In the case of an agreement entered into by the Secretary under subsection (a) for partial collection of a tax liability, the Secretary shall review the agreement at least once every 2 years.

(e) Administrative review.

The Secretary shall establish procedures for an independent administrative review of terminations of installment agreements under this section for taxpayers who request such a review.

(f) Cross reference.

For rights to administrative review and appeal, see section 7122(e).

In 2006, P.L. 109-222, Sec. 509(c), substituted "section 7122(e)" for "section 7122(d)" in subsec. (f), effective for offers-in-compromise submitted on and after the date which is 60 days after 5/17/2006.

In 2004, P.L. 108-357, Sec. 843(a)(1)(A), substituted "make payment on" for "satisfy liability for payment of" in subsec. (a) . . . Sec. 843(a)(1)(B), added "full or partial" after "facilitate" in subsec. (a) . . . Sec. 843(a)(2), added "full" before "payment" in matter before para. (c)(1) of subsec. (c) . . . Sec. 843(b), redesignated subsecs. (d) and (e) as subsecs. (e) and (f) and added subsec. (d), effective for agreements entered into on or after 10/22/2004.

In 2000, P.L. 106-554, Sec. 1(a)(7), [which enacted into law Sec. 302(a) of P.L. 106-554] substituted "September 1, 2001" for "July 1, 2000" in Sec. 3506 of P.L. 105-206, see below.

In 1998, P.L. 105-277, Sec. 4002(g), redesignated subsec. (d) [sic (e)] as (e), effective 7/22/98.

—P.L. 105-206, Sec. 3462(c)(2), added subsec. (d) [sic (e)], effective for proposed offers-in-compromise and installment agreements submitted after 7/22/98.

—P.L. 105-206, Sec. 3467(a), redesignated subsec. (c) as subsec. (d), and added new subsec. (c), effective 7/22/98.

—P.L. 105-206, Sec. 3506, of this Act, provides:

"SEC. 3506. STATEMENTS REGARDING INSTALLMENT AGREEMENTS.

"The Secretary of the Treasury or the Secretary's delegate shall, beginning not later than September 1, 2001, provide each taxpayer who has an installment agreement in effect under section 6159 of the Internal Revenue Code of 1986 an annual statement setting forth the initial balance at the beginning of the year, the payments made during the year, and the remaining balance as of the end of the year."

In 1996, P.L. 104-168, Sec. 201(a), added para. (b)(5) . . . Sec. 201(b), amended para. (b)(3), effective on the date 6 months after 7/30/96.

Prior to amendment, para. (b)(3) read as follows:

"(3) Subsequent change in financial conditions.

"(A) In general. If the Secretary makes a determination that the financial condition of a taxpayer with whom the Secretary has entered into an agreement under subsection (a) has significantly changed, the Secretary may alter, modify, or terminate such agreement.

"(B) Notice. Action may be taken by the Secretary under subparagraph (A) only if—

"(i) notice of such determination is provided to the taxpayer no later than 30 days prior to the date of such action, and

"(ii) such notice includes the reasons why the Secretary believes a significant change in the financial condition of the taxpayer has occurred."

—P.L. 104-168, Sec. 202(a), added subsec. (c), effective 1/1/97.

In 1988, P.L. 100-647, Sec. 6234(a), added Code Sec. 6159, effective for agreements entered into after 11/10/88.

Subchapter B — Payment of tax

Subchapter B.—Extensions of Time for Payment

Sec.
6161. Extension of time for paying tax.
6163. Extension of time for payment of estate tax on value of reversionary or remainder interest in property.
6164. Extension of time for payment of taxes by corporations expecting carrybacks.
6165. Bonds where time to pay tax or deficiency has been extended.
6166. Extension of time for payment of estate tax where estate consists largely of interest in closely held business.
6167. Extension of time for payment of tax attributable to recovery of foreign expropriation losses.

In **1981**, P.L. 97-34, Sec. 422(e)(5)(C), deleted items 6166 and 6166A and added new item 6166.
Prior to deletion, items 6166 and 6166A read as follows:
"6166. Alternate extension of time for payment of estate tax where estate consists largely of interest in closely held business.
"6166A. Extension of time for payment of estate tax where estate consists largely of interest in closely held business."
In **1976**, P.L. 94-455, Sec. 1906(b)(4), deleted the item for Code Sec. 6162, effective 2/1/77.
—P.L. 94-455, Sec. 2004(f)(5), redesignated the item for Code Sec. 6166 as the item for Code Sec. 6166A . . . added a new item for Code Sec. 6166.
In **1966**, added item 6167.
In **1958**, added item 6166.

Sec. 6161. Extension of time for paying tax.
(a) Amount determined by taxpayer on return.

(1) **General rule.** The Secretary, except as otherwise provided in this title, may extend the time for payment of the amount of the tax shown or required to be shown, on any return or declaration required under authority of this title (or any installment thereof), for a reasonable period not to exceed 6 months (12 months in the case of estate tax) from the date fixed for payment thereof. Such extension may exceed 6 months in the case of a taxpayer who is abroad.

(2) **Estate tax.** The Secretary may, for reasonable cause, extend the time for payment of—

(A) any part of the amount determined by the executor as the tax imposed by chapter 11, or

(B) any part of any installment under section 6166 (including any part of a deficiency prorated to any installment under such section),

for a reasonable period not in excess of 10 years from the date prescribed by section 6151(a) for payment of the tax (or, in the case of an amount referred to in subparagraph (B), if later, not beyond the date which is 12 months after the due date for the last installment).

(b) Amount determined as deficiency.

(1) **Income, gift, and certain other taxes.** Under regulations prescribed by the Secretary, the Secretary may extend the time for the payment of the amount determined as a deficiency of a tax imposed by chapter 1, 12, 41, 42, 43, or 44 for a period not to exceed 18 months from the date fixed for the payment of the deficiency, and in exceptional cases, for a further period not to exceed 12 months. An extension under this paragraph may be granted only where it is shown to the satisfaction of the Secretary that payment of a deficiency upon the date fixed for the payment thereof will result in undue hardship to the taxpayer in the case of a tax imposed by chapter 1, 41, 42, 43, or 44, or to the donor in the case of a tax imposed by chapter 12.

(2) **Estate tax.** Under regulations prescribed by the Secretary, the Secretary may, for reasonable cause, extend the time for the payment of any deficiency of a tax imposed by chapter 11 for a reasonable period not to exceed 4 years from the date otherwise fixed for the payment of the deficiency.

(3) **No extension for certain deficiencies.** No extension shall be granted under this subsection for any deficiency if the deficiency is due to negligence, to intentional disregard of rules and regulations, or to fraud with intent to evade tax.

(c) Claims in cases under title 11 of the United States Code or in receivership proceedings.

Extensions of time for payment of any portion of a claim for tax under chapter 1 or chapter 12, allowed in cases under title 11 of the United States Code or in receivership proceedings, which is unpaid, may be had in the same manner and subject to the same provisions and limitations as provided in subsection (b) in respect of a deficiency in such tax.

(d) Cross references.

(1) **Period of limitation.** For extension of the period of limitation in case of an extension under subsection (a)(2) or subsection (b)(2), see section 6503(d).

(2) **Security.** For authority of the Secretary to require security in case of an extension under subsection (a)(2) or subsection (b), see section 6165.

(3) **Postponement of certain acts.** For time for performing certain acts postponed by reason of war, see section 7508, and by reason of Presidentially declared disaster or terroristic or military action, see section 7508A.

In **2002**, P.L. 107-134, Sec. 112(d)(3), added para. (d)(3), effective for disasters and terroristic or military actions occurring on or after 9/11/2001, with respect to any action of the Secretary of the Treasury, the Secretary of Labor, or the Pension Benefit Guaranty Corporation occurring on or after 1/23/2002.
In **1988**, P.L. 100-418, Sec. 1941(b)(2)(B)(viii), substituted "or 44" for "44, or 45" each place it appeared in para. (b)(1), effective for crude oil removed from the premises on or after 8/23/88.
In **1981**, P.L. 97-34, Sec. 422(e)(1), deleted "or 6166A" after "section 6166" in subpara. (a)(2)(B), effective for estates of decedents dying after 12/31/81.
In **1980**, P.L. 96-589, Sec. 6(i)(8), substituted "in cases under title 11 of the United States Code or in receivership proceedings" for "in bankruptcy or receivership proceedings" in subsec. (c) and substituted "cases under title 11 of the United States Code or in receivership proceedings" for "bankruptcy or receivership proceedings" in the heading of subsec. (c), effective 10/1/79, except for any proceedings under the Bankruptcy Act begun before 10/1/79. Sec. 7(g) of this Act provides:
"(g) Definitions.
"For purposes of this section—
"(1) Bankruptcy case. The term 'bankruptcy case' means any case under title 11 of the United States Code (as recodified by P.L. 95-598).
"(2) Similar judicial proceeding. The term 'similar judicial proceeding' means a receivership, foreclosure, or similar proceeding in a Federal or State court (as modified by section 368(a)(3)(D) of the Internal Revenue Code of 1954)."
—P.L. 96-223, Sec. 101(f)(1)(H), substituted "44, or 45" for "or 44" each place it appeared in para. (b)(1), effective for periods after 2/29/80.
In **1976**, P.L. 94-455, Sec. 1906(b)(13)(A), substituted "Secretary" for "Secretary or his delegate" each place it appeared in Code Sec. 6161, effective 2/1/77.
—P.L. 94-455, Sec. 2004(c)(1), amended para. (a)(2), effective for estates of decedents dying after 12/31/76.
Prior to amendment, para. (a)(2), read as follows:
"(2) Estate tax. If the Secretary or his delegate finds—
"(A) that the payment, on the due date, of any part of the amount determined by the executor as the tax imposed by chapter 11, or
"(B) that the payment, on the date fixed for the payment of any installment under section 6166, of any part of such installment (including any part of a deficiency prorated to an installment the date for payment of which had not arrived), or
"(C) that the payment upon notice and demand of any part of a deficiency prorated under the provisions of section 6166 to installments the date for payment of which had arrived,
would result in undue hardship to the estate, he may extend the time for payment for a reasonable period not in excess of 10 years from the date prescribed by section 6151(a) for payment of the tax."
—P.L. 94-455, Sec. 2004(c)(2), amended subsec. (b), effective for estates of decedents dying after '76. Sec. 1307(d)(2)(C) made amendments to subsec. (b) with respect to chapters 41 and 44, prior to amendment by this section, for tax. yrs. begin. after '76. Sec. 1605(b)(3) of the Act, made amendments with respect to chapters 41 and 44, prior to amendment by this section, for tax. yrs. of real estate investment trusts begin. after 10/4/76.

Payment of tax Code Sec. 6164(c)

Prior to the amendment, subsec. (b) read as follows:
"(b) Amount determined as deficiency.

"Under regulations prescribed by the Secretary or his delegate, the Secretary or his delegate may extend, to the extent provided below, the time for payment of the amount determined as a deficiency:

"(1) In the case of a tax imposed by chapter 1, 12, 42 or 43, for a period not to exceed 18 months from the date fixed for payment of the deficiency, and, in exceptional cases, for a further period not to exceed 12 months;

"(2) In the case of a tax imposed by chapter 11, for a period not to exceed 4 years from the date otherwise fixed for payment of the deficiency.

An extension under this subsection may be granted only where it is shown to the satisfaction of the Secretary or his delegate that the payment of a deficiency upon the date fixed for the payment thereof will result in undue hardship to the taxpayer in the case of a tax imposed by chapter 1, 42, or chapter 43, to the estate in the case of a tax imposed by chapter 11, or to the donor in the case of a tax imposed by chapter 12. No extension shall be granted if the deficiency is due to negligence, to intentional disregard of rules and regulations, or to fraud with intent to evade tax."

In 1974, P.L. 93-406, Sec. 1016(a)(7), substituted "42 or 43" for "or 42" in para. (b)(1), and substituted ", 42, or chapter 43" for "or 42" in the second sentence of subsec. (b), effective 9/2/74 or other date as specified in Sec. 1017 of the Act (reproduced following Code Sec. 401).

In 1970, P.L. 91-614, Sec. 101(h), added "(12 months in the case of estate tax)" to the first sentence of para. (a)(1), effective for decedents dying after 12/31/70.

In 1969, P.L. 91-172, Sec. 101(j)(37), substituted "chapter 1, 12, or 42," for "chapter 1 or 12," in para. (b)(1) and substituted "chapter 1 or 42" for "chapter 1" the last place it appeared in subsec. (b), effective 1/1/70.

In 1958, P.L. 85-866, Sec. 206, amended para. (a)(2), effective for "estates of decedents with respect to which the date for the filing of the estate tax return (including extensions thereof) prescribed by section 6075(a) of the Internal Revenue Code of 1954 is after the date of the enactment of this Act [9/2/58]; except that (1) section 6166(i) of such Code as added by this section shall apply to estates of decedents dying after August 16, 1954, but only if the date for the filing of the estate tax return (including extensions thereof) expired on or before the date of the enactment of this Act and (2) notwithstanding section 6166(a) of such Code, if an election under such section is required to be made before the sixtieth day after the date of the enactment of this Act such an election shall be considered timely if made on or before such sixtieth day."

Prior to amendment, para. (a)(2) read as follows:

"(2) Estate tax.—If the Secretary or his delegate finds that the payment on the due date of any part of the amount determined by the executor as the tax imposed by chapter 11 would result in undue hardship to the estate, he may extend the time for payment for a reasonable period not in excess of 10 years from the date fixed for payment of the tax."

Sec. 6163. Extension of time for payment of estate tax on value of reversionary or remainder interest in property.

(a) Extension permitted.

If the value of a reversionary or remainder interest in property is included under chapter 11 in the value of the gross estate, the payment of the part of the tax under chapter 11 attributable to such interest may, at the election of the executor, be postponed until 6 months after the termination of the precedent interest or interests in the property, under such regulations as the Secretary may prescribe.

(b) Extension for reasonable cause.

At the expiration of the period of postponement provided for in subsection (a), the Secretary may, for reasonable cause, extend the time for payment for a reasonable period or periods not in excess of 3 years from the expiration of the period of postponement provided in subsection (a).

(c) Cross reference.

For authority of the Secretary to require security in the case of an extension under this section, see section 6165.

In 1976, P.L. 94-455, Sec. 1906(b)(13)(A), substituted "Secretary" for "Secretary or his delegate" each place it appeared in Code Sec. 6163, effective 2/1/77.

—P.L. 94-455, Sec. 2004(c)(3), amended subsec. (b), effective for estates of decedents dying after 12/31/76.

Prior to amendment, subsec. (b) read as follows:

"(b) Extension to prevent undue hardship.

"If the Secretary or his delegate finds that the payment of the tax at the expiration of the period of postponement provided for in subsection (a) would result in undue hardship to the estate, he may extend the time for payment for a reasonable period or periods of time not in excess of 3 years from the expiration of such period of postponement."

In 1975, P.L. 93-625, Sec. 7(d)(1), amended subsec. (c), effective for amounts outstanding on 7/1/75 or arising thereafter.

Prior to amendment, subsec. (c) read as follows:

"(c) Cross references.

"(1) Interest. For provisions requiring the payment of interest for the period of such extension, see section 6601(b).

"(2) Security. For authority of the Secretary or his delegate to require security in the case of such extension, see section 6165."

In 1964, P.L. 88-272, Sec. 240(a), substituted "or periods not in excess of 3" for "not in excess of 2" in subsec. (b), effective in the case of any reversionary or remainder interest only if the time for payment of the tax under chapter 11 of the Internal Revenue Code of 1954 attributable to such interest, including any extensions thereof, has not expired on the date of the enactment of this Act [2/26/64]."

In 1958, P.L. 85-866, Sec. 66(b)(1), added subsec. (b) and redesignated former subsec. (b) as (c), effective in the case of any reversionary or remainder interest only if the precedent interest or interests in the property did not terminate before the beginning of the 6-month period which ends on the date of the enactment of this Act [9/2/58]."

Sec. 6164. Extension of time for payment of taxes by corporations expecting carrybacks.

(a) In general.

If a corporation, in any taxable year, files with the Secretary a statement, as provided in subsection (b), with respect to an expected net operating loss carryback from such taxable year, the time for payment of all or part of any tax imposed by subtitle A for the taxable year immediately preceding such taxable year shall be extended, to the extent and subject to the conditions and limitations hereinafter provided in this section.

(b) Contents of statement.

The statement shall be filed at such time and in such manner and form as the Secretary may by regulations prescribe. Such statement shall set forth that the corporation expects to have a net operating loss carryback, as provided in section 172(b), from the taxable year in which such statement is made, and shall set forth, in such detail and with such supporting data and explanation as such regulations shall require—

(1) the estimated amount of the expected net operating loss;

(2) the reasons, facts, and circumstances which cause the corporation to expect such net operating loss;

(3) the amount of the reduction of the tax previously determined attributable to the expected carryback, such tax previously determined being ascertained in accordance with the method prescribed in section 1314(a); and such reduction being determined by applying the expected carryback in the manner provided by law to the items on the basis of which such tax was determined;

(4) the tax and the part thereof the time for payment of which is to be extended; and

(5) such other information for purposes of carrying out the provisions of this section as may be required by such regulations.

The Secretary shall, upon request, furnish a receipt for any statement filed, which shall set forth the date of such filing.

(c) Amount to which extension relates and installment payments.

The amount the time for payment of which may be extended under subsection (a) with respect to any tax shall not exceed the amount of such tax shown on the return, increased by any amount assessed as a deficiency (or as interest or addition to the tax) prior to the date of filing the statement and decreased by any amount paid or required to be paid prior to the date of such filing, and the total amount of the tax the time for payment of which may be extended shall not exceed the amount stated under subsection (b)(3). For purposes of this subsection, an amount shall not be considered as required to be paid unless shown on the return or assessed as a deficiency (or as interest or addition to the tax), and an amount assessed as a deficiency (or as interest or addition to the tax) shall be considered to be required to be paid prior to the date of filing of the statement if the 10th

3,617

day after notice and demand for its payment occurs prior to such date. If an extension of time under this section relates to only a part of the tax, the time for payment of the remainder shall be the date on which payment would have been required if such remainder had been the tax.

(d) Period of extension.

The extension of time for payment provided in this section shall expire—

(1) on the last day of the month in which falls the last date prescribed by law (including any extension of time granted the taxpayer) for the filing of the return for the taxable year of the expected net operating loss, or

(2) if an application for tentative carryback adjustment provided in section 6411 with respect to such loss is filed before the expiration of the period prescribed in paragraph (1), on the date on which notice is mailed by certified mail or registered mail by the Secretary to the taxpayer that such application is allowed or disallowed in whole or in part.

(e) Revised statements.

Each statement filed under subsection (a) with respect to any taxable year shall be in lieu of the last statement previously filed with respect to such year. If the amount the time for payment of which is extended under a statement filed is less than the amount under the last statement previously filed, the extension of time shall be terminated as to the difference between the two amounts.

(f) Termination.

The Secretary is not required to make any examination of the statement, but he may make such examination thereof as he deems necessary and practicable. The Secretary shall terminate the extension as to any part of the amount to which it relates which he deems should be terminated because, upon such examination, he believes that, as of the time such examination is made, all or any part of the statement clearly is in a material respect erroneous or unreasonable.

(g) Payments on termination.

If an extension of time is terminated under subsection (e) or (f) with respect to any amount, then—

(1) no further extension of time shall be made under this section with respect to such amount, and

(2) the time for payment of such amount shall be considered to be the date on which payment would have been required if there had been no extension with respect to such amount.

(h) Jeopardy.

If the Secretary believes that collection of the amount to which an extension under this section relates is in jeopardy, he shall immediately terminate such extension, and notice and demand shall be made by him for payment of such amount.

(i) Consolidated returns.

If the corporation seeking an extension of time under this section made or was required to make a consolidated return, either for the taxable year within which the net operating loss arises or for the preceding taxable year affected by such loss, the provisions of such section shall apply only to such extent and subject to such conditions, limitations, and exceptions as the Secretary may by regulations prescribe.

In 1982, P.L. 97-248, Sec. 234(b)(2)(C)(i), amended the last sentence of subsec. (c) . . . Sec. 234(b)(2)(C)(ii), amended para. (g)(2), effective for tax. yrs. begin. after 12/31/82.

Prior to amendment, the last sentence of subsec. (c) read as follows:
"If an extension of time under this section relates to only a part of the tax, the time for payment of the remainder shall be considered to be the dates on which payments would have been required if such remainder had been the tax and the taxpayer had elected to pay the tax in installments as provided in section 6152."

Prior to amendment, para. (g)(2) read as follows:
"(2) the time for payment for such amount shall be considered to be the dates on which payments would have been required if there had been no extension with respect to such amount and the taxpayer had elected to pay the tax in installments as provided in section 6152."

In 1976, P.L. 94-455, Sec. 1906(b)(13)(A), substituted "Secretary" for "Secretary or his delegate" each place it appeared in Code Sec. 6164, effective 2/1/77.

In 1958, P.L. 85-866, Sec. 89(b), added "certified mail or" before "registered mail" in para. (d)(2), effective for mailing after 9/2/58.

Sec. 6165. Bonds where time to pay tax or deficiency has been extended.

In the event the Secretary grants any extension of time within which to pay any tax or any deficiency therein, the Secretary may require the taxpayer to furnish a bond in such amount (not exceeding double the amount with respect to which the extension is granted) conditioned upon the payment of the amount extended in accordance with the terms of such extension.

In 1976, P.L. 94-455, Sec. 1906(b)(13)(A), substituted "Secretary" for "Secretary or his delegate" in Code Sec. 6165, effective 2/1/77.

Sec. 6166. Extension of time for payment of estate tax where estate consists largely of interest in closely held business.

(a) 5-year deferral; 10-year installment payment.

(1) **In general.** If the value of an interest in a closely held business which is included in determining the gross estate of a decedent who was (at the date of his death) a citizen or resident of the United States exceeds 35 percent of the adjusted gross estate, the executor may elect to pay part or all of the tax imposed by section 2001 in 2 or more (but not exceeding 10) equal installments.

(2) **Limitation.** The maximum amount of tax which may be paid in installments under this subsection shall be an amount which bears the same ratio to the tax imposed by section 2001 (reduced by the credits against such tax) as—

(A) the closely held business amount, bears to

(B) the amount of the adjusted gross estate.

(3) **Date for payment of installments.** If an election is made under paragraph (1), the first installment shall be paid on or before the date selected by the executor which is not more than 5 years after the date prescribed by section 6151(a) for payment of the tax, and each succeeding installment shall be paid on or before the date which is 1 year after the date prescribed by this paragraph for payment of the preceding installment.

(b) Definitions and special rules.

(1) **Interest in closely held business.** For purposes of this section, the term "interest in a closely held business" means—

(A) an interest as a proprietor in a trade or business carried on as a proprietorship;

(B) an interest as a partner in a partnership carrying on a trade or business, if—

(i) 20 percent or more of the total capital interest in such partnership is included in determining the gross estate of the decedent, or

• **Caution:** Code Sec. 6166(b)(1)(B)(ii), following, was amended by Sec. 571(a), P.L. 107-16, the Economic Growth and Tax Relief Reconciliation Act of 2001 (EGTRRA). These provisions generally sunset for tax years beginning after 12/31/2012. For specific sunset provisions, see Sec. 901, P.L. 107-16 (as

Payment of tax   Code Sec. 6166(b)(8)(B)(i)

amended) reproduced in history notes for this Code Sec.

(ii) such partnership had 45 or fewer partners; or (C) stock in a corporation carrying on a trade or business if—

(i) 20 percent or more in value of the voting stock of such corporation is included in determining the gross estate of the decedent, or

> • **Caution:** Code Sec. 6166(b)(1)(C)(ii), following, was amended by Sec. 571(a), P.L. 107-16, the Economic Growth and Tax Relief Reconciliation Act of 2001 (EGTRRA). These provisions generally sunset for tax years beginning after 12/31/2012. For specific sunset provisions see Sec. 901, P.L. 107-16 (as amended) reproduced in history notes for this Code Sec.

(ii) such corporation had 45 or fewer shareholders.

(2) Rules for applying paragraph (1). For purposes of paragraph (1)—

(A) Time for testing. Determinations shall be made as of the time immediately before the decedent's death.

(B) Certain interests held by husband and wife. Stock or a partnership interest which—

(i) is community property of a husband and wife (or the income from which is community income) under the applicable community property law of a State, or

(ii) is held by a husband and wife as joint tenants, tenants by the entirety, or tenants in common,

shall be treated as owned by one shareholder or one partner, as the case may be.

(C) Indirect ownership. Property owned, directly or indirectly, by or for a corporation, partnership, estate, or trust shall be considered as being owned proportionately by or for its shareholders, partners, or beneficiaries. For purposes of the preceding sentence, a person shall be treated as a beneficiary of any trust only if such person has a present interest in the trust.

(D) Certain interests held by members of decedent's family. All stock and all partnership interests held by the decedent or by any member of his family (within the meaning of section 267(c)(4)) shall be treated as owned by the decedent.

(3) Farmhouses and certain other structures taken into account. For purposes of the 35-percent requirement of subsection (a)(1), an interest in a closely held business which is the business of farming includes an interest in residential buildings and related improvements on the farm which are occupied on a regular basis by the owner or lessee of the farm or by persons employed by such owner or lessee for purposes of operating or maintaining the farm.

(4) Value. For purposes of this section, value shall be value determined for purposes of chapter 11 (relating to estate tax).

(5) Closely held business amount. For purposes of this section, the term "closely held business amount" means the value of the interest in a closely held business which qualifies under subsection (a)(1).

(6) Adjusted gross estate. For purposes of this section, the term "adjusted gross estate" means the value of the gross estate reduced by the sum of the amounts allowable as a deduction under section 2053 or 2054. Such sum shall be determined on the basis of the facts and circumstances in existence on the date (including extensions) for filing the return of tax imposed by section 2001 (or, if earlier, the date on which such return is filed).

(7) Partnership interests and stock which is not readily tradable.

(A) In general. If the executor elects the benefits of this paragraph (at such time and in such manner as the Secretary shall by regulations prescribe), then—

(i) for purposes of paragraph (1)(B)(i) or (1)(C)(i) (whichever is appropriate) and for purposes of subsection (c), any capital interest in a partnership and any non-readily-tradable stock which (after the application of paragraph (2)) is treated as owned by the decedent shall be treated as included in determining the value of the decedent's gross estate,

(ii) the executor shall be treated as having selected under subsection (a)(3) the date prescribed by section 6151(a), and

(iii) for purposes of applying section 6601(j), the 2-percent portion (as defined in such section) shall be treated as being zero.

(B) Non-readily-tradable stock defined. For purposes of this paragraph, the term "non-readily-tradable stock" means stock for which, at the time of the decedent's death, there was no market on a stock exchange or in an over-the-counter market.

(8) Stock in holding company treated as business company stock in certain cases.

(A) In general. If the executor elects the benefits of this paragraph, then—

(i) Holding company stock treated as business company stock. For purposes of this section, the portion of the stock of any holding company which represents direct ownership (or indirect ownership through 1 or more other holding companies) by such company in a business company shall be deemed to be stock in such business company.

(ii) 5-year deferral for principal not to apply. The executor shall be treated as having selected under subsection (a)(3) the date prescribed by section 6151(a).

(iii) 2-percent interest rate not to apply. For purposes of applying section 6601(j), the 2-percent portion (as defined in such section) shall be treated as being zero.

> • **Caution:** Code Sec. 6166(b)(8)(B), following, was amended by Sec. 573(a), P.L. 107-16, the Economic Growth and Tax Relief Reconciliation Act of 2001 (EGTRRA). These provisions generally sunset for tax years beginning after 12/31/2012. For specific sunset provisions see Sec. 901, P.L. 107-16 (as amended) reproduced in history notes for this Code Sec.

(B) All stock must be non-readily-tradable stock.

(i) In general. No stock shall be taken into account for purposes of applying this paragraph unless it is non-readily-tradable stock (within the meaning of paragraph (7)(B)).

3,619

(ii) Special application where only holding company stock is non-readily-tradable stock. If the requirements of clause (i) are not met, but all of the stock of each holding company taken into account is non-readily-tradable, then this paragraph shall apply, but subsection (a)(1) shall be applied by substituting "5" for "10".

(C) Application of voting stock requirement of paragraph (1)(C)(i). For purposes of clause (i) of paragraph (1)(C), the deemed stock resulting from the application of subparagraph (A) shall be treated as voting stock to the extent that voting stock in the holding company owns directly (or through the voting stock of 1 or more other holding companies) voting stock in the business company.

(D) Definitions. For purposes of this paragraph—
(i) Holding company. The term "holding company" means any corporation holding stock in another corporation.
(ii) Business company. The term "business company" means any corporation carrying on a trade or business.

(9) Deferral not available for passive assets.
(A) In general. For purposes of subsection (a)(1) and determining the closely held business amount (but not for purposes of subsection (g)), the value of any interest in a closely held business shall not include the value of that portion of such interest which is attributable to passive assets held by the business.

(B) Passive asset defined. For purposes of this paragraph—
(i) In general. The term "passive asset" means any asset other than an asset used in carrying on a trade or business.
(ii) Stock treated as passive asset. The term "passive asset" includes any stock in another corporation unless—
(I) such stock is treated as held by the decedent by reason of an election under paragraph (8), and
(II) such stock qualified under subsection (a)(1).
(iii) Exception for active corporations. If—

• *Caution:* Code Sec. 6166(b)(9)(B)(iii)(I), following, was amended by Sec. 571(a), P.L. 107-16, the Economic Growth and Tax Relief Reconciliation Act of 2001 (EGTRRA). These provisions generally sunset for tax years beginning after 12/31/2012. For specific sunset provisions see Sec. 901, P.L. 107-16 (as amended) reproduced in history notes for this Code Sec.

(I) a corporation owns 20 percent or more in value of the voting stock of another corporation, or such other corporation has 45 or fewer shareholders, and
(II) 80 percent or more of the value of the assets of each such corporation is attributable to assets used in carrying on a trade or business,
then such corporations shall be treated as 1 corporation for purposes of clause (ii). For purposes of applying subclause (II) to the corporation holding the stock of the other corporation, such stock shall not be taken into account.

• *Caution:* Code Sec. 6166(b)(10), following, was added by Sec. 572(a), P.L. 107-16, the Economic Growth and Tax Relief Reconciliation Act of 2001 (EGTRRA). These provisions generally sunset for tax years beginning after 12/31/2012. For specific sunset provisions see Sec. 901, P.L. 107-16 (as amended) reproduced in history notes for this Code Sec.

(10) Stock in qualifying lending and finance business treated as stock in an active trade or business company.
(A) In general. If the executor elects the benefits of this paragraph, then—
(i) Stock in qualifying lending and finance business treated as stock in an active trade or business company. For purposes of this section, any asset used in a qualifying lending and finance business shall be treated as an asset which is used in carrying on a trade or business.
(ii) 5-year deferral for principal not to apply. The executor shall be treated as having selected under subsection (a)(3) the date prescribed by section 6151(a).
(iii) 5 equal installments allowed. For purposes of applying subsection (a)(1), "5" shall be substituted for "10".

(B) Definitions. For purposes of this paragraph—
(i) Qualifying lending and finance business. The term "qualifying lending and finance business" means a lending and finance business, if—
(I) based on all the facts and circumstances immediately before the date of the decedent's death, there was substantial activity with respect to the lending and finance business, or
(II) during at least 3 of the 5 taxable years ending before the date of the decedent's death, such business had at least 1 full-time employee substantially all of whose services were the active management of such business, 10 full-time, nonowner employees substantially all of whose services were directly related to such business, and $5,000,000 in gross receipts from activities described in clause (ii).

(ii) Lending and finance business. The term "lending and finance business" means a trade or business of—
(I) making loans,
(II) purchasing or discounting accounts receivable, notes, or installment obligations,
(III) engaging in rental and leasing of real and tangible personal property, including entering into leases and purchasing, servicing, and disposing of leases and leased assets,
(IV) rendering services or making facilities available in the ordinary course of a lending or finance business, and
(V) rendering services or making facilities available in connection with activities described in subclauses (I) through (IV) carried on by the corporation rendering services or making facilities available, or another corporation which is a member of the same affiliated group (as defined in section 1504 without regard to section 1504(b)(3)).

(iii) Limitation. The term "qualifying lending and finance business" shall not include any interest in an entity, if the stock or debt of such entity or a controlled group (as defined in section 267(f)(1)) of which such entity was a member was readily tradable

Payment of tax

on an established securities market or secondary market (as defined by the Secretary) at any time within 3 years before the date of the decedent's death.

(c) Special rule for interests in 2 or more closely held businesses.

For purposes of this section, interests in 2 or more closely held businesses, with respect to each of which there is included in determining the value of the decedent's gross estate 20 percent or more of the total value of each such business, shall be treated as an interest in a single closely held business. For purposes of the 20-percent requirement of the preceding sentence, an interest in a closely held business which represents the surviving spouse's interest in property held by the decedent and the surviving spouse as community property or as joint tenants, tenants by the entirety, or tenants in common shall be treated as having been included in determining the value of the decedent's gross estate.

(d) Election.

Any election under subsection (a) shall be made not later than the time prescribed by section 6075(a) for filing the return of tax imposed by section 2001 (including extensions thereof), and shall be made in such manner as the Secretary shall by regulations prescribe. If an election under subsection (a) is made, the provisions of this subtitle shall apply as though the Secretary were extending the time for payment of the tax.

(e) Proration of deficiency to installments.

If an election is made under subsection (a) to pay any part of the tax imposed by section 2001 in installments and a deficiency has been assessed, the deficiency shall (subject to the limitation provided by subsection (a)(2)) be prorated to the installments payable under subsection (a). The part of the deficiency so prorated to any installment the date for payment of which has not arrived shall be collected at the same time as, and as a part of, such installment. The part of the deficiency so prorated to any installment the date for payment of which has arrived shall be paid upon notice and demand from the Secretary. This subsection shall not apply if the deficiency is due to negligence, to intentional disregard of rules and regulations, or to fraud with intent to evade tax.

(f) Time for payment of interest.

If the time for payment of any amount of tax has been extended under this section—

(1) Interest for first 5 years. Interest payable under section 6601 of any unpaid portion of such amount attributable to the first 5 years after the date prescribed by section 6151(a) for payment of the tax shall be paid annually.

(2) Interest for periods after first 5 years. Interest payable under section 6601 on any unpaid portion of such amount attributable to any period after the 5-year period referred to in paragraph (1) shall be paid annually at the same time as, and as a part of, each installment payment of the tax.

(3) Interest in the case of certain deficiencies. In the case of a deficiency to which subsection (e) applies which is assessed after the close of the 5-year period referred to in paragraph (1), interest attributable to such 5-year period, and interest assigned under paragraph (2) to any installment the date for payment of which has arrived on or before the date of the assessment of the deficiency, shall be paid upon notice and demand from the Secretary.

(4) Selection of shorter period. If the executor has selected a period shorter than 5 years under subsection (a)(3), such shorter period shall be substituted for 5 years in paragraphs (1), (2), and (3) of this subsection.

(g) Acceleration of payment.

(1) Disposition of interest; withdrawal of funds from business.

(A) If—

(i) any portion of an interest in a closely held business which qualifies under subsection (a)(1) is distributed, sold, exchanged, or otherwise disposed of, or

(II) money and other property attributable to such an interest is withdrawn from such trade or business, and

(ii) the aggregate of such distributions, sales, exchanges, or other dispositions and withdrawals equals or exceeds 50 percent of the value of such interest,

then the extension of time for payment of tax provided in subsection (a) shall cease to apply, and the unpaid portion of the tax payable in installments shall be paid upon notice and demand from the Secretary.

(B) In the case of a distribution in redemption of stock to which section 303 (or so much of section 304 as relates to section 303) applies—

(i) the redemption of such stock, and the withdrawal of money and other property distributed in such redemption, shall not be treated as a distribution or withdrawal for purposes of subparagraph (A), and

(ii) for purposes of subparagraph (A), the value of the interest in the closely held business shall be considered to be such value reduced by the value of the stock redeemed.

This subparagraph shall apply only if, on or before the date prescribed by subsection (a)(3) for the payment of the first installment which becomes due after the date of the distribution (or, if earlier, on or before the day which is 1 year after the date of the distribution), there is paid an amount of the tax imposed by section 2001 not less than the amount of money and other property distributed.

(C) Subparagraph (A)(i) does not apply to an exchange of stock pursuant to a plan of reorganization described in subparagraph (D), (E), or (F) of section 368(a)(1) nor to an exchange to which section 355 (or so much of section 356 as relates to section 355) applies; but any stock received in such an exchange shall be treated for purposes of subparagraph (A)(i) as an interest qualifying under subsection (a)(1).

(D) Subparagraph (A)(i) does not apply to a transfer of property of the decedent to a person entitled by reason of the decedent's death to receive such property under the decedent's will, the applicable law of descent and distribution, or a trust created by the decedent. A similar rule shall apply in the case of a series of subsequent transfers of the property by reason of death so long as each transfer is to a member of the family (within the meaning of section 267(c)(4)) of the transferor in such transfer.

(E) Changes in interest in holding company. If any stock in a holding company is treated as stock in a business company by reason of subsection (b)(8)(A)—

(i) any disposition of any interest in such stock in such holding company which was included in determining the gross estate of the decedent, or

(ii) any withdrawal of any money or other property from such holding company attributable to any interest included in determining the gross estate of the decedent, shall be treated for purposes of subparagraph (A) as a disposition of (or a withdrawal with respect to) the stock qualifying under subsection (a)(1).

(F) Changes in interest in business company. If any stock in a holding company is treated as stock in a business company by reason of subsection (b)(8)(A)—

(i) any disposition of any interest in such stock in the business company by such holding company, or

(ii) any withdrawal of any money or other property from such business company attributable to such stock by such holding company owning such stock,

shall be treated for purposes of subparagraph (A) as a disposition of (or a withdrawal with respect to) the stock qualifying under subsection (a)(1).

(2) Undistributed income of estate.

(A) If an election is made under this section and the estate has undistributed net income for any taxable year ending on or after the due date for the first installment, the executor shall, on or before the date prescribed by law for filing the income tax return for such taxable year (including extensions thereof), pay an amount equal to such undistributed net income in liquidation of the unpaid portion of the tax payable in installments.

(B) For purposes of subparagraph (A), the undistributed net income of the estate for any taxable year is the amount by which the distributable net income of the estate for such taxable year (as defined in section 643) exceeds the sum of—

(i) the amounts for such taxable year specified in paragraphs (1) and (2) of section 661(a) (relating to deductions for distributions, etc.);

(ii) the amount of tax imposed for the taxable year on the estate under chapter 1; and

(iii) the amount of the tax imposed by section 2001 (including interest) paid by the executor during the taxable year (other than any amount paid pursuant to this paragraph).

(C) For purposes of this paragraph, if any stock in a corporation is treated as stock in another corporation by reason of subsection (b)(8)(A), any dividends paid by such other corporation to the corporation shall be treated as paid to the estate of the decedent to the extent attributable to the stock qualifying under subsection (a)(1).

(3) Failure to make payment of principal or interest.

(A) In general. Except as provided in subparagraph (B), if any payment of principal or interest under this section is not paid on or before the date fixed for its payment by this section (including any extension of time), the unpaid portion of the tax payable in installments shall be paid upon notice and demand from the Secretary.

(B) Payment within 6 months. If any payment of principal or interest under this section is not paid on or before the date determined under subparagraph (A) but is paid within 6 months of such date

(i) the provisions of subparagraph (A) shall not apply with respect to such payment,

(ii) the provisions of section 6601(j) shall not apply with respect to the determination of interest on such payment, and

(iii) there is imposed a penalty in an amount equal to the product of

(I) 5 percent of the amount of such payment, multiplied by

(II) the number of months (or fractions thereof) after such date and before payment is made.

The penalty imposed under clause (iii) shall be treated in the same manner as a penalty imposed under subchapter B of chapter 68.

(h) Election in case of certain deficiencies.

(1) In general. If—

(A) a deficiency in the tax imposed by section 2001 is assessed,

(B) the estate qualifies under subsection (a)(1), and

(C) the executor has not made an election under subsection (a),

the executor may elect to pay the deficiency in installments. This subsection shall not apply if the deficiency is due to negligence, to intentional disregard of rules and regulations, or to fraud with intent to evade tax.

(2) Time of election. An election under this subsection shall be made not later than 60 days after issuance of notice and demand by the Secretary for the payment of the deficiency, and shall be made in such manner as the Secretary shall by regulations prescribe.

(3) Effect of election on payment. If an election is made under this subsection, the deficiency shall (subject to the limitation provided by subsection (a)(2)) be prorated to the installments which would have been due if an election had been timely made under subsection (a) at the time the estate tax return was filed. The part of the deficiency so prorated to any installment the date for payment of which would have arrived shall be paid at the time of the making of the election under this subsection. The portion of the deficiency so prorated to installments the date for payment of which would not have so arrived shall be paid at the time such installments would have been due if such an election had been made.

(i) Special rule for certain direct skips.

To the extent that an interest in a closely held business is the subject of a direct skip (within the meaning of section 2612(c)) occurring at the same time as and as a result of the decedent's death, then for purposes of this section any tax imposed by section 2601 on the transfer of such interest shall be treated as if it were additional tax imposed by section 2001.

(j) Regulations.

The Secretary shall prescribe such regulations as may be necessary to the application of this section.

(k) Cross references.

(1) Security. For authority of the Secretary to require security in the case of an extension under this section, see section 6165.

(2) Lien. For special lien (in lieu of bond) in the case of an extension under this section, see section 6324A.

(3) Period of limitation. For extension of the period of limitation in the case of an extension under this section, see Section 6503(d).

(4) Interest. For provisions relating to interest on tax payable in installments under this section, see subsection (j) of section 6601.

(5) Transfers within 3 years of death. For special rule of qualifying an estate under this section where property has been transferred within 3 years of decedent's death, see section 2035(c)(2).

In **2010,** P.L. 111-312, Sec. 101(a)(1), substituted "December 31, 2012" for "December 31, 2010" both places it appears in Sec. 901, P.L. 107-16, see below, effective as if included in the enactment of P.L. 107-16, EGTRRA, 6/7/2001.

In **2002,** P.L. 107-358, Sec. 2, added subsec. (c) in Sec. 901 of P.L. 107-16 [see below], effective 12/17/2002.

In **2001,** P.L. 107-16, Sec. 571(a), substituted "45" for "15" in clause (b)(1)(B)(ii), clause (b)(1)(C)(ii), and subclause (b)(9)(B)(iii)(I), effective for estates of decedents dying after 12/31/2001.

Payment of tax Code Sec. 6166A

—P.L. 107-16, Sec. 572(a), added para. (b)(10), effective for estates of decedents dying after 12/31/2001.
—P.L. 107-16, Sec. 573(a), amended subpara. (b)(8)(B), effective for estates of decedents dying after 12/31/2001.
Prior to amendment, subpara. (b)(8)(B) read as follows:
"(B) All stock must be non-readily-tradable stock. No stock shall be taken into account for purposes of applying this paragraph unless it is non-readily-tradable stock (within the meaning of paragraph (7)(B))."
—P.L. 107-16, Sec. 901, of this Act [as amended by Sec. 2, P.L. 107-358, and P.L. 111-312, see above], reads as follows:
"SEC. 901. SUNSET OF PROVISIONS OF ACT.
"(a) In general. All provisions of, and amendments made by, this Act shall not apply—
"(1) to taxable, plan, or limitation years beginning after December 31, 2012, or
"(2) in the case of title V, to estates of decedents dying, gifts made, or generation-skipping transfers, after December 31, 2012.
"(b) Application of certain laws. The Internal Revenue Code of 1986 and the Employee Retirement Income Security Act of 1974 shall be applied and administered to years, estates, gifts, and transfers described in subsection (a) as if the provisions and amendments described in subsection (a) had never been enacted.
"(c) Exception. Subsection (a) shall not apply to section 803 (relating to no federal income tax on restitution received by victims of the Nazi regime or their heirs or estates)."
In 2000, P.L. 106-554, Sec. 1(a)(7), [which enacted into law Sec. 319(18) of P.L. 106-554] substituted "2035(c)(2)" for "2035(d)(4)" in para. (k)(5), effective 12/21/2000.
In 1998, P.L. 105-206, Sec. 6007(c)(1), amended clause (b)(7)(A)(iii) ... Sec. 6007(c)(2), amended clause (b)(8)(A)(iii), effective for estates of decedents dying after 12/31/97. For Sec. 503(d)(2) of P.L. 105-34, see below.
Prior to amendment, clause (b)(7)(A)(iii) read as follows:
"(iii) section 6601(j) (relating to 2-percent rate of interest) shall not apply."
Prior to amendment, clause (b)(8)(A)(iii) read as follows:
"(iii) 2-percent interest rate not to apply. Section 6601(j) (relating to 2-percent rate of interest) shall not apply."
In 1997, P.L. 105-34, Sec. 503(a)(2)(B), substituted "2-percent" for "4-percent" in clause (b)(7)(A)(iii) and clause (b)(8)(A)(iii), effective for estates of decedents dying after 12/31/97. Sec. 503(d)(2) of this Act provides:
"(2) Election. In the case of the estate of any decedent dying before January 1, 1998, with respect to which there is an election under section 6166 of the Internal Revenue Code of 1986, the executor of the estate may elect to have the amendments made by this section apply with respect to installments due after the effective date of the election; except that the 2-percent portion of such installments shall be equal to the amount which would be the 4-percent portion of such installments without regard to such election. Such an election shall be made before January 1, 1999 in the manner prescribed by the Secretary of the Treasury and, once made, is irrevocable."
In 1996, P.L. 104-188, Sec. 1704(t)(15), deleted para. (k)(6), effective 8/20/96.
Prior to deletion, para. (k)(6) read as follows:
"(6) Payment of estate tax by employee stock ownership plan or eligible worker-owned cooperative. For provision allowing plan administrator or eligible worker-owned cooperative to elect to pay a certain portion of the estate tax in installments under the provisions of this section, see section 2210(c)."
In 1986, P.L. 99-514, Sec. 1432(e), redesignated subsecs. (i) and (j) as subsecs. (j) and (k), and added new subsec. (i), effective for any generation-skipping transfer (within the meaning of '86 Code Sec. 2611) made after 10/22/86, except as provided in Sec. 1433(b) of this Act reproduced in the note following Code Sec. 2601.
In 1984, P.L. 98-369, Sec. 544(b)(4), added para. (j)(6), effective for those estates of decedents which are required to file returns on a date (including any extensions) after 7/18/84.
—P.L. 98-369, Sec. 1021(a), added para. (b)(8) ... Sec. 1021(b), added para. (b)(9) ... Sec. 1021(c), added subparas. (g)(1)(E) and (F) ... Sec. 1021(d), added subpara. (g)(2)(C), effective for estates of decedents dying after 7/18/84. Sec. 1021(e)(2) of this Act provides a special rule as follows:
"(2) Special rule.—
"(A) In general.— At the election of the executor, if—
"(i) a corporation has 15 or fewer shareholders on June 22, 1984, and at all times thereafter before the date of the decedent's death, and
"(ii) stock of such corporation is included in the gross estate of the decedent, then all other corporations all of the stock of which is owned directly or indirectly by the corporation described in clauses (i) and (ii) shall be treated as one corporation for purposes of section 6166 of the Internal Revenue Code of 1954.
"(B) Effect of election.— Any executor who elects the application of this paragraph shall be treated as having made the election under paragraph (8) of section 6166(b) of such Code."
In 1983,
"Land Diverted Under 1983 Payment-in-Kind Program. Land diverted from production of agricultural commodities under a 1983 payment-in-kind program to be treated, for purposes of this section, as used during the 1983 crop year by qualified taxpayers in the active conduct of the trade or business of farming, with qualified taxpayers who materially participate in the diversion and devotion to conservation uses under a 1983 payment-in-kind program to be treated as materially participating in the operation of such land during the 1983 crop year, [see section 3 of Pub. L. 98-4, set out as a note under section 61 of this title.]"
—P.L. 97-448, Sec. 104(c)(1), substituted "35-percent requirement" for "65-percent requirement" in para. (b)(3) ... Sec. 104(c)(2), amended clauses (g)(1)(B)(i)

and (ii) ... Sec. 104(d)(1)(B), added para. (j)(5), effective for estates of decedents dying after 12/31/81.
Prior to amendment clauses (g)(1)(B)(i) and (ii) read as follows:
"(i) subparagraph (A)(i) does not apply with respect to the stock redeemed; and for purposes of such subparagraph the interest in the closely held business shall be considered to be such interest reduced by the value of the stock redeemed; and
"(ii) subparagraph (A)(ii) does not apply with respect to withdrawals of money and other property distributed; and for purposes of such subparagraph the value of the trade or business shall be considered to be such value reduced by the amount of money and other property distributed."
In 1981, P.L. 97-34, Sec. 422(a)(1), substituted "35 percent" for "65 percent" in para. (a)(1) ... Sec. 422(a)(2), substituted "20 percent or more" for "more than 20 percent" in subsec. (c) ... Sec. 422(c)(1), amended subpara. (g)(1)(A) ... Sec. 422(c)(2), amended para. (g)(3) ... Sec. 422(e)(5)(A), deleted para. (a)(4) ... Sec. 422(e)(5)(B), substituted "Extension" for "Alternate extension" in the heading of Code Sec. 6166, effective for the estates of decedents dying after 12/31/81.
Prior to amendment, subpara. (g)(1)(A) read as follows:
"(A) If —
"(i) one-third or more in value of an interest in a closely held business which qualifies under subsection (a)(1) is distributed, sold, exchanged, or otherwise disposed of, or
"(ii) aggregate withdrawals of money and other property from the trade or business, an interest in which qualifies under subsection (a)(1), made with respect to such interest, equal or exceed one-third of the value of such trade or business, then the extension of time for payment of tax provided in subsection (a) shall cease to apply, and any unpaid portion of the tax payable in installments shall be paid upon notice and demand from the Secretary."
Prior to amendment, para. (g)(3) read as follows:
"(3) Failure to pay installment. If any installment under this section is not paid on or before the date fixed for its payment by this section (including any extension of time for the payment of such installment), the unpaid portion of the tax payable in installments shall be paid upon notice and demand from the Secretary."
Prior to deletion, para. (a)(4) read as follows:
"(4) Eligibility for election. No election may be made under this section by the executor of the estate of any decedent if an election under section 6166A applies with respect to the estate of such decedent."
—P.L. 97-34, Sec. 422(c)(3), added a sentence to the end of subpara. (g)(1)(D), effective for transfers after 12/31/81.
In 1978, P.L. 95-600, Sec. 512(a), added subpara. (b)(2)(D) ... Sec. 512(b), added para. (b)(7), effective for estates of decedents dying after 11/6/78.
In 1976, P.L. 94-455, Sec. 2004(a), redesignated Code Sec. 6166 as Code Sec. 6166A, and added new Code Sec. 6166, effective for estates of decedents dying after 12/31/76.

Sec. 6166A. Repealed.

In 1981, P.L. 97-34, Sec. 422(d), repealed Code Sec. 6166A, effective for estates of decedents dying after 12/31/81.
Prior to repeal, Code Sec. 6166A read as follows:
"SEC. 6166A. EXTENSION OF TIME FOR PAYMENT OF ESTATE TAX WHERE ESTATE CONSISTS LARGELY OF INTEREST IN CLOSELY HELD BUSINESS.
"(a) Extension permitted.
"If the value of an interest in a closely held business which is included in determining the gross estate of a decedent who was (at the date of his death) a citizen or resident of the United States exceeds either—
"(1) 35 percent of the value of the gross estate of such decedent, or
"(2) 50 percent of the taxable estate of such decedent,
the executor may elect to pay part or all of the tax imposed by section 2001 in two or more (but not exceeding 10) equal installments. Any such election shall be made not later than the time prescribed by section 6075(a) for filing the return of such tax (including extensions thereof), and shall be made in such manner as the Secretary shall by regulations prescribe. If an election under this section is made, the provisions of this subtitle shall apply as though the Secretary were extending the time for payment of the tax. For purposes of this section, value shall be value determined for Federal estate tax purposes.
"(b) Limitation.
"The maximum amount of tax which may be paid in installments as provided in this section shall be an amount which bears the same ratio to the tax imposed by section 2001 (reduced by the credits against such tax) as the value of the interest in a closely held business which qualifies under subsection (a) bears to the value of the gross estate.
"(c) Closely held business.
"For purposes of this section, the term 'interest in a closely held business' means—
"(1) an interest as a proprietor in a trade or business carried on as a proprietorship,
"(2) an interest as a partner in a partnership carrying on a trade or business, if—
"(A) 20 percent or more of the total capital interest in such partnership is included in determining the gross estate of the decedent, or
"(B) such partnership had 10 or less partners,
"(3) stock in a corporation carrying on a trade or business, if—
"(A) 20 percent or more in value of the voting stock of such corporation is included in determining the gross estate of the decedent, or
"(B) such corporation had 10 or less shareholders.

Code Sec. 6166A — Payment of tax

For purposes of this subsection, determinations shall be made as of the time immediately before the decedent's death.

"(d) Special rule for interests in two or more closely held businesses.

"For purposes of subsections (a), (b), and (h)(1), interests in two or more closely held businesses, with respect to each of which there is included in determining the value of the decedent's gross estate more than 50 percent of the total value of each such business, shall be treated as an interest in a single closely held business. For purposes of the 50 percent requirement of the preceding sentence, an interest in a closely held business which represents the surviving spouse's interest in property held by the decedent and the surviving spouse as community property shall be treated as having been included in determining the value of the decedent's gross estate.

"(e) Date for payment of installments.

"If an election is made under subsection (a), the first installment shall be paid on or before the date prescribed by section 6151(a) for payment of the tax, and each succeeding installment shall be paid on or before the date which is one year after the date prescribed by this subsection for payment of the preceding installment.

"(f) Proration of deficiency to installments.

"If an election is made under subsection (a) to pay any part of the tax imposed by section 2001 in installments and a deficiency has been assessed, the deficiency shall (subject to the limitation provided by subsection (b)) be prorated to such installments. The part of the deficiency so prorated to any installment the date for payment of which has not arrived shall be collected at the same time as, and as a part of, such installment. The part of the deficiency so prorated to any installment the date for payment of which has arrived shall be paid upon notice and demand from the Secretary. This subsection shall not apply if the deficiency is due to negligence, to intentional disregard of rules and regulations, or to fraud with intent to evade tax.

"(g) Time for payment of interest.

"If the time for payment of any amount of tax has been extended under this section, interest payable under section 6601 on any unpaid portion of such amount shall be paid annually at the same time as, and as a part of, each installment payment of the tax. Interest, on that part of a deficiency prorated under this section to any installment the date for payment of which has not arrived, for the period before the date fixed for the last installment preceding the assessment of the deficiency, shall be paid upon notice and demand from the Secretary.

"(h) Acceleration of payment.

"(1) Withdrawal of funds from business; disposition of interest.

"(A) If—

"(i) aggregate withdrawals of money and other property from the trade or business, an interest in which qualifies under subsection (a), made with respect to such interest, equal or exceed 50 percent of the value of such trade or business, or

"(ii) 50 percent or more in value of an interest in a closely held business which qualifies under subsection (a) is distributed, sold, exchanged, or otherwise disposed of,

then the extension of time for payment of tax provided in this section shall cease to apply, and any unpaid portion of the tax payable in installments shall be paid upon notice and demand from the Secretary.

"(B) In the case of a distribution in redemption of stock to which section 303 (or so much of section 304 as relates to section 303) applies—

"(i) subparagraph (A)(i) does not apply with respect to withdrawals of money and other property distributed; and for purposes of such subparagraph the value of the trade or business shall be considered to be such value reduced by the amount of money and other property distributed, and

"(ii) subparagraph (A)(ii) does not apply with respect to the stock redeemed; and for purposes of such subparagraph the interest in the closely held business shall be considered to be such interest reduced by the value of the stock redeemed.

This subparagraph shall apply only if, on or before the date prescribed by subsection (e) for payment of the first installment which becomes due after the date of the distribution, there is paid an amount of the tax imposed by section 2001 not less than the amount of money and other property distributed.

"(C) Subparagraph (A)(ii) does not apply to an exchange of stock pursuant to a plan of reorganization described in subparagraph (D), (E), or (F) of section 368(a)(1) nor to an exchange to which section 355 (or so much of section 356 as relates to section 355) applies; but any stock received in such an exchange shall be treated for purposes of such subparagraph as an interest qualifying under subsection (a).

"(D) Subparagraph (A)(ii) does not apply to a transfer of property of the decedent by the executor to a person entitled to receive such property under the decedent's will or under the applicable law of descent and distribution.

"(2) Undistributed income of estate.

"(A) If an election is made under subsection (a) and the estate has undistributed net income for any taxable year after its fourth taxable year, the executor shall, on or before the date prescribed by law for filing the income tax return for such taxable year (including extensions thereof), pay an amount equal to such undistributed net income in liquidation of the unpaid portion of the tax payable in installments.

"(B) For purposes of subparagraph (A), the undistributed net income of the estate for any taxable year is the amount by which the distributable net income of the estate for such taxable year (as defined in section 643) exceeds the sum of—

"(i) the amounts for such taxable year specified in paragraphs (1) and (2) of section 661(a) (relating to deduction for distributions, etc.);

"(ii) the amount of tax imposed for the taxable year on the estate under chapter 1; and

"(iii) the amount of the Federal estate tax (including interest) paid by the executor during the taxable year (other than any amount paid pursuant to this paragraph).

"(3) Failure to pay installment. If any installment under this section is not paid on or before the date fixed for its payment by this section (including any extension of time for the payment of such installment), the unpaid portion of the tax payable in installments shall be paid upon notice and demand from the Secretary.

"(i) Transitional rules.

"(1) In general. If—

"(A) a deficiency in the tax imposed by section 2001 is assessed after the date of the enactment of this section, and

"(B) the estate qualifies under paragraph (1) or (2) of subsection (a),

the executor may elect to pay the deficiency in installments. This subsection shall not apply if the deficiency is due to negligence, to intentional disregard of rules and regulations, or to fraud with intent to evade tax.

"(2) Time of election. An election under this subsection shall be made not later than 60 days after issuance of notice and demand by the Secretary for the payment of the deficiency, and shall be made in such manner as the Secretary shall by regulations prescribe.

"(3) Effect of election on payment. If an election is made under this subsection, the deficiency shall (subject to the limitation provided by subsection (b)) be prorated to the installments which would have been due if an election had been timely made under this section at the time the estate tax return was filed. The part of the deficiency so prorated to any installment the date for payment of which would have arrived shall be paid at the time of the making of the election under this subsection. The portion of the deficiency so prorated to installments the date for payment of which would not have so arrived shall be paid at the time such installments would have been due if such an election had been made.

"(4) Application of subsection (h)(2). In the case of an election under this subsection, subsection (h)(2) shall not apply with respect to undistributed net income for any taxable year ending before January 1, 1960.

"(j) Regulations.

"The Secretary shall prescribe such regulations as may be necessary to the application of this section.

"(k) Cross references.

"(1) Security. For authority of the Secretary to require security in the case of an extension under this section, see section 6165.

"(2) Period of limitation. For extension of the period of limitation in the case of an extension under this section, see section 6503(d).”

In 1976, P.L. 94-455, Sec. 1906(b)(13)(A), substituted "Secretary" for "Secretary or his delegate" each place it appeared in Code Sec. 6166A, effective 2/1/77.

—P.L. 94-455, Sec. 2004(a), redesignated Code Sec. 6166 as Code Sec. 6166A, effective for estates of decedents dying after 12/31/76.

In 1975, P.L. 93-625, Sec. 7(d)(2), struck out the last sentence in subsec. (g), effective for amounts outstanding on or arising after 7/1/75.

Prior to amendment, the last sentence of subsec. (g) read as follows:

"In applying section 6601(b) (relating to the application of the 4-percent rate of interest in the case of certain extensions of time to pay estate tax) in the case of a deficiency, the entire amount which is prorated to installments under this section shall be treated as an amount of tax the payment of which is extended under this section."

—P.L. 93-625, Sec. 7(d)(3), deleted para. (k)(1) and redesignated paras. (k)(2) and (k)(3) as paras. (k)(1) and (k)(2), effective for amounts outstanding on or arising after 7/1/75.

Prior to deletion, para. (k)(1) read as follows:

"(1) Interest. For provisions requiring the payment of interest at the rate of 4 percent per annum for the period of an extension, see section 6601(b)."

In 1958, P.L. 85-866, Sec. 206(a), added Code Sec. 6166A, effective for "estates of decedents with respect to which the date for the filing of the estate tax return (including extensions thereof) prescribed by section 6075(a) of the Internal Revenue Code of 1954 is after the date of the enactment of this Act [9/2/58]; except that (1) section 6166(i) of such Code as added by this section shall apply to estates of decedents dying after August 16, 1954, but only if the date for the filing of the estate tax return (including extensions thereof) expired on or before the date of the enactment of this Act and (2) notwithstanding section 6166(a) of such Code, if an election under such section is required to be made before the sixtieth day after the date of the enactment of this Act such an election shall be considered timely if made on or before such sixtieth day."

Sec. 6167. Extension of time for payment of tax attributable to recovery of foreign expropriation losses.

(a) Extension allowed by election.

If—

(1) a corporation has a recovery of a foreign expropriation loss to which section 1351 applies, and

(2) the portion of the recovery received in money is less than 25 percent of the amount of such recovery (as defined in section 1351(c)) and is not greater than the tax attributable to such recovery,

the tax attributable to such recovery shall, at the election of the taxpayer, be payable in 10 equal installments on the 15th day of the third month of each of the taxable years following the taxable year of the recovery. Such election shall be made at such time and in such manner as the Secretary may prescribe by regulations. If an election is made under this subsection, the provisions of this subtitle shall apply as though the Secretary were extending the time for payment of such tax.

(b) Extension permitted by Secretary.

If a corporation has a recovery of a foreign expropriation loss to which section 1351 applies and if an election is not made under subsection (a), the Secretary may, upon finding that the payment of the tax attributable to such recovery at the time otherwise provided in this subtitle would result in undue hardship, extend the time for payment of such tax for a reasonable period or periods not in excess of 9 years from the date on which such tax is otherwise payable.

(c) Acceleration of payments.

If—
 (1) an election is made under subsection (a),
 (2) during any taxable year before the tax attributable to such recovery is paid in full—
  (A) any property (other than money) received on such recovery is sold or exchanged, or
  (B) any property (other than money) received on any sale or exchange described in subparagraph (A) is sold or exchanged, and
 (3) the amount of money received on such sale or exchange (reduced by the amount of the tax imposed under chapter 1 with respect to such sale or exchange), when added to the amount of money—
  (A) received on such recovery, and
  (B) received on previous sales or exchanges described in subparagraphs (A) and (B) of paragraph (2) (as so reduced),
exceeds the amount of money which may be received under subsection (a)(2),
an amount of the tax attributable to such recovery equal to such excess shall be payable on the 15th day of the third month of the taxable year following the taxable year in which such sale or exchange occurs. The amount of such tax so paid shall be treated, for purposes of this section, as a payment of the first unpaid installment or installments (or portion thereof) which become payable under subsection (a) following such taxable year.

(d) Proration of deficiency to installments.

If an election is made under subsection (a), and a deficiency attributable to the recovery of a foreign expropriation loss has been assessed, the deficiency shall be prorated to such installments. The part of the deficiency so prorated to any installment the date for payment of which has not arrived shall be collected at the same time as, and as part of, such installment. The part of the deficiency so prorated to any installment the date for payment of which has arrived shall be paid upon notice and demand from the Secretary. This subsection shall not apply if the deficiency is due to negligence, to intentional disregard of rules and regulations, or to fraud with intent to evade tax.

(e) Time for payment of interest.

If the time for payment for any amount of tax has been extended under this section, interest payable under section 6601 on any unpaid portion of such amount shall be paid annually at the same time as, and as part of, each installment payment of the tax. Interest, on that part of a deficiency prorated under this section to any installment the date for payment of which has not arrived, for the period before the date fixed for the last installment preceding the assessment of the deficiency, shall be paid upon notice and demand from the Secretary.

(f) Tax attributable to recovery of foreign expropriation loss.

For purposes of this section, the tax attributable to a recovery of a foreign expropriation loss is the sum of—
 (1) the additional tax imposed by section 1351(d)(1) on such recovery, and
 (2) the amount by which the tax imposed under subtitle A is increased by reason of the gain on such recovery which under section 1351(e) is considered as gain on the involuntary conversion of property.

(g) Failure to pay installment.

If any installment under this section is not paid on or before the date fixed for its payment by this section (including any extension of time for the payment of such installment), the unpaid portion of the tax payable in installments shall be paid upon notice and demand from the Secretary.

(h) Cross references.

 (1) Security. For authority of the Secretary to require security in the case of an extension under this section, see section 6165.
 (2) Period of limitation. For extension of the period of limitation in the case of an extension under this section, see section 6503(e).

In 1976, P.L. 94-455, Sec. 1902(b)(2)(B), substituted "section 6503(e)" for "section 6503(f)" in para. (h)(2), effective for estates of decedents dying after 10/4/76.
—P.L. 94-455, Sec. 1906(b)(13)(A), substituted "Secretary" for "Secretary or his delegate" each place it appeared in Code Se. 6167, effective 2/1/77.
In 1975, P.L. 93-625, Sec. 7(d)(2), deleted the last sentence of subsec. (e), effective 7/1/75, and applicable to amounts outstanding on 7/1/75, and arising thereafter.
Prior to amendment, the last sentence of subsec. (e) read as follows:
"In applying section 6601(j) (relating to the application of the 4 percent rate of interest in the case of recoveries of foreign expropriation losses to which this section applies) in the case of a deficiency, the entire amount which is prorated to installments under this section shall be treated as an amount of tax the payment of which is extended under this section."
—P.L. 93-625, Sec. 7(d)(3), deleted para. (h)(1) and redesignated paras. (h)(2) and (h)(3) as (h)(1) and (h)(2), effective 7/1/75, and applicable to amounts outstanding on 7/1/75, and arising thereafter.
Prior to amendment, para. (h)(1) read as follows:
 "(1) Interest. For provisions requiring the payment of interest at the rate of 4 percent per annum for the period of an extension, see section 6601(j)."
In 1966, P.L. 89-384, Sec. 1(d), added Code Sec. 6167, effective for amounts received after '64 in respect of foreign expropriation losses (as defined in Code Sec. 1351(b)) sustained after '58.

CHAPTER 63.—ASSESSMENT

Subchapter
A. In general.
B. Deficiency procedures in the case of income, estate, gift, and certain excise taxes.
C. Tax treatment of partnership items.
D. Treatment of electing large partnerships.

In 1997, P.L. 105-34, Sec. 1222(c), added item for Subchapter D
In 1982, P.L. 97-354, Sec. 4(b), added item D.
—P.L. 97-248, Sec. 402(b), added item C.
In 1969, P.L. 91-172, Sec. 101(j)(63), substituted "gift, and certain excise taxes" for "and gift taxes" in the item relating to subchapter B.

Subchapter A.—In General

Sec.
6201. Assessment authority.
6202. Establishment by regulations of mode or time of assessment.
6203. Method of assessment.
6204. Supplemental assessments.
6205. Special rules applicable to certain employment taxes.

Subchapter A

Payment of tax

6206. Special rules applicable to excessive claims under certain sections.
6207. Cross references.

In 2005, P.L. 109-59, Sec. 11163(d)(4), substituted "certain sections" for "sections 6420, 6421, and 6427" in item 6206.
In 1983, P.L. 97-424, Sec. 515(b)(3)(B), deleted "6424," after "6421" in item 6206.
In 1965, added 6424 in item 6206.
In 1956, substituted "sections 6420 and 6421" for "section 6420" in item "6206".
—added item 6206 and renumbered former item 6206 as 6207.

Sec. 6201. Assessment authority.
(a) Authority of Secretary.

The Secretary is authorized and required to make the inquiries, determinations, and assessments of all taxes (including interest, additional amounts, additions to the tax, and assessable penalties) imposed by this title, or accruing under any former internal revenue law, which have not been duly paid by stamp at the time and in the manner provided by law. Such authority shall extend to and include the following:

(1) Taxes shown on return. The Secretary shall assess all taxes determined by the taxpayer or by the Secretary as to which returns or lists are made under this title.

(2) Unpaid taxes payable by stamp.

(A) Omitted stamps. Whenever any article upon which a tax is required to be paid by means of a stamp is sold or removed for sale or use by the manufacturer thereof or whenever any transaction or act upon which a tax is required to be paid by means of a stamp occurs without the use of the proper stamp, it shall be the duty of the Secretary, upon such information as he can obtain, to estimate the amount of tax which has been omitted to be paid and to make assessment therefor upon the person or persons the Secretary determines to be liable for such tax.

(B) Check or money order not duly paid. In any case in which a check or money order received under authority of section 6311 as payment for stamps is not duly paid, the unpaid amount may be immediately assessed as if it were a tax imposed by this title, due at the time of such receipt, from the person who tendered such check or money order.

(3) Erroneous income tax prepayment credits. If on any return or claim for refund of income taxes under subtitle A there is an overstatement of the credit for income tax withheld at the source, or of the amount paid as estimated income tax, the amount so overstated which is allowed against the tax shown on the return or which is allowed as a credit or refund may be assessed by the Secretary in the same manner as in the case of a mathematical or clerical error appearing upon the return, except that the provisions of section 6213(b)(2) (relating to abatement of mathematical or clerical error assessments) shall not apply with regard to any assessment under this paragraph.

(4) Certain orders of criminal restitution.

(A) In general. The Secretary shall assess and collect the amount of restitution under an order pursuant to section 3556 of title 18, United States Code, for failure to pay any tax imposed under this title in the same manner as if such amount were such tax.

(B) Time of assessment. An assessment of an amount of restitution under an order described in subparagraph (A) shall not be made before all appeals of such order are concluded and the right to make all such appeals has expired.

(C) Restriction on challenge of assessment. The amount of such restitution may not be challenged by the person against whom assessed on the basis of the existence or amount of the underlying tax liability in any proceeding authorized under this title (including in any suit or proceeding in court permitted under section 7422).

(b) Amount not to be assessed.

(1) Estimated income tax. No unpaid amount of estimated income tax required to be paid under section 6654 or 6655 shall be assessed.

(2) Federal unemployment tax. No unpaid amount of Federal unemployment tax for any calendar quarter or other period of a calendar year, computed as provided in section 6157, shall be assessed.

(c) Compensation of child.

Any income tax under chapter 1 assessed against a child, to the extent attributable to amounts includible in the gross income of the child, and not of the parent, solely by reason of section 73(a), shall, if not paid by the child, for all purposes be considered as having also been properly assessed against the parent.

(d) Required reasonable verification of information returns.

In any court proceeding, if a taxpayer asserts a reasonable dispute with respect to any item of income reported on an information return filed with the Secretary under subpart B or C of part III of subchapter A of chapter 61 by a third party and the taxpayer has fully cooperated with the Secretary (including providing, within a reasonable period of time, access to and inspection of all witnesses, information, and documents within the control of the taxpayer as reasonably requested by the Secretary), the Secretary shall have the burden of producing reasonable and probative information concerning such deficiency in addition to such information return.

(e) Deficiency proceedings.

For special rules applicable to deficiencies of income, estate, gift, and certain excise taxes, see subchapter B.

In 2010, P.L. 111-237, Sec. 3(a), added para. (a)(4), effective for restitution ordered after 8/16/2010.
In 1996, P.L. 104-168, Sec. 602(a), redesignated subsec. (d) as (e) and added new subsec. (d), effective 7/30/96.
In 1988, P.L. 100-647, Sec. 1015(r)(1), deleted para. (a)(4), effective for notices of deficiencies mailed after 11/10/88.
Prior to deletion, para. (a)(4) read as follows:
"(4) Erroneous credit under section 32 or 34. If on any return or claim for refund of income taxes under subtitle A there is an overstatement of the credit allowable by section 34 (relating to certain uses of gasoline and special fuels), or section 32 (relating to earned income) the amount so overstated which is allowed against the tax shown on the return or which is allowed as a credit or refund may be assessed by the Secretary in the same manner as in the case of a mathematical or clerical error appearing upon the return, except that the provisions of section 6213(b)(2) (relating to abatement of mathematical or clerical error assessments) shall not apply with regard to any assessment under this paragraph."
—P.L. 100-647, Sec. 7106(c)(2), deleted "or tax imposed by section 3321" after "unemployment tax" in para. (b)(2), effective for renumeration paid after 12/31/88.
In 1987, P.L. 100-203, Sec. 10301(b)(3), substituted "section 6654 or 6655" for "section 6154 or 6654" in para. (b)(1), effective for tax. yrs. begin. after 12/31/87.
In 1984, P.L. 98-369, Sec. 412(b)(5), amended para. (b)(1), effective for tax. yrs. begin. after 12/31/84.
Prior to amendment, para. (b)(1) read as follows:
"(1) Estimated income tax. No unpaid amount of estimated tax under section 6153 or 6154 shall be assessed."
—P.L. 98-369, Sec. 474(r)(32)(A), and (B), substituted "section 34" for "section 39" and substituted "section 32" for "section 43" in para. (a)(4) . . . Sec. 474(r)(32)(C), substituted "section 32 or 34" for "section 39 or 43" in the heading of para. (a)(4), effective for tax. yrs. begin. after 12/31/83, and to carrybacks from tax. yrs. begin. after 12/31/83.
In 1983, P.L. 98-76, Sec. 231(b)(2)(A), substituted "Federal unemployment tax or tax imposed by section 3321" for "Federal unemployment tax" in para. (b)(2), effective for remuneration paid after 6/30/86.

Assessment Code Sec. 6205

—P.L. 97-424, Sec. 515(b)(6)(E), substituted "and special fuels" for ", special fuels and lubricating oil" in para. (a)(4), effective for articles sold after 1/6/83.

In 1978, P.L. 95-600, Sec. 103(a), changed the effective date for amendments made by Sec. 204(b)(2) of P.L. 94-12, to effective for tax. yrs. begin. after. 12/31/74, from effective for tax. yrs. begin. after 12/31/74 and before 1/1/79, see below.

In 1977, P.L. 95-30, Sec. 103(b), changed the effective date for amendments made by Sec. 204(b)(2) of P.L. 94-12, to effective for tax. yrs. begin. after. 12/31/74 and before 1/1/79, from effective for tax. yrs. begin. after 12/31/74 and before 1/1/78, see below.

In 1976, P.L. 94-455, Sec. 401(c), changed the effective date for amendments made by Sec. 204(b)(2) of P.L. 94-12, to effective for tax. yrs. begin. after. 12/31/74 and before 1/1/78, from effective for tax. yrs. begin. after 12/31/74 and before 1/1/77, see below.

—P.L. 94-455, Sec. 1206(c)(2)(A), substituted "mathematical or clerical error" for "mathematical error" in paras. (a)(3) and (4) . . . Sec. 1206(c)(2)(B), added ", except that the provisions of section 6213(b)(2) (relating to abatement of mathematical or clerical error assessments) shall not apply with regard to any assessment under this paragraph" before the period at the end of paras. (a)(3) and (4), effective for returns with the meaning of Code Sec. 6213(f)(1) filed after 12/31/76.

—P.L. 94-455, Sec. 1307(d)(2)(D), substituted "and certain excise taxes" for "chapter 42, and chapter 43 taxes" in subsec. (d), effective 10/4/76.

—P.L. 94-455, Sec. 1906(b)(13)(A), substituted "Secretary" for "Secretary or his delegate" each place it appeared in Code Sec. 6201, effective 2/1/77.

In 1975, P.L. 94-164, Sec. 2(f), changed the effective date for amendments made by Sec. 204(b)(2) of P.L. 94-12, to effective for tax. yrs. begin. after. 12/31/74 and before 1/1/77, from effective for tax. yrs. begin. after 12/31/74 and before 1/1/76, see below.

—P.L. 94-12, Sec. 204(b)(2), added "or 43" before the period at the end of the caption in para. (a)(4), and substituted "oil) or section 43 (relating to earned income," for "oil)," in para. (a)(4), effective [as amended by Sec. 2(f) of P.L. 94-164, Sec. 401(c) of P.L. 94-455, Sec. 103(b) of P.L. 95-30 and Sec. 103(a) of P.L. 95-600, see above] for tax. yrs. begin. after 12/31/74.

In 1974, P.L. 93-406, Sec. 1016(a)(8), substituted ", chapter 42, and chapter 43" for "and chapter 42" in subsec. (d), effective 9/2/74 or other date as specified in Sec. 1017 of the Act (reproduced following Code Sec. 401).

In 1970, P.L. 91-258, Sec. 207(d)(1), substituted "uses of gasoline, special fuels, and lubricating oil" for "uses of gasoline and lubricating oil" in subsec. (a)(4) . . . Sec. 207(d)(2), substituted "under section 39" for "for use of gasoline" in the heading of subsec. (a)(4), effective 7/1/70.

In 1969, P.L. 91-172, Sec. 101(j)(38), substituted "gift, and chapter 42 taxes" for "and gift taxes" in subsec. (d), effective 1/1/70.

—P.L. 91-53, Sec. 2(b), amended subsec. (b), effective for calendar yrs. begin. after 12/31/69.

Prior to amendment, subsec. (b) read as follows:

"(b) *Estimated income tax.*

"No unpaid amount of estimated tax under section 6153 or 6154 shall be assessed."

In 1965, P.L. 89-44, Sec. 809, added para. (a)(4), effective for tax. yrs. begin. after 6/30/65.

Sec. 6202. Establishment by regulations of mode or time of assessment.

If the mode or time for the assessment of any internal revenue tax (including interest, additional amounts, additions to the tax, and assessable penalties) is not otherwise provided for, the Secretary may establish the same by regulations.

In 1976, P.L. 94-455, Sec. 1906(b)(13)(A), substituted "Secretary" for "Secretary or his delegate" in Code Sec. 6202, effective 2/1/77.

Sec. 6203. Method of assessment.

The assessment shall be made by recording the liability of the taxpayer in the office of the Secretary in accordance with rules or regulations prescribed by the Secretary. Upon request of the taxpayer, the Secretary shall furnish the taxpayer a copy of the record of the assessment.

In 1976, P.L. 94-455, Sec. 1906(b)(13)(A), substituted "Secretary" for "Secretary or his delegate" each place it appeared in Code Sec. 6203, effective 2/1/77.

Sec. 6204. Supplemental assessments.
(a) General rule.

The Secretary may, at any time within the period prescribed for assessment, make a supplemental assessment whenever it is ascertained that any assessment is imperfect or incomplete in any material respect.

(b) Restrictions on assessment.

For restrictions on assessment of deficiencies in income, estate, gift, and certain excise taxes, see section 6213.

In 1976, P.L. 94-455, Sec. 1906(b)(13)(A), substituted "Secretary" for "Secretary or his delegate" each place it appeared in Code Sec. 6204, effective 2/1/77.

In 1974, P.L. 93-406, Sec. 1016(a)(27), substituted "gift, and certain excise taxes" for "and gift taxes" in subsec. (b), effective 9/2/74 or other date as specified in Sec. 1017 of this Act, reproduced in note following Code Sec. 401.

Sec. 6205. Special rules applicable to certain employment taxes.
(a) Adjustment of tax.

(1) General rule. If less than the correct amount of tax imposed by section 3101, 3111, 3201, 3221, or 3402 is paid with respect to any payment of wages or compensation, proper adjustments, with respect to both the tax and the amount to be deducted, shall be made, without interest, in such manner and at such times as the Secretary may by regulations prescribe.

(2) United States as employer. For purposes of this subsection, in the case of remuneration received from the United States or a wholly-owned instrumentality thereof during any calendar year, each head of a Federal agency or instrumentality who makes a return pursuant to section 3122 and each agent, designated by the head of a Federal agency or instrumentality, who makes a return pursuant to such section shall be deemed a separate employer.

(3) Guam or American Samoa as employer. For purposes of this subsection, in the case of remuneration received during any calendar year from the Government of Guam, the Government of American Samoa, a political subdivision of either, or any instrumentality of any one or more of the foregoing which is wholly owned thereby, the Governor of Guam, the Governor of American Samoa, and each agent designated by either who makes a return pursuant to section 3125 shall be deemed a separate employer.

(4) District of Columbia as employer. For purposes of this subsection, in the case of remuneration received during any calendar year from the District of Columbia or any instrumentality which is wholly owned thereby, the Mayor of the District of Columbia and each agent designated by him who makes a return pursuant to section 3125 shall be deemed a separate employer.

(5) States and political subdivisions as employer. For purposes of this subsection, in the case of remuneration received from a State or any political subdivision thereof (or any instrumentality of any one or more of the foregoing which is wholly owned thereby) during any calendar year, each head of an agency or instrumentality, and each agent designated by either, who makes a return pursuant to section 3125 shall be deemed a separate employer.

(b) Underpayments.

If less than the correct amount of tax imposed by section 3101, 3111, 3201, 3221, or 3402 is paid or deducted with respect to any payment of wages or compensation and the underpayment cannot be adjusted under subsection (a) of this section, the amount of the underpayment shall be assessed and collected in such manner and at such times (subject to the statute of limitations properly applicable thereto) as the Secretary may by regulations prescribe.

In 1986, P.L. 99-272, Sec. 13205(a)(2)(D), added para. (a)(5), effective for services performed after 3/31/86.

In 1976, P.L. 94-455, Sec. 1906(a)(13), substituted "Mayor of the District of Columbia and each agent designated by him" for "Commissioners of the District of Columbia and each agent designated by them" in para. (a)(4), effective 2/1/77.

—P.L. 94-455, Sec. 1906(b)(13)(A), substituted "Secretary" for "Secretary or his delegate" each place it appeared in Code Sec. 6205, effective 2/1/77.

3,627

Code Sec. 6205 — Assessment

In 1965, P.L. 89-97, Sec. 317(d), added para. (a)(4), effective for services performed after 9/30/65 and after the calendar quarter in which the Secretary of the Treasury receives a certification from the Commissioners of the District of Columbia expressing their desire to have the insurance system established by title II (and part A of title XVIII) of the Social Security Act extended to the officers and employees coming under the provisions of such amendments.

In 1960, P.L. 86-778, Sec. 103(r)(1), added para. (a)(3), effective for service in the employ of the Government of Guam or any political subdivision thereof, or any instrumentality of any one or more of the foregoing wholly owned thereby, which is performed after 1960 and after the calendar quarter in which the Secretary of the Treasury receives a certification by the Governor of Guam that legislation has been enacted by the Government of Guam expressing its desire to have the insurance system established by title II of the Social Security Act, section 401 *et seq.* of Title 42, extended to the officers and employees of such Government and such political subdivisions and instrumentalities, and (2) service in the employ of the Government of American Samoa or any political subdivision thereof or any instrumentality of any one or more of the foregoing wholly owned thereby, which is performed after 1960 and after the calendar quarter in which the Secretary of the Treasury receives a certification by the Governor of American Samoa that the Government of American Samoa desires to have the insurance system established by title II of the Social Security Act, section 401 *et seq.* of Title 42, extended to the officers and employees of such Government and such political subdivisions and instrumentalities.

Sec. 6206. Special rules applicable to excessive claims under certain sections.

Any portion of a refund made under section 6416(a)(4) and any portion of a payment made under section 6420, 6421, or 6427 which constitutes an excessive amount (as defined in section 6675(b)), and any civil penalty provided by section 6675, may be assessed and collected as if it were a tax imposed by section 4081 (with respect to refunds under section 6416(a)(4) and payments under sections 6420 and 6421), or 4041 or 4081 (with respect to payments under section 6427) and as if the person who made the claim were liable for such tax. The period for assessing any such portion, and for assessing any such penalty, shall be 3 years from the last day prescribed for the filing of the claim under section 6416(a)(4), 6420, 6421, or 6427, as the case may be.

In 2005, P.L. 109-59, Sec. 11163(d)(1)(A), substituted "Any portion of a refund made under section 6416(a)(4) and any portion" for "Any portion" in Code Sec. 6206 . . . Sec. 11163(d)(1)(B), substituted "refunds under section 6416(a)(4) and payments under sections 6420" for "payments under sections 6420" in Code Sec. 6206 . . . Sec. 11163(d)(1)(C), substituted "section 6416(a)(4), 6420" for "section 6420" in Code Sec. 6206 . . . Sec. 11163(d)(1)(D), substituted "certain sections" for "sections 6420, 6421, and 6427" in the heading of Code Sec. 6206, effective for sales after 12/31/2005.

In 2004, P.L. 108-357, Sec. 853(d)(2)(F), substituted "or 4081" for ", 4081, or 4091" in Code Sec. 6206, effective for aviation-grade kerosene removed, entered, or sold after 12/31/2004.

—P.L. 108-357, Sec. 853(f), of this Act, provides:

"*(f) Floor stocks tax.*

"(1) In general. There is hereby imposed on aviation-grade kerosene held on January 1, 2005, by any person a tax equal to—

"(A) the tax which would have been imposed before such date on such kerosene had the amendments made by this section been in effect at all times before such date, reduced by

"(B) the sum of—

"(i) the tax imposed before such date on such kerosene under section 4091 of the Internal Revenue Code of 1986, as in effect on such date, and

"(ii) in the case of kerosene held exclusively for such person's own use, the amount which such person would (but for this clause) reasonably expect (as of such date) to be paid as a refund under section 6427(l) of such Code with respect to such kerosene.

"(2) Exception for fuel held in aircraft fuel tank. Paragraph (1) shall not apply to kerosene held in the fuel tank of an aircraft on January 1, 2005.

"(3) Liability for tax and method of payment.

"(A) Liability for tax. The person holding the kerosene on January 1, 2005, to which the tax imposed by paragraph (1) applies shall be liable for such tax.

"(B) Method and time for payment. The tax imposed by paragraph (1) shall be paid at such time and in such manner as the Secretary of the Treasury (or the Secretary's delegate) shall prescribe, including the nonapplication of such tax on de minimis amounts of kerosene.

"(4) Transfer of floor stock tax revenues to trust funds. For purposes of determining the amount transferred to any trust fund, the tax imposed by this subsection shall be treated as imposed by section 4081 of the Internal Revenue Code of 1986—

"(A) in any case in which tax was not imposed by section 4091 of such Code, at the Leaking Underground Storage Tank Trust Fund financing rate under such section to the extent of 0.1 cents per gallon, and

"(B) at the rate under section 4081(a)(2)(A)(iv) of such Code to the extent of the remainder.

"(5) Held by a person. For purposes of this subsection, kerosene shall be considered as held by a person if title thereto has passed to such person (whether or not delivery to the person has been made).

"(6) Other laws applicable. All provisions of law, including penalties, applicable with respect to the tax imposed by section 4081 of such Code shall, insofar as applicable and not inconsistent with the provisions of this subsection, apply with respect to the floor stock tax imposed by paragraph (1) to the same extent as if such tax were imposed by such section."

In 1993, P.L. 103-66, Sec. 13242(d)(14), substituted "4041, 4081, or 4091" for "4041 or 4091" in Code Sec. 6206, effective 1/1/94.

In 1987, P.L. 100-203, Sec. 10502(d)(5), substituted "or 4041 or 4091" for "or 4041", effective for sales after 3/31/88.

In 1983, P.L. 97-424, Sec. 515(b)(3)(A), deleted "4091 (with respect to payments under section 6424)," after "6421)," and deleted "6424," each place it appeared in the heading and the text of Code Sec. 6206, for articles sold after 1/6/83.

In 1970, P.L. 91-258, Sec. 207(d)(3), substituted "6424, and 6427" for "and 6424", substituted "6424, or 6427" for "or 6424", substituted "by section 4081 (with respect to payments under sections 6420 and 6421), 4091 (with respect to payments under section 6424), or 4041 (with respect to payments under section 6427)" for "by section 4081 (or, in the case of lubricating oil, by section 4091)", effective 7/1/70.

In 1965, P.L. 89-44, Sec. 202, added the reference to 6424 in the heading and the text and added "(or, in the case of lubricating oil, by section 4091)" in the text of Code Sec. 6206 effective 1/1/66.

In 1956, ch. 462, Sec. 208(d)(1), added the reference 6421 in the heading and the text of Code Sec. 6206 effective 6/29/56.

—ch. 160, Sec. 4(b)(1), added Code Sec. 6206.

Sec. 6207. Cross references.

(1) For prohibition of suits to restrain assessment of any tax, see section 7421.

(2) For prohibition of assessment of taxes against insolvent banks, see section 7507.

(3) For assessment where property subject to tax has been sold in a distraint proceeding without the tax having been assessed prior to such sale, see section 6342.

(4) For assessment with respect to taxes required to be paid by chapter 52, see section 5703.

(5) For assessment in case of distilled spirits removed from place where distilled and not deposited in bonded warehouse, see section 5006(c).

(6) For period of limitation upon assessment, see chapter 66.

In 1976, P.L. 94-455, Sec. 1906(a)(14), deleted para. (7), effective 2/1/77. Prior to deletion, para. (7) read as follows:

"(7) For assessment under the provisions of the Tariff Act of 1930 of the taxes imposed by section 4501(b), and subchapters A, B, C, D, and E of chapter 38, see sections 4504 and 4601, respectively."

In 1958, P.L. 85-859, Sec. 204(2), changed para. (4) from "For assessment in case of sale or removal of tobacco, snuff, cigars, and cigarettes without the use of the proper stamps, see section 5703(d)" . . . Sec. 204(3), redesignated former paras. (8) and (9) as paras. (6) and (7), and deleted paras. (6) and (7) which contained cross references relating to assessments in case of certain spirits subject to excessive leakage, and to assessment of deficiencies in production of distilled spirits, effective 9/3/58.

In 1956, ch. 160, Sec. 4(b)(1), redesignated Code Sec. 6206 as Code Sec. 6207.

Subchapter B.—Deficiency Procedures in the Case of Income, Estate, Gift, and Certain Excise Taxes

Sec.
6211. Definition of a deficiency.
6212. Notice of deficiency.
6213. Restrictions applicable to deficiencies; petition to Tax Court.
6214. Determinations by Tax Court.
6215. Assessment of deficiency found by Tax Court.
6216. Cross references.

In 1969, P.L. 91-172, Sec. 101(j)(62), substituted "Gift, and Certain Excise Taxes" for "and Gift Taxes" in the heading of subchapter B.

Assessment

Sec. 6211. Definition of a deficiency.
(a) In general.

For purposes of this title in the case of income, estate, and gift taxes imposed by subtitles A and B and excise taxes imposed by chapters 41, 42, 43, and 44, the term "deficiency" means the amount by which the tax imposed by subtitle A or B, or chapter 41, 42, 43, or 44, exceeds the excess of—

(1) the sum of

(A) the amount shown as the tax by the taxpayer upon his return, if a return was made by the taxpayer and an amount was shown as the tax by the taxpayer thereon, plus

(B) the amounts previously assessed (or collected without assessment) as a deficiency, over—

(2) the amount of rebates, as defined in subsection (b)(2), made.

(b) Rules for application of subsection (a).

For purposes of this section—

(1) The tax imposed by Subtitle A and the tax shown on the return shall both be determined without regard to payments on account of estimated tax, without regard to the credit under section 31, without regard to the credit under section 33, and without regard to any credits resulting from the collection of amounts assessed under section 6851 or 6852 (relating to termination assessments).

(2) The term "rebate" means so much of an abatement, credit, refund, or other repayment, as was made on the ground that the tax imposed by subtitle A or B or chapter 41, 42, 43, or 44 was less than the excess of the amount specified in subsection (a)(1) over the rebates previously made.

(3) The computation by the Secretary, pursuant to section 6014, of the tax imposed by chapter 1 shall be considered as having been made by the taxpayer and the tax so computed considered as shown by the taxpayer upon his return.

(4) For purposes of subsection (a)—

⎡ • *Caution:* Code Sec. 6211(b)(4)(A), following, reflects the amendment made by Sec. 10909(b)(2)(N), P.L. 111-148. As provided in Sec. 10909(c), P.L. 111-148, as amended by Sec. 101(b)(2), P.L. 111-312, Code Sec. 6211(b)(4)(A) will read as if those amendments had never been enacted, effective for tax. yrs. begin. after 12/31/2011. Code Sec. 6211(b)(4)(A) is further amended by Sec. 10105(d), P.L. 111-148, effective for tax. yrs. end. after 12/31/2013. For Code Sec. 6211(b)(4)(A), reflecting the sunset, and generally effective after 12/31/2013, see below. ⎦

(A) any excess of the sum of the credits allowable under sections 24(d), 25A by reason of subsection (i)(6) thereof, 32, 34, 35, 36, 36A, 36C, 53(e), 168(k)(4), 6428, and 6431 over the tax imposed by subtitle A (determined without regard to such credits), and

⎡ • *Caution:* Code Sec. 6211(b)(4)(A), following, reflects the sunset of the amendments made by Sec. 10909(b)(2)(N), P.L. 111-148, and includes the amendment by Sec. 10105(d) of P.L. 111-148. For details of those amendments, effective date and sunset provisions, see the history for this Code Sec. ⎦

(A) any excess of the sum of the credits allowable under sections 24(d), 25A by reason of subsection (i)(6) thereof, 32, 34, 35, 36, 36A, 36B, 53(e), 168(k)(4), 6428, and 6431 over the tax imposed by subtitle A (determined without regard to such credits), and

(B) any excess of the sum of such credits as shown by the taxpayer on his return over the amount shown as the tax by the taxpayer on such return (determined without regard to such credits),

shall be taken into account as negative amounts of tax.

(c) Coordination with subchapters C and D.

In determining the amount of any deficiency for purposes of this subchapter, adjustments to partnership items shall be made only as provided in subchapters C and D.

In 2010, P.L. 111-312, Sec. 101(b)(1), amended Sec. 10909(c) of P.L. 111-148 [see below]

Prior to amendment, Sec. 10909(c) of P.L. 111-148, read as follows:

"(c) Application and Extension of EGTRRA Sunset. Notwithstanding section 901 of the Economic Growth and Tax Relief Reconciliation Act of 2001, such section shall apply to the amendments made by this section and the amendments made by section 202 of such Act by substituting 'December 31, 2011' for 'December 31, 2010' in subsection (a)(1) thereof."

—P.L. 111-312, Sec. 101(b)(2), substituted "Except as provided in subsection (c), the amendments" for "the amendments" in Sec. 10909(d), P.L. 111-148, (the effective date section for amendments made by Sec. 10909, P.L. 111-148), see below.

Prior to amendment, Sec. 10909(d), P.L. 111-148, read as follows:

"(d) Effective Date. The amendments made by this section shall apply to taxable years beginning after December 31, 2009."

—P.L. 111-148, Sec. 10105(d), added Sec. 1401(d)(3) of this Act, which provided for this amendment, by adding "36B," after "36A," in subpara. (b)(4)(A), effective for tax. yrs. end. after 12/31/2013, as provided in Sec. 1401(e) of this Act.

—P.L. 111-148, Sec. 10909(b)(2)(N), added "36C," before "53(e)" in subpara. (b)(4)(A), effective for tax. yrs. begin. after 12/31/2009.

—P.L. 111-148, Sec. 10909(c), of this Act, relating to the application and extension of the EGTRRA sunset provisions, [as amended by Sec. 101(b)(1) of P.L. 111-312, see above] provides:

"(c) Sunset provision. Each provision of law amended by this section is amended to read as such provision would read if this section had never been enacted. The amendments made by the preceding sentence shall apply to taxable years beginning after December 31, 2011."

—P.L. 111-148, Sec. 10909(d), of this Act [as amended by Sec. 101(b)(2), P.L. 111-312, see above] provides:

"(d) Effective Date. Except as provided in subsection (c) [Sec. 10909(c) of this Act], the amendments made by this section shall apply to taxable years beginning after December 31, 2009."

In 2009, P.L. 111-5, Sec. 1001(e)(1), added "36A," after "36," in subpara. (b)(4)(A), effective for tax. yrs. begin. after 12/31/2008.

—P.L. 111-5, Sec. 1004(b)(7), added "25A by reason of subsection (i)(6) thereof," after "24(d)," in subpara. (b)(4)(A), effective for tax. yrs. begin. after 12/31/2008.

—P.L. 111-5, Sec. 1201(a)(3)(B), added "168(k)(4)," after "53(e)," in subpara. (b)(4)(A) . . . Sec. 1201(b)(2), [Ed. Note: same amendment as Sec. 1201(a)(3)(B)], effective for tax. yrs. end. after 3/31/2008.

—P.L. 111-5, Sec. 1531(c)(4), substituted "6428, and 6431" for "and 6428" in subpara. (b)(4)(A), effective for obligations issued after 2/17/2009.

In 2008, P.L. 110-289, Sec. 3011(b)(2), substituted "34, 35, 36, 53(e), and 6428" for "34, and 35, 53(e), and 6428" in subpara. (b)(4)(A), effective for residences purchased on or after 4/9/2008, in tax. yrs. end. on or after such date.

—P.L. 110-185, Sec. 101(b)(1), substituted "53(e), and 6428" for "and 53(e)" in subpara. (d)(4)(A) [sic (b)(4)(A)], enacted 2/13/2008.

In 2007, P.L. 110-172, Sec. 11(a)(35), substituted "34, and 35" for "and 34 [sic 34]" in subpara. (b)(4)(A), enacted 12/29/2007.

In 2006, P.L. 109-432, Sec. 402(b)(1), substituted "34, and 53(e)" for "and 34" in subpara. (b)(4)(A), effective for tax. yrs. begin. after 12/20/2006.

In 2000, P.L. 106-554, Sec. 1(a)(7), [which enacted into law Sec. 314(a) of P.L. 106-554] substituted "sections 24(d), 32, and 34" for "sections 32 and 34" in para. (b)(4), effective for tax. yrs. begin. after 12/31/97.

In 1998, P.L. 105-206, Sec. 6012(f)(1), substituted "subchapters C and D" for "subchapter C" in the heading of subsec. (c) . . . Sec. 6012(f)(2), substituted "subchapters C and D" for "subchapter C" in subsec. (c), effective for partnership tax. yrs. end. after 8/5/97.

In 1997, P.L. 105-34, Sec. 1231(b), added subsec. (c), effective for partnership tax. yrs. end. after 8/5/97.

In 1988, P.L. 100-647, Sec. 1015(r)(2), amended para. (b)(4) effective for notices of deficiencies mailed after 11/10/88.

Prior to amendment, para. (b)(4) read as follows:

"(4) The tax imposed by subtitle A and the tax shown on the return shall both be determined without regard to the credit under section 34, unless, without regard to such credit, the tax imposed by subtitle A exceeds the excess of the amount specified in subsection (a)(1) over the amount specified in subsection (a)(2)."

—P.L. 100-418, Sec. 1941(b)(2)(B)(i), substituted "or 44" for "44, or 45" in subsec. (a) . . . Sec. 1941(b)(2)(B)(ii), substituted "or 44" for "44, or 45" in para. (b)(2) . . . Sec. 1941(b)(2)(C), substituted "and 44" for "44, and 45" in subsec. (a) . . . Sec. 1941(b)(2)(D), deleted paras. (b)(5) and (b)(6), effective for crude oil removed from the premises on or after 8/23/88.

Prior to deletion, paras. (b)(5) and (b)(6) read as follows:

"(5) The amount withheld under section 4995(a) from amounts payable to any producer for crude oil removed during any taxable period (as defined in section 4996(b)(7)) which is not otherwise shown on a return by such producer shall be treated as tax shown by the producer on a return for the taxable period.

"(6) Any liability to pay amounts required to be withheld under section 4995(a) shall not be treated as a tax imposed by chapter 45."

In 1987, P.L. 100-203, Sec. 10713(b)(2)(B), substituted "section 6851 or 6852" for "section 6851" in para. (b)(1), effective 12/22/87.

In 1984, P.L. 98-369, Sec. 474(r)(33)(A), substituted "without regard to the credit under section 33" for "without regard to so much of the credit under section 32 as exceeds 2 percent of the interest on obligations described in section 1451" in para. (b)(1) . . . Sec. 474(r)(33)(B), substituted "section 34" for "section 39" in para. (b)(4), effective for tax. yrs. begin. after 12/31/83, and to carrybacks from tax yrs. begin. after 12/31/83.

In 1980, P.L. 96-223, Sec. 101(f)(1)(A), substituted "44, or 45" for "or 44" each place it appeared in subsec. (a) . . . Sec. 101(f)(1)(B), substituted "44, or 45" for "or 44" each place it appeared in subsec. (b) . . . Sec. 101(f)(2), substituted "44, and 45" for "and 44" each place it appeared in subsec. (a) . . . Sec. 101(f)(3), added paras. (b)(5) and (b)(6), effective for periods after 2/29/80.

In 1976, P.L. 94-455, Sec. 1204(c)(4), deleted "and" after "31," and added ", and without regard to any credits resulting from the collection of amounts assessed under section 6851 (relating to termination assessments)" before the period at the end of para. (b)(1), for action taken under Code Sec. 6851, 6861 or 6862 where the notice and demand takes place after '76. Sec. 2(a) of P.L. 94-528, postponed the effective date to 2/28/77.

—P.L. 94-455, Sec. 1307(d)(2)(E), substituted "chapters 41, 42," for "chapters 42" in subsec. (a), effective 10/4/76.

—P.L. 94-455, Sec. 1307(d)(2)(F)(i), substituted "chapter 41, 42," for "chapter 42" in subsec. (a) and para. (b)(2), effective 10/4/76.

—P.L. 94-455, Sec. 1605(b)(4), substituted "43, and 44" for "and 43" in subsec. (a), substituted "43, or 44" for "or 43" in subsec. (a) and para. (b)(2), effective for tax. yrs. of real estate investment trusts begin. after 10/4/76.

—P.L. 94-455, Sec. 1906(b)(13)(A), substituted "Secretary" for "Secretary or his delegate" in para. (b)(3), effective 2/1/77.

In 1974, P.L. 93-406, Sec. 1016(a)(9)(A), amended the part of subsec. (a) preceding para. (1), effective 9/2/74 or other date as specified in Sec. 1017 of the Act (reproduced following Code Sec. 401).

Prior to amendment, subsec. (a) read as follows:

"(a) In general.

"For purposes of this title in the case of income, estate, gift and excise taxes, imposed by subtitles A and B, and chapter 42 the term 'deficiency' means the amount by which the tax imposed by subtitles A or B or chapter 42 exceeds the excess of—"

—P.L. 93-406, Sec. 1016(a)(9)(B), substituted "chapter 42 or 43" for "chapter 42" in subsec. (b)(2), effective 9/2/74 or other date as specified in Sec. 1017 of the Act (reproduced following Code Sec. 401).

In 1969, P.L. 91-172, Sec. 101(f)(1), added ", and excise" and "and chapter 42" and "or chapter 42" to subsec. (a) as precedes para. (1), effective 1/1/70.

—P.L. 91-172, Sec. 101(j)(39), substituted "subtitle A or B or chapter 42" for "subtitles A or B", effective 1/1/70.

In 1966, P.L. 89-368, Sec. 102, substituted "subtitle A" for "chapter 1." in para. (b)(1).

In 1965, P.L. 89-44, Sec. 809, added para. (b)(4) for max. yrs. begin. after 6/30/65.

Sec. 6212. Notice of deficiency.

(a) In general.

If the Secretary determines that there is a deficiency in respect of any tax imposed by subtitle A or B or chapter 41, 42, 43, or 44, he is authorized to send notice of such deficiency to the taxpayer by certified mail or registered mail. Such notice shall include a notice to the taxpayer of the taxpayer's right to contact a local office of the taxpayer advocate and the location and phone number of the appropriate office.

(b) Address for notice of deficiency.

(1) Income and gift taxes and certain excise taxes. In the absence of notice to the Secretary under section 6903 of the existence of a fiduciary relationship, notice of a deficiency in respect of a tax imposed by subtitle A, chapter 12, chapter 41, chapter 42, chapter 43, or chapter 44 if mailed to the taxpayer at his last known address, shall be sufficient for purposes of subtitle A, chapter 12, chapter 41, chapter 42, chapter 43, chapter 44, and this chapter even if such taxpayer is deceased, or is under a legal disability, or, in the case of a corporation, has terminated its existence.

(2) Joint income tax return. In the case of a joint income tax return filed by husband and wife, such notice of deficiency may be a single joint notice, except that if the Secretary has been notified by either spouse that separate residences have been established, then, in lieu of the single joint notice, a duplicate original of the joint notice shall be sent by certified mail or registered mail to each spouse at his last known address.

(3) Estate tax. In the absence of notice to the Secretary under section 6903 of the existence of a fiduciary relationship, notice of a deficiency in respect of a tax imposed by chapter 11, if addressed in the name of the decedent or other person subject to liability and mailed to his last known address, shall be sufficient for purposes of chapter 11 and of this chapter.

(c) Further deficiency letters restricted.

(1) General rule. If the Secretary has mailed to the taxpayer a notice of deficiency as provided in subsection (a), and the taxpayer files a petition with the Tax Court within the time prescribed in section 6213(a), the Secretary shall have no right to determine any additional deficiency of income tax for the same taxable year, of gift tax for the same calendar year, of estate tax in respect of the taxable estate of the same decedent, of chapter 41 tax for the same taxable year, of chapter 43 tax for the same taxable year, of chapter 44 tax for the same taxable year, of section 4940 tax for the same taxable year, or of chapter 42 tax (other than under section 4940) with respect to any act (or failure to act) to which such petition relates, except in the case of fraud, and except as provided in section 6214(a) (relating to assertion of greater deficiencies before the Tax Court), in section 6213(b)(1) (relating to mathematical or clerical errors), in section 6851 or 6852 (relating to termination assessments), or in section 6861(c) (relating to the making of jeopardy assessments).

(2) Cross references. For assessment as a deficiency notwithstanding the prohibition of further deficiency letters, in the case of—

(A) Deficiency attributable to change of treatment with respect to itemized deductions, see section 63(e)(3).

(B) Deficiency attributable to gain on involuntary conversion, see section 1033(a)(2)(C) and (D).

(C) Deficiency attributable to activities not engaged in for profit, see section 183(e)(4).

For provisions allowing determination of tax in title 11 cases, see section 505(a) of title 11 of the United States Code.

(d) Authority to rescind notice of deficiency with taxpayer's consent.

The Secretary may, with the consent of the taxpayer, rescind any notice of deficiency mailed to the taxpayer. Any notice so rescinded shall not be treated as a notice of deficiency for purposes of subsection (c)(1) (relating to further deficiency letters restricted), section 6213(a) (relating to restrictions applicable to deficiencies; petition to Tax Court), and section 6512(a) (relating to limitations in case of petition to Tax Court), and the taxpayer shall have no right to file a petition with the Tax Court based on such notice.

Nothing in this subsection shall affect any suspension of the running of any period of limitations during any period during which the rescinded notice was outstanding.

In 1998, P.L. 105-206, Sec. 1102(b), added a sentence at the end of subsec. (a), effective 7/22/98. Sec. 1102(f)(3) and (4) of this Act, provides:

"(3) National Taxpayer Advocate. Notwithstanding section 7803(c)(1)(B)(iv) of such Code, as added by this section, in appointing the first National Taxpayer Advocate after the date of the enactment of this Act, the Secretary of the Treasury—

"(A) shall not appoint any individual who was an officer or employee of the Internal Revenue Service at any time during the 2-year period ending on the date of appointment, and

"(B) need not consult with the Internal Revenue Service Oversight Board if the Oversight Board has not been appointed.

"(4) Current officers.

"(A) In the case of an individual serving as Commissioner of Internal Revenue on the date of the enactment of this Act who was appointed to such position before such date, the 5-year term required by section 7803(a)(1) of such Code, as added by this section, shall begin as of the date of such appointment.

"(B) Clauses (ii), (iii), and (iv) of section 7803(c)(1)(B) of such Code, as added by this section, shall not apply to the individual serving as Taxpayer Advocate on the date of the enactment of this Act."

—P.L. 105-206, Sec. 3463(a), of this Act, reads as follows:

"(a) In general. The Secretary of the Treasury or the Secretary's delegate shall include on each notice of deficiency under section 6212 of the Internal Revenue Code of 1986 the date determined by such Secretary (or delegate) as the last day on which the taxpayer may file a petition with the Tax Court."

—P.L. 105-206, Sec. 6005(e)(3), added "on or" before "before" each place it appeared in Sec. 312(d)(2) [sic (e)(2)] of P.L. 105-34 [see below].

In 1997, P.L. 105-34, Sec. 312(d)(12), deleted subpara. (c)(2)(C) and redesignated subpara. (c)(2)(E) [sic (D)] as (c)(2)(C), effective for sales and exchanges after 5/6/97, except as provided by Sec. 312(d)(2)-(4) [(e)(2)-(4)] of this Act [as amended by Sec. 6005(e)(3) of 105-206, see above], which reads as follows:

"(2) Sales on or before date of enactment. At the election of the taxpayer, the amendments made by this section shall not apply to any sale or exchange on or before the date of the enactment of this Act.

"(3) Certain sales within 2 years after date of enactment. Section 121 of the Internal Revenue Code of 1986 (as amended by this section) shall be applied without regard to subsection (c)(2)(B) thereof in the case of any sale or exchange of property during the 2-year period beginning on the date of the enactment of this Act if the taxpayer held such property on the date of the enactment of this Act and fails to meet the ownership and use requirements of subsection (a) thereof with respect to such property.

"(4) Binding contracts. At the election of the taxpayer, the amendments made by this section shall not apply to a sale or exchange after the date of the enactment of this Act, if—

"(A) such sale or exchange is pursuant to a contract which was binding on such date, or

"(B) without regard to such amendments, gain would not be recognized under section 1034 of the Internal Revenue Code of 1986 (as in effect on the day before the date of the enactment of this Act) on such sale or exchange by reason of a new residence acquired on or before such date or with respect to the acquisition of which by the taxpayer a binding contract was in effect on such date.

This paragraph shall not apply to any sale or exchange by an individual if the treatment provided by section 877(a)(1) of the Internal Revenue Code of 1986 applies to such individual."

Prior to deletion, subpara. (c)(2)(C) read as follows:

"(C) Deficiency attributable to gain on sale or exchange of principal residence, see section 1034(j)."

In 1988, P.L. 100-647, Sec. 1015(m), added the last sentence to subsec. (d), effective for notices of deficiency issued on or after 1/1/86.

—P.L. 100-418, Sec. 1941(b)(2)(B)(iii), substituted "or 44" for "44, or 45" in subsec. (a) . . . Sec. 1941(b)(2)(E)(i), substituted "or chapter 44" for "chapter 44, or chapter 45" in para. (b)(1) . . . Sec. 1941(b)(2)(E)(ii), substituted "chapter 44, and this chapter" for "chapter 44, chapter 45, and this chapter" in para. (b)(1) . . . Sec. 1941(b)(2)(F)(i), substituted "or of chapter 42 tax" for "of chapter 42 tax" in para. (c)(1) . . . Sec. 1941(b)(2)(F)(ii), deleted ", or of chapter 45 tax for the same taxable period" before "except in the case of fraud" in para. (c)(1), effective for crude oil removed from the premises on or after 8/23/88.

In 1987, P.L. 100-203, Sec. 10713(b)(2)(C), substituted "section 6851 or 6852" for "section 6851" in para. (c)(1), effective 12/22/87.

In 1986, P.L. 99-514, Sec. 104(b)(17), amended subpara. (c)(2)(A), effective for tax. yrs. begin. after 12/31/86.

Prior to amendment, subpara. (c)(2)(A) read as follows:

"(A) Deficiency attributable to change of treatment with respect to itemized deductions and zero bracket amounts, see section 63(g)(5)."

—P.L. 99-514, Sec. 1562(a), added subsec. (d), effective for notices of deficiency issued on or after 1/1/86.

In 1981, P.L. 97-34, Sec. 442(d)(4), substituted "calendar year" for "calendar quarter" in para. (c)(1), effective for gifts made after 12/31/81.

In 1980, P.L. 96-589, Sec. 6(d)(2), added the last sentence to para. (c)(2), effective 10/1/79, except for any proceeding under the Bankruptcy Act begun before 10/1/79. Sec. 7(g) of this Act provides:

"(g) Definitions.

"For purposes of this section—

"(1) Bankruptcy case. The term 'bankruptcy case' means any case under title 11 of the United States Code (as recodified by P.L. 95-598).

"(2) Similar judicial proceeding. The term 'similar judicial proceeding' means a receivership, foreclosure, or similar proceeding in a Federal or State court (as modified by section 368(a)(3)(D) of the Internal Revenue Code of 1954)."

—P.L. 96-223, Sec. 101(f)(1)(C), substituted "44, or 45" for "or 44" each place it appeared in subsec. (a) . . . Sec. 101(f)(4)(A), substituted "chapter 44, or chapter 45" for "or chapter 44" each place it appeared in para. (b)(1) . . . Sec. 101(f)(4)(B), substituted "chapter 44, chapter 45, and this chapter" for "chapter 44, and this chapter" in para. (b)(1) . . . Sec. 101(f)(4)(C), substituted "certain excise taxes" for "taxes imposed by chapter 42" in the heading for para. (b)(1) . . . Sec. 101(f)(5)(A), substituted "of chapter 42 tax" for "or of chapter 42 tax" in para. (c)(1) . . . Sec. 101(f)(5)(B), added ", or of chapter 45 tax for the same taxable period" after "to which such petition relates", in subsec. (c), effective for periods after 2/29/80.

In 1978, P.L. 95-600, Sec. 405(c)(5), substituted "principal residence" for "personal residence" in subpara. (c)(2)(C), effective for sales and exchanges of residences after 7/26/78, in tax. yrs. ending after 7/26/78.

—P.L. 95-600, Sec. 701(t)(3)(C), amended Sec. 1605(b)(5)(D) of P.L. 94-455, by substituting "of chapter 43 tax for the same taxable year, of chapter 44 tax for the same taxable year," for "of chapter 43 tax for the same taxable years," in para. (c)(1), effective 10/4/76.

In 1977, P.L. 95-30, Sec. 101(d)(15), amended subpara. (c)(2)(A), effective for tax. yrs. begin. after 12/31/76.

Prior to amendment, subpara. (c)(2)(A) read as follows:

"(A) Deficiency attributable to change of election with respect to the standard deduction where taxpayer and his spouse made separate returns, see section 144(b)."

In 1976, P.L. 94-528, Sec. 2(a), changed the effective date for amendments made by Sec. 1204(c)(5) of P.L. 94-455, from effective for action taken under Code Sec. 6851, 6862 or 6862 where the notice and demand take place after 12/31/76, to effective for action taken under Code Sec. 6851, 6862 or 6862 where the notice and demand take place after 2/28/77, see below.

—P.L. 94-455, Sec. 214(b), added subpara. (c)(2)(E), effective for tax. yrs. begin. after 12/31/69, but does not apply to any tax. yr. end. before 10/4/76 with respect to which the period for assessing a deficiency has expired before 10/4/76.

—P.L. 94-455, Sec. 1204(c)(5), added "in section 6851 (relating to termination assessments)," after "errors)," in para. (c)(1), effective [as amended by Sec. 2(a) of P.L. 94-528, see above] for action taken under Code Sec. 6851, 6861 or 6862 where the notice and demand takes place after 2/28/77.

—P.L. 94-455, Sec. 1206(c)(3), substituted "(relating to mathematical or clerical errors)" for "(relating to mathematical errors)" in para. (c)(1), effective for returns with the meaning of para. 6213(f)(1) filed after 12/31/76.

—P.L. 94-455, Sec. 1307(d)(2)(F)(ii), substituted "chapter 41, 42," for "chapter 42" in subsec. (a), effective 10/4/76.

—P.L. 94-455, Sec. 1307(d)(2)(G), substituted "chapter 41, chapter 42" for "chapter 42" each place it appeared in para. (b)(1) . . . substituted "of chapter 41 tax for the same taxable year, of chapter 43 tax for the same taxable year," for "of chapter 43 tax for the same taxable years," in para. (c)(1), effective 10/4/76.

—P.L. 94-455, Sec. 1605(b)(5)(A), substituted "43, or 44" for "or 43" in subsec. (a) . . . Sec. 1605(b)(5)(B), substituted "chapter 43, or chapter 44" for "or chapter 43" in para. (b)(1) . . . Sec. 1605(b)(5)(C), substituted "chapter 43, chapter 44, and this chapter" for "chapter 43, and this chapter" in para. (b)(1) . . . Sec. 1605(b)(5)(D), substituted "of chapter 43 tax for the same taxable years, of chapter 44 tax for the same taxable years," for "of chapter 43 tax for the same taxable years," [sic] in para. (c)(1), effective for tax. yrs. of real estate investment trusts begin. after 10/4/76.

—P.L. 94-455, Sec. 1901(b)(31)(C), substituted "1033(a)(2)(C) and (D)" for "1033(a)(3)(C) and (D)" in subpara. (c)(2)(B), effective for tax. yrs. begin. after 12/31/76.

—P.L. 94-455, Sec. 1901(b)(37)(C), deleted subpara. (c)(2)(D), for tax. yrs. begin. after 12/31/76.

Prior to amendment, subpara. (c)(2)(D) read as follows:

"(D) Deficiency attributable to war loss recoveries where prior benefit rule is elected, see section 1335."

—P.L. 94-455, Sec. 1906(b)(13)(A), substituted "Secretary" for "Secretary or his delegate" each place it appeared in Code Sec. 6212, effective 2/1/77.

In 1974, P.L. 93-406, Sec. 1016(a)(10), substituted "chapter 42 or 43" for "chapter 42" in subsec. (a), substituted "chapter 42, or chapter 43" for "or chapter 42" and "chapter 42, chapter 43, and this chapter" for "chapter 42, and this chapter", in para. (b)(1), substituted "of the same decedent, of chapter 43 tax for the same taxable years," for "of the same decedent," in subsec. (c), effective 9/2/74, except as provided in Sec. 1017 of this Act reproduced in note following Code Sec. 401.

In 1970, P.L. 91-614, Sec. 102(d)(5), substituted "calendar quarter" for "calendar year" in para. (c)(1), effective for gifts made after 12/31/70.

In 1969, P.L. 91-172, Sec. 101(f)(2), deleted "or" before "of estate tax" and after "the same decedent" added "of section 4940 tax for the same taxable year, or of chapter 42 tax (other than under section 4940) with respect to any act (or failure to act) to which such petition relates," in para. (c)(1), effective 1/1/70.

—P.L. 91-172, Sec. 101(j)(40), substituted "subtitle A or B or chapter 42" for "subtitles A or B" in subsec. (a) . . . Sec. 101(j)(41), added "and taxes imposed by chapter 42" in the heading of para. (b)(1), substituted "subtitle A, chapter 12 or chapter 42" for "subtitle A or chapter 12" in para. (b)(1); and added "chapter 42," after "chapter 12," the last place it appears in para. (b)(1), effective 1/1/70.

In 1964, P.L. 88-272, Sec. 112(d)(1), substituted "with respect to the" for "to take" in subpara. (c)(2)(A), effective for tax. yrs. begin. after '63.

In 1958, P.L. 85-866, Sec. 89, added "certified mail or" before "registered mail" in subsecs. (a) and (b)(2), effective for mailings after 9/2/58.
—P.L. 85-866, Sec. 76, substituted "subtitle A or chapter 12" for "chapter 1 or 12" and substituted "subtitle A, chapter 12," for "such chapter" in subsec. (b)(1), effective 8/17/54.

Sec. 6213. Restrictions applicable to deficiencies; petition to Tax Court.

(a) Time for filing petition and restriction on assessment.

Within 90 days, or 150 days if the notice is addressed to a person outside the United States, after the notice of deficiency authorized in section 6212 is mailed (not counting Saturday, Sunday, or a legal holiday in the District of Columbia as the last day), the taxpayer may file a petition with the Tax Court for a redetermination of the deficiency. Except as otherwise provided in section 6851, 6852, or 6861 no assessment of a deficiency in respect of any tax imposed by subtitle A or B, chapter 41, 42, 43, or 44 and no levy or proceeding in court for its collection shall be made, begun, or prosecuted until such notice has been mailed to the taxpayer, nor until the expiration of such 90-day or 150-day period, as the case may be, nor, if a petition has been filed with the Tax Court, until the decision of the Tax Court has become final. Notwithstanding the provisions of section 7421(a), the making of such assessment or the beginning of such proceeding or levy during the time such prohibition is in force may be enjoined by a proceeding in the proper court, including the Tax Court, and a refund may be ordered by such court of any amount collected within the period during which the Secretary is prohibited from collecting by levy or through a proceeding in court under the provisions of this subsection. The Tax Court shall have no jurisdiction to enjoin any action or proceeding or order any refund under this subsection unless a timely petition for a redetermination of the deficiency has been filed and then only in respect of the deficiency that is the subject of such petition. Any petition filed with the Tax Court on or before the last date specified for filing such petition by the Secretary in the notice of deficiency shall be treated as timely filed.

(b) Exceptions to restrictions on assessment.

(1) Assessments arising out of mathematical or clerical errors. If the taxpayer is notified that, on account of a mathematical or clerical error appearing on the return, an amount of tax in excess of that shown on the return is due, and that an assessment of the tax has been or will be made on the basis of what would have been the correct amount of tax but for the mathematical or clerical error, such notice shall not be considered as a notice of deficiency for the purposes of subsection (a) (prohibiting assessment and collection until notice of the deficiency has been mailed), or of section 6212(c)(1) (restricting further deficiency letters), or of section 6512(a) (prohibiting credits or refunds after petition to the Tax Court), and the taxpayer shall have no right to file a petition with the Tax Court based on such notice, nor shall such assessment or collection be prohibited by the provisions of subsection (a) of this section. Each notice under this paragraph shall set forth the error alleged and an explanation thereof.

(2) Abatement of assessment of mathematical or clerical errors.

(A) Request for abatement. Notwithstanding section 6404(b), a taxpayer may file with the Secretary within 60 days after notice is sent under paragraph (1) a request for an abatement of any assessment specified in such notice, and upon receipt of such request, the Secretary shall abate the assessment. Any reassessment of the tax with respect to which an abatement is made under this subparagraph shall be subject to the deficiency procedures prescribed by this subchapter.

(B) Stay of collection. In the case of any assessment referred to in paragraph (1), notwithstanding paragraph (1), no levy or proceeding in court for the collection of such assessment shall be made, begun, or prosecuted during the period in which such assessment may be abated under this paragraph.

(3) Assessments arising out of tentative carryback or refund adjustments. If the Secretary determines that the amount applied, credited, or refunded under section 6411 is in excess of the overassessment attributable to the carryback or the amount described in section 1341(b)(1) with respect to which such amount was applied, credited, or refunded, he may assess without regard to the provisions of paragraph (2) the amount of the excess as a deficiency as if it were due to a mathematical or clerical error appearing on the return.

(4) Assessment of amount paid. Any amount paid as a tax or in respect of a tax may be assessed upon the receipt of such payment notwithstanding the provisions of subsection (a). In any case where such amount is paid after the mailing of a notice of deficiency under section 6212, such payment shall not deprive the Tax Court of jurisdiction over such deficiency determined under section 6211 without regard to such assessment.

(5) Certain orders of criminal restitution. If the taxpayer is notified that an assessment has been or will be made pursuant to section 6201(a)(4)—

(A) such notice shall not be considered as a notice of deficiency for the purposes of subsection (a) (prohibiting assessment and collection until notice of the deficiency has been mailed), section 6212(c)(1) (restricting further deficiency letters), or section 6512(a) (prohibiting credits or refunds after petition to the Tax Court), and

(B) subsection (a) shall not apply with respect to the amount of such assessment.

(c) Failure to file petition.

If the taxpayer does not file a petition with the Tax Court within the time prescribed in subsection (a), the deficiency, notice of which has been mailed to the taxpayer, shall be assessed, and shall be paid upon notice and demand from the Secretary.

(d) Waiver of restrictions.

The taxpayer shall at any time (whether or not a notice of deficiency has been issued) have the right, by a signed notice in writing filed with the Secretary, to waive the restrictions provided in subsection (a) on the assessment and collection of the whole or any part of the deficiency.

(e) Suspension of filing period for certain excise taxes.

The running of the time prescribed by subsection (a) for filing a petition in the Tax Court with respect to the taxes imposed by section 4941 (relating to taxes on self-dealing), 4942 (relating to taxes on failure to distribute income), 4943 (relating to taxes on excess business holdings), 4944 (relating to investments which jeopardize charitable purpose), 4945 (relating to taxes on taxable expenditures), 4951 (relating to taxes on self-dealing), or 4952 (relating to taxes on taxable expenditures), 4955 (relating to taxes on political expenditures), 4958 (relating to private excess benefit), 4971 (relating to excise taxes on failure to meet minimum funding standard), [or] 4975 (relating to excise taxes on prohibited transactions) shall be suspended for any period during which the Secretary has extended the time allowed for making correction under section 4963(e).

(f) Coordination with title 11.

(1) Suspension of running of period for filing petition in title 11 cases. In any case under title 11 of the United

Assessment   Code Sec. 6213

States Code, the running of the time prescribed by subsection (a) for filing a petition in the Tax Court with respect to any deficiency shall be suspended for the period during which the debtor is prohibited by reason of such case from filing a petition in the Tax Court with respect to such deficiency, and for 60 days thereafter.

(2) Certain action not taken into account. For purposes of the second and third sentences of subsection (a), the filing of a proof of claim or request for payment (or the taking of any other action) in a case under title 11 of the United States Code shall not be treated as action prohibited by such second sentence.

(g) Definitions.

For purposes of this section—

(1) Return. The term "return" includes any return, statement, schedule, or list, and any amendment or supplement thereto, filed with respect to any tax imposed by subtitle A or B, or chapter 41, 42, 43, or 44.

(2) Mathematical or clerical error. The term "mathematical or clerical error" means—

(A) an error in addition, subtraction, multiplication, or division shown on any return,

(B) an incorrect use of any table provided by the Internal Revenue Service with respect to any return if such incorrect use is apparent from the existence of other information on the return,

(C) an entry on a return of an item which is inconsistent with another entry of the same or another item on such return,

(D) an omission of information which is required to be supplied on the return to substantiate an entry on the return,

(E) an entry on a return of a deduction or credit in an amount which exceeds a statutory limit imposed by subtitle A or B, or chapter 41, 42 43, or 44, if such limit is expressed—

(i) as a specified monetary amount, or

(ii) as a percentage, ratio, or fraction,

and if the items entering into the application of such limit appear on such return,

(F) an omission of a correct taxpayer identification number required under section 32 (relating to the earned income credit) to be included on a return,

(G) an entry on a return claiming the credit under section 32 with respect to net earnings from self-employment described in section 32(c)(2)(A) to the extent the tax imposed by section 1401 (relating to self-employment tax) on such net earnings has not been paid,

(H) an omission of a correct TIN required under section 21 (relating to expenses for household and dependent care services necessary for gainful employment) or section 151 (relating to allowance of deductions for personal exemptions),

(I) an omission of a correct TIN required under section 24(e) (relating to child tax credit) to be included on a return,

(J) an omission of a correct TIN required under section 25A(g)(1) (relating to higher education tuition and related expenses) to be included on a return,

• **Caution:** Code Sec. 6213(g)(2)(K) through (M), following, were amended by Sec. 303(g), P.L. 107-16, the Economic Growth and Tax Relief Reconciliation Act of 2001 (EGTRRA). These provisions generally sunset for tax years beginning after 12/31/2012. For specific sunset provisions, see Sec. 901, P.L. 107-16 (as amended) reproduced in history notes for this Code Sec.

(K) an omission of information required by section 32(k)(2) (relating to taxpayers making improper prior claims of earned income credit),

(L) the inclusion on a return of a TIN required to be included on the return under section 21, 24, 32, or 6428 if—

(i) such TIN is of an individual whose age affects the amount of the credit under such section, and

(ii) the computation of the credit on the return reflects the treatment of such individual as being of an age different from the individual's age based on such TIN,

(M) the entry on the return claiming the credit under section 32 with respect to a child if, according to the Federal Case Registry of Child Support Orders established under section 453(h) of the Social Security Act, the taxpayer is a noncustodial parent of such child,

(N) an omission of the reduction required under section 36A(c) with respect to the credit allowed under section 36A or an omission of the correct social security account number required under section 36A(d)(1)(B),

(O) an omission of any increase required under section 36(f) with respect to the recapture of a credit allowed under section 36, and

(P) an entry on a return claiming the credit under section 36 if—

(i) the Secretary obtains information from the person issuing the TIN of the taxpayer that indicates that the taxpayer does not meet the age requirement of section 36(b)(4),

(ii) information provided to the Secretary by the taxpayer on an income tax return for at least one of the 2 preceding taxable years is inconsistent with eligibility for such credit, or

(iii) the taxpayer fails to attach to the return the form described in section 36(d)(4).

A taxpayer shall be treated as having omitted a correct TIN for purposes of the preceding sentence if information provided by the taxpayer on the return with respect to the individual whose TIN was provided differs from the information the Secretary obtains from the person issuing the TIN.

(h) Cross references.

(1) For assessment as if a mathematical error on the return, in the case of erroneous claims for income tax prepayment credits, see section 6201(a)(3).

(2) For assessments without regard to restrictions imposed by this section in the case of—

(A) Recovery of foreign income taxes, see section 905(c).

(B) Recovery of foreign estate tax, see section 2016.

(3) For provisions relating to application of this subchapter in the case of certain partnership items, etc., see section 6230(a).

In 2010, P.L. 111-312, Sec. 101(a)(1), substituted "December 31, 2012" for "December 31, 2010" both places it appears in Sec. 901, P.L. 107-16 [see below], effective as if included in the enactment of P.L. 107-16, EGTRRA, 6/7/2001.
—P.L. 111-237, Sec. 3(b)(1), added para. (b)(5), effective for restitution ordered after 8/16/2010.

In 2009, P.L. 111-92, Sec. 11(h)(1), deleted "and" at the end of subpara. (g)(2)(M)... Sec. 11(h)(2), substituted ", and" for the period at the end of subpara. (g)(2)(N)... Sec. 11(h)(3), added subpara. (g)(2)(O), effective for tax. yrs. end. on or after 4/19/2008.

—P.L. 111-92, Sec. 12(d), deleted "and" at the end of subpara. (g)(2)(N), substituted ", and" for the period at the end of subpara. (g)(2)(O), and added subpara. (g)(2)(P), effective for tax. yrs. end. on or after 4/9/2008.
—P.L. 111-5, Sec. 1001(d), deleted "and" at the end of clause (g)(2)(L)(ii), substituted ", and" for the period at the end of subpara. (g)(2)(M), and added subpara. (g)(2)(N), effective for tax. yrs. begin. after 12/31/2008.

In 2008, P.L. 110-185, Sec. 101(b)(2), substituted "32, or 6428" for "or 32" in subpara. (g)(2)(L), enacted 2/13/2008.

In 2005, P.L. 109-135, Sec. 201(b)(4)(B), repealed Sec. 406 of P.L. 109-73.
Prior to repeal, Sec. 406 of P.L. 109-73 read as follows:

"SEC. 406. SPECIAL RULE FOR DETERMINING EARNED INCOME.

"(a) In general. In the case of a qualified individual, if the earned income of the taxpayer for the taxable year which includes August 25, 2005, is less than the earned income of the taxpayer for the preceding taxable year, the credits allowed under sections 24(d) and 32 of the Internal Revenue Code of 1986 may, at the election of the taxpayer, be determined by substituting—

"(1) such earned income for the preceding taxable year, for

"(2) such earned income for the taxable year which includes August 25, 2005.

"(b) Qualified individual. For purposes of this section, the term 'qualified individual' means any individual whose principal place of abode on August 25, 2005, was located—

"(1) in the core disaster area, or

"(2) in the Hurricane Katrina disaster area (but outside the core disaster area) and such individual was displaced from such principal place of abode by reason of Hurricane Katrina.

"(c) Earned income. For purposes of this section, the term 'earned income' has the meaning given such term under section 32(c) of such Code.

"(d) Special rules.

"(1) Application to joint returns. For purposes of subsection (a), in the case of a joint return for a taxable year which includes August 25, 2005—

"(A) such subsection shall apply if either spouse is a qualified individual, and

"(B) the earned income of the taxpayer for the preceding taxable year shall be the sum of the earned income of each spouse for such preceding taxable year.

"(2) Uniform application of election. Any election made under subsection (a) shall apply with respect to both section 24(d) and section 32 of such Code.

"(3) Errors treated as mathematical error. For purposes of section 6213 of such Code, an incorrect use on a return of earned income pursuant to subsection (a) shall be treated as a mathematical or clerical error.

"(4) No effect on determination of gross income, etc. Except as otherwise provided in this section, the Internal Revenue Code of 1986 shall be applied without regard to any substitution under subsection (a)."

In 2002, P.L. 107-358, Sec. 2, added subsec. (c) in Sec. 901 of P.L. 107-16 [see below], effective 12/17/2002.

In 2001, P.L. 107-16, Sec. 303(g), deleted "and" at the end of subpara. (g)(2)(K), substituted ", and" for the period at the end of subpara. (g)(2)(L), and added subpara. (g)(2)(M), effective 1/1/2004.

—P.L. 107-16, Sec. 901, of this Act [as amended by Sec. 2 of P.L. 107-358, and Sec. 101(a)(1) of P.L. 111-312, see above], reads as follows:

"SEC. 901. SUNSET OF PROVISIONS OF ACT.

"(a) In general. All provisions of, and amendments made by, this Act shall not apply—

"(1) to taxable, plan, or limitation years beginning after December 31, 2012, or

"(2) in the case of title V, to estates of decedents dying, gifts made, or generation skipping transfers, after December 31, 2012.

"(b) Application of certain laws. The Internal Revenue Code of 1986 and the Employee Retirement Income Security Act of 1974 shall be applied and administered to years, estates, gifts, and transfers described in subsection (a) as if the provisions and amendments described in subsection (a) had never been enacted.

"(c) Exception. Subsection (a) shall not apply to section 803 (relating to no federal income tax on restitution received by victims of the Nazi regime or their heirs or estates)."

In 1998, P.L. 105-277, Sec. 3003(a), added a flush sentence at the end of para. (g)(2) . . . Sec. 3003(b), deleted "and" at the end of subpara. (g)(2)(J), substituted ", and" for the period at the end of subpara. (g)(2)(K), and added subpara. (g)(2)(L), effective for tax. yrs. end. after 10/21/98.

—P.L. 105-206, Sec. 3463(b), added a sentence at the end of subsec. (a), effective for notices mailed after 12/31/98.

—P.L. 105-206, Sec. 3464(a)(1), substituted ", including the Tax Court, and a refund may be ordered by such court of any amount collected within the period during which the Secretary is prohibited from collecting by levy or through a proceeding in court under the provisions of this subsection," for ", including the Tax Court," in subsec. (a) . . . Sec. 3464(a)(2), substituted "to enjoin any action or proceeding or order any refund" for "to enjoin any action or proceeding" in subsec. (a), effective 7/22/98.

—P.L. 105-206, Sec. 6010(p)(3), amended Sec. 1085(a)(3) of P.L. 105-34 [see below], effective for tax. yrs. begin. after 12/31/96.

Prior to amendment, Sec. 1085(a)(3) of P.L. 105-34 read as follows:

"(3) Extension procedures applicable to mathematical or clerical errors. Paragraph (2) of section 6213(g) (relating to the definition of mathematical or clerical errors) is amended by striking 'and' at the end of subparagraph (H), by striking the period at the end of subparagraph (I) and inserting ', and', and by inserting after subparagraph (I) the following new subparagraph:

"'(J) an omission of information required by section 32(k)(2) (relating to taxpayers making improper prior claims of earned income credit).'."

In 1997, P.L. 105-34, Sec. 101(d)(2), deleted "and" at the end of subpara. (g)(2)(G), substituted ", and" for the period at the end of subpara. (g)(2)(H), and added subpara. (g)(2)(I), effective for tax. yrs. begin. after 12/31/97.

—P.L. 105-34, Sec. 201(b), deleted "and" at the end of subpara. (g)(2)(H) [as amended by Sec. 101(d)(2) of this Act, see above], substituted ", and" for the period at the end of subpara. (g)(2)(I) [as added by Sec. 101(d)(2) of this Act, see above], and added subpara. (g)(2)(J), effective for expenses paid after 12/31/97 (in tax. yrs. end. after 12/31/97), for education furnished in academic periods begin. after 12/31/97.

—P.L. 105-34, Sec. 1085(a)(3), [as amended by Sec. 6013(p)(3) of P.L. 105-206, see above] deleted "and" at the end of subpara. (g)(2)(I) substituted ", and" for the period at the end of subpara. (g)(2)(J), and added subpara. (g)(2)(K), effective for tax. yrs. begin. after 12/31/96.

In 1996, P.L. 104-193, Sec. 451(c), deleted "and" at the end of subpara. (g)(2)(D), substituted a comma for the period at the end of subpara. (g)(2)(E), and added subparas. (g)(2)(F) and (G), effective for returns the due date for which (without regard to extensions) is more than 30 days after date of enactment.

—P.L. 104-188, Sec. 1615(c), deleted "and" at the end of subpara. (g)(2)(F) [added by Sec. 451(c) of P.L. 104-193, see above] substituted ", and" for the period at the end of subpara. (g)(2)(G) [added by Sec. 451(c) of P.L. 104-193, see above] and added subpara. (g)(2)(H), effective for returns the due date for which (without regard to extensions) is on or after the 30th day after date of enactment. For special rules, see Sec. 1615(d)(2), of this Act, which reads as follows:

"(2) Special rule for 1995 and 1996. In the case of returns for taxable years beginning in 1995 or 1996, a taxpayer shall not be required by the amendments made by this section to provide a taxpayer identification number for a child who is born after October 31, 1995, in the case of a taxable year beginning in 1995 or November 30, 1996, in the case of a taxable year beginning in 1996."

—P.L. 104-168, Sec. 1311(c)(3), added "4958 (relating to private excess benefit)," before "4971" in subsec. (e), effective for excess benefit transactions occurring on or after 9/14/95. Sec. 1311(d)(2), of this Act, provides:

"(2) Binding contracts. The amendments referred to in paragraph (1) shall not apply to any benefit arising from a transaction pursuant to any written contract which was binding on September 13, 1995, and at all times thereafter before such transaction occurred."

In 1989, P.L. 101-239, Sec. 7811(k)(1), corrected Sec. 1015(r)(3) of P.L. 100-647, see below, so that it would amend Code Sec. 6213(h) instead of 6211(h).

In 1988, P.L. 100-647, Sec. 1015(r)(3), [as amended by Sec. 7811(k)(1) of P.L. 101-239, see above] deleted para. (h)(3) and redesignated para. (h)(4) as para. (h)(3), effective for notices of deficiencies mailed after 11/10/88.

Prior to deletion, para. (h)(3) read as follows:

"(3) For assessment as if a mathematical error on the return, in the case of erroneous claims for credits under section 32 or 34, see section 6201(a)(4)."

—P.L. 100-647, Sec. 6243(a), substituted ", including the Tax Court. The Tax Court shall have no jurisdiction to enjoin any action or proceeding under this subsection unless a timely petition for a redetermination of the deficiency has been filed and then only in respect of the deficiency that is the subject of such petition," for the period at the end of the last sentence in subsec. (a), effective for orders entered after 11/10/88.

—P.L. 100-418, Sec. 1941(b)(2)(B)(iv), and (v) substituted "or 44" for "44, or 45" in subsecs. (a) and (g), effective for crude oil removed from the premises on or after 8/23/88.

In 1987, P.L. 100-203, Sec. 10712(c)(1), substituted "4955 (relating to taxes on political expenditures), 4971" for "4971" in subsec. (e), effective for tax. yrs. begin. after 12/22/87.

—P.L. 100-203, Sec. 10713(b)(2)(D), substituted "section 6851, 6852, or 6861" for "section 6851 or section 6861" in subsec. (a), effective 12/22/87.

In 1986, P.L. 99-514, Sec. 1875(d)(2)(B)(i), amended para. (h)(4), effective for partnership tax. yrs. begin. after 9/3/82. For special rules, see Sec. 407(a)(3) of P.L. 97-248, reproduced below.

Prior to amendment, para. (h)(4) read as follows:

"(4) For provision that this subchapter shall not apply in the case of computational adjustments attributable to partnership items, see section 6230(a)."

In 1984, P.L. 98-369, Sec. 305(b)(4), substituted "section 4963(e)" for "section 4962(e)" in subsec. (e), effective for all taxable events occurring after 12/31/84.

—P.L. 98-369, Sec. 474(r)(34), substituted "section 32 or 34" for "section 39" in para. (h)(3), effective for tax. yrs. begin. after 12/31/83, and to carrybacks from tax. yrs. begin. after 12/31/83.

In 1982, P.L. 97-248, Sec. 402(c)(2), added para. (h)(4), effective for partnership tax. yrs. begin. after 9/3/82. Sec. 407(a)(3) of this Act provides:

"(3) The amendments made by sections 402, 403, and 404 [of this Act] shall apply to any partnership taxable year (or in the case of section 6232 of such Code, to any period) ending after the date of the enactment of this Act if the partnership, each partner, and each indirect partner requests such application and the Secretary of the Treasury or his delegate consents to such application."

In 1980, P.L. 96-596, Sec. 2(a)(4)(C), substituted "section 4962(e)" for "section 4941(e)(4), 4942(j)(2), 4943(d)(3), 4944(e)(3), [sic] 4945(i)(2), 4951(e)(4), 4952(e)(2), 4971(c)(3), or 4975(f)(6), [sic]." at the end of subsec. (e), effective as provided in Sec. 2(d) of this Act, reproduced in note following Code Sec. 4942.

—P.L. 96-589, Sec. 6(b)(1), redesignated subsecs. (f) and (g) as subsecs. (g) and (h) and added new subsec. (f), effective 10/1/79, except for any proceeding under the Bankruptcy Act begun before 10/1/79. Sec. 7(g) of this Act provides:

"(g) Definitions.

"For purposes of this section—

"(1) Bankruptcy case. The term 'bankruptcy case' means any case under title 11 of the United States Code (as recodified by P.L. 95-598).

"(2) Similar judicial proceeding. The term 'similar judicial proceeding' means a receivership, foreclosure, or similar proceeding in a Federal or State court (as modified by section 368(a)(3)(D) of the Internal Revenue Code of 1954)."

Assessment Code Sec. 6214

—P.L. 96-223, Sec. 101(f)(1)(D), substituted "44, or 45" for "or 44" in subsec. (a)... Sec. 101(f)(1)(E), substituted "44, or 45" for "or 44" in subsec. (f), effective for periods after 2/29/80.

In 1978, P.L. 95-600, Sec. 504(b)(2)(A), added "or refund" after "carryback" in the heading of para. (b)(3)... Sec. 504(b)(2)(B), added "or the amount described in section 1341(b)(1)" after "carryback" in para. (b)(3), effective for tentative refund claims filed on and after 11/6/78.

—P.L. 95-227, Sec. 4(d)(1), added ", 4951 (relating to taxes on self-dealing), or 4952 (relating to taxes on taxable expenditures)" after "4945 (relating to taxes on taxable expenditures)", added "4951(e)(4), 4952(e)(2)," after "4945(i)(2)," and substituted "4975(f)(6)" for "4975(f)(4)" in subsec. (e), effective for contributions, acts, and expenditures made after 12/31/77, in and for tax. yrs. begin. after 12/31/77.

—P.L. 95-227, Sec. 4(d)(2), substituted "or chapter 41, 42, 43, or 44" for "or chapter 42 or 43" each place it appeared in Code Sec. 6213, effective for contributions, acts, and expenditures made after 12/31/77, in and for tax. yrs. begin. after 12/31/77.

In 1976, P.L. 94-455, Sec. 1204(c)(6), added "section 6851 or" before "section 6861" in subsec. (a), effective for action taken under Code Sec. 6851, 6861 or 6862 where the notice and demand takes place after 12/31/76. Sec. 2(a) of P.L. 94-528, postponed the effective date to 2/28/77.

—P.L. 94-455, Sec. 1206(a), redesignated paras. (b)(2) and (3) as paras. (b)(3) and (4), deleted para. (b)(1) and added new paras. (b)(1) and (2), effective for returns within the meaning of Code Sec. 6213(f)(1) filed after 12/31/76.
Prior to amendment, para. (b)(1) read as follows:
"(b) Exceptions to restriction on assessment.
"(1) Mathematical errors. If the taxpayer is notified that, on account of a mathematical error appearing upon the return, an amount of tax in excess of that shown upon the return is due, and that an assessment of the tax has been or will be made on the basis of what would have been the correct amount of tax but for the mathematical error, such notice shall not be considered as a notice of deficiency for the purposes of subsection (a) (prohibiting assessment and collection until notice of the deficiency has been mailed), or of section 6212(c)(1) (restricting further deficiency letters), or section 6512(a) (prohibiting credits or refunds after petition to the Tax Court), and the taxpayer shall have no right to file a petition with the Tax Court based on such notice, nor shall such assessment or collection be prohibited by the provisions of subsection (a) of this section."

—P.L. 94-455, Sec. 1206(b), redesignated subsec. (f) as subsec. (g), and added new subsec. (f), effective for returns within the meaning of Code Sec. 6213(f)(1) filed after 12/31/76.

—P.L. 94-455, Sec. 1206(c)(1), substituted "he may assess without regard to the provisions of paragraph (2)" for "he may assess", and substituted "mathematical or clerical error" for "mathematical error" in para. (b)(3), as redesignated by this Act, effective for returns within the meaning of Code Sec. 6213(f)(1) filed after 12/31/76.

—P.L. 94-455, Sec. 1307(d)(2)(F)(iii), substituted "chapter 41, 42," for "chapter 42" in subsec. (a), effective 10/4/76.

—P.L. 94-455, Sec. 1605(b)(6), substituted "43, or 44" for "or 43" in subsec. (a), effective for tax. yrs. of real estate investment trusts begin. after 10/4/76.

—P.L. 94-455, Sec. 1906(a)(15), substituted "United States" for "States of the Union and the District of Columbia" in subsec. (a), effective 2/1/77.

—P.L. 94-455, Sec. 1906(b)(13)(A), substituted "Secretary" for "Secretary or his delegate" each place it appeared in Code Sec. 6213, effective 2/1/77.

In 1974, P.L. 93-406, Sec. 1016(a)(11)(A), substituted ", chapter 42 or 43" for "or chapter 42" in subsec. (a)... Sec. 1016(a)(11)(B), amended the heading of subsec. (e)... Sec. 1016(a)(11)(C), substituted "4945 (relating to taxes on taxable expenditures), 4971 (relating to excise taxes on failure to meet minimum funding standard), 4975 (relating to excise taxes on prohibited transactions)" for "or 4945 (relating to taxes on taxable expenditures)" in subsec. (e)... Sec. 1016(a)(11)(D), substituted ", 4945(i)(2), 4971(c)(3), or 4975(f)(4)," for "or 4945(h)(2)" in subsec. (e), effective as provided in Sec. 1017 of this Act, reproduced in note following Code Sec. 401.
Prior to amendment, the heading of subsec. (e) read as follows:
"(e) Suspension of filing period for certain chapter 42 taxes."

In 1969, P.L. 91-172, Sec. 101(f)(3), redesignated subsec. (e) as subsec. (f), and added new subsec. (e), effective 1/1/70.

—P.L. 91-172, Sec. 101(j)(42), added "or chapter 42" after "subtitle A or B" in subsec. (a), effective 1/1/70.

In 1965, P.L. 89-44, Sec. 809, added subsec. (e)(3).

Sec. 6214. Determinations by Tax Court.

(a) Jurisdiction as to increase of deficiency, additional amounts, or additions to the tax.

Except as provided by section 7463, the Tax Court shall have jurisdiction to redetermine the correct amount of the deficiency even if the amount so redetermined is greater than the amount of the deficiency, notice of which has been mailed to the taxpayer, and to determine whether any additional amount, or any addition to the tax should be assessed, if claim therefor is asserted by the Secretary at or before the hearing or a rehearing.

(b) Jurisdiction over other years and quarters.

The Tax Court in redetermining a deficiency of income tax for any taxable year or of gift tax for any calendar year or calendar quarter shall consider such facts with relation to the taxes for other years or calendar quarters as may be necessary correctly to redetermine the amount of such deficiency, but in so doing shall have no jurisdiction to determine whether or not the tax for any other year or calendar quarter has been overpaid or underpaid. Notwithstanding the preceding sentence, the Tax Court may apply the doctrine of equitable recoupment to the same extent that it is available in civil tax cases before the district courts of the United States and the United States Court of Federal Claims.

(c) Taxes imposed by section 507 or chapter 41, 42, 43, or 44.

The Tax Court, in redetermining a deficiency of any tax imposed by section 507 or chapter 41, 42, 43, or 44 for any period, act, or failure to act, shall consider such facts with relation to the taxes under chapter 41, 42, 43, or 44 for other periods, acts, or failures to act as may be necessary correctly to redetermine the amount of such deficiency, but in so doing shall have no jurisdiction to determine whether or not the taxes under chapter 41, 42, 43, or 44 for any other period, act, or failure to act have been overpaid or underpaid. The Tax Court, in redetermining a deficiency of any second tier tax (as defined in section 4963(b)), shall make a determination with respect to whether the taxable event has been corrected.

(d) Final decisions of Tax Court.

For purposes of this chapter, chapter 41, 42, 43, or 44, and subtitles A or B the date on which a decision of the Tax Court becomes final shall be determined according to the provisions of section 7481.

(e) Cross references.

For provisions giving Tax Court jurisdiction to order a refund of an overpayment and to award sanctions, see section 6512(b)(2).

In 2006, P.L. 109-280, Sec. 858(a), added "Notwithstanding the preceding sentence, the Tax Court may apply the doctrine of equitable recoupment to the same extent that it is available in civil tax cases before the district courts of the United States and the United States Court of Federal Claims." at the end of subsec. (b), effective for any action or proceeding in the United States Tax Court with respect to which a decision has not become final (as determined under Code Sec. 7481) as of 8/17/2006.

In 1996, P.L. 104-188, Sec. 1704(t)(16), amended subsec. (e), effective 8/20/96.
Prior to amendment, subsec. (e) read as follows:
"(e) Cross reference.
"(1) For provision giving Tax Court jurisdiction to determine whether any portion of deficiency is a substantial underpayment attributable to tax motivated transactions, see section 6621(c)(4).
"(2) For provision giving Tax Court jurisdiction to order a refund of an overpayment and to award sanctions, see section 6512(b)(2)."

In 1988, P.L. 100-647, Sec. 6244(b)(1), substituted "references-'" for "reference.-'" and designated the undesignated paragraph as para. (1) and added new para. (e)(2), effective for overpayments determined by the Tax Court which have not yet been refunded by the 90th day after 11/10/88.

—P.L. 100-418, Sec. 1941(b)(2)(B)(vi), substituted "or 44" for "44, or 45" each place it appeared in subsecs. (c) and (d), effective for crude oil removed from the premises on or after 8/23/88.

In 1986, P.L. 99-514, Sec. 1551(c)(8), substituted "section 6621(c)(4)" for "section 6621(d)(4)", in subsec. (e), effective for purposes of determining interest for periods after 12/31/86.

—P.L. 99-514, Sec. 1554(a), substituted "any addition to the tax" for "addition to the tax", in subsec. (a), effective for any action or proceeding in the Tax Court for which a decision has not become final (as determined under '54 Code Sec. 7481) before 10/22/86.

—P.L. 99-514, Sec. 1833, substituted "section 4963(b)" for "section 4962(b)", in subsec. (c), effective for taxable events occurring after 12/31/84.

In 1984, P.L. 98-369, Sec. 144(b), added subsec. (e), effective for interest accruing after 12/31/84.

In 1980, P.L. 96-596, Sec. 2(b), added the last sentence to subsec. (c), effective as provided in Sec. 2(d)(2) of this Act which reads as follows:
"(2) Second tier taxes. The amendments made by this section with respect to any second tier tax shall apply only with respect to taxes assessed after the date of

3,635

Code Sec. 6214 — Assessment

the enactment of this Act [12/24/80]. Nothing in the preceding sentence shall be construed to permit the assessment of a tax in a case to which, on the date of the enactment of this Act [12/24/80], the doctrine of res judicata applies."

—P.L. 96-223, Sec. 101(f)(1)(F), substituted "44, or 45" for "or 44" in subsec. (c)... Sec. 101(f)(1)(G), substituted "44, or 45" for "or 44" in subsec. (d), effective for periods after 2/29/80.

In **1976**, P.L. 94-455, Sec. 1307(d)(2)(F)(iv), substituted "chapter 41, 42," for "chapter 42" each place it appeared in subsecs. (c) and (d), effective 10/4/76.

—P.L. 94-455, Sec. 1307(d)(2)(H), substituted "chapter 41, 42," [sic] for "chapter 42" in the heading of subsec. (c), effective 10/4/76.

—P.L. 94-455, Sec. 1605(b)(7), substituted "43, or 44" for "or 43" in the heading of subsec. (c), substituted "43, or 44" for "or 43" each place it appeared in subsecs. (c) and (d), effective for tax. yrs. of real estate investment trusts begin. after 10/4/76.

—P.L. 94-455, Sec. 1906(b)(13)(A), substituted "Secretary" for "Secretary or his delegate" in Code Sec. 6214, effective 2/1/77.

In **1974**, P.L. 93-406, Sec. 1016(a)(12), inserted "or 43" after "chapter 42" each place it appeared in subsecs. (c) and (d), effective 9/2/74 or other date as specified in Sec. 1017 of the Act (reproduced following Code Sec. 401).

In **1970**, P.L. 91-614, Sec. 102(d)(6), amended subsec. (b), effective for gifts made after 12/31/70.

Prior to amendment, subsec. (b) read as follows:

"(b) Jurisdiction over other years.

"The Tax Court in redetermining a deficiency of income tax for any taxable year or of gift tax for any calendar year shall consider such facts with relation to the taxes for other years as may be necessary correctly to redetermine the amount of such deficiency, but in so doing shall have no jurisdiction to determine whether or not the tax for any other year has been overpaid or underpaid."

In **1969**, P.L. 91-172, Sec. 101(j)(43), redesignated subsec. (c) as subsec. (d) and added new subsec. (c)... Sec. 101(j)(44), added ", chapter 42," after "chapter" in subsec. (d), effective 1/1/70.

—P.L. 91-172, Sec. 960(a), substituted "Except as provided by section 7463, the Tax Court" for "The Tax Court" in subsec. (a), effective 12/30/70.

Sec. 6215. Assessment of deficiency found by Tax Court.

(a) General rule.

If the taxpayer files a petition with the Tax Court, the entire amount redetermined as the deficiency by the decision of the Tax Court which has become final shall be assessed and shall be paid upon notice and demand from the Secretary. No part of the amount determined as a deficiency by the Secretary but disallowed as such by the decision of the Tax Court which has become final shall be assessed or be collected by levy or by proceeding in court with or without assessment.

(b) Cross references.

(1) For assessment or collection of the amount of the deficiency determined by the Tax Court pending appellate court review, see section 7485.

(2) For dismissal of petition by Tax Court as affirmation of deficiency as determined by the Secretary, see section 7459(d).

(3) For decision of Tax Court that tax is barred by limitation as its decision that there is no deficiency, see section 7459(e).

(4) For assessment of damages awarded by Tax Court for instituting proceedings merely for delay, see section 6673.

(5) For treatment of certain deficiencies as having been paid, in connection with sale of surplus war-built vessels, see section 9(b)(8) of the Merchant Ship Sales Act of 1946 (50 U.S.C. App. 1742).

(6) For rules applicable to Tax Court proceedings, see generally subchapter C of chapter 76.

(7) For extension of time for paying amount determined as deficiency, see section 6161(b).

In **1986**, P.L. 99-514, Sec. 1404(c)(2), deleted para. (b)(7) and redesignated para. (b)(8) as para. (b)(7), effective for tax. yrs. begin. after 12/31/86.

Prior to amendment, para. (b)(7) read as follows:

"(7) For proration of deficiency to installments, see section 6152(c)."

In **1976**, P.L. 94-455, Sec. 1906(a)(16), deleted "60 Stat. 48;", before "50 U.S.C. App. 1742", in para. (b)(5), effective 2/1/77.

—P.L. 94-455, Sec. 1906(b)(13)(A), substituted "Secretary" for "Secretary or his delegate" each place it appeared in Code Sec. 6215, effective 2/1/77.

Sec. 6216. Cross references.

(1) For procedures relating to receivership proceedings, see subchapter B of chapter 70.

(2) For procedures relating to jeopardy assessments, see subchapter A of chapter 70.

(3) For procedures relating to claims against transferees and fiduciaries, see chapter 71.

(4) For procedures relating to partnership items, see subchapter C.

In **1982**, P.L. 97-248, Sec. 402(c)(3), added para. (4), effective for partnership tax. yrs. begin. after 9/3/82. Sec. 407(a)(3) of this Act provides:

"(3) The amendments made by sections 402, 403, and 404 [of this Act] shall apply to any partnership taxable year (or in the case of section 6232 of such Code, to any period) ending after the date of the enactment of this Act [9/3/82] if the partnership, each partner, and each indirect partner requests such application and the Secretary of the Treasury or his delegate consents to such application."

In **1980**, P.L. 96-589, Sec. 6(i)(9), amended para. (1), effective 10/1/79, except for any proceeding under the Bankruptcy Act begun before 10/1/79. Sec. 7(g) of this Act provides:

"(g) Definitions.

"For purposes of this section—

"(1) Bankruptcy case. The term 'bankruptcy case' means any case under title 11 of the United States Code (as recodified by P.L. 95-598).

"(2) Similar judicial proceeding. The term 'similar judicial proceeding' means a receivership, foreclosure, or similar proceeding in a Federal or State court (as modified by section 368(a)(3)(D) of the Internal Revenue Code of 1954)."

Prior to amendment para. (1) read as follows:

"(1) For procedures relating to bankruptcy and receivership, see subchapter B of chapter 70."

Subchapter C.—Tax Treatment of Partnership Items

Sec.
6221. Tax treatment determined at partnership level.
6222. Partner's return must be consistent with partnership return or Secretary notified of inconsistency.
6223. Notice to partners of proceedings.
6224. Participation in administrative proceedings; waivers; agreements.
6225. Assessments made only after partnership level proceedings are completed.
6226. Judicial review of final partnership administrative adjustments.
6227. Administrative adjustment requests.
6228. Judicial review where administrative adjustment request is not allowed in full.
6229. Period of limitations for making assessments.
6230. Additional administrative provisions.
6231. Definitions and special rules.
6233. Extension to entities filing partnership returns, etc.
6234. Declaratory judgment relating to treatment of items other than partnership items with respect to an oversheltered return.

In **1997**, P.L. 105-34, Sec. 1231(c), added item 6234.
In **1988**, P.L. 100-418, Sec. 1941(b)(3)(D), deleted item 6232.
Prior to deletion, item 6232 read as follows:
"6232. Extension of subchapter to windfall profit tax."
In **1984**, P.L. 98-369, Sec. 714(p)(2)(E), added item 6233.

Sec. 6221. Tax treatment determined at partnership level.

Except as otherwise provided in this subchapter, the tax treatment of any partnership item (and the applicability of any penalty, addition to tax, or additional amount which relates to an adjustment to a partnership item) shall be determined at the partnership level.

In 1997, P.L. 105-34, Sec. 1238(a), substituted "item (and the applicability of any penalty, addition to tax, or additional amount which relates to an adjustment to a partnership item)" for "item" in Code Sec. 6221, effective for partnership tax. yrs. end. after 8/5/97.

In 1982, P.L. 97-248, Sec. 402(a), added Code Sec. 6221, effective for partnership tax. yrs. begin. after 9/3/82. Sec. 407(a)(3) of this Act provides:

"(3) The amendments made by sections 402, 403 and 404 [of this Act] shall apply to any partnership taxable year (or in the case of section 6232 of such Code, to any period) ending after the date of the enactment of this Act [9/3/82] if the partnership, each partner, and each indirect partner requests such application and the Secretary of the Treasury or his delegate consents to such application."

Sec. 6222. Partner's return must be consistent with partnership return or Secretary notified of inconsistency.

(a) In general.

A partner shall, on the partner's return, treat a partnership item in a manner which is consistent with the treatment of such partnership item on the partnership return.

(b) Notification of inconsistent treatment.

(1) **In general.** In the case of any partnership item, if—

(A)(i) the partnership has filed a return but the partner's treatment on his return is (or may be) inconsistent with the treatment of the item on the partnership return, or

(ii) the partnership has not filed a return, and

(B) the partner files with the Secretary a statement identifying the inconsistency,

subsection (a) shall not apply to such item.

(2) **Partner receiving incorrect information.** A partner shall be treated as having complied with subparagraph (B) of paragraph (1) with respect to a partnership item if the partner—

(A) demonstrates to the satisfaction of the Secretary that the treatment of the partnership item on the partner's return is consistent with the treatment of the item on the schedule furnished to the partner by the partnership, and

(B) elects to have this paragraph apply with respect to that item.

(c) Effect of failure to notify.

In any case—

(1) described in paragraph (1)(A)(i) of subsection (b), and

(2) in which the partner does not comply with paragraph (1)(B) of subsection (b),

section 6225 shall not apply to any part of a deficiency attributable to any computational adjustment required to make the treatment of the items by such partner consistent with the treatment of the items on the partnership return.

(d) Addition to tax for failure to comply with section.

For addition to tax in the case of a partner's disregard of requirements of this section, see part II of subchapter A of chapter 68.

In 1989, P.L. 101-239, Sec. 7721(c)(7), substituted "part II of subchapter A of chapter 68" for "section 6653(a)" in subsec. (d), effective for returns the due date for which (determined without regard to extensions) is after 12/31/89.

In 1986, P.L. 99-514, Sec. 1503(c)(1), deleted "intentional or negligent" after "of a partner's" in subsec. (d), effective for returns the due date of which (determined without regard to extensions) is after 12/31/86.

In 1982, P.L. 97-248, Sec. 402(a), added Code Sec. 6222, effective for partnership tax. yrs. begin. after 9/3/82. Sec. 407(a)(3) of this Act provides:

"(3) The amendments made by sections 402, 403 and 404 [of this Act] shall apply to any partnership taxable year (or in the case of section 6232 of such Code, to any period) ending after the date of the enactment of this Act [9/3/82] if the partnership, each partner, and each indirect partner requests such application and the Secretary of the Treasury or his delegate consents to such application."

Sec. 6223. Notice to partners of proceedings.

(a) Secretary must give partners notice of beginning and completion of administrative proceedings.

The Secretary shall mail to each partner whose name and address is furnished to the Secretary notice of—

(1) the beginning of an administrative proceeding at the partnership level with respect to a partnership item, and

(2) the final partnership administrative adjustment resulting from any such proceeding.

A partner shall not be entitled to any notice under this subsection unless the Secretary has received (at least 30 days before it is mailed to the tax matters partner) sufficient information to enable the Secretary to determine that such partner is entitled to such notice and to provide such notice to such partner.

(b) Special rules for partnership with more than 100 partners.

(1) **Partner with less than 1 percent interest.** Except as provided in paragraph (2), subsection (a) shall not apply to a partner if—

(A) the partnership has more than 100 partners, and

(B) the partner has a less than 1 percent interest in the profits of the partnership.

(2) **Secretary must give notice to notice group.** If a group of partners in the aggregate having a 5 percent or more interest in the profits of a partnership so request and designate one of their members to receive the notice, the member so designated shall be treated as a partner to whom subsection (a) applies.

(c) Information base for Secretary's notices, etc.

For purposes of this subchapter—

(1) **Information on partnership return.** Except as provided in paragraphs (2) and (3), the Secretary shall use the names, addresses, and profits interests shown on the partnership return.

(2) **Use of additional information.** The Secretary shall use additional information furnished to him by the tax matters partner or any other person in accordance with regulations prescribed by the Secretary.

(3) **Special rule with respect to indirect partners.** If any information furnished to the Secretary under paragraph (1) or (2)—

(A) shows that a person has a profits interest in the partnership by reason of ownership of an interest through 1 or more pass-thru partners, and

(B) contains the name, address, and profits interest of such person,

then the Secretary shall use the name, address, and profits interest of such person with respect to such partnership interest (in lieu of the names, addresses, and profits interests of the pass-thru partners).

(d) Period for mailing notice.

(1) **Notice of beginning of proceedings.** The Secretary shall mail the notice specified in paragraph (1) of subsection (a) to each partner entitled to such notice not later than the 120th day before the day on which the notice specified in paragraph (2) of subsection (a) is mailed to the tax matters partner.

(2) **Notice of final partnership administrative adjustment.** The Secretary shall mail the notice specified in paragraph (2) of subsection (a) to each partner entitled to such notice not later than the 60th day after the day on which the notice specified in such paragraph (2) was mailed to the tax matters partner.

Code Sec. 6223(e)   **Partnership items**

(e) **Effect of Secretary's failure to provide notice.**
  (1) **Application of subsection.**
    (A) In general. This subsection applies where the Secretary has failed to mail any notice specified in subsection (a) to a partner entitled to such notice within the period specified in subsection (d).
    (B) Special rules for partnerships with more than 100 partners. For purposes of subparagraph (A), any partner described in paragraph (1) of subsection (b) shall be treated as entitled to notice specified in subsection (a). The Secretary may provide such notice—
      (i) except as provided in clause (ii), by mailing notice to the tax matters partner, or
      (ii) in the case of a member of a notice group which qualifies under paragraph (2) of subsection (b), by mailing notice to the partner designated for such purpose by the group.
  (2) **Proceedings finished.** In any case to which this subsection applies, if at the time the Secretary mails the partner notice of the proceeding—
    (A) the period within which a petition for review of a final partnership administrative adjustment under section 6226 may be filed has expired and no such petition has been filed, or
    (B) the decision of a court in an action begun by such a petition has become final,
the partner may elect to have such adjustment, such decision, or a settlement agreement described in paragraph (2) of section 6224(c) with respect to the partnership taxable year to which the adjustment relates apply to such partner. If the partner does not make an election under the preceding sentence, the partnership items of the partner for the partnership taxable year to which the proceeding relates shall be treated as nonpartnership items.
  (3) **Proceedings still going on.** In any case to which this subsection applies, if paragraph (2) does not apply, the partner shall be a party to the proceeding unless such partner elects—
    (A) to have a settlement agreement described in paragraph (2) of section 6224(c) with respect to the partnership taxable year to which the proceeding relates apply to the partner, or
    (B) to have the partnership items of the partner for the partnership taxable year to which the proceeding relates treated as nonpartnership items.
(f) **Only one notice of final partnership administrative adjustment.**
If the Secretary mails a notice of final partnership administrative adjustment for a partnership taxable year with respect to a partner, the Secretary may not mail another such notice to such partner with respect to the same taxable year of the same partnership in the absence of a showing of fraud, malfeasance, or misrepresentation of a material fact.
(g) **Tax matters partner must keep partners informed of proceedings.**
To the extent and in the manner provided by regulations, the tax matters partner of a partnership shall keep each partner informed of all administrative and judicial proceedings for the adjustment at the partnership level of partnership items.
(h) **Pass-thru partner required to forward notice.**
  (1) **In general.** If a pass-thru partner receives a notice with respect to a partnership proceeding from the Secretary, the tax matters partner, or another pass-thru partner, the pass-thru partner shall, within 30 days of receiving that notice, forward a copy of that notice to the person or persons holding an interest (through the pass-thru partner) in the profits or losses of the partnership for the partnership taxable year to which the notice relates.
  (2) **Partnership as pass-thru partner.** In the case of a pass-thru partner which is a partnership, the tax matters partner of such partnership shall be responsible for forwarding copies of the notice to the partners of such partnership.

In **1982,** P.L. 97-248, Sec. 402(a), added Code Sec. 6223, effective for partnership tax. yrs. begin. after 9/3/82. Sec. 407(a)(3) of this Act provides:
"(3) The amendments made by sections 402, 403, and 404 [of this Act] shall apply to any partnership taxable year (or in the case of section 6232 of such Code, to any period) ending after the date of the enactment of this Act [9/3/82] if the partnership, each partner, and each indirect partner requests such application and the Secretary of the Treasury or his delegate consents to such application."

Sec. 6224. Participation in administrative proceedings; waivers; agreements.
(a) **Participation in administrative proceedings.**
Any partner has the right to participate in any administrative proceeding relating to the determination of partnership items at the partnership level.
(b) **Partner may waive rights.**
  (1) **In general.** A partner may at any time waive—
    (A) any right such partner has under this subchapter, and
    (B) any restriction under this subchapter on action by the Secretary.
  (2) **Form.** Any waiver under paragraph (1) shall be made by a signed notice in writing filed with the Secretary.
(c) **Settlement agreement.**
In the absence of a showing of fraud, malfeasance, or misrepresentation of fact—
  (1) **Binds all parties.** A settlement agreement between the Secretary or the Attorney General (or his delegate) and 1 or more partners in a partnership with respect to the determination of partnership items for any partnership taxable year shall (except as otherwise provided in such agreement) be binding on all parties to such agreement with respect to the determination of partnership items for such partnership taxable year. An indirect partner is bound by any such agreement entered into by the pass-thru partner unless the indirect partner has been identified as provided in section 6223(c)(3).
  (2) **Other partners have right to enter into consistent agreements.** If the Secretary or the Attorney General (or his delegate) enters into a settlement agreement with any partner with respect to partnership items for any partnership taxable year, the Secretary or the Attorney General (or his delegate) shall offer to any other partner who so requests settlement terms for the partnership taxable year which are consistent with those contained in such settlement agreement. Except in the case of an election under paragraph (2) or (3) of section 6223(e) to have a settlement agreement described in this paragraph apply, this paragraph shall apply with respect to a settlement agreement entered into with a partner before notice of a final partnership administrative adjustment is mailed to the tax matters partner only if such other partner makes the request before the expiration of 150 days after the day on which such notice is mailed to the tax matters partner.
  (3) **Tax matters partner may bind certain other partners.**
    (A) In general. A partner who is not a notice partner (and not a member of a notice group described in subsection (b)(2) of section 6223) shall be bound by any settlement agreement—
      (i) which is entered into by the tax matters partner, and

(ii) in which the tax matters partner expressly states that such agreement shall bind the other partners.

(B) **Exception.** Subparagraph (A) shall not apply to any partner who (within the time prescribed by the Secretary) files a statement with the Secretary providing that the tax matters partner shall not have the authority to enter into a settlement agreement on behalf of such partner.

In 2002, P.L. 107-147, Sec. 416(d)(1)(A), added "or the Attorney General (or his delegate)" after "Secretary" each place it appeared in paras. (c)(1) and (2), effective for settlement agreements entered into after 3/9/2002.

In 1982, P.L. 97-248, Sec. 402(a), added Code Sec. 6224, effective for partnership tax. yrs. begin. after 9/3/82. Sec. 407(a)(3) of this Act provides:

"(3) The amendments made by sections 402, 403, and 404 [of this Act] shall apply to any partnership taxable year (or in the case of section 6232 of such Code, to any period) ending after the date of the enactment of this Act [9/3/82] if the partnership, each partner, and each indirect partner requests such application and the Secretary of the Treasury or his delegate consents to such application."

Sec. 6225. Assessments made only after partnership level proceedings are completed.

(a) Restriction on assessment and collection.

Except as otherwise provided in this subchapter, no assessment of a deficiency attributable to any partnership item may be made (and no levy or proceeding in any court for the collection of any such deficiency may be made, begun, or prosecuted) before—

(1) the close of the 150th day after the day on which a notice of a final partnership administrative adjustment was mailed to the tax matters partner, and

(2) if a proceeding is begun in the Tax Court under section 6226 during such 150-day period, the decision of the court in such proceeding has become final.

(b) Premature action may be enjoined.

Notwithstanding section 7421(a), any action which violates subsection (a) may be enjoined in the proper court, including the Tax Court. The Tax Court shall have no jurisdiction to enjoin any action or proceeding under this subsection unless a timely petition for a readjustment of the partnership items for the taxable year has been filed and then only in respect of the adjustments that are the subject of such petition.

(c) Limit where no proceeding begun.

If no proceeding under section 6226 is begun with respect to any final partnership administrative adjustment during the 150-day period described in subsection (a), the deficiency assessed against any partner with respect to the partnership items to which such adjustment relates shall not exceed the amount determined in accordance with such adjustment.

In 1997, P.L. 105-34, Sec. 1239(a), substituted "the proper court, including the Tax Court. The Tax Court shall have no jurisdiction to enjoin any action or proceeding under this subsection unless a timely petition for a readjustment of the partnership items for the taxable year has been filed and then only in respect of the adjustments that are the subject of such petition." for "the proper court." in subsec. (b), effective for partnership tax. yrs. end. after 8/5/97.

In 1982, P.L. 97-248, Sec. 402(a), added Code Sec. 6225, effective for partnership tax. yrs. begin. after 9/3/82. Sec. 407(a)(3) of this Act provides:

"(3) The amendments made by sections 402, 403, and 404 [of this Act] shall apply to any partnership taxable year (or in the case of section 6232 of such Code, to any period) ending after the date of the enactment of this Act [9/3/82] if the partnership, each partner, and each indirect partner requests such application and the Secretary of the Treasury or his delegate consents to such application."

Sec. 6226. Judicial review of final partnership administrative adjustments.

(a) Petition by tax matters partner.

Within 90 days after the day on which a notice of a final partnership administrative adjustment is mailed to the tax matters partner, the tax matters partner may file a petition for a readjustment of the partnership items for such taxable year with—

(1) the Tax Court,

(2) the district court of the United States for the district in which the partnership's principal place of business is located, or

(3) the Claims Court [Court of Federal Claims, see § 902(b), P.L. 102-572].

(b) Petition by partner other than tax matters partner.

(1) In general. If the tax matters partner does not file a readjustment petition under subsection (a) with respect to any final partnership administrative adjustment, any notice partner (and any 5-percent group) may, within 60 days after the close of the 90-day period set forth in subsection (a), file a petition for a readjustment of the partnership items for the taxable year involved with any of the courts described in subsection (a).

(2) Priority of the tax court action. If more than 1 action is brought under paragraph (1) with respect to any partnership for any partnership taxable year, the first such action brought in the Tax Court shall go forward.

(3) Priority outside the Tax Court. If more than 1 action is brought under paragraph (1) with respect to any partnership for any taxable year but no such action is brought in the Tax Court, the first such action brought shall go forward.

(4) Dismissal of other actions. If an action is brought under paragraph (1) in addition to the action which goes forward under paragraph (2) or (3), such action shall be dismissed.

(5) Treatment of premature petitions. If—

(A) a petition for a readjustment of partnership items for the taxable year involved is filed by a notice partner (or a 5-percent group) during the 90-day period described in subsection (a), and

(B) no action is brought under paragraph (1) during the 60-day period described therein with respect to such taxable year which is not dismissed,

such petition shall be treated for purposes of paragraph (1) as filed on the last day of such 60-day period.

(6) Tax matters partner may intervene. The tax matters partner may intervene in any action brought under this subsection.

(c) Partners treated as parties.

If an action is brought under subsection (a) or (b) with respect to a partnership for any partnership taxable year—

(1) each person who was a partner in such partnership at any time during such year shall be treated as a party to such action, and

(2) the court having jurisdiction of such action shall allow each such person to participate in the action.

(d) Partner must have interest in outcome.

(1) In order to be party to action. Subsection (c) shall not apply to a partner after the day on which—

(A) the partnership items of such partner for the partnership taxable year became nonpartnership items by reason of 1 or more of the events described in subsection (b) of section 6231, or

(B) the period within which any tax attributable to such partnership items may be assessed against that partner expired.

Notwithstanding subparagraph (B), any person treated under subsection (c) as a party to an action shall be permitted to participate in such action (or file a readjustment petition under subsection (b) or paragraph (2) of this subsection) solely for the purpose of asserting that the period of limitations for assessing any tax attributable to partnership items has expired with respect to such person, and the court having jurisdiction of such action shall have jurisdiction to consider such assertion.

(2) To file petition. No partner may file a readjustment petition under subsection (b) unless such partner would be treated as a party to the proceeding.

(e) Jurisdictional requirement for bringing action in District Court or Claims Court [Court of Federal Claims, see § 902(b), P.L. 102-572].

(1) In general. A readjustment petition under this section may be filed in a district court of the United States or the Claims Court [Court of Federal Claims, see § 902(b), P.L. 102-572] only if the partner filing the petition deposits with the Secretary, on or before the day the petition is filed, the amount by which the tax liability of the partner would be increased if the treatment of partnership items on the partner's return were made consistent with the treatment of partnership items on the partnership return, as adjusted by the final partnership administrative adjustment. In the case of a petition filed by a 5-percent group, the requirement of the preceding sentence shall apply to each member of the group. The court may by order provide that the jurisdictional requirements of this paragraph are satisfied where there has been a good faith attempt to satisfy such requirements and any shortfall in the amount required to be deposited is timely corrected.

(2) Refund on request. If an action brought in a district court of the United States or in the Claims Court [Court of Federal Claims, see § 902(b), P.L. 102-572] is dismissed by reason of the priority of a Tax Court action under paragraph (2) of subsection (b), the Secretary shall, at the request of the partner who made the deposit, refund the amount deposited under paragraph (1).

(3) Interest payable. Any amount deposited under paragraph (1), while deposited, shall not be treated as a payment of tax for purposes of this title (other than chapter 67).

(f) Scope of judicial review.

A court with which a petition is filed in accordance with this section shall have jurisdiction to determine all partnership items of the partnership for the partnership taxable year to which the notice of final partnership administrative adjustment relates, the proper allocation of such items among the partners, and the applicability of any penalty, addition to tax, or additional amount which relates to an adjustment to a partnership item.

(g) Determination of court reviewable.

Any determination by a court under this section shall have the force and effect of a decision of the Tax Court or a final judgment or decree of the district court or the Claims Court [Court of Federal Claims, see § 902(b), P.L. 102-572], as the case may be, and shall be reviewable as such. With respect to the partnership, only the tax matters partner, a notice partner, or a 5-percent group may seek review of a determination by a court under this section.

(h) Effect of decision dismissing action.

If an action brought under this section is dismissed (other than under paragraph (4) of subsection (b)), the decision of the court dismissing the action shall be considered as its decision that the notice of final partnership administrative adjustment is correct, and an appropriate order shall be entered in the records of the court.

In **1997**, P.L. 105-34, Sec. 1238(b)(1)(A), substituted "relates," for "relates or" in subsec. (f) . . . Sec. 1238(b)(1)(B), added ", and the applicability of any penalty, addition to tax, or additional amount which relates to an adjustment to a partnership item" before the period at the end of subsec. (f), effective for tax. yrs. end. after 8/5/97.

—P.L. 105-34, Sec. 1239(c), added a flush sentence at the end of para. (d)(1), effective for partnership tax. yrs. end. after 8/5/97.

—P.L. 105-34, Sec. 1240(a), redesignated para. (b)(5) as (b)(6) and added a new para. (b)(5), effective for petitions filed after 8/5/97.

In **1992**, P.L. 102-572, Sec. 902(b), effective 10/29/92, relating to Court designation provides as follows:

"(b) Other provisions of law. Reference in any other Federal law or documents to—

"(1) the 'United States Claims Court' shall be deemed to refer to the 'United States Court of Federal Claims'; and

"(2) the 'Claims Court' shall be deemed to refer to the 'Court of Federal Claims'"

In **1983**, P.L. 97-448, Sec. 306(c)(1)(A), substituted 'With respect to the partnership, only the tax matters partner' for 'Only the tax matters partner' in subsec. (g), effective for partnership tax yrs. begin. after 9/3/82.

In **1982**, P.L. 97-248, Sec. 402(a), added Code Sec. 6226, effective for partnership tax. yrs. begin. after 9/3/82. Sec. 407(a)(3) of this Act provides:

"(3) The amendments made by sections 402, 403, and 404 [of this Act] shall apply to any partnership taxable year (or in the case of section 6232 of such Code, to any period) ending after the date of the enactment of this Act [9/3/82] if the partnership, each partner, and each indirect partner requests such application and the Secretary of the Treasury or his delegate consents to such application."

Sec. 6227. Administrative adjustment requests.
(a) General rule.

A partner may file a request for an administrative adjustment of partnership items for any partnership taxable year at any time which is—

(1) within 3 years after the later of—

(A) the date on which the partnership return for such year is filed, or

(B) the last day for filing the partnership return for such year (determined without regard to extensions), and

(2) before the mailing to the tax matters partner of a notice of final partnership administrative adjustment with respect to such taxable year.

(b) Special rule in case of extension of period of limitations under section 6229.

The period prescribed by subsection (a)(1) for filing of a request for an administrative adjustment shall be extended—

(1) for the period within which an assessment may be made pursuant to an agreement (or any extension thereof) under section 6229(b), and

(2) for 6 months thereafter.

(c) Requests by tax matters partner on behalf of partnership.

(1) Substituted return. If the tax matters partner—

(A) files a request for an administrative adjustment, and

(B) asks that the treatment shown on the request be substituted for the treatment of partnership items on the partnership return to which the request relates,

the Secretary may treat the changes shown on such request as corrections of mathematical or clerical errors appearing on the partnership return.

(2) Requests not treated as substituted returns.

(A) In general. If the tax matters partner files an administrative adjustment request on behalf of the partnership which is not treated as a substituted return under paragraph (1), the Secretary may, with respect to all or any part of the requested adjustments—

(i) without conducting any proceeding, allow or make to all partners the credits or refunds arising from the requested adjustments,

(ii) conduct a partnership proceeding under this subchapter, or

(iii) take no action on the request.

(B) Exceptions. Clause (i) of subparagraph (A) shall not apply with respect to a partner after the day on which the partnership items become nonpartnership items by reason of 1 or more of the events described in subsection (b) of section 6231.

(3) Request must show effect on distributive shares. The tax matters partner shall furnish with any administrative adjustment request on behalf of the partnership revised schedules showing the effect of such request on the distributive shares of the partners and such other information as may be required under regulations.

(d) Other requests.

If any partner files a request for an administrative adjustment (other than a request described in subsection (c)), the Secretary may—

(1) process the request in the same manner as a claim for credit or refund with respect to items which are not partnership items,

(2) assess any additional tax that would result from the requested adjustments,

(3) mail to the partner, under subparagraph (A) of section 6231(b)(1) (relating to items becoming nonpartnership items), a notice that all partnership items of the partner for the partnership taxable year to which such request relates shall be treated as nonpartnership items, or

(4) conduct a partnership proceeding.

(e) Requests with respect to bad debts or worthless securities.

In the case of that portion of any request for an administrative adjustment which relates to the deductibility by the partnership under section 166 of a debt as a debt which became worthless, or under section 165(g) of a loss from worthlessness of a security, the period prescribed in subsection (a)(1) shall be 7 years from the last day for filing the partnership return for the year with respect to which such request is made (determined without regard to extensions).

In 2002, P.L. 107-147, Sec. 417(19)(A), substituted "subsection (c)" for "subsection (b)" in subsec. (d), effective 3/9/2002.

In 1997, P.L. 105-34, Sec. 1236(a), redesignated subsecs. (b) and (c) as subsecs. (c) and (d) and added a new subsec. (b), effective as if included in the amendments made by Sec. 402 of P.L. 97-248, see below.

—P.L. 105-34, Sec. 1243(a), added subsec. (e), , effective as if included in the amendments made by Sec. 402 of P.L. 97-248, see below. Sec. 1243(b)(2) of this Act provides:

"(2) Treatment of requests filed before date of enactment.— In the case of that portion of any request (filed before the date of the enactment of this Act) for an administrative adjustment which relates to the deductibility of a debt as a debt which became worthless or the deductibility of a loss from the worthlessness of a security—

"(A) paragraph (2) of section 6227(a) of the Internal Revenue Code of 1986 shall not apply,

"(B) the period for filing a petition under section 6228 of the Internal Revenue Code of 1986 with respect to such request shall not expire before the date 6 months after the date of the enactment of this Act, and

"(C) such a petition may be filed without regard to whether there was a notice of the beginning of an administrative proceeding or a final partnership administrative adjustment."

In 1982, P.L. 97-248, Sec. 402(a), added Code Sec. 6227, effective for partnership tax. yrs. begin. after 9/3/82. Sec. 407(a)(3) of this Act provides:

"(3) The amendments made by sections 402, 403 and 404 [of this Act] shall apply to any partnership taxable year (or in the case of section 6232 of such Code, to any period) ending after the date of the enactment of this Act [9/3/82] if the partnership, each partner, and each indirect partner requests such application and the Secretary of the Treasury or his delegate consents to such application."

Sec. 6228. Judicial review where administrative adjustment request is not allowed in full.

(a) Request on behalf of partnership.

(1) In general. If any part of an administrative adjustment request filed by the tax matters partner under subsection (c) of section 6227 is not allowed by the Secretary, the tax matters partner may file a petition for an adjustment with respect to the partnership items to which such part of the request relates with—

(A) the Tax Court,

(B) the district court of the United States for the district in which the principal place of business of the partnership is located, or

(C) the Claims Court [Court of Federal Claims, see § 902(b), P.L. 102-572].

(2) Period for filing petition.

(A) In general. A petition may be filed under paragraph (1) with respect to partnership items for a partnership taxable year only—

(i) after the expiration of 6 months from the date of filing of the request under section 6227, and

(ii) before the date which is 2 years after the date of such request.

(B) No petition after notice of beginning of administrative proceeding. No petition may be filed under paragraph (1) after the day the Secretary mails to the partnership a notice of the beginning of an administrative proceeding with respect to the partnership taxable year to which such request relates.

(C) Failure by secretary to issue timely notice of adjustment. If the Secretary—

(i) mails the notice referred to in subparagraph (B) before the expiration of the 2-year period referred to in clause (ii) of subparagraph (A), and

(ii) fails to mail a notice of final partnership administrative adjustment with respect to the partnership taxable year to which the request relates before the expiration of the period described in section 6229(a) (including any extension by agreement),

subparagraph (B) shall cease to apply with respect to such request, and the 2-year period referred to in clause (ii) of subparagraph (A) shall not expire before the date 6 months after the expiration of the period described in section 6229(a) (including any extension by agreement).

(D) Extension of time. The 2-year period described in subparagraph (A)(ii) shall be extended for such period as may be agreed upon in writing between the tax matters partner and the Secretary.

(3) Coordination with administrative adjustment.

(A) Administrative adjustment before filing of petition. No petition may be filed under this subsection after the Secretary mails to the tax matters partner a notice of final partnership administrative adjustment for the partnership taxable year to which the request under section 6227 relates.

(B) Administrative adjustment after filing but before hearing of petition. If the Secretary mails to the tax matters partner a notice of final partnership administrative adjustment for the partnership taxable year to which the request under section 6227 relates after the filing of a petition under this subsection but before the hearing of such petition, such petition shall be treated as an action brought under section 6226 with respect to that administrative adjustment, except that subsection (e) of section 6226 shall not apply.

(C) Notice must be before expiration of statute of limitations. A notice of final partnership administrative adjustment for the partnership taxable year shall be taken into account under subparagraphs (A) and (B) only if such notice is mailed before the expiration of the period prescribed by section 6229 for making assessments of tax attributable to partnership items for such taxable year.

(4) Partners treated as party to action.

(A) In general. If an action is brought by the tax matters partner under paragraph (1) with respect to any request for an adjustment of a partnership item for any taxable year—

(i) each person who was a partner in such partnership at any time during the partnership taxable year involved shall be treated as a party to such action, and

(ii) the court having jurisdiction of such action shall allow each such person to participate in the action.

(B) Partners must have interest in outcome. For purposes of subparagraph (A), rules similar to the rules of paragraph (1) of section 6226(d) shall apply.

(5) Scope of judicial review. Except in the case described in subparagraph (B) of paragraph (3), a court with which a petition is filed in accordance with this subsection shall have jurisdiction to determine only those partnership items to which the part of the request under section 6227 not allowed by the Secretary relates and those items with respect to which the Secretary asserts adjustments as offsets to the adjustments requested by the tax matters partner.

(6) Determination of court reviewable. Any determination by a court under this subsection shall have the force and effect of a decision of the Tax Court or a final judgment or decree of the district court or the Claims Court [Court of Federal Claims, see § 902(b), P.L. 102-572], as the case may be, and shall be reviewable as such. With respect to the partnership, only the tax matters partner, a notice partner, or a 5-percent group may seek review of a determination by a court under this subsection.

(b) Other requests.

(1) Notice providing that items become nonpartnership items. If the Secretary mails to a partner, under subparagraph (A) of section 6231(b)(1) (relating to items ceasing to be partnership items), a notice that all partnership items of the partner for the partnership taxable year to which a timely request for administrative adjustment under subsection (d) of section 6227 relates shall be treated as nonpartnership items—

(A) such request shall be treated as a claim for credit or refund of an overpayment attributable to nonpartnership items, and

(B) the partner may bring an action under section 7422 with respect to such claim at any time within 2 years of the mailing of such notice.

(2) Other cases.

(A) In general. If the Secretary fails to allow any part of an administrative adjustment request filed under subsection (d) of section 6227 by a partner and paragraph (1) does not apply—

(i) such partner may, pursuant to section 7422, begin a civil action for refund of any amount due by reason of the adjustments described in such part of the request, and

(ii) on the beginning of such civil action, the partnership items of such partner for the partnership taxable year to which such part of such request relates shall be treated as nonpartnership items for purposes of this subchapter.

(B) Period for filing petition.

(i) In general. An action may be begun under subparagraph (A) with respect to an administrative adjustment request for a partnership taxable year only—

(I) after the expiration of 6 months from the date of filing of the request under section 6227, and

(II) before the date which is 2 years after the date of filing of such request.

(ii) Extension of time. The 2-year period described in subclause (II) of clause (i) shall be extended for such period as may be agreed upon in writing between the partner and the Secretary.

(C) Action barred after partnership proceeding has begun. No petition may be filed under subparagraph (A) with respect to an administrative adjustment request for a partnership taxable year after the Secretary mails to the partnership a notice of the beginning of a partnership proceeding with respect to such year.

(D) Failure by Secretary to issue timely notice of adjustment. If the Secretary—

(i) mails the notice referred to in subparagraph (C) before the expiration of the 2-year period referred to in clause (i)(II) of subparagraph (B), and

(ii) fails to mail a notice of final partnership administrative adjustment with respect to the partnership taxable year to which the request relates before the expiration of the period described in section 6229(a) (including any extension by agreement),

subparagraph (C) shall cease to apply with respect to such request, and the 2-year period referred to in clause (i)(II) of subparagraph (B) shall not expire before the date 6 months after the expiration of the period described in section 6229(a) (including any extension by agreement).

In 2002, P.L. 107-147, Sec. 417(19)(B)(i), substituted "subsection (c) of section 6227" for "subsection (b) of section 6227" in para. (a)(1) . . . Sec. 417(19)(B)(ii), deleted "subsection (b) of" before "section 6227" in subpara. (a)(3)(A) . . . Sec. 417(19)(B)(iii), substituted "subsection (d) of section 6227" for "subsection (c) of section 6227" in para. (b)(1) and subpara. (b)(2)(A), effective 3/9/2002.

In 1992, P.L. 102-572, Sec. 902(b), effective 10/29/92, relating to Court designation provides as follows:

"(b) Other provisions of law. Reference in any other Federal law or documents to—

"(1) the 'United States Claims Court' shall be deemed to refer to the 'United States Court of Federal Claims'; and

"(2) the 'Claims Court' shall be deemed to refer to the 'Court of Federal Claims'"

In 1983, P.L. 97-448, Sec. 306(c)(1)(B), substituted "With respect to the partnership, only" for "Only" in the second sentence of para. (a)(6), effective for partnership tax. yrs. begin. after 9/3/82.

In 1982, P.L. 97-248, Sec. 402(a), added Code Sec. 6228, effective for partnership tax. yrs. begin. after 9/3/82. Sec. 407(a)(3) of this Act provides:

"(3) The amendments made by sections 402, 403 and 404 [of this Act] shall apply to any partnership taxable year (or in the case of section 6232 of such Code, to any period) ending after the date of the enactment of this Act [9/3/82] if the partnership, each partner, and each indirect partner requests such application and the Secretary of the Treasury or his delegate consents to such application."

Sec. 6229. Period of limitations for making assessments.

(a) General rule.

Except as otherwise provided in this section, the period for assessing any tax imposed by subtitle A with respect to any person which is attributable to any partnership item (or affected item) for a partnership taxable year shall not expire before the date which is 3 years after the later of—

(1) the date on which the partnership return for such taxable year was filed, or

(2) the last day for filing such return for such year (determined without regard to extensions).

(b) Extension by agreement.

(1) In general. The period described in subsection (a) (including an extension period under this subsection) may be extended—

(A) with respect to any partner, by an agreement entered into by the Secretary and such partner, and

(B) with respect to all partners, by an agreement entered into by the Secretary and the tax matters partner (or any other person authorized by the partnership in writing to enter into such an agreement),

before the expiration of such period.

(2) Special rule with respect to debtors in title 11 cases. Notwithstanding any other law or rule of law, if an agreement is entered into under paragraph (1)(B) and the agree-

Partnership items   Code Sec. 6229

ment is signed by a person who would be the tax matters partner but for the fact that, at the time that the agreement is executed, the person is a debtor in a bankruptcy proceeding under title 11 of the United States Code, such agreement shall be binding on all partners in the partnership unless the Secretary has been notified of the bankruptcy proceeding in accordance with regulations prescribed by the Secretary.

(3) Coordination with section 6501(c)(4). Any agreement under section 6501(c)(4) shall apply with respect to the period described in subsection (a) only if the agreement expressly provides that such agreement applies to tax attributable to partnership items.

(c) Special rule in case of fraud, etc.

(1) False return. If any partner has, with the intent to evade tax, signed or participated directly or indirectly in the preparation of a partnership return which includes a false or fraudulent item—

(A) in the case of partners so signing or participating in the preparation of the return, any tax imposed by subtitle A which is attributable to any partnership item (or affected item) for the partnership taxable year to which the return relates may be assessed at any time, and

(B) in the case of all other partners, subsection (a) shall be applied with respect to such return by substituting "6 years" for "3 years."

(2) Substantial omission of income. If any partnership omits from gross income an amount properly includible therein and such amount is described in clause (i) or (ii) of section 6501(e)(1)(A), subsection (a) shall be applied by substituting "6 years" for "3 years."

(3) No return. In the case of a failure by a partnership to file a return for any taxable year, any tax attributable to a partnership item (or affected item) arising in such year may be assessed at any time.

(4) Return filed by secretary. For purposes of this section, a return executed by the Secretary under subsection (b) of section 6020 on behalf of the partnership shall not be treated as a return of the partnership.

(d) Suspension when secretary makes administrative adjustment.

If notice of a final partnership administrative adjustment with respect to any taxable year is mailed to the tax matters partner, the running of the period specified in subsection (a) (as modified by other provisions of this section) shall be suspended—

(1) for the period during which an action may be brought under section 6226 (and, if a petition is filed under section 6226 with respect to such administrative adjustment, until the decision of the court becomes final), and

(2) for 1 year thereafter.

(e) Unidentified partner.

If—

(1) the name, address, and taxpayer identification number of a partner are not furnished on the partnership return for a partnership taxable year, and

(2)

(A) the Secretary, before the expiration of the period otherwise provided under this section with respect to such partner, mails to the tax matters partner the notice specified in paragraph (2) of section 6223(a) with respect to such taxable year, or

(B) the partner has failed to comply with subsection (b) of section 6222 (relating to notification of inconsistent treatment) with respect to any partnership item for such taxable year,

the period for assessing any tax imposed by subtitle A which is attributable to any partnership item (or affected item) for such taxable year shall not expire with respect to such partner before the date which is 1 year after the date on which the name, address, and taxpayer identification number of such partner are furnished to the Secretary.

(f) Special rules.

(1) Items becoming nonpartnership items. If, before the expiration of the period otherwise provided in this section for assessing any tax imposed by subtitle A with respect to the partnership items of a partner for the partnership taxable year, such items become nonpartnership items by reason of 1 or more of the events described in subsection (b) of section 6231, the period for assessing any tax imposed by subtitle A which is attributable to such items (or any item affected by such items) shall not expire before the date which is 1 year after the date on which the items become nonpartnership items. The period described in the preceding sentence (including any extension period under this sentence) may be extended with respect to any partner by agreement entered into by the Secretary and such partner.

(2) Special rule for partial settlement agreements. If a partner enters into a settlement agreement with the Secretary or the Attorney General (or his delegate) with respect to the treatment of some of the partnership items in dispute for a partnership taxable year but other partnership items for such year remain in dispute, the period of limitations for assessing any tax attributable to the settled items shall be determined as if such agreement had not been entered into.

(g) Period of limitations for penalties.

The provisions of this section shall apply also in the case of any addition to tax or an additional amount imposed under subchapter A of chapter 68 which arises with respect to any tax imposed under subtitle A in the same manner as if such addition or additional amount were a tax imposed by subtitle A.

(h) Suspension during pendency of bankruptcy proceeding.

If a petition is filed naming a partner as a debtor in a bankruptcy proceeding under title 11 of the United States Code, the running of the period of limitations provided in this section with respect to such partner shall be suspended—

(1) for the period during which the Secretary is prohibited by reason of such bankruptcy proceeding from making an assessment, and

(2) for 60 days thereafter.

In 2010, P.L. 111-147, Sec. 513(a)(2)(B), substituted "and such amount is described in clause (i) or (ii) of section 6501(e)(1)(A)" for "which is in excess of 25 percent of the amount of gross income stated in its return" in para. (c)(2). Sec. 513(d) of this Act provides:

"(d) Effective date. The amendments made by this section shall apply to—

"(1) returns filed after the date of the enactment of this Act; and

" (2) returns filed on or before such date if the period specified in section 6501 of the Internal Revenue Code of 1986 (determined without regard to such amendments) for assessment of such taxes has not expired as of such date."

In 2002, P.L. 107-147, Sec. 416(d)(1)(B), added "or the Attorney General (or his delegate)" after "Secretary" in para. (f)(2), effective for settlement agreements entered into after 3/9/2002.

In 1997, P.L. 105-34, Sec. 1233(a), substituted "(and, if a petition is filed under section 6226 with respect to such administrative adjustment, until the decision of the court becomes final)," for "(and, if an action with respect to such administrative adjustment is brought during such period, until the decision of the court in such action becomes final), and" in para. (d)(1) . . . Sec. 1233(b), added subsec. (h), effective for partnership tax. yrs. for which the period under Code Sec. 6229 for assessing tax has not expired on or before 8/5/97

—P.L. 105-34, Sec. 1233(c), redesignated para. (b)(2) as para. (b)(3) and added para. (b)(2), effective for agreements entered into after 8/5/97.

—P.L. 105-34, Sec. 1235(a)(1), redesignated the heading and text of subsec. (f) as para. (f)(1), and added a new heading for subsec. (f)... Sec. 1235(a)(3), added para. (f)(2), effective for settlements entered into after 8/5/97.

In **1988,** P.L. 100-647, Sec. 1018(o)(3), added the last sentence to subsec. (f), effective for partnership tax. yrs. begin. after 9/3/82. For special rules see Sec. 407(a)(3) of P.L. 97-248, reproduced below.

In **1986,** P.L. 99-514, Sec. 1875(d)(1), added subsec. (g), effective for partnership tax. yrs. begin. after 9/3/82. For special rules see Sec. 407(a)(3) of P.L. 97-248, reproduced below.

In **1982,** P.L. 97-248, Sec. 402(a), added Code Sec. 6229, effective for partnership tax. yrs. begin. after 9/3/82. Sec. 407(a)(3) of this Act provides:

"(3) The amendments made by sections 402, 403 and 404 [of this Act] shall apply to any partnership taxable year (or in the case of section 6232 of such Code, to any period) ending after the date of the enactment of this Act [9/3/82] if the partnership, each partner, and each indirect partner requests such application and the Secretary of the Treasury or his delegate consents to such application."

Sec. 6230. Additional administrative provisions.

(a) Coordination with deficiency proceedings.

(1) In general. Except as provided in paragraph (2) or (3), subchapter B of this chapter shall not apply to the assessment or collection of any computational adjustment.

(2) Deficiency proceedings to apply in certain cases.

(A) Subchapter B shall apply to any deficiency attributable to—

(i) affected items which require partner level determinations (other than penalties, additions to tax, and additional amounts that relate to adjustments to partnership items), or

(ii) items which have become nonpartnership items (other than by reason of section 6231(b)(1)(C)) and are described in section 6231(e)(1)(B).

(B) Subchapter B shall be applied separately with respect to each deficiency described in subparagraph (A) attributable to each partnership.

(C) Notwithstanding any other law or rule of law, any notice or proceeding under subchapter B with respect to a deficiency described in this paragraph shall not preclude or be precluded by any other notice, proceeding, or determination with respect to a partner's tax liability for a taxable year.

(3) Special rule in case of assertion by partner's spouse of innocent spouse relief.

(A) Notwithstanding section 6404(b), if the spouse of a partner asserts that section 6015 applies with respect to a liability that is attributable to any adjustment to a partnership item (including any liability for any penalties, additions to tax, or additional amounts relating to such adjustment), then such spouse may file with the Secretary within 60 days after the notice of computational adjustment is mailed to the spouse a request for abatement of the assessment specified in such notice. Upon receipt of such request, the Secretary shall abate the assessment. Any reassessment of the tax with respect to which an abatement is made under this subparagraph shall be subject to the deficiency procedures prescribed by subchapter B. The period for making any such reassessment shall not expire before the expiration of 60 days after the date of such abatement.

(B) If the spouse files a petition with the Tax Court pursuant to section 6213 with respect to the request for abatement described in subparagraph (A), the Tax Court shall only have jurisdiction pursuant to this section to determine whether the requirements of section 6015 have been satisfied. For purposes of such determination, the treatment of partnership items (and the applicability of any penalties, additions to tax, or additional amounts) under the settlement, the final partnership administrative adjustment, or the decision of the court (whichever is appropriate) that gave rise to the liability in question shall be conclusive.

(C) Rules similar to the rules contained in subparagraphs (B) and (C) of paragraph (2) shall apply for purposes of this paragraph.

(b) Mathematical and clerical errors appearing on partnership return.

(1) In general. Section 6225 shall not apply to any adjustment necessary to correct a mathematical or clerical error (as defined in section 6213(g)(2)) appearing on the partnership return.

(2) Exception. Paragraph (1) shall not apply to a partner if, within 60 days after the day on which notice of the correction of the error is mailed to the partner, such partner files with the Secretary a request that the correction not be made.

(c) Claims arising out of erroneous computations, etc.

(1) In general. A partner may file a claim for refund on the grounds that—

(A) the Secretary erroneously computed any computational adjustment necessary—

(i) to make the partnership items on the partner's return consistent with the treatment of the partnership items on the partnership return, or

(ii) to apply to the partner a settlement, a final partnership administrative adjustment, or the decision of a court in an action brought under section 6226 or section 6228(a),

(B) the Secretary failed to allow a credit or to make a refund to the partner in the amount of the overpayment attributable to the application to the partner of a settlement, a final partnership administrative adjustment, or the decision of a court in an action brought under section 6226 or section 6228(a), or

(C) the Secretary erroneously imposed any penalty, addition to tax, or additional amount which relates to an adjustment to a partnership item.

(2) Time for filing claim.

(A) Under paragraph (1)(A) or (C). Any claim under subparagraph (A) or (C) of paragraph (1) shall be filed within 6 months after the day on which the Secretary mails the notice of computational adjustment to the partner.

(B) Under paragraph (1)(B). Any claim under paragraph (1)(B) shall be filed within 2 years after whichever of the following days is appropriate:

(i) the day on which the settlement is entered into,

(ii) the day on which the period during which an action may be brought under section 6226 with respect to the final partnership administrative adjustment expires, or

(iii) the day on which the decision of the court becomes final.

(3) Suit if claim not allowed. If any portion of a claim under paragraph (1) is not allowed, the partner may bring suit with respect to such portion within the period specified in subsection (a) of section 6532 (relating to periods of limitations on refund suits).

(4) No review of substantive issues. For purposes of any claim or suit under this subsection, the treatment of partnership items on the partnership return, under the settlement, under the final partnership administrative adjustment, or under the decision of the court (whichever is appropriate) shall be conclusive. In addition, the determination under the final partnership administrative adjustment or under the decision of the court (whichever is appropriate) concerning the applicability of any penalty, addition to tax, or additional amount which relates to an adjustment to a partnership item shall also be conclusive.

Partnership items

Notwithstanding the preceding sentence, the partner shall be allowed to assert any partner level defenses that may apply or to challenge the amount of the computational adjustment.

(5) Rules for seeking innocent spouse relief.

(A) In general. The spouse of a partner may file a claim for refund on the ground that the Secretary failed to relieve the spouse under section 6015 from a liability that is attributable to an adjustment to a partnership item (including any liability for any penalties, additions to tax, or additional amounts relating to such adjustment).

(B) Time for filing claim. Any claim under subparagraph (A) shall be filed within 6 months after the day on which the Secretary mails to the spouse the notice of computational adjustment referred to in subsection (a)(3)(A).

(C) Suit if claim not allowed. If the claim under subparagraph (B) is not allowed, the spouse may bring suit with respect to the claim within the period specified in paragraph (3).

(D) Prior determinations are binding. For purposes of any claim or suit under this paragraph, the treatment of partnership items (and the applicability of any penalties, additions to tax, or additional amounts) under the settlement, the final partnership administrative adjustment, or the decision of the court (whichever is appropriate) that gave rise to the liability in question shall be conclusive.

(d) Special rules with respect to credits or refunds attributable to partnership items.

(1) In general. Except as otherwise provided in this subsection, no credit or refund of an overpayment attributable to a partnership item (or an affected item) for a partnership taxable year shall be allowed or made to any partner after the expiration of the period of limitation prescribed in section 6229 with respect to such partner for assessment of any tax attributable to such item.

(2) Administrative adjustment request. If a request for an administrative adjustment under section 6227 with respect to a partnership item is timely filed, credit or refund of any overpayment attributable to such partnership item (or an affected item) may be allowed or made at any time before the expiration of the period prescribed in section 6228 for bringing suit with respect to such request.

(3) Claim under subsection (c). If a timely claim is filed under subsection (c) for a credit or refund of an overpayment attributable to a partnership item (or affected item), credit or refund of such overpayment may be allowed or made at any time before the expiration of the period specified in section 6532 (relating to periods of limitations on suits) for bringing suit with respect to such claim.

(4) Timely suit. Paragraph (1) shall not apply to any credit or refund of any overpayment attributable to a partnership item (or an item affected by such partnership item) if a partner brings a timely suit with respect to a timely administrative adjustment request under section 6228 or a timely claim under subsection (c) relating to such overpayment.

(5) Overpayments refunded without requirement that partner file claim. In the case of any overpayment by a partner which is attributable to a partnership item (or an affected item) and which may be refunded under this subchapter, to the extent practicable credit or refund of such overpayment shall be allowed or made without any requirement that the partner file a claim therefor.

(6) Subchapter B of chapter 66 not applicable. Subchapter B of chapter 66 (relating to limitations on credit or refund) shall not apply to any credit or refund of an overpayment attributable to a partnership item.

(e) Tax matters partner required to furnish names of partners to Secretary.

If the Secretary mails to any partnership the notice specified in paragraph (1) of section 6223(a) with respect to any partnership taxable year, the tax matters partner shall furnish to the Secretary the name, address, profits interest, and taxpayer identification number of each person who was a partner in such partnership at any time during such taxable year. If the tax matters partner later discovers that the information furnished to the Secretary was incorrect or incomplete, the tax matters partner shall furnish such revised or additional information as may be necessary.

(f) Failure of tax matters partner, etc., to fulfill responsibility does not affect applicability of proceeding.

The failure of the tax matters partner, a pass-thru partner, the representative of a notice group, or any other representative of a partner to provide any notice or perform any act required under this subchapter or under regulations prescribed under this subchapter on behalf of such partner does not affect the applicability of any proceeding or adjustment under this subchapter to such partner.

(g) Date decision of court becomes final.

For purposes of section 6229(d)(1) and section 6230(c)(2)(B), the principles of section 7481(a) shall be applied in determining the date on which a decision of a district court or the Claims Court [Court of Federal Claims, see § 902(b), P.L. 102-572] becomes final.

(h) Examination authority not limited.

Nothing in this subchapter shall be construed as limiting the authority granted to the Secretary under section 7602.

(i) Time and manner of filing statements, making elections, etc.

Except as otherwise provided in this subchapter, each—

(1) statement,

(2) election,

(3) request, and

(4) furnishing of information,

shall be filed or made at such time, in such manner, and at such place as may be prescribed in regulations.

(j) Partnerships having principal place of business outside the United States.

For purposes of sections 6226 and 6228, a principal place of business located outside the United States shall be treated as located in the District of Columbia.

(k) Regulations.

The Secretary shall prescribe such regulations as may be necessary to carry out the purposes of this subchapter. Any reference in this subchapter to regulations is a reference to regulations prescribed by the Secretary.

(l) Court rules.

Any action brought under any provision of this subchapter shall be conducted in accordance with such rules of practice and procedure as may be prescribed by the Court in which the action is brought.

In **2007**, P.L. 110-172, Sec. 11(a)(36), substituted "section 6015" for "section 6013(e)" in subpara. (a)(3)(A) and (B), enacted 12/29/2007.

In **1998**, P.L. 105-206, Sec. 3201(e)(2), substituted "section 6015" for "section 6013(e)" in subpara. (c)(5)(A), effective for any liability for tax arising after 7/22/98 and any liability for tax arising on or before 7/22/98 but remaining unpaid as of 7/22/98.

Sec. 3202(g)(2), of this Act, provides:

"(2) 2-year period. The 2-year period under subsection (b)(1)(E) or (c)(3)(B) of section 6015 of the Internal Revenue Code of 1986 shall not expire before the date which is 2 years after the date of the first collection activity after the date of the enactment of this Act."

Code Sec. 6230   Partnership items

In 1997, P.L. 105-34, Sec. 1237(a), added para. (a)(3)...Sec. 1237(b), added para. (c)(5)...Sec. 1237(c)(1), substituted "paragraph (2) or (3)" for " paragraph (2)" in para. (a)(1), effective for partnership tax. yrs. begin. after 9/3/82. For special rules, see Sec. 407(a)(3) of P.L. 97-248, reproduced below.

—P.L. 105-34, Sec. 1238(b)(2), amended clause (a)(2)(A)(i)...Sec. 1238(b)(3)(A), added "(including any liability for any penalties, additions to tax, or additional amounts relating to such adjustment)" after "partnership item" in subpara. (A)(3)(A)...Sec. 1238(b)(3)(B), added "(and the applicability of any penalties, additions to tax, or additional amounts)" after "partnership items" in para. (a)(3)(B)...Sec. 1237(b)(3)(C), added "(including any liability for any penalties, additions to tax, or additional amounts relating to such adjustment)" before the period in subpara. (c)(5)(A)...Sec. 1238(b)(3)(D), added "(and the applicability of any penalties, additions to tax, or additional amounts)" after "partnership items" in subpara. (c)(5)(D)...Sec. 1238(b)(4), deleted "or" at the end of subpara. (c)(1)(A), substituted ", or" for the period at the end of subpara. (c)(1)(B), and added subpara. (c)(1)(C)...Sec. 1238(b)(5), substituted "(A) Under paragraph (1)(A) or (C). Any claim under subparagraph (A) or (C) of paragraph (1)" for "(A) Under paragraph (1)(A). Any claim under paragraph (1)(A)" in para. (c)(2)(A)...Sec. 1238(b)(6), added the last two sentences at the end of para. (c)(4), effective for partnership tax. yrs. end. after 8/5/97.

Prior to amendment, clause (a)(2)(A)(i) read as follows:
"(i) affected items which require partner level determinations, or"

—P.L. 105-34, Sec. 1239(c)(1), deleted "(or an affected item)" after "partnership item" in para. (d)(6), effective for partnership tax. yrs. end. after 8/5/97.

In 1992, P.L. 102-572, Sec. 902(b), effective 10/29/92, relating to Court designation provides as follows:

"(b) Other provisions of law. Reference in any other Federal law or documents to—

"(1) the 'United States Claims Court' shall be deemed to refer to the 'United States Court of Federal Claims'; and

"(2) the 'Claims Court' shall be deemed to refer to the 'Court of Federal Claims'."

In 1988, P.L. 100-647, Sec. 1018(o)(1), substituted 'nonpartnership items (other than by reason of section 6231(b)(1)(C))' for 'nonpartnership items', in clause (a)(2)(A)(ii), effective for partnership tax. yrs. begin. after 9/3/82. For special rules see Sec. 407(a)(3) of P.L. 97-248, reproduced below.

In 1986, P.L. 99-514, Sec. 1875(d)(2)(A), amended subsec. (a), effective for partnership tax. yrs. begin. after 9/3/82. For special rules see Sec. 407(a)(3) of P.L. 97-248, reproduced below.

Prior to amendment, subsec. (a) read as follows:

"(a) Normal deficiency proceedings do not apply to computational adjustments. Subchapter B of this chapter shall not apply to the assessment or collection of any computational adjustment."

In 1984, P.L. 98-369, Sec. 714(p)(2)(A), deleted "(or erroneously computed the amount of any such credit or refund)" from the end of subpara. (c)(1)(B), effective for partnership tax. yrs. begin. after 9/3/82.

In 1982, P.L. 97-248, Sec. 402(a), added Code Sec. 6230, effective for partnership tax. yrs. begin. after 9/3/82. Sec. 407(a)(3) of this Act provides:

"(3) The amendments made by sections 402, 403 and 404 [of this Act] shall apply to any partnership taxable year (or in the case of section 6232 of such Code, to any period) ending after the date of the enactment of this Act [9/3/82] if the partnership, each partner, and each indirect partner requests such application and the Secretary of the Treasury or his delegate consents to such application."

Sec. 6231. Definitions and special rules.
(a) Definitions.

For purposes of this subchapter—

(1) Partnership.

(A) In general. Except as provided in subparagraph (B), the term "partnership" means any partnership required to file a return under section 6031(a).

(B) Exception for small partnerships.

(i) In general. The term "partnership" shall not include any partnership having 10 or fewer partners each of whom is an individual (other than a nonresident alien), a C corporation, or an estate of a deceased partner. For purposes of the preceding sentence, a husband and wife (and their estates) shall be treated as 1 partner.

(ii) Election to have subchapter apply. A partnership (within the meaning of subparagraph (A)) may for any taxable year elect to have clause (i) not apply. Such election shall apply for such taxable year and all subsequent taxable years unless revoked with the consent of the Secretary.

(2) Partner. The term "partner" means—

(A) a partner in the partnership, and

(B) any other person whose income tax liability under subtitle A is determined in whole or in part by taking into account directly or indirectly partnership items of the partnership.

(3) Partnership item. The term "partnership item" means, with respect to a partnership, any item required to be taken into account for the partnership's taxable year under any provision of subtitle A to the extent regulations prescribed by the Secretary provide that, for purposes of this subtitle, such item is more appropriately determined at the partnership level than at the partner level.

(4) Nonpartnership item. The term "nonpartnership item" means an item which is (or is treated as) not a partnership item.

(5) Affected item. The term "affected item" means any item to the extent such item is affected by a partnership item.

(6) Computational adjustment. The term "computational adjustment" means the change in the tax liability of a partner which properly reflects the treatment under this subchapter of a partnership item. All adjustments required to apply the results of a proceeding with respect to a partnership under this subchapter to an indirect partner shall be treated as computational adjustments.

(7) Tax matters partner. The tax matters partner of any partnership is—

(A) the general partner designated as the tax matters partner as provided in regulations, or

(B) if there is no general partner who has been so designated, the general partner having the largest profits interest in the partnership at the close of the taxable year involved (or, where there is more than 1 such partner, the 1 of such partners whose name would appear first in an alphabetical listing).

If there is no general partner designated under subparagraph (A) and the Secretary determines that it is impracticable to apply subparagraph (B), the partner selected by the Secretary shall be treated as the tax matters partner. The Secretary shall, within 30 days of selecting a tax matters partner under the preceding sentence, notify all partners required to receive notice under section 6223(a) of the name and address of the person selected.

(8) Notice partner. The term "notice partner" means a partner who, at the time in question, would be entitled to notice under subsection (a) of section 6223 (determined without regard to subsections (b)(2) and (e)(1)(B) thereof).

(9) Pass-thru partner. The term "pass-thru partner" means a partnership, estate, trust, S corporation, nominee, or other similar person through whom other persons hold an interest in the partnership with respect to which proceedings under this subchapter are conducted.

(10) Indirect partner. The term "indirect partner" means a person holding an interest in a partnership through 1 or more pass-thru partners.

(11) 5-percent group. A 5-percent group is a group of partners who for the partnership taxable year involved had profits interests which aggregated 5 percent or more.

(12) Husband and wife. Except to the extent otherwise provided in regulations, a husband and wife who have a joint interest in a partnership shall be treated as 1 person.

(b) Items cease to be partnership items in certain cases.

(1) In general. For purposes of this subchapter, the partnership items of a partner for a partnership taxable year shall become nonpartnership items as of the date—

(A) the Secretary mails to such partner a notice that such items shall be treated as nonpartnership items,

(B) the partner files suit under section 6228(b) after the Secretary fails to allow an administrative adjustment request with respect to any of such items,

Partnership items   **Code Sec. 6231**

(C) the Secretary or the Attorney General (or his delegate) enters into a settlement agreement with the partner with respect to such items, or

(D) such change occurs under subsection (e) of section 6223 (relating to effect of Secretary's failure to provide notice) or under subsection (c) of this section.

(2) Circumstances in which notice is permitted. The Secretary may mail the notice referred to in subparagraph (A) of paragraph (1) to a partner with respect to partnership items for a partnership taxable year only if—

(A) such partner—

(i) has complied with subparagraph (B) of section 6222(b)(1) (relating to notification of inconsistent treatment) with respect to one or more of such items, and

(ii) has not, as of the date on which the Secretary mails the notice, filed a request for administrative adjustments which would make the partner's treatment of the item or items with respect to which the partner complied with subparagraph (B) of section 6222(b)(1) consistent with the treatment of such item or items on the partnership return, or

(B)(i) such partner has filed a request under section 6227(d) for administrative adjustment of one or more of such items, and

(ii) the adjustments requested would not make such partner's treatment of such items consistent with the treatment of such items on the partnership return.

(3) Notice must be mailed before beginning of partnership proceeding. Any notice to a partner under subparagraph (A) of paragraph (1) with respect to partnership items for a partnership taxable year shall be mailed before the day on which the Secretary mails to the tax matters partner a notice of the beginning of an administrative proceeding at the partnership level with respect to such items.

(c) Regulations with respect to certain special enforcement areas.

(1) Applicability of subsection. This subsection applies in the case of—

(A) assessments under section 6851 (relating to termination assessments of income tax) or section 6861 (relating to jeopardy assessments of income, estate, gift, and certain excise taxes),

(B) criminal investigations,

(C) indirect methods of proof of income,

(D) foreign partnerships, and

(E) other areas that the Secretary determines by regulation to present special enforcement considerations.

(2) Items may be treated as nonpartnership items. To the extent that the Secretary determines and provides by regulations that to treat items as partnership items will interfere with the effective and efficient enforcement of this title in any case described in paragraph (1), such items shall be treated as nonpartnership items for purposes of this subchapter.

(3) Special rules. The Secretary may prescribe by regulation such special rules as the Secretary determines to be necessary to achieve the purposes of this subchapter in any case described in paragraph (1).

(d) Time for determining partner's profits interest in partnership.

(1) In general. For purposes of section 6223(b) (relating to special rules for partnerships with more than 100 partners) and paragraph (11) of subsection (a) (relating to 5-percent group), the interest of a partner in the profits of a partnership for a partnership taxable year shall be determined—

(A) in the case of a partner whose entire interest in the partnership is disposed of during such partnership taxable year, as of the moment immediately before such disposition, or

(B) in the case of any other partner, as of the close of the partnership taxable year.

(2) Indirect partners. The Secretary shall prescribe regulations consistent with the principles of paragraph (1) to be applied in the case of indirect partners.

(e) Effect of judicial decisions in certain proceedings.

(1) Determinations at partner level. No judicial determination with respect to the income tax liability of any partner not conducted under this subchapter shall be a bar to any adjustment in such partner's income tax liability resulting from—

(A) a proceeding with respect to partnership items under this subchapter, or

(B) a proceeding with respect to items which become nonpartnership items—

(i) by reason of 1 or more of the events described in subsection (b), and

(ii) after the appropriate time for including such items in any other proceeding with respect to nonpartnership items.

(2) Proceedings under section 6228(a). No judicial determination in any proceeding under subsection (a) of section 6228 with respect to any partnership item shall be a bar to any adjustment in any other partnership item.

(f) Special rule for deductions, losses, and credits of foreign partnerships.

Except to the extent otherwise provided in regulations, in the case of any partnership the tax matters partner of which resides outside the United States or the books of which are maintained outside the United States, no deduction, loss, or credit shall be allowable to any partner unless section 6031 is complied with for the partnership's taxable year in which such deduction, loss, or credit arose at such time as the Secretary prescribes by regulations.

(g) Partnership return to be determinative of whether subchapter applies.

(1) Determination that subchapter applies. If, on the basis of a partnership return for a taxable year, the Secretary reasonably determines that this subchapter applies to such partnership for such year but such determination is erroneous, then the provisions of this subchapter are hereby extended to such partnership (and its items) for such taxable year and to partners of such partnership.

(2) Determination that subchapter does not apply. If, on the basis of a partnership return for a taxable year, the Secretary reasonably determines that this subchapter does not apply to such partnership for such year but such determination is erroneous, then the provisions of this subchapter shall not apply to such partnership (and its items) for such taxable year or to partners of such partnership.

In **2002**, P.L. 107-147, Sec. 416(d)(1)(C), added "or the Attorney General (or his delegate)" after "Secretary" in subpara. (b)(1)(C), effective for settlement agreements entered into after 3/9/2002.

—P.L. 107-147, Sec. 417(19)(C), substituted "section 6227(d)" for "section 6227(c)" in clause (b)(2)(B)(i), effective 3/9/2002.

In **1998**, P.L. 105-206, Sec. 3507(a), added a sentence at the end of para. (a)(7), effective for selections of tax matters partners made by the Secretary of the Treasury after 7/22/98.

In **1997**, P.L. 105-34, Sec. 1141(b)(1), substituted "deductions, losses, and" for "losses and" in the heading of subsec. (f) . . . Sec. 1141(b)(2), substituted "deduction, loss, or" for "loss of" each place it appeared in subsec. (f), effective for tax. yrs. begin. after 8/5/97.

—P.L. 105-34, Sec. 1232(a), added subsec. (g), effective for tax. yrs. end. after 8/5/97.

3,647

—P.L. 105-34, Sec. 1234(a), amended clause (a)(1)(B)(i), effective for partnership tax. yrs. end. after 8/5/97.

Prior to amendment, clause (a)(1)(B)(i) read as follows:

"(i) In general. The term 'partnership' shall not include any partnership if—

"(I) such partnership has 10 or fewer partners each of whom is a natural person (other than a nonresident alien) or an estate, and

"(II) each partner's share of each partnership item is the same as his share of every other item.

For purposes of the preceding sentence, a husband and wife (and their estates) shall be treated as 1 partner."

In 1984, P.L. 98-369, Sec. 714(p)(2)(B), substituted "S corporation" for "electing small business corporation" in para. (a)(9)...Sec. 714(p)(2)(C), amended subpara. (d)(1)(A)...Sec. 714(p)(2)(D), substituted "such loss or credit" for "such deduction or credit" in subsec. (f)...Sec. 714(p)(2)(I), substituted "section 6227(c)" for "section 6227(b)" in subpara. (b)(2)(B), for partnership tax. yrs. begin. after 9/3/82.

Prior to amendment, subpara. (d)(1)(A) read as follows:

"(A) in the case of a partner whose entire interest in the partnership is liquidated, sold, or exchanged during such partnership taxable year, as of the moment immediately before such liquidation, sale, or exchange, or"

In 1982, P.L. 97-248, Sec. 402(a), added Code Sec. 6231, effective for partnership tax. yrs. begin. after 9/3/82. Sec. 407(a)(3) of this Act provides:

"(3) The amendments made by sections 402, 403, and 404 [of this Act] shall apply to any partnership taxable year (or in the case of section 6232 of such Code, to any period) ending after the date of the enactment of this Act [9/3/82] if the partnership, each partner, and each indirect partner requests such application and the Secretary of the Treasury or his delegate consents to such application."

Sec. 6232. Repealed.

In 1988, P.L. 100-418, Sec. 1941(b)(1), repealed Code Sec. 6232, effective for crude oil removed from the premises on or after 8/23/88.

Prior to repeal, Code Sec. 6232 read as follows:

"SEC. 6232. EXTENSION OF SUBCHAPTER TO WINDFALL PROFIT TAX.

"(a) Inclusion as partnership item.

"For purposes of applying this subchapter to the tax imposed by chapter 45 (relating to the windfall profit tax), the term 'partnership item' means any item relating to the determination of the tax imposed by chapter 45 to the extent regulations prescribed by the Secretary provide that, for purposes of this subtitle, such item is more appropriately determined at the partnership level than at the partner level.

"(b) Separate application.

"This subchapter shall be applied separately with respect to—

"(1) partnership items described in subsection (a), and

"(2) partnership items described in section 6231(a)(3).

"(c) Partnership authorized to act for partners.

"(1) In general. For purposes of chapter 45 and so much of this subtitle as relates to chapter 45, to the extent and in the manner provided in regulations, a partnership shall be treated as authorized to act for each partner with respect to the determination, assessment, or collection of the tax imposed by chapter 45.

"(2) Partners entitled to 5 percent or more of income may elect out of subsection. Paragraph (1) shall not apply to any partnership if partners entitled to 5 percent or more of the income of the partnership elect (at the time and in the manner provided in regulations) not to have paragraph (1) apply to the partnership.

"(3) Partner's rights preserved. Nothing in paragraph (1) shall be construed to take away from any person any right granted to such person by the foregoing sections of this subchapter."

In 1982, P.L. 97-248, Sec. 402(a), added Code Sec. 6232, effective for periods after 12/31/82. Sec. 407(a)(3) of this Act provides:

"(3) The amendments made by sections 402, 403, and 404 shall apply to any partnership taxable year (or in the case of section 6232 of such Code, to any period) ending after the date of the enactment of this Act [9/3/82] if the partnership, each partner, and each indirect partner requests such application and the Secretary of the Treasury or his delegate consents to such application."

Sec. 6233. Extension to entities filing partnership returns, etc.

(a) General rule.

If a partnership return is filed by an entity for a taxable year but it is determined that the entity is not a partnership for such year, then, to the extent provided in regulations, the provisions of this subchapter are hereby extended in respect of such year to such entity and its items and to persons holding an interest in such entity.

(b) Similar rules in certain cases.

If a partnership return is filed for any taxable year but it is determined that there is no entity for such taxable year, to the extent provided in regulations, rules similar to the rules of subsection (a) shall apply.

In 1996, P.L. 104-188, Sec. 1307(c)(3)(B), amended subsec. (b), effective for tax. yrs. begin. after 12/31/96.

Prior to amendment, subsec. (b) read as follows:

"(b) Similar rules in certain cases.

"If for any taxable year—

"(1) an entity files a return as an S corporation but it is determined that the entity was not an S corporation for such year, or

"(2) a partnership return or S corporation return is filed but it is determined that there is no entity for such taxable year,

then, to the extent provided in regulations, rules similar to the rules of subsection (a) shall apply."

In 1984, P.L. 98-369, Sec. 714(p)(1), added Code Sec. 6233, effective for partnership tax. yrs. begin after 9/3/82. For special rules, see Sec. 407(a)(3) of P.L. 97-248, reproduced in note following Code Sec. 6232.

Sec. 6234. Declaratory judgment relating to treatment of items other than partnership items with respect to an oversheltered return.

(a) General rule.

If—

(1) a taxpayer files an oversheltered return for a taxable year,

(2) the Secretary makes a determination with respect to the treatment of items (other than partnership items) of such taxpayer for such taxable year, and

(3) the adjustments resulting from such determination do not give rise to a deficiency (as defined in section 6211) but would give rise to a deficiency if there were no net loss from partnership items,

the Secretary is authorized to send a notice of adjustment reflecting such determination to the taxpayer by certified or registered mail.

(b) Oversheltered return.

For purposes of this section, the term "oversheltered return" means an income tax return which—

(1) shows no taxable income for the taxable year, and

(2) shows a net loss from partnership items.

(c) Judicial review in the Tax Court.

Within 90 days, or 150 days if the notice is addressed to a person outside the United States, after the day on which the notice of adjustment authorized in subsection (a) is mailed to the taxpayer, the taxpayer may file a petition with the Tax Court for redetermination of the adjustments. Upon the filing of such a petition, the Tax Court shall have jurisdiction to make a declaration with respect to all items (other than partnership items and affected items which require partner level determinations as described in section 6230(a)(2)(A)(i)) for the taxable year to which the notice of adjustment relates, in accordance with the principles of section 6214(a). Any such declaration shall have the force and effect of a decision of the Tax Court and shall be reviewable as such.

(d) Failure to file petition.

(1) In general. Except as provided in paragraph (2), if the taxpayer does not file a petition with the Tax Court within the time prescribed in subsection (c), the determination of the Secretary set forth in the notice of adjustment that was mailed to the taxpayer shall be deemed to be correct.

(2) Exception. Paragraph (1) shall not apply after the date that the taxpayer—

(A) files a petition with the Tax Court within the time prescribed in subsection (c) with respect to a subsequent notice of adjustment relating to the same taxable year, or

(B) files a claim for refund of an overpayment of tax under section 6511 for the taxable year involved.

If a claim for refund is filed by the taxpayer, then solely for purposes of determining (for the taxable year involved) the amount of any computational adjustment in connection with a partnership proceeding under this subchapter (other than under this section) or the amount of any deficiency attributable to affected items in a proceeding under section 6230(a)(2), the items that are the subject of the notice of adjustment shall be presumed to have been correctly reported on the taxpayer's return during the pendency of the refund claim (and, if within the time prescribed by section 6532 the taxpayer commences a civil action for refund under section 7422, until the decision in the refund action becomes final).

(e) Limitations period.

(1) In general. Any notice to a taxpayer under subsection (a) shall be mailed before the expiration of the period prescribed by section 6501 (relating to the period of limitations on assessment).

(2) Suspension when Secretary mails notice of adjustment. If the Secretary mails a notice of adjustment to the taxpayer for a taxable year, the period of limitations on the making of assessments shall be suspended for the period during which the Secretary is prohibited from making the assessment (and, in any event, if a proceeding in respect of the notice of adjustment is placed on the docket of the Tax Court, until the decision of the Tax Court becomes final), and for 60 days thereafter.

(3) Restrictions on assessment. Except as otherwise provided in section 6851, 6852, or 6861, no assessment of a deficiency with respect to any tax imposed by subtitle A attributable to any item (other than a partnership item or any item affected by a partnership item) shall be made—

(A) until the expiration of the applicable 90-day or 150-day period set forth in subsection (c) for filing a petition with the Tax Court, or

(B) if a petition has been filed with the Tax Court, until the decision of the Tax Court has become final.

(f) Further notices of adjustment restricted.

If the Secretary mails a notice of adjustment to the taxpayer for a taxable year and the taxpayer files a petition with the Tax Court within the time prescribed in subsection (c), the Secretary may not mail another such notice to the taxpayer with respect to the same taxable year in the absence of a showing of fraud, malfeasance, or misrepresentation of a material fact.

(g) Coordination with other proceedings under this subchapter.

(1) In general. The treatment of any item that has been determined pursuant to subsection (c) or (d) shall be taken into account in determining the amount of any computational adjustment that is made in connection with a partnership proceeding under this subchapter (other than under this section), or the amount of any deficiency attributable to affected items in a proceeding under section 6230(a)(2), for the taxable year involved. Notwithstanding any other law or rule of law pertaining to the period of limitations on the making of assessments, for purposes of the preceding sentence, any adjustment made in accordance with this section shall be taken into account regardless of whether any assessment has been made with respect to such adjustment.

(2) Special rule in case of computational adjustment. In the case of a computational adjustment that is made in connection with a partnership proceeding under this subchapter (other than under this section), the provisions of paragraph (1) shall apply only if the computational adjustment is made within the period prescribed by section 6229 for assessing any tax under subtitle A which is attributable to any partnership item or affected item for the taxable year involved.

(3) Conversion to deficiency proceeding. If—

(A) after the notice referred to in subsection (a) is mailed to a taxpayer for a taxable year but before the expiration of the period for filing a petition with the Tax Court under subsection (c) (or, if a petition is filed with the Tax Court, before the Tax Court makes a declaration for that taxable year), the treatment of any partnership item for the taxable year is finally determined, or any such item ceases to be a partnership item pursuant to section 6231(b), and

(B) as a result of that final determination or cessation, a deficiency can be determined with respect to the items that are the subject of the notice of adjustment,

the notice of adjustment shall be treated as a notice of deficiency under section 6212 and any petition filed in respect of the notice shall be treated as an action brought under section 6213.

(4) Finally determined. For purposes of this subsection, the treatment of partnership items shall be treated as finally determined if—

(A) the Secretary or the Attorney General (or his delegate) enters into a settlement agreement (within the meaning of section 6224) with the taxpayer regarding such items,

(B) a notice of final partnership administrative adjustment has been issued and—

(i) no petition has been filed under section 6226 and the time for doing so has expired, or

(ii) a petition has been filed under section 6226 and the decision of the court has become final, or

(C) the period within which any tax attributable to such items may be assessed against the taxpayer has expired.

(h) Special rules if Secretary incorrectly determines applicable procedure.

(1) Special rule if Secretary erroneously mails notice of adjustment. If the Secretary erroneously determines that subchapter B does not apply to a taxable year of a taxpayer and consistent with that determination timely mails a notice of adjustment to the taxpayer pursuant to subsection (a) of this section, the notice of adjustment shall be treated as a notice of deficiency under section 6212 and any petition that is filed in respect of the notice shall be treated as an action brought under section 6213.

(2) Special rule if Secretary erroneously mails notice of deficiency. If the Secretary erroneously determines that subchapter B applies to a taxable year of a taxpayer and consistent with that determination timely mails a notice of deficiency to the taxpayer pursuant to section 6212, the notice of deficiency shall be treated as a notice of adjustment under subsection (a) and any petition that is filed in respect of the notice shall be treated as an action brought under subsection (c).

In 2002, P.L. 107-147, Sec. 416(d)(1)(D), added "or the Attorney General (or his delegate)" after "Secretary" in subpara. (g)(4)(A), effective for settlement agreements entered into after 3/9/2002.

In 1997, P.L. 105-34, Sec. 1231(a), added Code Sec. 6234, effective for partnership tax. yrs. end. after 8/5/97.

Subchapter D.—Repealed. [Tax Treatment of Subchapter S Items]

Sec.

6241. Repealed. [Tax treatment determined at corporate level.]

6242. Repealed. [Shareholder's return must be consistent with corporate return or Secretary notified of inconsistency.]

6243. Repealed. [All shareholders to be notified of proceedings and given opportunity to participate.]

Subchapter D — Partnership items

6244. Repealed. [Certain partnership provisions made applicable.]

6245. Repealed. [Subchapter S item defined.]

In 1996, P.L. 104-188, Sec. 1307(c)(3)(C), repealed Subchapter D.
Prior to repeal, Subchapter D. read as follows:
"Subchapter D. Tax Treatment of Subchapter S Items
"Sec. 6241. Tax treatment determined at corporate level.
"Sec. 6242. Shareholder's return must be consistent with corporate return or Secretary notified of inconsistency.
"Sec. 6243. All shareholders to be notified of proceedings and given opportunity to participate.
"Sec. 6244. Certain partnership provisions made applicable.
"Sec. 6245. Subchapter S item defined."
In 1982, P.L. 97-354, Sec. 4(a), added Subchapter D.

"SEC. 6241. TAX TREATMENT DETERMINED AT CORPORATE LEVEL.

In 1996, P.L. 104-188, Sec. 1307(c)(1), repealed Code Sec. 6241, effective for tax. yrs. begin. after 12/31/96.
Prior to repeal, Code Sec. 6241 read as follows:
"SEC. 6241. TAX TREATMENT DETERMINED AT CORPORATE LEVEL.
"Except as otherwise provided in regulations prescribed by the Secretary, the tax treatment of any subchapter S item shall be determined at the corporate level."
In 1982, P.L. 97-354, Sec. 4(a), added Code Sec. 6241, effective for tax. yrs. begin. after 12/31/82.

"SEC. 6242. SHAREHOLDER'S RETURN MUST BE CONSISTENT WITH CORPORATE RETURN OR SECRETARY NOTIFIED OF INCONSISTENCY.

In 1996, P.L. 104-188, Sec. 1307(c)(1), repealed Code Sec. 6242, effective for tax. yrs. begin. after 12/31/96.
Prior to repeal, Code Sec. 6242 read as follows:
"SEC. 6242. SHAREHOLDER'S RETURN MUST BE CONSISTENT WITH CORPORATE RETURN OR SECRETARY NOTIFIED OF INCONSISTENCY.
"A shareholder of an S corporation shall, on such shareholder's return, treat a subchapter S item in a manner which is consistent with the treatment of such item on the corporate return unless the shareholder notifies the Secretary (at the time and in the manner prescribed by regulations) of the inconsistency."
In 1982, P.L. 97-354, Sec. 4(a), added Code Sec. 6242, effective for tax. yrs. begin. after 12/31/82.

"SEC. 6243. ALL SHAREHOLDERS TO BE NOTIFIED OF PROCEEDINGS AND GIVEN OPPORTUNITY TO PARTICIPATE.

In 1996, P.L. 104-188, Sec. 1307(c)(1), repealed Code Sec. 6243, effective for tax. yrs. begin. after 12/31/96.
Prior to repeal, Code Sec. 6243 read as follows:
"SEC. 6243. ALL SHAREHOLDERS TO BE NOTIFIED OF PROCEEDINGS AND GIVEN OPPORTUNITY TO PARTICIPATE.
"In the manner and at the time prescribed in regulations, each shareholder in a corporation shall be given notice of, and the right to participate in, any administrative or judicial proceeding for the determination at the corporate level of any subchapter S item."
In 1982, P.L. 97-354, Sec. 4(a), added Code Sec. 6243, effective for tax. yrs. begin. after 12/31/82.

"SEC. 6244. CERTAIN PARTNERSHIP PROVISIONS MADE APPLICABLE.

In 1996, P.L. 104-188, Sec. 1307(c)(1), repealed Code Sec. 6244, effective for tax. yrs. begin. after 12/31/96.
Prior to repeal, Code Sec. 6244 read as follows:
"SEC. 6244. CERTAIN PARTNERSHIP PROVISIONS MADE APPLICABLE.
"The provisions of—
"(1) subchapter C which relate to—
"(A) assessing deficiencies, and filing claims for credit or refund, with respect to partnership items, and
"(B) judicial determination of partnership items, and
"(2) so much of the other provisions of this subtitle as relate to partnership items,
are (except to the extent modified or made inapplicable in regulations) hereby extended to and made applicable to subchapter S items."
In 1982, P.L. 97-354, Sec. 4(a), added Code Sec. 6244, effective for tax. yrs. begin. after 12/31/82.

"SEC. 6245. SUBCHAPTER S ITEM DEFINED.

In 1996, P.L. 104-188, Sec. 1307(c)(1), repealed Code Sec. 6245, effective for tax. yrs. begin. after 12/31/96.
Prior to repeal, Code Sec. 6245 read as follows:
"SEC. 6245. SUBCHAPTER S ITEM DEFINED.
"For purposes of this subchapter, the term 'subchapter S item' means any item of an S corporation to the extent regulations prescribed by the Secretary provide that, for purposes of this subtitle, such item is more appropriately determined at the corporate level than at the shareholder level."
In 1982, P.L. 97-354, Sec. 4(a), added Code Sec. 6245, effective for tax. yrs. begin. after 12/31/82.

Subchapter D.—Treatment of Electing Large Partnerships

Part
  I. Treatment of partnership items and adjustments.
  II. Partnership level adjustments.
  III. Definitions and special rules.

In 1997, P.L. 105-34, Sec. 1222(a), amended Chapter 63 by adding Subchapter D.

PART I.—TREATMENT OF PARTNERSHIP ITEMS AND ADJUSTMENTS

Sec.
6240. Application of subchapter.
6241. Partner's return must be consistent with partnership return.
6242. Procedures for taking partnership adjustments into account.

In 1997, P.L. 105-34, Sec. 1222(a), amended Chapter 63 by adding Part I of Subchapter D.

Sec. 6240. Application of subchapter.
(a) General rule.

This subchapter shall only apply to electing large partnerships and partners in such partnerships.

(b) Coordination with other partnership audit procedures.

(1) In general. Subchapter C of this chapter shall not apply to any electing large partnership other than in its capacity as a partner in another partnership which is not an electing large partnership.

(2) Treatment where partner in other partnership. If an electing large partnership is a partner in another partnership which is not an electing large partnership—

(A) subchapter C of this chapter shall apply to items of such electing large partnership which are partnership items with respect to such other partnership, but

(B) any adjustment under such subchapter C shall be taken into account in the manner provided by section 6242.

In 1998, P.L. 105-206, Sec. 6012(e), substituted "beginning" for "ending on or" in Sec. 1226 of P.L. 105-34, the effective date for amendments made by Sec. 1222 of P.L. 105-34, [see below].
In 1997, P.L. 105-34, Sec. 1222(a), added Code Sec. 6240 of Part I of Subchapter D of Chapter 63 of Subtitle F, effective for partnership tax. yrs. beginning after 12/31/97.

Sec. 6241. Partner's return must be consistent with partnership return.
(a) General rule.

A partner of any electing large partnership shall, on the partner's return, treat each partnership item attributable to such partnership in a manner which is consistent with the treatment of such partnership item on the partnership return.

(b) Underpayment due to inconsistent treatment assessed as math error.

Any underpayment of tax by a partner by reason of failing to comply with the requirements of subsection (a) shall be assessed and collected in the same manner as if such underpayment were on account of a mathematical or clerical error appearing on the partner's return. Paragraph (2) of section 6213(b) shall not apply to any assessment of an underpayment referred to in the preceding sentence.

Partnership items   Code Sec. 6242(b)(4)

(c) Adjustments not to affect prior year of partners.

(1) In general. Except as provided in paragraph (2), subsections (a) and (b) shall apply without regard to any adjustment to the partnership item under part II.

(2) Certain changes in distributive share taken into account by partner.

(A) In general. To the extent that any adjustment under part II involves a change under section 704 in a partner's distributive share of the amount of any partnership item shown on the partnership return, such adjustment shall be taken into account in applying this title to such partner for the partner's taxable year for which such item was required to be taken into account.

(B) Coordination with deficiency procedures.

(i) In general. Subchapter B shall not apply to the assessment or collection of any underpayment of tax attributable to an adjustment referred to in subparagraph (A).

(ii) Adjustment not precluded. Notwithstanding any other law or rule of law, nothing in subchapter B (or in any proceeding under subchapter B) shall preclude the assessment or collection of any underpayment of tax (or the allowance of any credit or refund of any overpayment of tax) attributable to an adjustment referred to in subparagraph (A) and such assessment or collection or allowance (or any notice thereof) shall not preclude any notice, proceeding, or determination under subchapter B.

(C) Period of limitations. The period for—

(i) assessing any underpayment of tax, or

(ii) filing a claim for credit or refund of any overpayment of tax,

attributable to an adjustment referred to in subparagraph (A) shall not expire before the close of the period prescribed by section 6248 for making adjustments with respect to the partnership taxable year involved.

(D) Tiered structures. If the partner referred to in subparagraph (A) is another partnership or an S corporation, the rules of this paragraph shall also apply to persons holding interests in such partnership or S corporation (as the case may be); except that, if such partner is an electing large partnership, the adjustment referred to in subparagraph (A) shall be taken into account in the manner provided by section 6242.

(d) Addition to tax for failure to comply with section.

For addition to tax in case of partner's disregard of requirements of this section, see part II of subchapter A of chapter 68.

In 1998, P.L. 105-206, Sec. 6012(e), substituted "beginning" for "ending on or" in Sec. 1226 of P.L. 105-34, the effective date for amendments made by Sec. 1222 of P.L. 105-34, [see below].

In 1997, P.L. 105-34, Sec. 1222(a), added Code Sec. 6241 of Part I of Subchapter D of Chapter 63 of Subtitle F, effective for partnership tax. yrs. end. on or after 12/31/97.

Sec. 6242. Procedures for taking partnership adjustments into account.

(a) Adjustments flow through to partners for year in which adjustment takes effect.

(1) In general. If any partnership adjustment with respect to any partnership item takes effect (within the meaning of subsection (d)(2)) during any partnership taxable year and if an election under paragraph (2) does not apply to such adjustment, such adjustment shall be taken into account in determining the amount of such item for the partnership taxable year in which such adjustment takes effect. In applying this title to any person who is (directly or indirectly) a partner in such partnership during such partnership taxable year, such adjustment shall be treated as an item actually arising during such taxable year.

(2) Partnership liable in certain cases. If—

(A) a partnership elects under this paragraph to not take an adjustment into account under paragraph (1),

(B) a partnership does not make such an election but in filing its return for any partnership taxable year fails to take fully into account any partnership adjustment as required under paragraph (1), or

(C) any partnership adjustment involves a reduction in a credit which exceeds the amount of such credit determined for the partnership taxable year in which the adjustment takes effect,

the partnership shall pay to the Secretary an amount determined by applying the rules of subsection (b)(4) to the adjustments not so taken into account and any excess referred to in subparagraph (C).

(3) Offsetting adjustments taken into account. If a partnership adjustment requires another adjustment in a taxable year after the adjusted year and before the partnership taxable year in which such partnership adjustment takes effect, such other adjustment shall be taken into account under this subsection for the partnership taxable year in which such partnership adjustment takes effect.

(4) Coordination with part II. Amounts taken into account under this subsection for any partnership taxable year shall continue to be treated as adjustments for the adjusted year for purposes of determining whether such amounts may be readjusted under part II.

(b) Partnership liable for interest and penalties.

(1) In general. If a partnership adjustment takes effect during any partnership taxable year and such adjustment results in an imputed underpayment for the adjusted year, the partnership—

(A) shall pay to the Secretary interest computed under paragraph (2), and

(B) shall be liable for any penalty, addition to tax, or additional amount as provided in paragraph (3).

(2) Determination of amount of interest. The interest computed under this paragraph with respect to any partnership adjustment is the interest which would be determined under chapter 67—

(A) on the imputed underpayment determined under paragraph (4) with respect to such adjustment,

(B) for the period beginning on the day after the return due date for the adjusted year and ending on the return due date for the partnership taxable year in which such adjustment takes effect (or, if earlier, in the case of any adjustment to which subsection (a)(2) applies, the date on which the payment under subsection (a)(2) is made).

Proper adjustments in the amount determined under the preceding sentence shall be made for adjustments required for partnership taxable years after the adjusted year and before the year in which the partnership adjustment takes effect by reason of such partnership adjustment.

(3) Penalties. A partnership shall be liable for any penalty, addition to tax, or additional amount for which it would have been liable if such partnership had been an individual subject to tax under chapter 1 for the adjusted year and the imputed underpayment determined under paragraph (4) were an actual underpayment (or understatement) for such year.

(4) Imputed underpayment. For purposes of this subsection, the imputed underpayment determined under this paragraph with respect to any partnership adjustment is the underpayment (if any) which would result—

3,651

(A) by netting all adjustments to items of income, gain, loss, or deduction and by treating any net increase in income as an underpayment equal to the amount of such net increase multiplied by the highest rate of tax in effect under section 1 or 11 for the adjusted year, and

(B) by taking adjustments to credits into account as increases or decreases (whichever is appropriate) in the amount of tax.

For purposes of the preceding sentence, any net decrease in a loss shall be treated as an increase in income and a similar rule shall apply to a net increase in a loss.

(c) Administrative provisions.

(1) In general. Any payment required by subsection (a)(2) or (b)(1)(A)—

(A) shall be assessed and collected in the same manner as if it were a tax imposed by subtitle C, and

(B) shall be paid on or before the return due date for the partnership taxable year in which the partnership adjustment takes effect.

(2) Interest. For purposes of determining interest, any payment required by subsection (a)(2) or (b)(1)(A) shall be treated as an underpayment of tax.

(3) Penalties.

(A) In general. In the case of any failure by any partnership to pay on the date prescribed therefor any amount required by subsection (a)(2) or (b)(1)(A), there is hereby imposed on such partnership a penalty of 10 percent of the underpayment. For purposes of the preceding sentence, the term "underpayment" means the excess of any payment required under this section over the amount (if any) paid on or before the date prescribed therefor.

(B) Accuracy-related and fraud penalties made applicable. For purposes of part II of subchapter A of chapter 68, any payment required by subsection (a)(2) shall be treated as an underpayment of tax.

(d) Definitions and special rules.

For purposes of this section—

(1) Partnership adjustment. The term "partnership adjustment" means any adjustment in the amount of any partnership item of an electing large partnership.

(2) When adjustment takes effect. A partnership adjustment takes effect—

(A) in the case of an adjustment pursuant to the decision of a court in a proceeding brought under part II, when such decision becomes final,

(B) in the case of an adjustment pursuant to any administrative adjustment request under section 6251, when such adjustment is allowed by the Secretary, or

(C) in any other case, when such adjustment is made.

(3) Adjusted year. The term "adjusted year" means the partnership taxable year to which the item being adjusted relates.

(4) Return due date. The term "return due date" means, with respect to any taxable year, the date prescribed for filing the partnership return for such taxable year (determined without regard to extensions).

(5) Adjustments involving changes in character. Under regulations, appropriate adjustments in the application of this section shall be made for purposes of taking into account partnership adjustments which involve a change in the character of any item of income, gain, loss, or deduction.

(e) Payments nondeductible.

No deduction shall be allowed under subtitle A for any payment required to be made by an electing large partnership under this section.

In **1998**, P.L. 105-206, Sec. 6012(e), substituted "beginning" for "ending on or" in Sec. 1226 of P.L. 105-34, the effective date for amendments made by Sec. 1222 of P.L. 105-34, see below.

In **1997**, P.L. 105-34, Sec. 1222(a), added Code Sec. 6242 of Part I of Subchapter D of Chapter 63 of Subtitle F, effective for partnership tax. yrs. end. on or after 12/31/97.

PART II.—PARTNERSHIP LEVEL ADJUSTMENTS

Subpart
A. Adjustments by Secretary.
B. Claims for adjustments by partnership.

In **1997**, P.L. 105-34, Sec. 1222(a), amended Chapter 63 by adding Part II of Subchapter D.

SUBPART A.—ADJUSTMENTS BY SECRETARY

Sec.
6245. Secretarial authority.
6246. Restrictions on partnership adjustments.
6247. Judicial review of partnership adjustment.
6248. Period of limitations for making adjustments.

In **1997**, P.L. 105-34, Sec. 1222(a), amended Chapter 63 by adding Subpart A of Part II of Subchapter D.

Sec. 6245. Secretarial authority.

(a) General rule.

The Secretary is authorized and directed to make adjustments at the partnership level in any partnership item to the extent necessary to have such item be treated in the manner required.

(b) Notice of partnership adjustment.

(1) In general. If the Secretary determines that a partnership adjustment is required, the Secretary is authorized to send notice of such adjustment to the partnership by certified mail or registered mail. Such notice shall be sufficient if mailed to the partnership at its last known address even if the partnership has terminated its existence.

(2) Further notices restricted. If the Secretary mails a notice of a partnership adjustment to any partnership for any partnership taxable year and the partnership files a petition under section 6247 with respect to such notice, in the absence of a showing of fraud, malfeasance, or misrepresentation of a material fact, the Secretary shall not mail another such notice to such partnership with respect to such taxable year.

(3) Authority to rescind notice with partnership consent. The Secretary may, with the consent of the partnership, rescind any notice of a partnership adjustment mailed to such partnership. Any notice so rescinded shall not be treated as a notice of a partnership adjustment, for purposes of this section, section 6246, and section 6247, and the taxpayer shall have no right to bring a proceeding under section 6247 with respect to such notice. Nothing in this subsection shall affect any suspension of the running of any period of limitations during any period during which the rescinded notice was outstanding.

In **1998**, P.L. 105-206, Sec. 6012(e), substituted "beginning" for "ending on or" in Sec. 1226 of P.L. 105-34, the effective date for amendments made by Sec. 1222 of P.L. 105-34, see below.

In **1997**, P.L. 105-34, Sec. 1222(a), added Code Sec. 6245 Subpart A of Part II of Subchapter D of Chapter 63 of Subtitle F, effective for partnership tax. yrs. end. on or after 12/31/97.

Sec. 6246. Restrictions on partnership adjustments.

(a) General rule.

Except as otherwise provided in this chapter, no adjustment to any partnership item may be made (and no levy or

Partnership items   Code Sec. 6248(b)

proceeding in any court for the collection of any amount resulting from such adjustment may be made, begun or prosecuted) before—
  (1) the close of the 90th day after the day on which a notice of a partnership adjustment was mailed to the partnership, and
  (2) if a petition is filed under section 6247 with respect to such notice, the decision of the court has become final.

(b) Premature action may be enjoined.
Notwithstanding section 7421(a), any action which violates subsection (a) may be enjoined in the proper court, including the Tax Court. The Tax Court shall have no jurisdiction to enjoin any action under this subsection unless a timely petition has been filed under section 6247 and then only in respect of the adjustments that are the subject of such petition.

(c) Exceptions to restrictions on adjustments.
  (1) Adjustments arising out of math or clerical errors.
    (A) In general. If the partnership is notified that, on account of a mathematical or clerical error appearing on the partnership return, an adjustment to a partnership item is required, rules similar to the rules of paragraphs (1) and (2) of section 6213(b) shall apply to such adjustment.
    (B) Special rule. If an electing large partnership is a partner in another electing large partnership, any adjustment on account of such partnership's failure to comply with the requirements of section 6241(a) with respect to its interest in such other partnership shall be treated as an adjustment referred to in subparagraph (A), except that paragraph (2) of section 6213(b) shall not apply to such adjustment.
  (2) Partnership may waive restrictions. The partnership shall at any time (whether or not a notice of partnership adjustment has been issued) have the right, by a signed notice in writing filed with the Secretary, to waive the restrictions provided in subsection (a) on the making of any partnership adjustment.

(d) Limit where no proceeding begun.
If no proceeding under section 6247 is begun with respect to any notice of a partnership adjustment during the 90-day period described in subsection (a), the amount for which the partnership is liable under section 6242 (and any increase in any partner's liability for tax under chapter 1 by reason of any adjustment under section 6242(a)) shall not exceed the amount determined in accordance with such notice.

In 1998, P.L. 105-206, Sec. 6012(e), substituted "beginning" for "ending on or" in Sec. 1226 of P.L. 105-34, the effective date for amendments made by Sec. 1222 of P.L. 105-34, see below.
In 1997, P.L. 105-34, Sec. 1222(a), added Code Sec. 6246 of Subpart A of Part II of Subchapter D of Chapter 63 of Subtitle F, effective for partnership tax. yrs. end. on or after 12/31/97.

Sec. 6247. Judicial review of partnership adjustment.
(a) General rule.
Within 90 days after the date on which a notice of a partnership adjustment is mailed to the partnership with respect to any partnership taxable year, the partnership may file a petition for a readjustment of the partnership items for such taxable year with—
  (1) the Tax Court,
  (2) the district court of the United States for the district in which the partnership's principal place of business is located, or
  (3) the Claims Court.

(b) Jurisdictional requirement for bringing action in district court or Claims Court.
  (1) In general. A readjustment petition under this section may be filed in a district court of the United States or the Claims Court only if the partnership filing the petition deposits with the Secretary, on or before the date the petition is filed, the amount for which the partnership would be liable under section 6242(b) (as of the date of the filing of the petition) if the partnership items were adjusted as provided by the notice of partnership adjustment. The court may by order provide that the jurisdictional requirements of this paragraph are satisfied where there has been a good faith attempt to satisfy such requirement and any shortfall of the amount required to be deposited is timely corrected.
  (2) Interest payable. Any amount deposited under paragraph (1), while deposited, shall not be treated as a payment of tax for purposes of this title (other than chapter 67).

(c) Scope of judicial review.
A court with which a petition is filed in accordance with this section shall have jurisdiction to determine all partnership items of the partnership for the partnership taxable year to which the notice of partnership adjustment relates and the proper allocation of such items among the partners (and the applicability of any penalty, addition to tax, or additional amount for which the partnership may be liable under section 6242(b)).

(d) Determination of court reviewable.
Any determination by a court under this section shall have the force and effect of a decision of the Tax Court or a final judgment or decree of the district court or the Claims Court, as the case may be, and shall be reviewable as such. The date of any such determination shall be treated as being the date of the court's order entering the decision.

(e) Effect of decision dismissing action.
If an action brought under this section is dismissed other than by reason of a rescission under section 6245(b)(3), the decision of the court dismissing the action shall be considered as its decision that the notice of partnership adjustment is correct, and an appropriate order shall be entered in the records of the court.

In 1998, P.L. 105-206, Sec. 6012(e), substituted "beginning" for "ending on or" in Sec. 1226 of P.L. 105-34, the effective date for amendments made by Sec. 1222 of P.L. 105-34, see below.
In 1997, P.L. 105-34, Sec. 1222(a), added Code Sec. 6247 of Subpart A of Part II of Subchapter D of Chapter 63 of Subtitle F, effective for partnership tax. yrs. end. on or after 12/31/97.

Sec. 6248. Period of limitations for making adjustments.
(a) General rule.
Except as otherwise provided in this section, no adjustment under this subpart to any partnership item for any partnership taxable year may be made after the date which is 3 years after the later of—
  (1) the date on which the partnership return for such taxable year was filed, or
  (2) the last day for filing such return for such year (determined without regard to extensions).

(b) Extension by agreement.
The period described in subsection (a) (including an extension period under this subsection) may be extended by an agreement entered into by the Secretary and the partnership before the expiration of such period.

3,653

Code Sec. 6248(c) — Partnership items

(c) **Special rule in case of fraud, etc.**
(1) **False return.** In the case of a false or fraudulent partnership return with intent to evade tax, the adjustment may be made at any time.
(2) **Substantial omission of income.** If any partnership omits from gross income an amount properly includible therein which is in excess of 25 percent of the amount of gross income stated in its return, subsection (a) shall be applied by substituting "6 years" for "3 years".
(3) **No return.** In the case of a failure by a partnership to file a return for any taxable year, the adjustment may be made at any time.
(4) **Return filed by Secretary.** For purposes of this section, a return executed by the Secretary under subsection (b) of section 6020 on behalf of the partnership shall not be treated as a return of the partnership.

(d) **Suspension when Secretary mails notice of adjustment.**
If notice of a partnership adjustment with respect to any taxable year is mailed to the partnership, the running of the period specified in subsection (a) (as modified by the other provisions of this section) shall be suspended—
(1) for the period during which an action may be brought under section 6247 (and, if a petition is filed under section 6247 with respect to such notice, until the decision of the court becomes final), and
(2) for 1 year thereafter.

In **1998**, P.L. 105-206, Sec. 6012(e), substituted "beginning" for "ending on or" in Sec. 1226 of P.L. 105-34, the effective date for amendments made by Sec. 1222 of P.L. 105-34, see below.
In **1997**, P.L. 105-34, Sec. 1222(a), added Code Sec. 6248 of Subpart A of Part II of Subchapter D of Chapter 63 of Subtitle F, effective for partnership tax. yrs. end. on or after 12/31/97.

SUBPART B.—CLAIMS FOR ADJUSTMENTS BY PARTNERSHIP
Sec.
6251. Administrative adjustment requests.
6252. Judicial review where administrative adjustment request is not allowed in full.

In **1997**, P.L. 105-34, Sec. 1222(a), amended Chapter 63 by adding Subpart B of Part II of Subchapter D.

Sec. 6251. Administrative adjustment requests.
(a) **General rule.**
A partnership may file a request for an administrative adjustment of partnership items for any partnership taxable year at any time which is—
(1) within 3 years after the later of—
(A) the date on which the partnership return for such year is filed, or
(B) the last day for filing the partnership return for such year (determined without regard to extensions), and
(2) before the mailing to the partnership of a notice of a partnership adjustment with respect to such taxable year.
(b) **Secretarial action.**
If a partnership files an administrative adjustment request under subsection (a), the Secretary may allow any part of the requested adjustments.
(c) **Special rule in case of extension under section 6248.**
If the period described in section 6248(a) is extended pursuant to an agreement under section 6248(b), the period prescribed by subsection (a)(1) shall not expire before the date 6 months after the expiration of the extension under section 6248(b).

In **1998**, P.L. 105-206, Sec. 6012(e), substituted "beginning" for "ending on or" in Sec. 1226 of P.L. 105-34, the effective date for amendments made by Sec. 1222 of P.L. 105-34, see below.
In **1997**, P.L. 105-34, Sec. 1222(a), added Code Sec. 6251 of Subpart B of Part II of Subchapter D of Chapter 63 of Subtitle F, effective for partnership tax. yrs. end. on or after 12/31/97.

Sec. 6252. Judicial review where administrative adjustment request is not allowed in full.
(a) **In general.**
If any part of an administrative adjustment request filed under section 6251 is not allowed by the Secretary, the partnership may file a petition for an adjustment with respect to the partnership items to which such part of the request relates with—
(1) the Tax Court,
(2) the district court of the United States for the district in which the principal place of business of the partnership is located, or
(3) the Claims Court.
(b) **Period for filing petition.**
A petition may be filed under subsection (a) with respect to partnership items for a partnership taxable year only—
(1) after the expiration of 6 months from the date of filing of the request under section 6251, and
(2) before the date which is 2 years after the date of such request.
The 2-year period set forth in paragraph (2) shall be extended for such period as may be agreed upon in writing by the partnership and the Secretary.
(c) **Coordination with subpart A.**
(1) **Notice of partnership adjustment before filing of petition.** No petition may be filed under this section after the Secretary mails to the partnership a notice of a partnership adjustment for the partnership taxable year to which the request under section 6251 relates.
(2) **Notice of partnership adjustment after filing but before hearing of petition.** If the Secretary mails to the partnership a notice of a partnership adjustment for the partnership taxable year to which the request under section 6251 relates after the filing of a petition under this subsection but before the hearing of such petition, such petition shall be treated as an action brought under section 6247 with respect to such notice, except that subsection (b) of section 6247 shall not apply.
(3) **Notice must be before expiration of statute of limitations.** A notice of a partnership adjustment for the partnership taxable year shall be taken into account under paragraphs (1) and (2) only if such notice is mailed before the expiration of the period prescribed by section 6248 for making adjustments to partnership items for such taxable year.
(d) **Scope of judicial review.**
Except in the case described in paragraph (2) of subsection (c), a court with which a petition is filed in accordance with this section shall have jurisdiction to determine only those partnership items to which the part of the request under section 6251 not allowed by the Secretary relates and those items with respect to which the Secretary asserts adjustments as offsets to the adjustments requested by the partnership.
(e) **Determination of court reviewable.**
Any determination by a court under this section shall have the force and effect of a decision of the Tax Court or a final judgment or decree of the district court or the Claims Court, as the case may be, and shall be reviewable as such. The

date of any such determination shall be treated as being the date of the court's order entering the decision.

In 1998, P.L. 105-206, Sec. 6012(e), substituted "beginning" for "ending on or" in Sec. 1226 of P.L. 105-34, the effective date for amendments made by Sec. 1222 of P.L. 105-34, see below.

In 1997, P.L. 105-34, Sec. 1222(a), added Code Sec. 6252 of Subpart B of Part II of Subchapter D of Chapter 63 of Subtitle F, effective for partnership tax. yrs. end. on or after 12/31/97.

PART III.—DEFINITIONS AND SPECIAL RULES
Sec.
6255. Definitions and special rules.

In 1997, P.L. 105-34, Sec. 1222(a), amended Chapter 63 by adding Part III of Subchapter D.

Sec. 6255. Definitions and special rules.
(a) Definitions.
For purposes of this subchapter—
(1) Electing large partnership. The term "electing large partnership" has the meaning given to such term by section 775.
(2) Partnership item. The term "partnership item" has the meaning given to such term by section 6231(a)(3).
(b) Partners bound by actions of partnership, etc.
(1) Designation of partner. Each electing large partnership shall designate (in the manner prescribed by the Secretary) a partner (or other person) who shall have the sole authority to act on behalf of such partnership under this subchapter. In any case in which such a designation is not in effect, the Secretary may select any partner as the partner with such authority.
(2) Binding effect. An electing large partnership and all partners of such partnership shall be bound—
(A) by actions taken under this subchapter by the partnership, and
(B) by any decision in a proceeding brought under this subchapter.
(c) Partnerships having principal place of business outside the United States.
For purposes of sections 6247 and 6252, a principal place of business located outside the United States shall be treated as located in the District of Columbia.
(d) Treatment where partnership ceases to exist.
If a partnership ceases to exist before a partnership adjustment under this subchapter takes effect, such adjustment shall be taken into account by the former partners of such partnership under regulations prescribed by the Secretary.
(e) Date decision becomes final.
For purposes of this subchapter, the principles of section 7481(a) shall be applied in determining the date on which a decision of a district court or the Claims Court becomes final.
(f) Partnerships in cases under title 11 of the United States Code.
(1) Suspension of period of limitations on making adjustment, assessment, or collection. The running of any period of limitations provided in this subchapter on making a partnership adjustment (or provided by section 6501 or 6502 on the assessment or collection of any amount required to be paid under section 6242) shall, in a case under title 11 of the United States Code, be suspended during the period during which the Secretary is prohibited by reason of such case from making the adjustment (or assessment or collection) and—
(A) for adjustment or assessment, 60 days thereafter, and
(B) for collection, 6 months thereafter.
A rule similar to the rule of section 6213(f)(2) shall apply for purposes of section 6246.
(2) Suspension of period of limitation for filing for judicial review. The running of the period specified in section 6247(a) or 6252(b) shall, in a case under title 11 of the United States Code, be suspended during the period during which the partnership is prohibited by reason of such case from filing a petition under section 6247 or 6252 and for 60 days thereafter.
(g) Regulations.
The Secretary shall prescribe such regulations as may be necessary to carry out the provisions of this subchapter, including regulations—
(1) to prevent abuse through manipulation of the provisions of this subchapter, and
(2) providing that this subchapter shall not apply to any case described in section 6231(c)(1) (or the regulations prescribed thereunder) where the application of this subchapter to such a case would interfere with the effective and efficient enforcement of this title.
In any case to which this subchapter does not apply by reason of paragraph (2), rules similar to the rules of sections 6229(f) and 6255(f) shall apply.

In 1998, P.L. 105-206, Sec. 6012(e), substituted "beginning" for "ending on or" in Sec. 1226 of P.L. 105-34, the effective date for amendments made by Sec. 1222 of P.L. 105-34, see below.

In 1997, P.L. 105-34, Sec. 1222(a), added Code Sec. 6255 of Part III of Subchapter D of Chapter 63 of Subtitle F, effective for partnership tax. yrs. end. on or after 12/31/97.

CHAPTER 64.—COLLECTION
Subchapter
A. General provisions.
B. Receipt of payment.
C. Lien for taxes.
D. Seizure of property for collection of taxes.
E. Repealed [Collection of State Individual Income Taxes]

In 1990, P.L. 101-508, Sec. 11801(b)(14), deleted the item for subchapter E. Prior to deletion, the item for subchapter E read as follows: "E. Collection of State individual income taxes."

Subchapter A.—General Provisions
Sec.
6301. Collection authority.
6302. Mode or time of collection.
6303. Notice and demand for tax.
6304. Fair tax collection practices.
6305. Collection of certain liability.
6306. Qualified tax collection contracts.

In 2004, P.L. 108-357, Sec. 881(a)(2)(B), added item 6306.
In 1998, P.L. 105-206, Sec. 3466(b), added item 6304.
In 1975, P.L. 93-647, Sec. 101(b)(2), added item 6305.

Sec. 6301. Collection authority.
The Secretary shall collect the taxes imposed by the internal revenue laws.

In 1976, P.L. 94-455, Sec. 1906(b)(13)(A), substituted "Secretary" for "Secretary or his delegate" in Code Sec. 6301, effective 2/1/77.

Sec. 6302. Mode or time of collection.
(a) Establishment by regulations.
If the mode or time for collecting any tax is not provided for by this title, the Secretary may establish the same by regulations.
(b) Discretionary method.
Whether or not the method of collecting any tax imposed by chapter 21, 31, 32, or 33, or by section 4481 is specifically provided for by this title, any such tax may, under regulations prescribed by the Secretary, be collected by means of returns, stamps, coupons, tickets, books, or such other reasonable devices or methods as may be necessary or helpful in securing a complete and proper collection of the tax.
(c) Use of government depositaries.
The Secretary may authorize Federal Reserve banks, and incorporated banks, trust companies, domestic building and loan associations, or credit unions which are depositaries or financial agents of the United States, to receive any tax imposed under the internal revenue laws, in such manner, at such times, and under such conditions as he may prescribe; and he shall prescribe the manner, times, and conditions under which the receipt of such tax by such banks, trust companies, domestic building and loan associations, and credit unions is to be treated as payment of such tax to the Secretary.
(d) Time for payment of manufacturers' excise tax on recreational equipment.
The taxes imposed by subchapter D of chapter 32 of this title (relating to taxes on recreational equipment) shall be due and payable on the date for filing the return for such taxes.
(e) Time for deposit of taxes on communications services and airline tickets.
(1) In general. Except as provided in paragraph (2), if, under regulations prescribed by the Secretary, a person is required to make deposits of any tax imposed by section 4251 or subsection (a) or (b) of section 4261 with respect to amounts considered collected by such person during any semimonthly period, such deposit shall be made not later than the 3rd day (not including Saturdays, Sundays, or legal holidays) after the close of the 1st week of the 2nd semimonthly period following the period to which such amounts relate.
(2) Special rule for tax due in September.
(A) Amounts considered collected. In the case of a person required to make deposits of the tax imposed by—
(i) section 4251, or
(ii) effective on January 1, 1997, section 4261 or 4271,
with respect to amounts considered collected by such person during any semimonthly period, the amount of such tax included in bills rendered or tickets sold during the period beginning on September 1 and ending on September 11 shall be deposited not later than September 29.
(B) Special rule where September 29 is on Saturday or Sunday. If September 29 falls on a Saturday or Sunday, the due date under subparagraph (A) shall be—
(i) in the case of Saturday, the preceding day, and
(ii) in the case of Sunday, the following day.
(C) Taxpayers not required to use electronic funds transfer. In the case of deposits not required to be made by electronic funds transfer, subparagraphs (A) and (B) shall be applied by substituting "September 10" for "September 11" and "September 28" for "September 29."

(f) Time for deposit of certain excise taxes.
(1) General rule. Except as otherwise provided in this subsection and subsection (e), if any person is required under regulations to make deposits of taxes under subtitle D with respect to semi-monthly periods, such person shall make deposits of such taxes for the period beginning on September 16 and ending on September 26 not later than September 29. In the case of taxes imposed by sections 4261 and 4271, this paragraph shall not apply to periods before January 1, 1997.
(2) Taxes on ozone depleting chemicals. If any person is required under regulations to make deposits of taxes under subchapter D of chapter 38 with respect to semimonthly periods, in lieu of paragraph (1), such person shall make deposits of such taxes for—
(A) the second semimonthly period in August, and
(B) the period beginning on September 1 and ending on September 11,
not later than September 29.
(3) Taxpayers not required to use electronic funds transfer. In the case of deposits not required to be made by electronic funds transfer, paragraphs (1) and (2) shall be applied by substituting "September 25" for "September 26", "September 10" for "September 11", and "September 28" for "September 29".
(4) Special rule where due date on Saturday or Sunday. If, but for this paragraph, the due date under paragraph (1), (2), or (3) would fall on a Saturday or Sunday, such due date shall be deemed to be—
(A) in the case of Saturday, the preceding day, and
(B) in the case of Sunday, the following day.
(g) Deposits of Social Security taxes and withheld income taxes.
If, under regulations prescribed by the Secretary, a person is required to make deposits of taxes imposed by chapters 21, 22, and 24 on the basis of eighth-month periods, such person shall make deposits of such taxes on the 1st banking day after any day on which such person has $100,000 or more of such taxes for deposit.
(h) Use of electronic fund transfer system for collection of certain taxes.
(1) Establishment of system.
(A) In general. The Secretary shall prescribe such regulations as may be necessary for the development and implementation of an electronic fund transfer system which is required to be used for the collection of depository taxes. Such system shall be designed in such manner as may be necessary to ensure that such taxes are credited to the general account of the Treasury on the date on which such taxes would otherwise have been required to be deposited under the Federal tax deposit system.
(B) Exemptions. The regulations prescribed under subparagraph (A) may contain such exemptions as the Secretary may deem appropriate.
(2) Phase-in requirements.
(A) In general. Except as provided in subparagraph (B), the regulations referred to in paragraph (1)—
(i) shall contain appropriate procedures to assure that an orderly conversion from the Federal tax deposit system to the electronic fund transfer system is accomplished, and
(ii) may provide for a phase-in of such electronic fund transfer system by classes of taxpayers based on the aggregate undeposited taxes of such taxpayers at the close of specified periods and any other factors the Secretary may deem appropriate.

(B) Phase-in requirements. The phase-in of the electronic fund transfer system shall be designed in such manner as may be necessary to ensure that—

(i) during each fiscal year beginning after September 30, 1993, at least the applicable required percentage of the total depository taxes imposed by chapters 21, 22, and 24 shall be collected by means of electronic fund transfer, and

(ii) during each fiscal year beginning after September 30, 1993, at least the applicable required percentage of the total other depository taxes shall be collected by means of electronic fund transfer.

(C) Applicable required percentage.

(i) In the case of the depository taxes imposed by chapters 21, 22, and 24, the applicable required percentage is—

(I) 3 percent for fiscal year 1994,

(II) 16.9 percent for fiscal year 1995,

(III) 20.1 percent for fiscal year 1996,

(IV) 58.3 percent for fiscal years 1997 and 1988, and

(V) 94 percent for fiscal year 1999 and all fiscal years thereafter.

(ii) In the case of other depository taxes, the applicable required percentage is—

(I) 3 percent for fiscal year 1994,

(II) 20 percent for fiscal year 1995,

(III) 30 percent for fiscal year 1996,

(IV) 60 percent for fiscal years 1997 and 1998, and

(V) 94 percent for fiscal year 1999 and all fiscal years thereafter.

(3) **Definitions.** For purposes of this subsection—

(A) Depository tax. The term "depository tax" means any tax if the Secretary is authorized to require deposits of such tax.

(B) Electronic fund transfer. The term "electronic fund transfer" means any transfer of funds, other than a transaction originated by check, draft, or similar paper instrument, which is initiated through an electronic terminal, telephonic instrument, or computer or magnetic tape so as to order, instruct, or authorize a financial institution or other financial intermediary to debit or credit an account.

(4) **Coordination with other electronic fund transfer requirements.**

(A) Coordination with certain excise taxes. In determining whether the requirements of subparagraph (B) of paragraph (2) are met, taxes required to be paid by electronic fund transfer under sections 5061(e) and 5703(b) shall be disregarded.

(B) Additional requirement. Under regulations, any tax required to be paid by electronic fund transfer under section 5061(e) or 5703(b) shall be paid in such a manner as to ensure that the requirements of the second sentence of paragraph (1)(A) of this subsection are satisfied.

(i) Repealed.

In 2010, P.L. 111-237, Sec. 2(a), amended subsec. (d), effective for articles sold by the manufacturer, producer, or importer after 8/16/2010.

Prior to amendment, subsec. (d) read as follows:

"(d) Time for payment of manufacturers' excise tax on recreational equipment. The taxes imposed by subchapter D of chapter 32 of this title (relating to taxes on recreational equipment) shall be due and payable on the date for filing the return for such taxes."

—P.L. 111-226, Sec. 219(e)(2), deleted subsec. (i), effective for tax. yrs. begin. after 12/31/2010.

Prior to deletion, subsec. (i) read as follows:

"(i) Cross references. For treatment of earned income advance amounts as payment of withholding and FICA taxes, see section 3507(d)."

In 2002, P.L. 107-134, Sec. 114(a), amended Sec. 301(a)(3) of P.L. 107-42 [see below], effective 9/22/2001.

In 2001, P.L. 107-42, Sec. 301, of this Act, reads as follows:

"Sec. 301. Extension of due date for excise tax deposits; treatment of loss compensation.

"(a) Extension of due date for excise tax deposits.

"(1) In general. In the case of an eligible air carrier, any airline-related deposit required under section 6302 of the Internal Revenue Code of 1986 to be made after September 10, 2001, and before November 15, 2001, shall be treated for purposes of such Code as timely made if such deposit is made on or before November 15, 2001. If the Secretary of the Treasury so prescribes, the preceding sentence shall be applied by substituting for 'November 15, 2001' each place it appears—

"(A) 'January 15, 2002'; or

"(B) such earlier date after November 15, 2001, as such Secretary may prescribe.

"(2) Eligible air carrier. For purposes of this subsection, the term 'eligible air carrier' means any domestic corporation engaged in the trade or business of transporting (for hire) persons by air if such transportation is available to the general public.

"(3) Airline-related deposit. For purposes of this subsection, the term 'airline-related deposit' means any deposit of taxes imposed by subchapter C of chapter 33 of such Code (relating to transportation by air).

"(b) Treatment of loss compensation. Nothing in any provision of law shall be construed to exclude from gross income under the Internal Revenue Code of 1986 any compensation received under section 101(a)(2) of this Act."

In 1997, P.L. 105-34, Sec. 901(e), of this Act provides:

"(e) Delayed deposits of highway motor fuel tax revenues. Notwithstanding section 6302 of the Internal Revenue Code of 1986, in the case of deposits of taxes imposed by section 4041 and 4081 (other than subsection (a)(2)(A)(ii)) of the Internal Revenue Code of 1986, the due date for any deposit which would (but for this subsection) be required to be made after July 31, 1998, and before October 1, 1998, shall be October 5, 1998."

—P.L. 105-34, Sec. 931, of this Act provides:

"SEC. 931. WAIVER OF PENALTY THROUGH JUNE 30, 1998 ON SMALL BUSINESSES FAILING TO MAKE ELECTRONIC FUND TRANSFERS OF TAXES.

"No penalty shall be imposed under the Internal Revenue Code of 1986 solely by reason of a failure by a person to use the electronic fund transfer system established under section 6302(h) of such Code if—

"(1) such person is a member of a class of taxpayers first required to use such system on or after July 1, 1997, and

"(2) such failure occurs before July 1, 1998."

—P.L. 105-2, Sec. 2(f), of this Act, provides:

"(f) Application of look-back safe harbor for deposits. Nothing in the look-back safe harbor prescribed in Treasury Regulation section 40.6302(c)-1(c)(2) shall be construed to permit such safe harbor to be used with respect to any tax unless such tax was imposed through the look-back period."

In 1996, P.L. 104-188, Sec. 1702(c)(3), added ", 22," after "chapters 21" in subsec. (g), effective for amounts required to be deposited after 12/31/90.

—P.L. 104-188, Sec. 1704(t)(52), corrected Sec. 11801(c)(22)(A) of P.L. 101-508, so that "chapters 21" appeared in the material to be deleted, rather than "chapter 21", see below.

—P.L. 104-188, Sec. 1809, of this Act provides:

"SEC. 1809. 6-MONTH DELAY OF ELECTRONIC FUND TRANSFER REQUIREMENT. Notwithstanding any other provision of law, the increase in the applicable required percentages for fiscal year 1997 in clauses (i)(IV) and (ii)(IV) of section 6302(h)(2)(C) of the Internal Revenue Code of 1986 shall not take effect before July 1, 1997."

In 1994, P.L. 103-465, Sec. 712(a), amended subsec. (f) . . . Sec. 712(d), amended subsec. (e), effective 1/1/95.

Prior to amendment, subsec. (f) read as follows:

"(f) Time for deposit of taxes on gasoline and diesel fuel.

"(1) General rule. Notwithstanding section 518 of the Highway Revenue Act of 1982, any person whose liability for tax under section 4081 is payable with respect to semimonthly periods shall, not later than September 27, make deposits of such tax for the period beginning on September 16 and ending on September 22.

"(2) Special rule where due date falls on Saturday, Sunday, or holiday. If, but for this paragraph, the due date under paragraph (1) would fall on a Saturday, Sunday, or holiday in the District of Columbia, such due date shall be deemed to be the immediately preceding day which is not a Saturday, Sunday, or such a holiday."

Prior to amendment, subsec. (e) read as follows:

"(e) Time for deposit of taxes on communications services and airline tickets.

"If, under regulations prescribed by the Secretary, a person is required to make deposits of any tax imposed by section 4251 or subsection (a) or (b) of section 4261 with respect to amounts considered collected by such person during any semimonthly period, such deposit shall be made not later than the 3rd day (not including Saturdays, Sundays, or legal holidays) after the close of the 1st week of the 2nd semimonthly period following the period to which such amounts relate."

In 1993, P.L. 103-182, Sec. 523(a), redesignated subsec. (h) as subsec. (i) and added subsec. (h), effective as provided in Sec. 523(b) of this Act reads as follows:

"(1) In general. The amendments made by this section shall take effect on the date of the Agreement [North American Free Trade Agreement] enters into force with respect to the United States.

Code Sec. 6302 — Collection

"(2) Regulations. Not later than 210 days after the enactment of this Act, the Secretary of the Treasury shall prescribe temporary regulations under section 6302(h) of the Internal Revenue Code of 1986 (as added by this section)."

— P.L. 103-66, Sec. 13242(d)(15), added "and diesel fuel" after "gasoline" in the heading of subsec. (f), effective 1/1/94.

In 1990, P.L. 101-508, Sec. 11217(b)(1)(A), added "communications services and" before "airline" in the heading of subsec. (e) . . . Sec. 11217(b)(1)(B), added "section 4251 or" before "subsection (a) or (b)" in subsec. (e), effective for payments of taxes considered collected during semimonthly periods begin. after 12/31/90.

— P.L. 101-508, Sec. 11334(a), amended subsec. (g), effective for amounts required to be deposited after 12/31/90.

Prior to amendment, subsec. (g) read as follows:

"(g) Deposits of social security taxes and withheld income taxes.

"(1) In general. If, under regulations prescribed by the Secretary, a person is required to make deposits of taxes imposed by chapters 21 and 24 on the basis of eighth-month periods, such person shall, for the years specified in paragraph (2), make deposits of such taxes on the applicable banking day after any day on which such person has $100,000 or more of such taxes for deposit.

"(2) Specified years. For purposes of paragraph (1)—

In the case of:	The applicable banking day is:
1990	1st
1991	2nd
1992	3rd
1993	1st
1994	1st".

— P.L. 101-508, Sec. 11334(b), deleted Sec. 7632(b)(2) of P.L. 101-239, part of the effective date for changes made by Sec. 7632(a) of P.L. 101-239, see below.

Prior to deletion, Sec. 7632(b)(2) of P.L. 101-239 read as follows:

"(2) Rule for 1995 and thereafter.—For calendar year 1995 and thereafter, the Secretary of the Treasury shall prescribe regulations with respect to the date on which deposits of such taxes shall be made in order to minimize the unevenness in the revenue effects of the amendment made by subsection (a) [Sec. 7632(a)] ."

— P.L. 101-508, Sec. 11801(c)(22)(A), [as corrected by Sec. 1704(t)(52) of P.L. 104-188, see above] substituted "chapter 21, 31, 32, or 33, or by section 4481" for "chapters 21, 31, 32, 33, section 4481 of chapter 36, section 4501(a) of chapter 37" in subsec. (b), effective 11/5/90, except as provided in Sec. 11821(b) of this Act, reproduced in note following Code Sec. 6428.

In 1989, P.L. 101-239, Sec. 7502(a), redesignated subsec. (e) as subsec. (f) and added new subsec. (e), effective for payments of taxes considered collected for semimonthly periods begin. after 6/30/90.

— P.L. 101-239, Sec. 7507(a), redesignated subsec. (f) as subsec. (g) [as redesignated by Sec. 7502(a) of this Act] and added new subsec. (f), effective for payments of taxes for tax periods begin. after 12/31/89.

— P.L. 101-239, Sec. 7632(a), redesignated subsec. (g) as subsec. (h) [as redesignated by Sec. 7507(a) of this Act] and added new subsec. (g), effective for amounts required to be deposited after 7/31/90 [amended by Sec. 11334(b) of P.L. 101-508, see above].

In 1988, P.L. 100-647, Sec. 6107(a), amended subsec. (d), effective for articles sold by the manufacturer, producer, or importer after 12/31/88.

Prior to amendment, subsec. (d) read as follows:

"(d) Time for payment of manufacturers excise tax on sport fishing equipment.

"The tax imposed by section 4161(a) (relating to manufacturers excise tax on sport fishing equipment) shall be due and payable on the date for filing the return for such tax."

— P.L. 100-418, Sec. 1941(b)(2)(G)(i), substituted "For" for "(1) For" in para. (e)(1) . . . Sec. 1941(b)(2)(G)(ii), deleted para. (e)(2), effective for crude oil removed from the premises on or after 8/23/88.

Prior to deletion, para. (e)(2) read as follows:

"(2) For depositary requirements applicable to the windfall profit tax imposed by section 4986, see section 4995(b)."

In 1984, P.L. 98-369, Sec. 734(i), amended Sec. 518(a) of P.L. 97-424 (reproduced below), by substituting "any Federal Reserve Bank" for "any government depository authorized under section 6302 of such Code."

— P.L. 98-369, Sec. 1015(c), redesignated subsec. (d) as subsec. (e) and added new subsec. (d), effective for articles sold by the manufacturer, producer, or importer after 9/30/84.

In 1983, P.L. 98-76, Sec. 226, provides:

"SEC. 226. DEPOSITARY SCHEDULES.

"Effective on and after January 1, 1984, the times for making payments prescribed under section 6302 of the Internal Revenue Code of 1954 with respect to the taxes imposed by chapter 22 of such Code shall be the same as the times prescribed under such section which apply to the taxes imposed by chapters 21 and 24 of such Code."

— P.L. 97-424, Sec. 518, [as amended by Sec. 734(i) of P.L. 98-369, see above] provides:

"SEC. 518 EXTENSION OF PAYMENT DUE DATE FOR CERTAIN FUEL TAXES.

"(a) 14-Day extension.— The Secretary shall prescribe regulations which permit any qualified person whose liability for tax under section 4081 of the Internal Revenue Code of 1954 is payable with respect to semi-monthly periods to pay such tax on or before the day which is 14 days after the close of such semimonthly period if such payment is made by wire transfer to any Federal Reserve Bank.

"(b) Qualified person defined.— For purposes of this section—

"(1) In general. The term 'qualified person' means—

"(A) any person other than any person whose average daily production of crude oil for the preceding calendar quarter exceeds 1,000 barrels, and

"(B) any independent refiner (within the meaning of section 4995(b)(4) of such Code).

"(2) Aggregation rules. For purposes of paragraph (1), in determining whether any person's production exceeds 1,000 barrels per day, rules similar to the rules of section 4992(e) of the Internal Revenue Code of 1954 shall apply.

"(c) Special rule where 14th day falls on Saturday, Sunday, or holiday.— If, but for this subsection, the due date under subsection (a) would fall on a Saturday, Sunday, or a holiday in the District of Columbia, such due date shall be deemed to be the immediately preceding day which is not a Saturday, Sunday, or such a holiday."

In 1980, P.L. 96-223, Sec. 101(c)(2), amended subsec. (d), effective for periods after 2/29/80.

Prior to amendment, subsec. (d) read as follows:

"(d) Cross reference. For treatment of payment of earned income advance amounts as payment of withholding and FICA taxes, see section 3507(d)."

— P.L. 96-222, Sec. 101(a)(2)(D), changed the effective date for amendments made by Sec. 105(e) of P.L. 95-600 to remuneration paid after 6/30/79, from effective for remuneration paid after 6/30/78.

In 1978, P.L. 95-600, Sec. 105(e), added new subsec. (d), for remuneration paid after 6/30/79.

In 1977, P.L. 95-147, Sec. 3(a), substituted ", trust companies, domestic building and loan associations, or credit unions" for "or trust companies" and substituted ", trust companies, domestic building and loan associations, and credit unions" for "and trust companies" in subsec. (c), effective for amounts deposited after 10/28/77.

In 1976, P.L. 94-455, Sec. 1906(a)(17), substituted "section 4501(a) of chapter 37" for "section 4501(a) or 4511 of chapter 37, or section 4701 or 4721 of chapter 39" in subsec. (b), effective 2/1/77.

— P.L. 94-455, Sec. 1906(b)(13)(A), substituted "Secretary" for "Secretary or his delegate" each place it appeared in Code Sec. 6302, effective 2/1/77.

In 1956, P.L. 627, Sec. 206(b), added "section 4481 of chapter 36" after "33" in subsec. (b), effective 7/1/56.

Sec. 6303. Notice and demand for tax.

(a) General rule.

Where it is not otherwise provided by this title, the Secretary shall, as soon as practicable, and within 60 days, after the making of an assessment of a tax pursuant to section 6203, give notice to each person liable for the unpaid tax, stating the amount and demanding payment thereof. Such notice shall be left at the dwelling or usual place of business of such person, or shall be sent by mail to such person's last known address.

(b) Assessment prior to last date for payment.

Except where the Secretary believes collection would be jeopardized by delay, if any tax is assessed prior to the last date prescribed for payment of such tax, payment of such tax shall not be demanded under subsection (a) until after such date.

In 1976, P.L. 94-455, Sec. 1906(b)(13)(A), substituted "Secretary" for "Secretary or his delegate" each place it appeared in Code Sec. 6303, effective 2/1/77.

Sec. 6304. Fair tax collection practices.
(a) Communication with the taxpayer.

Without the prior consent of the taxpayer given directly to the Secretary or the express permission of a court of competent jurisdiction, the Secretary may not communicate with a taxpayer in connection with the collection of any unpaid tax—

(1) at any unusual time or place or a time or place known or which should be known to be inconvenient to the taxpayer;

(2) if the Secretary knows the taxpayer is represented by any person authorized to practice before the Internal Revenue Service with respect to such unpaid tax and has knowledge of, or can readily ascertain, such person's name and address, unless such person fails to respond within a reasonable period of time to a communication from the Secretary or unless such person consents to direct communication with the taxpayer; or

(3) at the taxpayer's place of employment if the Secretary knows or has reason to know that the taxpayer's employer prohibits the taxpayer from receiving such communication. In the absence of knowledge of circumstances to the contrary, the Secretary shall assume that the convenient time for communicating with a taxpayer is after 8 a.m. and before 9 p.m., local time at the taxpayer's location.

(b) Prohibition of harassment and abuse.

The Secretary may not engage in any conduct the natural consequence of which is to harass, oppress, or abuse any person in connection with the collection of any unpaid tax. Without limiting the general application of the foregoing, the following conduct is a violation of this subsection:

(1) The use or threat of use of violence or other criminal means to harm the physical person, reputation, or property of any person.

(2) The use of obscene or profane language or language the natural consequence of which is to abuse the hearer or reader.

(3) Causing a telephone to ring or engaging any person in telephone conversation repeatedly or continuously with intent to annoy, abuse, or harass any person at the called number.

(4) Except as provided under rules similar to the rules in section 804 of the Fair Debt Collection Practices Act (15 U.S.C. 1692b), the placement of telephone calls without meaningful disclosure of the caller's identity.

(c) Civil action for violations of section.

For civil action for violations of this section, see section 7433.

In **1998**, P.L. 105-206, Sec. 3466(a), added Code Sec. 6304, effective 7/22/98.

Sec. 6305. Collection of certain liability.
(a) In general.

Upon receiving a certification from the Secretary of Health and Human Services, under section 452(b) of the Social Security Act with respect to any individual, the Secretary shall assess and collect the amount certified by the Secretary of Health and Human Services, in the same manner, with the same powers, and (except as provided in this section) subject to the same limitations as if such amount were a tax imposed by subtitle C the collection of which would be jeopardized by delay, except that—

(1) no interest or penalties shall be assessed or collected,

(2) for such purposes, paragraphs (4), (6), and (8) of section 6334(a) (relating to property exempt from levy) shall not apply.

(3) there shall be exempt from levy so much of the salary, wages, or other income of an individual as is being withheld therefrom in garnishment pursuant to a judgment entered by a court of competent jurisdiction for the support of his minor children,

(4) in the case of the first assessment against an individual for delinquency under a court or administrative order against such individual for a particular person or persons, the collection shall be stayed for a period of 60 days immediately following notice and demand as described in section 6303, and

(5) no additional fee may be assessed for adjustments to an amount previously certified pursuant to such section 452(b) with respect to the same obligor.

(b) Review of assessments and collections.

No court of the United States, whether established under article I or article III of the Constitution, shall have jurisdiction of any action, whether legal or equitable, brought to restrain or review the assessment and collection of amounts by the Secretary under subsection (a), nor shall any such assessment and collection be subject to review by the Secretary in any proceeding. This subsection does not preclude any legal, equitable, or administrative action against the State by an individual in any State court or before any State agency to determine his liability for any amount assessed against him and collected, or to recover any such amount collected from him, under this section.

In **1996**, P.L. 104-193, Sec. 361(a)(1), deleted "and" at the end of para. (a)(3)... Sec. 361(a)(2), substituted ", and" for the period at the end of para. (a)(4)... Sec. 361(a)(3), added para. (a)(5)... Sec. 361(a)(4), substituted "Secretary of Health and Human Services" for "Secretary of Health, Education, and Welfare" each place it appeared in subsec. (a), effective 10/1/97.

—P.L. 104-193, Sec. 395(a)-(c), of this Act provides:

"(a) In general. Except as otherwise specifically provided (but subject to subsections (b) and (c))—

"(1) the provisions of this title requiring the enactment of State laws under section 466 of the Social Security Act, or revision of State plans under section 454 of such Act, shall be effective with respect to periods beginning on and after October 1, 1996; and

"(2) all other provisions of this title shall become effective upon the date of the enactment of this Act.

"(b) Grace period for State law changes. The provisions of this title shall become effective with respect to a State on the later of —

"(1) the date specified in this title, or

"(2) the effective date of laws enacted by the legislature of such State implementing such provisions,

but in no event later than the 1st day of the 1st calendar quarter beginning after the close of the 1st regular session of the State legislature that begins after the date of the enactment of this Act. For purposes of the previous sentence, in the case of a State that has a 2-year legislative session, each year of such session shall be deemed to be a separate regular session of the State legislature.

"(c) Grace period for State constitutional amendment. A State shall not be found out of compliance with any requirement enacted by this title if the State is unable to so comply without amending the State constitution until the earlier of—

"(1) 1 year after the effective date of the necessary State constitutional amendment; or

"(2) 5 years after the date of the enactment of this Act."

In **1981**, P.L. 97-35, Sec. 2332(g), substituted "court or administrative order" for "court order" in para. (a)(4), effective 10/1/81.

In **1976**, P.L. 94-455, Sec. 1906(b)(13)(A), substituted "Secretary" for "Secretary or his delegate" each place it appeared in Code Sec. 6305, effective 2/1/77.

In **1975**, P.L. 94-46, Sec. 2, changed the effective date for amendments made by Sec. 101(b)(1) of P.L. 93-647, from 7/1/75 to 8/1/75, see below.

—P.L. 93-647, Sec. 101(b)(1), added new Code Sec. 6305, effective [as amended by Sec. 101(f) of P.L. 94-46, see above] 7/1/75.

Sec. 6306. Qualified tax collection contracts.
(a) In general.

Nothing in any provision of law shall be construed to prevent the Secretary from entering into a qualified tax collection contract.

(b) Qualified tax collection contract.

For purposes of this section, the term "qualified tax collection contract" means any contract which—

(1) is for the services of any person (other than an officer or employee of the Treasury Department)—

(A) to locate and contact any taxpayer specified by the Secretary,

(B) to request full payment from such taxpayer of an amount of Federal tax specified by the Secretary and, if such request cannot be met by the taxpayer, to offer the taxpayer an installment agreement providing for full payment of such amount during a period not to exceed 5 years, and

(C) to obtain financial information specified by the Secretary with respect to such taxpayer,

(2) prohibits each person providing such services under such contract from committing any act or omission which employees of the Internal Revenue Service are prohibited from committing in the performance of similar services,

(3) prohibits subcontractors from—

(A) having contacts with taxpayers,

(B) providing quality assurance services, and

(C) composing debt collection notices, and
(4) permits subcontractors to perform other services only with the approval of the Secretary.
(c) Fees.
The Secretary may retain and use—
(1) an amount not in excess of 25 percent of the amount collected under any qualified tax collection contract for the costs of services performed under such contract, and
(2) an amount not in excess of 25 percent of such amount collected for collection enforcement activities of the Internal Revenue Service.
The Secretary shall keep adequate records regarding amounts so retained and used. The amount credited as paid by any taxpayer shall be determined without regard to this subsection.
(d) No Federal liability.
The United States shall not be liable for any act or omission of any person performing services under a qualified tax collection contract.
(e) Application of Fair Debt Collection Practices Act.
The provisions of the Fair Debt Collection Practices Act (15 U.S.C. 1692 et seq.) shall apply to any qualified tax collection contract, except to the extent superseded by section 6304, section 7602(c), or by any other provision of this title.
(f) Cross references.
(1) For damages for certain unauthorized collection actions by persons performing services under a qualified tax collection contract, see section 7433A.
(2) For application of Taxpayer Assistance Orders to persons performing services under a qualified tax collection contract, see section 7811(g).

In 2009, P.L. 111-8, Sec. 106, of this Act provides:
"None of the funds made available in this Act may be used to enter into, renew, extend, administer, implement, enforce, or provide oversight of any qualified tax collection contract (as defined in section 6306 of the Internal Revenue Code of 1986)."
In 2004, P.L. 108-357, Sec. 881(a)(1), added Code Sec. 6306, effective 10/22/2004.

Subchapter B.—Receipt of Payment
Sec.
6311. Payment of tax by commercially acceptable means.
6313. Fractional parts of a cent.
6314. Receipt for taxes.
6315. Payments of estimated income tax.
6316. Payment by foreign currency.
6317. Payments of Federal unemployment tax for calendar quarter.

In 1997, P.L. 105-34, Sec. 1205(b), amended item 6311.
Prior to amendment, item 6311 read as follows:
"6311. Payment by check or money order."
In 1969, P.L. 91-53, Sec. 2(f)(2), added item 6317.

Sec. 6311. Payment of tax by commercially acceptable means.
(a) Authority to receive.
It shall be lawful for the Secretary to receive for internal revenue taxes (or in payment for internal revenue stamps) any commercially acceptable means that the Secretary deems appropriate to the extent and under the conditions provided in regulations prescribed by the Secretary.
(b) Ultimate liability.
If a check, money order, or other method of payment, including payment by credit card, debit card, or charge card so received is not duly paid, or is paid and subsequently charged back to the Secretary, the person by whom such check, or money order, or other method of payment has been tendered shall remain liable for the payment of the tax or for the stamps, and for all legal penalties and additions, to the same extent as if such check, money order, or other method of payment had not been tendered.
(c) Liability of banks and others.
If any certified, treasurer's, or cashier's check (or other guaranteed draft), or any money order, or any other means of payment that has been guaranteed by a financial institution (such as a credit card, debit card, or charge card transaction which has been guaranteed expressly by a financial institution) so received is not duly paid, the United States shall, in addition to its right to exact payment from the party originally indebted therefor, have a lien for—
(1) the amount of such check (or draft) upon all assets of the financial institution on which drawn,
(2) the amount of such money order upon all the assets of the issuer thereof, or
(3) the guaranteed amount of any other transaction upon all the assets of the institution making such guarantee,
and such amount shall be paid out of such assets in preference to any other claims whatsoever against such financial institution, issuer, or guaranteeing institution, except the necessary costs and expenses of administration and the reimbursement of the United States for the amount expended in the redemption of the circulating notes of such financial institution.
(d) Payment by other means.
(1) **Authority to prescribe regulations.** The Secretary shall prescribe such regulations as the Secretary deems necessary to receive payment by commercially acceptable means, including regulations that—
(A) specify which methods of payment by commercially acceptable means will be acceptable,
(B) specify when payment by such means will be considered received,
(C) identify types of nontax matters related to payment by such means that are to be resolved by persons ultimately liable for payment and financial intermediaries, without the involvement of the Secretary, and
(D) ensure that tax matters will be resolved by the Secretary, without the involvement of financial intermediaries.
(2) **Authority to enter into contracts.** Notwithstanding section 3718(f) of title 31, United States Code, the Secretary is authorized to enter into contracts to obtain services related to receiving payment by other means where cost beneficial to the Government. The Secretary may not pay any fee or provide any other consideration under any such contract for the use of credit, debit, or charge cards for the payment of taxes imposed by subtitle A.
(3) **Special provisions for use of credit cards.** If use of credit cards is accepted as a method of payment of taxes pursuant to subsection (a)—
(A) a payment of internal revenue taxes (or a payment for internal revenue stamps) by a person by use of a credit card shall not be subject to section 161 of the Truth in Lending Act (15 U.S.C. 1666), or to any similar provisions of State law, if the error alleged by the person is an error relating to the underlying tax liability, rather than an error relating to the credit card account such as a computational error or numerical transposition in the credit card transaction or an issue as to whether the person authorized payment by use of the credit card,
(B) a payment of internal revenue taxes (or a payment for internal revenue stamps) shall not be subject to sec-

tion 170 of the Truth in Lending Act (15 U.S.C. 1666i), or to any similar provisions of State law,

(C) a payment of internal revenue taxes (or a payment for internal revenue stamps) by a person by use of a debit card shall not be subject to section 908 of the Electronic Fund Transfer Act (15 U.S.C. 1693f), or to any similar provisions of State law, if the error alleged by the person is an error relating to the underlying tax liability, rather than an error relating to the debit card account such as a computational error or numerical transposition in the debit card transaction or an issue as to whether the person authorized payment by use of the debit card,

(D) the term "creditor" under section 103(f) of the Truth in Lending Act (15 U.S.C. 1602(f)) shall not include the Secretary with respect to credit card transactions in payment of internal revenue taxes (or payment for internal revenue stamps), and

(E) notwithstanding any other provision of law to the contrary, in the case of payment made by credit card or debit card transaction of an amount owed to a person as the result of the correction of an error under section 161 of the Truth in Lending Act (15 U.S.C. 1666) or section 908 of the Electronic Fund Transfer Act (15 U.S.C. 1693f), the Secretary is authorized to provide such amount to such person as a credit to that person's credit card or debit card account through the applicable credit card or debit card system.

(e) Confidentiality of information.

(1) In general. Except as otherwise authorized by this subsection, no person may use or disclose any information relating to credit or debit card transactions obtained pursuant to section 6103(k)(9) other than for purposes directly related to the processing of such transactions, or the billing or collection of amounts charged or debited pursuant thereto.

(2) Exceptions.

(A) Debit or credit card issuers or others acting on behalf of such issuers may also use and disclose such information for purposes directly related to servicing an issuer's accounts.

(B) Debit or credit card issuers or others directly involved in the processing of credit or debit card transactions or the billing or collection of amounts charged or debited thereto may also use and disclose such information for purposes directly related to—

(i) statistical risk and profitability assessment;

(ii) transferring receivables, accounts, or interest therein;

(iii) auditing the account information;

(iv) complying with Federal, State, or local law;

(v) properly authorized civil, criminal, or regulatory investigation by Federal, State, or local authorities.

(3) Procedures. Use and disclosure of information under this paragraph shall be made only to the extent authorized by written procedures promulgated by the Secretary.

(4) Cross reference. For provision providing for civil damages for violation of paragraph (1), see section 7431.

In **1998**, P.L. 105-277, Sec. 4003(c), substituted "under any such contract for the use of credit, debit, or charge cards for the payment of taxes imposed by subtitle A" for "under such contracts" in para. (d)(2), effective 9 months after 8/5/97.
—P.L. 105-206, Sec. 6012(b)(1), substituted "section 6103(k)(9)" for "section 6103(k)(8)" in para. (e)(1), effective 9 months after 8/5/97.

In **1997**, P.L. 105-34, Sec. 1205(a), amended Code Sec. 6311, effective 9 months after 8/5/97.

Prior to amendment, Code Sec. 6311 read as follows:
"SEC. 6311. PAYMENT BY CHECK OR MONEY ORDER.

"(a) Authority to receive. It shall be lawful for the Secretary to receive for internal revenue taxes, or in payment for internal revenue stamps, checks or money orders, to the extent and under the conditions provided in regulations prescribed by the Secretary.

"(b) Check or money order unpaid.

"(1) Ultimate liability. If a check or money order so received is not duly paid, the person by whom such check or money order has been tendered shall remain liable for the payment of the tax or for the stamps, and for all legal penalties and additions, to the same extent as if such check or money order had not been tendered.

"(2) Liability of banks and others. If any certified, treasurer's, or cashier's check (or other guaranteed draft) or any money order so received is not duly paid, the United States shall, in addition to its right to exact payment from the party originally indebted therefor, have a lien for the amount of such check (or draft) upon all the assets of the financial institution on which drawn or for the amount of such money order upon all the assets of the issuer thereof; and such amount shall be paid out of such assets in preference to any other claims whatsoever against such financial institution or issuer except the necessary costs and expenses of administration and the reimbursement of the United States for the amount expended in the redemption of the circulating notes of such financial institution."

In **1996**, P.L. 104-168, Sec. 1202, of this Act, provides:
"Sec. 1202. Required notice of certain payments.

"If any payment is received by the Secretary of the Treasury or his delegate from any taxpayer and the Secretary cannot associate such payment with such taxpayer, the Secretary shall make reasonable efforts to notify the taxpayer of such inability within 60 days after the receipt of such payment."

In **1984**, P.L. 98-369, Sec. 448(a), added "(or other guaranteed draft)" after "or cashier's check", added "(or draft)" after "the amount of such check", substituted "the financial institution" for "the bank or trust company", and substituted "such financial institution" for "such bank" in para. (b)(2), effective 7/18/84.

In **1976**, P.L. 94-455, Sec. 1906(b)(13)(A), substituted "Secretary" for "Secretary or his delegate" each place it appeared in Code Sec. 6311, effective 2/1/77.

Sec. 6313. Fractional parts of a cent.

In the payment of any tax imposed by this title, a fractional part of a cent shall be disregarded unless it amounts to one-half cent or more, in which case it shall be increased to 1 cent.

In **1976**, P.L. 94-455, Sec. 1906(a)(19), deleted "not payable by stamp" after "by this title" in Code Sec. 6313, effective 2/1/77.

Sec. 6314. Receipt for taxes.

(a) General rule.

The Secretary shall, upon request, give receipts for all sums collected by him, excepting only when the same are in payment for stamps sold and delivered; but no receipt shall be issued in lieu of a stamp representing a tax.

(b) Duplicate receipts for payment of estate taxes.

The Secretary shall, upon request, give to the person paying the tax under chapter 11 (relating to the estate tax) duplicate receipts, either of which shall be sufficient evidence of such payment, and shall entitle the executor to be credited and allowed the amount thereof by any court having jurisdiction to audit or settle his accounts.

(c) Cross references.

(1) For receipt required to be furnished by employer to employee with respect to employment taxes, see section 6051.

(2) For receipt of discharge of fiduciary from personal liability, see section 2204.

In **1976**, P.L. 94-455, Sec. 1906(b)(13)(A), substituted "Secretary" for "Secretary or his delegate" each place it appeared in Code Sec. 6314, effective 2/1/77.
In **1970**, P.L. 91-614, Sec. 101(d)(2), substituted "fiduciary" for "executor" in para. (c)(2), effective for decedents dying after 12/31/70.

Sec. 6315. Payments of estimated income tax.

Payment of the estimated income tax, or any installment thereof, shall be considered payment on account of the income taxes imposed by subtitle A for the taxable year.

Sec. 6316. Payment by foreign currency.

The Secretary is authorized in his discretion to allow payment of taxes in the currency of a foreign country under such circumstances and subject to such conditions as the Secretary may by regulations prescribe.

3,661

In 1976, P.L. 94-455, Sec. 1906(b)(13)(A), substituted "Secretary" for "Secretary or his delegate" in Code Sec. 6316, effective 2/1/77.

Sec. 6317. Payments of federal unemployment tax for calendar quarter.

Payment of Federal unemployment tax for a calendar quarter or other period within a calendar year pursuant to section 6157 shall be considered payment on account of the tax imposed by chapter 23 of such calendar year.

In 1988, P.L. 100-647, Sec. 7106(c)(3)(A), deleted "or tax imposed by section 3321" after "unemployment tax" . . . Sec. 7106(c)(3)(B), deleted "and 23A, as the case may be," after "chapter 23" effective for remuneration paid after 12/31/88.

In 1983, P.L. 98-76, Sec. 231(b)(2)(B), substituted "Federal unemployment tax or tax imposed by section 3321" for "Federal unemployment tax" and substituted "chapter 23 and 23A, as the case may be," for "chapter 23" in Code Sec. 6317, effective for remuneration paid after 6/30/86.

In 1969, P.L. 91-53, Sec. 2(c), added Code Sec. 6317, effective for calendar years begin 12/31/69.

Subchapter C.—Lien for Taxes
Part
  I. Due process for liens.
  II. Liens.

In 1998, P.L. 105-206, Sec. 3401(a), amended Subchapter C by adding Part I and redesignating the rest of Subchapter C as Part II.

PART I.—DUE PROCESS FOR LIENS
Sec.
6320. Notice and opportunity for hearing before filing of notice of lien.

In 1998, P.L. 105-206, Sec. 3401(a), added Part I to Subchapter C.

Sec. 6320. Notice and opportunity for hearing upon filing of notice of lien.
(a) Requirement of notice.
(1) In general. The Secretary shall notify in writing the person described in section 6321 of the filing of a notice of lien under section 6323.
(2) Time and method for notice. The notice required under paragraph (1) shall be—
  (A) given in person;
  (B) left at the dwelling or usual place of business of such person; or
  (C) sent by certified or registered mail to such person's last known address,
not more than 5 business days after the day of the filing of the notice of lien.
(3) Information included with notice. The notice required under paragraph (1) shall include in simple and nontechnical terms—
  (A) the amount of unpaid tax;
  (B) the right of the person to request a hearing during the 30-day period beginning on the day after the 5-day period described in paragraph (2);
  (C) the administrative appeals available to the taxpayer with respect to such lien and the procedures relating to such appeals; and
  (D) the provisions of this title and procedures relating to the release of liens on property.
(b) Right to fair hearing.
(1) In general. If the person requests a hearing in writing under subsection (a)(3)(B) and states the grounds for the requested hearing, such hearing shall be held by the Internal Revenue Service Office of Appeals.

(2) One hearing per period. A person shall be entitled to only one hearing under this section with respect to the taxable period to which the unpaid tax specified in subsection (a)(3)(A) relates.
(3) Impartial officer. The hearing under this subsection shall be conducted by an officer or employee who has had no prior involvement with respect to the unpaid tax specified in subsection (a)(3)(A) before the first hearing under this section or section 6330. A taxpayer may waive the requirement of this paragraph.
(4) Coordination with section 6330. To the extent practicable, a hearing under this section shall be held in conjunction with a hearing under section 6330.
(c) Conduct of hearing; review; suspensions.
For purposes of this section, subsections (c), (d) (other than paragraph (2)(B) thereof), (e), and (g) of section 6330 shall apply.

In 2006, P.L. 109-432, Sec. 407(c)(1), substituted "in writing under subsection (a)(3)(B) and states the grounds for the requested hearing" for "under subsection (a)(3)(B)" in para. (b)(1) . . . Sec. 407(c)(2), substituted "(e), and (g)" for "and (e)" in subsec. (c), effective for submissions made and issues raised after the date on which the Secretary first prescribes a list under Code Sec. 6702(c), as amended by Sec. 407(a) of P.L. 109-432.

In 1998, P.L. 105-206, Sec. 3401(a), added Code Sec. 6320, effective for collection actions initiated after the date which is 180 days after 7/22/98.

PART II.—LIENS
Sec.
6321. Lien for taxes.
6322. Period of lien.
6323. Validity and priority against certain persons.
6324. Special liens for estate and gift taxes.
6324A. Special lien for estate tax deferred under section 6166.
6324B. Special lien for additional estate tax attributable to farm, etc., valuation.
6325. Release of lien or discharge of property.
6326. Administrative appeal of liens.
6327. Cross references.

In 1998, P.L. 105-206, Sec. 3401(a), redesignated the Code Sections in Subchapter C as Part II of Subchapter C.

In 1988, P.L. 100-647, Sec. 6238(c), redesignated item 6326 as item 6327 and added new item 6326.

In 1981, P.L. 97-34, Sec. 442(e)(6)(D), deleted "or 6166A" following "section 6166" in item 6324A.

In 1976, P.L. 94-455, Sec. 2003(d)(2), added the item for Code Sec. 6324B.
—P.L. 94-455, Sec. 2004(f)(1), added the item for Code Sec. 6324A.

In 1966, amended item 6323 from "Validity against mortgagees, pledgees, purchasers, and judgment creditors" . . . deleted "partial" before "discharge" in item 6325.

Sec. 6321. Lien for taxes.
If any person liable to pay any tax neglects or refuses to pay the same after demand, the amount (including any interest, additional amount, addition to tax, or assessable penalty, together with any costs that may accrue in addition thereto) shall be a lien in favor of the United States upon all property and rights to property, whether real or personal, belonging to such person.

Sec. 6322. Period of lien.
Unless another date is specifically fixed by law, the lien imposed by section 6321 shall arise at the time the assessment is made and shall continue until the liability for the amount so assessed (or a judgment against the taxpayer arising out of such liability) is satisfied or becomes unenforceable by reason of lapse of time.

In 1966, P.L. 89-719, Sec. 113, added "(or a judgment against the taxpayer arising out of such liability)" after "liability for the amount so assessed" effective after 11/2/66, regardless of when a lien or a title of the U.S. arose or when the lien or interest of any other person was acquired. For a special exception included in Sec. 114 of P.L. 89-719 see the note to Code Sec. 6323.

Sec. 6323. Validity and priority against certain persons.
(a) Purchasers, holders of security interests, mechanic's lienors, and judgment lien creditors.
The lien imposed by section 6321 shall not be valid as against any purchaser, holder of a security interest, mechanic's lienor, or judgment lien creditor until notice thereof which meets the requirements of subsection (f) has been filed by the Secretary.
(b) Protection for certain interests even though notice filed.
Even though notice of a lien imposed by section 6321 has been filed, such lien shall not be valid—
   (1) Securities. With respect to a security (as defined in subsection (h)(4))—
      (A) as against a purchaser of such security who at the time of purchase did not have actual notice or knowledge of the existence of such lien; and
      (B) as against a holder of a security interest in such security who, at the time such interest came into existence, did not have actual notice or knowledge of the existence of such lien.
   (2) Motor vehicles. With respect to a motor vehicle (as defined in subsection (h)(3)), as against a purchaser of such motor vehicle, if—
      (A) at the time of the purchase such purchaser did not have actual notice or knowledge of the existence of such lien, and
      (B) before the purchaser obtains such notice or knowledge, he has acquired possession of such motor vehicle and has not thereafter relinquished possession of such motor vehicle to the seller or his agent.
   (3) Personal property purchased at retail. With respect to tangible personal property purchased at retail, as against a purchaser in the ordinary course of the seller's trade or business, unless at the time of such purchase such purchaser intends such purchase to (or knows such purchase will) hinder, evade, or defeat the collection of any tax under this title.
   (4) Personal property purchased in casual sale. With respect to household goods, personal effects, or other tangible personal property described in section 6334(a) purchased (not for resale) in a casual sale for less than $1,000, as against the purchaser, but only if such purchaser does not have actual notice or knowledge (A) of the existence of such lien, or (B) that this sale is one of a series of sales.
   (5) Personal property subject to possessory lien. With respect to tangible personal property subject to a lien under local law securing the reasonable price of the repair or improvement of such property, as against a holder of such a lien, if such holder is, and has been, continuously in possession of such property from the time such lien arose.
   (6) Real property tax and special assessment liens. With respect to real property, as against a holder of a lien upon such property, if such lien is entitled under local law to priority over security interests in such property which are prior in time, and such lien secures payment of—
      (A) a tax of general application levied by any taxing authority based upon the value of such property;
      (B) a special assessment imposed directly upon such property by any taxing authority, if such assessment is imposed for the purpose of defraying the cost of any public improvement; or
      (C) charges for utilities or public services furnished to such property by the United States, a State or political subdivision thereof, or an instrumentality of any one or more of the foregoing.
   (7) Residential property subject to a mechanic's lien for certain repairs and improvements. With respect to real property subject to a lien for repair or improvement of a personal residence (containing not more than four dwelling units) occupied by the owner of such residence, as against a mechanic's lienor, but only if the contract price on the contract with the owner is not more than $5,000.
   (8) Attorneys' liens. With respect to a judgment or other amount in settlement of a claim or of a cause of action, as against an attorney who, under local law, holds a lien upon or a contract enforcible against such judgment or amount, to the extent of his reasonable compensation for obtaining such judgment or procuring such settlement, except that this paragraph shall not apply to any judgment or amount in settlement of a claim or of a cause of action against the United States to the extent that the United States offsets such judgment or amount against any liability of the taxpayer to the United States.
   (9) Certain insurance contracts. With respect to a life insurance, endowment, or annuity contract, as against the organization which is the insurer under such contract, at any time—
      (A) before such organization had actual notice or knowledge of the existence of such lien;
      (B) after such organization had such notice or knowledge, with respect to advances required to be made automatically to maintain such contract in force under an agreement entered into before such organization had such notice or knowledge; or
      (C) after satisfaction of a levy pursuant to section 6332(b), unless and until the Secretary delivers to such organization a notice, executed after the date of such satisfaction, of the existence of such lien.
   (10) Deposit-secured loans. With respect to a savings deposit, share, or other account with an institution described in section 581 or 591, to the extent of any loan made by such institution without actual notice or knowledge of the existence of such lien, as against such institution, if such loan is secured by such account.
(c) Protection for certain commercial transactions financing agreements, etc.
   (1) In general. To the extent provided in this subsection, even though notice of a lien imposed by section 6321 has been filed, such lien shall not be valid with respect to a security interest which came into existence after tax lien filing but which—
      (A) is in qualified property covered by the terms of a written agreement entered into before tax lien filing and constituting—
         (i) a commercial transactions financing agreement,
         (ii) a real property construction or improvement financing agreement, or
         (iii) an obligatory disbursement agreement, and
      (B) is protected under local law against a judgment lien arising, as of the time of tax lien filing, out of an unsecured obligation.
   (2) Commercial transactions financing agreement. For purposes of this subsection—

(A) Definition. The term "commercial transactions financing agreement" means an agreement (entered into by a person in the course of his trade or business)—
(i) to make loans to the taxpayer to be secured by commercial financing security acquired by the taxpayer in the ordinary course of his trade or business, or
(ii) to purchase commercial financing security (other than inventory) acquired by the taxpayer in the ordinary course of his trade or business;

but such an agreement shall be treated as coming within the term only to the extent that such loan or purchase is made before the 46th day after the date of tax lien filing or (if earlier) before the lender or purchaser had actual notice or knowledge of such tax lien filing.

(B) Limitation on Qualified Property. The term "qualified property", when used with respect to a commercial transactions financing agreement, includes only commercial financing security acquired by the taxpayer before the 46th day after the date of tax lien filing.

(C) Commercial Financing Security Defined. The term "commercial financing security" means (i) paper of a kind ordinarily arising in commercial transactions, (ii) accounts receivable, (iii) mortgages on real property, and (iv) inventory.

(D) Purchaser treated as acquiring security interest. A person who satisfies subparagraph (A) by reason of clause (ii) thereof shall be treated as having acquired a security interest in commercial financing security.

(3) Real property construction or improvement financing agreement. For purposes of this subsection—
(A) Definition. The term "real property construction or improvement financing agreement" means an agreement to make cash disbursements to finance—
(i) the construction or improvement of real property,
(ii) a contract to construct or improve real property, or
(iii) the raising or harvesting of a farm crop or the raising of livestock or other animals.

For purposes of clause (iii), the furnishing of goods and services shall be treated as the disbursement of cash.

(B) Limitation on qualified property. The term "qualified property", when used with respect to a real property construction or improvement financing agreement, includes only—
(i) in the case of subparagraph (A)(i), the real property with respect to which the construction or improvement has been or is to be made,
(ii) in the case of subparagraph (A)(ii), the proceeds of the contract described therein, and
(iii) in the case of subparagraph (A)(iii), property subject to the lien imposed by section 6321 at the time of tax lien filing and the crop or the livestock or other animals referred to in subparagraph (A)(iii).

(4) Obligatory disbursement agreement. For purposes of this subsection—
(A) Definition. The term "obligatory disbursement agreement" means an agreement (entered into by a person in the course of his trade or business) to make disbursements, but such an agreement shall be treated as coming within the term only to the extent of disbursements which are required to be made by reason of the intervention of the rights of a person other than the taxpayer.

(B) Limitation on qualified property. The term "qualified property", when used with respect to an obligatory disbursement agreement, means property subject to the lien imposed by section 6321 at the time of tax lien filing and (to the extent that the acquisition is directly traceable to the disbursements referred to in subparagraph (A)) property acquired by the taxpayer after tax lien filing.

(C) Special rules for surety agreements. Where the obligatory disbursement agreement is an agreement ensuring the performance of a contract between the taxpayer and another person—
(i) the term "qualified property" shall be treated as also including the proceeds of the contract the performance of which was ensured, and
(ii) If the contract the performance of which was ensured was a contract to construct or improve real property, to produce goods, or to furnish services, the term "qualified property" shall be treated as also including any tangible personal property used by the taxpayer in the performance of such ensured contract.

(d) 45-day period for making disbursements.
Even though notice of a lien imposed by section 6321 has been filed, such lien shall not be valid with respect to a security interest which came into existence after tax lien filing by reason of disbursements made before the 46th day after the date of tax lien filing, or (if earlier) before the person making such disbursements had actual notice or knowledge of tax lien filing, but only if such security interest—

(1) is in property (A) subject, at the time of tax lien filing, to the lien imposed by section 6321, and (B) covered by the terms of a written agreement entered into before tax lien filing, and

(2) is protected under local law against a judgment lien arising, as of the time of tax lien filing, out of an unsecured obligation.

(e) Priority of interest and expenses.
If the lien imposed by section 6321 is not valid as against a lien or security interest, the priority of such lien or security interest shall extend to—

(1) any interest or carrying charges upon the obligation secured,

(2) the reasonable charges and expenses of an indenture trustee or agent holding the security interest for the benefit of the holder of the security interest,

(3) the reasonable expenses, including reasonable compensation for attorneys, actually incurred in collecting or enforcing the obligation secured,

(4) the reasonable costs of insuring, preserving, or repairing the property to which the lien or security interest relates,

(5) the reasonable costs of insuring payment of the obligation secured, and

(6) amounts paid to satisfy any lien on the property to which the lien or security interest relates, but only if the lien so satisfied is entitled to priority over the lien imposed by section 6321,

to the extent that, under local law, any such item has the same priority as the lien or security interest to which it relates.

(f) Place for filing notice; form.
(1) Place for filing. The notice referred to in subsection (a) shall be filed—
(A) Under State laws.
(i) Real property. In the case of real property, in one office within the State (or the county, or other governmental subdivision), as designated by the laws of such State, in which the property subject to the lien is situated; and

(ii) **Personal property.** In the case of personal property, whether tangible or intangible, in one office within the State (or the county, or other governmental subdivision), as designated by the laws of such State, in which the property subject to the lien is situated, except that State law merely conforming to or reenacting Federal law establishing a national filing system does not constitute a second office for filing as designated by the laws of such State; or

(B) **With clerk of district court.** In the office of the clerk of the United States district court for the judicial district in which the property subject to the lien is situated, whenever the State has not by law designated one office which meets the requirements of subparagraph (A); or

(C) **With recorder of deeds of the District of Columbia.** In the office of the Recorder of Deeds of the District of Columbia, if the property subject to the lien is situated in the District of Columbia.

(2) **Situs of property subject to lien.** For purposes of paragraphs (1) and (4), property shall be deemed to be situated—

(A) **Real property.** In the case of real property, at its physical location; or

(B) **Personal property.** In the case of personal property, whether tangible or intangible, at the residence of the taxpayer at the time the notice of lien is filed.

For purposes of paragraph (2)(B), the residence of a corporation or partnership shall be deemed to be the place at which the principal executive office of the business is located, and the residence of a taxpayer whose residence is without the United States shall be deemed to be in the District of Columbia.

(3) **Form.** The form and content of the notice referred to in subsection (a) shall be prescribed by the Secretary. Such notice shall be valid notwithstanding any other provision of law regarding the form or content of a notice of lien.

(4) **Indexing required with respect to certain real property.** In the case of real property, if—

(A) under the laws of the State in which the real property is located, a deed is not valid as against a purchaser of the property who (at the time of purchase) does not have actual notice or knowledge of the existence of such deed unless the fact of filing of such deed has been entered and recorded in a public index at the place of filing in such a manner that a reasonable inspection of the index will reveal the existence of the deed, and

(B) there is maintained (at the applicable office under paragraph (1)) an adequate system for the public indexing of Federal tax liens,

then the notice of lien referred to in subsection (a) shall not be treated as meeting the filing requirements under paragraph (1) unless the fact of filing is entered and recorded in the index referred to in subparagraph (B) in such a manner that a reasonable inspection of the index will reveal the existence of the lien.

(5) **National filing systems.** The filing of a notice of lien shall be governed solely by this title and shall not be subject to any other Federal law establishing a place or places for the filing of liens or encumbrances under a national filing system.

(g) **Refiling of notice.**

For purposes of this section—

(1) **General rule.** Unless notice of lien is refiled in the manner prescribed in paragraph (2) during the required refiling period, such notice of lien shall be treated as filed on the date on which it is filed (in accordance with subsection (f)) after the expiration of such refiling period.

(2) **Place for filing.** A notice of lien refiled during the required refiling period shall be effective only—

(A) if—

(i) such notice of lien is refiled in the office in which the prior notice of lien was filed, and

(ii) in the case of real property, the fact of refiling is entered and recorded in an index to the extent required by subsection (f)(4); and

(B) in any case in which, 90 days or more prior to the date of a refiling of notice of lien under subparagraph (A), the Secretary received written information (in the manner prescribed in regulations issued by the Secretary) concerning a change in the taxpayer's residence, if a notice of such lien is also filed in accordance with subsection (f) in the State in which such residence is located.

(3) **Required refiling period.** In the case of any notice of lien, the term "required refiling period" means—

(A) the one-year period ending 30 days after the expiration of 10 years after the date of the assessment of the tax, and

(B) the one-year period ending with the expiration of 10 years after the close of the preceding required refiling period for such notice of lien.

(4) **Transitional rule.** Notwithstanding paragraph (3), if the assessment of the tax was made before January 1, 1962, the first required refiling period shall be the calendar year 1967.

(h) **Definitions.**

For purposes of this section and section 6324—

(1) **Security interest.** The term "security interest" means any interest in property acquired by contract for the purpose of securing payment or performance of an obligation or indemnifying against loss or liability. A security interest exists at any time (A) if, at such time, the property is in existence and the interest has become protected under local law against a subsequent judgment lien arising out of an unsecured obligation, and (B) to the extent that, at such time, the holder has parted with money or money's worth.

(2) **Mechanic's lienor.** The term "mechanic's lienor" means any person who under local law has a lien on real property (or on the proceeds of a contract relating to real property) for services, labor, or materials furnished in connection with the construction or improvement of such property. For purposes of the preceding sentence, a person has a lien on the earliest date such lien becomes valid under local law against subsequent purchasers without actual notice, but not before he begins to furnish the services, labor, or materials.

(3) **Motor vehicle.** The term "motor vehicle" means a self-propelled vehicle which is registered for highway use under the laws of any State or foreign country.

(4) **Security.** The term "security" means any bond, debenture, note, or certificate or other evidence of indebtedness, issued by a corporation or a government or political subdivision thereof, with interest coupons or in registered form, share of stock, voting trust certificate, or any certificate of interest or participation in, certificate of deposit or receipt for, temporary or interim certificate for, or warrant or right to subscribe to or purchase, any of the foregoing; negotiable instrument; or money.

(5) Tax lien filing. The term "tax lien filing" means the filing of notice (referred to in subsection (a)) of the lien imposed by section 6321.

(6) Purchaser. The term "purchaser" means a person who, for adequate and full consideration in money or money's worth, acquires an interest (other than a lien or security interest) in property which is valid under local law against subsequent purchasers without actual notice. In applying the preceding sentence for purposes of subsection (a) of this section, and for purposes of section 6324—

(A) a lease of property,

(B) a written executory contract to purchase or lease property,

(C) an option to purchase or lease property or any interest therein, or

(D) an option to renew or extend a lease of property,

which is not a lien or security interest shall be treated as an interest in property.

(i) Special rules.

(1) Actual notice or knowledge. For purposes of this subchapter, an organization shall be deemed for purposes of a particular transaction to have actual notice or knowledge of any fact from the time such fact is brought to the attention of the individual conducting such transaction, and in any event from the time such fact would have been brought to such individual's attention if the organization had exercised due diligence. An organization exercises due diligence if it maintains reasonable routines for communicating significant information to the person conducting the transaction and there is reasonable compliance with the routines. Due diligence does not require an individual acting for the organization to communicate information unless such communication is part of his regular duties or unless he has reason to know of the transaction and that the transaction would be materially affected by the information.

(2) Subrogation. Where, under local law, one person is subrogated to the rights of another with respect to a lien or interest, such person shall be subrogated to such rights for purposes of any lien imposed by section 6321 or 6324.

(3) Forfeitures. For purposes of this subchapter, a forfeiture under local law of property seized by a law enforcement agency of a State, county, or other local governmental subdivision shall relate back to the time of seizure, except that this paragraph shall not apply to the extent that under local law the holder of an intervening claim or interest would have priority over the interest of the State, county, or other local governmental subdivision in the property.

(4) Cost-of-living adjustment. In the case of notices of liens imposed by section 6321 which are filed in any calendar year after 1998, each of the dollar amounts under paragraph (4) or (7) of subsection (b) shall be increased by an amount equal to—

(A) such dollar amount, multiplied by

(B) the cost-of-living adjustment determined under section 1(f)(3) for the calendar year, determined by substituting "calendar year 1996" for "calendar year 1992" in subparagraph (B) thereof.

If any amount as adjusted under the preceding sentence is not a multiple of $10, such amount shall be rounded to the nearest multiple of $10.

(j) Withdrawal of notice in certain circumstances.

(1) In general. The Secretary may withdraw a notice of a lien filed under this section and this chapter shall be applied as if the withdrawn notice had not been filed, if the Secretary determines that—

(A) the filing of such notice was premature or otherwise not in accordance with administrative procedures of the Secretary,

(B) the taxpayer has entered into an agreement under section 6159 to satisfy the tax liability for which the lien was imposed by means of installment payments, unless such agreement provides otherwise,

(C) the withdrawal of such notice will facilitate the collection of the tax liability, or

(D) with the consent of the taxpayer or the National Taxpayer Advocate, the withdrawal of such notice would be in the best interests of the taxpayer (as determined by the National Taxpayer Advocate) and the United States.

Any such withdrawal shall be made by filing notice at the same office as the withdrawn notice. A copy of such notice of withdrawal shall be provided to the taxpayer.

(2) Notice to credit agencies, etc. Upon written request by the taxpayer with respect to whom a notice of a lien was withdrawn under paragraph (1), the Secretary shall promptly make reasonable efforts to notify credit reporting agencies, and any financial institution or creditor whose name and address is specified in such request, of the withdrawal of such notice. Any such request shall be in such form as the Secretary may prescribe.

In 1998, P.L. 105-206, Sec. 1102(d)(1)(A), substituted "National Taxpayer Advocate" for "Taxpayer Advocate" each place it appeared in subpara. (j)(1)(D), effective 7/22/98.

—P.L. 105-206, Sec. 3435(a)(1)(A), substituted "$1,000" for "$250" in para. (b)(4) ... Sec. 3435(a)(1)(B), substituted "$5,000" for "$1,000" in para. (b)(7) ... Sec. 3435(a)(2), added para. (i)(4) ... Sec. 3435(b)(1), substituted "Deposit-secured loans" for "Passbook loans" in the heading of para. (b)(10) ... Sec. 3435(b)(2), deleted ", evidenced by a passbook," after "other account" in para. (b)(10) ... Sec. 3435(b)(3), substituted a period for "and if such institution has been continuously in possession of such passbook from the time the loan is made." in para. (b)(10), effective 7/22/98.

In 1996, P.L. 104-168, Sec. 501(a), added subsec. (j), effective 7/30/96.

In 1990, P.L. 101-508, Sec. 11317(b), substituted "10 years" for "6 years" each place it appeared in para. (g)(3), effective for taxes assessed after 11/5/90, and as provided in Sec. 11317(c)(2) of this Act which reads as follows:

"(2) taxes assessed on or before such date [11/5/90] if the period specified in section 6502 of the Internal Revenue Code of 1986 (determined without regard to the amendments made by subsection (a)) for collection of such taxes has not expired as of such date."

—P.L. 101-508, Sec. 11704(a)(26), substituted "Purchasers" for "Purchases" in the heading of subsec. (a), effective 11/5/90.

In 1988, P.L. 100-647, Sec. 1015(s)(1)(A), added ", except that State law merely conforming to or reenacting Federal law establishing a national filing system does not constitute a second office for filing as designated by the laws of such State" after "situated" in the last sentence of clause (f)(1)(A)(ii) ... Sec. 1015(s)(1)(B), added para. (f)(5), effective 11/10/88.

In 1986, P.L. 99-514, Sec. 1569(a), added para. (i)(3), effective 10/22/86.

In 1978, P.L. 95-600, Sec. 702(q)(1), amended para. (f)(4) ... Sec. 702(q)(2), amended subpara. (g)(2)(A), effective for liens, other security interests, and other interests in real property acquired after 11/6/78. Sec. 702(q)(3)(B) of this Act provides as follows:

"(B) If, after the date of the enactment of this Act, there is a change in the application (or nonapplication) of section 6323(f)(4) of the Internal Revenue Code of 1954 (as amended by paragraph (1)) with respect to any filing jurisdiction, such change shall apply only with respect to liens, other security interests, and other interests in real property acquired after the date of such change."

Prior to amendment, para. (f)(4) read as follows:

"(4) Index. The notice of lien referred to in subsection (a) shall not be treated as meeting the filing requirements under paragraph (1) unless the fact of filing is entered and recorded in a public index at the district office of the Internal Revenue Service for the district in which the property subject to the lien is situated."

Prior to amendment, subpara. (g)(2)(A) read as follows:

"(A) if such notice of lien is refiled in the office in which the prior notice of lien was filed and the fact of refiling is entered and recorded in an index in accordance with subsection (f)(4); and"

In 1976, P.L. 94-455, Sec. 1202(h)(2), deleted para. (i)(3), effective 1/1/77.

Prior to deletion para. (i)(3) read as follows:

"(3) Disclosure of amount of outstanding lien. If a notice of lien has been filed pursuant to subsection (f), the Secretary or his delegate is authorized to provide

by regulations the extent to which, and the conditions under which, information as to the amount of the outstanding obligation secured by the lien may be disclosed."
—P.L. 94-455, Sec. 1906(b)(13)(A), substituted "Secretary" for "Secretary or his delegate" each place it appeared in Code Sec. 6323, effective 2/1/77.
—P.L. 94-455, Sec. 2008(c)(1)(A), added para. (f)(4), effective for liens filed before 10/4/76 on 7/1/77, and for liens filed on or after 10/4/76 on 2/1/77.
—P.L. 94-455, Sec. 2008(c)(1)(B), substituted "paragraphs (1) and (4)" for "paragraph (1)", in para. (f)(2), effective for liens filed before 10/4/76 on 7/1/77, and for liens filed on or after 10/4/76 on 2/1/77.
—P.L. 94-455, Sec. 2008(c)(2), amended subpara. (g)(2)(A), effective for liens filed before 10/4/76 on 7/1/77, and for liens filed on or after 10/4/76.
Prior to amendment, subpara. (g)(2)(A) read as follows:
"(A) if such notice of lien is refiled in the office in which the prior notice of lien was filed; and",
In 1966, P.L. 89-719, Sec. 101(a), amended Code Sec. 6323, effective after 11/2/66, regardless of when a lien or title of the U.S. arose or the lien or interest of any other person was acquired, except that Sec. 114 of P.L. 89-719 provided that it does not apply in any case
"(1) in which a lien or a title derived from enforcement of a lien held by the United States has been enforced by a civil action or suit which has become final by judgment, sale, or agreement before the date of enactment of this Act; or
"(2) in which such amendments would—
"(A) impair a priority enjoyed by any person (other than the United States) holding a lien or interest prior to the date of enactment of this Act;
"(B) operate to increase the liability of any such person; or
"(C) shorten the time for bringing suit with respect to transactions occurring before the date of enactment of this Act."
Prior to amendment, Code Sec. 6323 read as follows:
"SEC. 6323. VALIDITY AGAINST MORTGAGEES, PLEDGEES, PURCHASERS, AND JUDGMENT CREDITORS.
"(a) Invalidity of lien without notice.
"Except as otherwise provided in subsections (c) and (d), the lien imposed by section 6321 shall not be valid as against any mortgagee, pledgee, purchaser, or judgment creditor until notice thereof has been filed by the Secretary or his delegate—
"(1) Under State or Territorial laws. In the office designated by the law of the State or Territory in which the property subject to the lien is situated, whenever the State or Territory has by law designated an office within the State or Territory for the filing of such notice; or
"(2) With clerk of district court. In the office of the clerk of the United States district court for the judicial district in which the property subject to the lien is situated, whenever the State or Territory has not by law designated an office within the State or Territory for the filing of such notice; or
"(3) With Recorder of Deeds of the District of Columbia. In the office of the Recorder of Deeds of the District of Columbia, if the property subject to the lien is situated in the District of Columbia.
"(b) Form of notice.
"If the notice filed pursuant to subsection (a)(1) is in such form as would be valid if filed with the clerk of the United States district court pursuant to subsection (a)(2), such notice shall be valid notwithstanding any law of the State or Territory regarding the form or content of a notice of lien.
"(c) Exception in case of securities.
"(1) Exception. Even though notice of a lien provided in section 6321 has been filed in the manner prescribed in subsection (a) of this section, the lien shall not be valid with respect to a security, as defined in paragraph (2) of this subsection, as against any mortgagee, pledgee, or purchaser of such security, for an adequate and full consideration in money or money's worth, if at the time of such mortgage, pledge, or purchase such mortgagee, pledgee, or purchaser is without notice or knowledge of the existence of such lien.
"(2) Definition of security. As used in this subsection, the term 'security' means any bond, debenture, note, or certificate or other evidence of indebtedness, issued by any corporation (including one issued by a government or political subdivision thereof), with interest coupons or in registered form, share of stock, voting trust certificate, or any certificate of interest or participation in, certificate of deposit or receipt for, temporary or interim certificate for, or warrant or right to subscribe to or purchase, any of the foregoing; negotiable instrument; or money.
"(d) Exception in case of motor vehicles.
"(1) Exception. Even though notice of a lien provided in section 6321 has been filed in the manner prescribed in subsection (a) of this section, the lien shall not be valid with respect to a motor vehicle, as defined in paragraph (2) of this subsection, as against any purchaser of such motor vehicle for an adequate and full consideration in money or money's worth if—
"(A) at the time of the purchase the purchaser is without notice or knowledge of the existence of such lien, and
"(B) before the purchaser obtains such notice or knowledge, he has acquired possession of such motor vehicle and has not thereafter relinquished possession of such motor vehicle to the seller or his agent.
"(2) Definition of motor vehicle. As used in this subsection, the term 'motor vehicle' means a self-propelled vehicle which is registered for highway use under the laws of any State of foreign country.
"(e) Disclosure of amount of outstanding lien.
"If a notice of lien has been filed under subsection (a), the Secretary or his delegate is authorized to provide by rules or regulations the extent to which, and the conditions under which, information as to the amount of the outstanding obligation secured by the lien may be disclosed."
—P.L. 88-493, Sec. 17(a), substituted "the recorder of deeds of the District of Columbia" for "the clerk of the United States District Court for the District of Columbia" in para. (a)(3), effective on the first day of the first month which is at least 90 days after 7/5/66.
In 1964, P.L. 88-272, Sec. 236(a), added subsec. (d) and redesignated subsec. (d) as (e)... Sec. 236(c)(1), substituted "subsections (c) and (d)" for "subsection (c)" in subsec. (a), effective for purchases after 2/26/64.

Sec. 6324. Special liens for estate and gift taxes.
(a) Liens for estate tax.

Except as otherwise provided in subsection (c)—

(1) Upon gross estate. Unless the estate tax imposed by chapter 11 is sooner paid in full, or becomes unenforceable by reason of lapse of time, it shall be a lien upon the gross estate of the decedent for 10 years from the date of death, except that such part of the gross estate as is used for the payment of charges against the estate and expenses of its administration, allowed by any court having jurisdiction thereof, shall be divested of such lien.

(2) Liability of transferees and others. If the estate tax imposed by chapter 11 is not paid when due, then the spouse, transferee, trustee (except the trustee of an employees' trust which meets the requirements of section 401(a)), surviving tenant, person in possession of the property by reason of the exercise, nonexercise, or release of a power of appointment, or beneficiary, who receives, or has on the date of the decedent's death, property included in the gross estate under sections 2034 to 2042, inclusive, to the extent of the value, at the time of the decedent's death, of such property, shall be personally liable for such tax. Any part of such property transferred by (or transferred by a transferee of) such spouse, transferee, trustee, surviving tenant, person in possession, or beneficiary, to a purchaser or holder of a security interest shall be divested of the lien provided in paragraph (1) and a like lien shall then attach to all the property of such spouse, transferee, trustee, surviving tenant, person in possession, or beneficiary, or transferee of any such person, except any part transferred to a purchaser or a holder of a security interest.

(3) Continuance after discharge of fiduciary. The provisions of section 2204 (relating to discharge of fiduciary from personal liability) shall not operate as a release of any part of the gross estate from the lien for any deficiency that may thereafter be determined to be due, unless such part of the gross estate (or any interest therein) has been transferred to a purchaser or a holder of a security interest, in which case such part (or such interest) shall not be subject to a lien or to any claim or demand for any such deficiency, but the lien shall attach to the consideration received from such purchaser or holder of a security interest, by the heirs, legatees, devisees, or distributees.

(b) Lien for gift tax.

Except as otherwise provided in subsection (c), unless the gift tax imposed by chapter 12 is sooner paid in full or becomes unenforceable by reason of lapse of time, such tax shall be a lien upon all gifts made during the period for which the return was filed, for 10 years from the date the gifts are made. If the tax is not paid when due, the donee of any gift shall be personally liable for such tax to the extent of the value of such gift. Any part of the property comprised in the gift transferred by the donee (or by a transferee of the donee) to a purchaser or holder of a security interest shall be divested of the lien imposed by this subsection and such lien, to the extent of the value of such gift, shall attach to all the property (including after-acquired property) of the donee (or the transferee) except any part transferred to a purchaser or holder of a security interest.

(c) Exceptions.

(1) The lien imposed by subsection (a) or (b) shall not be valid as against a mechanic's lienor and, subject to the conditions provided by section 6323(b) (relating to protection for certain interests even though notice filed), shall not be valid with respect to any lien or interest described in section 6323(b).

(2) If a lien imposed by subsection (a) or (b) is not valid as against a lien or security interest, the priority of such lien or security interest shall extend to any item described in section 6323(e) (relating to priority of interest and expenses) to the extent that, under local law, such item has the same priority as the lien or security interest to which it relates.

In 1970, P.L. 91-614, Sec. 101(d)(2), substituted "fiduciary" for "executor" each place it appeared in para. (a)(3), effective for decedents dying after 12/31/70.
—P.L. 91-614, Sec. 102(d)(7), substituted "period for which the return was filed," for "calendar year," in the first sentence of subsec. (b), effective for gifts made after 12/31/70.

In 1966, P.L. 89-719, Sec. 102, amended Code Sec. 6324, effective after 11/2/66 regardless of when a lien or title of the U.S. arose or a lien or interest of any other person was acquired. For a special exception included in Sec. 114 of P.L. 89-719 see the note to Code Sec. 6323.
Prior to amendment, Code Sec. 6324 read as follows:
"Sec. 6324. Special liens for estate and gift taxes.
"(a) Liens for estate tax.
"Except as otherwise provided in subsection (c) (relating to transfers of securities) and subsection (d) (relating to purchases of motor vehicles)—
"(1) Upon gross estate. Unless the estate tax imposed by chapter 11 is sooner paid in full, it shall be a lien for 10 years upon the gross estate of the decedent, except that such part of the gross estate as is used for the payment of charges against the estate and expenses of its administration, allowed by any court having jurisdiction thereof, shall be divested of such lien.
"(2) Liability of transferees and others. If the estate tax imposed by chapter 11 is not paid when due, then the spouse, transferee, trustee (except the trustee of an employee's trust which meets the requirements of section 401(a)), surviving tenant, person in possession of the property by reason of the exercise, nonexercise, or release of a power of appointment, or beneficiary, who receives, or has on the date of the decedent's death, property included in the gross estate under sections 2034 to 2042, inclusive, to the extent of the value, at the time of the decedent's death, of such property, shall be personally liable for such tax. Any part of such property transferred by (or transferred by a transferee of) such spouse, transferee, trustee, surviving tenant, person in possession of property by reason of the exercise, nonexercise, or release of a power of appointment, or beneficiary, to a bona fide purchaser, mortgagee, or pledgee for an adequate and full consideration in money or money's worth shall be divested of the lien provided in paragraph (1) and a like lien shall then attach to all the property of such spouse, transferee, trustee, surviving tenant, person in possession, beneficiary, or transferee of any such person, except any part transferred to a bona fide purchaser, mortgagee, or pledgee for an adequate and full consideration in money or moneys worth.
"(3) Continuance after discharge of executor. The provisions of section 2204 (relating to discharge of executor from personal liability) shall not operate as a release of any part of the gross estate from the lien for any deficiency that may thereafter be determined to be due, unless such part of the gross estate (or any interest therein) has been transferred to a bona fide purchaser, mortgagee, or pledgee for an adequate and full consideration in money, or money's worth, in which case such part (or such interest) shall not be subject to a lien or to any claim or demand for any such deficiency, but the lien shall attach to the consideration received from such purchaser, mortgagee, or pledgee by the heirs, legatees, devisees, or distributees.
"(b) Lien for gift tax.
Except as otherwise provided in subsection (c) (relating to transfers of securities) and subsection (d) (relating to purchases of motor vehicles), the gift tax imposed by chapter 12 shall be a lien upon all gifts made during the calendar year, for 10 years from the time the gifts are made. If the tax is not paid when due, the donee of any gift shall be personally liable for such tax to the extent of the value of such gift. Any part of the property comprised in the gift transferred by the donee (or by a transferee of the donee) to a bona fide purchaser, mortgagee, or pledgee for an adequate and full consideration in money or money's worth shall be divested of the lien herein imposed and the lien, to the extent of the value of such gift, shall attach to all the property (including after-acquired property) of the donee (or the transferee) except any part transferred to a bona fide purchaser, mortgagee, or pledgee for an adequate and full consideration in money or in money's worth.
"(c) Exception in case of securities.
"The lien imposed by subsection (a) or (b) shall not be valid with respect to a security, as defined in section 6323(c)(2), as against any mortgagee, pledgee, or purchaser of any such security, for an adequate and full consideration in money or money's worth, if, at the time of such mortgage, pledge, or purchase such mortgagee, pledgee, or purchaser is without notice or knowledge of the existence of such lien.
"(d) Exception in case of motor vehicles.

"The lien imposed by subsection (a) or (b) shall not be valid with respect to a motor vehicle, as defined in section 6323(d)(2), as against any purchaser of such motor vehicle for an adequate and full consideration in money or money's worth if—
"(1) at the time of the purchase the purchaser is without notice or knowledge of the existence of such lien, and
"(2) before the purchaser obtains such notice or knowledge, he has acquired possession of such motor vehicle and has not thereafter relinquished possession of such motor vehicle to the seller or his agent."
In 1964, P.L. 88-272, Sec. 236, added "and subsection (d) (relating to purchases of motor vehicles)" in subsecs. (a) and (b) and added subsec. (d), effective for purchases made after 2/26/64.

Sec. 6324A. Special lien for estate tax deferred under section 6166.

(a) General rule.
In the case of any estate with respect to which an election has been made under section 6166 if the executor makes an election under this section (at such time and in such manner as the Secretary shall by regulations prescribe) and files the agreement referred to in subsection (c), the deferred amount (plus any interest, additional amount, addition to tax, assessable penalty, and costs attributable to the deferred amount) shall be a lien in favor of the United States on the section 6166 lien property.

(b) Section 6166 lien property.

(1) In general. For purposes of this section, the term "section 6166 lien property" means interests in real and other property to the extent such interests—

(A) can be expected to survive the deferral period, and

(B) are designated in the agreement referred to in subsection (c).

(2) Maximum value of required property. The maximum value of the property which the Secretary may require as section 6166 lien property with respect to any estate shall be a value which is not greater than the sum of—

(A) the deferred amount, and

(B) the required interest amount.

For purposes of the preceding sentence, the value of any property shall be determined as of the date prescribed by section 6151(a) for payment of the tax imposed by chapter 11 and shall be determined by taking into account any encumbrance such as a lien under section 6324B.

(3) Partial substitution of bond for lien. If the value required as section 6166 lien property pursuant to paragraph (2) exceeds the value of the interests in property covered by the agreement referred to in subsection (c), the Secretary may accept bond in an amount equal to such excess conditioned on the payment of the amount extended in accordance with the terms of such extension.

(c) Agreement.
The agreement referred to in this subsection is a written agreement signed by each person in being who has an interest (whether or not in possession) in any property designated in such agreement—

(1) consenting to the creation of the lien under this section with respect to such property, and

(2) designating a responsible person who shall be the agent for the beneficiaries of the estate and for the persons who have consented to the creation of the lien in dealings with the Secretary on matters arising under section 6166 or this section.

(d) Special rules.

(1) Requirement that lien be filed. The lien imposed by this section shall not be valid as against any purchaser, holder of a security interest, mechanic's lien, or judgment lien creditor until notice thereof which meets the requirements of section 6323(f) has been filed by the Secretary. Such notice shall not be required to be refiled.

Collection   Code Sec. 6324B

(2) Period of lien. The lien imposed by this section shall arise at the time the executor is discharged from liability under section 2204 (or, if earlier, at the time notice is filed pursuant to paragraph (1)) and shall continue until the liability for the deferred amount is satisfied or becomes unenforceable by reason of lapse of time.

(3) Priorities. Even though notice of a lien imposed by this section has been filed as provided in paragraph (1), such lien shall not be valid.—

    (A) Real property tax and special assessment liens. To the extent provided in section 6323(b)(6).

    (B) Real property subject to a mechanic's lien for repairs and improvements. In the case of any real property subject to a lien for repair or improvement, as against a mechanic's lienor.

    (C) Real property construction or improvement financing agreement. As against any security interest set forth in paragraph (3) of section 6323(c) (whether such security interest came into existence before or after tax lien filing).

Subparagraphs (B) and (C) shall not apply to any security interest which came into existence after the date on which the Secretary filed notice (in a manner similar to notice filed under section 6323(f)) that payment of the deferred amount has been accelerated under section 6166(g).

(4) Lien to be in lieu of section 6324 lien. If there is a lien under this section on any property with respect to any estate, there shall not be any lien under section 6324 on such property with respect to the same estate.

(5) Additional lien property required in certain cases. If at any time the value of the property covered by the agreement is less than the unpaid portion of the deferred amount and the required interest amount, the Secretary may require the addition of property to the agreement (but he may not require under this paragraph that the value of the property covered by the agreement exceed such unpaid portion). If property having the required value is not added to the property covered by the agreement (or if other security equal to the required value is not furnished) within 90 days after notice and demand therefor by the Secretary, the failure to comply with the preceding sentence shall be treated as an act accelerating payment of the installments under section 6166(g).

(6) Lien to be in lieu of bond. The Secretary may not require under section 6165 the furnishing of any bond for the payment of any tax to which an agreement which meets the requirements of subsection (c) applies.

(e) Definitions.

For purposes of this section—

(1) Deferred amount. The term "deferred amount" means the aggregate amount deferred under section 6166 (determined as of the date prescribed by section 6151(a) for payment of the tax imposed by chapter 11).

(2) Required interest amount. The term "required interest amount" means the aggregate amount of interest which will be payable over the first 4 years of the deferral period with respect to the deferred amount (determined as of the date prescribed by section 6151(a) for the payment of the tax imposed by chapter 11).

(3) Deferral period. The term "deferral period" means the period for which the payment of tax is deferred pursuant to the election under section 6166.

(4) Application of definitions in case of deficiencies. In the case of a deficiency, a separate deferred amount, required interest amount, and deferral period shall be determined as of the due date of the first installment after the deficiency is prorated to installments under section 6166.

In 1981, P.L. 97-34, Sec. 422(e)(6)(A), deleted "or 6166A" after "section 6166" in subsec. (a), para. (c)(2) and subsec. (e)... Sec. 422(e)(6)(B), deleted "or 6166A(h)" after "section 6166(g)" in paras. (d)(3) and (d)(5)... Sec. 422(e)(6)(C), deleted "or 6166A" after "section 6166" from the title of Code Sec. 6324A, effective for estates of decedents dying after 12/31/81.

In 1978, P.L. 95-600, Sec. 702(e)(1)(A), amended para. (e)(2)... Sec. 702(e)(1)(B), substituted "required interest amount" for "aggregate interest amount" in subpara. (b)(2)(B)... Sec. 702(e)(1)(C), substituted "required interest amount" for "aggregate interest amount" in para. (d)(5)... Sec. 702(e)(1)(D), substituted "required interest amount" for "aggregate interest amount" in para. (e)(4), effective for estates of decedents dying after 12/31/76.

Prior to amendment, para. (e)(2) read as follows:

"(2) Aggregate interest amount. The term 'aggregate interest amount' means the aggregate amount of interest which will be payable over the deferral period with respect to the deferred amount (determined as of the date prescribed by section 6151(a) for payment of the tax imposed by chapter 11)."

In 1976, P.L. 94-455, Sec. 2004(d)(1), added Code Sec. 6324A, effective for estates of decedents dying after 12/31/76.

Sec. 6324B. Special lien for additional estate tax attributable to farm, etc., valuation.

(a) General rule.

In the case of any interest in qualified real property (within the meaning of section 2032A(b)), an amount equal to the adjusted tax difference attributable to such interest (within the meaning of section 2032A(c)(2)(B)) shall be a lien in favor of the United States on the property in which such interest exists.

(b) Period of lien.

The lien imposed by this section shall arise at the time an election is filed under section 2032A and shall continue with respect to any interest in the qualified real property—

    (1) until the liability for tax under subsection (c) of section 2032A with respect to such interest has been satisfied or has become unenforceable by reason of lapse of time, or

    (2) until it is established to the satisfaction of the Secretary that no further tax liability may arise under section 2032A(c) with respect to such interest.

(c) Certain rules and definitions made applicable.

    (1) In general. The rule set forth in paragraphs (1), (3), and (4) of section 6324A(d) shall apply with respect to the lien imposed by this section as if it were a lien imposed by section 6324A.

    (2) Qualified real property. For purposes of this section, the term "qualified real property" includes qualified replacement property (within the meaning of section 2032A(h)(3)(B)) and qualified exchange property (within the meaning of section 2032A(i)(3)).

(d) Substitution of security for lien.

To the extent provided in regulations prescribed by the Secretary, the furnishing of security may be substituted for the lien imposed by this section.

In 1981, P.L. 97-34, Sec. 421(d)(2)(B), added "and qualified exchange property (within the meaning of section 2032A(i)(3))" before the period in para. (c)(2), effective for exchanges made after 12/31/81.

In 1980, P.L. 96-222, Sec. 108(d), amended subsec. (c), effective for estates of decedents dying after 12/31/80.

Prior to amendment, subsec. (c) read as follows:

"(c) Certain rules made applicable.

"The rules set forth in paragraphs (1), (3), and (4) of section 6324A(d) shall apply with respect to the lien imposed by this section as if it were a lien imposed by section 6324A."

In 1978, P.L. 95-600, Sec. 703(r)(4), substituted "qualified real property" for "qualified farm real property" in subsec. (b), effective for estates of decedents dying after 12/31/76.

In 1976, P.L. 94-455, Sec. 2003(b), added Code Sec. 6324B, effective for estates of decedents dying after 12/31/76.

Sec. 6325. Release of lien or discharge of property.
(a) Release of lien.

Subject to such regulations as the Secretary may prescribe, the Secretary shall issue a certificate of release of any lien imposed with respect to any internal revenue tax not later than 30 days after the day on which—

(1) Liability satisfied or unenforceable. The Secretary finds that the liability for the amount assessed, together with all interest in respect thereof, has been fully satisfied or has become legally unenforceable; or

(2) Bond accepted. There is furnished to the Secretary and accepted by him a bond that is conditioned upon the payment of the amount assessed, together with all interest in respect thereof, within the time prescribed by law (including any extension of such time), and that is in accordance with such requirements relating to terms, conditions, and form of the bond and sureties thereon, as may be specified by such regulations.

(b) Discharge of property.

(1) Property double the amount of the liability. Subject to such regulations as the Secretary may prescribe, the Secretary may issue a certificate of discharge of any part of the property subject to any lien imposed under this chapter if the Secretary finds that the fair market value of that part of such property remaining subject to the lien is at least double the amount of the unsatisfied liability secured by such lien and the amount of all other liens upon such property which have priority over such lien.

(2) Part payment; interest of United States valueless. Subject to such regulations as the Secretary may prescribe, the Secretary may issue a certificate of discharge of any part of the property subject to the lien if—

(A) there is paid over to the Secretary in partial satisfaction of the liability secured by the lien an amount determined by the Secretary, which shall not be less than the value, as determined by the Secretary, of the interest of the United States in the part to be so discharged, or

(B) the Secretary determines at any time that the interest of the United States in the part to be so discharged has no value.

In determining the value of the interest of the United States in the part to be so discharged, the Secretary shall give consideration to the value of such part and to such liens thereon as have priority over the lien of the United States.

(3) Substitution of proceeds of sale. Subject to such regulations as the Secretary may prescribe, the Secretary may issue a certificate of discharge of any part of the property subject to the lien if such part of the property is sold and, pursuant to an agreement with the Secretary, the proceeds of such sale are to be held, as a fund subject to the liens and claims of the United States, in the same manner and with the same priority as such liens and claims had with respect to the discharged property.

(4) Right of substitution of value.

(A) In general. At the request of the owner of any property subject to any lien imposed by this chapter, the Secretary shall issue a certificate of discharge of such property if such owner—

(i) deposits with the Secretary an amount of money equal to the value of the interest of the United States (as determined by the Secretary) in the property; or

(ii) furnishes a bond acceptable to the Secretary in a like amount.

(B) Refund of deposit with interest and release of bond. The Secretary shall refund the amount so deposited (and shall pay interest at the overpayment rate under section 6621), and shall release such bond, to the extent that the Secretary determines that—

(i) the unsatisfied liability giving rise to the lien can be satisfied from a source other than such property; or

(ii) the value of the interest of the United States in the property is less than the Secretary's prior determination of such value.

(C) Use of deposit, etc., if action to contest lien not filed. If no action is filed under section 7426(a)(4) within the period prescribed therefor, the Secretary shall, within 60 days after the expiration of such period—

(i) apply the amount deposited, or collect on such bond, to the extent necessary to satisfy the unsatisfied liability secured by the lien; and

(ii) refund (with interest as described in subparagraph (B)) any portion of the amount deposited which is not used to satisfy such liability.

(D) Exception. Subparagraph (A) shall not apply if the owner of the property is the person whose unsatisfied liability gave rise to the lien.

(c) Estate or gift tax.

Subject to such regulations as the Secretary may prescribe, the Secretary may issue a certificate of discharge of any or all of the property subject to any lien imposed by section 6324 if the Secretary finds that the liability secured by such lien has been fully satisfied or provided for.

(d) Subordination of lien.

Subject to such regulations as the Secretary may prescribe, the Secretary may issue a certificate of subordination of any lien imposed by this chapter upon any part of the property subject to such lien if—

(1) there is paid over to the Secretary an amount equal to the amount of the lien or interest to which the certificate subordinates the lien of the United States,

(2) the Secretary believes that the amount realizable by the United States from the property to which the certificate relates, or from any other property subject to the lien, will ultimately be increased by reason of the issuance of such certificate and that the ultimate collection of the tax liability will be facilitated by such subordination, or

(3) in the case of any lien imposed by section 6324B, if the Secretary determines that the United States will be adequately secured after such subordination.

(e) Nonattachment of lien.

If the Secretary determines that, because of confusion of names or otherwise, any person (other than the person against whom the tax was assessed) is or may be injured by the appearance that a notice of lien filed under section 6323 refers to such person, the Secretary may issue a certificate that the lien does not attach to the property of such person.

(f) Effect of certificate.

(1) Conclusiveness. Except as provided in paragraphs (2) and (3), if a certificate is issued pursuant to this section by the Secretary and is filed in the same office as the notice of lien to which it relates (if such notice of lien has been filed) such certificate shall have the following effect:

(A) in the case of a certificate of release, such certificate shall be conclusive that the lien referred to in such certificate is extinguished;

(B) in the case of a certificate of discharge, such certificate shall be conclusive that the property covered by such certificate is discharged from the lien;

(C) in the case of subordination, such certificate shall be conclusive that the lien or interest to which the lien of the United States is subordinated is superior to the lien of the United States; and

(D) in the case of a certificate of nonattachment, such certificate shall be conclusive that the lien of the United States does not attach to the property of the person referred to in such certificate.

(2) Revocation of certificate of release or nonattachment. If the Secretary determines that a certificate of release or nonattachment of a lien imposed by section 6321 was issued erroneously or improvidently, or if a certificate of release of such lien was issued pursuant to a collateral agreement entered into in connection with a compromise under section 7122 which has been breached, and if the period of limitation on collection after assessment has not expired, the Secretary may revoke such certificate and reinstate the lien—

(A) by mailing notice of such revocation to the person against whom the tax was assessed at his last known address, and

(B) by filing notice of such revocation in the same office in which the notice of lien to which it relates was filed (if such notice of lien had been filed).

Such reinstated lien (i) shall be effective on the date notice of revocation is mailed to the taxpayer in accordance with the provisions of subparagraph (A), but not earlier than the date on which any required filing of notice of revocation is filed in accordance with the provisions of subparagraph (B), and (ii) shall have the same force and effect (as of such date), until the expiration of the period of limitation on collection after assessment, as a lien imposed by section 6321 (relating to lien for taxes).

(3) Certificates void under certain conditions. Notwithstanding any other provision of this subtitle, any lien imposed by this chapter shall attach to any property with respect to which a certificate of discharge has been issued if the person liable for the tax reacquires such property after such certificate has been issued.

(g) Filing of certificates and notices.

If a certificate or notice issued pursuant to this section may not be filed in the office designated by State law in which the notice of lien imposed by section 6321 is filed, such certificate or notice shall be effective if filed in the office of the clerk of the United States district court for the judicial district in which such office is situated.

(h) Cross reference.

For provisions relating to bonds, see chapter 73 (sec. 7101 and following).

In 1998, P.L. 105-206, Sec. 3106(a), added para. (b)(4), effective 7/22/98.

In 1982, P.L. 97-248, Sec. 348(a), substituted "Subject to such regulations as the Secretary may prescribe, the Secretary shall issue a certificate of release of any lien imposed with respect to any internal revenue tax not later than 30 days after the day on which—" for "Subject to such regulations as the Secretary may prescribe, the Secretary may issue a certificate of release of any lien imposed with respect to any internal revenue tax if—" preceding para. (a)(1), effective as provided in Sec. 348(b) of this Act which reads as follows:

"(b) Effective date.

"The amendment made by subsection (a) [of the Act] shall apply with respect to liens—

(1) which are filed after December 31, 1982,

(2) which are satisfied after December 31, 1982, or

(3) with respect to which the taxpayer after December 31, 1982, requests the Secretary of the Treasury or his delegate to issue a certificate of release on the grounds that the liability was satisfied or legally unenforceable."

In 1978, P.L. 95-600, Sec. 513(a), deleted "or" at the end of para. (d)(1) . . . substituted ", or" for the period at the end of para. (d)(2) . . . added new para. (d)(3), with respect to the estates of decedents dying after 12/31/76.

In 1976, P.L. 94-455, Sec. 1906(b)(13)(A), substituted "Secretary" for "Secretary or his delegate" each place it appeared in subsecs. (a) through (f), effective 2/1/77.

In 1966, P.L. 89-719, Sec. 103, amended, Code Sec. 6325 applicable from 11/2/66 regardless of when a lien or title of the U.S. arose or a lien or interest of any other person was acquired. For a special exception included in Sec. 114 of P.L. 89-719 see the note to Code Sec. 6323.

Prior to amendment, the Code Sec. read as follows:

"SEC. 6325. RELEASE OF LIEN OR PARTIAL DISCHARGE OF PROPERTY.

"(a) Release of lien.

"Subject to such rules or regulations as the Secretary or his delegate may prescribe, the Secretary or his delegate may issue a certificate of release of any lien imposed with respect to any internal revenue tax if—

"(1) Liability satisfied or unenforceable. The Secretary or his delegate finds that the liability for the amount assessed, together with all interest in respect thereof, has been fully satisfied or has become legally unenforceable; or

"(2) Bond accepted. There is furnished to the Secretary or his delegate and accepted by him a bond that is conditioned upon the payment of the amount assessed, together with all interest in respect thereof, within the time prescribed by law (including any extension of such time), and that is in accordance with such requirements relating to terms, conditions, and form of the bond and sureties thereon, as may be specified by such rules or regulations.

"(b) Partial discharge of property.

"(1) Property double the amount of the liability. Subject to such rules or regulations as the Secretary or his delegate may prescribe, the Secretary or his delegate may issue a certificate of discharge of any part of the property subject to any lien imposed under this chapter if the Secretary or his delegate finds that the fair market value of such property remaining subject to the lien is at least double the amount of the unsatisfied liability secured by such lien and the amount of all other liens upon such property which have priority to such lien.

"(2) Part payment or interest of United States valueless. Subject to such rules or regulations as the Secretary or his delegate may prescribe, the Secretary or his delegate may issue a certificate of discharge of any part of the property subject to the lien if—

"(A) there is paid over to the Secretary or his delegate in part satisfaction of the liability secured by the lien an amount determined by the Secretary or his delegate, which shall not be less than the value, as determined by the Secretary or his delegate, of the interest of the United States in the part to be so discharged, or

"(B) the Secretary or his delegate determines at any time that the interest of the United States in the part to be so discharged has no value.

"In determining the value of the interest of the United States in the part to be so discharged, the Secretary or his delegate shall give consideration to the fair market value of such part and to such liens thereon as have priority to the lien of the United States.

"(c) Estate or gift tax.

"Subject to such rules or regulations as the Secretary or his delegate may prescribe, the Secretary or his delegate may issue a certificate of discharge of any or all of the property subject to any lien imposed by section 6324 if the Secretary or his delegate finds that the liability secured by such lien has been fully satisfied or provided for.

"(d) Effect of certificate of release or discharge.

"A certificate of release or of discharge issued under this section shall be held conclusive that the lien upon the property covered by the certificate is extinguished.

"(e) Cross references.

"(1) For single bond complying with the requirements of both subsection (a)(2) and section 6165, see section 7102.

"(2) For other provisions relating to bonds, see generally chapter 73.

"(3) For provisions relating to suits to enforce lien, see section 7403.

"(4) For provisions relating to suits to clear title to realty, see section 7424."

In 1958, P.L. 85-866, Sec. 77, substituted in subsec. (a)(1) "or" for "," following "satisfied" and deleted ", or, in the case of the estate tax imposed by chapter 11 or the gift tax imposed by chapter 12, has been fully satisfied or provided for" following "unenforceable" . . . added subsec. (c) and redesignated former subsec. (c) as (d) and deleted preceding "discharge" in the catchline and text the word "partial"

redesignated former subsec. (d) as (e), effective 8/17/54.

Sec. 6326. Administrative appeal of liens.

(a) In general.

In such form and at such time as the Secretary shall prescribe by regulations, any person shall be allowed to appeal to the Secretary after the filing of a notice of a lien under this subchapter on the property or the rights to property of such person for a release of such lien alleging an error in the filing of the notice of such lien.

(b) Certificate of release.

If the Secretary determines that the filing of the notice of any lien was erroneous, the Secretary shall expeditiously (and, to the extent practicable, within 14 days after such determination) issue a certificate of release of such lien and shall include in such certificate a statement that such filing was erroneous.

In 1988, P.L. 100-647, Sec. 6238(a), added Code Sec. 6326, effective 60 days after the date regulations are issued [T.D. 8250, 5/5/89] under Sec. 6238(b) of this Act which reads as follows:

Code Sec. 6326 — Collection

"(b) Regulations. The Secretary of the Treasury or the Secretary's delegate shall prescribe the regulations necessary to implement the administrative appeal provided for in the amendment made by subsection (a) [Sec. 6238(a)] within 180 days after the date of the enactment of this Act."

Sec. 6327. Cross references.

(1) For lien in case of tax on distilled spirits, see section 5004.

(2) For exclusion of tax liability from discharge in cases under title 11 of the United States Code, see section 523 of such title 11.

(3) For recognition of tax liens in cases under title 11 of the United States Code, see sections 545 and 724 of such title 11.

(4) For collection of taxes in connection with plans for individuals with regular income in cases under title 11 of the United States Code, see section 1328 of such title 11.

(5) For provisions permitting the United States to be made party defendant in a proceeding in a State court for the foreclosure of a lien upon real estate where the United States may have a claim upon the premises involved, see section 2410 of Title 28 of the United States Code.

(6) For priority of lien of the United States in case of insolvency, see section 3713(a) of title 31, United States Code.

In 1988, P.L. 100-647, Sec. 6238(a), redesignated Code Sec. 6326 as Code Sec. 6327, effective 60 days after the date regulations are issued [T.D. 8250, 5/5/89] under Sec. 6238(b) of this Act which reads as follows:

"(b) Regulations. The Secretary of the Treasury or the Secretary's delegate shall prescribe the regulations necessary to implement the administrative appeal provided for in the amendment made by subsection (a) [Sec. 6238(a)] within 180 days after the date of the enactment of this Act [11/10/88]."

In 1982, P.L. 97-258, Sec. 3(f)(7), substituted "section 3713(a) of title 31, United States Code" for "R.S. 3466 (31 U.S.C. 191)" in para. (6), effective 9/13/82.

In 1980, P.L. 96-589, Sec. 6(i)(10)(A), deleted paras. (2), (3), (4) and (5) and added new paras. (2), (3) and (4)...Sec. (6)(i)(10)(B), redesignated paras. (6) and (4) as paras (5) and (6), effective 10/1/79, except for any proceeding under the Bankruptcy Act begun before 10/1/79. Sec. 7(g) of this Act provides:

"(g) Definitions.

"For purposes of this section—

"(1) Bankruptcy case. The term 'bankruptcy case' means any case under title 11 of the United States Code (as recodified by P.L. 95-598).

"(2) Similar judicial proceeding. The term 'similar judicial proceeding' means a receivership, foreclosure, or similar proceeding in a Federal or State court (as modified by section 368(a)(3)(D) of the Internal Revenue Code of 1954)."

Prior to deletion, paras. (2), (3), (4) and (5) read as follows:

"(2) For exclusion of tax liability from discharge in bankruptcy, see section 17 of the Bankruptcy Act, as amended (11 U.S.C. 35).

"(3) For limit on amount allowed in bankruptcy proceedings on debts owing to the United States, see section 57(j) of the Bankruptcy Act, as amended (11 U.S.C. 93).

"(4) For recognition of tax liens in proceedings under the Bankruptcy Act, see section 67(b) and (c) of that act, as amended (11 U.S.C. 107).

"(5) For collection of taxes in connection with wage earners' plans in bankruptcy courts, see section 680 of the Bankruptcy Act, as added by the act of June 22, 1938 (11 U.S.C. 1080)."

In 1976, P.L. 94-455, Sec. 1906(a)(20)(A), deleted "52 Stat. 851;" before "11 U.S.C. 35" in para. (2)...Sec. 1906(a)(20)(B), deleted "52 Stat. 867;" before "11 U.S.C. 93" in para. (3)...Sec. 1906(a)(2)(C), deleted "52 Stat. 877-877;" before "11 U.S.C. 107" in para. (4)...Sec. 1906(a)(20)(D), deleted "52 Stat. 938;" before "11 U.S.C. 1080" in para. (5), effective 2/1/77.

Subchapter D.—Seizure of Property for Collection of Taxes

Part

I. Due process for collections.

II. Levy.

In 1998, P.L. 105-206, Sec. 3401(b), redesignated Subchapter D as Part II and added Part I.

PART I.—DUE PROCESS FOR COLLECTIONS

Sec.

6330. Notice and opportunity for hearing before levy

In 1998, P.L. 105-206, Sec. 3401(a), added Part I

Sec. 6330. Notice and opportunity for hearing before levy.

(a) Requirement of notice before levy.

(1) In general. No levy may be made on any property or right to property of any person unless the Secretary has notified such person in writing of their right to a hearing under this section before such levy is made. Such notice shall be required only once for the taxable period to which the unpaid tax specified in paragraph (3)(A) relates.

(2) Time and method for notice. The notice required under paragraph (1) shall be—

(A) given in person;

(B) left at the dwelling or usual place of business of such person; or

(C) sent by certified or registered mail, return receipt requested, to such person's last known address;

not less than 30 days before the day of the first levy with respect to the amount of the unpaid tax for the taxable period.

(3) Information included with notice. The notice required under paragraph (1) shall include in simple and nontechnical terms—

(A) the amount of unpaid tax;

(B) the right of the person to request a hearing during the 30-day period under paragraph (2); and

(C) the proposed action by the Secretary and the rights of the person with respect to such action, including a brief statement which sets forth—

(i) the provisions of this title relating to levy and sale of property;

(ii) the procedures applicable to the levy and sale of property under this title;

(iii) the administrative appeals available to the taxpayer with respect to such levy and sale and the procedures relating to such appeals;

(iv) the alternatives available to taxpayers which could prevent levy on property (including installment agreements under section 6159); and

(v) the provisions of this title and procedures relating to redemption of property and release of liens on property.

(b) Right to fair hearing.

(1) In general. If the person requests a hearing in writing under subsection (a)(3)(B) and states the grounds for the requested hearing, such hearing shall be held by the Internal Revenue Service Office of Appeals.

(2) One hearing per period. A person shall be entitled to only one hearing under this section with respect to the taxable period to which the unpaid tax specified in subsection (a)(3)(A) relates.

(3) Impartial officer. The hearing under this subsection shall be conducted by an officer or employee who has had no prior involvement with respect to the unpaid tax specified in subsection (a)(3)(A) before the first hearing under this section or section 6320. A taxpayer may waive the requirement of this paragraph.

(c) Matters considered at hearing.

In the case of any hearing conducted under this section—

(1) Requirement of investigation. The appeals officer shall at the hearing obtain verification from the Secretary

that the requirements of any applicable law or administrative procedure have been met.

(2) **Issues at hearing.**

(A) In general. The person may raise at the hearing any relevant issue relating to the unpaid tax or the proposed levy, including—

(i) appropriate spousal defenses;

(ii) challenges to the appropriateness of collection actions; and

(iii) offers of collection alternatives, which may include the posting of a bond, the substitution of other assets, an installment agreement, or an offer-in-compromise.

(B) Underlying liability. The person may also raise at the hearing challenges to the existence or amount of the underlying tax liability for any tax period if the person did not receive any statutory notice of deficiency for such tax liability or did not otherwise have an opportunity to dispute such tax liability.

(3) **Basis for the determination.** The determination by an appeals officer under this subsection shall take into consideration—

(A) the verification presented under paragraph (1);

(B) the issues raised under paragraph (2); and

(C) whether any proposed collection action balances the need for the efficient collection of taxes with the legitimate concern of the person that any collection action be no more intrusive than necessary.

(4) **Certain issues precluded.** An issue may not be raised at the hearing if—

(A)(i) the issue was raised and considered at a previous hearing under section 6320 or in any other previous administrative or judicial proceeding; and

(ii) the person seeking to raise the issue participated meaningfully in such hearing or proceeding; or

(B) the issue meets the requirement of clause (i) or (ii) of section 6702(b)(2)(A).

This paragraph shall not apply to any issue with respect to which subsection (d)(2)(B) applies.

(d) **Proceeding after hearing.**

(1) **Judicial review of determination.** The person may, within 30 days of a determination under this section, appeal such determination to the Tax Court (and the Tax Court shall have jurisdiction with respect to such matter).

(2) **Jurisdiction retained at IRS Office of Appeals.** The Internal Revenue Service Office of Appeals shall retain jurisdiction with respect to any determination made under this section, including subsequent hearings requested by the person who requested the original hearing on issues regarding—

(A) collection actions taken or proposed with respect to such determination; and

(B) after the person has exhausted all administrative remedies, a change in circumstances with respect to such person which affects such determination.

(e) **Suspension of collections and statute of limitations.**

(1) **In general.** Except as provided in paragraph (2), if a hearing is requested under subsection (a)(3)(B), the levy actions which are the subject of the requested hearing and the running of any period of limitations under section 6502 (relating to collection after assessment), section 6531 (relating to criminal prosecutions), or section 6532 (relating to other suits) shall be suspended for the period during which such hearing, and appeals therein, are pending. In no event shall any such period expire before the 90th day after the day on which there is a final determination in such hearing. Notwithstanding the provisions of section 7421(a), the beginning of a levy or proceeding during the time the suspension under this paragraph is in force may be enjoined by a proceeding in the proper court, including the Tax Court. The Tax Court shall have no jurisdiction under this paragraph to enjoin any action or proceeding unless a timely appeal has been filed under subsection (d)(1) and then only in respect of the unpaid tax or proposed levy to which the determination being appealed relates.

(2) **Levy upon appeal.** Paragraph (1) shall not apply to a levy action while an appeal is pending if the underlying tax liability is not at issue in the appeal and the court determines that the Secretary has shown good cause not to suspend the levy.

(f) **Exceptions.**

If—

(1) the Secretary has made a finding under the last sentence of section 6331(a) that the collection of tax is in jeopardy,

(2) the Secretary has served a levy on a State to collect a Federal tax liability from a State tax refund,

(3) the Secretary has served a disqualified employment tax levy, or

(4) the Secretary has served a Federal contractor levy

this section shall not apply, except that the taxpayer shall be given the opportunity for the hearing described in this section within a reasonable period of time after the levy.

(g) **Frivolous requests for hearing, etc.**

Notwithstanding any other provision of this section, if the Secretary determines that any portion of a request for a hearing under this section or section 6320 meets the requirement of clause (i) or (ii) of section 6702(b)(2)(A), then the Secretary may treat such portion as if it were never submitted and such portion shall not be subject to any further administrative or judicial review.

(h) **Definitions related to exceptions.**

For purposes of subsection (f)—

(1) **Disqualified employment tax levy.** A disqualified employment tax levy is any levy in connection with the collection of employment taxes for any taxable period if the person subject to the levy (or any predecessor thereof) requested a hearing under this section with respect to unpaid employment taxes arising in the most recent 2-year period before the beginning of the taxable period with respect to which the levy is served. For purposes of the preceding sentence, the term "employment taxes" means any taxes under chapter 21, 22, 23, or 24.

(2) **Federal contractor levy.** A Federal contractor levy is any levy if the person whose property is subject to the levy (or any predecessor thereof) is a Federal contractor.

In 2010, P.L. 111-240, Sec. 2104(a), struck out "or" at the end of para. (f)(2), added "or" at the end of para. (f)(3), and added para. (f)(4) . . . Sec. 2104(b)(1), amended subsec. (h). . . . Sec. 2104(b)(2), added para. (h)(2) . . . Sec. 2104(c), substituted "exceptions" for "jeopardy and State refund collection" in the heading of subsec. (f), effetive for levies issued after 9/27/2010.

Prior to amendment subsec. (h) read as follows:

"(h) Disqualified employment tax levy.

"For purposes of subsection (f), a disqualified employment tax levy is any levy in connection with the collection of employment taxes for any taxable period if the person subject to the levy (or any predecessor thereof) requested a hearing under this section with respect to unpaid employment taxes arising in the most recent 2-year period before the beginning of the taxable period with respect to which the levy is served. For purposes of the preceding sentence, the term 'employment taxes' means any taxes under chapter 21, 22, 23, or 24."

In 2007, P.L. 110-28, Sec. 8243(a)(1), substituted a comma for "; or" at the end of para. (f)(1) . . . Sec. 8243(a)(2), added "or" at the end of para. (f)(2) . . . Sec. 8243(a)(3), added para. (f)(3) . . . Sec. 8243(b), added subsec. (h), effective for levies served on or after the date that is 120 days after 5/25/2007.

Code Sec. 6330   Collection

In **2006,** P.L. 109-432, Sec. 407(b)(1), added subsec. (g)... Sec. 407(b)(2)(A), redesignated subpara. (c)(4)(A) as clause (c)(4)(A)(i)... Sec. 407(b)(2)(B), redesignated subpara. (c)(4)(B) as clause (c)(4)(A)(ii)... Sec. 407(b)(2)(C), substituted "; or" for the period at the end of the first sentence of para. (c)(4)... Sec. 407(b)(2)(D), added subpara. (c)(4)(B)... Sec. 407(b)(3), substituted "in writing under subsection (a)(3)(B) and states the grounds for the requested hearing" for "under subsection (a)(3)(B)" in para. (b)(1), effective for submissions made and issues raised after the date on which the Secretary first prescribes a list under Code Sec. 6702(c), as amended by Sec. 407(a) of this Act.

—P.L. 109-280, Sec. 855(a), amended para. (d)(1), effective for determinations made after the date which is 60 days after 8/17/2006.

Prior to amendment, (d)(1) read as follows:

"(1) Judicial review of determination. The person may, within 30 days of a determination under this section, appeal such determination—

"(A) to the Tax Court (and the Tax court shall have jurisdiction with respect to such matter); or

"(B) if the Tax Court does not have jurisdiction of the underlying tax liability, to the district court of the United States.

"If a court determines that the appeal was to an incorrect court, a person shall have 30 days after the court determination to file such appeal with the correct court."

In **2000,** P.L. 106-554, Sec. 1(a)(7), [which enacted into law Sec. 313(b)(2)(A) of P.L. 106-554] added the last sentence in para. (e)(1), effective 12/21/2000.

—P.L. 106-554, Sec. 1(a)(7), [which enacted into law Sec. 313(d) of P.L. 106-554] substituted "with respect to" for "to hear" in subpara. (d)(1)(A), effective for collection actions initiated after 1/18/99.

In **1998,** P.L. 105-206, Sec. 3401(b), added Code Sec. 6330, effective for collection actions initiated after the date which is 180 days after 7/22/98.

PART II.—LEVY

Sec.

6331. Levy and distraint.
6332. Surrender of property subject to levy.
6333. Production of books.
6334. Property exempt from levy.
6335. Sale of seized property.
6336. Sale of perishable goods.
6337. Redemption of property.
6338. Certificate of sale; deed of real property.
6339. Legal effect of certificate of sale of personal property and deed of real property.
6340. Records of sale.
6341. Expense of levy and sale.
6342. Application of proceeds of levy.
6343. Authority to release levy and return property.
6344. Cross references.

In **1998,** P.L. 105-206, Sec. 3401(b), redesignated the Code Sections in Subchapter D as Part II of Subchapter D.

In **1966,** added "and return property" in item 6343.

Sec. 6331. Levy and distraint.
(a) Authority of Secretary.

If any person liable to pay any tax neglects or refuses to pay the same within 10 days after notice and demand, it shall be lawful for the Secretary to collect such tax (and such further sum as shall be sufficient to cover the expenses of the levy) by levy upon all property and rights to property (except such property as is exempt under section 6334) belonging to such person or on which there is a lien provided in this chapter for the payment of such tax. Levy may be made upon the accrued salary or wages of any officer, employee, or elected official, of the United States, the District of Columbia, or any agency or instrumentality of the United States or the District of Columbia, by serving a notice of levy on the employer (as defined in section 3401(d)) of such officer, employee, or elected official. If the Secretary makes a finding that the collection of such tax is in jeopardy, notice and demand for immediate payment of such tax may be made by the Secretary and, upon failure or refusal to pay such tax, collection thereof by levy shall be lawful without regard to the 10-day period provided in this section.

(b) Seizure and sale of property.

The term "levy" as used in this title includes the power of distraint and seizure by any means. Except as otherwise provided in subsection (e), a levy shall extend only to property possessed and obligations existing at the time thereof. In any case in which the Secretary may levy upon property or rights to property, he may seize and sell such property or rights to property (whether real or personal, tangible or intangible).

(c) Successive seizures.

Whenever any property or right to property upon which levy has been made by virtue of subsection (a) is not sufficient to satisfy the claim of the United States for which levy is made, the Secretary may, thereafter, and as often as may be necessary, proceed to levy in like manner upon any other property liable to levy of the person against whom such claim exists, until the amount due from him, together with all expenses, is fully paid.

(d) Requirement of notice before levy.

(1) In general. Levy may be made under subsection (a) upon the salary or wages or other property of any person with respect to any unpaid tax only after the Secretary has notified such person in writing of his intention to make such levy.

(2) 30-day requirement. The notice required under paragraph (1) shall be—

(A) given in person,

(B) left at the dwelling or usual place of business of such person, or

(C) sent by certified or registered mail to such person's last known address,

no less than 30 days before the day of the levy.

(3) Jeopardy. Paragraph (1) shall not apply to a levy if the Secretary has made a finding under the last sentence of subsection (a) that the collection of tax is in jeopardy.

(4) Information included with notice. The notice required under paragraph (1) shall include a brief statement which sets forth in simple and nontechnical terms—

(A) the provisions of this title relating to levy and sale of property,

(B) the procedures applicable to the levy and sale of property under this title,

(C) the administrative appeals available to the taxpayer with respect to such levy and sale and the procedures relating to such appeals,

(D) the alternatives available to taxpayers which could prevent levy on the property (including installment agreements under section 6159),

(E) the provisions of this title relating to redemption of property and release of liens on property, and

(F) the procedures applicable to the redemption of property and the release of a lien on property under this title.

(e) Continuing levy on salary and wages.

The effect of a levy on salary or wages payable to or received by a taxpayer shall be continuous from the date such levy is first made until such levy is released under section 6343.

(f) Uneconomical levy.

No levy may be made on any property if the amount of the expenses which the Secretary estimates (at the time of levy) would be incurred by the Secretary with respect to the levy and sale of such property exceeds the fair market value of such property at the time of levy.

(g) Levy on appearance date of summons.

(1) In general. No levy may be made on the property of any person on any day on which such person (or officer

3,674

or employee of such person) is required to appear in response to a summons issued by the Secretary for the purpose of collecting any underpayment of tax.

(2) **No application in case of jeopardy.** This subsection shall not apply if the Secretary finds that the collection of tax is in jeopardy.

(h) **Continuing levy on certain payments.**

(1) **In general.** If the Secretary approves a levy under this subsection, the effect of such levy on specified payments to or received by a taxpayer shall be continuous from the date such levy is first made until such levy is released. Notwithstanding section 6334, such continuous levy shall attach to up to 15 percent of any specified payment due to the taxpayer.

(2) **Specified payment.** For the purposes of paragraph (1), the term "specified payment" means—

(A) any Federal payment other than a payment for which eligibility is based on the income or assets (or both) of a payee,

(B) any payment described in paragraph (4), (7), (9), or (11) of section 6334(a), and

(C) any annuity or pension payment under the Railroad Retirement Act or benefit under the Railroad Unemployment Insurance Act.

(3) **Increase in levy for certain payments.** Paragraph (1) shall be applied by substituting "100 percent" for "15 percent" in the case of any specified payment due to a vendor of goods or services sold or leased to the Federal Government.

(i) **No levy during pendency of proceedings for refund of divisible tax.**

(1) **In general.** No levy may be made under subsection (a) on the property or rights to property of any person with respect to any unpaid divisible tax during the pendency of any proceeding brought by such person in a proper Federal trial court for the recovery of any portion of such divisible tax which was paid by such person if—

(A) the decision in such proceeding would be res judicata with respect to such unpaid tax; or

(B) such person would be collaterally estopped from contesting such unpaid tax by reason of such proceeding.

(2) **Divisible tax.** For purposes of paragraph (1), the term "divisible tax" means—

(A) any tax imposed by subtitle C; and

(B) the penalty imposed by section 6672 with respect to any such tax.

(3) **Exceptions.**

(A) Certain unpaid taxes. This subsection shall not apply with respect to any unpaid tax if—

(i) the taxpayer files a written notice with the Secretary which waives the restriction imposed by this subsection on levy with respect to such tax; or

(ii) the Secretary finds that the collection of such tax is in jeopardy.

(B) Certain levies. This subsection shall not apply to—

(i) any levy to carry out an offset under section 6402; and

(ii) any levy which was first made before the date that the applicable proceeding under this subsection commenced.

(4) **Limitation on collection activity; authority to enjoin collection.**

(A) Limitation on collection. No proceeding in court for the collection of any unpaid tax to which paragraph (1) applies shall be begun by the Secretary during the pendency of a proceeding under such paragraph. This subparagraph shall not apply to—

(i) any counterclaim in a proceeding under such paragraph; or

(ii) any proceeding relating to a proceeding under such paragraph.

(B) Authority to enjoin. Notwithstanding section 7421(a), a levy or collection proceeding prohibited by this subsection may be enjoined (during the period such prohibition is in force) by the court in which the proceeding under paragraph (1) is brought.

(5) **Suspension of statute of limitations on collection.** The period of limitations under section 6502 shall be suspended for the period during which the Secretary is prohibited under this subsection from making a levy.

(6) **Pendency of proceeding.** For purposes of this subsection, a proceeding is pending beginning on the date such proceeding commences and ending on the date that a final order or judgment from which an appeal may be taken is entered in such proceeding.

(j) **No levy before investigation of status of property.**

(1) **In general.** For purposes of applying the provisions of this subchapter, no levy may be made on any property or right to property which is to be sold under section 6335 until a thorough investigation of the status of such property has been completed.

(2) **Elements in investigation.** For purposes of paragraph (1), an investigation of the status of any property shall include—

(A) a verification of the taxpayer's liability;

(B) the completion of an analysis under subsection (f);

(C) the determination that the equity in such property is sufficient to yield net proceeds from the sale of such property to apply to such liability; and

(D) a thorough consideration of alternative collection methods.

(k) **No levy while certain offers pending or installment agreement pending or in effect.**

(1) **Offer-in-compromise pending.** No levy may be made under subsection (a) on the property or rights to property of any person with respect to any unpaid tax—

(A) during the period that an offer-in-compromise by such person under section 7122 of such unpaid tax is pending with the Secretary; and

(B) if such offer is rejected by the Secretary, during the 30 days thereafter (and, if an appeal of such rejection is filed within such 30 days, during the period that such appeal is pending).

For purposes of subparagraph (A), an offer is pending beginning on the date the Secretary accepts such offer for processing.

(2) **Installment agreements.** No levy may be made under subsection (a) on the property or rights to property of any person with respect to any unpaid tax—

(A) during the period that an offer by such person for an installment agreement under section 6159 for payment of such unpaid tax is pending with the Secretary;

(B) if such offer is rejected by the Secretary, during the 30 days thereafter (and, if an appeal of such rejection is filed within such 30 days, during the period that such appeal is pending);

(C) during the period that such an installment agreement for payment of such unpaid tax is in effect; and

(D) if such agreement is terminated by the Secretary, during the 30 days thereafter (and, if an appeal of such termination is filed within such 30 days, during the period that such appeal is pending).

(3) Certain rules to apply. Rules similar to the rules of—

(A) paragraphs (3) and (4) of subsection (i), and

(B) except in the case of paragraph (2)(C), paragraph (5) of subsection (i),

shall apply for purposes of this subsection.

(l) Cross references.

(1) For provisions relating to jeopardy, see subchapter A of chapter 70.

(2) For proceedings applicable to sale of seized property, see section 6335.

(3) For release and notice of release of levy, see section 6343.

In **2004**, P.L. 108-357, Sec. 887(a), added para. (h)(3), effective 10/22/2004.
In **2002**, P.L. 107-147, Sec. 416(e)(1), amended para. (k)(3), effective 3/9/2002. Prior to amendment, para. (k)(3) read as follows:
  "(3) Certain rules to apply. Rules similar to the rules of paragraphs (3) and (4) of subsection (i) shall apply for purposes of this subsection."
In **2000**, P.L. 106-554, Sec. 1(a)(7), [which enacted into law Sec. 313(b)(3) of P.L. 106-554] substituted "(3) and (4)" for "(3), (4), and (5)" in para. (k)(3), effective 12/21/2000.
In **1998**, P.L. 105-206, Sec. 3433(a), redesignated subsec. (i) as (j) and added subsec. (i), effective for unpaid tax attributable to tax. periods begin. after 12/31/98.
— P.L. 105-206, Sec. 3444(a), redesignated subsec. (j) [as redesignated by Sec. 3433(a) of this Act, see above] as (k) and added subsec. (j), effective 7/22/98.
— P.L. 105-206, Sec. 3462(b), redesignated subsec. (k) [as redesignated by Sec. 3444(a) of this Act, see above] as (l) and added subsec. (k), effective for offers-in-compromise pending on or made after 12/31/99.
— P.L. 105-206, Sec. 6010(f), substituted "If the Secretary approves a levy under this subsection, the effect of such levy" for "The effect of a levy" in para. (h)(1), effective for levies issued after 8/5/97.
In **1997**, P.L. 105-34, Sec. 1024(a)(1), redesignated subsec. (h) as (i)... Sec. 1024(a)(2), added a new subsec. (h), effective for levies issued after 8/5/97.
In **1988**, P.L. 100-647, Sec. 6236(a)(1), substituted "30 days" for "10 days" in para. (d)(2)... Sec. 6236(a)(2), substituted "30-day" for "10-day" in heading of para. (d)(2)... Sec. 6236(a)(3), added para. (d)(4)... Sec. 6236(b)(1),... Sec. 6236(b)(2), added para. (f)(3)... Sec. 6236(d), redesignated subsec. (f) as subsec. (h) and added new subsecs. (f) and (g), effective for levies issued on or after 7/1/89.
Prior to amendment, subsec. (e) read as follows:
  "(e) Continuing levy on salary and wages.
  "(1) Effect of levy. The effect of a levy on salary or wages payable to or received by a taxpayer shall be continuous from the date such levy is first made until the liability out of which such levy arose is satisfied or becomes unenforceable by reason of lapse of time.
  "(2) Release and notice of release. With respect to a levy described in paragraph (1), the Secretary shall promptly release the levy when the liability out of which such levy arose is satisfied or becomes unenforceable by reason of lapse of time, and shall promptly notify the person upon whom such levy was made that such levy has been released."
In **1984**, P.L. 98-369, Sec. 714(o), substituted "subsection (e)" for "subsection (d)(3)" in subsec. (b), effective for levies made after 12/31/82.
In **1982**, P.L. 97-248, Sec. 349(a), amended subsec. (d), redesignated subsec. (e) as subsec. (f), and added new subsec. (e), effective for levies made after 12/31/82. Prior to amendment, subsec. (d) read as follows:
  "(d) Salary and wages.
  "(1) In general. Levy may be made under subsection (a) upon the salary or wages of an individual with respect to any unpaid tax only after the Secretary has notified such individual in writing of his intention to make such levy. Such notice shall be given in person, left at the dwelling or usual place of business of such individual, or shall be sent by mail to such individual's last known address, no less than 10 days before the day of levy.
  "(2) Jeopardy. Paragraph (1) shall not apply to a levy if the Secretary has made a finding under the last sentence of subsection (a) that the collection of tax is in jeopardy.
  "(3) Continuing levy on salary and wages.
  "(A) Effect of levy. The effect of a levy on salary or wages payable to or received by a taxpayer shall be continuous from the date such levy is first made until the liability out of which such levy arose is satisfied or becomes unenforceable by reason of lapse of time.
  "(B) Release and notice of release. With respect to a levy described in subparagraph (A), the Secretary shall promptly release the levy when the liability out of which such levy arose is satisfied or becomes unenforceable by reason of lapse of time, and shall promptly notify the person upon whom such levy was made that such levy has been released."
In **1976**, P.L. 94-528, Sec. 2(c), changed the effective date for amendments made by Sec. 1209(d) of P.L. 94-455 from, effective for levies made after 12/31/76 to, effective for levies made after 2/28/77, see below.
— P.L. 94-455, Sec. 1209(d)(1), added para. (d)(3)... Sec. 1209(d)(2), substituted "Except as otherwise provided in subsection (d)(3), a levy" for "A levy" in the second sentence of subsec. (b), for levies made... Sec. 1209(d)(4), deleted the last sentence of para. (d)(1), effective [as amended by Sec. 2(c) of P.L. 94-528, see above] for levies made after 2/28/77.
Prior to deletion, the last sentence of para. (d)(1) read as follows:
  "No additional notice shall be required in the case of successive levies with respect to such tax."
— P.L. 94-455, Sec. 1906(b)(13)(A), substituted "Secretary" for "Secretary or his delegate" each place it appeared in Code Sec. 6331, effective 2/1/77.
In **1971**, P.L. 92-178, Sec. 211, redesignated subsec. (d) as (e), and added new subsec. (d), effective for levies made after 3/31/72.
In **1966**, P.L. 89-719, Sec. 104(a), added the second sentence of subsec. (b), effective after 11/2/66, regardless of when a lien or title of the U.S. arose or a lien or interest of any other person was acquired.

Sec. 6332. Surrender of property subject to levy.

(a) Requirement.

Except as otherwise provided in this section, any person in possession of (or obligated with respect to) property or rights to property subject to levy upon which a levy has been made shall, upon demand of the Secretary, surrender such property or rights (or discharge such obligation) to the Secretary, except such part of the property or rights as is, at the time of such demand, subject to an attachment or execution under any judicial process.

(b) Special rule for life insurance and endowment contracts.

(1) In general. A levy on an organization with respect to a life insurance or endowment contract issued by such organization shall, without necessity for the surrender of the contract document, constitute a demand by the Secretary for payment of the amount described in paragraph (2) and the exercise of the right of the person against whom the tax is assessed to the advance of such amount. Such organization shall pay over such amount 90 days after service of notice of levy. Such notice shall include a certification by the Secretary that a copy of such notice has been mailed to the person against whom the tax is assessed at his last known address.

(2) Satisfaction of levy. Such levy shall be deemed to be satisfied if such organization pays over to the Secretary the amount which the person against whom the tax is assessed could have had advanced to him by such organization on the date prescribed in paragraph (1) for the satisfaction of such levy, increased by the amount of any advance (including contractual interest thereon) made to such person on or after the date such organization had actual notice or knowledge (within the meaning of section 6323(i)(1)) of the existence of the lien with respect to which such levy is made, other than an advance (including contractual interest thereon) made automatically to maintain such contract in force under an agreement entered into before such organization had such notice or knowledge.

(3) Enforcement proceedings. The satisfaction of a levy under paragraph (2) shall be without prejudice to any civil action for the enforcement of any lien imposed by this title with respect to such contract.

(c) Special rule for banks.

Any bank (as defined in section 408(n)) shall surrender (subject to an attachment or execution under judicial process) any deposits (including interest thereon) in such bank only after 21 days after service of levy.

(d) Enforcement of levy.

(1) Extent of personal liability. Any person who fails or refuses to surrender any property or rights to property, subject to levy, upon demand by the Secretary, shall be liable in his own person and estate to the United States in a sum equal to the value of the property or rights not so surrendered, but not exceeding the amount of taxes for the collection of which such levy has been made, together with costs and interest on such sum at the underpayment rate established under section 6621 from the date of such levy (or, in the case of a levy described in section 6331(d)(3), from the date such person would otherwise have been obligated to pay over such amounts to the taxpayer). Any amount (other than costs) recovered under this paragraph shall be credited against the tax liability for the collection of which such levy was made.

(2) Penalty for violation. In addition to the personal liability imposed by paragraph (1), if any person required to surrender property or rights to property fails or refuses to surrender such property or rights to property without reasonable cause, such person shall be liable for a penalty equal to 50 percent of the amount recoverable under paragraph (1). No part of such penalty shall be credited against the tax liability for the collection of which such levy was made.

(e) Effect of honoring levy.

Any person in possession of (or obligated with respect to) property or rights to property subject to levy upon which a levy has been made who, upon demand by the Secretary, surrenders such property or rights to property (or discharges such obligation) to the Secretary (or who pays a liability under subsection (d)(1)) shall be discharged from any obligation or liability to the delinquent taxpayer and any other person with respect to such property or rights to property arising from such surrender or payment.

(f) Person defined.

The term "person," as used in subsection (a), includes an officer or employee of a corporation or a member or employee of a partnership, who as such officer, employee, or member is under a duty to surrender the property or rights to property, or to discharge the obligation.

In **1990,** P.L. 101-508, Sec. 11704(a)(27), substituted "this section" for "subsections (b) and (c)" in subsec. (a), effective 11/5/90.

In **1988,** P.L. 100-647, Sec. 1015(t)(1), added "and any other person" after "delinquent taxpayer" and deleted the last sentence of subsec. (d), effective for levies issued after 11/10/88.
Prior to deletion, the last sentence of subsec. (d) read as follows:
"In the case of a levy which is satisfied pursuant to subsection (b), such organization shall also be discharged from any obligation or liability to any beneficiary arising from such surrender or payment."
—P.L. 100-647, Sec. 6236(e)(1), redesignated subsecs. (c), (d) and (e) as subsecs. (d), (e) and (f) and added new subsec. (c)... Sec. 6236(e)(2)(A), substituted "subsections (b) and (c)" for "subsection (b)", in subsec. (a)... Sec. 6236(e)(2)(B), substituted "subsection (d)(1)" for "subsection (c)(1)" in subsec. (e), effective for levies issued on or after 7/1/89.

In **1986,** P.L. 99-514, Sec. 1511(c)(9), substituted "the underpayment rate" for "an annual rate" in para. (c)(1), effective for purposes of determining interest for periods after 12/31/86.

In **1976,** P.L. 94-528, Sec. 2(c), changed the effective date for amendments made by Sec. 1209(d)(3) of P.L. 94-455, from effective for levies made after 12/31/76, to effective for levies made after 2/28/77, see below.
—P.L. 94-455, Sec. 1209(d)(3), substituted "from the date of such levy (or, in the case of a levy described in section 6331(d)(3), from the date such person would otherwise have been obligated to pay over such amounts to the taxpayer)" for "from the date of such levy" in para. (c)(1), effective [as amended by Sec. 2(c) of P.L. 94-528, see above] for levies made after 2/28/77.
—P.L. 94-455, Sec. 1906(b)(13)(A), substituted "Secretary" for "Secretary or his delegate" each place it appeared in Code Sec. 6332, effective 2/1/77.

In **1975,** P.L. 93-625, Sec. 7(a)(2)(D), substituted "an annual rate established under section 6621" for "the rate of 6 percent per annum" in para. (c)(1), effective with respect to amounts outstanding on or arising after 7/1/75.

In **1966,** P.L. 89-719, Sec. 104(a), substituted "Except as otherwise provided in subsection (b), any person" for "Any person" in subsec. (a)... Sec. 104(b), amended subsec. (b), redesignated subsec. (c) as subsec. (e), and added new subsecs. (c) and (d), effective after 11/2/66, regardless of when a lien or title of the U.S. arose or when the lien or interest of any other person was acquired. For a special exception included in Sec. 114 of P.L. 89-719 see the note to Code Sec. 6323.

Prior to amendment, subsec. (b) read as follows:
"(b) Penalty for violation.
"Any person who fails or refuses to surrender as required by subsection (a) any property or rights to property, subject to levy, upon demand by the Secretary or his delegate, shall be liable in his own person and estate to the United States in a sum equal to the value of the property or rights not so surrendered, but not exceeding the amount of the taxes for the collection of which such levy has been made, together with costs and interest on such sum at the rate of 6 percent per annum from the date of such levy."

Sec. 6333. Production of books.

If a levy has been made or is about to be made on any property, or right to property, any person having custody or control of any books or records, containing evidence or statements relating to the property or right to property subject to levy, shall, upon demand of the Secretary, exhibit such books or records to the Secretary.

In **1976,** P.L. 94-455, Sec. 1906(b)(13)(A), substituted "Secretary" for "Secretary or his delegate" each place it appeared in Code Sec. 6333, effective 2/1/77.

Sec. 6334. Property exempt from levy.
(a) Enumeration.

There shall be exempt from levy—

(1) Wearing apparel and school books. Such items of wearing apparel and such school books as are necessary for the taxpayer or for members of his family;

(2) Fuel, provisions, furniture, and personal effects. So much of the fuel, provisions, furniture, and personal effects in the taxpayer's household, and of the arms for personal use, livestock, and poultry of the taxpayer, as does not exceed $6,250 in value;

(3) Books and tools of a trade, business, or profession. So many of the books and tools necessary for the trade, business, or profession of the taxpayer as do not exceed in the aggregate $3,125 in value;

(4) Unemployment benefits. Any amount payable to an individual with respect to his unemployment (including any portion thereof payable with respect to dependents) under an unemployment compensation law of the United States, of any State, or of the District of Columbia or of the Commonwealth of Puerto Rico.

(5) Undelivered mail. Mail, addressed to any person, which has not been delivered to the addressee.

(6) Certain annuity and pension payments. Annuity or pension payments under the Railroad Retirement Act, benefits under the Railroad Unemployment Insurance Act, special pension payments received by a person whose name has been entered on the Army, Navy, Air Force, and Coast Guard Medal of Honor roll (38 U.S.C. 562), and annuities based on retired or retainer pay under chapter 73 of title 10 of the United States Code.

(7) Workmen's compensation. Any amount payable to an individual as workmen's compensation (including any portion thereof payable with respect to dependents) under a workmen's compensation law of the United States, any State, the District of Columbia, or the Commonwealth of Puerto Rico.

(8) Judgments for support of minor children. If the taxpayer is required by judgment of a court of competent jurisdiction, entered prior to the date of levy, to contribute to the support of his minor children, so much of his salary, wages, or other income as is necessary to comply with such judgment.

(9) Minimum exemption for wages, salary, and other income. Any amount payable to or received by an individual as wages or salary for personal services, or as income derived from other sources, during any period, to the extent that the total of such amounts payable to or received by him during such period does not exceed the applicable exempt amount determined under subsection (d).

(10) Certain service-connected disability payments. Any amount payable to an individual as a service-connected (within the meaning of section 101(16) of title 38, United States Code) disability benefit under—

(A) subchapter II, III, IV, V, or VI of chapter 11 of such title 38, or

(B) chapter 13, 21, 23, 31, 32, 34, 35, 37, or 39 of such title 38.

(11) Certain public assistance payments. Any amount payable to an individual as a recipient of public assistance under—

(A) title IV or title XVI (relating to supplemental security income for the aged, blind, and disabled) of the Social Security Act, or

(B) State or local government public assistance or public welfare programs for which eligibility is determined by a needs or income test.

(12) Assistance under job training partnership act. Any amount payable to a participant under the Job Training Partnership Act (29 U.S.C. 1501 et seq.) from funds appropriated pursuant to such Act.

(13) Residences exempt in small deficiency cases and principal residences and certain business assets exempt in absence of certain approval or jeopardy.

(A) Residences in small deficiency cases. If the amount of the levy does not exceed $5,000—

(i) any real property used as a residence by the taxpayer; or

(ii) any real property of the taxpayer (other than real property which is rented) used by any other individual as a residence.

(B) Principal residences and certain business assets. Except to the extent provided in subsection (e)—

(i) the principal residence of the taxpayer (within the meaning of section 121); and

(ii) tangible personal property or real property (other than real property which is rented) used in the trade or business of an individual taxpayer.

(b) Appraisal.

The officer seizing property of the type described in subsection (a) shall appraise and set aside to the owner the amount of such property declared to be exempt. If the taxpayer objects at the time of the seizure to the valuation fixed by the officer making the seizure, the Secretary shall summon three disinterested individuals who shall make the valuation.

(c) No other property exempt.

Notwithstanding any other law of the United States (including section 207 of the Social Security Act), no property or rights to property shall be exempt from levy other than the property specifically made exempt by subsection (a).

(d) Exempt amount of wages, salary, or other income.

(1) Individuals on weekly basis. In the case of an individual who is paid or receives all of his wages, salary, and other income on a weekly basis, the amount of the wages, salary, and other income payable to or received by him during any week which is exempt from levy under subsection (a)(9) shall be the exempt amount.

(2) Exempt amount. For purposes of paragraph (1), the term "exempt amount" means an amount equal to—

(A) the sum of—

(i) the standard deduction, and

(ii) the aggregate amount of the deductions for personal exemptions allowed the taxpayer under section 151 in the taxable year in which such levy occurs, divided by

(B) 52.

Unless the taxpayer submits to the Secretary a written and properly verified statement specifying the facts necessary to determine the proper amount under subparagraph (A), subparagraph (A) shall be applied as if the taxpayer were a married individual filing a separate return with only 1 personal exemption.

(3) Individuals on basis other than weekly. In the case of any individual not described in paragraph (1), the amount of the wages, salary, and other income payable to or received by him during any applicable pay period or other fiscal period (as determined under regulations prescribed by the Secretary) which is exempt from levy under subsection (a)(9) shall be an amount (determined under such regulations) which as nearly as possible will result in the same total exemption from levy for such individual over a period of time as he would have under paragraph (1) if (during such period of time) he were paid or received such wages, salary, and other income on a regular weekly basis.

(e) Levy allowed on principal residences and certain business assets in certain circumstances.

(1) Principal residences.

(A) Approval required. A principal residence shall not be exempt from levy if a judge or magistrate of a district court of the United States approves (in writing) the levy of such residence.

(B) Jurisdiction. The district courts of the United States shall have exclusive jurisdiction to approve a levy under subparagraph (A).

(2) Certain business assets. Property (other than a principal residence) described in subsection (a)(13)(B) shall not be exempt from levy if—

(A) a district director or assistant district director of the Internal Revenue Service personally approves (in writing) the levy of such property; or

(B) the Secretary finds that the collection of tax is in jeopardy.

An official may not approve a levy under subparagraph (A) unless the official determines that the taxpayer's other assets subject to collection are insufficient to pay the amount due, together with expenses of the proceedings.

(f) Levy allowed on certain specified payments.

Any payment described in subparagraph (B) or (C) of section 6331(h)(2) shall not be exempt from levy if the Secretary approves the levy thereon under section 6331(h).

(g) Inflation adjustment.

(1) In general. In the case of any calendar year beginning after 1999, each dollar amount referred to in paragraphs (2) and (3) of subsection (a) shall be increased by an amount equal to—

(A) such dollar amount, multiplied by

(B) the cost-of-living adjustment determined under section 1(f)(3) for such calendar year, by substituting "calendar year 1998" for "calendar year 1992" in subparagraph (B) thereof.

(2) Rounding. If any dollar amount after being increased under paragraph (1) is not a multiple of $10, such dollar amount shall be rounded to the nearest multiple of $10.

In 1998, P.L. 105-206, Sec. 3431(a), substituted "$6,250" for "$2,500" in para. (a)(2)... Sec. 3431(b), substituted "$3,125" for "$1,250" in para. (a)(3)... Sec. 3431(c)(1), substituted "1999" for "1997" in para. (g)(1)... Sec. 3431(c)(2), substituted "1998" for "1996" in subpara. (g)(1)(B), effective for levies issued after 7/22/98.

—P.L. 105-206, Sec. 3445(a), amended para. (a)(13)...Sec. 3445(b), amended subsec. (e), effective 7/22/98.

Prior to amendment, para. (a)(13) read as follows:

"(13) Principal residence exempt in absence of certain approval or jeopardy. Except to the extent provided in subsection (e), the principal residence of the taxpayer (within the meaning of section 121)."

Prior to amendment, subsec (e) read as follows:

"(e) Effect of honoring levy.

"Any person in possession of (or obligated with respect to) property or rights to property subject to levy upon which a levy has been made who, upon demand by the Secretary, surrenders such property or rights to property (or discharges such obligation) to the Secretary (or who pays a liability under subsection (d)(1)) shall be discharged from any obligation or liability to the delinquent taxpayer and any other person with respect to such property or rights to property arising from such surrender or payment."

Sec. 3445(c) of this Act, relating to State fish and wildlife permits provides:

"(c) State fish and wildlife permits.

"(1) In general. With respect to permits issued by a State and required under State law for the harvest of fish or wildlife in the trade or business of an individual taxpayer, the term 'other assets' as used in section 6334(e)(2) of the Internal Revenue Code of 1986 shall include future income which may be derived by such taxpayer from the commercial sale of fish or wildlife under such permit.

"(2) Construction. Paragraph (1) shall not be construed to invalidate or in any way prejudice any assertion that the privilege embodied in permits described in paragraph (1) is not property or a right to property under the Internal Revenue Code of 1986."

—P.L. 105-206, Sec. 6005(e)(3), added "on or" before "before" each place it appeared in Sec. 312(d)(2) [sic (e)(2)] of P.L. 105-34 [see below].

In 1997, P.L. 105-34, Sec. 312(d)(1), substituted "section 121" for "section 1034" in para. (a)(13), effective for sales and exchanges after 5/6/97, except as provided by Secs. 312(d)(2)-(4) [sic (e)(2)-(4)] of this Act [as amended by Sec. 6005(e)(3) of 105-206, see above], which read as follows:

"(2) Sales on or before date of enactment.—At the election of the taxpayer, the amendments made by this section shall not apply to any sale or exchange on or before the date of the enactment of this Act.

"(3) Certain sales within 2 years after date of enactment. Section 121 of the Internal Revenue Code of 1986 (as amended by this section) shall be applied without regard to subsection (c)(2)(B) thereof in the case of any sale or exchange of property during the 2-year period beginning on the date of the enactment of this Act if the taxpayer held such property on the date of the enactment of this Act and fails to meet the ownership and use requirements of subsection (a) thereof with respect to such property.

"(4) Binding contracts.—At the election of the taxpayer, the amendments made by this section shall not apply to a sale or exchange after the date of the enactment of this Act, if—

"(A) such sale or exchange is pursuant to a contract which was binding on such date, or

"(B) without regard to such amendments, gain would not be recognized under section 1034 of the Internal Revenue Code of 1986 (as in effect on the day before the date of the enactment of this Act) on such sale or exchange by reason of a new residence acquired on or before such date or with respect to the acquisition of which by the taxpayer a binding contract was in effect on such date.

This paragraph shall not apply to any sale or exchange by an individual if the treatment provided by section 877(a)(1) of the Internal Revenue Code of 1986 applies to such individual."

—P.L. 105-34, Sec. 1025(a), redesignated subsec. (f) as (g) and added subsec. (f), effective for levies issued after 8/5/97.

In 1996, P.L. 104-193, Sec. 110(l)(6), deleted "(relating to aid to families with dependent children)" after "title IV" in subpara. (a)(11)(A), effective 7/1/97.

—P.L. 104-168, Sec. 502(a)(1), substituted "So" for "If the taxpayer is the head of a family, so" in para. (a)(2)...Sec. 502(a)(2), substituted "the taxpayer's household" for "his household" in para. (a)(2)...Sec. 502(a)(3), substituted "$2,500" for "$1,650 ($1,550 in the case of levies issued during 1989)" in para. (a)(2)...Sec. 502(b), substituted "$1,250" for "$1,100 ($1,050 in the case of levies issued during 1989)" in para. (a)(3)...Sec. 502(c), added subsec. (f), effective for levies issued after 12/31/96.

In 1988, P.L. 100-647, Sec. 1015(o)(1)(A), substituted "III, IV, V," for "IV[,]" in subpara. (a)(10)(A)...Sec. 1015(o)(1)(B), added "or" at end of subpara. (a)(10)(A)...Sec. 1015(o)(2), substituted "13, 21, 23," for "21," in subpara. (a)(10)(C)...Sec. 1015(o)(3), deleted subpara. (a)(10)(B) and redesignated subpara. (a)(10)(C) as (a)(10)(B), effective for amounts payable after 12/31/86.

Prior to deletion, subpara. (a)(10)(B) read as follows:

"(B) subchapter I, II, or III of chapter 19 of such title 38, or"

—P.L. 100-647, Sec. 6236(c)(1), substituted "$1,650 ($1,550 in the case of levies issued during 1989)" for "$1,550" in para. (a)(2)...Sec. 6236(c)(2), substituted "1,100 ($1,050 in the case of levies issued during 1989)" for "1,000" in para. (a)(3)...Sec. 6236(c)(3)(A), amended para. (d)(1)...Sec. 6236(c)(3)(B), redesignated para. (d)(2) as (d)(3) and added new para. (d)(2)...Sec. 6236(c)(4)(A), added paras. (a)(11), (12) and (13)...Sec. 6236(c)(4)(B), added subsec. (e), effective for levies issued on or after 7/1/89.

Prior to amendment, para. (d)(1) read as follows:

"(1) Individuals on weekly basis. In the case of an individual who is paid or receives all of his wages, salary, and other income on a weekly basis, the amount of the wages, salary, and other income payable to or received by him during any week which is exempt from levy under subsection (a)(9) shall be—

"(A) $75, plus

"(B) $25 for each individual who is specified in a written statement which is submitted to the person on whom notice of levy is served and which is verified in such manner as the Secretary shall prescribe by regulations and—

"(i) over half of whose support for the payroll period was received from the taxpayer.

"(ii) who is the spouse of the taxpayer, or who bears a relationship to the taxpayer specified in paragraphs (1) through (9) of section 152(a) (relating to definition of dependents), and

"(iii) who is not a minor child of the taxpayer with respect to whom amounts are exempt from levy under subsection (a)(8) for the payroll period.

For purposes of subparagraph (B)(ii) of the preceding sentence, 'payroll period' shall be substituted for 'taxable year' each place it appears in paragraph (9) of section 152(a)."

In 1986, P.L. 99-514, Sec. 1565(a), added para. (a)(10), effective for amounts payable after 12/31/86.

In 1984, P.L. 98-369, Sec. 2661(o)(5), added "(including section 207 of the Social Security Act)" after "any other law of the United States" in subsec. (c), effective for benefits payable or rights existing under the Social Security Act on or after 4/20/83.

In 1982, P.L. 97-248, Sec. 347(a)(1), substituted "$1,500" for "$500" in para. (a)(2)...Sec. 347(a)(2), substituted "$1,000" for "$250" in para. (a)(3)...Sec. 347(a)(3)(A), substituted "$75" for "$50" in subpara. (d)(1)(A)...Sec. 347(a)(3)(B), substituted "$25" for "$15" in subpara. (d)(1)(B), effective for levies made after 12/31/82.

In 1976, P.L. 94-528, Sec. 2(c), changed the effective date for amendments made by Sec. 1209 of P.L. 94-455 from "effective for levies made after 12/31/76" to "effective for levies made after 2/28/77", see below.

—P.L. 94-455, Sec. 1209(a), added para. (a)(9)...Sec. 1209(b), added subsec. (d)...Sec. 1209(c), substituted "(8) Judgments for support of minor children." for "(8) Salary, wages, or other income." in the heading of para. (a)(8) [as amended by Sec. 2(c) of P.L. 94-528, see above], effective for levies made 2/28/77.

—P.L. 94-455, Sec. 1906(b)(13)(A), substituted "Secretary" for "Secretary or his delegate" each place it appeared in Code Sec. 6334, effective 2/1/77.

In 1969, P.L. 91-172, Sec. 945, added para. (a)(8), effective for levies made 30 days or more after 12/30/69.

In 1966, P.L. 89-719, Sec. 104(c), added paras. (a)(6) and (7), effective after 11/2/66 regardless of when a lien or title of the U.S. arose or when a lien or interest of any other person was acquired.

In 1965, P.L. 89-44, Sec. 812(a), added para. (a)(5), effective 6/21/65.

In 1958, P.L. 85-840, Sec. 406, added para. (a)(4), effective 8/28/58.

Sec. 6335. Sale of seized property.

(a) Notice of seizure.

As soon as practicable after seizure of property, notice in writing shall be given by the Secretary to the owner of the property (or, in the case of personal property, the possessor thereof), or shall be left at his usual place of abode or business if he has such within the internal revenue district where the seizure is made. If the owner cannot be readily located, or has no dwelling or place of business within such district, the notice may be mailed to his last known address. Such notice shall specify the sum demanded and shall contain, in the case of personal property, an account of the property seized and, in the case of real property, a description with reasonable certainty of the property seized.

(b) Notice of sale.

The Secretary shall as soon as practicable after the seizure of the property give notice to the owner, in the manner prescribed in subsection (a), and shall cause a notification to be published in some newspaper published or generally circulated within the county wherein such seizure is made, or, if there be no newspaper published or generally circulated in such county, shall post such notice at the post office nearest the place where the seizure is made, and in not less than two other public places. Such notice shall specify the property to be sold, and the time, place, manner, and conditions of the sale thereof. Whenever levy is made without regard to the 10-day period provided in section 6331(a), public notice of sale of the property seized shall not be made within such 10-day period unless section 6336 (relating to sale of perishable goods) is applicable.

(c) Sale of indivisible property.

If any property liable to levy is not divisible, so as to enable the Secretary by sale of a part thereof to raise the whole amount of the tax and expenses, the whole of such property shall be sold.

(d) Time and place of sale.

The time of sale shall not be less than 10 days nor more than 40 days from the time of giving public notice under subsection (b). The place of sale shall be within the county in which the property is seized, except by special order of the Secretary.

(e) Manner and conditions of sale.

(1) **In general.**

(A) Determinations relating to minimum price. Before the sale of property seized by levy, the Secretary shall determine—

(i) a minimum price below which such property shall not be sold (taking into account the expense of making the levy and conducting the sale), and

(ii) whether, on the basis of criteria prescribed by the Secretary, the purchase of such property by the United States at such minimum price would be in the best interest of the United States.

(B) Sale to highest bidder at or above minimum price. If, at the sale, one or more persons offer to purchase such property for not less than the amount of the minimum price, the property shall be declared sold to the highest bidder.

(C) Property deemed sold to United States at minimum price in certain cases. If no person offers the amount of the minimum price for such property at the sale and the Secretary has determined that the purchase of such property by the United States would be in the best interest of the United States, the property shall be declared to be sold to the United States at such minimum price.

(D) Release to owner in other cases. If, at the sale, the property is not declared sold under subparagraph (B) or (C), the property shall be released to the owner thereof and the expense of the levy and sale shall be added to the amount of tax for the collection of which the levy was made. Any property released under this subparagraph shall remain subject to any lien imposed by subchapter C.

(2) **Additional rules applicable to sale.** The Secretary shall by regulations prescribe the manner and other conditions of the sale of property seized by levy. If one or more alternative methods or conditions are permitted by regulations, the Secretary shall select the alternatives applicable to the sale. Such regulations shall provide:

(A) That the sale shall not be conducted in any manner other than—

(i) by public auction, or

(ii) by public sale under sealed bids.

(B) In the case of the seizure of several items of property, whether such items shall be offered separately, in groups, or in the aggregate; and whether such property shall be offered both separately (or in groups) and in the aggregate, and sold under whichever method produces the highest aggregate amount.

(C) Whether the announcement of the minimum price determined by the Secretary may be delayed until the receipt of the highest bid.

(D) Whether payment in full shall be required at the time of acceptance of a bid, or whether a part of such payment may be deferred for such period (not to exceed 1 month) as may be determined by the Secretary to be appropriate.

(E) The extent to which methods (including advertising) in addition to those prescribed in subsection (b) may be used in giving notice of the sale.

(F) Under what circumstances the Secretary may adjourn the sale from time to time (but such adjournments shall not be for a period to exceed in all 1 month).

(3) **Payment of amount bid.** If payment in full is required at the time of acceptance of a bid and is not then and there paid, the Secretary shall forthwith proceed to again sell the property in the manner provided in this subsection. If the conditions of the sale permit part of the payment to be deferred, and if such part is not paid within the prescribed period, suit may be instituted against the purchaser for the purchase price or such part thereof as has not been paid, together with interest at the rate of 6 percent per annum from the date of the sale; or, in the discretion of the Secretary, the sale may be declared by the Secretary to be null and void for failure to make full payment of the purchase price and the property may again be advertised and sold as provided in subsections (b) and (c) and this subsection. In the event of such readvertisement and sale any new purchaser shall receive such property or rights to property, free and clear of any claim or right of the former defaulting purchaser, of any nature whatsoever, and the amount paid upon the bid price by such defaulting purchaser shall be forfeited.

(4) **Cross reference.** For provision providing for civil damages for violation of paragraph (1)(A)(i), see section 7433.

(f) Right to request sale of seized property within 60 days.

The owner of any property seized by levy may request that the Secretary sell such property within 60 days after such request (or within such longer period as may be specified by the owner). The Secretary shall comply with such request unless the Secretary determines (and notifies the owner within such period) that such compliance would not be in the best interests of the United States.

(g) Stay of sale of seized property pending Tax Court decision.

For restrictions on sale of seized property pending Tax Court decision, see section 6863(b)(3).

In **1998**, P.L. 105-206, Sec. 3441(a), substituted "a minimum price below which such property shall not be sold" for "a minimum price for which such property shall be sold" in clause (e)(1)(A)(i) . . . Sec. 3441(b), added para. (e)(4), effective for sales made after 7/22/98.

—P.L. 105-206, Sec. 3443, of this Act, provides:

"SEC. 3443. UNIFORM ASSET DISPOSAL MECHANISM.

"Not later than the date which is 2 years after the date of the enactment of this Act, the Secretary of the Treasury or the Secretary's delegate shall implement a uniform asset disposal mechanism for sales under section 6335 of the Internal Revenue Code of 1986. The mechanism should be designed to remove any participation in such sales by revenue officers of the Internal Revenue Service and should consider the use of outsourcing."

In **1988**, P.L. 100-647, Sec. 6236(g), redesignated subsec. (f) as subsec. (g), and added new subsec. (f), effective for requests made on or after 1/1/89.

In **1986**, P.L. 99-514, Sec. 1570(a), amended para. (e)(1), effective for property seized after 10/22/86, and for property seized on or before 10/22/86 which is held by the United States on 10/22/86.

Prior to amendment, para. (e)(1) read as follows:

"(1) Minimum price. Before the sale the Secretary shall determine a minimum price for which the property shall be sold, and if no person offers for such property at the sale the amount of the minimum price, the property shall be declared to be purchased at such price for the United States; otherwise the property shall be declared to be sold to the highest bidder. In determining the minimum price, the Secretary shall take into account the expense of making the levy and sale."

In **1976**, P.L. 94-455, Sec. 1906(b)(13)(A), substituted "Secretary" for "Secretary or his delegate" each place it appeared in Code Sec. 6335, effective 2/1/77.

In **1966**, P.L. 89-719, Sec. 104(d), amended the first sentence of subsec. (b), effective after 11/2/66, regardless of when the title or lien of the United States arose or when the lien or interest of another person was acquired.

Prior to amendment, the first sentence of subsec. (b) read as follows:

"The Secretary or his delegate shall as soon as practicable after the seizure of the property give notice to the owner, in the same manner as that prescribed in subsection (a), and shall cause a notification to be published in some newspaper within the county wherein such seizure is made, or, if there be no newspaper published in such county, shall post such notice at the post office nearest the place where the seizure is made, and in not less than two other public places."

Sec. 6336. Sale of perishable goods.

If the Secretary determines that any property seized is liable to perish or become greatly reduced in price or value by keeping, or that such property cannot be kept without great expense, he shall appraise the value of such property and—

(1) **Return to owner.** If the owner of the property can be readily found, the Secretary shall give him notice of such determination of the appraised value of the property. The property shall be returned to the owner if, within such time as may be specified in the notice, the owner—

(A) Pays to the Secretary an amount equal to the appraised value, or

(B) Gives bond in such form, with such sureties, and in such amount as the Secretary shall prescribe, to pay the appraised amount at such time as the Secretary determines to be appropriate in the circumstances.

(2) **Immediate sale.** If the owner does not pay such amount or furnish such bond in accordance with this section, the Secretary shall as soon as practicable make public sale of the property in accordance with such regulations as may be prescribed by the Secretary.

In **1976,** P.L. 94-455, Sec. 1906(b)(13)(A), substituted "Secretary" for "Secretary or his delegate" each place it appeared in Code Sec. 6336, effective 2/1/77.

Sec. 6337. Redemption of property.
(a) **Before sale.**

Any person whose property has been levied upon shall have the right to pay the amount due, together with the expenses of the proceeding, if any, to the Secretary at any time prior to the sale thereof, and upon such payment the Secretary shall restore such property to him, and all further proceedings in connection with the levy on such property shall cease from the time of such payment.

(b) **Redemption of real estate after sale.**

(1) **Period.** The owners of any real property sold as provided in section 6335, their heirs, executors, or administrators, or any person having any interest therein, or a lien thereon, or any person in their behalf, shall be permitted to redeem the property sold, or any particular tract of such property, at any time within 180 days after the sale thereof.

(2) **Price.** Such property or tract of property shall be permitted to be redeemed upon payment to the purchaser, or in case he cannot be found in the county in which the property is to be redeemed is situated, then to the Secretary, for the use of the purchaser, his heirs, or assigns, the amount paid by such purchaser and interest thereon at the rate of 20 percent per annum.

(c) **Record.**

When any lands sold are redeemed as provided in this section, the Secretary shall cause entry of the fact to be made upon the record mentioned in section 6340, and such entry shall be evidence of such redemption.

In **1982,** P.L. 97-248, Sec. 349A(a), substituted "180 days" for "120 days" in para. (b)(1), effective for property sold after 9/3/82.

In **1976,** P.L. 94-455, Sec. 1906(b)(13)(A), substituted "Secretary" for "Secretary or his delegate" each place it appeared in Code Sec. 6337, effective 2/1/77.

In **1966,** P.L. 89-719, Sec. 104(e), substituted "120 days" for "1 year" in para. (b)(1), effective after 11/2/66, regardless of when a lien or a title to the U.S. arose or when the lien or interest of any other person was acquired. For a special exception included in Sec. 114 of P.L. 89-719 see the note to Code Sec. 6323.

Sec. 6338. Certificate of sale; deed of real property.
(a) **Certificate of sale.**

In the case of property sold as provided in section 6335, the Secretary shall give to the purchaser a certificate of sale upon payment in full of the purchase price. In the case of real property, such certificate shall set forth the real property purchased, for whose taxes the same was sold, the name of the purchaser, and the price paid therefor.

(b) **Deed to real property.**

In the case of any real property sold as provided in section 6335 and not redeemed in the manner and within the time provided in section 6337, the Secretary shall execute (in accordance with the laws of the State in which such real property is situated pertaining to sales of real property under execution) to the purchaser of such real property at such sale, upon his surrender of the certificate of sale, a deed of the real property so purchased by him, reciting the facts set forth in the certificate.

(c) **Real property purchased by United States.**

If real property is declared purchased by the United States at a sale pursuant to section 6335, the Secretary shall at the proper time execute a deed therefor, and without delay cause such deed to be duly recorded in the proper registry of deeds.

In **1976,** P.L. 94-455, Sec. 1906(b)(13)(A), substituted "Secretary" for "Secretary or his delegate" each place it appeared in Code Sec. 6338, effective 2/1/77.

In **1966,** P.L. 89-719, Sec. 104(f), substituted "and without delay cause such deed" for "after its preparation and the endorsement of approval as to its form by the United States attorney for the district in which the property is situated, and the Secretary or his delegate shall, without delay, cause the deed" in subsec. (c), effective after 11/2/66, regardless of when a lien or a title of the U. S. arose or when the lien or interest of any other person was acquired.

In **1958,** P.L. 85-866, Sec. 78, deleted "district" preceding "attorney" in subsec. (c), effective 8/17/54.

Sec. 6339. Legal effect of certificate of sale of personal property and deed of real property.
(a) **Certificate of sale of property other than real property.**

In all cases of sale pursuant to section 6335 of property (other than real property), the certificate of such sale—

(1) **As evidence.** Shall be prima facie evidence of the right of the officer to make such sale, and conclusive evidence of the regularity of his proceedings in making the sale; and

(2) **As conveyances.** Shall transfer to the purchaser all right, title, and interest of the party delinquent in and to the property sold; and

(3) **As authority for transfer of corporate stock.** If such property consists of stocks, shall be notice, when received, to any corporation, company, or association of such transfer, and shall be authority to such corporation, company, or association to record the transfer on its books and records in the same manner as if the stocks were transferred or assigned by the party holding the same, in lieu of any original or prior certificate, which shall be void, whether canceled or not; and

(4) **As receipts.** If the subject of sale is securities or other evidences of debt, shall be a good and valid receipt to the person holding the same, as against any person holding or claiming to hold possession of such securities or other evidences of debt; and

(5) **As authority for transfer of title to motor vehicle.** If such property consists of a motor vehicle, shall be notice, when received, to any public official charged with the registration of title to motor vehicles, of such transfer and shall be authority to such official to record the transfer on his books and records in the same manner as if the certifi-

cate of title to such motor vehicle were transferred or assigned by the party holding the same, in lieu of any original or prior certificate, which shall be void, whether canceled or not.

(b) Deed of real property.
In the case of the sale of real property pursuant to section 6335—

(1) Deed as evidence. The deed of sale given pursuant to section 6338 shall be prima facie evidence of the facts therein stated; and

(2) Deed as conveyance of title. If the proceedings of the Secretary as set forth have been substantially in accordance with the provisions of law, such deed shall be considered and operate as a conveyance of all the right, title, and interest the party delinquent had in and to the real property thus sold at the time the lien of the United States attached thereto.

(c) Effect of junior encumbrances.
A certificate of sale of personal property given or a deed to real property executed pursuant to section 6338 shall discharge such property from all liens, encumbrances, and titles over which the lien of the United States with respect to which the levy was made had priority.

(d) Cross references.

(1) For distribution of surplus proceeds, see section 6342(b).

(2) For judicial procedure with respect to surplus proceeds, see section 7426(a)(2).

In **1976**, P.L. 94-455, Sec. 1906(b)(13)(A), substituted "Secretary" or his delegate" each place it appeared in Code Sec. 6339, effective 2/1/77.

In **1966**, P.L. 89-719, Sec. 104(g), added subsecs. (c) and (d), effective after 11/2/66, regardless of when a lien or a title of the U.S. arose or when the lien or interest of any other person was acquired. For a special exception included in Sec. 114 of P.L. 89-719 see the note to Code Sec. 6323.

In **1958**, P.L. 85-866, Sec. 79, substituted "as" for "of" following in the heading of para. (b)(2), effective 8/17/54.

Sec. 6340. Records of sale.
(a) Requirement.
The Secretary shall, for each internal revenue district, keep a record of all sales of property under section 6335 and of redemptions of such property. The record shall set forth the tax for which any such sale was made, the dates of seizure and sale, the name of the party assessed and all proceedings in making such sale, the amount of expenses, the names of the purchasers, and the date of the deed or certificate of sale of personal property.

(b) Copy as evidence.
A copy of such record, or any part thereof, certified by the Secretary shall be evidence in any court of the truth of the facts therein stated.

(c) Accounting to taxpayer.
The taxpayer with respect to whose liability the sale was conducted or who redeemed the property shall be furnished—

(1) the record under subsection (a) (other than the names of the purchasers);

(2) the amount from such sale applied to the taxpayer's liability; and

(3) the remaining balance of such liability.

In **1998**, P.L. 105-206, Sec. 3442(a)(1)(A), deleted "real" after "all sales of" in subsec. (a) . . . Sec. 3442(a)(1)(B), added "or certificate of sale of personal property" after "deed" in subsec. (a) . . . Sec. 3442(a)(2), added subsec. (c), effective for seizures occurring after 7/22/98.

In **1976**, P.L. 94-455, Sec. 1906(b)(13)(A), substituted "Secretary" for "Secretary or his delegate" each place it appeared in Code Sec. 6340, effective 2/1/77.

Sec. 6341. Expense of levy and sale.
The Secretary shall determine the expenses to be allowed in all cases of levy and sale.

In **1976**, P.L. 94-455, Sec. 1906(b)(13)(A), substituted "Secretary" for "Secretary or his delegate" in Code Sec. 6341, effective 2/1/77.

Sec. 6342. Application of proceeds of levy.
(a) Collection of liability.
Any money realized by proceedings under this subchapter (whether by seizure, by surrender under section 6332 (except pursuant to subsection (c)(2) thereof), or by sale of seized property) or by sale of property redeemed by the United States (if the interest of the United States in such property was a lien arising under the provisions of this title) shall be applied as follows:

(1) Expense of levy and sale. First, against the expenses of the proceedings;

(2) Specific tax liability on seized property. If the property seized and sold is subject to a tax imposed by any internal revenue law which has not been paid, the amount remaining after applying paragraph (1) shall then be applied against such tax liability (and, if such tax was not previously assessed, it shall then be assessed);

(3) Liability of delinquent taxpayer. The amount, if any, remaining after applying paragraphs (1) and (2) shall then be applied against the liability in respect of which the levy was made or the sale was conducted.

(b) Surplus proceeds.
Any surplus proceeds remaining after the application of subsection (a) shall, upon application and satisfactory proof in support thereof, be credited or refunded by the Secretary to the person or persons legally entitled thereto.

In **1976**, P.L. 94-455, Sec. 1906(b)(13)(A), substituted "Secretary" for "Secretary or his delegate" each place it appeared in Code Sec. 6342, effective 2/1/77.

In **1966**, P.L. 89-719, Sec. 104(h), amended so much of subsec. (a) as preceded para. (a)(1), deleted "under this subchapter" from para. (a)(1), and added "or the sale was conducted" after "levy was made" in para. (a)(3), effective after 11/2/66 regardless of when a lien or a title of the U. S. arose or when the lien or interest of any other person was acquired.

Prior to amendment, the introduction of subsec. (a) read as follows:
"Any money realized by proceedings under this subchapter (whether by seizure, by surrender under section 6332, or by the sale of seized property) shall be applied as follows:"

Sec. 6343. Authority to release levy and return property.
(a) Release of levy and notice of release.

(1) In general. Under regulations prescribed by the Secretary, the Secretary shall release the levy upon all, or part of, the property or rights to property levied upon and shall promptly notify the person upon whom such levy was made (if any) that such levy has been released if—

(A) the liability for which such levy was made is satisfied or becomes unenforceable by reason of lapse of time,

(B) release of such levy will facilitate the collection of such liability,

(C) the taxpayer has entered into an agreement under section 6159 to satisfy such liability by means of installment payments, unless such agreement provides otherwise,

(D) the Secretary has determined that such levy is creating an economic hardship due to the financial condition of the taxpayer, or

(E) the fair market value of the property exceeds such liability and release of the levy on a part of such property could be made without hindering the collection of such liability.

For purposes of subparagraph (C), the Secretary is not required to release such levy if such release would jeopardize the secured creditor status of the Secretary.

(2) Expedited determination on certain business property. In the case of any tangible personal property essential in carrying on the trade or business of the taxpayer, the Secretary shall provide for an expedited determination under paragraph (1) if levy on such tangible personal property would prevent the taxpayer from carrying on such trade or business.

(3) Subsequent levy. The release of levy on any property under paragraph (1) shall not prevent any subsequent levy on such property.

(b) Return of property.

If the Secretary determines that property has been wrongfully levied upon, it shall be lawful for the Secretary to return—

(1) the specific property levied upon,

(2) an amount of money equal to the amount of money levied upon, or

(3) an amount of money equal to the amount of money received by the United States from a sale of such property.

Property may be returned at any time. An amount equal to the amount of money levied upon or received from such sale may be returned at any time before the expiration of 9 months from the date of such levy. For purposes of paragraph (3), if property is declared purchased by the United States at a sale pursuant to section 6335(e) (relating to manner and conditions of sale), the United States shall be treated as having received an amount of money equal to the minimum price determined pursuant to such section or (if larger) the amount received by the United States from the resale of such property.

(c) Interest.

Interest shall be allowed and paid at the overpayment rate established under section 6621—

(1) in a case described in subsection (b)(2), from the date the Secretary receives the money to a date (to be determined by the Secretary) preceding the date of return by not more than 30 days, or

(2) in a case described in subsection (b)(3), from the date of the sale of the property to a date (to be determined by the Secretary) preceding the date of return by not more than 30 days.

(d) Return of property in certain cases.

If—

(1) any property has been levied upon, and

(2) the Secretary determines that—

(A) the levy on such property was premature or otherwise not in accordance with administrative procedures of the Secretary,

(B) the taxpayer has entered into an agreement under section 6159 to satisfy the tax liability for which the levy was imposed by means of installment payments, unless such agreement provides otherwise,

(C) the return of such property will facilitate the collection of the tax liability, or

(D) with the consent of the taxpayer or the National Taxpayer Advocate, the return of such property would be in the best interests of the taxpayer (as determined by the National Taxpayer Advocate) and the United States,

the provisions of subsection (b) shall apply in the same manner as if such property had been wrongly levied upon, except that no interest shall be allowed under subsection (c).

(e) Release of levy upon agreement that amount is not collectible.

In the case of a levy on the salary or wages payable to or received by the taxpayer, upon agreement with the taxpayer that the tax is not collectible, the Secretary shall release such levy as soon as practicable.

In **1998**, P.L. 105-206, Sec. 1102(d)(1)(B), substituted "National Taxpayer Advocate" for "Taxpayer Advocate" each place it appeared in subpara. (d)(2)(D), effective 7/22/98.

—P.L. 105-206, Sec. 3432(a), added subsec (e), effective for levies imposed after 12/31/99.

In **1996**, P.L. 104-168, Sec. 501(b), added subsec. (d), effective 7/30/96.

In **1988**, P.L. 100-647, Sec. 6236(f), amended subsec. (a), effective for levies issued on or after 7/1/89.

Prior to amendment, subsec. (a) read as follows:

"(a) Release of levy.

"It shall be lawful for the Secretary, under regulations prescribed by the Secretary, to release the levy upon all or part of the property or rights to property levied upon where the Secretary determines that such action will facilitate the collection of the liability, but such release shall not operate to prevent any subsequent levy."

In **1986**, P.L. 99-514, Sec. 1511(c)(10), substituted "the overpayment rate established under section 6621" for "an annual rate established under section 6621" in subsec. (c), effective for purposes of determining interest for periods after 12/31/86.

In **1979**, P.L. 96-167, Sec. 4(a), added new subsec. (c), effective for levies made after 12/29/79.

In **1976**, P.L. 94-455, Sec. 1906(b)(13)(A), substituted "Secretary" for "Secretary or his delegate" each place it appeared in subsecs. (a) and (b), effective 2/1/77.

In **1966**, P.L. 89-719, Sec. 104, added "and return property" after "levy" in the heading of Code Sec. 6343, added "(a) Release of levy" before "It shall be lawful" in code Sec. 6343, and added subsec. (b), effective after 11/2/66, regardless of when a lien or a title of the U.S. arose and when the lien or interest of any other person was acquired.

Sec. 6344. Cross references.

(a) Length of period.

For period within which levy may be begun in case of—

(1) Income, estate, and gift taxes, and taxes imposed by chapter 41, 42, 43, or 44, see sections 6502(a) and 6503(a)(1).

(2) Employment and miscellaneous excise taxes, see section 6502(a).

(b) Delinquent collection officers.

For distraint proceedings against delinquent internal revenue officers, see section 7804(c).

(c) Other references.

For provisions relating to—

(1) Stamps, marks and brands, see section 6807.

(2) Administration of real estate acquired by the United States, see section 7506.

In **1998**, P.L. 105-206, Sec. 1104(b)(1), substituted "section 7804(c)" for "section 7803(d)" in subsec. (b), effective 7/22/98.

In **1988**, P.L. 100-418, Sec. 1941(b)(2)(B)(ix), substituted "or 44" for "44, or 45" in para. (a)(1), effective for crude oil removed from the premises on or after 8/23/88.

In **1980**, P.L. 96-223, Sec. 101(f)(1)(I), substituted "44, or 45" for "or 44" in para. (a)(1), effective for periods after 2/29/80.

In **1976**, P.L. 94-455, Sec. 1307(d)(2)(F)(v), substituted "chapter 41, 42," for "chapter 42" in para. (a)(1), effective on and after 10/4/76.

—P.L. 94-455, Sec. 1605(b)(8), substituted "43, or 44" for "or 43" in para. (a)(1), effective for tax. yrs. of real estate investment trusts begin. after 10/4/76.

In **1974**, P.L. 93-406, Sec. 1016(a)(13), substituted "chapter 42 or 43" for "chapter 42" in para. (a)(1), effective 9/2/74 or other date as specified in Sec. 1017 of the Act (reproduced following Code Sec. 401).

In **1969**, P.L. 91-172, Sec. 101(j)(45), added "and taxes imposed by chapter 42" after "gift taxes" in para. (a)(1), effective 1/1/70.

Subchapter E.—Collection of State Individual Income Taxes [Repealed]

Sec.

6361. Repealed [General rules].

6362. Repealed [Qualified State individual income taxes].

Subchapter E — Collection

6363. Repealed [State agreements; other procedures].
6364. Repealed [Regulations].
6365. Repealed [Definitions and special rules].

In 1990, P.L. 101-508, Sec. 11801(a)(45), repealed Subchapter E of chapter 64.
In 1972, P.L. 92-512, Sec. 202, added Subchapter E.

Sec. 6361. Repealed.

In 1990, P.L. 101-508, Sec. 11801(a)(45), repealed Code Sec. 6361, effective 11/5/90 except as provided in Sec. 11821(b) of this Act, which reads as follows:
"(b) Savings provision.
"If—
"(1) any provision amended or repealed by this part applied to—
"(A) any transaction occurring before the date of the enactment of this Act [11/5/90],
"(B) any property acquired before such date of enactment [11/5/90], or
"(C) any item of income, loss, deduction, or credit taken into account before such date of enactment [11/5/90], and
"(2) the treatment of such transaction, property, or item under such provision would (without regard to the amendments made by this part) affect liability for tax for periods ending after such date of enactment [11/5/90],
nothing in the amendments made by this part shall be construed to affect the treatment of such transaction, property, or item for purposes of determining liability for tax for periods ending after such date of enactment [11/5/90]."
Prior to repeal, Code Sec. 6361 read as follows:
"SEC. 6361. GENERAL RULES.
"(a) Collection and administration.
In the case of any State which has in effect an agreement with the Secretary entered into under section 6363, the Secretary shall collect and administer the qualified State individual income taxes of such State. No fee or other charge shall be imposed upon any State for the collection or administration of the qualified State individual income taxes of such State or any other State. All provisions of this subtitle, subtitle G, and chapter 24 relating to the collection and administration of the taxes imposed by chapter 1 on the incomes of individuals (and all civil and criminal sanctions provided by this subtitle or by title 18 of the United States Code with respect to such collection and administration) shall apply to the collection and administration of qualified State individual income taxes as if such taxes were imposed by chapter 1, except to the extent that their application is modified by the Secretary by regulations necessary or appropriate to reflect the provisions of this subchapter, or to reflect differences in the taxes or differences in the situations in which liability for such taxes arises.
"(b) Civil proceedings.
Any person shall have, with respect to a qualified State individual income tax (including the current collection thereof), the same right to bring or contest a civil action and obtain review thereof, in the same court or courts and subject to the same requirements and procedures, as he would have under chapter 76, and under title 28 of the United States Code, if the tax were imposed by section 1 (or were for the current collection of the tax imposed by section 1). To the extent that the preceding sentence provides judicial procedures (including review procedures) with respect to any matter, such procedures shall replace judicial procedures under State law, except that nothing in this subchapter shall be construed in any way to affect the right or power of a State court to pass on matters involving the constitution of that State.
"(c) Transfers to States.
"(1) Prompt transfers. Any amount collected under this subchapter which is apportioned to a qualified State individual income tax shall be promptly transferred to the State on the basis of estimates by the Secretary. In the case of amounts collected under chapter 24, the estimated amount due the State shall be transferred to the State not later than the close of the third business day after the amount is deposited in a Federal Reserve bank. In the case of amounts collected pursuant to a return, a declaration of estimated tax, an amendment of such a declaration, or otherwise, the estimated amount due the State shall be transferred to the State not later than the close of the 30th day after the amount is received by the Secretary.
"(2) Adjustments. Not less often than once each fiscal year the difference between collections (adjusted for credits and refunds) made under this subchapter during the preceding fiscal year and the transfers to the States made on account of estimates of such collections shall be determined, and such difference shall be a charge against, or in addition to, the amounts otherwise payable.
"(d) Special rules.
"(1) United States to represent state interest.
"(A) General rule. In all administrative proceedings, and in all judicial proceedings (whether civil or criminal), relating to the administration and collection of a State qualified individual income tax the interests of the State imposing such tax shall be represented by the United States in the same manner in which the interests of the United States are represented by corresponding proceedings involving the taxes imposed by chapter 1.
"(B) Exceptions. Subparagraph (A) shall not apply to—
"(i) proceedings in a State court involving the constitution of that State, and
"(ii) proceedings involving the relationship between the United States and the State.
"(2) Allocation of overpayments and underpayments. If the combined amount collected in respect of a qualified State individual income tax for any period and the taxes imposed by chapter 1 for such period with respect to the income of any individual is greater or less than the combined amount required to be paid for such period, the collected amount shall be divided between the accounts for such taxes on the basis of the respective amounts required to be paid.
"(3) Finality of administrative determinations. Administrative determinations of the Secretary as to tax liabilities of, or refunds owing to, individuals with respect to qualified State individual income taxes shall not be reviewed by or enforced by any officer or employee of any State or political subdivision of a State."
In 1976, P.L. 94-455, Sec. 1906(b)(13)(A), substituted "Secretary" for "Secretary or his delegate" each place it appeared in Code Sec. 6361, effective 2/1/77.
— P.L. 94-455, Sec. 2116(c), added the second sentence of subsec. (a), effective 10/4/76.
In 1972, P.L. 92-512, Sec. 202(a), added Code Sec. 6361, effective on whichever of the following is later: (1) January 1, 1974, or (2) the first January 1 which is more than one year after the first date on which at least 2 States having residents who in the aggregate filed 5 percent of the Federal individual income tax returns filed during 1972 have notified the Secretary of the Treasury or his delegate of an election to enter into an agreement under Code Sec. 6363.

Sec. 6362. Repealed.

In 1990, P.L. 101-508, Sec. 11801(a)(45), repealed Code Sec. 6362, effective 11/5/90 except as provided in Sec. 11821(b) of this Act, is reproduced in note following Code Sec. 6361.
Prior to repeal, Code Sec. 6362 read as follows:
"SEC. 6362. QUALIFIED STATE INDIVIDUAL INCOME TAXES.
"(a) Qualified state individual income taxes defined.
"For purposes of this subchapter—
"(1) In general. The term 'qualified State individual income tax' means—
"(A) a qualified resident tax, and
"(B) a qualified nonresident tax.
"(2) Qualified resident tax. The term 'qualified resident tax' means a tax imposed by a State on the income of individuals who are residents of such State which is either—
"(A) a tax based on taxable income which meets the requirements of subsection (b), or
"(B) a tax which is a percentage of the Federal tax which meets the requirements of subsection (c),
and which, in addition, meets the requirements of subsections (e) and (f).
"(3) Qualified nonresident tax. The term 'qualified nonresident tax' means a tax which is imposed by a State on the wage and other business income of individuals who are not residents of such State and which meets the requirements of subsections (d), (e), and (f).
"(b) Qualified resident tax based on taxable income.
"(1) In general. A tax meets the requirements of this subsection only if it is imposed on an amount equal to the individual's taxable income (as defined in section 63) for the taxable year, adjusted—
"(A) by subtracting an amount equal to the amount of his interest on obligations of the United States which was included in his gross income for the year,
"(B) by adding an amount equal to his net State income tax deduction for the year,
"(C) by adding an amount equal to his net tax-exempt income for the year, and
"(D) if a credit is allowed against such tax for State or local sales tax in accordance with paragraph (2)(C), by adding an amount equal to the amount of his deduction under section 164(a)(4) for such sales tax.
"(2) Permitted adjustments. A tax which otherwise meets the requirements of paragraph (1) shall not be deemed to fail to meet such requirements solely because it provides for one or more of the following adjustments:
"(A) There is imposed a tax on the amount taxed under section 55 (relating to the minimum tax for tax preferences).
"(B) A credit determined under rules prescribed by the Secretary is allowed against such tax for income tax paid to another State or a political subdivision thereof.
"(C) A credit is allowed against such tax for all or a portion of any general sales tax imposed by the same State or a political subdivision thereof with respect to sales to the taxpayer or his dependents.
"(3) Net State income tax deduction. For purposes of this subsection and subsection (c), the term 'net State income tax deduction' means the excess (if any) of (A) the amount deducted from income under section 164(a)(3) as taxes paid to a State or a political subdivision thereof, over (B) amounts included in income as recoveries of prior income taxes paid to a State or a political subdivision thereof which had been deducted under section 164(a)(3).
"(4) Net tax-exempt income. For purposes of this subsection and subsection (c), the term 'net tax-exempt income' means the excess (if any) of—
"(A) the interest on obligations described in section 103(a) other than obligations of the State and its political subdivisions, and
"(B) the interest on obligations described in such section of the State and its political subdivision which under the law of the State is subject to the individual income tax imposed by the State, over
the sum of the amount of deductions allocable to such interest which is disallowed by application of section 265, and the amount of the proper adjustment to basis allocable to such obligations which is required to be made for the taxable year under section 1016(a)(5) or (6).
"(c) Qualified resident tax which is a percentage of the federal tax.
"(1) In general. A tax meets the requirements of this subsection only if it is imposed as a specified percentage of the excess of the taxes imposed by chapter 1 over the sum of the credits allowable under part IV of subchapter A of chapter 1 (other than the credits allowable by sections 31 and 34).

"(2) Required adjustments. A tax meets the requirements of this subsection only if the liability for tax is decreased by the decrease in such liability which would result from excluding from gross income an amount equal to the interest on obligations of the United States which was included in gross income for such year.

"(3) Permitted adjustments. A tax which otherwise meets the requirements of paragraphs (1) and (2) shall not be deemed to fail to meet such requirements solely because it provides for all of the following adjustments:

"(A) the liability for tax is increased by the increase in such liability which would result from including as an item of gross income an amount equal to the net tax exempt income for the year,

"(B) the liability for tax is increased by the increase in such liability which would result from including as an item of gross income an amount equal to the net State income tax deduction for the year, and

"(C) if a credit is allowed against such tax for State or local sales tax in accordance with paragraph (4)(B), the liability for tax is increased by the increase in such liability which would result from including as an item of income an amount equal to the amount of his deduction under section 164(a)(4) for such sales tax.

"(4) Further permitted adjustments. A tax which otherwise meets the requirements of paragraphs (1) and (2) shall not be deemed to fail to meet such requirements solely because it provides for one or both of the following adjustments:

"(A) A credit determined under rules prescribed by the Secretary is allowed against such tax for income tax paid to another State or a political subdivision thereof.

"(B) A credit is allowed against such tax for all or a portion of any general sales tax imposed by the same State or a political subdivision thereof with respect to sales to the taxpayer or his dependents.

"(d) Qualified nonresident tax.

"(1) In general. A tax imposed by a State meets the requirements of this subsection only if it has the following characteristics—

"(A) such tax is imposed by the State on the wage and other business income of individuals who are not residents of such State,

"(B) such tax applies only with respect to wage and other business income derived from sources within such State,

"(C) such tax applies only if 25 percent or more of the individual's wage and other business income for the taxable year is derived from sources within such State,

"(D) the amount of such tax imposed with respect to any individual who is not a resident does not exceed the amount of tax for which he would be liable under such State's qualified resident tax if he were a resident of such State and if his taxable income were an amount equal to the excess of—

"(i) the amount of his wage and other business income derived from sources within such State, over

"(ii) that portion of the nonbusiness deductions taken into account for purposes of the State's qualified resident tax which bears the same ratio to the amount of such deductions as the income referred to in clause (i) bears to his adjusted gross income, and

"(E) the State has in effect for the same period a qualified resident tax.

"(2) Wage and other business income. The term 'wage and other business income' means—

"(A) wages, as defined in section 3401(a),

"(B) net earnings from self-employment (within the meaning of section 1402(a)), and

"(C) the distributive share of income of any trade or business carried on by a trust, estate, or an S corporation to the extent such share (i) is includible in the gross income of the individual for the taxable year, and (ii) would constitute net earnings from self-employment (within the meaning of section 1402(a)) if such trade or business were carried on by a partnership.

"(e) Requirements relating to residence.

A tax imposed by a State meets the requirements of this subsection only if for purposes of such tax—

"(1) Resident individual. An individual (other than a trust or estate) is treated as a resident of such State with respect to a taxable year only if—

"(A) his principle place of residence has been within such State for a period of at least 135 consecutive days and at least 30 days of such period are in such taxable year, or

"(B) in the case of a citizen or resident of the United States who is not a resident (determined in the manner provided in subparagraph (A)) of any State with respect to such taxable year, such individual is domiciled in such State for at least 30 days during such taxable year.

"Nothing in this subchapter shall be construed to require or authorize the treatment of a Senator, Representative, Delegate, or Resident Commissioner as a resident of a State other than the State which he represents in Congress.

"(2) Estate. An estate of an individual is treated as a resident of the last State of which such individual was a resident (within the meaning of paragraph (1)) before his death.

"(3) Trusts.

"(A) Testamentary trust. A trust with respect to which a deceased individual is the principal contributor by reason of property passing on his death is treated as a resident of the last State of which such individual was a resident (within the meaning of paragraph (1)) before his death.

"(B) Nontestamentary trust. A trust (other than a trust described in subparagraph (A)) is treated as a resident of such State with respect to a taxable year only if the principal contributor to the trust, during the 3-year period ending on the date of the creation of the trust, resided in the State for an aggregate number of days longer than the aggregate number of days he resided in any other State.

"(C) Special rules. For purposes of this paragraph—

"(i) If on any day before the close of the taxable year an existing trust received assets having a value greater than the aggregate value of all assets theretofore contributed to the trust, such trust shall be treated as created on such day. For purposes of this subparagraph, the value of any asset taken into account shall be its fair market value on the day it is contributed to the trust.

"(ii) The principal contributor to the trust is the individual who contributed more (in value) of the assets contributed on the date of the creation of the trust (determined after applying clause (i)) than any other individual.

"(iii) If the foregoing rules would create more than one State of residence (or no State of residence) for a trust, such trust shall be treated as a resident of the State determined under similar principles prescribed by the Secretary by regulations.

"(4) Liability for tax on change of residence. With respect to a taxable year, in the case of an individual (other than an individual who comes into being or ceases to exist) who becomes a resident, or ceases to be a resident, of the State, his liability to such State for the resident tax is determined by multiplying the amount which would be his liability for tax (after the nonrefundable credits allowed against such tax) if he had been a resident of such State for the entire taxable year by a fraction the numerator of which is the number of days he was a resident of such State and the denominator of which is the total number of days in the taxable year. In the case of an individual who is treated as a resident of a State with respect to a taxable year by reason of paragraph (1)(B), the preceding sentence shall be applied by substituting days of domicile for days of residence.

"(5) Current collection of tax. In applying chapter 24 (relating to withholding) and provisions relating to estimated income tax (and amendments thereto)—

"(A) in the case of a resident tax, an individual is treated as subject to the tax if he reasonably expects to reside in the State for 30 days or more or if such individual is a resident of the State (within the meaning of paragraph (1), (2), or (3)), and

"(B) in the case of a nonresident tax, an individual is treated as subject to the tax if he reasonably expects to receive wage and other business income (within the meaning of subsection (d)(2)) for 30 days or more during the taxable year.

"(f) Additional requirements.

A tax imposed by a State shall meet the requirements of this subsection only if—

"(1) State agreement must be in effect for period concerned. A State agreement entered into under section 6363 is in effect with respect to such tax for the taxable period in question.

"(2) State laws must contain certain provisions. Under the laws of such State—

"(A) the provisions of this subchapter (and of the regulations prescribed thereunder) as in effect from time to time are made applicable for the period for which the State agreement is in effect, and

"(B) any change made by the State in the tax imposed by the State will not apply to taxable years beginning in any calendar year for which the State agreement is in effect unless such change is enacted before November 1 of such calendar year.

"(3) State laws taxing incomes of individuals can only be of certain kinds. The State does not impose any tax on the income of individuals other than—

"(A) a qualified resident tax,

"(B) a qualified nonresident tax, and

"(C) a separate tax on income which is not wage and other business income and which is received or accrued by individuals who are domiciled in the State but who are not residents of the State within the meaning of subsection (e)(1).

"(4) Taxable years must coincide. The taxable years of individuals under such tax coincide with taxable years for purposes of the taxes imposed by chapter 1.

"(5) Married individuals. A married individual (within the meaning of section 7703)—

"(A) who files a joint return for purposes of the taxes imposed by chapter 1 shall not file a separate return for purposes of such State tax, and

"(B) who files a separate return for purposes of the taxes imposed by chapter 1, shall not file a joint return for purposes of such State tax.

"(6) No double jeopardy under state law. The laws of such State do not provide criminal or civil sanctions for an act (or omission to act) with respect to a qualified resident tax or qualified nonresident tax other than the criminal or civil sanctions to which an individual is subjected by reason of section 6361.

"(7) Partnerships, trusts, and other conduct entities. Under the State law the tax treatment of—

"(A) partnerships and partners,

"(B) trusts and their beneficiaries,

"(C) estates and their beneficiaries,

"(D) S corporations and their shareholders, and

"(E) any other entity and the individuals having beneficial interests therein, to the extent that such entity is treated as a conduit for purposes of the taxes imposed by chapter 1,

shall correspond to the tax treatment provided therefor in the case of the taxes imposed by chapter 1.

"(8) Members of Armed Forces. The relief provided to any member of the Armed Forces of the United States by section 514 of the Soldiers' and Sailors' Civil Relief Act (50 U.S.C. App. sec. 574) is in no way diminished.

"(9) Withholding on compensation of employees of railroads, motor carriers, airlines, and water carriers. There is no contravention of the provisions of section [sic] section 11504 of title 49 or of section 1112 of the Federal Aviation Act of 1958 with respect to the withholding of compensation to which such sections apply for purposes of the nonresident tax."

In 1986, P.L. 99-514, Sec. 1301(j)(8), substituted "section 7703" for "section 143" in para. (f)(5), effective for bonds issued after 8/15/86.

In 1984, P.L. 98-369, Sec. 412(b)(6), substituted "and provisions relating to estimated income tax" for "and section 6015 and other provisions relating to declarations of estimated income" in para. (e)(5), effective for tax. yrs. begin. after 12/31/84.

—P.L. 98-369, Sec. 474(r)(35), substituted "sections 31 and 34" for "sections 31 and 39" in para. (c)(1), effective for tax. yrs. begin. after 12/31/83, and to carrybacks from tax yrs. begin. after 12/31/83.

—P.L. 98-369, Sec. 721(x)(5), substituted "an S corporation" for "electing small business corporation (within the meaning of section 1371(a))" in subpara. (d)(2)(C), effective for tax. yrs. begin. after 12/31/82.

In **1983**, P.L. 97-448, Sec. 306(a)(1)(A)(i), redesignated the second Sec. 201(c) of P.L. 97-248 as Sec. 201(d) of P.L. 97-248, see below.

—P.L. 97-424, Sec. 547(b)(5), substituted "103(a)" for "103(a)(1)" in para. (b)(4), effective 1/6/83.

In **1982**, P.L. 97-354, Sec. 5(a)(41)(A), substituted "S corporations" for "electing small business corporations (within the meaning of section 1371(a))" in subpara. (f)(7)(D) . . . Sec. 5(a)(41)(B), deleted "subchapter S corporations," after "trusts," in the heading of para. (f)(7), effective for tax. yrs. begin. after 12/31/82.

—P.L. 97-248, Sec. 201(d)(7), deleted "or 56" after "section 55" in subpara. (b)(2)(A), effective for tax. yrs. begin. after 12/31/82.

In **1978**, P.L. 95-600, Sec. 421(e)(8), substituted "section 55 or 56" for "section 56" in subpara. (b)(2)(A), effective for tax. yrs. begin. after 12/31/78.

—P.L. 95-473, Sec. 2(a)(2)(H), substituted "section [sic] 11504 of title 49" for "26, 226A, or 324 of the Interstate Commerce Act" in para. (f)(9), effective 10/17/78.

In **1976**, P.L. 94-455, Sec. 1906(b)(13)(A), substituted "Secretary" for "Secretary or his delegate" each place it appeared in Code Sec. 6362, effective 2/1/77.

—P.L. 94-455, Sec. 2116(b)(1)(A), deleted "and" at the end of subpara. (b)(1)(B), substituted ", and" for the period at the end of subpara. (b)(1)(C), and added subpara. (b)(1)(D) . . . Sec. 2116(b)(1)(B), added subpara. (b)(2)(C) . . . Sec. 2116(b)(2)(A), substituted "all" for "both" in para. (c)(3), deleted "and" at the end of subpara. (c)(3)(A), substituted ", and" for the period at the end of subpara. (c)(3)(B), and added subpara. (c)(3)(C) . . . Sec. 2116(b)(2)(B), amended para. (c)(4), effective 10/4/76.

Prior to amendment, para. (c)(4) read as follows:

"(4) Further permitted adjustment. A tax which otherwise meets the requirements of paragraphs (1) and (2) shall not be deemed to fail to meet such requirements solely because a credit determined under rules prescribed by the Secretary or his delegate is allowed against such tax for income tax paid to another State or a political subdivision thereof."

In **1972**, P.L. 92-512, Sec. 202(a), added Code Sec. 6362, effective 10/20/72.

Sec. 6363. Repealed.

In **1990**, P.L. 101-508, Sec. 11801(a)(45), repealed Code Sec. 6363, effective 11/5/90 except as provided in Sec. 11821(b) of this Act, reproduced in note following Code Sec. 6363.

Prior to repeal, Code Sec. 6363 read as follows:

"SEC. 6363. STATE AGREEMENTS; OTHER PROCEDURES.

"(a) State agreement.

If a State elects to enter into an agreement with the United States to have its individual income taxes collected and administered as provided in this subchapter, it shall file notice of such election in such manner and with such supporting information as the Secretary may prescribe by regulations. The Secretary shall enter into an agreement with such State unless the Secretary notifies the Governor of the State within 90 days after the date of the filing of notice of the election that the State does not have a qualified State individual income tax (determined without regard to section 6362(f)(1)). The provisions of this subchapter shall apply on and after the date (not earlier than the first January 1 which is more than 6 months after the date of the notice) specified for this purpose in the agreement.

"(b) Withdrawal.

"(1) By notification. If a State wishes to withdraw from the agreement, it shall notify the Secretary of its intention to withdraw in such manner as the Secretary may prescribe by regulations. The provisions of this subchapter (other than this section) shall not apply on or after the date specified for this purpose in the notification. Except as provided in regulations, the date so specified shall not be earlier than the first January 1 which is more than 6 months after the date on which the Secretary or his delegate is so notified.

"(2) By change in state law. Any change in State law which would (but for this subchapter) have the effect of causing a tax to cease to be a qualified State individual income tax shall be treated as an intention to withdraw from the agreement. Notification by the Secretary to the Governor of such State that the change in State law will be treated as an intention to withdraw shall be made by the Secretary in such manner as the Secretary shall by regulations prescribe. Such notification shall have the same effect as a notice under paragraph (1) of an intention to withdraw from the agreement received on the effective date of the change in State law.

"(c) Transition years.

"(1) Subchapter ceases to apply during taxpayer's year. If the provisions of this subchapter cease to apply on a day other than the last day of the taxpayer's taxable year, then amounts previously paid to the United States on account of the State's qualified individual income tax for that taxable year (whether paid by withholding, estimated tax, credit in lieu of refund, or otherwise) shall be treated as having been paid on account of the State's individual income tax for that taxable year. Such amounts shall be transferred to the State as though the State had not withdrawn from the agreement. Returns, applications, elections, and other forms previously filed with the Secretary for that taxable year, which are thereafter required to be filed with the appropriate State official shall be treated as having been filed with the appropriate State official.

"(2) Prevention of unintended hardships or benefits. The State may by law provide for the transition to a qualified State individual income tax or from such a tax to the extent necessary to prevent double taxation or other unintended hardships, or to prevent unintended benefits, under State law.

"(3) Administration of subsection. The provisions of this subsection shall be administered by the Secretary, by the State, or jointly, to the extent provided in regulations prescribed by the Secretary.

"(d) Judicial review.

"(1) In general. Whenever under this section the Secretary determines that a State does not have a qualified State individual income tax, such State may, within 60 days after the Governor of the State has been notified of such action, file with the United States court of appeals for the circuit in which such State is located, or with the United States Court of Appeals for the District of Columbia, a petition for review of such action. A copy of the petition shall be forthwith transmitted by the clerk of the court to the Secretary. The Secretary thereupon shall file in the court the record of the proceedings on which he based his action as provided in section 2112 of title 28, United States Code.

"(2) Jurisdiction of court; review. The court shall have jurisdiction to affirm the action of the Secretary or to set it aside in whole or in part and to issue such other orders as may be appropriate with regard to taxable years which include any part of the period of litigation. The judgment of the court shall be subject to review by the Supreme Court of the United States upon certiorari or certification as provided in section 1254 of title 28, United States Code.

"(3) Stay of decision.

"(A) If judgment on a petition to review a determination under subsection (a) includes a determination that the State has a qualified State individual income tax, then the provisions of this subchapter shall apply on and after the first January 1 which is more than 6 months after the date of the judgment.

"(B) If judgment on a petition to review a determination by the Secretary under subsection (b)(2) includes a determination that the State does not have a qualified State individual income tax, then the provisions of this subchapter (other than this section) shall not apply on and after the first January 1 which is more than 6 months after the date of the judgment."

In **1984**, P.L. 98-620, Sec. 402(28)(C), deleted para. (d)(4), effective 11/8/84 except for cases pending on 11/8/84.

Prior to deletion, para. (d)(4) read as follows:

"(4) Preference. Any judicial proceedings under this section shall be entitled to, and, upon request of the Secretary or the State, shall receive a preference and shall be heard and determined as expeditiously as possible."

In **1976**, P.L. 94-455, Sec. 1906(b)(13)(A), substituted "Secretary" for "Secretary or his delegate" each place it appeared in Code Sec. 6363, effective 2/1/77.

In **1972**, P.L. 92-512, Sec. 202(a), added Code Sec. 6363, effective 10/20/72.

Sec. 6364. Repealed.

In **1990**, P.L. 101-508, Sec. 11801(a)(45), repealed Code Sec. 6364, effective 11/5/90 except as provided in Sec. 11821(b) of this Act, reproduced in note following Code Sec. 6361.

Prior to repeal, Code Sec. 6364 read as follows:

"SEC. 6364. REGULATIONS.

The Secretary shall prescribe such regulations as may be necessary or appropriate to carry out the purposes of this subchapter."

In **1976**, P.L. 94-455, Sec. 1906(b)(13)(A), substituted "Secretary" for "Secretary or his delegate" in Code Sec. 6364, effective 2/1/77.

In **1972**, P.L. 92-512, Sec. 202(a), added Code Sec. 6364, effective 10/20/72.

Sec. 6365. Repealed.

In **1990**, P.L. 101-508, Sec. 11801(a)(45), repealed Code Sec. 6365, effective 11/5/90 except as provided in Sec. 11821(b) of this Act, reproduced in note following Code Sec. 6365.

Prior to repeal, Code Sec. 6365 read as follows:

"SEC. 6365. DEFINITIONS AND SPECIAL RULES.

"(a) State.

For purposes of this subchapter, the term 'State' includes the District of Columbia.

"(b) Governor.

For purposes of this subchapter, the term 'Governor' includes the Mayor of the District of Columbia.

"(c) Application of subchapter.

Whenever this subchapter begins to apply or ceases to apply, to any State tax on any January 1—

"(1) except as provided in paragraph (2), such change shall apply to taxable years beginning on or after such date, and

"(2) for purposes of chapter 24, such change shall apply to wages paid on or after such date."

In **1976**, P.L. 94-455, Sec. 1906(a)(21), substituted "Mayor of the District of Columbia" for "Commissioner of the District of Columbia" in subsec. (b), effective 2/1/77.

In **1972**, P.L. 92-512, Sec. 202(a), added Code Sec. 6365, effective 10/20/72.

CHAPTER 65.—ABATEMENTS, CREDITS, AND REFUNDS

Subchapter

A. Procedure in general.

B. Rules of special application.

Abatements, credits, refunds

Code Sec. 6401

Subchapter A.—Procedure in General

Sec.
6401. Amounts treated as overpayments.
6402. Authority to make credits or refunds.
6403. Overpayment of installment.
6404. Abatements.
6405. Reports of refunds and credits.
6406. Prohibition of administrative review of decisions.
6407. Date of allowance of refund or credit.
6408. State escheat laws not to apply.
6409. Refunds disregarded in the administration of federal programs and federally assisted programs.

In 2010, P.L. 111-312, Sec. Sec 728(a), added Code Sec. 6409, effective for apply to amounts received after 12/31/2009.
In 1987, P.L. 100-203, Sec. 10621(b), added item 6408.

Sec. 6401. Amounts treated as overpayments.
(a) Assessment and collection after limitation period.
The term "overpayment" includes that part of the amount of the payment of any internal revenue tax which is assessed or collected after the expiration of the period of limitation properly applicable thereto.

(b) Excessive credits.

(1) In general. If the amount allowable as credits under subpart C of part IV of subchapter A of chapter 1 (relating to refundable credits) exceeds the tax imposed by subtitle A (reduced by the credits allowable under subparts A, B, D, G, H, I, and J of such part IV), the amount of such excess shall be considered an overpayment.

(2) Special rule for credit under section 33. For purposes of paragraph (1), any credit allowed under section 33 (relating to withholding of tax on nonresident aliens and on foreign corporations) for any taxable year shall be treated as a credit allowable under subpart C of part IV of subchapter A of chapter 1 only if an election under subsection (g) or (h) of section 6013 is in effect for such taxable year. The preceding sentence shall not apply to any credit so allowed by reason of section 1446.

(c) Rule where no tax liability.
An amount paid as tax shall not be considered not to constitute an overpayment solely by reason of the fact that there was no tax liability in respect of which such amount was paid.

In 2009, P.L. 111-5, Sec. 1531(c)(5), substituted "I, and J" for "and I" in para. (b)(1), effective for obligations issued after 2/17/2009.
In 2008, P.L. 110-246, Sec. 4, Repeals the duplicative enactment and provides effective date provisions of the Act entitled "An Act to provide for the continuation of agricultural programs through fiscal year 2012, and for other purposes" Sec. 4, P.L. 110-246 reads as follows:

"Sec. 4. Repeal of duplicative enactment.
"(a) In General- The Act entitled 'An Act to provide for the continuation of agricultural programs through fiscal year 2012, and for other purposes' (H.R. 2419 of the 110th Congress), and the amendments made by that Act, are repealed, effective on the date of enactment of that Act.
"(b) Effective Date- Except as otherwise provided in this Act, this Act and the amendments made by this Act shall take effect on the earlier of--
"(1) the date of enactment of this Act; or
"(2) the date of the enactment of the Act entitled 'An Act to provide for the continuation of agricultural programs through fiscal year 2012, and for other purposes' (H.R. 2419 of the 110th Congress)."
—P.L. 110-246, Sec. 15316(c)(3), substituted "H, and I" for "and H" in para. (b)(1), effective for obligations issued after 5/22/2008. [Ed. Note: May 22, 2008 was the date of enactment for H.R. 2419 (PL 110-234), which was repealed by (2008 Farm Act § 4(a)) (PL 110-246, 6/18/2008), in connection with the reenactment of the farm bill to correct a technical deficiency in its original passage.]
In 2005, P.L. 109-135, Sec. 402(c)(2), amended Sec. 1303(e) of the Energy Policy Act of 2005, P.L. 109-58, to read as follows:
"(e) Effective dates.
"(1) In general. Except as provided in paragraph (2), the amendments made by this section shall apply to bonds issued after December 31, 2005.

"(2) Subsection (c). The amendments made by subsection (c) shall apply to taxable years beginning after December 31, 2005."
Prior to amendment, Sec. 1303(e) of P.L. 109-58 read as follows:
"(e) Effective date. The amendments made by this section shall apply to bonds issued after December 31, 2005."
—P.L. 109-58, Sec. 1303(c)(4), substituted "G, and H" for "and G" in para. (b)(1), effective for tax. yrs. begin. after 12/31/2005 [as amended by Sec. 402(c)(2) of P.L. 109-135, see above].
In 1998, P.L. 105-206, Sec. 6022(a), substituted "D, and G" for "and D" in para. (b)(1), effective for tax. yrs. begin. after 12/31/86.
In 1988, P.L. 100-647, Sec. 1012(s)(1)(B), substituted "The preceding sentence shall not apply to any credit so allowed by reason of section 1446." for "The preceding sentence shall not apply to any amount deducted and withheld under section 1446.", in para. (b)(2), effective as provided in Sec. 1012(s)(1)(D) of this Act which reads:
"(D) The amendments made by this paragraph shall apply to taxable years beginning after December 31, 1987. No amount shall be required to be deducted and withheld under section 1446 of the 1986 Code (as in effect before the amendment made by subparagraph (A))."
In 1986, P.L. 99-514, Sec. 1246(b), added the last sentence to para. (b)(2), effective as provided in Sec. 1246(d) of this Act which reads as follows:
"(d) Effective date.—
"The amendment made by this section shall apply to distributions after December 31, 1987 (or, if earlier, the effective date (which shall not be earlier than January 1, 1987) of the initial regulations issued under section 1446 of the Internal Revenue Code of 1986 as added by this section)."
In 1984, P.L. 98-369, Sec. 474(r)(36), amended subsec. (b), effective for tax. yrs. begin. after 12/31/83, and to carrybacks from tax. yrs. begin. after 12/31/83. Prior to amendment, subsec. (b) read as follows:
"(b) Excessive credits.
"If the amount allowable as credits under sections 31 (relating to tax withheld on wages) and 39 (relating to certain uses of gasoline, and special fuels) exceeds the tax imposed by subtitle A (reduced by the credits allowable under subpart A of part IV of subchapter A of chapter 1, other than the credits allowable under sections 31 and 39), the amount of such excess shall be considered an overpayment. For purposes of the preceding sentence, any credit allowed under paragraph (1) of section 32 (relating to withholding of tax on nonresident aliens and on foreign corporations) to a nonresident alien individual for a taxable year with respect to which an election under section 6013(g) or (h) is in effect shall be treated as an amount allowable as a credit under section 31."
—P.L. 98-369, Sec. 735(c)(16), substituted "and special fuels" for ", special fuels, and lubricating oil", in subsec. (b) (prior amendment by Sec. 474(r)(36) of this Act), effective for articles sold after 1/6/83.
In 1980, P.L. 96-223, Sec. 223(b)(2), deleted subsec. (d), to apply to qualified investments for tax. yrs. begin. after 12/31/79.
Prior to amendment, subsec. (d) read as follows:
"(d) Cross reference.
"For rule allowing refund for excess investment credit attributable to solar or wind energy property, see section 46(a)(9)(C)."
—P.L. 96-222, Sec. 103(a)(2)(B)(iv), substituted "(9)" for "(10)" in subsec. (d), for tax yrs begin. after 12/31/78.
In 1978, P.L. 95-618, Sec. 301(c)(2), added subsec. (d), effective for property placed in service after 9/30/78.
—P.L. 95-600, Sec. 103(a), changed the effective date for amendments made by Sec. 204(b)(1) of P.L. 94-12, to effective for tax. yrs. begin. after. 12/31/74, from effective for tax. yrs. begin. after 12/31/74 and before 1/1/79, see below.
—P.L. 95-600, Sec. 701(u)(15)(D), added a sentence to the end of subsec. (b). Sec. 701(u)(15)(E) provides as follows:
"(E) Effective dates. The amendments made by this paragraph—
"(i) to the extent that they relate to chapter 1 or 5 of the Internal Revenue Code of 1954, shall apply to taxable years ending on or after December 31, 1975, and
"(ii) to the extent they relate to wage withholding under chapter 24 of such Code, shall apply to remuneration paid on or after the first day of the first month which begins more than 90 days after the date of enactment of this Act."
In 1977, P.L. 95-30, Sec. 103(b), changed the effective date for amendments made by Sec. 204(b)(1) of P.L. 94-12, to effective for tax. yrs. begin. after. 12/31/74 and before 1/1/79, from effective for tax. yrs. begin. after 12/31/74 and before 1/1/78, see below.
In 1976, P.L. 94-455, Sec. 401(c), changed the effective date for amendments made by Sec. 204(b)(1) of P.L. 94-12, to effective for tax. yrs. begin. after. 12/31/74 and before 1/1/78, from effective for tax. yrs. begin. after 12/31/74 and before 1/1/77, see below.
—P.L. 94-455, Sec. 701(f)(2), substituted "wages" for "wages),", and deleted "and 667(b) (relating to taxes paid by certain trusts)" in subsec. (b), effective for distributions made in tax. yrs. begin. after 12/31/75.
—P.L. 94-455, Sec. 701(f)(3), substituted "lubricating oil), and" for "lubricating oil)," and deleted "and section 667(b) (relating to taxes paid by certain trusts)" in subsec. (b), as amended by P.L. 94-12, effective for distributions made in tax. yrs. begin. after 12/31/75.
In 1975, P.L. 94-164, Sec. 2(f), changed the effective date for amendments made by Sec. 204(b)(1) of P.L. 94-12, to effective for tax. yrs. begin. after. 12/31/74 and before 1/1/77, from effective for tax. yrs. begin. after 12/31/74 and before 1/1/76, see below.
—P.L. 94-12, Sec. 204(b)(1), added "43 (relating to earned income credit)," before "and 667(b)" and substituted ", 39, and 43" for "and 39" in subsec. (b), effective [as amended by Sec. 2(f) of P.L. 94-164, Sec. 401(c) of P.L. 94-455,

3,687

Sec. 103(b) of P.L. 95-30 and Sec. 103(a) of P.L. 95-600, see above] for tax. yrs. begin. after 12/31/74.

In 1970, P.L. 91-258, Sec. 207(d)(1), substituted "uses of gasoline, special fuels, and lubricating oil" for "uses of gasoline and lubricating oil" in subsec. (b), effective 7/1/70.

In 1969, P.L. 91-172, Sec. 331(c), deleted "under sections 31 and 39" in the heading, substituted ", 39 (relating) for "and 39 (relating)" and added "and 667(b) (relating to taxes paid by certain trusts)" after "lubricating oil)" in subsec. (b), effective for tax. yrs. begin. after 12/31/68.

In 1965, P.L. 89-44, Sec. 809, amended subsec. (b), effective for tax. yrs. begin. after 6/30/65.

Prior to amendment, subsec. (b) read as follows:
"*(b) Excessive withholding.*
"If the amount allowable as a credit under section 31 (relating to credit for tax withheld at the source under chapter 24) exceeds the taxes imposed by chapter 1 against which such credit is allowable, the amount of such excess shall be considered an overpayment."

Sec. 6402. Authority to make credits or refunds.
(a) General rule.

In the case of any overpayment, the Secretary, within the applicable period of limitations, may credit the amount of such overpayment, including any interest allowed thereon, against any liability in respect of an internal revenue tax on the part of the person who made the overpayment and shall, subject to subsections (c), (d), (e), and (f) refund any balance to such person.

(b) Credits against estimated tax.

The Secretary is authorized to prescribe regulations providing for the crediting against the estimated income tax for any taxable year of the amount determined by the taxpayer or the Secretary to be an overpayment of the income tax for a preceding taxable year.

(c) Offset of past-due support against overpayments.

The amount of any overpayment to be refunded to the person making the overpayment shall be reduced by the amount of any past-due support (as defined in section 464(c) of the Social Security Act) owed by that person of which the Secretary has been notified by a State in accordance with section 464 of such Act. The Secretary shall remit the amount by which the overpayment is so reduced to the State collecting such support and notify the person making the overpayment that so much of the overpayment as was necessary to satisfy his obligation for past-due support has been paid to the State. The Secretary shall apply a reduction under this subsection first to an amount certified by the State as past due support under section 464 of the Social Security Act before any other reductions allowed by law. This subsection shall be applied to an overpayment prior to its being credited to a person's future liability for an internal revenue tax.

(d) Collection of debts owed to federal agencies.

(1) *In general.* Upon receiving notice from any Federal agency that a named person owes a past-due legally enforceable debt (other than past-due support subject to the provisions of subsection (c)) to such agency, the Secretary shall—

(A) reduce the amount of any overpayment payable to such person by the amount of such debt;

(B) pay the amount by which such overpayment is reduced under subparagraph (A) to such agency; and

(C) notify the person making such overpayment that such overpayment has been reduced by an amount necessary to satisfy such debt.

(2) *Priorities for offset.* Any overpayment by a person shall be reduced pursuant to this subsection after such overpayment is reduced pursuant to subsection (c) with respect to past-due support collected pursuant to an assignment under section 402(a)(26) of the Social Security Act and before such overpayment is reduced pursuant to subsection (e) and (f) and before such overpayment is credited to the future liability for tax of such person pursuant to subsection (b). If the Secretary receives notice from a Federal agency or agencies of more than one debt subject to paragraph (1) that is owed by a person to such agency or agencies, any overpayment by such person shall be applied against such debts in the order in which such debts accrued.

(3) *Treatment of OASDI overpayments.*

(A) Requirements. Paragraph (1) shall apply with respect to an OASDI overpayment only if the requirements of paragraphs (1) and (2) of section 3720A(f) of title 31, United States Code, are met with respect to such overpayment.

(B) Notice; protection of other persons filing joint return.

(i) Notice. In the case of a debt consisting of an OASDI overpayment, if the Secretary determines upon receipt of the notice referred to in paragraph (1) that the refund from which the reduction described in paragraph (1)(A) would be made is based upon a joint return, the Secretary shall—

(I) notify each taxpayer filing such joint return that the reduction is being made from a refund based upon such return, and

(II) include in such notification a description of the procedures to be followed, in the case of a joint return, to protect the share of the refund which may be payable to another person.

(ii) Adjustments based on protections given to other taxpayers on joint return. If the other person filing a joint return with the person owing the OASDI overpayment takes appropriate action to secure his or her proper share of the refund subject to reduction under this subsection, the Secretary shall pay such share to such other person. The Secretary shall deduct the amount of such payment from amounts which are derived from subsequent reductions in refunds under this subsection and are payable to a trust fund referred to in subparagraph (C).

(C) Deposit of amount of reduction into appropriate trust fund. In lieu of payment, pursuant to paragraph (1)(B), of the amount of any reduction under this subsection to the Commissioner of Social Security, the Secretary shall deposit such amount in the Federal Old-Age and Survivors Insurance Trust Fund or the Federal Disability Insurance Trust Fund, whichever is certified to the Secretary as appropriate by the Commissioner of Social Security.

(D) OASDI overpayment. For purposes of this paragraph, the term "OASDI overpayment" means any overpayment of benefits made to an individual under title II of the Social Security Act.

(e) Collection of past-due, legally enforceable State income tax obligations.

(1) *In general.* Upon receiving notice from any State that a named person owes a past-due, legally enforceable State income tax obligation to such State, the Secretary shall, under such conditions as may be prescribed by the Secretary—

(A) reduce the amount of any overpayment payable to such person by the amount of such State income tax obligation;

(B) pay the amount by which such overpayment is reduced under subparagraph (A) to such State and notify such State of such person's name, taxpayer identification number, address, and the amount collected; and

(C) notify the person making such overpayment that the overpayment has been reduced by an amount necessary to satisfy a past-due, legally enforceable State income tax obligation.

If an offset is made pursuant to a joint return, the notice under subparagraph (B) shall include the names, taxpayer identification numbers, and addresses of each person filing such return.

(2) Offset permitted only against residents of State seeking offset. Paragraph (1) shall apply to an overpayment by any person for a taxable year only if the address shown on the Federal return for such taxable year of the overpayment is an address within the State seeking the offset.

(3) Priorities for offset. Any overpayment by a person shall be reduced pursuant to this subsection—

(A) after such overpayment is reduced pursuant to—
(i) subsection (a) with respect to any liability for any internal revenue tax on the part of the person who made the overpayment;
(ii) subsection (c) with respect to past-due support; and
(iii) subsection (d) with respect to any past-due, legally enforceable debt owed to a Federal agency; and
(B) before such overpayment is credited to the future liability for any Federal internal revenue tax of such person pursuant to subsection (b).

If the Secretary receives notice from one or more agencies of the State of more than one debt subject to paragraph (1) or subsection (f) that is owed by such person to such an agency, any overpayment by such person shall be applied against such debts in the order in which such debts accrued.

(4) Notice; consideration of evidence. No State may take action under this subsection until such State—
(A) notifies by certified mail with return receipt the person owing the past-due State income tax liability that the State proposes to take action pursuant to this section;
(B) gives such person at least 60 days to present evidence that all or part of such liability is not past-due or not legally enforceable;
(C) considers any evidence presented by such person and determines that an amount of such debt is past-due and legally enforceable; and
(D) satisfies such other conditions as the Secretary may prescribe to ensure that the determination made under subparagraph (C) is valid and that the State has made reasonable efforts to obtain payment of such State income tax obligation.

(5) Past-due, legally enforceable State income tax obligation. For purposes of this subsection, the term "past-due, legally enforceable State income tax obligation" means a debt—
(A)(i) which resulted from—
(I) a judgment rendered by a court of competent jurisdiction which has determined an amount of State income tax to be due; or
(II) a determination after an administrative hearing which has determined an amount of State income tax to be due; and
(ii) which is no longer subject to judicial review; or
(B) which resulted from a State income tax which has been assessed but not collected, the time for redetermination of which has expired, and which has not been delinquent for more than 10 years.

For purposes of this paragraph, the term "State income tax" includes any local income tax administered by the chief tax administration agency of the State.

(6) Regulations. The Secretary shall issue regulations prescribing the time and manner in which States must submit notices of past-due, legally enforceable State income tax obligations and the necessary information that must be contained in or accompany such notices. The regulations shall specify the types of State income taxes and the minimum amount of debt to which the reduction procedure established by paragraph (1) may be applied. The regulations may require States to pay a fee to reimburse the Secretary for the cost of applying such procedure. Any fee paid to the Secretary pursuant to the preceding sentence shall be used to reimburse appropriations which bore all or part of the cost of applying such procedure.

(7) Erroneous payment to State. Any State receiving notice from the Secretary that an erroneous payment has been made to such State under paragraph (1) shall pay promptly to the Secretary, in accordance with such regulations as the Secretary may prescribe, an amount equal to the amount of such erroneous payment (without regard to whether any other amounts payable to such State under such paragraph have been paid to such State).

(f) Collection of unemployment compensation debts.

(1) In general. Upon receiving notice from any State that a named person owes a covered unemployment compensation debt to such State, the Secretary shall, under such conditions as may be prescribed by the Secretary—
(A) reduce the amount of any overpayment payable to such person by the amount of such covered unemployment compensation debt;
(B) pay the amount by which such overpayment is reduced under subparagraph (A) to such State and notify such State of such person's name, taxpayer identification number, address, and the amount collected; and
(C) notify the person making such overpayment that the overpayment has been reduced by an amount necessary to satisfy a covered unemployment compensation debt.

If an offset is made pursuant to a joint return, the notice under subparagraph (C) shall include information related to the rights of a spouse of a person subject to such an offset.

(2) Priorities for offset. Any overpayment by a person shall be reduced pursuant to this subsection—
(A) after such overpayment is reduced pursuant to—
(i) subsection (a) with respect to any liability for any internal revenue tax on the part of the person who made the overpayment;
(i) subsection (c) with respect to past-due support; and
(iii) subsection (d) with respect to any past-due, legally enforceable debt owed to a Federal agency; and
(B) before such overpayment is credited to the future liability for any Federal internal revenue tax of such person pursuant to subsection (b).

If the Secretary receives notice from a State or States of more than one debt subject to paragraph (1) or subsection (e) that is owed by a person to such State or States, any overpayment by such person shall be applied against such debts in the order in which such debts accrued.

(3) Notice; consideration of evidence. No State may take action under this subsection until such State—
(A) notifies the person owing the covered unemployment compensation debt that the State proposes to take action pursuant to this section;

(B) provides such person at least 60 days to present evidence that all or part of such liability is not legally enforceable or is not a covered unemployment compensation debt;

(C) considers any evidence presented by such person and determines that an amount of such debt is legally enforceable and is a covered unemployment compensation debt; and

(D) satisfies such other conditions as the Secretary may prescribe to ensure that the determination made under subparagraph (C) is valid and that the State has made reasonable efforts to obtain payment of such covered unemployment compensation debt.

(4) Covered unemployment compensation debt. For purposes of this subsection, the term "covered unemployment compensation debt" means—

(A) a past-due debt for erroneous payment of unemployment compensation due to fraud or the person's failure to report earnings which has become final under the law of a State certified by the Secretary of Labor pursuant to section 3304 and which remains uncollected ;

(B) contributions due to the unemployment fund of a State for which the State has determined the person to be liable and which remain uncollected ; and

(C) any penalties and interest assessed on such debt.

(5) Regulations.

(A) In general. The Secretary may issue regulations prescribing the time and manner in which States must submit notices of covered unemployment compensation debt and the necessary information that must be contained in or accompany such notices. The regulations may specify the minimum amount of debt to which the reduction procedure established by paragraph (1) may be applied.

(B) Fee payable to secretary. The regulations may require States to pay a fee to the Secretary, which may be deducted from amounts collected, to reimburse the Secretary for the cost of applying such procedure. Any fee paid to the Secretary pursuant to the preceding sentence shall be used to reimburse appropriations which bore all or part of the cost of applying such procedure.

(C) Submission of notices through secretary of labor— The regulations may include a requirement that States submit notices of covered unemployment compensation debt to the Secretary via the Secretary of Labor in accordance with procedures established by the Secretary of Labor. Such procedures may require States to pay a fee to the Secretary of Labor to reimburse the Secretary of Labor for the costs of applying this subsection. Any such fee shall be established in consultation with the Secretary of the Treasury. Any fee paid to the Secretary of Labor may be deducted from amounts collected and shall be used to reimburse the appropriation account which bore all or part of the cost of applying this subsection.

(6) Erroneous payment to state. Any State receiving notice from the Secretary that an erroneous payment has been made to such State under paragraph (1) shall pay promptly to the Secretary, in accordance with such regulations as the Secretary may prescribe, an amount equal to the amount of such erroneous payment (without regard to whether any other amounts payable to such State under such paragraph have been paid to such State).

(7) Redesignated.
(8) Deleted.
(g) Review of reductions.

No court of the United States shall have jurisdiction to hear any action, whether legal or equitable, brought to restrain or review a reduction authorized by subsection (c), (d), (e), or (f). No such reduction shall be subject to review by the Secretary in an administrative proceeding. No action brought against the United States to recover the amount of any such reduction shall be considered to be a suit for refund of tax. This subsection does not preclude any legal equitable, or administrative action against the Federal agency or State to which the amount of such reduction was paid or any such action against the Commissioner of Social Security which is otherwise available with respect to recoveries of overpayments of benefits under section 204 of the Social Security Act.

(h) Federal agency.

For purposes of this section, the term "Federal agency" means a department, agency, or instrumentality of the United States, and includes a Government corporation (as such term is defined in section 103 of title 5, United States Code).

(i) Treatment of payments to States.

The Secretary may provide that, for purposes of determining interest, the payment of any amount withheld under subsection (c), (e), or (f) to a State shall be treated as a payment to the person or persons making the overpayment.

(j) Cross reference.

For procedures relating to agency notification of the Secretary, see section 3721 of title 31, United States Code.

(k) Refunds to certain fiduciaries of insolvent members of affiliated groups.

Notwithstanding any other provision of law, in the case of an insolvent corporation which is a member of an affiliated group of corporations filing a consolidated return for any taxable year and which is subject to a statutory or court-appointed fiduciary, the Secretary may by regulation provide that any refund for such taxable year may be paid on behalf of such insolvent corporation to such fiduciary to the extent that the Secretary determines that the refund is attributable to losses or credits of such insolvent corporation.

(l) Explanation of reason for refund disallowance.

In the case of a disallowance of a claim for refund, the Secretary shall provide the taxpayer with an explanation for such disallowance.

In 2010, P.L. 111-312, Sec. 503(a), substituted "is a covered unemployment compensation debt" for "is not a covered unemployment compensation debt" in subpara. (f)(3)(C), effective for refunds payable under section 6402 of the Internal Revenue Code of 1986 on or after 12/8/2008 [as if included in Sec. 801 of P.L. 111-291, see below].
—P.L. 111-291, Sec. 801(a)(1), deleted "resulting from fraud" before the period at the end of the heading of subsec. (f) . . . Sec. 801(a)(2), deleted paras. (f)(3) and (f)(8) and redesignated paras. (f)(4)-(f)(7) as paras. (f)(3)-(f)(6), respectively . . . Sec. 801(a)(3)(A), deleted "by certified mail with return receipt" after "notifies" in subpara. (f)(3)(A) [as redesignated by Sec. 801(a)(2) of this Act, see above] . . . Sec. 801(a)(3)(B), substituted "is not a covered unemployment compensation debt" for "due to fraud" in subpara. (f)(3)(B) [as redesignated by Sec. 801(a)(2) of this Act, see above] . . . Sec. 801(a)(3)(C), substituted "is not a covered unemployment compensation debt" for "due to fraud" in subpara. (f)(3)(C) [as redesignated by Sec. 801(a)(2) of this Act, see above] . . . Sec. 801(a)(4)(A)(i), added "or the person's failure to report earnings" after "due to fraud" in subpara. (f)(4)(A) [as redesignated by Sec. 801(a)(2) of this Act, see above] . . . Sec. 801(a)(4)(A)(ii), deleted "for not more than 10 years" before the semicolon at the end of subpara. (f)(4)(A) [as redesignated by Sec. 801(a)(2) of this Act, see above] . . . Sec. 801(a)(4)(B)(i), deleted "due to fraud" after "person to be liable" in subpara. (f)(4)(B) [as redesignated by Sec. 801(a)(2) of this Act, see above] . . . Sec. 801(a)(4)(B)(ii), deleted "for not more than 10 years" after "remain uncollected" in subpara. (f)(4)(B) [as redesignated by Sec. 801(a)(2) of this Act, see above], effective for refunds payable under section 6402 of the Internal Revenue Code of 1986 on or after 12/8/2008.
Prior to deletion, para. (f)(3) read as follows:
"(3) Offset permitted only against residents of state seeking offset. Paragraph (1) shall apply to an overpayment by any person for a taxable year only if the ad-

Abatements, credits, refunds
Code Sec. 6403

dress shown on the Federal return for such taxable year of the overpayment is an address within the State seeking the offset."
Prior to deletion, para. (f)(8) read as follows:
"(8) Termination. This section shall not apply to refunds payable after the date which is 10 years after the date of the enactment of this subsection."
In 2008, P.L. 110-328, Sec. 3(a), redesignated subsec. (f)-(k) as (g)-(l) and added subsec. (f)... Sec. 3(d)(1), substituted "(c), (d), (e), and (f)" for "(c), (d), and (e)," in subsec. (a)... Sec. 3(d)(2), substituted "and before such overpayment is reduced pursuant to subsections (e) and (f)," for "and before such overpayment is reduced pursuant to subsection (e)" in para. (d)(2)... Sec. 3(d)(3), added "or subsection (f)" after "paragraph (1)" in para. (e)(3)... Sec. 3(d)(4), substituted "(c), (d), (e), or (f)" for "(c), (d), or (e)," in subsec. (g) [as redesignated by Sec. 3(a) of this Act, see above]... Sec. 3(d)(5), substituted "subsection (c), (e), or (f)" for "subsection (c) or (e)" in subsec. (i) [as redesignated by Sec. 3(a) of this Act], effective for refunds payable under section 6402 of the Internal Revenue Code of 1986 on or after 9/30/2008.

In 2006, P.L. 109-171, Sec. 7301(d)(1), substituted "of such Act." for "the Social Security Act." in subsec. (c)... Sec. 7301(d)(2), substituted "The Secretary shall apply a reduction under this subsection first to an amount certified by the State as past due support under section 464 of the Social Security Act before any other reductions allowed by law." for "A reduction under this subsection shall be applied first to satisfy any past-due support which has been assigned to the State under section 402(a)(26) or 471(a)(17) of the Social Security Act, and shall be applied to satisfy any other past-due support after any other reductions allowed by law (but before a credit against future liability for an internal revenue tax) have been made." in subsec. (c), effective 10/1/2009, and for payments under parts A and D of title IV of the Social Security Act for calendar quarters begin. on or after 10/1/2009, and without regard to whether regulations to implement the amendments (in the case of State programs operated under such part D) are promulgated by 10/1/2009, except as provided in Sec. 7301(e)(2) of this Act, which reads as follows:
"(2) State option to accelerate effective date. Notwithstanding paragraph (1), a State may elect to have the amendments made by the preceding provisions of this section apply to the State and to amounts collected by the State (and the payments under parts A and D), on and after such date as the State may select that is not earlier than October 1, 2008, and not later than September 30, 2009."

In 1998, P.L. 105-206, Sec. 3505(a), added subsec. (j), effective for disallowances after the 180th day after date of enactment.
— P.L. 105-206, Sec. 3711(a), redesignated subsec. (e)-(j) as (f)-(k) and added subsec. (e)... Sec. 3711(c)(1), substituted "(c), (d), and (e)" for "(c) and (d)" in subsec. (a)... Sec. 3711(c)(2), added "and before such overpayment is reduced pursuant to subsection (e) and before such overpayment" for "and before such overpayment" in para. (d)(2)... Sec. 3711(c)(3)(A), substituted "(c), (d), or (e)" for "(c) or (d)" in subsec. (f) [as redesignated by Sec. 3711(a), of this Act, see above]... Sec. 3711(c)(3)(B), substituted "Federal agency or State" for "Federal agency" in subsec. (f) [as redesignated by Sec. 3711(a), of this Act, see above] ... Sec. 3711(c)(4), substituted "subsection (c) or (e)" for "subsection (c)" in subsec. (h) [as redesignated by Sec. 3711(a), of this Act, see above], effective for refunds payable under Code Sec. 6402 after 12/31/99.
— P.L. 105-33, Sec. 5514(a)(1), deleted Sec. 110(l)(7) of P.L. 104-193 [see below] as if those provisions had never been enacted, effective 7/1/97.

In 1996, P.L. 104-193, Sec. 110(l)(7)(A), substituted "(c), (d), and (e)" for "(c) and (d)" in subsec. (a) [prior to deletion by Sec. 5514(a)(1) of P.L. 105-33, see above] ... Sec. 110(l)(7)(B), redesignated subsecs. (e)-(i) as subsec. (f)-(j) [prior to deletion by Sec. 5514(a)(1) of P.L. 105-33, see above]... Sec. 110(l)(7)(C), added subsec. (e) [prior to deletion by Sec. 5514(a)(1) of P.L. 105-33, see above], effective 7/1/97.
— P.L. 104-134, Sec. 31001(u)(2), amended subsec. (f), effective 4/26/96.
Prior to amendment, subsec. (f) read as follows:
"(f) Federal agency.
"For purposes of this section, the term 'Federal agency' means a department, agency, or instrumentality of the United States (other than an agency subject to section 9 of the Act of May 18, 1933 (48 Stat. 63, chapter 32; 16 U.S.C. 831h)), and includes a Government corporation (as such term is defined in section 103 of title 5, United States Code)."

In 1994, P.L. 103-296, Sec. 108(h)(7), substituted "Commissioner of Social Security" for "Secretary of Health and Human Services" in subpara. (d)(3)(C) and subsec. (e), effective 3/31/95.

In 1991, P.L. 102-164, Sec. 401(a), amended Sec. 2653(c) of P.L. 98-369, so that the amendments are effective for refunds payable under Code Sec. 6402 after 12/31/85, rather than effective for refunds payable under Code Sec. 6402 after 12/31/85 and on or before 1/10/94.

In 1990, P.L. 101-508, Sec. 5129(c)(1)(A), deleted "any OASDI overpayment and" after "debt (other than" in para. (d)(1)... Sec. 5129(c)(1)(B), amended para. (d)(3)... Sec. 5129(c)(2), added "or any such action against the Secretary of Health and Human Services which is otherwise available with respect to recoveries of overpayments of benefits under section 204 of the Social Security Act" before the period at the end of subsec. (e), effective 1/1/91 except as provided in Sec. 5129(d)(2) of this Act, which reads as follows:
"(2) shall not apply to refunds to which the amendments made by section 2653 of the Deficit Reduction Act of 1984 (98 Stat. 1153) do not apply."
Prior to amendment, para. (d)(3) read as follows:
"(3) Definitions. For purposes of this subsection, the term 'OASDI overpayment' means any overpayment of benefits made to an individual under title II of the Social Security Act."

In 1988, P.L. 100-647, Sec. 6276, added subsec. (i), effective 11/10/88.
— P.L. 100-485, Sec. 701(a), amended Sec. 2653(c) of P.L. 98-369, the effective date for changes made by Sec. 2653(b)(1) of P.L. 98-369, by substituting "on or before January 10, 1994" for "before July 1, 1988", see below.

In 1987, P.L. 100-203, Sec. 9402(a), amended Sec. 2653(c) of P.L. 98-369, the effective date for changes made by Sec. 2653(b)(1) and (2) of P.L. 98-369, by substituting "July 1, 1988" for "January 1, 1988", see below. Sec. 9402(b) of this Act provides:
"(b) Clarification of Congressional intent as to scope of provision.
"(1) Nothing in the amendments made by section 2653 of the Deficit Reduction Act of 1984 shall be construed as exempting debts of corporations or any other category of persons from the application of such amendments.
"(2) It is the intent of the Congress that, to the extent practicable, the amendments made by section 2653 of the Deficit Reduction Act of 1984 shall extend to all Federal agencies (as defined in the amendments made by such section).
"(3) The Secretary of the Treasury shall issue regulations to carry out the purposes of this subsection."

In 1984, P.L. 98-378, Sec. 21(e)(1)(A), substituted "collecting such support" for "to which such support has been assigned" in subsec. (c)... Sec. 21(e)(1)(B), added "A reduction under this subsection shall be applied first to satisfy any past-due support which has been assigned to the State under section 402(a)(26) or 471(a)(17) of the Social Security Act, and shall be applied to satisfy any other past-due support after any other reductions allowed by law (but before a credit against future liability for an internal revenue tax) have been made." before the last sentence in subsec. (c)... Sec. 21(e)(2), redesignated subsec. (g) (as added by Sec. 2653(b)(1) of P.L. 98-369) as subsec. (h) and added new subsec. (g), effective for refunds payable under Code Sec. 6402 after 12/31/85.
— P.L. 98-369, Sec. 2653(b)(1), added subsecs. (d), (e), (f), and (g)... Sec. 2653(b)(2), substituted "subsections (c) and (d)" for "subsection (c)" in subsec. (a), effective for refunds payable under Code Sec. 6402 after 12/31/85 [as amended by Sec. 401(a) of P.L. 102-164, Sec. 701(a) of P.L. 100-485, Sec. 9402(a) of P.L. 100-203, see above].

In 1981, P.L. 97-35, Sec. 2331(c)(1), substituted "shall, subject to subsection (c), refund" for "shall refund" in subsec. (a)... Sec. 2331(c)(2), added subsec. (c), effective 10/1/81, except as provided in Sec. 2336(b) of this Act, which reads:
"(b) If a State agency administering a plan approved under part D of title IV of the Social Security Act demonstrates, to the satisfaction of the Secretary of Health and Human Services, that it cannot, by reason of State law, comply with the requirements of an amendment made by this chapter to which the effective date specified in subsection (a) applies, the Secretary may prescribe that, in the case of such State, the amendment will become effective beginning with the first month beginning after the close of the first session of such State's legislature ending on or after October 1, 1981. For purposes of the preceding sentence, the term 'session of a State's legislature' includes any regular, special, budget, or other session of a State legislature."

In 1976, P.L. 94-455, Sec. 1906(b)(13)(A), substituted "Secretary" for "Secretary or his delegate" each place it appeared in Code Sec. 6402, effective 2/1/77.
— P.L. 94-455, Sec. 1906(b)(13)(K), deleted "(or his delegate)", which followed "or the Secretary", in subsec. (b), effective 2/1/77.

In 1973, P.L. 93-53, Sec. 3, amended Sec. 22 of the Second Liberty Bond Act as follows effective with respect to refunds made after December 31, 1973:
"Second Liberty Bond Act
* * *
"Sec. 22. United States savings bonds and Treasury savings certificates — Authority to issue; use of proceeds.
* * *
"(j)(1) The Secretary of the Treasury is authorized to prescribe by regulations that checks issued to individuals (other than trusts and estates) as refunds made in respect of the taxes imposed by subtitle A of the Internal Revenue Code of 1954 may, at the time and in the manner provided in such regulations, become United States savings bonds of Series E. Except as provided in paragraph (2), bonds issued under this subsection shall be treated for all purposes of law as series E bonds issued under this section. This subsection shall apply only if the claim for refund was filed on or before the last day prescribed by law for filing the return (determined without extensions thereof) for the taxable year in respect of which the refund is made.
"(2) Any check-bond issued under this subsection shall bear an issue date of the first day of the first calendar month beginning after the close of the taxable year for which issued.
"(3) In the case of any check-bond issued under this subsection to joint payees, the regulations prescribed under this subsection may provide that either payee may redeem the bond upon his request."

Sec. 6403. Overpayment of installment.

In the case of a tax payable in installments, if the taxpayer has paid as an installment of the tax more than the amount determined to be the correct amount of such installment, the overpayment shall be credited against the unpaid installments, if any. If the amount already paid, whether or not on the basis of installments, exceeds the amount determined to be the correct amount of the tax, the overpayment shall be credited or refunded as provided in section 6402.

Sec. 6404. Abatements.

(a) General rule.

The Secretary is authorized to abate the unpaid portion of the assessment of any tax or any liability in respect thereof, which—

(1) is excessive in amount, or

(2) is assessed after the expiration of the period of limitation properly applicable thereto, or

(3) is erroneously or illegally assessed.

(b) No claim for abatement of income, estate, and gift taxes.

No claim for abatement shall be filed by a taxpayer in respect of an assessment of any tax imposed under subtitle A or B.

(c) Small tax balances.

The Secretary is authorized to abate the unpaid portion of the assessment of any tax, or any liability in respect thereof, if the Secretary determines under uniform rules prescribed by the Secretary that the administration and collection costs involved would not warrant collection of the amount due.

(d) Assessments attributable to certain mathematical errors by Internal Revenue Service.

In the case of an assessment of any tax imposed by chapter 1 attributable in whole or in part to a mathematical error described in section 6213(g)(2)(A), if the return was prepared by an officer or employee of the Internal Revenue Service acting in his official capacity to provide assistance to taxpayers in the preparation of income tax returns, the Secretary is authorized to abate the assessment of all or any part of any interest on such deficiency for any period ending on or before the 30th day following the date of notice and demand by the Secretary for payment of the deficiency.

(e) Abatement of interest attributable to *unreasonable* errors and delays by Internal Revenue Service.

(1) In general. In the case of any assessment of interest on —

(A) any deficiency attributable in whole or in part to any unreasonable error or delay by an officer or employee of the Internal Revenue Service (acting in his official capacity) in performing a ministerial or managerial act, or

(B) any payment of any tax described in section 6212(a) to the extent that any unreasonable error or delay in such payment is attributable to such an officer or employee being erroneous or dilatory in performing a ministerial or managerial act,

the Secretary may abate the assessment of all or any part of such interest for any period. For purposes of the preceding sentence, an error or delay shall be taken into account only if no significant aspect of such error or delay can be attributed to the taxpayer involved, and after the Internal Revenue Service has contacted the taxpayer in writing with respect to such deficiency or payment.

(2) Interest abated with respect to erroneous refund check. The Secretary shall abate the assessment of all interest on any erroneous refund under section 6602 until the date demand for repayment is made, unless—

(A) the taxpayer (or a related party) has in any way caused such erroneous refund, or

(B) such erroneous refund exceeds $50,000.

(f) Abatement of any penalty or addition to tax attributable to erroneous written advice by the Internal Revenue Service.

(1) In general. The Secretary shall abate any portion of any penalty or addition to tax attributable to erroneous advice furnished to the taxpayer in writing by an officer or employee of the Internal Revenue Service, acting in such officer's or employee's official capacity.

(2) Limitations. Paragraph (1) shall apply only if—

(A) the written advice was reasonably relied upon by the taxpayer and was in response to a specific written request of the taxpayer, and

(B) the portion of the penalty or addition to tax did not result from a failure by the taxpayer to provide adequate or accurate information.

(3) Initial regulations. Within 180 days after the date of the enactment of this subsection, the Secretary shall prescribe such initial regulations as may be necessary to carry out this subsection.

(g) Suspension of interest and certain penalties where Secretary fails to contact taxpayer.

(1) Suspension.

(A) In general. In the case of an individual who files a return of tax imposed by subtitle A for a taxable year on or before the due date for the return (including extensions), if the Secretary does not provide a notice to the taxpayer specifically stating the taxpayer's liability and the basis for the liability before the close of the 36-month period beginning on the later of—

(i) the date on which the return is filed; or

(ii) the due date of the return without regard to extensions,

the Secretary shall suspend the imposition of any interest, penalty, addition to tax, or additional amount with respect to any failure relating to the return which is computed by reference to the period of time the failure continues to exist and which is properly allocable to the suspension period.

(B) Separate application. This paragraph shall be applied separately with respect to each item or adjustment. If, after the return for a taxable year is filed, the taxpayer provides to the Secretary 1 or more signed written documents showing that the taxpayer owes an additional amount of tax for the taxable year, clause (i) shall be applied by substituting the date the last of the documents was provided for the date on which the return is filed.

(2) Exceptions. Paragraph (1) shall not apply to—

(A) any penalty imposed by section 6651;

(B) any interest, penalty, addition to tax, or additional amount in a case involving fraud;

(C) any interest, penalty, addition to tax, or additional amount with respect to any tax liability shown on the return;

(D) any interest, penalty, addition to tax, or additional amount with respect to any gross misstatement;

(E) any interest, penalty, addition to tax, or additional amount with respect to any reportable transaction with respect to which the requirement of section 6664(d)(2)(A) is not met and any listed transaction (as defined in 6707A(c)); or

(F) any criminal penalty.

(3) Suspension period. For purposes of this subsection, the term "suspension period" means the period—

(A) beginning on the day after the close of the 36-month period under paragraph (1); and

(B) ending on the date which is 21 days after the date on which notice described in paragraph (1)(A) is provided by the Secretary.

(h) Review of denial of request for abatement of interest.

(1) In general. The Tax Court shall have jurisdiction over any action brought by a taxpayer who meets the requirements referred to in section 7430(c)(4)(A)(ii) to determine

Abatements, credits, refunds   Code Sec. 6405(a)

whether the Secretary's failure to abate interest under this section was an abuse of discretion, and may order an abatement, if such action is brought within 180 days after the date of the mailing of the Secretary's final determination not to abate such interest.

(2) Special rules.

(A) Date of mailing. Rules similar to the rules of section 6213 shall apply for purposes of determining the date of the mailing referred to in paragraph (1).

(B) Relief. Rules similar to the rules of section 6512(b) shall apply for purposes of this subsection.

(C) Review. An order of the Tax Court under this subsection shall be reviewable in the same manner as a decision of the Tax Court, but only with respect to the matters determined in such order.

(i) Cross reference.

For authority to suspend running of interest, etc. by reason of Presidentially declared disaster or terroristic or military action, see section 7508A.

In 2007, P.L. 110-28, Sec. 8242(a), substituted "36-month period" for "18-month period" in subparas. (g)(1)(A) and (g)(3)(A), effective for notices provided by the Secretary of the Treasury, or his delegate, after the date which is 6 months after 5/25/2007.

In 2006, P.L. 109-432, Sec. 426(b)(1), added "of the Secretary's delegate" after "the Secretary of the Treasury," in Sec. 903(d)(2)(B)(iii), P.L. 108-357, the effective date for changes made by Sec. 903(c) of P.L. 108-357, as amended by Sec. 303(a)(1) of P.L. 109-135, see below.

In 2005, P.L. 109-135, Sec. 303(a)(1), amended Sec. 903(d)(2) of P.L. 108-357, the effective date for changes made by Sec. 903(c) of P.L. 108-357, see below: Prior to amendment, Sec. 903(d)(2) of P.L. 108-357, read as follows:

"(2) Exception for reportable or listed transactions. The amendments made by subsection (c) shall apply with respect to interest accruing after October 3, 2004."

—P.L. 109-135, Sec. 303(b)(1), added "If, after the return for a taxable year is filed, the taxpayer provides to the Secretary 1 or more signed written documents showing that the taxpayer owes an additional amount of tax for the taxable year, clause (i) shall be applied by substituting the date the last of the documents was provided for the date on which the return is filed." at the end of para. (g)(1), effective for documents provided on or after 12/21/2005.

In 2004, P.L. 108-357, Sec. 903(a), substituted "18-month period" for "1-year period (18-month period in the case of taxable years beginning before January 1, 2004)" each place it appeared in subsec. (g)... Sec. 903(b), deleted "or" at the end of subpara. (g)(2)(C), redesignated subpara. (g)(2)(D) as (g)(2)(E), and added subpara. (g)(2)(D), effective for tax. yrs. begin. after 12/31/2003.

—P.L. 108-357, Sec. 903(c), deleted "or" at the end of subpara. (g)(2)(D) [as added by Sec. 903(b) of this Act, see above], redesignated subpara. (g)(2)(E) as (g)(2)(F) [as redesignated by Sec. 903(b) of this Act, see above], and added subpara. (g)(2)(E), effective as provided in Sec. 903(c)(2) of this Act, [as amended by Sec. 303(a)(1) of P.L. 109-135, and Sec. 426(b)(1) of P.L. 109-432, see above] which reads as follows:

"(2) Exception for reportable or listed transactions.

"(A) In general. The amendments made by subsection (c) shall apply with respect to interest accruing after October 3, 2004.

"(B) Special rule for certain listed and reportable transactions.

"(i) In general. Except as provided in clauses (ii), (iii), and (iv), the amendments made by subsection (c) shall also apply with respect to interest accruing on or before October 3, 2004.

"(ii) Participants in settlement initiatives. Clause (i) shall not apply to any transaction if, as of January 23, 2006—

"(I) the taxpayer is participating in a settlement initiative described in Internal Revenue Service Announcement 2005-80 with respect to such transaction, or

"(II) the taxpayer has entered into a settlement agreement pursuant to such an initiative.

Subclause (I) shall not apply to any taxpayer if, after January 23, 2006, the taxpayer withdraws from, or terminates, participation in the initiative or the Secretary of the Treasury or the Secretary's delegate determines that a settlement agreement will not be reached pursuant to the initiative within a reasonable period of time.

"(iii) Taxpayers acting in good faith. The Secretary of the Treasury or the Secretary's delegate may except from the application of clause (i) any transaction in which the taxpayer has acted reasonably and in good faith.

"(iv) Closed transactions. Clause (i) shall not apply to a transaction if, as of December 14, 2005—

"(I) the assessment of all Federal income taxes for the taxable year in which the tax liability to which the interest relates arose is prevented by the operation of any law or rule of law, or

"(II) a closing agreement under section 7121 has been entered into with respect to the tax liability arising in connection with the transaction."

In 2002, P.L. 107-134, Sec. 112(d)(1)(A), deleted subsec. (h)... Sec. 112(d)(1)(B), redesignated subsec. (i) as (h)... Sec. 112(d)(1)(C), added subsec. (i), effective for disasters and terroristic or military actions occurring on or after 9/11/2001, with respect to any action of the Secretary of the Treasury, the Secretary of Labor, or the Pension Benefit Guaranty Corporation occurring on or after 1/23/2002.

Prior to deletion, subsec. (h) read as follows:

"(h) Abatement of interest on underpayments by taxpayers in Presidentially declared disaster areas.

"(1) In general. If the Secretary extends for any period the time for filing income tax returns under section 6081 and the time for paying income tax with respect to such returns under section 6161 for any taxpayer located in a Presidentially declared disaster area, the Secretary shall abate for such period the assessment of any interest prescribed under section 6601 on such income tax.

"(2) Presidentially declared disaster area. For purposes of paragraph (1), the term 'Presidentially declared disaster area' means, with respect to any taxpayer, any area which the President has determined warrants assistance by the Federal Government under the Robert T. Stafford Disaster Relief and Emergency Assistance Act."

In 1998, P.L. 105-277, Sec. 4003(e)(2), added "Robert T. Stafford" before "Disaster" in para. (h)(2), effective for disasters declared after 12/31/96.

—P.L. 105-206, Sec. 3305(a), redesignated subsec. (g) as (h) and added subsec. (g), effective for tax. yrs. end. after 7/22/98.

—P.L. 105-206, Sec. 3309(a), redesignated subsec. (h) [as redesignated by Sec. 3305(a), of this Act, see above] as (i) and added subsec. (h), effective for disasters declared after 12/31/97, with respect to tax. yrs. begin. after 12/31/97.

—P.L. 105-206, Sec. 3309(c), of this Act, reads as follows:

"(c) Emergency designation.

"(1) For the purposes of section 252(e) of the Balanced Budget and Emergency Deficit Control Act, Congress designates the provisions of this section as an emergency requirement.

"(2) The amendments made by subsections (a) and (b) of this section shall only take effect upon the transmittal by the President to the Congress of a message designating the provisions of subsections (a) and (b) as an emergency requirement pursuant to section 252(e) of the Balanced Budget and Emergency Deficit Control Act."

In 1996, P.L. 104-168, Sec. 301(a)(1), added "unreasonable" before "error" each place it appeared in subparas. (e)(1)(A) and (e)(1)(B)... Sec. 301(a)(2), substituted "in performing a ministerial or managerial act" for "in performing a ministerial act" each place it appeared in para. (e)(1)... Sec. 301(b)(1), substituted "Abatement" for "Assessments" in the heading of subsec. (e)... Sec. 301(b)(2), added "unreasonable" before "errors" in the heading of subsec. (e), effective for interest accruing with respect to deficiencies or payments for tax. yrs. begin. after 7/30/96.

—P.L. 104-168, Sec. 302(a), added subsec. (g), effective for requests for abatement after 7/30/96.

—P.L. 104-168, Sec. 701(c)(3), substituted "section 7430(c)(4)(A)(ii)" for "section 7430(c)(4)(A)(iii)" in subsec. (g) [as added by Sec. 302(a) of this Act, see above], effective for proceedings commenced after 7/30/96.

In 1988, P.L. 100-647, Sec. 1015(n)(1), added "error or" before "delay" in subpara. (e)(1)(B)... Sec. 1015(n)(2), added "erroneous or" before "dilatory" in subpara. (e)(1)(B), effective for interest accruing for deficiencies or payments for tax. yrs. begin. after 12/31/78. For special rules see Sec. 1563(b)(2) of P.L. 99-514, reproduced below.

—P.L. 100-647, Sec. 6229(a), added subsec. (f), effective for advice requested on or after 1/1/89.

In 1986, P.L. 99-514, Sec. 1563(a), added subsec. (e), effective for interest accruing for deficiencies or payments for tax. yrs. begin. after 12/31/78. Sec. 1563(b)(2) of this Act provides:

"(2) Statute of limitations. If refund or credit of any amount resulting from the application of the amendment made by subsection (a) is prevented at any time before the close of the date which is 1 year after the date of the enactment of this Act by the operation of any law or rule of law (including res judicata), refund or credit of such amount (to the extent attributable to the application of the amendment made by subsection (a)) may, nevertheless, be made or allowed if claim therefore is filed before the close of such 1-year period."

In 1980, P.L. 96-589, Sec. 6(b)(2), substituted "section 6213(g)(2)(A)" for "section 6213(f)(2)(A)" in subsec. (d), effective 10/1/79, except for any proceeding under the Bankruptcy Act begun before 10/1/79. Sec. 7(g) of this Act provides:

"(g) Definitions.

"For purposes of this section—

"(1) Bankruptcy case. The term 'bankruptcy case' means any case under title 11 of the United States Code (as recodified by P.L. 95-598).

"(2) Similar judicial proceeding. The term 'similar judicial proceeding' means a receivership, foreclosure, or similar proceeding in a Federal or State court (as modified by section 368(a)(3)(D) of the Internal Revenue Code of 1954)."

In 1976, P.L. 94-455, Sec. 1212(a), added subsec. (d), effective for returns filed for tax. yrs. end. after 10/4/76.

—P.L. 94-455, Sec. 1906(b)(13)(A), substituted "Secretary" for "Secretary or his delegate" each place it appeared in Code Sec. 6404, effective 2/1/77.

Sec. 6405. Reports of refunds and credits.
(a) By Treasury to Joint Committee.

No refund or credit of any income, war profits, excess profits, estate, or gift tax, or any tax imposed with respect to public charities, private foundations, operators' trust funds, pension plans, or real estate investment trusts under chapter 41, 42, 43, or 44, in excess of $2,000,000 shall be made until after the expiration of 30 days from the date upon which

3,693

a report giving the name of the person to whom the refund or credit is to be made, the amount of such refund or credit, and a summary of the facts and the decision of the Secretary, is submitted to the Joint Committee on Taxation.

(b) Tentative adjustments.

Any credit or refund allowed or made under section 6411 shall be made without regard to the provisions of subsection (a) of this section. In any such case, if the credit or refund, reduced by any deficiency in such tax thereafter assessed and by deficiencies in any other tax resulting from adjustments reflected in the determination of the credit or refund, is in excess of $2,000,000, there shall be submitted to such committee a report containing the matter specified in subsection (a) at such time after the making of the credit or refund as the Secretary shall determine the correct amount of the tax.

(c) Refunds attributable to certain disaster losses.

If any refund or credit of income taxes is attributable to the taxpayer's election under section 165(i) to deduct a disaster loss for the taxable year immediately preceding the taxable year in which the disaster occurred, the Secretary is authorized in his discretion to make the refund or credit, to the extent attributable to such election, without regard to the provisions of subsection (a) of this section. If such refund or credit is made without regard to subsection (a), there shall thereafter be submitted to such Joint Committee a report containing the matter specified in subsection (a) as soon as the Secretary shall determine the correct amount of the tax for the taxable year for which the refund or credit is made.

In 2000, P.L. 106-554, Sec. 1(a)(7), [which enacted into law Sec. 305(a) of P.L. 106-554] substituted "$2,000,000" for "$1,000,000" in subsecs. (a) and (b), effective 12/21/2000, except for any refund or credit with respect to a report that has been made before such date of the enactment under section 6405.

In 1990, P.L. 101-508, Sec. 11801(c)(21)(A), repealed subsec. (d), effective 11/5/90, except as provided in Sec. 11821(b) of this Act reproduced in note following Code Sec. 6361.

Prior to deletion, subsec. (d) read as follows:

"*(d) Qualified State individual income taxes.*

"For purposes of this section, a refund or credit made under subchapter E of chapter 64 (relating to Federal collection of qualified State individual income taxes) for a taxable year shall be treated as a portion of a refund or credit of the income tax for that taxable year."

—P.L. 101-508, Sec. 11834(a), substituted "$1,000,000" for "$200,000" in subsecs. (a) and (b), effective 11/5/90, except that such amendment shall not apply for any refund or credit for a report [which] has been made before 11/5/90 under Code Sec. 6405.

In 1986, P.L. 99-514, Sec. 1879(e), deleted subsec. (b), and redesignated subsecs. (c), (d) and (e) as subsecs. (b), (c) and (d), effective for tax. yrs. begin. after 12/31/82. For exception see note for amendments made by Sec. 711(c)(3) of P.L. 98-369 reproduced below:

Prior to deletion, subsec. (b) read as follows:

"*(b) By Joint Committee to Congress.*

"A report to Congress shall be made annually by such committee of such refunds and credits, including the names of all persons and corporations to whom amounts are credited or payments are made, together with the amounts credited or paid to each."

In 1984, P.L. 98-369, Sec. 711(c)(3), substituted "section 165(i)" for "section 165(h)" in subsec. (d), effective for tax. yrs. begin. after 12/31/82, except that "[s]uch amendments shall also apply to the taxpayer's last taxable year beginning before January 1, 1983, solely for purposes of determining the amount allowable as a deduction with respect to any loss taken into account for such year by reason of an election under section 165(i) of the Internal Revenue Code of 1954 (as amended by this section)."

In 1978, P.L. 95-227, Sec. 4(d)(3), substituted "public charities, private foundations, operators' trust funds, pension plans, or real estate investment trusts under chapters 41, 42, 43, or 44" for "private foundations and pension plans under chapters 42 and 43" in subsec. (a), effective for contributions, acts, and expenditures made after 12/31/77, in and for tax. yrs. begin. after 12/31/77.

In 1976, P.L. 94-455, Sec. 1210(a), amended subsec. (a), effective 10/4/76 except for any refund or credit with respect to which a report has been made before 10/4/76 under Code Sec. 6405(a) or 6405(c).

Prior to amendment, subsec. (a) read as follows:

"*(a) By Treasury to Joint Committee.*

"No refund or credit of any income, war profits, excess profits, estate, or gift tax in excess of $100,000 shall be made until after the expiration of 30 days from the date upon which a report giving the name of the person to whom the refund or credit is to be made, the amount of such refund or credit, and a summary of the facts and the decision of the Secretary or his delegate, is submitted to the Joint Committee on Internal Revenue Taxation."

—P.L. 94-455, Sec. 1210(b), substituted "$200,000" for "$100,000" in subsec. (c), effective 10/4/76 except for any refund or credit with respect to which a report has been made before 10/4/76 under Code Sec. 6405(a) or 6405(c).

—P.L. 94-455, Sec. 1906(b)(13)(A), substituted "Secretary" for "Secretary or his delegate" each place it appeared in Code Sec. 6405, effective 2/1/77.

In 1972, P.L. 92-512, Sec. 203(a), added subsec. (e), effective 10/20/72.

—P.L. 92-418, Sec. 2(b), added subsec. (d), effective for refunds or credits made after 7/1/72.

Sec. 6406. Prohibition of administrative review of decisions.

In the absence of fraud or mistake in mathematical calculation, the findings of fact in and the decision of the Secretary upon the merits of any claim presented under or authorized by the internal revenue laws and the allowance or nonallowance by the Secretary of interest on any credit or refund under the internal revenue laws shall not, except as provided in subchapters C and D of chapter 76 (relating to the Tax Court), be subject to review by any other administrative or accounting officer, employee, or agent of the United States.

In 1976, P.L. 94-455, Sec. 1906(b)(13)(A), substituted "Secretary" for "Secretary or his delegate" each place it appeared in Code Sec. 6406, effective 2/1/77.

Sec. 6407. Date of allowance of refund or credit.

The date on which the Secretary first authorizes the scheduling of an overassessment in respect of any internal revenue tax shall be considered as the date of allowance of refund or credit in respect of such tax.

In 1976, P.L. 94-455, Sec. 1906(b)(13)(A), substituted "Secretary" for "Secretary or his delegate" Code Sec. 6407, effective 2/1/77.

Sec. 6408. State escheat laws not to apply.

No overpayment of any tax imposed by this title shall be refunded (and no interest with respect to any such overpayment shall be paid) if the amount of such refund (or interest) would escheat to a State or would otherwise become the property of a State under any law relating to the disposition of unclaimed or abandoned property. No refund (or payment of interest) shall be made to the estate of any decedent unless it is affirmatively shown that such amount will not escheat to a State or otherwise become the property of a State under such a law.

In 1987, P.L. 100-203, Sec. 10621(a), added Code Sec. 6408, effective 12/22/87.

Sec. 6409. Refunds disregarded in the administration of federal programs and federally assisted programs.

(a) In general.

Notwithstanding any other provision of law, any refund (or advance payment with respect to a refundable credit) made to any individual under this title shall not be taken into account as income, and shall not be taken into account as resources for a period of 12 months from receipt, for purposes of determining the eligibility of such individual (or any other individual) for benefits or assistance (or the amount or extent of benefits or assistance) under any Federal program or under any State or local program financed in whole or in part with Federal funds.

(b) Termination.

Subsection (a) shall not apply to any amount received after December 31, 2012.

In 2010, P.L. 111-312, Sec. 728(a), added Code Sec. 6409, effective for amounts received after 12/31/2009.

Abatements, credits, refunds
Code Sec. 6411(b)

Subchapter B.—Rules of Special Application
Sec.
6411. Tentative carryback and refund adjustments.
6412. Floor stocks refunds.
6413. Special rules applicable to certain employment taxes.
6414. Income tax withheld.
6415. Credits or refunds to persons who collected certain taxes.
6416. Certain taxes on sales and services.
6419. Excise tax on wagering.
6420. Gasoline used on farms.
6421. Gasoline used for certain nonhighway purposes, used by local transit systems, or sold for certain exempt purposes.
6422. Cross references.
6423. Conditions to allowance in the case of alcohol and tobacco taxes.
6424. Repealed.
6425. Adjustment of overpayment of estimated income tax by corporation.
6426. Credit for alcohol fuel, biodiesel, and alternative fuel mixtures.
6426. Repealed.
6427. Fuels not used for taxable purposes.
6428. 2008 recovery rebates for individuals.
6429. Advance payment of portion of increased child credit for 2003.
6430. Treatment of tax imposed at Leaking Underground Storage Tank Trust Fund financing rate.
6431. Credit for qualified bonds allowed to issuer.
6432. COBRA premium assistance.

In 2009, P.L. 111-5, Sec. 1531(b), added item 6431.... Sec. 3001(a)(12)(A), added item 6432.
In 2008, P.L. 110-185, Sec. 101(f)(3), amended item 6428.
Prior to amendment, item 6428 read as follows:
"6428. Acceleration of 10 percent income tax rate bracket benefit for 2001."
In 2005, P.L. 109-58, Sec. 1362(b)(3)(B), added item 6430.
—P.L. 109-59, Sec. 1113(b)(3)(B), substituted "alcohol fuel, biodiesel, and alternative fuel" for "alcohol fuel and biodiesel" in item 6426.
In 2004, P.L. 108-357, Sec. 301(c)(14), added item 6426.
In 2003, P.L. 108-27, Sec. 101(b)(2), added item 6429.
In 2001, P.L. 107-16, Sec. 101(b)(2), added item 6428.
In 1990, P.L. 101-508, Sec. 11801(c)(22)(B)(ii), deleted item 6418.
Prior to deletion, item 6418 read as follows:
"6418. Sugar."
—P.L. 101-508, Sec. 11801(b)(15), deleted item 6428.
Prior to deletion, item 6428 read as follows:
"6428. 1981 rate reduction tax credit."
In 1988, P.L. 100-418, Sec. 1941(b)(3)(E), deleted items 6429 and 6430.
Prior to deletion, items 6429 and 6430 read as follows:
"6429. Credit and refund of Chapter 45 taxes paid by royalty owners.
"6430. Credit or refund of windfall profit taxes to certain trust beneficiaries."
In 1986, P.L. 99-514, Sec. 1703(c)(2)(E), amended item 6421.
Prior to amendment, item 6421 read as follows:
"6421. Gasoline used for certain nonhighway purposes or by local transit system."
In 1983, P.L. 97-424, Sec. 515(b)(14), deleted item 6424.
Prior to deletion item 6424 read as follows:
"6424. Lubricating oil used for certain nontaxable purposes."
—P.L. 97-448, Sec. 106(a)(4)(D), added item 6430.
In 1982, P.L. 97-248, Sec. 280(c)(2)(H), deleted item 6426.
Prior to deletion item 6426 read as follows:
"6426. Refund of aircraft use tax where plane transports for hire in foreign air commerce."
In 1981, P.L. 97-34, Sec. 101(b)(2)(A), amended item 6428.
Prior to amendment, item 6428 read as follows:
"6428. Refund of 1974 individual income taxes."
In 1980, P.L. 96-499, Sec. 1131(b)(1), added item 6429.
In 1978, P.L. 95-618, Sec. 233(b)(2)(B), substituted "used for certain nontaxable purposes," for "not used in highway motor vehicles" in item 6424.
—P.L. 95-600, Sec. 504(b)(1)(B), added "and refund" after "carryback" in item 6411.

In 1975, P.L. 94-12, Sec. 101(c), added new item 6428.
In 1970, added items 6426 and 6427.
In 1968, added item 6425.
In 1965, added item 6424.
In 1958, added item 6423.
In 1956, added item "6421" and renumbered former item "6421" as item "6422."
—added item "6420", and renumbered former item "6420. Cross references" as item "6421".

Sec. 6411. Tentative carryback and refund adjustments.
(a) Application for adjustment.

A taxpayer may file an application for a tentative carryback adjustment of the tax for the prior taxable year affected by a net operating loss carryback provided in section 172(b), by a business credit carryback provided in section 39, or by a capital loss carryback provided in subsection (a)(1) or (c) of section 1212, from any taxable year. The application shall be verified in the manner prescribed by section 6065 in the case of a return of such taxpayer and shall be filed, on or after the date of filing for the return for the taxable year of the net operating loss, net capital loss, or unused business credit from which the carryback results and within a period of 12 months after such taxable year or, with respect to any portion of a business credit carryback attributable to a net operating loss carryback or a net capital loss carryback from a subsequent taxable year, within a period of 12 months from the end of such subsequent taxable year, in the manner and form required by regulations prescribed by the Secretary. The application shall set forth in such detail and with such supporting data and explanation as such regulations shall require—

(1) The amount of the net operating loss, net capital loss, or unused business credit;

(2) The amount of the tax previously determined for the prior taxable year affected by such carryback, the tax previously determined being ascertained in accordance with the method prescribed in section 1314(a);

(3) The amount of decrease in such tax, attributable to such carryback, such decrease being determined by applying the carryback in the manner provided by law to the items on the basis of which such tax was determined;

(4) The unpaid amount of such tax, not including any amount required to be shown under paragraph (5);

(5) The amount, with respect to the tax for the taxable year immediately preceding the taxable year from which the carryback is made, as to which an extension of time for payment under section 6164 is in effect; and

(6) Such other information for purposes of carrying out the provisions of this section as may be required by such regulations.

Except for purposes of applying section 6611(f)(4)(B), an application under this subsection shall not constitute a claim for credit or refund.

(b) Allowance of adjustments.

Within a period of 90 days from the date on which an application for a tentative carryback adjustment is filed under subsection (a), or from the last day of the month in which falls the last date prescribed by law (including any extension of time granted the taxpayer) for filing the return for the taxable year of the net operating loss, net capital loss, or unused business credit from which such carryback results, whichever is the later, the Secretary shall make, to the extent he deems practicable in such period, a limited examination of the application, to discover omissions and errors of computation therein, and shall determine the amount of the decrease in the tax attributable to such carryback upon the basis of the application and the examination, except that the Secretary may disallow, without further action, any applica-

3,695

tion which he finds contains errors of computation which he deems cannot be corrected by him within such 90-day period or material omissions. Such decrease shall be applied against any unpaid amount of the tax decreased (including any amount of such tax as to which an extension of time under section 6164 is in effect) and any remainder shall be credited against any unsatisfied amount of any tax for the taxable year immediately preceding the taxable year of the net operating loss, net capital loss, or unused business credit the time for payment of which tax is extended under section 6164. Any remainder shall, within such 90-day period, be either credited against any tax or installment thereof then due from the taxpayer, or refunded to the taxpayer.

(c) Consolidated returns.

If the corporation seeking a tentative carryback adjustment under this section, made or was required to make a consolidated return, either for the taxable year within which the net operating loss, net capital loss, or unused business credit arises, or for the preceding taxable year affected by such loss or credit, the provisions of this section shall apply only to such extent and subject to such conditions, limitations, and exceptions as the Secretary may by regulations prescribe.

(d) Tentative refund of tax under claim of right adjustment.

(1) Application. A taxpayer may file an application for a tentative refund of any amount treated as an overpayment of tax for the taxable year under section 1341(b)(1). Such application shall be in such manner and form as the Secretary may prescribe by regulation and shall—

(A) be verified in the same manner as an application under subsection (a),

(B) be filed during the period beginning on the date of filing the return for such taxable year and ending on the date 12 months from the last day of such taxable year, and

(C) set forth in such detail and with such supporting data such regulations prescribe—

(i) the amount of the tax for such taxable year computed without regard to the deduction described in section 1341(a)(2),

(ii) the amount of the tax for all prior taxable years for which the decrease in tax provided in section 1341(a)(5)(B) was computed,

(iii) the amount determined under section 1341(a)(5)(B),

(iv) the amount of the overpayment determined under section 1341(b)(1); and

(v) such other information as the Secretary may require.

(2) Allowance of adjustments. Within a period of 90 days from the date on which an application is filed under paragraph (1) or from the date of the overpayment (determined under section 1341(b)(1)), whichever is later, the Secretary shall—

(A) review the application,

(B) determine the amount of the overpayment, and

(C) apply, credit, or refund such overpayment,

in a manner similar to the manner provided in subsection (b).

(3) Consolidated returns. The provisions of subsection (c) shall apply to an adjustment under this subsection to the same extent and manner as the Secretary may by regulations provide.

In **2005**, P.L. 109-135, Sec. 409(a)(1), substituted "6611(f)(4)(B)" for "6611(f)(3)(B)" in subsec. (a), effective for foreign tax credit carrybacks arising in tax. yrs. begin. after 8/5/97 as if included in Sec. 1055 of the Taxpayer Relief Act of 1997, P.L. 105-34.

In **2004**, P.L. 108-311, Sec. 403(b)(2), of this Act provides:

"(2) In the case of a net operating loss for a taxable year ending during 2001 or 2002—

"(A) an application under section 6411(a) of the Internal Revenue Code of 1986 with respect to such loss shall not fail to be treated as timely filed if filed before November 1, 2002,

"(B) any election made under section 172(b)(3) of such Code may (notwithstanding such section) be revoked before November 1, 2002, and

"(C) any election made under section 172(j) of such Code shall (notwithstanding such section) be treated as timely made if made before November 1, 2002."

In **2000**, P.L. 106-554, Sec. 1(a)(7), [which enacted into law Sec. 318(d)(1) of P.L. 106-554] substituted "subsection (a)(1) or (c) of section 1212" for "section 1212(a)(1)" in subsec. (a), effective for property acquired and positions established by the taxpayer after 6/23/81, in tax. yrs. ending after such date.

In **1988**, P.L. 100-647, Sec. 1002(h)(2), deleted "unused research credit," which followed "net capital loss," in subsec. (c) effective for tax. yrs. begin. after 12/31/85.

In **1986**, P.L. 99-514, Sec. 231(a)(2), amended Sec. 221(d) of P.L. 97-34, the effective date for changes made by Sec. 221(b)(2)(B) of P.L. 97-34, by substituting "amounts paid or incurred after June 30, 1981 and before January 1, 1986" [see below].

—P.L. 99-514, Sec. 231(d)(3)(H)(i), deleted "by a research credit carryback provided in section 30(g)(2)" following "provided in section 39" in subsec. (a) . . . Sec. 231(d)(3)(H)(ii), deleted "a research credit carryback or" following "with respect to any portion", in subsec. (a) . . . Sec. 231(d)(3)(H)(iii), deleted "(or, with respect to any portion of a business credit carryback attributable to a research credit carryback from a subsequent taxable year within a period of 12 months from the end of such subsequent taxable year)" following "such subsequent taxable year" in subsec. (a) . . . Sec. 231(d)(3)(H)(iv), deleted "unused research credit" each place it appeared in subsecs. (a) and (b), effective for tax. yrs. begin. after 12/31/85.

—P.L. 99-514, Sec. 1847(b)(10), substituted "unused research credit, or unused business credit" for "unused business credit", in the second sentence of subsec. (a) [amended by Sec. 231(d)(3) of this Act, see above], effective for tax. yrs. begin. after 12/31/83.

—P.L. 99-514, Sec. 1875(d)(3), of this Act provided that notwithstanding Sec. 715 of P.L. 98-369, the amendments made by Sec. 714(n)(2) of P.L. 98-369, are effective for applications filed after 7/18/84.

In **1984**, P.L. 98-369, Sec. 474(r)(37)(A), amended the matter preceding para. (a)(2) . . . Sec. 474(r)(37)(B), substituted "unused research credit, or unused business credit" for "unused investment credit, unused work incentive program credit, unused new employee credit, unused research credit, or unused employee stock ownership credit" in subsecs. (b) and (c), effective for tax. yrs. begin. after 12/31/83, and for carrybacks from tax. yrs. begin. after 12/31/83.

Prior to amendment, the matter preceding para. (a)(2) read as follows:

"(a) Application for adjustment.

"A taxpayer may file an application for a tentative carryback adjustment of the tax for the prior taxable year affected by a net operating loss carryback provided in section 172(b), by an investment credit carryback provided in section 46(b), by a work incentive program carryback provided in section 50A(b), by a new employee credit carryback provided in section 53(b), by a research credit carryback provided in section 44F(g)(2), by an employee stock ownership credit carryback provided by section 44G(b)(2) or by a capital loss carryback provided in section 1212(a)(1), from any taxable year. The application shall be verified in the manner prescribed by section 6065 in the case of a return of such taxpayer, and shall be filed, on or after the date of filing of the return for the taxable year of the net operating loss, net capital loss, unused investment credit, unused work incentive program credit, unused new employee credit, unused research credit, or unused employee stock ownership credit from which the carryback results and within a period of 12 months from the end of such taxable year (or, with respect to any portion of an investment credit carryback, a work incentive program carryback, a new employee credit carryback, a research credit carryback, or employee stock ownership credit carryback from a taxable year attributable to a net operating loss carryback or a capital loss carryback (or, in the case of a work incentive program carryback, to an investment credit carryback, or, in the case of a new employee credit carryback to an investment credit carryback or a work incentive program carryback, or, in the case of a research credit carryback, to an investment credit carryback, a work incentive program carryback, or a new employee credit carryback) from a subsequent taxable year, within a period of 12 months from the end of such subsequent taxable year), in the manner and form required by regulations prescribed by the Secretary.

The application shall set forth in such detail and with such supporting data and explanation as such regulations shall require—

"(1) The amount of net operating loss, net capital loss, unused investment credit, unused work incentive program credit, unused new employee credit, unused research credit, or unused employee stock ownership credit;"

—P.L. 98-369, Sec. 714(n)(2)(B), substituted "Except for purposes of applying section 6611(f)(3)(B), an" for "An" in the last sentence of subsec. (a), effective [as provided in Sec. 1875(d)(3) of P.L. 99-514, see above] for applications filed after 7/18/84.

In **1981**, P.L. 97-34, Sec. 221(b)(2)(B)(i), substituted "unused new employee credit, or unused research credit" for "or unused new employee credit", each time it appeared in Code Sec. 6411 ... Sec. 221(b)(2)(B)(ii), added "by a research credit carryback provided in section 44F(g)(2)" after "53(b)," in subsec. (a) ... Sec. 221(b)(2)(B)(iii), substituted "a new employee credit carryback, or a research credit carryback from" for "or a new employee credit carryback from" each time it appeared in Code Sec. 6411 ... Sec. 221(b)(2)(B)(iv), substituted "work incentive program carryback, or, in the case of a research credit carryback, to an investment credit carryback, a work incentive program carryback, or a new employee credit carryback)" for "work incentive program carryback)" in subsec. (a), effective [as amended by Sec. 231(a)(2) of P.L. 99-514, see above] for amounts paid or incurred after 6/30/81. For transitional rule see Sec. 221(d)(2) of this Act reproduced in note following Code Sec. 44F.

— P.L. 97-34, Sec. 331(d)(2)(B)(i), substituted "unused research credit, or unused employee stock ownership credit" for "or unused research credit" each place it appeared in Code Sec. 6411 ... Sec. 331(d)(2)(B)(ii), added "by and employee stock ownership credit carryback provided by section 44G(b)(2)" after "section 44F(g)(2)" in subsec. (a) ... Sec. 331(d)(2)(B)(iii), substituted "a research credit carryback, or employee stock ownership credit carryback from" for "or a research credit carryback from" each time it appeared in Code Sec. 6411 ... Sec. 331(d)(2)(B)(iv), substituted "new employee credit carryback, or, in the case of an employee stock ownership credit carryback, to an investment credit carryback, a new employee credit carryback or a research and experimental credit carryback)" for "new employee credit carryback)" in the second sentence of subsec. (a), for tax. yrs. begin. after 12/31/81.

In 1980, P.L. 96-222, Sec. 103(a)(6)(G)(xiii), substituted "section 53(b)" for "section 53(c)" in subsec. (a), effective for tax. yrs. begin. after 12/31/78.

— P.L. 96-222, Sec. 105(a)(2), amended para. (d)(2), for tentative refund claims filed on or after 11/6/78.

Prior to amendment, para. (d)(2) read as follows:

"(2) Allowance of adjustments. Within a period of 90 days from the date on which an application is filed under paragraph (1), or from the last day of the month in which falls the last date prescribed by law (including any extension of time granted the taxpayer) for filing the return for taxable year in which the overpayment occurs, whichever is later, the Secretary shall—

"(A) review the application,

"(B) determine the amount of the overpayment, and

"(C) apply, credit, or refund such overpayment in a manner similar to the manner provided in subsection (b)."

In 1978, P.L. 95-600, Sec. 504(a), added new subsec. (d) ... Sec. 504(b)(1)(A), added "and refund" after "carryback" in the heading of Code Sec. 6411, effective for tentative refund claims filed on and after 11/6/78.

In 1977, P.L. 95-30, Sec. 202(d)(5)(A), substituted "unused work incentive program credit, or unused new employee credit" for "or unused work incentive program credit" each place it appeared in Code Sec. 6411 ... added "by a new employee credit carryback provided in section 53(c)," after "section 50A(b)" in the first sentence of subsec. (a) ... substituted ", a work incentive program carryback, or a new employee credit carryback from" for "or a work incentive program carryback from" in the second sentence of subsec. (a) ... substituted "investment credit carryback, or, in the case of a new employee credit carryback, to an investment credit carryback or a work incentive program carryback)" for "investment credit carryback)" in the second sentence of subsec. (a), effective for tax. yrs. begin. after 12/31/76. and to credit carrybacks from such yrs.

In 1976, P.L. 94-455, Sec. 1906(b)(13)(A), substituted "Secretary" for "Secretary or his delegate" each place it appeared in Code Sec. 6411, effective 2/1/77.

— P.L. 94-455, Sec. 2107(g)(1), added "(or, in the case of a work incentive program carryback, to an investment credit carryback)" after "capital loss carryback" in the second sentence of subsec. (a), effective 10/4/76.

In 1971, P.L. 92-178, Sec. 601(e)(1), substituted "unused investment credit, or unused work incentive program credit" for "or unused investment credit" each place it appeared in Code Sec. 6411 ... added "by a work incentive program carryback provided in section 50A(b)," after "section 46(b)," in the first sentence of subsec. (a) ... added "or a work incentive program carryback" after "investment credit carryback" in the second sentence of subsec. (a), effective for tax. yrs. begin. after 12/31/71.

In 1969, P.L. 91-172, Sec. 512(d)(1), amended the first two sentences of subsec. (a) ... Sec. 512(d)(2), substituted "net operating loss, net capital loss, or unused investment credit" for "net operating loss or unused investment credit" wherever it appeared in para. (a)(1), subsec. (b) and subsec. (c), effective for net capital losses sustained in tax. yrs. begin. after 12/31/69.

Prior to amendment, the first two sentences of subsec. (a) read as follows:

"A taxpayer may file an application for a tentative carryback adjustment of the tax for the prior taxable year affected by a net operating loss carryback provided in section 172(b), or by an investment credit carryback provided in section 46(b), from any taxable year. The application shall be verified in the manner prescribed by section 6065 in the case of a return of such taxpayer, and shall be filed, on or after the date of filing of the return for that taxable year of the net operating loss or unused investment credit from which the carryback results and within a period of 12 months from the end of such taxable year (or, with respect to any portion of an investment credit carryback from a taxable year attributable to a net operating loss carryback from a subsequent taxable year, with a period of 12 months from the end of such subsequent taxable year) in the manner and form required by regulations prescribed by the Secretary or his delegate."

In 1967, P.L. 90-225, Sec. 2(b), added "(or, with respect to any portion of an investment credit carryback from a taxable year attributable to a net operating loss carryback from a subsequent taxable year, with a period of 12 months from the end of such subsequent taxable year), effective for investment credit carrybacks attributable to net operating loss carrybacks from tax. yrs. end. after 7/31/67.

In 1966, P.L. 89-721, Sec. 2(a)-(c), provided in introductory text for a tentative carryback adjustment based on an investment credit carryback as provided for in section 46 (b) of this title and and added 'or unused investment credit' after 'the taxable year of the net operating loss', added in para. (a)(1) 'or unused investment' after 'net operating loss', and deleted in para. (a)(5) 'of such loss' and added in lieu thereof 'from which the carryback is made' ... Sec. 2(d), added 'or unused investment credit' after "net operating loss' in two places in subsec. (b) ... Sec. 2(d), (e), added 'or unused investment credit' after 'net operating loss' and 'or credit' after 'such loss' in subsec. (c).

Sec. 6412. Floor stocks refunds.

(a) In general.

(1) Tires and taxable fuel. Where before October 1, 2011, any article subject to the tax imposed by section 4071 or 4081 has been sold by the manufacturer, producer, or importer and on such date is held by a dealer and has not been used and is intended for sale, there shall be credited or refunded (without interest) to the manufacturer, producer, or importer an amount equal to the difference between the tax paid by such manufacturer, producer, or importer on his sale of the article and the amount of tax made applicable to such article on and after October 1, 2011, if claim for such credit or refund is filed with the Secretary on or before March 31, 2012, based upon a request submitted to the manufacturer, producer, or importer before January 1, 2012, by the dealer who held the article in respect of which the credit or refund is claimed, and, on or before March 31, 2012, reimbursement has been made to such dealer by such manufacturer, producer, or importer for the tax reduction on such article or written consent has been obtained from such dealer to allowance of such credit or refund. No credit or refund shall be allowable under this paragraph with respect to taxable fuel in retail stocks held at the place where intended to be sold at retail, nor with respect to taxable fuel held for sale by a producer or importer of taxable fuel.

(2) Definitions. For purposes of this section—

(A) The term "dealer" includes a wholesaler, jobber, distributor, or retailer.

(B) An article shall be considered as "held by a dealer" if title thereto has passed to such dealer (whether or not delivery to him has been made), and if for purposes of consumption title to such article or possession thereof has not at any time been transferred to any person other than a dealer.

(b) Limitation on eligibility for credit or refund.

No manufacturer, producer, or importer shall be entitled to credit or refund under subsection (a) unless he has in his possession such evidence of the inventories with respect to which the credit or refund is claimed as may be required by regulations prescribed under this section.

(c) Other laws applicable.

All provisions of law, including penalties, applicable in respect of the taxes imposed by sections 4071 and 4081 shall, insofar as applicable and not inconsistent with subsections (a) and (b) of this section, apply in respect of the credits and refunds provided for in subsection (a) to the same extent as if such credits or refunds constituted overpayments of such taxes.

In 2005, P.L. 109-59, Sec. 11101(a)(3)(A), substituted "2011" for "2005" each place it appeared in para. (a)(1) ... Sec. 11101(a)(3)(B), substituted "2012" for "2006" each place it appeared in para. (a)(1), effective 8/10/2005.

In 1998, P.L. 105-178, Sec. 9002(a)(2)(A)(i), substituted "2005" for "1999" each place it appeared in para. (a)(1) ... Sec. 9002(a)(2)(A)(ii), substituted "2006" for "2000" each place it appeared in para. (a)(1), effective 6/9/98.

In 1993, P.L. 103-66, Sec. 13242(d)(16), substituted "taxable fuel" for "gasoline" each place it appeared in para. (a)(1), effective 1/1/94.

In 1991, P.L. 102-240, Sec. 8002(c)(1)(A), substituted "1999" for "1995" each place it appeared in para. (a)(1) ... Sec. 8002(c)(1)(B), substituted "2000" for "1996" each place it appeared in para. (a)(1), effective 12/18/91.

In 1990, P.L. 101-508, Sec. 11211(f)(1)(A), substituted "1995" for "1993" each place it appeared in para. (a)(1) . . . Sec. 11211(f)(1)(B), substituted "1996" for "1994" each place it appeared in para. (a)(1), effective 11/5/90.

In 1987, P.L. 100-17, Sec. 502(d)(1)(A), substituted "1993" for "1988" each place it appeared in para. (a)(1) . . . Sec. 502(d)(1)(B), substituted "1994" for "1989" each place it appeared in para. (a)(1), effective 4/2/87.

In 1984, P.L. 98-369, Sec. 734(a)(1), amended Sec. 523(b) of P.L. 97-424 (reproduced below), by adding "(or will be subject to a lower rate of tax under such section)" after "and which will not be subject to tax under such section" in Sec. 523(b)(1) of P.L. 97-424. . . . Sec. 734(a)(2), amended Sec. 523(b) of P.L. 97-424 (reproduced below), by adding Sec. 523(b)(3) to P.L. 97-424 and by substituting "Except as provided in paragraph (3), in the case of" for "In the case of" in Sec. 523(b)(2) of P.L. 97-424 . . . Sec. 734(d), amended Sec. 523(b)(1) of P.L. 97-424 (reproduced below), by adding the last sentence.

—P.L. 98-369, Sec. 735(c)(12)(A), amended the material preceding "there shall be credited or refunded" in para. (a)(1) . . . Sec. 735(c)(12)(B), deleted the last sentence in para. (a)(1) . . . Sec. 735(c)(12)(C), amended subpara. (a)(2)(A) . . . Sec. 735(c)(12)(D), substituted "4071" for "4061, 4071," in subsec. (c), effective for articles sold on or after 1/1/84.

Prior to amendment, amended material of para. (a)(1) read as follows:

"(1) Trucks, tires, tubes, tread rubber, and gasoline. Where before October 1, 1988, any article subject to the tax imposed by section 4061(a)(1), 4071(a)(1), (3), or (4), or 4081 has been sold by the manufacturer, producer, or importer and on such date is held by a dealer and has not been used and is intended for sale (or, in the case of tread rubber, is intended for sale or is held for use)".

Prior to deletion, last sentence of (a)(1) read as follows:

No credit or refund shall be allowable under this paragraph with respect to inner tubes for bicycle tires (as defined in section 4221(e)(4)(B))."

Prior to amendment, subpara. (a)(2)(A) read as follows:

"(A) The term 'dealer' includes a wholesaler, jobber, distributor, or retailer, or, in the case of tread rubber subject to tax under section 4071(a)(4), includes any person (other than the manufacturer, producer, or importer thereof) who holds such tread rubber for sale or use."

In 1983, P.L. 97-424, Sec. 516(a)(5)(A), substituted "1989" for "1985" each place it appeared in para. (a)(1) . . . Sec. 516(a)(5)(B), substituted "1988" for "1984" each place it appeared in para. (a)(1), effective 1/6/83.

—P.L. 97-424, Sec. 522(a)-(d), provides as follows:

SEC. 522. FLOOR STOCKS REFUNDS.

"(a) General rule.

"(1) In general. Where, before the day after the date of the enactment of this Act, any tax-repealed article has been sold by the manufacturer, producer, or importer and on such day is held by a dealer and has not been used and is intended for sale, there shall be credited or refunded (without interest) to the manufacturer, producer, or importer an amount equal to the tax paid by such manufacturer, producer, or importer on his sale of the article if —

"(A) claim for such credit or refund is filed with the Secretary of the Treasury or his delegate before October 1, 1983, based on a request submitted to the manufacturer, producer, or importer before July 1, 1983, by the dealer who held the article in respect of which the credit or refund is claimed, and

"(B) on or before October 1, 1983, reimbursement has been made to the dealer by the manufacturer, producer, or importer in an amount equal to the tax paid on the article or written consent has been obtained from the dealer to allowance of the credit or refund.

"(2) Limitation on eligibility for credit or refund. No manufacturer, producer, or importer shall be entitled to credit or refund under paragraph (1) unless he has in his possession such evidence of the inventories with respect to which the credit or refund is claimed as may be required by regulations prescribed by the Secretary of the Treasury or his delegate under this subsection.

"(3) Other laws applicable. All provisions of law, including penalties, applicable with respect to the taxes imposed by section 4061, 4071, or 4091 (whichever is appropriate) shall, insofar as applicable and not inconsistent with paragraphs (1) and (2) of this subsection, apply in respect of the credits and refunds provided for in paragraph (1) to the same extent as if the credits or refunds constituted overpayments of the tax."

"(b) Refunds with respect to certain consumer purchases of trucks and trailers.

"(1) In general. Except as otherwise provided in paragraph (2), where after December 2, 1982, and before the day after the date of the enactment of this Act, a tax-repealed article on which tax was imposed by section 4061(a) has been sold to an ultimate purchaser, there shall be credited or refunded (without interest) to the manufacturer, producer, or importer of such article an amount equal to the tax paid by such manufacturer, producer, or importer on his sale of the article.

"(2) Limitation of eligibility for credit or refund. No manufacturer, producer, or importer shall be entitled to a credit or refund under paragraph (1) with respect to an article unless—

"(A) he has in his possession such evidence of the sale of the article to an ultimate purchaser, and of the reimbursement of the tax to such purchaser, as may be required by regulations prescribed by the Secretary of the Treasury or his delegate under this subsection.

"(B) claim for such credit or refund is filed with the Secretary of the Treasury or his delegate before October 1, 1983, based on information submitted to the manufacturer, producer, or importer before July 1, 1983, by the person who sold the article (in respect of which the credit or refund is claimed) to the ultimate purchaser, and

"(C) on or before October 1, 1983, reimbursement has been made to the ultimate purchaser in an amount equal to the tax paid on the article.

"(3) Other laws applicable. All provisions of law, including penalties, applicable with respect to the taxes imposed by section 4061(a) shall, insofar as applicable and not inconsistent with paragraph (1) or (2) of this subsection, apply in respect of the credits and refunds provided for in paragraph (1) to the same extent as if the credits or refunds constituted overpayments of the tax.

"(c) Certain uses by manufacturer, etc. In the case of any article which was subject to the tax imposed by section 4061(a) (as in effect on the day before the date of the enactment of this Act), any tax paid by reason of section 4218(a) (relating to use by manufacturer or importer considered sale) with respect to a tax-repealed article shall be deemed to be an overpayment of such tax if tax was imposed on such article after December 2, 1982, by reason of section 4218(a).

"(d) Transfer of floor stocks refunds from highway trust fund. The Secretary of the Treasury shall pay from time to time from the Highway Trust Fund into the general fund of the Treasury amounts equivalent to the floor stocks refunds made under this section."

—P.L. 97-424, Sec. 523(a), and (b) [as amended by Secs. 734(a)(1), (a)(2) and (d) of P.L. 98-369, see above] provide as follows:

"SEC. 523. DEFINITIONS AND SPECIAL RULE.

"(a) In general. For purposes of this subtitle —

"(1) The term 'dealer' includes a wholesaler, jobber, distributor, or retailer.

"(2) An article shall be considered as 'held by a dealer' if title thereto has passed to such dealer (whether or not delivery to him has been made) and if for purposes of consumption title to such article or possession thereof has not at any time been transferred to any person other than a dealer.

"(3) The term 'tax-repealed article' means any article on which a tax was imposed by section 4061(a), 4061(b), or section 4091 as in effect on the day before the date of the enactment of this Act, and which will not be subject to tax under section 4061(a), 4061(b), or 4091 as in effect on the day after the date of the enactment of this Act.

"(4) Except as otherwise expressly provided herein, any reference in this subtitle to a section or other provision shall be treated as a reference to a section or other provision of the Internal Revenue Code of 1954.

"(b) 1984 extension of floor stocks refund to tires.

"(1) In general. In the case of an article on which a tax was imposed by section 4071(a) as in effect on December 31, 1983, and which will not be subject to tax under such section (or will be subject to a lower rate of tax under such section) as in effect on January 1, 1984, such article shall be treated as a tax-repealed article for purposes of subsection (a) of section 522 Any tread rubber which was subject to tax under section 4071(a)(4) as in effect on December 31, 1983, and which on January 1, 1984, is part of a retread tire which is held by a dealer and has not been used and is intended for sale shall be treated as a tax-repealed article for purposes of subsection (a) of section 522.

"(2) Allowance of refund. Except as provided in paragraph (3), in the case of tax-repealed article to which paragraph (1) applies, subsection (a) of section 522 shall be applied—

"(A) by treating January 1, 1984, as the day after the date of the enactment of this Act, and

"(B) by substituting '1984' for '1983' each place it appears in paragraph (1) of such subsection (a).

"(3) Special rules for tires taxed at lower rate after January 1, 1984. In the case of any tire which is a tax-repealed article solely by reason of the amendment made by subsection (a)(1) or (d) of section 734 of the Tax Reform Act of 1984 —

"(A) the amount of the credit or refund under subsection (a) shall not exceed the excess of —

"(i) the tax imposed with respect to such tire by section 4071(a) as in effect on December 31, 1983, over

"(ii) the tax which would have been imposed with respect to such tire by section 4071(a) on January 1, 1984, and

"(B) paragraph (1) of section 522(a) shall be applied —

"(i) by substituting 'January 1, 1985' for 'July 1, 1983', and

"(ii) by substituting 'April 1, 1985' for 'October 1, 1983' each place it appears."

In 1978, P.L. 95-618, Sec. 231(f)(1), deleted "and buses" following "Trucks" in the heading of para. (a)(1), effective for articles sold after 11/9/78.

—P.L. 95-599, Sec. 502(c)(1), substituted "1984" for "1979" each place it appeared in para. (a)(1) . . . Sec. 502(c)(2), substituted "1985" for "1980" each place it appeared in para. (a)(1), effective 11/6/78.

In 1976, P.L. 94-455, Sec. 1906(a)(22), redesignated paras. (a)(2) and (a)(4) as paras. (a)(1) and (a)(2) respectively . . . Sec. 1906(b)(13)(A), substituted "Secretary" for "Secretary or his delegate" in subsec. (a), effective 2/1/77.

—P.L. 94-280, Sec. 303(b)(1), substituted "1979" for "1977" each place it appeared in para. (a)(2) . . . Sec. 303(b)(2), substituted "1980" for "1978" each place it appeared in para. (a)(2), effective 5/5/76.

In 1971, P.L. 92-178, Sec. 401(b), provided as follows:

"(b) Floor stocks refunds.

"(1) In general. Where, before the day after the date of the enactment of this Act [date of enactment is 12/10/71], any tax-repealed article (as defined in subsection (e)) has been sold by the manufacturer, producer, or importer and on such day is held by a dealer and has not been used and is intended for sale, there shall be credited or refunded (without interest) to the manufacturer, producer, or importer an amount equal to the tax paid by such manufacturer, producer, or importer on his sale of the article, if —

"(A) claim for such credit or refund is filed with the Secretary of the Treasury or his delegate before the first day of the 10th calendar month beginning after the day after the date of the enactment of this Act [date of enactment is 12/10/71] based upon a request submitted to the manufacturer, producer, or importer before the first day of the 7th calendar month beginning after the day after the date of the enactment of this Act [date of enactment is 12/10/71] by the dealer who held the article in respect of which the credit or refund is claimed: and

"(B) on or before the first day of such 10th calendar month reimbursement has been made to the dealer by the manufacturer, producer, or importer in an amount equal to the tax paid on the article or written consent has been obtained from the dealer to allowance of the credit or refund.

"(2) Limitation on eligibility for credit or refund. No manufacturer, producer, or importer shall be entitled to credit or refund under paragraph (1) unless he has in his possession such evidence of the inventories with respect to which the credit or refund is claimed as may be required by regulations prescribed by the Secretary of the Treasury or his delegate under this subsection.

"(3) Other laws applicable. All provisions of law, including penalties, applicable with respect to the taxes imposed by section 4061(a) of the Internal Revenue Code of 1954 shall, insofar as applicable and not inconsistent with paragraphs (1) and (2) of this subsection, apply in respect of the credits and refunds provided for in paragraph (1) to the same extent as if the credits or refunds constituted overpayments of the tax."

—P.L. 92-178, Sec. 401(e), provided as follows:

"(e) Definitions. For purposes of this section—

"(1) The term 'dealer' includes a wholesaler, jobber, distributor, or retailer.

"(2) An article shall be considered as 'held by a dealer' if title thereto has passed to such dealer (whether or not delivery to him has been made) and if for purposes of consumption title to such article or possession thereof has not at any time been transferred to any person other than a dealer.

"(3) The term 'tax-repealed article' means an article on which a tax was imposed by section 4061(a) of the Internal Revenue Code of 1954 as in effect on the day before the date of the enactment of this Act [date of enactment is 12/10/71] and is not imposed (without regard to the amendment made by paragraph (2) of subsection (a) of this section) under such section 4061(a) as in effect on the day after the date of the enactment of this Act [date of enactment is 12/10/71]."

—P.L. 92-178, Sec. 401(g)(5), deleted para. (a)(1), effective for articles sold on or after 12/11/71.

Prior to amendment, para. (a)(1) as follows:

"(1) Passenger automobiles, etc. Where before the day after the date of the enactment of the Excise Tax Reduction Act of 1965 [6/22/65], or before January 1, 1966, January 1, of 1973, 1974, 1978, 1979, 1980, 1981, or 1982, any article subject to the tax imposed by section 4061(a)(2) has been sold by the manufacturer, producer, or importer and on such day or such date is held by a dealer and has not been used and is intended for sale, there shall be credited or refunded (without interest) to the manufacturer, producer, or importer an amount equal to the difference between the tax paid by the manufacturer, producer, or importer on his sale of the article and the amount of tax made applicable to the article on such day or such date, if—

"(A) claim for such credit or refund is filed with the Secretary or his delegate on or before the 10th day of the 8th calendar month beginning after such day or such date based upon a request submitted to the manufacturer, producer, or importer before the first day of the 7th calendar month beginning after such day or such date by the dealer who held the article in respect of which the credit or refund is claimed; and

"(B) on or before such 10th day reimbursement has been made to the dealer by the manufacturer, producer, or importer for the tax reduction on the article or written consent has been obtained from the dealer to allowance of the credit or refund."

In 1970, P.L. 91-605, Sec. 303(b)(1), substituted "1977" for "1972" each place it appeared in para. (a)(2) . . . Sec. 303(b)(2), substituted "January 1, 1978" for "January 1, 1973" each place it appeared in para. (a)(2) . . . Sec. 303(b)(3), substituted "March 31, 1978" for "February 10, 1973" each place it appeared in para. (a)(2), effective 12/31/70.

—P.L. 91-614, Sec. 201(a)(2), substituted "January 1 of 1973, 1974, 1978, 1979, 1980, 1981, or 1982" for "January 1, 1971, January 1, 1972, January 1, 1973, or January 1, 1974," in para. (a)(1).

In 1969, P.L. 91-172, Sec. 702(a)(2), substituted "January 1, 1971, January 1, 1972, January 1, 1973, or January 1, 1974" for "January 1, 1970, January 1, 1971, January 1, 1972, or January 1, 1973" in para. (a)(1).

In 1968, P.L. 90-364, Sec. 105(a)(2), substituted, "January 1, 1970, January 1, 1971, January 1, 1972, or January 1, 1973," for "May 1, 1968, or January 1, 1969," in para. (a)(1), effective 4/30/68.

—P.L. 90-285, Sec. 1(a)(2), substituted "April 30, 1968" for "March 31, 1968" and substituted "May 1, 1968" for "April 1, 1968" in para. (a)(1), effective 3/31/68.

In 1966, P.L. 89-368, Sec. 201(b), substituted "January 1, 1966, April 1, 1968, or January 1, 1969" for "January 1, 1966, 1967, 1968, or 1969" in para. (a)(1), effective for articles sold after 3/15/66.

In 1965, P.L. 89-44, Sec. 209(a), amended para. (a)(1) . . . Sec. 209(d), deleted subsec. (e), effective 6/21/65.

Prior to amendment, para. (a)(1) read as follows:

"(1) Passenger automobiles, etc. Where before July 1, 1965, any article subject to the tax imposed by section 4061(a)(2) has been sold by the manufacturer, producer, or importer and on such date is held by a dealer and has not been used and is intended for sale, there shall be credited or refunded (without interest) to the manufacturer, producer, or importer an amount equal to the difference between the tax paid by such manufacturer, producer, or importer on his sale of the article and the amount of tax made applicable to such article on and after July 1, 1965, if claim for such credit or refund is filed with the Secretary or his delegate on or before November 10, 1965, based upon a request submitted to the manufacturer, producer, or importer before October 1, 1965, by the dealer who held the article in respect of which the credit or refund is claimed, and, on or before November 10, 1965, reimbursement has been made to such dealer by such manufacturer, producer, or importer for the tax reduction on such article or written consent has been obtained from such dealer to allowance of such credit or refund."

Prior to deletion, subsec (e) read as follows:

"(e) Cross reference. For floor stocks refunds in case of certain alcohol and tobacco taxes, see sections 5063 and 5707".

—P.L. 89-44, Sec. 209, included the following provision:

"(b) Floor stock refunds; other manufacturers excise taxes and tax on playing cards.

"(1) In general. Where before the day after the date of the enactment of this Act, any article subject to the tax imposed by section 4111, 4121, 4141, 4151, 4161, 4171, 4191, or 4451 of the Internal Revenue Code of 1954 (hereinafter in this Act referred to as the 'Code'), or where before January 1, 1966, any article subject to the tax imposed by section 4061(b), 4091(1), or 4131 of the Code, has been sold by the manufacturer, producer, or importer, and on such day or such date is held by a dealer and has not been used and is intended for sale, there shall be credited or refunded (without interest) to the manufacturer, producer, or importer an amount equal to the difference between the tax paid by the manufacturer, producer, or importer on his sale of the article and the amount of tax made applicable to the article on such day or such date, if—

"(A) claim for such credit or refund is filed with the Secretary of the Treasury or his delegate on or before February 10, 1966 (or August 10, 1966, in the case of an article subject to the tax imposed by section 4061(b), 4091(1), or 4131 of the Code), based upon a request submitted to the manufacturer, producer, or importer before January 1, 1966 (or July 1, 1966, in the case of an article subject to the tax imposed by section 4061(b), 4091(1), or 4131 of the Code), by the dealer who held the article in respect of which the credit or refund is claimed; and

"(B) on or before such February 10 (or such August 10 in the case of an article subject to the tax imposed by section 4061(b), 4091(1), or 4131 of the Code) reimbursement has been made to the dealer by the manufacturer, producer, or importer for the tax reduction on the article or written consent has been obtained from the dealer to allowance of the credit or refund.

"(2) Definitions. For purposes of this subsection—

"(A) The term 'dealer' includes a wholesaler, jobber, distributor, or retailer.

"(B) An article shall be considered as 'held by a dealer' if title thereto has passed to the dealer (whether or not delivery to him has been made), and if for purposes of consumption title to the article or possession thereof has not at any time been transferred to any person other than a dealer. For purposes of paragraph (1) and notwithstanding the preceding sentence, an article shall be considered as 'held by a dealer' and not to have been used, although possession of such article has been transferred to another person, if such article is returned to the dealer in a transaction under which any amount paid or deposited by the transferee for such article is refunded to him (other than amounts retained by the dealer to cover damage to the article). Moreover, such an article shall be considered as held by a dealer on the day after the date of the enactment of this Act even though it is in the possession of the transferee on such day, if it is returned to the dealer (in a transaction described in the preceding sentence) before August 1, 1965.

"(C) In the case of an article subject to the tax imposed by section 4451 (relating to playing cards)—

"(i) an article shall be treated as having been sold by the manufacturer before the day after the date of the enactment of this Act if it has been removed for consumption or sale before such day, and

"(ii) if an article has been removed for consumption or sale, but has not been sold, by the manufacturer before such day, the manufacturer shall be treated as the dealer.

"(3) Limitation on eligibility for credit or refund. No manufacturer, producer, or importer shall be entitled to credit or refund under paragraph (1) unless he has in his possession such evidence of the inventories with respect to which the credit or refund is claimed as may be required by regulations prescribed by the Secretary of the Treasury or his delegate under this subsection.

"(4) Other laws applicable. All provisions of law, including penalties, applicable in respect of the taxes imposed by sections 4061(b), 4091(1), 4111, 4121, 4131, 4141, 4151, 4161, 4171, 4191, and 4451 of the Code shall, insofar as applicable and not inconsistent with paragraphs (1), (2), and (3) of this subsection, apply in respect of the credits and refunds provided for in paragraph (1) to the same extent as if the credits or refunds constituted overpayments of the taxes.

"(c) Refunds with respect to certain consumer purchases.

"(1) In general. Where after May 14, 1965, and before the day after the date of the enactment of this Act, a new automotive item subject to the tax imposed by section 4061(a)(2) of the Code, or a new self-contained air-conditioning unit subject to the tax imposed by section 4111 of the Code, has been sold to an ultimate purchaser, there shall be credited or refunded (without interest) to the manufacturer, producer, or importer of such article an amount equal to the difference between the tax paid by such manufacturer, producer, or importer on his sale of the article, and the tax made applicable to the article on such day, if—

"(A) claim for such credit or refund is filed with the Secretary of the Treasury or his delegate on or before February 10, 1966, based upon information submitted to the manufacturer, producer, or importer before January 1, 1966, by the person who sold the article (in respect to which the credit or refund is claimed) to the ultimate purchaser; and

"(B) on or before February 10, 1966, reimbursement has been made to the ultimate purchaser for the tax reduction on the article.

"(2) Limitation on eligibility for credit or refund. No manufacturer, producer, or importer shall be entitled to a credit or refund under paragraph (1) with respect to an article unless he has in his possession such evidence of the sale of the article to an ultimate purchaser, and of the reimbursement of the tax to such purchaser, as may be required by regulations prescribed by the Secretary of the Treasury or his delegate under this subsection.

"(3) Other laws applicable. All provisions of law, including penalties, applicable in respect to the taxes imposed by sections 4061(a)(2) and 4111 of the Code shall, insofar as applicable and not inconsistent with paragraphs (1) and (2) of this subsection, apply in respect of the credits and refunds provided for in paragraph (1) to the same extent as if the credits or refunds constituted overpayments of the tax."

In 1964, P.L. 88-348, Sec. 2(b)(1)(C), substituted "July 1, 1965" for "July 1, 1964" and substituted "October 1, 1965" for "October 1, 1964" and substituted "November 10, 1965" for "November 10, 1964" each place they appeared in para. (a)(1).

In 1963, P.L. 88-52, Sec. 3(b)(1)(C), substituted "July 1, 1964" for "July 1, 1963", and substituted "October 1, 1964" for "October 1, 1963", and substituted "November 10, 1964" for "November 10, 1963" each place they appeared in para. (a)(1).

In 1962, P.L. 87-508, Sec. 3(b)(3), substituted "July 1, 1963" for "July 1, 1962", and substituted "October 1, 1963" for "October 1, 1962", and substituted "November 10, 1963" for "November 10, 1962" each place they appeared in para. (a)(1).

—P.L. 87-456, Sec. 302(d), deleted subsec. (d), effective for articles entered or withdrawn from warehouse for consumption after 8/30/63.

Prior to deletion subsec. (d) read as follows:

"(d) Sugar. With respect to any sugar or articles composed in chief value of sugar upon which tax imposed under section 4501(b) has been paid and which, on June 30, 1967, are held by the importer and intended for sale or other disposition, there shall be refunded (without interest) to such importer, subject to such regulations as may be prescribed by the Secretary or his delegate, an amount equal to the tax paid with respect to such sugar or articles composed in chief value of sugar, if claim for such refund is filed with the Secretary or his delegate on or before September 30, 1967."

—P.L. 87-535, Sec. 18(b), substituted "June 30, 1967" for "December 31, 1962", and substituted "September 30, 1967" for "March 31, 1963" in subsec. (d) effective 1/1/62.

In 1961, P.L. 87-72, Sec. 3(b)(3), substituted "July 1, 1962" for "July 1, 1961", and substituted "October 1, 1962" for "October 1, 1961", and substituted "November 10, 1962" for "November 10, 1961" in para. (a)(1).

—P.L. 87-61, Sec. 206(c)(1), added "tubes" after "tires" in the heading of para. (a)(2) . . . Sec. 206(c)(2), substituted "4071(a)(1), (3), or (4)," for "4071(a)(1) or (4)," in para. (a)(2) . . . Sec. 206(c)(3), substituted "October 1, 1972" for "July 1, 1972" each place it appeared in para. (a)(2) . . . Sec. 206(c)(4), substituted "February 10, 1973" for "November 10, 1972" each place it appeared in para. (a)(2) . . . Sec. 206(c)(5), substituted "January 1, 1973" for "October 1, 1972" in para. (a)(2) . . . Sec. 206(c)(6), added the last sentence to para. (a)(2) . . . Sec. 206(d), deleted para. (a)(3), effective 6/29/61.

Prior to deletion, para (a)(3) read as follows:

"(3) Gasoline held on July 1, 1961. Where before July 1, 1961, any gasoline subject to the tax imposed by section 4081 has been sold by the producer or importer and on such date is held by a dealer and is intended for sale, there shall be credited or refunded (without interest) to the producer or importer an amount equal to the difference between the tax paid by such producer or importer on his sale of the gasoline and the amount of tax made applicable to such gasoline on and after July 1, 1961, if claim for such credit or refund is filed with the Secretary or his delegate on or before November 10, 1961, based upon a request submitted to the producer or importer before October 1, 1961, by the dealer who held the gasoline in respect of which the credit or refund is claimed, and, on or before November 10, 1961, reimbursement has been made to such dealer by such producer or importer for the tax reduction on such gasoline or written consent has been obtained from such dealer to allowance of such credit or refund. No credit or refund shall be allowable under this paragraph with respect to gasoline in retail stocks held at the place where intended to be sold at retail, nor with respect to gasoline held for sale by a producer or importer of gasoline."

—P.L. 87-15, Sec. 2(b), substituted "December 31, 1962" for "September 30, 1961" where it first appeared in subsec. (d), and substituted "March 31, 1963" for "September 30, 1961" the second place it appeared in subsec. (d).

In 1960, P.L. 86-564, Sec. 201(b)(3), substituted "July 1, 1961" for "July 1, 1960", and substituted "October 1, 1961" for "October 1, 1960", and substituted "November 10, 1961" for "November 10, 1960" each place they appeared in para. (a)(1).

—P.L. 86-592, Sec. 2, substituted "September 30, 1961" for "June 30, 1961" in subsec. (d).

In 1959, P.L. 86-75, Sec. 3(b)(3), substituted "July 1, 1960" for "July 1, 1959", and substituted "October 1, 1960" for "October 1, 1959", and substituted "November 10, 1960" for "November 10, 1959" each place they appeared in para. (a)(1).

—P.L. 86-342, Sec. 201(c)(4), redesignated para. (a)(3) as para. (a)(4), and added new para. (a)(3).

In 1958, P.L. 85-475, Sec. 3(b)(4), substituted "July 1, 1959" for "July 1, 1958", and substituted "October 1, 1959" for "October 1, 1958", and substituted "November 10, 1959" for "November 10, 1958" each place they appeared in para. (a)(1).

—P.L. 85-859, Sec. 162(a), added ", if claim for such refund is filed with the Secretary or his delegate on or before September 30, 1961" before the period at the end of subsec. (d), effective for the first day of the first calendar quarter which begins more than 60 days after 9/2/58.

In 1957, P.L. 85-12, Sec. 3(b)(4), substituted "July 1, 1958" for "April 1, 1957", and substituted "October 1, 1958" for "July 1, 1957", and substituted "November 10, 1958" for "August 10, 1957" each place they appeared in para. (a)(1).

In 1956, P.L. 627, Sec. 808(a), amended subsecs. (a), (b) and (c), effective 6/29/56.

Prior to amendment subsecs. (a), (b) and (c) read as follows:

"(a) Motor vehicles.

"(1) In general. Where before April 1, 1957, any article subject to the tax imposed by section 4061(a) or (b) has been sold by the manufacturer, producer, or importer, and on such date is held by a dealer and has not been used and is intended for sale, there shall be credited or refunded (without interest) to the manufacturer, producer, or importer an amount equal to the difference between the tax paid by such manufacturer, producer, or importer on his sale of the article and the amount of tax made applicable to such article on and after April 1, 1957.

"(2) Definitions. For purposes of this subsection—

"(A) The term 'dealer' includes a wholesaler, jobber, distributor, or retailer.

"(B) An article shall be considered as 'held by a dealer' if title thereto has passed to such dealer (whether or not delivery to him has been made), and if for purposes of consumption title to such article or possession thereof has not at any time been transferred to any person other than a dealer.

"(3) Refunds to dealers. Under regulations prescribed by the Secretary or his delegate, the refund provided by this subsection may be made to the dealer instead of the manufacturer, producer, or importer, if the manufacturer, producer, or importer waives any claim for the amount so to be refunded.

"(4) Reimbursement of dealers. When the credit or refund provided for in this subsection has been allowed to the manufacturer, producer, or importer, he shall remit to the dealer to whom was sold the article in respect of which the credit or refund was allowed so much of that amount of the tax corresponding to the credit or refund as was included in or added to the price paid or agreed to be paid by the dealer.

"(5) Limitation on eligibility for credit or refund. No person shall be entitled to credit or refund under this subsection unless (A) he has in his possession such evidence of the inventories with respect to which the credit or refund is claimed as may be required by regulations prescribed under this subsection, and (B) claim for such credit or refund is filed with the Secretary or his delegate before July 1, 1957.

"(b) Gasoline.

"(1) In general. With respect to any gasoline taxable under section 4081, upon which tax (including floor stocks tax) at the applicable rate has been paid, and which, on April 1, 1957, is held and intended for sale by any person, there shall be credited or refunded (without interest) to the producer or importer who paid the tax, subject to such regulations as may be prescribed by the Secretary or his delegate, an amount equal to so much of the difference between the tax so paid and the amount of tax made applicable to such gasoline on and after April 1, 1957, as has been paid by such producer or importer to such person as reimbursement for the tax reduction on such gasoline, if claim for such credit or refund is filed with the Secretary or his delegate prior to July 1, 1957. No credit or refund shall be allowable under this subsection with respect to gasoline in retail stocks held at the place where intended to be sold at retail, nor with respect to gasoline held for sale by a producer or importer of gasoline.

"(2) Limitation on eligibility for credit or refund. No producer or importer shall be entitled to a credit or refund under paragraph (1) unless he has in his possession satisfactory evidence of the inventories with respect to which he has made the reimbursements described in such paragraph, and establishes to the satisfaction of the Secretary or his delegate with respect to the quantity of gasoline as to which credit or refund is claimed under such paragraph, that on or after April 1, 1957, such quantity of gasoline was sold to the ultimate consumer at a price which reflected the amount of the tax reduction.

"(c) Other laws applicable to certain floor stocks refunds. All provisions of law, including penalties, applicable in respect of the taxes imposed by sections 4061 and 4081 shall, insofar as applicable and not inconsistent with subsections (a) and (b) of this section, be applicable in respect of the credits and refunds provided for in such subsections to the same extent as if such credits or refunds constituted overpayments of such taxes."

—P.L. 458, Sec. 3(b)(4), substituted "April 1, 1957" for "April 1, 1956", and substituted "July 1, 1957" for "July 1, 1956" each place they appeared in subsecs. (a) and (b).

—P.L. 545, Sec. 19, substituted "1961" for "1957" in subsec. (d), effective 1/1/56.

In 1955, P.L. 18, Sec. 3(b)(4), substituted "April 1, 1956" for "April 1, 1955", and substituted "July 1, 1956" for "July 1, 1955" each place they appeared in subsecs. (a) and (b).

Sec. 6413. Special rules applicable to certain employment taxes.

(a) Adjustment of tax.

(1) General rule. If more than the correct amount of tax imposed by section 3101, 3111, 3201, 3221, or 3402 is paid with respect to any payment of remuneration, proper adjustments, with respect to both the tax and the amount to be deducted, shall be made, without interest, in such manner and at such times as the Secretary may by regulations prescribe.

(2) United States as employer. For purposes of this subsection, in the case of remuneration received from the United States or a wholly-owned instrumentality thereof during any calendar year, each head of a Federal agency or instrumentality who makes a return pursuant to section 3122 and each agent, designated by the head of a Federal agency or instrumentality who makes a return pursuant to such section shall be deemed a separate employer.

(3) **Guam or American Samoa as employer.** For purposes of this subsection, in the case of remuneration received during any calendar year from the Government of Guam, the Government of American Samoa, a political subdivision of either, or any instrumentality of any one or more of the foregoing which is wholly owned thereby, the Governor of Guam, the Governor of American Samoa, and each agent designated by either who makes a return pursuant to section 3125 shall be deemed a separate employer.

(4) **District of Columbia as employer.** For purposes of this subsection, in the case of remuneration received during any calendar year from the District of Columbia or any instrumentality which is wholly owned thereby, the Mayor of the District of Columbia and each agent designated by him who makes a return pursuant to section 3125 shall be deemed a separate employer.

(5) **States and political subdivisions as employer.** For purposes of this subsection, in the case of remuneration received from a State or any political subdivision thereof (or any instrumentality of any one or more of the foregoing which is wholly owned thereby) during any calendar year, each head of an agency or instrumentality, and each agent designated by either, who makes a return pursuant to section 3125 shall be deemed a separate employer.

(b) **Overpayments of certain employment taxes.**

If more than the correct amount of tax imposed by section 3101, 3111, 3201, 3221, or 3402 is paid or deducted with respect to any payment of remuneration and the overpayment cannot be adjusted under subsection (a) of this section, the amount of the overpayment shall be refunded in such manner and at such times (subject to the statute of limitations properly applicable thereto) as the Secretary may by regulations prescribe.

(c) **Special refunds.**

(1) **In general.** If by reason of an employee receiving wages from more than one employer during a calendar year the wages received by him during such year exceed the contribution and benefit base (as determined under section 230 of the Social Security Act) which is effective with respect to such year, the employee shall be entitled (subject to the provisions of section 31(b)) to a credit or refund of any amount of tax, with respect to such wages, imposed by section 3101(a) or section 3201(a) (to the extent of so much of the rate applicable under section 3201(a) as does not exceed the rate of tax in effect under section 3101(a)), or by both such sections, and deducted from the employee's wages (whether or not paid to the Secretary), which exceeds the tax with respect to the amount of such wages received in such year which is equal to such contribution and benefit base. The term "wages" as used in this paragraph shall, for purposes of this paragraph, include "compensation" as defined in section 3231(e).

(2) **Applicability in case of Federal and State employees, employees of certain foreign affiliates, and governmental employees in Guam, American Samoa, and the District of Columbia.**

(A) Federal employees. In the case of remuneration received from the United States or a wholly-owned instrumentality thereof during any calendar year, each head of a Federal agency or instrumentality who makes a return pursuant to section 3122 and each agent, designated by the head of a Federal agency or instrumentality, who makes a return pursuant to such section shall, for purposes of this subsection, be deemed a separate employer, and the term "wages" includes for purposes of this subsection the amount, not to exceed an amount equal to the contribution and benefit base (as determined under section 230 of the Social Security Act) for any calendar year with respect to which such contribution and benefit base is effective, determined by each such head or agent as constituting wages paid to an employee.

(B) State employees. For purposes of this subsection, in the case of remuneration received during any calendar year, the term "wages" includes such remuneration for services covered by an agreement made pursuant to section 218 of the Social Security Act as would be wages if such services constituted employment; the term "employer" includes a State or any political subdivision thereof, or any instrumentality of any one or more of the foregoing; the term "tax" or "tax imposed by section 3101(a)" includes, in the case of services covered by an agreement made pursuant to section 218 of the Social Security Act, an amount equivalent to the tax which would be imposed by section 3101(a), if such services constituted employment as defined in section 3121; and the provisions of this subsection shall apply whether or not any amount deducted from the employee's remuneration as a result of an agreement made pursuant to section 218 of the Social Security Act has been paid to the Secretary.

(C) Employees of certain foreign affiliates. For purposes of paragraph (1) of this subsection, the term "wages" includes such remuneration for services covered by an agreement made pursuant to section 3121(l) as would be wages if such services constituted employment; the term "employer" includes any American employer which has entered into an agreement pursuant to section 3121(l); the term "tax" or "tax imposed by section 3101(a)," includes, in the case of services covered by an agreement entered into pursuant to section 3121(l), an amount equivalent to the tax which would be imposed by section 3101(a), if such services constituted employment as defined in section 3121; and the provisions of paragraph (1) of this subsection shall apply whether or not any amount deducted from the employee's remuneration as a result of the agreement entered into pursuant to section 3121(l) has been paid to the Secretary.

(D) Governmental employees in Guam. In the case of remuneration received from the Government of Guam or any political subdivision thereof or from any instrumentality of any one or more of the foregoing which is wholly owned thereby, during any calendar year, the Governor of Guam and each agent designated by him who makes a return pursuant to section 3125(b) shall, for purposes of this subsection, be deemed a separate employer.

(E) Governmental employees in American Samoa. In the case of remuneration received from the Government of American Samoa or any political subdivision thereof or from any instrumentality of any one or more of the foregoing which is wholly owned thereby, during any calendar year, the Governor of American Samoa and each agent designated by him who makes a return pursuant to section 3125(c) shall, for purposes of this subsection, be deemed a separate employer.

(F) **Governmental employees in the District of Columbia.** In the case of remuneration received from the District of Columbia or any instrumentality wholly owned thereby, during any calendar year, the Mayor of the District of Columbia and each agent designated by him who makes a return pursuant to section 3125(d) shall, for purposes of this subsection, be deemed a separate employer.

(G) **Employees of States and political subdivisions.** In the case of remuneration received from a State or any political subdivision thereof (or any instrumentality of any one or more of the foregoing which is wholly owned thereby) during any calendar year, each head of an agency or instrumentality, and each agent designated by either, who makes a return pursuant to section 3125(a) shall, for purposes of this subsection, be deemed a separate employer.

(d) Refund or credit of Federal unemployment tax.

Any credit allowable under section 3302, to the extent not previously allowed, shall be considered an overpayment, but no interest shall be allowed or paid with respect to such overpayment.

In 1993, P.L. 103-66, Sec. 13207(d)(1), substituted "section 3101(a) or section 3201(a) (to the extent of so much of the rate applicable under section 3201(a) as does not exceed the rate of tax in effect under section 3101(a))" for "section 3101 or section 3201" in para. (c)(1) . . . Sec. 13207(d)(2), substituted "section 3101(a)" for "section 3101" each place it appeared in subparas. (c)(2)(B) and (C) . . . Sec. 13207(d)(3), deleted para. (c)(3), effective for 1994 and later calendar yrs.

Prior to deletion, para. (c)(3) read as follows:

"(3) **Separate application for hospital insurance taxes.** In applying this subsection with respect to—

"(A) the tax imposed by section 3101(b) (or any amount equivalent to such tax), and

"(B) so much of the tax imposed by section 3201 as is determined at a rate not greater than the rate in effect under section 3101(b),

the applicable contribution base determined under section 3121(x)(2) for any calendar year shall be substituted for 'contribution and benefit base (as determined under section 230 of the Social Security Act)' each place it appears."

In 1990, P.L. 101-508, Sec. 11331(d)(1), amended para. (c)(3), effective for 1991 and later calendar years.

Prior to amendment, para. (c)(3) read as follows:

"(3) **Applicability with respect to compensation of employees subject to the railroad retirement tax act.** In the case of any individual who, during any calendar year, receives wages from one or more employers and also receives compensation which is subject to the tax imposed by section 3201 or 3211, such compensation shall, solely for purposes of applying paragraph (1) with respect to the tax imposed by section 3101(b), be treated as wages received from an employer with respect to which the tax imposed by section 3101(b) was deducted."

In 1986, P.L. 99-272, Sec. 13205(a)(2)(E)(i), added para. (a)(5) . . . Sec. 13205(a)(2)(E)(ii), substituted "3125(b)" for "3125(a)" in subpara. (c)(2)(D), substituted "3125(c)" for "3125(b)" in subpara. (c)(2)(E), substituted "3125(d)" for "3125(c)" in subpara. (c)(2)(F), and added subpara. (c)(2)(G), effective for services performed after 3/31/86.

In 1983, P.L. 98-21, Sec. 321(e)(4)(A)(i), substituted "foreign affiliates" for "foreign corporations" in subpara. (c)(2)(C) . . . Sec. 321(e)(4)(A)(ii), substituted "American employer" for "domestic corporations" in subpara. (c)(2)(C) . . . Sec. 321(e)(4)(B), substituted "foreign affiliates" for "foreign corporations" in the heading of para. (c)(2), effective for agreements entered into after 4/20/83. Sec. 321(f)(1)(B) provides as follows:

"(B) At the election of any American employer, the amendments made by this section (other than subsection (d)) shall also apply to any agreement entered into on or before the date of the enactment of this Act. Any such election shall be made at such time and in such manner as the Secretary may by regulations prescribe."

In 1976, P.L. 94-455, Sec. 1906(a)(23)(A), substituted "Mayor of the District of Columbia and each agent designated by him" for "Commissioners of the District of Columbia and each agent designated by them" in para. (a)(4) . . . Sec. 1906(a)(23)(C), substituted "Mayor of the District of Columbia and each agent designated by him" for "Commissioners of the District of Columbia and each agent designated by them" in subpara. (c)(2)(F) . . . Sec. 1906(a)(23)(D), deleted "after 1967" after "any calendar year" in para. (c)(3), effective 2/1/77.

—P.L. 94-455, Sec. 1906(a)(23)(B)(i), amended para. (c)(1) . . . Sec. 1906(a)(23)(B)(ii), amended subpara. (c)(2)(A), effective for remuneration paid after 12/31/76.

Prior to amendment, para. (c)(1) read as follows:

"(1) **In general.** If by reason of an employee receiving wages from more than one employer during a calendar year after the calendar year 1950 and prior to the calendar year 1955, the wages received by him during such year exceed $3,600, the employee shall be entitled (subject to the provisions of section 31(b)) to a credit or refund of any amount of tax, with respect to such wages, imposed by section 1400 of the Internal Revenue Code of 1939 and deducted from the employee's wages (whether or not paid to the Secretary or his delegate), which exceeds the tax with respect to the first $3,600 of such wages received; or if by reason of an employee receiving wages from more than one employer (A) during any calendar year after the calendar year 1954 and prior to the calendar year 1959, the wages received by him during such year exceed $4,200, or (B) during any calendar year after the calendar year 1958 and prior to the calendar year 1966, the wages received by him during such year exceed $4,800, or (C) during any calendar year after the calendar year 1965 and prior to the calendar year 1968, the wages received by him during each year exceed $6,600 or (D) during any calendar year after the calendar year 1967 and prior to the calendar year 1972, the wages received by him during such year exceed $7,800 or (E) during any calendar year after the calendar year 1971 and prior to the calendar year 1973, the wages received by him during such year exceed $9,000, or (F) during any calendar year after the calendar year 1972 and prior to the calendar year 1974, the wages received by him during such year exceed $10,800, or (G) during any calendar year after the calendar year 1973 and prior to the calendar year 1975, the wages received by him during such year exceed $13,200, or (H) during any calendar year after 1974, the wages received by him during such year exceed the contribution and benefit base (as determined under section 230 of the Social Security Act) which is effective with respect to such year, the employee shall be entitled (subject to the provisions of section 31(b)) to a credit or refund of any amount of tax, with respect to such wages, imposed by section 3101 or section 3201, or by both such sections, and deducted from the employee's wages (whether or not paid to the Secretary or his delegate), which exceeds the tax with respect to the first $4,200 of such wages received in such calendar year after 1954 and before 1959, or which exceeds the tax with respect to the first $4,800 of such wages received in such calendar year after 1958, and before 1966, or which exceeds the tax with respect to the first $6,600 of such wages received in such calendar year after 1965 and before 1968, or which exceeds the tax with respect to the first $7,800 of such wages received in such calendar year after 1967 and before 1972, or which exceeds the tax with respect to the first $9,000 of such wages received in such calendar year after 1971 and before 1973, or which exceeds the tax with respect to the first $10,800 of such wages received in such calendar year after 1972 and before 1974, or which exceeds the tax with respect to the first $13,200 of such wages received in such calendar year after 1973 and before 1975, or which exceeds the tax with respect to an amount of such wages received in such calendar year after 1974 equal to the contribution and benefit base (as determined under section 230 of the Social Security Act) which is effective with respect to such year. The term 'wages' as used in this paragraph shall, for purposes of this paragraph, include 'compensation' as defined in section 3231(e)."

Prior to amendment, subpara. (c)(2)(A) read as follows:

"(A) **Federal employees.** In the case of remuneration received from the United States or a wholly-owned instrumentality thereof during any calendar year, each head of a Federal agency or instrumentality who makes a return pursuant to section 3122 and each agent, designated by the head of a Federal agency or instrumentality, who makes a return pursuant to such section shall, for purposes of this subsection, be deemed a separate employer, and the term 'wages' includes for the purposes of this subsection the amount not to exceed $3,600 for the calendar year 1951, 1952, 1953, or 1954, $4,200 for the calendar year 1955, 1956, 1957, or 1958, $5,800 for the calendar year 1959, 1960, 1961, 1962, 1963, 1964, or 1965, $6,600 for the calendar year 1966 or 1967, $7,800 for the calendar year 1968, 1969, 1970 or 1971, $9,000 for the calendar year 1972, $10,800 for the calendar year 1973, $13,200 for the calendar year 1974, or an amount equal to the contribution and benefit base (as determined under section 230 of the Social Security Act) for any calendar year after 1974 with respect to which such contribution and benefit base is effective, determined by each such head or agent as constituting wages paid to an employee."

—P.L. 94-455, Sec. 1906(b)(13)(A), substituted "Secretary" for "Secretary or his delegate" each place it appeared in Code Sec. 6413, effective 2/1/77.

In 1974, P.L. 93-445, Sec. 502(a), added "or section 3201, or by both such sections," after "section 3101" in paragraph (c)(1), effective 1/1/75 for compensation paid for services rendered on or after that date.

—P.L. 93-445, Sec. 502(b), added the sentence at the end of paragraph (c)(1), effective 1/1/75 for compensation paid for services rendered on or after that date.

In 1973, P.L. 93-233, Sec. 5(b)(5) and (6), substituted "$13,200" for "$12,600" each place it appeared in paragraph (c)(1) and subpara. (c)(2)(A), effective for remuneration paid after, and tax. yrs. begin. after 1973.

—P.L. 93-66, Sec. 203(b)(5) and (6), substituted "$12,600" for "$12,000" each place it appeared in para. (c)(1) and subpara. (c)(2)(A), effective for remuneration paid after, and tax. yrs. begin. after 1973.

In 1972, P.L. 92-336, Sec. 203(b)(5), amended para. (c)(1), effective for remuneration paid after 12/72.

Prior to amendment, para. (c)(1) read as follows:

"(1) **In general.** If by reason of an employee receiving wages from more than one employer during a calendar year after the calendar year 1950 and prior to the calendar year 1955, the wages received by him during such year exceed $3,600, the employee shall be entitled (subject to the provisions of section 31(b)) to a credit or refund of any amount of tax, with respect to such wages, imposed by section 1400 of the Internal Revenue Code of 1939 and deducted from the employee's wages (whether or not paid to the Secretary or his delegate), which exceeds the tax with respect to the first $3,600 of such wages received; or if by reason of an employee receiving wages from more than one employer (A) during any calendar year after the calendar year 1954 and prior to the calendar year 1959, the wages received by him during such year exceed $4,200, or (B) during any calendar year after the calendar year 1958 and prior to the calendar year 1966, the

Abatements, credits, refunds Code Sec. 6415

wages received by him during such year exceed $4,800, or (C) during any calendar year after the calendar year 1965 and prior to the calendar year 1968, the wages received by him during each year exceed $6,600 or (D) during any calendar year after the calendar year 1967 and prior to the calendar year 1972, the wages received by him during such year exceed $7,800 or (E) during any calendar year after the calendar year 1971, the wages received by him during such year exceed $9,000, the employee shall be entitled (subject to the provisions of section 31(b)) to a credit or refund of any amount of tax, with respect to such wages, imposed by section 3101 and deducted from the employee's wages (whether or not paid to the Secretary or his delegate), which exceeds the tax with respect to the first $4,200 of such wages received in such calendar year after 1954 and before 1959, or which exceeds the tax with respect to the first $4,800 of such wages received in such calendar year after 1958, and before 1966, or which exceeds the tax with respect to the first $6,600 of such wages received in such calendar year after 1965 and before 1968, or which exceeds the tax with respect to the first $7,800 of such wages received in such calendar year after 1967 and before 1972, or which exceeds the tax with respect to the first $9,000 of such wages received in such calendar year after 1971."

—P.L. 92-336, Sec. 203(b)(6), substituted "$9,000 for the calendar year 1972, $10,800 for the calendar year 1973, $12,000 for the calendar year 1974, or an amount equal to the contribution and benefit base (as determined under section 230 of the Social Security Act) for any calendar year after 1974 with respect to which such contribution and benefit base is effective" for "or $9,000 for any calendar year after 1971" in subpara. (c)(2)(A), effective for remuneration paid after 12/72. (Note that P.L. 92-336 erroneously amended subpara. (a)(2)(A) instead of subpara. (c)(2)(A).)

In **1971**, P.L. 92-5, Sec. 203(b)(5), added "and prior to the calendar years 1972" after "after the calendar year 1967" in para. (c)(1), added "or (E) during any calendar year after the calendar year 1971, the wages received by him during such year exceed $9,000," after "exceed $7,800" in para. (c)(1), added "and before 1972, or which exceeds the tax with respect to the first $9,000 of such wages received in such calendar year after 1971," at the end of para. (c)(1), effective for remuneration paid after 12/71.

—P.L. 92-5, Sec. 203(b)(6), substituted "$7,800 for the calendar years 1968, 1969, 1970, or 1971, or $9,000 for any calendar year after 1971" for "or $7,800 for any calendar year after 1967" in subpara. (c)(2)(A), effective for remuneration paid after 12/71.

In **1967**, P.L. 90-248, Sec. 108(b)(5)(A), added "and prior to the calendar year 1968" after "the calendar year 1965" in para. (c)(1) ... Sec. 108(b)(5)(B), added "or (D) during any calendar year after the calendar year 1967, the wages received by him during such year exceed $7,800," after "exceed $6,600" in para. (c)(1) ... Sec. 108(b)(5)(C), added "and before 1968, or which exceeds the tax with respect to the first $7,800 of such wages received in such calendar year after 1967" before the period at the end of the para. (c)(1) ... Sec. 108(b)(6), substituted "$6,600 for the calendar year 1966 or 1967, or $7,800 for any calendar year after 1967" for "or $6,600 for any calendar year after 1965" in subpara. (c)(2)(A), effective for remuneration paid after 1967.

—P.L. 90-248, Sec. 502(a), added para. (c)(3), effective 1/2/68.

In **1965**, P.L. 89-97, Sec. 317, added para. (a)(4) and subpara. (c)(2)(F) and added the reference to District of Columbia in the catchline of subsec. (c)(2) for service performed after 7/30/65 and after the calendar quarter in which the Secretary of the Treasury receives a certification from the Commissioners of the District of Columbia expressing their desire to have the insurance system established by title II (and part A of title XVIII) of the Social Security Act extended to the officers and employees coming under the provisions of such amendments.

—P.L. 89-97, Sec. 320, added the provision for coverage of $6,600 of wages after '65 in para. (c)(1) and subpara. (c)(2)(A), effective for remuneration paid after 1965.

In **1960**, P.L. 86-778, Sec. 103(r)(2)-(4), added para. (a)(3) and included governmental employees in Guam and American Samoa in the catchline, and added subpars. (D) and (E) in subsec. (c)(3), effective for (1) service in the employ of the Government of Guam or any political subdivision thereof, or any instrumentality of any one or more of the foregoing wholly owned thereby, which is performed after 1960 and after the calendar quarter in which the Secretary of the Treasury receives a certification by the Governor of Guam that legislation has been enacted by the Government of Guam expressing its desire to have the insurance system established by title II of the Social Security Act, section 401 et seq. of Title 42, extended to the officers and employees of such Government and such political subdivisions and instrumentalities, and (2) service in the employ of the Government of American Samoa or any political subdivision thereof or any instrumentality of any one or more of the foregoing wholly owned thereby, which is performed after 1960 and after the calendar quarter in which the Secretary of the Treasury receives a certification by the Governor of American Samoa that the Government of American Samoa desires to have the insurance system established by title II of the Social Security Act, section 401 et seq. of Title 42, extended to the officers and employees of such Government and such political subdivisions and instrumentalities.

In **1958**, P.L. 85-840, Sec. 402(d)(1), conformed the special-refund provisions to the increase in the limitation on wages from $4,200 to $4,800 for calendar years after 1958 in para. (c)(1) ... Sec. 402(d)(2), substituted "$4,200 for the calendar year 1955, 1956, 1957, or 1958, or $4,800 for any calendar year after 1958" for "$4,200 for any calendar year after 1954" in subpara. (c)(2)(A), effective for remuneration paid after 1958.

In **1954**, P.L. 761, Sec. 202, conformed the special-refund provisions to the increase made by said act Sept. 1, 1954, in the limitation on wages from $3,600 to $4,200 for calendar years after 1954 in para. (c)(1), added "and employees of certain foreign corporations" at the end of the heading of para. (c)(2), substituted "$3,600 for the calendar year 1951, 1952, 1953, or 1954, or $4,200 for any calendar year after 1954" for "$3,600" in subpara. (c)(2)(A) and added subpara. (c)(2)(C), effective for remuneration paid after 1954.

Sec. 6414. Income tax withheld.

> • **Caution:** Code Sec. 6414, following, is effective for payments made before 1/1/2013. For Code Sec. 6414, effective for payments made after 12/31/2012, see below.

In the case of an overpayment of tax imposed by chapter 24, or by chapter 3, refund or credit shall be made to the employer or to the withholding agent, as the case may be, only to the extent that the amount of such overpayment was not deducted and withheld by the employer or withholding agent.

Sec. 6414. Income tax withheld.

> • **Caution:** Code Sec. 6414, following, is effective for payments made after 12/31/2012. For Code Sec. 6414, effective for payments made before 1/1/2013, see above.

In the case of an overpayment of tax imposed by chapter 24, or by chapter 3 or 4, refund or credit shall be made to the employer or to the withholding agent, as the case may be, only to the extent that the amount of such overpayment was not deducted and withheld by the employer or withholding agent.

Sec. 6415. Credits or refunds to persons who collected certain taxes.

(a) Allowance of credits or refunds.

Credit or refund of any overpayment of tax imposed by section 4251, 4261, or 4271 may be allowed to the person who collected the tax and paid it to the Secretary if such person establishes, under such regulations as the Secretary may prescribe, that he has repaid the amount of such tax to the person from whom he collected it, or obtains the consent of such person to the allowance of such credit or refund.

(b) Credit on returns.

Any person entitled to a refund of tax imposed by section 4251, 4261 or 4271 paid, or collected and paid, to the Secretary by him may, instead of filing a claim for refund, take credit therefor against taxes imposed by such section due upon any subsequent return.

(c) Refund of overcollections.

In case any person required under section 4251, 4261, or 4271 to collect any tax shall make an overcollection of such tax, such person shall, upon proper application, refund such overcollection to the person entitled thereto.

(d) Refund of taxable payment.

Any person making a refund of any payment on which tax imposed by section 4251, 4261 or 4271 has been collected may repay therewith the amount of tax collected on such payment.

In **1976**, P.L. 94-455, Sec. 1906(b)(13)(A), substituted "Secretary" for "Secretary or his delegate" each place it appeared in Code Sec. 6415, effective 2/1/77.

In **1970**, P.L. 91-258, Sec. 205(b)(2), substituted "4251, 4261, or 4271" for "4251 or 4261" each place it appeared in Code Sec. 6415, effective 7/1/70.

In **1965**, P.L. 89-44, Sec. 601, substituted "4251 or 4261" for "4231(1), 4231(2), 4231(3), 4241, 4251, 4261 or 4286" in the first sentence of subsec. (a) and deleted the last sentence of subsec. (a)

Prior to deletion, the last sentence of subsec. (a) read as follows:

"For purposes of this subsection, in the case of any payment outside the United States in respect of which tax is imposed under paragraph (1), (2), or (3) of sec-

3,703

tion 4231, the person who paid for the admission or for the use of the box or seat shall be considered the person from whom the tax was collected."
In 1958, P.L. 85-859, Sec. 163(d), added the last sentence of subsec. (a), effective 1/1/59.
— P.L. 85-475, Sec. 4(b)(4), struck out references to section 4271 in former listing of sections imposing taxes.

Sec. 6416. Certain taxes on sales and services.
(a) Condition to allowance.
(1) **General rule.** No credit or refund of any overpayment of tax imposed by chapter 31 (relating to retail excise taxes), or chapter 32 (manufacturers taxes) shall be allowed or made unless the person who paid the tax establishes, under regulations prescribed by the Secretary, that he —

(A) has not included the tax in the price of the article with respect to which it was imposed and has not collected the amount of the tax from the person who purchased such article;

(B) has repaid the amount of the tax to the ultimate purchaser of the article;

(C) in the case of an overpayment under subsection (b)(2) of this section —

(i) has repaid or agreed to repay the amount of the tax to the ultimate vendor of the article, or

(ii) has obtained the written consent of such ultimate vendor to the allowance of the credit or the making of the refund; or

(D) has filed with the Secretary the written consent of the person referred to in subparagraph (B) to the allowance of the credit or the making of the refund.

(2) **Exceptions.** This subsection shall not apply to —

(A) the tax imposed by section 4041 (relating to tax on special fuels) on the use of any liquid, and

(B) an overpayment of tax under paragraph (1), (3)(A), (4), (5), or (6) of subsection (b) of this section.

(3) **Special rule.** For purposes of this subsection, in any case in which the Secretary determines that an article is not taxable, the term "ultimate purchaser" (when used in paragraph (1)(B) of this subsection) includes a wholesaler, jobber, distributor, or retailer who, on the 15th day after the date of such determination, holds such article for sale; but only if claim for credit or refund by reason of this paragraph is filed on or before the date for filing the return with respect to the taxes imposed under chapter 32 for the first period which begins more than 60 days after the date on such determination.

(4) **Registered ultimate vendor or credit card issuer to administer credits and refunds of gasoline tax.**

(A) In general. For purposes of this subsection, except as provided in subparagraph (B), if an ultimate vendor purchases any gasoline on which tax imposed by section 4081 has been paid and sells such gasoline to an ultimate purchaser described in subparagraph (C) or (D) of subsection (b)(2) (and such gasoline is for a use described in such subparagraph), such ultimate vendor shall be treated as the person (and the only person) who paid such tax, but only if such ultimate vendor is registered under section 4101.

(B) Credit card issuer. For purposes of this subsection, if the purchase of gasoline described in subparagraph (A) (determined without regard to the registration status of the ultimate vendor) is made by means of a credit card issued to the ultimate purchaser, paragraph (1) shall not apply and the person extending the credit to the ultimate purchaser shall be treated as the person (and the only person) who paid the tax, but only if such person —

(i) is registered under section 4101, and

(ii) has established, under regulations prescribed by the Secretary, that such person —

(I) has not collected the amount of the tax from the person who purchased such article, or

(II) has obtained the written consent from the ultimate purchaser to the allowance of the credit or refund, and

(iii) has so established that such person —

(I) has repaid or agreed to repay the amount of the tax to the ultimate vendor,

(II) has obtained the written consent of the ultimate vendor to the allowance of the credit or refund, or

(III) has otherwise made arrangements which directly or indirectly provides the ultimate vendor with reimbursement of such tax.

If clause (i), (ii), or (iii) is not met by such person extending the credit to the ultimate purchaser, then such person shall collect an amount equal to the tax from the ultimate purchaser and only such ultimate purchaser may claim such credit or payment.

(C) Timing of claims. The procedure and timing of any claim under subparagraph (A) or (B) shall be the same as for claims under section 6427(i)(4), except that the rules of section 6427(i)(3)(B) regarding electronic claims shall not apply unless the ultimate vendor or credit card issuer has certified to the Secretary for the most recent quarter of the taxable year that all ultimate purchasers of the vendor or credit card issuer are certified and entitled to a refund under subparagraph (C) or (D) of subsection (b)(2).

(b) Special cases in which tax payments considered overpayments.

Under regulations prescribed by the Secretary, credit or refund (without interest) shall be allowed or made in respect of the overpayments determined under the following paragraphs:

(1) **Price readjustments.**

(A) In general. Except as provided in subparagraph (B) or (C), if the price of any article in respect of which a tax, based on such price, is imposed by chapter 31 or 32, is readjusted by reason of the return or repossession of the article or a covering or container, or by a bona fide discount, rebate, or allowance, including a readjustment for local advertising (but only to the extent provided in section 4216(e)(2) and (3)), the part of the tax proportionate to the part of the price repaid or credited to the purchaser shall be deemed to be an overpayment.

(B) Further manufacture. Subparagraph (A) shall not apply in the case of an article in respect of which tax was computed under section 4223(b)(2); but if the price for which such article was sold is readjusted by reason of the return or repossession of the article, the part of the tax proportionate to the part of such price repaid or credited to the purchaser shall be deemed to be an overpayment.

(C) Adjustment of tire price. No credit or refund of any tax imposed by subsection (a) or (b) of section 4071 shall be allowed or made by reason of an adjustment of a tire pursuant to a warranty or guarantee.

Abatements, credits, refunds   Code Sec. 6416(b)(5)(C)

> • *Caution:* Code Sec. 6416(b)(2), following, is effective for sales before 12/31/2012. For Code Sec. 6416(b)(2), effective for sales after 12/31/2012, see below.

(2) Specified uses and resales. The tax paid under chapter 32 (or under subsection (a) or (d) of section 4041 in respect of sales or under section 4051) in respect of any article shall be deemed to be an overpayment if such article was, by any person—

(A) exported;

(B) used or sold for use as supplies for vessels or aircraft;

(C) sold to a State or local government for the exclusive use of a State or local government;

(D) sold to a nonprofit educational organization for its exclusive use;

(E) sold to a qualified blood collector organization (as defined in section 7701(a)(49)) for such organization's exclusive use in the collection, storage, or transportation of blood;

(F) in the case of any tire taxable under section 4071(a), sold to any person for use as described in section 4221(e)(3); or

(G) in the case of gasoline, used or sold for use in the production of special fuels referred to in section 4041.

Subparagraphs (C), (D), and (E) shall not apply in the case of any tax paid under section 4064. In the case of the tax imposed by section 4131, subparagraphs (B), (C), (D), and (E) shall not apply and subparagraph (A) shall apply only if the use of the exported vaccine meets such requirements as the Secretary may by regulations prescribe. This paragraph shall not apply in the case of any tax imposed under section 4041(a)(1) or 4081 on diesel fuel or kerosene and any tax paid under section 4121. Subparagraphs (C) and (D) shall not apply in the case of any tax imposed on gasoline under section 4081 if the requirements of subsection (a)(4) are not met. In the case of taxes imposed by subchapter C or D of chapter 32, subparagraph (E) shall not apply.

> • *Caution:* Code Sec. 6416(b)(2), following, is effective for sales after 12/31/2012. For Code Sec. 6416(b)(2), effective for sales before 12/31/2012, see above.

(2) Specified uses and resales. The tax paid under chapter 32 (or under subsection (a) or (d) of section 4041 in respect of sales or under section 4051) in respect of any article shall be deemed to be an overpayment if such article was, by any person—

(A) exported;

(B) used or sold for use as supplies for vessels or aircraft;

(C) sold to a State or local government for the exclusive use of a State or local government;

(D) sold to a nonprofit educational organization for its exclusive use;

(E) sold to a qualified blood collector organization (as defined in section 7701(a)(49)) for such organization's exclusive use in the collection, storage, or transportation of blood;

(F) in the case of any tire taxable under section 4071(a), sold to any person for use as described in section 4221(e)(3); or

(G) in the case of gasoline, used or sold for use in the production of special fuels referred to in section 4041.

Subparagraphs (C), (D), and (E) shall not apply in the case of any tax paid under section 4064. In the case of the tax imposed by section 4131, subparagraphs (B), (C), (D), and (E) shall not apply and subparagraph (A) shall apply only if the use of the exported vaccine meets such requirements as the Secretary may by regulations prescribe. This paragraph shall not apply in the case of any tax imposed under section 4041(a)(1) or 4081 on diesel fuel or kerosene and any tax paid under section 4121. Subparagraphs (C) and (D) shall not apply in the case of any tax imposed on gasoline under section 4081 if the requirements of subsection (a)(4) are not met. In the case of taxes imposed by subchapter C or D of chapter 32, subparagraph (E) shall not apply. In the case of the tax imposed by section 4191, subparagraphs (B), (C), (D), and (E) shall not apply.

(3) Tax-paid articles used for further manufacture, etc. If the tax imposed by chapter 32 has been paid with respect to the sale of any article (other than coal taxable under section 4121) by the manufacturer, producer, or importer thereof and such article is sold to a subsequent manufacturer or producer before being used, such tax shall be deemed to be an overpayment by such subsequent manufacturer or producer if—

(A) in the case of any article other than any fuel taxable under section 4081, such article is used by the subsequent manufacturer or producer as material in the manufacture or production of, or as a component part of—

(i) another article taxable under chapter 32, or

(ii) an automobile bus chassis or an automobile bus body,

manufactured or produced by him; or

(B) in the case of any fuel taxable under section 4081, such fuel is used by the subsequent manufacturer or producer, for nonfuel purposes, as a material in the manufacture or production of any other article manufactured or produced by him.

(4) Tires. If—

(A) the tax imposed by section 4071 has been paid with respect to the sale of any tire by the manufacturer, producer, or importer thereof, and

(B) such tire is sold by any person on or in connection with, or with the sale of, any other article, such tax shall be deemed to be an overpayment by such person if such other article is—

(i) an automobile bus chassis or an automobile bus body,

(ii) by such person exported, sold to a State or local government for the exclusive use of a State or local government, sold to a nonprofit educational organization for its exclusive use, or used or sold for use as supplies for vessels or aircraft, or

(iii) sold to a qualified blood collector organization for its exclusive use in connection with a vehicle the organization certifies will be primarily used in the collection, storage, or transportation of blood.

(5) Return of certain installment accounts. If—

(A) tax was paid under section 4216(d)(1) in respect of any installment account,

(B) such account is, under the agreement under which the account was sold, returned to the person who sold such account, and

(C) the consideration is readjusted as provided in such agreement, the part of the tax paid under section 4216(d)(1) allocable to the part of the consideration repaid or credited to the purchaser of such account shall be deemed to be an overpayment.

(6) Truck chassis, bodies, and semitrailers used for further manufacture If—

(A) the tax imposed by section 4051 has been paid with respect to the sale of any article, and

(B) before any other use, such article is by any person used as a component part of another article taxable under section 4051 manufactured or produced by him, such tax shall be deemed to be an overpayment by such person. For purposes of the preceding sentence, an article shall be treated as having been used as a component part of another article if, had it not been broken or rendered useless in the manufacture or production of such other article, it would have been so used.

This subsection shall apply in respect of an article only if the exportation or use referred to in the applicable provision of this subsection occurs before any other use, or, in the case of a sale or resale, the use referred to in the applicable provision of this subsection is to occur before any other use.

(c) Refund to exporter or shipper.

Under regulations prescribed by the Secretary the amount of any tax imposed by chapter 31, or chapter 32 erroneously or illegally collected in respect of any article exported to a foreign country or shipped to a possession of the United States may be refunded to the exporter or shipper thereof, if the person who paid such tax waives his claim to such amount.

(d) Credit on returns.

Any person entitled to a refund of tax imposed by chapter 31 or 32, paid to the Secretary may, instead of filing a claim for refund, take credit therefor against taxes imposed by such chapter due on any subsequent return. The preceding sentence shall not apply to the tax imposed by section 4081 in the case of refunds described in section 4081(e).

(e) Accounting procedures for like articles.

Under regulations prescribed by the Secretary, if any person uses or resells like articles, then for purposes of this section the manufacturer, producer, or importer of any such article may be identified, and the amount of tax paid under chapter 32 in respect of such article may be determined—

(1) on a first-in-first-out basis,

(2) on a last-in-first-out basis, or

(3) in accordance with any other consistent method approved by the Secretary.

(f) Meaning of terms.

For purposes of this section, any term used in this section has the same meaning as when used in chapter 31, 32, or 33, as the case may be.

In **2010**, P.L. 111-152, Sec. 1405(b)(2), added "In the case of the tax imposed by section 4191, subparagraphs (B), (C), (D), and (E) shall not apply." at the end of para. (b)(2), effective for sales after 12/31/2012.

In **2007**, P.L. 110-172, Sec. 11(d)(1)(A), substituted "ultimate vendor or credit card issuer has certified" for "ultimate vendor" and all that follows through "has certified" in subpara. (a)(4)(C). . . . Sec. 11(d)(1)(B), substituted "all ultimate purchasers of the vendor or credit card issuer are certified" for "all ultimate purchasers of the vendor" and all that follows through "are certified" in subpara. (a)(4)(C), effective for sales after 12/31/2005.

In **2006**, P.L. 109-280, Sec. 1207(e)(1)(A), redesignated subparas. (b)(2)(E) and (F) as (b)(2)(F) and (G) and added subpara. (b)(2)(E). . . . Sec. 1207(e)(1)(B), added "In the case of taxes imposed by subchapter C or D of chapter 32, subparagraph (E) shall not apply." before the period at the end of para. (b)(2). . . . Sec. 1207(e)(1)(C)(i), substituted "Subparagraphs (C), (D), and (E)" for "Subparagraphs (C) and (D)" in para. (b)(2). . . . Sec. 1207(e)(1)(C)(ii), substituted "(B), (C), (D), and (E)" for "(B), (C), and (D)" in para. (b)(2). . . . Sec. 1207(e)(2), deleted "or" at the end of clause (b)(4)(B)(i), substituted ", or" for the period at the end of clause (b)(4)(B)(ii), and added clause (b)(4)(B)(iii), effective 1/1/2007.

In **2005**, P.L. 109-59, Sec. 11163(b)(1)(A), added "except as provided in subparagraph (B)," after "For purposes of this subsection," in subpara. (a)(4)(A) . . . Sec. 11163(b)(1)(B), redesignated subpara. (a)(4)(B) as (C) and added subpara. (a)(4)(B) . . . Sec. 11163(b)(1)(C), substituted "subparagraph (A) or (B)" for "sub-paragraph (A)" in subpara. (a)(4)(C) [as redesignated by Sec. 11163(b)(1)(B) of this Act, see above] . . . Sec. 11163(b)(1)(D), added "or credit card issuer" after "vendor" in subpara. (a)(4)(C) [as redesignated by Sec. 11163(b)(1)(B) of this Act, see above] . . . Sec. 11163(b)(1)(E), added "or credit card issuer" after "vendor" in the heading of para. (a)(4) . . . Sec. 11163(b)(2), added "Subparagraphs (C) and (D) shall not apply in the case of any tax imposed on gasoline under section 4081 if the requirements of subsection (a)(4) are not met." at the end of para. (b)(2), effective for sales after 12/31/2005.

In **2004**, P.L. 108-357, Sec. 853(d)(2)(G), deleted "4091 or" after "tax paid under section" in para. (b)(2) . . . Sec. 853(d)(2)(H), deleted "or 4091" after "section 4081" each place it appeared in para. (b)(3) . . . Sec. 853(d)(2)(I), deleted "or to the tax imposed by section 4091 in the case of refunds described in section 4091(d)" after "section 4081(e)" in subsec. (d), effective for aviation-grade kerosene removed, entered, or sold after 12/31/2004.

—P.L. 108-357, Sec. 853(f), of this Act, provides:

"(f) Floor stocks tax.

"(1) In general. There is hereby imposed on aviation-grade kerosene held on January 1, 2005, by any person a tax equal to—

"(A) the tax which would have been imposed before such date on such kerosene had the amendments made by this section been in effect at all times before such date, reduced by

"(B) the sum of—

"(i) the tax imposed before such date on such kerosene under section 4091 of the Internal Revenue Code of 1986, as in effect on such date, and

"(ii) in the case of kerosene held exclusively for such person's own use, the amount which such person would (but for this clause) reasonably expect (as of such date) to be paid as a refund under section 6427(l) of such Code with respect to such kerosene.

"(2) Exception for fuel held in aircraft fuel tank. Paragraph (1) shall not apply to kerosene held in the fuel tank of an aircraft on January 1, 2005.

"(3) Liability for tax and method of payment.

"(A) Liability for tax. The person holding the kerosene on January 1, 2005, to which the tax imposed by paragraph (1) applies shall be liable for such tax.

"(B) Method and time for payment. The tax imposed by paragraph (1) shall be paid at such time and in such manner as the Secretary of the Treasury (or the Secretary's delegate) shall prescribe, including the nonapplication of such tax on de minimis amounts of kerosene.

"(4) Transfer of floor stock tax revenues to trust funds. For purposes of determining the amount transferred to any trust fund, the tax imposed by this subsection shall be treated as imposed by section 4081 of the Internal Revenue Code of 1986—

"(A) in any case in which tax was not imposed by section 4091 of such Code, at the Leaking Underground Storage Tank Trust Fund financing rate under such section to the extent of 0.1 cents per gallon, and

"(B) at the rate under section 4081(a)(2)(A)(iv) of such Code to the extent of the remainder.

"(5) Held by a person. For purposes of this subsection, kerosene shall be considered as held by a person if title thereto has passed to such person (whether or not delivery to the person has been made).

"(6) Other laws applicable. All provisions of law, including penalties, applicable with respect to the tax imposed by section 4081 of such Code shall, insofar as applicable and not inconsistent with the provisions of this subsection, apply with respect to the floor stock tax imposed by paragraph (1) to the same extent as if such tax were imposed by such section."

—P.L. 108-357, Sec. 865(a), amended para. (a)(4), effective 1/1/2005. Prior to amendment, para. (a)(4) read as follows:

"(4) Wholesale distributors to administer credits and refunds of gasoline tax.

"(A) In general. For purposes of this subsection, a wholesale distributor who purchases any gasoline on which tax imposed by section 4081 has been paid and who sells the gasoline to its ultimate purchaser shall be treated as the person (and the only person) who paid such tax.

"(B) Wholesale distributor. For purposes of subparagraph (A), the term 'wholesale distributor' has the meaning given such term by section 4093(b)(2) (determined by substituting 'any gasoline taxable under section 4081' for 'aviation fuel' therein). Such term includes any person who makes retail sales of gasoline at 10 or more retail motor fuel outlets."

In **1998**, P.L. 105-206, Sec. 6023(23), substituted "section 4216(d)(1)" for "section 4216(e)(1)" each place it appeared in para. (b)(5), effective 7/22/98.

In **1997**, P.L. 105-34, Sec. 905(a), added a sentence at the end of subpara. (a)(4)(B), effective for sales after 8/5/97.

—P.L. 105-34, Sec. 1032(e)(6), added "or kerosene" after "diesel fuel" in the flush matter at the end of para. (b)(2), effective 7/1/98.

—P.L. 105-34, Sec. 1436(b), added "or to the tax imposed by section 4091 in the case of refunds described in section 4091(d)" before the period at the end of subsec. (d), effective for fuel acquired by the producer after 9/30/97.

In **1996**, P.L. 104-188, Sec. 1702(b)(3), substituted "chapter 31 or 32" for "chapter 32 or section 4051" in para. (b)(1), effective 7/1/91.

In **1993**, P.L. 103-66, Sec. 13242(d)(17)(A), substituted "gasoline" for "product" each place it appeared in subpara. (a)(4)(A) . . . Sec. 13242(d)(17)(B)(i), substituted "section 4093(b)(2)" for "section 4092(b)(2)" in subpara. (a)(4)(B) . . . Sec. 13242(d)(17)(B)(ii), substituted "any gasoline taxable under section 4081" for 'aviation fuel' therein)." for "'any product taxable under section 4081' for 'a ble fuel therein)." in subpara. (a)(4)(B) . . . Sec. 13242(d)(18), added "any tax imposed under section 4041(a)(1) or 4081 on diesel fuel and" after "This paragraph shall not apply in the case of" in the material following the first sentence of para. (b)(2) . . . Sec. 13242(d)(19)(A), substituted "any fuel taxable under section 4081 or 4091" for "gasoline taxable under section 4081 and other than any fuel taxable

Abatements, credits, refunds — Code Sec. 6416

under section 4091" in subpara. (b)(3)(A) . . . Sec. 13242(d)(19)(B), substituted "any fuel taxable under section 4081 or 4091, such fuel" for "gasoline taxable under section 4081 or any fuel taxable under section 4091, such gasoline or fuel" in subpara. (b)(3)(B), effective 1/1/94.

In 1990, P.L. 101-508, Sec. 11212(d)(2), added the last sentence to subsec. (d), effective 7/1/91.

In 1988, P.L. 100-647, Sec. 2001(d)(1)(B), substituted "(or under subsection (a) or (d) of section 4041 in respect of sales or under section 4051)" for "(or under paragraph (1)(A) or (2)(A) of section 4041(a) or under paragraph (1)(A) or (2)(A) of section 4041(d) or under section 4051)" in para. (b)(2), effective 1/1/87.

—P.L. 100-647, Sec. 6102(a), added para. (a)(4), effective for fuel sold by wholesale distributors (as defined in Code Sec. 6416(a)(4)(B)) after 9/30/88.

In 1987, P.L. 100-203, Sec. 9201(b)(2), added the last sentence to para. (b)(2), effective 1/1/88.

—P.L. 100-203, Sec. 10502(d)(6)(A), deleted "(other than coal taxable under section 4121)" after "in respect of any article" in para. (b)(2) . . . Sec. 10502(d)(6)(B), added the last sentence to para. (b)(2) [as amended by Sec. 9201(b)(2) of this Act, see above] . . . Sec. 10502(d)(7), added "and other than any fuel taxable under section 4091" after "section 4081" in subpara. (b)(3)(A) . . . Sec. 10502(d)(8), substituted "or any fuel taxable under section 4091, such gasoline or fuel" for ", such gasoline" in subpara. (b)(3)(B), effective for sales after 3/31/87.

In 1986, P.L. 99-499, Sec. 521(d)(5), added "or under paragraph (1)(A) or (2)(A) of section 404(d)" after "section 4041(a)" in para. (b)(2), effective 1/1/87.

In 1984, P.L. 98-369, Sec. 734(i)(1)(A), added para. (b)(6) . . . Sec. 734(b)(1)(B), substituted "(5), or (6)" for "or (5)" in subpara. (a)(2)(B), effective 4/1/83.

—P.L. 98-369, Sec. 734(b)(2)(A), amended para. (b)(4) . . . Sec. 734(b)(2)(B)(i), deleted subpara. (b)(2)(E) . . . Sec. 734(b)(2)(B)(ii), deleted subpara. (b)(3)(C) . . . Sec. 734(b)(2)(B)(iii), deleted ", (b)(3)(C) or (D), or (b)(4)" after "subsection (b)(2)" in subpara. (a)(1)(C) . . . Sec. 734(b)(2)(B)(iv), added "(4)," before "(5)" in subpara. (a)(2)(B) . . . Sec. 734(b)(2)(B)(v), amended para. (a)(3), effective for articles sold on or after 1/1/84.

Prior to amendment, para. (b)(4) read as follows:

"(4) Tires and inner tubes. If —

"(A) a tire or inner tube taxable under section 4071, or a recapped or retreaded tire in respect of which tax under section 4071(a)(4) was paid on the tread rubber used in the recapping or retreading, is sold by the manufacturer, producer, or importer thereof on or in connection with, or with the sale of, any other article manufactured or produced by him; and

"(B) such other article is —

"(i) an automobile bus chassis or an automobile bus body, or

"(ii) by any person exported, sold to a State or local government for the exclusive use of a State or local government, sold to a nonprofit educational organization for its exclusive use, or used or sold for use as supplies for vessels or aircraft,

any tax imposed by chapter 32 in respect of such tire or inner tube which has been paid by the manufacturer, producer, or importer thereof shall be deemed to be an overpayment by him."

Prior to deletion, subpara. (b)(2)(E) read as follows:

"(E) In the case of a tire or inner tube, resold for use as provided in subparagraph (C) of paragraph (3) (or in the case of the tread rubber on a recapped or retreaded tire, resold for use as provided in subparagraph (D) of paragraph (3)), and the other article referred to in such subparagraph is by any person exported or sold as provided in such subparagraph;"

Prior to deletion, subpara. (b)(3)(C) read as follows:

"(C) In the case of a tire or inner tube taxable under section 4071, such article is sold by the subsequent manufacturer or producer on or in connection with, or with the sale of, any other article manufactured or produced by him and such other article is —

"(i) an automobile bus chassis or an automobile bus body, or

"(ii) by any person exported, sold to a State or local government for the exclusive use of a State or local government, sold to a nonprofit educational organization for its exclusive use, or used or sold for use as supplies for vessels or aircraft;"

Prior to amendment, para. (a)(3) read as follows:

"(3) Special rules. For purposes of this subsection —

"(A) in any case in which the Secretary determines that an article is not taxable, the term 'ultimate purchaser' (when used in paragraph (1)(B) of this subsection) includes a wholesaler, jobber, distributor, or retailer who, on the 15th day after the date of such determination, holds such article for sale; but only if claim for credit or refund by reason of this subparagraph is filed on or before the day for filing the return with respect to the taxes imposed under chapter 32 for the first period which begins more than 60 days after the date of such determination; and

"(B) in applying paragraph (1)(C) to any overpayment under paragraph (2)(F), (3)(C), or (4) of subsection (b), the term 'ultimate vendor' means the ultimate vendor of the other article."

—P.L. 98-369, Sec. 734(j), added "or by section 4051" after "chapter 32" in subpara. (b)(1)(A), effective 4/1/83.

—P.L. 98-369, Sec. 735(c)(13)(A), substituted "subsection (a) or (b) of section 4071" for "section 4071(a)(1) or (2) or section 4071(b)" in subpara. (b)(1)(C) . . . Sec. 735(c)(13)(B), deleted subparas. (b)(2)(F) and (b)(2)(H)–(K) and added new subpara. (b)(2)(F), effective 1/7/83, and deleted subparas. (b)(2)(G), (b)(2)(L), and (b)(2)(M) and added new subpara. (b)(2)(E), effective for articles sold on or after 1/1/84.

Prior to deletion, subparas. (b)(2)(F)–(M) read as follows:

"(F) In the case of any article taxable under section 4061(b) (other than spark plugs and storage batteries), used or sold for use as repair or replacement parts or

accessories for farm equipment (other than equipment taxable under section 4061(a);

"(G) In the case of tread rubber in respect of which tax was paid under section 4071(a)(4) —

"(i) used or sold for use otherwise than in the recapping or retreading of tires of the type used on highway vehicles (as defined in section 4072(c)),

"(ii) destroyed, scrapped, wasted, or rendered unless in the recapping or retreading process,

"(iii) used in the recapping or retreading of a tire the sale of which is later adjusted pursuant to a warranty or guarantee, in which case the overpayment shall be in proportion to the adjustment in the sales price of such tire, or

"(iv) used in the recapping or retreading of a tire, if such tire is by any person exported, used or sold for use as supplies for vessels or aircraft, sold to a State or local government for the exclusive use of a State or local government, or sold to a nonprofit educational organization for its exclusive use,

unless credit or refund of such tax is allowable under paragraph (3);

"(H) In the case of gasoline, used or sold for use in production of special fuels referred to in section 4041;

"(I) In the case of any article taxable under section 4061(b), sold for use by the purchaser or in connection with an automobile bus;

"(J) In the case of a box, container, receptacle, bin, or other similar article taxable under section 4061(a), sold to any person for use as described in section 4063(a)(7); or

"(K) In the case of any article taxable under section 4061(b), sold on or in connection with the first retail sale of a light-duty truck, as described in section 4061(a)(2), if credit or refund of such tax is not available under any other provisions of law;

"(L) In the case of any tire or inner tube taxable under paragraph (1) or (3) of section 4071(a), sold to any person for use as described in section 4221(e)(5)(A); or

"(M) In the case of tread rubber taxable under paragraph (4) of section 4071(a), used in the recapping or retreading of a tire sold to any person for use on or in connection with a qualified bus (as defined in section 4221(d)(7)."

—P.L. 98-369, Sec. 735(c)(13)(C), deleted subparas. (b)(3)(A), (b)(3)(D), (b)(3)(E), and the matter following (b)(3)(F), effective for articles sold on or after 1/1/84; deleted subpara. (b)(3)(B), effective 1/7/83; and deleted subpara. (b)(3)(F) and added new subparas. (b)(3)(A) and (B), effective 4/1/83.

Prior to deletion, subparas. (b)(3)(A) and (B) read as follows:

"(A) In the case of any article other than an article to which subparagraph (B), (C), (D), or (E) applies, such article is used by the subsequent manufacturer or producer as material in the manufacture or production of, or as a component part of —

"(i) another article taxable under chapter 32, or

"(ii) an automobile bus chassis or an automobile bus body, manufactured or produced by him;

"(B) In the case of a part or accessory taxable under section 4061(b), such article is used by the subsequent manufacturer or producer as material in the manufacture or production of, or as a component part of, any other article manufactured or produced by him;"

Prior to deletion, subparas. (b)(3)(D)–(F) and the matter following subpara. (b)(3)(F) read as follows:

"(D) In the case of tread rubber in respect of which tax was paid under section 4071(a)(4) used in the recapping or retreading of a tire, such tire is sold by the subsequent manufacturer or producer on or in connection with, or with the sale of, any other article manufactured or produced by him and such other article is by any person exported, sold to a State or local government for the exclusive use of a State or local government, sold to a nonprofit educational organization for its exclusive use, or used or sold for use as supplies for vessels or aircraft, unless credit or refund of such tax is allowable under subparagraph (C);

"(E) In the case of —

"(i) a bicycle tire (as defined in section 4221(e)(4)(B)), or

"(ii) an inner tube for such a tire, such article is used by the subsequent manufacturer or producer as material in the manufacture or production of, or as a component part of, a bicycle (other than a rebuilt or reconditioned bicycle); or

"(F) In the case of gasoline taxable under section 4081, such gasoline is used by the subsequent manufacturer or producer, for nonfuel purposes, as a material in the manufacture or production of any other article manufactured or produced by him.

For purposes of subparagraphs (A) and (B), an article shall be treated as having been used as a component part of another article if, had it not been broken or rendered useless in the manufacture or production of such other article, it would have been so used."

—P.L. 98-369, Sec. 735(c)(13)(D), deleted "or (B)" in subpara. (a)(2)(B), effective 1/7/83.

—P.L. 98-369, Sec. 735(c)(13)(E), deleted subsec. (c), effective for articles sold on or after 1/1/84, deleted subsec. (g), effective 1/7/83, and redesignated subsecs. (e), (f), (h), and (i) as subsecs. (c), (d), (e), and (f), respectively.

Prior to deletion, subsec. (c) read as follows:

"(c) Credit for tax paid on tires or inner tubes.

"If tires or inner tubes on which tax has been paid under chapter 32 are sold on or in connection with, or with the sale of, another article taxable under chapter 32, there shall be credited (under regulations prescribed by the Secretary) be credited (without interest) against the tax imposed on the sale of such other article, an amount determined by multiplying the applicable percentage rate of tax for such other article by —

"(1) the purchase price (less, in the case of tires, the part of such price attributable to the metal rim or rim base), if such tires or inner tubes were taxable under section 4071 (relating to tax on tires and inner tubes); or

3,707

"(2) if such tires or inner tubes were taxable under section 4218 (relating to use by manufacturer, producer, or importer), the price (less, in the case of tires, the part of such price attributable to the metal rim or rim base) at which such or similar tires or inner tubes are sold, in the ordinary course of trade, by manufacturers, producers, or importers thereof, as determined by the Secretary."

Prior to deletion, subsec. (g) read as follows:

"(g) Trucks, buses, tractors, etc.

"Under regulations prescribed by the Secretary, subsection (b)(2)(A) shall apply, in the case of any article subject to the tax imposed by section 4061(a) only if the article with respect to which the tax was paid was sold by the manufacturer, producer, or importer for export after receipt by him of notice of intent to export or to resell for export."

—P.L. 98-369, Sec. 735(c)(13)(F), deleted "(except in any case to which subsection (g) applies)" after "exported" in subpara. (b)(2)(A), effective 1/7/83.

In 1983, P.L. 97-424, Sec. 511(g)(2)(A), substituted "paragraph (1)(A) or (2)(A) of section 4041(a)" for "section 4041(a)(1) or (b)(1)" in para. (b)(2) . . . Sec. 512(b)(2)(C), added "or under section 4051" after "section 4041(a)" in para. (b)(2) [as amended by Sec. 511(g)(2)(A) of the Act, see above] . . . Sec. 512(b)(2)(D), substituted "chapter 31 (relating to retail excise taxes)" for "chapter 31 (special fuels)" in para. (a)(1), effective 4/1/83.

—P.L. 97-424, Sec. 515(b)(4)(A), deleted subpara. (b)(2)(N) . . . Sec. 515(b)(4)(B), deleted the second to last sentence in para. (b)(2) . . . Sec. 515(b)(4)(C), added "or" to the end of subpara. (b)(2)(L) . . . Sec. 515(b)(4)(D), substituted a period for "; or" at the end of subpara (b)(2)(M), effective for articles sold after 1/6/83.

Prior to deletion, subpara. (b)(2)(N) read as follows:

"(N) In the case of lubricating oil taxable under section 4091 which is contained in a mixture which is rerefined oil (as defined in section 4093(b)(3)), used or sold."

Prior to deletion, the second to last sentence of para. (b)(2) read as follows:

"The amount of the credit or refund under subparagraph (N) with respect to any lubricating oil shall be the amount which would be exempt from tax under section 4093."

—P.L. 97-424, Sec. 521(a)-(e), provided provisions on floor stocks taxes which are reproduced in the note following Code Sec. 4081.

In 1980, P.L. 96-598, Sec. 1(a), amended subpara. (b)(2)(G) . . . Sec. 1(b)(1), added new subpara. (b)(3)(D) . . . Sec. 1(b)(2)(A), added "(or in the case of the tread rubber on a recapped or retreaded tire, resold for use as provided in subparagraph (D) of paragraph (3))," after "paragraph (3)" in subpara. (b)(2)(E) . . . Sec. 1(b)(2)(B), substituted "(b)(3)(C) or (D)" for "(b)(3)(C)" in subpara. (a)(1)(C) . . . Sec. 1(b)(2)(C), added "(D)," after "(C)," in subpara. (b)(3)(A) . . . Sec. 1(b)(2)(D), substituted "section 4071, or a recapped or retreaded tire in respect of which tax under section 4071(a)(4) was paid on the tread rubber used in the recapping or retreading," for "section 4071" in subpara. (b)(4)(A), effective on the first day of the first calendar month which begins more than 10 days after 12/24/80.

Prior to amendment, subpara. (b)(2)(G) read as follows:

"(G) in the case of tread rubber in respect of which tax was paid under section 4071(a)(4), used or sold for use otherwise than in the recapping or retreading of tires of the type used on highway vehicles (as defined in section 4072(c)), unless credit or refund of such tax is allowable under subsection (b)(3);"

—P.L. 96-596, Sec. 4(c)(1), amended para. (b)(1), effective for adjustments to any tire after 12/31/82.

Prior to amendment, para. (b)(1) read as follows:

"(1) Price readjustments. If the price of any article in respect of which a tax, based on such price, is imposed by chapter 32, is readjusted by reason of the return or repossession of the article or a covering or container, or by a bona fide discount, rebate, or allowance including a readjustment for local advertising (but only to the extent provided in section 4216(e)(2) and (3)), the part of the tax proportionate to the part of the price repaid or credited to the purchaser shall be deemed to be an overpayment. The preceding sentence shall not apply in the case of an article in respect of which tax was computed under section 4223(b)(2); but if the price for which such article was sold is readjusted by reason of the return or repossession of the article, the part of the tax proportionate to the part of such price repaid or credited to the purchaser shall be deemed to be an overpayment."

—P.L. 96-222, Sec. 108(c)(2)(A), amended subpara. (b)(3)(C) . . . Sec. 108(c)(2)(B), amended subpara. (b)(4)(B) . . . Sec. 108(c)(3), deleted "or" at the end of subpara. (b)(2)(L), substituted "; or" for the period at the end of subpara. (b)(2)(M), and added subpara. (b)(2)(N) . . . Sec. 108(c)(4), amended subpara. (b)(3)(A), effective the first day of the first calendar month which begins more than 10 days after 11/9/78.

Prior to amendment, subpara. (b)(3)(C) read as follows:

"(C) in the case of a tire or inner tube taxable under section 4071, such article is sold by the subsequent manufacturer or producer on or in connection with, or with the sale of, any other article manufactured or produced by him and such other article is by any person exported, sold to a State or local government for the exclusive use of a State or local government, sold to a nonprofit educational organization for its exclusive use, or used or sold for use as supplies for vessels or aircraft;"

Prior to amendment, subpara. (b)(4)(B) read as follows:

"(B) such other article is by any person exported, sold to a State or local government for the exclusive use of a State or local government, sold to a nonprofit educational organization for its exclusive use, or used or sold for use as supplies for vessels or aircraft, any tax imposed by chapter 32 in respect of such tire or inner tube which has been paid by the manufacturer, producer, or importer thereof shall be deemed to be an overpayment by him;"

Prior to amendment, subpara. (b)(3)(A) read as follows:

"(A) in the case of any article other than an article to which subparagraph (B), (C), or (E) applies, such article is used by the subsequent manufacturer or producer as material in the manufacture or production of, or as a component part of, another article taxable under chapter 32 manufactured or produced by him;"

In 1978, P.L. 95-618, Sec. 201(c)(3), added the last sentence of para. (b)(2), effective for 1980 and later model year automobiles (as defined in Code Sec. 4064(b)).

—P.L. 95-618, Sec. 232(b), amended subpara. (b)(2)(I), effective for sales on or after the first day of the first calendar month beginning more than 10 days after 11/9/78.

Prior to amendment, subpara. (b)(2)(I) read as follows:

"(I) in the case of a bus chassis or body taxable under section 4061(a), sold to any person for use as described in section 4063(a)(6) or 4221(e)(5);"

—P.L. 95-618, Sec. 233(c)(3), substituted a semicolon for the period at the end of subpara. (b)(2)(K), and added subparas. (b)(2)(L) and (b)(2)(M), effective the first day of the first calendar month which begins more than 10 days after 11/9/78.

—P.L. 95-227, Sec. 2(b)(4), added "(other than coal taxable under section 4121)" after "in respect of any article" in para (b)(2) and added "(other than coal taxable under section 4121)" after "with respect to the sale of any article" in para. (b)(3), effective for sales after 3/31/78. Sec. 5 of P.L. 95-227 provides general reservation, see note following Code Sec. 192.

In 1976, P.L. 94-455, Sec. 1904(b)(1)(A), substituted "(special fuels)" for "(retailers taxes)" in para. (a)(1) . . . Sec. 1904(b)(1)(B), deleted "subchapter E of", after "tax imposed by" in subsec. (e), effective 2/1/77.

—P.L. 94-455, Sec. 1904(b)(2), substituted "section 4216(e)(2) and (3)" for "section 4216(f)(2) and (3)" in para. (b)(1) . . . Sec. 1906(a)(24)(A), redesignated subparas. (a)(3)(C) and (a)(3)(D) as subparas. (a)(3)(A) and (a)(3)(B), effective 2/1/77.

—P.L. 94-455, Sec. 1906(a)(24)(B)(i), deleted subparas. (b)(2)(G), (b)(2)(H), (b)(2)(I) and (b)(2)(J), and redesignated subparas. (b)(2)(F), (b)(2)(K), (b)(2)(L), (b)(2)(M), (b)(2)(R), (b)(2)(S) and (b)(2)(T) [as added by Sec. 2108(a)(3) of this Act, see below] as subparas. (b)(2)(E), (b)(2)(F), (b)(2)(G), (b)(2)(H), (b)(2)(I), (b)(2)(J) and (b)(2)(K), effective for the use or resale for use of liquids after 12/31/76.

Prior to amendment, subparas. (b)(2)(G), (H), (I) and (J) read as follows:

"(G) in the case of a liquid taxable under section 4041, sold for use as fuel in a diesel-powered highway vehicle or as fuel for the propulsion of a motor vehicle, motorboat, or airplane, if before July 1, 1970 (i) the vendee used such liquid otherwise than as fuel in such a vehicle, motorboat, or airplane or resold such liquid, or (ii) such liquid was (within the meaning of paragraphs (1), (2), and (3) of section 6420(c)) used on a farm for farming purposes;

"(H) in the case of a liquid in respect of which tax was paid under section 4041 at the rate of 3 cents or 4 cents a gallon, used during any calendar quarter beginning before July 1, 1970 in vehicles while engaged in furnishing scheduled common carrier public passenger land transportation service along regular routes; except that (i) this subparagraph shall apply only if the 60 percent passenger fare revenue test set forth in section 6421(b)(2) is met with respect for such quarter, and (ii) the amount of such overpayment for such quarter shall be an amount determined by multiplying 1 cent (where tax was paid at the 3-cent rate) or 2 cents (where tax was paid at the 4-cent rate) for each gallon of liquid so used by the percentage which such person's tax-exempt passenger fare revenue (as defined in section 6421(d)(2)) derived from such scheduled service during such quarter was of his total passenger fare revenue (not including tax imposed by section 4261, relating to the tax on transportation of persons) derived from such scheduled service during such quarter;

"(I) in the case of a liquid in respect of which tax was paid under section 4041(a)(1) at the rate of 3 cents or 4 cents a gallon, used or resold for use before July 1, 1970, as a fuel in a diesel-powered highway vehicle (i) which (at the time of such use or resale) is not registered, and is not required to be registered for highway use under the laws of any State or foreign country, or (ii) which, in the case of a diesel-powered highway vehicle owned by the United States, is not used on the highway; except that the amount of any overpayment by reason of this subparagraph shall not exceed an amount computed at the rate of 1 cent a gallon where tax was paid at the 3-cent rate or at the rate of 2 cents a gallon where tax was paid at the 4-cent rate;

"(J) in the case of a liquid in respect of which tax was paid under section 4041(b)(1) at the rate of 3 cents or 4 cents a gallon, used or resold for use before July 1, 1970, otherwise than as a fuel for the propulsion of a highway vehicle (i) which (at the time of such use or resale) is registered, or is required to be registered, for highway use under the laws of any State or foreign country, or (ii) which, in the case of a highway vehicle owned by the United States, is used on the highway; except that the amount of any overpayment by reason of this subparagraph shall not exceed an amount computed at the rate of one cent a gallon where tax was paid at the 3-cent rate or at the rate of 2 cents a gallon where tax was paid at the 4-cent rate;"

—P.L. 94-455, Sec. 1906(b)(13)(A), substituted "Secretary" for "Secretary or his delegate" each place it appeared in Code Sec. 6416, effective 2/1/77.

—P.L. 94-455, Sec. 2108(a)(1), deleted "or" at the end of subpara. (b)(2)(R) . . . Sec. 2108(a)(2), substituted "; or" for the period at the end of subpara. (b)(2)(S) . . . Sec. 2108(a)(3), added subpara. (b)(2)(T), effective for parts and accessories sold after 10/4/76.

In 1971, P.L. 92-178, Sec. 401(a)(3)(C)(i), substituted "described in section 4063(a)(6) or 4221(e)(5); or" for "described in section 4221(e)(5)," . . . Sec. 401(a)(3)(C)(ii), added subpara. (b)(2)(S) . . . Sec. 401(g)(6), substituted "Trucks, buses, tractors, etc." for "automobiles, etc.", effective for articles sold on or after 12/10/71.

Abatements, credits, refunds Code Sec. 6416

In 1970, P.L. 91-614, Sec. 302(a)(1)(A), substituted "and such article is sold to a subsequent manufacturer or producer before being used, such tax shall be deemed to be an overpayment by such subsequent manufacturer or producer if" for "to a second manufacturer or producer, such tax shall be deemed to be an overpayment by such second manufacturer or producer if" in para. (b)(3) . . . Sec. 302(a)(1)(B), substituted "the subsequent manufacturer" for "the second manufacturer" each place it appeared in subparas. (b)(3)(A), (b)(3)(B), (b)(3)(C), (b)(3)(E) and (b)(3)(F) . . . Sec. 302(a)(2), deleted the last sentence of subsec. (c) . . . Sec. 302(b), deleted subpara. (b)(2)(E), effective for claims for credit or refund filed after 12/31/70, but only if the filing of the claim is not barred on 1/1/71 by any law or rule of law.

Prior to deletion, the last sentence of subsec. (c) read as follows:

"The credit provided by this subsection shall be allowable only in respect of the first sale on or in connection with, or with the sale of, another article on the sale of which tax is imposed under chapter 32."

Prior to deletion, subpara. (b)(2)(E) read as follows:

"(E) resold to a manufacturer or producer for use by him as provided in subparagraph (A), (B), (E), or (F) of paragraph (3)."

—P.L. 91-258, Sec. 205(b)(3), substituted "section 4041 (relating to tax on special fuels) on the use of any liquid" for "section 4041(a)(2) or (b)(2) (use of diesel and special motor fuels)" in subpara. (a)(2)(A). . . . Sec. 205(b)(4), amended subpara. (b)(2)(M), . . . Sec. 207(d)(4), added "before July 1, 1970" after "if" in subpara. (b)(2)(G). . . . Sec. 207(d)(5), added "beginning before July 1, 1970," after "during any calendar quarter" in subpara. (b)(2)(H) . . . Sec. 207(d)(6), added "before July 1, 1970," after "used or resold for use" in subpara. (b)(2)(I) . . . Sec. 207(d)(7), added "before July 1, 1970," after "used or resold for use" in subpara. (b)(2)(J) effective 7/1/70.

Prior to amendment subsec. (b)(2)(M) read as follows:

"(M) in the case of gasoline, used or sold for use in production of special motor fuels referred to in section 4041(b);"

In 1965, P.L. 89-44, Sec. 206(c), substituted "allocable" for "proportionate" in para. (b)(5) [as amended by Sec. 601(c)(12) of this Act, see below], effective for articles sold on or after 6/22/65.

—P.L. 89-44, Sec. 601(c)(1), deleted "section 4231(4), (5), or (6) (cabarets, etc.)," from the material preceding subpara. (a)(1)(A) in para. (a)(1) . . . Sec. 601(c)(2), deleted ", admission, or service" each place it appeared in subpara. (a)(1)(A) . . . Sec. 601(c)(3), amended subpara. (a)(1)(B) . . . Sec. 601(c)(4), deleted "or (D)" in subpara. (a)(1)(C) . . . Sec. 601(c)(5), deleted "(i), (ii), or (iii), as the case may be," in subpara. (a)(1)(D) . . . Sec. 601(c)(6), deleted subparas. (a)(3)(A) and (a)(3)(B), and deleted "(ii)" in subpara. (a)(3)(C), and deleted "or (D)" in subpara. (a)(3)(D) . . . Sec. 601(c)(7), deleted "31 or" and "(in the case of a tax imposed by chapter 32)" in para. (b)(1) . . . Sec. 601(c)(8), amended subpara. (b)(2)(F) . . . Sec. 601(c)(9), deleted subparas. (b)(2)(N), (b)(2)(O), (b)(2)(P) and (b)(2)(Q) . . . Sec. 601(c)(10), deleted "(D)," in subpara. (b)(3)(A), and deleted subpara. (b)(3)(D), and amended subparas. (b)(3)(B) and (b)(3)(C) . . . Sec. 601(c)(11), amended para. (b)(4) . . . Sec. 601(c)(12), deleted "4053(b)(1) or" each place it appeared in para. (b)(5) . . . Sec. 601(c)(13), amended subsec. (c) . . . Sec. 601(c)(14), deleted subsec. (d) . . . Sec. 601(c)(15), substituted "section 4061(a)," for "sections 4061(a), 4111, 4121, 4141," in subsec. (g), effective 6/21/65.

Prior to amendment, subpara. (a)(1)(B) read as follows:

"(B) has repaid the amount of the tax

"(i) in the case of any tax imposed by chapter 31 (other than the tax imposed by section 4041(a)(1) or (b)(1)), to the purchaser of the article,

"(ii) in the case of any tax imposed by chapter 32 and the tax imposed by section 4041(a)(1) or (b)(1) (diesel and special motor fuels), to the ultimate purchaser of the article, or

"(iii) in the case of any tax imposed by section 4231(4), (5), or (6) (cabarets, etc.) to the person who paid for the admission, refreshment, service, or merchandise."

Prior to deletion, subparas. (a)(3)(A) and (a)(3)(B) read as follows:

"(A) any tax collected under section 4231(6) from a concessionaire and paid to the Secretary or his delegate shall be treated as paid by the concessionaire;

"(B) if tax under chapter 31 was paid by a supplier pursuant to an agreement under section 6011(c), either the person who (without regard to section 6011(c)) was required to return and pay the tax or the supplier may be treated as the person who paid the tax;"

Prior to amendment, subpara. (b)(2)(F) read as follows:

"(F) in the case of a tire, inner tube, or receiving set, resold for use as provided in subparagraph (C) or (D) of paragraph (3) and the other article referred to in such subparagraph is by any person exported or sold as provided in such subparagraphs;"

Prior to deletion, subparas. (b)(2)(N), (b)(2)(O), (b)(2)(P) and (b)(2)(Q) read as follows:

"(N) in the case of lubricating oil, used or sold for nonlubricating purposes;

"(O) in the case of lubricating oil in respect of which tax was paid at the rate of 6 cents a gallon, used or sold for use as cutting oils (within the meaning of section 4092(b)); except that the amount of such overpayment shall not exceed an amount computed at the rate of 3 cents a gallon;

"(P) in the case of any musical instrument taxable under section 4151, sold to a religious institution for exclusively religious purposes;

"(Q) in the case of unexposed motion picture film, used or sold for use in the making of newsreel motion picture film."

Prior to deletion, subpara. (b)(3)(D) read as follows:

"(D) in the case of a radio receiving set or an automobile radio receiving set—

"(i) such set is used by the second manufacturer or producer as a component part of any other article manufactured or produced by him, and

"(ii) such other article is by any person exported, sold to a State or local government for the exclusive use of a State or local government, sold to a nonprofit educational organization for its exclusive use, or used or sold for use as supplies for vessels or aircraft;"

Prior to amendment, subparas. (b)(3)(B) and (b)(3)(C) read as follows:

"(B) in the case of—

"(i) a part or accessory taxable under section 4061(b),

"(ii) a radio or television component taxable under section 4141, or

"(iii) a camera lens taxable under section 4171,

such article is used by the second manufacturer or producer as material in the manufacture or production of, or as a component part of, any other article manufactured or produced by him;

"(C) in the case of—

"(i) a tire or inner tube taxable under section 4071, or

"(ii) an automobile radio or television receiving set taxable under section 4141, such article is sold by the second manufacturer or producer on or in connection with, or with the sale of, any other article manufactured or produced by him and such other article is by any person exported, sold to a State or local government for the exclusive use of a State or local government, sold to a nonprofit educational organization for its exclusive use, or used or sold for use as supplies for vessels or aircraft;"

Prior to amendment, para. (b)(4) read as follows:

"(4) Tires, inner tubes, and automobile radio and television receiving sets. If

"(A)(i) a tire or inner tube taxable under section 4071, or automobile radio or television receiving set taxable under section 4141, is sold by the manufacturer, producer, or importer thereof on or in connection with, or with the sale of, any other article manufactured or produced by him, or

"(ii) a radio receiving set or an automobile radio receiving set is used by the manufacturer thereof as a component part of any other article manufactured or produced by him; and

"(B) such other article is by any person exported, sold to a State or local government for the exclusive use of a State or local government, sold to a nonprofit educational organization for its exclusive use, or used or sold for use as supplies for vessels or aircraft, any tax imposed by chapter 32 in respect of such tire, inner tube, or receiving set which has been paid by the manufacturer, producer, or importer thereof shall be deemed to be an overpayment by him."

Prior to amendment, subsec. (c) read as follows:

"(c) Credit for tax paid on tires, inner tubes, or radio or television receiving sets.

"If tires, inner tubes, or automobile radio or television receiving sets on which tax has been paid under chapter 32 are sold on or in connection with, or with the sale of, another article taxable under chapter 32, there shall (under regulations prescribed by the Secretary or his delegate) be credited (without interest) against the tax imposed on the sale of such other article, an amount determined by multiplying the applicable percentage rate of tax for such other article by—

"(1) the purchase price (less, in the case of tires, the part of such price attributable to the metal rim or rim base) if such tires or inner tubes were taxable under section 4071 (relating to tax on tires and inner tubes) or, in the case of automobile radio or television receiving sets, if such sets were taxable under section 4141; or

"(2) if such tires, inner tubes, or automobile radio or television receiving sets were taxable under section 4218 (relating to use by manufacturer, producer, or importer), the price (less, in the case of tires, the part of such price attributable to the metal rim or rim base) at which such or similar tires, inner tubes, or sets are sold, in the ordinary course of trade, by manufacturers, producers, or importers thereof, as determined by the Secretary or his delegate.

"The credit provided by this subsection shall be allowable only in respect of the first sale on or in connection with, or with the sale of, another article on the sale of which tax is imposed under chapter 32."

Prior to deletion, subsec. (d) read as follows:

"(d) Mechanical pencils taxable as jewelry.

"If any article, on the sale of which tax has been paid under section 4201, is further manufactured or processed resulting in an article taxable under section 4001, the person who sells such article at retail shall, in the computation of the retailers' excise tax due on such sale, be entitled to a credit or refund, without interest, in an amount equal to the tax paid under section 4201."

—P.L. 89-44, Sec. 801(d)(2), added subpara. (b)(2)(R), effective for articles sold on or after 6/22/65.

In 1962, P.L. 87-508, Sec. 5(c)(3)(A), substituted "commuter fare revenue" for "tax-exempt passenger fare revenue" in subpara. (b)(2)(H) . . . Sec. 5(c)(3)(B), deleted "(not including the tax imposed by section 4261, relating to the tax on transportation of persons)" in subpara. (b)(2)(H), effective for the use or sale of special fuels made on or after 11/16/62.

In 1961, P.L. 87-61, Sec. 205(c)(1), deleted "or" at the end of subpara. (b)(3)(D) . . . Sec. 205(c)(2), substituted "; or" for the period at the end of subpara. (b)(3)(E) . . . Sec. 205(c)(3), added subpara. (b)(3)(F) . . . Sec. 205(d), substituted "(E), or (F)" for "or (E)" in subpara. (b)(2)(E), effective 10/1/61.

In 1960, P.L. 86-781, Sec. 2, added "including (in the case of a tax imposed by chapter 32) a readjustment for local advertising (but only to the extent provided in section 4216(f)(2) and (3))," in after "or allowances" in the first sentence of para. (b)(1), effective for articles sold on or after the first day of the first calendar quarter beginning more than 20 days after 9/14/60.

—P.L. 86-418, Sec. 3(a), substituted "subparagraph (A), (B), or (E)" for "subparagraph (A) or (B)" in subpara. (b)(2)(E) . . . Sec. 3(b)(1), substituted "subparagraph (B), (C), (D), or (E)" for "subparagraph (B), (C), or (D)," in para. (b)(3) . . . Sec. 3(b)(2), deleted "or" at the end of subpara. (b)(3)(C), and substituted "; or" for the period at the end of subpara. (b)(3)(D), and added subpara. (b)(3)(E), effective for bicycle tires and tubes sold by the manufacturer, producer, or importer thereof on or after the first day of the first month after 4/8/60.

In 1959, P.L. 86-342, Sec. 201(d)(1)(A), substituted "at the rate of 3 cents or 4 cents a gallon" for "at the rate of 3 cents a gallon" each place it appeared in subparas. (b)(2)(H), (b)(2)(I) and (b)(2)(J) . . . Sec. 201(d)(1)(B), substituted "1 cent (where tax was paid at the 3-cent rate) or 2 cents (where tax was paid at the 4-cent rate) for each gallon" for "1 cent for each gallon" in subpara. (b)(2)(H) . . . Sec. 201(d)(1)(C), substituted "at the rate of 1 cent a gallon where tax was paid at the 3-cent rate or at the rate of 2 cents a gallon where tax was paid at the 4-cent rate;" for "at the rate of 1 cent a gallon;" at the end of subparas. (b)(2)(I) and (b)(2)(J).

In 1958, P.L. 85-859, Sec. 163(a), amended subsecs. (a), (b) and (c) . . . Sec. 163(c), added subsecs. (g), (h) and (i), effective 1/1/59. Sec. 163(b) and 1(c) of this Act provide exceptions to amendments made to subsec. (b) as follows:

"(b) Effective Date. — Section 6416 (b) of the Internal Revenue Code of 1954, as amended by this Act, shall apply only with respect to articles exported, sold, or resold, as the case may be, on or after the effective date specified in section 1 (c) of this Act.

"(c) Effective Date. — Except as otherwise provided, the amendments and repeals made by title I of this Act shall take effect on the first day of the first calendar quarter which begins more than 60 days after the date on which this Act is enacted. For effective dates of amendments made by title II of this Act, see section 210."

Prior to amendment subsecs. (a), (b) and (c) read as follows:

"(a) Condition to Allowance.

"No credit or refund of any overpayment of tax imposed by section 4231(6) or by chapter 31 (other than section 4041(a)(2) or (b)(2)) or chapter 32 (except an overpayment of tax under paragraph (1) or (3) of subsection (b) of this section) shall be allowed unless the person who paid the tax establishes under regulations prescribed by the Secretary or his delegate —

"(1) That he has not included the tax in the price of the article or service with respect to which it was imposed or has not collected the amount of the tax from the vendee; or

"(2) Has repaid the amount of the tax to the purchaser (in case of retailers' taxes) or to the ultimate purchaser (in the case of manufacturers' taxes and the tax under section 4041(a)(1) or (b)(1)) of the article or service or, in any case within subsection (b)(2), has repaid or has agreed to repay the amount of the tax to the ultimate vendor of the article; or

"(3) Has filed with the Secretary or his delegate the written consent of such purchaser, ultimate purchaser, or ultimate vendor, as the case may be, to the allowance of the credit or refund or has obtained the written consent of such ultimate vendor thereto."

"(b) Special Cases in Which Tax Payments Considered Overpayments.

"Under regulations prescribed by the Secretary or his delegate credit or refund, without interest, shall be made of the overpayments determined under the following paragraphs:

"(1) Price readjustments. If the price of any article in respect of which a tax, based on such price, is imposed by chapter 31 or 32, is readjusted by reason of the return or repossession of the article or a covering or container, or by a bona fide discount, rebate or allowance, the part of the tax proportionate to the part of the price repaid or credited to the purchaser shall be deemed to be an overpayment.

"(2) Specified uses and resales. The tax paid under subchapter E of chapter 31 or chapter 32 in respect of any article shall be deemed to be an overpayment if such article was, by any person —

"(A) Resold for the exclusive use of any State, Territory of the United States, or any political subdivision of the foregoing, or the District of Columbia, or, in the case of musical instruments embraced in section 4151, resold for the use of any religious or nonprofit educational institution for exclusively religious or educational purposes;

"(B) Used or resold for use for any of the purposes, but subject to the conditions, provided in section 4222;

"(C) In the case of a liquid taxable under section 4041, sold for use as fuel in a diesel-powered highway vehicle or as fuel for the propulsion of a motor vehicle, motorboat, or airplane, if (i) the vendee used such liquid otherwise than as fuel in such a vehicle, motorboat, or airplane or resold such liquid, or (ii) such liquid was (within the meaning of paragraphs (1), (2), and (3) of section 6420(c)) used on a farm for farming purposes;

"(D) In the case of lubricating oils, used or resold for nonlubricating purposes;

"(E) In the case of unexposed motion picture films, used or resold for use in the making of newsreel motion picture films;

"(F) In the case of articles taxable under section 406(b) other than spark plugs, storage batteries, leaf springs, coils, timers, and tire chains), used or resold for use as repair or replacement parts or accessories for farm equipment (other than equipment taxable under section 4061(a));

"(H) In the case of gasoline, used in production of special motor fuels referred to in section 4041(b);

"(I) In the case of lubricating oils in respect to which tax was paid at the rate of 6 cents a gallon, used or resold for use on or after the effective date of this subparagraph as cutting oils (within the meaning of section 4092(b)) except that the amount of such overpayment shall not exceed an amount computed at the rate of 3 cents a gallon;

"(J) In the case of a liquid in respect of which tax was paid under section 4041(a)(1) at the rate of 3 cents a gallon, used or resold for use as a fuel in a diesel-powered highway vehicle (i) which (at the time of such use or resale) is not registered, and not required to be registered, for highway use under the laws of any State or foreign country, or (ii) which, in the case of a diesel-powered highway vehicle owned by the United States, is not used on the highway; except that the amount of any overpayment by reason of this subparagraph shall not exceed an amount computed at the rate of 1 cent a gallon;

"(K) In the case of a liquid in respect of which tax was paid under section 4041(b)(1) at the rate of 3 cents a gallon, used or resold for use otherwise than as a fuel for the propulsion of a highway vehicle (i) which (at the time of such use or resale) is registered, or is required to be registered, for highway use under the laws of any State or foreign country, or (ii) which, in the case of a highway vehicle owned by the United States, is used on the highway; except that the amount of any overpayment by reason of this subparagraph shall not exceed an amount computed at the rate of 1 cent a gallon;

"(L) In the case of a liquid in respect of which tax was paid under section 4041 at the rate of 3 cents a gallon, used during any calendar quarter in vehicles while engaged in furnishing scheduled common carrier public passenger land transportation service along regular routes; except that (i) this subparagraph shall apply only if the 60 percent passenger fare revenue test set forth in section 6421(b)(2) is met with respect to such quarter, and (ii) the amount of such overpayment for such quarter shall be an amount determined by multiplying 1 cent for each gallon of liquid so used by the percentage which such person's tax-exempt passenger fare revenue (as defined in section 6421(d)(2)) derived from such scheduled service during such quarter was of his total passenger fare revenue (not including the tax imposed by section 4261, relating to the tax on transportation of persons) derived from such scheduled service during such quarter;

"(M) In the case of tread rubber in respect of which tax was paid under section 4071(a)(4), used or resold for use otherwise than in the recapping or retreading of tires of the type used on highway vehicles (as defined in section 4072(c)), unless credit or refund of such tax is allowable under subsection (b)(3).

"(3) Tax-paid articles used for further manufacture. — If the tax imposed by chapter 32 has been paid with respect to the sale of —

"(A) Any article (other than a tire, inner tube, or automobile radio or television receiving set taxable under section 4141 and other than an automobile part or accessory taxable under section 4061(b), a refrigerator component taxable under section 4111, a radio or television component taxable under section 4141, or a camera lens taxable under section 4171) purchased by a manufacturer or producer and used by him as material in the manufacture or production of, or as a component part of, an article with respect to which tax under chapter 32 has been paid, or which has been sold free of tax by virtue of section 4220 or 4224, relating to tax-free sales;

"(B) An automobile part or accessory taxable under section 4061(b), a refrigerator component taxable under section 4111, a radio or television component taxable under section 4141, or a camera lens taxable under section 4171, purchased by a manufacturer or producer and used by him as material in the manufacture of, production of, or as a component part of, any article; such tax shall be deemed an overpayment by such manufacturer or producer."

"(c) Credit for Tax Paid on Tires, Inner Tubes, Radios or Television Receiving Sets.

"If tires, inner tubes, or automobile radio or television receiving sets on which tax has been imposed under chapter 32 are sold on or in connection with, or with the sale of, an article taxable under section 4061(a) (relating to automobiles, trucks, etc.), there shall (under regulations prescribed by the Secretary or his delegate) be credited, without interest, against the tax under section 4061 an amount equal to, in the case of an article taxable under paragraphs (1) or (2) of subsection (a) of section 4061, the applicable percentage rate of tax provided in such subsections —

"(1) Of the purchase price (less, in the case of tires, the part of such price attributable to the metal rim or rim base) if such tires or inner tubes were taxable under section 4071 (relating to tax on tires and inner tubes) or, in the case of automobile radio or television receiving sets, if such sets were taxable under section 4141; or

"(2) If such tires, inner tubes, or automobile radio or television receiving sets were taxable under section 4218 (relating to use by manufacturer, producer, or importer), then of the price (less, in the case of tires, the part of such price attributable to the metal rim or rim base) at which such or similar tires, inner tubes, or sets are sold, in the ordinary course of trade, by manufacturers, producers, or importers thereof, as determined by the Secretary or his delegate."

— P.L. 85-859, Sec. 163(e)(1)-(2), provides as follows: "If —

"(1) a radio receiving set, an automobile radio receiving set, or a radio or television component was (before any other use) used as a component part of any other article, and

"(2) such other article was (before any other use) by any person exported, or sold to a State or local government for the exclusive use of a State or local government, then any tax imposed by chapter 32 of the Internal Revenue Code of 1954 (or the corresponding provisions of prior revenue law) in respect of such set or component which has been paid shall be deemed to have been an overpayment, by the manufacturer, producer, or importer of such other article, at the time paid. No credit or refund shall be allowed or made under this subsection unless the manufacturer, producer, or importer of such other article establishes to the satisfaction of the Secretary of the Treasury or his delegate that he did not include the amount of the tax in the price of such other article (and has not collected the amount of the tax from the purchaser of such other article), that the amount of the tax has been repaid to the ultimate purchaser of such other article, or that he has obtained the written consent of such ultimate purchaser to the allowance of the credit or the making of the refund. No interest shall be allowed or paid in respect of any such overpayment."

— P.L. 85-475, Sec. 4(b)(6), deleted "or section 4281", and substituted "by such chapter" for "by such chapter or section" in subsec. (f), effective only for amounts paid on or after 8/1/58.

In 1956, P.L. 466, Sec. 2(b)(1), amended subpara. (b)(2)(C), effective for liquid sold after 12/31/55.

Prior to amendment, subpara. (b)(2)(C) read as follows:

"(C) In the case of a liquid taxable under section 4041, sold for use as fuel in a diesel-powered highway vehicle or as fuel for the propulsion of a motor vehicle, motorboat, or airplane, if the vendee used such liquid otherwise than as fuel in such a vehicle, motorboat, or airplane or resold such liquid;"

—P.L. 627, Sec. 208(b), substituted a semicolon for the period at the end of subpara. (b)(2)(I), and added subparas. (b)(2)(J), (b)(2)(K), (b)(2)(L) and (b)(2)(M) effective 6/29/56.

In 1955, P.L. 367, Sec. 1(h), added "and other than an automobile part or accessory taxable under section 4061(b), a refrigerator component taxable under section 4111, a radio or television component taxable under section 4141, a camera lens taxable under section 4171" after "section 4141" in subpara. (b)(3)(A), effective for the first day of the first month which begins more than ten days after 8/11/55.

—P.L. 367, Sec. 1(i), amended subpara. (b)(3)(B), effective for articles used by the manufacturer or producer as material in the manufacture of, production of, or as a component part of, another article on or after the first day of the first month which begins more than 10 days after 8/11/55.

Prior to amendment, subpara. (b)(3)(B) read as follows:

"(B) Any article described in sections 4142 and 4143(b) purchased by a manufacturer or producer and used by him as material in the manufacture or production of, or as a component part of, communication, detection, or navigation receivers of the type used in commercial, military, or marine installations if such receivers have been sold by him to the United States for its exclusive use."

—P.L. 367, Sec. 2(b), deleted subpara. (b)(2)(G), effective for articles sold by the manufacturer, producer, or importer on or after the first day of the first month which begins more than 10 days after 8/11/55.

Prior to deletion, subpara. (b)(2)(G) read as follows:

"(G) In the case of a communication, detection, or navigation receiver of the type used in commercial, military, or marine installations, resold to the United States for its exclusive use."

—P.L. 355, Sec. 2, substituted a semicolon for the period at the end of subpara. (b)(2)(H), and added subpara. (b)(2)(I), effective on the first day of the first calendar quarter which begins more than 10 days after 8/11/55.

Sec. 6418. Repealed.

In 1990, P.L. 101-508, Sec. 11801(c)(22)(B)(i), repealed Code Sec. 6418, effective 11/5/90 except as provided in Sec. 11821(b) of this Act, which reads as follows:

"(b) Savings provision.

"If—

"(1) any provision amended or repealed by this part applied to—

"(A) any transaction occurring before the date of the enactment of this Act [11/5/90],

"(B) any property acquired before such date of enactment [11/5/90], or

"(C) any item of income, loss, deduction, or credit taken into account before such date of enactment [11/5/90], and

"(2) the treatment of such transaction, property, or item under such provision would (without regard to the amendments made by this part) affect liability for tax for periods ending after such date of enactment [11/5/90],

nothing in the amendments made by this part shall be construed to affect the treatment of such transaction, property, or item for purposes of determining liability for tax for periods ending after such date of enactment [11/5/90]."

Prior to repeal, Code Sec. 6418 read as follows:

"SEC. 6418. SUGAR.

"(a) Use as livestock feed or for distillation or production of alcohol.

"Upon the use of any manufactured sugar, or article manufactured therefrom, as livestock feed, or in the production of livestock feed, or for the distillation of alcohol, or for the production of alcohol (other than alcohol produced for human food consumption), there shall be paid by the Secretary to the person so using such manufactured sugar, or article manufactured therefrom, the amount of any tax paid under section 4501 with respect thereto.

"(b) Exportation.

Upon the exportation from the United States to a foreign country, or the shipment from the United States to any possession of the United States except Puerto Rico, of any manufactured sugar, or any article manufactured wholly or partly from manufactured sugar, with respect to which tax under the provisions of section 4501(a) has been paid, the amount of such tax shall be paid by the Secretary to the consignor named in the bill of lading under which the article was exported or shipped to a possession, or to the shipper, or to the manufacturer of the manufactured sugar or of the articles exported, if the consignor waives any claim thereto in favor of such shipper or manufacturer."

In 1976, P.L. 94-455, Sec. 1906(b)(13)(A), substituted "Secretary" for "Secretary or his delegate" each place it appeared in Code Sec. 6418, effective 2/1/77.

In 1965, P.L. 89-331, Sec. 9(b), added "or production" in the heading of subsec. (a), and added "or for the production of alcohol (other than alcohol produced for human food consumption)" in subsec. (a), effective 11/8/65.

In 1962, P.L. 87-456, Sec. 302(c), eliminated in subsec. (b) provisions which prohibited the Secretary or his delegate from making payment of the tax with respect to any manufactured sugar, or article, upon which, through substitution or otherwise, a drawback of any tax paid under section 4501(b) has been or is to be claimed under any provisions of law made applicable by section 4504, effective 8/31/63.

In 1956, ch. 342, Sec. 21(b), substituted "4501" for "4501(a)" in subsection (a).

Sec. 6419. Excise tax on wagering.
(a) Credit or refund generally.

No overpayment of tax imposed by chapter 35 shall be credited or refunded (otherwise than under subsection (b)), in pursuance of a court decision or otherwise, unless the person who paid the tax establishes, in accordance with regulations prescribed by the Secretary, (1) that he has not collected (whether as a separate charge or otherwise) the amount of the tax from the person who placed the wager on which the tax was imposed, or (2) that he has repaid the amount of the tax to the person who placed such wager, or unless he files with the Secretary written consent of the person who placed such wager to the allowance of the credit or the making of the refund. In the case of any laid-off wager, no overpayment of tax imposed by chapter 35 shall be so credited or refunded to the person with whom such laid-off wager was placed unless he establishes, in accordance with regulations prescribed by the Secretary, that the provisions of the preceding sentence have been complied with both with respect to the person who placed the laid-off wager with him and with respect to the person who placed the original wager.

(b) Credit or refund on wagers laid-off by taxpayer.

Where any taxpayer lays off part or all of a wager with another person who is liable for tax imposed by chapter 35 on the amount so laid off, a credit against such tax shall be allowed, or a refund shall be made to, the taxpayer laying off such amount. Such credit or refund shall be in an amount which bears the same ratio to the amount of tax which such taxpayer paid on the original wager as the amount so laid off bears to the amount of the original wager. Credit or refund under this subsection shall be allowed or made only in accordance with regulations prescribed by the Secretary; and no interest shall be allowed with respect to any amount so credited or refunded.

In 1976, P.L. 94-455, Sec. 1906(b)(13)(A), substituted "Secretary" for "Secretary or his delegate" each place it appeared in Code Sec. 6419, effective 2/1/77.

Sec. 6420. Gasoline used on farms.
(a) Gasoline.

Except as provided in subsection (g), if gasoline is used on a farm for farming purposes, the Secretary shall pay (without interest) to the ultimate purchaser of such gasoline the amount determined by multiplying—

(1) the number of gallons so used, by

(2) the rate of tax on gasoline under section 4081 which applied on the date he purchased such gasoline.

(b) Time for filing claims; period covered.

Not more than one claim may be filed under this section by any person with respect to gasoline used during this taxable year, and no claim shall be allowed under this section with respect to gasoline used during any taxable year unless filed by such person not later than the time prescribed by law for filing a claim for credit or refund of overpayment of income tax for such taxable year. For purposes of this subsection, a person's taxable year shall be his taxable year for purposes of subtitle A.

(c) Meaning of terms.

For purposes of this section—

(1) Use on a farm for farming purposes. Gasoline shall be treated as used on a farm for farming purposes only if used (A) in carrying on a trade or business, (B) on a farm situated in the United States, and (C) for farming purposes.

(2) Farm. The term "farm" includes stock, dairy, poultry, fruit, fur-bearing animal, and truck farms, plantations, ranches, nurseries, ranges, greenhouses or other similar structures used primarily for the raising of agricultural or horticultural commodities, and orchards.

(3) Farming purposes. Gasoline shall be treated as used for farming purposes only if used—

(A) by the owner, tenant, or operator of a farm, in connection with cultivating the soil, or in connection with raising or harvesting any agricultural or horticultural commodity, including the raising, shearing, feeding, caring for, training, and management of livestock, bees, poultry, and fur-bearing animals and wildlife, on a farm of which he is the owner, tenant, or operator;

(B) by the owner, tenant, or operator of a farm, in handling, drying, packing, grading, or storing any agricultural or horticultural commodity in its unmanufactured state; but only if such owner, tenant or operator produced more than one-half of the commodity which he so treated during the period with respect to which claim is filed;

(C) by the owner, tenant, or operator of a farm, in connection with—

(i) the planting, cultivating, caring for, or cutting of trees, or

(ii) the preparation (other than milling) of trees for market, incidental to farming operations; or

(D) by the owner, tenant, or operator of a farm, in connection with the operation, management, conservation, improvement, or maintenance of such farm and its tools and equipment.

(4) Certain farming use other than by owner, etc. In applying paragraph (3)(A) to a use on a farm for any purpose described in paragraph (3)(A) by any person other than the owner, tenant, or operator of such farm—

(A) the owner, tenant, or operator of such farm shall be treated as the user and ultimate purchaser of the gasoline, except that

(B) if the person so using the gasoline is an aerial or other applicator of fertilizers or other substances and is the ultimate purchaser of the gasoline, then subparagraph (A) of this paragraph shall not apply and the aerial or other applicator shall be treated as having used such gasoline on a farm for farming purposes.

In the case of an aerial applicator, gasoline shall be treated as used on a farm for farming purposes if the gasoline is used for the direct flight between the airfield and one or more farms.

(5) Gasoline. The term "gasoline" has the meaning given to such term by section 4083(a).

(d) Exempt sales; other payments or refunds available.

No amount shall be payable under this section with respect to any gasoline which the Secretary determines was exempt from the tax imposed by section 4081. The amount which (but for this sentence) would be payable under this section with respect to any gasoline shall be reduced by any other amount which the Secretary determines is payable under this section, or is refundable under any provision of this title, to any person with respect to such gasoline.

(e) Applicable laws.

(1) In general. All provisions of law, including penalties, applicable in respect of the tax imposed by section 4081 shall, insofar as applicable and not inconsistent with this section, apply in respect of the payments provided for in this section to the same extent as if such payments constituted refunds of overpayments of the tax so imposed.

(2) Examination of books and witnesses. For the purpose of ascertaining the correctness of any claim made under this section, or the correctness of any payment made in respect of any such claim, the Secretary shall have the authority granted by paragraphs (1), (2), and (3) of section 7602(a) (relating to examination of books and witnesses) as if the claimant were the person liable for tax.

(3) Fractional parts of a dollar. Section 7504 (granting the Secretary discretion with respect to fractional parts of a dollar) shall not apply.

(f) Regulations.

The Secretary may by regulations prescribe the conditions, not inconsistent with the provisions of this section, under which payments may be made under this section.

(g) Income tax credit in lieu of payment.

(1) Persons not subject to income tax. Payment shall be made under subsection (a) only to—

(A) the United States or an agency or instrumentality thereof, a State, a political subdivision of a State, or an agency or instrumentality of one or more States or political subdivisions, or

(B) an organization exempt from tax under section 501(a) (other than an organization required to make a return of the tax imposed under subtitle A for its taxable year).

(2) Allowance of credit against income tax. For allowance of credit against the tax imposed by subtitle A, see section 34.

(h) Repealed.

(i) Cross references.

(1) For exemption from tax in case of special fuels used on a farm for farming purposes see section 4041(f).

(2) For civil penalty for excessive claim under this section see section 6675.

(3) For fraud penalties, etc., see chapter 75 (section 7201 and following, relating to crimes, other offenses, and forfeitures).

(4) For treatment of an Indian tribal government as a State [sic (] and a subdivision of an Indian tribal government as a political subdivision of a State), see section 7871.

In 2006, P.L. 109-432, Sec. 420(d), Sec. 420 of this Act relating to modification of refunds for kerosene used in aviation, reads as follows:

"Sec. 420. Modification of refunds for kerosene used in aviation.

"(d) Special rule for kerosene used in aviation on a farm for farming purposes.

"(1) Refunds for purchases after December 31, 2004, and before October 1, 2005.

"The Secretary of the Treasury shall pay to the ultimate purchaser of any kerosene which is used in aviation on a farm for farming purposes and which was purchased after December 31, 2004, and before October 1, 2005, an amount equal to the aggregate amount of tax imposed on such fuel under section 4041 or 4081 of the Internal Revenue Code of 1986, as the case may be, reduced by any payment to the ultimate vendor under section 6427(l)(5)(C) of such Code (as in effect on the day before the date of the enactment of the Safe, Accountable, Flexible, Efficient Transportation Equity Act: a Legacy for Users).

"(2) Use on a farm for farming purposes. For purposes of paragraph (1), kerosene shall be treated as used on a farm for farming purposes if such kerosene is used for farming purposes (within the meaning of section 6420(c)(3) of the Internal Revenue Code of 1986) in carrying on a trade or business on a farm situated in the United States. For purposes of the preceding sentence, rules similar to the rules of section 6420(c)(4) of such Code shall apply.

"(3) Time for filing claims. No claim shall be allowed under paragraph (1) unless the ultimate purchaser files such claim before the date that is 3 months after the date of the enactment of this Act.

"(4) No double benefit. No amount shall be paid under paragraph (1) or section 6427(l) of the Internal Revenue Code of 1986 with respect to any kerosene described in paragraph (1) to the extent that such amount is in excess of the tax imposed on such kerosene under section 4041 or 4081 of such Code, as the case may be.

"(5) Applicable laws. For purposes of this subsection, rules similar to the rules of section 6427(j) of the Internal Revenue Code of 1986 shall apply.

In 2005, P.L. 109-59, Sec. 11121(a), amended subpara. (c)(4)(B)... Sec. 11121(b), added 'In the case of an aerial applicator, gasoline shall be treated as used on a farm for farming purposes if the gasoline is used for the direct flight between the airfield and one or more farms.' as a flush sentence at the end of para. (c)(4), effective for fuel use or air transportation after 9/30/2005.

Prior to amendment, subpara. (c)(4)(B) read as follows:

"(B) if—

Abatements, credits, refunds Code Sec. 6421(b)(1)(B)

"(i) the person so using the gasoline is an aerial or other applicator of fertilizers or other substances and is the ultimate purchaser of the gasoline, and

"(ii) the person described in subparagraph (A) waives (at such time and in such form and manner as the Secretary shall prescribe) his right to be treated as the user and ultimate purchaser of the gasoline,

then subparagraph (A) of this paragraph shall not apply and the aerial or other applicator shall be treated as having used such gasoline on a farm for farming purposes."

In 1993, P.L. 103-66, Sec. 13241(f)(5), deleted subsec. (h), effective 10/1/93.

Prior to deletion, subsec. (h) read as follows:

"(h) Termination. Except with respect to taxes imposed by section 4081 at the Leaking Underground Storage Tank Trust Fund financing rate, this section shall apply only with respect to gasoline purchased before October 1, 1999."

—P.L. 103-66, Sec. 13242(d)(20), substituted "section 4083(a)" for "section 4082(b)" in para. (c)(5), effective 1/1/94.

In 1991, P.L. 102-240, Sec. 8002(b)(5), substituted "1999" for "1995" in subsec. (h), effective 12/18/91.

In 1990, P.L. 101-508, Sec. 11211(d)(5), substituted "1995" for "1993" in subsec. (h), effective 11/5/90.

In 1989, P.L. 101-239, Sec. 7841(d)(20), substituted "section 7602(a)" for "section 7602" in para. (e)(2), effective 12/19/89.

In 1987, P.L. 100-17, Sec. 502(b)(6), substituted "1993" for "1988" in subsec. (h), effective 4/2/87.

In 1986, P.L. 99-499, Sec. 521(c)(1), substituted "Except with respect to taxes imposed by section 4081 at the Leaking Underground Storage Tank Trust Fund financing rate, this section" for "This section" in subsec. (h), effective 1/1/87.

In 1984, P.L. 98-369, Sec. 474(r)(38), substituted "section 34" for "section 39" in para. (g)(2), effective for tax. yrs. begin. after 12/31/83, and for carrybacks from tax. yrs. begin. after 12/31/83.

In 1983, P.L. 97-473, Sec. 202(b)(12), added para. (h)(4) [sic (i)(4)].

—P.L. 97-424, Sec. 511(f), amended para. (c)(4), effective 4/1/83.

Prior to amendment, para. (c)(4) read as follows:

"(4) Certain farming use other than by owner, etc. In applying paragraph (3)(A) to a use on a farm for any purpose described in paragraph (3)(A) by any person other than the owner, tenant, or operator of such farm—

"(A) the owner, tenant, or operator of such farm shall be treated as the user and ultimate purchaser of the gasoline, except that

"(B) if the person so using the gasoline is an aerial applicator who is the ultimate purchaser of the gasoline and the person described in subparagraph (A) waives (at such time and in such form and manner as the Secretary shall prescribe) his right to be treated as the user and ultimate purchaser of the gasoline, then subparagraph (A) of this paragraph shall not apply and the aerial applicator shall be treated as having used such gasoline on a farm for farming purposes."

—P.L. 97-424, Sec. 516(b)(4), redesignated subsec. (h) as subsec. (i) and added new subsec. (h), effective 1/6/83.

In 1978, P.L. 95-458, Sec. 3(a), redesignated para. (c)(4) as para. (c)(5) and added new para. (c)(4) . . . Sec. 3(c), amended subpara. (c)(3)(A), effective 4/1/79 (the first day of the first calendar quarter which begins more than 90 days after 10/14/78, the date of enactment).

Prior to amendment, subpara. (c)(3)(A) read as follows:

"(A) by the owner, tenant, or operator of a farm, in connection with cultivating the soil, or in connection with raising or harvesting any agricultural or horticultural commodity, including the raising, shearing, feeding, caring for, training, and management of livestock, bees, poultry, and fur-bearing animals and wildlife, on a farm of which he is the owner, tenant, or operator; except that if such use is by any person other than the owner, tenant, or operator of such farm, then for purposes of this subparagraph, in applying subsection (a) to this subparagraph, the owner, tenant, or operator of the farm on which gasoline or a liquid taxable under section 4041 issued shall be treated as the user and ultimate purchaser of such gasoline or liquid;"

In 1976, P.L. 94-455, Sec. 1906(a)(26), amended subsec. (b) . . . substituted "apply in respect" for "apply in respect" in para. (e)(1) . . . deleted subsec. (g) and redesignated subsecs. (h) and (i) as subsecs. (g) and (h) . . . substituted "subsection (g)" for "subsection (h)" in subsec. (a) . . . deleted "with respect to gasoline used after June 30, 1965," after "subsection (a)", and deleted "for gasoline used after June 30, 1965," after "subtitle A", in redesignated subsec. (g), effective 2/1/77.

Prior to amendment, subsec. (b) read as follows:

"(b) Time for filing claim; period covered.

"(1) Gasoline used before July 1, 1965. Except as provided in paragraph (2), not more than one claim may be filed under this section by any person with respect to gasoline used during the one-year period ending on June 30 of any year. No claim shall be allowed under this paragraph with respect to any one-year period unless filed on or before September 30 of the year in which such one-year period ends.

"(2) Gasoline used after June 30, 1965. In the case of gasoline used after June 30, 1965—

"(A) not more than one claim may be filed under this section by any person with respect to gasoline used during this taxable year; and

"(B) no claim shall be allowed under this section with respect to gasoline used during any taxable year unless filed by such person not later than the time prescribed by law for filing a claim for credit or refund, of overpayment of income tax for such taxable year.

For purposes of this paragraph, a person's taxable year shall be his taxable year for purposes of subtitle A, except that a person's first taxable year beginning after

June 30, 1965, shall include the period after June 30, 1965, and before the beginning of such first taxable year."

Prior to amendment, subsec. (g) read as follows:

"(g) Effective date.

"This section shall apply only with respect to gasoline purchased after December 31, 1955."

—P.L. 94-455, Sec. 1906(b)(6), amended subpara. (c)(3)(A), effective for the use of liquids after 12/31/70.

Prior to amendment, subpara. (c)(3)(A) read as follows:

"(A) by the owner, tenant, or operator of a farm, in connection with cultivating the soil, or in connection with raising or harvesting any agricultural or horticultural commodity, including the raising, shearing, feeding, caring for, training, and management of livestock, bees, poultry, and fur-bearing animals and wildlife, on a farm of which he is the owner, tenant, or operator; except that if such use is by any person other than the owner, tenant, or operator of such farm, then (i) for purposes of this subparagraph, in applying subsection (a) to this subparagraph, and for purposes of section 6416(b)(2)(G)(ii) (but not for purposes of section 4041), the owner, tenant, or operator of the farm on which gasoline or a liquid taxable under section 4041 is used shall be treated as the user and ultimate purchaser of such gasoline or liquid, and (ii) for purposes of applying section 6416(b)(2)(G)(ii), any tax paid under section 4041 in respect of a liquid used on a farm for farming purposes (within the meaning of this subparagraph) shall be treated as having been paid by the owner, tenant, or operator of the farm on which such liquid is used;"

—P.L. 94-455, Sec. 1906(b)(13)(A), substituted "Secretary" for "Secretary or his delegate" each place it appeared in Code Sec. 6420, effective 2/1/77.

In 1970, P.L. 91-258, Sec. 205(c)(7), substituted "special fuels" for "diesel fuel and special motor fuels" and substituted "section 4041(f)" for "section 4041(d)" in subsec. (i)(1), effective 7/1/70.

—P.L. 91-258, Sec. 207(b), substituted "time prescribed by law for filing a claim for credit or refund of overpayment of income tax for such taxable year" for "time prescribed by law for filing an income tax return for such taxable year" in subpara. (b)(2)(B), effective for tax. yrs. end. after 6/30/70.

In 1965, P.L. 89-44, Sec. 809, substituted "Except as provided in subsection (h), if" for "If" in subsec. (a) . . . amended subsec. (b) . . . substituted "payable" for "paid" in the first sentence of subsec. (d) . . . added subsec. (h) . . . redesignated subsec. (h) as (i), effective for gasoline used on or after 7/1/65.

Prior to amendment, subsec. (b) read as follows:

"(b) Time for filing claim; period covered. Not more than one claim may be filed under this section by any person with respect to gasoline used during the one-year period ending on June 30 of any year. No claim shall be allowed under this section with respect to any one-year period unless filed on or before September 30 of the year in which such one-year period ends."

In 1958, P.L. 85-859, Sec. 163(d)(2), substituted "section 6416(b)(2)(G)(ii)" for "section 6416(b)(2)(C)(ii)" each place it appeared in subpara. (c)(3)(A), effective 1/1/59.

In 1956, ch. 160, Sec. 1, added Code Sec. 6420, effective for gasoline purchased after '55.

Sec. 6421. Gasoline used for certain nonhighway purposes, used by local transit systems, or sold for certain exempt purposes.

(a) Nonhighway uses.

Except as provided in subsection (i), if gasoline is used in an off-highway business use, the Secretary shall pay (without interest) to the ultimate purchaser of such gasoline an amount equal to the amount determined by multiplying the number of gallons so used by the rate at which tax was imposed on such gasoline under section 4081. Except as provided in paragraph (2) of subsection (f) of this section, in the case of gasoline used as a fuel in an aircraft, the Secretary shall pay (without interest) to the ultimate purchaser of such gasoline an amount equal to the amount determined by multiplying the number of gallons of gasoline so used by the rate at which tax was imposed on such gasoline under section 4081.

(b) Intercity, local, or school buses.

(1) Allowance. Except as provided in paragraph (2) and subsection (i), if gasoline is used in an automobile bus while engaged in—

  (A) furnishing (for compensation) passenger land transportation available to the general public, or

  (B) the transportation of students and employees of schools (as defined in the last sentence of section 4221(d)(7)(C)),

the Secretary shall pay (without interest) to the ultimate purchaser of such gasoline an amount equal to the product of the number of gallons of gasoline so used multiplied by

3,713

the rate at which tax was imposed on such gasoline by section 4081.

(2) Limitation in case of nonscheduled intercity or local buses. Paragraph (1)(A) shall not apply in respect of gasoline used in any automobile bus while engaged in furnishing transportation which is not scheduled and not along regular routes unless the seating capacity of such bus is at least 20 adults (not including the driver).

(c) Exempt purposes.

If gasoline is sold to any person for any purpose described in paragraph (2), (3), (4), (5), or (6) of section 4221(a), the Secretary shall pay (without interest) to such person an amount equal to the product of the number of gallons of gasoline so sold multiplied by the rate at which tax was imposed on such gasoline by section 4081. The preceding sentence shall apply notwithstanding paragraphs (2) and (3) of subsection (f). Subsection (a) shall not apply to gasoline to which this subsection applies.

(d) Time for filing claims; period covered.

(1) In general. Except as provided in paragraph (2), not more than one claim may be filed under subsection (a), and not more than one claim may be filed under subsection (b), and not more than one claim may be filed under subsection (c), by any person with respect to gasoline used during his taxable year; and no claim shall be allowed under this paragraph with respect to gasoline used during any taxable year unless filed by such person not later than the time prescribed by law for filing a claim for credit or refund of overpayment of income tax for such taxable year. For purposes of this subsection, a person's taxable year shall be his taxable year for purposes of subtitle A.

(2) Exception. For payments per quarter based on aggregate amounts payable under this section and section 6427, see section 6427(i)(2).

(3) Application to sales under subsection (c). For purposes of this subsection, gasoline shall be treated as used for a purpose referred to in subsection (c) when it is sold for such a purpose.

(e) Definitions.

For purposes of this section—

(1) Gasoline. The term "gasoline" has the meaning given to such term by section 4083(a).

(2) Off-highway business use.

(A) In general. The term "off-highway business use" means any use by a person in a trade or business of such person or in an activity of such person described in section 212 (relating to production of income) otherwise than as a fuel in a highway vehicle—

(i) which (at the time of such use), is registered, or is required to be registered, for highway use under the laws of any State or foreign country, or

(ii) which, in the case of a highway vehicle owned by the United States, is used on the highway.

(B) Uses in boats.

(i) In general. Except as otherwise provided in this subparagraph, the term "off-highway business use" does not include any use in a motorboat.

(ii) Fisheries and whaling. The term "off-highway business use" shall include any use in a vessel employed in the fisheries or in the whaling business.

(C) Uses in mobile machinery.

(i) In general. The term "off-highway business use" shall include any use in a vehicle which meets the requirements described in clause (ii).

(ii) Requirements for mobile machinery. The requirements described in this clause are—

(I) the design-based test, and

(II) the use-based test.

(iii) Design-based test. For purposes of clause (ii)(I), the design-based test is met if the vehicle consists of a chassis—

(I) to which there has been permanently mounted (by welding, bolting, riveting, or other means) machinery or equipment to perform a construction, manufacturing, processing, farming, mining, drilling, timbering, or similar operation if the operation of the machinery or equipment is unrelated to transportation on or off the public highways,

(II) which has been specially designed to serve only as a mobile carriage and mount (and a power source, where applicable) for the particular machinery or equipment involved, whether or not such machinery or equipment is in operation, and

(III) which, by reason of such special design, could not, without substantial structural modification, be used as a component of a vehicle designed to perform a function of transporting any load other than that particular machinery or equipment or similar machinery or equipment requiring such a specially designed chassis.

(iv) Use-based test. For purposes of clause (ii)(II), the use-based test is met if the use of the vehicle on public highways was less than 7,500 miles during the taxpayer's taxable year. This clause shall be applied without regard to use of the vehicle by any organization which is described in section 501(c) and exempt from tax under section 501(a).

(f) Exempt sales; other payments or refunds available.

(1) Gasoline used on farms. This section shall not apply in respect of gasoline which was (within the meaning of paragraphs (1), (2), and (3) of section 6420(c)) used on a farm for farming purposes.

(2) Gasoline used in aviation. This section shall not apply in respect of gasoline which is used as a fuel in an aircraft—

(A) in aviation which is not commercial aviation (as defined in section 4083(b)), or

(B) in commercial aviation (as so defined) with respect to the tax imposed by section 4081 at the Leaking Underground Storage Tank Trust Fund financing rate and, in the case of fuel purchased after September 30, 1995, at so much of the rate specified in section 4081(a)(2)(A) as does not exceed 4.3 cents per gallon.

(3) Gasoline used in trains. In the case of gasoline used as a fuel in a train, this section shall not apply with respect to—

(A) the Leaking Underground Storage Tank Trust Fund financing rate under section 4081, and

(B) so much of the rate specified in section 4081(a)(2)(A) as does not exceed the rate applicable under section 4041(a)(1)(C)(ii).

(g) Applicable laws.

(1) In general. All provisions of law, including penalties, applicable in respect to the tax imposed by section 4081 shall, insofar as applicable and not inconsistent with this section, apply in respect of the payments provided for in this section to the same extent as if such payments constituted refunds of overpayments of the tax so imposed.

(2) Examination of books and witnesses. For the purpose of ascertaining the correctness of any claim made under this section, or the correctness of any payment made in respect of any such claim, the Secretary shall have the authority granted by paragraphs (1), (2), and (3)

Abatements, credits, refunds   Code Sec. 6421

of section 7602(a) (relating to examination of books and witnesses) as if the claimant were the person liable for tax.

(h) Regulations.

The Secretary may by regulations prescribe the conditions, not inconsistent with the provisions of this section, under which payments may be made under this section.

(i) Income tax credit in lieu of payment.

(1) **Persons not subject to income tax.** Payment shall be made under subsections (a) and (b), only to—

(A) the United States or an agency or instrumentality thereof, a State, a political subdivision of a State, or an agency or instrumentality of one or more States or political subdivisions, or

(B) an organization exempt from tax under section 501(a) (other than an organization required to make a return of the tax imposed under subtitle A for its taxable year).

(2) **Exception.** Paragraph (1) shall not apply to a payment of a claim filed under subsection (d)(2).

(3) **Allowance of credit against income tax.** For allowance of credit against the tax imposed by subtitle A, see section 34.

(j) Cross references.

(1) For civil penalty for excessive claims under this section, see section 6675.

(2) For fraud penalties, etc., see chapter 75 (section 7201 and following, relating to crimes, other offenses, and forfeitures).

(3) For treatment of an Indian tribal government as a State and a subdivision of an Indian tribal government as a political subdivision of a State, see section 7871.

In 2006, P.L. 109-280, Sec. 1207(b)(3)(B), substituted "(5), or (6)" for "or (5)" in subsec. (c), effective 1/1/2007.

In 2005, P.L. 109-59, Sec. 11151(b)(3)(A), substituted "aviation which is not commercial aviation (as defined in section 4083(b))" for "noncommercial aviation (as defined in section 4041(c)(2))" in subpara. (f)(2)(A) . . . Sec. 11151(b)(3)(B), substituted "commercial aviation" for "aviation which is not noncommercial aviation" in subpara. (f)(2)(B), effective for aviation-grade kerosene removed, entered, or sold after 12/31/2004 (as if included in Sec. 853 of P.L. 108-357, the American Jobs Creation Act of 2004, 10/22/2004).

In 2004, P.L. 108-357, Sec. 241(a)(2)(C), amended subpara. (f)(3)(B), effective 1/1/2005.

Prior to amendment, subpara. (f)(3)(B) read as follows:

"(B) so much of the rate specified in section 4081(a)(2)(A) as does not exceed—

"(i) 6.8 cents per gallon after September 30, 1993, and before October 1, 1995,

"(ii) 5.55 cents per gallon after September 30, 1995, and before November 1, 1998, and

"(iii) 4.3 cents per gallon after October 31, 1998."

—P.L. 108-357, Sec. 851(d)(1), added subpara. (e)(2)(C), effective for tax. yrs. begin. after 10/22/2004.

In 1998, P.L. 105-206, Sec. 6010(g)(3)(A), substituted "(2)" for "(2)(A)" in subsec. (c) . . . Sec. 6010(g)(3)(B), added a sentence at the end of subsec. (c), effective 10/1/97.

—P.L. 105-206, Sec. 6023(24)(A), redesignated subsecs. (j) and (k) as (i) and (j) . . . Sec. 6023(24)(C), substituted "subsection (i)" for "subsection (j)" in subsecs. (a) and (b), effective 7/22/98.

—P.L. 105-178, Sec. 9006(b)(1)(A), substituted "November 1, 1998" for "October 1, 1999" in clause (f)(3)(B)(ii) . . . Sec. 9006(b)(1)(B), substituted "October 31, 1998" for "September 30, 1999" in clause (f)(3)(B)(iii), effective 6/9/98.

—P.L. 105-178, Sec. 9009(b)(3), amended para. (d)(2), effective 10/1/98.

Prior to amendment, para. (d)(2) read as follows:

"(2) Exception. If $1,000 or more is payable under this section to any person with respect to gasoline used during any of the first three quarters of his taxable year, a claim may be filed under this section by such person with respect to gasoline used during such quarter. No claim filed under this paragraph shall be allowed unless filed on or before the last day of the first quarter following the quarter for which the claim is filed."

In 1997, P.L. 105-34, Sec. 902(a), deleted clauses (e)(2)(B)(iii) and (iv), effective 1/1/98.

Prior to deletion, clauses (e)(2)(B)(iii) and (iv) read as follows:

"(iii) Exception for diesel fuel. The term 'off-highway business use' shall include the use of diesel fuel in a boat in the active conduct of—

"(I) a trade or business of commercial fishing or transporting persons or property for compensation or hire, and

"(II) except as provided in clause (iv), any other trade or business.

"(iv) Noncommercial boats. In the case of a boat used predominantly in any activity which is of a type generally considered to constitute entertainment, amusement, or recreation, clause (iii)(II) shall not apply to—

"(I) the taxes under sections 4041(a)(1) and 4081 for the period after December 31, 1993, and before January 1, 2000, and

"(II) so much of the tax under sections 4041(a)(1) and 4081 as does not exceed 4.3 cents per gallon for the period after December 31, 1999."

In 1996, P.L. 104-188, Sec. 1609(g)(4)(C), substituted "section 4041(c)(2)" for "section 4041(c)(4)", in subpara. (f)(2)(A), effective on the 7th calendar day after 8/20/96.

In 1993, P.L. 103-66, Sec. 13163(b), amended subpara. (e)(2)(B), effective 1/1/94. Prior to amendment, subpara. (e)(2)(B) read as follows:

"(B) Exception for use in motorboats. The term 'off-highway business use' does not include any use in a motorboat. The preceding sentence shall not apply to use in a vessel employed in the fisheries or in the whaling business."

—P.L. 103-66, Sec. 13241(f)(6), added "and at the deficit reduction rate" after "financing rate" in para. (f)(3) and added "and deficit reduction tax" after "tax" in the heading to para. (f)(3) . . . Sec. 13241(f)(7), deleted subsec. (i), effective 10/1/93.

Prior to deletion, subsec. (i) read as follows:

"(i) Effective date. Except with respect to taxes imposed by section 4081 at the Leaking Underground Storage Tank Trust Fund financing rate, this section shall apply only with respect to gasoline purchased before October 1, 1999."

—P.L. 103-66, Sec. 13242(d)(20), substituted "section 4083(a)" for "section 4082(b)" in para. (e)(1) . . . Sec. 13242(d)(22), added "The preceding sentence shall apply notwithstanding paragraphs (2)(A) and (3) of subsection (f)." at the end of subsec. (c) . . . Sec. 13242(d)(23), added "and, in the case of fuel purchased after September 30, 1995, at so much of the rate specified in section 4081(a)(2)(A) as does not exceed 4.3 cents per gallon" before the period in subpara. (f)(2)(B) . . . Sec. 13242(d)(24), amended para. (f)(3) [as amended by Sec. 13241(f)(6) of this Act, see above], effective 1/1/94.

Prior to amendment, para. (f)(3) [as amended by Sec. 13241(f)(6) of this Act] read as follows:

"(3) Leaking/underground storage tank trust fund tax and deficit reduction tax on gasoline used in trains. This section shall not apply with respect to the tax imposed by section 4081 at the Leaking Underground Storage Tank Trust Fund financing rate and at the deficit reduction rate on gasoline used as a fuel in a train."

In 1991, P.L. 102-240, Sec. 8002(b)(6), substituted "1999" for "1995" in subsec. (i), effective 12/18/91.

In 1990, P.L. 101-508, Sec. 11211(d)(6), substituted "1995" for "1993" in subsec. (i), effective 11/5/90.

In 1989, P.L. 101-239, Sec. 7841(d)(20), substituted "section 7602(a)" for "section 7602" in para. (g)(2), effective 12/19/89.

In 1988, P.L. 100-647, Sec. 1017(c)(6), redesignated subsec. (i) (relating to income tax credit) and subsec. (j) as subsecs. (j) and (k) . . . Sec. 1017(c)(7), substituted "subsection (j)" for "subsection (i)" in subsec. (a) and para (b)(1) . . . Sec. 1017(c)(8), substituted "subsection (d)(2)" for "subsection (c)(2)" in para. (j)(2) . . . Sec. 1017(c)(15), added para. (d)(3), effective for gasoline removed (as defined in Code Sec. 4082) after 12/31/87.

—P.L. 100-647, Sec. 2001(d)(3)(E), amended all that followed para. (f)(1) (paras. (f)(2) and (f)(4)) . . . Sec. 2001(d)(3)(F), substituted "paragraph (2) of subsection (f)" for "paragraph (3) of subsection (e)" in the second sentence of subsec. (a), effective 1/1/87.

Prior to amendment all that followed para. (f)(1) (paras. (f)(2) and (f)(4) read as follows:

"(2) Gasoline used in noncommercial aviation. This section shall not apply in respect of gasoline which is used as a fuel in an aircraft in noncommercial aviation (as defined in section 4041(c)(4)).

"(4) Section not to apply to certain off-highway business uses with respect to the tax imposed by section 4081 at the leaking underground storage tank trust fund financing rate. This section shall not apply with respect to the tax imposed by section 4081 at the Leaking Underground Storage Tank Trust Fund financing rate on gasoline used in any off-highway business use other than use in a vessel employed in the fisheries or in the whaling business."

In 1987, P.L. 100-203, Sec. 10502(d)(9), deleted subpara. (e)(2)(C) . . . Sec. 10502(d)(10), deleted para. (j)(1) and redesignated paras. (j)(2)-(j)(4) as (j)(1)-(3), effective for sales after 3/31/88.

Prior to deletion, subpara. (e)(2)(C) read as follows:

"(C) Commercial fishing vessels. For provisions exempting from tax gasoline and special motor fuels used for commercial fishing vessels, see—

"(i) subsections (a)(3) and (d)(3) of section 4221 (relating to certain tax-free sales),

"(ii) section 6416(b)(2)(B) (relating to refund or credit in case of certain uses), and

"(iii) section 4041(g)(1) (relating to exemptions from tax on special fuels)."

Prior to deletion, para. (j)(1) read as follows:

"(1) For rate of tax in case of special fuels used in noncommercial aviation or for nonhighway purposes, see section 4041."

—P.L. 100-17, Sec. 502(b)(7), substituted "1993" for "1988" in subsec. (h), effective 4/2/87.

In 1986, P.L. 99-514, Sec. 1703(c)(1), redesignated subsecs. (c), (d), (e), (f), (g), and (h) as subsecs. (d), (e), (f), (g), (h), and (i), and added new subsec. (c) . . . Sec. 1703(c)(2)(A), substituted "not more than one claim may be filed under subsection (b), and not more than one claim may be filed under subsection (c)" for "and not more than one claim may be filed under subsection (b)" in para. (d)(1) . . . Sec. 1703(c)(2)(B), deleted para. (f)(1) and redesignated paras. (f)(2) and

3,715

Code Sec. 6421 — Abatements, credits, refunds

(f)(3) as paras. (f)(1) and (f)(2)... Sec. 1703(c)(2)(D), amended the heading of Code Sec. 6421, effective for gasoline removed (as defined in Code Sec. 4082) after 12/31/87.

Prior to deletion, para. (f)(1) read as follows:

"(1) Exempt sales. No amount shall be payable under this section with respect to any gasoline which the Secretary determines was exempt from the tax imposed by section 4081. The amount which (but for this sentence) would be payable under this section with respect to any gasoline shall be reduced by any other amount which the Secretary determines is payable under this section, or is refundable under any provision of this title, to any person with respect to such gasoline."

Prior to amendment, the heading of Code Sec. 6421 read as follows:

"SEC. 6421. GASOLINE USED FOR CERTAIN NONHIGHWAY PURPOSES OR BY LOCAL TRANSIT SYSTEMS."

—P.L. 99-499, Sec. 521(c)(2)(A), substituted "Except with respect to taxes imposed by section 4081 at the Leaking Underground Storage Tank Trust Fund financing rate, this section" for "This section", in subsec. (h)... Sec. 521(c)(2)(B), added para. (e)(4), effective 1/1/87.

In 1984, P.L. 98-369, Sec. 474(r)(38), substituted "section 34" for "section 39" in para. (i)(3), effective for tax. yrs. begin. after 12/31/83, and for carrybacks from tax. yrs. begin. after 12/31/83.

In 1983, P.L. 97-473, Sec. 202(b)(12), added para. (j)(4).

—P.L. 97-424, Sec. 511(c)(1), amended the first sentence of subsec. (a)... Sec. 511(c)(3)(A), substituted "off-highway business use" for "qualified business use" in subparas. (d)(2)(A) and (B)... Sec. 511(c)(3)(B), substituted "Off-highway" for "Qualified" in the heading of para. (d)(2), effective 4/1/83.

Prior to amendment, the first sentence of subsec. (a) read as follows:

"Except as provided in subsection (i), if gasoline is used in a qualified business use, the Secretary shall pay (without interest) to the ultimate purchaser of such gasoline an amount equal to 1 cent for each gallon of gasoline so used on which tax was paid at the rate of 3 cents a gallon and 2 cents for each gallon of gasoline so used on which tax was paid at the rate of 4 cents a gallon."

—P.L. 97-424, Sec. 515(b)(7), substituted "and special motor fuels" for ", special motor fuels, and lubricating oil" in subpara. (d)(2)(C), effective for articles sold after 1/6/83.

—P.L. 97-424, Sec. 516(a)(6), substituted "1988" for "1984" in subsec. (h), effective 1/6/83.

In 1980, P.L. 96-222, Sec. 108(c)(1), added a sentence to the end of subpara. (d)(2)(B), effective 12/1/78 [the first day of the first calendar month which begins more than 10 days after 11/9/78, date of enactment].

In 1978, P.L. 95-618, Sec. 222(a)(1)(A), substituted "Except as provided in subsection (i), if gasoline is used in a qualified business use," for

"Except as provided in subsection (i), if gasoline is used otherwise than as a fuel in a highway vehicle (1) which (at the time of such use) is registered, or is required to be registered, for highway use under the laws of any State or foreign country, or (2) which, in the case of a highway vehicle owned by the United States, is used on the highway,' in subsec. (a)... Sec. 222(a)(1)(B), added para. (d)(3), effective for uses after 12/31/78.

—P.L. 95-618, Sec. 233(a)(1), amended subsec. (b)... Sec. 233(a)(3)(A), deleted para. (d)(2) and redesignated para. (d)(3), [as added by Sec. 222(a)(1)(B) of this Act] as para. (d)(2), effective 12/1/78 (the first day of the first calendar month which begins more than 10 days after 11/9/78, date of enactment).

Prior to amendment, subsec. (b) read as follows:

"(b) Local transit systems.

"(1) Allowance. Except as provided in subsection (i), if gasoline is used during any calendar quarter in vehicles while engaged in furnishing scheduled common carrier public passenger land transportation service along regular routes, the Secretary shall, subject to the provisions of paragraph (2), pay (without interest) to the ultimate purchaser of such gasoline the amount determined by multiplying—

"(A) 1 cent for each gallon of gasoline so used on which tax was paid at the rate of 3 cents a gallon and 2 cents for each gallon of gasoline so used on which tax was paid at the rate of 4 cents a gallon, by

"(B) the percentage which the ultimate purchaser's commuter fare revenue derived from such scheduled service during such quarter was of his total passenger fare revenue derived from such scheduled service during such quarter.

"(2) Limitation. Paragraph 1 shall apply in respect of gasoline used during any calendar quarter only if at least 60 percent of the total passenger fare revenue derived during such quarter from scheduled service described in paragraph (1) by the person filing the claim was attributable to commuter fare revenue derived during such quarter by such person from such scheduled service."

Prior to deletion, para. (d)(2) read as follows:

"(2) Commuter fare revenue. The term 'commuter fare revenue' means revenue attributable to fares derived from the transportation of persons and attributable to—

"(A) amounts paid for transportation which do not exceed 60 cents,

"(B) amounts paid for commutation or season tickets for single trips of less than 30 miles, or

"(C) amounts paid for commutation tickets for one month or less."

—P.L. 95-599, Sec. 502(a)(10), substituted "1984" for "1979" in subsec. (h), effective 11/6/78.

In 1976, P.L. 94-455, Sec. 1906(a)(27)(A), deleted "after June 30, 1970," before "in the case of gasoline used", in subsec. (a) ... deleted "after June 30, 1970," after "gasoline which is used" in para. (e)(3), effective for gasoline used as a fuel after 6/30/76.

—P.L. 94-455, Sec. 1906(a)(27)(B), amended subsec. (c), effective 2/1/77.

Prior to amendment, subsec. (c) read as follows:

"(c) Time for filing claims; period covered.

"(1) Gasoline used before July 1, 1965. Except as provided in paragraphs (2) and (3), not more than one claim may be filed under subsection (a), and not more than one claim may be filed under subsection (b), by any person with respect to gasoline used during the one-year period ending on June 30 of any year. No claim shall be allowed under this paragraph with respect to any one-year period unless filed on or before September 30 of the year in which such one-year period ends.

"(2) Exception. Except as provided in paragraph (3), if $1,000 or more is payable under this section to any person with respect to gasoline used during a calendar quarter, a claim may be filed under this section by such person with respect to gasoline used during such quarter. No claim filed under this paragraph shall be allowed unless filed on or before the last day of the first calendar quarter following the calendar quarter for which the claim is filed.

"(3) Gasoline used after June 30, 1965.

"(A) In general. In the case of gasoline used after June 30, 1965—

"(i) except as provided in subparagraph (B), not more than one claim may be filed under subsection (a), and not more than one claim may be filed under subsection (b), by any person with respect to gasoline used during his taxable year; and

"(ii) no claim shall be allowed under this subparagraph with respect to gasoline used during any taxable year unless filed by such person not later than the time prescribed by law for filing a claim for credit or refund of overpayment of income tax for such taxable year.

For purposes of this paragraph, a person's taxable year shall be his taxable year for purposes of subtitle A, except that a person's first taxable year beginning after June 30, 1965, shall include the period after June 30, 1965, and before the beginning of such first taxable year.

"(B) Exception. If $1,000 or more is payable under this section to any person with respect to gasoline used during any of the first three quarters of his taxable year, a claim may be filed under this section by such person with respect to gasoline used during such quarter. No claim filed under this subparagraph shall be allowed unless filed on or before the last day of the first quarter following the quarter for which the claim is filed."

—P.L. 94-455, Sec. 1906(a)(27)(C), deleted "after June 30, 1956, and", after "gasoline purchased", in subsec. (h), effective 2/1/77.

—P.L. 94-455, Sec. 1906(a)(27)(D), deleted "with respect to gasoline used after June 30, 1965," after "subsections (a) and (b)", in para. (i)(1) ... substituted "subsection (c)(2)" for "subsection (c)(3)(B)" in para. (i)(2) ... deleted "for gasoline used after June 30, 1965. [sic]" after "subtitle A", in para. (i)(3), effective 2/1/77.

In 1976, P.L. 94-455, Sec. 1906(b)(13)(A), substituted "Secretary" for "Secretary or his delegate" each place it appeared in Code Sec. 6421, effective 2/1/77.

—P.L. 94-280, Sec. 303(a)(11), substituted "1979" for "1977" in subsec. (h), effective 5/5/76.

In 1970, P.L. 91-605, Sec. 303(a)(11), substituted "1977" for "1972" in subsec. (h).

—P.L. 91-258, Sec. 205(b)(1), added the sentence at the end of subsec. (a), and added para. (e)(3)... Sec. 205(c)(8), amended subsec. (j), effective 7/1/70.

Prior to amendment, subsec. (j) read as follows:

"(j) Cross references.

"(1) For reduced rate of tax in case of diesel fuel and special motor fuels used for certain nonhighway purposes, see subsections (a) and (b) of section 4041.

"(2) For partial refund of tax in case of diesel fuel and special motor fuels used for certain nonhighway purposes, see section 6416(b)(2)(I) and (J).

"(3) For partial refund of tax in case of diesel fuel and special motor fuels used by local transit systems, see section 6416(b)(2)(H).

"(4) For civil penalty for excessive claims under this section, see section 6675.

"(5) For fraud penalties, etc., see chapter 75 (section 7201 and following, relating to crimes, other offenses, and forfeitures)."

—P.L. 91-258, Sec. 207(b), substituted "time prescribed by law for filing a claim for credit or refund of overpayment of income tax for such taxable year" for "time prescribed by law for filing an income tax return for such taxable year" in clause. (c)(3)(A)(ii), effective for tax. yrs. end. after 6/30/70.

In 1965, P.L. 89-44, Sec. 809, substituted "Except as provided in subsection (i), if" for "If" in paras. (a)(1) and (b)(1) ... changed the heading of para. (c)(1) from "General rule" ... substituted, "Except as provided in paragraph (3), if" for "If" in para. (c)(2), substituted "payable" for "paid" in the first sentence of para. (e)(1) ... added para. (c)(3) and (i) ... redesignated subsec. (i) as (j), effective for gasoline used on or after 7/1/65.

In 1962, P.L. 87-508, Sec. 5, amended subsecs. (b) and para. (d)(2), effective for claims filed after 11/15/62.

Prior to amendment, subsec. (b) read as follows:

"(b) Local transit systems.

"(1) Allowance. If gasoline is used during any calendar quarter in vehicles while engaged in furnishing scheduled common carrier public passenger land transportation service along regular routes, the Secretary or his delegate shall, subject to the provisions of paragraph (2), pay (without interest) to the ultimate purchaser of such gasoline the amount determined by multiplying—

"(A) 1 cent for each gallon of gasoline so used on which tax was paid at the rate of 3 cents a gallon and 2 cents for each gallon of gasoline so used on which tax was paid at the rate of 4 cents a gallon, by

"(B) the percentage which the ultimate purchaser's tax-exempt passenger fare revenue derived from such scheduled service during such quarter was of his total passenger fare revenue (not including the tax imposed by section 4261, relating to the tax on transportation of persons) derived from such scheduled service during such quarter.

"(2) Limitation. Paragraph (1) shall apply in respect of gasoline used during any calendar quarter only if at least 60 percent of the total passenger fare revenue

Abatements, credits, refunds Code Sec. 6423(d)(1)(A)

(not including the tax imposed by section 4261, relating to the tax on transportation of persons) derived during such quarter from scheduled service described in paragraph (1) by the person filing the claim was attributable to tax-exempt passenger fare revenue derived during such quarter by such person from such scheduled service."

Prior to amendment, para. (d)(2) read as follows:

"(2) Tax-exempt passenger fare revenue. The term 'tax-exempt passage for revenue' means revenue attributable to fares which were exempt from the tax imposed by section 4261 by reason of section 4263(a) (relating to the exemption for commutation travel, etc.)."

In **1961**, P.L. 87-61, Sec. 201(e), substituted "October 1, 1972" for "July 1, 1972" in subsec. (h).

In **1959**, P.L. 86-342, Sec. 201(d)(2), substituted "1 cent for each gallon of gasoline so used on which tax was paid at the rate of 3 cents a gallon and 2 cents for each gallon of gasoline so used on which tax was paid at the rate of 4 cents a gallon" for "1 cent for each gallon of gasoline so used" in subsec. (a) and subpara. (b)(1)(A).

In **1958**, P.L. 85-859, Sec. 164(a), amended subsec. (c), effective for claims, the last day of filing of which occurs after 1/1/59

—P.L. 85-859, Sec. 163(d)(3), substituted "section 6416(b)(2)(I) and (j)" for "section 6416(b)(2)(J) and (K)" in para. (i)(2), and substituted "section 6416(b)(2)(H)" for "section 6416(b)(2)(L) in para. (i)(3), effective on the first day of the first calendar quarter which begins more than 60 days after 9/2/58.

In **1956**, ch. 725, Sec. 2, substituted '4263(a)' for '4262(b)' in para. (d)(2), effective 10/1/56.

—ch. 462, title II, Sec. 208(c), added Code Sec. 6421, effective 7/1/56.

Sec. 6422. Cross references.

(1) For limitations on credits and refunds, see subchapter B of chapter 66.

(2) For overpayment in case of adjustments to accrued foreign taxes, see section 905(c).

(3) For credit or refund in case of deficiency dividends paid by a personal holding company, see section 547.

(4) For refund, credit, or abatement of amounts disallowed by courts upon review of Tax Court decision, see section 7486.

(5) For refund or redemption of stamps, see chapter 69.

(6) For abatement, credit, or refund in case of jeopardy assessments, see chapter 70.

(7) For treatment of certain overpayments as having been refunded, in connection with sale of surplus war-built vessels, see section 9(b)(8) of the Merchant Ship Sales Act of 1946 (50 U. S. C. App. 1742).

(8) For restrictions on transfers and assignments of claims against the United States, see section 3727 of title 31, United States Code.

(9) For set-off of claims against amounts due the United States, see section 3728 of title 31, United States Code.

(10) For special provisions relating to alcohol and tobacco taxes, see subtitle E.

(11) for [sic]credit or refund in case of deficiency dividends paid by a regulated investment company or real estate investment trust, see section 860.

(12) For special rules in the case of a credit or refund attributable to partnership items, see section 6227 and subsections (c) and (d) of section 6230.

In **1997**, P.L. 105-34, Sec. 1131(c)(3), deleted para. (5) and redesignated paras. (6)-(13) as paras. (5)-(12), effective 8/5/97.

Prior to deletion, para. (5) read as follows:

"(5) For abatement or refund of tax on transfers to avoid income tax, see section 1494(b)."

In **1990**, P.L. 101-508, Sec. 11801(c)(17)(A), deleted para. (6) and redesignated paras. (7)-(15) as paras. (6)-(13), effective 11/5/90, except as provided in Sec. 11821(b) of this Act reproduced in note following Code Sec. 1481.

In **1982**, P.L. 97-258, Sec. 3(f)(8), substituted "section 3727 of title 31, United States Code" for "R.S. 3477 (31 U.S.C. 203)" in para. (10) . . . Sec. 3(f)(9), substituted "section 3728 of title 31, United States Code" for "the Act of March 3, 1875, as amended by section 13 of the Act of March 3, 1933 (31 U.S.C. 227)" in para. (11), effective 9/13/82.

—P.L. 97-248, Sec. 402(c)(4), added para. (15), effective for partnership tax. yrs. begin. after 9/3/82 and for any partnership tax. yr. ending after 9/3/82 if the partnership, each partner, and each indirect partner requests such application and the Secretary of the Treasury or his delegate consents to such application.

In **1980**, P.L. 96-222, Sec. 103(a)(11)(A), amended Sec. 362(e) of P.L. 95-600, the effective date for changes made by Sec. 362 of P.L. 95-600 by substituting "860(e)" for "860(d)" [see below].

In **1978**, P.L. 95-600, Sec. 362(d)(4)(A), added "regulated investment company or" before "real estate investment trust" in para. (14) . . . Sec. 362(d)(4)(B), substituted "860" for "859" in para. (14), effective for determinations (as defined in Code Sec. 860(e)) after 11/6/78.

In **1976**, P.L. 94-455, Sec. 1601(f)(1), added para. (14), effective for determinations as defined in subsec. 859(c) occurring after 10/4/76.

—P.L. 94-455, Sec. 1901(b)(36)(B), deleted para. (2), and redesignated paras. (3) through (13) as paras. (2) through (12), effective for tax. yrs. begin. after 12/31/76.

Prior to amendment, para. (2) read as follows:

"(2) For overpayment arising out of adjustments incident to involuntary liquidation of inventory, see section 1321."

—P.L. 94-455, Sec. 1906(a)(28), deleted "60 Stat. 48;", before "50 U.S.C. App. 1742", in redesignated para. (9), and deleted "47 Stat. 1516;", before "31 U.S.C. 227", in redesignated para. (11), effective 2/1/77.

In **1963**, P.L. 88-36, Sec. 201(c), deleted para. (7) which was cross reference provision for abatement or refund in case of tax on silver bullion to section 4894 and redesignated paras. (8)-(14) as paras. (7)-(13), respectively, effective for transfers after 6/4/63.

In **1958**, P.L. 85-859, Sec. 204(4), substituted "subtitle E" for "sections 5011, 5044, 5057, 5063, 5705, and 5707" in para. (14), effective 9/3/58.

In **1956**, ch. 462, Sec. 208(c), renumbered Code Sec. 6421 as Code Sec. 6422.

—ch. 160, Sec. 1, redesignated Code Sec. 6420 as Code Sec. 6421.

In **1954**, ch. 736, added Code Sec. 6420.

Sec. 6423. Conditions to allowance in the case of alcohol and tobacco taxes.

(a) Conditions.

No credit or refund shall be allowed or made, in pursuance of a court decision or otherwise, of any amount paid or collected as an alcohol or tobacco tax unless the claimant establishes (under regulations prescribed by the Secretary)—

(1) that he bore the ultimate burden of the amount claimed; or

(2) that he has unconditionally repaid the amount claimed to the person who bore the ultimate burden of such amount; or

(3) that (A) the owner of the commodity furnished him the amount claimed for payment of the tax, (B) he has filed with the Secretary the written consent of such owner to the allowance to the claimant of the credit or refund, and (C) such owner satisfies the requirements of paragraph (1) or (2).

(b) Filing of claims.

No credit or refund of any amount to which subsection (a) applies shall be allowed or made unless a claim therefor has been filed by the person who paid the amount claimed, and unless such claim is filed within the time prescribed by law and in accordance with regulations prescribed by the Secretary. All evidence relied upon in support of such claim shall be clearly set forth and submitted with the claim.

(c) Application of section.

This section shall apply only if the credit or refund is claimed on the grounds that an amount of alcohol or tobacco tax was assessed or collected erroneously, illegally, without authority, or in any manner wrongfully, or on the grounds that such amount was excessive. This section shall not apply to—

(1) any claim for drawback, and

(2) any claim made in accordance with any law expressly providing for credit or refund where a commodity is withdrawn from the market, returned to bond, or lost or destroyed.

(d) Meaning of terms.

For purposes of this section—

(1) Alcohol or tobacco tax. The term "alcohol or tobacco tax" means—

(A) any tax imposed by chapter 51 (other than part II of subchapter A, relating to occupational taxes) or by

Code Sec. 6423(d)(1)(A) — Abatements, credits, refunds

chapter 52 or by any corresponding provision of prior internal revenue laws, and

(B) in the case of any commodity of a kind subject to a tax described in subparagraph (A), any tax equal to any such tax, any additional tax, or any floor stocks tax.

(2) Tax. The term "tax" includes a tax and an exaction denominated a "tax", and any penalty, addition to tax, additional amount, or interest applicable to any such tax.

(3) Ultimate burden. The claimant shall be treated as having borne the ultimate burden of an amount of an alcohol or tobacco tax for purposes of subsection (a)(1), and the owner referred to in subsection (a)(3) shall be treated as having borne such burden for purposes of such subsection, only if—

(A) he has not, directly or indirectly, been relieved of such burden or shifted such burden to any other person,

(B) no understanding or agreement exists for any such relief or shifting, and

(C) if he has neither sold nor contracted to sell the commodities involved in such claim, he agrees that there will be no such relief or shifting, and furnishes such bond as the Secretary may require to insure faithful compliance with his agreement.

In **1976**, P.L. 94-455, Sec. 1906(a)(29)(A), amended subsec. (b) . . . Sec. 1906(a)(29)(B), deleted subsec. (c) and redesignated subsecs. (d) and (e) as subsecs. (c) and (d), . . . Sec. 1906(a)(29)(C), added "and" at the end of para. (c)(1), as redesignated by this Act, substituted a period for ", and" at the end of para. (c)(2), and deleted para. (c)(3), effective 2/1/77.

Prior to amendment, subsec. (b) read as follows:

"(b) Filing of claims.

"No credit or refund of any amount to which subsection (a) applies shall be allowed or made unless a claim therefor has been filed by the person who paid the amount claimed, and, except as hereinafter provided in this subsection, unless such claim is filed after April 30, 1958, and within the time prescribed by law, and in accordance with regulations prescribed by the Secretary or his delegate. All evidence relied upon in support of such claim shall be clearly set forth and submitted with the claim. Any claimant who has on or before April 30, 1958, filed a claim for any amount to which subsection (a) applies may, if such claim was not barred from allowance on April 30, 1958, file a superseding claim after April 30, 1958, and on or before April 30, 1959, conforming to the requirements of this section and covering the amount (or any part thereof) claimed in such prior claim. No claim filed before May 1, 1958, for the credit or refund of any amount to which subsection (a) applies shall be held to constitute a claim for refund or credit within the meaning of, or for purposes of, section 7422(a); except that any claimant who instituted a suit before June 15, 1957, for recovery of any amount to which subsection (a) applies shall not be barred by this subsection from the maintenance of such suit as to any amount claimed in such suit on such date if in such suit he establishes the conditions to allowance required under subsection (a) with respect to such amount."

Prior to deletion, subsec. (c) read as follows:

"(c) Period not extended.

"Any suit or proceeding, with respect to any amount to which subsection (a) applies, which is barred on April 30, 1958, shall remain barred. No claim for credit or refund of any such amount which is barred from allowance on April 30, 1958, shall be allowed after such date in any amount."

Prior to amendment, redesignated para. (c)(3) read as follows:

"(3) any amount claimed with respect to a commodity which has been lost, where a suit or proceeding was instituted before June 15, 1957."

—P.L. 94-455, Sec. 1906(b)(13)(A), substituted "Secretary" for "Secretary or his delegate" each place it appeared in Code Sec. 6423, effective 2/1/77.

In **1958**, P.L. 85-323, Sec. 1, added Code Sec. 6423, effective for credits or refunds allowed or made after 4/30/58.

Sec. 6424. Repealed.

In **1983**, P.L. 97-473, Sec. 202(b)(13), added para. (g)(3).

—P.L. 97-424, Sec. 515(b)(5), repealed Code Sec. 6424, effective for articles sold after 1/6/83.

Prior to repeal, Code Sec. 6424 read as follows:

"SEC. 6424. LUBRICATING OIL USED FOR CERTAIN NONTAXABLE PURPOSES.

"(a) Payments.

"Except as provided in subsection (f), if lubricating oil (other than cutting oils, as defined in section 4092(b), and other oil which has previously been used) is used—

"(1) in a qualified business use (as defined in section 6421(d) (2)), or

"(2) in a qualified bus (as defined in section 4221(d)(7)), the Secretary shall pay (without interest) to the ultimate purchaser of such lubricating oil an amount equal to 6 cents for each gallon of lubricating oil so used.

"(b) Time for filing claims; period covered.

"(1) General rule. Except as provided in paragraph (2), not more than one claim may be filed under subsection (a) by any person with respect to lubricating oil used during his taxable year. No claim shall be allowed under this paragraph with respect to lubricating oil used during any taxable year unless filed by such person not later than the time prescribed by law for filing a claim for credit or refunds of overpayment of income tax for such taxable year. For purposes of this subsection, a person's taxable year shall be his taxable year for purposes of subtitle A.

"(2) Exception. If $1,000 or more is payable under this section to any person with respect to lubricating oil used during any of the first three quarters of his taxable year, a claim may be filed under this section by such person with respect to lubricating oil used during such quarter. No claim filed under this paragraph shall be allowed unless filed on or before the last day of the first quarter following the quarter for which the claim is filed.

"(c) Exempt sales.

"No amount shall be payable under this section with respect to any lubricating oil which the Secretary determines was exempt from the tax imposed by section 4091. The amount which (but for this sentence) would be payable under this section with respect to any lubricating oil shall be reduced by any other amount which the Secretary determines is payable under this section, or is refundable under any provision of this title, to any person with respect to such lubricating oil.

"(d) Applicable laws.

"(1) In general. All provisions of law, including penalties, applicable in respect of the tax imposed by section 4091 shall, insofar as applicable and not inconsistent with this section, apply in respect of the payments provided for in this section to the same extent as if such payments constituted refunds of overpayments of the tax so imposed.

"(2) Examination of books and witnesses. For the purpose of ascertaining the correctness of any claim made under this section, or the correctness of any payment made in respect of any such claim, the Secretary shall have the authority granted by paragraphs (1), (2), and (3) of section 7602 (relating to examination of books and witnesses) as if the claimant were the person liable for tax.

"(e) Regulations.

"The Secretary may by regulations prescribe the conditions, not inconsistent with the provisions of this section, under which payments may be made under this section.

"(f) Income tax credit in lieu of payment.

"(1) Persons not subject to income tax. Payment shall be made under subsection (a) only to—

"(A) the United States or an agency or instrumentality thereof, a State, a political subdivision of a State, or an agency or instrumentality of one or more States or political subdivisions, or

"(B) an organization exempt from tax under section 501(a) (other than an organization required to make a return of the tax imposed under subtitle A for its taxable year).

"(2) Exception. Paragraph (1) shall not apply to a payment of a claim filed under subsection (b)(2).

"(3) Allowance of Credit against income tax. For allowance of credit against the tax imposed by subtitle A for lubricating oil used, see section 39.

"(g) Cross references.

"(1) For civil penalty for excessive claims under this section, see section 6675.

"(2) For fraud penalties etc., see chapter 75 (section 7201 and following, relating to crimes, other offenses, and forfeitures).

"(3) For treatment of an Indian tribal government as a State (and a subdivision of an Indian tribal government as a political subdivision of a State), see section 7871."

In **1978**, P.L. 95-618, Sec. 222(a)(3), substituted "is used in a qualified business use (within the meaning of section 6421(d)(3))" for "is used otherwise than in a highway motor vehicle" in subsec. (a), effective for uses after 12/31/78.

—P.L. 95-618, Sec. 233(b)(1), amended subsec. (a) . . . Sec. 233(b)(2)(A), substituted "used for certain nontaxable purposes" for "not used in highway motor vehicles" in the heading of Code Sec. 6424, effective 12/1/78 (the first day of the first calendar month which begins 10 days after 11/9/78, date of enactment).

Prior to amendment, subsec. (a), as amended by Sec. 222(a)(3) of this Act (see above), read as follows:

"(a) Payments.

"Except as provided in subsection (g), if lubricating oil (other than cutting oils, as defined in section 4092(b), and other oil which has previously been used) is used in a qualified business use (within the meaning of section 6421(d)(3)), the Secretary shall pay (without interest) to the ultimate purchaser of such lubricating oil an amount equal to 6 cents for each gallon of lubricating oil so used."

In **1976**, P.L. 94-455, Sec. 1906(a)(30)(A), deleted ", except that a person's first taxable year beginning after December 31, 1965, shall include the period after December 31, 1965, and before the beginning of such first taxable year" after "subtitle A", in para. (b)(1) . . . Sec. 1906(a)(30)(B), deleted subsec. (f) and redesignated subsecs. (g) and (h) as subsecs. (f) and (g), effective 2/1/77.

Prior to amendment, subsec. (f) read as follows:

"(f) Effective date.

"This section shall apply only with respect to lubricating oil placed in use after December 31, 1965."

—P.L. 94-455, Sec. 1906(b)(13)(A), substituted "Secretary" for "Secretary or his delegate" each place it appeared in Code Sec. 6424, effective 2/1/77.

In **1970**, P.L. 91-258, Sec. 207(b), substituted "time prescribed by law for filing a claim for credit or refund of overpayment of income tax for such taxable year" for "time prescribed by law for filing an income tax return for such taxable year" in para. (b)(1), effective for tax. yrs. end. after 6/30/70.

In 1965, P.L. 89-44, Sec. 202, added Code Sec. 6424, effective 1/1/66.

Sec. 6425. Adjustment of overpayment of estimated income tax by corporation.

(a) Application for adjustment.

(1) Time for filing. A corporation may, after the close of the taxable year and on or before the 15th day of the third month thereafter, and before the day on which it files a return for such taxable year, file an application for an adjustment of an overpayment by it of estimated income tax for such taxable year. An application under this subsection shall not constitute a claim for credit or refund.

(2) Form of application, etc. An application under this subsection shall be verified in the manner prescribed by section 6065 in the case of a return of the taxpayer, and shall be filed in the manner and form required by regulations prescribed by the Secretary. The application shall set forth—

(A) the estimated income tax paid by the corporation during the taxable year,

(B) the amount which, at the time of filing the application, the corporation estimates as its income tax liability for the taxable year,

(C) the amount of the adjustment, and

(D) such other information for purposes of carrying out the provisions of this section as may be required by such regulations.

(b) Allowance of adjustment.

(1) Limited examination of application. Within a period of 45 days from the date on which an application for an adjustment is filed under subsection (a), the Secretary shall make, to the extent he deems practicable in such period, a limited examination of the application to discover omissions and errors therein, and shall determine the amount of the adjustment upon the basis of the application and the examination; except that the Secretary may disallow, without further action, any application which he finds contains material omissions or errors which he deems cannot be corrected within such 45 days.

(2) Adjustment credited or refunded. The Secretary, within the 45-day period referred to in paragraph (1), may credit the amount of the adjustment against any liability in respect of an internal revenue tax on the part of the corporation and shall refund the remainder to the corporation.

(3) Limitation. No application under this section shall be allowed unless the amount of the adjustment equals or exceeds (A) 10 percent of the amount estimated by the corporation on its application as its income tax liability for the taxable year, and (B) $500.

(4) Effect of adjustment. For purposes of this title (other than section 6655), any adjustment under this section shall be treated as a reduction, in the estimated income tax paid, made on the day the credit is allowed or the refund is paid.

(c) Definitions.

For purposes of this section and section 6655(h) (relating to excessive adjustment)—

(1) The term "income tax liability" means the excess of—

(A) The sum of —

(i) the tax imposed by section 11 or 1201(a), or subchapter L of chapter 1, whichever is applicable,

(ii) the tax imposed by section 55, plus

(iii) the tax imposed by section 59A, over

(B) the credits against tax provided by part IV of subchapter A of chapter 1.

(2) The amount of an adjustment under this section is equal to the excess of—

(A) the estimated income tax paid by the corporation during the taxable year, over

(B) the amount which, at the time of filing the application, the corporation estimates as its income tax liability for the taxable year.

(d) Consolidated returns.

If the corporation seeking an adjustment under this section paid its estimated income tax on a consolidated basis or expects to make a consolidated return for the taxable year, this section shall apply only to such extent and subject to such conditions, limitations, and exceptions as the Secretary may by regulations prescribe.

In **1987**, P.L. 100-203, Sec. 10301(b)(4), substituted "6655(h)" for "6655(g)" in subsec. (c), effective for tax. yrs. begin. after 12/31/87.

In **1986**, P.L. 99-514, Sec. 701(d)(2), amended subpara. (c)(1)(A), effective for tax. yrs. begin. after 12/31/86.

Prior to amendment, subpara. (c)(1)(A) read as follows:

"(A) the tax imposed by section 11 or 1201(a), or subchapter L of chapter 1, whichever is applicable, over"

—P.L. 99-499, Sec. 516(b)(4)(C), deleted "plus" from the end of clause (c)(1)(A)(i) [as amended by Sec. 701(d)(2) of P.L. 99-514, see above], substituted "plus" for "over" at the end of clause (c)(1)(A)(ii) [as amended by Sec. 701(d)(2) of P.L. 99-514, see above], and added clause (c)(1)(A)(iii), effective for tax. yrs. begin. after 12/31/86.

In **1976**, P.L. 94-455, Sec. 1906(b)(13)(A), substituted "Secretary" for "Secretary or his delegate" each place it appeared in Code Sec. 6425, effective 2/1/77.

In **1968**, P.L. 90-364, Sec. 103, added Code Sec. 6425, applicable generally for tax. yrs. begin. after 12/31/67.

Sec. 104 of the '68 Revenue and Expenditure Control Act also provides as follows:

"SEC. 104. SPECIAL RULES FOR APPLICATION OF SECTIONS 102 AND 103.

"(a) Payment of estimated tax for taxable years beginning before date of enactment.

"In determining whether any taxpayer is required to make a declaration or amended declaration of estimated tax, or to pay any amount or additional amount of estimated tax, by reason of the amendments made by sections 102 and 103—

"(1) such amendments shall apply (A) in the case of an individual, only if the taxable year ends on or after September 30, 1968, and (B) in the case of a corporation, only if the taxable year ends on or after June 30, 1968,

"(2) in applying sections 6015, 6073, and 6654 of the Internal Revenue Code of 1954, such amendments shall first be taken into account as of September 1, 1968, and

"(3) in applying sections 6016, 6074, 6154, and 6655 of such Code, such amendments shall first be taken into account as of May 31, 1968.

"In the case of any amount or additional amount of estimated tax payable, by reason of such amendments, by a corporation on or after June 15, 1968, and before the 15th day after the date of the enactment of this Act, the time prescribed for payment of such amount or additional amount shall not expire before such date (not earlier than the 15th day after the date of the enactment of this Act) as the Secretary of the Treasury or his delegate shall prescribe.

"(b) Payment of tax surcharge for taxable years ending before date of enactment.

In the case of a taxable year ending before the date of the enactment of this Act, the time prescribed for payment of the tax imposed by section 51 of the Internal Revenue Code of 1954 shall not expire before September 15, 1968."

Sec. 6426. Credit for alcohol fuel, biodiesel and alternative fuel mixtures.

(a) Allowance of credits.

There shall be allowed as a credit—

(1) against the tax imposed by section 4081 an amount equal to the sum of the credits described in subsections (b), (c), and (e), and

(2) against the tax imposed by section 4041 an amount equal to the sum of the credits described in subsection (d).

No credit shall be allowed in the case of the credits described in subsections (d) and (e) unless the taxpayer is registered under section 4101.

(b) Alcohol fuel mixture credit.

(1) In general. For purposes of this section, the alcohol fuel mixture credit is the product of the applicable amount and the number of gallons of alcohol used by the taxpayer in producing any alcohol fuel mixture for sale or use in a trade or business of the taxpayer.

(2) Applicable amount. For purposes of this subsection—
(A) In general. Except as provided in subparagraphs (B) and (C), the applicable amount is—
(i) in the case of calendar years beginning before 2009, 51 cents, and
(ii) in the case of calendar years beginning after 2008, 45 cents.
(B) Mixtures not containing ethanol. In the case of an alcohol fuel mixture in which none of the alcohol consists of ethanol, the applicable amount is 60 cents.
(C) Reduction delayed until annual production or importation of 7,500,000,000 gallons. In the case of any calendar year beginning after 2008, if the Secretary makes a determination described in section 40(h)(3)(B) with respect to all preceding calendar years beginning after 2007, subparagraph (A)(ii) shall be applied by substituting "51 cents" for "45 cents".

(3) Alcohol fuel mixture. For purposes of this subsection, the term "alcohol fuel mixture" means a mixture of alcohol and a taxable fuel which—
(A) is sold by the taxpayer producing such mixture to any person for use as a fuel, or
(B) is used as a fuel by the taxpayer producing such mixture.

For purposes of subparagraph (A), a mixture produced by any person at a refinery prior to a taxable event which includes ethyl tertiary butyl ether or other ethers produced from alcohol shall be treated as sold at the time of its removal from the refinery (and only at such time) to another person for use as a fuel.

(4) Other definitions. For purposes of this subsection—
(A) Alcohol. The term "alcohol" includes methanol and ethanol but does not include—
(i) alcohol produced from petroleum, natural gas, or coal (including peat), or
(ii) alcohol with a proof of less than 190 (determined without regard to any added denaturants).

Such term also includes an alcohol gallon equivalent of ethyl tertiary butyl ether or other ethers produced from such alcohol.
(B) Taxable fuel. The term "taxable fuel" has the meaning given such term by section 4083(a)(1).

(5) Volume of alcohol. For purposes of determining under subsection (a) the number of gallons of alcohol with respect to which a credit is allowable under subsection (a), the volume of alcohol shall include the volume of any denaturant (including gasoline) which is added under any formulas approved by the Secretary to the extent that such denaturants do not exceed 2 percent of the volume of such alcohol (including denaturants).

(6) Termination. This subsection shall not apply to any sale, use, or removal for any period after December 31, 2011.

(c) Biodiesel mixture credit.
(1) In general. For purposes of this section, the biodiesel mixture credit is the product of the applicable amount and the number of gallons of biodiesel used by the taxpayer in producing any biodiesel mixture for sale or use in a trade or business of the taxpayer.

(2) Applicable amount. For purposes of this subsection, the applicable amount is $1.00.

(3) Biodiesel mixture. For purposes of this section, the term "biodiesel mixture" means a mixture of biodiesel and diesel fuel (as defined in section 4083(a)(3)), determined without regard to any use of kerosene, which—

(A) is sold by the taxpayer producing such mixture to any person for use as a fuel, or
(B) is used as a fuel by the taxpayer producing such mixture.

(4) Certification for biodiesel. No credit shall be allowed under this subsection unless the taxpayer obtains a certification (in such form and manner as prescribed by the Secretary) from the producer of the biodiesel which identifies the product produced and the percentage of biodiesel and agri-biodiesel in the product.

(5) Other definitions. Any term used in this subsection which is also used in section 40A shall have the meaning given such term by section 40A.

(6) Termination. This subsection shall not apply to any sale, use, or removal for any period after December 31, 2011.

(d) Alternative fuel credit.
(1) In general. For purposes of this section, the alternative fuel credit is the product of 50 cents and the number of gallons of an alternative fuel or gasoline gallon equivalents of a nonliquid alternative fuel sold by the taxpayer for use as a fuel in a motor vehicle or motorboat, sold by the taxpayer for use as a fuel in aviation, or so used by the taxpayer.

(2) Alternative fuel. For purposes of this section, the term "alternative fuel" means—
(A) liquefied petroleum gas,
(B) P Series Fuels (as defined by the Secretary of Energy under section 13211(2) of title 42, United States Code),
(C) compressed or liquefied natural gas,
(D) liquefied hydrogen,
(E) any liquid fuel which meets the requirements of paragraph (4) and which is derived from coal (including peat) through the Fischer-Tropsch process,
(F) compressed or liquefied gas derived from biomass (as defined in section 45K(c)(3)), and
(G) liquid fuel derived from biomass (as defined in section 45K(c)(3)).

Such term does not include ethanol, methanol, biodiesel, or any fuel (including lignin, wood residues, or spent pulping liquors) derived from the production of paper or pulp.

(3) Gasoline gallon equivalent. For purposes of this subsection, the term "gasoline gallon equivalent" means, with respect to any nonliquid alternative fuel, the amount of such fuel having a Btu content of 124,800 (higher heating value).

(4) Carbon capture requirement.
(A) In general. The requirements of this paragraph are met if the fuel is certified, under such procedures as required by the Secretary, as having been derived from coal produced at a gasification facility which separates and sequesters not less than the applicable percentage of such facility's total carbon dioxide emissions.
(B) Applicable percentage. For purposes of subparagraph (A), the applicable percentage is—
(i) 50 percent in the case of fuel produced after September 30, 2009, and on or before December 30, 2009, and
(ii) 75 percent in the case of fuel produced after December 30, 2009.

(5) Termination. This subsection shall not apply to any sale or use for any period after December 31, 2011 (September 30, 2014, in the case of any sale or use involving liquefied hydrogen).

Abatements, credits, refunds   Code Sec. 6426

(e) Alternative fuel mixture credit.
  (1) In general. For purposes of this section, the alternative fuel mixture credit is the product of 50 cents and the number of gallons of alternative fuel used by the taxpayer in producing any alternative fuel mixture for sale or use in a trade or business of the taxpayer.
  (2) Alternative fuel mixture. For purposes of this section, the term "alternative fuel mixture" means a mixture of alternative fuel and taxable fuel (as defined in subparagraph (A), (B), or (C) of section 4083(a)(1)) which—
    (A) is sold by the taxpayer producing such mixture to any person for use as fuel, or
    (B) is used as a fuel by the taxpayer producing such mixture.
  (3) Termination. This subsection shall not apply to any sale or use for any period after December 31, 2011 (September 30, 2014, in the case of any sale or use involving liquefied hydrogen).
(f) Mixture not used as a fuel, etc.
  (1) Imposition of tax. If—
    (A) any credit was determined under this section with respect to alcohol or biodiesel used in the production of any alcohol fuel mixture or biodiesel mixture, respectively, and
    (B) any person—
      (i) separates the alcohol or biodiesel from the mixture, or
      (ii) without separation, uses the mixture other than as a fuel,
    then there is hereby imposed on such person a tax equal to the product of the applicable amount and the number of gallons of such alcohol or biodiesel.
  (2) Applicable laws. All provisions of law, including penalties, shall, insofar as applicable and not inconsistent with this section, apply in respect of any tax imposed under paragraph (1) as if such tax were imposed by section 4081 and not by this section.
(g) Coordination with exemption from excise tax.
  Rules similar to the rules under section 40(c) shall apply for purposes of this section.
(h) Denial of double benefit.
  No credit shall be determined under subsection (d) or (e) with respect to any fuel with respect to which credit may be determined under subsection (b) or (c) or under section 40 or 40A.
(i) Limitation to fuels with connection to the United States.
  (1) Alcohol. No credit shall be determined under this section with respect to any alcohol which is produced outside the United States for use as a fuel outside the United States.
  (2) Biodiesel and alternative fuels. No credit shall be determined under this section with respect to any biodiesel or alternative fuel which is produced outside the United States for use as a fuel outside the United States.
For purposes of this subsection, the term "United States" includes any possession of the United States.

In 2010, P.L. 111-312, Sec. 701(b)(1), substituted "December 31, 2011" for "December 31, 2009" in para. (c)(6), effective for fuel sold or used after 12/31/2009.
—P.L. 111-312, Sec. 701(c), of this Act, provides:
"(c) Special rule for 2010.
"Notwithstanding any other provision of law, in the case of any biodiesel mixture credit properly determined under section 6426(c) of the Internal Revenue Code of 1986 for periods during 2010, such credit shall be allowed, and any refund or payment attributable to such credit (including any payment under section 6427(e) of such Code) shall be made, only in such manner as the Secretary of the Treasury (or the Secretary's delegate) shall provide. Such Secretary shall issue guidance within 30 days after the date of the enactment of this Act providing for a one-time submission of claims covering periods during 2010. Such guidance shall provide for a 180-day period for the submission of such claims (in such manner as prescribed by such Secretary) to begin not later than 30 days after such guidance is issued. Such claims shall be paid by such Secretary not later than 60 days after receipt. If such Secretary has not paid pursuant to a claim filed under this subsection within 60 days after the date of the filing of such claim, the claim shall be paid with interest from such date determined by using the overpayment rate and method under section 6621 of such Code."
—P.L. 111-312, Sec. 704(a), substituted "December 31, 2011" for "December 31, 2009" in paras. (d)(5) and (e)(3) . . . Sec. 704(b), substituted "biodiesel, or any fuel (including lignin, wood residues, or spent pulping liquors) derived from the production of paper or pulp" for "or biodiesel" in para. (d)(2), effective for fuel sold or used after 12/31/2009.
—P.L. 111-312, Sec. 704(c), of this Act, provides:
"(c) Special rule for 2010. Notwithstanding any other provision of law, in the case of any alternative fuel credit or any alternative fuel mixture credit properly determined under subsection (d) or (e) of section 6426 of the Internal Revenue Code of 1986 for periods during 2010, such credit shall be allowed, and any refund or payment attributable to such credit (including any payment under section 6427(e) of such Code) shall be made, only in such manner as the Secretary of the Treasury (or the Secretary's delegate) shall provide. Such Secretary shall issue guidance within 30 days after the date of the enactment of this Act providing for a one-time submission of claims covering periods during 2010. Such guidance shall provide for a 180-day period for the submission of such claims (in such manner as prescribed by such Secretary) to begin not later than 30 days after such guidance is issued. Such claims shall be paid by such Secretary not later than 60 days after receipt. If such Secretary has not paid pursuant to a claim filed under this subsection within 60 days after the date of the filing of such claim, the claim shall be paid with interest from such date determined by using the overpayment rate and method under section 6621 of such Code."
—P.L. 111-312, Sec. 708(b)(1), substituted "December 31, 2011" for "December 31, 2010" in para. (b)(6), effective for periods after 12/31/2010.

In 2008, P.L. 110-343, Sec. 202(a)DivB, substituted "December 31, 2009" for "December 31, 2008" in para. (c)(6) . . . Sec. 202(b)(2)DivB, amended para. (c)(2), effective for fuel produced, and sold or used, after 12/31/2008
Prior to amendment, para. (c)(2) read as follows:
"(2) Applicable amount. For purposes of this subsection—
"(A) In general. Except as provided in subparagraph (B), the applicable amount is 50 cents.
"(B) Amount for agri-biodiesel. In the case of any biodiesel which is agri-biodiesel, the applicable amount is $1.00.
—P.L. 110-343, Sec. 203(c)(1)DivB, added subsec. (i), effective for claims for credit or payment made on or after 5/15/2008.
—P.L. 110-343, Sec. 204(a)(1)DivB, substituted 'December 31, 2009' for 'September 30, 2009' in para. (d)(4) . . . Sec. 204(a)(2)DivB, substituted 'December 31, 2009' for 'September 30, 2009' in para. (e)(3) . . . Sec. 204(b)(1)DivB, deleted 'and' at the end of subpara. (d)(2)(E), redesignated subpara. (d)(2)(F) as subpara. (d)(2)(G), and added a new subpara. (d)(2)(F) . . . Sec. 204(b)(2)DivB, inserted 'sold by the taxpayer for use as a fuel in aviation,' after 'motorboat,' in para. (d)(1) . . . Sec. 204(c)(1)DivB, redesignated para. (d)(4) [as amended] as para. (d)(5) and added a new para. (d)(4) . . . Sec. 204(c)(2)DivB, inserted 'which meets the requirements of paragraph (4) and which is' after 'any liquid fuel' in subpara. (d)(2)(E), effective for fuel sold or used after 10/3/2008.
—P.L. 110-246, Sec. 4, Repeals the duplicative enactment and provides effective date provisions of the Act entitled 'An Act to provide for the continuation of agricultural programs through fiscal year 2012, and for other purposes' Sec. 4, P.L. 110-246 reads as follows:
"Sec. 4. Repeal of duplicative enactment.
"(a) In General- The Act entitled 'An Act to provide for the continuation of agricultural programs through fiscal year 2012, and for other purposes' (H.R. 2419 of the 110th Congress), and the amendments made by that Act, are repealed, effective on the date of enactment of that Act.
"(b) Effective Date- Except as otherwise provided in this Act, this Act and the amendments made by this Act shall take effect on the earlier of—
"(1) the date of enactment of this Act; or
"(2) the date of the enactment of the Act entitled 'An Act to provide for the continuation of agricultural programs through fiscal year 2012, and for other purposes' (H.R. 2419 of the 110th Congress)."
—P.L. 110-246, Sec. 15331(b)(1), substituted "the applicable amount is—
"(i) in the case of calendar years beginning before 2009, 51 cents, and
"(ii) in the case of calendar years beginning after 2008, 45 cents." for "the applicable amount is 51 cents" in subpara. (b)(2)(A) . . . Sec. 15331(b)(2), added subpara. (b)(2)(C) . . . Sec. 15331(b)(3), substituted "subparagraphs (B) and (C)" for "subparagraph (B)" in subpara. (b)(2)(A), effective 10/3/2008.
—P.L. 110-246, Sec. 15332(b), redesignated para. (b)(5) as para. (b)(6) and added new para. (b)(5), effective for fuel sold or used after 12/31/2008. [Ed. Note: May 22, 2008 was the date of enactment for H.R. 2419 (PL 110-234), which was repealed by (2008 Farm Act § 4(a)) (PL 110-246, 6/18/2008), in connection with the reenactment of the farm bill to correct a technical deficiency in its original passage.]

In 2007, P.L. 110-172, Sec. 5(a)(2), substituted "fuel" for "hydrocarbons" in Sec. 6426(d)(2)(F). . . . Sec. 5(a)(3), added subsec. (h), effective for any sale or use for any period after 9/30/2006.

In 2005, P.L. 109-59, Sec. 11113(b)(1), amended subsec. (a) . . . Sec. 11113(b)(2), redesignated subsecs. (d) and (e) as subsecs. (f) and (g), and added subsecs. (d) and (e) . . . Sec. 11113(b)(3)(A), substituted "alcohol fuel, biodiesel, and alternative fuel" for "alcohol fuel and biodiesel" in the heading of Code Sec. 6426, effective for any sale or use for any period after 9/30/2006.

3,721

Prior to amendment, subsec. (a) read as follows:
"(a) Allowance of credits. There shall be allowed as a credit against the tax imposed by section 4081 an amount equal to the sum of—
"(1) the alcohol fuel mixture credit, plus
"(2) the biodiesel mixture credit."
—P.L. 109-59, Sec. 11151(e)(2), substituted "section 45K(c)(3)" for "section 29(c)(3)" in subpara. (d)(2)(F) [as added by Sec. 11113(b)(2) of this Act, see above], effective for credits determined under the Internal Revenue Code of 1986 for tax. yrs. end. after 12/31/2005 [as if included in the provision of the Energy Tax Incentives Act of 2005 to which the amendment relates].
—P.L. 109-58, Sec. 1344(a), substituted "2008" for "2006" in para. (c)(6), effective 8/8/2005.
In 2004, P.L. 108-357, Sec. 301(a), added Code Sec. 6426, effective for fuel sold or used after 12/31/2004.

Sec. 6426. Repealed.

In 1982, P.L. 97-248, Sec. 280(c)(2)(G), repealed Code Sec. 6426, effective for transportation begin after 8/31/82, but not for any amount paid on or before 8/31/82.
Prior to repeal, Code Sec. 6426 read as follows:
"SEC. 6426. REFUND OF AIRCRAFT USE TAX WHERE PLANE TRANSPORTS FOR HIRE IN FOREIGN AIR COMMERCE.
"(a) General rule.
"In the case of any aircraft used in the business of transporting persons or property for compensation or hire by air, if any of such transportation during any period is transportation in foreign air commerce, the Secretary shall pay (without interest) to the person who paid the tax under the section 4491 for such period the amount determined by multiplying that portion of the amount so paid for such period which is determined under section 4491(a)(2) with respect to such aircraft by a fraction—
"(1) the numerator of which is the number of airport-to-airport miles such aircraft traveled in foreign air commerce during such period while engaged in such business, and
"(2) the denominator of which is the total number of airport-to-airport miles such aircraft traveled during such period.
"(b) Definitions.
"For purposes of this section—
"(1) Foreign air commerce. The term 'foreign air commerce' means any movement by air of the aircraft which does not begin and end in the United States; except that any segment of such movement in which the aircraft traveled between two ports or stations in the United States shall be treated as travel which is not foreign air commerce.
"(2) Airport-to-airport miles. The term 'airport-to-airport miles' means the official mileage distance between airports as determined under regulations prescribed by the Secretary.
"(c) Payments to persons paying tentative tax.
"In the case of any person who paid a tentative tax determined under section 4493(b) with respect to any aircraft for any period, the amount payable under subsection (a) with respect to such aircraft for such period—
"(1) shall be computed with reference to that portion of the tax imposed under section 4491 for such period which is determined under section 4491(a)(2), and
"(2) as so computed, shall be reduced by an amount equal to—
"(A) the amount by which that portion of the tax imposed under section 4491 for such period which is determined under section 4491(a)(2), exceeds
"(B) the amount of the tentative tax determined under section 4493(b) paid for such period.
"(d) Time for filing claim.
"Not more than one claim may be filed under this section by any person with respect to any year. No claim shall be allowed under this subsection with respect to any year unless filed on or before the first September 30 after the end of such year.
"(e) Regulations.
"The Secretary may by regulations prescribe the conditions, not inconsistent with the provisions of this section, under which payments may be made under this section or the amount to which any person is entitled under this section with respect to any period may be treated by such person as an overpayment which may be credited against the tax imposed by section 4491 with respect to such period."
In 1976, P.L. 94-455, Sec. 1906(b)(13)(A), substituted "Secretary" for "Secretary or his delegate" each place it appeared in Code Sec. 6426, effective 2/1/77.
In 1970, P.L. 91-258, Sec. 206(c), added Code Sec. 6426, effective 7/1/70.

Sec. 6427. Fuels not used for taxable purposes.
(a) Nontaxable uses.

Except as provided in subsection (k), if tax has been imposed under paragraph (2) or (3) of section 4041(a) or section 4041(c) on the sale of any fuel and the purchaser uses such fuel other than for the use for which sold, or resells such fuel, the Secretary shall pay (without interest) to him an amount equal to—

(1) the amount of tax imposed on the sale of the fuel to him, reduced by

(2) if he uses the fuel, the amount of tax which would have been imposed under section 4041 on such use if no tax under section 4041 had been imposed on the sale of the fuel.

(b) Intercity, local, or school buses.

(1) Allowance. Except as otherwise provided in this subsection and subsection (k), if any fuel other than gasoline (as defined in section 4083(a)) on the sale of which tax was imposed by section 4041(a) or 4081 is used in an automobile bus while engaged in—

(A) furnishing (for compensation) passenger land transportation available to the general public, or

(B) the transportation of students and employees of schools (as defined in the last sentence of section 4221(d)(7)(C)),

the Secretary shall pay (without interest) to the ultimate purchaser of such fuel an amount equal to the product of the number of gallons of such fuel so used multiplied by the rate at which tax was imposed on such fuel by section 4041(a) or 4081, as the case may be.

(2) Reduction in refund in certain cases.

(A) in general. Except as provided in subparagraphs (B) and (C), the rate of tax taken into account under paragraph (1) shall be 7.4 cents per gallon less than the aggregate rate at which tax was imposed on such fuel by section 4041(a) or 4081, as the case may be.

(B) Exception for school bus transportation. Subparagraph (A) shall not apply to fuel used in an automobile bus while engaged in the transportation described in paragraph (1)(B).

(C) Exception for certain intracity transportation. Subparagraph (A) shall not apply to fuel used in any automobile bus while engaged in furnishing (for compensation) intracity passenger land transportation—

(i) which is available to the general public, and

(ii) which is scheduled and along regular routes,

but only if such bus is a qualified local bus.

(D) Qualified local bus. For purposes of this paragraph, the term "qualified local bus" means any local bus—

(i) which has a seating capacity of at least 20 adults (not including the driver), and

(ii) which is under contract (or is receiving more than a nominal subsidy) from any State or local government (as defined in section 4221(d)) to furnish such transportation.

(3) Limitation in case of nonscheduled intercity or local buses. Paragraph (1)(A) shall not apply in respect of fuel used in any automobile bus while engaged in furnishing transportation which is not scheduled and not along regular routes unless the seating capacity of such bus is at least 20 adults (not including the driver).

(4) Refunds for use of diesel fuel in certain intercity buses. With respect to any fuel to which paragraph (2)(A) applies, if the ultimate purchaser of such fuel waives (at such time and in such form and manner as the Secretary shall prescribe) the right to payment under paragraph (1) and assigns such right to the ultimate vendor, then the Secretary shall pay the amount which would be paid under paragraph (1) to such ultimate vendor, but only if such ultimate vendor—

(A) is registered under section 4101, and

(B) meets the requirements of subparagraph (A), (B), or (D) of section 6416(a)(1).

(c) Use for farming purposes.

Except as provided in subsection (k), if any fuel on the sale of which tax was imposed under paragraph (2) or (3) of section 4041(a) or section 4041(c) is used on a farm for farming purposes (within the meaning of section 6420(c)), the Secretary shall pay (without interest) to the purchaser an amount equal to the amount of the tax imposed on the sale of the fuel. For purposes of this subsection, if fuel is used on a farm by any person other than the owner, tenant, or operator of such farm, the rules of paragraph (4) of section 6420(c) shall be applied (except that "liquid taxable under section 4041" shall be substituted for "gasoline" each place it appears in such paragraph (4)).

(d) Use by certain aircraft museums or in certain other aircraft uses.

Except as provided in subsection (k), if—

(1) any gasoline on which tax was imposed by section 4081, or

(2) any fuel on the sale of which tax was imposed under section 4041,

is used by an aircraft museum (as defined in section 4041(h)(2)) in an aircraft or vehicle owned by such museum and used exclusively for purposes set forth in section 4041(h)(2)(C), or is used in a helicopter or a fixed-wing aircraft for a purpose described in section 4041(l), the Secretary shall pay (without interest) to the ultimate purchaser of such gasoline or fuel an amount equal to the aggregate amount of the tax imposed on such gasoline or fuel.

(e) Alcohol, biodiesel, or alternative fuel.

Except as provided in subsection (k)—

(1) Used to produce a mixture. If any person produces a mixture described in section 6426 in such person's trade or business, the Secretary shall pay (without interest) to such person an amount equal to the alcohol fuel mixture credit or the biodiesel mixture credit or the alternative fuel mixture credit with respect to such mixture.

(2) Alternative fuel. If any person sells or uses an alternative fuel (as defined in section 6426(d)(2)) for a purpose described in section 6426(d)(1) in such person's trade or business, the Secretary shall pay (without interest) to such person an amount equal to the alternative fuel credit with respect to such fuel.

(3) Coordination with other repayment provisions. No amount shall be payable under paragraph (1) or (2) with respect to any mixture or alternative fuel with respect to which an amount is allowed as a credit under section 6426.

(4) Registration requirement for alternative fuels. The Secretary shall not make any payment under this subsection to any person with respect to any alternative fuel credit or alternative fuel mixture credit unless the person is registered under section 4101.

(5) Limitation to fuels with connection to the United States. No amount shall be payable under paragraph (1) or (2) with respect to any mixture or alternative fuel if credit is not allowed with respect to such mixture or alternative fuel by reason of section 6426(i).

(6) Termination. This subsection shall not apply with respect to—

(A) any alcohol fuel mixture (as defined in section 6426(b)(3)) sold or used after December 31, 2011,

(B) any biodiesel mixture (as defined in section 6426(c)(3)) sold or used after December 31, 2011,

(C) except as provided in subparagraph (D), any alternative fuel or alternative fuel mixture (as defined in subsection (d)(2) or (e)(3) of section 6426) sold or used after December 31, 2011, and

(D) any alternative fuel or alternative fuel mixture (as so defined) involving liquefied hydrogen sold or used after September 30, 2014.

(f) Repealed.
(g) Repealed.
(h) Blend stocks not used for producing taxable fuel.

(1) Gasoline blend stocks or additives not used for producing gasoline. Except as provided in subsection (k), if any gasoline blend stock or additive (within the meaning of section 4083(a)(2)) is not used by any person to produce gasoline and such person establishes that the ultimate use of such gasoline blend stock or additive is not to produce gasoline, the Secretary shall pay (without interest) to such person an amount equal to the aggregate amount of the tax imposed on such person with respect to such gasoline blend stock or additive.

(2) Diesel fuel blend stocks or additives not used for producing diesel. Except as provided in subsection (k), if any diesel fuel blend stock is not used by any person to produce diesel fuel and such person establishes that the ultimate use of such diesel fuel blend stock is not to produce diesel fuel, the Secretary shall pay (without interest) to such person an amount equal to the aggregate amount of the tax imposed on such person with respect to such diesel fuel blend stock.

(i) Time for filing claims; period covered.

(1) General rule. Except as otherwise provided in this subsection, not more than one claim may be filed under subsection (a), (b), (c), (d), (h), (l), (m), or (o) by any person with respect to fuel used (or a qualified diesel powered highway vehicle purchased) during his taxable year; and no claim shall be allowed under this paragraph with respect to fuel used during any taxable year unless filed by the purchaser not later than the time prescribed by law for filing a claim for credit or refund of overpayment of income tax for such taxable year. For purposes of this paragraph, a person's taxable year shall be his taxable year for purposes of subtitle A.

(2) Exceptions.

(A) In general. If, at the close of any quarter of the taxable year of any person, at least $750 is payable in the aggregate under subsections (a), (b), (d), (h), (l), (m), and (o) of this section and section 6421 to such person with respect to fuel used during—

(i) such quarter, or

(ii) any prior quarter (for which no other claim has been filed) during such taxable year,

a claim may be filed under this section with respect to such fuel.

(B) Time for filing claim. No claim filed under this paragraphshall be allowed unless filed during the 1st quarter following the last quarter included in the claim.

(C) Nonapplication of paragraph. This paragraph shall not apply to any fuel used solely in any off-highway business use described in section 6421(e)(2)(C).

(3) Special rule for mixture credits and the alternative fuel credit.

(A) In general. A claim may be filed under subsection (e)(1) by any person with respect to a mixture described in section 6426 or under subsection (e)(2) by any person with respect to an alternative fuel (as defined in section 6426(d)(2)) for any period—

(i) for which $200 or more is payable under such subsection (e)(1) or (e)(2), and

(ii) which is not less than 1 week.

In the case of an electronic claim, this subparagraph shall be applied without regard to clause (i).

(B) Payment of claim. Notwithstanding subsection (e)(1) or (e)(2), if the Secretary has not paid pursuant to a claim filed under this section within 45 days of the date of the filing of such claim (20 days in the case of an electronic claim), the claim shall be paid with interest from such date determined by using the overpayment rate and method under section 6621.

(C) Time for filing claim. No claim filed under this paragraph shall be allowed unless filed on or before the last day of the first quarter following the earliest quarter included in the claim.

(4) Special rule for vendor refunds.

(A) In general. A claim may be filed under subsections (b)(4) and paragraph (4)(C), or (5), of subsection (l) by any person with respect to fuel sold by such person for any period—

(i) for which $200 or more ($100 or more in the case of kerosene) is payable under paragraph (4)(C), or (5), of subsection (l), and

(ii) which is not less than 1 week.

Notwithstanding subsection (l)(1), paragraph (3)(B) shall apply to claims filed under subsections (b)(4), (l)(4)(C)(ii), and (l)(5).

(B) Time for filing claim. No claim filed under this paragraph shall be allowed unless filed on or before the last day of the first quarter following the earliest quarter included in the claim.

(j) Applicable laws.

(1) In general. All provisions of law, including penalties, applicable in respect of the taxes imposed by sections 4041 and 4081 shall, insofar as applicable and not inconsistent with this section, apply in respect of the payments provided for in this section to the same extent as if such payments constituted refunds of overpayments of the tax so imposed.

(2) Examination of books and witnesses. For the purpose of ascertaining the correctness of any claim made under this section, or the correctness of any payment made in respect of any such claim, the Secretary shall have the authority granted by paragraphs (1), (2), and (3) of section 7602(a) (relating to examination of books and witnesses) as if the claimant were the person liable for tax.

(k) Income tax credit in lieu of payment.

(1) Persons not subject to income tax. Payment shall be made under this section only to—

(A) the United States or an agency or instrumentality thereof, a State, a political subdivision of a State, or any agency or instrumentality of one or more States or political subdivisions, or

(B) an organization exempt from tax under section 501(a) (other than an organization required to make a return of the tax imposed under subtitle A for its taxable year).

(2) Exception. Paragraph (1) shall not apply to a payment of a claim filed under paragraph (2), (3), or (4) of subsection (i).

(3) Allowance of credit against income tax. For allowances of credit against the income tax imposed by subtitle A for fuel used or resold by the purchaser, see section 34.

(l) Nontaxable uses of diesel fuel, and kerosene.

(1) In general. Except as otherwise provided in this subsection and in subsection (k), if any diesel fuel or kerosene on which tax has been imposed by section 4041 or 4081 is used by any person in a nontaxable use, the Secretary shall pay (without interest) to the ultimate purchaser of such fuel an amount equal to the aggregate amount of tax imposed on such fuel under section 4041 or 4081, as the case may be, reduced by any payment made to the ultimate vendor under paragraph (4)(C)(i).

(2) Nontaxable use. For purposes of this subsection, the term "nontaxable use" means any use which is exempt from the tax imposed by section 4041(a)(1) other than by reason of a prior imposition of tax.

(3) Refund of certain taxes on fuel used in diesel-powered trains. For purposes of this subsection, the term "nontaxable use" includes fuel used in a diesel-powered train. The preceding sentence shall not apply with respect to—

(A) the Leaking Underground Storage Tank Trust Fund financing rate under sections 4041 and 4081, and

(B) so much of the rate specified in section 4081(a)(2)(A) as does not exceed the rate applicable under section 4041(a)(1)(C)(ii).

The preceding sentence shall not apply in the case of fuel sold for exclusive use by a State or any political subdivision thereof.

(4) Refunds for kerosene used in aviation.

(A) Kerosene used in commercial aviation. In the case of kerosene used in commercial aviation (as defined in section 4083(b)) (other than supplies for vessels or aircraft within the meaning of section 4221(d)(3)), paragraph (1) shall not apply to so much of the tax imposed by section 4041 or 4081, as the case may be, as is attributable to—

(i) the Leaking Underground Storage Tank Trust Fund financing rate imposed by such section, and

(ii) so much of the rate of tax specified in section 4041(c) or section 4081(a)(2)(A)(iii), as the case may be, as does not exceed 4.3 cents per gallon.

(B) Kerosene used in noncommercial aviation. In the case of kerosene used in aviation that is not commercial aviation (as so defined) (other than any use which is exempt from the tax imposed by section 4041(c) other than by reason of a prior imposition of tax), paragraph (1) shall not apply to—

(i) any tax imposed by subsection (c) or (d)(2) of section 4041, and

(ii) so much of the tax imposed by section 4081 as is attributable to—

(I) the Leaking Underground Storage Tank Trust Fund financing rate imposed by such section, and

(II) so much of the rate of tax specified in section 4081(a)(2)(A)(iii) as does not exceed the rate specified in section 4081(a)(2)(C)(ii).

(C) Payments to ultimate, registered vendor.

(i) In general. With respect to any kerosene used in aviation (other than kerosene described in clause (ii) or kerosene to which paragraph (5) applies), if the ultimate purchaser of such kerosene waives (at such time and in such form and manner as the Secretary shall prescribe) the right to payment under paragraph (1) and assigns such right to the ultimate vendor, then the Secretary shall pay the amount which would be paid under paragraph (1) to such ultimate vendor, but only if such ultimate vendor—

(I) is registered under section 4101, and

(II) meets the requirements of subparagraph (A), (B), or (D) of section 6416(a)(1).

(ii) Payments for kerosene used in noncommercial aviation. The amount which would be paid under paragraph (1) with respect to any kerosene to which subparagraph (B) applies shall be paid only to the ultimate vendor of such kerosene. A payment shall be made to such vendor if such vendor—

(I) is registered under section 4101, and
(II) meets the requirements of subparagraph (A), (B), or (D) of section 6416(a)(1).

(5) Registered vendors to administer claims for refund of diesel fuel or kerosene sold to state and local governments.

(A) In general. Paragraph (1) shall not apply to diesel fuel or kerosene used by a State of local government.

(B) Sales of kerosene not for use in motor fuel. Paragraph (1) shall not apply to kerosene (other than kerosene used in aviation) sold by a vendor—

(i) for any use if such sale is from a pump which (as determined under regulations prescribed by the Secretary) is not suitable for use in fueling any diesel-powered highway vehicle or train, or

(ii) to the extent provided by the Secretary, for blending with heating oil to be used during periods of extreme or unseasonable cold.

(C) Payment to ultimate, registered, vendor. Except as provided in subparagraph (D), the amount which would (but for subparagraph (A) or (B)) have been paid under paragraph (1) with respect to any fuel shall be paid to the ultimate vendor of such fuel, if such vendor—

(i) is registered under section 4101, and
(ii) meets the requirements of subparagraph (A), (B), or (D) of section 6416(a)(1).

(D) Credit card issuer. For purposes of this paragraph, if the purchase of any fuel described in subparagraph (A) (determined without regard to the registration status of the ultimate vendor) is made by means of a credit card issued to the ultimate purchaser, the Secretary shall pay to the person extending the credit to the ultimate purchaser the amount which would have been paid under paragraph (1) (but for subparagraph (A)), but only if such person meets the requirements of clauses (i), (ii), and (iii) of section 6416(a)(4)(B). If such clause (i), (ii), or (iii) is not met by such person extending the credit to the ultimate purchaser, then such person shall collect an amount equal to the tax from the ultimate purchaser and only such ultimate purchaser may claim such amount.

(m) Diesel fuel used to produce emulsion.

(1) In general. Except as provided in subsection (k), if any diesel fuel on which tax was imposed by section 4081 at the regular tax rate is used by any person in producing an emulsion described in section 4081(a)(2)(D) which is sold or used in such person's trade or business, the Secretary shall pay (without interest) to such person an amount equal to the excess of the regular tax rate over the incentive tax rate with respect to such fuel.

(2) Definitions. For purposes of paragraph (1)—

(A) Regular tax rate. The term "regular tax rate" means the aggregate rate of tax imposed by section 4081 determined without regard to section 4081(a)(2)(D).

(B) Incentive tax rate. The term "incentive tax rate" means the aggregate rate of tax imposed by section 4081 determined with regard to section 4081(a)(2)(D).

(n) Regulations.

The Secretary may by regulations prescribe the conditions, not inconsistent with the provisions of this section, under which payments may be made under this section.

(o) Payments for taxes imposed by section 4041(d).

For purposes of subsections (a), (b), and (c), the taxes imposed by section 4041(d) shall be treated as imposed by section 4041(a).

(p) Cross references.

(1) For civil penalty for excessive claims under this section, see section 6675.

(2) For fraud penalties, etc., see chapter 75 (section 7201 and following, relating to crimes, other offenses, and forfeitures).

(3) For treatment of an Indian tribal government as a State (and a subdivision of an Indian tribal government as a political subdivision of a State), see section 7871.

In 2010, P.L. 111-312, Sec. 701(b)(2), substituted "December 31, 2011" for "December 31, 2009" in subpara. (e)(6)(B), effective for fuel sold or used after 12/31/2009.

—P.L. 111-312, Sec. 701(c), of this Act, provides:

"(c) Special rule for 2010.

"Notwithstanding any other provision of law, in the case of any biodiesel mixture credit properly determined under section 6426(c) of the Internal Revenue Code of 1986 for periods during 2010, such credit shall be allowed, and any refund or payment attributable to such credit (including any payment under section 6427(e) of such Code) shall be made, only in such manner as the Secretary of the Treasury (or the Secretary's delegate) shall provide. Such Secretary shall issue guidance within 30 days after the date of the enactment of this Act providing for a one-time submission of claims covering periods during 2010. Such guidance shall provide for a 180-day period for the submission of such claims (in such manner as prescribed by such Secretary) to begin not later than 30 days after such guidance is issued. Such claims shall be paid by such Secretary not later than 60 days after receipt. If such Secretary has not paid pursuant to a claim filed under this subsection within 60 days after the date of the filing of such claim, the claim shall be paid with interest from such date determined by using the overpayment rate and method under section 6621 of such Code."

—P.L. 111-312, Sec. 704(a), substituted "December 31, 2011" for "December 31, 2009" in subpara. (e)(6)(C), effective for fuel sold or used after 12/31/2009.

—P.L. 111-312, Sec. 704(c), of this Act, provides:

"(c) Special rule for 2010. Notwithstanding any other provision of law, in the case of any alternative fuel credit or any alternative fuel mixture credit properly determined under subsection (d) or (e) of section 6426 of the Internal Revenue Code of 1986 for periods during 2010, such credit shall be allowed, and any refund or payment attributable to such credit (including any payment under section 6427(e) of such Code) shall be made, only in such manner as the Secretary of the Treasury (or the Secretary's delegate) shall provide. Such Secretary shall issue guidance within 30 days after the date of the enactment of this Act providing for a one-time submission of claims covering periods during 2010. Such guidance shall provide for a 180-day period for the submission of such claims (in such manner as prescribed by such Secretary) to begin not later than 30 days after such guidance is issued. Such claims shall be paid by such Secretary not later than 60 days after receipt. If such Secretary has not paid pursuant to a claim filed under this subsection within 60 days after the date of the filing of such claim, the claim shall be paid with interest from such date determined by using the overpayment rate and method under section 6621 of such Code."

—P.L. 111-312, Sec. 708(c)(1), substituted "December 31, 2011" for "December 31, 2010" in subpara. (e)(6)(A), effective for sales and uses after 12/31/2010.

In 2008, P.L. 110-343, Sec. 202(a)DivB, substituted "December 31, 2009" for "December 31, 2008" in subpara. (e)(6)(B) [as redesignated by Sec. 203(e)(2) Div B of this Act, see above], effective for fuel produced, and sold or used, after 12/31/2008.

—P.L. 110-343, Sec. 203(e)(2)DivB, redesignated para. (e)(5) as para. (e)(6), and added para. (e)(5), effective for claims for credit or payment made on or after 5/15/2008.

—P.L. 110-343, Sec. 204(a)(3)DivB, substituted "December 31, 2009" for "September 30, 2009" in subpara. (e)(5)(C) [sic (e)(6)(C)] [as redesignated by Sec. 203(c)(2) Div B of this Act, see above], effective for fuel sold or used after 10/3/2008.

In 2007, P.L. 110-172, Sec. 5(a)(1)(A), added "or under subsection (e)(2) by any person with respect to an alternative fuel (as defined in section 6426(d)(2))" after "section 6426" in subpara. (i)(3)(A)... Sec. 5(a)(1)(B), added "or (e)(2)" after "subsection (e)(1)" in clause (i)(3)(A)(i) and subpara. (i)(3)(B)... Sec. 5(a)(1)(C), substituted "mixture credits and the alternative fuel credit" for "alcohol fuel and biodiesel mixture credit" in the heading of para. (i)(3), effective for any sale or use for any period after 9/30/2006.

—P.L. 110-172, Sec. 11(a)(37), redesignated para. (e)(3) [as added by Sec. 11113 of P.L. 109-59, see below]as para. (e)(5)... Sec. 11(a)(38), substituted "section 4081(a)(2)(A)(iii)" for "section 4081(a)(2)(iii)" in clause (I)(4)(A)(ii) [as amended by Sec. 11161(b)(3)(E)(ii) of P.L. 109-59, see below]... Sec. 11(a)(39)(A), deleted subsec. (p) and redesignated subsec. (q) as subsec. (p). Sec. 11(a)(39)(B) provides:

"(B) The Internal Revenue Code of 1986 shall be applied and administered as if the amendments made by paragraph (2) of section 11151(a) of the SAFETEA-LU [P.L. 109-59] had never been enacted."

—P.L. 110-172, Sec. 11(e)(1), substituted "2008" for "2006" in subpara. (e)(5)(B), effective 8/8/2005.

In 2006, P.L. 109-432, Sec. 420(a), amended para. (l)(4)... Sec. 420(b)(1), deleted para. (l)(5) and redesignated para. (l)(6) as para. (l)(5)... Sec. 420(b)(3)(A), substituted "paragraph (4)(B), (5), or (6)" for "paragraph (4)(C) or (5)" each place it appeared in subpara. (i)(4)(A)... Sec. 420(b)(3)(B), substituted "(l)(4)(C)(ii),

Code Sec. 6427 — Abatements, credits, refunds

and (l)(5)" for "(l)(5), and (l)(6)" in subpara. (i)(4)(A) ... Sec. 420(b)(4), substituted "(4)(B)" for "(4)(C)(i)" in para. (l)(1), effective for kerosene sold after 9/30/2005, except as provided in Sec. 420(c)(2) of this Act, which reads as follows:

"(2) Special rule for pending claims. In the case of kerosene sold for use in aviation (other than kerosene to which section 6427(l)(4)(C)(ii) of the Internal Revenue Code of 1986 (as added by subsection (a)) applies or kerosene to which section 6427(l)(5) of such Code (as redesignated by subsection (b)) applies) after September 30, 2005, and before the date of the enactment of this Act, the ultimate purchaser shall be treated as having waived the right to payment under section 6427(l)(1) of such Code and as having assigned such right to the ultimate vendor if such ultimate vendor has met the requirements of subparagraph (A), (B), or (D) of section 6416(a)(1) of such Code."

Prior to amendment, para. (l)(4) read as follows:

"(4) Refunds for kerosene used in commercial aviation.

"(A) No refund of certain taxes on fuel used in commercial aviation. In the case of kerosene used in commercial aviation (as defined in section 4083(b)) (other than supplies for vessels or aircraft within the meaning of section 4221(d)(3)), paragraph (1) shall not apply to so much of the tax imposed by section 4081 as is attributable to

"(i) the Leaking Underground Storage Tank Trust Fund financing rate imposed by such section, and

"(ii) so much of the rate of tax specified in section 4081(a)(2)(iii) as does not exceed 4.3 cents per gallon.

"(B) Payment to ultimate, registered vendor. With respect to kerosene used in commercial aviation as described in subparagraph (A) , if the ultimate purchaser of such kerosene waives (at such time and in such form and manner as the Secretary shall prescribe) the right to payment under paragraph (1) and assigns such right to the ultimate vendor, then the Secretary shall pay the amount which would be paid under paragraph

"(1) to such ultimate vendor, but only if such ultimate vendor

"(i) is registered under section 4101 , and

"(ii) meets the requirements of subparagraph (A), (B), or (D) of section 6416(a)(1)."

Prior to repeal, para. (l)(5) read as follows:

"(5) Refunds for kerosene used in noncommercial aviation.

"(A) In general. In the case of kerosene used in aviation not described in paragraph (4)(A) (other than any use which is exempt from the tax imposed by section 4041(c) other than by reason of a prior imposition of tax), paragraph (1) shall not apply to so much of the tax imposed by section 4081 as is attributable to

"(i) the Leaking Underground Storage Tank Trust Fund financing rate imposed by such section, and

"(ii) so much of the rate of tax specified in section 4081(a)(2)(A)(iii) as does not exceed the rate specified in section 4081(a)(2)(C)(ii).

"(B) Payment to ultimate, registered vendor. The amount which would be paid under paragraph (1) with respect to any kerosene shall be paid only to the ultimate vendor of such kerosene. A payment shall be made to such vendor if such vendor

"(i) is registered under section 4101, and

"(ii) meets the requirements of subparagraph (A)), (B) , or (D) of section 6416(a)(1) ."

—P.L. 109-432, Sec. 420(d), of this Act, reads as follows:

" Special Rule For Kerosene Used In Aviation On A Farm for Farming Purposes.

"(1) Refunds For Purchases After December 31, 2004, and before October 1, 2005.

"The Secretary of the Treasury shall pay to the ultimate purchaser of any kerosene which is used in aviation on a farm for farming purposes and which was purchased after December 31, 2004, and before October 1, 2005, an amount equal to the aggregate amount of tax imposed on such fuel under section 4041 or 4081 of the Internal Revenue Code of 1986, as the case may be, reduced by any payment to the ultimate vendor under section 6427(l)(5)(C) of such Code (as in effect on the day before the date of the enactment of the Safe, Accountable, Flexible, Efficient Transportation Equity Act: a Legacy for Users).

"(2) Use on a farm for purposes. For purposes of paragraph (1), kerosene shall be treated as used on a farm for farming purposes if such kerosene is used for farming purposes (within the meaning of section 6420(c)(3) of the Internal Revenue Code of 1986) in carrying on a trade or business on a farm situated in the United States. For purposes of the preceding sentence, rules similar to the rules of section 6420(c)(4) of such Code shall apply.

"(3) Time for filing claims. No claim shall be allowed under paragraph (1) unless the ultimate purchaser files such claim before the date that is 3 months after the date of the enactment of this Act.

"(4) No double benefit. No amount shall be paid under paragraph (1) or section 6427(l) of the Internal Revenue Code of 1986 with respect to any kerosene described in paragraph (1) to the extent that such amount is in excess of the tax imposed on such kerosene under section 4041 or 4081 of such Code, as the case may be.

" (5) Applicable laws. For purposes of this subsection, rules similar to the rules of section 6427(j) of the Internal Revenue Code of 1986 shall apply. "

In 2005, P.L. 109-59, Sec. 11113(b)(3)(C)(i), added "or the alternative fuel mixture credit" after "biodiesel mixture credit" in para. (e)(1) ... Sec. 11113(b)(3)(C)(ii), redesignated para. (e)(2) as para. (e)(3) and para. (e)(4) as para. (e)(5) ... Sec. 11113(b)(3)(C)(iii), added para. (e)(2) ... Sec. 11113(b)(3)(C)(iv), substituted "under paragraph (1) or (2) with respect to any mixture or alternative fuel" for "under paragraph (1) with respect to any mixture" in para. (e)(3) [as redesignated by Sec. 11113(b)(3)(C)(ii) of this Act, see above] ...

Sec. 11113(b)(3)(C)(v), added para. (e)(4) ... Sec. 11113(b)(3)(C)(vi), deleted "and" at the end of subpara. (e)(5)(A) [as redesignated by Sec. 11113(b)(3)(C)(ii) of this Act, see above] ... Sec. 11113(b)(3)(C)(vii), substituted a comma for the period at the end of subpara. (e)(5)(B) [as redesignated by Sec. 11113(b)(3)(C)(ii) of this Act, see above] ... Sec. 11113(b)(3)(C)(viii), added subparas. (e)(5)(C) and (e)(5)(D) ... Sec. 11113(b)(3)(C)(ix), substituted ", biodiesel, or alternative fuel" for "or biodiesel used to produce alcohol fuel and biodiesel mixtures" in the heading of subsec. (e), effective for any sale or use for any period after 9/30/2006.

—P.L. 109-59, Sec. 11151(a)(1), deleted subsec. (f) ... Sec. 11151(a)(2), deleted subsec. (o) and redesignated subsec. (p) as subsec. (o), effective for fuel sold or used after 12/31/2004 as if included in Sec. 301 of P.L. 108-357, the American Jobs Creation Act of 2004.

Prior to deletion, subsec. (f) read as follows:

"(f) Gasoline, diesel fuel, kerosene, and aviation fuel used to produce certain alcohol fuels.

"(1) In general. Except as provided in subsection (k), if any gasoline, diesel fuel, kerosene, or aviation fuel on which tax was imposed by section 4081 or 4091 at the regular tax rate is used by any person in producing a mixture described in section 4081(c) or 4091(c)(1)(A) (as the case may be) which is sold or used in such person's trade or business the Secretary shall pay (without interest) to such person an amount equal to the excess of the regular tax rate over the incentive tax rate with respect to such fuel.

"(2) Definitions. For purposes of paragraph (1)—

"(A) Regular tax rate. The term 'regular tax rate' means—

"(i) in the case of gasoline, diesel fuel, or kerosene, the aggregate rate of tax imposed by section 4081 determined without regard to subsection (c) thereof, and

"(ii) in the case of aviation fuel, the aggregate rate of tax imposed by section 4091 determined without regard to subsection (c) thereof.

"(B) Incentive tax rate. The term 'incentive tax rate' means—

"(i) in the case of gasoline, diesel fuel, or kerosene, the aggregate rate of tax imposed by section 4081 with respect to fuel described in subsection (c)(2) thereof, and

"(ii) in the case of aviation fuel, the aggregate rate of tax imposed by section 4091 with respect to fuel described in subsection (c)(2) thereof.

"(3) Coordination with other repayment provisions. No amount shall be payable under paragraph (1) with respect to any gasoline, diesel fuel, or aviation fuel with respect to which an amount is payable under subsection (d) or (l) of this section or under section 6420 or 6421.

"(4) Termination. This subsection shall not apply with respect to any mixture sold or used after September 30, 2007."

Prior to deletion, subsec. (o) read as follows:

"(o) Gasohol used in noncommercial aviation. Except as provided in subsection (k), if—

"(1) any tax is imposed by section 4081at a rate determined under subsection (c) thereof on gasohol (as defined in such subsection), and

"(2) such gasohol is used as a fuel in any aircraft in noncommercial aviation (as defined in section 4041(c)(2)),

the Secretary shall pay (without interest) to the ultimate purchaser of such gasohol an amount equal to 1.4 cents (2 cents in the case of a mixture none of the alcohol in which consists of ethanol) multiplied by the number of gallons of gasohol so used."

—P.L. 109-59, Sec. 11161(b)(2)(A), amended para. (l)(2) ... Sec. 11161(b)(2)(B), redesignated para. (l)(5) as para. (l)(6), and added para. (l)(5) ... Sec. 11161(b)(3)(B), substituted "and kerosene" for ", kerosene, and aviation fuel" in the heading of subsec. (l) ... Sec. 11161(b)(3)(D)(i), substituted "paragraph (4)(B), (5), or (6)" for "paragraph (4)(B) or (5)" each place it appeared in subpara. (i)(4)(B) ... Sec. 11161(b)(3)(D)(ii), substituted "subsections (b)(4), (l)(5), and (l)(6)" for "subsection (b)(4) and subsection (l)(5)" in subpara. (i)(4)(A) ... Sec. 11161(b)(3)(E)(i), deleted "aviation-grade" in subpara. (l)(4)(A) ... Sec. 11161(b)(3)(E)(ii), substituted "section 4081(a)(2)(iii)" for "section 4081(a)(2)(A)(iv)" in para. (l)(4) ... Sec. 11161(b)(3)(E)(iii), substituted "kerosene used in commercial aviation as described in subparagraph (A)" for "aviation-grade kerosene" in subpara. (l)(4)(B) ... Sec. 11161(b)(3)(E)(iv), substituted "kerosene used in commercial aviation" for "aviation-grade kerosene" in the heading of para. (l)(4) ... Sec. 11161(b)(3)(F), substituted "kerosene used in aviation" for "aviation-grade kerosene" in subpara. (l)(6)(B) [as redesignated by Sec. 11161(b)(2)(B) of this Act, see above], effective for fuels or liquids removed, entered, or sold after 9/30/2005.

Prior to amendment, para. (l)(2) read as follows:

"(2) Nontaxable use. For purposes of this subsection, the term 'nontaxable use' means—

"(A) in the case of diesel fuel or kerosene, any use which is exempt from the tax imposed by section 4041(a)(1) other than by reason of a prior imposition of tax, and

"(B) in the case of aviation-grade kerosene—

"(i) any use which is exempt from the tax imposed by section 4041(c) other than by reason of a prior imposition of tax, or

"(ii) any use in commercial aviation (within the meaning of section 4083(b))."

—P.L. 109-59, Sec. 11162(a), amended subpara. (l)(6)(A) [as redesignated by Sec. 11161(b)(2)(B) of this Act, see above] ... Sec. 11162(b), deleted "farmers and" in the heading of para. (l)(6) [as redesignated by Sec. 11161(b)(2)(B) of this Act, see above], effective for sales after 9/30/2005.

Prior to amendment, subpara. (l)(6)(A) [as redesignated by Sec. 11161(b)(2)(B) of this Act, see above] read as follows:

"(A) In general. Paragraph (1) shall not apply to diesel fuel or kerosene used—

"(i) on a farm for farming purposes (within the meaning of section 6420(c)), or

"(ii) by a State or local government."

Abatements, credits, refunds   Code Sec. 6427

—P.L. 109-59, Sec. 11163(c)(1), substituted "Except as provided in subparagraph (D), the amount" for "The amount" in subpara. (l)(6)(C) [as redesignated by Sec. 11161(b)(2)(B) of this Act, see above] . . . Sec. 11163(c)(2), added subpara. (l)(6)(D), effective for sales after 12/31/2005.

—P.L. 109-58, Sec. 1343(b)(1); redesignated subsecs. (m)-(p) as subsecs. (n)-(q), and added subsec. (m) . . . Sec. 1343(b)(3), added "(m)," after "(l)," in paras. (i)(1) and (2), effective 1/1/2006.

—P.L. 109-58, Sec. 1344(a), substituted "2008" for "2006" in subpara. (e)(4)(B) [sic (e)(3)(B)], effective 8/8/2005.

In 2004, P.L. 108-357, Sec. 241(a)(2)(D), amended subpara. (l)(3)(B), effective 1/1/2005.

Prior to amendment, subpara. (l)(3)(B) read as follows:

"(B) so much of the rate specified in section 4081(a)(2)(A) as does not exceed—

"(i) 6.8 cents per gallon after September 30, 1993, and before October 1, 1995,

"(ii) 5.55 cents per gallon after September 30, 1995, and before November 1, 1998, and

"(iii) 4.3 cents per gallon after October 31, 1998."

—P.L. 108-357, Sec. 301(c)(9), added subsec. (e) . . . Sec. 301(c)(10)(A), substituted "subsection (e)(1)" for "subsection (f)" each place it appeared in subpara. (i)(3)(A) . . . Sec. 301(c)(10)(B), substituted "a mixture described in section 6426" for "gasoline, diesel fuel, or kerosene used to produce a qualified alcohol mixture (as defined in section 4081(c)(3))" in subpara. (i)(3)(A) . . . Sec. 301(c)(10)(C), added a flush sentence at the end of subpara. (i)(3)(A) . . . Sec. 301(c)(10)(D), substituted "subsection (e)(1)" for "subsection (f)(1)" in subpara. (i)(3)(B) . . . Sec. 301(c)(10)(E), substituted "45 days of the date of the filing of such claim (20 days in the case of an electronic claim)" for "20 days of the date of the filing of such claim" in subpara. (i)(3)(B) . . . Sec. 301(c)(10)(F), substituted "alcohol fuel and biodiesel mixture" for "alcohol mixture" in the heading of para. (i)(3), effective for fuel sold or used after 12/31/2004.

—P.L. 108-357, Sec. 301(e), of this Act, reads as follows:

"(e) Format for filing. The Secretary of the Treasury shall describe the electronic format for filing claims described in section 6427(i)(3)(B) of the Internal Revenue Code of 1986 (as amended by subsection (c)(10)(C)) not later than December 31, 2004."

—P.L. 108-357, Sec. 851(d)(3), added subpara. (i)(2)(C), effective for tax. yrs. begin. after 10/22/2004.

—P.L. 108-357, Sec. 853(c)(1), amended para. (l)(4) . . . Sec. 853(c)(2)(A), substituted "paragraph (4)(B) or (5) of subsection (l)" for "subsection (l)(5)" each place it appeared in subpara. (i)(4)(A) . . . Sec. 853(c)(2)(B), substituted "subsection (l)(5)" for "the preceding sentence" in subpara. (i)(4)(A) . . . Sec. 853(c)(3), amended subpara. (l)(2)(B) . . . Sec. 853(d)(2)(J), substituted "and 4081" for ", 4081, and 4091" in para. (j)(1) . . . Sec. 853(d)(2)(K)(i), amended para. (l)(1) . . . Sec. 853(d)(2)(K)(ii), substituted "Paragraph (1) shall not apply to kerosene (other than aviation-grade kerosene)" for "Paragraph (1)(A) shall not apply to kerosene" in subpara. (l)(5)(B), effective for aviation-grade kerosene removed, entered, or sold after 12/31/2004.

Prior to amendment, para. (l)(1) read as follows:

"(1) In general. Except as otherwise provided in this subsection and in subsection (k), if—

"(A) any diesel fuel or kerosene on which tax has been imposed by section 4041 or 4081, or

"(B) any aviation fuel on which tax has been imposed by section 4091,

is used by any person in a nontaxable use, the Secretary shall pay (without interest) to the ultimate purchaser of such fuel an amount equal to the aggregate amount of tax imposed on such fuel under section 4041, 4081, or 4091, as the case may be."

Prior to amendment, subpara. (l)(2)(B) read as follows:

"(B) in the case of aviation fuel, any use which is exempt from the tax imposed by section 4041(c)(1) other than by reason of a prior imposition of tax."

Prior to amendment, para. (l)(4) read as follows:

"(4) No refund of certain taxes on fuel used in commercial aviation. In the case of fuel used in commercial aviation (as defined in section 4092(b)) (other than supplies for vessels or aircraft within the meaning of section 4221(d)(3)), paragraph (1) shall not apply to so much of the tax imposed by section 4091 as is attributable to—

"(A) the Leaking Underground Storage Tank Trust Fund financing rate imposed by such section, and

"(B) in the case of fuel purchased after September 30, 1995, as so much of the rate of tax specified in section 4091(b)(1) as does not exceed 4.3 cents per gallon."

—P.L. 108-357, Sec. 853(f), of this Act, reads as follows:

"(f) Floor stocks tax.

"(1) In general. There is hereby imposed on aviation-grade kerosene held on January 1, 2005, by any person a tax equal to—

"(A) the tax which would have been imposed before such date on such kerosene had the amendments made by this section been in effect at all times before such date, reduced by

"(B) the sum of—

"(i) the tax imposed before such date on such kerosene under section 4091 of the Internal Revenue Code of 1986, as in effect on such date, and

"(ii) in the case of kerosene held exclusively for such person's own use, the amount which such person would (but for this clause) reasonably expect (as of such date) to be paid as a refund under section 6427(l) of such Code with respect to such kerosene.

"(2) Exception for fuel held in aircraft fuel tank. Paragraph (1) shall not apply to kerosene held in the fuel tank of an aircraft on January 1, 2005.

"(3) Liability for tax and method of payment.

"(A) Liability for tax. The person holding the kerosene on January 1, 2005, to which the tax imposed by paragraph (1) applies shall be liable for such tax.

"(B) Method and time for payment. The tax imposed by paragraph (1) shall be paid at such time and in such manner as the Secretary of the Treasury (or the Secretary's delegate) shall prescribe, including the nonapplication of such tax on de minimis amounts of kerosene.

"(4) Transfer of floor stock tax revenues to trust funds. For purposes of determining the amount transferred to any trust fund, the tax imposed by this subsection shall be treated as imposed by section 4081 of the Internal Revenue Code of 1986—

"(A) in any case in which tax was not imposed by section 4091 of such Code, at the Leaking Underground Storage Tank Trust Fund financing rate under such section to the extent of 0.1 cents per gallon, and

"(B) at the rate under section 4081(a)(2)(A)(iv) of such Code to the extent of the remainder.

"(5) Held by a person. For purposes of this subsection, kerosene shall be considered as held by a person if title thereto has passed to such person (whether or not delivery to the person has been made).

"(6) Other laws applicable. All provisions of law, including penalties, applicable with respect to the tax imposed by section 4081 of such Code shall, insofar as applicable and not inconsistent with the provisions of this subsection, apply with respect to the floor stock tax imposed by paragraph (1) to the same extent as if such tax were imposed by such section."

—P.L. 108-357, Sec. 857(b), added para. (b)(4) . . . Sec. 857(c), added "subsections (b)(4) and" after "filed under" in subpara. (i)(4)(A), effective for fuel sold after 12/31/2004.

—P.L. 108-357, Sec. 870(b), amended subsec. (h), effective for fuel removed, sold, or used after 12/31/2004.

Prior to amendment, subsec. (h) read as follows:

"(h) Gasoline blend stocks or additives not used for producing gasoline. Except as provided in subsection (k), if any gasoline blend stock or additive (within the meaning of section 4083(a)(2)) is not used by any person to produce gasoline and such person establishes that the ultimate use of such gasoline blend stock or additive is not to produce gasoline, the Secretary shall pay (without interest) to such person an amount equal to the aggregate amount of the tax imposed on such person with respect to such gasoline blend stock or additive."

In 1998, P.L. 105-206, Sec. 6016(b)(1), substituted "other aircraft uses" for "helicopters" in the heading of subsec. (d) . . . Sec. 6016(b)(2), added "or a fixed-wing aircraft" after "helicopter" in subsec. (d), effective on the 7th calendar day after 8/20/96.

—P.L. 105-206, Sec. 6017(a), amended subpara. (i)(2)(B), effective 10/1/98.

Prior to amendment, subpara. (i)(2)(B) read as follows:

"(B) Time for filing claim. No claim filed under this paragraph shall be allowed unless filed on or before the last day of the first quarter following the quarter for which the claim is filed."

—P.L. 105-206, Sec. 6023(16), substituted "section 4041(c)(2)" for "section 4041(c)(4)" in para. (q)(2) . . . Sec. 6023(25), deleted ", (e)," after "(d)," in para. (f)(3) . . . Sec. 6023(26)(A), redesignated subsecs. (n), (p), (q), and (r) as subsecs. (m)-(p) . . . Sec. 6023(26)(B), substituted "(o)" for "(q)" in para. (i)(1) and subpara. (i)(2)(A), effective 7/22/98.

In 1998, P.L. 105-178, Sec. 9003(a)(2), substituted "2007" for "1999" in para. (f)(4) . . . Sec. 9006(b)(2)(A), substituted "November 1, 1998" for "October 1, 1999" in clause (l)(3)(B)(ii) . . . Sec. 9006(b)(2)(B), substituted "October 31, 1998" for "September 30, 1999" in clause (l)(3)(B)(iii), effective 6/9/98.

—P.L. 105-178, Sec. 9009(a), amended subpara. (i)(2)(A) . . . Sec. 9009(b)(1), deleted para. (i)(4) and redesignated para. (i)(5) as (4) . . . Sec. 9009(b)(2), amended para. (k)(2), effective 10/1/98.

Prior to amendment, subpara. (i)(2)(A) read as follows:

"(A) In general. If $1,000 or more is payable under subsections (a), (b), (d), (h), and (o) to any person with respect to fuel used during any of the first 3 quarters of his taxable year, a claim may be filed under this section with respect to fuel used, during such quarter."

Prior to deletion, para. (i)(4) read as follows:

"(4) Special rule for refunds under subsection (l).

"(A) In general. If at the close of any of the 1st 3 quarters of the taxable year of any person, at least $750 is payable under subsection (l) to such person with respect to fuel used during such quarter or any prior quarter during the taxable year (and for which no other claim has been filed), a claim may be filed under subsection (l) with respect to such fuel.

"(B) Time for filing claim. No claim filed under this paragraph shall be allowed unless filed during the 1st quarter following the last quarter included in the claim."

Prior to amendment, para. (k)(2) read as follows:

"(2) Exception. Paragraph (1) shall not apply to a payment of a claim filed under paragraph (2), (3), (4), or (5) of subsection (i)."

In 1997, P.L. 105-34, Sec. 1032(c)(3)(A), added "or kerosene" after "diesel fuel" each place it appeared in paras. (l)(1), (2), and (5) . . . Sec. 1032(c)(3)(B), redesignated subpara. (l)(5)(B) as subpara. (l)(5)(C), and added a new subpara. (l)(5)(B) . . . Sec. 1032(c)(3)(C), substituted "subparagraph (A) or (B)" for "subparagraph (A)" in subpara. (l)(5)(C) [as redesignated by Sec. 1032(c)(3)(B) of this Act, see above] . . . Sec. 1032(c)(3)(D), added ", kerosene," after "diesel fuel" in the heading of subsec. (l) . . . Sec. 1032(c)(3)(E), added "($100 or more in the case of kerosene)" after "$200 or more" in clause (i)(5)(A)(i) . . . Sec. 1032(e)(7), added "kerosene," after "diesel fuel," in the heading of subsec. (f), and paras. (f)(1) and (f)(3) . . . Sec. 1032(e)(8), substituted ", diesel fuel, or kerosene" for "or diesel fuel" each place it appeared in para. (f)(2) . . . Sec. 1032(e)(9), substi-

3,727

tuted ", diesel fuel, or kerosene" for "or diesel fuel" in subpara. (i)(3)(A) . . . Sec. 1032(e)(10), amended the heading of para. (i)(4), effective 7/1/98.
Prior to amendment, the heading of para. (i)(4) read as follows:
"(4) Special rule for nontaxable uses of diesel fuel and aviation fuel taxed under section 4081 or 4091."
—P.L. 105-34, Sec. 1601(g)(1), of this Act, regarding amendments to Subtitle G of P.L. 104-188, reads as follows:
"(1) Extension of period for claiming refunds for alcohol fuels. Notwithstanding section 6427(i)(3)(C) of the Internal Revenue Code of 1986, a claim filed under section 6427(f) of such Code for any period after September 30, 1995, and before October 1, 1996, shall be treated as timely filed if filed before the 60th day after the date of the enactment of this Act."
In 1996, P.L. 104-188, Sec. 1606(a), deleted subsec. (g) . . . Sec. 1606(b)(2)(A), deleted "(g)," after "(d)," in para. (i)(1) and subpara. (i)(2)(A) . . . Sec. 1606(b)(2)(B), deleted "(or a qualified diesel powered highway vehicle purchased)" after "fuel used" each place it appeared in para. (i)(1) and subpara. (i)(2)(A), effective for vehicles purchased after 8/20/96.
Prior to deletion, subsec. (g) read as follows:
"(g) Advance repayment of increased diesel fuel tax to original purchasers of diesel-powered automobiles and light trucks.
"(1) In general. Except as provided in subsection (k), the Secretary shall pay (without interest) to the original purchaser of any qualified diesel-powered highway vehicle an amount equal to the diesel fuel differential amount.
"(2) Qualified diesel-powered highway vehicle. For purposes of this subsection, the term 'qualified diesel-powered highway vehicle' means any diesel-powered highway vehicle which—
"(A) has at least 4 wheels,
"(B) has a gross vehicle weight rating of 10,000 pounds or less, and
"(C) is registered for highway use in the United States under the laws of any State.
"(3) Diesel fuel differential amount. For purposes of this subsection, the term 'diesel fuel differential amount' means—
"(A) except as provided in subparagraph (B), $102, or
"(B) in the case of a truck or van, $198.
"(4) Original purchaser. For purposes of this subsection—
"(A) In general. Except as provided in subparagraph (B), the term 'original purchaser' means the first person to purchase the qualified diesel-powered vehicle for use other than resale.
"(B) Exception for certain persons not subject to fuels tax. The term 'original purchaser' shall not include any State or local government (as defined in section 4221(d)(4)) or any nonprofit educational organization (as defined in section 4221(d)(5)).
"(C) Treatment of demonstration use by dealer. For purposes of subparagraph (A), use as a demonstrator by a dealer shall not be taken into account.
"(5) Vehicles to which subsection applies. Except as provided in paragraph (6), this subsection shall only apply to qualified diesel-powered highway vehicles originally purchased after January 1, 1985, and before January 1, 1999.
"(6) Special rule for certain vehicles held on January 1, 1985.
"(A) In general. In the case of any person holding a qualified diesel-powered highway vehicle on January 1, 1985—
"(i) such person shall be treated as if he originally purchased such vehicle on December 31, 1984, but
"(ii) the amount payable under paragraph (1) to such person for such vehicle shall be the applicable fraction of the diesel fuel differential amount.
"(B) Applicable fraction. For purposes of subparagraph (A), the applicable fraction is the fraction determined in accordance with the following table:

If the model year of the vehicle is:	The applicable fraction is:
1984 or 1985	1
1983	5/6
1982	4/6
1981	3/6
1980	2/6
1979	1/6

In the case of a 1978 or earlier model year vehicle, the applicable fraction shall be zero.
"(7) Basis reduction. For the purposes of subtitle A, the basis of any qualified diesel-powered highway vehicle shall be reduced by the amount payable under this subsection with respect to such vehicle."
—P.L. 104-188, Sec. 1702(b)(2)(B), added "unless such fuel was used by a State or any political subdivision thereof" before the period at the end of para. (l)(4) [prior to amendment by Sec. 13241(f)(9) of P.L. 103-66, see below, effective 12/1/90.
—P.L. 104-188, Sec. 1703(k), substituted "1999" for "1995" in para. (f)(4), effective 1/1/94.
In 1993, P.L. 103-66, Sec. 13241(f)(8)(A), substituted "7.4 cents" for "3.1 cents" in subpara. (b)(2)(A) . . . Sec. 13241(f)(8)(B), substituted "Reduction" for "3-cent reduction" in the heading of para. (b)(2) . . . Sec. 13241(f)(9), amended paras. (l)(3) and (4) . . . Sec. 13241(f)(10), deleted subsecs. (m) and (o), effective 10/1/93.
Prior to amendment, paras. (l)(3) and (4) read as follows:
"(3) No refund of Leaking Underground Storage Tank Trust Fund financing tax. Paragraph (1) shall not apply to so much of the tax imposed by section 4091 as is attributable to the Leaking Underground Storage Tank Trust Fund financing rate imposed by such section in the case of—
"(A) fuel used in a diesel-powered train, and
"(B) fuel used in any aircraft (except as supplies for vessels or aircraft within the meaning of section 4221(d)(3)).
"(4) No refund of deficit reduction tax on fuel used in trains. In the case of fuel used in a diesel-powered train, paragraph (1) also shall not apply to so much of the tax imposed by section 4091 as is attributable to the diesel fuel deficit reduction rate imposed by such section unless such fuel was used by a State or any political subdivision thereof." [amended by Sec. 1702(b)(2)(B) of P.L. 104-188, see above]
Prior to deletion, subsecs. (m) and (o) read as follows:
"(m) Special rules with respect to noncommercial aviation. For purposes of subsection (a), in the case of gasoline—
"(1) on which tax was imposed under section 4041(c)(2),
"(2) on which tax was not imposed under section 4081, and
"(3) which was not used as an off-highway business use (within the meaning of section 6421(e)(2)),
the amount of the payment under subsection (a) shall be an amount equal to the amount of gasoline used as described in subsection (a) or resold multiplied by the rate equal to the excess of the rate of tax imposed by section 4041(c)(2) over the rate of tax imposed by section 4081." * * *
"(o) Termination of certain provisions. Except with respect to taxes imposed by section 4041(d) and sections 4081 and 4091 at the Leaking Underground Storage Tank Trust Fund financing rate, subsections (a), (b), (c), (d), (g), (h), and (l) shall only apply with respect to fuels purchased before October 1, 1999."
—P.L. 103-66, Sec. 13242(c)(1), added para. (l)(5) . . . Sec. 13242(c)(2)(A), added para. (i)(5) . . . Sec. 13242(c)(2)(B), substituted "otherwise provided in this subsection" for "provided in paragraphs (2), (3), and (4)" in para. (i)(1) . . . Sec. 13242(c)(2)(C), substituted "(4), or (5)" for "or (4)" in para. (k)(2) . . . Sec. 13242(c)(2)(D), added subpara. (i)(3)(C) . . . Sec. 13242(d)(21), substituted "paragraph (2) or (3) of section 4041(a) or section 4041(c)" for "section 4041(a) or (c)" in subsecs. (a) and (c) . . . Sec. 13242(d)(25)(A), substituted "if any fuel other than gasoline (as defined in section 4083(a))" for "if any fuel" in para. (b)(1) . . . Sec. 13242(d)(25)(B), substituted "4081" for "4091" each place it appeared in subsec. (b) . . . Sec. 13242(d)(26)(A), substituted "or 4091(c)(1)(A)" for ", 4091(c)(1)(A), or 4091(d)(1)(A)" in para. (f)(1) . . . Sec. 13242(d)(26)(B), amended para. (f)(2) . . . Sec. 13242(d)(27), substituted "section 4083(a)(2)" for "section 4082(b)" in subsec. (h) . . . Sec. 13242(d)(28)(A), substituted "alcohol mixture" for "gasohol" in the heading of para. (i)(3) . . . Sec. 13242(d)(28)(B), substituted "gasoline or diesel fuel used to produce a qualified alcohol mixture (as defined in section 4081(c)(3))" for "gasoline used to produce gasohol (as defined in section 4081(c)(1))" in subpara. (i)(3)(A) . . . Sec. 13242(d)(29), substituted "sections 4041, 4081, and 4091" for "section 4041" in para. (j)(1) . . . Sec. 13242(d)(30), added "4081 or" before "4091" in the heading of para. (i)(4) . . . Sec. 13242(d)(31), amended so much of subsec. (l) [as amended by Sec. 13241(f)(9) of this Act] as preceded para. (l)(5) [as added by Sec. 13242(c)(1) of this Act], effective 1/1/94.
Prior to amendment, para. (f)(2) read as follows:
"(2) Definitions. For purposes of paragraph (1)—
"(A) Regular tax rate. The term 'regular tax rate' means—
"(i) in the case of gasoline, the aggregate rate of tax imposed by section 4081 determined without regard to subsection (c)(1) thereof,
"(ii) in the case of diesel fuel, the aggregate rate of tax imposed by section 4091 on such fuel determined without regard to subsection (c) thereof, and
"(iii) in the case of aviation fuel, the aggregate rate of tax imposed by section 4091 on such fuel determined without regard to subsection (d) thereof.
"(B) Incentive tax rate. The term 'incentive tax rate' means—
"(i) in the case of gasoline, the aggregate rate of tax imposed by section 4081 with respect to fuel described in subsection (c)(1) thereof,
"(ii) in the case of diesel fuel, the aggregate rate of tax imposed by section 4091 with respect to fuel described in subsection (c)(1)(B) thereof, and
"(iii) in the case of aviation fuel, the aggregate rate of tax imposed by section 4091 with respect to fuel described in subsection (d)(1)(B) thereof."
Prior to amendment, paras. (l)(1)-(4) [as amended by Sec. 13241(f)(9) of this Act] read as follows:
"(l) Nontaxable uses of diesel fuel and aviation fuel taxed under section 4091.
"(1) In general. Except as provided in subsection (k) and in paragraphs (3) and (4) of this subsection, if any fuel on which tax has been imposed by section 4091 is used by any person in a nontaxable use, the Secretary shall pay (without interest) to the ultimate purchaser of such fuel an amount equal to the aggregate amount of tax imposed on such fuel under section 4091.
"(2) Nontaxable use. For purposes of this subsection, the term 'nontaxable use' means, with respect to any fuel, any use of such fuel if such use is exempt under section 4041 from the taxes imposed by subsections (a)(1) and (c)(1) of section 4041 (other than by reason of the imposition of tax on any sale thereof).
"(3) No refund of certain taxes on fuel used in diesel-powered trains. In the case of fuel used in a diesel-powered train, paragraph (1) shall not apply to so much of the tax imposed by section 4091 as is attributable to the Leaking Underground Storage Tank Trust Fund financing rate and the diesel fuel deficit reduction rate imposed by such section. The preceding sentence shall not apply in the case of fuel sold for exclusive use by a State or any political subdivision thereof.
"(4) No refund of leaking underground storage tank trust fund taxes on fuel used in commercial aviation. In the case of fuel used in commercial aviation (as defined in section 4093(c)(2)(B)) (other than supplies for vessels or aircraft within the meaning of section 4221(d)(3)), paragraph (1) shall not apply to so much of the tax imposed by section 4091 as is attributable to the Leaking Underground Storage Tank Trust Fund financing rate imposed by such section."

Abatements, credits, refunds — Code Sec. 6427

In 1991, P.L. 102-240, Sec. 8002(b)(7), substituted "1999" for "1995" in para. (g)(5)... Sec. 8002(b)(8), substituted "1999" for "1995" in subsec. (o), effective 12/18/91.

In 1990, P.L. 101-508, Sec. 11211(b)(4)(B)(i), added para. (1)(4)... Sec. 11211(b)(4)(B)(ii), substituted "paragraphs (3) and (4)" for "paragraph (3)" in para. (l)(1)... Sec. 11211(b)(5), substituted "shall be 3.1 cents per gallon less than the aggregate rate at which tax was imposed on such fuel by section 4041(a) or 4091, as the case may be" for "shall not exceed 12 cents" in subpara. (b)(2)(A)... Sec. 11211(b)(6)(E)(ii), amended subsec. (q), effective 12/1/90.

Prior to amendment, subsec. (q) read as follows:

"(q) Gasoline used in noncommercial aviation during period rate reduction in effect. Except as provided in subsection (k), if—

"(1) any tax is imposed by section 4081 on any gasoline,

"(2) such gasoline is used during 1991 as a fuel in any aircraft in noncommercial aviation (as defined in section 4041(c)(4)), and

"(3) no tax is imposed by section 4041(c)(2) on taxable events occurring during 1991 by reason of section 4283,

the Secretary shall pay (without interest) to the ultimate purchaser of such gasoline an amount equal to the excess of the aggregate amount of tax paid under section 4081 on the gasoline so used over an amount equal to 6 cents multiplied by the number of gallons of gasoline so used."

—P.L. 101-508, Sec. 11211(d)(7), substituted "1995" for "1993" each place it appeared in para. (g)(5)... Sec. 11211(d)(8), substituted "1995" for "1993" in subsec. (o), effective 11/5/90.

—P.L. 101-508, Sec. 11213(b)(3), amended subsec. (f), effective 12/1/90.

Prior to amendment, subsec. (f) read as follows:

"(f) Gasoline, diesel fuel, and aviation fuel used to produce certain alcohol fuels. Except as provided in subsection (k)—

"(1) Gasoline and diesel fuels.

"(A) In general. If any gasoline or diesel fuel on which tax was imposed by section 4081 or 4091 at the regular tax rate is used by any person in producing a mixture described in section 4081(c) or in section 4091(c)(1)(A) (as the case may be) which is sold or used in such person's trade or business, the Secretary shall pay (without interest) to such person an amount equal to the excess of the regular tax rate over the incentive tax rate with respect to such fuel.

"(B) Definitions. For purposes of subparagraph (A)—

"(i) Regular tax rate. The term 'regular tax rate' means—

"(I) in the case of gasoline, the aggregate rate of tax imposed by section 4081 determined without regard to subsection (c) thereof, and

"(II) in the case of diesel fuel, the aggregate rate of tax imposed by section 4091 on such fuel determined without regard to subsection (c) thereof,

"(ii) Incentive tax rate. The term 'incentive tax rate' means—

"(I) in the case of gasoline, the aggregate rate of tax imposed by section 4081 with respect to fuel described in subsection (c)(1) thereof, and

"(II) in the case of diesel fuel, the aggregate rate of tax imposed by section 4091 with respect to fuel described in subsection (c)(1)(B) thereof.

"(C) Coordination with other repayment provisions. No amount shall be payable under subparagraph (A) with respect to any gasoline or diesel fuel with respect to which an amount is payable under subsection (d), (e), or (l) of this section or under section 6420 or 6421.

"(2) Aviation fuel. If any aviation fuel on which tax was imposed by section 4091 is used by any person in producing a mixture at least 10 percent of which is alcohol (as defined in section 4081(c)(3)) which is sold or used in such person's trade or business, the Secretary shall pay (without interest) to such person an amount equal to the aggregate amount of tax (attributable to the Airport and Airway Trust Fund financing rate) imposed on such fuel under section 4091.

"(3) Termination. Paragraphs (1) and (2) shall not apply with respect to any mixture sold or used after September 30, 1993."

—P.L. 101-508, Sec. 11801(a)(46), repealed subsec. (e)... Sec. 11801(c)(23)(A), deleted "(e)," in para. (i)(1)... Sec. 11801(c)(23)(B), amended subpara. (i)(2)(A)... Sec. 11801(c)(23)(C), deleted subpara. (i)(2)(B) and redesignated subpara. (i)(2)(C) as (i)(2)(B), effective 11/5/90, except as provided in Sec. 11821(b) of this Act, reproduced in note following Code Sec. 6428.

Prior to repeal, subsec. (e) read as follows:

"(e) Use in certain taxicabs.

"(1) In general. Except as provided in subsection (k), if—

"(A) any gasoline on which tax is imposed by section 4081, or

"(B) any fuel on the sale of which tax is imposed by section 4041 or 4091,

is used in a qualified taxicab while engaged exclusively in furnishing qualified taxicab services, the Secretary shall pay (without interest) to the ultimate purchaser of such gasoline or fuel an amount determined at the rate of 4 cents a gallon.

"(2) Definitions. For purposes of this subsection—

"(A) Qualified taxicab services. The term 'qualified taxicab services' means the furnishing of nonscheduled passenger land transportation for a fixed fare by a taxicab which is operated by a person who—

"(i) is licensed to engage in the trade or business of furnishing such transportation by a Federal, State, or local authority having jurisdiction over a substantial portion of such transportation furnished by such person, and

"(ii) is not prohibited under the laws, regulations, or procedures of such Federal, State, or local authority, and is not prohibited by company policy, from furnishing (with consent of the passengers) shared transportation.

"(B) Qualified taxicab. Except as provided by subparagraph (C), the term 'qualified taxicab' means any land vehicle the passenger capacity of which is less than 10 adults, including the driver.

"(C) Certain gas-guzzling taxicabs excluded. The term 'qualified taxicab' does not include any vehicle if—

"(i) such vehicle was acquired by the person operating such vehicle after 1978,

"(ii) the model year of such vehicle is 1978 or later, and

"(iii) the fuel economy of the model type of such vehicle is less than or equal to the average fuel economy standard applicable under section 502(a) of the Motor Vehicle Information and Cost Savings Act to the model year of such vehicle. The preceding sentence shall not apply to any vehicle manufactured by a manufacturer to which an exemption under section 502(c) of the Motor Vehicle Information and Cost Savings Act was granted (or on application could have been granted) for the model year of such vehicle. Terms used in this subparagraph shall have the same meaning as when used in title V of the Motor Vehicle Information and Cost Savings Act.

"(3) Termination. This subsection shall not apply after September 30, 1988."

Prior to amendment, subpara. (i)(2)(A) read as follows:

"(A) In general. If—

"(i) $1,000 or more is payable under subsections (a), (b), (d), (e), (g), (h) and (q), or

"(ii) $50 or more is payable under subsection (e), to any person with respect to fuel used (or a qualified diesel powered highway vehicle purchased) during any of the first three quarters of his taxable year, a claim may be filed under this section by the purchaser with respect to fuel used (or a qualified diesel powered highway vehicle purchased) during such quarter."

Prior to deletion, subpara. (i)(2)(B) read as follows:

"(B) Special rule. If the requirements of subparagraph (A)(ii) are met by any person for any quarter but the requirements of subparagraph (A)(i) are not met by such person for such quarter, such person may file a claim under subparagraph (A) for such quarter only with respect to amounts referred to in subparagraph (A)(ii)."

In 1989, P.L. 101-239, Sec. 7501(b)(3), substituted "1991" for "1990" each place it appeared in subsec. (q), effective 12/19/89.

—P.L. 101-239, Sec. 7812(a), corrected Sec. 2001(d)(7)(C) of P.L. 100-647, so that it amended subpara. (f)(1)(B), instead of subpara. (g)(1)(B), see below.

—P.L. 101-239, Sec. 7822(b)(1), substituted "subsection (a), (b), (c), (d), (e), (g), (h), (l) or (q) by any person" for "subsection (a), (b), (c), (d), (e), (g), (h), or (l) by any person" in para. (i)(1)... Sec. 7822(b)(2), amended clause (i)(2)(A)(i)... Sec. 7822(b)(3), amended subpara. (i)(2)(B)... Sec. 7822(b)(4), redesignated the subsec. relating to payments for taxes imposed by section 4041(d) as subsec. (p), effective for sales after 3/31/88.

Prior to amendment, clause (i)(2)(A)(i) read as follows:

"(i) $1,000 or more is payable under subsections (a), (b), (d), (e), (g), (h) and (q), or".

Prior to amendment, subpara. (i)(2)(B) read as follows:

"(B) Special rule. If the requirements of clause (ii) of subparagraph (A) are met by any person for any quarter but the requirements of subparagraph (A)(i) are not met by such person for such quarter, such person may file a claim under subparagraph (A) for such quarter only with respect to amounts referred to in the clause of subparagraph (A) the requirements of which are met such such person for such quarter."

—P.L. 101-239, Sec. 7841(d)(20), substituted "section 7602(a)" for "section 7602" in para. (j)(2), effective 12/19/89.

In 1988, P.L. 100-647, Sec. 1017(c)(3), substituted "section 6421(e)(2)" for "6421(d)(2)" in para. (m)(3)... Sec. 1017(c)(10), substituted "paragraph (2) or (3) of subsection (i)." for "subsection (i)(2) or (h)(3)." in para. (k)(2), effective for gasoline removed (as defined in Code Sec. 4082) after 12/31/87.

—P.L. 100-647, Sec. 2001(d)(7)(A), changed the effective date for changes made by Sec. 10502(c)(4) of P.L. 100-203 from "sales after 3/31/88" to "gasoline removed (as defined in Code Sec. 4082) after 12/31/87, except that references to Code Sec. 4091 [in subsec. (f)] do not apply to sales before 1/1/88, see below.

—P.L. 100-647, Sec. 2001(d)(7)(B)(i), substituted "regular tax rate" for "regular Highway Trust Fund financing rate" each place it appeared in subpara. (f)(1)(A), ... Sec. 2001(d)(7)(B)(ii), substituted 'incentive tax rate' for 'incentive Highway Trust Fund financing rate' in subpara. (f)(1)(A)... Sec. 2001(d)(7)(C), [as amended by Sec. 7812(a) of P.L. 101-239, see above] amended subpara. (f)(1)(B) ... Sec. 2001(d)(7)(D), added 'under section 4041' after 'exempt' in para (1)(2), effective for sales after 3/31/88.

Prior to amendment, subpara. (f)(1)(B) read as follows:

"(B) Definitions. For purposes of subparagraph (A)—

"(i) Regular highway trust fund financing rate. The term 'regular Highway Trust Fund financing rate' means—

"(I) 9 cents per gallon in the case of gasoline, and

"(II) 15 cents per gallon in the case of diesel fuel.

"(ii) Incentive highway trust fund financing rate".

The term "incentive Highway Trust Fund Financing rate" means—

"(I) 3⅓ cents per gallon in the case of gasoline, and

"(II) 10 cents per gallon in the case of diesel fuel."

—P.L. 100-647, Sec. 2004(s)(2), added "(except as supplies for vessels or aircraft within the meaning of section 4221(d)(3)" after "aircraft" in subpara. (l)(3)(B)... Sec. 2004(s)(3), redesignated subsec. (p), relating to gasoline used in noncommercial aviation during period rate reduction in effect, as subsec. (q) [sic (p)], and redesignated subsec. (q), dealing with cross references, as subsec. (r), effective for sales after 3/31/88.

—P.L. 100-647, Sec. 3002(a), added para. (i)(4)... Sec. 3002(b), substituted "paragraph (2), (3), or (4)" for "paragraph (2) or (3)" in para. (k)(2) [as amended by Sec. 1017(c)(10) of this Act, see above]... Sec. 3002(c)(1), substituted "paragraph (2), (3), and (4)" for "paragraph (2)" in para. (i)(1)... Sec. 3002(c)(2), deleted "(l)," from subpara. (i)(2)(A), effective for fuel used after 12/31/88.

In 1987, P.L. 100-223, Sec. 405(b)(1), redesignated subsec. (p) as subsec. (q) and added new subsec. (p)... Sec. 405(b)(2)(A), substituted "(h), or (p)" for "or (h)"

3,729

Code Sec. 6427 Abatements, credits, refunds

in para. (i)(1) . . . Sec. 405(b)(2)(B), substituted "(h), and (p)" [sic (h), (l) and (p)] for "and (h)" [sic (h) and (l)] in clause (i)(2)(A)(i), effective 12/30/87.

—P.L. 100-203, Sec. 10502(c)(1), redesignated subsecs. (l)-(p) as subsecs. (m)-(q) respectively and added new subsec. (l) . . . Sec. 10502(c)(2)(A), substituted "section 4041(a) or 4091" for "subsection (a) of section 4041" the first place it appeared in para. (b)(1) . . . Sec. 10502(c)(2)(B), substituted "section 4041(a) or 4091, as the case may be" for "subsection (a) of section 4041" at the end of para. (b)(1) . . . Sec. 10502(c)(3), added "or 4091" after "section 4041" in subpara. (e)(1)(B) . . . Sec. 10502(c)(5)(A), substituted "(h), or (l)" for "or (h)" in para. (i)(1) . . . Sec. 10502(c)(5)(B), substituted "(h), and (l)" for "and (h)" in clause (i)(2)(A)(i) . . . Sec. 10502(c)(6), amended subsec. (o) [as redesignated by Sec. 10502(c)(1) of the Act, see above], effective for sales after 3/31/88.

—P.L. 100-203, Sec. 10502(c)(4), amended subsec. (f), effective for gasoline remove as defined in Code Sec. 4082) after 12/31/87, except that references to Code Sec. 4091 [in subsec. (f)] do not apply to sales before 1/1/88 [as amended by Sec. 2001(d)(7)(A) of P.L. 100-647].

Prior to amendment, subsec. (f) read as follows:

"(f) Gasoline used to produce certain alcohol fuels.

"(1) In general. Except as provided in subsection (k), if any gasoline on which a tax is imposed by section 4081 at the rate of 9 cents a gallon is used by any person in producing a mixture described in section 4081(c) which is sold or used in such person's trade or business, the Secretary shall pay (without interest) to such person an amount equal to the amount determined at the Highway Trust Fund financing rate of 5⅔ cents a gallon. The preceding sentence shall not apply with respect to any mixture sold or used after December 31, 1992.

"(2) Coordination with other repayment provisions. No amount shall be payable under paragraph (l) with respect to any gasoline with respect to which an amount is payable under subsection (d) or (e) of this section or under section 6420 or 6421."

Prior to amendment, subsec. (o) (as redesignated by Sec. 10502(c)(1) of the Act) read as follows:

"(o) Termination of subsections (a), (b), (c), (d), (g), and (h). Except with respect to taxes imposed by section 4041(d) and section 4081 at the Leaking Underground Storage Tank Trust Fund financing rate, subsections (a), (b), (c), (d), (g), and (h) shall only apply with respect to fuels purchased before October 1, 1993.".

—P.L. 100-17, Sec. 502(b)(8), substituted "1993" for "1988" each place it appeared in para. (g)(5) . . . Sec. 502(b)(9), substituted "1993" for "1988" in subsec. (m), effective 4/2/87.

In 1986, P.L. 99-514, Sec. 422(b), substituted "September 30, 1988" for "September 30, 1985" in para. (e)(3), effective 10/22/86.

—P.L. 99-514, Sec. 1703(d)(1), added para. (h)(3) [as so designated before amendment by Sec. 1703(e)(1) of this Act, see below] . . . Sec. 1703(d)(1)(B)(i), deleted "(f)" after "(d), (e)," in para. (h)(1) [as so designated before amendment by Sec. 1703(e)(1) of this Act] . . . Sec. 1703(d)(1)(B)(ii), added "or" at the end of clause (h)(2)(A)(i), deleted "or" at the end of clause (h)(2)(A)(ii), deleted clause (h)(2)(A)(iii), and deleted "(or clauses)" after "referred to in the clause" in subpara. (h)(2)(A) [sic (h)(2)(B)] [before amendment by Sec. 1703(e)(1) of this Act] . . . Sec. 1703(d)(1)(B)(iii), deleted "or clause (iii)" after "clause (ii)" in para. (f)(2)(B) [sic (h)(2)(B), as so designated before amendment by Sec. 1703(e)(1) of this Act] . . . Sec. 1703(d)(1)(B)(iv), substituted "subsection (h)(2) or (h)(3)" for "subsection (h)(2)" in para. (j)(2) [as so designated before amendment by Sec. 1703(e)(1) of this Act] . . . Sec. 1703(e)(1)(A), redesignated subsecs. (h)-(n) [sic (h)-(o), after amendment by P.L. 99-499, Sec. 521(c)(3)(B), see below] as subsecs. (i)-(p), . . . Sec. 1703(e)(1)(B), added new subsec. (h) . . . Sec. 1703(e)(2)(A), substituted "subsection (k)" for "subsection (j)" in subsecs. (a), (c), and (d), and in paras. (b)(1), (e)(1), (f)(1), and (g)(1) . . . Sec. 1703(e)(2)(B), substituted "(g), or (h)" for "or (g)" in para. (i)(1) [as so redesignated, see above] . . . Sec. 1703(e)(2)(C), substituted "(g), and (h)" for "and (g)" in clause (i)(2)(A)(i) and in subsec. (n) [as so redesignated] . . . Sec. 1703(e)(2)(D), substituted "(g), and (h)" for "and (g)" in the heading of subsec. (n) [as so redesignated] . . . Sec. 1703(e)(2)(E), substituted "(i)(2)" [sic "subsection (i)(2)"] for "subsection (h)(2)" in para. (i)(2) [sic (k)(2), as so redesignated], effective for gasoline removed (as defined in Code Sec. 4082) after 12/31/87.

Prior to deletion, clause (h)(2)(A)(iii) read as follows:

"(iii) $200 or more is payable under subsection (f),"

—P.L. 99-514, Sec. 1877(b)(1), redesignated subpara. (b)(2)(B) and (b)(2)(C) as subparas. (b)(2)(C) and (b)(2)(D) and added new subpara. (b)(2)(B) . . . Sec. 1877(b)(2), substituted "subparagraphs (B) and (C)" for "subparagraph (B)" in subpara. (b)(2)(A) . . . Sec. 1877(b)(3), substituted "Exception for certain intracity transportation" for "Exception" in the heading of subpara. (b)(2)(C) [as redesignated by Sec. 1877(b)(1) of this Act, see above], effective 8/1/84.

—P.L. 99-514, Sec. 1899A(55), substituted "otherwise provided in this subsection" for "provided in paragraph (2)" in para. (b)(1) . . . Sec. 1899A(56), substituted "amount" for "anount" in para. (g)(1), effective 10/22/86.

—P.L. 99-499, Sec. 521(c)(3)(A), substituted "Except with respect to taxes imposed by section 4041(d) and section 4081 at the Leaking Underground Storage Tank Trust Fund financing rate, subsections" for "Subsections" in subsec. (m) . . . Sec. 521(c)(3)(B)(i), redesignated subsec. (n) as (o) and added new subsec. (n) . . . Sec. 521(c)(3)(C), substituted "at the Highway Trust Fund financing rate" for "at the rate" in para. (f)(1), effective 1/1/87.

In 1984, P.L. 98-369, Sec. 474(r)(38), substituted "section 34" for "section 39" in para. (i)(3), effective for tax. yrs. begin. after 12/31/83, and for carrybacks from tax. yrs. begin. after 12/31/83.

—P.L. 98-369, Sec. 732(a)(3), substituted "4 5/9 cents" for "5 cents" in para. (f)(1), effective 4/1/83.

—P.L. 98-369, Sec. 734(c)(2), redesignated subsecs. (j), (k), and (l) as subsecs. (k), (l), and (m), and added new subsec. (j), effective 10/1/84.

—P.L. 98-369, Sec. 911(b), redesignated subsecs. (g)-(m) [as previously redesignated by Sec. 734(c)(2) of this Act, see above] as subsecs. (h)-(n), and added new subsec. (g) . . . Sec. 911(d)(2)(B), substituted "(j)" [sic , (k)] for "(i)" in subsecs. (a), (c) and (d), and paras. (b)(1), (e)(1) and (f)(1) . . . Sec. 911(d)(2)(C), substituted "(f), or (g)" for "or (f)", and substituted "fuel used (or a qualified diesel powered highway vehicle purchased)" for "fuel used" each place it appeared in para. (h)(1) [as redesignated by Sec. 911(b) of this Act, see above] . . . Sec. 911(d)(2)(D), substituted "(e), and (g)" for "and (e)", and substituted "fuel used (or a qualified diesel powered highway vehicle purchased)" for "fuel used" each place it appeared in subpara. (h)(2)(A) [as redesignated by Sec. 911(b) of the Act, see above] . . . Sec. 911(d)(2)(E), substituted "(h)(2)" for "(g)(2)" in para. (k)(2) [sic (j)(2), as redesignated by Sec. 911(b) of this Act, see above] . . . Sec. 911(d)(2)(F), substituted "(d), and (g)" for "and (d)" each place it appeared in subsec. (m) [as redesignated by Sec. 911(b) of this Act, see below], effective 8/1/84.

—P.L. 98-369, Sec. 912(d), substituted "5 2/3 cents" for "4 5/9 cents" in para. (f)(1) [as amended by Sec. 732(a)(3) of this Act, see below], effective 1/1/85.

—P.L. 98-369, Sec. 914, substituted "September 30, 1985" for "September 30, 1984" in para. (e)(3), effective 7/18/84.

—P.L. 98-369, Sec. 915(a), redesignated para. (b)(2) as para. (b)(3), and added new para. (b)(2), effective on 8/1/84.

In 1983, P.L. 97-473, Sec. 202(b)(13), added para. (k)(3) [sic , subsec. (k) redesignated (l) by P.L. 97-424, Sec. 516(b)(5), see below].

—P.L. 97-424, Sec. 511(d)(4), amended subsec. (f) . . . Sec. 511(e)(1), substituted "an amount determined at the rate of 4 cents a gallon" for "an amount equal to the aggregate amount of the tax imposed on such gasoline or fuel" in para. (e)(1), effective 4/1/83.

Prior to amendment, subsec. (f) read as follows:

"(f) Gasoline used to produce certain alcohol fuels.

"(1) In general. Except as provided in subsection (i), if any gasoline on which tax is imposed by section 4081 is used by any person in producing a mixture described in section 4081(c) which is sold or used in such person's trade or business, the Secretary shall pay (without interest) to such person an amount equal to the aggregate amount of the tax imposed on such gasoline. The preceding sentence shall not apply with respect to any mixture sold or used after December 31, 1992.

"(2) Coordination with other repayment provisions. No amount shall be payable under subsection (d) or (e) of this section or under section 6420 or 6421 with respect to any gasoline with respect to which an amount is payable under paragraph (1)."

—P.L. 97-424, Sec. 511(e)(2), substituted "September 30, 1984" for "December 31, 1982" in para. (e)(3), effective 1/1/83.

—P.L. 97-424, Sec. 511(e)(3), amended clause (e)(2)(A)(ii), effective for fuel purchased after 12/31/82 and before 1/1/84.

Prior to amendment clause (e)(2)(A)(ii) read as follows:

"(ii) is not prohibited under the laws, regulations, or procedures of such Federal, State, or local authority, and is not prohibited by company policy, from furnishing (with consent of the passengers) shared transportation."

—P.L. 97-424, Sec. 511(e)(4), provides:

"(4) Study. The Secretary of the Treasury or his delegate shall conduct a study of the reduced rate of fuels taxes provided for taxicabs by section 6427(e) of the Internal Revenue Code of 1954. Not later than January 1, 1984, the Secretary shall transmit a report on the study conducted under the preceding sentence to the Congress, together with such recommendations as he may deem advisable."

—P.L. 97-424, Sec. 511(g)(2)(B), substituted "section 4041(a) or (c)" for "section 4041(a), (b), or (c)" in subsec. (a) . . . Sec. 511(g)(2)(C), substituted "subsection (a) of section 4041" for "subsection (a) or (b) of section 4041" in para. (b)(1) . . . Sec. 511(g)(2)(D), substituted "section 4041(a) or (c)" for "section 4041(a), (b) or (c)" in subsec. (c) . . . Sec. 516(b)(5), redesignated subsec. (k) as subsec. (l) and added new subsec. (k), effective 1/6/83.

In 1982, P.L. 97-248, Sec. 279(b)(2)(A), added "or is used in a helicopter for a purpose described in section 4041(1)," after "section 4041(h)(2)(C)," in subsec. (d) . . . Sec. 279(b)(2)(B), added "or in certain helicopters" after "museums" in the heading of subsec. (d), effective 9/1/82.

In 1980, P.L. 96-541, Sec. 4, substituted "1982" for "1980" in para. (e)(3) effective 12/17/80.

—P.L. 96-223, Sec. 232(d)(1)(A), redesignated subsecs. (f), (g), (h), (i), and (j) as subsecs. (g), (h), (i), (j), and (k), respectively . . . Sec. 232(d)(1)(B), added new subsec. (f) . . . Sec. 232(d)(2)(A), deleted "or" at the end of clause (g)(2)(A)(i) [as redesignated by Sec. 232(d)(1)(A) of this Act, see above], inserted "or" at the end of clause (g)(2)(A)(ii), and added new clause (g)(2)(A)(iii) . . . Sec. 232(d)(2)(B), amended subpara. (g)(2)(B) [as redesignated by Sec. 232(d)(1)(A) of this Act, see above] . . . Sec. 232(d)(4)(B), substituted "(i)" for "(h)" in subsecs. (a), (c), (d), and paras. (b)(1) and (e)(1) . . . Sec. 232(d)(4)(C), substituted "(a), (b), (c), (d), (e), or (f)" for "(a), (b), (c), (d), or (e)" in subsec. (g)(1) [as redesignated by Sec. 232(d)(1)(A) of this Act, see above] . . . Sec. 232(d)(4)(D), substituted "(g)(2)" for "(f)(2)" in para. (i)(2) [as redesignated by Sec. 232(d)(1)(A) of this Act, see above], effective 1/1/79. Sec. 232(h)(2)(B) of the Act provides:

"(B) Transitional rule. Any mixture sold or used on or after January 1, 1979, and before the date of the enactment of this Act which is described in section 6427(f)(1) of the Internal Revenue Code of 1954 (as amended by subsection (d)) shall, for purposes of section 6427 of such Code, be treated as sold or used on the date of the enactment of this Act."

Prior to amendment, subpara. (g)(2)(B) read as follows:

"(B) Special rule. If a claim may be filed by any person under subparagraph (A)(ii) but not under subparagraph (A)(i) for any quarter, such person may file a claim under subparagraph (A) for such quarter only with respect to amounts payable under subsection (e)."

Abatements, credits, refunds   Code Sec. 6428(f)(2)

In **1978**, P.L. 95-618, Sec. 233(a)(2), amended subsec. (b), effective on the first day of the first calendar month which begins more than 10 days after 11/9/78. Prior to amendment, subsec. (b) read as follows:

"(b) Local transit systems.

"(1) Allowance. Except as provided in subsection (g) is any fuel on the sale of which tax was imposed under section 4041(a) or (b) is used by the purchaser during any calendar quarter in vehicles while engaged in furnishing scheduled common carrier public passenger land transportation service along regular routes, the Secretary shall, subject to the provisions of paragraph (2), pay (without interest) to the purchaser the amount determined by multiplying —

"(A) 2 cents for each gallon of fuel so used on which tax was imposed at the rate of 4 cents a gallon, by

"(B) the percentage which the purchaser's commuter fare revenue (as defined in section 6421(d)(2)) derived from such scheduled service during the quarter was of his total passenger fare revenue derived from such scheduled service during the quarter.

"(2) Limitation. Paragraph (1) shall apply in respect of fuel used during any calendar quarter only if at least 60 percent of the total passenger fare revenue derived during the quarter from scheduled service described in paragraph (1) by the purchaser was attributable to commuter fare revenue derived during the quarter by the purchaser from such scheduled service."

—P.L. 95-600, Sec. 703(1)(3), substituted "Secretary" for "Secretary or his delegate" in subsec. (d), effective 10/4/76.

—P.L. 95-599, Sec. 505(a)(1), redesignated subsecs. (e), (f), (g), (h) and (i) as subsecs. (f), (g), (h), (i) and (j) respectively . . . Sec. 505(a)(2), added new subsec. (e) . . . Sec. 505(b), amended para. (f)(2), [as redesignated by Sec. 505(a)(1) of this Act, see above] . . . Sec. 505(c)(2), substituted "(h)" for "(g)" in subsecs. (a), (c), (d) and para. (b)(1) . . . Sec. 505(c)(3), substituted "(a), (b), (c), (d), or (e)" for "(a), (b), (c), or (d)" in para. (f)(1) [as redesignated by Sec. 505(a)(1) of this Act, see above] . . . Sec. 505(c)(4), substituted "(f)(2)" for "(e)(2)" in para. (h)(2) [as redesignated by Sec. 505(a)(1) of this Act, see above], effective 1/1/79.

Prior to amendment, para. (f)(2) read as follows:

"(2) Exception. If $1,000 or more is payable under subsections (a), (b), and (d) to any person with respect to fuel used during any of the first three quarters of his taxable year, a claim may be filed under this section by the purchaser with respect to fuel used during such quarter. No claim filed under this paragraph shall be allowed unless filed on or before the last day of the first quarter following the quarter for which the claim is filed."

—P.L. 95-458, Sec. 3(b), amended the second sentence of subsec. (c), effective on the first day of the first calendar quarter which begins more than 90 days after 10/14/78.

Prior to amendment, the second sentence of subsec. (c) read as follows:

"For purposes of this subsection, if fuel is used on a farm by any person other than the owner, tenant, or operator of such farm, such owner, tenant, or operator shall be treated as the user and purchaser of such fuel."

In **1976**, P.L. 94-530, Sec. 1(b), redesignated subsecs. (d) through (h) as subsecs. (e) through (i), respectively, and added new subsec. (d), effective 10/1/76.

—P.L. 94-530, Sec. 1(c)(2), substituted "(g)" for "(f)" in subsecs. (a) and (c) and para. (b)(1), effective 10/1/76.

—P.L. 94-530, Sec. 1(c)(3), substituted "(a), (b), (c), or (d)" for "(a), (b), or (c)" in para. (e)(1), [as redesignated by Sec. 1(b) of this Act, see above], effective 10/1/76.

—P.L. 94-530, Sec. 1(c)(4), substituted "(a), (b), and (d)" for "(a) and (b)" in para. (e)(2), [as redesignated by Sec. 1(b) of this Act, see above], effective 10/1/76.

—P.L. 94-530, Sec. 1(c)(5), substituted "(e)(2)" for "(d)(2)" in para. (g)(2) [as redesignated by Sec. 1(b) of, this Act see above], effective 10/1/76.

—P.L. 94-455, Sec. 1906(a)(31)(A), deleted ", after June 30, 1970,", in subsecs. (a), (b) and (c), effective only for fuel used or resold after 6/30/70.

—P.L. 94-455, Sec. 1906(b)(13)(A), substituted "Secretary" for "Secretary or his delegate" each place it appeared in Code Sec. 6427, effective 2/1/77.

In **1970**, P.L. 91-258, Sec. 207(a), added Code Sec. 6427, effective for tax. yrs. end. after 6/30/70.

Sec. 6428. 2008 Recovery rebates for individuals

(a) In general.

In the case of an eligible individual, there shall be allowed as a credit against the tax imposed by subtitle A for the first taxable year beginning in 2008 an amount equal to the lesser of—

(1) net income tax liability, or

(2) $600 ($1,200 in the case of a joint return).

(b) Special rules.

(1) In general. In the case of a taxpayer described in paragraph (2)—

(A) the amount determined under subsection (a) shall not be less than $300 ($600 in the case of a joint return), and

(B) the amount determined under subsection (a) (after the application of subparagraph (A)) shall be increased by the product of $300 multiplied by the number of qualifying children (within the meaning of section 24(c)) of the taxpayer.

(2) Taxpayer described. A taxpayer is described in this paragraph if the taxpayer—

(A) has qualifying income of at least $3,000, or

(B) has—

(i) net income tax liability which is greater than zero, and

(ii) gross income which is greater than the sum of the basic standard deduction plus the exemption amount (twice the exemption amount in the case of a joint return).

(c) Treatment of credit.

The credit allowed by subsection (a) shall be treated as allowed by subpart C of part IV of subchapter A of chapter 1.

(d) Limitation based on adjusted gross income.

The amount of the credit allowed by subsection (a) (determined without regard to this subsection and subsection (f)) shall be reduced (but not below zero) by 5 percent of so much of the taxpayer's adjusted gross income as exceeds $75,000 ($150,000 in the case of a joint return).

(e) Definitions.

For purposes of this section—

(1) Qualifying income. The term "qualifying income" means—

(A) earned income,

(B) social security benefits (within the meaning of section 86(d)), and

(C) any compensation or pension received under chapter 11, chapter 13, or chapter 15 of title 38, United States Code.

(2) Net income tax liability. The term "net income tax liability" means the excess of—

(A) the sum of the taxpayer's regular tax liability (within the meaning of section 26(b)) and the tax imposed by section 55 for the taxable year, over

(B) the credits allowed by part IV (other than section 24 and subpart C thereof) of subchapter A of chapter 1.

(3) Eligible individual. The term "eligible individual" means any individual other than—

(A) any nonresident alien individual,

(B) any individual with respect to whom a deduction under section 151 is allowable to another taxpayer for a taxable year beginning in the calendar year in which the individual's taxable year begins, and

(C) an estate or trust.

(4) Earned income. The term "earned income" has the meaning set forth in section 32(c)(2) except that such term shall not include net earnings from self-employment which are not taken into account in computing taxable income.

(5) Basic standard deduction; exemption amount. The terms "basic standard deduction" and "exemption amount" shall have the same respective meanings as when used in section 6012(a).

(f) Coordination with advance refunds of credit.

(1) In general. The amount of credit which would (but for this paragraph) be allowable under this section shall be reduced (but not below zero) by the aggregate refunds and credits made or allowed to the taxpayer under subsection (g). Any failure to so reduce the credit shall be treated as arising out of a mathematical or clerical error and assessed according to section 6213(b)(1).

(2) Joint returns. In the case of a refund or credit made or allowed under subsection (g) with respect to a joint return, half of such refund or credit shall be treated as having been made or allowed to each individual filing such return.

(g) Advance refunds and credits.

(1) In general. Each individual who was an eligible individual for such individual's first taxable year beginning in 2007 shall be treated as having made a payment against the tax imposed by chapter 1 for such first taxable year in an amount equal to the advance refund amount for such taxable year.

(2) Advance refund amount. For purposes of paragraph (1), the advance refund amount is the amount that would have been allowed as a credit under this section for such first taxable year if this section (other than subsection (f) and this subsection) had applied to such taxable year.

(3) Timing of payments. The Secretary shall, subject to the provisions of this title, refund or credit any overpayment attributable to this section as rapidly as possible. No refund or credit shall be made or allowed under this subsection after December 31, 2008.

(4) No interest. No interest shall be allowed on any overpayment attributable to this section.

(h) Identification number requirement.

(1) In general. No credit shall be allowed under subsection (a) to an eligible individual who does not include on the return of tax for the taxable year—

(A) such individual's valid identification number,

(B) in the case of a joint return, the valid identification number of such individual's spouse, and

(C) in the case of any qualifying child taken into account under subsection (b)(1)(B), the valid identification number of such qualifying child.

(2) Valid identification number. For purposes of paragraph (1), the term "valid identification number" means a social security number issued to an individual by the Social Security Administration. Such term shall not include a TIN issued by the Internal Revenue Service.

(3) Special rule for members of the Armed Forces. Paragraph (1) shall not apply to a joint return where at least 1 spouse was a member of the Armed Forces of the United States at any time during the taxable year.

In 2010, P.L. 111-312, Sec. 101(a)(1), substituted "December 31, 2012" for "December 31, 2010" both places it appeared in Sec. 901 of P.L. 107-16, [see below] effective as if included in the enactment of P.L. 107-16, EGTRRA, 6/7/2001.

In 2008, P.L. 110-289, Sec. 3027, of this Act, provides:

"SEC. 3027. TRANSFER OF FUNDS APPROPRIATED TO CARRY OUT 2008 RECOVERY REBATES FOR INDIVIDUALS. Of the funds made available by section 101(e)(1)(A) of the Economic Stimulus Act of 2008 (Public Law 110-185) [see below], the Secretary of the Treasury may transfer funds among the accounts specified in such section to carry out section 6428 of the Internal Revenue Code of 1986. The Secretary shall provide advance notification of any such transfer to the Committees on Appropriations of the House of Representatives and the Senate, and any transfer greater than $5,000,000 shall be subject to the approval of such Committees."

— P.L. 110-245, Sec. 101(a), added para. (h)(3), effective 2/13/2008, as if included in the amendments made by Sec. 101 of the Economic Stimulus Act of 2008 [P.L. 110-185].

— P.L. 110-245, Sec. 102(b), substituted "except that such term shall" for "except that—" and all that follows through "(B) such term shall" in para. (e)(4), effective for tax. yrs. end. after 12/31/2007.

— P.L. 110-185, Sec. 101(a), amended Code Sec. 6428, enacted 2/13/2008.

Prior to amendment, Code Sec. 6428 read as follows:

"Code Sec. 6428. Acceleration of 10 percent income tax rate bracket benefit for 2001.

"(a) In general. In the case of an eligible individual, there shall be allowed as a credit against the tax imposed by chapter 1 for the taxpayer's first taxable year beginning in 2001 an amount equal to 5 percent of so much of the taxpayer's taxable income as does not exceed the initial bracket amount (as defined in section 1(i)(1)(B)).

"(b) Credit treated as nonrefundable personal credit. For purposes of this title, the credit allowed under this section shall be treated as a credit allowable under subpart A of part IV of subchapter A of chapter 1.

"(c) Eligible individual. For purposes of this section, the term 'eligible individual' means any individual other than—

"(1) any estate or trust,

"(2) any nonresident alien individual, and

"(3) any individual with respect to whom a deduction under section 151 is allowable to another taxpayer for a taxable year beginning in the calendar year in which the individual's taxable year begins.

"(d) Coordination with advance refunds of credit.

"(1) In general. The amount of credit which would (but for this paragraph) be allowable under this section shall be reduced (but not below zero) by the aggregate refunds and credits made or allowed to the taxpayer under subsection (e). Any failure to so reduce the credit shall be treated as arising out of a mathematical or clerical error and assessed according to section 6213(b)(1).

"(2) Joint returns. In the case of a refund or credit made or allowed under subsection (e) with respect to a joint return, half of such refund or credit shall be treated as having been made or allowed to each individual filing such return.

"(e) Advance refunds of credit based on prior year data.

"(1) In general. Each individual who was an eligible individual for such individual's first taxable year beginning in 2000 shall be treated as having made a payment against the tax imposed by chapter 1 for such first taxable year in an amount equal to the advance refund amount for such taxable year.

"(2) Advance refund amount. For purposes of paragraph (1), the advance refund amount is the amount that would have been allowed as a credit under this section for such first taxable year if—

"(A) this section (other than subsections (b) and (d) and this subsection) had applied to such taxable year, and

"(B) the credit for such taxable year were not allowed to exceed the excess (if any) of—

"(i) the sum of the regular tax liability (as defined in section 26(b)) plus the tax imposed by section 55, over

"(ii) the sum of the credits allowable under part IV of subchapter A of chapter 1 (other than the credits allowable under subpart C thereof, relating to refundable credits).

"(3) Timing of payments. In the case of any overpayment attributable to this subsection, the Secretary shall, subject to the provisions of this title, refund or credit such overpayment as rapidly as possible and, to the extent practicable, before October 1, 2001. No refund or credit shall be made or allowed under this subsection after December 31, 2001.

"(4) No interest. No interest shall be allowed on any overpayment attributable to this subsection."

—P.L. 110-185, Sec. 101(c), through (e) reads as follows:

"(c) Treatment of possessions.

"(1) Payment to possession.

"(A) Mirror code possession. The Secretary of the Treasury shall make a payment to each possession of the United States with a mirror code tax system in an amount equal to the loss to that possession by reason of the amendments made by this section. Such amount shall be determined by the Secretary of the Treasury based on information provided by the government of the respective possession.

"(B) Other possessions. The Secretary of the Treasury shall make a payment to each possession of the United States which does not have a mirror code tax system in an amount estimated by the Secretary of the Treasury as being equal to the aggregate benefits that would have been provided to residents of such possession by reason of the amendments made by this section if a mirror code tax system had been in effect in such possession. The preceding sentence shall not apply with respect to any possession of the United States unless such possession has a plan, which has been approved by the Secretary of the Treasury, under which such possession will promptly distribute such payment to the residents of such possession.

"(2) Coordination with credit allowed against united states income taxes. No credit shall be allowed against United States income taxes under section 6428 of the Internal Revenue Code of 1986 (as amended by this section) to any person—

"(A) to whom a credit is allowed against taxes imposed by the possession by reason of the amendments made by this section, or

"(B) who is eligible for a payment under a plan described in paragraph (1)(B).

"(3) Definitions and special rules.

"(A) Possession of the united states. For purposes of this subsection, the term 'possession of the United States' includes the Commonwealth of Puerto Rico and the Commonwealth of the Northern Mariana Islands.

"(B) Mirror code tax system. For purposes of this subsection, the term 'mirror code tax system' means, with respect to any possession of the United States, the income tax system of such possession if the income tax liability of the residents of such possession under such system is determined by reference to the income tax laws of the United States as if such possession were the United States.

"(C) Treatment of payments. For purposes of section 1324(b)(2) of title 31, United States Code, the payments under this subsection shall be treated in the same manner as a refund due from the credit allowed under section 6428 of the Internal Revenue Code of 1986 (as amended by this section).

"(d) Refunds Disregarded in the Administration of Federal Programs and Federally Assisted Programs. Any credit or refund allowed or made to any individual by reason of section 6428 of the Internal Revenue Code of 1986 (as amended by this section) or by reason of subsection (c) of this section shall not be taken into account as income and shall not be taken into account as resources for the month of receipt and the following 2 months, for purposes of determining the eligibility of such individual or any other individual for benefits or assistance, or the amount or extent of benefits or assistance, under any Federal program or under any State or local program financed in whole or in part with Federal funds.

"(e) Appropriations To Carry Out Rebates.

"(1) In general. Immediately upon the enactment of this Act, the following sums are appropriated, out of any money in the Treasury not otherwise appropriated, for the fiscal year ending September 30, 2008:

"(A) Department of the treasury.

Abatements, credits, refunds   Code Sec. 6428

"(i) For an additional amount for 'Department of the Treasury--Financial Management Service--Salaries and Expenses', $64,175,000, to remain available until September 30, 2009.

"(ii) For an additional amount for 'Department of the Treasury--Internal Revenue Service--Taxpayer Services', $50,720,000, to remain available until September 30, 2009.

"(iii) For an additional amount for 'Department of the Treasury--Internal Revenue Service--Operations Support', $151,415,000, to remain available until September 30, 2009.

"(B) Social security administration. For an additional amount for 'Social Security Administration--Limitation on Administrative Expenses', $31,000,000, to remain available until September 30, 2008.

"(2) Reports. No later than 15 days after enactment of this Act, the Secretary of the Treasury shall submit a plan to the Committees on Appropriations of the House of Representatives and the Senate detailing the expected use of the funds provided by paragraph (1)(A). Beginning 90 days after enactment of this Act, the Secretary of the Treasury shall submit a quarterly report to the Committees on Appropriations of the House of Representatives and the Senate detailing the actual expenditure of funds provided by paragraph (1)(A) and the expected expenditure of such funds in the subsequent quarter."

In 2002, P.L. 107-358, Sec. 2, added subsec. (c) in Sec. 901 of P.L. 107-16 [see below], effective 12/17/2002.

—P.L. 107-147, Sec. 411(a)(1), amended subsec. (b)... Sec. 411(a)(2)(A), amended subsec. (d)... Sec. 411(a)(2)(B), amended para. (e)(2), effective for tax. yrs. begin. after 12/31/2000.

Prior to amendment, subsec. (b) read as follows:

"(b) Limitation based on amount of tax. The credit allowed by subsection (a) shall not exceed the excess (if any) of—

"(1) the sum of the regular tax liability (as defined in section 26(b) plus the tax imposed by section 55, over

"(2) the sum of the credits allowable under part IV of subchapter A of chapter 1 (other than the credits allowable under subpart C thereof, relating to refundable credits)."

Prior to amendment, subsec. (d) read as follows:

"(d) Special rules.

"(1) Coordination with advance refunds of credit.

"(A) In general. The amount of credit which would (but for this paragraph) be allowable under this section shall be reduced (but not below zero) by the aggregate refunds and credits made or allowed to the taxpayer under subsection (e). Any failure to so reduce the credit shall be treated as arising out of a mathematical or clerical error and assessed according to section 6213(b)(1).

"(B) Joint returns. In the case of a refund or credit made or allowed under subsection (e) with respect to a joint return, half of such refund or credit shall be treated as having been made or allowed to each individual filing such return.

"(2) Coordination with estimated tax.

"The credit under this section shall be treated for purposes of section 6654(f) in the same manner as a credit under subpart A of part IV of subchapter A of chapter 1."

Prior to amendment, para. (e)(2) read as follows:

"(2) Advance refund amount. For purposes of paragraph (1), the advance refund amount is the amount that would have been allowed as a credit under this section for such first taxable year if this section (other than subsection (d) and this subsection) had applied to such taxable year."

In 2001, P.L. 107-16, Sec. 101(b)(1), added Code Sec. 6428, effective for tax. yrs. begin. after 12/31/2000.

—P.L. 107-16, Sec. 901, of this Act [as amended by Sec. 2 of P.L. 107-358, and Sec. 101(a)(1) of P.L. 111-312, see above], reads as follows:

"SEC. 901. SUNSET OF PROVISIONS OF ACT.

"(a) In general. All provisions of, and amendments made by, this Act shall not apply—

"(1) to taxable, plan, or limitation years beginning after December 31, 2012, or

"(2) in the case of title V, to estates of decedents dying, gifts made, or generation skipping transfers, after December 31, 2012.

"(b) Application of certain laws. The Internal Revenue Code of 1986 and the Employee Retirement Income Security Act of 1974 shall be applied and administered to years, estates, gifts, and transfers described in subsection (a) as if the provisions and amendments described in subsection (a) had never been enacted.

"(c) Exception. Subsection (a) shall not apply to section 803 (relating to no federal income tax on restitution received by victims of the Nazi regime or their heirs or estates)."

Sec. 6428. Repealed.

In 1990, P.L. 101-508, Sec. 11801(a)(47), repealed Code Sec. 6428, effective 11/5/90 except as provided in Sec. 11821(b) of this Act, which reads as follows:

"(b) Savings provision. If

"(1) any provision amended or repealed by this part applied to

"(A) any transaction occurring before the date of enactment of this Act [11/5/90],

"(B) any property acquired before such date of enactment [11/5/90], or

"(C) any item of income, loss, deduction, or credit taken into account before such date of enactment [11/5/90], and

"(2) the treatment of such transaction, property, or item under such provision would (without regard to the amendments made by this part) affect liability for tax for periods ending after such date of enactment [11/5/90],

nothing in the amendments made by this part shall be construed to affect the treatment of such transaction, property, or item for purposes of determining liability for tax for periods ending after such date of enactment [11/5/90]."

Prior to repeal, Code Sec. 6428 read as follows:

"SEC. 6428. 1981 RATE REDUCTION TAX CREDIT.

"(a) Allowance of credit.

"There shall be allowed as a credit against the tax imposed by section 1, or against a tax imposed in lieu of the tax imposed by section 1, for any taxable year beginning in 1981, an amount equal to the product of

"(1) 1.25 percent, multiplied by

"(2) the amount of tax imposed by section 1 (or in lieu thereof) for such taxable year.

"(b) Special rules for application of this section.

"(1) Application with other credits. In determining any credit allowed under subpart A of part IV of subchapter A of chapter 1 (other than under sections 31, 39, and 43), the tax imposed by chapter 1 shall (before any other reductions) be reduced by the credit allowed under subsection (a).

"(2) Credit treated as subpart A credit. For purposes of this title, the credit allowed under subsection (a) shall be treated as a credit allowed under subpart A of part IV of subchapter A of chapter 1.

"(c) Tables to reflect credit.

"(1) Section 3 tables. The tables prescribed by the Secretary under section 3 shall reflect the credit allowed under subsection (a).

"(2) Other tables. In order to reflect the amount of the credit under subsection (a) for different levels of tax or taxable income, the Secretary may

"(A) modify the tables under section 1, or

"(B) prescribe such other tables as he determines necessary.

"(d) Special rules.

"For purposes of this section—

"(1) Individuals to whom 50 percent maximum rate or 20 percent capital gain rate applies.

"(A) In general. In the case of any individual to whom this paragraph applies, in determining the amount of the credit allowable under subsection (a)—

"(i) the portion of the tax imposed by section 1 determined under section 1348(a)(2) (as in effect before its repeal by the Economic Recovery Tax Act of 1981), and

"(ii) the portion of the tax imposed by section 1 determined under subsection (a)(2)(B) of section 102 of the Economic Recovery Tax Act of 1981,

shall not be taken into account.

"(B) Individuals to whom paragraph applies. This paragraph applies to any individual if the tax imposed by section 1 for the taxable year is determined under—

"(i) section 1348 (as in effect before its repeal by the Economic Recovery Tax Act of 1981), or

"(ii) section 102(a)(2) of the Economic Recovery Tax Act of 1981.

"(2) Special rule for tax imposed by section 402(e). The tax imposed by subsection (e) of section 402 shall be treated as a tax imposed by section 1."

In 1983, P.L. 97-448, Sec. 101(a)(2), added subsec. (d).

In 1981, P.L. 97-34, Sec. 101(b)(1), amended Code Sec. 6428.

Prior to amendment, Code Sec. 6428 read as follows:

"SEC. 6428. REFUND OF 1974 INDIVIDUAL INCOME TAXES.

"(a) General rule.

"Except as otherwise provided in this section, each individual shall be treated as having made a payment against the tax imposed by chapter 1 for his first taxable year beginning in 1974 in an amount equal to 10 percent of the amount of his liability for tax for such taxable year.

"(b) Minimum payment.

"The amount treated as paid by reason of this section shall not be less than the lesser of—

"(1) the amount of the taxpayer's liability for tax for his first taxable year beginning in 1974, or

"(2) $100 ($50 in the case of a married individual filing a separate return).

"(c) Maximum payment.

"(1) In general. The amount treated as paid by reason of this section shall not exceed $200 ($100 in the case of a married individual filing a separate return).

"(2) Limitation based on adjusted gross income. The excess (if any) of—

"(A) the amount which would (but for this paragraph) be treated as paid by reason of this section, over

"(B) the applicable minimum payment provided by subsection (b),

shall be reduced (but not below zero) by an amount which bears the same ratio to such excess as the adjusted gross income for the taxable year in excess of $20,000 bears to $10,000. In the case of a married individual filing a separate return, the preceding sentence shall be applied by substituting '$10,000' for '$20,000' and by substituting '$5,000' for '$10,000'.

"(d) Liability for tax.

"For purposes of this section, the liability for tax for the taxable year shall be the sum of—

"(1) the tax imposed by chapter 1 for such year, reduced by the sum of the credits allowable under—

"(A) section 33 (relating to foreign tax credit),

"(B) section 37 (relating to retirement income),

"(C) section 38 (relating to investment in certain depreciable property),

"(D) section 40 (relating to expenses of work incentive programs), and

"(E) section 41 (relating to contributions to candidates for public office), plus

"(2) the tax on amounts described in section 3102(c) or 3202(c) which are required to be shown on the taxpayer's return of the chapter 1 tax for the taxable year.

3,733

Code Sec. 6428 — Abatements, credits, refunds

"(e) *Date payment deemed made.*

"The payment provided by this section shall be deemed made on whichever of the following dates is the later:

"(1) the date prescribed by law (determined without extensions) for filing the return of tax under chapter 1 for the taxable year, or

"(2) the date on which the taxpayer files his return of tax under chapter 1 for the taxable year.

"(f) *Joint return.*

"For purposes of this section, in the case of a joint return under section 6013 both spouses shall be treated as one individual.

"(g) *Marital status.*

"The determination of marital status for purposes of this section shall be made under section 143.

"(h) *Certain persons not eligible.*

"This section shall not apply to any estate or trust, nor shall it apply to any nonresident alien individual."

In **1975,** P.L. 94-12, Sec. 101(a), added Code Sec. 6428, effective 3/29/75.

Sec. 6429. Advance payment of portion of increased child credit for 2003.

(a) In general.

Each taxpayer who was allowed a credit under section 24 on the return for the taxpayer's first taxable year beginning in 2002 shall be treated as having made a payment against the tax imposed by chapter 1 for such taxable year in an amount equal to the child tax credit refund amount (if any) for such taxable year.

(b) Child tax credit refund amount.

For purposes of this section, the child tax credit refund amount is the amount by which the aggregate credits allowed under part IV of subchapter A of chapter 1 for such first taxable year would have been increased if—

(1) the per child amount under section 24(a)(2) for such year were $1,000,

(2) only qualifying children (as defined in section 24(c)) of the taxpayer for such year who had not attained age 17 as of December 31, 2003, were taken into account, and

(3) section 24(d)(1)(B)(ii) did not apply.

(c) Timing of payments.

In the case of any overpayment attributable to this section, the Secretary shall, subject to the provisions of this title, refund or credit such overpayment as rapidly as possible and, to the extent practicable, before October 1, 2003. No refund or credit shall be made or allowed under this section after December 31, 2003.

(d) Coordination with child tax credit.

(1) In general. The amount of credit which would (but for this subsection and section 26) be allowed under section 24 for the taxpayer's first taxable year beginning in 2003 shall be reduced (but not below zero) by the payments made to the taxpayer under this section. Any failure to so reduce the credit shall be treated as arising out of a mathematical or clerical error and assessed according to section 6213(b)(1).

(2) Joint returns. In the case of a payment under this section with respect to a joint return, half of such payment shall be treated as having been made to each individual filing such return.

(e) No interest.

No interest shall be allowed on any overpayment attributable to this section.

In **2003,** P.L. 108-27, Sec. 101(b)(1), added Code Sec. 6429, effective 5/28/2003.
—P.L. 108-27, Sec. 107, of this Act, reads as follows:

"SEC. 107. APPLICATION OF EGTRRA SUNSET TO THIS TITLE. Each amendment made by this title [Secs. 101-106] shall be subject to title IX of the Economic Growth and Tax Relief Reconciliation Act of 2001 to the same extent and in the same manner as the provision of such Act to which such amendment relates."

Sec. 6429. Repealed.

In **1988,** P.L. 100-418, Sec. 1941(b)(1), repealed Code Sec. 6429, effective for crude oil removed from the premises on or after 8/23/88.

Prior to repeal, Code Sec. 6429 read as follows:

"Sec. 6429. Credit and refund of chapter 45 taxes paid by royalty owners.

"(a) *Treatment as overpayment.*

"In the case of a qualified royalty owner, that portion of the tax imposed by section 4986 which is paid in connection with qualified royalty production removed from the premises during calendar year 1981 shall be treated as an overpayment of the tax imposed by section 4986.

"(b) *Credits and refunds.*

"(1) In general. Under regulations prescribed by the Secretary, any amount treated as an overpayment of tax under subsection (a) shall be credited against the tax imposed by section 4986 or refunded to the qualified royalty owner.

"(2) Claim for credit or refund. Any claim for credit or refund under this section shall be filed in such form and manner, and at such time, as the Secretary may prescribe by regulations.

"(c) *$2,500 limitation on credit or refund.*

"(1) In general. The aggregate amount which may be treated as an overpayment under subsection (a) with respect to any qualified royalty owner for production removed from the premises during calendar year 1981 shall not exceed $2,500.

"(2) Allocation within a family. In the case of individuals who are members of the same family (within the meaning of section 4992(e)(3)(C)) at any time during the qualified period, the $2,500 amount in paragraph (1) shall be reduced for each such individual by allocating such amount among all such individuals in proportion to their respective qualified royalty production.

"(3) Allocation between corporations and individuals.

"(A) In general. In the case of an individual who owns at any time during the calendar year stock in a qualified family farm corporation, the $2,500 amount in paragraph (1) applicable to such individual shall be reduced by the amount which bears the same ratio to the credit or refund allowable to the corporation under this section (determined after the application of paragraph (4)) as the fair market value of the shares owned by such individual during such period bears to the fair market value of all shares of the corporation.

"(B) Special rule for family members. In the case of individuals who are members of the same family (within the meaning of section 4992(e)(3)(C)) at any time during the calendar year—

"(i) for purposes of subparagraph (A), all such individuals shall be treated as 1 individual, and

"(ii) the amount allocated among such individuals under paragraph (2) shall be $2,500, reduced by the amount determined under subparagraph (A).

"(4) Allocation between corporations. If at any time after June 24, 1980, any individual owns stock in two or more qualified family farm corporations, the $2,500 amount in paragraph (1) shall be reduced for each such corporation by allocating such amount among all such corporations in proportion to their respective qualified royalty production.

"(d) *Definitions and special rules.*

"For purposes of this section—

"(1) Qualified royalty owner. The term 'qualified royalty owner' means a producer (within the meaning of section 4996(a)(1)), but only if such producer is an individual, an estate, or a qualified family farm corporation.

"(2) Qualified royalty production. The term 'qualified royalty production' means, with respect to any qualified royalty owner, taxable crude oil which is attributable to an economic interest of such royalty owner other than an operating mineral interest (within the meaning of section 614(d)). Such term does not include taxable crude oil attributable to any overriding royalty interest, production payment, net profits interest, or similar interest of the qualified royalty owner which

"(A) is created after June 9, 1981, out of an operating mineral interest in property which is proven oil or gas property (within the meaning of section 613A(c)(9)(A)) on the date such interest is created, and

"(B) is not created pursuant to a binding contract entered into prior to June 10, 1981.

"(3) Production from transferred property.

"(A) In general. In the case of a transfer of an interest in any property, the qualified royalty production of the transferee shall not include any production attributable to an interest that has been transferred after June 9, 1981, in a transfer which

"(i) is described in section 613A(c)(9)(A), and

"(ii) is not described in section 613A(c)(9)(B).

"(B) Exceptions. Subparagraph (A) shall not apply in the case of any transfer so long as the transferor and the transferee are required by paragraph (3) or (4) of subsection (c) to share the $2,500 amount in subsection (c)(1). The preceding sentence shall apply to the case of any property only if the production from the property was qualified royalty production of the transferor.

"(C) Transfers include subleases. For purposes of this paragraph, a sublease shall be treated as a transfer.

"(4) Qualified family farm corporation. The term 'qualified family farm corporation' means a corporation—

"(A) all the outstanding shares of stock of which at all times during the calendar year are held by members of the same family (within the meaning of section 2032A(e)(2)), and

"(B) 80 percent in value of the assets of which (other than royalty interests from which there is qualified royalty production determined by treating such corporation as a qualified royalty owner) are held by the corporation at all times during such calendar year for use for farming purposes (within the meaning of section 2032A(e)(5)).

"(e) Cross reference.

"For the holder of the economic interest in the case of a production payment, see section 636."

In **1983**, P.L. 97-448, Sec. 106(a)(1), deleted subpara. (d)(3)(D) ... Sec. 106(a)(3), substituted "other than royalty interests from which there is qualified royalty production determined by treating such corporation as a qualified royalty owner" for "other than royalty interests described in paragraph (2)(A)" in subpara. (d)(4)(B), effective 1/1/81.

Prior to amendment, subpara. (d)(3)(D) read as follows:

"(D) Estates. For purposes of this paragraph, property held by any estate shall be treated as owned both by such estate and proportionately by the beneficiaries of such estate."

In **1981**, P.L. 97-34, Sec. 601(a)(1), amended subsec. (a) ... Sec. 601(a)(2), amended para. (c)(1) ... Sec. 601(a)(3), substituted "$2,500" for "$1,000" and "calendar year" for "qualified period" in subsec. (c) ... Sec. 601(a)(4), amended paras. (d)(2) and (d)(3) ... Sec. 601(a)(5), amended para. (d)(4), effective 1/1/81.

Prior to amendment, subsec. (a) read as follows:

"(a) Treatment as overpayment.

"In the case of a qualified royalty owner, that portion of the tax imposed by section 4986 which is paid in connection with qualified royalty production shall be treated as an overpayment of the tax imposed by section 4986."

Prior to amendment, para. (c)(1) read as follows:

"(1) In general. The aggregate amount which may be treated as an overpayment under subsection (a) with respect to any qualified royalty owner shall not exceed $1,000."

Prior to amendment, paras. (d)(2) and (d)(3) read as follows:

"(2) Qualified royalty production. The term 'qualified royalty production' means, with respect to any qualified royalty owner, taxable crude oil which—

"(A) is attributable to an economic interest of such royalty owner other than an operating mineral interest (within the meaning of section 614(d)), and

"(B) is removed from the premises during the qualified period.

"(3) Qualified period. The term 'qualified period' means the period beginning March 1, 1980, and ending December 31, 1980."

Prior to amendment, para. (d)(4) read as follows:

"(4) Qualified family farm corporation. The term 'qualified family farm corporation' means a corporation—

"(A) which was in existence on June 25, 1980,

"(B) all of the outstanding shares of stock of which at all times after June 24, 1980, and before January 1, 1981, were held by members of the same family (within the meaning of section 2032A(e)(2)), and

"(C) 80 percent in value of the assets of which (other than royalty interests described in paragraph (2)(A)) were held by the corporation on such date for use for farming purposes (within the meaning of section 2032A(e)(5))."

In **1980**, P.L. 96-499, Sec. 1131(a)(1), added Code Sec. 6429.

Sec. 6430. Treatment of tax imposed at Leaking Underground Storage Tank Trust fund financing rate.

No refunds, credits, or payments shall be made under this subchapter for any tax imposed at the Leaking Underground Storage Tank Trust Fund financing rate, except in the case of fuels—

(1) which are exempt from tax under section 4081(a) by reason of section 4082(f)(2),

(2) which are exempt from tax under section 4041(d) by reason of the last sentence of paragraph (5) thereof, or

(3) with respect to which the rate increase under section 4081(a)(2)(B) is zero by reason of section 4082(e)(2).

In **2007**, P.L. 110-172, Sec. 6(d)(1)(C), of this Act, provides:

"(C) Notwithstanding section 6430 of the Internal Revenue Code of 1986, a refund, credit, or payment may be made under subchapter B of chapter 65 of such Code for taxes imposed with respect to any liquid after September 30, 2005, and before the date of the enactment of this Act under section 4041(d)(1) or 4042 of such Code at the Leaking Underground Storage Tank Trust Fund financing rate to the extent that tax was imposed with respect to such liquid under section 4081 at the Leaking Underground Storage Tank Trust Fund financing rate."

—P.L. 110-172, Sec. 6(d)(2)(D), amended Code Sec. 6430, effective for fuel entered, removed, or sold after 9/30/2005.

Prior to amendment, Code Sec. 6430 read as follows:

"Sec. 6430. Treatment of tax imposed at Leaking Underground Storage Tank Trust Fund financing rate.

"No refunds, credits, or payments shall be made under this subchapter for any tax imposed at the Leaking Underground Storage Tank Trust Fund financing rate, except in the case of fuels destined for export."

In **2005**, P.L. 109-58, Sec. 1362(b)(3)(A), added Code Sec. 6430, effective for fuel entered, removed, or sold after 9/30/2005.

Sec. 6430. Repealed.

In **1988**, P.L. 100-418, Sec. 1941(b)(1), repealed Code Sec. 6430, effective for crude oil removed from the premises on or after 8/23/88.

Prior to repeal, Code Sec. 6430 read as follows:

"SEC. 6430. CREDIT OR REFUND OF WINDFALL PROFIT TAXES TO CERTAIN TRUST BENEFICIARIES.

"(a) General rule.

"That portion of the tax imposed by section 4986 (relating to crude oil windfall profit tax) which is paid by any trust with respect to any qualified beneficiary's allocable trust production shall be treated as an overpayment of such tax by such qualified beneficiary. Any such overpayment shall be credited against the tax imposed by section 4986 or refunded to such qualified beneficiary.

"(b) Coordination with royalty exemption.

"(1) In general. If the aggregate amount of the allocable trust production of any qualified beneficiary for any calendar year exceeds such beneficiary's unused exempt royalty limit for such calendar year, then the amount treated as an overpayment under subsection (a) with respect to such qualified beneficiary shall be reduced by an amount which bears the same ratio to the amount which (but for this paragraph) would be so treated as—

"(A) the amount of such excess, bears to

"(B) the aggregate amount of such allocable trust production.

"(2) Unused exempt royalty limit. The unused exempt royalty limit of any qualified beneficiary for any calendar year is the excess of—

"(A) the number of days in such calendar year, multiplied by the limitation in barrels determined under the table contained in section 4994(f)(2)(A)(ii), over

"(B) the amount of exempt royalty oil (within the meaning of section 4994(f))—

"(i) with respect to which such qualified beneficiary is the producer, and

"(ii) which is removed from the premises during such calendar year.

"(3) Allocation. Rules similar to the rules of paragraphs (2), (3), and (4) of section 6429(c) shall apply to the amount determined under paragraph (2)(A).

"(c) Allocable trust production.

"For purposes of this section—

"(1) In general. The term 'allocable trust production' means, with respect to any qualified beneficiary, the qualified royalty production of any trust which—

"(A) is removed from the premises during the calendar year, and

"(B) is allocated to such qualified beneficiary under paragraph (2).

"(2) Allocation of production.

"(A) In general. The qualified royalty production of a trust for any calendar year shall be allocated between the trust and its income beneficiaries as follows:

"(i) there shall be allocated to the trust an amount of production based on the amount of any reserve for depletion for the calendar year with respect to qualified royalty production, and

"(ii) production not allocated under clause (i) shall be allocated between the trust and the income beneficiaries in accordance with their respective shares of the adjusted distributable net income for the calendar year.

"(B) Definition and special rule. For purposes of this paragraph—

"(i) Adjusted distributable net income. The term 'adjusted distributable net income' means distributable net income (as defined in section 643) for the calendar year reduced by the excess (if any) of—

"(I) any reserve for depletion for such year with respect to qualified royalty production, over

"(II) the amount allowable as a deduction for depletion to the trust for such year with respect to qualified royalty production.

"(ii) Allocation pro rata from each unit of production. Allocations under subparagraph (A) shall be treated as made pro rata from each unit of the qualified royalty production.

"(3) Production from transferred property.

"(A) In general. The allocable trust production of any qualified beneficiary shall not include any production attributable to an interest in property which has been transferred after June 9, 1981, in a transfer which—

"(i) is described in section 613A(c)(9)(A), and

"(ii) is not described in section 613A(c)(9)(B).

"(B) Exceptions. Subparagraph (A) shall not apply in the case of any transfer so long as the transferor and the qualified beneficiary are required by subsection (b)(3) to share the amount determined under subsection (b)(2)(A). The preceding sentence shall apply to the transfer of any property only if the production attributable to the property was allocable trust production or qualified royalty production of the transferor.

"(d) Definitions.

"For purposes of this section—

"(1) Qualified beneficiary. The term 'qualified beneficiary' means any individual or estate which is a beneficiary of any trust which is a producer.

"(2) Qualified royalty production. The term 'qualified royalty production' means, with respect to any person, taxable crude oil (within the meaning of section 4991(a)) which is attributable to an economic interest of such person other than an operating mineral interest (within the meaning of section 614(d)). Such term does not include taxable crude oil attributable to any overriding royalty interest, production payment, net profits interest, or similar interest of the person which—

"(A) is created after June 9, 1981, out of an operating mineral interest in property which is proven oil or gas property (within the meaning of section 613A(c)(9)(A)) on the date such interest is created, and

"(B) is not created pursuant to a binding contract entered into before June 10, 1981.

Code Sec. 6430

"(3) Producer. The term 'producer' has the meaning given to such term by section 4996(a)(1).
"(e) Regulations.
"The Secretary shall prescribe such regulations as may be necessary or appropriate to carry out the purposes of this section."
In 1983, P.L. 97-448, Sec. 106(a)(4)(A), added Code Sec. 6430, effective for calendar years begin. after 12/31/81.

Sec. 6431. Credit for qualified bonds allowed to issuer.
(a) In general.
In the case of a qualified bond issued before January 1, 2011, the issuer of such bond shall be allowed a credit with respect to each interest payment under such bond which shall be payable by the Secretary as provided in subsection (b).
(b) Payment of credit.
The Secretary shall pay (contemporaneously with each interest payment date under such bond) to the issuer of such bond (or to any person who makes such interest payments on behalf of the issuer) 35 percent of the interest payable under such bond on such date.
(c) Application of arbitrage rules.
For purposes of section 148, the yield on a qualified bond shall be reduced by the credit allowed under this section.
(d) Interest payment date.
For purposes of this subsection, the term "interest payment date" means each date on which interest is payable by the issuer under the terms of the bond.
(e) Qualified bond.
For purposes of this subsection, the term "qualified bond" has the meaning given such term in section 54AA(g).
(f) Application of section to certain qualified tax credit bonds.
　(1) **In general.** In the case of any specified tax credit bond—
　　(A) such bond shall be treated as a qualified bond for purposes of this section,
　　(B) subsection (a) shall be applied without regard to the requirement that the qualified bond be issued before January 1, 2011,
　　(C) the amount of the payment determined under subsection (b) with respect to any interest payment due under such bond shall be equal to the lesser of—
　　　(i) the amount of interest payable under such bond on such date, or
　　　(ii) the amount of interest which would have been payable under such bond on such date if such interest were determined at the applicable credit rate determined under section 54A(b)(3),
　　(D) interest on any such bond shall be includible in gross income for purposes of this title,
　　(E) no credit shall be allowed under section 54A with respect to such bond,
　　(F) any payment made under subsection (b) shall not be includible as income for purposes of this title, and
　　(G) the deduction otherwise allowed under this title to the issuer of such bond with respect to interest paid under such bond shall be reduced by the amount of the payment made under this section with respect to such interest.
　(2) **Special rule for new clean renewable energy bonds and qualified energy conservation bonds.** In the case of any specified tax credit bond described in clause (i) or (ii) of paragraph (3)(A), the amount determined under paragraph (1)(C)(ii) shall be 70 percent of the amount so determined without regard to this paragraph and sections 54C(b) and 54D(b).

　(3) **Specified tax credit bond.** For purposes of this subsection, the term "specified tax credit bond" means any qualified tax credit bond (as defined in section 54A(d)) if—
　　(A) such bond is—
　　　(i) a new clean renewable energy bond (as defined in section 54C),
　　　(ii) a qualified energy conservation bond (as defined in section 54D),
　　　(iii) a qualified zone academy bond (as defined in section 54E) determined without regard to any allocation relating to the national zone academy bond limitation for 2011 or any carryforward of such allocation, or
　　　(iv) a qualified school construction bond (as defined in section 54F), and
　　(B) the issuer of such bond makes an irrevocable election to have this subsection apply.

In 2010, P.L. 111-312, Sec. 758(b), added "determined without regard to any allocation relating to the national zone academy bond limitation for 2011 or any carryforward of such allocation" after "54E)" in subpara. (f)(3)(A)(iii), effective for obligations issued after 12/31/2010.
—P.L. 111-147, Sec. 301(a), added subsec. (f), effective for bonds issued after 3/18/2010.
In 2009, P.L. 111-5, Sec. 1531(b), added Code Sec. 6431, effective for obligations issued after 2/17/2009.

Sec. 6432. COBRA premium assistance.
(a) In general.
The person to whom premiums are payable under COBRA continuation coverage shall be reimbursed as provided in subsection (c) for the amount of premiums not paid by assistance eligible individuals by reason of section 3001(a) of title III of division B of the American Recovery and Reinvestment Act of 2009.
(b) Person entitled to reimbursement.
For purposes of subsection (a), except as otherwise provided by the Secretary, the person to whom premiums are payable under COBRA continuation coverage shall be treated as being—
　(1) in the case of any group health plan which is a multiemployer plan (as defined in section 3(37) of the Employee Retirement Income Security Act of 1974), the plan,
　(2) in the case of any group health plan not described in paragraph (1)—
　　(A) which is subject to the COBRA continuation provisions contained in—
　　　(i) the Internal Revenue Code of 1986,
　　　(ii) the Employee Retirement Income Security Act of 1974,
　　　(iii) the Public Health Service Act, or
　　　(iv) title 5, United States Code, or
　　(B) under which some or all of the coverage is not provided by insurance, the employer maintaining the plan, and
　(3) in the case of any group health plan not described in paragraph (1) or (2), the insurer providing the coverage under the group health plan.
(c) Method of reimbursement.
Except as otherwise provided by the Secretary—
　(1) **Treatment as payment of payroll taxes.** Each person entitled to reimbursement under subsection (a) (and filing a claim for such reimbursement at such time and in such manner as the Secretary may require) shall be treated for purposes of this title and section 1324(b)(2) of title 31, United States Code, as having paid to the Secretary, on the date that the assistance eligible individual's premium

Abatements, credits, refunds   **Code Sec. 6432**

payment is received, payroll taxes in an amount equal to the portion of such reimbursement which relates to such premium. To the extent that the amount treated as paid under the preceding sentence exceeds the amount of such person's liability for such taxes, the Secretary shall credit or refund such excess in the same manner as if it were an overpayment of such taxes.

(2) Overstatements. Any overstatement of the reimbursement to which a person is entitled under this section (and any amount paid by the Secretary as a result of such overstatement) shall be treated as an underpayment of payroll taxes by such person and may be assessed and collected by the Secretary in the same manner as payroll taxes.

(3) Reimbursement contingent on payment of remaining premium. No reimbursement may be made under this section to a person with respect to any assistance eligible individual until after the reduced premium required under section 3001(a)(1)(A) of title III of division B of the American Recovery and Reinvestment Act of 2009.

(d) Definitions.

For purposes of this section—

(1) Payroll taxes. The term "payroll taxes" means—

(A) amounts required to be deducted and withheld for the payroll period under section 3402 (relating to wage withholding),

(B) amounts required to be deducted for the payroll period under section 3102 (relating to FICA employee taxes), and

(C) amounts of the taxes imposed for the payroll period under section 3111 (relating to FICA employer taxes).

(2) Person. The term "person" includes any governmental entity.

(e) Employer Determination of Qualifying Event as Involuntary Termination

For purposes of this section, in any case in which--

(1) based on a reasonable interpretation of section 3001(a)(3)(C) of division B of the American Recovery and Reinvestment Act of 2009 and administrative guidance thereunder, an employer determines that the qualifying event with respect to COBRA continuation coverage for an individual was involuntary termination of a covered employee's employment, and

(2) the employer maintains supporting documentation of the determination, including an attestation by the employer of involuntary termination with respect to the covered employee,

the qualifying event for the individual shall be deemed to be involuntary termination of the covered employee's employment.

(f) Reporting.

Each person entitled to reimbursement under subsection (a) for any period shall submit such reports (at such time and in such manner as the Secretary may require, including—

(1) an attestation of involuntary termination of employment for each covered employee on the basis of whose termination entitlement to reimbursement is claimed under subsection (a),

(2) a report of the amount of payroll taxes offset under subsection (a) for the reporting period and the estimated offsets of such taxes for the subsequent reporting period in connection with reimbursements under subsection (a), and

(3) a report containing the TINs of all covered employees, the amount of subsidy reimbursed with respect to each covered employee and qualified beneficiaries, and a designation with respect to each covered employee as to whether the subsidy reimbursement is for coverage of 1 individual or 2 or more individuals.

(g) Regulations.

The Secretary shall issue such regulations or other guidance as may be necessary or appropriate to carry out this section, including—

(1) the requirement to report information or the establishment of other methods for verifying the correct amounts of reimbursements under this section, and

(2) the application of this section to group health plans that are multiemployer plans (as defined in section 3(37) of the Employee Retirement Income Security Act of 1974).

In 2010, P.L. 111-157, Sec. 3(a), substituted "May 31, 2010" for "March 31, 2010" in Sec. 3001(a)(3)(A), Div B of P.L. 111-5 [see below]; . . . Sec. 3(b), added para. (18) to Sec. 3001(a), Div B of P.L. 111-5 [see below];
—P.L. 111-144, Sec. 3(a), substituted "March 31, 2010" for "February 28, 2010" in Sec. 3001(a)(3)(A) DivB of P.L. 111-5 [see below]; . . . Sec. 3(b)(1)(A), added "or consists of a reduction of hours followed by such an involuntary termination of employment during such period (as described in paragraph (17)(C))" before the period at the end of Sec. 3001(a)(3)(C) DivB of P.L. 111-5 [see below]; . . . Sec. 3(b)(1)(B), added para. (17) to Sec. 3001(a) DivB of P.L. 111-5 [see below]; . . . Sec. 3(b)(2)(A), amended clause (ii) of Sec. 3001(a)(16)(A) DivB of P.L. 111-5 [see below]; . . . Sec. 3(b)(2)(B), amended subcl. (I) of Sec. 3001(a)(16)(C)(i) DivB of P.L. 111-5 [see below];
Prior to amendment, Sec. 3001(a)(16)(A)(ii) of P.L. 111-5 [see below], read as follows:
"(ii) such individual pays, not later than 60 days after the date of the enactment of this paragraph (or, if later, 30 days after the date of provision of the notification required under subparagraph (D)(ii)), the amount of such premium, after the application of paragraph (1)(A)."
Prior to amendment, Sec. 3001(a)(16)(C)(i)(I) of P.L. 111-5 [see below], read as follows:
"(I) such period begins before the date of the enactment of this paragraph, and"
—P.L. 111-144, Sec. 3(b)(3), deleted "of the first month" after "15 months after the first day" in Sec. 3001(a)(2)(A)(ii)(I) DivB of P.L. 111-5 [see below]; . . . Sec. 3(b)(4), added the last 2 sentences at the end of Sec. 3001(a)(5) DivB of P.L. 111-5 [see below];
—P.L. 111-144, Sec. 3(b)(5)(C)(i), substituted "section 3001(a) of title III of division B of the American Recovery and Reinvestment Act of 2009" for "section 3002(a) of the Health Insurance Assistance for the Unemployed Act of 2009" in subsec. (a); . . . Sec. 3(b)(5)(C)(ii), substituted "section 3001(a) of title III of division B of the American Recovery and Reinvestment Act of 2009" for "section 3002(a) of the Health Insurance Assistance for the Unemployed Act of 2009" in para. (c)(3); . . . Sec. 3(b)(5)(C)(iii), added subsec. (e), redesignated subsec. (e) as subsec. (f), and redesignated subsec. (f) as subsec. (g) effective or tax. yrs. end. after 02/17/2009.
—P.L. 111-144, Sec. 3(c), of this Act, reads as follows:
"(c) Effective Date. The amendments made by this section shall take effect as if included in the provisions of section 3001 of division B of the American Recovery and Reinvestment Act of 2009 [P.L. 111-5, see below] to which they relate, except that—
"(1) the amendments made by subsection (b)(1) shall apply to periods of coverage beginning after the date of the enactment of this Act [3/3/2010];
"(2) the amendments made by subsection (b)(2) shall take effect as if included in the amendments made by section 1010 of division B of the Department of Defense Appropriations Act, 2010 [P.L. 111-118, see below]; and
"(3) the amendments made by subsections (b)(3) and (b)(4) shall take effect on the date of the enactment of this Act [3/3/2010]."
In 2009, P.L. 111-118, Sec. 1010(a)DivB, substituted "February 28, 2010" for "December 31, 2009" in Sec. 3001(a)(3)(A) of P.L. 111-5 [see below] . . . Sec. 1010(b)DivB, substituted "15 months" for "9 months" in Sec. 3001(a)(2)(A)(ii)(I) of P.L. 111-5 [see below] . . . Sec. 1010(c)DivB, added para. (a)(16) to Sec. 3001 of P.L. 111-5 [see below] . . . Sec. 1010(d)(1)(A)DivB, substituted "such qualified beneficiary is eligible for COBRA continuation coverage related to a qualifying event occurring;" for "at any time" in Sec. 3001(a)(3)(A) of P.L. 111-5 [see below] . . . Sec. 1010(d)(1)(B)DivB, deleted ", such qualified beneficiary is eligible for COBRA continuation coverage" before the comma at the end of Sec. 3001(a)(3)(A) of P.L. 111-5 [see below] . . . Sec. 1010(d)(2)DivB, substituted "have a qualifying event relating to COBRA continuation coverage" for "become entitled to elect COBRA continuation coverage" in Sec. 3001(a)(7)(A)(i) of P.L. 111-5 [see below], effective for premiums to which Sec. 3001(a)(1)(A) [of P.L. 111-5, see below] applies.
—P.L. 111-5, Sec. 3001(a)(12)(A), added Code Sec. 6432, effective for premiums to which subsec. (a)(1)(A) [of Sec. 3001 of this Act, see below] applies. Sec. 3001(a) of this Act [as amended by Sec. 1010(a)-(d) Div B, of P.L. 111-118, Sec. 3(a)-(b)(4) of P.L. 111-144, and Sec. 3(a) of P.L. 111-157, see above], reads as follows:
"Sec. 3001. Premium assistance for COBRA benefits.
"(a) Premium assistance for COBRA continuation coverage for individuals and their families.
"(1) Provision of premium assistance.

3,737

"(A) Reduction of premiums payable. In the case of any premium for a period of coverage beginning on or after the date of the enactment of this Act [2/17/2009] for COBRA continuation coverage with respect to any assistance eligible individual, such individual shall be treated for purposes of any COBRA continuation provision as having paid the amount of such premium if such individual pays (or a person other than such individual's employer pays on behalf of such individual) 35 percent of the amount of such premium (as determined without regard to this subsection)."

"(B) Plan enrollment option.

"(i) In general. Notwithstanding the COBRA continuation provisions, an assistance eligible individual may, not later than 90 days after the date of notice of the plan enrollment option described in this subparagraph, elect to enroll in coverage under a plan offered by the employer involved, or the employee organization involved (including, for this purpose, a joint board of trustees of a multiemployer trust affiliated with one or more multiemployer plans), that is different than coverage under the plan in which such individual was enrolled at the time the qualifying event occurred, and such coverage shall be treated as COBRA continuation coverage for purposes of the applicable COBRA continuation coverage provision.

"(ii) Requirements. An assistance eligible individual may elect to enroll in different coverage as described in clause (i) only if—

"(I) the employer involved has made a determination that such employer will permit assistance eligible individuals to enroll in different coverage as provided for this subparagraph;

"(II) the premium for such different coverage does not exceed the premium for coverage in which the individual was enrolled at the time the qualifying event occurred;

"(III) the different coverage in which the individual elects to enroll is coverage that is also offered to the active employees of the employer at the time at which such election is made; and

"(IV) the different coverage is not— (aa) coverage that provides only dental, vision, counseling, or referral services (or a combination of such services);

"(bb) a flexible spending arrangement (as defined in section 106(c)(2) of the Internal Revenue Code of 1986); or

"(cc) coverage that provides coverage for services or treatments furnished in an on-site medical facility maintained by the employer and that consists primarily of first-aid services, prevention and wellness care, or similar care (or a combination of such care).

"(C) Premium reimbursement. For provisions providing the balance of such premium, see section 6432 of the Internal Revenue Code of 1986, as added by paragraph (12).

"(2) Limitation of period of premium assistance.

"(A) In general. Paragraph (1)(A) shall not apply with respect to any assistance eligible individual for months of coverage beginning on or after the earlier of—

"(i) the first date that such individual is eligible for coverage under any other group health plan (other than coverage consisting of only dental, vision, counseling, or referral services (or a combination thereof), coverage under a flexible spending arrangement (as defined in section 106(c)(2) of the Internal Revenue Code of 1986), or coverage of treatment that is furnished in an on-site medical facility maintained by the employer and that consists primarily of first-aid services, prevention and wellness care, or similar care (or a combination thereof)) or is eligible for benefits under title XVIII of the Social Security Act, or

"(ii) the earliest of—

"(I) the date which is 15 months after the first day that paragraph (1)(A) applies with respect to such individual,

"(II) the date following the expiration of the maximum period of continuation coverage required under the applicable COBRA continuation coverage provision, or

"(III) the date following the expiration of the period of continuation coverage allowed under paragraph (4)(B)(ii).

"(B) Timing of eligibility for additional coverage. For purposes of subparagraph (A)(i), an individual shall not be treated as eligible for coverage under a group health plan before the first date on which such individual could be covered under such plan.

"(C) Notification requirement. An assistance eligible individual shall notify in writing the group health plan with respect to which paragraph (1)(A) applies if such paragraph ceases to apply by reason of subparagraph (A)(i). Such notice shall be provided to the group health plan in such time and manner as may be specified by the Secretary of Labor.

"(3) Assistance eligible individual. For purposes of this section, the term 'Assistance eligible individual' means any qualified beneficiary if—

"(A) such qualified beneficiary is eligible for COBRA continuation coverage related to a qualifying event occurring during the period that begins with September 1, 2008, and ends with May 31, 2010,

"(B) such qualified beneficiary elects such coverage, and

"(C) the qualifying event with respect to the COBRA continuation coverage consists of the involuntary termination of the covered employee's employment and occurred during such period or consists of a reduction of hours followed by such an involuntary termination of employment during such period (as described in paragraph (17)(C)).

"(4) Extension of election period and effect on coverage.

"(A) In general. For purposes of applying section 605(a) of the Employee Retirement Income Security Act of 1974, section 4980B(f)(5)(A) of the Internal Revenue Code of 1986, section 2205(a) of the Public Health Service Act, and section 8905a(c)(2) of title 5, United States Code, in the case of an individual who does not have an election of COBRA continuation coverage in effect on the date of the enactment of this Act [2/17/2009] but who would be an assistance eligible individual if such election were so in effect, such individual may elect the COBRA continuation coverage under the COBRA continuation coverage provisions containing such sections during the period beginning on the date of the enactment of this Act [2/17/2009] and ending 60 days after the date on which the notification required under paragraph (7)(C) is provided to such individual.

"(B) Commencement of coverage; no reach-back. Any COBRA continuation coverage elected by a qualified beneficiary during an extended election period under subparagraph (A)—

"(i) shall commence with the first period of coverage beginning on or after the date of the enactment of this Act [2/17/2009], and

"(ii) shall not extend beyond the period of COBRA continuation coverage that would have been required under the applicable COBRA continuation coverage provision if the coverage had been elected as required under such provision.

"(C) Preexisting conditions. With respect to a qualified beneficiary who elects COBRA continuation coverage pursuant to subparagraph (A), the period—

"(i) beginning on the date of the qualifying event, and

"(ii) ending with the beginning of the period described in subparagraph (B)(i), shall be disregarded for purposes of determining the 63-day periods referred to in section 701(c)(2) of the Employee Retirement Income Security Act of 1974, section 9801(c)(2) of the Internal Revenue Code of 1986, and section 2701(c)(2) of the Public Health Service Act.

"(5) Expedited review of denials of premium assistance. In any case in which an individual requests treatment as an assistance eligible individual and is denied such treatment by the group health plan, the Secretary of Labor (or the Secretary of Health and Human Services in connection with COBRA continuation coverage which is provided other than pursuant to part 6 of subtitle B of title I of the Employee Retirement Income Security Act of 1974), in consultation with the Secretary of the Treasury, shall provide for expedited review of such denial. An individual shall be entitled to such review upon application to such Secretary in such form and manner as shall be provided by such Secretary. Such Secretary shall make a determination regarding such individual's eligibility within 15 business days after receipt of such individual's application for review under this paragraph. Either Secretary's determination upon review of the denial shall be de novo and shall be the final determination of such Secretary. A reviewing court shall grant deference to such Secretary's determination. The provisions of this paragraph, paragraphs (1) through (4), and paragraph (7) shall be treated as provisions of title I of the Employee Retirement Income Security Act of 1974 for purposes of part 5 of subtitle B of such title. In addition to civil actions that may be brought to enforce applicable provisions of such Act or other laws, the appropriate Secretary or an affected individual may bring a civil action to enforce such determinations and for appropriate relief. In addition, such Secretary may assess a penalty against a plan sponsor or health insurance issuer of not more than $110 per day for each failure to comply with such determination of such Secretary after 10 days after the date of the plan sponsor's or issuer's receipt of the determination.

"(6) Disregard of subsidies for purposes of federal and state programs. Notwithstanding any other provision of law, any premium reduction with respect to an assistance eligible individual under this subsection shall not be considered income or resources in determining eligibility for, or the amount of assistance or benefits provided under, any other public benefit provided under Federal law or the law of any State or political subdivision thereof.

"(7) Notices to individuals.

"(A) General notice.

"(i) In general. In the case of notices provided under section 606(a)(4) of the Employee Retirement Income Security Act of 1974 (29 U.S.C. 1166(4)), section 4980B(f)(6)(D) of the Internal Revenue Code of 1986, section 2206(4) of the Public Health Service Act (42 U.S.C. 300bb-6(4)), or section 8905a(f)(2)(A) of title 5, United States Code, with respect to individuals who, during the period described in paragraph (3)(A), have a qualifying event relating to COBRA continuation coverage, the requirements of such sections shall not be treated as met unless such notices include an additional notification to the recipient of—

"(I) the availability of premium reduction with respect to such coverage under this subsection, and

"(II) the option to enroll in different coverage if the employer permits assistance eligible individuals to elect enrollment in different coverage (as described in paragraph (1)(B)).

"(ii) Alternative notice. In the case of COBRA continuation coverage to which the notice provision under such sections does not apply, the Secretary of Labor, in consultation with the Secretary of the Treasury and the Secretary of Health and Human Services, shall, in consultation with administrators of the group health plans (or other entities) that provide or administer the COBRA continuation coverage involved, provide rules requiring the provision of such notice.

"(iii) Form. The requirement of the additional notification under this subparagraph may be met by amendment of existing notice forms or by inclusion of a separate document with the notice otherwise required.

"(B) Specific requirements. Each additional notification under subparagraph (A) shall include—

"(i) the forms necessary for establishing eligibility for premium reduction under this subsection,

"(ii) the name, address, and telephone number necessary to contact the plan administrator and any other person maintaining relevant information in connection with such premium reduction,

"(iii) a description of the extended election period provided for in paragraph (4)(A),

"(iv) a description of the obligation of the qualified beneficiary under paragraph (2)(C) to notify the plan providing continuation coverage of eligibility for subsequent coverage under another group health plan or eligibility for benefits under title XVIII of the Social Security Act and the penalty provided under section 6720C of the Internal Revenue Code of 1986 for failure to so notify the plan, "(v) a description, displayed in a prominent manner, of the qualified beneficiary's right to a reduced premium and any conditions on entitlement to the reduced premium, and

"(vi) a description of the option of the qualified beneficiary to enroll in different coverage if the employer permits such beneficiary to elect to enroll in such different coverage under paragraph (1)(B).

"(C) Notice in connection with extended election periods. In the case of any assistance eligible individual (or any individual described in paragraph (4)(A)) who became entitled to elect COBRA continuation coverage before the date of the enactment of this Act [2/17/2009], the administrator of the group health plan (or other entity) involved shall provide (within 60 days after the date of enactment of this Act) for the additional notification required to be provided under subparagraph (A) and failure to provide such notice shall be treated as a failure to meet the notice requirements under the applicable COBRA continuation provision.

"(D) Model notices. Not later than 30 days after the date of enactment of this Act—

"(i) the Secretary of the Labor, in consultation with the Secretary of the Treasury and the Secretary of Health and Human Services, shall prescribe models for the additional notification required under this paragraph (other than the additional notification described in clause (ii)), and

"(ii) in the case of any additional notification provided pursuant to subparagraph (A) under section 8905a(f)(2)(A) of title 5, United States Code, the Office of Personnel Management shall prescribe a model for such additional notification.

"(8) Regulations. The Secretary of the Treasury may prescribe such regulations or other guidance as may be necessary or appropriate to carry out the provisions of this subsection, including the prevention of fraud and abuse under this subsection, except that the Secretary of Labor and the Secretary of Health and Human Services may prescribe such regulations (including interim final regulations) or other guidance as may be necessary or appropriate to carry out the provisions of paragraphs (5), (7), and (9).

"(9) Outreach. The Secretary of Labor, in consultation with the Secretary of the Treasury and the Secretary of Health and Human Services, shall provide outreach consisting of public education and enrollment assistance relating to premium reduction provided under this subsection. Such outreach shall target employers, group health plan administrators, public assistance programs, States, insurers, and other entities as determined appropriate by such Secretaries. Such outreach shall include an initial focus on those individuals electing continuation coverage who are referred to in paragraph (7)(C). Information on such premium reduction, including enrollment, shall also be made available on websites of the Departments of Labor, Treasury, and Health and Human Services.

"(10) Definitions. For purposes of this section—

"(A) Administrator. The term 'administrator' has the meaning given such term in section 3(16)(A) of the Employee Retirement Income Security Act of 1974.

"(B) COBRA continuation coverage. The term 'COBRA continuation coverage' means continuation coverage provided pursuant to part 6 of subtitle B of title I of the Employee Retirement Income Security Act of 1974 (other than under section 609), title XXII of the Public Health Service Act, section 4980B of the Internal Revenue Code of 1986 (other than subsection (f)(1) of such section insofar as it relates to pediatric vaccines), or section 8905a of title 5, United States Code, or under a State program that provides comparable continuation coverage. Such term does not include coverage under a health flexible spending arrangement under a cafeteria plan within the meaning of section 125 of the Internal Revenue Code of 1986.

"(C) COBRA continuation provision. The term 'COBRA continuation provision' means the provisions of law described in subparagraph (B).

"(D) Covered employee. The term 'covered employee' has the meaning given such term in section 607(2) of the Employee Retirement Income Security Act of 1974.

"(E) Qualified beneficiary. The term 'qualified beneficiary' has the meaning given such term in section 607(3) of the Employee Retirement Income Security Act of 1974.

"(F) Group health plan. The term 'group health plan' has the meaning given such term in section 607(1) of the Employee Retirement Income Security Act of 1974.

"(G) State. The term 'State' includes the District of Columbia, the Commonwealth of Puerto Rico, the Virgin Islands, Guam, American Samoa, and the Commonwealth of the Northern Mariana Islands.

"(H) Period of coverage. Any reference in this subsection to a period of coverage shall be treated as a reference to a monthly or shorter period of coverage with respect to which premiums are charged with respect to such coverage.

"(11) Reports.

"(A) Interim report. The Secretary of the Treasury shall submit an interim report to the Committee on Education and Labor, the Committee on Ways and Means, and the Committee on Energy and Commerce of the House of Representatives and the Committee on Health, Education, Labor, and Pensions and the Committee on Finance of the Senate regarding the premium reduction provided under this subsection that includes—

"(i) the number of individuals provided such assistance as of the date of the report; and

"(ii) the total amount of expenditures incurred (with administrative expenditures noted separately) in connection with such assistance as of the date of the report.

"(B) Final report. As soon as practicable after the last period of COBRA continuation coverage for which premium reduction is provided under this section, the Secretary of the Treasury shall submit a final report to each Committee referred to in subparagraph (A) that includes—

"(i) the number of individuals provided premium reduction under this section;

"(ii) the average dollar amount (monthly and annually) of premium reductions provided to such individuals; and

"(iii) the total amount of expenditures incurred (with administrative expenditures noted separately) in connection with premium reduction under this section."
—P.L. 111-5, Sec. 3001(a)(12)(B), of this Act, provides:

"(B) Social security trust funds held harmless. In determining any amount transferred or appropriated to any fund under the Social Security Act, section 6432 of the Internal Revenue Code of 1986 shall not be taken into account."
—P.L. 111-5, Sec. 3001(a)(12)(E), of this Act, provides:

"(E) Special rule.

"(i) In general. In the case of an assistance eligible individual who pays, with respect to the first period of COBRA continuation coverage to which subsection (a)(1)(A) applies or the immediately subsequent period, the full premium amount for such coverage, the person to whom such payment is payable shall—

"(I) make a reimbursement payment to such individual for the amount of such premium paid in excess of the amount required to be paid under subsection (a)(1)(A); or

"(II) provide credit to the individual for such amount in a manner that reduces one or more subsequent premium payments that the individual is required to pay under such subsection for the coverage involved.

"(ii) Reimbursing employer. A person to which clause (i) applies shall be reimbursed as provided for in section 6432 of the Internal Revenue Code of 1986 for any payment made, or credit provided, to the employee under such clause.

"(iii) Payment of credits. Unless it is reasonable to believe that the credit for the excess payment in clause (i)(II) will be used by the assistance eligible individual within 180 days of the date on which the person receives from the individual the payment of the full premium amount, a person to which clause (i) applies shall make the payment required under such clause to the individual within 60 days of such payment of the full premium amount. If, as of any day within the 180-day period, it is no longer reasonable to believe that the credit will be used during that period, payment equal to the remainder of the credit outstanding shall be made to the individual within 60 days of such day."
—P.L. 111-5, Sec. 3001(a)(16), of this Act [as added by Sec. 1010(c) Div B, of P.L. 111-118, and as amended by Sec. 3(b)(2)(A)-(B) Div B, of P.L. 111-144, see above], provides:

"(16) Rules related to 2009 extension.

"(A) Election to pay premiums retroactively and maintain COBRA coverage. In the case of any premium for a period of coverage during an assistance eligible individual's transition period, such individual shall be treated for purposes of any COBRA continuation provision as having timely paid the amount of such premium if—

"(i) such individual was covered under the COBRA continuation coverage to which such premium relates for the period of coverage immediately preceding such transition period, and

"(ii) such individual pays, the amount of such premium, after the application of paragraph (1)(A), by the latest of—

"(I) 60 days after the date of the enactment of this paragraph,

"(II) 30 days after the date of provision of the notification required under subparagraph (D)(ii), or

"(III) the end of the period described in section 4980B(f)(2)(B)(iii) of the Internal Revenue Code of 1986.

"(B) Refunds and credits for retroactive premium assistance eligibility. In the case of an assistance eligible individual who pays, with respect to any period of COBRA continuation coverage during such individual's transition period, the premium amount for such coverage without regard to paragraph (1)(A), rules similar to the rules of paragraph (12)(E) shall apply.

"(C) Transition period.

"(i) In general. For purposes of this paragraph, the term 'transition period' means, with respect to any assistance eligible individual, any period of coverage if—

"(I) such assistance eligible individual experienced an involuntary termination that was a qualifying event prior to the date of enactment of the Department of Defense Appropriations Act, 2010; and

"(II) paragraph (1)(A) applies to such period by reason of the amendment made by section 1010(b) of the Department of Defense Appropriations Act, 2010.

"(ii) Construction. Any period during the period described in subclauses (I) and (II) of clause (i) for which the applicable premium has been paid pursuant to subparagraph (A) shall be treated as a period of coverage referred to in such paragraph, irrespective of any failure to timely pay the applicable premium (other than pursuant to subparagraph (A)) for such period.

"(D) Notification.

"(i) In general. In the case of an individual who was an assistance eligible individual at any time on or after October 31, 2009, or experiences a qualifying event (consisting of termination of employment) relating to COBRA continuation coverage on or after such date, the administrator of the group health plan (or other entity) involved shall provide an additional notification with information regarding the amendments made by section 1010 of the Department of Defense Appropriations Act, 2010, within 60 days after the date of the enactment of such Act or, in the case of a qualifying event occurring after such date of enactment, consistent with the timing of notifications under paragraph (7)(A).

"(ii) To individuals who lost assistance. In the case of an assistance eligible individual described in subparagraph (A)(i) who did not timely pay the premium for any period of coverage during such individual's transition period or paid the premium for such period without regard to paragraph (1)(A), the administrator of the group health plan (or other entity) involved shall provide to such individual, within the first 60 days of such individual's transition period, an additional notification with information regarding the amendments made by section 1010 of the Department of Defense Appropriations Act, 2010, including information on the ability under subparagraph (A) to make retroactive premium payments with respect to the transition period of the individual in order to maintain COBRA continuation coverage.

"(iii) Application of rules. Rules similar to the rules of paragraph (7) shall apply with respect to notifications under this subparagraph."

—P.L. 111-5, Sec. 3001(a)(17), of this Act [as added by Sec. 3(b)(1)(B) Div B, of P.L. 111-144, see above], provides:

"(17) Special rules in case of individuals losing coverage because of a reduction of hours.

"(A) New election period.

"(i) In general. For the purposes of the COBRA continuation provisions, in the case of an individual described in subparagraph (C) who did not make (or who made and discontinued) an election of COBRA continuation coverage on the basis of the reduction of hours of employment, the involuntary termination of employment of such individual on or after the date of the enactment of this paragraph shall be treated as a qualifying event.

"(ii) Counting COBRA Duration period from previous qualifying event. In any case of an individual referred to in clause (i), the period of such individual's continuation coverage shall be determined as though the qualifying event were the reduction of hours of employment.

"(iii) Construction. Nothing in this paragraph shall be construed as requiring an individual referred to in clause (i) to make a payment for COBRA continuation coverage between the reduction of hours and the involuntary termination of employment.

"(iv) Preexisting conditions. With respect to an individual referred to in clause (i) who elects COBRA continuation coverage pursuant to such clause, rules similar to the rules in paragraph (4)(C) shall apply.

"(B) Notices. In the case of an individual described in subparagraph (C), the administrator of the group health plan (or other entity) involved shall provide, during the 60-day period beginning on the date of such individual's involuntary termination of employment, an additional notification described in paragraph (7)(A), including information on the provisions of this paragraph. Rules similar to the rules of paragraph (7) shall apply with respect to such notification.

"(C) Individuals described. Individuals described in this subparagraph are individuals who are assistance eligible individuals on the basis of a qualifying event consisting of a reduction of hours occurring during the period described in paragraph (3)(A) followed by an involuntary termination of employment insofar as such involuntary termination of employment occurred on or after the date of the enactment of this paragraph."

—P.L. 111-5, Sec. 3001(a)(18), of this Act [as added by Sec. 3(b) of P.L. 111-157, see above], provides:

"(18) Rules related to April and May 2010 extension. In the case of an individual who, with regard to coverage described in paragraph (10)(B), experiences a qualifying event related to a termination of employment on or after April 1, 2010 and prior to the date of the enactment of this paragraph, rules similar to those in paragraphs (4)(A) and (7)(C) shall apply with respect to all continuation coverage, including State continuation coverage programs."

CHAPTER 66.—LIMITATIONS

Subchapter
A. Limitations on assessment and collection.
B. Limitations on credit or refund.
C. Mitigation of effect of period of limitations.
D. Periods of limitation in judicial proceedings.

Subchapter A.—Limitations on Assessment and Collection

Sec.
6501. Limitations on assessment and collection.
6502. Collection after assessment.
6503. Suspension of running of period of limitation.
6504. Cross references.

Sec. 6501. Limitations on assessment and collection.
(a) General rule.

Except as otherwise provided in this section, the amount of any tax imposed by this title shall be assessed within 3 years after the return was filed (whether or not such return was filed on or after the date prescribed) or, if the tax is payable by stamp, at any time after such tax became due and before the expiration of 3 years after the date on which any part of such tax was paid, and no proceeding in court without assessment for the collection of such tax shall be begun after the expiration of such period. For purposes of this chapter, the term "return" means the return required to be filed by the taxpayer (and does not include a return of any person from whom the taxpayer has received an item of income, gain, loss, deduction, or credit).

(b) Time return deemed filed.

• *Caution:* Sec. 6501(b)(1)-(2), following, is effective for payments made before 1/1/2013. For sec. 6501(b)(1)-(2), effective for payments made after 12/31/2012, see below.

(1) Early return. For purposes of this section, a return of tax imposed by this title, except tax imposed by chapter 3, 21, or 24, filed before the last day prescribed by law or by regulations promulgated pursuant to law for the filing thereof, shall be considered as filed on such last day.

(2) Return of certain employment taxes and tax imposed by chapter 3. For purposes of this section, if a return of tax imposed by chapter 3, 21, or 24 for any period ending with or within a calendar year is filed before April 15 of the succeeding calendar year, such return shall be considered filed on April 15 of such calendar year.

• *Caution:* Sec. 6501(b)(1)-(2), following, is effective for payments made after 12/31/2012. For sec. 6501(b)(1)-(2), effective for payments made before 1/1/2013, see above.

(1) Early return. For purposes of this section, a return of tax imposed by this title, except tax imposed by chapter 3, 4, 21, or 24, filed before the last day prescribed by law or by regulations promulgated pursuant to law for the filing thereof, shall be considered as filed on such last day.

(2) Return of certain employment and withholding taxes. For purposes of this section, if a return of tax imposed by chapter 3, 4, 21, or 24 for any period ending with or within a calendar year is filed before April 15 of the succeeding calendar year, such return shall be considered filed on April 15 of such calendar year.

(3) Return executed by Secretary. Notwithstanding the provisions of paragraph (2) of section 6020(b), the execution of a return by the Secretary pursuant to the authority conferred by such section shall not start the running of the period of limitations on assessment and collection.

(4) Return of excise taxes. For purposes of this section, the filing of a return for a specified period on which an entry has been made with respect to a tax imposed under a provision of subtitle D (including a return on which an entry has been made showing no liability for such tax for such period) shall constitute the filing of a return of all amounts of such tax which, if properly paid, would be required to be reported on such return for such period.

(c) Exceptions.

(1) False return. In the case of a false or fraudulent return with the intent to evade tax, the tax may be assessed, or a proceeding in court for collection of such tax may be begun without assessment, at any time.

(2) Willful attempt to evade tax. In case of a willful attempt in any manner to defeat or evade tax imposed by this title (other than tax imposed by subtitle A or B), the tax may be assessed, or a proceeding in court for the collection of such tax may be begun without assessment, at any time.

(3) No return. In the case of failure to file a return, the tax may be assessed, or a proceeding in court for the collection of such tax may be begun without assessment, at any time.

Limitations on assessment and collection

(4) Extension by agreement.
(A) In general. Where, before the expiration of the time prescribed in this section for the assessment of any tax imposed by this title, except the estate tax provided in chapter 11, both the Secretary and the taxpayer have consented in writing to its assessment after such time, the tax may be assessed at any time prior to the expiration of the period agreed upon. The period so agreed upon may be extended by subsequent agreements in writing made before the expiration of the period previously agreed upon.
(B) Notice to taxpayer of right to refuse or limit extension. The Secretary shall notify the taxpayer of the taxpayer's right to refuse to extend the period of limitations, or to limit such extension to particular issues or to a particular period of time, on each occasion when the taxpayer is requested to provide such consent.

(5) Tax resulting from changes in certain income tax or estate tax credits. For special rules applicable in cases where the adjustment of certain taxes allowed as a credit against income taxes or estate taxes results in additional tax, see section 905(c) (relating to the foreign tax credit for income tax purposes) and section 2016 (relating to taxes of foreign countries, States, etc., claimed as credit against estate taxes).

(6) Termination of private foundation status. In the case of a tax on termination of private foundation status under section 507, such tax may be assessed, or a proceeding in court for the collection of such tax may be begun without assessment, at any time.

(7) Special rule for certain amended returns. Where, within the 60-day period ending on the day on which the time prescribed in this section for the assessment of any tax imposed by subtitle A for any taxable year would otherwise expire, the Secretary receives a written document signed by the taxpayer showing that the taxpayer owes an additional amount of such tax for such taxable year, the period for the assessment of such additional amount shall not expire before the day 60 days after the day on which the Secretary receives such document.

(8) Failure to notify Secretary of certain foreign transfers.
(A) In general. In the case of any information which is required to be reported to the Secretary pursuant to an election under section 1295(b) or under section 1298(f), 6038, 6038A, 6038B, 6038D, 6046, 6046A, or 6048, the time for assessment of any tax imposed by this title with respect to any tax return, event, or period to which such information relates shall not expire before the date which is 3 years after the date on which the Secretary is furnished the information required to be reported under such section.
(B) Application to failures due to reasonable cause. If the failure to furnish the information referred to in subparagraph (A) is due to reasonable cause and not willful neglect, subparagraph (A) shall apply only to the item or items related to such failure.

(9) Gift tax on certain gifts not shown on return. If any gift of property the value of which (or any increase in taxable gifts required under section 2701(d) which) is required to be shown on a return of tax imposed by chapter 12 (without regard to section 2503(b)), and is not shown on such return, any tax imposed by chapter 12 on such gift may be assessed, or a proceeding in court for the collection of such tax may be begun without assessment, at any time. The preceding sentence shall not apply to any item which is disclosed in such return, or in a statement attached to the return, in a manner adequate to apprise the Secretary of the nature of such item.

(10) Listed transactions. If a taxpayer fails to include on any return or statement for any taxable year any information with respect to a listed transaction (as defined in section 6707A(c)(2)) which is required under section 6011 to be included with such return or statement, the time for assessment of any tax imposed by this title with respect to such transaction shall not expire before the date which is 1 year after the earlier of—
(A) the date on which the Secretary is furnished the information so required, or
(B) the date that a material advisor meets the requirements of section 6112 with respect to a request by the Secretary under section 6112(b) relating to such transaction with respect to such taxpayer.

(11) Certain orders of criminal restitution. In the case of any amount described in section 6201(a)(4), such amount may be assessed, or a proceeding in court for the collection of such amount may be begun without assessment, at any time.

(d) Request for prompt assessment.
Except as otherwise provided in subsection (c), (e), or (f), in the case of any tax (other than the tax imposed by chapter 11 of subtitle B, relating to estate taxes) for which return is required in the case of a decedent, or by his estate during the period of administration, or by a corporation, the tax shall be assessed, and any proceeding in court without assessment for the collection of such tax shall be begun, within 18 months after written request therefor (filed after the return is made and filed in such manner and such form as may be prescribed by regulations of the Secretary) by the executor, administrator, or other fiduciary representing the estate of such decedent, or by the corporation, but not after the expiration of 3 years after the return was filed. This subsection shall not apply in the case of a corporation unless—

(1) (A) such written request notifies the Secretary that the corporation contemplates dissolution at or before the expiration of such 18-month period, (B) the dissolution is in good faith begun before the expiration of such 18-month period, and (C) the dissolution is completed;

(2) (A) such written request notifies the Secretary that a dissolution has in good faith been begun, and (B) the dissolution is completed; or

(3) a dissolution has been completed at the time such written request is made.

(e) Substantial omission of items.
Except as otherwise provided in subsection (c)—
(1) Income taxes. In the case of any tax imposed by subtitle A—
(A) General rule. If the taxpayer omits from gross income an amount properly includible therein and—
(i) such amount is in excess of 25 percent of the amount of gross income stated in the return, or
(ii) such amount—
(I) is attributable to one or more assets with respect to which information is required to be reported under section 6038D (or would be so required if such section were applied without regard to the dollar threshold specified in subsection (a) thereof and without regard to any exceptions provided pursuant to subsection (h)(1) thereof), and
(II) is in excess of $5,000,

the tax may be assessed, or a proceeding in court for collection of such tax may be begun without assessment, at any time within 6 years after the return was filed.

(B) Determination of gross income. For purposes of subparagraph (A)—
  (i) in the case of a trade or business, the term "gross income" means the total of the amounts received or accrued from the sale of goods or services (if such amounts are required to be shown on the return) prior to diminution by the cost of such sales or services; and
  (ii) in determining the amount omitted from gross income, there shall not be taken into account any amount which is omitted from gross income stated in the return if such amount is disclosed in the return, or in a statement attached to the return, in a manner adequate to apprise the Secretary of the nature and amount of such item.
(C) Constructive dividends. If the taxpayer omits from gross income an amount properly includible therein under section 951(a), the tax may be assessed, or a proceeding in court for the collection of such tax may be done without assessing, at any time within 6 years after the return was filed.

(2) Estate and gift taxes. In the case of a return of estate tax under chapter 11 or a return of gift tax under chapter 12, if the taxpayer omits from the gross estate or from the total amount of the gifts made during the period for which the return was filed items includible in such gross estate or such total gifts, as the case may be, as exceed in amount 25 percent of the gross estate stated in the return or the total amount of gifts stated in the return, the tax may be assessed, or a proceeding in court for the collection of such tax may be begun without assessment, at any time within 6 years after the return was filed. In determining the items omitted from the gross estate or the total gifts, there shall not be taken into account any item which is omitted from the gross estate or from the total gifts stated in the return if such item is disclosed in the return, or in a statement attached to the return, in a manner adequate to apprise the Secretary of the nature and amount of such item.

(3) Excise taxes. In the case of a return of a tax imposed under a provision of subtitle D, if the return omits an amount of such tax properly includible thereon which exceeds 25 percent of the amount of such tax reported thereon, the tax may be assessed, or a proceeding in court for the collection of such tax may be begun without assessment, at any time within 6 years after the return is filed. In determining the amount of tax omitted on a return, there shall not be taken into account any amount of tax imposed by chapter 41, 42, 43, or 44 which is omitted from the return if the transaction giving rise to such tax is disclosed in the return, or in a statement attached to the return, in a manner adequate to apprise the Secretary of the existence and nature of such item.

(f) Personal holding company tax.
If a corporation which is a personal holding company for any taxable year fails to file with its return under chapter 1 for such year a schedule setting forth—
(1) the items of gross income and adjusted ordinary gross income, described in section 543, received by the corporation during such year, and
(2) the names and addresses of the individuals who owned, within the meaning of section 544 (relating to rules for determining stock ownership), at any time during the last half of such year more than 50 percent in value of the outstanding capital stock of the corporation,
the personal holding company tax for such year may be assessed, or a proceeding in court for the collection of such tax may be begun without assessment, at any time within 6 years after the return for such year was filed.

(g) Certain income tax returns of corporations.
(1) Trusts or partnerships. If a taxpayer determines in good faith that it is a trust or partnership and files a return as such under subtitle A, and if such taxpayer is thereafter held to be a corporation for the taxable year for which the return is filed, such return shall be deemed the return of the corporation for purposes of this section.
(2) Exempt organizations. If a taxpayer determines in good faith that it is an exempt organization and files a return as such under section 6033, and if such taxpayer is thereafter held to be a taxable organization for the taxable year for which the return is filed, such return shall be deemed the return of the organization for purposes of this section.
(3) DISC. If a corporation determines in good faith that it is a DISC (as defined in section 992(a)) and files a return as such under section 6011(c)(2) and if such corporation is thereafter held to be a corporation which is not a DISC for the taxable year for which the return is filed, such return shall be deemed the return of a corporation which is not a DISC for purposes of this section.

(h) Net operating loss carryback or capital loss carrybacks.
In the case of a deficiency attributable to the application to the taxpayer of a net operating loss carryback or a capital loss carryback (including deficiencies which may be assessed pursuant to the provisions of section 6213(b)(3)), such deficiency may be assessed at any time before the expiration of the period within which a deficiency for the taxable year of the net operating loss or net capital loss which results in such carryback may be assessed.

(i) Foreign tax carrybacks.
In the case of a deficiency attributable to the application to the taxpayer of a carryback under section 904(c) (relating to carryback and carryover of excess foreign taxes) or under section 907(f) (relating to carryback and carryover of disallowed foreign oil and gas taxes), such deficiency may be assessed at any time before the expiration of one year after the expiration of the period within which a deficiency may be assessed for the taxable year of the excess taxes described in section 904(c) or 907(f) which result in such carryback.

(j) Certain credit carrybacks.
(1) In general. In the case of a deficiency attributable to the application to the taxpayer of a credit carryback (including deficiencies which may be assessed pursuant to the provisions of section 6213(b)(3)), such deficiency may be assessed at any time before the expiration of the period within which a deficiency for the taxable year of the unused credit which results in such carryback may be assessed, or with respect to any portion of a credit carryback from a taxable year attributable to a net operating loss carryback, capital loss carryback, or other credit carryback from a subsequent taxable year, at any time before the expiration of the period within which a deficiency for such subsequent taxable year may be assessed.
(2) Credit carryback defined. For purposes of this subsection, the term "credit carryback" has the meaning given such term by section 6511(d)(4)(C).

(k) Tentative carryback adjustment assessment period.
In a case where an amount has been applied, credited, or refunded under section 6411 (relating to tentative carryback and refund adjustments) by reason of a net operating loss carryback, a capital loss carryback, or a credit carryback (as defined in Section 6511(d)(4)(C)) to a prior taxable year, the period described in subsection (a) of this section for assess-

Limitations on assessment and collection   Code Sec. 6501

ing a deficiency for such prior taxable year shall be extended to include the period described in subsection (h) or (j), whichever is applicable; except that the amount which may be assessed solely by reason of this subsection shall not exceed the amount so applied, credited, or refunded under section 6411, reduced by any amount which may be assessed solely by reason of subsection (h) or (j), as the case may be.

(l) Special rule for chapter 42 and similar taxes.

(1) In general. For purposes of any tax imposed by section 4912, by chapter 42 (other than section 4940), or by section 4975, the return referred to in this section shall be the return filed by the private foundation, plan, trust, or other organization (as the case may be) for the year in which the act (or failure to act) giving rise to liability for such tax occurred. For purposes of section 4940, such return is the return filed by the private foundation for the taxable year for which the tax is imposed.

(2) Certain contributions to section 501(c)(3) organizations. In the case of a deficiency of tax of a private foundation making a contribution in the manner provided in section 4942(g)(3) (relating to certain contributions to section 501(c)(3) organizations) attributable to the failure of a section 501(c)(3) organization to make the distribution prescribed by section 4942(g)(3), such deficiency may be assessed at any time before the expiration of one year after the expiration of the period within which a deficiency may be assessed for the taxable year with respect to which the contribution was made.

(3) Certain set-asides described in section 4942(g)(2). In the case of a deficiency attributable to the failure of an amount set aside by a private foundation for a specific project to be treated as a qualifying distribution under the provisions of section 4942(g)(2)(B)(ii), such deficiency may be assessed at any time before the expiration of 2 years after the expiration of the period within which a deficiency may be assessed for the taxable year to which the amount set aside relates.

(m) Deficiencies attributable to election of certain credits. The period for assessing a deficiency attributable to any election under section 30(e)(6), 30B(h)(9), 30C(e)(5), [**Ed. Note: See history for Code Sec. 6501] 30D(e)(4), 40(f), 43, 45B, 45C(d)(4), 45H(g), or 51(j) (or any revocation thereof) shall not expire before the date 1 year after the date on which the Secretary is notified of such election (or revocation).

(n) Cross references.

(1) For period of limitations for assessment and collection in the case of a joint income return filed after separate returns have been filed, see section 6013(b)(3) and (4).

(2) For extension of period in the case of partnership items (as defined in section 6231(a)(3)), see section 6229.

(3) For declaratory judgment relating to treatment of items other than partnership items with respect to an oversheltered return, see section 6234.

In 2010, P.L. 111-240, Sec. 2103, of this Act, reads as follows:

"Sec. 2103. Report on tax shelter penalties and certain other enforcement actions."

"(a) In general. The Commissioner of Internal Revenue, in consultation with the Secretary of the Treasury, shall submit to the Committee on Ways and Means of the House of Representatives and the Committee on Finance of the Senate an annual report on the penalties assessed by the Internal Revenue Service during the preceding year under each of the following provisions of the Internal Revenue Code of 1986:

"(1) Section 6662A (relating to accuracy-related penalty on understatements with respect to reportable transactions).

"(2) Section 6700(a) (relating to promoting abusive tax shelters).

"(3) Section 6707 (relating to failure to furnish information regarding reportable transactions).

"(4) Section 6707A (relating to failure to include reportable transaction information with return).

"(5) Section 6708 (relating to failure to maintain lists of advisees with respect to reportable transactions).

"(b) Additional information. The report required under subsection (a) shall also include information on the following with respect to each year:

"(1) Any action taken under section 330(b) of title 31, United States Code, with respect to any reportable transaction (as defined in section 6707A(c) of the Internal Revenue Code of 1986).

"(2) Any extension of the time for assessment of tax enforced, or assessment of any amount under such an extension, under paragraph (10) of section 6501(c) of the Internal Revenue Code of 1986.

"(c) Date of report. The first report required under subsection (a) shall be submitted not later than December 31, 2010."

—P.L. 111-237, Sec. 3(b)(2), added para. (c)(11), effective for restitution ordered after 8/16/2010.

—P.L. 111-226, Sec. 218(a)(1), substituted "(A) In general. In the case of any information" for "In the case of any information" in para. (c)(8) . . . Sec. 218(a)(2), added subpara. (c)(8)(B), effective for returns filed after 3/18/2010, as if included in Sec. 513 of P.L. 111-147 [see below].

—P.L. 111-147, Sec. 501(c)(2), added "4," after "chapter 3," in para. (b)(1) . . . Sec. 501(c)(3)(A), added "4," after "chapter 3," in para. (b)(2) . . . Sec. 501(c)(3)(B), substituted "and withholding taxes" for "taxes and tax imposed by chapter 3" in the heading of para. (b)(2), effective for payments made after 12/31/2012. Sec. 501(d)(2) of this Act, provides:

"(2) Grandfathered treatment of outstanding obligations. The amendments made by this section shall not require any amount to be deducted or withheld from any payment under any obligation outstanding on the date which is 2 years after the date of the enactment of this Act or from the gross proceeds from any disposition of such an obligation."

—P.L. 111-147, Sec. 513(a)(1), redesignated subparas. (e)(1)(A)-(B) as subparas. (e)(1)(B)-(C), respectively, and added subpara. (e)(1)(A) . . . Sec. 513(a)(2)(A), substituted "(B) Determination of gross income. For purposes of subparagraph (A)—" for "(B) General rule. If the taxpayer omits from gross income an amount properly includible therein which is in excess of 25 percent of the amount of gross income stated in the return, the tax may be assessed, or a proceeding in court for the collection of such tax may be begun without assessment, at any time within 6 years after the return was filed. For purposes of this subparagraph—" in subpara. (e)(1)(B) [as redes. by Sec. 513(a)(1) of this Act, see above] . . . Sec. 513(b)(1), added "pursuant to an election under section 1295(b) or" before "under section 6038" in para. (c)(8) . . . Sec. 513(b)(2), added "1298(f)," before "6038" in para. (c)(8) . . . Sec. 513(b)(3), added "6038D," after "6038B," in para. (c)(8) . . . Sec. 513(c), substituted "tax return, event," for "event" in para. (c)(8), effective for returns filed after 3/18/2010. Sec. 513(d)(2) of this Act, provides:

"(2) returns filed on or before such date if the period specified in section 6501 of the Internal Revenue Code of 1986 (determined without regard to such amendments) for assessment of such taxes has not expired as of such date."

In 2009, P.L. 111-5, Sec. 1141(b)(4), substituted "section 30(e)(6)" for "section 30(d)(4)" in subsec. (m), effective for vehicles acquired after 2/17/2009.

—P.L. 111-5, Sec. 1142(b)(7), substituted "section 30D(e)(4)" for "section 30D(e)(9)" in subsec. (m), effective for vehicles acquired after 12/31/2009.

[**Ed. Note. We believe that Congress intended to substitute "30D(e)(4)" for "30D(e)(9)."]

In 2008, P.L. 110-343, Sec. 205(d)(3)DivB, added "30D(e)(9)," after "30C(e)(5)," in subsec. (m), effective for tax. yrs. begin. after 12/31/2008.

—P.L. 110-343, Sec. 402(d)DivB, substituted "foreign oil and gas taxes" for "oil and gas extraction taxes" in subsec. (i), effective for tax. yrs. begin. after 12/31/2008.

In 2007, P.L. 110-172, Sec. 7(a)(2)(B), added "45H(g)," after "45C(d)(4)," in subsec. (m), effective for expenses paid or incurred after 12/31/2002, in tax. yrs. end. after such date.

In 2005, P.L. 109-135, Sec. 403(y), deleted "(as defined in section 6111)" after "material advisor" in subpara. (c)(10)(B), effective for tax. yrs. with respect to which the period for assessing a deficiency did not expire before 10/22/2004, as if included in Sec. 814 of the American Jobs Creation Act of 2004, P.L. 108-357.

—P.L. 109-58, Sec. 1341(b)(4), added "30B(h)(9)," after "30(d)(4)," in subsec. (m), effective for property placed in service after 12/31/2005, in tax. yrs. end. after 12/31/2005.

—P.L. 109-58, Sec. 1342(b)(4), added "30C(e)(5)," after "30B(h)(9)," in subsec. (m) [as amended by Sec. 1341(b)(4) of this Act, see above], effective for property placed in service after 12/31/2005, in tax. yrs. end. after 12/31/2005.

In 2004, P.L. 108-357, Sec. 413(c)(28), amended subpara. (e)(1)(B), effective for tax. yrs. of foreign corporations begin. after 12/31/2004, and for tax. yrs. of United States shareholders with or within which such tax. yrs. of foreign corporations end.

Prior to amendment, subpara. (e)(1)(B) read as follows:

"(B) Constructive dividends. If the taxpayer omits from gross income an amount properly includible therein under section 551(b) (relating to the inclusion in the gross income of United States shareholders of their distributive shares of the undistributed foreign personal holding company income), the tax may be assessed, or a proceeding in court for the collection of such tax may be begun without assessment, at any time within 6 years after the return was filed."

—P.L. 108-357, Sec. 814(a), added para. (c)(10), effective for tax. yrs. with respect to which the period for assessing a deficiency did not expire before 10/22/2004.

In 1998, P.L. 105-206, Sec. 3461(b)(1), substituted "(A) In general. Where" for "Where" in para. (c)(4) . . . Sec. 3461(b)(2), added subpara. (c)(4)(B), effective for requests to extend the period of limitations made after 12/31/99.

3,743

—P.L. 105-206, Sec. 6007(e)(2)(A), deleted "The value of any item which is so disclosed may not be redetermined by the Secretary after the expiration of the period under subsection (a)." at the end of para. (c)(9), effective for gifts made in calendar yrs. end. after 8/5/97.
—P.L. 105-206, Sec. 6023(27), substituted "election under section 30(d)(4), 40(f), 43, 45B, 45C(d)(4), or 51(j) (or any" for "election under section 30(d)(4), 40(f), 43, 45B or 51(j) (or any" in subsec. (m), effective 7/22/98

In 1997, P.L. 105-34, Sec. 506(b), amended para. (c)(9), effective for gifts made in calendar yrs. end. after 8/5/97.
Prior to amendment, para. (c)(9) read as follows:
"(9) Gift tax on certain gifts not shown on return. If any gift of property the value of which is determined under section 2701 or 2702 (or any increase in taxable gifts required under section 2701(d)) is required to be shown on a return of tax imposed by chapter 12 (without regard to section 2503(b)), and is not shown on such return, any tax imposed by chapter 12 on such gift may be assessed, or a proceeding in court for the collection of such tax may be begun without assessment, at any time. The preceding sentence shall not apply to any item not shown as a gift on such return if such item is disclosed in such return, or in a statement attached to the return, in a manner adequate to apprise the Secretary of the nature of such item."
—P.L. 105-34, Sec. 1145(a), amended para. (c)(8), effective for information the due date for reporting of which is after 8/5/97.
Prior to amendment, para. (c)(8) read as follows:
"(8) Failure to notify Secretary under section 6038B. In the case of any tax imposed on any exchange or distribution by reason of subsection (a), (d) or (e) of section 367, the time for assessment of such tax shall not expire before the date which is 3 years after the date on which the Secretary is notified of such exchange or distribution under section 6038B(a)."
—P.L. 105-34, Sec. 1239(e)(2), added para. (o)(3) [sic (n)(3)], effective for partnership tax. yrs. end. after 8/5/97.
—P.L. 105-34, Sec. 1284(a), added a sentence at the end of subsec. (a), effective for tax. yrs. begin. after 8/5/97.

In 1996, P.L. 104-188, Sec. 1702(e)(3)(A), repealed subsec. (m) [repealed previously by Sec. 1941(b)(2)(H) of P.L. 100-418, see below] and redesignated subsecs. (n) and (o) as (m) and (n) . . . Sec. 1702(e)(3)(B), substituted "section 40(f), 43, or 51(j)" for "section 40(f) or 51(j)" in subsec. (m) [as redesignated by Sec. 1702(e)(3)(A) of this Act, see above] effective for costs paid or incurred in tax. yrs. begin. after 12/31/90, except as provided in Sec. 11511(c)(2) of P.L. 101-508, reproduced below.
—P.L. 104-188, Sec. 1703(n)(8), substituted "45B, or 51(j)" for "or 51(j)" in subsec. (m) [as redesignated by Sec. 1702(e)(3)(A) of this Act, see above], effective for taxes paid after 12/31/93.
—P.L. 104-188, Sec. 1704(t)(4)(B), substituted "section 30(d)(4), 40(f)" for "section 40(f)" in subsec. (m) [as redesignated by Sec. 1702(e)(3)(A) of this Act, see above], effective 8/20/96.

In 1990, P.L. 101-508, Sec. 11511(c)(2), provides:
"(2) Subsection (m) of section 6501 is amended by striking '44B' each place it appears and inserting '43 or 44B'."
However, Sec. 1941(b)(2)(H) of P.L. 100-418, repealed subsec. (m), see below.
Prior to repeal, subsec. (m) contained no references to section "44B".
—P.L. 101-508, Sec. 11602(b), added para. (c)(9), effective for gifts after 10/8/90.

In 1989, P.L. 101-239, Sec. 7814(e)(2)(E), deleted ", 41(h)" following "section 40(f)" in subsec. (n), effective for tax. yrs. begin. after 12/31/88.
In 1988, P.L. 100-647, Sec. 1008(j)(1), deleted para. (o)(3), effective for amounts received after 12/31/86, in tax. yrs. end. after such date.
Prior to deletion para. (o)(3) read as follows:
"(3) For extension of period in the case of certain contributions in aid of construction, see section 118(c)."
—P.L. 100-647, Sec. 4008(c)(2), substituted ", 41(h), or 51(j)" for "or 51(j)" in subsec. (n) effective for tax. yrs. begin. after 12/31/88.
—P.L. 100-418, Sec. 1941(b)(2)(H), repealed subsec. (m), effective for crude oil removed from the premises on or after 8/23/88.
Prior to repeal, subsec. (m) read as follows:
"(m) Special rules for windfall profit tax.
"(1) Oil subject to withholding.
"(A) In general. In the case of any oil to which section 4995(a) applies and with respect to which no return is required, the return referred to in this section shall be the return (of the person liable for the tax imposed by section 4986) of the taxes imposed by subtitle A for the taxable year in which the removal year ends.
"(B) Removal year. For purposes of subparagraph (A), the term 'removal year' means the calendar year in which the oil is removed from the premises.
"(2) Extension of liability attributable to DOE reclassification.
"(A) In general. In the case of the tax imposed by chapter 45, if a Department of Energy change becomes final, the period for assessing any deficiency attributable to such change shall not expire before the date which is 1 year after the date on which such change becomes final.
"(B) Department of Energy Change. For purposes of subparagraph (A) and section 6511(h)(2), the term 'Department of Energy change' means any change by the Department of Energy in the classification under the June 1979 energy regulations (as defined in section 4996(b)(8)(C)) of a property or of domestic crude oil from a property.
"(3) Cross reference.
For extension of period for windfall profit tax items of partnerships, see section 6229 as made applicable by section 6232."

In 1987, P.L. 100-203, Sec. 10712(c)(2), substituted "plan, trust or other organization" for "plan, or trust" in para. (l)(1) . . . Sec. 10714(c), substituted "by section 4912, by chapter 42 (other than section 4940)," for "by chapter 42 (other than section 4940)" in para. (l)(1), effective for tax. yrs. begin. after 12/22/87.
In 1986, P.L. 99-514, Sec. 1810(g)(3)(A), substituted "(a), (d), or (e)" for "(a) or (d)" in para. (c)(8) . . . Sec. 1810(g)(3)(B), substituted "exchange or distribution" for "exchange" each time it appeared in para. (c)(8), effective for transfers or exchanges after 12/31/84 in tax. yrs. end. after 12/31/84. For special rules, see Sec. 131(g)(2) and (3) of P.L. 98-369 reproduced in note following Code Sec. 367.
—P.L. 99-514, Sec. 1847(b)(13), redesignated subsec. (n) as subsec. (o), and added new subsec. (n) . . . Sec. 1847(b)(14), substituted "or a credit carryback (as defined in section 6511(d)(4)(C)" for "an investment credit carryback, a work incentive program carryback, or a new employee credit carryback" in subsec. (k), effective for tax. yrs. begin. after 12/31/83, and to carrybacks from tax. yrs. begin. after 12/31/86.
In 1984, P.L. 98-369, Sec. 131(d)(2), added para. (c)(8), for transfers or exchanges after 12/31/84 in tax. yrs. end. after 12/31/84. For special rules, see Sec. 131(g)(2) and (3) of the Act reproduced in note following Code Sec. 367.
—P.L. 98-369, Sec. 163(b)(1), deleted subsecs. (l) and (o), redesignated subsecs. (m), (n) and (p) as subsecs. (k), (l) and (m) and added new subsec. (n), effective for expenditures for which the second tax. yr. described in Code Sec. 118(b)(2)(B) ends after 12/31/84.
Prior to deletion subsec. (l) read as follows:
"(l) Joint income return after separate return.
"For period of limitations for assessment and collection in the case of a joint income return filed after separate returns have been filed, see section 6013(b)(3) and (4)."
Prior to deletion subsec. (o) read as follows:
"(o) Special rules for partnership items.
"For extension of period in the case of partnership items (as defined in section 6231(a)(3)), see section 6229."
—P.L. 98-369, Sec. 211(b)(24)(A), deleted para. (c)(6) and redesignated para. (c)(7) as (c)(6) . . . Sec. 211(b)(24)(B), deleted subsec. (k), effective for tax. yrs. begin. after 12/31/83.
Prior to deletion, para. (c)(6) read as follows:
"(6) Tax resulting from certain distributions or from termination as life insurance company. In the case of any tax imposed under section 802(a) by reason of section 802(b)(3) on account of a termination of the taxpayer as an insurance company or as a life insurance company to which section 815(d)(2)(A) applies, or on account of a distribution by the taxpayer to which section 815(d)(2)(B) applies, such tax may be assessed within 3 years after the return was filed (whether or not such return was filed on or after the date prescribed) for the taxable year for which the taxpayer ceases to be an insurance company, the second taxable year for which the taxpayer is not a life insurance company, or the taxable year in which the distribution is actually made, as the case may be."
Prior to deletion, subsec. (k) read as follows:
"(k) Reductions of policyholders surplus account of life insurance companies.
"In the case of a deficiency attributable to the application to the taxpayer of section 815(d)(5) (relating to reductions of policyholders surplus account of life insurance companies for certain unused deductions), such deficiency may be assessed at any time before the expiration of the period within which a deficiency for the last taxable year to which the loss described in section 815(d)(5)(A) is carried under section 812(d)(2) may be assessed."
—P.L. 98-369, Sec. 314(a)(3), substituted "section 4942(g)(2)(B)(ii)" for "4942(g)(2)(B)(i)(II)" in para. (n)(3) (before redesignation as para. (l) by Sec. 163(b)(1) of the Act), effective 7/18/84.
—P.L. 98-369, Sec. 447(a), added para. (c)(7), effective for documents received by the Secretary of the Treasury or his delegate after 7/18/84.
—P.L. 98-369, Sec. 474(r)(39), deleted subsec. (p) and redesignated subsec. (q) as subsec. (p) for tax. yrs. begin. after 12/31/83, and to carrybacks from such years.
Prior to deletion, subsec. (p) read as follows:
"(p) Deficiency attributable to election under section 44B.
"The period for assessing a deficiency attributable to any election under section 44B (or any revocation thereof) shall not expire before the date 1 year after the date on which the Secretary is notified of such election (or revocation)."
—P.L. 98-369, Sec. 714(p)(2)(F), amended para. (q)(3) (before redesignation by Sec. 474(r)(39) of this Act), effective for tax. yrs. begin. after 9/3/82.
Prior to amendment, para. (q)(3) read as follows:
"(3) Partnership items of federally registered partnerships. Under regulations prescribed by the Secretary, rules similar to the rules of subsection (o) shall apply to the tax imposed by section 4986."
—P.L. 98-369, Sec. 801(d)(14), substituted "section 6011(c)(2)" for "section 6011(e)(2)" in para. (g)(3), effective for transactions after 12/31/84, in tax. yrs. end. after 12/31/84.
In 1982, P.L. 97-248, Sec. 402(c)(5), amended subsec. (o), effective for partnership tax. yrs. begin. after 9/3/82. Sec. 407(a)(3) of this Act provides:
"(3) The amendments made by sections 402, 403, and 404 [of this Act] shall apply to any partnership taxable year (or in the case of section 6232 of such Code, to any period) ending after the date of the enactment of this Act [9/3/82] if the partnership, each partner, and each indirect partner requests such application and the Secretary of the Treasury or his delegate consents to such application."
Prior to amendment, subsec. (o) read as follows:
"(o) Special rules for partnership items of federally registered partnerships.
"(1) In general. In the case of any tax imposed by subtitle A with respect to any person, the period for assessing a deficiency attributable to any partnership item of a federally registered partnership shall not expire before the later of—

"(A) the date which is 4 years after the date on which the partnership return of the federally registered partnership for the partnership taxable year in which the item arose was filed (or, later, if the date prescribed for filing the return), or

"(B) if the name or address of such person does not appear on the partnership return, the date which is 1 year after the date on which such information is furnished to the Secretary in such manner and at such place as he may prescribe by regulations.

"(2) Partnership item defined. For purposes of this subsection, the term 'partnership item' means—

"(A) any item required to be taken into account for the partnership taxable year under any provision of subchapter K of chapter 1 to the extent that regulations prescribed by the Secretary provide that for purposes of this subtitle such item is more appropriately determined at the partnership level than at the partner level, and

"(B) any other item to the extent affected by an item described in subparagraph (A).

"(3) Extension by agreement. The extensions referred to in subsection (c)(4), insofar as they relate to partnership items, may, with respect to any person, be consented to—

"(A) except to the extent the Secretary is otherwise notified by the partnership, by a general partner of the partnership, or

"(B) by any person authorized to do so by the partnership in writing.

"(4) Federally registered partnership. For purposes of this subsection, the term 'federally registered partnership' means, with respect to any partnership taxable year, any partnership—

"(A) interests in which have been offered for sale at any time during such taxable year or a prior taxable year in any offering required to be registered with the Securities and Exchange Commission, or

"(B) which, at any time during such taxable year or a prior taxable year, was subject to the annual reporting requirements of the Securities and Exchange Commission which relate to the protection of investors in the partnership."

In 1980, P.L. 96-223, Sec. 101(g)(1), added new subsec. (q) effective for periods after 2/29/80.

—P.L. 96-222, Sec. 102(a)(2)(A), redesignated subsec. (q) as added by Sec. 212(a) of P.L. 95-600 as subsec. (o) . . . Sec. 103(a)(6)(G)(x), redesignated subsec. (q) [as added by Sec. 321(b)(2) of P.L. 95-600] as subsec. (p), effective for amounts paid or incurred after 12/31/78, in tax. yrs. end. after 12/31/78.

—P.L. 96-222, Sec. 103(a)(6)(B), added new para. (d)(5) to Sec. 321(d) of P.L. 95-600, the effective date for changes made by Sec. 321(b) of P.L. 95-600 [see below].

In 1978, P.L. 95-628, Sec. 8(c)(1)(A), amended subsec. (j) . . . Sec. 8(c)(1)(B), substituted "subsection (h) or (j)" for "subsection (h), (j), (o) or (p)" each place it appeared in subsec. (m) . . . Sec. 8(c)(1)(C), deleted subsecs. (o) and (p), effective for carrybacks arising in tax. yrs. begin. after 11/10/78.

Prior to amendment, subsecs. (j), (o) and (p) read as follows:

"(j) Investment credit carrybacks.

"In the case of a deficiency attributable to the application to the taxpayer of an investment credit carryback (including deficiencies which may be assessed pursuant to the provisions of section 6213(b)(3)), such deficiency may be assessed at any time before the expiration of the period within which a deficiency for the taxable year of the unused investment credit which results in such carryback may be assessed, or, with respect to any portion of an investment credit carryback from a taxable year attributable to a net operating loss carryback or a capital loss carryback from a subsequent taxable year, at any time before the expiration of the period within which a deficiency for such subsequent taxable year may be assessed.

"(o) Work incentive program credit carrybacks.

"In the case of a deficiency attributable to the application to the taxpayer of a work incentive program credit carryback (including deficiencies which may be assessed pursuant to the provisions of section 6213(b)(3)), such deficiency may be assessed at any time before the expiration of the period within which a deficiency for the taxable year of the unused work incentive program credit which results in such carryback may be assessed, or, with respect to any portion of a work incentive program credit carryback from a taxable year attributable to a net operating loss carryback, an investment credit carryback, or a capital loss carryback from a subsequent taxable year, at any time before the expiration of the period within which a deficiency for such subsequent taxable year may be assessed.

"(p) New employee credit carrybacks.

"In the case of a deficiency attributable to the application to the taxpayer of a new employee credit carryback (including deficiencies which may be assessed pursuant to the provisions of section 6213(b)(3)), such deficiency may be assessed at any time before the expiration of the period within which a deficiency for the taxable year of the unused new employee credit which results in such carryback may be assessed, or, with respect to any portion of a new employee credit carryback from a taxable year attributable to a net operating loss carryback, an investment credit carryback, a work incentive program credit carryback, or a capital loss carryback from a subsequent taxable year, at any time before the expiration of the period within which a deficiency for such subsequent taxable year may be assessed."

—P.L. 95-600, Sec. 212(a), added new subsec. (q), effective for partnership items arising in partnership tax. yrs. begin. after 12/31/78.

—P.L. 95-600, Sec. 321(b)(2), added new subsec. (q), effective for amounts paid or incurred after 12/31/78, in tax. yrs. end. after 12/31/78.

—P.L. 95-600, Sec. 504(b)(3), added "and refund" after "carryback" the first place it appears in subsec. (m), effective for tentative refund claims filed on and after 11/6/78.

—P.L. 95-600, Sec. 701(t)(3)(A), substituted "43, or 44" for "or 43" in para. (e)(3), effective 10/4/76.

—P.L. 95-600, Sec. 703(n), substituted "section 6213(b)(3)" for "Section 6213(b)(2)" in subsecs. (h), (j), and (o), effective 10/4/76.

—P.L. 95-600, Sec. 703(p)(2), deleted the last sentence of subsec. (h), effective for losses sustained in tax. yrs. ending after 11/6/78.

Prior to amendment, the last sentence of subsec. (h) read as follows:

"In the case of a deficiency attributable to the application of a net operating loss carryback, such deficiency may be assessed within 18 months after the date on which the taxpayer files in accordance with section 172(b)(3) a copy of the certification (with respect to the taxable year of the net operating loss) issued under section 317 of the Trade Expansion Act of 1962, if later than the date prescribed by the preceding sentence."

—P.L. 95-227, Sec. 4(d)(4), para. (e)(3), substituted "43, or 44" for "or 43", in the second sentence of para. (e)(3), effective for contributions, acts, and expenditures made after 12/31/77, in and for tax. yrs. begin. after 12/31/77.

—P.L. 95-227, Sec. 4(d)(5), para. (n)(1) substitutes "For purposes of any tax imposed by chapter 42 (other than section 4940) or by section 4975, the return referred to in this section shall be the return filed by the private foundation, plan, or trust (as the case may be) for the year in which the act (or failure to act) giving rise to liability for such tax occurred" for the first sentence in para. (n)(1), effective for contributions, acts and expenditures made after 12/31/77, in and for tax. yrs. begin. after 12/31/77.

In 1977, P.L. 95-30, Sec. 202(d)(4)(A), added subsec. (p), effective for tax. yrs. begin. after 12/31/76 and to credit carrybacks from such yrs.

—P.L. 95-30, Sec. 202(d)(5)(B), substituted "a work incentive program carryback, or a new employee credit carryback" for "or a work incentive program carryback" in subsec. (m) and substituted "(j), (o), or (p)" for "(j), or (o)" each place it appeared in subsec. (m), effective for tax. yrs. begin. after 12/31/76 and to credit carrybacks from such yrs.

In 1976, P.L. 94-455, Sec. 1031(b)(5), substituted "section 904(c)" for "section 904(d)" each place it appeared in subsec. (i), effective for tax. yrs. begin. after 12/31/75.

—P.L. 94-455, Sec. 1035(d)(3), substituted "excess foreign taxes) or under section 907(f) (relating to carryback and carryover of disallowed oil and gas extraction taxes)" for "excess foreign taxes)" and substituted "section 904(c) or 907(f)" for "section 904(c)" in subsec. (i), as previously amended by this Act, effective for taxes paid or accrued during tax. yrs. end. after 10/4/76.

—P.L. 94-455, Sec. 1302(b), added para. (n)(3), effective for tax. yrs. begin. after 12/31/74.

—P.L. 94-455, Sec. 1307(d)(2)(F)(vi), substituted "chapter 41, 42," for "chapter 42" in para. (e)(3), effective 10/4/76.

—P.L. 94-455, Sec. 1906(b)(13)(A), substituted "Secretary" for "Secretary or his delegate" each place it appeared in Code Sec. 6501, effective 2/1/77.

—P.L. 94-455, Sec. 2107(g)(2)(A), added ", and investment credit carryback," after "net operating loss carryback" in subsec. (o), effective 10/4/76.

In 1974, P.L. 93-406, Sec. 1016(a)(14), substituted "chapter 42 or 43" for "chapter 42" in para. (e)(3), effective 9/2/74 or other date as specified in Sec. 1017 of the Act (reproduced following Code Sec. 401).

In 1971, P.L. 92-178, Sec. 504(c), added para. (g)(3), for tax. yrs. end. after 12/31/71, except that a corporation may be a DISC for any tax. yr. begin. before 1/1/72.

—P.L. 92-178, Sec. 601(d)(1), added subsec. (o) . . . Sec. 601(e)(2), substituted "an investment credit carryback, or a work incentive program carryback" for "or an investment credit carryback" in subsec. (m) and substituted "(h), (j), or (o)" for "(h) or (j)" in subsec. (m), effective for tax. yrs. begin. after 12/31/71.

In 1970, P.L. 91-614, Sec. 102(d)(8), substituted "during the period for which the return was filed" for "during the year," in the first sentence of para. (e)(2) effective for gifts made after 12/31/70.

In 1969, P.L. 91-172, Sec. 101(g)(1), added new subsec. (n) . . . Sec. 101(g)(2), added para. (c)(7) . . . Sec. 101(g)(3), added new sentence to end of subsec. (e)(3), effective 1/1/70.

—P.L. 91-172, Sec. 512(e)(1), amended subsec. (h), substituted "loss carryback or a capital loss carryback" for "loss carryback" in subsec. (j) and substituted "net operating loss carryback, a capital loss carryback, or an investment credit carryback" for "net operating loss carryback or an investment credit carryback" in subsec. (m), effective for net capital losses sustained in tax. yrs. begin. after 12/31/69.

Prior to amendment subsec. (h) read as follows:

"(h) Net operating loss carrybacks.

"In the case of a deficiency attributable to the application to the taxpayer of a net operating loss carryback (including deficiencies which may be assessed pursuant to the provisions of section 6213(b)(2), such deficiency may be assessed at any time before the expiration of the period within which a deficiency for the taxable year of the net operating loss which results in such carryback may be assessed, or within 18 months after the date on which the taxpayer files in accordance with section 172(b)(3) a copy of the certification (with respect to such taxable year) issued under section 317 of the Trade Expansion Act of 1962, whichever is later."

In 1967, P.L. 90-225, Sec. 2(c), amended subsec. (j) by adding the last phrase beginning "or with respect to any", effective with respect to investment credit carrybacks attributable to net operating loss carrybacks from tax. yrs. end. after 7/31/67.

In 1966, P.L. 89-809, Sec. 105(f)(3), substituted "chapter 3, 21, or 24" for "Chapter 21 or 24" in paras. (b)(1) and (2) and added "and tax imposed by chapter 3" to heading of subsec. (b)(2), effective 11/13/66.

—P.L. 89-721, Sec. 2(f), added "concluding deficiencies which may be assessed pursuant to the provisions of section 6213(b)(2))" after "investment credit car-

Code Sec. 6501 — Limitations on assessment and collection

ryback", in subsec. (j), effective for tax. yrs. end. after 12/31/61, but only in the case of applications filed after 11/2/66.

—P.L. 89-721, Sec. 3(a), added subsec. (m) to apply to any case where the application under Code Sec. 6411 is filed after 11/2/66.

In 1965, P.L. 89-44, Sec. 810(a), added para. (b)(4)... Sec. 810(b)(1), added para. (e)(3)... Sec. 810(b)(2), substituted "Substantial omission of items" for "Omission from gross income" in the heading of subsec. (e), effective for returns filed after 6/30/65.

In 1964, P.L. 88-272, Sec. 225(c)(6), substituted "gross income and adjusted ordinary gross income, described in section 543" for "gross income, described in section 543(a)" in subsec. (f) for tax. yrs. begin. after 12/31/63.

—P.L. 88-571, Sec. 3(b), added subsec. (k) and redesignated former subsec. (k) as (l) effective for amounts added to policyholders surplus accounts for tax. yrs. begin. after 12/31/58.

In 1962, P.L. 87-858, Sec. 3(b)(4), substituted "802(a)" for "802(a)(1)" in subsec. (c)(6), effective for tax. yrs. begin. after 12/31/61.

—P.L. 87-794, Sec. 317(a), amended subsec. (h), effective for net operating losses for tax. yrs. end. after 12/31/61.

Prior to amendment, subsec. (h) read as follows:

"(h) Net Operating Loss Carrybacks. In the case of a deficiency attributable to the application to the taxpayer of a net operating loss carryback (including deficiencies which may be assessed pursuant to the provisions of section 6213(b)(2)), such deficiency may be assessed at any time before the expiration of the period within which a deficiency for the taxable year of the net operating loss which results in such carryback may be assessed."

—P.L. 87-834, Sec. 2, added subsec. (j) and redesignated former subsec. (j) as (k), effective for tax. yrs. end. after 12/31/61.

In 1960, P.L. 86-780, Sec. 3(c), added subsec. (i) and redesignated former subsec. (i) as (j), effective for tax. yrs. begin. after 12/31/57.

In 1959, P.L. 86-69, Sec. 3(g), added subsec. (c)(6), effective for tax. yrs. begin. after 12/31/57.

In 1958, P.L. 85-859, Sec. 165(a), substituted "at any time after such tax became due and before the expiration of 3 years after the date on which any part of such tax was paid" for "within 3 years after such tax became due" in subsec. (a), effective 1/1/59.

—P.L. 85-866, Sec. 80(a), substituted "subsection (c), (e), or (f)," for "subsection (c)," in the first sentence of subsec. (d)... Sec. 80(b), amended the second sentence of subsec. (d)... Sec. 81(a), substituted "organization" for "corporation" each place it appeared in para. (g)(2)... Sec. 81(b), redesignated subsec. (h) as subsec. (i) and added new subsec. (h), effective 8/17/54.

Sec. 6502. Collection after assessment.

(a) Length of period.

Where the assessment of any tax imposed by this title has been made within the period of limitation properly applicable thereto, such tax may be collected by levy or by a proceeding in court, but only if the levy is made or the proceeding begun—

(1) within 10 years after the assessment of the tax, or

(2) if—

(A) there is an installment agreement between the taxpayer and the Secretary, prior to the date which is 90 days after the expiration of any period for collection agreed upon in writing by the Secretary and the taxpayer at the time the installment agreement was entered into; or

(B) there is a release of levy under section 6343 after such 10-year period, prior to the expiration of any period for collection agreed upon in writing by the Secretary and the taxpayer before such release.

If a timely proceeding in court for the collection of a tax is commenced, the period during which such tax may be collected by levy shall be extended and shall not expire until the liability for the tax (or a judgment against the taxpayer arising from such liability) is satisfied or becomes unenforceable.

(b) Date when levy is considered made.

The date on which a levy on property or rights to property is made shall be the date on which the notice of seizure provided in section 6335(a) is given.

In 1998, P.L. 105-206, Sec. 3461(a)(1), amended para. (a)(2).... Sec. 3461(a)(2), deleted "The period so agreed upon may be extended by subsequent agreements in writing made before the expiration of the period previously agreed upon." following para. (a)(2), effective for requests to extend the period of limitations made after 12/31/99. Sec. 3461(c)(2), of this Act, provides:

"(2) Prior request. If, in any request to extend the period of limitations made on or before December 31, 1999, a taxpayer agreed to extend such period beyond the 10-year period referred to in section 6502(a) of the Internal Revenue Code of 1986, such extension shall expire on the later of—

"(A) the last day of such 10-year period;

"(B) December 31, 2002; or

"(C) in the case of an extension in connection with an installment agreement, the 90th day after the end of the period of such extension."

Prior to amendment, para. (a)(2) read as follows:

"(2) prior to the expiration of any period for collection agreed upon in writing by the Secretary and the taxpayer before the expiration of such 10-year period (or, if there is a release of levy under section 6343 after such 10-year period, then before such release)."

In 1990, P.L. 101-508, Sec. 11317(a)(1), substituted "10 years" for "6 years" in para. (a)(1)... Sec. 11317(a)(2), substituted "10-year period" for "6-year period" each place it appeared in para. (a)(2), effective as provided in Sec. 11317(c) of this Act which reads as follows:

"(1) taxes assessed after the date of the enactment [11/5/90] of this Act, and

"(2) taxes assessed on or before such date if the period specified in section 6502 of the Internal Revenue Code of 1986 (determined without regard to the amendments made by subsection (a)) for collection of such taxes has not expired as of such date."

In 1989, P.L. 101-239, Sec. 7811(k)(2), substituted "unenforceable" for "enforceable" in the last sentence of subsec. (a), effective for levies issued after 11/10/88.

In 1988, P.L. 100-647, Sec. 1015(u)(1), amended the last sentence of subsec. (a), effective for levies issued after 11/10/88.

Prior to amendment, the last sentence of subsec. (a) read as follows:

"The period provided by this subsection during which a tax may be collected by levy shall not be extended or curtailed by reason of a judgment against the taxpayer."

In 1976, P.L. 94-455, Sec. 1906(b)(13)(A), substituted "Secretary" for "Secretary or his delegate" in Code Sec. 6502, effective 2/1/77.

In 1966, P.L. 89-719, Sec. 113, added the last sentence in subsec. (a), effective after 11/2/66, regardless of when a lien or a title of the U.S. arose or when the lien or interest of any other person was acquired. For a special exception included in Sec. 114 of P.L. 89-719 see the note to Code Sec. 6323.

Sec. 6503. Suspension of running of period of limitation.

(a) Issuance of statutory notice of deficiency.

(1) General rule. The running of the period of limitations provided in section 6501 or 6502 (or section 6229, but only with respect to a deficiency described in paragraph (2)(A) or (3) of section 6230(a)) on the making of assessments or the collection by levy or a proceeding in court, in respect of any deficiency as defined in section 6211 (relating to income, estate, gift and certain excise taxes), shall (after the mailing of a notice under section 6212(a)) be suspended for the period during which the Secretary is prohibited from making the assessment or from collecting by levy or a proceeding in court (and in any event, if a proceeding in respect of the deficiency is placed on the docket of the Tax Court, until the decision of the Tax Court becomes final), and for 60 days thereafter.

(2) Corporation joining in consolidated income tax return. If a notice under section 6212(a) in respect of a deficiency in tax imposed by subtitle A for any taxable year is mailed to a corporation, the suspension of the running of the period of limitations provided in paragraph (1) of this subsection shall apply in the case of corporations with which such corporation made a consolidated income tax return for such taxable year.

(b) Assets of taxpayer in control or custody of court.

The period of limitations on collection after assessment prescribed in section 6502 shall be suspended for the period the assets of the taxpayer are in the control or custody of the court in any proceeding before any court of the United States or of any State or of the District of Columbia, and for 6 months thereafter.

(c) Taxpayer outside United States.

The running of the period of limitations on collection after assessment prescribed in section 6502 shall be suspended for the period during which the taxpayer is outside the United States if such period of absence is for a continuous period of at least 6 months. If the preceding sentence applies and at the time of the taxpayer's return to the United States the period of limitations on collection after assessment prescribed in section 6502 would expire before the expiration of 6 months from the date of his return, such period shall not expire before the expiration of such 6 months.

(d) Extensions of time for payment of estate tax.

The running of the period of limitation for collection of any tax imposed by chapter 11 shall be suspended for the period of any extension of time for payment granted under the provisions of section 6161(a)(2) or (b)(2) or under the provisions of section 6163 or 6166.

(e) Extensions of time for payment of tax attributable to recoveries of foreign expropriation losses.

The running of the period of limitations for collection of the tax attributable to a recovery of a foreign expropriation loss (within the meaning of section 6167(f)) shall be suspended for the period of any extension of time for payment under subsection (a) or (b) of section 6167.

(f) Wrongful seizure of or lien on property of third party.

(1) **Wrongful seizure.** The running of the period under section 6502 shall be suspended for a period equal to the period from the date property (including money) of a third party is wrongfully seized or received by the Secretary to the date the Secretary returns property pursuant to section 6343(b) or the date on which a judgment secured pursuant to section 7426 with respect to such property becomes final, and for 30 days thereafter. The running of such period shall be suspended under this paragraph only with respect to the amount of such assessment equal to the amount of money or the value of specific property returned.

(2) **Wrongful lien.** In the case of any assessment for which a lien was made on any property, the running of the period under section 6502 shall be suspended for a period equal to the period beginning on the date any person becomes entitled to a certificate under section 6325(b)(4) with respect to such property and ending on the date which is 30 days after the earlier of—

(A) the earliest date on which the Secretary no longer holds any amount as a deposit or bond provided under section 6325(b)(4) by reason of such deposit or bond being used to satisfy the unpaid tax or being refunded or released; or

(B) the date that the judgment secured under section 7426(b)(5) becomes final.

The running of such period shall be suspended under this paragraph only with respect to the amount of such assessment equal to the value of the interest of the United States in the property plus interest, penalties, additions to the tax, and additional amounts attributable thereto.

(g) Suspension pending correction.

The running of the periods of limitations provided in sections 6501 and 6502 on the making of assessments or the collection by levy or a proceeding in court in respect of any tax imposed by chapter 42 or section 507, 4971, or 4975 shall be suspended for any period described in section 507(g)(2) or during which the Secretary has extended the time for making correction under section 4963(e).

(h) Cases under title 11 of the United States Code.

The running of the period of limitations provided in section 6501 or 6502 on the making of assessments or collection shall, in a case under title 11 of the United States Code, be suspended for the period during which the Secretary is prohibited by reason of such case from making the assessment or from collecting and—

(1) for assessment, 60 days thereafter, and

(2) for collection, 6 months thereafter.

(i) Extension of time for payment of undistributed PFIC earnings tax liability.

The running of any period of limitations for collection of any amount of undistributed PFIC earnings tax liability (as defined in section 1294(b)) shall be suspended for the period of any extension of time under section 1294 for payment of such amount.

(j) Extension in case of certain summonses.

(1) **In general.** If any designated summons is issued by the Secretary to a corporation (or to any other person to whom the corporation has transferred records) with respect to any return of tax by such corporation for a taxable year (or other period) for which such corporation is being examined under the coordinated examination program (or any successor program) of the Internal Revenue Service, the running of any period of limitations provided in section 6501 on the assessment of such tax shall be suspended—

(A) during any judicial enforcement period—

(i) with respect to such summons, or

(ii) with respect to any other summons which is issued during the 30-day period which begins on the date on which such designated summons is issued and which relates to the same return as such designated summons, and

(B) if the court in any proceeding referred to in paragraph (3) requires any compliance with a summons referred to in subparagraph (A), during the 120-day period beginning with the 1st day after the close of the suspension under subparagraph (A).

If subparagraph (B) does not apply, such period shall in no event expire before the 60th day after the close of the suspension under subparagraph (A).

(2) **Designated summons.** For purposes of this subsection—

(A) In general. The term "designated summons" means any summons issued for purposes of determining the amount of any tax imposed by this title if—

(i) the issuance of such summons is preceded by a review of such issuance by the regional counsel of the Office of Chief Counsel for the region in which the examination of the corporation is being conducted,

(ii) such summons is issued at least 60 days before the day on which the period prescribed in section 6501 for the assessment of such tax expires (determined with regard to extensions), and

(iii) such summons clearly states that it is a designated summons for purposes of this subsection.

(B) Limitation. A summons which relates to any return shall not be treated as a designated summons if a prior summons which relates to such return was treated as a designated summons for purposes of this subsection.

(3) **Judicial enforcement period.** For purposes of this subsection, the term "judicial enforcement period" means, with respect to any summons, the period—

(A) which begins on the day on which a court proceeding with respect to such summons is brought, and

(B) which ends on the day on which there is a final resolution as to the summoned person's response to such summons.

(k) Cross references.

For suspension in case of—

(1) Deficiency dividends of a personal holding company, see section 547(f).

(2) Receiverships, see subchapter B of chapter 70.

(3) Claims against transferees and fiduciaries, see chapter 71.
(4) Tax return preparers, see section 6694(c)(3).
(5) Deficiency dividends in the case of a regulated investment company or a real estate investment trust, see section 860(h).

In 2007, P.L. 110-28, Sec. 8246(a)(2)(E), substituted "Tax return preparers" for "Income tax return preparers" in para. (k)(4), effective for returns prepared after 5/25/2007.

In 1998, P.L. 105-206, Sec. 3106(b)(3), amended subsec. (f), effective 7/22/98. Prior to amendment, subsec. (f) read as follows:

"(f) Wrongful seizure of property of third party.

"The running of the period of limitations on collection after assessment prescribed in section 6502 shall be suspended for a period equal to the period from the date property (including money) of a third party is wrongfully seized or received by the Secretary to the date the Secretary returns property pursuant to section 6343(b) or the date on which a judgment secured pursuant to section 7426 with respect to such property becomes final, and for 30 days thereafter. The running of the period of limitations on collection after assessment shall be suspended under this subsection only with respect to the amount of such assessment equal to the amount of money or the value of specific property returned."

In 1997, P.L. 105-34, Sec. 1237(c)(2), substituted "paragraph (2)(A) or (3) of section 6230(a)" for "section 6230(a)(2)(A)" in subsec. (a), effective for partnership tax. yrs. begin. after 9/3/82. See Sec. 407(a)(3) of P.L. 97-248 reproduced in note following Code Sec. 6230.

In 1996, P.L. 104-188, Sec. 1702(h)(17)(A), redesignated subsec. (k), which related to extension in case of certain summonses, as subsec. (j) [this amendment was previously made by Sec. 1002(c) of P.L. 104-168, see below] . . . Sec. 1702(h)(17)(B), redesignated subsec. (l), which related to cross references, as subsec. (k) [this amendment was previously made by Sec. 1002(c) of P.L. 104-168, see below], effective for any tax (whether imposed before, on, or after 11/5/90) if the period prescribed by Code Sec. 6501 for the assessment of such tax (determined with regard to extensions) has not expired on 11/5/90.

—P.L. 104-168, Sec. 1002(a), redesignated clauses (k)[sic (j)](2)(A)(i) and (ii) as clauses (k)[sic (j)](2)(A)(ii) and (iii), and added a new clause (k)[sic (j)](2)(A)(i) . . . Sec. 1002(b), substituted "to a corporation (or to any other person to whom the corporation has transferred records) with respect to any return of tax by such corporation for a taxable year (or other period) for which such corporation is being examined under the coordinated examination program (or any successor program) of the Internal Revenue Service" for "with respect to any return of tax by a corporation" in para. (k)[sic (j)](1) . . . Sec. 1002(c), redesignated subsecs. (k) [sic (j)] and (l) [sic (k)] as subsecs. (j) and (k), effective for summonses issued after 7/30/96.

—P.L. 104-168, Sec. 1003, of this Act, provides:

"Sec. 1003. Annual report to Congress concerning designated summonses.

"Not later than December 31 of each calendar year after 1995, the Secretary of the Treasury or his delegate shall report to the Committee on Ways and Means of the House of Representatives and the Committee on Finance of the Senate on the number of designated summonses (as defined in section 6503(j) of the Internal Revenue Code of 1986) which were issued during the preceding 12 months."

In 1990, P.L. 101-508, Sec. 11311(a), added subsec. (k) [sic (j)] and redesignated subsec. (k) [as redesignated by Sec. 11801(c)(20)(A) of this Act, see below] as subsec. (l) [sic (k)], effective for any tax (whether imposed before, on, or after the date of the enactment of this Act) [11/5/90] if the period prescribed by Sec. 6501 of the Internal Revenue Code of 1986 for the assessment of such tax (determined with regard to extensions) has not expired on such date of the enactment.

—P.L. 101-508, Sec. 11801(c)(20)(A), deleted subsec. (h) and redesignated subsecs. (i), (j), and (k) as subsecs. (h), (i), and (j), effective 11/5/90, except as provided in Sec. 11821(b) of this Act, which reads as follows:

"(b) Savings provision.

"If—

"(1) any provision amended or repealed by this part applied to—

"(A) any transaction occurring before the date of the enactment of this Act [11/5/90],

"(B) any property acquired before such date of enactment [11/5/90], or

"(C) any item of income, loss, deduction, or credit taken into account before such date of enactment [11/5/90], and

"(2) the treatment of such transaction, property, or item under such provision would (without regard to the amendments made by this part) affect liability for tax for periods ending after such date of enactment [11/5/90],

nothing in the amendments made by this part shall be construed to affect the treatment of such transaction, property, or item for purposes of determining liability for tax for periods ending after such date of enactment [11/5/90]."

Prior to deletion, subsec. (h) read as follows:

"(h) Extension of time for collecting tax attributable to divestitures pursuant to Bank Holding Company Act amendments of 1970. The running of the period of limitations for collection of the tax attributable to a sale with respect to which the taxpayer makes an election under section 6158(a) shall be suspended for the period during which there are any unpaid installments of such tax."

In 1987, P.L. 100-203, Sec. 10712(c)(3), deleted "4951, 4952," after "507" in subsec. (g), effective for tax. yrs. begin. after 12/22/87.

In 1986, P.L. 99-514, Sec. 1235(d)(2)(B)(ii), redesignated subsec. (i) [sic j] as subsec. (k) and added new subsec. (j), effective for tax. yrs. of foreign corporations begin. after 12/31/86.

—P.L. 99-514, Sec. 1875(d)(2)(B)(ii), substituted "section 6501 or 6502 (or section 6229, but only with respect to a deficiency described in section 6230(a)(2)(A))" for "section 6501 or 6502" in para. (a)(1), effective for partnership tax. yrs. begin. after 9/3/82.

In 1984, P.L. 98-369, Sec. 305(b)(4), substituted "section 4963(e)" for "4962(e)" in subsec. (g), effective for tax. events occurring after 12/31/84.

In 1981, P.L. 97-34, Sec. 422(e)(7), substituted "6163 or 6166" for "6163, 6166, or 6166A" in subsec. (d), effective for estates of decedents dying after 12/31/81.

In 1980, P.L. 96-596, Sec. 2(a)(4)(D), substituted "4962(e)" for "4941(e)(4), 4942(j)(2), 4943(d)(3), 4944(e)(3), 4945(i)(2), 4951(e)(4), 4952(e)(2), 4971(c)(3), or 4975(f)(6)" in subsec. (g) . . . Sec. 2(a)(4)(E), redesignated subsec. (j) as subsec. (i) [sic , Sec. 6(a) of P.L. 96-589 added new subsec. (i), see below], effective as provided in Sec. 2(d)(2) of this Act which reads as follows:

"(2) Second tier taxes. The amendments made by this section with respect to any second tier tax shall apply only with respect to taxes assessed after the date of the enactment of this Act [12/24/80]. Nothing in the preceding sentence shall be construed to permit the assessment of a tax in a case to which, on the date of enactment of this Act [12/24/80], the doctrine of res judicata applies."

—P.L. 96-596, Sec. 2(a)(4)(F), provides:

"(F) The amendments made by sections 1203(h)(1) and 1601(f)(2) of the Tax Reform Act of 1976 [P.L. 94-455, see below] and the amendment made by section 362(d)(5) of the Revenue Act of 1978 [P.L. 95-600, see below], shall be deemed to be amendments to section 6503(i) [sic] of the Internal Revenue Code of 1954 (as redesignated by [Sec. 2(a)(4)(E) of this Act])."

—P.L. 96-589, Sec. 6(a), redesignated subsec. (i) as subsec. (j) [sic , there is no subsec. (i)] and added new subsec. (i) . . . Sec. 6(i)(11), amended para. (i)(2) [sic , para. (j)(2)], effective 10/1/79, except for any proceeding under the Bankruptcy Act begun before 10/1/79. Sec. 7(g) of this Act provides:

"(g) Definitions.

"For purposes of this section—

"(1) Bankruptcy case. The term 'bankruptcy case' means any case under title 11 of the United States Code (as recodified by P.L. 95-598).

"(2) Similar judicial proceeding. The term 'similar judicial proceeding' means a receivership, foreclosure, or similar proceeding in a Federal or State court (as modified by section 368(a)(3)(D) of the Internal Revenue Code of 1954)."

Prior to amendment, para. (i)(2) [sic para. (j)(2)] read as follows:

"(2) Bankruptcy and receiverships, see subchapter B of chapter 70."

—P.L. 96-222, Sec. 103(a)(11)(A), amended Sec. 362(e) of P.L. 95-600, the effective date for changes made by Sec. 362 of P.L. 95-600, by substituting "860(e)" for "860(d)" [see below].

—P.L. 96-222, Sec. 108(b)(1)(A)(i), substituted "4951, 4952, 4971, or 4975" for "4971, 4975, 4985, or 4986" in subsec. (g) . . . Sec. 108(b)(1)(A)(ii), substituted "4951(e)(4), 4952(e)(2), 4971(c)(3), or 4975(f)(6)" for "4971(c)(3), 4975(f)(6), 4985(e)(4), or 4986(e)(2)" in subsec. (g), effective for contributions, acts, and expenditures made after '77, in and for tax. yrs. begin. after '77.

In 1978, P.L. 95-600, Sec. 362(d)(5), amended para. (h)(5) [sic (j)(5)], with respect to determinations (as defined in Code Sec. 860(e)) after 11/6/78.

Prior to the amendment, para. (h)(5) read as follows:

"(5) Deficiency dividends of a real estate investment trust, see section 859(f)."

—P.L. 95-227, Sec. 4(d)(6), substituted "or section 507, 4971, 4975, 4985, or 4986" for "or section 507 or section 4971 or section 4975", and substituted "4975(f)(6), 4985(e)(4), or 4986(e)(2)" for "or 4975(f)(4)" in subsec. (g), effective for contributions, acts, and expenditures made after '77, in and for tax. yrs. begin. after '77.

In 1976, P.L. 94-455, Sec. 1203(h)(1), added para. (4) to redesignated subsec. (h), [sic , subsec. (j)] for documents prepared after '76.

—P.L. 94-455, Sec. 1601(f)(2), added para. (5) to "Section 6503(i)" [sic ; amendment was apparently intended for redesignated subsec. (h)], for determinations as defined in subsec. 859(e) occurring after 10/4/76.

—P.L. 94-455, Sec. 1902(b)(2)(A), deleted subsec. (e), and redesignated subsecs. (f), (g), (h) and (i) as subsecs. (e), (f), (g) and (h), effective for estates of decedents dying after 10/4/76.

Prior to deletion, subsec. (e) read as follows:

"(e) Certain powers of appointment.

"The running of the period of limitations for assessment or collection of any tax imposed by chapter 11 shall be suspended in respect of the estate of a decedent claiming a deduction under section 2055(b)(2) until 30 days after the expiration of the period for assessment or collection of the tax imposed by chapter 11 on the estate of the surviving spouse."

—P.L. 94-455, Sec. 1906(b)(13)(A), substituted "Secretary" for "Secretary or his delegate" each place it appeared in Code Sec. 6503, effective 2/1/77.

—P.L. 94-455, Sec. 2004(c)(4), substituted "section 6163, 6166, or 6166A" for "section 6166" in subsec. (d), effective for estates of decedents dying after 12/31/76.

—P.L. 94-452, Sec. 3(b), redesignated subsec. (i) as subsec. (j) and added new subsec. (i), effective 10/1/77 for sales after 7/7/70 in tax. yrs. end. after 7/7/70, but only in the case of qualified bank holding corps. with the meaning of subsec. 1103(b), as amended by this Act.

In 1974, P.L. 93-406, Sec. 1016(a)(15)(A), substituted "certain excise" for "chapter 42" in para. (a)(1), effective 9/2/74 or other date as specified in Sec. 1017 of the Act (reproduced following Code Sec. 401).

—P.L. 93-406, Sec. 1016(a)(15)(B), added "or section 4971 or section 4975" after "section 507" and substituted "4945(i)(2), 4971(c)(3), or 4975(f)(4)" for "or 4945(h)(2)" in subsec. (h), effective 9/2/74 or other date as specified in Sec. 1017 of the Act (reproduced following Code Sec. 401).

In 1969, P.L. 91-172, Sec. 101(g)(4), redesignated subsec. (h) as subsec. (i) and added new subsec. (h), effective 1/1/70.

Limitations on assessment and collection   Code Sec. 6504

—P.L. 91-172, Sec. 101(j)(46), added "and chapter 42" to the parenthetical phrase in para. (a)(1), effective 1/1/70.

In **1966**, P.L. 89-719, Sec. 106, deleted "(other than the estate of a decedent or of an incompetent)" and "or Territory" in subsec. (b), amended subsec. (c), redesignated subsec. (g) as subsec. (h), and added new subsec. (g), effective after 11/2/66, regardless of when a lien or a title of the U.S. arose or when the lien or interest of any other person was acquired. For a special exception included in Sec. 114 of P.L. 89-719 see the note to Code Sec. 6323.

Prior to amendment, subsec. (c) read as follows:

"(c) Location of property outside the United States or removal of property from the United States.

"In case collection is hindered or delayed because property of the taxpayer is situated or held outside the United States or is removed from the United States, the period of limitations on collection after assessment prescribed in section 6502 shall be suspended for the period collection is so hindered or delayed. The total suspension of time under this subsection shall not in the aggregate exceed 6 years."

—P.L. 89-384, Sec. 1(e), redesignated subsec. (f) as subsec. (g) and added, new subsec. (f), effective for amounts received after 12/31/64 for foreign expropriation losses (as defined in Code Sec. 1351(b)) sustained after 12/31/58.

In **1958**, P.L. 85-866, Sec. 206(d), eliminated "assessment or" following "period of limitations for" and added "or under the provisions of section 6166" in subsec. (d), effective as provided in Sec. 206(f) of this Act, which provides:

"(f) Effective date. The amendments made by this section shall apply to estates of decedents with respect to which the date for the filing of the estate tax return (including extensions thereof) prescribed by section 6075(a) of the Internal Revenue Code of 1954 is after the date of the enactment of this Act (9/2/58); except that (1) section 6166(i) of such Code as added by this section shall apply to estates of decedents dying after August 16, 1954, but only if the date for the filing of the estate tax return (including extensions thereof) expired on or before the date of the enactment of this Act and (2) notwithstanding section 6166(a) of such Code, if an election under such section is required to be made before the sixtieth day after the date of the enactment of this Act such an election shall be considered timely if made on or before such sixtieth day."

In **1956**, P.L. 1011, Sec. 2, added subsec. (e) and redesignated subsec. (e) as subsec. (f), effective for decedent dying after 8/16/54.

Sec. 6504. Cross references.

For limitation period in case of—

(1) Adjustments to accrued foreign taxes, see section 905(c).

(2) Change of treatment with respect to itemized deductions where taxpayer and his spouse make separate returns, see section 63(e)(3).

(3) Involuntary conversion of property, see section 1033(a)(2)(C) and (D).

(4) Application by fiduciary for discharge from personal liability for estate tax, see section 2204.

(5) Insolvent banks and trust companies, see section 7507.

(6) Service in a combat zone, etc., see section 7508.

(7) Claims against transferees and fiduciaries, see chapter 71.

(8) Assessments to recover excessive amounts paid under section 6420 (relating to gasoline used on farms), 6421 (relating to gasoline used for certain nonhighway purposes or by local transit systems), or 6427 (relating to fuels not used for taxable purposes) and assessments of civil penalties under section 6675 for excessive claims under section 6420, 6421, or 6427, see section 6206.

(9) Assessment and collection of interest, see section 6601(g).

(10) Assessment of civil penalties under section 6694 or 6695, see section 6696(d)(1).

(11) Assessments of tax attributable to partnership items, see section 6229.

In **1998**, P.L. 105-206, Sec. 6005(e)(3), added "on or" before "before" each place it appeared in the heading and text of Sec. 312(d)(2)[sic (e)] of P.L. 105-34, see below.

In **1997**, P.L. 105-34, Sec. 312(d)(13), deleted para. (4) and redesignated paras. (5)-(12) as paras. (4)-(11), effective for sales and exchanges after 5/6/97, except as provided by Secs. 312(d)(2)-(4) [sic (e)(2)-(4)] of this Act [as amended by Sec. 6005(e)(3), 105-206, see above], which read as follows:

"(2) Sales on or before date of enactment [8/5/97].—At the election of the taxpayer, the amendments made by this section shall not apply to any sale or exchange on or before the date of the enactment [8/5/97] of this Act.

"(3) Certain sales within 2 years after date of enactment. Section 121 of the Internal Revenue Code of 1986 (as amended by this section) shall be applied without regard to subsection (c)(2)(B) thereof in the case of any sale or exchange of property during the 2-year period beginning on the date of the enactment [8/5/97] of this Act if the taxpayer held such property on the date of the enactment [8/5/97] of this Act and fails to meet the ownership and use requirements of subsection (a) thereof with respect to such property.

"(4) Binding contracts.—At the election of the taxpayer, the amendments made by this section shall not apply to a sale or exchange after the date of the enactment [8/5/97] of this Act, if—

"(A) such sale or exchange is pursuant to a contract which was binding on such date, or

"(B) without regard to such amendments, gain would not be recognized under section 1034 of the Internal Revenue Code of 1986 (as in effect on the day before the date of the enactment [8/5/97] of this Act) on such sale or exchange by reason of a new residence acquired on or before such date or with respect to the acquisition of which by the taxpayer a binding contract was in effect on such date.

This paragraph shall not apply to any sale or exchange by an individual if the treatment provided by section 877(a)(1) of the Internal Revenue Code of 1986 applies to such individual."

Prior to deletion, para. (4) read as follows:

"(4) Gain upon sale or exchange of principal residence, see section 1034(j)."

In **1986**, P.L. 99-514, Sec. 104(b)(18), amended para. (2), effective for tax. yrs. begin. after 12/31/86.

Prior to amendment, para. (2) read as follows:

"(2) Change of treatment with respect to itemized deductions and zero bracket amount where taxpayer and his spouse make separate returns, see section 63(g)(5)."

In **1983**, P.L. 97-424, Sec. 515(b)(10), deleted "6424 (relating to lubricating oil used for certain nontaxable purposes)," after "systems)," and deleted "6424" after "6421,", in para. (9), effective for articles sold after 1/6/83.

In **1982**, P.L. 97-248, Sec. 402(c)(6), added para. (12), effective for partnership tax. yrs. begin. after 9/3/82. Sec. 407(a)(3) of this Act provides:

"(3) The amendments made by sections 402, 403, and 404 [of this Act] shall apply to any partnership taxable year (or in the case of section 6232 of such Code, to any period) ending after the date of the enactment of this Act [9/3/82] if the partnership, each partner, and each indirect partner requests such application and the Secretary of the Treasury or his delegate consents to such application."

In **1978**, P.L. 95-618, Sec. 233(b)(2)(D), substituted "used for certain nontaxable purposes" for "not used in highway motor vehicles" in para. (9), effective 12/1/78 (the first day of the first calendar month which begins more than 10 days after 11/9/78).

—P.L. 95-600, Sec. 405(c)(6), substituted "principal residence" for "residence" in para. (4), effective for sales and exchanges of residences after 7/26/78, in tax. yrs. ending after 7/26/78.

—P.L. 95-600, Sec. 703(j)(10), amended Sec. 1901(b)(37)(D) of P.L. 94-455, to delete para. (6), of Code Sec. 6504 (instead of Code Sec. 6515) see below.

In **1977**, P.L. 95-30, Sec. 101(d)(16), amended para. (2), effective for tax. yrs. begin. after 12/31/76.

Prior to amendment, para. (2) read as follows:

"(2) Change of election with respect to the standard deduction where taxpayer and his spouse make separate returns, see section 144(b)."

In **1976**, P.L. 94-455, Sec. 1203(h)(2), added para. (11), effective for documents prepared after 12/31/76.

—P.L. 94-455, Sec. 1901(b)(31)(D), substituted "1033(a)(2)(C) and (D)" for "1033(a)(3)(C) and (D)" in para. (3) ... Sec. 1901(b)(36)(D), deleted para. (1), effective for tax. yrs. begin. after 12/31/76.

Prior to deletion, para. (1) read as follows:

"(1) Adjustments incident to involuntary liquidation of inventory, see section 1321."

—P.L. 94-455, Sec. 1901(b)(37)(D), deleted para. (6), effective for tax. yrs. begin after 12/31/76.

Prior to deletion, para. (6) read as follows:

"(6) War loss recovered where prior benefit rule is elected, see section 1335."

—P.L. 94-455, Sec. 1901(b)(39)(B), deleted para. (7), effective for tax. yrs. begin. after 12/31/76.

Prior to amendment, para. (7) read as follows:

"(7) Recovery of unconstitutional Federal taxes, see section 1346."

—P.L. 94-455, Sec. 1906(a)(32), deleted paras. (13) and (14), added new para. (13) and redesignated paras. (2), (3), (4), (5), (9), (10), (11), (12), (13), and (15) as paras. (1), (2), (3), (4), (5), (6), (7), (8), (9), and (10), effective 2/1/77.

Prior to deletion, paras. (13) and (14) read as follows:

"(13) Assessments to recover excessive amounts paid under section 6420 (relating to gasoline used on farms) and assessments of civil penalties under section 6675 for excessive claims under section 6420, see section 6206."

"(14) Assessments to recover excessive amounts paid under section 6421 (relating to gasoline used for certain nonhighway purposes or by local transit systems) and assessments of civil penalties under section 6675 for excessive claims under section 6421, see section 6206."

In **1975**, P.L. 93-625, Sec. 7(d)(4), substituted "6601(g)" for "6601(h)" in para. (15), effective 7/1/75 and applicable to amounts outstanding on or arising after 7/1/75.

In **1970**, P.L. 91-614, Sec. 101(d)(2), substituted "fiduciary" for "executor" in para. (9), effective for decedents dying after 12/31/70.

In **1969**, P.L. 91-172, Sec. 213(c)(3), deleted para. (8), effective for tax. yrs. begin. after 12/31/69.

Prior to amendment, para. (8) read as follows:

3,749

Code Sec. 6504 — Limitations on assessment and collection

"(8) Limitations on deductions allowable to individuals in certain cases, see sec. 270(d).".

In 1964, P.L. 88-272, Sec. 112(d)(2), substituted "with respect to the" for "to take" in para. (3), effective for tax. yrs. begin after 12/31/63.

In 1958, P.L. 85-866, Sec. 84(b), added para. (15), effective 8/17/54.

In 1956, ch. 462, Sec. 208(e)(5), added para. (14).

—ch. 160, Sec. 4(d), added para. (13).

Subchapter B.—Limitations on Credit or Refund

Sec.
6511. Limitations on credit or refund.
6512. Limitations in case of petition to Tax Court.
6513. Time return deemed filed and tax considered paid.
6514. Credits or refunds after period of limitation.
6515. Cross references.

Sec. 6511. Limitations on credit or refund.

(a) Period of limitation on filing claim.

Claim for credit or refund of an overpayment of any tax imposed by this title in respect of which tax the taxpayer is required to file a return shall be filed by the taxpayer within 3 years from the time the return was filed or 2 years from the time the tax was paid, whichever of such periods expires the later, or if no return was filed by the taxpayer, within 2 years from the time the tax was paid. Claim for credit or refund of an overpayment of any tax imposed by this title which is required to be paid by means of a stamp shall be filed by the taxpayer within 3 years from the time the tax was paid.

(b) Limitation on allowance of credits and refunds.

(1) **Filing of claim within prescribed period.** No credit or refund shall be allowed or made after the expiration of the period of limitation prescribed in subsection (a) for the filing of a claim for credit or refund, unless a claim for credit or refund is filed by the taxpayer within such period.

(2) **Limit on amount of credit or refund.**

(A) Limit where claim filed within 3-year period. If the claim was filed by the taxpayer during the 3-year period prescribed in subsection (a), the amount of the credit or refund shall not exceed the portion of the tax paid within the period, immediately preceding the filing of the claim, equal to 3 years plus the period of any extension of time for filing the return. If the tax was required to be paid by means of a stamp, the amount of the credit or refund shall not exceed the portion of the tax paid within the 3 years immediately preceding the filing of the claim.

(B) Limit where claim not filed within 3-year period. If the claim was not filed within such 3-year period, the amount of the credit or refund shall not exceed the portion of the tax paid during the 2 years immediately preceding the filing of the claim.

(C) Limit if no claim filed. If no claim was filed, the credit or refund shall not exceed the amount which would be allowable under subparagraph (A) or (B), as the case may be, if claim was filed on the date the credit or refund is allowed.

(c) Special rules applicable in case of extension of time by agreement.

If an agreement under the provisions of section 6501(c)(4) extending the period for assessment of a tax imposed by this title is made within the period prescribed in subsection (a) for the filing of a claim for credit or refund—

(1) **Time for filing claim.** The period for filing claim for credit or refund or for making credit or refund if no claim is filed, provided in subsections (a) and (b)(1), shall not expire prior to 6 months after the expiration of the period within which an assessment may be made pursuant to the agreement or any extension thereof under section 6501(c)(4).

(2) **Limit on amount.** If a claim is filed, or a credit or refund is allowed when no claim was filed, after the execution of the agreement and within 6 months after the expiration of the period within which an assessment may be made pursuant to the agreement or any extension thereof, the amount of the credit or refund shall not exceed the portion of the tax paid after the execution of the agreement and before the filing of the claim or the making of the credit or refund, as the case may be, plus the portion of the tax paid within the period which would be applicable under subsection (b)(2) if a claim had been filed on the date the agreement was executed.

(3) **Claims not subject to special rule.** This subsection shall not apply in the case of a claim filed, or credit or refund allowed if no claim is filed, either—

(A) prior to the execution of the agreement or

(B) more than 6 months after the expiration of the period within which an assessment may be made pursuant to the agreement or any extension thereof.

(d) Special rules applicable to income taxes.

(1) **Seven-year period of limitation with respect to bad debts and worthless securities.** If the claim for credit or refund relates to an overpayment of tax imposed by subtitle A on account of—

(A) The deductibility by the taxpayer, under section 166 or section 832(c), of a debt as a debt which became worthless, or, under section 165(g), of a loss from worthlessness of a security, or

(B) The effect that the deductibility of a debt or loss described in subparagraph (A) has on the application to the taxpayer of a carryover,

in lieu of the 3-year period of limitation prescribed in subsection (a), the period shall be 7 years from the date prescribed by law for filing the return for the year with respect to which the claim is made. If the claim for credit or refund relates to an overpayment on account of the effect that the deductibility of such a debt or loss has on the application to the taxpayer of a carryback, the period shall be either 7 years from the date prescribed by law for filing the return for the year of the net operating loss which results in such carryback or the period prescribed in paragraph (2) of this subsection, whichever expires the later. In the case of a claim described in this paragraph the amount of the credit or refund may exceed the portion of the tax paid within the period prescribed in subsection (b)(2) or (c), whichever is applicable, to the extent of the amount of the overpayment attributable to the deductibility of items described in this paragraph.

(2) **Special period of limitation with respect to net operating loss or capital loss carrybacks.**

(A) Period of limitation. If the claim for credit or refund relates to an overpayment attributable to a net operating loss carryback or a capital loss carryback, in lieu of the 3-year period of limitation prescribed in subsection (a), the period shall be that period which ends 3 years after the time prescribed by law for filing the return (including extensions thereof) for the taxable year of the net operating loss or net capital loss which results in such carryback, or the period prescribed in subsection (c) in respect of such taxable year, whichever expires later. In the case of such a claim, the amount of the credit or refund may exceed the portion of the tax paid within the period provided in subsection (b)(2) or (c), whichever is applicable to the extent of the amount of the overpayment attributable to such carryback.

(B) Applicable rules.

(i) In general. If the allowance of a credit or refund of an overpayment of tax attributable to a net operating loss carryback or a capital loss carryback is otherwise prevented by the operation of any law or rule of law other than section 7122 (relating to compromises), such credit or refund may be allowed or made, if claim therefor is filed within the period provided in subparagraph (A) of this paragraph.

(ii) Tentative carryback adjustments. If the allowance of an application, credit, or refund of a decrease in tax determined under section 6411(b) is otherwise prevented by the operation of any law or rule of law other than section 7122, such application, credit, or refund may be allowed or made if application for a tentative carryback adjustment is made within the period provided in section 6411(a).

(iii) Determinations by courts to be conclusive. In the case of any such claim for credit or refund or any such application for a tentative carryback adjustment, the determination by any court, including the Tax Court, in any proceeding in which the decision of the court has become final, shall be conclusive except with respect to—

(I) the net operating loss deduction and the effect of such deduction, and

(II) the determination of a short-term capital loss and the effect of such short-term capital loss, to the extent that such deduction or short-term capital loss is affected by a carryback which was not an issue in such proceeding.

(3) Special rules relating to foreign tax credit.

(A) Special period of limitation with respect to foreign taxes paid or accrued. If the claim for credit or refund relates to an overpayment attributable to any taxes paid or accrued to any foreign country or to any possession of the United States for which credit is allowed against the tax imposed by subtitle A in accordance with the provisions of section 901 or the provisions of any treaty to which the United States is a party, in lieu of the 3-year period of limitation prescribed in subsection (a), the period shall be 10 years from the date prescribed by law for filing the return for the year in which such taxes were actually paid or accrued.

(B) Exception in the case of foreign taxes paid or accrued. In the case of a claim described in subparagraph (A), the amount of the credit or refund may exceed the portion of the tax paid within the period provided in subsection (b) or (c), whichever is applicable, to the extent of the amount of the overpayment attributable to the allowance of a credit for the taxes described in subparagraph (A).

(4) Special period of limitation with respect to certain credit carrybacks.

(A) Period of limitation. If the claim for credit or refund relates to an overpayment attributable to a credit carryback, in lieu of the 3-year period of limitation prescribed in subsection (a), the period shall be that period which ends 3 years after the time prescribed by law for filing the return (including extensions thereof) for the taxable year of the unused credit which results in such carryback (or, with respect to any portion of a credit carryback from a taxable year attributable to a net operating loss carryback, capital loss carryback, or other credit carryback from a subsequent taxable year, the period shall be that period which ends 3 years after the time prescribed by law for filing the return, including extensions thereof, for such subsequent taxable year) or the period prescribed in subsection (c) in respect of such taxable year, whichever expires later. In the case of such a claim, the amount of the credit or refund may exceed the portion of the tax paid within the period provided in subsection (b)(2) or (c), whichever is applicable, to the extent of the amount of the overpayment attributable to such carryback.

(B) Applicable rules. If the allowance of a credit or refund of an overpayment of tax attributable to a credit carryback is otherwise prevented by the operation of any law or rule of law other than section 7122, relating to compromises, such credit or refund may be allowed or made, if claim therefor is filed within the period provided in subparagraph (A) of this paragraph. In the case of any such claim for credit or refund, the determination by any court, including the Tax Court, in any proceeding in which the decision of the court has become final, shall not be conclusive with respect to any credit, and the effect of such credit, to the extent that such credit is affected by a credit carryback which was not in issue in such proceeding.

(C) Credit carryback defined. For purposes of this paragraph, the term "credit carryback" means any business carryback under section 39.

(5) Special period of limitation with respect to self-employment tax in certain cases. If the claim for credit or refund relates to an overpayment of the tax imposed by chapter 2 (relating to the tax on self-employment income) attributable to an agreement, or modification of an agreement, made pursuant to section 218 of the Social Security Act (relating to coverage of State and local employees), and if the allowance of a credit or refund of such overpayment is otherwise prevented by the operation of any law or rule of law other than section 7122 (relating to compromises), such credit or refund may be allowed or made if claim therefor is filed on or before the last day of the second year after the calendar year in which such agreement (or modification) is agreed to by the State and the Commissioner of Social Security.

(6) Special period of limitation with respect to amounts included in income subsequently recaptured under qualified plan termination. If the claim for credit or refund relates to an overpayment of tax imposed by subtitle A on account of the recapture, under section 4045 of the Employee Retirement Income Security Act of 1974, of amounts included in income for a prior taxable year, the 3-year period of limitation prescribed in subsection (a) shall be extended, for purposes of permitting a credit or refund of the amount of the recapture, until the date which occurs one year after the date on which such recaptured amount is paid by the taxpayer.

(7) Special period of limitation with respect to self-employment tax in certain cases. If—

(A) the claim for credit or refund relates to an overpayment of the tax imposed by chapter 2 (relating to the tax on self-employment income) attributable to Tax Court determination in a proceeding under section 7436, and

(B) the allowance of a credit or refund of such overpayment is otherwise prevented by the operation of any law or rule of law other than section 7122 (relating to compromises),

such credit or refund may be allowed or made if claim therefor is filed on or before the last day of the second

Code Sec. 6511(d)(7)(B)   **Limitations on assessment and collection**

year after the calendar year in which such determination becomes final.

(8) Special rules when uniformed services retired pay is reduced as a result of award of disability compensation.

(A) Period of limitation on filing claim. If the claim for credit or refund relates to an overpayment of tax imposed by subtitle A on account of—

(i) the reduction of uniformed services retired pay computed under section 1406 or 1407 of title 10, United States Code, or

(ii) the waiver of such pay under section 5305 of title 38 of such Code,

as a result of an award of compensation under title 38 of such Code pursuant to a determination by the Secretary of Veterans Affairs, the 3-year period of limitation prescribed in subsection (a) shall be extended, for purposes of permitting a credit or refund based upon the amount of such reduction or waiver, until the end of the 1-year period beginning on the date of such determination.

(B) Limitation to 5 taxable years. Subparagraph (A) shall not apply with respect to any taxable year which began more than 5 years before the date of such determination.

(e) Repealed.

(f) Special rule for chapter 42 and similar taxes.

For purposes of any tax imposed by section 4912, chapter 42, or section 4975, the return referred to in subsection (a) shall be the return specified in section 6501(l)(1).

(g) Special rule for claims with respect to partnership items.

In the case of any tax imposed by subtitle A with respect to any person which is attributable to any partnership item (as defined in section 6231(a)(3)), the provisions of section 6227 and subsections (c) and (d) of section 6230 shall apply in lieu of the provisions of this subchapter.

(h) Running of periods of limitation suspended while taxpayer is unable to manage financial affairs due to disability.

(1) In general. In the case of an individual, the running of the periods specified in subsections (a), (b), and (c) shall be suspended during any period of such individual's life that such individual is financially disabled.

(2) Financially disabled.

(A) In general. For purposes of paragraph (1), an individual is financially disabled if such individual is unable to manage his financial affairs by reason of a medically determinable physical or mental impairment of the individual which can be expected to result in death or which has lasted or can be expected to last for a continuous period of not less than 12 months. An individual shall not be considered to have such an impairment unless proof of the existence thereof is furnished in such form and manner as the Secretary may require.

(B) Exception where individual has guardian, etc. An individual shall not be treated as financially disabled during any period that such individual's spouse or any other person is authorized to act on behalf of such individual in financial matters.

(i) Cross references.

(1) For time return deemed filed and tax considered paid, see section 6513.

• *Caution:* Code Sec. 6511(i)(2), following, was amended by Sec. 532(c)(11), P.L. 107-16, the Economic Growth and Tax Relief Reconciliation Act of 2001 (EGTRRA). These provisions generally sunset for tax years beginning after 12/31/2012. For specific sunset provisions, see Sec. 901, P.L. 107-16 (as amended) reproduced in history notes for this Code Sec.

---

(2) For limitations with respect to certain credits against estate tax, see sections 2014(b) and 2015.

(3) For limitations in case of floor stocks refunds, see section 6412.

(4) For a period of limitations for credit or refund in the case of joint income returns after separate returns have been filed, see section 6013(b)(3).

(5) For limitations in case of payments under section 6420 (relating to gasoline used on farms), see section 6420(b).

(6) For limitations in case of payments under section 6421 (relating to gasoline used for certain nonhighway purposes or by local transit systems), see section 6421(d).

(7) For a period of limitations for refund of an overpayment of penalties imposed under section 6694 or 6695, see section 6696(d)(2).

In 2010, P.L. 111-312, Sec. 101(a)(1), substituted "December 31, 2012" for "December 31, 2010" both places it appears in Sec. 901, P.L. 107-16 [see below], effective as if included in the enactment of P.L. 107-16, EGTRRA, 6/7/2001.

In 2008, P.L. 110-245, Sec. 106(a), added para. (d)(8), effective for claims for credit or refund filed after 6/17/2008.

—P.L. 110-245, Sec. 106(c), of this Act provides:

"(c) Transition Rules- In the case of a determination described in paragraph (8) of section 6511(d) of the Internal Revenue Code of 1986 (as added by this section) which is made by the Secretary of Veterans Affairs after December 31, 2000, and before the date of the enactment of this Act, such paragraph—

"(1) shall not apply with respect to any taxable year which began before January 1, 2001, and

"(2) shall be applied by substituting for 'the date of such determination' in subparagraph (A) thereof."

In 2002, P.L. 107-358, Sec. 2, added subsec. (c) in Sec. 901 of P.L. 107-16 [see below], effective 12/17/2002.

In 2001, P.L. 107-16, Sec. 532(c)(11), substituted "2014(b)" for "2011(c), 2014(b)," in para. (i)(2), effective for estates of decedents dying, and generation-skipping transfers, after 12/31/2004.

—P.L. 107-16, Sec. 901, of this Act [as amended by Sec. 2 of P.L. 107-358, and Sec. 101(a)(1) of P.L. 111-312, see above], reads as follows:

"SEC. 901. SUNSET OF PROVISIONS OF ACT.

"(a) In general. All provisions of, and amendments made by, this Act shall not apply—

"(1) to taxable, plan, or limitation years beginning after December 31, 2012, or

"(2) in the case of title V, to estates of decedents dying, gifts made, or generation skipping transfers, after December 31, 2012.

"(b) Application of certain laws. The Internal Revenue Code of 1986 and the Employee Retirement Income Security Act of 1974 shall be applied and administered to years, estates, gifts, and transfers described in subsection (a) as if the provisions and amendments described in subsection (a) had never been enacted.

"(c) Exception. Subsection (a) shall not apply to section 803 (relating to no federal income tax on restitution received by victims of the Nazi regime or their heirs or estates)."

In 1998, P.L. 105-206, Sec. 3202(a), redesignated subsec. (h) as subsec. (i) and added new subsec. (h), effective for periods of disability before, on, or after 7/22/98 but shall not apply to any claim for credit or refund which (without regard to such amendment) is barred by the operation of any law or rule of law (including res judicata) as of 7/22/98.

In 1997, P.L. 105-34, Sec. 1056(a), substituted "for the year in which such taxes were actually paid or accrued" for "for the year with respect to which the claim is made" in subpara. (d)(3)(A), effective for taxes paid or accrued in tax. yrs. begin. after 8/5/97.

—P.L. 105-34, Sec. 1454(b)(1), added para. (d)(7), effective 8/5/97.

In 1994, P.L. 103-296, Sec. 108(h)(8), substituted "Commissioner of Social Security" for "Secretary of Health and Human Services" in para. (d)(5), effective 3/31/95.

In 1990, P.L. 101-508, Sec. 11801(c)(17)(B), deleted "; except that with respect to an overpayment attributable to the creation of or an increase in a net operating loss carryback as a result of the elimination of excessive profits by a renegotiation (as defined in section 1481(a)(1)(A)), the period shall not expire before the expiration of the 12th month following the month in which the agreement or order for the elimination of such excessive profits becomes final" after "whichever expires

later" in subpara. (d)(2)(A) . . . Sec. 11801(c)(22)(C), deleted subsec. (e), effective 11/5/90 except as provided in Sec. 11821(b) of this Act, which reads as follows:
"(b) Savings provision. If

"(1) any provision amended or repealed by this part applied to—

"(A) any transaction occurring before the date of enactment of this Act [11/5/90],

"(B) any property acquired before such date of enactment [11/5/90], or

"(C) any item of income, loss, deduction, or credit taken into account before such date of enactment [11/5/90], and

"(2) the treatment of such transaction, property, or item under such provision would (without regard to the amendments made by this part) affect liability for part tax for periods ending after such date of enactment [11/5/90],
nothing in the amendments made by this part shall be construed to affect the treatment of such transaction, property, or item for purposes of determining liability for tax for periods ending after such date of enactment [11/5/90]."
Prior to deletion, subsec. (e) read as follows:
(e) Special rules in case of manufactured sugar.

"(1) Use as livestock feed or for distillation or production of alcohol. No payment shall be allowed under section 6418(a) unless within 2 years after the right to such payment has accrued a claim therefor is filed by the person entitled thereto.

"(2) Exportation. No payment shall be allowed under section 6418(b) unless within 2 years after the right to such payment has accrued a claim therefor is filed by the person entitled thereto."

In 1988, P.L. 100-647, Sec. 1017(c)(11), substituted "section 6421(d)" for "section 6421(c)" in para. (i) [sic (h)](6), effective for gasoline removed (as defined in Code Sec. 4082) after 12/31/87.

—P.L. 100-647, Sec. 1018(u)(21), corrected Sec. 231(d)(3)(I) of P.L. 99-514, to amend para. (d)(4) instead of para. (d)(6), see below.

—P.L. 100-647, Sec. 1018(u)(51)(A), substituted "section 4912, chapter 42," for "chapter 42" in subsec. (f) . . . Sec. 1018(u)(51)(B), substituted "similar taxes" for "certain chapter 43 taxes" in the heading of subsec. (f), effective for tax. yrs. begin. after 12/22/87.

In 1988, P.L. 100-418, Sec. 1941(b)(2)(I), deleted subsec. (h) and redesignated subsec. (i) as subsec. (h), effective for crude oil removed from the premises on or after 8/23/88.
Prior to deletion, subsec. (h) read as follows:
"(h) Special rules for windfall profit taxes.

"(1) Oil subject to withholding. In the case of any oil to which section 4995(a) applies and with respect to which no return is required, the return referred to in subsection (a) shall be the return (of the person liable for the tax imposed by section 4986) of the taxes imposed by subtitle A for the taxable year in which the removal year (as defined in section 6501(m)(1)(B)) ends.

"(2) Special rule for DOE reclassification. In the case of any tax imposed by chapter 45, if a Department of Energy change (as defined in section 6501(m)(2)(B)) becomes final, the period for filing a claim for credit or refund for any overpayment attributable to such change shall not expire before the date which is 1 year after the date on which such change becomes final.

"(3) Cross reference.
For period of limitation for windfall profit tax items of partnerships, see section 6227(a) and subsections (c) and (d) of section 6230 as made applicable by section 6232."

In 1986, P.L. 99-514, Sec. 141(b)(3), amended subpara. (d)(2)(B), effective for tax. yrs. begin. after 12/31/86.
Prior to amendment, subpara. (d)(2)(B) read as follows:

"(B) Applicable rules.

"(i) If the allowance of a credit or refund of an overpayment of tax attributable to a net operating loss carryback or a capital loss carryback is otherwise prevented by the operation of any law or rule of law other than section 7122, relating to compromises, such credit or refund may be allowed or made, if claim therefor is filed within the period provided in subparagraph (A) of this paragraph. If the allowance of an application, credit, or refund of a decrease in tax determined under section 6411(b) is otherwise prevented by the operation of any law or rule of law other than section 7122, such application, credit, or refund may be allowed or made if application for a tentative carryback adjustment is made within the period provided in section 6411(a). In the case of any such claim for credit or refund or any such application for a tentative carryback adjustment, the determination by any court, including the Tax Court, in any proceeding in which the decision of the court has become final, shall be conclusive except with respect to the net operating loss deduction, and the effect of such deduction, or with respect to the determination of a short-term capital loss, and the effect of such short-term capital loss, to the extent that such deduction is affected by a carryback which was not an issue in such proceeding.

"(ii) A claim for credit or refund for a computation year (as defined in section 1302(c)(1)) shall be determined to relate to an overpayment attributable to a net operating loss carryback or a capital loss carryback, as the case may be, when such carryback relates to any base period year (as defined in section 1302(c)(3))."

—P.L. 99-514, Sec. 231(a)(2), amended Sec. 221(b)(2)(A) of P.L. 97-34, the effective date for changes made by Sec. 221(b)(1)(A) of P.L. 97-34, by substituting "amounts paid or incurred after June 30, 1981" for "amounts paid or incurred after June 30, 1981 and before January 1, 1986" [see below].

—P.L. 99-514, Sec. 231(d)(3)(I), [as amended by Sec. 1018(u)(21) of P.L. 100-647, see above] deleted "and any research credit carryback under section 30(g)(2)" from the end of subpara. (d)(4)(C), effective for tax. yrs. begin. after 12/31/85.

—P.L. 99-514, Sec. 1847(b)(15)(A), substituted "section 6501(m)(1)(B)" for "section 6501(q)(1)(B)" in para. (h)(1) . . . Sec. 1847(b)(15)(B), substituted "section 6501(m)(2)(B)" for "section 6501(q)(2)(B)" in para. (h)(2), effective for tax. yrs. begin. after 12/31/83 and carrybacks from tax. yrs. begin. after 12/31/83.

In 1984, P.L. 98-369, Sec. 163(b)(2), substituted "section 6501(l)(1)" for "section 6501(n)(1)" in subsec. (f), effective for expenditures for which the second tax. yr. described in Code Sec. 118(b)(2)(B) ends after 12/31/84.

—P.L. 98-369, Sec. 211(b)(25), deleted para. (d)(6) and redesignated para. (d)(7) as para. (d)(6), effective for tax. yrs. begin. after 12/31/83.
Prior to deletion, para. (d)(6) read as follows:
"(6) Special period of limitation with respect to reduction of policyholders surplus account of life insurance companies.

"(A) Period of limitation. If the claim for credit or refund relates to an overpayment arising by operation of section 815(d)(5) (relating to reduction of policyholders surplus account of life insurance companies for certain unused deductions), in lieu of the 3-year period of limitation prescribed in subsection (a), the period shall be that period which ends with the expiration of the 15th day of the 39th month following the end of the last taxable year to which the loss described in section 815(d)(5)(A) is carried under section 812(b)(2), or the period prescribed in subsection (c), in respect of such taxable year, whichever expires later. In the case of such a claim, the amount of the credit or refund may exceed the portion of the tax paid within the period provided in subsection (b)(2) or (c), whichever is applicable, to the extent of the amount of overpayment arising by operation of section 815(d)(5).

"(B) Applicable rules. If the allowance of a credit or refund of an overpayment arising by operation of section 815(d)(5) is otherwise prevented by operation of any law or rule of law, other than section 7122 (relating to compromises), such credit or refund may be allowed or made, if claim therefor is filed within the period provided in subparagraph (A) of this paragraph. In the case of any such claim for credit or refund, the determination by any court, including the Tax Court, in any proceeding in which the decision of the court has become final, shall be conclusive except with respect to the effect of the operation of section 815(d)(5), to the extent such effect of the operation of section 815(d)(5) was not in issue in such proceeding."

—P.L. 98-369, Sec. 474(r)(40), amended subpara. (d)(4)(C), effective for tax. yrs. begin. after 12/31/83 and to carrybacks from tax. yrs. begin. after 12/31/83.
Prior to amendment, subpara. (d)(4)(C) read as follows:

"(C) Credit carryback defined. For purposes of this paragraph, the term 'credit carryback' means any investment credit carryback, work incentive program credit carryback, and new employee credit carryback, research credit carryback, and employee stock ownership credit carryback."

—P.L. 98-369, Sec. 714(p)(2)(G), amended para. (h)(3), effective for periods after 12/31/82.
Prior to amendment, para. (h)(3) read as follows:

"(3) Partnership items of federally registered partnerships. Under regulations prescribed by the Secretary, rules similar to the rules of subsection (g) shall apply to the tax imposed by section 4986."

—P.L. 98-369, Sec. 735(c)(14), deleted subsec. (i) and redesignated subsec. (j) as subsec. (i), effective for articles sold on or after 4/1/84.
Prior to deletion, subsec. (i) read as follows:
"(i) Special rule for certain tread rubber tax credits or refunds.

The period for allowing a credit or making a refund of any overpayment of tax arising by reason of subparagraph (G)(iii) of section 6416(b)(2) with respect to any adjustment of sales price of a tire pursuant to a warranty or guarantee shall not expire if claim therefor is filed before the date which is one year after the day on which such adjustment is made."

—P.L. 98-369, Sec. 2663(j)(5)(F), substituted "Health and Human Services" for "Health, Education, and Welfare" in para. (d)(5), effective 7/18/84, but this amendment is not be construed as changing or affecting any right, liability, status or interpretation which existed before 7/18/84.

In 1982, P.L. 97-248, Sec. 402(c)(7), amended subsec. (g), effective for partnership tax. yrs. begin. after 9/3/82. Sec. 407(a)(3) of this Act provides:

"(3) The amendments made by sections 402, 403, and 404 [of this Act] shall apply to any partnership taxable year (or in the case of section 6232 of such Code, to any period) ending after the date of the enactment of this Act [9/3/82] if the partnership, each partner, and each indirect partner requests such application and the Secretary of the Treasury or his delegate consents to such application."
Prior to amendment, subsec. (g) read as follows:
"(g) Special rule for partnership items of federally registered partnerships.

"(1) In general. In the case of any tax imposed by subtitle A with respect to any person, the period for filing a claim for credit or refund of any overpayment attributable to any partnership item of a federally registered partnership shall not expire before the later of—

"(A) the date which is 4 years after the date prescribed by law (including extensions thereof) for filing the partnership return for the partnership taxable year in which the item arose, or

"(B) if an agreement under the provisions of section 6501(c)(4) extending the period for the assessment of any deficiency attributable to such partnership item is made before the date specified in subparagraph (A), the date 6 months after the expiration of such extension.
In any case to which the preceding sentence applies, the amount of the credit or refund may exceed the portion of the tax paid within the period provided in subsection (b)(2) or (c), whichever is applicable.

"(2) Definitions. For purposes of this subsection, the terms 'partnership item' and 'federally registered partnership' have the same meanings as such terms have when used in section 6501(o)."

In 1981, P.L. 97-34, Sec. 221(b)(2)(A), substituted "new employee credit carryback, and research credit carryback" for "and new employee credit carryback" in subpara. (d)(4)(C), effective for amounts paid or incurred after 6/30/81. For transitional rule see Sec. 221(d)(2) of this Act, reproduced in note following Code Sec. 44F.

—P.L. 97-34, Sec. 331(d)(2)(A), substituted "research credit carryback, and employee stock ownership credit carryback" for "and research credit carryback" in subpara. (d)(4)(C), effective for tax. yrs. begin. after 12/31/81.

In 1980, P.L. 96-598, Sec. 1(c), redesignated subsec (i) as (j) and added new subsec. (i), effective 2/1/81.

—P.L. 96-223, Sec. 101(g)(2), redesignated subsec. (h) as subsec. (i) and added new subsec. (h), for periods after 2/29/80. Sec. 101(i)(2) of this Act, provides as follows:

"(2) Transitional rules.—For the period ending June 30, 1980, the Secretary of the Treasury or his delegate shall prescribe rules relating to the administration of chapter 45 of the Internal Revenue Code of 1954. To the extent provided in such rules, such rules shall supplement or supplant for such period the administrative provisions contained in chapter 45 of such Code (or in so much of subtitle F of such Code as relates to such chapter 45)."

—P.L. 96-222, Sec. 102(a)(2)(B), substituted "6501(o)" for "6501(q)" in para. (g)(2), effective for partnership items arising in partnership tax. yrs. begin. after 12/31/78.

—P.L. 96-222, Sec. 108(b)(1)(B)(i), added "or section 4975" after "chapter 42" in subsec. (f) . . . Sec. 108(b)(1)(B)(ii), substituted "chapter 42 and certain chapter 43" for "chapter 42" in the heading of subsec. (f), effective for contributions, acts and expenditures made after 12/31/77, in and for tax. yrs. begin. after 12/31/77.

In 1978, P.L. 95-628, Sec. 8(a), substituted "3 years after the time prescribed by law for filing the return (including extensions thereof) for" for "with the expiration of the 15th day of the 40th month (or the 39th month, in the case of a corporation) following the end of" following "shall be that period which ends" in subpara. (d)(2)(A) . . . Sec. 8(b)(1), amended para. (d)(4) . . . Sec. 8(b)(2), deleted paras. (d)(7) and (d)(9) and redesignated para. (d)(8) as (d)(7), effective for carrybacks arising in tax. yrs. begin. after 11/10/78.

Prior to amendment, para. (d)(4) read as follows:

"(4) Special period of limitation with respect to investment credit carrybacks.

"(A) Period of limitation. If the claim for credit or refund relates to an overpayment attributable to an investment credit carryback, in lieu of the 3-year period of limitation prescribed in subsection (a), the period shall be that period which ends with the expiration of the 15th day of the 40th month (or 39th month, in the case of a corporation) following the end of the taxable year of the unused investment credit which results in such carryback (or, with respect to any portion of an investment credit carryback from a taxable year attributable to a net operating loss carryback or a capital loss carryback from a subsequent taxable year, the period shall be that period which ends with the expiration of the 15th day of the 40th month, or 39th month, in the case of a corporation, following the end of such subsequent taxable year), or the period prescribed in subsection (c) in respect of such taxable year, whichever expires later. In the case of such a claim, the amount of the credit or refund may exceed the portion of the tax paid within the period provided in subsection (b)(2) or (c), whichever is applicable, to the extent of the amount of the overpayment attributable to such carryback.

"(B) Applicable rules. If the allowance of a credit or refund of an overpayment of tax attributable to an investment credit carryback is otherwise prevented by the operation of any law or rule of law other than section 7122, relating to compromises, such credit or refund may be allowed or made, if claim therefor is filed within the period provided in subparagraph (A) of this paragraph. In the case of any such claim for credit or refund, the determination by any court, including the Tax Court, in any proceeding in which the decision of the court has become final, shall not be conclusive with respect to the investment credit, and the effect of such credit, to the extent that such credit is affected by a carryback which was not in issue in such proceeding."

Prior to deletion, para. (d)(7) read as follows:

"(7) Special period of limitation with respect to work incentive program credit carrybacks.

"(A) Period of limitation. If the claim for credit or refund relates to an overpayment attributable to a work incentive program credit carryback, in lieu of the 3-year period of limitation prescribed in subsection (a), the period shall be that period which ends with the expiration of the 15th day of the 40th month (or 39th month, in the case of a corporation) following the end of the taxable year of the unused work incentive program credit which results in such carryback (or, with respect to any portion of a work incentive program credit carryback from a taxable year attributable to a net operating loss carryback, an investment credit carryback, or a capital loss carryback from a subsequent taxable year, the period shall be that period which ends with the expiration of the 15th day of the 40th month, or 39th month, in the case of a corporation, following the year of such taxable year) or the period prescribed in subsection (c) in respect of such taxable year, whichever expires later. In the case of such a claim, the amount of the credit or refund may exceed the portion of the tax paid within the period provided in subsection (b)(2) or (c), whichever is applicable, to the extent of the amount of the overpayment attributable to such carryback.

"(B) Applicable rules. If the allowance of a credit or refund of an overpayment of tax attributable to a work incentive program credit carryback is otherwise prevented by the operation of any law or rule of law other than section 7122, relating to compromises, such credit or refund may be allowed or made, if claim therefor is filed within the period provided in subparagraph (A) of this paragraph. In the case of any such claim for credit or refund, the determination by any court, including the Tax Court, in any proceeding in which the decision of the court has become final, shall not be conclusive with respect to the work incentive program credit, and the effect of such credit, to the extent that such credit is affected by a carryback which was not in issue in such proceeding."

Prior to deletion, para. (d)(9) read as follows:

"(9) Special period of limitation with respect to new employee credit carrybacks.

"(A) Period of limitations. If the claim for credit or refund relates to an overpayment attributable to a new employee credit carryback, in lieu of the 3-year period of limitation prescribed in subsection (a), the period shall be that period which ends with the expiration of the 15th day of the 40th month (or 39th month, in the case of a corporation) following the end of the taxable year of the unused new employee credit which results in such carryback (or, with respect to any portion of a new employee credit carryback from a taxable year attributable to a net operating loss carryback, an investment credit carryback, a work incentive program credit carryback, or a capital loss carryback from a subsequent taxable year, the period shall be that period which ends with the expiration of the 15th day of the 40th month, or 39th month, in the case of a corporation, following the end of such taxable year) or the period prescribed in subsection (c) in respect of such taxable year, whichever expires later. In the case of such a claim, the amount of the credit or refund may exceed the portion of the tax paid within the period provided in subsection (b)(2) or (c), whichever is applicable, to the extent of the amount of the overpayment attributable to such carryback.

"(B) Applicable rules. If the allowance of a credit or refund of an overpayment of tax attributable to a new employee credit carryback is otherwise prevented by the operation of any law or rule of law other than section 7122, relating to compromises, such credit or refund may be allowed or made, if claim therefor is filed within the period provided in subparagraph (A) of this paragraph. In the case of any such claim for credit or refund, the determination by any court, including the Tax Court, in any proceeding in which the decision of the court has become final shall not be conclusive with respect to the new employee credit, and the effect of such credit, to the extent that such credit is affected by a carryback which was not in issue in such proceeding."

—P.L. 95-600, Sec. 212(b)(1), redesignated subsec. (g) as subsec. (h), and added new subsec. (g), effective for partnership items arising in partnership tax. yrs. begin. after 12/31/78.

—P.L. 95-600, Sec. 703(p)(3), amended the first sentence of subpara. (d)(2)(A), effective for losses sustained in tax. yrs. ending after 11/6/78.

Prior to amendment, the first sentence of subpara. (d)(2)(A) read as follows:

"If the claim for credit or refund relates to an overpayment attributable to a net operating loss carryback or a capital loss carryback, in lieu of the 3-year period of limitation prescribed in subsection (a), the period shall be that period which ends with the expiration of the 15th day of the 40th month (or the 39th month, in the case of a corporation) following the end of the taxable year of the net operating loss or net capital loss which results in such carryback, or the period prescribed in subsection (c) in respect of such taxable year, whichever expires later; except that—

"(i) with respect to an overpayment attributable to a net operating loss carryback to any year on account of a certification issued to the taxpayer under section 317 of the Trade Expansion Act of 1962, the period shall not expire before the expiration of the sixth month following the month in which such certification is issued to the taxpayer, and

"(ii) with respect to an overpayment attributable to the creation of, or an increase in, a net operating loss carryback as a result of the elimination of excessive profits by a renegotiation (as defined in section 1481(a)(1)(A)), the period shall not expire before the expiration of the twelfth month following the month in which the agreement or order for the elimination of such excessive profits becomes final."

In 1977, P.L. 95-30, Sec. 202(d)(4)(B), added para. (d)(9), effective for tax. yrs. begin. after 12/31/76 and to credit carrybacks from 12/31/76.

In 1976, P.L. 94-455, Sec. 1203(h)(3), added para. (g)(7), effective for documents prepared after 12/31/76.

—P.L. 94-455, Sec. 1906(a)(33)(A), deleted "September 1, 1959, or", which preceded "the expiration of the twelfth month", and deleted ", whichever is the later", which preceded the period, in clause (d)(2)(A)(ii) . . . Sec. 1906(a)(33)(B), deleted "the later of the following dates: (A)", which followed "is filed on or before", and deleted ", or (B) December 31, 1965", which preceded the period, in para. (d)(5), effective 2/1/77.

—P.L. 94-455, Sec. 2107(g)(2)(B), added ", an investment credit carryback," after "net operating loss carryback" in subpara. (d)(7)(A), effective 10/4/76.

In 1974, P.L. 93-406, Sec. 4081(b), added para. (d)(8), effective 9/2/74.

In 1971, P.L. 92-178, Sec. 601(d)(2), added para. (d)(7), for tax. yrs. begin. after 12/31/71.

In 1969, P.L. 91-172, Sec. 101(h), redesignated subsec. (f) as subsec. (g) and adding new subsec. (f), effective 1/1/70.

—P.L. 91-172, Sec. 311(d)(3)(A), substituted "1302(c)(1)" for "1302(e)(1)" in clause (d)(2)(B)(ii) . . . Sec. 311(d)(3)(B), substituted "1302(c)(3)" for "1302(e)(3)" in clause (d)(2)(B)(ii), effective for computation yrs. (within the meaning of sec. 1302(c)(1) of the Internal Revenue Code of 1954) begin. after 12/31/69, and to base period yrs. (within the meaning of sec. 1302(c)(3) of such Code) applicable to such computation years.

—P.L. 91-172, Sec. 512(e)(2)(A), substituted "loss or capital loss carrybacks" for "loss carrybacks" in the heading of para. (d)(2) . . . Sec. 512(e)(2)(B), substituted "loss carryback or a capital loss carryback" for "loss carryback" in that part of subpara. (d)(2)(A) that precedes clause (d)(2)(A)(i) . . . Sec. 512(e)(2)(C), substituted "operating loss or net capital loss which" for "operating loss which" in that part of subpara. (d)(2)(A) that precedes clause (d)(2)(A)(i) . . . Sec. 512(e)(2)(D), substituted "loss carryback or a capital loss carryback" for "loss carryback" in the first sentence of clause (d)(2)(B)(i) . . . Sec. 512(e)(2)(E), amended the last sentence of clause (d)(2)(B)(i) . . . Sec. 512(e)(2)(F), substituted "loss carryback or a capital loss carryback, as the case may be," for "loss carryback" in clause (d)(2)(B)(ii) . . . Sec. 512(e)(2)(G), substituted "loss carryback

Limitations on assessment and collection

Code Sec. 6512(b)(1)

or a capital loss carryback" for "loss carryback" in subpara. (d)(4)(A), effective for net capital losses sustained in tax. yrs. begin. after 12/31/69.

Prior to amendment, the last sentence of clause (d)(2)(B)(i) read as follows:

"In the case of any such claim for credit or refund or any such application for a tentative carryback adjustment, the determination by any court, including the Tax Court, in any proceeding in which the decision of the court has become final, shall be conclusive except with respect to the net operating loss deduction, and the effect of such deduction, to the extent that such deduction is affected by a carryback which was not in issue in such proceeding."

In 1967, P.L. 90-225, Sec. 2(d), added "(or, with respect to any portion of an investment credit carryback from a taxable year attributable to a net operating loss carryback from a subsequent taxable year, the period shall be that period which ends with the expiration of the 15th day of the 40th month, or 39th month, in the case of a corporation, following the end of such subsequent taxable year)" following "which results in such carryback" in subpara. (d)(4)(A), effective for investment credit carrybacks attributable to net operating loss carrybacks from tax. yrs. end. after 7/31/67.

In 1965, P.L. 89-331, Sec. 9(c), added "or production" in the heading of para. (e)(1), effective 11/8/65.

In 1964, P.L. 88-571, Sec. 3(c), added para. (d)(6), effective for additions to policyholder surplus account in tax. yrs. begin. after 12/31/58.

—P.L. 88-272, Sec. 232(d), amended subpara. (d)(2)(B) . . . Sec. 239, added para. (d)(5), effective for tax. yrs. begin. after 12/31/63.

Prior to amendment, subpara. (d)(2)(B) read as follows:

"(B) Applicable rules.

"If the allowance of a credit or refund of an overpayment of tax attributable to a net operating loss carryback is otherwise prevented by the operation of any law or rule of law other than section 7122, relating to compromises, such credit or refund may be allowed or made, if claim therefor is filed within the period provided in subparagraph (A) of this paragraph. If the allowance of an application, credit, or refund of a decrease in tax determined under section 6411(b) is otherwise prevented by the operation of any law or rule of law other than section 7122, such application, credit, or refund may be allowed or made if application for a tentative carryback adjustment is made within the period provided in section 6411(a). In the case of any such claim for credit or refund or any such application for a tentative carryback adjustment, the determination by any court, including the Tax Court, in any proceeding in which the decision of the court has become final, shall be conclusive except with respect to the net operating loss deduction, and the effect of such deduction, to the extent that such deduction is affected by a carryback which was not in issue in such proceeding."

In 1962, P.L. 87-834, Sec. 2(e)(2), added para. (d)(4), effective for tax. yrs. end. after 12/31/61.

—P.L. 87-794, Sec. 317(d), amended subpara. (d)(2)(A), effective for net operating losses for tax. yrs. ending after 12/31/55.

Prior to amendment, subpara. (d)(2)(A) read as follows:

"(A) Period of limitation. If the claim for credit or refund relates to an overpayment attributable to a net operating loss carryback, in lieu of the 3-year period of limitation prescribed in subsection (a), the period shall be that period which ends with the expiration of the 15th day of the 40th month (or 39th month, in the case of a corporation) following the end of the taxable year of the net operating loss which results in such carryback, or the period prescribed in subsection (c) in respect of such taxable year, whichever expires later; except that, with respect to an overpayment attributable to the creation of or an increase in a net operating loss carryback as a result of the elimination of excessive profits by a renegotiation (as defined in section 1481(a)(1)(A)), the period shall not expire before September 1, 1959, or the expiration of the twelfth month following the month in which the agreement or order for the elimination of such excessive profits becomes final, whichever is the later. In the case of such a claim, the amount of the credit or refund may exceed the portion of the tax paid within the period provided in subsection (b)(2) or (c), whichever is applicable, to the extent of the amount of the overpayment attributable to such carryback."

In 1959, P.L. 86-280, Sec. 1(a), added "; except that, with respect to an overpayment attributable to the creation of or an increase in a net operating loss carryback as a result of the elimination of excessive profits by a renegotiation (as defined in section 1481(a)(1)(A)), the period shall not expire before September 1, 1959, or the expiration of the twelfth month following the month in which the agreement or order for the elimination of such excessive profits becomes final, whichever is the later" before the period at the end of the first sentence in subpara. (d)(2)(A), effective as provided in the first sentence of Sec. 1(c) of this Act, which reads as follows:

"(c) The amendment made by subsection (a) shall apply with respect to claims for credit or refund resulting from the elimination of excessive profits by renegotiation to which section 6511(d)(2) of the Internal Revenue Code of 1954 applies."

In 1958, P.L. 85-866, Sec. 82(a), amended the first sentence of subsec. (a) . . . Sec. 82(b), amended the heading and the first sentence of subpara. (b)(2)(A) . . . Sec. 82(c), amended the heading of subpara. (b)(2)(B) . . . Sec. 82(d), substituted "15th day of the 40th month (or 39th month, in the case of a corporation)" for "15th day of the 39th month" in subpara. (d)(2)(A), effective 8/17/54 and as provided in Code Sec. 7851.

Prior to amendment, the first sentence of subsec. (a) read as follows:

"Claim for credit or refund of an overpayment of any tax imposed by this title in respect of which tax the taxpayer is required to file a return shall be filed by the taxpayer within 3 years from the time the return was required to be filed (determined without regard to any extension of time) or 2 years from the time the tax was paid, whichever of such periods expires the later, or if no return was filed by the taxpayer, within 2 years from the time the tax was paid."

Prior to amendment, the heading and the first sentence of subpara. (b)(2)(A) read as follows:

"(A) Limit to amount paid within 3 years. — If the claim was filed by the taxpayer during the 3-year period prescribed in subsection (a), the amount of the credit or refund shall not exceed the portion of the tax paid within 3 years immediately preceding the filing of the claim."

Prior to amendment, the heading of subpara. (b)(2)(B) read as follows:

"(B) Limit to amount paid within 2 years. — "

—P.L. 85-866, Sec. 96, provided that,

"If refund or credit of any overpayment of income tax —

"(1) for any taxable year beginning after December 31, 1953, and ending after August 16, 1954, and

"(2) resulting from the application of section 162 of the Internal Revenue Code of 1954 (relating to trade or business expenses) insofar as such section relates to expenses described in Income Tax Regulations § 1.162-5 (relating to expenses for education) as promulgated by Treasury Decision 6291 (23 Federal Register 2244), is prevented on the date of the enactment of this Act [9/2/58], or within 60 days after such date, by the operation of any law or rule of law (other than chapter 74 of the Internal Revenue Code of 1954, relating to closing agreements and compromises), refund or credit of such overpayment may, nevertheless, be made if claim therefor has been filed on or before such date or is filed within 60 days after such date."

In 1956, P.L. 627, Sec. 208(e)(6), added para. (f)(6), effective 6/29/56

—P.L. 466, Sec. 4(e), added para. (f)(5), effective 4/2/56.

Sec. 6512. Limitations in case of petition to Tax Court.
(a) Effect of petition to Tax Court.

If the Secretary has mailed to the taxpayer a notice of deficiency under section 6212(a) (relating to deficiencies of income, estate, gift, and certain excise taxes) and if the taxpayer files a petition with the Tax Court within the time prescribed in section 6213(a) (or 7481(c) with respect to a determination of statutory interest or section 7481(d) solely with respect to a determination of estate tax by the Tax Court) no credit or refund of income tax for the same taxable year, of gift tax for the same calendar year or calendar quarter, of estate tax in respect of the taxable estate of the same decedent, or of tax imposed by chapter 41, 42, 43, or 44 with respect to any act (or failure to act) to which such petition relates in respect of which the Secretary has determined the deficiency shall be allowed or made and no suit by the taxpayer for the recovery of any part of the tax shall be instituted in any court except—

(1) As to overpayments determined by a decision of the Tax Court which has become final, and

(2) As to any amount collected in excess of an amount computed in accordance with the decision of the Tax Court which has become final, and

(3) As to any amount collected after the period of limitation upon the making of levy or beginning a proceeding in court for collection has expired; but in any such claim for credit or refund or in any such suit for refund the decision of the Tax Court which has become final, as to whether such period has expired before the notice of deficiency was mailed, shall be conclusive, and

(4) As to overpayments attributable to partnership items, in accordance with subchapter C of chapter 63, and

(5) As to any amount collected within the period during which the Secretary is prohibited from making the assessment or from collecting by levy or through a proceeding in court under the provisions of section 6213(a), and

(6) As to overpayments the Secretary is authorized to refund or credit pending appeal as provided in subsection (b).

(b) Overpayment determined by Tax Court.

(1) Jurisdiction to determine. Except as provided by paragraph (3) and by section 7463, if the Tax Court finds that there is no deficiency and further finds that the taxpayer has made an overpayment of income tax for the same taxable year, of gift tax for the same calendar year or calendar quarter, of estate tax in respect of the taxable estate of the same decedent, or of tax imposed by chapter 41, 42, 43, or 44 with respect to any act (or failure to act) to

3,755

Code Sec. 6512(b)(1) Limitations on assessment and collection

which such petition relates, in respect of which the Secretary determined the deficiency, or finds that there is a deficiency but that the taxpayer has made an overpayment of such tax, the Tax Court shall have jurisdiction to determine the amount of such overpayment, and such amount shall, when the decision of the Tax Court has become final, be credited or refunded to the taxpayer. If a notice of appeal in respect of the decision of the Tax Court is filed under section 7483, the Secretary is authorized to refund or credit the overpayment determined by the Tax Court to the extent the overpayment is not contested on appeal.

(2) Jurisdiction to enforce. If, after 120 days after a decision of the Tax Court has become final, the Secretary has failed to refund the overpayment determined by the Tax Court, together with the interest thereon as provided in subchapter B of chapter 67, then the Tax Court, upon motion by the taxpayer, shall have jurisdiction to order the refund of such overpayment and interest. An order of the Tax Court disposing of a motion under this paragraph shall be reviewable in the same manner as a decision of the Tax Court, but only with respect to the matters determined in such order.

(3) Limit on amount of credit or refund. No such credit or refund shall be allowed or made of any portion of the tax unless the Tax Court determines as part of its decision that such portion was paid—

(A) after the mailing of the notice of deficiency,

(B) within the period which would be applicable under section 6511(b)(2), (c), or (d), if on the date of the mailing of the notice of deficiency a claim had been filed (whether or not filed) stating the grounds upon which the Tax Court finds that there is an overpayment, or

(C) within the period which would be applicable under section 6511(b)(2), (c), or (d), in respect of any claim for refund filed within the applicable period specified in section 6511 and before the date of the mailing of the notice of deficiency—

  (i) which had not been disallowed before that date,

  (ii) which had been disallowed before that date and in respect of which a timely suit for refund could have been commenced as of that date, or

  (iii) in respect of which a suit for refund had been commenced before that date and within the period specified in section 6532.

In the case of a credit or refund relating to an affected item (within the meaning of section 6231(a)(5)), the preceding sentence shall be applied by substituting the periods under sections 6229 and 6230(d) for the periods under section 6551(b)(2), (c), and (d). In a case described in subparagraph (B) where the date of the mailing of the notice of deficiency is during the third year after the due date (with extensions) for filing the return of tax and no return was filed before such date, the applicable period under subsections (a) and (b)(2) of section 6511 shall be 3 years.

(4) Denial of jurisdiction regarding certain credits and reductions. The Tax Court shall have no jurisdiction under this subsection to restrain or review any credit or reduction made by the Secretary under section 6402.

(c) Cross references.

(1) For provisions allowing determination of tax in title 11 cases, see section 505(a) of title 11 of the United States Code.

(2) For provision giving the Tax Court jurisdiction to award reasonable litigation costs in proceedings to enforce

an overpayment determined by such court, see section 7430.

In **2000**, P.L. 106-554, Sec. 1(a)(7) , [which enacted into law Sec. 319(19) of P.L. 106-554] substituted ", and" for "; and" at the end of paras. (a)(1), (2) and (5), effective 12/21/2000..

In **1998**, P.L. 105-206, Sec. 3464(b), substituted ", and" for the period at the end of para. (a)(4), and added paras. (a)(5) and (6) . . . Sec. 3464(c), added a sentence at the end of para. (b)(1), effective 7/22/98.

In **1997**, P.L. 105-34, Sec. 1239(c)(2), added a sentence at the end of para. (b)(3), effective for partnership tax. yrs. end. after 8/5/97.

—P.L. 105-34, Sec. 1282(a), added a flush sentence at the end of para. (b)(3), effective for claims for credit or refund for tax. yrs. end. after 8/5/97.

—P.L. 105-34, Sec. 1451(a), added a sentence at the end of para. (b)(2) . . . Sec. 1451(b), added para. (b)(4), effective 8/5/97.

In **1988**, P.L. 100-647, Sec. 6244(a), substituted "paragraph (3)" for "paragraph (2)" in para. (b)(1), and redesignated para. (b)(3) as para. (b)(3), and added new para. (b)(2) . . . Sec. 6244(b)(2), substituted "references" for "reference" in the heading of subsec. (c), and designated the undesignated para. as para. (c)(1), and added para. (c)(2), effective for overpayments determined by the Tax Court which have not yet been refunded by the 90th day after 11/10/88.

—P.L. 100-647, Sec. 6246(b)(1), added "(or 7481(c) with respect to a determination of statutory interest)" after "section 6213(a)" in subsec. (a), effective for assessments of deficiencies redetermined by the Tax Court made after 11/10/88.

—P.L. 100-647, Sec. 6247(b)(1), substituted "interest or section 7481(d) solely with respect to a determination of estate tax by the Tax Court)" for "interest)" in subsec. (a), [as amended by Sec. 6246(b)(1) of this Act, see above], effective for Tax Court cases for which the decision is not final on 11/10/88.

—P.L. 100-418, Sec. 1941(b)(2)(J)(i), substituted "or of tax imposed by chapter 41" for "of tax imposed by chapter 41" in subsec. (a) . . . Sec. 1941(b)(2)(J)(ii), deleted ", or of tax imposed by chapter 45 for the same taxable period" following "to which such petition relates" in subsec. (a) . . . Sec. 1941(b)(2)(K)(i), substituted "or of tax imposed by chapter 41" for "of tax imposed by chapter 41" in para. (b)(1) . . . Sec. 1941(b)(2)(K)(ii), deleted ", or of tax imposed by chapter 45 for the same taxable period" following "to which such petition relates" in para. (b)(1), effective for crude oil removed from the premises on or after 8/23/88.

In **1982**, P.L. 97-248, Sec. 402(c)(8), substituted ", and" for the period at the end of para. (a)(3) and added para. (a)(4) . . . Sec. 402(c)(9), substituted "(c), or (d)" for "(c), (d), or (g)" each place it appeared in para. (b)(2), effective for partnership tax. yrs. begin. after 9/3/82. Sec. 407(a)(3) of this Act provides:

"(3) The amendments made by sections 402, 403, and 404 [of this Act] shall apply to any partnership taxable year (or in the case of section 6232 of such Code, to any period) ending after the date of the enactment of this Act [9/3/82] if the partnership, each partner, and each indirect partner requests such application and the Secretary of the Treasury or his delegate consents to such application."

In **1980**, P.L. 96-589, Sec. 6(d)(3), added subsec. (c), effective 10/1/79, except for any proceeding under the Bankruptcy Act begun before 10/1/79. Sec. 7(g) of this Act provides:

"(g) Definitions.

"For purposes of this section—

"(1) Bankruptcy case. The term 'bankruptcy case' means any case under title 11 of the United States Code (as recodified by P.L. 95-598).

"(2) Similar judicial proceeding. The term 'similar judicial proceeding' means a receivership, foreclosure, or similar proceeding in a Federal or State court (as modified by section 368(a)(3)(D) of the Internal Revenue Code of 1954)."

—P.L. 96-223, Sec. 101(f)(6)(A)(i), substituted "certain excise taxes" for "chapter 41, 42, 43, or 44 taxes" in subsec. (a) . . . Sec. 101(f)(6)(A)(ii), substituted "of tax imposed by chapter 41" for "or of tax imposed by chapter 41" in subsec. (a) . . . Sec. 101(f)(6)(A)(iii), added ", or of tax imposed by chapter 45 for the same taxable period" after "to which such petition relates" in subsec. (a) . . . Sec. 101(f)(6)(B)(i), substituted "of tax imposed by chapter 41" for "or of tax imposed by chapter 41" in para. (b)(1) . . . Sec. 101(f)(6)(B)(ii), added ", or of tax imposed by chapter 45 for the same taxable period" after "to which such petition relates" in para. (b)(1), effective for periods after 2/29/80.

In **1978**, P.L. 95-600, Sec. 212(b)(2), substituted "(c), (d), or (g)" for "(c), or (d)" each place it appeared in para. (b)(2), effective for partnership items arising in partnership tax. yrs. begin. after 12/31/78.

In **1976**, P.L. 94-455, Sec. 1307(d)(2)(F)(vii), substituted "chapter 41, 42," for "chapter 42" each place it appeared in subsec. (a) and para. (b)(1), effective 10/4/76.

—P.L. 94-455, Sec. 1605(b)(9), substituted "43, or 44" for "or 43" each place it appeared in subsec. (a) or para. (b)(1), effective for tax. yrs. of real estate investment trusts begin. after 10/4/76.

—P.L. 94-455, Sec. 1906(b)(13)(A), substituted "Secretary" for "Secretary or his delegate" each place it appeared in subsec. (a) and para. (b)(1), effective 2/1/77.

In **1974**, P.L. 93-406, Sec. 1016(a)(16), substituted "chapter 42 or 43" for "chapter 42" each place it appeared in Code Sec. 6512, effective 9/2/74 or other date as specified in Sec. 1017 of the Act (see the note following Code Sec. 401).

In **1970**, P.L. 91-614, Sec. 102(d)(9), substituted "the same calendar year or calendar quarter" for "the same calendar year" each place it appeared in Sec. 6512, effective for gifts made after 12/31/70.

In **1969**, P.L. 91-172, Sec. 101(j)(47)(A), substituted "gift, and chapter 42 taxes" for "and gift taxes" in subsec. (a) . . . Sec. 101(j)(47)(B), substituted "of estate tax in respect of the taxable estate of the same decedent, or of tax imposed by chapter 42 with respect to any act (or failure to act) to which such petition relates," for "or of estate tax in respect of the taxable estate of the same decedent," in subsec.

3,756

Limitations on assessment and collection Code Sec. 6513

(a) ... Sec. 101(j)(48), substituted "of estate tax in respect of the taxable estate of the same decedent, or of tax imposed by chapter 42 with respect to any act (or failure to act) to which such petition relates," for "or of estate tax in respect of the taxable estate of the same decedent," in para. (b)(1), effective 1/1/70.

—P.L. 91-172, Sec. 960(b), substituted "Except as provided by paragraph (2) and by section 7463, if the Tax Court" for "If the Tax Court" in para. (b)(1), effective 12/30/70.

In 1962, P.L. 87-870, Sec. 4, deleted "or" at the end of subpara. (b)(2)(A), substituted ", or" for the period at the end of subpara. (b)(2)(B), and added subpara. (b)(2)(C), effective 10/24/62.

Sec. 6513. Time return deemed filed and tax considered paid.
(a) Early return or advance payment of tax.

For purposes of section 6511, any return filed before the last day prescribed for the filing thereof shall be considered as filed on such last day. For purposes of section 6511(b)(2) and (c) and section 6512, payment of any portion of the tax made before the last day prescribed for the payment of the tax shall be considered made on such last day. For purposes of this subsection, the last day prescribed for filing the return or paying the tax shall be determined without regard to any extension of time granted the taxpayer and without regard to any election to pay the tax in installments.

(b) Prepaid income tax.

For purposes of section 6511 or 6512—

(1) Any tax actually deducted and withheld at the source during any calendar year under chapter 24 shall, in respect of the recipient of the income, be deemed to have been paid by him on the 15th day of the fourth month following the close of his taxable year with respect to which such tax is allowable as a credit under section 31.

(2) Any amount paid as estimated income tax for any taxable year shall be deemed to have been paid on the last day prescribed for filing the return under section 6012 for such taxable year (determined without regard to any extension of time for filing such return).

> • **Caution:** Sec. 6513(b)(3), following, is effective for payments made before 1/1/2013. For sec. 6513(b)(3), effective for payments made after 12/31/2012, see below.

(3) Any tax withheld at the source under chapter 3 shall, in respect of the recipient of the income, be deemed to have been paid by such recipient on the last day prescribed for filing the return under section 6012 for the taxable year (determined without regard to any extension of time for filing) with respect to which such tax is allowable as a credit under section 1462. For this purpose, any exemption granted under section 6012 from the requirement of filing a return shall be disregarded.

> • **Caution:** Sec. 6513(b)(3), following, is effective for payments made after 12/31/2012. For sec. 6513(b)(3), effective for payments made before 1/1/2013, see above.

(3) Any tax withheld at the source under chapter 3 or 4 shall, in respect of the recipient of the income, be deemed to have been paid by such recipient on the last day prescribed for filing the return under section 6012 for the taxable year (determined without regard to any extension of time for filing) with respect to which such tax is allowable as a credit under section 1462 or 1474(b). For this purpose, any exemption granted under section 6012 from the requirement of filing a return shall be disregarded.

> • **Caution:** Sec. 6513(c), following, is effective for payments made before 1/1/2013. For sec. 6513(c), effective for payments made after 12/31/2012, see below.

(c) Return and payment of social security taxes and income tax withholding.

Notwithstanding subsection (a), for purposes of section 6511 with respect to any tax imposed by chapter 3, 21, or 24—

(1) If a return for any period ending with or within a calendar year is filed before April 15 of the succeeding calendar year, such return shall be considered filed on April 15 of such succeeding calendar year; and

(2) If a tax with respect to remuneration or other amount paid during any period ending with or within a calendar year is paid before April 15 of the succeeding calendar year, such tax shall be considered paid on April 15 of such succeeding calendar year.

> • **Caution:** Sec. 6513(c), following, is effective for payments made after 12/31/2012. For sec. 6513(c), effective for payments made before 1/1/2013, see above.

(c) Return and payment of social security taxes and income tax withholding.

Notwithstanding subsection (a), for purposes of section 6511 with respect to any tax imposed by chapter 3, 4, 21, or 24—

(1) If a return for any period ending with or within a calendar year is filed before April 15 of the succeeding calendar year, such return shall be considered filed on April 15 of such succeeding calendar year; and

(2) If a tax with respect to remuneration or other amount paid during any period ending with or within a calendar year is paid before April 15 of the succeeding calendar year, such tax shall be considered paid on April 15 of such succeeding calendar year.

(d) Overpayment of income tax credited to estimated tax.

If any overpayment of income tax is, in accordance with section 6402(b), claimed as a credit against estimated tax for the succeeding taxable year, such amount shall be considered as a payment of the income tax for the succeeding taxable year (whether or not claimed as a credit in the return of estimated tax for such succeeding taxable year), and no claim for credit or refund of such overpayment shall be allowed for the taxable year in which the overpayment arises.

(e) Payments of Federal unemployment tax.

Notwithstanding subsection (a), for purposes of section 6511 any payment of tax imposed by chapter 23 which, pursuant to section 6157, is made for a calendar quarter or other period within a calendar year shall, if made before the last day prescribed for filing the return for the calendar year (determined without regard to any extension of time for filing), be considered made on such last day.

In 2010, P.L. 111-147, Sec. 501(c)(4)(A), added "or 4" after "chapter 3" in para. (b)(3) ... Sec. 501(c)(4)(B), added "or 1474(b)" after "section 1462" in para. (b)(3) ... Sec. 501(c)(5), added "4," after "chapter 3," in subsec. (c), effective for payments made after 12/31/2012. Sec. 501(d)(2) of this Act, provides:

"(2) Grandfathered treatment of outstanding obligations. The amendments made by this section shall not require any amount to be deducted or withheld from any payment under any obligation outstanding on the date which is 2 years after the

3,757

date of the enactment of this Act or from the gross proceeds from any disposition of such an obligation."
In 1988, P.L. 100-647, Sec. 7106(c)(4), deleted the last sentence of subsec. (e), effective for remuneration paid after 12/31/88.
Prior to deletion, the last sentence of subsec. (e) read as follows:
"Notwithstanding subsection (a), for purposes of section 6511, any payment of tax imposed by chapter 23A which, pursuant to section 6157, is made for a calendar quarter within a taxable period shall, if made before the last day prescribed for filing the return for the taxable period (determined without regard to any extension of time for filing), be considered made on such last day."
In 1983, P.L. 98-76, Sec. 231(b)(2)(C), added the last sentence of subsec. (e), effective for remuneration paid after 6/30/86.
In 1969, P.L. 91-53, Sec. 2(d), added subsec. (e), effective for calendar yrs. begin. after 12/31/69.
In 1966, P.L. 89-809, Sec. 105, designated existing provisions of subsec. (b) as paras. (b)(1) and (2) and added para. (b)(3), and amended subsec. (c) by adding reference to chapter 3 and by inserting "or other amount" after "remuneration" in para. (c)(2), effective 11/13/66.

Sec. 6514. Credits or refunds after period of limitation.
(a) Credits or refunds after period of limitation.
A refund of any portion of an internal revenue tax shall be considered erroneous and a credit of any such portion shall be considered void—
(1) Expiration of period for filing claim. If made after the expiration of the period of limitation for filing claim therefor, unless within such period claim was filed; or
(2) Disallowance of claim and expiration of period for filing suit. In the case of a claim filed within the proper time and disallowed by the Secretary, if the credit or refund was made after the expiration of the period of limitation for filing suit, unless within such period suit was begun by the taxpayer.
(3) Recovery of erroneous refunds. For procedure by the United States to recover erroneous refunds, see sections 6532(b) and 7405.
(b) Credit after period of limitation.
Any credit against a liability in respect of any taxable year shall be void if any payment in respect of such liability would be considered an overpayment under section 6401(a).

In 1976, P.L. 94-455, Sec. 1906(b)(13)(A), substituted "Secretary" for "Secretary or his delegate" in Code Sec. 6514, effective 2/1/77.

Sec. 6515. Cross references.
For limitations in case of—
(1) Deficiency dividends of a personal holding company, see section 547.
(2) Tentative carry-back adjustments, see section 6411.
(3) Service in a combat zone, etc., see section 7508.
(4) Suits for refund by taxpayers, see section 6532(a).
(5) Deficiency dividends of a regulated investment company or real estate investment trust, see section 860.
(6) Refunds or credits attributable to partnership items, see section 6227 and subsections (c) and (d) of section 6230.

In 1990, P.L. 101-508, Sec. 11801(c)(17)(C), deleted para. (2), and redesignated paras. (3), (4), (5), (6) and (7) as paras. (2), (3), (4), (5) and (6), effective 11/5/90, except as provided in Sec. 11821(b) of this Act reproduced in note following Code Sec. 1481.
Prior to deletion, para. (2) read as follows:
"(2) Overpayment in certain renegotiations of war contracts, see section 1481."
In 1982, P.L. 97-248, Sec. 402(c)(10), added para. (7), effective for partnership tax. yrs. begin. after 9/3/82. P.L. Sec. 407(a)(3) of this Act provides:
"(3) The amendments made by sections 402, 403, and 404 [of this Act] shall apply to any partnership taxable year (or in the case of section 6232 of such Code, to any period) ending after the date of the enactment of this Act [9/3/82] if the partnership, each partner, and each indirect partner requests such application and the Secretary of the Treasury or his delegate consents to such application."
In 1980, P.L. 96-222, Sec. 103(a)(11)(A), amended Sec. 362(e) of P.L. 95-600, the effective date for changes made by Sec. 362 of P.L. 95-600, by substituting "860(e)" for "860(d)" [see below].
In 1978, P.L. 95-600, Sec. 362(d)(4)(A), added "regulated investment company or" before "real estate investment trust" in para. (5) [sic (6)] ... Sec. 362(d)(4)(B), substituted "860" for "859" in para. (5) [sic (6)], effective for determinations (as defined in Code Sec. 860(e)) after 11/6/78.

—P.L. 95-600, Sec. 703(j)(10), deleted the amendment made by Sec. 1901(b)(37)(D) of P.L. 94-455 [reinstated former para. (6), redesignated para. (4)], effective 10/4/76, see below.
In 1976, P.L. 94-455, Sec. 1601(f)(3), added para. (8), subsequently redesignated by this Act, for determinations as defined in subsec. 859(c) occurring after 10/4/76.
—P.L. 94-455, Sec. 1901(b)(36)(D), deleted para. (1), for tax. yrs. begin. after '76.
Prior to amendment, para. (1) read as follows:
"(1) Adjustments incident to involuntary liquidation of inventory, see section 1321."
—P.L. 94-455, Sec. 1901(b)(37)(D), deleted para. (6), for tax. yrs. begin. after '76.
Prior to amendment, para. (6) read as follows:
"(6) Service in a combat zone, etc., see section 7508."
—P.L. 94-455, Sec. 1901(b)(37)(E), deleted para. (2), and further amended Code Sec. 6515 "by redesignating paragraphs (3), (4), (5), (6), [sic] (7), and (8) as paragraphs (1), (2), (3), (4), (5), and (6) respectively", for tax. yrs. begin. after '76.
Prior to amendment, para. (2) read as follows:
"(2) War loss recoveries where prior benefit rule is elected, see section 1335."

Subchapter C.—Mitigation of Effect of Period of Limitations
Sec.
6521. Mitigation of effect of limitation in case of related taxes under different chapters.

Sec. 6521. Mitigation of effect of limitation in case of related taxes under different chapters.
(a) Self-employment tax and tax on wages.
In the case of the tax imposed by chapter 2 (relating to tax on self-employment income) and the tax imposed by section 3101 (relating to tax on employees under the Federal Insurance Contributions Act)—
(1) If an amount is erroneously treated as self-employment income, or if an amount is erroneously treated as wages, and
(2) If the correction of the error would require an assessment of one such tax and the refund or credit of the other tax, and
(3) If at any time the correction of the error is authorized as to one such tax but is prevented as to the other tax by any law or rule of law (other than section 7122, relating to compromises),
then, if the correction authorized is made, the amount of the assessment, or the amount of the credit or refund, as the case may be, authorized as to the one tax shall be reduced by the amount of the credit or refund, or the amount of the assessment, as the case may be, which would be required with respect to such other tax for the correction of the error if such credit or refund, or such assessment, of such other tax were not prevented by any law or rule of law (other than section 7122, relating to compromises).
(b) Definitions.
For purposes of subsection (a), the terms "self-employment income" and "wages" shall have the same meaning as when used in section 1402(b).

Subchapter D.—Periods of Limitation in Judicial Proceedings
Sec.
6531. Periods of limitation on criminal prosecutions.
6532. Periods of limitation on suits.
6533. Cross references.

Sec. 6531. Periods of limitation on criminal prosecutions.
No person shall be prosecuted, tried, or punished for any of the various offenses arising under the internal revenue laws unless the indictment is found or the information instituted within 3 years next after the commission of the offense, except that the period of limitation shall be 6 years—

Limitations on assessment and collection — Code Sec. 6533(3)

(1) for offenses involving the defrauding or attempting to defraud the United States or any agency thereof, whether by conspiracy or not, and in any manner;

(2) for the offense of willfully attempting in any manner to evade or defeat any tax or the payment thereof;

(3) for the offense of willfully aiding or assisting in, or procuring, counseling, or advising, the preparation or presentation under, or in connection with any matter arising under, the internal revenue laws, of a false or fraudulent return, affidavit, claim, or document (whether or not such falsity or fraud is with the knowledge or consent of the person authorized or required to present such return, affidavit, claim, or document);

(4) for the offense of willfully failing to pay any tax, or make any return (other than a return required under authority of part III of subchapter A of chapter 61) at the time or times required by law or regulations;

(5) for offenses described in sections 7206(1) and 7207 (relating to false statements and fraudulent documents);

(6) for the offense described in section 7212(a) (relating to intimidation of officers and employees of the United States);

(7) for offenses described in section 7214(a) committed by officers and employees of the United States; and

(8) for offenses arising under section 371 of Title 18 of the United States Code, where the object of the conspiracy is to attempt in any manner to evade or defeat any tax or the payment thereof.

The time during which the person committing any of the various offenses arising under the internal revenue laws is outside the United States or is a fugitive from justice within the meaning of section 3290 of Title 18 of the United States Code, shall not be taken as any part of the time limited by law for the commencement of such proceedings. (The preceding sentence shall also be deemed an amendment to section 3748(a) of the Internal Revenue Code of 1939, and shall apply in lieu of the sentence in section 3748(a) which relates to the time during which a person committing an offense is absent from the district wherein the same is committed, except that such amendment shall apply only if the period of limitations under section 3748 would, without the application of such amendment, expire more than 3 years after the date of enactment of this title, and except that such period shall not, with the application of this amendment, expire prior to the date which is 3 years after the date of enactment of this title.) Where a complaint is instituted before a commissioner of the United States within the period above limited, the time shall be extended until the date which is 9 months after the date of the making of the complaint before the commissioner of the United States. For the purpose of determining the periods of limitation on criminal prosecutions, the rules of section 6513 shall be applicable.

Sec. 6532. Periods of limitation on suits.

(a) Suits by taxpayers for refund.

(1) **General rule.** No suit or proceeding under section 7422(a) for the recovery of any internal revenue tax, penalty, or other sum, shall be begun before the expiration of 6 months from the date of filing the claim required under such section unless the Secretary renders a decision thereon within that time, nor after the expiration of 2 years from the date of mailing by certified mail or registered mail by the Secretary to the taxpayer of a notice of the disallowance of the part of the claim to which the suit or proceeding relates.

(2) **Extension of time.** The 2-year period prescribed in paragraph (1) shall be extended for such period as may be agreed upon in writing between the taxpayer and the Secretary.

(3) **Waiver of notice of disallowance.** If any person files a written waiver of the requirement that he be mailed a notice of disallowance, the 2-year period prescribed in paragraph (1) shall begin on the date such waiver is filed.

(4) **Reconsideration after mailing of notice.** Any consideration, reconsideration, or action by the Secretary with respect to such claim following the mailing of a notice by certified mail or registered mail of disallowance shall not operate to extend the period within which suit may be begun.

(5) **Cross reference.** For substitution of 120-day period for the 6-month period contained in paragraph (1) in a title 11 case, see section 505(a)(2) of title 11 of the United States Code.

(b) Suits by United States for recovery of erroneous refunds.

Recovery of an erroneous refund by suit under section 7405 shall be allowed only if such suit is begun within 2 years after the making of such refund, except that such suit may be brought at any time within 5 years from the making of the refund if it appears that any part of the refund was induced by fraud or misrepresentation of a material fact.

(c) Suits by persons other than taxpayers.

(1) **General rule.** Except as provided by paragraph (2), no suit or proceeding under section 7426 shall be begun after the expiration of 9 months from the date of the levy or agreement giving rise to such action.

(2) **Period when claim is filed.** If a request is made for the return of property described in section 6343(b), the 9-month period prescribed in paragraph (1) shall be extended for a period of 12 months from the date of filing of such request or for a period of 6 months from the date of mailing by registered or certified mail by the Secretary to the person making such request of a notice of disallowance of the part of the request to which the action relates, whichever is shorter.

In 1980, P.L. 96-589, Sec. 6(d)(4), added para. (a)(5), effective 10/1/79, except for any proceeding under the Bankruptcy Act begun before October 1, '79. Sec. 7(g) of this Act provides:

"(g) Definitions.

"For purposes of this section—

"(1) Bankruptcy case. The term 'bankruptcy case' means any case under title 11 of the United States Code (as recodified by P.L. 95-598).

"(2) Similar judicial proceeding. The term 'similar judicial proceeding' means a receivership, foreclosure, or similar proceeding in a Federal or State court (as modified by section 368(a)(3)(D) of the Internal Revenue Code of 1954)."

In 1976, P.L. 94-455, Sec. 1906(b)(13)(A), substituted "Secretary" for "Secretary or his delegate" each place it appeared in Code Sec. 6532, effective 2/1/77.

In 1966, P.L. 89-719, Sec. 110, added subsec. (c), effective after 11/2/66, regardless of when a lien or a title of the U.S. arose or when the lien or interest of any other person was acquired. For a special exception included in Sec. 114 of P.L. 89-719 see the note to Code Sec. 6323.

In 1958, P.L. 85-866, Sec. 89(b), inserted "certified mail or" before "registered mail", each place it appeared in paras. (a)(1) and (4), effective for mailings after 9/2/58.

Sec. 6533. Cross references.

(1) For period of limitation in respect of civil actions for fines, penalties, and forfeitures, see section 2462 of Title 28 of the United States Code.

(2) For extensions of time by reason of armed service in a combat zone, see section 7508.

(3) For suspension of running of statute until 3 years after termination of hostilities, see section 3287 of Title 18.

Chapter 67

CHAPTER 67.—INTEREST

Subchapter
A. Interest on underpayments.
B. Interest on overpayments.
C. Determination of interest rate; compounding of interest.
D. Notice requirements.

In **1998**, P.L. 105-206, Sec. 3308(b), added item D.
In **1982**, P.L. 97-248, Sec. 433(b)(3)(B), added "; compounding of interest" after "rate" in item C.
In **1975**, P.L. 93-625, Sec. 7(d)(5), added item C.

Subchapter A.—Interest on Underpayments

Sec.
6601. Interest on underpayment, nonpayment, or extensions of time for payment, of tax.
6602. Interest on erroneous refund recoverable by suit.
6603. Deposits made to suspend running of interest on potential underpayments, etc.

In **2004**, P.L. 108-357, Sec. 842(b), added item 6603.

Sec. 6601. Interest on underpayment, nonpayment, or extensions of time for payment, of tax.

(a) General rule.

If any amount of tax imposed by this title (whether required to be shown on a return, or to be paid by stamp or by some other method) is not paid on or before the last date prescribed for payment, interest on such amount at the underpayment rate established under section 6621 shall be paid for the period from such last date to the date paid.

(b) Last date prescribed for payment.

For purposes of this section, the last date prescribed for payment of the tax shall be determined under chapter 62 with the application of the following rules:

(1) Extensions of time disregarded. The last date prescribed for payment shall be determined without regard to any extension of time for payment or any installment agreement entered into under section 6159.

(2) Installment payments. In the case of an election under section 6156(a) to pay the tax in installments—

(A) The date prescribed for payment of each installment of the tax shown on the return shall be determined under section 6156(b), and

(B) The last date prescribed for payment of the first installment shall be deemed the last date prescribed for payment of any portion of the tax not shown on the return.

(3) Jeopardy. The last date prescribed for payment shall be determined without regard to any notice and demand for payment issued, by reason of jeopardy (as provided in chapter 70), prior to the last date otherwise prescribed for such payment.

(4) Accumulated earnings tax. In the case of the tax imposed by section 531 for any taxable year, the last date prescribed for payment shall be deemed to be the due date (without regard to extensions) for the return of tax imposed by subtitle A for such taxable year.

(5) Last date for payment not otherwise prescribed. In the case of taxes payable by stamp and in all other cases in which the last date for payment is not otherwise prescribed, the last date for payment shall be deemed to be the date the liability for tax arises (and in no event shall be later than the date notice and demand for the tax is made by the Secretary).

(c) Suspension of interest in certain income, estate, gift, and certain excise tax cases.

In the case of a deficiency as defined in section 6211 (relating to income, estate, gift and certain excise taxes), if a waiver of restrictions under section 6213(d) on the assessment of such deficiency has been filed, and if notice and demand by the Secretary for payment of such deficiency is not made within 30 days after the filing of such waiver, interest shall not be imposed on such deficiency for the period beginning immediately after such 30th day and ending with the date of notice and demand and interest shall not be imposed during such period on any interest with respect to such deficiency for any prior period. In the case of a settlement under section 6224(c) which results in the conversion of partnership items to nonpartnership items pursuant to section 6231(b)(1)(C), the preceding sentence shall apply to a computational adjustment resulting from such settlement in the same manner as if such adjustment were a deficiency and such settlement were a waiver referred to in the preceding sentence.

(d) Income tax reduced by carryback or adjustment for certain unused deductions.

(1) Net operating loss or capital loss carryback. If the amount of any tax imposed by subtitle A is reduced by reason of a carryback of a net operating loss or net capital loss such reduction in tax shall not affect the computation of interest under this section for the period ending with the filing date for the taxable year in which the net operating loss or net capital loss arises.

(2) Foreign tax credit carrybacks. If any credit allowed for any taxable year is increased by reason of a carryback of tax paid or accrued to foreign countries or possessions of the United States, such increase shall not affect the computation of interest under this section for the period ending with the filing date for the taxable year in which such taxes were in fact paid or accrued, or, with respect to any portion of such credit carryback from a taxable year attributable to a net operating loss carryback or a capital loss carryback from a subsequent taxable year, such increase shall not affect the computation of interest under this section for the period ending with the filing date for such subsequent taxable year.

(3) Certain credit carrybacks.

(A) In general. If any credit allowed for any taxable year is increased by reason of a credit carryback, such increase shall not affect the computation of interest under this section for the period ending with the filing date for the taxable year in which the credit carryback arises, or, with respect to any portion of a credit carryback from a taxable year attributable to a net operating loss carryback, capital loss carryback, or other credit carryback from a subsequent taxable year, such increase shall not affect the computation of interest under this section for the period ending with the filing date for such subsequent taxable year.

(B) Credit carryback defined. For purposes of this paragraph, the term "credit carryback" has the meaning given such term by section 6511(d)(4)(C).

(4) Filing date. For purposes of this subsection, the term "filing date" has the meaning given to such term by section 6611(f)(4)(A).

(e) Applicable rules.

Except as otherwise provided in this title—

(1) Interest treated as tax. Interest prescribed under this section on any tax shall be paid upon notice and demand, and shall be assessed, collected, and paid in the same manner as taxes. Any reference in this title (except sub-

Interest
Code Sec. 6601

chapter B of chapter 63, relating to deficiency procedures) to any tax imposed by this title shall be deemed also to refer to interest imposed by this section on such tax.

(2) Interest on penalties, additional amounts, or additions to the tax.

(A) In general. Interest shall be imposed under subsection (a) in respect of any assessable penalty, additional amount, or addition to the tax (other than an addition to tax imposed under section 6651(a)(1) or 6653 or under part II of subchapter A of chapter 68) only if such assessable penalty, additional amount, or addition to the tax is not paid within 21 calendar days from the date of notice and demand therefor (10 business days if the amount for which such notice and demand is made equals or exceeds $100,000), and in such case interest shall be imposed only for the period from the date of the notice and demand to the date of payment.

(B) Interest on certain additions to tax. Interest shall be imposed under this section with respect to any addition to tax imposed by section 6651(a)(1) or 6653 or under part II of subchapter A of chapter 68 for the period which—

(i) begins on the date on which the return of the tax with respect to which such addition to tax is imposed is required to be filed (including any extensions), and

(ii) ends on the date of payment of such addition to tax.

(3) Payments made within specified period after notice and demand. If notice and demand is made for payment of any amount and if such amount is paid within 21 calendar days (10 business days if the amount for which such notice and demand is made equals or exceeds $100,000) after the date of such notice and demand, interest under this section on the amount so paid shall not be imposed for the period after the date of such notice and demand.

(f) Satisfaction by credits.

If any portion of a tax is satisfied by credit of an overpayment, then no interest shall be imposed under this section on the portion of the tax so satisfied for any period during which, if the credit had not been made, interest would have been allowable with respect to such overpayment. The preceding sentence shall not apply to the extent that section 6621(d) applies.

(g) Limitation on assessment and collection.

Interest prescribed under this section on any tax may be assessed and collected at any time during the period within which the tax to which such interest relates may be collected.

(h) Exception as to estimated tax.

This section shall not apply to any failure to pay any estimated tax required to be paid by section 6654 or 6655.

(i) Exception as to federal unemployment tax.

This section shall not apply to any failure to make a payment of tax imposed by section 3301 for a calendar quarter or other period within a taxable year required under authority of section 6157.

(j) 2-percent rate on certain portion of estate tax extended under section 6166.

(1) In general. If the time for payment of an amount of tax imposed by chapter 11 is extended as provided in section 6166, then in lieu of the annual rate provided by subsection (a)—

(A) interest on the 2-percent portion of such amount shall be paid at the rate of 2 percent, and

(B) interest on so much of such amount as exceeds the 2-percent portion shall be paid at a rate equal to 45 percent of the annual rate provided by subsection (a).

For purposes of this subsection, the amount of any deficiency which is prorated to installments payable under section 6166 shall be treated as an amount of tax payable in installments under such section.

(2) 2-percent portion. For purposes of this subsection, the term "2-percent portion" means the lesser of—

(A)(i) the amount of the tentative tax which would be determined under the rate schedule set forth in section 2001(c) if the amount with respect to which such tentative tax is to be computed were the sum of $1,000,000 and the applicable exclusion amount in effect under section 2010(c), reduced by

(ii) the applicable credit amount in effect under section 2010(c), or

(B) the amount of the tax imposed by chapter 11 which is extended as provided in section 6166.

(3) Inflation adjustment. In the case of estates of decedents dying in a calendar year after 1998, the $1,000,000 amount contained in paragraph (2)(A) shall be increased by an amount equal to—

(A) $1,000,000, multiplied by

(B) the cost-of-living adjustment determined under section 1(f)(3) for such calendar year by substituting "calendar year 1997" for "calendar year 1992" in subparagraph (B) thereof.

If any amount as adjusted under the preceding sentence is not a multiple of $10,000, such amount shall be rounded to the next lowest multiple of $10,000.

(4) Treatment of payments. If the amount of tax imposed by chapter 11 which is extended as provided in section 6166 exceeds the 2-percent portion, any payment of a portion of such amount shall, for purposes of computing interest for periods after such payment, be treated as reducing the 2-percent portion by an amount which bears the same ratio to the amount of such payment as the amount of the 2-percent portion (determined without regard to this paragraph) bears to the amount of the tax which is extended as provided in section 6166.

(k) No interest on certain adjustments.

For provisions prohibiting interest on certain adjustments in tax, see section 6205(a).

In 2005, P.L. 109-135, Sec. 409(a)(2), substituted "6611(f)(4)(A)" for "6611(f)(3)(A)" in para. (d)(4), effective for foreign tax credit carrybacks arising in tax. yrs. begin. after 8/5/97 as if included in Sec. 1055 of the Taxpayer Relief Act of 1997, P.L. 105-34.

In 1998, P.L. 105-277, Sec. 4002(d), substituted "Subject to any applicable statute of limitation not having expired with regard to either a tax underpayment or a tax overpayment, the amendments" for "The amendments" in Sec. 3301(c)(2) of P.L. 105-206 [see below], effective 10/21/98.

—P.L. 105-277, Sec. 4003(e)(1), added "or 1998" after "1997" in Sec. 915(b) of P.L. 105-34.

"(d) Effective date. This section shall apply to disasters declared after December 31, 1996."

—P.L. 105-206, Sec. 3301(b), added a sentence at the end of subsec. (f), effective for interest for periods begin. after 7/22/98. Sec. 3301(c)(2) of this Act [as amended by Sec. 4002(d) of P.L. 105-277, see above] provides:

"(2) Special rule. Subject to any applicable statute of limitation not having expired with regard to either a tax underpayment or a tax overpayment, the amendments made by this section shall apply to interest for periods beginning before the date of the enactment of this Act if the taxpayer—

"(A) reasonably identifies and establishes periods of such tax overpayments and underpayments for which the zero rate applies; and

"(B) not later than December 31, 1999, requests the Secretary of the Treasury to apply section 6621(d) of the Internal Revenue code of 1986, as added by subsection (a), to such periods."

In 1997, P.L. 105-34, Sec. 501(e), redesignated para. (j)(3) as (j)(4) and added new para. (j)(3), effective for estates of decedents dying, and gifts made, after 12/31/97.

—P.L. 105-34, Sec. 503(a), amended paras. (j)(1) and (2) . . . Sec. 503(c)(2), substituted "2-percent" for "4-percent" each place it appeared including the heading and text of para. (j)(4) [as redesignated by Sec. 501(e) of this Act, see above.]. . . . Sec. 503(c)(3), substituted "2-percent" for "4-percent" in the heading of subsec. (j).

(j), effective for estates of decedents dying after 12/31/97, except as provided by Sec. 503(d)(2) of this Act, which reads as follows:

"(2) Election. In the case of the estate of any decedent dying before January 1, 1998, with respect to which there is an election under section 6166 of the Internal Revenue Code of 1986, the executor of the estate may elect to have the amendments made by this section apply with respect to installments due after the effective date of the election; except that the 2-percent portion of such installments shall be equal to the amount which would be the 4-percent portion of such installments without regard to such election. Such an election shall be made before January 1, 1999 in the manner prescribed by the Secretary of the Treasury and, once made, is irrevocable."

Prior to amendment, paras. (j)(1) and (2) read as follows:

"(1) In general. If the time for payment of an amount of tax imposed by chapter 11 is extended as provided in section 6166, interest on the 4-percent portion of such amount shall (in lieu of the annual rate provided by subsection (a)) be paid at the rate of 4 percent. For purposes of this subsection, the amount of any deficiency which is prorated to installments payable under section 6166 shall be treated as an amount of tax payable in installments under such section.

"(2) 4-percent portion. For purposes of this subsection, the term '4-percent portion' means the lesser of—

"(A) $345,800 reduced by the amount of the credit allowable under section 2010(a); or

"(B) the amount of the tax imposed by chapter 11 which is extended as provided in section 6166."

—P.L. 105-34, Sec. 915, of this Act [as amended by Sec. 403(e)(1) of P.L. 105-277, see above], relating to the abatement of interest on underpayments by taxpayers in presidentially declared disaster areas, provides:

"SEC. 915. ABATEMENT OF INTEREST ON UNDERPAYMENTS BY TAXPAYERS IN PRESIDENTIALLY DECLARED DISASTER AREAS.

"(a) In general. If the Secretary of the Treasury extends for any period the time for filing income tax returns under section 6081 of the Internal Revenue Code of 1986 and the time for paying income tax with respect to such returns under section 6161 of such Code (and waives any penalties relating to the failure to so file or so pay) for any individual located in a Presidentially declared disaster area, the Secretary shall, notwithstanding section 7508A(b) of such Code, abate for such period the assessment of any interest prescribed under section 6601 of such Code on such income tax.

"(b) Presidentially declared disaster area. For purposes of subsection (a), the term 'Presidentially declared disaster area' means, with respect to any individual, any area which the President has determined during 1997 or 1998 warrants assistance by the Federal Government under the Robert T. Stafford Disaster Relief and Emergency Assistance Act.

"(c) Individual. For purposes of this section, the term 'individual' shall not include any estate or trust.

"(d) Effective date. This section shall apply to disasters declared after December 31, 1996."

—P.L. 105-34, Sec. 1055(a), redesignated paras. (d)(2) and (3) as paras. (d)(3) and (4), and added new para. (d)(2), effective for foreign tax credit carrybacks arising in tax. yrs. begin. after 8/5/97.

—P.L. 105-34, Sec. 1242(a), added a sentence at the end of subsec. (c), effective for adjustments for partnership tax. yrs. begin. after 8/5/97.

In 1996, P.L. 104-168, Sec. 303(a), amended para. (e)(3) . . . Sec. 303(b)(1), substituted "21 calendar days from the date of notice and demand therefor (10 business days if the amount for which such notice and demand is made equals or exceeds $100,000)" for "10 days from the date of notice and demand therefor" in subpara. (e)(2)(A), effective for any notice and demand given after 12/31/96.

Prior to amendment, para. (e)(3) read as follows:

"(3) Payments made within 10 days after notice and demand.

"If notice and demand is made for payment of any amount, and if such amount is paid within 10 days after the date of such notice and demand, interest under this section on the amount so paid shall not be imposed for the period after the date of such notice and demand."

In 1992, P.L. 102-244, Sec. 4, provides:

"SEC. 4. EXTENSION OF TIME FOR PAYMENT OF ADDITIONAL FUTA TAXES.

"(a) In general. Notwithstanding any other provision of law, if a qualified taxpayer is required to pay additional taxes for taxable years beginning in 1991 with respect to any employment in any State by reason of such State being declared a credit reduction State, such taxpayer may elect to defer the filing and payment of such additional taxes to a date no later than June 30, 1992.

"(b) Interest. Notwithstanding subsection (a), for purposes of section 6601(a) of the Internal Revenue Code of 1986, the last date prescribed for payment of any additional taxes for which an election is made under subsection (a) shall be January 31, 1992.

"(c) Definitions. For purposes of this section—

"(1) Qualified taxpayer. The term 'qualified taxpayer' means a taxpayer—

"(A) in a State which has been declared a credit reduction State for taxable years beginning in 1991, and

"(B) who did not receive notice of such credit reduction before December 1, 1991 from either the State unemployment compensation agency or the Internal Revenue Service.

"(2) Credit reduction state. The term 'credit reduction State' means a State with respect to which the Internal Revenue Service has determined that a reduction in credits is applicable for taxable years beginning in 1991 pursuant to the provisions of section 3302 of the Internal Revenue Code of 1986.

"(d) Time and manner for making election. An election under this section shall be made at such time and in such manner as the Secretary of the Treasury shall prescribe."

In 1990, P.L. 101-508, Sec. 11801(c)(20)(B)(i), deleted "or 6158(a)" after "6156(a)" in the material preceding subpara. (b)(2)(A) . . . Sec. 11801(c)(20)(B)(ii), deleted "or 6158(a)" [sic "or 6158(a), as the case may be"] after "6156(b)" in subpara. (b)(2)(A) . . . Sec. 11801(c)(20)(B)(iii), deleted the last sentence of para. (b)(2), effective 11/5/90 except as provided in Sec. 11821(b) of this Act, reproduced in note following Code Sec. 6158.

Prior to deletion, the last sentence of para. (b)(2) read as follows:

"For purposes of subparagraph (A), section 6158(a) shall be treated as providing that the date prescribed for payment of each installment shall not be later than the date prescribed for payment of the 1985 installment".

In 1989, P.L. 101-239, Sec. 7721(c)(8), substituted "section 6651(a)(1) or 6653 or under part II of subchapter A of chapter 68" for "section 6651(a)(1), 6653, 6659, 6660, or 6661" each place it appeared in para. (e)(2), effective for returns the due date for which (determined without regard to extensions) is after 12/31/89.

In 1988, P.L. 100-647, Sec. 1015(b)(2)(C), substituted "6653, 6659" for "6659" in para. (e)(2), effective for returns the due date for which (determined without regard to extensions) is after 12/31/88.

—P.L. 100-647, Sec. 1018(u)(42), amended Sec. 1404(c)(3) of P.L. 99-514, part of the changes made to Code Sec. 6601, by substituting "section 6601(b)" for "section 6601", see below.

—P.L. 100-647, Sec. 6234(b)(1), added "or any installment agreement entered into under section 6159" after "time for payment" in para. (b)(1), effective for agreements entered into after 11/10/88.

—P.L. 100-647, Sec. 7106(c)(5), deleted "or 3321" after "3301" in subsec. (i), effective for remuneration paid after 12/31/88.

In 1987, P.L. 100-203, Sec. 10301(b)(5), substituted "6654 or 6655" for "6154 or 6654" in subsec. (h), effective for tax. yrs. begin. after 12/31/87.

In 1986, P.L. 99-514, Sec. 1404(c)(3)(A), [as amended by 1018(u)(42) of P.L. 100-647, see above.], substituted "section 6156(a) or 6158(a)" for "section 6152(a), 6156(a) or 6158(a)" in para. (b)(2) . . . Sec. 1404(c)(3)(B), substituted "section 6156(b) or 6158(a)" for "section 6152(b), 6156(b), or 6158(a)" in subpara. (b)(2)(A), effective for tax. yrs. begin. after 12/31/86.

—P.L. 99-514, Sec. 1511(c)(11), substituted "the underpayment rate" for "annual rate" in subsec. (a), effective for purposes of determining interest for periods after 12/31/86.

—P.L. 99-514, Sec. 1512(a), redesignated para. (b)(4) as (b)(5) and added new para. (b)(4), effective for returns the due date for which (determined without regard to extensions) is after 12/31/85.

—P.L. 99-514, Sec. 1564(a), added "and interest shall not be imposed during such period on any interest with respect to such deficiency for any prior period" before the period at the end of subsec. (c), effective for interest accruing after 12/31/82. Sec. 1564(b)(2) of this Act provides:

"(2) Statute of limitations.—If refund or credit of any amount resulting from the application of the amendment made by subsection (a) is prevented at any time before the close of the date which is 1 year after the date of the enactment of this Act by the operation of any law or rule of law (including res judicata), refund or credit of such amount (to the extent attributable to the application of the amendment made by subsection (a)), may nevertheless, be made or allowed if claim therefore is filed before the close of such 1-year period."

In 1984, P.L. 98-369, Sec. 158(a), amended para. (e)(2), effective for interest accrued after 7/18/84, except for additions to tax for which notice and demand is made before 7/18/84.

Prior to amendment, para. (e)(2) read as follows:

"(2) Interest on penalties, additional amounts, or additions to the tax. Interest shall be imposed under subsection (a) in respect of any assessable penalty, additional amount, or addition to the tax only if such assessable penalty, additional amount, or addition to the tax is not paid within 10 days from the date of notice and demand therefor, and in such case interest shall be imposed only for the period from the date of the notice and demand to the date of payment."

—P.L. 98-369, Sec. 211(b)(26), deleted para. (d)(3) and redesignated para. (d)(4) as para. (d)(3), effective for tax. yrs. begin. after 12/31/83.

Prior to deletion, para. (d)(3) read as follows:

"(3) Adjustment for certain unused deductions of life insurance companies. If the amount of any tax imposed by subtitle A is reduced by operation of section 815(d)(5) (relating to reduction of policyholders surplus account of life insurance companies for certain unused deductions), such reduction in tax shall not affect the computation of interest under this section for the period ending with the last day of the last taxable year to which the loss described in section 815(d)(5)(A) is carried under section 812(b)(2)."

—P.L. 98-369, Sec. 412(b)(7), amended subsec. (h), effective for tax. yrs. begin. after 12/31/84.

Prior to amendment, subsec. (h) read as follows:

"(h) Exception as to estimated tax.

"This section shall not apply to any failure to pay estimated tax required by section 6153 or section 6154."

—P.L. 98-369, Sec. 714(n)(1), corrected Sec. 346(c)(2)(B) of P.L. 97-248 to read substitute "the filing date for" for "the last day of" rather than for "the last day of the" each place it appeared in subpara. (d)(2)(A), see below.

In 1983, P.L. 98-76, Sec. 231(b)(2)(D), substituted "3301 or 3321" for "3301" in subsec. (i), effective for remuneration paid after 6/30/86.

In 1982, P.L. 97-248, Sec. 344(b)(1), deleted para. (e)(2) and redesignated paras. (e)(3) and (4) as paras. (e)(2) and (3), effective for interest accruing after 12/31/82.

Prior to amendment, para. (e)(2) read as follows:

"(2) No interest on interest. No interest under this section shall be imposed on the interest provided by this section."

—P.L. 97-248, Sec. 346(c)(2)(A), substituted "the filing date for the taxable year" for "the last day of the taxable year" in para. (d)(1)... Sec. 346(c)(2)(B), substituted "the filing date for" for "the last day of" each place it appeared in subpara. (d)(2)(A)... Sec. 346(c)(2)(C), added para. (d)(4), effective for interest accruing after 10/3/82 [30th day after date of enactment (9/3/82)].

In 1980, P.L. 96-223, Sec. 101(f)(7), substituted "certain excise tax" for "chapter 41, 42, 43, or 44 tax" in the heading of subsec. (c), effective for periods after 2/29/80.

In 1978, P.L. 95-628, Sec. 8(c)(2), amended para. (d)(2) and deleted paras. (d)(4) and (d)(5), effective for carrybacks arising in tax. yrs. begin. after 11/10/78.

Prior to amendment, para. (d)(2), read as follows:

"(2) Investment credit carryback. If the credit allowed by section 38 for any taxable year is increased by reason of an investment credit carryback, such increase shall not affect the computation of interest under this section for the period ending with the last day of the taxable year in which the investment credit carryback arises, or with respect to any portion of an investment credit carryback from a taxable year attributable to a net operating loss carryback or a capital loss carryback from a subsequent taxable year, such increase shall not affect the computation of interest under this section for the period ending with the last day of such subsequent taxable year."

Prior to deletion, paras. (d)(4) and (d)(5) read as follows:

"(4) Work incentive program credit carryback. If the credit allowed by section 40 for any taxable year is increased by reason of a work incentive program credit carryback, such increase shall not affect the computation of interest under this section for the period ending with the last day of the taxable year in which the work incentive program credit carryback arises, or, with respect to any portion of a work incentive program credit carryback from a taxable year attributable to a net operating loss carryback, an investment credit carryback, or a capital loss carryback from a subsequent taxable year, such increase shall not affect the computation of interest under this section for the period ending with the last day of such subsequent taxable year.

"(5) New employee credit carryback. If the credit allowed by section 44B for any taxable year is increased by reason of a new employee credit carryback, such increase shall not affect the computation of interest under this section for the period ending with the last day of the taxable year in which the new employee credit carryback arises, or, with respect to any portion of a new employee credit carryback from a taxable year attributable to a net operating loss carryback, an investment credit carryback, a work incentive program carryback, or a capital loss carryback from a subsequent taxable year, such increase shall not affect the computation of interest under this section for the period ending with the last day of such subsequent taxable year."

In 1977, P.L. 95-30, Sec. 202(d)(4)(C), added para. (d)(5), effective for tax. yrs. begin. after 12/31/76 and for credit carrybacks from such yrs.

—P.L. 95-30, Sec. 305, provided as follows:

"SEC. 305. INTEREST ON UNDERPAYMENTS OF TAX.

"No interest shall be payable for any period before April 16, 1977 (March 16, 1977, in the case of a corporation), on any underpayment of a tax imposed by the Internal Revenue Code of 1954, to the extent that such underpayment was created or increased by any provision of the Tax Reform Act of 1976."

In 1976, P.L. 94-455, Sec. 1307(d)(2)(H), substituted "Chapter 41, 42. [sic]" for "Chapter 42" in the heading of subsec. (c), effective 10/4/76.

—P.L. 94-455, Sec. 1605(b)(10), substituted "43, or 44" for "or 43" in the heading of subsec. (c), effective for tax. yrs. of real estate investment trusts begin. after 10/4/76.

—P.L. 94-455, Sec. 1906(a)(34), deleted "(or section 59 of the Internal Revenue Code of 1939)", after "section 6153", in subsec. (h), effective 2/1/77.

—P.L. 94-455, Sec. 1906(b)(13)(A), substituted "Secretary" for "Secretary or his delegate" each place it appeared in Code Sec. 6601, effective 2/1/77.

—P.L. 94-455, Sec. 2004(b), redesignated subsec. (j) as subsec. (k), and added new subsec. (j), effective for estates of decedents dying after 12/31/76.

—P.L. 94-455, Sec. 2107(g)(2)(C), added ", an investment credit carryback," after "net operating loss carryback" in para. (d)(4), effective 10/4/76.

—P.L. 94-452, Sec. 3(c)(3), substituted ", 6156(a), or 6158(a)" for "or 6156(a)" in para. (b)(2) ... substituted ", 6156(a), or 6158(a)" for "or 6165(b)" in subpara. (b)(2)(A) ... added the last sentence in para. (b)(2), effective 10/1/77 for sales after 7/7/70 in tax. yrs. end. after 7/7/70, but only in the case of qualified bank holding corps. within the meaning of Code Sec. 1103(b), as amended by this Act.

In 1975, P.L. 93-625, Sec. 7(b)(1), deleted subsecs. (b) and (j) and redesignated subsecs. (c), (d), (e), (f), (g), (h), (i), (k), and (l) as (b), (c), (d), (e), (f), (g), (h), (i), and (j), effective 7/1/75, and applicable to amounts outstanding on or arising after 7/1/75.

Prior to deletion, subsecs. (b) and (j) read as follows:

"(b) Extensions of time for payment of estate tax.

"If the time for payment of an amount of tax imposed by chapter 11 is extended as provided in section 6161(a)(2) or 6166, or if the time for payment of an amount of such tax is postponed or extended as provided by section 6163, interest shall be paid at the rate of 4 percent, in lieu of 6 percent as provided in subsection (a).

* * *

"(j) Extensions of time for payment of tax attributable to recoveries of foreign expropriation losses.

"If the time for payment of an amount of the tax attributable to a recovery of a foreign expropriation loss (within the meaning of section 6167(f)) is extended as provided in subsection (a) or (b) of section 6167, interest shall be paid at the rate of 4 percent, in lieu of 6 percent as provided in subsection (a)."

—P.L. 93-625, Sec. 7(a)(2)(A), substituted "an annual rate established under section 6621" for "the rate of 6 percent per annum" in subsec. (a), effective 7/1/75, and applicable to amounts outstanding on or arising after 7/1/75.

In 1974, P.L. 93-406, Sec. 1016(a)(17), inserted "or 43" after "chapter 42" in the heading of subsec. (d), and substituted "certain excise" for "chapter 42" in subsec. (d), effective 9/2/74 or other date as specified in Sec. 1017 of the Act (reproduced following Code Sec. 401).

In 1971, P.L. 92-178, Sec. 601(d)(3), added para. (e)(4), effective for tax. yrs. begin. after 12/31/71.

In 1969, P.L. 91-172, Sec. 101(j)(49), substituted "gift, and chapter 42 taxes" for "and gift taxes" and substituted "gift and chapter 42 taxes" for "and gift taxes" in subsec. (d), effective 1/1/70.

—P.L. 91-172, Sec. 512(e)(3), substituted "loss or capital loss carryback" for "loss carryback" in the heading of para. (e)(1) ... substituted "net operating loss or net capital loss" for "net operating loss" wherever it appeared in para. (e)(1) ... substituted "loss carryback or a capital loss carryback" for "loss carryback" in para. (e)(2), effective for net capital losses sustained in tax. yrs. begin. after 12/31/69. Sec. 946 of this Act provides as follows:

"(a) Interest on Underpayment.

"Notwithstanding section 6601 of the Internal Revenue Code of 1954, in the case of any taxable year ending before the date of the enactment of this Act, no interest on any underpayment of tax, to the extent such underpayment is attributable to the amendments made by this Act, shall be assessed or collected for any period before the 90th day after such date.

"(b) Declarations of Estimated Tax.

"In the case of a taxable year beginning before the date of enactment of this Act, if any taxpayer is required to make a declaration or amended declaration of estimated tax, or to pay any amount or additional amount of estimated tax, by reason of the amendments made by this Act, such amount or additional amount shall be paid ratably on or before each of the remaining installment dates for the taxable year beginning with the first installment date on or after the 30th day after such date of enactment. With respect to any declaration or payment of estimated tax before such first installment date, sections 6015, 6154, 6654, and 6655 of the Internal Revenue Code of 1954 shall be applied without regard to the amendments made by this Act. For purposes of this subsection, the term 'installment date' means any date on which, under section 6153 or 6154 of such Code (whichever is applicable), an installment payment of estimated tax is required to be made by the taxpayer."

—P.L. 91-53, Sec. 2(e), redesignated subsec. (k) as subsec. (l) and added new subsec. (k), effective for calendar years begin. after '69.

In 1967, P.L. 90-225, Sec. 2(e), added "or with respect to any portion of an investment credit carryback from a taxable year attributable to a net operating loss carryback from a subsequent taxable year, such increase shall not affect the computation of interest under this section for the period ending with the last day of such subsequent taxable year" at the end of para. (e)(2), effective for investment credit carrybacks attributable to net operating loss carrybacks from tax. yrs. end. after 7/31/67.

In 1966, P.L. 89-384, Sec. 1(f), redesignated subsec. (j) as subsec. (k) and added new subsec. (j), effective for amounts received after 12/31/64 for foreign expropriation losses (as defined in Code Sec. 1351(b)) sustained in tax yrs. begin. after 12/31/58.

In 1964, P.L. 88-571, Sec. 3(d), added para. (e)(3) and added "or adjustment for certain unused deductions" in the heading of subsec. (e), effective for amounts added to policyholders surplus accounts, effective for tax. yrs. begin. after 12/31/58.

In 1962, P.L. 87-834, Sec. 2(e)(3), designated existing provisions as para. (e)(1) and added para. (e)(2), effective for tax. yrs. end. after 12/31/61.

In 1961, P.L. 87-61, Sec. 203(c)(2), provided for determinations in the case of elections under section 6156(a) in subsec. (c)(2), effective 7/1/61.

In 1958, P.L. 85-866, Sec. 66, substituted "if the time for payment of an amount of such tax is postponed or extended as provided by section 6163" for "if postponement of the payment of an amount of such tax is permitted by section 6163(a)" in subsec. (b), ... Sec. 84, redesignated subsec. (h) as subsec. (j), and added new subsec. (h), effective 8/17/54.

—P.L. 85-866, Sec. 206(e), substituted "section 6161(a)(2) or 6166" for "section 6161(a)(2)" in subsec. (b), effective for estates of decedents dying with respect to which the date for the filing the state tax return (including extensions) prescribed by Code Sec. 6075(a) is after 9/2/58.

—P.L. 85-866, Sec. 83, added subsec. (g) and redesignated subsec. (g) as (i), effective for overpayments credited after '57.

Sec. 6602. Interest on erroneous refund recoverable by suit.

Any portion of an internal revenue tax (or any interest, assessable penalty, additional amount, or addition to tax) which has been erroneously refunded, and which is recoverable by suit pursuant to section 7405, shall bear interest at the underpayment rate established under section 6621 from the date of the payment of the refund.

In 1986, P.L. 99-514, Sec. 1511(c)(12), substituted "the underpayment rate" for "an annual rate" in Code Sec. 6602, effective for purposes of determining interest for periods after 12/31/86.

In 1975, P.L. 93-625, Sec. 7(a)(2)(B), substituted "an annual rate established under section 6621" for "the rate of 6 percent per annum" in Code Sec. 6602, effective 7/1/75, and applicable to amounts outstanding on or arising after 7/1/75.

Sec. 6603. Deposits made to suspend running of interest on potential underpayments, etc.

(a) Authority to make deposits other than as payment of tax.

A taxpayer may make a cash deposit with the Secretary which may be used by the Secretary to pay any tax imposed under subtitle A or B or chapter 41, 42, 43, or 44 which has not been assessed at the time of the deposit. Such a deposit shall be made in such manner as the Secretary shall prescribe.

(b) No interest imposed.

To the extent that such deposit is used by the Secretary to pay tax, for purposes of section 6601 (relating to interest on underpayments), the tax shall be treated as paid when the deposit is made.

(c) Return of deposit.

Except in a case where the Secretary determines that collection of tax is in jeopardy, the Secretary shall return to the taxpayer any amount of the deposit (to the extent not used for a payment of tax) which the taxpayer requests in writing.

(d) Payment of interest.

(1) In general. For purposes of section 6611 (relating to interest on overpayments), except as provided in paragraph (4), a deposit which is returned to a taxpayer shall be treated as a payment of tax for any period to the extent (and only to the extent) attributable to a disputable tax for such period. Under regulations prescribed by the Secretary, rules similar to the rules of section 6611(b)(2) shall apply.

(2) Disputable tax.

(A) In general. For purposes of this section, the term "disputable tax" means the amount of tax specified at the time of the deposit as the taxpayer's reasonable estimate of the maximum amount of any tax attributable to disputable items.

(B) Safe harbor based on 30-day letter. In the case of a taxpayer who has been issued a 30-day letter, the maximum amount of tax under subparagraph (A) shall not be less than the amount of the proposed deficiency specified in such letter.

(3) Other definitions. For purposes of paragraph (2)—

(A) Disputable item. The term "disputable item" means any item of income, gain, loss, deduction, or credit if the taxpayer—

(i) has a reasonable basis for its treatment of such item, and

(ii) reasonably believes that the Secretary also has a reasonable basis for disallowing the taxpayer's treatment of such item.

(B) 30-day letter. The term "30-day letter" means the first letter of proposed deficiency which allows the taxpayer an opportunity for administrative review in the Internal Revenue Service Office of Appeals.

(4) Rate of interest. The rate of interest under this subsection shall be the Federal short-term rate determined under section 6621(b), compounded daily.

(e) Use of deposits.

(1) Payment of tax. Except as otherwise provided by the taxpayer, deposits shall be treated as used for the payment of tax in the order deposited.

(2) Returns of deposits. Deposits shall be treated as returned to the taxpayer on a last-in, first-out basis.

In 2004, P.L. 108-357, Sec. 842(a), added Code Sec. 6603, effective for deposits made after 10/22/2004. Sec. 842(c)(2) of this Act, provides:

"(2) Coordination with deposits made under Revenue Procedure 84-58. In the case of an amount held by the Secretary of the Treasury or his delegate on the date of the enactment of this Act as a deposit in the nature of a cash bond deposit pursuant to Revenue Procedure 84-58, the date that the taxpayer identifies such amount as a deposit made pursuant to section 6603 of the Internal Revenue Code (as added by this Act) shall be treated as the date such amount is deposited for purposes of such section 6603."

Subchapter B.—Interest on Overpayments

Sec.
6611. Interest on overpayments.
6612. Cross references.

Sec. 6611. Interest on overpayments.

(a) Rate.

Interest shall be allowed and paid upon any overpayment in respect of any internal revenue tax at the overpayment rate established under section 6621.

(b) Period.

Such interest shall be allowed and paid as follows:

(1) Credits. In the case of a credit, from the date of the overpayment to the due date of the amount against which the credit is taken.

(2) Refunds. In the case of a refund, from the date of the overpayment to a date (to be determined by the Secretary) preceding the date of the refund check by not more than 30 days, whether or not such refund check is accepted by the taxpayer after tender of such check to the taxpayer. The acceptance of such check shall be without prejudice to any right of the taxpayer to claim any additional overpayment and interest thereon.

(3) Late returns. Notwithstanding paragraph (1) or (2) in the case of a return of tax which is filed after the last date prescribed for filing such return (determined with regard to extensions), no interest shall be allowed or paid for any day before the date on which the return is filed.

(c) Repealed.

(d) Advance payment of tax, payment of estimated tax, and credit for income tax withholding.

The provisions of section 6513 (except the provisions of subsection (c) thereof), applicable in determining the date of payment of tax for purposes of determining the period of limitation on credit or refund, shall be applicable in determining the date of payment for purposes of subsection (a).

(e) Disallowance of interest on certain overpayments.

(1) Refunds within 45 days after return is filed. If any overpayment of tax imposed by this title is refunded within 45 days after the last day prescribed for filing the return of such tax (determined without regard to any extension of time for filing the return) or, in the case of a return filed after such last date, is refunded within 45 days after the date the return is filed, no interest shall be allowed under subsection (a) on such overpayment.

(2) Refunds after claim for credit or refund. If—

(A) the taxpayer files a claim for a credit or refund for any overpayment of tax imposed by this title, and

(B) such overpayment is refunded within 45 days after such claim is filed,

no interest shall be allowed on such overpayment from the date the claim is filed until the day the refund is made.

(3) IRS initiated adjustments. If an adjustment initiated by the Secretary, results in a refund or credit of an overpayment, interest on such overpayment shall be computed by subtracting 45 days from the number of days interest

Interest
Code Sec. 6611

would otherwise be allowed with respect to such overpayment.

(4) Certain withholding taxes. In the case of any overpayment resulting from tax deducted and withheld under chapter 3 or 4, paragraphs (1), (2), and (3) shall be applied by substituting "180 days" for "45 days" each place it appears.

(f) Refund of income tax caused by carryback or adjustment for certain unused deductions.

(1) Net operating loss or capital loss carryback. For purposes of subsection (a), if any overpayment of tax imposed by subtitle A results from a carryback of a net operating loss or net capital loss, such overpayment shall be deemed not to have been made prior to the filing date for the taxable year in which such net operating loss or net capital loss arises.

(2) Foreign tax credit carrybacks. For purposes of subsection (a), if any overpayment of tax imposed by subtitle A results from a carryback of tax paid or accrued to foreign countries or possessions of the United States, such overpayment shall be deemed not to have been made before the filing date for the taxable year in which such taxes were in fact paid or accrued, or, with respect to any portion of such credit carryback from a taxable year attributable to a net operating loss carryback or a capital loss carryback from a subsequent taxable year, such overpayment shall be deemed not to have been made before the filing date for such subsequent taxable year.

(3) Certain credit carrybacks.

(A) In general. For purposes of subsection (a), if any overpayment of tax imposed by subtitle A results from a credit carryback, such overpayment shall be deemed not to have been made before the filing date for the taxable year in which such credit carryback arises, or, with respect to any portion of a credit carryback from a taxable year attributable to a net operating loss carryback, capital loss carryback, or other credit carryback from a subsequent taxable year, such overpayment shall be deemed not to have been made before the filing date for such subsequent taxable year.

(B) Credit carryback defined. For purposes of this paragraph, the term "credit carryback" has the meaning given such term by section 6511(d)(4)(C).

(4) Special rules for paragraphs (1), (2), and (3).

(A) Filing date. For purposes of this subsection, the term "filing date" means the last date prescribed for filing the return of tax imposed by subtitle A for the taxable year (determined without regard to extensions).

(B) Coordination with subsection (e).

(i) In general. For purposes of subsection (e)—

(I) any overpayment described in paragraph (1), (2), or (3) shall be treated as an overpayment for the loss year, and

(II) such subsection shall be applied with respect to such overpayment by treating the return for the loss year as not filed before claim for such overpayment is filed.

(ii) Loss year. For purposes of this subparagraph, the term "loss year" means—

(I) in the case of a carryback of a net operating loss or net capital loss, the taxable year in which such loss arises,

(II) in the case of a carryback of taxes paid or accrued to foreign countries or possessions of the United States, the taxable year in which such taxes were in fact paid or accrued (or, with respect to any portion of such carryback from a taxable year

attributable to a net operating loss carryback or a capital loss carryback from a subsequent taxable year, such subsequent taxable year), and

(III) in the case of a credit carryback (as defined in paragraph (3)(B)), the taxable year in which such credit carryback arises (or, with respect to any portion of a credit carryback from a taxable year attributable to a net operating loss carryback, a capital loss carryback, or other credit carryback from a subsequent taxable year, such subsequent taxable year).

(C) Application of subparagraph (B) where section 6411(a) claim filed. For purposes of subparagraph (B)(i)(II), if a taxpayer—

(i) files a claim for refund of any overpayment described in paragraph (1), (2), or (3) with respect to the taxable year to which a loss or credit is carried back, and

(ii) subsequently files an application under section 6411(a) with respect to such overpayment,

then the claim for overpayment shall be treated as having been filed on the date the application under section 6411(a) was filed.

(g) No interest until return in processible form.

(1) For purposes of subsections (b)(3) and (e), a return shall not be treated as filed until it is filed in processible form.

(2) For purposes of paragraph (1), a return is in a processible form if—

(A) such return is filed on a permitted form, and

(B) such return contains—

(i) the taxpayer's name, address, and identifying number and the required signature, and

(ii) sufficient required information (whether on the return or on required attachments) to permit the mathematical verification of tax liability shown on the return.

(h) Prohibition of administrative review.

For prohibition of administrative review, see section 6406.

In 2010, P.L. 111-147, Sec. 501(b), added para. (e)(4), effective as provided in Sec. 501(d)(2)-(3) of this Act, which reads as follows:

"(2) Grandfathered treatment of outstanding obligations. The amendments made by this section shall not require any amount to be deducted or withheld from any payment under any obligation outstanding on the date which is 2 years after the date of the enactment of this Act or from the gross proceeds from any disposition of such an obligation.

"(3) Interest on overpayments. The amendment made by subsection (b) shall apply—

"(A) in the case of such amendment's application to paragraph (1) of section 6611(e) of the Internal Revenue Code of 1986, to returns the due date for which (determined without regard to extensions) is after the date of the enactment of this Act,

"(B) in the case of such amendment's application to paragraph (2) of such section, to claims for credit or refund of any overpayment filed after the date of the enactment of this Act (regardless of the taxable period to which such refund relates), and

"(C) in the case of such amendment's application to paragraph (3) of such section, to refunds paid after the date of the enactment of this Act (regardless of the taxable period to which such refund relates)."

In 2000, P.L. 106-554, Sec. 1(a)(7), [which enacted into law Sec. 319(20) of P.L. 106-554] deleted the comma after "(b)(3)" in para. (g)(1), effective 12/21/2000.

In 1998, P.L. 105-206, Sec. 6010(l), substituted "and (e)" for "(e), and (h)" in para. (g)(1), effective for foreign tax credit carrybacks arising in tax. yrs. begin. after 8/5/97.

In 1997, P.L. 105-34, Sec. 1055(b)(1), redesignated paras. (f)(2) and (3) as paras. (f)(3) and (4) and added new para. (f)(2)... Sec. 1055(b)(2)(A)(i), substituted "paragraphs (1), (2), and (3)" for "paragraphs (1) and (2)" in the heading of para. (f)(4) [as redesignated by Sec. 1055(b)(1) of this Act, see above]... Sec. 1055(b)(2)(A)(ii), substituted "paragraph (1), (2), or (3)" for "paragraph (1) or (2)" in subclause (f)(4)(B)(i)(I) and clause (f)(4)(C)(i) [as redesignated by Sec. 1055(b)(1) of this Act, see above]... Sec. 1055(b)(2)(B), deleted "and" at the end of subclause (f)(4)(B)(ii)(I) [as redesignated by Sec. 1055(b)(1) of this Act, see above], redesignated subclause (f)(4)(B)(ii)(II) as (f)(4)(B)(ii)(III) [as redesignated by Sec. 1055(b)(1) of this Act, see above] and added subclause (f)(4)(B)(ii)(II) [as redesignated by Sec. 1055(b)(1) of this Act, see above]... Sec. 1055(b)(2)(C), added "(as defined in paragraph (3)(B))" after "in the case of a credit carryback" the first place it appears in subclause (f)(4)(B)(ii)(III) [as redesignated by Sec. 1055(b)(1) and (b)(2)(B) of this Act, see above]... Sec. 1055(b)(2)(D), deleted subsec. (g) and redes. subsecs. (h) and (i) as subsecs. (g) and (h), effective for foreign tax credit carrybacks arising in tax. yrs. begin. after 8/5/97.

Prior to deletion, subsec. (g) read as follows:

"(g) Refund of income tax caused by carryback of foreign taxes. For purposes of subsection (a), if any overpayment of tax results from a carryback of tax paid or accrued to foreign countries or possessions of the United States, such overpayment shall be deemed not to have been paid or accrued prior to the filing date (as defined in subsection (f)(3)) for the taxable year under this subtitle in which such taxes were in fact paid or accrued."

In 1993, P.L. 103-66, Sec. 13271(a), amended subsec. (e), effective as provided in Sec. 13271(b) of this Act, which reads as follows:

"(b) Effective dates.

"(1) Paragraph (1) of section 6611(e) of the Internal Revenue Code of 1986 (as amended by subsection (a)) shall apply in the case of returns the due date for which (determined without regard to extensions) is on or after January 1, 1994.

"(2) Paragraph (2) of section 6611(e) of such Code (as so amended) shall apply in the case of claims for credit or refund of any overpayment filed on or after January 1, 1995, regardless of the taxable period to which such refund relates.

"(3) Paragraph (3) of section 6611(e) of such Code (as so amended) shall apply in the case of any refund paid on or after January 1, 1995, regardless of the taxable period to which such refund relates."

Prior to amendment, subsec. (e) read as follows:

"(e) Income tax refund within 45 days after return is filed. If any overpayment of tax imposed by subtitle A is refunded within 45 days after the last date prescribed for filing the return of such tax (determined without regard to any extension of time for filing the return) or, in case the return is filed after such last date, is refunded within 45 days after the date the return is filed, no interest shall be allowed under subsection (a) on such overpayment."

In 1988, P.L. 100-418, Sec. 1941(b)(2)(L), deleted subsec. (h) and redesignated subsecs. (i) and (j) as (h) and (i), effective for crude oil removed from the premises on or after 8/23/88.

Prior to deletion, subsec. (h) read as follows:

"(h) Special rule for windfall profit tax.

"(1) In general. If any overpayment of tax imposed by section 4986 is refunded within 45 days after—

"(A) the last date (determined without regard to any extension of time for filing the return) prescribed for filing the return of the tax imposed by section 4986 for the taxable period with respect to which the overpayment was made, or

"(B) if such return is filed after such last date, the date on which the return is filed,

no interest shall be allowed under subsection (a) on such overpayment.

"(2) Special rule where no return is required. In the case of any oil for which no return of the tax imposed by section 4986 is required, the return referred to in paragraph (1) shall be the return of the tax imposed by subtitle A for the taxable year of the producer in which the removal year (with respect to which the overpayment was made) ends. For purposes of the preceding sentence, the term 'removal year' means the calendar year in which the oil is removed from the premises."

In 1986, P.L. 99-514, Sec. 1511(c)(13), substituted "the overpayment rate established under section 6621" for "an annual rate established under section 6621" in subsec. (a), effective for purposes of determining interest for periods after 12/31/86.

—P.L. 99-514, Sec. 1875(d)(3), of this Act provided that notwithstanding Sec. 715 of P.L. 98-369, the amendments made by Sec. 714(n)(2) of P.L. 98-369, are effective for applications filed after 7/18/84.

In 1984, P.L. 98-369, Sec. 211(b)(27), deleted para. (f)(4), effective for tax. yrs. begin. after 12/31/83.

Prior to deletion, para. (f)(4) read as follows:

"(4) Adjustment for certain unused deductions of life insurance companies. For purposes of subsection (a), if any overpayment of tax imposed by subtitle A arises by operation of section 815(d)(5) (relating to reduction of policyholders surplus account of life insurance companies for certain unused deductions), such overpayment shall be deemed not to have been made prior to the close of the last taxable year to which the loss described in section 815(d)(5)(A) is carried under section 812(b)(2)."

—P.L. 98-369, Sec. 714(n)(2)(A), added subpara. (f)(3)(C), effective [as provided in Sec. 1875(d)(3) of P.L. 99-514, see above] for applications filed after 7/18/84.

In 1982, P.L. 97-248, Sec. 346(a), added para. (b)(3) ... Sec. 346(b), redesignated subsec. (i) as subsec. (j) and added new subsec. (i), effective for returns filed after 10/3/82.

—P.L. 97-248, Sec. 346(c)(1)(A), substituted "the filing date for the taxable year" for "the close of the taxable year" in para. (f)(1) ... Sec. 346(c)(1)(B), substituted "the filing date for" for "the close of" each place it appeared in subpara. (f)(2)(A) ... Sec. 346(c)(1)(C), redesignated para. (f)(3) as para. (f)(4) and added new para. (f)(3) ... Sec. 346(c)(1)(D), substituted "the filing date (as defined in subsection (f)(3)) for the taxable year" for "the close of the taxable year", in subsec. (g), effective for interest accruing after 10/3/82.

In 1980, P.L. 96-223, Sec. 101(h), redesignated subsec. (h) as subsec. (i) and added new subsec. (h), effective for periods after 2/29/80. Sec. 101(i)(2) of this Act, provides:

"(2) Transitional rules. For the period ending June 30, 1980, the Secretary of the Treasury or his delegate shall prescribe rules relating to the administration of

chapter 45 of the Internal Revenue Code of 1954. To the extent provided in such rules, such rules shall supplement or supplant for such period the administrative provisions contained in chapter 45 of such Code (or in so much of subtitle F of such Code as relates to such chapter 45)."

In 1978, P.L. 95-628, Sec. 8(c)(3)(A), amended para. (f)(3) [sic (f)(2)] ... Sec. 8(c)(3)(B), deleted paras. (f)(4) and (f)(5), effective for carrybacks arising in tax. yrs. begin. after 11/10/78.

Prior to amendment, para. (f)(3) [sic (f)(2)], read as follows:

"(2) Investment credit carryback. For purposes of subsection (a), if any overpayment of tax imposed by subtitle A results from an investment credit carryback, such overpayment shall be deemed not to have been made prior to the close of the taxable year in which such investment credit carryback arises, or, with respect to any portion of an investment credit carryback from a taxable year attributable to a net operating loss carryback or a capital loss carryback from a subsequent taxable year, such overpayment shall be deemed not to have been made prior to the close of such subsequent taxable year."

Prior to deletion, paras. (f)(4) and (f)(5)

"(4) Work incentive program credit carryback. For purposes of subsection (a), if any overpayment of tax imposed by subtitle A results from a work incentive program credit carryback, such overpayment shall be deemed not to have been made prior to the close of the taxable year in which such work incentive program credit carryback arises, or, with respect to any portion of a work incentive program credit carryback from a taxable year attributable to a net operating loss carryback, an investment credit carryback, or a capital loss carryback from a subsequent taxable year, such overpayment shall be deemed not to have been made prior to the close of such subsequent taxable year.

"(5) New employee credit carryback. For purposes of subsection (a), if any overpayment of tax imposed by subtitle A results from a new employee credit carryback, such overpayment shall be deemed not to have been made before the close of the taxable year in which such new employee credit carryback arises, or, with respect to any portion of a new employee credit carryback from a taxable year attributable to a net operating loss carryback, an investment credit carryback, a work incentive program credit carryback, or a capital loss carryback from a subsequent taxable year, such overpayment shall be deemed not to have been made before the close of such subsequent taxable year."

In 1977, P.L. 95-30, Sec. 202(d)(4)(D), added para. (f)(5), effective for tax. yrs. begin. after 12/31/76 and to credit carrybacks from such yrs.

In 1976, P.L. 94-455, Sec. 1904(b)(10)(A)(iv), deleted subsec. (h) and redesignated subsec. (i) as subsec. (h), effective for acquisitions of stock or debt obligations made after 6/30/74.

Prior to deletion, subsec. (h) read as follows:

"(h) Refund within 45 days after filing claim for refund of interest equalization tax paid on securities sold to foreigners.

"No interest shall be allowed under subsection (a) on any overpayment of the tax imposed by section 4911, arising by reason of section 4919(a), if the overpayment is refunded within 45 days after the filing of a claim for refund for that overpayment of tax with respect to a prior quarter."

—P.L. 94-455, Sec. 1906(b)(13)(A), substituted "Secretary" for "Secretary or his delegate" in Code Sec. 6611, effective 2/1/77.

—P.L. 94-455, Sec. 2107(g)(2)(D), added ", an investment credit carryback," after "net operating loss carryback" in para. (f)(4), effective 10/4/76.

In 1975, P.L. 94-12, Sec. 101(b), of this Act provides:

"(b) No Interest on Individual Income Tax Refunds for 1974 Refunded Within 60 Days After Return Is Filed. In applying section 6611(e) of the Internal Revenue Code of 1954 (relating to income tax refund within 45 days after return is filed) in the case of any overpayment of tax imposed by subtitle A of such Code by an individual (other than an estate or trust and other than a nonresident alien individual) for a taxable year beginning in 1974, '60 days' shall be substituted for '45 days' each place it appears in such section 6611(e)."

—P.L. 93-625, Sec. 7(a)(2)(C), substituted "an annual rate established under section 6621" for "the rate of 6 percent per annum" in subsec. (a), effective 7/1/75, and applicable to amounts outstanding on or arising after 7/1/75.

In 1973, P.L. 93-17, Sec. 3(i)(2), redesignated subsec. (h) as subsec. (i) and added new subsec. (h), effective 4/10/73.

In 1971, P.L. 92-178, Sec. 601(d)(4), added para. (f)(4), effective for tax. yrs. begin. after 12/31/71.

In 1969, P.L. 91-172, Sec. 512(e)(4), substituted "loss or capital loss carryback" for "loss carryback" in heading of para. (f)(1) ... substituted "net operating loss or net capital loss" for "net operating loss" in para. (f)(1) ... substituted "loss carryback or a capital loss carryback" for "loss carryback" in para. (f)(2), effective for net capital losses sustained in tax. yrs. begin. after 12/31/69.

In 1967, P.L. 90-225, Sec. 2(f), added ", or, with respect to any portion of an investment credit carryback from a taxable year attributable to a net operating loss carryback from a subsequent taxable year, such overpayment shall be deemed not to have been made prior to the close of such subsequent taxable year" after "such investment credit carryback arises" in para. (f)(2), effective for investment credit carrybacks attributable to net operating loss carrybacks from tax. yrs. end. after 7/31/67.

In 1966, P.L. 89-721, Sec. 1(a), added "or, in case the return is filed after such last date, is refunded within 45 days after the date the return is filed" in subsec. (e), effective for refunds made more than 45 days after 11/2/66.

In 1964, P.L. 88-571, Sec. 3(e), added para. (f)(3) and added "or adjustment for certain unused deductions" in the heading of subsec. (f), effective for amounts added to policyholders surplus accounts, for tax. yrs. begin. after 12/31/58.

In 1962, P.L. 87-834, Sec. 2(e)(4), designated existing provisions in subsec. (f) as para. (f)(1), and added para. (f)(2), effective for tax. yrs. end. after 12/31/61.

Interest   **Code Sec. 6621(c)(2)(A)(i)**

In 1958, P.L. 85-866, Sec. 83, deleted "but if the amount against which the credit is taken as an additional assessment, then to the date of the assessment of that amount" after "taken", in para. (b)(1), and deleted subsec. (c), effective for overpayments credited after 12/31/57.
Prior to deletion, subsec. (c) read as follows:
"(c) Additional assessment defined.
"As used in this section, the term 'additional assessment' means a further assessment for a tax of the same character previously paid in part, and includes the assessment of a deficiency (as defined in section 6211)."
— P.L. 85-866, Sec. 42, added subsec. (g) and redesignated subsec. (g) as subsec. (h), effective for tax. yrs. begin. after 12/31/57.
— P.L. 85-866, Sec. 83(e), provides as follows:
"(e) Interest attributable to net operating loss carryback for certain taxable years ending in 1954.
"If by reason of enactment of section 172(b)(1)(A) of the Internal Revenue Code of 1954—
"(1) a deficiency resulted for the first taxable year preceding a taxable year ending after December 31, 1953, and before August 17, 1954, and
"(2) an overpayment resulted for the second preceding taxable year,
no interest shall be payable with respect to any portion of such deficiency for any period during which there existed a corresponding amount of such overpayment with respect to which interest is not payable."

Sec. 6612. Cross references.
(a) Interest on judgments for overpayments.
For interest on judgments for overpayments, see 28 U. S. C. 2411(a).
(b) Adjustments.
For provisions prohibiting interest on certain adjustments in tax, see section 6413(a).

• *Caution:* Code Sec. 6612(c), following, was amended by Sec. 532(c)(12), P.L. 107-16, the Economic Growth and Tax Relief Reconciliation Act of 2001 (EGTRRA). These provisions generally sunset for tax years beginning after 12/31/2012. For specific sunset provisions, see Sec. 901, P.L. 107-16 (as amended) reproduced in history notes for this Code Sec.

(c) Other restrictions on interest.
For other restrictions on interest, see [sections] 2014(e) (relating to refunds attributable to foreign tax credits), 6412 (relating to floor stock refunds), 6413(d) (relating to taxes under the Federal Unemployment Tax Act), 6416 (relating to certain taxes on sales and services), 6419 (relating to the excise tax on wagering), and 6420 (relating to payments in the case of gasoline used on the farm for farming purposes), and 6421 (relating to payments in the case of gasoline used for certain nonhighway purposes or by local transit systems).

In 2010, P.L. 111-312, Sec. 101(a)(1), substituted "December 31, 2012" for "December 31, 2010" both places it appears in Sec. 901, P.L. 107-16 [see below], effective as if included in the enactment of P.L. 107-16, EGTRRA, 6/7/2001.
In 2002, P.L. 107-358, Sec. 2, added subsec. (c) in Sec. 901 of P.L. 107-16 [see below], effective 12/17/2002.
In 2001, P.L. 107-16, Sec. 532(c)(12), deleted "section 2011(c) (relating to refunds due to credit for State taxes)," after "on interest, see" in subsec. (c), effective for estates of decedents dying, and generation-skipping transfers, after 12/31/2004.
— P.L. 107-16, Sec. 901, of this Act [as amended by Sec. 2 of P.L. 107-358, and Sec. 101(a)(1) of P.L. 111-312, see above], reads as follows:
"SEC. 901. SUNSET OF PROVISIONS OF ACT.
"(a) In general. All provisions of, and amendments made by, this Act shall not apply—
"(1) to taxable, plan, or limitation years beginning after December 31, 2012, or
"(2) in the case of title V, to estates of decedents dying, gifts made, or generation skipping transfers, after December 31, 2012.
"(b) Application of certain laws. The Internal Revenue Code of 1986 and the Employee Retirement Income Security Act of 1974 shall be applied and administered to years, estates, gifts, and transfers described in subsection (a) as if the provisions and amendments described in subsection (a) had never been enacted.
"(c) Exception. Subsection (a) shall not apply to section 803 (relating to no federal income tax on restitution received by victims of the Nazi regime or their heirs or estates)."
In 1956, ch. 462, title II, Sec. 208(e)(7), inserted reference to section 6421 of this title.

— ch. 160, Sec. 4(f), inserted reference to section 6420 of this title.

Subchapter C.—Determination of Interest Rate; Compounding of Interest

Sec.
6621. Determination of rate of interest.
6622. Interest compounded daily.

In 1982, P.L. 97-248, Sec. 344(b)(2), added item 6621 . . . Sec. 344(b)(3), added "; Compounding of Interest" after "Rate" in the subchapter title.

Sec. 6621. Determination of rate of interest.
(a) General rule.
(1) Overpayment rate. The overpayment rate established under this section shall be the sum of—
(A) the Federal short-term rate determined under subsection (b), plus
(B) 3 percentage points (2 percentage points in the case of a corporation).
To the extent that an overpayment of tax by a corporation for any taxable period (as defined in subsection (c)(3), applied by substituting "overpayment" for "underpayment") exceeds $10,000, subparagraph (B) shall be applied by substituting "0.5 percentage point" for "2 percentage points".
(2) Underpayment rate. The underpayment rate established under this section shall be the sum of—
(A) the Federal short-term rate determined under subsection (b), plus
(B) 3 percentage points.
(b) Federal short-term rate.
For purposes of this section—
(1) General rule. The Secretary shall determine the Federal short-term rate for the first month in each calendar quarter.
(2) Period during which rate applies.
(A) In general. Except as provided in subparagraph (B), the Federal short-term rate determined under paragraph (1) for any month shall apply during the first calendar quarter beginning after such month.
(B) Special rule for individual estimated tax. In determining the addition to tax under section 6654 for failure to pay estimated tax for any taxable year, the Federal short-term rate which applies during the 3rd month following such taxable year shall also apply during the first 15 days of the 4th month following such taxable year.
(3) Federal short-term rate. The federal short-term rate for any month shall be the Federal short-term rate determined during such month by the Secretary in accordance with section 1274(d). Any such rate shall be rounded to the nearest full percent (or, if a multiple of ½ of 1 percent, such rate shall be increased to the next highest full percent).
(c) Increase in underpayment rate for large corporate underpayments.
(1) In general. For purposes of determining the amount of interest payable under section 6601 on any large corporate underpayment for periods after the applicable date, paragraph (2) of subsection (a) shall be applied by substituting "5 percentage points" for "3 percentage points".
(2) Applicable date. For purposes of this subsection—
(A) In general. The applicable date is the 30th day after the earlier of —
(i) the date on which the 1st letter of proposed deficiency which allows the taxpayer an opportunity for

3,767

administrative review in the Internal Revenue Service Office of Appeals is sent, or

(ii) the date on which the deficiency notice under section 6212 is sent.

The preceding sentence shall be applied without regard to any such letter or notice which is withdrawn by the Secretary.

(B) Special rules.

(i) Nondeficiency procedures. In the case of any underpayment of any tax imposed by this title to which the deficiency procedures do not apply, subparagraph (A) shall be applied by taking into account any letter or notice provided by the Secretary which notifies the taxpayer of the assessment or proposed assessment of the tax.

(ii) Exception where amounts paid in full. For purposes of subparagraph (A), a letter or notice shall be disregarded if, during the 30-day period beginning on the day on which it was sent, the taxpayer makes a payment equal to the amount shown as due in such letter or notice, as the case may be.

(iii) Exception for letters or notices involving small amounts. For purposes of this paragraph, any letter or notice shall be disregarded if the amount of the deficiency or proposed deficiency (or the assessment or proposed assessment) set forth in such letter or notice is not greater than $100,000 (determined by not taking into account any interest, penalties, or additions to tax).

(3) Large corporate underpayment. For purposes of this subsection—

(A) In general. The term "large corporate underpayment" means any underpayment of a tax by a C corporation for any taxable period if the amount of such underpayment for such period exceeds $100,000.

(B) Taxable period. For purposes of subparagraph (A), the term "taxable period" means—

(i) in the case of any tax imposed by subtitle A, the taxable year, or

(ii) in the case of any other tax, the period to which the underpayment relates.

(d) Elimination of interest on overlapping periods of tax overpayments and underpayments.

To the extent that, for any period, interest is payable under subchapter A and allowable under subchapter B on equivalent underpayments and overpayments by the same taxpayer of tax imposed by this title, the net rate of interest under this section on such amounts shall be zero for such period.

In 2010, P.L. 111-312, Sec. 704(c), of this Act provides:

"(c) Special rule for 2010. Notwithstanding any other provision of law, in the case of any alternative fuel credit or any alternative fuel mixture credit properly determined under subsection (d) or (e) of section 6426 of the Internal Revenue Code of 1986 for periods during 2010, such credit shall be allowed, and any refund or payment attributable to such credit (including any payment under section 6427(e) of such Code) shall be made, only in such manner as the Secretary of the Treasury (or the Secretary's delegate) shall provide. Such Secretary shall issue guidance within 30 days after the date of the enactment of this Act providing for a one-time submission of claims covering periods during 2010. Such guidance shall provide for a 180-day period for the submission of such claims (in such manner as prescribed by such Secretary) to begin not later than 30 days after such guidance is issued. Such claims shall be paid by such Secretary not later than 60 days after receipt. If such Secretary has not paid pursuant to a claim filed under this subsection within 60 days after the date of the filing of such claim, the claim shall be paid with interest from such date determined by using the overpayment rate and method under section 6621 of such Code."

In 1998, P.L. 105-277, Sec. 4002(d), substituted "Subject to any applicable statute of limitation not having expired with regard to either a tax underpayment or a tax overpayment, the amendments" for "The amendments" in Sec. 3301(c)(2) of P.L. 105-206 [see below], effective 10/21/98.

—P.L. 105-206, Sec. 3301(a), added subsec. (d), effective for interest for periods begin. after 7/22/98. Sec. 3301(c)(2) of this Act [as amended by Sec. 402(d) of P.L. 105-277, see above] provides:

"(2) Special rule. Subject to any applicable statute of limitation not having expired with regard to either a tax underpayment or a tax overpayment, the amendments made by this section shall apply to interest for periods beginning before the date of the enactment of this Act if the taxpayer—

"(A) reasonably identifies and establishes periods of such tax overpayments and underpayments for which the zero rate applies; and

"(B) not later than December 31, 1999, requests the Secretary of the Treasury to apply section 6621(d) of the Internal Revenue Code of 1986, as added by subsection (a), to such periods."

—P.L. 105-206, Sec. 3302(a), amended subpara. (a)(1)(B), effective for interest for the second and succeeding calendar quarters begin. after 7/22/98. Prior to amendment, subpara. (a)(1)(B) read as follows:

"(B) 2 percentage points."

In 1997, P.L. 105-34, Sec. 1463(a), added clause (c)(2)(B)(iii), effective for purposes of determining interest for periods after 12/31/97.

—P.L. 105-34, Sec. 1604(b)(1), substituted "subsection (c)(3), applied by substituting 'overpayment' for 'underpayment')" for "subsection(c)(3))" in para. (a)(1), effective for purposes of determining interest for periods after 12/31/94.

In 1996, P.L. 104-188, Sec. 1702(c)(6), added the sentence at the end of subpara. (c)(2)(A)... Sec. 1702(c)(7), substituted "this title" for "this subtitle" in clause (c)(2)(B)(i), effective for purposes of determining interest for periods after 12/31/90.

In 1994, P.L. 103-465, Sec. 713(a), added the last sentence at the end of para. (a)(1), effective for purposes of determining interest for periods after 12/31/94.

In 1990, P.L. 101-508, Sec. 11341(a), added subsec. (c), effective for purposes of determining interest for periods after 12/31/90.

In 1989, P.L. 101-239, Sec. 7721(b), repealed subsec. (c), effective for returns the due date for which (determined without regard to extensions) is after 12/31/89. Prior to repeal, subsec. (c) read as follows:

"(c) Interest on substantial underpayments attributable to tax motivated transactions.

"(1) In general. In the case of interest payable under section 6601 with respect to any substantial underpayment attributable to tax motivated transactions, the rate of interest established under this section shall be 120 percent of the underpayment rate established under this section.

"(2) Substantial underpayment attributable to tax motivated transactions. For purposes of this subsection, the term 'substantial underpayment attributable to tax motivated transactions' means any underpayment of taxes imposed by subtitle A for any taxable year which is attributable to 1 or more tax motivated transactions if the amount of the underpayment for such year so attributable exceeds $1,000.

"(3) Tax motivated transactions.

"(A) In general. For purposes of this subsection, the term 'tax motivated transaction' means—

"(i) any valuation overstatement (within the meaning of section 6659(c)),

"(ii) any loss disallowed by reason of section 465(a) and any credit disallowed under section 46(c)(8),

"(iii) any straddle (as defined in section 1092(c) without regard to subsections (d) and (e) of section 1092),

"(iv) any use of an accounting method specified in regulations prescribed by the Secretary as a use which may result in a substantial distortion of income for any period, and

"(v) any sham or fraudulent transaction.

"(B) Regulatory authority. The Secretary may by regulations specify other types of transactions which will be treated as tax motivated for purposes of this subsection and may by regulations provide that specified transactions being treated as tax motivated will no longer be so treated. In prescribing regulations under the preceding sentence, the Secretary shall take into account—

"(i) the ratio of tax benefits to cash invested,

"(ii) the methods of promoting the use of this type of transaction, and

"(iii) other relevant considerations.

"(C) Effective date for regulations. Any regulations prescribed under subparagraph (A)(iv) or (B) shall apply only to interest accruing after a date (specified in such regulations) which is after the date on which such regulations are prescribed.

"(4) Jurisdiction of tax court. In the case of any proceeding in the Tax Court for a redetermination of a deficiency, the Tax Court shall also have jurisdiction to determine the portion (if any) of such deficiency which is a substantial underpayment attributable to tax motivated transactions."

In 1988, P.L. 100-647, Sec. 1015(d)(1), substituted "Federal short-term rate" for "short-term Federal rate" each place it appeared subsec. (a) and para. (b)(1)... Sec. 1015(d)(2), substituted "Federal Short-Term Rate" for "Short-Term Federal Rate" in heading of subsec. (b), effective for Purposes of determining interest for periods after 12/31/86.

In 1986, P.L. 99-514, Sec. 1511(a), deleted subsecs. (a), (b), and (c), and added new subsecs. (a) and (b), effective for purposes of determining interest for periods after 12/31/86.

Prior to deletion, subsecs. (a)-(c) read as follows:

"(a) In general.

"The annual rate established under this section shall be such adjusted rate as is established by the Secretary under subsection (b).

"(b) Adjustment of interest rate.

"(1) Establishment of adjusted rate. If the adjusted prime rate charged by banks (rounded to the nearest full percent)—

Interest Part I

"(A) during the 6-month period ending on September 30 of any calendar year, or

"(B) during the 6-month period ending on March 31 of any calendar year, differs from the interest rate in effect under this section on either such date, respectively, then the Secretary shall establish, within 15 days after the close of the applicable 6-month period, an adjusted rate of interest equal to such adjusted prime rate.

"(2) Effective date of adjustment. Any adjusted rate of interest established under paragraph (1) shall become effective—

"(A) on January 1 of the succeeding year in the case of an adjustment attributable to paragraph (1)(A), and

"(B) on July 1 of the same year in the case of an adjustment attributable to paragraph (1)(B).

"(c) Definition of prime rate.

"For purposes of subsection (b), the term 'adjusted prime rate charged by banks' means the average predominant prime rate quoted by commercial banks to large businesses, as determined by the Board of Governors of the Federal Reserve System."

—P.L. 99-514, Sec. 1511(c)(1)(A), redesignated subsec. (d) as subsec. (c)... Sec. 1511(c)(1)(B), substituted "the underpayment rate established under this section" for "the adjusted rate established under subsection (b)" in para. (c)(1) [as redesignated]... Sec. 1511(c)(1)(C), deleted "annual" before "rate of interest" in para. (c)(1) [as redesignated], effective for purposes of determining interest for periods after 12/31/86. Sec. 1511(b) of this Act provides:

"(b) Coordination by regulation.—

"The Secretary of the Treasury or his delegate may issue regulations to coordinate section 6621 of the Internal Revenue Code of 1954 (as amended by this section) with section 6601(f) of such Code. Such regulations shall not apply to any period after the date 3 years after the date of the enactment of this Act."

—P.L. 99-514, Sec. 1535(a), deleted "and" from the end of clause (c)(3)(A)(iii), substituted ", and" for the period at the end of clause (c)(3)(A)(iv), and added clause (c)(3)(A)(v), effective for interest accruing after 12/31/84; except in the case of any underpayment with respect to which there was a final court decision before 10/22/86.

In 1984, P.L. 98-369, Sec. 144(c), added subsec. (d), effective for interest accruing after 12/31/84.

—P.L. 98-369, Sec. 714(m), amended Sec. 345(b) of P.L. 97-248, the effective date for changes made by Sec. 345(a) of P.L. 97-248, by substituting "taking effect on or after" for "taking effect on" (see below).

In 1982, P.L. 97-248, Sec. 345(a), amended subsec. (b), effective [as amended by Sec. 714(m) of P.L. 98-369, see above] for adjustments taking effect on or after 1/1/83.

Prior to amendment, subsec. (b) read as follows:

"(b) Adjustment of interest rate.

"The Secretary shall establish an adjusted rate of interest for the purpose of subsection (a) not later than October 15 of any year if the adjusted prime rate charged by banks during September of that year, rounded to the nearest full percent, is at least a full percentage point more or less than the interest rate which is then in effect. Any such adjusted rate of interest shall be equal to the adjusted prime rate charged by banks, rounded to the nearest full percent, and shall become effective on January 1 of the immediately succeeding year."

In 1981, P.L. 97-34, Sec. 711(a), deleted the last sentence of subsec. (b)... Sec. 711(b), deleted "90 percent of" before "the average predominate prime rate" in subsec. (c), effective for adjustments made after 8/13/81.

Prior to deletion, the last sentence of subsec. (b) read as follows:

"An adjustment provided for under this subsection may not be made prior to the expiration of 23 months following the date of any preceding adjustment under this subsection which changes the rate of interest."

—P.L. 97-34, Sec. 711(c), substituted "January 1" for "February 1" in subsec. (b), effective for adjustments made for periods after '82.

In 1979, P.L. 96-167, Sec. 4(b), amended subsec. (a), effective 12/29/79.

Prior to amendment, subsec. (a) read as follows:

"(a) In general. The rate of interest under sections 6601(a), 6602, 6611(a), 6332(c)(1), and 7426(g) of this title, and under section 2411(a) of title 28 is 9 percent per annum, or such adjusted rate as is established by the Secretary under subsection (b)."

In 1976, P.L. 94-455, Sec. 1906(b)(13)(A), substituted "Secretary" for "Secretary or his delegate" each place it appeared in Code Sec. 6621, effective 2/1/77.

In 1975, P.L. 93-625, Sec. 7(a)(1), added Code Sec. 6621, effective for amounts outstanding on or arising after 7/1/75.

Sec. 6622. Interest compounded daily.
(a) General rule.

In computing the amount of any interest required to be paid under this title or sections 1961(c)(1) or 2411 of title 28, United States Code, by the Secretary or by the taxpayer, or any other amount determined by reference to such amount of interest, such interest and such amount shall be compounded daily.

(b) Exception for penalty for failure to file estimated tax.

Subsection (a) shall not apply for purposes of computing the amount of any addition to tax under section 6654 or 6655.

In 1982, P.L. 97-248, Sec. 344(a), added Code Sec. 6622, effective for interest accruing after 12/31/82.

Subchapter D.—Notice Requirements
Sec.
6631. Notice requirements.

In 1998, P.L. 105-206, Sec. 3308(a), added Subchapter D and Sec. 6631.

Sec. 6631. Notice requirements.

The Secretary shall include with each notice to an individual taxpayer which includes an amount of interest required to be paid by such taxpayer under this title information with respect to the section of this title under which the interest is imposed and a computation of the interest.

In 2000, P.L. 106-554, Sec. 1(a)(7), [which enacted into law Sec. 302(c) of P.L. 106-554] substituted "June 30, 2001" for "December 31, 2000" and added "In the case of any notice issued after June 30, 2001, and before July 1, 2003, to which section 6631 of the Internal Revenue Code of 1986 applies, the requirements of section 6631 of such Code shall be treated as met if such notice contains a telephone number at which the taxpayer can request a copy of the taxpayer's payment history relating to interest amounts included in such notice." in Sec. 3308(c) of P.L. 105-206, see below.

In 1998, P.L. 105-206, Sec. 3308(a), added Code Sec. 6631, effective for notices issued after June 30, 2001. In the case of any notice issued after June 30, 2001, and before July 1, 2003, to which section 6631 of the Internal Revenue Code of 1986 applies, the requirements of section 6631 of such Code shall be treated as met if such notice contains a telephone number at which the taxpayer can request a copy of the taxpayer's payment history relating to interest amounts included in such notice.

CHAPTER 68.—ADDITIONS TO THE TAX, ADDITIONAL AMOUNTS, AND ASSESSABLE PENALTIES

Subchapter
A. Additions to the tax and additional amounts.
B. Assessable penalties.
C. Procedural requirements.

In 1998, P.L. 105-206, Sec. 3306(b), added item C.

Subchapter A.—Additions to the Tax and Additional Amounts

Part
  I. General provisions.
  II. Accuracy-related and fraud penalties.
  III. Applicable rules.

PART I.—GENERAL PROVISIONS

Sec.
6651. Failure to file tax return or to pay tax.
6652. Failure to file certain information returns, registration statements, etc.
6653. Failure to pay stamp tax.
6654. Failure by individual to pay estimated income tax.
6655. Failure by corporation to pay estimated income tax.
6656. Failure to make deposit of taxes.
6657. Bad checks.
6658. Coordination with title 11.
6659. Repealed.
6659A. Repealed.
6660. Repealed.
6661. Repealed.
6662. Repealed.

In 1996, P.L. 104-188, Sec. 1704(t)(19), deleted item 6662.
Prior to deletion, item 6662 read as follows:
"Sec. 6662. Applicable rules."

3,769

In **1989**, P.L. 101-239, Sec. 7721(c)(13), added after the heading for Subchapter A, the items for Parts I, II, and III and added the heading for Part I.
— P.L. 101-239, Sec. 7721(c)(14)(A), deleted items 6659, 6659A, 6660, 6661.
Prior to deletion, items 6659, 6659A, 6669 and 6661 read as follows:
"6659. Addition to tax in the case of valuation overstatements for purposes of the income tax.
"6659A. Addition to tax in case of overstatements of pension liabilities.
"6660. Addition to tax in the case of valuation understatement for purposes of estate or gift taxes.
"6661. Substantial understatement of liability."
— P.L. 101-239, Sec. 7721(c)(14)(B), amended item 6653.
Prior to amendment, item 6653 read as follows:
"6653. Additions to tax for negligence and fraud."
— P.L. 101-239, Sec. 7742(b), amended item 6656.
Prior to amendment, item 6656 read as follows:
"6656. Failure to make deposit of taxes or overstatement of deposits."
In **1986**, P.L. 99-514, Sec. 1138(a), added item 6659A.... Sec. 1503(d)(2), amended item 6653.
Prior to amendment, item 6653 read as follows:
"6653. Failure to pay tax."
In **1984**, P.L. 98-369, Sec. 155(c)(2)(B), added item 6660.
In **1982**, P.L. 97-248, Sec. 323(c), substituted items 6661 and 6662 for item 6660.
Prior to amendment item 6660 read as follows:
"6660. Applicable rules."
In **1981**, P.L. 97-34, Sec. 722(a)(2), redesignated item 6659 as item 6660 and added new item 6659 ... Sec. 724(b)(2), amended item 6656.
Prior to amendment, item 6656 read as follows:
"6656. Failure to make deposit of taxes."
In **1980**, P.L. 96-589, Sec. 6(e)(2), added item 6658.
In **1979**, P.L. 96-167, Sec. 6(b), repealed item 6658.
Prior to repeal, item 6658 read as follows:
"6658. ADDITION TO TAX IN CASE OF JEOPARDY."
In **1974**, P.L. 93-406, Sec. 1031(b)(1)(B)(ii), added ", registration statements, etc." before the period in item 6652.
In **1969**, P.L. 91-172, Sec. 943(c)(5), added "or pay tax" to item 6651.

Sec. 6651. Failure to file tax return or to pay tax.
(a) Addition to the tax.
In case of failure—
(1) to file any return required under authority of subchapter A of chapter 61 (other than part III thereof), subchapter A of chapter 51 (relating to distilled spirits, wines, and beer), or of subchapter A of chapter 52 (relating to tobacco, cigars, cigarettes, and cigarette papers and tubes), or of subchapter A of chapter 53 (relating to machine guns and certain other firearms), on the date prescribed therefor (determined with regard to any extension of time for filing), unless it is shown that such failure is due to reasonable cause and not due to willful neglect, there shall be added to the amount required to be shown as tax on such return 5 percent of the amount of such tax if the failure is for not more than 1 month, with an additional 5 percent for each additional month or fraction thereof during which such failure continues, not exceeding 25 percent in the aggregate;
(2) to pay the amount shown as tax on any return specified in paragraph (1) on or before the date prescribed for payment of such tax (determined with regard to any extension of time for payment), unless it is shown that such failure is due to reasonable cause and not due to willful neglect, there shall be added to the amount shown as tax on such return 0.5 percent of the amount of such tax if the failure is for not more than 1 month, with an additional 0.5 percent for each additional month or fraction thereof during which such failure continues, not exceeding 25 percent in the aggregate; or
(3) to pay any amount in respect of any tax required to be shown on a return specified in paragraph (1) which is not so shown (including an assessment made pursuant to section 6213(b)) within 21 calendar days from the date of notice and demand therefor (10 business days if the amount for which such notice and demand is made equals or exceeds $100,000), unless it is shown that such failure is due to reasonable cause and not due to willful neglect,

there shall be added to the amount of tax stated in such notice and demand 0.5 percent of the amount of such tax if the failure is for not more than 1 month, with an additional 0.5 percent for each additional month or fraction thereof during which such failure continues, not exceeding 25 percent in the aggregate.

In the case of a failure to file a return of tax imposed by chapter 1 within 60 days of the date prescribed for filing of such return (determined with regard to any extensions of time for filing), unless it is shown that such failure is due to reasonable cause and not due to willful neglect, the addition to tax under paragraph (1) shall not be less than the lesser of $135 or 100 percent of the amount required to be shown as tax on such return.

(b) Penalty imposed on net amount due.
For purposes of—
(1) subsection (a)(1), the amount of tax required to be shown on the return shall be reduced by the amount of any part of the tax which is paid on or before the date prescribed for payment of the tax and by the amount of any credit against the tax which may be claimed on the return,
(2) subsection (a)(2), the amount of tax shown on the return shall, for purposes of computing the addition for any month, be reduced by the amount of any part of the tax which is paid on or before the beginning of such month and by the amount of any credit against the tax which may be claimed on the return, and
(3) subsection (a)(3), the amount of tax stated in the notice and demand shall, for the purpose of computing the addition for any month, be reduced by the amount of any part of the tax which is paid before the beginning of such month.

(c) Limitations and special rule.
(1) Additions under more than one paragraph. With respect to any return, the amount of the addition under paragraph (1) of subsection (a) shall be reduced by the amount of the addition under paragraph (2) of subsection (a) for any month (or fraction thereof) to which an addition to tax applies under both paragraphs (1) and (2). In any case described in the last sentence of subsection (a), the amount of the addition under paragraph (1) of subsection (a) shall not be reduced under the preceding sentence below the amount provided in such last sentence.
(2) Amount of tax shown more than amount required to be shown. If the amount required to be shown as tax on a return is less than the amount shown as tax on such return, subsections (a)(2) and (b)(2) shall be applied by substituting such lower amount.

(d) Increase in penalty for failure to pay tax in certain cases.
(1) In general. In the case of each month (or fraction thereof) beginning after the day described in paragraph (2) of this subsection, paragraphs (2) and (3) of subsection (a) shall be applied by substituting "1 percent" for "0.5 percent" each place it appears.
(2) Description. For purposes of paragraph (1), the day described in this paragraph is the earlier of—
(A) the day 10 days after the date on which notice is given under section 6331(d), or
(B) the day on which notice and demand for immediate payment is given under the last sentence of section 6331(a).

(e) Exception for estimated tax.
This section shall not apply to any failure to pay any estimated tax required to be paid by section 6654 or 6655.

3,770

(f) Increase in penalty for fraudulent failure to file.

If any failure to file any return is fraudulent, paragraph (1) of subsection (a) shall be applied—

(1) by substituting "15 percent" for "5 percent" each place it appears, and

(2) by substituting "75 percent" for "25 percent".

(g) Treatment of returns prepared by Secretary under section 6020(b).

In the case of any return made by the Secretary under section 6020(b)—

(1) such return shall be disregarded for purposes of determining the amount of the addition under paragraph (1) of subsection (a), but

(2) such return shall be treated as the return filed by the taxpayer for purposes of determining the amount of the addition under paragraphs (2) and (3) of subsection (a).

(h) Limitation on penalty on individual's failure to pay for months during period of installment agreement.

In the case of an individual who files a return of tax on or before the due date for the return (including extensions), paragraphs (2) and (3) of subsection (a) shall each be applied by substituting "0.25" for "0.5" each place it appears for purposes of determining the addition to the tax for any month during which an installment agreement under section 6159 is in effect for the payment of such tax.

In **2008**, P.L. 110-245, Sec. 303(a), substituted "$135" for "$100" in subsec. (a), effective for returns required to be filed after 12/31/2008.

In **1998**, P.L. 105-206, Sec. 3303(a), added subsec. (h), effective for purposes of determining additions to the tax for months begin. after 12/31/99.

—P.L. 105-206, Sec. 3707, of this Act, reads as follows:

"SEC. 3707. ILLEGAL TAX PROTESTER DESIGNATION.

"(a) Prohibition. The officers and employees of the Internal Revenue Service—

"(1) shall not designate taxpayers as illegal tax protesters (or any similar designation); and

"(2) in the case of any such designation made on or before the date of the enactment of this Act—

"(A) shall remove such designation from the individual master file; and

"(B) shall disregard any such designation not located in the individual master file.

"(b) Designation of nonfilers allowed. An officer or employee of the Internal Revenue Service may designate any appropriate taxpayer as a nonfiler, but shall remove such designation once the taxpayer has filed income tax returns for 2 consecutive taxable years and paid all taxes shown on such returns.

"(c) Effective date. The provisions of this section shall take effect on the date of the enactment of this Act, except that the removal of any designation under subsection (a)(2)(A) shall not be required to begin before January 1, 1999."

In **1996**, P.L. 104-168, Sec. 303(b)(2), substituted "21 calendar days from the date of notice and demand therefor (10 business days if the amount for which such notice and demand is made equals or exceeds $100,000)" for "10 days of the date of the notice and demand therefor" in para. (a)(3), effective for any notice and demand given after 12/31/96.

—P.L. 104-168, Sec. 1301(a), added subsec. (g), effective for any return the due date for which (determined without regard to extensions) is after 7/30/96.

In **1992**, P.L. 102-244, Sec. 4, regarding the extension of time for payment of additional FUTA taxes, is reproduced in note following Code Sec. 6601.

In **1989**, P.L. 101-239, Sec. 7741(a), added subsec. (f), effective in case of failures to file returns the due date for which (determined without regard to extensions) is after 12/31/89.

In **1987**, P.L. 100-203, Sec. 10301(b)(6), substituted "section 6654 or 6655" for "section 6154 or 6654" in subsec. (e), effective for tax. yrs. begin. after 12/31/87.

In **1986**, P.L. 99-514, Sec. 1502(a), redesignated subsec. (d) as subsec. (e), and added new subsec. (d), effective as provided in Sec. 1502(c)(1) of this Act which reads as follows:

"(1) Subsection (a). The amendments made by subsection (a) shall apply—

"(A) to failures to pay which begin after December 31, 1986, and

"(B) to failures to pay which begin on or before December 31, 1986, if after December 31, 1986—

"(i) notice (or renotice) under section 6331(d) of the Internal Revenue Code of 1954 is given with respect to such failure, or

"(ii) notice and demand for immediate payment of the underpayment is made under the last sentence of section 6331(a) of such Code.

In the case of a failure to pay described in subparagraph (B), paragraph (2) of section 6651(d) of such Code (as added by subsection (a)) shall be applied by taking into account the first notice (or renotice) after December 31, 1986."

—P.L. 99-514, Sec. 1502(b), amended para. (c)(1), effective for amounts assessed after 12/31/86, for failures to pay which begin before, on, or after 12/31/86.

Prior to amendment, para. (c)(1) read as follows:

"(1) Additions under more than one paragraph.

"(A) With respect to any return, the amount of the addition under paragraph (1) of subsection (a) shall be reduced by the amount of the addition under paragraph (2) of subsection (a) for any month to which an addition to tax applies under both paragraphs (1) and (2). In any case described in the last sentence of subsection (a), the amount of the addition under paragraph (1) of subsection (a) shall not be reduced under the preceding sentence below the amount provided in such last sentence.

"(B) With respect to any return, the maximum amount of the addition permitted under paragraph (3) of subsection (a) shall be reduced by the amount of the addition under paragraph (1) of subsection (a) (determined without regard to the last sentence of such subsection) which is attributable to the tax for which the notice and demand is made and which is not paid within 10 days of notice and demand."

In **1984**, P.L. 98-369, Sec. 412(b)(8), amended subsec. (d), effective for tax. yrs. begin. after 12/31/84.

Prior to amendment, subsec. (d) read as follows:

"(d) Exception for declarations of estimated tax.

"This section shall not apply to any failure to file a declaration of estimated tax required by section 6015 or to pay any estimated tax required to be paid by section 6153 or 6154."

In **1982**, P.L. 97-248, Sec. 318(a), added the last sentence of subsec. (a) . . . Sec. 318(b)(1), added the last sentence of subpara. (c)(1)(A) . . . Sec. 318(b)(2), added "(determined without regard to the last sentence of such subsection)" after "paragraph (1) of subsection (a)" in subpara. (c)(1)(B), effective for returns whose filing due date (including extensions) is after 12/31/82.

In **1976**, P.L. 94-455, Sec. 1904(b)(10)(A)(v), deleted subsec. (e), effective for acquisitions of stock or debt obligations made after 6/30/74.

Prior to deletion, subsec. (e) read as follows:

"(e) Certain interest equalization tax returns.

The provisions of this section shall apply with respect to returns of amounts withheld under section 4918(e)(7) (relating to withholding of interest equalization tax by participating firms) in the same manner and to the same extent as they apply with respect to returns specified in subsection (a)(1)."

In **1971**, P.L. 92-9, Sec. 3(j)(1), added subsec. (e), effective for returns required to be filed on or after 4/1/71.

In **1969**, P.L. 91-172, Sec. 943(a), amended Code Sec. 6651, effective for returns the date prescribed by law (without regard to any extension of time) for filing of which is after 12/31/69, and with respect to notices and demands for payment of tax made after 12/31/69.

Prior to amendment, Code Sec. 6651 read as follows:

"SEC. 6651. FAILURE TO FILE TAX RETURN.

"(a) Addition to the tax.

"In case of failure to file any return required under authority of subchapter A of chapter 61 (other than part III thereof), of subchapter A of chapter 51 (relating to distilled spirits, wines, and beer), or of subchapter A of chapter 52 (relating to tobacco, cigars, cigarettes, and cigarette papers and tubes), or of subchapter A of chapter 53 (relating to machine guns and certain other firearms), on the date prescribed therefor (determined with regard to any extension of time for filing), unless it is shown that such failure is due to reasonable cause and not due to willful neglect, there shall be added to the amount required to be shown as tax on such return 5 percent of the amount of such tax if the failure is for not more than 1 month, with an additional 5 percent for each additional month or fraction thereof during which such failure continues, not exceeding 25 percent in the aggregate.

"(b) Penalty imposed on net amount due.

"For purposes of subsection (a), the amount of tax required to be shown on the return shall be reduced by the amount of any part of the tax which is paid on or before the date prescribed for payment of the tax and by the amount of any credit against the tax which may be claimed upon the return.

"(c) Exception for declarations of estimated tax.

"This section shall not apply to any failure to file a declaration of estimated tax required by section 6015."

In **1968**, P.L. 90-364, Sec. 103, deleted "or section 6016" from the end of subsec. (c), effective for tax. yrs. begin. after 12/31/67. For special provision on effective date, see Sec. 104 of the P.L., reproduced after Code Sec. 6425.

Sec. 6652. Failure to file certain information returns, registration statements, etc.

(a) Returns with respect to certain payments aggregating less than $10.

In the case of each failure to file a statement of a payment to another person required under the authority of—

(1) section 6042(a)(2) (relating to payments of dividends aggregating less than $10), or

(2) section 6044(a)(2) (relating to payments of patronage dividends aggregating less than $10),

on the date prescribed therefor (determined with regard to any extension of time for filing), unless it is shown that such failure is due to reasonable cause and not to willful neglect, there shall be paid (upon notice and demand by the Secretary and in the same manner as tax) by the person failing to so file the statement, $1 for each such statement not so filed,

3,771

but the total amount imposed on the delinquent person for all such failures during the calendar year shall not exceed $1,000.

(b) Failure to report tips.

In the case of failure by an employee to report to his employer on the date and in the manner prescribed therefor any amount of tips required to be so reported by section 6053(a) which are wages (as defined in section 3121(a)) or which are compensation (as defined in section 3231(e)), unless it is shown that such failure is due to reasonable cause and not due to willful neglect, there shall be paid by the employee, in addition to the tax imposed by section 3101 or section 3201 (as the case may be) with respect to the amount of tips which he so failed to report, an amount equal to 50 percent of such tax.

(c) Returns by exempt organizations and by certain trusts.

(1) Annual returns under 6033(a)(1) or 6012(a)(6).

(A) Penalty on organization. In the case of—

(i) a failure to file a return required under 6033(a)(1) (relating to returns by exempt organizations) or section 6012(a)(6) (relating to returns by political organizations) on the date and in the manner prescribed therefor (determined with regard to any extension of time for filing), or

(ii) a failure to include any of the information required to be shown on a return filed under 6033(a)(1) or section 6012(a)(6) or to show the correct information,

there shall be paid by the exempt organization $20 for each day during which such failure continues. The maximum penalty under this subparagraph on failures with respect to any 1 return shall not exceed the lesser of $10,000 or 5 percent of the gross receipts of the organization for the year. In the case of an organization having gross receipts exceeding $1,000,000 for any year, with respect to the return required under 6033(a)(1) or section 6012(a)(6) for such year, the first sentence of this subparagraph shall be applied by substituting "100" for "20" and, in lieu of applying the second sentence of this subparagraph, the maximum penalty under this subparagraph shall not exceed $50,000.

(B) Managers.

(i) In general. The Secretary may make a written demand on any organization subject to penalty under subparagraph (A) specifying therein a reasonable future date by which the return shall be filed (or the information furnished) for purposes of this subparagraph.

(ii) Failure to comply with demand. If any person fails to comply with any demand under clause (i) on or before the date specified in such demand, there shall be paid by the person failing to so comply $10 for each day after the expiration of the time specified in such demand during which such failure continues. The maximum penalty imposed under this subparagraph on all persons for failures with respect to any 1 return shall not exceed $5,000.

(C) Public inspection of annual returns and reports. In the case of a failure to comply with the requirements of section 6104(d) with respect to any annual return on the date and in the manner prescribed therefor (determined with regard to any extension of time for filing) or report required under section 527(j), there shall be paid by the person failing to meet such requirements $20 for each day during which such failure continues. The maximum penalty imposed under this subparagraph on all persons for failures with respect to any 1 return or report shall not exceed $10,000.

(D) Public inspection of applications for exemption and notice of status. In the case of a failure to comply with the requirements of section 6104(d) with respect to any exempt status application materials (as defined in such section) or notice materials (as defined in such section) on the date and in the manner prescribed therefor, there shall be paid by the person failing to meet such requirements $20 for each day during which such failure continues.

(E) No penalty for certain annual notices. This paragraph shall not apply with respect to any notice required under section 6033(i).

(2) Returns under section 6034 or 6043(b).

(A) Penalty on organization or trust. In the case of a failure to file a return required under section 6034 (relating to returns by certain trusts) or section 6043(b) (relating to terminations, etc., of exempt organizations), on the date and in the manner prescribed therefor (determined without regard to any extension of time for filing), there shall be paid by the exempt organization or trust failing so to file $10 for each day during which such failure continues, but the total amount imposed under this subparagraph on any organization or trust for failure to file any 1 return shall not exceed $5,000.

(B) Managers. The Secretary may make written demand on an organization or trust failing to file under subparagraph (A) specifying therein a reasonable future date by which such filing shall be made for purposes of this subparagraph. If such filing is not made on or before such date, there shall be paid by the person failing so to file $10 for each day after the expiration of the time specified in the written demand during which such failure continues, but the total amount imposed under this subparagraph on all persons for failure to file any 1 return shall not exceed $5,000.

(C) Split-interest trusts. In the case of a trust which is required to file a return under section 6034(a), subparagraphs (A) and (B) of this paragraph shall not apply and paragraph (1) shall apply in the same manner as if such return were required under section 6033, except that—

(i) the 5 percent limitation in the second sentence of paragraph (1)(A) shall not apply,

(ii) in the case of any trust with gross income in excess of $250,000, the first sentence of paragraph (1)(A) shall be applied by substituting "$100" for "$20", and the second sentence thereof shall be applied by substituting "$50,000" for "$10,000", and

(iii) the third sentence of paragraph (1)(A) shall be disregarded.

In addition to any penalty imposed on the trust pursuant to this subparagraph, if the person required to file such return knowingly fails to file the return, such penalty shall also be imposed on such person who shall be personally liable for such penalty.

(3) Disclosure under section 6033(a)(2).

(A) Penalty on entities. In the case of a failure to file a disclosure required under section 6033(a)(2), there shall be paid by the tax-exempt entity (the entity manager in the case of a tax-exempt entity described in paragraph (4), (5), (6), or (7) of section 4965(c)) $100 for each day during which such failure continues. The maximum penalty under this subparagraph on failures with respect to any 1 disclosure shall not exceed $50,000.

(B) Written demand.

(i) In general. The Secretary may make a written demand on any entity or manager subject to penalty under subparagraph (A) specifying therein a reasonable future date by which the disclosure shall be filed for purposes of this subparagraph.

(ii) Failure to comply with demand. If any entity or manager fails to comply with any demand under clause (i) on or before the date specified in such demand, there shall be paid by such entity or manager failing to so comply $100 for each day after the expiration of the time specified in such demand during which such failure continues. The maximum penalty imposed under this subparagraph on all entities and managers for failures with respect to any 1 disclosure shall not exceed $10,000.

(C) Definitions. Any term used in this section which is also used in section 4965 shall have the meaning given such term under section 4965.

(4) Reasonable cause exception. No penalty shall be imposed under this subsection with respect to any failure if it is shown that such failure is due to reasonable cause.

(5) Other special rules.

(A) Treatment as tax. Any penalty imposed under this subsection shall be paid on notice and demand of the Secretary and in the same manner as tax.

(B) Joint and several liability. If more than 1 person is liable under this subsection for any penalty with respect to any failure, all such persons shall be jointly and severally liable with respect to such failure.

(C) Person. For purposes of this subsection, the term "person" means any officer, director, trustee, employee, or other individual who is under a duty to perform the act in respect of which the violation occurs.

(d) Annual registration and other notification by pension plan.

(1) Registration. In the case of any failure to file a registration statement required under section 6057(a) (relating to annual registration of certain plans) which includes all participants required to be included in such statement, on the date prescribed therefor (determined without regard to any extension of time for filing), unless it is shown that such failure is due to reasonable cause, there shall be paid (on notice and demand by the Secretary and in the same manner as tax) by the person failing so to file, an amount equal to $1 for each participant with respect to whom there is a failure to file, multiplied by the number of days during which such failure continues, but the total amount imposed under this paragraph on any person for any failure to file with respect to any plan year shall not exceed $5,000.

(2) Notification of change of status. In the case of failure to file a notification required under section 6057(b) (relating to notification of change of status) on the date prescribed therefor (determined without regard to any extension of time for filing), unless it is shown that such failure is due to reasonable cause, there shall be paid (on notice and demand by the Secretary and in the same manner as tax) by the person failing so to file, $1 for each day during which such failure continues, but the total amounts imposed under this paragraph on any person for failure to file any notification shall not exceed $1,000.

(e) Information required in connection with certain plans of deferred compensation; etc.

In the case of failure to file a return or statement required under section 6058 (relating to information required in connection with certain plans of deferred compensation), 6047 (relating to information relating to certain trusts and annuity and bond purchase plans), or 6039D (relating to returns and records with respect to certain fringe benefit plans) on the date and in the manner prescribed therefor (determined with regard to any extension of time for filing), unless it is shown that such failure is due to reasonable cause, there shall be paid (on notice and demand by the Secretary and in the same manner as tax) by the person failing so to file, $25 for each day during which such failure continues, but the total amount imposed under this subsection on any person for failure to file any return shall not exceed $15,000. This subsection shall not apply to any return or statement which is an information return described in section 6724(d)(1)(C)(ii) or a payee statement described in section 6724(d)(2)(Y).

(f) Returns required under section 6039C.

(1) In general. In the case of each failure to make a return required by section 6039C which contains the information required by such section on the date prescribed therefor (determined with regard to any extension of time for filing), unless it is shown that such failure is due to reasonable cause and not to willful neglect, the amount determined under paragraph (2) shall be paid (upon notice and demand by the Secretary and in the same manner as tax) by the person failing to make such return.

(2) Amount of penalty. For purposes of paragraph (1), the amount determined under this paragraph with respect to any failure shall be $25 for each day during which such failure continues.

(3) Limitation. The amount determined under paragraph (2) with respect to any person for failing to meet the requirements of section 6039C for any calendar year shall not exceed the lesser of—

(A) $25,000, or

(B) 5 percent of the aggregate of the fair market value of the United States real property interests owned by such person at any time during such year.

For purposes of the preceding sentence, fair market value shall be determined as of the end of the calendar year (or, in the case of any property disposed of during the calendar year, as of the date of such disposition).

(g) Information required in connection with deductible employee contributions.

In the case of failure to make a report required by section 219(f)(4) which contains the information required by such section on the date prescribed therefor (determined with regard to any extension of time for filing), there shall be paid (on notice and demand by the Secretary and in the same manner as tax) by the person failing so to file, an amount equal to $25 for each participant with respect to whom there was a failure to file such information, multiplied by the number of years during which such failure continues, but the total amount imposed under this subsection on any person for failure to file shall not exceed $10,000. No penalty shall be imposed under this subsection on any failure which is shown to be due to reasonable cause and not willful neglect.

(h) Failure to give notice to recipients of certain pension, etc., distributions.

In the case of each failure to provide notice as required by section 3405(e)(10)(B), at the time prescribed therefor, unless it is shown that such failure is due to reasonable cause and not to willful neglect, there shall be paid, on notice and demand of the Secretary and in the same manner as tax, by the person failing to provide such notice, an amount equal to $10 for each such failure, but the total amount imposed on such person for all such failures during any calendar year shall not exceed $5,000.

Code Sec. 6652(i) — Penalties

(i) Failure to give written explanation to recipients of certain qualifying rollover distributions.

In the case of each failure to provide a written explanation as required by section 402(f), at the time prescribed therefor, unless it is shown that such failure is due to reasonable cause and not to willful neglect, there shall be paid, on notice and demand of the Secretary and in the same manner as tax, by the person failing to provide such written explanation, an amount equal to the $100 for each such failure, but the total amount imposed on such person for all such failures during any calendar year shall not exceed $50,000.

(j) Failure to file certification with respect to certain residential rental projects.

In the case of each failure to provide a certification as required by section 142(d)(7) at the time prescribed therefor, unless it is shown that such failure is due to reasonable cause and not to willful neglect, there shall be paid, on notice and demand of the Secretary and in the same manner as tax, by the person failing to provide such certification, an amount equal to $100 for each such failure.

(k) Failure to make reports required under section 1202.

In the case of a failure to make a report required under section 1202(d)(1)(C) which contains the information required by such section on the date prescribed therefor (determined with regard to any extension of time for filing), there shall be paid (on notice and demand by the Secretary and in the same manner as tax) by the person failing to make such report, an amount equal to $50 for each report with respect to which there was such a failure. In the case of any failure due to negligence or intentional disregard, the preceding sentence shall be applied by substituting "$100" for "$50". In the case of a report covering periods in 2 or more years, the penalty determined under preceding provisions of this subsection shall be multiplied by the number of such years. No penalty shall be imposed under this subsection on any failure which is shown to be due to reasonable cause and not willful neglect.

(l) Failure to file return with respect to certain corporate transactions.

In the case of any failure to make a return required under section 6043(c) containing the information required by such section on the date prescribed therefor (determined with regard to any extension of time for filing), unless it is shown that such failure is due to reasonable cause, there shall be paid (on notice and demand by the Secretary and in the same manner as tax) by the person failing to file such return, an amount equal to $500 for each day during which such failure continues, but the total amount imposed under this subsection with respect to any return shall not exceed $100,000.

(m) Alcohol and tobacco taxes.

For penalties for failure to file certain information returns with respect to alcohol and tobacco taxes, see generally, subtitle E.

In 2006, P.L. 109-280, Sec. 1201(b)(2), added subpara. (c)(2)(C), effective for returns for tax. yrs. begin. after 12/31/2006.

— P.L. 109-280, Sec. 1223(d), added subpara. (c)(1)(E), effective for notices and returns with respect to annual periods begin. after 2006.

— P.L. 109-222, Sec. 516(c)(1), redesignated paras. (c)(3) and (4) as paras. (c)(4) and (5) and added para. (c)(3) ... Sec. 516(c)(2), substituted "6033(a)(1)" for "6033" each place it appeared in para. (c)(1), effective for disclosures the due date for which are after 5/17/2006.

In 2000, P.L. 106-230, Sec. 1(c)(1), added "or notice materials (as defined in such section)" after "section)" in subpara. (c)(1)(D) ... Sec. 1(c)(2), added "and notice of status" after "exemption" in the heading in subpara. (c)(1)(D), effective 7/1/2000. ... Sec. 2(c)(1), added "or report required under section 527(j)" after "filing)" in subpara. (c)(1)(C) ... Sec. 2(c)(2), added "or report" after "1 return" in subpara. (c)(1)(C) ... Sec. 2(c)(3), added "and reports" after "returns" in the heading in subpara. (c)(1)(C), effective 7/1/2000. ... Sec. 3(c)(1), added "or section 6012(a)(6) (relating to returns by political organizations)" after "organizations)" in para. (c)(1) ... Sec. 3(c)(2), added "or section 6012(a)(6)" after "section 6033" in subpara. (c)(1)(A)(ii) ... Sec. 3(c)(3), added "or section 6012(a)(6)" after "section 6033" in the third sentence of subpara. (c)(1)(A) ... Sec. 3(c)(4), added "or 6012(a)(6)" after "section 6033" in the heading in para. (c)(1), effective for tax. yrs. begin. after 6/30/2000.

In 1998, P.L. 105-277, Sec. 1004(b)(2)(B), substituted "section 6104(d) with respect to any annual return" for "subsection (d) or (e)(1) of section 6104 (relating to public inspection of annual returns)" in subpara. (c)(1)(C) ... Sec. 1004(b)(2)(C), substituted "section 6104(d) with respect to any exempt status application materials (as defined in such section)" for "section 6104(e)(2) (relating to public inspection of applications for exemption)" in subpara. (c)(1)(D), effective as provided in Sec. 104(b)(3), of this Act, which reads as follows:

"(3) Effective date.

"(A) In general. Except as provided in subparagraph (B), the amendments made by this subsection shall apply to requests made after the later of December 31, 1998, or the 60th day after the Secretary of the Treasury first issues the regulations referred to in section 6104(d)(4) of the Internal Revenue Code of 1986, as amended by this section.

"(B) Publication of annual returns. Section 6104(d) of such Code, as in effect before the amendments made by this subsection, shall not apply to any return the due date for which is after the date such amendments take effect under subparagraph (A)."

In 1997, P.L. 105-34, Sec. 1281(a), added the sentence at the end of subsec. (g) ... Sec. 1281(b), added the sentence at the end of subsec. (k), effective for tax. yrs. begin. after 8/5/97.

— P.L. 105-34, Sec. 1602(d)(2)(B), substituted "section 6724(d)(2)(Y)" for "section 6724(d)(2)(X)" in subsec. (e), effective for benefits paid after 12/31/96.

In 1996, P.L. 104-188, Sec. 1455(c)(1), substituted "$100" for "$10" in subsec. (i) ... Sec. 1455(c)(2), substituted "$50,000" for "$5,000" in subsec. (i) ... Sec. 1455(d), added the sentence to the end of subsec. (e), effective for returns, reports, and other statements the due date for which (determined without regard to extensions) is after 12/31/96.

— P.L. 104-188, Sec. 1704(s)(1), substituted "$20" for "$10" and substituted "$10,000" for "$5,000" in subpara (c)(1)(C) ... Sec. 1704(s)(2), substituted "$20" for "$10" in subpara. (c)(1)(D), effective 8/20/96.

— P.L. 104-168, Sec. 1314(a), substituted "$20" for "$10" and "$10,000" for "$5,000" in subpara. (c)(1)(A) ... Sec. 1314(b), added a sentence at the end of subpara. (c)(1)(A), effective for tax. yrs. end. on or after 7/30/96.

In 1993, P.L. 103-66, Sec. 13113(c), added subsec. (k), effective for stock issued after 8/10/93.

In 1992, P.L. 102-318, Sec. 522(b)(2)(F), substituted "section 3405(e)(10)(B)" for "section 3405(d)(10)(B)" in subsec. (h), effective for distributions after 12/31/92, except as provided in Sec. 522(d)(2) of this Act which reads as follows:

"(2) Transition rule for certain annuity contracts. If, as of July 1, 1992, a State law prohibits a direct trustee-to-trustee transfer from an annuity contract described in section 403(b) of the Internal Revenue Code of 1986 which was purchased for an employee by an employer which is a State or a political subdivision thereof (or an agency or instrumentality of any 1 or more of either), the amendments made by this section shall not apply to distributions before the earlier of—

"(A) 90 days after the first day after July 1, 1992, on which such transfer is allowed under State law, or

"(B) January 1, 1994."

In 1989, P.L. 101-239, Sec. 7208(b)(2), redesignated subsec. (l) as subsec. (m) and added new subsec. (l), effective for transactions after 3/31/90.

— P.L. 101-239, Sec. 7841(d)(5)(A), redesignated the subsec. relating to information with respect to includible employee benefits as subsec. (k) [inoperative, see Sec. 203(a)(1) of P.L. 101-140, below] ... Sec. 7841(d)(5)(B), redesignated the subsec. relating to alcohol and tobacco taxes as subsec. (l) [inoperative, see Sec. 203(a)(1) of P.L. 101-140, below], effective 12/19/89.

— P.L. 101-140, Sec. 203(a)(1), repealed as if not enacted Sec. 1151(b) of P.L. 99-514, which redesignated subsec. (l) as subsec. (m) [which was redesignated as subsec. (l) by Sec. 10502(d)(1) of P.L. 100-203, see below] and added new subsec. (l) [which was redesignated as subsec. (k) by Sec. 10502(d)(1) of P.L. 100-203, see below].

In 1988, P.L. 100-647, Sec. 1011B(a)(10), Sec. 1018(u)(36) and Sec. 3021(a)(1), amended subsec. (k) [as redesignated from subsec. (l) by Sec. 10502(d)(11) of P.L. 100-203, see below] which had been added as subsec. (l) by Sec. 1151(b) of P.L. 99-514 which has been repealed as if not enacted, see above.

— P.L. 100-647, Sec. 1017(b), added "(and the corresponding provision of section 4041(d)(1)" after "section 4041(a)(1)" in subsec. (j) [added by Sec. 1702(b) of P.L. 99-514, see below], effective for sales after the first calendar quarter beginning after 10/22/86.

In 1987, P.L. 100-203, Sec. 10502(d)(11), deleted subsec. (j) added by Sec. 1702(b) of P.L. 99-514 and redesignated subsecs. (l) and (m) [as added and redesignated by Sec. 1151(b) of P.L. 99-514 which is repealed as if not enacted by Sec. 203(a)(1) of P.L. 101-140, see above] as subsecs. (k) and (l), respectively, effective for sales after 3/31/88.

Prior to deletion, subsec. (j) read as follows:

"(j) Failure to give written notice to certain sellers of diesel fuel.

"(1) In general. If any qualified retailer fails to provide the notice described in section 4041(n)(3)(A)(ii) to any seller of diesel fuel to such retailer, unless it is shown that such failure is due to reasonable cause and not to willful neglect, there shall be paid, on notice and demand of the Secretary and in the same manner as tax, by such retailer with respect to each sale of diesel fuel to such retailer by such seller to which section 4041(n)(4) applies an amount equal to 5 percent of the tax imposed by section 4041(a)(1) (and the corresponding provision of section

4041(d)(1)) on such sale by reason of paragraphs (3) and (4)(A) of section 4041(n).

"(2) Definitions. For purposes of paragraph (1), the terms 'qualified retailer' and 'diesel fuel' have the respective meanings given such terms by section 4041(n)."

—P.L. 100-203, Sec. 10704(a), amended subsec. (c), effective as provided by Sec. 10704(d) which reads:

"Effective date.

"The amendments made by this section shall apply—

"(1) to returns for years beginning after December 31, 1986, and

"(2) on and after the date of the enactment of this Act in the case of applications submitted to the Internal Revenue Service—

"(A) after July 15, 1987, or

"(B) on or before July 15, 1987, if the organization has a copy of the application on July 15, 1987."

Prior to amendment, subsec. (c) read as follows:

"(c) Returns by exempt organizations and by certain trusts.

"(1) Penalty on organization or trust. In the case of a failure to file a return required under section 6033 (relating to returns by exempt organizations), section 6034 (relating to returns by certain trusts), or section 6043(b) (relating to exempt organizations), on the date and in the manner prescribed therefor (determined with regard to any extension of time for filing), unless it is shown that such failure is due to reasonable cause there shall be paid (on notice and demand by the Secretary and in the same manner as tax) by the exempt organization or trust failing so to file, $10 for each day during which such failure continues, but the total amount imposed hereunder on any organization for failure to file any return shall not exceed $5,000.

"(2) Managers. The Secretary may make written demand upon an organization failing to file under paragraph (1) specifying therein a reasonable future date by which such filing shall be made, and if such filing is not made on or before such date, and unless it is shown that failure so to file is due to reasonable cause, there shall be paid (on notice and demand by the Secretary and in the same manner as tax) by the person failing so to file, $10 for each day after the expiration of the time specified in the written demand during which such failure continues, but the total amount imposed hereunder on all persons for such failure to file shall not exceed $5,000. If more than one person is liable under this paragraph for a failure to file, all such persons shall be jointly and severally liable with respect to such failure. The term 'person' as used herein means any officer, director, trustee, employee, member, or other individual who is under a duty to perform the act in respect of which the violation occurs.

"(3) Annual returns. In the case of a failure to comply with the requirements of section 6104(d) (relating to public inspection of private foundations' annual returns), on the date and in the manner prescribed therefor (determined with regard to any extension of time for filing), unless it is shown that such failure is due to reasonable cause, there shall be paid (on notice and demand by the Secretary and in the same manner as tax) by the person failing to meet such requirement, $10 for each day during which such failure continues, but the total amount imposed hereunder on all such persons for such failure with respect to any one annual return shall not exceed $5,000. If more than one person is liable under this paragraph for a failure to file or comply with the requirements of section 6104(d), all such persons shall be jointly and severally liable with respect to such failure. The term person as used herein means any officer, director, trustee, employee, member, or other individual who is under a duty to perform the act in respect of which the violation occurs.".

In **1986**, P.L. 99-514, Sec. 1301(g), redesignated subsec. (j) as subsec. (k), and added new subsec. (j), effective for bonds issued after 8/15/86.

—P.L. 99-514, Sec. 1501(d)(1)(A)(i), deleted subsec. (a), and redesignated subsecs. (b)-(k) as subsecs. (a)-(j) . . . Sec. 1501(d)(1)(A)(ii), substituted "Returns with respect to certain payments aggregating less than $10." for "Other returns." in the heading of subsec. (a) [as redesignated by Sec. 1501(d)(1)(A)(i), see above], effective for returns with due dates (determined without regard to extensions) after 12/31/86.

Prior to repeal, subsec. (a) read as follows:

"(a) Returns relating to information at source, payments of dividends, etc., and certain transfers of stock.

"(1) In general. In the case of each failure—

"(A) to file a statement of the amount of payments to another person required by—

"(i) section 6041(a) or (b) (relating to certain information at source),

"(ii) section 6050A(a) (relating to reporting requirements of certain fishing boat operators), or

"(iii) section 6051(d) (relating to information returns with respect to income tax withheld),

"(B) to make a return required by—

"(i) subsection (a) or (b) of section 6041A (relating to returns of direct sellers),

"(ii) section 6045 (relating to returns of brokers),

"(iii) section 6052(a) (relating to reporting payment of wages in the form of group term life insurance), or

"(iv) section 6053(c)(1) (relating to reporting with respect to certain tips),

"(v) section 6050H(a) (relating to mortgage interest received in trade or business from individuals),

"(vi) section 6050I(a) (relating to cash received in trade or business),

"(vii) section 6050J(a) (relating to foreclosures and abandonments of security),

"(viii) section 6050K (relating to exchanges of certain partnership interest), or

"(ix) section 6050L (relating to returns relating to certain dispositions of donated property).

"[(C)](3) [sic , see Sec. 201(i)(2)(A) & (B) of P.L. 97-448 in note] to make a return required by section 4997(a) (relating to information with respect to windfall profit tax on crude oil),

on the date prescribed therefor (determined with regard to any extension of time for filing), unless it is shown that such failure is due to reasonable cause and not to willful neglect, there shall be paid (upon notice and demand by the Secretary and in the same manner as tax), by the person failing to file a statement referred to in subparagraph (A) or failing to make a return referred to in subparagraph (B) [or (C)], $50 for each such failure, but the total amount imposed on the delinquent person for all such failures during any calendar year shall not exceed $50,000.

"(2) Failure to file returns on interest, dividends, and patronage dividends.

"(A) In general. In the case of each failure to file a statement of the amount of payments to another person required by—

"(i) section 6042(a)(1) (relating to payments of dividends),

"(ii) section 6044(a)(1) (relating to payments of patronage dividends), or

"(iii) section 6049(a) (relating to payments of interest),

on the date prescribed therefor (determined with regard to any extension of time for filing), there shall be paid by the person failing to file such statement a penalty of $50 for each such failure unless it is shown that such person exercised due diligence in attempting to satisfy the requirement with respect to such statement.

"(B) Self-assessment. Any penalty imposed under subparagraph (A) on any person —

"(i) for purposes of this subtitle, shall be treated as an excise tax imposed by subtitle D, and

"(ii) shall be due and payable on April 1 of the calendar year following the calendar year for which such statement is required.

"(C) Deficiency procedures not to apply. Subchapter B of chapter 63 (relating to deficiency procedures for income, estate, gift, and certain excise taxes) shall not apply in respect of the assessment or collection of any penalty imposed by subparagraph (A).

"(3) Penalty in case of intentional disregard. If 1 or more failures to which paragraph (1) or (2) applies are due to intentional disregard of the filing requirement, then with respect to such failures—

"(A) the penalty imposed under paragraph (1) or (2) shall be not less than an amount equal to—

"(i) in the case of a return not described in clauses (ii) and (iii), 10 percent of the aggregate amount of the items required to be reported,

"(ii) in the case of a return required to be filed by section 6045 (other than by subsection (d) of such section), 5 percent of the gross proceeds required to be reported, and

"(iii) in the case of a return required to be filed by section 6041A(b), 6050H, 6050I, or 6050J, $100 for each such failure, and

"(B) the $50,000 limitation under paragraph (1) shall not apply."

—P.L. 99-514, Sec. 1702(b), redesignated subsec. (j) [sic (k) see Sec. 1301(g) of this Act] as subsec. (k), and added new subsec. (j), effective for sales after the first calendar quarter begin. more than 60 days after 10/22/86.

—P.L. 99-514, Sec. 1810(f)(9)(A), amended para. (g)(1) [before redesignation as para. (f)(1) by Sec. 1501(d)(1)(A)(i) of this Act] . . . Sec. 1810(f)(9)(B), amended para. (g)(3) [before redesignation as para. (f)(3) by Sec. 1501(d)(1)(A)(i) of this Act.] . . . Sec. 1810(f)(9)(C), deleted ", etc.," from the heading of subsec. (g) [before redesignation as subsec. (f) by Sec. 1501(d)(1)(A)(i) of this Act], effective 12/31/84.

Prior to amendment, para. (g)(1) read as follows:

"(1) In general. In the case of each failure—

"(A) to make a return required by section 6039C which contains the information required by such section, or

"(B) to furnish a statement required by section 6039C(b)(3), on the date prescribed therefor (determined with regard to any extension of time for filing), unless it is shown that such failure is due to reasonable cause and not to willful neglect the amount determined under paragraph (2) shall be paid (upon notice and demand by the Secretary and in the same manner as tax) by the person failing to make such return or furnish such statement."

Prior to amendment, para. (g)(3) read as follows:

"(3) Limitations.

"(A) For failure to meet requirements of subsection (A) or (B) of section 6039C. The amount determined under paragraph (2) with respect to any person for failing to meet the requirements of subsection (a) or (b) of section 6039C for any calendar year shall not exceed $25,000 with respect to each such subsection.

"(B) For failure to meet requirements of section 6039C(c). The amount determined under paragraph (2) with respect to any person for failing to meet the requirements of subsection (c) of section 6039C for any calendar year shall not exceed the lesser of $25,000 or 5 percent of the aggregate of the fair market value of the United States real property interests owned by such person at any time during such year. For purposes of the preceding sentence, fair market value shall be determined as of the end of the calendar year, or, in the case of any property disposed of during the calendar year, as of the date of such disposition)."

—P.L. 99-514, Sec. 1811(a)(2), substituted "section 6676" for "section 6652" in Sec. 145(d)(2) of P.L. 98-369 [reproduced below as part of the effective date for the amendments made by Sec. 145(b)(2) of P.L. 98-369] . . . Sec. 1811(c)(2), added "(other than by subsection (d) of such section)," after "section 6045" in clause (a)(3)(A)(ii), [before deletion by Sec. 1501(d)(1)(A)(i) of this Act], effective after "section 6045" for amounts received after 12/31/84.

In **1984**, P.L. 98-612, Sec. 1(b)(2), amended subsec. (d), effective 1/1/85. [Inoperative, same amendment made by Sec. 1(d)(2) of P.L. 98-611, below.]

—P.L. 98-611, Sec. 1(d)(2), substituted "6039D (relating to returns and records with respect to certain fringe benefit plans)" for "125(h) (relating to information with respect to cafeteria plans)" in subsec. (f), effective 1/1/85.

—P.L. 98-397, Sec. 207(b), redesignated subsec. (j) as subsec. (k) and added new subsec. (j), effective for distributions after 12/31/84. See Sec. 302(c) of this Act.

—P.L. 98-369, Sec. 145(b)(1)(A), deleted "or" at the end of clause (a)(1)(B)(iii) . . . Sec. 145(b)(1)(B), added "or" to the end of clause (a)(1)(B)(iv) . . . Sec. 145(b)(1)(C), added clause (a)(1)(B)(v) . . . Sec. 145(b)(2), added "or section 6050H" after "section 6041A(b)" in clause (a)(3)(A)(iii), effective for amounts received after 12/31/84. Sec. 145(d)(2) [as amended by Sec. 1811(a)(2) of P.L. 99-514, see above] of the Act provides:

"(2) Special rule for obligations in existence on December 31, 1984.—In the case of any obligation in existence on December 31, 1984, no penalty shall be imposed under section 6676 of the Internal Revenue Code of 1954 by reason of the amendments made by this section on any failure to supply a taxpayer identification number with respect to amounts received before January 1, 1986."

—P.L. 98-369, Sec. 146(b)(1)(A), deleted "or" at the end of clause (a)(1)(B)(iv) . . . Sec. 146(b)(1)(B), added "or" to the end of clause (a)(1)(B)(v) . . . Sec. 146(b)(1)(C), added clause (a)(1)(B)(vi) . . . Sec. 146(b)(2), substituted ", 6050H or 6050I" for "or section 6050H" in clause (a)(3)(A)(iii), effective for amounts received after 12/31/84.

—P.L. 98-369, Sec. 148(b)(1)(A), deleted "or" at the end of clause (a)(1)(B)(v) . . . Sec. 148(b)(1)(B), added "or" to the end of clause (a)(1)(B)(vi) . . . Sec. 148(b)(1)(C), added clause (a)(1)(B)(vii) . . . Sec. 148(b)(2), substituted ", 6050I, or 6050J" for "or 6050I" in clause (a)(3)(A)(iii), effective for acquisitions of property and abandonments of property after 12/31/84.

—P.L. 98-369, Sec. 149(b)(1), deleted "or" at the end of clause (a)(1)(B)(vi), added "or" to the end of clause (a)(1)(B)(vii), and added clause (a)(1)(B)(viii), effective for exchanges after 12/31/84.

—P.L. 98-369, Sec. 155(b)(2)(A)(i), deleted "or" at the end of clause (a)(1)(B)(vii) . . . Sec. 155(b)(2)(A)(ii), added "or" to the end of clause (a)(1)(B)(viii) . . . Sec. 155(b)(2)(A)(iii), added clause (a)(1)(B)(ix), effective for contributions made after 12/31/84, in tax. yrs. end. after 12/31/84.

—P.L. 98-369, Sec. 491(d)(50), deleted "and bond purchase" after "certain trusts and annuity" in subsec. (f), effective for obligations issued after 12/31/83.

—P.L. 98-369, Sec. 531(b)(4)(B)(i), substituted ", 6047 (relating to information relating to certain trusts and annuity and bond purchase plans), or 125(h) (relating to information with respect to cafeteria plans)" for "or 6047 (relating to information relating to certain trusts and annuity and bond purchase plans)" in subsec. (f) . . . Sec. 531(b)(4)(B)(ii), substituted "deferred compensation; etc.—" for "deferred compensation.—" in the heading of subsec. (f), effective 1/1/85.

—P.L. 98-369, Sec. 714(j)(3), redesignated subsec. (i) as subsec. (j), and added new subsec. (i), effective for returns or statements whose filing due date (without regard to extensions) is after 12/31/82.

In 1983, P.L. 98-67, Sec. 105(b)(1)(A), redesignated para. (a)(2) as para. (a)(3) and added new para. (a)(2) . . . Sec. 105(b)(1)(B)(i), deleted clauses (a)(1)(A)(ii), (a)(1)(A)(iii) and (a)(1)(A)(iv), and redesignated clauses (a)(1)(A)(v) and (a)(1)(A)(vi) as clauses (a)(1)(A)(ii) and (a)(1)(A)(iii) . . . Sec. 105(b)(1)(B)(ii), deleted "6042(e), 6044(f), 6049(e), or" in clause (a)(1)(A)(iii) [as redesignated by Sec. 105(b)(1)(B)(i), see above] . . . Sec. 105(b)(1)(C), substituted "paragraph (1) or (2)" for "paragraph (1)" in the matter preceding subpara. (a)(3)(A) and in subpara. (a)(3)(A) [as redesignated by made after 12/31/83.

Prior to deletion, clauses (a)(1)(A)(ii), (a)(1)(A)(iii) and (a)(1)(A)(iv) read as follows:

"(ii) section 6042(a)(1) (relating to payments of dividends),

"(iii) section 6044(a)(1) (relating to payments of patronage dividends),

"(iv) section 6049(a) (relating to payments of interest),"

—P.L. 97-448, Sec. 201(i)(2)(A), deleted "or" at the end of subpara. (a)(1)(F), added "or" at the end of para. (a)(2), and added para. (a)(3) . . . Sec. 201(i)(2)(B), substituted "paragraph (2) or (3)" for "paragraph (2)" in subsec. (a), effective for returns and statements the due dates for which (without regard to extensions) are after 1/12/83.

In 1982, P.L. 97-248, Sec. 309(b)(2), added "or" at the end of para. (b)(1), and deleted paras. (b)(3) and (b)(4), effective for amounts paid (or treated as paid) after 12/31/82.

Prior to deletion, paras. (b)(3) and (b)(4) read as follows:

"(3) section 6049(a)(2) (relating to payments of interest aggregating less than $10), or

"(4) section 6049(a)(3) (relating to other payments of interest by corporations),"

—P.L. 97-248, Sec. 315(a), amended subsec. (a) . . . Sec. 315(b), substituted "$25" for "$10" and substituted "$15,000" for "$5,000" in subsec. (f), effective for returns or statements whose filing due date (without regard to extensions) is after 12/31/82.

Prior to amendment, subsec. (a) read as follows:

"(a) Returns relating to information at source, payments of dividends, etc., and certain transfers of stock.

"In the case of each failure—

"(1) to file a statement of the aggregate amount of payments to another person required by—

"(A) section 6041(a) or (b) (relating to certain information at source),

"(B) section 6042(a)(1) (relating to payments of dividends aggregating $10 or more),

"(C) section 6044(a)(1) (relating to payments of patronage dividends aggregating $10 or more),

"(D) section 6049(a)(1) (relating to payments of interest aggregating $10 or more),

"(E) section 6050A(a) (relating to reporting requirements of certain fishing boat operators), or

"(F) section 6051(d) (relating to information returns with respect to income tax withheld), or

"(2) to make a return required by section 6052(a) (relating to reporting payment of wages in the form of group-term life insurance) with respect to group-term life insurance on the life of an employee,

on the date prescribed therefor (determined with regard to any extension of time for filing), unless it is shown that such failure is due to reasonable cause and not to willful neglect, there shall be paid (upon notice and demand by the Secretary and in the same manner as tax), by the person failing to file a statement referred to in paragraph (1) or failing to make a return referred to in paragraph (2), $10 for each such failure, but the total amount imposed on the delinquent person for all such failures during any calendar year shall not exceed $25,000."

In 1981, P.L. 97-34, Sec. 311(f), redesignated subsec. (h) as subsec. (i) and added new subsec. (h), effective for tax. yrs. begin. after 12/31/81. For transitional rule, see Sec. 311(i)(2) of this Act reproduced in note following Code Sec. 219.

—P.L. 97-34, Sec. 723(a)(1), amended para. (a)(1) . . . Sec. 723(a)(3), amended subsec. (b) . . . Sec. 723(a)(4), added "information at source," before "payments of dividends" in the heading of subsec. (a), effective for returns and statements required to be furnished after 12/31/81.

Prior to amendment, para. (a)(1) read as follows:

"(1) to file a statement of the aggregate amount of payments to another person required by section 6042(a)(1) (relating to payments of dividends aggregating $10 or more), section 6044(a)(1) (relating to payments of patronage dividends aggregating $10 or more), or section 6049(a)(1) (relating to payments of interest aggregating $10 or more), or"

Prior to amendment, subsec. (b) read as follows:

"(b) Other returns.

"In the case of each failure to file a statement of a payment to another person required under authority of section 6041 (relating to certain information at source), section 6042(a)(2) (relating to payments of dividends aggregating less than $10), section 6044(a)(2) (relating to payments of patronage dividends aggregating less than $10), section 6049(a)(2) (relating to payments of interest aggregating less than $10), section 6049(a)(3) (relating to other payments of interest by corporations), or section 6051(d) (relating to information returns with respect to income tax withheld), in the case of each failure to make a return required by section 6050A(a) (relating to reporting requirements of certain fishing boat operators), and in the case of each failure to furnish a statement required by section 6053(b) (relating to statements furnished by employers with respect to tips), section 6050A(b) (relating to statements furnished by certain fishing boat operators), or section 6050C (relating to information regarding windfall profit tax on crude oil) on the date prescribed therefor (determined with regard to any extension of time for filing), unless it is shown that such failure is due to reasonable cause and not to willful neglect, there shall be paid (upon notice and demand by the Secretary and in the same manner as tax) by the person failing to so file the statement, $1 for each such statement not so filed, but the total amount imposed on the delinquent person for all such failures during the calendar year shall not exceed $1,000."

In 1980, P.L. 96-603, Sec. 1(d)(2)(A), amended the first sentence of para. (d)(3) . . . Sec. 1(d)(2)(B), substituted "returns" for "reports" in the heading of para. (d)(3), effective for tax. yrs. begin. after 12/31/80.

Prior to amendment, the first sentence of para. (d)(3) read as follows:

"In the case of a failure to file a report required under section 6056 (relating to annual reports by private foundations) or to comply with the requirements of section 6104(d) (relating to public inspection of private foundations' annual reports), on the date and in the manner prescribed therefor (determined with regard to any extension of time for filing), unless it is shown that such failure is due to reasonable cause, there shall be paid (on notice and demand by the Secretary and in the same manner as tax) by the person failing so to file or meet the publicity requirement, $10 for each day during which such failure continues, but the total amount imposed hereunder on all such persons for such failure to file or comply with the requirements of section 6104(d) with regard to any one annual report shall not exceed $5,000."

—P.L. 96-499, Sec. 1123(b), redesignated subsec. (g) as subsec. (h), and added new subsec. (g), effective for calendar year 1980 and subsequent calendar years. Calendar year 1980 is treated as beginning on 6/19/80, and ending on 12/31/80.

—P.L. 96-223, Sec. 101(d)(2)(A), substituted ", section 6050A" for "or section 6050A", and added ", or section 6050C (relating to information regarding windfall profit tax on crude oil)" after "fishing boat operators)" in subsec. (b) effective for periods after 2/29/80.

In 1979, P.L. 96-167, Sec. 7(b)(1)(A), added "or" at the end of para. (a)(1) . . . Sec. 7(b)(1)(B), deleted para. (a)(2) and redesignated para. (a)(3) as para. (a)(2) . . . Sec. 7(b)(1)(C), substituted "return referred to in paragraph (2)" for "return referred to in paragraph (2) or (3)" in subsec. (a) effective for calendar yrs. begin. after 12/31/79.

Prior to deletion, para. (a)(2) read as follows:

"(2) to make a return required by section 6039(a) (relating to reporting information in connection with certain options) with respect to a transfer of stock or a transfer of legal title to stock, or"

In 1976, P.L. 94-455, Sec. 1207(e)(3)(B), added "in the case of each failure to make a return required by section 6050A(a) (relating to reporting requirements of certain fishing boat operators)," after "withheld)," in subsec. (b), . . . Sec. 1207(e)(3)(C), added "or section 6050A(b) (relating to statements furnished by certain fishing boat operators)," after "tips," in subsec. (b), effective for calendar yrs. begin. after 10/4/76, except as provided in Sec. 1207(f)(4)(B) of the Act, which reads as follows:

Penalties   Code Sec. 6653

"(B) Notwithstanding subparagraph (A), if the owner or operator of any boat treated a share of the boat's catch of fish or other aquatic animal life (or a share of the proceeds therefrom) received by an individual after December 31, 1971, and before the date of the enactment of this Act for services performed by such individual after December 31, 1971, on such boat as being subject to the tax under chapter 21 of the Internal Revenue Code of 1954, then the amendments made by paragraphs (1) (A) and (B) and (2) of subsection (e) shall not apply with respect to such services performed by such individual (and the share of the catch, or proceeds therefrom, received by him for such services)."

—P.L. 94-455, Sec. 1906(b)(13)(A), substituted "Secretary" for "Secretary or his delegate" each place it appeared in Code Sec. 6652, effective 2/1/77.

In 1974, P.L. 93-406, Sec. 1031(b)(1)(B)(i), added ", registration statements, etc." before the period at the end of the heading of Code Sec. 6652 . . . Sec. 1031(b)(1)(A), redesignated subsec. (e) as subsec. (g) and added new subsecs. (e) and (f), effective 9/2/74.

In 1969, P.L. 91-172, Sec. 101(d)(4), redesignated subsec. (d) as subsec. (e) and added new subsec. (d), effective for tax yrs. begin. after 12/31/69.

In 1965, P.L. 89-212, Sec. 2(e)(1), added "or which are compensation (as defined in section 3231(e))" after "which are wages (as defined in section 3121(a))" . . . Sec. 2(e)(2), added "or section 3201 (as the case may be)" after "section 3101" in subsec. (c), effective for tips received after 1965.

—P.L. 89-97, Sec. 313(e)(2)(B), added "and in the case of each failure to furnish a statement required by section 6053(b) (relating to statements furnished by employers with respect to tips)," after "income tax withheld," in subsec. (b) . . . Sec. 313(e)(3), redesignated subsec. (b) as subsec. (d), and added new subsec. (c), effective for tips received by employees after 1965.

In 1964, P.L. 88-272, Sec. 221(b)(2), amended subsec. (a), effective for tax. yrs. end. after 12/31/63.

Prior to amendment, subsec. (a) read as follows:
"(a) Returns Relating to Payments of Dividends, Interest, and Patronage Dividends.

"In the case of each failure to file a statement of the aggregate amount of payments to another person required by section 6042(a)(1) (relating to payments of dividends aggregating $10 or more), section 6044(a)(1) (relating to payments of patronage dividends aggregating $10 or more), or section 6049(a)(1) (relating to payments of interest aggregating $10 or more), on the date prescribed therefor (determined with regard to any extension of time for filing), unless it is shown that such failure is due to reasonable cause and not to willful neglect, there shall be paid (upon notice and demand by the Secretary or his delegate and in the same manner as tax), by the person failing to so file the statement, $10 for each such statement not so filed, but the total amount imposed on the delinquent person for all such failures during any calendar year shall not exceed $25,000."

In 1962, P.L. 87-834, Sec. 19(d), amended Code Sec. 6652, effective for payments of dividends and interest made on or after 1/1/63. Sec. 19(h)(2) of this Act provides as follows:

"(2) Patronage dividends.—The amendments made by this section shall apply to payments of amounts described in section 6044 (b) of the Internal Revenue Code of 1954 made on or after January 1, 1963, with respect to patronage occurring on or after the first day of the first taxable year of the cooperative beginning on or after January 1, 1963."

Prior to amendment, Code Sec. 6652 read as follows:
"(a) Additional Amount.

"In case of each failure to file a statement of a payment to another person, required under authority of section 6041 (relating to information at source), section 6042(1) (relating to payments of corporate dividends), section 6044 (relating to patronage dividends), or section 6051(d) (relating to information returns with respect to income tax withheld), on the date prescribed therefor (determined with regard to any extension of time for filing), unless it is shown that such failure is due to reasonable cause and not to willful neglect, there shall be paid (upon notice and demand by the Secretary or his delegate and in the same manner as tax), by the person failing to so file the statement, $1 for each such statement not so filed, but the total amount imposed on the delinquent person for all such failures during any calendar year shall not exceed $1,000."
"(b) Alcohol and Tobacco Taxes.

"For penalties for failure to file certain information returns with respect to alcohol and tobacco taxes, see, generally, subtitle E."

In 1958, P.L. 85-866, Sec. 85, amended subsec. (a), effective 8/17/54, as provided in Code Sec. 7851.

Prior to amendment, subsec. (a) read as follows:
"(a) Additional Amount.

"In case of each failure to file a statement of a payment to another person, required under authority of section 6041 (relating to information at source), section 6042 (relating to payments of corporate dividends), section 6044 (relating to patronage dividends), section 6045 (relating to returns of brokers), or section 6051(d) (relating to information returns with respect to income tax withheld), unless it is shown that such failure is due to reasonable cause and not to willful neglect, there shall be paid by the person failing to file the statement, upon notice and demand by the Secretary or his delegate and in the same manner as tax, $1 for each such statement not filed, but the total amount imposed on the delinquent person for all such failures during any calendar year shall not exceed $1,000."

Sec. 6653. Failure to pay stamp tax.

Any person (as defined in section 6671(b)) who—

(1) willfully fails to pay any tax imposed by this title which is payable by stamp, coupons, tickets, books, or other devices or methods prescribed by this title or by regulations under the authority of this title, or

(2) willfully attempts in any manner to evade or defeat any such tax or the payment thereof,

shall, in addition to other penalties provided by law, be liable for a penalty of 50 percent of the total amount of the underpayment of the tax.

In 1989, P.L. 101-239, Sec. 7721(c)(1), amended Code Sec. 6653, effective for returns the due date for which (determined without regard to extensions) is after 12/31/89.

Prior to amendment, Code Sec. 6653 read as follows:
"SEC. 6653. ADDITIONS TO TAX FOR NEGLIGENCE AND FRAUD.
"(a) Negligence.

"(1) In general. If any part of any underpayment (as defined in subsection (c)) of tax required to be shown on a return is due to negligence (or disregard of rules or regulations), there shall be added to the tax an amount equal to 5 percent of the underpayment.

"(2) Underpayment taken into account reduced by portion attributable to fraud. There shall not be taken into account under this subsection any portion of an underpayment attributable to fraud with respect to which a penalty is imposed under subsection (b).

"(3) Negligence. For purposes of this subsection, the term negligence includes any failure to make a reasonable attempt to comply with the provisions of this title, and the term 'disregard' includes any careless, reckless, or intentional disregard.

"(b) Fraud.

"(1) In general. If any part of any underpayment (as defined in subsection (c)) of tax required to be shown on a return is due to fraud, there shall be added to the tax an amount equal to 75 percent of the portion of the underpayment which is attributable to fraud.

"(2) Determination of portion attributable to fraud. If the Secretary establishes that any portion of an underpayment is attributable to fraud, the entire underpayment shall be treated as attributable to fraud, except with respect to any portion of the underpayment which the taxpayer establishes is not attributable to fraud.

"(3) Special rule for joint returns. In the case of a joint return, this subsection shall not apply with respect to a spouse unless some part of the underpayment is due to the fraud of such spouse.

"(c) Definition of underpayment.

For purposes of this section, the term 'underpayment' means—

"(1) Income, estate, gift, and certain excise taxes. In the case of a tax to which section 6211 (relating to income, estate, gift, and certain excise taxes) is applicable, a deficiency as defined in that section (except that, for this purpose, the tax shown on a return referred to in section 6211(a)(1)(A) shall be taken into account only if such return was filed on or before the last day prescribed for the filing of such return, determined with regard to any extension of time for such filing), and

"(2) Other taxes. In the case of any other tax, the amount by which such tax imposed by this title exceeds the excess of—

"(A) The sum of—

"(i) The amount shown as the tax by the taxpayer upon his return (determined without regard to any credit for an overpayment for any prior period, and without regard to any adjustment under authority of sections 6205(a) and 6413(a)), if a return was made by the taxpayer within the time prescribed for filing such return (determined with regard to any extension of time for such filing) and an amount was shown as the tax by the taxpayer thereon, plus

"(ii) Any amount, not shown on the return, paid in respect of such tax, over—

"(B) The amount of rebates made.

For purposes of subparagraph (B), the term 'rebate' means so much of an abatement, credit, refund, or other repayment, as was made on the ground that the tax imposed was less than the excess of the amount specified in subparagraph (A) over the rebates previously made.

"(d) No delinquency penalty if fraud assessed.

If any penalty is assessed under subsection (b) (relating to fraud) for an underpayment of tax which is required to be shown on a return, no penalty under section 6651 (relating to failure to file such return or pay tax) shall be assessed with respect to the portion of the underpayment which is attributable to fraud.

"(e) Failure to pay stamp tax.

Any person (as defined in section 6671(b)) who willfully fails to pay any tax imposed by this title which is payable by stamp, coupons, tickets, books, or other devices or methods prescribed by this title or by regulations under authority of this title, or willfully attempts in any manner to evade or defeat any such tax or the payment thereof, shall, in addition to other penalties provided by law, be liable to a penalty of 50 percent of the total amount of the underpayment of the tax.

"(f) Special rule in cases of failure to report unrecognized gain on position in personal property.

If—

"(1) a taxpayer fails to make the report required under section 1092(a)(3)(B) in the manner prescribed by such section and such failure is not due to reasonable cause, and

"(2) such taxpayer has an underpayment of any tax attributable (in whole or in part) to the denial of a deduction of a loss with respect to any position (within the meaning of section 1092(d)(2)),

then such underpayment shall, for purposes of subsection (a), be treated as an underpayment due to negligence.

"(g) Special rule for amounts shown on information returns.

3,777

Code Sec. 6653

If—

"(1) any amount is shown on—

"(A) an information return (as defined in section 6724(d)(1)), or

"(B) a return filed under section 6031, section 6037, section 6012(a) by an estate or trust, section 6050B, or section 6050E, and

"(2) the payee (or other person with respect to whom the return is made) fails to properly show such amount on his return,

any portion of an underpayment attributable to such failure shall be treated, for purposes of subsection (a), as due to negligence in the absence of clear and convincing evidence to the contrary. If any penalty is imposed under subsection (a) by reason of the preceding sentence, only the portion of the underpayment which is attributable to the failure described in the preceding sentence shall be taken into account in determining the amount of the penalty under subsection (a)."

In 1988, P.L. 100-647, Sec. 1015(b)(2)(A), amended para. (a)(1)... Sec. 1015(b)(2)(B), amended para. (b)(1), effective for returns the due date for which (determined without regard to extensions) is after 12/31/88.

Prior to amendment, para. (a)(1) read as follows:

"(1) In general. If any part of any underpayment (as defined in subsection (c)) is due to negligence or disregard of rules or regulations, there shall be added to the tax an amount equal to the sum of—

"(A) 5 percent of the underpayment, and

"(B) an amount equal to 50 percent of the interest payable under section 6601 was respect to the portion of such underpayment which is attributable to negligence for the period beginning on the last date prescribed by law for payment of such underpayment (determined without regard to any extension) and ending on the date of the assessment of the tax (or, if earlier, the date of the payment of the tax)."

Prior to amendment para. (b)(1) read as follows:

"(1) In general. If any part of any underpayment (as defined in subsection (c)) of tax required to be shown on a return is due to fraud, there shall be added to the tax an amount equal to the sum of—

"(A) 75 percent of the portion of the underpayment which is attributable to fraud, and

"(B) an amount equal to 50 percent of the interest payable under section 6601 with respect to such portion for the period beginning on the last day prescribed by law for payment of such underpayment (determined without regard to any extension) and ending on the date of the assessment of the tax or, if earlier, the date of the payment of the tax."

—P.L. 100-647, Sec. 1015(b)(3), added a new sentence to the end of subsec. (g), effective for returns the due date for which (determined without regard to extensions) is after 12/31/86.

In 1986, P.L. 99-514, Sec. 1503(a), amended subsecs. (a) and (b)... Sec. 1503(b), amended subsec. (g)... Sec. 1503(c)(2), substituted "portion of the underpayment which is attributable to fraud" for "same underpayment" in subsec. (d)... Sec. 1503(c)(3), deleted "or intentional disregard of rules and regulations (but without intent to defraud)" after "negligence" in subsec. (f)... Sec. 1503(d)(1), amended the heading for the Code Sec. 6653, effective for returns the due date for which (determined without regard to extensions) after is 12/31/86.

Prior to amendment, subsecs. (a) and (b) read as follows:

"(a) Negligence or intentional disregard of rules and regulations with respect to income, gift, or Windfall Profit taxes.

"(1) In general. If any part of any underpayment (as defined in subsection (c)(1)) of any tax imposed by subtitle A, by chapter 12 of subtitle B, or by chapter 45 (relating to windfall profit tax) is due to negligence or intentional disregard of rules or regulations (but without intent to defraud), there shall be added to the tax an amount equal to 5 percent of the underpayment.

"(2) Additional amount for portion attributable to negligence, etc. There shall be added to the tax (in addition to the amount determined under paragraph (1)) an amount equal to 50 percent of the interest payable under section 6601—

"(A) with respect to the portion of the underpayment described in paragraph (1) which is attributable to the negligence or intentional disregard referred to in paragraph (1), and

"(B) for the period beginning on the last date prescribed by law for payment of such underpayment (determined without regard to any extension) and ending on the date of the assessment of the tax (or, if earlier, the date of the payment of the tax).

"(b) Fraud.

"(1) In general. If any part of any underpayment (as defined in subsection (c)) of tax required to be shown on a return is due to fraud, there shall be added to the tax an amount equal to 50 percent of the underpayment.

"(2) Additional amount for portion attributable to fraud. There shall be added to the tax (in addition to the amount determined under paragraph (1)) an amount equal to 50 percent of the interest payable under section 6601—

"(A) with respect to the portion of the underpayment described in paragraph (1) which is attributable to fraud, and

"(B) for the period beginning on the last day prescribed by law for payment of such underpayment (determined without regard to any extension) and ending on the date of the assessment of the tax (or, if earlier, the date of the payment of the tax).

"(3) No negligence addition when there is addition for fraud. The addition to tax under this subsection shall be in lieu of any amount determined under subsection (a).

"(4) Special rule for joint returns. In the case of a joint return under section 6013, this subsection shall not apply with respect to the tax of the spouse unless some part of the underpayment is due to the fraud of such spouse."

Prior to amendment, subsec. (g) read as follows:

"(g) Special rule in the case of interest or dividend payments.

Penalties

"(1) In general. If—

"(A) any payment is shown on a return made by the payor under section 6042(a), 6044(a), or 6049(a), and

"(B) the payee fails to include any portion of such payment in gross income, any portion of an underpayment attributable to such failure shall be treated, for purposes of subsection (a), as due to negligence in the absence of clear and convincing evidence to the contrary.

"(2) Penalty to apply only to portion of underpayment due to failure to include interest or dividend payment. If any penalty is imposed under subsection (a) by reason of paragraph (1), the amount of the penalty imposed by paragraph (1) of subsection (a) shall be 5 percent of the portion of the underpayment which is attributable to the failure described in paragraph (1)."

Prior to amendment, the heading for Code Sec. 6653 read as follows:

"SEC. 6653. FAILURE TO PAY TAX."

In 1985, P.L. 99-44, Sec. 1(b), repealed Sec. 179(b)(3) of P.L. 98-369 (see below) to take effect as if included in the amendments made by Sec. 179(b) of P.L. 98-369. Sec. 1(b) of this Act also provides that the "... Internal Revenue Code of 1954 shall be applied and administered as if such [Sec. 179(b)(2) 98-369] and the amendments made by [Sec. 179(b)(2) of P.L. 98-369] had not been enacted". Sec. 1(c) of this Act provides:

"(c) Repeal of regulations.

Regulations issued before the date of the enactment of this Act [5/24/85] to carry out the amendments made by paragraphs (1)(C), (2), and (3) of section 179(b) of the Tax Reform Act of 1984 [P.L. 98-369] shall have no force and effect."

In 1984, P.L. 98-369, Sec. 179(b)(3), added subsec. (h), effective for tax. yrs. begin. after 12/31/84, but repealed retroactively by Sec. 1(b) of P.L. 99-44 (see above).

Prior to repeal subsec. (h) as added by Sec. 179 (b)(3) of P.L. 98-369 read as follows:

"(h) Special rule in the case of underpayment attributable to failure to meet certain substantiation requirements.

"(1) In general. Any portion of an underpayment attributable to a failure to comply with the requirements of section 274(d) shall be treated, for purposes of subsection (a), as due to negligence in the absence of clear and convincing evidence to the contrary.

"(2) Penalty to apply only to portion of underpayment due to failure to meet substantiation requirements. If any penalty is imposed under subsection (a) by reason of paragraph (1), the amount of the penalty imposed by paragraph (1) of subsection (a) will be 5 percent of the portion of the underpayment which is attributable to the failure described in paragraph (1)."

In 1983, P.L. 98-67, Sec. 106, added subsec. (g), effective for payments made after 12/31/83.

—P.L. 97-448, Sec. 105(a)(1)(D)(i), redesignated subsec. (g) as subsec. (f)... Sec. 105(a)(1)(D)(ii), substituted "unrecognized" for "unrealized" in the heading of subsec. (f) (as redesignated by Sec. 105(a)(1)(D)(i) of the Act), effective for property acquired and positions established by the taxpayer after 6/23/81, in tax yrs. end. after 6/23/81.

—P.L. 97-448, Sec. 107(a)(3), added "(or, if earlier, the date of the payment of the tax)" after "assessment of the tax" in subpara. (a)(2)(B), effective for taxes the last date prescribed for payment of which is after 12/31/81.

In 1982, P.L. 97-248, Sec. 325(a), amended subsec. (b), effective for taxes the last day prescribed by law for payment of which (determined without regard to any extension) is after 9/3/82.

Prior to amendment, subsec. (b) read as follows:

"(b) Fraud.

If any part of any underpayment (as defined in subsection (c)) of tax required to be shown on a return is due to fraud, there shall be added to the tax an amount equal to 50 percent of the underpayment. In the case of income taxes and gift taxes, this amount shall be in lieu of any amount determined under subsection (a). In the case of a joint return under section 6013, this subsection shall not apply with respect to the tax of a spouse unless some part of the underpayment is due to the fraud of such spouse."

In 1981, P.L. 97-34, Sec. 501(b), added subsec. (g), for property acquired and positions established by the taxpayer after 6/23/81, in tax. yrs. end. after 6/23/81. For election with respect to property held on 6/23/81, see Sec. 508(c) of this Act reproduced in note following Code Sec. 1092.

—P.L. 97-34, Sec. 722(b)(1), amended subsec. (a), effective for taxes the last date prescribed for payment of which is after 12/31/81.

Prior to amendment, subsec. (a) read as follows:

"(a) Negligence or intentional disregard of rules and regulations with respect to income, gift, or windfall profit taxes.

"If any part of any underpayment (as defined in subsection (c)(1)) of any tax imposed by subtitle A, by chapter 12 of subtitle B (relating to income taxes and gift taxes), or by chapter 45 (relating to windfall profit tax) is due to negligence or intentional disregard of rules and regulations (but without intent to defraud), there shall be added to the tax an amount equal to 5 percent of the underpayment."

In 1980, P.L. 96-223, Sec. 101(f)(8)(A), substituted ", by chapter 12" for "or by chapter 12" in subsec. (a)... Sec. 101(f)(8)(B), substituted ", or by chapter 45 (relating to windfall profit tax) is due" for "is due" in subsec. (a)... Sec. 101(f)(8)(C), substituted ", gift, or windfall profit" for "or gift" in the heading of subsec. (a), effective for periods after 2/29/80.

In 1974, P.L. 93-406, Sec. 1016(a)(18), substituted "certain excise" for "chapter 42" each time it appeared in para. (c)(1), effective 9/2/74 or other date as specified in Sec. 1017 of the Act (reproduced following Code Sec. 401).

Penalties
Code Sec. 6654(d)(1)(D)(ii)

In 1971, P.L. 91-679, Sec. 2, added a new sentence to the end of subsec. (b), effective for all tax. yrs. to which the Internal Revenue Code of 1954 applies. Corresponding provisions shall be deemed to be included in the Internal Revenue Code of 1939 and shall apply to all tax. yrs. to which such Code applies.

In 1969, P.L. 91-172, Sec. 101(j)(50), substituted "gift and chapter 42 taxes" for "and gift taxes" in the heading of para. (c)(1), and substituted "gift and chapter 42 taxes" for "and gift taxes" the last place it appeared in para. (c)(1), effective 1/1/70.

—P.L. 91-172, Sec. 943(c)(6), added "or pay tax" after "such return" in subsec. (d), for returns the date prescribed by law (without regard to any extension of time) for filing of which is after 12/31/69, and with respect to notices and demands for payment of tax made after 12/31/69.

In 1958, P.L. 85-866, Sec. 86, added "on or" after "such return was filed" in para. (c)(1), effective 8/17/54.

Sec. 6654. Failure by individual to pay estimated income tax.

> • **Caution:** Code Sec. 6654(a), following is effective for tax. yrs. before 1/1/2013. For Code Sec. 6654(a) effective for tax yrs begin after 12/31/2012, see below.

(a) Addition to the tax.

Except as otherwise provided in this section, in the case of any underpayment of estimated tax by an individual, there shall be added to the tax under chapter 1 and the tax under chapter 2 for the taxable year an amount determined by applying—

(1) the underpayment rate established under section 6621,
(2) to the amount of the underpayment,
(3) for the period of the underpayment.

> • **Caution:** Code Sec. 6654(a), following, is effective for tax. yrs. begin. after 12/31/2012. For Code Sec. 6654(a) effective for tax. yrs. begin. after 1/1/2013, see above.

(a) Addition to the tax.

Except as otherwise provided in this section, in the case of any underpayment of estimated tax by an individual, there shall be added to the tax under chapter 1 the tax under chapter 2, and the tax under chapter 2A for the taxable year an amount determined by applying—

(1) the underpayment rate established under section 6621,
(2) to the amount of the underpayment,
(3) for the period of the underpayment.

(b) Amount of underpayment; period of underpayment.

For purposes of subsection (a)—

(1) **Amount.** The amount of the underpayment shall be the excess of—
  (A) the required installment, over
  (B) the amount (if any) of the installment paid on or before the due date for the installment.

(2) **Period of underpayment.** The period of the underpayment shall run from the due date for the installment to whichever of the following dates is the earlier—
  (A) the 15th day of the 4th month following the close of the taxable year, or
  (B) with respect to any portion of the underpayment, the date on which such portion is paid.

(3) **Order of crediting payments.** For purposes of paragraph (2)(B), a payment of estimated tax shall be credited against unpaid required installments in the order in which such installments are required to be paid.

(c) Number of required installments; due dates.

For purposes of this section—

(1) **Payable in 4 installments.** There shall be 4 required installments for each taxable year.

(2) **Time for payment of installments.**

In the case of the following required installments:	The due date is:
1st	April 15
2nd	June 15
3rd	September 15
4th	January 15 of the following taxable year.

(d) Amount of required installments.

For purposes of this section—

(1) **Amount.**

(A) In general. Except as provided in paragraph (2), the amount of any required installment shall be 25 percent of the required annual payment.

(B) Required annual payment. For purposes of subparagraph (A), the term "required annual payment" means the lesser of—
  (i) 90 percent of the tax shown on the return for the taxable year (or, if no return is filed, 90 percent of the tax for such year), or
  (ii) 100 percent of the tax shown on the return of the individual for the preceding taxable year.

Clause (ii) shall not apply if the preceding taxable year was not a taxable year of 12 months or if the individual did not file a return for such preceding taxable year.

(C) Limitation on use of preceding year's tax.
  (i) In general. If the adjusted gross income shown on the return of the individual for the preceding taxable year beginning in any calendar year exceeds $150,000, clause (ii) of subparagraph (B) shall be applied by substituting the applicable percentage for "100 percent". For purposes of the preceding sentence, the applicable percentage shall be determined in accordance with the following table:

If the preceding taxable year begins in:	The applicable percentage is:
1998	105
1999	108.6
2000	110
2001	112
2002 or thereafter	110

This clause shall not apply in the case of a preceding taxable year beginning in calendar year 1997.

(ii) Separate returns. In the case of a married individual (within the meaning of section 7703) who files a separate return for the taxable year for which the amount of the installment is being determined, clause (i) shall be applied by substituting "$75,000" for "$150,000".

(iii) Special rule. In the case of an estate or trust, adjusted gross income shall be determined as provided in section 67(e).

(D) Special rule for 2009.
  (i) In general. Notwithstanding subparagraph (C), in the case of any taxable year beginning in 2009, clause (ii) of subparagraph (B) shall be applied to any qualified individual by substituting "90 percent" for "100 percent".
  (ii) Qualified individual. For purposes of this subparagraph, the term "qualified individual" means any individual if—

(I) the adjusted gross income shown on the return of such individual for the preceding taxable year is less than $500,000, and

(II) such individual certifies that more than 50 percent of the gross income shown on the return of such individual for the preceding taxable year was income from a small business.

A certification under subclause (II) shall be in such form and manner and filed at such time as the Secretary may by regulations prescribe.

(iii) Income from a small business. For purposes of clause (ii), income from a small business means, with respect to any individual, income from a trade or business the average number of employees of which was less than 500 employees for the calendar year ending with or within the preceding taxable year of the individual.

(iv) Separate returns. In the case of a married individual (within the meaning of section 7703) who files a separate return for the taxable year for which the amount of the installment is being determined, clause (ii)(I) shall be applied by substituting "$250,000" for "$500,000".

(v) Estates and trusts. In the case of an estate or trust, adjusted gross income shall be determined as provided in section 67(e).

(2) Lower required installment where annualized income installment is less than amount determined under paragraph (1).

(A) In general. In the case of any required installment, if the individual establishes that the annualized income installment is less than the amount determined under paragraph (1)—

(i) the amount of such required installment shall be the annualized income installment, and

(ii) any reduction in a required installment resulting from the application of this subparagraph shall be recaptured by increasing the amount of the next required installment determined under paragraph (1) by the amount of such reduction (and by increasing subsequent required installments to the extent that the reduction has not previously been recaptured under this clause).

(B) Determination of annualized income installment. In the case of any required installment, the annualized income installment is the excess (if any) of—

(i) an amount equal to the applicable percentage of the tax for the taxable year computed by placing on an annualized basis the taxable income, alternative minimum taxable income, and adjusted self-employment income for months in the taxable year ending before the due date for the installment, over

(ii) the aggregate amount of any prior required installments for the taxable year.

(C) Special rules. For purposes of this paragraph—

(i) Annualization. The taxable income, alternative minimum taxable income, and adjusted self-employment income shall be placed on an annualized basis under regulations prescribed by the Secretary.

(ii) Applicable percentage.

In the case of the following required installments:	The applicable percentage is:
1st	22.5
2nd	45
3rd	67.5
4th	90

(iii) Adjusted self-employment income. The term "adjusted self-employment income" means self-employment income (as defined in section 1402(b)); except that section 1402(b) shall be applied by placing wages (within the meaning of section 1402(b)) for months in the taxable year ending before the due date for the installment on an annualized basis consistent with clause (i).

(D) Treatment of subpart F and section 936 income.

(i) In general. Any amounts required to be included in gross income under section 936(h) or 951(a) (and credits properly allocable thereto) shall be taken into account in computing any annualized income installment under subparagraph (B) in a manner similar to the manner under which partnership income inclusions (and credits properly allocable thereto) are taken into account.

(ii) Prior year safe harbor. If a taxpayer elects to have this clause apply to any taxable year—

(I) clause (i) shall not apply, and

(II) for purposes of computing any annualized income installment for such taxable year, the taxpayer shall be treated as having received ratably during such taxable year items of income and credit described in clause (i) in an amount equal to the amount of such items shown on the return of the taxpayer for the preceding taxable year (the second preceding taxable year in the case of the first and second required installments for such taxable year).

(e) Exceptions.

(1) Where tax is small amount. No addition to tax shall be imposed under subsection (a) for any taxable year if the tax shown on the return for such taxable year (or, if no return is filed, the tax), reduced by the credit allowable under section 31, is less than $1,000.

(2) Where no tax liability for preceding taxable year. No addition to tax shall be imposed under subsection (a) for any taxable year if—

(A) the preceding taxable year was a taxable year of 12 months,

(B) the individual did not have any liability for tax for the preceding taxable year, and

(C) the individual was a citizen or resident of the United States throughout the preceding taxable year.

(3) Waiver in certain cases.

(A) In general. No addition to tax shall be imposed under subsection (a) with respect to any underpayment to the extent the Secretary determines that by reason of casualty, disaster, or other unusual circumstances the imposition of such addition to tax would be against equity and good conscience.

(B) Newly retired or disabled individuals. No addition to tax shall be imposed under subsection (a) with respect to any underpayment if the Secretary determines that—

(i) the taxpayer—

(I) retired after having attained age 62, or

(II) became disabled,

in the taxable year for which estimated payments were required to be made or in the taxable year preceding such taxable year, and

(ii) such underpayment was due to reasonable cause and not to willful neglect.

Penalties   Code Sec. 6654(l)(2)(B)(i)

> • *Caution:* Code Sec. 6654(f), following is effective for tax. yrs. before 1/1/2013. For Code Sec. 6654(f) effective for tax yrs begin after 12/31/2012, see below.

(f) Tax computed after application of credits against tax. For purposes of this section, the term "tax" means—
(1) the tax imposed by chapter 1 (other than any increase in such tax by reason of section 143(m)), plus
(2) the tax imposed by chapter 2, minus
(3) the credits against tax provided by part IV of subchapter A of chapter 1, other than the credit against tax provided by section 31 (relating to tax withheld on wages).

> • *Caution:* Code Sec. 6654(f), following, is effective for tax. yrs. begin. after 12/31/2012. For Code Sec. 6654(f) effective for tax. yrs. begin. after 1/1/2013, see above.

(f) Tax computed after application of credits against tax. For purposes of this section, the term "tax" means—
(1) the tax imposed by chapter 1 (other than any increase in such tax by reason of section 143(m)), plus
(2) the tax imposed by chapter 2, plus
(3) the taxes imposed by chapter 2A, minus
(4) the credits against tax provided by part IV of subchapter A of chapter 1, other than the credit against tax provided by section 31 (relating to tax withheld on wages).

(g) Application of section in case of tax withheld on wages.
(1) **In general.** For purposes of applying this section, the amount of the credit allowed under section 31 for the taxable year shall be deemed a payment of estimated tax, and an equal part of such amount shall be deemed paid on each due date for such taxable year, unless the taxpayer establishes the dates on which all amounts were actually withheld, in which case the amounts so withheld shall be deemed payments of estimated tax on the dates on which such amounts were actually withheld.
(2) **Separate application.** The taxpayer may apply paragraph (1) separately with respect to—
(A) wage withholding, and
(B) all other amounts withheld for which credit is allowed under section 31.

(h) Special rule where return filed on or before January 31. If, on or before January 31 of the following taxable year, the taxpayer files a return for the taxable year and pays in full the amount computed on the return as payable, then no addition to tax shall be imposed under subsection (a) with respect to any underpayment of the 4th required installment for the taxable year.

(i) Special rules for farmers and fishermen. For purposes of this section—
(1) **In general.** If an individual is a farmer or fisherman for any taxable year—
(A) there shall be only 1 required installment for the taxable year,
(B) the due date for such installment shall be January 15 of the following taxable year,
(C) the amount of such installment shall be equal to the required annual payment determined under subsection (d)(1)(B) by substituting "66 ⅔ percent" for "90 percent" and without regard to subparagraph (C) of subsection (d)(1), and
(D) subsection (h) shall be applied—
(i) by substituting "March 1" for "January 31", and
(ii) by treating the required installment described in subparagraph (A) of this paragraph as the 4th required installment.
(2) **Farmer or fisherman defined.** An individual is a farmer or fisherman for any taxable year if—
(A) the individual's gross income from farming or fishing (including oyster farming) for the taxable year is at least 66 ⅔ percent of the total gross income from all sources for the taxable year, or
(B) such individual's gross income from farming or fishing (including oyster farming) shown on the return of the individual for the preceding taxable year is at least 66 ⅔ percent of the total gross income from all sources shown on such return.

(j) Special rules for nonresident aliens. In the case of a nonresident alien described in section 6072(c):
(1) **Payable in 3 installments.** There shall be 3 required installments for the taxable year.
(2) **Time for payment of installments.** The due dates for required installments under this subsection shall be determined under the following table:

In the case of the following required installments:	The due date is:
1st	June 15
2nd	September 15
3rd	January 15 of the following taxable year.

(3) **Amount of required installments.**
(A) First required installment. In the case of the first required installment, subsection (d) shall be applied by substituting "50 percent" for "25 percent" in subsection (d)(1)(A)
(B) Determination of applicable percentage. The applicable percentage for purposes of subsection (d)(2) shall be determined under the following table:

In the case of the following required installments:	The applicable percentage is:
1st	45
2nd	67.5
3rd	90.

(k) Fiscal years and short years.
(1) **Fiscal years.** In applying this section to a taxable year beginning on any date other than January 1, there shall be substituted, for the months specified in this section, the months which correspond thereto.
(2) **Short taxable year.** This section shall be applied to taxable years of less than 12 months in accordance with regulations prescribed by the Secretary.

(l) Estates and trusts.
(1) **In general.** Except as otherwise provided in this subsection, this section shall apply to any estate or trust.
(2) **Exception for estates and certain trusts.** With respect to any taxable year ending before the date 2 years after the date of the decedent's death, this section shall not apply to—
(A) the estate of such decedent, or
(B) any trust—
(i) all of which was treated (under subpart E of part I of subchapter J of chapter 1) as owned by the decedent, and

(ii) to which the residue of the decedent's estate will pass under his will (or, if no will is admitted to probate, which is the trust primarily responsible for paying debts, taxes, and expenses of administration).

(3) Exception for charitable trusts and private foundations. This section shall not apply to any trust which is subject to the tax imposed by section 511 or which is a private foundation.

(4) Special rule for annualizations. In the case of any estate or trust to which this section applies, subsection (d)(2)(B)(i)shall be applied by substituting "ending before the date 1 month before the due date for the installment" for "ending before the due date for the installment".

• *Caution:* Code Sec. 6654(m), following, is effective for tax. yrs. begin. before 1/1/2013. For Code Sec. 6654(m) effective for tax. yrs. begin. after 12/31/2012, see below.

(m) Regulations.
The Secretary shall prescribe such regulations as may be necessary to carry out the purposes of this section.

• *Caution:* Code Sec. 6654(m), following, is effective for tax. yrs. begin. after 12/31/2012. For Code Sec. 6654(m) effective for tax. yrs. begin. before 1/1/2013, see above.

(m) Special rule for medicare tax.
For purposes of this section, the tax imposed under section 3101(b)(2) (to the extent not withheld) shall be treated as a tax imposed under chapter 2.

(n) Regulations.
The Secretary shall prescribe such regulations as may be necessary to carry out the purposes of this section.

In 2010, P.L. 111-152, Sec. 1402(a)(2)(A), substituted "the tax under chapter 2, and the tax under chapter 2A" for "and the tax under chapter 2" in subsec. (a) . . . Sec. 1402(a)(2)(B)(i), substituted "plus" for "minus" at the end of para. (f)(2) . . . Sec. 1402(a)(2)(B)(ii), added para. (f)(3) and redesignated para. (f)(3) as (f)(4), effective for tax. yrs. begin after 12/31/2012. . . . Sec. 1402(b)(2), added subsec. (m), and redesignated subsec. (m) as (n), effective with respect to remuneration received, and tax. yrs. begin. after, 12/31/2012.

In 2009, P.L. 111-5, Sec. 1212, added subpara. (d)(1)(D), effective 2/17/2009.

In 1999, P.L. 106-170, Sec. 531(a), amended the table in clause (d)(1)(C)(i), effective for any installment payment for tax. yrs. begin. after 12/31/99.
Prior to amendment, the table in clause (d)(1)(C)(i) read as follows:

"If the preceding taxable year begins in:	The applicable percentage is:
1998	105
1999 or 2000	106
2001	112
2002 or thereafter	110"

In 1998, P.L. 105-277, Sec. 2003(a), amended the table in clause (d)(1)(C)(i), effective for any installment payment for tax. yrs. begin. after 12/31/99.
Prior to amendment, the table in clause (d)(1)(C)(i) read as follows:

"If the preceding taxable year begins in:	The applicable percentage is:
1998, 1999, or 2000	105
2001	112
2002 or thereafter	110"

—P.L. 105-206, Sec. 1(c), of this Act, reads as follows:
"(c) Waiver of estimated tax penalties. No addition to tax shall be made under section 6654 or 6655 of the Internal Revenue Code of 1986 with respect to any underpayment of an installment required to be paid on or before the 30th day after the date of the enactment of this Act to the extent such underpayment was created or increased by any provision of this Act."

In 1997, P.L. 105-34, Sec. 1(d), of this Act provides:
"(d) Waiver of Estimated Tax Penalties. No addition to tax shall be made under section 6654 or 6655 of the Internal Revenue Code of 1986 for any period before January 1, 1998, for any payment the due date of which is before January 16, 1998, with respect to any underpayment attributable to such period to the extent such underpayment was created or increased by any provision of this Act."
—P.L. 105-34, Sec. 1091(a), amended clause (d)(1)(C)(i), effective for any installment payment for tax. yrs. begin. after 12/31/97.
Prior to amendment, clause (d)(1)(C)(i) read as follows:
"(i) In general. If the adjusted gross income shown on the return of the individual for the preceding taxable year exceeds $150,000, clause (ii) of subparagraph (B) shall be applied by substituting '110 percent' for '100 percent'."
—P.L. 105-34, Sec. 1202(a), substituted "$1,000" for "$500" in para. (e)(1), effective for tax. yrs. begin. after 12/31/97.

In 1996, P.L. 104-188, Sec. 1102, of this Act, provides:
"Sec. 1102. Underpayments of estimated tax.
"No addition to the tax shall be made under section 6654 or 6655 of the Internal Revenue Code of 1986 (relating to failure to pay estimated tax) with respect to any underpayment of an installment required to be paid before the date of the enactment of this Act to the extent such underpayment was created or increased by any provision of this title."

In 1994, P.L. 103-465, Sec. 711(b), added subpara. (d)(2)(D), effective for purposes of determining underpayments of estimated tax for tax. yrs. begin. after 12/31/94.

In 1993, P.L. 103-66, Sec. 13001(d), of this Act provides:
"(d) Waiver of estimated tax penalties. No addition to tax shall be made under section 6654 or 6655 of the Internal Revenue Code of 1986 for any period before April 16, 1994 (March 16, 1994, in the case of a corporation), with respect to any underpayment to the extent such underpayment was created or increased by any provision of this chapter."
—P.L. 103-66, Sec. 13214(a), deleted subparas. (d)(1)(C) through (F), and added new subpara. (d)(1)(C) . . . Sec. 13214(b)(1), deleted "and subsection (d)(1)(C)(iii) shall not apply", after "in subsection (d)(1)(A)" in subpara. (j)(3)(A) . . . Sec. 13214(b)(2), substituted "subsection (d)(2)(B)(i)" for "paragraphs (1)(C)(iv) and (2)(B)(i) of subsection (d)" in para. (l)(4), effective for tax. yrs. begin. after 12/31/93.
Prior to deletion, subparas. (d)(1)(C) through (F) read as follows:
"(C) Limitation on use of preceding year's tax.
"(i) In general. In any case to which this subparagraph applies, clause (ii) of subparagraph (B) shall be applied as if it read as follows:
"(ii) the greater of—
"(I) 100 percent of the tax shown on the return of the individual for the preceding taxable year, or
"(II) 90 percent of the tax shown on the return for the current year, determined by taking into account the adjustments set forth in subparagraph (D).'
"(ii) Cases to which subparagraph applies. This subparagraph shall apply if—
"(I) the modified adjusted gross income for the current year exceeds the amount of the adjusted gross income shown on the return of the individual for the preceding taxable year by more than $40,000 ($20,000 in the case of a separate return for the current year by a married individual),
"(II) the adjusted gross income shown on the return for the current year exceeds $75,000 ($37,500 in the case of a married individual filing a separate return), and
"(III) the taxpayer has made a payment of estimated tax (determined without regard to subsection (g) and section 6402(b)) with respect to any of the preceding 3 taxable years (or a penalty has been previously assessed under this section for a failure to pay estimated tax with respect to any of such 3 preceding taxable years).
This subparagraph shall not apply to any taxable year beginning after December 31, 1996.
"(iii) May use preceding year's tax for first installment. This subparagraph shall not apply for purposes of determining the amount of the 1st required installment for any taxable year. Any reduction in an installment by reason of the preceding sentence shall be recaptured by increasing the amount of the 1st succeeding required installment (with respect to which the requirements of clause (iv) are not met) by the amount of such reduction.
"(iv) Annualization exception. This subparagraph shall not apply to any required installment if the individual establishes that the requirements of subclauses (I) and (II) of clause (ii) would not have been satisfied if such subclauses were applied on the basis of—
"(I) the annualized amount of the modified adjusted gross income for months in the current year ending before the due date for the installment determined by assuming that all items referred to in clause (i) of subparagraph (D) accrued ratably during the current year, and
"(II) the annualized amount of the adjusted gross income for months in the current year ending before the due date for the installment.
Any reduction in an installment under the preceding sentence shall be recaptured by increasing the amount of the 1st succeeding required installment (with respect to which the requirements of the preceding sentence are not met) by the amount of such reduction.
"(D) Modified adjusted gross income for current year. For purposes of this paragraph, the term 'modified adjusted gross income' means the amount of the adjusted gross income shown on the return for the current year determined with the following modifications:
"(i) The qualified pass-thru items shown on the return for the preceding taxable year shall be treated as also shown on the return for the current year (and the actual qualified pass-thru items (if any) for the current year shall be disregarded).
"(ii) The amount of any gain from any involuntary conversion (within the meaning of section 1033) which is shown on the return for the current year shall be disregarded.

"(iii) The amount of any gain from the sale or exchange of a principal residence (within the meaning of section 1034) which is shown on the return for the current year shall be disregarded.

"(E) Qualified pass-thru item. For purposes of this paragraph—

"(i) In general. Except as otherwise provided in this subparagraph, the term 'qualified pass-thru item' means any item of income, gain, loss, deduction, or credit attributable to an interest in a partnership or S corporation. Such term shall not include any gain or loss from the disposition of an interest in an entity referred to in the preceding sentence.

"(ii) 10-percent owners and general partners excluded. The term 'qualified pass-thru item' shall not include, with respect to any year, any item attributable to—

"(I) an interest in an S corporation, if at any time during such year the individual was a 10-percent owner in such corporation, or

"(II) an interest in a partnership, if at any time during such year the individual was a 10-percent owner or general partner in such partnership.

"(iii) 10-percent owner. The term '10-percent owner' means—

"(I) in the case of an S corporation, an individual who owns 10 percent or more (by vote or value) of the stock in such corporation, and

"(II) in the case of a partnership, an individual who owns 10 percent or more of the capital interest (or the profits interest) in such partnership.

"(F) Other definitions and special rules. For purposes of this paragraph—

"(i) Current year. The term 'current year' means the taxable year for which the amount of the installment is being determined.

"(ii) Special rule. If no return is filed for the current year, any reference in subparagraph (C) or (D) to an item shown on the return for the current year shall be treated as a reference to the actual amount of such item for such year.

"(iii) Marital status. Marital status shall be determined under section 7703."

In **1991**, P.L. 102-164, Sec. 403(a), added subparas. (d)(1)(C), (D), (E) and (F) . . . Sec. 403(b)(1), amended subpara. (i)(1)(C) . . . Sec. 403(b)(2), added "and subsection (d)(1)(C)(iii) shall not apply" before the period at the end of subpara. (j)(3)(A) . . . Sec. 403(b)(3), substituted "paragraphs (1)(C)(iv) and (2)(B)(i) of subsection (d)" for "subsection (d)(2)(B)(i)", effective for tax. yrs. begin. after 12/31/91.

Prior to amendment, subpara. (i)(1)(C) read as follows:

"(C) the amount of such installment shall be equal to the required annual payment (determined under subsection (d)(1)(B) by substituting '66⅔ percent' for '90 percent', and"

In **1989**, P.L. 101-239, Sec. 7811(j)(5), substituted "this section shall" for "this subsection shall" in para. (l)(1) . . . Sec. 7811(j)(6), added "(or, if no will is admitted to probate, which is the trust primarily responsible for paying debts, taxes, and expenses of administration)" before the comma in clause (1)(2)(B)(ii), effective for tax. yrs. begin. after 12/31/86, except as provided in Sec. 1019(b)(2) of P.L. 100-647 reproduced below.

In **1988**, P.L. 100-647, Sec. 1014(d)(1)(A), and (B) corrected Sec. 1404(a) of P.L. 99-514, so that Sec. 1404(a) of P.L. 99-514 amended Code Sec. 6654(l) as amended by Sec. 1841 of P.L. 99-514, rather than Code Sec. 6654(k).

—P.L. 100-647, Sec. 1014(d)(2), amended subsec. (l), effective for tax. yrs. begin. after 12/31/86, except as provided in Sec. 1019(b)(2) of this Act, which reads:

"(b) Waiver of estimated tax penalties.

No addition to tax shall be made under section 6654 or 6655 of the 1986 Code for any period before April 16, 1989 (March 16, 1989 in the case of a taxpayer subject to section 6655 of the 1986 Code) with respect to any underpayment to the extent such underpayment was created or increased by any provision of this title [title I] or title II."

Prior to amendment, subsec. (l) read as follows:

"(l) Trusts and certain estates.

This section shall apply to—

"(1) any trust, and

"(2) any estate with respect to any taxable year ending 2 or more years after the date of the death of the decedent's death.

—P.L. 100-647, Sec. 4005(g)(5), added '(other than any increase in such tax by reason of section 143(m))" after 'chapter (1)' in para. (f)(1), effective for financing provided, and mortgage certificates issued, after 12/31/90, except as provided in Sec. 4005(h)(3)(B) of this Act reproduced in note following Code Sec. 143.

—P.L. 100-418, Sec. 1941(b)(6)(A), amended para. (f)(3), effective for crude oil removed from premises on or after 8/23/88.

Prior to amendment, para. (f)(3) read as follows:

"(3) the sum of—

"(A) the credits against tax allowed by part IV of subchapter A of chapter 1, other than the credit against tax provided by section 31 (relating to tax withheld on wages), plus

"(B) to the extent allowed under regulations prescribed by the Secretary, any overpayment of the tax imposed by section 4986 (determined without regard to section 4995(a)(4)(B))."

—P.L. 100-360, Sec. 111(e)(2), provides:

"(2) Waiver of estimated tax requirement for years beginning in 1989. In the case of a taxable year beginning in 1989, the premium imposed by section 59B of the Internal Revenue Code of 1986 (as added by this section) shall not be treated as a tax for purposes of applying section 6654 of such Code."

In **1987**, P.L. 100-203, Sec. 10303(a), changed the effective date for amendments made by Sec. 1541 of P.L. 99-514, from effective for tax. yrs. begin. after 12/31/86 to effective for tax. yrs. begin. after 12/31/87.

In **1986**, P.L. 99-514, Sec. 1404(a), [as amended by Sec. 1014(d)(1)(A) and (B) of P.L. 100-647, see above] amended subsec. (l), as amended by Sec. 1841 of this Act, see below, effective for tax. yrs. begin. after 12/31/86.

Prior to amendment, subsec. (l) read as follows:

"(l) Estates and trusts.

"This section shall not apply to any estate or trust."

—P.L. 99-514, Sec. 1511(c)(14), substituted "underpayment" for "applicable annual" in para. (a)(1), effective for purposes of determining interest for periods after 12/31/86.

—P.L. 99-514, Sec. 1541(a), substituted "90 percent" for "80 percent" each place it appeared in clause (d)(1)(B)(i) . . . Sec. 1541(b)(1)(A), substituted "22.5" for "20" in clause (d)(2)(C)(ii) . . . Sec. 1541(b)(1)(B), substituted "45" for "40" in clause (d)(2)(C)(ii) . . . Sec. 1541(b)(1)(C), substituted "67.5" for "60" in clause (d)(2)(C)(ii) . . . Sec. 1541(b)(1)(D), substituted "90" for "80" in clause (d)(2)(C)(ii) . . . Sec. 1541(b)(2), substituted "90 percent" for "80 percent" in subpara. (i)(1)(C) . . . Sec. 1541(b)(3)(A), substituted "45" for "40" in subpara. (j)(3)(B) [as added by Sec. 1841 of this Act, see below] . . . Sec. 1541(b)(3)(B), substituted "67.5" for "60" in subpara. (j)(3)(B) . . . Sec. 1541(b)(3)(C), substituted "90" for "80" in subpara. (j)(3)(B), [amendments made by Sec. 1541(b)(3) are inoperative; already made by Sec. 1841 of this Act, see below] effective for tax. yrs. begin. after 12/31/87 [as amended by Sec. 10303(a) of P.L. 100-203, see above].

—P.L. 99-514, Sec. 1543, provides:

"Sec. 1543. Waiver of estimated penalties for 1986 underpayments attributable to this act.

"No addition to tax shall be made under section 6654 or 6655 of the Internal Revenue Code of 1986 (relating to failure to pay estimated tax) for any period before April 16, 1987 (March 16, 1987, in the case of a taxpayer subject to section 6655 of such Code), with respect to any underpayment, to the extent such underpayment was created or increased by any provision of this Act."

—P.L. 99-514, Sec. 1841, redesignated subsecs. (j), (k), and (l) as (k), (l), and (m), respectively, and added new subsec. (j), effective for tax. yrs. begin. after 12/31/84, with special rules provided by Secs. 414(a)(2) and 413 of P.L. 98-369, see below.

—P.L. 99-514, Sec. 1879(a), provides:

"(a) Waiver of estimated tax penalties. —

"No addition to tax shall be made under section 6654 or 6655 of the Internal Revenue Code of 1954 (relating to failure to pay estimated income tax) for any period before April 16, 1985 (March 16, 1985 in the case of a taxpayer subject to section 6655 of such Code), with respect to any underpayment, to the extent that such underpayment was created or increased by any provision of the Tax Reform Act of 1984."

In **1984**, P.L. 98-369, Sec. 411, amended Code Sec. 6654, effective for tax. yrs. begin. after 12/31/84. Sec. 414(a)(2) and 413 of the Act provide:

"(2) Waiver authority. The provisions of paragraph (3) of section 6654(e) of the Internal Revenue Code of 1954 (as amended by section 411) shall also apply with respect to underpayments for taxable years beginning in 1984."

"Sec. 413. Crediting of income tax overpayment against estimated tax liability.

"The application of the Internal Revenue Code of 1954 with respect to the crediting of a prior year overpayment of income tax against the estimated tax shall be determined—

"(1) without regard to Revenue Ruling 83-111 (and without regard to any other regulation, ruling, or decision reaching the same result as, or a result similar to, the result set forth in such Revenue Ruling); and

"(2) with full regard to the rules (including Revenue Ruling 77-475) before Revenue Ruling 83-111."

Prior to amendment, Code Sec. 6654 read as follows:

"Sec. 6654. Failure by individual to pay estimated income tax.

"(a) Addition to the tax.

"In the case of any underpayment of estimated tax by an individual, except as provided in subsection (d), there shall be added to the tax under chapter 1 and the tax under chapter 2 for the taxable year an amount determined at an annual rate established under section 6621 upon the amount of the underpayment (determined under subsection (b)) for the period of the underpayment (determined under subsection (c)).

"(b) Amount of underpayment.

"For purposes of subsection (a), the amount of the underpayment shall be the excess of—

"(1) The amount of the installment which would be required to be paid if the estimated tax were equal to 80 percent (66⅔ percent in the case of individuals referred to in section 6073(b), relating to income from farming or fishing) of the tax shown on the return for the taxable year or, if no return was filed, 80 percent (66⅔ percent in the case of individuals referred to in section 6073(b), relating to income from farming or fishing) of the tax for such year, over

"(2) The amount, if any, of the installment paid on or before the last date prescribed for such payment.

"(c) Period of underpayment.

"The period of the underpayment shall run from the date the installment was required to be paid to whichever of the following dates is the earlier—

"(1) The 15th day of the fourth month following the close of the taxable year.

"(2) With respect to any portion of the underpayment, the date on which such portion is paid. For purposes of this paragraph, a payment of estimated tax on any installment date shall be considered a payment of any previous underpayment only to the extent such payment exceeds the amount of the installment determined under subsection (b)(1) for such installment date.

"(d) Exception.

"Notwithstanding the provisions of the preceding subsections the addition to the tax with respect to any underpayment of any installment shall not be imposed if the total amount of all payments of estimated tax made on or before the last date prescribed for the payment of such installment equals or exceeds the amount which would have been required to be paid on or before such date if the estimated tax were whichever of the following is the least —

"(1) The tax shown on the return of the individual for the preceding taxable year, if a return showing a liability for tax was filed by the individual for the preceding taxable year and such preceding year was a taxable year of 12 months.

"(2) An amount equal to 80 percent (66⅔ percent in the case of individuals referred to in section 6073(b), relating to income from farming or fishing) of the tax for the taxable year computed by placing on an annualized basis the taxable income for the months in the taxable year ending before the month in which the installment is required to be paid and by taking into account the adjusted self-employment income (if the net earnings from self-employment (as defined in section 1402(a)) for the taxable year equal or exceed $400). For purposes of this paragraph —

"(A) The taxable income shall be placed on an annualized basis under regulations prescribed by the Secretary.

"(B) The term 'adjusted self-employment income' means —

"(i) the net earnings from self-employment (as defined in section 1402(a)) for the months in the taxable year ending before the month in which the installment is required to be paid, but not more than

"(ii) the excess of (I) an amount equal to the contribution and benefit base (as determined under section 230 of the Social Security Act) which is effective for the calendar year in which the taxable year begins, over (II) the amount determined by placing the wages (within the meaning of section 1402(b)) for the months in the taxable year ending before the month in which the installment is required to be paid on an annualized basis in a manner consistent with clauses (i) and (ii) of subparagraph (A).

"(3) An amount equal to 90 percent of the tax computed, at the rates applicable year, on the basis of the actual taxable income and the actual self-employment income for the months in the taxable year ending before the month in which the installment is required to be paid as if such months constituted the taxable year.

"(4) An amount equal to the tax computed, at the rates applicable to the taxable year, on the basis of the taxpayer's status with respect to personal exemptions under section 151 for the taxable year, but otherwise on the basis of the facts shown on his return for, and the law applicable to, the preceding taxable year.

"(e) Application of section in case of tax withheld on wages.

"For purposes of applying this section —

"(1) The estimated tax shall be computed without any reduction for the amount which the individual estimates as his credit under section 31 (relating to tax withheld at source on wages), and

"(2) the amount of the credit allowed under section 31 for the taxable year shall be deemed a payment of estimated tax, and an equal part of such amount shall be deemed paid on each installment date (determined under section 6153) for such taxable year, unless the taxpayer establishes the dates on which all amounts were actually withheld, in which case the amounts so withheld shall be deemed payments of estimated tax on the dates on which such amounts were actually withheld.

"(f) Exception where tax is small amount.

"(1) In general. No addition to tax shall be imposed under subsection (a) for any taxable year if the tax shown on the return for such taxable year (or, if no return is filed, the tax), reduced by the credit allowable under section 31, is less than the amount determined under the following table:

"In the case of taxable years beginning in:	The amount is:
1981	$ 100
1982	200
1983	300
1984	400
1985 and thereafter	500.

"(2) Special rule. For purposes of subsection (b), the amount of any installment required to be paid shall be determined without regard to subsection (b) of section 6015.

"(g) Tax computed after application of credits against tax.

"For purposes of subsections (b), (d) [,] (f), and (h) the term tax means —

"(1) the tax imposed by this chapter 1 (other than by section 55), plus

"(2) the tax imposed by chapter 2, minus

"(3) the sum of —

"(A) the credits against tax allowed by part IV of subchapter A of chapter 1, other than the credit against tax provided by section 31 (relating to tax withheld on wages), plus

"(B) to the extent allowed under regulations prescribed by the Secretary, any overpayment of the tax imposed by section 4986 (determined without regard to section 4995(a)(4)(B)).

"(h) Exception where no tax liability for preceding taxable year

"No addition to tax shall be imposed under subsection (a) for any taxable year if —

"(1) the individual did not have any liability for tax for the preceding taxable year,

"(2) the preceding taxable year was a taxable year of 12 months, and

"(3) the individual was a citizen or resident of the United States throughout the preceding taxable year.

"(i) Short taxable year.

"The application of this section to taxable years of less than 12 months shall be in accordance with regulations prescribed by the Secretary."

In **1983**, P.L. 97-448, Sec. 106(a)(4)(C), amended subpara. (g)(3)(B), effective 1/1/82. [See Sec. 201(j)(3) of this Act below.]

Prior to amendment, subpara. (g)(3)(B) read as follows:

"(B) to the extent allowed under regulations prescribed by the Secretary, any amount which is treated under section 6429 as an overpayment of the tax imposed by section 4986."

—P.L. 97-448, Sec. 107(c)(1), substituted ", reduced by the credit allowable under section 31, is less than" for "is less than" in para. (f)(1), effective for estimated tax for tax. yrs. begin. after 12/31/80.

—P.L. 97-448, Sec. 201(j)(3), amended subpara. (g)(3)(B), for periods after 2/29/80.

Prior to amendment, subpara. (g)(3)(B) read as follows:

"(B) to the extent allowed under regulations prescribed by the Secretary, any amount which is treated under section 6429 or 6430 as an overpayment of the tax imposed by section 4986."

—P.L. 97-448, Sec. 306(a)(1)(A)(i), redesignated the second Sec. 201(c) of P.L. 97-248 as Sec. 201(d) of P.L. 97-248, see below.

In **1982**, P.L. 97-248, Sec. 201(d)(7), deleted "or 56" after "section 55" in para. (g)(1), effective for tax. yrs. begin. after 12/31/82.

—P.L. 97-248, Sec. 328(a)(1), redesignated subsec. (h) as subsec. (i) and added new subsec. (h) . . . Sec. 328(a)(2), substituted "[,] (f), and (h)" for "and (f)" in subsec. (g), effective for tax. yrs. begin. after 12/31/82.

In **1981**, P.L. 97-34, Sec. 601(a)(6)(A), amended para. (f)(3) [redesignated para. (g)(3) by Sec. 725(b) of this Act], effective 1/1/80.

Prior to amendment, para. (f)(3) read as follows:

"(3) the credits against tax allowed by part IV of subchapter A of chapter 1, other than the credit against tax provided by section 31 (relating to tax withheld on wages)."

—P.L. 97-34, Sec. 725(b), redesignated subsecs. (f) and (g) as subsecs. (g) and (h) and added new subsec. (f) . . . Sec. 725(c)(5), substituted "subsections (b), (d) and (f)" for "subsections (b) and (d)" in subsec. (g) (as redesignated), effective for estimated tax. yrs. begin. after 12/31/80.

In **1978**, P.L. 95-600, Sec. 421(e)(9), substituted "section 55 or 56" for "section 56" in para. (f)(1), for tax. yrs. begin. after 12/31/78.

In **1977**, P.L. 95-30, Sec. 102(b)(16), amended subpara. (d)(2)(A), for tax. yrs. begin. after '76.

Prior to amendment, subpara. (d)(2)(A) read as follows:

"(A) The taxable income shall be placed on an annualized basis by —

"(i) multiplying by 12 (or, in the case of a taxable year of less than 12 months, the number of months in the taxable year) the taxable income (computed without deduction of personal exemptions) for the months in the taxable year ending before the month in which the installment is required to be paid,

"(ii) dividing the resulting amount by the number of months in the taxable year ending before the month in which such installment date falls, and

"(iii) deducting from such amount the deductions for personal exemptions allowable for the taxable year (such personal exemptions being determined as of the last date prescribed for payment of the installment)."

—P.L. 95-30, Sec. 303, provided as follows with respect to underpayments of estimated tax.

"Sec. 303. Underpayments of estimated tax.

"No addition to the tax shall be made under section 6654 or 6655 of the Internal Revenue Code of 1954 (relating to failure to pay estimated income tax) for any period before April 16, 1977 (March 16, 1977, in the case of a taxpayer subject to section 6655), with respect to any underpayment, to the extent that such underpayment was created or increased by any provision of the Tax Reform Act of 1976."

In **1976**, P.L. 94-455, Sec. 1906(a)(35), deleted subsec. (h), effective 2/1/77.

Prior to amendment, subsec. (h) read as follows:

"(h) Applicability.

"This section shall apply only with respect to taxable years beginning after December 31, 1954; and section 294(d) of the Internal Revenue Code of 1939 shall continue in force with respect to taxable years beginning before January 1, 1955."

—P.L. 94-455, Sec. 1906(b)(13)(A), substituted "Secretary" for "Secretary or his delegate" in subsec. (g), effective 2/1/77.

In **1975**, P.L. 93-625, Sec. 7(c), substituted "an annual rate established under section 6621" for "the rate of 6 percent per annum" in subsec. (a), effective with respect to amounts outstanding on or arising after 7/1/75.

In **1973**, P.L. 93-66, Sec. 203(b)(7), substituted "$12,600" for "$12,000" in subpara. (d)(2)(B)(ii), effective for tax. yrs. begin. after 1972 . . . Sec. 203(d), amended Sec. 203(b)(7)(C) of P.L. 92-336 (see below) by substituting "$12,600" for "$12,000".

—P.L. 93-233, Sec. 5(b)(7), substituted "$13,200" for "$12,600" in clause. (d)(2)(B)(ii), effective for tax. yrs. begin. after 1973 . . . Sec. 5(d), amended Sec. 203(b)(7)(C) of P.L. 92-336 (see below) by substituting "$13,200" for "$12,600".

In **1972**, P.L. 92-336, Sec. 203(b)(7), substituted "$10,800" for "$9,000", in subpara. (d)(2)(B)(ii), effective for tax. yrs. begin. after 1972 . . . substituted "$12,000" [$12,600 as amended in '73 by Sec. 203(d) of P.L. 93-66, see above] for "$10,800", in subpara. (d)(2)(B)(ii), effective for tax. yrs. begin. after 1973 . . . substituted "(I) an amount equal to the contribution and benefit base (as determined under section 230 of the Social Security Act) which is effective for the calendar year in which the taxable year begins, over (II)" for "$12,000 [$12,600 as amended in '73 by Sec. 203(d) of P.L. 93-66, see above and $13,200 as amended in '73 by Sec. 5(d) of P.L. 93-233, see above] over", in subpara. (d)(2)(B)(ii), effective for tax. yrs. begin. after 1974.

In **1971**, P.L. 92-178, Sec. 207, of this Act, provided as follows:

"Sec. 207. Waiver of Penalty for Underpayment of 1971 Estimated Income Tax.

"(a) Waiver of Penalty.

"Notwithstanding any other provision of law, section 6654(a) of the Internal Revenue Code of 1954 (relating to addition to tax for failure by individual to pay estimated income tax) shall not apply to any taxable year beginning after December 31, 1970, and ending before January 1, 1972—

"(1) if gross income for the taxable year does not exceed $10,000 in the case of—

"(A) a single individual other than a head of a household (as defined in section 2(b) of such Code) or a surviving spouse (as defined in section 2(a) of such Code); or

"(B) a married individual not entitled under section 6013 of such Code to file a joint return for the taxable year; or

"(2) if gross income for the taxable year does not exceed $20,000 in the case of—

"(A) a head of a household (as defined in section 2(b) of such Code); or

"(B) a surviving spouse (as defined in section 2(a) of such Code); or

"(3) in the case of a married individual entitled under section 6013 of such Code to file a joint return for the taxable year, if the aggregate gross income of such individual and his spouse for the taxable year does not exceed $20,000.

"(b) Limitation.

"Subsection (a) shall not apply if the taxpayer has income from sources other than wages (as defined in section 3401(a) of such Code) in excess of $200 for the taxable year ($400 in the case of a husband and wife entitled to file a joint return under section 6013 of such Code for the taxable year)."

—P.L. 92-5, Sec. 203(b)(7), substituted "$9,000" for "$6,600" in subpara. (d)(2)(B)(ii), effective for tax. yrs. begin. after 1971.

In 1969, P.L. 91-172, Sec. 301(b)(13), inserted "(other than by section 56)" after "chapter 1" in subsec. (f)(1), for tax. yrs. end. after 12/31/69.

In 1966, P.L. 89-368, Sec. 102(b)(1), added "and the tax under chapter 2" in subsec. (a)...Sec. 103(a), substituted "80 percent" for "70 percent" in subsecs. (b) and (d)...Sec. 102(b)(2), amended subsec. (d)...Sec. 102(c)(3), amended subsec. (f), effective for tax. yrs. begin. after 12/31/66.

Prior to amendment, subsecs. (d) and (f) read as follows:

"(d) Exception.

"Notwithstanding the provisions of the preceding subsections, the addition to the tax with respect to any underpayment of any installment shall not be imposed if the total amount of all payments of estimated tax made on or before the last date prescribed for the payment of such installment equals or exceeds whichever of the following is the lesser—

"(1) The amount which would have been required to be paid on or before such date if the estimated tax were whichever of the following is the least—

"(A) The tax shown on the return of the individual for the preceding taxable year, if a return showing a liability for tax was filed by the individual for the preceding taxable year and such preceding taxable year was a taxable year of 12 months, or

"(B) An amount equal to the tax computed, at the rates applicable to the taxable year, on the basis of the taxpayer's status with respect to personal exemptions under section 151 for the taxable year, but otherwise on the basis of the facts shown on his return for, and the law applicable to, the preceding taxable year, or

"(C) An amount equal to 70 percent (66⅔ percent in the case of individuals referred to in section 6073(b), relating to income from farming or fishing) of the tax for the taxable year computed by placing on an annualized basis the taxable income for the months in the taxable year ending before the month in which the installment is required to be paid. For purposes of this subparagraph, the taxable income shall be placed on an annualized basis by—

"(i) multiplying by 12 (or, in the case of a taxable year of less than 12 months, the number of months in the taxable year) the taxable income (computed without deduction of personal exemptions) for the months in the taxable year ending before the month in which the installment is required to be paid,

"(ii) dividing the resulting amount by the number of months in the taxable year ending before the month in which such installment date falls, and

"(iii) deducting from such amount the deductions for personal exemptions allowable for the taxable year (such personal exemptions being determined as of the last date prescribed for payment of the installment); or

"(2) An amount equal to 90 percent of the tax computed, at the rates applicable to the taxable year, on the basis of the actual taxable income for the months in the taxable year ending before the month in which the installment is required to be paid."

"(f) Tax computed after application of credits against tax.

"For purposes of subsections (b) and (d), the term 'tax' means the tax imposed by chapter 1 reduced by the credits against tax allowed by part IV of subchapter A of chapter 1, other than the credit against tax provided by section 31 (relating to tax withheld on wages)."

In 1962, P.L. 87-682, Sec. 1(a)(4), inserted "or fishing" after "from farming" in subsec. (b) and subpara. (d)(1)(C) for tax. yrs. begin. after '62.

Sec. 6655. Failure by corporation to pay estimated income tax.

(a) Addition to tax.

Except as otherwise provided in this section, in the case of any underpayment of estimated tax by a corporation, there shall be added to the tax under chapter 1 for the taxable year an amount determined by applying—

(1) the underpayment rate established under section 6621,

(2) to the amount of the underpayment,

(3) for the period of the underpayment.

(b) Amount of underpayment; period of underpayment.

For purposes of subsection (a)—

(1) Amount. The amount of the underpayment shall be the excess of—

(A) the required installment, over

(B) the amount (if any) of the installment paid on or before the due date for the installment.

(2) Period of underpayment. The period of the underpayment shall run from the due date for the installment to whichever of the following dates is the earlier—

(A) the 15th day of the 3rd month following the close of the taxable year, or

(B) with respect to any portion of the underpayment, the date on which such portion is paid.

(3) Order of crediting payments. For purposes of paragraph (2)(B), a payment of estimated tax shall be credited against unpaid required installments in the order in which such installments are required to be paid.

(c) Number of required installments; due dates.

For purposes of this section—

(1) Payable in 4 installments. There shall be 4 required installments for each taxable year.

(2) Time for payment of installments.

In the case of the following required installments:	The due date is:
1st	April 15
2nd	June 15
3rd	September 15
4th	December 15

(d) Amount of required installments.

For purposes of this section—

(1) Amount.

(A) In general. Except as otherwise provided in this section, the amount of any required installment shall be 25 percent of the required annual payment.

(B) Required annual payment. Except as otherwise provided in this subsection, the term "required annual payment" means the lesser of—

(i) 100 percent of the tax shown on the return for the taxable year (or, if no return is filed, 100 percent of the tax for such year), or

(ii) 100 percent of the tax shown on the return of the corporation for the preceding taxable year.

Clause (ii) shall not apply if the preceding taxable year was not a taxable year of 12 months, or the corporation did not file a return for such preceding taxable year showing a liability for tax.

(2) Large corporations required to pay 100 percent of current year tax.

(A) In general. Except as provided in subparagraph (B), clause (ii) of paragraph (1)(B) shall not apply in the case of a large corporation.

(B) May use last year's tax for 1st installment. Subparagraph (A) shall not apply for purposes of determining the amount of the 1st required installment for any taxable year. Any reduction in such 1st installment by reason of the preceding sentence shall be recaptured by increasing the amount of the next required installment determined under paragraph (1) by the amount of such reduction.

(e) Lower required installment where annualized income installment or adjusted seasonal installment is less than amount determined under Subsection (d).

(1) In general. In the case of any required installment, if the corporation establishes that the annualized income installment or the adjusted seasonal installment is less than the amount determined under subsection (d)(1) (as modified by paragraphs (2) and (3) of subsection (d))

(A) the amount of such required installment shall be the annualized income installment (or, if lesser, the adjusted seasonal installment), and

(B) any reduction in a required installment resulting from the application of this paragraph shall be recaptured by increasing the amount of the next required installment determined under subsection (d)(1) (as so modified) by the amount of such reduction (and by increasing subsequent required installments to the extent that the reduction has not previously been recaptured under this subparagraph).

(2) Determination of annualized income installment.

(A) In general. In the case of any required installment, the annualized income installment is the excess (if any) of—

(i) an amount equal to the applicable percentage of the tax for the taxable year computed by placing on an annualized basis the taxable income, alternative minimum taxable income, and modified alternative minimum taxable income—

(I) for the first 3 months of the taxable year, in the case of the 1st required installment,

(II) for the first 3 months of the taxable year, in the case of the 2nd required installment,

(III) for the first 6 months of the taxable year in the case of the 3rd required installment, and

(IV) for the first 9 months of the taxable year, in the case of the 4th required installment, over

(ii) the aggregate amount of any prior required installments for the taxable year.

(B) Special rules. For purposes of this paragraph—

(i) Annualization. The taxable income, alternative minimum taxable income, and modified alternative minimum taxable income shall be placed on an annualized basis under regulations prescribed by the Secretary.

(ii) Applicable percentage.

In the case of the following required installments:	The applicable percentage is:
1st	25
2nd	50
3rd	75
4th	100

(iii) Modified alternative minimum taxable income. The term "modified alternative minimum taxable income" has the meaning given to such term by section 59A(b).

(C) Election for different annualization periods.

(i) If the taxpayer makes an election under this clause—

(I) subclause (I) of subparagraph (A)(i) shall be applied by substituting "2 months" for "3 months",

(II) subclause (II) of subparagraph (A)(i) shall be applied by substituting "4 months" for "3 months",

(III) subclause (III) of subparagraph (A)(i) shall be applied by substituting "7 months" for "6 months", and

(IV) subclause (IV) of subparagraph (A)(i) shall be applied by substituting "10 months" for "9 months".

(ii) If the taxpayer makes an election under this clause—

(I) subclause (II) of subparagraph (A)(i) shall be applied by substituting "5 months" for "3 months",

(II) subclause (III) of subparagraph (A)(i) shall be applied by substituting "8 months" for "6 months", and

(III) subclause (IV) of subparagraph (A)(i) shall be applied by substituting "11 months" for "9 months".

(iii) An election under clause (i) or (ii) shall apply to the taxable year for which made and such an election shall be effective only if made on or before the date required for the payment of the first required installment for such taxable year.

(3) Determination of adjusted seasonal installment.

(A) In general. In the case of any required installment, the amount of the adjusted seasonal installment is the excess (if any) of—

(i) 100 percent of the amount determined under subparagraph (C), over

(ii) the aggregate amount of all prior required installments for the taxable year.

(B) Limitation on application of paragraph. This paragraph shall apply only if the base period percentage for any 6 consecutive months of the taxable year equals or exceeds 70 percent.

(C) Determination of amount. The amount determined under this subparagraph for any installment shall be determined in the following manner—

(i) take the taxable income for all months during the taxable year preceding the filing month,

(ii) divide such amount by the base period percentage for all months during the taxable year preceding the filing month,

(iii) determine the tax on the amount determined under clause (ii), and

(iv) multiply the tax computed under clause (iii) by the base period percentage for the filing month and all months during the taxable year preceding the filing month.

(D) Definitions and special rules. For purposes of this paragraph—

(i) Base period percentage. The base period percentage for any period of months shall be the average percent which the taxable income for the corresponding months in each of the 3 preceding taxable years bears to the taxable income for the 3 preceding taxable years.

(ii) Filing month. The term "filing month" means the month in which the installment is required to be paid.

(iii) Reorganization, etc. The Secretary may by regulations provide for the determination of the base period percentage in the case of reorganizations, new corporations, and other similar circumstances.

(4) Treatment of subpart F and section 936 income.

(A) In general. Any amounts required to be included in gross income under section 936(h) or 951(a) (and credits properly allocable thereto) shall be taken into account in computing any annualized income installment under paragraph (2) in a manner similar to the manner under which partnership income inclusions (and credits properly allocable thereto) are taken into account.

(B) Prior year safe harbor.

(i) In general. If a taxpayer elects to have this subparagraph apply for any taxable year—

(I) subparagraph (A) shall not apply, and

(II) for purposes of computing any annualized income installment for such taxable year, the taxpayer shall be treated as having received ratably during such taxable year items of income and credit described in subparagraph (A) in an amount equal to 115 percent of the amount of such items shown on the return of the taxpayer for the preceding taxable year (the second preceding taxable year in the case of the first and second required installments for such taxable year).

(ii) Special rule for noncontrolling shareholder.

(I) In general. If a taxpayer making the election under clause (i) is a noncontrolling shareholder of a corporation, clause (i)(II) shall be applied with respect to items of such corporation by substituting "100 percent" for "115 percent".

(II) Noncontrolling shareholder. For purposes of subclause (I), the term "noncontrolling shareholder" means, with respect to any corporation, a shareholder which (as of the beginning of the taxable year for which the installment is being made) does not own (within the meaning of section 958(a)), and is not treated as owning (within the meaning of section 958(b)), more than 50 percent (by vote or value) of the stock in the corporation.

(5) Treatment of certain REIT dividends.

(A) In general. Any dividend received from a closely held real estate investment trust by any person which owns (after application of subsection (d)(5) of section 856) 10 percent or more (by vote or value) of the stock or beneficial interests in the trust shall be taken into account in computing annualized income installments under paragraph (2) in a manner similar to the manner under which partnership income inclusions are taken into account.

(B) Closely held REIT. For purposes of subparagraph (A), the term "closely held real estate investment trust" means a real estate investment trust with respect to which 5 or fewer persons own (after application of subsection (d)(5) of section 856) 50 percent or more (by vote or value) of the stock or beneficial interests in the trust.

(f) Exception where tax is small amount.

No addition to tax shall be imposed under subsection (a) for any taxable year if the tax shown on the return for such taxable year (or, if no return is filed, the tax) is less than $500.

(g) Definitions and special rules.

(1) Tax. For purposes of this section, the term "tax" means the excess of—

(A) the sum of—

(i) the tax imposed by section 11 or 1201(a), or subchapter L of chapter 1, whichever applies,

(ii) the tax imposed by section 55,

(iii) the tax imposed by section 59A, plus

(iv) the tax imposed by section 887, over

(B) the credits against tax provided by part IV of subchapter A of chapter 1.

For purposes of the preceding sentence, in the case of a foreign corporation subject to taxation under section 11 or 1201(a), or under subchapter L of chapter 1, the tax imposed by section 881 shall be treated as a tax imposed by section 11.

(2) Large corporation.

(A) In general. For purposes of this section, the term "large corporation" means any corporation if such corporation (or any predecessor corporation) had taxable income of $1,000,000 or more for any taxable year during the testing period.

(B) Rules for applying subparagraph (A).

(i) Testing period. For purposes of subparagraph (A), the term "testing period" means the 3 taxable years immediately preceding the taxable year involved.

(ii) Members of controlled group. For purposes of applying subparagraph (A) to any taxable year in the testing period with respect to corporations which are component members of a controlled group of corporations for such taxable year, the $1,000,000 amount specified in subparagraph (A) shall be divided among such members under rules similar to the rules of section 1561.

(iii) Certain carrybacks and carryovers not taken into account. For purposes of subparagraph (A), taxable income shall be determined without regard to any amount carried to the taxable year under section 172 or 1212(a).

(3) Certain tax-exempt organizations. For purposes of this section—

(A) Any organization subject to the tax imposed by section 511, and any private foundation, shall be treated as a corporation subject to tax under section 11.

(B) Any tax imposed by section 511, and any tax imposed by section 1 or 4940 on a private foundation, shall be treated as a tax imposed by section 11.

(C) Any reference to taxable income shall be treated as including a reference to unrelated business taxable income or net investment income (as the case may be).

In the case of any organization described in subparagraph (A), subsection (b)(2)(A) shall be applied by substituting "5th month" for "3rd month", subsection (e)(2)(A) shall be applied by substituting "2 months" for "3 months" in clause (i)(I), the election under clause (i) of subsection (e)(2)(C) may be made separately for each installment, and clause (ii) of subsection (e)(2)(C) shall not apply. In the case of a private foundation, subsection (c)(2) shall be applied by substituting "May 15" for "April 15".

(4) Application of section to certain taxes imposed on S corporations. In the case of an S corporation, for purposes of this section—

(A) The following taxes shall be treated as imposed by section 11:

(i) The tax imposed by section 1374(a) (or the corresponding provisions of prior law).

(ii) The tax imposed by section 1375(a).

(iii) Any tax for which the S corporation is liable by reason of section 1371(d)(2).

(B) Paragraph (2) of subsection (d) shall not apply.

(C) Clause (ii) of subsection (d)(1)(B) shall be applied as if it read as follows:

"(ii) the sum of—

"(I) the amount determined under clause (i) by only taking into account the taxes referred to in clauses (i) and (iii) of subsection (g)(4)(A), and

"(II) 100 percent of the tax imposed by section 1375(a) which was shown on the return of the corporation for the preceding taxable year."

(D) The requirement in the last sentence of subsection (d)(1)(B) that the return for the preceding taxable year show a liability for tax shall not apply.

(E) Any reference in subsection (e) to taxable income shall be treated as including a reference to the net recognized built-in gain or the excess passive income (as the case may be).

(h) Excessive adjustment under section 6425.

(1) **Addition to tax.** If the amount of an adjustment under section 6425 made before the 15th day of the 3rd month following the close of the taxable year is excessive, there shall be added to the tax under chapter 1 for the taxable year an amount determined at the underpayment rate established under section 6621 upon the excessive amount from the date on which the credit is allowed or the refund is paid to such 15th day.

(2) **Excessive amount.** For purposes of paragraph (1), the excessive amount is equal to the amount of the adjustment or (if smaller) the amount by which—

(A) the income tax liability (as defined in section 6425(c)) for the taxable year as shown on the return for the taxable year, exceeds

(B) the estimated income tax paid during the taxable year, reduced by the amount of the adjustment.

(i) Fiscal years and short years.

(1) **Fiscal years.** In applying this section to a taxable year beginning on any date other than January 1, there shall be substituted, for the months specified in this section, the months which correspond thereto.

(2) **Short taxable year.** This section shall be applied to taxable years of less than 12 months in accordance with regulations prescribed by the Secretary.

(j) Regulations.

The Secretary shall prescribe such regulations as may be necessary to carry out the purposes of this section.

In **2010**, P.L. 111-344, Sec. 10002, substituted "163.75" for "159.25" in Sec. 561(2) of P.L. 111-147 [see below]

—P.L. 111-240, Sec. 2131, substituted "159.25" for "123.25" in Sec. 561(2) of P.L. 111-147 [see below]

—P.L. 111-237, Sec. 4(a), substituted "123.25" for "123" in Sec. 561(2) of P.L. 111-147 [see below]

—P.L. 111-227, Sec. 4002, substituted "123" for "122.50" in Sec. 561(2) of P.L. 111-147 [see below]

—P.L. 111-210, Sec. 3, substituted "122.50" for "122.25" in Sec. 561(2) of P.L. 111-147 [see below]

—P.L. 111-171, Sec. 12(a), substituted "135.50" for "134.75" in Sec. 202(b)(1) of P.L. 111-42 [see below]

—P.L. 111-171, Sec. 12(b), substituted "122.25" for "121.5" in Sec. 561(2) of P.L. 111-147 [see below]

—P.L. 111-152, Sec. 1410, of this Act, reads as follows:

" Sec. 1410. Time for Payment of Corporate Estimated Taxes.

"The percentage under paragraph (1) of section 202(b) of the Corporate Estimated Tax Shift Act of 2009 in effect on the date of the enactment of this Act is increased by 15.75 percentage points.

—P.L. 111-147, Sec. 561, of this Act [as amended by Sec. 12(b) of P.L. 111-171, Sec. 3 of P.L. 111-210, Sec. 4002 of P.L. 111-227, Sec. 4(a) of P.L. 111-237, Sec. 2131 of P.L. 111-240, and Sec. 10002 of P.L. 111-344, see above], reads as follows:

"Sec. 561. Time for Payment of Corporate Estimated Taxes.

"Notwithstanding section 6655 of the Internal Revenue Code of 1986, in the case of a corporation with assets of not less than $1,000,000,000 (determined as of the end of the preceding taxable year)—

"(1) the percentage under paragraph (1) of section 202(b) of the Corporate Estimated Tax Shift Act of 2009 [P.L. 111-42] in effect on the date of the enactment of this Act is increased by 23 percentage points,

"(2) the amount of any required installment of corporate estimated tax which is otherwise due in July, August, or September of 2015 shall be 163.75 percent of such amount,

"(3) the amount of any required installment of corporate estimated tax which is otherwise due in July, August, or September of 2019 shall be 106.5 percent of such amount, and

"(4) the amount of the next required installment after an installment referred to in paragraph (2) or (3) shall be appropriately reduced to reflect the amount of the increase by reason of such paragraph."

In **2009**, P.L. 111-124, Sec. 4, which affects the interest rate (as previously affected by Sec. 18, P.L. 111-92, see below) in Sec. 202(b)(1), P.L. 111-42 (see below), reads as follows:

"Sec. 4. Time for Payment of Corporate Estimated Taxes.

"The percentage under paragraph (1) of section 202(b) of the Corporate Estimated Tax Shift Act of 2009 in effect on the date of the enactment of this Act is increased by 1.5 percentage points."

—P.L. 111-92, Sec. 18, which affects the interest rate provided in Sec. 202(b)(1), P.L. 111-42, reproduced below:

"Sec. 18. Time for Payment of Corporate Estimated Taxes. The percentage under paragraph (1) of section 202(b) of the Corporate Estimated Tax Shift Act of 2009 [P.L. 111-42, see below] in effect on the date of the enactment of this Act is increased by 33.0 percentage points."

—P.L. 111-42, Sec. 202, of this Act [Enacted 7/28/2009] [as affected by Sec. 18 of P.L. 111-92, Sec. 4 of P.L. 111-124, and Sec. 12(a) of P.L. 111-171, see above], reads as follows:

"Sec. 202. Time for Payment of Corporate Estimated Taxes.

"(a) Repeal of adjustments for 2010, 2011, and 2013. Section 401 of the Tax Increase Prevention and Reconciliation Act of 2005 (and any modification of such section contained in any other provision of law) shall not apply with respect to any installment of corporate estimated tax which (without regard to such section) would otherwise be due after December 31, 2009.

"(b) Adjustment for 2014. Notwithstanding section 6655 of the Internal Revenue Code of 1986—

"(1) in the case of a corporation with assets of not less than $1,000,000,000 (determined as of the end of the preceding taxable year), the amount of any required installment of corporate estimated tax which is otherwise due in July, August, or September of 2014 shall be 135.50 percent of such amount; and

"(2) the amount of the next required installment after an installment referred to in paragraph (1) shall be appropriately reduced to reflect the amount of the increase by reason of such paragraph."

—P.L. 111-3, Sec. 704, of this Act, increases the amount in Sec. 401(1)(C), P.L. 109-222 [reproduced below] [Ed. note: Sec. 202, P.L. 111-42, 7/28/2009, see above, repeals and provides adjustments under Sec. 401, P.L. 109-222, see below] as in effect 2/4/2009, by 0.5 percentage points [Ed. Note: This increases the amount to 120.00 percent.] Sec. 704, P.L. 111-3, reads as follows:

Sec. 704. Time for Payment of Corporate Estimated Taxes.

"The percentage under subparagraph (C) of section 401(1) of the Tax Increase Prevention and Reconciliation Act of 2005 in effect on the date of the enactment of this Act is increased by 0.5 percentage point."

In **2008**, P.L. 110-436, Sec. 6, of this Act, increases the amount in Sec. 401(1)(C), P.L. 109-222 [reproduced below] by 2.0 percentage points. [Ed. note: This increases the amount to 119.50 percent.] [Ed. note: Sec. 202, P.L. 111-42, 7/28/2009, see above, repeals and provides adjustments under Sec. 401, P.L. 109-222, see below] Sec. 6, P.L. 110-436, by reads as follows:

"Sec. 6. Time for Payment of Corporate Estimated Taxes. The percentage under subparagraph (C) of section 401(1) of the Tax Increase Prevention and Reconciliation Act of 2005 in effect on the date of the enactment of this Act is increased by 2 percentage points."

—P.L. 110-289, Sec. 3094, of this Act, [Ed. note: Sec. 202, P.L. 111-42, 7/28/2009, see above, repeals and provides adjustments under Sec. 401, P.L. 109-222, see below] reads as follows:

Sec. 3094. Time for Payment of Corporate Estimated Taxes.

"(a) Repeal of adjustment for 2012. Subparagraph (B) of section 401(1) of the Tax Increase Prevention and Reconciliation Act of 2005 [P.L. 109-222, see below] is amended by striking the percentage contained therein and inserting '100 percent'. No other provision of law which would change such percentage shall have any force and effect."

"(b) Modification of adjustment for 2013. The percentage under subparagraph (C) of section 401(1) of the Tax Increase Prevention and Reconciliation Act of 2005 [P.L. 109-222, see below] in effect on the date of the enactment of this Act is increased by 16.75 percentage points."

—P.L. 110-287, Sec. 3, substituted "101.25 percent" for "101 percent" in Sec. 401(1)(C) of P.L. 109-222 [Ed. note: Sec. 202, P.L. 111-42, 7/28/2009, see above, repeals and provides adjustments under Sec. 401, P.L. 109-222, see below].

—P.L. 110-246, Sec. 4, Repeals the duplicative enactment and provides effective date provisions of the Act entitled "An Act to provide for the continuation of agricultural programs through fiscal year 2012, and for other purposes" Sec, 4, P.L. 110-246 reads as follows:

"Sec. 4. Repeal of duplicative enactment.

"(a) In General. The Act entitled 'An Act to provide for the continuation of agricultural programs through fiscal year 2012, and for other purposes' (H.R. 2419 of the 110th Congress), and the amendments made by that Act, are repealed, effective on the date of enactment of that Act.

"(b) Effective Date- Except as otherwise provided in this Act, this Act and the amendments made by this Act shall take effect on the earlier of--

"(1) the date of enactment of this Act; or

"(2) the date of the enactment of the Act entitled 'An Act to provide for the continuation of agricultural programs through fiscal year 2012, and for other purposes' (H.R. 2419 of the 110th Congress)."

—P.L. 110-246, Sec. 15202, substituted "125 percent" for "117.25 percent" in Sec. 401(1)(B) of P.L. 109-222 [Ed. note: Sec. 202, P.L. 111-42, 7/28/2009, see above, repeals and provides adjustments under Sec. 401, P.L. 109-222, see below].

—P.L. 110-191, Sec. 10, substituted "101 percent" for "100.75 percent" in Sec. 401(1)(C) of P.L. 109-222 [Ed. note: Sec. 202, P.L. 111-42, 7/28/2009, see above, repeals and provides adjustments under Sec. 401, P.L. 109-222, see below].

Penalties   Code Sec. 6655

In 2007, P.L. 110-142, Sec. 10, substituted "117.25 percent" for "115.75 percent" in Sec. 401(1)(B) of P.L. 109-222 [Ed. note: Sec. 202, P.L. 111-42, 7/28/2009, see above, repeals and provides adjustments under Sec. 401, P.L. 109-222, see below].

—P.L. 110-138, Sec. 602, substituted "115.75 percent" for "115 percent" in Sec. 401(1)(B) of P.L. 109-222 [Ed. note: Sec. 202, P.L. 111-42, 7/28/2009, see above, repeals and provides adjustments under Sec. 401, P.L. 109-222, see below].

—P.L. 110-89, Sec. 2(a), substituted "115 percent" for "114.75 percent" in Sec. 401(1)(B) of P.L. 109-222 [Ed. note: Sec. 202, P.L. 111-42, 7/28/2009, see above, repeals and provides adjustments under Sec. 401, P.L. 109-222, see below].

—P.L. 110-52, Sec. 3, substituted "114.75 percent" for "114.50 percent" in Sec. 401(1)(B) of P.L. 109-222 [Ed. note: Sec. 202, P.L. 111-42, 7/28/2009, see above, repeals and provides adjustments under Sec. 401, P.L. 109-222, see below].

—P.L. 110-42, Sec. 4, substituted "114.50 percent" for "114.25 percent" in Sec. 401(1)(B) of P.L. 109-222 [Ed. note: Sec. 202, P.L. 111-42, 7/28/2009, see above, repeals and provides adjustments under Sec. 401, P.L. 109-222, see below].

—P.L. 110-28, Sec. 8248, substituted "114.25 percent" for "106.25 percent" in Sec. 401(1)(B) of P.L. 109-222 [Ed. note: Sec. 202, P.L. 111-42, 7/28/2009, see above, repeals and provides adjustments under Sec. 401, P.L. 109-222, see below].

In 2006, P.L. 109-222, Sec. 401, of this Act [As amended by Sec. 7248 of P.L. 110-28, Sec. 4 of P.L. 110-42, Sec. 3 of P.L. 110-52, Sec. 2(a) of P.L. 110-89, Sec. 602 of P.L. 110-138, and Sec. 3094(a) and (b) of 110-289, and as affected by Sec. 6, P.L. 110-436, Sec. 704, P.L. 111-3, and Sec. 202, P.L. 111-42 see above], reads as follows:

"SEC. 401. TIME FOR PAYMENT OF CORPORATE ESTIMATED TAXES.

"(1) in the case of a corporation with assets of not less than $1,000,000,000 (determined as of the end of the preceding taxable year)—

"(A) the amount of any required installment of corporate estimated tax which is otherwise due in July, August, or September of 2006 shall be 105 percent of such amount,

"(B) the amount of any required installment of corporate estimated tax which is otherwise due in July, August, or September of 2012 shall be 100 percent of such amount,

"(C) the amount of any required installment of corporate estimated tax which is otherwise due in July, August, or September of 2013 shall be 117.50 [120.00, see Sec. 6, P.L. 110-436 and Sec. 704, P.L. 111-3] percent of such amount, and

"(D) the amount of the next required installment after an installment referred to in subparagraph (A), (B), or (C) shall be appropriately reduced to reflect the amount of the increase by reason of such subparagraph,

"(2) 20.5 percent of the amount of any required installment of corporate estimated tax which is otherwise due in September 2010 shall not be due until October 1, 2010, and

"(3) 27.5 percent of the amount of any required installment of corporate estimated tax which is otherwise due in September 2011 shall not be due until October 1, 2011."

In 2003, P.L. 108-27, Sec. 501, of this Act, reads as follows:

"SEC. 501. TIME FOR PAYMENT OF CORPORATE ESTIMATED TAXES. Notwithstanding section 6655 of the Internal Revenue Code of 1986, 25 percent of the amount of any required installment of corporate estimated tax which is otherwise due in September 2003 shall not be due until October 1, 2003."

In 2001, P.L. 107-16, Sec. 801, of this Act, reads as follows:

"SEC. 801. TIME FOR PAYMENT OF CORPORATE ESTIMATED TAXES. Notwithstanding section 6655 of the Internal Revenue Code of 1986—

"(1) 100 percent of the amount of any required installment of corporate estimated tax which is otherwise due in September 2001 shall not be due until October 1, 2001; and

"(2) 20 percent of the amount of any required installment of corporate estimated tax which is otherwise due in September 2004 shall not be due until October 1, 2004."

In 2000, P.L. 106-554, Sec. 1(a)(7), [which enacted into law Sec. 319(21) of P.L. 106-554] substituted "subsection (d)(5)" for "subsections (d)(5) and (l)(3)(B)" in subparas. (e)(5)(A) and (B), effective 12/21/2000.

In 1999, P.L. 106-170, Sec. 571(a), added para. (e)(5), effective for estimated tax payments due on or after 12/15/99.

In 1998, P.L. 105-206, Sec. 1(c), of this Act, reads as follows:

"(c) Waiver of estimated tax penalties. No addition to tax shall be made under section 6654 or 6655 of the Internal Revenue Code of 1986 with respect to any underpayment of an installment required to be paid on or before the 30th day after the date of the enactment of this Act to the extent such underpayment was created or increased by any provision of this Act."

In 1997, P.L. 105-34, Sec. 1(d), of this Act, relating to the waiver of estimated tax penalties, is reproduced in the notes following Code Sec. 6654.

—P.L. 105-34, Sec. 1461(a), added the sentence at the end of para. (g)(3), effective for purposes of determining underpayments of estimated tax for tax. yrs. begin. after 8/5/97.

In 1996, P.L. 104-188, Sec. 1102, of this Act provides:

"Sec. 1102. Underpayments of estimated tax.

"No addition to the tax shall be made under section 6654 or 6655 of the Internal Revenue Code of 1986 (relating to failure to pay estimated tax) with respect to any underpayment of an installment required to be paid before the date of enactment of this Act to the extent such underpayment was created or increased by any provisions of this title."

—P.L. 104-188, Sec. 1703(h), substituted ", subsection (e)(2)(A) shall be applied by substituting '2 months' for '3 months' in clause (i)(I), the election under clause (i) of subsection (e)(2)(C) may be made separately for each installment, and clause (iii) of subsection (e)(2)(C) shall not apply," for "and, except in the case of an election under subsection (e)(2)(C), subsection (e)(2)(A) shall be applied by substituting '2 months' for '3 months' and in clause (i)(I), by substituting '4 months' for '5 months' in clause (i)(II), by substituting '7 months' for '8 months' in clause (i)(III), and by substituting '10 months' for '11 months' in clause (i)(IV)." in the sentence following subpara. (g)(3)(C), effective for tax. yrs. begin. after 12/31/93.

In 1994, P.L. 103-465, Sec. 711(a), added para. (e)(4), effective for purposes of determining underpayments of estimated tax for tax. yrs. begin. after 12/31/94.

In 1993, P.L. 103-66, Sec. 13001(d), of this Act, provides:

"(d) Waiver of estimated tax penalties. No addition to tax shall be made under section 6654 or 6655 of the Internal Revenue Code of 1986 for any period before April 16, 1994 (March 16, 1994, in the case of a corporation), with respect to any underpayment to the extent such underpayment was created or increased by any provision of this chapter."

—P.L. 103-66, Sec. 13225(a)(1), substituted "100 percent" for "91 percent" each place it appeared in clause (d)(1)(B)(i)...Sec. 13225(a)(2)(A)(i), deleted para. (d)(3)...Sec. 13225(a)(2)(A)(ii), substituted "100 percent" for "91 percent" in the heading of para. (d)(2)...Sec. 13225(a)(2)(B), amended the table in clause (e)(2)(B)(ii)...Sec. 13225(a)(2)(C), substituted "100 percent" for "91 percent" in clause (e)(3)(A)(i)...Sec. 13225(b)(1)(A), deleted "or for the first 5 months" after "for the first 3 months" in subclause (e)(2)(A)(i)(II)...Sec. 13225(b)(1)(B), deleted "or for the first 8 months" after "for the first 6 months" in subclause (e)(2)(A)(i)(III)...Sec. 13225(b)(1)(C), deleted "or for the first 11 months" after "for the first 9 months" in subclause (e)(2)(A)(i)(IV)...Sec. 13225(b)(2), added subpara. (e)(2)(C)...Sec. 13225(b)(3), substituted "and, except in the case of an election under subsection (e)(2)(C), subsection (e)(2)(A)" for "and subsection (e)(2)(A)" in the last sentence of para. (g)(3), effective for tax. yrs. begin. after 12/31/93.

Prior to deletion, para. (d)(3) read as follows:

"(3) Temporary increase in amount of installment based on current year tax. In the case of any taxable year beginning after June 30, 1992, and before 1997—

"(A) paragraph (l)(B)(i) and subsection (e)(3)(A)(i) shall be applied by substituting '97 percent' for '91 percent' each place it appears, and

"(B) the table contained in subsection (e)(2)(B)(ii) shall be applied by substituting '24.25', '48.50', '72.75', and '97' for '22.75', '45.50', '68.25', and '91.00', respectively."

Prior to amendment, the table in clause (e)(2)(B)(ii) read as follows:

"In the case of the following required installments:	The applicable percentage is:
1st	22.75
2nd	45.50
3rd	68.25
4th	91.00

In 1992, P.L. 102-318, Sec. 512(a)(1), substituted "91 percent" for "90 percent" each place is appeared in clause (d)(1)(B)(i)...Sec. 512(a)(2), substituted "91 percent" for "90 percent" in the heading of para. (d)(2)...Sec. 512(a)(3), amended para. (d)(3)...Sec. 512(b)(1), amended table in clause (e)(2)(B)(ii)...Sec. 512(b)(2), substituted "91 percent" for "90 percent" in clause (e)(3)(A)(i), effective for tax. yrs. begin. after 6/30/92.

Prior to amendment, para. (d)(3) read as follows:

"(3) Temporary increase in amount of installment based on current year tax. In the case of any taxable year beginning after 1991 and before 1997—

"(A) Paragraph (1)(B)(i) and subsection (e)(3)(A)(i) shall be applied by substituting for '90 percent' each place it appears the current year percentage determined under the following table:

In the case of a taxable year beginning in:	The current year percentage is:
1992	93
1993 through 1996	95

"(B) Appropriate adjustments to the table contained in subsection (e)(2)(B)(ii) shall be made to reflect the provisions of subparagraph (A)."

Prior to amendment, table in clause (e)(2)(B)(ii) read as follows:

"In the case of the following required installments:	The applicable percentage is:
1st	22.5
2nd	45
3rd	67.5
4th	90"

—P.L. 102-244, Sec. 3(a), amended the table in subpara. (d)(3)(A), effective for tax. yrs. begin. after 12/31/92.

Prior to amendment, the table in subpara. (d)(3)(A) read as follows:

3,789

"In the case of a taxable year beginning in	The current year percentage in:
1992	93
1993 or 1994	94
1995 or 1996	95"

In **1991**, P.L. 102-227, Sec. 201(a), added para. (d)(3), effective for tax. yrs. begin. after 12/31/91.

—P.L. 102-227, Sec. 201(b), substituted "modified by paragraphs (2) and (3) of subsection (d)" for "modified by subsection (d)(2)" in para. (e)(1), effective for tax. yrs. begin. after 12/31/91.

In **1990**, P.L. 101-508, Sec. 11307, of this Act provides:

"Sec. 11307. Waiver of estimated tax penalties.

No addition to tax shall be made under section 6655 of the Internal Revenue Code of 1986 for any period before March 16, 1991, with respect to any underpayment to the extent such underpayment was created or increased by any provision of this part [part I of Subtitle C]."

—P.L. 101-508, Sec. 11704(a)(28), substituted "in clause (i)(IV)." for "in clause (i)(IV)" in the last sentence of para. (g)(3), effective 11/5/90.

In **1989**, P.L. 101-239, Sec. 7209(a), added para. (g)(4), effective for tax. yrs. begin. after 12/31/89.

—P.L. 101-239, Sec. 7822(a), substituted "subsection (d)(1)" for "section (d)(1)" in para. (e)(1), effective for tax. yrs. begin. after 12/31/87.

In **1988**, P.L. 100-647, Sec. 1019(b), of this Act provides:

"(b) Waiver of estimated tax penalties. No addition to tax shall be made under section 6654 or 6655 of the 1986 Code for any period before April 16, 1989 (March 16, 1989 in the case of a taxpayer subject to section 6655 of the 1986 Code) with respect to any underpayment to the extent such underpayment was created or increased by any provision of this title or title II."

—P.L. 100-647, Sec. 2004(r), amended subpara. (g)(3)(C), effective for tax. yrs. begin. 12/31/87. For other provisions see Sec. 10303(b)(2) of P.L. 100-203 [reproduced below].

Prior to amendment, subpara. (g)(3)(C) read as follows:

"(C) Any reference to taxable income shall be treated as including a reference to unrelated business taxable income or net investment income (as the case may be).

In the case of any organization described in subparagraph (A), subsection (b)(2)(A) shall be applied by substituting 5th month for 3rd month."

—P.L. 100-647, Sec. 5001(a), deleted the last sentence of para. (e)(1), effective for installments required to be made after 12/31/88.

Prior to deletion, the last sentence of para. (e)(1) read as follows:

"Reduction shall be treated as recaptured for purposes of subparagraph (B) if 90 percent of the reduction is recaptured."

—P.L. 100-418, Sec. 1941(b)(6)(B), amended subpara. (g)(1)(B), effective for crude oil removed from the premises on or after 8/23/88.

Prior to amendment, subpara. (g)(1)(B) read as follows:

"(B) the sum of—

"(i) the credits against tax provided by part IV of subchapter A of chapter 1, plus

"(ii) to the extent allowed under regulations prescribed by the Secretary, any overpayment of the tax imposed by section 4986 (determined without regard to section 4995(a)(4)(B))."

In **1987**, P.L. 100-203, Sec. 10301(a), amended Code Sec. 6655, effective for tax. yrs. begin. after 12/31/87. See Sec. 10303(b)(2) of the Act provides:

"(2) Corporations also may use 1986 tax to determine amount of certain estimated tax installments due on or before June 15, 1987.

"(A) In general. In the case of a large corporation, no addition to tax shall be imposed by section 6655 of the Internal Revenue Code of 1986 with respect to any underpayment of an estimated tax installment to which this subsection applies if no addition would be imposed with respect to such underpayment by reason of section 6655(d)(1) of such Code if such corporation were not a large corporation. The preceding sentence shall apply only to the extent the underpayment is paid on or before the last date prescribed for payment of the most recent installment of estimated tax due on or before September 15, 1987.

"(B) Installment to which subsection applies. This subsection applies to any installment of estimated tax for a taxable year beginning after December 31, 1986, which is due on or before June 15, 1987.

"(C) Large corporation. For purposes of this subsection, the term 'large corporation' has the meaning given such term by section 6655(i)(2) of such Code (as in effect on the day before the date of the enactment of this Act)."

Prior to amendment, Code Sec. 6655 read as follows:

"Sec. 6655. Failure by corporation to pay estimated income tax.

"(a) Addition to tax.

"Except as provided in subsections (d) and (e), in the case of any underpayment of tax by a corporation—

"(1) In general. There shall be added to the tax under chapter 1 for the taxable year an amount determined at the underpayment rate established under section 6621 on the amount of the underpayment for the period of the underpayment.

"(2) Special rule where corporation paid 80 percent or more of tax. In any case in which there would be no underpayment if subsection (b) were applied by substituting '80 percent' for '90 percent' each place it appears, the addition to tax under paragraph (1) shall be equal to 75 percent of the amount otherwise determined under paragraph (1).

"(b) Amount of underpayment.

"For purposes of subsection (a), the amount of the underpayment shall be the excess of—

"(1) The amount of the installment which would be required to be paid if the estimated tax were equal to 90 percent of the tax shown on the return for the taxable year or, if no return was filed, 90 percent of the tax for such year, over

"(2) The amount, if any, of the installment paid on or before the last date prescribed for payment.

"(c) Period of underpayment.

"The period of the underpayment shall run from the date the installment was required to be paid to whichever of the following dates is the earlier—

"(1) The 15th day of the third month following the close of the taxable year.

"(2) With respect to any portion of the underpayment, the date on which such portion is paid. For purposes of this paragraph, a payment of estimated tax on any installment date shall be considered a payment of any previous underpayment only to the extent such payment exceeds the amount of the installment determined under subsection (b)(1) for such installment date.

"(d) Exception.

"Notwithstanding the provisions of the preceding subsections, the addition to the tax with respect to any underpayment of any installment shall not be imposed if the total amount of all payments of estimated tax made on or before the last date prescribed for payment of such installment equals or exceeds the amount which would have been required to be paid on or before such date if the estimated tax were whichever of the following is the lesser—

"(1) The tax shown on the return of the corporation for the preceding taxable year, if a return showing a liability for tax was filed by the corporation for the preceding taxable year and such preceding year was a taxable year of 12 months.

"(2) An amount equal to the tax computed at the rates applicable to the taxable year but otherwise on the basis of the facts shown on the return of the corporation for, and the law applicable to, the preceding taxable year.

"(3)(A) An amount equal to 90 percent of the tax for the taxable year computed by placing on an annualized basis the taxable income:

"(i) for the first three months of the taxable year, in the case of the installment required to be paid in the 4th month.

"(ii) for the first 3 months or for the first 5 months of the taxable year, in the case of the installment required to be paid in the 6th month,

"(iii) for the first 6 months or for the first 8 months of the taxable year in the case of the installment required to be paid in the 9th month, and

"(iv) for the first 9 months or for the first 11 months of the taxable year, in the case of the installment required to be paid in the 12th month of the taxable year.

"(B) For purposes of this paragraph, the taxable income shall be placed on an annualized basis by—

"(i) multiplying by 12 the taxable income referred to in subparagraph (A), and

"(ii) dividing the resulting amount by the number of months in the taxable year (3, 5, 6, 8, 9, or 11, as the case may be) referred to in subparagraph (A).

"(e) Additional exception for recurring seasonal income.

"(1) In general. Notwithstanding the preceding subsections, the addition to the tax with respect to any underpayment of any installment shall not be imposed if the total amount of all payments of estimated tax made on or before the last date prescribed for the payment of such installment equals or exceeds 90 percent of the amount determined under paragraph (2).

"(2) Determination of amount. The amount determined under this paragraph for any installment shall be determined in the following manner—

"(A) take the taxable income for all months during the taxable year preceding the filing month,

"(B) divide such amount by the base period percentage for all months during the taxable year preceding the filing month,

"(C) determine the tax on the amount determined under subparagraph (B), and

"(D) multiply the tax computed under subparagraph (C) by the base period percentage for the filing month and all months during the taxable year preceding the filing month.

"(3) Definitions and special rules. For purposes of this subsection—

"(A) Base period percentage. The base period percentage for any period of months shall be the average percent which the taxable income for the corresponding months in each of the 3 preceding taxable years bears to the taxable income for the 3 preceding taxable years.

"(B) Filing month. The term 'filing month' means the month in which the installment is required to be paid.

"(C) Limitation on application of subsection. This subsection shall only apply if the base period percentage for any 6 consecutive months of the taxable year equals or exceeds 70 percent.

"(D) Reorganizations, etc. The Secretary may by regulations provide for the determination of the base period percentage in the case of reorganizations, new corporations, and other similar circumstances.

"(f) Definition of tax.

"For purposes of subsections (b),(d),(e), and (i), the term 'tax' means the excess of—

"(1) the sum of—

"(A) the tax imposed by section 11 or 1201(a), or subchapter L of chapter 1, whichever is applicable,

"(B) the tax imposed by section 55, plus

"(C) the tax imposed by section 59A, over

"(2) the sum of—

"(A) the credits against tax provided by part IV of subchapter A of chapter 1, plus

"(B) to the extent allowed under regulations prescribed by the Secretary, any overpayment of the tax imposed by section 4986 (determined without regard to section 4995(a)(4)(B)).

"(g) Short taxable year.

"The application of this section to taxable years of less than 12 months shall be in accordance with regulations prescribed by the Secretary.

"(h) Excessive adjustment under section 6425.

"(1) Addition to tax. If the amount of an adjustment under section 6425 made before the 15th day of the third month following the close of the taxable year is excessive, there shall be added to the tax under chapter 1 for the taxable year an amount determined at an annual rate established under section 6621 upon the excessive amount from the date on which the credit is allowed or the refund is paid to such 15th day.

"(2) Excessive amount. For purposes of paragraph (1), the excessive amount is equal to the amount of the adjustments or (if smaller) the amount by which—

"(A) the income tax liability (as defined in section 6425(c)) for the taxable year as shown on the return for the taxable year, exceeds

"(B) the estimated income tax paid during the taxable year, reduced by the amount of the adjustment.

"(i) Large corporations required to pay minimum percentage of current year tax.

"(1) Minimum percentage.

"(A) In general. Except as provided in subparagraph (B), in the case of a large corporation, paragraphs (1) and (2) of subsection (d) shall not apply.

"(B) Transition rule. For taxable years beginning before 1984, in the case of a large corporation, the amount treated as the estimated tax for the taxable year under paragraphs (1) and (2) of subsection (d) shall in no event be less than the applicable percentage of—

"(i) the tax shown on the return for the taxable year, or

"(ii) if no return was filed, the tax for such year.

"(C) Applicable percentage. For purposes of subparagraph (B), the applicable percentage shall be determined in accordance with the following table:

If the taxable year begins in:	The applicable percentage is:
1982	65
1983	75

"(2) Large corporation. For purposes of this subsection, the term 'large corporation' means any corporation if such corporation (or any predecessor corporation) had taxable income of $1,000,000 or more for any taxable year during the testing period.

"Rules for applying paragraph (2).

"(A) Testing period. For purposes of this subsection, the term 'testing period' means the 3 taxable years immediately preceding the taxable year involved.

"(B) Members of controlled groups. For purposes of applying paragraph (2) to any taxable year in the testing period with respect to corporations which are component members of a controlled group of corporations for such taxable year, the $1,000,000 amount specified in paragraph (2) shall be divided among such members under rules similar to the rules of section 1561."

In **1986**, P.L. 99-514, Sec. 701(d)(3), amended para. (f)(1), effective for tax. yrs. begin. after 12/31/86.

Prior to amendment, para. (f)(1) read as follows:

"(1) the tax imposed by section 11 or 1201(a), or subchapter L of chapter 1, whichever is applicable, over"

—P.L. 99-514, Sec. 1511(c)(15), substituted "the underpayment rate" for "the rate" in para. (a)(1), effective for purposes of determining interest for periods after 12/31/86.

—P.L. 99-514, Sec. 1543, provides:

"Sec. 1543. Waiver of estimated penalties for 1986 underpayments attributable to this act.

"No addition to tax shall be made under section 6654 or 6655 of the Internal Revenue Code of 1986 (relating to failure to pay estimated tax) for any period before April 16, 1987 (March 16, 1987, in the case of a taxpayer subject to section 6655 of such Code), with respect to any underpayment, to the extent such underpayment was created or increased by any provision of this Act."

—P.L. 99-514, Sec. 1824, repealed Sec. 218 of P.L. 98-369, which, prior to repeal, provided as follows:

"Sec. 218. Underpayments of estimated tax for 1984.

"No addition to the tax shall be made under section 6655 of the Internal Revenue Code of 1954 (relating to failure by corporation to pay estimated tax) with respect to any underpayment of an installment required to be paid before the date of the enactment of this Act to the extent—

"(1) such underpayment was created or increased by any provision of this subtitle, and

"(2) such underpayment is paid in full on or before the last date prescribed for payment of the first installment of estimated tax required to be paid after the date of the enactment of this Act."

—P.L. 99-499, Sec. 516(b)(4)(D), deleted "plus" from the end of subpara. (f)(1)(A), substituted "plus" for "over" at the end of subpara. (f)(1)(B), and added subpara. (f)(1)(C), effective for tax. yrs. begin. after 12/31/86.

In **1984**, P.L. 98-369, Sec. 218, provided rules regarding underpayments of estimated tax for 1984, repealed by Sec. 1824 of P.L. 99-514, see above.

—P.L. 98-369, Sec. 413, makes a provision regarding crediting of income tax overpayment against estimated tax liability, reproduced in note following Code Sec. 6654.

In **1983**, P.L. 97-448, Sec. 201(j)(4), amended subpara. (e)(2)(B), [sic . (f)(2)(B)] effective for tax. yrs. begin. after 12/31/82.

Prior to amendment, subpara. (e)(2)(B) read as follows:

"(B) to the extent allowed under regulations prescribed by the Secretary, any amount which is treated under section 6429 as an overpayment of the tax imposed by section 4986."

In **1982**, P.L. 97-248, Sec. 208(d)(6), [sic (d)(7)], provides as follows:

"(6) Underpayments of tax for 1982. No addition to the tax shall be made under section 6655 of the Internal Revenue Code of 1954 (relating to failure by corporation to pay estimated income tax) for any period before October 15, 1982, with respect to any underpayment of estimated tax by a taxpayer with respect to any tax imposed by chapter 1 of such Code, to the extent that such underpayment was created or increased by any provision of this section."

—P.L. 97-248, Sec. 234(a)(1), substituted "90" for "80" each place it appeared in para. (b)(1) . . . Sec. 234(a)(2), substituted "90" for "80" in para. (d)(3) . . . Sec. 234(c), amended subsec. (a) . . . Sec. 234(d)(1), redesignated subsecs. (e), (f), (g) and (h) as subsecs. (f), (g), (h) and (i), and added new subsec (e) . . . Sec. 234(d)(2), substituted "(d), (e) and (f)" for "(d) and (h)" in subsec. (f) (as redesignated by Sec. 234(d)(1) of the Act), effective for tax. yrs. begin. after 12/31/82.

Prior to amendment, subsec. (a) read as follows:

"(a) Addition to the tax.

"In case of any underpayment of estimated tax by a corporation, except as provided in subsection (d), there shall be added to the tax under chapter 1 for the taxable year an amount determined at an annual rate established under section 6621 upon the amount of the underpayment (determined under subsection (b)) for the period of the underpayment (determined under subsection (c))."

—P.L. 97-248, Sec. 268, provides as follows:

"Sec. 268. Underpayments of estimated tax for 1982.

"No addition to the tax shall be made under section 6655 of the Internal Revenue Code of 1954 (relating to failure by corporation to pay estimated income tax) for any period before December 15, 1982, with respect to any underpayment of estimated tax by a taxpayer with respect to any tax imposed by section 802(a), to the extent that such underpayment was created or increased by any provisions of this subtitle."

In **1981**, P.L. 97-34, Sec. 601(a)(6)(B), amended para. (e)(2), effective 1/1/80.

Prior to amendment, para. (e)(2) read as follows:

"(2) the credits against tax provided by part IV of subchapter A of chapter 1."

—P.L. 97-34, Sec. 731(a), amended para. (h)(1) . . . Sec. 731(b), amended the heading of subsec. (h), effective for tax. yrs. begin after 12/31/81.

Prior to amendment, the heading of subsec. (h) and para. (h)(1) read as follows:

"(h) Large corporations required to pay at least 60 percent of current year tax.

"(1) In general. In the case of a large corporation, the amount treated as the estimated tax for the taxable year under paragraphs (1) and (2) of subsection (d) shall in no event be less than 60 percent of—

"(A) the tax shown on the return for the taxable year, or

"(B) if no return was filed, the tax for such year."

In **1980**, P.L. 96-499, Sec. 1111(a), added subsec. (h) . . . Sec. 1111(b), substituted "subsections (b), (d), and (h)" for "subsections (b) and (d)" in subsec. (e), effective for tax. yrs. begin. after 12/31/80.

In **1978**, P.L. 95-600, Sec. 301(b)(20)(B), amended subsec. (e), effective for tax. yrs. begin. after 12/31/78.

Prior to amendment, subsec. (e) read as follows:

"(e) Definition of tax.

"(1) In general. For purposes of subsections (b) and (d), the term 'tax' means the excess of—

"(A) the tax imposed by section 11 or 1201(a), or subchapter L of chapter 1, whichever is applicable, over

"(B) the sum of—

"(i) the credits against tax provided by part IV of subchapter A of chapter 1, and

"(ii) in the case of a taxable year beginning before January 1, 1977, the amount of the corporation's temporary estimated tax exemption for such year.

"(2) Temporary estimated tax exemption. For purposes of clause (ii) of paragraph (1)(B), the amount of a corporation's temporary estimated tax exemption for a taxable year equals the applicable percentage (determined under section 6154(c)(2)(B)) multiplied by the lesser of—

"(A) an amount equal to 22 percent of the corporation's surtax exemption (as defined in section 11(d)) for such year, or

"(B) the excess determined under paragraph (1) without regard to clause (ii) of paragraph (1)(B).

"(3) Special rule for subsection (d)(1) and (2). In applying this subsection for purposes of subsection (d)(1) and (2), the applicable percentage and the exclusion percentage shall be the percentage for the taxable year for which the underpayment is being determined."

In **1977**, P.L. 95-30, Sec. 303, made certain provisions with respect to underpayments of estimated tax. See note at Code Sec. 6654.

In **1976**, P.L. 94-455, Sec. 803(g), provided rules for the waiver of penalty for underpayment of estimated tax, which read as follows:

"(g) Waiver of penalty for underpayment of estimated tax. If—

"(1) a corporation made underpayments of estimated tax for a taxable year of the corporation which includes August 1, 1975, because the corporation intended to elect to have the provisions of subparagraph (B) of section 46(a)(1) of the Internal Revenue Code of 1954 (as it existed before the date of enactment of this Act) apply for such taxable year, and

"(2) the corporation does not elect to have the provisions of such subparagraph apply for such taxable year because this Act does not contain the amendments made by section 804(a)(2) (relating to flowthrough of investment credit), or the provisions of subsection (f) of such section (relating to grace period for certain plan transfers), of the bill H.R. 10612 (94th Congress, 2d Session), as amended by the Senate,

then the provisions of section 6655 of such Code (relating to failure by corporation to pay estimated income tax) shall not apply to so much of any such underpayment as the corporation can establish, to the satisfaction of the Secretary of the Treasury, is properly attributable to the inapplicability of such subparagraph (B) for such taxable year."

—P.L. 94-455, Sec. 1906(b)(3)(A), added "and" at the end of clause (e)(1)(B)(i), deleted clauses (e)(1)(B)(ii) and (iii), and added new clause (e)(1)(B)(ii), effective 2/1/77.

Prior to amendment, clauses (e)(1)(B)(ii) and (iii) read as follows:

"(ii) in the case of a taxable year beginning after December 31, 1967, and before January 1, 1977, the amount of the corporation's temporary estimated tax exemption for such year, and

"(iii) in the case of a taxable year beginning after December 31, 1967, and before January 1, 1972, the amount of the corporation's transitional exemption for such year."

—P.L. 94-455, Sec. 1906(a)(3)(B), substituted "clause (ii)" for "clauses (ii) and (iii)" in subpara. (e)(2)(B), effective 2/1/77.

—P.L. 94-455, Sec. 1906(b)(3)(C)(i), deleted para. (e)(3) and redesignated para. (e)(4) as (e)(3), effective 2/1/77.

Prior to deletion, para. (e)(3) read as follows:

"(3) Transitional exemption. For purposes of clause (iii) of paragraph (1)(B), the amount of a corporation's transitional exemption for a taxable year equals the exclusion percentage (determined under section 6154(c)(3)(B)) multiplied by the lesser of—

"(A) $100,000, reduced by the amount of the corporation's temporary estimated tax exemption for such year, or

"(B) the excess determined under paragraph (1) without regard to clause (iii) of paragraph (1)(B)."

—P.L. 94-455, Sec. 1906(b)(13)(A), substituted "Secretary" for "Secretary or his delegate" in Code Sec. 6655, effective 2/1/77.

In 1975, P.L. 93-625, Sec. 7(c), substituted "an annual rate established under section 6621" for "the rate of 6 percent per annum" in subsecs. (a) and (g), effective for amounts outstanding on or arising after 7/1/75.

In 1968, P.L. 90-364, Sec. 103, substituted "80 percent" for "70 percent" each place it appeared in subsec. (b) and para. (d)(3) ... deleted the phrase "reduced by $100,000" after "for the preceding taxable year" at the beginning of para. (d)(1) ... added new subsec. (g) ... amended subsec. (e), effective for tax. yrs. begin. after 12/31/67. For special provision on effective date, see Sec. 104 of the P. L., reproduced after Code Sec. 6425.

Prior to amendment, subsec. (e) read as follows:

"(e) Definition of tax.

"For purposes of subsections (b), (d)(2), and (d)(3), the term 'tax' means the excess of—

"(1) the tax imposed by section 11 or 1201(a), or subchapter L of chapter 1, whichever is applicable, over

"(2) the sum of—

"(A) $100,000, and

"(B) the credits against tax provided in part IV of subchapter A of chapter 1."

In 1964, P.L. 88-272, Sec. 122, substituted "any installment date" and "such installment date" for "the 15th day of the 12th month." in paras. (c)(2) and (d)(3), redesignated clauses (A)(i) and (ii) as (A)(iii) and (iv), respectively, and added (A)(i) and (ii), and substituted "(3, 5, 6, 8, 9,)" for "(6 or 8, or 9)" in subpara. (B)(ii), effective for tax. yrs. begin. after '63.

In 1959, P.L. 86-69, Sec. 3(h), provided that: "In the case of any taxpayer subject to tax under section 811 of the Internal Revenue Code of 1954 (as such section was in effect before the enactment of this Act [6/25/59]), no addition to the tax shall be made under section 6655 of such Code (relating to failure by corporation to pay estimated tax) with respect to estimated tax for a taxable year beginning in 1958."

Sec. 6656. Failure to make deposit of taxes.

(a) Underpayment of deposits.

In the case of any failure by any person to deposit (as required by this title or by regulations of the Secretary under this title) on the date prescribed therefor any amount of tax imposed by this title in such government depository as is authorized under section 6302(c) to receive such deposit, unless it is shown that such failure is due to reasonable cause and not due to willful neglect, there shall be imposed upon such person a penalty equal to the applicable percentage of the amount of the underpayment.

(b) Definitions.

For purposes of subsection (a)—

(1) Applicable percentage.—

(A) In general. Except as provided in subparagraph (B), the term "applicable percentage" means—

(i) 2 percent if the failure is for not more than 5 days,

(ii) 5 percent if the failure is for more than 5 days but not more than 15 days, and

(iii) 10 percent if the failure is for more than 15 days.

(B) Special rule. In any case where the tax is not deposited on or before the earlier of—

(i) the day 10 days after the date of the first delinquency notice to the taxpayer under section 6303, or

(ii) the day on which notice and demand for immediate payment is given under section 6861 or 6862 or the last sentence of section 6331(a),

the applicable percentage shall be 15 percent.

(2) Underpayment. The term "underpayment" means the excess of the amount of the tax required to be deposited over the amount, if any, thereof deposited on or before the date prescribed therefor.

(c) Exception for first-time depositors of employment taxes.

The Secretary may waive the penalty imposed by subsection (a) on a person's inadvertent failure to deposit any employment tax if—

(1) such person meets the requirements referred to in section 7430(c)(4)(A)(ii),

(2) such failure—

(A) occurs during the first quarter that such person was required to deposit any employment tax; or

(B) if such person is required to change the frequency of deposits of any employment tax, relates to the first deposit to which such change applies, and

(3) the return of such tax was filed on or before the due date.

For purposes of this subsection, the term "employment taxes" means the taxes imposed by subtitle C.

(d) Authority to abate penalty where deposit sent to Secretary.

The Secretary may abate the penalty imposed by subsection (a) with respect to the first time a depositor is required to make a deposit if the amount required to be deposited is inadvertently sent to the Secretary instead of to the appropriate government depository.

(e) Designation of periods to which deposits apply.

(1) In general. A deposit made under this section shall be applied to the most recent period or periods within the specified tax period to which the deposit relates, unless the person making such deposit designates a different period or periods to which such deposit is to be applied.

(2) Time for making designation. A person may make a designation under paragraph (1) only during the 90-day period beginning on the date of a notice that a penalty under subsection (a) has been imposed for the specified tax period to which the deposit relates.

In 1998, P.L. 105-206, Sec. 3304(a), added subsec. (e) ... Sec. 3304(b)(1), amended para. (c)(2), effective for deposits required to be made after the 180th day after 7/22/98.

Prior to amendment, para. (c)(2) read as follows:

"(2) such failure occurs during the 1st quarter that such person was required to deposit any employment tax, and"

—P.L. 105-206, Sec. 3304(c), amended para. (e)(1), effective for deposits required to be made after 12/31/2001.

Prior to amendment, para. (e)(1) read as follows:

"(1) In general. A person may, with respect to any deposit of tax to be reported on such person's return for a specified tax period, designate the period or periods within such specified tax period to which the deposit is to be applied for purposes of this section."

In 1996, P.L. 104-168, Sec. 304(a), added subsecs. (c) and (d), effective for deposits required to be made after 7/30/96.

—P.L. 104-168, Sec. 701(c)(3), substituted "section 7430(c)(4)(A)(ii)" for "section 7430(c)(4)(A)(iii)" in para. (c)(1) [as added by Sec. 304(a) of this Act, see above], effective for proceedings commenced after 7/30/96.

In 1989, P.L. 101-239, Sec. 7742(a), amended Code Sec. 6656, effective for deposits required to be made after 12/31/89.

Prior to amendment, Code Sec. 6656 read as follows:

"Sec. 6656. Failure to make deposit of taxes overstatement of deposits.

"(a) Under payment of deposits.

Penalties   Code Sec. 6659

"In case of failure by any person required by this title or by regulation of the Secretary under this title to deposit on the date prescribed therefor any amount of tax imposed by this title in such government depositary as is authorized under section 6302(c) to receive such deposit, unless it is shown that such failure is due to reasonable cause and not due to willful neglect, there shall be imposed upon such person a penalty of 10 percent of the amount of the underpayment. For purposes of this subsection, the term 'underpayment' means the excess of the amount of the tax required to be so deposited over the amount, if any, thereof deposited on or before the date prescribed therefor.

"(b) Overstated deposit claims.

"(1) Imposition of penalty. Any person who makes an overstated deposit claim shall be subject to a penalty equal to 25 percent of such claim.

"(2) Overstated deposit claim defined. For purposes of this subsection, the term overstated deposit claim means the excess of —

"(A) the amount of tax under this title which any person claims, in a return filed with the Secretary, that such person has deposited in a government depositary under section 6302(c) for any period, over

"(B) the aggregate amount such person has deposited in a government depositary under section 6302(c), for such period, on or before the date such return is filed.

"(3) Penalty not imposed in certain cases. The penalty under paragraph (2) shall not apply if it is shown that the excess described in paragraph (2) is due to reasonable cause and not due to willful neglect.

"(4) Penalty in addition to other penalties. The penalty under paragraph (1) shall be in addition to any other penalty provided by law."

In 1986, P.L. 99-509, Sec. 8001(a), substituted "10 percent" for "5 percent" in subsec. (a), effective for penalties assessed after 10/21/86.

In 1981, P.L. 97-34, Sec. 724(a), amended subsec. (b).... Sec. 724(b)(1), added "overstatement of deposits" after "taxes" in the heading of Code Sec. 6656 ... Sec. 724(b)(3), substituted "Underpayment of deposits" for "Penalty" in the heading of subsec. (a), effective for returns filed after 8/13/81.

Prior to amendment, subsec. (b) read as follows:

"(b) Penalty not imposed after due date for return.

"For purposes of subsection (a), the failure shall be deemed not to continue beyond the last day (determined without regard to any extension of time) prescribed for payment of the tax required to be deposited or beyond the date the tax is paid, whichever is earlier."

In 1976, P.L. 94-455, Sec. 1906(b)(13)(A), substituted "Secretary" for "Secretary or his delegate" in subsec. (a), effective 2/1/77.

In 1969, P.L. 91-172, Sec. 943(b), amended first sentence of subsec. (a), effective for deposits the time for making of which is after 12/31/69.

Prior to amendment, the first sentence of subsec. (a) read as follows:

"In case of failure by any person required by this title or by regulation of the Secretary or his delegate under this title to deposit on the date prescribed therefor any amount of tax imposed by this title in such government depositary as is authorized under section 6302(c) to receive such deposit, unless it is shown that such failure is due to reasonable cause and not due to willful neglect, there shall be imposed upon such person a penalty of 1 percent of the amount of the underpayment if the failure is for not more than 1 month, with an additional 1 percent for each additional month or fraction thereof during which such failure continues, not exceeding 6 percent in the aggregate."

Sec. 6657. Bad checks.

If any instrument in payment, by any commercially acceptable means, of any amount receivable under this title is not duly paid, in addition to any other penalties provided by law, there shall be paid as a penalty by the person who tendered , upon notice and demand by the Secretary, in the same manner as tax, an amount equal to 2 percent of the amount of such check, except that if the amount of such instrument is less than $1,250, the penalty under this section shall be $25 or the amount of such instrument, whichever is the lesser. This section shall not apply if the person tendered such instrument in good faith and with reasonable cause to believe that it would be duly paid.

In 2010, P.L. 111-198, Sec. 3(a)(1), substituted "If any instrument in payment, by any commercially acceptable means, of any amount" for "If any check or money order in payment of any amount" in Code Sec. 6657.... Sec. 3(a)(2), substituted "such instrument" for "such check" each place it appears in Code Sec. 6657, effective for instruments tendered after 7/2/2010.

In 2007, P.L. 110-28, Sec. 8245(a)(1), substituted "$1,250" for "$750" in Code Sec. 6657.... Sec. 8245(a)(2), substituted "$25" for "$15" in Code Sec. 6657, effective for checks or money orders received after 5/25/2007.

In 1988, P.L. 100-647, Sec. 5071(a)(1), substituted "2 percent" for "1 percent". ... Sec. 5071(a)(2), substituted "$750" for "$500".... Sec. 5071(a)(3), substituted "$15" for "$5" in Code Sec. 6657, effective for checks or money orders received after 11/10/88.

In 1976, P.L. 94-455, Sec. 1906(b)(13)(A), substituted "Secretary" for "Secretary or his delegate" in Code Sec. 6657, effective 2/1/77.

Sec. 6658. Coordination with title 11.

(a) Certain failures to pay tax.

No addition to the tax shall be made under section 6651, 6654, or 6655 for failure to make timely payment of tax with respect to a period during which a case is pending under title 11 of the United States Code—

(1) if such tax was incurred by the estate and the failure occurred pursuant to an order of the court finding probable insufficiency of funds of the estate to pay administrative expenses, or

(2) if—

(A) such tax was incurred by the debtor before the earlier of the order for relief or (in the involuntary case) the appointment of a trustee, and

(B)(i) the petition was filed before the due date prescribed by law (including extensions) for filing a return of such tax, or

(ii) the date for making the addition to the tax occurs on or after the day on which the petition was filed.

(b) Exception for collected taxes.

Subsection (a) shall not apply to any liability for an addition to the tax which arises from the failure to pay or deposit a tax withheld or collected from others and required to be paid to the United States.

In 1980, P.L. 96-589, Sec. 6(e)(1), added Code Sec. 6658, effective 10/1/79, except for any proceeding under the Bankruptcy Act begun before 10/1/79. Sec. 7(g) of this Act provides:

"(g) Definitions.

"For purposes of this section—

"(1) Bankruptcy case. The term 'bankruptcy case' means any case under title 11 of the United States Code (as recodified by P.L. 95-598).

"(2) Similar judicial proceeding. The term 'similar judicial proceeding' means a receivership, foreclosure, or similar proceeding in a Federal or State court (as modified by section 368(a)(3)(D) of the Internal Revenue Code of 1954)."

Sec. 6658. Repealed.

In 1979, P.L. 96-167, Sec. 6(a), repealed Code Sec. 6658, effective for violations (or attempted violations) occurring after 12/29/79.

Prior to repeal, Code Sec. 6658 read as follows:

"Sec. 6658. Addition to tax in case of jeopardy.

"If a taxpayer violates or attempts to violate section 6851 (relating to termination of taxable year) there shall, in addition to all other penalties, be added as part of the tax 25 percent of the total amount of the tax or deficiency in the tax."

Sec. 6659. Repealed.

In 1989, P.L. 101-239, Sec. 7721(c)(2), repealed Code Sec. 6659, effective for returns the due date for which (determined without regard to extensions) is after 12/31/89.

Prior to repeal, Code Sec. 6659 read as follows:

"Sec. 6659. Addition to tax in the case of valuation overstatements for purposes of the income tax.

"(a) Addition to the tax.

"If —

"(1) an individual, or

"(2) a closely held corporation or a personal service corporation,

has an underpayment of the tax imposed by chapter 1 for the taxable year which is attributable to a valuation overstatement, then there shall be added to the tax an amount equal to the applicable percentage of the underpayment so attributable.

"(b) Applicable percentage defined.

"For purposes of subsection (a), the applicable percentage shall be determined under the following table:

"If the valuation claimed is the following percent of the correct valuation—	The applicable percentage is:
"150 percent or more but not more than 200 percent	10
"More than 200 percent but not more than 250 percent	20
"More than 250 percent	30

"(c) Valuation overstatement defined.

"For purposes of this section, there is a valuation overstatement if the value of any property, or the adjusted basis of any property, claimed on any return is 150 percent or more of the amount determined to be the correct amount of such valuation or adjusted basis (as the case may be).

"(d) Underpayment must be at least $1,000.

"This section shall not apply if the underpayment for the taxable year attributable to valuation overstatements is less than $1,000.

"(e) Authority to waive.

"The Secretary may waive all or any part of the addition to the tax provided by this section on a showing by the taxpayer that there was a reasonable basis for the valuation or adjusted basis claimed on the return and that such claim was made in good faith.

"(f) Special rules for overstatement of charitable deduction.

"(1) Amount of applicable percentage. In the case of any underpayment attributable to a valuation overstatement with respect to charitable deduction property, the applicable percentage for purposes of subsection (a) shall be 30 percent.

"(2) Limitation on authority to waive. In the case of any underpayment attributable to a valuation overstatement with respect to charitable deduction property, the Secretary may not waive any portion of the addition to tax provided by this section unless the Secretary determines that—

"(A) the claimed value of the property was based on a qualified appraisal made by a qualified appraiser, and

"(B) in addition to obtaining such appraisal, the taxpayer made a good faith investigation of the value of the contributed property.

"(3) Definitions. For purposes of this subsection—

"(A) Charitable deduction property. The term 'charitable deduction property' means any property contributed by the taxpayer in a contribution for which a deduction was claimed under section 170. For purposes of paragraph (2), such term shall not include any securities for which (as of the date of the contribution) market quotations are readily available on an established securities market.

"(B) Qualified appraiser. The term 'qualified appraiser' means any appraiser meeting the requirements of the regulations prescribed under section 170(a)(1).

"(C) Qualified appraisal. The term 'qualified appraisal' means any appraisal meeting the requirements of the regulations prescribed under section 170(a)(1).

"(g) Other definitions.

"For purposes of this section—

"(1) Underpayment. The term 'underpayment' has the meaning given to such term by section 6653(c)(1).

"(2) Closely held corporation. The term 'closely held corporation' means any corporation described in section 465(a)(1)(B).

"(3) Personal service corporation. The term 'personal service corporation' means any corporation which is a service organization (within the meaning of section 414(m)(3))."

In **1984**, P.L. 98-369, Sec. 155(c)(1)(A), amended subsec. (c)... Sec. 155(c)(1)(B), redesignated subsec. (f) as subsec. (g) and added new subsec. (f), effective for returns filed after 12/31/84.

Prior to amendment, subsec. (c) read as follows:

"(c) Valuation overstatement defined.

"(1) In general. For purposes of this section, there is a valuation overstatement if the value of any property, or the adjusted basis of any property, claimed on any return is 150% or more of the amount determined to be the correct amount of such valuation or adjusted basis (as the case may be).

"(2) Property must have been acquired within last 5 years. This section shall not apply to any property which, as of the close of the taxable year for which there is a valuation overstatement, has been held by the taxpayer for more than 5 years."

—P.L. 98-369, Sec. 721(x)(4), substituted "section 465(a)(1)(B)" for "section 465(a)(1)(C)" in para. (f)(2) (before redesignation by Sec. 155(c)(1)(B) of the Act), effective for tax. yrs. begin. after 12/31/82.

In **1983**, P.L. 97-448, Sec. 107(a)(1), substituted "valuation overstatements" for "the valuation overstatement" in subsec. (d)... Sec. 107(a)(2), substituted "is 150% or more of" for "exceeds 150 percent of", in para. (c)(1), effective for returns filed after 12/31/81.

In **1981**, P.L. 97-34, Sec. 722(a)(1), added Code Sec. 6659, effective for returns filed after 12/31/81.

Sec. 6659A. Repealed.

In **1989**, P.L. 101-239, Sec. 7721(c)(2), repealed Code Sec. 6659A, effective for returns the due date for which (determined without regard to extensions) is after 12/31/89.

Prior to repeal, Code Sec. 6659A read as follows:

"SEC. 6659A. ADDITION TO TAX IN CASE OF OVERSTATEMENTS OF PENSION LIABILITIES.

"(a) Addition to tax.

"In the case of an underpayment of the tax imposed by chapter 1 on any taxpayer for the taxable year which is attributable to an overstatement of pension liabilities, there shall be added to such tax an amount equal to the applicable percentage of the underpayment so attributable.

"(b) Applicable percentage defined.

"For purposes of subsection (a), the applicable percentage shall be determined under the following table:

"If the valuation claimed is the following percent of the correct valuation—	The applicable percentage is:
"150 percent or more but not more than 200 percent	10
"More than 200 percent but not more than 250 percent	20
"More than 250 percent	30

"(c) Overstatement of pension liabilities.

"For purposes of this section, there is an overstatement of pension liabilities if the actuarial determination of the liabilities taken into account for purposes of computing the deduction under paragraph (1) or (2) of section 404(a) exceeds the amount determined to be the correct amount of such liability.

"(d) Underpayment must be at least $1,000.

"This section shall not apply if the underpayment for the taxable year attributable to valuation overstatements is less than $1,000.

"(e) Authority to waive.

"The Secretary may waive all or any part of the addition to the tax provided by this section on a showing by the taxpayer that there was a reasonable basis for the valuation claimed on the return and that such claim was made in good faith."

In **1986**, P.L. 99-514, Sec. 1138(a), added Code Sec. 6659A, effective for overstatements made after 10/22/86.

Sec. 6660. Repealed.

In **1989**, P.L. 101-239, Sec. 7721(c)(2), repealed Code Sec. 6660, effective for returns the due date for which (determined without regard to extensions) is after 12/31/89.

Prior to repeal, Code Sec. 6660 read as follows:

"SEC. 6660. ADDITION TO TAX IN THE CASE OF VALUATION UNDERSTATEMENT FOR PURPOSES OF ESTATE OR GIFT TAXES.

"(a) Addition to the tax.

"In the case of any underpayment of a tax imposed by subtitle B (relating to estate and gift taxes) which is attributable to a valuation understatement, there shall be added to the tax an amount equal to the applicable percentage of the underpayment so attributed.

"(b) Applicable percentage.

"For purposes of subsection (a), the applicable percentage shall be determined under the following table:

"If the valuation claimed is the following percent of the correct valuation—	The applicable percentage is:
"50 percent or more but not more than 66 ⅔ percent	10
"40 percent or more but less than 50 percent	20
"Less than 40 percent	30

"(c) Valuation understatement defined.

"For purposes of this section, there is a valuation understatement if the value of any property claimed on any return is 66⅔ percent or less of the amount determined to be the correct amount of such valuation.

"(d) Underpayment must be at least $1,000.

"This section shall not apply if the underpayment is less than $1,000 for any taxable period (or, in the case of the tax imposed by chapter 11, with respect to the estate of the decedent).

"(e) Authority to waive.

"The Secretary may waive all or any part of the addition to the tax provided by this section on a showing by the taxpayer that there was a reasonable basis for the valuation claimed on the return and that such claim was made in good faith.

"(f) Underpayment defined.

"For purposes of this section, the term 'underpayment' has the meaning given to such term by section 6653(c)(1)."

In **1986**, P.L. 99-514, Sec. 1811(d), added subsec. (f), effective for returns filed after 12/31/84.

—P.L. 99-514, Sec. 1899A(57), substituted "estate" for "the estate" in the heading of Code Sec. 6660, effective 10/22/86.

In **1984**, P.L. 98-369, Sec. 155(c)(2)(A), added Code Sec. 6660, effective for returns filed after 12/31/84.

Sec. 6661. Repealed.

In **1989**, P.L. 101-239, Sec. 7721(c)(2), repealed Code Sec. 6661, effective for returns the due date for which (determined without regard to extensions) is after 12/31/89.

Prior to repeal, Code Sec. 6661 read as follows:

"SEC. 6661. SUBSTANTIAL UNDERSTATEMENT OF LIABILITY.

"(a) Addition to tax.

"If there is a substantial understatement of income tax for any taxable year, there shall be added to the tax an amount equal to 25 percent of the amount of any underpayment attributable to such understatement.

"(b) Definition and special rule.

"(1) Substantial understatement.

"(A) In general. For purposes of this section, there is a substantial understatement of income tax for any taxable year if the amount of the understatement for the taxable year exceeds the greater of—

"(i) 10 percent of the tax required to be shown on the return for the taxable year, or

"(ii) $5,000.

"(B) Special rule for corporations. In the case of a corporation other than an S corporation or a personal holding company (as defined in section 542), paragraph (1) shall be applied by substituting '$10,000' for '$5,000'.

"(2) Understatement.

"(A) In general. For purposes of paragraph (1), the term 'understatement' means the excess of—

"(i) the amount of the tax required to be shown on the return for the taxable year, over

"(ii) the amount of the tax imposed which is shown on the return, reduced by any rebate (within the meaning of section 6211(b)(2)).

"(B) Reduction for understatement due to position of taxpayer or disclosed item. The amount of the understatement under subparagraph (A) shall be reduced by that portion of the understatement which is attributable to—

"(i) the tax treatment of any item by the taxpayer if there is or was substantial authority for such treatment, or

"(ii) any item with respect to which the relevant facts affecting the item's tax treatment are adequately disclosed in the return or in a statement attached to the return.

"(C) Special rules in cases involving tax shelters.

"(i) In general. In the case of any item attributable to a tax shelter—

"(I) subparagraph (B)(ii) shall not apply, and

"(II) subparagraph (B)(i) shall not apply unless (in addition to meeting the requirements of such subparagraph) the taxpayer reasonably believed that the tax treatment of such item by the taxpayer was more likely than not the proper treatment.

"(ii) Tax shelter. For purposes of clause (i), the term 'tax shelter' means—

"(I) a partnership or other entity;

"(II) any investment plan or arrangement, or

"(III) any other plan or arrangement,

"if the principal purpose of such partnership, entity, plan, or arrangement is the avoidance or evasion of Federal income tax.

"(3) Coordination with penalty imposed by section 6659. For purposes of determining the amount of the addition to tax assessed under subsection (a), there shall not be taken into account that portion of the substantial understatement on which a penalty is imposed under section 6659 (relating to addition to tax in the case of valuation overstatements).

"(c) Authority to waive.

"The Secretary may waive all or any part of the addition to tax provided by this section on a showing by the taxpayer that there was reasonable cause for the understatement (or part thereof) and that the taxpayer acted in good faith."

In 1988, P.L. 100-647, Sec. 1015(c), provides:

"(c) Amendment related to section 1504 of the reform act. The repeal made by section 8002(c) of the Omnibus Budget Reconciliation Act of 1986 [P.L. 99-509] shall take effect as if the Tax Reform Act of 1986 had been enacted on the day before the date of the enactment of the Omnibus Budget Reconciliation Act of 1986."

In 1986, P.L. 99-514, Sec. 1504(a), [repealed by Sec. 8002(c) of P.L. 99-509, see below], substituted "20 percent" for "10 percent" in subsec. (a), effective for returns having a due date (determined without regard to exceptions) after 12/31/86.

—P.L. 99-509, Sec. 8002(a), amended subsec. (a), effective for penalties assessed after 10/21/86.

Prior to amendment, subsec. (a) read as follows:

"(a) Addition to tax.

"If there is a substantial understatement of income tax for any taxable year, there shall be added to the tax an amount equal to 10 percent of the amount of any underpayment attributable to such understatement."

—P.L. 100-647, Sec. 1015(c) [see P.L. 99-509, Sec. 8002(c), of P.L. 100-647, above] repealed Sec. 1504(a) of P.L. 99-514 [see above].

In 1984, P.L. 98-369, Sec. 714(h)(3), added ", reduced by any rebate (within the meaning of section 6211(b)(2))" after "return" in clause (b)(2)(A)(ii), effective for returns whose filing due date (determined without regard to extensions) is after 12/31/84.

In 1982, P.L. 97-354, Sec. 5(a)(42), substituted "an S corporation" for "an electing small business corporation (as defined by section 1371(b))" in subpara. (b)(1)(B), effective for tax yrs. begin. after 12/31/82.

—P.L. 97-248, Sec. 323(a), added Code Sec. 6661 effective for returns whose filing due date (determined without regard to extensions) is after 12/31/82.

Sec. 6662. Repealed.

In 1989, P.L. 101-239, Sec. 7721(a), as part of the amendments to subchapter A of chapter 68, repealed Code Sec 6662 effective for returns for the due date for which (determined without regard to extensions) is after 12/31/89.

Prior to repeal, Code Sec 6662 read as follows:

"Sec. 6662. Applicable rules.

"(a) Additions treated as tax.

"Except as otherwise provided in this title—

"(1) The additions to the tax, additional amounts, and penalties provided by this chapter shall be paid upon notice and demand and shall be assessed, collected, and paid in the same manner as taxes;

"(2) Any reference in this title to 'tax' imposed by this title shall be deemed also to refer to the additions to the tax, additional amounts, and penalties provided by this chapter.

"(b) Procedure for assessing certain additions to tax.

"For purposes of subchapter B of chapter 63 (relating to deficiency procedures for income, estate, gift, and certain excise taxes), subsection (a) shall not apply to any addition to tax under section 6651, 6654, or 6655; except that it shall apply—

"(1) in the case of an addition described in section 6651, to that portion of such addition which is attributable to a deficiency in tax described in section 6211; or

"(2) to an addition described in section 6654 or 6655, if no return is filed for the taxable year."

In 1982, P.L. 97-248, Sec. 323(a), redesignated Code Sec. 6661 [sic , 6660] as Code Sec. 6662, for returns whose filing due date (determined without regard to extensions) is after 12/31/82.

In 1981, P.L. 97-34, Sec. 722(a)(1), redesignated Code Sec. 6659 as Code Sec. 6660, for returns filed after 12/31/81.

In 1974, P.L. 93-406, Sec. 1016(a)(19), substituted "certain excise" for "chapter 42" in subsec. (b), effective 9/2/74 or other date as specified in Sec. 1017 of the Act (reproduced following Code Sec. 401).

In 1969, P.L. 91-172, Sec. 101(j)(51), substituted in subsec. (b) "gift and chapter 42 taxes" for "and gift taxes," effect. 1/1/70.

In 1960, P.L. 86-470, Sec. 1, rewrote subsec. (b) effective "with respect to assessments made after [5/14/60].... Any addition to tax under section 6651, 6654, or 6655 of the Internal Revenue Code of 1954, assessed and collected on or before the date of the enactment of this Act, shall not be considered an overpayment solely on the ground that such assessment was invalid, if such assessment would not have been invalid had the amendment made by the first section of this Act applied with respect to such assessment."

Prior to amendment, subsec. (b) read as follows:

"(b) Additions to tax for failure to file return or pay tax.

"Any addition under section 6651 or section 6653 to a tax imposed by another subtitle of this title shall be considered a part of such tax for the purpose of applying the provisions of this title relating to the assessment and collection of such tax (including the provisions of subchapter B of chapter 63, relating to deficiency procedures for income, estate, and gift taxes)."

PART II.—ACCURACY-RELATED AND FRAUD PENALTIES

Sec.

6662. Imposition of accuracy-related penalty on underpayments.

6662A. Imposition of accuracy-related penalty on understatements with respect to reportable transactions.

6663. Imposition of fraud penalty.

6664. Definitions and special rules.

In 2004, P.L. 108-357, Sec. 812(e)(2), deleted item 6662 and added items 6662 and 6662A.

Prior to deletion, item 6662 read as follows:

"6662. Imposition of accuracy-related penalty."

Sec. 6662. Imposition of accuracy-related penalty on underpayments.

(a) Imposition of penalty.

If this section applies to any portion of an underpayment of tax required to be shown on a return, there shall be added to the tax an amount equal to 20 percent of the portion of the underpayment to which this section applies.

(b) Portion of underpayment to which section applies.

This section shall apply to the portion of any underpayment which is attributable to 1 or more of the following:

(1) Negligence or disregard of rules or regulations.

(2) Any substantial understatement of income tax.

(3) Any substantial valuation misstatement under chapter 1.

(4) Any substantial overstatement of pension liabilities.

(5) Any substantial estate or gift tax valuation understatement.

(6) [Ed. Note] We believe Congress intended to add paragraph (b)(6) in another Public Law.

(6) Any disallowance of claimed tax benefits by reason of a transaction lacking economic substance (within the meaning of section 7701(o)) or failing to meet the requirements of any similar rule of law.

(7) Any undisclosed foreign financial asset understatement.

This section shall not apply to any portion of an underpayment on which a penalty is imposed under section 6663. Except as provided in paragraph (1) or (2)(B) of section 6662A(e), this section shall not apply to the portion of any underpayment which is attributable to a reportable transaction understatement on which a penalty is imposed under section 6662A.

(c) **Negligence.**

For purposes of this section, the term "negligence" includes any failure to make a reasonable attempt to comply with the provisions of this title, and the term "disregard" includes any careless, reckless, or intentional disregard.

(d) **Substantial understatement of income tax.**

(1) Substantial understatement.—

(A) In general. For purposes of this section, there is a substantial understatement of income tax for any taxable year if the amount of the understatement for the taxable year exceeds the greater of—

(i) 10 percent of the tax required to be shown on the return for the taxable year, or

(ii) $5,000.

(B) Special rule for corporations. In the case of a corporation other than an S corporation or a personal holding company (as defined in section 542), there is a substantial understatement of income tax for any taxable year if the amount of the understatement for the taxable year exceeds the lesser of—

(i) 10 percent of the tax required to be shown on the return for the taxable year (or, if greater, $10,000), or

(ii) $10,000,000.

(2) **Understatement.**

(A) In general. For purposes of paragraph (1), the term "understatement" means the excess of—

(i) the amount of the tax required to be shown on the return for the taxable year, over

(ii) the amount of the tax imposed which is shown on the return, reduced by any rebate (within the meaning of section 6211(b)(2)).

The excess under the preceding sentence shall be determined without regard to items to which section 6662A applies.

(B) Reduction for understatement due to position of taxpayer or disclosed item. The amount of the understatement under subparagraph (A) shall be reduced by that portion of the understatement which is attributable to—

(i) the tax treatment of any item by the taxpayer if there is or was substantial authority for such treatment, or

(ii) any item if—

(I) the relevant facts affecting the item's tax treatment are adequately disclosed in the return or in a statement attached to the return, and

(II) there is a reasonable basis for the tax treatment of such item by the taxpayer.

For purposes of clause (ii)(II), in no event shall a corporation be treated as having a reasonable basis for its tax treatment of an item attributable to a multiple-party financing transaction if such treatment does not clearly reflect the income of the corporation.

(C) Reduction not to apply to tax shelters.

(i) In general. Subparagraph (B) shall not apply to any item attributable to a tax shelter.

(ii) Tax shelter. For purposes of clause (i), the term "tax shelter" means—

(I) a partnership or other entity,

(II) any investment plan or arrangement, or

(III) any other plan or arrangement,

if a significant purpose of such partnership, entity, plan, or arrangement is the avoidance or evasion of Federal income tax.

(D) Repealed.

(3) **Secretarial list.** The Secretary may prescribe a list of positions which the Secretary believes do not meet 1 or more of the standards specified in paragraph (2)(B)(i), section 6664(d)(2), and section 6694(a)(1). Such list (and any revisions thereof) shall be published in the Federal Register or the Internal Revenue Bulletin.

(e) **Substantial valuation misstatement under chapter 1.**

(1) **In general.** For purposes of this section, there is a substantial valuation misstatement under chapter 1 if—

(A) the value of any property (or the adjusted basis of any property) claimed on any return of tax imposed by chapter 1 is 150 percent or more of the amount determined to be the correct amount of such valuation or adjusted basis (as the case may be), or

(B)(i) the price for any property or services (or for the use of property) claimed on any such return in connection with any transaction between persons described in section 482 is 200 percent or more (or 50 percent or less) of the amount determined under section 482 to be the correct amount of such price, or

(ii) the net section 482 transfer price adjustment for the taxable year exceeds the lesser of $5,000,000 or 10 percent of the taxpayer's gross receipts.

(2) **Limitation.** No penalty shall be imposed by reason of subsection (b)(3) unless the portion of the underpayment for the taxable year attributable to substantial valuation misstatements under chapter 1 exceeds $5,000 ($10,000 in the case of a corporation other than an S corporation or a personal holding company (as defined in section 542)).

(3) **Net section 482 transfer price adjustment.** For purposes of this subsection—

(A) In general. The term "net section 482 transfer price adjustment" means, with respect to any taxable year, the net increase in taxable income for the taxable year (determined without regard to any amount carried to such taxable year from another taxable year) resulting from adjustments under section 482 in the price for any property or services (or for the use of property).

(B) Certain adjustments excluded in determining threshold. For purposes of determining whether the threshold requirements of paragraph (1)(B)(ii) are met, the following shall be excluded:

(i) Any portion of the net increase in taxable income referred to in subparagraph (A) which is attributable to any redetermination of a price if—

(I) it is established that the taxpayer determined such price in accordance with a specific pricing method set forth in the regulations prescribed under section 482 and that the taxpayer's use of such method was reasonable,

(II) the taxpayer has documentation (which was in existence as of the time of filing the return) which sets forth the determination of such price in accordance with such a method and which establishes that the use of such method was reasonable, and

(III) the taxpayer provides such documentation to the Secretary within 30 days of a request for such documentation.

(ii) Any portion of the net increase in taxable income referred to in subparagraph (A) which is attributable to a redetermination of price where such price was not determined in accordance with such a specific pricing method if—

(I) the taxpayer establishes that none of such pricing methods was likely to result in a price that would clearly reflect income, the taxpayer used another pricing method to determine such price and such other pricing method was likely to result in a price that would clearly reflect income,

(II) the taxpayer has documentation (which was in existence as of the time of filing the return) which sets forth the determination of such price in accordance with such other method and which establishes that the requirements of subclause (I) were satisfied, and

(III) the taxpayer provides such documentation to the Secretary within 30 days of request for such documentation.

(iii) Any portion of such net increase which is attributable to any transaction solely between foreign corporations unless, in the case of any such corporations, the treatment of such transaction affects the determination of income from sources within the United States or taxable income effectively connected with the conduct of a trade or business within the United States.

(C) Special rule. If the regular tax (as defined in section 55(c)) imposed by chapter 1 on the taxpayer is determined by reference to an amount other than taxable income, such amount shall be treated as the taxable income of such taxpayer for purposes of this paragraph.

(D) Coordination with reasonable cause exception. For purposes of section 6664(c) the taxpayer shall not be treated as having reasonable cause for any portion of an underpayment attributable to a net section 482 transfer price adjustment unless such taxpayer meets the requirements of clause (i), (ii), or (iii) of subparagraph (B) with respect to such portion.

(f) Substantial overstatement of pension liabilities.

(1) In general. For purposes of this section, there is a substantial overstatement of pension liabilities if the actuarial determination of the liabilities taken into account for purposes of computing the deduction under paragraph (1) or (2) of section 404(a) is 200 percent or more of the amount determined to be the correct amount of such liabilities.

(2) Limitation. No penalty shall be imposed by reason of subsection (b)(4) unless the portion of the underpayment for the taxable year attributable to substantial overstatements of pension liabilities exceeds $1,000.

(g) Substantial estate or gift tax valuation understatement.

(1) In general. For purposes of this section, there is a substantial estate or gift tax valuation understatement if the value of any property claimed on any return of tax imposed by subtitle B is 65 percent or less of the amount determined to be the correct amount of such valuation.

(2) Limitation. No penalty shall be imposed by reason of subsection (b)(5) unless the portion of the underpayment attributable to substantial estate or gift tax valuation understatements for the taxable period (or, in the case of the tax imposed by chapter 11, with respect to the estate of the decedent) exceeds $5,000.

(h) Increase in penalty in case of gross valuation misstatements.

(1) In general. To the extent that a portion of the underpayment to which this section applies is attributable to one or more gross valuation misstatements, subsection (a)shall be applied with respect to such portion by substituting "40 percent" for "20 percent".

(2) Gross valuation misstatements. The term "gross valuation misstatements" means—

(A) any substantial valuation misstatement under chapter 1 as determined under subsection (e) by substituting—

(i) in paragraph (1)(A), "200 percent" for "150 percent",

(ii) in paragraph (1)(B)(i)—

(I) "400 percent" for "200 percent", and

(II) "25 percent" for "50 percent", and

(iii) in paragraph (1)(B)(ii)—

(I) "$20,000,000" for "$5,000,000" and

(II) "20 percent" for "10 percent".

(B) any substantial overstatement of pension liabilities as determined under subsection (f) by substituting "400 percent" for "200 percent", and

(C) any substantial estate or gift tax valuation understatement as determined under subsection (g) by substituting "40 percent" for "65 percent".

(i) Increase in penalty in case of nondisclosed noneconomic substance transactions.

(1) In general. In the case of any portion of an underpayment which is attributable to one or more nondisclosed noneconomic substance transactions, subsection (a) shall be applied with respect to such portion by substituting "40 percent" for "20 percent".

(2) Nondisclosed noneconomic substance transactions. For purposes of this subsection, the term "nondisclosed noneconomic substance transaction" means any portion of a transaction described in subsection (b)(6) with respect to which the relevant facts affecting the tax treatment are not adequately disclosed in the return nor in a statement attached to the return.

(3) Special rule for amended returns. In no event shall any amendment or supplement to a return of tax be taken into account for purposes of this subsection if the amendment or supplement is filed after the earlier of the date the taxpayer is first contacted by the Secretary regarding the examination of the return or such other date as is specified by the Secretary.

(j) Undisclosed foreign financial asset understatement.

(1) In general. For purposes of this section, the term "undisclosed foreign financial asset understatement" means, for any taxable year, the portion of the understatement for such taxable year which is attributable to any transaction involving an undisclosed foreign financial asset.

(2) Undisclosed foreign financial asset. For purposes of this subsection, the term "undisclosed foreign financial asset" means, with respect to any taxable year, any asset with respect to which information was required to be provided under section 6038, 6038B, 6038D, 6046A, or 6048 for such taxable year but was not provided by the taxpayer as required under the provisions of those sections.

(3) Increase in penalty for undisclosed foreign financial asset understatements. In the case of any portion of an underpayment which is attributable to any undisclosed foreign financial asset understatement, subsection (a)shall be applied with respect to such portion by substituting "40 percent" for "20 percent".

In 2010, P.L. 111-152, Sec. 1409(b)(1), added para. (b)(6)

—P.L. 111-152, Sec. 1409(b)(2), added subsec. (i), effective for underpayments attributable for transactions entered into after 3/30/2010.

—P.L. 111-147, Sec. 512(a)(1), added para. (b)(7) . . . Sec. 512(a)(2), added subsec. (j), effective for tax. yrs. begin. after 3/18/2010.

In 2006, P.L. 109-280, Sec. 1219(a)(1)(A), substituted "150 percent" for "200 percent" in subpara. (e)(1)(A) . . . Sec. 1219(a)(1)(B), substituted "65 percent" for "50 percent" in para. (g)(1) . . . Sec. 1219(a)(2)(A), amended clauses (h)(2)(A)(i) and (ii) . . . Sec. 1219(a)(2)(B), substituted "40 percent" for "65 percent" for "25 percent" for "50 percent" in subpara (h)(2)(C), effective for returns filed after

8/17/2006, except as provided in para. 1219(e)(3), of this Act, which reads as follows:

"(3) Special rule for certain easements. In the case of a contribution of a qualified real property interest which is a restriction with respect to the exterior of a building described in section 170(h)(4)(C)(ii) of the Internal Revenue Code of 1986, and an appraisal with respect to the contribution, the amendments made by subsections (a) and (b) shall apply to returns filed after July 25, 2006."

Prior to amendment, Clauses (h)(2)(A)(i) and (ii) read as follows:

"(i) '400 percent' for '200 percent' each place it appears,

"(ii) '25 percent' for '50 percent', and"

In 2005, P.L. 109-135, Sec. 403(x)(1), added a flush sentence at the end of subsec. (b), effective for tax. yrs. end. after 10/22/2004 as if included in Sec. 812 of the American Jobs Creation Act of 2004, P.L. 108-357 [as amended by Sec. 403(x)(3) of this Act, see below].

—P.L. 109-135, Sec. 403(x)(3), of this Act, which amends Sec. 812(f) of P.L. 108-357, reads as follows:

"(f) Effective dates.

"(1) In general. Except as provided in paragraph (2), the amendments made by this section shall apply to taxable years ending after the date of the enactment of this Act.

"(2) Disqualified opinions. Section 6664(d)(3)(B) of the Internal Revenue Code of 1986 (as added by subsection (c)) shall not apply to the opinion of a tax advisor if—

"(A) the opinion was provided to the taxpayer before the date of the enactment of this Act,

"(B) the opinion relates to one or more transactions all of which were entered into before such date, and

"(C) the tax treatment of items relating to each such transaction was included on a return or statement filed by the taxpayer before such date."

—P.L. 109-135, Sec. 412(aaa), deleted "the" before "1 or more" in para. (d)(3), effective 12/21/2005.

In 2004, P.L. 108-357, Sec. 812(b), added a flush sentence at the end of subpara. (d)(2)(A) . . . Sec. 812(d), amended subpara. (d)(2)(C) . . . Sec. 812(e)(1), amended the heading of Code Sec. 6662, effective for tax. yrs. end. after 10/22/2004. For special rule, see Sec. 403(x)(3) of P.L. 109-135, reproduced above.

Prior to amendment, the heading of Code Sec. 6662 read as follows:

"Sec. 6662. Imposition of accuracy-related penalty."

Prior to amendment, subpara. (d)(2)(C) read as follows:

"(C) Special rules in cases involving tax shelters.

"(i) In general. In the case of any item of a taxpayer other than a corporation which is attributable to a tax shelter—

"(I) subparagraph (B)(ii) shall not apply, and

"(II) subparagraph (B)(i) shall not apply unless (in addition to meeting the requirements of such subparagraph) the taxpayer reasonably believed that the tax treatment of such item by the taxpayer was more likely than not the proper treatment.

"(ii) Subparagraph (B) not to apply to corporations. Subparagraph (B) shall not apply to any item of a corporation which is attributable to a tax shelter.

"(iii) Tax shelter. For purposes of this subparagraph, the term 'tax shelter' means—

"(I) a partnership or other entity,

"(II) any investment plan or arrangement, or

"(III) any other plan or arrangement,

"if a significant purpose of such partnership, entity, plan, or arrangement is the avoidance or evasion of Federal income tax."

—P.L. 108-357, Sec. 819(a), amended subpara. (d)(1)(B) . . . Sec. 819(b)(1), added para. (d)(3) . . . Sec. 819(b)(2), deleted subpara. (d)(2)(D), effective for tax. yrs. begin. after 10/22/2004.

Prior to amendment, subpara. (d)(1)(B) read as follows:

"(B) Special rule for corporations. In the case of a corporation other than an S corporation or a personal holding company (as defined in section 542), paragraph (1) shall be applied by substituting '$10,000' for '$5,000'."

Prior to deletion, subpara. (d)(2)(D) read as follows:

"(D) Secretarial list. The Secretary shall prescribe (and revise not less frequently than annually) a list of positions—

"(i) for which the Secretary believes there is not substantial authority, and

"(ii) which affect a significant number of taxpayers.

"Such list (and any revision thereof) shall be published in the Federal Register."

In 1997, P.L. 105-34, Sec. 1028(c)(1), added sentence at end of subpara. (d)(2)(B). . . . Sec. 1028(c)(2), substituted "a significant purpose" for "the principal purpose" in clause (d)(2)(C)(iii), effective for items with respect to transactions entered into after 8/5/97.

In 1994, P.L. 103-465, Sec. 744(a), redesignated clause (d)(2)(C)(ii) as clause (d)(2)(C)(iii) and added new clause (d)(2)(C)(ii) . . . Sec. 744(b)(1), substituted "In the case of any item of a taxpayer other than a corporation which is" for "In the case of any item" in clause (d)(2)(C)(i) . . . Sec. 744(b)(2), substituted "this subparagraph" for "clause (i)" in clause (d)(2)(C)(iii) [as redesignated by Sec. 744(a) of this Act, see above], effective for items related to transactions occurring after 12/8/94.

In 1993, P.L. 103-66, Sec. 13236(a), amended clause (e)(1)(B)(ii) . . . Sec. 13236(b), amended subpara. (e)(3)(B) . . . Sec. 13236(c), added subpara. (e)(3)(D) . . . Sec. 13236(d), amended clause (h)(2)(A)(iii), effective for tax. yrs. begin. after 12/31/93.

Prior to amendment, clause (e)(1)(B)(ii) read as follows:

"(ii) the net section 482 transfer price adjustment for the taxable year exceeds $10,000,000."

Prior to amendment, subpara. (e)(3)(B) read as follows:

"(B) Certain adjustments excluded in determining threshold. For purposes of determining whether the $10,000,000 threshold requirement of paragraph (1)(B)(ii) is met, there shall be excluded—

"(i) any portion of the net increase in taxable income referred to in subparagraph (A) which is attributable to any redetermination of a price if it is shown that there was a reasonable cause for the taxpayer's determination of such price and that the taxpayer acted in good faith with respect to such price, and

"(ii) any portion of such net increase which is attributable to any transaction solely between foreign corporations unless, in the case of any of such corporations, the treatment of such transaction affects the determination of income from sources within the United States or taxable income effectively connected with the conduct of a trade or business within the United States."

Prior to amendment, clause (h)(2)(A)(iii) reads as follows:

"(iii) '$20,000,000' for '$10,000,000',"

—P.L. 103-66, Sec. 13251(a), amended clause (d)(2)(B)(ii), effective for returns the due dates for which (determined without regard to extensions) are after 12/31/93.

Prior to amendment, clause (d)(2)(B)(ii) read as follows:

"(ii) any item with respect to which the relevant facts affecting the item's tax treatment are adequately disclosed in the return or in a statement attached to the return."

In 1990, P.L. 101-508, Sec. 11312(a), amended subsec. (e) . . . Sec. 11312(b)(1), amended para. (b)(3) . . . Sec. 11312(b)(2), amended subpara. (h)(2)(A), effective for tax. yrs. end. after 11/5/90.

Prior to amendment, subsec. (e) read as follows:

"'(e) Substantial valuation overstatement under chapter 1.

"(1) In general. For purposes of this section, there is a substantial valuation overstatement under chapter 1 if the value of any property (or the adjusted basis of any property) claimed on any return of tax imposed by chapter 1 is 200 percent or more of the amount determined to be the correct amount of such valuation or adjusted basis (as the case may be).

"(2) Limitation. No penalty shall be imposed by reason of subsection (b)(3) unless the portion of the underpayment for the taxable year attributable to substantial valuation overstatements under chapter 1 exceeds $5,000 ($10,000 in the case of a corporation other than an S corporation or a personal holding company (as defined in section 542))."

Prior to amendment, para. (b)(3) read as follows:

"(3) Any substantial valuation overstatement under chapter 1."

Prior to amendment, subpara. (h)(2)(A) read as follows:

"(A) any substantial valuation overstatement under chapter 1 as determined under subsection (e) by substituting '400 percent' for '200 percent'."

In 1989, P.L. 101-239, Sec. 7721(a), added Code Sec. 6662, as part of Part II of subchapter A of chapter 68, effective for returns the due date for which (determined without regard to extensions) is after 12/31/89.

Sec. 6662A. Imposition of accuracy-related penalty on understatements with respect to reportable transactions.

(a) Imposition of penalty.

If a taxpayer has a reportable transaction understatement for any taxable year, there shall be added to the tax an amount equal to 20 percent of the amount of such understatement.

(b) Reportable transaction understatement.

For purposes of this section—

(1) In general. The term "reportable transaction understatement" means the sum of—

(A) the product of—

(i) the amount of the increase (if any) in taxable income which results from a difference between the proper tax treatment of an item to which this section applies and the taxpayer's treatment of such item (as shown on the taxpayer's return of tax), and

(ii) the highest rate of tax imposed by section 1 (section 11 in the case of a taxpayer which is a corporation), and

(B) the amount of the decrease (if any) in the aggregate amount of credits determined under subtitle A which results from a difference between the taxpayer's treatment of an item to which this section applies (as shown on the taxpayer's return of tax) and the proper tax treatment of such item.

For purposes of subparagraph (A), any reduction of the excess of deductions allowed for the taxable year over gross income for such year, and any reduction in the amount of capital losses which would (without regard to

Penalties Code Sec. 6664(a)(1)

section 1211) be allowed for such year, shall be treated as an increase in taxable income.

(2) Items to which section applies. This section shall apply to any item which is attributable to—

(A) any listed transaction, and

(B) any reportable transaction (other than a listed transaction) if a significant purpose of such transaction is the avoidance or evasion of Federal income tax.

(c) Higher penalty for nondisclosed listed and other avoidance transactions.

Subsection (a) shall be applied by substituting "30 percent" for "20 percent" with respect to the portion of any reportable transaction understatement with respect to which the requirement of section 6664(d)(2)(A) is not met.

(d) Definitions of reportable and listed transactions.

For purposes of this section, the terms "reportable transaction" and "listed transaction" have the respective meanings given to such terms by section 6707A(c).

(e) Special rules.

(1) Coordination with penalties, etc., on other understatements. In the case of an understatement (as defined in section 6662(d)(2))—

(A) the amount of such understatement (determined without regard to this paragraph) shall be increased by the aggregate amount of reportable transaction understatements for purposes of determining whether such understatement is a substantial understatement under section 6662(d)(1), and

(B) the addition to tax under section 6662(a) shall apply only to the excess of the amount of the substantial understatement (if any) after the application of subparagraph (A) over the aggregate amount of reportable transaction understatements.

(2) Coordination with other penalties.

(A) Coordination with fraud penalty. This section shall not apply to any portion of an understatement on which a penalty is imposed under section 6663.

(B) Coordination with certain increased underpayment penalties. This section shall not apply to any portion of an understatement on which a penalty is imposed under section 6662 if the rate of the penalty is determined under subsections (h) or (i) of section 6662.

(3) Special rule for amended returns. Except as provided in regulations, in no event shall any tax treatment included with an amendment or supplement to a return of tax be taken into account in determining the amount of any reportable transaction understatement if the amendment or supplement is filed after the earlier of the date the taxpayer is first contacted by the Secretary regarding the examination of the return or such other date as is specified by the Secretary.

In 2010, P.L. 111-240, Sec. 2103, of this Act, reads as follows:

"SEC. 2103. Report on Tax Shelter Penalties and Certain Other Enforcement Actions.

"(a) In general. The Commissioner of Internal Revenue, in consultation with the Secretary of the Treasury, shall submit to the Committee on Ways and Means of the House of Representatives and the Committee on Finance of the Senate an annual report on the penalties assessed by the Internal Revenue Service during the preceding year under each of the following provisions of the Internal Revenue Code of 1986:

"(1) Section 6662A (relating to accuracy-related penalty on understatements with respect to reportable transactions).

"(2) Section 6700(a) (relating to promoting abusive tax shelters).

"(3) Section 6707 (relating to failure to furnish information regarding reportable transactions).

"(4) Section 6707A (relating to failure to include reportable transaction information with return).

"(5) Section 6708 (relating to failure to maintain lists of advisees with respect to reportable transactions).

"(b) Additional information. The report required under subsection (a) shall also include information on the following with respect to each year:

"(1) Any action taken under section 330(b) of title 31, United States Code, with respect to any reportable transaction (as defined in section 6707A(c) of the Internal Revenue Code of 1986).

"(2) Any extension of the time for assessment of tax enforced, or assessment of any amount under such an extension, under paragraph (10) of section 6501(c) of the Internal Revenue Code of 1986.

"(c) Date of report. The first report required under subsection (a) shall be submitted not later than December 31, 2010."

—P.L. 111-152, Sec. 1409(b)(3)(A), substituted "subsections (h) or (i) of section 6662" for "section 6662(h)" in subpara (e)(2)(B)

—P.L. 111-152, Sec. 1409(b)(3)(B), substituted "certain increased underpayment penalties" for "gross valuation misstatement penalty" in the heading to subpara. (e)(2)(B), effective for underpayments attributable to transactions entered into after 3/30/2010.

In 2005, P.L. 109-135, Sec. 403(x)(2), amended para. (e)(2), effective for tax. yrs. end. after 10/22/2004 as if included in Sec. 812 of the American Jobs Creation Act of 2004, P.L. 108-357 [as amended by Sec. 403(x)(3) of this Act, see below]. Prior to amendment, para. (e)(2) read as follows:

"(2) Coordination with other penalties.

"(A) Application of fraud penalty. References to an underpayment in section 6663 shall be treated as including references to a reportable transaction understatement.

"(B) No double penalty. This section shall not apply to any portion of an understatement on which a penalty is imposed under section 6663.

"(C) Coordination with valuation penalties.

"(i) Section 6662(e). Section 6662(e) shall not apply to any portion of an understatement on which a penalty is imposed under this section.

"(ii) Section 6662(h). This section shall not apply to any portion of an understatement on which a penalty is imposed under section 6662(h)."

—P.L. 109-135, Sec. 403(x)(3), amended Sec. 812(f) of P.L. 108-357 [which provides the effective date for the amendment made by Sec. 812(a) of P.L. 108-357, see below], to read as follows:

"(f) Effective dates.

"(1) In general. Except as provided in paragraph (2), the amendments made by this section shall apply to taxable years ending after the date of the enactment of this Act.

"(2) Disqualified opinions. Section 6664(d)(3)(B) of the Internal Revenue Code of 1986 (as added by subsection (c)) shall not apply to the opinion of a tax advisor if—

"(A) the opinion was provided to the taxpayer before the date of the enactment of this Act,

"(B) the opinion relates to one or more transactions all of which were entered into before such date, and

"(C) the tax treatment of items relating to each such transaction was included on a return or statement filed by the taxpayer before such date."

In 2004, P.L. 108-357, Sec. 812(a), added Code Sec. 6662A, effective for tax. yrs. end. after 10/22/2004. For special rule, see Sec. 403(x)(3) of P.L. 109-135, reproduced above.

Sec. 6663. Imposition of fraud penalty.

(a) Imposition of penalty.

If any part of any underpayment of tax required to be shown on a return is due to fraud, there shall be added to the tax an amount equal to 75 percent of the portion of the underpayment which is attributable to fraud.

(b) Determination of portion attributable to fraud.

If the Secretary establishes that any portion of an underpayment is attributable to fraud, the entire underpayment shall be treated as attributable to fraud, except with respect to any portion of the underpayment which the taxpayer establishes (by a preponderance of the evidence) is not attributable to fraud.

(c) Special rule for joint returns.

In the case of a joint return, this section shall not apply with respect to a spouse unless some part of the underpayment is due to the fraud of such spouse.

In 1989, P.L. 101-239, Sec. 7721(a), added Code Sec. 6663, effective for returns the due date for which (determined without regard to extensions) is after 12/31/89.

Sec. 6664. Definitions and special rules.

(a) Underpayment.

For purposes of this part, the term "underpayment" means the amount by which any tax imposed by this title exceeds the excess of—

(1) the sum of—

3,799

(A) the amount shown as the tax by the taxpayer on his return, plus
(B) amounts not so shown previously assessed (or collected without assessment), over
(2) the amount of rebates made.

For purposes of paragraph (2), the term "rebate" means so much of an abatement, credit, refund, or other repayment, as was made on the ground that the tax imposed was less than the excess of the amount specified in paragraph (1) over the rebates previously made.

(b) Penalties applicable only where return filed.
The penalties provided in this part shall apply only in cases where a return of tax is filed (other than a return prepared by the Secretary under the authority of section 6020(b)).

(c) Reasonable cause exception for underpayments.
(1) **In general.** No penalty shall be imposed under section 6662 or 6663 with respect to any portion of an underpayment if it is shown that there was a reasonable cause for such portion and that the taxpayer acted in good faith with respect to such portion.
(2) **Exception.** Paragraph (1) shall not apply to any portion of an underpayment which is attributable to one or more transactions described in section 6662(b)(6).
(3) **Special rule for certain valuation overstatements.** In the case of any underpayment attributable to a substantial or gross valuation overstatement under chapter 1 with respect to charitable deduction property, paragraph (1) shall not apply. The preceding sentence shall not apply to a substantial valuation overstatement under chapter 1 if—
(A) the claimed value of the property was based on a qualified appraisal made by a qualified appraiser, and
(B) in addition to obtaining such appraisal, the taxpayer made a good faith investigation of the value of the contributed property.
(4) **Definitions.** For purposes of this subsection—
(A) Charitable deduction property. The term "charitable deduction property" means any property contributed by the taxpayer in a contribution for which a deduction was claimed under section 170. For purposes of paragraph (3), such term shall not include any securities for which (as of the date of the contribution) market quotations are readily available on an established securities market.
(B) Qualified appraisal. The term "qualified appraisal" has the meaning given such term by section 170(f)(11)(E)(i).
(C) Qualified appraiser. The term "qualified appraiser" has the meaning given such term by section 170(f)(11)(E)(ii).

(d) Reasonable cause exception for reportable transaction understatements.
(1) **In general.** No penalty shall be imposed under section 6662A with respect to any portion of a reportable transaction understatement if it is shown that there was a reasonable cause for such portion and that the taxpayer acted in good faith with respect to such portion.
(2) **Exception.** Paragraph (1) shall not apply to any portion of a reportable transaction understatement which is attributable to one or more transactions described in section 6662(b)(6).
(3) **Special rules.** Paragraph (1) shall not apply to any reportable transaction understatement unless—
(A) the relevant facts affecting the tax treatment of the item are adequately disclosed in accordance with the regulations prescribed under section 6011,

(B) there is or was substantial authority for such treatment, and
(C) the taxpayer reasonably believed that such treatment was more likely than not the proper treatment.

A taxpayer failing to adequately disclose in accordance with section 6011 shall be treated as meeting the requirements of subparagraph (A) if the penalty for such failure was rescinded under section 6707A(d).

(4) **Rules relating to reasonable belief.** For purposes of paragraph (3)(C)—
(A) In general. A taxpayer shall be treated as having a reasonable belief with respect to the tax treatment of an item only if such belief—
(i) is based on the facts and law that exist at the time the return of tax which includes such tax treatment is filed, and
(ii) relates solely to the taxpayer's chances of success on the merits of such treatment and does not take into account the possibility that a return will not be audited, such treatment will not be raised on audit, or such treatment will be resolved through settlement if it is raised.
(B) Certain opinions may not be relied upon.
(i) In general. An opinion of a tax advisor may not be relied upon to establish the reasonable belief of a taxpayer if—
(I) the tax advisor is described in clause (ii), or
(II) the opinion is described in clause (iii).
(ii) Disqualified tax advisors. A tax advisor is described in this clause if the tax advisor—
(I) is a material advisor (within the meaning of section 6111(b)(1)) and participates in the organization, management, promotion, or sale of the transaction or is related (within the meaning of section 267(b) or 707(b)(1)) to any person who so participates,
(II) is compensated directly or indirectly by a material advisor with respect to the transaction,
(III) has a fee arrangement with respect to the transaction which is contingent on all or part of the intended tax benefits from the transaction being sustained, or
(IV) as determined under regulations prescribed by the Secretary, has a disqualifying financial interest with respect to the transaction.
(iii) Disqualified opinions. For purposes of clause (i), an opinion is disqualified if the opinion—
(I) is based on unreasonable factual or legal assumptions (including assumptions as to future events),
(II) unreasonably relies on representations, statements, findings, or agreements of the taxpayer or any other person,
(III) does not identify and consider all relevant facts, or
(IV) fails to meet any other requirement as the Secretary may prescribe.

In 2010, P.L. 111-152, Sec. 1409(c)(1)(A), redesignated paras. (c)(2) and (c)(3) as paras. (c)(3) and (c)(4)... Sec. 1409(c)(1)(B), substituted "paragraph (3)" for "paragraph (2)" in subpara. (c)(4)(A) [as redesignated by Sec. 1409(c)(1)(A) of this Act]... Sec. 1409(c)(1)(C), added para. (c)(2), effective for underpayments attributable to transactions entered into after 3/30/2010.... Sec. 1409(d)(1)(A), redesignated paras. (d)(2) and (d)(3) as paras. (d)(3) and (d)(4)... Sec. 1409(d)(1)(B), substituted "paragraph (3)(C)" for "paragraph (2)(C)" in subpara. (d)(4) [as redesignated by Sec. 1409(d)(1)(A) of this Act]... Sec. 1409(d)(1)(C), added para. (d)(2), effective for understatements attributable to transactions entered into after 3/30/2010.

Penalties   Part I

In 2006, P.L. 109-280, Sec. 1219(a)(3), substituted "paragraph (1) shall not apply. The preceding sentence shall not apply to a substantial valuation overstatement under chapter 1 if" for "paragraph (1) shall not apply unless" in para. (c)(2), effective for returns filed after 8/17/2006, except as provided in Sec. 1219(e)(3) of this Act, which reads as follows:

"(3) Special rule for certain easements. In the case of a contribution of a qualified real property interest which is a restriction with respect to the exterior of a building described in section 170(h)(4)(C)(ii) of the Internal Revenue Code of 1986, and an appraisal with respect to the contribution, the amendments made by subsections (a) and (b) shall apply to returns filed after July 25, 2006."

—P.L. 109-280, Sec. 1219(c)(2), amended subparas. (c)(3)(B) and (C), effective for appraisals prepared with respect to returns or submissions files after 8/17/2006, except as provided in Sec. 1219(e)(3) of this Act, which reads as follows:

"(3) Special rule for certain easements. In the case of a contribution of a qualified real property interest which is a restriction with respect to the exterior of a building described in section 170(h)(4)(C)(ii) of the Internal Revenue Code of 1986, and an appraisal with respect to the contribution, the amendments made by subsections (a) and (b) shall apply to returns filed after July 25, 2006."

Prior to amendment, subparas. (c)(3)(B) and (C) read as follows:

"(B) Qualified appraiser. The term 'qualified appraiser' means any appraiser meeting the requirements of the regulations prescribed under section 170(a)(1).

"(C) Qualified appraisal. The term 'qualified appraisal' means any appraisal meeting the requirements of the regulations prescribed under section 170(a)(1)."

In 2005, P.L. 109-135, Sec. 403(x)(3), amended Sec. 812(f) of P.L. 108-357, which provides the effective date for the amendments made by Sec. 812(c)(1), (c)(2)(A) and (c)(2)(B) of P.L. 108-357, see below.

As amended, Sec. 812(f) of P.L. 108-357 reads as follows:

"(f) Effective dates.

"(1) In general. Except as provided in paragraph (2), the amendments made by this section shall apply to taxable years ending after the date of the enactment of this Act.

"(2) Disqualified opinions. Section 6664(d)(3)(B) of the Internal Revenue Code of 1986 (as added by subsection (c)) shall not apply to the opinion of a tax advisor if—

"(A) the opinion was provided to the taxpayer before the date of the enactment of this Act,

"(B) the opinion relates to one or more transactions all of which were entered into before such date, and

"(C) the tax treatment of items relating to each such transaction was included on a return or statement filed by the taxpayer before such date."

In 2004, P.L. 108-357, Sec. 812(c)(1), added subsec. (d) . . . Sec. 812(c)(2)(A), substituted "section 6662 or 6663" for "this part" in para. (c)(1) . . . Sec. 812(c)(2)(B), added "for underpayments" after "exception" in the heading of subsec. (c), effective for tax. yrs. end. after 10/22/2004 as provided in Sec. 403(x)(3) of P.L. 109-135, see above. For special exception, see Sec. 403(x)(3) of P.L. 109-135, reproduced above.

In 1989, P.L. 101-239, Sec. 7721(a), added Code Sec. 6664, effective for returns the due date for which (determined without regard to extensions) is after 12/31/89.

PART III.—APPLICABLE RULES

Sec.
6665. Applicable rules.

Sec. 6665. Applicable rules.
(a) Additions treated as tax.

Except as otherwise provided in this title—

(1) the additions to the tax, additional amounts, and penalties provided by this chapter shall be paid upon notice and demand and shall be assessed, collected, and paid in the same manner as taxes; and

(2) any reference in this title to "tax" imposed by this title shall be deemed also to refer to the additions to the tax, additional amounts, and penalties provided by this chapter.

(b) Procedure for assessing certain additions to tax.

For purposes of subchapter B of chapter 63 (relating to deficiency procedures for income, estate, gift, and certain excise taxes), subsection (a) shall not apply to any addition to tax under section 6651, 6654, or 6655; except that it shall apply—

(1) in the case of an addition described in section 6651, to that portion of such addition which is attributable to a deficiency in tax described in section 6211; or

(2) to an addition described in section 6654 or 6655, if no return is filed for the taxable year.

In 1989, P.L. 101-239, Sec. 7721(a), added Code Sec. 6665, effective for returns the due date for which (determined without regard to extensions) is after 12/31/89.

Subchapter B.—Assessable Penalties

Part.
I. General Provisions.
II. Failure to comply with certain information reporting requirements.

In 1986, P.L. 99-514, Sec. 1501(d)(3), added items for Part I and Part II.

PART I.—GENERAL PROVISIONS

Sec.
6671. Rules for application of assessable penalties.
6672. Failure to collect and pay over tax, or attempt to evade or defeat tax.
6673. Sanctions and costs awarded by courts.
6674. Fraudulent statement or failure to furnish statement to employee.
6675. Excessive claims with respect to the use of certain fuels.
6676. Erroneous claim for refund or credit.
6677. Failure to file information with respect to certain foreign trusts.
6679. Failure to file returns, etc., with respect to foreign corporations or foreign partnerships.
6682. False information with respect to withholding.
6683. Repealed [Failure of foreign corporation to file return of personal holding company tax.]
6684. Assessable penalties with respect to liability for tax under chapter 42.
6685. Assessable penalty with respect to public inspection requirements for certain tax-exempt organizations.
6686. Failure to file returns or supply information by DISC or former FSC.
6687. Repealed.
6688. Assessable penalties with respect to information required to be furnished under section 7654.
6689. Failure to file notice of redetermination of foreign tax.
6690. Fraudulent statement or failure to furnish statement to plan participant.
6692. Failure to file actuarial report.
6693. Failure to provide reports on certain tax-favored accounts or annuities; penalties relating to designated nondeductible contributions.
6694. Understatement of taxpayer's liability by tax return preparer.
6695. Other assessable penalties with respect to the preparation of tax returns for other persons.
6695A. Substantial and gross valuation misstatements attributable to incorrect appraisals.
6696. Rules applicable with respect to sections 6694, 6695, and 6695A
6697. Repealed.
6698. Failure to file partnership return.
6698A. Repealed.
6699. Failure to file S corporation return.
6700. Promoting abusive tax shelters, etc.
6701. Penalties for aiding and abetting understatement of tax liability.
6702. Frivolous income tax return.

3,801

Part I

Penalties

6703. Rules applicable to penalties under sections 6700, 6701, and 6702.
6704. Failure to keep records necessary to meet reporting requirements under section 6047(d).
6705. Failure by broker to provide notice to payors.
6706. Original issue discount information requirements.
6707. Failure to furnish information regarding reportable transactions.
6707A. Penalty for failure to include reportable transaction information with return.
6708. Failure to maintain lists of advisees with respect to reportable transactions.
6709. Penalties with respect to mortgage credit certificates.
6710. Failure to disclose that contributions are nondeductible.
6711. Failure by tax-exempt organization to disclose that certain information or service available from Federal Government.
6712. Failure to disclose treaty-based return positions.
6713. Disclosure or use of information by preparers of returns.
6714. Failure to meet disclosure requirements applicable to quid pro quo contributions.
6715. Dyed fuel sold for use or used in taxable use, etc.
6715A. Tampering with or failing to maintain security requirements for mechanical dye injection systems.
6716. Failure to file information with respect to certain transfers at death and gifts.
6717. Refusal of entry.
6718. Failure to display tax registration on vessels.
6719. Failure to register or reregister.
6720. Fraudulent acknowledgments with respect to donations of motor vehicles, boats, and airplanes.
6720A. Penalty with respect to certain adulterated fuels.
6720B. Fraudulent identification of exempt use property.
6720C. Penalty for failure to notify health plan of cessation of eligibility for COBRA premium assistance.

In **2010,** P.L. 111-325, Sec. 501(a), amended item 6697.
Prior to amendment, item 6697 read as follows:
"Sec. 6697. Assessable penalties with respect to liability for tax of regulated investment companies. . . ."
In **2009,** P.L. 111-5, Sec. 3001(a)(13)(A), added item 6720C.
In **2007,** P.L. 110-172, Sec. 11(g)(21), added "former" before "FSC" in item 6686.
—P.L. 110-142, Sec. 9(b), added item 6699.
—P.L. 110-28, Sec. 8246(a)(2)(F)(ii), amended item 6694.
Prior to amendment, item 6694 read as follows:
"Sec. 6694. Understatement of taxpayer's liability by income tax return preparer."
—P.L. 110-28, Sec. 8246(a)(2)(G)(iii), amended item 6695.
Prior to amendment, item 6695 read as follows:
"Sec. 6695. Other assessable penalties with respect to the preparation of income tax returns for other persons."
—P.L. 110-28, Sec. 8247(b), added item 6676.
In **2006,** P.L. 109-280, Sec. 1215(c)(2), added item 6720B.
—P.L. 109-280, Sec. 1219(b)(3), added item 6695A and amended item 6696.
Prior to amendment, item 6696 read as follows:
"Sec. 6696. Rules applicable with respect to sections 6694 and 6695."
In **2005,** P.L. 109-135, Sec. 403(n)(3)(B), repealed item 6683.
Prior to repeal, item 6683 read as follows:
"6683. Failure of foreign corporation to file return of personal holding company tax."
—P.L. 109-59, Sec. 1164(b)(4), added "or reregister" after "register" in item 6719.
—P.L. 109-59, Sec. 1167(c), added item 6720A.
In **2004,** P.L. 108-357, Sec. 811(b), added item 6707A. . . . Sec. 815(b)(5)(B), amended item 6708. . . . Sec. 816(b), substituted "reportable transactions" for "tax shelters" in item 6707. . . . Sec. 854(c)(2), added item 6715A. . . . Sec. 859(b)(2),
added item 6717. . . . Sec. 861(b)(2), added item 6718. . . . Sec. 863(c)(2), added item 6719. . . . Sec. 884(b)(2), added item 6720.
Prior to amendment, item 6708 read as follows:
"6708. Failure to maintain lists of investors in potentially abusive tax shelters."
In **2001,** P.L. 107-16, Sec. 542(b)(5)(A), added item 6716.
In **1997,** P.L. 105-34, Sec. 211(e)(2)(D), substituted "certain tax-favored" for "individual retirement" in item 6693.
In **1996,** P.L. 104-188, Sec. 1703(n)(9)(B), changed item 6714 regarding dye fuel to item 6715 . . . Sec. 1901(c)(3), amended item 6677.
Prior to amendment, item 6677 read as follows:
"Sec. 6677. Failure to file information returns with respect to certain foreign trusts."
In **1993,** P.L. 103-66, Sec. 13173(c)(2), added item 6714 . . . Sec. 13242(b)(2), added item 6714 [sic 6715]
In **1989,** P.L. 101-239, Sec. 7711(b)(4), deleted item 6676.
Prior to deletion, item 6676 read as follows:
"6676. Failure to supply identifying numbers."
—P.L. 101-239, Sec. 7711(b)(4), deleted item 6687.
Prior to deletion, item 6687 read as follows:
"6687. Failure to supply information with respect to place of residence."
—P.L. 101-239, Sec. 7816(v)(2), deleted the item added by Sec. 6242 of P.L. 100-647 and added item 6713.
In **1988,** P.L. 100-647, Sec. 1011(b)(4)(B)(ii), substituted "penalties relating to" for "overstatement of" in item 6693 . . . Sec. 1012(aa)(5)(C)(ii), added new item 6712 [sic] . . . Sec. 6242(c), added new item 6712 [sic].
In **1987,** P.L. 100-203, Sec. 10701(c)(2), added item 6710 . . . Sec. 10704(b)(2), amended item 6685.
Prior to amendment, item 6685 read as follows:
"6685. Assessable penalties with respect to private foundation annual returns."
—P.L. 100-203, Sec. 10705(b), added item 6711.
In **1986,** P.L. 99-514, Sec. 667(b), substituted "regulated" for "qualified" in item 6697 . . . Sec. 1102(d)(2)(C), added "overstatement of designated nondeductible contributions" after "annuities" in item 6693 . . . Sec. 1171(b)(7)(B), deleted item 6699 . . . Sec. 1501(d)(4), deleted item 6678 . . . Sec. 1848(e)(3), substituted "section 6047(d)" for "section 6047(e)" in item 6704 . . . Sec. 1862(d)(3), redesignated item 6708 relating to penalties with respect to mortgage credit certificates as item 6709. Prior to deletion item 6699 read as follows:
"6699. Assessable penalties relating to tax credit employee stock ownership plan."
Prior to deletion item 6678 read as follows:
"6678. Failure to furnish certain statements."
In **1984,** P.L. 98-369, Sec. 41(c)(2), added item 6706 . . . Sec. 141(c)(2), added item 6707 . . . Sec. 142(c)(2), added item 6708 . . . Sec. 612(d)(2), added item 6708 [sic 6709] . . . Sec. 801(d)(15)(B), amended item 6686.
Prior to amendment, item 6686 read as follows:
"6686. Failure of DISC to file returns."
In **1983,** P.L. 97-424, Sec. 515(b)(11)(D), deleted "or lubricating oil" from after "certain gasoline" in item 6675.
—P.L. 97-448, Sec. 306(c)(2)(B), corrected Sec. 405(c)(2) & (3) of P.L. 97-248, (which amended the heading of Code Sec. 6679 to read "Failure to file returns, etc., with respect to foreign corporations or foreign partnerships."
In **1982,** P.L. 97-248, Sec. 292(d)(2)(B), substituted "primarily for delay, etc." for "merely for delay." in item 6673.
—97-248, Sec. 320(b), added item 6700.
—97-248, Sec. 322(b), added item 6703.
—97-248, Sec. 324(b), added item 6701.
—97-248, Sec. 326(b), added item 6702.
—97-248, Sec. 334(c)(2), added item 6704.
—97-248, Sec. 340(b)(3), amended item 6679. Prior to amendment item 6679 read as follows:
"6679. Failure to file returns as to organization or reorganization of foreign corporations and as to acquisitions of their stock."
—97-248, Sec. 405(c)(3), amended item 6679. Prior to amendment item 6679 (as amended by Sec. 340(b)(3) of this Act, see above) read as follows:
"6679. Failure to file returns or supply information under section 6035 or 6046."
In **1981,** P.L. 97-34, Sec. 721(c), amended item 6682.
Prior to amendment, item 6682 read as follows:
"6682. False information with respect to withholding allowances based on itemized deductions."
In **1980,** P.L. 96-603, Sec. 1(e)(3), substituted "returns" for "reports" in item 6685.
—P.L. 96-603, Sec. 2(d)(2), added item 6689.
—P.L. 96-223, Sec. 401(a), repealed Sec. 2005(e)(4) of P.L. 96-223 and repealed Sec. 702(r)(1)(C) of P.L. 95-600 and the amendments made by Secs. 2004(e)(4) and 702(r)(1)(C) [see below].
—P.L. 96-223, Sec. 107(a)(2)(E), redesignated item 6698 [Failure to file information with respect to carryover basis property] as 6698A [inoperative, see Sec. 401(a) of P.L. 96-223, above].
—P.L. 96-222, Sec. 101(a)(7)(L)(v)(X), substituted "tax credit employee stock ownership plan" for "ESOP" in item 6699.
In **1978,** P.L. 95-600, Sec. 141(c)(2), added item 6699.
—P.L. 95-600, Sec. 211(b), added item 6698 [sic]. (P.L. 95-600, created two Code Secs. 6698.)
—P.L. 95-600, Sec. 362(d)(9), amended item 6697.
Prior to amendment, item for 6697 read as follows:

"Assessable penalties with respect to liability for tax of real estate investment trusts."
—P.L. 95-600, Sec. 702(r)(1)(C), redesignated item 6694 as item 6698, but Sec. 702(r)(1)(c) was repealed by Sec. 401(a) of P.L. 96-223 [see above].
In **1976**, P.L. 94-455, Sec. 1203(i)(3), added item 6694 through 6696 [P.L. 94-455 added two Code Secs. 6694].
—P.L. 94-455, Sec. 1601(b)(2), added item 6697.
—P.L. 94-455, Sec. 2005(e)(4), added item 6694, but Sec. 2005(e)(4) was repealed by Sec. 401(a) of P.L. 96-223 [see above]. Item 6694 added by Sec. 2005(e)(4) read as follows:
"6694. Failure to file information with respect to carryover basis property."
In **1974**, P.L. 93-406, Sec. 1016(b)(3), substituted "6688" for "6687" as the section number for that section entitled "Assessable penalties with respect to information required to be furnished under section 7654."
—P.L. 93-406, Sec. 1031(b)(2)(B), 1033(d), and 2002(h)(4) added items 6690, 6692, and 6693, respectively, to this table.
In **1973**, P.L. 93-17, Sec. 3(d)(3)(B), added item 6689.
In **1972**, P.L. 92-606, Sec. 1(f)(7), added item 6687.
—added item 6687.
In **1971**, added item 6686.
In **1969**, P.L. 91-172, Sec. 101(j)(60), added items 6684 and 6685.
In **1966**, P.L. 89-809, Sec. 104, added item 6683.
—added item 6682.
In **1965**, added "or lubricating oil" in item 6675.
In **1964**, inserted items 6680 and 6681.
In **1962**, added items 6677-6679.
In **1961**, added item 6676.
In **1956**, substituted "Excessive claims with respect to the use of certain gasoline" for "Excessive claims for gasoline used on farms" in item "6675."
—inserted item "6675. Excessive claims for gasoline used on farms."

Sec. 6671. Rules for application of assessable penalties.
(a) Penalty assessed as tax.

The penalties and liabilities provided by this subchapter shall be paid upon notice and demand by the Secretary, and shall be assessed and collected in the same manner as taxes. Except as otherwise provided, any reference in this title to "tax" imposed by this title shall be deemed also to refer to the penalties and liabilities provided by this subchapter.

(b) Person defined.

The term "person", as used in this subchapter, includes an officer or employee of a corporation, or a member or employee of a partnership, who as such officer, employee, or member is under a duty to perform the act in respect of which the violation occurs.

In **1976**, P.L. 94-455, Sec. 1906(b)(13)(A), substituted "Secretary" for "Secretary or his delegate" in Code Sec. 6671, effective 2/1/77.

Sec. 6672. Failure to collect and pay over tax, or attempt to evade or defeat tax.
(a) General rule.

Any person required to collect, truthfully account for, and pay over any tax imposed by this title who willfully fails to collect such tax, or truthfully account for and pay over such tax, or willfully attempts in any manner to evade or defeat any such tax or the payment thereof, shall, in addition to other penalties provided by law, be liable to a penalty equal to the total amount of the tax evaded, or not collected, or not accounted for and paid over. No penalty shall be imposed under section 6653 or part II of subchapter A of chapter 68 for any offense to which this section is applicable.

(b) Preliminary notice requirement.

(1) In general. No penalty shall be imposed under subsection (a) unless the Secretary notifies the taxpayer in writing by mail to an address as determined under section 6212(b) or in person that the taxpayer shall be subject to an assessment of such penalty.

(2) Timing of notice. The mailing of the notice described in paragraph (1) (or, in the case of such a notice delivered in person, such delivery) shall precede any notice and demand of any penalty under subsection (a) by at least 60 days.

(3) Statute of limitations. If a notice described in paragraph (1) with respect to any penalty is mailed or delivered in person before the expiration of the period provided by section 6501 for the assessment of such penalty (determined without regard to this paragraph), the period provided by such section for the assessment of such penalty shall not expire before the later of—

(A) the date 90 days after the date on which such notice was mailed or delivered in person, or

(B) if there is a timely protest of the proposed assessment, the date 30 days after the Secretary makes a final administrative determination with respect to such protest.

(4) Exception for jeopardy. This subsection shall not apply if the Secretary finds that the collection of the penalty is in jeopardy.

(c) Extension of period of collection where bond is filed.

(1) In general. If, within 30 days after the day on which notice and demand of any penalty under subsection (a) is made against any person, such person—

(A) pays an amount which is not less than the minimum amount required to commence a proceeding in court with respect to his liability for such penalty,

(B) files a claim for refund of the amount so paid, and

(C) furnishes a bond which meets the requirements of paragraph (3),

no levy or proceeding in court for the collection of the remainder of such penalty shall be made, begun, or prosecuted until a final resolution of a proceeding begun as provided in paragraph (2). Notwithstanding the provisions of section 7421(a), the beginning of such proceeding or levy during the time such prohibition is in force may be enjoined by a proceeding in the proper court. Nothing in this paragraph shall be construed to prohibit any counterclaim for the remainder of such penalty in a proceeding begun as provided in paragraph (2).

(2) Suit must be brought to determine liability for penalty. If, within 30 days after the day on which his claim for refund with respect to any penalty under subsection (a) is denied, the person described in paragraph (1) fails to begin a proceeding in the appropriate United States district court (or in the Court of Claims) for the determination of his liability for such penalty, paragraph (1) shall cease to apply with respect to such penalty, effective on the day following the close of the 30-day period referred to in this paragraph.

(3) Bond. The bond referred to in paragraph (1) shall be in such form and with such sureties as the Secretary may by regulations prescribe and shall be in an amount equal to 1½ times the amount of excess of the penalty assessed over the payment described in paragraph (1).

(4) Suspension of running of period of limitations on collection. The running of the period of limitations provided in section 6502 on the collection by levy or by a proceeding in court in respect of any penalty described in paragraph (1) shall be suspended for the period during which the Secretary is prohibited from collecting by levy or a proceeding in court.

(5) Jeopardy collection. If the Secretary makes a finding that the collection of the penalty is in jeopardy, nothing in this subsection shall prevent the immediate collection of such penalty.

(d) Right of contribution where more than 1 person liable for penalty.

If more than 1 person is liable for the penalty under subsection (a) with respect to any tax, each person who paid such penalty shall be entitled to recover from other persons

Code Sec. 6672(d) — **Penalties**

who are liable for such penalty an amount equal to the excess of the amount paid by such person over such person's proportionate share of the penalty. Any claim for such a recovery may be made only in a proceeding which is separate from, and is not joined or consolidated with—

(1) an action for collection of such penalty brought by the United States, or

(2) a proceeding in which the United States files a counterclaim or third-party complaint for the collection of such penalty.

(e) **Exception for voluntary board members of tax-exempt organizations.**

No penalty shall be imposed by subsection (a) on any unpaid, volunteer member of any board of trustees or directors of an organization exempt from tax under subtitle A if such member—

(1) is solely serving in an honorary capacity,

(2) does not participate in the day-to-day or financial operations of the organization, and

(3) does not have actual knowledge of the failure on which such penalty is imposed.

The preceding sentence shall not apply if it results in no person being liable for the penalty imposed by subsection (a).

In **1998**, P.L. 105-206, Sec. 3307(a), added "or in person" after "section 6212(b)" in para. (b)(1) ... Sec. 3307(b)(1), added "(or, in the case of such a notice delivered in person, such delivery)" after "paragraph (1)" in para. (b)(2) ... Sec. 3307(b)(2), added "or delivered in person" after "mailed" each place it appeared in para. (b)(3), effective 7/22/98.

In **1996**, P.L. 104-168, Sec. 901(a), redesignated subsec. (b) as (c) and added new subsec. (b), effective for proposed assessments made after 6/30/96.

—P.L. 104-168, Sec. 903(a), added subsec. (d), effective for penalties assessed after 7/30/96.

—P.L. 104-168, Sec. 904(a), added subsec. (e), effective 7/30/96.

—P.L. 104-168, Sec. 904(b), of this Act, provides:

"(b) Public information requirements.

"(1) In general. The Secretary of the Treasury or the Secretary's delegate (hereafter in this subsection referred to as the 'Secretary') shall take such actions as may be appropriate to ensure that employees are aware of their responsibilities under the Federal tax depository system, the circumstances under which employees may be liable for the penalty imposed by section 6672 of the Internal Revenue Code of 1986, and the responsibility to promptly report to the Internal Revenue Service any failure referred to in subsection (a) of such section 6672. Such actions shall include—

"(A) printing of a warning on deposit coupon booklets and the appropriate tax returns that certain employees may be liable for the penalty imposed by such section 6672, and

"(B) the development of a special information packet.

"(2) Development of explanatory materials. The Secretary shall develop materials explaining the circumstances under which board members of tax-exempt organizations (including voluntary and honorary members) may be subject to penalty under section 6672 of such Code. Such materials shall be made available to tax-exempt organizations.

"(3) IRS instructions. The Secretary shall clarify the instructions to Internal Revenue Service employees on the application of the penalty under section 6672 of such Code with regard to voluntary members of boards of trustees or directors of tax-exempt organizations."

In **1989**, P.L. 101-239, Sec. 7721(c)(9), substituted "under section 6653 or part II of subchapter A of chapter 68" for "under section 6653" in subsec. (a), effective for returns for which (determined without regard to extensions) the due date is after 12/31/89.

—P.L. 101-239, Sec. 7737(a), added the last sentence to para. (b)(1), effective 12/19/89.

In **1982**, P.L. 97-248, Sec. 334(e)(4), provides:

"(6) Waiver of penalty.— No penalty shall be assessed under section 6672 with respect to any failure to withhold as required by the amendments made by this section [Code Sec. 3405] if such failure was before July 1, 1983, and if the person made a good faith effort to comply with such withholding requirements."

In **1978**, P.L. 95-628, Sec. 9(a), added "(a) General rule." before "Any person" and added subsec. (b), effective for penalties assessed more than 60 days after 11/10/78.

Sec. 6673. Sanctions and costs awarded by courts.

(a) **Tax court proceedings.**

(1) **Procedures instituted primarily for delay, etc.** Whenever it appears to the Tax Court that—

(A) proceedings before it have been instituted or maintained by the taxpayer primarily for delay,

(B) the taxpayer's position in such proceeding is frivolous or groundless, or

(C) the taxpayer unreasonably failed to pursue available administrative remedies,

the Tax Court, in its decision, may require the taxpayer to pay to the United States a penalty not in excess of $25,000.

(2) **Counsel's liability for excessive costs.** Whenever it appears to the Tax Court that any attorney or other person admitted to practice before the Tax Court has multiplied the proceedings in any case unreasonably and vexatiously, the Tax Court may require—

(A) that such attorney or other person pay personally the excess costs, expenses, and attorneys' fees reasonably incurred because of such conduct, or

(B) if such attorney is appearing on behalf of the Commissioner of Internal Revenue, that the United States pay such excess costs, expenses, and attorneys' fees in the same manner as such an award by a district court.

(b) **Proceedings in other courts.**

(1) **Claims under section 7433.** Whenever it appears to the court that the taxpayer's position in the proceedings before the court instituted or maintained by such taxpayer under section 7433 is frivolous or groundless, the court may require the taxpayer to pay to the United States a penalty not in excess of $10,000.

(2) **Collection of sanctions and costs.** In any civil proceeding before any court (other than the Tax Court) which is brought by or against the United States in connection with the determination, collection, or refund of any tax, interest, or penalty under this title, any monetary sanctions, penalties, or costs awarded by the court to the United States may be assessed by the Secretary and, upon notice and demand, may be collected in the same manner as a tax.

(3) **Sanctions and costs awarded by a court of appeals.** In connection with any appeal from a proceeding in the Tax Court or a civil proceeding described in paragraph (2), an order of a United States Court of Appeals or the Supreme Court awarding monetary sanctions, penalties or court costs to the United States may be registered in a district court upon filing a certified copy of such order and shall be enforceable as other district court judgments. Any such sanctions, penalties, or costs may be assessed by the Secretary and, upon notice and demand, may be collected in the same manner as a tax.

In **1989**, P.L. 101-239, Sec. 7731(a), amended Code Sec. 6673, effective for positions taken after 12/31/89, in proceedings which are pending on, or commenced after 12/31/89.

Prior to amendment, Code Sec. 6673 read as follows:

"SEC. 6673. DAMAGES ASSESSABLE FOR INSTITUTING PROCEEDINGS BEFORE THE COURT PRIMARILY FOR DELAY, ETC.

"(a) In general.

"Whenever it appears to the Tax Court that proceedings before it have been instituted or maintained by the taxpayer primarily for delay, that the taxpayer's position in such proceeding is frivolous or groundless, or that the taxpayer unreasonably failed to pursue available administrative remedies, damages in an amount not in excess of $5,000 shall be awarded to the United States by the Tax Court in its decision. Damages so awarded shall be assessed at the same time as the deficiency and shall be paid upon notice and demand from the Secretary and shall be collected as a part of the tax.

"(b) Claims under section 7433.

"Whenever it appears to the court that the taxpayer's position in proceedings before the court instituted or maintained by such taxpayer under section 7433 is frivolous or groundless, damages in an amount not in excess of $10,000 shall be awarded to the United States by the court in the court's decision. Damages so awarded shall be assessed at the same time as the decision and shall be paid upon notice and demand from the Secretary."

In **1988**, P.L. 100-647, Sec. 6241(b)(1), added "(a) In general.— " before "Whenever" and added subsec. (b) ... Sec. 6241(b)(2), deleted "tax" after "before the" in the heading Code Sec. 6673, effective for actions by officers or employees of the Internal Revenue Service after 11/10/88.

Penalties

Code Sec. 6677(a)(2)

In **1986**, P.L. 99-514, Sec. 1552(a), substituted ", that the taxpayer's position in such proceeding is frivolous or groundless, or that the taxpayer unreasonably failed to pursue available administrative remedies" for "or that the taxpayer's position in such proceedings is frivolous or groundless" in Code Sec. 6673, effective for proceedings commenced after 10/22/86. Sec. 1552(c) of this Act provides:

"(c) Report.—

"The Secretary of the Treasury or his delegate and the Tax Court shall each prepare a report for 1987 and for each 2-calendar year period thereafter on the inventory of cases in the Tax Court and the measures to close cases more efficiently. Such reports shall be submitted to the Committee on Ways and Means of the House of Representatives and the Committee on Finance of the Senate."

In **1984**, P.L. 98-369, Sec. 160, amended Sec. 292(e)(2) of P.L. 97-243, the effective date for amendments made by Secs. 292(b) and (d)(2) of P.L. 97-243, reproduced below.

Prior to amendment Sec. 292(e)(2) of P.L. 97-248 read as follows:

"(2) Penalty.—The amendments made by subsections (b) and (d)(2) shall apply to any action or proceeding in the Tax Court commenced after December 31, 1982."

In **1982**, P.L. 97-248, Sec. 292(b), substituted "Whenever it appears to the Tax Court that proceedings before it have been instituted or maintained by the taxpayer primarily for delay or that the taxpayer's position in such proceedings is frivolous or groundless, damages in an amount not in excess of $5,000 shall be awarded to the United States by the Tax Court in its decision." for "Whenever it appears to the Tax Court that proceedings before it have been instituted by the taxpayer merely for delay, damages in an amount not in excess of $500 shall be awarded to the United States by the Tax Court in its decision." in Code Sec. 6673 . . . Sec. 292(d)(2)(A), substituted "primarily for delay, etc." for "merely for delay." in the heading of Code Sec. 6673, effective as provided in Sec. 292(e)(2) of this Act which reads as follows:

"(2) Penalty.—The amendments made by subsections (b) and (d)(2) shall apply to any action or proceeding in the United States Tax Court which—

"(A) is commenced after December 31, 1982, or

"(B) is pending in the United States Tax Court on the day which is 120 days after the date of the enactment of the Tax Reform Act of 1984."

In **1976**, P.L. 94-455, Sec. 1906(b)(13)(A), substituted "Secretary" for "Secretary or his delegate" in Code Sec. 6673, effective 2/1/77.

Sec. 6674. Fraudulent statement or failure to furnish statement to employee.

In addition to the criminal penalty provided by section 7204, any person required under the provisions of section 6051 or 6053(b) to furnish a statement to an employee who willfully furnishes a false or fraudulent statement, or who willfully fails to furnish a statement in the manner, at the time, and showing the information required under section 6051 or 6053(b), or regulations prescribed thereunder, shall for each such failure be subject to a penalty under this subchapter of $50, which shall be assessed and collected in the same manner as the tax on employers imposed by section 3111.

In **1965**, P.L. 89-97, Sec. 313(e)(2)(C), substituted "6051 or 6053(b)" for "6051" each place it appeared in Code Sec. 6674, effective for tips received after 12/31/65.

Sec. 6675. Excessive claims with respect to the use of certain fuels.
(a) Civil penalty.

In addition to any criminal penalty provided by law, if a claim is made under section 6416(a)(4) (relating to certain sales of gasoline), section 6420 (relating to gasoline used on farms), 6421 (relating to gasoline used for certain nonhighway purposes or by local transit systems), or 6427 (relating to fuels not used for taxable purposes) for an excessive amount, unless it is shown that the claim for such excessive amount is due to reasonable cause, the person making such claim shall be liable to a penalty in an amount equal to whichever of the following is the greater:

(1) Two times the excessive amount; or
(2) $10.

(b) Excessive amount defined.

For purposes of this section, the term "excessive amount" means in the case of any person the amount by which—

(1) the amount claimed under section 6416(a)(4), 6420, 6421, or 6427 as the case may be, for any period, exceeds

(2) the amount allowable under such section for such period.

(c) Assessment and collection of penalty.

For assessment and collection of penalty provided by subsection (a), see section 6206.

In **2005**, P.L. 109-59, Sec. 11163(d)(2), added "section 6416(a)(4) (relating to certain sales of gasoline)," after "made under" in subsec. (a) . . . Sec. 11163(d)(3), added "6416(a)(4)," after "under section" in para. (b)(1), effective for sales after 12/31/2005.

In **1983**, P.L. 97-424, Sec. 515(b)(11)(A), deleted "6424 (relating to lubricating oil used for certain nontaxable purposes)," before "or 6427" in subsec. (a) . . . Sec. 515(b)(11)(B), deleted "6424" before "or 6427" in para. (b)(1) . . . Sec. 515(b)(11)(C), deleted "or lubricating oil" after "certain fuels" in the heading of Code Sec. 6675, effective for articles sold after 1/6/83.

In **1978**, P.L. 95-618, Sec. 233(b)(2)(D), substituted "used for certain nontaxable purposes" for "not used in highway motor vehicles" in subsec. (a), effective the first day of the first calendar month which begins more than 10 days after 11/9/78.

In **1970**, P.L. 91-258, Sec. 207(d)(8), substituted "fuels" for "gasoline" in the heading of Code Sec. 6675, deleted "or" before "6424" in subsec. (a) and added ", or 6427 (relating to fuels not used for taxable purposes)", after "motor vehicles)" in subsec. (a), effective 7/1/70.

In **1965**, P.L. 89-44, Sec. 202, added "or lubricating oil" to the catchline and included claims made under section 6424, effective 1/1/66.

In **1956**, ch. 462, Sec. 208(d)(2), substituted "with respect to the use of certain gasoline" for "for gasoline used on farms" in the catchline, included claims made under section 6421 in subsec. (a) and included amounts claimed under section 6421 in subsec. (b), effective 6/29/56.

—ch. 160, Sec. 3, added Code Sec. 6675, effective 4/2/56.

Sec. 6676. Erroneous claim for refund or credit.
(a) Civil penalty.

If a claim for refund or credit with respect to income tax (other than a claim for a refund or credit relating to the earned income credit under section 32) is made for an excessive amount, unless it is shown that the claim for such excessive amount has a reasonable basis, the person making such claim shall be liable for a penalty in an amount equal to 20 percent of the excessive amount.

(b) Excessive amount.

For purposes of this section, the term "excessive amount" means in the case of any person the amount by which the amount of the claim for refund or credit for any taxable year exceeds the amount of such claim allowable under this title for such taxable year.

(c) Noneconomic substance transactions treated as lacking reasonable basis.

For purposes of this section, any excessive amount which is attributable to any transaction described in section 6662(b)(6) shall not be treated as having a reasonable basis.

(d) Coordination with other penalties.

This section shall not apply to any portion of the excessive amount of a claim for refund or credit which is subject to a penalty imposed under part II of subchapter A of chapter 68.

In **2010**, P.L. 111-152, Sec. 1409(d), redesignated subsec. (c) as (d) and added subsec. (c), effective for transactions entered into after 3/30/2010.

In **2007**, P.L. 110-28, Sec. 8247(a), added Code Sec. 6676, effective for any claim filed or submitted after 5/25/2007.

Sec. 6677. Failure to file information with respect to certain foreign trusts.
(a) Civil penalty.

In addition to any criminal penalty provided by law, if any notice or return required to be filed by section 6048—

(1) is not filed on or before the time provided in such section, or

(2) does not include all the information required pursuant to such section or includes incorrect information,

the person required to file such notice or return shall pay a penalty equal to the greater of $10,000 or 35 percent of the

3,805

Code Sec. 6677(a)(2)

gross reportable amount. If any failure described in the preceding sentence continues for more than 90 days after the day on which the Secretary mails notice of such failure to the person required to pay such penalty, such person shall pay a penalty (in addition to the amount determined under the preceding sentence) of $10,000 for each 30-day period (or fraction thereof) during which such failure continues after the expiration of such 90-day period. At such time as the gross reportable amount with respect to any failure can be determined by the Secretary, any subsequent penalty imposed under this subsection with respect to such failure shall be reduced as necessary to assure that the aggregate amount of such penalties do not exceed the gross reportable amount (and to the extent that such aggregate amount already exceeds the gross reportable amount the Secretary shall refund such excess to the taxpayer).

(b) Special rules for returns under section 6048(b).

In the case of a return required under section 6048(b)—

(1) the United States person referred to in such section shall be liable for the penalty imposed by subsection (a), and

(2) subsection (a) shall be applied by substituting "5 percent" for "35 percent".

(c) Gross reportable amount.

For purposes of subsection (a), the term "gross reportable amount" means—

(1) the gross value of the property involved in the event (determined as of the date of the event) in the case of a failure relating to section 6048(a),

(2) the gross value of the portion of the trust's assets at the close of the year treated as owned by the United States person in the case of a failure relating to section 6048(b)(1), and

(3) the gross amount of the distributions in the case of a failure relating to section 6048(c).

(d) Reasonable cause exception.

No penalty shall be imposed by this section on any failure which is shown to be due to reasonable cause and not due to willful neglect. The fact that a foreign jurisdiction would impose a civil or criminal penalty on the taxpayer (or any other person) for disclosing the required information is not reasonable cause.

(e) Deficiency procedures not to apply.

Subchapter B of chapter 63 (relating to deficiency procedures for income, estate, gift, and certain excise taxes) shall not apply in respect of the assessment or collection of any penalty imposed by subsection (a).

In 2010, P.L. 111-147, Sec. 535(a)(1), added "the greater of $10,000 or" before "35 percent" in para. (a)(1) . . . Sec. 535(a)(2), substituted "At such time as the gross reportable amount with respect to any failure can be determined by the Secretary, any subsequent penalty imposed under this subsection with respect to such failure shall be reduced as necessary to assure that the aggregate amount of such penalties do not exceed the gross reportable amount (and to the extent that such aggregate amount already exceeds the gross reportable amount the Secretary shall refund such excess to the taxpayer)." for "In no event shall the penalty under this subsection with respect to any failure exceed the gross reportable amount." in the last sentence of para. (a)(1), effective for notices and returns required to be filed after 12/31/2009.

In 1996, P.L. 104-188, Sec. 1901(b), amended Code Sec. 6677, effective as provided in Sec. 1901(d) of this Act, which reads as follows:

"(d) Effective dates.—

"(1) Reportable events.—To the extent related to subsection (a) of section 6048 of the Internal Revenue Code of 1986, as amended by this section, the amendments made by this section shall apply to reportable events (as defined in such section 6048) occurring after the date of the enactment of this Act.

"(2) Grantor trust reporting.—To the extent related to subsection (b) of such section 6048, the amendments made by this section shall apply to taxable years of United States persons beginning after December 31, 1995.

"(3) Reporting by United States beneficiaries.—To the extent related to subsection (c) of such section 6048, the amendments made by this section shall apply to distributions received after the date of the enactment of this Act."

Prior to amendment, Code Sec. 6677 read as follows:

"Sec. 6677. Failure to file information returns with respect to certain foreign trusts.

"(a) Civil penalty.

"In addition to any criminal penalty provided by law, any person required to file a return under section 6048 who fails to file such return at the time provided in such section, or who files a return which does not show the information required pursuant to such section, shall pay a penalty equal to 5 percent of the amount transferred to a trust (or, in the case of a failure with respect to section 6048(c), equal to 5 percent of the value of the corpus of the trust at the close of the taxable year), but not more than $1,000, unless it is shown that such failure is due to reasonable cause.

"(b) Deficiency procedures not to apply.

"Subchapter B of chapter 63 (relating to deficiency procedures for income, estate, gift, and certain excise taxes) shall not apply in respect of the assessment or collection of any penalty imposed by subsection (a)."

In 1976, P.L. 94-455, Sec. 1013(d)(2), substituted "to a trust (or, in the case of a failure with respect to section 6048(c), equal to 5 percent of the value of the corpus of the trust at the close of the taxable year)" for "to a trust" in subsec. (a), effective for tax. yrs. end. after 12/31/75, but only in the case of (a) foreign trusts created after 5/21/74, and (b) transfers of property to foreign trust after 5/21/74.

In 1974, P.L. 93-406, Sec. 1016(a)(21), substituted "and certain excise" for "chapter 42" in subsec. (b), effective 9/2/74 or other date as specified in Sec. 1017 of the Act (reproduced following Code Sec. 401).

In 1969, P.L. 91-172, Sec. 101(j)(53), substituted "gift, and chapter 42 taxes" for "and gift taxes", in subsec. (b), effective 1/1/70.

In 1962, P.L. 87-834, Sec. 7(g), added Code Sec. 6677, effective 10/16/62.

Sec. 6678. Repealed.

In 1986, P.L. 99-514, Sec. 1501(d)(2), repealed Code Sec. 6678, effective for returns having a due date (determined without regard to extensions) after 12/31/86. Prior to repeal, Code Sec. 6678 read as follows:

"Sec. 6678. Failure to furnish certain statements.

"(a) In general.

"In the case of each failure—

"(1) to furnish a statement under sections 6041(d), 6041A(e), 6045(b), 6052(b), 6050H(d), 6050I(e), 6050J(e), 6050K(b), or 6050L(c), on the date prescribed therefor to a person with respect to whom a return has been made under section 6041(a), 6041A(a) or (b), 6045(a), 6052(a), 6050H(a), 6050I(a), 6050J(a), 6050K(a), or 6050L(a), respectively, or

"(2) to furnish a statement under section 6039(a) on the date prescribed therefor to a person with respect to whom such a statement is required,

"(3) to furnish a statement under—

"(A) section 4997(a) (relating to statements with respect to windfall profit tax on crude oil),

"(B) section 6050A(b) (relating to statements furnished by certain fishing boat operators),

"(C) section 6050C (relating to information regarding windfall profit tax on crude oil),

"(D) section 6051 (relating to information returns with respect to income tax withheld) if the statement is required to be furnished to the employee,

"(E) subsection (b) or (c) of Section 6053 (relating to statements furnished by employers with respect to tips),

"(F) section 6031(b), 6034A, or 6037(b) (relating to statements furnished by certain pass-thru entities), or

"(G) section 6045(d) (relating to statements required in the case of certain substitute payments), on the date prescribed therefor to a person with respect to whom such a statement is required,

unless it is shown that such failure is due to reasonable cause and not to willful neglect, there shall be paid (upon notice and demand by the Secretary and in the same manner as tax) by the person failing to so furnish the statement $50 for each such statement not so furnished, but the total amount imposed on the delinquent person for all such failures during any calendar year shall not exceed $50,000.

"(b) Failure to file interest and dividend statements.

"(1) In general. In the case of any person who fails to furnish a statement under section 6042(c), 6044(e), or 6049(c) on the date prescribed therefor to a person with respect to whom a return has been made under section 6042(a)(1), 6044(a)(1), or 6049(a), respectively, such person shall pay a penalty of $50 for each failure unless it is shown that such person exercised due diligence in attempting to satisfy the requirement with respect to such statement.

"(2) Self-assessment. Any penalty imposed under paragraph (1) on any person—

"(A) for purposes of this subtitle, shall be treated as an excise tax imposed by subtitle D, and

"(B) shall be due and payable on April 1 of the calendar year following the calendar year for which such statement is required.

"(3) Deficiency procedures not to apply. Subchapter B of chapter 63 (relating to deficiency procedures for income, estate, gift, and certain excise taxes) shall not apply in respect of the assessment or collection of any penalty imposed by paragraph (1).

"(c) Failure to notify partnership of exchange of partnership interest.

"In the case of any person who fails to furnish the notice required by section 6050K(c)(1) on the date prescribed therefor, unless it is shown that such failure is due to reasonable cause and not to willful neglect, such person shall pay a penalty of $50 for each such failure."

Penalties   Code Sec. 6679

—P.L. 99-514, Sec. 1811(c)(1), deleted "or" from the end of subpara. (a)(3)(E) [before repeal by Sec. 1501(d)(2) of this Act] added "or" to the end of subpara. (a)(3)(F) [before repeal by Sec. 1501(d)(2) of this Act] and added subpara. (a)(3)(G) [before repeal by Sec. 1501(d)(2) of this Act], effective for tax. yrs. begin. after 12/31/84.

In 1984, P.L. 98-369, Sec. 145(b)(3)(A), and (B), substituted "6052(b), or 6050H(d)" for "or 6052(b)" and substituted "6052(a), or 6050H(a)" for "or 6052(a)" in para. (a)(1), effective for amounts received after 12/31/84.

—P.L. 98-369, Sec. 146(b)(3)(A), and (B), substituted "6050H(d), or 6050I(e)" for "or 6050H(d)" and substituted "6050H(a), or 6050I(a)" for "or 6050H(a)" in para. (a)(1) (as amended by Sec. 145(b)(3)(A) and (B) of the Act), effective for amounts received after 12/31/84.

—P.L. 98-369, Sec. 148(b)(3)(A), and (B), substituted "6050I(e), or 6050J(e)" for "or 6050I(e)" and substituted "6050I(a), or 6050J(a)" for "or 6050I(a)" in para. (a)(1) (as amended by Sec. 146(b)(3)(A) & (B) of the Act), effective for acquisitions of property and abandonments of property after 12/31/84.

—P.L. 98-369, Sec. 149(b)(2)(A), and (B), substituted "6050J(e), or 6050K(b)" for "or 6050J(e)" and substituted "6050J(a), or 6050K(a)" for "or 6050J(a)" in para. (a)(1) (as amended by Sec. 148(b)(3)(A) and (B) of the Act)... Sec. 149(b)(3), added subsec. (c), effective for exchanges after 12/31/84.

—P.L. 98-369, Sec. 155(b)(2)(B)(i), and (ii), substituted "6050K(b), or 6050L(c)" for "or 6050K(b)" and substituted "6050K(a), or 6050L(a)" for "or 6050K(a)" in para. (a)(1) (as amended by Sec. 149(b)(2)(A) and (B) of the Act), effective for contributions made after 12/31/84, in tax. yrs. end. after 12/31/84.

—P.L. 98-369, Sec. 714(f), substituted "section 6053" for "section 6053(c)" in subpara. (a)(3)(E), effective for calendar yrs. begin. after 12/31/82.

—P.L. 98-369, Sec. 714(q)(3), deleted "or" at the end of subpara. (a)(3)(D), added "or" at the end of subpara. (a)(3)(E) and added subpara. (a)(3)(F), effective for tax. yrs. begin. after 12/31/84.

In 1983, P.L. 98-67, Sec. 105(b)(2), amended Code Sec. 6678 by adding "(a) In general." before "In the case of" in the matter preceding para. (1), by substituting "6045(b)," for "6042(c), 6044(e), 6045(b), 6049(c)," in para. (1), by substituting "6045(a)," for "6042(a)(1), 6044(a)(1), 6045(a), 6049(a)," in para. (1) and by adding subsec. (b), effective for payments made after 1/31/83.

—P.L. 97-448, Sec. 201(i)(3), redesignated subparas. (3)(A) through (D) as subparas. (3)(B) through (E), and added subpara. (3)(A), effective, for returns and statements the due dates for which (without regard to extensions) are after 1/12/83.

In 1982, P.L. 97-248, Sec. 309(b)(3), substituted "6049(a)" for "6049(a)(1)" in para. (1), effective for amounts paid (or treated as paid) after 12/31/82.

—P.L. 97-248, Sec. 311(a)(2), added "6045(b)" after "6044(e)", and added "6045(a)" after "6044(a)(1)" in para. (1), effective as provided in Sec. 311(c)(1) of this Act which reads as follows:

"(c) Effective Dates.—

"(1) Subsection (a).— The amendments made by subsection (a) shall take effect on the date of the enactment of this Act [9/3/82], except that—

"(A) regulations relating to reporting by commodities and securities brokers shall be issued under section 6045 of the Internal Revenue Code of 1954 (as amended by this Act) within 6 months after the date of the enactment of this Act, and

"(B) such regulations shall not apply to transactions occurring before January 1, 1983."

—P.L. 97-248, Sec. 312(b), added "6041A(e)" after "6041(d)", and added "6041A(a) or (b)" after "6041(a)" in para. (1), effective for payments and sales made after 12/31/82.

—P.L. 97-248, Sec. 314(b), substituted "subsection (b) or (c) of section 6053(c)" for "section 6053(b)" in subpara. (3)(D), effective for calendar yrs. begin. after 12/31/82.

—P.L. 97-248, Sec. 315(c)(1), and (2), substituted "$50" for "$10" and substituted "$50,000" for "$25,000", in Code Sec. 6678, effective for returns or statements whose filing due date (without regard to extensions) is after 12/31/82.

In 1981, P.L. 97-34, Sec. 723(a)(2), deleted "or" at the end of para. (1), added "or" at the end of para. (2), and added para. (3)... Sec. 723(b)(2), added "6041(d)," before "6042(c)" and added "6041(a)," before "6042(a)(1)" in para. (1), effective for returns and statements required to be furnished after 12/31/81.

In 1979, P.L. 96-167, Sec. 7(b)(2), amended Code Sec. 6678 effective for calendar yrs. after '79.

Prior to amendment, Code Sec. 6678 read as follows:

"In the case of each failure to furnish a statement under section 6039(b), 6042(c), 6044(e), 6049(c), or 6052(b) on the date prescribed therefor to a person with respect to whom a return has been made under section 6039(a), 6042(a)(1), 6044(a)(1), 6049(a)(1), or 6052(a), respectively, unless it is shown that such failure is due to reasonable cause and not to willful neglect, there shall be paid (upon notice and demand by the Secretary and in the same manner as tax), by the person failing to so furnish the statement, $10 for each such statement not so furnished, but the total amount imposed on the delinquent person for all such failures during any calendar year shall not exceed $25,000."

In 1976, P.L. 94-455, Sec. 1906(b)(13)(A), substituted "Secretary" for "Secretary or his delegate" in Code Sec. 6678, effective 2/1/77.

In 1964, P.L. 88-272, Sec. 204(c)(2), 221(b)(3), inserted references to sections 6039(a), 6039(b), 6052(a), and 6052(b), applicable to group-term life insurance provided after Dec. 31, 1963, in taxable years ending after such date, and applicable to stock transferred pursuant to options exercised on or after Jan. 1, 1964.

In 1962, P.L. 87-834, Sec. 19(e), added Code Sec. 6678, applicable to payments of dividends, patronage dividends, and interest made on or after '63, with respect to patronage occurring on or after the first day of the first taxable year of the cooperative, beginning on or after '63.

Sec. 6679. Failure to file returns, etc., with respect to foreign corporations or foreign partnerships.

(a) Civil penalty.

(1) In general. In addition to any criminal penalty provided by law, any person required to file a return under section 6046 and 6046A who fails to file such return at the time provided in such section, or who files a return which does not show the information required pursuant to such section, shall pay a penalty of $10,000, unless it is shown that such failure is due to reasonable cause.

(2) Increase in penalty where failure continues after notification. If any failure described in paragraph (1) continues for more than 90 days after the day on which the Secretary mails notice of such failure to the United States person, such person shall pay a penalty (in addition to the amount required under paragraph (1)) of $10,000 for each 30-day period (or fraction thereof) during which such failure continues after the expiration of such 90-day period. The increase in any penalty under this paragraph shall not exceed $50,000.

(3) Repealed.

(b) Deficiency procedures not to apply.

Subchapter B of chapter 63 (relating to deficiency procedure for income, estate, gift, and certain excise taxes) shall not apply in respect of the assessment or collection of any penalty imposed by subsection (a).

In 2004, P.L. 108-357, Sec. 413(c)(29)(A), substituted "6046 and 6046A" for "6035, 6046, or 6046A" in para. (a)(1) ... Sec. 413(c)(29)(B), deleted para. (a)(3), effective for tax. yrs. of foreign corporations begin. after 12/31/2004, and for tax. yrs. of United States shareholders with or within which such tax. yrs. of foreign corporations end.

Prior to deletion, para. (a)(3) read as follows:

"(3) Reduced penalty for returns relating to foreign personal holding companies. In the case of a return required under section 6035, paragraph (1) shall be applied by substituting '$1,000' for '$10,000', and paragraph (2) shall not apply."

In 1997, P.L. 105-34, Sec. 1143(b), amended subsec. (a), effective for transfers and changes after 8/5/97.

Prior to amendment, subsec. (a) read as follows:

"(a) Civil penalty.

"In addition to any criminal penalty provided by law, any person required to file a return under section 6035, 6046 or 6046A who fails to file such return at the time provided in such section, or who files a return which does not show the information required pursuant to such section, shall pay a penalty of $1,000, unless it is shown that such failure is due to reasonable cause."

In 1983, P.L. 97-448, Sec. 306(c)(2)(A), corrected Sec. 405(b) of P.L. 97-248 to amend subsec. (a) as amended by Sec. 340(b)(1) of P.L. 97-248 by substituting "section 6035, 6046 or 6046A" for "section 6035 or 6046'", see below.

—P.L. 97-448, Sec. 306(c)(2)(B), corrected Sec. 405(c)(2) and (3) of P.L. 97-248, which amended the heading of Code. Sec. 6679 to read "Failure to file returns, etc., with respect to foreign corporations or foreign partnerships."

In 1982, P.L. 97-248, Sec. 340(b)(1), substituted "section 6035 or 6046" for "section 6046" in subsec. (a) ... Sec. 340(b)(2), amended the heading of Code Sec. 6679, effective for tax. yrs. of foreign corporations begin. after 9/3/82.

Prior to amendment, the heading of Code Sec. 6679 read as follows:

"SEC. 6679. FAILURE TO FILE RETURNS, ETC. AS TO ORGANIZATION OR REORGANIZATION OF FOREIGN CORPORATIONS AND AS TO ACQUISITIONS OF THEIR STOCK."

—P.L. 97-248, Sec. 405(b), substituted "section 6035, 6046 or 6046A" for "section 6035 or 6046" in subsec. (a) ... Sec. 405(c)(2), amended the heading of Code Sec. 6679, effective for acquisitions or dispositions of, or substantial changes in, interests on foreign partnerships occurring after 9/3/82.

Prior to amendment, the heading of Code Sec. 6679 read as follows:

"SEC. 6679. FAILURE TO FILE RETURNS, ETC., OR SUPPLY INFORMATION UNDER SECTION 6035 OR 6046."

In 1974, P.L. 93-406, Sec. 1016(a)(22), substituted "and certain excise" for "chapter 42" in subsec. (b), effective 9/2/74 or other date as specified in Sec. 1017 of the Act (reproduced following Code Sec. 401).

In 1969, P.L. 91-172, Sec. 101(j)(54), substituted in subsec. (b) "gift and chapter 42 taxes" for "and gift taxes", in subsec. (b), effective 1/1/70.

In 1962, P.L. 87-834, Sec. 20(c), added Code Sec. 6679, effective 10/16/62.

3,807

Sec. 6682. False information with respect to withholding.

(a) Civil penalty.

In addition to any criminal penalty provided by law, if—

(1) any individual makes a statement under section 3402 or section 3406 which results in a decrease in the amounts deducted and withheld under chapter 24, and

(2) as of the time such statement was made, there was no reasonable basis for such statement,

such individual shall pay a penalty of $500 for such statement.

(b) Exception.

The Secretary may waive (in whole or in part) the penalty imposed under subsection (a) if the taxes imposed with respect to the individual under subtitle A for the taxable year are equal to or less than the sum of—

(1) the credits against such taxes allowed by part IV of subchapter A of chapter 1, and

(2) the payments of estimated tax which are considered payments on account of such taxes.

(c) Deficiency procedures not to apply.

Subchapter B of chapter 63 (relating to deficiency procedures for income, estate, gift, and certain excise taxes) shall not apply in respect to the assessment or collection of any penalty imposed by subsection (a).

In **1983**, P.L. 98-67, Sec. 107(a), added "or section 3406" after "section 3402" in para. (a)(1), effective 8/5/83.

In **1981**, P.L. 97-34, Sec. 721(a), amended Code Sec. 6682, effective for acts and failures to act after 12/31/81.

Prior to amendment, Code Sec. 6682 read as follows:

"SEC. 6682. FALSE INFORMATION WITH RESPECT TO WITHHOLDING ALLOWANCES BASED ON ITEMIZED DEDUCTIONS.

"(a) Civil penalty.

"In addition to any criminal penalty provided by law, if any individual in claiming a withholding allowance under section 3402(f)(1)(F) states (1) as the amount of the wages (within the meaning of chapter 24) shown on his return for any taxable year an amount less than such wages actually shown, or (2) as the amount of the itemized deductions referred to in section 3402(m) shown on the return for any taxable year an amount greater than such deductions actually shown, he shall pay a penalty of $50 for such statement, unless (1) such statement did not result in a decrease in the amounts deducted and withheld under chapter 24, or (2) the taxes imposed with respect to the individual under subtitle A for the succeeding taxable year do not exceed the sum of (A) the credits against such taxes allowed by part IV of subchapter A of chapter 1, and (B) the payments of estimated tax which are considered payments on account of such taxes.

"(b) Deficiency procedures not to apply.

"Subchapter B of chapter 63 (relating to deficiency procedures for income, estate, gift, and [sic] certain excise taxes) shall not apply in respect of the assessment or collection of any penalty imposed by subsection (a)."

In **1974**, P.L. 93-406, Sec. 1016(a)(23), substituted "and certain excise" for "chapter 42" in subsec. (b), effective 9/2/74 or other date as specified in Sec. 1017 of the Act (reproduced following Code Sec. 401).

In **1969**, P.L. 91-172, Sec. 101(j)(55), substituted "gift, and chapter 42 taxes" for "and gift taxes", in subsec. (b), effective 1/1/70.

In **1966**, P.L. 89-368, Sec. 101, added Code Sec. 6682.

Sec. 6683. Repealed.

In **2005**, P.L. 109-135, Sec. 403(n)(3)(A), repealed Code Sec. 6683, effective for tax. yrs. of foreign corporations begin. after 12/31/2004, and for tax. yrs. of United States shareholders with or within which such tax. yrs. of foreign corporations end, as if included in Sec. 413 of the American Jobs Creation Act of 2004, P.L. 108-357.

Prior to repeal, Code Sec. 6683 read as follows:

"SEC. 6683. FAILURE OF FOREIGN CORPORATION TO FILE RETURN OF PERSONAL HOLDING COMPANY TAX.

"Any foreign corporation which—

"(1) is a personal holding company for any taxable year, and

"(2) fails to file or to cause to be filed with the Secretary a true and accurate return of the tax imposed by section 541,

shall, in addition to other penalties provided by law, pay a penalty equal to 10 percent of the taxes imposed by chapter 1 (including the tax imposed by section 541) on such foreign corporation for such taxable year. No penalty shall be imposed under this section on any failure which is shown to be due to reasonable cause and not willful neglect."

In **1997**, P.L. 105-34, Sec. 1281(c), added the sentence at the end of Code Sec. 6683, effective for tax. yrs. begin. after 8/5/97.

In **1976**, P.L. 94-455, Sec. 1906(b)(13)(A), substituted "Secretary" for "Secretary or his delegate" in Code Sec. 6683, effective 2/1/77.

In **1966**, P.L. 89-809, Sec. 104, added Code Sec. 6683, effective for tax. yrs. begin. after 12/31/66.

Sec. 6684. Assessable penalties with respect to liability for tax under chapter 42.

If any person becomes liable for tax under any section of chapter 42 (relating to private foundations and certain other tax-exempt organizations) by reason of any act or failure to act which is not due to reasonable cause and either—

(1) such person has theretofore been liable for tax under such chapter, or

(2) such act or failure to act is both willful and flagrant,

then such person shall be liable for a penalty equal to the amount of such tax.

In **1987**, P.L. 100-203, Sec. 10712(c)(4), substituted "private foundations and certain other tax-exempt organizations" for "private foundations" in Code Sec. 6684, effective for tax. yrs. begin. after 12/22/87.

In **1969**, P.L. 91-172, Sec. 101(c), added Code Sec. 6684, effective 1/1/70.

Sec. 6685. Assessable penalty with respect to public inspection requirements for certain tax-exempt organizations.

In addition to the penalty imposed by section 7207 (relating to fraudulent returns, statements, or other documents), any person who is required to comply with the requirements of subsection (d) of section 6104 and who fails to so comply with respect to any return or application, if such failure is willful, shall pay a penalty of $5,000 with respect to each such return or application.

In **1998**, P.L. 105-277, Sec. 1004(b)(2)(D), deleted "or (e)" after "subsection (d)" in Code Sec. 6685, effective as provided in Sec. 1004(b)(3), of this Act, which reads as follows:

"(3) Effective date.

"(A) In general. Except as provided in subparagraph (B), the amendments made by this subsection shall apply to requests made after the later of December 31, 1998, or the 60th day after the Secretary of the Treasury first issues the regulations referred to in section 6104(d)(4) of the Internal Revenue Code of 1986, as amended by this section.

"(B) Publication of annual returns. Section 6104(d) of such Code, as in effect before the amendments made by this subsection, shall not apply to any return the due date for which is after the date such amendments take effect under subparagraph (A)."

In **1996**, P.L. 104-168, Sec. 1313(b), substituted "$5,000" for "$1,000" in Code Sec. 6685, effective for requests made on or after the 60th day after the Secretary of the Treasury first issues the regulations referred to [in] section 6104(e)(3) of the Internal Revenue Code of 1986 [as added by Sec. 1313(a)(3) of this Act, see Code Sec. 6104].

In **1987**, P.L. 100-203, Sec. 10704(b)(1), amended Code Sec. 6685, effective as provided in Sec. 10704(d) which reads as follows:

"(d) Effective date. — The amendments made by this section shall apply—

"(1) to returns for years beginning after December 31, 1986, and

"(2) on and after the date of the enactment of this Act in the case of applications submitted to the Internal Revenue Service—

"(A) after July 15, 1987, or

"(B) on or before July 15, 1987, if the organization has a copy of the application on July 15, 1987."

Prior to amendment, Code Sec. 6685 read as follows:

"SEC. 6685. ASSESSABLE PENALTIES WITH RESPECT TO PRIVATE FOUNDATION ANNUAL RETURNS.

"In addition to the penalty imposed by section 7207 (relating to fraudulent returns, statements, or other documents), any person who is required to comply with the requirements of section 6104(d) (relating to private foundations' annual returns) and who fails to so comply with respect to any return, if such failure is willful, shall pay a penalty of $1,000 with respect to each such return."

In **1980**, P.L. 96-603, Sec. 1(d)(4), amended Code Sec. 6685, effective for tax. yrs. begin. after 12/31/80.

Prior to amendment, Code Sec. 6685 read as follows:

"SEC. 6685. ASSESSABLE PENALTIES WITH RESPECT TO PRIVATE FOUNDATION ANNUAL REPORTS.

"In addition to the penalty imposed by section 7207 (relating to fraudulent returns, statements, or other documents), any person who is required to file the report and the notice required under section 6056 (relating to annual reports by private foundations) or to comply with the requirements of section 6104(d) (relating to public inspection of private foundations' annual reports) and who fails so to file or comply, if such failure is willful, shall pay a penalty of $1,000 with respect to each such report or notice."

Penalties

Code Sec. 6693(a)(2)(C)

In 1969, P.L. 91-172, Sec. 101(e)(4), added Code Sec. 6685, effective 1/1/70.

Sec. 6686. Failure to file returns or supply information by DISC or former FSC.

In addition to the penalty imposed by section 7203 (relating to willful failure to file return, supply information, or pay tax) any person required to supply information or to file a return under section 6011(c) who fails to supply such information or file such return at the time prescribed by the Secretary, or who files a return which does not show the information required, shall pay a penalty of $100 for each failure to supply information (but the total amount imposed on the delinquent person for all such failures during any calendar year shall not exceed $25,000) or a penalty of $1,000 for each failure to file a return, unless it is shown that such failure is due to reasonable cause.

In 2007, P.L. 110-172, Sec. 11(g)(21), added "former" before "FSC" in the heading of Sec. 6686, enacted 12/29/2007.

In 1984, P.L. 98-369, Sec. 801(d)(15)(A)(i), substituted "section 6011(c) for 'section 6011(e)' in Code Sec. 6686 . . . Sec. 801(d)(15)(A)(ii), amended the heading of Code Sec. 6686, effective for transactions after 12/31/84, in tax. yrs. end. after 12/31/84.

Prior to amendment, the heading of Code Sec. 6686 read as follows:
"Sec. 6686. Failure of DISC to file returns."

In 1976, P.L. 94-455, Sec. 1906(b)(13)(A), substituted "Secretary" for "Secretary or his delegate" in Code Sec. 6686, effective 2/1/77.

In 1971, P.L. 92-178, Sec. 504(d), added Sec. 6686, effective for tax. yrs. end. after 12/31/71, except that a corporation may not be a DISC for any tax. yr. begin. before 1/1/72.

Sec. 6687. Repealed.

In 1989, P.L. 101-239, Sec. 7711(b)(1), repealed Code Sec. 6687, effective for returns and statements that due date for which (determined without regard to extensions) is after 12/31/89.

Prior to repeal, Code Sec. 6687 read as follows:
"Sec. 6687. Failure to supply information with respect to place of residence.

"(a) Civil penalty.

"If any person fails to include on his return any information required under section 6017A with respect to his place of residence, he shall pay a penalty of $5 for each such failure, unless it is shown that such failure is due to reasonable cause.

"(b) Deficiency procedures not to apply.

"Subchapter B of chapter 63 (relating to deficiency procedures for income, estate, gift, and chapter 42 taxes) shall not apply in respect of the assessment or collection of any penalty imposed by subsection (a)."

In 1972, P.L. 92-512, Sec. 144(b), added Code Sec. 6687, effective 10/20/72. In P. L. 92-606, Congress enacted another penalty Code Section with the same number, see below.

Sec. 6688. Assessable penalties with respect to information required to be furnished under section 7654.

In addition to any criminal penalty provided by law, any person described in section 7654(a) who is required under section 937(c) or by regulations prescribed under section 7654 to furnish information and who fails to comply with such requirement at the time prescribed by such regulations unless it is shown that such failure is due to reasonable cause and not to willful neglect, shall pay (upon notice and demand by the Secretary and in the same manner as tax) a penalty of $1,000 for each such failure.

In 2004, P.L. 108-357, Sec. 908(b)(1), added "under section 937(c) or" before "by regulations" in Code Sec. 6688 . . . Sec. 908(b)(2), substituted "$1,000" for "$100" in Code Sec. 6688, effective for tax. yrs. end. after 10/22/2004.

In 1976, P.L. 94-455, Sec. 1906(b)(13)(A), substituted "Secretary" for "Secretary or his delegate" in Code Sec. 6688, effective 2/1/77.

In 1974, P.L. 93-406, Sec. 1016(b)(4), substituted "6688" for "6687" in the heading of the above Code Section, effective 9/2/74 or other date as specified in Sec. 1017 of the Act (reproduced following Code Sec. 401).

In 1972, P.L. 92-606, Sec. 1(c), added Code Sec. 6687, effective for tax yrs. begin. after 10/4/72. In P. L. 92-512, Congress enacted another penalty Code Section with the same number, see above.

Sec. 6689. Failure to file notice of redetermination of foreign tax.

(a) Civil penalty.

If the taxpayer fails to notify the Secretary (on or before the date prescribed by regulations for giving such notice) of a foreign tax redetermination, unless it is shown that such failure is due to reasonable cause and not due to willful neglect, there shall be added to the deficiency attributable to such redetermination an amount (not in excess of 25 percent of the deficiency) determined as follows—

(1) 5 percent of the deficiency if the failure is for not more than 1 month, with

(2) an additional 5 percent of the deficiency for each month (or fraction thereof) during which the failure continues.

(b) Foreign tax redetermination defined.

For purposes of this section, the term "foreign tax redetermination" means any redetermination for which a notice is required under subsection (c) of section 905 or paragraph (2) of section 404A(g).

In 1980, P.L. 96-603, Sec. 2(c)(2), added Code Sec. 6689, effective for employer contributions or accruals in tax. yrs. begin. after 12/31/79.

Sec. 6690. Fraudulent statement or failure to furnish statement to plan participant.

Any person required under section 6057(e) to furnish a statement to a participant who willfully furnishes a false or fraudulent statement, or who willfully fails to furnish a statement in the manner, at the time, and showing the information required under section 6057(e), or regulations prescribed thereunder, shall for each such act, or for each such failure, be subject to a penalty under this subchapter of $50, which shall be assessed and collected in the same manner as the tax on employers imposed by section 3111.

In 1974, P.L. 93-406, Sec. 1031(b)(2)(A), added Code Sec. 6690, effective 9/2/74.

Sec. 6692. Failure to file actuarial report.

The plan administrator (as defined in section 414(g)) of each defined benefit plan to which section 412 applies who fails to file the report required by section 6059 at the time and in the manner required by section 6059, shall pay a penalty of $1,000 for each such failure unless it is shown that such failure is due to reasonable cause.

In 1974, P.L. 93-406, Sec. 1033(b), added Code Sec. 6692, effective 9/2/74.

Sec. 6693. Failure to provide reports on certain tax-favored accounts or annuities; penalties relating to designated nondeductible contributions.

(a) Reports.

(1) **In general.** If a person required to file a report under a provision referred to in paragraph (2) fails to file such report at the time and in the manner required by such provision, such person shall pay a penalty of $50 for each failure unless it is shown that such failure is due to reasonable cause.

(2) **Provisions.** The provisions referred to in this paragraph are—

(A) subsections (i) and (l) of section 408 (relating to individual retirement plans),

(B) section 220(h) (relating to Archer MSAs),

(C) section 223(h) (relating to health savings accounts),

• **Caution:** Code Sec. 6693(a)(2)(D), following, was amended by P.L. 107-16, the Economic Growth and Tax

3,809

Relief Reconciliation Act of 2001 (EGTRRA). These provisions generally sunset for tax years beginning after 12/31/2012. For specific sunset provisions, see Sec. 901, P.L. 107-16 (as amended) reproduced in history notes for this Code Sec.

(D) section 529(d) (relating to qualified tuition programs), and

(E) section 530(h) (relating to Coverdell education savings accounts).

This subsection shall not apply to any report which is an information return described in section 6724(d)(1)(C)(i) or a payee statement described in section 6724(d)(2)(X).

(b) Penalties relating to nondeductible contributions.

(1) Overstatement of designated nondeductible contributions. Any individual who—

(A) is required to furnish information under section 408(o)(4) as to the amount of designated nondeductible contributions made for any taxable year, and

(B) overstates the amount of such contributions made for such taxable year,

shall pay a penalty of $100 for each such overstatement unless it is shown that such overstatement is due to reasonable cause.

(2) Failure to file form. Any individual who fails to file a form required to be filed by the Secretary under section 408(o)(4) shall pay a penalty of $50 for each such failure unless it is shown that such failure is due to reasonable cause.

(c) Penalties relating to simple retirement accounts.

(1) Employer penalties. An employer who fails to provide 1 or more notices required by section 408(l)(2)(C) shall pay a penalty of $50 for each day on which such failures continue.

(2) Trustee and issuer penalties. A trustee or issuer who fails—

(A) to provide 1 or more statements required by the last sentence of section 408(i) shall pay a penalty of $50 for each day on which such failures continue, or

(B) to provide 1 or more summary descriptions required by section 408(l)(2)(B) shall pay a penalty of $50 for each day on which such failures continue.

(3) Reasonable cause exception. No penalty shall be imposed under this subsection with respect to any failure which the taxpayer shows was due to reasonable cause.

(d) Deficiency procedures not to apply.

Subchapter B of chapter 63 (relating to deficiency procedures for income, estate, gift, and certain excise taxes) does not apply to the assessment or collection of any penalty imposed by this section.

In 2010, P.L. 111-312, Sec. 101(a)(1), substituted "December 31, 2012" for "December 31, 2010" both places it appeared in Sec. 901 of P.L. 107-16, [see below] effective as if included in the enactment of P.L. 107-16, EGTRRA, 6/7/2001.

In 2006, P.L. 109-280, Sec. 1304(a), Sec. 1304 of this Act, provides:
"Sec. 1304. Qualified tuition programs.
"(a) Permanent extension of modifications. Section 901 of the Economic Growth and Tax Relief Reconciliation Act of 2001 (relating to sunset provisions) shall not apply to section 402 of such Act (relating to modifications to qualified tuition programs)."

In 2003, P.L. 108-173, Sec. 1201(g), redesignated subparas. (a)(2)(C) and (D) as (a)(2)(D) and (E), and added subpara. (a)(2)(C), effective for tax. yrs. begin. after 12/31/2003.

In 2002, P.L. 107-358, Sec. 2, added subsec. (c) in Sec. 901 of P.L. 107-16 [see below], effective 12/17/2002.

In 2001, P.L. 107-22, Sec. 1(b)(2)(C), substituted "Coverdell education savings" for "education individual retirement" in subpara. (a)(2)(D), effective 7/26/2001.

—P.L. 107-16, Sec. 402(a)(4)(A), substituted "qualified tuition" for "qualified State tuition" in subpara. (a)(2)(C), effective for tax. yrs. begin. after 12/31/2001.

—P.L. 107-16, Sec. 901, of this Act [as amended by Sec. 2 of P.L. 107-358, and Sec. 101(a)(1) of P.L. 111-312, see above], reads as follows:
"SEC. 901. SUNSET OF PROVISIONS OF ACT.
"(a) In general. All provisions of, and amendments made by, this Act shall not apply—
"(1) to taxable, plan, or limitation years beginning after December 31, 2012, or
"(2) in the case of title V, to estates of decedents dying, gifts made, or generation skipping transfers, after December 31, 2012.
"(b) Application of certain laws. The Internal Revenue Code of 1986 and the Employee Retirement Income Security Act of 1974 shall be applied and administered to years, estates, gifts, and transfers described in subsection (a) as if the provisions and amendments described in subsection (a) had never been enacted.
"(c) Exception. Subsection (a) shall not apply to section 803 (relating to no federal income tax on restitution received by victims of the Nazi regime or their heirs or estates)."

In 2000, P.L. 106-554, Sec. 1(a)(7), [which enacted into law Sec. 202(b)(2)(E) of P.L. 106-554] substituted "Archer MSAs" for "medical savings accounts" in subpara. (a)(2)(B), effective 12/21/2000.

In 1998, P.L. 105-277, Sec. 4006(c)(4), substituted "section" for "Section" in subparas. (a)(2)(C) and (D), effective 10/21/98.

In 1997, P.L. 105-34, Sec. 211(e)(2)(B), deleted "and" at the end of subpara. (a)(2)(A), substituted ", and" for the period at the end of subpara. (a)(2)(B), and added subpara. (a)(2)(C)... Sec. 211(e)(2)(C), substituted "certain tax-favored" for "individual retirement" in the heading of Code Sec. 6693, effective 1/1/98.

—P.L. 105-34, Sec. 213(c), deleted "and" at the end of subpara. (a)(2)(A), substituted ", and" for the period at the end of subpara. (a)(2)(C), and added subpara. (a)(2)(D), effective for tax. yrs. begin. after 12/31/97.

—P.L. 105-34, Sec. 1601(d)(1)(C)(ii)(I), added "or issuer" after "trustee" in para. (c)(2)... Sec. 1601(d)(1)(C)(ii)(II), added "and issuer" after "Trustee" in the heading of para. (c)(2), effective for tax. yrs. begin. after 12/31/96.

—P.L. 105-34, Sec. 1602(a)(4), added a sentence at the end of subsec. (a), effective for tax. yrs. begin. after 12/31/96.

In 1996, P.L. 104-191, Sec. 301(g)(1), amended subsec. (a), effective for tax. yrs. begin. after 12/31/96.

Prior to amendment, subsec. (a) read as follows:
"(a) The person required by subsection (i) or (l) of section 408 to file a report regarding an individual retirement account or individual retirement annuity at the time and in the manner required by such subsection shall pay a penalty of $50 for each failure unless it is shown that such failure is due to reasonable cause. This subsection shall not apply to any report which is an information return described in section 6724(d)(1)(C)(i) or a payee statement described in section 6724(d)(2)(W). "

—P.L. 104-188, Sec. 1421(b)(4)(B), redesignated subsec. (c) as subsec. (d) and added new subsec. (c), effective for tax. yrs. begin. after 12/31/96.

—P.L. 104-188, Sec. 1455(d)(3), added the sentence at the end of subsec. (a), effective for returns, reports, and other statements the due date for which (determined without regard to extensions) is after 12/31/96.

In 1988, P.L. 100-647, Sec. 1011(b)(4)(A), amended subsec. (b)... Sec. 1011(b)(4)(B)(i), substituted "penalties relating to" for "overstatement of" in the heading of Code Sec. 6693, effective for contributions and distributions for tax yrs. begin. after 12/31/86.

Prior to amendment, subsec. (b) read as follows:
"(b) Overstatement of designated nondeductible contributions.
"Any individual who—
"(1) is required to furnish information under section 408(o)(4) as to the amount of designated nondeductible contributions made for any taxable year, and
"(2) overstates the amount of such contributions made for such taxable year,
"shall pay a penalty of $100 for each such overstatement unless it is shown that overstatement is due to reasonable cause."

In 1986, P.L. 99-514, Sec. 1102(d)(1), redesignated subsec. (b) as subsec. (c) and added new subsec. (b)... Sec. 1102(d)(2)(A), substituted "than this section" for "(I) subsection (a)" in subsec. (c)... Sec. 1102(d)(2)(B), added "; overstatement of designated nondeductible contributions" after "annuities" in the heading of Code Sec. 6693, effective for contributions and distributions for tax. yrs. begin. after 12/31/86.

In 1984, P.L. 98-369, Sec. 147(b), substituted "$50" for "$10" in subsec. (a), effective for failures occurring after 7/18/84.

In 1980, P.L. 96-222, Sec. 101(a)(10)(H)(i), substituted "subsection (i) or (l) of section 408" for "section 408(i)" the first place it appeared in subsec. (a)... Sec. 101(a)(10)(H)(ii), substituted "such subsection" for "section 408(i)" the second place it appeared in subsec. (a), presumably intended by Congress to be effective with respect to failures occurring after 4/1/80 [Sec. 101(b)(1)(F)] although technically effective as if included in the provisions of P.L. 95-600 [Sec. 101(b)(2)].

In 1974, P.L. 93-406, Sec. 2002(f), added Code Sec. 6693, effective 1/1/75.

Sec. 6694. Understatement of taxpayer's liability by tax return preparer.

(a) Understatement due to unreasonable positions.

(1) In general. If a tax return preparer—

(A) prepares any return or claim of refund with respect to which any part of an understatement of liability is due to a position described in paragraph (2), and

(B) knew (or reasonably should have known) of the position,

such tax return preparer shall pay a penalty with respect to each such return or claim in an amount equal to the greater of $1,000 or 50 percent of the income derived (or to be derived) by the tax return preparer with respect to the return or claim.

(2) Unreasonable position.

(A) In general. Except as otherwise provided in this paragraph, a position is described in this paragraph unless there is or was substantial authority for the position.

(B) Disclosed positions. If the position was disclosed as provided in section 6662(d)(2)(B)(ii)(I) and is not a position to which subparagraph (C) applies, the position is described in this paragraph unless there is a reasonable basis for the position.

(C) Tax shelters and reportable transactions. If the position is with respect to a tax shelter (as defined in section 6662(d)(2)(C)(ii)) or a reportable transaction to which section 6662A applies, the position is described in this paragraph unless it is reasonable to believe that the position would more likely than not be sustained on its merits.

(3) Reasonable cause exception. No penalty shall be imposed under this subsection if it is shown that there is reasonable cause for the understatement and the tax return preparer acted in good faith.

(b) Understatement due to willful or reckless conduct.

(1) In general. Any tax return preparer who prepares any return or claim for refund with respect to which any part of an understatement of liability is due to a conduct described in paragraph (2) shall pay a penalty with respect to each such return or claim in an amount equal to the greater of—

(A) $5,000, or

(B) 50 percent of the income derived (or to be derived) by the tax return preparer with respect to the return or claim.

(2) Willful or reckless conduct. Conduct described in this paragraph is conduct by the tax return preparer which is—

(A) a willful attempt in any manner to understate the liability for tax on the return or claim, or

(B) a reckless or intentional disregard of rules or regulations.

(3) Reduction in penalty. The amount of any penalty payable by any person by reason of this subsection for any return or claim for refund shall be reduced by the amount of the penalty paid by such person by reason of subsection (a).

(c) Extension of period of collection where preparer pays 15 percent of penalty.

(1) In general. If, within 30 days after the day on which notice and demand of any penalty under subsection (a) or (b) is made against any person who is a tax return preparer, such person pays an amount which is not less than 15 percent of the amount of such penalty and files a claim for refund of the amount so paid, no levy or proceeding in court for the collection of the remainder of such penalty shall be made, begun, or prosecuted until the final resolution of a proceeding begun as provided in paragraph (2). Notwithstanding the provisions of section 7421(a), the beginning of such proceeding or levy during the time such prohibition is in force may be enjoined by a proceeding in the proper court. Nothing in this paragraph shall be construed to prohibit any counterclaim for the remainder of such penalty in a proceeding begun as provided in paragraph (2).

(2) Preparer must bring suit in district court to determine his liability for penalty. If, within 30 days after the day on which his claim for refund of any partial payment of any penalty under subsection (a) or (b) is denied (or, if earlier, within 30 days after the expiration of 6 months after the day on which he filed the claim for refund), the tax return preparer fails to begin a proceeding in the appropriate United States district court for the determination of his liability for such penalty, paragraph (1) shall cease to apply with respect to such penalty, effective on the day following the close of the applicable 30-day period referred to in this paragraph.

(3) Suspension of running of period of limitations on collection. The running of the period of limitations provided in section 6502 on the collection by levy or by a proceeding in court in respect of any penalty described in paragraph (1) shall be suspended for the period during which the Secretary is prohibited from collecting by levy or a proceeding in court.

(d) Abatement of penalty where taxpayer's liability not understated.

If at any time there is a final administrative determination or a final judicial decision that there was no understatement of liability in the case of any return or claim for refund with respect to which a penalty under subsection (a) or (b) has been assessed, such assessment shall be abated, and if any portion of such penalty has been paid the amount so paid shall be refunded to the person who made such payment as an overpayment of tax without regard to any period of limitations which, but for this subsection, would apply to the making of such refund.

(e) Understatement of liability defined.

For purposes of this section, the term "understatement of liability" means any understatement of the net amount payable with respect to any tax imposed by this title or any overstatement of the net amount creditable or refundable with respect to any such tax. Except as otherwise provided in subsection (d), the determination of whether or not there is an understatement of liability shall be made without regard to any administrative or judicial action involving the taxpayer.

(f) Cross reference.

For definition of tax return preparer, see section 7701(a)(36).

In 2008, P.L. 110-343, Sec. 506(a)DivC, amended subsec. (a), effective as provided in Sec. 506(b) Div C, which reads as follows:

"(b) Effective date. The amendment made by this section shall apply—

"(1) in the case of a position other than a position described in subparagraph (C) of section 6694(a)(2) of the Internal Revenue Code of 1986 (as amended by this section), to returns prepared after May 25, 2007, and

"(2) in the case of a position described in such subparagraph (C), to returns prepared for taxable years ending after the date of the enactment of this Act [10/3/2008]."

Prior to amendment, subsec. (a) read as follows:

"(a) Understatement due to unreasonable positions.

"(1) In general.

"Any tax return preparer who prepares any return or claim for refund with respect to which any part of an understatement of liability is due to a position described in paragraph (2) shall pay a penalty with respect to each such return or claim in an amount equal to the greater of—

"(A) $1,000, or

"(B) 50 percent of the income derived (or to be derived) by the tax return preparer with respect to the return or claim.

"(2) Unreasonable position.

"A position is described in this paragraph if—

"(A) the tax return preparer knew (or reasonably should have known) of the position;

"(B) there was not a reasonable belief that the position would more likely than not be sustained on its merits, and

"(C)(i) the position was not disclosed as provided in section 6662(d)(2)(B)(ii), or

"(ii) there was no reasonable basis for the position.

"(3) Reasonable cause exception.
"No penalty shall be imposed under this subsection if it is shown that there is reasonable cause for the understatement and the tax return preparer acted in good faith."

In 2007, P.L. 110-28, Sec. 8246(a)(2)(F)(i)(I), substituted "tax return preparer" for "income tax return preparer" in the heading of Sec. 6694... Sec. 8246(a)(2)(F)(i)(II), substituted "a tax return preparer" for "an income tax return preparer" each place it appears in Sec. 6694... Sec. 8246(a)(2)(F)(i)(III), substituted "the tax return preparer" for "the income tax return preparer" in para. (c)(2)... Sec. 8246(a)(2)(F)(i)(IV), substituted "this title" for "subtitle A" in subsec. (e)... Sec. 8246(a)(2)(F)(i)(V), substituted "tax return preparer" for "income tax return preparer" in subsec. (f)... Sec. 8246(b), amended subsecs. (a) and (b), effective for returns prepared after 5/25/2007.

Prior to amendment, subsecs. (a) and (b) read as follows:
"(a) Understatements due to unrealistic positions.
"(1) any part of any understatement of liability with respect to any return or claim for refund is due to a position for which there was not a realistic possibility of being sustained on its merits,
"(2) any person who is an income tax return preparer with respect to such return or claim knew (or reasonably should have known) of such position, and
"(3) such position was not disclosed as provided in section 6662(d)(2)(B)(ii) or was frivolous,
"such person shall pay a penalty of $250 with respect to such return or claim unless it is shown that there is reasonable cause for the understatement and such person acted in good faith.
"(b) Willful or reckless conduct. If any part of any understatement of liability with respect to any return or claim for refund is due—
"(1) to a willful attempt in any manner to understate the liability for tax by a person who is an income tax return preparer with respect to such return or claim, or
"(2) to any reckless or intentional disregard of rules or regulations by any such person,
"such person shall pay a penalty of $1,000 with respect to such return or claim. With respect to any return or claim, the amount of the penalty payable by any person by reason of this subsection shall be reduced by the amount of the penalty paid by such person by reason of subsection (a)."

In 1989, P.L. 101-239, Sec. 7732(a), amended subsecs. (a) and (b), effective for documents prepared after 12/31/89.

Prior to amendment, subsecs. (a) and (b) read as follows:
"(a) Negligent or intentional disregard of rules and regulations.
"If any part of any understatement of liability with respect to any return or claim for refund is due to the negligent or intentional disregard of rules and regulations by any person who is an income tax return preparer with respect to such return or claim, such person shall pay a penalty of $100 with respect to such return or claim.
"(b) Willful understatement of liability.
"If any part of any understatement of liability with respect to any return or claim for refund is due to a willful attempt in any manner to understate the liability for a tax by a person who is an income tax return preparer with respect to such return or claim, such person shall pay a penalty of $500 with respect to such return or claim. With respect to any return or claim, the amount of the penalty payable by any person by reason of this subsection shall be reduced by the amount of the penalty paid by such person by reason of subsection (a)."
—P.L. 101-239, Sec. 7737(a), added the last sentence to para. (c)(1), effective 12/19/89.

In 1976, P.L. 94-455, Sec. 1203(b)(1), added Code Sec. 6694, effective for documents prepared after 12/31/76.

Sec. 6695. Other assessable penalties with respect to the preparation of tax returns for other persons.

(a) Failure to furnish copy to taxpayer.

Any person who is a tax return preparer with respect to any return or claim for refund who fails to comply with section 6107(a) with respect to such return or claim shall pay a penalty of $50 for such failure, unless it is shown that such failure is due to reasonable cause and not due to willful neglect. The maximum penalty imposed under this subsection on any person with respect to documents filed during any calendar year shall not exceed $25,000.

(b) Failure to sign return.

Any person who is a tax return preparer with respect to any return or claim for refund, who is required by regulations prescribed by the Secretary to sign such return or claim, and who fails to comply with such regulations with respect to such return or claim shall pay a penalty of $50 for such failure, unless it is shown that such failure is due to reasonable cause and not due to willful neglect. The maximum penalty imposed under this subsection on any person with respect to documents filed during any calendar year shall not exceed $25,000.

(c) Failure to furnish identifying number.

Any person who is a tax return preparer with respect to any return or claim for refund and who fails to comply with section 6109(a)(4) with respect to such return or claim shall pay a penalty of $50 for such failure, unless it is shown that such failure is due to reasonable cause and not due to willful neglect. The maximum penalty imposed under this subsection on any person with respect to documents filed during any calendar year shall not exceed $25,000.

(d) Failure to retain copy or list.

Any person who is a tax return preparer with respect to any return or claim for refund who fails to comply with section 6107(b) with respect to such return or claim shall pay a penalty of $50 for each such failure, unless it is shown that such failure is due to reasonable cause and not due to willful neglect. The maximum penalty imposed under this subsection on any person with respect to any return period shall not exceed $25,000.

(e) Failure to file correct information returns.

Any person required to make a return under section 6060 who fails to comply with the requirements of such section shall pay a penalty of $50 for—

(1) each failure to file a return as required under such section, and

(2) each failure to set forth an item in the return as required under section,

unless it is shown that such failure is due to reasonable cause and not due to willful neglect. The maximum penalty imposed under this subsection on any person with respect to any return period shall not exceed $25,000.

(f) Negotiation of check.

Any person who is a tax return preparer who endorses or otherwise negotiates (directly or through an agent) any check made in respect of the taxes imposed by this title which is issued to a taxpayer (other than the tax return preparer) shall pay a penalty of $500 with respect to each such check. The preceding sentence shall not apply with respect to the deposit by a bank (within the meaning of section 581) of the full amount of the check in the taxpayer's account in such bank for the benefit of the taxpayer.

(g) Failure to be diligent in determining eligibility for earned income credit.

Any person who is a tax return preparer with respect to any return or claim for refund who fails to comply with due diligence requirements imposed by the Secretary by regulations with respect to determining eligibility for, or the amount of, the credit allowable by section 32 shall pay a penalty of $100 for each such failure.

In 2007, P.L. 110-28, Sec. 8246(a)(2)(G)(i)(I), deleted "income" from the heading of Code Sec. 6695... Sec. 8246(a)(2)(G)(i)(II), substituted "a tax return preparer" for "an income tax return preparer" each place it appeared in Code Sec. 6695... Sec. 8246(a)(2)(G)(ii)(I), substituted "this title" for "subtitle A" in subsec. (f)... Sec. 8246(a)(2)(G)(ii)(II), substituted "the tax return preparer" for "the income tax return preparer" in subsec. (f), effective for returns prepared after 5/25/2007.

In 1997, P.L. 105-34, Sec. 1085(a)(2), added subsec. (g), effective for tax. yrs. begin. after 12/31/96.

In 1989, P.L. 101-239, Sec. 7733(a)(1), substituted "$50" for "$25" in subsec. (a)... Sec. 7733(a)(2), added the last sentence to subsec. (a)... Sec. 7733(b)(1), substituted "$50" for "$25" in subsec. (b)... Sec. 7733(b)(2), added the last sentence to subsec. (b)... Sec. 7733(c)(1), substituted "$50" for "$25" in subsec. (c)... Sec. 7733(c)(2), added the last sentence to subsec. (c)... Sec. 7733(d), amended subsec. (e), effective for documents prepared after 12/31/89.

Prior to amendment, subsec. (e) read as follows:
"(e) Failure to file correct information return.
"Any person required to make a return under section 6060 who fails to comply with the requirements of such section shall pay a penalty of—
"(1) $100 for each failure to file a return as required under such section, and
"(2) $5 for each failure to set forth an item in the return as required under such section,

Penalties   Code Sec. 6696

unless it is shown that such failure is due to reasonable cause and not due to willful neglect. The maximum penalty imposed under this subsection on any person with respect to any return period shall not exceed $20,000."

In **1985**, P.L. 99-44, Sec. 1(b), repealed Sec. 179(b)(2) of P.L. 98-369 (see below) to take effect as if included in the amendments made by Sec. 179(b) of P.L. 98-369. Sec. 1(b) of this Act also provides that the " . . . Internal Revenue Code of 1954 shall be applied and administered as if such [Sec. 179(b)(2) of P.L. 98-369] (and the amendments made by such Sec. 179(b)(2) of P.L. 98-369]) had not been enacted". Sec. 1(c) of this Act provides:

"(c) Repeal of regulations.

Regulations issued before the date of the enactment of this Act [5/24/85] to carry out the amendments made by paragraphs (1)(C), (2), and (3) of section 179(b) of the Tax Reform Act of 1984 [P.L. 98-369] shall have no force and effect."

In **1984**, P.L. 98-369, Sec. 179(b)(2), deleted subsec. (b), effective for tax. yrs. begin. after 12/31/84, but repealed retroactively by Sec. 1(b) of P.L. 99-44 (see above).

Prior to deletion, subsec. (b) [as amended by Sec. 179(b)(2) of P.L. 98-369] read as follows:

"(b) Failure to inform taxpayer of certain recordkeeping requirements or to sign return.

"Any person who is an income tax return preparer with respect to any return or claim for refund and who is required by regulations to sign such return or claim—

"(1) shall advise the taxpayer of the substantiation requirements of section 274(d) and obtain written confirmation from the taxpayer that such requirements were met with respect to any deduction or credit claimed on such return or claim for refund, and

"(2) shall sign such return or claim for refund.

Any person who fails to comply with the requirements of the preceding sentence with respect to any return or claim shall pay a penalty of $25 for such failure, unless it is shown that such failure is due to reasonable cause and not to willful neglect."

In **1978**, P.L. 95-600, Sec. 701(cc)(1), added a sentence at the end of subsec. (f), effective for documents prepared after 12/31/76.

In **1976**, P.L. 94-455, Sec. 1203(f), added Code Sec. 6695, effective for documents prepared after 12/31/76.

Sec. 6695A. Substantial and gross valuation misstatements attributable to incorrect appraisals.

(a) Imposition of penalty.

If—

(1) a person prepares an appraisal of the value of property and such person knows, or reasonably should have known, that the appraisal would be used in connection with a return or a claim for refund, and

(2) the claimed value of the property on a return or claim for refund which is based on such appraisal results in a substantial valuation misstatement under chapter 1 (within the meaning of section 6662(e)), a substantial estate or gift tax valuation understatement (within the meaning of section 6662(g)), or a gross valuation misstatement (within the meaning of section 6662(h)), with respect to such property,

then such person shall pay a penalty in the amount determined under subsection (b).

(b) Amount of penalty.

The amount of the penalty imposed under subsection (a) on any person with respect to an appraisal shall be equal to the lesser of—

(1) the greater of—

(A) 10 percent of the amount of the underpayment (as defined in section 6664(a)) attributable to the misstatement described in subsection (a)(2), or

(B) $1,000, or

(2) 125 percent of the gross income received by the person described in subsection (a)(1) from the preparation of the appraisal.

(c) Exception.

No penalty shall be imposed under subsection (a) if the person establishes to the satisfaction of the Secretary that the value established in the appraisal was more likely than not the proper value.

In **2007**, P.L. 110-172, Sec. 3(e)(1), added "a substantial estate or gift tax valuation understatement (within the meaning of section 6662(g))," before "or a gross valuation misstatement" in para. (a)(2), effective for appraisals prepared for returns or submissions filed after 8/17/2006, except as provided in Sec. 1219(e)(3) of P.L. 109-280, which reads as follows:

"(3) Special rule for certain easements. In the case of a contribution of a qualified real property interest which is a restriction with respect to the exterior of a building described in section 170(h)(4)(C)(ii) of the Internal Revenue Code of 1986, and an appraisal with respect to the contribution, the amendments made by subsections (a) and (b) shall apply to returns filed after July 25, 2006."

—P.L. 110-172, Sec. 11(a)(40), substituted "then such person" for "then such person" in para. (a)(2), enacted 12/29/2007.

In **2006**, P.L. 109-280, Sec. 1219(b)(1), added Code Sec. 6695A, effective for appraisals prepared for returns or submissions filed after 8/17/2006, except as provided in Sec. 1219(e)(3) of this Act, which reads as follows:

"(3) Special rule for certain easements. In the case of a contribution of a qualified real property interest which is a restriction with respect to the exterior of a building described in section 170(h)(4)(C)(ii) of the Internal Revenue Code of 1986, and an appraisal with respect to the contribution, the amendments made by subsections (a) and (b) shall apply to returns filed after July 25, 2006."

Sec. 6696. Rules applicable with respect to sections 6694, 6695, and 6695A.

(a) Penalties to be additional to any other penalties.

The penalties provided by section 6694, 6695, and 6695A shall be in addition to any other penalties provided by law.

(b) Deficiency procedures not to apply.

Subchapter B of chapter 63 (relating to deficiency procedures for income, estate, gift, and certain excise taxes) shall not apply with respect to the assessment or collection of the penalties provided by sections 6694, 6695, and 6695A.

(c) Procedure for claiming refund.

Any claim for credit or refund of any penalty paid under section 6694, 6695, or 6695A shall be filed in accordance with regulations prescribed by the Secretary.

(d) Periods of limitation.

(1) Assessment. The amount of any penalty under section 6694(a), section 6695, or 6695A shall be assessed within 3 years after the return or claim for refund with respect to which the penalty is assessed was filed, and no proceeding in court without assessment for the collection of such tax shall be begun after the expiration of such period. In the case of any penalty under section 6694(b), the penalty may be assessed, or a proceeding in court for the collection of the penalty may be begun without assessment, at any time.

(2) Claim for refund. Except as provided in section 6694(d), any claim for refund of an overpayment of any penalty assessed under section 6694, 6695, or 6695A shall be filed within 3 years from the time the penalty was paid.

(e) Definitions.

For purposes of sections 6694, 6695, and 6695A—

(1) Return. The term "return" means any return of any tax imposed by this title.

(2) Claim for refund. The term "claim for refund" means a claim for refund of, or credit against, any tax imposed by this title.

In **2007**, P.L. 110-172, Sec. 3(e)(2), substituted ", section 6695, or 6695A" for "or under section 6695" in para. (d)(1), effective for appraisals prepared for returns or submissions filed after the 8/17/2006, except as provided in Sec. 1219(e)(3) of P.L. 109-280, see below.

—P.L. 110-28, Sec. 8246(a)(2)(H), substituted "this title" for "subtitle A" each place it appeared in subsec. (e), effective for returns prepared after 5/25/2007.

In **2006**, P.L. 109-280, Sec. 1219(b)(2)(A), substituted "6694, 6695, and 6695A" for "6694 and 6695" each place it appeared in the text and heading of Code Sec. 6696 . . . Sec. 1219(b)(2)(B), substituted "6694, 6695, or 6695A" for "6694 or 6695" each place it appeared in the text of Code Sec. 6696, effective for appraisals prepared for returns or submissions filed after the 8/17/2006, except as provided in Sec. 1219(e)(3) of this Act, which reads as follows:

"(3) Special rule for certain easements. In the case of a contribution of a qualified real property interest which is a restriction with respect to the exterior of a building described in section 170(h)(4)(C)(ii) of the Internal Revenue Code of

3,813

Code Sec. 6696

1986, and an appraisal with respect to the contribution, the amendments made by subsections (a) and (b) shall apply to returns filed after July 25, 2006.
In 1976, P.L. 94-455, Sec. 1203(f), added Code Sec. 6696, effective for documents prepared after 12/31/76.

Sec. 6697. Repealed.

In 2010, P.L. 111-325, Sec. 501(a), repealed Sec. 6697, effective for tax. yrs. begin. after 12/22/2010.
Prior to repeal, Sec. 6697 read as follows:
"SEC. 6697. ASSESSABLE PENALTIES WITH RESPECT TO LIABILITY FOR TAX OF REGULATED INVESTMENT COMPANIES.
Penalties
" (a) Civil Penalty.
"In addition to any other penalty provided by law, any regulated investment company whose tax liability for any taxable year is deemed to be increased pursuant to section 860(c)(1)(A) shall pay a penalty in an amount equal to the amount of the interest (for which such company is liable) which is attributable solely to such increase.
"(b) 50-Percent limitation.
"The penalty payable under this section with respect to any determination shall not exceed one-half of the amount of the deduction allowed by section 860(a) for such taxable year.
"(c) Deficiency procedures not to apply.
"Subchapter B of chapter 63 (relating to deficiency procedure for income, estate, gift, and certain excise taxes) shall not apply in respect of the assessment or collection of any penalty imposed by subsection (a)."
In 1986, P.L. 99-514, Sec. 667(a), amended the heading of Code Sec. 6697, and amended subsec. (a), effective for tax. yrs. begin. after 12/31/86.
Prior to amendment, the section heading and subsec. (a) read as follows:
"SEC. 6697. ASSESSABLE PENALTIES WITH RESPECT TO LIABILITY FOR TAX OF QUALIFIED INVESTMENT ENTITIES.
"(a) Civil penalty.
"In addition to any other penalty provided by law, any qualified investment entity (as defined in section 860(b)) whose tax liability for any taxable year is deemed to be increased pursuant to section 860(c)(1)(A) (relating to interest and additions to tax determined with respect to the amount of the deduction for deficiency dividends allowed) shall pay a penalty in an amount equal to the amount of interest (for which such entity is liable) which is attributable solely to such increase."
In 1980, P.L. 96-222, Sec. 103(a)(11)(A), amended Sec. 362(e) of P.L. 95-600, the effective date for changes made by Sec. 362 of P.L. 95-600, by substituting "860(e)" for "860(d)" [see below].
In 1978, P.L. 95-600, Sec. 362(b), amended Code Sec. 6697, effective for determinations (as defined in Code Sec. 860(e)) after 11/6/78.
Prior to amendment, Code Sec. 6697 read as follows:
"SEC. 6697. ASSESSABLE PENALTIES WITH RESPECT TO LIABILITY FOR TAX OF REAL ESTATE INVESTMENT TRUSTS.
"(a) Civil penalty.
"In addition to any other penalty provided by law, any real estate investment trust whose tax liability for any taxable year is deemed to be increased pursuant to section 859(b)(2)(A) (relating to interest and additions to tax determined with respect to the amount of the deduction for deficiency dividends allowed) shall pay a penalty in an amount equal to the amount of interest for which such trust is liable that is attributable solely to such increase.
"(b) 50-percent limitation.
"The penalty payable under this section with respect to any determination shall not exceed one-half of the amount of the deduction allowed by section 859(a) for such taxable year.
"(c) Deficiency procedures not to apply.
"Subchapter B of chapter 63 (relating to deficiency procedure for income, estate, gift, and certain excise taxes) shall not apply in respect of the assessment or collection of any penalty imposed by subsection (a)."
In 1976, P.L. 94-455, Sec. 1601(b)(1), added Code Sec. 6697. Sec. 1608(a) of the Act provides:
"(a) Deficiency dividend procedures.—
"The amendments made by section 1601 shall apply with respect to determinations (as defined in section 859(c) of the Internal Revenue Code of 1954) occurring after the date of the enactment of this Act [10/4/76]. If the amendments made by section 1601 apply to a taxable year ending on or before the date of enactment of this Act—
"(1) the reference to section 857(b)(3)(A)(ii) in sections 857(b)(3)(C) and 859(b)(1)(B) of such Code, as amended, shall be considered to be a reference to section 857(b)(3)(A) of such Code, as in effect immediately before the enactment of this Act, and
"(2) the reference to section 857(b)(2)(B) in section 859(a) of such Code, as amended, shall be considered to be a reference to section 857(b)(2)(C) of such Code, as in effect immediately before the enactment of this Act."

Sec. 6698. Failure to file partnership return.
(a) General rule.

In addition to the penalty imposed by section 7203 (relating to willful failure to file return, supply information, or pay tax), if any partnership required to file a return under section 6031 for any taxable year—

(1) fails to file such return at the time prescribed therefor (determined with regard to any extension of time for filing), or

(2) files a return which fails to show the information required under section 6031,

such partnership shall be liable for a penalty determined under subsection (b) for each month (or fraction thereof) during which such failure continues (but not to exceed 12 months), unless it is shown that such failure is due to reasonable cause.

(b) Amount per month.

For purposes of subsection (a), the amount determined under this subsection for any month is the product of—

(1) $195, multiplied by

(2) the number of persons who were partners in the partnership during any part of the taxable year

(c) Assessment of penalty.

The penalty imposed by subsection (a) shall be assessed against the partnership.

(d) Deficiency procedures not to apply.

Subchapter B of chapter 63 (relating to deficiency procedures for income, estate, gift, and certain excise taxes) shall not apply in respect of the assessment or collection of any penalty imposed by subsection (a).

In 2009, P.L. 111-92, Sec. 16(a), substituted "$195" for "$89" in para. (b)(1), effective for returns for tax. yrs. begin. after 12/31/2009.
In 2008, P.L. 110-458, Sec. 127(a), substituted "$89" for "$85" in subsec. (b)(1), effective for returns required to be filed after 12/31/2008.
In 2007, P.L. 110-141, Sec. 2, of this Act, reads as follows:
"Sec. 2. Modification of penalty for failure to file partnership returns. For any return of a partnership required to be filed under section 6031 of the Internal Revenue Code of 1986 for a taxable year beginning in 2008, the dollar amount in effect under section 6698(b)(1) of such Code shall be increased by $1."
—P.L. 110-142, Sec. 8(a), substituted "12 months" for "5 months" in subsec. (a) . . . Sec. 8(b), substituted "$85" for "$50" in para. (b)(1), effective for returns required to be filed after 12/20/2007.
In 1978, P.L. 95-600, Sec. 211(a), added Code Sec. 6698, effective for returns for tax. yrs. begin. after 12/31/78.

Sec. 6698A. Repealed.

In 1980, P.L. 96-223, Sec. 401(a), repealed Sec. 2005(d)(2) of P.L. 94-455 and Secs. 702(r)(1)(A) and (B) of P.L. 95-600 and the amendments made by Secs. 2005(d)(2) and 702(r)(1)(A) and (B), effective for decedents dying after '76 [see below]. Sec. 401(b) of P.L. 96-223 provides as follows:
"(b) Revival of prior law.
"Except to the extent necessary to carry out subsection (d), the Internal Revenue Code of 1954 shall be applied and administered as if the provisions repealed by subsection (a), and the amendments made by those provisions, had not been enacted."
—P.L. 96-222, Sec. 107(a)(2)(D), redesignated Code Sec. 6698 as Code Sec. 6698A, effective for estates of decedents dying after 12/31/79.
In 1978, P.L. 95-600, Sec. 515(6), postponed the effective date for changes made by Sec. 2005(d) of P.L. 94-455 from '76 to '79. [inoperative]
—P.L. 95-600, Sec. 702(r)(1)(A), redesignated Code Sec. 6694 (as added by Sec. 2005(d)(2) in P.L. 94-455) as Code Sec. 6698 . . . Sec. 702(r)(1)(B), added new subsec. (c), for estates of decedents dying after 12/31/76, but Secs. 702(r)(1)(A) and (B) were repealed by Sec. 401(a) of P.L. 96-223 [see above]. Subsec. (c) added by Sec. 702(r)(1)(B) read as follows:
"(c) Deficiency procedures not to apply.
"Subchapter B of chapter 63 (relating to deficiency procedures for income, estate, gift, and certain excise taxes) shall not apply in respect of the assessment or collection of any penalty imposed by subsection (a)."
In 1976, P.L. 94-455, Sec. 2005(d)(2), added Code Sec. 6694, for decedents dying after '76, but Sec. 2005(d)(2) was repealed by Sec. 401(a) of P.L. 96-223 [see above]. For Code Sec. 6694 added by Sec. 2005(d)(2) see note for Sec. 401(d) of P.L. 96-223 following Code Sec. 1014.

Sec. 6699. Failure to file S corporation return.
(a) General rule.

In addition to the penalty imposed by section 7203 (relating to willful failure to file return, supply information, or

Penalties Code Sec. 6700(a)(2)(A)

pay tax), if any S corporation required to file a return under section 6037 for any taxable year—

(1) fails to file such return at the time prescribed therefor (determined with regard to any extension of time for filing), or

(2) files a return which fails to show the information required under section 6037,

such S corporation shall be liable for a penalty determined under subsection (b) for each month (or fraction thereof) during which such failure continues (but not to exceed 12 months), unless it is shown that such failure is due to reasonable cause.

(b) Amount per month.

For purposes of subsection (a), the amount determined under this subsection for any month is the product of—

(1) $195, multiplied by

(2) the number of persons who were shareholders in the S corporation during any part of the taxable year.

(c) Assessment of penalty.

The penalty imposed by subsection (a) shall be assessed against the S corporation.

(d) Deficiency procedures not to apply.

Subchapter B of chapter 63 (relating to deficiency procedures for income, estate, gift, and certain excise taxes) shall not apply in respect of the assessment or collection of any penalty imposed by subsection (a).

In 2009, P.L. 111-92, Sec. 16(a), substituted "$195" for "$89" in para. (b)(1), effective for returns for tax. yrs. begin. after 12/31/2009.

In 2008, P.L. 110-458, Sec. 128(a), substituted "$89" for "$85" in para. (b)(1), effective for returns required to be filed after 12/31/2008.

In 2007, P.L. 110-142, Sec. 9(a), added new Code Sec. 6699, effective for returns required to be filed after 12/20/2007.

Sec. 6699. Repealed.

In 1986, P.L. 99-514, Sec. 1171(b)(7)(A), repealed Code Sec. 6699 [as amended by Sec. 1847(b)(9) of this Act, see below], effective for compensation paid or accrued after 12/31/86, in tax. yrs. end. after 12/31/86, except as provided in Sec. 1171(c)(2) of this Act which reads as follows:

"(2) Sections 404(i) and 6699 to continue to apply to pre-1987 credits.— The provisions of sections 404(i) and 6699 of the Internal Revenue Code of 1986 shall continue to apply with respect to credits under section 41 of such Code attributable to compensation paid or accrued before January 1, 1987 (or under section 38 of such Code with respect to qualified investment before January 1, 1983)."

Prior to repeal, Code Sec. 6699 read as follows:

"SEC. 6699. ASSESSABLE PENALTIES RELATING TO TAX CREDIT EMPLOYEE STOCK OWNERSHIP PLAN.

"(a) In general.

"If a taxpayer who has claimed an employee plan credit or a credit allowable under section 41 (relating to the employee stock ownership credit) for any taxable year—

"(1) fails to satisfy any requirement provided by section 409 with respect to a qualified investment made before January 1, 1983,

"(2) fails to make any contribution which is required under section 48(n) within the period required for making such contribution,

"(3) fails to satisfy any requirement provided under section 409 with respect to a credit claimed under section 41 in taxable years ending after December 31, 1982, or

"(4) fails to make any contribution which is required under section 44G(c)(1)(B) within the period required for making such contribution.

the taxpayer shall pay a penalty in an amount equal to the amount involved in such failure.

"(b) No penalty where there is timely correction of failure.

"Subsection (a) shall not apply with respect to any failure if the employer corrects such failure (as determined by the Secretary) within 90 days after the Secretary notifies him of such failure.

"(c) Amount involved defined.

"(1) In general. For purposes of this section, the term 'amount involved' means an amount determined by the Secretary.

"(2) Maximum and minimum amount.

"(A) The amount determined under paragraph (1) with respect to a failure described in paragraph (1) or (2) of subsection (a)—

"(i) shall not exceed the amount of the employee plan credit claimed by the employer to which such failure relates, and

"(ii) shall not be less than the product of one-half of 1 percent of the amount referred to in clause (i), multiplied by the number of months (or parts thereof) during which such failure continues.

"(B) The amount determined under paragraph (1) with respect to a failure described in paragraph (3) or (4) of subsection (a)—

"(i) shall not exceed the amount of the credit claimed by the employer under section 41 to which such failure relates, and

"(ii) shall not be less than the product of one-half of 1 percent of the amount referred to in clause (i), multiplied by the number of months (or parts thereof) during which such failure continues."

—P.L. 99-514, Sec. 1847(b)(9)(A), substituted "section 41" for "section 44G" each place it appeared in subsec. (a) and subpara. (c)(2)(B) . . . Sec. 1847(b)(9)(B), substituted "section 44G(c)(1)(B)" for "section 44G(c)(1)(B)" in para. (a)(4), effective for tax. yrs. begin. after 12/31/83, and to carrybacks from tax. yrs. begin. after 12/31/83.

In 1984, P.L. 98-369, Sec. 491(e)(9), substituted "section 409" for "section 409A" in paras. (a)(1) and (3), effective for obligations issued after 12/31/83.

In 1983, P.L. 97-448, Sec. 103(g)(2)(B), corrected Sec. 331(c)(4) of P.L. 97-34 to amend para. (c)(2) instead of para (2), [see below].

—P.L. 97-448, Sec. 103(g)(2)(C), substituted "clause (i)" for "subparagraph (A)" in clause (c)(2)(A)(ii) . . . Sec. 103(g)(2)(D), substituted "clause (i)" for "subparagraph (A)", in clause (c)(2)(B)(ii), effective for tax yrs. end. after 12/31/82.

In 1981, P.L. 97-34, Sec. 331(c)(3)(A)-(C), added "or a credit allowable under section 44G (relating to the employee stock ownership credit)" after "employee plan credit", substituted "section 409A with respect to a qualified investment made before January 1, 1983," for "section 409A, or", and added paras. (a)(3) and (4) . . . Sec. 331(c)(4), amended para. (c)(2), effective for tax. yrs. end. after 12/31/82.

Prior to amendment, para. (c)(2) read as follows:

"(2) Maximum and minimum amount. The amount determined under paragraph (1)—

"(A) shall not exceed the amount determined by multiplying the qualified investment of the employer for the taxable year to which the failure relates by the employee plan percentage claimed by the employer for such year, and

"(B) shall not be less than the product of one-half of 1 percent of the amount referred to in subparagraph (A), multiplied by the number of months (or parts thereof) during which such failure continues."

In 1980, P.L. 96-222, Sec. 101(a)(7)(B), corrected Sec. 141(g) of P.L. 95-600 [see below].

Prior to corrections, Sec. 141(g) of P.L. 95-600 read as follows:

"(g) Effective dates.—

"(1) In general.— The amendments made by this section (other than by subsection (f)(3)) shall apply with respect to qualified investment for taxable years beginning after December 31, 1978. The amendment made by subsection (f)(7) shall apply to years beginning after December 31, 1978."

—P.L. 96-222, Sec. 101(a)(7)(L)(iii)(VI), substituted "employee plan" for "ESOP" each place it appeared . . . Sec. 101(a)(7)(L)(v)(IX), substituted "tax credit employee stock ownership plan" for "ESOP" in the heading of Code Sec. 6699, presumably intended by Congress to be effective with respect to qualified investment for tax. yrs. begin. after 12/31/78 [Sec. 101(b)(2)] although technically effective with respect to the estates of decedents dying after 4/1/80 (date of enactment) [Sec. 101(b)(1)(D)].

In 1978, P.L. 95-600, Sec. 141(c)(1), added new Code Sec. 6699, with respect to qualified investment for tax. yrs. begin. after 12/31/78. Sec. 141(g)(2) of this Act provides:

"(2) Election to have amendments apply during 1978. At the election of the taxpayer, paragraph (1) shall be applied by substituting 'December 31, 1977' for 'December 31, 1978'; except that in the case of a plan in existence before December 31, 1978, any such election shall not affect the required allocation of employer securities attributable to qualified investment for taxable years beginning before January 1, 1979. An election under the preceding sentence shall be made at such time and in such manner as the Secretary of the Treasury or his delegate shall prescribe. Such an election, once made, shall be irrevocable."

Sec. 6700. Promoting abusive tax shelters, etc.

(a) Imposition of penalty.

Any person who—

(1)(A) organizes (or assists in the organization of)—

    (i) a partnership or other entity,

    (ii) any investment plan or arrangement, or

    (iii) any other plan or arrangement, or

(B) participates (directly or indirectly) in the sale of any interest in an entity or plan or arrangement referred to in subparagraph (A), and

(2) makes or furnishes or causes another person to make or furnish (in connection with such organization or sale)—

(A) a statement with respect to the allowability of any deduction or credit, the excludability of any income, or the securing of any other tax benefit by reason of holding an interest in the entity or participating in the plan or arrangement which the person knows or has reason to know is false or fraudulent as to any material matter, or

(B) a gross valuation overstatement as to any material matter,

shall pay, with respect to each activity described in paragraph (1), a penalty equal to the $1,000 or, if the person establishes that it is lesser, 100 percent of the gross income derived (or to be derived) by such person from such activity. For purposes of the preceding sentence, activities described in paragraph (1)(A) with respect to each entity or arrangement shall be treated as a separate activity and participation in each sale described in paragraph (1)(B) shall be so treated. Notwithstanding the first sentence, if an activity with respect to which a penalty imposed under this subsection involves a statement described in paragraph (2)(A), the amount of the penalty shall be equal to 50 percent of the gross income derived (or to be derived) from such activity by the person on which the penalty is imposed.

(b) Rules relating to penalty for gross valuation overstatements.

(1) Gross valuation overstatement defined. For purposes of this section, the term "gross valuation overstatement" means any statement as to the value of any property or services if—

(A) the value so stated exceeds 200 percent of the amount determined to be the correct valuation, and

(B) the value of such property or services is directly related to the amount of any deduction or credit allowable under chapter 1 to any participant.

(2) Authority to waive. The Secretary may waive all or any part of the penalty provided by subsection (a) with respect to any gross valuation overstatement on a showing that there was a reasonable basis for the valuation and that such valuation was made in good faith.

(c) Penalty in addition to other penalties.

The penalty imposed by this section shall be in addition to any other penalty provided by law.

In **2010**, P.L. 111-240, Sec. 2103, of this act provides:
Sec. 2103. Report on tax shelter penalties and certain other enforcement actions.
(a) In general. The Commissioner of Internal Revenue, in consultation with the Secretary of the Treasury, shall submit to the Committee on Ways and Means of the House of Representatives and the Committee on Finance of the Senate an annual report on the penalties assessed by the Internal Revenue Service during the preceding year under each of the following provisions of the Internal Revenue Code of 1986:
(1) Section 6662A (relating to accuracy-related penalty on understatements with respect to reportable transactions).
(2) Section 6700(a) (relating to promoting abusive tax shelters).
(3) Section 6707 (relating to failure to furnish information regarding reportable transactions).
(4) Section 6707A (relating to failure to include reportable transaction information with return).
(5) Section 6708 (relating to failure to maintain lists of advisees with respect to reportable transactions).
(b) Additional information. The report required under subsection (a) shall also include information on the following with respect to each year:
(1) Any action taken under section 330(b) of title 31, United States Code, with respect to any reportable transaction (as defined in section 6707A(c) of the Internal Revenue Code of 1986).
(2) Any extension of the time for assessment of tax enforced, or assessment of any amount under such an extension, under paragraph (10) of section 6501(c) of the Internal Revenue Code of 1986.
(c) Date of report. The first report required under subsection (a) shall be submitted not later than December 31, 2010.
In **2004**, P.L. 108-357, Sec. 818(a), added "Notwithstanding the first sentence, if an activity with respect to which a penalty imposed under this subsection involves a statement described in paragraph (2)(A), the amount of the penalty shall be equal to 50 percent of the gross income derived (or to be derived) from such activity by the person on which the penalty is imposed." at the end of subsec. (a), effective for activities after 10/22/2004.
In **1989**, P.L. 101-239, Sec. 7734(a)(1), added "(directly or indirectly)" after "participates" in subpara. (a)(1)(B) . . . Sec. 7734(a)(2), added "or causes another person to make or furnish" after "makes or furnishes" in para. (a)(2) . . . Sec. 7734(a)(3), substituted "shall pay, with respect to each activity described in paragraph (1), a penalty equal to the $1,000 or, if the person establishes that it is lesser, 100 percent of the gross income derived (or to be derived) by such person from such activity. For purposes of the preceding sentence, activities described in paragraph (1)(A) with respect to each entity or arrangement shall be treated as a separate activity and participation in each sale described in paragraph (1)(B) shall be so treated." for "shall pay a penalty equal to the greater of $1,000 or 20 percent of the gross income derived or to be derived by such person from such activity." in para. (a)(2), effective for activities after 12/31/89.
In **1984**, P.L. 98-369, Sec. 143(a), substituted "20 percent" for "10 percent" in subsec. (a), effective 7/19/84.
In **1982**, P.L. 97-248, Sec. 320(a), added Code Sec. 6700, effective 9/4/82.

Sec. 6701. Penalties for aiding and abetting understatement of tax liability.

(a) Imposition of penalty.

Any person—

(1) who aids or assists in, procures, or advises with respect to, the preparation or presentation of any portion of a return, affidavit, claim, or other document,

(2) who knows (or has reason to believe) that such portion will be used in connection with any material matter arising under the internal revenue laws, and

(3) who knows that such portion (if so used) would result in an understatement of the liability for tax of another person,

shall pay a penalty with respect to each such document in the amount determined under subsection (b).

(b) Amount of penalty.

(1) In general. Except as provided in paragraph (2), the amount of the penalty imposed by subsection (a) shall be $1,000.

(2) Corporations. If the return, affidavit, claim, or other document relates to the tax liability of a corporation, the amount of the penalty imposed by subsection (a) shall be $10,000.

(3) Only 1 penalty per person per period. If any person is subject to a penalty under subsection (a) with respect to any document relating to any taxpayer for any taxable period (or where there is no taxable period, any taxable event), such person shall not be subject to a penalty under subsection (a) with respect to any other document relating to such taxpayer for such taxable period (or event).

(c) Activities of subordinates.

(1) In general. For purposes of subsection (a), the term "procures" includes—

(A) ordering (or otherwise causing) a subordinate to do an act, and

(B) knowing of, and not attempting to prevent, participation by a subordinate in an act.

(2) Subordinate. For purposes of paragraph (1), the term "subordinate" means any other person (whether or not a director, officer, employee, or agent of the taxpayer involved) over whose activities the person has direction, supervision, or control.

(d) Taxpayer not required to have knowledge.

Subsection (a) shall apply whether or not the understatement is with the knowledge or consent of the persons authorized or required to present the return, affidavit, claim, or other document.

(e) Certain actions not treated as aid or assistance.

For purposes of subsection (a)(1), a person furnishing typing, reproducing, or other mechanical assistance with respect to a document shall not be treated as having aided or assisted in the preparation of such document by reason of such assistance.

(f) Penalty in addition to other penalties.

(1) In general. Except as provided by paragraphs (2) and (3), the penalty imposed by this section shall be in addition to any other penalty provided by law.

(2) Coordination with return preparer penalties. No penalty shall be assessed under subsection (a) or (b) of section 6694 on any person with respect to any document for which a penalty is assessed on such person under subsection (a).

(3) Coordination with section 6700. No penalty shall be assessed under section 6700 on any person with respect to any document for which a penalty is assessed on such person under subsection (a).

In 1989, P.L. 101-239, Sec. 7735(a)(1), deleted "in connection with any matter arising under the internal revenue laws" after "or other document" in para. (a)(1) . . . Sec. 7735(a)(2), substituted "who knows (or has reason to believe)" for "who knows" in para. (a)(2) . . . Sec. 7735(a)(3), substituted "would result" for "will result" in para. (a)(3) . . . Sec. 7735(b)(1), added para. (f)(3) . . . Sec. 7735(b)(2), substituted "paragraphs (2) and (3)" for "paragraph (2)" in para. (f)(1), effective 12/31/89.

In 1982, P.L. 97-248, Sec. 324(a), added Code Sec. 6701, effective 9/4/82. Sec. 324(d) of this Act provides as follows:

"(d) *Cross references.* For provisions relating to burden of proof and prepayment forum, see section 6703 of the Internal Revenue Code of 1954, as added by section 333 [sic , 322] of this Act."

Sec. 6702. Frivolous tax submissions.
(a) Civil penalty for frivolous tax returns.

A person shall pay a penalty of $5,000 if—

(1) such person files what purports to be a return of a tax imposed by this title but which—

(A) does not contain information on which the substantial correctness of the self-assessment may be judged, or

(B) contains information that on its face indicates that the self-assessment is substantially incorrect, and

(2) the conduct referred to in paragraph (1)—

(A) is based on a position which the Secretary has identified as frivolous under subsection (c), or

(B) reflects a desire to delay or impede the administration of Federal tax laws.

(b) Civil penalty for specified frivolous submissions.

(1) **Imposition of penalty.** Except as provided in paragraph (3), any person who submits a specified frivolous submission shall pay a penalty of $5,000.

(2) **Specified frivolous submission.** For purposes of this section—

(A) Specified Frivolous Submission. The term "specified frivolous submission" means a specified submission if any portion of such submission—

(i) is based on a position which the Secretary has identified as frivolous under subsection (c), or

(ii) reflects a desire to delay or impede the administration of Federal tax laws.

(B) Specified submission. The term "specified submission" means—

(i) a request for a hearing under—

(I) section 6320 (relating to notice and opportunity for hearing upon filing of notice of lien), or

(II) section 6330 (relating to notice and opportunity for hearing before levy), and

(ii) an application under—

(I) section 6159 (relating to agreements for payment of tax liability in installments),

(II) section 7122 (relating to compromises), or

(III) section 7811 (relating to taxpayer assistance orders).

(3) **Opportunity to withdraw submission.** If the Secretary provides a person with notice that a submission is a specified frivolous submission and such person withdraws such submission within 30 days after such notice, the penalty imposed under paragraph (1) shall not apply with respect to such submission.

(c) Listing of frivolous positions.

The Secretary shall prescribe (and periodically revise) a list of positions which the Secretary has identified as being frivolous for purposes of this subsection. The Secretary shall not include in such list any position that the Secretary determines meets the requirement of section 6662(d)(2)(B)(ii)(II).

(d) Reduction of Penalty.

The Secretary may reduce the amount of any penalty imposed under this section if the Secretary determines that such reduction would promote compliance with and administration of the Federal tax laws.

(e) Penalties in addition to other penalties.

The penalties imposed by this section shall be in addition to any other penalty provided by law.

In 2006, P.L. 109-432, Sec. 407(a), amended Sec. 6702, effective for submissions made and issues raised after the date on which the Secretary first prescribes a list under Code Sec. 6702(c), as amended by Sec. 407(a) of P.L. 109-432.

Prior to amendment, Sec. 6702 read as follows:

"Sec. 6702. Frivolous income tax return.

"(a) Civil penalty. If—

"(1) any individual files what purports to be a return of the tax imposed by subtitle A but which—

"(A) does not contain information on which the substantial correctness of the self-assessment may be judged, or

"(B) contains information that on its face indicates that the self-assessment is substantially incorrect; and

"(2) the conduct referred to in paragraph (1) is due to—

"(A) a position which is frivolous, or

"(B) a desire (which appears on the purported return) to delay or impede the administration of Federal income tax laws,

then such individual shall pay a penalty of $500.

"(b) Penalty in addition to other penalties. The penalty imposed by subsection (a) shall be in addition to any other penalty provided by law."

In 1982, P.L. 97-248, Sec. 326(a), added Code Sec. 6702, effective for documents filed after 9/3/82. Sec. 326(d) of this Act provides as follows:

"(d) *Cross reference.* For provisions relating to burden of proof and prepayment forum, see section 6703 of the Internal Revenue Code of 1954, as added by section 333 [sic , 322] of this Act."

Sec. 6703. Rules applicable to penalties under sections 6700, 6701, and 6702.
(a) Burden of proof.

In any proceeding involving the issue of whether or not any person is liable for a penalty under section 6700, 6701, or 6702, the burden of proof with respect to such issue shall be on the Secretary.

(b) Deficiency procedures not to apply.

Subchapter B of chapter 63 (relating to deficiency procedures) shall not apply with respect to the assessment or collection of the penalties provided by sections 6700, 6701, and 6702.

(c) Extension of period of collection where person pays 15 percent of penalty.

(1) **In general.** If, within 30 days after the day on which notice and demand of any penalty under section 6700 or 6701 is made against any person, such person pays an amount which is not less than 15 percent of the amount of such penalty and files a claim for refund of the amount so paid, no levy or proceeding in court for the collection of the remainder of such penalty shall be made, begun, or prosecuted until the final resolution of a proceeding begun as provided in paragraph (2). Notwithstanding the provisions of section 7421(a), the beginning of such proceeding or levy during the time such prohibition is in force may be enjoined by a proceeding in the proper court. Nothing in this paragraph shall be construed to prohibit any counterclaim for the remainder of such penalty in a proceeding begun as provided in paragraph (2).

(2) **Person must bring suit in district court to determine his liability for penalty.** If, within 30 days after the day on which his claim for refund of any partial payment

of any penalty under section 6700 or 6701 is denied (or, if earlier, within 30 days after the expiration of 6 months after the day on which he filed the claim for refund), the person fails to begin a proceeding in the appropriate United States district court for the determination of his liability for such penalty, paragraph (1) shall cease to apply with respect to such penalty, effective on the day following the close of the applicable 30-day period referred to in this paragraph.

(3) Suspension of running of period of limitations on collection. The running of the period of limitations provided in section 6502 on the collection by levy or by a proceeding in court in respect of any penalty described in paragraph (1) shall be suspended for the period during which the Secretary is prohibited from collecting by levy or a proceeding in court.

In 1989, P.L. 101-239, Sec. 7736(a), substituted "section 6700 or 6701" for "section 6700, 6701, or 6702" each place it appeared in subsec. (c), effective for returns filed after 12/31/89.

—P.L. 101-239, Sec. 7737(a), added the sentence at the end of para. (c)(1), effective 12/19/89.

In 1982, P.L. 97-248, Sec. 322(a), added Code Sec. 6703, effective 9/4/82.

Sec. 6704. Failure to keep records necessary to meet reporting requirements under section 6047(d).
(a) Liability for penalty.
Any person who—
(1) has a duty to report or may have a duty to report any information under section 6047(d), and
(2) fails to keep such records as may be required by regulations prescribed under section 6047(d) for the purpose of providing the necessary data base for either current reporting or future reporting,
shall pay a penalty for each calendar year for which there is any failure to keep such records.
(b) Amount of penalty.
(1) In general. The penalty of any person for any calendar year shall be $50, multiplied by the number of individuals with respect to whom such failure occurs in such year.
(2) Maximum amount. The penalty under this section of any person for any calendar year shall not exceed $50,000.
(c) Exceptions.
(1) Reasonable cause. No penalty shall be imposed by this section on any person for any failure which is shown to be due to reasonable cause and not to willful neglect.
(2) Inability to correct previous failure. No penalty shall be imposed by this section on any failure by a person if such failure is attributable to a prior failure which has been penalized under this section and with respect to which the person has made all reasonable efforts to correct the failure.
(3) Pre-1983 failures. No penalty shall be imposed by this section on any person for any failure which is attributable to a failure occurring before January 1, 1983, if the person has made all reasonable efforts to correct such pre-1983 failure.

In 1986, P.L. 99-514, Sec. 1848(e)(1)(A), substituted "section 6047(d)" for "section 6047(e)" each place it appeared in subsec. (a) ... Sec. 1848(e)(1)(B), substituted "section 6047(d)" for "section 6047(e)" in the heading of Code Sec. 6704, effective for obligations issued after 12/31/83.

In 1982, P.L. 97-248, Sec. 334(c)(1), added Code Sec. 6704, effective 1/1/85.

Sec. 6705. Failure by broker to provide notice to payors.
(a) In general.
Any person required under section 3406(d)(2)(B) to provide notice to any payor who willfully fails to provide such notice to such payor shall pay a penalty of $500 for each such failure.
(b) Penalty in addition to other penalties.
Any penalty imposed by this section shall be in addition to any other penalty provided by law.

In 1983, P.L. 98-67, Sec. 104(c)(1), added Code Sec. 6705, effective for payments made after 12/31/83.

Sec. 6706. Original issue discount information requirements.
(a) Failure to show information on debt instrument.
In the case of a failure to set forth on a debt instrument the information required to be set forth on such instrument under section 1275(c)(1), unless it is shown that such failure is due to reasonable cause and not to willful neglect, the issuer shall pay a penalty of $50 for each instrument with respect to which such a failure exists.
(b) Failure to furnish information to Secretary.
Any issuer who fails to furnish information required under section 1275(c)(2) with respect to any issue of debt instruments on the date prescribed therefor (determined with regard to any extension of time for filing) shall pay a penalty equal to 1 percent of the aggregate issue price of such issue, unless it is shown that such failure is due to reasonable cause and not willful neglect. The amount of the penalty imposed under the preceding sentence with respect to any issue of debt instruments shall not exceed $50,000 for such issue.
(c) Deficiency procedures not to apply.
Subchapter B of chapter 63 (relating to deficiency procedures for income, estate, gift, and certain excise taxes) shall not apply in respect of the assessment or collection of any penalty imposed by this section.

In 1984, P.L. 98-369, Sec. 41(c)(1), added Code Sec. 6706, effective 8/17/84.

Sec. 6707. Failure to furnish information regarding reportable transactions.
(a) In general.
If a person who is required to file a return under section 6111(a) with respect to any reportable transaction—
(1) fails to file such return on or before the date prescribed therefor, or
(2) files false or incomplete information with the Secretary with respect to such transaction,
such person shall pay a penalty with respect to such return in the amount determined under subsection (b).
(b) Amount of penalty.
(1) In general. Except as provided in paragraph (2), the penalty imposed under subsection (a) with respect to any failure shall be $50,000.
(2) Listed transactions. The penalty imposed under subsection (a) with respect to any listed transaction shall be an amount equal to the greater of—
(A) $200,000, or
(B) 50 percent of the gross income derived by such person with respect to aid, assistance, or advice which is provided with respect to the listed transaction before the date the return is filed under section 6111.
Subparagraph (B) shall be applied by substituting "75 percent" for "50 percent" in the case of an intentional failure or act described in subsection (a).

Penalties

Code Sec. 6707A(c)(2)

(c) Rescission authority.

The provisions of section 6707A(d) (relating to authority of Commissioner to rescind penalty) shall apply to any penalty imposed under this section.

(d) Reportable and listed transactions.

For purposes of this section, the terms "reportable transaction" and "listed transaction" have the respective meanings given to such terms by section 6707A(c).

In 2010, P.L. 111-240, Sec. 2103, of this Act, reads as follows:
"SEC. 2103. REPORT ON TAX SHELTER PENALTIES AND CERTAIN OTHER ENFORCEMENT ACTIONS."
"(a) In general. The Commissioner of Internal Revenue, in consultation with the Secretary of the Treasury, shall submit to the Committee on Ways and Means of the House of Representatives and the Committee on Finance of the Senate an annual report on the penalties assessed by the Internal Revenue Service during the preceding year under each of the following provisions of the Internal Revenue Code of 1986:
"(1) Section 6662A (relating to accuracy-related penalty on understatements with respect to reportable transactions).
"(2) Section 6700(a) (relating to promoting abusive tax shelters).
"(3) Section 6707 (relating to failure to furnish information regarding reportable transactions).
"(4) Section 6707A (relating to failure to include reportable transaction information with return).
"(5) Section 6708 (relating to failure to maintain lists of advisees with respect to reportable transactions).
"(b) Additional information. The report required under subsection (a) shall also include information on the following with respect to each year:
"(1) Any action taken under section 330(b) of title 31, United States Code, with respect to any reportable transaction (as defined in section 6707A(c) of the Internal Revenue Code of 1986).
"(2) Any extension of the time for assessment of tax enforced, or assessment of any amount under such an extension, under paragraph (10) of section 6501(c) of the Internal Revenue Code of 1986.
"(c) Date of report. The first report required under subsection (a) shall be submitted not later than December 31, 2010."
In 2004, P.L. 108-357, Sec. 816(a), amended Code Sec. 6707, effective for returns the due date for which is after 10/22/2004.
Prior to amendment, Code Sec. 6707 read as follows:
"SEC. 6707. FAILURE TO FURNISH INFORMATION REGARDING TAX SHELTERS.
"(a) Failure to register tax shelter.
"(1) Imposition of penalty. If a person who is required to register a tax shelter under section 6111(a)—
"(A) fails to register such tax shelter on or before the date described in section 6111(a)(1), or
"(B) files false or incomplete information with the Secretary with respect to such registration,
such person shall pay a penalty with respect to such registration in the amount determined under paragraph (2) or (3), as the case may be.
"No penalty shall be imposed under the preceding sentence with respect to any failure which is due to reasonable cause.
"(2) Amount of penalty. Except as provided in paragraph (3), the penalty imposed under paragraph (1) with respect to any tax shelter shall be an amount equal to the greater of—
"(A) 1 percent of the aggregate amount invested in such tax shelter, or
"(B) $500.
"(3) Confidential arrangements.
"(A) In general. In the case of a tax shelter (as defined in section 6111(d)), the penalty imposed under paragraph (1) shall be an amount equal to the greater of—
"(i) 50 percent of the fees paid to all promoters of the tax shelter with respect to offerings made before the date such shelter is registered under section 6111, or
"(ii) $10,000.
"Clause (i) shall be applied by substituting '75 percent' for '50 percent' in the case of an intentional failure or act described in paragraph (1).
"(B) Special rule for participants required to register shelter. In the case of a person required to register such a tax shelter by reason of section 6111(d)(3)—
"(i) such person shall be required to pay the penalty under paragraph (1) only if such person actually participated in such shelter,
"(ii) the amount of such penalty shall be determined by taking into account under subparagraph (A)(i) only the fees paid by such person, and
"(iii) such penalty shall be in addition to the penalty imposed on any other person for failing to register such shelter.
"(b) Failure to furnish tax shelter identification number.
"(1) Sellers, etc. Any person who fails to furnish the identification number of a tax shelter which such person is required to furnish under section 6111(b)(1) shall pay a penalty of $100 for each such failure.
"(2) Failure to include number on return. Any person who fails to include an identification number on a return on which such number is required to be included under section 6111(b)(2) shall pay a penalty of $250 for each such failure, unless such failure is due to reasonable cause."
In 1997, P.L. 105-34, Sec. 1028(b), added para. (a)(3) . . . Sec. 1028(d)(1), substituted "Except as provided in paragraph (3), the penalty" for "The penalty" in para. (a)(2) . . . Sec. 1028(d)(2), substituted "paragraph (2) or (3), as the case may be" for "paragraph (2)" in subpara. (a)(1)(A) [sic para. (a)(1), ed. note: Amendment cannot be made as stated, but can be made to para. (a)(1)], effective for any tax shelter (as defined in Code Sec. 6111(d) [as amended by Sec. 1028(a) of this Act]) interests in which are offered to potential participants after the Secretary of the Treasury prescribes guidance with respect to meeting requirements added by such amendments.
In 1986, P.L. 99-514, Sec. 1532(a), amended para. (a)(2), effective for failures for tax shelters, interests in which are first offered for sale after 10/22/86.
Prior to amendment, para. (a)(2) read as follows:
"(2) Amount of penalty. The penalty imposed under paragraph (1) with respect to any tax shelter shall be an amount equal to the greater of—
"(A) $500, or
"(B) the lesser of (i) 1 percent of the aggregate amount invested in such tax shelter, or (ii) $10,000.
The $10,000 limitation in subparagraph (B) shall not apply where there is an intentional disregard of the requirements of section 6111(a)."
—P.L. 99-514, Sec. 1533(a), substituted "$250" for "$50" in para. (b) (2), effective for returns filed after 10/22/86.
In 1984, P.L. 98-369, Sec. 141(b), added Code Sec. 6707, effective for any tax shelter (within the meaning of Code Sec. 6111) any interest in which is first sold to any investor after 8/31/84. Sec. 141(d)(2) and (3) of the Act provide:
"(2) Substantial investment test.—For purposes of determining whether any investment is a tax shelter by reason of section 6111(c)(1)(B)(iii) of such Code (as added by this section), only offers for sale after August 31, 1984, shall be taken into account.
"(3) Furnishing of shelter identification number for interests sold before September 1, 1984.—With respect to interests sold before September 1, 1984, any liability to act under paragraph (1) of section 6111(b) of such Code (as added by this section) which would (but for this sentence) arise before such date shall be deemed to arise on December 31, 1984."

Sec. 6707A. Penalty for failure to include reportable transaction information with return.

(a) Imposition of penalty.

Any person who fails to include on any return or statement any information with respect to a reportable transaction which is required under section 6011 to be included with such return or statement shall pay a penalty in the amount determined under subsection (b).

(b) Amount of penalty.

(1) In general. Except as otherwise provided in this subsection, the amount of the penalty under subsection (a) with respect to any reportable transaction shall be 75 percent of the decrease in tax shown on the return as a result of such transaction (or which would have resulted from such transaction if such transaction were respected for Federal tax purposes).

(2) Maximum penalty. The amount of the penalty under subsection (a) with respect to any reportable transaction shall not exceed—

(A) in the case of a listed transaction, $200,000 ($100,000 in the case of a natural person), or

(B) in the case of any other reportable transaction, $50,000 ($10,000 in the case of a natural person).

(3) Minimum penalty. The amount of the penalty under subsection (a) with respect to any transaction shall not be less than $10,000 ($5,000 in the case of a natural person).

(c) Definitions.

For purposes of this section—

(1) Reportable transaction. The term "reportable transaction" means any transaction with respect to which information is required to be included with a return or statement because, as determined under regulations prescribed under section 6011, such transaction is of a type which the Secretary determines as having a potential for tax avoidance or evasion.

(2) Listed transaction. The term "listed transaction" means a reportable transaction which is the same as, or substantially similar to, a transaction specifically identified by the Secretary as a tax avoidance transaction for purposes of section 6011.

3,819

(d) Authority to rescind penalty.
(1) In general. The Commissioner of Internal Revenue may rescind all or any portion of any penalty imposed by this section with respect to any violation if—
(A) the violation is with respect to a reportable transaction other than a listed transaction, and
(B) rescinding the penalty would promote compliance with the requirements of this title and effective tax administration.
(2) No judicial appeal. Notwithstanding any other provision of law, any determination under this subsection may not be reviewed in any judicial proceeding.
(3) Records. If a penalty is rescinded under paragraph (1), the Commissioner shall place in the file in the Office of the Commissioner the opinion of the Commissioner with respect to the determination, including—
(A) a statement of the facts and circumstances relating to the violation,
(B) the reasons for the rescission, and
(C) the amount of the penalty rescinded.
(e) Penalty reported to SEC.
In the case of a person—
(1) which is required to file periodic reports under section 13 or 15(d) of the Securities Exchange Act of 1934 or is required to be consolidated with another person for purposes of such reports, and
(2) which—
(A) is required to pay a penalty under this section with respect to a listed transaction,
(B) is required to pay a penalty under section 6662A with respect to any reportable transaction at a rate prescribed under section 6662A(c), or
(C) is required to pay a penalty under section 6662(h) with respect to any reportable transaction and would (but for section 6662A(e)(2)(B)) have been subject to penalty under section 6662A at a rate prescribed under section 6662A(c),
the requirement to pay such penalty shall be disclosed in such reports filed by such person for such periods as the Secretary shall specify. Failure to make a disclosure in accordance with the preceding sentence shall be treated as a failure to which the penalty under subsection (b)(2) applies.
(f) Coordination with other penalties.
The penalty imposed by this section shall be in addition to any other penalty imposed by this title.

In **2010**, P.L. 111-240, Sec. 2041(a), amended subsec. (b), effective for penalties assessed after 12/31/2006.
Prior to amendment, subsec. (b) read as follows:
"(b) Amount of penalty.
"(1) In general. Except as provided in paragraph (2), the amount of the penalty under subsection (a) shall be—
"(A) $10,000 in the case of a natural person, and
"(B) $50,000 in any other case.
"(2) Listed transaction. The amount of the penalty under subsection (a) with respect to a listed transaction shall be—
"(A) $100,000 in the case of a natural person, and
"(B) $200,000 in any other case."
—P.L. 111-240, Sec. 2103, of this Act provides:
"SEC. 2103. REPORT ON TAX SHELTER PENALTIES AND CERTAIN OTHER ENFORCEMENT ACTIONS.
"(a) IN GENERAL. The Commissioner of Internal Revenue, in consultation with the Secretary of the Treasury, shall submit to the Committee on Ways and Means of the House of Representatives and the Committee on Finance of the Senate an annual report on the penalties assessed by the Internal Revenue Service during the preceding year under each of the following provisions of the Internal Revenue Code of 1986:
"(1) Section 6662A (relating to accuracy-related penalty on understatements with respect to reportable transactions).
"(2) Section 6700(a) (relating to promoting abusive tax shelters).
"(3) Section 6707 (relating to failure to furnish information regarding reportable transactions).
"(4) Section 6707A (relating to failure to include reportable transaction information with return).
"(5) Section 6708 (relating to failure to maintain lists of advisees with respect to reportable transactions).
"(b) ADDITIONAL INFORMATION. The report required under subsection (a) shall also include information on the following with respect to each year:
"(1) Any action taken under section 330(b) of title 31, United States Code, with respect to any reportable transaction (as defined in section 6707A(c) of the Internal Revenue Code of 1986).
"(2) Any extension of the time for assessment of tax enforced, or assessment of any amount under such an extension, under paragraph (10) of section 6501(c) of the Internal Revenue Code of 1986.
"(c) DATE OF REPORT. The first report required under subsection (a) shall be submitted not later than December 31, 2010."
In **2007**, P.L. 110-172, Sec. 11(a)(41), substituted "section 6662A(e)(2)(B)" for "section 6662A(e)(2)(C)", enacted 12/29/2007.
In **2005**, P.L. 109-135, Sec. 403(w), added "and which were not filed before such date" before the period at the end of Sec. 811(c) of P.L. 108-357, which provides the effective date for the amendment made by Sec. 811(a) of such Act, see below.
In **2004**, P.L. 108-357, Sec. 811(a), added Code Sec. 6707A, effective for returns and statements the due date for which is after 10/22/2004 and which were not filed before such date.
—P.L. 108-357, Sec. 811(d), of this Act, provides:
"(d) Report. The Commissioner of Internal Revenue shall annually report to the Committee on Ways and Means of the House of Representatives and the Committee on Finance of the Senate—
"(1) a summary of the total number and aggregate amount of penalties imposed, and rescinded, under section 6707A of the Internal Revenue Code of 1986, and
"(2) a description of each penalty rescinded under section 6707(c) of such Code and the reasons therefor."

Sec. 6708. Failure to maintain lists of advisees with respect to reportable transactions.
(a) Imposition of penalty.
(1) In general. If any person who is required to maintain a list under section 6112(a) fails to make such list available upon written request to the Secretary in accordance with section 6112(b) within 20 business days after the date of such request, such person shall pay a penalty of $10,000 for each day of such failure after such 20th day.
(2) Reasonable cause exception. No penalty shall be imposed by paragraph (1) with respect to the failure on any day if such failure is due to reasonable cause.
(b) Penalty in addition to other penalties.
The penalty imposed by this section shall be in addition to any other penalty provided by law.

In **2010**, P.L. 111-240, Sec. 2103, of this Act, reads as follows:
"SEC. 2103. Report on Tax Shelter Penalties and Certain Other Enforcement Actions.
"(a) In general. The Commissioner of Internal Revenue, in consultation with the Secretary of the Treasury, shall submit to the Committee on Ways and Means of the House of Representatives and the Committee on Finance of the Senate an annual report on the penalties assessed by the Internal Revenue Service during the preceding year under each of the following provisions of the Internal Revenue Code of 1986:
"(1) Section 6662A (relating to accuracy-related penalty on understatements with respect to reportable transactions).
"(2) Section 6700(a) (relating to promoting abusive tax shelters).
"(3) Section 6707 (relating to failure to furnish information regarding reportable transactions).
"(4) Section 6707A (relating to failure to include reportable transaction information with return).
"(5) Section 6708 (relating to failure to maintain lists of advisees with respect to reportable transactions).
"(b) Additional information. The report required under subsection (a) shall also include information on the following with respect to each year:
"(1) Any action taken under section 330(b) of title 31, United States Code, with respect to any reportable transaction (as defined in section 6707A(c) of the Internal Revenue Code of 1986).
"(2) Any extension of the time for assessment of tax enforced, or assessment of any amount under such an extension, under paragraph (10) of section 6501(c) of the Internal Revenue Code of 1986.
"(c) Date of report. The first report required under subsection (a) shall be submitted not later than December 31, 2010."
In **2004**, P.L. 108-357, Sec. 815(b)(5)(A), amended the heading of Code Sec. 6708, effective for transactions with respect to which material aid, assistance, or advice referred to in Code Sec. 6111(b)(1)(A)(i) (as added by this section) is provided after 10/22/2004.
Prior to amendment, the heading of Code Sec. 6708 read as follows:

Penalties

"SEC. 6708. FAILURE TO MAINTAIN LISTS OF INVESTORS IN POTENTIALLY ABUSIVE TAX SHELTERS."
—P.L. 108-357, Sec. 817(a), amended subsec. (a), effective for requests made after 10/22/2004.
Prior to amendment, subsec. (a) read as follows:
"(a) In general. Any person who fails to meet any requirement imposed by section 6112 shall pay a penalty of $50 for each person with respect to whom there is such a failure, unless it is shown that such failure is due to reasonable cause and not due to willful neglect. The maximum penalty imposed under this subsection for any calendar year shall not exceed $100,000."
In 1986, P.L. 99-514, Sec. 1534(a), substituted "$100,000" for "$50,000" in subsec. (a), effective for failures occurring or continuing after 10/22/86.
In 1984, P.L. 98-369, Sec. 142(b), added Code Sec. 6708, effective for any interest which is first sold to any investor after 8/31/84.
—P.L. 98-369, Sec. 632, provided various exceptions to the amendments made by Title VI of this Act. See note following Code Sec. 103A.

Sec. 6709. Penalties with respect to mortgage credit certificates.

(a) Negligence.

If—

(1) any person makes a material misstatement in any verified written statement made under penalties of perjury with respect to the issuance of a mortgage credit certificate, and

(2) such misstatement is due to the negligence of such person,

such person shall pay a penalty of $1,000 for each mortgage credit certificate with respect to which such a misstatement was made.

(b) Fraud.

If a misstatement described in subsection (a)(1) is due to fraud on the part of the person making such misstatement, in addition to any criminal penalty, such person shall pay a penalty of $10,000 for each mortgage credit certificate with respect to which such a misstatement is made.

(c) Reports.

Any person required by section 25(g) to file a report with the Secretary who fails to file the report with respect to any mortgage credit certificate at the time and in the manner required by the Secretary shall pay a penalty of $200 for such failure unless it is shown that such failure is due to reasonable cause and not to willful neglect. In the case of any report required under the second sentence of section 25(g), the aggregate amount of the penalty imposed by the preceding sentence shall not exceed $2,000.

(d) Mortgage credit certificate.

The term "mortgage credit certificate" has the meaning given to such term by section 25(c).

In 1986, P.L. 99-514, Sec. 1862(d)(2), redesignated Code Sec. 6708 relating to penalties with respect to mortgage credit certificates as Code Sec. 6709, effective for interest paid or accrued after 12/31/84, on indebtedness incurred after 12/31/84.
In 1984, P.L. 98-369, Sec. 612(d)(1), added Code Sec. 6708 [sic 6709], effective for interest paid or accrued after 12/31/84, on indebtedness incurred after 12/31/84.

Sec. 6710. Failure to disclose that contributions are nondeductible.

(a) Imposition of penalty.

If there is a failure to meet the requirement of section 6113 with respect to a fundraising solicitation by (or on behalf of) an organization to which section 6113 applies, such organization shall pay a penalty of $1,000 for each day on which such a failure occurred. The maximum penalty imposed under this subsection on failures by any organization during any calendar year shall not exceed $10,000.

(b) Reasonable cause exception.

No penalty shall be imposed under this section with respect to any failure if it is shown that such failure is due to reasonable cause.

(c) $10,000 Limitation not to apply where intentional disregard.

If any failure to which subsection (a) applies is due to intentional disregard of the requirement of section 6113—

(1) the penalty under subsection (a) for the day on which such failure occurred shall be the greater of—

(A) $1,000, or

(B) 50 percent of the aggregate cost of the solicitations which occurred on such day and with respect to which there was such a failure,

(2) the $10,000 limitation of subsection (a) shall not apply to any penalty under subsection (a) for the day on which such failure occurred, and

(3) such penalty shall not be taken into account in applying such limitation to other penalties under subsection (a).

(d) Day on which failure occurs.

For purposes of this section, any failure to meet the requirement of section 6113 with respect to a solicitation—

(1) by television or radio, shall be treated as occurring when the solicitation was telecast or broadcast,

(2) by mail, shall be treated as occurring when the solicitation was mailed,

(3) not by mail but in written or printed form, shall be treated as occurring when the solicitation was distributed, or

(4) by telephone, shall be treated as occurring when the solicitation was made.

In 1987, P.L. 100-203, Sec. 10701(b), added Code Sec. 6710, effective for solicitations after 1/31/88.

Sec. 6711. Failure by tax-exempt organization to disclose that certain information or service available from Federal Government.

(a) Imposition of penalty.

If—

(1) a tax-exempt organization offers to sell (or solicits money for) specific information or a routine service for any individual which could be readily obtained by such individual free of charge (or for a nominal charge) from an agency of the Federal Government,

(2) the tax-exempt organization, when making such offer or solicitation, fails to make an express statement (in a conspicuous and easily recognizable format) that the information or service can be so obtained, and

(3) such failure is due to intentional disregard of the requirements of this subsection,

such organization shall pay a penalty determined under subsection (b) for each day on which such a failure occurred.

(b) Amount of penalty.

The penalty under subsection (a) for any day on which a failure referred to in such subsection occurred shall be the greater of—

(1) $1,000, or

(2) 50 percent of the aggregate cost of the offers and solicitations referred to in subsection (a)(1) which occurred on such day and with respect to which there was such a failure.

(c) Definitions.

For purposes of this section—

(1) Tax-exempt organization. The term "tax-exempt organization" means any organization which—

(A) is described in subsection (c) or (d) of section 501 and exempt from taxation under section 501(a), or

(B) is a political organization (as defined in section 527(e)).

(2) **Day on which failure occurs.** The day on which any failure referred to in subsection (a) occurs shall be determined under rules similar to the rules of section 6710(d).

In **1987,** P.L. 100-203, Sec. 10705(a), added Code Sec. 6711, effective for offers and solicitations after 1/31/88.

Sec. 6712. Failure to disclose treaty-based return positions.
(a) General rule.
If a taxpayer fails to meet the requirements of section 6114 there is hereby imposed a penalty equal to $1,000 ($10,000 in the case of a C corporation) on each such failure.
(b) Authority to waive.
The Secretary may waive all or any part of the penalty provided by this section on a showing by the taxpayer that there was reasonable cause for the failure and that the taxpayer acted in good faith.
(c) Penalty in addition to other penalties.
The penalty imposed by this section shall be in addition to any other penalty imposed by law.

In **1988,** P.L. 100-647, Sec. 1012(aa)(5)(B), added Code Sec. 6712, effective for tax periods the due date for filing returns for which (without extension) occurs after 12/31/88.

Sec. 6713. Disclosure or use of information by preparers of returns.
(a) Imposition of penalty.
If any person who is engaged in the business of preparing or providing services in connection with the preparation of, returns of tax imposed by chapter 1, or any person who for compensation prepares any such return for any other person, and who—
  (1) discloses any information furnished to him for, or in connection with, the preparation of any such return, or
  (2) uses any such information for any purpose other than to prepare, or assist in preparing, any such return,
shall pay a penalty of $250 for each such disclosure or use, but the total amount imposed under this subsection on such a person for any calendar year shall not exceed $10,000.
(b) Exceptions.
The rules of section 7216(b) shall apply for purposes of this section.
(c) Deficiency procedures not to apply.
Subchapter B of chapter 63 (relating to deficiency procedures for income, estate, gift, and certain excise taxes) shall not apply in respect of the assessment or collection of any penalty imposed by this section.

In **1989,** P.L. 101-239, Sec. 7816(v)(1), redesignated Code Sec. 6712 (relating to disclosure or use of information by preparers of returns, added by Sec. 6242(a) of P.L. 100-647, see below) as Code Sec. 6713, effective for disclosures or uses after 12/31/88.
In **1988,** P.L. 100-647, Sec. 6242(a), added Code Sec. 6712, [6713] effective for disclosures or uses after 12/31/88.

Sec. 6714. Failure to meet disclosure requirements applicable to quid pro quo contributions.
(a) Imposition of penalty.
If an organization fails to meet the disclosure requirement of section 6115 with respect to a quid pro quo contribution, such organization shall pay a penalty of $10 for each contribution in respect of which the organization fails to make the required disclosure, except that the total penalty imposed by this subsection with respect to a particular fundraising event or mailing shall not exceed $5,000.

(b) Reasonable cause exception.
No penalty shall be imposed under this section with respect to any failure if it is shown that such failure is due to reasonable cause.

In **1993,** P.L. 103-66, Sec. 13173(b), added Code Sec. 6714, effective for quid pro quo contributions made on or after 1/1/94.

Sec. 6715. Dyed fuel sold for use or used in taxable use.
(a) Imposition of penalty.
If—
  (1) any dyed fuel is sold or held for sale by any person for any use which such person knows or has reason to know is not a nontaxable use of such fuel,
  (2) any dyed fuel held for use or used by any person for a use other than a nontaxable use and such person knew, or had reason to know, that such fuel was so dyed,
  (3) any person willfully alters, chemically or otherwise, or attempts to so alter, the strength or composition of any dye or marking done pursuant to section 4082 in any dyed fuel, or
  (4) any person who has knowledge that a dyed fuel which has been altered as described in paragraph (3) sells or holds for sale such fuel for any use which the person knows or has reason to know is not a nontaxable use of such fuel,
then, such person shall pay a penalty in addition to the tax (if any).
(b) Amount of penalty.
  (1) **In general.** Except as provided in paragraph (2), the amount of the penalty under subsection (a) on each act shall be the greater of—
    (A) $1,000, or
    (B) $10 for each gallon of the dyed fuel involved.
  (2) **Multiple violations.** In determining the penalty under subsection (a) on any person, paragraph (1) shall be applied by increasing the amount in paragraph (1)(A) by the product of such amount and the number of prior penalties (if any) imposed by this section on such person (or a related person or any predecessor of such person or related person).
(c) Definitions.
For purposes of this section—
  (1) **Dyed fuel.** The term "dyed fuel" means any dyed diesel fuel or kerosene, whether or not the fuel was dyed pursuant to section 4082.
  (2) **Nontaxable use.** The term "nontaxable use" has the meaning given such term by section 4082(b).
(d) Joint and several liability of certain officers and employees.
If a penalty is imposed under this section on any business entity, each officer, employee, or agent of such entity who willfully participated in any act giving rise to such penalty shall be jointly and severally liable with such entity for such penalty.
(e) No administrative appeal for third and subsequent violations.
In the case of any person who is found to be subject to the penalty under this section after a chemical analysis of such fuel and who has been penalized under this section at least twice after the date of the enactment of this subsection, no administrative appeal or review shall be allowed with respect to such finding except in the case of a claim regarding—
  (1) fraud or mistake in the chemical analysis, or
  (2) mathematical calculation of the amount of the penalty.

Penalties

Code Sec. 6716

In 2004, P.L. 108-357, Sec. 855(a), added subsec. (e), effective for penalties assessed after 10/22/2004.
—P.L. 108-357, Sec. 856(a), deleted "or" at the end of para. (a)(2), added "or" at the end of para. (a)(3), and added para. (a)(4)... Sec. 856(b), substituted "alters, chemically or otherwise, or attempts to so alter," for "alters, or attempts to alter," in para. (a)(3), effective 10/22/2004.
In 1997, P.L. 105-34, Sec. 1032(e)(11), added "or kerosene" after "diesel fuel" in para. (c)(1), effective 7/1/98.
In 1996, P.L. 104-188, Sec. 1703(n)(9)(A), redesignated Code Sec. 6714, as added by Sec. 13242(b)(1) of P.L. 103-66, as Code Sec. 6715, effective 1/1/94.
In 1993, P.L. 103-66, Sec. 13242(b)(1), added Code Sec. 6714 [sic 6715], effective 1/1/94.

Sec. 6715A. Tampering with or failing to maintain security requirements for mechanical dye injection systems.

(a) Imposition of penalty.

(1) **Tampering.** If any person tampers with a mechanical dye injection system used to indelibly dye fuel for purposes of section 4082, such person shall pay a penalty in addition to the tax (if any).

(2) **Failure to maintain security requirements.** If any operator of a mechanical dye injection system used to indelibly dye fuel for purposes of section 4082 fails to maintain the security standards for such system as established by the Secretary, then such operator shall pay a penalty in addition to the tax (if any).

(b) Amount of penalty.

The amount of the penalty under subsection (a) shall be—
(1) for each violation described in paragraph (1), the greater of—
  (A) $25,000, or
  (B) $10 for each gallon of fuel involved, and
(2) for each—
  (A) failure to maintain security standards described in paragraph (2), $1,000, and
  (B) failure to correct a violation described in paragraph (2), $1,000 per day for each day after which such violation was discovered or such person should have reasonably known of such violation.

(c) Joint and several liability.

(1) **In general.** If a penalty is imposed under this section on any business entity, each officer, employee, or agent of such entity or other contracting party who willfully participated in any act giving rise to such penalty shall be jointly and severally liable with such entity for such penalty.

(2) **Affiliated groups.** If a business entity described in paragraph (1) is part of an affiliated group (as defined in section 1504(a)), the parent corporation of such entity shall be jointly and severally liable with such entity for the penalty imposed under this section.

In 2004, P.L. 108-357, Sec. 854(c)(1), added Code Sec. 6715A, effective as provided in Sec. 854(d) of this Act, which reads as follows:
"(d) Effective date. The amendments made by subsections (a) and (c) shall take effect on the 180th day after the date on which the Secretary issues the regulations described in subsection (b)."
Sec. 854(b) of this Act, provides:
"(b) Dye injector security. Not later than 180 days after the date of the enactment of this Act, the Secretary of the Treasury shall issue regulations regarding mechanical dye injection systems described in the amendment made by subsection (a), and such regulations shall include standards for making such systems tamper resistant."

• **Caution:** Code Sec. 6716, was added by Sec. 542(b)(4), P.L. 107-16, EGTRRA. As provided in Sec. 301(a), P.L. 111-312, this amendment will apply as if never enacted, effective for estates of decedents dying, and transfers made, after 12/31/2009.

Sec. 6716. Failure to file information with respect to certain transfers at death and gifts.

(a) Information required to be furnished to the Secretary.

Any person required to furnish any information under section 6018 who fails to furnish such information on the date prescribed therefor (determined with regard to any extension of time for filing) shall pay a penalty of $10,000 ($500 in the case of information required to be furnished under section 6018(b)(2)) for each such failure.

(b) Information required to be furnished to beneficiaries.

Any person required to furnish in writing to each person described in section 6018(e) or 6019(b) the information required under such section who fails to furnish such information shall pay a penalty of $50 for each such failure.

(c) Reasonable cause exception.

No penalty shall be imposed under subsection (a) or (b) with respect to any failure if it is shown that such failure is due to reasonable cause.

(d) Intentional disregard.

If any failure under subsection (a) or (b) is due to intentional disregard of the requirements under sections 6018 and 6019(b), the penalty under such subsection shall be 5 percent of the fair market value (as of the date of death or, in the case of section 6019(b), the date of the gift) of the property with respect to which the information is required.

(e) Deficiency procedures not to apply.

Subchapter B of chapter 63 (relating to deficiency procedures for income, estate, gift, and certain excise taxes) shall not apply in respect of the assessment or collection of any penalty imposed by this section.

In 2010, P.L. 111-312, Sec. 101(a)(1), substituted "December 31, 2012" for "December 31, 2010" both places it appears in Sec. 901, P.L. 107-16 [see below], effective as if included in the enactment of P.L. 107-16, EGTRRA, 6/7/2001.
—P.L. 111-312, Sec. 301(a), provides that Code Sec. 6716, as amended by Sec. 542(b)(4), P.L. 107-16, EGTRRA, 6/7/2001 (added Code Sec. 6716, see below) will read as if such provision had never been enacted, effective for estates of decedents dying, and transfers made, after 12/31/2009.
Sec. 301(a), P.L. 111-312, 12/17/2010, provides:
"(a) In general. Each provision of law amended by subtitle A or E of title V of the Economic Growth and Tax Relief Reconciliation Act of 2001 is amended to read as such provision would read if such subtitle had never been enacted."
—P.L. 111-312, Sec. 301(c), of this Act, provides:
"(c) Special election with respect to estates of decedents dying in 2010. Notwithstanding subsection (a), in the case of an estate of a decedent dying after December 31, 2009, and before January 1, 2011, the executor (within the meaning of section 2203 of the Internal Revenue Code of 1986) may elect to apply such Code as though the amendments made by subsection (a) do not apply with respect to chapter 11 of such Code and with respect to property acquired or passing from such decedent (within the meaning of section 1014(b) of such Code). Such election shall be made at such time and in such manner as the Secretary of the Treasury or the Secretary's delegate shall provide. Such an election once made shall be revocable only with the consent of the Secretary of the Treasury or the Secretary's delegate. For purposes of section 2652(a)(1) of such Code, the determination of whether any property is subject to the tax imposed by such chapter 11 shall be made without regard to any election made under this subsection."
—P.L. 111-312, Sec. 301(d), of this Act, provides:
"(d) Extension of time for performing certain acts.
"(1) Estate tax. In the case of the estate of a decedent dying after December 31, 2009, and before the date of the enactment of this Act, the due date for—
"(A) filing any return under section 6018 of the Internal Revenue Code of 1986 (including any election required to be made on such a return) as such section is in effect after the date of the enactment of this Act without regard to any election under subsection (c),
"(B) making any payment of tax under chapter 11 of such Code, and
"(C) making any disclaimer described in section 2518(b) of such Code of an interest in property passing by reason of the death of such decedent, shall not be earlier than the date which is 9 months after the date of the enactment of this Act.
"(2) Generation-skipping tax. In the case of any generation-skipping transfer made after December 31, 2009, and before the date of the enactment of this Act, the due date for filing any return under section 2662 of the Internal Revenue Code

Code Sec. 6716 — Penalties

of 1986 (including any election required to be made on such a return) shall not be earlier than the date which is 9 months after the date of the enactment of this Act."

In 2002, P.L. 107-358, Sec. 2, added subsec. (c) in Sec. 901 of P.L. 107-16 [see below], effective 12/17/2002.

In 2001, P.L. 107-16, Sec. 542(b)(4), added Code Sec. 6716, effective for estates of decedents dying after 12/31/2009.

— P.L. 107-16, Sec. 901, of this Act [as amended by Sec. 2 of P.L. 107-358, and Sec. 101(a)(1), P.L. 111-312, see above], reads as follows:

"SEC. 901. SUNSET OF PROVISIONS OF ACT.

"(a) In general. All provisions of, and amendments made by, this Act shall not apply—

"(1) to taxable, plan, or limitation years beginning after December 31, 2012, or

"(2) in the case of title V, to estates of decedents dying, gifts made, or generation skipping transfers, after December 31, 2012.

"(b) Application of certain laws. The Internal Revenue Code of 1986 and the Employee Retirement Income Security Act of 1974 shall be applied and administered to years, estates, gifts, and transfers described in subsection (a) as if the provisions and amendments described in subsection (a) had never been enacted.

"(c) Exception. Subsection (a) shall not apply to section 803 (relating to no federal income tax on restitution received by victims of the Nazi regime or their heirs or estates)."

Sec. 6717. Refusal of entry.
(a) In general.

In addition to any other penalty provided by law, any person who refuses to admit entry or refuses to permit any other action by the Secretary authorized by section 4083(d)(1) shall pay a penalty of $1,000 for such refusal.

(b) Joint and several liability.

(1) In general. If a penalty is imposed under this section on any business entity, each officer, employee, or agent of such entity or other contracting party who willfully participated in any act giving rise to such penalty shall be jointly and severally liable with such entity for such penalty.

(2) Affiliated groups. If a business entity described in paragraph (1) is part of an affiliated group (as defined in section 1504(a)), the parent corporation of such entity shall be jointly and severally liable with such entity for the penalty imposed under this section.

(c) Reasonable cause exception.

No penalty shall be imposed under this section with respect to any failure if it is shown that such failure is due to reasonable cause.

In 2004, P.L. 108-357, Sec. 859(a), added Code Sec. 6717, effective 1/1/2005.

Sec. 6718. Failure to display tax registration on vessels.
(a) Failure to display registration.

Every operator of a vessel who fails to display proof of registration pursuant to section 4101(a)(3) shall pay a penalty of $500 for each such failure. With respect to any vessel, only one penalty shall be imposed by this section during any calendar month.

(b) Multiple violations.

In determining the penalty under subsection (a) on any person, subsection (a) shall be applied by increasing the amount in subsection (a) by the product of such amount and the aggregate number of penalties (if any) imposed with respect to prior months by this section on such person (or a related person or any predecessor of such person or related person).

(c) Reasonable cause exception.

No penalty shall be imposed under this section with respect to any failure if it is shown that such failure is due to reasonable cause.

In 2004, P.L. 108-357, Sec. 861(b)(1), added Code Sec. 6718, effective for penalties imposed after 12/31/2004.

— P.L. 108-357, Sec. 862(c), substituted "section 4101(a)(3)" for "section 4101(a)(2)" in subsec. (a) [as added by Sec. 861(b)(1) of this Act, see above], effective 1/1/2005.

Sec. 6719. Failure to register or reregister.
(a) Failure to register or reregister.

Every person who is required to register or reregister under section 4101 and fails to do so shall pay a penalty in addition to the tax (if any).

(b) Amount of penalty.

The amount of the penalty under subsection (a) shall be—

(1) $10,000 for each initial failure to register or reregister, and

(2) $1,000 for each day thereafter such person fails to register or reregister.

(c) Reasonable cause exception.

No penalty shall be imposed under this section with respect to any failure if it is shown that such failure is due to reasonable cause.

In 2005, P.L. 109-59, Sec. 11164(b)(1)(A), added "or reregister" after "register" each place it appeared in Code Sec. 6719 ... Sec. 11164(b)(1)(B), added "or reregister" after "register" in the heading of subsec. (a) ... Sec. 11164(b)(1)(C), added "or reregister" after "register" in the heading of Code Sec. 6719, effective for actions, or failures to act, after 8/10/2005.

In 2004, P.L. 108-357, Sec. 863(c)(1), added Code Sec. 6719, effective for penalties imposed after 12/31/2004.

Sec. 6720. Fraudulent acknowledgments with respect to donations of motor vehicles, boats, and airplanes.

Any donee organization required under section 170(f)(12)(A) to furnish a contemporaneous written acknowledgment to a donor which knowingly furnishes a false or fraudulent acknowledgment, or which knowingly fails to furnish such acknowledgment in the manner, at the time, and showing the information required under section 170(f)(12), or regulations prescribed thereunder, shall for each such act, or for each such failure, be subject to a penalty equal to—

(1) in the case of an acknowledgment with respect to a qualified vehicle to which section 170(f)(12)(A)(ii) applies, the greater of—

(A) the product of the highest rate of tax specified in section 1 and the sales price stated on the acknowledgment, or

(B) the gross proceeds from the sale of such vehicle, and

(2) in the case of an acknowledgment with respect to any other qualified vehicle to which section 170(f)(12) applies, the greater of—

(A) the product of the highest rate of tax specified in section 1 and the claimed value of the vehicle, or

(B) $5,000.

In 2004, P.L. 108-357, Sec. 884(b)(1), added Code Sec. 6720, effective for contributions made after 12/31/2004.

Sec. 6720A. Penalty with respect to certain adulterated fuels.
(a) In general.

Any person who knowingly transfers for resale, sells for resale, or holds out for resale any liquid for use in a diesel-powered highway vehicle or a diesel-powered train which does not meet applicable EPA regulations (as defined in section 45H(c)(3)), shall pay a penalty of $10,000 for each such transfer, sale, or holding out for resale, in addition to the tax on such liquid (if any).

(b) Penalty in the case of retailers.

Any person who knowingly holds out for sale (other than for resale) any liquid described in subsection (a), shall pay a penalty of $10,000 for each such holding out for sale, in addition to the tax on such liquid (if any).

Penalties   Part II

In 2005, P.L. 109-59, Sec. 11167(a), added Code Sec. 6720A, effective for any transfer, sale, or holding out for sale or resale occurring after 8/10/2005.

Sec. 6720B. Fraudulent identification of exempt use property.

In addition to any criminal penalty provided by law, any person who identifies applicable property (as defined in section 170(e)(7)(C)) as having a use which is related to a purpose or function constituting the basis for the donee's exemption under section 501 and who knows that such property is not intended for such a use shall pay a penalty of $10,000.

In 2006, P.L. 109-280, Sec. 1215(c)(1), added Code Sec. 6720B, effective for identifications made after 8/17/2006.

Sec. 6720C. Penalty for failure to notify health plan of cessation of eligibility for COBRA premium assistance.
(a) In general.

Any person required to notify a group health plan under section 3001(a)(2)(C) of title III of division B of the American Recovery and Reinvestment Act of 2009 who fails to make such a notification at such time and in such manner as the Secretary of Labor may require shall pay a penalty of 110 percent of the premium reduction provided under such section after termination of eligibility under such subsection.
(b) Reasonable cause exception.

No penalty shall be imposed under subsection (a) with respect to any failure if it is shown that such failure is due to reasonable cause and not to willful neglect.

In 2010, P.L. 111-144, Sec. 3(b)(5)(D), substituted "section 3001(a)(2)(C) of title III of division B of the American Recovery and Reinvestment Act of 2009" for "section 3002(a)(2)(C) of the Health Insurance Assistance for the Unemployed Act of 2009" in subsec. (a), effective for tax. yrs. end. after 02/17/2009.

In 2009, P.L. 111-5, Sec. 3001(a)(13)(A), added Code Sec. 6720C, effective for failures occurring after 2/17/2009.

PART II.—FAILURE TO COMPLY WITH CERTAIN INFORMATION REPORTING REQUIREMENTS

Sec.
6721. Failure to file correct information returns.
6722. Failure to furnish correct payee statements.
6723. Failure to comply with other information reporting requirements.
6724. Waiver; definitions and special rules.
6725. Failure to report information under section 4101.

In 2004, P.L. 108-357, Sec. 863(d)(2), added item 6725.

In 1989, P.L. 101-239, Sec. 7711(a), amended Part II of subchapter B of chapter 68.

Prior to amendment part II of subchapter B of chapter 68 read as follows:

"PART II—FAILURE TO FILE CERTAIN INFORMATION RETURNS OR STATEMENTS
"Sec.
"6721. Failure to file certain information returns.
"6722. Failure to furnish certain payee statements.
"6723. Failure to include correct information.
"6724. Waiver; definitions and special rules.

In 1986, P.L. 99-514, Sec. 1501(a), added part II of Subchapter B of chapter 68.

"SEC. 6721. FAILURE TO FILE CERTAIN INFORMATION RETURNS.
"(a) General rule.

"In the case of each failure to file an information return with the Secretary on the date prescribed therefor (determined with regard to any extension of time for filing), the person failing to so file such return shall pay $50 for each such failure, but the total amount imposed on such person for all such failures during any calendar year shall not exceed $100,000.
"(b) Penalty in case of intentional disregard.

"If 1 or more failures to which subsection (a) applies are due to intentional disregard of the filing requirement, then, with respect to each such failure—
"(1) the penalty imposed under subsection (a) shall be $100, or, if greater—
"(A) in the case of a return other than a return required under section 6045(a), 6041A(b), 6050H, 6050J, 6050K, or 6050L, 10 percent of the aggregate amount of the items required to be reported (or, if greater, in the case of a return filed under section 6050I, 10 percent of the taxable income derived from the transaction), or
"(B) in the case of a return required to be filed by section 6045(a), 6050K, or 6050L, 5 percent of the aggregate amount of the items required to be reported, and
"(2) in the case of any penalty determined under paragraph (1)—
"(A) the $100,000 limitation under subsection (a) shall not apply, and
"(B) such penalty shall not be taken into account in applying the $100,000 limitation to penalties not determined under paragraph (1)."

In 1988, P.L. 100-690, Sec. 7601(a)(2)(A), inserted "(or, if greater, in the case of a return filed under section 6050I, 10 percent of the taxable income derived from the transaction)" after "reported" in subpara. (b)(1)(A), effective for actions after 11/18/88.

In 1986, P.L. 99-514, Sec. 1501(a), added Code Sec. 6721, part of part II of Subchapter B of chapter 68, effective for returns the due date of which (determined without regard to extensions) is after 12/31/86.

"SEC. 6722. FAILURE TO FURNISH CERTAIN PAYEE STATEMENTS.
"(a) General rule.

"In the case of each failure to furnish a payee statement on the date prescribed therefor to the person to whom such statement is required to be furnished, the person failing to so furnish such statement shall pay $50 for each such failure, but the total amount imposed on such person for all such failures during any calendar year shall not exceed $100,000.
"(b) Failure to notify partnership of exchange of partnership interest.

"In the case of any person who fails to furnish the notice required by section 6050K(c)(1) on the date prescribed therefor, such person shall pay a penalty of $50 for each such failure.

In 1986, P.L. 99-514, Sec. 1501(a), added Code Sec. 6722, part of part II of Subchapter B of chapter 68, effective for for returns the due date of which (determined without regard to extensions) is after 12/31/86.

"SEC. 6723. FAILURE TO INCLUDE CORRECT INFORMATION.
"(a) General rule.
"If—
"(1) any person files an information return or furnishes a payee statement, and
"(2) such person does not include all of the information required to be shown on such return or statement or includes incorrect information,
"such person shall pay $5 for each return or statement with respect to which such failure occurs, but the total amount imposed on such person for all such failures during any calendar year shall not exceed $20,000.
"(b) Penalty in case of intentional disregard.

"If 1 or more failures to which subsection (a) applies are due to intentional disregard of the correct information reporting requirement, then, with respect to each such failure—
"(1) the penalty imposed under subsection (a) shall be $100, or, if greater—
"(A) in the case of a return other than a return required under section 6045(a), 6041A(b), 6050H, 6050J, 6050K, or 6050L, 10 percent of the aggregate amount of the items required to be reported correctly, or
"(B) in the case of a return required to be filed by section 6045(a), 6050K, or 6050L, 5 percent of the aggregate amount of the items required to be reported correctly, and
"(2) in the case of any penalty determined under paragraph (1)—
"(A) the $20,000 limitation under subsection (a) shall not apply, and
"(B) such penalty shall not be taken into account in applying the $20,000 limitation to penalties not determined under paragraph (1).
"(c) Coordination with section 6676.

"No penalty shall be imposed under subsection (a) or (b) with respect to any return or statement if a penalty is imposed under section 6676 (relating to failure to supply identifying number) with respect to such return or statement.

In 1986, P.L. 99-514, Sec. 1501(a), added Code Sec. 6723, part of Part II of Subchapter B of chapter 68, effective for returns the due date of which (determined without regard to extensions) is after 12/31/86.

"SEC. 6724. WAIVER; DEFINITIONS AND SPECIAL RULES.
"(a) Reasonable cause waiver.

"No penalty shall be imposed under this part with respect to any failure if it is shown that such failure is due to reasonable cause and not to willful neglect.
"(b) Payment of penalty.

"Any penalty imposed by this part shall be paid on notice and demand by the Secretary and in the same manner as tax.
"(c) Special rules for failure to file interest and dividend returns or statements.
"(1) Higher standards for waiver. In the case of any interest or dividend return or statement—
"(A) subsection (a) shall not apply, but

3,825

"(B) no penalty shall be imposed under this part if it is shown that the person otherwise liable for such penalty exercised due diligence in attempting to satisfy the requirement with respect to such return or statement.

"(2) Limitations not to apply. In the case of any interest or dividend return or statement—

"(A) the $100,000 limitations of sections 6721(a) and 6722(a) and the $20,000 limitation of section 6723(a) shall not apply (and any penalty imposed on any failure involving such a return or statement shall not be taken into account in applying such limitations to other penalties), and

"(B) penalties imposed with respect to such returns or statements shall not be taken into account for purposes of applying such limitations with respect to other returns or statements.

"(3) Self assessment. Any penalty imposed under this part on any person with respect to an interest or dividend return or statement—

"(A) shall be assessed and collected in the same manner as an excise tax imposed by subtitle D, and

"(B) shall be due and payable on April 1 of the calendar year following the calendar year for which such return or statement is required.

"(4) Deficiency procedures not to apply. Subchapter B of chapter 63 (relating to deficiency procedures for income, estate, gift, and certain excise taxes) shall not apply in respect of the assessment or collection of any penalty imposed under this part with respect to an interest or dividend return or statement.

"(5) Interest or dividend return or statement. For purposes of this subsection, the term 'interest or dividend return or statement' means—

"(A) any return required by section 6042(a)(1), 6044(a)(1), or 6049(a), and

"(B) any statement required under section 6042(c), 6044(e), or 6049(c).

"(d) Definitions.

"For purposes of this part—

"(1) Information return. The term 'information return' means—

"(A) any statement of the amount of payments to another person required by—

"(i) section 6041 (a) or (b) (relating to certain information at source),

"(ii) section 6042(a)(1) (relating to payments of dividends),

"(iii) section 6044(a)(1) (relating to payments of patronage dividends),

"(iv) section 6049(a) (relating to payments of interest),

"(v) section 6050A(a) (relating to reporting requirements of certain fishing boat operators),

"(vi) section 6050N(a) (relating to payments of royalties), or

"(vii) section 6051(d) (relating to information returns with respect to income tax withheld), and

"(B) any return required by—

"(i) section 6041A (a) or (b) (relating to returns of direct sellers),

"(ii) section 6045 (a) or (d) (relating to returns of brokers),

"(iii) section 6050H(a) (relating to mortgage interest received in trade or business from individuals),

"(iv) section 6050I(a) (relating to cash received in trade or business),

"(v) section 6050J(a) (relating to foreclosures and abandonments of security),

"(vi) section 6050K(a) (relating to exchanges of certain partnership interests),

"(vii) section 6050L(a) (relating to returns relating to certain dispositions of donated property),

"(viii) section 6052(a) (relating to reporting payment of wages in the form of group-term life insurance),

"(ix) section 6053(c)(1) (relating to reporting with respect to certain tips),

"(x) section 1060(b) (relating to reporting requirements of transferors and transferees in certain asset acquisitions), or

"(xi) subparagraph (A) or (C) of subsection (c)(4), or subsection (e), of section 4093 (relating to information reporting with respect to tax on diesel and aviation fuel).

"(2) Payee statement. The term 'payee statement' means any statement required to be furnished under—

"(A) section 6031(b) or (c), 6034A, or 6037(c) (relating to statements furnished by certain pass-thru entities),

"(B) section 6039(c) (relating to information required in connection with certain options),

"(C) section 6041(d) (relating to information at source),

"(D) section 6041A(e) (relating to returns regarding payments of remuneration for services and direct sales),

"(E) section 6042(c) (relating to returns regarding payments of dividends and corporate earnings and profits),

"(F) section 6044(e) (relating to returns regarding payments of patronage dividends),

"(G) section 6045(b) or (d) (relating to returns of brokers),

"(H) section 6049(c) (relating to returns regarding payments of interest),

"(I) section 6050A(b) (relating to reporting requirements of certain fishing boat operators),

"(J) section 6050H(d) (relating to returns relating to mortgage interest received in trade or business from individuals),

"(K) section 6050I(e) (relating to returns relating to cash received in trade or business),

"(L) section 6050J(e) (relating to returns relating to foreclosures and abandonments of security),

"(M) section 6050K(b) (relating to returns relating to exchanges of certain partnership interests),

"(N) section 6050L(c) (relating to returns relating to certain dispositions of donated property),

"(O) section 6050N(b) (relating to returns regarding payments of royalties),

"(P) section 6051 (relating to receipts for employees),

"(Q) section 6052(b) (relating to returns regarding payment of wages in the form of group-term life insurance),

"(R) section 6053 (b) or (c) (relating to reports of tips), or

"(S) section 4093(c)(4)(B) (relating to certain purchasers of diesel and aviation fuels).

In **1989**, P.L. 101-239, Sec. 7811(c)(3), amended clauses (viii)-(xi) in subpara. (d)(1)(B), for any acquisition of assets after 5/6/86, unless such acquisition is pursuant to a binding contract which was in effect on 5/6/86, and at all times thereafter.

Prior to amendment clauses (d)(1)(B)(viii)-(xi) read as follows:

"(viii) section 6052(a) (relating to reporting payment of wages in the form of group-term life insurance),

"(ix) section 6053(c)(1) (relating to reporting with respect to certain tips).

"(xi) [sic (x)] section 1060(b) (relating to reporting requirements of transferors and transferees in certain asset acquisitions), or

"(xi) subparagraph (A) or (C) of subsection (c)(4), or subsection (d), of section 4093 (relating to information reporting with respect to tax on diesel and aviation fuels)."

—P.L. 101-239, Sec. 7813(a), redesignated subpara. (d)(12)(U) as (d)(2)(S), deleted "or" at the end of subpara. (d)(2)(Q) and substituted ", or" for the period at the end of subpara. (d)(2)(R), effective 1/1/89.

In **1988**, P.L. 100-647, Sec. 1006(h)(3)(A), deleted "or" from clause (d)(1)(B) (ix [sic viii]); substituted ", or" for the period at end of clause (d)(1)(B)(x [sic ix]), and added new clause (d)(1)(B)(xi [sic x]), effective for any acquisition of assets after 5/6/86, unless such acquisition is pursuant to a binding contract which was in effect on 5/6/86, and at all times thereafter

—P.L. 100-647, Sec. 1015(a), substituted "6031(b) or (c)" for "6031(b)" in subpara. (d)(2)(B [sic A]), effective for returns the due date of which (determined without regard to extensions) is after 12/31/86.

—P.L. 100-647, Sec. 3001(b)(1), added new clause (d)(1)(B)(xi) ... Sec. 3001(b)(2), deleted ", or" at end of subpara. (d)(2)(S [sic Q]); substituted "or" for the period at end of subpara. (d)(2)(T [sic R]), [corrected by Sec. 7813(a) of P.L. 101-239, see above], and added new subpara. (U [sic S]), effective 1/1/89. Sec. 3001(c)(2) of this Act Provides:

"(2) Refunds with interest for pre-effective date purchases.—

"(A) In general.—In the case of fuel—

"(i) which is purchased from a producer or importer during the period beginning on April 1, 1988, and ending on December 31, 1988,

"(ii) which is used (before the claim under this subparagraph is filed) by any person in a nontaxable use (as defined in section 6427(l)(2) of the 1986 Code), and

"(iii) with respect to which a claim is not permitted to be filed for any quarter under section 6427(i) of the 1986 Code,

the Secretary of the Treasury or the Secretary's delegate shall pay (with interest) to such person the amount of tax imposed on such fuel under section 4091 of the 1986 Code (to the extent not attributable to amounts described in section 6427(l)(3) of the 1986 Code) if claim therefor is filed not later than June 30, 1989. Not more than 1 claim may be filed under the preceding sentence and such claim shall not be taken into account under section 6427(i) of the 1986 Code. Any claim for refund filed under this paragraph shall be considered a claim for refund under section 6427(l) of the 1986 Code.

"(B) Interest.—The amount of interest payable under subparagraph (A) shall be determined under section 6611 of the 1986 Code except that the date of the overpayment with respect to fuel purchased during any month shall be treated as being the 1st day of the succeeding month. No interest shall be paid under this paragraph with respect to fuel used by any agency of the United States.

"(C) Registration procedures required to be specified.—Not later than the 30th day after the date of the enactment of this Act, the Secretary of the Treasury or the Secretary's delegate shall prescribe the procedures for complying with the requirements of section 4093(c)(3) of the 1986 Code (as added by this section)."

In **1988**, P.L. 100-418, Sec. 1941(b)(2)(M)(i), deleted clause (d)(1)(B)(i) and redesignated clauses (d)(1)(B)(ii)-(x) as clauses (d)(1)(B)(i)-(ix) ... Sec. 1941(b)(2)(M)(ii), deleted subparas. (d)(2)(A) and (d)(2)(K) and redesignated subparas. (d)(2)(B)-(T) as subparas. (d)(2)(A)-(R), effective for crude oil removed from the premises on or after 8/23/88.

Prior to deletion clause (d)(1)(B)(i) read as follows:

"(i) section 4997(a) (relating to information with respect to windfall profit tax on crude oil),"

Prior to deletion subpara. (d)(2)(A) read as follows:

"(A) section 4997(a) (relating to records and information; regulations),"

Prior to deletion subpara. (d)(2)(K) read as follows:

"(K) section 6050C (relating to information regarding windfall profit tax on domestic crude oil),"

In **1986**, P.L. 99-514, Sec. 1501, added Code Sec. 6724, part of Part II of Subchapter B of Chapter 68, effective for returns the due date of which (determined without regard to extensions) is after 12/31/86.

Sec. 6721. Failure to file correct information returns.
(a) Imposition of penalty.

(1) In general. In the case of a failure described in paragraph (2) by any person with respect to an information return, such person shall pay a penalty of $100 for each return with respect to which such a failure occurs, but the total amount imposed on such person for all such failures during any calendar year shall not exceed $1,500,000.

(2) **Failures subject to penalty.** For purposes of paragraph (1), the failures described in this paragraph are—
   (A) any failure to file an information return with the Secretary on or before the required filing date, and
   (B) any failure to include all of the information required to be shown on the return or the inclusion of incorrect information.

(b) **Reduction where correction in specified period.**
   (1) **Correction within 30 days.** If any failure described in subsection (a)(2) is corrected on or before the day 30 days after the required filing date—
      (A) the penalty imposed by subsection (a) shall be $30 in lieu of $100, and
      (B) the total amount imposed on the person for all such failures during any calendar year which are so corrected shall not exceed $250,000.
   (2) **Failures corrected on or before August 1.** If any failure described in subsection (a)(2) is corrected after the 30th day referred to in paragraph (1) but on or before August 1 of the calendar year in which the required filing date occurs—
      (A) the penalty imposed by subsection (a) shall be $60 in lieu of $100, and
      (B) the total amount imposed on the person for all such failures during the calendar year which are so corrected shall not exceed $500,000.

(c) **Exception for de minimis failures to include all required information.**
   (1) **In general.** If—
      (A) an information return is filed with the Secretary,
      (B) there is a failure described in subsection (a)(2)(B) (determined after the application of section 6724(a)) with respect to such return, and
      (C) such failure is corrected on or before August 1 of the calendar year in which the required filing date occurs,
   for purposes of this section, such return shall be treated as having been filed with all of the correct required information.
   (2) **Limitation.** The number of information returns to which paragraph (1) applies for any calendar year shall not exceed the greater of—
      (A) 10, or
      (B) one-half of 1 percent of the total number of information returns required to be filed by the person during the calendar year.

(d) **Lower limitations for persons with gross receipts of not more than $5,000,000.**
   (1) **In general.** If any person meets the gross receipts test of paragraph (2) with respect to any calendar year, with respect to failures during such calendar year—
      (A) subsection (a)(1) shall be applied by substituting "$500,000" for "$1,500,000",
      (B) subsection (b)(1)(B) shall be applied by substituting "$75,000" for "$250,000", and
      (C) subsection (b)(2)(B) shall be applied by substituting "$200,000" for "$500,000".
   (2) **Gross receipts test.**
      (A) In general. A person meets the gross receipts test of this paragraph for any calendar year if the average annual gross receipts of such person for the most recent 3 taxable years ending before such calendar year do not exceed $5,000,000.

      (B) Certain rules made applicable. For purposes of subparagraph (A), the rules of paragraphs (2) and (3) of section 448(c) shall apply.

(e) **Penalty in case of intentional disregard.**
   If 1 or more failures described in subsection (a)(2) are due to intentional disregard of the filing requirement (or the correct information reporting requirement), then, with respect to each such failure—
   (1) subsections (b), (c), and (d) shall not apply,
   (2) the penalty imposed under subsection (a) shall be $250, or, if greater—
      (A) in the case of a return other than a return required under section 6045(a), 6041A(b), 6050H, 6050I, 6050J, 6050K, or 6050L, 10 percent of the aggregate amount of the items required to be reported correctly,
      (B) in the case of a return required to be filed by section 6045(a), 6050K, or 6050L, 5 percent of the aggregate amount of the items required to be reported correctly,
      (C) in the case of a return required to be filed under section 6050I(a) with respect to any transaction (or related transactions), the greater of—
         (i) $25,000, or
         (ii) the amount of cash (within the meaning of section 6050I(d)) received in such transaction (or related transactions) to the extent the amount of such cash does not exceed $100,000, or
      (D) in the case of a return required to be filed under section 6050V, 10 percent of the value of the benefit of any contract with respect to which information is required to be included on the return, and
   (3) in the case of any penalty determined under paragraph (2)—
      (A) the $1,500,000 limitation under subsection (a) shall not apply, and
      (B) such penalty shall not be taken into account in applying such limitation (or any similar limitation under subsection (b)) to penalties not determined under paragraph (2).

(f) **Adjustment for inflation.**
   (1) **In general.** For each fifth calendar year beginning after 2012, each of the dollar amounts under subsections (a), (b), (d) (other than paragraph (2)(A) thereof), and (e) shall be increased by such dollar amount multiplied by the cost-of-living adjustment determined under section 1(f)(3) determined by substituting "calendar year 2011" for "calendar year 1992" in subparagraph (B) thereof.
   (2) **Rounding.** If any amount adjusted under paragraph (1)—
      (A) is not less than $75,000 and is not a multiple of $500, such amount shall be rounded to the next lowest multiple of $500, and
      (B) is not described in subparagraph (A) and is not a multiple of $10, such amount shall be rounded to the next lowest multiple of $10.

In 2010, P.L. 111-240, Sec. 2102(a)(1), substituted "$100" for "$50" in para. (a)(1) and subparas. (b)(1)(A) and (b)(2)(A); ... Sec. 2102(a)(2), substituted "$1,500,000" for "$250,000" in para. (a)(1) and subparas. (d)(1)(A), and (e)(3)(A); ... Sec. 2102(b)(1), substituted "$30" for "$15" in subpara. (b)(1)(A); ... Sec. 2102(b)(2), substituted "$250,000" for "$75,000" in subparas. (b)(1)(B) and (d)(1)(B); ... Sec. 2102(c)(1), substituted "$60" for "$30" in subpara. (b)(2)(A); ... Sec. 2102(c)(2), substituted "$500,000" for "$150,000" in subparas. (b)(2)(B) and (d)(1)(C); ... Sec. 2102(d)(1)(A), substituted "$500,000" for "$100,000" in subpara. (d)(1)(A); ... Sec. 2102(d)(1)(B), substituted "$75,000" for "$25,000" in subpara. (d)(1)(B); ... Sec. 2102(d)(1)(C), substituted "$200,000" for "$50,000" in subpara. (d)(1)(C); ... Sec. 2102(d)(2), substituted "such calendar year" for "such taxable year" in para. (d)(1); ... Sec. 2102(e), substituted "$250" for "$100" in para. (e)(2); ... Sec. 2102(f), added subsec. (f),

Code Sec. 6721 — Penalties

effective with respect to information returns required to be filed on or after 1/1/2011.

In 2006, P.L. 109-280, Sec. 1211(b)(2), deleted "or" at the end of subpara. (e)(2)(B), substituted "or" for "and" at the end of subpara. (e)(2)(C) and added subpara. (e)(2)(D), effective for acquisitions of contracts after 8/17/2006.

In 1990, P.L. 101-508, Sec. 11318(b)(1), added "6050I" after "6050H" in subpara. (e)(2)(A)... Sec. 11318(b)(2), deleted "or" at the end of subpara. (e)(2)(A)... Sec. 11318(b)(3), substituted "or" for "and" at the end of subpara. (e)(2)(B)... Sec. 11318(b)(4), added subpara. (e)(2)(C), effective for amounts received after 11/5/90.

In 1989, P.L. 101-239, Sec. 7711(a), amended Code Sec. 6721 as part of the amendments to part II of subchapter B of chapter 68, effective for returns and statements the due date for which (determined without regard to extensions) is after 12/31/89. For text of Code Sec. 6721 prior to amendment, see notes to part II of subchapter B of chapter 68.

Sec. 6722. Failure to furnish correct payee statements.

(a) Imposition of penalty.

(1) **General rule.** In the case of each failure described in paragraph (2) by any person with respect to a payee statement, such person shall pay a penalty of $100 for each statement with respect to which such a failure occurs, but the total amount imposed on such person for all such failures during any calendar year shall not exceed $1,500,000.

(2) **Failures subject to penalty.** For purposes of paragraph (1), the failures described in this paragraph are—

  (A) any failure to furnish a payee statement on or before the date prescribed therefor to the person to whom such statement is required to be furnished, and

  (B) any failure to include all of the information required to be shown on a payee statement or the inclusion of incorrect information.

(b) Reduction where correction in specified period.

(1) **Correction within 30 days.** If any failure described in subsection (a)(2) is corrected on or before the day 30 days after the required filing date—

  (A) the penalty imposed by subsection (a) shall be $30 in lieu of $100, and

  (B) the total amount imposed on the person for all such failures during any calendar year which are so corrected shall not exceed $250,000.

(2) **Failures corrected on or before August 1.** If any failure described in subsection (a)(2) is corrected after the 30th day referred to in paragraph (1) but on or before August 1 of the calendar year in which the required filing date occurs—

  (A) the penalty imposed by subsection (a) shall be $60 in lieu of $100, and

  (B) the total amount imposed on the person for all such failures during the calendar year which are so corrected shall not exceed $500,000.

(c) Exception for de minimis failures.

(1) **In general.** If—

  (A) a payee statement is furnished to the person to whom such statement is required to be furnished,

  (B) there is a failure described in subsection (a)(2)(B) (determined after the application of section 6724(a)) with respect to such statement, and

  (C) such failure is corrected on or before August 1 of the calendar year in which the required filing date occurs, for purposes of this section, such statement shall be treated as having been furnished with all of the correct required information.

(2) **Limitation.** The number of payee statements to which paragraph (1) applies for any calendar year shall not exceed the greater of—

  (A) 10, or

  (B) one-half of 1 percent of the total number of payee statements required to be filed by the person during the calendar year.

(d) Lower limitations for persons with gross receipts of not more than $5,000,000.

(1) **In general.** If any person meets the gross receipts test of paragraph (2) with respect to any calendar year, with respect to failures during such calendar year—

  (A) subsection (a)(1) shall be applied by substituting "$500,000" for "$1,500,000",

  (B) subsection (b)(1)(B) shall be applied by substituting "$75,000" for "$250,000", and

  (C) subsection (b)(2)(B) shall be applied by substituting "$200,000" for "$500,000".

(2) **Gross receipts test.** A person meets the gross receipts test of this paragraph if such person meets the gross receipts test of section 6721(d)(2).

(e) Penalty in case of intentional disregard.

If 1 or more failures to which subsection (a) applies are due to intentional disregard of the requirement to furnish a payee statement (or the correct information reporting requirement), then, with respect to each such failure—

(1) subsections (b), (c), and (d) shall not apply,

(2) the penalty imposed under subsection (a)(1) shall be $250, or, if greater—

  (A) in the case of a payee statement other than a statement required under section 6045(b), 6041A(e) (in respect of a return required under section 6041A(b)), 6050H(d), 6050J(e), 6050K(b), or 6050L(c), 10 percent of the aggregate amount of the items required to be reported correctly, or

  (B) in the case of a payee statement required under section 6045(b), 6050K(b), or 6050L(c), 5 percent of the aggregate amount of the items required to be reported correctly, and

(3) in the case of any penalty determined under paragraph (2)—

  (A) the $1,500,000 limitation under subsection (a) shall not apply, and

  (B) such penalty shall not be taken into account in applying such limitation to penalties not determined under paragraph (2).

(f) Adjustment for inflation.

(1) **In general.** For each fifth calendar year beginning after 2012, each of the dollar amounts under subsections (a), (b), (d)(1), and (e) shall be increased by such dollar amount multiplied by the cost-of-living adjustment determined under section 1(f)(3) determined by substituting "calendar year 2011" for "calendar year 1992" in subparagraph (B) thereof.

(2) **Rounding.** If any amount adjusted under paragraph (1)—

  (A) is not less than $75,000 and is not a multiple of $500, such amount shall be rounded to the next lowest multiple of $500, and

  (B) is not described in subparagraph (A) and is not a multiple of $10, such amount shall be rounded to the next lowest multiple of $10.

In 2010, P.L. 111-240, Sec. 2102(g), amended Code Sec. 6722, effective with respect to information returns required to be filed on or after 1/1/2011. Prior to amendment, Code Sec. 6722 read as follows:

"Sec. 6722. Failure to furnish correct payee statements.

"(a) General rule. In the case of each failure described in subsection (b) by any person with respect to a payee statement, such person shall pay a penalty of $50 for each statement with respect to which such a failure occurs, but the total amount imposed on such person for all such failures during any calendar year shall not exceed $100,000.

"(b) Failures subject to penalty. For purposes of subsection (a), the failures described in this subsection are—

"(1) any failure to furnish a payee statement on or before the date prescribed therefor to the person to whom such statement is required to be furnished, and

Penalties   Code Sec. 6724(d)(1)(B)(xxi)

"(2) any failure to include all of the information required to be shown on a payee statement or the inclusion of incorrect information.

"(c) Penalty in case of intentional disregard. If 1 or more failures to which subsection (a) applies are due to intentional disregard of the requirement to furnish a payee statement (or the correct information reporting requirement), then, with respect to each failure—

"(1) the penalty imposed under subsection (a) shall be $100, or, if greater—

"(A) in the case of a payee statement other than a statement required under section 6045(b), 6041A(e) (in respect of a return required under section 6041A(b)), 6050H(d), 6050J(e), 6050K(b), or 6050L(c), 10 percent of the aggregate amount of the items required to be reported correctly, or

"(B) in the case of a payee statement required under section 6045(b), 6050K(b), or 6050L(c), 5 percent of the aggregate amount of the items required to be reported correctly, and

"(2) in the case of any penalty determined under paragraph (1)—

"(A) the $100,000 limitation under subsection (a) shall not apply, and

"(B) such penalty shall not be taken into account in applying such limitation to penalties not determined under paragraph (1).".

In 1989, P.L. 101-239, Sec. 7711(a), amended Code Sec. 6722 as part of the amendments to part II of subchapter B of chapter 68, effective for returns and statements the due date for which (determined without regard to extensions) is after 12/31/89. For text of Code Sec. 6722 prior to amendment, see notes to part II of subchapter B of chapter 68.

Sec. 6723. Failure to comply with other information reporting requirements.

In the case of a failure by any person to comply with a specified information reporting requirement on or before the time prescribed therefor, such person shall pay a penalty of $50 for each such failure, but the total amount imposed on such person for all such failures during any calendar year shall not exceed $100,000.

In 1989, P.L. 101-239, Sec. 7711(a), amended Code Sec. 6723 as part of the amendments to part II of subchapter B of chapter 68, effective for returns and statements the due date for which (determined without regard to extensions) is after 12/31/89. For text of Code Sec. 6723 prior to amendment, see notes to part II of subchapter B of chapter 68.

Sec. 6724. Waiver; definitions and special rules.

(a) Reasonable cause waiver.

No penalty shall be imposed under this part with respect to any failure if it is shown that such failure is due to reasonable cause and not to willful neglect.

(b) Payment of penalty.

Any penalty imposed by this part shall be paid on notice and demand by the Secretary and in the same manner as tax.

(c) Special rule for failure to meet magnetic media requirements.

No penalty shall be imposed under section 6721 solely by reason of any failure to comply with the requirements of the regulations prescribed under section 6011(e)(2), except to the extent that such a failure occurs with respect to more than 250 information returns (more than 100 information returns in the case of a partnership having more than 100 partners) or with respect to a return described in section 6011(e)(4).

(d) Definitions.

For purposes of this part—

(1) Information return. The term "information return" means—

(A) any statement of the amount of payments to another person required by—

(i) section 6041(a) or (b) (relating to certain information at source),

(ii) section 6042(a)(1) (relating to payments of dividends),

(iii) section 6044(a)(1) (relating to payments of patronage dividends),

(iv) section 6049(a) (relating to payments of interest),

(v) section 6050A(a) (relating to reporting requirements of certain fishing boat operators),

(vi) section 6050N(a) (relating to payments of royalties),

(vii) section 6051(d) (relating to information returns with respect to income tax withheld),

(viii) section 6050R (relating to returns relating to certain purchases of fish), and [Ed. note: P.L. 105-34 does not replace "and" with "or"] or

(ix) section 110(d) (relating to qualified lessee construction allowances for short-term leases),

(B) any return required by-

(i) section 6041A(a) or (b) (relating to returns of direct sellers),

(ii) section 6043A(a) (relating to returns relating to taxable mergers and acquisitions),

(iii) section 6045(a) or (d) (relating to returns of brokers),

(iv) section 6045B(a) (relating to returns relating to actions affecting basis of specified securities),

(v) section 6050H(a) (relating to mortgage interest received in trade or business from individuals),

(vi) section 6050I(a) or (g)(1) (relating to cash received in trade or business, etc.),

(vii) section 6050J(a) (relating to foreclosures and abandonments of security),

(viii) section 6050K(a) (relating to exchanges of certain partnership interests),

(ix) section 6050L(a) (relating to returns relating to certain dispositions of donated property),

(x) section 6050P (relating to returns relating to the cancellation of indebtedness by certain financial entities),

(xi) section 6050Q (relating to certain long-term care benefits),

(xii) section 6050S (relating to returns relating to payments for qualified tuition and related expenses),

(xiii) section 6050T (relating to returns relating to credit for health insurance costs of eligible individuals),

(xiv) section 6052(a) (relating to reporting payment of wages in the form of group [term] life insurance),

(xv) section 6050V (relating to returns relating to applicable insurance contracts in which certain exempt organizations hold interests),

(xvi) section 6053(c)(1) (relating to reporting with respect to certain tips),

(xvii) subsection (b) or (e) of section 1060 (relating to reporting requirements of transferors and transferees in certain asset acquisitions),

(xviii) section 4101(d) (relating to information reporting with respect to fuels taxes),

(xix) subparagraph (C) of section 338(h)(10) (relating to information required to be furnished to the Secretary in case of elective recognition of gain or loss),

(xx) section 264(f)(5)(A)(iv) (relating to reporting with respect to certain life insurance and annuity contracts),

(xxi) section 6050U (relating to charges or payments for qualified long-term care insurance contracts under combined arrangements),

> • **Caution:** Code Sec. 6724(d)(1)(B)(xxii)-(xxiii), following, is generally effective after 12/31/2010, and before 1/1/2014. For Code Sec. 6724(d)(1)(B)(xxii)-(xxiii), effective after 12/31/2013, see below.

3,829

(xxii) section 6039(a) (relating to returns required with respect to certain options), or
(xxiii) section 6050W (relating to returns to payments made in settlement of payment card transactions), and

> • **Caution:** Code Sec. 6724(d)(1)(B)(xxii)-(xxv), following, is generally effective after 12/31/2013. For Code Sec. 6724(d)(1)(B)(xxii)-(xxiii), effective after 12/31/2010, and before 1/1/2014, see above.

(xxii) section 6039(a) (relating to returns required with respect to certain options),
(xxiii) section 6050W (relating to returns to payments made in settlement of payment card transactions),
(xxiv) section 6055 (relating to returns relating to information regarding health insurance coverage),
(xxv) section 6056 (relating to returns relating to certain employers required to report on health insurance coverage), and
(C) any statement of the amount of payments to another person required to be made to the Secretary under—
(i) section 408(i)(relating to reports with respect to individual retirement accounts or annuities), or
(ii) section 6047(d) (relating to reports by employers, plan administrators, etc.).

> • **Caution:** The closing para. for Code Sec. 6724(d)(1), following, is effective for payments made before 1/1/2013. For the closing para. for Code Sec. 6724(d)(1), effective for payments made after 12/31/2012, see below.

Such term also includes any form, statement, or schedule required to be filed with the Secretary with respect to any amount from which tax was required to be deducted and withheld under chapter 3 (or from which tax would be required to be so deducted and withheld but for an exemption under this title or any treaty obligation of the United States).

> • **Caution:** The closing para. for Code Sec. 6724(d)(1), following, is effective for payments made after 12/31/2012. For the closing para. for Code Sec. 6724(d)(1), effective for payments made before 1/1/2013, see above.

Such term also includes any form, statement, or schedule required to be filed with the Secretary under chapter 4 or with respect to any amount from which tax was required to be deducted and withheld under chapter 3 (or from which tax would be required to be so deducted and withheld but for an exemption under this title or any treaty obligation of the United States).

(2) Payee statement. The term "payee statement" means any statement required to be furnished under—
(A) section 6031(b) or (c), 6034A, or 6037(b) (relating to statements furnished by certain pass-thru entities),
(B) section 6039(b) (relating to information required in connection with certain options),
(C) section 6041(d) (relating to information at source),
(D) section 6041A(e) (relating to returns regarding payments of remuneration for services and direct sales),
(E) section 6042(c) (relating to returns regarding payments of dividends and corporate earnings and profits),
(F) subsections (b) and (d) of section 6043A (relating to returns relating to taxable mergers and acquisitions).[,]
(G) section 6044(e) (relating to returns regarding payments of patronage dividends),
(H) section 6045(b) or (d) (relating to returns of brokers),
(I) section 6045A (relating to information required in connection with transfers of covered securities to brokers),
(J) subsections (c) and (e) of section 6045B (relating to returns relating to actions affecting basis of specified securities),
(K) section 6049(c) (relating to returns regarding payments of interest),
(L) section 6050A(b) (relating to reporting requirements of certain fishing boat operators),
(M) section 6050H(d) or (h)(2) (relating to returns relating to mortgage interest received in trade or business from individuals),
(N) section 6050I(e) or paragraph (4) or (5) of section 6050I(g) (relating to cash received in trade or business, etc.),
(O) section 6050J(e) (relating to returns relating to foreclosures and abandonments of security),
(P) section 6050K(b) (relating to returns relating to exchanges of certain partnership interests),
(Q) section 6050L(c) (relating to returns relating to certain dispositions of donated property),
(R) section 6050N(b) (relating to returns regarding payments of royalties),
(S) section 6050P(d) (relating to returns relating to the cancellation of indebtedness by certain financial entities),
(T) section 6050Q(b) (relating to certain long-term care benefits),
(U) section 6050R(c) (relating to returns relating to certain purchases of fish),
(V) section 6051 (relating to receipts for employees),
(W) section 6052(b) (relating to returns regarding payment of wages in the form of group-term life insurance),
(X) section 6053(b) or (c) (relating to reports of tips),
(Y) section 6048(b)(1)(B) (relating to foreign trust reporting requirements),
(Z) section 408(i) (relating to reports with respect to individual retirement plans) to any person other than the Secretary with respect to the amount of payments made to such person,
(AA) section 6047(d) (relating to reports by plan administrators) to any person other than the Secretary with respect to the amount of payments made to such person,
(BB) section 6050S (relating to returns relating to qualified tuition and related expenses),
(CC) section 264(f)(5)(A)(iv) relating to reporting with respect to certain life insurance and annuity contracts),
(DD) section 6050T (relating to returns relating to credit for health insurance costs of eligible individuals),

(EE) section 6050U (relating to charges or payments for qualified long-term care insurance contracts under combined arrangements), or
(FF) section 6050W(c) (relating to returns relating to payments made in settlement of payment card transactions).

• *Caution:* Code Sec. 6724(d)(2)(EE)-(HH), following, are generally effective after 12/31/2013.

(EE) section 6050U (relating to charges or payments for qualified long-term care insurance contracts under combined arrangements),
(FF) section 6050W(c) (relating to returns relating to payments made in settlement of payment card transactions),
(GG) section 6055(c) (relating to statements relating to information regarding health insurance coverage), or
(HH) section 6056(c) (relating to statements relating to certain employers required to report on health insurance coverage).

• *Caution:* The closing para. for Code Sec. 6724(d)(2), following, is effective for payments made before 1/1/2013. For the closing para. for Code Sec. 6724(d)(2), effective for payments made after 12/31/2012, see below.

Such term also includes any form, statement, or schedule required to be furnished to the recipient of any amount from which tax was required to be deducted and withheld under chapter 3 (or from which tax would be required to be so deducted and withheld but for an exemption under this title or any treaty obligation of the United States).

• *Caution:* The closing para. for Code Sec. 6724(d)(2), following, is effective for payments made after 12/31/2012. For the closing para. for Code Sec. 6724(d)(2); effective for payments made before 1/1/2013, see above.

Such term also includes any form, statement, or schedule required to be furnished to the recipient of any amount from which tax was required to be deducted and withheld under chapter 3 or 4 (or from which tax would be required to be so deducted and withheld but for an exemption under this title or any treaty obligation of the United States).

(3) Specified information reporting requirement. The term "specified information reporting requirement" means—

(A) the notice required by section 6050K(c)(1) (relating to requirement that transferor notify partnership of exchange),
(B) any requirement contained in the regulations prescribed under section 6109 that a person—

(i) include his TIN on any return, statement, or other document (other than an information return or payee statement),
(ii) furnish his TIN to another person, or
(iii) include on any return, statement, or other document (other than an information return or payee statement) made with respect to another person the TIN of such person,
(C) any requirement contained in the regulations prescribed under section 215 that a person—
(i) furnish his TIN to another person, or
(ii) include on his return the TIN of another person, and
(D) any requirement under section 6109(h) that—
(i) a person include on his return the name, address, and TIN of another person, or
(ii) a person furnish his TIN to another person.

(4) Required filing date. The term "required filing date" means the date prescribed for filing an information return with the Secretary (determined with regard to any extension of time for filing).

(e) Special rule for certain partnership returns.

In any partnership return under section 6031(a) is required under section 6011(e) to be filed on magnetic media or in other machine-readable form, for purposes of this part, each schedule required to be included with such return with respect to each partner shall be treated as a separate information return.

In **2010,** P.L. 111-148, Sec. 1502(b)(1), deleted "or" at the end of clause (d)(1)(B)(xxii), substituted "or" for "and" at the end of clause (d)(1)(B)(xxiii) and added clause (d)(1)(B)(xxiv) . . . Sec. 1502(b)(2), deleted "or" at the end of subpara. (d)(2)(EE), substituted ", or" for the period at the end of subpara. (d)(2)(FF) and added subpara. (d)(2)(GG), effective for calendar yrs. begin. after 2013.
—P.L. 111-148, Sec. 1514(b)(1), deleted "or" at the end of clause (d)(1)(B)(xxiii) [as amended by Sec. 1502(b)(1) of this Act, see above], substituted "or" for "and" at the end of clause (d)(1)(B)(xxiv) [as added by Sec. 1502(b)(1) of this Act, see above] and added clause (d)(1)(B)(xxv) . . . Sec. 1514(b)(2), deleted "or" at the end of subpara. (d)(2)(FF) [as amended by Sec. 1502(b)(2) of this Act, see above] substituted ", or" for the period at the end of subpara. (d)(2)(GG) [as added by Sec. 1502(b)(2) of this Act, see above] and added subpara. (d)(2)(HH), effective for periods begin. after 12/31/2013.
—P.L. 111-148, Sec. 10108(j)(3)(E), substituted "certain" for "large" in clause (d)(1)(B)(xxv) [as added by Sec. 1514(b)(1) of this Act, see above] . . . Sec. 10108(j)(3)(F), substituted "certain" for "large" in subpara. (d)(2)(HH) [as added by Sec. 1514(b)(2) of this Act, see above], effective for periods begin. after 12/31/2013.
—P.L. 111-147, Sec. 501(c)(6), added "under chapter 4 or" after "filed with the Secretary" in the last sentence of para. (d)(1) . . . Sec. 501(c)(7), added "or 4" after "chapter 3" in para. (d)(2), effective for payments made after 12/31/2012. Sec. 501(d)(2) of this Act, provides:
"(2) Grandfathered treatment of outstanding obligations. The amendments made by this section shall not require any amount to be deducted or withheld from any payment under any obligation outstanding on the date which is 2 years after the date of the enactment of this Act or from the gross proceeds from any disposition of such an obligation."
—P.L. 111-147, Sec. 522(b), added "or with respect to a return described in section 6011(e)(4)" before the period at the end of subsec. (c), effective for returns the due date for which (determined without regard to extensions) is after 3/18/2010.

In **2008,** P.L. 110-343, Sec. 403(c)(2)DivB, added subpara. (d)(2)(I) and redesignated subparas. (d)(2)(I)-(d)(2)(DD) as subparas. (d)(2)(J)-(d)(2)(EE) . . . Sec. 403(d)(2)(A)DivB, added clause (d)(1)(B)(iv) and redesignated clauses (d)(1)(B)(iv)-(xxii) as clauses (d)(1)(B)(v)-(xxiii) . . . Sec. 403(d)(2)(B)DivB, added subpara. (d)(2)(J) and redesignated subparas. (d)(2)(J)-(d)(2)(EE) as subparas. (d)(2)(K)-(d)(2)(FF), effective 1/1/2011.
—P.L. 110-289, Sec. 3091(b)(1)(A), deleted "or" at the end of clause (d)(1)(B)(xx) . . . Sec. 3091(b)(1)(B), redesignated clause (d)(1)(B)(xix) that follows clause (d)(1)(B)(xx) as clause (d)(1)(B)(xxi) . . . Sec. 3091(b)(1)(C), substituted "or" for "and" at the end of clause (d)(1)(B)(xxi) [as redes. by (d)(1)(B) of this Act] . . . Sec. 3091(b)(1)(D), added clause (d)(1)(B)(xxii) . . . Sec. 3091(b)(2), deleted "or" at the end of subpara. (d)(2)(BB), substituted ", or" for the period at the end of subpara. (d)(2)(CC), and added subpara. (d)(2)(DD), effective for returns due after 12/31/2010.
—P.L. 110-289, Sec. 3091(e)(2)(B), of this Act, reads as follows:
"(B) Eligibility for TIN matching program. Solely for purposes of carrying out any TIN matching program established by the Secretary under section 3406(i) of the Internal Revenue Code of 1986—

"(i) the amendments made this section shall be treated as taking effect on the date of the enactment of this Act, and

"(ii) each person responsible for setting the standards and mechanisms referred to in section 6050W(d)(2)(C) of such Code, as added by this section, for settling transactions involving payment cards shall be treated in the same manner as a payment settlement entity."

In **2007**, P.L. 110-172, Sec. 11(b)(2)(A), added "or" after "section 6050H(a)" in clause (d)(1)(B)(iv).... Sec. 11(b)(2)(B), added "or (h)(2)" after "section 6050H(d)" in subpara. (d)(2)(K), effective for amounts paid or accrued after 12/31/2006.

In **2006**, P.L. 109-432, Sec. 403(c)(1), deleted "or" at the end of clause (d)(1)(B)(xvii) [(xix)], substituted "or" for "and" at the end of clause (d)(1)(B)(xviii) [(xx)], and added clause (d)(1)(B)(xix) [(xxi)]... Sec. 403(c)(2), substituted "section 6039(b)" for "section 6039(a)" in subpara. (d)(2)(B), effective for calendar yrs. begin. after 12/20/2006.

— P.L. 109-280, Sec. 844(d)(2)(A), deleted "or" at the end of cl. (d)(1)(B)(xvii), substituted "or" for "and" at the end of cl. (d)(1)(B)(xviii) and added cl. (d)(1)(B)(xix), effective for charges made after 12/31/2009.... Sec. 844(d)(2)(B), deleted "or" at the end of subpara. (d)(2)(AA), deleted the period at the end of subpara. (d)(2)(BB), and added subpara (d)(2)(CC), effective for charges made after 12/31/2009.

— P.L. 109-280, Sec. 1211(b)(1), redesignated clauses (d)(1)(B)(xiv)-(xix) [as amended by Sec. 844(d)(2)(A), of this Act, see above] as clauses (d)(1)(B)(xv)-(xx) and added clause (d)(1)(B)(xiv), effective for acquisitions of contracts after 8/17/2006.

In **2004**, P.L. 108-357, Sec. 805(b)(1), redesignated clauses (d)(1)(B)(ii)-(xviii) as clauses (d)(1)(B)(iii)-(xix), and added clause (d)(1)(B)(ii)... Sec. 805(b)(2), redesignated subparas. (d)(2)(F)-(BB) as subparas. (d)(2)(G)-(CC) respectively, and added subpara. (d)(2)(F), effective for acquisitions after 10/22/2004.

— P.L. 108-357, Sec. 853(d)(2)(L), deleted clause (d)(1)(B)(xvi) and redesignated clauses (d)(1)(B)(xvii)-(xix) as clauses (d)(1)(B)(xvi)-(xviii)... Sec. 853(d)(2)(M), deleted subpara. (d)(2)(X) and redesignated subparas. (d)(2)(Y)-(CC) as subparas. (d)(2)(X)-(BB), effective for aviation-grade kerosene removed, entered, or sold after 12/31/2004.

— P.L. 108-357, Sec. 853(f), of this Act, provides:

"(f) *Floor stocks tax.*

"(1) In general. There is hereby imposed on aviation-grade kerosene held on January 1, 2005, by any person a tax equal to—

"(A) the tax which would have been imposed before such date on such kerosene had the amendments made by this section been in effect at all times before such date, reduced by

"(B) the sum of—

"(i) the tax imposed before such date on such kerosene under section 4091 of the Internal Revenue Code of 1986, as in effect on such date, and

"(ii) in the case of kerosene held exclusively for such person's own use, the amount which such person would (but for this clause) reasonably expect (as of such date) to be paid as a refund under section 6427(l) of such Code with respect to such kerosene.

"(2) Exception for fuel held in aircraft fuel tank. Paragraph (1) shall not apply to kerosene held in the fuel tank of an aircraft on January 1, 2005.

"(3) Liability for tax and method of payment.

"(A) Liability for tax. The person holding the kerosene on January 1, 2005, to which the tax imposed by paragraph (1) applies shall be liable for such tax.

"(B) Method and time for payment. The tax imposed by paragraph (1) shall be paid at such time and in such manner as the Secretary of the Treasury (or the Secretary's delegate) shall prescribe, including the nonapplication of such tax on de minimis amounts of kerosene.

"(4) Transfer of floor stock tax revenues to trust funds. For purposes of determining the amount transferred to any trust fund, the tax imposed by this subsection shall be treated as imposed by section 4081 of the Internal Revenue Code of 1986—

"(A) in any case in which tax was not imposed by section 4091 of such Code, at the Leaking Underground Storage Tank Trust Fund financing rate under such section to the extent of 0.1 cents per gallon, and

"(B) at the rate under section 4081(a)(2)(A)(iv) of such Code to the extent of the remainder.

"(5) Held by a person. For purposes of this subsection, kerosene shall be considered as held by a person if title thereto has passed to such person (whether or not delivery to the person has been made).

"(6) Other laws applicable. All provisions of law, including penalties, applicable with respect to the tax imposed by section 4081 of such Code shall, insofar as applicable and not inconsistent with the provisions of this subsection, apply with respect to the floor stock tax imposed by paragraph (1) to the same extent as if such tax were imposed by such section."

In **2002**, P.L. 107-210, Sec. 202(c)(2)(A), redesignated clauses (d)(1)(B)(xi)-(xvii) as clauses (d)(1)(B)(xii)-(xviii) and added clause (d)(1)(B)(xi)... Sec. 202(c)(2)(B), deleted "or" at the end of subpara. (d)(2)(Z), substituted ", or" for the period at the end of subpara. (d)(2)(AA), and added subpara. (d)(2)(BB), effective 8/6/2002.

In **2000**, P.L. 106-554, Sec. 1(a)(7), [which enacted into law Sec. 319(23) of P.L. 106-554] amended clauses (d)(1)(B)(xiv)–(xvii), effective 12/21/2000.

Prior to amendment, clauses (d)(1)(B)(xiv)–(xvii) read as follows:

"(xiv) subparagraph (A) or (C) of subsection (c)(4) of section 4093 (relating to information reporting with respect to tax on diesel and aviation fuels),

"(xv) section 4101(d) (relating to information reporting with respect to fuels taxes),

"(xvi) subparagraph (C) of section 338(h)(10) (relating to information required to be furnished to the Secretary in case of elective recognition of gain or loss); or

"(xvii) section 264(f)(5)(A)(iv) (relating to reporting with respect to certain life insurance and annuity contracts)."

— P.L. 106-554, Sec. 1(a)(7), [which enacted into law Sec. 319(23)(B) of P.L. 106-554] substituted "inserting ', or', and by adding after subparagraph (Z)" for "inserting 'or', and by adding at the end" in Sec. 6010(o)(4)(C) of P.L. 105-206, see below.

In **1998**, P.L. 105-206, Sec. 6004(a)(3), amended Sec. 201(c)(2)(A) of P.L. 105-34 [see below] by redesignating clauses (d)(1)(B)(x)-(xv) as (d)(1)(B)(xi)-(xvi) and adding clause (d)(1)(B)(x), effective for expenses paid after 12/31/97 (in tax. yrs. end. after 12/31/97), for education furnished in academic periods begin. after 12/31/97.

— P.L. 105-206, Sec. 6010(o)(4)(B), deleted 'or' at the end of clause (d)(1)(B)(xv) [as redesignated by Sec. 6004(a)(3) of this Act, see above]; substituted '; or' for the period at the end of clause (d)(1)(B)(xvi) [as redesignated by Sec. 6004(a)(3) of this Act, see above], and added clause (d)(1)(B)(xvii)... Sec. 6010(o)(4)(C), deleted 'or' at the end of subpara. (d)(2)(Y), substituted ', or' for the period [sic ', and'] at the end of subpara. (d)(2)(Z), and added subpara. (d)(2)(AA), effective as provided in Sec. 1084(d) [sic (f)] of P.L. 105-34, which reads as follows:

"(d) Effective date. The amendments made by this section shall apply to contracts issued after June 8, 1997, in taxable years ending after such date. For purposes of the preceding sentence, any material increase in the death benefit or other material change in the contract shall be treated as a new contract but the addition of covered lives shall be treated as a new contract only with respect to such additional covered lives. For purposes of this subsection, an increase in the death benefit under a policy or contract issued in connection with a lapse described in section 501(d)(2) of the Health Insurance Portability and Accountability of 1996 shall not be treated as a new contract."

— P.L. 105-206, Sec. 6012(b)(5), substituted "section 6724(d)(1)" for "section 6724(d)(1)(A)" in Sec. 1213(b) of P.L. 105-34 [see below].

— P.L. 105-206, Sec. 6012(d), added "(more than 100 information returns in the case of a partnership having more than 100 partners)" before the period at the end of subsec. (c), effective for partnership tax. yrs. begin. after 12/31/97.

— P.L. 105-206, Sec. 6012(e), substituted "beginning" for "ending on or" in Sec. 1226 of P.L. 105-34 [see below].

In **1997**, P.L. 105-34, Sec. 201(c)(2)(A), redesignated clauses (d)(1)(B)(ix)-(xiv) as clauses (d)(1)(B)(x)-(xv) and added new clause (d)(1)(B)(ix)... Sec. 201(c)(2)(B), deleted "or" at the end of (d)(2)(X) [as amended by Sec. 1502(d)(2)(A), see below], substituted ", or" for the period at the end of (d)(2)(Y) [as amended by Sec. 1502(d)(2)(A), see below] and added subpara. (d)(2)(Z), effective for expenses paid after 12/31/97 (in tax. yrs. end. after 12/31/97), for education furnished in academic periods begin. after 12/31/97.

— P.L. 105-34, Sec. 1213(b), deleted "or" at the end of clause (d)(1)(A)(vii), added "or" at the end of clause (d)(1)(A)(viii) [ed. note: added "or" without removing "and"], and added clause (d)(1)(A)(ix), effective for leases entered into after 8/5/97.

— P.L. 105-34, Sec. 1223(b), added subsec. (e), effective [as amended by Sec. 6012(d) of 105-206, see above] for partnership tax. yrs. begin. after 12/31/97.

— P.L. 105-34, Sec. 1602(d)(2)(A), amended subparas. (d)(2)(R)-(X)[sic (Y)][see Sec. 323(b)(2) of P.L. 104-191, and P.L. 104-188, Secs. 1116(b)(2)(B), 1455(a)(2), and 1901(c)(1), below], effective for benefits paid after 12/31/96.

Prior to amendment, subparas. (c)(2)(R)-(X)[sic (Y)], [see Sec. 323(b)(2) of P.L. 104-191, and P.L. 104-188, Secs. 1116(b)(2)(B), 1455(a)(2), and 1901(c)(1), below], read as follows:

"(R) section 6051 (relating to receipts for employees),

"(S) section 6050R(c) (relating to returns relating to certain purchases of fish),

"(T) section 6052(b) (relating to returns regarding payment of wages in the form of group-term life insurance),

"(U) section 6053(b) or (c) (relating to reports of tips),

"(U)[sic V] section 4093(c)(4)(B) (relating to certain purchasers of diesel and aviation fuels),

"(V)[sic W] section 6048(b)(1)(B) (relating to foreign trust reporting requirements)

"(W)[sic X] section 408(i) (relating to reports with respect to individual retirement plans) to any person other than the Secretary with respect to the amount of payments made to such person,

"(X)[sic Y] section 6047(d) (relating to reports to plan administrators) to any person other than the Secretary with respect to the amount of payments made to such person,"

In **1996**, P.L. 104-191, Sec. 323(b)(1), redesignated clauses (d)(1)(B)(ix) through (xiv) as clauses (d)(1)(B)(x) through (xv) and added new clause (d)(1)(B)(ix)... Sec. 323(b)(2), redesignated subparas. (d)(2)(Q) through (T) [as redesignated by Secs. 1116(b)(2)(B) and 1455(a)(2) of P.L. 104-188, see below] as subparas. (d)(2)(R) through (U) and added new subpara. (d)(2)(Q), effective for benefits paid after 12/31/96.

— P.L. 104-188, Sec. 1116(b)(2)(A), deleted "or" at the end of clause (d)(1)(A)(vi), substituted "or" for "and" at the end of clause (d)(1)(A)(vii) and added clause (d)(1)(A)(viii)... Sec. 1116(b)(2)(B), redesignated subparas. (d)(2)(R) – (U) [as added by Sec. 1901(c)(1) of this Act, see below] as subparas. (d)(2)(S) – (V) and added new subpara. (d)(2)(R), effective for payments made after 12/31/97.

— P.L. 104-188, Sec. 1455(a)(1), deleted "and" at the end of subpara. (d)(1)(A), substituted a period for "and" at the end of subpara. (d)(1)(B), and added subpara. (d)(1)(C)... Sec. 1455(a)(2), deleted "or" at the end of subpara. (d)(2)(U) [as redesignated by Sec. 1116(b)(2)(B) of this Act, see above], deleted the period at the end of subpara. (d)(2)(V) [as redesignated by Sec. 1116(b)(2)(B) of this

Penalties Chapter 69

Act, see above], and added subparas. (d)(2)(W) and (X), effective for returns, reports, and other statements the due date for which (determined without regard to extensions) is after 12/31/96.

—P.L. 104-188, Sec. 1615(a)(2)(B), added "and" to the end of subpara. (d)(3)(C), deleted subpara. (d)(3)(D), and redesignated subpara. (d)(3)(E) as subpara. (d)(3)(D), effective for returns the due date for which (without regard to extensions) is on or after the 30th day after 8/20/96. For special rules, see Sec. 1615(d)(2), of this Act, which reads as follows:

"(2) Special rule for 1995 and 1996. In the case of returns for taxable years beginning in 1995 or 1996, a taxpayer shall not be required by the amendments made by this section to provide a taxpayer identification number for a child who is born after October 31, 1995, in the case of a taxable year beginning in 1995 or November 30, 1996, in the case of a taxable year beginning in 1996."

Prior to deletion, subpara. (d)(3)(D) read as follows:

"(D) the requirement of section 6109(e) that a person include the TIN of any dependent on his return, and"

—P.L. 104-188, Sec. 1702(b)(1), amended Sec. 11212(e)(1) of P.L. 101-508 by substituting "Subparagraph (B) of section 6724(d)(1)" for "Paragraph (1) of section 6724(d)", see below.

—P.L. 104-188, Sec. 1702(c)(2)(A), deleted "or" at the end of clause (d)(1)(B)(xii) ... Sec. 1702(c)(2)(B), substituted ", or" for the period at the end of clause (d)(1)(B)(xiii), effective for acquisitions after 10/9/90, except as provided in Sec. 11323(d)(2), of this Act, reproduced below.

—P.L. 104-188, Sec. 1704(j)(3), substituted "section 6109(h)" for "section 6109(f)" in subpara. (d)(3)(E) [redesignated subpara. (d)(3)(D) by Sec. 1615(a)(2)(B) of this Act, see above], effective 8/20/96.

—P.L. 104-188, Sec. 1901(c)(1), deleted "or" at the end of subpara. (d)(2)(S), substituted ", or" for the period at the end of subpara. (d)(2)(T), and added subpara. (d)(2)(U), effective as provided in Sec. 1901(d), of this Act, which reads as follows:

"(d) Effective dates.

"(1) Reportable events. To the extent related to subsection (a) of section 6048 of the Internal Revenue Code of 1986, as amended by this section, the amendments made by this section shall apply to reportable events (as defined in such section 6048) occurring after the date of the enactment of this Act.

"(2) Grantor trust reporting. To the extent related to subsection (b) of such section 6048, the amendments made by this section shall apply to taxable years of United States persons beginning after December 31, 1995.

"(3) Reporting by United States beneficiaries. To the extent related to subsection (c) of such section 6048, the amendments made by this section shall apply to distributions received after the date of the enactment of this Act."

In 1994, P.L. 103-322, Sec. 20415(b)(1), amended clause (d)(1)(B)(iv) ... Sec. 20415(b)(2), amended subpara. (d)(2)(K), effective on the 60th day after the date on which the temporary regulations are prescribed under subsection (c) [Sec. 20415(c) of this Act]. Sec. 20415(c) of this Act regarding regulations, reads as follows:

"(c) Regulations. The Secretary of the Treasury or the Secretary's delegate shall prescribe temporary regulations under the amendments made by this section [Sec. 20415 of this Act] within 90 days after the date of enactment of this Act [9/13/94]."

Prior to amendment, clause (d)(1)(B)(iv) read as follows:

"(iv) section 6050I(a) (relating to cash received in trade or business),"

Prior to amendment, subpara. (d)(2)(K) read as follows:

"(K) section 6050I(e) relating to returns relating to cash received in trade or business),"

In 1993, P.L. 103-66, Sec. 13252(b)(1), added clause (d)(1)(B)(viii) and redesignated clauses (d)(1)(B)(viii)–(xiv) [sic xiii)] as clauses (d)(1)(B)(ix)–(xiv) ... Sec. 13252(b)(2), redesignated subparas. (d)(2)(P)–(S) as subparas. (d)(2)(Q)–(T) and added new subpara. (d)(2)(P), effective for discharges of indebtedness after 12/31/93.

In 1992, P.L. 102-486, Sec. 1933(b), deleted "and" at the end of subpara. (d)(3)(C), substituted ", and" for the period at the end of subpara. (d)(3)(D), and added subpara. (d)(3)(E), effective for tax. yrs. begin. after 12/31/91.

In 1990, P.L. 101-508, Sec. 11212(e)(1), [as amended by Sec. 1702(b)(1) of P.L. 104-188, see above] deleted "or" at the end of clause (d)(1)(B)(x), deleted ", or subsection (e)," in clause (d)(1)(B)(xi), substituted ", or" for the period at the end of clause (d)(1)(B)(xii), and added clause (d)(1)(B)(xii), effective 12/1/90.

—P.L. 101-508, Sec. 11323(b)(2), substituted "subsection (b) or (e) of section 1060" for "section 1060(b)" in clause (d)(1)(B)(x) ... Sec. 11323(c)(2), deleted "or" at the end of clause (d)(1)(B)(x), added ", or" for the period at the end of clause (d)(1)(B)(xi) [see Sec. 11212(e)(1) above], and added clause (d)(1)(B)(xii)[sic xiii], effective for acquisitions after 10/9/90, except as provided in Sec. 11323(d)(2) of this Act, which reads as follows:

"(2) Binding contract exception. The amendments made by this section shall not apply to any acquisition pursuant to a written binding contract in effect on October 9, 1990, and at all times thereafter before such acquisition."

In 1989, P.L. 101-239, Sec. 7711(a), amended Code Sec. 6724 as part of the amendments to part II of subchapter B of chapter 68, effective for returns and statements the due date for which (determined without regard to extensions) is after 12/31/89. For text of Code Sec. 6724 prior to amendment, see notes to part II of subchapter B of chapter 68.

Sec. 6725. Failure to report information under section 4101.

(a) In general.

In the case of each failure described in subsection (b) by any person with respect to a vessel or facility, such person shall pay a penalty of $10,000 in addition to the tax (if any).

(b) Failures subject to penalty.

For purposes of subsection (a), the failures described in this subsection are—

(1) any failure to make a report under section 4101(d) on or before the date prescribed therefor, and

(2) any failure to include all of the information required to be shown on such report or the inclusion of incorrect information.

(c) Reasonable cause exception.

No penalty shall be imposed under this section with respect to any failure if it is shown that such failure is due to reasonable cause.

In 2004, P.L. 108-357, Sec. 863(d)(1), added Code Sec. 6725, effective for penalties imposed after 12/31/2004.

Subchapter C.—Procedural Requirements

Sec.
6751. Procedural requirements.

In 1998, P.L. 105-206, Sec. 3306(a), added item 6751.

Sec. 6751. Procedural requirements.

(a) Computation of penalty included in notice.

The Secretary shall include with each notice of penalty under this title information with respect to the name of the penalty, the section of this title under which the penalty is imposed, and a computation of the penalty.

(b) Approval of assessment.

(1) In general. No penalty under this title shall be assessed unless the initial determination of such assessment is personally approved (in writing) by the immediate supervisor of the individual making such determination or such higher level official as the Secretary may designate.

(2) Exceptions. Paragraph (1) shall not apply to—

(A) any addition to tax under section 6651, 6654, or 6655; or

(B) any other penalty automatically calculated through electronic means.

(c) Penalties.

For purposes of this section, the term "penalty" includes any addition to tax or any additional amount.

In 2000, P.L. 106-554, Sec. 1(a)(7), [which enacted into law Sec. 302(b) of P.L. 106-554] substituted "June 30, 2001" for "December 31, 2000" and added "In the case of any notice of penalty issued after June 30, 2001, and before July 1, 2003, the requirements of section 6751(a) of the Internal Revenue Code of 1986 shall be treated as met if such notice contains a telephone number at which the taxpayer can request a copy of the taxpayer's assessment and payment history with respect to such penalty." in Sec. 3306(c) of P.L. 105-206, see below.

In 1998, P.L. 105-206, Sec. 3306(a), added Code Sec. 6751, effective for notices issued, and penalties assessed, after June 30, 2001. In the case of any notice of penalty issued after June 30, 2001, and before July 1, 2003, the requirements of section 6751(a) of the Internal Revenue Code of 1986 shall be treated as met if such notice contains a telephone number at which the taxpayer can request a copy of the taxpayer's assessment and payment history with respect to such penalty.

CHAPTER 69.—GENERAL PROVISIONS RELATING TO STAMPS

Sec.
6801. Authority for establishment, alteration, and distribution.
6802. Supply and distribution.

6803. Accounting and safeguarding.
6804. Attachment and cancellation.
6805. Redemption of stamps.
6806. Occupational tax stamps.
6807. Stamping, marking, and branding seized goods.
6808. Special provisions relating to stamps.

Sec. 6801. Authority for establishment, alteration, and distribution.
(a) Establishment and alteration.
The Secretary may establish, and from time to time alter, renew, replace, or change the form, style, character, material, and device of any stamp, mark, or label under any provision of the laws relating to internal revenue.
(b) Preparation and distribution of regulations, forms, stamps and dies.
The Secretary shall prepare and distribute all the instructions, regulations, directions, forms, blanks, and stamps; and shall provide proper and sufficient adhesive stamps and other stamps or dies for expressing and denoting the several stamp taxes.

In **1984**, P.L. 98-369, Sec. 454(c)(13), substituted "several stamp taxes." for "several stamp taxes; except that stamps required by or prescribed pursuant to the provisions of section 5205 or section 5235 may be prepared and distributed by persons authorized by the Secretary, under such controls for the protection of the revenue as shall be deemed necessary." in subsec. (b), effective 7/1/85.
In **1976**, P.L. 94-569, Sec. 2, substituted all that follows "several stamp taxes" for the period at the end of subsec. (b), effective 10/20/76.
— P.L. 94-455, Sec. 1906(b)(13)(A), substituted "Secretary" for "Secretary or his delegate" each place it appeared in Code Sec. 6801, effective 2/1/77.

Sec. 6802. Supply and distribution.
The Secretary shall furnish, without prepayment, to—
(1) Postmaster General. The Postmaster General a suitable quantity of adhesive stamps, coupons, tickets, or such other devices as may be prescribed by the Secretary pursuant to section 6302(b) or this chapter, to be distributed to, and kept on sale by, the various postmasters in the United States in all post offices of the first and second classes, and such post offices of the third and fourth classes as—
(A) are located in county seats, or
(B) are certified by the Secretary to the Postmaster General as necessary.
(2) Designated depositary of the United States. Any designated depositary of the United States a suitable quantity of adhesive stamps to be kept on sale by such designated depositary.

In **1976**, P.L. 94-455, Sec. 1906(a)(36), substituted a period for the semicolon at the end of para. (2), effective 2/1/77. The Act apparently meant for the amendment to be made at the end of subpara. (1)(B), and has been corrected thusly.
— P.L. 94-455, Sec. 1906(b)(13)(A), substituted "Secretary" for "Secretary or his delegate" each place it appeared in Code Sec. 6802, effective 2/1/77.
In **1965**, P.L. 89-44, Sec. 601(d)(1), deleted "(other than stamps on playing cards)" after "adhesive stamps" in para. (1), effective 6/22/65.
— P.L. 89-44, Sec. 601(d)(2), deleted para. (3), effective 1/1/66.
Prior to deletion, para. (3) read as follows:
"(3) State agents. Any person who is—
"(A) duly appointed and acting as agent of any State for the sale of stock transfer stamps of such State, and
"(B) designated by the Secretary or his delegate for the purpose, a suitable quantity of such adhesive stamps as are required by section 4301, to be kept on sale by such person."

Sec. 6803. Accounting and safeguarding.
(a) Bond.
In cases coming within the provisions of paragraph (2) of section 6802, the Secretary may require a bond, with sufficient sureties, in a sum to be fixed by the Secretary, conditioned for the faithful return, whenever so required, of all quantities or amounts undisposed of and for the payment monthly for all quantities or amounts sold or not remaining on hand.
(b) Regulations.
The Secretary may from time to time make such regulations as he may find necessary to insure the safekeeping or prevent the illegal use of all adhesive stamps referred to in paragraph (2) of section 6802.

In **1976**, P.L. 94-455, Sec. 1906(a)(37), amended Code Sec. 6803.
Prior to amendment, Code Sec. 6803 read as follows:
"SEC. 6803. ACCOUNTING AND SAFEGUARDING.
"(b) Depositaries and State agents.
"(1) Bond. In cases coming within the provisions of paragraph (2) or (3) of section 6802, the Secretary or his delegate may require a bond, with sufficient sureties, in a sum to be fixed by the Secretary or his delegate, conditioned for the faithful return, whenever so required, of all quantities or amounts undisposed of and for the payment monthly for all quantities or amounts sold or not remaining on hand.
"(2) Regulations. The Secretary or his delegate may from time to time make such regulations as he may find necessary to insure the safekeeping or prevent the illegal use of all adhesive stamps referred to in paragraphs (2) and (3) of section 6802."
In **1972**, P.L. 92-310, Sec. 230(a), deleted subsec. (a), effective 6/6/72.
Prior to deletion, subsec. (a) read as follows:
"(a) The Postmaster General.
"(1) Bond and accounting. The Postmaster General may require each postmaster under paragraph (1) of section 6802 to furnish bond in such increased amount as he may from time to time determine, and each such postmaster shall deposit the receipts from the sale of such stamps, coupons, tickets, books, or other devices, to the credit of, and render accounts to the Postmaster General at such times and in such form as the Postmaster General may by regulations prescribe.
"(2) Deposit of receipts. The Postmaster General shall at least once a month transfer to the Treasury as internal revenue collections all receipts so deposited."

Sec. 6804. Attachment and cancellation.
Except as otherwise expressly provided in this title, the stamps referred to in section 6801 shall be attached, protected, removed, canceled, obliterated, and destroyed, in such manner and by such instruments or other means as the Secretary may prescribe by rules or regulations.

In **1976**, P.L. 94-455, Sec. 1906(b)(13)(A), substituted "Secretary" for "Secretary or his delegate" in Code Sec. 6804, effective 2/1/77.

Sec. 6805. Redemption of stamps.
(a) Authorization.
The Secretary, subject to regulations prescribed by him, may, upon receipt of satisfactory evidence of the facts, make allowance for or redeem such of the stamps, issued under authority of any internal revenue law, as may have been spoiled, destroyed, or rendered useless or unfit for the purpose intended, or for which the owner may have no use.
(b) Method and conditions of allowance.
Such allowance or redemption may be made, either by giving other stamps in lieu of the stamps so allowed for or redeemed, or by refunding the amount or value to the owner thereof, deducting therefrom, in case of repayment, the percentage, if any, allowed to the purchaser thereof; but no allowance or redemption shall be made in any case until the stamps so spoiled or rendered useless shall have been returned to the Secretary, or until satisfactory proof has been made showing the reason why the same cannot be returned; or, if so required by the Secretary, when the person presenting the same cannot satisfactorily trace the history of said stamps from their issuance to the presentation of his claim as aforesaid.
(c) Time for filing claims.
No claim for the redemption of, or allowance for, stamps shall be allowed under this section unless presented within 3 years after the purchase of such stamps from the Government.

Jeopardy, bankruptcy, receivership — Code Sec. 6851(a)(1)

(d) Finality of decisions.

The findings of fact in and the decision of the Secretary upon the merits of any claim presented under or authorized by this section shall, in the absence of fraud or mistake in mathematical calculation, be final and not subject to revision by any accounting officer.

In **1976**, P.L. 94-455, Sec. 1906(b)(13)(A), substituted "Secretary" for "Secretary or his delegate" each place it appeared in Code Sec. 6805, effective 2/1/77.

In **1958**, P.L. 85-859, Sec. 165(b), deleted ", or which through mistake may have been improperly or unnecessarily used, or where the rates or duties represented thereby have been excessive in amount, paid in error, or in any manner wrongfully collected" in subsec. (a) . . . Sec. 165(c), added "under this section" after following "shall be allowed" in subsec. (c), effective on the first day of the first calendar quarter which begins more than 60 days after 9/2/58.

Sec. 6806. Occupational tax stamps.

Every person engaged in any business, avocation, or employment, who is thereby made liable to a special tax (other than a special tax under subchapter B of chapter 35, under subchapter B of chapter 36, or under subtitle E) shall place and keep conspicuously in his establishment or place of business all stamps denoting payment of such special tax.

In **1968**, P.L. 90-448, Sec. 204, amended Code Sec. 6806, effective 10/22/68.
Prior to amendment, Code Sec. 6806 read as follows:
"SEC. 6806. POSTING OCCUPATIONAL TAX STAMPS.
"(a) General rule.
"Every person engaged in any business avocation, or employment, who is thereby made liable to a special tax shall place and keep conspicuously in his establishment or place of business all stamps denoting payment of said special tax.
"(b) Coin operated gaming devices.
"The Secretary or his delegate may by regulations require that the stamps denoting the payment of the special tax imposed by section 4461 shall be posted on or in each device in such a manner that it will be visible to any person operating the device.
"(c) Occupational wagering tax.
"Every person liable for special tax under section 4411 shall place and keep conspicuously in his principal place of business the stamp denoting the payment of such special tax; except that if he has no such place of business, he shall keep such stamp on his person, and exhibit it, upon request, to any officer or employee of the Treasury Department."
In **1965**, P.L. 89-44, Sec. 601(e), deleted "amusement and" before "gaming" in the heading of subsec. (b), effective 7/1/65.

Sec. 6807. Stamping, marking, and branding seized goods.

If any article of manufacture or produce requiring brands, stamps, or marks of whatever kind to be placed thereon, is sold upon levy, forfeiture (except as provided in section 5688 with respect to distilled spirits), or other process provided by law, the same not having been branded, stamped, or marked, as required by law, the officer selling the same shall, upon sale thereof, fix or cause to be affixed the brands, stamps, or marks so required.

Sec. 6808. Special provisions relating to stamps.

For special provisions on stamps relating to—
(1) Distilled spirits and fermented liquors, see chapter 51.
(2) Machine guns and short-barrelled firearms, see chapter 53.
(3) Tobacco, snuff, cigars and cigarettes, see chapter 52.

In **1976**, P.L. 94-455, Sec. 1904(b)(5)(B), deleted para. (4), effective 2/1/77.
Prior to deletion, para. (4) read as follows:
"(4) Documents and other instruments, see chapter 34."
—P.L. 94-455, Sec. 1904(b)(7)(A), deleted para. (7), effective 2/1/77.
Prior to deletion, para. (7) read as follows:
"(7) Oleomargarine, see subchapter F of chapter 38."
—P.L. 94-455, Sec. 1904(b)(8)(B), deleted para. (12), effective 2/1/77.
Prior to deletion, para. (12) read as follows:
"(12) White phosphorous matches, see subchapter B of chapter 39."
—P.L. 94-455, Sec. 1904(b)(9)(A), deleted para. (10), effective 2/1/77.
Prior to deletion, para. (10) read as follows:
"(10) Process, renovated, or adulterated butter, see subchapter C of chapter 39."
—P.L. 94-455, Sec. 1952(n)(1), deleted para. (2), and redesignated paras. (3), (6) and (11) as paras. (1), (2) and (3), effective 2/1/77.
Prior to deletion, para. (2) read as follows:

"(2) Cotton futures, see subchapter D of chapter 39."
In **1974**, P.L. 93-490, Sec. 3(b)(6), repealed para. (5), effective for filled cheese manufactured, imported, or sold after 10/26/74.
Prior to deletion, para. (5) read as follows:
"(5) Filled cheese, see subchapter C of chapter 39."
In **1970**, P.L. 91-513, Sec. 1102(c), deleted para. (8), effective 5/1/71.
Prior to deletion, para. (8) read as follows:
"(8) Opium, opium for smoking, opiates and coca leaves, and marihuana, subchapter A of chapter 39."
In **1965**, P.L. 89-44, Sec. 601(f), deleted para. (1), which was a cross reference provision for capital stock, to chapter 34, effective 1/1/66, and deleted para. (9), which was a cross reference provision for playing cards, to subchapter A of chapter 36, effective 6/22/65.
In **1963**, P.L. 88-36, Sec. 201(d), redesignated para. (12) as para. (11) and deleted para. (11), which was a cross reference provision for silver bullion, to subchapter F of chapter 9, and redesignated para. (13) as para. (12), effective transfers after 6/4/63.

CHAPTER 70.— JEOPARDY, RECEIVERSHIP, ETC.

Subchapter
A. Jeopardy.
B. Receiverships, etc.

In **1980**, P.L. 96-589, Sec. 6(g)(3)(C), amended the item for Subchapter B.
Prior to amendment, the item for Subchapter B read as follows:
"B. BANKRUPTCY AND RECEIVERSHIPS."
—P.L. 96-589, Sec. 6(g)(3)(D), amended the heading of Chapter 70.
Prior to amendment, the heading read as follows:
"CHAPTER 70.—JEOPARDY, BANKRUPTCY AND RECEIVERSHIPS"

Subchapter A.— Jeopardy

Part
  I. Termination of taxable year.
 II. Jeopardy assessments.
III. Special rules with respect to certain cash.

In **1982**, P.L. 97-248, Sec. 330(b), added item III.

PART I.— TERMINATION OF TAXABLE YEAR

Sec.
6851. Termination assessments of income tax.
6852. Termination assessments in case of flagrant political expenditures of section 501(c)(3) organizations.

In **1987**, P.L. 100-203, Sec. 10713(b)(2)(H), added item 6852.
In **1976**, P.L. 94-455, Sec. 1204(b)(12), amended item 6851.
Prior to amendment, item 6851 read as follows:
"6851. Termination of taxable year."

Sec. 6851. Termination assessments of income tax.
(a) Authority for making.

(1) In general. If the Secretary finds that a taxpayer designs quickly to depart from the United States or to remove his property therefrom, or to conceal himself or his property therein, or to do any other act (including in the case of a corporation distributing all or a part of its assets in liquidation or otherwise) tending to prejudice or to render wholly or partially ineffectual proceedings to collect the income tax for the current or the immediately preceding taxable year unless such proceeding be brought without delay, the Secretary shall immediately make a determination of tax for the current taxable year or for the preceding taxable year, or both, as the case may be, and notwithstanding any other provision of law, such tax shall become immediately due and payable. The Secretary shall immediately assess the amount of the tax so determined (together with all interest, additional amounts, and additions to the tax provided by law) for the current taxable year or such preceding taxable year, or both, as the case may be, and shall cause notice of such determination and

3,835

assessment to be given the taxpayer, together with a demand for immediate payment of such tax.

(2) Computation of tax. In the case of a current taxable year, the Secretary shall determine the tax for the period beginning on the first day of such current taxable year and ending on the date of the determination under paragraph (1) as though such period were a taxable year of the taxpayer, and shall take into account any prior determination made under this subsection with respect to such current taxable year.

(3) Treatment of amounts collected. Any amounts collected as a result of any assessments under this subsection shall, to the extent thereof, be treated as a payment of tax for such taxable year.

(4) This section inapplicable where section 6861 applies. This section shall not authorize any assessment of tax for the preceding taxable year which is made after the due date of the taxpayer's return for such taxable year (determined with regard to any extensions).

(b) Notice of deficiency.

If an assessment of tax is made under the authority of subsection (a), the Secretary shall mail a notice under section 6212(a) for the taxpayer's full taxable year (determined without regard to any action taken under subsection (a)) with respect to which such assessment was made within 60 days after the later of (i) the due date of the taxpayer's return for such taxable year (determined with regard to any extensions), or (ii) the date such taxpayer files such return. Such deficiency may be in an amount greater or less than the amount assessed under subsection (a).

(c) Citizens.

In the case of a citizen of the United States or of a possession of the United States about to depart from the United States, the Secretary may, at his discretion, waive any or all of the requirements placed on the taxpayer by this section.

(d) Departure of alien.

Subject to such exceptions as may, by regulations, be prescribed by the Secretary—

(1) No alien shall depart from the United States unless he first procures from the Secretary a certificate that he has complied with all the obligations imposed upon him by the income tax laws.

(2) Payment of taxes shall not be enforced by any proceedings under the provisions of this section prior to the expiration of the time otherwise allowed for paying such taxes if, in the case of an alien about to depart from the United States, the Secretary determines that the collection of the tax will not be jeopardized by the departure of the alien.

(e) Sections 6861(f) and (g) to apply.

The provisions of section 6861(f) (relating to collection of unpaid amounts) and 6861(g) (relating to abatement if jeopardy does not exist) shall apply with respect to any assessment made under subsection (a).

(f) Cross references.

(1) For provisions permitting immediate levy in case of jeopardy, see section 6331(a).

(2) For provisions relating to the review of jeopardy, see section 7429.

In 1976, P.L. 94-528, Sec. 2(a), changed the effective date for amendments made by Sec. 1204(b)(1) of P.L. 94-455, to effective for action taken under Code Secs. 6851, 6861 or 6862 where the notice and demand takes place after 2/28/77, from effective for action taken under Code Secs. 6851, 6861 or 6862 where the notice and demand takes place after 12/31/76, see below.

—P.L. 94-455, Sec. 1204(b)(1), amended so much of Code Sec. 6851 as precedes subsec. (c), effective [as amended by Sec. 2(a) of P.L. 94-528, see above] for action taken under Code Secs. 6851, 6861 or 6862 where the notice and demand takes place after 2/28/77.

Prior to amendment, that part of Code Sec. 6851 read as follows:
"SEC. 6851. TERMINATION OF TAXABLE YEAR.
"(a) Income tax in jeopardy.

"(1) In general. If the Secretary or his delegate finds that a taxpayer designs quickly to depart from the United States or to remove his property therefrom, or to conceal himself or his property therein, or to do any other act tending to prejudice or to render wholly or partly ineffectual proceedings to collect the income tax for the current or the preceding taxable year unless such proceedings be brought without delay, the Secretary or his delegate shall declare the taxable period for such taxpayer immediately terminated, and shall cause notice of such finding and declaration to be given the taxpayer, together with a demand for immediate payment of the tax for the taxable period so declared terminated and of the tax for the preceding taxable year or so much of such tax as is unpaid, whether or not the time otherwise allowed by law for filing return and paying the tax has expired; and such taxes shall thereupon become immediately due and payable. In any proceeding in court brought to enforce payment of taxes made due and payable by virtue of the provisions of this section, the finding of the Secretary or his delegate, made as herein provided, whether made after notice to the taxpayer or not, shall be for all purposes presumptive evidence of jeopardy.

"(2) Corporation in liquidation. If the Secretary or his delegate finds that the collection of the income tax of a corporation for the current or the preceding taxable year will be jeopardized by the distribution of all or a portion of the assets of such corporation in the liquidation of the whole or any part of its capital stock, the Secretary or his delegate shall declare the taxable period for such taxpayer immediately terminated and shall cause notice of such finding and declaration to be given the taxpayer, together with a demand for immediate payment of the tax for the taxable period so declared terminated and of the tax for the preceding taxable year or so much of such tax as is unpaid, whether or not the time otherwise allowed by law for filing return and paying the tax has expired; and such taxes shall thereupon become immediately due and payable.

"(b) Reopening of taxable period.

"Notwithstanding the termination of the taxable period of the taxpayer by the Secretary or his delegate, as provided in subsection (a), the Secretary or his delegate may reopen such taxable period each time the taxpayer is found by the Secretary or his delegate to have received income, within the current taxable year, since a termination of the period under subsection (a). A taxable period so terminated by the Secretary or his delegate may be reopened by the taxpayer (other than a nonresident alien) if he files with the Secretary or his delegate a true and accurate return of the items of gross income and of the deductions and credits allowed under this title for such taxable period, together with such other information as the Secretary or his delegate may by regulations prescribe. If the taxpayer is a nonresident alien the taxable period so terminated may be reopened by him if he files, or causes to be filed, with the Secretary or his delegate a true and accurate return of his total income derived from all sources within the United States, in the manner prescribed in this title."

—P.L. 94-455, Sec. 1204(b)(2), deleted subsec. (e) and added new subsecs. (e) and (f), for action taken under Code Secs. 6851, 6861 or 6862 where the notice and demand takes place after '76. Sec. 2(a) of P.L. 94-528, postponed the effective date for this amendment to be for notices and demands taking place after 2/28/77.

Prior to amendment, subsec. (e) read as follows:
"(e) Furnishing of bond where taxable year is closed by the Secretary or his delegate.

"Payment of taxes shall not be enforced by any proceedings under the provisions of this section prior to the expiration of the time otherwise allowed for paying such taxes if the taxpayer furnishes, under regulations prescribed by the Secretary or his delegate, a bond to insure the timely making of returns with respect to, and payment of, such taxes or any income or excess profits taxes for prior years."

—P.L. 94-455, Sec. 1906(b)(13)(A), substituted "Secretary" for "Secretary or his delegate" each place it appeared in Code Sec. 6851, effective 2/1/77.

In 1958, P.L. 85-866, Sec. 87, designated existing provisions of subsec. (d) as para. (d)(1), added opening provisions and para. (d)(2), effective 8/17/54.

Sec. 6852. Termination assessments in case of flagrant political expenditures of section 501(c)(3) organizations.

(a) Authority to make.

(1) In general. If the Secretary finds that—

(A) a section 501(c)(3) organization has made political expenditures, and

(B) such expenditures constitute a flagrant violation of the prohibition against making political expenditures,

the Secretary shall immediately make a determination of any income tax payable by such organization for the current or immediately preceding taxable year, or both, and shall immediately make a determination of any tax payable under section 4955 by such organization or any manager thereof with respect to political expenditures during the current or preceding taxable year, or both. Notwithstanding any other provision of law, any such tax shall become immediately due and payable. The Secretary shall immediately assess the amount of tax so determined (together with all interest, additional amounts, and additions to the tax provided by law) for the current year or the preceding taxable year, or both, and shall cause notice of such determination and assessment to be given to the organization or any manager thereof, as the case may be, together with a demand for immediate payment of such tax.

(2) Computation of tax. In the case of a current taxable year, the Secretary shall determine the taxes for the period beginning on the 1st day of such current taxable year and ending on the date of the determination under paragraph (1) as though such period were a taxable year of the organization, and shall take into account any prior determination made under this subsection with respect to such current taxable year.

(3) Treatment of amounts collected. Any amounts collected as a result of any assessments under this subsection shall, to the extent thereof, be treated as a payment of income tax for such taxable year, or tax under section 4955 with respect to the expenditure, as the case may be.

(4) Section inapplicable to assessments after due date. This section shall not authorize any assessment of tax for the preceding taxable year which is made after the due date of the organization's return for such taxable year (determined with regard to any extensions).

(b) Definitions and special rules.

(1) Definitions. For purposes of this section, the terms "section 501(c)(3) organization", "political expenditure", and "organization manager" have the respective meanings given to such terms by section 4955.

(2) Certain rules made applicable. The provisions of sections 6851(b), 6861(f), and 6861(g) shall apply with respect to any assessment made under subsection (a), except that determinations under section 6861(g) shall be made on the basis of whether the requirements of subsection (a)(1)(B) of this section are met in lieu of whether jeopardy exists.

In **1987**, P.L. 100-203, Sec. 10713(b)(1), added Code Sec. 6582, effective 12/22/87.

PART II.—JEOPARDY ASSESSMENTS

Sec.
6861. Jeopardy assessments of income, estate, gift, and certain excise taxes.
6862. Jeopardy assessment of taxes other than income, estate, gift, and certain excise taxes.
6863. Stay of collection of jeopardy assessments.
6864. Termination of extended period for payment in case of carryback.

In **1974**, P.L. 93-406, Sec. 1016(b)(5), substituted "gift, and certain excise taxes" for "and gift taxes" in items 6861 and 6862.

Sec. 6861. Jeopardy assessments of income, estate, gift, and certain excise taxes.

(a) Authority for making.

If the Secretary believes that the assessment or collection of a deficiency, as defined in section 6211, will be jeopardized by delay, he shall, notwithstanding the provisions of section 6213(a), immediately assess such deficiency (together with all interest, additional amounts, and additions to the tax provided for by law), and notice and demand shall be made by the Secretary for the payment thereof.

(b) Deficiency letters.

If the jeopardy assessment is made before any notice in respect of the tax to which the jeopardy assessment relates has been mailed under section 6212(a), then the Secretary shall mail a notice under such subsection within 60 days after the making of the assessment.

(c) Amount assessable before decision of Tax Court.

The jeopardy assessment may be made in respect of a deficiency greater or less than that notice of which has been mailed to the taxpayer, despite the provisions of section 6212(c) prohibiting the determination of additional deficiencies, and whether or not the taxpayer has theretofore filed a petition with the Tax Court. The Secretary may, at any time before the decision of the Tax Court is rendered, abate such assessment, or any unpaid portion thereof, to the extent that he believes the assessment to be excessive in amount. The Secretary shall notify the Tax Court of the amount of such assessment, or abatement, if the petition is filed with the Tax Court before the making of the assessment or is subsequently filed, and the Tax Court shall have jurisdiction to redetermine the entire amount of the deficiency and of all amounts assessed at the same time in connection therewith.

(d) Amount assessable after decision of Tax Court.

If the jeopardy assessment is made after the decision of the Tax Court is rendered, such assessment may be made only in respect of the deficiency determined by the Tax Court in its decision.

(e) Expiration of right to assess.

A jeopardy assessment may not be made after the decision of the Tax Court has become final or after the taxpayer has filed a petition for review of the decision of the Tax Court.

(f) Collection of unpaid amounts.

When the petition has been filed with the Tax Court and when the amount which should have been assessed has been determined by a decision of the Tax Court which has become final, then any unpaid portion, the collection of which has been stayed by bond as provided in section 6863(b) shall be collected as part of the tax upon notice and demand from the Secretary, and any remaining portion of the assessment shall be abated. If the amount already collected exceeds the amount determined as the amount which should have been assessed, such excess shall be credited or refunded to the taxpayer as provided in section 6402, without the filing of claim therefor. If the amount determined as the amount which should have been assessed is greater than the amount actually assessed, then the difference shall be assessed and shall be collected as part of the tax upon notice and demand from the Secretary.

(g) Abatement if jeopardy does not exist.

The Secretary may abate the jeopardy assessment if he finds that jeopardy does not exist. Such abatement may not be made after a decision of the Tax Court in respect of the deficiency has been rendered or, if no petition is filed with the Tax Court, after the expiration of the period for filing such petition. The period of limitation on the making of assessments and levy or a proceeding in court for collection, in respect of any deficiency, shall be determined as if the jeopardy assessment so abated had not been made, except that the running of such period shall in any event be suspended for the period from the date of such jeopardy assessment until the expiration of the 10th day after the day on which such jeopardy assessment is abated.

(h) Cross references.

(1) For the effect of the furnishing of security for payment, see section 6863.
(2) For provision permitting immediate levy in case of jeopardy, see section 6331(a).

In **1976**, P.L. 94-455, Sec. 1906(b)(13)(A), substituted "Secretary" for "Secretary or his delegate" each place it appeared in Code Sec. 6861, effective 2/1/77.

In **1974**, P.L. 93-406, Sec. 1016(a)(24), substituted ", gift, and certain excise taxes." for "and gift taxes." in the heading of Code Sec. 6861, effective 9/2/74 or

3,837

other date as specified in Sec. 1017 of the Act (reproduced following Code Sec. 401).

Sec. 6862. Jeopardy assessment of taxes other than income, estate, gift, and certain excise taxes.
(a) Immediate assessment.

If the Secretary believes that the collection of any tax (other than income tax, estate tax, gift tax, and the excise taxes imposed by chapters 41, 42, 43, and 44) under any provision of the internal revenue laws will be jeopardized by delay, he shall, whether or not the time otherwise prescribed by law for making return and paying such tax has expired, immediately assess such tax (together with all interest, additional amounts, and additions to the tax provided for by law). Such tax, additions to the tax, and interest shall thereupon become immediately due and payable, and immediate notice and demand shall be made by the Secretary for the payment thereof.
(b) Immediate levy.

For provision permitting immediate levy in case of jeopardy, see section 6331(a).

In 1988, P.L. 100-418, Sec. 1941(b)(2)(N), substituted "and 44" for "44, and 45" in subsec. (a), effective for crude oil removed from the premises on or after 8/23/88.
In 1980, P.L. 96-223, Sec. 101(f)(9), substituted "the excise taxes imposed by chapters 41, 42, 43, 44, and 45" for "certain excise taxes" in subsec. (a), effective for periods after 2/29/80.
—P.L. 96-222, Sec. 108(b)(1)(C), substituted "the taxes imposed by chapters 41, 42, 43, and 44" for "certain excise taxes" in subsec. (a), effective for contributions, acts and expenditures made after 12/31/77, in and for tax. yrs. begin. after such date.
In 1976, P.L. 94-455, Sec. 1906(b)(13)(A), substituted "Secretary" for "Secretary or his delegate" each place it appeared in Code Sec. 6862, effective 2/1/77.
In 1974, P.L. 93-406, Sec. 1016(a)(25), substituted ", gift, and certain excise taxes" for "and gift taxes" in the heading of Code Sec. 6862, and substituted "gift tax, and certain excise taxes)" for "and gift tax)" in subsec. (a), effective 9/2/74 or other date as specified in Sec. 1017 of the Act (reproduced following Code Sec. 401)

Sec. 6863. Stay of collection of jeopardy assessments.
(a) Bond to stay collection.

When an assessment has been made under section 6851, 6852, 6861 or 6862, the collection of the whole or any amount of such assessment may be stayed by filing with the Secretary, within such time as may be fixed by regulations prescribed by the Secretary, a bond in an amount equal to the amount as to which the stay is desired, conditioned upon the payment of the amount (together with interest thereon) the collection of which is stayed, at the time at which, but for the making of such assessment, such amount would be due. Upon the filing of the bond the collection of so much of the amount assessed as is covered by the bond shall be stayed. The taxpayer shall have the right to waive such stay at any time in respect of the whole or any part of the amount covered by the bond, and if as a result of such waiver any part of the amount covered by the bond is paid, then the bond shall, at the request of the taxpayer, be proportionately reduced. If any portion of such assessment is abated, the bond shall, at the request of the taxpayer, be proportionately reduced.
(b) Further conditions in case of income, estate, or gift taxes.

In the case of taxes subject to the jurisdiction of the Tax Court—

(1) Prior to petition to Tax Court. If the bond is given before the taxpayer has filed his petition under section 6213(a), the bond shall contain a further condition that if a petition is not filed within the period provided in such section, then the amount, the collection of which is stayed by the bond, will be paid on notice and demand at any time after the expiration of such period, together with interest thereon from the date of the jeopardy notice and demand to the date of notice and demand under this paragraph.

(2) Effect of Tax Court decision. The bond shall be conditioned upon the payment of so much of such assessment (collection of which is stayed by the bond) as is not abated by a decision of the Tax Court which has become final. If the Tax Court determines that the amount assessed is greater than the amount which should have been assessed, then when the decision of the Tax Court is rendered the bond shall, at the request of the taxpayer, be proportionately reduced.

(3) Stay of sale of seized property pending Tax Court decision.

(A) General rule. Where, notwithstanding the provisions of section 6213(a), an assessment has been made under section 6851, 6852, or 6861, the property seized for collection of the tax shall not be sold—

(i) before the expiration of the periods described in subsection (c)(1)(A) and (B),

(ii) before the issuance of the notice of deficiency described in section 6851(b) or 6861(b), and the expiration of the period provided in section 6213(a) for filing a petition with the Tax Court, and

(iii) if a petition is filed with the Tax Court (whether before or after the making of such assessment), before the expiration of the period during which the assessment of the deficiency would be prohibited if neither sections 6851(a), 6852(a), nor 6861(a) were applicable.

Clauses (ii) and (iii) shall not apply in the case of a termination assessment under section 6851 if the taxpayer does not file a return for the taxable year by the due date (determined with regard to any extensions).

(B) Exceptions. Such property may be sold if—
 (i) the taxpayer consents to the sale,
 (ii) the Secretary determines that the expenses of conservation and maintenance will greatly reduce the net proceeds, or
 (iii) the property is of the type described in section 6336.

(C) Review by tax court. If, but for the application of subparagraph (B), a sale would be prohibited by subparagraph (A)(iii), then the Tax Court shall have jurisdiction to review the Secretary's determination under subparagraph (B) that the property may be sold. Such review may be commenced upon motion by either the Secretary or the taxpayer. An order of the Tax Court disposing of a motion under this paragraph shall be reviewable in the same manner as a decision of the Tax Court.

(c) Stay of sale of seized property pending district court determination under section 7429.

(1) General rule. Where a jeopardy assessment has been made under section 6862(a), the property seized for the collection of the tax shall not be sold—

(A) if a civil action is commenced in accordance with section 7429(b), on or before the day on which the district court judgment in such action becomes final, or

(B) if subparagraph (A) does not apply, before the day after the expiration of the period provided in section 7429(a) for requesting an administrative review, and if such review is requested, before the day after the expiration of the period provided in section 7429(b), for commencing an action in the district court.

Jeopardy, bankruptcy, receivership Code Sec. 6871(a)

(2) **Exceptions.** With respect to any property described in paragraph (1), the exceptions provided by subsection (b)(3)(B) shall apply.

In 1989, P.L. 101-239, Sec. 7822(d)(2), corrected Sec. 10713(b)(2)(E)(iii) of P.L. 100-203, see below, so that it would substitute "6851(a), 6852(a), nor 6861(a)" for "6851(a) nor 6861(a)" instead of substituting "6851(a), 6852(a) or 6861(a)" for "6851(a) or 6861(a)" in clause (a)(3)(A)(iii), see below.

In 1988, P.L. 100-647, Sec. 6245(a), added subpara. (b)(3)(C), effective 90 days after 11/10/88.

In 1987, P.L. 100-203, Sec. 10713(b)(2)(E)(i), substituted "6851, 6852" for "6851" in subsec. (a)... Sec. 10713(b)(2)(E)(ii), substituted "6851, 6852, or 6861" for "6851 or 6861" in subpara. (b)(3)(A)... Sec. 10713(b)(2)(E)(iii), [as amended by Sec. 7822(d)(2) of P.L. 101-239, see above] substituted "6851(a), 6852(a), nor 6861(a)" for "6851(a), nor 6861(a)", in clause (a)(3)(A)(iii), effective 12/22/87.

In 1976, P.L. 94-528, Sec. 2(a), changed the effective date for amendments made by Sec. 1204(c)(8) and (9) of P.L. 94-455, from effective for action taken under Code Sec. 6851, 6861 or 6862 where the notice and demand take place after 12/31/76, to effective for action taken under Code Sec. 6851, 6861 or 6862 where the notice and demand take place after 2/28/77, see below.

—P.L. 94-455, Sec. 1204(c)(7), substituted "6851, 6861," for "6861" in subsec. (a) ... substituted "an assessment" for "a jeopardy assessment" in the first sentence of subsec. (a) ... substituted "such assessment" for "the jeopardy assessment" each place it appeared in subsec. (a), for action taken under Code Secs. 6851, 6861 or 6862 where the notice and demand takes place after '76. Sec. 2(a) of P.L. 94-528, postponed the effective date for this amendment to be for notices and demands taking place after 2/28/77.

—P.L. 94-455, Sec. 1204(c)(8), amended subpara. (b)(3)(A), effective [as amended by Sec. 2(a) of P.L. 94-528, see above] for action taken under Code Secs. 6851, 6861 or 6862 where the notice and demand takes place after 2/28/77. Prior to amendment, subpara. (b)(3)(A) read as follows:

"(A) General rule. Where, notwithstanding the provisions of section 6213(a), jeopardy assessment has been made under section 6861 the property seized for the collection of the tax shall not be sold—

"(i) if section 6861(b) is applicable, prior to the issuance of the notice of deficiency and the expiration of the time provided in section 6213(a) for filing petition with the Tax Court, and

"(ii) if petition is filed with the Tax Court (whether before or after the making of such jeopardy assessment under section 6861), prior to the expiration of the period during which the assessment of the deficiency would be prohibited if section 6861(a) were not applicable."

—P.L. 94-455, Sec. 1204(c)(9), added subsec. (c), effective [as amended by Sec. 2(a) of P.L. 94-528, see above] for action taken under Code Secs. 6851, 6861 or 6862 where the notice and demand takes place after 2/28/77.

—P.L. 94-455, Sec. 1906(a)(38), deleted subpara. (b)(3)(C), effective 2/1/77. Prior to amendment, subpara. (b)(3)(C) read as follows:

"(C) Applicability. Subparagraphs (A) and (B) shall be applicable only with respect to a jeopardy assessment made on or after January 1, 1955, and shall apply with respect to taxes imposed by this title and with respect to taxes imposed by the Internal Revenue Code of 1939."

—P.L. 94-455, Sec. 1906(b)(13)(A), substituted "Secretary" for "Secretary or his delegate" each place it appeared in Code Sec. 6863, effective 2/1/77.

Sec. 6864. Termination of extended period for payment in case of carryback.

For termination of extensions of time for payment of income tax granted to corporations expecting carrybacks in case of jeopardy, see section 6164(h).

PART III.—SPECIAL RULES WITH RESPECT TO CERTAIN CASH

Sec.
6867. Presumptions where owner of large amount of cash is not identified.

Sec. 6867. Presumptions where owner of large amount of cash is not identified.

(a) **General rule.**

If the individual who is in physical possession of cash in excess of $10,000 does not claim such cash—

(1) as his, or

(2) as belonging to another person whose identity the Secretary can readily ascertain and who acknowledges ownership of such cash,

then, for purposes of sections 6851 and 6861, it shall be presumed that such cash represents gross income of a single individual for the taxable year in which the possession occurs, and that the collection of tax will be jeopardized by delay.

(b) **Rules for assessing.**

In the case of any assessment resulting from the application of subsection (a)—

(1) the entire amount of the cash shall be treated as taxable income for the taxable year in which the possession occurs,

(2) such income shall be treated as taxable at the highest rate of tax specified in section 1, and

(3) except as provided in subsection (c), the possessor of the cash shall be treated (solely with respect to such cash) as the taxpayer for purposes of chapters 63 and 64 and section 7429(a)(1).

(c) **Effect of later substitution of true owner.**

If, after an assessment resulting from the application of subsection (a), such assessment is abated and replaced by an assessment against the owner of the cash, such later assessment shall be treated for purposes of all laws relating to lien, levy and collection as relating back to the date of the original assessment.

(d) **Definitions.**

For purposes of this section—

(1) **Cash.** The term "cash" includes any cash equivalent.

(2) **Cash equivalent.** The term "cash equivalent" means—

(A) foreign currency,

(B) any bearer obligation, and

(C) any medium of exchange which—

(i) is of a type which has been frequently used in illegal activities, and

(ii) is specified as a cash equivalent for purposes of this part in regulations prescribed by the Secretary.

(3) **Value of cash equivalent.** Any cash equivalent shall be taken into account—

(A) in the case of a bearer obligation, at its face amount, and

(B) in the case of any other cash equivalent, at its fair market value.

In 1988, P.L. 100-647, Sec. 1001(a)(1), substituted "at the highest rate of tax specified in section 1" for "at a 50-percent rate" in para. (b)(2), effective for tax. yrs. begin. after 12/31/86.

In 1982, P.L. 97-248, Sec. 330(a), added Code Sec. 6867, effective 9/4/82.

Subchapter B.—Receiverships, Etc.

Sec.
6871. Claims for income, estate, gift, and certain excise taxes in receivership proceedings, etc.
6872. Suspension of period on assessment.
6873. Unpaid claims.

In 1980, P.L. 96-589, Sec. 6(g)(3)(A), amended item 6871.
Prior to amendment, item 6871 read as follows:
"6871. Claims for income, estate, and gift taxes in bankruptcy and receivership proceedings."
—P.L. 96-589, Sec. 6(g)(3)(B), amended the heading of Subchapter B of Chapter 70.
Prior to amendment, the heading of Subchapter B read as follows:
"SUBCHAPTER B. BANKRUPTCY AND RECEIVERSHIPS."

Sec. 6871. Claims for income, estate, gift, and certain excise taxes in receivership proceedings, etc.

(a) **Immediate assessment in receivership proceedings.**

On the appointment of a receiver for the taxpayer in any receivership proceeding before any court of the United States or of any State or of the District of Columbia, any deficiency (together with all interest, additional amounts, and additions to the tax provided by law) determined by the Secretary in respect of a tax imposed by subtitle A or B or by

3,839

chapter 41, 42, 43, or 44 on such taxpayer may, despite the restrictions imposed by section 6213(a) on assessments, be immediately assessed if such deficiency has not theretofore been assessed in accordance with law.

(b) Immediate assessment with respect to certain title 11 cases.

Any deficiency (together with all interest, additional amounts, and additions to the tax provided by law) determined by the Secretary in respect of a tax imposed by subtitle A or B or by chapter 41, 42, 43, or 44 on—

(1) the debtor's estate in a case under title 11 of the United States Code, or

(2) the debtor, but only if liability for such tax has become res judicata pursuant to a determination in a case under title 11 of the United States Code,

may, despite the restrictions imposed by section 6213(a) on assessments, be immediately assessed if such deficiency has not theretofore been assessed in accordance with law.

(c) Claim filed despite pendency of tax court proceedings.

In the case of a tax imposed by subtitle A or B or by chapter 41, 42, 43, or 44—

(1) claims for the deficiency and for interest, additional amounts, and additions to the tax may be presented, for adjudication in accordance with law, to the court before which the receivership proceeding (or the case under title 11 of the United States Code) is pending, despite the pendency of proceedings for the redetermination of the deficiency pursuant to a petition to the Tax Court; but

(2) in the case of a receivership proceeding, no petition for any such redetermination shall be filed with the Tax Court after the appointment of the receiver.

In **1989**, P.L. 101-239, Sec. 7841(d)(2), substituted "or 44" for "44, or 45" each place it appeared in Sec. 6871, effective 12/19/89.

In **1980**, P.L. 96-589, Sec. 6(g)(1), amended Code Sec. 6871, effective 10/1/79, except for any proceeding under the Bankruptcy Act begun before 10/1/79. Sec. 7(g) of this Act provides:

"(g) Definitions.

"For purposes of this section—

"(1) Bankruptcy case. The term 'bankruptcy case' means any case under title 11 of the United States Code (as recodified by P.L. 95-598).

"(2) Similar judicial proceeding. The term 'similar judicial proceeding' means a receivership, foreclosure, or similar proceeding in a Federal or State court (as modified by section 368(a)(3)(D) of the Internal Revenue Code of 1954)."

Prior to amendment, Code Sec. 6871 read as follows:

"SEC. 6871. CLAIMS FOR INCOME, ESTATE, AND GIFT TAXES IN BANKRUPTCY AND RECEIVERSHIP PROCEEDINGS.

"(a) Immediate assessment.

"Upon the adjudication of bankruptcy of any taxpayer in any liquidating proceeding, the filing in (where approval is required by the Bankruptcy Act) the approval of a petition of, or the approval of a petition against, any taxpayer in any other bankruptcy proceeding, or the appointment of a receiver for any taxpayer in any receivership proceeding before any court of the United States or of any State or of the District of Columbia, any deficiency (together with all interest, additional amounts, or additions to the tax provided by law) determined by the Secretary in respect of a tax imposed by subtitle A or B upon such taxpayer shall, despite the restrictions imposed by section 6213(a) on assessments, be immediately assessed if such deficiency has not theretofore been assessed in accordance with law.

"(b) Claim filed despite pendency of Tax Court proceedings.

"In the case of a tax imposed by subtitle A or B claims for the deficiency and such interest, additional amounts, and additions to the tax may be presented, for adjudication in accordance with law, to the court before which the bankruptcy or receivership proceeding is pending, despite the pendency of proceedings for the redetermination of the deficiency in pursuance of a petition to the Tax Court; but no petition for any such redetermination shall be filed with the Tax Court after the adjudication of bankruptcy, the filing or (where approval is required by the Bankruptcy Act) the approval of a petition of, or the approval of a petition against, any taxpayer in any other bankruptcy proceeding, or the appointment of the receiver."

In **1976**, P.L. 94-455, Sec. 1906(b)(13)(A), substituted "Secretary" for "Secretary or his delegate" in Code Sec. 6871 . . . Sec. 1906(c)(1), deleted "or Territory", after "of any State", in subsec. (a), effective 2/1/77.

In **1958**, P.L. 85-866, Sec. 88, substituted "the filing or (where approval is required by the Bankruptcy Act) the approval of a petition of, or the approval of a petition against, any taxpayer" for "the approval of a petition of, or against, any taxpayer" in subsec. (a), substituted "the filing or (where approval is required

by the Bankruptcy Act) the approval of a petition of, or the approval of a petition against, any taxpayer" for "approval of the petition" in subsec. (b), effective 8/17/54.

Sec. 6872. Suspension of period on assessment.

If the regulations issued pursuant to section 6036 require the giving of notice by any fiduciary in any case under title 11 of the United States Code, or by a receiver in any other court proceeding, to the Secretary of his qualification as such, the running of the period of limitations on the making of assessments shall be suspended for the period from the date of the institution of the proceeding to a date 30 days after the date upon which the notice from the receiver or other fiduciary is received by the Secretary; but the suspension under this sentence shall in no case be for a period in excess of 2 years.

In **1980**, P.L. 96-589, Sec. 6(i)(12), substituted "any case under title 11 of the United States Code" for "any proceeding under the Bankruptcy Act", effective 10/1/79, except for any proceeding under the Bankruptcy Act begun before 10/1/79. Sec. 7(g) of this Act provides:

"(g) Definitions.

"For purposes of this section—

"(1) Bankruptcy case. The term 'bankruptcy case' means any case under title 11 of the United States Code (as recodified by P.L. 95-598).

"(2) Similar judicial proceeding. The term 'similar judicial proceeding' means a receivership, foreclosure, or similar proceeding in a Federal or State court (as modified by section 368(a)(3)(D) of the Internal Revenue Code of 1954)."

In **1976**, P.L. 94-455, Sec. 1906(b)(13)(A), substituted "Secretary" for "Secretary or his delegate" each place it appeared in Code Sec. 6872, effective 2/1/77.

Sec. 6873. Unpaid claims.

(a) General rule.

Any portion of a claim for taxes allowed in a receivership proceeding which is unpaid shall be paid by the taxpayer upon notice and demand from the Secretary after the termination of such proceeding.

(b) Cross references.

(1) For suspension of running of period of limitations on collection, see section 6503(b).

(2) For extension of time for payment, see section 6161(c).

In **1980**, P.L. 96-589, Sec. 6(g)(2), deleted "or any proceeding under the Bankruptcy Act" after "receivership" in subsec. (a), effective 10/1/79, except for any proceeding under the Bankruptcy Act begun before 10/1/79. Sec. 7(g) of this Act provides:

"(g) Definitions.

"For purposes of this section—

"(1) Bankruptcy case. The term 'bankruptcy case' means any case under title 11 of the United States Code (as recodified by P.L. 95-598).

"(2) Similar judicial proceeding. The term 'similar judicial proceeding' means a receivership, foreclosure, or similar proceeding in a Federal or State court (as modified by section 368(a)(3)(D) of the Internal Revenue Code of 1954)."

In **1976**, P.L. 94-455, Sec. 1906(b)(13)(A), substituted "Secretary" for "Secretary or his delegate" in subsec. (a), effective 2/1/77.

CHAPTER 71.—TRANSFEREES AND FIDUCIARIES

Sec.
6901. Transferred assets.
6902. Provisions of special application to transferees.
6903. Notice of fiduciary relationship.
6904. Prohibition of injunctions.
6905. Discharge of executor from personal liability for decedent's income and gift taxes.

In **1970**, P.L. 91-614, Sec. 101(e)(2), added item 6905.

Sec. 6901. Transferred assets.

(a) Method of collection.

The amounts of the following liabilities shall, except as hereinafter in this section provided, be assessed, paid, and collected in the same manner and subject to the same provisions and limitations as in the case of the taxes with respect to which the liabilities were incurred:

(1) Income, estate, and gift taxes.
  (A) Transferees. The liability, at law or in equity, of a transferee of property—
    (i) of a taxpayer in the case of a tax imposed by subtitle A (relating to income taxes),
    (ii) of a decedent in the case of a tax imposed by chapter 11 (relating to estate taxes), or
    (iii) of a donor in the case of a tax imposed by chapter 12 (relating to gift taxes),
  in respect of the tax imposed by subtitle A or B.
  (B) Fiduciaries. The liability of a fiduciary under section 3713(b) of title 31, United States Code in respect of the payment of any tax described in subparagraph (A) from the estate of the taxpayer, the decedent, or the donor, as the case may be.

(2) Other taxes. The liability, at law or in equity of a transferee of property of any person liable in respect of any tax imposed by this title (other than a tax imposed by subtitle A or B), but only if such liability arises on the liquidation of a partnership or corporation, or on a reorganization within the meaning of section 368(a).

(b) Liability.
Any liability referred to in subsection (a) may be either as to the amount of tax shown on a return or as to any deficiency or underpayment of any tax.

(c) Period of limitations.
The period of limitations for assessment of any such liability of a transferee or a fiduciary shall be as follows:

(1) Initial transferee. In the case of the liability of an initial transferee, within 1 year after the expiration of the period of limitation for assessment against the transferor;

(2) Transferee of transferee. In the case of the liability of a transferee of a transferee, within 1 year after the expiration of the period of limitation for assessment against the preceding transferee, but not more than 3 years after the expiration of the period of limitation for assessment against the initial transferor;

except that if, before the expiration of the period of limitation for the assessment of the liability of the transferee, a court proceeding for the collection of the tax or liability in respect thereof has been begun against the initial transferor or the last preceding transferee, respectively, then the period of limitation for assessment of the liability of the transferee shall expire 1 year after the return of execution in the court proceeding.

(3) Fiduciary. In the case of the liability of a fiduciary, not later than 1 year after the liability arises or not later than the expiration of the period for collection of the tax in respect of which such liability arises, whichever is the later.

(d) Extension by agreement.

(1) Extension of time for assessment. If before the expiration of the time prescribed in subsection (c) for the assessment of the liability, the Secretary and the transferee or fiduciary have both consented in writing to its assessment after such time, the liability may be assessed at any time prior to the expiration of the period agreed upon. The period so agreed upon may be extended by subsequent agreements in writing made before the expiration of the period previously agreed upon. For the purpose of determining the period of limitation on credit or refund to the transferee or fiduciary of overpayments of tax made by such transferee or fiduciary or overpayments of tax made by the transferor of which the transferee or fiduciary is legally entitled to credit or refund, such agreement and any extension thereof shall be deemed an agreement and extension thereof referred to in section 6511(c).

(2) Extension of time for credit or refund. If the agreement is executed after the expiration of the period of limitation for assessment against the taxpayer with reference to whom the liability of such transferee or fiduciary arises, then in applying the limitations under section 6511(c) on the amount of the credit or refund, the periods specified in section 6511(b)(2) shall be increased by the period from the date of such expiration to the date of the agreement.

(e) Period for assessment against transferor.
For purposes of this section, if any person is deceased, or is a corporation which has terminated its existence, the period of limitation for assessment against such person shall be the period that would be in effect had death or termination of existence not occurred.

(f) Suspension of running of period of limitations.
The running of the period of limitations upon the assessment of the liability of a transferee or fiduciary shall, after the mailing to the transferee or fiduciary of the notice provided for in section 6212 (relating to income, estate, and gift taxes), be suspended for the period during which the Secretary is prohibited from making the assessment in respect of the liability of the transferee or fiduciary (and in any event, if a proceeding in respect of the liability is placed on the docket of the Tax Court, until the decision of the Tax Court becomes final), and for 60 days thereafter.

(g) Address for notice of liability.
In the absence of notice to the Secretary under section 6903 of the existence of a fiduciary relationship, any notice of liability enforceable under this section required to be mailed to such person, shall, if mailed to the person subject to the liability at his last known address, be sufficient for purposes of this title, even if such person is deceased, or is under a legal disability, or, in the case of a corporation, has terminated its existence.

(h) Definition of transferee.
As used in this section, the term "transferee" includes donee, heir, legatee, devisee, and distributee, and with respect to estate taxes, also includes any person who, under section 6324(a)(2), is personally liable for any part of such tax.

(i) Extension of time.
For extensions of time by reason of armed service in a combat zone, see section 7508.

In 1982, P.L. 97-258, Sec. 3(f)(10), substituted "section 3713(b) of title 31, United States Code" for "section 3467 of the Revised Statutes (31 U.S.C. 192)" in subpara. (a)(1)(B), effective 9/13/82.
In 1976, P.L. 94-455, Sec. 1906(b)(13)(A), substituted "Secretary" for "Secretary or his delegate" each place it appeared in Code Sec. 6901, effective 2/1/77.

Sec. 6902. Provisions of special application to transferees.

(a) Burden of proof.
In proceedings before the Tax Court the burden of proof shall be upon the Secretary to show that a petitioner is liable as a transferee of property of a taxpayer, but not to show that the taxpayer was liable for the tax.

(b) Evidence.
Upon application to the Tax Court, a transferee of property of a taxpayer shall be entitled, under rules prescribed by the Tax Court, to a preliminary examination of books, papers, documents, correspondence, and other evidence of the taxpayer or a preceding transferee of the taxpayer's property, if the transferee making the application is a petitioner before the Tax Court for the redetermination of his liability in respect of the tax (including interest, additional amounts, and additions to the tax provided by law) imposed upon the tax-

payer. Upon such application, the Tax Court may require by subpoena, ordered by the Tax Court or any division thereof and signed by a judge, the production of all such books, papers, documents, correspondence, and other evidence within the United States the production of which, in the opinion of the Tax Court or division thereof, is necessary to enable the transferee to ascertain the liability of the taxpayer or preceding transferee and will not result in undue hardship to the taxpayer or preceding transferee. Such examination shall be had at such time and place as may be designated in the subpoena.

In 1976, P.L. 94-455, Sec. 1906(b)(13)(A), substituted "Secretary" for "Secretary or his delegate" in subsec. (a), effective 2/1/77.

Sec. 6903. Notice of fiduciary relationship.
(a) Rights and obligations of fiduciary.

Upon notice to the Secretary that any person is acting for another person in a fiduciary capacity, such fiduciary shall assume the powers, rights, duties, and privileges of such other person in respect of a tax imposed by this title (except as otherwise specifically provided and except that the tax shall be collected from the estate of such other person), until notice is given that the fiduciary capacity has terminated.

(b) Manner of notice.

Notice under this section shall be given in accordance with regulations prescribed by the Secretary.

In 1976, P.L. 94-455, Sec. 1906(b)(13)(A), substituted "Secretary" for "Secretary or his delegate" each place it appeared in Code Sec. 6903, effective 2/1/77.

Sec. 6904. Prohibition of injunctions.

For prohibition of suits to restrain enforcement of liability of transferee, or fiduciary, see section 7421(b).

Sec. 6905. Discharge of executor from personal liability for decedent's income and gift taxes.
(a) Discharge of liability.

In the case of liability of a decedent for taxes imposed by subtitle A or by chapter 12, if the executor makes written application (filed after the return with respect to such taxes is made and filed in such manner and such form as may be prescribed by regulations of the Secretary) for release from personal liability for such taxes, the Secretary may notify the executor of the amount of such taxes. The executor, upon payment of the amount of which he is notified, or 9 months after receipt of the application if no notification is made by the Secretary before such date, shall be discharged from personal liability for any deficiency in such tax thereafter found to be due and shall be entitled to a receipt or writing showing such discharge.

(b) Definition of executor.

For purposes of this section, the term "executor" means the executor or administrator of the decedent appointed, qualified, and acting within the United States.

(c) Cross reference.

For discharge of executor from personal liability for taxes imposed under chapter 11, see section 2204.

In 1976, P.L. 94-455, Sec. 1906(b)(13)(A), substituted "Secretary" for "Secretary or his delegate" each place it appeared in Code Sec. 6905, effective 2/1/77.
In 1970, P.L. 91-614, Sec. 101(e)(1), added Code Sec. 6905, effective for decedents dying after 12/31/70.
—P.L. 91-614, Sec. 101(f), substituted "9 months" for "1 year" in subsec. (a), effective for estates of decedents dying after 12/31/73.

CHAPTER 72.—LICENSING AND REGISTRATION
Subchapter
A. Licensing.
B. Registration.

Subchapter A.—Licensing
Sec.
7001. Collection of foreign items.

Sec. 7001. Collection of foreign items.
(a) License.

All persons undertaking as a matter of business or for profit the collection of foreign payments of interest or dividends by means of coupons, checks, or bills of exchange shall obtain a license from the Secretary and shall be subject to such regulations enabling the Government to obtain the information required under subtitle A (relating to income taxes) as the Secretary shall prescribe.

(b) Penalty for failure to obtain license.

For penalty for failure to obtain the license provided for in this section, see section 7231.

In 1976, P.L. 94-455, Sec. 1906(b)(13)(A), substituted "Secretary" for "Secretary or his delegate" each place it appeared in Code Sec. 7001, effective 2/1/77.

Subchapter B.—Registration
Sec.
7011. Registration—persons paying a special tax.
7012. Cross references.

Sec. 7011. Registration—persons paying a special tax.
(a) Requirement.

Every person engaged in any trade or business on which a special tax is imposed by law shall register with the Secretary his name or style, place of residence, trade or business, and the place where such trade or business is to be carried on. In case of a firm or company, the names of the several persons constituting the same, and the places of residence, shall be so registered.

(b) Registration in case of death or change of location.

Any person exempted under the provisions of section 4905 from the payment of a special tax, shall register with the Secretary in accordance with regulations prescribed by the Secretary.

In 1976, P.L. 94-455, Sec. 1906(b)(13)(A), substituted "Secretary" for "Secretary or his delegate" each place it appeared in Code Sec. 7011, effective 2/1/77.

Sec. 7012. Cross references.

(1) For provisions relating to registration in connection with firearms, see sections 5802, 5841, and 5861.
(2) For special rules with respect to registration by persons engaged in receiving wagers, see section 4412.
(3) For provisions relating to registration in relation to the taxes on gasoline and diesel fuel, see section 4101.
(4) For provisions relating to registration by dealers in distilled spirits, wines, and beer, see section 5124.
(5) For penalty for failure to register, see section 7272.
(6) For other penalties for failure to register with respect to wagering, see section 7262.

In 2005, P.L. 109-59, Sec. 11125(b)(9), redesignated paras. (4) and (5) as paras. (5) and (6), and added para. (4), effective 7/1/2008, but not for taxes imposed for periods before 7/1/2008.
In 1996, P.L. 104-188, Sec. 1702(b)(4)(A), substituted "taxes on gasoline and diesel fuel" for "production or importation of gasoline" in para. (3)... Sec. 1702(b)(4)(B), deleted para. (4) and redesignated paras. (5) and (6) as paras. (4) and (5), effective 12/1/90.
Prior to deletion, para. (4) read as follows:
"(4) For provisions relating to registration in relation to the manufacture or production of lubricating oils, see section 4101."
In 1976, P.L. 94-455, Sec. 1906(a)(39), amended Code Sec. 7012, effective 2/1/77.
Prior to amendment, Code Sec. 7012 read as follows:
"SEC. 7012. CROSS REFERENCES.
"(c) Firearms.

"For provisions relating to registration in connection with firearms, see sections 5802, 5841, and 5854.

"(f) For special rules with respect to registration by persons engaged in receiving wagers, see section 4412.

"(g) For provisions relating to registration in relation to the production or importation of gasoline, see section 4101.

"(h) For provisions relating to registration in relation to the manufacture or production of lubricating oils, see section 4101.

"(i) Penalty.

"(1) For penalty for failure to register, see section 7272.

"(2) For other penalties for failure to register with respect to wagering, see section 7262."

—P.L. 94-455, Sec. 1904(b)(8)(C), deleted subsec. (e), effective 2/1/77.
Prior to deletion subsec. (e) read as follows:
"(e) For provisions relating to registration in relation to the manufacture of white phosphorous matches, see section 4804(d)."

In 1970, P.L. 91-513, Sec. 1102(d), deleted subsecs. (a) and (b), effective 5/1/71.
Prior to deletion, subsecs. (a) and (b) read as follows:
"(a) Narcotic drugs.
"For provisions relating to registration in relation to narcotic drugs, see section 4722.
"(b) Marihuana.
"For provisions relating to registration in relation to marihuana, see section 4753."

In 1965, P.L. 89-44, Sec. 601(g), deleted subsec. (d) relating to registration in relation to the manufacturer of playing cards, with a cross reference to section 4455, effective 6/22/65.

In 1958, P.L. 85-475, Sec. 4(b)(7), redesignated subsec. (j) as (i) and deleted subsec. (i) which referred to section 4273, effective 8/1/58.

CHAPTER 73.—BONDS

Sec.
7101. Form of bonds.
7102. Single bond in lieu of multiple bonds.
7103. Cross references—other provisions for bonds.

Sec. 7101. Form of bonds.

Whenever, pursuant to the provisions of this title (other than section 7485), or rules or regulations prescribed under authority of this title, a person is required to furnish a bond or security—

(1) General rule. Such bond or security shall be in such form and with such surety or sureties as may be prescribed by regulations issued by the Secretary.

(2) United States bonds and notes in lieu of surety bonds. The person required to furnish such bond or security may, in lieu thereof, deposit bonds or notes of the United States as provided in section 9303 of title 31, United States Code.

In 1982, P.L. 97-258, Sec. 3(f)(11), substituted "section 9303 of title 31, United States Code" for "6 U.S.C. 15" in para. (2), effective 9/13/82.
In 1976, P.L. 94-455, Sec. 1906(b)(13)(A), substituted "Secretary" for "Secretary or his delegate" in para. (1), effective 2/1/77.
In 1972, P.L. 92-310, Sec. 230(b), substituted "section 7485" for "sections 7485 and 6803(a)(i)" in Code Sec. 7101, effective 6/6/72.

Sec. 7102. Single bond in lieu of multiple bonds.

In any case in which two or more bonds are required or authorized, the Secretary may provide for the acceptance of a single bond complying with the requirements for which the several bonds are required or authorized.

In 1976, P.L. 94-455, Sec. 1906(b)(13)(A), substituted "Secretary" for "Secretary or his delegate" in Code Sec. 7102, effective 2/1/77.

Sec. 7103. Cross references—other provisions for bonds.

(a) Extensions of time.

(1) For bond where time to pay tax or deficiency has been extended, see section 6165.

(2) For bond to stay collection of a jeopardy assessment, see section 6863.

(3) For bond to stay assessment and collection prior to review of a Tax Court decision, see section 7485.

(4) For a bond to stay collection of a penalty assessed under section 6672, see section 6672(b).

(5) For bond in case of an election to postpone payment of estate tax where the value of a reversionary or remainder interest is included in the gross estate, see section 6165.

(b) Release of lien or seized property.

(1) For the release of the lien provided for in section 6325 by furnishing the Secretary a bond, see section 6325(a)(2).

(2) For bond to obtain release of perishable goods which have been seized under forfeiture proceeding, see section 7324(3).

(3) For bond to release perishable goods under levy, see section 6336.

(4) For bond executed by claimant of seized goods valued at $100,000 or less, see section 7325(3).

(c) Miscellaneous.

(1) For bond as a condition precedent to the allowance of the credit for accrued foreign taxes, see section 905(c).

(2) For bonds relating to alcohol and tobacco taxes, see generally subtitle E.

In 1986, P.L. 99-514, Sec. 1566(c), substituted "$100,000" for "$1,000" in para. (b)(4), effective 10/22/86.

In 1978, P.L. 95-628, Sec. 9(b)(2), added para. (a)(4), effective for penalties assessed more than 60 days after 11/10/78.

In 1976, P.L. 94-528, Sec. 2(a), changed the effective date for amendments made by Sec. 1204(c)(10) of P.L. 94-455, from effective for action taken under Code Sec. 6851, 6861 or 6862 where the notice and demand take place after 12/31/76, to effective for action taken under Code Sec. 6851, 6861 or 6862 where the notice and demand take place after 2/28/77, see below.

—P.L. 94-455, Sec. 1204(c)(10), deleted para. (a)(4), effective [as amended by Sec. 2(a) of P.L. 94-528, see above] for action taken under Code Secs. 6851, 6861, or 6862, where the notice and demand takes place after 2/28/77.
Prior to deletion, para. (a)(4) read as follows:
"(4) For furnishing of bond where taxable year is closed by the Secretary or his delegate, see section 6851(e)."

—P.L. 94-455, Sec. 1906(a)(40), deleted subsec. (d), effective 2/1/77.
Prior to deletion, subsec. (d) read as follows:
"(d) Bonds required with respect to certain products.
"(1) For bond in case of articles taxable under subchapter B of chapter 37 processed for exportation without payment of the tax provided therein, see section 4513(c) [sic].
"(2) For bond in case of oleomargarine removed from the place of manufacture for exportation to a foreign country, see section 4593(b).
"(3) For requirement of bonds with respect to certain industries see—
"(A) section 4596 relating to a manufacturer of oleomargarine;
"(B) section 4814(c) relating to a manufacturer of process or renovated butter or adulterated butter;
"(C) [repealed]
"(E) section 4804(c) relating to a manufacturer of white phosphorous matches."
—P.L. 94-455, Sec. 1906(b)(13)(A), substituted "Secretary" for "Secretary or his delegate" in Code Sec. 7103, effective 2/1/77.

In 1974, P.L. 93-490, Sec. 3(b)(7), deleted subpara. (d)(3)(C), effective for filled cheese manufactured, imported, or sold after 10/26/74.
Prior to deletion, subpara. (d)(3)(C) read as follows:
"(C) section 4833(c) relating to a manufacturer of filled cheese;"

In 1972, P.L. 92-310, Sec. 230(c), deleted subsec. (e), effective 6/6/72.
Prior to deletion, subsec. (e) read as follows:
"(e) Personnel bonds."
"(1) For bonds of internal revenue personnel to insure faithful performance of duties, see section 7803(c)."
"(2) For jurisdiction of United States district courts, concurrently with the courts of the several States, in an action on the official bond of any internal revenue officer or employee, see section 7402(d)."
"(3) For bonds of postmasters to whom stamps have been furnished under section 6802(1), see section 6803(a)(1)."
"(4) For bonds in cases coming within the provisions of section 6802(2) or (3), relating to stamps furnished a designated depositary of the United States or State agent, see section 6803(b)(1)."

In 1970, P.L. 91-513, Sec. 1102(e), deleted subpara. (d)(3)(D), effective 5/1/71.
Prior to deletion, subpara. (d)(3)(D) read as follows:
"(D) section 4713(b) relating to a manufacturer of opium suitable for smoking purposes;".

In 1965, P.L. 89-44, Sec. 802(b)(3), deleted subpara. (d)(3)(F) which was a cross reference to section 4101 relating to a producer or importer of gasoline or a manufacturer or producer of lubricating oils subject to tax under chapter 32, effective for articles sold on or after 7/1/65.

CHAPTER 74.—CLOSING AGREEMENTS AND COMPROMISES

Sec.
7121. Closing agreements.
7122. Compromises.
7123. Appeals dispute resolution procedures.
7124. Cross references.

In 1998, P.L. 105-206, Sec. 3465(a)(2), deleted item 7123 and added items 7123 and 7124.
Prior to deletion, item 7123 read as follows:
"7123. Cross references."

Sec. 7121. Closing agreements.
(a) Authorization.

The Secretary is authorized to enter into an agreement in writing with any person relating to the liability of such person (or of the person or estate for whom he acts) in respect of any internal revenue tax for any taxable period.

(b) Finality.

If such agreement is approved by the Secretary (within such time as may be stated in such agreement, or later agreed to) such agreement shall be final and conclusive, and, except upon a showing of fraud or malfeasance, or misrepresentation of a material fact—

(1) the case shall not be reopened as to the matters agreed upon or the agreement modified by any officer, employee, or agent of the United States, and

(2) in any suit, action, or proceeding, such agreement, or any determination, assessment, collection, payment, abatement, refund, or credit made in accordance therewith, shall not be annulled, modified, set aside, or disregarded.

In 1976, P.L. 94-455, Sec. 1906(b)(13)(A), substituted "Secretary" for "Secretary or his delegate" each place it appeared in Code Sec. 7121, effective 2/1/77.

Sec. 7122. Compromises.
(a) Authorization.

The Secretary may compromise any civil or criminal case arising under the internal revenue laws prior to reference to the Department of Justice for prosecution or defense; and the Attorney General or his delegate may compromise any such case after reference to the Department of Justice for prosecution or defense.

(b) Record.

Whenever a compromise is made by the Secretary in any case, there shall be placed on file in the office of the Secretary the opinion of the General Counsel for the Department of the Treasury or his delegate, with his reasons therefor, with a statement of—

(1) The amount of tax assessed,

(2) The amount of interest, additional amount, addition to the tax, or assessable penalty, imposed by law on the person against whom the tax is assessed, and

(3) The amount actually paid in accordance with the terms of the compromise.

Notwithstanding the foregoing provisions of this subsection, no such opinion shall be required with respect to the compromise of any civil case in which the unpaid amount of tax assessed (including any interest, additional amount, addition to the tax, or assessable penalty) is less than $50,000. However, such compromise shall be subject to continuing quality review by the Secretary.

(c) Rules for submission of offers-in-compromise.

(1) **Partial payment required with submission.**

(A) Lump-sum offers.

(i) In general. The submission of any lump-sum offer-in-compromise shall be accompanied by the payment of 20 percent of the amount of such offer.

(ii) Lump-sum offer-in-compromise. For purposes of this section, the term "lump-sum offer-in-compromise" means any offer of payments made in 5 or fewer installments.

(B) Periodic payment offers.

(i) In general. The submission of any periodic payment offer-in-compromise shall be accompanied by the payment of the amount of the first proposed installment.

(ii) Failure to make installment during pendency of offer. Any failure to make an installment (other than the first installment) due under such offer-in-compromise during the period such offer is being evaluated by the Secretary may be treated by the Secretary as a withdrawal of such offer-in-compromise.

(2) **Rules of application.**

(A) Use of payment. The application of any payment made under this subsection to the assessed tax or other amounts imposed under this title with respect to such tax may be specified by the taxpayer.

(B) Application of user fee. In the case of any assessed tax or other amounts imposed under this title with respect to such tax which is the subject of an offer-in-compromise to which this subsection applies, such tax or other amounts shall be reduced by any user fee imposed under this title with respect to such offer-in-compromise.

(C) Waiver authority. The Secretary may issue regulations waiving any payment required under paragraph (1) in a manner consistent with the practices established in accordance with the requirements under subsection (d)(3).

(d) Standards for evaluation of offers.

(1) **In general.** The Secretary shall prescribe guidelines for officers and employees of the Internal Revenue Service to determine whether an offer-in-compromise is adequate and should be accepted to resolve a dispute.

(2) **Allowances for basic living expenses.**

(A) In general. In prescribing guidelines under paragraph (1), the Secretary shall develop and publish schedules of national and local allowances designed to provide that taxpayers entering into a compromise have an adequate means to provide for basic living expenses.

(B) Use of schedules. The guidelines shall provide that officers and employees of the Internal Revenue Service shall determine, on the basis of the facts and circumstances of each taxpayer, whether the use of the schedules published under subparagraph (A) is appropriate and shall not use the schedules to the extent such use would result in the taxpayer not having adequate means to provide for basic living expenses.

(3) **Special rules relating to treatment of offers.** The guidelines under paragraph (1) shall provide that—

(A) an officer or employee of the Internal Revenue Service shall not reject an offer-in-compromise from a low-income taxpayer solely on the basis of the amount of the offer,

(B) in the case of an offer-in-compromise which relates only to issues of liability of the taxpayer—

(i) such offer shall not be rejected solely because the Secretary is unable to locate the taxpayer's return or return information for verification of such liability; and

(ii) the taxpayer shall not be required to provide a financial statement, and

(C) any offer-in-compromise which does not meet the requirements of subparagraph (A)(i) or (B)(i), as the case may be, of subsection (c)(1) may be returned to the taxpayer as unprocessable.

(e) Administrative review.

The Secretary shall establish procedures—

(1) for an independent administrative review of any rejection of a proposed offer-in-compromise or installment agreement made by a taxpayer under this section or section 6159 before such rejection is communicated to the taxpayer; and

(2) which allow a taxpayer to appeal any rejection of such offer or agreement to the Internal Revenue Service Office of Appeals.

(f) Deemed acceptance of offer not rejected within certain period.

Any offer-in-compromise submitted under this section shall be deemed to be accepted by the Secretary if such offer is not rejected by the Secretary before the date which is 24 months after the date of the submission of such offer. For purposes of the preceding sentence, any period during which any tax liability which is the subject of such offer-in-compromise is in dispute in any judicial proceeding shall not be taken into account in determining the expiration of the 24-month period.

(f [(g)]) Frivolous submissions, etc.

Notwithstanding any other provision of this section, if the Secretary determines that any portion of an application for an offer-in-compromise or installment agreement submitted under this section or section 6159 meets the requirement of clause (i) or (ii) of section 6702(b)(2)(A), then the Secretary may treat such portion as if it were never submitted and such portion shall not be subject to any further administrative or judicial review.

In 2006, P.L. 109-432, Sec. 407(d), added subsec. (f) [sic (g)], effective for submissions made and issues raised after the date on which the Secretary first prescribes a list under Code Sec. 6702(c), as amended by Sec. 407(a) of P.L. 109-432.

—P.L. 109-222, Sec. 509(a), redesignated subsecs. (c) and (d) as subsecs. (d) and (e), and added subsec. (c) . . . Sec. 509(b)(1), substituted a comma for "; and" at the end of subpara. (d)(3)(A) [as redesignated by Sec. 509(a) of this Act, see above], substituted ", and" for the period at the end of subpara. (d)(3)(B) [as redesignated by Sec. 509(a) of this Act, see above], and added subpara. (d)(3)(C) . . . Sec. 509(b)(2), added subsec. (f), effective for offers-in-compromise submitted on and after the date which is 60 days after 5/17/2006.

In 1998, P.L. 105-206, Sec. 3462(a), added subsec. (c) . . . Sec. 3462(c)(1), added subsec. (d), effective for proposed offers-in-compromise and installment agreements submitted after 7/22/98.

In 1996, P.L. 104-168, Sec. 503(a), substituted "$50,000. However, such compromise shall be subject to continuing quality review by the Secretary." for "$500." in subsec. (b), effective 7/30/96.

In 1976, P.L. 94-455, Sec. 1906(b)(13)(A), substituted "Secretary" for "Secretary or his delegate" each place it appeared in Code Sec. 7122, effective 2/1/77.

Sec. 7123. Appeals dispute resolution procedures.

(a) Early referral to appeals procedures.

The Secretary shall prescribe procedures by which any taxpayer may request early referral of 1 or more unresolved issues from the examination or collection division to the Internal Revenue Service Office of Appeals.

(b) Alternative dispute resolution procedures.

(1) Mediation. The Secretary shall prescribe procedures under which a taxpayer or the Internal Revenue Service Office of Appeals may request non-binding mediation on any issue unresolved at the conclusion of—

(A) appeals procedures; or

(B) unsuccessful attempts to enter into a closing agreement under section 7121 or a compromise under section 7122.

(2) Arbitration. The Secretary shall establish a pilot program under which a taxpayer and the Internal Revenue Service Office of Appeals may jointly request binding arbitration on any issue unresolved at the conclusion of—

(A) appeals procedures; or

(B) unsuccessful attempts to enter into a closing agreement under section 7121 or a compromise under section 7122.

In 1998, P.L. 105-206, Sec. 3465(a)(1), added Code Sec. 7123, effective 7/22/98.
—P.L. 105-206, Sec. 3465(b) and (c), of this Act, reads as follows:

"(b) Appeals officers in each State. The Commissioner of Internal Revenue shall ensure that an appeals officer is regularly available within each State.

"(c) Appeals videoconferencing alternative for rural areas. The Commissioner of Internal Revenue shall consider the use of the videoconferencing of appeals conferences between appeals officers and taxpayers seeking appeals in rural or remote areas."

Sec. 7124. Cross references.

For criminal penalties for concealment of property, false statement, or falsifying and destroying records, in connection with any closing agreement, compromise, or offer of compromise, see section 7206.

In 1998, P.L. 105-206, Sec. 3465(a)(1), redesignated Code Sec. 7123 as Code Sec. 7124, effective 7/22/98.
In 1982, P.L. 97-258, Sec. 3(f)(12), deleted "(a) Criminal penalties[.]" and repealed subsec. (b), effective 9/13/82.
Prior to repeal, subsec. (b) read as follows:
"(b) *Compromises after judgment.* For compromises after judgment, see R.S. 3469 (31 U.S.C. 194)."

CHAPTER 75.—CRIMES, OTHER OFFENSES, AND FORFEITURES

Subchapter

A. Crimes.

B. Other offenses.

C. Forfeitures.

D. Miscellaneous penalty and forfeiture provisions.

Subchapter A.—Crimes

Part

I. General provisions.

II. Penalties applicable to certain taxes.

PART I.—GENERAL PROVISIONS

Sec.

7201. Attempt to evade or defeat tax.

7202. Willful failure to collect or pay over tax.

7203. Willful failure to file return, supply information, or pay tax.

7204. Fraudulent statement or failure to make statement to employees.

7205. Fraudulent withholding exemption certificate or failure to supply information.

7206. Fraud and false statements.

7207. Fraudulent returns, statements, or other documents.

7208. Offenses relating to stamps.

7209. Unauthorized use or sale of stamps.

7210. Failure to obey summons.

7211. False statements to purchasers or lessees relating to tax.

7212. Attempts to interfere with administration of internal revenue laws.

7213. Unauthorized disclosure of information.

Part I   Closing agreements, compromises

7213A. Unauthorized inspection of returns or return information.
7214. Offenses by officers and employees of the United States.
7215. Offenses with respect to collected taxes.
7216. Disclosure or use of information by preparers of returns.
7217. Prohibition on executive branch influence over taxpayer audits and other investigations.
7217. Repealed.

In **1998**, P.L. 105-206, Sec. 1105(b), added item 7217.
In **1997**, P.L. 105-35, Sec. 2(b)(2), added item 7213A
In **1982**, P.L. 97-248, Sec. 357(b)(2), deleted item 7217.
Prior to deletion item 7217 read as follows:
"7217. Civil damages for unauthorized disclosure of returns and return information."
In **1976**, P.L. 94-455, Sec. 1202(e)(2), added item 7217.
In **1971**, P.L. 92-178, Sec. 316(b), added item 7216.
In **1958**, added item 7215. (Chapter 78 is effective as set forth in Code Sec. 7851(a)(6)).

Sec. 7201. Attempt to evade or defeat tax.

Any person who willfully attempts in any manner to evade or defeat any tax imposed by this title or the payment thereof shall, in addition to other penalties provided by law, be guilty of a felony and, upon conviction thereof, shall be fined not more than $100,000 ($500,000 in the case of a corporation), or imprisoned not more than 5 years, or both, together with the costs of prosecution.

In **1982**, P.L. 97-248, Sec. 329(a), substituted "$100,000 ($500,000 in the case of a corporation)" for "$10,000" in Code Sec. 7201, effective for offenses committed after 9/3/82.

Sec. 7202. Willful failure to collect or pay over tax.

Any person required under this title to collect, account for, and pay over any tax imposed by this title who willfully fails to collect or truthfully account for and pay over such tax shall, in addition to other penalties provided by law, be guilty of a felony and, upon conviction thereof, shall be fined not more than $10,000, or imprisoned not more than 5 years, or both, together with the costs of prosecution.

Sec. 7203. Willful failure to file return, supply information, or pay tax.

Any person required under this title to pay any estimated tax or tax, or required by this title or by regulations made under authority thereof to make a return, keep any records, or supply any information, who willfully fails to pay such estimated tax or tax, make such return, keep such records, or supply such information, at the time or times required by law or regulations, shall, in addition to other penalties provided by law, be guilty of a misdemeanor and, upon conviction thereof, shall be fined not more than $25,000 ($100,000 in the case of a corporation), or imprisoned not more than 1 year, or both, together with the costs of prosecution. In the case of any person with respect to whom there is a failure to pay any estimated tax, this section shall not apply to such person with respect to such failure if there is no addition to tax under section 6654 or 6655 with respect to such failure. In the case of a willful violation of any provision of section 6050I, the first sentence of this section shall be applied by substituting "felony" for "misdemeanor" and "5 years" for "1 year".

In **1990**, P.L. 101-647, Sec. 3303(a), substituted "by substituting 'felony' for "by substituting" in the last sentence of Code Sec. 7203, effective for actions and failures to act occurring after 11/29/90.
In **1988**, P.L. 100-690, Sec. 7601(a)(2)(B), added the last sentence of Code Sec. 7203, effective for actions after 11/18/88.

In **1984**, P.L. 98-369, Sec. 412(b)(9), deleted "(other than a return required under authority of section 6015)" after "to make a return" in Code Sec. 7203, effective for tax. yrs. begin. after 12/31/84.
In **1982**, P.L. 97-248, Sec. 327, added the last sentence to Code Sec. 7203, effective 9/3/82.
—P.L. 97-248, Sec. 329(b), substituted "$25,000 ($100,000 in the case of a corporation)" for "$10,000" in Code Sec. 7203, effective for offenses committed after 9/3/82.
In **1968**, P.L. 90-364, Sec. 103, deleted "or section 6016" at end of parenthetical phrase, effective for tax. yrs. begin, after 12/31/67. For special provision on effective date, see Sec. 104 of this Act, reproduced after Code Sec. 6425.

Sec. 7204. Fraudulent statement or failure to make statement to employees.

In lieu of any other penalty provided by law (except the penalty provided by section 6674) any person required under the provisions of section 6051 to furnish a statement who willfully furnishes a false or fraudulent statement or who willfully fails to furnish a statement in the manner, at the time, and showing the information required under section 6051, or regulations prescribed thereunder, shall, for each such offense, upon conviction thereof, be fined not more than $1,000, or imprisoned not more than 1 year, or both.

Sec. 7205. Fraudulent withholding exemption certificate or failure to supply information.

(a) Withholding on wages.

Any individual required to supply information to his employer under section 3402 who willfully supplies false or fraudulent information, or who willfully fails to supply information thereunder which would require an increase in the tax to be withheld under section 3402, shall, in addition to any other penalty provided by law, upon conviction thereof, be fined not more than $1,000, or imprisoned not more than 1 year, or both.

(b) Backup withholding on interest and dividends.

If any individual willfully makes a false certification under paragraph (1) or (2)(C) of section 3406(d), then such individual shall, in addition to any other penalty provided by law, upon conviction thereof, be fined not more than $1,000, or imprisoned not more than 1 year, or both.

In **1989**, P.L. 101-239, Sec. 7711(b)(2), amended subsec. (b), effective for returns and statements the due date for which (determined without regard to extensions) is after 12/31/89.
Prior to amendment subsec. (b) read as follows:
"(b) Backup withholding on interest and dividends.
"If any individual willfully makes—
"(1) any false certification or affirmation on any statement required by a payor in order to meet the due diligence requirements of section 6676(b), or
"(2) a false certification under paragraph (1) or (2)(C) of section 3406(d),
then such individual shall, in addition to any other penalty provided by law, upon conviction thereof, be fined not more than $1,000, or imprisoned not more than 1 year, or both."
In **1984**, P.L. 98-369, Sec. 159(a)(1), and (2), substituted "in addition to" for "in lieu of" each place it appeared in Code Sec. 7205, and deleted "(except the penalty provided by section 6682)" each place it appeared in Code Sec. 7205, effective for actions and failures to act occurring after 7/18/84.
In **1983**, P.L. 98-67, Sec. 107(b)(1), substituted "(a) Withholding on wages. Any individual" for "Any individual" in Code Sec. 7205 . . . Sec. 107(b)(2), added subsec. (b), effective 8/5/83.
In **1981**, P.L. 97-34, Sec. 721(b), substituted "$1,000" for "$500" in Code Sec. 7205, effective for acts and failures to act after 12/31/81.
In **1966**, P.L. 89-368, Sec. 101(e)(5), substituted "3402" for "3402(f)", and substituted "other penalty provided by law (except the penalty provided in section 6682)" for "penalty otherwise provided." in Code Sec. 7205, effective for remuneration paid after 4/30/66.

Sec. 7206. Fraud and false statements.

Any person who—

(1) Declaration under penalties of perjury. Willfully makes and subscribes any return, statement, or other document, which contains or is verified by a written declaration that it is made under the penalties of perjury, and which he does not believe to be true and correct as to every material matter; or

(2) Aid or assistance. Willfully aids or assists in, or procures, counsels, or advises the preparation or presentation under, or in connection with any matter arising under, the internal revenue laws, of a return, affidavit, claim, or other document, which is fraudulent or is false as to any material matter, whether or not such falsity or fraud is with the knowledge or consent of the person authorized or required to present such return, affidavit, claim, or document; or

(3) Fraudulent bonds, permits, and entries. Simulates or falsely or fraudulently executes or signs any bond, permit, entry, or other document required by the provisions of the internal revenue laws, or by any regulation made in pursuance thereof, or procures the same to be falsely or fraudulently executed, or advises, aids in, or connives at such execution thereof; or

(4) Removal or concealment with intent to defraud. Removes, deposits, or conceals, or is concerned in removing, depositing, or concealing, any goods or commodities for or in respect whereof any tax is or shall be imposed, or any property upon which levy is authorized by section 6331, with intent to evade or defeat the assessment or collection of any tax imposed by this title; or

(5) Compromises and closing agreements. In connection with any compromise under section 7122, or offer of such compromise, or in connection with any closing agreement under section 7121, or offer to enter into any such agreement, willfully—

  (A) Concealment of property. Conceals from any officer or employee of the United States any property belonging to the estate of a taxpayer or other person liable in respect of the tax, or

  (B) Withholding, falsifying, and destroying records. Receives, withholds, destroys, mutilates, or falsifies any book, document, or record, or makes any false statement, relating to the estate or financial condition of the taxpayer or other person liable in respect of the tax;

shall be guilty of a felony and, upon conviction thereof, shall be fined not more than $100,000 ($500,000 in the case of a corporation), or imprisoned not more than 3 years, or both, together with the costs of prosecution.

In 1982, P.L. 97-248, Sec. 329(c), substituted "$100,000 ($500,000 in the case of a corporation)" for "$5,000" in Code Sec. 7206, effective for offenses committed after 9/3/82.

Sec. 7207. Fraudulent returns, statements, or other documents.

Any person who willfully delivers or discloses to the Secretary any list, return, account, statement, or other document, known by him to be fraudulent or to be false as to any material matter, shall be fined not more than $10,000 ($50,000 in the case of a corporation), or imprisoned not more than 1 year, or both. Any person required pursuant to section 6047(b), section 6104(d), or subsection (i) or (j) of section 527 to furnish any information to the Secretary or any other person who willfully furnishes to the Secretary or such other person any information known by him to be fraudulent or to be false as to any material matter shall be fined not more than $10,000 ($50,000 in the case of a corporation), or imprisoned not more than 1 year, or both.

In 2002, P.L. 107-276, Sec. 6(d), substituted "pursuant to section 6047(b), section 6104(d); or subsection (i) or (j) of section 527" for "pursuant to subsection (b) of section 6047 or pursuant to subsection (d) of section 6104" in Code Sec. 7207, effective for reports and notices required to be filed on or after 11/2/2002.

In 1998, P.L. 105-277, Sec. 1004(b)(2)(E), deleted "or (e)" after "subsection (d)" in Code Sec. 7207, effective as provided in Sec. 1004(b)(3), of this Act, which reads as follows:

  "(3) Effective date.

  "(A) In general. Except as provided in subparagraph (B), the amendments made by this subsection shall apply to requests made after the later of December 31, 1998, or the 60th day after the Secretary of the Treasury first issues the regulations referred to in section 6104(d)(4) of the Internal Revenue Code of 1986, as amended by this section.

  "(B) Publication of annual returns. Section 6104(d) of such Code, as in effect before the amendments made by this subsection, shall not apply to any return the due date for which is after the date such amendments take effect under subparagraph (A)."

In 1987, P.L. 100-203, Sec. 10704(c), substituted "subsection (d) or (e) of section 6104" for "subsection (d) of section 6104", effective as provided in Sec. 10704(d) which reads:

  "(1) to returns for years beginning after December 31, 1986, and

  "(2) on and after the date of the enactment of this Act in the case of applications submitted to the Internal Revenue Service—

  "(A) after July 15, 1987, or

  "(B) on or before July 15, 1987, if the organization has a copy of the application on July 15, 1987."

In 1984, P.L. 98-369, Sec. 491(d)(51), deleted "or (c)" after "pursuant to subsection (b)" in Code Sec. 7207, effective for obligations issued after 12/31/83.

In 1982, P.L. 97-248, Sec. 329(d), substituted "$10,000 ($50,000 in the case of a corporation)" for "$1,000" each place it appeared in Code Sec. 7207, effective for offenses committed after 9/3/82.

In 1980, P.L. 96-603, Sec. 1(d)(5), substituted "subsection (b) or (c) of section 6047 or pursuant to subsection (d) of section 6104" for "sections 6047(b) or (c), 6056, or 6104(d)", effective for tax. yrs. begin. after 12/31/80.

In 1976, P.L. 94-455, Sec. 1906(b)(13)(A), substituted "Secretary" for "Secretary or his delegate" in Code Sec. 7207, effective 2/1/77.

In 1969, P.L. 91-172, Sec. 101(e)(5), substituted "sections 6047(b) or (c), 6056, or 6104(d)" for "section 6047(b) or (c)", effective 1/1/70.

In 1962, P.L. 87-792, Sec. 7(m)(3), inserted sentence providing that any person required pursuant to section 6047(b) or (c) to furnish any information to the Secretary or any other person who willfully furnishes to the Secretary or such other person any information known by him to be fraudulent or to be false as to any material matter shall be fined not more than $1,000, or imprisoned not more than 1 year, or both, effective for tax. yrs. begin. after 12/31/62.

Sec. 7208. Offenses relating to stamps.

Any person who—

(1) Counterfeiting. With intent to defraud, alters, forges, makes, or counterfeits any stamp, coupon, ticket, book, or other device prescribed under authority of this title for the collection or payment of any tax imposed by this title, or sells, lends, or has in his possession any such altered, forged, or counterfeited stamp, coupon, ticket, book, or other device, or makes, uses, sells, or has in his possession any material in imitation of the material used in the manufacture of such stamp, coupon, ticket, book, or other device; or

(2) Mutilation or removal. Fraudulently cuts, tears, or removes from any vellum, parchment, paper, instrument, writing, package, or article, upon which any tax is imposed by this title, any adhesive stamp or the impression of any stamp, die, plate, or other article provided, made, or used in pursuance of this title; or

(3) Use of mutilated, insufficient, or counterfeited stamps. Fraudulently uses, joins, fixes, or places to, with, or upon any vellum, parchment, paper, instrument, writing, package, or article, upon which any tax is imposed by this title,

  (A) any adhesive stamp, or the impression of any stamp, die, plate, or other article, which has been cut, torn, or removed from any other vellum, parchment, paper, instrument, writing, package, or article, upon which any tax is imposed by this title; or

  (B) any adhesive stamp or the impression of any stamp, die, plate, or other article of insufficient value; or

  (C) any forged or counterfeited stamp, or the impression of any forged or counterfeited stamp, die, plate, or other article; or

(4) Reuse of stamps.

  (A) Preparation for reuse. Willfully removes, or alters the cancellation or defacing marks of, or otherwise prepares, any adhesive stamp, with intent to use, or cause the same to be used, after it has already been used; or

(B) Trafficking. Knowingly or willfully buys, sells, offers for sale, or gives away, any such washed or restored stamp to any person for use, or knowingly uses the same; or

(C) Possession. Knowingly and without lawful excuse (the burden of proof of such excuse being on the accused) has in possession any washed, restored, altered stamp, which has been removed from any vellum, parchment, paper, instrument, writing, package, or article; or

(5) Emptied stamped packages. Commits the offense described in section 7271 (relating to disposal and receipt of stamped packages) with intent to defraud the revenue, or to defraud any person;

shall be guilty of a felony and, upon conviction thereof, shall be fined not more than $10,000, or imprisoned not more than 5 years, or both.

Sec. 7209.   Unauthorized use or sale of stamps.

Any person who buys, sells, offers for sale, uses, transfers, takes or gives in exchange, or pledges or gives in pledge, except as authorized in this title or in regulations made pursuant thereto, any stamp, coupon, ticket, book, or other device prescribed by the Secretary under this title for the collection or payment of any tax imposed by this title, shall, upon conviction thereof, be fined not more than $1,000, or imprisoned not more than 6 months, or both.

In 1976, P.L. 94-455, Sec. 1906(b)(13)(A), substituted "Secretary" for "Secretary or his delegate" in Code Sec. 7209, effective 2/1/77.

Sec. 7210.   Failure to obey summons.

Any person who, being duly summoned to appear to testify, or to appear and produce books, accounts, records, memoranda, or other papers, as required under sections 6420(e)(2), 6421(g)(2), 6427(j)(2), 7602, 7603, and 7604(b), neglects to appear or to produce such books, accounts, records, memoranda, or other papers, shall, upon conviction thereof, be fined not more than $1,000, or imprisoned not more than 1 year, or both, together with costs of prosecution.

In 1988, P.L. 100-647, Sec. 1017(c)(9), substituted "6421(g)(2)" for "6421(f)(2)" in Code Sec. 7210, effective for gasoline removed (as defined in Code Sec. 4082) after 12/31/87.

In 1986, P.L. 99-514, Sec. 1703(e)(2)(G), substituted "6427(j)(2)" for "6427(i)(2)" in Code Sec. 7210, effective for gasoline removed (as defined in Code Sec. 4082) after 12/31/87.

In 1984, P.L. 98-369, Sec. 911(d)(2)(G), substituted "6427(i)(2)" for "6427(h)(2)" in Code Sec. 7210, effective 8/1/84.

In 1983, P.L. 97-424, Sec. 515(b)(12), deleted "6424(d)(2)" after "6421(f)(2)" in Code Sec. 7210, effective for articles sold after 1/6/83.

In 1980, P.L. 96-223, Sec. 232(d)(4)(E), substituted "6427(h)(2)" for "6427(g)(2)" in Code Sec. 7210, effective 1/1/79.

In 1978, P.L. 95-599, Sec. 505(c)(5), substituted "6427(g)(2)" for "6427(f)(2)" in Code Sec. 7210, effective 1/1/79.

In 1976, P.L. 94-530, Sec. 1(c)(6), substituted "6427(f)(2)" for "6427(e)(2)" in Code Sec. 7210, effective 10/1/76.

In 1970, P.L. 91-258, Sec. 207(d)(9), added "6427(e)(2)" in Code Sec. 7210, effective 7/1/70.

In 1965, P.L. 89-44, Sec. 202(c)(4), added reference to section 6424(d)(2) of this title, effective 1/1/66.

In 1956, ch. 462, Sec. 208(d)(3), inserted reference to section 6421(f)(2) of this title, effective 6/29/56.

—ch. 160, Sec. 4(h), inserted reference to section 6420(e)(2) of this title.

Sec. 7211.   False statements to purchasers or lessees relating to tax.

Whoever in connection with the sale or lease, or offer for sale or lease, of any article, or for the purpose of making such sale or lease, makes any statement, written or oral—

(1) intended or calculated to lead any person to believe that any part of the price at which such article is sold or leased, or offered for sale or lease, consists of a tax imposed under the authority of the United States, or

(2) ascribing a particular part of such price to a tax imposed under the authority of the United States,

knowing that such statement is false or that the tax is not so great as the portion of such price ascribed to such tax, shall be guilty of a misdemeanor and, upon conviction thereof, shall be punished by a fine of not more than $1,000, or by imprisonment for not more than 1 year, or both.

Sec. 7212.   Attempts to interfere with administration of Internal Revenue laws.

(a) Corrupt or forcible interference.

Whoever corruptly or by force or threats of force (including any threatening letter or communication) endeavors to intimidate or impede any officer or employee of the United States acting in an official capacity under this title, or in any other way corruptly or by force or threats of force (including any threatening letter or communication) obstructs or impedes, or endeavors to obstruct or impede, the due administration of this title, shall, upon conviction thereof, be fined not more than $5,000, or imprisoned not more than 3 years, or both, except that if the offense is committed only by threats of force, the person convicted thereof shall be fined not more than $3,000, or imprisoned not more than 1 year, or both. The term "threats of force", as used in this subsection, means threats of bodily harm to the officer or employee of the United States or to a member of his family.

(b) Forcible rescue of seized property.

Any person who forcibly rescues or causes to be rescued any property after it shall have been seized under this title, or shall attempt or endeavor so to do, shall, excepting in cases otherwise provided for, for every such offense, be fined not more than $500, or not more than double the value of the property so rescued, whichever is the greater, or be imprisoned not more than 2 years.

Sec. 7213.   Unauthorized disclosure of information.

(a) Returns and return information.

(1) Federal employees and other persons. It shall be unlawful for any officer or employee of the United States or any person described in section 6103(n) (or an officer or employee of any such person), or any former officer or employee, willfully to disclose to any person, except as authorized in this title, any return or return information (as defined in section 6103(b)). Any violation of this paragraph shall be a felony punishable upon conviction by a fine in any amount not exceeding $5,000, or imprisonment of not more than 5 years, or both, together with the costs of prosecution, and if such offense is committed by any officer or employee of the United States, he shall, in addition to any other punishment, be dismissed from office or discharged from employment upon conviction for such offense.

(2) State and other employees. It shall be unlawful for any person (not described in paragraph (1)) willfully to disclose to any person, except as authorized in this title, any return or return information (as defined in section 6103(b)) acquired by him or another person under subsection (d), (i)(3)(B)(i) or (7)(A)(ii), (l)(6), (7), (8), (9), (10), (12), (15), (16), (19), (20) or (21), or (m)(2), (4), (5), (6), or (7) of section 6103 or under section 6104(c). Any violation of this paragraph shall be a felony punishable by a fine in any amount not exceeding $5,000, or imprisonment of not more than 5 years, or both, together with the costs of prosecution.

(3) Other persons. It shall be unlawful for any person to whom any return or return information (as defined in section 6103(b)) is disclosed in a manner unauthorized by this title thereafter willfully to print or publish in any manner not provided by law any such return or return information. Any violation of this paragraph shall be a felony punishable by a fine in any amount not exceeding $5,000, or imprisonment of not more than 5 years, or both, together with the costs of prosecution.

(4) Solicitation. It shall be unlawful for any person willfully to offer any item of material value in exchange for any return or return information (as defined in section 6103(b)) and to receive as a result of such solicitation any such return or return information. Any violation of this paragraph shall be a felony punishable by a fine in any amount not exceeding $5,000, or imprisonment of not more than 5 years, or both, together with the costs of prosecution.

(5) Shareholders. It shall be unlawful for any person to whom a return or return information (as defined in section 6103(b)) is disclosed pursuant to the provisions of section 6103(e)(1)(D)(iii) willfully to disclose such return or return information in any manner not provided by law. Any violation of this paragraph shall be a felony punishable by a fine in any amount not to exceed $5,000, or imprisonment of not more than 5 years, or both, together with the costs of prosecution.

(b) Disclosure of operations of manufacturer or producer.

Any officer or employee of the United States who divulges or makes known in any manner whatever not provided by law to any person the operations, style of work, or apparatus of any manufacturer or producer visited by him in the discharge of his official duties shall be guilty of a misdemeanor and, upon conviction thereof, shall be fined not more than $1,000, or imprisoned not more than 1 year, or both, together with the costs of prosecution; and the offender shall be dismissed from office or discharged from employment.

(c) Disclosures by certain delegates of Secretary.

All provisions of law relating to the disclosure of information, and all provisions of law relating to penalties for unauthorized disclosure of information, which are applicable in respect of any function under this title when performed by an officer or employee of the Treasury Department are likewise applicable in respect of such function when performed by any person who is a "delegate" within the meaning of section 7701(a)(12)(B).

(d) Disclosure of software.

Any person who willfully divulges or makes known software (as defined in section 7612(d)(1)) to any person in violation of section 7612 shall be guilty of a felony and, upon conviction thereof, shall be fined not more than $5,000, or imprisoned not more than 5 years, or both, together with the costs of prosecution.

(e) Cross references.

(1) Penalties for disclosure of information by preparers of returns. For penalty for disclosure or use of information by preparers of returns, see section 7216.

(2) Penalties for disclosure of confidential information. For penalties for disclosure of confidential information by any officer or employee of the United States or any department or agency thereof, see 18 U.S.C. 1905.

In **2010**, P.L. 111-148, Sec. 1414(d), substituted "(20), or (21)" for "or (20)" in para. (a)(2), effective 3/23/2010.

In **2006**, P.L. 109-280, Sec. 1224(b)(5), added "or under section 6104(c)" after "6103" in para. (a)(2), effective 8/17/2006 but not for requests made before 8/17/2006.

In **2003**, P.L. 108-173, Sec. 105(e)(4), substituted "(16), or (19)" for "or (16)" in para. (a)(2), effective 12/8/2003.

—P.L. 108-173, Sec. 811(c)(2)(C), substituted "(19), or (20)" for "or (19)" in para. (a)(2) [as amended by Sec. 105(e)(4) of this Act, see above], effective 12/8/2003.

In **2002**, P.L. 107-134, Sec. 201(c)(10), substituted "(i)(3)(B)(i) or (7)(A)(ii)," for "(i)(3)(B)(i)," in para. (a)(2), effective for disclosures made on or after 1/23/2002.

In **1998**, P.L. 105-206, Sec. 3413(b), redesignated subsec. (d) as (e) and added subsec. (d), effective for summonses issued, and software acquired, after 7/22/98. Sec. 3413(e)(2) of P.L. 105-206, provides:

"(2) Software protection. In the case of any software acquired on or before such date of enactment, the requirements of section 7612(a)(2) of the Internal Revenue Code of 1986 (as added by such amendments) shall apply after the 90th day after such date. The preceding sentence shall not apply to the requirement under section 7612(c)(2)(G)(ii) of such Code (as so added)."

In **1997**, P.L. 105-33, Sec. 11024(b)(8), substituted "(15), or (16)" for "or (15)," in para. (a)(2), effective 8/5/97.

—P.L. 105-35, Sec. 2(c), added "(5)," after "(m)(2), (4)," in para. (a)(2), effective for violations occurring on and after 8/5/97.

In **1996**, P.L. 104-168, Sec. 1206(b)(5), substituted "(12), or (15)" for "or (12)" in para. (a)(2), effective 7/30/96.

In **1991**, P.L. 102-164, Sec. 401(a), amended Sec. 2653(c) of P.L. 98-369, [as amended by Sec. 701(a) of P.L. 100-485, see below and as amended by Sec. 9402(a) of P.L. 100-203, see below,] the effective date for amendments made by Sec. 2653(b) of P.L. 98-369, so that the amendments are effective for refunds payable under Code Sec. 6402 after 12/31/85, rather than effective for refunds payable under Code Sec. 6402 after 12/31/85 and on or before 1/10/94.

In **1990**, P.L. 101-508, Sec. 5111(b)(3), substituted "(m)(2), (4), (6), or (7)" for "(m)(2), (4), or (6)" in para. (a)(2), effective 11/5/90.

In **1989**, P.L. 101-239, Sec. 6202(a)(1)(C), substituted "(10), or (12)" for "or (10)", in para. (a)(2), effective 12/19/89.

In **1988**, P.L. 100-647, Sec. 8008(c)(2)(B), substituted "(m)(2), (4), or (6)" for "(m)(2) or (4)" in para. (a)(2), effective for 11/10/88.

—P.L. 100-485, Sec. 701(a), amended Sec. 2653(c) of P.L. 98-369, [as amended by Sec. 9402(a) of P.L. 100-203, see below] the effective date for amendments made by Sec. 2653(b) of P.L. 98-369, so that the amendments are effective for refunds payable under Code Sec. 6402 after 12/31/85 and on or before 1/10/94 rather than effective for refunds payable under Code Sec. 6402 after 12/31/85 and before 7/1/88.

—P.L. 100-647, Sec. 701(b)(2)(C), substituted "(9) or (10)" for "(9), (10) or (11)" in para. (a)(2), effective 10/13/88.

In **1987**, P.L. 100-203, Sec. 9402(a), amended Sec. 2653(c) of P.L. 98-369, the effective date for amendments made by Sec. 2653(b) of P.L. 98-369, so that the amendments are effective for refunds payable under Code Sec. 6402 after 12/31/85 and before 7/1/88 rather than effective for refunds payable under Code Sec. 6402 after 12/31/85 and before 1/1/88, see below.

In **1984**, P.L. 98-378, Sec. 21(f)(5), substituted "(10), or (11)" for "or (10)" in para. (a)(2), effective for refunds payable under Code Sec. 6402 after 12/31/85.

—P.L. 98-369, Sec. 453(b)(4), substituted "8, or 9" for "or 8" in para. (a)(2), effective on the first day of the first calendar month which begins more than 90 days after 7/18/84.

—P.L. 98-369, Sec. 2653(b)(4), substituted "(l)(6), (7), (8), (9), or (10)" for "(l)(6), (7), (8), or (9)" in para. (a)(2), effective for refunds payable under Code Sec. 6402 after 12/31/85, [as amended by Sec. 401(a) of P.L. 102-164, Sec. 701(a) of P.L. 100-485, and Sec. 9402(a) of P.L. 100-203, see above].

In **1983**, P.L. 97-437, Sec. 2, added Sec. 3111(c)(2) of title 5, United States Code, which makes Code Sec. 7213(a) applicable to student interns of IRS. See note following Code Sec. 6103.

In **1982**, P.L. 97-365, Sec. 8(c)(2), substituted "(m)(2) or (4)" for "(m)(4)" in para. (a)(2), effective 10/25/82.

—P.L. 97-248, Sec. 356(b)(2), substituted "(d), (i)(3)(B)(i)," for "(d)" in para. (a)(2), effective 9/3/82.

In **1980**, P.L. 96-611, Sec. 11(a)(4)(A), substituted "(l)(6), (7), or (8)" for "(1)(6) or (7)" in the first sentence of para. (a)(2) as amended by Sec. 302(b) of P.L. 96-499, see below, effective 12/5/80.

—P.L. 96-499, Sec. 302(b), amended the first sentence of para. (a)(2), effective 12/5/80.

Prior to amendment the first sentence of para. (a)(2) read as follows:

"It shall be unlawful for any officer, employee, or agent, or former officer, employee, or agent, of any State (as defined in section 6103(b)(5)), any local child support enforcement agency, any educational institution, or any State food stamp agency (as defined in section 6103(1)(7)(C) [section 6103(i)(7)(c)]) willfully to disclose to any person, except as authorized in this title, any return or return information (as defined in section 6103(b)) acquired by him or another person under subsection (d), (1)(6) or (7), (m)(4)(B) or section 6103."

—P.L. 96-265, Sec. 408(a)(2)(D), substituted "subsection (d), (1)(6) or (7), or (m)(4)(B)" for "subsection (d), (1)(6), or (m)(4)(B)" in para. (a)(2), effective 6/9/80.

—P.L. 96-249, Sec. 127(a)(2)(D)(i), substituted "any educational institution, or any State food stamp agency (as defined in section 6103(1)(7)(C))" [reference should be to section 6103(i)(7)(C)] for "any education institution" . . . Sec. 127(a)(2)(D)(ii), substituted "subsection (d), (1)(6) or (7), [sic (i)(7)] or (m)(4)(B)" for "subsection (d), (1)(6), or (m)(4)(B)" in the first sentence of para. (a)(2), effective 5/26/80.

In **1978**, P.L. 95-600, Sec. 701(bb)(1)(C), substituted ", any local" for "or any local" in para. (a)(2), and added ", or any educational institution" after "enforce-

Code Sec. 7213 — Crimes and forfeitures

ment agency" in para. (a)(2), and substituted "subsection (d), (1)(6), or (m)(4)(B) of section 6103" for "section 6103(d) or (1)(6)" in para. (a)(2)... Sec. 701(bb)(6), substituted "willfully to disclose" for "to disclose" in paras. (a)(1), (a)(2) and (a)(5), and substituted "thereafter willfully to print or publish" for "to thereafter print or publish" in para. (a)(3), and substituted "willfully to offer" for "to offer" in para. (a)(4), effective 1/1/77.

In **1976,** P.L. 94-455, Sec. 1202(d), deleted subsec. (c), and redesignated subsecs. (d) and (e) as subsecs. (c) and (d), and amended subsec. (a), effective 1/1/77.

Prior to deletion, subsec. (c) read as follows:

"(c) Offenses relating to reproduction of documents.

"Any person who uses any film or photoimpression, or reproduction therefrom, or who discloses any information contained in any such film, photoimpression, or reproduction, in violation of any provision of the regulations prescribed pursuant to section 7513(b), shall be fined not more than $1,000, or imprisoned not more than 1 year, or both."

Prior to amendment subsec. (a) read as follows:

"(a) Income returns.

"(1) Federal employees and other persons. It shall be unlawful for any officer or employee of the United States to divulge or to make known in any manner whatever not provided by law to any person the amount or source of income, profits, losses, expenditures, or any particular thereof, set forth or disclosed in any income return, or to permit any income return or copy thereof or any book containing any abstract or particulars thereof to be seen or examined by any person except as provided by law; and it shall be unlawful for any person to print or publish in any manner whatever not provided by law any income return, or any part thereof or source of income, profits, losses, or expenditures appearing in any income return; and any person committing an offense against the foregoing provision shall be guilty of a misdemeanor and, upon conviction thereof, shall be fined not more than $1,000, or imprisoned not more than 1 year, or both, together with the costs of prosecution; and if the offender be an officer or employee of the United States he shall be dismissed from office or discharged from employment.

"(2) State employees. Any officer, employee, or agent of any State or political subdivision, who divulges (except as authorized in section 6103(b), or when called upon to testify in any judicial or administrative proceeding to which the State or political subdivision, or such State or local official, body, or commission, as such, is a party), or who makes known to any person in any manner whatever not provided by law, any information acquired by him through an inspection permitted him or another under section 6103(b), or who permits any income return or copy thereof or any book containing any abstract or particulars thereof, or any other information, acquired by him through an inspection permitted him or another under section 6103(b), to be seen or examined by any person except as provided by law, shall be guilty of a misdemeanor and, upon conviction thereof, shall be fined not more than $1,000, or imprisoned not more than 1 year, or both, together with the costs of prosecution.

"(3) Shareholders. Any shareholder who pursuant to the provisions of section 6103(c) is allowed to examine the return of any corporation, and who makes known in any manner whatever not provided by law letter or communication obstructs or impedes, or endeavors to obstruct or impede, the due administration of this title, shall, upon conviction thereof, be fined not more than $5,000, or imprisoned not more than 3 years, or both, except that if the offense is committed only by threats of force, the person convicted thereof shall be fined not more than $3,000, or imprisoned not more than 1 year, or both. The term 'threats of force', as used in this subsection, means threats of bodily harm to the officer or employee of the United States or to a member of his family."

—P.L. 94-455, Sec. 1202(h)(3), amended para. (d)(1), effective 1/1/77.

Prior to amendment para. (d)(1) read as follows:

"(1) Returns of Federal unemployment tax. For special provisions applicable to returns of tax under chapter 23 (relating to Federal Unemployment Tax), see section 6106."

In **1960,** P.L. 86-778, Sec. 103(s), added subsec. (d) and redesignated former subsec. (d) as (e), effective 9/13/60.

In **1958,** P.L. 85-866, Sec. 90(c), added subsec. (c) and redesignated former subsec. (c) as (d), effective 8/17/54.

Sec. 7213A. Unauthorized inspection of returns or return information.

(a) Prohibitions.

(1) Federal employees and other persons. It shall be unlawful for—

(A) any officer or employee of the United States, or

(B) any person described in subsection (l)(18) or (n) of section 6103 or an officer or employee of any such person,

willfully to inspect, except as authorized in this title, any return or return information.

(2) State and other employees. It shall be unlawful for any person (not described in paragraph (1)) willfully to inspect, except as authorized in this title, any return or return information acquired by such person or another person under a provision of section 6103 referred to in section 7213(a)(2) or under section 6104(c).

(b) Penalty.

(1) In general. Any violation of subsection (a) shall be punishable upon conviction by a fine in any amount not exceeding $1,000, or imprisonment of not more than 1 year, or both, together with the costs of prosecution.

(2) Federal officers or employees. An officer or employee of the United States who is convicted of any violation of subsection (a) shall, in addition to any other punishment, be dismissed from office or discharged from employment.

(c) Definitions.

For purposes of this section, the terms "inspect", "return", and "return information" have the respective meanings given such terms by section 6103(b).

In **2006,** P.L. 109-280, Sec. 1224(b)(6), added "or under section 6104(c)" after "7213(a)(2)" in para. (a)(2), effective 8/17/2006 but not for requests made before 8/17/2006.

In **2002,** P.L. 107-210, Sec. 202(b)(3), substituted "subsection (l)(18) or (n) of section 6103" for "section 6103(n)" in subpara. (a)(1)(B), effective 8/6/2002.

In **1997,** P.L. 105-35, Sec. 2(a), added Code Sec. 7213A, effective for violations occurring on and after 8/5/97.

Sec. 7214. Offenses by officers and employees of the United States.

(a) Unlawful acts of revenue officers or agents.

Any officer or employee of the United States acting in connection with any revenue law of the United States—

(1) who is guilty of any extortion or willful oppression under color of law; or

(2) who knowingly demands other or greater sums than are authorized by law, or receives any fee, compensation, or reward, except as by law prescribed, for the performance of any duty; or

(3) who with intent to defeat the application of any provision of this title fails to perform any of the duties of his office or employment; or

(4) who conspires or colludes with any other person to defraud the United States; or

(5) who knowingly makes opportunity for any person to defraud the United States; or

(6) who does or omits to do any act with intent to enable any other person to defraud the United States; or

(7) who makes or signs any fraudulent entry in any book, or makes or signs any fraudulent certificate, return, or statement; or

(8) who, having knowledge or information of the violation of any revenue law by any person, or of fraud committed by any person against the United States under any revenue law, fails to report, in writing, such knowledge or information to the Secretary; or

(9) who demands, or accepts, or attempts to collect, directly or indirectly as payment or gift, or otherwise, any sum of money or other thing of value for the compromise, adjustment, or settlement of any charge or complaint for any violation or alleged violation of law, except as expressly authorized by law so to do;

shall be dismissed from office or discharged from employment and, upon conviction thereof, shall be fined not more than $10,000, or imprisoned not more than 5 years, or both. The court may in its discretion award out of the fine so imposed an amount, not in excess of one-half thereof, for the use of the informer, if any, who shall be ascertained by the judgment of the court. The court also shall render judgment against the said officer or employee for the amount of damages sustained in favor of the party injured, to be collected by execution.

(b) Interest of internal revenue officer or employee in tobacco or liquor production.

Any internal revenue officer or employee interested, directly or indirectly, in the manufacture of tobacco, snuff, or cigarettes, or in the production, rectification, or redistillation of distilled spirits, shall be dismissed from office; and each such officer or employee so interested in any such manufacture or production, rectification, or redistillation or production of fermented liquors shall be fined not more than $5,000.

(c) Cross reference.

For penalty on collecting or disbursing officers trading in public funds or debts or property, see 18 U.S.C. 1901.

In **1976**, P.L. 94-455, Sec. 1906(b)(13)(A), substituted "Secretary" for "Secretary or his delegate" each place it appeared in Code Sec. 7214, effective 2/1/77.

In **1958**, P.L. 85-859, Sec. 204(5), eliminated a cross reference in subsec. (c) that related to penalty imposed for unlawfully removing or permitting to be removed distilled spirits from a bonded warehouse, effective on 9/3/58.

Sec. 7215. Offenses with respect to collected taxes.
(a) Penalty.

Any person who fails to comply with any provision of section 7512(b) shall, in addition to any other penalties provided by law, be guilty of a misdemeanor, and, upon conviction thereof, shall be fined not more than $5,000, or imprisoned not more than one year, or both, together with the costs of prosecution.

(b) Exceptions.

This section shall not apply—

(1) to any person, if such person shows that there was reasonable doubt as to (A) whether the law required collection of tax, or (B) who was required by law to collect tax, and

(2) to any person, if such person shows that the failure to comply with the provisions of section 7512(b) was due to circumstances beyond his control.

For purposes of paragraph (2), a lack of funds existing immediately after the payment of wages (whether or not created by the payment of such wages) shall not be considered to be circumstances beyond the control of a person.

In **1983**, P.L. 98-67, Sec. 102(a), repealed the amendment made by Sec. 307(a)(15) of P.L. 97-248, as if the amendment had never been enacted, except as provided in Sec. 102(c) and (d) reproduced in note following Code Sec. 3451.

Prior to the repeal of the amendment made by Sec. 307(a)(15) of P.L. 97-248, the last sentence of subsec. (b) read as follows:

"For purposes of paragraph (2), a lack of funds existing immediately after the payment of wages or amounts subject to withholding under subchapter B of chapter 24 (whether or not created by the payment of such wages or amounts) shall not be considered to be circumstances beyond the control of the person."

In **1982**, P.L. 97-248, Sec. 307(a)(15), amended the last sentence of subsec. (b), effective for payments of interest, dividends, and patronage dividends paid or credited after 6/30/83.

Prior to amendment, the last sentence subsec. (b) read as follows:

"For purposes of paragraph (2), a lack of funds existing immediately after the payment of wages (whether or not created by the payment of such wages) shall not be considered to be circumstances beyond the control of a person."

In **1958**, P.L. 85-321, Sec. 2, added section 7215, effective 2/12/58.

Sec. 7216. Disclosure or use of information by preparers of returns.

(a) General rule.

Any person who is engaged in the business of preparing, or providing services in connection with the preparation of, returns of the tax imposed by chapter 1, or any person who for compensation prepares any such return for any other person, and who knowingly or recklessly—

(1) discloses any information furnished to him for, or in connection with, the preparation of any such return, or

(2) uses any such information for any purpose other than to prepare, or assist in preparing, any such return,

shall be guilty of a misdemeanor, and, upon conviction thereof, shall be fined not more than $1,000, or imprisoned not more than 1 year, or both together with the costs of prosecution.

(b) Exceptions.

(1) Disclosure. Subsection (a) shall not apply to a disclosure of information if such disclosure is made—

(A) pursuant to any other provision of this title, or

(B) pursuant to an order of a court.

(2) Use. Subsection (a) shall not apply to the use of information in the preparation of, or in connection with the preparation of, State and local tax returns and declarations of estimated tax of the person to whom the information relates.

(3) Regulations. Subsection (a) shall not apply to a disclosure or use of information which is permitted by regulations prescribed by the Secretary under this section. Such regulations shall permit (subject to such conditions as such regulations shall provide) the disclosure or use of information for quality or peer reviews.

In **1989**, P.L. 101-239, Sec. 7739(a), added the last sentence to para. (b)(3), effective 12/19/89.

In **1988**, P.L. 100-647, Sec. 6242(b), added "knowingly or recklessly" after "and who" in subsec. (a), effective for disclosures or uses after 12/31/88.

—P.L. 100-647, Sec. 6242(b), added "knowingly or recklessly" after "and who" in subsec. (a), effective for disclosures or uses after 12/31/88.

In **1984**, P.L. 98-369, Sec. 412(b)(10)(A), deleted "or declarations or amended declarations of estimated tax under section 6015," after "imposed by chapter 1," in subsec. (a) . . . Sec. 412(b)(10)(B), substituted "return" for "return or declaration" each place it appeared in subsec. (a), effective for tax. yrs. begin. after 12/31/84.

In **1976**, P.L. 94-455, Sec. 1906(b)(13)(A), substituted "Secretary" for "Secretary or his delegate" in Code Sec. 7216, effective 2/1/77.

In **1971**, P.L. 92-178, Sec. 316(a), added Code Sec. 7216, effective 1/1/72.

Sec. 7217. Prohibition on executive branch influence over taxpayer audits and other investigations.

(a) Prohibition.

It shall be unlawful for any applicable person to request, directly or indirectly, any officer or employee of the Internal Revenue Service to conduct or terminate an audit or other investigation of any particular taxpayer with respect to the tax liability of such taxpayer.

(b) Reporting requirement.

Any officer or employee of the Internal Revenue Service receiving any request prohibited by subsection (a) shall report the receipt of such request to the Treasury Inspector General for Tax Administration.

(c) Exceptions.

Subsection (a) shall not apply to any written request made—

(1) to an applicable person by or on behalf of the taxpayer and forwarded by such applicable person to the Internal Revenue Service;

(2) by an applicable person for disclosure of return or return information under section 6103 if such request is made in accordance with the requirements of such section; or

(3) by the Secretary of the Treasury as a consequence of the implementation of a change in tax policy.

(d) Penalty.

Any person who willfully violates subsection (a) or fails to report under subsection (b) shall be punished upon conviction by a fine in any amount not exceeding $5,000, or imprisonment of not more than 5 years, or both, together with the costs of prosecution.

(e) Applicable person.

For purposes of this section, the term "applicable person" means—

(1) the President, the Vice President, any employee of the executive office of the President, and any employee of the executive office of the Vice President; and

(2) any individual (other than the Attorney General of the United States) serving in a position specified in section 5312 of title 5, United States Code.

In **1998**, P.L. 105-206, Sec. 1105(a), added Code Sec. 7217, effective for requests made after 7/22/98.

Sec. 7217. Repealed.

In **1982**, P.L. 97-248, Sec. 357(b)(1), repealed Code Sec. 7217, effective for disclosures made after 9/3/82.

Prior to repeal, Code Sec. 7217 read as follows:

"Sec. 7217. Civil damages for unauthorized disclosure of returns and return information.

"(a) General rule.

"Whenever any person knowingly, or by reason of negligence, discloses a return or return information (as defined in section 6103(b)) with respect to a taxpayer in violation of the provisions of section 6103, such taxpayer may bring a civil action for damages against such person, and the district courts of the United States shall have jurisdiction of any action commenced under the provisions of this section.

"(b) *No liability for good faith but erroneous interpretation.*

"No liability shall arise under this section with respect to any disclosure which results from a good faith, but erroneous, interpretation of section 6103.

"(c) *Damages.*

"In any suit brought under the provisions of subsection (a), upon a finding of liability on the part of the defendant, the defendant shall be liable to the plaintiff in an amount equal to the sum of—

"(1) actual damages sustained by the plaintiff as a result of the unauthorized disclosure of the return or return information and, in the case of a willful disclosure or a disclosure which is the result of gross negligence, punitive damages, but in no case shall a plaintiff entitled to recovery receive less than the sum of $1,000 with respect to each instance of such unauthorized disclosure; and

"(2) the costs of the action.

"(d) *Period for bringing action.*

"An action to enforce any liability created under this section may be brought, without regard to the amount in controversy, within 2 years from the date on which the cause of action arises or at any time within 2 years after discovery by the plaintiff of the unauthorized disclosure."

In **1978**, P.L. 95-600, Sec. 701(bb)(7)(A), redesignated subsecs. (b) and (c) as subsecs. (c) and (d) . . . Sec. 701(bb)(7)(B), added new subsec. (b) . . . Sec. 701(bb)(7)(C), added "Period for bringing action" to the beginning of subsec. (d), effective for disclosures made after 11/6/78.

In **1976**, P.L. 94-455, Sec. 1202(e)(1), added Code Sec. 7217, effective 1/1/77.

PART II.—PENALTIES APPLICABLE TO CERTAIN TAXES

Sec.

7231. Failure to obtain license for collection of foreign items.

7232. Failure to register or reregister under sectio 4101, false representations of registration status, etc.

7233 to 7239. Repealed

7240. Repealed [Officials investing or speculating in sugar]

7241. Repealed [Willful failure to furnish certain information regarding windfall profit tax on domestic crude oil]

In **2005**, P.L. 109-59, Sec. 11164(b)(4), added "or reregister" after "register" in item 7232.

In **1997**, P.L. 105-34, Sec. 1032(e)(12)(C), amended item 7232.

Prior to amendment, item 7232 read as follows:

"7232. Failure to register, or false statement by manufacturer or producer of gasoline, diesel fuel, or aviation fuel."

In **1996**, P.L. 104-188, Sec. 1704(t)(20)(B), deleted "lubricating oil" after "gasoline," in item 7232.

In **1990**, P.L. 101-508, Sec. 11801(c)(22)(D)(ii), deleted item 7240.

Prior to deletion, item 7240 read as follows:

"7240. Officials investing or speculating in sugar."

In **1988**, substituted ", lubricating oil, diesel fuel, or aviation fuel" for "or lubricating oil" in item 7232.

—P.L. 100-418, Sec. 1941(b)(3)(F), deleted item 7241.

Prior to deletion, item 7241 read as follows:

"7241. Willful failure to furnish certain information regarding windfall profit tax on domestic crude oil."

In **1980**, P.L. 96-223, Sec. 101(e)(2), added item 7241.

In **1965**, deleted "or give bond" after "register" in item 7232.

In **1964**, added item 7240.

Sec. 7231. Failure to obtain license for collection of foreign items.

Any person required by section 7001 (relating to collection of certain foreign items) to obtain a license who knowingly undertakes to collect the payments described in section 7001 without having obtained a license therefor, or without complying with regulations prescribed under section 7001, shall be guilty of a misdemeanor and, upon conviction thereof, shall be fined not more than $5,000, or imprisoned not more than 1 year, or both.

Sec. 7232. Failure to register or reregister under section 4101, false representations of registration status, etc.

Every person who fails to register or reregister as required by section 4101, or who in connection with any purchase of any taxable fuel (as defined in section 4083), or aviation fuel falsely represents himself to be registered as provided by section 4101, or who willfully makes any false statement in an application for registration or reregistration under section 4101, shall, upon conviction thereof, be fined not more than $10,000, or imprisoned not more than 5 years, or both, together with the costs of prosecution.

In **2005**, P.L. 109-59, Sec. 11164(b)(2)(A), added "or reregister" after "register" in Code Sec. 7232 . . . Sec. 11164(b)(2)(B), added "or reregistration" after "registration" in Code Sec. 7232 . . . Sec. 11164(b)(2)(C), added "or reregister" after "register" in the heading of Code Sec. 7232, effective for actions, or failures to act, after 8/10/2005.

In **2004**, P.L. 108-357, Sec. 863(b), substituted "$10,000" for "$5,000" in Code Sec. 7232, effective for penalties imposed after 12/31/2004.

In **1998**, P.L. 105-206, Sec. 6010(h)(2), substituted "gasoline, diesel fuel" for "gasoline, lubricating oil, diesel fuel" in Sec. 1032(e)(12)(A) of P.L. 105-34, see below.

In **1997**, P.L. 105-34, Sec. 1032(e)(12)(A), substituted "any taxable fuel (as defined in section 4083)" for "gasoline, diesel fuel" in Code Sec. 7232 [amended by Sec. 6010(h)(2) of 105-206, see above] . . . Sec. 1032(e)(12)(B), amended the heading of Code Sec. 7232, effective 7/1/98.

Prior to amendment, the heading of Code Sec. 7232 read as follows:

"SEC. 7232. FAILURE TO REGISTER, OR FALSE STATEMENT BY MANUFACTURER OR PRODUCER OF GASOLINE, DIESEL FUEL, OR AVIATION FUEL."

In **1996**, P.L. 104-188, Sec. 1704(t)(20)(A)(i), deleted "lubricating oil," after "of gasoline," in the heading of Code Sec. 7232 . . . Sec. 1704(t)(20)(A)(ii), deleted "lubricating oil," after "of gasoline," in Code Sec. 7232, effective 8/20/96.

In **1988**, P.L. 100-647, Sec. 3001(b)(3)(A), substituted, ", lubricating oil, diesel fuel, or aviation fuel" for "or lubricating oil" in Code Sec. 7232 . . . Sec. 3001(b)(3)(B), substituted ", lubricating oil, diesel fuel, or aviation fuel" for "or lubricating oil" in the heading of Code Sec. 7232, effective 1/1/89. Sec. 3001(c)(2) of this Act provides:

"(2) Refunds with interest for pre-effective date purchases.—

"(A) In general.— In the case of fuel—

"(i) which is purchased from a producer or importer during the period beginning on April 1, 1988, and ending on December 31, 1988,

"(ii) which is used (before the claim under this subparagraph is filed) by any person in a nontaxable use (as defined in section 6427(l)(2) of the 1986 Code), and

"(iii) with respect to which a claim is not permitted to be filed for any quarter under section 6427(i) of the 1986 Code,

the Secretary of the Treasury or the Secretary's delegate shall pay (with interest) to such person the amount of tax imposed on such fuel under section 4091 of the 1986 Code (to the extent not attributable to amounts described in section 6427(l)(3) of the 1986 Code) if claim therefor is filed not later than June 30, 1989. Not more than 1 claim may be filed under the preceding sentence and such claim shall not be taken into account under section 6427(i) of the 1986 Code. Any claim for refund filed under this paragraph shall be considered a claim for refund under section 6427(l) of the 1986 Code.

"(B) *Interest.*— The amount of interest payable under subparagraph (A) shall be determined under section 6611 of the 1986 Code except that the date of the overpayment with respect to fuel purchased during any month shall be treated as being the 1st day of the succeeding month. No interest shall be paid under this paragraph with respect to fuel used by any agency of the United States.

"(C) *Registration procedures required to be specified.*— Not later than the 30th day after the date of the enactment of this Act, the Secretary of the Treasury or the Secretary's delegate shall prescribe the procedures for complying with the requirements of section 4093(c)(3) of the 1986 Code (as added by this section)."

In **1965**, P.L. 89-44, Sec. 802(b)(4), deleted "or give bond" after "register" in both heading and text of Code Sec. 7032, after "registered" in the body of Code Sec. 7232, effective 7/1/65.

Crimes and forfeitures

Sec. 7240. Repealed.

In 1990, P.L. 101-508, Sec. 11801(c)(22)(D)(i), repealed Code Sec. 7240, effective 11/5/90 except as provided in Sec. 11821(b) of this Act, which reads as follows:

"*(b) Savings provision.*

"If—

"(1) any provision amended or repealed by this part applied to—

"(A) any transaction occurring before the date of the enactment of this Act [11/5/90],

"(B) any property acquired before such date of enactment [11/5/90], or

"(C) any item of income, loss, deduction, or credit taken into account before such date of enactment [11/5/90], and

"(2) the treatment of such transaction, property, or item under such provision would (without regard to the amendments made by this part) affect liability for tax for periods ending after such date of enactment [11/5/90],

nothing in the amendments made by this part shall be construed to affect the treatment of such transaction, property, or item for purposes of determining liability for tax for periods ending after such date of enactment [11/5/90]."

Prior to repeal, Code Sec. 7420 read as follows:

"SEC. 7240. OFFICIALS INVESTING OR SPECULATING IN SUGAR.

"Any person, while acting in any official capacity in the administration of chapter 37, relating to manufactured sugar, who invests or speculates in sugar or liquid sugar, contracts relating thereto, or the stock or membership interests of any association or corporation engaged in the production or manufacture of sugar or liquid sugar, shall be dismissed from office or discharged from employment and shall be guilty of a felony and, upon conviction thereof, be fined not more than $10,000, or imprisoned not more than 2 years, or both."

In 1976, P.L. 94-455, Sec. 1904(b)(6)(A), deleted "subchapter A of" after "the administration of" in Code Sec. 7240, effective 2/1/77.

Sec. 7241. Repealed.

In 1988, P.L. 100-418, Sec. 1941(b)(1), repealed Code Sec. 7241, effective for crude oil removed from the premises on or after 8/23/88.

Prior to repeal, Code Sec. 7241 read as follows:

"SEC. 7241. WILLFUL FAILURE TO FURNISH CERTAIN INFORMATION REGARDING WINDFALL PROFIT TAX ON DOMESTIC CRUDE OIL.

"Any person who is required under section 6050C (or regulations thereunder) to furnish any information or certification to any other person and who willfully fails to furnish such information or certification at the time or times required by law or regulations, shall, in addition to other penalties provided by law, be guilty of a misdemeanor and upon conviction thereof, shall be fined not more than $10,000, or imprisoned not more than 1 year, or both, together with the costs of prosecution."

In 1980, P.L. 96-223, Sec. 101(e)(1), added Code Sec. 7241, effective for periods after 2/29/80.

Subchapter B.—Other Offenses

Sec.
7261. Representation that retailers' excise tax is excluded from price of article.
7262. Violation of occupational tax laws relating to wagering—failure to pay special tax.
7268. Possession with intent to sell in fraud of law or to evade tax.
7269. Failure to produce records.
7270. Insurance policies.
7271. Penalties for offenses relating to stamps.
7272. Penalty for failure to register or reregister.
7273. Penalties for offenses relating to special taxes.
7275. Penalty for offenses relating to certain airline tickets and advertising.

In 2005, P.L. 109-59, Sec. 11164(b)(4), added "or reregister" after "register" in item 7272.

In 1970, P.L. 91-258, Sec. 203(c)(2), added item 7275.

Sec. 7261. Representation that retailers' excise tax is excluded from price of article.

Whoever, in connection with the sale or lease, or offer for sale or lease, of any article taxable under chapter 31, makes any statement, written or oral, in an advertisement or otherwise, intended or calculated to lead any person to believe that the price of the article does not include the tax imposed by chapter 31, shall on conviction thereof be fined not more than $1,000.

Sec. 7262. Violation of occupational tax laws relating to wagering—failure to pay special tax.

Any person who does any act which makes him liable for special tax under subchapter B of chapter 35 without having paid such tax, shall, besides being liable to the payment of the tax, be fined not less than $1,000 and not more than $5,000.

Sec. 7268. Possession with intent to sell in fraud of law or to evade tax.

Every person who shall have in his custody or possession any goods, wares, merchandise, articles, or objects on which taxes are imposed by law, for the purpose of selling the same in fraud of the internal revenue laws, or with design to avoid payment of the taxes imposed thereon, shall be liable to a penalty of $500 or not less than double the amount of taxes fraudulently attempted to be evaded.

Sec. 7269. Failure to produce records.

Whoever fails to comply with any duty imposed upon him by section 6018, 6036 (in the case of an executor), or 6075(a), or, having in his possession or control any record, file, or paper, containing or supposed to contain any information concerning the estate of the decedent, or, having in his possession or control any property comprised in the gross estate of the decedent, fails to exhibit the same upon request to the Secretary who desires to examine the same in the performance of his duties under chapter 11 (relating to estate taxes), shall be liable to a penalty of not exceeding $500, to be recovered, with costs of suit, in a civil action in the name of the United States.

In 1976, P.L. 94-455, Sec. 1906(b)(13)(A), substituted "Secretary" for "Secretary or his delegate" in Code Sec. 7269, effective 2/1/77.

Sec. 7270. Insurance policies.

Any person who fails to comply with the requirements of section 4374 (relating to liability for tax on policies issued by foreign insurers), with intent to evade the tax shall, in addition to other penalties provided therefor, pay a fine of double the amount of the tax.

In 1976, P.L. 94-455, Sec. 1904(b)(5)(A), substituted "liability for tax on policies issued by foreign insurers" for "the affixing of stamps on insurance policies, etc." in Code Sec. 7270, effective 2/1/77.

Sec. 7271. Penalties for offenses relating to stamps.

Any person who with respect to any tax payable by stamps—

(1) Failure to attach or cancel stamps, etc. Fails to comply with rules or regulations prescribed pursuant to section 6804 (relating to attachment, cancellation, etc., of stamps), unless such failure is shown to be due to reasonable cause and not willful neglect; or

(2) Instruments. Makes, signs, issues, or accepts, or causes to be made, signed, issued, or accepted, any instrument, document, or paper of any kind or description whatsoever without the full amount of tax thereon being duly paid; or

(3) Disposal and receipt of stamped packages. In the case of any container which is stamped, branded, or marked (whether or not under authority of law) in such manner as to show that the provisions of the internal revenue laws with respect to the contents or intended contents thereof have been complied with, and which is empty or contains any contents other than contents therein when the container was lawfully stamped, branded, or marked—

(A) Transfers or receives (whether by sale, gift, or otherwise) such container knowing it to be empty or to contain such other contents; or

(B) Stamps, brands, or marks such container, or otherwise produces such a stamped, branded, or marked container, knowing it to be empty or to contain such other contents;

shall be liable for each such offense to a penalty of $50.

In **1976**, P.L. 94-455, Sec. 1906(a)(41), deleted para. (2) and redesignated paras. (3) and (4) as paras. (2) and (3), effective 2/1/77.
Prior to deletion, para. (2) read as follows:
"(2) Manufacture or offer for sale. Manufactures or imports and sells, or offers for sale, or causes to be manufactured or imported and sold, or offered for sale, any playing cards, package, or other article without the full amount of tax being duly paid; or"

Sec. 7272. Penalty for failure to register or reregister.
(a) In general.

Any person (other than persons required to register under subtitle E, or persons engaging in a trade or business on which a special tax is imposed by such subtitle) who fails to register with the Secretary as required by this title or by regulations issued thereunder shall be liable to a penalty of $50 ($10,000 in the case of a failure to register or reregister under section 4101).

(b) Cross references.

For provisions relating to persons required by this title to register, see sections 4101, 4412, and 7011.

In **2005**, P.L. 109-59, Sec. 11164(b)(3)(A), added "or reregister" after "failure to register" in subsec. (a)... Sec. 11164(b)(3)(B), added "or reregister" after "register" in the heading of Code Sec. 7272, effective for actions, or failures to act, after 8/10/2005.
In **2004**, P.L. 108-357, Sec. 863(a), added "($10,000 in the case of a failure to register under section 4101)" after "$50" in subsec. (a), effective for penalties imposed after 12/31/2004.
In **1976**, P.L. 94-455, Sec. 1904(b)(8)(F), deleted "4804(d)," before "and 7011." in subsec. (b)... Sec. 1906(a)(42), deleted "4722, 4753," after "sections 4101, 4412," in subsec. (b)... Sec. 1906(a)(13)(A), substituted "Secretary" for "Secretary or his delegate" in Code Sec. 7272, effective 2/1/77.
In **1965**, P.L. 89-44, Sec. 601(h), eliminated from subsec. (b) reference to section 4455, effective 6/22/65.
In **1958**, P.L. 85-859, Sec. 204(7), excluded from subsec. (a) persons required to register under subtitle E and persons engaging in a trade or business on which a special tax is imposed by such subtitle;... Sec. 204(7), eliminated from subsec. (b) references to sections 5802 and 5841 of this title, effective 9/3/58.
— P.L. 85-475, Sec. 4(b)(8), deleted a reference to section 4273 from subsec. (b), effective 8/1/58.

Sec. 7273. Penalties for offenses relating to special taxes.

Any person who shall fail to place and keep stamps denoting the payment of the special tax as provided in section 6806 shall be liable to a penalty (not less than $10) equal to the special tax for which his business rendered him liable, unless such failure is shown to be due to reasonable cause. If such failure to comply with section 6806 is through willful neglect or refusal, then the penalty shall be double the amount above prescribed.

In **1968**, P.L. 90-618, Sec. 205, amended Code Sec. 7273, effective 10/22/68.
Prior to amendment, Code Sec 7273 read as follows:
"(a) General rule.
"Any person who shall fail to place and keep stamps denoting the payment of the special tax as provided in section 6806(a) or (b) (whichever is applicable) shall be liable to a penalty equal to the special tax for which his business rendered him liable (unless such failure is shown to be due to reasonable cause), but in no case shall said penalty be less than $10. Where the failure to comply with the provisions of section 6806(a) or (b) shall be through willful neglect or refusal then the penalty shall be double the amount above prescribed. Nothing in this subsection shall in any way affect the liability of any person for exercising or carrying on any trade, business, or profession or doing any act for the exercising, carrying on, or doing of which a special tax is imposed by law, without the payment thereof.
"(b) Failure to post or exhibit special wagering tax stamp.

"Any person who, through negligence, fails to comply with section 6806(c) relating to the posting or exhibiting of the special wagering tax stamp, shall be liable to a penalty of $50. Any person who, through willful neglect or refusal, fails to comply with section 6806(c) shall be liable to a penalty of $100."

Sec. 7275. Penalty for offenses relating to certain airline tickets and advertising.
(a) Tickets.

In the case of transportation by air all of which is taxable transportation (as defined in section 4262), the ticket for such transportation shall show the total of—

(1) the amount paid for such transportation, and

(2) the taxes imposed by subsections (a) and (b) of section 4261.

(b) Advertising.

In the case of transportation by air all of which is taxable transportation (as defined in section 4262) or would be taxable transportation if section 4262 did not include subsection (b) thereof, any advertising made by or on behalf of any person furnishing such transportation (or offering to arrange such transportation) which states the cost of such transportation shall—

(1) state such cost as the total of (A) the amount to be paid for such transportation, and (B) the taxes imposed by sections 4261(a), (b), and (c), and

(2) if any such advertising states separately the amount to be paid for such transportation or the amount of such taxes, shall state such total at least as prominently as the more prominently stated of the amount to be paid for such transportation or the amount of such taxes and shall describe such taxes substantially as: "user taxes to pay for airport construction and airway safety and operations."

(c) Penalty.

Any person who violates any provision of subsection (a) or (b) is, for each violation, guilty of a misdemeanor, and upon conviction thereof shall be fined not more than $100.

In **1984**, P.L. 98-369, Sec. 714(b), corrected Sec. 281A(b)(2) of P.L. 97-248 to be the effective date for changes made by Sec. 281A(b)(1) rather than Sec. 281A(a) of P.L. 97-248, see below.
In **1982**, P.L. 97-248, Sec. 281A(b)(1), amended subsec. (a), effective for transportation begin. after 7/3/82.
Prior to amendment, subsec. (a) read as follows:
"(a) Tickets.
"In the case of transportation by air all of which is taxable transportation (as defined in section 4262), the ticket for such transportation
"(1) shall show the total of (A) the amount paid for such transportation and (B) the taxes imposed by sections 4261(a) and (b), and
"(2) if the ticket shows amounts paid with respect to any segment of such transportation, shall comply with paragraph (1) with respect to such segments as well as with respect to the sum of the segments."
In **1971**, P.L. 91-680, Sec. 3(a), and (b), added "and" at the end of para. (a)(1), deleted para. (a)(2), redesignated para. (a)(3) as para. (a)(2), and substituted "paragraph (1)" for "paragraphs (1) and (2)" in subsec. (a), deleted "only" in para. (b)(1) and amended para. (b)(2), effective for transportation begin. after 6/30/70.
Prior to deletion, para. (a)(2) read as follows:
"(2) shall not show separately the amount paid for such transportation nor the amount of such taxes, and."
Prior to deletion, subsec. (b)(2) read as follows:
"(2) shall not state separately the amount to be paid for such transportation nor the amount of such taxes."
In **1970**, P.L. 91-258, Sec. 203(c), added Code Sec. 7275, effective for transportation begin. after 6/30/70.

Subchapter C. — Forfeitures
Part
  I. Property subject to forfeiture.
  II. Provisions common to forfeitures.

PART I. — PROPERTY SUBJECT TO FORFEITURE

Sec.
7301. Property subject to tax.
7302. Property used in violation of internal revenue laws.

Crimes and forfeitures — Code Sec. 7304

7303. Other property subject to forfeiture.
7304. Penalty for fraudulently claiming drawback.

Sec. 7301. Property subject to tax.

(a) Taxable articles.

Any property on which, or for or in respect whereof, any tax is imposed by this title which shall be found in the possession or custody or within the control of any person, for the purpose of being sold or removed by him in fraud of the internal revenue laws, or with design to avoid payment of such tax, or which is removed, deposited, or concealed, with intent to defraud the United States of such tax or any part thereof, may be seized, and shall be forfeited to the United States.

(b) Raw materials.

All property found in the possession of any person intending to manufacture the same into property of a kind subject to tax for the purpose of selling such taxable property in fraud of the internal revenue laws, or with design to evade the payment of such tax, may also be seized, and shall be forfeited to the United States.

(c) Equipment.

All property whatsoever, in the place or building, or any yard or enclosure, where the property described in subsection (a) or (b) is found, or which is intended to be used in the making of property described in subsection (a), with intent to defraud the United States of tax or any part thereof, on the property described in subsection (a) may also be seized, and shall be forfeited to the United States.

(d) Packages.

All property used as a container for, or which shall have contained, property described in subsection (a) or (b) may also be seized, and shall be forfeited to the United States.

(e) Conveyances.

Any property (including aircraft, vehicles, vessels, or draft animals) used to transport or for the deposit or concealment of property described in subsection (a) or (b), or any property used to transport or for the deposit or concealment of property which is intended to be used in the making or packaging of property described in subsection (a), may also be seized, and shall be forfeited to the United States.

In 1958, P.L. 85-859, Sec. 204(8), included in subsec. (e) property used to transport or for the deposit or concealment of property which is intended to be used in the making or packaging of property described in subsec. (a), effective 9/3/58.

Sec. 7302. Property used in violation of internal revenue laws.

It shall be unlawful to have or possess any property intended for use in violating the provisions of the internal revenue laws, or regulations prescribed under such laws, or which has been so used, and no property rights shall exist in any such property. A search warrant may issue as provided in chapter 205 of title 18 of the United States Code and the Federal Rules of Criminal Procedure for the seizure of such property. Nothing in this section shall in any manner limit or affect any criminal or forfeiture provision of the internal revenue laws, or of any other law. The seizure and forfeiture of any property under the provisions of this section and the disposition of such property subsequent to seizure and forfeiture, or the disposition of the proceeds from the sale of such property, shall be in accordance with existing laws or those hereafter in existence relating to seizures, forfeitures, and disposition of property or proceeds, for violation of the internal revenue laws.

Sec. 7303. Other property subject to forfeiture.

There may be seized and forfeited to the United States the following:

(1) Counterfeit stamps. Every stamp involved in the offense described in section 7208 (relating to counterfeit, reused, cancelled, etc., stamps), and the vellum, parchment, document, paper, package, or article upon which such stamp was placed or impressed in connection with such offense.

(2) False stamping of packages. Any container involved in the offense described in section 7271 (relating to disposal of stamped packages), and of the contents of such container.

(3) Fraudulent bonds, permits, and entries. All property to which any false or fraudulent instrument involved in the offense described in section 7207 relates.

In 1976, P.L. 94-455, Sec. 1904(b)(8)(G), deleted para. (6), effective 2/1/77. Prior to amendment, para. (6) read as follows:
"(6) White phosphorus matches.
"(A) All packages of white phosphorus matches subject to tax under subchapter B of chapter 39 and found without the stamps required by subchapter B of chapter 39.
"(B) All the white phosphorus matches owned by any manufacturer of white phosphorus matches, or any importer or exporter of matches, or in which he has any interest as owner if he shall omit, neglect, or refuse to do or cause to be done any of the things required by law in carrying on or conducting his business, or shall do anything prohibited by subchapter B of chapter 39, if there be no specific penalty or punishment imposed by any other provision of subchapter B of chapter 39 for the neglecting, omitting, or refusing to do, or for the doing or causing to be done, the thing required or prohibited."
—P.L. 94-455, Sec. 1904(b)(9)(D), deleted paras. (3), (4), and (5), and redesignated paras. (7) and (8) as paras. (2) and (3), effective 2/1/77.
Prior to amendment, paras. (3), (4), and (5), read as follows:
"(3) Offenses by manufacturer or importer of or wholesale dealer in oleomargarine or adulterated butter. All oleomargarine or adulterated butter owned by any manufacturer or importer of or wholesale dealer in oleomargarine or adulterated butter, or in which he has any interest as owner, if he shall knowingly or willfully omit, neglect, or refuse to do, or cause to be done, any of the things required by law in the carrying on or conducting of his business, or if he shall do anything prohibited by subchapter F of chapter 38, or subchapter C of chapter 39.
"(4) Purchase or receipt of adulterated butter. All articles of adulterated butter (or the full value thereof) knowingly purchased or received by any person from any manufacturer or importer who has not paid the special tax provided in section 4821.
"(5) Packages of oleomargarine. All packages of oleomargarine subject to the tax under subchapter F of chapter 38 that shall be found without the stamps or marks provided for in that chapter."
In 1974, P.L. 93-490, Sec. 3(b)(5), amended paras. (4) and (5), effective for filled cheese manufactured, imported, or sold after 10/26/74.
Prior to amendment, paras. (4) and (5) read as follows:
"(4) Purchase or receipt of filled cheese or adulterated butter. All articles of filled cheese or adulterated butter (or the full value thereof) knowingly purchased or received by any person from any manufacturer or importer who has not paid the special tax provided in section 4821 or 4841.
"(5) Packages of oleomargarine or filled cheese. All packages of oleomargarine or filled cheese subject to the tax under subchapter F of chapter 38, or part II of subchapter C of chapter 39, whichever is applicable, that shall be found without the stamps or marks provided for in the applicable subchapter or part thereof."
In 1958, P.L. 85-881, Sec. 1(c), deleted para. (2), effective 9/2/58.
Prior to deletion, para. (2) read as follows:
"(2) Oleomargarine and filled cheese. Any oleomargarine, filled cheese, or adulterated butter, intended for human consumption which contains any ingredient adjudged, as provided in section 4817, 4818, or 4835, whichever is applicable, to be deleterious to the public health."

Sec. 7304. Penalty for fraudulently claiming drawback.

Whenever any person fraudulently claims or seeks to obtain an allowance of drawback on goods, wares, or merchandise on which no internal tax shall have been paid, or fraudulently claims any greater allowance of drawback than the tax actually paid, he shall forfeit triple the amount wrongfully or fraudulently claimed or sought to be obtained, or the sum of $500, at the election of the Secretary.

In 1976, P.L. 94-455, Sec. 1906(b)(13)(A), substituted "Secretary" for "Secretary or his delegate" in Code Sec. 7304, effective 2/1/77.

PART II.—PROVISIONS COMMON TO FORFEITURES
Sec.
7321. Authority to seize property subject to forfeiture.
7322. Delivery of seized personal property to United States marshal.
7323. Judicial action to enforce forfeiture.
7324. Special disposition of perishable goods.
7325. Personal property valued at $100,000 or less.
7326. Disposal of forfeited or abandoned property in special cases.
7327. Customs laws applicable.
7328. Cross references.

In **1986**, P.L. 99-514, Sec. 1565(d), substituted "$100,000" for "$2,500" in item 7325.
In **1976**, P.L. 94-455, Sec. 1904(b)(8)(H)(ii), redesignated the item for Code Sec. 7329, as the item for Code Sec. 7328.
In **1958**, substituted "$2,500" for "$1,000" in item 7325.

Sec. 7321. Authority to seize property subject to forfeiture.

Any property subject to forfeiture to the United States under any provision of this title may be seized by the Secretary.

In **1976**, P.L. 94-455, Sec. 1906(b)(13)(A), substituted "Secretary" for "Secretary or his delegate" in Code Sec. 7321, effective 2/1/77.

Sec. 7322. Delivery of seized personal property to United States marshal.

Any forfeitable property which may be seized under the provisions of this title may, at the option of the Secretary, be delivered to the United States marshal of the district, and remain in the care and custody and under the control of such marshal, pending disposal thereof as provided by law.

In **1976**, P.L. 94-455, Sec. 1906(b)(13)(A), substituted "Secretary" for "Secretary or his delegate" in Code Sec. 7322, effective 2/1/77.

Sec. 7323. Judicial action to enforce forfeiture.
(a) Nature and venue.

The proceedings to enforce such forfeitures shall be in the nature of a proceeding in rem in the United States District Court for the district where such seizure is made.
(b) Service of process when property has been returned under bond.

In case bond as provided in section 7324(3) shall have been executed and the property returned before seizure thereof by virtue of process in the proceedings in rem authorized in subsection (a) of this section, the marshal shall give notice of pendency of proceedings in court to the parties executing said bond, by personal service or publication, and in such manner and form as the court may direct, and the court shall thereupon have jurisdiction of said matter and parties in the same manner as if such property had been seized by virtue of the process aforesaid.
(c) Cost of seizure taxable.

The cost of seizure made before process issues shall be taxable by the court.

Sec. 7324. Special disposition of perishable goods.

When any property which is seized under the provisions of section 7301 or section 7302 is liable to perish or become greatly reduced in price or value by keeping, or when it cannot be kept without great expense—

(1) **Application for examination.** The owner thereof, or the United States marshal of the district, may apply to the Secretary to examine it; and

(2) **Appraisal.** If, in the opinion of the Secretary, it shall be necessary that such property should be sold to prevent such waste or expense, the Secretary shall appraise the same; and thereupon

(3) **Return to owner under bond.** The owner shall have such property returned to him upon giving bond in an amount equal to such appraised value to abide the final order, decree, or judgment of the court having cognizance of the case, and to pay the amount of said appraised value to the Secretary, the United States marshal, or otherwise, as may be ordered and directed by the court, which bond shall be filed by the Secretary with the United States attorney for the district in which the proceedings in rem authorized in section 7323 may be commenced.

(4) **Sale in absence of bond.**
(A) Order to sell. If such owner shall neglect or refuse to give such bond, the Secretary shall issue to any Treasury officer or employee or to the United States marshal an order to sell the same.
(B) Manner of sale. Such Treasury officer or employee or the marshal shall as soon as practicable make public sale of such property in accordance with such regulations as may be prescribed by the Secretary.
(C) Disposition of proceeds. The proceeds of the sale, after deducting the reasonable costs of the seizure and sale, shall be paid to the court to abide its final order, decree, or judgment.

(5) **Form of bond and sureties.** For provisions relating to form and sureties on bonds, see section 7101.

In **1976**, P.L. 94-455, Sec. 1906(b)(13)(A), substituted "Secretary" for "Secretary or his delegate" each place it appeared in Code Sec. 7324, effective 2/1/77.
In **1958**, P.L. 85-866, Sec. 78, deleted "district" before "attorney" in para. (3), effective 8/17/54.
—P.L. 85-859, Sec. 204(9), included property seized under section 7302 of this title, effective 9/3/58.

Sec. 7325. Personal property valued at $100,000 or less.

In all cases of seizure of any goods, wares, or merchandise as being subject to forfeiture under any provision of this title which, in the opinion of the Secretary, are of the appraised value of $100,000 or less, the Secretary shall, except in cases otherwise provided, proceed as follows:

(1) **List and appraisement.** The Secretary shall cause a list containing a particular description of the goods, wares, or merchandise seized to be prepared in duplicate, and an appraisement thereof to be made by three sworn appraisers, to be selected by the Secretary who shall be respectable and disinterested citizens of the United States residing within the internal revenue district wherein the seizure was made. Such list and appraisement shall be properly attested by the Secretary and such appraisers. Each appraiser shall be allowed for his services such compensation as the Secretary shall by regulations prescribe, to be paid in the manner similar to that provided for other necessary charges incurred in collecting internal revenue.

(2) **Notice of seizure.** If such goods are found by such appraisers to be of the value of $100,000 or less, the Secretary shall publish a notice for 3 weeks, in some newspaper of the district where the seizure was made, describing the articles and stating the time, place, and cause of their seizure, and requiring any person claiming them to appear and make such claim within 30 days from the date of the first publication of such notice.

(3) **Execution of bond by claimant.** Any person claiming the goods, wares, or merchandise so seized, within the time specified in the notice, may file with the Secretary a claim, stating his interest in the articles seized, and may

Crimes and forfeitures — Chapter 76

execute a bond to the United States in the penal sum of $2,500, conditioned that, in case of condemnation of the articles so seized, the obligors shall pay all the costs and expenses of the proceedings to obtain such condemnation; and upon the delivery of such bond to the Secretary, he shall transmit the same, with the duplicate list or description of the goods seized, to the United States attorney for the district, and such attorney shall proceed thereon in the ordinary manner prescribed by law.

(4) Sale in absence of bond. If no claim is interposed and no bond is given within the time above specified, the Secretary shall give reasonable notice of the sale of the goods, wares, or merchandise by publication, and, at the time and place specified in the notice, shall, unless otherwise provided by law, sell the articles so seized at public auction, or upon competitive bids, in accordance with such regulations as may be prescribed by the Secretary.

In **1986**, P.L. 99-514, Sec. 1566(a), substituted "$100,000" for "$2,500" each place it appeared in Code Sec. 7325 . . . Sec. 1566(b), substituted "$2,500" for "$250" in para. (3), effective 10/22/86.

In **1976**, P.L. 94-455, Sec. 1906(b)(13)(A), substituted "Secretary" for "Secretary or his delegate" each place it appeared in Code Sec. 7325, effective 2/1/77.

In **1958**, P.L. 85-866, Sec. 78, deleted "district" before "attorney" in para. (3), effective 8/17/54.

—P.L. 85-859, Sec. 204(10), (12), substituted "$2,500" for "$1,000" each place it appeared in Code Sec. 7325, and added ", unless otherwise provided by law," before "sell the articles" in para. (4), effective 9/3/58.

Sec. 7326. Disposal of forfeited or abandoned property in special cases.

(a) Coin-operated gaming devices.

Any coin-operated gaming device as defined in section 4462 upon which a tax is imposed by section 4461 and which has been forfeited under any provision of this title shall be destroyed, or otherwise disposed of, in such manner as may be prescribed by the Secretary.

(b) Firearms.

For provisions relating to disposal of forfeited firearms, see section 5872(b).

In **1976**, P.L. 94-455, Sec. 1906(a)(43), substituted "section 5872(b)" for "section 5862(b)" subsec. (b), as redesignated , and redesignated subsec. (c) as subsec. (b), effective 2/1/77.

—P.L. 94-455, Sec. 1906(b)(13)(A), substituted "Secretary" for "Secretary or his delegate" in subsec. (a), effective 2/1/77.

In **1970**, P.L. 91-513, Sec. 1102(f), deleted subsec. (b), effective 5/1/71. Prior to deletion, subsec. (b) read as follows:

"(b) Narcotic drugs. For provisions relating to disposal of forfeited narcotic drugs, see sections 4714, 4733, and 4745(d)."

In **1965**, P.L. 89-44, Sec. 601(j), substituted "section 4462", for "section 4462(a)(2)" in subsec. (a), effective 7/1/65.

In **1958**, P.L. 85-859, Sec. 204(13), added subsec. (a), and redesignated former paras. (1) and (2) as subsecs. (b) and (c), respectively, effective 9/3/58.

Sec. 7327. Customs laws applicable.

The provisions of law applicable to the remission or mitigation by the Secretary of forfeitures under the customs laws shall apply to forfeitures incurred or alleged to have been incurred under the internal revenue laws.

In **1976**, P.L. 94-455, Sec. 1906(b)(13)(A), substituted "Secretary" for "Secretary or his delegate" in Code Sec. 7327, effective 2/1/77.

Sec. 7328. Cross references.

(1) For the issuance of certificates of probable cause relieving officers making seizures of responsibility for damages, see 28 U.S.C. 2465.

(2) For provisions relating to forfeitures generally in connection with alcohol taxes, see chapter 51.

(3) For provisions relating to forfeitures generally in connection with tobacco taxes, see chapter 52.

(4) For provisions relating to forfeitures generally in connection with taxes on certain firearms, see chapter 53.

In **1976**, P.L. 94-455, Sec. 1904(b)(8)(H)(i), redesignated Code Sec. 7329 as Code Sec. 7328, effective 2/1/77.

Subchapter D.—Miscellaneous Penalty and Forfeiture Provisions

Sec.
7341. Penalty for sales to evade tax.
7342. Penalty for refusal to permit entry or examination.
7343. Definition of term "person."
7344. Extended application of penalties relating to officers of the Treasury Department.

Sec. 7341. Penalty for sales to evade tax.

(a) Nonenforceability of contract.

Whenever any person who is liable to pay any tax imposed by this title upon, for, or in respect of, any property sells or causes or allows the same to be sold before such tax is paid, with intent to avoid such tax, or in fraud of the internal revenue laws, any debt contracted in such sale, and any security given therefor, unless the same shall have been bona fide transferred to an innocent holder, shall be void, and the collection thereof shall not be enforced in any court.

(b) Forfeiture of sum paid on contract.

If such property has been paid for, in whole or in part, the sum so paid shall be deemed forfeited.

(c) Moiety.

Any person who shall sue for the sum so paid (in an action of debt) shall recover from the seller the amount so paid, one-half to his own use and the other half to the use of the United States.

Sec. 7342. Penalty for refusal to permit entry or examination.

Any owner of any building or place, or person having the agency or superintendence of the same, who refuses to admit any officer or employee of the Treasury Department acting under the authority of section 7606 (relating to entry of premises for examination of taxable articles) or refuses to permit him to examine such article or articles, shall, for every such refusal, forfeit $500.

Sec. 7343. Definition of term "person."

The term "person" as used in this chapter includes an officer or employee of a corporation, or a member or employee of a partnership, who as such officer, employee, or member is under a duty to perform the act in respect of which the violation occurs.

Sec. 7344. Extended application of penalties relating to officers of the Treasury Department.

All provisions of law imposing fines, penalties, or other punishment for offenses committed by an internal revenue officer or other officer of the Department of the Treasury, or under any agency or office thereof, shall apply to all persons whomsoever, employed, appointed, or acting under the authority of any internal revenue law, or any revenue provision of any law of the United States, when such persons are designated or acting as officers or employees in connection with such law, or are persons having the custody or disposition of any public money.

CHAPTER 76.—JUDICIAL PROCEEDINGS

Subchapter
A. Civil actions by the United States.
B. Proceedings by taxpayers and third parties.
C. The Tax Court.
D. Court review of Tax Court decisions.
E. Burden of proof.

Chapter 76   Crimes and forfeitures

In **1998**, P.L. 105-206, Sec. 3001(b), added item E.

Subchapter A.—Civil Actions by the United States

Sec.
7401. Authorization.
7402. Jurisdiction of district courts.
7403. Action to enforce lien or to subject property to payment of tax.
7404. Authority to bring civil action for estate taxes.
7405. Action for recovery of erroneous refunds.
7406. Disposition of judgments and moneys recovered.
7407. Action to enjoin tax return preparers.
7408. Actions to enjoin specified conduct related to tax shelters and reportable transactions.
7409. Action to enjoin flagrant political expenditures of section 501(c)(3) organizations.
7410. Cross references.

In **2007**, P.L. 110-28, Sec. 8246(a)(2)(I)(ii), amended item 7407.
Prior to deletion, item 7407 read as follows:
"7407. Action to enjoin income tax return preparers."
In **2004**, P.L. 108-357, Sec. 820(b)(2), deleted item 7408 and added item 7408.
Prior to deletion, item 7408 read as follows:
"7408. Action to enjoin promoters of abusive tax shelters, etc."
In **1987**, P.L. 100-203, Sec. 10713(a)(2), amended item 7409 and added new item 7410.
Prior to amendment, item 7409 read as follows:
"7409. Cross references."
In **1982**, P.L. 97-248, Sec. 321(b), redesignated item 7408 as 7409 and added a new item 7408.
In **1976**, P.L. 94-455, Sec. 1203(i)(4), redesignated the item for Code Sec. 7407 as the item for Code Sec. 7408 ... added a new item for Code Sec. 7407.

Sec. 7401. Authorization.

No civil action for the collection or recovery of taxes, or of any fine, penalty, or forfeiture, shall be commenced unless the Secretary authorizes or sanctions the proceedings and the Attorney General or his delegate directs that the action be commenced.

In **1976**, P.L. 94-455, Sec. 1906(b)(13)(A), substituted "Secretary" for "Secretary or his delegate" in Code Sec. 7401, effective 2/1/77.

Sec. 7402. Jurisdiction of district courts.

(a) To issue orders, processes, and judgments.

The district courts of the United States at the instance of the United States shall have such jurisdiction to make and issue in civil actions, writs and orders of injunction, and of *ne exeat republica*, orders appointing receivers, and such other orders and processes, and to render such judgments and decrees as may be necessary or appropriate for the enforcement of the internal revenue laws. The remedies hereby provided are in addition to and not exclusive of any and all other remedies of the United States in such courts or otherwise to enforce such laws.

(b) To enforce summons.

If any person is summoned under the internal revenue laws to appear, to testify, or to produce books, papers, or other data, the district court of the United States for the district in which such person resides or may be found shall have jurisdiction by appropriate process to compel such attendance, testimony, or production of books, papers, or other data.

(c) For damages to United States officers or employees.

Any officer or employee of the United States acting under authority of this title, or any person acting under or by authority of any such officer or employee, receiving any injury to his person or property in the discharge of his duty shall be entitled to maintain an action for damages therefor, in the district court of the United States, in the district wherein the party doing the injury may reside or shall be found.

(d) Repealed.

(e) To quiet title.

The United States district courts shall have jurisdiction of any action brought by the United States to quiet title to property if the title claimed by the United States to such property was derived from enforcement of a lien under this title.

(f) General jurisdiction.

For general jurisdiction of the district courts of the United States in civil actions involving internal revenue, see section 1340 of title 28 of the United States Code.

In **1972**, P.L. 92-310, Sec. 230(d), deleted subsec. (d) effective 6/6/72.
Prior to deletion, subsec. (d) read as follows:
"(d) Action on bonds. The United States district courts, concurrently with the courts of the several States, shall have jurisdiction of any action brought on the official bond of any internal revenue officer or employee required to give bond under regulations promulgated by authority of section 7803."
In **1966**, P.L. 89-719, Sec. 107(a), redesignated subsec. (e) as (f) and added subsec. (e), applicable after 11/2/66, regardless of when a lien or a title of the U.S. arose or when the lien or interest of any other person was acquired; except that, if, before 11/2/66, any person has commenced a civil action to clear title of property pursuant to Code Sec. 7424 as in effect immediately before 11/2/66, such action shall be determined in accordance with Code Sec. 7424 as in effect immediately before that date.

Sec. 7403. Action to enforce lien or to subject property to payment of tax.

(a) Filing.

In any case where there has been a refusal or neglect to pay any tax, or to discharge any liability in respect thereof, whether or not levy has been made, the Attorney General or his delegate, at the request of the Secretary, may direct a civil action to be filed in a district court of the United States to enforce the lien of the United States under this title with respect to such tax or liability or to subject any property, of whatever nature, of the delinquent, or in which he has any right, title, or interest, to the payment of such tax or liability. For purposes of the preceding sentence, any acceleration of payment under section 6166(g) shall be treated as a neglect to pay tax.

(b) Parties.

All persons having liens upon or claiming any interest in the property involved in such action shall be made parties thereto.

(c) Adjudication and decree.

The court shall, after the parties have been duly notified of the action, proceed to adjudicate all matters involved therein and finally determine the merits of all claims to and liens upon the property, and, in all cases where a claim or interest of the United States therein is established, may decree a sale of such property, by the proper officer of the court, and a distribution of the proceeds of such sales according to the findings of the court in respect to the interests of the parties and of the United States. If the property is sold to satisfy a first lien held by the United States, the United States may bid at the sale such sum, not exceeding the amount of such lien with expenses of sale, as the Secretary directs.

(d) Receivership.

In any such proceeding, at the instance of the United States, the court may appoint a receiver to enforce the lien, or, upon certification by the Secretary during the pendency of such proceedings that it is in the public interest, may appoint a receiver with all the powers of a receiver in equity.

Judicial proceedings   Code Sec. 7408(b)(2)

In 1981, P.L. 97-34, Sec. 422(e)(8), deleted "or 6166A(h)" after "section 6166(g)" in subsec. (a), effective for estates of decedents dying after 12/31/81.

In 1976, P.L. 94-455, Sec. 1906(b)(13)(A), substituted "Secretary" for "Secretary or his delegate" each place it appeared in Code Sec. 7403, effective 2/1/77.

—P.L. 94-455, Sec. 2004(f)(2), added the sentence at the end of subsec. (a), effective for estates of decedents dying after 12/31/76.

In 1966, P.L. 89-719, Sec. 107, added the last sentence in subsec. (c), effective after 11/2/66, regardless of when a lien or a title of the U.S. arose or when the lien or interest of any other person was acquired.

Sec. 7404. Authority to bring civil action for estate taxes.

If the estate tax imposed by chapter 11 is not paid on or before the due date thereof, the Secretary shall proceed to collect the tax under the provisions of general law; or appropriate proceedings in the name of the United States may be commenced in any court of the United States having jurisdiction to subject the property of the decedent to be sold under the judgment or decree of the court. From the proceeds of such sale the amount of the tax, together with the costs and expenses of every description to be allowed by the court, shall be first paid, and the balance shall be deposited according to the order of the court, to be paid under its direction to the person entitled thereto. This section insofar as it applies to the collection of a deficiency shall be subject to the provisions of sections 6213 and 6601.

In 1976, P.L. 94-455, Sec. 1906(b)(13)(A), substituted "Secretary" for "Secretary or his delegate" in Code Sec. 7404, effective 2/1/77.

Sec. 7405. Action for recovery of erroneous refunds.
(a) Refunds after limitation period.

Any portion of a tax imposed by this title, refund of which is erroneously made, within the meaning of section 6514, may be recovered by civil action brought in the name of the United States.

(b) Refunds otherwise erroneous.

Any portion of a tax imposed by this title which has been erroneously refunded (if such refund would not be considered as erroneous under section 6514) may be recovered by civil action brought in the name of the United States.

(c) Interest.

For provision relating to interest on erroneous refunds, see section 6602.

(d) Periods of limitation.

For periods of limitations on actions under this section, see section 6532(b).

Sec. 7406. Disposition of judgments and moneys recovered.

All judgments and moneys recovered or received for taxes, costs, forfeitures, and penalties shall be paid to the Secretary as collections of internal revenue taxes.

In 1976, P.L. 94-455, Sec. 1906(b)(13)(A), substituted "Secretary" for "Secretary or his delegate" in Code Sec. 7406, effective 2/1/77.

Sec. 7407. Action to enjoin tax return preparers.
(a) Authority to seek injunction.

A civil action in the name of the United States to enjoin any person who is a tax return preparer from further engaging in any conduct described in subsection (b) or from further acting as a tax return preparer may be commenced at the request of the Secretary. Any action under this section shall be brought in the District Court of the United States for the district in which the tax return preparer resides or has his principal place of business or in which the taxpayer with respect to whose tax return the action is brought resides. The court may exercise its jurisdiction over such action (as provided in section 7402(a)) separate and apart from any other action brought by the United States against such tax return preparer or any taxpayer.

(b) Adjudication and decrees.

In any action under subsection (a), if the court finds—

(1) that a tax return preparer has—

(A) engaged in any conduct subject to penalty under section 6694 or 6695, or subject to any criminal penalty provided by this title,

(B) misrepresented his eligibility to practice before the Internal Revenue Service, or otherwise misrepresented his experience or education as a tax return preparer,

(C) guaranteed the payment of any tax refund or the allowance of any tax credit, or

(D) engaged in any other fraudulent or deceptive conduct which substantially interferes with the proper administration of the Internal Revenue laws, and

(2) that injunctive relief is appropriate to prevent the recurrence of such conduct,

the court may enjoin such person from further engaging in such conduct. If the court finds that a tax return preparer has continually or repeatedly engaged in any conduct described in subparagraphs (A) through (D) of this subsection and that an injunction prohibiting such conduct would not be sufficient to prevent such person's interference with the proper administration of this title, the court may enjoin such person from acting as a tax return preparer.

In 2007, P.L. 110-28, Sec. 8246(a)(2)(I)(i)(I), substituted "tax return preparers" for "income tax return preparers" in the heading of Code Sec. 7407...Sec. 8246(a)(2)(I)(i)(II), substituted "a tax return preparer" for "an income tax return preparer" each place it appeared in Code Sec. 7407...Sec. 8246(a)(2)(I)(i)(III), substituted "tax return preparer" for "income tax preparer" both places it appeared in subsec. (a)...Sec. 8246(a)(2)(I)(i)(IV), substituted "tax return" for "income tax return" in subsec. (a), effective for returns prepared after 5/25/2007.

In 1989, P.L. 101-239, Sec. 7738(a), deleted subsec. (c)...Sec. 7738(b), substituted "A civil" for "Except as provided in subsection (c), a civil" in subsec. (a), effective for actions commenced after 12/31/89.

Prior to deletion, subsec. (c) read as follows:

"(c) Bond to stay injunction. No action to enjoin under subsection (b)(1)(A) shall be commenced or pursued with respect to any income tax return preparer who files and maintains, with the Secretary in the internal revenue district in which is located such preparer's legal residence or principal place of business, a bond in a sum of $50,000 as surety for the payment of penalties under section 6694 and 6695."

In 1976, P.L. 94-455, Sec. 1203(g), added Code Sec. 7407, effective for documents prepared after 12/31/76.

Sec. 7408. Actions to enjoin specified conduct related to tax shelters and reportable transactions.
(a) Authority to seek injunction.

A civil action in the name of the United States to enjoin any person from further engaging in specified conduct may be commenced at the request of the Secretary. Any action under this section shall be brought in the district court of the United States for the district in which such person resides, has his principal place of business, or has engaged in specified conduct. The court may exercise its jurisdiction over such action (as provided in section 7402(a)) separate and apart from any other action brought by the United States against such person.

(b) Adjudication and decree.

In any action under subsection (a), if the court finds—

(1) that the person has engaged in any specified conduct, and

(2) that injunctive relief is appropriate to prevent recurrence of such conduct,

the court may enjoin such person from engaging in such conduct or in any other activity subject to penalty under this title.

3,859

(c) Specified conduct.
For purposes of this section, the term "specified conduct" means any action, or failure to take action, which is—
(1) subject to penalty under section 6700, 6701, 6707, or 6708, or
(2) in violation of any requirement under regulations issued under section 330 of title 31, United States Code.

(d) Citizens and residents outside the United States.
If any citizen or resident of the United States does not reside in, and does not have his principal place of business in, any United States judicial district, such citizen or resident shall be treated for purposes of this section as residing in the District of Columbia.

In 2004, P.L. 108-357, Sec. 820(a), redesignated subsec. (c) as subsec. (d), deleted subsecs. (a) and (b), and added subsecs. (a)-(c)... Sec. 820(b)(1), amended the heading of Code Sec. 7408, effective on the day after 10/22/2004.
Prior to amendment, the heading of Code Sec. 7408 read as follows:
"Sec. 7408. Action to enjoin promoters of abusive tax shelters, etc."
Prior to deletion, subsecs. (a) and (b) read as follows:
"(a) Authority to seek injunction. A civil action in the name of the United States to enjoin any person from further engaging in conduct subject to penalty under section 6700 (relating to penalty for promoting abusive tax shelters, etc.) or section 6701 (relating to penalties for aiding and abetting understatement of tax liability) may be commenced at the request of the Secretary. Any action under this section shall be brought in the district court of the United States for the district in which such person resides, has his principal place of business, or has engaged in conduct subject to penalty under section 6700 or section 6701. The court may exercise its jurisdiction over such action (as provided in section 7402(a)) separate and apart from any other action brought by the United States against such person.
"(b) Adjudication and decree. In any action under subsection (a), if the court finds—
"(1) that the person has engaged in any conduct subject to penalty under section 6700 (relating to penalty for promoting abusive tax shelters, etc.) or section 6701 (relating to penalties for aiding and abetting understatement of tax liability), and
"(2) that injunctive relief is appropriate to prevent recurrence of such conduct, the court may enjoin such person from engaging in such conduct or in any other activity subject to penalty under section 6700 or section 6701."
In 1984, P.L. 98-369, Sec. 143(b)(1), added "or section 6701 (relating to penalties for aiding and abetting understatement of tax liability)" after "etc.)" in subsecs. (a) and (b)... Sec. 143(b)(2), added "or section 6701" after "has engaged in conduct subject to penalty under section 6700" in subsec. (a)... Sec. 143(b)(3), added "or section 6701" before the period at the end of subsec. (b), effective 7/19/84.
In 1982, P.L. 97-248, Sec. 321(a), added Code Sec. 7408, effective 9/4/82.

Sec. 7409. Action to enjoin flagrant political expenditures of section 501(c)(3) organizations.

(a) Authority to seek injunction.
(1) **In general.** If the requirements of paragraph (2) are met, a civil action in the name of the United States may be commenced at the request of the Secretary to enjoin any section 501(c)(3) organization from further making political expenditures and for such other relief as may be appropriate to ensure that the assets of such organization are preserved for charitable or other purposes specified in section 501(c)(3). Any action under this section shall be brought in the district court of the United States for the district in which such organization has its principal place of business or for any district in which it has made political expenditures. The court may exercise its jurisdiction over such action (as provided in section 7402(a)) separate and apart from any other action brought by the United States against such organization.

(2) **Requirements.** An action may be brought under subsection (a) only if—
(A) the Internal Revenue Service has notified the organization of its intention to seek an injunction under this section if the making of political expenditures does not immediately cease, and
(B) the Commissioner of Internal Revenue has personally determined that—

(i) such organization has flagrantly participated in, or intervened in (including the publication or distribution of statements), any political campaign on behalf of (or in opposition to) any candidate for public office, and
(ii) injunctive relief is appropriate to prevent future political expenditures.

(b) Adjudication and decree.
In any action under subsection (a), if the court finds on the basis of clear and convincing evidence that—
(1) such organization has flagrantly participated in, or intervened in (including the publication or distribution of statements), any political campaign on behalf of (or in opposition to) any candidate for public office, and
(2) injunctive relief is appropriate to prevent future political expenditures,
the court may enjoin such organization from making political expenditures and may grant such other relief as may be appropriate to ensure that the assets of such organization are preserved for charitable or other purposes specified in section 501(c)(3).

(c) Definitions.
For purposes of this section, the terms "section 501(c)(3) organization" and "political expenditures" have the respective meanings given to such terms by section 4955.

In 1987, P.L. 100-203, Sec. 10713(a)(1), added Code Sec. 7409, effective 12/22/87.

Sec. 7410. Cross references.
(1) For provisions for collecting taxes in general, see chapter 64.
(2) For venue in a civil action for the collection of any tax, see section 1396 of Title 28 of the United States Code.
(3) For venue of a proceeding for the recovery of any fine, penalty, or forfeiture, see section 1395 of Title 28 of the United States Code.

In 1987, P.L. 100-203, Sec. 10713(a)(1), redesignated Code Sec. 7409 as Code Sec. 7410, effective 12/22/87.
In 1982, P.L. 97-248, Sec. 321(a), redesignated Code Sec. 7408 as Code Sec. 7409, effective 9/4/82.
In 1976, P.L. 94-455, Sec. 1203(g), redesignated Code Sec. 7407 as Code Sec. 7408, effective for documents prepared after 12/31/76.

Subchapter B.—Proceedings by Taxpayers and Third Parties

Sec.
7421. Prohibition of suits to restrain assessment or collection.
7422. Civil actions for refund.
7423. Repayments to officers or employees.
7424. Intervention.
7425. Discharge of liens.
7426. Civil actions by persons other than taxpayers.
7427. Tax return preparers.
7428. Declaratory judgments relating to status and classification of organizations under section 501(c)(3), etc.
7429. Review of jeopardy levy or assessment procedures.
7430. Awarding of costs and certain fees.
7431. Civil damages for unauthorized inspection or disclosure of returns and return information.
7432. Civil damages for failure to release lien.
7433. Civil damages for certain unauthorized collection actions.

Judicial proceedings Code Sec. 7422(e)

7433A. Civil damages for certain unauthorized collection actions by persons performing services under qualified tax collection contracts.

7434. Civil damages for fraudulent filing of information returns.

7435. Civil damages for unauthorized enticement of information disclosure.

7436. Proceedings for determination of employment status.

7437. Cross references.

In **2007,** P.L. 110-28, Sec. 8246(a)(2)(J)(ii), amended item 7427.
Prior to amendment, item 7427 read as follows:
"7427. Income tax return preparers."

In **2004,** P.L. 108-357, Sec. 881(b)(2), added item 7433A.

In **1997,** P.L. 105-34, Sec. 1454(b)(4), amended item 7436 and added item 7437.
Prior to amendment, item 7436 read as follows:
"7436. Cross references."

In **1996,** P.L. 104-168, Sec. 601(b), amended item 7434 and added item 7435.
Prior to amendment, item 7434 read as follows:
"Sec. 7434. Cross references."
—P.L. 104-468, Sec. 1203(b), amended item 7435 [as added by Sec. 601(b) of this Act, see above] and added item 7436.
Prior to amendment, item 7435 read as follows:
"Sec. 7435. Cross references."

In **1988,** P.L. 100-647, Sec. 6237(e)(4), inserted "levy or" after "jeopardy" in item 7429... Sec. 6239(c), deleted "court" before "costs and" in item 7430... Sec. 6240(b), redesignated item 7432 as item 7433 and added new item 7432... Sec. 6241(c), further redesignated item 7433 as 7434 and added new item 7433.

In **1982,** P.L. 97-248, Sec. 292(d)(1), redesignated item 7430 as 7431 and added a new item 7430.
—97-248, Sec. 357(b)(3), redesignated item 7431 (as redesignated by Sec. 292(d)(1) of the Act) as item 7432 and added a new item 7431.

In **1976,** P.L. 94-455, Sec. 1203(b)(2)(B), redesignated the item for 7427 as 7428... added a new item for 7427.
—P.L. 94-455, Sec. 1204(c)(13), added the item for Code Sec. 7429.
—P.L. 94-455, Sec. 1306(b)(6), redesignated the item for 7428, previously redesignated by the Act, as 7430... added a new item for 7428.

In **1966,** added "and third parties" to heading of subchapter B, redesignated former item 7425 to 7427, changed item 7424 from "civil action to clear title to property" and added items 7425 and 7426.

Sec. 7421. Prohibition of suits to restrain assessment or collection.

(a) Tax.

Except as provided in sections 6015(e), 6212(a) and (c), 6213(a), 6225(b), 6246(b), 6330(e)(1), 6331(i), 6672(c), 6694(c), and 7426(a) and (b)(1), 7429(b), and 7436, no suit for the purpose of restraining the assessment or collection of any tax shall be maintained in any court by any person, whether or not such person is the person against whom such tax was assessed.

(b) Liability of transferee or fiduciary.

No suit shall be maintained in any court for the purpose of restraining the assessment or collection (pursuant to the provisions of chapter 71) of—

(1) the amount of the liability, at law or in equity, of a transferee of property of a taxpayer in respect of any internal revenue tax, or

(2) the amount of the liability of a fiduciary under section 3713(b) of title 31, United States Code in respect of any such tax.

In **2000,** P.L. 106-554, Sec. 1(a)(7), [which enacted into law Sec. 313(b)(2)(B) of P.L. 106-554] added "6330(e)(1)," after "6246(b)," in subsec. (a), effective 12/21/2000.
—P.L. 106-554, Sec. 1(a)(7), [which enacted into law Sec. 319(24) of P.L. 106-554] substituted "6672(c)" for "6672(b)" in subsec. (a), effective 12/21/2000.

In **1998,** P.L. 105-277, Sec. 4002(c)(1), substituted "6015(e)" for "6015(d)" in subsec. (a), effective for any liability for tax arising after 7/22/98, and any liability for tax on or before 7/22/98 but remaining unpaid as of 7/22/98, except as provided in Sec. 3201(g)(2) of P.L. 105-206 [see below].
—P.L. 105-277, Sec. 4002(f), added "6246(b)," after "6331(i)," in subsec. (a), effective for unpaid tax attributable to tax. periods begin. after 12/31/98.
—P.L. 105-206, Sec. 3201(e)(3), added "6015(d)," after "sections" in subsec. (a), effective for any liability for tax arising after 7/22/98, and any liability for tax

arising on or before 7/22/98 but remaining unpaid as of 7/22/98, except as provided in Sec. 3201(g)(2), of this Act, which reads as follows:
"(2) 2-year period. The 2-year period under subsection (b)(1)(E) or (c)(3)(B) of section 6015 of the Internal Revenue Code of 1986 shall not expire before the date which is 2 years after the date of the first collection activity after the date of the enactment of this Act."
—P.L. 105-206, Sec. 6012(e), substituted "beginning" for "ending on or" in Sec. 1226 of P.L. 105-34, which provides the effective date for amendments made by Sec. 1222 of P.L. 105-34 [see below]

In **1997,** P.L. 105-34, Sec. 1222(b)(1), added "6246(b)," after "6213(a)," in subsec. (a), effective [as amended by Sec. 6012(e), 105-206, see above] for partnership tax. yrs. begin. after 12/31/97.
—P.L. 105-34, Sec. 1239(e)(3), added "6225(b)," after "6213(a)," in subsec. (a) [as amended by Sec. 1222(b)(1) of this Act, see above], effective for partnership tax. yrs. end. after 8/5/97.
—P.L. 105-34, Sec. 1454(b)(2), substituted "7429(b), and 7436" for "and 7429(b)" in subsec. (a), effective 8/5/97.

In **1982,** P.L. 97-258, Sec. 3(f)(13), substituted "section 3713(b) of title 31, United States Code" for "section 3467 of the Revised Statutes (31 U.S.C. 192)" in para. (b)(2), effective 9/13/82.

In **1978,** P.L. 95-628, Sec. 9(b)(1), added "6672(c), 6694(c)," after "6213(a)," in subsec. (a), effective for penalties assessed more than 60 days after date of enactment [11/10/78].

In **1976,** P.L. 94-455, Sec. 1204(c)(11), substituted "and 7426(a) and (b)(1), and 7429(b)" for "7426(a) and (b)(1)" in subsec. (a), for actions taken under section 6851, 6861, or 6862 of the Internal Revenue Code of 1954 where the notice and demand takes place after '76. Sec. 2(a) of P.L. 94-528, postponed the effective date for this amendment to be for notices and demands taking place after 2/28/77.

In **1966,** P.L. 89-719, Sec. 110, added the reference to Code Sec. "7426(a) and (b)(1)" and all after "maintained in any court" in subsec. (a).

Sec. 7422. Civil actions for refund.

(a) No suit prior to filing claim for refund.

No suit or proceeding shall be maintained in any court for the recovery of any internal revenue tax alleged to have been erroneously or illegally assessed or collected, or of any penalty claimed to have been collected without authority, or of any sum alleged to have been excessive or in any manner wrongfully collected, until a claim for refund or credit has been duly filed with the Secretary, according to the provisions of law in that regard, and the regulations of the Secretary established in pursuance thereof.

(b) Protest or duress.

Such suit or proceeding may be maintained whether or not such tax, penalty, or sum has been paid under protest or duress.

(c) Suits against collection officer a bar.

A suit against any officer or employee of the United States (or former officer or employee) or his personal representative for the recovery of any internal revenue tax alleged to have been erroneously or illegally assessed or collected, or of any penalty claimed to have been collected without authority, or of any sum alleged to have been excessive or in any manner wrongfully collected shall be treated as if the United States had been a party to such suit in applying the doctrine of res judicata in all suits, in respect of any internal revenue tax, and in all proceedings in the Tax Court and on review of decisions of the Tax Court.

(d) Credit treated as payment.

The credit of an overpayment of any tax in satisfaction of any tax liability shall, for the purpose of any suit for refund of such tax liability so satisfied, be deemed to be a payment in respect of such tax liability at the time such credit is allowed.

(e) Stay of proceedings.

If the Secretary prior to the hearing of a suit brought by a taxpayer in a district court or the United States Claims Court [Court of Federal Claims, see § 902(b), P.L. 102-572] for the recovery of any income tax, estate tax, gift tax, or tax imposed by chapter 41, 42, 43, or 44 (or any penalty relating to such taxes) mails to the taxpayer a notice that a deficiency has been determined in respect of the tax which is the subject matter of taxpayer's suit, the proceedings in taxpayer's suit shall be stayed during the period of time in which the taxpayer may file a petition with the Tax Court for a redetermination of the asserted deficiency, and for 60 days thereafter. If the taxpayer files a petition with the Tax Court, the district court or the United States Claims Court [United States Court of Federal Claims, see § 902(b), P.L. 102-572], as the case may be, shall lose jurisdiction of taxpayer's suit to whatever extent jurisdiction is acquired by the Tax Court of the subject matter of taxpayer's suit for refund. If the taxpayer does not file a petition with the Tax Court for a redetermination of the asserted deficiency, the United States may counterclaim in the taxpayer's suit, or intervene in the event of a suit as described in subsection (c) (relating to suits against officers or employees of the United States), within the period of the stay of proceedings notwithstanding that the time for such pleading may have otherwise expired. The taxpayer shall have the burden of proof with respect to the issues raised by such counterclaim or intervention of the United States except as to the issue of whether the taxpayer has been guilty of fraud with intent to evade tax. This subsection shall not apply to a suit by a taxpayer which, prior to the date of enactment of this title, is commenced, instituted, or pending in a district court or the United States Claims Court [United States Court of Federal Claims, see § 902(b), P.L. 102-572] for the recovery of any income tax, estate tax, or gift tax (or any penalty relating to such taxes).

(f) Limitation on right of action for refund.

(1) **General rule.** A suit or proceeding referred to in subsection (a) may be maintained only against the United States and not against any officer or employee of the United States (or former officer or employee) or his personal representative. Such suit or proceeding may be maintained against the United States notwithstanding the provisions of section 2502 of title 28 of the United States Code (relating to aliens' privilege to sue) and notwithstanding the provisions of section 1502 of such title 28 (relating to certain treaty cases).

(2) **Misjoinder and change of venue.** If a suit or proceeding brought in a United States district court against an officer or employee of the United States (or former officer or employee) or his personal representative is improperly brought solely by virtue of paragraph (1), the court shall order, upon such terms as are just, that the pleadings be amended to substitute the United States as a party for such officer or employee as of the time such action commenced, upon proper service of process on the United States. Such suit or proceeding shall upon request by the United States be transferred to the district or division where it should have been brought if such action initially had been brought against the United States.

(g) Special rules for certain excise taxes imposed by chapter 42 or 43.

(1) **Right to bring actions.**

(A) **In general.** With respect to any taxable event, payment of the full amount of the first tier tax shall constitute sufficient payment in order to maintain an action under this section with respect to the second tier tax.

(B) **Definitions.** For purposes of subparagraph (A), the terms "taxable event", "first tier tax", and "second tier tax" have the respective meanings given to such terms by section 4963.

(2) **Limitation on suit for refund.** No suit may be maintained under this section for the credit or refund of any tax imposed under section 4941, 4942, 4943, 4944, 4945, 4951, 4952, 4955, 4958, 4971, or 4975 with respect to any act (or failure to act) giving rise to liability for tax under such sections, unless no other suit has been maintained for credit or refund of, and no petition has been filed in the Tax Court with respect to a deficiency in, any other tax imposed by such sections with respect to such act (or failure to act).

(3) **Final determination of issues.** For purposes of this section, any suit for the credit or refund of any tax imposed under section 4941, 4942, 4943, 4944, 4945, 4951, 4952, 4955, 4958, 4971, or 4975 with respect to any act (or failure to act) giving rise to liability for tax under such sections, shall constitute a suit to determine all questions with respect to any other tax imposed with respect to such act (or failure to act) under such sections, and failure by the parties to such suit to bring any such question before the Court shall constitute a bar to such question.

(h) Special rule for actions with respect to partnership items.

No action may be brought for a refund attributable to partnership items (as defined in section 6231(a)(3)) except as provided in section 6228(b) or section 6230(c).

(i) Special rule for actions with respect to tax shelter promoter and understatement penalties.

No action or proceeding may be brought in the United States Claims Court [United States Court of Federal Claims, see § 902(b), P.L. 102-572] for any refund or credit of a penalty imposed by section 6700 (relating to penalty for promoting abusive tax shelters, etc.) or section 6701 (relating to penalties for aiding and abetting understatement of tax liability).

(j) Special rule for actions with respect to estates for which an election under section 6166 is made.

(1) **In general.** The district courts of the United States and the United States Court of Federal Claims shall not fail to have jurisdiction over any action brought by the representative of an estate to which this subsection applies to determine the correct amount of the estate tax liability of such estate (or for any refund with respect thereto) solely because the full amount of such liability has not been paid by reason of an election under section 6166 with respect to such estate.

(2) **Estates to which subsection applies.** This subsection shall apply to any estate if, as of the date the action is filed—

(A) no portion of the installments payable under section 6166 have been accelerated;

(B) all such installments the due date for which is on or before the date the action is filed have been paid;

(C) there is no case pending in the Tax Court with respect to the tax imposed by section 2001 on the estate and, if a notice of deficiency under section 6212 with respect to such tax has been issued, the time for filing a petition with the Tax Court with respect to such notice has expired; and

(D) no proceeding for declaratory judgment under section 7479 is pending.

(3) **Prohibition on collection of disallowed liability.** If the court redetermines under paragraph (1) the estate tax liability of an estate, no part of such liability which is disallowed by a decision of such court which has become final may be collected by the Secretary, and amounts paid in excess of the installments determined by the court as currently due and payable shall be refunded.

(k) Cross references.

(1) For provisions relating generally to claims for refund or credit, see chapter 65 (relating to abatements, credit, and refund) and chapter 66 (relating to limitations).

(2) For duty of United States attorneys to defend suits, see section 507 of Title 28 of the United States Code.

Judicial proceedings

Code Sec. 7424

(3) For jurisdiction of United States district courts, see section 1346 of Title 28 of the United States Code.

(4) For payment by the Treasury of judgments against internal revenue officers or employees, upon certificate of probable cause, see section 2006 of Title 28 of the United States Code.

In 1998, P.L. 105-206, Sec. 3104(a), redesignated subsec. (j) as (k) and added subsec. (j), effective for any claim for refund filed after 7/22/98.

In 1996, P.L. 104-168, Sec. 1311(c)(4), added "4958," after "4955," in paras. (g)(2) and (3), effective for excess benefit transactions occurring on or after 9/14/95. Sec. 1311(d)(2) of this Act provides:

"(2) Binding contracts. The amendments referred to in paragraph (1) shall not apply to any benefit arising from a transaction pursuant to any written contract which was binding on September 13, 1995, and at all times thereafter before such transaction occurred."

In 1992, P.L. 102-572, Sec. 902(b), effective 10/29/92, relating to Court designation provides as follows:

"(b) Other provisions of law. Reference in any other Federal law or documents to —

"(1) the 'United States Claims Court' shall be deemed to refer to the 'United States Court of Federal Claims'; and

"(2) the 'Claims Court' shall be deemed to refer to the 'Court of Federal Claims'."

In 1988, P.L. 100-418, Sec. 1941(b)(2)(B)(x), substituted "or 44" for "44, or 45" in subsec. (e), effective for crude oil removed from the premises on or after 8/23/88.

In 1987, P.L. 100-203, Sec. 10712(c)(5), substituted "4952, 4955" for "4952" in paras. (g)(2) and (g)(3), effective for tax. yrs. begin. after 12/22/87.

In 1986, P.L. 99-514, Sec. 1899A(58), substituted "section 4963" for "section 4962" in subpara. (g)(1)(B), effective 10/22/86.

In 1984, P.L. 98-369, Sec. 714(g)(1), redesignated subsec. (i) as (j) and added subsec. (i), effective for any claim for refund or credit filed after 7/18/84.

—P.L. 98-369, Sec. 714(p)(2)(H), substituted "section 6231(a)(3)" for "section 6131(a)(3)" in subsec. (h), effective for partnership tax. yrs. begin. after 9/3/82.

In 1982, P.L. 97-248, Sec. 402(c)(11), redesignated subsec. (h) as (i) and added subsec. (h), effective for partnership tax. yrs. begin. after 9/3/82. Sec. 407(a)(3) of the Act provides:

"(3) The amendments made by sections 402, 403, and 404 [of this Act] shall apply to any partnership taxable year (or in the case of section 6232 of such Code, to any period) ending after the date of the enactment [9/3/82] of this Act if the partnership, each partner, and each indirect partner requests such application and the Secretary of the Treasury or his delegate consents to such application."

In 1982, P.L. 97-164, Sec. 151, substituted "United States Claims Court" for "Court of Claims" each place it appeared in subsec. (e), effective 10/1/82.

In 1980, P.L. 96-596, Sec. 2(c)(2), amended para. (g)(1), effective as provided in Sec. 2(d)(2) of this Act which reads as follows:

"(2) Second tier taxes. The amendments made by this section with respect to any second tier tax shall apply only with respect to taxes assessed after the date of the enactment of this Act [12/24/80]. Nothing in the preceding sentence shall be construed to permit the assessment of a tax in a case to which, on the date of enactment of this Act [12/24/80], the doctrine of res judicata applies."

Prior to amendment, para. (g)(1) read as follows:

"(1) Right to bring actions. With respect to any act (or failure to act) giving rise to liability under section 4941, 4942, 4943, 4944, 4945, 4951, 4952, 4971, or 4975, payment of the full amount of tax imposed under section 4941(a) (relating to initial taxes on self-dealing), section 4942(a) (relating to initial tax on failure to distribute income), section 4943(a) (relating to initial tax on excess business holdings), section 4944(a) (relating to initial taxes on investments which jeopardize charitable purpose), section 4945(a) (relating to initial taxes on taxable expenditures), section 4951(a) (relating to initial taxes on self-dealing), 4952(a) (relating to initial taxes on taxable expenditures), 4971(a) (relating to initial tax on failure to meet minimum funding standard), 4975(a) (relating to initial tax on prohibited transactions), section 4941(b) (relating to additional tax on self-dealing), section 4942(b) (relating to additional tax on failure to distribute income), section 4943(b) (relating to additional tax on excess business holdings), section 4944(b) (relating to additional taxes on investments which jeopardize charitable purpose), section 4945(b) (relating to additional taxes on taxable expenditures), section 4951(b) (relating to additional taxes on self-dealing), 4952(b) (relating to additional taxes on taxable expenditures), section 4971(b) (relating to additional tax on failure to meet minimum funding standard), or section 4975(b) (relating to additional tax on prohibited transactions) shall constitute sufficient payment in order to maintain an action under this section with respect to such act (or failure to act)."

—P.L. 96-223, Sec. 101(f)(1)(J), substituted "44, or 45" for "or 44" in subsec. (e), effective for periods after 2/29/80.

—P.L. 96-222, Sec. 108(b)(1)(D), substituted "4944, 4945, 4951, 4952" for "4944, 4945" each place it appeared in subsec. (g)... Sec. 108(b)(1)(E), substituted "section 4945(a) (relating to initial taxes on taxable expenditures), section 4951(a) (relating to initial taxes on self-dealing), 4952(a) (relating to initial taxes on taxable expenditures)" for "section 4945(a) (relating to initial taxes on taxable expenditures)" in para. (g)(1)... Sec. 108(b)(1)(F), substituted "section 4945(b) (relating to additional taxes on taxable expenditures), section 4951(b) (relating to additional taxes on self-dealing), 4952(b) (relating to additional taxes on taxable expenditures)" for "section 4945(b) (relating to additional taxes on taxable ex-

penditures)" in para. (g)(1), effective for contributions, acts and expenditures made after 12/31/77, in and for tax. yrs. begin. after such date.

In 1976, P.L. 94-455, Sec. 1307(d)(2)(F)(viii), substituted "chapter 41, 42," for "chapter 42", in subsec. (e), effective 10/4/76.

—P.L. 94-455, Sec. 1605(b)(11), substituted "43, or 44" for "or 43" in subsec. (e), effective for tax. yrs. of real estate investment trusts begin. after 10/4/76.

—P.L. 94-455, Sec. 1906(a)(44), deleted "instituted after June 15, 1942," after "res judicata in all suits", and deleted "where the petition to the Tax Court was filed after such date" after "on review of decisions of the Tax Court" in subsec. (c)... Sec. 1906(b)(13)(A), substituted "Secretary" for "Secretary or his delegate" each place it appeared in Code Sec. 7422, effective 2/1/77.

In 1974, P.L. 93-406, Sec. 1016(a)(26), amended Code Sec. 7422, effective 9/2/74 or other date as specified in Sec. 1017 of the Act (reproduced following Code Sec. 401), by substituting as follows:

... in subsec. (e), "chapter 42 or 43" for "chapter 42";

... in subsec. (g), "chapter 42 or 43" for "chapter 42" in the heading;

... in paras. (g)(1), (2), and (3), "4945, 4971, or 4975" for "or 4945";

... in para. (g)(1), "section 4945(a) (relating to initial taxes on taxable expenditures), 4971(a) (relating to initial tax on failure to meet minimum funding standard), 4975(a) (relating to initial tax on prohibited transactions)" for "section 4945(a) (relating to initial taxes on taxable expenditures)";

... in para. (g)(1), "section 4945(b) (relating to additional taxes on taxable expenditures), section 4971(b) (relating to additional tax on failure to meet minimum funding standard), or section 4975(b) (relating to additional tax on prohibited transactions)" for "section 4945(b) (relating to additional taxes on taxable expenditures)".

In 1971, P.L. 92-178, Sec. 309, added "and notwithstanding the provisions of section 1502 of such title 28 (relating to certain treaty cases)" to the end of the second sentence in para. (f)(1), effective for suits or proceedings which are instituted after 1/30/67.

In 1969, P.L. 91-172, Sec. 101(j)(56), substituted "gift tax, or tax imposed by Chapter 42" for "or gift tax," in subsec. (e), effective 1/1/70.

—P.L. 91-172, Sec. 101(i), redesignated subsec. (g) as (h) and added subsec. (g), effective 1/1/70.

In 1966, P.L. 89-713, Sec. 3(a), redesignated subsec. (f) as subsec. (g) and added subsec. (f), effective for suits brought against officers, employees or personal representatives referred to therein which are instituted 90 days or more after 11/2/66.

In 1958, P.L. 85-866, Sec. 78, deleted "district" before "attorneys" in para. (f)(2), effective 8/17/54.

Sec. 7423. Repayments to officers or employees.

The Secretary, subject to regulations prescribed by the Secretary is authorized to repay—

(1) Collections recovered. To any officer or employee of the United States the full amount of such sums of money as may be recovered against him in any court, for any internal revenue taxes collected by him, with the cost and expense of suit; also

(2) Damages and costs. All damages and costs recovered against any officer or employee of the United States in any suit brought against him by reason of anything done in the due performance of his official duty under this title.

In 1983, P.L. 97-437, Sec. 2, added Sec. 3111(c)(2) of title 5, United States Code, which makes Code Sec. 7423 applicable to student interns of IRS. See note following Code Sec. 6103.

In 1976, P.L. 94-455, Sec. 1906(b)(13)(A), substituted "Secretary" for "Secretary or his delegate" in Code Sec. 7423, effective 2/1/77.

Sec. 7424. Intervention.

If the United States is not a party to a civil action or suit, the United States may intervene in such action or suit to assert any lien arising under this title on the property which is the subject of such action or suit. The provisions of section 2410 of title 28 of the United States Code (except subsection (b)) and of section 1444 of title 28 of the United States Code shall apply in any case in which the United States intervenes as if the United States had originally been named a defendant in such action or suit. In any case in which the application of the United States to intervene is denied, the adjudication in such civil action or suit shall have no effect upon such lien.

In 1966, P.L. 89-719, Sec. 108, amended Code Sec. 7424, effective after 11/2/66, regardless of when a lien or a title of the U.S. arose or when the lien or interest of any other person was acquired, except that if, before 11/2/66 any person has commenced a civil action to clear title to property pursuant to Code Sec. 7424 as

3,863

in effect immediately before 11/2/66 such action shall be determined in accordance with Code Sec. 7424 as in effect immediately before such date.

Prior to amendment, Code Sec. 7424 read as follows:

"SEC. 7424. CIVIL ACTION TO CLEAR TITLE TO PROPERTY.

"(a) *Obtaining leave to file.*

"(1) Request for institution of proceedings by United States.— Any person having a lien upon or any interest in the property referred to in section 7403, notice of which has been duly filed of record in the jurisdiction in which the property is located, prior to the filing of notice of the lien of the United States as provided in section 6323, or any person purchasing the property at a sale to satisfy such prior lien or interest, may make written request to the Secretary or his delegate to authorize the filing of a civil action as provided in section 7403.

"(2) Petition to court.— If the Secretary or his delegate fails to authorize the filing of such civil action within 6 months after receipt of such written request, such person or purchaser may, after giving notice to the Secretary or his delegate, file a petition in the district court of the United States for the district in which the property is located, praying leave to file a civil action for a final determination of all claims to or liens upon the property in question.

"(3) Court order.— After a full hearing in open court, the district court may in its discretion enter an order granting leave to file such civil action, in which the United States and all persons having liens upon or claiming any interest in the property shall be made parties.

"(b) *Adjudication.*

"Upon the filing of such civil action, the district court shall proceed to adjudicate the matters involved therein, in the same manner as in the case of civil actions filed under section 7403. For the purpose of such adjudication, the assessment of the tax upon which the lien of the United States is based shall be conclusively presumed to be valid.

"(c) *Costs.*

"All costs of the proceedings on the petition and the civil action shall be borne by the person filing the civil action."

Sec. 7425. Discharge of liens.
(a) Judicial proceedings.

If the United States is not joined as a party, a judgment in any civil action or suit described in subsection (a) of section 2410 of title 28 of the United States Code, or a judicial sale pursuant to such a judgment, with respect to property on which the United States has or claims a lien under the provisions of this title—

(1) shall be made subject to and without disturbing the lien of the United States, if notice of such lien has been filed in the place provided by law for such filing at the time such action or suit is commenced, or

(2) shall have the same effect with respect to the discharge or divestment of such lien of the United States as may be provided with respect to such matters by the local law of the place where such property is situated, if no notice of such lien has been filed in the place provided by law for such filing at the time such action or suit is commenced or if the law makes no provision for such filing.

If a judicial sale of property pursuant to a judgment in any civil action or suit to which the United States is not a party discharges a lien of the United States arising under the provisions of this title, the United States may claim, with the same priority as its lien had against the property sold, the proceeds (exclusive of costs) of such sale at any time before the distribution of such proceeds is ordered.

(b) Other sales.

Notwithstanding subsection (a) a sale of property on which the United States has or claims a lien, or a title derived from enforcement of a lien, under the provisions of this title, made pursuant to an instrument creating a lien on such property, pursuant to a confession of judgment on the obligation secured by such an instrument, or pursuant to a nonjudicial sale under a statutory lien on such property—

(1) shall, except as otherwise provided, be made subject to and without disturbing such lien or title, if notice of such lien was filed or such title recorded in the place provided by law for such filing or recording more than 30 days before such sale and the United States is not given notice of such sale in the manner prescribed in subsection (c)(1); or

(2) shall have the same effect with respect to the discharge or divestment of such lien or such title of the United States, as may be provided with respect to such matters by the local law of the place where such property is situated, if—

(A) notice of such lien or such title was not filed or recorded in the place provided by law for such filing more than 30 days before such sale,

(B) the law makes no provision for such filing, or

(C) notice of such sale is given in the manner prescribed in subsection (c)(1).

(c) Special rules.

(1) **Notice of sale.** Notice of a sale to which subsection (b) applies shall be given (in accordance with regulations prescribed by the Secretary) in writing, by registered or certified mail or by personal service, not less than 25 days prior to such sale, to the Secretary.

(2) **Consent to sale.** Notwithstanding the notice requirement of subsection (b)(2)(C), a sale described in subsection (b) of property shall discharge or divest such property of the lien or title of the United States if the United States consents to the sale of such property free of such lien or title.

(3) **Sale of perishable goods.** Notwithstanding the notice requirement of subsection (b)(2)(C), a sale described in subsection (b) of property liable to perish or become greatly reduced in price or value by keeping, or which cannot be kept without great expense, shall discharge or divest such property of the lien or title of the United States if notice of such sale is given (in accordance with regulations prescribed by the Secretary) in writing, by registered or certified mail or by personal service, to the Secretary before such sale. The proceeds (exclusive of costs) of such sale shall be held as a fund subject to the liens and claims of the United States, in the same manner and with the same priority as such liens and claims had with respect to the property sold, for not less than 30 days after the date of such sale.

(4) **Forfeitures of land sales contracts.** For purposes of subsection (b), a sale of property includes any forfeiture of a land sales contract.

(d) Redemption by United States.

(1) **Right to redeem.** In the case of a sale of real property to which subsection (b) applies to satisfy a lien prior to that of the United States, the Secretary may redeem such property within the period of 120 days from the date of such sale or the period allowable for redemption under local law, whichever is longer.

(2) **Amount to be paid.** In any case in which the United States redeems real property pursuant to paragraph (1), the amount to be paid for such property shall be the amount prescribed by subsection (d) of section 2410 of title 28 of the United States Code.

(3) **Certificate of redemption.**

(A) In General. In any case in which real property is redeemed by the United States pursuant to this subsection, the Secretary shall apply to the officer designated by local law, if any, for the documents necessary to evidence the fact of redemption and to record title to such property in the name of the United States. If no such officer is designated by local law or if such officer fails to issue such documents, the Secretary shall execute a certificate of redemption therefor.

(B) Filing. The Secretary shall, without delay, cause such documents or certificate to be duly recorded in the proper registry of deeds. If the State in which the real property redeemed by the United States is situated has

Judicial proceedings   Code Sec. 7426(g)(1)

not by law designated an office in which such certificate may be recorded, the Secretary shall file such certificate in the office of the clerk of the United States district court for the judicial district in which such property is situated.

(C) Effect. A certificate of redemption executed by the Secretary shall constitute prima facie evidence of the regularity of such redemption and shall, when recorded, transfer to the United States all the rights, title, and interest in and to such property acquired by the person from whom the United States redeems such property by virtue of the sale of such property.

In 1986, P.L. 99-514, Sec. 1572(a), added para. (c)(4), effective for forfeitures after the 30th day after 10/22/86.

In 1976, P.L. 94-455, Sec. 1906(b)(13)(A), substituted "Secretary" for "Secretary or his delegate" each place it appeared in Code Sec. 7425, effective 2/1/77.

In 1966, P.L. 89-719, Sec. 109, redesignated Code Sec. 7425 as 7427 and added Code Sec. 7425, effective after 11/2/66 regardless of when a lien or a title of the U.S. arose or when a lien or interest of any other person was acquired. For a special exception included in Sec. 114 of P.L. 89-719 see the note to Code Sec. 6323.

Sec. 7426. Civil actions by persons other than taxpayers.

(a) Actions permitted.

(1) Wrongful levy. If a levy has been made on property or property has been sold pursuant to a levy, any person (other than the person against whom is assessed the tax out of which such levy arose) who claims an interest in or lien on such property and that such property was wrongfully levied upon may bring a civil action against the United States in a district court of the United States. Such action may be brought without regard to whether such property has been surrendered to or sold by the Secretary.

(2) Surplus proceeds. If property has been sold pursuant to a levy, any person (other than the person against whom is assessed the tax out of which such levy arose) who claims an interest in or lien on such property junior to that of the United States and to be legally entitled to the surplus proceeds of such sale may bring a civil action against the United States in a district court of the United States.

(3) Substituted sale proceeds. If property has been sold pursuant to an agreement described in section 6325(b)(3) (relating to substitution of proceeds of sale), any person who claims to be legally entitled to all or any part of the amount held as a fund pursuant to such agreement may bring a civil action against the United States in a district court of the United States.

(4) Substitution of value. If a certificate of discharge is issued to any person under section 6325(b)(4) with respect to any property, such person may, within 120 days after the day on which such certificate is issued, bring a civil action against the United States in a district court of the United States for a determination of whether the value of the interest of the United States (if any) in such property is less than the value determined by the Secretary. No other action may be brought by such person for such a determination.

(b) Adjudication.

The district court shall have jurisdiction to grant only such of the following forms of relief as may be appropriate in the circumstances:

(1) Injunction. If a levy or sale would irreparably injure rights in property which the court determines to be superior to rights of the United States in such property, the court may grant an injunction to prohibit the enforcement of such levy or to prohibit such sale.

(2) Recovery of property. If the court determines that such property has been wrongfully levied upon, the court may—

(A) order the return of specific property if the United States is in possession of such property;

(B) grant a judgment for the amount of money levied upon; or

(C) if such property was sold, grant a judgment for an amount not exceeding the greater of—

(i) the amount received by the United States from the sale of such property, or

(ii) the fair market value of such property immediately before the levy.

For the purposes of subparagraph (C), if the property was declared purchased by the United States at a sale pursuant to section 6335(e) (relating to manner and conditions of sale), the United States shall be treated as having received an amount equal to the minimum price determined pursuant to such section or (if larger) the amount received by the United States from the resale of such property.

(3) Surplus proceeds. If the court determines that the interest or lien of any party to an action under this section was transferred to the proceeds of a sale of such property, the court may grant a judgment in an amount equal to all or any part of the amount of the surplus proceeds of such sale.

(4) Substituted sale proceeds. If the court determines that a party has an interest in or lien on the amount held as a fund pursuant to an agreement described in section 6325(b)(3) (relating to substitution of proceeds of sale), the court may grant a judgment in an amount equal to all or any part of the amount of such fund.

(5) Substitution of value. If the court determines that the Secretary's determination of the value of the interest of the United States in the property for purposes of section 6325(b)(4) exceeds the actual value of such interest, the court shall grant a judgment ordering a refund of the amount deposited, and a release of the bond, to the extent that the aggregate of the amounts thereof exceeds such value determined by the court.

(c) Validity of assessment.

For purposes of an adjudication under this section, the assessment of tax upon which the interest or lien of the United States is based shall be conclusively presumed to be valid.

(d) Limitation on rights of action.

No action may be maintained against any officer or employee of the United States (or former officer or employee) or his personal representative with respect to any acts for which an action could be maintained under this section.

(e) Substitution of United States as party.

If an action, which could be brought against the United States under this section, is improperly brought against any officer or employee of the United States (or former officer or employee) or his personal representative, the court shall order, upon such terms as are just, that the pleadings be amended to substitute the United States as a party for such officer or employee as of the time such action was commenced upon proper service of process on the United States.

(f) Provision inapplicable.

The provisions of section 7422(a) (relating to prohibition of suit prior to filing claim for refund) shall not apply to actions under this section.

(g) Interest.

Interest shall be allowed at the overpayment rate established under section 6621—

(1) in the case of a judgment pursuant to subsection (b)(2)(B), from the date the Secretary receives the money wrongfully levied upon to the date of payment of such judgment;

(2) in the case of a judgment pursuant to subsection (b)(2)(C), from the date of the sale of the property wrongfully levied upon to the date of payment of such judgment; and

(3) in the case of a judgment pursuant to subsection (b)(5) which orders a refund of any amount, from the date the Secretary received such amount to the date of payment of such judgment.

(h) **Recovery of damages permitted in certain cases.**

(1) **In general.** Notwithstanding subsection (b), if, in any action brought under this section, there is a finding that any officer or employee of the Internal Revenue Service recklessly or intentionally, or by reason of negligence, disregarded any provision of this title the defendant shall be liable to the plaintiff in an amount equal to the lesser of $1,000,000 ($100,000 in the case of negligence) or the sum of—

(A) actual, direct economic damages sustained by the plaintiff as a proximate result of the reckless or intentional or negligent disregard of any provision of this title by the officer or employee (reduced by any amount of such damages awarded under subsection (b)); and

(B) the costs of the action.

(2) **Requirement that administrative remedies be exhausted; mitigation; period.** The rules of section 7433(d) shall apply for purposes of this subsection.

(3) **Payment authority.** Claims pursuant to this section shall be payable out of funds appropriated under section 1304 of title 31, United States Code.

(i) **Cross reference.**

For period of limitation, see section 6532(c).

In **1998**, P.L. 105-206, Sec. 3102(b), redesignated subsec. (h) as (i) and added subsec. (h), effective for actions of officers or employees of the IRS after 7/22/98. —P.L. 105-206, Sec. 1906(b)(1), added para. (a)(4) . . . Sec. 3106(b)(2)(A), added para. (b)(5) . . . Sec. 3106(b)(2)(B), deleted "and" at the end of para. (g)(1), substituted "; and" for the period at the end of para. (g)(2), and added para. (g)(3), effective 7/22/98.

In **1986**, P.L. 99-514, Sec. 1511(c)(16), substituted "the overpayment rate established under section 6621" for "an annual rate established under section 6621", effective for purposes of determining interest for periods after 12/31/86.

In **1982**, P.L. 97-248, Sec. 350(a), amended subpara. (b)(2)(C), effective for levies made after 12/31/82.

Prior to amendment, subpara. (b)(2)(C) read as follows:

"(C) grant a judgment for an amount not exceeding the amount received by the United States from the sale of such property."

In **1976**, P.L. 94-455, Sec. 1906(b)(13)(A), substituted "Secretary" for "Secretary or his delegate" each place it appeared in Code Sec. 7426, effective 2/1/77.

In **1975**, P.L. 93-625, Sec. 7(a)(2)(E), substituted "an annual rate established under section 6621" for "the rate of 6 percent per annum" in subsec. (g), effective 7/1/75, and applicable to amounts outstanding on or arising after 7/1/75.

In **1966**, P.L. 89-719, Sec. 110, added Code Sec. 7426, effective after 11/2/66 regardless of when a lien or a title of the U.S. arose or when a lien or interest of any other person was acquired. For a special exception included in Sec. 114 of P.L. 89-719 see the note to Sec. 6323.

Sec. 7427. Tax return preparers.

In any proceeding involving the issue of whether or not a tax return preparer has willfully attempted in any manner to understate the liability for tax (within the meaning of section 6694(b)), the burden of proof in respect to such issue shall be upon the Secretary.

In **2007**, P.L. 110-28, Sec. 8246(a)(2)(J)(i)(I), substituted "Tax return preparers" for "Income tax return preparers" in the heading of Code Sec. 7427 . . . Sec. 8246(a)(2)(J)(i)(II), substituted "a tax return preparer" for "an income tax return preparer" in Code Sec. 7427, effective for returns prepared after 5/25/2007.

In **1976**, P.L. 94-455, Sec. 1203(b)(2)(A), added Code Sec. 7427, effective for documents prepared after 12/31/76.

Sec. 7428. Declaratory judgments relating to status and classification of organizations under section 501(c)(3), etc.

(a) **Creation of remedy.**

In a case of actual controversy involving—

(1) a determination by the Secretary—

(A) with respect to the initial qualification or continuing qualification of an organization as an organization described in section 501(c)(3) which is exempt from tax under section 501(a) or as an organization described in section 170(c)(2),

(B) with respect to the initial classification or continuing classification of an organization as a private foundation (as defined in section 509(a)),

(C) with respect to the initial classification or continuing classification of an organization as a private operating foundation (as defined in section 4942(j)(3)), or

(D) with respect to the initial classification or continuing classification of a cooperative as an organization described in section 521(b) which is exempt from tax under section 521(a), or

(2) a failure by the Secretary to make a determination with respect to an issue referred to in paragraph (1),

upon the filing of an appropriate pleading, the United States Tax Court, the United States Claims Court [United States Court of Federal Claims, see § 902(b), P.L. 102-572], or the district court of the United States for the District of Columbia may make a declaration with respect to such initial qualification or continuing qualification or with respect to such initial classification or continuing classification. Any such declaration shall have the force and effect of a decision of the Tax Court or a final judgment or decree of the district court or the Claims Court [Court of Federal Claims, see § 902(b), P.L. 102-572], as the case may be, and shall be reviewable as such. For purposes of this section, a determination with respect to a continuing qualification or continuing classification includes any revocation of or other change in a qualification or classification.

(b) **Limitations.**

(1) **Petitioner.** A pleading may be filed under this section only by the organization the qualification or classification of which is at issue.

(2) **Exhaustion of administrative remedies.** A declaratory judgment or decree under this section shall not be issued in any proceeding unless the Tax Court, the Claims Court [Court of Federal Claims, see § 902(b), P.L. 102-572], or the district court of the United States for the District of Columbia determines that the organization involved has exhausted administrative remedies available to it within the Internal Revenue Service. An organization requesting the determination of an issue referred to in subsection (a)(1) shall be deemed to have exhausted its administrative remedies with respect to a failure by the Secretary to make a determination with respect to such issue at the expiration of 270 days after the date on which the request for such determination was made if the organization has taken, in a timely manner, all reasonable steps to secure such determination.

(3) **Time for bringing action.** If the Secretary sends by certified or registered mail notice of his determination with respect to an issue referred to in subsection (a)(1) to the organization referred to in paragraph (1), no proceeding may be initiated under this section by such organization unless the pleading is filed before the 91st day after the date of such mailing.

(4) Nonapplication for certain revocations. No action may be brought under this section with respect to any revocation of status described in section 6033(j)(1).

(c) Validation of certain contributions made during pendency of proceedings.

(1) In general. If

(A) the issue referred to in subsection (a)(1) involves the revocation of a determination that the organization is described in section 170(c)(2),

(B) a proceeding under this section is initiated within the time provided by subsection (b)(3), and

(C) either—

(i) a decision of the Tax Court has become final (within the meaning of section 7481), or

(ii) a judgment of the district court of the United States for the District of Columbia has been entered, or

(iii) a judgment of the Claims Court [Court of Federal Claims, see § 902(b), P.L. 102-572] has been entered,

and such decision or judgment, as the case may be, determines that the organization was not described in section 170(c)(2),

then, notwithstanding such decision or judgment, such organization shall be treated as having been described in section 170(c)(2) for purposes of section 170 for the period beginning on the date on which the notice of the revocation was published and ending on the date on which the court first determined in such proceeding that the organization was not described in section 170(c)(2).

(2) Limitation. Paragraph (1) shall apply only—

(A) with respect to individuals, and only to the extent that the aggregate of the contributions made by any individual to or for the use of the organization during the period specified in paragraph (1) does not exceed $1,000 (for this purpose treating a husband and wife as one contributor), and

(B) with respect to organizations described in section 170(c)(2) which are exempt from tax under section 501(a) (for this purpose excluding any such organization with respect to which there is pending a proceeding to revoke the determination under section 170(c)(2)).

(3) Exception. This subsection shall not apply to any individual who was responsible, in whole or in part, for the activities (or failures to act) on the part of the organization which were the basis for the revocation.

(d) Subpoena power for district court for District of Columbia.

In any action brought under this section in the district court of the United States for the District of Columbia, a subpoena requiring the attendance of a witness at a trial or hearing may be served at any place in the United States.

In **2006**, P.L. 109-280, Sec. 1223(c), added para. (b)(4), effective for notices and returns with respect to annual periods begin. after 12/31/2006.

In **2004**, P.L. 108-357, Sec. 317(a), deleted "or" at the end of subpara. (a)(1)(B) and added subpara. (a)(1)(D), effective for pleadings filed after 10/22/2004.

In **1992**, P.L. 102-572, Sec. 902(b), effective 10/29/92, relating to Court designation provides as follows:

"(b) Other provisions of law. Reference in any other Federal law or documents to—

"(1) the 'United States Claims Court' shall be deemed to refer to the 'United States Court of Federal Claims'; and

"(2) the 'Claims Court' shall be deemed to refer to the 'Court of Federal Claims'"

In **1984**, P.L. 98-369, Sec. 1033(b), added subsec. (d), effective for inquiries and examinations begin. after 12/31/84.

In **1982**, P.L. 97-164, Sec. 152, substituted "Claims Court" for "Court of Claims" each place it appeared in Code Sec. 7428, effective 10/1/82.

In **1978**, P.L. 95-600, Sec. 701(dd)(2), added a new sentence to the end of subsec. (a), effective at the time Code Sec. 7428 was added. See below.

In **1976**, P.L. 94-455, Sec. 1306(a), added new Code Sec. 7428, effective for pleadings filed with the United States Tax Court, the district court of the United States for the District of Columbia, or the United States Court of Claims more than 6 months after 10/4/76 but only with respect to determinations (or requests for determinations) made after January 1, 1976.

Sec. 7429. Review of jeopardy levy or assessment procedures.

(a) Administrative review.

(1) Administrative review.

(A) Prior approval required. No assessment may be made under section 6851(a), 6852(a), 6861(a), or 6862, and no levy may be made under section 6331(a) less than 30 days after notice and demand for payment is made, unless the Chief Counsel for the Internal Revenue Service (or such Counsel's delegate) personally approves (in writing) such assessment or levy.

(B) Information to taxpayer. Within 5 days after the day on which such an assessment or levy is made, the Secretary shall provide the taxpayer with a written statement of the information upon which the Secretary relied in making such assessment or levy.

(2) Request for review. Within 30 days after the day on which the taxpayer is furnished the written statement described in paragraph (1), or within 30 days after the last day of the period within which such statement is required to be furnished, the taxpayer may request the Secretary to review the action taken.

(3) Redetermination by Secretary. After a request for review is made under paragraph (2), the Secretary shall determine—

(A) whether or not—

(i) the making of the assessment under section 6851, 6861, or 6862, as the case may be, is reasonable under the circumstances, and

(ii) the amount so assessed or demanded as a result of the action taken under section 6851, 6861, or 6862 is appropriate under the circumstances, or

(B) whether or not the levy described in subsection (a)(1) is reasonable under the circumstances.

(b) Judicial review.

(1) Proceedings permitted. Within 90 days after the earlier of—

(A) the day the Secretary notifies the taxpayer of the Secretary's determination described in subsection (a)(3), or

(B) the 16th day after the request described in subsection (a)(2) was made,

the taxpayer may bring a civil action against the United States for a determination under this subsection in the court with jurisdiction determined under paragraph (2).

(2) Jurisdiction for determination.

(A) In general. Except as provided in subparagraph (B), the district courts of the United States shall have exclusive jurisdiction over any civil action for a determination under this subsection.

(B) Tax court. If a petition for a redetermination of a deficiency under section 6213(a) has been timely filed with the Tax Court before the making of an assessment or levy that is subject to the review procedures of this section, and 1 or more of the taxes and taxable periods before the Tax Court because of such petition is also included in the written statement that is provided to the taxpayer under subsection (a), then the Tax Court also shall have jurisdiction over any civil action for a determination under this subsection with respect to all the taxes and taxable periods included in such written statement.

(3) Determination by court. Within 20 days after a proceeding is commenced under paragraph (1), the court shall determine—

    (A) whether or not—

        (i) the making of the assessment under section 6851, 6861, or 6862, as the case may be, is reasonable under the circumstances, and

        (ii) the amount so assessed or demanded as a result of the action taken under section 6851, 6861, or 6862 is appropriate under the circumstances, or

    (B) whether or not the levy described in subsection (a)(1) is reasonable under the circumstances.

If the court determines that proper service was not made on the United States or on the Secretary, as may be appropriate, within 5 days after the date of the commencement of the proceeding, then the running of the 20-day period set forth in the preceding sentence shall not begin before the day on which proper service was made on the United States or on the Secretary, as may be appropriate.

(4) Order of court. If the court determines that the making of such levy is unreasonable, that the making of such assessment is unreasonable, or that the amount assessed or demanded is inappropriate, then the court may order the Secretary to release such levy, to abate such assessment, to redetermine (in whole or in part) the amount assessed or demanded, or to take such other action as the court finds appropriate.

(c) Extension of 20-day period where taxpayer so requests.

If the taxpayer requests an extension of the 20-day period set forth in subsection (b)(2) and establishes reasonable grounds why such extension should be granted, the court may grant an extension of not more than 40 additional days.

(d) Computation of days.

For purposes of this section, Saturday, Sunday, or a legal holiday in the District of Columbia shall not be counted as the last day of any period.

(e) Venue.

(1) District Court. A civil action in a district court under subsection (b) shall be commenced only in the judicial district described in section 1402(a)(1) or (2) of title 28, United States Code.

(2) Transfer of actions. If a civil action is filed under subsection (b) with the Tax Court and such court finds that there is want of jurisdiction because of the jurisdiction provisions of subsection (b)(2), then the Tax Court shall, if such court determines it is in the interest of justice, transfer the civil action to the district court in which the action could have been brought at the time such action was filed. Any civil action so transferred shall proceed as if such action had been filed in the district court to which such action is transferred on the date on which such action was actually filed in the Tax Court from which such action is transferred.

(f) Finality of determination.

Any determination made by a court under this section shall be final and conclusive and shall not be reviewed by any other court.

(g) Burden of proof.

(1) Reasonableness of levy, termination, or jeopardy assessment. In a proceeding under subsection (b) involving the issue of whether the making of a levy described in subsection (a)(1) or the making of an assessment under section 6851, 6852, 6861, or 6862 is reasonable under the circumstances, the burden of proof in respect to such issue shall be upon the Secretary.

(2) Reasonableness of amount of assessment. In a proceeding under subsection (b) involving the issue of whether an amount assessed or demanded as a result of action taken under section 6851, 6852, 6861, or 6862 is appropriate under the circumstances, the Secretary shall provide a written statement which contains any information with respect to which his determination of the amount assessed was based, but the burden of proof in respect of such issue shall be upon the taxpayer.

In **1998**, P.L. 105-206, Sec. 3434(a), amended para. (a)(1), effective for taxes assessed and levies made after 7/22/98.
Prior to amendment, para. (a)(1) read as follows:
"(1) Information to taxpayer. Within 5 days after the day on which an assessment is made under section 6851(a), 6852(a), 6861(a), or 6862, or levy is made under section 6331(a) less than 30 days after notice and demand for payment is made under section 6331(a), the Secretary shall provide the taxpayer with a written statement of the information upon which the Secretary relies in making such assessment or levy."

In **1988**, P.L. 100-647, Sec. 6237(a)(1), added "or levy is made under section 6331(a) less than 30 days after notice and demand for payment is made under section 6331(a)," after "6862," in para. (a)(1) . . . Sec. 6237(a)(2), added "or levy" after "such assessment" in para. (a)(1) . . . Sec. 6237(b), amended para. (a)(3) . . . Sec. 6237(c), amended subsec. (b) . . . Sec. 6237(d), amended subsec. (e) . . . Sec. 6237(e)(1), deleted "district" before "court" each place it appeared in subsecs. (c) and (f) . . . Sec. 6237(e)(2)(A), added "the making of a levy described in subsection (a)(1) or" after "whether" in para. (g)(1) . . . Sec. 6237(a)(2)(B), substituted "levy, termination," for "termination" in the heading of para. (g)(1) . . . Sec. 6237(e)(2)(C), substituted "a proceeding" for "an action" in paras. (g)(1) and (g)(2) . . . Sec. 6237(e)(3), added "levy or" after "jeopardy" in the heading of Code Sec. 7429, effective for jeopardy levies issued and assessments made on or after 7/1/89.

Prior to amendment, para. (a)(3) read as follows:
"(3) Redetermination by Secretary. After a request for review is made under paragraph (2), the Secretary shall determine whether or not—
"(A) the making of the assessment under section 6851, 6852, 6861, or 6862, as the case may be, is reasonable under the circumstances, and
"(B) the amount so assessed or demanded as a result of the action taken under section 6851, 6852, or 6861 or 6862 is appropriate under the circumstances."

Prior to amendment, subsec. (b) read as follows:
"(b) Judicial review.
"(1) Actions permitted. Within 30 days after the earlier of—
"(A) the day the Secretary notifies the taxpayer of his determination described in subsection (a)(3), or
"(B) the 16th day after the request described in subsection (a)(2) was made, the taxpayer may bring a civil action against the United States in a district court of the United States for a determination under this subsection.
"(2) Determination by district court. Within 20 days after an action is commenced under paragraph (1), the district court shall determine whether or not—
"(A) the making of the assessment under section 6851, 6852, 6861, or 6862, as the case may be, is reasonable under the circumstances, and
"(B) the amount so assessed or demanded as a result of the action taken under section 6851, 6852, 6861, or 6862, is appropriate under the circumstances.
If the court determines that proper service was not made on the United States within 5 days after the date of the commencement of the action, the running of the 20-day period set forth in the preceding sentence shall not begin before the day on which proper service was made on the United States.
"(3) Order of district court. If the court determines that the making of such assessment is unreasonable or that the amount assessed or demanded is inappropriate, the court may order the Secretary to abate such assessment, to redetermine (in whole or in part) the amount assessed or demanded, or to take such other action as the court finds appropriate."

Prior to amendment, subsec. (e) read as follows:
"(e) Venue.
"A civil action under subsection (b) shall be commenced only in the judicial district described in section 1402(a)(1) or (2) of title 28, United States Code."

In **1987**, P.L. 100-203, Sec. 10712(b)(2)(F), substituted "6851(a), 6852(a)," for "6851(a)," in para. (a)(1), and substituted "6851, 6852," for "6851," each place it appeared in Code Sec. 7429, effective 12/22/87.

In **1984**, P.L. 98-369, Sec. 446(a), added the last sentence in para. (b)(2), effective for actions commenced after 7/18/84.

In **1976**, P.L. 94-528, Sec. 2(a), changed the effective date for amendments made by Sec. 1204(a) of P.L. 94-455, from effective for action taken under Code Sec. 6851, 6861 or 6862 where the notice and demand take place after 12/31/76, to effective for action taken under Code Sec. 6851, 6861 or 6862 where the notice and demand take place after 2/28/77, see below.

—P.L. 94-455, Sec. 1204(a), added Code Sec. 7429, effective [as amended by Sec. 2(a) of P.L. 94-528, see above] for action taken under section 6851, 6861, or 6862 of the Internal Revenue Code of 1954 where the notice and demand takes place after 2/28/77.

Judicial proceedings

Sec. 7430. Awarding of costs and certain fees.
(a) In general.

In any administrative or court proceeding which is brought by or against the United States in connection with the determination, collection, or refund of any tax, interest, or penalty under this title, the prevailing party may be awarded a judgment or a settlement for—

(1) reasonable administrative costs incurred in connection with such administrative proceeding within the Internal Revenue Service, and

(2) reasonable litigation costs incurred in connection with such court proceeding.

(b) Limitations.

(1) Requirement that administrative remedies be exhausted. A judgment for reasonable litigation costs shall not be awarded under subsection (a) in any court proceeding unless the court determines that the prevailing party has exhausted the administrative remedies available to such party within the Internal Revenue Service. Any failure to agree to an extension of the time for the assessment of any tax shall not be taken into account for purposes of determining whether the prevailing party meets the requirements of the preceding sentence.

(2) Only costs allocable to the United States. An award under subsection (a) shall be made only for reasonable litigation and administrative costs which are allocable to the United States and not to any other party.

(3) Costs denied where party prevailing protracts proceedings. No award for reasonable litigation and administrative costs may be made under subsection (a) with respect to any portion of the administrative or court proceeding during which the prevailing party has unreasonably protracted such proceeding.

(4) Period for applying to IRS for administrative costs. An award may be made under subsection (a) by the Internal Revenue Service for reasonable administrative costs only if the prevailing party files an application with the Internal Revenue Service for such costs before the 91st day after the date on which the final decision of the Internal Revenue Service as to the determination of the tax, interest, or penalty is mailed to such party.

(c) Definitions.

For purposes of this section—

(1) Reasonable litigation costs. The term "reasonable litigation costs" includes—

(A) reasonable court costs, and

(B) based upon prevailing market rates for the kind or quality of services furnished—

(i) the reasonable expenses of expert witnesses in connection with a court proceeding, except that no expert witness shall be compensated at a rate in excess of the highest rate of compensation for expert witnesses paid by the United States,

(ii) the reasonable cost of any study, analysis, engineering report, test, or project which is found by the court to be necessary for the preparation of the party's case, and

(iii) reasonable fees paid or incurred for the services of attorneys in connection with the court proceeding, except that such fees shall not be in excess of $125 per hour unless the court determines that a special factor, such as the limited availability of qualified attorneys for such proceeding, the difficulty of the issues presented in the case, or the local availability of tax expertise, justifies a higher rate.

In the case of any calendar year beginning after 1996, the dollar amount referred to in clause (iii) shall be increased by an amount equal to such dollar amount multiplied by the cost-of-living adjustment determined under section 1(f)(3) for such calendar year, by substituting "calendar year 1995" for "calendar year 1992" in subparagraph (B) thereof. If any dollar amount after being increased under the preceding sentence is not a multiple of $10, such dollar amount shall be rounded to the nearest multiple of $10.

(2) Reasonable administrative costs. The term "reasonable administrative costs" means—

(A) any administrative fees or similar charges imposed by the Internal Revenue Service, and

(B) expenses, costs, and fees described in paragraph (1)(B), except that any determination made by the court under clause (ii) or (iii) thereof shall be made by the Internal Revenue Service in cases where the determination under paragraph (4)(C) of the awarding of reasonable administrative costs is made by the Internal Revenue Service.

Such term shall only include costs incurred on or after whichever of the following is the earliest: (i) the date of the receipt by the taxpayer of the notice of the decision of the Internal Revenue Service Office of Appeals; (ii) the date of the notice of deficiency; or (iii) the date on which the first letter of proposed deficiency which allows the taxpayer an opportunity for administrative review in the Internal Revenue Service Office of Appeals is sent.

(3) Attorneys' fees.

(A) In general. For purposes of paragraphs (1) and (2), fees for the services of an individual (whether or not an attorney) who is authorized to practice before the Tax Court or before the Internal Revenue Service shall be treated as fees for the services of an attorney.

(B) Pro bono services. The court may award reasonable attorneys' fees under subsection (a) in excess of the attorneys' fees paid or incurred if such fees are less than the reasonable attorneys' fees because an individual is representing the prevailing party for no fee or for a fee which (taking into account all the facts and circumstances) is no more than a nominal fee. This subparagraph shall apply only if such award is paid to such individual or such individual's employer.

(4) Prevailing party.

(A) In general. The term "prevailing party" means any party in any proceeding to which subsection (a) applies (other than the United States or any creditor of the taxpayer involved)—

(i) which—

(I) has substantially prevailed with respect to the amount in controversy, or

(II) has substantially prevailed with respect to the most significant issue or set of issues presented, and

(ii) which meets the requirements of the 1st sentence of section 2412(d)(1)(B) of title 28, United States Code (as in effect on October 22, 1986) except to the extent differing procedures are established by rule of court and meets the requirements of section 2412(d)(2)(B) of such title 28 (as so in effect).

(B) Exception if United States establishes that its position was substantially justified.

(i) General rule. A party shall not be treated as the prevailing party in a proceeding to which subsection (a) applies if the United States establishes that the position of the United States in the proceeding was substantially justified.

(ii) Presumption of no justification if Internal Revenue Service did not follow certain published guidance. For purposes of clause (i), the position of the United States shall be presumed not to be substantially justified if the Internal Revenue Service did not follow its applicable published guidance in the administrative proceeding. Such presumption may be rebutted.

(iii) Effect of losing on substantially similar issues. In determining for purposes of clause (i) whether the position of the United States was substantially justified, the court shall take into account whether the United States has lost in courts of appeal for other circuits on substantially similar issues.

(iv) Applicable published guidance. For purposes of clause (ii), the term "applicable published guidance" means—

(I) regulations, revenue rulings, revenue procedures, information releases, notices, and announcements, and

(II) any of the following which are issued to the taxpayer: private letter rulings, technical advice memoranda, and determination letters.

(C) Determination as to prevailing party. Any determination under this paragraph as to whether a party is a prevailing party shall be made by agreement of the parties or—

(i) in the case where the final determination with respect to the tax, interest, or penalty is made at the administrative level, by the Internal Revenue Service, or

(ii) in the case where such final determination is made by a court, the court.

(D) Special rules for applying net worth requirement. In applying the requirements of section 2412(d)(2)(B) of title 28, United States Code, for purposes of subparagraph (A)(ii) of this paragraph—

(i) the net worth limitation in clause (i) of such section shall apply to—

(I) an estate but shall be determined as of the date of the decedent's death, and

(II) a trust but shall be determined as of the last day of the taxable year involved in the proceeding, and

(ii) individuals filing a joint return shall be treated as separate individuals for purposes of clause (i) of such section.

(E) Special rules where judgment less than taxpayer's offer.

(i) In general. A party to a court proceeding meeting the requirements of subparagraph (A)(ii) shall be treated as the prevailing party if the liability of the taxpayer pursuant to the judgment in the proceeding (determined without regard to interest) is equal to or less than the liability of the taxpayer which would have been so determined if the United States had accepted a qualified offer of the party under subsection (g).

(ii) Exceptions. This subparagraph shall not apply to—

(I) any judgment issued pursuant to a settlement; or

(II) any proceeding in which the amount of tax liability is not in issue, including any declaratory judgment proceeding, any proceeding to enforce or quash any summons issued pursuant to this title,

and any action to restrain disclosure under section 6110(f).

(iii) Special rules. If this subparagraph applies to any court proceeding—

(I) the determination under clause (i) shall be made by reference to the last qualified offer made with respect to the tax liability at issue in the proceeding; and

(II) reasonable administrative and litigation costs shall only include costs incurred on and after the date of such offer.

(iv) Coordination. This subparagraph shall not apply to a party which is a prevailing party under any other provision of this paragraph.

(5) Administrative proceedings. The term "administrative proceeding" means any procedure or other action before the Internal Revenue Service.

(6) Court proceedings. The term "court proceeding" means any civil action brought in a court of the United States (including the Tax Court and the United States Claims Court [United States Court of Federal Claims, see § 902(b), P.L. 102-572]).

(7) Position of United States. The term "position of the United States" means—

(A) the position taken by the United States in a judicial proceeding to which subsection (a) applies, and

(B) the position taken in an administrative proceeding to which subsection (a) applies as of the earlier of—

(i) the date of the receipt by the taxpayer of the notice of the decision of the Internal Revenue Service Office of Appeals, or

(ii) the date of the notice of deficiency.

(d) Special rules for payment of costs.

(1) Reasonable administrative costs. An award for reasonable administrative costs shall be payable out of funds appropriated under section 1304 of title 31, United States Code.

(2) Reasonable litigation costs. An award for reasonable litigation costs shall be payable in the case of the Tax Court in the same manner as such an award by a district court.

(e) Multiple actions.

For purposes of this section, in the case of —

(1) multiple actions which could have been joined or consolidated, or

(2) a case or cases involving a return or returns of the same taxpayer (including joint returns of married individuals) which could have been joined in a single court proceeding in the same court,

such actions or cases shall be treated as 1 court proceeding regardless of whether such joinder or consolidation actually occurs, unless the court in which such action is brought determines, in its discretion, that it would be inappropriate to treat such actions or cases as joined or consolidated.

(f) Right of appeal.

(1) Court proceedings. An order granting or denying (in whole or in part) an award for reasonable litigation or administrative costs under subsection (a) in a court proceeding, may be incorporated as a part of the decision or judgment in the court proceeding and shall be subject to appeal in the same manner as the decision or judgment.

(2) Administrative proceedings. A decision granting or denying (in whole or in part) an award for reasonable administrative costs under subsection (a) by the Internal Revenue Service shall be subject to the filing of a petition for review with the Tax Court under rules similar to the rules under section 7463 (without regard to the amount in dispute). If the Secretary sends by certified or registered mail a notice of such decision to the petitioner, no proceeding in the Tax Court may be initiated under this paragraph unless such petition is filed before the 91st day after the date of such mailing.

(3) Appeal of Tax Court decision. An order of the Tax Court disposing of a petition under paragraph (2) shall be reviewable in the same manner as a decision of the Tax Court, but only with respect to the matters determined in such order.

(g) Qualified offer.

For purposes of subsection (c)(4)—

(1) In general. The term "qualified offer" means a written offer which—

(A) is made by the taxpayer to the United States during the qualified offer period;

(B) specifies the offered amount of the taxpayer's liability (determined without regard to interest);

(C) is designated at the time it is made as a qualified offer for purposes of this section; and

(D) remains open during the period beginning on the date it is made and ending on the earliest of the date the offer is rejected, the date the trial begins, or the 90th day after the date the offer is made.

(2) Qualified offer period. For purposes of this subsection, the term "qualified offer period" means the period—

(A) beginning on the date on which the first letter of proposed deficiency which allows the taxpayer an opportunity for administrative review in the Internal Revenue Service Office of Appeals is sent, and

(B) ending on the date which is 30 days before the date the case is first set for trial.

In 2000, P.L. 106-554, Sec. 1(a)(7), [which enacted into law Sec. 319(25)(A) of P.L. 106-554] substituted "Attorneys'" for "Attorneys" in the heading of para. (c)(3)... Sec. 1(a)(7), [which enacted into law Sec. 319(25)(B) of P.L. 106-554] substituted "attorneys' fees" for "attorneys fees" each place it appeared in subpara. (c)(3)(B), effective 12/21/2000.

In 1998, P.L. 105-206, Sec. 3101(a)(1), substituted "$125" for "$110" in clause (c)(1)(B)(iii)... Sec. 3101(a)(2), added "the difficulty of the issues presented in the case, or the local availability of tax expertise," before "justifies a higher rate" in clause (c)(1)(B)(iii)... Sec. 3101(b), amended the last sentence of para. (c)(2) ... Sec. 3101(c), amended para. (c)(3)... Sec. 3101(d), redesignated clause (c)(4)(B)(iii) as (iv) and added clause (c)(4)(B)(iii)... Sec. 3101(e)(1), added subpara. (c)(4)(E)... Sec. 3101(e)(2), added subsec. (g), effective for costs incurred (and, in the case of the amendment made by subsec. (c), services performed) more than 180 days after 7/22/98.

Prior to amendment, clause (c)(1)(B)(iii) read as follows:

"(iii) reasonable fees paid or incurred for the services of attorneys in connection with the court proceeding, except that such fees shall not be in excess of $110 per hour unless the court determines that a special factor, such as the limited availability of qualified attorneys for such proceeding, justifies a higher rate."

Prior to amendment, the last sentence of para. (c)(2) read as follows:

"Such term shall only include costs incurred on or after the earlier of (i) the date of the receipt by the taxpayer of the notice of the decision of the Internal Revenue Service Office of Appeals, or (ii) the date of the notice of deficiency."

Prior to amendment, para. (c)(3) read as follows:

"(3) Attorney's fees. For purposes of paragraphs (1) and (2), fees for the services of an individual (whether or not an attorney) who is authorized to practice before the Tax Court or before the Internal Revenue Service shall be treated as fees for the services of an attorney."

—P.L. 105-206, Sec. 6012(h), redesignated para. (b)(5) as (b)(4), effective for civil actions or proceedings commenced after 8/5/97.

—P.L. 105-206, Sec. 6014(e), substituted "subparagraph (A)(ii)" for "subparagraph (A)(iii)" in subpara. (c)(4)(D), effective for proceedings commenced after 8/5/97.

In 1997, P.L. 105-34, Sec. 1285(a), added para. (f)(3)... Sec. 1285(b), added para. (b)(5)... Sec. 1285(c)(1), substituted "the filing of a petition for review with" for "appeal to" in para. (f)(2)... Sec. 1285(c)(2), added a sentence at the end of para. (f)(2), effective for civil actions or proceedings commenced after 8/5/97.

—P.L. 105-34, Sec. 1453(a), added subpara. (c)(4)(D), effective for proceedings commenced after 8/5/97.

In 1996, P.L. 104-168, Sec. 701(a), deleted clause (c)(4)(A)(i) and redesignated clauses (c)(4)(A)(ii) and (iii) as clauses (c)(4)(A)(i) and (ii)... Sec. 701(b), redesignated subpara. (c)(4)(B) as (C) and added subpara. (c)(4)(B)... Sec. 701(c)(1), substituted "paragraph (4)(C)" for "paragraph (4)(B)" in subpara.

(c)(2)(B)... Sec. 701(c)(2), substituted "this paragraph" for "subparagraph (A)" in subpara. (c)(4)(C) [as redesignated by Sec. 701(b) of this Act], effective for proceedings commenced after 7/30/96.

Prior to deletion, clause (c)(4)(A)(i) read as follows:

"(i) which establishes that the position of the United States in the proceeding was not substantially justified,"

—P.L. 104-168, Sec. 702(a)(1), substituted "$110" for "$75" in clause (c)(1)(B)(iii)... Sec. 702(a)(2), deleted "an increase in the cost of living or" after "court determines that" in clause (c)(1)(B)(iii)... Sec. 702(a)(3), added two sentences at the end of subpara. (c)(1)(B), effective for proceedings commenced after 7/30/96.

—P.L. 104-168, Sec. 703, added the sentence at the end of para. (b)(1), effective for proceedings commenced after 7/30/96.

—P.L. 104-168, Sec. 704, deleted para. (b)(3) and redesignated para. (b)(4) as para. (b)(3), effective for proceedings commenced after 7/30/96.

Prior to deletion, para. (b)(3) read as follows:

"(3) Exclusion of declaratory judgment proceedings.

"(A) In general. No award for reasonable litigation costs may be made under subsection (a) with respect to any declaratory judgment proceeding.

"(B) Exception for section 501(c)(3) determination revocation proceedings. Subparagraph (A) shall not apply to any proceeding which involves the revocation of a determination that the organization is described in section 501(c)(3)."

In 1992, P.L. 102-572, Sec. 902(b), effective 10/29/92, relating to Court designation provides as follows:

"(b) Other provisions of law. Reference in any other Federal law or documents to—

"(1) the 'United States Claims Court' shall be deemed to refer to the 'United States Court of Federal Claims'; and

"(2) the 'Claims Court' shall be deemed to refer to the 'Court of Federal Claims'."

In 1988, P.L. 100-647, Sec. 1015(i), amended clause (c)(2)(A)(iii), effective for amounts paid after 9/30/86, in civil actions or proceedings, commenced after 12/31/85. See Sec. 1551(h)(3) of P.L. 99-514, reproduced below.

Prior to amendment, clause (c)(2)(A)(iii) read as follows:

"(iii) meets the requirements of section 504(b)(1)(B) of title 5, United States Code (as in effect on the date of the enactment of the Tax Reform Act of 1986 and applied by taking into account the commencement of the proceeding described in subsection (a) in lieu of the initiation of the adjudication referred to in such section)."

—P.L. 100-647, Sec. 6239(a), amended Code Sec. 7430, effective for proceedings commencing after 11/10/88.

Prior to amendment, Code Sec. 7430 read as follows:

"SEC. 7430. AWARDING OF COURT COSTS AND CERTAIN FEES.

"(a) In general.

In the case of any civil proceeding which is—

"(1) brought by or against the United States in connection with the determination, collection, or refund of any tax, interest, or penalty under this title, and

"(2) brought in a court of the United States (including the Tax Court and the United States Claims Court),

the prevailing party may be awarded a judgment (payable in the case of the Tax Court in the same manner as such an award by a district court) for reasonable litigation costs incurred in such proceeding.

"(b) Limitations.

"(1) Requirement that administrative remedies be exhausted. A judgment for reasonable litigation costs shall not be awarded under subsection (a) unless the court determines that the prevailing party has exhausted the administrative remedies available to such party within the Internal Revenue Service.

"(2) Only costs allocable to the United States. An award under subsection (a) shall be made only for reasonable litigation costs which are allocable to the United States and not to any other party to the action or proceeding.

"(3) Exclusion of declaratory judgment proceedings.

"(A) In general. No award for reasonable litigation costs may be made under subsection (a) with respect to any declaratory judgment proceeding.

"(B) Exception for section 501(c)(3) determination revocation proceedings. Subparagraph (A) shall not apply to any proceeding which involves the revocation of a determination that the organization is described in section 501(c)(3).

"(4) Costs denied where party prevailing protracts proceedings. No award for reasonable litigation costs may be made under subsection (a) with respect to any portion of the civil proceeding during which the prevailing party has unreasonably protracted such proceeding.

"(c) Definitions.

For purposes of this section

"(1) Reasonable litigation costs.

"(A) In general. The term 'reasonable litigation costs' includes—

"(i) reasonable court costs, and

"(ii) based upon prevailing market rates for the kind or quality of services furnished—

"(I) the reasonable expenses of expert witnesses in connection with the civil proceeding, except that no expert witness shall be compensated at a rate in excess of the highest rate of compensation for expert witnesses paid by the United States,

"(II) the reasonable cost of any study, analysis, engineering report, test, or project which is found by the court to be necessary for the preparation of the party's case, and

"(III) reasonable fees paid or incurred for the services of attorneys in connection with the civil proceeding, except that such fees shall not be in excess of $75 per hour unless the court determines that an increase in the cost of living or a special factor, such as the limited availability of qualified attorneys for such proceeding, justifies a higher rate.

"(B) Attorney's fees. In the case of any proceeding in the Tax Court, fees for the services of an individual (whether or not an attorney) who is authorized to practice before the Tax Court shall be treated as fees for the services of an attorney.

"(2) Prevailing party.

"(A) In general. The term 'prevailing party' means any party to any proceeding described in subsection (a) (other than the United States or any creditor of the taxpayer involved) which—

"(i) establishes that the position of the United States in the civil proceeding was not substantially justified

"(ii)(I) has substantially prevailed with respect to the amount in controversy, or

"(II) has substantially prevailed with respect to the most significant issue or set of issues presented

"(iii) meets the requirements of section 504(b)(1)(B) of title 5, United States Code (as in effect on the date of the enactment of the Tax Reform Act of 1986 and applied by taking into account the commencement of the proceeding described in subsection (a) in lieu of the initiation of the adjudication referred to in such section).

"(B) Determination as to prevailing party. Any determination under subparagraph (A) as to whether a party is a prevailing party shall be made—

"(i) by the court, or

"(ii) by agreement of the parties.

"(3) Civil actions. The term 'civil proceeding' includes a civil action.

"(4) Position of United States. The term 'position of the United States' includes—

"(A) the position taken by the United States in the civil proceeding, and

"(B) any administrative action or inaction by the District Counsel of the Internal Revenue Service (and all subsequent administrative action or inaction) upon which such proceeding is based.

"(d) Multiple actions.

For purposes of this section, in the case of—

"(1) multiple actions which could have been joined or consolidated, or

"(2) a case or cases involving a return or returns of the same taxpayer (including joint returns of married individuals) which could have been joined in a single proceeding in the same court,

such actions or cases shall be treated as one civil proceeding regardless of whether such joinder or consolidation actually occurs, unless the court in which such action is brought determines, in its discretion, that it would be inappropriate to treat such actions or cases as joined or consolidated for purposes of this section.

"(e) Right of appeal.

An order granting or denying an award for reasonable litigation costs under subsection (a), in whole or in part, shall be incorporated as a part of the decision or judgment in the case and shall be subject to appeal in the same manner as the decision or judgment."

In **1986**, P.L. 99-514, Sec. 1551(a), deleted para. (b)(1), and redesignated paras. (b)(2), (b)(3) and (b)(4) as paras. (b)(1), (b)(2) and (b)(3) . . . Sec. 1551(b), added para. (b)(4) . . . Sec. 1551(c), amended subpara. (c)(1)(A) . . . Sec. 1551(d)(1), substituted "was unreasonable" for "was not substantially justified" in clause (c)(2)(A)(i) . . . Sec. 1551(d)(2), deleted "and" from the end of clause (c)(2)(A)(i), substituted "and" for the period at the end of clause (c)(2)(A)(ii), and added clause (c)(2)(A)(iii) . . . Sec. 1551(e), added para. (c)(4), effective for amounts paid after 9/30/86, in civil actions or proceedings, commenced after 12/31/85. Sec. 1551(h)(3) of this Act provides:

"(3) Applicability of amendments to certain prior cases. The amendments made by this section shall apply to any case commenced after December 31, 1985, and finally disposed of before the date of the enactment of this Act, except that in any such case, the 30-day period referred to in section 2412(d)(1)(B) of title 28, United States Code, or Rule 231 of the Tax Court, as the case may be, shall be deemed to commence on the date of the enactment of this Act."

Prior to deletion, para. (b)(1) read as follows:

"(1) Maximum dollar amount. The amount of reasonable litigation costs which may be awarded under subsection (a) with respect to any prevailing party in any civil proceeding shall not exceed $25,000."

Prior to amendment, subpara. (c)(1)(A) read as follows:

"(A) in general. The term 'reasonable litigation costs' includes

"(i) reasonable court costs,

"(ii) the reasonable expenses of expert witnesses in connection with the civil proceeding,

"(iii) the reasonable cost of any study, analysis, engineering report, test, or project which is found by the court to be necessary for the preparation of the party's case, and

"(iv) reasonable fees paid or incurred for the services of attorneys in connection with the civil proceeding."

—P.L. 99-514, Sec. 1551(f), added "(payable in the case of the Tax Court in the same manner as such an award by a district court)" after "awarded a judgment" in subsec. (a), effective for civil actions or proceedings commenced after 2/28/83.

—P.L. 99-514, Sec. 1551(g), deleted subsec. (f), effective for amounts paid after 9/30/86, in civil actions or proceedings, commenced after 12/31/85. For special rules, see Sec. 1551(h)(3) of this Act, reproduced above.

Prior to deletion, subsec. (f) read as follows:

"(f) Termination. This section shall not apply to any proceeding commenced after December 31, 1985."

In **1984**, P.L. 98-369, Sec. 714(c), substituted "including the Tax Court and the United States Claims Court" for "including the Tax Court" in para. (a)(2), effective for civil actions or proceedings commenced after 2/28/83.

In **1982**, P.L. 97-248, Sec. 292(a), added Code Sec. 7430, effective for civil actions or proceedings commenced after 2/28/83.

Sec. 7431. Civil damages for unauthorized inspection or disclosure of returns and return information.

(a) In general.

(1) Inspection or disclosure by employee of United States. If any officer or employee of the United States knowingly, or by reason of negligence, inspects or discloses any return or return information with respect to a taxpayer in violation of any provision of section 6103, such taxpayer may bring a civil action for damages against the United States in a district court of the United States.

(2) Inspection or disclosure by a person who is not an employee of United States. If any person who is not an officer or employee of the United States knowingly, or by reason of negligence, inspects or discloses any return or return information with respect to a taxpayer in violation of any provision of section 6103 or in violation of section 6104(c), such taxpayer may bring a civil action for damages against such person in a district court of the United States.

(b) Exceptions.

No liability shall arise under this section with respect to any inspection or disclosure—

(1) which results from a good faith, but erroneous, interpretation of section 6103, or

(2) which is requested by the taxpayer.

(c) Damages.

In any action brought under subsection (a), upon a finding of liability on the part of the defendant, the defendant shall be liable to the plaintiff in an amount equal to the sum of—

(1) the greater of—

(A) $1,000 for each act of unauthorized inspection or disclosure of a return or return information with respect to which such defendant is found liable, or

(B) the sum of—

(i) the actual damages sustained by the plaintiff as a result of such unauthorized inspection or disclosure, plus

(ii) in the case of a willful inspection or disclosure or an inspection or disclosure which is the result of gross negligence, punitive damages, plus

(2) the costs of the action, plus

(3) in the case of a plaintiff which is described in section 7430(c)(4)(A)(ii), reasonable attorneys fees, except that if the defendant is the United States, reasonable attorneys fees may be awarded only if the plaintiff is the prevailing party (as determined under section 7430(c)(4)).

(d) Period for bringing action.

Notwithstanding any other provision of law, an action to enforce any liability created under this section may be brought, without regard to the amount in controversy, at any time within 2 years after the date of discovery by the plaintiff of the unauthorized inspection or disclosure.

(e) Notification of unlawful inspection and disclosure.

If any person is criminally charged by indictment or information with inspection or disclosure of a taxpayer's return or return information in violation of—

(1) paragraph (1) or (2) of section 7213(a),

(2) section 7213A(a), or

(3) subparagraph (B) of section 1030(a)(2) of title 18, United States Code,

Judicial proceedings

Code Sec. 7433(d)(2)

the Secretary shall notify such taxpayer as soon as practicable of such inspection or disclosure.

(f) Definitions.

For purposes of this section, the terms "inspect", "inspection", "return", and "return information" have the respective meanings given such terms by section 6103(b).

(g) Extension to information obtained under section 3406.

For purposes of this section—

(1) any information obtained under section 3406 (including information with respect to any payee certification failure under subsection (d) thereof) shall be treated as return information, and

(2) any inspection or use of such information other than for purposes of meeting any requirement under section 3406 or (subject to the safeguards set forth in section 6103) for purposes permitted under section 6103 shall be treated as a violation of section 6103.

For purposes of subsection (b), the reference to section 6103 shall be treated as including a reference to section 3406.

(h) Special rule for information obtained under section 6103(k)(9).

For purposes of this section, any reference to section 6103 shall be treated as including a reference to section 6311(e).

In **2006**, P.L. 109-280, Sec. 1224(b)(7), added "or in violation of section 6104(c)" after "6103" in para. (a)(2), effective 8/17/2006, but not for requests made before 8/17/2006.

In **1998**, P.L. 105-206, Sec. 3101(f), substituted ", plus" for the period at the end of para. (c)(2) and added para. (c)(3), effective for costs incurred more than 180 days after 7/22/98.

—P.L. 105-206, Sec. 6012(b)(3), redesignated subsec. (g) [sic (h)] [as added by Sec. 1205(c)(2) of P.L. 105-34, see below] as subsec. (h), and substituted "(9)" for "(8)" in the heading of subsec. (h) [as redesignated], effective on the day 9 months after 8/5/97.

In **1997**, P.L. 105-34, Sec. 1205(c)(2), added subsec. (g) [sic (h)], effective on the day 9 months after 8/5/97.

—P.L. 105-35, Sec. 3(a)(1), substituted "Inspection or disclosure" for "Disclosure" in the headings of paras. (a)(1) and (a)(2) . . . Sec. 3(a)(2), substituted "inspects or discloses" for "discloses" in paras. (a)(1) and (a)(2) . . . Sec. 3(b), redesignated subsecs. (e) and (f) as (f) and (g) and added subsec. (e) . . . Sec. 3(c), amended subsec. (b) . . . Sec. 3(d)(1), added "inspection or" before "disclosure" in subpara. (c)(1)(A), clause (c)(1)(B)(i), and subsec. (d) . . . Sec. 3(d)(2), substituted "willful inspection or disclosure or an inspection or disclosure" for "willful disclosure or a disclosure" in clause (c)(1)(B)(ii) . . . Sec. 3(d)(3), amended subsec. (f) [as redesignated by Sec. 3(b) of this Act, see above] . . . Sec. 3(d)(4), added "inspection or" before "disclosure" in the heading of Code Sec. 7431 . . . Sec. 3(d)(6), substituted "any inspection or use" for "any use" in subsec. (g) [as redesignated by Sec. 3(b) of this Act, see above], effective for inspections and disclosures occurring on and after 8/5/97.

Prior to amendment, subsec. (b) read as follows:

"(b) No liability for good faith but erroneous interpretation. No liability shall arise under this section with respect to any disclosure which results from a good faith, but erroneous, interpretation of section 6103."

Prior to amendment, subsec. (f) [as redesignated by Sec. 3(b) of this Act, see above] read as follows:

"(f) Return; return information. For purposes of this section, the terms 'return' and 'return information' have the respective meanings given such terms in section 6103(b)."

In **1983**, P.L. 98-67, Sec. 104(b), added subsec. (f), effective 8/5/83.

—P.L. 97-437, Sec. 2, added Sec. 3111(c)(2) of title 5, United States Code, which makes Code Sec. 7431 applicable to student interns of IRS. See note following Code Sec. 6103.

In **1982**, P.L. 97-248, Sec. 357(a), added Code Sec. 7431, effective for disclosures made after 9/3/82.

Sec. 7432. Civil damages for failure to release lien.

(a) In general.

If any officer or employee of the Internal Revenue Service knowingly, or by reason of negligence, fails to release a lien under section 6325 on property of the taxpayer, such taxpayer may bring a civil action for damages against the United States in a district court of the United States.

(b) Damages.

In any action brought under subsection (a), upon a finding of liability on the part of the defendant, the defendant shall be liable to the plaintiff in an amount equal to the sum of—

(1) actual, direct economic damages sustained by the plaintiff which, but for the actions of the defendant, would not have been sustained, plus

(2) the costs of the action.

(c) Payment authority.

Claims pursuant to this section shall be payable out of funds appropriated under section 1304 of title 31, United States Code.

(d) Limitations.

(1) Requirement that administrative remedies be exhausted. A judgment for damages shall not be awarded under subsection (b) unless the court determines that the plaintiff has exhausted the administrative remedies available to such plaintiff within the Internal Revenue Service.

(2) Mitigation of damages. The amount of damages awarded under subsection (b)(1) shall be reduced by the amount of such damages which could have reasonably been mitigated by the plaintiff.

(3) Period for bringing action. Notwithstanding any other provision of law, an action to enforce liability created under this section may be brought without regard to the amount in controversy and may be brought only within 2 years after the date the right of action accrues.

(e) Notice of failure to release lien.

The Secretary shall by regulation prescribe reasonable procedures for a taxpayer to notify the Secretary of the failure to release a lien under section 6325 on property of the taxpayer.

In **1988**, P.L. 100-647, Sec. 6240(a), added Code Sec. 7432, effective for notices provided by taxpayer of the failure to release a lien, and damages arising, after 12/31/88.

Sec. 7433. Civil damages for certain unauthorized collection actions.

(a) In general.

If, in connection with any collection of Federal tax with respect to a taxpayer, any officer or employee of the Internal Revenue Service recklessly or intentionally, or by reason of negligence, disregards any provision of this title, or any regulation promulgated under this title, such taxpayer may bring a civil action for damages against the United States in a district court of the United States. Except as provided in section 7432, such civil action shall be the exclusive remedy for recovering damages resulting from such actions.

(b) Damages.

In any action brought under subsection (a), or petition filed under subsection (e) upon a finding of liability on the part of the defendant, the defendant shall be liable to the plaintiff in an amount equal to the lesser of $1,000,000 ($100,000, in the case of negligence) or the sum of—

(1) actual, direct economic damages sustained by the plaintiff as a proximate result of the reckless or intentional or negligent actions of the officer or employee, and

(2) the costs of the action.

(c) Payment authority.

Claims pursuant to this section shall be payable out of funds appropriated under section 1304 of title 31, United States Code.

(d) Limitations.

(1) Requirement that administrative remedies be exhausted. A judgment for damages shall not be awarded under subsection (b) unless the court determines that the plaintiff has exhausted the administrative remedies available to such plaintiff within the Internal Revenue Service.

(2) Mitigation of damages. The amount of damages awarded under subsection (b)(1) shall be reduced by the amount of such damages which could have reasonably been mitigated by the plaintiff.

(3) Period for bringing action. Notwithstanding any other provision of law, an action to enforce liability created under this section may be brought without regard to the amount in controversy and may be brought only within 2 years after the date the right of action accrues.

(e) Actions for violations of certain bankruptcy procedures.

(1) In general. If, in connection with any collection of Federal tax with respect to a taxpayer, any officer or employee of the Internal Revenue Service willfully violates any provision of section 362 (relating to automatic stay) or 524 (relating to effect of discharge) of title 11, United States Code (or any successor provision), or any regulation promulgated under such section, such taxpayer may petition the bankruptcy court to recover damages against the United States.

(2) Remedy to be exclusive.

(A) In general. Except as provided in subparagraph (B), notwithstanding section 105 of such title 11, such petition shall be the exclusive remedy for recovering damages resulting from such actions.

(B) Certain other actions permitted. Subparagraph (A) shall not apply to an action under section 362(h) of such title 11 for a violation of a stay provided by section 362 of such title; except that—

(i) administrative and litigation costs in connection with such an action may only be awarded under section 7430; and

(ii) administrative costs may be awarded only if incurred on or after the date that the bankruptcy petition is filed.

In 1998, P.L. 105-206, Sec. 3102(a)(1)(A), added ", or by reason of negligence," after "recklessly or intentionally" in subsec. (a) . . . Sec. 3102(a)(1)(B)(i), added "($100,000, in the case of negligence)" after "$1,000,000" in the matter preceding para. (b)(1) . . . Sec. 3102(a)(1)(B)(ii), added "or negligent" after "reckless or intentional" in para. (b)(1) . . . Sec. 3102(a)(2), amended para. (d)(1) . . . Sec. 3102(c)(1), added subsec. (e) . . . Sec. 3102(c)(2), added "or petition filed under subsection (e)" after "subsection (a)" in subsec. (b), effective for actions of officers or employees of the Internal Revenue Service after 7/22/98.

Prior to amendment, para. (d)(1) read as follows:

"(1) Award for damages may be reduced if administrative remedies not exhausted.

"The amount of damages awarded under subsection (b) may be reduced if the court determines that the plaintiff has not exhausted the administrative remedies available to such plaintiff within the Internal Revenue Service."

In 1996, P.L. 104-168, Sec. 801(a), substituted "$1,000,000" for "$100,000" in subsec. (b), effective for actions by officers or employees of the Internal Revenue Service after 7/30/96.

—P.L. 104-168, Sec. 802(a), amended para. (d)(1), effective for proceedings commenced after 7/30/96.

Prior to amendment, para. (d)(1) read as follows:

"(1) Requirement that administrative remedies be exhausted. A judgment for damages shall not be awarded under subsection (b) unless the court determines that the plaintiff has exhausted the administrative remedies available to such plaintiff within the Internal Revenue Service."

In 1988, P.L. 100-647, Sec. 6241(a), added Code Sec. 7433, effective for actions of officers or employees of the Internal Revenue Service after 11/10/88.

Sec. 7433A. Civil damages for certain unauthorized collection actions by persons performing services under qualified tax collection contracts.

(a) In general.

Subject to the modifications provided by subsection (b), section 7433 shall apply to the acts and omissions of any person performing services under a qualified tax collection contract (as defined in section 6306(b)) to the same extent and in the same manner as if such person were an employee of the Internal Revenue Service.

(b) Modifications.

For purposes of subsection (a)—

(1) Any civil action brought under section 7433 by reason of this section shall be brought against the person who entered into the qualified tax collection contract with the Secretary and shall not be brought against the United States.

(2) Such person and not the United States shall be liable for any damages and costs determined in such civil action.

(3) Such civil action shall not be an exclusive remedy with respect to such person.

(4) Subsections (c), (d)(1), and (e) of section 7433 shall not apply.

In 2004, P.L. 108-357, Sec. 881(b)(1), added Code Sec. 7433A, effective 10/22/2004.

Sec. 7434. Civil damages for fraudulent filing of information returns.

(a) In general.

If any person willfully files a fraudulent information return with respect to payments purported to be made to any other person, such other person may bring a civil action for damages against the person so filing such return.

(b) Damages.

In any action brought under subsection (a), upon a finding of liability on the part of the defendant, the defendant shall be liable to the plaintiff in an amount equal to the greater of $5,000 or the sum of—

(1) any actual damages sustained by the plaintiff as a proximate result of the filing of the fraudulent information return (including any costs attributable to resolving deficiencies asserted as a result of such filing),

(2) the costs of the action, and

(3) in the court's discretion, reasonable attorneys' fees.

(c) Period for bringing action.

Notwithstanding any other provision of law, an action to enforce the liability created under this section may be brought without regard to the amount in controversy and may be brought only within the later of—

(1) 6 years after the date of the filing of the fraudulent information return, or

(2) 1 year after the date such fraudulent information return would have been discovered by exercise of reasonable care.

(d) Copy of complaint filed with IRS.

Any person bringing an action under subsection (a) shall provide a copy of the complaint to the Internal Revenue Service upon the filing of such complaint with the court.

(e) Finding of court to include correct amount of payment.

The decision of the court awarding damages in an action brought under subsection (a) shall include a finding of the correct amount which should have been reported in the information return.

(f) Information return.

For purposes of this section, the term "information return" means any statement described in section 6724(d)(1)(A).

In 1998, P.L. 105-206, Sec. 6023(29), substituted "attorneys' fees" for "attorneys fees" in para. (b)(3), effective 7/22/98.

In 1996, P.L. 104-168, Sec. 601(a), added Code Sec. 7434, effective for fraudulent returns filed after 7/30/96.

Judicial proceedings

Sec. 7435. Civil damages for unauthorized enticement of information disclosure.

(a) In general.

If any officer or employee of the United States intentionally compromises the determination or collection of any tax due from an attorney, certified public accountant, or enrolled agent representing a taxpayer in exchange for information conveyed by the taxpayer to the attorney, certified public accountant, or enrolled agent for purposes of obtaining advice concerning the taxpayer's tax liability, such taxpayer may bring a civil action for damages against the United States in a district court of the United States. Such civil action shall be the exclusive remedy for recovering damages resulting from such actions.

(b) Damages.

In any action brought under subsection (a), upon a finding of liability on the part of the defendant, the defendant shall be liable to the plaintiff in an amount equal to the lesser of $500,000 or the sum of—

(1) actual, direct economic damages sustained by the plaintiff as a proximate result of the information disclosure, and

(2) the costs of the action.

Damages shall not include the taxpayer's liability for any civil or criminal penalties, or other losses attributable to incarceration or the imposition of other criminal sanctions.

(c) Payment authority.

Claims pursuant to this section shall be payable out of funds appropriated under section 1304 of title 31, United States Code.

(d) Period for bringing action.

Notwithstanding any other provision of law, an action to enforce liability created under this section may be brought without regard to the amount in controversy and may be brought only within 2 years after the date the actions creating such liability would have been discovered by exercise of reasonable care.

(e) Mandatory stay.

Upon a certification by the Commissioner or the Commissioner's delegate that there is an ongoing investigation or prosecution of the taxpayer, the district court before which an action under this section is pending shall stay all proceedings with respect to such action pending the conclusion of the investigation or prosecution.

(f) Crime-fraud exception.

Subsection (a) shall not apply to information conveyed to an attorney, certified public accountant, or enrolled agent for the purpose of perpetrating a fraud or crime.

In 1996, P.L. 104-168, Sec. 1203(a), added Code Sec. 7435, effective for actions after 7/30/96.

Sec. 7436. Proceedings for determination of employment status.

(a) Creation of remedy.

If, in connection with an audit of any person, there is an actual controversy involving a determination by the Secretary as part of an examination that—

(1) one or more individuals performing services for such person are employees of such person for purposes of subtitle C, or

(2) such person is not entitled to the treatment under subsection (a) of section 530 of the Revenue Act of 1978 with respect to such an individual,

upon the filing of an appropriate pleading, the Tax Court may determine whether such a determination by the Secretary is correct and the proper amount of employment tax under such determination. Any such redetermination by the Tax Court shall have the force and effect of a decision of the Tax Court and shall be reviewable as such.

(b) Limitations.

(1) **Petitioner.** A pleading may be filed under this section only by the person for whom the services are performed.

(2) **Time for filing action.** If the Secretary sends by certified or registered mail notice to the petitioner of a determination by the Secretary described in subsection (a), no proceeding may be initiated under this section with respect to such determination unless the pleading is filed before the 91st day after the date of such mailing.

(3) **No adverse inference from treatment while action is pending.** If, during the pendency of any proceeding brought under this section, the petitioner changes his treatment for employment tax purposes of any individual whose employment status as an employee is involved in such proceeding (or of any individual holding a substantially similar position) to treatment as an employee, such change shall not be taken into account in the Tax Court's determination under this section.

(c) Small case procedures.

(1) **In general.** At the option of the petitioner, concurred in by the Tax Court or a division thereof before the hearing of the case, proceedings under this section may (notwithstanding the provisions of section 7453) be conducted subject to the rules of evidence, practice, and procedure applicable under section 7463 if the amount of employment taxes placed in dispute is $50,000 or less for each calendar quarter involved.

(2) **Finality of decisions.** A decision entered in any proceeding conducted under this subsection shall not be reviewed in any other court and shall not be treated as a precedent for any other case not involving the same petitioner and the same determinations.

(3) **Certain rules to apply.** Rules similar to the rules of the last sentence of subsection (a), and subsections (c), (d), and (e), of section 7463 shall apply to proceedings conducted under this subsection.

(d) Special rules.

(1) **Restrictions on assessment and collection pending action, etc.** The principles of subsections (a), (b), (c), (d) and (f) of section 6213, section 6214(a), section 6215, section 6503(a), section 6512, and section 7481 shall apply to proceedings brought under this section in the same manner as if the Secretary's determination described in subsection (a) were a notice of deficiency.

(2) **Awarding of costs and certain fees.** Section 7430 shall apply to proceedings brought under this section.

(e) Employment tax.

The term "employment tax" means any tax imposed by subtitle C.

In 2000, P.L. 106-554, Sec. 1(a)(7), [which enacted into law Sec. 314(f) of P.L. 106-554] added "and the proper amount of employment tax under such determination" after "Secretary is correct" in subsec. (a), effective 8/5/97.

In 1998, P.L. 105-206, Sec. 3103(b)(1), substituted "$50,000" for "$10,000" in para. (c)(1), effective for proceedings commenced after 7/22/98.

In 1997, P.L. 105-34, Sec. 1454(a), added Code Sec. 7436, effective 8/5/97.

Sec. 7437. Cross references.

(1) For determination of amount of any tax, additions to tax, etc., in title 11 cases, see section 505 of title 11 of the United States Code.

(2) For exclusion of tax liability from discharge in cases under title 11 of the United States Code, see section 523 of such title 11.

Code Sec. 7437(3) — Judicial proceedings

(3) For recognition of tax liens in cases under title 11 of the United States Code, see sections 545 and 724 of such title 11.

(4) For collection of taxes in connection with plans for individuals with regular income in cases under title 11 of the United States Code, see section 1328 of such title 11.

(5) For provisions permitting the United States to be made party defendant in a proceeding in a State court for the foreclosure of a lien upon real estate where the United States may have claim upon the premises involved, see section 2410 of Title 28 of the United States Code.

(6) For priority of lien of the United States in case of insolvency, see section 3713(a) of title 31, United States Code.

(7) For interest on judgments for overpayments, see section 2411(a) of Title 28 of the United States Code.

(8) For review of a Tax Court decision, see section 7482.

(9) For statute prohibiting suits to replevy property taken under revenue laws, see section 2463 of Title 28 of the United States Code.

In **1997**, P.L. 105-34, Sec. 1454(a), redesignated Code Sec. 7436 as Code Sec. 7437, effective 8/5/97.

In **1996**, P.L. 104-168, Sec. 601(a), redesignated Code Sec. 7434 as Code Sec. 7435, effective for fraudulent information returns filed after 7/30/96.

—P.L. 104-168, Sec. 1203(a), redesignated Code Sec. 7435 [as redesignated by Sec. 601(a) of this Act, see above] as Code Sec. 7436, effective for actions after 7/30/96.

In **1988**, P.L. 100-647, Sec. 6240(a), redesignated Code Sec. 7432 as Code Sec. 7433, effective for notices provided by the taxpayer of the failure to release a lien, and damages arising, after 12/31/88.

—P.L. 100-647, Sec. 6241(a), redesignated Code Sec. 7433 [as redesignated by Sec. 6240(a) of this Act, above] as Code Sec. 7434, effective for actions by officers or employees of the Internal Revenue Service after 11/10/88.

In **1982**, P.L. 97-258, Sec. 3(f)(14), substituted "section 3713(a) of title 31, United States Code" for "R.S. 3466 (31 U.S.C. 191)" in Code Sec. 7430(6) [sic Code Sec. 7430 redesignated as Code Sec. 7432 by P.L. 97-248, see below], effective 9/13/82.

—P.L. 97-248, Sec. 292(a), redesignated Code Sec. 7430 as Code Sec. 7431, effective for civil actions or proceedings commenced after 2/28/83.

—P.L. 97-248, Sec. 357(a), redesignated Code Sec. 7431 as Code Sec. 7432, effective for disclosures made after 9/3/82.

In **1980**, P.L. 96-589, Sec. 6(d)(1), amended para. (1) and deleted paras. (2), (3) and ... Sec. 6(i)(13), added paras. (2), (3) and (4), effective 10/1/79, except for any proceeding under the Bankruptcy Act begun before 10/1/79. Sec. 7(g) of this Act provides:

"(g) Definitions.

"For purposes of this section—

"(1) Bankruptcy case. The term 'bankruptcy case' means any case under title 11 of the United States Code (as recodified by P.L. 95-598).

"(2) Similar judicial proceeding. The term 'similar judicial proceeding' means a receivership, foreclosure, or similar proceeding in a Federal or State court (as modified by section 368(a)(3)(D) of the Internal Revenue Code of 1954)."

Prior to amendment, paras. (1), (2), (3) and (4) read as follows:

"(1) For exclusion of tax liability from discharge in bankruptcy, see section 17 of the Bankruptcy Act, as amended (11 U.S.C. 35).

"(2) For limit on amount allowed in bankruptcy proceedings on debts owing to the United States, see section 57(j) of the Bankruptcy Act, as amended (11 U.S.C. 93).

"(3) For recognition of tax liens in proceedings under the Bankruptcy Act, see section 67(b) and (c) of that act, as amended (11 U.S.C. 107).

"(4) For collection of taxes in connection with wage earners' plans in bankruptcy courts, see section 680 of the Bankruptcy Act, as added June 22, 1938 (11 U.S.C. 1080)."

In **1976**, P.L. 94-455, Sec. 1203(b)(2)(A), redesignated Code Sec. 7427 as Code Sec. 7428, effective for documents prepared after 12/31/76.

—P.L. 94-455, Sec. 1306(a), redesignated Code Sec. 7428 [as redesignated by Sec. 1203(b)(2)(A) of this Act, see above] as Code Sec. 7430, effective for pleadings filed more than 6 months after 10/4/76, but only with respect to determinations (or requests for determinations) made after 1/1/77.

—P.L. 94-455, Sec. 1906(a)(45), deleted "52 Stat. 851;" after the parenthesis at the end of para. (1) ... deleted "52 Stat. 867;" following the parenthesis at the end of para. (2) ... deleted "52 Stat. 876, 877;" following the parenthesis at the end of para. (3) ... deleted "52 Stat. 938;" following the parenthesis at the end of para. (4), effective 2/1/77.

In **1966**, P.L. 89-719, Sec. 109, redesignated Code Sec. 7425 as Code Sec. 7427.

Subchapter C.—The Tax Court

Part

I. Organization and jurisdiction.
II. Procedure.
III. Miscellaneous provisions.
IV. Declaratory judgments.

PART I.—ORGANIZATION AND JURISDICTION

Sec.

7441. Status.
7442. Jurisdiction.
7443. Membership.
7443A. Special trial judges.
7444. Organization.
7445. Offices.
7446. Times and places of sessions.
7447. Retirement.
7448. Annuities to surviving spouses and dependent children of judges and special trial judges.

In **2008**, P.L. 110-458, Sec. 108(l), repealed item 7443B.
Prior to repeal, item 7443B read as follows:
"7443B. Recall of special trial judges of the tax court."

In **2006**, P.L. 109-280, Sec. 854(c)(2), added "and special trial judges" after "judges" in item 7448.

—P.L. 109-280, Sec. 856(b), added item 7443B.

In **1986**, P.L. 99-514, Sec. 1556(b)(3), added item 7443A.

In **1976**, P.L. 94-455, Sec. 1906(b)(10), substituted "surviving spouses" for "widows" in the item for Code Sec. 7448.

In **1961**, added item 7448.

Sec. 7441. Status.

There is hereby established, under article I of the Constitution of the United States, a court of record to be known as the United States Tax Court. The members of the Tax Court shall be the chief judge and the judges of the Tax Court.

In **1969**, P.L. 91-172, Sec. 951, amended Code Sec. 7441, effective 12/30/69.
Prior to amendment, Code Sec. 7441 read as follows:
"SEC. 7441. STATUS.
"The Board of Tax Appeals shall be continued as an independent agency in the Executive Branch of the Government, and shall be known as the Tax Court of the United States. The members thereof shall be known as the chief judge and the judges of the Tax Court."

Sec. 7442. Jurisdiction.

The Tax Court and its divisions shall have such jurisdiction as is conferred on them by this title, by chapters 1, 2, 3, and 4 of the Internal Revenue Code of 1939, by title II and title III of the Revenue Act of 1926 (44 Stat. 10-87), or by laws enacted subsequent to February 26, 1926.

Sec. 7443. Membership.

(a) Number.

The Tax Court shall be composed of 19 members.

(b) Appointment.

Judges of the Tax Court shall be appointed by the President, by and with the advice and consent of the Senate, solely on the grounds of fitness to perform the duties of the office.

(c) Salary.

(1) Each judge shall receive salary at the same rate and in the same installments as judges of the district courts of the United States.

(2) For rate of salary and frequency of installment see section 135, title 28, United States Code, and section 5505, title 5, United States Code.

(d) Expenses for travel and subsistence.

Judges of the Tax Court shall receive necessary traveling expenses, and expenses actually incurred for subsistence while traveling on duty and away from their designated sta-

Judicial proceedings   Code Sec. 7443B

tions, subject to the same limitations in amount as are now or may hereafter be applicable to the United States Court of International Trade.

(e) Term of office.

The term of office of any judge of the Tax Court shall expire 15 years after he takes office.

(f) Removal from office.

Judges of the Tax Court may be removed by the President, after notice and opportunity for public hearing, for inefficiency, neglect of duty, or malfeasance in office, but for no other cause.

(g) Disbarment of removed judges.

A judge of the Tax Court removed from office in accordance with subsection (f) shall not be permitted at any time to practice before the Tax Court.

In **1980**, P.L. 96-439, Sec. 1, substituted "19" for "16" in subsec. (a), and deleted the last sentence of subsec. (b), effective 2/1/81.
Prior to amendment the last sentence of subsec. (b) read as follows:
"No individual shall be a judge of the Tax Court unless he is appointed to that office before attaining the age of 65."
—P.L. 96-417, Sec. 601(10), substituted "Court of International Trade" for "Customs Court" in subsec. (d), effective 11/1/80.
In **1975**, P.L. 94-91, Title IV, provided that travel expenses of the judges shall be paid upon the written certificate of the judge, effective 8/9/75.
In **1969**, P.L. 91-172, Sec. 952(a), added a sentence to the end of subsec. (b), effective for judges appointed after 12/30/69.
—P.L. 91-172, Sec. 952(b), amended subsec. (e), effective for 12/30/69 except, as provided in Sec. 962(c) of this Act, which reads as follows:
"(1) the term of office being served by a judge of the Tax Court on that date shall expire on the date it would have expired under the law in effect on the date preceding the date of enactment of this Act; and
"(2) a judge of the Tax Court on the date of enactment of this Act may be reappointed in the same manner as a judge of the Tax Court hereafter appointed.
Prior to amendment, subsec. (e) read as follows:
"The terms of office of all judges of the Tax Court shall expire 12 years after the expiration of the terms for which their predecessors were appointed; but any judge appointed to fill a vacancy occurring prior to the expiration of the term for which his predecessor was appointed shall be appointed only for the unexpired term of his predecessor."
—P.L. 91-172, Sec. 953, amended subsec. (c), effective 12/30/69.
Prior to amendment, subsec. (c) read as follows:
"(c) Salary. Each judge shall receive salary at the rate of $30,000 per annum, to be paid in monthly installments."
In **1964**, P.L. 88-426, Sec. 403(i), increased the salary of the judges from $22,500 to $30,000 in subsec. (c) effective on the first day of the first pay period which begins on or after 7/1/64, except to the extent provided in Sec. 501(c) of P.L. 88-426, see Sec. 501 of P.L. 88-426.
In **1955**, ch. 9, Sec. 1(h), increased the salary of the judges from "$15,000" a year to "$22,500" in subsec. (c), effective 3/1/55.

Sec. 7443A. Special trial judges.

(a) Appointment.

The chief judge may, from time to time, appoint special trial judges who shall proceed under such rules and regulations as may be promulgated by the Tax Court.

(b) Proceedings which may be assigned to special trial judges.

The chief judge may assign—

(1) any declaratory judgment proceeding,

(2) any proceeding under section 7463,

(3) any proceeding where neither the amount of the deficiency placed in dispute (within the meaning of section 7463) nor the amount of any claimed overpayment exceeds $50,000,

(4) any proceeding under section 6320 or 6330,

(5) any proceeding under section 7436(c),

(6) any proceeding under section 7623(b)(4), and

(7) any other proceeding which the chief judge may designate,

to be heard by the special trial judges of the court.

(c) Authority to make court decision.

The court may authorize a special trial judge to make the decision of the court with respect to any proceeding described in paragraph (1), (2), (3), (4), (5), or (6) of subsection (b), subject to such conditions and review as the court may provide.

(d) Salary.

Each special trial judge shall receive salary—

(1) at a rate equal to 90 percent of the rate for judges of the Tax Court, and

(2) in the same installments as such judges.

(e) Expenses for travel and subsistence.

Subsection (d) of section 7443 shall apply to special trial judges subject to such rules and regulations as may be promulgated by the Tax Court.

In **2006**, P.L. 109-432, Sec. 406(a)(2)(A), deleted "and" at the end of para. (b)(5), redesignated para. (b)(6) as para. (b)(7) and added para. (b)(6) . . . Sec. 406(a)(2)(B), substituted "(5), or (6)" for "or (5)" in subsec. (c), effective for information provided on or after 12/20/2006.
—P.L. 109-280, Sec. 857(a), deleted "and" at the end of para. (b)(4), redesignated para. (b)(5) as (b)(6), and added para. (b)(5) . . . Sec. 857(b), substituted "(4), or (5)" for "or (4)" in subsec. (c), effective for any proceeding under Code Sec. 7436(c) for which a decision has not become final (as determined under Code Sec. 7481) before 8/17/2006.
In **1998**, P.L. 105-277, Sec. 4002(e)(1), substituted "7443A(b)" for "7443(b)" in Sec. 3401(c)(1) of P.L. 105-206 [see below] . . . Sec. 4002(e)(2), substituted "7443A(c)" for "7443(b)" in Sec. 3401(c)(2) of P.L. 105-206 [see below], effective 10/21/98.
—P.L. 105-206, Sec. 3103(b)(1), substituted "$50,000" for "$10,000" in para. (b)(3), effective for proceedings commenced after 7/22/98.
—P.L. 105-206, Sec. 3401(c)(1), deleted "and" at the end of para. (b)(3), redesignated para. (b)(4) as (b)(5) and added para. (b)(4) [as clarified by Sec. 4002(e)(1) of P.L. 105-277, see above] . . . Sec. 3401(c)(2), substituted "(3), or (4)" for "or (3)" in subsec. (c) [as clarified by Sec. 4002(e)(2) of P.L. 105-277, see above], effective for collection actions initiated after the date which is 180 days after 7/22/98.
In **1988**, P.L. 100-647, Sec. 1015(j), of this Act provides:
"(j) Provision related to section 1556 of the reform act.
"To the extent the salary recommendations submitted by the President on January 5, 1987, are inconsistent with the provisions of section 7443A(d)(1) of the 1986 Code, such recommendations shall not be effective for any period."
In **1986**, P.L. 99-514, Sec. 1556(a), added Code Sec. 7443A, effective 10/22/86. Sec. 1556(c)(2) and (c)(3) of this Act provide:
"(2) Salary. Subsection (d) of section 7443A of the Internal Revenue Code of 1954 (as added by this section) shall take effect on the 1st day of the 1st month beginning after the date of the enactment of this Act.
"(3) New appointments not required. Nothing in the amendments made by this section shall be construed to require the reappointment of any individual serving as a special trial judge of the Tax Court on the day before the date of the enactment of this Act."

Sec. 7443B. Repealed.

> • *Caution:* Sec. 108(l), P.L. 110-458, repealed as if not enacted Sec. 856, P.L. 109-280, which added Code Sec. 7443B. For text of Code Sec. 7443B prior to the repeal of Sec. 856, P.L. 109-280 see history notes for this Code Sec.

In **2008**, P.L. 110-458, Sec. 108(l), repealed Sec. 856, P.L. 109-280 as if never enacted. Sec. 856(a), P.L. 109-280 added Code Sec. 7443B. Code Sec. 7443B as added by Sec. 856(a), P.L. 109-280 read as follows:
Prior to repeal of Sec. 856(a), P.L. 109-280, Code Sec. 7443B read as follows:
"SEC. 7443B. RECALL OF SPECIAL TRIAL JUDGES OF THE TAX COURT.
"(a) Recalling of retired special trial judges.
Any individual who has retired pursuant to the applicable provisions of title 5, United States Code, upon reaching the age and service requirements established therein, may at or after retirement be called upon by the chief judge of the Tax Court to perform such judicial duties with the Tax Court as may be requested of such individual for any period or periods specified by the chief judge; except that in the case of any such individual—
"(1) the aggregate of such periods in any 1 calendar year shall not (without such individual's consent) exceed 90 calendar days, and
"(2) such individual shall be relieved of performing such duties during any period in which illness or disability precludes the performance of such duties.
"Any act, or failure to act, by an individual performing judicial duties pursuant to this subsection shall have the same force and effect as if it were the act (or failure to act) of a special trial judge of the Tax Court.
"(b) Compensation. For the year in which a period of recall occurs, the special trial judge shall receive, in addition to the annuity provided under the applicable provisions of title 5, United States Code, an amount equal to the difference be-

3,877

tween that annuity and the current salary of the office to which the special trial judge is recalled.

"(c) Rulemaking authority. The provisions of this section may be implemented under such rules as may be promulgated by the Tax Court."

In 2006, P.L. 109-280, Sec. 856(a), added Code Sec. 7443B. Sec. 108(l), P.L. 110-458, repealed Sec. 856 of this act, and its amendments, as if never enacted.

Sec. 7444. Organization.

(a) Seal.

The Tax Court shall have a seal which shall be judicially noticed.

(b) Designation of chief judge.

The Tax Court shall at least biennially designate a judge to act as chief judge.

(c) Divisions.

The chief judge may from time to time divide the Tax Court into divisions of one or more judges, assign the judges of the Tax Court thereto, and in case of a division of more than one judge, designate the chief thereof. If a division, as a result of a vacancy or the absence or inability of a judge assigned thereto to serve thereon, is composed of less than the number of judges designated for the division, the chief judge may assign other judges to the division or direct the division to proceed with the transaction of business without awaiting any additional assignment of judges thereto.

(d) Quorum.

A majority of the judges of the Tax Court or of any division thereof shall constitute a quorum for the transaction of the business of the Tax Court or of the division, respectively. A vacancy in the Tax Court or in any division thereof shall not impair the powers nor affect the duties of the Tax Court or division nor of the remaining judges of the Tax Court or division, respectively.

Sec. 7445. Offices.

The principal office of the Tax Court shall be in the District of Columbia, but the Tax Court or any of its divisions may sit at any place within the United States.

Sec. 7446. Times and places of sessions.

The times and places of the sessions of the Tax Court and of its divisions shall be prescribed by the chief judge with a view to securing reasonable opportunity to taxpayers to appear before the Tax Court or any of its divisions, with as little inconvenience and expense to taxpayers as is practicable.

Sec. 7447. Retirement.

(a) Definitions.

For purposes of this section—

(1) The term "Tax Court" means the United States Tax Court.

(2) The term "judge" means the chief judge or a judge of the Tax Court; but such term does not include any individual performing judicial duties pursuant to subsection (c).

(3) In any determination of length of service as judge there shall be included all periods (whether or not consecutive) during which an individual served as judge, as judge of the Tax Court of the United States, or as a member of the Board of Tax Appeals.

(b) Retirement.

(1) Any judge shall retire upon attaining the age of 70.

(2) Any judge who meets the age and service requirements set forth in the following table may retire:

The judge has attained age:	And the years of service as a judge are at least:
65	15
66	14
67	13
68	12
69	11
70	10

(3) Any judge who is not reappointed following the expiration of the term of his office may retire upon the completion of such term, if (A) he has served as a judge of the Tax Court for 15 years or more and (B) not earlier than 9 months preceding the date of the expiration of the term of his office and not later than 6 months preceding such date, he advised the President in writing that he was willing to accept reappointment to the Tax Court.

(4) Any judge who becomes permanently disabled from performing his duties shall retire.

Section 8335(a) of title 5 of the United States Code (relating to automatic separation from the service) shall not apply in respect of judges. Any judge who retires shall be designated "senior judge".

(c) Recalling of retired judges.

At or after his retirement, any individual who has elected to receive retired pay under subsection (d) may be called upon by the chief judge of the Tax Court to perform such judicial duties with the Tax Court as may be requested of him for any period or periods specified by the chief judge; except that in the case of any such individual—

(1) the aggregate of such periods in any one calendar year shall not (without his consent) exceed 90 calendar days; and

(2) he shall be relieved of performing such duties during any period in which illness or disability precludes the performance of such duties.

Any act, or failure to act, by an individual performing judicial duties pursuant to this subsection shall have the same force and effect as if it were the act (or failure to act) of a judge of the Tax Court; but any such individual shall not be counted as a judge of the Tax Court for purposes of section 7443(a). Any individual who is performing judicial duties pursuant to this subsection shall be paid the same compensation (in lieu of retired pay) and allowances for travel and other expenses as a judge.

(d) Retired pay.

Any individual who—

(1) retires under paragraph (1), (2), or (3) of subsection (b) and elects under subsection (e) to receive retired pay under this subsection shall receive retired pay during any period at a rate which bears the same ratio to the rate of the salary payable to a judge during such period as the number of years he has served as judge bears to 10; except that the rate of such retired pay shall not be more than the rate of such salary for such period; or

(2) retires under paragraph (4) of subsection (b) and elects under subsection (e) to receive retired pay under this subsection shall receive retired pay during any period at a rate—

(A) equal to the rate of the salary payable to a judge during such period if before he retired he had served as a judge not less than 10 years; or

(B) one-half of the rate of the salary payable to a judge during such period if before he retired he had served as a judge less than 10 years.

Such retired pay shall begin to accrue on the day following the day on which his salary as judge ceases to accrue, and shall continue to accrue during the remainder of his life. Retired pay under this subsection shall be paid in the same manner as the salary of a judge. In computing the rate of the retired pay under paragraph (1) of this subsection for any individual who is entitled thereto, that portion of the aggregate number of years he has served as a judge which is a fractional part of 1 year shall be eliminated if it is less than 6 months, or shall be counted as a full year if it is 6 months or more. In computing the rate of the retired pay under paragraph (1) of this subsection for any individual who is entitled thereto, any period during which such individual performs services under subsection (c) on a substantially full-time basis shall be treated as a period during which he has served as a judge.

(e) Election to receive retired pay.

Any judge may elect to receive retired pay under subsection (d). Such an election—

(1) may be made only while an individual is a judge (except that in the case of an individual who fails to be reappointed as judge at the expiration of a term of office, it may be made at any time before the day after the day on which his successor takes office);

(2) once made, shall be irrevocable;

(3) in the case of any judge other than the chief judge, shall be made by filing notice thereof in writing with the chief judge; and

(4) in the case of the chief judge, shall be made by filing notice thereof in writing with the Office of Personnel Management.

The chief judge shall transmit to the Office of Personnel Management a copy of each notice filed with him under this subsection.

(f) Retired pay affected in certain cases.

In the case of an individual for whom an election to receive retired pay under subsection (d) is in effect—

(1) 1-year forfeiture for failure to perform judicial duties. If such individual during any calendar year fails to perform judicial duties required of him by subsection (c), such individual shall forfeit all rights to retired pay under subsection (d) for the 1-year period which begins on the 1st day on which he so fails to perform such duties.

(2) Permanent forfeiture of retired pay where certain non-government services performed. If such individual performs (or supervises or directs the performance of) legal or accounting services in the field of Federal taxation for his client, his employer, or any of his employer's clients, such individual shall forfeit all rights to retired pay under subsection (d) for all periods beginning on or after the 1st day on which he engages in any such activity. The preceding sentence shall not apply to any civil office or employment under the Government of the United States.

(3) Suspension of retired pay during period of compensated Government service. If such individual accepts compensation for civil office or employment under the Government of the United States (other than the performance of judicial duties pursuant to subsection (c)), such individual shall forfeit all rights to retired pay under subsection (d) for the period for which such compensation is received.

(4) Forfeitures of retired pay under paragraphs (1) and (2) not to apply where individual elects to freeze amount of retired pay.

(A) In general. If any individual makes an election under this paragraph—

(i) paragraphs (1) and (2) (and subsection (c)) shall not apply to such individual beginning on the date such election takes effect, and

(ii) the retired pay under subsection (d) payable to such individual for periods beginning on or after the date such election takes effect shall be equal to the retired pay to which such individual would be entitled without regard to this clause at the time of such election.

(B) Election. An election under this paragraph—

(i) may be made by an individual only if such individual meets the age and service requirements for retirement under paragraph (2) of subsection (b),

(ii) may be made only during the period during which the individual may make an election to receive retired pay or while the individual is receiving retired pay, and

(iii) shall be made in the same manner as the election to receive retired pay.

Such an election, once it takes effect, shall be irrevocable.

(C) When election takes effect. Any election under this paragraph shall take effect on the 1st day of the 1st month following the month in which the election is made.

(g) Coordination with Civil Service retirement.

(1) General rule. Except as otherwise provided in this subsection, the provisions of the civil service retirement laws (including the provisions relating to the deduction and withholding of amounts from basic pay, salary, and compensation) shall apply in respect of service as a judge (together with other service as an officer or employee to whom such civil service retirement laws apply) as if this section had not been enacted.

(2) Effect of electing retired pay. In the case of any individual who has filed an election to receive retired pay under subsection (d)—

(A) no annuity or other payment shall be payable to any person under the civil service retirement laws with respect to any service performed by such individual (whether performed before or after such election is filed and whether performed as judge or otherwise);

(B) no deduction for purposes of the Civil Service Retirement and Disability Fund shall be made from retired pay payable to him under subsection (d) or from any other salary, pay, or compensation payable to him, for any period beginning after the day on which such election is filed; and

(C) such individual shall be paid the lump-sum credit computed under section 8331(8) of title 5 of the United States Code upon making application therefor with the Office of Personnel Management.

(h) Retirement for disability.

(1) Any judge who becomes permanently disabled from performing his duties shall certify to the President his disability in writing. If the chief judge retires for disability, his retirement shall not take effect until concurred in by the President. If any other judge retires for disability, he shall furnish to the President a certificate of disability signed by the chief judge.

(2) Whenever any judge who becomes permanently disabled from performing his duties does not retire and the President finds that such judge is unable to discharge efficiently all the duties of his office by reason of permanent mental or physical disability and that the appointment of an additional judge is necessary for the efficient dispatch of business, the President shall declare such judge to be retired.

(i) Revocation of election to receive retired pay.

(1) In general. Notwithstanding subsection (e)(2), an individual who has filed an election to receive retired pay under subsection (d) may revoke such election at any time before the first day on which retired pay (or compensation under subsection (c) in lieu of retired pay) would (but for such revocation) begin to accrue with respect to such individual.

(2) **Manner of revoking.** Any revocation under this subsection shall be made by filing a notice thereof in writing with the Civil Service Commission. The Civil Service Commission shall transmit to the chief judge a copy of each notice filed under this subsection.

(3) **Effect of revocation.** In the case of any revocation under this subsection—

(A) for purposes of this section, the individual shall be treated as not having filed an election to receive retired pay under subsection (d),

(B) for purposes of section 7448—

(i) the individual shall be treated as not having filed an election under section 7448(b), and

(ii) section 7448(g) shall not apply, and the amount credited to such individual's account (together with interest at 4 percent per annum to December 31, 1947, and 3 percent per annum thereafter, compounded on December 31 of each year to the date on which the revocation is filed) shall be returned to such individual,

(C) no credit shall be allowed for any service as a judge of the Tax Court unless with respect to such service either there has been deducted and withheld the amount required by the civil service retirement laws or there has been deposited in the Civil Service Retirement and Disability Fund an amount equal to the amount so required, with interest,

(D) the Tax Court shall deposit in the Civil Service Retirement and Disability Fund an amount equal to the additional amount it would have contributed to such Fund but for the election under subsection (e), and

(E) if subparagraph (D) is complied with, service on the Tax Court shall be treated as service with respect to which deductions and contributions had been made during the period of service.

(j) **Thrift savings plan.**

(1) **Election to contribute.**

(A) In general. A judge of the Tax Court may elect to contribute to the Thrift Savings Fund established by section 8437 of title 5, United States Code.

(B) Period of Election. An election may be made under this paragraph only during a period provided under section 8432(b) of title 5, United States Code, for individuals subject to chapter 84 of such title.

(2) **Applicability of title 5 provisions.** Except as otherwise provided in this subsection, the provisions of subchapters III and VII of chapter 84 of title 5, United States Code, shall apply with respect to a judge who makes an election under paragraph (1).

(3) **Special rules.**

(A) Amount contributed. The amount contributed by a judge to the Thrift Savings Fund in any pay period shall not exceed the maximum percentage of such judge's basic pay for such period as allowable under section 8440f of title 5, United States Code. Basic pay does not include any retired pay paid pursuant to this section.

(B) Contributions for benefit of judge. No contributions may be made for the benefit of a judge under section 8432(c) of title 5, United States Code.

(C) Applicability of section 8433(b) of title 5 whether or not judge retires. Section 8433(b) of title 5, United States Code, applies with respect to a judge who makes an election under paragraph (1) and who either—

(i) retires under subsection (b), or

(ii) ceases to serve as a judge of the Tax Court but does not retire under subsection (b).

Retirement under subsection (b) is a separation from service for purposes of subchapters III and VII of chapter 84 of that title.

(D) Applicability of section 8351(b)(5) of title 5. The provisions of section 8351(b)(5) of title 5, United States Code, shall apply with respect to a judge who makes an election under paragraph (1).

(E) Exception. Notwithstanding subparagraph (C), if any judge retires under this section, or resigns without having met the age and service requirements set forth under subsection (b)(2), and such judge's nonforfeitable account balance is less than an amount that the Executive Director of the Federal Retirement Thrift Investment Board prescribes by regulation, the Executive Director shall pay the non-forfeitable account balance to the participant in a single payment.

In **2006**, P.L. 109-280, Sec. 853(a), added subsec. (j), effective 8/17/2006, except that U.S. Tax Court judges may only begin to participate in the Thrift Savings Plan at the next open season beginning after such date.

In **1988**, P.L. 100-647, Sec. 1015(k)(1), added the last sentence to subsec. (d), effective for purposes of determining the amount of retired pay for months beginning after the date of enactment of this Act regardless of when services under Code Sec. 7447(c) were performed.

In **1986**, P.L. 99-514, Sec. 1557(a), amended para. (b)(2) . . . Sec. 1557(b), amended subsec. (f) . . . Sec. 1557(d)(1), deleted para. (a)(2), and redesignated paras. (a)(3) and (a)(5), as paras. (a)(2) and (a)(3) . . . Sec. 1557(d)(2), substituted "Office of Personnel Management" for "Civil Service Commission" each place it appeared in subsec. (e) . . . Sec. 1557(d)(3), substituted "Office of Personnel Management" for "Civil Service Commission" in subpara. (g)(2)(C), effective 10/22/86. Sec. 1557(e)(2) of this Act provides:

"(2) Forfeiture of retired pay.—The amendments made by this section shall not apply to any individual who, before the date of the enactment of this Act, forfeited his rights to retired pay under section 7447(d) of the Internal Revenue Code of 1954 by reason of the 1st sentence of section 7447(f) of such Code (as in effect on the day before such date)."

Prior to amendment, para. (b)(2) read as follows:

"(2) Any judge who has attained the age of 65 may retire any time after serving as judge for 15 years or more."

Prior to amendment, subsec. (f) read as follows:

"(f) Individuals receiving retired pay to be available for recall.

"Any individual who has elected to receive retired pay under subsection (d) who thereafter—

"(1) accepts civil office or employment under the Government of the United States (other than the performance of judicial duties pursuant to subsection (c)); or

"(2) performs (or supervises or directs the performance of) legal or accounting services in the field of Federal taxation or in the field of the renegotiation of Federal contracts for his client, his employer, or any of his employer's clients,

shall forfeit all rights to retired pay under subsection (d) for all periods beginning on or after the first day on which he accepts such office or employment or engages in any activity described in paragraph (2). Any individual who has elected to receive retired pay under subsection (d) who thereafter during any calendar year fails to perform judicial duties required of him by subsection (c) shall forfeit all rights to retired pay under subsection (d) for the 1-year period which begins on the first day on which he so fails to perform such duties."

Prior to deletion, para. (a)(2) read as follows:

"(2) The term 'Civil Service Commission' means the United States Civil Service Commission."

In **1982**, P.L. 97-362, Sec. 106(d), added the last sentence to subsec. (b), effective 10/25/82.

In **1978**, P.L. 95-472, Sec. 1, added subsec. (i), effective for revocations made after 10/17/78. Sec. 2(b) of the Act provides as follows:

"(b) Any individual who elects to revoke under section 7447(i) of the Internal Revenue Code of 1954 within one year after the date of enactment of this Act shall be treated as having the requisite current service for purposes of redepositing funds in the Civil Service Retirement and Disability Fund and for purposes of reviving creditable service under subchapter III of chapter 83 of title 5 of the United States Code."

In **1971**, P.L. 92-41, Sec. 4(a), substituted "At or after his retirement, any individual who has elected to receive" for "Any individual who is receiving" in the first sentence of subsec. (c), effective as if included in the Internal Revenue Code of 1954 on the date of its enactment. Provisions having the same effect as such amendment shall be treated as having been included in the Internal Revenue Code of 1939 effective on and after 8/7/53.

In **1969**, P.L. 91-172, Sec. 954(a), amended subsec. (b) . . . Sec. 954(b), amended subsec. (d) . . . Sec. 954(c), deleted paras. (g)(2), (3), and (4) and added para. (g)(2) . . . Sec. 954(d), added subsec. (h) . . . Sec. 954(e), repealed para. (a)(4), and substituted "civil service retirement laws" for "Civil Service Retirement Act" and substituted "such civil service retirement laws apply" for "civil service retirement laws" in para. (g)(1), effective 12/30/69, except as provided in Sec. 962(d) of this Act, which reads as follows:

"(1) all judges of the Tax Court retiring on or after the date of enactment of this Act, and

"(2) all individuals performing judicial duties pursuant to section 7447(c) or receiving retired pay pursuant to section 7447(d) on the day preceding the date of enactment of this Act.

Any individual who has served as a judge of the Tax Court for 18 years or more by the end of one year after the date of the enactment of this Act may retire in accordance with the provisions of section 7447 of the Internal Revenue Code of 1954 as in effect on the day preceding the date of the enactment of this Act. Any individual who is a judge of the Tax Court on the date of the enactment of this Act may retire under provisions of section 7447 of such Code upon the completion of the term of his office, if he is not reappointed as a judge of the Tax Court and gives notice to the President within the time prescribed by section 7447(b) of such Code (or if his term expires within 6 months after the date of enactment of this Act, gives notice to the President before the expiration of 3 months after the date of enactment of this Act), and shall receive retired pay at a rate which bears the same ratio to the rate of the salary payable to a judge as the number of years he has served as a judge of the Tax Court bears to 15; except that the rate of such retired pay shall not exceed the rate of the salary of a judge of the Tax Court. For purposes of the preceding sentence the years of service as a judge of the Tax Court shall be determined in the manner set forth in section 7447(d) of such Code."

Prior to amendment, para. (a)(4) read as follows:

"(4) The term 'Civil Service Act' means the Civil Service Act of May 29, 1930, as amended."

Prior to amendment, para. (b) read as follows:

"(b) Retirement.

"(1) Any judge who has served as judge for 18 years or more may retire at any time.

"(2) Any judge who has served as judge for 10 years or more and has attained the age of 70 shall retire not later than the close of the third month beginning after whichever of the following months is the latest:

"(A) The month in which he attained age 70;
"(B) The month in which he completed 10 years of service as judge; or
"(C) August 1953.

Section 2(a) of the Civil Service Retirement Act (relating to automatic separation from the service) shall not apply in respect of judges."

Prior to amendment, subsec. (d) read as follows:

"(d) Retired pay.

"Any individual who after August 7, 1953—

"(1) ceases to be a judge by reason of paragraph (2) of subsection (b), or ceases to be a judge after having served as judge for 18 years or more; and

"(2) elects under subsection (e) to receive retired pay under this subsection, shall receive retired pay during any period at a rate which bears the same ratio to the rate of the salary payable to a judge during such period as the number of years he has served as judge bears to 24; except that the rate of such retired pay shall be not less than one-half of the rate of such salary for such period and not more than the rate of such salary for such period. Such retired pay shall begin to accrue on the day following the day on which his salary as judge ceases to accrue, and shall continue to accrue during the remainder of his life. Retired pay under this subsection shall be paid in the same manner as the salary of a judge. In computing the rate of the retired pay under this subsection for any individual who is entitled thereto, that portion of the aggregate number of years he has served as a judge which is a fractional part of 1 year shall be eliminated if it is less than 6 months, or shall be counted as a full year if it is 6 months or more.

Prior to deletion, paras. (g)(2), (3) and (4) read as follows:

"(2) Effect of electing retired pay. In the case of any individual who has filed an election to receive retired pay under subsection (d) and who has not filed a waiver under paragraph (3) of this subsection—

"(A) he shall not be entitled to any annuity under section 1, 2, 3A, 6, or 7 of the Civil Service Retirement Act for any period beginning on or after the day on which he files such election;

"(B) no amount shall be returned to him under section 7(a) of such Act;

"(C) subsections (b) and (c) of section 4 of such Act, and subsection (c) of section 12 of such Act, shall apply in respect of such individual as if he were retiring or had retired under section 1 of such Act on the date on which his retired pay under subsection (d) of this section began to accrue; except that—

"(i) the amount of any annuity payable to a survivor of such individual under subsection (b) or (c) of such section 4 or under subsection (c) of such section 12 shall be based on a life annuity for such individual computed as provided in subsection (a) of such section 4, and

"(ii) if such individual makes the election provided by subsection (b) or (c) of such section 4, his retired pay under subsection (d) of this section shall be reduced by the amount by which a life annuity computed as provided in subsection (a) of such section 4 would be reduced;

"(D) in computing the aggregate amount of the annuity paid for purposes of section 12(g) of such Act, any retired pay which has accrued under subsection (d) of this section (including any such retired pay forfeited under subsection (f)) shall be included as if it were an annuity payable to him under such Act; and

"(E) no deduction for purposes of the civil service retirement and disability fund shall be made from the retired pay payable to him under subsection (d) of this section, or from any other salary, pay, or compensation payable to him, for any period after the date on which such retired pay began to accrue.

"(3) Waiver of civil service benefits.

"(A) Any individual who has elected to receive retired pay under subsection (d) of this section may (at any time thereafter during the period prescribed by subsection (e)(1)) waive all benefits under the Civil Service Retirement Act. Such a waiver—

"(i) once made, shall be irrevocable, and

"(ii) shall be made in the same manner as is provided for an election by such individual under subsection (e). The chief judge shall transmit to the Civil Service Commission a copy of each notice of waiver filed with him under this paragraph.

"(B) In the case of any individual who has made a waiver under this paragraph—

"(i) no annuity shall be payable to any person under the Civil Service Retirement Act with respect to any service performed by such individual (whether performed before or after such waiver is filed and whether performed as judge or otherwise);

"(ii) no deduction shall be made from any salary, pay, or compensation of such individual for purposes of the civil service retirement and disability fund for any period beginning after the day on which such waiver is filed;

"(iii) except as provided in clause (iv), no refund shall be made under the Civil Service Retirement Act of any amount credited to the account of such individual or of any interest on any amount so credited;

"(iv) additional sums voluntarily deposited by such individual under the second paragraph of section 10 of the Civil Service Retirement Act shall be promptly refunded, together with interest on such additional sums at 3 percent per annum (compounded on December 31 of each year) to the day of such filing; and

"(v) subsections (e) and (g) of section 12 of the Civil Service Retirement Act shall not apply.

"(4) Employees' compensation. The fourth and sixth paragraphs of section 6 of the Civil Service Retirement Act shall apply in respect of retired pay accruing under subsection (d) of this section as if such retired pay were an annuity payable under such act."

—P.L. 91-172, Sec. 960(c), substituted "United States Tax Court" for "Tax Court of the United States" in para. (a)(1) . . . Sec. 960(d), substituted ", or as judge of the Tax Court of the United States, or as a member of the Board of Tax Appeals" for "or as a member of the Board" in para. (a)(5), effective 12/30/69.

In 1966, P.L. 89-354, Sec. 1, substituted "during any period at a rate which bears the same ratio to the rate of the salary payable to a judge during such period" for "at a rate which bears the same ratio to the rate of the salary payable to him as judge at the time he ceases to be a judge" and "the rate of such salary for such period" for "the rate of such salary" wherever appearing in subsec. (d), effective on or after the first day of the first calendar month which begins after 2/2/66.

Sec. 7448. Annuities to surviving spouses and dependent children of judges and special trial judges.

(a) Definitions.

For purposes of this section—

(1) The term "Tax Court" means the United States Tax Court.

(2) The term "judge" means the chief judge or a judge of the Tax Court, including any individual receiving retired pay (or compensation in lieu of retired pay) under section 7447 or under section 1106 of the Internal Revenue Code of 1939 whether or not performing judicial duties pursuant to section 7447(c) or pursuant to section 1106(d) of the Internal Revenue Code of 1939.

(3) The term "chief judge" means the chief judge of the Tax Court.

(4) The term "judge's salary" means the salary of a judge received under section 7443(c), retired pay received under section 7447(d), and compensation (in lieu of retired pay) received under section 7447(c).

(5) The term "special trial judge" means a judicial officer appointed pursuant to section 7443A, including any individual receiving an annuity under chapters 83 or 84 of title 5, United States Code, whether or not performing judicial duties under section 7443B.

(6) The term "special trial judge's salary" means the salary of a special trial judge received under section 7443A(d), any amount received as an annuity under chapters 83 or 84 of title 5, United States Code, and compensation received under section 7443B.

(7) The term "survivors annuity fund" means the Tax Court judges survivors annuity fund established by this section.

(8) The term "surviving spouse" means a surviving spouse of an individual, who either (A) shall have been

3,881

married to such individual for at least 2 years immediately preceding his death or (B) is a parent of issue by such marriage, and who has not remarried.

(9) The term "dependent child" means an unmarried child, including a dependent stepchild or an adopted child, who is under the age of 18 years or who because of physical or mental disability is incapable of self-support.

(b) Election.

(1) **Judges.** Any judge may by written election filed while he is a judge (except that in the case of an individual who is not reappointed following expiration of his term of office, it may be made at any time before the day after the day on which his successor takes office) bring himself within the purview of this section. In the case of any judge other than the chief judge the election shall be filed with the chief judge; in the case of the chief judge the election shall be filed as prescribed by the Tax Court.

(2) **Special trial judges.** Any special trial judge may by written election filed with the chief judge bring himself or herself within the purview of this section. Such election shall be filed not later than the later of 6 months after—

(A) 6 months after the date of the enactment of this paragraph,
(B) the date the judge takes office, or
(C) the date the judge marries.

(c) Survivors annuity fund.

(1) **Salary deductions.** There shall be deducted and withheld from the salary of each judge or special trial judge electing under subsection (b) a sum equal to 3.5 percent of such judge's or special trial judge's salary. The amounts so deducted and withheld from such judge's or special trial judge's salary shall, in accordance with such procedure as may be prescribed by the Comptroller General of the United States, be deposited in the Treasury of the United States to the credit of a fund to be known as the "Tax Court judicial officers survivors annuity fund" and said fund is appropriated for the payment of annuities, refunds, and allowances as provided by this section. Each judge or special trial judge electing under subsection (b) shall be deemed thereby to consent and agree to the deductions from his salary as provided in this subsection, and payment less such deductions shall be a full and complete discharge and acquittance of all claims and demands whatsoever for all judicial services rendered by such judge or special trial judge during the period covered by such payment, except the right to the benefits to which he or his survivors shall be entitled under the provisions of this section.

(2) **Appropriations where unfunded liability.**

(A) In general. Not later than the close of each fiscal year, there shall be deposited in the Treasury of the United States to the credit of the survivors annuity fund, in accordance with such procedures as may be prescribed by the Comptroller General of the United States, amounts required to reduce to zero the unfunded liability (if any) of such fund. Subject to appropriation Acts, such deposits shall be taken from sums available for such fiscal year for the payment of amounts described in subsection (a)(4) and section 7443A(d), and shall immediately become an integrated part of such fund.

(B) Exception. The amount required by subparagraph (A) to be deposited in any fiscal year shall not exceed an amount equal to 11 percent of the aggregate amounts described in subsection[s] (a)(4) and (a)(6) paid during such fiscal year.

(C) Unfunded liability defined. For purposes of subparagraph (A), the term "unfunded liability" means the amount estimated by the Secretary to be equal to the excess (as of the close of the fiscal year involved) of—

(i) the present value of all benefits payable from the survivors annuity fund (determined on an annual basis in accordance with section 9503 of title 31, United States Code), over

(ii) the sum of—

(I) the present values of future deductions under subsection (c) and future deposits under subsection (d), plus

(II) the balance in such fund as of the close of such fiscal year.

(D) Amounts not credited to individual accounts. Amounts appropriated pursuant to this paragraph shall not be credited to the account of any individual for purposes of subsection (g).

(d) Deposits in survivors annuity fund.

Each judge or special trial judge electing under subsection (b) shall deposit, with interest at 4 percent per annum to December 31, 1947, and 3 percent per annum thereafter, compounded on December 31 of each year, to the credit of the survivors annuity fund, a sum equal to 3.5 percent of his judge's or special trial judge's salary and of his basic salary, pay, or compensation for service as a Senator, Representative, Delegate, or Resident Commissioner in Congress, and for any other civilian service within the purview of section 8332 of title 5 of the United States Code. Each such judge or special trial judge may elect to make such deposits in installments during the continuance of his service as a judge or special trial judge in such amount and under such conditions as may be determined in each instance by the chief judge. Notwithstanding the failure of a judge or special trial judge to make such deposit, credit shall be allowed for the service rendered, but the annuity of the surviving spouse of such judge or special trial judge shall be reduced by an amount equal to 10 percent of the amount of such deposit, computed as of the date of the death of such judge or special trial judge, unless such surviving spouse shall elect to eliminate such service entirely from credit under subsection (n), except that no deposit shall be required from a judge or special trial judge for any year with respect to which deductions from his salary were actually made under the civil service retirement laws and no deposit shall be required for any honorable service in the Army, Navy, Air Force, Marine Corps, or Coast Guard of the United States.

(e) Investment of survivors annuity fund.

The Secretary of the Treasury shall invest from time to time, in interest-bearing securities of the United States or Federal farm loan bonds, such portions of the survivors annuity fund as in his judgment may not be immediately required for the payment of the annuities, refunds, and allowances as provided in this section. The income derived from such investments shall constitute a part of said fund for the purpose of paying annuities and of carrying out the provisions of subsections (g), (h), and (j).

(f) Crediting of deposits.

The amount deposited by or deducted and withheld from the salary of each judge or special trial judge electing to bring himself within the purview of this section for credit to the survivors annuity fund shall be credited to an individual account of such judge or special trial judge.

(g) Termination.

If the service of any judge or special trial judge electing under subsection (b) terminates other than pursuant to the provisions of section 7447 or other than pursuant to section

1106 of the Internal Revenue Code of 1939 or if any judge or special trial judge ceases to be married after making the election under subsection (b) and revokes (in a writing filed as provided in subsection (b)) such election, the amount credited to his individual account, together with interest at 4 percent per annum to December 31, 1947, and 3 percent per annum thereafter, compounded on December 31 of each year, to the date of his relinquishment of office, shall be returned to him. For the purpose of this section, the service of any judge or special trial judge electing under subsection (b) who is not reappointed following expiration of his term but who, at the time of such expiration, is eligible for and elects to receive retired pay under section 7447 shall be deemed to have terminated pursuant to said section.

(h) Entitlement to annuity.

In case any judge or special trial judge electing under subsection (b) shall die while a judge or special trial judge after having rendered at least 5 years of civilian service computed as prescribed in subsection (n), for the last 5 years of which the salary deductions provided for by subsection (c)(1) or the deposits required by subsection (d) have actually been made or the salary deductions required by the civil service retirement laws have actually been made—

(1) if such judge or special trial judge is survived by a surviving spouse but not by a dependent child, there shall be paid to such surviving spouse an annuity beginning with the day of the death of the judge or special trial judge or following the surviving spouse's attainment of the age of 50 years, whichever is the later, in an amount computed as provided in subsection (m); or

(2) if such judge or special trial judge is survived by a surviving spouse and a dependent child or children, there shall be paid to such surviving spouse an immediate annuity in an amount computed as provided in subsection (m), and there shall also be paid to or on behalf of each such child an immediate annuity equal to the lesser of—

(A) 10 percent of the average annual salary of such judge or special trial judge (determined in accordance with subsection (m)), or

(B) 20 percent of such average annual salary, divided by the number of such children; or

(3) if such judge or special trial judge leaves no surviving spouse but leaves a surviving dependent child or children, there shall be paid to or on behalf of each such child an immediate annuity equal to the lesser of—

(A) 20 percent of the average annual salary of such judge or special trial judge (determined in accordance with subsection (m)), or

(B) 40 percent of such average annual salary, divided by the number of such children.

The annuity payable to a surviving spouse under this subsection shall be terminable upon such surviving spouse's death or such surviving spouse's remarriage before attaining age 55. The annuity payable to a child under this subsection shall be terminable upon (A) his attaining the age of 18 years, (B) his marriage, or (C) his death, whichever first occurs, except that if such child is incapable of self-support by reason of mental or physical disability his annuity shall be terminable only upon death, marriage, or recovery from such disability. In case of the death of a surviving spouse of a judge or special trial judge leaving a dependent child or children of the judge or special trial judge surviving such spouse, the annuity of such child or children shall be recomputed and paid as provided in paragraph (3) of this subsection. In any case in which the annuity of a dependent child is terminated under this subsection, the annuities of any remaining dependent child or children, based upon the service of the same judge or special trial judge, shall be recomputed and paid as though the child whose annuity was so terminated had not survived such judge or special trial judge.

(i) Determination of dependency and disability.

Questions of dependency and disability arising under this section shall be determined by the chief judge subject to review only by the Tax Court, the decision of which shall be final and conclusive. The chief judge may order or direct at any time such medical or other examinations as he shall deem necessary to determine the facts relative to the nature and degree of disability of any dependent child who is an annuitant or applicant for annuity under this section, and may suspend or deny any such annuity for failure to submit to any examination so ordered or directed.

(j) Payments in certain cases.

(1) In any case in which—

(A) a judge or special trial judge electing under subsection (b) shall die while in office (whether in regular active service, retired from such service under section 7447, or receiving any annuity under chapters 83 or 84 of title 5, United 23 States Code,), before having rendered 5 years of civilian service computed as prescribed in subsection (n), or after having rendered 5 years of such civilian service but without a survivor or survivors entitled to annuity benefits provided by subsection (h), or

(B) the right of all persons entitled to annuity under subsection (h) based on the service of such judge or special trial judge shall terminate before a valid claim therefor shall have been established,

the total amount credited to the individual account of such judge or special trial judge, with interest at 4 percent per annum to December 31, 1947, and 3 percent per annum thereafter, compounded on December 31 of each year, to the date of the death of such judge or special trial judge, shall be paid, upon the establishment of a valid claim therefor, to the person or persons surviving at the date title to the payment arises, in the following order of precedence, and such payment shall be a bar to recovery by any other person:

(i) to the beneficiary or beneficiaries whom the judge or special trial judge may have designated by a writing filed prior to his death with the chief judge, except that in the case of the chief judge such designation shall be by a writing filed by him, prior to his death, as prescribed by the Tax Court;

(ii) if there be no such beneficiary, to the surviving spouse of such judge or special trial judge;

(iii) if none of the above, to the child or children of such judge or special trial judge and the descendants of any deceased children by representation;

(iv) if none of the above, to the parents of such judge or special trial judge or the survivor of them;

(v) if none of the above, to the duly appointed executor or administrator of the estate of such judge or special trial judge; and

(vi) if none of the above, to such other next of kin of such judge or special trial judge as may be determined by the chief judge to be entitled under the laws of the domicile of such judge or special trial judge at the time of his death.

Determination as to the surviving spouse, child, or parent of a judge or special trial judge for the purposes of this paragraph shall be made by the chief judge without regard to the definitions in paragraphs (8) and (9) of subsection (a).

(2) In any case in which the annuities of all persons entitled to annuity based upon the service of a judge or special trial judge shall terminate before the aggregate amount of annuity paid equals the total amount credited to the individual account of such judge or special trial judge, with interest at 4 percent per annum to December 31, 1947, and 3 percent per annum thereafter, compounded on December 31 of each year, to the date of the death of such judge or special trial judge, the difference shall be paid, upon establishment of a valid claim therefor, in the order of precedence prescribed in paragraph (1).

(3) Any accrued annuity remaining unpaid upon the termination (other than by death) of the annuity of any person based upon the service of a judge or special trial judge shall be paid to such person. Any accrued annuity remaining unpaid upon the death of any person receiving annuity based upon the service of a judge or special trial judge shall be paid, upon the establishment of a valid claim therefor, in the following order of precedence:

(A) to the duly appointed executor or administrator of the estate of such person;

(B) if there is no such executor or administrator payment may be made, after the expiration of thirty days from the date of the death of such person, to such individual or individuals as may appear in the judgment of the chief judge to be legally entitled thereto, and such payment shall be a bar to recovery by any other individual.

(k) Payments to persons under legal disability.

Where any payment under this section is to be made to a minor, or to a person mentally incompetent or under other legal disability adjudged by a court of competent jurisdiction, such payment may be made to the person who is constituted guardian or other fiduciary by the law of the State of residence of such claimant or is otherwise legally vested with the care of the claimant or his estate. Where no guardian or other fiduciary of the person under legal disability has been appointed under the laws of the State of residence of the claimant, the chief judge shall determine the person who is otherwise legally vested with the care of the claimant or his estate.

(l) Method of payment of annuities.

Annuities granted under the terms of this section shall accrue monthly and shall be due and payable in monthly installments on the first business day of the month following the month or other period for which the annuity shall have accrued. None of the moneys mentioned in this section shall be assignable, either in law or in equity, or subject to execution, levy, attachment, garnishment, or other legal process.

(m) Computation of annuities.

The annuity of the surviving spouse of a judge or special trial judge electing under subsection (b) shall be an amount equal to the sum of (1) 1.5 percent of the average annual salary (whether judge's or special trial judge's salary or compensation for other allowable service) received by such judge or special trial judge for judicial service (including periods in which he received retired pay under section 7447(d) or any annuity under chapters 83 or 84 of title 5, United States Code) or for any other prior allowable service during the period of 3 consecutive years in which he received the largest such average annual salary, multiplied by the sum of his years of such judicial service, his years of prior allowable service as a Senator, Representative, Delegate, or Resident Commissioner in Congress, his years of prior allowable service performed as a member of the Armed Forces of the United States, and his years, not exceeding 15, of prior allowable service performed as a congressional employee (as defined in section 2107 of title 5 of the United States Code), and (2) three-fourths of 1 percent of such average annual salary multiplied by his years of any other prior allowable service, except that such annuity shall not exceed an amount equal to 50 percent of such average annual salary, nor be less than an amount equal to 25 percent of such average annual salary, and shall be further reduced in accordance with subsection (d) (if applicable). In determining the period of 3 consecutive years referred to in the preceding sentence, there may not be taken into account any period for which an election under section 7447(f)(4) is in effect.

(n) Includible service.

Subject to the provisions of subsection (d), the years of service of a judge or special trial judge which are allowable as the basis for calculating the amount of the annuity of his surviving spouse shall include his years of service as a member of the United States Board of Tax Appeals, as a judge or special trial judge of the Tax Court of the United States, and as a judge or special trial judge of the Tax Court, his years of service pursuant to any appointment under section 7443A, his years of service as a Senator, Representative, Delegate, or Resident Commissioner in Congress, his years of active service as a member of the Armed Forces of the United States not exceeding 5 years in the aggregate and not including any such service for which credit is allowed for the purposes of retirement or retired pay under any other provision of law, and his years of any other civilian service within the purview of section 8332 of title 5 of the United States Code.

(o) Simultaneous entitlement.

Nothing contained in this section shall be construed to prevent a surviving spouse eligible therefor from simultaneously receiving an annuity under this section and any annuity to which such spouse would otherwise be entitled under any other law without regard to this section, but in computing such other annuity service used in the computation of such spouse's annuity under this section shall not be credited.

(p) Estimates of expenditures.

The chief judge shall submit to the President annual estimates of the expenditures and appropriations necessary for the maintenance and operation of the survivors annuity fund, and such supplemental and deficiency estimates as may be required from time to time for the same purposes, according to law. The chief judge shall cause periodic examinations of the survivors annuity fund to be made by an actuary, who may be an actuary employed by another department of the Government temporarily assigned for the purpose, and whose findings and recommendations shall be transmitted by the chief judge to the Tax Court.

(q) Transitional provision.

In the case of a judge who dies within 6 months after the date of enactment of this section after having rendered at least 5 years of civilian service computed as prescribed in subsection (n), but without having made an election as provided in subsection (b), an annuity shall be paid to his surviving spouse and surviving dependents as is provided in this section, as if such judge had elected on the day of his death to bring himself within the purview of this section but had not made the deposit provided for by subsection (d). An annuity shall be payable under this section computed upon the basis of the actual length of service as a judge and other allowable service of the judge and subject to the reduction required by subsection (d) even though no deposit has been made, as required by subsection (h) with respect to any of such service.

Judicial proceedings
Code Sec. 7448

(r) Waiver of civil service benefits.

Any judge electing under subsection (b) shall, at the time of such election, waive all benefits under the civil service retirement laws. Such a waiver shall be made in the same manner and shall have the same force and effect as an election filed under section 7447(e).

(s) Increases in survivor annuities.

Each time that an increase is made under section 8340(b) of title 5, United States Code, in annuities payable under subchapter III of chapter 83 of that title, each annuity payable from the survivors annuity fund under this sectionshall be increased at the same time by the same percentage by which annuities are increased under such section 8340(b).

(t) Authorization of appropriation.

Funds necessary to carry out the provisions of this section may be appropriated out of any money in the Treasury not otherwise appropriated.

In 2006, P.L. 109-280, Sec. 851(a), amended subsec. (s), effective with respect to increases made under section 8340(b) of title 5, United States Code, in annuities payable under subchapter III of chapter 83 of that title, taking effect after 8/17/2006.
Prior to amendment, subsec. (s) read as follows:
"(s) Increases attributable to increased pay.
"Whenever the salary of a judge under section 7443(c) is increased, each annuity payable from the survivors annuity fund which is based, in whole or in part, upon a deceased judge having rendered some portion of his or her final 18 months of service as a judge of the Tax Court, shall also be increased. The amount of the increase in such an annuity shall be determined by multiplying the amount of the annuity, on the date on which the increase in salary becomes effective, by 3 percent for each full 5 percent by which such salary has been increased."
—P.L. 109-280, Sec. 854(a), redesignated para. (a)(5), (6) and (7) as para. (a)(7), (8) and (9) and added new para. (a)(5) and (6)... Sec. 854(b)(1), added "and special trial judges" after "judges" in the heading for subsec. (b)... Sec. 854(b)(3), added para. (b)(2)... Sec. 854(c)(1), added matter to the heading of Sec. 7448... Sec. 854(c)(3)(A), inserted inserting "or special trial judge" after "judge [sic]" each place it appears in subsec. (c)(1), (d), (f), (g), (h), (j), (m), (n), and (u) other than in the phrase "chief judge"... Sec. 854(c)(3)(B), inserted inserting "or special trial judge's" after "judge's" each place it appears in subsec. (c)(1), (d), (f), (g), (h), (j), (m), (n), and (u)... Sec. 854(c)(4)(A), substituted "Tax Court judicial officers" for "Tax Court judges" in para. (c)(1)... Sec. 854(c)(4)(B)(i), inserted "and section 7443A(d)" after "(a)(4)" in para. (c)(2)(A)... Sec. 854(c)(4)(B)(ii), substituted "subsections (a)(4) and (a)(6)" for "subsection (a)(4)" in para. (c)(2)(B)... Sec. 854(c)(5)(A), substituted "service, retired" for "service or retired" and inserted ", or receiving any annuity under chapters 83 or 84 of title 5, United States Code," after "section 7447", in subpara. (j)(1)(A)... Sec. 854(c)(5)(B), substituted "paragraphs (8) and (9) of subsection (a)" for "subsections (a) (6) and (7)" in para. (j)(1)(A)... Sec. 854(c)(6), inserted "or any annuity under chapters 83 or 84 of title 5, United States Code" after "7447(d)" in para. (m)(1)... Sec. 854(c)(7), inserted "his years of service pursuant to any appointment under section 7443A," after "of the Tax Court," in subsec. (n), enacted 8/17/2006.

In 1986, P.L. 99-514, Sec. 1557(c), added the last sentence to subsec. (m), effective 10/22/86. Sec. 1557(e)(2) of this Act provides:
"(2) Forfeiture of retired pay. The amendments made by this section shall not apply to any individual who, before the date of the enactment of this Act, forfeited his rights to retired pay under section 7447(d) of the Internal Revenue Code of 1954 by reason of the 1st sentence of section 7447(f) of such Code (as in effect on the day before such date)."
—P.L. 99-514, Sec. 1559(a)(1)(A), substituted "3.5 percent" for "3 percent" in subsec. (c) (as so designated before redesignation as para. (c)(1) by Sec. 1559(a)(2)(A) of this Act, see below), effective for amounts paid after 11/1/86.
—P.L. 99-514, Sec. 1559(a)(1)(B), substituted "3.5 percent" for "3 percent" the second place it appeared in subsec. (d), effective for service after 11/1/86.
—P.L. 99-514, Sec. 1559(a)(2)(A), redesignated subsec. (c) as para. (c)(1), added new subsec. (c) heading "(c) Survivors annuity fund" and added para. (c)(2)... Sec. 1559(a)(2)(B), substituted "subsec. (c)(1)" for "subsec. (c)", in subsec. (h), effective for fiscal yrs. begin. after 12/31/86.
—P.L. 99-514, Sec. 1559(b)(1)(A)(i), substituted "1.5 percent" for "1¼ percent" in subsec. (m)... Sec. 1559(b)(1)(A)(ii), substituted "except that such amount shall not exceed an amount equal to 50 percent of such average annual salary, nor be less than an amount equal to 25 percent of such average annual salary, and shall be further reduced in accordance with subsection (d) (if applicable)." for "but such annuity shall not exceed 40 percent of such average annual salary and shall be further reduced in accordance with subsection (d), if applicable." in subsec. (m)... Sec. 1559(b)(1)(B), substituted "or such surviving spouse's remarriage before attaining age 55" for "or remarriage", in the second sentence of subsec. (h)... Sec. 1559(b)(2)(A), substituted "the lesser of—
"(A) 10 percent of the average annual salary of such judge (determined in accordance with subsection (m)), or
"(B) 20 percent of such average annual salary, divided by the number of such children; or" for 'one-half the amount of the annuity of such surviving spouse, but not to exceed $4,644 per year divided by the number of such children or $1,548 per year, whichever is lesser; or' in para. (h)(2)... Sec. 1559(b)(2)(B), substituted 'the lesser of—
"(A) 20 percent of the average annual salary of such judge (determined in accordance with subsection (m)), or
"(B) 40 percent of such average annual salary, divided by the number of such children.' for 'the amount of the annuity to which such surviving spouse would have been entitled under paragraph (2) of this subsection had such spouse survived, but not to exceed $5,580 per year divided by the number of such children or $1,860 per year, whichever is lesser.' in para. (h)(3), effective for annuities the starting date of which is after 11/1/86. Sec. 1559(d)(4) and (d)(5) of this Act provide:
"(4) Opportunity to revoke survivor annuity election.—
"(A) In general.—Any individual who before November 1, 1986, made an election under subsection (b) of section 7448 of the Internal Revenue Code of 1954 may revoke such election. Such a revocation shall constitute a complete withdrawal from the survivor annuity program provided for in such section and shall be filed as provided for elections under such subsection.
"(B) Effect of revocation.—Any revocation under subparagraph (A) shall have the same effect as if there were a termination to which section 7448(g) of such Code applies on the date such revocation is filed.
"(C) Period revocation permitted.—Any revocation under subparagraph (A) may be made only during the 180-day period beginning on the date of the enactment of this Act.
"(5) Opportunity to elect survivor annuity where prior revocation.—Any individual who under paragraph (4) revoked an election under subsection (b) of section 7448 of such Code may thereafter make such an election only if such individual deposits to the credit of the survivors annuity fund under subsection (c) of such section the entire amount paid to such individual under paragraph (4), together with interest computed as provided in subsection (d) of such section."
—P.L. 99-514, Sec. 1559(c), added "or if any judge ceases to be married after making the election under subsection (b) and revokes (in a writing filed as provided in subsection (b)) such election" after "1939" and deleted "of service" in the heading of subsec. (g), effective 11/1/86.

In 1984, P.L. 98-369, Sec. 462(a)(1), substituted "$4,644 per year divided by the number of such children or $1,548 per year," for "$900 per year divided by the number of such children or $360 per year," in para. (h)(2)... Sec. 462(a)(2), substituted "$5,580 per year divided by the number of such children or $1,860 per year, whichever is lesser" for "$480 per year" in para. (h)(3), effective for annuities payable for months begin. after 7/18/84.
—P.L. 98-216, Sec. 3(c)(1), substituted "President" for "Bureau of the Budget" in subsec. (p), effective 2/14/84.

In 1983, P.L. 97-448, Sec. 305(e), substituted "the amendment made by subsection (b)" for "the amendment made by subsection (a)" in Sec. 105(c) of P.L. 97-362, reproduced below.

In 1982, P.L. 97-362, Sec. 105(a)(1), substituted "3 consecutive years" for "5 consecutive years" in subsec. (m)... Sec. 105(a)(2), substituted "40" for "37½" in subsec. (m), effective for annuities payable for judges dying after 10/25/82.
—P.L. 97-362, Sec. 105(b), redesignated subsec. (s) as (t) and added subsec. (s), effective for increases in the salary of judges of the United States Tax Court taking effect after 10/25/82. Sec. 105(c) [as amended by Sec. 305(e) of P.L. 97-448, see above] of this Act provides:
"(c) Catchup for survivors annuities in pay status on date of enactment.
"If an annuity payable under section 7448(h) of the Internal Revenue Code of 1954 (relating to entitlement to annuity) to the surviving spouse of a judge of the United States Tax Court is being paid on the date of the enactment of this Act, then the amount of that annuity shall be adjusted, as of the first day of the first month beginning more than 30 days after such date, to reflect the amount of the annuity which would have been payable if the amendment made by subsection (b) applied with respect to increases in the salary of a judge under section 7443(c) of such Code taking effect after December 31, 1963."

In 1976, P.L. 94-455, Sec. 1906(a)(46)(A), substituted "The term 'surviving spouse'" means a surviving spouse of" for "The term 'widow' means a surviving wife of", and substituted "a parent of issue" for "the mother of issue" in para. (a)(6), ... Sec. 1906(a)(46)(B), amended subsec. (h), effective 2/1/77.
Prior to amendment, subsec. (h) read as follows:
"(h) Entitlement to annuity.
"In case any judge electing under subsection (b) shall die while a judge after having rendered at least 5 years of civilian service computed as prescribed in subsection (n), for the last 5 years of which the salary deductions provided for by subsection (c) or the deposits required by subsection (d) have actually been made or the salary deductions required by the civil service retirement laws have actually been made—
"(1) if such judge is survived by a widow but not by a dependent child, there shall be paid to such widow an annuity beginning with the day of the death of the judge or following the widow's attainment of the age of 50 years, whichever is the later, in an amount computed as provided in subsection (m); or
"(2) if such judge is survived by a widow and a dependent child or children, there shall be paid to such widow an immediate annuity in an amount computed as provided in subsection (m), and there shall also be paid to or on behalf of each such child an immediate annuity equal to one-half the amount of the annuity of such widow, but not to exceed $900 per year divided by the number of such children or $360 per year, whichever is lesser; or
"(3) if such judge leaves no surviving widow or widower but leaves a surviving dependent child or children, there shall be paid to or on behalf of each such child an immediate annuity equal to the amount of the annuity to which such widow

3,885

would have been entitled under paragraph (2) of this subsection had she survived, but not to exceed $480 per year.

"The annuity payable to a widow under this subsection shall be terminable upon such widow's death or remarriage. The annuity payable to a child under this subsection shall be terminable upon (A) his attaining the age of 18 years, (B) his marriage, or (C) his death, whichever first occurs, except that if such child is incapable of self-support by reason of mental or physical disability his annuity shall be terminable only upon death, marriage, or recovery from such disability. In case of the death of a widow of a judge leaving a dependent child or children of the judge surviving her, the annuity of such child or children shall be recomputed and paid as provided in paragraph (3) of this subsection. In any case in which the annuity of a dependent child is terminated under this subsection, the annuities of any remaining dependent child or children, based upon the service of the same judge, shall be recomputed and paid as though the child whose annuity was so terminated had not survived such judge."

—P.L. 94-455, Sec. 1906(a)(46)(C), substituted "such spouse" for "she" in subsecs. (h) and (o), effective 2/1/77. (See note above for subsec. (h) and note below for subsec. (o) before P.L. 94-455.)

—P.L. 94-455, Sec. 1906(a)(46)(D), substituted "such spouse's" for "her" in subsec. (o), effective 2/1/77.

—P.L. 94-455, Sec. 1906(a)(46)(E), substituted "surviving spouse" for "widow" each place it appeared in subsecs. (d), (j), (m), (n), (o) and (q), effective 2/1/77. (See note above for subsec. (o) before P.L. 94-455 amendments.)

—P.L. 94-455, Sec. 1906(a)(46)(F), substituted "surviving spouses" for "widows" in the heading of Code Sec. 7448, effective 2/1/77.

In **1971**, P.L. 92-41, Sec. 4(b), amended subsec. (m), only with respect to judges of the U.S. Tax Court dying on or after 7/1/71.

Prior to amendment, subsec. (m) read as follows:

"The annuity of the widow of a judge electing under subsection (b) shall be an amount equal to the sum of (1) 1¼ percent of the average annual salary received by such judge for judicial service and any other prior allowable service during the last 5 years of such service prior to his death, or prior to his receiving retired pay under section 7447(d), whichever first occurs, multiplied by the sum of his years of prior allowable service as a Senator, Representative, Delegate, or Resident Commissioner in Congress, his years of prior allowable service performed as a member of the Armed Forces of the United States, and his years, not exceeding 15, of prior allowable service performed as a congressional employee (as defined in section 2107 of title 5 of the United States Code), and (2) three-fourths of 1 percent of such average annual salary multiplied by his years of any other prior allowable service, but such annuity shall not exceed 37½ percent of such average annual salary and shall be further reduced in accordance with subsection (d), if applicable."

In **1969**, P.L. 91-172, Sec. 955(a), amended subsec. (b) . . . Sec. 955(b)(1), substituted "civil service retirement laws" for "Civil Service Retirement Act" the last place it appears in subsecs. (d), (h), and (r) . . . substituted "section 8332 of title 5 of the United States Code" for "section 3 of the Civil Service Retirement Act (5 U.S.C. 2253)" in subsecs. (d) and (n) . . . substituted "section 2107 of title 5 of the United States Code" for "section 1(c) of the Civil Service Retirement Act (5 U.S.C. 2251(c))" in subsec. (m) . . . substituted "an election filed under section 7447(e)" for "a waiver filed under section 7447(g)(3)" in subsec. (r), effective 12/30/69.

Prior to amendment, subsec. (b) read as follows:

"(b) Election.

"Any judge may by written election filed with the chief judge within 6 months after the date on which he takes office after appointment or any reappointment, or within 6 months after the date upon which he first becomes eligible for retirement under section 7447(b), or within 6 months after the enactment of this section, bring himself within the purview of this section, except that, in the case of such election by the chief judge, the election shall be filed as prescribed by the Tax Court subject to the preceding requirements as to the time of filing."

—P.L. 91-172, Sec. 960(c), substituted "United States Tax Court" for "Tax Court of the United States" . . . Sec. 960(e), added ", as a judge of the Tax Court of the United States", after "Tax Appeals" in subsec. (n), effective 12/30/69.

In **1961**, P.L. 87-370, Sec. 1, added Code Sec. 7448.

PART II.—PROCEDURE

Sec.
7451. Fee for filing petition.
7452. Representation of parties.
7453. Rules of practice, procedure, and evidence.
7454. Burden of proof in fraud, foundation manager, and transferee cases.
7455. Service of process.
7456. Administration of oaths and procurement of testimony.
7457. Witness fees.
7458. Hearings.
7459. Reports and decisions.
7460. Provisions of special application to divisions.
7461. Publicity of proceedings.
7462. Publication of reports.
7463. Disputes involving $50,000 or less.
7464. Intervention by trustee of debtor's estate.
7465. Provisions of special application to transferees.

In **1998**, P.L. 105-206, Sec. 3103(b)(2), substituted "$50,000" for "10,000" in item 7463.
In **1984**, P.L. 98-369, Sec. 461(a)(2)(B), substituted "$10,000" for "$5,000" in item 7463.
In **1980**, P.L. 96-589, Sec. 6(c)(2), amended item 7464 and added new item 7465. Prior to amendment, item 7464 read as follows:
"7464. Provisions of special application to transferees."
In **1978**, P.L. 95-600, Sec. 502(a)(2)(B), substituted "$5,000" for "$1,500" in item 7463.
In **1969**, P.L. 91-172, Sec. 957(b), renumbered item 7463 as 7464 and added new item 7463.

Sec. 7451. Fee for filing petition.

The Tax Court is authorized to impose a fee in an amount not in excess of $60 to be fixed by the Tax Court for the filing of any petition.

In **2006**, P.L. 109-280, Sec. 859(a), deleted "for the redetermination of a deficiency or for a declaratory judgment under part IV of this subchapter or under section 7428 or for judicial review under section 6226 or section 6228(a)." after "petition" and inserted a period in Code Sec. 7451, effective 8/17/2006.
In **1982**, P.L. 97-248, Sec. 402(c)(12), added "or for judicial review under section 6226 or section 6228(a)" at the end of Code Sec. 7451, effective for partnership tax. yrs. begin. after 9/3/82. Sec. 407(a)(3) of the Act provides:
"(3) The amendments made by sections 402, 403, and 404 [of this Act] shall apply to any partnership taxable year (or in the case of section 6232 of such Code, to any period) ending after the date of the enactment of this Act [9/3/82] if the partnership, each partner, and each indirect partner requests such application and the Secretary of the Treasury or his delegate consents to such application."
In **1981**, P.L. 97-34, Sec. 751(a), substituted "$60" for "$10", effective for petitions filed after 12/31/81.
In **1976**, P.L. 94-455, Sec. 1306(b)(1), added "or under section 7428" before the period at the end of Code Sec. 7451, effective for pleadings filed with the United States Tax Court, the district court of the United States for the District of Columbia or the United States Court of Claims more than 6 months after 10/4/76, but only with respect to determinations (or requests for determinations) made after 1/1/76.
In **1974**, P.L. 93-406, Sec. 1041(b)(1), substituted "deficiency or for a declaratory judgment under part IV of this subchapter" for "deficiency" in Code Sec. 7451, effective for pleadings filed more than one year after 9/2/74.

Sec. 7452. Representation of parties.

The Secretary shall be represented by the Chief Counsel for the Internal Revenue Service or his delegate in the same manner before the Tax Court as he has heretofore been represented in proceedings before such Court. The taxpayer shall continue to be represented in accordance with the rules of practice prescribed by the Court. No qualified person shall be denied admission to practice before the Tax Court because of his failure to be a member of any profession or calling.

In **1976**, P.L. 94-455, Sec. 1906(b)(13)(A), substituted "Secretary" for "Secretary or his delegate" in Code Sec. 7452, effective 2/1/77.
In **1959**, P.L. 86-368, Sec. 2(a), substituted "Chief Counsel for the Internal Revenue Service or his delegate" for "Assistant General Counsel of the Treasury Department serving as Chief Counsel of the Internal Revenue Service, or the delegate of such Chief Counsel", effective when the Chief Counsel for the Internal Revenue Service first appointed pursuant to Code Sec. 7801, as amended by Sec. 1 of P.L. 86-368, qualifies and takes office.

Sec. 7453. Rules of practice, procedure, and evidence.

Except in the case of proceedings conducted under section 7436(c) or 7463, the proceedings of the Tax Court and its divisions shall be conducted in accordance with such rules of practice and procedure (other than rules of evidence) as the Tax Court may prescribe and in accordance with the rules of evidence applicable in trials without a jury in the United States District Court of the District of Columbia.

Judicial proceedings Code Sec. 7456(c)(1)

In 1997, P.L. 105-34, Sec. 1454(b)(3), substituted "section 7436(c) or 7463" for "section 7463" in Code Sec. 7453, effective 8/5/97.

In 1969, P.L. 91-172, Sec. 960(f), substituted "Except in the case of proceedings conducted under section 7463, the" for "The" in Code Sec. 7453, effective 12/30/70.

Sec. 7454. Burden of proof in fraud, foundation manager, and transferee cases.
(a) Fraud.

In any proceeding involving the issue whether the petitioner has been guilty of fraud with intent to evade tax, the burden of proof in respect of such issue shall be upon the Secretary.

(b) Foundation managers.

In any proceeding involving the issue whether a foundation manager (as defined in section 4946(b)) has "knowingly" participated in an act of self-dealing (within the meaning of section 4941), participated in an investment which jeopardizes the carrying out of exempt purposes (within the meaning of section 4944), or agreed to the making of a taxable expenditure (within the meaning of section 4945), or whether the trustee of a trust described in section 501(c)(21) has "knowingly" participated in an act of self-dealing (within the meaning of section 4951) or agreed to the making of a taxable expenditure (within the meaning of section 4952), or whether an organization manager (as defined in section 4955(f)(2)) has "knowingly" agreed to the making of a political expenditure (within the meaning of section 4955), or whether an organization manager (as defined in section 4912(d)(2)) has "knowingly" agreed to the making of disqualifying lobbying expenditures within the meaning of section 4912(b), or whether an organization manager (as defined in section 4958(f)(2)) has "knowingly" participated in an excess benefit transaction (as defined in section 4958(c)), the burden of proof in respect of such issue shall be upon the Secretary.

(c) Cross reference.

For provisions relating to burden of proof as to transferee liability, see section 6902(a).

In 1996, P.L. 104-188, Sec. 1704(t)(43), substituted "section 4955(f)(2)" for "section 4955(e)(2)" in subsec. (b), effective 8/20/96.

—P.L. 104-168, Sec. 1311(c)(5), added "or whether an organization manager (as defined in section 4958(f)(2)) has 'knowingly' participated in an excess benefit transaction (as defined in section 4958(c))," after "section 4912(b)," in subsec. (b), effective for excess benefit transactions occurring on or after 9/14/95. Sec. 1311(d)(2), of this Act, provides:

"(2) Binding contracts. The amendments referred to in paragraph (1) shall not apply to any benefit arising from a transaction pursuant to any written contract which was binding on September 13, 1995, and at all times thereafter before such transaction occurred."

In 1987, P.L. 100-203, Sec. 10712(c)(6), substituted "or whether an organization manager (as defined in section 4955(e)(2)) has 'knowingly' agreed to the making of a political expenditure (within the meaning of section 4955), the burden of proof" for "the burden of proof" in subsec. (b) . . . Sec. 10714(b), substituted ", or whether an organization manager (as defined in section 4912(d)(2)) has 'knowingly' agreed to the making of disqualifying lobbying expenditures within the meaning of section 4912(b), the burden of proof" for "the burden of proof" in subsec. (b) [as amended by Sec. 10712(c)(6), see above], effective for tax. yrs. begin. after 12/22/87.

In 1980, P.L. 96-222, Sec. 108(b)(3)(B), substituted "501(c)(21)" for "502(c)(21)" in subsec. (b), effective for contributions, acts, and expenditures made after 12/31/77, in and for tax. yrs. begin. after 12/31/77.

In 1978, P.L. 95-227, Sec. 4(d)(7), added "or whether the trustee of a trust described in section 502(c)(21) has 'knowingly' participated in an act of self-dealing (within the meaning of section 4951) or agreed to the making of a taxable expenditure (within the meaning of section 4952), after "section 4945)," in subsec. (b), effective for contributions, acts, and expenditures made after 12/31/77, in and for tax. yrs. begin. after 12/31/77.

In 1976, P.L. 94-455, Sec. 1906(b)(13)(A), substituted "Secretary" for "Secretary or his delegate" each place it appeared in Code Sec. 7454, effective 2/1/77.

In 1969, P.L. 91-172, Sec. 101(j)(57), substituted "fraud, foundation manager, and transferee cases" for "fraud and transferee cases" in the heading of Code Sec. 7454, redesignated subsec. (b) as (c) and added subsec. (b), effective 1/1/70.

Sec. 7455. Service of process.

The mailing by certified mail or registered mail of any pleading, decision, order, notice, or process in respect of proceedings before the Tax Court shall be held sufficient service of such pleading, decision, order, notice, or process.

In 1958, P.L. 85-866, Sec. 89(b), added "certified mail or" before "registered mail" in Code Sec. 7455, effective only if mailing occurred after 9/2/58.

Sec. 7456. Administration of oaths and procurement of testimony.
(a) In general.

For the efficient administration of the functions vested in the Tax Court or any division thereof, any judge or special trial judge of the Tax Court, the clerk of the court or his deputies, as such, or any other employee of the Tax Court designated in writing for the purpose by the chief judge, may administer oaths, and any judge or special trial judge of the Tax Court may examine witnesses and require, by subpoena ordered by the Tax Court or any division thereof and signed by the judge or special trial judge (or by the clerk of the Tax Court or by any other employee of the Tax Court when acting as deputy clerk)—

(1) the attendance and testimony of witnesses, and the production of all necessary returns, books, papers, documents, correspondence, and other evidence, from any place in the United States at any designated place of hearing, or

(2) the taking of a deposition before any designated individual competent to administer oaths under this title. In the case of a deposition the testimony shall be reduced to writing by the individual taking the deposition or under his direction and shall then be subscribed by the deponent.

(b) Production of records in the case of foreign corporations, foreign trusts or estates and nonresident alien individuals.

The Tax Court or any division thereof, upon motion and notice by the Secretary, and upon good cause shown therefor, shall order any foreign corporation, foreign trust or estate, or nonresident alien individual, who has filed a petition with the Tax Court, to produce, or, upon satisfactory proof to the Tax Court or any of its divisions, that the petitioner is unable to produce, to make available to the Secretary, and, in either case, to permit the inspection, copying, or photographing of such books, records, documents, memoranda, correspondence and other papers, wherever situated, as the Tax Court or any division thereof, may deem relevant to the proceedings and which are in the possession, custody or control of the petitioner, or of any person directly or indirectly under his control or having control over him or subject to the same common control. If the petitioner fails or refuses to comply with any of the provisions of such order, after reasonable time for compliance has been afforded to him, the Tax Court or any division thereof, upon motion, shall make an order striking out pleadings or parts thereof, or dismissing the proceeding or any part thereof, or rendering a judgment by default against the petitioner. For the purpose of this subsection, the term "foreign trust or estate" includes an estate or trust, any fiduciary of which is a foreign corporation or nonresident alien individual; and the term "control" is not limited to legal control.

(c) Incidental powers.

The Tax Court and each division thereof shall have power to punish by fine or imprisonment, at its discretion, such contempt of its authority, and none other, as—

(1) misbehavior of any person in its presence or so near thereto as to obstruct the administration of justice;

(2) misbehavior of any of its officers in their official transactions; or

(3) disobedience or resistance to its lawful writ, process, order, rule, decree, or command.

It shall have such assistance in the carrying out of its lawful writ, process, order, rule, decree, or command as is available to a court of the United States. The United States marshal for any district in which the Tax Court is sitting shall, when requested by the chief judge of the Tax Court, attend any session of the Tax Court in such district and may otherwise provide, when requested by the chief judge of the Tax Court, for the security of the Tax Court, including the personal protection of Tax Court judges, court officers, witnesses, and other threatened persons in the interests of justice, where criminal intimidation impedes on the functioning of the judicial process or any other official proceeding. The United States Marshals Service retains final authority regarding security requirements for the Tax Court.

In 1986, P.L. 110-177, Sec. 102(b), added matter to the end of the language following para. (c)(3), enacted 1/7/2008. Sec. 102(c) of this Act provides:

"(c) Reimbursement. The United States Tax Court shall reimburse the United States Marshals Service for protection provided under the amendments made by this section."

In 1986, P.L. 99-514, Sec. 1555(a), added the last sentence to subsec. (e), effective 10/22/86.

—P.L. 99-514, Sec. 1556(b)(1), deleted subsecs. (c) and (d), and redesignated subsec. (e) as subsec. (c), effective 10/22/86. Secs. 1556(c)(2) and (c)(3) of this Act provide:

"(2) Salary. Subsection (d) of section 7443A of the Internal Revenue Code of 1954 (as added by this section) shall take effect on the 1st day of the 1st month beginning after the date of the enactment of this Act."

"(3) New appointments not required. Nothing in the amendments made by this section shall be construed to require the reappointment of any individual serving as a special trial judge of the Tax Court on the day before the date of the enactment of this Act."

Prior to deletion, subsecs. (c) and (d) read as follows:

"(c) Special trial judges.

"The chief judge may from time to time appoint special trial judges who shall proceed under such rules and regulations as may be promulgated by the Tax Court. Each special trial judge shall receive pay at an annual rate determined under section 225 of the Federal Salary Act of 1967 (2 U.S.C. 351-361), as adjusted by section 461 of title 28, United States Code, and also necessary traveling expenses and per diem allowances, as provided in subchapter I of chapter 57 of title 5, United States Code, while traveling on official business and away from Washington, District of Columbia.

"(d) Proceedings which may be assigned to special trial judges.

"The chief judge may assign—

"(1) any declaratory judgment proceeding,

"(2) any proceeding under section 7463,

"(3) any proceeding where neither the amount of the deficiency placed in dispute (within the meaning of section 7463) nor the amount of any claimed overpayment exceeds $10,000; and

"(4) any other proceeding which the chief judge may designate,

to be heard by the special trial judges of the court, and the court may authorize a special trial judge to make the decision of the court with respect to any proceeding described in paragraph (1), (2), or (3), subject to such conditions and review as the court may provide."

In 1984, P.L. 98-369, Sec. 463(a), amended subsec. (d), effective 10/25/85.

Prior to amendment, subsec. (d) read as follows:

"(d) Proceeding which may be assigned to commissioners.

"The chief judge may assign—

"(1) any declaratory judgment proceeding,

"(2) any proceeding under section 7463, and

"(3) any other proceeding where neither the amount of the deficiency placed in dispute (within the meaning of section 7463) nor the amount of any claimed overpayment exceeds $5,000,

to be heard by the commissioners of the court, and the court may authorize a commissioner to make the decision of the court with respect to any such proceeding, subject to such conditions and review as the court may provide."

—P.L. 98-369, Sec. 464(a), substituted "special trial judge" for "commissioner" each place it appeared in subsec. (a)...Sec. 464(b)(1), substituted "Special Trial Judges" for "Commissioners" in the heading of subsec. (c)...Sec. 464(b)(2), substituted "special trial judges" for "commissioners" in subsec. (c)...Sec. 464(b)(3), substituted "special trial judge" for "commissioner" in subsec. (c)...Sec. 464(c)(1), substituted "Special Trial Judges" for "Commissioners" in the heading of subsec. (d) [as amended by Sec. 463(a) of this Act, see above]...Sec. 464(c)(2), substituted "special trial judges" for "commissioners" in subsec. (d) [as amended by Sec. 463(a) of this Act, see above]...Sec. 464(c)(3), substituted "special trial judge" for "commissioner" in subsec. (d) [as amended by Sec.

463(a) of this Act, see above], effective 7/18/84. Sec. 464(e)(2) of the Act also provides that:

"(2) Any reference in any law to a commissioner of the Tax Court shall be treated as a reference to a special trial judge of the Tax Court."

In 1982, P.L. 97-362, Sec. 106(c)(1), redesignated subsec. (d) as (e) and added subsec. (d)...Sec. 106(c)(2), deleted the last sentence of subsec. (c), effective 10/25/82.

Prior to deletion, the last sentence of subsec. (c) read as follows:

"The chief judge may assign proceedings under sections 6226, 6228(a), 7428, 7463, 7476, 7477, and 7478 to be heard by the commissioners of the court, and the court may authorize a commissioner to make the decision of the court with respect to such proceedings, subject to such conditions and review as the court may by rule provide."

—P.L. 97-248, Sec. 402(c)(13), added "6226, 6228(a)," before "7428" in subsec. (c), effective for partnership tax. yrs. begin. after 9/3/82. Sec. 407(a)(3) of this Act provides:

"(3) The amendments made by sections 402, 403, and 404 [of this Act] shall apply to any partnership taxable year (or in the case of section 6232 of such Code, to any period) ending after the date of the enactment of this Act [9/3/82] if the partnership, each partner, and each indirect partner requests such application and the Secretary of the Treasury or his delegate consents to such application."

In 1982, P.L. 97-164, Sec. 153(a), amended the second sentence of subsec. (c), effective 10/1/82. Sec. 153(b) of this Act provides:

"(b) Notwithstanding the amendment made by subsection (a) [P.L. 97-164], until such time as a change in the salary rate of a commissioner of the United States Tax Court occurs in accordance with section 7456(c) of the Internal Revenue Code of 1954, the salary of such commissioner shall be equal to the salary of a commissioner of the Court of Claims immediately prior to the effective date of this Act."

Prior to amendment, the second sentence of subsec. (c) read as follows:

"Each commissioner shall receive the same compensation and travel and subsistence allowances provided by law for commissioners of the United States Court of Claims."

In 1980, P.L. 96-222, Sec. 105(a)(1)(B), substituted "sections 7428, 7463" for "sections 7428" in subsec. (c), effective for requests for determinations made after 12/31/78.

In 1978, P.L. 95-600, Sec. 336(b)(1), added a new sentence to the end of subsec. (c), effective for requests for determinations made after 12/31/78.

—P.L. 95-600, Sec. 502(c), substituted "any judge or commissioner of the Tax Court" for "any judge of the Tax Court" each place it appeared in subsec. (a), and substituted "by the judge or commissioner" for "by the judge" in subsec. (a), effective 11/6/78.

In 1976, P.L. 94-455, Sec. 1906(b)(13)(A), substituted "Secretary" for "Secretary or his delegate" each place it appeared in Code Sec. 7456, effective 2/1/77.

In 1969, P.L. 91-172, Sec. 956, added subsec. (d)...Sec. 958, amended subsec. (c), effective 12/30/69.

Prior to amendment, subsec. (c) read as follows:

"(c) Commissioners.

"The chief judge may from time to time by written order designate an attorney from the legal staff of the Tax Court to act as a commissioner in a particular case. The commissioner so designated shall proceed under such rules and regulations as may be promulgated by the Tax Court. The commissioner shall receive the same travel and subsistence allowances now or hereafter provided by law for commissioners of the United States Court of Claims."

Sec. 7457. Witness fees.

(a) Amount.

Any witness summoned or whose deposition is taken under section 7456 shall receive the same fees and mileage as witnesses in courts of the United States.

(b) Payment.

Such fees and mileage and the expenses of taking any such deposition shall be paid as follows:

(1) Witnesses for Secretary. In the case of witnesses for the Secretary, such payments shall be made by the Secretary out of any moneys appropriated for the collection of internal revenue taxes, and may be made in advance.

(2) Other witnesses. In the case of any other witnesses, such payments shall be made, subject to rules prescribed by the Tax Court, by the party at whose instance the witness appears or the deposition is taken.

In 1976, P.L. 94-455, Sec. 1906(b)(13)(A), substituted "Secretary" for "Secretary or his delegate" each place it appeared in Code Sec. 7457, effective 2/1/77.

Sec. 7458. Hearings.

Notice and opportunity to be heard upon any proceeding instituted before the Tax Court shall be given to the taxpayer and the Secretary. If an opportunity to be heard upon the proceeding is given before a division of the Tax Court,

Judicial proceedings

neither the taxpayer nor the Secretary shall be entitled to notice and opportunity to be heard before the Tax Court upon review, except upon a specific order of the chief judge. Hearings before the Tax Court and its divisions shall be open to the public, and the testimony, and, if the Tax Court so requires, the argument, shall be stenographically reported. The Tax Court is authorized to contract (by renewal of contract or otherwise) for the reporting of such hearings, and in such contract to fix the terms and conditions under which transcripts will be supplied by the contractor to the Tax Court and to other persons and agencies.

In 1976, P.L. 94-455, Sec. 1906(b)(13)(A), substituted "Secretary" for "Secretary or his delegate" each place it appeared in Code Sec. 7458, effective 2/1/77.
— P.L. 94-455, Sec. 1906(b)(13)(L), deleted "nor his delegate" after "Secretary" in Code Sec. 7458, effective 2/1/77.

Sec. 7459. Reports and decisions.
(a) Requirement.

A report upon any proceeding instituted before the Tax Court and a decision thereon shall be made as quickly as practicable. The decision shall be made by a judge in accordance with the report of the Tax Court, and such decision so made shall, when entered, be the decision of the Tax Court.

(b) Inclusion of findings of fact or opinions in report.

It shall be the duty of the Tax Court and of each division to include in its report upon any proceeding its findings of fact or opinion or memorandum opinion. The Tax Court shall report in writing all its findings of fact, opinions, and memorandum opinions. Subject to such conditions as the Tax Court may by rule provide, the requirements of this subsection and of section 7460 are met if findings of fact or opinion are stated orally and recorded in the transcript of the proceedings.

(c) Date of decision.

A decision of the Tax Court (except a decision dismissing a proceeding for lack of jurisdiction) shall be held to be rendered upon the date that an order specifying the amount of the deficiency is entered in the records of the Tax Court or, in the case of a declaratory judgment proceeding under part IV of this subchapter or under section 7428 or in the case of an action brought under section 6226, 6228(a), or 6234(c), 6247, or 6252 the date of the court's order entering the decision. If the Tax Court dismisses a proceeding for reasons other than lack of jurisdiction and is unable from the record to determine the amount of the deficiency determined by the Secretary, or if the Tax Court dismisses a proceeding for lack of jurisdiction, an order to that effect shall be entered in the records of the Tax Court, and the decision of the Tax Court shall be held to be rendered upon the date of such entry.

(d) Effect of decision dismissing petition.

If a petition for a redetermination of a deficiency has been filed by the taxpayer, a decision of the Tax Court dismissing the proceeding shall be considered as its decision that the deficiency is the amount determined by the Secretary. An order specifying such amount shall be entered in the records of the Tax Court unless the Tax Court cannot determine such amount from the record in the proceeding, or unless the dismissal is for lack of jurisdiction.

(e) Effect of decision that tax is barred by limitation.

If the assessment or collection of any tax is barred by any statute of limitations, the decision of the Tax Court to that effect shall be considered as its decision that there is no deficiency in respect of such tax.

(f) Findings of fact as evidence.

The findings of the Board of Tax Appeals made in connection with any decision prior to February 26, 1926, shall, notwithstanding the enactment of the Revenue Act of 1926 (44 Stat. 9), continue to be prima facie evidence of the facts therein stated.

(g) Penalty.

For penalty for taxpayer instituting proceedings before Tax Court merely for delay, see section 6673.

In 1998, P.L. 105-206, Sec. 6012(e), substituted "beginning" for "ending on or" in Sec. 1226 of P.L. 105-34, the effective date for amendments made by Sec. 1222 [see below].
In 1997, P.L. 105-34, Sec. 1222(b)(2), substituted ", 6228(a), 6247, or 6252" for "or section 6228(a)" in subsec. (c), effective [as amended by Sec. 6012(d) of 105-206, see above] for partnership tax. yrs. begin. after 12/31/97.
— P.L. 105-34, Sec. 1239(e)(1), substituted ", 6228(a), or 6234(c)" for "or section 6228(a)" [amendment made by substituting for ", 6228(a)" as added by Sec. 1222(b)(2) of this Act, see above], effective for partnership tax. yrs. end. after 8/5/97.
In 1982, P.L. 97-362, Sec. 106(b), added the last sentence to subsec. (b), effective 10/25/82.
— P.L. 97-248, Sec. 402(c)(14), added "or in the case of an action brought under section 6226 or section 6228(a)" after "or under section 7428" in subsec (c), effective for partnership tax. yrs. begin. after 9/3/82. Sec. 407(a)(3) of this Act provides:
"(3) The amendments made by sections 402, 403, and 404 [of this Act] shall apply to any partnership taxable year (or in the case of section 6232 of such Code, to any period) ending after the date of the enactment of this Act [9/3/82] if the partnership, each partner, and each indirect partner requests such application and the Secretary of the Treasury or his delegate consents to such application."
In 1976, P.L. 94-455, Sec. 1306(b)(2), added "or under section 7428" after "under part IV of this subchapter," in subsec. (c), effective for pleadings filed with the United States Tax Court, the district court of the United States for the District of Columbia, or the United States Court of Claims, more than 6 months after 10/4/76, but only with respect to determinations (or requests for determinations) made after 1/1/76.
— P.L. 94-455, Sec. 1906(b)(13)(A), substituted "Secretary" for "Secretary or his delegate" each place it appeared in Code Sec. 7459, effective 2/1/77.
In 1974, P.L. 93-406, Sec. 1041(b)(2), added before the period at the end of the first sentence in subsec. (c) "or, in the case of a declaratory judgment proceeding under part IV of the subchapter, the date of the court's order entering the decision", effective for pleadings filed more than one year after 9/2/74.

Sec. 7460. Provisions of special application to divisions.
(a) Hearings, determinations, and reports.

A division shall hear, and make a determination upon, any proceeding instituted before the Tax Court and any motion in connection therewith, assigned to such division by the chief judge, and shall make a report of any such determination which constitutes its final disposition of the proceeding.

(b) Effect of action by a division.

The report of the division shall become the report of the Tax Court within 30 days after such report by the division, unless within such period the chief judge has directed that such report shall be reviewed by the Tax Court. Any preliminary action by a division which does not form the basis for the entry of the final decision shall not be subject to review by the Tax Court except in accordance with such rules as the Tax Court may prescribe. The report of a division shall not be a part of the record in any case in which the chief judge directs that such report shall be reviewed by the Tax Court.

Sec. 7461. Publicity of proceedings.
(a) General rule.

Except as provided in subsection (b), all reports of the Tax Court and all evidence received by the Tax Court and its divisions, including a transcript of the stenographic report of the hearings, shall be public records open to the inspection of the public.

(b) Exceptions.

(1) Trade secrets or other confidential information. The Tax Court may make any provision which is necessary to prevent the disclosure of trade secrets or other confidential information, including a provision that any document or information be placed under seal to be opened only as directed by the court.

(2) Evidence, etc. After the decision of the Tax Court in any proceeding has become final, the Tax Court may, upon motion of the taxpayer or the Secretary, permit the withdrawal by the party entitled thereto of originals of books, documents, and records, and of models, diagrams, and other exhibits, introduced in evidence before the Tax Court or any division; or the Tax Court may, on its own motion, make such other disposition thereof as it deems advisable.

In 1984, P.L. 98-369, Sec. 465(a), amended Code Sec. 7461, effective 7/18/84. Prior to amendment, Code Section 7461 read as follows:

"SEC. 7461. PUBLICITY OF PROCEEDINGS.

"All reports of the Tax Court and all evidence received by the Tax Court and its divisions, including a transcript of the stenographic report of the hearings, shall be public records open to the inspection of the public; except that after the decision of the Tax Court in any proceeding has become final the Tax Court may, upon motion of the taxpayer or the Secretary, permit the withdrawal by the party entitled thereto of originals of books, documents, and records, and of models, diagrams, and other exhibits, introduced in evidence before the Tax Court or any division; or the Tax Court may, on its own motion, make such other disposition thereof as it deems advisable."

In 1976, P.L. 94-455, Sec. 1906(b)(13)(A), substituted "Secretary" for "Secretary or his delegate" each place it appeared in Code Sec. 7461, effective 2/1/77.

Sec. 7462. Publication of reports.

The Tax Court shall provide for the publication of its reports at the Government Printing Office in such form and manner as may be best adapted for public information and use, and such authorized publication shall be competent evidence of the reports of the Tax Court therein contained in all courts of the United States and of the several States without any further proof or authentication thereof. Such reports shall be subject to sale in the same manner and upon the same terms as other public documents.

Sec. 7463. Disputes involving $50,000 or less.
(a) In general.

In the case of any petition filed with the Tax Court for a redetermination of a deficiency where neither the amount of the deficiency placed in dispute, nor the amount of any claimed overpayment, exceeds—

(1) $50,000 for any one taxable year, in the case of the taxes imposed by subtitle A,

(2) $50,000, in the case of the tax imposed by chapter 11,

(3) $50,000 for any one calendar year, in the case of the tax imposed by chapter 12, or

(4) $50,000 for any 1 taxable period (or, if there is no taxable period, taxable event) in the case of any tax imposed by subtitle D which is described in section 6212(a) (relating to a notice of deficiency),

at the option of the taxpayer concurred in by the Tax Court or a division thereof before the hearing of the case, proceedings in the case shall be conducted under this section. Notwithstanding the provisions of section 7453, such proceedings shall be conducted in accordance with such rules of evidence, practice, and procedure as the Tax Court may prescribe. A decision, together with a brief summary of the reasons therefor, in any such case shall satisfy the requirements of sections 7459(b) and 7460.

(b) Finality of decisions.

A decision entered in any case in which the proceedings are conducted under this section shall not be reviewed in any other court and shall not be treated as a precedent for any other case.

(c) Limitation of jurisdiction.

In any case in which the proceedings are conducted under this section, notwithstanding the provisions of sections 6214(a) and 6512(b), no decision shall be entered redetermining the amount of a deficiency, or determining an overpayment, except with respect to amounts placed in dispute within the limits described in subsection (a) and with respect to amounts conceded by the parties.

(d) Discontinuance of proceedings.

At any time before a decision entered in a case in which the proceedings are conducted under this section becomes final, the taxpayer or the Secretary may request that further proceedings under this section in such case be discontinued. The Tax Court, or the division thereof hearing such case, may, if it finds that (1) there are reasonable grounds for believing that the amount of the deficiency placed in dispute, or the amount of an overpayment, exceeds the applicable jurisdictional amount described in subsection (a), and (2) the amount of such excess is large enough to justify granting such request, discontinue further proceedings in such case under this section. Upon any such discontinuance, proceedings in such case shall be conducted in the same manner as cases to which the provisions of sections 6214(a) and 6512(b) apply.

(e) Amount of deficiency in dispute.

For purposes of this section, the amount of any deficiency placed in dispute includes additions to the tax, additional amounts, and penalties imposed by chapter 68, to the extent that the procedures described in subchapter B of chapter 63 apply.

(f) Additional cases in which proceedings may be conducted under this section.

At the option of the taxpayer concurred in by the Tax Court or a division thereof before the hearing of the case, proceedings may be conducted under this section (in the same manner as a case described in subsection (a)) in the case of—

(1) a petition to the Tax Court under section 6015(e) in which the amount of relief sought does not exceed $50,000, and

(2) an appeal under section 6330(d)(1)(A) to the Tax Court of a determination in which the unpaid tax does not exceed $50,000.

In 2000, P.L. 106-554, Sec. 1(a)(7), [which enacted into law Sec. 313(b)(1) of P.L. 106-554] added subsec. (f), effective 12/21/2000.

In 1998, P.L. 105-206, Sec. 3103(a), substituted "$50,000" for "$10,000" each place it appeared in Code Sec. 7463, effective for proceedings commenced after 7/22/98.

In 1990, P.L. 101-508, Sec. 11801(c)(21)(B), deleted subsec. (f), effective 11/5/90, except as provided in Sec. 11821(b) of this Act, which reads as follows:

"(b) Savings provision. If —

"(1) any provision amended or repealed by this part applied to—

"(A) any transaction occurring before the date of the enactment of this Act [11/5/90],

"(B) any property acquired before such date of enactment [11/5/90], or

"(C) any item of income, loss, deduction, or credit taken into account before such date of enactment [11/5/90], and

"(2) the treatment of such transaction, property, or item under such provision would (without regard to the amendments made by this part) affect liability for tax for periods ending after such date of enactment [11/5/90],

nothing in the amendments made by this part shall be construed to affect the treatment of such transaction, property, or item for purposes of determining liability for tax for periods ending after such date of enactment [11/5/90]."

Prior to deletion, subsec. (f) read as follows:

"(f) Qualified state individual income taxes. For purposes of this section, a deficiency placed in dispute or claimed overpayment with regard to a qualified State individual income tax to which subchapter E of chapter 64 applies, for a taxable year, shall be treated as a portion of a deficiency placed in dispute or claimed overpayment of the income tax for that taxable year."

In 1984, P.L. 98-369, Sec. 461(a)(1), substituted "$10,000" for "$5,000" each place it appeared in subsec. (a) . . . Sec. 461(a)(2)(A), substituted "$10,000" for "$5,000" in the heading of Code Sec. 7463, effective 7/18/84.

In 1982, P.L. 97-362, Sec. 106(a)(1)(A), deleted "or" from the end of para. (a)(2) . . . Sec. 106(a)(1)(B), added "or" to the end of para. (a)(3) . . . Sec. 106(a)(1)(C), added para. (a)(4), effective for petitions filed after 10/25/82.

In 1980, P.L. 96-222, Sec. 105(a)(1)(A), deleted subsec. (g), effective 4/1/80.

Prior to deletion, subsec. (g) read as follows:

"(g) Commissioners. The chief judge of the Tax Court may assign proceedings conducted under this section to be heard by the Commissioners of the court, and the court may authorize a commissioner to make the decision of the court with re-

Judicial proceedings   Code Sec. 7472

spect to any such proceeding, subject to such conditions and review as the court may by rule provide."
In 1978, P.L. 95-600, Sec. 502(a)(1), substituted paras. (a)(1), (2) and (3) for paras. (a)(1) and (2), effective the first day of the first calendar month beginning more than 180 days after 11/6/78.
Prior to amendment, paras. (a)(1) and (2) read as follows:
"(1) $1,500 for any one taxable year, in the case of the taxes imposed by subtitle A and chapter 12, or
"(2) $1,500, in the case of the tax imposed by chapter 11,"
—P.L. 95-600, Sec. 502(b), added subsec. (g), effective 11/6/78.
In 1976, P.L. 94-455, Sec. 1906(b)(13)(A), substituted "Secretary" for "Secretary or his delegate" in Code Sec. 7463, effective 2/1/77.
In 1972, P.L. 92-512, Sec. 203(b)(1), added subsec. (f) . . . Sec. 203(b)(2), substituted "$1,500" for "$1,000" in the heading of subsec. (a), and in paras. (a)(1) and (2), effective 1/1/74.
In 1969, P.L. 91-172, Sec. 957(a), added Code Sec. 7463, effective 12/30/70.

Sec. 7464. Intervention by trustee of debtor's estate.

The trustee of the debtor's estate in any case under title 11 of the United States Code may intervene, on behalf of the debtor's estate, in any proceeding before the Tax Court to which the debtor is a party.

In 1980, P.L. 96-589, Sec. 6(c)(1), added Code Sec. 7464, effective 10/1/79 except for any proceeding under the Bankruptcy Act begun before 10/1/79. Sec. 7(g) of this Act provides:
"(g) Definitions.
"For purposes of this section—
"(1) Bankruptcy case. The term 'bankruptcy case' means any case under title 11 of the United States Code (as recodified by P.L. 95-598).
"(2) Similar judicial proceeding. The term 'similar judicial proceeding' means a receivership, foreclosure, or similar proceeding in a Federal or State court (as modified by section 368(a)(3)(D) of the Internal Revenue Code of 1954)."

Sec. 7465. Provisions of special application to transferees.

(1) For rules of burden of proof in transferee proceedings, see section 6902(a).
(2) For authority of Tax Court to prescribe rules by which a transferee of property of a taxpayer shall be entitled to examine books, records and other evidence, see section 6902(b).

In 1980, P.L. 96-589, Sec. 6(c)(1), redesignated Code Sec. 7464 as Code Sec. 7465, effective 10/1/79 except for any proceeding under the Bankruptcy Act begun before 10/1/79. Sec. 7(g) of this Act provides:
"(g) Definitions.
For purposes of this section—
"(1) Bankruptcy case. The term 'bankruptcy case' means any case under title 11 of the United States Code (as recodified by P.L. 95-598).
"(2) Similar judicial proceeding. The term 'similar judicial proceeding' means a receivership, foreclosure, or similar proceeding in a Federal or State court (as modified by section 368(a)(3)(D) of the Internal Revenue Code of 1954)."
In 1969, P.L. 91-172, Sec. 957(a), redesignated Code Sec. 7463 as Code Sec. 7464, effective 12/30/70.

PART III.—MISCELLANEOUS PROVISIONS

Sec.
7471. Employees.
7472. Expenditures.
7473. Disposition of fees.
7474. Fee for transcript of record.
7475. Practice fee.

In 1988, added item 7475.

Sec. 7471. Employees.
(a) Appointment and compensation.

The Tax Court is authorized to appoint, in accordance with the provisions of title 5, United States Code, governing appointment in the competitive service, and to fix the basic pay of, in accordance with chapter 51 and subchapter III of chapter 53 of such title, such employees as may be necessary efficiently to execute the functions vested in the Tax Court.

(b) Expenses for travel and subsistence.

The employees of the Tax Court shall receive their necessary traveling expenses, and expenses for subsistence while traveling on duty and away from their designated stations, as provided in chapter 57 of title 5, United States Code.
(c) Special trial judges.

For compensation and travel and subsistence allowances of special trial judges of the Tax Court, see subsections (d) and (e) of section 7443A.

In 1986, P.L. 99-514, Sec. 1556(b)(2), substituted "subsections (d) and (e) of section 7443A" for "section 7456(c)" in subsec. (c), effective 10/22/86. Sec. 1556(c)(3) of this Act provides:
"(3) New appointments not required. Nothing in the amendments made by this section shall be construed to require the reappointment of any individual serving as a special trial judge of the Tax Court on the day before the date of the enactment of this Act.".
In 1984, P.L. 98-369, Sec. 464(d), substituted "Special trial judges" for "Commissioners" in the heading of subsec. (c) and substituted "special trial judges" for "commissioners" in subsec. (c), effective 7/18/84. Sec. 464(e)(2) of this Act provides:
"(2) Any reference in any law to a commissioner of the Tax Court shall be treated as a reference to a special trial judge of the Tax Court.".
In 1976, P.L. 94-455, Sec. 1906(a)(47)(A), substituted "is authorized to appoint, in accordance with the provisions of title 5, United States Code, governing appointment in the competitive service, and to fix the basic pay of, in accordance with chapter 51 and subchapter III of chapter 53 of such title" for "is authorized in accordance with the civil service laws to appoint, and in accordance with the Classification Act of 1949 (63 Stat. 954; 5 U.S.C. chapter 21), as amended to fix the compensation of," in subsec. (a) . . . Sec. 1906(a)(47)(B), substituted "as provided in chapter 57 of title 5, United States Code." for "as provided in the Travel Expense Act of 1949 (63 Stat. 166; 5 U.S.C. chapter 16)." in subsec. (b), effective the first day of the first month which begins more than 90 days after 10/4/76.
In 1969, P.L. 91-172, Sec. 960(g), amended subsec. (c), effective 12/30/69.
Prior to amendment, subsec. (c) read as follows:
"(c) Commissioners.
"For travel and subsistence allowances of commissioners of the Tax Court, see section 7456(c)."

Sec. 7472. Expenditures.

The Tax Court is authorized to make such expenditures (including expenditures for personal services and rent at the seat of Government and elsewhere, and for law books, books of reference, and periodicals), as may be necessary efficiently to execute the functions vested in the Tax Court. Notwithstanding any other provision of law, the Tax Court is authorized to pay on behalf of its judges, age 65 or over, any increase in the cost of Federal Employees' Group Life Insurance imposed after April 24, 1999, that is incurred after the date of the enactment of the Pension Protection Act of 2006, including any expenses generated by such payments, as authorized by the chief judge in a manner consistent with such payments authorized by the Judicial Conference of the United States pursuant to section 604(a)(5) of title 28, United States Code. Except as provided in section 7475, all expenditures of the Tax Court shall be allowed and paid, out of any moneys appropriated for purposes of the Tax Court, upon presentation of itemized vouchers therefor signed by the certifying officer designated by the chief judge.

In 2009, P.L. 111-8, Sec. 618(a), added "after April 24, 1999, that is incurred" after the word "imposed" in Code Sec. 7472, effective 8/17/2006.
In 2006, P.L. 109-280, Sec. 852, added "Notwithstanding any other provision of law, the Tax Court is authorized to pay on behalf of its judges, age 65 or over, any increase in the cost of Federal Employees' Group Life Insurance imposed after the date of the enactment of the Pension Protection Act of 2006, including any expenses generated by such payments, as authorized by the chief judge in a manner consistent with such payments authorized by the Judicial Conference of the United States pursuant to section 604(a)(5) of title 28, United States Code." after the first sentence of Code Sec. 7472, enacted 8/17/2006.
In 1986, P.L. 99-514, Sec. 1553(b)(1), substituted "Except as provided in section 7475, all" for "All" in the second sentence of Code Sec. 7472, effective 1/1/87.

3,891

Sec. 7473. Disposition of fees.

Except as provided in section 7475, all fees received by the Tax Court shall be covered into the Treasury as miscellaneous receipts.

In 1986, P.L. 99-514, Sec. 1553(b)(2), substituted "Except as provided in section 7475, all" for "All" in Code Sec. 7473, effective 1/1/87.

Sec. 7474. Fee for transcript of record.

The Tax Court is authorized to fix a fee, not in excess of the fee fixed by law to be charged and collected therefor by the clerks of the district courts, for comparing, or for preparing and comparing, a transcript of the record, or for copying any record, entry, or other paper and the comparison and certification thereof.

Sec. 7475. Practice fee.
(a) In general.

The Tax Court is authorized to impose a periodic registration fee on practitioners admitted to practice before such Court. The frequency and amount of such fee shall be determined by the Tax Court, except that such amount may not exceed $30 per year.

(b) Use of fees.

The fees described in subsection (a) shall be available to the Tax Court to employ independent counsel to pursue disciplinary matters and to provide services to pro se taxpayers.

In 2006, P.L. 109-280, Sec. 860(a), added "and to provide services to pro se taxpayers" before the period at the end of subsec. (b), effective 8/17/2006.
In 1986, P.L. 99-514, Sec. 1553(a), added Code Sec. 7475, effective 1/1/87.

PART IV.—DECLARATORY JUDGMENTS
Sec.
7476. Declaratory judgments relating to qualification of certain retirement plans.
7477. Declaratory judgments relating to value of certain gifts.
7478. Declaratory judgments relating to status of certain governmental obligations.
7479. Declaratory judgments relating to eligibility of estate with respect to installment payments under section 6166.

In 1997, P.L. 105-34, Sec. 505(b), added item 7479.
—P.L. 105-34, Sec. 506(c)(2), added item 7477.
In 1984, P.L. 98-369, Sec. 131(e)(2)(B), deleted item 7477.
Prior to deletion, item 7477 read as follows:
"7477. Declaratory judgments relating to transfers of property from the United States."
In 1978, P.L. 95-600, Sec. 336(c)(2), added item 7478.
In 1976, P.L. 94-455, Sec. 1042(d)(2)(D), amended the item for Code Sec. 7476 ... added the item for Code Sec. 7477.
—P.L. 94-455, Sec. 1042(d)(2)(E), substituted "DECLARATORY JUDGMENTS" for "DECLARATORY JUDGMENTS RELATING TO QUALIFICATION OF CERTAIN RETIREMENT PLANS" in the heading of Part IV of chapter 76.
In 1974, P.L. 93-406, Sec. 1041(a), added Part IV.

Sec. 7476. Declaratory judgments relating to qualification of certain retirement plans.
(a) Creation of remedy.

In a case of actual controversy involving—

(1) a determination by the Secretary with respect to the initial qualification or continuing qualification of a retirement plan under subchapter D of chapter 1, or

(2) a failure by the Secretary to make a determination with respect to—

(A) such initial qualification, or

(B) such continuing qualification if the controversy arises from a plan amendment or plan termination,

upon the filing of an appropriate pleading, the Tax Court may make a declaration with respect to such initial qualification or continuing qualification. Any such declaration shall have the force and effect of a decision of the Tax Court and shall be reviewable as such. For purposes of this section, a determination with respect to a continuing qualification includes any revocation of or other change in a qualification.

(b) Limitations.

(1) Petitioner. A pleading may be filed under this section only by a petitioner who is the employer, the plan administrator, an employee who has qualified under regulations prescribed by the Secretary as an interested party for purposes of pursuing administrative remedies within the Internal Revenue Service, or the Pension Benefit Guaranty Corporation.

(2) Notice. For purposes of this section, the filing of a pleading by any petitioner may be held by the Tax Court to be premature, unless the petitioner establishes to the satisfaction of the court that he has complied with the requirements prescribed by regulations of the Secretary with respect to notice to other interested parties of the filing of the request for a determination referred to in subsection (a).

(3) Exhaustion of administrative remedies. The Tax Court shall not issue a declaratory judgment or decree under this section in any proceeding unless it determines that the petitioner has exhausted administrative remedies available to him within the Internal Revenue Service. A petitioner shall not be deemed to have exhausted his administrative remedies with respect to a failure by the Secretary to make a determination with respect to initial qualification or continuing qualification of a retirement plan before the expiration of 270 days after the request for such determination was made.

(4) Plan put into effect. No proceeding may be maintained under this section unless the plan (and, in the case of a controversy involving the continuing qualification of the plan because of an amendment to the plan, the amendment) with respect to which a decision of the Tax Court is sought has been put into effect before the filing of the pleading. A plan or amendment shall not be treated as not being in effect merely because under the plan the funds contributed to the plan may be refunded if the plan (or the plan as so amended) is found to be not qualified.

(5) Time for bringing action. If the Secretary sends by certified or registered mail notice of his determination with respect to the qualification of the plan to the persons referred to in paragraph (1) (or, in the case of employees referred to in paragraph (1), to any individual designated under regulations prescribed by the Secretary as a representative of such employee), no proceeding may be initiated under this section by any person unless the pleading is filed before the ninety-first day after the day after such notice is mailed to such person (or to his designated representative, in the case of an employee).

(c) Retirement plan.

For purposes of this section, the term "retirement plan" means—

(1) a pension, profit-sharing, or stock bonus plan described in section 401(a) or a trust which is part of such a plan, or

(2) an annuity plan described in section 403(a).

(d) Cross reference.

For provisions concerning intervention by Pension Benefit Guaranty Corporation and Secretary of Labor in actions brought under this section and right of Pension Benefit

Judicial proceedings — Code Sec. 7477

Guaranty Corporation to bring action, see section 3001(c) of subtitle A of title III of the Employee Retirement Income Security Act of 1974.

In **1986**, P.L. 99-514, Sec. 1899A(59), substituted "plan, or" for "plan,, or" at the end of para. (c)(1) effective 10/22/86.
In **1984**, P.L. 98-369, Sec. 491(d)(52), deleted para. (c)(3), substituted a period for ", or" at the end of para. (c)(2), and substituted ", or" for the comma at the end of para. (c)(1), effective for obligations issued after 12/31/83.
Prior to deletion, para. (c)(3) read as follows:
"(3) a bond purchase plan described in section 405(a)."
In **1978**, P.L. 95-600, Sec. 336(b)(2)(A), deleted subsec. (c) and redesignated subsecs. (d) and (e) as subsecs. (c) and (d), effective for requests for determinations made after 12/31/78.
Prior to deletion, subsec. (c) read as follows:
"(c) Commissioners.
 The chief judge of the Tax Court may assign proceedings under this section or section 7428 to be heard by the commissioners of the court, and the court may authorize a commissioner to make the decision of the court with respect to such proceeding, subject to such conditions and review as the court may by rule provide."
—P.L. 95-600, Sec. 701(dd)(1), added a new sentence at the end of subsec. (a), effective with respect to pleadings filed more than one year after 9/2/74.
In **1976**, P.L. 94-455, Sec. 1306(b)(3), substituted "this section or section 7428" for "this section" following "may assign proceedings under" in subsec. (c), for pleadings filed more than 6 months after 10/4/76, but only with respect to determinations (or requests for determinations) made after 1/1/76.
—P.L. 94-455, Sec. 1042(d)(2)(C), substituted "Sec. 7476. Declaratory judgments relating to qualification of certain retirement plans." for "Sec. 7476. Declaratory judgments." in the heading of Code Sec. 7476, for pleadings filed with the Tax Court after 10/4/76, but only with respect to transfers begin. after 10/9/75.
—P.L. 94-455, Sec. 1906(a)(48), substituted "upon the filing of an appropriate pleading, the Tax Court may make a declaration with respect to such initial qualification or continuing qualification. Any such declaration shall have the force and effect of a decision of the Tax Court and shall be reviewable as such." for "upon the filing of an appropriate pleading, the United States Tax Court may make a declaration with respect to such initial qualification or continuing qualification. Any such declaration shall have the force and effect of a decision of the Tax Court and shall be reviewable as such." at the end of subsec. (a), effective on the first day of the first month which begins more than 90 days after 10/4/76 [date of enactment].
—P.L. 94-455, Sec. 1906(b)(13)(A), substituted "Secretary" for "Secretary or his delegate" each time it appeared in subsecs. (a) and (b), effective 2/1/77.
In **1974**, P.L. 93-406, Sec. 1041(a), added Code Sec. 7476, effective with respect to pleadings filed more than one year after 9/2/74.

Sec. 7477. Declaratory judgments relating to value of certain gifts.
(a) Creation of remedy.
 In a case of an actual controversy involving a determination by the Secretary of the value of any gift shown on the return of tax imposed by chapter 12 or disclosed on such return or in any statement attached to such return, upon the filing of an appropriate pleading, the Tax Court may make a declaration of the value of such gift. Any such declaration shall have the force and effect of a decision of the Tax Court and shall be reviewable as such.
(b) Limitations.
 (1) Petitioner. A pleading may be filed under this section only by the donor.
 (2) Exhaustion of administrative remedies. The court shall not issue a declaratory judgment or decree under this section in any proceeding unless it determines that the petitioner has exhausted all available administrative remedies within the Internal Revenue Service.
 (3) Time for bringing action. If the Secretary sends by certified or registered mail notice of his determination as described in subsection (a) to the petitioner, no proceeding may be initiated under this section unless the pleading is filed before the 91st day after the date of such mailing.

In **1997**, P.L. 105-34, Sec. 506(c)(1), added Code Sec. 7477, effective for gifts made after 8/5/97.

Sec. 7477. Repealed.

In **1984**, P.L. 98-369, Sec. 131(e)(1), repealed Code Sec. 7477, effective for transfers or exchanges after 12/31/84, in tax. yrs. end. after 12/31/84.
Secs. 131(g)(2) and (g)(3) of the Act provide the following special rule and ruling request:
"(2) Special rule for certain transfers of intangibles. —
"(A) In general. — If, after June 6, 1984, and before January 1, 1985, a United States person transfers any intangible property (within the meaning of section 936(h)(3)(B) of the Internal Revenue Code of 1954) to a foreign corporation or in a transfer described in section 1491, such transfer shall be treated for purposes of sections 367(a), 1492(2), and 1494(b) of such Code as pursuant to a plan having as 1 of its principal purposes the avoidance of Federal income tax.
"(B) Waiver. — Subject to such terms and conditions as the Secretary of the Treasury or his delegate may prescribe, the Secretary may waive the application of subparagraph (A) with respect to any transfer.
"(3) Ruling request before March 1, 1984. — The amendments made by this section (and the provisions of paragraph (2) of this subsection) shall not apply to any transfer or exchange of property described in a request filed before March 1, 1984, under section 367(a), 1492(2), or 1494(b) of the Internal Revenue Code of 1954 (as in effect before such amendments)."
Prior to repeal, Code Sec. 7477 read as follows:
"Sec. 7477. Declaratory judgments relating to transfers of property from the United States.
"(a) Creation of remedy.
 "(1) In general. In a case of actual controversy involving—
 "(A) a determination by the Secretary—
  "(i) that an exchange described in section 367(a)(1) is in pursuance of a plan having as one of its principal purposes the avoidance of Federal income taxes, or
  "(ii) of the terms and conditions pursuant to which an exchange described in section 367(a)(1) will be determined not to be in pursuance of a plan having as one of its principal purposes the avoidance of Federal income taxes, or
 "(B) a failure by the Secretary to make a determination as to whether an exchange described in section 367(a)(1) is in pursuance of a plan having as one of its principal purposes the avoidance of Federal income taxes, upon the filing of an appropriate pleading, the Tax Court may make the appropriate declaration referred to in paragraph (2). Such declaration shall have the force and effect of a decision of the Tax Court and shall be reviewable as such.
 "(2) Scope of declaration. The declaration referred to in paragraph (1) shall be—
 "(A) in the case of a determination referred to in subparagraph (A) of paragraph (1), whether or not such determination is reasonable, and, if it is not reasonable, a determination of the issue set forth in subparagraph (A)(ii) of paragraph (1), and
 "(B) in the case of a failure described in subparagraph (B) of paragraph (1), the determination of the issues set forth in subparagraph (A) of paragraph (1).
"(b) Limitations.
 "(1) Petitioner. A pleading may be filed under this section only by a petitioner who is a transferor or transferee of stock, securities, or property transferred in an exchange described in section 367(a)(1).
 "(2) Exhaustion of administrative remedies. The Tax Court shall not issue a declaratory judgment or decree under this section in any proceeding unless it determines that the petitioner has exhausted administrative remedies available to him within the Internal Revenue Service. A petitioner shall not be deemed to have exhausted his administrative remedies with respect to a failure by the Secretary to make a determination with respect to whether or not an exchange described in section 367(a)(1) is in pursuance of a plan having as one of its principal purposes the avoidance of Federal income taxes before the expiration of 270 days after the request for such determination was made.
 "(3) Exchange shall have begun. No proceeding may be maintained under this section unless the exchange is described in section 367(a)(1) with respect to which a decision of the Tax Court is sought has begun before the filing of the pleading.
 "(4) Time for bringing action. If the Secretary sends by certified or registered mail to the petitioners referred to in paragraph (1) notice of his determination with respect to whether or not an exchange described in section 367(a)(1) is in pursuance of a plan having as one of its principal purposes the avoidance of Federal income taxes or with respect to the terms and conditions pursuant to which such an exchange will be determined not to be made in pursuance of such a plan, no proceeding may be initiated under this section by any petitioner unless the pleading is filed before the 91st day after the day such notice is mailed to such petitioner."
In **1978**, P.L. 95-600, Sec. 336(b)(2)(B), repealed subsec. (c), effective for requests for determinations made after 12/31/78.
Prior to repeal, subsec. (c) read as follows:
"(c) Commissioners.
 "The chief judge of the Tax Court may assign proceedings under this section to be heard by the commissioners of the court, and the court may authorize a commissioner to make the decision of the court with respect to such proceeding, subject to such conditions and review as the court may by rule provide."
In **1976**, P.L. 94-455, Sec. 1042(d)(1), added Code Sec. 7477, effective for pleadings filed with the Tax Court after 10/4/76, but only for transfers begin. after 10/9/75.

Sec. 7478. Declaratory judgments relating to status of certain governmental obligations.
(a) Creation of remedy.

In a case of actual controversy involving—

(1) a determination by the Secretary whether interest on prospective obligations will be excludable from gross income under section 103(a), or

(2) a failure by the Secretary to make a determination with respect to any matter referred to in paragraph (1),

upon the filing of an appropriate pleading, the Tax Court may make a declaration whether interest on such prospective obligations will be excludable from gross income under section 103(a). Any such declaration shall have the force and effect of a decision of the Tax Court and shall be reviewable as such.

(b) Limitations.

(1) Petitioner. A pleading may be filed under this section only by the prospective issuer.

(2) Exhaustion of administrative remedies. The court shall not issue a declaratory judgment or decree under this section in any proceeding unless it determines that the petitioner has exhausted all available administrative remedies within the Internal Revenue Service. A petitioner shall be deemed to have exhausted its administrative remedies with respect to a failure of the Secretary to make a determination with respect to an issue of obligations at the expiration of 180 days after the date on which the request for such determination was made if the petitioner has taken, in a timely manner, all reasonable steps to secure such determination.

(3) Time for bringing action. If the Secretary sends by certified or registered mail notice of his determination as described in subsection (a)(1) to the petitioner, no proceeding may be initiated under this section unless the pleading is filed before the 91st day after the date of such mailing.

In 1988, P.L. 100-647, Sec. 1013(a)(42)(A), substituted "whether interest on prospective obligations will be excludable from gross income under section 103(a)" for "whether prospective obligations are described in section 103(a)" in para. (a)(1) . . . Sec. 1013(a)(42)(B), substituted "whether interest on such prospective obligations will be excludable from gross income under section 103(a)" for "whether such prospective obligations are described in section 103(a)" in subsec. (a), effective for bonds issued after 8/15/86.

In 1978, P.L. 95-600, Sec. 336(a), added Code Sec. 7478, effective for requests for determinations made after 12/31/78.

Sec. 7479. Declaratory judgments relating to eligibility of estate with respect to installment payments under section 6166.
(a) Creation of remedy.

In a case of actual controversy involving a determination by the Secretary of (or a failure by the Secretary to make a determination with respect to)—

(1) whether an election may be made under section 6166 (relating to extension of time for payment of estate tax where estate consists largely of interest in closely held business) with respect to an estate (or with respect to any property included therein), or

(2) whether the extension of time for payment of tax provided in section 6166(a) has ceased to apply with respect to an estate (or with respect to any property included therein),

upon the filing of an appropriate pleading, the Tax Court may make a declaration with respect to whether such election may be made or whether such extension has ceased to apply. Any such declaration shall have the force and effect of a decision of the Tax Court and shall be reviewable as such.

(b) Limitations.

(1) Petitioner. A pleading may be filed under this section, with respect to any estate, only—

(A) by the executor of such estate, or

(B) by any person who has assumed an obligation to make payments under section 6166 with respect to such estate (but only if each other such person is joined as a party).

(2) Exhaustion of administrative remedies. The court shall not issue a declaratory judgment or decree under this section in any proceeding unless it determines that the petitioner has exhausted all available administrative remedies within the Internal Revenue Service. A petitioner shall be deemed to have exhausted its administrative remedies with respect to a failure of the Secretary to make a determination at the expiration of 180 days after the date on which the request for such determination was made if the petitioner has taken, in a timely manner, all reasonable steps to secure such determination.

(3) Time for bringing action. If the Secretary sends by certified or registered mail notice of his determination as described in subsection (a) to the petitioner, no proceeding may be initiated under this section unless the pleading is filed before the 91st day after the date of such mailing.

(c) Extension of time to file refund suit.

The 2-year period in section 6532(a)(1) for filing suit for refund after disallowance of a claim shall be suspended during the 90-day period after the mailing of the notice referred to in subsection (b)(3) and, if a pleading has been filed with the Tax Court under this section, until the decision of the Tax Court has become final.

In 1998, P.L. 105-206, Sec. 3104(b), added subsec. (c), effective for any claim for refund filed after 7/22/98.

—P.L. 105-206, Sec. 6007(d), substituted "an estate (or with respect to any property included therein)," for "an estate," each place it appeared in paras. (a)(1) and (2), effective for estates of decedents dying after 8/5/97.

In 1997, P.L. 105-34, Sec. 505(a), added Code Sec. 7479, effective for estates of decedents dying after 8/5/97.

Subchapter D.—Court Review of Tax Court Decisions

Sec.
7481. Date when Tax Court decision becomes final.
7482. Courts of review.
7483. Notice of appeal.
7484. Change of incumbent in office.
7485. Bond to stay assessment and collection.
7486. Refund, credit, or abatement of amounts disallowed.
7487. Cross references.

In 1969, P.L. 91-172, Sec. 959(b), amended item 7483, which formerly read "Petition for review."

Sec. 7481. Date when Tax Court decision becomes final.
(a) Reviewable decisions.

Except as provided in subsections (b), (c), and (d), the decision of the Tax Court shall become final—

(1) Timely notice of appeal not filed. Upon the expiration of the time allowed for filing a notice of appeal, if no such notice has been duly filed within such time; or

(2) Decision affirmed or appeal dismissed.

(A) Petition for certiorari not filed on time. Upon the expiration of the time allowed for filing a petition for certiorari, if the decision of the Tax Court has been affirmed or the appeal dismissed by the United States Court of Appeals and no petition for certiorari has been duly filed; or

(B) Petition for certiorari denied. Upon the denial of a petition for certiorari, if the decision of the Tax Court has been affirmed or the appeal dismissed by the United States Court of Appeals; or

(C) After mandate of Supreme Court. Upon the expiration of 30 days from the date of issuance of the mandate of the Supreme Court, if such Court directs that the decision of the Tax Court be affirmed or the appeal dismissed.

(3) Decision modified or reversed.

(A) Upon mandate of Supreme Court. If the Supreme Court directs that the decision of the Tax Court be modified or reversed, the decision of the Tax Court rendered in accordance with the mandate of the Supreme Court shall become final upon the expiration of 30 days from the time it was rendered, unless within such 30 days either the Secretary or the taxpayer has instituted proceedings to have such decision corrected to accord with the mandate, in which event the decision of the Tax Court shall become final when so corrected.

(B) Upon mandate of the Court of Appeals. If the decision of the Tax Court is modified or reversed by the United States Court of Appeals, and if—

(i) the time allowed for filing a petition for certiorari has expired and no such petition has been duly filed, or

(ii) the petition for certiorari has been denied, or

(iii) the decision of the United States Court of Appeals has been affirmed by the Supreme Court, then the decision of the Tax Court rendered in accordance with the mandate of the United States Court of Appeals shall become final on the expiration of 30 days from the time such decision of the Tax Court was rendered, unless within such 30 days either the Secretary or the taxpayer has instituted proceedings to have such decision corrected so that it will accord with the mandate, in which event the decision of the Tax Court shall become final when so corrected.

(4) Rehearing. If the Supreme Court orders a rehearing; or if the case is remanded by the United States Court of Appeals to the Tax Court for a rehearing, and if—

(A) the time allowed for filing a petition for certiorari has expired and no such petition has been duly filed, or

(B) the petition for certiorari has been denied, or

(C) the decision of the United States Court of Appeals has been affirmed by the Supreme Court,

then the decision of the Tax Court rendered upon such rehearing shall become final in the same manner as though no prior decision of the Tax Court has been rendered.

(5) Definition of "mandate." As used in this section, the term "mandate", in case a mandate has been recalled prior to the expiration of 30 days from the date of issuance thereof, means the final mandate.

(b) Nonreviewable decisions.

The decision of the Tax Court in a proceeding conducted under section 7436(c) or 7463 shall become final upon the expiration of 90 days after the decision is entered.

(c) Jurisdiction over interest determinations.

(1) In general. Notwithstanding subsection (a), if, within 1 year after the date the decision of the Tax Court becomes final under subsection (a) in a case to which this subsection applies, the taxpayer files a motion in the Tax Court for a redetermination of the amount of interest involved, then the Tax Court may reopen the case solely to determine whether the taxpayer has made an overpayment of such interest or the Secretary has made an underpayment of such interest and the amount thereof.

(2) Cases to which this subsection applies. This subsection shall apply where—

(A)(i) an assessment has been made by the Secretary under section 6215 which includes interest as imposed by this title, and

(ii) the taxpayer has paid the entire amount of the deficiency plus interest claimed by the Secretary, and

(B) the Tax Court finds under section 6512(b) that the taxpayer has made an overpayment.

(3) Special rules. If the Tax Court determines under this subsection that the taxpayer has made an overpayment of interest or that the Secretary has made an underpayment of interest, then that determination shall be treated under section 6512(b)(1) as a determination of an overpayment of tax. An order of the Tax Court redetermining interest, when entered upon the records of the court, shall be reviewable in the same manner as a decision of the Tax Court.

(d) Decisions relating to estate tax extended under section 6166.

If with respect to a decedent's estate subject to a decision of the Tax Court—

(1) the time for payment of an amount of tax imposed by chapter 11 is extended under section 6166, and

(2) there is treated as an administrative expense under section 2053 either—

(A) any amount of interest which a decedent's estate pays on any portion of the tax imposed by section 2001 on such estate for which the time of payment is extended under section 6166, or

(B) interest on any estate, succession, legacy, or inheritance tax imposed by a State on such estate during the period of the extension of time for payment under section 6166,

then, upon a motion by the petitioner in such case in which such time for payment of tax has been extended under section 6166, the Tax Court may reopen the case solely to modify the Court's decision to reflect such estate's entitlement to a deduction for such administration expenses under section 2053 and may hold further trial solely with respect to the claim for such deduction if, within the discretion of the Tax Court, such a hearing is deemed necessary. An order of the Tax Court disposing of a motion under this subsection shall be reviewable in the same manner as a decision of the Tax Court, but only with respect to the matters determined in such order.

In **1997**, P.L. 105-34, Sec. 1452(a), amended subsec. (c), effective 8/5/97. Prior to amendment, subsec. (c) read as follows:

"(c) Jurisdiction over interest determinations. Notwithstanding subsection (a), if—

"(1) an assessment has been made by the Secretary under section 6215 which includes interest as imposed by this title,

"(2) the taxpayer has paid the entire amount of the deficiency plus interest claimed by the Secretary, and

"(3) within 1 year after the date the decision of the Tax Court becomes final under subsection (a), the taxpayer files a petition in the Tax Court for a determination that the amount of interest claimed by the Secretary exceeds the amount of interest imposed by this title,

then the Tax Court may reopen the case solely to determine whether the taxpayer has made an overpayment of such interest and the amount of any such overpayment. If the Tax Court determines under this subsection that the taxpayer has made an overpayment of interest, then that determination shall be treated under section 6512(b)(1) as a determination of an overpayment of tax. An order of the Tax Court redetermining the interest due, when entered upon the records of the court, shall be reviewable in the same manner as a decision of the Tax Court."

—P.L. 105-34, Sec. 1454(b)(3), substituted "section 7436(c) or 7463" for "section 7463" in subsec. (b), effective 8/5/97.

Code Sec. 7481

In 1988, P.L. 100-647, Sec. 6246(a), added subsec. (c) ... Sec. 6246(b)(2), substituted "subsections (b) and (c)" for "subsection (b)", in subsec. (a), effective on assessments of deficiencies redetermined by the Tax Court made after 11/10/88.
—P.L. 100-647, Sec. 6247(a), added subsec. (d) ... Sec. 6247(b)(2), substituted "subsections (b), (c), and (d)" for "subsections (b) and (c)", in subsec. (a), as amended by Sec. 6246(b)(2) of this Act, effective for Tax Court cases for which the decision is not final on 11/10/88.
In 1976, P.L. 94-455, Sec. 1906(b)(13)(A), substituted "Secretary" for "Secretary or his delegate" in Code Sec. 7481, effective 2/1/77.
In 1969, P.L. 91-172, Sec. 960(h)(1), amended so much as precedes para. (2) ... substituted "appeal" for "petition for review" in the heading of para. (2) and each place it appears in the text of para. (2) ... added subsec. (b), to take effect 30 days after the date of the enactment of this Act. In the case of any decision of the Tax Court entered before the 30th day after the date of the enactment of this Act, the United States Courts of Appeals shall have jurisdiction to hear an appeal from such decision. If such appeal was filed within the time prescribed by Rule 13(a) of the Federal Rules of Appellate Procedure or by section 7483 of the Internal Revenue Code of 1954, as in effect at the time the decision of the Tax Court was entered, as provided in Sec. 962(f).
Prior to amendment, that part of Sec. 7481, as preceded para. (2) read as follows: "The decision of the Tax Court shall become final—
"(1) Timely petition for review not filed. Upon the expiration of the time allowed for filing a petition for review, if no such petition has been duly filed within such time; or"

Sec. 7482. Courts of review.
(a) Jurisdiction.
(1) In general. The United States Courts of Appeals (other than the United States Court of Appeals for the Federal Circuit) shall have exclusive jurisdiction to review the decisions of the Tax Court, except as provided in section 1254 of Title 28 of the United States Code, in the same manner and to the same extent as decisions of the district courts in civil actions tried without a jury; and the judgment of any such court shall be final, except that it shall be subject to review by the Supreme Court of the United States upon certiorari, in the manner provided in section 1254 of Title 28 of the United States Code.
(2) Interlocutory orders.
(A) In general. When any judge of the Tax Court includes in an interlocutory order a statement that a controlling question of law is involved with respect to which there is a substantial ground for difference of opinion and that an immediate appeal from that order may materially advance the ultimate termination of the litigation, the United States Court of Appeals may, in its discretion, permit an appeal to be taken from such order, if application is made to it within 10 days after the entry of such order. Neither the application for nor the granting of an appeal under this paragraph shall stay proceedings in the Tax Court, unless a stay is ordered by a judge of the Tax Court or by the United States Court of Appeals which has jurisdiction of the appeal or a judge of that court.
(B) Order treated as tax court decision. For purposes of subsections (b) and (c), an order described in this paragraph shall be treated as a decision of the Tax Court.
(C) Venue for review of subsequent proceedings. If a United States Court of Appeals permits an appeal to be taken from an order described in subparagraph (A), except as provided in subsection (b)(2), any subsequent review of the decision of the Tax Court in the proceeding shall be made by such Court of Appeals.
(3) Certain orders entered under section 6213(a). An order of the Tax Court which is entered under authority of section 6213(a) and which resolves a proceeding to restrain assessment or collection shall be treated as a decision of the Tax Court for purposes of this section and shall be subject to the same review by the United States Court of Appeals as a similar order of a district court.

(b) Venue.
(1) In general. Except as otherwise provided in paragraphs (2) and (3), such decisions may be reviewed by the United States court of appeals for the circuit in which is located—
(A) in the case of a petitioner seeking redetermination of tax liability other than a corporation, the legal residence of the petitioner,
(B) in the case of a corporation seeking redetermination of tax liability, the principal place of business or principal office or agency of the corporation, or, if it has no principal place of business or principal office or agency in any judicial circuit, then the office to which was made the return of the tax in respect of which the liability arises,
(C) in the case of a person seeking a declaratory decision under section 7476, the principal place of business, or principal office or agency of the employer,
(D) in the case of an organization seeking a declaratory decision under section 7428, the principal office or agency of the organization,
(E) in the case of a petition under section 6226, 6228(a), 6247, or 6252 the principal place of business of the partnership, or
(F) in the case of a petition under section 6234(c)—
(i) the legal residence of the petitioner if the petitioner is not a corporation, and
(ii) the place or office applicable under subparagraph (B) if the petitioner is a corporation.
If for any reason no subparagraph of the preceding sentence applies, then such decisions may be reviewed by the Court of Appeals for the District of Columbia. For purposes of this paragraph, the legal residence, principal place of business, or principal office or agency referred to herein shall be determined as of the time the petition seeking redetermination of tax liability was filed with the Tax Court or as of the time the petition seeking a declaratory decision under section 7428 or 7476, or the petition under section 6226, 6228(a) or 6234(c), was filed with the Tax Court.
(2) By agreement. Notwithstanding the provisions of paragraph (1), such decisions may be reviewed by any United States Court of Appeals which may be designated by the Secretary and the taxpayer by stipulation in writing.
(3) Declaratory judgment actions relating to status of certain governmental obligations. In the case of any decision of the Tax Court in a proceeding under section 7478, such decision may only be reviewed by the Court of Appeals for the District of Columbia.
(c) Powers.
(1) To affirm, modify, or reverse. Upon such review, such courts shall have power to affirm or, if the decision of the Tax Court is not in accordance with law, to modify or to reverse the decision of the Tax Court, with or without remanding the case for a rehearing, as justice may require.
(2) To make rules. Rules for review of decisions of the Tax Court shall be those prescribed by the Supreme Court under section 2072 of Title 28 of the United States Code.
(3) To require additional security. Nothing in section 7483 shall be construed as relieving the petitioner from making or filing such undertakings as the court may require as a condition of or in connection with the review.
(4) To impose penalties. The United States Court of Appeals and the Supreme Court shall have power to require the taxpayer to pay to the United States a penalty in any

Judicial proceedings Code Sec. 7485(a)(2)

case where the decision of the Tax Court is affirmed and it appears that the appeal was instituted or maintained primarily for delay or that the taxpayer's position in the appeal is frivolous or groundless.

In 1998, P.L. 105-206, Sec. 6012(e), substituted "beginning" for "ending on or" in Sec. 1226 of P.L. 105-34, the effective date for amendments made by Sec. 1222 of P.L. 105-34, see below.

In 1997, P.L. 105-34, Sec. 1222(b)(3), substituted ", 6228(a), 6247, or 6252" for "or 6228(a)" in subpara. (b)(1)(E), effective for partnership tax. yrs. begin. after 12/31/97.

—P.L. 105-34, Sec. 1239(d)(1), deleted "or" at the end of subpara. (b)(1)(D), substituted ", or" for the period at the end of subpara. (b)(1)(E) and added subpara. (b)(1)(F) ... Sec. 1239(d)(2), substituted ", 6228(a), or 6234(c)" for "or 6228(a)" at the end of para. (b)(1), effective for partnership tax. yrs. end. after 8/5/97.

In 1989, P.L. 101-239, Sec. 7731(b), amended para. (c)(4), effective for positions taken after 12/31/89, in proceedings which are pending on, or commenced after 12/31/89.

Prior to amendment, para. (c)(4) reads as follows:

"(4) To impose damages. The United States Court of Appeals and the Supreme Court shall have power to impose damages in any case where the decision of the Tax Court is affirmed and it appears that the notice of appeal was filed merely for delay."

In 1988, P.L. 100-647, Sec. 6243(b), added para. (a)(3), effective for orders entered 11/10/88.

In 1986, P.L. 99-514, Sec. 1558(a), added para. (a)(2) ... Sec. 1558(b), added "(1) In general." before the "The United States" in the material before para. (a)(2), effective for any order of the Tax Court entered after 10/22/86.

—P.L. 99-514, Sec. 1810(g)(2), substituted "section 7428 or 7476" for "section 7428, 7476, or 7477" in para. (b)(1), effective for transfers or exchanges after 12/31/84, in tax. yrs. end. after 12/31/84. See Secs. 131(g)(2) and (g)(3) of P.L. 98-369 for special rules, reproduced in the note following Code Sec. 7477.

— Sec. 1899A(60), substituted "partnership." for "partnership," in subpara. (b)(1)(E), effective 10/22/86.

In 1984, P.L. 98-369, Sec. 131(e)(2)(A), deleted subpara. (b)(1)(D) and redesignated subparas. (b)(1)(E) and (F) as subparas. (b)(1)(D) and (E), respectively, effective for transfers or exchanges after 12/31/84, in tax. yrs. end. after 12/31/84. See Secs. 131(g)(2) and (g)(3) of the Act for special rules, reproduced in note following Code Sec. 7477.

Prior to deletion, subpara. (b)(1)(D) read as follows:

"(D) in the case of a person seeking a declaratory judgment under section 7477, the legal residence of such person if such person is not a corporation, or the principal place of business or principal office or agency of such person if such person is a corporation.

In 1982, P.L. 97-248, Sec. 402(c)(15)(A)-(D), amended para. (b)(1) by deleting 'or' at the end of subpara. (b)(1)(D), substituting ', or' for the period and the end of subpara. (b)(1)(E), adding new subpara. (b)(1)(F), inserting ', or the petition under section 6225 or 6228(a),' after 'or 7477' in para. (b)(1), effective for partnership tax. yrs. begin. after 9/3/82. Sec. 407(a)(3) of this Act provides:

"(3) The amendments made by sections 402, 403, and 404 [of this Act] shall apply to any partnership taxable year (or in the case of section 6232 of such Code, to any period) ending after the date of the enactment of this Act [9/3/82] if the partnership, each partner, and each indirect partner requests such application and the Secretary of the Treasury or his delegate consents to such application."

In 1982, P.L. 97-164, Sec. 154, added "(other than the United States Court of Appeals for the Federal Circuit)" after "United States Court of Appeals" in subsec. (a), effective 10/1/82.

In 1978, P.L. 95-600, Sec. 336(c)(1), substituted "provided in paragraphs (2) and (3)" for "provided in paragraph (2)" in para. (b)(1), added a new para. (b)(3), effective for requests for determinations made after 12/31/78.

In 1976, P.L. 94-455, Sec. 1042(d)(2)(A), deleted "or" at the end of subpara. (b)(1)(B), substituted ", or" for the period at the end of subpara. (b)(1)(C), added subpara. (b)(1)(D), for pleadings filed with the Tax Court after 10/4/76, but only with respect to transfers begin. after 10/9/75.

—P.L. 94-455, Sec. 1042(d)(2)(B), substituted "no subparagraph of the preceding sentence applies" for "subparagraph (A), (B), and (C) do not apply" in the second sentence of para. (b)(1) ... added "or 7477" following "section 7476" in the last sentence of para. (b)(1), for pleadings filed with the Tax Court after 10/4/76, but only with respect to transfers begin. after 10/9/75.

—P.L. 94-455, Sec. 1306(b)(4), deleted "or" at the end of subpara. (b)(1)(C), substituted ", or" for the period at the end of new subpara. (b)(1)(D), as previously amended by the Act, added new subpara. (b)(1)(E), effective for pleadings filed more than 6 months after 10/4/76, but only with respect to determinations (or requests for determinations) made after 1/1/76.

—P.L. 94-455, Sec. 1306(b)(5), substituted "section 7428, 7476" for "section 7476" in the last sentence of para. (b)(1) as previously amended by the Act, for pleadings filed more than 6 months after 10/4/76, but only with respect to determinations (or requests for determinations) made after 1/1/76.

—P.L. 94-455, Sec. 1906(b)(13)(A), substituted "Secretary" for "Secretary or his delegate" in para. (b)(2), effective 2/1/77.

In 1974, P.L. 93-406, Sec. 1041(b)(3), amended para. (b)(1), effective with respect to pleadings filed more than one year after 9/2/74, as follows:

... in subpara. (b)(1)(B), by substituting ", or" for the period at the end thereof;
... subpara. (b)(1)(C) was added;

... by substituting "subparagraph (A), (B), and (C) do not apply" for "neither (A) nor (B) applies";
... by inserting before the period at the end of the last sentence thereof "or as of the time the petition seeking a declaratory decision under section 7476 was filed with the Tax Court".

In 1969, P.L. 91-172, Sec. 960(h)(2), substituted "section 2072 of title 28" for "section 2074 of title 28" in para. (c)(2) ... struck out "Until such rules become effective the rules adopted under authority of section 1141(c)(2) of the Internal Revenue Code of 1939 shall remain in effect." from the end of para. (c)(2) ... substituted "notice of appeal" for "petition" in para. (c)(4). For effective date, see note following Code Sec. 7481.

In 1966, P.L. 89-713, Sec. 3(c), amended para. (b)(1), effective for decisions of the Tax Court entered after 11/2/66.

Prior to amendment the subsec. read as follows:

"(1) In general. Except as provided in paragraph (2), such decisions may be reviewed by the United States Court of Appeals for the circuit in which is located the office to which was made the return of the tax in respect of which the liability arises, or, if no return was made, then by the United States Court of Appeals for the District of Columbia."

Sec. 7483. Notice of appeal.

Review of a decision of the Tax Court shall be obtained by filing a notice of appeal with the clerk of the Tax Court within 90 days after the decision of the Tax Court is entered. If a timely notice of appeal is filed by one party, any other party may take an appeal by filing a notice of appeal within 120 days after the decision of the Tax Court is entered.

In 1969, P.L. 91-172, Sec. 959, amended Code Sec. 7483, effective 30 days after 12/30/69. In the case of any decision of the Tax Court entered before the 30th day after the date of the enactment of this Act, the United States Courts of Appeals shall have jurisdiction to hear an appeal from such decision, if such appeal was filed within the time prescribed by Rule 13(a) of the Federal Rules of Appellate Procedure or by section 7483 of the Internal Revenue Code of 1954, as in effect at the time the decision of the Tax Court was entered, as provided in Sec. 962(f).

Prior to amendment, Code Sec. 7483 read as follows:

"Sec. 7483. Petition for review.

"The decision of the Tax Court may be reviewed by a United States Court of Appeals as provided in section 7482 if a petition for such review is filed by either the Secretary (or his delegate) or the taxpayer within 3 months after the decision is rendered. If, however, a petition for such review is so filed by one party to the proceeding, a petition for review of the decision of the Tax Court may be filed by any other party to the proceeding within 4 months after such decision is rendered."

Sec. 7484. Change of incumbent in office.

When the incumbent of the office of Secretary changes, no substitution of the name of his successor shall be required in proceedings pending before any appellate court reviewing the action of the Tax Court.

In 1976, P.L. 94-455, Sec. 1906(b)(13)(A), substituted "Secretary" for "Secretary or his delegate" in Code Sec. 7484, effective 2/1/77.

Sec. 7485. Bond to stay assessment and collection.
(a) Upon notice of appeal.

Notwithstanding any provision of law imposing restrictions on the assessment and collection of deficiencies, the review under section 7483 shall not operate as a stay of assessment or collection of any portion of the amount of the deficiency determined by the Tax Court unless a notice of appeal in respect of such portion is duly filed by the taxpayer, and then only if the taxpayer—

(1) on or before the time his notice of appeal is filed has filed with the Tax Court a bond in a sum fixed by the Tax Court not exceeding double the amount of the portion of the deficiency in respect of which the notice of appeal is filed, and with surety approved by the Tax Court, conditioned upon the payment of the deficiency as finally determined, together with any interest, additional amounts, or additions to the tax provided for by law, or

(2) has filed a jeopardy bond under the income or estate tax laws.

If as a result of a waiver of the restrictions on the assessment and collection of a deficiency any part of the amount determined by the Tax Court is paid after the filing of the

Code Sec. 7485(a)(2)

appeal bond, such bond shall, at the request of the taxpayer, be proportionately reduced.

(b) Bond in case of appeal of certain partnership-related decisions.

The condition of subsection (a) shall be satisfied if a partner duly files notice of appeal from a decision under section 6226, 6228(a), 6247, or 6252 and on or before the time the notice of appeal is filed with the Tax Court, a bond in an amount fixed by the Tax Court is filed, and with surety approved by the Tax Court, conditioned upon the payment of deficiencies attributable to the partnership items to which that decision relates as finally determined, together with any interest, penalties, additional amounts, or additions to the tax provided by law. Unless otherwise stipulated by the parties, the amount fixed by the Tax Court shall be based upon its estimate of the aggregate liability of the parties to the action.

(c) Cross references.

(1) For requirement of additional security notwithstanding this section, see section 7482(c)(3).

(2) For deposit of United States bonds or notes in lieu of sureties, see section 9303 of title 31, United States Code.

In 1998, P.L. 105-206, Sec. 6012(e), substituted "beginning" for "ending on or" in Sec. 1226 of P.L. 105-34, the effective date for amendments made by Sec. 1222 of P.L. 105-34, see below.

In 1997, P.L. 105-34, Sec. 1222(b)(4)(A), substituted ", 6228(a), 6247, or 6252" for "or 6228(a)" in subsec. (b)... Sec. 1222(b)(4)(B), amended the heading of subsec. (b), effective for partnership tax. yrs. begin. after 12/31/97.

Prior to amendment, the heading of subsec. (b) read as follows:

"(b) Bond in case of appeal of decision under section 6226 or section 6228(a)."
—P.L. 105-34, Sec. 1241(a)(1), added "penalties," after "any interest," in subsec. (b)... Sec. 1421(a)(2), substituted "aggregate liability of the parties to the action" for "aggregate of such deficiencies" in subsec. (b), effective for partnership tax. yrs. begin. after 9/3/82. See Sec. 407(a)(3) of P.L. 97-248 reproduced below.

In 1982, P.L. 97-258, Sec. 3(f)(15), substituted "section 9303 of title 31, United States Code" for "6 U.S.C. 15" in para. (b)(2), [sic , para. (b)(2) was redesignated as para. (c)(2) by P.L. 97-248, see below], effective 9/13/82.
—P.L. 97-248, Sec. 402(c)(16), redesignated subsec. (b) as (c) and added subsec. (b), effective for partnership tax. yrs. begin. after 9/3/82. Sec. 407(a)(3) of this Act provides:

"(3) The amendments made by sections 402, 403, and 404 [of this Act] shall apply to any partnership taxable year (or in the case of section 6232 of such Code, to any period) ending after the date of the enactment of this Act [9/3/82] if the partnership, each partner, and each indirect partner requests such application and the Secretary of the Treasury or his delegate consents to such application."

In 1969, P.L. 91-172, Sec. 960(h)(3), substituted "notice of appeal" for "petition of review" in the heading of subsec. (a) and each place it appeared in subsec. (a), substituted "appeal bond" for "review bond" in para. (a)(2). For effective date, see note following Code Sec. 7481.

Sec. 7486. Refund, credit, or abatement of amounts disallowed.

In cases where assessment or collection has not been stayed by the filing of a bond, then if the amount of the deficiency determined by the Tax Court is disallowed in whole or in part by the court of review, the amount so disallowed shall be credited or refunded to the taxpayer, without the making of claim therefor, or, if collection has not been made, shall be abated.

Sec. 7487. Cross references.

(1) Nonreviewability. For nonreviewability of Tax Court decisions in small claims cases, see section 7463(b).

(2) Transcripts. For authority of the Tax Court to fix fees for transcript of records, see section 7474.

In 1969, P.L. 91-172, Sec. 960(i), amended Code Sec. 7487, effective 12/30/70. Prior to amendment, Code Sec. 7487 read as follows:

"Sec. 7487. Cross reference.

"For authority of the Tax Court to fix fees for transcripts of records, see section 7474."

Judicial proceedings

Subchapter E.—Burden of Proof

Sec.
7491. Burden of proof.

In 1998, P.L. 105-206, Sec. 3001(a), added Subchapter E to Chapter 76.

Sec. 7491. Burden of proof.

(a) Burden shifts where taxpayer produces credible evidence.

(1) General rule. If, in any court proceeding, a taxpayer introduces credible evidence with respect to any factual issue relevant to ascertaining the liability of the taxpayer for any tax imposed by subtitle A or B, the Secretary shall have the burden of proof with respect to such issue.

(2) Limitations. Paragraph (1) shall apply with respect to an issue only if—

(A) the taxpayer has complied with the requirements under this title to substantiate any item;

(B) the taxpayer has maintained all records required under this title and has cooperated with reasonable requests by the Secretary for witnesses, information, documents, meetings, and interviews; and

(C) in the case of a partnership, corporation, or trust, the taxpayer is described in section 7430(c)(4)(A)(ii).

Subparagraph (C) shall not apply to any qualified revocable trust (as defined in section 645(b)(1)) with respect to liability for tax for any taxable year ending after the date of the decedent's death and before the applicable date (as defined in section 645(b)(2)).

(3) Coordination. Paragraph (1) shall not apply to any issue if any other provision of this title provides for a specific burden of proof with respect to such issue.

(b) Use of statistical information on unrelated taxpayers.

In the case of an individual taxpayer, the Secretary shall have the burden of proof in any court proceeding with respect to any item of income which was reconstructed by the Secretary solely through the use of statistical information on unrelated taxpayers.

(c) Penalties.

Notwithstanding any other provision of this title, the Secretary shall have the burden of production in any court proceeding with respect to the liability of any individual for any penalty, addition to tax, or additional amount imposed by this title.

In 1998, P.L. 105-277, Sec. 4002(b), added a flush sentence at the end of para. (a)(2), effective for court proceedings arising in connection with examinations commencing after 7/22/98 [For Sec. 3001(c)(2) of P.L. 105-206, see below].
—P.L. 105-206, Sec. 3001(a), added Code Sec. 7491, effective for court proceedings arising in connection with examinations commencing after 7/22/98.

Sec. 3001(c)(2) of P.L. 105-206, provides:

"(2) Taxable periods or events after date of enactment. In any case in which there is no examination, such amendments shall apply to court proceedings arising in connection with taxable periods or events beginning or occurring after such date of enactment [7/22/98]."

Subchapter E. Repealed.

Sec.
7492. Repealed.

In 1976, P.L. 94-455, Sec. 1952(n)(4)(A), repealed subchapter E.
In 1970, repealed item 7491.
— repealed item 7493.
In 1976, P.L. 94-455, Sec. 1952(n)(4)(A), repealed Code Sec. 7492, effective 1/1/77.

Prior to amendment, Code Sec. 7492 read as follows:

"Sec. 7492. Enforceability of cotton futures contracts.

"No contract of sale of cotton for future delivery mentioned in section 4851(a), which does not conform to the requirements of section 4833 and has not the necessary stamps affixed thereto as required by section 4871, shall be enforceable in

Miscellaneous provisions — Code Sec. 7502(b)

any court of the United States by, or on behalf of, any party to such contract or his privies.

CHAPTER 77.—MISCELLANEOUS PROVISIONS

Sec.
7501. Liability for taxes withheld or collected.
7502. Timely mailing treated as timely filing and paying.
7503. Time for performance of acts where last day falls on Saturday, Sunday, or legal holiday.
7504. Fractional parts of a dollar.
7505. Sale of personal property acquired by the United States.
7506. Administration of real estate acquired by the United States.
7507. Exemption of insolvent banks from tax.
7508. Time for performing certain acts postponed by reason of service in combat zone or contingency operation.
7508A. Authority to postpone certain deadlines by reason of Presidentially declared disaster or terroristic or military actions.
7509. Expenditures incurred by the United States Postal Service.
7510. Exemption from tax of domestic goods purchased for the United States.
7512. Separate accounting for certain collected taxes, etc.
7513. Reproduction of returns and other documents.
7514. Authority to prescribe or modify seals.
7515. [Repealed] Special statistical studies and compilations and other services on request.
7516. Supplying training and training aids on request.
7517. Furnishing on request of statement explaining estate or gift valuation.
7518. Tax incentives relating to merchant marine capital construction funds.
7519. Required payments for entities electing not to have required taxable year.
7520. Valuation tables.
7521. Procedures involving taxpayer interviews.
7522. Content of tax due, deficiency, and other notices.
7523. Graphic presentation of major categories of Federal outlays and income.
7524. Annual notice of tax delinquency.
7525. Confidentiality privileges relating to taxpayer communications.
7526. Low-income taxpayer clinics.
7527. Advance payment of credit for health insurance costs of eligible individuals.
7528. Internal Revenue Service user fees.

In **2003**, P.L. 108-121, Sec. 104(b)(3), amended item 7508.
Prior to amendment, item 7508 read as follows:
 "Sec. 7508. Time for performing certain acts postponed by reason of service in combat zone."
—P.L. 108-89, Sec. 202(b)(1), added item 7528.
In **2002**, P.L. 107-210, Sec. 202(d)(1), added item 7527.
—P.L. 107-134, Sec. 112(e)(1), amended item 7508A.
Prior to amendment, item 7508A read as follows:
 "Sec. 7508A. Authority to postpone certain tax-related deadlines by reason of Presidentially declared disaster."
In **1998**, P.L. 105-206, Sec. 3411(b), added item 7525.
—P.L. 105-206, Sec. 3601(b), added item 7526.
In **1997**, P.L. 105-34, Sec. 911(b), added item 7508A.
In **1996**, P.L. 104-168, Sec. 1204(b), added item 7524.
In **1990**, P.L. 101-508, Sec. 11704(a)(31), redesignated item 7521 as 7522.
—P.L. 101-508, Sec. 11622(b), added item 7523.

In **1989**, P.L. 101-239, Sec. 7816(u)(2), substituted "Sec. 7521. Procedures involving taxpayer interviews." for "7520. Procedures involving taxpayer interviews."
In **1988**, P.L. 100-647, Sec. 5031(b), added new item 7520[sic] ... Sec. 6228(c), added new item 7520[sic] ... Sec. 6233(b), added new item 7521.
In **1987**, P.L. 100-203, Sec. 10206(b)(2), added item 7519.
In **1986**, P.L. 99-514, Sec. 261(f), added item 7518.
In **1976**, P.L. 94-455, Sec. 1906(b)(11), amended the item for Code Sec. 7508.
—P.L. 94-455, Sec. 1906(b)(12), amended the item for Code Sec. 7509.
In **1976**, P.L. 94-455, Sec. 2008(a)(2)(C), added the item for Code Sec. 7517.
In **1966**, added "and paying" in item 7502.
In **1962**, added items 7515 and 7516.
—repealed item 7511 dealing with exemption of consular officers and employees of foreign states from payment of internal revenue taxes on imported articles.
In **1958**, added items 7513 and 7514.
—added item 7512.

Sec. 7501. Liability for taxes withheld or collected.

(a) General rule.

Whenever any person is required to collect or withhold any internal revenue tax from any other person and to pay over such tax to the United States, the amount of tax so collected or withheld shall be held to be a special fund in trust for the United States. The amount of such fund shall be assessed, collected, and paid in the same manner and subject to the same provisions and limitations (including penalties) as are applicable with respect to the taxes from which such fund arose.

(b) Penalties.

For penalties applicable to violations of this section, see sections 6672 and 7202.

Sec. 7502. Timely mailing treated as timely filing and paying.

(a) General rule.

(1) Date of delivery. If any return, claim, statement, or other document required to be filed, or any payment required to be made, within a prescribed period or on or before a prescribed date under authority of any provision of the internal revenue laws is, after such period or such date, delivered by United States mail to the agency, officer, or office with which such return, claim, statement, or other document is required to be filed, or to which such payment is required to be made, the date of the United States postmark stamped on the cover in which such return, claim, statement, or other document, or payment, is mailed shall be deemed to be the date of delivery or the date of payment, as the case may be.

(2) Mailing requirements. This subsection shall apply only if—

(A) the postmark date falls within the prescribed period or on or before the prescribed date—

(i) for the filing (including any extension granted for such filing) of the return, claim, statement, or other document, or

(ii) for making the payment (including any extension granted for making such payment), and

(B) the return, claim, statement, or other document, or payment was, within the time prescribed in subparagraph (A), deposited in the mail in the United States in an envelope or other appropriate wrapper, postage prepaid, properly addressed to the agency, officer, or office with which the return, claim, statement, or other document is required to be filed, or to which such payment is required to be made.

(b) Postmarks.

This section shall apply in the case of postmarks not made by the United States Postal Service only if and to the extent provided by regulations prescribed by the Secretary.

(c) Registered and certified mailing; electronic filing.
   (1) Registered mail. For purposes of this section, if any return, claim, statement, or other document, or payment, is sent by United States registered mail—
      (A) such registration shall be prima facie evidence that the return, claim, statement, or other document was delivered to the agency, officer, or office to which addressed; and
      (B) the date of registration shall be deemed the postmark date.
   (2) Certified mail; electronic filing. The Secretary is authorized to provide by regulations the extent to which the provisions of paragraph (1) with respect to prima facie evidence of delivery and the postmark date shall apply to certified mail and electronic filing.
(d) Exceptions.
This section shall not apply with respect to—
   (1) the filing of a document in, or the making of a payment to, any court other than the Tax Court,
   (2) currency or other medium of payment unless actually received and accounted for, or
   (3) returns, claims, statements, or other documents, or payments, which are required under any provision of the internal revenue laws or the regulations thereunder to be delivered by any method other than by mailing.
(e) Mailing of deposits.
   (1) Date of deposit. If any deposit required to be made (pursuant to regulations prescribed by the Secretary under section 6302(c)) on or before a prescribed date is, after such date, delivered by the United States mail to the bank, trust company, domestic building and loan association, or credit union authorized to receive such deposit, such deposit shall be deemed received by such bank, trust company, domestic building and loan association, or credit union on the date the deposit was mailed.
   (2) Mailing requirements. Paragraph (1) shall apply only if the person required to make the deposit establishes that—
      (A) the date of mailing falls on or before the second day before the prescribed date for making the deposit (including any extension of time granted for making such deposit), and
      (B) the deposit was, on or before such second day, mailed in the United States in an envelope or other appropriate wrapper, postage prepaid, properly addressed to the bank, trust company, domestic building and loan association, or credit union authorized to receive such deposit.
In applying subsection (c) for purposes of this subsection, the term "payment" includes "deposit", and the reference to the postmark date refers to the date of mailing.
   (3) No application to certain deposits. Paragraph (1) shall not apply with respect to any deposit of $20,000 or more by any person who is required to deposit any tax more than once a month.
(f) Treatment of private delivery services.
   (1) In general. Any reference in this section to the United States mail shall be treated as including a reference to any designated delivery service, and any reference in this section to a postmark by the United States Postal Service shall be treated as including a reference to any date recorded or marked as described in paragraph (2)(C) by any designated delivery service.
   (2) Designated delivery service. For purposes of this subsection, the term "designated delivery service" means any delivery service provided by a trade or business if such service is designated by the Secretary for purposes of this section. The Secretary may designate a delivery service under the preceding sentence only if the Secretary determines that such service—
      (A) is available to the general public,
      (B) is at least as timely and reliable on a regular basis as the United States mail,
      (C) records electronically to its data base, kept in the regular course of its business, or marks on the cover in which any item referred to in this section is to be delivered, the date on which such item was given to such trade or business for delivery, and
      (D) meets such other criteria as the Secretary may prescribe.
   (3) Equivalents of registered and certified mail. The Secretary may provide a rule similar to the rule of paragraph (1) with respect to any service provided by a designated delivery service which is substantially equivalent to United States registered or certified mail.

In **1998**, P.L. 105-206, Sec. 2003(b), amended subsec. (c), effective 7/22/98. Prior to amendment, subsec. (c) read as follows:
"(c) Registered and certified mailing.
"(1) Registered mail. For purposes of this section, if any such return, claim, statement, or other document, or payment, is sent by United States registered mail—
"(A) such registration shall be prima facie evidence that the return, claim, statement, or other document was delivered to the agency, officer, or office to which addressed, and
"(B) the date of registration shall be deemed the postmark date.
"(2) Certified mail. The Secretary is authorized to provide by regulations the extent to which the provisions of paragraph (1) of this subsection with respect to prima facie evidence of delivery and the postmark date shall apply to certified mail."
In **1996**, P.L. 104-168, Sec. 1210, added subsec. (f), effective 7/30/96.
In **1986**, P.L. 99-514, Sec. 1811(e), substituted "any tax" for "the tax" in para. (e)(3), effective 7/18/84.
In **1984**, P.L. 98-369, Sec. 157(a), added para. (e)(3), effective 7/31/84.
In **1977**, P.L. 95-147, Sec. 3(b), substituted ", trust company, domestic building and loan association, or credit union" for "or trust company" each place it appeared in subsec. (e), effective for amounts deposited after 10/28/77.
In **1976**, P.L. 94-455, Sec. 1906(a)(49), substituted "United States Postal Service" for "United States Post Office" in subsec. (b), effective 2/1/77.
— P.L. 94-455, Sec. 1906(b)(13)(A), substituted "Secretary" for "Secretary or his delegate" each place it appeared in Code Sec. 7502, effective 2/1/77.
In **1968**, P.L. 90-364, Sec. 106(a), added subsec. (e), effective for mailing occurring after 6/28/68.
In **1966**, P.L. 89-713, Sec. 5(a), amended Code Sec. 7502, effective for mailing after 11/2/66.
Prior to amendment, Code Sec. 7502 read as follows:
"SEC. 7502. TIMELY MAILING TREATED AS TIMELY FILING.
"(a) General rule.
"If any claim, statement, or other document (other than a return or other document required under authority of chapter 61), required to be filed within a prescribed period or on or before a prescribed date under authority of any provision of the internal revenue laws is, after such period or such date, delivered by United States mail to the agency, officer, or office with which such claim, statement, or other document is required to be filed, the date of the United States postmark stamped on the cover in which such claim, statement, or other document is mailed shall be deemed to be the date of delivery. This subsection shall apply only if the postmark date falls within the prescribed period or on or before the prescribed date for the filing of the claim, statement, or other document, determined with regard to any extension granted for such filing, and only if the claim, statement, or other document was, within the prescribed time, deposited in the mail in the United States in an envelope or other appropriate wrapper, postage prepaid, properly addressed to the agency, office, or officer with which the claim, statement, or other document is required to be filed.
"(b) Stamp machine.
"This section shall apply in the case of postmarks not made by the United States Post Office only if and to the extent provided by regulations prescribed by the Secretary or his delegate.
"(c) Registered and certified mail.
"(1) Registered mail. If any such claim, statement, or other document is sent by United States registered mail, such registration shall be prima facie evidence that the claim, statement, or other document was delivered to the agency, office, or officer to which addressed, and the date of registration shall be deemed the postmark date.
"(2) Certified mail. The Secretary or his delegate is authorized to provide by regulations the extent to which the provisions of paragraph (1) of this subsection

Miscellaneous provisions   Code Sec. 7507(b)

with respect to prima facie evidence of delivery and the postmark date shall apply to certified mail.

"(d) Exception.

"This section shall not apply with respect to the filing of a document in any court other than the Tax Court."

In 1958, P.L. 85-866, Sec. 89(a), designated existing provisions of subsec. (c) as para. (c)(1) and added para. (c)(2), effective for mailings after 9/2/58.

Sec. 7503. Time for performance of acts where last day falls on Saturday, Sunday, or legal holiday.

When the last day prescribed under authority of the internal revenue laws for performing any act falls on Saturday, Sunday, or a legal holiday, the performance of such act shall be considered timely if it is performed on the next succeeding day which is not a Saturday, Sunday, or a legal holiday. For purposes of this section, the last day for the performance of any act shall be determined by including any authorized extension of time; the term "legal holiday" means a legal holiday in the District of Columbia; and in the case of any return, statement, or other document required to be filed, or any other act required under authority of the internal revenue laws to be performed, at any office of the Secretary or at any other office of the United States or any agency thereof, located outside the District of Columbia but within an internal revenue district, the term "legal holiday" also means a Statewide legal holiday in the State where such office is located.

In 1988, P.L. 100-647, Sec. 6278, of this Act provides:

"Section 7503 of the 1986 Code shall apply for purposes of determining whether any disposition meets the requirements of section 10222(b)(2)(B) of the Revenue Act of 1987. If any disposition meets the requirements of such section by reason of the preceding sentence, for all purposes of the 1986 Code, such disposition shall be deemed to have occurred on December 31, 1988."

In 1976, P.L. 94-455, Sec. 1906(b)(13)(A), substituted "Secretary" for "Secretary or his delegate" in Code Sec. 7503, effective 2/1/77.

Sec. 7504. Fractional parts of a dollar.

The Secretary may by regulations provide that in the allowance of any amount as a credit or refund, or in the collection of any amount as a deficiency or underpayment, of any tax imposed by this title, a fractional part of a dollar shall be disregarded, unless it amounts to 50 cents or more, in which case it shall be increased to 1 dollar.

In 1976, P.L. 94-455, Sec. 1906(b)(13)(A), substituted "Secretary" for "Secretary or his delegate" in Code Sec. 7504, effective 2/1/77.

Sec. 7505. Sale of personal property acquired by the United States.

(a) Sale.

Any personal property acquired by the United States in payment of or as security for debts arising under the internal revenue laws may be sold by the Secretary in accordance with such regulations as may be prescribed by the Secretary.

(b) Accounting.

In case of the resale of such property, the proceeds of the sale shall be paid into the Treasury as internal revenue collections, and there shall be rendered a distinct account of all charges incurred in such sales.

In 1976, P.L. 94-455, Sec. 1906(b)(13)(A), substituted "Secretary" for "Secretary or his delegate" each place it appeared in Code Sec. 7505, effective 2/1/77.

In 1966, P.L. 89-719, Sec. 111, substituted "acquired by the United States in payment of or as security for debts arising under the internal revenue laws" for "purchased by the United States under the authority of section 6335(e) (relating to purchase for the account of the United States of property sold under levy)" in subsec. (a), and substituted "acquired" for "purchased" in the heading of Code Sec. 7505, effective after 11/2/66 regardless of when a lien or a title of the U.S. arose or when the lien or interest of any other person was acquired.

Sec. 7506. Administration of real estate acquired by the United States.

(a) Person charged with.

The Secretary shall have charge of all real estate which is or shall become the property of the United States by judgment of forfeiture under the internal revenue laws, or which has been or shall be assigned, set off, or conveyed by purchase or otherwise to the United States in payment of debts or penalties arising under the laws relating to internal revenue, or which has been or shall be vested in the United States by mortgage or other security for the payment of such debts, or which has been redeemed by the United States, and of all trusts created for the use of the United States in payment of such debts due them.

(b) Sale.

The Secretary, may, at public sale, and upon not less than 20 days' notice, sell and dispose of any real estate owned or held by the United States as aforesaid.

(c) Lease.

Until such sale, the Secretary may lease such real estate owned as aforesaid on such terms and for such period as the Secretary shall deem proper.

(d) Release to debtor.

In cases where real estate has or may become the property of the United States by conveyance or otherwise, in payment of or as security for a debt arising under the laws relating to internal revenue, and such debt shall have been paid, together with the interest thereon, at the rate of 1 percent per month, to the United States, within 2 years from the date of the acquisition of such real estate, it shall be lawful for the Secretary to release by deed or otherwise convey such real estate to the debtor from whom it was taken, or to his heirs or other legal representatives.

In 1976, P.L. 94-455, Sec. 1906(b)(13)(A), substituted "Secretary" for "Secretary or his delegate" each place it appeared in Code Sec. 7506, effective 2/1/77.

In 1966, P.L. 89-719, Sec. 111(b), added "or which has been redeemed by the United States" after "of such debts," in subsec. (a), effective after 11/2/66 regardless of when a lien or a title of the U.S. arose or when the lien or interest of any other person was acquired.

Sec. 7507. Exemption of insolvent banks from tax.

(a) Assets in general.

Whenever and after any bank or trust company, a substantial portion of the business of which consists of receiving deposits and making loans and discounts, has ceased to do business by reason of insolvency or bankruptcy, no tax shall be assessed or collected, or paid into the Treasury of the United States, on account of such bank or trust company, which shall diminish the assets thereof necessary for the full payment of all its depositors; and such tax shall be abated from such national banks as are found by the Comptroller of the Currency to be insolvent; and the Secretary, when the facts shall appear to him, is authorized to remit so much of the said tax against any such insolvent banks and trust companies organized under State law as shall be found to affect the claims of their depositors.

(b) Segregated assets; earnings.

Whenever any bank or trust company, a substantial portion of the business of which consists of receiving deposits and making loans and discounts, has been released or discharged from its liability to its depositors for any part of their claims against it, and such depositors have accepted, in lieu thereof, a lien upon subsequent earnings of such bank or trust company, or claims against assets segregated by such bank or trust company or against assets transferred from it to an individual or corporate trustee or agent, no tax shall be assessed or collected, or paid into the Treasury of the United

States, on account of such bank or trust company, such individual or corporate trustee or such agent, which shall diminish the assets thereof which are available for the payment of such depositor claims and which are necessary for the full payment thereof. The term "agent", as used in this subsection, shall be deemed to include a corporation acting as a liquidating agent.

(c) Refund; reassessment; statutes of limitation.

(1) Any such tax collected shall be deemed to be erroneously collected, and shall be refunded subject to all provisions and limitations of law, so far as applicable, relating to the refunding of taxes.

(2) Any tax, the assessment, collection, or payment of which is barred under subsection (a), or any such tax which has been abated or remitted, shall be assessed or reassessed whenever it shall appear that payment of the tax will not diminish the assets as aforesaid.

(3) Any tax, the assessment, collection, or payment of which is barred under subsection (b), or any such tax which has been refunded, shall be assessed or reassessed after full payment of such claims of depositors to the extent of the remaining assets segregated or transferred as described in subsection (b).

(4) The running of the statute of limitations on the making of assessment and collection shall be suspended during, and for 90 days beyond, the period for which, pursuant to this section, assessment or collection may not be made, and a tax may be reassessed as provided in paragraphs (2) and (3) of this subsection and collected, during the time within which, had there been no abatement, collection might have been made.

(d) Exception of employment taxes.

This section shall not apply to any tax imposed by chapter 21 or chapter 23.

In 1976, P.L. 94-455, Sec. 1906(a)(50), deleted "after May 28, 1938," after "abated or remitted" in para. (c)(2), and after "been refunded" in para. (c)(3), effective for tax. yrs. begin 2/1/77.

—P.L. 94-455, Sec. 1906(b)(13)(A), substituted "Secretary" for "Secretary or his delegate" in Code Sec. 7507, effective 2/1/77.

Sec. 7508. Time for performing certain acts postponed by reason of service in combat zone or contingency operation.

(a) Time to be disregarded.

In the case of an individual serving in the Armed Forces of the United States, or serving in support of such Armed Forces, in an area designated by the President of the United States by Executive order as a "combat zone" for purposes of section 112 , or when deployed outside the United States away from the individual's permanent duty station while participating in an operation designated by the Secretary of Defense as a contingency operation (as defined in section 101(a)(13) of title 10, United States Code) or which became such a contingency operation by operation of law, at any time during the period designated by the President by Executive order as the period of combatant activities in such zone for purposes of such section or at any time during the period of such contingency operation, or hospitalized as a result of injury received while serving in such an area or operation during such time, the period of service in such area or operation, plus the period of continuous qualified hospitalization attributable to such injury, and the next 180 days thereafter, shall be disregarded in determining, under the internal revenue laws, in respect of any tax liability (including any interest, penalty, additional amount, or addition to the tax) of such individual—

(1) Whether any of the following acts was performed within the time prescribed therefor:

(A) Filing any return of income, estate, gift, employment, or excise tax;

(B) Payment of any income, estate, gift, employment, or excise tax or any installment thereof or of any other liability to the United States in respect thereof;

(C) Filing a petition with the Tax Court for redetermination of a deficiency, or for review of a decision rendered by the Tax Court;

(D) Allowance of a credit or refund of any tax;

(E) Filing a claim for credit or refund of any tax;

(F) Bringing suit upon any such claim for credit or refund;

(G) Assessment of any tax;

(H) Giving or making any notice or demand for the payment of any tax, or with respect to any liability to the United States in respect of any tax;

(I) Collection, by the Secretary, by levy or otherwise, of the amount of any liability in respect of any tax;

(J) Bringing suit by the United States, or any officer on its behalf, in respect of any liability in respect of any tax; and

(K) Any other act required or permitted under the internal revenue laws specified by the Secretary;

(2) The amount of any credit or refund.

(b) Special rule for overpayments.

(1) **In general.** Subsection (a) shall not apply for purposes of determining the amount of interest on any overpayment of tax.

(2) **Special rules.** If an individual is entitled to the benefits of subsection (a) with respect to any return and such return is timely filed (determined after the application of such subsection), subsections (b)(3) and (e) of section 6611 shall not apply.

(c) Application to spouse.

The provisions of this section shall apply to the spouse of any individual entitled to the benefits of subsection (a). Except in the case of the combat zone designated for purposes of the Vietnam conflict, the preceding sentence shall not cause this section to apply for any spouse for any taxable year beginning more than 2 years after the date designated under section 112 as the date of termination of combatant activities in a combat zone.

(d) Missing status.

The period of service in the area or contingency operation referred to in subsection (a) shall include the period during which an individual entitled to benefits under subsection (a) is in a missing status, within the meaning of section 6013(f)(3).

(e) Exceptions.

(1) **Tax in jeopardy; cases under title 11 of the United States Code and receiverships; and transferred assets.** Notwithstanding the provisions of subsection (a), any action or proceeding authorized by section 6851 (regardless of the taxable year for which the tax arose), chapter 70, or 71, as well as any other action or proceeding authorized by law in connection therewith, may be taken, begun, or prosecuted. In any other case in which the Secretary determines that collection of the amount of any assessment would be jeopardized by delay, the provisions of subsection (a) shall not operate to stay collection of such amount by levy or otherwise as authorized by law. There shall be excluded from any amount assessed or collected pursuant to this paragraph the amount of interest, penalty, additional amount, and addition to the tax, if any, in respect of

Miscellaneous provisions
Code Sec. 7508

the period disregarded under subsection (a). In any case to which this paragraph relates, if the Secretary is required to give any notice to or make any demand upon any person, such requirement shall be deemed to be satisfied if the notice or demand is prepared and signed, in any case in which the address of such person last known to the Secretary is in an area for which United States post offices under instructions of the Postmaster General are not, by reason of the combatant activities, accepting mail for delivery at the time the notice or demand is signed. In such case the notice or demand shall be deemed to have been given or made upon the date it is signed.

(2) Action taken before ascertainment of right to benefits. The assessment or collection of any internal revenue tax or of any liability to the United States in respect of any internal revenue tax, or any action or proceeding by or on behalf of the United States in connection therewith, may be made, taken, begun, or prosecuted in accordance with law, without regard to the provisions of subsection (a), unless prior to such assessment, collection, action, or proceeding it is ascertained that the person concerned is entitled to the benefits of subsection (a).

(f) Treatment of individuals performing Desert Shield services.

(1) In general. Any individual who performed Desert Shield services (and the spouse of such individual) shall be entitled to the benefits of this section in the same manner as if such services were services referred to in subsection (a).

(2) Desert Shield services. For purposes of this subsection, the term "Desert Shield services" means any services in the Armed Forces of the United States or in support of such Armed Forces if—

(A) such services are performed in the area designated by the President pursuant to this subparagraph as the "Persian Gulf Desert Shield area", and

(B) such services are performed during the period beginning on August 2, 1990, and ending on the date on which any portion of the area referred to in subparagraph (A) is designated by the President as a combat zone pursuant to section 112.

(g) Qualified hospitalization.

For purposes of subsection (a), the term "qualified hospitalization" means—

(1) any hospitalization outside the United States, and

(2) any hospitalization inside the United States, except that not more than 5 years of hospitalization may be taken into account under this paragraph.

Paragraph (2) shall not apply for purposes of applying this section with respect to the spouse of an individual entitled to the benefits of subsection (a).

In **2005,** P.L. 109-73, Sec. 403(a), amended subparas. (a)(1)(A) and (B), effective for any period for performing an act which has not expired before 8/25/2005.
Prior to amendment, subparas. (a)(1)(A) and (B) read as follows:
"(A) Filing any return of income, estate, or gift tax (except income tax withheld at source and income tax imposed by subtitle C or any law superseded thereby);"
"(B) Payment of any income, estate, or gift tax (except income tax withheld at source and income tax imposed by subtitle C or any law superseded thereby) or any installment thereof or of any other liability to the United States in respect thereof;"

In **2003,** P.L. 108-121, Sec. 104(a)(1), added ", or when deployed outside the United States away from the individual's permanent duty station while participating in an operation designated by the Secretary of Defense as a contingency operation (as defined in section 101(a)(13) of title 10, United States Code) or which became such a contingency operation by operation of law" after "section 112" in subsec. (a)... Sec. 104(a)(2), added "or at any time during the period of such contingency operation" after "for purposes of such section" in the first sentence of subsec. (a)... Sec. 104(a)(3), added "or operation" after "such an area" in subsec. (a)... Sec. 104(a)(4), added "or operation" after "such area" in subsec. (a)... Sec. 104(b)(1), added "or contingency operation" after "area" in subsec.

(d) ... Sec. 104(b)(2), added "or contingency operation" after "combat zone" in the heading of Code Sec. 7508, effective for any period for performing an act which has not expired before 11/11/2003.

In **2002,** P.L. 107-134, Sec. 112(b), deleted "in regulations prescribed under this section" after "laws specified" in subpara. (a)(1)(K), effective for disasters and terroristic or military actions occurring on or after 9/11/2001, with respect to any action of the Secretary of the Treasury, the Secretary of Labor, or the Pension Benefit Guaranty Corporation occurring on or after 1/23/2002.

In **1999,** P.L. 106-170, Sec. 522, of this Act, provides:
"SEC. 522. AUTHORITY TO POSTPONE CERTAIN TAX-RELATED DEAD-LINES BY REASON OF Y2K FAILURES.
"(a) In general. In the case of a taxpayer determined by the Secretary of the Treasury (or the Secretary's delegate) to be affected by a Y2K failure, the Secretary may disregard a period of up to 90 days in determining, under the internal revenue laws, in respect of any tax liability (including any interest, penalty, additional amount, or addition to the tax) of such taxpayer—
"(1) whether any of the acts described in paragraph (1) of section 7508(a) of the Internal Revenue Code of 1986 (without regard to the exceptions in parentheses in subparagraphs (A) and (B)) were performed within the time prescribed therefor, and
"(2) the amount of any credit or refund.
"(b) Applicability of certain rules. For purposes of this section, rules similar to the rules of subsections (b) and (e) of section 7508 of the Internal Revenue Code of 1986 shall apply."

In **1996,** P.L. 104-117, Sec. 1(a)(8) and (b), of this Act, regarding treatment of certain individuals performing services in certain hazardous duty areas, effective 11/21/95, provides:
"(a) General rule. For purposes of the following provisions of the Internal Revenue Code of 1986, a qualified hazardous duty area shall be treated in the same manner as if it were a combat zone (as determined under section 112 of such Code):
* * *
"(8) Section 7508 (relating to time for performing certain acts postponed by reason of service in combat zone).
* * *
"(b) Qualified hazardous duty area. For purposes of this section, the term 'qualified hazardous duty area' means Bosnia and Herzegovina, Croatia, or Macedonia, if as of the date of the enactment [3/20/96] of this section any member of the Armed Forces of the United States is entitled to special pay under section 310 of title 37, United States Code (relating to special pay; duty subject to hostile fire or imminent danger) for services performed in such country. Such term includes any such country only during the period such entitlement is in effect. Solely for purposes of applying section 7508 of the Internal Revenue Code of 1986, in the case of an individual who is performing services as part of Operation Joint Endeavor outside the United States while deployed away from such individual's permanent duty station, the term 'qualified hazardous duty area' includes, during the period for which such entitlement is in effect, any area in which such services are performed."

In **1991,** P.L. 102-2, Sec. 1(a), added subsec. (f) ... Sec. 1(b)(1), redesignated subsecs. (b), (c) and (d) as subsecs. (c), (d) and (e) and added subsec. (b) ... Sec. 1(b)(2), deleted "(including interest)" after "credit or refund" in para. (a)(2) ... Sec. 1(c)(1)(A), deleted "outside the United States" after "or hospitalized" in subsec. (a) ... Sec. 1(c)(1)(B), substituted "the period of continuous qualified hospitalization" for "the period of continuous hospitalization outside the United States" in subsec. (a) ... Sec. 1(c)(2), added subsec. (g), effective 8/2/90.

In **1986,** P.L. 99-514, Sec. 1708(a)(4), amended the last sentence of subsec. (b), effective for tax. yrs. begin. after 12/31/82.
Prior to amendment, the last sentence of subsec. (b) read as follows:
"The preceding sentence shall not cause this section to apply to any spouse for any taxable year beginning—
"(1) after December 31, 1982, in the case of service in the combat zone designated for purposes of the Vietnam conflict, or
"(2) more than 2 years after the date designated under section 112 as of the date of termination of combatant activities in that zone, in the case of any combat zone other than that referred to in paragraph (1)."

In **1983,** P.L. 97-448, Sec. 307(d), substituted "December 31, 1982" for "January 2, 1978" in para. (b)(1).

In **1980,** P.L. 96-589, Sec. 6(i)(14), substituted "cases under title 11 of the United States Code and receiverships" for "bankruptcy and receiverships" in the heading of para. (d)(1), effective 10/1/79, except for any proceeding under the Bankruptcy Act begun before 10/1/79. Sec. 7(g) of this Act provides:
"(g) Definitions.
"For purposes of this section—
"(1) Bankruptcy case. The term 'bankruptcy case' means any case under title 11 of the United States Code (as recodified by P.L. 95-598).
"(2) Similar judicial proceeding. The term 'similar judicial proceeding' means a receivership, foreclosure, or similar proceeding in a Federal or State court (as modified by section 368(a)(3)(D) of the Internal Revenue Code of 1954)."
"Sec. 204. Time for performing certain acts postponed by reason of captive status.
"(a) General rule.
"In the case of any individual who was at any time an American hostage, any period during which he was in captive status (and any period during which he was outside the United States and hospitalized as a result of captive status), and the next 180 days thereafter, shall be disregarded in determining, under the internal revenue laws, in respect of any tax liability (including any interest, penalty, additional amount, or addition to the tax) of such individual—

3,903

"(1) whether any of the acts specified in paragraph (1) of section 7508(a) of the Internal Revenue Code of 1954 was performed within the time prescribed therefor, and

"(2) the amount of any credit or refund (including interest).

"(b) Application to Spouse.

"The provisions of this section shall apply to the spouse of any individual entitled to the benefits of subsection (a). The preceding sentence shall not cause this section to apply to any spouse for any taxable year beginning more than 2 years after the date on which the hostage period ends.

"(c) Section 7508(d) Made Applicable.

"Subsection (d) of section 7508 of the Internal Revenue Code of 1954 shall apply to subsection (a) in the same manner as if the benefits of subsection (a) were provided by subsection (a) of such section 7508."

For definitions and special rules see Sec. 205 of P.L. 96-449 reproduced in note following Code Sec. 1.

In 1976, P.L. 94-569, Sec. 3(e), amended subsec. (b), effective 10/20/76.

Prior to amendment, subsec. (b) read as follows:

"The preceding sentence shall not cause this section to apply to any spouse for any taxable year beginning more than 2 years after—

"(1) the date of the enactment of this subsection, in the case of service in the combat zone designated for purposes of the Vietnam conflict, or

"(2) the date designated under section 112 as the date of termination of combatant activities in that zone, in the case of any combat zone other than that referred to in paragraph (1)."

—P.L. 94-455, Sec. 1906(a)(51), substituted "by reason of service in combat zone" for "by reason of war" in the heading of Code Sec. 7508, and substituted "United States" for "States of the Union and the District of Columbia" each place it appeared in subsec. (a), effective 2/1/77.

—P.L. 94-455, Sec. 1906(b)(13)(A), substituted "Secretary" for "Secretary or his delegate" each place it appeared in Code Sec. 7508, effective 2/1/77.

In 1975, P.L. 93-597, Sec. 5(a), redesignated subsec. (b) as (d) and added subsecs. (b) and (c), effective for tax. yrs. end. on or after 2/28/61.

Sec. 7508A.

> • **Caution:** Code Sec. 7508A, following, was amended by P.L. 107-16, the Economic Growth and Tax Relief Reconciliation Act of 2001 (EGTRRA). These provisions generally sunset for tax years beginning after 12/31/2012. For specific sunset provisions, see Sec. 901, P.L. 107-16 (as amended) reproduced in history notes for this Code Sec.

Authority to postpone certain deadlines by reason of Presidentially declared disaster or terroristic or military actions.

(a) In general.

In the case of a taxpayer determined by the Secretary to be affected by a federally declared disaster (as defined by section 165(h)(3)(C)(i)) or a terroristic or military action (as defined in section 692(c)(2)), the Secretary may specify a period of up to one year that may be disregarded in determining, under the internal revenue laws, in respect of any tax liability of such taxpayer—

(1) whether any of the acts described in paragraph (1) of section 7508(a) were performed within the time prescribed therefor (determined without regard to extension under any other provision of this subtitle for periods after the date (determined by the Secretary) of such disaster or action),

(2) the amount of any interest, penalty, additional amount, or addition to the tax for periods after such date, and

(3) the amount of any credit or refund.

(b) Special rules regarding pensions, etc.

In the case of a pension or other employee benefit plan, or any sponsor, administrator, participant, beneficiary, or other person with respect to such plan, affected by a disaster or action described in subsection (a), the Secretary may specify a period of up to one year which may be disregarded in determining the date by which any action is required or permitted to be completed under this title. No plan shall be treated as failing to be operated in accordance with the terms of the plan solely as the result of disregarding any period by reason of the preceding sentence.

(c) Special rules for overpayments.

The rules of section 7508(b) shall apply for purposes of this section.

In 2010, P.L. 111-312, Sec. 101(a)(1), substituted "December 31, 2012" for "December 31, 2010" both places it appeared in Sec. 901 of P.L. 107-16, [see below] effective as if included in the enactment of P.L. 107-16, EGTRRA, 6/7/2001.

In 2008, P.L. 110-343, Sec. 706(a)(2)(D)(vii)DivC, substituted "federally declared disaster (as defined by section 165(h)(3)(C)(i))" for "Presidentially declared disaster (as defined in section 1033(h)(3))" in subsec. (a), effective for disasters declared in tax. yrs. begin. after 12/31/2007.

In 2005, P.L. 109-135, Sec. 201(b)(4)(B), repealed Sec. 403(b) of P.L. 109-73.

Prior to repeal, Sec. 403(b) of P.L. 109-73 read as follows:

"(b) Application with respect to Hurricane Katrina. In the case of any taxpayer determined by the Secretary of the Treasury to be affected by the Presidentially declared disaster relating to Hurricane Katrina, any relief provided by the Secretary of the Treasury under section 7508A of the Internal Revenue Code of 1986 shall be for a period ending not earlier than February 28, 2006, and shall be treated as applying to the filing of returns relating to, and the payment of, employment and excise taxes."

In 2002, P.L. 107-358, Sec. 2, added subsec. (c) in Sec. 901 of P.L. 107-16 [see below], effective 12/17/2002.

—P.L. 107-134, Sec. 112(a), amended Code Sec. 7508A, effective for disasters and terroristic or military actions occurring on or after 9/11/2001, with respect to any action of the Secretary of the Treasury, the Secretary of Labor, or the Pension Benefit Guaranty Corporation occurring on or after 1/23/2002.

Prior to amendment, Code Sec. 7508A read as follows:

"SEC. 7508A. AUTHORITY TO POSTPONE CERTAIN TAX-RELATED DEADLINES BY REASON OF PRESIDENTIALLY DECLARED DISASTER.

"(a) In general. In the case of a taxpayer determined by the Secretary to be affected by a Presidentially declared disaster (as defined by section 1033(h)(3)), the Secretary may prescribe regulations under which a period of up to 120 days may be disregarded in determining, under the internal revenue laws, in respect of any tax liability (including any penalty, additional amount, or addition to the tax) of such taxpayer—

"(1) whether any of the acts described in paragraph (1) of section 7508(a) were performed within the time prescribed therefor, and

"(2) the amount of any credit or refund.

"(b) Interest on overpayments and underpayments. Subsection (a) shall not apply for the purpose of determining interest on any overpayment or underpayment."

In 2001, P.L. 107-16, Sec. 802(a), substituted "120 days" for "90 days" in subsec. (a), effective 6/7/2001.

—P.L. 107-16, Sec. 901, of this Act [as amended by Sec. 2 of P.L. 107-358, and Sec. 101(a)(1) of P.L. 111-312, see above], reads as follows:

"SEC. 901. SUNSET OF PROVISIONS OF ACT.

"(a) In general. All provisions of, and amendments made by, this Act shall not apply—

"(1) to taxable, plan, or limitation years beginning after December 31, 2012, or

"(2) in the case of title V, to estates of decedents dying, gifts made, or generation skipping transfers, after December 31, 2012.

"(b) Application of certain laws. The Internal Revenue Code of 1986 and the Employee Retirement Income Security Act of 1974 shall be applied and administered to years, estates, gifts, and transfers described in subsection (a) as if the provisions and amendments described in subsection (a) had never been enacted.

"(c) Exception. Subsection (a) shall not apply to section 803 (relating to no federal income tax on restitution received by victims of the Nazi regime or their heirs or estates)."

In 1997, P.L. 105-34, Sec. 911(a), added Code Sec. 7508A, effective for any period for performing an act that has not expired before 8/5/97.

—P.L. 105-34, Sec. 915, of this Act, relating to abatement of interest on underpayments by taxpayers in Presidentially declared disaster areas, is reproduced in notes following Code Sec. 6601.

Sec. 7509. Expenditures incurred by the United States Postal Service.

The Postmaster General or his delegate shall at least once a month transfer to the Treasury of the United States a statement of the additional expenditures in the District of Columbia and elsewhere incurred by the United States Postal Service in performing the duties, if any, imposed upon such Service with respect to chapter 21, relating to the tax under the Federal Insurance Contributions Act, and the Secretary shall be authorized and directed to advance from time to time to the credit of the United States Postal Service, from appropriations made for the collection of the taxes imposed by chapter 21, such sums as may be required for such additional expenditures incurred by the United States Postal Service.

Miscellaneous provisions   Code Sec. 7514

In 1976, P.L. 94-455, Sec. 1906(a)(52), substituted "United States Postal Service" for "Post Office Department" in the heading of Code Sec. 7509, substituted "United States Postal Service" for "Post Office Department" each place it appeared in Code Sec. 7509, substituted "such service" for "such Department" following "imposed upon" in Code Sec. 7509, and deleted "together with the receipts required to be deposited under section 6803(a)," after "to the Treasury of the United States," . . . Sec. 1906(b)(13)(A), substituted "Secretary" for "Secretary or his delegate" in Code Sec. 7509, effective 2/1/77.

Sec. 7510. Exemption from tax of domestic goods purchased for the United States.

The privilege existing by provision of law on December 1, 1873, or thereafter of purchasing supplies of goods imported from foreign countries for the use of the United States, duty free, shall be extended, under such regulations as the Secretary may prescribe, to all articles of domestic production which are subject to tax by the provisions of this title.

In 1976, P.L. 94-455, Sec. 1906(b)(13)(A), substituted "Secretary" for "Secretary or his delegate" in Code Sec. 7510, effective 2/1/77.

Sec. 7511. Repealed.

In 1962, P.L. 87-456, Sec. 302(d), repealed Code Sec. 7511, effective for articles entered, or withdrawn from warehouse, for consumption on or after 8/31/63. Prior to repeal, Code Sec. 7511 read as follows:

"SEC. 7511. EXEMPTION OF CONSULAR OFFICERS AND EMPLOYEES OF FOREIGN STATES FROM PAYMENT OF INTERNAL REVENUE TAXES ON IMPORTED ARTICLES.

"(a) Rule of exemption.

"No internal revenue tax shall be imposed with respect to articles imported by a consular officer of a foreign state or by an employee of a consulate of a foreign state, whether such articles accompany the officer or employee to his post in the United States, its insular possessions, or the Panama Canal Zone, or are imported by him at any time during the exercise of his functions therein, if—

"(1) such officer or employee is a national of the state appointing him and not engaged in any profession, business, or trade within the territory specified in this subsection;

"(2) the articles are imported by the officer or employee for his personal or official use; and

"(3) the foreign state grants an equivalent exemption to corresponding officers or employees of the Government of the United States stationed in such foreign state.

"(b) Certificates by Secretary of State.

"The Secretary of State shall certify to the Secretary of the Treasury the names of the foreign states which grant an equivalent exemption to the consular officers or employees of the Government of the United States stationed in such foreign states."

Sec. 7512. Separate accounting for certain collected taxes, etc.

(a) General rule.

Whenever any person who is required to collect, account for, and pay over any tax imposed by subtitle C, or chapter 33—

(1) at the time and in the manner prescribed by law or regulations (A) fails to collect, truthfully account for, or pay over such tax, or (B) fails to make deposits, payments, or returns of such tax, and

(2) is notified, by notice delivered in hand to such person, of any such failure,

then all the requirements of subsection (b) shall be complied with. In the case of a corporation, partnership, or trust, notice delivered in hand to an officer, partner, or trustee, shall, for purposes of this section, be deemed to be notice delivered in hand to such corporation, partnership or trust and to all officers, partners, trustees, and employees thereof.

(b) Requirements.

Any person who is required to collect, account for, and pay over any tax imposed by subtitle C or chapter 33, if notice has been delivered to such person in accordance with subsection (a), shall collect the taxes imposed by subtitle C or chapter 33 which become collectible after delivery of such notice, shall (not later than the end of the second banking day after any amount of such taxes is collected) deposit such amount in a separate account in a bank (as defined in section 581), and shall keep the amount of such taxes in such account until payment over to the United States. Any such account shall be designated as a special fund in trust for the United States, payable to the United States by such person as trustee.

(c) Relief from further compliance with subsection (b).

Whenever the Secretary is satisfied, with respect to any notification made under subsection (a), that all requirements of law and regulations with respect to the taxes imposed by subtitle C or chapter 33, as the case may be, will henceforth be complied with, he may cancel such notification. Such cancellation shall take effect at such time as is specified in the notice of such cancellation.

In 1988, P.L. 100-418, Sec. 1941(b)(2)(O)(i), substituted "or chapter 33" for ", by chapter 33, or by section 4986" in subsecs. (a) and (b) . . . Sec. 1941(b)(2)(O)(ii), substituted "or chapter 33" for ", chapter 33, or section 4986" in subsecs. (b) and (c), effective for crude oil removed from the premises on or after 8/23/88.

In 1980, P.L. 96-223, Sec. 101(c)(3)(A), substituted ", by chapter 33, or by section 4986" for "or by chapter 33" in subsecs. (a) and (b) . . . Sec. 101(c)(3)(B), substituted ", chapter 33, or section 4986" for "or chapter 33" in subsecs. (b) and (c), effective for periods after 2/29/80.

In 1976, P.L. 94-455, Sec. 1906(b)(13)(A), substituted "Secretary" for "Secretary or his delegate" in Code Sec. 7512, effective 2/1/77.

In 1958, P.L. 85-321, Sec. 1, added Code Sec. 7512.

—P.L. 85-321, Sec. 4, [as amended by P.L. 99-514, Sec. 2], provides: "Notification may be made under section 7512(a) of the Internal Revenue Code of 1986 (as added by the first section of this Act)—

"(1) in the case of taxes imposed by subtitle C of such Code, only with respect to pay periods beginning after the date of the enactment of this Act [2/11/58]; and

"(2) in the case of taxes imposed by chapter 33 of such Code, only with respect to taxes so imposed after the date of the enactment of this Act [2/11/58]."

Sec. 7513. Reproduction of returns and other documents.

(a) In general.

The Secretary is authorized to have any Federal agency or any person process films or other photoimpressions of any return, document, or other matter, and make reproductions from films or photoimpressions of any return, document or other matter.

(b) Regulations.

The Secretary shall prescribe regulations which shall provide such safeguards as in the opinion of the Secretary are necessary or appropriate to protect the film, photoimpressions, and reproductions made therefrom, against any unauthorized use, and to protect the information contained therein against any unauthorized disclosure.

(c) Penalty.

For penalty for violation of regulations for safeguarding against unauthorized use of any film or photoimpression, or reproduction made therefrom, and against unauthorized disclosure of information contained therein, see section 7213.

In 1976, P.L. 94-455, Sec. 1202(f), deleted subsec. (c), and redesignated subsec. (d) as subsec. (c), effective 2/1/77.

Prior to deletion, subsec. (c) read as follows:

"(c) Use of reproductions.

"Any reproduction of any return, document, or other matter made in accordance with this section shall have the same legal status as the original; and any such reproduction shall, if properly authenticated, be admissible in evidence in any judicial or administrative proceeding, as if it were the original, whether or not the original was in existence."

—P.L. 94-455, Sec. 1906(b)(13)(A), substituted "Secretary" for "Secretary or his delegate" each place it appeared in Code Sec. 7513, effective 2/1/77.

In 1958, P.L. 85-866, Sec. 90(a), added Code Sec. 7513, effective 8/17/54.

Sec. 7514. Authority to prescribe or modify seals.

The Secretary is authorized to prescribe or modify seals of office for the district directors of internal revenue and other officers or employees of the Treasury Department to whom any of the functions of the Secretary of the Treasury shall have been or may be delegated. Each seal so prescribed shall contain such device as the Secretary may select. Each seal shall remain in the custody of any officer or employee whom the Secretary may designate, and, in accordance with the regulations approved by the Secretary, may be affixed in lieu of the seal of the Treasury Department to any certificate or attestation (except for material to be published in the Federal Register) that may be required of such officer or employee. Judicial notice shall be taken of any seal prescribed in accordance with this authority, a facsimile of which has been published in the Federal Register together with the regulations prescribing such seal and the affixation thereof.

In 1976, P.L. 94-455, Sec. 1906(b)(13)(A), substituted "Secretary" for "Secretary or his delegate" each place it appeared in Code Sec. 7514, effective 2/1/77.
—P.L. 94-455, Sec. 1906(b)(13)(M), substituted "functions of the Secretary of the Treasury" for "functions of the Secretary", in Code Sec. 7514, effective 2/1/77.
In 1958, P.L. 85-866, Sec. 91(a), added Code Sec. 7514, effective 8/17/54.

Sec. 7515. Repealed.

In 1976, P.L. 94-455, Sec. 1202(h)(4), repealed Code Sec. 7515, effective 1/1/77. Prior to repeal, Code Sec. 7515 read as follows:
"Sec. 7515. Special statistical studies and compilations and other services on request.
"The Secretary or his delegate is authorized within his discretion, upon written request, to make special statistical studies and compilations involving data from any returns, declarations, statements, or other documents required by this title or by regulations or from any records established or maintained in connection with the administration and enforcement of this title, to engage in any such special study or compilation, upon the payment, by the party or parties making the request, of the cost of the work or services performed for such party or parties."
In 1962, P.L. 87-870, Sec. 3(a)(1), added Code Sec. 7515, effective 10/24/62.

Sec. 7516. Supplying training and training aids on request.

The Secretary is authorized within his discretion, upon written request, to admit employees and officials of any State, the Commonwealth of Puerto Rico, any possession of the United States, any political subdivision or instrumentality of any of the foregoing, the District of Columbia, or any foreign government to training courses conducted by the Internal Revenue Service, and to supply them with texts and other training aids. The Secretary may require payment from the party or parties making the request of a reasonable fee not to exceed the cost of the training and training aids supplied pursuant to such request.

In 1976, P.L. 94-455, Sec. 1906(b)(13)(A), substituted "Secretary" for "Secretary or his delegate" each place it appeared in Code Sec. 7516, effective 2/1/77.
In 1962, P.L. 87-870, Sec. 3(a)(1), added Code Sec. 7516, effective 10/24/62.

Sec. 7517. Furnishing on request of statement explaining estate or gift evaluation.

(a) General rule.

If the Secretary makes a determination or a proposed determination of the value of an item of property for purposes of the tax imposed under chapter 11, 12, or 13, he shall furnish, on the written request of the executor, donor, or the person required to make the return of the tax imposed by chapter 13 (as the case may be), to such executor, donor, or person a written statement containing the material required by subsection (b). Such statement shall be furnished not later than 45 days after the later of the date of such request or the date of such determination or proposed determination.

(b) Contents of statement.

A statement required to be furnished under subsection (a) with respect to the value of an item of property shall—

(1) explain the basis on which the valuation was determined or proposed,

(2) set forth any computation used in arriving at such value, and

(3) contain a copy of any expert appraisal made by or for the Secretary.

(c) Effect of statement.

Except to the extent otherwise provided by law, the value determined or proposed by the Secretary with respect to which a statement is furnished under this section, and the method used in arriving at such value, shall not be binding on the Secretary.

In 1976, P.L. 94-455, Sec. 2008(a)(1), added Code Sec. 7517, effective as provided in Sec. 2008(d)(1) this Act which reads as follows:
"(1) The amendments made by subsection (a)—
"(A) insofar as they relate to the tax imposed under chapter 11 of the Internal Revenue Code of 1954, shall apply to the estates of decedents dying after December 31, 1976, and
"(B) insofar as they relate to the tax imposed under chapter 12 of such Code, shall apply to gifts made after December 31, 1976."

Sec. 7518. Tax incentives relating to Merchant Marine capital construction funds.

(a) Ceiling on deposits.

(1) In general. The amount deposited in a fund established under chapter 535 of title 46 of the United States Code (hereinafter in this section referred to as a "capital construction fund") shall not exceed for any taxable year the sum of:

(A) that portion of the taxable income of the owner or lessee for such year (computed as provided in chapter 1 but without regard to the carryback of any net operating loss or net capital loss and without regard to this section) which is attributable to the operation of the agreement vessels in the foreign or domestic commerce of the United States or in the fisheries of the United States,

(B) the amount allowable as a deduction under section 167 for such year with respect to the agreement vessels,

(C) if the transaction is not taken into account for purposes of subparagraph (A), the net proceeds (as defined in joint regulations) from—

(i) the sale or other disposition of any agreement vessel, or

(ii) insurance or indemnity attributable to any agreement vessel, and

(D) the receipts from the investment or reinvestment of amounts held in such fund.

(2) Limitations on deposits by lessees. In the case of a lessee, the maximum amount which may be deposited with respect to an agreement vessel by reason of paragraph (1)(B) for any period shall be reduced by any amount which, under an agreement entered into under chapter 535 of title 46, United States Code, the owner is required or permitted to deposit for such period with respect to such vessel by reason of paragraph (1)(B).

(3) Certain barges and containers included. For purposes of paragraph (1), the term "agreement vessel" includes barges and containers which are part of the complement of such vessel and which are provided for in the agreement.

(b) Requirements as to investments.

(1) In general. Amounts in any capital construction fund shall be kept in the depository or depositories specified in the agreement and shall be subject to such trustee and other fiduciary requirements as may be specified by the Secretary.

(2) Limitation on fund investments. Amounts in any capital construction fund may be invested only in interest-bearing securities approved by the Secretary; except that,

Miscellaneous provisions Code Sec. 7518(f)(2)

if such Secretary consents thereto, an agreed percentage (not in excess of 60 percent) of the assets of the fund may be invested in the stock of domestic corporations. Such stock must be currently fully listed and registered on an exchange registered with the Securities and Exchange Commission as a national securities exchange, and must be stock which would be acquired by prudent men of discretion and intelligence in such matters who are seeking a reasonable income and the preservation of their capital. If at any time the fair market value of the stock in the fund is more than the agreed percentage of the assets in the fund, any subsequent investment of amounts deposited in the fund, and any subsequent withdrawal from the fund, shall be made in such a way as to tend to restore the fund to a situation in which the fair market value of the stock does not exceed such agreed percentage.

(3) Investment in certain preferred stock permitted. For purposes of this subsection, if the common stock of a corporation meets the requirements of this subsection and if the preferred stock of such corporation would meet such requirements but for the fact that it cannot be listed and registered as required because it is nonvoting stock, such preferred stock shall be treated as meeting the requirements of this subsection.

(c) Nontaxability for deposits.

(1) In general. For purposes of this title—

(A) taxable income (determined without regard to this section and chapter 535 of title 46, United States Code) for the taxable year shall be reduced by an amount equal to the amount deposited for the taxable year out of amounts referred to in subsection (a)(1)(A),

(B) gain from a transaction referred to in subsection (a)(1)(C) shall not be taken into account if an amount equal to the net proceeds (as defined in joint regulations) from such transaction is deposited in the fund,

(C) the earnings (including gains and losses) from the investment and reinvestment of amounts held in the fund shall not be taken into account,

(D) the earnings and profits (within the meaning of section 316) of any corporation shall be determined without regard to this section and chapter 535 of title 46, United States Code, and

(E) in applying the tax imposed by section 531 (relating to the accumulated earnings tax), amounts while held in the fund shall not be taken into account.

(2) Only qualified deposits eligible for treatment. Paragraph (1) shall apply with respect to any amount only if such amount is deposited in the fund pursuant to the agreement and not later than the time provided in joint regulations.

(d) Establishment of accounts.

For purposes of this section—

(1) In general. Within a capital construction fund 3 accounts shall be maintained:

(A) the capital account,

(B) the capital gain account, and

(C) the ordinary income account.

(2) Capital account. The capital account shall consist of—

(A) amounts referred to in subsection (a)(1)(B),

(B) amounts referred to in subsection (a)(1)(C) other than that portion thereof which represents gain not taken into account by reason of subsection (c)(1)(B),

(C) the percentage applicable under section 243(a)(1) of any dividend received by the fund with respect to which the person maintaining the fund would (but for subsection (c)(1)(C)) be allowed a deduction under section 243, and

(D) interest income exempt from taxation under section 103.

(3) Capital gain account. The capital gain account shall consist of—

(A) amounts representing capital gains on assets held for more than 6 months and referred to in subsection (a)(1)(C) or (a)(1)(D), reduced by

(B) amounts representing capital losses on assets held in the fund for more than 6 months.

(4) Ordinary income account. The ordinary income account shall consist of—

(A) amounts referred to in subsection (a)(1)(A),

(B)(i) amounts representing capital gains on assets held for 6 months or less and referred to in subsection (a)(1)(C) or (a)(1)(D), reduced by

(ii) amounts representing capital losses on assets held in the fund for 6 months or less,

(C) interest (not including any tax-exempt interest referred to in paragraph (2)(D)) and other ordinary income (not including any dividend referred to in subparagraph (E)) received on assets held in the fund,

(D) ordinary income from a transaction described in subsection (a)(1)(C), and

(E) the portion of any dividend referred to in paragraph (2)(C) not taken into account under such paragraph.

(5) Capital losses only allowed to offset certain gains. Except on termination of a capital construction fund, capital losses referred to in paragraph (3)(B) or in paragraph (4)(B)(ii) shall be allowed only as an offset to gains referred to in paragraph (3)(A) or (4)(B)(i), respectively.

(e) Purposes of qualified withdrawals.

(1) In general. A qualified withdrawal from the fund is one made in accordance with the terms of the agreement but only if it is for:

(A) the acquisition, construction, or reconstruction of a qualified vessel,

(B) the acquisition, construction, or reconstruction of barges and containers which are part of the complement of a qualified vessel, or

(C) the payment of the principal on indebtedness incurred in connection with the acquisition, construction, or reconstruction of a qualified vessel or a barge or container which is part of the complement of a qualified vessel.

Except to the extent provided in regulations prescribed by the Secretary, subparagraph (B), and so much of subparagraph (C) as relates only to barges and containers, shall apply only with respect to barges and containers constructed in the United States.

(2) Penalty for failing to fulfill any substantial obligation. Under joint regulations, if the Secretary determines that any substantial obligation under any agreement is not being fulfilled, he may, after notice and opportunity for hearing to the person maintaining the fund, treat the entire fund or any portion thereof as an amount withdrawn from the fund in a nonqualified withdrawal.

(f) Tax treatment of qualified withdrawals.

(1) Ordering rule. Any qualified withdrawal from a fund shall be treated—

(A) first as made out of the capital account,

(B) second as made out of the capital gain account, and

(C) third as made out of the ordinary income account.

(2) Adjustment to basis of vessel, etc., where withdrawal from ordinary income account. If any portion of a qualified withdrawal for a vessel, barge, or container is made out of the ordinary income account, the basis of such vessel, barge, or container shall be reduced by an amount equal to such portion.

(3) Adjustment to basis of vessel, etc., where withdrawal from capital gain account. If any portion of a qualified withdrawal for a vessel, barge, or container is made out of the capital gain account, the basis of such vessel, barge, or container shall be reduced by an amount equal to such portion.

(4) Adjustment to basis of vessels, etc., where withdrawals pay principal on debt. If any portion of a qualified withdrawal to pay the principal on any indebtedness is made out of the ordinary income account or the capital gain account, then an amount equal to the aggregate reduction which would be required by paragraphs (2) and (3) if this were a qualified withdrawal for a purpose described in such paragraphs shall be applied, in the order provided in joint regulations, to reduce the basis of vessels, barges, and containers owned by the person maintaining the fund. Any amount of a withdrawal remaining after the application of the preceding sentence shall be treated as a nonqualified withdrawal.

(5) Ordinary income recapture of basis reduction. If any property the basis of which was reduced under paragraph (2), (3), or (4) is disposed of, any gain realized on such disposition, to the extent it does not exceed the aggregate reduction in the basis of such property under such paragraphs, shall be treated as an amount referred to in subsection (g)(3)(A) which was withdrawn on the date of such disposition. Subject to such conditions and requirements as may be provided in joint regulations, the preceding sentence shall not apply to a disposition where there is a redeposit in an amount determined under joint regulations which will, insofar as practicable, restore the fund to the position it was in before the withdrawal.

(g) Tax treatment of nonqualified withdrawals.

(1) In general. Except as provided in subsection (h), any withdrawal from a capital construction fund which is not a qualified withdrawal shall be treated as a nonqualified withdrawal.

(2) Ordering rule. Any nonqualified withdrawal from a fund shall be treated—

(A) first as made out of the ordinary income account,
(B) second as made out of the capital gain account, and
(C) third as made out of the capital account.

For purposes of this section, items withdrawn from any account shall be treated as withdrawn on a first-in-first-out basis; except that (i) any nonqualified withdrawal for research, development, and design expenses incident to new and advanced ship design, machinery and equipment, and (ii) any amount treated as a nonqualified withdrawal under the second sentence of subsection (f)(4), shall be treated as withdrawn on a last-in-first-out basis.

(3) Operating rules. For purposes of this title—

(A) any amount referred to in paragraph (2)(A) shall be included in income as an item of ordinary income for the taxable year in which the withdrawal is made,
(B) any amount referred to in paragraph (2)(B) shall be included in income for the taxable year in which the withdrawal is made as an item of gain realized during such year from the disposition of an asset held for more than 6 months, and
(C) for the period on or before the last date prescribed for payment of tax for the taxable year in which this withdrawal is made—

(i) no interest shall be payable under section 6601 and no addition to the tax shall be payable under section 6651,
(ii) interest on the amount of the additional tax attributable to any item referred to in subparagraph (A) or (B) shall be paid at the applicable rate (as defined in paragraph (4)) from the last date prescribed for payment of the tax for the taxable year for which such item was deposited in the fund, and
(iii) no interest shall be payable on amounts referred to in clauses (i) and (ii) of paragraph (2) or in the case of any nonqualified withdrawal arising from the application of the recapture provision of section 606(5) of the Merchant Marine Act, 1936, as in effect on December 31, 1969.

(4) Interest rate. For purposes of paragraph (3)(C)(ii), the applicable rate of interest for any nonqualified withdrawal—

(A) made in a taxable year beginning in 1970 or 1971 is 8 percent, or
(B) made in a taxable year beginning after 1971, shall be determined and published jointly by the Secretary of the Treasury or his delegate and the applicable Secretary and shall bear a relationship to 8 percent which the Secretaries determine under joint regulations to be comparable to the relationship which the money rates and investment yields for the calendar year immediately preceding the beginning of the taxable year bear to the money rates and investment yields for the calendar year 1970.

(5) Amount not withdrawn from fund after 25 years from deposit taxed as nonqualified withdrawal.

(A) In general. The applicable percentage of any amount which remains in a capital construction fund at the close of the 26th, 27th, 28th, 29th, or 30th taxable year following the taxable year for which such amount was deposited shall be treated as a nonqualified withdrawal in accordance with the following table:

If the amount remains in the fund at the close of the—	The applicable percentage is—
26th taxable year	20 percent
27th taxable year	40 percent
28th taxable year	60 percent
29th taxable year	80 percent
30th taxable year	100 percent.

(B) Earnings treated as deposits. The earnings of any capital construction fund for any taxable year (other than net gains) shall be treated for purposes of this paragraph as an amount deposited for such taxable year.
(C) Amounts committed treated as withdrawn. For purposes of subparagraph (A), an amount shall not be treated as remaining in a capital construction fund at the close of any taxable year to the extent there is a binding contract at the close of such year for a qualified withdrawal of such amount with respect to an identified item for which such withdrawal may be made.
(D) Authority to treat excess funds as withdrawn. If the Secretary determines that the balance in any capital construction fund exceeds the amount which is appropriate to meet the vessel construction program objectives of the person who established such fund, the amount of such excess shall be treated as a nonqualified withdrawal under subparagraph (A) unless such person

Miscellaneous provisions Code Sec. 7519(c)(3)(A)(i)

develops appropriate program objectives within 3 years to dissipate such excess.

(E) Amounts in fund on January 1, 1987. For purposes of this paragraph, all amounts in a capital construction fund on January 1, 1987, shall be treated as deposited in such fund on such date.

(6) Nonqualified withdrawals taxed at highest marginal rate.

> • *Caution:* Code Sec. 7518(g)(6)(A), following, was amended by Sec. 301(a)(2)(D), P.L. 108-27. These provisions generally sunset for tax years beginning after 12/31/2012. For specific sunset provisions see Sec. 303, P.L. 108-27 reproduced in history notes for this Code Sec.

(A) In general. In the case of any taxable year for which there is a nonqualified withdrawal (including any amount so treated under paragraph (5)), the tax imposed by chapter 1 shall be determined—

(i) by excluding such withdrawal from gross income, and

(ii) by increasing the tax imposed by chapter 1 by the product of the amount of such withdrawal and the highest rate of tax specified in section 1 (section 11 in the case of a corporation).

With respect to the portion of any nonqualified withdrawal made out of the capital gain account during a taxable year to which section 1(h) or 1201(a) applies, the rate of tax taken into account under the preceding sentence shall not exceed 15 percent (34 percent in the case of a corporation).

(B) Tax benefit rule. If any portion of a nonqualified withdrawal is properly attributable to deposits (other than earnings on deposits) made by the taxpayer in any taxable year which did not reduce the taxpayer's liability for tax under chapter 1 for any taxable year preceding the taxable year in which such withdrawal occurs—

(i) such portion shall not be taken into account under subparagraph (A), and

(ii) an amount equal to such portion shall be treated as allowed as a deduction under section 172 for the taxable year in which such withdrawal occurs.

(C) Coordination with deduction for net operating losses. Any nonqualified withdrawal excluded from gross income under subparagraph (A) shall be excluded in determining taxable income under section 172(b)(2).

(h) Certain corporate reorganizations and changes in partnerships.

Under joint regulations—

(1) a transfer of a fund from one person to another person in a transaction to which section 381 applies may be treated as if such transaction did not constitute a nonqualified withdrawal, and

(2) a similar rule shall be applied in the case of a continuation of a partnership.

(i) Definitions.

For purposes of this section, any term defined in section 607(k) of the Merchant Marine Act, 1936 which is also used in this section (including the definition of "Secretary") shall have the meaning given such term by such section 607(k) as in effect on the date of the enactment of this section.

In **2010**, P.L. 111-312, Sec. 102(a), substituted "December 31, 2012" for "December 31, 2010" in Sec. 303, P.L. 108-27 [see below], effective as if included in the enactment of P.L. 108-27, 5/28/2003.

In **2006**, P.L. 109-304, Sec. 17(e)(6)(A), substituted "chapter 535 of title 46 of the United States Code" for "section 607 of the Merchant Marine Act, 1936" in para. (a)(1) . . . Sec. 17(e)(6)(B), substituted "chapter 535 of title 46, United States Code" for "section 607 of the Merchant Marine Act, 1936" in para. (a)(2) and subparas. (c)(1)(A) and (D) . . . Sec. 17(e)(6)(C), substituted "Merchant Marine Act, 1936," for "Merchant Marine Act of 1936" in clause (g)(3)(C)(iii), enacted 10/6/2006.

—P.L. 109-222, Sec. 102, substituted "December 31, 2010" for "December 31, 2008" in Sec. 303 of P.L. 108-27 [see below], effective 5/17/2006.

In **2003**, P.L. 108-27, Sec. 301(a)(2)(D), substituted "15 percent" for "20 percent" in subpara. (g)(6)(A), effective for tax. yrs. end. on or after 5/6/2003.

—P.L. 108-27, Sec. 303, of this Act [as amended by Sec. 102 of P.L. 109-222, and Sec. 102(a), P.L. 111-312, see above], reads as follows:

"Sec. 303. Sunset of title. All provisions of, and amendments made by, this title [Secs. 301 and 302] shall not apply to taxable years beginning after December 31, 2012, and the Internal Revenue Code of 1986 shall be applied and administered to such years as if such provisions and amendments had never been enacted."

In **1997**, P.L. 105-34, Sec. 311(c)(2), substituted "20 percent" for "28 percent" in subpara. (g)(6)(A), effective for tax. yrs. end. after 5/6/97.

In **1990**, P.L. 101-508, Sec. 11101(d)(7)(A), substituted "1(h)" for "1(j)" in subpara. (g)(6)(A), effective for tax. yrs. begin. after 12/31/90.

In **1988**, P.L. 100-647, Sec. 1002(m)(1), substituted "section 1(i)" for "section 1(j)", in subpara. (g)(6)(A) effective for tax. yrs. begin. after 12/31/86.

—P.L. 100-647, Sec. 1018(u)(23), substituted "not a qualified withdrawal" for "not qualified withdrawal" in para. (g)(1), effective for tax. yrs. begin. after 12/31/86.

In **1986**, P.L. 99-514, Sec. 261(b), added Code Sec. 7518, effective for tax. yrs. begin. after 12/31/86.

Sec. 7519. Required payments for entities electing not to have required taxable year.

(a) General rule.

This section applies to a partnership or S corporation for any taxable year, if—

(1) an election under section 444 is in effect for the taxable year, and

(2) the required payment determined under subsection (b) for such taxable year (or any preceding taxable year) exceeds $500.

(b) Required payment.

For purposes of this section, the term "required payment" means, with respect to any applicable election year of a partnership or S corporation, an amount equal to—

(1) the excess of the product of—

(A) the applicable percentage of the adjusted highest section 1 rate, multiplied by

(B) the net base year income of the entity, over

(2) the net required payment balance.

For purposes of paragraph (1)(A), the term "adjusted highest section 1 rate" means the highest rate of tax in effect under section 1 as of the end of the base year plus 1 percentage point (or, in the case of applicable election years beginning in 1987, 36 percent).

(c) Refund of payments.—

(1) In general. If, for any applicable election year, the amount determined under subsection (b)(2) exceeds the amount determined under subsection (b)(1), the entity shall be entitled to a refund of such excess for such year.

(2) Termination of elections, etc. If—

(A) an election under section 444 is terminated effective with respect to any year, or

(B) the entity is liquidated during any year, the entity shall be entitled to a refund of the net required payment balance.

(3) Date on which refund payable. Any refund under this subsection shall be payable on the later of —

(A) April 15 of the calendar year following—

(i) in the case of the year referred to in paragraph (1), the calendar year in which it begins,

3,909

(ii) in the case of the year referred to in paragraph (2), the calendar year in which it ends, or

(B) the day 90 days after the day on which claim therefor is filed with the Secretary.

(d) Net base year income.

For purposes of this section—

(1) In general. An entity's net base year income shall be equal to the sum of—

(A) the deferral ratio multiplied by the entity's net income for the base year, plus

(B) the excess (if any) of—

(i) the deferral ratio multiplied by the aggregate amount of applicable payments made by the entity during the base year, over

(ii) the aggregate amount of such applicable payments made during the deferral period of the base year.

For purposes of this paragraph, the term "deferral ratio" means the ratio which the number of months in the deferral period of the base year bears to the number of months in the partnership's or S corporation's taxable year.

(2) Net income. Net income is determined by taking into account the aggregate amount of the following items—

(A) Partnerships. In the case of a partnership, net income shall be the amount (not below zero) determined by taking into account the aggregate amount of the partnership's items described in section 702(a) (other than credits and tax-exempt income).

(B) S corporations. In the case of an S corporation, net income shall be the amount (not below zero) determined by taking into account the aggregate amount of the S corporation's items described in section 1366(a) (other than credits and tax exempt income). If the S corporation was a C corporation for the base year, its taxable income for such year shall be treated as its net income for such year (and such corporation shall be treated as an S corporation for such taxable year for purposes of paragraph (3)).

(C) Certain limitations disregarded. For purposes of subparagraph (A) or (B), any limitation on the amount of any item described in either such paragraph which may be taken into account for purposes of computing the taxable income of a partner or shareholder shall be disregarded.

(3) Applicable payments.

(A) In general. The term "applicable payment" means amounts paid by a partnership or S corporation which are includible in gross income of a partner or shareholder.

(B) Exceptions. The term "applicable payment" shall not include any—

(i) gain from the sale or exchange of property between the partner or shareholder and the partnership or S corporation, and

(ii) dividend paid by the S corporation.

(4) Applicable percentage. The applicable percentage is the percentage determined in accordance with the following table:

If the applicable election year of the partnership or S corporation begins during:	The applicable percentage is:
1987	25
1988	50
1989	75
1990 or thereafter	100

Notwithstanding the preceding provisions of this paragraph, the applicable percentage for any partnership or S corporation shall be 100 percent unless more than 50 percent of such entity's net income for the short taxable year which would have resulted if the entity had not made an election under section 444 would have been allocated to partners or shareholders who would have been entitled to the benefits of section 806(e)(2)(C) of the Tax Reform Act of 1986 with respect to such income.

(5) Treatment of guaranteed payments.

(A) In general. Any guaranteed payment by a partnership shall not be treated as an applicable payment, and the amount of the net income of the partnership shall be determined by not taking such guaranteed payment into account.

(B) Guaranteed payment. For purposes of subparagraph (A), the term "guaranteed payment" means any payment referred to in section 707(c).

(e) Other definitions and special rules.

For purposes of this section—

(1) Deferral period. The term "deferral period" has the meaning given to such term by section 444(b)(4).

(2) Years.

(A) Base year. The term "base year" means, with respect to any applicable election year, the taxable year of the partnership or S corporation preceding such applicable election year.

(B) Applicable election year. The term "applicable election year" means any taxable year of a partnership or S corporation with respect to which an election is in effect under section 444.

(3) Requirement of reporting. Each partnership or S corporation which makes an election under section 444 shall include on any required return or statement such information as the Secretary shall prescribe as is necessary to carry out the provisions of this section.

(4) Net required payment balance. The term "net required payment balance" means the excess (if any) of—

(A) the aggregate of the required payments under this section for all preceding applicable election years, over

(B) the aggregate amount allowable as a refund to the entity under subsection (c) for all preceding applicable election years.

(f) Administrative provisions.

(1) In general. Except as otherwise provided in this subsection or in regulations prescribed by the Secretary, any payment required by this section shall be assessed and collected in the same manner as if it were a tax imposed by subtitle C.

(2) Due date. The amount of any payment required by this section shall be paid on or before April 15 of the calendar year following the calendar year in which the applicable election year begins (or such later date as may be prescribed by the Secretary).

(3) Interest. For purposes of determining interest, any payment required by this section shall be treated as a tax; except that no interest shall be allowed with respect to any refund of a payment made under this section.

(4) Penalties.

(A) In general. In the case of any failure by any person to pay on the date prescribed therefor any amount required by this section, there shall be imposed on such person a penalty of 10 percent of the underpayment. For purposes of the preceding sentence, the term "underpayment" means the excess of the amount of the payment required under this section over the amount (if any) of such payment paid on or before the date prescribed therefor. No penalty shall be imposed under this subparagraph on any failure which is shown to be due to reasonable cause and not willful neglect.

(B) Negligence and fraud penalties made applicable. For purposes of part II of subchapter A of chapter 68, any payment required by this section shall be treated as a tax.

(C) Willful failure. If any partnership or S corporation willfully fails to comply with the requirements of this section, section 444 shall cease to apply with respect to such partnership or S corporation.

(g) Regulations.

The Secretary shall prescribe such regulations as may be necessary or appropriate to carry out the provisions of this section and section 280H, including regulations providing for appropriate adjustments in the application of this section and sections 280H and 444 in cases where—

(1) 2 or more applicable election years begin in the same calendar year, or

(2) the base year is a taxable year of less than 12 months.

In **1997**, P.L. 105-34, Sec. 1281(d), added a sentence at the end of subpara. (f)(4)(A), effective for tax. yrs. begin. after 8/5/97.

In **1990**, P.L. 101-508, Sec. 11704(a)(29), substituted "payable on the later of" for "payable on later of" in para. (c)(3), effective 11/5/90.

In **1989**, P.L. 101-239, Sec. 7721(c)(12), substituted "part II of subchapter A of chapter 68" for "section 6653" in subpara. (f)(4)(B), effective for returns the due date for which (determined without regard to extensions) is after 12/31/89.

—P.L. 101-239, Sec. 7821(b)(1), deleted "for taxable years beginning after 1987," after "this paragraph" in para. (d)(4)... Sec. 7821(b)(2), substituted "unless more than 50 percent" for "if more than 50 percent" in para. (d)(4)... Sec. 7821(b)(3), substituted "who would have been entitled" for "who would not have been entitled" in para. (d)(4), effective for tax. yrs. begin. after 12/31/88.

In **1988**, P.L. 100-647, Sec. 2004(e)(4)(A), amended para. (b)(2)... Sec. 2004(e)(4)(B), added para. (e)(4)... Sec. 2004(e)(5), amended subsec. (c)... Sec. 2004(e)(6), amended subsec. (g)... Sec. 2004(e)(7), added "(and such corporation shall be treated as an S corporation for such taxable year for purposes of paragraph (3))" at the end of subpara. (d)(2)(B)... Sec. 2004(e)(8), added para. (d)(5)... Sec. 2004(e)(9), added the last sentence to para. (d)(4)... Sec. 2004(e)(10), substituted "(other than credits and tax-exempt income)" for "(other than credits)" in subparas. (d)(2)(A) and (B)... Sec. 2004(e)(14)(B), deleted "or incurred" after "amounts paid", in subpara. (d)(3)(A) effective for applicable election yrs. begin. after 12/31/86.

Prior to amendment, para. (b)(2) read as follows:

"(2) the amount of the required payment for the preceding applicable election year."

Prior to amendment, subsec. (g) read as follows:

"*(g) Regulations.*

The Secretary shall prescribe such regulations as may be necessary or appropriate to carry out the provisions of this section and section 28011, including regulations for annualizing the income and applicable payments of an entity if the base year is a taxable year of less than 12 months."

Prior to amendment, subsec. (c) read as follows:

"*(c) Refund of payments.*

If the amount determined under subsection (b)(2) exceeds the amount determined under subsection (b)(1), then the entity shall be entitled to a refund of such excess."

In **1987**, P.L. 100-203, Sec. 10206(b)(1), added Code Sec. 7519, effective for applicable election years begin. after 12/31/86.

Sec. 7520. Valuation tables.
(a) General rule.

For purposes of this title, the value of any annuity, any interest for life or a term of years, or any remainder or reversionary interest shall be determined—

(1) under tables prescribed by the Secretary, and

(2) by using an interest rate (rounded to the nearest ²⁄₁₀ths of 1 percent) equal to 120 percent of the Federal midterm rate in effect under section 1274(d)(1) for the month in which the valuation date falls.

If an income, estate, or gift tax charitable contribution is allowable for any part of the property transferred, the taxpayer may elect to use such Federal midterm rate for either of the 2 months preceding the month in which the valuation date falls for purposes of paragraph (2). In the case of transfers of more than 1 interest in the same property with respect to which the taxpayer may use the same rate under paragraph (2), the taxpayer shall use the same rate with respect to each such interest.

(b) Section not to apply for certain purposes.

This section shall not apply for purposes of part I of subchapter D of chapter 1 or any other provision specified in regulations.

(c) Tables.

(1) **In general.** The tables prescribed by the Secretary for purposes of subsection (a) shall contain valuation factors for a series of interest rate categories.

(2) **Initial table.** Not later than the day 3 months after the date of the enactment of this section, the Secretary shall prescribe initial tables for purposes of subsection (a). Such tables may be based on the same mortality experience as used for purposes of section 2031 on the date of the enactment of this section.

(3) **Revision for recent mortality charges.** Not later than December 31, 1989, the Secretary shall revise the initial tables prescribed for purposes of subsection (a) to take into account the most recent mortality experience available as of the time of such revision. Such tables shall be revised not less frequently than once each 10 years thereafter to take into account the most recent mortality experience available as of the time of the revision.

(d) Valuation date.

For purposes of this section, the term "valuation date" means the date as of which the valuation is made.

(e) Tables to include formulas.

For purposes of this section, the term "tables" includes formulas.

In **1988**, P.L. 100-647, Sec. 5031(a), added Code 7520, effective for cases where the date as of which the valuation is to be made occurs on or after the 1st day of the 6th calendar month beginning after 11/10/88.

Sec. 7521. Procedures involving taxpayer interviews.
(a) Recording of interviews.

(1) **Recording by taxpayer.** Any officer or employee of the Internal Revenue Service in connection with any in-person interview with any taxpayer relating to the determination or collection of any tax shall, upon advance request of such taxpayer, allow the taxpayer to make an audio recording of such interview at the taxpayer's own expense and with the taxpayer's own equipment.

(2) **Recording by IRS officer or employee.** An officer or employee of the Internal Revenue Service may record any interview described in paragraph (1) if such officer or employee—

(A) informs the taxpayer of such recording prior to the interview, and

(B) upon request of the taxpayer, provides the taxpayer with a transcript or copy of such recording but only if the taxpayer provides reimbursement for the cost of the transcription and reproduction of such transcript or copy.

(b) Safeguards.

(1) **Explanations of processes.** An officer or employee of the Internal Revenue Service shall before or at an initial interview provide to the taxpayer—

(A) in the case of an in-person interview with the taxpayer relating to the determination of any tax, an explanation of the audit process and the taxpayer's rights under such process, or

(B) in the case of an in-person interview with the taxpayer relating to the collection of any tax, an explanation of the collection process and the taxpayer's rights under such process.

(2) Right of consultation. If the taxpayer clearly states to an officer or employee of the Internal Revenue Service at any time during any interview (other than an interview initiated by an administrative summons issued under subchapter A of chapter 78) that the taxpayer wishes to consult with an attorney, certified public accountant, enrolled agent, enrolled actuary, or any other person permitted to represent the taxpayer before the Internal Revenue Service, such officer or employee shall suspend such interview regardless of whether the taxpayer may have answered one or more questions.

(c) Representatives holding power of attorney.

Any attorney, certified public accountant, enrolled agent, enrolled actuary, or any other person permitted to represent the taxpayer before the Internal Revenue Service who is not disbarred or suspended from practice before the Internal Revenue Service and who has a written power of attorney executed by the taxpayer may be authorized by such taxpayer to represent the taxpayer in any interview described in subsection (a). An officer or employee of the Internal Revenue Service may not require a taxpayer to accompany the representative in the absence of an administrative summons issued to the taxpayer under subchapter A of chapter 78. Such an officer or employee, with the consent of the immediate supervisor of such officer or employee, may notify the taxpayer directly that such officer or employee believes such representative is responsible for unreasonable delay or hindrance of an Internal Revenue Service examination or investigation of the taxpayer.

(d) Section not to apply to certain investigations.

This section shall not apply to criminal investigations or investigations relating to the integrity of any officer or employee of the Internal Revenue Service.

In 1998, P.L. 105-206, Sec. 3502, of this Act, reads as follows:
"SEC. 3502. EXPLANATION OF TAXPAYERS' RIGHTS IN INTERVIEWS WITH THE INTERNAL REVENUE SERVICE.
"The Secretary of the Treasury or the Secretary's delegate shall, as soon as practicable, but not later than 180 days after the date of the enactment of this Act, revise the statement required by section 6227 of the Omnibus Taxpayer Bill of Rights (Internal Revenue Service Publication No. 1) to more clearly inform taxpayers of their rights—
"(1) to be represented at interviews with the Internal Revenue Service by any person authorized to practice before the Internal Revenue Service; and
"(2) to suspend an interview pursuant to section 7521(b)(2) of the Internal Revenue Code of 1986."

In 1989, P.L. 101-239, Sec. 7816(u)(1), redesignated Code Sec. 7520 (as added by Sec. 6228(a) of P.L. 100-647) as Code Sec. 7521, effective for interviews conducted on or after 90 days after 11/10/88.
In 1988, P.L. 100-647, Sec. 6228(a), added Code Sec. 7520, effective for interviews conducted on or after 90 days after 11/10/88.
— P.L. 100-647, Sec. 6228(b), of this Act provides:
"(b) Regulations with respect to time and place of examination.— The Secretary of the Treasury or the Secretary's delegate shall issue regulations to implement subsection (a) of section 7605 of the 1986 Code (relating to time and place of examination) within 1 year after the date of the enactment of this Act [11/10/88]."

Sec. 7522. Content of tax due, deficiency, and other notices.

(a) General rule.

Any notice to which this section applies shall describe the basis for, and identify the amounts (if any) of, the tax due, interest, additional amounts, additions to the tax, and assessable *penalties* included in such notice. An inadequate description under the preceding sentence shall not invalidate such notice.

(b) Notices to which section applies.

This section shall apply to —
(1) any tax due notice or deficiency notice described in section 6155, 6212, or 6303,
(2) any notice generated out of any information return matching program, and
(3) the 1st letter of proposed deficiency which allows the taxpayer an opportunity for administrative review in the Internal Revenue Service Office of Appeals.

In 1990, P.L. 101-508, Sec. 11704(a)(30), redesignated Code Sec. 7521 relating to content of tax due, deficiency, and other notices [as added by Sec. 6233(a) of P.L. 100-647] as Code Sec. 7522, effective 11/5/90.
In 1988, P.L. 100-647, Sec. 6233(a), added Code Sec. 7521, effective for mailings made on or after 1/1/90.

Sec. 7523. Graphic presentation of major categories of federal outlays and income.

(a) General rule.

In the case of any booklet of instructions for Form 1040, 1040A, or 1040EZ prepared by the Secretary for filing individual income tax returns for taxable years beginning in any calendar year, the Secretary shall include in a prominent place—

(1) a pie-shaped graph showing the relative sizes of the major outlay categories, and
(2) a pie-shaped graph showing the relative sizes of the major income categories.

(b) Definitions and special rules.

For purposes of subsection (a)—
(1) Major outlay categories. The term "major outlay categories" means the following:
(A) Defense, veterans, and foreign affairs.
(B) Social security, medicare, and other retirement.
(C) Physical, human, and community development.
(D) Social programs.
(E) Law enforcement and general government.
(F) Interest on the debt.

(2) Major income categories. The term "major income categories" means the following:
(A) Social security, medicare, and unemployment and other retirement taxes.
(B) Personal income taxes.
(C) Corporate income taxes.
(D) Borrowing to cover the deficit.
(E) Excise, customs, estate, gift, and miscellaneous taxes.

(3) Required footnotes. The pie-shaped graph showing the major outlay categories shall include the following footnotes:

(A) A footnote to the category referred to in paragraph (1)(A) showing the percentage of the total outlays which is for defense, the percentage of total outlays which is for veterans, and the percentage of total outlays which is for foreign affairs.

(B) A footnote to the category referred to in paragraph (1)(C) showing that such category consists of agriculture, natural resources, environment, transportation, education, job training, economic development, space, energy, and general science.

(C) A footnote to the category referred to in paragraph (1)(D) showing the percentage of the total outlays which is for medicaid, supplemental nutrition assistance program benefits, and assistance under a State program funded under part A of title IV of the Social Security Act and the percentage of total outlays which is for

Miscellaneous provisions   Code Sec. 7526(b)(2)(A)

public health, unemployment, assisted housing, and social services.

(4) Data on which graphs are based. The graphs required under subsection (a) shall be based on data for the most recent fiscal year for which complete data is available as of the completion of the preparation of the instructions by the Secretary.

In 2008, P.L. 110-246, Sec. 4, Repeals the duplicative enactment and provides effective date provisions of the Act entitled "An Act to provide for the continuation of agricultural programs through fiscal year 2012, and for other purposes" Sec. 4, P.L. 110-246 reads as follows:

"Sec. 4. Repeal of duplicative enactment.

"(a) In General- The Act entitled 'An Act to provide for the continuation of agricultural programs through fiscal year 2012, and for other purposes' (H.R. 2419 of the 110th Congress), and the amendments made by that Act, are repealed, effective on the date of enactment of that Act.

"(b) Effective Date- Except as otherwise provided in this Act, this Act and the amendments made by this Act shall take effect on the earlier of—

"(1) the date of enactment of this Act; or

"(2) the date of the enactment of the Act entitled 'An Act to provide for the continuation of agricultural programs through fiscal year 2012, and for other purposes' (H.R. 2419 of the 110th Congress)."

—P.L. 110-246, Sec. 4002(b)(1)(E), substituted "supplemental nutrition assistance program benefits" for "food stamps" in subpara. (b)(1)(D), effective 5/22/2008. [Ed. Note: May 22, 2008 was the date of enactment for H.R. 2419 (PL 110-234), which was repealed by (2008 Farm Act § 4(a)) (PL 110-246, 6/18/2008), in connection with the reenactment of the farm bill to correct a technical deficiency in its original passage.]

In 1996, P.L. 104-193, Sec. 110(l)(8), substituted "assistance under a State program funded under part A of title IV of the Social Security Act" for "aid to families with dependent children" in subpara. (b)(3)(C), effective 7/1/97.

In 1990, P.L. 101-508, Sec. 11622(a), added Code Sec. 7523 as part of the amendment to chap. 77, effective for instructions prepared for tax. yrs. begin. after '90.

Sec. 7524. Annual notice of tax delinquency.

Not less often than annually, the Secretary shall send a written notice to each taxpayer who has a tax delinquent account of the amount of the tax delinquency as of the date of the notice.

In 1996, P.L. 104-168, Sec. 1204(a), added Code Sec. 7524, effective for calendar yrs. after 1996.

Sec. 7525. Confidentiality privileges relating to taxpayer communications.

(a) Uniform application to taxpayer communications with federally authorized practitioners.

(1) General rule. With respect to tax advice, the same common law protections of confidentiality which apply to a communication between a taxpayer and an attorney shall also apply to a communication between a taxpayer and any federally authorized tax practitioner to the extent the communication would be considered a privileged communication if it were between a taxpayer and an attorney.

(2) Limitations. Paragraph (1) may only be asserted in—

(A) any noncriminal tax matter before the Internal Revenue Service; and

(B) any noncriminal tax proceeding in Federal court brought by or against the United States.

(3) Definitions. For purposes of this subsection—

(A) Federally authorized tax practitioner. The term "federally authorized tax practitioner" means any individual who is authorized under Federal law to practice before the Internal Revenue Service if such practice is subject to Federal regulation under section 330 of title 31, United States Code.

(B) Tax advice. The term "tax advice" means advice given by an individual with respect to a matter which is within the scope of the individual's authority to practice described in subparagraph (A).

(b) Section not to apply to communications regarding tax shelters.

The privilege under subsection (a) shall not apply to any written communication which is—

(1) between a federally authorized tax practitioner and—

(A) any person,

(B) any director, officer, employee, agent, or representative of the person, or

(C) any other person holding a capital or profits interest in the person, and

(2) in connection with the promotion of the direct or indirect participation of the person in any tax shelter (as defined in section 6662(d)(2)(C)(ii)).

In 2004, P.L. 108-357, Sec. 813(a), amended subsec. (b), effective for communications made on or after 10/22/2004.

Prior to amendment, subsec. (b) read as follows:

"(b) Section not to apply to communications regarding corporate tax shelter. The privilege under subsection (a) shall not apply to any written communication between a federally authorized tax practitioner and a director, shareholder, officer, or employee, agent, or representative of a corporation in connection with the promotion of the direct or indirect participation of such corporation in any tax shelter (as defined in section 6662(d)(2)(C)(iii))."

In 1998, P.L. 105-206, Sec. 3411(a), added Code Sec. 7525, effective for communications made on or after 7/22/98.

—P.L. 105-206, Sec. 3468, of this Act, reads as follows:

"SEC. 3468. PROHIBITION ON REQUESTS TO TAXPAYERS TO GIVE UP RIGHTS TO BRING ACTIONS.

"(a) Prohibition. No officer or employee of the United States may request a taxpayer to waive the taxpayer's right to bring a civil action against the United States or any officer or employee of the United States for any action taken in connection with the internal revenue laws.

"(b) Exceptions. Subsection (a) shall not apply in any case where—

"(1) a taxpayer waives the right described in subsection (a) knowingly and voluntarily; or

"(2) the request by the officer or employee is made in person and the taxpayer's attorney or other federally authorized tax practitioner (within the meaning of section 7525(a)(3)(A) of the Internal Revenue Code of 1986) is present, or the request is made in writing to the taxpayer's attorney or other representative."

Sec. 7526. Low income taxpayer clinics.

(a) In general.

The Secretary may, subject to the availability of appropriated funds, make grants to provide matching funds for the development, expansion, or continuation of qualified low income taxpayer clinics.

(b) Definitions.

For purposes of this section—

(1) Qualified low income taxpayer clinic.

(A) In general. The term "qualified low income taxpayer clinic" means a clinic that—

(i) does not charge more than a nominal fee for its services (except for reimbursement of actual costs incurred); and

(ii)(I) represents low-income taxpayers in controversies with the Internal Revenue Service; or

(II) operates programs to inform individuals for whom English is a second language about their rights and responsibilities under this title.

(B) Representation of low income taxpayers. A clinic meets the requirements of subparagraph (A)(ii)(I) if—

(i) at least 90 percent of the taxpayers represented by the clinic have incomes which do not exceed 250 percent of the poverty level, as determined in accordance with criteria established by the Director of the Office of Management and Budget; and

(ii) the amount in controversy for any taxable year generally does not exceed the amount specified in section 7463.

(2) Clinic. The term "clinic" includes—

(A) a clinical program at an accredited law, business, or accounting school in which students represent low in-

3,913

come taxpayers in controversies arising under this title; and

(B) an organization described in section 501(c) and exempt from tax under section 501(a) which satisfies the requirements of paragraph (1) through representation of taxpayers or referral of taxpayers to qualified representatives.

(3) **Qualified representative.** The term "qualified representative" means any individual (whether or not an attorney) who is authorized to practice before the Internal Revenue Service or the applicable court.

(c) **Special rules and limitations.**

(1) **Aggregate limitation.** Unless otherwise provided by specific appropriation, the Secretary shall not allocate more than $6,000,000 per year (exclusive of costs of administering the program) to grants under this section.

(2) **Limitation on annual grants to a clinic.** The aggregate amount of grants which may be made under this section to a clinic for a year shall not exceed $100,000.

(3) **Multi-year grants.** Upon application of a qualified low income taxpayer clinic, the Secretary is authorized to award a multi-year grant not to exceed 3 years.

(4) **Criteria for awards.** In determining whether to make a grant under this section, the Secretary shall consider—

(A) the numbers of taxpayers who will be served by the clinic, including the number of taxpayers in the geographical area for whom English is a second language;

(B) the existence of other low income taxpayer clinics serving the same population;

(C) the quality of the program offered by the low-income taxpayer clinic, including the qualifications of its administrators and qualified representatives, and its record, if any, in providing service to low-income taxpayers; and

(D) alternative funding sources available to the clinic, including amounts received from other grants and contributions, and the endowment and resources of the institution sponsoring the clinic.

(5) **Requirement of matching funds.** A low-income taxpayer clinic must provide matching funds on a dollar for dollar basis for all grants provided under this section. Matching funds may include—

(A) the salary (including fringe benefits) of individuals performing services for the clinic; and

(B) the cost of equipment used in the clinic.

Indirect expenses, including general overhead of the institution sponsoring the clinic, shall not be counted as matching funds.

In **1998,** P.L. 105-206, Sec. 3601(a), added Code Sec. 7526, effective 7/22/98.

Sec. 7527. Advance payment of credit for health insurance costs of eligible individuals.

(a) **General rule.**

Not later than August 1, 2003, the Secretary shall establish a program for making payments on behalf of certified individuals to providers of qualified health insurance (as defined in section 35(e)) for such individuals.

(b) **Limitation on advance payments during any taxable year.**

The Secretary may make payments under subsection (a) only to the extent that the total amount of such payments made on behalf of any individual during the taxable year does not exceed 65 percent (80 percent in the case of eligible coverage months beginning before February 13, 2011) of the amount paid by the taxpayer for coverage of the taxpayer and qualifying family members under qualified health insurance for eligible coverage months beginning in the taxable year.

(c) **Certified individual.**

For purposes of this section, the term "certified individual" means any individual for whom a qualified health insurance costs credit eligibility certificate is in effect.

(d) **Qualified health insurance costs eligibility certificate.**

(1) **In general.** For purposes of this section, the term "qualified health insurance costs eligibility certificate" means any written statement that an individual is an eligible individual (as defined in section 35(c)) if such statement provides such information as the Secretary may require for purposes of this section and—

(A) in the case of an eligible TAA recipient (as defined in section 35(c)(2)) or an eligible alternative TAA recipient (as defined in section 35(c)(3)), is certified by the Secretary of Labor (or by any other person or entity designated by the Secretary), or

(B) in the case of an eligible PBGC pension recipient (as defined in section 35(c)(4)), is certified by the Pension Benefit Guaranty Corporation (or by any other person or entity designated by the Secretary).

(2) **Inclusion of certain information.** In the case of any statement described in paragraph (1) which is issued before February 13, 2011, such statement shall not be treated as a qualified health insurance costs credit eligibility certificate unless such statement includes—

(A) the name, address, and telephone number of the State office or offices responsible for providing the individual with assistance with enrollment in qualified health insurance (as defined in section 35(e)),

(B) a list of the coverage options that are treated as qualified health insurance (as so defined) by the State in which the individual resides, and

(C) in the case of a TAA-eligible individual (as defined in section 4980B(f)(5)(C)(iv)(II)), a statement informing the individual that the individual has 63 days from the date that is 7 days after the date of the issuance of such certificate to enroll in such insurance without a lapse in creditable coverage (as defined in section 9801(c)).

(e) **Payment for premiums due prior to commencement of advance payments.**

In the case of eligible coverage months beginning before February 13, 2011—

(1) **In general.** The program established under subsection (a) shall provide that the Secretary shall make 1 or more retroactive payments on behalf of a certified individual in an aggregate amount equal to 80 percent of the premiums for coverage of the taxpayer and qualifying family members under qualified health insurance for eligible coverage months (as defined in section 35(b)) occurring prior to the first month for which an advance payment is made on behalf of such individual under subsection (a).

(2) **Reduction of payment for amounts received under national emergency grants.** The amount of any payment determined under paragraph (1) shall be reduced by the amount of any payment made to the taxpayer for the purchase of qualified health insurance under a national emergency grant pursuant to section 173(f) of the Workforce Investment Act of 1998 for a taxable year including the eligible coverage months described in paragraph (1).

In **2010,** P.L. 111-344, Sec. 111(b), substituted "February 13, 2011" for "January 1, 2011" in subsec. (b), effective for coverage months begin. after 12/31/2010.
—P.L. 111-344, Sec. 112(a), substituted "February 13, 2011" for "January 1, 2011" in subsec. (e), effective for coverage months begin. after 12/31/2010.

Miscellaneous provisions   Subchapter A

—P.L. 111-344, Sec. 118(a), substituted "February 13, 2011" for "January 1, 2011" in subsec. (d)(2), effective for certificates issued after 12/31/2010.

In **2009**, P.L. 111-5, Sec. 1899A(a)(2), added "(80 percent in the case of eligible coverage months beginning before January 1, 2011)" after "65 percent" in subsec. (b), effective for coverage months begin. on or after the first day of the first month begin. 60 days after 2/17/2009.

—P.L. 111-5, Sec. 1899B(a), added subsec. (e), effective for coverage months begin. after 12/31/2008.

—P.L. 111-5, Sec. 1899B(c), of this Act provides:

"(c) Transitional rule. The Secretary of the Treasury shall not be required to make any payments under section 7527(e) of the Internal Revenue Code of 1986, as added by this section, until after the date that is 6 months after the date of the enactment of this Act."

—P.L. 111-5, Sec. 1899H(a), amended subsec. (d), effective for certificates issued after the date that is 6 months after 2/17/2009.

Prior to amendment, subsec. (d) read as follows:

"(d) Qualified health insurance costs credit eligibility certificate. For purposes of this section, the term 'qualified health insurance costs credit eligibility certificate' means any written statement that an individual is an eligible individual (as defined in section 35(c)) if such statement provides such information as the Secretary may require for purposes of this section and—

"(1) in the case of an eligible TAA recipient (as defined in section 35(c)(2)) or an eligible alternative TAA recipient (as defined in section 35(c)(3)), is certified by the Secretary of Labor (or by any other person or entity designated by the Secretary), or

"(2) in the case of an eligible PBGC pension recipient (as defined in section 35(c)(4)), is certified by the Pension Benefit Guaranty Corporation (or by any other person or entity designated by the Secretary)."

In **2002**, P.L. 107-210, Sec. 202(a), added Code Sec. 7527, effective 8/6/2002.

Sec. 7528. Internal Revenue Service user fees.

(a) General rule.

The Secretary shall establish a program requiring the payment of user fees for—

(1) requests to the Internal Revenue Service for ruling letters, opinion letters, and determination letters, and

(2) other similar requests.

(b) Program criteria.

(1) **In general.** The fees charged under the program required by subsection (a)—

(A) shall vary according to categories (or subcategories) established by the Secretary,

(B) shall be determined after taking into account the average time for (and difficulty of) complying with requests in each category (and subcategory), and

(C) shall be payable in advance.

(2) **Exemptions, etc.**

(A) In general. The Secretary shall provide for such exemptions (and reduced fees) under such program as the Secretary determines to be appropriate.

(B) Exemption for certain requests regarding pension plans. The Secretary shall not require payment of user fees under such program for requests for determination letters with respect to the qualified status of a pension benefit plan maintained solely by 1 or more eligible employers or any trust which is part of the plan. The preceding sentence shall not apply to any request—

(i) made after the later of—

(I) the fifth plan year the pension benefit plan is in existence, or

(II) the end of any remedial amendment period with respect to the plan beginning within the first 5 plan years, or

(ii) made by the sponsor of any prototype or similar plan which the sponsor intends to market to participating employers.

(C) Definitions and special rules. For purposes of subparagraph (B)—

(i) Pension benefit plan. The term "pension benefit plan" means a pension, profit-sharing, stock bonus, annuity, or employee stock ownership plan.

(ii) Eligible employer. The term "eligible employer" means an eligible employer (as defined in section 408(p)(2)(C)(i)(I)) which has at least 1 employee who is not a highly compensated employee (as defined in section 414(q)) and is participating in the plan. The determination of whether an employer is an eligible employer under subparagraph (B) shall be made as of the date of the request described in such subparagraph.

(iii) Determination of average fees charged. For purposes of any determination of average fees charged, any request to which subparagraph (B) applies shall not be taken into account.

(3) **Average fee requirement.** The average fee charged under the program required by subsection (a) shall not be less than the amount determined under the following table:

Category	Average Fee
Employee plan ruling and opinion	$ 250
Exempt organization ruling	$ 350
Employee plan determination	$ 300
Exempt organization determination	$ 275
Chief counsel ruling	$ 200

In **2007**, P.L. 110-28, Sec. 8244, deleted subsec. (c), enacted 5/25/2007.

Prior to deletion, subsec. (c) read as follows:

"(c) Termination. No fee shall be imposed under this section with respect to requests made after September 30, 2014."

In **2004**, P.L. 108-357, Sec. 891(a), substituted "September 30, 2014" for "December 31, 2004" in subsec. (c), effective for requests after 10/22/2004.

In **2003**, P.L. 108-89, Sec. 202(a), added Code Sec. 7528, effective for requests made after 10/1/2003.

—P.L. 108-89, Sec. 202(c), of this Act, reads as follows:

"(c) Limitations. Notwithstanding any other provision of law, any fees collected pursuant to section 7528 of the Internal Revenue Code of 1986, as added by subsection (a), shall not be expended by the Internal Revenue Service unless provided by an appropriations Act."

CHAPTER 78.—DISCOVERY OF LIABILITY AND ENFORCEMENT OF TITLE

Subchapter

A. Examination and inspection.

B. General powers and duties.

C. [Repealed] Supervision of operations of certain manufacturers.

D. Possessions.

Subchapter A.—Examination and Inspection

Sec.

7601. Canvass of districts for taxable persons and objects.

7602. Examination of books and witnesses.

7603. Service of summons.

7604. Enforcement of summons.

7605. Time and place of examination.

7606. Entry of premises for examination of taxable objects.

7608. Authority of internal revenue enforcement officers.

7609. Special procedures for third-party summonses.

7610. Fees and costs for witnesses.

7611. Restrictions on church tax inquiries and examinations.

7612. Special procedures for summonses for computer software.

7613. Cross references.

In **1998**, P.L. 105-206, Sec. 3413(d), deleted item 7612 and added items 7612 and 7613.

Prior to deletion, item 7612 read as follows:

"7612. Cross references."

Subchapter A   **Miscellaneous provisions**

In 1984, P.L. 98-573, Sec. 213(b)(2), deleted item 7607.
Prior to deletion the item 7607 read as follows:
"7607. Additional authority for Bureau of Customs."
—P.L. 98-369, Sec. 1033(c)(2), redesignated item 7611 as 7612 and added new item 7611.
In 1976, P.L. 94-455, Sec. 1205(b), redesignated item 7609 as 7611 and added new items 7609 and 7610.
In 1970, P.L. 91-513, Sec. 1102(g), deleted from item 7607 "Bureau of Narcotics and" after "authority for", effective 5/1/71.
In 1958, added item 7608, and redesignated former item 7608 as 7609.
In 1956, renumbered item 7607, as item 7608, and added item 7607.

Sec. 7601. Canvass of districts for taxable persons and objects.
(a) General rule.
The Secretary shall, to the extent he deems it practicable, cause officers or employees of the Treasury Department to proceed, from time to time, through each internal revenue district and inquire after and concerning all persons therein who may be liable to pay any internal revenue tax, and all persons owning or having the care and management of any objects with respect to which any tax is imposed.
(b) Penalties.
For penalties applicable to forcible obstruction or hindrance of Treasury officers or employees in the performance of their duties, see section 7212.

In 1976, P.L. 94-455, Sec. 1906(b)(13)(A), substituted "Secretary" for "Secretary or his delegate" each place it appeared in Code Sec. 7601, effective 2/1/77.

Sec. 7602. Examination of books and witnesses.
(a) Authority to summon, etc.
For the purpose of ascertaining the correctness of any return, making a return where none has been made, determining the liability of any person for any internal revenue tax or the liability at law or in equity of any transferee or fiduciary of any person in respect of any internal revenue tax, or collecting any such liability, the Secretary is authorized—
(1) To examine any books, papers, records, or other data which may be relevant or material to such inquiry;
(2) To summon the person liable for tax or required to perform the act, or any officer or employee of such person, or any person having possession, custody, or care of books of account containing entries relating to the business of the person liable for tax or required to perform the act, or any other person the Secretary may deem proper, to appear before the Secretary at a time and place named in the summons and to produce such books, papers, records, or other data, and to give such testimony, under oath, as may be relevant or material to such inquiry; and
(3) To take such testimony of the person concerned, under oath, as may be relevant or material to such inquiry.
(b) Purpose may include inquiry into offense.
The purposes for which the Secretary may take any action described in paragraph (1), (2), or (3) of subsection (a) include the purpose of inquiring into any offense connected with the administration or enforcement of the internal revenue laws.
(c) Notice of contact of third parties.
(1) General notice. An officer or employee of the Internal Revenue Service may not contact any person other than the taxpayer with respect to the determination or collection of the tax liability of such taxpayer without providing reasonable notice in advance to the taxpayer that contacts with persons other than the taxpayer may be made.
(2) Notice of specific contacts. The Secretary shall periodically provide to a taxpayer a record of persons contacted during such period by the Secretary with respect to the determination or collection of the tax liability of such taxpayer. Such record shall also be provided upon request of the taxpayer.
(3) Exceptions. This subsection shall not apply—
(A) to any contact which the taxpayer has authorized;
(B) if the Secretary determines for good cause shown that such notice would jeopardize collection of any tax or such notice may involve reprisal against any person; or
(C) with respect to any pending criminal investigation.
(d) No administrative summons when there is Justice Department referral.
(1) Limitation of authority. No summons may be issued under this title, and the Secretary may not begin any action under section 7604 to enforce any summons, with respect to any person if a Justice Department referral is in effect with respect to such person.
(2) Justice Department referral in effect. For purposes of this subsection—
(A) In general. A Justice Department referral is in effect with respect to any person if —
(i) the Secretary has recommended to the Attorney General a grand jury investigation of, or the criminal prosecution of, such person for any offense connected with the administration or enforcement of the internal revenue laws, or
(ii) any request is made under section 6103(h)(3)(B) for the disclosure of any return or return information (within the meaning of section 6103(b)) relating to such person.
(B) Termination. A Justice Department referral shall cease to be in effect with respect to a person when—
(i) the Attorney General notifies the Secretary, in writing, that—
(I) he will not prosecute such person for any offense connected with the administration or enforcement of the internal revenue laws,
(II) he will not authorize a grand jury investigation of such person with respect to such an offense, or
(III) he will discontinue such a grand jury investigation,
(ii) a final disposition has been made of any criminal proceeding pertaining to the enforcement of the internal revenue laws which was instituted by the Attorney General against such person, or
(iii) the Attorney General notifies the Secretary, in writing, that he will not prosecute such person for any offense connected with the administration or enforcement of the internal revenue laws relating to the request described in subparagraph (A)(ii).
(3) Taxable years, etc., treated separately. For purposes of this subsection, each taxable period (or, if there is no taxable period, each taxable event) and each tax imposed by a separate chapter of this title shall be treated separately.
(e) Limitation on examination on unreported income.
The Secretary shall not use financial status or economic reality examination techniques to determine the existence of unreported income of any taxpayer unless the Secretary has a reasonable indication that there is a likelihood of such unreported income.

In 1998, P.L. 105-206, Sec. 3412, added subsec. (d), effective 7/22/98.
—P.L. 105-206, Sec. 3417(a), redesignated subsecs. (c) and (d) [as added by Sec. 3412 of this Act, see above] as subsecs. (d) and (e), and added subsec. (c), effective for contacts made after the 180th day after 7/22/98.
In 1982, P.L. 97-248, Sec. 333(a), amended Code Sec. 7602, effective 9/4/82.
Prior to amendment, Code Sec. 7602 read as follows:
"SEC. 7602. EXAMINATION OF BOOKS AND WITNESSES."

Miscellaneous provisions — Code Sec. 7604

"For the purpose of ascertaining the correctness of any return, making a return where none has been made, determining the liability of any person for any internal revenue tax or the liability at law or in equity of any transferee or fiduciary of any person in respect of any internal revenue tax, or collecting any such liability, the Secretary is authorized—

"(1) To examine any books, papers, records, or other data which may be relevant or material to such inquiry;

"(2) To summon the person liable for tax or required to perform the act, or any officer or employee of such person, or any person having possession, custody, or care of books of account containing entries relating to the business of the person liable for tax or required to perform the act, or any other person the Secretary may deem proper, to appear before the Secretary at a time and place named in the summons and to produce such books, papers, records, or other data, and to give such testimony, under oath, as may be relevant or material to such inquiry; and

"(3) To take such testimony of the person concerned, under oath, as may be relevant or material to such inquiry."

In 1976, P.L. 94-455, Sec. 1906(b)(13)(A), substituted "Secretary" for "Secretary or his delegate" each place it appeared in Code Sec. 7602, effective 2/1/77.

Sec. 7603. Service of summons.
(a) In general.

A summons issued under section 6420(e)(2), 6421(g)(2), 6427(j)(2), or 7602 shall be served by the Secretary, by an attested copy delivered in hand to the person to whom it is directed, or left at his last and usual place of abode; and the certificate of service signed by the person serving the summons shall be evidence of the facts it states on the hearing of an application for the enforcement of the summons. When the summons requires the production of books, papers, records, or other data, it shall be sufficient if such books, papers, records, or other data are described with reasonable certainty.

(b) Service by mail to third-party recordkeepers.

(1) In general. A summons referred to in subsection (a) for the production of books, papers, records, or other data by a third-party recordkeeper may also be served by certified or registered mail to the last known address of such recordkeeper.

(2) Third-party recordkeeper. For purposes of paragraph (1), the term "third-party recordkeeper" means—

(A) any mutual savings bank, cooperative bank, domestic building and loan association, or other savings institution chartered and supervised as a savings and loan or similar association under Federal or State law, any bank (as defined in section 581), or any credit union (within the meaning of section 501(c)(14)(A)),

(B) any consumer reporting agency (as defined under section 603(f) of the Fair Credit Reporting Act (15 U.S.C. 1681a(f))),

(C) any person extending credit through the use of credit cards or similar devices,

(D) any broker (as defined in section 3(a)(4) of the Securities Exchange Act of 1934 (15 U.S.C. 78c(a)(4))),

(E) any attorney,

(F) any accountant,

(G) any barter exchange (as defined in section 6045(c)(3)),

(H) any regulated investment company (as defined in section 851) and any agent of such regulated investment company when acting as an agent thereof,

(I) any enrolled agent, and

(J) any owner or developer of a computer software source code (as defined in section 7612(d)(2)).

Subparagraph (J) shall apply only with respect to a summons requiring the production of the source code referred to in subparagraph (J) or the program and data described in section 7612(b)(1)(A)(ii) to which such source code relates.

In 2000, P.L. 106-554, Sec. 1(a)(7), [which enacted into law Sec. 319(26) of P.L. 106-554 substituted a comma for the semicolon at the end of subparas. (b)(2)(A)–(G), effective 12/21/2000.

In 1998, P.L. 105-206, Sec. 3413(c), deleted "and" at the end of subpara. (b)(2)(H) [as added by Sec. 3416(a) of this Act, see below], substituted ", and" for the period at the end of subpara. (b)(2)(I) [as added by Sec. 3416(a) of this Act, see below] and added subpara. (b)(2)(J), effective for summonses issued, and software acquired, after 7/22/98.

—P.L. 105-206, Sec. 3416(a), substituted "(a) In general. A summons issued" for "A summons issued" in Code Sec. 7603 and added subsec. (b), effective for summonses served after 7/22/98.

In 1988, P.L. 100-647, Sec. 1017(c)(9), substituted "6421(g)(2)" for "6421(f)(2)" effective for gasoline removed (as defined in section 4082 of the Internal Revenue Code of 1986, as amended by Sec. 1703(a) of P.L. 99-514) after 12/31/87.

In 1986, P.L. 99-514, Sec. 1703(e)(2)(G), substituted "section 6427(j)(2)" for "section 6427(i)(2)" in Code Sec. 7603, effective for gasoline removed (as defined in section 4082 of the Internal Revenue Code of 1986, as amended by Sec. 1703(a) of this Act) after 12/31/87.

In 1984, P.L. 98-369, Sec. 911(d)(2)(G), substituted "6427(i)(2)" for "6427(h)(2)" in Code Sec. 7603, effective 8/1/84.

In 1983, P.L. 97-424, Sec. 515(b)(12), deleted "6424(d)(2)," after "6421(f)(2)," in Code Sec. 7603, effective for articles sold after 1/6/83.

In 1980, P.L. 96-223, Sec. 232(d)(4)(E), substituted "6427(h)(2)" for "6427(g)(2)", effective 1/1/79.

In 1978, P.L. 95-599, Sec. 505(c)(5), substituted "6427(g)(2)" for "6427(f)(2)" in Code Sec. 7603, effective 1/1/79.

In 1976, P.L. 94-530, Sec. 1(c)(6), substituted "6427(f)(2)" for "6427(e)(2)", in Code Sec. 7603, effective 10/1/76.

—P.L. 94-455, Sec. 1906(b)(13)(A), substituted "Secretary" for "Secretary or his delegate" in Code Sec. 7603, effective 2/1/77.

In 1970, P.L. 91-258, Sec. 207(d)(9), added "6427(e)(2)" in Code Sec. 7603, effective 7/1/70.

In 1965, P.L. 89-44, Sec. 202(c)(4), included any summons issued under section 6424(d)(2), effective 1/1/66.

In 1956, ch. 462, Sec. 208(d)(4), included any summons issued under section 6421(f)(2), effective 6/29/56.

—ch. 160, Sec. 4(i), included any summons issued under section 6420(e)(2).

Sec. 7604. Enforcement of summons.
(a) Jurisdiction of district court.

If any person is summoned under the internal revenue laws to appear, to testify, or to produce books, papers, records, or other data, the United States district court for the district in which such person resides or is found shall have jurisdiction by appropriate process to compel such attendance, testimony, or production of books, papers, records, or other data.

(b) Enforcement.

Whenever any person summoned under section 6420(e)(2), 6421(g)(2), 6427(j)(2) or 7602 neglects or refuses to obey such summons, or to produce books, papers, records, or other data, or to give testimony, as required, the Secretary may apply to the judge of the district court or to a United States commissioner for the district within which the person so summoned resides or is found for an attachment against him as for a contempt. It shall be the duty of the judge or commissioner to hear the application, and, if satisfactory proof is made, to issue an attachment, directed to some proper officer, for the arrest of such person, and upon his being brought before him to proceed to a hearing of the case; and upon such hearing the judge or the United States commissioner shall have power to make such order as he shall deem proper, not inconsistent with the law for the punishment of contempts, to enforce obedience to the requirements of the summons and to punish such person for his default or disobedience.

(c) Cross references.

(1) Authority to issue orders, processes, and judgments. For authority of district courts generally to enforce the provisions of this title, see section 7402.

(2) Penalties. For penalties applicable to violation of section 6420(e)(2), 6421(g)(2), 6427(j)(2), or 7602, see section 7210.

In 1988, P.L. 100-647, Sec. 1017(c)(9), substituted "6421(g)(2)" for "6421(f)(2)" in subsec. (b) and para. (c)(2), effective for gasoline removed (as defined in section 4082 of the Internal Revenue Code of 1986, as amended by Sec. 1703(a) of P.L. 99-514) after 12/31/87.

Code Sec. 7604

In 1986, P.L. 99-514, Sec. 1703(e)(2)(G), substituted "section 6427(j)(2)" for "section 6427(i)(2)" in subsec. (b) and para. (c)(2), effective for gasoline removed (as defined in section 4082 of the Internal Revenue Code of 1986, as amended by Sec. 1703(a) of this Act) after 12/31/87.
In 1984, P.L. 98-369, Sec. 911(d)(2)(G), substituted "6427(i)(2)" for "6427(h)(2)" in subsec. (b) and para. (c)(2), effective 8/1/84.
In 1983, P.L. 97-424, Sec. 515(b)(12), deleted "6424(d)(2)," after "6421(f)(2)," each place it appeared in Code Sec. 7604, effective for articles sold after 1/6/83.
In 1980, P.L. 96-223, Sec. 232(d)(4)(E), substituted "6427(h)(2)" for "6427(g)(2)" in subsec. (b) and para. (c)(2), effective 1/1/79.
In 1978, P.L. 95-599, Sec. 505(c)(5), substituted "6427(g)(2)", for "6427(f)(2)" in subsec. (a) . . . Sec. 505(c)(6), substituted "6427(g)(2)" for "6427(e)(2)" in para. (c)(2), effective 1/1/79.
In 1976, P.L. 94-530, Sec. 1(c)(6), substituted "6427(f)(2)" for "6427(e)(2)" in subsec. (b), effective 10/1/76.
—P.L. 94-455, Sec. 1906(b)(13)(A), substituted "Secretary" for "Secretary or his delegate" in Code Sec. 7604, effective 2/1/77.
In 1970, P.L. 91-258, Sec. 207(d)(9), added "6427(e)(2)" in subsec. (b) and para. (c)(2), effective 7/1/70.
In 1965, P.L. 89-44, Sec. 202(c)(4), added references to section 6424(d)(2), effective 1/1/66.
In 1956, ch. 462, Sec. 208(d)(4), added references to section 6421(f)(2), effective 6/29/56.
—ch. 160, Sec. 4(i), added references to section 6420(e)(2).

Sec. 7605. Time and place of examination.
(a) Time and place.

The time and place of examination pursuant to the provisions of section 6420(e)(2), 6421(g)(2), 6427(j)(2), or 7602 shall be such time and place as may be fixed by the Secretary and as are reasonable under the circumstances. In the case of a summons under authority of paragraph (2) of section 7602, or under the corresponding authority of section 6420(e)(2), 6421(g)(2), or 6427(j)(2), the date fixed for appearance before the Secretary shall not be less than 10 days from the date of the summons.

(b) Restrictions on examination of taxpayer.

No taxpayer shall be subjected to unnecessary examination or investigations, and only one inspection of a taxpayer's books of account shall be made for each taxable year unless the taxpayer requests otherwise or unless the Secretary, after investigation, notifies the taxpayer in writing that an additional inspection is necessary.

(c) Cross reference.

For provisions restricting church tax inquiries and examinations, see section 7611.

In 1988, P.L. 100-647, Sec. 1017(c)(9), substituted "6421(g)(2)" for "6421(f)(2)" in subsec. (a), effective for gasoline removed (as defined in section 4082 of the Internal Revenue Code of 1986, as amended by Sec. 1703(a) of P.L. 99-514) after 12/31/87.
In 1986, P.L. 99-514, Sec. 1703(e)(2)(G), substituted "section 6427(j)(2)" for "section 6427(i)(2)" in subsec. (a), effective for gasoline removed (as defined in section 4082 of the Internal Revenue Code of 1986, as amended by Sec. 1703(a) of this Act) after 12/31/87.
In 1984, P.L. 98-369, Sec. 911(d)(2)(G), substituted "6427(i)(2)" for "6427(h)(2)" in subsec. (a), effective 8/1/84.
—P.L. 98-369, Sec. 1033(c)(1), amended subsec. (c), effective for inquiries and examinations begin. after 12/31/84.
Prior to amendment, subsec. (c) read as follows:
"(c) Restriction on examination of churches.
"No examination of the books of account of a church or convention or association of churches shall be made to determine whether such organization may be engaged in the carrying on of an unrelated trade or business or may be otherwise engaged in activities which may be subject to tax under part III of subchapter F of chapter 1 of this title (sec. 511 and following, relating to taxation of business income of exempt organizations) unless the Secretary (such officer being no lower than a principal internal revenue officer for an internal revenue region) believes that such organization may be so engaged and so notifies the organization in advance of the examination. No examination of the religious activities of such an organization shall be made except to the extent necessary to determine whether such organization is a church or a convention or association of churches, and no examination of the books of account of such an organization shall be made other than to the extent necessary to determine the amount of tax imposed by this title."
In 1983, P.L. 97-424, Sec. 515(b)(12), deleted "6424(d)(2)," after "6421(f)(2)," each place it appeared in subsec. (a), effective for articles sold after 1/6/83.
In 1980, P.L. 96-223, Sec. 232(d)(4)(E), substituted "6427(h)(2)" for "6427(g)(2)" in subsec. (a), effective 1/1/79.

Miscellaneous provisions

In 1978, P.L. 95-599, Sec. 505(c)(5), substituted "6427(g)(2)" for "6427(f)(2)" in subsec. (a), effective 1/1/79.
In 1976, P.L. 94-530, Sec. 1(c)(6), substituted "6427(f)(2)" for "6427(e)(2)" in subsec. (a), effective 10/1/76.
—P.L. 94-455, Sec. 1906(b)(13)(A), substituted "Secretary" for "Secretary or his delegate" each place it appeared in Code Sec. 7605, effective 2/1/77.
In 1970, P.L. 91-258, Sec. 207(d)(9), added "6427(e)(2)" to the first sentence of subsec. (a), and substituted "6424(d)(2), or 6427(e)(2)" for "or 6424(d)(2)" in the second of subsec. (a), effective 7/1/70.
In 1969, P.L. 91-172, Sec. 121(f), added subsec. (c), effective for tax. yrs. begin after 12/31/69.
In 1965, P.L. 89-44, Sec. 202(c)(4), added references to section 6424(d)(2) in subsec. (a), effective 1/1/66.
In 1956, ch. 462, Sec. 208(d)(4), added references to section 6421(f)(2) in subsec. (a), effective 6/29/56.
—ch. 160, Sec. 4(i), added references to section 6420(e)(2) in the second sentence.

Sec. 7606. Entry of premises for examination of taxable objects.
(a) Entry during day.

The Secretary may enter, in the daytime, any building or place where any articles or objects subject to tax are made, produced, or kept, so far as it may be necessary for the purpose of examining said articles or objects.

(b) Entry at night.

When such premises are open at night, the Secretary may enter them while so open, in the performance of his official duties.

(c) Penalties.

For penalty for refusal to permit entry or examination, see section 7342.

In 1976, P.L. 94-455, Sec. 1906(b)(13)(A), substituted "Secretary" for "Secretary or his delegate" each place it appeared in Code Sec. 7606, effective 2/1/77.

Sec. 7607. Repealed.

In 1984, P.L. 98-573, Sec. 213(b)(1), repealed Code Sec. 7607, effective 10/15/84.
Prior to repeal, Code Sec. 7607 read as follows:
"SEC. 7607. ADDITIONAL AUTHORITY FOR BUREAU OF CUSTOMS.
"Officers of the customs (as defined in section 401(1) of the Tariff Act of 1930, as amended; 19 U.S.C., sec. 1401(1)), may—
"(1) carry firearms, execute and serve search warrants and arrest warrants, and serve subpoenas and summonses issued under the authority of the United States, and
"(2) make arrests without warrant for violations of any law of the United States relating to narcotic drugs (as defined in section 102(16) of the Controlled Substances Act) or marihuana (as defined in section 102(15) of the Controlled Substances Act) where the violation is committed in the presence of the person making the arrest or where such person has reasonable grounds to believe that the person to be arrested has committed or is committing such violation."
—P.L. 98-473, Sec. 320(b), also repealed Code Sec. 7607.
In 1970, P.L. 91-513, Sec. 1102(g), amended Code Sec. 7607, effective 5/1/71.
Prior to amendment, Code Sec. 7607 read as follows:
"The Commissioner, Deputy Commissioner, Assistant to the Commissioner, and agents, of the Bureau of Narcotics of the Department of the Treasury, and officers of the customs (as defined in section 401(1) of the Tariff Act of 1930, as amended; 19 U. S. C., sec. 1401(1)), may—
"(1) carry firearms, execute and serve search warrants and arrest warrants, and serve subpoenas and summonses issued under the authority of the United States, and
"(2) make arrests without warrant for violations of any law of the United States relating to narcotic drugs (as defined in section 4731) or marihuana (as defined in section 4761) where the violation is committed in the presence of the person making the arrest or where such person has reasonable grounds to believe that the person to be arrested has committed or is committing such violation."
In 1956, July 18, 1956, ch. 629, title I, Sec. 104(a), added Code Sec 7607, effective 7/19/56.

Sec. 7608. Authority of internal revenue enforcement officers.
(a) Enforcement of subtitle E and other laws pertaining to liquor, tobacco, and firearms.

Any investigator, agent, or other internal revenue officer by whatever term designated, whom the Secretary charges with the duty of enforcing any of the criminal, seizure, or forfeiture provisions of subtitle E or of any other law of the

Miscellaneous provisions   Code Sec. 7608(c)(4)(B)(iv)

United States pertaining to the commodities subject to tax under such subtitle for the enforcement of which the Secretary is responsible may—

(1) carry firearms;

(2) execute and serve search warrants and arrest warrants, and serve subpoenas and summonses issued under authority of the United States;

(3) in respect to the performance of such duty, make arrests without warrant for any offense against the United States committed in his presence, or for any felony cognizable under the laws of the United States if he has reasonable grounds to believe that the person to be arrested has committed, or is committing, such felony; and

(4) in respect to the performance of such duty, make seizures of property subject to forfeiture to the United States.

(b) Enforcement of laws relating to internal revenue other than subtitle E.

(1) Any criminal investigator of the Intelligence Division of the Internal Revenue Service whom the Secretary charges with the duty of enforcing any of the criminal provisions of the internal revenue laws, any other criminal provisions of law relating to internal revenue for the enforcement of which the Secretary is responsible, or any other law for which the Secretary has delegated investigatory authority to the Internal Revenue Service, is, in the performance of his duties, authorized to perform the functions described in paragraph (2).

(2) The functions authorized under this subsection to be performed by an officer referred to in paragraph (1) are—

(A) to execute and serve search warrants and arrest warrants, and serve subpoenas and summonses issued under authority of the United States;

(B) to make arrests without warrant for any offense against the United States relating to the internal revenue laws committed in his presence, or for any felony cognizable under such laws if he has reasonable grounds to believe that the person to be arrested has committed or is committing any such felony; and

(C) to make seizures of property subject to forfeiture under the internal revenue laws.

(c) Rules relating to undercover operations.

(1) Certification required for exemption of undercover operations from certain laws. With respect to any undercover investigative operation of the Internal Revenue Service (hereinafter in this subsection referred to as the "Service") which is necessary for the detection and prosecution of offenses under the internal revenue laws, any other criminal provisions of law relating to internal revenue, or any other law for which the Secretary has delegated investigatory authority to the Internal Revenue Service—

(A) sums authorized to be appropriated for the Service may be used—

(i) to purchase property, buildings, and other facilities, and to lease space, within the United States, the District of Columbia, and the territories and possessions of the United States without regard to—

(I) sections 1341 and 3324 of title 31, United States Code,

(II) sections 11(a) and 22 of title 41, United States Code,

(III) section 255 of title 41, United States Code,

(IV) section 8141 of title 40, United States Code, and

(V) section 254(a) and (c) of title 41, United States Code, and

(ii) to establish or to acquire proprietary corporations or business entities as part of the undercover operation, and to operate such corporations or business entities on a commercial basis, without regard to sections 9102 and 9103 of title 31, United States Code;

(B) sums authorized to be appropriated for the Service and the proceeds from the undercover operations may be deposited in banks or other financial institutions without regard to the provisions of section 648 of title 18, United States Code, and section 3302 of title 31, United States Code, and

(C) the proceeds from the undercover operation may be used to offset necessary and reasonable expenses incurred in such operation without regard to the provisions of section 3302 of title 31, United States Code.

This paragraph shall apply only upon the written certification of the Commissioner of Internal Revenue (or, if designated by the Commissioner, the Deputy Commissioner or an Assistant Commissioner of Internal Revenue) that any action authorized by subparagraph (A), (B), or (C) is necessary for the conduct of such undercover operation.

(2) Liquidation of corporations and business entities. If a corporation or business entity established or acquired as part of an undercover operation under subparagraph (B) of paragraph (1) with a net value over $50,000 is to be liquidated, sold, or otherwise disposed of, the Service, as much in advance as the Commissioner or his delegate determines is practicable, shall report the circumstances to the Secretary. The proceeds of the liquidation, sale, or other disposition, after obligations are met, shall be deposited in the Treasury of the United States as miscellaneous receipts.

(3) Deposit of proceeds. As soon as the proceeds from an undercover investigative operation with respect to which an action is authorized and carried out under subparagraphs (B) and (C) of paragraph (1) are no longer necessary for the conduct of such operation, such proceeds or the balance of such proceeds remaining at the time shall be deposited into the Treasury of the United States as miscellaneous receipts.

(4) Audits.

(A) The Service shall conduct a detailed financial audit of each undercover investigative operation which is closed in each fiscal year; and

(i) submit the results of the audit in writing to the Secretary; and

(ii) not later than 180 days after such undercover operation is closed, submit a report to the Congress concerning such audit.

(B) The Service shall also submit a report annually to the Congress specifying as to its undercover investigative operations—

(i) the number, by programs, of undercover investigative operations pending as of the end of the 1-year period for which such report is submitted;

(ii) the number, by programs, of undercover investigative operations commenced in the 1-year period for which such report is submitted;

(iii) the number, by programs, of undercover investigative operations closed in the 1-year period for which such report is submitted, and

(iv) the following information with respect to each undercover investigative operation pending as of the end of the 1-year period for which such report is submitted or closed during such 1-year period—

(I) the date the operation began and the date of the certification referred to in the last sentence of paragraph (1),

(II) the total expenditures under the operation and the amount and use of the proceeds from the operation,

(III) a detailed description of the operation including the potential violation being investigated and whether the operation is being conducted under grand jury auspices, and

(IV) the results of the operation including the results of criminal proceedings.

(5) **Definitions.** For purposes of paragraph (4)—

(A) Closed. The term "closed" means the date on which the later of the following occurs;

(i) all criminal proceedings (other than appeals) are concluded, or

(ii) covert activities are concluded, whichever occurs later.

(B) Employees. The term "employees" has the meaning given such term by section 2105 of title 5, United States Code.

(C) Undercover investigative operation. The term "undercover investigative operation" means any undercover investigative operation of the Service; except that, for purposes of subparagraphs (A) and (C) of paragraph (4), such term only includes an operation which is exempt from section 3302 or 9102 of title 31, United States Code.

In 2008, P.L. 110-343, Sec. 401(a)DivC, deleted para. (c)(6), effective for operations conducted after 10/3/2008.
Prior to deletion, para. (c)(6) read as follows:
"(6) Application of section.
"The provisions of this subsection—
"(A) shall apply after November 17, 1988, and before January 1, 1990, and
"(B) shall apply after the date of the enactment of this paragraph and before January 1, 2008.
"All amounts expended pursuant to this subsection during the period described in subparagraph (B) shall be recovered to the extent possible, and deposited in the Treasury of the United States as miscellaneous receipts, before January 1, 2008."
In 2006, P.L. 109-432, Sec. 121, substituted "2008" for "2007" each place it appeared in para. (c)(6), enacted 12/20/2006.
In 2005, P.L. 109-135, Sec. 304, substituted "January 1, 2007" for "January 1, 2006" each place it appeared in para. (c)(6), effective 12/21/2005.
In 2003, P.L. 108-178, Sec. 4(e), substituted "title 40, United States Code" for "title 40" in subclause (c)(1)(A)(i)(IV), effective 8/21/2002.
In 2002, P.L. 107-217, Sec. 3(f), substituted "section 8141 of title 40" for "section 34 of title 40, United States Code" in subclause (c)(1)(A)(i)(IV), effective 8/21/2002.
In 2000, P.L. 106-554, Sec. 1(a)(7), [which enacted into law Sec. 301 of P.L. 106-554] of this Act, reads as follows:
"Section 3003(a)(1) of the Federal Reports Elimination and Sunset Act of 1995 (31 U.S.C. 1113 note) shall not apply to any report required to be submitted under any of the following provisions of law:"

* * * * * *

"15(B) Section 7608"
—P.L. 106-554, Sec. 1(a)(7), [which enacted into law Sec. 303 of P.L. 106-554] substituted "January 1, 2006" for "January 1, 2001" in subsec. (c) and subpara. (c)(6)(B), effective 12/21/2000.
In 1998, P.L. 105-206, Sec. 1103(e)(4), deleted "or of the Internal Security Division" after "Intelligence Division" in para. (b)(1), effective 7/22/98.
In 1996, P.L. 104-316, Sec. 113, deleted "and the Comptroller General of the United States" after "Secretary" in para. (c)(2), effective 10/19/96.
—P.L. 104-168, Sec. 1205(a), amended Sec. 7601(c)(3) of P.L. 100-690, see below, the effective date for changes made by Sec. 7601(c)(1) and (2) of P.L. 100-690, effective date of enactment. The effect of this amendment is to reinstate the changes made by para. (b)(1) and the addition of subsec. (c) made by Sec. 7601(c) of P.L. 100-690, see below.
Prior to amendment, Sec. 7601(c)(3) of P.L. 100-690 [as amended by Sec. 3301(a) of P.L. 101-647, see below] read as follows:
"(3) Effective date.—The amendments made by this subsection [Sec. 7601(c)] shall take effect on the date of the enactment of this Act [11/18/88] and shall

cease to apply after December 31, 1991; and all amounts expended pursuant to such amendments shall be recovered to the extent possible, and deposited in the Treasury of the United States as miscellaneous receipts, before January 1, 1992."
—P.L. 104-168, Sec. 1205(b), added para. (c)(6)... Sec. 1205(c)(1)(A), deleted "preceding the period" following "1-year period" in clause (c)(4)(B)(ii)... Sec. 1205(c)(1)(B), deleted "and" at the end of clause (c)(4)(B)(ii)... Sec. 1205(c)(1)(C), amended clause (c)(4)(B)(iii) and added clause (c)(4)(B)(iv)... Sec. 1205(c)(2), amended subpara. (c)(5)(C), effective 7/30/96.
Prior to amendment, clause (c)(4)(B)(iii) read as follows:
"(iii) the number, by programs, of undercover investigative operations closed in the 1-year period preceding the period for which such report is submitted and, with respect to each such closed undercover operation, the results obtained and any civil claims made with respect thereto."
Prior to amendment, subpara. (c)(5)(C) read as follows:
"(C) Undercover investigative operation. The terms 'undercover investigative operation' and 'undercover operation' mean any undercover investigative operation of the Service—
"(i) in which—
"(I) the gross receipts (excluding interest earned) exceed $50,000; or
"(II) expenditures, both recoverable and nonrecoverable (other than expenditures for salaries of employees, exceed $150,000; and
"(ii) which is exempt from section 3302 or 9102 of title 31, United States Code.
Clauses (i) and (ii) shall not apply with respect to the report required under subparagraph (B) of paragraph (4)."
In 1990, P.L. 101-647, Sec. 3301(a), amended Sec. 7601(c)(3) of P.L. 100-690, the effective date for changes made by Sec. 7601(c) of P.L. 100-690, by substituting "1990" for "1989" and "1992" for "1991", see below.
—P.L. 101-647, Sec. 3301(b), of this Act provides:
"(b) GAO Study.
"(1) In general. The Comptroller General of the United States shall conduct a study of undercover investigative operations of the Internal Revenue Service which were conducted using any authority provided in subsection (c) of section 7608 of the Internal Revenue Code of 1986. The study shall include an evaluation of—
"(A) the use of the proceeds of such operations,
"(B) the results of such operations, and
"(C) the financial audits conducted by the Internal Revenue Service under such subsection.
"(2) Report. Not later than July 1, 1991, the Comptroller General shall submit to the Committee on Ways and Means of the House of Representatives and the Committee on Finance of the Senate the results of the study required in paragraph (1)."
—P.L. 101-508, Sec. 11704(a)(32), deleted the comma after "operations", in subpara. (c)(1)(B) [reproduced in note to P.L. 100-690, see below]... Sec. 11704(a)(33)(A), substituted "interest" for "interested", in subclause (c)(5)(C)(i)(I) [reproduced in note to P.L. 100-690, see below]... Sec. 11704(a)(33)(B), substituted "title 31" for "title 3", in clause (c)(5)(C)(ii), [reproduced in note to P.L. 100-690, see below], effective 11/5/90.
In 1988, P.L. 100-690, Sec. 7601(c)(1), substituted a comma for "or" before "any other" in para. (b)(1)... Sec. 7601(c)(1), added ", or any other law for which the Secretary has delegated investigatory authority to the Internal Revenue Service," after "responsible" in para. (b)(1)... Sec. 7601(c)(2), added subsec. (c), effective 11/18/88 [as amended by Sec. 3301(a) of P.L. 101-647, and Sec. 1205(a) of P.L. 104-168, see above].
In 1976, P.L. 94-455, Sec. 1906(b)(13)(A), substituted "Secretary" for "Secretary or his delegate" each place it appeared in Code Sec. 7608, effective 2/1/77.
In 1962, P.L. 87-863, Sec. 6(a), redesignated existing provisions as subsec. (a), added heading of subsec. (a) and added subsec. (b), effective 10/24/62.
In 1958, P.L. 85-859, Sec. 204(14), added Code Sec. 7608, effective 9/3/58.

Sec. 7609. Special procedures for third-party summonses.

(a) Notice.

(1) In general. If any summons to which this section applies requires the giving of testimony on or relating to, the production of any portion of records made or kept on or relating to, or the production of any computer software source code (as defined in 7612(d)(2)) with respect to, any person (other than the person summoned) who is identified in the summons, then notice of the summons shall be given to any person so identified within 3 days of the day on which such service is made, but no later than the 23rd day before the day fixed in the summons as the day upon which such records are to be examined. Such notice shall be accompanied by a copy of the summons which has been served and shall contain an explanation of the right under subsection (b)(2) to bring a proceeding to quash the summons.

(2) Sufficiency of notice. Such notice shall be sufficient if, on or before such third day, such notice is served in the manner provided in section 7603 (relating to service of summons) upon the person entitled to notice, or is mailed by certified or registered mail to the last known address of such person, or, in the absence of a last known address, is left with the person summoned. If such notice is mailed, it shall be sufficient if mailed to the last known address of the person entitled to notice or, in the case of notice to the Secretary under section 6903 of the existence of a fiduciary relationship, to the last known address of the fiduciary of such person, even if such person or fiduciary is then deceased, under a legal disability, or no longer in existence.

(3) **Nature of summons.** Any summons to which this subsection applies (and any summons in aid of collection described in subsection (c)(2)(D)) shall identify the taxpayer to whom the summons relates or the other person to whom the records pertain and shall provide such other information as will enable the person summoned to locate the records required under the summons.

(b) Right to intervene; right to proceeding to quash.

(1) **Intervention.** Notwithstanding any other law or rule of law, any person who is entitled to notice of a summons under subsection (a) shall have the right to intervene in any proceeding with respect to the enforcement of such summons under section 7604.

(2) **Proceeding to quash.**

(A) In general. Notwithstanding any other law or rule of law, any person who is entitled to notice of a summons under subsection (a) shall have the right to begin a proceeding to quash such summons not later than the 20th day after the day such notice is given in the manner provided in subsection (a)(2). In any such proceeding, the Secretary may seek to compel compliance with the summons.

(B) Requirement of notice to person summoned and to Secretary. If any person begins a proceeding under subparagraph (A) with respect to any summons, not later than the close of the 20-day period referred to in subparagraph (A) such person shall mail by registered or certified mail a copy of the petition to the person summoned and to such office as the Secretary may direct in the notice referred to in subsection (a)(1).

(C) Intervention; etc. Notwithstanding any other law or rule of law, the person summoned shall have the right to intervene in any proceeding under subparagraph (A). Such person shall be bound by the decision in such proceeding (whether or not the person intervenes in such proceeding).

(c) Summons to which section applies.

(1) **In general.** Except as provided in paragraph (2), this section shall apply to any summons issued under paragraph (2) of section 7602(a) or under section 6420(e)(2), 6421(g)(2), 6427(j)(2), or 7612.

(2) **Exceptions.** This section shall not apply to any summons—

(A) served on the person with respect to whose liability the summons is issued, or any officer or employee of such person;

(B) issued to determine whether or not records of the business transactions or affairs of an identified person have been made or kept;

(C) issued solely to determine the identity of any person having a numbered account (or similar arrangement) with a bank or other institution described in section 7603(b)(2)(A);

(D) issued in aid of the collection of—

(i) an assessment made or judgment rendered against the person with respect to whose liability the summons is issued; or

(ii) the liability at law or in equity of any transferee or fiduciary of any person referred to in clause (i); or

(E)(i) issued by a criminal investigator of the Internal Revenue Service in connection with the investigation of an offense connected with the administration or enforcement of the internal revenue laws; and

(ii) served on any person who is not a third-party recordkeeper (as defined in section 7603(b)).

(3) **John Doe and certain other summonses.** Subsection (a) shall not apply to any summons described in subsection (f) or (g).

(4) **Records.** For purposes of this section, the term "records" includes books, papers, and other data.

(d) Restriction on examination of records.

No examination of any records required to be produced under a summons as to which notice is required under subsection (a) may be made—

(1) before the close of the 23rd day after the day notice with respect to the summons is given in the manner provided in subsection (a)(2), or

(2) where a proceeding under subsection (b)(2)(A) was begun within the 20-day period referred to in such subsection and the requirements of subsection (b)(2)(B) have been met, except in accordance with an order of the court having jurisdiction of such proceeding or with the consent of the person beginning the proceeding to quash.

(e) Suspension of statute of limitations.

(1) **Subsection (b) action.** If any person takes any action as provided in subsection (b) and such person is the person with respect to whose liability the summons is issued (or is the agent, nominee, or other person acting under the direction or control of such person), then the running of any period of limitations under section 6501 (relating to the assessment and collection of tax) or under section 6531 (relating to criminal prosecutions) with respect to such person shall be suspended for the period during which a proceeding, and appeals therein, with respect to the enforcement of such summons is pending.

(2) **Suspension after 6 months of service of summons.** In the absence of the resolution of the summoned party's response to the summons, the running of any period of limitations under section 6501 or under section 6531 with respect to any person with respect to whose liability the summons is issued (other than a person taking action as provided in subsection (b)) shall be suspended for the period—

(A) beginning on the date which is 6 months after the service of such summons, and

(B) ending with the final resolution of such response.

(f) Additional requirement in the case of a John Doe summons.

Any summons described in subsection (c)(1) which does not identify the person with respect to whose liability the summons is issued may be served only after a court proceeding in which the Secretary establishes that—

(1) the summons relates to the investigation of a particular person or ascertainable group or class of persons,

(2) there is a reasonable basis for believing that such person or group or class of persons may fail or may have failed to comply with any provision of any internal revenue law, and

(3) the information sought to be obtained from the examination of the records or testimony (and the identity of the

person or persons with respect to whose liability the summons is issued) is not readily available from other sources.

(g) Special exception for certain summonses.

A summons is described in this subsection if, upon petition by the Secretary, the court determines, on the basis of the facts and circumstances alleged, that there is reasonable cause to believe the giving of notice may lead to attempts to conceal, destroy, or alter records relevant to the examination, to prevent the communication of information from other persons through intimidation, bribery, or collusion, or to flee to avoid prosecution, testifying, or production of records.

(h) Jurisdiction of District Court; etc.

(1) Jurisdiction. The United States district court for the district within which the person to be summoned resides or is found shall have jurisdiction to hear and determine any proceeding brought under subsection (b)(2), (f), or (g). An order denying the petition shall be deemed a final order which may be appealed.

(2) Special rule for proceedings under subsections (f) and (g). The determinations required to be made under subsections (f) and (g) shall be made ex parte and shall be made solely on the petition and supporting affidavits.

(i) Duty of summoned party.

(1) Recordkeeper must assemble records and be prepared to produce records. On receipt of a summons to which this section applies for the production of records, the summoned party shall proceed to assemble the records requested, or such portion thereof as the Secretary may prescribe, and shall be prepared to produce the records pursuant to the summons on the day on which the records are to be examined.

(2) Secretary may give summoned party certificate. The Secretary may issue a certificate to the summoned party that the period prescribed for beginning a proceeding to quash a summons has expired and that no such proceeding began within such period, or that the taxpayer consents to the examination.

(3) Protection for summoned party who discloses. Any summoned party, or agent or employee thereof, making a disclosure of records or testimony pursuant to this section in good faith reliance on the certificate of the Secretary or an order of a court requiring production of records or the giving of such testimony shall not be liable to any customer or other person for such disclosure.

(4) Notice of suspension of statute of limitations in the case of a John Doe summons. In the case of a summons described in subsection (f) with respect to which any period of limitations has been suspended under subsection (e)(2), the summoned party shall provide notice of such suspension to any person described in subsection (f).

(j) Use of summons not required.

Nothing in this section shall be construed to limit the Secretary's ability to obtain information, other than by summons, through formal or informal procedures authorized by sections 7601 and 7602.

In 2005, P.L. 109-135, Sec. 408(a)(1), added "or" at the end of subpara. (c)(2)(D), substituted a period for "; or" at the end of subpara. (c)(2)(E), and deleted subpara. (c)(2)(F)... Sec. 408(a)(2), redesignated para. (c)(3) as para. (c)(4) and added para. (c)(3), effective for summonses served after 7/22/98 as if included in Sec. 3415 of the IRS Restructuring and Reform Act of 1998, P.L. 105-206.
Prior to deletion, subpara. (c)(2)(F) read as follows:
"(F) described in subsection (f) or (g)."

In 1998, P.L. 105-206, Sec. 3415(a), amended para. (a)(1)... Sec. 3415(b), added subsec. (j)... Sec. 3415(c)(1), deleted paras. (a)(3) and (4), redesignated para. (a)(5) as para. (a)(3), and substituted "subsection (c)(2)(D)" for "subsection (c)(2)(B)" in newly redesignated para. (a)(3)... Sec. 3415(c)(2), amended subsec. (c)... Sec. 3415(c)(3), substituted "summoned party's response to the summons"

for "third-party recordkeeper's response to the summons described in subsection (c), or the summoned party's response to a summons described in subsection (f)" in para. (e)(2)... Sec. 3415(c)(4)(A), substituted "described in subsection (c)(1)" for "described in subsection (c)" in subsec. (f)... Sec. 3415(c)(4)(B), added "or testimony" after "records" in para. (f)(3)... Sec. 3415(c)(5), substituted "A summons is described in this section if" for "In the case of any summons described in subsection (c), the provisions of subsections (a)(1) and (b) shall not apply if" in subsec. (g)... Sec. 3415(c)(6)(A), deleted "third-party recordkeeper and" after "Duty of" in the heading of subsec. (i)... Sec. 3415(c)(6)(B), substituted "to which this section applies for the production of records, the summoned party" for "described in subsection (c), the third-party recordkeeper" in para. (i)(1)... Sec. 3415(c)(6)(C)(i), substituted "summoned party" for "recordkeeper" in the heading of para. (i)(2)... Sec. 3415(c)(6)(C)(ii), substituted "the summoned party" for "the third-party recordkeeper" in para. (i)(2)... Sec. 3415(c)(6)(D), amended para. (i)(3), effective for summonses served after 7/22/98.
Prior to amendment, para. (a)(1) read as follows:
"(1) In general. If—
"(A) any summons described in subsection (c) is served on any person who is a third-party recordkeeper, and
"(B) the summons requires the production of any portion of records made or kept of the business transactions or affairs of any person (other than the person summoned) who is identified in the description of the records contained in the summons,
then notice of the summons shall be given to any person so identified within 3 days of the day on which such service is made, but no later than the 23rd day before the day fixed in the summons as the day upon which such records are to be examined. Such notice shall be accompanied by a copy of the summons which has been served and shall contain an explanation of the right under subsection (b)(2) to bring a proceeding to quash the summons."
Prior to deletion, paras. (a)(3) and (4) read as follows:
"(3) Third-party recordkeeper defined. For purposes of this subsection, the term 'third-party recordkeeper' means—
"(A) any mutual savings bank, cooperative bank, domestic building and loan association, or other savings institution chartered and supervised as a savings and loan or similar association under Federal or State law, any bank (as defined in section 581), or any credit union (within the meaning of section 501(c)(14)(A));
"(B) any consumer reporting agency (as defined under section 603(d) of the Fair Credit Reporting Act (15 U.S.C. 1681a(f)));
"(C) any person extending credit through the use of credit cards or similar devices;
"(D) any broker (as defined in section 3(a)(4) of the Securities Exchange Act of 1934 (15 U.S.C. 78c(a)(4)));
"(E) any attorney;
"(F) any accountant;
"(G) any barter exchange (as defined in section 6045(c)(3));
"(H) any regulated investment company (as defined in section 851) and any agent of such regulated investment company when acting as an agent thereof; and
"(I) any enrolled agent."
"(4) Exceptions. Paragraph (1) shall not apply to any summons—
"(A) served on the person with respect to whose liability the summons is issued, or any officer or employee of such person,
"(B) to determine whether or not records of the business transactions or affairs of an identified person have been made or kept, or
"(C) described in subsection (f)."
Prior to amendment, subsec. (c) read as follows:
"(c) Summons to which section applies.
"(1) In general. Except as provided in paragraph (2), a summons is described in this subsection if it is issued under paragraph (2) of section 7602(a) or under section 6420(e)(2), 6421(g)(2), or 6427(j)(2) and requires the production of records.
"(2) Exceptions. A summons shall not be treated as described in this subsection if—
"(A) it is solely to determine the identity of any person having a numbered account (or similar arrangement) with a bank or other institution described in subsection (a)(3)(A), or
"(B) it is in aid of the collection of—
"(i) the liability of any person against whom an assessment has been made or judgment rendered, or
"(ii) the liability at law or in equity of any transferee or fiduciary of any person referred to in clause (i).
"(3) Records; certain related testimony. For purposes of this section—
"(A) the term 'records' includes books, papers, or other data, and
"(B) a summons requiring the giving of testimony relating to records shall be treated as a summons requiring the production of such records."
Prior to amendment, para. (i)(3) read as follows:
"(3) Protection for recordkeeper who discloses. Any third-party recordkeeper, or agent or employee thereof, making a disclosure of records pursuant to this section in good-faith reliance on the certificate of the Secretary or an order of a court requiring production of records shall not be liable to any customer or other person for such disclosure."

In 1996, P.L. 104-168, Sec. 1001(a), deleted "and" at the end of subpara. (a)(3)(G), substituted "; and" for the period at the end of subpara. (a)(3)(H) and added subpara. (a)(3)(I), effective for summonses issued after 7/30/96.

In 1988, P.L. 100-647, Sec. 1015(1)(1)(A) and (B), added "or the summoned party's response to a summons described in section (f)" after "the summons described in subsection (c)" and substituted "the summons is issued" for "the summons is issued other" in subsec. (e)(2)... Sec. 1015(1)(2)(A), substituted "the summoned party" for "the third-party recordkeeper" in para. (i)(4)... Sec.

Miscellaneous provisions   Code Sec. 7611(a)(2)(A)

1015(1)(2)(B), added "and summoned party" after "recordkeeper" in the subsec. (i) heading, effective 11/10/88.

— P.L. 100-647, Sec. 1017(c)(9), substituted "6421(g)(2)" for "6421(f)(2)" in para. (c)(1), effective for gasoline removed (as defined in Code Sec. 4082, as amended by Sec. 1703 of P.L. 99-514) after 12/31/87.

In **1986**, P.L. 99-514, Sec. 656(a), deleted "and" at the end of subpara. (a)(3)(F), substituted "; and" for the period at the end of subpara. (a)(3)(G), and added subpara. (a)(3)(H), effective for summonses served after 10/22/86.

— P.L. 99-514, Sec. 1561(a), amended subsec. (e) . . . Sec. 1561(b), added para. (i)(4), effective on 10/22/86.

Prior to amendment, subsec. (e) read as follows:

"(e) Suspension of statute of limitations.

"If any person takes any action as provided in subsection (b) and such person is the person with respect to whose liability the summons is issued (or is the agent, nominee, or other person acting under the direction or control of such person), then the running of any period of limitations under section 6501 (relating to the assessment and collection of tax) or under section 6531 (relating to criminal prosecutions) with respect to such person shall be suspended for the period during which a proceeding, and appeals therein, with respect to the enforcement of such summons is pending."

— P.L. 99-514, Sec. 1703(e)(2)(G), substituted "6427(j)(2)" for "6427(i)(2)", effective for gasoline removed (as defined in Code Sec. 4082, as amended by Sec. 1703 of this Act) after 12/31/87.

In **1984**, P.L. 98-620, Sec. 402(28)(D), deleted para. (h)(3), effective 11/8/84 except for cases pending on 11/8/84.

Prior to deletion para. (h)(3) read as follows:

"(3) Priority. Except as to cases the court considers of greater importance, a proceeding brought for the enforcement of any summons, or a proceeding under this section, and appeals, takes precedence on the docket over all other cases and shall be assigned for hearing and decided at the earliest practicable date."

— P.L. 98-369, Sec. 714(i), substituted "section 7602(a)" for "section 7602" in para. (c)(1), effective 9/4/82.

— P.L. 98-369, Sec. 911(d)(2)(G), substituted "6427(i)(2)" for "6427(h)(2)" in para. (c)(1), effective 8/1/84.

In **1983**, P.L. 97-424, Sec. 515(b)(12), deleted "6424(d)(2)," after "6421(f)(2)," in para. (c)(1), effective for articles sold after 1/6/83.

In **1982**, P.L. 97-248, Sec. 311(b), deleted "and" at the end of subpara. (a)(3)(E), substituted "; and" for the period at the end of subpara. (a)(3)(F), and added subpara. (a)(3)(G), effective for summonses served after 12/31/82.

— P.L. 97-248, Sec. 331(a), amended para. (b)(2) . . . Sec. 331(b), amended subsec. (d) . . . Sec. 331(c), amended subsec. (h) . . . Sec. 331(d)(1)(A), and (B), substituted "23rd day" for "14th day" in para. (a)(1) and amended the last sentence of para. (a)(1) . . . Sec. 331(d)(2), amended the heading of subsec. (b), effective for summonses served after 12/31/82.

Prior to amendment, para. (b)(2) read as follows:

"(2) Right to stay compliance. Notwithstanding any other law or rule of law, any person who is entitled to notice of a summons under subsection (a) shall have the right to stay compliance with the summons if, not later than the 14th day after the day such notice is given in the manner provided in subsection (a)(2)—

"(A) notice in writing is given to the person summoned not to comply with the summons, and

"(B) a copy of such notice not to comply with the summons is mailed by registered or certified mail to such person and to such office as the Secretary may direct in the notice referred to in subsection (a)(1)."

Prior to amendment, subsec. (d) read as follows:

"(d) Restriction on examination of records.

"No examination of any records required to be produced under a summons as to which notice is required under subsection (a) may be made —

"(1) before the expiration of the 14-day period allowed for the notice not to comply under subsection (b)(2), or

"(2) when the requirements of subsection (b)(2) have been met, except in accordance with an order issued by a court of competent jurisdiction authorizing examination of such records or with the consent of the person staying compliance."

Prior to amendment, subsec. (h) read as follows:

"(h) Jurisdiction of district court.

"(1) The United States district court for the district within which the person to be summoned resides or is found shall have jurisdiction to hear and determine proceedings brought under subsections (f) or (g). The determinations required to be made under subsections (f) and (g) shall be made ex parte and shall be made solely upon the petition and supporting affidavits. An order denying the petition shall be deemed a final order which may be appealed.

"(2) Except as to cases the court considers of greater importance, a proceeding brought for the enforcement of any summons, or a proceeding under this section, and appeals, take precedence on the docket over all cases and shall be assigned for hearing and decided at the earliest practicable date."

Prior to amendment, the last sentence of para. (a)(1) read as follows:

"Such notice shall be accompanied by a copy of the summons which has been served and shall contain directions for staying compliance with the summons under subsection (b)(2)."

Prior to amendment, the heading for subsec. (b) read as follows:

"(b) Right to intervene; right to stay compliance."

— P.L. 97-248, Sec. 332(a), added subsec. (i), effective for summonses served after 12/31/82.

In **1980**, P.L. 96-223, Sec. 232(d)(4)(E), substituted "6427(h)(2)" for "6427(g)(2)" in para. (c)(1), effective 1/1/79.

In **1978**, P.L. 95-600, Sec. 703(1)(4), substituted "6427(f)(2)" for "6427(e)(2)" in para. (c)(1), effective 10/4/76.

— P.L. 95-599, Sec. 505(c)(6), substituted "6427(g)(2)" for "6427(e)(2)" in para. (c)(1), effective 1/1/79.

In **1976**, P.L. 94-528, Sec. 2(b), changed the effective for amendments made by Sec. 1205(a) of P.L. 94-455, from effective for any summons issued after 12/31/76, to effective for any summons issued after 2/28/77, see below.

— P.L. 94-455, Sec. 1205(a), added Code Sec. 7609, effective [as amended by Sec. 2(b) of P.L. 94-528, see above] for any summons issued after 2/28/77.

Sec. 7610. Fees and costs for witnesses.
(a) In general.

The Secretary shall by regulations establish the rates and conditions under which payment may be made of—

(1) fees and mileage to persons who are summoned to appear before the Secretary, and

(2) reimbursement for such costs that are reasonably necessary which have been directly incurred in searching for, reproducing, or transporting books, papers, records, or other data required to be produced by summons.

(b) Exceptions.

No payment may be made under paragraph (2) of subsection (a) if—

(1) the person with respect to whose liability the summons is issued has a proprietary interest in the books, papers, records or other data required to be produced, or

(2) the person summoned is the person with respect to whose liability the summons is issued or an officer, employee, agent, accountant, or attorney of such person who, at the time the summons is served, is acting as such.

(c) Summons to which section applies.

This section applies with respect to any summons authorized under section 6420(e)(2), 6421(g)(2), 6427(j)(2), or 7602.

In **1988**, P.L. 100-647, Sec. 1017(c)(9), substituted "6421(g)(2)" for "6421(f)(2)" in subsec. (c), effective for gasoline removed (as defined in Code Sec. 4082 as amended by Sec. 1703 of P.L. 99-514) after 12/31/87.

In **1986**, P.L. 99-514, Sec. 1703(e)(2)(G), substituted "6427(j)(2)" for "6427(i)(2)" in subsec. (c), effective for gasoline removed as defined in Code Sec. 4082 as amended by Sec. 1703 of this Act) after 12/31/87.

In **1984**, P.L. 98-369, Sec. 911(d)(2)(G), substituted "6427(i)(2)" for "6427(h)(2)" in subsec. (c), effective 8/1/84.

In **1983**, P.L. 97-424, Sec. 515(b)(12), deleted "6424(d)(2)," after "6421(f)(2)," in subsec. (c), effective for articles sold after 1/6/83.

In **1980**, P.L. 96-223, Sec. 232(d)(4)(E), substituted "6427(h)(2)" for "6427(g)(2)" in subsec. (c), effective 1/1/79.

In **1978**, P.L. 95-599, Sec. 505(c)(6), substituted "6427(g)(2)" for "6427(e)(2)" in subsec. (c), effective 1/1/79.

In **1976**, P.L. 94-528, Sec. 2(b), changed the effective date for amendments made by Sec. 1205(a) of P.L. 94-455, from effective for any summons issued after 12/31/76, to effective for any summons issued after 2/28/77, see below.

— P.L. 94-455, Sec. 1205(a), added Code Sec. 7610, effective [as amended by Sec. 2(b) of P.L. 94-528, see above] for any summons issued after 2/28/77.

Sec. 7611. Restrictions on church tax inquiries and examinations.

(a) Restrictions on inquiries.

(1) In general. The Secretary may begin a church tax inquiry only if—

(A) the reasonable belief requirements of paragraph (2), and

(B) the notice requirements of paragraph (3), have been met.

(2) Reasonable belief requirements. The requirements of this paragraph are met with respect to any church tax inquiry if an appropriate high-level Treasury official reasonably believes (on the basis of facts and circumstances recorded in writing) that the church—

(A) may not be exempt, by reason of its status as a church, from tax under section 501(a), or

3,923

(B) may be carrying on an unrelated trade or business (within the meaning of section 513) or otherwise engaged in activities subject to taxation under this title.

(3) Inquiry notice requirements.
(A) In general. The requirements of this paragraph are met with respect to any church tax inquiry if, before beginning such inquiry, the Secretary provides written notice to the church of the beginning of such inquiry.
(B) Contents of inquiry notice. The notice required by this paragraph shall include—
  (i) an explanation of—
    (I) the concerns which gave rise to such inquiry, and
    (II) the general subject matter of such inquiry, and
  (ii) a general explanation of the applicable—
    (I) administrative and constitutional provisions with respect to such inquiry (including the right to a conference with the Secretary before any examination of church records), and
    (II) provisions of this title which authorize such inquiry or which may be otherwise involved in such inquiry.

(b) Restrictions on examinations.
(1) In general. The Secretary may begin a church tax examination only if the requirements of paragraph (2) have been met and such examination may be made only—
(A) in the case of church records, to the extent necessary to determine the liability for, and the amount of, any tax imposed by this title, and
(B) in the case of religious activities, to the extent necessary to determine whether an organization claiming to be a church is a church for any period.

(2) Notice of examination; opportunity for conference. The requirements of this paragraph are met with respect to any church tax examination if—
(A) at least 15 days before the beginning of such examination, the Secretary provides the notice described in paragraph (3) to both the church and the appropriate regional counsel of the Internal Revenue Service, and
(B) the church has a reasonable time to participate in a conference described in paragraph (3)(A)(iii), but only if the church requests such a conference before the beginning of the examination.

(3) Contents of examination notice, et cetera.
(A) In general. The notice described in this paragraph is a written notice which includes—
  (i) a copy of the church tax inquiry notice provided to the church under subsection (a),
  (ii) a description of the church records and activities which the Secretary seeks to examine,
  (iii) an offer to have a conference between the church and the Secretary in order to discuss, and attempt to resolve, concerns relating to such examination, and
  (iv) a copy of all documents which were collected or prepared by the Internal Revenue Service for use in such examination and the disclosure of which is required by the Freedom of Information Act (5 U.S.C. 552).
(B) Earliest day examination notice may be provided. The examination notice described in subparagraph (A) shall not be provided to the church before the 15th day after the date on which the church tax inquiry notice was provided to the church under subsection (a).
(C) Opinion of regional counsel with respect to examination. Any regional counsel of the Internal Revenue Service who receives an examination notice under paragraph (1) may, within 15 days after such notice is provided, submit to the regional commissioner for the region an advisory objection to the examination.

(4) Examination of records and activities not specified in notice. Within the course of a church tax examination which (at the time the examination begins) meets the requirements of paragraphs (1) and (2), the Secretary may examine any church records or religious activities which were not specified in the examination notice to the extent such examination meets the requirement of subparagraph (A) or (B) of paragraph (1) (whichever applies).

(c) Limitation on period of inquiries and examinations.
(1) Inquiries and examinations must be completed within 2 years.
(A) In general. The Secretary shall complete any church tax status inquiry or examination (and make a final determination with respect thereto) not later than the date which is 2 years after the examination notice date.
(B) Inquiries not followed by examinations. In the case of a church tax inquiry with respect to which there is no examination notice under subsection (b), the Secretary shall complete such inquiry (and make a final determination with respect thereto) not later than the date which is 90 days after the inquiry notice date.

(2) Suspension of 2-year period. The running of the 2-year period described in paragraph (1)(A) and the 90-day period in paragraph (1)(B) shall be suspended—
(A) for any period during which—
  (i) a judicial proceeding brought by the church against the Secretary with respect to the church tax inquiry or examination is pending or being appealed,
  (ii) a judicial proceeding brought by the Secretary against the church (or any official thereof) to compel compliance with any reasonable request of the Secretary in a church tax examination for examination of church records or religious activities is pending or being appealed, or
  (iii) the Secretary is unable to take actions with respect to the church tax inquiry or examination by reason of an order issued in any judicial proceeding brought under section 7609,
(B) for any period in excess of 20 days (but not in excess of 6 months) in which the church or its agents fail to comply with any reasonable request of the Secretary for church records or other information, or
(C) for any period mutually agreed upon by the Secretary and the church.

(d) Limitations on revocation of tax-exempt status, etc.
(1) In general. The Secretary may—
(A) determine that an organization is not a church which—
  (i) is exempt from taxation by reason of section 501(a), or
  (ii) is described in section 170(c), or
(B)(i) send a notice of deficiency of any tax involved in a church tax examination, or
  (ii) in the case of any tax with respect to which subchapter B of chapter 63 (relating to deficiency procedures) does not apply, assess any underpayment of such tax involved in a church tax examination,
only if the appropriate regional counsel of the Internal Revenue Service determines in writing that there has been substantial compliance with the requirements of this section and approves in writing of such revocation, notice of deficiency, or assessment.

Miscellaneous provisions   Code Sec. 7611(i)(3)

(2) Limitations on period of assessment.
  (A) Revocation of tax-exempt status.
    (i) 3-year statute of limitations generally. In the case of any church tax examination with respect to the revocation of tax-exempt status under section 501(a), any tax imposed by chapter 1 (other than section 511) may be assessed, or a proceeding in court for collection of such tax may be begun without assessment, only for the 3 most recent taxable years ending before the examination notice date.
    (ii) 6-year statute of limitations where tax-exempt status revoked. If an organization is not a church exempt from tax under section 501(a) for any of the 3 taxable years described in clause (i), clause (i) shall be applied by substituting "6 most recent taxable years" for "3 most recent taxable years".
  (B) Unrelated business tax. In the case of any church tax examination with respect to the tax imposed by section 511 (relating to unrelated business income), such tax may be assessed, or a proceeding in court for the collection of such tax may be begun without assessment, only with respect to the 6 most recent taxable years ending before the examination notice date.
  (C) Exception where shorter statute of limitations otherwise applicable. Subparagraphs (A) and (B) shall not be construed to increase the period otherwise applicable under subchapter A of chapter 66 (relating to limitations on assessment and collection).

(e) Information not collected in substantial compliance with procedures to stay summons proceeding.
  (1) In general. If there has not been substantial compliance with—
    (A) the notice requirements of subsection (a) or (b),
    (B) the conference requirement described in subsection (b)(3)(A)(iii), or
    (C) the approval requirement of subsection (d)(1) (if applicable),
  with respect to any church tax inquiry or examination, any proceeding to compel compliance with any summons with respect to such inquiry or examination shall be stayed until the court finds that all practicable steps to correct the noncompliance have been taken. The period applicable under paragraph (1) or subsection (c) shall not be suspended during the period of any stay under the preceding sentence.
  (2) Remedy to be exclusive. No suit may be maintained, and no defense may be raised in any proceeding (other than as provided in paragraph (1)), by reason of any noncompliance by the Secretary with the requirements of this section.

(f) Limitations on additional inquiries and examinations.
  (1) In general. If any church tax inquiry or examination with respect to any church is completed and does not result in—
    (A) a revocation, notice of deficiency, or assessment described in subsection (d)(1), or
    (B) a request by the Secretary for any significant change in the operational practices of the church (including the adequacy of accounting practices),
  no other church tax inquiry or examination may begin with respect to such church during the applicable 5-year period unless such inquiry or examination is approved in writing by the Secretary or does not involve the same or similar issues involved in the preceding inquiry or examination. For purposes of the preceding sentence, an inquiry or examination shall be treated as completed not later than the expiration of the applicable period under paragraph (1) of subsection (c).
  (2) Applicable 5-year period. For purposes of paragraph (1), the term "applicable 5-year period" means the 5-year period beginning on the date the notice taken into account for purposes of subsection (c)(1) was provided. For purposes of the preceding sentence, the rules of subsection (c)(2) shall apply.

(g) Treatment of final report of revenue agent.
Any final report of an agent of the Internal Revenue Service shall be treated as a determination of the Secretary under paragraph (1) of section 7428(a), and any church receiving such a report shall be treated for purposes of sections 7428 and 7430 as having exhausted the administrative remedies available to it.

(h) Definitions.
For purposes of this section—
  (1) Church. The term "church" includes—
    (A) any organization claiming to be a church, and
    (B) any convention or association of churches.
  (2) Church tax inquiry. The term "church tax inquiry" means any inquiry to a church (other than an examination) to serve as a basis for determining whether a church—
    (A) is exempt from tax under section 501(a) by reason of its status as a church, or
    (B) is carrying on an unrelated trade or business (within the meaning of section 513) or otherwise engaged in activities which may be subject to taxation under this title.
  (3) Church tax examination. The term "church tax examination" means any examination for purposes of making a determination described in paragraph (2) of—
    (A) church records at the request of the Internal Revenue Service, or
    (B) the religious activities of any church.
  (4) Church records.
    (A) In general. The term "church records" means all corporate and financial records regularly kept by a church, including corporate minute books and lists of members and contributors.
    (B) Exception. Such term shall not include records acquired—
      (i) pursuant to a summons to which section 7609 applies, or
      (ii) from any governmental agency.
  (5) Inquiry notice date. The term "inquiry notice date" means the date the notice with respect to a church tax inquiry is provided under subsection (a).
  (6) Examination notice date. The term "examination notice date" means the date the notice with respect to a church tax examination is provided under subsection (b) to the church.
  (7) Appropriate high-level Treasury official. The term "appropriate high-level Treasury official" means the Secretary of the Treasury or any delegate of the Secretary whose rank is no lower than that of a principal Internal Revenue officer for an internal revenue region.

(i) Section not to apply to criminal investigations, etc.
This section shall not apply to—
  (1) any criminal investigation,
  (2) any inquiry or examination relating to the tax liability of any person other than a church,
  (3) any assessment under section 6851 (relating to termination assessments of income tax), section 6852 (relating to termination assessments in case of flagrant political expenditures of section 501(c)(3) organizations), or section

3,925

6861 (relating to jeopardy assessments of income taxes, etc.),
(4) any willful attempt to defeat or evade any tax imposed by this title, or
(5) any knowing failure to file a return of tax imposed by this title.

In **1998**, P.L. 105-206, Sec. 1102(e)(3), substituted "Secretary" for "Assistant Commissioner for Employee Plans and Exempt Organizations of the Internal Revenue Service" in para. (f)(1), effective 7/22/98.
In **1996**, P.L. 104-188, Sec. 1704(t)(59), substituted "appropriate" for "appropriate" in para. (h)(7), effective 8/20/96.
In **1989**, P.L. 101-239, Sec. 7822(d)(1), amended Sec. 10713(b)(2)(G) of P.L. 100-203, which amended para. (i)(3), see below.
Prior to amendment, Sec. 10713(b)(2)(G) of P.L. 100-203 substituted "section 6852 relating to termination assessments in case of political expenditures of section 501(c)(3), or 6861" for "or section 6861" in para. (i)(3).
In **1988**, P.L. 100-647, Sec. 1018(u)(49), substituted "this title" for "the title" in para. (i)(5), effective 10/22/86.
In **1987**, P.L. 100-203, Sec. 10713(b)(2)(G), [as amended by Sec. 7822(d)(1) of P.L. 101-239, see above], substituted "section 6852 (relating to termination assessments in case of flagrant political expenditures of section 501(c)(3) organizations), or section 6861 (relating to jeopardy assessments of income taxes, etc.),", for "or section 6861 (relating to jeopardy assessments of income taxes, etc.)," in para. (i)(3), effective 12/22/87.
In **1986**, P.L. 99-514, Sec. 1899A(61)(A), redesignated subparas. (i)(A) through (i)(E) as paras. (i)(1) through (i)(5) . . . Sec. 1899A(61)(B), substituted "etc." for "etc" at the end of para. (i)(3) (as redesignated) . . . Sec. 1899A(61)(C), substituted "the title" for "the title" [sic], in para. (i)(5) (as redesignated) . . . Sec. 1899A(62), deleted all the matter that followed subpara. (a)(1)(A) and added subpara. (a)(1)(B) [inoperative amendment], effective 10/22/86.
In **1984**, P.L. 98-369, Sec. 1033(a), added Code Sec. 7611, for inquiries and examinations begin. after 12/31/84.

Sec. 7612. Special procedures for summonses for computer software.
(a) **General rule.**
For purposes of this title—
(1) except as provided in subsection (b), no summons may be issued under this title, and the Secretary may not begin any action under section 7604 to enforce any summons to produce or analyze any tax-related computer software source code; and
(2) any software and related materials which are provided to the Secretary under this title shall be subject to the safeguards under subsection (c).
(b) **Circumstances under which computer software source code may be provided.**
(1) **In general.** Subsection (a)(1) shall not apply to any portion, item, or component of tax-related computer software source code if—
(A) the Secretary is unable to otherwise reasonably ascertain the correctness of any item on a return from—
(i) the taxpayer's books, papers, records, or other data; or
(ii) the computer software executable code (and any modifications thereof) to which such source code relates and any associated data which, when executed, produces the output to ascertain the correctness of the item;
(B) the Secretary identifies with reasonable specificity the portion, item, or component of such source code needed to verify the correctness of such item on the return; and
(C) the Secretary determines that the need for the portion, item, or component of such source code with respect to such item outweighs the risks of unauthorized disclosure of trade secrets.
(2) **Exceptions.** Subsection (a)(1) shall not apply to—
(A) any inquiry into any offense connected with the administration or enforcement of the internal revenue laws;
(B) any tax-related computer software source code acquired or developed by the taxpayer or a related person primarily for internal use by the taxpayer or such person rather than for commercial distribution;
(C) any communications between the owner of the tax-related computer software source code and the taxpayer or related persons; or
(D) any tax-related computer software source code which is required to be provided or made available pursuant to any other provision of this title.
(3) **Cooperation required.** For purposes of paragraph (1), the Secretary shall be treated as meeting the requirements of subparagraphs (A) and (B) of such paragraph if—
(A) the Secretary determines that it is not feasible to determine the correctness of an item without access to the computer software executable code and associated data described in paragraph (1)(A)(ii);
(B) the Secretary makes a formal request to the taxpayer for such code and data and to the owner of the computer software source code for such executable code; and
(C) such code and data is not provided within 180 days of such request.
(4) **Right to contest summons.** In any proceeding brought under section 7604 to enforce a summons issued under the authority of this subsection, the court shall, at the request of any party, hold a hearing to determine whether the applicable requirements of this subsection have been met.
(c) **Safeguards to ensure protection of trade secrets and other confidential information.**
(1) **Entry of protective order.** In any court proceeding to enforce a summons for any portion of software, the court may receive evidence and issue any order necessary to prevent the disclosure of trade secrets or other confidential information with respect to such software, including requiring that any information be placed under seal to be opened only as directed by the court.
(2) **Protection of software.** Notwithstanding any other provision of this section, and in addition to any protections ordered pursuant to paragraph (1), in the case of software that comes into the possession or control of the Secretary in the course of any examination with respect to any taxpayer—
(A) the software may be used only in connection with the examination of such taxpayer's return, any appeal by the taxpayer to the Internal Revenue Service Office of Appeals, any judicial proceeding (and any appeals therefrom), and any inquiry into any offense connected with the administration or enforcement of the internal revenue laws;
(B) the Secretary shall provide, in advance, to the taxpayer and the owner of the software a written list of the names of all individuals who will analyze or otherwise have access to the software;
(C) the software shall be maintained in a secure area or place, and, in the case of computer software source code, shall not be removed from the owner's place of business unless the owner permits, or a court orders, such removal;
(D) the software may not be copied except as necessary to perform such analysis, and the Secretary shall number all copies made and certify in writing that no other copies have been (or will be) made;
(E) at the end of the period during which the software may be used under subparagraph (A)—

Miscellaneous provisions   Code Sec. 7621(a)

(i) the software and all copies thereof shall be returned to the person from whom they were obtained and any copies thereof made under subparagraph (D) on the hard drive of a machine or other mass storage device shall be permanently deleted; and

(ii) the Secretary shall obtain from any person who analyzes or otherwise had access to such software a written certification under penalty of perjury that all copies and related materials have been returned and that no copies were made of them;

(F) the software may not be decompiled or disassembled;

(G) the Secretary shall provide to the taxpayer and the owner of any interest in such software, as the case may be, a written agreement, between the Secretary and any person who is not an officer or employee of the United States and who will analyze or otherwise have access to such software, which provides that such person agrees not to—

(i) disclose such software to any person other than persons to whom such information could be disclosed for tax administration purposes under section 6103; or

(ii) participate for 2 years in the development of software which is intended for a similar purpose as the software examined; and

(H) the software shall be treated as return information for purposes of section 6103. For purposes of subparagraph (C), the owner shall make available any necessary equipment or materials for analysis of computer software source code required to be conducted on the owner's premises. The owner of any interest in the software shall be considered a party to any agreement described in subparagraph (G).

(d) Definitions.

For purposes of this section—

(1) Software. The term "software" includes computer software source code and computer software executable code.

(2) Computer software source code. The term "computer software source code" means—

(A) the code written by a programmer using a programming language which is comprehensible to appropriately trained persons and is not capable of directly being used to give instructions to a computer;

(B) related programmers' notes, design documents, memoranda, and similar documentation; and

(C) related customer communications.

(3) Computer software executable code. The term "computer software executable code" means—

(A) any object code, machine code, or other code readable by a computer when loaded into its memory and used directly by such computer to execute instructions; and

(B) any related user manuals.

(4) Owner. The term "owner" shall, with respect to any software, include the developer of the software.

(5) Related person. A person shall be treated as related to another person if such persons are related persons under section 267 or 707(b).

(6) Tax-related computer software source code. The term "tax-related computer software source code" means the computer source code for any computer software program intended for accounting, tax return preparation or compliance, or tax planning.

In **1998,** P.L. 105-206, Sec. 3413(a), added Code Sec. 7612, effective for summonses issued, and software acquired, after 7/22/98. Sec. 3413(e)(2), of this Act, provides:

"(2) Software protection. In the case of any software acquired on or before such date of enactment, the requirements of section 7612(a)(2) of the Internal Revenue Code of 1986 (as added by such amendments) shall apply after the 90th day after such date. The preceding sentence shall not apply to the requirement under section 7612(c)(2)(G)(ii) of such Code (as so added)."

Sec. 7613.   Cross references.
(a) Inspection of books, papers, records, or other data.

For inspection of books, papers, records, or other data in the case of—

(1) Wagering, see section 4423.

(2) Alcohol, tobacco, and firearms taxes, see subtitle E.

(b) Search warrants.

For provisions relating to—

(1) Searches and seizures, see Rule 41 of the Federal Rules of Criminal Procedure.

(2) Issuance of search warrants with respect to subtitle E, see section 5557.

(3) Search warrants with respect to property used in violation of the internal revenue laws, see section 7302.

In **1998,** P.L. 105-206, Sec. 3413(a), redesignated Code Sec. 7612 as Code Sec. 7613, effective for summonses issued, and software acquired, after 7/22/98.
In **1984,** P.L. 98-369, Sec. 1033(a), redesignated Code Sec. 7611 as Code Sec. 7612, effective for inquiries and examinations begin. after 12/31/84.
In **1976,** P.L. 94-528, Sec. 2(b), changed the effective date for changes made by Sec. 1205(a) of P.L. 94-455, to effective for any summons issued after 2/28/77, from any summons issued after 12/31/76, see below.
—P.L. 94-455, Sec. 1205(a), redesignated Code Sec. 7609 as Code Sec. 7611, effective [as amended by Sec. 2(b) of P.L. 94-528, see above] for any summons issued after 2/28/77.
—P.L. 94-455, Sec. 1904(b)(7)(D), deleted para. (a)(1), effective 2/1/77.
Prior to deletion, para. (a)(1) read as follows:
"(1) Wholesale dealers in oleomargarine, see section 4597."
—P.L. 94-455, Sec. 1904(b)(9)(E), deleted para. (a)(2) and redesignated paras. (a)(5) and (6) as paras. (a)(1) and (2), effective 2/1/77.
Prior to deletion, para. (a)(2) read as follows:
"(2) Wholesale dealers in process or renovated butter or adulterated butter, see section 4815(b)."
In **1970,** P.L. 91-513, Sec. 1102(h), deleted paras. (a)(3) and (4), effective 5/1/71.
Prior to deletion, paras. (a)(3) and (4) read as follows:
"(3) Opium, opiates, and coca leaves, see sections 4702(a), 4705, 4721, 4773.
"(4) Marihuana, see sections 4742, 4753(b), and 4773."
In **1958,** P.L. 85-859, Sec. 204(15), added para. (a)(6); substituted in para. (b)(2) "with respect to subtitle E, see section 5557" for "in connection with industrial alcohol, etc., see sections 5314 and 7302," and added para. (b)(3), effective 9/3/58.

Subchapter B.—General Powers and Duties

Sec.
7621. Internal revenue districts.
7622. Authority to administer oaths and certify.
7623. Expenses of detection of underpayments and fraud, etc.
7624. Reimbursement to State and local law enforcement agencies.

In **1996,** P.L. 104-168, Sec. 1209(b), amended item 7623.
Prior to amendment, item 7623 read as follows:
"Sec. 7623. Expenses of detection and punishment of frauds."
In **1988,** P.L. 100-690, Sec. 7602(d)(1), added item 7624.

Sec. 7621.   Internal revenue districts.
(a) Establishment and alteration.

The President shall establish convenient internal revenue districts for the purpose of administering the internal revenue laws. The President may from time to time alter such districts.

3,927

(b) Boundaries.

For the purpose mentioned in subsection (a), the President may subdivide any State or the District of Columbia, or may unite into one district two or more States.

In 1976, P.L. 94-455, Sec. 1906(a)(53), amended subsec. (b), effective 2/1/77. Prior to amendment, subsec. (b) read as follows:
"(b) Boundaries.
"For the purpose mentioned in subsection (a), the President may subdivide any State, Territory, or the District of Columbia, or may unite into one district two or more States or a Territory and one or more States."
In 1959, P.L. 86-70, Sec. 22(e), substituted "may unite into one district two or more States or a Territory and one or more States" for "may unite two or more States or Territories into one district", effective 1/3/59.

Sec. 7622. Authority to administer oaths and certify.
(a) Internal revenue personnel.

Every officer or employee of the Treasury Department designated by the Secretary for that purpose is authorized to administer such oaths or affirmations and to certify to such papers as may be necessary under the internal revenue laws or regulations made thereunder.

(b) Others.

Any oath or affirmation required or authorized under any internal revenue law or under any regulations made thereunder may be administered by any person authorized to administer oaths for general purposes by the law of the United States, or of any State or possession of the United States, or of the District of Columbia, wherein such oath or affirmation is administered. This subsection shall not be construed as an exclusive enumeration of the persons who may administer such oaths or affirmations.

In 1976, P.L. 94-455, Sec. 1906(b)(13)(A), substituted "Secretary" for "Secretary or his delegate" in Code Sec. 7622 ... Sec. 1906(c)(2), deleted ", Territory,", after "or of any State", in subsec. (b), effective 2/1/77.

Sec. 7623. Expenses of detection of underpayments and fraud, etc.
(a) In general.

The Secretary, under regulations prescribed by the Secretary, is authorized to pay such sums as he deems necessary for—

(1) detecting underpayments of tax, or

(2) detecting and bringing to trial and punishment persons guilty of violating the internal revenue laws or conniving at the same,

in cases where such expenses are not otherwise provided for by law. Any amount payable under the preceding sentence shall be paid from the proceeds of amounts collected by reason of the information provided, and any amount so collected shall be available for such payments.

(b) Awards to Whistleblowers.

(1) In general. If the Secretary proceeds with any administrative or judicial action described in subsection (a) based on information brought to the Secretary's attention by an individual, such individual shall, subject to paragraph (2), receive as an award at least 15 percent but not more than 30 percent of the collected proceeds (including penalties, interest, additions to tax, and additional amounts) resulting from the action (including any related actions) or from any settlement in response to such action. The determination of the amount of such award by the Whistleblower Office shall depend upon the extent to which the individual substantially contributed to such action.

(2) Award in case of less substantial contribution.

(A) In general. In the event the action described in paragraph (1) is one which the Whistleblower Office determines to be based principally on disclosures of specific allegations (other than information provided by the individual described in paragraph (1)) resulting from a judicial or administrative hearing, from a governmental report, hearing, audit, or investigation, or from the news media, the Whistleblower Office may award such sums as it considers appropriate, but in no case more than 10 percent of the collected proceeds (including penalties, interest, additions to tax, and additional amounts) resulting from the action (including any related actions) or from any settlement in response to such action, taking into account the significance of the individual's information and the role of such individual and any legal representative of such individual in contributing to such action.

(B) Nonapplication of paragraph where individual is original source of information. Subparagraph (A) shall not apply if the information resulting in the initiation of the action described in paragraph (1) was originally provided by the individual described in paragraph (1).

(3) Reduction in or denial of award. If the Whistleblower Office determines that the claim for an award under paragraph (1) or (2) is brought by an individual who planned and initiated the actions that led to the underpayment of tax or actions described in subsection (a)(2), then the Whistleblower Office may appropriately reduce such award. If such individual is convicted of criminal conduct arising from the role described in the preceding sentence, the Whistleblower Office shall deny any award.

(4) Appeal of award determination. Any determination regarding an award under paragraph (1), (2), or (3) may, within 30 days of such determination, be appealed to the Tax Court (and the Tax Court shall have jurisdiction with respect to such matter).

(5) Application of this subsection. This subsection shall apply with respect to any action—

(A) against any taxpayer, but in the case of any individual, only if such individual's gross income exceeds $200,000 for any taxable year subject to such action, and

(B) if the tax, penalties, interest, additions to tax, and additional amounts in dispute exceed $2,000,000.

(6) Additional rules.

(A) No contract necessary. No contract with the Internal Revenue Service is necessary for any individual to receive an award under this subsection.

(B) Representation. Any individual described in paragraph (1) or (2) may be represented by counsel.

(C) Submission of information. No award may be made under this subsection based on information submitted to the Secretary unless such information is submitted under penalty of perjury.

In 2006, P.L. 109-432, Sec. 406(a)(1)(A), substituted "(a) In general. The Secretary" for "The Secretary" in Code Sec. 7623 ... Sec. 406(a)(1)(B), substituted "or" for "and" at the end of para. (1) ... Sec. 406(a)(1)(C), deleted "(other than interest)" in Code Sec. 7623 ... Sec. 406(a)(1)(D), added subsec. (b), effective for to information provided on or after 12/20/2006.
—P.L. 109-432, Sec. 406(b), of this Act, reads as follows:
"(b) Whistleblower office.
"(1) In general. Not later than the date which is 12 months after the date of the enactment of this Act, the Secretary of the Treasury shall issue guidance for the operation of a whistleblower program to be administered in the Internal Revenue Service by an office to be known as the "Whistleblower Office" which—
"(A) shall at all times operate at the direction of the Commissioner of Internal Revenue and coordinate and consult with other divisions in the Internal Revenue Service as directed by the Commissioner of Internal Revenue,
"(B) shall analyze information received from any individual described in section 7623(b) of the Internal Revenue Code of 1986 and either investigate the matter itself or assign it to the appropriate Internal Revenue Service office, and

Miscellaneous provisions Code Sec. 7651(1)

"(C) in its sole discretion, may ask for additional assistance from such individual or any legal representative of such individual.

"(2) Request for assistance. The guidance

"issued under paragraph (1) shall specify that any assistance requested under paragraph (1)(C) shall be under the direction and control of the Whistleblower Office or the office assigned to investigate the matter under paragraph (1)(A). No individual or legal representative whose assistance is so requested may by reason of such request represent himself or her self as an employee of the Federal Government.

—P.L. 109-432, Sec. 406(c), of this Act, reads as follows:

"(c) Report by Secretary. The Secretary of the Treasury shall each year conduct a study and report to Congress on the use of section 7623 of the Internal Revenue Code of 1986, including—

"(1) an analysis of the use of such section during the preceding year and the results of such use, and

"(2) any legislative or administrative recommendations regarding the provisions of such section and its application.

In 1998, P.L. 105-206, Sec. 3804, of this Act, reads as follows:

"SEC. 3804. STUDY OF PAYMENTS MADE FOR DETECTION OF UNDERPAYMENTS AND FRAUD.

"Not later than 1 year after the date of the enactment of this Act, the Secretary of the Treasury shall conduct a study and report to Congress on the use of section 7623 of the Internal Revenue Code of 1986 including—

"(1) an analysis of the present use of such section and the results of such use; and

"(2) any legislative or administrative recommendations regarding the provisions of such section and its application."

In 1996, P.L. 104-168, Sec. 1209(a), amended Code Sec. 7623, effective on the date which is 6 months after 7/30/96.

Prior to amendment, Code Sec. 7623 read as follows:

"SEC. 7623. EXPENSES OF DETECTION AND PUNISHMENT OF FRAUDS.

"The Secretary, under regulations prescribed by the Secretary, is authorized to pay such sums, not exceeding in the aggregate the sum appropriated therefor, as he may deem necessary for detecting and bringing to trial and punishment persons guilty of violating the internal revenue laws, or conniving at the same, in cases where such expenses are not otherwise provided for by law."

—P.L. 104-168, Sec. 1209(d), of this Act, reads as follows:

"(d) Report. The Secretary of the Treasury or his delegate shall submit an annual report to the Committee on Ways and Means of the House of Representatives and the Committee on Finance of the Senate on the payments under section 7623 of the Internal Revenue Code of 1986 during the year and on the amounts collected for which such payments were made."

In 1976, P.L. 94-455, Sec. 1906(b)(13)(A), substituted "Secretary" for "Secretary or his delegate" each place it appeared in Code Sec. 7623, effective 2/1/77.

Sec. 7624. Reimbursement to State and local law enforcement agencies.

(a) Authorization of reimbursement.

Whenever a State or local law enforcement agency provides information to the Internal Revenue Service that substantially contributes to the recovery of Federal taxes imposed with respect to illegal drug-related activities (or money laundering in connection with such activities), such agency may be reimbursed by the Internal Revenue Service for costs incurred in the investigation (including but not limited to reasonable expenses, per diem, salary, and overtime) not to exceed 10 percent of the sum recovered.

(b) Records; 10 percent limitation.

The Internal Revenue Service shall maintain records of the receipt of information from a contributing agency and shall notify the agency when monies have been recovered as the result of such information. Following such notification, the agency shall submit a statement detailing the investigative costs it incurred. Where more than 1 State or local agency has given information that substantially contributes to the recovery of Federal taxes, the Internal Revenue Service shall equitably allocate investigative costs among such agencies not to exceed an aggregate amount of 10 percent of the taxes recovered.

(c) No reimbursement where duplicative.

No State or local agency may receive reimbursement under this section if reimbursement has been received by such agency under a Federal or State forfeiture program or under State revenue laws.

In 1988, P.L. 100-690, Sec. 7602(a), added Code Sec. 7624, effective for information first provided more than 90 days after 11/18/88. Sec. 7602(f) and (g) of this Act provides:

"(f) Authorization of appropriations.

"There is authorized to be appropriated from the account referred to in section 7809(d) of the Internal Revenue Code of 1986 such sums as may be necessary to make the payments authorized by section 7624 of such Code.

"(g) Regulations.

"The Secretary of the Treasury shall, not later than 90 days after the date of enactment of this Act [11/18/88], prescribe such rules and regulations as shall be necessary and proper to carry out the provisions of this section, including regulations relating to the definition of information which substantially contributes to the recovery of Federal taxes and the substantiation of expenses required in order to receive a reimbursement."

Subchapter C.—Supervision of Operations of Certain Manufacturers [Repealed]

Sec.

7641. Repealed [Supervision of operations of certain manufacturers]

In 1976, P.L. 94-455, Sec. 1906(a)(54), repealed subchapter C of chapter 78, effective on the first day of the first month which begins more than 90 days after the date of the enactment of this Act. [10/4/76]

Sec. 7641. Repealed.

In 1976, P.L. 94-455, Sec. 1906(a)(54), repealed section 7641 of subchapter C of chapter 78, effective on the first day of the first month which begins more than 90 days after the date of the enactment of this Act. [10/4/76]

Prior to repeal, Code Sec. 7641 read as follows:

"SEC. 7641. SUPERVISION OF OPERATIONS OF CERTAIN MANUFACTURERS.

"Every manufacturer of oleomargarine, process or renovated butter or adulterated butter, or white phosphorous matches shall conduct his business under such surveillance of officers or employees of the Treasury Department as the Secretary or his delegate may by regulations require."

In 1974, P.L. 93-490, Sec. 3(b)(8), deleted "filled cheese" after "Every manufacturer of", effective with respect to filled cheese manufactueres, imported, or sold after 10/26/74.

In 1970, P.L. 91-513, Sec. 1102(i), deleted "opium, suitable for smoking purposes," after "oleomargarine", effective 5/1/71.

Subchapter D.—Possessions

Sec.

7651. Administration and collection of taxes in possessions.

7652. Shipments to the United States.

7653. Shipments from the United States.

7654. Coordination of United States and certain possession individual income taxes.

7655. Cross references.

In 1986, P.L. 99-514, Sec. 1276(b), substituted "certain possession" for "Guam" in item 7654.

In 1972, P.L. 92-606, Sec. 1(f)(6), amended item 7654.

Prior to amendment item 7654 read as follows: "Payment to Guam and American Samoa of proceeds of tax on coconut and other vegetable oils." [sic]

Sec. 7651. Administration and collection of taxes in possessions.

Except as otherwise provided in this subchapter, and except as otherwise provided in section 28(a) of the Revised Organic Act of the Virgin Islands and section 30 of the Organic Act of Guam (relating to the covering of the proceeds of certain taxes into the treasuries of the Virgin Islands and Guam, respectively)—

(1) Applicability of administrative provisions. All provisions of the laws of the United States applicable to the assessment and collection of any tax imposed by this title or of any other liability arising under this title (including penalties) shall, in respect of such tax or liability, extend to and be applicable in any possession of the United States in the same manner and to the same extent as if such possession were a State, and as if the term "United States" when used in a geographical sense included such possession.

3,929

(2) Tax imposed in possession. In the case of any tax which is imposed by this title in any possession of the United States—

(A) Internal revenue collections. Such tax shall be collected under the direction of the Secretary, and shall be paid into the Treasury of the United States as internal revenue collections; and

(B) Applicable laws. All provisions of the laws of the United States applicable to the administration, collection, and enforcement of such tax (including penalties) shall, in respect of such tax, extend to and be applicable in such possession of the United States in the same manner and to the same extent as if such possession were a State, and as if the term "United States" when used in a geographical sense included such possession.

(3) Other laws relating to possessions. This section shall apply notwithstanding any other provision of law relating to any possession of the United States.

(4) Virgin Islands.

(A) For purposes of this section, the reference in section 28(a) of the Revised Organic Act of the Virgin Islands to "any tax specified in section 3811 of the Internal Revenue Code" shall be deemed to refer to any tax imposed by chapter 2 or by chapter 21.

(B) For purposes of this section, section 28(a) of the Revised Organic Act of the Virgin Islands shall be effective as if such section 28(a) had been enacted before the enactment of this title and such section 28(a) shall have no effect on the amount of income tax liability required to be paid by any person to the United States.

In 2007, P.L. 110-172, Sec. 11(a)(34)(B), deleted para. (4) and redes. para. (5) as para. (4), enacted 12/29/2007.

Prior to deletion, para. (4) read as follows:

"(4) Canal Zone. For purposes of this section, the term 'possession of the United States' includes the Canal Zone."

In 1986, P.L. 99-514, Sec. 1275(b), amended subpara. (5)(B), effective as provided in Sec. 1277(c)(2) of this Act, which reads as follows:

"(2) Section 1275(b).—

"(A) In general.— The amendment made by section 1275(b) shall apply with respect to—

"(i) any taxable year beginning after December 31, 1986, and

"(ii) any pre-1987 open year.

"(B) Special rules.— In the case of any pre-1987 open year—

"(i) the amendment made by section 1275(b) shall not apply to income from sources in the Virgin Islands or income effectively connected with the conduct of a trade or business in the Virgin Islands, and

"(ii) the taxpayer shall be allowed a credit—

"(I) against any additional tax imposed by subtitle A of the Internal Revenue Code of 1954 (by reason of the amendment made by section 1275(b)) on income not described in clause (i),

"(II) for any tax paid to the Virgin Islands before the date of the enactment of this Act and attributable to such income.

For purposes of clause (ii)(II), any tax paid before January 1, 1987, pursuant to a process in effect before August 16, 1986, shall be treated as paid before the date of the enactment of this Act.

"(C) Pre-1987 open year.— For purposes of this paragraph, the term 'pre-1987 open year' means any taxable year beginning before January 1, 1987, if on the date of the enactment of this Act the assessment of a deficiency of income tax for such taxable year is not barred by any law or rule of law.

"(D) Exception.— In the case of any pre-1987 open year, the amendment made by section 1275(b) shall not apply to any domestic corporation if—

"(i) during the fiscal year which ended May 31, 1986, such corporation was actively engaged directly or through a subsidiary in the conduct of a trade or business in the Virgin Islands and such trade or business consists of business related to marine activities, and

"(ii) such corporation was incorporated on March 31, 1983, in Delaware.

"(E) Exception for certain transactions.—

"(i) In general.— In the case of any pre-1987 open year, the amendment made by section 1275(b) shall not apply to any income derived from transactions described in clause (ii) by 1 or more corporations which were formed in Delaware on or about March 6, 1981, and which have owned 1 or more office buildings in St. Thomas, United States Virgin Islands, for at least 5 years before the date of the enactment of this Act.

"(ii) Description of transactions.— The transactions described in this clause are—

"(I) the redemptions of limited partnership interests for cash and property described in an agreement (as amended) dated March 12, 1981,

"(II) the subsequent disposition of the properties distributed in such redemptions, and

"(III) interest earned before January 1, 1987, on bank deposits of proceeds received from such redemptions to the extent such deposits are located in the United States Virgin Islands.

"(iii) Limitation.— The aggregate reduction in tax by reason of this subparagraph shall not exceed $8,312,000. If the taxes which would be payable as the result of the application of the amendment made by section 1275(b) to pre-1987 open years exceeds the limitation of the preceding sentence, such excess shall be treated as attributable to income received in taxable years in reverse chronological order."

Prior to amendment, subpara. (5)(B) read as follows:

"(B) For purposes of this title (other than section 881(b)(1) or subpart C of part III of subchapter N or chapter 1), section 28(a) of the Revised Organic Act of the Virgin Islands shall be effective as if such section had been enacted subsequent to the enactment of this title."

In 1984, P.L. 98-369, Sec. 130(c), added "(other than section 881(b)(1))" after "For purposes of this title" in subpara. (5)(B), effective for payments made after 3/1/84, in tax. yrs. end. after 3/1/84.

—P.L. 98-369, Sec. 801(d)(9), added "or subpart C of part III of subchapter N of chapter 1" after "881(b)(1)" in subpara. (5)(B), as amended by Sec. 130(c) of this Act, effective for transactions after 12/31/84, in tax. yrs. end. after 12/31/84.

In 1976, P.L. 94-455, Sec. 1906(b)(13)(A), substituted "Secretary" for "Secretary or his delegate" in Code Sec. 7651, effective 2/1/77.

In 1970, P.L. 91-513, Sec. 1102(j), deleted "and in sections 4705(b), 4735, and 4762 (relating to taxes on narcotic drugs and marihuana" after "Except as otherwise provided in this subchapter" in Code Sec. 7651, effective 5/1/71.

Sec. 7652. Shipments to the United States.

(a) Puerto Rico.

(1) Rate of tax. Except as provided in section 5314, articles of merchandise of Puerto Rican manufacture coming into the United States and withdrawn for consumption or sale shall be subject to a tax equal to the internal revenue tax imposed in the United States upon the like articles of merchandise of domestic manufacture.

(2) Payment of tax. The Secretary shall by regulations prescribe the mode and time for payment and collection of the tax described in paragraph (1), including any discretionary method described in section 6302(b) and (c). Such regulations shall authorize the payment of such tax before shipment from Puerto Rico, and the provisions of section 7651(2)(B) shall be applicable to the payment and collection of such tax in Puerto Rico.

(3) Deposit of internal revenue collections. All taxes collected under the internal revenue laws of the United States on articles produced in Puerto Rico and transported to the United States (less the estimated amount necessary for payment of refunds and drawbacks), or consumed in the island, shall be covered into the treasury of Puerto Rico.

(b) Virgin Islands.

(1) Taxes imposed in the United States. Except as provided in section 5314, there shall be imposed in the United States, upon articles coming into the United States from the Virgin Islands, a tax equal to the internal revenue tax imposed in the United States upon like articles of domestic manufacture.

(2) Exemption from tax imposed in the Virgin Islands. Such articles shipped from such islands to the United States shall be exempt from the payment of any tax imposed by the internal revenue laws of such islands.

(3) Disposition of internal revenue collections. The Secretary shall determine the amount of all taxes imposed by, and collected under the internal revenue laws of the United States on articles produced in the Virgin Islands and transported to the United States. The amount so determined less 1 percent and less the estimated amount of refunds or credits shall be subject to disposition as follows:

(A) The payment of an estimated amount shall be made to the government of the Virgin Islands before the com-

Miscellaneous provisions   Code Sec. 7652

mencement of each fiscal year as set forth in section 4(c)(2) of the Act entitled "An Act to authorize appropriations for certain insular areas of the United States, and for other purposes", approved August 18, 1978 (48 U.S.C. 1645), as in effect on the date of the enactment [5/18/2000] of the Trade and Development Act of 2000. The payment so made shall constitute a separate fund in the treasury of the Virgin Islands and may be expended as the legislature may determine.

(B) Any amounts remaining shall be deposited in the Treasury of the United States as miscellaneous receipts. If at the end of any fiscal year the total of the Federal contribution made under subparagraph (A) with respect to the four calendar quarters immediately preceding the beginning of that fiscal year has not been obligated or expended for an approved purpose, the balance shall continue available for expenditure during any succeeding fiscal year, but only for emergency relief purposes and essential public projects. The aggregate amount of moneys available for expenditure for emergency relief purposes and essential public projects only shall not exceed the sum of $5,000,000 at the end of any fiscal year. Any unobligated or unexpended balance of the Federal contribution remaining at the end of a fiscal year which would cause the moneys available for emergency relief purposes and essential public projects only to exceed the sum of $5,000,000 shall thereupon be transferred and paid over to the Treasury of the United States as miscellaneous receipts.

(c) Articles containing distilled spirits.

For purposes of subsections (a)(3) and (b)(3), any article containing distilled spirits shall in no event be treated as produced in Puerto Rico or the Virgin Islands unless at least 92 percent of the alcoholic content in such article is attributable to rum.

(d) Articles other than articles containing distilled spirits.

For purposes of subsections (a)(3) and (b)(3)—

(1) Value added requirement for Puerto Rico. Any article, other than an article containing distilled spirits, shall in no event be treated as produced in Puerto Rico unless the sum of—

(A) the cost or value of the materials produced in Puerto Rico, plus

(B) the direct costs of processing operations performed in Puerto Rico,

equals or exceeds 50 percent of the value of such article as of the time it is brought into the United States.

(2) Prohibition of federal excise tax subsidies.

(A) In general. No amount shall be transferred under subsection (a)(3) or (b)(3) in respect of taxes imposed on any article, other than an article containing distilled spirits, if the Secretary determines that a Federal excise tax subsidy was provided by Puerto Rico or the Virgin Islands (as the case may be) with respect to such article.

(B) Federal excise tax subsidy. For purposes of this paragraph, the term "Federal excise tax subsidy" means any subsidy—

(i) of a kind different from, or

(ii) in an amount per value or volume of production greater than,

the subsidy which Puerto Rico or the Virgin Islands offers generally to industries producing articles not subject to Federal excise taxes.

(3) Direct costs of processing operations. For purposes of this subsection, the term "direct cost of processing operations" has the same meaning as when used in section 213 of the Caribbean Basin Economic Recovery Act.

(e) Shipments of rum to the United States

(1) Excise taxes on rum covered into treasuries of Puerto Rico and Virgin Islands. All taxes collected under section 5001(a)(1) on rum imported into the United States (less the estimated amount necessary for payment of refunds and drawbacks) shall be covered into the treasuries of Puerto Rico and the Virgin Islands.

(2) Secretary prescribes formula. The Secretary shall, from time to time, prescribe by regulation a formula for the division of such tax collections between Puerto Rico and the Virgin Islands and the timing and methods for transferring such tax collections.

(3) Rum defined. For purposes of this subsection, the term "rum" means any article classified under subheading 2208.40.00 of the Harmonized Tariff Schedule of the United States (19 U.S.C. 1202).

(4) Coordination with subsections (a) and (b). Paragraph (1) shall not apply with respect to any rum subject to tax under subsection (a) or (b).

(f) Limitation on cover over of tax on distilled spirits.

For purposes of this section, with respect to taxes imposed under section 5001 or this section on distilled spirits, the amount covered into the treasuries of Puerto Rico and the Virgin Islands shall not exceed the lesser of the rate of—

(1) $10.50 ($13.25 in the case of distilled spirits brought into the United States after June 30, 1999, and before January 1, 2012), or

(2) the tax imposed under section 5001(a)(1), on each proof gallon.

(g) Drawback for medicinal alcohol, etc.

In the case of medicines, medicinal preparations, food products, flavors, flavoring extracts, or perfume containing distilled spirits, which are unfit for beverage purposes and which are brought into the United States from Puerto Rico or the Virgin Islands—

(1) subpart B of part II of subchapter A of chapter 51 shall be applied as if—

(A) the use and tax determination described in section 5111 had occurred in the United States by a United States person at the time the article is brought into the United States, and

(B) the rate of tax were the rate applicable under subsection (f) of this section, and

(2) no amount shall be covered into the treasuries of Puerto Rico or the Virgin Islands.

(h) Manner of cover over of tax must be derived from this title.

No amount shall be covered into the treasury of Puerto Rico or the Virgin Islands with respect to taxes for which cover over is provided under this section unless made in the manner specified in this section without regard to—

(1) any provision of law which is not contained in this title or in a revenue Act; and

(2) whether such provision of law is a subsequently enacted provision or directly or indirectly seeks to waive the application of this subsection.

In 2010, P.L. 111-312, Sec. 755(a), substituted "January 1, 2012" for "January 1, 2010" in para. (f)(1), effective for distilled spirits brought into the United States after 12/31/2009.

In 2008, P.L. 110-343, Sec. 308(a)DivC, substituted "January 1, 2010" for "January 1, 2008" in para. (f)(1), effective for distilled spirits brought into the United States after 12/31/2007.

In 2006, P.L. 109-432, Sec. 114(a), substituted "2008" for "2006" in subsection (a), which shall apply to articles brought into the United States after 12/31/2005.

Code Sec. 7652   Miscellaneous provisions

In 2005, P.L. 109-59, Sec. 11125(b)(22)(A), substituted "subpart B" for "subpart F" in para. (g)(1) . . . Sec. 11125(b)(22)(B), substituted "section 5111" for "section 5131(a)" in para. (g)(1), effective 7/1/2008, but not for taxes imposed for periods before 7/1/2008.

In 2004, P.L. 108-311, Sec. 305(a), substituted "January 1, 2006" for "January 1, 2004" in para. (f)(1), effective for articles brought into the United States after 12/31/2003.

In 2002, P.L. 107-147, Sec. 609(a), substituted "January 1, 2004" for "January 1, 2002" in para. (f)(1), effective for articles brought into the United States after 12/31/2001.

In 2000, P.L. 106-200, Sec. 602(b), amended so much of para. (b)(3) that preceded subpara. (b)(3)(B) . . . Sec. 602(c), added subsec. (h), effective for transfers or payments made after 5/18/2000.

Prior to amendment, so much of para. (b)(3) that preceded subpara. (b)(3)(B), read as follows:

"(3) Disposition of internal revenue collections. Beginning with the calendar quarter ending September 30, 1975, and quarterly thereafter, the Secretary shall determine the amount of all taxes imposed by, and collected during the quarter under, the internal revenue laws of the United States on articles produced in the Virgin Islands and transported to the United States. The amount so determined less 1 percent and less the estimated amount of refunds or credits shall be subject to disposition as follows:

"(A) There shall be transferred and paid over, as soon as practicable after the close of the quarter, to the Government of the Virgin Islands from the amounts so determined a sum equal to the total amount of the revenue collected by the Government of the Virgin Islands during the quarter, as certified by the Government Comptroller of the Virgin Islands. The moneys so transferred and paid over shall constitute a separate fund in the treasury of the Virgin Islands and may be expended as the legislature may determine."

In 1999, P.L. 106-170, Sec. 512(a), amended para. (f)(1), effective 7/1/99.

Prior to amendment, para. (f)(1) read as follows:

"(1) $10.50 ($11.30 in the case of distilled spirits brought into the United States during the 5-year period beginning on October 1, 1993), or"

—P.L. 106-170, Sec. 512(b), of this Act, provides:

"(b) Special cover over transfer rules. Notwithstanding section 7652 of the Internal Revenue Code of 1986, the following rules shall apply with respect to any transfer before the first day of the month within which the date of the enactment of the Trade and Development Act of 2000 occurs, of amounts relating to the increase in the cover over of taxes by reason of the amendment made by subsection (a):

"Initial transfer of incremental increase in cover over. The Secretary of the Treasury shall, within 15 days after the date of the enactment of this Act, transfer an amount equal to the lesser of—

"(A) the amount of such increase otherwise required to be covered over after June 30, 1999, and before the date of the enactment of this Act, or

"(B) $20,000,000.

"(2) Second transfer of incremental increase in cover over attributable to periods before resumption of regular payments. The Secretary of the Treasury shall transfer on the first payment date after the date of the enactment of the Trade and Development Act of 2000 an amount equal to the excess of—

"(A) the amount of such increase otherwise required to be covered over after June 30, 1999, and before the first day of the month within which such date of enactment occurs, over

"(B) the amount of the transfer described in paragraph (1)."

In 1994, P.L. 103-465, Sec. 136(b), substituted "flavoring extracts, or perfume" for "or flavoring extracts" in subsec. (g), effective 1/1/95.

In 1993, P.L. 103-66, Sec. 13227(e), amended para. (f)(1), effective 10/1/93.

Prior to amendment, para. (f)(1) read as follows:

"(1) $10.50, or"

In 1990, P.L. 101-508, Sec. 11201(e), regarding floor stocks taxes, is reproduced in note following Code Sec. 5001.

—P.L. 101-508, Sec. 11218, regarding floor stocks tax treatment of articles in foreign trade zones, is reproduced in note following Code Sec. 5001.

In 1988, P.L. 100-418, Sec. 1214(p)(1), substituted "subheading 2208.40.00 of the Harmonized Tariff Schedule of the United States" for "item 169.13 or 169.14 of the Tariff Schedules of the United States" in para (e)(3), effective for crude oil removed from premises on or after 8/23/88.

In 1986, P.L. 99-514, Sec. 1879(i)(1), added subsec. (g), effective for articles brought into the United States after 10/22/86. Sec. 1879(i)(3)(A) and (B) of this Act, provide:

"(3)(A) Section 7652 of the Internal Revenue Code of 1954 (other than subsection (f) thereof) shall not prevent the payment to Puerto Rico or the Virgin Islands of amounts with respect to medicines, medicinal preparations, food products, flavors, or flavoring extracts containing distilled spirits, which are unfit for beverage purposes and which are brought into the United States from Puerto Rico or the Virgin Islands on or before the date of the enactment of this Act.

"(B) With respect to articles brought into the United States after September 27, 1985, subparagraph (A) shall apply only if the Secretary of the Treasury or his delegate is satisfied that the amounts paid to Puerto Rico or the Virgin Islands under subparagraph (A) are being repaid to the proper persons who used the distilled spirits in such articles."

In 1984, P.L. 98-369, Sec. 2681(a), redesignated subsec. (c) as subsec. (e) and added new subsecs. (c) and (d), effective for articles brought into the United States on or after 3/1/84. Sec. 2681(b)(2) and (3) of the Act provide:

"(2) Exception for Puerto Rico for periods before January 1, 1985.

"(A) In general. Subject to the limitations of subparagraphs (B) and (C), the amendments made by subsection (a) shall not apply with respect to articles containing distilled spirits brought into the United States from Puerto Rico after February 29, 1984, and before January 1, 1985.

"(B) $130,000,000 Limitation. In the case of such articles brought into the United States after February 29, 1984, and before July 1, 1984, the aggregate amount payable to Puerto Rico by reason of subparagraph (A) shall not exceed the excess of—

"(i) $130,000,000, over

"(ii) the aggregate amount payable to Puerto Rico under section 7652(a) of the Internal Revenue Code of 1954 with respect to such articles which were brought into the United States after June 30, 1983, and before March 1, 1984, and which would not meet the requirements of section 7652(c) of such Code.

"(C) $75,000,000 Limitation. The aggregate amount payable to Puerto Rico by reason of subparagraph (A) shall not exceed $75,000,000 in the case of articles—

"(i) brought into the United States after June 30, 1984, and before January 1, 1985,

"(ii) which would not meet the requirements of section 7652(c) of such Code,

"(iii) which have been redistilled in Puerto Rico, and

"(iv) which do not contain distilled spirits derived from cane.

"(3) Limitation on incentive payments to United States distillers.

"(A) In general. In the case of articles to which this paragraph applies, the aggregate amount of incentive payments paid to any United States distiller with respect to such articles shall not exceed the limitation described in subparagraph (C).

"(B) Articles to which paragraph applies. This paragraph shall apply to any article containing distilled spirits described in clauses (i) through (iv) of paragraph (2)(C).

"(C) Limitation.

"(i) In general. The limitation described in this subparagraph is $1,500,000.

"(ii) Special rule. The limitation described in this subparagraph shall be zero with respect to any distiller who was not entitled to or receiving incentive payments as of March 1, 1984.

"(D) Payments in excess of limitation. If any United States distiller receives any incentive payment with respect to articles to which this paragraph applies in excess of the limitation described in subparagraph (C), such distiller shall pay to the United States the total amount of such incentive payments with respect to such articles in the same manner, and subject to the same penalties, as if such amount were tax due and payable under section 5001 of such Code on the date such payments were received.

"(E) Incentive payments.

"(i) In general. For purposes of this paragraph, the term 'incentive payment' means any payment made directly or indirectly by the commonwealth of Puerto Rico to any United States distiller as an incentive to engage in redistillation operations.

"(ii) Transportation payments excluded. Such term shall not include any payment of a direct cost of transportation to or from Puerto Rico with respect to any article to which this paragraph applies."

—P.L. 98-369, Sec. 2682(a), added subsec. (f), effective for articles containing distilled spirits brought into the United States after 9/30/85.

In 1983, P.L. 98-213, Sec. 5(c), added Sec. 1906(a)(55)(D) of P.L. 94-455, see below.

—P.L. 98-67, Sec. 221(a), added subsec. (c), effective for articles imported into the United States after 6/30/83.

In 1976, P.L. 94-455, Sec. 1906(a)(55)(A), deleted subpara. (b)(3)(B) and redesignated subpara. (b)(3)(C) as subpara. (b)(3)(B) . . . Sec. 1906(a)(55)(B), [as amended by Sec. 5(c) of P.L. 98-213, see above] substituted "emergency relief purposes and essential public projects" for "approved emergency relief purposes and essential public projects as provided in subparagraph (B)" in para. (b)(3) . . . Sec. 1906(a)(55)(C), deleted "including payments under subparagraph (B)," after "public projects only," in para. (b)(3) . . . Sec. 1906(a)(55)(D), [as added by Sec. 5(c) of P.L. 98-213, see above], substituted a period for the colon after "determine" in subpara. (b)(3)(A) and deleted the last sentence of subpara. (b)(3)(A), effective 2/1/77.

Prior to amendment, subpara. (b)(3)(B), read as follows:

"(B) There shall also be transferred and paid over to the government of the Virgin Islands during each of the fiscal years ending June 30, 1955, and June 30, 1956, the sum of $1,000,000 or the balance of the internal revenue collections available under this paragraph (3) after payments are made under subparagraph (A), whichever amount is greater. The moneys so transferred and paid over shall be deposited in the separate fund established by subparagraph (A), but shall be obligated or expended for emergency purposes and essential public projects only with the prior approval of the President or his designated representative."

Prior to deletion, the last sentence of subpara. (b)(3)(A) read as follows:

"Provided, That the approval of the President or his designated representative shall be obtained before such moneys may be obligated or expended."

—P.L. 94-455, Sec. 1906(b)(13)(A), substituted "Secretary" for "Secretary or his delegate" each place it appeared in Code Sec. 7652, effective 2/1/77.

In 1976, P.L. 94-202, Sec. 10(a)(1), amended the first sentence of para. (b)(3) . . . Sec. 10(a)(2), amended the first sentence of subpara. (b)(3)(A), effective for all taxes imposed by, and collected after June 30, 1975, under, the internal revenue laws of the United States on articles produced in the Virgin Islands and transported to the United States.

Prior to amendment, the first sentence of para. (b)(3) read as follows:

"Beginning with the fiscal year ending June 30, 1954, and annually thereafter, the Secretary or his delegate shall determine the amount of all taxes imposed by, and collected during the fiscal year under, the internal revenue laws of the United

Miscellaneous provisions   Code Sec. 7654

States on articles produced in the Virgin Islands and transported to the United States."

Prior to amendment, the first sentence of subpara. (b)(3)(A) read as follows:
  "There shall be transferred and paid over to the government of the Virgin Islands from the amounts so determined a sum equal to the total amount of the revenue collected by the government of the Virgin Islands during the fiscal year, as certified by the Government Comptroller of the Virgin Islands."
—P.L. 94-202, Sec. 10(a)(3), substituted "with respect to the four calendar quarters immediately preceding the beginning" for "at the beginning" in the sentence immediately following subpara. (b)(3)(C), effective 1/2/76.

In 1965, P.L. 89-44, Sec. 808(b)(3), added "(less the estimated amount necessary for payment of refunds and drawbacks)" in para. (a)(3), effective 7/1/65.

In 1958, P.L. 85-859, Sec. 204(17), substituted "section 5314" for "section 5318" in para. (a)(1)... Sec. 204(18), substituted "section 5314" for "section 5318" in para. (b)(1), effective 7/1/59.

Sec. 7653. Shipments from the United States.

(a) Tax imposed.

  (1) Puerto Rico. All articles of merchandise of United States manufacture coming into Puerto Rico shall be entered at the port of entry upon payment of a tax equal in rate and amount to the internal revenue tax imposed in Puerto Rico upon the like articles of Puerto Rican manufacture.

  (2) Virgin Islands. There shall be imposed in the Virgin Islands upon articles imported from the United States a tax equal to the internal revenue tax imposed in such islands upon like articles there manufactured.

(b) Exemption from tax imposed in the United States.

  Articles, goods, wares, or merchandise going into Puerto Rico, the Virgin Islands, Guam, and American Samoa from the United States shall be exempted from the payment of any tax imposed by the internal revenue laws of the United States.

(c) Drawback of tax paid in the United States.

  All provisions of law for the allowance of drawback of internal revenue tax on articles exported from the United States are, so far as applicable, extended to like articles upon which an internal revenue tax has been paid when shipped from the United States to Puerto Rico, the Virgin Islands, Guam, or American Samoa.

(d) Cross reference.

  For the disposition of the proceeds of all taxes collected under the internal revenue laws of the United States on articles produced in Guam and transported into the United States or its possessions, or consumed in Guam, see the Act of August 1, 1950 (48 U. S. C. 1421h).

In 1976, P.L. 94-455, Sec. 1906(a)(56), deleted "c. [sic] 512, 64 Stat. 392, section 30;" following the parenthesis in subsec. (d), effective 2/1/77.

In 1960, P.L. 86-624, Sec. 18(h), substituted "or its possessions" for ", its possessions or the Territory of Hawaii" in subsec. (d), effective 8/21/59.

In 1959, P.L. 86-70, Sec. 22(f), substituted "its possessions or the Territory of Hawaii" for "its Territories or possessions." in subsec. (d), effective 1/3/59.

Sec. 7654. Coordination of United States and certain possession individual income taxes.

(a) General rule.

  The net collection of taxes imposed by chapter 1 for each taxable year with respect to an individual to whom section 931 or 932(c) applies shall be covered into the Treasury of the specified possession of which such individual is a bona fide resident.

(b) Definition and special rule.

  For purposes of this section—

  (1) Net collections. In determining net collections for a taxable year, an appropriate adjustment shall be made for credits allowed against the tax liability and refunds made of income taxes for the taxable year.

  (2) Specified possession. The term "specified possession" means Guam, American Samoa, the Northern Mariana Islands, and the Virgin Islands.

(c) Transfers.

  The transfers of funds between the United States and any specified possession required by this section shall be made not less frequently than annually.

(d) Federal personnel.

  In addition to the amount determined under subsection (a), the United States shall pay to each specified possession at such times and in such manner as determined by the Secretary—

  (1) the amount of the taxes deducted and withheld by the United States under chapter 24 with respect to compensation paid to members of the Armed Forces who are stationed in such possession but who have no income tax liability to such possession with respect to such compensation by reason of the Servicemembers Civil Relief Act (50 App. U.S.C. 501 *et seq.*), and

  (2) the amount of the taxes deducted and withheld under chapter 24 with respect to amounts paid for services performed as an employee of the United States (or any agency thereof) in a specified possession with respect to an individual unless section 931 or 932(c) applies.

(e) Regulations.

  The Secretary shall prescribe such regulations as may be necessary to carry out the provisions of this section and sections 931 and 932, including regulations prohibiting the rebate of taxes covered over which are allocable to United States source income and prescribing the information which the individuals to whom such sections may apply shall furnish to the Secretary.

In 2003, P.L. 108-189, Sec. 2(d), substituted "Servicemembers Civil Relief Act" for "Soldiers' and Sailors' Civil Relief Act" in para. (d)(1), effective 12/19/2003.

In 1988, P.L. 100-647, Sec. 1012(y), substituted "an individual to whom" for "an individual to which" in subsec. (a), effective for tax. yrs. begin. after 12/31/86, except as provided in Sec. 1277(b) of P.L. 99-514, reproduced below.

In 1986, P.L. 99-514, Sec. 1276(a), amended Code Sec. 7654, effective for tax. yrs. begin. after 12/31/86, except as provided in Sec. 1277(b) of this Act, which reads as follows:

"(b) Special rule for Guam, American Samoa, and the Northern Mariana Islands.—

  "The amendments made by subtitle [Subtitle G of Title XII, P.L. 99-514] shall apply with respect to Guam, American Samoa, or the Northern Mariana Islands (and to residents thereof and corporations created or organized therein) only if (and so long as) an implementing agreement under section 1271 is in effect between the United States and such possession."

Prior to amendment, Code Sec. 7654 read as follows:

"Sec. 7654. Coordination of United States and Guam individual income taxes.

"(a) General rule.

  "The net collections of the income taxes imposed for each taxable year with respect to any individual to whom this subsection applies for such year shall be divided between the United States and Guam according to the following rules:

  "(1) net collections attributable to United States source income shall be covered into the Treasury of the United States;

  "(2) net collections attributable to Guam source income shall be covered into the treasury of Guam; and

  "(3) all other net collections of such taxes shall be covered into the treasury of the jurisdiction (either the United States or Guam) with which such individual is required by section 935(b) to file his return for such year.

This subsection applies to an individual for a taxable year if section 935 applies to such individual for such year and if such individual has (or, in the case of a joint return, such individual and his spouse have (A) adjusted gross income of $50,000 or more and (B) gross income of $5,000 or more derived from sources within the jurisdiction (either the United States or Guam) with which the individual is not required under section 935(b) to file his return for the year.

"(b) Definitions and special rules.

  "For purposes of this section—

  "(1) Net collections. In determining net collections for a taxable year, appropriate adjustment shall be made for credits allowed against the tax liability for such year and refunds made of income taxes for such year.

  "(2) Income taxes. The term 'income taxes' means—

  "(A) with respect to taxes imposed by the United States, the taxes imposed by chapter 1, and

  "(B) with respect to Guam, the Guam territorial income tax.

  "(3) Source. The determination of the source of income shall be based on the principles contained in part I of subchapter N of chapter 1 (section 861 and following).

3,933

"(c) *Transfers.*
"The transfers of funds between the United States and Guam required by this section shall be made not less frequently than annually.
"(d) *Military personnel in Guam.*
"In addition to any amount determined under subsection (a), the United States shall pay to Guam at such times and in such manner as determined by the Secretary or his delegate the amount of the taxes deducted and withheld by the United States under chapter 24 with respect to compensation paid to members of the Armed Forces who are stationed in Guam but who have no income tax liability to Guam with respect to such compensation by reason of the Soldiers and Sailors Civil Relief Act (50 App. U.S.C., sec. 501 *et seq.*).
"(e) *Regulations.*
"The Secretary shall prescribe such regulations as may be necessary to carry out the provisions of this section and section 935, including (but not limited to)—
"(1) such regulations as are necessary to insure that the provisions of this title, as made applicable in Guam by section 31 of the Organic Act of Guam, apply in a manner which is consistent with this section and section 935, and
"(2) regulations prescribing the information which the individuals to whom section 935 may apply shall furnish to the Secretary."
In 1976, P.L. 94-455, Sec. 1906(b)(13)(A), substituted "Secretary" for "Secretary or his delegate" each place it appeared in Code Sec. 7654, effective 2/1/77.
In 1972, P.L. 92-606, Sec. 1(b), amended Code Sec. 7654, effective for tax. yrs. begin. after 12/31/72.
Prior to amendment, Code Sec. 7654 read as follows:
"Sec. 7654. Payment to Guam and American Samoa of Proceeds of Tax on Coconut and Palm Oil.
"All taxes collected under subchapter B of chapter 37 with respect to coconut oil wholly of the production of Guam or American Samoa, or produced from materials wholly of the growth or production of Guam or American Samoa, shall be held as separate funds and paid to the treasury of Guam or American Samoa, respectively. No part of the money from such funds shall be used, directly or indirectly, to pay a subsidy to the producers or processors of copra, coconut oil, or allied products, except that this sentence shall not be construed as prohibiting the use of such money, in accordance with regulations prescribed by the Secretary or his delegate, for the acquisition or construction of facilities for the better curing of copra or for bona fide loans to copra producers of Guam or American Samoa."

Sec. 7655. Cross references.
(a) Imposition of tax in possessions.
For provisions imposing tax in possessions, see—
(1) Chapter 2, relating to self-employment tax;
(2) Chapter 21, relating to the tax under the Federal Insurance Contributions Act.
(b) Other provisions.
For other provisions relating to possessions of the United States, see—
(1) Section 931, relating to income tax on residents of Guam, American Samoa, or the Northern Mariana Islands;
(2) Section 933, relating to income tax on residents of Puerto Rico.

In 1990, P.L. 101-508, Sec. 11801(c)(22)(E)(i), substituted a period for the comma at the end of para. (a)(2) and deleted para. (a)(3)... Sec. 11801(c)(22)(E)(ii), substituted a period for the comma at the end of para. (b)(2) and deleted para. (b)(3), effective 11/5/90, except as provided in Sec. 11821(b) of this Act reproduced in note following Code Sec. 6418.
Prior to deletion, para. (a)(3) read as follows:
"(3) Chapter 37, relating to tax on sugar."
Prior to deletion, para. (b)(3) read as follows:
"(3) Section 6418(b), relating to exportation of sugar to Puerto Rico."
In 1986, P.L. 99-514, Sec. 1272(d)(11), redesignated paras. (b)(1) and (b)(2) as paras. (b)(2) and (b)(3), and added para. (b)(1), effective for tax. yrs. begin. after 12/31/86, except as provided in Sec. 1277(b) of this Act, which reads as follows:
"(b) Special rule for Guam, American Samoa, and the Northern Mariana Islands.—
"The amendments made by this subtitle shall apply with respect to Guam, American Samoa, or the Northern Mariana Islands (and to residents thereof and corporations created or organized therein) only if (and so long as) an implementing agreement under section 1271 is in effect between the United States and such possession."
In 1976, P.L. 94-455, Sec. 1904(b)(6), substituted "Chapter 37" for "Subchapter A of chapter 37" in para. (a)(5), and redesignated para. (a)(5) as para. (a)(3), effective 2/1/77.
In 1970, P.L. 91-513, Sec. 1102(k), deleted paras. (a)(3) and (4), effective 5/1/71.
Prior to deletion, paras. (a)(3) and (4) read as follows:
"(3) Parts I and III of subchapter A of chapter 39, relating to taxes in respect of narcotic drugs;
"(4) Parts II and III of subchapter A of chapter 39, relating to taxes in respect of marihuana."

In 1958, P.L. 85-859, Sec. 204(19), redesignated para. (a)(6) as para. (a)(5) and deleted para. (a)(5), containing a cross reference to chapter 51 of this title, effective 9/3/58.

CHAPTER 79.—DEFINITIONS
Sec.
7701. Definitions.
7702. Life insurance contract defined.
7702A. Modified endowment contract defined.
7702B. Treatment of qualified long-term care insurance.
7703. Determination of marital status.
7704. Certain publicly traded partnerships treated as corporations.

In 1996, P.L. 104-191, Sec. 321(e), added item 7702B.
In 1988, P.L. 100-647, Sec. 5012(c)(2), added item 7702A.
In 1987, P.L. 100-203, Sec. 10211(b), added item 7704.
In 1986, P.L. 99-514, Sec. 1301(j)(2)(B), added item 7703.
In 1984, P.L. 98-369, Sec. 221(c), added item 7702.

Sec. 7701. Definitions.
(a) When used in this title, where not otherwise distinctly expressed or manifestly incompatible with the intent thereof—
(1) Person. The term "person" shall be construed to mean and include an individual, a trust, estate, partnership, association, company or corporation.
(2) Partnership and partner. The term "partnership" includes a syndicate, group, pool, joint venture, or other unincorporated organization, through or by means of which any business, financial operation, or venture is carried on, and which is not, within the meaning of this title, a trust or estate or a corporation; and the term "partner" includes a member in such a syndicate, group, pool, joint venture, or organization.
(3) Corporation. The term "corporation" includes associations, joint-stock companies, and insurance companies.
(4) Domestic. The term "domestic" when applied to a corporation or partnership means created or organized in the United States or under the law of the United States or of any State unless, in the case of a partnership, the Secretary provides otherwise by regulations.
(5) Foreign. The term "foreign" when applied to a corporation or partnership means a corporation or partnership which is not domestic.
(6) Fiduciary. The term "fiduciary" means a guardian, trustee, executor, administrator, receiver, conservator, or any person acting in any fiduciary capacity for any person.
(7) Stock. The term "stock" includes shares in an association, joint-stock company, or insurance company.
(8) Shareholder. The term "shareholder" includes a member in an association, joint-stock company, or insurance company.
(9) United States. The term "United States" when used in a geographical sense includes only the States and the District of Columbia.
(10) State. The term "State" shall be construed to include the District of Columbia, where such construction is necessary to carry out provisions of this title.
(11) Secretary of the Treasury and Secretary.
(A) Secretary of the Treasury. The term "Secretary of the Treasury" means the Secretary of the Treasury, personally, and shall not include any delegate of his.
(B) Secretary. The term "Secretary" means the Secretary of the Treasury or his delegate.

(12) Delegate.
  (A) In general. The term "or his delegate"—
    (i) when used with reference to the Secretary of the Treasury, means any officer, employee, or agency of the Treasury Department duly authorized by the Secretary of the Treasury directly, or indirectly by one or more redelegations of authority, to perform the function mentioned or described in the context; and
    (ii) when used with reference to any other official of the United States, shall be similarly construed.
  (B) Performance of certain functions in Guam or American Samoa. The term "delegate," in relation to the performance of functions in Guam or American Samoa with respect to the taxes imposed by chapters 1, 2, and 21, also includes any officer or employee of any other department or agency of the United States, or of any possession thereof, duly authorized by the Secretary (directly, or indirectly by one or more redelegations of authority) to perform such functions.

(13) Commissioner. The term "Commissioner" means the Commissioner of Internal Revenue.

(14) Taxpayer. The term "taxpayer" means any person subject to any internal revenue tax.

(15) Military or naval forces and armed forces of the United States. The term "military or naval forces of the United States" and the term "Armed Forces of the United States" each includes all regular and reserve components of the uniformed services which are subject to the jurisdiction of the Secretary of Defense, the Secretary of the Army, the Secretary of the Navy, or the Secretary of the Air Force, and each term also includes the Coast Guard. The members of such forces include commissioned officers and personnel below the grade of commissioned officers in such forces.

(16) Withholding agent. The term "withholding agent" means any person required to deduct and withhold any tax under the provisions of sections 1441, 1442, 1443, or 1461.

(17) Husband and wife. As used in sections 682 and 2516, if the husband and wife therein referred to are divorced, wherever appropriate to the meaning of such sections, the term "wife" shall be read "former wife" and the term "husband" shall be read "former husband"; and, if the payments described in such sections are made by or on behalf of the wife or former wife to the husband or former husband instead of vice versa, wherever appropriate to the meaning of such sections, the term "husband" shall be read "wife" and the term "wife" shall be read "husband."

(18) International organization. The term "international organization" means a public international organization entitled to enjoy privileges, exemptions, and immunities as an international organization under the International Organizations Immunities Act (22 U.S.C. 288–288f).

(19) Domestic building and loan association. The term "domestic building and loan association" means a domestic building and loan association, a domestic savings and loan association, and a Federal savings and loan association—
  (A) which either (i) is an insured institution within the meaning of section 401(a) of the National Housing Act (12 U.S.C., sec. 1724(a)), or (ii) is subject by law to supervision and examination by State or Federal authority having supervision over such associations;
  (B) the business of which consists principally of acquiring the savings of the public and investing in loans; and
  (C) at least 60 percent of the amount of the total assets of which (at the close of the taxable year) consists of—
    (i) cash,
    (ii) obligations of the United States or of a State or political subdivision thereof, and stock or obligations of a corporation which is an instrumentality of the United States or of a State or political subdivision thereof, but not including obligations the interest on which is excludable from gross income under section 103,
    (iii) certificates of deposit in, or obligations of, a corporation organized under a State law which specifically authorizes such corporation to insure the deposits or share accounts of member associations,
    (iv) loans secured by a deposit or share of a member,
    (v) loans (including redeemable ground rents, as defined in section 1055) secured by an interest in real property which is (or, from the proceeds of the loan, will become) residential real property or real property used primarily for church purposes, loans made for the improvement of residential real property or real property used primarily for church purposes, provided that for purposes of this clause, residential real property shall include single or multifamily dwellings, facilities in residential developments dedicated to public use or property used on a nonprofit basis for residents, and mobile homes not used on a transient basis,
    (vi) loans secured by an interest in real property located within an urban renewal area to be developed for predominantly residential use under an urban renewal plan approved by the Secretary of Housing and Urban Development under part A or part B of title I of the Housing Act of 1949, as amended, or located within any area covered by a program eligible for assistance under section 103 of the Demonstration Cities and Metropolitan Development Act of 1966, as amended, and loans made for the improvement of any such real property,
    (vii) loans secured by an interest in educational, health, or welfare institutions or facilities, including structures designed or used primarily for residential purposes for students, residents, and persons under care, employees, or members of the staff of such institutions or facilities,
    (viii) property acquired through the liquidation of defaulted loans described in clause (v), (vi), or (vii),
    (ix) loans made for the payment of expenses of college or university education or vocational training, in accordance with such regulations as may be prescribed by the Secretary,
    (x) property used by the association in the conduct of the business described in subparagraph (B), and
    (xi) any regular or residual interest in a REMIC, but only in the proportion which the assets of such REMIC consist of property described in any of the preceding clauses of this subparagraph; except that if 95 percent or more of the assets of such REMIC are assets described in clauses (i) through (x), the entire interest in the REMIC shall qualify.

At the election of the taxpayer, the percentage specified in this subparagraph shall be applied on the basis of the average assets outstanding during the taxable year, in lieu of the close of the taxable year, computed under regulations prescribed by the Secretary. For purposes of clause (v), if a multifamily structure securing a loan is used in part for nonresidential purposes, the entire loan is deemed a residential real property loan if the planned residential use exceeds 80 percent of the property's planned use (determined as of the time the loan is made). For purposes of clause (v), loans made to finance the acquisition or development of land shall be deemed to be loans secured by an interest in residential real property if, under regulations prescribed by the Secretary, there is reasonable assurance that the property will become residential real property within a period of 3 years from the date of acquisition of such land; but this sentence shall not apply for any taxable year unless, within such 3-year period, such land becomes residential real property. For purposes of determining whether any interest in a REMIC qualifies under clause (xi), any regular interest in another REMIC held by such REMIC shall be treated as a loan described in a preceding clause under principles similar to the principles of clause (xi); except that, if such REMIC's are part of a tiered structure, they shall be treated as 1 REMIC for purposes of clause (xi).

(20) Employee. For the purpose of applying the provisions of section 79 with respect to group-term life insurance purchased for employees, for the purpose of applying the provisions of sections 104, 105, and 106 with respect to accident and health insurance or accident and health plans, and for the purpose of applying the provisions of subtitle A with respect to contributions to or under a stock bonus, pension, profit-sharing, or annuity plan, and with respect to distributions under such a plan, or by a trust forming part of such a plan, and for purposes of applying section 125 with respect to cafeteria plans, the term "employee" shall include a full-time life insurance salesman who is considered an employee for the purpose of chapter 21, or in the case of services performed before January 1, 1951, who would be considered an employee if his services were performed during 1951.

(21) Levy. The term "levy" includes the power of distraint and seizure by any means.

(22) Attorney General. The term "Attorney General" means the Attorney General of the United States.

(23) Taxable year. The term "taxable year" means the calendar year, or the fiscal year ending during such calendar year, upon the basis of which the taxable income is computed under subtitle A. "Taxable year" means, in the case of a return made for a fractional part of a year under the provisions of subtitle A or under regulations prescribed by the Secretary, the period for which such return is made.

(24) Fiscal year. The term "fiscal year" means an accounting period of 12 months ending on the last day of any month other than December.

(25) Paid or incurred, paid or accrued. The terms "paid or incurred" and "paid or accrued" shall be construed according to the method of accounting upon the basis of which the taxable income is computed under subtitle A.

(26) Trade or business. The term "trade or business" includes the performance of the functions of a public office.

(27) Tax Court. The term "Tax Court" means the United States Tax Court.

(28) Other terms. Any term used in this subtitle with respect to the application of, or in connection with, the provisions of any other subtitle of this title shall have the same meaning as in such provisions.

(29) Internal Revenue Code. The term "Internal Revenue Code of 1986" means this title, and the term "Internal Revenue Code of 1939" means the Internal Revenue Code enacted February 10, 1939, as amended.

(30) United States person. The term "United States person" means—
(A) a citizen or resident of the United States,
(B) a domestic partnership,
(C) a domestic corporation,
(D) any estate (other than a foreign estate, within the meaning, of paragraph (31)), and
(E) any trust if—
  (i) a court within the United States is able to exercise primary supervision over the administration of the trust, and
  (ii) one or more United States persons have the authority to control all substantial decisions of the trust.

(31) Foreign estate or trust.
(A) Foreign estate. The term "foreign estate" means an estate the income of which, from sources without the United States which is not effectively connected with the conduct of a trade or business within the United States, is not includible in gross income under subtitle A.
(B) Foreign trust. The term "foreign trust" means any trust other than a trust described in subparagraph (E) of paragraph (30).

(32) Cooperative bank. The term "cooperative bank" means an institution without capital stock organized and operated for mutual purposes and without profit, which—
(A) either—
  (i) is an insured institution within the meaning of section 401(a) of the National Housing Act (12 U.S.C., sec. 1724(a)), or
  (ii) is subject by law to supervision and examination by State or Federal authority having supervision over such institutions, and
(B) meets the requirements of subparagraphs (B) and (C) of paragraph (19) of this subsection (relating to definition of domestic building and loan association).
In determining whether an institution meets the requirements referred to in subparagraph (B) of this paragraph, any reference to an association or to a domestic building and loan association contained in paragraph (19) shall be deemed to be a reference to such institution.

(33) Regulated public utility. The term "regulated public utility" means—
(A) A corporation engaged in the furnishing or sale of—
  (i) electric energy, gas, water, or sewerage disposal services, or
  (ii) transportation (not included in subparagraph (C)) on an intrastate, suburban, municipal, or interurban electric railroad, on an intrastate, municipal, or suburban trackless trolley system, or on a municipal or suburban bus system, or
  (iii) transportation (not included in clause (ii)) by motor vehicle—
if the rates for such furnishing or sale, as the case may be, have been established or approved by a State or political subdivision thereof, by an agency or instrumentality of the United States, by a public service or public utility commission or other similar body of the District of Columbia or of any State or political subdivision thereof, or by a foreign country or an agency or instrumentality or political subdivision thereof.
(B) A corporation engaged as a common carrier in the furnishing or sale of transportation of gas by pipe line, if subject to the jurisdiction of the Federal Energy Regulatory Commission.

(C) A corporation engaged as a common carrier (i) in the furnishing or sale of transportation by railroad, if subject to the jurisdiction of the Surface Transportation Board, or (ii) in the furnishing or sale of transportation of oil or other petroleum products (including shale oil) by pipe line, if subject to the jurisdiction of the Federal Energy Regulatory Commission or if the rates for such furnishing or sale are subject to the jurisdiction of a public service or public utility commission or other similar body of the District of Columbia or of any State.

(D) A corporation engaged in the furnishing or sale of telephone or telegraph service, if the rates for such furnishing or sale meet the requirements of subparagraph (A).

(E) A corporation engaged in the furnishing or sale of transportation as a common carrier by air, subject to the jurisdiction of the Secretary of Transportation.

(F) A corporation engaged in the furnishing or sale of transportation by a water carrier subject to jurisdiction under subchapter II of chapter 135 of title 49.

(G) A rail carrier subject to part A of subtitle IV of title 49, if (i) substantially all of its railroad properties have been leased to another such railroad corporation or corporations by an agreement or agreements entered into before January 1, 1954, (ii) each lease is for a term of more than 20 years, and (iii) at least 80 percent or more of its gross income (computed without regard to dividends and capital gains and losses) for the taxable year is derived from such leases and from sources described in subparagraphs (A) through (F), inclusive. For purposes of the preceding sentence, an agreement for lease of railroad properties entered into before January 1, 1954, shall be considered to be a lease including such term as the total number of years of such agreement may, unless sooner terminated, be renewed or continued under the terms of the agreement, and any such renewal or continuance under such agreement shall be considered part of the lease entered into before January 1, 1954.

(H) A common parent corporation which is a common carrier by railroad subject to part A of subtitle IV of title 49 if at least 80 percent of its gross income (computed without regard to capital gains or losses) is derived directly or indirectly from sources described in subparagraphs (A) through (F), inclusive. For purposes of the preceding sentence, dividends and interest, and income from leases described in subparagraph (G), received from a regulated public utility shall be considered as derived from sources described in subparagraphs (A) through (F), inclusive, if the regulated public utility is a member of an affiliated group (as defined in section 1504) which includes the common parent corporation.

The term "regulated public utility" does not (except as provided in subparagraphs (G) and (H)) include a corporation described in subparagraphs (A) through (F), inclusive, unless 80 percent or more of its gross income (computed without regard to dividends and capital gains and losses) for the taxable year is derived from sources described in subparagraphs (A) through (F), inclusive. If the taxpayer establishes to the satisfaction of the Secretary that (i) its revenue from regulated rates described in subparagraph (A) or (D) and its revenue derived from unregulated rates are derived from the operation of a single interconnected and coordinated system or from the operation of more than one such system, and (ii) the unregulated rates have been and are substantially as favorable to users and consumers as are the regulated rates, then such revenue from such unregulated rates shall be considered, for purposes of the preceding sentence, as income derived from sources described in subparagraph (A) or (D).

(34) Repealed.

(35) Enrolled actuary. The term "enrolled actuary" means a person who is enrolled by the Joint Board for the Enrollment of Actuaries established under subtitle C of the title III of the Employee Retirement Income Security Act of 1974.

(36) Tax return preparer.

(A) In general. The term " tax return preparer" means any person who prepares for compensation, or who employs one or more persons to prepare for compensation, any return of tax imposed by this title or any claim for refund of tax imposed by this title. For purposes of the preceding sentence, the preparation of a substantial portion of a return or claim for refund shall be treated as if it were the preparation of such return or claim for refund.

(B) Exceptions. A person shall not be an " tax return preparer" merely because such person—

(i) furnishes typing, reproducing, or other mechanical assistance,

(ii) prepares a return or claim for refund of the employer (or of an officer or employee of the employer) by whom he is regularly and continuously employed,

(iii) prepares as a fiduciary a return or claim for refund for any person, or

(iv) prepares a claim for refund for a taxpayer in response to any notice of deficiency issued to such taxpayer or in response to any waiver of restriction after the commencement of an audit of such taxpayer or another taxpayer if a determination in such audit of such other taxpayer directly or indirectly affects the tax liability of such taxpayer.

(37) Individual retirement plan. The term "individual retirement plan" means—

(A) an individual retirement account described in section 408(a), and

(B) an individual retirement annuity described in section 408(b).

(38) Joint return. The term "joint return" means a single return made jointly under section 6013 by a husband and wife.

(39) Persons residing outside United States. If any citizen or resident of the United States does not reside in (and is not found in) any United States judicial district, such citizen or resident shall be treated as residing in the District of Columbia for purposes of any provision of this title relating to—

(A) jurisdiction of courts, or

(B) enforcement of summons.

(40) Indian tribal government.

(A) In general. The term "Indian tribal government" means the governing body of any tribe, band, community, village, or group of Indians, or (if applicable) Alaska Natives, which is determined by the Secretary, after consultation with the Secretary of the Interior, to exercise governmental functions.

(B) Special rule for Alaska natives. No determination under subparagraph (A) with respect to Alaska Natives shall grant or defer any status or powers other than those enumerated in section 7871. Nothing in the Indian Tribal Governmental Tax Status Act of 1982, or in the amendments made thereby, shall validate or invalidate any claim by Alaska Natives of sovereign authority over lands or people.

(41) TIN. The term "TIN" means the identifying number assigned to a person under section 6109.

(42) Substituted basis property. The term "substituted basis property" means property which is—
(A) transferred basis property, or
(B) exchanged basis property.

(43) Transferred basis property. The term "transferred basis property" means property having a basis determined under any provision of subtitle A (or under any corresponding provision of prior income tax law) providing that the basis shall be determined in whole or in part by reference to the basis in the hands of the donor, grantor, or other transferor.

(44) Exchanged basis property. The term "exchanged basis property" means property having a basis determined under any provision of subtitle A (or under any corresponding provision of prior income tax law) providing that the basis shall be determined in whole or in part by reference to other property held at any time by the person for whom the basis is to be determined.

(45) Nonrecognition transaction. The term "nonrecognition transaction" means any disposition of property in a transaction in which gain or loss is not recognized in whole or in part for purposes of subtitle A.

(46) Determination of whether there is a collective bargaining agreement. In determining whether there is a collective bargaining agreement between employee representatives and 1 or more employers, the term "employee representatives" shall not include any organization more than one-half of the members of which are employees who are owners, officers, or executives of the employer. An agreement shall not be treated as a collective bargaining agreement unless it is a bona fide agreement between bona fide employee representatives and 1 or more employers.

• *Caution:* Code Sec. 7701(a)(47), following, was added by Sec. 542(e)(2), P.L. 107-16, EGTRRA. As provided in Sec. 301(a), P.L. 111-312, this amendment will apply as if never enacted, effective for estates of decedents dying, and transfers made, after 12/31/2009.

(47) Executor. The term "executor" means the executor or administrator of the decedent, or, if there is no executor or administrator appointed, qualified, and acting within the United States, then any person in actual or constructive possession of any property of the decedent.

(48) Off-highway vehicles.
(A) Off-highway transportation vehicles.
(i) In general. A vehicle shall not be treated as a highway vehicle if such vehicle is specially designed for the primary function of transporting a particular type of load other than over the public highway and because of this special design such vehicle's capability to transport a load over the public highway is substantially limited or impaired.
(ii) Determination of vehicle's design. For purposes of clause (i), a vehicle's design is determined solely on the basis of its physical characteristics.
(iii) Determination of substantial limitation or impairment. For purposes of clause (i), in determining whether substantial limitation or impairment exists, account may be taken of factors such as the size of the vehicle, whether such vehicle is subject to the licensing, safety, and other requirements applicable to highway vehicles, and whether such vehicle can transport a load at a sustained speed of at least 25 miles per hour. It is immaterial that a vehicle can transport a greater load off the public highway than such vehicle is permitted to transport over the public highway.
(B) Nontransportation trailers and semitrailers. A trailer or semitrailer shall not be treated as a highway vehicle if it is specially designed to function only as an enclosed stationary shelter for the carrying on of an off-highway function at an off-highway site.

(49) Qualified blood collector organization. The term "qualified blood collector organization" means an organization which is—
(A) described in section 501(c)(3) and exempt from tax under section 501(a),
(B) primarily engaged in the activity of the collection of human blood,
(C) registered with the Secretary for purposes of excise tax exemptions, and
(D) registered by the Food and Drug Administration to collect blood.

(50) Termination of United States citizenship.
(A) In general. An individual shall not cease to be treated as a United States citizen before the date on which the individual's citizenship is treated as relinquished under section 877A(g)(4).
(B) Dual citizen. Under regulations prescribed by the Secretary, subparagraph (A) shall not apply to an individual who became at birth a citizen of the United States and a citizen of another country.

(b) Definition of resident alien and nonresident alien.
(1) In general. For purposes of this title (other than subtitle B)—
(A) Resident alien. An alien individual shall be treated as a resident of the United States with respect to any calendar year if (and only if) such individual meets the requirements of clause (i), (ii), or (iii):
(i) Lawfully admitted for permanent residence. Such individual is a lawful permanent resident of the United States at any time during such calendar year.
(ii) Substantial presence test. Such individual meets the substantial presence test of paragraph (3).
(iii) First year election. Such individual makes the election provided in paragraph (4).
(B) Nonresident alien. An individual is a nonresident alien if such individual is neither a citizen of the United States nor a resident of the United States (within the meaning of subparagraph (A)).

(2) Special rules for first and last year of residency.
(A) First year of residency.
(i) In general. If an alien individual is a resident of the United States under paragraph (1)(A) with respect to any calendar year, but was not a resident of the United States at any time during the preceding calendar year, such alien individual shall be treated as a resident of the United States only for the portion of such calendar year which begins on the residency starting date.

(ii) Residency starting date for individuals lawfully admitted for permanent residence. In the case of an individual who is a lawfully permanent resident of the United States at any time during the calendar year, but does not meet the substantial presence test of paragraph (3), the residency starting date shall be the first day in such calendar year on which he was present in the United States while a lawful permanent resident of the United States.

(iii) Residency starting date for individuals meeting substantial presence test. In the case of an individual who meets the substantial presence test of paragraph (3) with respect to any calendar year, the residency starting date shall be the first day during such calendar year on which the individual is present in the United States.

(iv) Residency starting date for individuals making first year election. In the case of an individual who makes the election provided by paragraph (4) with respect to any calendar year, the residency starting date shall be the 1st day during such calendar year on which the individual is treated as a resident of the United States under that paragraph.

(B) Last year of residency. An alien individual shall not be treated as a resident of the United States during a portion of any calendar year if—

(i) such portion is after the last day in such calendar year on which the individual was present in the United States (or, in the case of an individual described in paragraph (1)(A)(i), the last day on which he was so described),

(ii) during such portion the individual has a closer connection to a foreign country than to the United States, and

(iii) the individual is not a resident of the United States at any time during the next calendar year.

(C) Certain nominal presence disregarded.

(i) In general. For purposes of subparagraphs (A)(iii) and (B), an individual shall not be treated as present in the United States during any period for which the individual establishes that he has a closer connection to a foreign country than to the United States.

(ii) Not more than 10 days disregarded. Clause (i) shall not apply to more than 10 days on which the individual is present in the United States.

(3) Substantial presence test.

(A) In general. Except as otherwise provided in this paragraph, an individual meets the substantial presence test of this paragraph with respect to any calendar year (hereinafter in this subsection referred to as the "current year") if—

(i) such individual was present in the United States on at least 31 days during the calendar year, and

(ii) the sum of the number of days on which such individual was present in the United States during the current year and the 2 preceding calendar years (when multiplied by the applicable multiplier determined under the following table) equals or exceeds 183 days:

In the case of days in:	The applicable multiplier is:
Current year	1
1st preceding year	1/3
2nd preceding year	1/6

(B) Exception where individual is present in the United States during less than one-half of current year and closer connection to foreign country is established. An individual shall not be treated as meeting the substantial presence test of this paragraph with respect to any current year if—

(i) such individual is present in the United States on fewer than 183 days during the current year, and

(ii) it is established that for the current year such individual has a tax home (as defined in section 911(d)(3) without regard to the second sentence thereof) in a foreign country and has a closer connection to such foreign country than to the United States.

(C) Subparagraph (B) not to apply in certain cases. Subparagraph (B) shall not apply to any individual with respect to any current year if at any time during such year—

(i) such individual had an application for adjustment of status pending, or

(ii) such individual took other steps to apply for status as a lawful permanent resident of the United States.

(D) Exception for exempt individuals or for certain medical conditions. An individual shall not be treated as being present in the United States on any day if—

(i) such individual is an exempt individual for such day, or

(ii) such individual was unable to leave the United States on such day because of a medical condition which arose while such individual was present in the United States.

(4) First-year election.

(A) An alien individual shall be deemed to meet the requirements of this subparagraph if such individual—

(i) is not a resident of the United States under clause (i) or (ii) of paragraph (1)(A) with respect to a calendar year (hereinafter referred to as the "election year"),

(ii) was not a resident of the United States under paragraph (1)(A) with respect to the calendar year immediately preceding the election year,

(iii) is a resident of the United States under clause (ii) of paragraph (1)(A) with respect to the calendar year immediately following the election year, and

(iv) is both—

(I) present in the United States for a period of at least 31 consecutive days in the election year, and

(II) present in the United States during the period beginning with the first day of such 31-day period and ending with the last day of the election year (hereinafter referred to as the "testing period") for a number of days equal to or exceeding 75 percent of the number of days in the testing period (provided that an individual shall be treated for purposes of this subclause as present in the United States for a number of days during the testing period not exceeding 5 days in the aggregate, notwithstanding his absence from the United States on such days).

(B) An alien individual who meets the requirements of subparagraph (A) shall, if he so elects, be treated as a resident of the United States with respect to the election year.

(C) An alien individual who makes the election provided by subparagraph (B) shall be treated as a resident of the United States for the portion of the election year which begins on the 1st day of the earliest testing period during such year with respect to which the individual meets the requirements of clause (iv) of subparagraph (A).

(D) The rules of subparagraph (D)(i) of paragraph (3) shall apply for purposes of determining an individual's presence in the United States under this paragraph.

(E) An election under subparagraph (B) shall be made on the individual's tax return for the election year, provided that such election may not be made before the individual has met the substantial presence test of paragraph (3) with respect to the calendar year immediately following the election year.

(F) An election once made under subparagraph (B) remains in effect for the election year, unless revoked with the consent of the Secretary.

(5) Exempt individual defined. For purposes of this subsection—

(A) In general. An individual is an exempt individual for any day if, for such day, such individual is—
  (i) a foreign government-related individual,
  (ii) a teacher or trainee,
  (iii) a student, or
  (iv) a professional athlete who is temporarily in the United States to compete in a charitable sports event described in section 274(l)(1)(B).

(B) Foreign government-related individual. The term "foreign government-related individual" means any individual temporarily present in the United States by reason of—
  (i) diplomatic status, or a visa which the Secretary (after consultation with the Secretary of State) determines represents full-time diplomatic or consular status for purposes of this subsection,
  (ii) being a full-time employee of an international organization, or
  (iii) being a member of the immediate family of an individual described in clause (i) or (ii).

(C) Teacher or trainee. The term "teacher or trainee" means any individual—
  (i) who is temporarily present in the United States under subparagraph (J) or (Q) of section 101(15) of the Immigration and Nationality Act (other than as a student), and
  (ii) who substantially complies with the requirements for being so present.

(D) Student. The term "student" means any individual—
  (i) who is temporarily present in the United States—
    (I) under subparagraph (F) or (M) of section 101(15) of the Immigration and Nationality Act, or
    (II) as a student under subparagraph (J) or (Q) of such section 101(15), and
  (ii) who substantially complies with the requirements for being so present.

(E) Special rules for teachers, trainees, and students.
  (i) Limitation on teachers and trainees. An individual shall not be treated as an exempt individual by reason of clause (ii) of subparagraph (A) for the current year if, for any 2 calendar years during the preceding 6 calendar years, such person was an exempt person under clause (ii) or (iii) of subparagraph (A). In the case of an individual all of whose compensation is described in section 872(b)(3), the preceding sentence shall be applied by substituting "4 calendar years" for "2 calendar years".

  (ii) Limitation on students. For any calendar year after the 5th calendar year for which an individual was an exempt individual under clause (ii) or (iii) of subparagraph (A), such individual shall not be treated as an exempt individual by reason of clause (iii) of subparagraph (A), unless such individual establishes to the satisfaction of the Secretary that such individual does not intend to permanently reside in the United States and that such individual meets the requirements of subparagraph (D)(ii).

(6) Lawful permanent resident. For purposes of this subsection, an individual is a lawful permanent resident of the United States at any time if—

(A) such individual has the status of having been lawfully accorded the privilege of residing permanently in the United States as an immigrant in accordance with the immigration laws, and

(B) such status has not been revoked (and has not been administratively or judicially determined to have been abandoned).

An individual shall cease to be treated as a lawful permanent resident of the United States if such individual commences to be treated as a resident of a foreign country under the provisions of a tax treaty between the United States and the foreign country, does not waive the benefits of such treaty applicable to residents of the foreign country, and notifies the Secretary of the commencement of such treatment.

(7) Presence in the United States. For purposes of this subsection—

(A) In general. Except as provided in subparagraph (B), (C), or (D), an individual shall be treated as present in the United States on any day if such individual is physically present in the United States at any time during such day.

(B) Commuters from Canada or Mexico. If an individual regularly commutes to employment (or self-employment) in the United States from a place of residence in Canada or Mexico, such individual shall not be treated as present in the United States on any day during which he so commutes.

(C) Transit between 2 foreign points. If an individual, who is in transit between 2 points outside the United States, is physically present in the United States for less than 24 hours, such individual shall not be treated as present in the United States on any day during such transit.

(D) Crew members temporarily present. An individual who is temporarily present in the United States on any day as a regular member of the crew of a foreign vessel engaged in transportation between the United States and a foreign country or a possession of the United States shall not be treated as present in the United States on such day unless such individual otherwise engages in any trade or business in the United States on such day.

(8) Annual statements. The Secretary may prescribe regulations under which an individual who (but for subparagraph (B) or (D) of paragraph (3)) would meet the substantial presence test of paragraph (3) is required to submit an annual statement setting forth the basis on which such individual claims the benefits of subparagraph (B) or (D) of paragraph (3), as the case may be.

(9) Taxable year.

(A) In general. For purposes of this title, an alien individual who has not established a taxable year for any prior period shall be treated as having a taxable year which is the calendar year.

Miscellaneous provisions

(B) Fiscal year taxpayer. If—
  (i) an individual is treated under paragraph (1) as a resident of the United States for any calendar year, and
  (ii) after the application of subparagraph (A), such individual has a taxable year other than a calendar year,

he shall be treated as a resident of the United States with respect to any portion of a taxable year which is within such calendar year.

(10) Coordination with section 877. If—
  (A) an alien individual was treated as a resident of the United States during any period which includes at least 3 consecutive calendar years (hereinafter referred to as the "initial residency period"), and
  (B) such individual ceases to be treated as a resident of the United States but subsequently becomes a resident of the United States before the close of the 3rd calendar year beginning after the close of the initial residency period,

such individual shall be taxable for the period after the close of the initial residency period and before the day on which he subsequently became a resident of the United States in the manner provided in section 877(b). The preceding sentence shall apply only if the tax imposed pursuant to section 877(b) exceeds the tax which, without regard to this paragraph, is imposed pursuant to section 871.

(11) Regulations. The Secretary shall prescribe such regulations as may be necessary or appropriate to carry out the purposes of this subsection.

(c) Includes and including.

The terms "includes" and "including" when used in a definition contained in this title shall not be deemed to exclude other things otherwise within the meaning of the term defined.

(d) Commonwealth of Puerto Rico.

Where not otherwise distinctly expressed or manifestly incompatible with the intent thereof, references in this title to possessions of the United States shall be treated as also referring to the Commonwealth of Puerto Rico.

(e) Treatment of certain contracts for providing services, etc.

For purposes of chapter 1—

(1) In general. A contract which purports to be a service contract shall be treated as a lease of property if such contract is properly treated as a lease of property, taking into account all relevant factors including whether or not—
  (A) the service recipient is in physical possession of the property,
  (B) the service recipient controls the property,
  (C) the service recipient has a significant economic or possessory interest in the property,
  (D) the service provider does not bear any risk of substantially diminished receipts or substantially increased expenditures if there is nonperformance under the contract,
  (E) the service provider does not use the property concurrently to provide significant services to entities unrelated to the service recipient, and
  (F) the total contract price does not substantially exceed the rental value of the property for the contract period.

(2) Other arrangements. An arrangement (including a partnership or other pass-thru entity) which is not described in paragraph (1) shall be treated as a lease if such arrangement is properly treated as a lease, taking into account all relevant factors including factors set forth in paragraph (1).

(3) Special rules for contracts or arrangements involving solid waste disposal, energy, and clean water facilities.
  (A) In general. Notwithstanding paragraphs (1) and (2), and except as provided in paragraph (4), any contract or arrangement between a service provider and a service recipient—
    (i) with respect to—
      (I) the operation of a qualified solid waste disposal facility,
      (II) the sale to the service recipient of electrical or thermal energy produced at a cogeneration or alternative energy facility, or
      (III) the operation of a water treatment works facility, and
    (ii) which purports to be a service contract, shall be treated as a service contract.
  (B) Qualified solid waste disposal facility. For purposes of subparagraph (A), the term "qualified solid waste disposal facility" means any facility if such facility provides solid waste disposal services for residents of part or all of 1 or more governmental units and substantially all of the solid waste processed at such facility is collected from the general public.
  (C) Cogeneration facility. For purposes of subparagraph (A), the term "cogeneration facility" means a facility which uses the same energy source for the sequential generation of electrical or mechanical power in combination with steam, heat, or other forms of useful energy.
  (D) Alternative energy facility. For purposes of subparagraph (A), the term "alternative energy facility" means a facility for producing electrical or thermal energy if the primary energy source for the facility is not oil, natural gas, coal, or nuclear power.
  (E) Water treatment works facility. For purposes of subparagraph (A), the term "water treatment works facility" means any treatment works within the meaning of section 212(2) of the Federal Water Pollution Control Act.

(4) Paragraph (3) not to apply in certain cases.
  (A) In general. Paragraph (3) shall not apply to any qualified solid waste disposal facility, cogeneration facility, alternative energy facility, or water treatment works facility used under a contract or arrangement if—
    (i) the service recipient (or a related entity) operates such facility,
    (ii) the service recipient (or a related entity) bears any significant financial burden if there is nonperformance under the contract or arrangement (other than for reasons beyond the control of the service provider),
    (iii) the service recipient (or a related entity) receives any significant financial benefit if the operating costs of such facility are less than the standards of performance or operation under the contract or arrangement, or
    (iv) the service recipient (or a related entity) has an option to purchase, or may be required to purchase, all or a part of such facility at a fixed and determinable price (other than for fair market value).

Miscellaneous provisions

Code Sec. 7701(e)

For purposes paragraph, the term "related entity" has meaning as when used in section 168(h) sales for application of subparagraph (A) (B) ct to certain rights and allocations under the wi... For purposes of subparagraph (A), there shall be taken into account—

(i) any right of a service recipient to inspect any facility, to exercise any sovereign power the service recipient may possess, or to act in the event of a breach of contract by the service provider, or

(ii) any allocation of any financial burden or benefits in the event of any change in any law.

(C) Special rules for application of subparagraph (A) in the case of certain events.

(i) Temporary shut-downs, etc. For purposes of clause (ii) of subparagraph (A), there shall not be taken into account any temporary shut-down of the facility for repairs, maintenance, or capital improvements, or any financial burden caused by the bankruptcy or similar financial difficulty of the service provider.

(ii) Reduced costs. For purposes of clause (iii) of subparagraph (A), there shall not be taken into account any significant financial benefit merely because payments by the service recipient under the contract or arrangement are decreased by reason of increased production or efficiency or the recovery of energy or other products.

(5) Exception for certain low-income housing. This subsection shall not apply to any property described in clause (i), (ii), (iii), or (iv) of section 1250(a)(1)(B) (relating to low-income housing) if—

(A) such property is operated by or for an organization described in paragraph (3) or (4) of section 501(c), and

(B) at least 80 percent of the units in such property are leased to low-income tenants (within the meaning of section 167(k)(3)(B) (as in effect on the day before the date of the enactment [11/5/90] of the Revenue Reconciliation Act of 1990).

(6) Regulations. The Secretary may prescribe such regulations as may be necessary or appropriate to carry out the provisions of this subsection.

(f) Use of related persons or pass-thru entities.

The Secretary shall prescribe such regulations as may be necessary or appropriate to prevent the avoidance of those provisions of this title which deal with—

(1) the linking of borrowing to investment, or

(2) diminishing risks,

through the use of related persons, pass-thru entities, or other intermediaries.

(g) Clarification of fair market value in the case of nonrecourse indebtedness.

For purposes of subtitle A, in determining the amount of gain or loss (or deemed gain or loss) with respect to any property, the fair market value of such property shall be treated as being not less than the amount of any nonrecourse indebtedness to which such property is subject.

(h) Motor vehicle operating leases.

(1) In general. For purposes of this title, in the case of a qualified motor vehicle operating agreement which contains a terminal rental adjustment clause—

(A) such agreement shall be treated as a lease if (but for such terminal rental adjustment clause) such agreement would be treated as a lease under this title, and

(B) the lessee shall not be treated as the owner of the property subject to an agreement during any period such agreement is in effect.

(2) Qualified motor vehicle operating agreement defined. For purposes of this subsection—

(A) In general. The term "qualified motor vehicle operating agreement" means any agreement with respect to a motor vehicle (including a trailer) which meets the requirements of subparagraphs (B), (C), and (D) of this paragraph.

(B) Minimum liability of lessor. An agreement meets the requirements of this subparagraph if under such agreement the sum of—

(i) the amount the lessor is personally liable to repay, and

(ii) the net fair market value of the lessor's interest in any property pledged as security for property subject to the agreement,

equals or exceeds all amounts borrowed to finance the acquisition of property subject to the agreement. There shall not be taken into account under clause (ii) any property pledged which is property subject to the agreement or property directly or indirectly financed by indebtedness secured by property subject to the agreement.

(C) Certification by lessee; notice of tax ownership. An agreement meets the requirements of this subparagraph if such agreement contains a separate written statement separately signed by the lessee—

(i) under which the lessee certifies, under penalty of perjury, that it intends that more than 50 percent of the use of the property subject to such agreement is to be in a trade or business of the lessee, and

(ii) which clearly and legibly states that the lessee has been advised that it will not be treated as the owner of the property subject to the agreement for Federal income tax purposes.

(D) Lessor must have no knowledge that certification is false. An agreement meets the requirements of this subparagraph if the lessor does not know that the certification described in subparagraph (C)(i) is false.

(3) Terminal rental adjustment clause defined.

(A) In general. For purposes of this subsection, the term "terminal rental adjustment clause" means a provision of an agreement which permits or requires the rental price to be adjusted upward or downward by reference to the amount realized by the lessor under the agreement upon sale or other disposition of such property.

(B) Special rule for lessee dealers. The term "terminal rental adjustment clause" also includes a provision of an agreement which requires a lessee who is a dealer in motor vehicles to purchase the motor vehicle for a predetermined price and then resell such vehicle where such provision achieves substantially the same results as a provision described in subparagraph (A).

(i) Taxable mortgage pools.

(1) Treated as separate corporations. A taxable mortgage pool shall be treated as a separate corporation which may not be treated as an includible corporation with any other corporation for purposes of section 1501.

(2) Taxable mortgage pool defined. For purposes of this title—

(A) In general. Except as otherwise provided in this paragraph, a taxable mortgage pool is any entity (other than a REMIC) if—

Miscellaneous provisions

(i) substantially all of the assets of such entity consists of debt obligations (or interests therein) and more than 50 percent of such debt obligations (or interests) consists of real estate mortgages (or interests therein),

(ii) such entity is the obligor under debt obligations with 2 or more maturities, and

(iii) under the terms of the debt obligations referred to in clause (ii) (or underlying arrangement), payments on such debt obligations bear a relationship to payments on the debt obligations (or interests) referred to in clause (i).

(B) Portion of entities treated as pools. Any portion of an entity which meets the definition of subparagraph (A) shall be treated as a taxable mortgage pool.

(C) Exception for domestic building and loan. Nothing in this subsection shall be construed to treat any domestic building and loan association (or portion thereof) as a taxable mortgage pool.

(D) Treatment of certain equity interests. To the extent provided in regulations, equity interest of varying classes which correspond to maturity classes of debt shall be treated as debt for purposes of this subsection.

(3) Treatment of certain REIT's. If—

(A) a real estate investment trust is a taxable mortgage pool, or

(B) a qualified REIT subsidiary (as defined in section 856(i)(2)) of a real estate investment trust is a taxable mortgage pool,

under regulations prescribed by the Secretary, adjustments similar to the adjustments provided in section 860E(d) shall apply to the shareholders of such real estate investment trust.

(j) Tax treatment of Federal Thrift Savings Fund.

(1) In general. For purposes of this title—

(A) the Thrift Savings Fund shall be treated as a trust described in section 401(a) which is exempt from taxation under section 501(a);

(B) any contribution to, or distribution from, the Thrift Savings Fund shall be treated in the same manner as contributions to or distributions from such a trust; and

(C) subject to section 401(k)(4)(B) and any dollar limitation on the application of section 402(e)(3), contributions to the Thrift Savings Fund shall not be treated as distributed or made available to an employee or Member nor as a contribution made to the Fund by an employee or Member merely because the employee or Member has, under the provisions of subchapter III of chapter 84 of title 5, United States Code, and section 8351 of such title 5, an election whether the contribution will be made to the Thrift Savings Fund or received by the employee or Member in cash.

(2) Nondiscrimination requirements. Notwithstanding any other provision of law, the Thrift Savings Fund is not subject to the nondiscrimination requirements applicable to arrangements described in section 401(k) or to matching contributions (as described in section 401(m)), so long as it meets the requirements of this section.

(3) Coordination with Social Security Act. Paragraph (1) shall not be construed to provide that any amount of the employee's or Member's basic pay which is contributed to the Thrift Savings Fund shall not be included in the term "wages" for the purposes of section 209 of the Social Security Act or section 3121(a) of this title.

(4) Definitions. For purposes of this subsection, the terms "Member", "employee", and "Thrift Savings Fund" shall have the same respective meanings chapter III of chapter 84 of title 5, U.

(5) Coordination with other provisions used in subvision of law not contained in this title tes Code. purposes of determining the treatment under No pro- the Thrift Savings Fund or any contribution to, oply for tion from, such Fund.

(k) Treatment of certain amounts paid to charity.

In the case of any payment which, except for section 501(b) of the Ethics in Government Act of 1978, might be made to any officer or employee of the Federal Government but which is made instead on behalf of such officer or employee to an organization described in section 170(c)—

(1) such payment shall not be treated as received by such officer or employee for all purposes of this title and for all purposes of any tax law of a State or political subdivision thereof, and

(2) no deduction shall be allowed under any provision of this title (or of any tax law of a State or political subdivision thereof) to such officer or employee by reason of having such payment made to such organization.

For purposes of this subsection, a Senator, a Representative in, or a Delegate or Resident Commissioner to, the Congress shall be treated as an officer or employee of the Federal Government.

(l) Regulations relating to conduit arrangements.

The Secretary may prescribe regulations recharacterizing any multiple-party financing transaction as a transaction directly among any 2 or more of such parties where the Secretary determines that such recharacterization is appropriate to prevent avoidance of any tax imposed by this title.

(m) Designation of contract markets.

Any designation by the Commodity Futures Trading Commission of a contract market which could not have been made under the law in effect on the day before the date of the enactment [12/21/2000] of the Commodity Futures Modernization Act of 2000 shall apply for purposes of this title except to the extent provided in regulations prescribed by the Secretary.

(n) Convention or association of churches.

For purposes of this title, any organization which is otherwise a convention or association of churches shall not fail to so qualify merely because the membership of such organization includes individuals as well as churches or because individuals have voting rights in such organization.

(o) Clarification of economic substance doctrine.

(1) Application of doctrine. In the case of any transaction to which the economic substance doctrine is relevant, such transaction shall be treated as having economic substance only if—

(A) the transaction changes in a meaningful way (apart from Federal income tax effects) the taxpayer's economic position, and

(B) the taxpayer has a substantial purpose (apart from Federal income tax effects) for entering into such transaction.

(2) Special rule where taxpayer relies on profit potential.

(A) In general. The potential for profit of a transaction shall be taken into account in determining whether the requirements of subparagraphs (A) and (B) of paragraph (1) are met with respect to the transaction only if the present value of the reasonably expected pre-tax profit from the transaction is substantial in relation to the present value of the expected net tax benefits that would be allowed if the transaction were respected.

Miscellaneous provisions

Code Sec. 7701(o)(2)

and foreign taxes. Fees and other transaction expenses shall be taken into account as expenses in determining pre-tax profit under subparagraph (A). The Secretary shall issue regulations requiring foreign taxes to be treated as expenses in determining pre-tax profit in appropriate cases.

(3) **State and local tax benefits.** For purposes of paragraph (1), any State or local income tax effect which is related to a Federal income tax effect shall be treated in the same manner as a Federal income tax effect.

(4) **Financial accounting benefits.** For purposes of paragraph (1)(B), achieving a financial accounting benefit shall not be taken into account as a purpose for entering into a transaction if the origin of such financial accounting benefit is a reduction of Federal income tax.

(5) **Definitions and special rules.** For purposes of this subsection—

(A) Economic substance doctrine. The term "economic substance doctrine" means the common law doctrine under which tax benefits under subtitle A with respect to a transaction are not allowable if the transaction does not have economic substance or lacks a business purpose.

(B) Exception for personal transactions of individuals. In the case of an individual, paragraph (1) shall apply only to transactions entered into in connection with a trade or business or an activity engaged in for the production of income.

(C) Determination of application of doctrine not affected. The determination of whether the economic substance doctrine is relevant to a transaction shall be made in the same manner as if this subsection had never been enacted.

(D) Transaction. The term "transaction" includes a series of transactions.

(p) **Cross references.**

(1) **Other definitions.** For other definitions, see the following sections of Title 1 of the United States Code:

(1) Singular as including plural, section 1.

(2) Plural as including singular, section 1.

(3) Masculine as including feminine, section 1.

(4) Officer, section 1.

(5) Oath as including affirmation, section 1.

(6) County as including parish, section 2.

(7) Vessel as including all means of water transportation, section 3.

(8) Vehicle as including all means of land transportation, section 4.

(9) Company or association as including successors and assigns, section 5.

(2) **Effect of cross references.** For effect of cross references in this title, see section 7806(a).

In 2010, P.L. 111-312, Sec. 101(a)(1), substituted "December 31, 2012" for "December 31, 2010" both places it appeared in Sec. 901 of P.L. 107-16 [see below], effective as if included in the enactment of P.L. 107-16, EGTRRA, 6/7/2001.

—P.L. 111-312, Sec. 301(a), provides that Code Sec. 7701, as amended by Sec. 542(e)(3), P.L. 107-16, EGTRRA, 6/7/2001 [see below] will read as if such provision had never been enacted, effective for estates of decedents dying, and transfers made, after 12/31/2009.

Sec. 301(a), P.L. 111-312, 12/17/2010 provides:

"(a) In general. Each provision of law amended by subtitle A or E of title V of the Economic Growth and Tax Relief Reconciliation Act of 2001 is amended to read as such provision would read if such subtitle had never been enacted."

Prior to deletion, para. (a)(47) read as follows:

"(47) Executor. The term 'executor' means the executor or administrator of the decedent, or, if there is no executor or administrator appointed, qualified, and acting within the United States, then any person in actual or constructive possession of any property of the decedent."

—P.L. 111-152, Sec. 1409(a), redesignated subsec. (o) as (p) and added subsec. (o), effective for transactions entered into after 3/30/2010.

In 2008, P.L. 110-245, Sec. 301(c)(1), added para. (a)(50) ... Sec. 301(c)(2)(B), added matter at the end of para. (b)(6) ... Sec. 301(c)(2)(C), deleted subsec. (n), redesignated subsec. (o) and (p) as subsec. (n) and (o), effective for any individual whose expatriation date (as so defined) is on or after 6/17/2008.

Prior to deletion, subsec. (n) read as follows:

"(n) Special rules for determining when an individual is no longer a United States citizen or long-term resident. For purposes of this chapter—

"(1) United States citizens. An individual who would (but for this paragraph) cease to be treated as a citizen of the United States shall continue to be treated as a citizen of the United States until such individual—

"(A) gives notice of an expatriating act (with the requisite intent to relinquish citizenship) to the Secretary of State, and

"(B) provides a statement in accordance with section 6039G (if such a statement is otherwise required).

"(2) Long-term residents. A long-term resident (as defined in section 877(e)(2)) who would (but for this paragraph) be described in section 877(e)(1) shall be treated as a lawful permanent resident of the United States and as not described in section 877(e)(1) until such individual—

"(A) gives notice of termination of residency (with the requisite intent to terminate residency) to the Secretary of Homeland Security, and

"(B) provides a statement in accordance with section 6039G (if such a statement is otherwise required)."

In 2007, P.L. 110-28, Sec. 8246(a)(1)(A), deleted "Income" in the heading of para. (a)(36), and deleted "income" before "tax return" in subpara. (a)(36)(A), before "tax return" in subpara. (a)(36)(B). ... Sec. 8246(a)(1)(B), substituted "this title" for "subtitle A" in subpara. (a)(36)(A), effective for returns prepared after 5/25/2007.

In 2006, P.L. 109-280, Sec. 830, of this Act, provides:

"SEC. 830. DIRECT PAYMENT OF TAX REFUNDS TO INDIVIDUAL RETIREMENT PLANS.

"(a) In general. The Secretary of the Treasury (or the Secretary's delegate) shall make available a form (or modify existing forms) for use by individuals to direct that a portion of any refund of overpayment of tax imposed by chapter 1 of the Internal Revenue Code of 1986 be paid directly to an individual retirement plan (as defined in section 7701(a)(37) of such Code) of such individual.

"(b) Effective date. The form required by subsection (a) shall be made available for taxable years beginning after December 31, 2006."

—P.L. 109-280, Sec. 1207(f), added para. (a)(49), effective 1/1/2007.

—P.L. 109-280, Sec. 1222, redesignated subsec. (o) as subsec. (p) and added subsec. (o), enacted 8/17/2006.

In 2005, P.L. 109-135, Sec. 403(v)(2), amended subsec. (n), effective for individuals who expatriate after 6/3/2004 as if included in Sec. 804 of the American Jobs Creation Act of 2004, P.L. 108-357.

Prior to amendment, subsec. (n) read as follows:

"(n) Special rules for determining when an individual is no longer a United States citizen or long-term resident. An individual who would (but for this subsection) cease to be treated as a citizen or resident of the United States shall continue to be treated as a citizen or resident of the United States, as the case may be, until such individual—

"(1) gives notice of an expatriating act or termination of residency (with the requisite intent to relinquish citizenship or terminate residency) to the Secretary of State or the Secretary of Homeland Security, and

"(2) provides a statement in accordance with section 6039G."

In 2004, P.L. 108-357, Sec. 804(b), redesignated subsec. (n) as (o) and added subsec. (n), effective for individuals who expatriate after 6/3/2004.

—P.L. 108-357, Sec. 835(b)(10)(A), deleted "and any regular interest in a FASIT," before "but only in the proportion" in clause (a)(19)(C)(xi) ... Sec. 835(b)(10)(B), deleted "or FASIT" after "REMIC" each place it appeared in clause (a)(19)(C)(xi) ... Sec. 835(b)(11), deleted "or a FASIT" after "REMIC" in subpara. (i)(2)(A), effective 1/1/2005, except as provided in Sec. 835(c)(2) of this Act, which reads as follows:

"(2) Exception for existing FASITs. Paragraph (1) shall not apply to any FASIT in existence on the date of the enactment of this Act to the extent that regular interests issued by the FASIT before such date continue to remain outstanding in accordance with the original terms of issuance."

—P.L. 108-357, Sec. 852(a), added para. (a)(48), effective 10/22/2004, except as provided in Sec. 852(c)(2) [sic (b)(2)] of this Act, which reads as follows:

"(2) Fuel taxes. With respect to taxes imposed under subchapter B of chapter 31 and part III of subchapter A of chapter 32, the amendment made by this section shall apply to taxable periods beginning after the date of the enactment of this Act."

—P.L. 108-311, Sec. 207(24), substituted "682" for "152(b)(4), 682," in para. (a)(17), effective for tax. yrs. begin. after 12/31/2004.

In 2002, P.L. 107-358, Sec. 2, added subsec. (c) in Sec. 901 of P.L. 107-16 [see below], effective 12/17/2002.

In 2001, P.L. 107-16, Sec. 542(e)(3), added para. (a)(47), effective for estates of decedents dying after 12/31/2009.

—P.L. 107-16, Sec. 901, of this Act [as amended by Sec. 2 of P.L. 107-358, and Sec. 101(a)(1), P.L. 111-312, see above], reads as follows:

"SEC. 901. SUNSET OF PROVISIONS OF ACT.

"(a) In general. All provisions of, and amendments made by, this Act shall not apply—

"(1) to taxable, plan, or limitation years beginning after December 31, 2012, or

"(2) in the case of title V, to estates of decedents dying, gifts made, or generation skipping transfers, after December 31, 2012.

Miscellaneous provisions

Code Sec. 7701

"(b) Application of certain laws. The Internal Revenue Code of 1986 and the Employee Retirement Income Security Act of 1974 shall be applied and administered to years, estates, gifts, and transfers described in subsection (a) as if the provisions and amendments described in subsection (a) had never been enacted.

"(c) Exception. Subsection (a) shall not apply to section 803 (relating to no federal income tax on restitution received by victims of the Nazi regime or their heirs or estates)."

In 2000, P.L. 106-554, Sec. 1(a)(7), [which enacted into law Sec. 401(i) of P.L. 106-554] redesignated subsec. (m) as (n) and added subsec. (m), effective 12/21/2000.

In 1997, P.L. 105-34, Sec. 1151(a), added "unless, in the case of a partnership, the Secretary provides otherwise by regulations" before the period at the end of para. (a)(4), effective for partnerships created or organized after the date determined under Code Sec. 7805(b) (without regard to paragraph (2) thereof) with respect to such regulations.

— P.L. 105-34, Sec. 1161(a), added a flush sentence at the end of Sec. 1907(a)(3) of P.L. 104-188 [see below]

— P.L. 105-34, Sec. 1174(b)(1), added subpara. (b)(7)(D) . . . Sec. 1174(b)(2), substituted ", (C), or (D)" for "or (C)" in subpara. (b)(7)(A), effective for tax. yrs. begin. after 12/31/97.

— P.L. 105-34, Sec. 1601(i)(3)(A), substituted "persons" for "fiduciaries" in clause (a)(30)(E)(ii), effective as provided in Sec. 1907(a)(3) of P.L. 104-188 [see below]

— P.L. 105-34, Sec. 1601(i)(4), of this Act, provides:

"(4) Effective date related to Subtitle I. [of P.L. 104-188] The Secretary of the Treasury may by regulations or other administrative guidance provide that the amendments made by section 1907(a) of the Small Business Job Protection Act of 1996 shall not apply to a trust with respect to a reasonable period beginning on the date of the enactment of such Act, if —

"(A) such trust is in existence on August 20, 1996, and is a United States person for purposes of the Internal Revenue Code of 1986 on such date (determined without regard to such amendments),

"(B) no election is in effect under section 1907(a)(3)(B) of such Act with respect to such trust,

"(C) before the expiration of such reasonable period, such trust makes the modifications necessary to be treated as a United States person for purposes of such Code (determined with regard to such amendments), and

"(D) such trust meets such other conditions as the Secretary may require."

In 1996, P.L. 104-188, Sec. 1402(b)(3), deleted ", for the purpose of applying the provisions of section 101(b) with respect to employees' death benefits" after "and health plans" in para. (a)(2), effective for decedents dying after 8/20/96.

— P.L. 104-188, Sec. 1621(b)(8), amended clause (a)(19)(C)(xi) . . . Sec. 1621(b)(9), added "or a FASIT" after "a REMIC" in subpara. (i)(2)(A), effective 9/1/97.

Prior to amendment, clause (a)(19)(C)(xi) read as follows:

"(xi) any regular or residual interest in a REMIC, but only in the proportion which the assets of such REMIC consist of property described in any of the preceding clauses of this subparagraph; except that if 95 percent or more of the assets of such REMIC are assets described in clauses (i) through (x), the entire interest in the REMIC shall qualify." . . . Sec. 1907(a)(1), deleted "and" at the end of subpara. (a)(30)(C), deleted subpara. (a)(30)(D), and added subparas. (a)(30)(D) and (E) . . . Sec. 1907(a)(2), amended para. (a)(31), effective as provided in Sec. 1907(a)(3) of this Act [as amended by Sec. 1161(a) of P.L. 105-34, see above], which reads as follows:

"(3) Effective date. The amendments made by this subsection shall apply —

"(A) to taxable years beginning after December 31, 1996, or

"(B) at the election of the trustee of a trust, to taxable years ending after the date of the enactment of this Act.

Such an election, once made, shall be irrevocable.

To the extent prescribed in regulations by the Secretary of the Treasury or his delegate, a trust which was in existence on August 20, 1996 (other than a trust treated as owned by the grantor under subpart E of part I of subchapter J of chapter 1 of the Internal Revenue Code of 1986), and which was treated as a United States person on the day before the date of the enactment of this Act may elect to continue to be treated as a United States person notwithstanding section 7701(a)(30)(E) of such Code."

Prior to deletion, subpara. (a)(30)(D) read as follows:

"(D) any estate or trust (other than a foreign estate or foreign trust, within the meaning of section 7701(a)(31))."

Prior to amendment, para. (a)(31) read as follows:

"(31) Foreign estate or trust.

"The terms 'foreign estate' and 'foreign trust' mean an estate or trust, as the case may be, the income of which, from sources without the United States which is not effectively connected with the conduct of a trade or business within the United States, is not includible in gross income under subtitle A."

In 1995, P.L. 104-88, Sec. 304(e)(1), substituted "Federal Energy Regulatory Commission" for "Federal Power Commission" in subpara. (a)(33)(B) . . . Sec. 304(e)(2), substituted "Surface Transportation Board" for "Interstate Commerce Commission" in subpara. (a)(33)(C), substituted "Federal Energy Regulatory Commission" for "Interstate Commerce Commission" in subpara. (a)(33)(C) . . . Sec. 304(e)(4), substituted "a water carrier subject to jurisdiction under subchapter II of chapter 135 of title 49" for "common carrier by water, subject to the jurisdiction of the Interstate Commerce Commission under subchapter III of chapter 105 of title 49, or subject to the jurisdiction of the Federal Maritime Board under the Intercoastal Shipping Act, 1933" in subpara. (a)(33)(F) . . . Sec. 304(e)(5), substituted "rail carrier subject to part A of subtitle IV" for "railroad corporation subject to subchapter I of chapter 105" in subpara.

(a)(33)(G) . . . Sec. 304(e)(6), substituted "part A of subtitle IV" for "subchapter I of chapter 105" in subpara. (a)(33)(H), effective 12/29/95.

In 1994, P.L. 103-296, Sec. 320(a)(3), substituted "subparagraph (J) or (Q)" for "subparagraph (J)" in clause (b)(5)(C)(i) and subclause (b)(5)(D)(i)(II), effective with the calendar quarter following 8/15/94.

In 1993, P.L. 103-66, Sec. 13238, redesignated subsec. (l) as (m) and added subsec. (l), effective 8/10/93.

In 1992, P.L. 102-318, Sec. 521(b)(43), substituted "section 402(e)(3)" for "section 402(a)(8)", in subpara. (j)(1)(C), effective for distributions after 12/31/92. For special rule, see Sec. 521(e)(2) of this Act which reads as follows:

"(2) Special rule for partial distributions. For purposes of section 402(a)(5)(D)(i)(II) of the Internal Revenue Code of 1986 (as in effect before the amendments made by this section), a distribution before January 1, 1993, which is made before or at the same time as a series of periodic payments shall not be treated as one of such series if it is not substantially equal in amount to other payments in such series."

In 1991, P.L. 102-90, Sec. 314(e), amended the sentence at the end of subsec. (k), effective 1/1/92.

Prior to amendment, the sentence at the end of subsec. (k) read as follows:

"For purposes of this subsection, a Representative in, or a Delegate or Resident Commissioner to, the Congress shall be treated as an officer or employee of the Federal Government and a Senator or officer (except the Vice President) or employee of the Senate shall not be treated as an officer or employee of the Federal Government."

In 1990, P.L. 101-508, Sec. 11704(a)(34), substituted "(C) subject to section 401(k)(4)(B) and any dollar limitation on the application of section 402(a)(8)," for "(C) subject to, section 401(k)(4)(B), [and] any dollar limitation on the application of section 402(a)(8)," in subpara. (j)(1)(C), effective 11/5/90.

— P.L. 101-508, Sec. 11812(b)(13), added "(as in effect on the day before the date of the enactment of the Revenue Reconciliation Act of 1990)" before the period at the end of subpara. (e)(5)(B), effective for property placed in service after 11/5/90, except as provided in Sec. 11812(c)(2) of this Act reproduced in note following Code Sec. 42.

In 1989, P.L. 101-194, Sec. 602, redesignated subsec. (k) as (l), and added subsec. (k), effective as provided in Sec. 603 of this Act, which reads as follows:

"SEC. 603. EFFECTIVE DATE.

"The amendments made by this title shall take effect on January 1, 1991. Such amendments shall cease to be effective if the provisions of section 703 [of P.L. 101-194] are subsequently repealed, in which case the laws in effect before such amendments shall be deemed to be reenacted."

In 1988, P.L. 100-647, Sec. 1(c), substituted "of 1986" for "of 1954" in para. (a)(29).

— P.L. 100-647, Sec. 1001(d)(2)(D), substituted "subparagraph (F) or (M)" for subparagraph (F)" in subclause (b)(5)(D)(i)(I), effective for tax. yrs. begin. after 12/31/86, but only in the case of scholarships and fellowships granted after 8/16/86.

— P.L. 100-647, Sec. 1002(a)(2), amended Sec. 201(d)(14)(B) of P.L. 99-514, by substituting "within the meaning of section 168(c)(2)(F)" for "section 168(c)(2)(F)" see below.

— P.L. 100-647, Sec. 1002(e)(3), of this Act provides:

"(3) Notwithstanding section 203 of the Reform Act, the amendments made by section 201 of the Reform Act shall apply to any real property which was acquired before January 1, 1987, and was converted on or after such date from personal use to a use for which depreciation is allowable."

— P.L. 100-647, Sec. 1006(t)(12), substituted "are assets described" for "are loans described" in clause (a)(19)(C)(xi) . . . Sec. 1006(t)(25)(A), added the sentence at the end of para. (a)(19), effective for tax. yrs. begin. after 12/31/86.

— P.L. 100-647, Sec. 1006(w)(1), amended Sec. 675(a) of P.L. 99-514, the effective date for changes made by Sec. 671(b)(3) of P.L. 99-514, by substituting "the amendments made by this subtitle shall take effect on January 1, 1987" for "the amendments made by this part shall apply to taxable years beginning after December 31, 1986," see below.

— P.L. 100-647, Sec. 1011A(m)(1), added ", section 401(k)(4)(B)" after "paragraph (2)" in subpara. (j)(1)(C), effective 10/22/87.

— P.L. 100-647, Sec. 1011B(e)(1), substituted "and 106" for "106, and 125," in para. (a)(20) . . . Sec. 1011B(e)(2), added "and for purposes of applying section 125 with respect to cafeteria plans," before "the term" in para. (a)(20), effective for tax. yrs. begin. after 12/31/85.

— P.L. 100-647, Sec. 1018(g)(3), substituted "section 274(1)(1)(B)" for "section 274(k)(2)" in clause (b)(5)(A)(iv), effective for periods after 10/22/86.

— P.L. 100-647, Sec. 6138(a), and (b) of this Act provide:

"(a) In general. The Secretary of the Treasury or his delegate shall conduct a study of section 7701(b) of the Internal Revenue Code of 1986, relating to the determination as to whether a person is a United States resident for purposes of Federal tax laws. Such study shall include an examination of —

"(1) the effect such determination has on Federal tax administration and investment flows between the United States and other countries,

"(2) the coordination of such determination with any treaty obligations of the United States,

"(3) how such determination compares with the way such determination is made by our major trading partners, and

"(4) any estimated revenue gain or loss which would result from modifying such determination.

"(b) Report. The Secretary of the Treasury or his delegate shall report before May 1, 1989, the results of the study conducted under subsection (a) to the Committee on Finance of the Senate and the Committee on Ways and Means of the House of Representatives."

3,945

Code Sec. 7701 — Miscellaneous provisions

In 1987, P.L. 100-202, Sec. 101(m)(1), deleted "the provisions of paragraph (2) and" following "subject to" in subpara. (j)(1)(C) ... Sec. 101(m)(2), amended para. (j)(2) effective 12/22/87.
Prior to amendment, para. (j)(2) read as follows:

"(2) Nondiscrimination requirements. Paragraph (1)(C) shall not apply to the Thrift Savings Fund unless the Fund meets the antidiscrimination requirements (other than any requirement relating to coverage) applicable to arrangements described in section 401(k) and to matching contributions. Rules similar to the rules of sections 401(k)(8) and 401(m)(8) (relating to no disqualification if excess contributions distributed) shall apply for purposes of the preceding sentence."

In 1986, P.L. 99-514, Sec. 201(c), redesignated subsec. (h) as (i) and added subsec. (h) ... Sec. 201(d)(14)(A), substituted "section 168(h)" for "section 168(j)" in subpara. (e)(4)(A) [as amended by Sec. 1802(a)(9)(C) of this Act, see below] ... Sec. 201(d)(14)(B), [as amended by Sec. 1002(a)(2) of P.L. 100-647, see above] substituted "property described in clause (i), (ii), (iii), or (iv) of section 1250(a)(1)(B) (relating to low-income housing)" for "low-income housing (within the meaning of section 168(c)(2)(F))" in para. (e)(5) [as amended by Sec. 1899A (64) of this Act, see below], effective for property placed in service after 12/31/86, in tax. yrs. ending after 12/31/86. For transitional rules see Sec. 203(b)-(e) of this Act reproduced in note following Code Sec. 168. Sec. 203(a)(1)(B) of this Act provides:

"(B) Election to have amendments made by section 201 apply. A taxpayer may elect (at such time and in such manner as the Secretary of the Treasury or his delegate may prescribe) to have the amendments made by section 201 apply to any property placed in service after July 31, 1986, and before January 1, 1987."
— P.L. 99-514, Sec. 671(b)(3), [as amended by Sec. 1006(w)(1) of P.L. 100-647, see above] deleted "and" at the end of clause (a)(19)(C)(ix), substituted "and" for the period at the end of the clause (a)(19)(C)(x), and added clause (a)(19)(C)(xi), effective for tax. yrs. begin. after 12/31/86.
— P.L. 99-514, Sec. 673, redesignated subsec. (i) [as redesignated by Sec. 201(c) of this Act, see above] as subsec. (j), and added subsec. (i), effective 1/1/92. Secs. 675(c)(2) and (c)(3) of this Act provides special rules as follows:

"(2) Treatment of existing entities.— The amendment made by section 673 shall not apply to any entity in existence on December 31, 1991. The preceding sentence shall cease to apply with respect to any entity as of the 1st day after December 31, 1991, on which there is a substantial transfer of cash or other property to such entity.

"(3) Special rule for coordination with wash-sale rules.— Notwithstanding paragraphs (1) and (2), for purposes of applying section 860F(d) of the Internal Revenue Code of 1986 (as added by this part), the amendment made by section 673 shall apply to taxable years beginning after December 31, 1986."
— P.L. 99-514, Sec. 1137, added the sentence at the end of para. (a)(46), effective 10/22/86.
— P.L. 99-514, Sec. 1147(a), redesignated subsec. (j) [as redesignated by Sec. 673 of this Act, see above] as subsec. (k), and added new subsec. (j), effective 10/22/86.
— P.L. 99-514, Sec. 1166(a), substituted "106, and 125" for "and 106" in para. (a)(20), effective for tax. yrs. begin. after 12/31/85.
— P.L. 99-514, Sec. 1802(a)(9)(C), added the sentence at the end of subpara. (e)(4)(A) ... Sec. 1810(1)(1), added the sentence at the end of subpara. (b)(4)(E)(i) ... Sec. 1810(1)(2)(A), substituted "the requirements of clause (i), (ii), or (iii)" for "the requirements of clause (i) or (ii)" in subpara. (b)(4)(A) ... Sec. 1810(1)(2)(B), added clause (b)(1)(A)(iii) ... Sec. 1810(1)(3), added clause (b)(2)(A)(iv) ... Sec. 1810(1)(4), redesignated paras. (b)(4) through (b)(10) as paras. (b)(5) through (b)(11) respectively, and added para. (b)(4), effective for tax. yrs. begin. after 12/31/84.
— P.L. 99-514, Sec. 1804(b)(2), amended Sec. 53(e) of P.L. 98-369, which provides the effective date for amendments made by Sec. 53(c) of P.L. 98-369, by adding special rules, see below.
— P.L. 99-514, Sec. 1810(1)(5)(A), deleted "or" at the end of clause (b)(4)(A)(ii), substituted ", or" for the period at the end of clause (b)(4)(A)(iii), and added clause (b)(4)(A)(iv), effective for periods after 10/22/86.
— P.L. 99-514, Sec. 1842(b), substituted ", 682, and 2516" for "and 682" in para. (a)(17), effective for transfers after 7/18/84 and for transfers after 7/18/63, and on or before 7/18/84, if both parties elect.
— P.L. 99-514, Sec. 1899A(63), substituted "preceding" for "preceeding" in clause (b)(4)(E)(i) [before redesignation as (b)(5)(E)(i) by Sec. 1810(1)(4) of this Act, see above] ... Sec. 1899A(64), substituted "section 168(c)(2)(F))" for "section 168(C)(2)(F))" in para. (e)(5) [before amendment by Sec. 201(d)(14)(B) of this Act, see above], effective 10/22/86.

In 1984, P.L. 98-443, Sec. 9(q), substituted "Secretary of Transportation" for "Civil Aeronautics Board" in subpara. (a)(33)(E), effective 1/1/85.
— P.L. 98-369, Sec. 31(e), redesignated subsec. (e) as (f) and added subsec. (e), effective for property placed in service by the taxpayer after 5/23/83, in tax. yrs. end. after 5/23/83, and to property placed in service by the taxpayer on or before 5/23/83, if the lease to the tax-exempt entity is entered into after 5/23/83, except for the special rule provided in Sec. 31(g)(19) of the Act (following) and subject to the special provisions in Sec. 31(g) of this Act reproduced in the note following Code Sec. 168. Sec. 31(g)(19) provides:

"(19) Special rule for certain energy management contracts.—

"(A) In general.— The amendments made by subsection (e) [Sec. 31(e) of P.L. 98-369] shall not apply to property used pursuant to an energy management contract that was entered into prior to May 1, 1984.

"(B) Definition of energy management contract.— For purposes of subparagraph (A), the term 'energy management contract' means a contract for the providing of energy conservation or energy management services."

— P.L. 98-369, Sec. 43(a)(1), added paras. (a)(42), (43), (44) and (45), effective for tax. yrs. end. after 7/18/84.
— P.L. 98-369, Sec. 53(c), redesignated subsec. (f) [as redesignated by Sec. 31(e) of the Act, see above] as subsec. (g), and added new subsec. (f), effective [as amended by Sec. 1804(b)(2) of P.L. 99-514, see above] 7/18/84. Sec. 53(e)(3)(B)-(D) of this Act provides:

"(B) Special rule for purposes of section 265(2).— The amendment made by subsection (c) insofar as it relates to section 265(2) of the Internal Revenue Code of 1954 shall apply to —

"(i) term loans made after July 18, 1984, and

"(ii) demand loans outstanding after July 18, 1984 (other than any loan outstanding on July 18, 1984, and repaid before September 18, 1984).

"(C) Treatment of renegotiations, etc.— For purposes of this paragraph, any loan renegotiated, extended, or revised after July 18, 1984, shall be treated as a loan made after such date.

"(D) Definition of term and demand loans.— For purposes of this paragraph, the terms 'demand loan' and 'term loan' have the respective meanings given such terms by paragraphs (5) and (6) of section 7872(f) of the Internal Revenue Code of 1954, except that the second sentence of such paragraph (5) shall not apply."
— P.L. 98-369, Sec. 75(c), redesignated subsec. (g) [as redesignated by Sec. 53(c) of this Act, see above] as subsec. (h), and added new subsec. (g), effective for distributions, sales, and exchanges made after 3/31/84 in tax. yrs. end. after 3/31/84.
— P.L. 98-369, Sec. 138(a), redesignated subsecs. (b), (c) and (d) as subsecs. (c), (d) and (e), and added subsec. (b), effective for tax. yrs. begin. after 12/31/84. Secs. 138(b)(2)-(3) of the Act provide transitional rules as follows:

"(2) Transitional rule for applying substantial presence test.—

"(A) If an alien individual was not a resident of the United States as of the close of calendar year 1984, the determination of whether such individual meets the substantial presence test of section 7701(b)(3) of the Internal Revenue Code of 1954 (as added by this section) shall be made by only taking into account presence after 1984.

"(B) If an alien individual was a resident of the United States as of the close of calendar year 1984, but was not a resident of the United States as of the close of calendar year 1983, the determination of whether such individual meets such substantial presence test shall be made by only taking into account presence in the United States after 1983.

"(3) Transitional rule for applying lawful residence test.— In the case of any individual who—

"(A) was a lawful permanent resident of the United States (within the meaning of section 7701(b)(5) of the Internal Revenue Code of 1954, as added by this section) throughout calendar year 1984, or

"(B) was present in the United States at any time during 1984 while such individual was a lawful permanent resident of the United States (within the meaning of such section 7701(b)(5)),
for purposes of section 7701(b)(2)(A) of such Code (as so added), such individual shall be treated as a resident of the United States during 1984."
— P.L. 98-369, Sec. 412(b)(11), deleted para. (a)(34), effective for tax. yrs. begin. after 12/31/84.
Prior to deletion, para. (a)(34) read as follows:

"(34) Estimated income tax. The term 'estimated income tax' means—

"(A) in the case of an individual, the estimated tax as defined in section 6015(d), or

"(B) in the case of a corporation, the estimated tax as defined in section 6154(c)."
— P.L. 98-369, Sec. 422(d)(3), substituted "152(b)(4) and 682" for "71, 152(b)(4), 215, and 682" in para. (a)(17), effective for divorce or separation instruments (as defined in Code Sec. 71(b)(2)) executed after 12/31/84. Sec. 422(e)(2) of this Act provides as follows:

"(2) Modifications of instruments executed before January 1, 1985.— The amendments made by this section shall also apply to any divorce or separation instrument (as so defined) executed before January 1, 1985, but modified on or after such date if the modification expressly provides that the amendments made by this section shall apply to such modification."
— P.L. 98-369, Sec. 474(r)(29)(K), deleted "1451," from para. (a)(16), effective as provided in Sec. 475(b) of this Act, which reads as follows:

"(b) Tax-free covenant bonds. The amendments made by subsections (j) and (r)(29) of section 474 [P.L. 98-369] shall not apply with respect to obligations issued before January 1, 1984."
— P.L. 98-369, Sec. 491(d)(53), deleted subpara. (a)(37)(C), substituted a period for ", and" at the end of subpara. (a)(37)(B) and added "and" at the end of subpara. (a)(37)(A), effective for obligations issued after 12/31/83.
Prior to deletion, subpara. (a)(37)(C) read as follows:

"(C) a retirement bond described in section 409."
— P.L. 98-369, Sec. 526(c)(1), added para. (a)(46), effective 4/1/84.
— P.L. 98-216, Sec. 3(c)(2), substituted "subchapter I of chapter 105 of title 49" for "part I of the Interstate Commerce Act" in subpara. (a)(33)(G), effective 2/14/84.

In 1983, P.L. 98-67, Sec. 104(d)(1), added para. (a)(41), effective for payments made after 12/31/83.
— P.L. 97-473, Sec. 202(b)(2), added para. (a)(40).
— P.L. 97-449, Sec. 5(e)(1), substituted "subchapter III of chapter 105 of title 49" for "part III of the Interstate Commerce Act" in subpara. (a)(33)(F) ... Sec. 5(e)(2), substituted "subchapter I of chapter 105 of title 49" for "part I of the Interstate Commerce Act" in subpara. (a)(33)(H).
— P.L. 97-448, Sec. 306(a)(1)(A)(i), redesignated the second Sec. 201(c) of P.L. 97-248 as Sec. 201(d) of P.L. 97-248, see below.

—P.L. 97-448, Sec. 306(b)(3), redesignated para. (a)(38) [as added by Sec. 336 of P.L. 97-248, see below] as para. (a)(39), effective 9/4/82.

In 1982, P.L. 97-248, Sec. 201(d)(10), [as redesignated by Sec. 306(a)(1)(A)(i) of P.L. 97-448, see above], added para. (a)(38), effective for tax. yrs. begin. after 12/31/82.

—P.L. 97-248, Sec. 336(a), added para. (a)(39) [as redesignated by Sec. 306(b)(3) of P.L. 97-448, see above], effective 9/4/82.

In 1981, P.L. 97-34, Sec. 725(c)(4), substituted "6015(d)" for "6015(c)" in subpara. (a)(34)(A), effective for estimated tax for tax. yrs. begin. after 12/31/80.

In 1980, P.L. 96-605, Sec. 402, provides:

"SEC. 402. TREATMENT OF AUTHORS AND ARTISTS AS EMPLOYEES.

"(a) In general.

"An author or artist performing services under contract with a corporation shall be considered as an employee of the corporation for the purpose of applying the provisions specified in section 7701(a)(20) of the Internal Revenue Code of 1954, if, on December 31, 1977, such author or artist was a participant in one or more of the pension, profit-sharing or annuity plans of such corporation which are described in subsection (b)(2).

"(b) Definitions.

"For purposes of this section—

"(1) Contract. The term 'contract' means a contract which during its term—

"(A) requires such author or artist to give the corporation first reading or first refusal on writings or drawings of specified types, and prohibits him from offering any such writing or drawing to any other publication unless it has been offered to and rejected by the corporation; or

"(B) requires such author or artist to use his best efforts to produce work of specified types for the corporation.

"(2) Corporation. The term 'corporation' means a corporation which for at least 15 years prior to January 1, 1978, had in effect one or more pension, profit-sharing and annuity plans, each of which—

"(A) had contained from its inception a definition of the term 'employee' that included the category of 'authors and artists under contract', and

"(B) had been determined by the Secretary of the Treasury (taking into account the definition described in subparagraph (A)) to be a qualified plan within part I of subchapter D of chapter 1 of subtitle A of the Internal Revenue Code of 1954 for all of such years.

"(c) Effective date.

"The provisions of this section shall apply to taxable years ending after December 31, 1980."

In 1978, P.L. 95-600, Sec. 701(cc)(2), amended clause (a)(36)(B)(iii), effective for documents prepared after 12/31/76.

Prior to amendment, clause (a)(36)(B)(iii) read as follows:

"(iii) prepares a return or claim for refund for any trust or estate with respect to which he is a fiduciary, or".

—P.L. 95-600, Sec. 157(k)(2), added para. (a)(37), effective for tax. yrs. begin. after 12/31/74.

In 1976, P.L. 94-455, Sec. 1203(a), added para. (a)(36), effective for documents prepared after 12/31/76.

—P.L. 94-455, Sec. 1906(a)(57)(A), amended para. (a)(11) . . . Sec. 1906(a)(57)(B), amended subpara. (a)(12)(A) . . . Sec. 1906(b)(13)(A), substituted "Secretary" for "Secretary or his delegate" each place it appeared in Code Sec. 7701 . . . Sec. 1906(c)(3), deleted "or Territory" after "of any State" in para. (a)(4), effective 2/1/77.

Prior to amendment, para. (a)(11) read as follows:

"(11) Secretary. The term 'Secretary' means the Secretary of the Treasury."

Prior to amendment, subpara. (a)(12)(A) read as follows:

"(A) In general. The term Secretary or his delegate means the Secretary of the Treasury, or any officer, employee, or agency of the Treasury Department duly authorized by the Secretary (directly, or indirectly by one or more redelegations of authority) to perform the function mentioned or described in the context, and the term or his delegate when used in connection with any other official of the United States shall be similarly construed."

In 1974, P.L. 93-406, Sec. 3043, added para. (a)(35), effective 9/2/74.

In 1972, P.L. 92-606, Sec. 1(f)(4), substituted "chapters 1, 2," for "chapters 2" in subpara. (a)(12)(B), effective for tax. yrs. begin. after 12/31/72.

In 1969, P.L. 91-172, Sec. 432(c), amended para. (a)(19) . . . Sec. 432(d)(1), amended subpara. (a)(32)(B) . . . Sec. 432(d)(2), deleted the third sentence of para. (a)(32) effective for tax. yrs. begin. after 7/11/69.

Prior to amendment, para. (a)(19) read as follows:

"(19) Domestic building and loan association.

"The term 'domestic building and loan association' means a domestic building and loan association, a domestic savings and loan association, and a Federal savings and loan association—

"(A) which either (i) is an insured institution within the meaning of section 401(a) of the National Housing Act (12 U.S.C., sec. 1724(a)), or (ii) is subject by law to supervision and examination by State or Federal authority having supervision over such associations;

"(B) substantially all of the business of which consists of acquiring the savings of the public and investing in loans described in subparagraph (C);

"(C) at least 90 percent of the amount of the total assets of which (as of the close of the taxable year) consists of (i) cash, (ii) obligations of the United States or of a State or political subdivision thereof, stock or obligations of a corporation which is an instrumentality of the United States or of a State or political subdivision thereof, and certificates of deposit in, or obligations of, a corporation organized under a State law which specifically authorizes such corporation to insure the deposits or share accounts of member associations, (iii) loans secured by an interest in real property and loans made for the improvement of real property, (iv) loans secured by a deposit or share of a member, (v) property acquired through the liquidation of defaulted loans described in clause (iii), and (vi) property used by the association in the conduct of the business described in subparagraph (B);

"(D) of the assets of which taken into account under subparagraph (C) as assets constituting the 90 percent of total assets—

"(i) at least 80 percent of the amount of such assets consists of assets described in clauses (i), (ii), (iv), and (vi) of such subparagraph and of loans secured by an interest in real property which is (or, from the proceeds of the loan, will become) residential real property or real property used primarily for church purposes, loans made for the improvement of residential real property or real property used primarily for church purposes, or property acquired through the liquidation of defaulted loans described in this clause; and

"(ii) at least 60 percent of the amount of such assets consists of assets described in clauses (i), (ii), (iv), and (vi) of such subparagraph and of loans secured by an interest in real property which is (or, from the proceeds of the loan, will become) residential real property containing 4 or fewer family units or real property used primarily for church purposes, loans made for the improvement of residential real property containing 4 or fewer family units or real property used primarily for church purposes, or property acquired through the liquidation of defaulted loans described in this clause;

"(E) not more than 18 percent of the amount of the total assets of which (as of the close of the taxable year) consists of assets other than those described in clause (i) of subparagraph (D), and not more than 36 percent of the amount of the total assets of which (as of the close of the taxable year) consists of assets other than those described in clause (ii) of subparagraph (D); and

"(F) except for property described in subparagraph (C), not more than 3 percent of the assets of which consists of stock of any corporation.

"The term 'domestic building and loan association' also includes any association which, for the taxable year, would satisfy the requirements of the first sentence of this subparagraph if '41 percent' were substituted for '36 percent' in subparagraph (E). Except in the case of the taxpayer's first taxable year beginning after the date of the enactment of the Revenue Act of 1962, the second sentence of this paragraph shall not apply to an association for the taxable year unless such association (i) was a domestic building and loan association within the meaning of the first sentence of this paragraph for the first taxable year preceding the taxable year, or (ii) was a domestic building and loan association solely by reason of the second sentence of this paragraph for the first taxable year preceding the taxable year (but not for the second preceding taxable year). At the election of the taxpayer, the percentages specified in this paragraph shall be applied on the basis of the average assets outstanding during the taxable year, in lieu of the close of the taxable year, computed under regulations prescribed by the Secretary or his delegate."

Prior to amendment, subpara. (a)(32)(B) read as follows:

"(B) meets the requirements of subparagraphs (B), (C), (D), (E), and (F) of paragraph (19) of this subsection (relating to definition of domestic building and loan association) determined with the application of the second, third, and fourth sentences of paragraph (19).

"In determining whether an institution meets the requirements referred to in subparagraph (B) of this paragraph, any reference to an association or to a domestic building and loan association contained in paragraph (19) shall be deemed to be a reference to such institution. In the case of an institution which, for the taxable year, is a co-operative bank within the meaning of the first sentence of this paragraph by reason of the application of the second and third sentences of paragraph (19) of this subsection, the deduction otherwise allowable under section 166(c) for a reasonable addition to the reserve for bad debts shall, under regulations prescribed by the Secretary or his delegate, be reduced in a manner consistent with the reductions provided by the table contained in section 593(b)(5)."

—P.L. 91-172, Sec. 960(j), substituted "United States Tax Court" for "Tax Court of the United States" in para. (a)(27), effective 12/30/69.

In 1968, P.L. 90-364, Sec. 103(e)(6), substituted "section 6154(c)" for "section 6016(b)" in subpara. (a)(34)(B), effective for tax. yrs. begin. after 12/31/67 except as provided in Sec. 104 of this Act, reproduced in note following Code Sec. 6425.

In 1966, P.L. 89-809, Sec. 103(l)(1), substituted ", from sources without the United States which is not effectively connected with the conduct of a trade or business within the United States," for "from sources without the United States" in para. (a)(31), effective for tax. yrs. begin. after 12/31/66.

—P.L. 89-368, Sec. 102(b)(5), added para. (a)(34), effective for tax. yrs. begin. after 12/31/66.

In 1964, P.L. 88-272, Sec. 204(a)(3), substituted "For the purpose of applying the provisions of section 79 with respect to group-term life insurance purchased for employees, for the purpose of applying the provisions of sections 104" for "For the purpose of applying the provisions of sections 104" in para. (a)(20), effective for group-term life insurance provided after 12/31/63 in tax. yrs. end. after 12/31/63.

—P.L. 88-272, Sec. 234(b)(3), added para. (a)(33), effective for tax. yrs. begin. after 12/31/63.

In 1962, P.L. 87-834, Sec. 6(c), amended para. (a)(19), effective for tax. yrs. begin. after 10/16/62.

Prior to amendment, para. (a)(19) read as follows:

"(19) Domestic building and loan association. The term 'domestic building and loan association' means a domestic building and loan association, a domestic savings and loan association, and a Federal savings and loan association, substantially all the business of which is confined to making loans to members."

—P.L. 87-834, Sec. 7(h), added paras. (a)(30) and (31), effective 10/17/62.

—P.L. 87-870, Sec. 5(a), added para. (a)(32), effective for tax. yrs. begin. after 10/16/62.

In 1960, P.L. 86-624, Sec. 18(i), deleted ", the Territory of Hawaii," in para. (a)(9)... Sec. 18(j), deleted "the Territory of Hawaii and" in para. (a)(10), effective 8/21/59.

—P.L. 86-778, Sec. 103(t), amended para. (a)(12), effective as provided in the sentence at the end of Sec. 103(v)(1) of this Act, which reads as follows:

"The amendments made by subsections (j), (s), and (t) shall take effect on the date of the enactment of this Act [9/13/60]; and there are authorized to be appropriated such sums as may be necessary for the performance by any officer or employee of functions delegated to him by the Secretary of the Treasury in accordance with the amendment made by such subsection (t)."

Prior to amendment, para. (a)(12) read as follows:

"(12) Delegate. The term 'Secretary or his delegate' means the Secretary of the Treasury, or any officer, employee, or agency of the Treasury Department duly authorized by the Secretary (directly, or indirectly by one or more redelegations of authority) to perform the function mentioned or described in the context, and the term 'or his delegate' when used in connection with any other official of the United States shall be similarly construed."

In 1959, P.L. 86-70, Sec. 22(g), substituted "the Territory of Hawaii" for "the Territories of Alaska and Hawaii" in para. (a)(9)... Sec. 22(h), substituted "Territory of Hawaii" for "Territories" in para. (a)(10), effective 1/3/59.

Sec. 7702. Life insurance contract defined.

(a) General rule.

For purposes of this title, the term "life insurance contract" means any contract which is a life insurance contract under the applicable law, but only if such contract—

(1) meets the cash value accumulation test of subsection (b), or

(2)(A) meets the guideline premium requirements of subsection (c), and

(B) falls within the cash value corridor of subsection (d).

(b) Cash value accumulation test for subsection (a)(1).

(1) **In general.** A contract meets the cash value accumulation test of this subsection if, by the terms of the contract, the cash surrender value of such contract may not at any time exceed the net single premium which would have to be paid at such time to fund future benefits under the contract.

(2) **Rules for applying paragraph (1).** Determinations under paragraph (1) shall be made—

(A) on the basis of interest at the greater of an annual effective rate of 4 percent or the rate or rates guaranteed on issuance of the contract,

(B) on the basis of the rules of subparagraph (B)(i) (and, in the case of qualified additional benefits, subparagraph (B)(ii)) of subsection (c)(3), and

(C) by taking into account under subparagraphs (A) and (D) of subsection (e)(1) only current and future death benefits and qualified additional benefits.

(c) Guideline premium requirements.

For purposes of this section—

(1) **In general.** A contract meets the guideline premium requirements of this subsection if the sum of the premiums paid under such contract does not at any time exceed the guideline premium limitation as of such time.

(2) **Guideline premium limitation.** The term "guideline premium limitation" means, as of any date, the greater of—

(A) the guideline single premium, or

(B) the sum of the guideline level premiums to such date.

(3) **Guideline single premium.**

(A) In general. The term "guideline single premium" means the premium at issue with respect to future benefits under the contract.

(B) Basis on which determination is made. The determination under subparagraph (A) shall be based on

(i) reasonable mortality charges which meet the requirements (if any) prescribed in regulations and which (except as provided in regulations) do not exceed the mortality charges specified in the prevailing commissioners' standard tables (as defined in section 807(d)(5)) as of the time the contract is issued,

(ii) any reasonable charges (other than mortality charges) which (on the basis of the company's experience, if any, with respect to similar contracts) are reasonably expected to be actually paid, and

(iii) interest at the greater of an annual effective rate of 6 percent or the rate or rates guaranteed on issuance of the contract.

(C) When determination made. Except as provided in subsection (f)(7), the determination under subparagraph (A) shall be made as of the time the contract is issued.

(D) Special rules for subparagraph (B)(ii).—

(i) Charges not specified in the contract. If any charge is not specified in the contract, the amount taken into account under subparagraph (B)(ii) for such charge shall be zero.

(ii) New companies, etc. If any company does not have adequate experience for purposes of the determination under subparagraph (B)(ii), to the extent provided in regulations, such determination shall be made on the basis of the industry-wide experience.

(4) **Guideline level premium.** The term "guideline level premium" means the level annual amount, payable over a period not ending before the insured attains age 95, computed on the same basis as the guideline single premium, except that paragraph (3)(B)(iii) shall be applied by substituting "4 percent" for "6 percent".

(d) Cash value corridor for purposes of subsection (a)(2)(B).

For purposes of this section—

(1) **In general.** A contract falls within the cash value corridor of this subsection if the death benefit under the contract at any time is not less than the applicable percentage of the cash surrender value.

(2) **Applicable percentage.**

In the case of an insured with an attained age as of the beginning of the contract year of:		The applicable percentage shall decrease by a ratable portion for each full year:	
More than:	But not more than:	From:	To:
0	40	250	250
40	45	250	215
45	50	215	185
50	55	185	150
55	60	150	130
60	65	130	120
65	70	120	115
70	75	115	105
75	90	105	105
90	95	105	100

(e) Computational rules.

(1) **In general.** For purposes of this section (other than subsection (d))—

(A) the death benefit (and any qualified additional benefit) shall be deemed not to increase,

(B) the maturity date, including the date on which any benefit described in subparagraph (C) is payable, shall be deemed to be no earlier than the day on which the insured attains age 95, and no later than the day on which the insured attains age 100,

(C) the death benefits shall be deemed to be provided until the maturity date determined by taking into account subparagraph (B), and

(D) the amount of any endowment benefit (or sum of endowment benefits, including any cash surrender value on the maturity date determined by taking into account subparagraph (B)) shall be deemed not to exceed the least amount payable as a death benefit at any time under the contract.

(2) Limited increases in death benefit permitted. Notwithstanding paragraph (1)(A)—

(A) for purposes of computing the guideline level premium, an increase in the death benefit which is provided in the contract may be taken into account but only to the extent necessary to prevent a decrease in the excess of the death benefit over the cash surrender value of the contract,

(B) for purposes of the cash value accumulation test, the increase described in subparagraph (A) may be taken into account if the contract will meet such test at all times assuming that the net level reserve (determined as if level annual premiums were paid for the contract over a period not ending before the insured attains age 95) is substituted for the net single premium

(C) for purposes of the cash value accumulation test, the death benefit increases may be taken into account if the contract—

(i) has an initial death benefit of $5,000 or less and a maximum death benefit of $25,000 or less,

(ii) provides for a fixed predetermined annual increase not to exceed 10 percent of the initial death benefit or 8 percent of the death benefit at the end of the preceding year, and

(iii) was purchased to cover payment of burial expenses or in connection with prearranged funeral expenses.

For purposes of subparagraph (C), the initial death benefit of a contract shall be determined by treating all contracts issued to the same contract owner as 1 contract.

(f) Other definitions and special rules.

For purposes of this section—

(1) Premiums paid.

(A) In general. The term "premiums paid" means the premiums paid under the contract less amounts (other than amounts includible in gross income) to which section 72(e) applies and less any excess premiums with respect to which there is a distribution described in subparagraph (B) or (E) of paragraph (7) and any other amounts received with respect to the contract which are specified in regulations.

(B) Treatment of certain premiums returned to policyholder. If, in order to comply with the requirements of subsection (a)(2)(A), any portion of any premium paid during any contract year is returned by the insurance company (with interest) within 60 days after the end of a contract year, the amount so returned (excluding interest) shall be deemed to reduce the sum of the premiums paid under the contract during such year.

(C) Interest returned includible in gross income. Notwithstanding the provisions of section 72(e), the amount of any interest returned as provided in subparagraph (B) shall be includible in the gross income of the recipient.

(2) Cash values.

(A) Cash surrender value. The cash surrender value of any contract shall be its cash value determined without regard to any surrender charge, policy loan, or reasonable termination dividends.

(B) Net surrender value. The net surrender value of any contract shall be determined with regard to surrender charges but without regard to any policy loan.

(3) Death benefit. The term "death benefit" means the amount payable by reason of the death of the insured (determined without regard to any qualified additional benefits).

(4) Future benefits. The term "future benefits" means death benefits and endowment benefits.

(5) Qualified additional benefits.

(A) In general. The term "qualified additional benefits" means any—

(i) guaranteed insurability,

(ii) accidental death or disability benefit,

(iii) family term coverage,

(iv) disability waiver benefit, or

(v) other benefit prescribed under regulations.

(B) Treatment of qualified additional benefits. For purposes of this section, qualified additional benefits shall not be treated as future benefits under the contract, but the charges for such benefits shall be treated as future benefits.

(C) Treatment of other additional benefits. In the case of any additional benefit which is not a qualified additional benefit—

(i) such benefit shall not be treated as a future benefit, and

(ii) any charge for such benefit which is not prefunded shall not be treated as a premium.

(6) Premium payments not disqualifying contract. The payment of a premium which would result in the sum of the premiums paid exceeding the guideline premium limitation shall be disregarded for purposes of subsection (a)(2) if the amount of such premium does not exceed the amount necessary to prevent the termination of the contract on or before the end of the contract year (but only if the contract will have no cash surrender value at the end of such extension period).

(7) Adjustments.

(A) In general. If there is a change in the benefits under (or in other terms of) the contract which was not reflected in any previous determination or adjustment made under this section, there shall be proper adjustments in future determinations made under this section.

(B) Rule for certain changes during first 15 years. If—

(i) a change described in subparagraph (A) reduces benefits under the contract,

(ii) the change occurs during the 15-year period beginning on the issue date of the contract, and

(iii) a cash distribution is made to the policyholder as a result of such change,

section 72 (other than subsection (e)(5) thereof) shall apply to such cash distribution to the extent it does not exceed the recapture ceiling determined under subparagraph (C) or (D) (whichever applies).

(C) Recapture ceiling where change occurs during first 5 years. If the change referred to in subparagraph (B)(ii) occurs during the 5-year period beginning on the issue date of the contract, the recapture ceiling is—

(i) in the case of a contract to which subsection (a)(1) applies, the excess of—

(I) the cash surrender value of the contract, immediately before the reduction, over

(II) the net single premium (determined under subsection (b)), immediately after the reduction, or

3,949

(ii) in the case of a contract to which subsection (a)(2) applies, the greater of—
(I) the excess of the aggregate premiums paid under the contract, immediately before the reduction, over the guideline premium limitation for the contract (determined under subsection (c)(2), taking into account the adjustment described in subparagraph (A)), or
(II) the excess of the cash surrender value of the contract, immediately before the reduction, over the cash value corridor of subsection (d) (determined immediately after the reduction).
(D) Recapture ceiling where change occurs after 5th year and before 16th year. If the change referred to in subparagraph (B) occurs after the 5-year period referred to under subparagraph (C), the recapture ceiling is the excess of the cash surrender value of the contract, immediately before the reduction, over the cash value corridor of subsection (d) (determined immediately after the reduction and whether or not subsection (d) applies to the contract).
(E) Treatment of certain distributions made in anticipation of benefit reductions. Under regulations prescribed by the Secretary, subparagraph (B) shall apply also to any distribution made in anticipation of a reduction in benefits under the contract. For purposes of the preceding sentence, appropriate adjustments shall be made in the provisions of subparagraphs (C) and (D); and any distribution which reduces the cash surrender value of a contract and which is made within 2 years before a reduction in benefits under the contract shall be treated as made in anticipation of such reduction.

(8) **Correction of errors.** If the taxpayer establishes to the satisfaction of the Secretary that—
(A) the requirements described in subsection (a) for any contract year were not satisfied due to reasonable error, and
(B) reasonable steps are being taken to remedy the error,
the Secretary may waive the failure to satisfy such requirements.

(9) **Special rule for variable life insurance contracts.** In the case of any contract which is a variable contract (as defined in section 817), the determination of whether such contract meets the requirements of subsection (a) shall be made whenever the death benefits under such contract change but not less frequently than once during each 12-month period.

(g) **Treatment of contracts which do not meet subsection (a) test.**
(1) **Income inclusion.**
(A) In general. If at any time any contract which is a life insurance contract under the applicable law does not meet the definition of life insurance contract under subsection (a), the income on the contract for any taxable year of the policyholder shall be treated as ordinary income received or accrued by the policyholder during such year.
(B) Income on the contract. For purposes of this paragraph, the term "income on the contract" means, with respect to any taxable year of the policyholder, the excess of—
(i) the sum of
(I) the increase in the net surrender value of the contract during the taxable year, and
(II) the cost of life insurance protection provided under the contract during the taxable year, over
(ii) the premiums paid (as defined in subsection (f)(1)) under the contract during the taxable year.
(C) Contracts which cease to meet definition. If, during any taxable year of the policyholder, a contract which is a life insurance contract under the applicable law ceases to meet the definition of life insurance contract under subsection (a), the income on the contract for all prior taxable years shall be treated as received or accrued during the taxable year in which such cessation occurs.
(D) Cost of life insurance protection. For purposes of this paragraph, the cost of life insurance protection provided under the contract shall be the lesser of—
(i) the cost of individual insurance on the life of the insured as determined on the basis of uniform premiums (computed on the basis of 5-year age brackets) prescribed by the Secretary by regulations, or
(ii) the mortality charge (if any) stated in the contract.

(2) **Treatment of amount paid on death of insured.** If any contract which is a life insurance contract under the applicable law does not meet the definition of life insurance contract under subsection (a), the excess of the amount paid by the reason of the death of the insured over the net surrender value of the contract shall be deemed to be paid under a life insurance contract for purposes of section 101 and subtitle B.

(3) **Contract continues to be treated as insurance contract.** If any contract which is a life insurance contract under the applicable law does not meet the definition of life insurance contract under subsection (a), such contract shall, notwithstanding such failure, be treated as an insurance contract for purposes of this title.

(h) **Endowment contracts receive same treatment.**
(1) **In general.** References in subsections (a) and (g) to a life insurance contract shall be treated as including references to a contract which is an endowment contract under the applicable law.
(2) **Definition of endowment contract.** For purposes of this title (other than paragraph (1)), the term "endowment contract" means a contract which is an endowment contract under the applicable law and which meets the requirements of subsection (a).

(i) **Transitional rule for certain 20-pay contracts.**
(1) **In general.** In the case of a qualified 20-pay contract, this section shall be applied by substituting "3 percent" for "4 percent" in subsection (b)(2).
(2) **Qualified 20-pay contract.** For purposes of paragraph (1), the term "qualified 20-pay contract" means any contract which—
(A) requires at least 20 nondecreasing annual premium payments, and
(B) is issued pursuant to an existing plan of insurance.
(3) **Existing plan of insurance.** For purposes of this subsection, the term "existing plan of insurance" means, with respect to any contract, any plan of insurance which was filed by the company issuing such contract in 1 or more States before September 28, 1983, and is on file in the appropriate State for such contract.

(j) **Certain church self-funded death benefit plans treated as life insurance.—**
(1) **In general.** In determining whether any plan or arrangement described in paragraph (2) is a life insurance contract, the requirement of subsection (a) that the con-

Miscellaneous provisions
Code Sec. 7702

tract be a life insurance contract under applicable law shall not apply.

(2) Description. For purposes of this subsection, a plan or arrangement is described in this paragraph if—

(A) such plan or arrangement provides for the payment of benefits by reason of the death of the individuals covered under such plan or arrangement, and

(B) such plan or arrangement is provided by a church for the benefit of its employees and their beneficiaries, directly or through an organization described in section 414(e)(3)(A) or an organization described in section 414(e)(3)(B)(ii).

(3) Definitions. For purposes of this subsection—

(A) Church. The term "church" means a church or a convention or association of churches.

(B) Employee. The term "employee" includes an employee described in section 414(e)(3)(B).

(k) Regulations.

The Secretary shall prescribe such regulations as may be necessary or appropriate to carry out the purposes of this section.

In 2004, P.L. 108-476, Sec. 1, of this Act, provides:
"SECTION 1. CERTAIN ARRANGEMENTS MAINTAINED BY THE YMCA RETIREMENT FUND TREATED AS CHURCH PLANS.
"(a) Retirement plans.
"(1) In general. For purposes of sections 401(a) and 403(b) of the Internal Revenue Code of 1986, any retirement plan maintained by the YMCA Retirement Fund as of January 1, 2003, shall be treated as a church plan (within the meaning of section 414(e) of such Code) which is maintained by an organization described in section 414(e)(3)(A) of such Code.
"(2) Tax-deferred retirement plan. In the case of a retirement plan described in paragraph (1) which allows contributions to be made under a salary reduction agreement—
"(A) such treatment shall not apply for purposes of section 415(c)(7) of such Code, and
"(B) any account maintained for a participant or beneficiary of such plan shall be treated for purposes of such Code as a retirement income account described in section 403(b)(9) of such Code, except that such account shall not, for purposes of section 403(b)(12) of such Code, be treated as a contract purchased by a church for purposes of section 403(b)(1)(D) of such Code.
"(3) Money purchase pension plan. In the case of a retirement plan described in paragraph (1) which is subject to the requirements of section 401(a) of such Code—
"(A) such plan (but not any reserves held by the YMCA Retirement Fund)—
"(i) shall be treated for purposes of such Code as a defined contribution plan which is a money purchase pension plan, and
"(ii) shall be treated as having made an election under section 410(d) of such Code for plan years beginning after December 31, 2005, except that notwithstanding the election—
"(I) nothing in the Employee Retirement Income Security Act of 1974 or such Code shall prohibit the YMCA Retirement Fund from commingling for investment purposes the assets of the electing plan with the assets of such Fund and with the assets of any employee benefit plan maintained by such Fund, and
"(II) nothing in this section shall be construed as subjecting any assets described in subclause (I), other than the assets of the electing plan, to any provision of such Act,
"(B) notwithstanding section 401(a)(11) or 417 of such Code or section 205 of such Act, such plan may offer a lump-sum distribution option to participants who have not attained age 55 without offering such participants an annuity option, and
"(C) any account maintained for a participant or beneficiary of such plan shall, for purposes of section 401(a)(9) of such Code, be treated as a retirement income account described in section 403(b)(9) of such Code.
"(4) Self-funded death benefit plan. For purposes of section 7702(j) of such Code, a retirement plan described in paragraph (1) shall be treated as an arrangement described in section 7702(j)(2).
"(b) YMCA retirement fund. For purposes of this section, the term 'YMCA Retirement Fund' means the Young Men's Christian Association Retirement Fund, a corporation created by an Act of the State of New York which became law on April 30, 1921.
"(c) Effective date. This section shall apply to plan years beginning after December 31, 2003."

In 1988, P.L. 100-647, Sec. 1018(j), changed the effective date for changes made by Sec. 1825(a)(4) of P.L. 99-514, from "effective for contracts issued after 12/31/84, in tax. yrs. end. and as provided in Sec. 221(d)(2) of P.L. 98-369," to "effective for contracts entered into after 10/22/86," see below.
—P.L. 100-647, Sec. 5011(a), amended clauses (c)(3)(B)(i) and (c)(3)(B)(ii) . . . Sec. 5011(b), added subpara. (c)(3)(D), effective for contracts entered into on or after 10/21/88.
Prior to amendments, clauses (c)(3)(B)(i) and (c)(3)(B)(ii) read as follows:

"(i) the mortality charges specified in the contract (or, if none is specified, the mortality charges used in determining the statutory reserves for such contract).
"(ii) any charges (not taken into account under clause (i)) specified in the contract (the amount of any charge not so specified shall be treated as zero), and"
—P.L. 100-647, Sec. 5011(c), of this Act provides:
"(c) Interim rules.—
"(1) Regulations.— Not later than January 1, 1990, the Secretary of the Treasury (or his delegate) shall issue regulations under section 7702(c)(3)(B)(i) of the 1986 Code (as amended by subsection (a)).
"(2) Standards before regulations take effect.— In the case of any contract to which the amendments made by this section apply and which is issued before the effective date of the regulations required under paragraph (1), mortality charges which do not differ materially from the charges actually expected to be imposed by the company (taking into account any relevant characteristic of the insured of which the company is aware) shall be treated as meeting the requirements of clause (i) of section 7702(c)(3)(B) of the 1986 Code (as amended by subsection (a))."
—P.L. 100-647, Sec. 6078(a), redesignated subsec. (j) as subsec. (k) and added subsec. (j), effective for contracts issued after 12/31/84, in tax. yrs. end. after 12/31/84. For special rules see Sec. 221(d)(2)-(5) [as amended by Sec. 1825(c)(1) of P.L. 99-514, see above] of P.L. 98-369, reproduced below.
In 1986, P.L. 99-514, Sec. 1825(a)(1)(A), substituted "shall be deemed to be no earlier than" for "shall be no earlier than" in subpara. (e)(1)(B) . . . Sec. 1825(a)(1)(B), deleted "and" at the end of subpara. (e)(1)(B) . . . Sec. 1825(a)(1)(C), redesignated subpara. (e)(1)(C) as (D), and added subpara. (e)(1)(C) . . . Sec. 1825(a)(1)(D), substituted "the maturity date determined by taking into account subparagraph (B)" for "the maturity date described in subparagraph (B)", in subpara. (e)(1)(D) [as redesignated by Sec. 1825(a)(1)(C), see above] . . . Sec. 1825(a)(2), substituted "subparagraphs (A) and (D)" for "subparagraphs (A) and (C)" in subpara. (b)(2)(C) . . . Sec. 1825(a)(3), added "(other than subsection (d))" after "section" in para. (e)(1) . . . Sec. 1825(b)(1), amended para. (f)(7) . . . Sec. 1825(b)(2), substituted "less any excess premiums with respect to which there is a distribution described in subparagraph (B) or (E) of paragraph (7) and any other amounts received" for "less any other amount received" in subpara. (f)(1)(A) . . . Sec. 1825(c), amended clause (g)(1)(B)(ii), effective for contracts issued after 12/31/84 in tax. yrs. end. after 12/31/84. For special rules see Sec. 221(d)(2)-(5) [as amended by Sec. 1825(c)(1) of P.L. 99-514, see below] of P.L. 98-369, reproduced below.
Prior to amendment, para. (f)(7) read as follows:
"(7) Adjustments.
"(A) In general. In the event of a change in the future benefits or any qualified additional benefit (or in any other terms) under the contract which was not reflected in any previous determination made under this section, under regulations prescribed by the Secretary, there shall be proper adjustments in future determinations made under this section.
"(B) Certain changes treated as exchange. In the case of any change which reduces the future benefits under the contract, such change shall be treated as an exchange of the contract for another contract."
Prior to amendment, clause (g)(1)(B)(ii) read as follows:
"(ii) the amount of premiums paid under the contract during the taxable year reduced by any policyholder dividends received during such taxable year."
—P.L. 99-514, Sec. 1825(a)(4)(A), [as amended by Sec. 1018(j) of P.L. 100-647, see above], deleted "and" at the end of subpara. (e)(2)(A) . . . Sec. 1825(a)(4)(B), [as amended by Sec. 1018(j) of P.L. 100-647, see above], substituted ", and" for the period at the end of subpara. (e)(2)(B) . . . Sec. 1825(a)(4)(C), [as amended by Sec. 1018(j) of P.L. 100-647, see above], added subpara. (e)(2)(C), effective for contracts entered into after 10/22/86.
—P.L. 99-514, Sec. 1825(e), amended Sec. 221(d)(2)(C)(i) of P.L. 98-369 [reproduced below], special rules for changes made by Sec. 221(a) of P.L. 98-369, by deleting "in clause (i) thereof" after "June 30, 1984" in clause (d)(2)(C)(i) and by substituting "any mortality charges and any initial excess interest guarantees" for "any mortality charges" in subclause (d)(2)(C)(i)(I), see below.
In 1984, P.L. 98-369, Sec. 221(a), added Code Sec. 7702, effective for contracts issued after 12/31/84 in tax. yrs. ending after 12/31/84. For special rules, Sec. 221(d)(2)-(5) [as amended by Sec. 1825(e)(1) of P.L. 99-514 above] of the Act provides as follows:
"(2) Special rule for certain contracts issued after June 30, 1984.—
"(A) General rule.— Except as otherwise provided in this paragraph, the amendments made by this section shall apply also to any contract issued after June 30, 1984, which provides an increasing death benefit and has premium funding more rapid that 10-year level premium payments.
"(B) Exception for certain contracts.— Subparagraph (A) shall not apply to any contract if—
"(i) such contract (whether or not a flexible premium contract) would meet the requirements of section 101(f) of the Internal Revenue Code of 1954,
"(ii) such contract is not a flexible premium life insurance contract (within the meaning of section 101(f) of such Code) and would meet the requirements of section 7702 of such Code determined by—
"(I) substituting '3 percent' for '4 percent' in section 7702(b)(2) of such Code, and
"(II) treating subparagraph (B) of section 7702(e)(1) of such Code as if it read as follows: 'the maturity date shall be the latest maturity date permitted under the contract, but not less than 20 years after the date of issue or (if earlier) age 95', or
"(iii) under such contract—
"(I) the premiums (including any policy fees) will be adjusted from time-to-time to reflect the level amount necessary (but not less than zero) at the time of

3,951

such adjustment to provide a level death benefit assuming interest crediting and an annual effective interest rate of not less than 3 percent, or

"(II) at the option of the insured, in lieu of an adjustment under subclause (I) there will be a comparable adjustment in the amount of the death benefit.

"(C) Certain contracts issued before October 1, 1984.—

"(i) In general.—Subparagraph (A) shall be applied by substituting 'September 30, 1984' for 'June 30, 1984' in the case of a contract—

"(I) which would meet the requirements of section 7702 of such Code if '3 percent' were substituted for '4 percent' in section 7702(b)(2) of such Code, and the rate or rates guaranteed on issuance of the contract were determined without regard to any mortality charges and any initial excess interest guarantees, and

"(II) the cash surrender value of which does not at any time exceed the net single premium which would have to be paid at such time to fund future benefits under the contract.

"(ii) Definitions.—For purposes of clause (i)—

"(I) In general.—Except as provided in subclause (II), terms used in clause (i) shall have the same meanings as when used in section 7702 of such Code.

"(II) Net single premium.—The term 'net single premium' shall be determined by substituting '3 percent' for '4 percent' in section 7702(b)(2) of such Code, by using the 1958 standard ordinary mortality and morbidity tables of the National Association of Insurance Commissioners, and by assuming a level death benefit.

"(3) Transitional rule for certain existing plans of insurance.—A plan of insurance on file in 1 or more States before September 28, 1983, shall be treated for purposes of section 7702(i)(3) of such Code as a plan of insurance on file in 1 or more States before September 28, 1983, without regard to whether such plan of insurance is modified after September 28, 1983, to permit the crediting of excess interest or similar amounts annually and not monthly under contracts issued pursuant to such plan of insurance.

"(4) Extension of flexible premium contract provisions.—The amendments made by subsection (b) shall take effect on January 1, 1984.

"(5) Special rule for master contract.—For purposes of this subsection, in the case of a master contract, the date taken into account with respect to any insured shall be the first date on which such insured is covered under such contract."

Sec. 7702A. Modified endowment contract defined.

(a) General rule.

For purposes of section 72, the term "modified endowment contract" means any contract meeting the requirements of section 7702—

(1) which—

(A) is entered into on or after June 21, 1988, and

(B) fails to meet the 7-pay test of subsection (b), or

(2) which is received in exchange for a contract described in paragraph (1) or this paragraph.

(b) 7-pay test.

For purposes of subsection (a), a contract fails to meet the 7-pay test of this subsection if the accumulated amount paid under the contract at any time during the 1st 7 contract years exceeds the sum of the net level premiums which would have been paid on or before such time if the contract provided for paid-up future benefits after the payment of 7 level annual premiums.

(c) Computational rules.

(1) In general. Except as provided in this subsection, the determination under subsection (b) of the 7 level annual premiums shall be made—

(A) as of the time the contract is issued, and

(B) by applying the rules of section 7702(b)(2) and of section 7702(e) (other than paragraph (2)(C) thereof), except that the death benefit provided for the 1st contract year shall be deemed to be provided until the maturity date without regard to any scheduled reduction after the 1st 7 contract years.

(2) Reduction in benefits during 1st 7 years.

(A) In general. If there is a reduction in benefits under the contract within the 1st 7 contract years, this section shall be applied as if the contract had originally been issued at the reduced benefit level.

(B) Reductions attributable to nonpayment of premiums. Any reduction in benefits attributable to the nonpayment of premiums due under the contract shall not be taken into account under subparagraph (A) if the benefits are reinstated within 90 days after the reduction in such benefits.

(3) Treatment of material changes.

(A) In general. If there is a material change in the benefits under (or in other terms of) the contract which was not reflected in any previous determination under this section, for purposes of this section—

(i) such contract shall be treated as a new contract entered into on the day on which such material change takes effect, and

(ii) appropriate adjustments shall be made in determining whether such contract meets the 7-pay test of subsection (b) to take into account the cash surrender value under the contract.

(B) Treatment of certain benefit increases. For purposes of subparagraph (A), the term "material change" includes any increase in the death benefit under the contract or any increase in, or addition of, a qualified additional benefit under the contract. Such term shall not include—

(i) any increase which is attributable to the payment of premiums necessary to fund the lowest level of the death benefit and qualified additional benefits payable in the 1st 7 contract years (determined after taking into account death benefit increases described in subparagraph (A) or (B) of section 7702(e)(2)) or to crediting of interest or other earnings (including policyholder dividends) in respect of such premiums, and

(ii) to the extent provided in regulations, any cost-of-living increase based on an established broad-based index if such increase is funded ratably over the remaining period during which premiums are required to be paid under the contract.

(4) Special rule for contracts with death benefits of $10,000 or less. In the case of a contract—

(A) which provides an initial death benefit of $10,000 or less, and

(B) which requires at least 7 nondecreasing annual premium payments, each of the 7 level annual premiums determined under subsection (b) (without regard to this paragraph) shall be increased by $75. For purposes of this paragraph, the contract involved and all contracts previously issued to the same policyholder by the same company shall be treated as one contract.

(5) Regulatory authority for certain collection expenses. The Secretary may by regulations prescribe rules for taking into account expenses solely attributable to the collection of premiums paid more frequently than annually.

(6) Treatment of certain contracts with more than one insured. If—

(A) a contract provides a death benefit which is payable only upon the death of 1 insured following (or occurring simultaneously with) the death of another insured, and

(B) there is a reduction in such death benefit below the lowest level of such death benefit provided under the contract during the 1st 7 contract years,

this section shall be applied as if the contract had originally been issued at the reduced benefit level.

(d) Distributions affected.

If a contract fails to meet the 7-pay test of subsection (b), such contract shall be treated as failing to meet such requirements only in the case of—

(1) distributions during the contract year in which the failure takes effect and during any subsequent contract year, and

Miscellaneous provisions   Code Sec. 7702B(b)(1)(E)

(2) under regulations prescribed by the Secretary, distributions (not described in paragraph (1)) in anticipation of such failure.

For purposes of the preceding sentence, any distribution which is made within 2 years before the failure to meet the 7-pay test shall be treated as made in anticipation of such failure.

(e) Definitions.

For purposes of this section—

(1) Amount paid.

(A) In general. The term "amount paid" means—

(i) the premiums paid under the contract, reduced by

(ii) amounts to which section 72(e) applies (determined without regard to paragraph (4)(A) thereof) but not including amounts includible in gross income.

(B) Treatment of certain premiums returned. If, in order to comply with the requirements of subsection (b), any portion of any premium paid during any contract year is returned by the insurance company (with interest) within 60 days after the end of such contract year, the amount so returned (excluding interest) shall be deemed to reduce the sum of the premiums paid under the contract during such contract year.

(C) Interest returned includible in gross income. Notwithstanding the provisions of section 72(e), the amount of any interest returned as provided in subparagraph (B) shall be includible in the gross income of the recipient.

(2) Contract year. The term "contract year" means the 12-month period beginning with the 1st month for which the contract is in effect, and each 12-month period beginning with the corresponding month in subsequent calendar years.

(3) Other terms. Except as otherwise provided in this section, terms used in this section shall have the same meaning as when used in section 7702.

In **2002**, P.L. 107-147, Sec. 416(f), repealed Sec. 318(a)(2) of P.L. 106-554 [as enacted into law by P.L. 106-554, see below] as if the provision had never been enacted. See below for amendment.

In **2000**, P.L. 106-554, Sec. 1(a)(7), [which enacted into law Sec. 318(a)(1) of P.L. 106-554] added "or this paragraph" after "paragraph (1)" in para. (a)(2) . . . Sec. 1(a)(7), [which enacted into law Sec. 318(a)(2) of P.L. 106-554] substituted "under the old contract" for "under the contract" in clause (c)(3)(A)(ii), effective 12/21/2000. [Caution: Sec. 416(f) of P.L. 107-147, above, repealed this provision as if it had never been enacted.]

In **1989**, P.L. 101-239, Sec. 7647(a), added para. (c)(6), effective for contracts entered into on or after 9/14/89.

— P.L. 101-239, Sec. 7815(a)(1), amended subpara. (c)(3)(B) . . . Sec. 7815(a)(4)(A), substituted "of $10,000 or less" for "under $10,000" in the heading of para. (c)(4) . . . Sec. 7815(a)(4)(B), substituted "the same policyholder" for "the same insurer" in para. (c)(4), effective for contracts entered into on or after 6/21/88.

Prior to amendment, subpara. (c)(3)(B) read as follows:

"(B) Treatment of certain increases in future benefits. For purposes of subparagraph (A), the term 'material change' includes any increase in future benefits under the contract. Such terms shall not include—

"(i) any increase which is attributable to the payment of premiums necessary to fund the lowest level of future benefits payable in the 1st 7 contract years (determined after taking into account death benefit increases described in subparagraph (A) or (B) of section 7702(e)(2)) or to crediting of interest or other earnings (including policyholder dividends) in respect of such premiums, and

"(ii) to the extent provided in regulations, any cost-of-living increase based on an established broad-based index if such increase is funded ratably over the remaining life of the the contract."

— P.L. 101-239, Sec. 7815(a)(2), amended Sec. 5012(e)(2) of P.L. 100-647 [reproduced below], part of the special rules for changes made by Sec. 5012(c)(1) of P.L. 100-647, by substituting "makes at least 7 level annual premium payments:" for "continues to make level annual premium payments over the life of the contract", see below.

In **1988**, P.L. 100-647, Sec. 5012(c)(1), added Code Sec. 7702A, effective for contracts entered into on or after 6/21/88. Sec. 5012(e)(2)-(4) [as amended by Sec. 7815(a)(2) of P.L. 101-239, see above] of this Act provides:

"(2) Special rule where death benefit increases by more than $150,000. If the death benefit under the contract increases by more than $150,000 over the death benefit under the contract in effect on October 20, 1988, the rules of section 7702A(c)(3) of the 1986 Code (as added by this section) shall apply in determining whether such contract is issued on or after June 21, 1988. The preceding sentence shall not apply in the case of a contract which, as of June 21, 1988, required at least 7 level annual premium payments and under which the policyholder makes at least 7 level annual premium payments.

"(3) Certain other material changes taken into account. A contract entered into before June 21, 1988, shall be treated as entered into after such date if—

"(A) on or after June 21, 1988, the death benefit under the contract is increased (or a qualified additional benefit is increased or added) and before June 21, 1988, the owner of the contract did not have a unilateral right under the contract to obtain such increase or addition without providing additional evidence of insurability, or

"(B) the contract is converted after June 20, 1988, from a term life insurance contract to a life insurance contract providing coverage other than term life insurance coverage without regard to any right of the owner of the contract to such conversion.

"(4) Certain exchanges permitted. In the case of a modified endowment contract which—

"(A) required at least 7 annual level premium payments,

"(B) is entered into after June 20, 1988, and before the date of the enactment of this Act, and

"(C) is exchanged within 3 months after such date of enactment for a life insurance contract which meets the requirements of section 7702A(b),

the contract which is received in exchange for such contract shall not be treated as a modified endowment contract if the taxpayer elects, notwithstanding section 1035 of the 1986 Code, to recognize gain on such exchange."

Sec. 7702B. Treatment of qualified long-term care insurance.

(a) In general.

For purposes of this title—

(1) a qualified long-term care insurance contract shall be treated as an accident and health insurance contract,

(2) amounts (other than policyholder dividends, as defined in section 808, or premium refunds) received under a qualified long-term care insurance contract shall be treated as amounts received for personal injuries and sickness and shall be treated as reimbursement for expenses actually incurred for medical care (as defined in section 213(d),

(3) any plan of an employer providing coverage under a qualified long-term care insurance contract shall be treated as an accident and health plan with respect to such coverage,

(4) except as provided in subsection (e)(3), amounts paid for a qualified long-term care insurance contract providing the benefits described in subsection (b)(2)(A) shall be treated as payments made for insurance for purposes of section 213(d)(1)(D), and

(5) a qualified long-term care insurance contract shall be treated as a guaranteed renewable contract subject to the rules of section 816(e).

(b) Qualified long-term care insurance contract.

For purposes of this title—

(1) In general. The term "qualified long-term care insurance contract" means any insurance contract if—

(A) the only insurance protection provided under such contract is coverage of qualified long-term care services,

(B) such contract does not pay or reimburse expenses incurred for services or items to the extent that such expenses are reimbursable under title XVIII of the Social Security Act or would be so reimbursable but for the application of a deductible or coinsurance amount,

(C) such contract is guaranteed renewable,

(D) such contract does not provide for a cash surrender value or other money that can be—

(i) paid, assigned, or pledged as collateral for a loan, or

(ii) borrowed,

other than as provided in subparagraph (E) or paragraph (2)(C),

(E) all refunds of premiums, and all policyholder dividends or similar amounts, under such contract are to be applied as a reduction in future premiums or to increase future benefits, and

(F) such contract meets the requirements of subsection (g).

(2) Special rules.

(A) Per diem, etc. payments permitted. A contract shall not fail to be described in subparagraph (A) or (B) of paragraph (1) by reason of payments being made on a per diem or other periodic basis without regard to the expenses incurred during the period to which the payments relate.

(B) Special rules relating to medicare.

(i) Paragraph (1)(B) shall not apply to expenses which are reimbursable under title XVIII of the Social Security Act only as a secondary payor.

(ii) No provision of law shall be construed or applied so as to prohibit the offering of a qualified long-term care insurance contract on the basis that the contract coordinates its benefits with those provided under such title.

(C) Refunds of premiums. Paragraph (1)(E) shall not apply to any refund on the death of the insured, or on a complete surrender or cancellation of the contract, which cannot exceed the aggregate premiums paid under the contract. Any refund on a complete surrender or cancellation of the contract shall be includible in gross income to the extent that any deduction or exclusion was allowable with respect to the premiums.

(c) Qualified long-term care services.

For purposes of this section—

(1) In general. The term "qualified long-term care services" means necessary diagnostic, preventive, therapeutic, curing, treating, mitigating, and rehabilitative services, and maintenance or personal care services, which—

(A) are required by a chronically ill individual, and

(B) are provided pursuant to a plan of care prescribed by a licensed health care practitioner.

(2) Chronically ill individual.

(A) In general. The term "chronically ill individual" means any individual who has been certified by a licensed health care practitioner as—

(i) being unable to perform (without substantial assistance from another individual) at least 2 activities of daily living for a period of at least 90 days due to a loss of functional capacity,

(ii) having a level of disability similar (as determined under regulations prescribed by the Secretary in consultation with the Secretary of Health and Human Services) to the level of disability described in clause (i), or

(iii) requiring substantial supervision to protect such individual from threats to health and safety due to severe cognitive impairment.

Such term shall not include any individual otherwise meeting the requirements of the preceding sentence unless within the preceding 12-month period a licensed health care practitioner has certified that such individual meets such requirements.

(B) Activities for daily living. For purposes of subparagraph (A), each of the following is an activity of daily living:

(i) Eating.
(ii) Toileting.
(iii) Transferring.
(iv) Bathing.
(v) Dressing.
(vi) Continence.

A contract shall not be treated as a qualified long-term care insurance contract unless the determination of whether an individual is a chronically ill individual described in subparagraph (A)(i) takes into account at least 5 of such activities.

(3) Maintenance or personal care services. The term "maintenance or personal care services" means any care the primary purpose of which is the provision of needed assistance with any of the disabilities as a result of which the individual is a chronically ill individual (including the protection from threats to health and safety due to severe cognitive impairment).

(4) Licensed health care practitioner. The term "licensed health care practitioner" means any physician (as defined in section 1861(r)(1) of the Social Security Act) and any registered professional nurse, licensed social worker, or other individual who meets such requirements as may be prescribed by the Secretary.

(d) Aggregate payments in excess of limits.

(1) In general. If the aggregate of—

(A) the periodic payments received for any period under all qualified long-term care insurance contracts which are treated as made for qualified long-term care services for an insured, and

(B) the periodic payments received for such period which are treated under section 101(g) as paid by reason of the death of such insured,

exceeds the per diem limitation for such period, such excess shall be includible in gross income without regard to section 72. A payment shall not be taken into account under subparagraph (B) if the insured is a terminally ill individual (as defined in section 101(g)) at the time the payment is received.

(2) Per diem limitation. For purposes of paragraph (1), the per diem limitation for any period is an amount equal to the excess (if any) of—

(A) the greater of—

(i) the dollar amount in effect for such period under paragraph (4), or

(ii) the costs incurred for qualified long-term care services provided for the insured for such period, over

(B) the aggregate payments received as reimbursements (through insurance or otherwise) for qualified long-term care services provided for the insured during such period.

(3) Aggregation rules. For purposes of this subsection—

(A) all persons receiving periodic payments described in paragraph (1) with respect to the same insured shall be treated as 1 person, and

(B) the per diem limitation determined under paragraph (2) shall be allocated first to the insured and any remaining limitation shall be allocated among the other such persons in such manner as the Secretary shall prescribe.

(4) Dollar amount. The dollar amount in effect under this subsection shall be $175 per day (or the equivalent amount in the case of payments on another periodic basis).

(5) Inflation adjustment. In the case of a calendar year after 1997, the dollar amount contained in paragraph (4) shall be increased at the same time and in the same manner as amounts are increased pursuant to section 213(d)(10).

Miscellaneous provisions Code Sec. 7702B(g)(1)(C)

(6) Periodic payments. For purposes of this subsection, the term "periodic payment" means any payment (whether on a periodic basis or otherwise) made without regard to the extent of the costs incurred by the payee for qualified long-term care services.

> • **Caution:** Code Sec. 7702B(e), following, is effective prior to amendment by Sec. 844(c), P.L. 109-280. For Code Sec. 7702B(e) effective after amendments made by Sec. 844(c), P.L. 109-280, see below. For effective date of amendments made by Sec. 844(c), P.L. 109-280, see note following this Code Sec.

(e) Treatment of coverage provided as part of a life insurance contract.

Except as otherwise provided in regulations prescribed by the Secretary, in the case of any long-term care insurance coverage (whether or not qualified) provided by a rider on or as part of a life insurance contract—

 (1) In general. This title shall apply as if the portion of the contract providing such coverage is a separate contract.

 (2) Application of section 7702. Section 7702(c)(2) (relating to the guideline premium limitation) shall be applied by increasing the guideline premium limitation with respect to a life insurance contract, as of any date—

  (A) by the sum of any charges (but not premium payments) against the life insurance contract's cash surrender value (within the meaning of section 7702(f)(2)(A)) for such coverage made to that date under the contract, less

  (B) any such charges the imposition of which reduces the premiums paid for the contract (within the meaning of section 7702(f)(1)).

 (3) Application of section 213. No deduction shall be allowed under section 213(a) for charges against the life insurance contract's cash surrender value described in paragraph (2), unless such charges are includible in income as a result of the application of section 72(e)(10) and the rider is a qualified long-term care insurance contract under subsection (b).

 (4) Portion defined. For purposes of this subsection, the term "portion" means only the terms and benefits under a life insurance contract that are in addition to the terms and benefits under the contract without regard to long-term care insurance coverage.

> • **Caution:** Code Sec. 7702B(e), following, is effective after amendment by Sec. 844(c), P.L. 109-280. For Code Sec. 7702B(e) effective before amendments made by Sec. 844(c), P.L. 109-280, see above. For effective date of amendments made by Sec. 844(c), P.L. 109-280, see note following this Code Sec.

(e) Treatment of coverage provided as part of a life insurance or annuity contract.

Except as otherwise provided in regulations prescribed by the Secretary, in the case of any long-term care insurance coverage (whether or not qualified) provided by a rider on or as part of a life insurance contract or an annuity contract—

 (1) In general. This title shall apply as if the portion of the contract providing such coverage is a separate contract.

 (2) Denial of deduction under section 213. No deduction shall be allowed under section 213(a) for any payment made for coverage under a qualified long-term care insurance contract if such payment is made as a charge against the cash surrender value of a life insurance contract or the cash value of an annuity contract.

 (3) Portion defined. For purposes of this subsection, the term "portion" means only the terms and benefits under a life insurance contract or annuity contract that are in addition to the terms and benefits under the contract without regard to long term care insurance coverage.

 (4) Annuity contracts to which paragraph (1) does not apply. For purposes of this subsection, none of the following shall be treated as an annuity contract:

  (A) A trust described in section 401(a) which is exempt from tax under section 501(a).

  (B) A contract—

   (i) purchased by a trust described in subparagraph (A),

   (ii) purchased as part of a plan described in section 403(a),

   (iii) described in section 403(b),

   (iv) provided for employees of a life insurance company under a plan described in section 818(a)(3), or

   (v) from an individual retirement account or an individual retirement annuity.

  (C) A contract purchased by an employer for the benefit of the employee (or the employee's spouse).

Any dividend described in section 404(k) which is received by a participant or beneficiary shall, for purposes of this paragraph, be treated as paid under a separate contract to which subparagraph (B)(i) applies.

(f) Treatment of certain state-maintained plans.

 (1) In general. If—

  (A) an individual receives coverage for qualified long-term care services under a State long-term care plan, and

  (B) the terms of such plan would satisfy the requirements of subsection (b) were such plan an insurance contract,

 such plan shall be treated as a qualified long-term care insurance contract for purposes of this title.

 (2) State long-term care plan. For purposes of paragraph (1), the term "State long-term care plan" means any plan—

  (A) which is established and maintained by a State or an instrumentality of a State,

  (B) which provides coverage only for qualified long-term care services, and

  (C) under which such coverage is provided only to—

   (i) employees and former employees of a State (or any political subdivision or instrumentality of a State),

   (ii) the spouses of such employees, and

   (iii) individuals bearing a relationship to such employees or spouses which is described in any of subparagraphs (A) through (G) of section 152(d)(2).

(g) Consumer protection provisions.

 (1) In general. The requirements of this subsection are met with respect to any contract if the contract meets—

  (A) the requirements of the model regulation and model Act described in paragraph (2),

  (B) the disclosure requirement of paragraph (3), and

  (C) the requirements relating to nonforfeitability under paragraph (4).

(2) Requirements of model regulation and Act.
(A) In general. The requirements of this paragraph are met with respect to any contract if such contract meets—
 (i) Model regulation. The following requirements of the model regulation:
  (I) Section 7A (relating to guaranteed renewal or noncancellability), and the requirements of section 6B of the model Act relating to such section 7A.
  (II) Section 7B (relating to prohibitions on limitations and exclusions).
  (III) Section 7C (relating to extension of benefits).
  (IV) Section 7D (relating to continuation or conversion of coverage).
  (V) Section 7E (relating to discontinuance and replacement of policies).
  (VI) Section 8 (relating to unintentional lapse).
  (VII) Section 9 (relating to disclosure), other than section 9F thereof.
  (VIII) Section 10 (relating to prohibitions against post-claims underwriting).
  (IX) Section 11 (relating to minimum standards).
  (X) Section 12 (relating to requirement to offer inflation protection, except that any requirement for a signature on a rejection of inflation protection shall permit the signature to be on an application or on a separate form.
  (XI) Section 23 (relating to prohibition against preexisting conditions and probationary periods in replacement policies or certificates).
 (ii) Model act. The following requirements of the model Act:
  (I) Section 6C (relating to preexisting conditions).
  (II) Section 6D (relating to prior hospitalization).
(B) Definitions. For purposes of this paragraph—
 (i) Model provisions. The terms "model regulation" and "model Act" mean the long-term care insurance model regulation, and the long-term care insurance model Act, respectively, promulgated by the National Association of Insurance Commissioners (as adopted as of January 1993).
 (ii) Coordination. Any provision of the model regulation or model Act listed under clause (i) or (ii) of subparagraph (A) shall be treated as including any other provision of such regulation or Act necessary to implement the provision.
 (iii) Determination. For purposes of this section and section 4980C, the determination of whether any requirement of a model regulation or the model Act has been met shall be made by the Secretary.

(3) Disclosure requirement. The requirement of this paragraph is met with respect to any contract if such contract meets the requirements of section 4980C(d).

(4) Nonforfeiture requirements.
(A) In general. The requirements of this paragraphare met with respect to any level premium contract, if the issuer of such contract offers to the policyholder, including any group policyholder, a nonforfeiture provision meeting the requirements of subparagraph (B).
(B) Requirements of provision. The nonforfeiture provision required under subparagraph (A) shall meet the following requirements:
 (i) The nonforfeiture provision shall be appropriately captioned.
 (ii) The nonforfeiture provision shall provide for a benefit available in the event of a default in the payment of any premiums and the amount of the benefit may be adjusted subsequent to being initially granted only as necessary to reflect changes in claims, persistency, and interest as reflected in changes in rates for premium paying contracts approved by the appropriate State regulatory agency for the same contract form.
 (iii) The nonforfeiture provision shall provide at least one of the following:
  (I) Reduced paid-up insurance.
  (II) Extended term insurance.
  (III) Shortened benefit period.
  (IV) Other similar offerings approved by the appropriate State regulatory agency.

(5) Cross reference. For coordination of the requirements of this subsectionwith State requirements, see section 4980C(f).

In 2006, P.L. 109-280, Sec. 844(c), amended subsec. (e), effective for contracts issued after 12/31/1996, but only for tax. yrs. begin. after 12/31/2009.
—P.L. 109-280, Sec. 844(f), substituted "title" for "section" in para. (e)(1), effective 8/21/96 [as if included in Sec. 321(a) of P.L. 104-191].
Prior to amendment, subsec. (e) read as follows:
 "(e) Treatment of coverage provided as part of a life insurance contract. Except as otherwise provided in regulations prescribed by the Secretary, in the case of any long-term care insurance coverage (whether or not qualified) provided by a rider on or as part of a life insurance contract—
 "(1) In general. This section shall apply as if the portion of the contract providing such coverage is a separate contract.
 "(2) Application of section 7702.
 "Section 7702(c)(2) (relating to the guideline premium limitation) shall be applied by increasing the guideline premium limitation with respect to a life insurance contract, as of any date—
 "(A) by the sum of any charges (but not premium payments) against the life insurance contract's cash surrender value (within the meaning of section 7702(f)(2)(A)) for such coverage made to that date under the contract, less
 "(B) any such charges the imposition of which reduces the premiums paid for the contract (within the meaning of section 7702(f)(1)).
 "(3) Application of section 213. No deduction shall be allowed under section 213(a) for charges against the life insurance contract's cash surrender value described in paragraph (2), unless such charges are includible in income as a result of the application of section 72(e)(10) and the rider is a qualified long-term care insurance contract under subsection (b).
 "(4) Portion defined. For purposes of this subsection, the term "portion" means only the terms and benefits under a life insurance contract that are in addition to the terms and benefits under the contract without regard to long-term care insurance coverage."

In 2004, P.L. 108-311, Sec. 207(25), substituted "subparagraphs (A) through (G) of section 152(d)(2)" for "paragraphs (1) through (8) of section 152(a)" in clause (f)(2)(C)(iii), effective for tax. yrs. begin. after 12/31/2004.
Prior to amendment, subsec. (e) read as follows:
 "(e) Treatment of coverage provided as part of a life insurance contract. Except as otherwise provided in regulations prescribed by the Secretary, in the case of any long-term care insurance coverage (whether or not qualified) provided by a rider on or as part of a life insurance contract—
 "(1) In general. This section shall apply as if the portion of the contract providing such coverage is a separate contract.
 "(2) Application of section 7702. Section 7702(c)(2) (relating to the guideline premium limitation) shall be applied by increasing the guideline premium limitation with respect to a life insurance contract, as of any date—
 "(A) by the sum of any charges (but not premium payments) against the life insurance contract's cash surrender value (within the meaning of section 7702(f)(2)(A)) for such coverage made to that date under the contract, less
 "(B) any such charges the imposition of which reduces the premiums paid for the contract (within the meaning of section 7702(f)(1)).
 "(3) Application of section 213. No deduction shall be allowed under section 213(a) for charges against the life insurance contract's cash surrender value described in paragraph (2), unless such charges are includible in income as a result of the application of section 72(e)(10) and the rider is a qualified long-term care insurance contract under subsection (b).
 "(4) Portion defined. For purposes of this subsection, the term "portion" means only the terms and benefits under a life insurance contract that are in addition to the terms and benefits under the contract without regard to long-term care insurance coverage."

In 1998, P.L. 105-206, Sec. 6023(28), added "section" after "Application of" in the heading of para. (e)(2), effective 7/22/98.
In 1997, P.L. 105-34, Sec. 1602(b), added "described in subparagraph (A)(i)" after "chronically ill individual" in subpara. (c)(2)(B). . . . Sec. 1602(e), substituted "appropriate State regulatory agency" for "Secretary" in clauses (g)(4)(B)(ii) and (iii), effective for contracts issued after 12/31/96.

Miscellaneous provisions   Code Sec. 7704(d)(1)(E)

In 1996, P.L. 104-191, Sec. 321(a), added Code Sec. 7702B, effective for contracts issued after 12/31/96. Sec. 321(f)(2)-(5), of this Act, reads as follows:

"(2) Continuation of existing policies. In the case of any contract issued before January 1, 1997, which met the long-term care insurance requirements of the State in which the contract was sitused at the time the contract was issued—

"(A) such contract shall be treated for purposes of the Internal Revenue Code of 1986 as a qualified long-term care insurance contract (as defined in section 7702B(b) of such Code), and

"(B) services provided under, or reimbursed by, such contract shall be treated for such purposes as qualified long-term care services (as defined in section 7702B(c) of such Code).

In the case of an individual who is covered on December 31, 1996, under a State long-term care plan (as defined in section 7702B(f)(2) of such Code), the terms of such plan on such date shall be treated for purposes of the preceding sentence as a contract issued on such date which met the long-term care insurance requirements of such State.

"(3) Exchanges of existing policies. If, after the date of enactment of this Act and before January 1, 1998, a contract providing for long-term care insurance coverage is exchanged solely for a qualified long-term care insurance contract (as defined in section 7702B(b) of such Code), no gain or loss shall be recognized on the exchange. If, in addition to a qualified long-term care insurance contract, money or other property is received in the exchange, then any gain shall be recognized to the extent of the sum of the money and the fair market value of the other property received. For purposes of this paragraph, the cancellation of a contract providing for long-term care insurance coverage and reinvestment of the cancellation proceeds in a qualified long-term care insurance contract within 60 days thereafter shall be treated as an exchange.

"(4) Issuance of certain riders permitted. For purposes of applying sections 101(f), 7702, and 7702A of the Internal Revenue Code of 1986 to any contract—

"(A) the issuance of a rider which is treated as a qualified long-term care insurance contract under section 7702B, and

"(B) the addition of any provision required to conform any other long-term care rider to be so treated,

shall not be treated as a modification or material change of such contract.

"(5) Application of per diem limitation to existing contracts. The amount of per diem payments made under a contract issued on or before July 31, 1996, with respect to an insured which are excludable from gross income by reason of section 7702B of the Internal Revenue Code of 1986 (as added by this section) shall not be reduced under subsection (d)(2)(B) thereof by reason of reimbursements received under a contract issued on or before such date. The preceding sentence shall cease to apply as of the date (after July 31, 1996) such contract is exchanged or there is any contract modification which results in an increase in the amount of such per diem payments or the amount of such reimbursements."

—P.L. 104-191, Sec. 325, added subsec. (g), effective for contracts issued after 12/31/96.

Sec. 7703.   Determination of marital status.
(a) General rule.

For purposes of part V of subchapter B of chapter 1 and those provisions of this title which refer to this subsection—

(1) the determination of whether an individual is married shall be made as of the close of his taxable year; except that if his spouse dies during his taxable year such determination shall be made as of the time of such death; and

(2) an individual legally separated from his spouse under a decree of divorce or of separate maintenance shall not be considered as married.

(b) Certain married individuals living apart.

For purposes of those provisions of this title which refer to this subsection, if—

(1) an individual who is married (within the meaning of subsection (a)) and who files a separate return maintains as his home a household which constitutes for more than one-half of the taxable year the principal place of abode of a child (within the meaning of section 152(f)(1)) with respect to whom such individual is entitled to a deduction for the taxable year under section 151 (or would be so entitled but for section 152(e)),

(2) such individual furnishes over one-half of the cost of maintaining such household during the taxable year, and

(3) during the last 6 months of the taxable year, such individual's spouse is not a member of such household,

such individual shall not be considered as married.

In 2004, P.L. 108-311, Sec. 207(26)(A), substituted "152(f)(1)" for "151(c)(3)" in para. (b)(1) . . . Sec. 207(26)(B), deleted "paragraph (2) or (4) of" after "so entitled but for" in para. (b)(1), effective for tax. yrs. begin. after 12/31/2004.

In 1988, P.L. 100-647, Sec. 1018(u)(41), substituted "151(c)(3)" for "151(e)(3)" in subsec. (b), effective for bonds issued after 8/15/86. For transitional rules, see Secs. 1311-1319 of P.L. 99-514, reproduced in note following Code Sec. 103.

In 1986, P.L. 99-514, Sec. 1301(j)(2)(A), added Code Sec. 7703, effective for bonds issued after 8/15/86. [Provisions relating to determination of marital status were formerly contained in Code Sec. 143, prior to the enactment of this section by this Act.] For transitional rules, see Secs. 1311-1319 of this Act reproduced in note following Code Sec. 103.

Sec. 7704.   Certain publicly traded partnerships treated as corporations.
(a) General rule.

For purposes of this title, except as provided in subsection (c), a publicly traded partnership shall be treated as a corporation.

(b) Publicly traded partnership.

For purposes of this section, the term "publicly traded partnership" means any partnership if—

(1) interests in such partnership are traded on an established securities market, or

(2) interests in such partnership are readily tradable on a secondary market (or the substantial equivalent thereof).

(c) Exception for partnerships with passive-type income.

(1) In general. Subsection (a) shall not apply to any publicly traded partnership for any taxable year if such partnership met the gross income requirements of paragraph (2) for such taxable year and each preceding taxable year beginning after December 31, 1987, during which the partnership (or any predecessor) was in existence. For purposes of the preceding sentence, a partnership shall not be treated as being in existence during any period before the 1st taxable year in which such partnership (or a predecessor) was a publicly traded partnership.

(2) Gross income requirements. A partnership meets the gross income requirements of this paragraph for any taxable year if 90 percent or more of the gross income of such partnership for such taxable year consists of qualifying income.

(3) Exception not to apply to certain partnerships which could qualify as regulated investment companies. This subsection shall not apply to any partnership which would be described in section 851(a) if such partnership were a domestic corporation. To the extent provided in regulations, the preceding sentence shall not apply to any partnership a principal activity of which is the buying and selling of commodities (not described in section 1221(a)(1)), or options, futures, or forwards with respect to commodities.

(d) Qualifying income.

For purposes of this section—

(1) In general. Except as otherwise provided in this subsection, the term "qualifying income" means—

(A) interest,

(B) dividends,

(C) real property rents,

(D) gain from the sale or other disposition of real property (including property described in section 1221(a)(1)),

(E) income and gains derived from the exploration, development, mining or production, processing, refining, transportation (including pipelines transporting gas, oil, or products thereof), or the marketing of any mineral or natural resource (including fertilizer, geothermal energy, and timber), industrial source carbon dioxide, or the transportation or storage of any fuel described in subsection (b), (c), (d), or (e) of section 6426, or any alcohol fuel defined in section 6426(b)(4)(A) or any biodiesel fuel as defined in section 40A(d)(1),

3,957

(F) any gain from the sale or disposition of a capital asset (or property described in section 1231(b)) held for the production of income described in any of the foregoing subparagraphs of this paragraph, and

(G) in the case of a partnership described in the second sentence of subsection (c)(3), income and gains from commodities (not described in section 1221(a)(1)) or futures, forwards, and options with respect to commodities.

For purposes of subparagraph (E), the term "mineral or natural resource" means any product of a character with respect to which a deduction for depletion is allowable under section 611; except that such term shall not include any product described in subparagraph (A) or (B) of section 613(b)(7).

(2) Certain interest not qualified. Interest shall not be treated as qualifying income if—

(A) such interest is derived in the conduct of a financial or insurance business, or

(B) such interest would be excluded from the term "interest" under section 856(f).

(3) Real property rent. The term "real property rent" means amounts which would qualify as rent from real property under section 856(d) if—

(A) such section were applied without regard to paragraph (2)(C) thereof (relating to independent contractor requirements), and

(B) stock owned, directly or indirectly, by or for a partner would not be considered as owned under section 318(a)(3)(A) by the partnership unless 5 percent or more (by value) of the interests in such partnership are owned, directly or indirectly, by or for such partner.

(4) Certain income qualifying under regulated investment company or real estate trust provisions. The term "qualifying income" also includes any income which would qualify under section 851(b)(2)(A) or 856(c)(2).

(5) Special rule for determining gross income from certain real property sales. In the case of the sale or other disposition of real property described in section 1221(a)(1), gross income shall not be reduced by inventory costs.

(e) Inadvertent terminations.

If—

(1) a partnership fails to meet the gross income requirements of subsection (c)(2),

(2) the Secretary determines that such failure was inadvertent,

(3) no later than a reasonable time after the discovery of such failure, steps are taken so that such partnership once more meets such gross income requirements, and

(4) such partnership agrees to make such adjustments (including adjustments with respect to the partners) or to pay such amounts as may be required by the Secretary with respect to such period,

then, notwithstanding such failure, such entity shall be treated as continuing to meet such gross income requirements for such period.

(f) Effect of becoming corporation.

As of the 1st day that a partnership is treated as a corporation under this section, for purposes of this title, such partnership shall be treated as—

(1) transferring all of its assets (subject to its liabilities) to a newly formed corporation in exchange for the stock of the corporation, and

(2) distributing such stock to its partners in liquidation of their interests in the partnership.

(g) Exception for electing 1987 partnerships.

(1) In general. Subsection (a) shall not apply to an electing 1987 partnership.

(2) Electing 1987 partnership. For purposes of this subsection, the term "electing 1987 partnership" means any publicly traded partnership if—

(A) such partnership is an existing partnership (as defined in section 10211(c)(2) of the Revenue Reconciliation Act of 1987),

(B) subsection (a) has not applied (and without regard to subsection (c)(1) would not have applied) to such partnership for all prior taxable years beginning after December 31, 1987, and before January 1, 1998, and

(C) such partnership elects the application of this subsection, and consents to the application of the tax imposed by paragraph (3), for its first taxable year beginning after December 31, 1997.

A partnership which, but for this sentence, would be treated as an electing 1987 partnership shall cease to be so treated (and the election under subparagraph (C) shall cease to be in effect) as of the 1st day after December 31, 1997, on which there has been an addition of a substantial new line of business with respect to such partnership.

(3) Additional tax on electing partnerships.

(A) Imposition of tax. There is hereby imposed for each taxable year on the income of each electing 1987 partnership a tax equal to 3.5 percent of such partnership's gross income for the taxable year from the active conduct of trades and businesses by the partnership.

(B) Adjustments in the case of tiered partnerships. For purposes of this paragraph, in the case of a partnership which is a partner in another partnership, the gross income referred to in subparagraph (A) shall include the partnership's distributive share of the gross income of such other partnership from the active conduct of trades and businesses of such other partnership. A similar rule shall apply in the case of lower-tiered partnerships.

(C) Treatment of tax. For purposes of this title, the tax imposed by this paragraph shall be treated as imposed by chapter 1 other than for purposes of determining the amount of any credit allowable under chapter 1 and shall be paid by the partnership. Section 6655 shall be applied to such partnership with respect to such tax in the same manner as if the partnership were a corporation, such tax were imposed by section 11, and references in such section to taxable income were references to the gross income referred to in subparagraph (A).

(4) Election. An election and consent under this subsection shall apply to the taxable year for which made and all subsequent taxable years unless revoked by the partnership. Such revocation may be made without the consent of the Secretary, but, once so revoked, may not be reinstated.

In 2008, P.L. 110-343, Sec. 116(a)DivB, added "or industrial source carbon dioxide" after "timber)" in subpara. (d)(1)(E), effective 10/3/2008 in tax. yrs. end. after 10/3/2008.

—P.L. 110-343, Sec. 208(a)DivB, substituted ", industrial source carbon dioxide, or the transportation or storage of any fuel described in subsection (b), (c), (d), or (e) of section 6426, or any alcohol fuel defined in section 6426(b)(4)(A) or any biodiesel fuel as defined in section 40A(d)(1)" for "or industrial source carbon dioxide" in subpara (d)(1)(E), effective 10/3/2008 in tax. yrs. end. after 10/3/2008.

In 2004, P.L. 108-357, Sec. 331(e), substituted "section 851(b)(2)(A)" for "section 851(b)(2)" in para. (d)(4), effective for tax. yrs. begin. after 10/22/2004.

In 1999, P.L. 106-170, Sec. 532(c)(2)(V), substituted "section 1221(a)(1)" for "section 1221(1)" in para. (c)(3) . . . Sec. 532(c)(2)(W), substituted "section 1221(a)(1)" for "section 1221(1)" in subpara. (d)(1)(D) . . . Sec. 532(c)(2)(X), substituted "section 1221(a)(1)" for "section 1221(1)" in subpara. (d)(1)(G) . . . Sec. 532(c)(2)(Y), substituted "section 1221(a)(1)" for "section 1221(1)" in para. (d)(5), effective for any instrument held, acquired, or entered into, any transaction entered into, and supplies held or acquired on or after 12/17/99.

Miscellaneous provisions Code Sec. 7801

In 1998, P.L. 105-206, Sec. 6009(b)(1), substituted "and shall be paid by the partnership. Section 6655 shall be applied to such partnership with respect to such tax in the same manner as if the partnership were a corporation, such tax were imposed by section 11, and references in such section to taxable income were references to the gross income referred to in subparagraph (A)." for the period at the end of subpara. (g)(3)(C), effective for tax. yrs. begin. after 7/22/98.

In 1997, P.L. 105-34, Sec. 964(a), added subsec. (g), effective for tax. yrs. begin. after 12/31/97.

In 1988, P.L. 100-647, Sec. 2004(f)(1), substituted "or to pay such amounts as may be required" for "as may be required" in para. (e)(4), effective as provided in Sec. 10211(c) of P.L. 100-203, reproduced below.

— P.L. 100-647, Sec. 2004(f)(2), added Sec. 10211(c)(2)(C) of P.L. 100-203 [reproduced below], part of the effective date for changes made by Sec. 10211(a) of P.L. 100-203, see below.

— P.L. 100-647, Sec. 2004(f)(3), added a sentence to the end of para. (c)(1) . . . Sec. 2004(f)(4), added a sentence to the end of para. (d)(1) . . . Sec. 2004(f)(5), amended para. (d)(3), effective as provided in Sec. 10211(c) of P.L. 100-203, reproduced below

Prior to amendment, para. (d)(3) read as follows:

"(3) Real property rent. The term 'real property rent' means amounts which would qualify as rent from real property under section 856(d) if such section were applied without regard to paragraph (2)(C) thereof (relating to independent contractor requirements)."

In 1987, P.L. 100-203, Sec. 10211(a), added Code Sec. 7704, effective as provided in Sec. 10211(c) [as amended by Sec. 2004(f)(2) of P.L. 100-647] of this Act which reads:

"(1) In general.— The amendments made by this section shall apply—

"(A) except as provided in subparagraph (B), to taxable years beginning after December 31, 1987, or

"(B) in the case of an existing partnership, to taxable years beginning after December 31, 1997.

"(2) Existing partnership.— For purposes of this subsection —

"(A) In general.— The term 'existing partnership' means any partnership if—

"(i) such partnership was a publicly traded partnership on December 17, 1987,

"(ii) a registration statement indicating that such partnership was to be a publicly traded partnership was filed with the Securities and Exchange Commission with respect to such partnership on or before such date, or

"(iii) with respect to such partnership, an application was filed with a State regulatory commission on or before such date seeking permission to restructure a portion of a corporation as a publicly traded partnership.

"(B) Special rule where substantial new line of business added after December 17, 1987.— A partnership which, but for this subparagraph, would be treated as an existing partnership shall cease to be treated as an existing partnership as of the 1st day after December 17, 1987, on which there has been an addition of a substantial new line of business with respect to such partnership."

"(C) Coordination with passive-type income requirements.— In the case of an existing partnership, paragraph (1) of section 7704(c) of the Internal Revenue Code of 1986 (as added by this section) shall be applied by substituting for 'December 31, 1987' the earlier of —

"(i) December 31, 1997, or

"(ii) the day (if any) as of which such partnership ceases to be treated as an existing partnership by reason of subparagraph (B)."

CHAPTER 80.—GENERAL RULES

Subchapter

A. Application of internal revenue laws.

B. Effective date and related provisions.

C. Provisions affecting more than one subtitle.

In 1983, added Subchapter C.

Subchapter A.—Application of Internal Revenue Laws

Sec.

7801. Authority of Department of the Treasury.

7802. Internal Revenue Service Oversight Board.

7803. Commissioner of Internal Revenue; other officials.

7804. Other personnel.

7805. Rules and regulations.

7806. Construction of title.

7807. Rules in effect upon enactment of this title.

7808. Depositaries for collections.

7809. Deposit of collections.

7810. Revolving fund for redemption of real property.

7811. Taxpayer Assistance Orders.

In 1998, P.L. 105-206, Sec. 1101(c)(2), amended item 7802.

Prior to amendment, item 7802 read as follows:

"7802. Commissioner of Internal Revenue; Assistant Commissioners; Taxpayer Advocate."

— P.L. 105-206, Sec. 1102(e)(1), amended item 7803.

Prior to amendment, item 7803 read as follows:

"7803. Other personnel."

— P.L. 105-206, Sec. 1104(b)(2), amended item 7804.

Prior to amendment, item 7804 read as follows:

"7804. Effect of reorganization plans."

In 1996, P.L. 104-168, Sec. 101(b)(3), amended item 7802.

Prior to amendment, item 7802 read as follows:

"Sec. 7802. Commissioner of Internal Revenue; Assistant Commissioner (Employee Plans and Exempt Organizations)."

In 1988, P.L. 100-647, Sec. 6230(b), added item 7811.

In 1974, P.L. 93-406, Sec. 1051(c), inserted "; Assistant Commissioner (Employee Plans and Exempt Organizations)" before the period in item 7802.

In 1966, P.L. 89-719, Sec. 112, added item 7810.

Sec. 7801. Authority of Department of the Treasury.

(a) Powers and duties of Secretary.

(1) In general. Except as otherwise expressly provided by law, the administration and enforcement of this title shall be performed by or under the supervision of the Secretary of the Treasury.

(2) Administration and enforcement of certain provisions by Attorney General.

(A) In general. The administration and enforcement of the following provisions of this title shall be performed by or under the supervision of the Attorney General; and the term "Secretary" or "Secretary of the Treasury" shall, when applied to those provisions, mean the Attorney General; and the term "internal revenue officer" shall, when applied to those provisions, mean any officer of the Bureau of Alcohol, Tobacco, Firearms, and Explosives so designated by the Attorney General:

(i) Chapter 53.

(ii) Chapters 61 through 80, to the extent such chapters relate to the enforcement and administration of the provisions referred to in clause (i).

(B) Use of existing rulings and interpretations. Nothing in this Act alters or repeals the rulings and interpretations of the Bureau of Alcohol, Tobacco, and Firearms in effect on the effective date of the Homeland Security Act of 2002, which concern the provisions of this title referred to in subparagraph (A). The Attorney General shall consult with the Secretary to achieve uniformity and consistency in administering provisions under chapter 53 of title 26, United States Code.

(b) Repealed.

(c) Functions of Department of Justice unaffected.

Nothing in this section or section 301(f) of title 31 shall be considered to affect the duties, powers, or functions imposed upon, or vested in, the Department of Justice, or any officer thereof, by law existing on May 10, 1934.

In 2002, P.L. 107-296, Sec. 1112(k)(1), substituted "Secretary. (1) In general. Except" for "Secretary. Except" in subsec. (a) . . . Sec. 1112(k)(2), added para. (a)(2), effective 60 days after 11/25/2002.

In 1988, P.L. 100-647, Sec. 6227, of this Act provides:

"SEC. 6227. DISCLOSURE OF RIGHTS OF TAXPAYERS.

"(a) In General.

"The Secretary of the Treasury shall, as soon as practicable, but not later than 180 days after the date of the enactment of this Act, prepare a statement which sets forth in simple and nontechnical terms—

"(1) the rights of a taxpayer and the obligations of the Internal Revenue Service (hereinafter in this section referred to as the 'Service') during an audit;

"(2) the procedures by which a taxpayer may appeal any adverse decision of the Service (including administrative and judicial appeals);

"(3) the procedures for prosecuting refund claims and filing of taxpayer complaints; and

"(4) the procedures which the Service may use in enforcing the internal revenue laws (including assessment, jeopardy assessment, levy and distraint, and enforcement of liens).

3,959

Code Sec. 7801   **Miscellaneous provisions**

"(b) Transmission to Committees of Congress.

"The Secretary of the Treasury shall transmit drafts of the statement required under subsection (a) (or proposed revisions of any such statement) to the Committee on Ways and Means of the House of Representatives, the Committee on Finance of the Senate, and the Joint Committee on Taxation on the same day.

"(c) Distribution.

"The statement prepared in accordance with subsections (a) and (b) shall be distributed by the Secretary of the Treasury to all taxpayers the Secretary contacts with respect to the determination or collection of any tax (other than by providing tax forms). The Secretary shall take such actions as the Secretary deems necessary to ensure that such distribution does not result in multiple statements being sent to any one taxpayer."

In 1982, P.L. 97-258, Sec. 2(f)(1), added "or section 301(f) of title 31" after "in this section" in subsec. (c), effective 9/13/82.

—P.L. 97-258, Sec. 5(b), repealed subsec. (b), enacted 9/13/1982

Prior to repeal, subsec. (b) read as follows:

"(b) Office of General Counsel for the Department.

"(1) General Counsel. There shall be in the Department of the Treasury the office of General Counsel for the Department of the Treasury. The General Counsel shall be appointed by the President, by and with the advice and consent of the Senate. The General Counsel shall be the chief law officer of the Department and shall perform such duties as may be prescribed by the Secretary of the Treasury.

"(2) Assistant General Counsels. The President is authorized to appoint, by and with the advice and consent of the Senate, an Assistant General Counsel who shall be the Chief Counsel for the Internal Revenue Service. The Chief Counsel shall be the chief law officer for the Internal Revenue Service and shall perform such duties as may be prescribed by the Secretary of the Treasury. The Secretary of the Treasury may appoint, without regard to the provisions of the civil service laws, and fix the duties of not to exceed five other assistant General Counsels.

"(3) Attorneys. The Secretary of the Treasury may appoint and fix the duties of such other attorneys as he may deem necessary."

In 1976, P.L. 94-455, Sec. 1906(b)(13)(B), substituted "Secretary of the Treasury" for "Secretary" each place it appeared in subsec. (b), effective 2/1/77.

In 1964, P.L. 88-426, Sec. 305(39), deleted "and shall receive basic compensation at the annual rate of $19,000" from the first sentence of para. (b)(2), effective 7/1/64.

In 1959, P.L. 86-368, Sec. 1, amended subsec. (b), effective 9/22/59.

Prior to amendment, subsec. (b) read as follows:

"(b) General Counsel for the Department.

"There shall be in the Department of the Treasury the office of General Counsel for the Department of the Treasury. The General Counsel shall be appointed by the President, by and with the advice and consent of the Senate. The General Counsel shall be the chief law officer of the Department and shall perform such duties as may be prescribed by the Secretary. The Secretary must appoint and fix the duties of an Assistant General Counsel who shall serve as Chief Counsel of the Internal Revenue Service and may appoint and fix the duties of not to exceed five other Assistant General Counsels. All Assistant General Counsels shall be appointed without regard to the provisions of the civil service laws. The Secretary may also appoint and fix the duties of such other attorneys as he may deem necessary."

Sec. 7802. Internal Revenue Service Oversight Board.

(a) Establishment.

There is established within the Department of the Treasury the Internal Revenue Service Oversight Board (hereafter in this subchapter referred to as the "Oversight Board").

(b) Membership.

(1) Composition. The Oversight Board shall be composed of nine members, as follows:

(A) six members shall be individuals who are not otherwise Federal officers or employees and who are appointed by the President, by and with the advice and consent of the Senate.

(B) one member shall be the Secretary of the Treasury or, if the Secretary so designates, the Deputy Secretary of the Treasury.

(C) one member shall be the Commissioner of Internal Revenue.

(D) one member shall be an individual who is a full-time Federal employee or a representative of employees and who is appointed by the President, by and with the advice and consent of the Senate.

(2) Qualifications and terms.

(A) Qualifications. Members of the Oversight Board described in paragraph (1)(A) shall be appointed without regard to political affiliation and solely on the basis of their professional experience and expertise in one or more of the following areas:

(i) Management of large service organizations.

(ii) Customer service.

(iii) Federal tax laws, including tax administration and compliance.

(iv) Information technology.

(v) Organization development.

(vi) The needs and concerns of taxpayers.

(vii) The needs and concerns of small businesses.

In the aggregate, the members of the Oversight Board described in paragraph (1)(A) should collectively bring to bear expertise in all of the areas described in the preceding sentence.

(B) Terms. Each member who is described in subparagraph (A) or (D) of paragraph (1) shall be appointed for a term of 5 years, except that of the members first appointed under paragraph (1)(A)—

(i) two members shall be appointed for a term of 3 years,

(ii) two members shall be appointed for a term of 4 years, and

(iii) two members shall be appointed for a term of 5 years.

(C) Reappointment. An individual who is described in subparagraph (A) or (D) of paragraph (1) may be appointed to no more than two 5-year terms on the Oversight Board.

(D) Vacancy. Any vacancy on the Oversight Board shall be filled in the same manner as the original appointment. Any member appointed to fill a vacancy occurring before the expiration of the term for which the member's predecessor was appointed shall be appointed for the remainder of that term.

(3) Ethical considerations.

(A) Financial disclosure. During the entire period that an individual appointed under subparagraph (A) or (D) of paragraph (1) is a member of the Oversight Board, such individual shall be treated as serving as an officer or employee referred to in section 101(f) of the Ethics in Government Act of 1978 for purposes of title I of such Act, except that section 101(d) of such Act shall apply without regard to the number of days of service in the position.

(B) Restrictions on post-employment. For purposes of section 207(c) of title 18, United States Code, an individual appointed under subparagraph (A) or (D) of paragraph (1) shall be treated as an employee referred to in section 207(c)(2)(A)(i) of such title during the entire period the individual is a member of the Board, except that subsections (c)(2)(B) and (f) of section 207 of such title shall not apply.

(C) Members who are special government employees. If an individual appointed under subparagraph (A) or (D) or paragraph (1) is a special Government employee, the following additional rules apply for purposes of chapter 11 of title 18, United States Code:

(i) Restriction on representation. In addition to any restriction under section 205(c) of title 18, United States Code, except as provided in subsections (d) through (i) of section 205 of such title, such individual (except in the proper discharge of official duties) shall not, with or without compensation, represent anyone to or before any officer or employee of—

(I) the Oversight Board or the Internal Revenue Service on any matter;

(II) the Department of the Treasury on any matter involving the internal revenue laws or involving

3,960

the management or operations of the Internal Revenue Service; or

(III) the Department of Justice with respect to litigation involving a matter described in subclause (I) or (II).

(ii) Compensation for services provided by another. For purposes of section 203 of such title—

(I) such individual shall not be subject to the restrictions of subsection (a)(1) thereof for sharing in compensation earned by another for representations on matters covered by such section, and

(II) a person shall not be subject to the restrictions of subsection (a)(2) thereof for sharing such compensation with such individual.

(D) Waiver. The President may, only at the time the President nominates the member of the Oversight Board described in paragraph (1)(D), waive for the term of the member any appropriate provision of chapter 11 of title 18, United States Code, to the extent such waiver is necessary to allow such member to participate in the decisions of the Board while continuing to serve as a full-time Federal employee or a representative of employees. Any such waiver shall not be effective unless a written intent of waiver to exempt such member (and actual waiver language) is submitted to the Senate with the nomination of such member.

(4) Quorum. Five members of the Oversight Board shall constitute a quorum. A majority of members present and voting shall be required for the Oversight Board to take action.

(5) Removal.

(A) In general. Any member of the Oversight Board appointed under subparagraph (A) or (D) of paragraph (1) may be removed at the will of the President.

(B) Secretary and commissioner. An individual described in subparagraph (B) or (C) of paragraph (1) shall be removed upon termination of service in the office described in such subparagraph.

(6) Claims.

(A) In general. Members of the Oversight Board who are described in subparagraph (A) or (D) of paragraph (1) shall have no personal liability under Federal law with respect to any claim arising out of or resulting from an act or omission by such member within the scope of service as a member.

(B) Effect on other law. This paragraph shall not be construed—

(i) to affect any other immunities and protections that may be available to such member under applicable law with respect to such transactions;

(ii) to affect any other right or remedy against the United States under applicable law; or

(iii) to limit or alter in any way the immunities that are available under applicable law for Federal officers and employees.

(c) General responsibilities.

(1) Oversight.

(A) In general. The Oversight Board shall oversee the Internal Revenue Service in its administration, management, conduct, direction, and supervision of the execution and application of the internal revenue laws or related statutes and tax conventions to which the United States is a party.

(B) Mission of IRS. As part of its oversight functions described in subparagraph (A), the Oversight Board shall ensure that the organization and operation of the Internal Revenue Service allows it to carry out its mission.

(C) Confidentiality. The Oversight Board shall ensure that appropriate confidentiality is maintained in the exercise of its duties.

(2) Exceptions. The Oversight Board shall have no responsibilities or authority with respect to—

(A) the development and formulation of Federal tax policy relating to existing or proposed internal revenue laws, related statutes, and tax conventions,

(B) specific law enforcement activities of the Internal Revenue Service, including specific compliance activities such as examinations, collection activities, and criminal investigations,

(C) specific procurement activities of the Internal Revenue Service, or

(D) except as provided in subsection (d)(3), specific personnel actions.

(d) Specific responsibilities.

The Oversight Board shall have the following specific responsibilities:

(1) Strategic plans. To review and approve strategic plans of the Internal Revenue Service, including the establishment of—

(A) mission and objectives, and standards of performance relative to either, and

(B) annual and long-range strategic plans.

(2) Operational plans. To review the operational functions of the Internal Revenue Service, including—

(A) plans for modernization of the tax system,

(B) plans for outsourcing or managed competition, and

(C) plans for training and education.

(3) Management. To—

(A) recommend to the President candidates for appointment as the Commissioner of Internal Revenue and recommend to the President the removal of the Commissioner,

(B) review the Commissioner's selection, evaluation, and compensation of Internal Revenue Service senior executives who have program management responsibility over significant functions of the Internal Revenue Service, and

(C) review and approve the Commissioner's plans for any major reorganization of the Internal Revenue Service.

(4) Budget. To—

(A) review and approve the budget request of the Internal Revenue Service prepared by the Commissioner;

(B) submit such budget request to the Secretary of the Treasury; and

(C) ensure that the budget request supports the annual and long-range strategic plans.

(5) Taxpayer protection. To ensure the proper treatment of taxpayers by the employees of the Internal Revenue Service.

The Secretary shall submit the budget request referred to in paragraph (4)(B) for any fiscal year to the President who shall submit such request, without revision, to Congress together with the President's annual budget request for the Internal Revenue Service for such fiscal year.

(e) Board personnel matters.

(1) Compensation of members.

(A) In general. Each member of the Oversight Board who—

(i) is described in subsection (b)(1)(A); or

(ii) is described in subsection (b)(1)(D) and is not otherwise a Federal officer or employee, shall be compensated at a rate of $30,000 per year. All other members shall serve without compensation for such service.

(B) Chairperson. In lieu of the amount specified in subparagraph (A), the Chairperson of the Oversight Board shall be compensated at a rate of $50,000 per year.

(2) Travel expenses.

(A) In general. The members of the Oversight Board shall be allowed travel expenses, including per diem in lieu of subsistence, at rates authorized for employees of agencies under subchapter I of chapter 57 of title 5, United States Code, to attend meetings of the Oversight Board and, with the advance approval of the Chairperson of the Oversight Board, while otherwise away from their homes or regular places of business for purposes of duties as a member of the Oversight Board.

(B) Report. The Oversight Board shall include in its annual report under subsection (f)(3)(A) information with respect to the travel expenses allowed for members of the Oversight Board under this paragraph.

(3) Staff.

(A) In general. The Chairperson of the Oversight Board may appoint and terminate any personnel that may be necessary to enable the Board to perform its duties.

(B) Detail of government employees. Upon request of the Chairperson of the Oversight Board, a Federal agency shall detail a Federal Government employee to the Oversight Board without reimbursement. Such detail shall be without interruption or loss of civil service status or privilege.

(4) Procurement of temporary and intermittent services. The Chairperson of the Oversight Board may procure temporary and intermittent services under section 3109(b) of title 5, United States Code.

(f) Administrative matters.

(1) Chair.

(A) Term. The members of the Oversight Board shall elect for a 2-year term a chairperson from among the members appointed under subsection (b)(1)(A).

(B) Powers. Except as otherwise provided by a majority vote of the Oversight Board, the powers of the Chairperson shall include—

(i) establishing committees;

(ii) setting meeting places and times;

(iii) establishing meeting agendas; and

(iv) developing rules for the conduct of business.

(2) Meetings. The Oversight Board shall meet at least quarterly and at such other times as the Chairperson determines appropriate.

(3) Reports.

(A) Annual. The Oversight Board shall each year report with respect to the conduct of its responsibilities under this title to the President, the Committees on Ways and Means, Government Reform and Oversight, and Appropriations of the House of Representatives and the Committees on Finance, Governmental Affairs, and Appropriations of the Senate.

(B) Additional report. Upon a determination by the Oversight Board under subsection (c)(1)(B) that the organization and operation of the Internal Revenue Service are not allowing it to carry out its mission, the Oversight Board shall report such determination to the Committee on Ways and Means of the House of Representatives, and the Committee on Finance of the Senate.

In 2000, P.L. 106-554, Sec. 1(a)(7), [which enacted into law Sec. 301 of P.L. 106-554] of this Act, reads as follows:

"Section 3003(a)(1) of the Federal Reports Elimination and Sunset Act of 1995 (31 U.S.C. 1113 note) shall not apply to any report required to be submitted under any of the following provisions of law:"

* * * * * *

"15(C) Section 7802(f)(3)"

—P.L. 106-554, Sec. 1(a)(7), [which enacted into law Sec. 319(27) of P.L. 106-554] substituted ", and" for "; and" after "4 years" in clause (b)(2)(B)(ii), effective 12/21/2000.

In 1998, P.L. 105-206, Sec. 1101(a), amended Code Sec. 7802, effective 7/22/98. Sec. 1101(d)(2)-(3) of this Act provides:

"(2) Initial nominations to Internal Revenue Service Oversight Board. The President shall submit the initial nominations under section 7802 of the Internal Revenue Code of 1986, as added by this section, to the Senate not later than 6 months after the date of the enactment of this Act.

"(3) Effect on actions prior to appointment of Oversight Board. Nothing in this section shall be construed to invalidate the actions and authority of the Internal Revenue Service prior to the appointment of the members of the Internal Revenue Service Oversight Board."

Prior to amendment, Code Sec. 7802 read as follows:

"SEC. 7802. COMMISSIONER OF INTERNAL REVENUE; ASSISTANT COMMISSIONERS; TAXPAYER ADVOCATE.

"(a) Commissioner of Internal Revenue. There shall be in the Department of the Treasury a Commissioner of Internal Revenue, who shall be appointed by the President, by and with the advice and consent of the Senate. The Commissioner of Internal Revenue shall have such duties and powers as may be prescribed by the Secretary of the Treasury.

"(b) Assistant Commissioner for Employee Plans and Exempt Organizations.

"(1) Establishment of Office. There is established within the Internal Revenue Service an office to be known as the 'Office of Employee Plans and Exempt Organizations' to be under the supervision and direction of an Assistant Commissioner of Internal Revenue. As head of the Office, the Assistant Commissioner shall be responsible for carrying out such functions as the Secretary may prescribe with respect to organizations exempt from tax under section 501(a) and with respect to plans to which part I of subchapter D of chapter 1 applies (and with respect to organizations designed to be exempt under such section and plans designed to be plans to which such part applies).

"(2) Authorization of appropriations. There is authorized to be appropriated to the Department of the Treasury to carry out the functions of the Office an amount equal to the sum of—

"(A) so much of the collections from taxes imposed under section 4940 (relating to excise tax based on investment income) as would have been collected if the rate of tax under such section was 2 percent during the second preceding fiscal year; and

"(B) the greater of—

"(i) an amount equal to the amount described in paragraph (A); or

"(ii) $30,000,000.

"(c) Assistant Commissioner (taxpayer services). There is established within the Internal Revenue Service an office to be known as the 'Office for Taxpayer Services' to be under the supervision and direction of an Assistant Commissioner of the Internal Revenue. The Assistant Commissioner shall be responsible for taxpayer services such as telephone, walk-in, and taxpayer educational services, and the design and production of tax and informational forms.

"(d) Office of Taxpayer Advocate.

"(1) In general. There is established in the Internal Revenue Service an office to be known as the 'Office of the Taxpayer Advocate'. Such office shall be under the supervision and direction of an official to be known as the 'Taxpayer Advocate' who shall be appointed by and report directly to the Commissioner of Internal Revenue. The Taxpayer Advocate shall be entitled to compensation at the same rate as the highest level official reporting directly to the Deputy Commissioner of the Internal Revenue Service.

"(2) Functions of office.

"(A) In general. It shall be the function of the Office of Taxpayer Advocate to—

"(i) assist taxpayers in resolving problems with the Internal Revenue Service,

"(ii) identify areas in which taxpayers have problems in dealings with the Internal Revenue Service,

"(iii) to the extent possible, propose changes in the administrative practices of the Internal Revenue Service to mitigate problems identified under clause (ii), and

"(iv) identify potential legislative changes which may be appropriate to mitigate such problems.

"(B) Annual reports.

"(i) Objectives. Not later than June 30 of each calendar year after 1995, the Taxpayer Advocate shall report to the Committee on Ways and Means of the House of Representatives and the Committee on Finance of the Senate on the objectives of the Taxpayer Advocate for the fiscal year beginning in such calendar year. Any such report shall contain full and substantive analysis, in addition to statistical information.

"(ii) Activities. Not later than December 31 of each calendar year after 1995, the Taxpayer Advocate shall report to the Committee on Ways and Means of the House of Representatives and the Committee on Finance of the Senate on the activities of the Taxpayer Advocate during the fiscal year ending during such calendar year. Any such report shall contain full and substantive analysis, in addition to statistical information, and shall—

"(I) identify the initiatives the Taxpayer Advocate has taken on improving taxpayer services and Internal Revenue Service responsiveness,

"(II) contain recommendations received from individuals with the authority to issue Taxpayer Assistance Orders under section 7811,

"(III) contain a summary of at least 20 of the most serious problems encountered by taxpayers, including a description of the nature of such problems,

"(IV) contain an inventory of the items described in subclauses (I), (II), and (III) for which action has been taken and the result of such action,

"(V) contain an inventory of the items described in subclauses (I), (II), and (III) for which action remains to be completed and the period during which each item has remained on such inventory,

"(VI) contain an inventory of the items described in subclauses (II) and (III) for which no action has been taken, the period during which each item has remained on such inventory, the reasons for the inaction, and identify any Internal Revenue Service official who is responsible for such inaction,

"(VII) identify any Taxpayer Assistance Order which was not honored by the Internal Revenue Service in a timely manner, as specified under section 7811(b),

"(VIII) contain recommendations for such administrative and legislative action as may be appropriate to resolve problems encountered by taxpayers,

"(IX) describe the extent to which regional problem resolution officers participate in the selection and evaluation of local problem resolution officers, and

"(X) include such other information as the Taxpayer Advocate may deem advisable.

"(iii) Report to be submitted directly. Each report required under this subparagraph shall be provided directly to the Committees referred to in clauses (i) and (ii) without any prior review or comment from the Commissioner, the Secretary of the Treasury, any other officer or employee of the Department of the Treasury, or the Office of Management and Budget.

"(3) Responsibilities of Commissioner. The Commissioner of Internal Revenue shall establish procedures requiring a formal response to all recommendations submitted to the Commissioner by the Taxpayer Advocate within 3 months after submission to the Commissioner."

In 1996, P.L. 104-168, Sec. 101(a), added subsec. (d) . . . Sec. 101(b)(2), amended the heading of Code Sec. 7802, effective 7/30/96.

Prior to amendment, the heading of Code Sec. 7802 read as follows:

"Sec. 7802. Commissioner of Internal Revenue; Assistant Commissioner (Employee Plans and Exempt Organizations)."

In 1988, P.L. 100-647, Sec. 6235(a), added subsec. (c), effective on the date 180 days after 11/10/88.

In 1982, P.L. 97-258, Sec. 2(f)(2)(A), added "(1) Establishment of Office." before "There" in subsec. (b) . . . Sec. 2(f)(2)(B), added para. (b)(2), effective 9/13/82.

In 1976, P.L. 94-455, Sec. 1906(b)(13)(A), substituted "Secretary" for "Secretary or his delegate" in subsec. (b), effective 2/1/77.

—P.L. 94-455, Sec. 1906(b)(13)(B), substituted "Secretary of the Treasury" for "Secretary" in subsec. (a), effective 2/1/77.

In 1974, P.L. 93-406, Sec. 1051(a), amended Code Sec. 7802, effective the 90th day following 9/2/74.

Prior to amendment, Code Sec. 7802 read as follows:

"Sec. 7802. Commissioner of Internal Revenue.

"There shall be in the Department of the Treasury a Commissioner of Internal Revenue, who shall be appointed by the President, by and with the advice and consent of the Senate. The Commissioner of Internal Revenue shall leave such duties and powers as may be prescribed by the Secretary."

Sec. 7803. Commissioner of Internal Revenue; other officials.

(a) Commissioner of Internal Revenue.

(1) Appointment.

(A) In general. There shall be in the Department of the Treasury a Commissioner of Internal Revenue who shall be appointed by the President, by and with the advice and consent of the Senate. Such appointment shall be made from individuals who, among other qualifications, have a demonstrated ability in management.

(B) Term. The term of the Commissioner of Internal Revenue shall be a 5-year term, beginning with a term to commence on November 13, 1997. Each subsequent term shall begin on the day after the date on which the previous term expires.

(C) Vacancy. Any individual appointed as Commissioner of Internal Revenue during a term as defined in subparagraph (B) shall be appointed for the remainder of that term.

(D) Removal. The Commissioner may be removed at the will of the President.

(E) Reappointment. The Commissioner may be appointed to more than one term.

(2) Duties. The Commissioner shall have such duties and powers as the Secretary may prescribe, including the power to—

(A) administer, manage, conduct, direct, and supervise the execution and application of the internal revenue laws or related statutes and tax conventions to which the United States is a party; and

(B) recommend to the President a candidate for appointment as Chief Counsel for the Internal Revenue Service when a vacancy occurs, and recommend to the President the removal of such Chief Counsel.

If the Secretary determines not to delegate a power specified in subparagraph (A) or (B), such determination may not take effect until 30 days after the Secretary notifies the Committees on Ways and Means, Government Reform and Oversight, and Appropriations of the House of Representatives and the Committees on Finance, Governmental Affairs, and Appropriations of the Senate.

(3) Consultation with Board. The Commissioner shall consult with the Oversight Board on all matters set forth in paragraphs (2) and (3) (other than paragraph (3)(A)) of section 7802(d).

(b) Chief Counsel for the Internal Revenue Service.

(1) Appointment. There shall be in the Department of the Treasury a Chief Counsel for the Internal Revenue Service who shall be appointed by the President, by and with the consent of the Senate.

(2) Duties. The Chief Counsel shall be the chief law officer for the Internal Revenue Service and shall perform such duties as may be prescribed by the Secretary, including the duty—

(A) to be legal advisor to the Commissioner and the Commissioner's officers and employees;

(B) to furnish legal opinions for the preparation and review of rulings and memoranda of technical advice;

(C) to prepare, review, and assist in the preparation of proposed legislation, treaties, regulations, and Executive orders relating to laws which affect the Internal Revenue Service;

(D) to represent the Commissioner in cases before the Tax Court; and

(E) to determine which civil actions should be litigated under the laws relating to the Internal Revenue Service and prepare recommendations for the Department of Justice regarding the commencement of such actions.

If the Secretary determines not to delegate a power specified in subparagraph (A), (B), (C), (D), or (E), such determination may not take effect until 30 days after the Secretary notifies the Committees on Ways and Means, Government Reform and Oversight, and Appropriations of the House of Representatives and the Committees on Finance, Governmental Affairs, and Appropriations of the Senate.

(3) Persons to whom chief counsel reports. The Chief Counsel shall report directly to the Commissioner of Internal Revenue, except that—

(A) the Chief Counsel shall report to both the Commissioner and the General Counsel for the Department of the Treasury with respect to—

(i) legal advice or interpretation of the tax law not relating solely to tax policy;

(ii) tax litigation; and

(B) the Chief Counsel shall report to the General Counsel with respect to legal advice or interpretation of the tax law relating solely to tax policy.

If there is any disagreement between the Commissioner and the General Counsel with respect to any matter jointly referred to them under subparagraph (A), such matter shall be submitted to the Secretary or Deputy Secretary for resolution.

(4) Chief Counsel personnel. All personnel in the Office of Chief Counsel shall report to the Chief Counsel.

(c) Office of the Taxpayer Advocate.

(1) Establishment.

(A) In general. There is established in the Internal Revenue Service an office to be known as the "Office of the Taxpayer Advocate".

(B) National taxpayer advocate.

(i) In general. The Office of the Taxpayer Advocate shall be under the supervision and direction of an official to be known as the "National Taxpayer Advocate". The National Taxpayer Advocate shall report directly to the Commissioner of Internal Revenue and shall be entitled to compensation at the same rate as the highest rate of basic pay established for the Senior Executive Service under section 5382 of title 5, United States Code, or, if the Secretary of the Treasury so determines, at a rate fixed under section 9503 of such title.

(ii) Appointment. The National Taxpayer Advocate shall be appointed by the Secretary of the Treasury after consultation with the Commissioner of Internal Revenue and the Oversight Board and without regard to the provisions of title 5, United States Code, relating to appointments in the competitive service or the Senior Executive Service.

(iii) Qualifications. An individual appointed under clause (ii) shall have—

(I) a background in customer service as well as tax law; and

(II) experience in representing individual taxpayers.

(iv) Restriction on employment. An individual may be appointed as the National Taxpayer Advocate only if such individual was not an officer or employee of the Internal Revenue Service during the 2-year period ending with such appointment and such individual agrees not to accept any employment with the Internal Revenue Service for at least 5 years after ceasing to be the National Taxpayer Advocate. Service as an officer or employee of the Office of the Taxpayer Advocate shall not be taken into account in applying this clause.

(2) Functions of Office.

(A) In general. It shall be the function of the Office of Taxpayer Advocate to—

(i) assist taxpayers in resolving problems with the Internal Revenue Service;

(ii) identify areas in which taxpayers have problems in dealings with the Internal Revenue Service;

(iii) to the extent possible, propose changes in the administrative practices of the Internal Revenue Service to mitigate problems identified under clause (ii); and

(iv) identify potential legislative changes which may be appropriate to mitigate such problems.

(B) Annual reports.

(i) Objectives. Not later than June 30 of each calendar year, the National Taxpayer Advocate shall report to the Committee on Ways and Means of the House of Representatives and the Committee on Finance of the Senate on the objectives of the Office of the Taxpayer Advocate for the fiscal year beginning in such calendar year. Any such report shall contain full and substantive analysis, in addition to statistical information.

(ii) Activities. Not later than December 31 of each calendar year, the National Taxpayer Advocate shall report to the Committee on Ways and Means of the House of Representatives and the Committee on Finance of the Senate on the activities of the Office of the Taxpayer Advocate during the fiscal year ending during such calendar year. Any such report shall contain full and substantive analysis, in addition to statistical information, and shall—

(I) identify the initiatives the Office of the Taxpayer Advocate has taken on improving taxpayer services and Internal Revenue Service responsiveness;

(II) contain recommendations received from individuals with the authority to issue Taxpayer Assistance Orders under section 7811;

(III) contain a summary of at least 20 of the most serious problems encountered by taxpayers, including a description of the nature of such problems;

(IV) contain an inventory of the items described in subclauses (I), (II), and (III) for which action has been taken and the result of such action;

(V) contain an inventory of the items described in subclauses (I), (II), and (III) for which action remains to be completed and the period during which each item has remained on such inventory;

(VI) contain an inventory of the items described in subclauses (I), (II), and (III) for which no action has been taken, the period during which each item has remained on such inventory, the reasons for the inaction, and identify any Internal Revenue Service official who is responsible for such inaction;

(VII) identify any Taxpayer Assistance Order which was not honored by the Internal Revenue Service in a timely manner, as specified under section 7811(b);

(VIII) contain recommendations for such administrative and legislative action as may be appropriate to resolve problems encountered by taxpayers;

(IX) identify areas of the tax law that impose significant compliance burdens on taxpayers or the Internal Revenue Service, including specific recommendations for remedying these problems;

(X) identify the 10 most litigated issues for each category of taxpayers, including recommendations for mitigating such disputes; and

(XI) include such other information as the National Taxpayer Advocate may deem advisable.

(iii) Report to be submitted directly. Each report required under this subparagraph shall be provided directly to the committees described in clause (i) without any prior review or comment from the Commissioner, the Secretary of the Treasury, the Oversight Board, any other officer or employee of the Department of the Treasury, or the Office of Management and Budget.

(iv) Coordination with report of treasury inspector general for tax administration. To the extent that information required to be reported under clause (ii) is also required to be reported under paragraph (1) or (2) of subsection (d) by the Treasury Inspector General for Tax Administration, the National Taxpayer Advocate shall not contain such information in the report submitted under such clause.

(C) Other responsibilities. The National Taxpayer Advocate shall—
  (i) monitor the coverage and geographic allocation of local offices of taxpayer advocates;
  (ii) develop guidance to be distributed to all Internal Revenue Service officers and employees outlining the criteria for referral of taxpayer inquiries to local offices of taxpayer advocates;
  (iii) ensure that the local telephone number for each local office of the taxpayer advocate is published and available to taxpayers served by the office; and
  (iv) in conjunction with the Commissioner, develop career paths for local taxpayer advocates choosing to make a career in the Office of the Taxpayer Advocate.

(D) Personnel actions.
  (i) In general. The National Taxpayer Advocate shall have the responsibility and authority to—
    (I) appoint local taxpayer advocates and make available at least 1 such advocate for each State; and
    (II) evaluate and take personnel actions (including dismissal) with respect to any employee of any local office of a taxpayer advocate described in subclause (I).
  (ii) Consultation. The National Taxpayer Advocate may consult with the appropriate supervisory personnel of the Internal Revenue Service in carrying out the National Taxpayer Advocate's responsibilities under this subparagraph.

(3) **Responsibilities of Commissioner.** The Commissioner shall establish procedures requiring a formal response to all recommendations submitted to the Commissioner by the National Taxpayer Advocate within 3 months after submission to the Commissioner.

(4) **Operation of local offices.**
  (A) In general. Each local taxpayer advocate—
    (i) shall report to the National Taxpayer Advocate or delegate thereof;
    (ii) may consult with the appropriate supervisory personnel of the Internal Revenue Service regarding the daily operation of the local office of the taxpayer advocate;
    (iii) shall, at the initial meeting with any taxpayer seeking the assistance of a local office of the taxpayer advocate, notify such taxpayer that the taxpayer advocate offices operate independently of any other Internal Revenue Service office and report directly to Congress through the National Taxpayer Advocate; and
    (iv) may, at the taxpayer advocate's discretion, not disclose to the Internal Revenue Service contact with, or information provided by, such taxpayer.
  (B) Maintenance of independent communications. Each local office of the taxpayer advocate shall maintain a separate phone, facsimile, and other electronic communication access, and a separate post office address.

(d) **Additional duties of the Treasury Inspector General for Tax Administration.**
  (1) **Annual reporting.** The Treasury Inspector General for Tax Administration shall include in one of the semiannual reports under section 5 of the Inspector General Act of 1978—
    (A) an evaluation of the compliance of the Internal Revenue Service with—
      (i) restrictions under section 1204 of the Internal Revenue Service Restructuring and Reform Act of 1998 on the use of enforcement statistics to evaluate Internal Revenue Service employees;
      (ii) restrictions under section 7521 on directly contacting taxpayers who have indicated that they prefer their representatives be contacted;
      (iii) required procedures under section 6320 upon the filing of a notice of a lien;
      (iv) required procedures under subchapter D of chapter 64 for seizure of property for collection of taxes, including required procedures under section 6330 regarding levies; and
      (v) restrictions under section 3707 of the Internal Revenue Service Restructuring and Reform Act of 1998 on designation of taxpayers;
    (B) a review and a certification of whether or not the Secretary is complying with the requirements of section 6103(e)(8) to disclose information to an individual filing a joint return on collection activity involving the other individual filing the return;
    (C) information regarding extensions of the statute of limitations for assessment and collection of tax under section 6501 and the provision of notice to taxpayers regarding requests for such extension;
    (D) an evaluation of the adequacy and security of the technology of the Internal Revenue Service;
    (E) any termination or mitigation under section 1203 of the Internal Revenue Service Restructuring and Reform Act of 1998;
    (F) information regarding improper denial of requests for information from the Internal Revenue Service identified under paragraph (3)(A); and
    (G) information regarding any administrative or civil actions with respect to violations of the fair debt collection provisions of section 6304, including—
      (i) a summary of such actions initiated since the date of the last report; and
      (ii) a summary of any judgments or awards granted as a result of such actions.

  (2) **Semiannual reports.**
    (A) In general. The Treasury Inspector General for Tax Administration shall include in each semiannual report under section 5 of the Inspector General Act of 1978—
      (i) the number of taxpayer complaints during the reporting period;
      (ii) the number of employee misconduct and taxpayer abuse allegations received by the Internal Revenue Service or the Inspector General during the period from taxpayers, Internal Revenue Service employees, and other sources;
      (iii) a summary of the status of such complaints and allegations; and
      (iv) a summary of the disposition of such complaints and allegations, including the outcome of any Department of Justice action and any monies paid as a settlement of such complaints and allegations.
    (B) Clauses (iii) and (iv) of subparagraph (A) shall only apply to complaints and allegations of serious employee misconduct.

  (3) **Other responsibilities.** The Treasury Inspector General for Tax Administration shall—
    (A) conduct periodic audits of a statiscally valid sample of the total number of determinations made by the In-

ternal Revenue Service to deny written requests to disclose information to taxpayers on the basis of section 6103 of this title or section 552(b)(7) of title 5, United States Code;

(B) establish and maintain a toll-free telephone number for taxpayers to use to confidentially register complaints of misconduct by Internal Revenue Service employees and incorporate the telephone number in the statement required by section 6227 of the Omnibus Taxpayer Bill of Rights (Internal Revenue Service Publication No. 1); and

(C) not later than December 31, 2010, submit a written report to Congress on the implementation of section 6103(k)(10).

In 2008, P.L. 110-428, Sec. 2(c), deleted "and" at the end of clause (d)(3)(A), substituted "; and" for the period at the end of clause (d)(3)(B), and added subpara. (d)(3)(C), effective disclosures made after December 31, 2008.
—P.L. 110-428, Sec. 2(e), of this Act, provides:
"(e) Annual Reports. The Secretary of the Treasury shall annually submit to Congress and make publicly available a report on the filing of false and fraudulent returns by individuals incarcerated in Federal and State prisons. Such report shall include statistics on the number of false and fraudulent returns associated with each Federal and State prison."

In 2007, P.L. 110-176, Sec. 1(a), amended para. (a)(1), effective (as if included in PL 105-206, Sec. 1102(a)) 1/4/2008.
Prior to amendment, para. (a)(1) read as follows:
"(1) Appointment.
"(A) In general. There shall be in the Department of the Treasury a Commissioner of Internal Revenue who shall be appointed by the President, by and with the advice and consent of the Senate, to a 5-year term. Such appointment shall be made from individuals who, among other qualifications, have a demonstrated ability in management.
"(B) Vacancy. Any individual appointed to fill a vacancy in the position of Commissioner occurring before the expiration of the term for which such individual's predecessor was appointed shall be appointed only for the remainder of that term.
"(C) Removal. The Commissioner may be removed at the will of the President.
"(D) Reappointment. The Commissioner may be appointed to more than one 5-year term."

In 1998, P.L. 105-206, Sec. 1001, of this Act, reads as follows:
"SEC. 1001. REORGANIZATION OF THE INTERNAL REVENUE SERVICE.
"(a) In general. The Commissioner of Internal Revenue shall develop and implement a plan to reorganize the Internal Revenue Service. The plan shall—
"(1) supersede any organization or reorganization of the Internal Revenue Service based on any statute or reorganization plan applicable on the effective date of this section;
"(2) eliminate or substantially modify the existing organization of the Internal Revenue Service which is based on a national, regional, and district structure;
"(3) establish organizational units serving particular groups of taxpayers with similar needs; and
"(4) ensure an independent appeals function within the Internal Revenue Service, including the prohibition in the plan of ex parte communications between appeals officers and other Internal Revenue Service employees to the extent that such communications appear to compromise the independence of the appeals officers.
"(b) Savings provisions.
"(1) Preservation of specific tax rights and remedies. Nothing in the plan developed and implemented under subsection (a) shall be considered to impair any right or remedy, including trial by jury, to recover any internal revenue tax alleged to have been erroneously or illegally assessed or collected, or any penalty claimed to have been collected without authority, or any sum alleged to have been excessive or in any manner wrongfully collected under the internal revenue laws. For the purpose of any action to recover any such tax, penalty, or sum, all statutes, rules, and regulations referring to the collector of internal revenue, the principal officer for the internal revenue district, or the Secretary, shall be deemed to refer to the officer whose act or acts referred to in the preceding sentence gave rise to such action. The venue of any such action shall be the same as under existing law.
"(2) Continuing effect of legal documents. All orders, determinations, rules, regulations, permits, agreements, grants, contracts, certificates, licenses, registrations, privileges, and other administrative actions—
"(A) which have been issued, made, granted, or allowed to become effective by the President, any Federal agency or official thereof, or by a court of competent jurisdiction, in the performance of any function transferred or affected by the reorganization of the Internal Revenue Service or any other administrative unit of the Department of the Treasury under this section; and
"(B) which are in effect at the time this section takes effect, or were final before the effective date of this section and are to become effective on or after the effective date of this section,
shall continue in effect according to their terms until modified, terminated, superseded, set aside, or revoked in accordance with law by the President, the Secretary of the Treasury, the Commissioner of Internal Revenue, or other authorized official, a court of competent jurisdiction, or by operation of law.
"(3) Proceedings not affected. The provisions of this section shall not affect any proceedings, including notices of proposed rulemaking, or any application for any license, permit, certificate, or financial assistance pending before the Department of the Treasury (or any administrative unit of the Department, including the Internal Revenue Service) at the time this section takes effect, with respect to functions transferred or affected by the reorganization under this section but such proceedings and applications shall continue. Orders shall be issued in such proceedings, appeals shall be taken therefrom, and payments shall be made pursuant to such orders, as if this section had not been enacted, and orders issued in any such proceedings shall continue in effect until modified, terminated, superseded, or revoked by a duly authorized official, by a court of competent jurisdiction, or by operation of law. Nothing in this paragraph shall be deemed to prohibit the discontinuance or modification of any such proceeding under the same terms and conditions and to the same extent that such proceeding could have been discontinued or modified if this section had not been enacted.
"(4) Suits not affected. The provisions of this section shall not affect suits commenced before the effective date of this section, and in all such suits, proceedings shall be had, appeals taken, and judgments rendered in the same manner and with the same effect as if this section had not been enacted.
"(5) Nonabatement of actions. No suit, action, or other proceeding commenced by or against the Department of the Treasury (or any administrative unit of the Department, including the Internal Revenue Service), or by or against any individual in the official capacity of such individual as an officer of the Department of the Treasury, shall abate by reason of the enactment of this section.
"(6) Administrative actions relating to promulgation of regulations. Any administrative action relating to the preparation or promulgation of a regulation by the Department of the Treasury (or any administrative unit of the Department, including the Internal Revenue Service) relating to a function transferred or affected by the reorganization under this section may be continued by the Department of the Treasury through any appropriate administrative unit of the Department, including the Internal Revenue Service with the same effect as if this section had not been enacted.
"(c) Effective date. This section shall take effect on the date of the enactment of this Act."
—P.L. 105-206, Sec. 1102(a), amended Code Sec. 7803, effective 7/22/98. Sec. 1102(f)(2)-(4), of this Act, provides:
"(2) Chief Counsel. Section 7803(b)(3) of the Internal Revenue Code of 1986, as added by this section, shall take effect on the date that is 90 days after the date of the enactment of this Act.
"(3) National Taxpayer Advocate. Notwithstanding section 7803(c)(1)(B)(iv) of such Code, as added by this section, in appointing the first National Taxpayer Advocate after the date of the enactment of this Act, the Secretary of the Treasury—
"(A) shall not appoint any individual who was an officer or employee of the Internal Revenue Service at any time during the 2-year period ending on the date of appointment; and
"(B) need not consult with the Internal Revenue Service Oversight Board if the Oversight Board has not been appointed.
"(4) Current officers.
"(A) In the case of an individual serving as Commissioner of Internal Revenue on the date of the enactment of this Act who was appointed to such position before such date, the 5-year term required by section 7803(a)(1) of such Code, as added by this section, shall begin as of the date of such appointment.
"(B) Clauses (ii), (iii), and (iv) of section 7803(c)(1)(B) of such Code, as added by this section, shall not apply to the individual serving as Taxpayer Advocate on the date of the enactment of this Act."
Prior to amendment, Code Sec. 7803 read as follows:
"SEC. 7803. OTHER PERSONNEL.
"(a) Appointment and supervision. The Secretary is authorized to employ such number of persons as the Secretary deems proper for the administration and enforcement of the internal revenue laws, and the Secretary shall issue all necessary directions, instructions, orders, and rules applicable to such persons.
"(b) Posts of duty of employees in field service or traveling.
"(1) Designation of post of duty. The Secretary shall determine and designate the posts of duty of all such persons engaged in field work or traveling on official business outside of the District of Columbia.
"(2) Detail of personnel from field service. The Secretary may order any such person engaged in field work to duty in the District of Columbia, for such periods as the Secretary may prescribe, and to any designated post of duty outside the District of Columbia upon the completion of such duty.
"(c) Delinquent internal revenue officers and employees. If any officer or employee of the Treasury Department acting in connection with the internal revenue laws fails to account for and pay over any amount of money or property collected or received by him in connection with the internal revenue laws, the Secretary shall issue notice and demand to such officer or employee for payment of the amount which he failed to account for and pay over, and, upon failure to pay the amount demanded within the time specified in such notice, the amount so demanded shall be deemed imposed upon such officer or employee and assessed upon the date of such notice and demand, and the provisions of chapter 64 and all other provisions of law relating to the collection of assessed taxes shall be applicable in respect of such amount."
—P.L. 105-206, Sec. 3701, of this Act, reads as follows:
"SEC. 3701. CATALOGING COMPLAINTS. In collecting data for the report required under section 1211 of the Taxpayer Bill of Rights 2 (P.L. 104-168), the Secretary of the Treasury or the Secretary's delegate shall, not later than January 1, 2000, maintain records of taxpayer complaints of misconduct by Internal Revenue Service employees on an individual employee basis."

Miscellaneous provisions   Code Sec. 7805(b)(2)

—P.L. 105-206, Sec. 3705, of this Act, reads as follows:
"SEC. 3705. INTERNAL REVENUE SERVICE EMPLOYEE CONTACTS.
"(a) Notice. The Secretary of the Treasury or the Secretary's delegate shall provide that—
"(1) any manually generated correspondence received by a taxpayer from the Internal Revenue Service shall include in a prominent manner the name, telephone number, and unique identifying number of an Internal Revenue Service employee the taxpayer may contact with respect to the correspondence;
"(2) any other correspondence or notice received by a taxpayer from the Internal Revenue Service shall include in a prominent manner a telephone number that the taxpayer may contact; and
"(3) an Internal Revenue Service employee shall give a taxpayer during a telephone or personal contact the employee's name and unique identifying number.
"(b) Single contact. The Secretary of the Treasury or the Secretary's delegate shall develop a procedure under which, to the extent practicable and if advantageous to the taxpayer, one Internal Revenue Service employee shall be assigned to handle a taxpayer's matter until it is resolved.
"(c) Telephone helpline in Spanish. The Secretary of the Treasury or the Secretary's delegate shall provide, in appropriate circumstances, that taxpayer questions on telephone helplines of the Internal Revenue Service are answered in Spanish.
"(d) Other telephone helpline options. The Secretary of the Treasury or the Secretary's delegate shall provide, in appropriate circumstances, on telephone helplines of the Internal Revenue Service an option for any taxpayer to talk to an Internal Revenue Service employee during normal business hours. The person shall direct phone questions of the taxpayer to other Internal Revenue Service personnel who can provide assistance to the taxpayer.
"(e) Effective dates.
"(1) In general. Except as otherwise provided in this subsection, this section shall take effect 60 days after the date of the enactment of this Act.
"(2) Subsection (c). Subsection (c) shall take effect on January 1, 2000.
"(3) Subsection (d). Subsection (d) shall take effect on January 1, 2000.
"(4) Unique identifying number. Any requirement under this section to provide a unique identifying number shall take effect 6 months after the date of the enactment of this Act."
—P.L. 105-206, Sec. 3706, of this Act, reads as follows:
"SEC. 3706. USE OF PSEUDONYMS BY INTERNAL REVENUE SERVICE EMPLOYEES.
"(a) In general. Any employee of the Internal Revenue Service may use a pseudonym only if—
"(1) adequate justification for the use of a pseudonym is provided by the employee, including protection of personal safety; and
"(2) such use is approved by the employee's supervisor before the pseudonym is used.
"(b) Effective date. Subsection (a) shall apply to requests made after the date of the enactment of this Act."
—P.L. 105-206, Sec. 3709, of this Act, reads as follows:
"SEC. 3709. LISTING OF LOCAL INTERNAL REVENUE SERVICE TELEPHONE NUMBERS AND ADDRESSES. The Secretary of the Treasury or the Secretary's delegate shall, as soon as practicable, provide that the local telephone numbers and addresses of Internal Revenue Service offices located in any particular area be listed in a telephone book for that area."
In 1976, P.L. 94-455, Sec. 1906(a)(58), redesignated subsec. (d) as subsec. (c)... Sec. 1906(b)(13)(A), substituted "Secretary" for "Secretary or his delegate" each place it appeared in Code Sec. 7803, effective 2/1/77.
In 1972, P.L. 92-310, Sec. 230(e), deleted subsec. (c), effective 6/6/72.
Prior to deletion, subsec. (c) read as follows:
"(c) Bonds of employees. Whenever the Secretary or his delegate deems it proper, he may require any such officer or employee to furnish such bond, or he may purchase such blanket or schedule bonds, as the Secretary or his delegate deems appropriate. The premium of any such bond or bonds may, in the discretion of the Secretary or his delegate, be paid from the appropriation for expenses of the Internal Revenue Service."

Sec. 7804. Other personnel.
(a) Appointment and supervision.
Unless otherwise prescribed by the Secretary, the Commissioner of Internal Revenue is authorized to employ such number of persons as the Commissioner deems proper for the administration and enforcement of the internal revenue laws, and the Commissioner shall issue all necessary directions, instructions, orders, and rules applicable to such persons.
(b) Posts of duty of employees in field service or traveling.
Unless otherwise prescribed by the Secretary—
(1) Designation of post of duty. The Commissioner shall determine and designate the posts of duty of all such persons engaged in field work or traveling on official business outside of the District of Columbia.
(2) Detail of personnel from field service. The Commissioner may order any such person engaged in field work to duty in the District of Columbia, for such periods as the Commissioner may prescribe, and to any designated post of duty outside the District of Columbia upon the completion of such duty.
(c) Delinquent internal revenue officers and employees.
If any officer or employee of the Treasury Department acting in connection with the internal revenue laws fails to account for and pay over any amount of money or property collected or received by him in connection with the internal revenue laws, the Secretary shall issue notice and demand to such officer or employee for payment of the amount which he failed to account for and pay over, and, upon failure to pay the amount demanded within the time specified in such notice, the amount so demanded shall be deemed imposed upon such officer or employee and assessed upon the date of such notice and demand, and the provisions of chapter 64 and all other provisions of law relating to the collection of assessed taxes shall be applicable in respect of such amount.

In 2001, P.L. 107-67, Sec. 102, of this Act, reads as follows:
"Sec. 102. The Internal Revenue Service shall maintain a training program to ensure that Internal Revenue Service employees are trained in taxpayers' rights, in dealing courteously with the taxpayers, and in cross-cultural relations."
In 1998, P.L. 105-206, Sec. 1104(a), amended Code Sec. 7804, effective 7/22/98. Prior to amendment, Code Sec. 7804 read as follows:
"SEC. 7804. EFFECT OF REORGANIZATION PLANS.
"(a) Application. The provisions of Reorganization Plan Numbered 26 of 1950 and Reorganization Plan Numbered 1 of 1952 shall be applicable to all functions vested by this title, or by any act amending this title (except as otherwise expressly provided in such amending act), in any officer, employee, or agency, of the Department of the Treasury.
"(b) Preservation of existing rights and remedies. Nothing in Reorganization Plan Numbered 26 of 1950 or Reorganization Plan Numbered 1 of 1952 shall be considered to impair any right or remedy, including trial by jury, to recover any internal revenue tax alleged to have been erroneously or illegally assessed or collected, or any penalty claimed to have been collected without authority, or any sum alleged to have been excessive or in any manner wrongfully collected under the internal revenue laws. For the purpose of any action to recover any such tax, penalty, or sum, all statutes, rules, and regulations referring to the collector of internal revenue, the principal officer for the internal revenue district, or the Secretary, shall be deemed to refer to the officer whose act or acts referred to in the preceding sentence gave rise to such action. The venue of any such action shall be the same as under existing law."
In 1976, P.L. 94-455, Sec. 1906(b)(13)(A), substituted "Secretary" for "Secretary or his delegate" in Code Sec. 7804, effective 2/1/77.

Sec. 7805. Rules and regulations.
(a) Authorization.
Except where such authority is expressly given by this title to any person other than an officer or employee of the Treasury Department, the Secretary shall prescribe all needful rules and regulations for the enforcement of this title, including all rules and regulations as may be necessary by reason of any alteration of law in relation to internal revenue.
(b) Retroactivity of regulations.
(1) In general. Except as otherwise provided in this subsection, no temporary, proposed, or final regulation relating to the internal revenue laws shall apply to any taxable period ending before the earliest of the following dates:
(A) The date on which such regulation is filed with the Federal Register.
(B) In the case of any final regulation, the date on which any proposed or temporary regulation to which such final regulation relates was filed with the Federal Register.
(C) The date on which any notice substantially describing the expected contents of any temporary, proposed, or final regulation is issued to the public.
(2) Exception for promptly issued regulations. Paragraph (1) shall not apply to regulations issued within 18 months of the date of the enactment of the statutory provision to which the regulation relates.

(3) Prevention of abuse. The Secretary may provide that any regulation may take effect or apply retroactively to prevent abuse.

(4) Correction of procedural defects. The Secretary may provide that any regulation may apply retroactively to correct a procedural defect in the issuance of any prior regulation.

(5) Internal regulations. The limitation of paragraph (1) shall not apply to any regulation relating to internal Treasury Department policies, practices, or procedures.

(6) Congressional authorization. The limitation of paragraph (1) may be superseded by a legislative grant from Congress authorizing the Secretary to prescribe the effective date with respect to any regulation.

(7) Election to apply retroactively. The Secretary may provide for any taxpayer to elect to apply any regulation before the dates specified in paragraph (1).

(8) Application to rulings. The Secretary may prescribe the extent, if any, to which any ruling (including any judicial decision or any administrative determination other than by regulation) relating to the internal revenue laws shall be applied without retroactive effect.

(c) Preparation and distribution of regulations, forms, stamps, and other matters.

The Secretary shall prepare and distribute all the instructions, regulations, directions, forms, blanks, stamps, and other matters pertaining to the assessment and collection of internal revenue.

(d) Manner of making elections prescribed by Secretary.

Except to the extent otherwise provided by this title, any election under this title shall be made at such time and in such manner as the Secretary shall prescribe.

(e) Temporary regulations.

(1) Issuance. Any temporary regulation issued by the Secretary shall also be issued as a proposed regulation.

(2) 3-Year duration. Any temporary regulation shall expire within 3 years after the date of issuance of such regulation.

(f) Review of impact of regulations on small business.

(1) Submissions to small business administration. After publication of any proposed or temporary regulation by the Secretary, the Secretary shall submit such regulation to the Chief Counsel for Advocacy of the Small Business Administration for comment on the impact of such regulation on small business. Not later than the date 4 weeks after the date of such submission, the Chief Counsel for Advocacy shall submit comments on such regulation to the Secretary.

(2) Consideration of comments. In prescribing any final regulation which supersedes a proposed or temporary regulation which had been submitted under this subsection to the Chief Counsel for Advocacy of the Small Business Administration—

(A) the Secretary shall consider the comments of the Chief Counsel for Advocacy on such proposed or temporary regulation, and

(B) the Secretary shall discuss any response to such comments in the preamble of such final regulation.

(3) Submission of certain final regulations. In the case of the promulgation by the Secretary of any final regulation (other than a temporary regulation) which does not supersede a proposed regulation, the requirements of paragraphs (1) and (2) shall apply; except that—

(A) the submission under paragraph (1) shall be made at least 4 weeks before the date of such promulgation, and

(B) the consideration (and discussion) required under paragraph (2) shall be made in connection with the promulgation of such final regulation.

In **2006**, P.L. 109-280, Sec. 811, of this Act [relating to Sec. 901 of P.L. 107-16, see below], provides:

"SEC. 811. PENSIONS AND INDIVIDUAL RETIREMENT ARRANGEMENT PROVISIONS OF ECONOMIC GROWTH AND TAX RELIEF RECONCILIATION ACT OF 2001 MADE PERMANENT.

"Title IX of the Economic Growth and Tax Relief Reconciliation Act of 2001 shall not apply to the provisions of, and amendments made by, subtitles A through F of title VI of such Act (relating to pension and individual retirement arrangement provisions)."

In **2003**, P.L. 108-89, Sec. 202(b)(2), repealed Sec. 10511 of P.L. 100-203 [see below], effective for requests made after 10/1/2003.

— P.L. 108-89, Sec. 202(b)(3), repealed Sec. 620 of P.L. 107-16 [see below], effective for requests made after 10/1/2003.

In **2001**, P.L. 107-16, Sec. 620, of this Act [prior to repeal by Sec. 202(b)(3) of P.L. 108-89, see above], reads as follows:

"SEC. 620. ELIMINATION OF USER FEE FOR REQUESTS TO IRS REGARDING PENSION PLANS.

"(a) *Elimination of certain user fees.* The Secretary of the Treasury or the Secretary's delegate shall not require payment of user fees under the program established under section 10511 of the Revenue Act of 1987 for requests to the Internal Revenue Service for determination letters with respect to the qualified status of a pension benefit plan maintained solely by one or more eligible employers or any trust which is part of the plan. The preceding sentence shall not apply to any request—

"(1) made after the later of—

"(A) the fifth plan year the pension benefit plan is in existence; or

"(B) the end of any remedial amendment period with respect to the plan beginning within the first 5 plan years; or

"(2) made by the sponsor of any prototype or similar plan which the sponsor intends to market to participating employers.

"(b) *Pension benefit plan.* For purposes of this section, the term 'pension benefit plan' means a pension, profit-sharing, stock bonus, annuity, or employee stock ownership plan.

"(c) *Eligible employer.* For purposes of this section, the term 'eligible employer' means an eligible employer (as defined in section 408(p)(2)(C)(i)(I) of the Internal Revenue Code of 1986) which has at least one employee who is not a highly compensated employee (as defined in section 414(q)) and is participating in the plan. The determination of whether an employer is an eligible employer under this section shall be made as of the date of the request described in subsection (a).

"(d) *Determination of average fees charged.* For purposes of any determination of average fees charged, any request to which subsection (a) applies shall not be taken into account.

"(e) *Effective date.* The provisions of this section shall apply with respect to requests made after December 31, 2001."

In **1998**, P.L. 105-206, Sec. 3704, deleted "by regulations or forms" after "the Secretary shall" in subsec. (d), effective 7/22/98.

In **1996**, P.L. 104-168, Sec. 1101(a), amended subsec. (b), effective for regulations which relate to statutory provisions enacted on or after 7/30/96.

Prior to amendment, subsec. (b) read as follows:

"(b) Retroactivity of regulations or rulings. The Secretary may prescribe the extent, if any, to which any ruling or regulation, relating to the internal revenue laws, shall be applied without retroactive effect."

— P.L. 104-117, Sec. 2, substituted "October 1, 2003" for "October 1, 2000" in Sec. 10511(c) of P.L. 100-203, reproduced below [as amended by Sec. 743 of P.L. 103-465 and Sec. 11319(a) of P.L. 101-508, see below].

In **1994**, P.L. 103-465, Sec. 743, substituted "October 1, 2000" for "October 1, 1995" in Sec. 10511(c) of P.L. 100-203, reproduced below [as amended by Sec. 11319(a) of P.L. 101-508, see below].

In **1990**, P.L. 101-508, Sec. 11319(a), added the sentence at the end of Sec. 10511(c) of P.L. 100-203, reproduced below, effective 9/29/90, except that no advance payment shall be required for any fee for any requests filed after 9/29/90, and before the 30th day after 11/5/90.

— P.L. 101-508, Sec. 11621(a), amended subsec. (f), effective for regulations issued after the date which is 30 days after 11/5/90.

Prior to amendment, subsec. (f) read as follows:

"(f) Impact of regulations on small business reviewed. After the publication of any proposed regulation by the Secretary and before the promulgation of any final regulation by the Secretary which does not supersede a proposed regulation, the Secretary shall submit such regulation to the Administrator of the Small Business Administration for comment on the impact of such regulation on small business. The Administrator shall have 4 weeks from the date of submission to respond."

In **1988**, P.L. 100-647, Sec. 6232(a), added subsecs. (e) and (f), effective for any regulation issued after the date which is 10 days after 11/10/88.

In **1987**, P.L. 100-203, Sec. 10511, [as amended by Sec. 11319(a) of P.L. 101-508, Sec. 743 of P.L. 103-465, and Sec. 2 of P.L. 104-117, see above] but prior to repeal by Sec. 202(b)(2) of P.L. 108-89, see above], provides the following rules for tax-related user fees:

"SEC. 10511. FEES FOR REQUESTS FOR RULING, DETERMINATION, AND SIMILAR LETTERS.

Miscellaneous provisions   Code Sec. 7809(c)(1)

"(a) General rule. The Secretary of the Treasury or his delegate (hereinafter in this section referred to as the 'Secretary') shall establish a program requiring the payment of user fees for requests to the Internal Revenue Service for ruling letters, opinion letters, and determination letters and for similar requests.

"(b) Program criteria.

"(1) In general. The fees charged under the program required by subsection (a)—

"(A) shall vary according to categories (or subcategories) established by the Secretary,

"(B) shall be determined after taking into account the average time for (and difficulty of) complying with requests in each category (and subcategory), and

"(C) shall be payable in advance.

"(2) Exemptions, etc. The Secretary shall provide for such exemptions (and reduced fees) under such program as he determines to be appropriate.

"(3) Average fee requirement. The average fee charged under the program required by subsection (a) shall not be less than the amount determined under the following table:

"Category	Average Fee
Employee plan ruling and opinion	$ 250
Exempt organization ruling	$ 350
Employee plan determination	$ 300
Exempt organization determination	$ 275
Chief counsel ruling	$200.

"(c) Application of section. Subsection (a) shall apply with respect to requests made on or after the 1st day of the second calendar month beginning after the date of the enactment of this Act and before September 30, 1990. Subsection (a) shall also apply with respect to requests made after September 30, 1990, and before October 1, 2003."

In **1984**, P.L. 98-369, Sec. 43(b), added subsec. (d), effective for tax. yrs. end. after 7/18/84.

In **1976**, P.L. 94-455, Sec. 1906(b)(13)(A), substituted "Secretary" for "Secretary or his delegate" each place it appeared in Code Sec. 7805, effective 2/1/77.

Sec. 7806. Construction of title.
(a) Cross references.

The cross references in this title to other portions of the title, or other provisions of law, where the word "see" is used, are made only for convenience, and shall be given no legal effect.

(b) Arrangement and classification.

No inference, implication, or presumption of legislative construction shall be drawn or made by reason of the location or grouping of any particular section or provision or portion of this title, nor shall any table of contents, table of cross references, or similar outline, analysis, or descriptive matter relating to the contents of this title be given any legal effect. The preceding sentence also applies to the sidenotes and ancillary tables contained in the various prints of this Act before its enactment into law.

Sec. 7807. Rules in effect upon enactment of this title.
(a) Interim provision for administration of title.

Until regulations are promulgated under any provision of this title which depends for its application upon the promulgation of regulations (or which is to be applied in such manner as may be prescribed by regulations) all instructions, rules or regulations which are in effect immediately prior to the enactment of this title shall, to the extent such instructions, rules, or regulations could be prescribed as regulations under authority of such provision, be applied as if promulgated as regulations under such provision.

(b) Provisions of this title corresponding to prior internal revenue laws.

(1) Reference to law applicable to prior period. Any provision of this title which refers to the application of any portion of this title to a prior period (or which depends upon the application to a prior period of any portion of this title) shall, when appropriate and consistent with the purpose of such provision, be deemed to refer to (or depend upon the application of) the corresponding provision of the Internal Revenue Code of 1939 or of such other internal revenue laws as were applicable to the prior period.

(2) Elections or other acts. If an election or other act under the provisions of the Internal Revenue Code of 1939 would, if this title had not been enacted, be given effect for a period subsequent to the date of enactment of this title, and if corresponding provisions are contained in this title, such election or other act shall be given effect under the corresponding provisions of this title.

Sec. 7808. Depositaries for collections.

The Secretary is authorized to designate one or more depositaries in each State for the deposit and safe-keeping of the money collected by virtue of the internal revenue laws; and the receipt of the proper officer of such depositary to the proper officer or employee of the Treasury Department for the money deposited by him shall be a sufficient voucher for such Treasury officer or employee in the settlement of his accounts.

In **1976**, P.L. 94-455, Sec. 1906(b)(13)(A), substituted "Secretary" for "Secretary or his delegate" in Code Sec. 7808, effective 2/1/77.

Sec. 7809. Deposit of collections.
(a) General rule.

Except as provided in subsections (b) and (c) and in sections 6306, 7651, 7652, 7654, and 7810, the gross amount of all taxes and revenues received under the provisions of this title, and collections of whatever nature received or collected by authority of any internal revenue law, shall be paid daily into the Treasury of the United States under instructions of the Secretary as internal revenue collections, by the officer or employee receiving or collecting the same, without any abatement or deduction on account of salary, compensation, fees, costs, charges, expenses, or claims of any description. A certificate of such payment, stating the name of the depositor and the specific account on which the deposit was made, signed by the Treasurer of the United States, designated depositary, or proper officer of a deposit bank, shall be transmitted to the Secretary.

(b) Deposit funds.

In accordance with instructions of the Secretary, there shall be deposited with the Treasurer of the United States in a deposit fund account—

(1) Sums offered in compromise. Sums offered in compromise under the provisions of section 7122;

(2) Sums offered for purchase of real estate. Sums offered for the purchase of real estate under the provisions of section 7506;

(3) Surplus proceeds in sales under levy. Surplus proceeds in any sale under levy, after making allowance for the amount of the tax, interest, penalties, and additions thereto, and for costs and charges of the levy and sale; and

(4) Surplus proceeds in sales of redeemed property. Surplus proceeds in any sale under section 7506 of real property redeemed by the United States, after making allowance for the amount of the tax, interest, penalties, and additions thereto, and for the costs of sale.

Upon the acceptance of such offer in compromise or offer for the purchase of such real estate, the amount so accepted shall be withdrawn from such deposit fund account and deposited in the Treasury of the United States as internal revenue collections. Upon the rejection of any such offer, the Secretary shall refund to the maker of such offer the amount thereof.

(c) Deposit of certain receipts.

Moneys received in payment for—

(1) Work or services performed pursuant to section 6103(p) (relating to furnishing of copies of returns or of return information), and section 6108(b) (relating to special statistical studies and compilations);

(2) work or services performed (including materials supplied) pursuant to section 7516 (relating to the supplying of training and training aids on request);

(3) other work or services performed for a State or a department or agency of the Federal Government (subject to all provisions of law and regulations governing disclosure of information) in supplying copies of, or data from, returns, statements, or other documents filed under authority of this title or records maintained in connection with the administration and enforcement of this title; and

(4) work or services performed (including materials supplied) pursuant to section 6110 (relating to public inspection of written determinations),

shall be deposited in a separate account which may be used to reimburse appropriations which bore all or part of the costs of such work or services, or to refund excess sums when necessary.

(d) Deposit of funds for law enforcement agency account.

(1) **In general.** In the case of any amounts recovered as the result of information provided to the Internal Revenue Service by State and local law enforcement agencies which substantially contributed to such recovery, an amount equal to 10 percent of such amounts shall be deposited in a separate account which shall be used to make the reimbursements required under section 7624.

(2) **Deposit in Treasury as internal revenue collections.** If any amounts remain in such account after payment of any qualified costs incurred under section 7624, such amounts shall be withdrawn from such account and deposited in the Treasury of the United States as internal revenue collections.

In **2004**, P.L. 108-357, Sec. 881(a)(2)(A), added "6306," before "7651" in subsec. (a), effective 10/22/2004.

In **1988**, P.L. 100-690, Sec. 7602(b), added subsec. (d), effective for information first provided more than 90 days after 11/18/88.

In **1976**, P.L. 94-528, Sec. 2(d), deleted "and" at the end of para. (c)(2), substituted "; and" for the comma at the end of para. (c)(3), and added para. (c)(4), effective 10/4/76.

— P.L. 94-455, Sec. 1202(h)(5), substituted "section 6103(p) (relating to furnishing of copies of returns or of return information), and section 6108(b) (relating to special statistical studies and compilations)" for "section 7515 (relating to special statistical studies and compilations for other services on request)" in para. (c)(1), effective 1/1/77.

— P.L. 94-455, Sec. 1906(a)(59), deleted "4735, 4762,", after "(b) and (c) and in sections", in subsec. (a), effective 2/1/77.

— P.L. 94-455, Sec. 1906(b)(13)(A), substituted "Secretary" for "Secretary or his delegate" each place it appeared in Code Sec. 7809, effective 2/1/77.

In **1966**, P.L. 89-719, Sec. 112, added reference to Code Sec. 7809 in subsec. (a), and added para. (b)(4), effective after 11/2/66 regardless of when a lien or a title of the U.S. arose or when the lien or interest of any other person was acquired.

In **1962**, P.L. 87-870, Sec. 3(b), substituted "subsections (b) and (c) and in" for "subsection (b)," in subsec. (a), and added subsec. (c), effective 10/24/62.

Sec. 7810. Revolving fund for redemption of real property.

(a) Establishment of fund.

There is established a revolving fund, under the control of the Secretary, which shall be available without fiscal year limitation for all expenses necessary for the redemption (by the Secretary) of real property as provided in section 7425(d) and section 2410 of title 28 of the United States Code. There are authorized to be appropriated from time to time such sums (not to exceed $10,000,000 in the aggregate) as may be necessary to carry out the purposes of this section.

(b) Reimbursement of fund.

The fund shall be reimbursed from the proceeds of a subsequent sale of real property redeemed by the United States in an amount equal to the amount expended out of such fund for such redemption.

(c) System of accounts.

The Secretary shall maintain an adequate system of accounts for such fund and prepare annual reports on the basis of such accounts.

In **1984**, P.L. 98-369, Sec. 443, substituted "$10,000,000" for "$1,000,000" in subsec. (a), effective 7/18/84.

In **1976**, P.L. 94-455, Sec. 1906(b)(13)(A), substituted "Secretary" for "Secretary or his delegate" each place it appeared in Code Sec. 7810, effective 2/1/77.

In **1966**, P.L. 89-719, Sec. 112, added Code Sec. 7810, effective after 11/2/66 regardless of when a lien or a title of the U.S. arose or when the lien or interest of any other person was acquired.

Sec. 7811. Taxpayer Assistance Orders.

(a) Authority to issue.

(1) **In general.** Upon application filed by a taxpayer with the Office of the Taxpayer Advocate (in such form, manner, and at such time as the Secretary shall by regulations prescribe), the National Taxpayer Advocate may issue a Taxpayer Assistance Order if—

(A) The National Taxpayer Advocate determines the taxpayer is suffering or about to suffer a significant hardship as a result of the manner in which the internal revenue laws are being administered by the Secretary; or

(B) the Taxpayer meets such other requirements as are set forth in regulations prescribed by the Secretary.

(2) **Determination of hardship.** For purposes of paragraph (1), a significant hardship shall include—

(A) an immediate threat of adverse action;

(B) a delay of more than 30 days in resolving taxpayer account problems;

(C) the incurring by the taxpayer of significant costs (including fees for professional representation) if relief is not granted; or

(D) irreparable injury to, or a long-term adverse impact on, the taxpayer if relief is not granted.

(3) **Standard where administrative guidance not followed.** In cases where any Internal Revenue Service employee is not following applicable published administrative guidance (including the Internal Revenue Manual), the National Taxpayer Advocate shall construe the factors taken into account in determining whether to issue a Taxpayer Assistance Order in the manner most favorable to the taxpayer.

(b) Terms of a Taxpayer Assistance Order.

The terms of a Taxpayer Assistance Order may require the Secretary within a specified time period —

(1) to release property of the taxpayer levied upon, or

(2) to cease any action, take any action as permitted by law, or refrain from taking any action, with respect to the taxpayer under—

(A) chapter 64 (relating to collection),

(B) subchapter B of chapter 70 (relating to bankruptcy and receiverships),

(C) chapter 78 (relating to discovery of liability and enforcement of title), or

(D) any other provision of law which is specifically described by the National Taxpayer Advocate in such order.

(c) Authority to modify or rescind.

Any Taxpayer Assistance Order issued by the National Taxpayer Advocate under this section may be modified or rescinded—

(1) only by the National Taxpayer Advocate, the Commissioner of Internal Revenue, or the Deputy Commissioner of Internal Revenue, and

(2) only if a written explanation of the reasons for the modification or rescission is provided to the National Taxpayer Advocate.

(d) Suspension of running of period of limitation.
The running of any period of limitation with respect to any action described in subsection (b) shall be suspended for—
(1) the period beginning on the date of the taxpayer's application under subsection (a) and ending on the date of the National Taxpayer Advocate's decision with respect to such application, and
(2) any period specified by the National Taxpayer Advocate in a Taxpayer Assistance Order issued pursuant to such application.

(e) Independent action of National Taxpayer Advocate.
Nothing in this section shall prevent the National Taxpayer Advocate from taking any action in the absence of an application under subsection (a).

(f) National Taxpayer Advocate.
For purposes of this section, the term "National Taxpayer Advocate" includes any designee of the National Taxpayer Advocate.

(g) Application to persons performing services under a qualified tax collection contract.
Any order issued or action taken by the National Taxpayer Advocate pursuant to this section shall apply to persons performing services under a qualified tax collection contract (as defined in section 6306(b)) to the same extent and in the same manner as such order or action applies to the Secretary.

In 2004, P.L. 108-357, Sec. 881(c), added subsec. (g), effective 10/22/2004.
In 2000, P.L. 106-554, Sec. 1(a)(7), [which enacted into law Sec. 319(28) of P.L. 106-554] substituted "Taxpayer Assistance Order" for "taxpayer assistance order" in para. (a)(3)... Sec. 1(a)(7), [which enacted into law Sec.319(29) of P.L. 106-554] substituted "National Taxpayer Advocate's" for "Ombudsman's" in para. (d)(1), effective 12/21/2000.
In 1998, P.L. 105-206, Sec. 1102(c), amended subsec. (a)... Sec. 1102(d)(1)(C), substituted "National Taxpayer Advocate" for "Taxpayer Advocate" in subpara. (b)(2)(D)... Sec. 1102(d)(1)(D), substituted "National Taxpayer Advocate" for "Taxpayer Advocate" each place it appeared in subsec. (c)... Sec. 1102(d)(1)(E), substituted "National Taxpayer Advocate" for "Taxpayer Advocate" in para. (d)(2)... Sec. 1102(d)(1)(F), substituted "National Taxpayer Advocate" for "Taxpayer Advocate" in subsec. (e)... Sec. 1102(d)(1)(G), substituted "National Taxpayer Advocate" for "Taxpayer Advocate" each place it appeared in subsec. (f)... Sec. 1102(d)(2), substituted "National Taxpayer Advocate's" for "Taxpayer Advocate's" in para. (d)(1)... Sec. 1102(d)(3), substituted "National Taxpayer Advocate" for "Taxpayer Advocate" in the headings of subsecs. (e) and (f), effective 7/22/98.
Prior to amendment, subsec. (a) read as follows:
"(a) Authority to issue. Upon application filed by a taxpayer with the Office of the Taxpayer Advocate (in such form, manner, and at such time as the Secretary shall by regulations prescribe), the Taxpayer Advocate may issue a Taxpayer Assistance Order if, in the determination of the Taxpayer Advocate, the taxpayer is suffering or about to suffer a significant hardship as a result of the manner in which the internal revenue laws are being administered by the Secretary."
In 1996, P.L. 104-168, Sec. 101(b)(1)(A), substituted "the Office of the Taxpayer Advocate" for "the Office of Ombudsman" in subsec. (a)... Sec. 101(b)(1)(B), substituted "Taxpayer Advocate" for "Ombudsman" each place it appeared in Code Sec. 7811, effective 7/30/96.
—P.L. 104-168, Sec. 102(a)(1), added "within a specified time period" after "the Secretary" in subsec. (b)... Sec. 102(a)(2), added "take any action as permitted by law" after "cease any action," in subsec. (b)... Sec. 102(b), amended subsec. (c) [as amended by Sec. 101(b)(1)(B) of this Act, see above], effective 7/30/96.
Prior to amendment, subsec. (c) read as follows:
"(c) Authority to modify or rescind. Any Taxpayer Assistance Order issued by the Taxpayer Advocate under this section may be modified or rescinded only by the Taxpayer Advocate, a district director, a service center director, a compliance center director, a regional director of appeals, or any superior of any such person."
In 1988, P.L. 100-647, Sec. 6230(a), added Code Sec. 7811, effective 1/1/89.

Subchapter B.—Effective Date and Related Provisions
Sec.
7851. Applicability of revenue laws.
7852. Other applicable rules.

Sec. 7851. Applicability of revenue laws.
(a) General rules.
Except as otherwise provided in any section of this title—
(1) Subtitle A.
(A) Chapters 1, 2, 4, and 6 of this title shall apply only with respect to taxable years beginning after December 31, 1953, and ending after the date of enactment of this title, and with respect to such taxable years, chapters 1 (except sections 143 and 144) and 2, and section 3801, of the Internal Revenue Code of 1939 are hereby repealed.
(B) Chapters 3 and 5 of this title shall apply with respect to payments and transfers occurring after December 31, 1954, and as to such payments and transfers sections 143 and 144 and chapter 7 of the Internal Revenue Code of 1939 are hereby repealed.
(C) Any provision of subtitle A of this title the applicability of which is stated in terms of a specific date (occurring after December 31, 1953), or in terms of taxable years ending after a specific date (occurring after December 31, 1953), shall apply to taxable years ending after such specific date. Each such provision shall, in the case of a taxable year subject to the Internal Revenue Code of 1939, be deemed to be included in the Internal Revenue Code of 1939, but shall be applicable only to taxable years ending after such specific date. The provisions of the Internal Revenue Code of 1939 superseded by provisions of subtitle A of this title the applicability of which is stated in terms of a specific date (occurring after December 31, 1953) shall be deemed to be included in subtitle A of this title, but shall be applicable only to the period prior to the taking effect of the corresponding provision of subtitle A.
(D) Effective with respect to taxable years ending after March 31, 1954, and subject to tax under chapter 1 of the Internal Revenue Code of 1939—
(i) Sections 13(b)(3), 26(b)(2)(C), 26(h)(1)(C) (including the comma and the word "and" immediately preceding such section), 26(i)(3), 108(k), 207(a)(1)(C), 207(a)(3)(C), and the last sentence of section 362(b)(3) of such Code are hereby repealed; and
(ii) Sections 13(b)(2), 26(b)(2)(B), 26(h)(1)(B), 26(i)(2), 207(a)(1)(B), 207(a)(3)(B), 421(a)(1)(B), and the second sentence of section 362(b)(3) of such Code are hereby amended by striking out "and before April 1, 1954" (and any accompanying punctuation) wherever appearing therein.
(2) Subtitle B.
(A) Chapter 11 of this title shall apply with respect to estates of decedents dying after the date of enactment of this title, and with respect to such estates chapter 3 of the Internal Revenue Code of 1939 is hereby repealed.
(B) Chapter 12 of this title shall apply with respect to the calendar year 1955 and all calendar years thereafter, and with respect to such years chapter 4 of the Internal Revenue Code of 1939 is hereby repealed.
(3) Subtitle C. Subtitle C of this title shall apply only with respect to remuneration paid after December 31, 1954, except that chapter 22 of such subtitle shall apply only with respect to remuneration paid after December 31, 1954, which is for services performed after such date.

Chapter 9 of the Internal Revenue Code of 1939 is hereby repealed with respect to remuneration paid after December 31, 1954, except that subchapter B of such chapter (and subchapter E of such chapter to the extent it relates to subchapter B) shall remain in force and effect with respect to remuneration paid after December 31, 1954, for services performed on or before such date.

(4) Subtitle D. Subtitle D of this title shall take effect on January 1, 1955. Subtitles B and C of the Internal Revenue Code of 1939 (except chapters 7, 9, 15, 26, and 28, subchapter B of chapter 25, and parts VII and VIII of subchapter A of chapter 27 of such code) are hereby repealed effective January 1, 1955. Provisions having the same effect as section 6416(b)(2)(H), and so much of section 4082(c) as refers to special motor fuels, shall be considered to be included in the Internal Revenue Code of 1939 effective as of May 1, 1954. Section 2450(a) of the Internal Revenue Code of 1939 (as amended by the Excise Tax Reduction Act of 1954) applies to the period beginning on April 1, 1954, and ending on December 31, 1954.

(5) Subtitle E. Subtitle E shall take effect on January 1, 1955, except that the provisions in section 5411 permitting the use of a brewery under regulations prescribed by the Secretary for the purpose of producing and bottling soft drinks, section 5554, and chapter 53 shall take effect on the day after the date of enactment of this title. Subchapter B of chapter 25, and part VIII of subchapter A of chapter 27, of the Internal Revenue Code of 1939 are hereby repealed effective on the day after the date of enactment of this title. Chapters 15 and 26, and part VII of subchapter A of chapter 27, of the Internal Revenue Code of 1939 are hereby repealed effective January 1, 1955.

(6) Subtitle F.

(A) General rule. The provisions of subtitle F shall take effect on the day after the date of enactment of this title and shall be applicable with respect to any tax imposed by this title. The provisions of subtitle F shall apply with respect to any tax imposed by the Internal Revenue Code of 1939 only to the extent provided in subparagraphs (B) and (C) of this paragraph.

(B) Assessment, collection, and refunds. Notwithstanding the provisions of subparagraph (A), and notwithstanding any contrary provision of subchapter A of chapter 63 (relating to assessment), chapter 64 (relating to collection), or chapter 65 (relating to abatements, credits, and refunds) of this title, the provisions of part II of subchapter A of chapter 28 and chapters 35, 36, and 37 (except section 3777) of subtitle D of the Internal Revenue Code of 1939 shall remain in effect until January 1, 1955, and shall also be applicable to the taxes imposed by this title. On and after January 1, 1955, the provisions of subchapter A of chapter 63, chapter 64, and chapter 65 (except section 6405) of this title shall be applicable to all internal revenue taxes (whether imposed by this title or by the Internal Revenue Code of 1939), notwithstanding any contrary provision of part II of subchapter A of chapter 28, or of chapter 35, 36, or 37, of the Internal Revenue Code of 1939. The provisions of section 6405 (relating to reports of refunds and credits) shall be applicable with respect to refunds or credits allowed after the date of enactment of this title, and section 3777 of the Internal Revenue Code of 1939 is hereby repealed with respect to such refunds and credits.

(C) Taxes imposed under the 1939 Code. After the date of enactment of this title, the following provisions of subtitle F shall apply to the taxes imposed by the Internal Revenue Code of 1939, notwithstanding any contrary provisions of such code:

(i) Chapter 73, relating to bonds.

(ii) Chapter 74, relating to closing agreements and compromises.

(iii) Chapter 75, relating to crimes and other offenses, but only insofar as it relates to offenses committed after the date of enactment of this title, and in the case of such offenses, section 6531, relating to periods of limitation on criminal prosecution, shall be applicable. The penalties (other than penalties which may be assessed) provided by the Internal Revenue Code of 1939 shall not apply to offenses, committed after the date of enactment of this title, to which chapter 75 of this title is applicable.

(iv) Chapter 76, relating to judicial proceedings.

(v) Chapter 77, relating to miscellaneous provisions, except that section 7502 shall apply only if the mailing occurs after the date of enactment of this title, and section 7503 shall apply only if the last date referred to therein occurs after the date of enactment of this title.

(vi) Chapter 78, relating to discovery of liability and enforcement of title.

(vii) Chapter 79, relating to definitions.

(viii) Chapter 80, relating to application of internal revenue laws, effective date, and related provisions.

(D) Chapter 28 and subtitle D of 1939 Code. Except as otherwise provided in subparagraphs (B) and (C), the provisions of chapter 28 and of subtitle D of the Internal Revenue Code of 1939 shall remain in effect with respect to taxes imposed by the Internal Revenue Code of 1939.

(7) Other provisions. If the effective date of any provision of the Internal Revenue Code of 1954 is not otherwise provided in this section or in any other section of this title, such provision shall take effect on the day after the date of enactment of this title. If the repeal of any provision of the Internal Revenue Code of 1939 is not otherwise provided by this section or by any other section of this title, such provision is hereby repealed effective on the day after the date of enactment of this title.

(b) Effect of repeal of Internal Revenue Code of 1939.

(1) Existing rights and liabilities. The repeal of any provision of the Internal Revenue Code of 1939 shall not affect any act done or any right accruing or accrued, or any suit or proceeding had or commenced in any civil cause, before such repeal; but all rights and liabilities under such code shall continue, and may be enforced in the same manner, as if such repeal had not been made.

(2) Existing offices. The repeal of any provision of the Internal Revenue Code of 1939 shall not abolish, terminate, or otherwise change—

(A) any internal revenue district,

(B) any office, position, board, or committee, or

(C) the appointment or employment of any officer or employee,

existing immediately preceding the enactment of this title, the continuance of which is not manifestly inconsistent with any provision of this title, but the same shall continue unless and until changed by lawful authority.

(3) Existing delegations of authority. Any delegation of authority made pursuant to the provisions of Reorganization Plan Numbered 26 of 1950 or Reorganization Plan Numbered 1 of 1952, including any redelegation of authority made pursuant to any such delegation of authority, and in effect under the Internal Revenue Code of 1939

Miscellaneous provisions — Code Sec. 7871(a)(6)(C)

immediately preceding the enactment of this title shall, notwithstanding the repeal of such code, remain in effect for purposes of this title, unless distinctly inconsistent or manifestly incompatible with the provisions of this title. The preceding sentence shall not be construed as limiting in any manner the power to amend, modify, or revoke any such delegation or redelegation of authority.

(c) Crimes and forfeitures.

All offenses committed, and all penalties or forfeitures incurred, under any provision of law hereby repealed, may be prosecuted and punished in the same manner and with the same effect as if this title had not been enacted.

(d) Periods of limitation.

All periods of limitation, whether applicable to civil causes and proceedings, or to the prosecution of offenses, or for the recovery of penalties or forfeitures, hereby repealed shall not be affected thereby, but all suits, proceedings, or prosecutions, whether civil or criminal, for causes arising, or acts done or committed, prior to said repeal, may be commenced and prosecuted within the same time as if this title had not been enacted.

(e) Reference to other provisions.

For the purpose of applying the Internal Revenue Code of 1939 or the Internal Revenue Code of 1954 to any period, any reference in either such code to another provision of the Internal Revenue Code of 1939 or the Internal Revenue Code of 1954 which is not then applicable to such period shall be deemed a reference to the corresponding provision of the other code which is then applicable to such period.

Sec. 7852. Other applicable rules.

(a) Separability clause.

If any provision of this title, or the application thereof to any person or circumstances, is held invalid, the remainder of the title, and the application of such provision to other persons or circumstances, shall not be affected thereby.

(b) Reference in other laws to Internal Revenue Code of 1939.

Any reference in any other law of the United States or in any Executive order to any provision of the Internal Revenue Code of 1939 shall, where not otherwise distinctly expressed or manifestly incompatible with the intent thereof, be deemed also to refer to the corresponding provision of this title.

(c) Items not to be twice included in income or deducted therefrom.

Except as otherwise distinctly expressed or manifestly intended, the same item (whether of income, deduction, credit, or otherwise) shall not be taken into account both in computing a tax under subtitle A of this title and a tax under chapter 1 or 2 of the Internal Revenue Code of 1939.

(d) Treaty obligations.

(1) In general. For purposes of determining the relationship between a provision of a treaty and any law of the United States affecting revenue, neither the treaty nor the law shall have preferential status by reason of its being a treaty or law.

(2) Savings clause for 1954 treaties. No provision of this title (as in effect without regard to any amendment thereto enacted after August 16, 1954) shall apply in any case where its application would be contrary to any treaty obligation of the United States in effect on August 16, 1954.

(e) Privacy Act of 1974.

The provisions of subsections (d)(2), (3), and (4), and (g) of section 552a of title 5, United States Code, shall not be applied, directly or indirectly, to the determination of the existence or possible existence of liability (or the amount thereof) of any person for any tax, penalty, interest, fine, forfeiture, or other imposition or offense to which the provisions of this title apply.

In **1988**, P.L. 100-647, Sec. 1012(aa)(1)(A), amended subsec. (d), effective for any taxable period with respect to which the time for assessment of any deficiency has not expired by reason of any law or rule of law before 11/10/88.
Prior to amendment, subsec. (d) read as follows:
"(d) Treaty obligations.
"No provision of this title shall apply in any case where its application would be contrary to any treaty obligation of the United States in effect on the date of enactment of this title."
In **1976**, P.L. 94-455, Sec. 1202(g), added subsec. (e), effective 1/1/77.

Subchapter C.— Provisions Affecting More than One Subtitle

Sec.
7871. Indian tribal governments treated as States for certain purposes.
7872. Treatment of loans with below-market interest rates.
7873. Income derived by Indians from exercise of fishing rights.
7874. Rules relating to expatriated entities and their foreign parents.

In **2004**, P.L. 108-357, Sec. 801(b), added item 7874.
In **1988**, P.L. 100-647, Sec. 3041(b), added item 7873.
In **1984**, P.L. 98-369, Sec. 172(b), added item 7872.
In **1983**, P.L. 97-473, Sec. 202(a), added subchapter C.

Sec. 7871. Indian tribal governments treated as states for certain purposes.

(a) General rule.

An Indian tribal government shall be treated as a State—

(1) for purposes of determining whether and in what amount any contribution or transfer to or for the use of such government (or a political subdivision thereof) is deductible under—

(A) section 170 (relating to income tax deduction for charitable, etc., contributions and gifts),

(B) sections 2055 and 2106(a)(2) (relating to estate tax deduction for transfers of public, charitable, and religious uses), or

(C) section 2522 (relating to gift tax deduction for charitable and similar gifts);

(2) subject to subsection (b), for purposes of any exemption from, credit or refund of, or payment with respect to, an excise tax imposed by—

(A) chapter 31 (relating to tax on special fuels),

(B) chapter 32 (relating to manufacturers excise taxes),

(C) subchapter B of chapter 33 (relating to communications excise tax), or

(D) subchapter D of chapter 36 (relating to tax on use of certain highway vehicles);

(3) for purposes of section 164 (relating to deduction for taxes);

(4) subject to subsection (c), for purposes of section 103 (relating to state and local bonds);

(5) for purposes of section 511(a)(2)(B) (relating to the taxation of colleges and universities which are agencies or instrumentalities of governments or their political subdivisions);

(6) for purposes of—

(A) section 105(e) (relating to accident and health plans),

(B) section 403(b)(1)(A)(ii) (relating to the taxation of contributions of certain employers for employee annuities), and

(C) section 454(b)(2) (relating to discount obligations); and

3,973

(7) for purposes of—
   (A) chapter 41 (relating to tax on excess expenditures to influence legislation), and
   (B) subchapter A of chapter 42 (relating to private foundations).

(b) Additional requirements for excise tax exemptions.
Paragraph (2) of subsection (a) shall apply with respect to any transaction only if, in addition to any other requirement of this title applicable to similar transactions involving a State or political subdivision thereof, the transaction involves the exercise of an essential governmental function of the Indian tribal government.

(c) Additional requirements for tax-exempt bonds.
   (1) In general. Subsection (a) of section 103 shall apply to any obligation (not described in paragraph (2)) issued by an Indian tribal government (or subdivision thereof) only if such obligation is part of an issue substantially all of the proceeds of which are to be used in the exercise of any essential governmental function.
   (2) No exemption for private activity bonds. Except as provided in paragraph (3), subsection (a) of section 103 shall not apply to any private activity bond (as defined in section 141(a)) issued by an Indian tribal government (or subdivision thereof).
   (3) Exception for certain private activity bonds.
      (A) In general. In the case of an obligation to which this paragraph applies—
         (i) paragraph (2) shall not apply,
         (ii) such obligation shall be treated for purposes of this title as a qualified small issue bond, and
         (iii) section 146 shall not apply.
      (B) Obligations to which paragraph applies. This paragraph shall apply to any obligation issued as part of an issue if—
         (i) 95 percent or more of the net proceeds of the issue are to be used for the acquisition, construction, reconstruction, or improvement of property which is of a character subject to the allowance for depreciation and which is part of a manufacturing facility (as defined in section 144(a)(12)(C)),
         (ii) such issue is issued by an Indian tribal government or a subdivision thereof,
         (iii) 95 percent or more of the net proceeds of the issue are to be used to finance property which—
            (I) is to be located on land which, throughout the 5-year period ending on the date of issuance of such issue, is part of the qualified Indian lands of the issuer, and
            (II) is to be owned and operated by such issuer,
         (iv) such obligation would not be a private activity bond without regard to subparagraph (C),
         (v) it is reasonably expected (at the time of issuance of the issue) that the employment requirement of subparagraph (D)(i) will be met with respect to the facility to be financed by the net proceeds of the issue, and
         (vi) no principal user of such facility will be a person (or group of persons) described in section 144(a)(6)(B).
      For purposes of clause (iii), section 150(a)(5) shall apply.
      (C) Private activity bond rules to apply. An obligation to which this paragraph applies (other than an obligation described in paragraph (1)) shall be treated for purposes of this title as a private activity bond.
      (D) Employment requirements.
         (i) In general. The employment requirements of this subparagraph are met with respect to a facility financed by the net proceeds of an issue if, as of the close of each calendar year in the testing period, the aggregate face amount of all outstanding tax-exempt private activity bonds issued to provide financing for the establishment which includes such facility is not more than 20 times greater than the aggregate wages (as defined by section 3121(a)) paid during the preceding calendar year to individuals (who are enrolled members of the Indian tribe of the issuer or the spouse of any such member) for services rendered at such establishment.
         (ii) Failure to meet requirements.
            (I) In general. If, as of the close of any calendar year in the testing period, the requirements of this subparagraph are not met with respect to an establishment, section 103 shall cease to apply to interest received or accrued (on all private activity bonds issued to provide financing for the establishment) after the close of such calendar year.
            (II) Exception. Subclause (I) shall not apply if the requirements of this subparagraph would be met if the aggregate face amount of all tax-exempt private activity bonds issued to provide financing for the establishment and outstanding at the close of the 90th day after the close of the calendar year were substituted in clause (i) for such bonds outstanding at the close of such calendar year.
         (iii) Testing period. For purposes of this subparagraph, the term "testing period" means, with respect to an issue, each calendar year which begins more than 2 years after the date of issuance of the issue (or, in the case of a refunding obligation, the date of issuance of the original issue).
      (E) Definitions. For purposes of this paragraph—
         (i) Qualified Indian lands. The term "qualified Indian lands" means land which is held in trust by the United States for the benefit of an Indian tribe.
         (ii) Indian tribe. The term "Indian tribe" means any Indian tribe, band, nation, or other organized group or community which is recognized as eligible for the special programs and services provided by the United States to Indians because of their status as Indians.
         (iii) Net proceeds. The term "net proceeds" has the meaning given such term by section 150(a)(3).

(d) Treatment of subdivisions of Indian tribal governments as political subdivisions.
For the purposes specified in subsection (a), a subdivision of an Indian tribal government shall be treated as a political subdivision of a State if (and only if) the Secretary determines (after consultation with the Secretary of the Interior) that such subdivision has been delegated the right to exercise one or more of the substantial governmental functions of the Indian tribal government.

(e) Essential governmental function.
For purposes of this section, the term "essential governmental function" shall not include any function which is not customarily performed by State and local governments with general taxing powers.

(f) Tribal economic development bonds.
   (1) Allocation of limitation.
      (A) In general. The Secretary shall allocate the national tribal economic development bond limitation among the Indian tribal governments in such manner as the Secretary, in consultation with the Secretary of the Interior, determines appropriate.

Miscellaneous provisions Code Sec. 7872(c)(1)(B)(i)

(B) National limitation. There is a national tribal economic development bond limitation of $2,000,000,000.

(2) Bonds treated as exempt from tax. In the case of a tribal economic development bond—

(A) notwithstanding subsection (c), such bond shall be treated for purposes of this title in the same manner as if such bond were issued by a State,

(B) the Indian tribal government issuing such bond and any instrumentality of such Indian tribal government shall be treated as a State for purposes of section 141, and

(C) section 146 shall not apply.

(3) Tribal economic development bond.

(A) In general. For purposes of this section, the term "tribal economic development bond" means any bond issued by an Indian tribal government—

(i) the interest on which would be exempt from tax under section 103 if issued by a State or local government, and

(ii) which is designated by the Indian tribal government as a tribal economic development bond for purposes of this subsection.

(B) Exceptions. Such term shall not include any bond issued as part of an issue if any portion of the proceeds of such issue are used to finance—

(i) any portion of a building in which class II or class III gaming (as defined in section 4 of the Indian Gaming Regulatory Act) is conducted or housed or any other property actually used in the conduct of such gaming, or

(ii) any facility located outside the Indian reservation (as defined in section 168(j)(6)).

(C) Limitation on amount of bonds designated. The maximum aggregate face amount of bonds which may be designated by any Indian tribal government under subparagraph (A) shall not exceed the amount of national tribal economic development bond limitation allocated to such government under paragraph (1).

In 2009, P.L. 111-5, Sec. 1402(a), added subsec. (f), effective for obligations issued after 2/17/2009.

—P.L. 111-5, Sec. 1402(b), of this Act provides:

"Study. The Secretary of the Treasury, or the Secretary's delegate, shall conduct a study of the effects of the amendment made by subsection (a). Not later than 1 year after the date of the enactment of this Act, the Secretary of the Treasury, or the Secretary's delegate, shall report to Congress on the results of the study conducted under this paragraph, including the Secretary's recommendations regarding such amendment."

In 1993, P.L. 103-66, Sec. 13222(d), deleted subpara. (a)(6)(B) and redesignated subparas. (a)(6)(C) and (D) as subparas. (a)(6)(B) and (C), effective for amounts paid or incurred after 12/31/93.

Prior to deletion, subpara. (a)(6)(B) read as follows:

"(B) section 162(e) (relating to appearances, etc., with respect to legislation)."

In 1987, P.L. 100-203, Sec. 10632(a), added subsec. (e) . . . Sec. 10632(b)(1), added para. (c)(3) . . . Sec. 10632(b)(2), substituted "Except as provided in paragraph (3), subsection (a)" for "Subsection (a)" in para. (c)(2), effective for obligations issued after 10/13/87.

In 1986, P.L. 99-514, Sec. 112(b)(4), deleted subpara. (a)(6)(A) and redesignated subparas. (a)(6)(B), (C), (D), (E), and (F) as (A), (B), (C), (D), and (E), effective for tax. yrs. begin. after 12/31/86.

Prior to deletion, subpara. (a)(6)(A) read as follows:

"(A) section 24(c)(4) (defining State for purposes of credit for contribution to candidates for public offices),"

—P.L. 99-514, Sec. 123(b)(3), deleted subpara. (a)(6)(B) (as amended by Sec. 112(b)(4) of this Act), and redesignated subparas. (a)(6)(C), (D), and (E) as (B), (C), and (D), respectively, effective for tax. yrs. begin. after 12/31/86, but only in the case of scholarships and fellowships granted after 8/16/86.

Prior to deletion, subpara. (a)(6)(B) read as follows:

"(B) section 117(b)(2)(A) (relating to scholarships and fellowship grants),"

—P.L. 99-514, Sec. 1301(j)(6), substituted "State and local bonds" for "interest on certain governmental obligations" in para. (a)(4) . . . Sec. 1301(j)(7), amended para. (c)(2), effective for bonds issued after 8/15/86. For transitional rules, see Secs. 1312-1318 of P.L. 99-514 at note following Code Sec. 103.

Prior to amendment, para. (c)(2) read as follows:

"(2) No exemption for certain private-activity bonds. Subsection (a) of section 103 shall not apply to any of the following issued by an Indian tribal government (or subdivision thereof):

"(A) An industrial development bond (as defined in section 103(b)(2)).

"(B) An obligation described in section 103(1)(1)(A) (relating to scholarship bonds).

"(C) A mortgage subsidy bond (as defined in paragraph (1) of section 103A(b) without regard to paragraph (2) thereof)."

—P.L. 99-514, Sec. 1899A(65), substituted "; and" for the period at the end of subpara. (a)(6)(F) (as designated before amendment by Secs. 112 and 123 of this Act, see above), effective 10/22/86.

In 1984, P.L. 98-369, Sec. 474(r)(41), substituted "section 24(c)(4)" for "section 41(c)(4)" in subpara. (a)(6)(A), effective for tax. yrs. begin. after 12/31/83, and for carrybacks from tax. yrs. begin. after 12/31/83.

—P.L. 98-369, Sec. 1065(b), deleted subparas. (a)(6)(B) and (C) and added subparas. (a)(6)(B) – (F), effective for tax. yrs. begin. after 12/31/84.

Prior to deletion, subparas. (a)(6)(B) and (C) read as follows:

"(B) section 117(b)(2)(A) (relating to scholarships and fellowship grants), and

"(C) section 403(b)(1)(A)(ii) (relating to the taxation of contributions of certain employers for employee annuities); and"

In 1983, P.L. 98-21, Sec. 122(c)(6), deleted subpara. (a)(6)(A) and redesignated subparas. (a)(6)(B), (C) and (D) as subparas. (a)(6)(A), (B) and (C), effective for tax. yrs. begin. after 12/31/83.

Prior to deletion, subpara. (a)(6)(A) read as follows:

"(A) section 37(e)(9)(A) (relating to certain public retirement systems),"

—P.L. 97-473, Sec. 202(a), added Code Sec. 7871.

Sec. 7872. Treatment of loans with below-market interest rates.

(a) Treatment of gift loans and demand loans.

(1) In general. For purposes of this title, in the case of any below-market loan to which this section applies and which is a gift loan or a demand loan, the forgone interest shall be treated as—

(A) transferred from the lender to the borrower, and

(B) retransferred by the borrower to the lender as interest.

(2) Time when transfers made. Except as otherwise provided in regulations prescribed by the Secretary, any forgone interest attributable to periods during any calendar year shall be treated as transferred (and retransferred) under paragraph (1) on the last day of such calendar year.

(b) Treatment of other below-market loans.

(1) In general. For purposes of this title, in the case of any below-market loan to which this section applies and to which subsection (a)(1) does not apply, the lender shall be treated as having transferred on the date the loan was made (or, if later, on the first day on which this section applies to such loan), and the borrower shall be treated as having received on such date, cash in an amount equal to the excess of—

(A) the amount loaned, over

(B) the present value of all payments which are required to be made under the terms of the loan.

(2) Obligation treated as having original issue discount. For purposes of this title

(A) In general. Any below-market loan to which paragraph (1) applies shall be treated as having original issue discount in an amount equal to the excess described in paragraph (1).

(B) Amount in addition to other original issue discount. Any original issue discount which a loan is treated as having by reason of subparagraph (A) shall be in addition to any other original issue discount on such loan (determined without regard to subparagraph (A)).

(c) Below-market loans to which section applies.

(1) In general. Except as otherwise provided in this subsection, and subsection (g), this section shall apply to—

(A) Gifts. Any below-market loan which is a gift loan.

(B) Compensation-related loans. Any below-market loan directly or indirectly between—

(i) an employer and an employee, or

3,975

(ii) an independent contractor and a person for whom such independent contractor provides services.
(C) **Corporation-shareholder loans.** Any below-market loan directly or indirectly between a corporation and any shareholder of such corporation.
(D) **Tax avoidance loans.** Any below-market loan 1 of the principal purposes of the interest arrangements of which is the avoidance of any Federal tax.
(E) **Other below-market loans.** To the extent provided in regulations, any below-market loan which is not described in subparagraph (A), (B), (C), or (F) if the interest arrangements of such loan have a significant effect on any Federal tax liability of the lender or the borrower.
(F) **Loans to qualified continuing care facilities.** Any loan to any qualified continuing care facility pursuant to a continuing care contract.

(2) $10,000 de minimis exception for gift loans between individuals.
(A) **In general.** In the case of any gift loan directly between individuals, this section shall not apply to any day on which the aggregate outstanding amount of loans between such individuals does not exceed $10,000.
(B) **De minimis exception not to apply to loans attributable to acquisition of income-producing assets.** Subparagraph (A) shall not apply to any gift loan directly attributable to the purchase or carrying of income-producing assets.
(C) **Cross reference.** For limitation on amount treated as interest where loans do not exceed $100,000, see subsection (d)(1).

(3) $10,000 de minimis exception for compensation-related and corporate-shareholder loans.
(A) **In general.** In the case of any loan described in subparagraph (B) or (C) of paragraph (1), this section shall not apply to any day on which the aggregate outstanding amount of loans between the borrower and lender does not exceed $10,000.
(B) **Exception not to apply where 1 of principal purposes is tax avoidance.** Subparagraph (A) shall not apply to any loan the interest arrangements of which have as 1 of their principal purposes the avoidance of any Federal tax.

(d) Special rules for gift loans.

(1) Limitation on interest accrual for purposes of income taxes where loans do not exceed $100,000.
(A) **In general.** For purposes of subtitle A, in the case of a gift loan directly between individuals, the amount treated as retransferred by the borrower to the lender as of the close of any year shall not exceed the borrower's net investment income for such year.
(B) **Limitation not to apply where 1 of principal purposes is tax avoidance.** Subparagraph (A) shall not apply to any loan the interest arrangements of which have as 1 of their principal purposes the avoidance of any Federal tax.
(C) **Special rule where more than 1 gift loan outstanding.** For purposes of subparagraph (A), in any case in which a borrower has outstanding more than 1 gift loan, the net investment income of such borrower shall be allocated among such loans in proportion to the respective amounts which would be treated as retransferred by the borrower without regard to this paragraph.
(D) **Limitation not to apply where aggregate amount of loans exceed $100,000.** This paragraph shall not apply to any loan made by a lender to a borrower for any day on which the aggregate outstanding amount of loans between the borrower and lender exceeds $100,000.

(E) **Net investment income.** For purposes of this paragraph—
(i) **In general.** The term "net investment income" has the meaning given such term by section 163(d)(4).
(ii) **De minimis rule.** If the net investment income of any borrower for any year does not exceed $1,000, the net investment income of such borrower for such year shall be treated as zero.
(iii) **Additional amounts treated as interest.** In determining the net investment income of a person for any year, any amount which would be included in the gross income of such person for such year by reason of section 1272 if such section applied to all deferred payment obligations shall be treated as interest received by such person for such year.
(iv) **Deferred payment obligations.** The term "deferred payment obligation" includes any market discount bond, short-term obligation, United States savings bond, annuity, or similar obligation.

(2) Special rule for gift tax. In the case of any gift loan which is a term loan, subsection (b)(1) (and not subsection (a)) shall apply for purposes of chapter 12.

(e) Definitions of below-market loan and forgone interest.
For purposes of this section—
(1) Below-market loan. The term "below-market loan" means any loan if—
(A) in the case of a demand loan, interest is payable on the loan at a rate less than the applicable Federal rate, or
(B) in the case of a term loan, the amount loaned exceeds the present value of all payments due under the loan.

(2) Forgone interest. The term "forgone interest" means, with respect to any period during which the loan is outstanding, the excess of—
(A) the amount of interest which would have been payable on the loan for the period if interest accrued on the loan at the applicable Federal rate and were payable annually on the day referred to in subsection (a)(2), over
(B) any interest payable on the loan properly allocable to such period.

(f) Other definitions and special rules.
For purposes of this section—
(1) Present value. The present value of any payment shall be determined in the manner provided by regulations prescribed by the Secretary—
(A) as of the date of the loan, and
(B) by using a discount rate equal to the applicable Federal rate.

(2) Applicable federal rate.
(A) **Term loans.** In the case of any term loan, the applicable Federal rate shall be the applicable Federal rate in effect under section 1274(d) (as of the day on which the loan was made), compounded semiannually.
(B) **Demand loans.** In the case of a demand loan, the applicable Federal rate shall be the Federal short-term rate in effect under section 1274(d) for the period for which the amount of forgone interest is being determined, compounded semiannually.

(3) Gift loan. The term "gift loan" means any below-market loan where the forgoing of interest is in the nature of a gift.

(4) Amount loaned. The term "amount loaned" means the amount received by the borrower.

Miscellaneous provisions — Code Sec. 7872(h)(2)(B)

(5) Demand loan. The term "demand loan" means any loan which is payable in full at any time on the demand of the lender. Such term also includes (for purposes other than determining the applicable Federal rate under paragraph (2)) any loan if the benefits of the interest arrangements of such loan are not transferable and are conditioned on the future performance of substantial services by an individual. To the extent provided in regulations, such term also includes any loan with an indefinite maturity.

(6) Term loan. The term "term loan" means any loan which is not a demand loan.

(7) Husband and wife treated as 1 person. A husband and wife shall be treated as 1 person.

(8) Loans to which section 483, 643(i), or 1274 applies. This section shall not apply to any loan to which section 483, 643(i), or 1274 applies.

(9) No withholding. No amount shall be withheld under chapter 24 with respect to—

(A) any amount treated as transferred or retransferred under subsection (a), and

(B) any amount treated as received under subsection (b).

(10) Special rule for term loans. If this section applies to any term loan on any day, this section shall continue to apply to such loan notwithstanding paragraphs (2) and (3) of subsection (c). In the case of a gift loan, the preceding sentence shall only apply for purposes of chapter 12.

(11) Time for determining rate applicable to employee relocation loans.

(A) In general. In the case of any term loan made by an employer to an employee the proceeds of which are used by the employee to purchase a principal residence (within the meaning of section 121), the determination of the applicable Federal rate shall be made as of the date the written contract to purchase such residence was entered into.

(B) Paragraph only to apply to cases to which section 217 applies. Subparagraph (A) shall only apply to the purchase of a principal residence in connection with the commencement of work by an employee or a change in the principal place of work of an employee to which section 217 applies.

(g) Exception for certain loans to qualified continuing care facilities.

(1) In general. This section shall not apply for any calendar year to any below-market loan made by a lender to a qualified continuing care facility pursuant to a continuing care contract if the lender (or the lender's spouse) attains age 65 before the close of such year.

(2) $90,000 limit. Paragraph (1) shall apply only to the extent that the aggregate outstanding amount of any loan to which such paragraph applies (determined without regard to this paragraph), when added to the aggregate outstanding amount of all other previous loans between the lender (or the lender's spouse) and any qualified continuing care facility to which paragraph (1) applies, does not exceed $90,000.

(3) Continuing care contract. For purposes of this section, the term "continuing care contract" means a written contract between an individual and a qualified continuing care facility under which—

(A) the individual or individual's spouse may use a qualified continuing care facility for their life or lives,

(B) the individual or individual's spouse—

(i) will first—

(I) reside in a separate, independent living unit with additional facilities outside such unit for the providing of meals and other personal care, and

(II) not require long-term nursing care, and

(ii) then will be provided long-term and skilled nursing care as the health of such individual or individual's spouse requires, and

(C) no additional substantial payment is required if such individual or individual's spouse requires increased personal care services or long-term and skilled nursing care.

(4) Qualified continuing care facility.

(A) In general. For purposes of this section, the term "qualified continuing care facility" means 1 or more facilities—

(i) which are designed to provide services under continuing care contracts, and

(ii) substantially all of the residents of which are covered by continuing care contracts.

(B) Substantially all facilities must be owned or operated by borrower. A facility shall not be treated as a qualified continuing care facility unless substantially all facilities which are used to provide services which are required to be provided under a continuing care contract are owned or operated by the borrower.

(C) Nursing homes excluded. The term "qualified continuing care facility" shall not include any facility which is of a type which is traditionally considered a nursing home.

(5) Adjustment of limit for inflation.

(A) In general. In the case of any loan made during any calendar year after 1986 to which paragraph (1) applies, the dollar amount in paragraph (2) shall be increased by the inflation adjustment for such calendar year. Any increase under the preceding sentence shall be rounded to the nearest multiple of $100 (or, if such increase is a multiple of $50, such increase shall be increased to the nearest multiple of $100).

(B) Inflation adjustment. For purposes of subparagraph (A), the inflation adjustment for any calendar year is the percentage (if any) by which—

(i) the CPI for the preceding calendar year exceeds

(ii) the CPI for calendar year 1985.

For purposes of the preceding sentence, the CPI for any calendar year is the average of the Consumer Price Index as of the close of the 12-month period ending on September 30 of such calendar year.

(6) Suspension of application. Paragraph (1) shall not apply for any calendar year to which subsection (h) applies.

(h) Exception for loans to qualified continuing care facilities.

(1) In general. This section shall not apply for any calendar year to any below-market loan owed by a facility which on the last day of such year is a qualified continuing care facility, if such loan was made pursuant to a continuing care contract and if the lender (or the lender's spouse) attains age 62 before the close of such year.

(2) Continuing care contract. For purposes of this section, the term "continuing care contract" means a written contract between an individual and a qualified continuing care facility under which—

(A) the individual or individual's spouse may use a qualified continuing care facility for their life or lives,

(B) the individual or individual's spouse will be provided with housing, as appropriate for the health of such individual or individual's spouse—

(i) in an independent living unit (which has additional available facilities outside such unit for the provision of meals and other personal care), and

(ii) in an assisted living facility or a nursing facility, as is available in the continuing care facility, and

(C) the individual or individual's spouse will be provided assisted living or nursing care as the health of such individual or individual's spouse requires, and as is available in the continuing care facility.

The Secretary shall issue guidance which limits such term to contracts which provide only facilities, care, and services described in this paragraph.

(3) Qualified continuing care facility.

(A) In general. For purposes of this section, the term "qualified continuing care facility" means 1 or more facilities—

(i) which are designed to provide services under continuing care contracts,

(ii) which include an independent living unit, plus an assisted living or nursing facility, or both, and

(iii) substantially all of the independent living unit residents of which are covered by continuing care contracts.

(B) Nursing homes excluded. The term "qualified continuing care facility" shall not include any facility which is of a type which is traditionally considered a nursing home.

(4) Repealed.

(i) Regulations.

(1) In general. The Secretary shall prescribe such regulations as may be necessary or appropriate to carry out the purposes of this section, including—

(A) regulations providing that where, by reason of varying rates of interest, conditional interest payments, waivers of interest, disposition of the lender's or borrower's interest in the loan, or other circumstances, the provisions of this section do not carry out the purposes of this section, adjustments to the provisions of this section will be made to the extent necessary to carry out the purposes of this section,

(B) regulations for the purpose of assuring that the positions of the borrower and lender are consistent as to the application (or nonapplication) of this section, and

(C) regulations exempting from the application of this section any class of transactions the interest arrangements of which have no significant effect on any Federal tax liability of the lender or the borrower.

(2) Estate tax coordination. Under regulations prescribed by the Secretary, any loan which is made with donative intent and which is a term loan shall be taken into account for purposes of chapter 11 in a manner consistent with the provisions of subsection (b).

In **2006**, P.L. 109-432, Sec. 425(a), deleted para. (h)(4), effective for calendar yrs. begin. after 12/31/2005, for loans made before, on, or after 12/31/2005.

Prior to deletion, para. (h)(4) read as follows:

"(4) Termination.

"This subsection shall not apply to any calendar year after 2010."

—P.L. 109-222, Sec. 209(a), redesignated subsec. (h) as (i) and added subsec. (h) . . . Sec. 209(b)(1), added para. (g)(6), effective for calendar yrs. begin. after 12/31/2005, for loans made before, on, or after 12/31/2005.

In **2000**, P.L. 106-554, Sec. 1(a)(7), [which enacted into law Sec. 319(30) of P.L. 106-554] substituted "forgoing" for "foregoing" in para. (f)(3), effective 12/21/2000.

In **1998**, P.L. 105-206, Sec. 6005(e)(3), added "on or" before "before" each place it appeared in Sec. 312(d)(2) [sic (e)(2)] of P.L. 105-34, see below.

—P.L. 105-206, Sec. 6023(30), substituted "forgone" for "foregone" in subpara. (f)(2)(B), effective 7/22/98.

In **1997**, P.L. 105-34, Sec. 312(d)(1), substituted "section 121" for "section 1034" in subpara. (f)(11)(A), effective for sales and exchanges after 5/6/97, except as provided by Secs. 312(d)(2)-(4) [sic (e)(2)-(4)] of this Act, [as amended by Sec. 6005(e)(3) of 105-206, see above] which read as follows:

"(2) Sales on or before date of enactment. At the election of the taxpayer, the amendments made by this section shall not apply to any sale or exchange on or before the date of the enactment of this Act.

"(3) Certain sales within 2 years after date of enactment. Section 121 of the Internal Revenue Code of 1986 (as amended by this section) shall be applied without regard to subsection (c)(2)(B) thereof in the case of any sale or exchange of property during the 2-year period beginning on the date of the enactment of this Act if the taxpayer held such property on the date of the enactment of this Act and fails to meet the ownership and use requirements of subsection (a) thereof with respect to such property.

"(4) Binding contracts. At the election of the taxpayer, the amendments made by this section shall not apply to a sale or exchange after the date of the enactment of this Act, if—

"(A) such sale or exchange is pursuant to a contract which was binding on such date, or

"(B) without regard to such amendments, gain would not be recognized under section 1034 of the Internal Revenue Code of 1986 (as in effect on the day before the date of the enactment of this Act) on such sale or exchange by reason of a new residence acquired on or before such date or with respect to the acquisition of which by the taxpayer a binding contract was in effect on such date.

This paragraph shall not apply to any sale or exchange by an individual if the treatment provided by section 877(a)(1) of the Internal Revenue Code of 1986 applies to such individual."

In **1996**, P.L. 104-188, Sec. 1602(b)(7), deleted para. (f)(12), effective for loans made after 8/20/96, except as provided in Secs. 1602(c)(2) and (3) of this Act which read as follows:

"(2) Refinancings. The amendments made by this section shall not apply to loans made after the date of the enactment of this Act to refinance securities acquisition loans (determined without regard to section 133(b)(1)(B) of the Internal Revenue Code of 1986, as in effect on the day before the date of the enactment of this Act) made on or before such date or to refinance loans described in this paragraph if—

"(A) the refinancing loans meet the requirements of section 133 of such Code (as so in effect),

"(B) immediately after the refinancing the principal amount of the loan resulting from the refinancing does not exceed the principal amount of the refinanced loan (immediately before the refinancing), and

"(C) the term of such refinancing loan does not extend beyond the last day of the term of the original securities acquisition loan.

For purposes of this paragraph, the term 'securities acquisition loan' includes a loan from a corporation to an employee stock ownership plan described in section 133(b)(3) of such Code (as so in effect).

"(3) Exception. Any loan made pursuant to a binding written contract in effect before June 10, 1996, and at all times thereafter before such loan is made, shall be treated for purposes of paragraphs (1) and (2) as a loan made on or before the date of the enactment of this Act."

Prior to deletion, para. (f)(12) read as follows:

"(12) Special rule for certain employer security loans.

"This section shall not apply to any loan between a corporation (or any member of the controlled group of corporations which includes such corporation) and an employee stock ownership plan described in section 4975(e)(7) to the extent that the interest rate on such loan is equal to the interest rate paid on a related securities acquisition loan (as described in section 133(b)) to such corporation. "

—P.L. 104-188, Sec. 1704(t)(58)(A), substituted "forgone" for "foregone" each place it appeared in subsec. (a) and para. (e)(2) . . . Sec. 1704(t)(58)(B), substituted "Forgone" for "Foregone" in the heading of subsec. (e) and para. (e)(2), effective 8/20/96.

—P.L. 104-188, Sec. 1906(c)(2), added ", 643(i)," before "or 1274" each place it appeared in para. (f)(8), effective for loans of cash or marketable securities made after 9/19/95.

In **1989**, P.L. 101-179, Sec. 307(a)(1), amended Sec. 1812(b)(5) of P.L. 99-514 by adding "or Poland" after "Israel", see below . . . Sec. 307(a)(2), amended Sec. 1812(b)(5) of P.L. 99-514 by adding "or Polish" after "Israel" in the heading, see below, effective for obligations issued after 11/28/89.

In **1988**, P.L. 100-647, Sec. 1005(c)(15), substituted "section 163(d)(4)" for "section 163(d)(3)" in subpara. (d)(1)(E), effective 12/31/86. This amendment cannot be made to this Code Sec. as it currently exists. Sec. 1005(c)(13) of this Act, provides:

"(13) For purposes of applying the amendments made by this subsection [1005(c)] and the amendments made by section 10102 of the Revenue Act of 1987, the provisions of this subsection shall be treated as having been enacted immediately before the enactment of the Revenue Act of 1987.".

—P.L. 100-647, Sec. 1018(u)(48), redesignated para. (f)(11) [sic (12)] as para. (f)(12), effective for term loans made after 6/6/84, and demand loans outstanding after 6/6/84.

In **1986**, P.L. 99-514, Sec. 511(d)(1), [sic (c)(1)], substituted "section 163(d)(4)" for "section 163(d)(3)" in clause (d)(1)(E)(i), effective for tax. yrs. begin. after 12/31/86.

—P.L. 99-514, Sec. 1812(b)(2), amended para. (f)(9) . . . Sec. 1812(b)(3), amended para. (f)(5) . . . Sec. 1812(b)(4), added ", compounded semiannually" before the period at the end of subpara. (f)(2)(B) . . . Sec. 1854(c)(2)(B), added para. (f)(11) [sic (f)(12)], effective for term loans made after 6/6/84, and demand loans outstanding after 6/6/84. Sec. 1812(b)(5) [as amended by Sec. 307(a)(1) of P.L. 101-179, see above] of this Act provides:

Miscellaneous provisions

Code Sec. 7873(b)(3)(B)

"(5) Certain Israel or Polish bonds not subject to rules relating to below-market loans.—Section 7872 of the Internal Revenue Code of 1954 (relating to treatment of loans with below-market interest rates) shall not apply to any obligation issued by Israel or Poland if—

"(A) the obligation is payable in United States dollars, and

"(B) the obligation bears interest at an annual rate of not less than 4 percent."

For exceptions ad special rules, see P.L. 98-369, Secs. 172(c)(2) through (c)(6), reproduced below.

Prior to amendment, para. (f)(9) read as follows:

"(9) No withholding. No amount shall be withheld under chapter 24 with respect to any amount treated as transferred or retransferred under subsection (a)."

Prior to amendment, para. (f)(5) read as follows:

"(5) Demand loan. The term 'demand loan' means any loan which is payable in full at any time on the demand of the lender. Such term also includes (for purposes other than determining the applicable Federal rate under paragraph (2)) any loan which is not transferable and the benefits of the interest arrangements of which is conditioned on the future performance of substantial services by an individual."

In 1985, P.L. 99-121, Sec. 201(a), redesignated subsec. (g) as (h) and added subsec. (g) . . . Sec. 201(b), added subpara. (c)(1)(F) . . . Sec. 201(c)(1), added "and subsection (g)" after "subsection" in para. (c)(1) . . . Sec. 201(c)(2), substituted "(C), or (F)" for "or (C)" in subpara. (c)(1)(E), effective for loans made after 10/11/85, except as provided in Sec. 204(a)(2) of this Act which reads as follows:

"(2) Section 7872 not to apply to certain loans.—Section 7872 of the Internal Revenue Code of 1954 shall not apply to loans made on or before the date of the enactment of this Act to any qualified continuing care facility pursuant to a continuing care contract. For purposes of this paragraph, the terms 'qualified continuing care facility' and 'continuing care contract' have the meanings given such terms by section 7872(g) of such Code (as added by section 201)."

—P.L. 99-121, Sec. 202, added para. (f)(11), effective for contracts entered into after 6/30/85, in tax. yrs. end. after 6/30/85.

—P.L. 99-121, Sec. 203, contains provisions for non-loan payments to certain residential housing facilities for the elderly, effective for term loans made after 6/6/84 and demand loans outstanding after 6/6/84 (for exceptions and special rules see Secs. 172(c)(2)-(6) of P.L. 98-369, reproduced below). Sec. 203 of this Act provides:

"SEC. 203. Section 7872 of the Internal Revenue Code shall not apply to non-loan payments to certain residential housing facilities for the elderly.

"(a) General rule. For purposes of section 7872 of the Internal Revenue Code of 1954, payments made to a specified independent living facility for the elderly by a payor who is an individual at least 65 years old shall not be treated as loans provided—

"(1) the independent living facility is designed and operated to meet some substantial combination of the health, physical, emotional, recreational, social, religious and similar needs of persons over the age of 65;

"(2) in exchange for the payment, the payor obtains the right to occupy (or equivalent contractual right) independent living quarters located in the independent living facility;

"(3) the amount of the payment is equal to the fair market value of the right to occupy the independent living quarters;

"(4) upon leaving the independent living facility, the payor is entitled to receive a payment equal to at least 50 percent of the fair market value at that time of the right to occupy the independent living quarters, the timing of which payment may be contingent on the time when the independent living facility is able to locate a new occupant for such quarters; and

"(5) the excess, if any, of the fair market value of the independent living quarters at the time the payor leaves such quarters (less a reasonable amount to cover costs) over the amount paid to the payor is used by an organization described in section 501(c)(3) of such Code to provide housing and related services for needy elderly persons.

"(b) Specified independent living facility for the elderly. For purposes of this section—

"(1) In general.—The term 'specified independent living facility for the elderly' means—

"(A) the Our Lady of Life Apartments owned by a Missouri not-for-profit corporation with the same name,

"(B) the Laclede Oakes Manor owned by the Lutheran Health Care Association of St. Louis, Missouri, and

"(C) the Luther Center Northeast owned by the Lutheran Altenheim Society of Missouri.

"(2) Requirements.—A facility shall not be considered to be a specified independent living facility for the elderly—

"(A) if it is located at any site other than the site which it occupied (or was in the process of occupying through construction) on the date of the enactment of this Act, or

"(B) if its ownership is transferred after such date of enactment to a person other than an organization described in section 501(c)(3) of the Internal Revenue Code of 1954."

In 1984, P.L. 98-369, Sec. 172(a), added Code Sec. 7872, effective for term loans made after 6/6/84 and demand loans outstanding after 6/6/84. For exceptions and special rules, Secs. 172(c)(2) through (c)(6) of the Act provide as follows:

"(2) Exception for demand loans outstanding on June 6, 1984, and repaid within 60 days after date of enactment.—The amendments made by this section shall not apply to any demand loan which—

"(A) was outstanding on June 6, 1984, and

"(B) was repaid before the date 60 days after the date of the enactment of this Act.

"(3) Exception for certain existing loans to continuing care facilities.—Nothing in this subsection shall be construed to apply the amendments made by this section to any loan made before June 6, 1984, to a continuing care facility by a resident of such facility which is contingent on continued residence at such facility.

"(4) Applicable federal rate for periods before January 1, 1985.—For periods before January 1, 1985, the applicable Federal rate under paragraph (2) of section 7872(f) of the Internal Revenue Code of 1954, as added by this section, shall be 10 percent, compounded semiannually.

"(5) Treatment of renegotiations, etc.—For purposes of this subsection, any loan renegotiated, extended, or revised after June 6, 1984, shall be treated as a loan made after such date.

"(6) Definition of term and demand loans.—For purposes of this subsection, the terms 'demand loan' and 'term loan' have the respective meanings given such terms by paragraphs (5) and (6) of section 7872(f) of the Internal Revenue Code of 1954, as added by this section, but the second sentence of such paragraph (5) shall not apply."

Sec. 7873. Income derived by Indians from exercise of fishing rights.

(a) In general.

(1) Income and self-employment taxes. No tax shall be imposed by subtitle A on income derived—

(A) by a member of an Indian tribe directly or through a qualified Indian entity, or

(B) by a qualified Indian entity,

from a fishing rights-related activity of such tribe.

(2) Employment taxes. No tax shall be imposed by subtitle C on remuneration paid for services performed in a fishing rights-related activity of an Indian tribe by a member of such tribe for another member of such tribe or for a qualified Indian entity.

(b) Definitions.

For purposes of this section—

(1) Fishing rights-related activity. The term "fishing rights-related activity" means, with respect to an Indian tribe, any activity directly related to harvesting, processing, or transporting fish harvested in the exercise of a recognized fishing right of such tribe or to selling such fish but only if substantially all of such harvesting was performed by members of such tribe.

(2) Recognized fishing rights. The term "recognized fishing rights" means, with respect to an Indian tribe, fishing rights secured as of March 17, 1988, by a treaty between such tribe and the United States or by an Executive order or an Act of Congress.

(3) Qualified Indian entity.

(A) In general. The term "qualified Indian entity" means, with respect to an Indian tribe, any entity if—

(i) such entity is engaged in a fishing rights-related activity of such tribe,

(ii) all of the equity interests in the entity are owned by qualified Indian tribes, members of such tribes, or their spouses,

(iii) except as provided in regulations, in the case of an entity which engages to any extent in any substantial processing or transporting of fish, 90 percent or more of the annual gross receipts of the entity is derived from fishing rights-related activities of one or more qualified Indian tribes each of which owns at least 10 percent of the equity interests in the entity, and

(iv) substantially all of the management functions of the entity are performed by members of qualified Indian tribes.

For purposes of clause (iii), equity interests owned by a member (or the spouse of a member) of a qualified Indian tribe shall be treated as owned by the tribe.

(B) Qualified indian tribe. For purposes of subparagraph (A), an Indian tribe is a qualified Indian tribe with respect to an entity if such entity is engaged in a fishing rights-related activity of such tribe.

(c) Special rules.
(1) Distributions from qualified indian entity. For purposes of this section, any distribution with respect to an equity interest in a qualified Indian entity of an Indian tribe to a member of such tribe shall be treated as derived by such member from a fishing rights-related activity of such tribe to the extent such distribution is attributable to income derived by such entity from a fishing rights-related activity of such tribe.
(2) De minimis unrelated amounts may be excluded. If, but for this paragraph, all but a de minimis amount—
(A) derived by a qualified Indian tribal entity, or by an individual through such an entity, is entitled to the benefits of paragraph (1) of subsection (a), or
(B) paid to an individual for services is entitled to the benefits of paragraph (2) of subsection (a),
then the entire amount shall be entitled to the benefits of such paragraph.

In 1988, P.L. 100-647, Sec. 3041(a), added Code Sec. 7873, effective for all periods beginning before, on, or after 11/10/88. Sec. 3044(b) of this Act provides: "(b) No Inference Created. Nothing in the amendments made by this subtitle [Subtitle E] shall create any inference as to the existence or nonexistence or scope of any exemption from tax for income derived from fishing rights secured as of March 17, 1988, by any treaty, law, or Executive Order."

Sec. 7874. Rules relating to expatriated entities and their foreign parents.
(a) Tax on inversion gain of expatriated entities.
(1) In general. The taxable income of an expatriated entity for any taxable year which includes any portion of the applicable period shall in no event be less than the inversion gain of the entity for the taxable year.
(2) Expatriated entity. For purposes of this subsection—
(A) In general. The term "expatriated entity" means—
(i) the domestic corporation or partnership referred to in subparagraph (B)(i) with respect to which a foreign corporation is a surrogate foreign corporation, and
(ii) any United States person who is related (within the meaning of section 267(b) or 707(b)(1)) to a domestic corporation or partnership described in clause (i).
(B) Surrogate foreign corporation. A foreign corporation shall be treated as a surrogate foreign corporation if, pursuant to a plan (or a series of related transactions)—
(i) the entity completes after March 4, 2003, the direct or indirect acquisition of substantially all of the properties held directly or indirectly by a domestic corporation or substantially all of the properties constituting a trade or business of a domestic partnership,
(ii) after the acquisition at least 60 percent of the stock (by vote or value) of the entity is held—
(I) in the case of an acquisition with respect to a domestic corporation, by former shareholders of the domestic corporation by reason of holding stock in the domestic corporation, or
(II) in the case of an acquisition with respect to a domestic partnership, by former partners of the domestic partnership by reason of holding a capital or profits interest in the domestic partnership, and
(iii) after the acquisition the expanded affiliated group which includes the entity does not have substantial business activities in the foreign country in which, or under the law of which, the entity is created or organized, when compared to the total business activities of such expanded affiliated group.

An entity otherwise described in clause (i) with respect to any domestic corporation or partnership trade or business shall be treated as not so described if, on or before March 4, 2003, such entity acquired directly or indirectly more than half of the properties held directly or indirectly by such corporation or more than half of the properties constituting such partnership trade or business, as the case may be.
(3) Coordination with subsection (b). A corporation which is treated as a domestic corporation under subsection (b) shall not be treated as a surrogate foreign corporation for purposes of paragraph (2)(A).
(b) Inverted corporations treated as domestic corporations.
Notwithstanding section 7701(a)(4), a foreign corporation shall be treated for purposes of this title as a domestic corporation if such corporation would be a surrogate foreign corporation if subsection (a)(2) were applied by substituting "80 percent" for "60 percent".
(c) Definitions and special rules.
(1) Expanded affiliated group. The term "expanded affiliated group" means an affiliated group as defined in section 1504(a) but without regard to section 1504(b)(3), except that section 1504(a) shall be applied by substituting "more than 50 percent" for "at least 80 percent" each place it appears.
(2) Certain stock disregarded. There shall not be taken into account in determining ownership under subsection (a)(2)(B)(ii)—
(A) stock held by members of the expanded affiliated group which includes the foreign corporation, or
(B) stock of such foreign corporation which is sold in a public offering related to the acquisition described in subsection (a)(2)(B)(i).
(3) Plan deemed in certain cases. If a foreign corporation acquires directly or indirectly substantially all of the properties of a domestic corporation or partnership during the 4-year period beginning on the date which is 2 years before the ownership requirements of subsection (a)(2)(B)(ii) are met, such actions shall be treated as pursuant to a plan.
(4) Certain transfers disregarded. The transfer of properties or liabilities (including by contribution or distribution) shall be disregarded if such transfers are part of a plan a principal purpose of which is to avoid the purposes of this section.
(5) Special rule for related partnerships. For purposes of applying subsection (a)(2)(B)(ii) to the acquisition of a trade or business of a domestic partnership, except as provided in regulations, all partnerships which are under common control (within the meaning of section 482) shall be treated as 1 partnership.
(6) Regulations. The Secretary shall prescribe such regulations as may be appropriate to determine whether a corporation is a surrogate foreign corporation, including regulations—
(A) to treat warrants, options, contracts to acquire stock, convertible debt interests, and other similar interests as stock, and
(B) to treat stock as not stock.
(d) Other definitions.
For purposes of this section—
(1) Applicable period. The term "applicable period" means the period—
(A) beginning on the first date properties are acquired as part of the acquisition described in subsection (a)(2)(B)(i), and

(B) ending on the date which is 10 years after the last date properties are acquired as part of such acquisition.

(2) **Inversion gain.** The term "inversion gain" means the income or gain recognized by reason of the transfer during the applicable period of stock or other properties by an expatriated entity, and any income received or accrued during the applicable period by reason of a license of any property by an expatriated entity—

(A) as part of the acquisition described in subsection (a)(2)(B)(i), or

(B) after such acquisition if the transfer or license is to a foreign related person.

Subparagraph (B) shall not apply to property described in section 1221(a)(1) in the hands of the expatriated entity.

(3) **Foreign related person.** The term "foreign related person" means, with respect to any expatriated entity, a foreign person which—

(A) is related (within the meaning of section 267(b) or 707(b)(1)) to such entity, or

(B) is under the same common control (within the meaning of section 482) as such entity.

(e) Special rules.

(1) **Credits not allowed against tax on inversion gain.** Credits (other than the credit allowed by section 901) shall be allowed against the tax imposed by this chapter on an expatriated entity for any taxable year described in subsection (a) only to the extent such tax exceeds the product of—

(A) the amount of the inversion gain for the taxable year, and

(B) the highest rate of tax specified in section 11(b)(1).

For purposes of determining the credit allowed by section 901, inversion gain shall be treated as from sources within the United States.

(2) **Special rules for partnerships.** In the case of an expatriated entity which is a partnership—

(A) subsection (a)(1) shall apply at the partner rather than the partnership level,

(B) the inversion gain of any partner for any taxable year shall be equal to the sum of—

(i) the partner's distributive share of inversion gain of the partnership for such taxable year, plus

(ii) gain recognized for the taxable year by the partner by reason of the transfer during the applicable period of any partnership interest of the partner in such partnership to the surrogate foreign corporation, and

(C) the highest rate of tax specified in the rate schedule applicable to the partner under this chapter shall be substituted for the rate of tax referred to in paragraph (1).

(3) **Coordination with section 172 and minimum tax.** Rules similar to the rules of paragraphs (3) and (4) of section 860E(a) shall apply for purposes of subsection (a).

(4) **Statute of limitations.**

(A) In general. The statutory period for the assessment of any deficiency attributable to the inversion gain of any taxpayer for any pre-inversion year shall not expire before the expiration of 3 years from the date the Secretary is notified by the taxpayer (in such manner as the Secretary may prescribe) of the acquisition described in subsection (a)(2)(B)(i) to which such gain relates and such deficiency may be assessed before the expiration of such 3-year period notwithstanding the provisions of any other law or rule of law which would otherwise prevent such assessment.

(B) Pre-inversion year. For purposes of subparagraph (A), the term "pre-inversion year" means any taxable year if—

(i) any portion of the applicable period is included in such taxable year, and

(ii) such year ends before the taxable year in which the acquisition described in subsection (a)(2)(B)(i) is completed.

(f) Special rule for treaties.

Nothing in section 894 or 7852(d) or in any other provision of law shall be construed as permitting an exemption, by reason of any treaty obligation of the United States heretofore or hereafter entered into, from the provisions of this section.

(g) Regulations.

The Secretary shall provide such regulations as are necessary to carry out this section, including regulations providing for such adjustments to the application of this section as are necessary to prevent the avoidance of the purposes of this section, including the avoidance of such purposes through—

(1) the use of related persons, pass-through or other noncorporate entities, or other intermediaries, or

(2) transactions designed to have persons cease to be (or not become) members of expanded affiliated groups or related persons.

In 2005, P.L. 109-135, Sec. 403(u), amended para. (a)(3), effective for tax. yrs. end. after 3/4/2003 as if included in Sec. 801 of the American Jobs Creation Act of 2004, P.L. 108-357.
Prior to amendment, para. (a)(3) read as follows:
"(3) Coordination with subsection (b). Paragraph (1) shall not apply to any entity which is treated as a domestic corporation under subsection (b)."
In 2004, P.L. 108-357, Sec. 801(a), added Code Sec. 7874, effective for tax. yrs. end. after 3/4/2003.

Subtitle G.—The Joint Committee on Taxation

Chapter

91. Organization and membership of the Joint Committee.
92. Powers and duties of the Joint Committee.

In 1976, P.L. 94-455, Sec. 1907(b)(1), deleted "Internal Revenue", which preceded "Taxation", in the heading for Subtitle G.

CHAPTER 91.—ORGANIZATION AND MEMBERSHIP OF THE JOINT COMMITTEE

Sec.
8001. Authorization.
8002. Membership.
8003. Election of chairman and vice chairman.
8004. Appointment and compensation of staff.
8005. Payment of expenses.

Sec. 8001. Authorization.

There shall be a joint congressional committee known as the Joint Committee on Taxation (hereinafter in this subtitle referred to as the "Joint Committee").

In 1976, P.L. 94-455, Sec. 1907(a)(1), substituted "Joint Committee on Taxation" for "Joint Committee on Internal Revenue Taxation" in Code Sec. 8001, effective 2/1/77.

Sec. 8002. Membership.

(a) Number and selection.

The Joint Committee shall be composed of 10 members as follows:

(1) **From Committee on Finance.** Five members who are members of the Committee on Finance of the Senate, three from the majority and two from the minority party, to be chosen by such Committee; and

3,981

(2) From Committee on Ways and Means. Five members who are members of the Committee on Ways and Means of the House of Representatives, three from the majority and two from the minority party, to be chosen by such Committee.

(b) Tenure of office.

(1) General limitation. No person shall continue to serve as a member of the Joint Committee after he has ceased to be a member of the Committee by which he was chosen, except that—

(2) Exception. The members chosen by the Committee on Ways and Means who have been reelected to the House of Representatives may continue to serve as members of the Joint Committee notwithstanding the expiration of the Congress.

(c) Vacancies.

A vacancy in the Joint Committee—

(1) Effect. Shall not affect the power of the remaining members to execute the functions of the Joint Committee; and

(2) Manner of filling. Shall be filled in the same manner as the original selection, except that—

(A) Adjournment or recess of Congress. In case of a vacancy during an adjournment or recess of Congress for a period of more than 2 weeks, the members of the Joint Committee who are members of the Committee entitled to fill such vacancy may designate a member of such Committee to serve until his successor is chosen by such Committee; and

(B) Expiration of Congress. In the case of a vacancy after the expiration of a Congress which would be filled by the Committee on Ways and Means, the members of such Committee who are continuing to serve as members of the Joint Committee may designate a person who, immediately prior to such expiration, was a member of such Committee and who is reelected to the House of Representatives, to serve until his successor is chosen by such Committee.

(d) Allowances.

The members shall serve without compensation in addition to that received for their services as members of Congress; but they shall be reimbursed for travel, subsistence, and other necessary expenses incurred by them in the performance of the duties vested in the Joint Committee, other than expenses in connection with meetings of the Joint Committee held in the District of Columbia during such times as the Congress is in session.

Sec. 8003. Election of chairman and vice chairman.

The Joint Committee shall elect a chairman and vice chairman from among its members.

Sec. 8004. Appointment and compensation of staff.

Except as otherwise provided by law, the Joint Committee shall have power to appoint and fix the compensation of the Chief of Staff of the Joint Committee and such experts and clerical, stenographic, and other assistants as it deems advisable.

In 1976, P.L. 94-455, Sec. 1907(a)(2), substituted "compensation of the Chief of Staff of the Joint Committee" for "compensation of a clerk" in Code Sec. 8004, effective 2/1/77.

Sec. 8005. Payment of expenses.

The expenses of the Joint Committee shall be paid one-half from the contingent fund of the Senate and one-half from the contingent fund of the House of Representatives, upon vouchers signed by the chairman or the vice chairman.

CHAPTER 92.—POWERS AND DUTIES OF THE JOINT COMMITTEE

Sec.
8021. Powers.
8022. Duties.
8023. Additional powers to obtain data.

Sec. 8021. Powers.

(a) To obtain data and inspect income returns.

For powers of the Joint Committee to obtain and inspect income returns, see section 6103(f).

(b) Relating to hearings and sessions.

The Joint Committee, or any subcommittee thereof, is authorized—

(1) To hold. To hold hearings and to sit and act at such places and times;

(2) To require attendance of witnesses and production of books. To require by subpoena (to be issued under the signature of the chairman or vice chairman) or otherwise the attendance of such witnesses and the production of such books, papers, and documents;

(3) To administer oaths. To administer such oaths; and

(4) To take testimony. To take such testimony; as it deems advisable.

(c) To procure printing and binding.

The Joint Committee, or any subcommittee thereof, is authorized to have such printing and binding done as it deems advisable.

(d) To make expenditures.

The Joint Committee, or any subcommittee thereof, is authorized to make such expenditures as it deems advisable.

(e) Investigations.

The Joint Committee shall review all requests (other than requests by the chairman or ranking member of a committee or subcommittee) for investigations of the Internal Revenue Service by the Government Accountability Office, and approve such requests when appropriate, with a view towards eliminating overlapping investigations, ensuring that the Government Accountability Office has the capacity to handle the investigation, and ensuring that investigations focus on areas of primary importance to tax administration.

(f) Relating to joint reviews.

(1) In general. The Chief of Staff, and the staff of the Joint Committee, shall provide such assistance as is required for joint reviews described in paragraph (2).

(2) Joint reviews. Before June 1 of each calendar year after 1998 and before 2005, there shall be a joint review of the strategic plans and budget for the Internal Revenue Service and such other matters as the Chairman of the Joint Committee deems appropriate. Such joint review shall be held at the call of the Chairman of the Joint Committee and shall include two members of the majority and one member of the minority from each of the Committees on Finance, Appropriations, and Governmental Affairs of the Senate, and the Committees on Ways and Means, Appropriations, and Government Reform and Oversight of the House of Representatives.

In 2005, P.L. 109-135, Sec. 412(rr)(5), substituted "Government Accountability Office" for "General Accounting Office" each place it appeared in subsec. (e), effective 12/21/2005.

In 2004, P.L. 108-311, Sec. 321(a), substituted "2005" for "2004" in para. (f)(2), effective 10/4/2004.

—P.L. 108-311, Sec. 321(c), of this Act, provides:

"(c) Time for joint review. The joint review required by section 8021(f)(2) of the Internal Revenue Code of 1986 to be made before June 1, 2004, shall be treated as timely if made before June 1, 2005."

—P.L. 108-271, Sec. 8, of this Act, provides:

"SEC. 8. REDESIGNATION.

Miscellaneous provisions
Code Sec. 8023

"(a) In general. The General Accounting Office is hereby redesignated the Government Accountability Office.

"(b) References. Any reference to the General Accounting Office in any law, rule, regulation, certificate, directive, instruction, or other official paper in force on the date of enactment of this Act [7/7/2004] shall be considered to refer and apply to the Government Accountability Office."

In 1998, P.L. 105-206, Sec. 4001(a), added subsec. (e), effective for requests made after 7/22/98, and subsec. (f), effective 7/22/98.

In 1988, P.L. 100-647, Sec. 1018(s)(1), substituted "6103(f)" for "6103(d)" in subsec. (a), effective 2/1/77.

In 1976, P.L. 94-455, Sec. 1907(a)(3), amended subsec. (d), effective 2/1/77. Prior to amendment, subsec. (d) read as follows:

"(d) To make expenditures.

"(1) General authority. The Joint Committee, or any subcommittee thereof, is authorized to make such expenditures as it deems advisable.

"(2) Limitation. The cost of stenographic services in reporting such hearings as the Joint Committee may hold shall not be in excess of 25 cents per 100 words."

Sec. 8022. Duties.

It shall be the duty of the Joint Committee—

(1) Investigation.

(A) Operation and effects of law. To investigate the operation and effects of the Federal system of internal revenue taxes;

(B) Administration. To investigate the administration of such taxes by the Internal Revenue Service or any executive department, establishment, or agency charged with their administration; and

(C) Other investigations. To make such other investigations in respect of such system of taxes as the Joint Committee may deem necessary.

(2) Simplification of law.

(A) Investigation of methods. To investigate measures and methods for the simplification of such taxes, particularly the income tax; and

(B) Publication of proposals. To publish, from time to time, for public examination and analysis, proposed measures and methods for the simplification of such taxes.

(3) Reports.

(A) To report, from time to time, to the Committee on Finance and the Committee on Ways and Means, and, in its discretion, to the Senate or House of Representatives, or both, the results of its investigations, together with such recommendations as it may deem advisable.

(B) Subject to amounts specifically appropriated to carry out this subparagraph, to report, at least once each Congress, to the Committee on Finance and the Committee on Ways and Means on the overall state of the Federal tax system, together with recommendations with respect to possible simplification proposals and other matters relating to the administration of the Federal tax system as it may deem advisable.

(C) To report, for each calendar year after 1998 and before 2005, to the Committees on Finance, Appropriations, and Governmental Affairs of the Senate, and to the Committees on Ways and Means, Appropriations, and Government Reform and Oversight of the House of Representatives, with respect to the matters addressed in the joint review referred to in section 8021(f)(2).

(4) Cross reference. For duties of the Joint Committee relating to refunds of income and estate taxes, see section 6405.

In 2004, P.L. 108-311, Sec. 321(b)(1), substituted "2005" for "2004" in subpara. (3)(C) . . . Sec. 321(b)(2), substituted "with respect to the matters addressed in the joint review referred to in section 8021(f)(2)." for "with respect to—(i) strategic and business plans for the Internal Revenue Service; (ii) progress of the Internal Revenue Service in meeting its objectives; (iii) the budget for the Internal Revenue Service and whether it supports its objectives; (iv) progress of the Internal Revenue Service in improving taxpayer service and compliance; (v) progress of

the Internal Revenue Service on technology modernization; and (vi) the annual filing season." in subpara. (3)(C), effective 10/4/2004.

In 2000, P.L. 106-554, Sec. 1(a)(7), [which enacted into law Sec. 301 of P.L. 106-554] of this Act, reads as follows:

"Section 3003(a)(1) of the Federal Reports Elimination and Sunset Act of 1995 (31 U.S.C. 1113 note) shall not apply to any report required to be submitted under any of the following provisions of law:"

*   *   *   *   *   *

"15(D) Section 8022(3)"

In 1998, P.L. 105-206, Sec. 4002(a), amended para. (3), effective 7/22/98. Prior to amendment, para. (3) read as follows:

"(3) Reports. To report, from time to time, to the Committee on Finance and the Committee on Ways and Means, and, in its discretion, to the Senate or the House of Representatives, or both, the results of its investigations, together with such recommendation as it may deem advisable."

Sec. 8023. Additional powers to obtain data.
(a) Securing of data.

The Joint Committee or the Chief of Staff of the Joint Committee, upon approval of the Chairman or Vice Chairman, is authorized to secure directly from the Internal Revenue Service or the office of the Chief Counsel for the Internal Revenue Service or directly from any executive department, board, bureau, agency, independent establishment, or instrumentality of the Government, information, suggestions, rulings, data, estimates, and statistics, for the purpose of making investigations, reports, and studies relating to internal revenue taxation. In the investigation by the Joint Committee on Taxation of the administration of the internal revenue taxes by the Internal Revenue Service, the Chief of Staff of the Joint Committee on Taxation is authorized to secure directly from the Internal Revenue Service such tax returns, or copies of tax returns, and other relevant information, as the Chief of Staff deems necessary for such investigation, and the Internal Revenue Service is authorized and directed to furnish such tax returns and information to the Chief of Staff together with a brief report, with respect to each return, as to any action taken or proposed to be taken by the Service as a result of any audit of the return.

(b) Furnishing of data.

The Internal Revenue Service, the office of the Chief Counsel for the Internal Revenue Service, executive departments, boards, bureaus, agencies, independent establishments, and instrumentalities are authorized and directed to furnish such information, suggestions, rulings, data, estimates, and statistics directly to the Joint Committee or to the Chief of Staff of the Joint Committee, upon request made pursuant to this section.

(c) Application of subsections (a) and (b).

Subsections (a) and (b) shall be applied in accordance with their provisions without regard to any reorganization plan becoming effective on, before, or after the date of the enactment of this subsection.

In 1976, P.L. 94-455, Sec. 1210(c), added the last sentence in subsec. (a), effective 1/1/77.

—P.L. 94-455, Sec. 1907(a)(4), amended subsec. (c), effective 2/1/77. Prior to amendment, subsec. (c) read as follows:

"(c)

Subsections (a) and (b) shall be applied in accordance with their provisions without regard to Reorganization Plan Numbered 26 of 1950 or to any other reorganization plan becoming effective on, before, or after February 28, 1951."

In 1959, P.L. 86-368, Sec. 2(b), substituted "or the office of the Chief Counsel for the Internal Revenue Service" for "(including the Assistant General Counsel of the Treasury Department serving as the Chief Counsel of the Internal Revenue Service)" in subsec. (a), and substituted ", the office of the Chief Counsel for the Internal Revenue Service" for "(including the Assistant General Counsel of the Treasury Department serving as the Chief Counsel of the Internal Revenue Service)", in subsec. (b), effective when the Chief Counsel for the Internal Revenue Service first appointed pursuant to amendment of section 7801 of this title by P.L. 86-368 qualifies and takes office.

3,983

Subtitle H.—Financing of Presidential Election Campaigns

Chapter
95. Presidential election campaign fund.
96. Presidential primary matching payment account.

CHAPTER 95.—PRESIDENTIAL ELECTION CAMPAIGN FUND

Sec.
9001. Short title.
9002. Definitions.
9003. Condition for eligibility for payments.
9004. Entitlement of eligible candidates to payments.
9005. Certification by Commission.
9006. Payments to eligible candidates.
9007. Examinations and audits; repayments.
9008. Payments for presidential nominating conventions.
9009. Reports to Congress; regulations.
9010. Participation by Commission in judicial proceedings.
9011. Judicial review.
9012. Criminal penalties.
9013. Effective date of chapter.

In 1974, P.L. 93-443, Sec. 404(c)(6), substituted "Commission" for "Comptroller General" in item 9005.
—P.L. 93-443, Sec. 404(c)(14), substituted "Commission" for "Comptroller General" in item 9010.
—P.L. 93-443, Sec. 406(a), substituted new item 9008.
Prior to amendment, item 9008 read as follows:
"9008. Information on proposed expenses."

Sec. 9001. Short title.

This chapter may be cited as the "Presidential Election Campaign Fund Act".

In 1971, P.L. 92-178, Sec. 801, added Code Sec. 9001, effective 1/1/73.

Sec. 9002. Definitions.

For purposes of this chapter—

(1) The term "authorized committee" means, with respect to the candidates of a political party for President and Vice President of the United States, any political committee which is authorized in writing by such candidates to incur expenses to further the election of such candidates. Such authorization shall be addressed to the chairman of such political committee, and a copy of such authorization shall be filed by such candidates with the Commission. Any withdrawal of any authorization shall also be in writing and shall be addressed and filed in the same manner as the authorization.

(2) The term "candidate" means, with respect to any presidential election, an individual who (A) has been nominated for election to the office of President of the United States or the office of Vice President of the United States by a major party, or (B) has qualified to have his name on the election ballot (or to have the names of electors pledged to him on the election ballot) as the candidate of a political party for election to either such office in 10 or more States. For purposes of paragraphs (6) and (7) of this section and purposes of section 9004(a)(2), the term "candidate" means, with respect to any preceding presidential election, an individual who received popular votes for the office of President in such election. The term "candidate" shall not include any individual who has ceased actively to seek election to the office of President of the United States or to the office of Vice President of the United States, in more than one State.

(3) The term "Commission" means the Federal Election Commission established by section 306(a)(1) of the Federal Election Campaign Act of 1971.

(4) The term "eligible candidates" means the candidates of a political party for President and Vice President of the United States who have met all applicable conditions for eligibility to receive payments under this chapter set forth in section 9003.

(5) The term "fund" means the Presidential Election Campaign Fund established by section 9006(a).

(6) The term "major party" means, with respect to any presidential election, a political party whose candidate for the office of President in the preceding presidential election received, as the candidate of such party, 25 percent or more of the total number of popular votes received by all candidates for such office.

(7) The term "minor party" means, with respect to any presidential election, a political party whose candidate for the office of President in the preceding presidential election received, as the candidate of such party, 5 percent or more but less than 25 percent of the total number of popular votes received by all candidates for such office.

(8) The term "new party" means, with respect to any presidential election, a political party which is neither a major party nor a minor party.

(9) The term "political committee" means any committee, association, or organization (whether or not incorporated) which accepts contributions or makes expenditures for the purpose of influencing, or attempting to influence, the nomination or election of one or more individuals to Federal, State, or local elective public office.

(10) The term "presidential election" means the election of presidential and vice-presidential electors.

(11) The term "qualified campaign expense" means an expense—

(A) incurred (i) by the candidate of a political party for the office of President to further his election to such office or to further the election of the candidate of such political party for the office of Vice President, or both (ii) by the candidate of a political party for the office of Vice President to further his election to such office or to further the election of the candidate of such political party for the office of President, or both, or (iii) by an authorized committee of the candidates of a political party for the offices of President and Vice President to further the election of either or both of such candidates to such offices,

(B) incurred within the expenditure report period (as defined in paragraph (12)), or incurred before the beginning of such period to the extent such expense is for property, services, or facilities used during such period, and

(C) neither the incurring nor payment of which constitutes a violation of any law of the United States or of the State in which such expense is incurred or paid.

An expense shall be considered as incurred by a candidate or an authorized committee if it is incurred by a person authorized by such candidate or such committee, as the case may be, to incur such expense on behalf of such candidate or such committee. If an authorized committee of the candidates of a political party for President and Vice President of the United States also incurs expenses to further the election of one or more other individuals to Federal, State, or local elective public office, expenses incurred by such committee which are not specifically to further the election of such other individual or individuals shall be considered as incurred to further the election of such candidates for President and Vice President in such proportion as the Commission prescribes by rules or regulations.

(12) The term "expenditure report period" with respect to any presidential election means—

(A) in the case of a major party, the period beginning with the first day of September before the election, or, if earlier, with the date on which such major party at its national convention nominated its candidate for election to the office of President of the United States, and ending 30 days after the date of the presidential election; and

(B) in the case of a party which is not a major party, the same period as the expenditure report period of the major party which has the shortest expenditure report period for such presidential election under subparagraph (A).

In **2007**, P.L. 110-172, Sec. 11(a)(42)(A), substituted "section 306(a)(1)" for "section 309(a)(1), enacted 12/29/2007.
In **1976**, P.L. 94-283, Sec. 306(a)(1), added a sentence to the end of para. (2) . . . Sec. 115(c)(1), substituted '309(a)(1)' for '310(a)(1)' in para. (3), effective 5/11/76.
In **1974**, P.L. 93-443, Sec. 404(c)(2), substituted 'Commission' for 'Comptroller General' in para. (11) . . . Sec. 404(c)(1), amended para. (3), effective for tax. yrs. begin. after 12/31/74.
Prior to amendment, para. (3) read as follows:
"(3) The term 'Comptroller General' means the Comptroller General of the United States."
—P.L. 93-443, Sec. 404(c)(3), substituted "Commission" for "Comptroller General" in para. (11), effective for tax. yrs. begin. after 12/31/74.
In **1971**, P.L. 92-178, Sec. 801, added Code Sec. 9002, effective 1/1/73.

Sec. 9003. Condition for eligibility for payments.

(a) In general.

In order to be eligible to receive any payments under section 9006, the candidates of a political party in a presidential election shall, in writing—

(1) agree to obtain and furnish to the Commission such evidence as it may request of the qualified campaign expenses of such candidates,

(2) agree to keep and furnish to the Commission such records, books, and other information as it may request, and

(3) agree to an audit and examination by the Commission under section 9007 and to pay any amounts required to be paid under such section.

(b) Major parties.

In order to be eligible to receive any payments under section 9006, the candidates of a major party in a presidential election shall certify to the Commission, under penalty of perjury, that—

(1) such candidates and their authorized committees will not incur qualified campaign expenses in excess of the aggregate payments to which they will be entitled under section 9004, and

(2) no contributions to defray qualified campaign expenses have been or will be accepted by such candidates or any of their authorized committees except to the extent necessary to make up any deficiency in payments received out of the fund on account of the application of section 9006(d), and no contributions to defray expenses which would be qualified campaign expenses but for subparagraph (C) of section 9002(11) have been or will be accepted by such candidates or any of their authorized committees.

Such certification shall be made within such time prior to the day of the presidential election as the Commission shall prescribe by rules or regulations.

(c) Minor and new parties.

In order to be eligible to receive any payments under section 9006, the candidates of a minor or new party in a presidential election shall certify to the Commission under penalty of perjury, that—

(1) such candidates and their authorized committees will not incur qualified campaign expenses in excess of the aggregate payments to which the eligible candidates of a major party are entitled under section 9004, and

(2) such candidates and their authorized committees will accept and expend or retain contributions to defray qualified campaign expenses only to the extent that the qualified campaign expenses incurred by such candidates and their authorized committees certified to under paragraph (1) exceed the aggregate payments received by such candidates out of the fund pursuant to section 9006.

Such certification shall be made within such time prior to the day of the presidential election as the Commission shall prescribe by rules or regulations.

(d) Withdrawal by candidate.

In any case in which an individual ceases to be a candidate as a result of the operation of the last sentence of section 9002(2), such individual—

(1) shall no longer be eligible to receive any payments under section 9006, except that such individual shall be eligible to receive payments under such section to defray qualified campaign expenses incurred while actively seeking election to the office of President of the United States or to the office of Vice President of the United States in more than one State; and

(2) shall pay to the Secretary, as soon as practicable after the date upon which such individual ceases to be a candidate, an amount equal to the amount of payments received by such individual under section 9006 which are not used to defray qualified campaign expenses.

(e) Closed captioning requirement.

No candidate for the office of President or Vice President may receive amounts from the Presidential Election Campaign Fund under this chapter or chapter 96 unless such candidate has certified that any television commercial prepared or distributed by the candidate will be prepared in a manner which ensures that the commercial contains or is accompanied by closed captioning of the oral content of the commercial to be broadcast in line 21 of the vertical blanking interval, or is capable of being viewed by deaf and hearing impaired individuals via any comparable successor technology to line 21 of the vertical blanking interval.

In **1992**, P.L. 102-393, Sec. 534(a), added subsec. (e), effective for amounts made available under chapter 95 or 96 of the Internal Revenue Code of 1986 more than thirty days after 10/6/92.
In **1976**, P.L. 94-455, Sec. 1906(b)(13)(A), substituted "Secretary" for "Secretary or his delegate" in para. (d)(2), effective 2/1/77.
—P.L. 94-283, Sec. 306(a)(2), added subsec. (d), effective 5/11/76.
In **1974**, P.L. 93-443, Sec. 404(c)(4), substituted "Commission" for "Comptroller General" and "it" for "he" each place they appeared, effective with respect to tax. yrs. begin. after 12/31/74.
—P.L. 93-443, Sec. 405(b), substituted "of such candidates" for "with respect to which payment is sought" in para. (a)(1), added "and" at the end of para. (a)(2), substituted a period for ", and" at the end of para. (a)(3), and deleted para. (a)(4), effective with respect to tax. yrs. begin. after 12/31/74.
Prior to deletion, para. (a)(4) read as follows:
"(4) agree to furnish statements of qualified campaign expenses and proposed qualified campaign expenses required under section 9008."
In **1973**, P.L. 93-53, Sec. 6(c), substituted "section 9006(d)" for "section 9006(c)" in subsec. (b)(2).
In **1971**, P.L. 92-178, Sec. 801, added Code Sec. 9003, effective 1/1/73.

3,985

Sec. 9004. Entitlement of eligible candidates to payments.

(a) In general.

Subject to the provisions of this chapter—

(1) The eligible candidates of each major party in a presidential election shall be entitled to equal payments under section 9006 in an amount which, in the aggregate, shall not exceed the expenditure limitations applicable to such candidates under section 315(b)(1)(B) of the Federal Election Campaign Act of 1971.

(2)(A) The eligible candidates of a minor party in a presidential election shall be entitled to payments under section 9006 equal in the aggregate to an amount which bears the same ratio to the amount allowed under paragraph (1) for a major party as the number of popular votes received by the candidate for President of the minor party, as such candidate, in the preceding presidential election bears to the average number of popular votes received by the candidates for President of the major parties in the preceding presidential election.

(B) If the candidate of one or more political parties (not including a major party) for the office of President was a candidate for such office in the preceding presidential election and received 5 percent or more but less than 25 percent of the total number of popular votes received by all candidates for such office, such candidate and his running mate for the office of Vice President, upon compliance with the provisions of section 9003(a) and (c), shall be treated as eligible candidates entitled to payments under section 9006 in an amount computed as provided in subparagraph (A) by taking into account all the popular votes received by such candidate for the office of President in the preceding presidential election. If eligible candidates of a minor party are entitled to payments under this subparagraph, such entitlement shall be reduced by the amount of entitlement allowed under subparagraph (A).

(3) The eligible candidates of a minor party or a new party in a presidential election whose candidate for President in such election receives, as such candidate, 5 percent or more of the total number of popular votes cast for the office of President in such election shall be entitled to payments under section 9006 equal in the aggregate to an amount which bears the same ratio to the amount allowed under paragraph (1) for a major party as the number of popular votes received by such candidate in such election bears to the average number of popular votes received in such election by the candidates for President of the major parties. In the case of eligible candidates entitled to payments under paragraph (2), the amount allowable under this paragraph shall be limited to the amount, if any, by which the entitlement under the preceding sentence exceeds the amount of the entitlement under paragraph (2).

(b) Limitations.

The aggregate payments to which the eligible candidates of a political party shall be entitled under subsections (a)(2) and (3) with respect to a presidential election shall not exceed an amount equal to the lower of—

(1) the amount of qualified campaign expenses incurred by such eligible candidates and their authorized committees, reduced by the amount of contributions to defray qualified campaign expenses received and expended or retained by such eligible candidates and such committees, or

(2) the aggregate payments to which the eligible candidates of a major party are entitled under subsection (a)(1), reduced by the amount of contributions described in paragraph (1) of this subsection.

(c) Restrictions.

The eligible candidates of a political party shall be entitled to payments under subsection (a) only—

(1) to defray qualified campaign expenses incurred by such eligible candidates or their authorized committees, or

(2) to repay loans the proceeds of which were used to defray such qualified campaign expenses, or otherwise to restore funds (other than contributions to defray qualified campaign expenses received and expended by such candidates or such committees) used to defray such qualified campaign expenses.

(d) Expenditures from personal funds.

In order to be eligible to receive any payment under section 9006, the candidate of a major, minor, or new party in an election for the office of President shall certify to the Commission, under penalty of perjury, that such candidate will not knowingly make expenditures from his personal funds, or the personal funds of his immediate family, in connection with his campaign for election to the office of President in excess of, in the aggregate, $50,000. For purposes of this subsection, expenditures from personal funds made by a candidate of a major, minor, or new party for the office of Vice President shall be considered to be expenditures by the candidate of such party for the office of President.

(e) Definition of immediate family.

For purposes of subsection (d), the term "immediate family" means a candidate's spouse, and any child, parent, grandparent, brother, half-brother, sister, or half-sister of the candidate, and the spouses of such persons.

In **2007**, P.L. 110-172, Sec. 11(a)(42)(B), substituted "section 315(b)(1)(B)" for "section 320(b)(1)(B)" in para. (a)(1), enacted 12/29/2007.

In **1976**, P.L. 94-283, Sec. 307(d), substituted "320(b)(1)(B) of the Federal Election Campaign Act of 1971" for "608(c)(1)(B) of title 18, United States Code" in para. (a)(1), effective 5/11/76.

—P.L. 94-283, Sec. 301(a), added subsecs. (d) and (e), enacted 5/11/76. Sec. 301(b) of the Act provides: "For purposes of applying section 9004(d) of the Internal Revenue Code of 1954, as added by subsection (a), expenditures made by an individual after January 29, 1976, and before the date of the enactment of this Act [5/11/76] shall not be taken into account."

In **1974**, P.L. 93-443, Sec. 404(a), amended para. (a)(1), effective for tax. yrs. begin. after 12/31/74.

Prior to amendment, para. (a)(1) read as follows:

"(1) the eligible candidates of a major party in a presidential election shall be entitled to payments under section 9006 equal in the aggregate to 15 cents multiplied by the total number of residents within the United States who have attained the age of 18, as determine by the Bureau of the Census, as of the first day of June of the year preceding the year of the presidential election."

—P.L. 93-443, Sec. 404(b), substituted "allowed" for "computed" in paras. (a)(2) and (a)(3), effective for tax. yrs. begin. after 12/31/74.

In **1971**, P.L. 92-178, Sec. 801, added Code Sec. 9004, effective 1/1/73.

Sec. 9005. Certification by Commission.

(a) Initial certifications.

Not later than 10 days after the candidates of a political party for President and Vice President of the United States have met all applicable conditions for eligibility to receive payments under this chapter set forth in section 9003, the Commission shall certify to the Secretary of the Treasury for payment to such eligible candidates under section 9006 payment in full of amounts to which such candidates are entitled under section 9004.

(b) Finality of certifications and determinations.

Initial certifications by the Commission under subsection (a), and all determinations made by it under this chapter, shall be final and conclusive, except to the extent that they are subject to examination and audit by the Commission under section 9007 and judicial review under section 9011.

In 1976, P.L. 94-455, Sec. 1906(b)(13)(C), substituted "to the Secretary of the Treasury" for "to the Secretary" in subsec. (a), effective 2/1/77.

In 1974, P.L. 93-433, Sec. 404(c)(6), substituted "Commission" for "Comptroller General" in the heading of Code Sec. 9005 ... Sec. 404(c)(7), substituted "Commission" for "Comptroller", and substituted "it" for "he" each place it appeared in Code Sec. 9005, effective for tax. yrs. begin. after 12/31/74.

—P.L. 93-433, Sec. 405(a), amended subsec. (a), effective for tax. yrs. begin. after 12/31/74.

Prior to amendment, subsec. (a) read as follows:

"(a) Initial certifications.

"On the basis of the evidence, books, records, and information furnished by the eligible candidates of a political party and prior to examination and audit under section 9007, the Comptroller General shall certify from time to time to the Secretary for payment to such candidates under section 9006 the payments to which such candidates are entitled under section 9004."

In 1971, P.L. 92-178, Sec. 801, added Code Sec. 9005, effective 1/1/73.

Sec. 9006. Payments to eligible candidates.
(a) Establishment of campaign fund.

There is hereby established on the books of the Treasury of the United States a special fund to be known as the "Presidential Election Campaign Fund." The Secretary of the Treasury shall, from time to time, transfer to the fund an amount not in excess of the sum of the amounts designated (subsequent to the previous Presidential election) to the fund by individuals under section 6096. There is appropriated to the fund for each fiscal year, out of amounts in the general fund of the Treasury not otherwise appropriated, an amount equal to the amounts so designated during each fiscal year, which shall remain available to the fund without fiscal year limitation.

(b) Payments from the fund.

Upon receipt of a certification from the Commission under section 9005 for payment to the eligible candidates of a political party, the Secretary of the Treasury shall pay to such candidates out of the fund the amount certified by the Commission. Amounts paid to any such candidates shall be under the control of such candidates.

(c) Insufficient amounts in fund.

If at the time of a certification by the Commission under section 9005 for payment to the eligible candidates of a political party, the Secretary determines that the moneys in the fund are not, or may not be, sufficient to satisfy the full entitlements of the eligible candidates of all political parties, he shall withhold from such payment such amount as he determines to be necessary to assure that the eligible candidates of each political party will receive their pro rata share of their full entitlement. Amounts withheld by reason of the preceding sentence shall be paid when the Secretary determines that there are sufficient moneys in the fund to pay such amounts, or portions thereof, to all eligible candidates from whom amounts have been withheld, but, if there are not sufficient moneys in the fund to satisfy the full entitlement of the eligible candidates of all political parties, the amounts so withheld shall be paid in such manner that the eligible candidates of each political party receive their pro rata share of their full entitlement. In any case in which the Secretary determines that there are insufficient moneys in the fund to make payments under subsection (b), section 9008(b)(3), and section 9037(b), moneys shall not be made available from any other source for the purpose of making such payments.

In 2007, P.L. 110-172, Sec. 11(a)(43), substituted "Commission" for "Comptroller General" each place it appeared in Code Sec. 9006, enacted 12/29/2007.

In 1976, P.L. 94-455, Sec. 1906(b)(13)(A), substituted "Secretary" for "Secretary or his delegate" each place it appeared in subsec. (c), effective 2/1/77.

—P.L. 94-455, Sec. 1906(b)(13)(B), substituted "Secretary of the Treasury" for "Secretary" in subsecs. (a) and (b), effective 2/1/77.

—P.L. 94-283, Sec. 302(a), deleted subsec. (b), and redesignated subsecs. (c) and (d) as subsecs. (b) and (c) respectively ... Sec. 302(b), added the last sentence subsec. (c) [as redesignated by Sec. 302(a), see above], effective 5/11/76.

Prior to deletion, subsec. (b) read as follows:

"(b) Transfer to the general fund.

"If, after a presidential election and after all eligible candidates have been paid the amount which they are entitled to receive under this chapter, there are moneys remaining in the fund, the Secretary shall transfer the moneys so remaining to the general fund of the Treasury."

In 1974, P.L. 93-443, Sec. 403(a)(1), substituted "from time to time" for "as provided by appropriation Acts" in subsec. (a) ... Sec. 403(a)(2), added the final sentence in subsec. (a) ... Sec. 404(c)(8), substituted "Commission" for "Comptroller General" each place it appeared in subsecs. (c) and (d), effective for tax. yrs. begin. after 12/31/74.

In 1973, P.L. 93-53, Sec. 6(b), amended Code Sec. 9006, effective for tax. yrs. begin. after 12/31/72. Any designation made under Code Sec. 6096 (as in effect for tax. yrs. begin. before 1/1/73) for the account of the candidates of any specified political party shall, for purposes of section 9006(a) of such Code (as amended), be treated solely as a designation to the Presidential Election Campaign Fund.

Prior to amendment Code Sec. 9006 read as follows:

"(a) Establishment of campaign fund.

"There is hereby established on the books of the Treasury of the United States a special fund to be known as the 'Presidential Election Campaign Fund.' The Secretary shall maintain in the fund (1) a separate account for the candidates of each major party, each minor party, and each new party for which a specific designation is made under section 6096 for payment into an account in the fund and (2) a general account for which no specific designation is made. The Secretary shall, as provided by appropriation Acts, transfer to each account in the fund an amount not in excess of the sum of the amounts designated (subsequent to the previous presidential election) to such account by individuals under section 6096 for payment into such account of the fund.

"(b) Transfer to the general fund.

"If, after a presidential election and after all eligible candidates have been paid the amount which they are entitled to receive under this chapter, there are moneys remaining in any account in the fund, the Secretary shall transfer the moneys so remaining to the general fund of the Treasury.

"(c) Payments from the fund.

"Upon receipt of a certification from the Comptroller General under section 9005 for payment to the eligible candidates of a political party, the Secretary shall pay to such candidates out of the specific account in the fund for such candidates the amount certified by the Comptroller General. Payments to eligible candidates from the account designated for them shall be limited to the amounts in such account at the time of payment. Amounts paid to any such candidates shall be under the control of such candidates.

"(d) Transfers from general account to separate accounts.

"(1) If, on the 60th day prior to the presidential election, the moneys in any separate account in the fund are less than the aggregate entitlement under section 9004(a)(1) or (2) of the eligible candidates to which such account relates, 80 percent of the amount in the general account shall be transferred to the separate accounts (whether or not all the candidates to which such separate accounts relate are eligible candidates) in the ratio of the entitlement under section 9004(a)(1) or (2) of the candidates to which such accounts relate. No amount shall be transferred to any separate account under the preceding sentence which, when added to the moneys in that separate account prior to any payment out of that account during the calendar year, would be in excess of the aggregate entitlement under section 9004(a)(1) or (2) of the candidates to whom such account relates.

"(2) If, at the close of the expenditure report period, the moneys in any separate account in the fund are not sufficient to satisfy any unpaid entitlement of the eligible candidates to which such account relates, the balance in the general account shall be transferred to the separate accounts in the following manner:

"(A) For the separate account of the candidates of a major party, compute the percentage which the average number of popular votes received by the candidates for President of the major parties is of the total number of popular votes cast for the office of President in the election.

"(B) For the separate account of the candidates of a minor or new party, compute the percentage which the popular votes received for President by the candidate to which such account relates is of the total number of popular votes cast for the office of President in the election.

"(C) In the case of each separate account, multiply the applicable percentage obtained under subparagraph (A) or (B) for such account by the amount of the money in the general account prior to any distribution made under paragraph (1), and transfer to such separate account an amount equal to the excess of the product of such multiplication over the amount of any distribution made under such paragraph to such account."

In 1971, P.L. 92-178, Sec. 801, added Code Sec. 9006, effective 1/1/73.

Sec. 9007. Examinations and audits; repayments.
(a) Examinations and audits.

After each presidential election, the Commission shall conduct a thorough examination and audit of the qualified campaign expenses of the candidates of each political party for President and Vice President.

(b) Repayments.

(1) If the Commission determines that any portion of the payments made to the eligible candidates of a political party under section 9006 was in excess of the aggregate payments to which candidates were entitled under section 9004, it shall so notify such candidates, and such candidates shall pay to the Secretary of the Treasury an amount equal to such portion.

(2) If the Commission determines that the eligible candidates of a political party and their authorized committees incurred qualified campaign expenses in excess of the aggregate payments to which the eligible candidates of a major party were entitled under section 9004, it shall notify such candidates of the amount of such excess and such candidates shall pay to the Secretary of the Treasury an amount equal to such amount.

(3) If the Commission determines that the eligible candidates of a major party or any authorized committee of such candidates accepted contributions (other than contributions to make up deficiencies in payments out of the fund on account of the application of section 9006(c)) to defray qualified campaign expenses (other than qualified campaign expenses with respect to which payment is required under paragraph (2)), it shall notify such candidates of the amount of the contributions so accepted, and such candidates shall pay to the Secretary of the Treasury an amount equal to such amount.

(4) If the Commission determines that any amount of any payment made to the eligible candidates of a political party under section 9006 was used for any purpose other than—

(A) to defray the qualified campaign expenses with respect to which such payment was made, or

(B) to repay loans the proceeds of which were used, or otherwise to restore funds (other than contributions to defray qualified campaign expenses which were received and expended) which were used, to defray such qualified campaign expenses,

it shall notify such candidates of the amount so used, and such candidates shall pay to the Secretary of the Treasury an amount equal to such amount.

(5) No payment shall be required from the eligible candidates of a political party under this subsection to the extent that such payment, when added to other payments required from such candidates under this subsection, exceeds the amount of payments received by such candidates under section 9006.

(c) Notification.

No notification shall be made by the Commission under subsection (b) with respect to a presidential election more than 3 years after the day of such election.

(d) Deposit of repayments.

All payments received by the Secretary of the Treasury under subsection (b) shall be deposited by him in the general fund of the Treasury.

In 1976, P.L. 94-455, Sec. 1906(b)(13)(B), substituted "Secretary of the Treasury" for "Secretary" in subsec. (d), . . . Sec. 1906(b)(13)(C), substituted "to the Secretary of the Treasury" for "to the Secretary" each place it appeared in subsec. (b), effective 2/1/77.

In 1976, P.L. 94-283, Sec. 307(e), substituted "9006(c)" for "9006(d)", in para. (b)(3), effective 5/11/76.

In 1974, P.L. 93-443, Sec. 404(c)(9), (10), and (11), substituted "Commission" for "Comptroller General" and "it" for "he" each place they appeared in subsec. (a), (b), and (c), effective for tax. yrs. begin. after 12/31/74.

In 1973, P.L. 93-53, Sec. 6(c), substituted "section 9006(d)" for "section 9006(c)" in para. (b)(3), effective for tax. yrs. begin. after '72.

In 1971, P.L. 92-178, Sec. 801, added Code Sec. 9007, effective 1/1/73.

Sec. 9008. Payments for Presidential Nominating Conventions.

(a) Establishment of accounts.

The Secretary shall maintain in the fund, in addition to any account which he maintains under section 9006(a), a separate account for the national committee of each major party and minor party. The Secretary shall deposit in each such account an amount equal to the amount which each such committee may receive under subsection (b). Such deposits shall be drawn from amounts designated by individuals under section 6096 and shall be made before any transfer is made to any account for any eligible candidate under section 9006(a).

(b) Entitlement to payments from the fund.

(1) Major parties. Subject to the provisions of this section, the national committee of a major party shall be entitled to payments under paragraph (3), with respect to any presidential nominating convention, in amounts which, in the aggregate, shall not exceed $4,000,000.

(2) Minor parties. Subject to the provisions of this section, the national committee of a minor party shall be entitled to payments under paragraph (3), with respect to any presidential nominating convention, in amounts which, in the aggregate, shall not exceed an amount which bears the same ratio to the amount the national committee of a major party is entitled to receive under paragraph (1) as the number of popular votes received by the candidate for President of the minor party, as such candidate, in the preceding presidential election bears to the average number of popular votes received by the candidates for President of the United States of the major parties in the preceding presidential election.

(3) Payments. Upon receipt of certification from the Commission under subsection (g), the Secretary shall make payments from the appropriate account maintained under subsection (a) to the national committee of a major party or minor party which elects to receive its entitlement under this subsection. Such payments shall be available for use by such committee in accordance with the provisions of subsection (c).

(4) Limitation. Payments to the national committee of a major party or minor party under this subsection from the account designated for such committee shall be limited to the amounts in such account at the time of payment.

(5) Adjustment of entitlements. The entitlements established by this subsection shall be adjusted in the same manner as expenditure limitations established by section 315(b) and section 315(d) of the Federal Election Campaign Act of 1971 are adjusted pursuant to the provisions of section 315(c) of such Act.

(c) Use of funds.

No part of any payment made under subsection (b) shall be used to defray the expenses of any candidate or delegate who is participating in any presidential nominating convention. Such payments shall be used only—

(1) to defray expenses incurred with respect to a presidential nominating convention (including the payment of deposits) by or on behalf of the national committee receiving such payments; or

(2) to repay loans the proceeds of which were used to defray such expenses, or otherwise to restore funds (other than contributions to defray such expenses received by such committee) used to defray such expenses.

(d) Limitation of expenditures.

(1) Major parties. Except as provided by paragraph (3), the national committee of a major party may not make expenditures with respect to a presidential nominating con-

vention which, in the aggregate, exceed the amount of payments to which such committee is entitled under subsection (b)(1).

(2) Minor parties. Except as provided by paragraph (3), the national committee of a minor party may not make expenditures with respect to a presidential nominating convention which, in the aggregate, exceed the amount of the entitlement of the national committee of a major party under subsection (b)(1).

(3) Exception. The Commission may authorize the national committee of a major party or minor party to make expenditures which, in the aggregate, exceed the limitation established by paragraph (1) or paragraph (2) of this subsection. Such authorization shall be based upon a determination by the Commission that, due to extraordinary and unforeseen circumstances, such expenditures are necessary to assure the effective operation of the presidential nominating convention by such committee.

(4) Provision of legal or accounting services. For purposes of this section, the payment, by any person other than the national committee of a political party (unless the person paying for such services is a person other than the regular employer of the individual rendering such services) of compensation to any individual for legal or accounting services rendered to or on behalf of the national committee of a political party shall not be treated as an expenditure made by or on behalf of such committee with respect to its limitations on presidential nominating convention expenses.

(e) Availability of payments.

The national committee of a major party or minor party may receive payments under subsection (b)(3) beginning on July 1 of the calendar year immediately preceding the calendar year in which a presidential nominating convention of the political party involved is held.

(f) Transfer to the fund.

If, after the close of a presidential nominating convention and after the national committee of the political party involved has been paid the amount which it is entitled to receive under this section, there are moneys remaining in the account of such national committee, the Secretary shall transfer the moneys so remaining to the fund.

(g) Certification by Commission.

Any major party or minor party may file a statement with the Commission in such form and manner and at such times as it may require, designating the national committee of such party. Such statement shall include the information required by section 303(b) of the Federal Election Campaign Act of 1971, together with such additional information as the Commission may require. Upon receipt of a statement filed under the preceding sentences, the Commission promptly shall verify such statement according to such procedures and criteria as it may establish and shall certify to the Secretary for payment in full to any such committee of amounts to which such committee may be entitled under subsection (b). Such certifications shall be subject to an examination and audit which the Commission shall conduct no later than December 31 of the calendar year in which the presidential nominating convention involved is held.

(h) Repayments.

The Commission shall have the same authority to require repayments from the national committee of a major party or a minor party as it has with respect to repayments from any eligible candidate under section 9007(b). The provisions of section 9007(c) and section 9007(d) shall apply with respect to any repayment required by the Commission under this subsection.

In **1984,** P.L. 98-355, Sec. 1(a), substituted "$4,000,000" for "$3,000,000" in para. (b)(1) ... Sec. 1(b)(1), substituted "section 315(b) and section 315(d)" for "section 320(b) and section 320(d)" in para. (b)(5) ... Sec. 1(b)(2), substituted "section 315(c)" for "section 320(c)" in para. (b)(5), effective 1/1/84.

In **1980,** P.L. 96-187, Sec. 202, substituted "$3,000,000" for "$2,000,000" in subsec. (b), effective 1/8/80.

In **1976,** P.L. 94-283, Sec. 307(a), substituted "section 320(b) and section 320(d) of the Federal Election Campaign Act of 1971" for "section 608(c) and section 608(f) of title 18, United States Code," and "section 320(c) of such Act" for "section 608(d) of such title" in para. (b)(5), effective 5/11/76.

—P.L. 94-283, Sec. 303, added para. (d)(4), effective 5/11/76.

In **1974,** P.L. 93-443, Sec. 406(a), amended Code Sec. 9008, effective with respect to tax. yrs. begin. after 12/31/74.

Prior to amendment, Code Sec. 9008 read as follows:

"SEC. 9008. INFORMATION ON PROPOSED EXPENSES.

"(a) Reports by candidates.

"The candidates of a political party for President and Vice President in a presidential election shall, from time to time as the Comptroller General may require, furnish to the Comptroller General as detailed statement, in such form as the Comptroller General may prescribe, of—

"(1) the qualified campaign expenses incurred by them and their authorized committees prior to the date of such statement (whether or not evidence of such expenses has been furnished for purposes of section 9005), and

"(2) the qualified campaign expenses which they and their authorized committees propose to incur on or after the date of such statement.

"The Comptroller General shall require a statement under this subsection from such candidates of each political party at least once each week during the second, third, and fourth weeks preceding the day of the presidential election and at least twice during the week preceding such day.

"(b) Publication.

"The Comptroller General shall, as soon as possible after he receives each statement under subsection (a), prepare and publish a summary of such statement, together with any other data or information which he deems advisable, in the Federal Register. Such summary shall not include any information which identifies any individual who made a designation under section 6096."

In **1971,** P.L. 92-178, Sec. 801, added Code Sec. 9008, for 1/1/73.

Sec. 9009. Reports to Congress; regulations.
(a) Reports.

The Commission shall, as soon as practicable after each presidential election, submit a full report to the Senate and House of Representatives setting forth—

(1) the qualified campaign expenses (shown in such detail as the Commission determines necessary) incurred by the candidates of each political party and their authorized committees;

(2) the amounts certified by it under section 9005 for payment to the eligible candidates of each political party;

(3) the amount of payments, if any, required from such candidates under section 9007, and the reasons for each payment required; and

(4) the expenses incurred by the national committee of a major party or minor party with respect to a presidential nominating convention;

(5) the amounts certified by it under section 9008(g) for payment to each such committee; and

(6) the amount of payments, if any, required from such committees under section 9008(h), and the reasons for each such payment.

Each report submitted pursuant to this section shall be printed as a Senate document.

(b) Regulations, etc.

The Commission is authorized to prescribe such rules and regulations in accordance with the provisions of subsection (c), to conduct such examinations and audits (in addition to the examinations and audits required by section 9007(a)), to conduct such investigations, and to require the keeping and submission of such books, records, and information, as it deems necessary to carry out the functions and duties imposed on it by this chapter.

(c) Review of regulations.

(1) The Commission, before prescribing any rule or regulation under subsection (b), shall transmit a statement with respect to such rule or regulation to the Senate and to the

House of Representatives, in accordance with the provisions of this subsection. Such statement shall set forth the proposed rule or regulation and shall contain a detailed explanation and justification of such rule or regulation.

(2) If either such House does not, through appropriate action, disapprove the proposed rule or regulation set forth in such statement no later than 30 legislative days after receipt of such statement, then the Commission may prescribe such rule or regulation. Whenever a committee of the House of Representatives reports any resolution relating to any such rule or regulation, it is at any time thereafter in order (even though a previous motion to the same effect has been disagreed to) to move to proceed to the consideration of the resolution. The motion is highly privileged and is not debatable. An amendment to the motion is not in order, and it is not in order to move to reconsider the vote by which the motion is agreed to or disagreed to. The Commission may not prescribe any rule or regulation which is disapproved by either such House under this paragraph.

(3) For purposes of this subsection, the term "legislative days" does not include any calendar day on which both Houses of the Congress are not in session.

(4) For purposes of this subsection, the term "rule or regulation" means a provision or series of interrelated provisions stating a single separable rule of law.

In **1976,** P.L. 94-283, Sec. 304(a), amended para. (c)(2), and added para. (c)(4), effective 5/11/76.
Prior to amendment, para. (c)(2) read as follows:
"(2) If either such House does not, through appropriate action, disapprove the proposed rule or regulation set forth in such statement no later than 30 legislative days after receipt of such statement, then the Commission may prescribe such rule or regulation. The Commission may not prescribe any rule or regulation which is disapproved by either such House under this paragraph."
In **1974,** P.L. 93-443, Sec. 404(c)(12), substituted "Commission" for "Comptroller General" and "it" for "him" each place they appeared in subsec. (a) . . . Sec. 406(b)(1), deleted "and" in para. (a)(2), substituted "; and" for the period at the end of para. (a)(3) and added paras. (a)(4), (5), and (6) . . . Sec. 404(c)(13), substituted "Commission" for "Comptroller General", "it" for "he", and "it" for "him" each place they appeared in subsec. (b) . . . Sec. 409(b), added "in accordance with the provisions of subsection (c)" after "regulations" in subsec. (b) . . . Sec. 409(a), added subsec. (c), effective for tax. yrs. begin. after 12/31/74.
In **1971,** P.L. 92-178, Sec. 801, added Code Sec. 9009, effective 1/1/73.

Sec. 9010. Participation by Commission in judicial proceedings.
(a) Appearance by counsel.
The Commission is authorized to appear in and defend against any action filed under section 9011, either by attorneys employed in its office or by counsel whom it may appoint without regard to the provisions of title 5, United States Code, governing appointments in the competitive service, and whose compensation it may fix without regard to the provisions of chapter 51 and subchapter III of chapter 53 of such title.

(b) Recovery of certain payments.
The Commission is authorized through attorneys and counsel described in subsection (a) to appear in the district courts of the United States to seek recovery of any amounts determined to be payable to the Secretary of the Treasury as a result of examination and audit made pursuant to section 9007.

(c) Declaratory and injunctive relief.
The Commission is authorized through attorneys and counsel described in subsection (a) to petition the courts of the United States for declaratory or injunctive relief concerning any civil matter covered by the provisions of this subtitle or section 6096. Upon application of the Commission, an action brought pursuant to this subsection shall be heard and determined by a court of three judges in accordance with the provisions of section 2284 of title 28, United States Code, and any appeal shall lie to the Supreme Court.

(d) Appeal.
The Commission is authorized on behalf of the United States to appeal from, and to petition the Supreme Court for certiorari to review, judgments or decrees entered with respect to actions in which it appears pursuant to the authority provided in this section.

In **1984,** P.L. 98-620, Sec. 402(28)(E), deleted the last sentence of subsec. (c), effective 11/8/84, except for cases pending on 11/8/84.
Prior to deletion, the last sentence of subsec. (c) read as follows:
"It shall be the duty of the judges designated to hear the case to assign the case for hearing at the earliest practicable date, to participate in the hearing and determination thereof, and to cause the case to be in every way expedited."
In **1976,** P.L. 94-455, Sec. 1906(b)(13)(C), substituted "to the Secretary of the Treasury" for "to the Secretary" in subsec. (b), effective 2/1/77.
In **1974,** P.L. 93-443, Sec. 404(c)(14), (15), (16), (17), and (18), substituted "Commission" for "Comptroller General", "it" for "him", "it" for "he", and "its" for "his" each place they appeared in the heading and text of Code Sec. 9010, effective for tax. yrs. begin. after 12/31/74.
In **1971,** P.L. 92-178, Sec. 801, added Code Sec. 9010, effective 1/1/73.

Sec. 9011. Judicial review.
(a) Review of certification, determination, or other action by the Commission.
Any certification, determination, or other action by the Commission made or taken pursuant to the provisions of this chapter shall be subject to review by the United States Court of Appeals for the District of Columbia upon petition filed in such Court by any interested person. Any petition filed pursuant to this section shall be filed within thirty days after the certification, determination, or other action by the Commission for which review is sought.

(b) Suits to implement chapter.
(1) The Commission, the national committee of any political party, and individuals eligible to vote for President are authorized to institute such actions, including actions for declaratory judgment or injunctive relief, as may be appropriate to implement or construe any provision of this chapter.

(2) The district courts of the United States shall have jurisdiction of proceedings instituted pursuant to this subsection and shall exercise the same without regard to whether a person asserting rights under provisions of this subsection shall have exhausted any administrative or other remedies that may be provided at law. Such proceedings shall be heard and determined by a court of three judges in accordance with the provisions of section 2284 of title 28, United States Code, and any appeal shall lie to the Supreme Court.

In **1984,** P.L. 98-620, Sec. 402(28)(F), deleted the last sentence of para. (b)(2), effective 11/8/84, except for cases pending on 11/8/84.
Prior to deletion, the last sentence of para. (b)(2) read as follows:
"It shall be the duty of the judges designated to hear the case to assign the case for hearing at the earliest practical date, to participate in the hearing and determination thereof, and to cause the case to be in every way expedited."
In **1974,** P.L. 93-443, Sec. 404(c)(19), (20), and (21), substituted "Commission" for "Comptroller General" each place it appeared in Code Sec. 9011, effective for tax. yrs. begin. after 12/31/74.
In **1971,** P.L. 92-178, Sec. 801, added Code Sec. 9011, effective 1/1/73.

Sec. 9012. Criminal penalties.
(a) Excess expenses.
(1) It shall be unlawful for an eligible candidate of a political party for President and Vice President in a presidential election or any of his authorized committees knowingly and willfully to incur qualified campaign expenses in excess of the aggregate payments to which the eligible candidates of a major party are entitled under section 9004 with respect to such election. It shall be unlawful for the

national committee of a major party or minor party knowingly and willfully to incur expenses with respect to a presidential nominating convention in excess of the expenditure limitation applicable with respect to such committee under section 9008(d), unless the incurring of such expenses is authorized by the Commission under section 9008(d)(3).

(2) Any person who violates paragraph (1) shall be fined not more than $5,000, or imprisoned not more than one year or both. In the case of a violation by an authorized committee, any officer or member of such committee who knowingly and willfully consents to such violation shall be fined not more than $5,000, or imprisoned not more than one year, or both.

(b) Contributions.

(1) It shall be unlawful for an eligible candidate of a major party in a presidential election or any of his authorized committees knowingly and willfully to accept any contribution to defray qualified campaign expenses, except to the extent necessary to make up any deficiency in payments received out of the fund on account of the application of section 9006(c), or to defray expenses which would be qualified campaign expenses but for subparagraph (C) of section 9002(11).

(2) It shall be unlawful for an eligible candidate of a political party (other than a major party) in a presidential election or any of his authorized committees knowingly and willfully to accept and expend or retain contributions to defray qualified campaign expenses in an amount which exceeds the qualified campaign expenses incurred with respect to such election by such eligible candidate and his authorized committees.

(3) Any person who violates paragraph (1) or (2) shall be fined not more than $5,000, or imprisoned not more than one year, or both. In the case of a violation by an authorized committee, any officer or member of such committee who knowingly and willfully consents to such violation shall be fined not more than $5,000, or imprisoned not more than one year, or both.

(c) Unlawful use of payments.

(1) It shall be unlawful for any person who receives any payment under section 9006, or to whom any portion of any payment received under such section is transferred, knowingly and willfully to use, or authorize the use of, such payment or such portion for any purpose other than—

(A) to defray the qualified campaign expenses with respect to which such payment was made, or

(B) to repay loans the proceeds of which were used, or otherwise to restore funds (other than contributions to defray qualified campaign expenses which were received and expended) which were used, to defray such qualified campaign expenses.

(2) It shall be unlawful for the national committee of a major party or minor party which receives any payment under section 9008(b)(3) to use, or authorize the use of, such payment for any purpose other than a purpose authorized by section 9008(c).

(3) Any person who violates paragraph (1) shall be fined not more than $10,000, or imprisoned not more than five years, or both.

(d) False statements, etc.

(1) It shall be unlawful for any person knowingly and willfully—

(A) to furnish any false, fictitious, or fraudulent evidence, books, or information to the Commission under this subtitle, or to include in any evidence, books, or information so furnished any misrepresentation of a material fact, or to falsify or conceal any evidence, books, or information relevant to a certification by the Commission or an examination and audit by the Commission under this chapter; or

(B) to fail to furnish to the Commission any records, books, or information requested by it for purposes of this chapter.

(2) Any person who violates paragraph (1) shall be fined not more than $10,000, or imprisoned not more than five years, or both.

(e) Kickbacks and illegal payments.

(1) It shall be unlawful for any person knowingly and willfully to give or accept any kickback or any illegal payment in connection with any qualified campaign expense of eligible candidates or their authorized committees. It shall be unlawful for the national committee of a major party or minor party knowingly and willfully to give or accept any kickback or any illegal payment in connection with any expense incurred by such committee with respect to a presidential nominating convention.

(2) Any person who violates paragraph (1) shall be fined not more than $10,000, or imprisoned not more than five years, or both.

(3) In addition to the penalty provided by paragraph (2), any person who accepts any kickback or illegal payment in connection with any qualified campaign expense of eligible candidates or their authorized committees, or in connection with any expense incurred by the national committee of a major party or minor party with respect to a presidential nominating convention. [sic] shall pay to the Secretary of the Treasury, for deposit in the general fund of the Treasury, an amount equal to 125 percent of the kickback or payment received.

(f) Unauthorized expenditures and contributions.

(1) Except as provided in paragraph (2), it shall be unlawful for any political committee which is not an authorized committee with respect to the eligible candidates of a political party for President and Vice President in a presidential election knowingly and willfully to incur expenditures to further the election of such candidates, which would constitute qualified campaign expenses if incurred by an authorized committee of such candidates, in an aggregate amount exceeding $1,000.

(2) This subsection shall not apply to (A) expenditures by a broadcaster regulated by the Federal Communications Commission, or by a periodical publication, in reporting the news or in taking editorial positions, or (B) expenditures by any organization described in section 501(c) which is exempt from tax under section 501(a) in communicating to its members the views of that organization.

(3) Any political committee which violates paragraph (1) shall be fined not more than $5,000, and any officer or member of such committee who knowingly and willfully consents to such violation and any other individual who knowingly and willfully violates paragraph (1) shall be fined not more than $5,000, or imprisoned not more than one year, or both.

(g) Unauthorized disclosure of information.

(1) It shall be unlawful for any individual to disclose any information obtained under the provisions of this chapter except as may be required by law.

(2) Any person who violates paragraph (1) shall be fined not more than $5,000, or imprisoned not more than one year, or both.

In **1976,** P.L. 94-455, Sec. 1906(b)(13)(C), substituted "to the Secretary of the Treasury" for "to the Secretary" in para. (e)(3), effective 2/1/77.
— P.L. 94-283, Sec. 307(f); substituted "9006(c)" for "9006(d)" in para. (b)(1), effective 5/11/76.
In **1974,** P.L. 93-443, Sec. 404(c)(22)(A), substituted "Commission" for "Comptroller General" each place it appeared in para. (d)(1) . . . Sec. 404(c)(22)(B), substituted "it" for "him" in para. (d)(1) . . . Sec. 406(b)(2), deleted "Campaign" from the heading of subsec. (a) . . . Sec. 406(b)(3), added the sentence at the end of para. (a)(1) . . . Sec. 406(b)(4), redesignated para. (c)(2) as (3) and added para. (c)(2) . . . Sec. 406(b)(5), added the sentence at the end of para. (e)(1) . . . Sec. 406(b)(6), added ", or in connection with any expense incurred by the national committee of a major party or minor party with respect to a presidential nominating convention." after "their authorized committees" in para. (e)(3), effective for tax. yrs. begin. after 12/31/74.
In **1973,** P.L. 93-53, Sec. (6)(c), substituted "9006(d)" for "9006(c)" in subsec. (b)(1), effective for tax. yrs. begin. after 12/31/72.
In **1971,** P.L. 92-178, Sec. 801, added Code Sec. 9012, effective 1/1/73.

Sec. 9013. Effective date of chapter.

The provisions of this chapter shall take effect on January 1, 1973.

In **1971,** P.L. 92-178, Sec. 801, added Code Sec. 9013.

CHAPTER 96.—PRESIDENTIAL PRIMARY MATCHING PAYMENT ACCOUNT

Sec.
9031. Short title.
9032. Definitions.
9033. Eligibility for payments.
9034. Entitlement of eligible candidates to payments.
9035. Qualified campaign expense limitations.
9036. Certification by Commission.
9037. Payments to eligible candidates.
9038. Examinations and audits; repayments.
9039. Reports to Congress; regulations.
9040. Participation by Commission in judicial proceedings.
9041. Judicial review.
9042. Criminal penalties.

In **1976,** P.L. 94-283, Sec. 305(b), substituted "limitations" for "limitation" in the title of Sec. 9035, effective 5/11/76.
In **1974,** P.L. 93-443, Sec. 408(c), substituted a new chapter 96.
Prior to amendment, chapter 96 read as follows:
"CHAPTER 96. PRESIDENTIAL ELECTION CAMPAIGN FUND ADVISORY BOARD
"SEC. 9021. ESTABLISHMENT OF ADVISORY BOARD.
"(a) *Establishment of board.*
"There is hereby established an advisory board to be known as the Presidential Election Campaign Fund Advisory Board (hereinafter in this section referred to as the 'Board'). It shall be the duty and function of the Board to counsel and assist the Comptroller General of the United States in the performance of the duties and functions imposed on him under the Presidential Election Campaign Fund Act.
"(b) *Composition of board.*
"The Board shall be composed of the following members:
"(1) the majority leader and minority leader of the Senate and the Speaker and minority leader of the House of Representatives, who shall serve ex officio;
"(2) two members representing each political party which is a major party (as defined in section 9002(6)), which members shall be appointed by the Comptroller General from recommendations submitted by such political party; and
"(3) three members representing the general public, which members shall be selected by the members described in paragraphs (1) and (2).
"The terms of the first members of the Board described in paragraphs (2) and (3) shall expire on the sixtieth day after the date of the first presidential election following January 1, 1973, and the terms of subsequent members described in paragraphs (2) and (3) shall begin on the sixty-first day after the date of a presidential election and expire on the sixtieth day following the date of the subsequent presidential election. The Board shall elect a Chairman from its members.
"(c) *Compensation.*
"Members of the Board (other than members described in subsection (b)(1)) shall receive compensation at the rate of $75 a day for each day they are engaged in performing duties and functions as such members, including traveltime, and, while away from their homes or regular places of business, shall be allowed travel expenses, including per diem in lieu of subsistence, as authorized by law for persons in the Government service employed intermittently.
"(d) *Status.*

"Service by an individual as a member of the Board shall not, for purposes of any other law of the United States be considered as service as an officer or employee of the United States."

Sec. 9031. Short title.

This chapter may be cited as the "Presidential Primary Matching Payment Account Act".

In **1974,** P.L. 93-443, Sec. 408(c), added Code Sec. 9031, effective for tax. yrs. begin. after 12/31/74.

Sec. 9032. Definitions.

For purposes of this chapter—

(1) The term "authorized committee" means, with respect to the candidates of a political party for President and Vice President of the United States, any political committee which is authorized in writing by such candidates to incur expenses to further the election of such candidates. Such authorization shall be addressed to the chairman of such political committee, and a copy of such authorization shall be filed by such candidates with the Commission. Any withdrawal of any authorization shall also be in writing and shall be addressed and filed in the same manner as the authorization.

(2) The term "candidate" means an individual who seeks nomination for election to be President of the United States. For purposes of this paragraph, an individual shall be considered to seek nomination for election if he (A) takes the action necessary under the law of a State to qualify himself for nomination for election, (B) receives contributions or incurs qualified campaign expenses, or (C) gives his consent for any other person to receive contributions or to incur qualified campaign expenses on his behalf. The term "candidate" shall not include any individual who is not actively conducting campaigns in more than one State in connection with seeking nomination for election to be President of the United States.

(3) The term "Commission" means the Federal Election Commission established by section 306(a)(1) of the Federal Election Campaign Act of 1971.

(4) Except as provided by section 9034(a), the term "contribution"—

(A) means a gift, subscription, loan, advance, or deposit of money, or anything of value, the payment of which was made on or after the beginning of the calendar year immediately preceding the calendar year of the presidential election with respect to which such gift, subscription, loan, advance, or deposit of money, or anything of value, is made, for the purpose of influencing the result of a primary election,

(B) means a contract, promise, or agreement, whether or not legally enforceable, to make a contribution for any such purpose,

(C) means funds received by a political committee which are transferred to that committee from another committee, and

(D) means the payment by any person other than a candidate, or his authorized committee, of compensation for the personal services of another person which are rendered to the candidate or committee without charge, but

(E) does not include—

(i) except as provided in subparagraph (D), the value of personal services rendered to or for the benefit of a candidate by an individual who receives no compensation for rendering such service to or for the benefit of the candidate, or

(ii) payments under section 9037.

(5) The term "matching payment account" means the Presidential Primary Matching Payment Account established under section 9037(a).

(6) The term "matching payment period" means the period beginning with the beginning of the calendar year in which a general election for the office of President of the United States will be held and ending on the date on which the national convention of the party whose nomination a candidate seeks nominates its candidate for the office of President of the United States, or, in the case of a party which does not make such nomination by national convention, ending on the earlier of (A) the date such party nominates its candidate for the office of President of the United States, or (B) the last day of the last national convention held by a major party during such calendar year.

(7) The term "primary election" means an election, including a runoff election or a nominating convention or caucus held by a political party, for the selection of delegates to a national nominating convention of a political party, or for the expression of a preference for the nomination of persons for election to the office of President of the United States.

(8) The term "political committee" means any individual, committee, association, or organization (whether or not incorporated) which accepts contributions or incurs qualified campaign expenses for the purpose of influencing, or attempting to influence, the nomination of any person for election to the office of President of the United States.

(9) The term "qualified campaign expense" means a purchase, payment, distribution, loan, advance, deposit, or gift of money or of anything of value—

(A) incurred by a candidate, or by his authorized committee, in connection with his campaign for nomination for election, and

(B) neither the incurring nor payment of which constitutes a violation of any law of the United States or of the State in which the expense is incurred or paid.

For purposes of this paragraph, an expense is incurred by a candidate or by an authorized committee if it is incurred by a person specifically authorized in writing by the candidate or committee, as the case may be, to incur such expense on behalf of the candidate or the committee.

(10) The term "State" means each State of the United States and the District of Columbia.

In 2007, P.L. 110-172, Sec. 11(a)(42)(C), substituted "section 306(a)(1)" for "section 309(a)(1)" in para. (3), enacted 12/29/2007.

In 1976, P.L. 94-283, Sec. 306(b)(1), added a sentence to the end of para. (2), effective 5/11/76.

—P.L. 94-283, Sec. 115(c)(2), substituted "309(a)(1)" for "310(a)(1)" in para. (3), effective 5/11/76.

In 1974, P.L. 93-443, Sec. 408(c), added Code Sec. 9032, effective for tax. yrs. begin. after 12/31/74.

Sec. 9033. Eligibility for payments.
(a) Conditions.

To be eligible to receive payments under section 9037, a candidate shall, in writing—

(1) agree to obtain and furnish to the Commission any evidence it may request of qualified campaign expenses,

(2) agree to keep and furnish to the Commission any records, books, and other information it may request, and

(3) agree to an audit and examination by the Commission under section 9038 and to pay any amounts required to be paid under such section.

(b) Expense limitation; declaration of intent; minimum contributions.

To be eligible to receive payments under section 9037, a candidate shall certify to the Commission that—

(1) the candidate and his authorized committees will not incur qualified campaign expenses in excess of the limitations on such expenses under section 9035,

(2) the candidate is seeking nomination by a political party for election to the office of President of the United States,

(3) the candidate has received matching contributions which in the aggregate, exceed $5,000 in contributions from residents of each of at least 20 States, and

(4) the aggregate of contributions certified with respect to any person under paragraph (3) does not exceed $250.

(c) Termination of payments.

(1) General rule. Except as provided by paragraph (2), no payment shall be made to any individual under section 9037—

(A) if such individual ceases to be a candidate as a result of the operation of the last sentence of section 9032(2); or

(B) more than 30 days after the date of the second consecutive primary election in which such individual receives less than 10 percent of the number of votes cast for all candidates of the same party for the same office in such primary election, if such individual permitted or authorized the appearance of his name on the ballot, unless such individual certifies to the Commission that he will not be an active candidate in the primary involved.

(2) Qualified campaign expenses; payments to Secretary. Any candidate who is ineligible under paragraph (1) to receive any payments under section 9037 shall be eligible to continue to receive payments under section 9037 to defray qualified campaign expenses incurred before the date upon which such candidate becomes ineligible under paragraph (1).

(3) Calculation of voting percentage. For purposes of paragraph (1)(B), if the primary elections involved are held in more than one State on the same date, a candidate shall be treated as receiving that percentage of the votes on such date which he received in the primary election conducted on such date in which he received the greatest percentage vote.

(4) Reestablishment of eligibility.

(A) In any case in which an individual is ineligible to receive payments under section 9037 as a result of the operation of paragraph (1)(A), the Commission may subsequently determine that such individual is a candidate upon a finding that such individual is actively seeking election to the office of President of the United States in more than one State. The Commission shall make such determination without requiring such individual to reestablish his eligibility to receive payments under subsection (a).

(B) Notwithstanding the provisions of paragraph (1)(B), a candidate whose payments have been terminated under paragraph (1)(B) may again receive payments (including amounts he would have received but for paragraph (1)(B)) if he receives 20 percent or more of the total number of votes cast for candidates of the same party in a primary election held after the date on which the election was held which was the basis for terminating payments to him.

In 1976, P.L. 94-283, Sec. 305(c), substituted "limitations" for "limitation" in para. (b)(1), effective 5/11/76.
—P.L. 94-283, Sec. 306(b)(2), added subsec. (c), effective 5/11/76.
In 1974, P.L. 93-443, Sec. 408(c), added Code Sec. 9033, effective for tax. yrs. begin. after 12/31/74.

Sec. 9034. Entitlement of eligible candidates to payments.
(a) In general.

Every candidate who is eligible to receive payments under section 9033 is entitled to payments under section 9037 in an amount equal to the amount of each contribution received by such candidate on or after the beginning of the calendar year immediately preceding the calendar year of the presidential election with respect to which such candidate is seeking nomination, or by his authorized committees, disregarding any amount of contributions from any person to the extent that the total of the amounts contributed by such person on or after the beginning of such preceding calendar year exceeds $250. For purposes of this subsection and section 9033(b), the term "contribution" means a gift of money made by a written instrument which identifies the person making the contribution by full name and mailing address, but does not include a subscription, loan, advance, or deposit of money, or anything of value or anything described in subparagraph (B), (C), or (D) of section 9032(4).

(b) Limitations.

The total amount of payments to which a candidate is entitled under subsection (a) shall not exceed 50 percent of the expenditure limitation applicable under section 315(b)(1)(A) of the Federal Election Campaign Act of 1971.

In 2007, P.L. 110-172, Sec. 11(a)(42)(D), substituted "section 315(b)(1)(A)" for "section 302(b)(1)(A)" in subsec. (b), enacted 12/29/2007.
In 1976, P.L. 94-283, Sec. 307(b), substituted "section 320(b)(1)(A) of the Federal Election Campaign Act of 1971" for "section 608(c)(1)(A) of title 18, United States Code," [sic] in subsec. (b), effective 5/11/76.
In 1974, P.L. 93-443, Sec. 408(c), added Code Sec. 9034, effective for tax. yrs. begin. after 12/31/74.

Sec. 9035. Qualified campaign expense limitations.
(a) Expenditure limitations.

No candidate shall knowingly incur qualified campaign expenses in excess of the expenditure limitation applicable under section 320(b)(1)(A) of the Federal Election Campaign Act of 1971, and no candidate shall knowingly make expenditures from his personal funds, or the personal funds of his immediate family, in connection with his campaign for nomination for election to the office of President in excess of, in the aggregate, $50,000.

(b) Definition of immediate family.

For purposes of this section, the term "immediate family" means a candidate's spouse, and any child, parent, grandparent, brother, half-brother, sister, or half-sister of the candidate, and the spouses of such persons.

In 1976, P.L. 94-283, Sec. 305(a), substituted "limitations" for "limitation" in the heading of Code Sec. 9035 ... added "(a) Expenditure limitations." before "No candidate" to designate subsec. (a) ... added ", and no candidate shall knowingly make expenditures from his personal funds, or the personal funds of his immediate family, in connection with his campaign for nomination for election to the office of President in excess of, in the aggregate, $50,000" after "State Code" in subsec. (a) ... added subsec. (b), enacted 5/11/76. Sec. 305(d) of the Act provides: "For purposes of applying section 9035(a) of the Internal Revenue Code of 1954, as amended by subsection (a), expenditures made by an individual after January 29, 1976, and before the date of the enactment of this Act [5/11/76] shall not be taken into account."
—P.L. 94-283, Sec. 307(c), substituted "section 320(b)(1)(A) of the Federal Election Campaign Act of 1971" for "section 608(c)(1)(A) of title 18, United States Code," in subsec. (a), effective 5/11/76.
In 1974, P.L. 93-443, Sec. 408(c), added Code Sec. 9035, effective for tax. yrs. begin. after 12/31/74.

Sec. 9036. Certification by Commission.
(a) Initial certifications.

Not later than 10 days after a candidate establishes his eligibility under section 9033 to receive payments under section 9037, the Commission shall certify to the Secretary for payment to such candidate under section 9037 payment in full of amounts to which such candidate is entitled under section 9034. The Commission shall make such additional certifications as may be necessary to permit candidates to receive payments for contributions under section 9037.

(b) Finality of determinations.

Initial certifications by the Commission under subsection (a), and all determinations made by it under this chapter, are final and conclusive, except to the extent that they are subject to examination and audit by the Commission under section 9038 and judicial review under section 9041.

In 1974, P.L. 93-443, Sec. 408(c), added Code Sec. 9036, effective for tax. yrs. begin. after 12/31/74.

Sec. 9037. Payments to eligible candidates.
(a) Establishment of account.

The Secretary shall maintain in the Presidential Election Campaign Fund established by section 9006(a), in addition to any account which he maintains under such section, a separate account to be known as the Presidential Primary Matching Payment Account. The Secretary shall deposit into the matching payment account, for use by the candidate of any political party who is eligible to receive payments under section 9033, the amount available after the Secretary determines that amounts for payments under section 9006(c) and for payments under section 9008(b)(3) are available for such payments.

(b) Payments from the matching payment account.

Upon receipt of a certification from the Commission under section 9036, but not before the beginning of the matching payment period, the Secretary shall promptly transfer the amount certified by the Commission from the matching payment account to the candidate. In making such transfers to candidates of the same political party, the Secretary shall seek to achieve an equitable distribution of funds available under subsection (a), and the Secretary shall take into account, in seeking to achieve an equitable distribution, the sequence in which such certifications are received.

In 1976, P.L. 94-455, Sec. 1906(b)(13)(A), substituted "Secretary" for "Secretary or his delegate" each place it appeared in Code Sec. 9037, effective 2/1/77.
In 1974, P.L. 93-443, Sec. 408(c), added Code Sec. 9037, effective for tax. yrs. begin. after 12/31/74.

Sec. 9038. Examinations and audits; repayments.
(a) Examinations and audits.

After each matching payment period, the Commission shall conduct a thorough examination and audit of the qualified campaign expenses of every candidate and his authorized committees who received payments under section 9037.

(b) Repayments.

(1) If the Commission determines that any portion of the payments made to a candidate from the matching payment account was in excess of the aggregate amount of payments to which such candidate was entitled under section 9034, it shall notify the candidate, and the candidate shall pay to the Secretary an amount equal to the amount of excess payments.

(2) If the Commission determines that any amount of any payment made to a candidate from the matching payment account was used for any purpose other than—

   (A) to defray the qualified campaign expenses with respect to which such payment was made, or

(B) to repay loans the proceeds of which were used, or otherwise to restore funds (other than contributions to defray qualified campaign expenses which were received and expended) which were used, to defray qualified campaign expenses,

it shall notify such candidate of the amount so used, and the candidate shall pay to the Secretary an amount equal to such amount.

(3) Amounts received by a candidate from the matching payment account may be retained for the liquidation of all obligations to pay qualified campaign expenses incurred for a period not exceeding 6 months after the end of the matching payment period. After all obligations have been liquidated, that portion of any unexpended balance remaining in the candidate's accounts which bears the same ratio to the total unexpended balance as the total amount received from the matching payment account bears to the total of all deposits made into the candidate's accounts shall be promptly repaid to the matching payment account.

(c) Notification.

No notification shall be made by the Commission under subsection (b) with respect to a matching payment period more than 3 years after the end of such period.

(d) Deposit of repayments.

All payments received by the Secretary under subsection (b) shall be deposited by him in the matching payment account.

In 1976, P.L. 94-455, Sec. 1906(b)(13)(A), substituted "Secretary" for "Secretary or his delegate" each place it appeared in Code Sec. 9038, effective 2/1/77.
In 1974, P.L. 93-443, Sec. 408(c), added Code Sec. 9038, effective for tax. yrs. begin. after 12/31/74.

Sec. 9039. Reports to Congress; regulations.
(a) Reports.

The Commission shall, as soon as practicable after each matching payment period, submit a full report to the Senate and House of Representatives setting forth—

(1) the qualified campaign expenses (shown in such detail as the Commission determines necessary) incurred by the candidates of each political party and their authorized committees,

(2) the amounts certified by it under section 9036 for payment to each eligible candidate, and

(3) the amount of payments, if any, required from candidates under section 9038, and the reasons for each payment required.

Each report submitted pursuant to this section shall be printed as a Senate document.

(b) Regulations, etc.

The Commission is authorized to prescribe rules and regulations in accordance with the provisions of subsection (c), to conduct examinations and audits (in addition to the examinations and audits required by section 9038(a)), to conduct investigations, and to require the keeping and submission of any books, records, and information, which it determines to be necessary to carry out its responsibilities under this chapter.

(c) Review of regulations.

(1) The Commission, before prescribing any rule or regulation under subsection (b), shall transmit a statement with respect to such rule or regulation to the Senate and to the House of Representatives, in accordance with the provisions of this subsection. Such statement shall set forth the proposed rule or regulation and shall contain a detailed explanation and justification of such rule or regulation.

(2) If either such House does not, through appropriate action, disapprove the proposed rule or regulation set forth in such statement no later than 30 legislative days after receipt of such statement, then the Commission may prescribe such rule or regulation. Whenever a committee of the House of Representatives reports any resolution relating to any such rule or regulation, it is at any time thereafter in order (even though a previous motion to the same effect has been disagreed to) to move to proceed to the consideration of the resolution. The motion is highly privileged and is not debatable. An amendment to the motion is not in order, and it is not in order to move to reconsider the vote by which the motion is agreed to or disagreed to. The Commission may not prescribe any rule or regulation which is disapproved by either such House under this paragraph.

(3) For purposes of this subsection, the term "legislative days" does not include any calendar day on which both Houses of the Congress are not in session.

(4) For purposes of this subsection, the term "rule or regulation" means a provision or series of interrelated provisions stating a single separable rule of law.

In 1976, P.L. 94-283, Sec. 304(b), added three new sentences at the end of the first sentence in para. (c)(2), and added para. (c)(4), effective 5/11/76.
In 1974, P.L. 93-443, Sec. 408(c), added Code Sec. 9039, effective for tax. yrs. begin. after 12/31/74.

Sec. 9040. Participation by Commission in judicial proceedings.
(a) Appearance by counsel.

The Commission is authorized to appear in and defend against any action instituted under this section, either by attorneys employed in its office or by counsel whom it may appoint without regard to the provisions of title 5, United States Code, governing appointments in the competitive service, and whose compensation it may fix without regard to the provisions of chapter 51 and subchapter III of chapter 53 of such title.

(b) Recovery of certain payments.

The Commission is authorized, through attorneys and counsel described in subsection (a), to institute actions in the district courts of the United States to seek recovery of any amounts determined to be payable to the Secretary as a result of an examination and audit made pursuant to section 9038.

(c) Injunctive relief.

The Commission is authorized, through attorneys and counsel described in subsection (a), to petition the courts of the United States for such injunctive relief as is appropriate to implement any provision of this chapter.

(d) Appeal.

The Commission is authorized on behalf of the United States to appeal from, and to petition the Supreme Court for certiorari to review, judgments or decrees entered with respect to actions in which it appears pursuant to the authority provided in this section.

In 1976, P.L. 94-455, Sec. 1906(b)(13)(A), substituted "Secretary" for "Secretary or his delegate" in Code Sec. 9040, effective 2/1/77.
In 1974, P.L. 93-443, Sec. 408(c), added Code Sec. 9040, effective for tax. yrs. begin. after 12/31/74.

Sec. 9041. Judicial review.
(a) Review of agency action by the Commission.

Any agency action by the Commission made under the provisions of this chapter shall be subject to review by the United States Court of Appeals for the District of Columbia Circuit upon petition filed in such court within 30 days after the agency action by the Commission for which review is sought.

Code Sec. 9041(b) — Financing Presidential campaigns

(b) Review procedures.
The provisions of chapter 7 of title 5, United States Code, apply to judicial review of any agency action, as defined in section 551(13) of title 5, United States Code, by the Commission.

In 1974, P.L. 93-443, Sec. 408(c), added Code Sec. 9041, effective for tax. yrs. begin. after 12/31/74.

Sec. 9042. Criminal penalties.
(a) Excess campaign expenses.
Any person who violates the provisions of section 9035 shall be fined not more than $25,000, or imprisoned not more than 5 years, or both. Any officer or member of any political committee who knowingly consents to any expenditure in violation of the provisions of section 9035 shall be fined not more than $25,000, or imprisoned not more than 5 years, or both.

(b) Unlawful use of payments.
(1) It is unlawful for any person who receives any payment under section 9037, or to whom any portion of any such payment is transferred, knowingly and willfully to use, or authorize the use of, such payment or such portion for any purpose other than—
  (A) to defray qualified campaign expenses, or
  (B) to repay loans the proceeds of which were used, or otherwise to restore funds (other than contributions to defray qualified campaign expenses which were received and expended) which were used, to defray qualified campaign expenses.
(2) Any person who violates the provisions of paragraph (1) shall be fined not more than $10,000, or imprisoned not more than 5 years, or both.

(c) False statements, etc.
(1) It is unlawful for any person knowingly and willfully—
  (A) to furnish any false, fictitious, or fraudulent evidence, books, or information to the Commission under this chapter, or to include in any evidence, books, or information so furnished any misrepresentation of a material fact, or to falsify or conceal any evidence, books, or information relevant to a certification by the Commission or an examination and audit by the Commission under this chapter, or
  (B) to fail to furnish to the Commission any records, books, or information requested by it for purposes of this chapter.
(2) Any person who violates the provisions of paragraph (1) shall be fined not more than $10,000, or imprisoned not more than 5 years, or both.

(d) Kickbacks and illegal payments.
(1) It is unlawful for any person knowingly and willfully to give or accept any kickback or any illegal payment in connection with any qualified campaign expense of a candidate, or his authorized committees, who receives payments under section 9037.
(2) Any person who violates the provisions of paragraph (1) shall be fined not more than $10,000, or imprisoned not more than 5 years, or both.
(3) In addition to the penalty provided by paragraph (2), any person who accepts any kickback or illegal payment in connection with any qualified campaign expense of a candidate or his authorized committees shall pay to the Secretary for deposit in the matching payment account, an amount equal to 125 percent of the kickback or payment received.

In 1974, P.L. 93-443, Sec. 408(c), added Code Sec. 9042, effective for tax. yrs. begin. after 12/31/74.

Subtitle I.—Trust Fund Code
Chapter
98. Trust fund code.
Sec. 9500. Short title.
This subtitle may be cited as the "Trust Fund Code of 1981".

In 1981, P.L. 97-119, Sec. 103(a), added Code Sec. 9500, effective 1/1/82. Sec. 103(d)(2) of this Act provides:
"(2) Savings provisions. The Black Lung Disability Trust Fund established by the amendments made by this section shall be treated for all purposes of law as the continuation of the Black Lung Disability Trust Fund established by section 3 of the Black Lung Benefits Revenue Act of 1977. Any reference in any law to the Black Lung Disability Trust Fund established by such section 3 shall be deemed to include a reference to the Black Lung Disability Trust Fund established by the amendments made by this section."

CHAPTER 98.—TRUST FUND CODE
Subchapter
A. Establishment of Trust Funds.
B. General provisions.

Subchapter A.—Establishment of Trust Funds
Sec.
9501. Black Lung Disability Trust Fund.
9502. Airport and Airway Trust Fund.
9503. Highway Trust Fund.
9504. Sport Fish Restoration and Boating Resources Trust Fund
9505. Harbor Maintenance Trust Fund.
9506. Inland Waterways Trust Fund.
9507. Hazardous Substance Superfund.
9508. Leaking Underground Storage Tank Trust Fund.
9509. Oil Spill Liability Trust Fund.
9510. Vaccine Injury Compensation Trust Fund.
9511. [Repealed] National Recreational Trails Trust Fund
9511. Patient-centered outcomes research trust fund.

In 2010, P.L. 111-148, added item 9511.
In 2005, P.L. 109-59, Sec. 1115(b)(2)(E), substituted "Sport Fish Restoration and Boating" for "Aquatic resources" in item 9504, effective 10/1/2005.
In 1991, P.L. 102-240, Sec. 8003(c), added item 9511.
In 1987, P.L. 100-203, Sec. 9202(b), added item 9510.
In 1986, P.L. 99-662, Sec. 1403(c), added item 9505 . . . Sec. 1405(c), added item 9506.
— P.L. 99-509, Sec. 8033(c), added item 9509.
— P.L. 99-499, Sec. 517(d), added item 9507 . . . Sec. 522(b), added item 9508.
In 1984, P.L. 98-369, Sec. 1016(d), added item 9504.
In 1983, P.L. 97-448, Sec. 531(d), added item 9503.
In 1982, P.L. 97-248, Sec. 281(c)(1), amended item 9501 and added item 9502.
Prior to amendment item 9501 read as follows:
"9501. Establishment of Black Lung Disability Trust Fund."

Sec. 9501. Black Lung Disability Trust Fund.
(a) Creation of trust fund.
(1) **In general.** There is established in the Treasury of the United States a trust fund to be known as the "Black Lung Disability Trust Fund", consisting of such amounts as may be appropriated or credited to the Black Lung Disability Trust Fund.
(2) **Trustees.** The trustees of the Black Lung Disability Trust Fund shall be the Secretary of the Treasury, the Secretary of Labor, and the Secretary of Health and Human Services.

3,996

Establishment of trust funds
Code Sec. 9502(b)(2)

(b) Transfer of certain taxes; other receipts.
(1) Transfer to Black Lung Disability Trust Fund of amounts equivalent to certain taxes. There are hereby appropriated to the Black Lung Disability Trust Fund amounts equivalent to the taxes received in the Treasury under section 4121 or subchapter B of chapter 42.
(2) Certain repaid amounts, etc. The following amounts shall be credited to the Black Lung Disability Trust Fund:
  (A) Amounts repaid or recovered under subsection (b) of section 424 of the Black Lung Benefits Act (including interest thereon).
  (B) Amounts paid as fines or penalties, or interest thereon, under section 423, 431, or 432 of the Black Lung Benefits Act.
  (C) Amounts paid into the Black Lung Disability Trust Fund by a trust described in section 501(c)(21).

(c) Repayable advances.
(1) Authorization. There are authorized to be appropriated to the Black Lung Disability Trust Fund, as repayable advances, such sums as may from time to time be necessary to make the expenditures described in subsection (d).
(2) Repayment with interest. Repayable advances made to the Black Lung Disability Trust Fund shall be repaid, and interest on such advances shall be paid, to the general fund of the Treasury when the Secretary of the Treasury determines that moneys are available in the Black Lung Disability Trust Fund for such purposes.
(3) Rate of interest. Interest on advances made pursuant to this subsection shall be at a rate determined by the Secretary of the Treasury (as of the close of the calendar month preceding the month in which the advance is made) to be equal to the current average market yield on outstanding marketable obligations of the United States with remaining periods to maturity comparable to the anticipated period during which the advance will be outstanding.

(d) Expenditures from trust fund.
Amounts in the Black Lung Disability Trust Fund shall be available, as provided by appropriation Acts, for—
  (1) the payment of benefits under section 422 of the Black Lung Benefits Act in any case in which the Secretary of Labor determines that—
    (A) the operator liable for the payment of such benefits—
      (i) has not commenced payment of such benefits within 30 days after the date of an initial determination of eligibility by the Secretary of Labor, or
      (ii) has not made a payment within 30 days after that payment is due,
    except that, in the case of a claim filed on or after the date of the enactment of the Black Lung Benefits Revenue Act of 1981, amounts will be available under this subparagraph only for benefits accruing after the date of such initial determination, or
    (B) there is no operator who is liable for the payment of such benefits;
  (2) the payment of obligations incurred by the Secretary of Labor with respect to all claims of miners or their survivors in which the miner's last coal mine employment was before January 1, 1970,
  (3) the repayment into the Treasury of the United States of an amount equal to the sum of the amounts expended by the Secretary of Labor for claims under part C of the Black Lung Benefits Act which were paid before April 1, 1978, except that the Black Lung Disability Trust Fund shall not be obligated to pay or reimburse any such amounts which are attributable to periods of eligibility before January 1, 1974,
  (4) the repayment of, and the payment of interest on, repayable advances to the Black Lung Disability Trust Fund,
  (5) the payment of all expenses of administration on or after March 1, 1978—
    (A) incurred by the Department of Labor or the Department of Health and Human Services under part C of the Black Lung Benefits Act (other than under section 427(a) or 433), or
    (B) incurred by the Department of the Treasury in administering subchapter B of chapter 32 and in carrying out its responsibilities with respect to the Black Lung Disability Trust Fund,
  (6) the reimbursement of operators for amounts paid by such operators (other than as penalties or interest) before April 1, 1978, in satisfaction (in whole or in part) of claims of miners whose last employment in coal mines was terminated before January 1, 1970, and
  (7) the reimbursement of operators and insurers for amounts paid by such operators and insurers (other than amounts paid as penalties, interest, or attorney fees) at any time in satisfaction (in whole or in part) of any claim denied (within the meaning of section 402(i) of the Black Lung Benefits Act) before March 1, 1978, and which is or has been approved in accordance with the provisions of section 435 of the Black Lung Benefits Act.
For purposes of the preceding sentence, any reference to section 402(i), 422, or 435 of the Black Lung Benefits Act shall be treated as a reference to such section as in effect immediately after the enactment of this section.

In **1982**, P.L. 97-248, Sec. 281(c)(2), amended the heading of Code Sec. 9501, effective 9/1/82.
Prior to amendment, the heading of Code Sec. 9501 read as follows:
"Sec. 9501. Establishment of Black Lung Disability Trust Fund."
In **1981**, P.L. 97-119, Sec. 103(a), added Code Sec. 9501, effective 1/1/82, except for para. (c)(3) which is effective for advances made after 12/31/81. Sec. 103(d)(2) of this Act provides:
"(2) Savings provisions. The Black Lung Disability Trust Fund established by the amendments made by this section shall be treated for all purposes of law as the continuation of the Black Lung Disability Trust Fund established by section 3 of the Black Lung Benefits Revenue Act of 1977. Any reference in any law to the Black Lung Disability Trust Fund established by such section 3 shall be deemed to include a reference to the Black Lung Disability Trust Fund established by the amendments made by this section."

Sec. 9502. Airport and Airway Trust Fund.
(a) Creation of trust fund.
There is established in the Treasury of the United States a trust fund to be known as the "Airport and Airway Trust Fund", consisting of such amounts as may be appropriated, credited, or paid into the Airport and Airway Trust Fund as provided in this section, section 9503(c)(5), or section 9602(b).

(b) Transfers to Airport and Airway Trust Fund.
There are hereby appropriated to the Airport and Airway Trust Fund amounts equivalent to—
  (1) the taxes received in the Treasury under—
    (A) section 4041(c) (relating to aviation fuels),
    (B) sections 4261 and 4271 (relating to transportation by air), and
    (C) section 4081 with respect to aviation gasoline and kerosene to the extent attributable to the rate specified in section 4081(a)(2)(C), and
  (2) the amounts determined by the Secretary of the Treasury to be equivalent to the amounts of civil penalties collected under section 47107(n) of title 49, United States Code.

Code Sec. 9502(b)(2)   **Establishment of trust funds**

There shall not be taken into account under paragraph (1) so much of the taxes imposed by section 4081 as are determined at the rate specified in section 4081(a)(2)(B).

(c) Appropriation of additional sums.

There are hereby authorized to be appropriated to the Airport and Airway Trust Fund such additional sums as may be required to make the expenditures referred to in subsection (d) of this section.

(d) Expenditures from Airport and Airway Trust Fund.

(1) **Airport and airway program.** Amounts in the Airport and Airway Trust Fund shall be available, as provided by appropriation Acts, for making expenditures before July 23, 2011, to meet those obligations of the United States—

(A) incurred under title I of the Airport and Airway Development Act of 1970 or of the Airport and Airway Development Act Amendments of 1976 or of the Aviation Safety and Noise Abatement Act of 1979 or under the Fiscal Year 1981 Airport Development Authorization Act or the provisions of the Airport and Airway Improvement Act of 1982 or the Airport and Airway Safety and Capacity Expansion Act of 1987 or the Federal Aviation Administration Research, Engineering, and Development Authorization Act of 1990 or the Aviation Safety and Capacity Expansion Act of 1990 or the Airport and Airway Safety, Capacity, Noise Improvement, and Intermodal Transportation Act of 1992 or the Airport Improvement Program Temporary Extension Act of 1994 or the Federal Aviation Administration Authorization Act of 1994 or the Federal Aviation Reauthorization Act of 1996 or the provisions of the Omnibus Consolidated and Emergency Supplemental Appropriations Act, 1999 providing for payments from the Airport and Airway Trust Fund or the Interim Federal Aviation Administration Authorization Act or section 6002 of the 1999 Emergency Supplemental Appropriations Act, Public Law 106-59, or the Wendell H. Ford Aviation Investment and Reform Act for the 21st Century or the Aviation and Transportation Security Act or the Vision 100—Century of Aviation Reauthorization Act or any joint resolution making continuing appropriations for the fiscal year 2008 or the Department of Transportation Appropriations Act, 2008 or the Airport and Airway Extension Act of 2008 or the Federal Aviation Administration Extension Act of 2008 or the Federal Aviation Administration Extension Act of 2008, Part II or the Federal Aviation Administration Extension Act of 2009 or the Fiscal Year 2010 Federal Aviation Administration Extension Act or the Fiscal Year 2010 Federal Aviation Administration Extension Act, Part II or the Federal Aviation Administration Extension Act of 2010 or the Airport and Airway Extension Act of 2010 or the Airport and Airway Extension Act of 2010, Part II or the Airline Safety and Federal Aviation Administration Extension Act of 2010 or the Airport and Airway Extension Act of 2010, Part III or the Airport and Airway Extension Act of 2010, Part IV or the Airport and Airway Extension Act of 2011, Part II or the Airport and Airway Extension Act of 2011, Part III;

(B) heretofore or hereafter incurred under part A of subtitle VII of title 49, United States Code, which are attributable to planning, research and development, construction, or operation and maintenance of—

(i) air traffic control,
(ii) air navigation,
(iii) communications, or
(iv) supporting services,

for the airway system; or

(C) for those portions of the administrative expenses of the Department of Transportation which are attributable to activities described in subparagraph (A) or (B).

Any reference in subparagraph (A) to an Act shall be treated as a reference to such Act and the corresponding provisions (if any) of title 49, United States Code, as such Act and provisions were in effect on the date of the enactment of the last Act referred to in subparagraph (A).

(2) **Transfers from Airport and Airway Trust Fund on account of certain refunds.** The Secretary of the Treasury shall pay from time to time from the Airport and Airway Trust Fund into the general fund of the Treasury amounts equivalent to the amounts paid after August 31, 1982, in respect of fuel used in aircraft, under section 6420 (relating to amounts paid in respect of gasoline used on farms, 6421 (relating to amounts paid in respect of gasoline used for certain nonhighway purposes), or 6427 (relating to fuels not used for taxable purposes) (other than subsections (l)(4) thereof).

(3) **Transfers from the Airport and Airway Trust Fund on account of certain section 34 credits.** The Secretary of the Treasury shall pay from time to time from the Airport and Airway Trust Fund into the general fund of the Treasury amounts equivalent to the credits allowed under section 34 (other than payments made by reason of paragraph (4) of section 6427(l)) with respect to fuel used after August 31, 1982. Such amounts shall be transferred on the basis of estimates by the Secretary of the Treasury, and proper adjustments shall be made in amounts subsequently transferred to the extent prior estimates were in excess of or less than the credits allowed.

(4) **Transfers for refunds and credits not to exceed trust fund revenues attributable to fuel used.** The amounts payable from the Airport and Airway Trust Fund under paragraph (2) or (3) shall not exceed the amounts required to be appropriated to such Trust Fund with respect to fuel so used.

(5) **Transfers from Airport and Airway Trust Fund on account of refunds of taxes on transportation by air.** The Secretary of the Treasury shall pay from time to time from the Airport and Airway Trust Fund into the general fund of the Treasury amounts equivalent to the amounts paid after December 31, 1995, under section 6402 (relating to authority to make credits or refunds) or section 6415 (relating to credits or refunds to persons who collected certain taxes) in respect of taxes under sections 4261 and 4271.

(6) **Transfers from the Airport and Airway Trust Fund on account of certain airports.** The Secretary of the Treasury may transfer from the Airport and Airway Trust Fund to the Secretary of Transportation or the Administrator of the Federal Aviation Administration an amount to make a payment to an airport affect by a diversion that is the subject of an administrative action under paragraph (3) or a civil action under paragraph (4) of section 47107(n) of title 49, United States Code.

(e) Limitation on transfers to trust fund.

(1) **In general.** Except as provided in paragraph (2), no amount may be appropriated or credited to the Airport and Airway Trust Fund on and after the date of any expenditure from the Airport and Airway Trust Fund which is not permitted by this section. The determination of whether an expenditure is so permitted shall be made without regard to—

Establishment of trust funds Code Sec. 9502

(A) any provision of law which is not contained or referenced in this title or in a revenue Act; and

(B) whether such provision of law is a subsequently enacted provision or directly or indirectly seeks to waive the application of this subsection.

(2) Exception for prior obligations. Paragraph (1) shall not apply to any expenditure to liquidate any contract entered into (or for any amount otherwise obligated) before July 23, 2011 [Ed. Note. We believe that the intent of P.L. 110-190, Sec. 3(b) is to amend subsec. (e), not subsec. (f), as the law directs], in accordance with the provisions of this section.

In 2011, P.L. 112-21, Sec. 3(a)(1), substituted "July 23, 2011" for "July 1, 2011" in para. (d)(1)... Sec. 3(a)(2), added "or the Airport and Airway Extension Act of 2011, Part III" before the semicolon at the end of subpara. (d)(1)(A)... Sec. 3(b), substituted "July 23, 2011" for "July 1, 2011" in para. (e)(2), effective 7/1/2011.

— P.L. 112-16, Sec. 3(a)(1), substituted "July 1, 2011" for "June 1, 2011" in para. (d)(1)... Sec. 3(a)(2), added "or the Airport and Airway Extension Act of 2011, Part II" before the semicolon at the end of subpara. (d)(1)(A)... Sec. 3(b), substituted "July 1, 2011" for "June 1, 2011" in para. (e)(2), effective 6/1/2011.

— P.L. 112-7, Sec. 3(a)(1), substituted "June 1, 2011" for "April 1, 2011" in para. (d)(1)... Sec. 3(a)(2), added "or the Airport and Airway Extension Act of 2011" before the semicolon at the end of subpara. (d)(1)(A)... Sec. 3(b), substituted "June 1, 2011" for "April 1, 2011" in para. (e)(2), effective 4/1/2011.

In 2010, P.L. 111-329, Sec. 3(a)(1), substituted "April 1, 2011" for "January 1, 2011" in para. (d)(1)... Sec. 3(a)(2), added "or the Airport and Airway Extension Act of 2010, Part IV" before the semicolon at the end of subpara. (d)(1)(A)... Sec. 3(b), substituted "April 1, 2011" for "January 1, 2011" in para. (e)(2), effective 1/1/2011.

— P.L. 111-249, Sec. 3(a)(1), substituted "January 1, 2011" for "October 1, 2010" in para. (d)(1)... Sec. 3(a)(2), added "or the Airport and Airway Extension Act of 2010, Part III" before the semicolon at the end of subpara. (d)(1)(A)... Sec. 3(b), substituted "January 1, 2011" for "October 1, 2010" in para. (e)(2), effective 10/1/2010.

— P.L. 111-216, Sec. 102(a)(1), substituted "October 1, 2010" for "August 2, 2010" in para. (d)(1)... Sec. 102(a)(2), added "or the Airline Safety and Federal Aviation Administration Extension Act of 2010" before the semicolon at the end of subpara. (d)(1)(A)... Sec. 102(b), substituted "October 1, 2010" for "August 2, 2010" in para. (e)(2), effective 8/2/2010.

— P.L. 111-197, Sec. 3(a)(1), substituted "August 2, 2010" for "July 4, 2010" in para. (d)(1)... Sec. 3(a)(2), added "or the Airport and Airway Extension Act of 2010" before the semicolon at the end of subpara. (d)(1)(A)... Sec. 3(b), substituted "August 2, 2010" for "July 4, 2010" in para. (e)(2), effective 7/4/2010.

— P.L. 111-161, Sec. 3(a)(1), substituted "July 4, 2010" for "May 1, 2010" in para. (d)(1)... Sec. 3(a)(2), added added "or the Airport and Airway Extension Act of 2010" before the semicolon at the end of subpara. (d)(1)(A)... Sec. 3(b), substituted "July 4, 2010" for "May 1, 2010" in para. (e)(2), effective 5/1/2010.

— P.L. 111-153, Sec. 3(a)(1), substituted "May 1, 2010" for "April 1, 2010" in para. (d)(1)... Sec. 3(a)(2), added "or the Federal Aviation Administration Extension Act of 2010" before the semicolon at the end of subpara. (d)(1)(A)... Sec. 3(b), substituted "May 1, 2010" for "April 1, 2010" in para. (e)(2), effective 4/1/2010.

— P.L. 111-147, Sec. 444(b)(1), substituted "section 9503(c)(5)" for "section 9503(c)(7)" in subsec. (a), effective for transfers relating to amounts paid and credits allowed after 3/18/2010.

In 2009, P.L. 111-116, Sec. 3(a)(1), substituted "April 1, 2010" for "January 1, 2010" in para. (d)(1)... Sec. 3(a)(2), added "or the Fiscal Year 2010 Federal Aviation Administration Extension Act, Part II" before the semicolon at the end of subpara. (d)(1)(A)... Sec. 3(b), substituted "April 1, 2010" for "January 1, 2010" in para. (e)(2);, effective 1/1/2010.

— P.L. 111-69, Sec. 3(a)(1), substituted "January 1, 2010" for "October 1, 2009" in para. (d)(1)... Sec. 3(a)(2), added "or the Fiscal Year 2010 Federal Aviation Administration Extension Act" before the semicolon at the end of subpara. (d)(1)(A)... Sec. 3(b), substituted "January 1, 2010" for "October 1, 2009" in para. (e)(2), effective 10/1/2009.

— P.L. 111-12, Sec. 3(a)(1), substituted "October 1, 2009" for "April 1, 2009" in para. (d)(1)... Sec. 3(a)(2), added "or the Federal Aviation Administration Extension Act of 2009" before the semicolon at the end of subpara. (d)(1)(A)... Sec. 3(b), substituted "October 1, 2009" for "April 1, 2009" in para. (e)(2), effective 4/1/2009.

In 2008, P.L. 110-330, Sec. 3(a)(1), substituted "April 1, 2009" for "October 1, 2008" in para. (d)(1)... Sec. 3(a)(2), added "or the Federal Aviation Administration Extension Act of 2008, Part II" before the semicolon at the end of subpara. (d)(1)(A)... Sec. 3(b), substituted "April 1, 2009" for "October 1, 2008" in para. (e)(2), effective 10/1/2008.

— P.L. 110-253, Sec. 3(a)(1), substituted "October 1, 2008" for "July 1, 2008" in para. (d)(1)... Sec. 3(a)(2), added "or the Federal Aviation Administration Extension Act of 2008" before the semicolon at the end of subpara. (d)(1)(A)... Sec. 3(b), substituted "October 1, 2008" for the date specified in such paragraph [July 1, 2008], in para. (e)(2), effective 7/1/2008.

— P.L. 110-190, Sec. 3(a)(1), substituted "July 1, 2008" for "March 1, 2008" in para. (d)(1)... Sec. 3(a)(2), added "or the Airport and Airway Extension Act of 2008" before the semicolon at the end of subpara. (d)(1)(A)... Sec. 3(b), substituted "July 1, 2008" for "March 1, 2008" in para. (e)(2) [Ed. Note. We believe that the intent of P.L. 110-190, Sec. 3(b) is to amend subsec. (e), not subsec. (f), as the law directs], effective 3/1/2008.

In 2007, P.L. 110-172, Sec. 11(f)(1), deleted subsec. (e) and redesignated subsec. (f) as (e), effective for fuel sold or used after 12/31/2004.

Prior to deletion, subsec. (e) read as follows:

"*(e) Certain taxes on alcohol mixtures to remain in general fund.* For purposes of this section, the amounts which would (but for this subsection) be required to be appropriated under subparagraphs (A), (C), and (D) of subsection (b)(1) shall be reduced by —

"(1) 0.6 cent per gallon in the case of taxes imposed on any mixture at least 10 percent of which is alcohol (as defined in section 4081(c)(3)) if any portion of such alcohol is ethanol; and

"(2) 0.67 cent per gallon in the case of fuel used in producing a mixture described in paragraph (1)."

— P.L. 110-161, Sec. 116(c)(1)(A), substituted "March 1, 2008" for "October 1, 2007" in para. (d)(1)... Sec. 116(c)(1)(B), added "or the Department of Transportation Appropriations Act, 2008" after "Aviation Reauthorization Act" in subpara. (d)(1)(A)... Sec. 116(c)(2), substituted "March 1, 2008" for "October 1, 2007" in para. (f)(2), effective 10/1/2007.

— P.L. 110-92, Sec. 149(b), added "or any joint resolution making continuing appropriations for the fiscal year 2008" before the semicolon at the end of subpara. (d)(1)(A), effective 9/29/2007.

In 2006, P.L. 109-432, Sec. 420(b)(5)(A), deleted "and (l)(5)" after "(other than subsections (l)(4)" in para. (d)(2)... Sec. 420(b)(5)(B), deleted "or (5)" after "by reason of paragraph (4)" in para. (d)(3), effective for kerosene sold after 9/30/2005, except as provided by Sec. 420(c)(2) of this Act, which reads as follows:

"(2) Special rule for pending claims. In the case of kerosene sold for use in aviation (other than kerosene to which section 6427(l)(4)(C)(ii) of the Internal Revenue Code of 1986 (as added by subsection (a)) applies or kerosene to which section 6427(l)(5) of such Code (as redesignated by subsection (b)) applies) after September 30, 2005, and before the date of the enactment of this Act, the ultimate purchaser shall be treated as having waived the right to payment under section 6427(l)(1) of such Code and as having assigned such right to the ultimate vendor if such ultimate vendor has met the requirements of subparagraph (A), (B), or (D) of section 6416(a)(1) of such Code."

In 2005, P.L. 109-59, Sec. 11161(c)(2)(A), substituted "appropriated, credited, or paid into the Airport and Airway Trust Fund as provided in this section, section 9503(c)(7), or section 9602(b)" for "appropriated or credited to the Airport and Airway Trust Fund as provided in this section or section 9602(b)" in subsec. (a)... Sec. 11161(c)(2)(B)(i), substituted "section 4041(c)" for "subsections (c) and (e) of section 4041" in subpara. (b)(1)(A)... Sec. 11161(c)(2)(B)(ii), substituted "and kerosene to the extent attributable to the rate specified in section 4081(a)(2)(C)" for "and aviation-grade kerosene" in subpara. (b)(1)(C)... Sec. 11161(d)(1), added "(other than subsections (l)(4) and (l)(5) thereof)" after "or 6427 (relating to fuels not used for taxable purposes)" in para. (d)(2)... Sec. 11161(d)(2), added "(other than payments made by reason of paragraph (4) or (5) of section 6427(l))" after "section 34" in para. (d)(3), effective for fuels or liquids removed, entered, or sold after 9/30/2005.

In 2004, P.L. 108-357, Sec. 853(b)(1)(A), added "and" at the end of subpara. (b)(1)(B), deleted subparas. (b)(1)(C) and (D), and added subpara. (b)(1)(C)... Sec. 853(d)(2)(O), substituted "There shall not be taken into account under paragraph (1) so much of the taxes imposed by section 4081 as are determined at the rate specified in section 4081(a)(2)(B)." for "There shall not be taken into account under paragraph (1) so much of the taxes imposed by section 4081 and 4091 as are determined at the rates specified in section 4081(a)(2)(B) or 4091(b)(2).", at the end of subsec. (b), effective for aviation-grade kerosene removed, entered, or sold after 12/31/2004.

Prior to deletion, subparas. (b)(1)(C) and (D) read as follows:

"(C) section 4081 (relating to gasoline) with respect to aviation gasoline, and"

"(D) section 4091 (relating to aviation fuel), and"

— P.L. 108-357, Sec. 853(f), of this Act, provides:

"*(f) Floor stocks tax.*

"(1) In general. There is hereby imposed on aviation-grade kerosene held on January 1, 2005, by any person a tax equal to—

"(A) the tax which would have been imposed before such date on such kerosene had the amendments made by this section been in effect at all times before such date, reduced by

"(B) the sum of—

"(i) the tax imposed before such date on such kerosene under section 4091 of the Internal Revenue Code of 1986, as in effect on such date, and

"(ii) in the case of kerosene held exclusively for such person's own use, the amount which such person would (but for this clause) reasonably expect (as of such date) to be paid as a refund under section 6427(l) of such Code with respect to such kerosene.

"(2) Exception for fuel held in aircraft fuel tank. Paragraph (1) shall not apply to kerosene held in the fuel tank of an aircraft on January 1, 2005.

"(3) Liability for tax and method of payment.

"(A) Liability for tax. The person holding the kerosene on January 1, 2005, to which the tax imposed by paragraph (1) applies shall be liable for such tax.

"(B) Method and time for payment. The tax imposed by paragraph (1) shall be paid at such time and in such manner as the Secretary of the Treasury (or the Secretary's delegate) shall prescribe, including the nonapplication of such tax on de minimis amounts of kerosene.

"(4) Transfer of floor stock tax revenues to trust funds. For purposes of determining the amount transferred to any trust fund, the tax imposed by this subsection shall be treated as imposed by section 4081 of the Internal Revenue Code of 1986—

"(A) in any case in which tax was not imposed by section 4091 of such Code, at the Leaking Underground Storage Tank Trust Fund financing rate under such section to the extent of 0.1 cents per gallon, and

"(B) at the rate under section 4081(a)(2)(A)(iv) of such Code to the extent of the remainder.

"(5) Held by a person. For purposes of this subsection, kerosene shall be considered as held by a person if title thereto has passed to such person (whether or not delivery to the person has been made).

"(6) Other laws applicable. All provisions of law, including penalties, applicable with respect to the tax imposed by section 4081 of such Code shall, insofar as applicable and not inconsistent with the provisions of this subsection, apply with respect to the floor stock tax imposed by paragraph (1) to the same extent as if such tax were imposed by such section."

In 2003, P.L. 108-176, Sec. 901(a)(1), substituted "October 1, 2007" for "October 1, 2003" in para. (d)(1) . . . Sec. 901(a)(2), added "or the Vision 100 — Century of Aviation Reauthorization Act" before the semicolon at the end of subpara. (d)(1)(A) . . . Sec. 901(b), substituted "October 1, 2007" for "October 1, 2003" in para. (f)(2), effective 12/12/2003.

In 2001, P.L. 107-71, Sec. 123(b), added "or the Aviation and Transportation Security Act" after "21st Century" in subpara. (d)(1)(A), effective 11/19/2001.

In 2000, P.L. 106-181, Sec. 1001(a)(1), substituted "October 1, 2003" for "October 1, 1998" in para. (d)(1) . . . Sec. 1001(a)(2), added "or the provisions of the Omnibus Consolidated and Emergency Supplemental Appropriations Act, 1999 providing for payments from the Airport and Airway Trust Fund or the Interim Federal Aviation Administration Authorization Act or section 6002 of the 1999 Emergency Supplemental Appropriations Act, P.L. 106-59, or the Wendell H. Ford Aviation Investment and Reform Act for the 21st Century" before the semicolon at the end of subpara. (d)(1)(A) . . . Sec. 1001(b), added subsec. (f), effective 4/5/2000.

In 1998, P.L. 105-206, Sec. 6010(g)(2), deleted "There shall not be taken into account under paragraph (1) so much of the taxes imposed by section 4081 and 4091 as are determined at the rates specified in section 4081(a)(2)(B) or 4091(b)(2)." at the end of para. (b)(1) and added "There shall not be taken into account under paragraph (1) so much of the taxes imposed by section 4081 and 4091 as are determined at the rates specified in section 4081(a)(2)(B) or 4091(b)(2)." at the end of subsec. (b), effective for taxes received in the Treasury on and after 10/1/97.

— P.L. 105-206, Sec. 6023(31), amended subsec. (e), effective 7/22/98.

Prior to amendment, subsec. (e) read as follows:

"(e) Special rules for transfers into trust fund.

"(1) Increases in tax revenues before 1993 to remain in general fund. In the case of taxes imposed before January 1, 1993, the amounts required to be appropriated under paragraphs (1), (2), and (3) of subsection (b) shall be determined without regard to any increase in a rate of tax enacted by the Revenue Reconciliation Act of 1990.

"(2) Certain taxes on alcohol mixtures to remain in general fund. For purposes of this section, the amounts which would (but for this paragraph) be required to be appropriated under paragraphs (1), (2), and (3) of subsection (b) shall be reduced by —

"(A) 0.6 cent per gallon in the case of taxes imposed on any mixture at least 10 percent of which is alcohol (as defined in section 4081(c)(3)) if any portion of such alcohol is ethanol, and

"(B) 0.67 cent per gallon in the case of fuel used in producing a mixture described in subparagraph (A)."

In 1997, P.L. 105-34, Sec. 1031(d)(1)(A), deleted "(to the extent that the rate of the tax on such gasoline exceeds 4.2 cents per gallon)" in subpara. (b)(1)(C) . . . Sec. 1031(d)(1)(B), deleted "to the extent attributable to the Airport and Airway Trust Fund financing rate" in subpara. (b)(1)(D) . . . Sec. 1031(d)(1)(C), added a sentence at the end of para. (b)(1) . . . Sec. 1031(d)(2), deleted subsec. (f), effective for taxes received in the Treasury on and after 10/1/97.

Prior to deletion, subsec. (f) read as follows:

"(f) Definition of Airport and Airway Trust Fund financing rate.

"For purposes of this section —

"(1) In general. Except as otherwise provided in this subsection, the Airport and Airway Trust Fund financing rate is —

"(A) in the case of fuel used in an aircraft in noncommercial aviation (as defined in section 4041(c)(2)), 17.5 cents per gallon, and

"(B) in the case of fuel used in an aircraft other than in noncommercial aviation (as so defined), zero.

"(2) Alcohol fuels. If the rate of tax on any fuel is determined under section 4091(c), the Airport and Airway Trust Fund financing rate is the excess (if any) of the rate of tax determined under section 4091(c) over 4.4 cents per gallon (1⁹⁄₁₀ of 4.4 cents per gallon in the case of a rate of tax determined under section 4091(c)(2)).

"(3) Termination. Notwithstanding the preceding provisions of this subsection, the Airport and Airway Trust Fund financing rate shall be zero with respect to taxes imposed during any period that the rate of the tax imposed by section 4091(b)(1) is 4.3 cents per gallon."

— P.L. 105-34, Sec. 1604(g)(5), redesignated para. (d)(5) [sic (6)] as para. (d)(6), effective 8/5/97.

— P.L. 105-2, Sec. 2(c)(1), amended subsec. (b), effective 2/28/97. . . . Sec. 2(c)(2), amended para. (f)(3), effective 2/28/97.

Prior to amendment, subsec. (b) read as follows:

"(b) Transfer to airport and airway trust fund of amounts equivalent to certain taxes. There is hereby appropriated to the Airport and Airway Trust Fund —

"(1) amounts equivalent to the taxes received in the Treasury after August 31, 1982, and before January 1, 1997, under subsections (c) and (e) of section 4041 (taxes on aviation fuel) and under sections 4261 and 4271 (taxes on transportation by air);

"(2) amounts determined by the Secretary of the Treasury to be equivalent to the taxes received in the Treasury after August 31, 1982, and before January 1, 1997, under section 4081 (to the extent of 15 cents per gallon), with respect to gasoline used in aircraft;

"(3) amounts determined by the Secretary to be equivalent to the taxes received in the Treasury before January 1, 1997, under section 4091 (to the extent attributable to the Airport and Airway Trust Fund financing rate);

"(4) amounts determined by the Secretary of the Treasury to be equivalent to the taxes received in the Treasury after August 31, 1982, and before January 1, 1997, under section 4071 with respect to tires of the types used on aircraft, and

"(5) amounts determined by the Secretary of the Treasury to be equivalent to the amounts of civil penalties collected under section 47107(n) of title 49, United States Code."

Prior to amendment, para. (f)(3) read as follows:

"(3) Termination. Notwithstanding the preceding provisions of this subsection, the Airport and Airway Trust Fund financing rate shall be zero with respect to —

"(A) taxes imposed after December 31, 1995, and before the date which is 7 calendar days after the date of the enactment of the Small Business Job Protection Act of 1996 and

"(B) taxes imposed after December 31, 1996."

In 1996, P.L. 104-264, Sec. 806(1), deleted "and" at the end of para. (b)(3) . . . Sec. 806(2), substituted ", and" for the period at the end of para. (b)(4) . . . Sec. 806(3), added para. (b)(5) . . . Sec. 806(4), added para. (d)(5) [sic (6)] . . . Sec. 1001(a), substituted "October 1, 1998" for "October 1, 1996" in para. (d)(1) . . . Sec. 1001(b), added "or the Federal Aviation Reauthorization Act of 1996" before the semicolon at the end of subpara. (d)(1)(A), effective for fiscal yrs. begin. after 9/30/96. Sec. 3(b) of this Act provides:

"(b) Limitation on Statutory Construction. Nothing in this Act or any amendment made by this Act shall be construed as affecting funds made available for a fiscal year ending before October 1, 1996."

— P.L. 104-264, Sec. 1203, of this Act, reads as follows:

"SEC. 1203. AUTHORITY TO CLOSE AIRPORT LOCATED NEAR CLOSED OR REALIGNED MILITARY BASE.

"Notwithstanding any other provision of a law, rule, or grant assurance, an airport that is not a commercial service airport may be closed by its sponsor without any obligation to repay grants made under chapter 471 or title 49, United States Code, the Airport and Airway Improvement Act of 1982, or any other law if the airport is located within 2 miles of a United States Army depot which has been closed or realigned; except that in the case of a disposal of the land associated with the airport, the part of the proceeds from the disposal that is proportional to the Government's share of the cost of acquiring the land shall be paid to the Secretary of Transportation for deposit in the Airport and Airway Trust Fund established under section 9502 of the Internal Revenue Code of 1986 (26 U.S.C. 9502)."

— P.L. 104-188, Sec. 1609(c)(1), substituted "January 1, 1997" for "January 1, 1996" each place it appeared in subsec. (b) . . . Sec. 1609(c)(2), amended para. (f)(3) . . . Sec. 1609(c)(3), added para. (d)(5) . . . Sec. 1609(g)(4)(C), substituted "section 4041(c)(2)" for "section 4041(c)(4)" in subpara. (f)(1)(A) . . . Sec. 1609(g)(4)(D), substituted "15 cents" for "14 cents" in para. (b)(2), effective on the 7th calendar day after 8/20/96.

Prior to amendment, para. (f)(3) read as follows:

"(3) Termination.

"Notwithstanding the preceding provisions of this subsection, the Airport and Airway Trust Fund financing rate is zero with respect to tax received after December 31, 1995."

— P.L. 104-188, Sec. 1703(n)(3), added "and before" after "1982," in para. (b)(2) [There is no need to make this amendment as "and before" appeared after "1982," in para. (b)(2) before amended by this Act.], effective 1/1/94.

In 1994, P.L. 103-305, Sec. 401(1), substituted "October 1, 1996" for "October 1, 1995" in para. (d)(1) . . . Sec. 401(2), added "or the Airport and Airway Safety, Capacity, Noise Improvement, and Intermodal Transportation Act of 1992" after "Capacity Expansion Act of 1990" in subpara. (d)(1)(A) . . . Sec. 401(3), substituted "or the Federal Aviation Administration Authorization Act of 1994" for "(as such Acts were in effect on the date of the enactment of the Airport Improvement Program Temporary Extension Act of 1994)" in subpara. (d)(1)(A) . . . Sec. 401(4), added the sentence at the end of para. (d)(1), effective 8/23/94.

— P.L. 103-272, Sec. 5(g)(3), substituted "part A of subtitle VII of title 49, United States Code," for "the Federal Aviation Act of 1958, as amended (49 U.S.C. 1301 et seq.)," in subpara. (d)(1)(B), effective 7/5/94.

— P.L. 103-260, Sec. 108, substituted "or the Airport Improvement Program Temporary Extension Act of 1994 (as such Acts were in effect on the date of the enactment of the Airport Improvement Program Temporary Extension Act of 1994" for "(as such Acts were in effect on the date of the enactment of the Airport and Airway Safety, Capacity, Noise Improvement, and Intermodal Transportation Act of 1992)" in subpara. (d)(1)(A), effective 5/26/94.

In 1993, P.L. 103-66, Sec. 13242(d)(32), added subsec. (f) . . . Sec. 13242(d)(33), substituted "(to the extent of 14 cents per gallon)" for "(to the extent attributable to the Highway Trust Fund financing rate and the deficit reduction rate)" in para. (b)(2), effective 1/1/94.

In 1992, P.L. 102-581, Sec. 501(1), substituted "October 1, 1995" for "October 1, 1992" in para. (d)(1) . . . Sec. 501(2), substituted "(as such Acts were in effect

Establishment of trust funds Code Sec. 9503(c)(1)

on the date of the enactment of the Airport and Airway Safety, Capacity, Noise Improvement, and Intermodal Transportation Act of 1992)" for "(as such Acts were in effect on the date of the enactment of the Aviation Safety and Capacity Expansion Act of 1990)" in subpara. (d)(1)(A), effective 10/31/92.

—P.L. 102-581, Sec. 502(a), amended para. (e)(1), effective 11/5/90.

Prior to amendment, para. (e)(1) read as follows:

"(1) Increases in tax revenues before 1993 to remain in general fund. In the case of taxes imposed before January 1, 1993, the amounts which would (but for this paragraph) be required to be appropriated under paragraphs (1), (2), and (3) of subsection (b) shall be 3 cents per gallon less (3.5 cents per gallon less in the case of taxes imposed by section 4041(c)(1) and 4091) than the amounts which would (but for this sentence) be appropriated under such paragraphs."

In 1990, P.L. 101-508, Sec. 11211(b)(6)(G), added para. (d)(4), effective 12/1/90.

—P.L. 101-508, Sec. 11213(c)(1), added subsec. (e) ... Sec. 11213(c)(2), added "and the deficit reduction rate" after "financing rate" in para. (b)(2) ... Sec. 11213(d)(3), substituted "January 1, 1996" for "January 1, 1991" each place it appeared in subsec. (b) ... Sec. 11213(d)(4), amended subpara. (d)(1)(A), effective 11/5/90.

Prior to amendment, subpara. (d)(1)(A) read as follows:

"(A) incurred under title I of the Airport and Airway Development Act of 1970 or of the Airport and Airway Development Act Amendments of 1976 or of the Aviation Safety and Noise Abatement Act of 1979 or under the Fiscal Year 1981 Airport Development Authorization Act or the provisions of the Airport and Airway Improvement Act of 1982 or the Airport and Airway Safety and Capacity Expansion Act of 1987 (as such Acts were in effect on the date of the enactment of the Airport and Airway Safety and Capacity Expansion Act of 1987);"

In 1989, P.L. 101-239, Sec. 7822(b)(5), substituted "; and" for ", and" in para. (b)(3), effective for sales after 3/31/88.

In 1987, P.L. 100-223, Sec. 402(a)(3), substituted "January 1, 1991" for "January 1, 1988" in paras. (b)(1), (b)(2) and (b)(4) ... Sec. 403(a), substituted "October 1, 1992" for "October 1, 1987" in para. (d)(1) ... Sec. 403(b), substituted "(or the Airport and Airway Safety and Capacity Expansion Act of 1987 (as such Acts were in effect on the date of the enactment of the Airport and Airway Safety and Capacity Expansion Act of 1987))" for "(as such Acts were in effect on the date of the enactment of the Surface Transportation Assistance Act of 1982)" in subpara. (d)(1)(A), effective 12/30/87.

—P.L. 100-203, Sec. 10502(d)(12), deleted "and" at the end of para. (b)(2), redesignated para. (b)(3) as (4), and added para. (b)(3), effective for sales after 3/31/88.

—P.L. 100-203, Sec. 10502(g), substituted "January 1, 1991" for "January 1, 1988" in para. (b)(3) (as added by Sec. 10502(d)(12)), effective 12/31/87.

In 1986, P.L. 99-499, Sec. 521(b)(2), substituted "subsections (c) and (e) of section 4041" for "subsections (c) and (d) of section 4041" in para. (b)(1), and substituted "section 4081 (to the extent attributable to the Highway Trust Fund financing rate)" for "section 4081" in para. (b)(2), effective 1/1/87.

In 1984, P.L. 98-369, Sec. 474(r)(42)(A), and (B), substituted "section 34" for "section 39" in para. (d)(3) and in the para. heading, effective for tax. yrs. begin. after 12/31/83, and to carrybacks to tax. yrs. begin. after 12/31/83.

—P.L. 98-369, Sec. 735(c)(15), substituted "under section 4071 with respect to tires of the types used on aircraft" for "under paragraphs (2) and (3) of section 4071(a), with respect to tires and tubes of the types used on aircraft" in para. (b)(3), effective for articles sold on or after 1/1/84.

In 1982, P.L. 97-248, Sec. 281(a), added Code Sec. 9502, effective 9/1/82. Sec. 281(d)(2) of this Act provides:

"(2) Savings provisions. The Airport and Airway Trust Fund established by the amendments made by this section shall be treated for all purposes of law as the continuation of the Airport and Airway Trust Fund established by section 208 of the Airport and Airway Revenue Act of 1970. Any reference in any law to the Airport and Airway Trust Fund established by such section 208 shall be deemed to include a reference to the Airport and Airway Trust Fund established by the amendments made by this section."

Sec. 9503. Highway Trust Fund.
(a) Creation of trust fund.

There is established in the Treasury of the United States a trust fund to be known as the "Highway Trust Fund", consisting of such amounts as may be appropriated or credited to the Highway Trust Fund as provided in this section or section 9602(b).

(b) Transfer to Highway Trust Fund of amounts equivalent to certain taxes and penalties.

(1) **Certain taxes.** There are hereby appropriated to the Highway Trust Fund amounts equivalent to the taxes received in the Treasury before October 1, 2011, under the following provisions—

(A) section 4041 (relating to taxes on diesel fuels and special motor fuels),

(B) section 4051 (relating to retail tax on heavy trucks and trailers),

(C) section 4071 (relating to tax on tires),

(D) section 4081 (relating to tax on gasoline, diesel fuel, and kerosene), and

(E) section 4481 (relating to tax on use of certain vehicles).

For purposes of this paragraph, taxes received under sections 4041 and 4081 shall be determined without reduction for credits under section 6426.

(2) Liabilities incurred before October 1, 2011. There are hereby appropriated to the Highway Trust Fund amounts equivalent to the taxes which are received in the Treasury after September 30, 2011, and before July 1, 2012, and which are attributable to liability for tax incurred before October 1, 2011, under the provisions described in paragraph (1).

(3) Repealed.

(4) Certain taxes not transferred to Highway Trust Fund. For purposes of paragraph (1) and (2), there shall not be taken into account the taxes imposed by—

(A) section 4041(d),

(B) section 4081 to the extent attributable to the rate specified in section 4081(a)(2)(B),

(C) section 4041 or 4081 to the extent attributable to fuel used in a train, or

(D) in the case of gasoline and special motor fuels used as described in paragraph (3)(D) or (4)(B) of subsection (c), section 4041 or 4081 with respect to so much of the rate of tax as exceeds—

(i) 11.5 cents per gallon with respect to taxes imposed before October 1, 2001,

(ii) 13 cents per gallon with respect to taxes imposed after September 30, 2001, and before October 1, 2003, and

(iii) 13.5 cents per gallon with respect to taxes imposed after September 30, 2003, before October 1, 2005.

(5) Certain penalties. There are hereby appropriated to the Highway Trust Fund amounts equivalent to the penalties paid under sections 6715, 6715A, 6717, 6718, 6719, 6720A, 6725, 7232, and 7272 (but only with regard to penalties under such section related to failure to register under section 4101).

(6) Limitation on transfers to Highway Trust Fund.

(A) In general. Except as provided in subparagraph (B), no amount may be appropriated to the Highway Trust Fund on and after the date of any expenditure from the Highway Trust Fund which is not permitted by this section. The determination of whether an expenditure is so permitted shall be made without regard to—

(i) any provision of law which is not contained or referenced in this title or in a revenue Act, and

(ii) whether such provision of law is a subsequently enacted provision or directly or indirectly seeks to waive the application of this paragraph.

(B) Exception for prior obligations. Subparagraph (A) shall not apply to any expenditure to liquidate any contract entered into (or for any amount otherwise obligated) before October 1, 2011, in accordance with the provisions of this section.

(c) Expenditures from Highway Trust Fund.

(1) Federal-aid highway program. Except as provided in subsection (e), amounts in the Highway Trust Fund shall be available, as provided by appropriation Acts, for making expenditures before October 1, 2011, to meet those obligations of the United States heretofore or hereafter incurred which are authorized to be paid out of the Highway Trust Fund under the Surface Transportation Extension Act of 2011 or any other provision of law which was re-

4,001

ferred to in this paragraph before the date of the enactment of such Act (as such Act and provisions of law are in effect on the date of the enactment of such Act).

(2) Floor stocks refunds. The Secretary shall pay from time to time from the Highway Trust Fund into the general fund of the Treasury amounts equivalent to the floor stocks refunds made before July 1, 2012, under section 6412(a). The amounts payable from the Highway Trust Fund under the preceding sentence shall be determined by taking into account only the portion of the taxes which are deposited into the Highway Trust Fund.

(3) Transfers from the trust fund for motorboat fuel taxes.
  (A) Transfer to land and water conservation fund.
    (i) In general. The Secretary shall pay from time to time from the Highway Trust Fund into the land and water conservation fund provided for in title I of the Land and Water Conservation Fund Act of 1965 amounts (as determined by the Secretary) equivalent to the motorboat fuel taxes received on or after October 1, 2005, and before October 1, 2011.
    (ii) Limitation. The aggregate amount transferred under this subparagraph during any fiscal year shall not exceed $1,000,000.
  (B) Excess funds transferred to sport fish restoration and boating trust fund. Any amounts in the Highway Trust Fund—
    (i) which are attributable to motorboat fuel taxes, and
    (ii) which are not transferred from the Highway Trust Fund under subparagraph (A),
shall be transferred by the Secretary from the Highway Trust Fund into the Sport Fish Restoration and Boating Trust Fund.
  (C) Motorboat fuel taxes. For purposes of this paragraph, the term "motorboat fuel taxes" means the taxes under section 4041(a)(2) with respect to special motor fuels used as fuel in motorboats and under section 4081 with respect to gasoline used as fuel in motorboats, but only to the extent such taxes are deposited into the Highway Trust Fund.
  (D) Determination. The amount of payments made under this paragraph after October 1, 1986 shall be determined by the Secretary in accordance with the methodology described in the Treasury Department's Report to Congress of June 1986 entitled "Gasoline Excise Tax Revenues Attributable to Fuel Used in Recreational Motorboats."

(4) Transfers from the trust fund for small-engine fuel taxes.
  (A) In general. The Secretary shall pay from time to time from the Highway Trust Fund into the Sport Fish Restoration and Boating Trust Fund amounts (as determined by him) equivalent to the small-engine fuel taxes received on or after December 1, 1990, and before October 1, 2011.
  (B) Small-engine fuel taxes. For purposes of this paragraph, the term "small-engine fuel taxes" means the taxes under section 4081 with respect to gasoline used as a fuel in the nonbusiness use of small-engine outdoor power equipment, but only to the extent such taxes are deposited into the Highway Trust Fund.

(5) Transfers from the trust fund for certain aviation fuel taxes. The Secretary shall pay at least monthly from the Highway Trust Fund into the Airport and Airway Trust Fund amounts (as determined by the Secretary) equivalent to the taxes received on or after October 1, 2005, and before October 1, 2011, under section 4081

with respect to so much of the rate of tax as does not exceed—
  (A) 4.3 cents per gallon of kerosene subject to section 6427(l)(4)(A) with respect to which a payment has been made by the Secretary under section 6427(l), and
  (B) 21.8 cents per gallon of kerosene subject to section 6427(l)(4)(B) with respect to which a payment has been made by the Secretary under section 6427(l).

Transfers under the preceding sentence shall be made on the basis of estimates by the Secretary, and proper adjustments shall be made in the amounts subsequently transferred to the extent prior estimates were in excess of or less than the amounts required to be transferred. Any amount allowed as a credit under section 34 by reason of paragraph (4) of section 6427(l) shall be treated for purposes of subparagraphs (A) and (B) as a payment made by the Secretary under such paragraph.

(d) Adjustments of apportionments.

(1) Estimates of unfunded highway authorizations and net highway receipts. The Secretary of the Treasury, not less frequently than once in each calendar quarter, after consultation with the Secretary of Transportation, shall estimate—
  (A) the amount which would (but for this subsection) be the unfunded highway authorizations at the close of the next fiscal year, and
  (B) the net highway receipts for the 48-month period beginning at the close of such fiscal year.

(2) Procedure where there is excess unfunded highway authorizations. If the Secretary of the Treasury determines for any fiscal year that the amount described in paragraph (1)(A) exceeds the amount described in paragraph (1)(B)—
  (A) he shall so advise the Secretary of Transportation, and
  (B) he shall further advise the Secretary of Transportation as to the amount of such excess.

(3) Adjustment of apportionments where unfunded authorizations exceed 4 years' receipts.
  (A) Determination of percentage. If, before any apportionment to the States is made, in the most recent estimate made by the Secretary of the Treasury there is an excess referred to in paragraph (2)(B), the Secretary of Transportation shall determine the percentage which—
    (i) the excess referred to in paragraph (2)(B), is of
    (ii) the amount authorized to be appropriated from the Trust Fund for the fiscal year for apportionment to the States.
If, but for this sentence, the most recent estimate would be one which was made on a date which will be more than 3 months before the date of the apportionment, the Secretary of the Treasury shall make a new estimate under paragraph (1) for the appropriate fiscal year.
  (B) Adjustment of apportionments. If the Secretary of Transportation determines a percentage under subparagraph (A) for purposes of any apportionment, notwithstanding any other provision of law, the Secretary of Transportation shall apportion to the States (in lieu of the amount which, but for the provisions of this subsection, would be so apportioned) the amount obtained by reducing the amount authorized to be so apportioned by such percentage.

(4) Apportionment of amounts previously withheld from apportionment. If, after funds have been withheld from apportionment under paragraph (3)(B), the Secretary of the Treasury determines that the amount described in paragraph (1)(A) does not exceed the amount described in

Establishment of trust funds Code Sec. 9503(f)(4)

paragraph (1)(B) or that the excess described in paragraph (1)(B) is less than the amount previously determined, he shall so advise the Secretary of Transportation. The Secretary of Transportation shall apportion to the States such portion of the funds so withheld from apportionment as the Secretary of the Treasury has advised him may be so apportioned without causing the amount described in paragraph (1)(A) to exceed the amount described in paragraph (1)(B). Any funds apportioned pursuant to the preceding sentence shall remain available for the period for which they would be available if such apportionment took effect with the fiscal year in which they are apportioned pursuant to the preceding sentence.

(5) **Definitions.** For purposes of this subsection—

(A) Unfunded highway authorizations. The term "unfunded highway authorizations" means, at any time, the excess (if any) of—

(i) the total potential unpaid commitments at such time as a result of the apportionment to the States of the amounts authorized to be appropriated from the Highway Trust Fund, over

(ii) the amount available in the Highway Trust Fund at such time to defray such commitments (after all other unpaid commitments at such time which are payable from the Highway Trust Fund have been defrayed).

(B) Net highway receipts. The term "net highway receipts" means, with respect to any period, the excess of—

(i) the receipts (including interest) of the Highway Trust Fund during such period, over

(ii) the amounts to be transferred during such period from such Fund under subsection (c) (other than paragraph (1) thereof).

(6) **Measurement of net highway receipts.** For purposes of making any estimate under paragraph (1) of net highway receipts for periods ending after the date specified in subsection (b)(1), the Secretary shall treat—

(A) each expiring provision of subsection (b) which is related to appropriations or transfers to the Highway Trust Fund to have been extended through the end of the 48-month period referred to in paragraph (1)(B), and

(B) with respect to each tax imposed under the sections referred to in subsection (b)(1), the rate of such tax during the 48-month period referred to in paragraph (1)(B) to be the same as the rate of such tax as in effect on the date of such estimate.

(7) **Reports.** Any estimate under paragraph (1) and any determination under paragraph (2) shall be reported by the Secretary of the Treasury to the Committee on Ways and Means of the House of Representatives, the Committee on Finance of the Senate, the Committees on the Budget of both Houses, the Committee on Public Works and Transportation of the House of Representatives, and the Committee on Environment and Public Works of the Senate.

(e) **Establishment of mass transit account.**

(1) **Creation of account.** There is established in the Highway Trust Fund a separate account to be known as the "Mass Transit Account" consisting of such amounts as may be transferred or credited to the Mass Transit Account as provided in this section or section 9602(b).

(2) **Transfers to mass transit account.** The Secretary of the Treasury shall transfer to the Mass Transit Account the mass transit portion of the amounts appropriated to the Highway Trust Fund under subsection (b) which are attributable to taxes under sections 4041 and 4081, imposed after March 31, 1983. For purposes of the preceding sentence, the term "mass transit portion" means, for any fuel with respect to which tax was imposed under section 4041 or 4081 and otherwise deposited into the Highway Trust Fund, the amount determined at the rate of—

(A) except as otherwise provided in this sentence, 2.86 cents per gallon,

(B) 1.43 cents per gallon in the case of any partially exempt methanol or ethanol fuel (as defined in section 4041(m)) none of the alcohol in which consists of ethanol,

(C) 1.86 cents per gallon in the case of liquefied natural gas,

(D) 2.13 cents per gallon in the case of liquefied petroleum gas, and

(E) 9.71 cents per MCF (determined at standard temperature and pressure) in the case of compressed natural gas.

(3) **Expenditures from account.** Amounts in the Mass Transit Account shall be available, as provided by appropriation Acts, for making capital or capital related expenditures (including capital expenditures for new projects) before October 1, 2011, in accordance with the Surface Transportation Extension Act of 2011 or any other provision of law which was referred to in this paragraph before the date of the enactment of such Act (as such Act and provisions of law are in effect on the date of the enactment of such Act).

(4) **Limitation.** Rules similar to the rules of subsection (d) shall apply to the Mass Transit Account except that subsection (d)(1) shall be applied by substituting "12 month" for "24-month".

(5) **Portion of certain transfers to be made from account.**

(A) In general. Transfers under paragraphs (2) and (3) of subsection (c) shall be borne by the Highway Account and the Mass Transit Account in proportion to the respective revenues transferred under this section to the Highway Account (after the application of paragraph (2)) and the Mass Transit Account.

(B) Highway Account. For purposes of subparagraph (A), the term "Highway Account" means the portion of the Highway Trust Fund which is not the Mass Transit Account.

(f) **Determination of trust fund balances after September 30, 1998.**

(1) **In general.** For purposes of determining the balances of the Highway Trust Fund and the Mass Transit Account after September 30, 1998, the opening balance of the Highway Trust Fund (other than the Mass Transit Account) on October 1, 1998, shall be $8,000,000,000. The Secretary shall cancel obligations held by the Highway Trust Fund to reflect the reduction in the balance under this paragraph.

(2) **Restoration of foregone interest.** Out of money in the Treasury not otherwise appropriated, there is hereby appropriated—

(A) $14,700,000,000 to the Highway Account (as defined in subsection (e)(5)(B)) in the Highway Trust Fund; and

(B) $4,800,000,000 to the Mass Transit Account in the Highway Trust Fund.

(3) [Ed. Note: We believe that Congress intended to add the following paragraph as Code Sec. 9503(f)(3).]

(4) **Treatment of appropriated amounts.** Any amount appropriated under this subsection to the Highway Trust Fund shall remain available without fiscal year limitation.

Code Sec. 9503 — Establishment of trust funds

In 2011, P.L. 112-5, Sec. 401(a)(1), substituted "October 1, 2011" for "March 5, 2011" in subpara. (b)(6)(B) and para. (c)(1)... Sec. 401(a)(2), substituted "the Surface Transportation Extension Act of 2011" for "the Surface Transportation Extension Act of 2010, Part II" in para. (c)(1) and (e)(3)... Sec. 401(a)(3), substituted "October 1, 2011" for "March 5, 2011" in para. (e)(3), effective 3/4/2011.

In 2010, P.L. 111-322, Sec. 2401(a)(1), substituted "March 5, 2011" for "December 31, 2010 (January 1, 2011, in the case of expenditures for administrative expenses)" in subpara. (b)(6)(B) and para. (c)(1)... Sec. 2401(a)(2), substituted "the Surface Transportation Extension Act of 2010, Part II" for "the Surface Transportation Extension Act of 2010" in para. (c)(1) and para. (e)(3)... Sec. 2401(a)(3), substituted "March 5, 2011" for "January 1, 2011" in para. (e)(3), effective 12/31/2010.

—P.L. 111-147, Sec. 441(a), deleted subpara. (f)(1)(B).
Prior to deletion, subpara. (f)(1)(B) read as follows:

"(B) notwithstanding section 9602(b), obligations held by such Fund after September 30, 1998, shall be obligations of the United States which are not interest-bearing."... Sec. 441(b)(1), substituted a period for ", and" at the end of subpara. (f)(1)(A)... Sec. 441(b)(2), substituted "1998, the opening balance" for "1998" and all that follows through "the opening balance" in the matter preceding subpara. (f)(1)(A), effective 3/18/2010.

—P.L. 111-147, Sec. 442(a), amended para. (f)(2)... Sec. 442(b), substituted "this section" for "this subsection" in para. (e)(1), effective 3/18/2010.

—P.L. 111-147, Sec. 443(a), added para. (f)(4), effective 3/18/2010.

—P.L. 111-147, Sec. 444(a), deleted para. (c)(2), and redesignated paras. (c)(3)-(6) as paras. (c)(2)-(5), effective for transfers relating to amounts paid and credits allowed after 3/18/2010.

Prior to deletion, para. (c)(2) read as follows:

"(2) Transfers from Highway Trust Fund for certain repayments and credits.

"(A) In general. The Secretary shall pay from time to time from the Highway Trust Fund into the general fund of the Treasury amounts equivalent to—

"(i) the amounts paid before July 1, 2012, under—

"(I) section 6420 (relating to amounts paid in respect of gasoline used on farms),

"(II) section 6421 (relating to amounts paid in respect of gasoline used for certain nonhighway purposes or by local transit systems), and

"(III) section 6427 (relating to fuels not used for taxable purposes),

" on the basis of claims filed for periods ending before October 1, 2011, and

"(ii) the credits allowed under section 34 (relating to credit for certain uses of fuel) with respect to fuel used before October 1, 2011.

"The amounts payable from the Highway Trust Fund under this subparagraph or paragraph (3) shall be determined by taking into account only the portion of the taxes which are deposited in to the Highway Trust Fund. Clauses (i)(III) and (ii) shall not apply to claims under section 6427(e).

"(B) Transfers based on estimates. Transfers under subparagraph (A) shall be made on the basis of estimates by the Secretary, and proper adjustments shall be made in amounts subsequently transferred to the extent prior estimates were in excess or less than the amounts required to be transferred.

"(C) Exception for use in aircraft and motorboats. This paragraph shall not apply to amounts estimated by the Secretary as attributable to use of gasoline and special fuels in motorboats or in aircraft."

—P.L. 111-147, Sec. 444(b)(2), substituted "paragraph (3)(D) or (4)(B)" for "paragraph (4)(D) or (5)(B)" in subpara. (b)(4)(D)... Sec. 444(b)(3), added matter to the end of para. (c)(2), as redesignated by Sec. 444(a)... Sec. 444(b)(4), substituted "(2) and (3)" for "(2), (3), and (4)" in subpara. (e)(5)(A), effective for transfers relating to amounts paid and credits allowed after 3/18/2010.

—P.L. 111-147, Sec. 445(a)(1)(A), substituted "December 31, 2010 (January 1, 2011" for "September 30, 2009 (October 1, 2009" in para. (c)(1)... Sec. 445(a)(1)(B), substituted "under the Surface Transportation Extension Act of 2010 or any other provision of law which was referred to in this paragraph before the date of the enactment of such Act (as such Act and provisions of law are in effect on the date of the enactment of such Act)." for "under" and all that follows in para. (c)(1)... Sec. 445(a)(2)(A), substituted "January 1, 2011" for "October 1, 2009" in para. (e)(3)... Sec. 445(a)(2)(B), substituted "in accordance with the Surface Transportation Extension Act of 2010 or any other provision of law which was referred to in this paragraph before the date of the enactment of such Act (as such Act and provisions of law are in effect on the date of the enactment of such Act)." for "in accordance with" and all that follows in para. (e)(3)... Sec. 445(a)(3), substituted "December 31, 2010 (January 1, 2011" for "September 30, 2009 (October 1, 2009" in subpara. (b)(6)(B), effective 9/30/2009.

In 2009, P.L. 111-46, Sec. 1, deleted para. (f)(2), and added new para. (f)(2), enacted 8/7/2009.

Prior to amendment, para. (f)(2) read as follows:

"Restoration of fund balance. Out of money in the Treasury not otherwise appropriated, there is hereby appropriated to the Highway Trust Fund $8,017,000,000."

In 2008, P.L. 110-318, Sec. 1(a)(1), redesignated paras. (f)(1) and (2) as subparas. (f)(1)(A) and (B), respectively... Sec. 1(a)(2), substituted "(1) In general. For purposes" for "For purposes" in the opening sentence of subsec. (f)... Sec. 1(a)(3), indented the flush sentence at the end of para. (f)(1) [as amended by this Act, see above] to the right... Sec. 1(a)(4), added para. (f)(2)... Sec. 1(b), substituted "paragraph" for "subsection" in the last sentence of para. (f)(1) [as amended by this Act, see above], enacted 9/15/2008.

—P.L. 110-244, Sec. 121(c), substituted "SAFETEA-LU Technical Corrections Act of 2008" for "Safe, Accountable, Flexible, Efficient Transportation Equity Act: A Legacy for Users" in paras. (c)(1) and (e)(3), effective 6/6/2008.

In 2007, P.L. 110-172, Sec. 11(a)(44), redesignated para. (c)(7) as (6), enacted 12/29/2007.

In 2006, P.L. 109-432, Sec. 420(b)(6)(A), amended subparas. (c)(7)(A) and (B) ... Sec. 420(b)(6)(B), deleted "or (5)" after "by reason of paragraph (4)" in para. (c)(7), effective for kerosene sold after 9/30/2005. Sec. 420(c)(2) of this Act, provides:

"(2) Special rule for pending claims. In the case of kerosene sold for use in aviation (other than kerosene to which section 6427(l)(4)(C)(ii) of the Internal Revenue Code of 1986 (as added by subsection (a)) applies or kerosene to which section 6427(l)(5) of such Code (as redesignated by subsection (b)) applies) after September 30, 2005, and before the date of the enactment of this Act, the ultimate purchaser shall be treated as having waived the right to payment under section 6427(l)(1) of such Code and as having assigned such right to the ultimate vendor if such ultimate vendor has met the requirements of subparagraph (A), (B), or (D) of section 6416(a)(1) of such Code."

Prior to amendment, subparas. (c)(7)(A)-(B) read as follows:

"(A) 4.3 cents per gallon of kerosene with respect to which a payment has been made by the Secretary under section 6427(l)(4), and

"(B) 21.8 cents per gallon of kerosene with respect to which a payment has been made by the Secretary under section 6427(l)(5)."

In 2005, P.L. 109-59, Sec. 11101(c)(1)(A), substituted "2011" for "2005" each place it appeared in paras. (b)(1) and (2) and paras. (c)(1) and (3)... Sec. 11101(c)(1)(B), substituted "2012" for "2006" each place it appeared in paras. (b)(1) and (2) and paras. (c)(2) and (3)... Sec. 11101(c)(2)(A), substituted "2011" for "2005" in subpara. (c)(5)(A)... Sec. 11101(d)(1)(A), amended para. (c)(1)... Sec. 11101(d)(1)(B), amended para. (e)(3)... Sec. 11101(d)(1)(C), substituted "September 30, 2009 (October 1, 2009, in the case of expenditures for administrative expenses)" for "July 31, 2005" in subpara. (b)(6)(B), effective 8/10/2005.

Prior to amendment, para. (c)(1) read as follows:

"(1) Federal-aid highway program. Except as provided in subsection (e), amounts in the Highway Trust Fund shall be available, as provided by appropriation Acts, for making expenditures before August 15, 2005, to meet those obligations of the United States heretofore or hereafter incurred which are—

"(A) authorized by law to be paid out of the Highway Trust Fund established by section 209 of the Highway Revenue Act of 1956,

"(B) authorized to be paid out of the Highway Trust Fund under title I or II of the Surface Transportation Assistance Act of 1982,

"(C) authorized to be paid out of the Highway Trust Fund under the Surface Transportation and Uniform Relocation Assistance Act of 1987,

"(D) authorized to be paid out of the Highway Trust Fund under the Intermodal Surface Transportation Efficiency Act of 1991,

"(E) authorized to be paid out of the Highway Trust Fund under the Transportation Equity Act for the 21st Century,

"(F) authorized to be paid out of the Highway Trust Fund under the Surface Transportation Extension Act of 2003,

"(G) authorized to be paid out of the Highway Trust Fund under the Surface Transportation Extension Act of 2004,

"(H) authorized to be paid out of the Highway Trust Fund under the Surface Transportation Extension Act of 2004, Part II,

"(I) authorized to be paid out of the Highway Trust Fund under the Surface Transportation Extension Act of 2004, Part III,

"(J) authorized to be paid out of the Highway Trust Fund under the Surface Transportation Extension Act of 2004, Part IV,

"(K) authorized to be paid out of the Highway Trust Fund under the Surface Transportation Extension Act of 2004, Part V,

"(L) authorized to be paid out of the Highway Trust Fund under the Surface Transportation Extension Act of 2005,

"(M) authorized to be paid out of the Highway Trust Fund under the Surface Transportation Extension Act of 2005, Part II,

"(N) authorized to be paid out of the Highway Trust Fund under the Surface Transportation Extension Act of 2005, Part III,

"(O) authorized to be paid out of the Highway Trust Fund under the Surface Transportation Extension Act of 2005, Part IV,

"(P) authorized to be paid out of the Highway Trust Fund under the Surface Transportation Extension Act of 2005, Part V, or

"(Q) authorized to be paid out of the Highway Trust Fund under the Surface Transportation Extension Act of 2005, Part VI.

"In determining the authorizations under the Acts referred to in the preceding subparagraphs, such Acts shall be applied as in effect on the date of enactment of the Surface Transportation Extension Act of 2005, Part VI."

Prior to amendment, para. (e)(3) reads as follows:

"(3) Expenditures from account. Amounts in the Mass Transit Account shall be available, as provided by appropriation Acts, for making capital or capital-related expenditures before August 15, 2005 (including capital expenditures for new projects) in accordance with,

"(A) section 5338(a)(1) or (b)(1) of title 49,

"(B) the Intermodal Surface Transportation Efficiency Act of 1991,

"(C) the Transportation Equity Act for the 21st Century,

"(D) the Surface Transportation Extension Act of 2003,

"(E) the Surface Transportation Extension Act of 2004,

"(F) the Surface Transportation Extension Act of 2004, Part II,

"(G) the Surface Transportation Extension Act of 2004, Part III,

"(H) the Surface Transportation Extension Act of 2004, Part IV,

"(I) the Surface Transportation Extension Act of 2004, Part V,

"(J) the Surface Transportation Extension Act of 2005,

"(K) the Surface Transportation Extension Act of 2005, Part II,

Establishment of trust funds
Code Sec. 9503

"(L) the Surface Transportation Extension Act of 2005, Part III,
"(M) the Surface Transportation Extension Act of 2005, Part IV,
"(N) the Surface Transportation Extension Act of 2005, Part V, or
"(O) the Surface Transportation Extension Act of 2005, Part VI,
as such section and Acts are in effect on the date of the enactment of the Surface Transportation Extension Act of 2005, Part VI.'

—P.L. 109-59, Sec. 11102(a)(1), substituted '48-month' for '24-month' in subpara. (d)(1)(B)... Sec. 11102(a)(2), substituted '4 years'' for '2 years'' in the heading of para. (d)(3)... Sec. 11102(b), redesignated para. (d)(6) as (7) and added para. (d)(6), effective 8/10/2005.

—P.L. 109-59, Sec. 11115(a)(1)(A), deleted the heading of para. (c)(4) and deleted subparas. (c)(4)(A)-(C)... Sec. 11115(a)(1)(B), redesignated subparas. (c)(4)(D) and (E) as subparas. (c)(4)(C) and (D)... Sec. 11115(a)(1)(C), added the heading of para. (c)(4) and added new subparas. (c)(4)(A) and (B)... Sec. 11115(a)(2), substituted 'and Boating' for 'Account in the Aquatic Resources' in subpara. (c)(5)(A), effective 10/1/2005.

Prior to deletion, the heading of para. (c)(4) and subparas. (c)(4)(A)-(C) read as follows:

"(4) Transfers from the trust fund for motorboat fuel taxes.

"(A) Transfer to boat safety account.

"(i) In general. The Secretary shall pay from time to time from the Highway Trust Fund into the Boat Safety Account in the Aquatic Resources Trust Fund amounts (as determined by him) equivalent to the motorboat fuel taxes received on or after October 1, 1980, and before October 1, 2005.

"(ii) Limitations.

"(I) Limit on transfers during any fiscal year. The aggregate amount transferred under this subparagraph during any fiscal year shall not exceed $60,000,000 for each of fiscal years 1989 and 1990 and $70,000,000 for each fiscal year thereafter.

"(II) Limit on amount in fund. No amount shall be transferred under this subparagraph if the Secretary determines that such transfer would result in increasing the amount in the Boat Safety Account to a sum in excess of $60,000,000 for each of fiscal years 1989 and 1990 and $70,000,000 for each fiscal year thereafter.

In making the determination under subclause (II) for any fiscal year, the Secretary shall not take into account any amount appropriated from the Boat Safety Account in any preceding fiscal year but not distributed.

"(B) $1,000,000 per year of excess transferred to land and water conservation fund.

"(i) In general. Any amount received in the Highway Trust Fund—

"(I) which is attributable to motorboat fuel taxes, and

"(II) which is not transferred from the Highway Trust Fund under subparagraph (A),

shall be transferred (subject to the limitation of clause (ii)) by the Secretary from the Highway Trust Fund into the land and water conservation fund provided for in title I of the Land and Water Conservation Fund Act of 1965.

"(ii) Limitation. The aggregate amount transferred under this subparagraph during any fiscal year shall not exceed $1,000,000.

"(C) Excess funds transferred to sport fish restoration account. Any amount received in the Highway Trust Fund—

"(i) which is attributable to motorboat fuel taxes, and

"(ii) which is not transferred from the Highway Trust Fund under subparagraph (A) or (B),

shall be transferred by the Secretary from the Highway Trust Fund into the Sport Fish Restoration Account in the Aquatic Resources Trust Fund.'

—P.L. 109-59, Sec. 11161(c)(1), added para. (c)(7) [sic (6)]... Sec. 11161(c)(2)(C), deleted para. (b)(3), effective for fuels or liquids removed, entered, or sold after 9/30/2005.

Prior to deletion, para. (b)(3) read as follows:

"(3) Adjustments for aviation uses. The amounts described in paragraphs (1) and (2) with respect to any period shall (before the application of this subsection) be reduced by appropriate amounts to reflect any amounts transferred to the Airport and Airway Trust Fund under section 9502(b) with respect to such period."

—P.L. 109-59, Sec. 11167(b), added "6720A," after "6719," in para. (b)(5), effective for any transfer, sale, or holding out for sale or resale occurring after 8/10/2005.

—P.L. 109-42, Sec. 7(a)(1)(A), substituted "August 15, 2005" for "July 31, 2005" in matter before subpara. (c)(1)(A)... Sec. 7(a)(1)(B), deleted "or" at the end of subpara. (c)(1)(O)... Sec. 7(a)(1)(C), substituted ", or" for the period at the end of subpara. (c)(1)(P)... Sec. 7(a)(1)(D), added subpara. (c)(1)(Q)... Sec. 7(a)(1)(E), substituted "Surface Transportation Extension Act of 2005, Part VI" for "Surface Transportation Extension Act of 2005, Part V" in matter following subpara. (c)(1)(Q)... Sec. 7(a)(2)(A), substituted "August 15, 2005" for "July 31, 2005" in matter before subpara. (e)(3)(A)... Sec. 7(a)(2)(B), deleted "or" at the end of subpara. (e)(3)(M)... Sec. 7(a)(2)(C), added "or" at the end of subpara. (e)(3)(N)... Sec. 7(a)(2)(D), added subpara. (e)(3)(O)... Sec. 7(a)(2)(E), substituted "Surface Transportation Extension Act of 2005, Part VI" for "Surface Transportation Extension Act of 2005, Part V" in matter after subpara. (e)(3)(O) ... Sec. 7(a)(3), added "The preceding sentence shall be applied by substituting 'August 15, 2005' for the date therein." at the end of subpara. (b)(6)(B), effective 7/30/2005.

—P.L. 109-42, Sec. 7(c), of this Act, reads as follows:

"(c) Temporary rule regarding adjustments. During the period beginning on the date of the enactment of the Surface Transportation Extension Act of 2003 and ending on August 14, 2005, for purposes of making any estimate under section 9503(d) of the Internal Revenue Code of 1986 of receipts of the Highway Trust Fund, the Secretary of the Treasury shall treat—

"(1) each expiring provision of paragraphs (1) through (4) of section 9503(b) of such Code which is related to appropriations or transfers to such Fund to have been extended through the end of the 24-month period referred to in section 9503(d)(1)(B) of such Code, and

"(2) with respect to each tax imposed under the sections referred to in section 9503(b)(1) of such Code, the rate of such tax during the 24-month period referred to in section 9503(d)(1)(B) of such Code to be the same as the rate of such tax as in effect on the date of the enactment of the Surface Transportation Extension Act of 2003."

—P.L. 109-42, Sec. 7(d)(1), deleted "'The preceding sentence shall be applied by substituting "August 15, 2005" for the date therein.' at the end of subpara. (b)(6)(B), effective on the date of the enactment [8/10/2005] of the Safe, Accountable, Flexible, Efficient Transportation Equity Act: A Legacy for Users and shall be executed immediately before the amendments made by such Act.

—P.L. 109-40, Sec. 9(a)(1)(A), substituted 'July 31, 2005' for 'July 28, 2005' in matter before subpara. (c)(1)(A)... Sec. 9(a)(1)(B), deleted 'or' at the end of subpara. (c)(1)(N)... Sec. 9(a)(1)(C), substituted ', or' for the period at the end of subpara. (c)(1)(O)... Sec. 9(a)(1)(D), added subpara. (c)(1)(P)... Sec. 9(a)(1)(E), substituted 'Surface Transportation Extension Act of 2005, Part V' for 'Surface Transportation Extension Act of 2005, Part IV' in matter following subpara. (c)(1)(P)... Sec. 9(a)(2)(A), substituted 'July 31, 2005' for 'July 28, 2005' in matter before subpara. (e)(3)(A)... Sec. 9(a)(2)(B), deleted 'or' at the end of subpara. (e)(3)(L)... Sec. 9(a)(2)(C), added 'or' at the end of subpara. (e)(3)(M)... Sec. 9(a)(2)(D), added subpara. (e)(3)(N)... Sec. 9(a)(2)(E), substituted 'Surface Transportation Extension Act of 2005, Part V' for 'Surface Transportation Extension Act of 2005, Part IV' in matter after subpara. (e)(3)(N)... Sec. 9(a)(3), substituted 'July 31, 2005' for 'July 28, 2005' in subpara. (b)(6)(B), effective 7/28/2005.

—P.L. 109-40, Sec. 9(d), of this Act, reads as follows:

"(d) Temporary rule regarding adjustments. During the period beginning on the date of the enactment of the Surface Transportation Extension Act of 2003 and ending on July 30, 2005, for purposes of making any estimate under section 9503(d) of the Internal Revenue Code of 1986 of receipts of the Highway Trust Fund, the Secretary of the Treasury shall treat—

"(1) each expiring provision of paragraphs (1) through (4) of section 9503(b) of such Code which is related to appropriations or transfers to such Fund to have been extended through the end of the 24-month period referred to in section 9503(d)(1)(B) of such Code; and

"(2) with respect to each tax imposed under the sections referred to in section 9503(b)(1) of such Code, the rate of such tax during the 24-month period referred to in section 9503(d)(1)(B) of such Code to be the same as the rate of such tax as in effect on the date of the enactment of the Surface Transportation Extension Act of 2003."

—P.L. 109-37, Sec. 9(a)(1)(A), substituted "July 28, 2005" for "July 22, 2005" in matter before subpara. (c)(1)(A)... Sec. 9(a)(1)(B), deleted "or" at the end of subpara. (c)(1)(M)... Sec. 9(a)(1)(C), substituted ", or" for the period at the end of subpara. (c)(1)(N)... Sec. 9(a)(1)(D), added subpara. (c)(1)(O)... Sec. 9(a)(1)(E), substituted "Surface Transportation Extension Act of 2005, Part IV" for "Surface Transportation Extension Act of 2005, Part III" in matter following subpara. (c)(1)(O)... Sec. 9(a)(2)(A), substituted "July 28, 2005" for "July 22, 2005" in matter before subpara. (e)(3)(A)... Sec. 9(a)(2)(B), deleted "or" at the end of subpara. (e)(3)(K)... Sec. 9(a)(2)(C), added "or" at the end of subpara. (e)(3)(L)... Sec. 9(a)(2)(D), added subpara. (e)(3)(M)... Sec. 9(a)(2)(E), substituted "Surface Transportation Extension Act of 2005, Part IV" for "Surface Transportation Extension Act of 2005, Part III" in matter after subpara. (e)(3)(M)... Sec. 9(a)(3), substituted "July 28, 2005" for "July 22, 2005" in subpara. (b)(6)(B), effective 7/22/2005.

—P.L. 109-37, Sec. 9(d), of this Act, reads as follows:

"(d) Temporary rule regarding adjustments. During the period beginning on the date of the enactment of the Surface Transportation Extension Act of 2003 and ending on July 27, 2005, for purposes of making any estimate under section 9503(d) of the Internal Revenue Code of 1986 of receipts of the Highway Trust Fund, the Secretary of the Treasury shall treat—

"(1) each expiring provision of paragraphs (1) through (4) of section 9503(b) of such Code which is related to appropriations or transfers to such Fund to have been extended through the end of the 24-month period referred to in section 9503(d)(1)(B) of such Code; and

"(2) with respect to each tax imposed under the sections referred to in section 9503(b)(1) of such Code, the rate of such tax during the 24-month period referred to in section 9503(d)(1)(B) of such Code to be the same as the rate of such tax as in effect on the date of the enactment of the Surface Transportation Extension Act of 2003."

—P.L. 109-35, Sec. 9(a)(1)(A), substituted "July 22, 2005" for "July 20, 2005" in matter before subpara. (c)(1)(A)... Sec. 9(a)(1)(B), deleted "or" at the end of subpara. (c)(1)(L)... Sec. 9(a)(1)(C), substituted ", or" for the period at the end of subpara. (c)(1)(M)... Sec. 9(a)(1)(D), added subpara. (c)(1)(N)... Sec. 9(a)(1)(E), substituted "Surface Transportation Extension Act of 2005, Part III" for "Surface Transportation Extension Act of 2005, Part II" in matter following subpara. (c)(1)(N)... Sec. 9(a)(2)(A), substituted "July 22, 2005" for "July 20, 2005" in matter before subpara. (e)(3)(A)... Sec. 9(a)(2)(B), deleted "or" at the end of subpara. (e)(3)(J)... Sec. 9(a)(2)(C), added "or" at the end of subpara. (e)(3)(K)... Sec. 9(a)(2)(D), added subpara. (e)(3)(L)... Sec. 9(a)(2)(E), substituted "Surface Transportation Extension Act of 2005, Part III" for "Surface Transportation Extension Act of 2005, Part II" in matter after subpara. (e)(3)(L) ... Sec. 9(a)(3), substituted "July 22, 2005" for "July 20, 2005" in subpara. (b)(6)(B), effective 7/20/2005.

—P.L. 109-35, Sec. 9(d), of this Act, reads as follows:

"(d) Temporary rule regarding adjustments. During the period beginning on the date of the enactment of the Surface Transportation Extension Act of 2003 and ending on July 21, 2005, for purposes of making any estimate under section 9503(d) of the Internal Revenue Code of 1986 of receipts of the Highway Trust Fund, the Secretary of the Treasury shall treat—

"(1) each expiring provision of paragraphs (1) through (4) of section 9503(b) of such Code which is related to appropriations or transfers to such Fund to have been extended through the end of the 24-month period referred to in section 9503(d)(1)(B) of such Code; and

"(2) with respect to each tax imposed under the sections referred to in section 9503(b)(1) of such Code, the rate of such tax during the 24-month period referred to in section 9503(d)(1)(B) of such Code to be the same as the rate of such tax as in effect on the date of the enactment of the Surface Transportation Extension Act of 2003."

—P.L. 109-20, Sec. 9(a)(1)(A), substituted "July 20, 2005" for "July 1, 2005" in matter before subpara. (c)(1)(A) . . . Sec. 9(a)(1)(B), deleted "or" at the end of subpara. (c)(1)(K) . . . Sec. 9(a)(1)(C), substituted ", or" for the period at the end of subpara. (c)(1)(L) . . . Sec. 9(a)(1)(D), added subpara. (c)(1)(M) . . . Sec. 9(a)(1)(E), substituted "Surface Transportation Extension Act of 2005, Part II" for "Surface Transportation Extension Act of 2005" in matter following subpara. (c)(1)(M) . . . Sec. 9(a)(2)(A), substituted "July 20, 2005" for "July 1, 2005" in matter before subpara. (e)(3)(A) . . . Sec. 9(a)(2)(B), deleted "or" at the end of subpara. (e)(3)(I) . . . Sec. 9(a)(2)(C), added "or" at the end of subpara. (e)(3)(J) . . . Sec. 9(a)(2)(D), added subpara. (e)(3)(K) . . . Sec. 9(a)(2)(E), substituted "Surface Transportation Extension Act of 2005, Part II" for "Surface Transportation Extension Act of 2005" in matter after subpara. (e)(3)(K) . . . Sec. 9(a)(3), substituted "July 20, 2005" for "July 1, 2005" in subpara. (b)(6)(B), effective 7/1/2005.

—P.L. 109-20, Sec. 9(d), of this Act, reads as follows:

"(d) Temporary rule regarding adjustments. During the period beginning on the date of the enactment of the Surface Transportation Extension Act of 2003 and ending on July 19, 2005, for purposes of making any estimate under section 9503(d) of the Internal Revenue Code of 1986 of receipts of the Highway Trust Fund, the Secretary of the Treasury shall treat—

"(1) each expiring provision of paragraphs (1) through (4) of section 9503(b) of such Code which is related to appropriations or transfers to such Fund to have been extended through the end of the 24-month period referred to in section 9503(d)(1)(B) of such Code, and

"(2) with respect to each tax imposed under the sections referred to in section 9503(b)(1) of such Code, the rate of such tax during the 24-month period referred to in section 9503(d)(1)(B) of such Code to be the same as the rate of such tax as in effect on the date of the enactment of the Surface Transportation Extension Act of 2003."

—P.L. 109-14, Sec. 9(a)(1)(A), substituted "July 1, 2005" for "June 1, 2005" in matter before subpara. (c)(1)(A) . . . Sec. 9(a)(1)(B), deleted "or" at the end of subpara. (c)(1)(J) . . . Sec. 9(a)(1)(C), substituted ", or" for the period at the end of subpara. (c)(1)(K) . . . Sec. 9(a)(1)(D), added subpara. (c)(1)(L) . . . Sec. 9(a)(1)(E), substituted "Surface Transportation Extension Act of 2005" for "Surface Transportation Extension Act of 2004, Part V" in matter following subpara. (c)(1)(L) . . . Sec. 9(a)(2)(A), substituted "July 1, 2005" for "June 1, 2005" in matter before subpara. (e)(3)(A) . . . Sec. 9(a)(2)(B), deleted "or" at the end of subpara. (e)(3)(H) . . . Sec. 9(a)(2)(C), added "or" at the end of subpara. (e)(3)(I) . . . Sec. 9(a)(2)(D), added subpara. (e)(3)(J) . . . Sec. 9(a)(2)(E), substituted "Surface Transportation Extension Act of 2005" for "Surface Transportation Extension Act of 2004, Part V" in matter after subpara. (e)(3)(J) . . . Sec. 9(a)(3), substituted "July 1, 2005" for "June 1, 2005" in subpara. (b)(6)(B), effective 5/31/2005.

—P.L. 109-14, Sec. 9(e), of this Act, reads as follows:

"(e) Temporary Rule Regarding Adjustments. During the period beginning on the date of the enactment of the Surface Transportation Extension Act of 2003 and ending on June 30, 2005, for purposes of making any estimate under section 9503(d) of the Internal Revenue Code of 1986 of receipts of the Highway Trust Fund, the Secretary of the Treasury shall treat—

"(1) each expiring provision of paragraphs (1) through (4) of section 9503(b) of such Code which is related to appropriations or transfers to such Fund to have been extended through the end of the 24-month period referred to in section 9503(d)(1)(B) of such Code, and

"(2) with respect to each tax imposed under the sections referred to in section 9503(b)(1) of such Code, the rate of such tax during the 24-month period referred to in section 9503(d)(1)(B) of such Code to be the same as the rate of such tax as in effect on the date of the enactment of the Surface Transportation Extension Act of 2003."

In 2004, P.L. 108-357, Sec. 301(c)(11), added a flush sentence at the end of para. (b)(1), effective for fuel sold or used after 12/31/2004. . . . Sec. 301(c)(12)(A), added "or" at the end of subpara. (b)(4)(C) . . . Sec. 301(c)(12)(B), substituted a period for the comma at the end of clause (b)(4)(D)(iii) . . . Sec. 301(c)(12)(C), deleted subparas. (b)(4)(E) and (F), effective for fuel sold or used after 9/30/2004. . . . Sec. 301(c)(13), added the sentence at the end of subpara. (c)(2)(A), effective for fuel sold or used after 12/31/2004.

Prior to deletion, subparas. (b)(4)(E)-(F) read as follows:

"(E) in the case of fuels described in section 4041(b)(2)(A), 4041(k), or 4081(c), section 4041 or 4081 before October 1, 2003, and for the period beginning after September 30, 2004, and before October 1, 2005, with respect to a rate equal to 2.5 cents per gallon, or"

"(F) in the case of fuels described in section 4081(c)(2), such section before before October 1, 2003, and for the period beginning after September 30, 2004, and before October 1, 2005, with respect to a rate equal to 2.8 cents per gallon."

—P.L. 108-357, Sec. 868(a), redesignated para. (b)(5) as (b)(6), and added para. (b)(5) . . . Sec. 868(b)(1), added "and penalties" after "taxes" in the heading of subsec. (b) . . . Sec. 868(b)(2), substituted "Certain taxes" for "In general" in the heading of para. (b)(1), effective for penalties assessed on or after 10/22/2004.

—P.L. 108-310, Sec. 13(a)(1)(A), substituted "June 1, 2005" for "October 1, 2004" in matter before subpara. (c)(1)(A) . . . Sec. 13(a)(1)(B), deleted "or" at the end of subpara. (c)(1)(I) . . . Sec. 13(a)(1)(C), substituted ", or" for the period at the end of subpara. (c)(1)(J) . . . Sec. 13(a)(1)(D), added subpara. (c)(1)(K) . . . Sec. 13(a)(1)(E), substituted "Surface Transportation Extension Act of 2004, Part V" for "Surface Transportation Extension Act of 2004, Part IV" in matter following subpara. (c)(1)(K) . . . Sec. 13(a)(2)(A), substituted "June 1, 2005" for "October 1, 2004" in matter before subpara. (e)(3)(A) . . . Sec. 13(a)(2)(B), deleted "or" at the end of subpara. (e)(3)(G) . . . Sec. 13(a)(2)(C), added "or" at the end of subpara. (e)(3)(H) . . . Sec. 13(a)(2)(D), added subpara. (e)(3)(I) . . . Sec. 13(a)(2)(E), substituted "Surface Transportation Extension Act of 2004, Part V" for "Surface Transportation Extension Act of 2004, Part IV" in matter after subpara. (e)(3)(I) . . . Sec. 13(a)(3), substituted "June 1, 2005" for "October 1, 2004" in subpara. (b)(5)(B), effective 9/30/2004.

—P.L. 108-310, Sec. 13(c), added "before October 1, 2003, and for the period beginning after September 30, 2004, and" before "before October 1, 2005" in subparas. (b)(4)(E) and (F), effective for taxes imposed after 9/30/2003.

—P.L. 108-310, Sec. 13(a)(4), of this Act, reads as follows:

"(4) Conforming amendment. Subsection (a) of section 10 of the Surface Transportation Extension Act of 2004, Part IV is amended by striking paragraph (4)."

—P.L. 108-310, Sec. 13(e), of this Act, reads as follows:

"(e) Temporary rule regarding adjustments. During the period beginning on the date of the enactment of the Surface Transportation Extension Act of 2003 and ending on May 31, 2005, for purposes of making any estimate under section 9503(d) of the Internal Revenue Code of 1986 of receipts of the Highway Trust Fund, the Secretary of the Treasury shall treat—

"(1) each expiring provision of paragraphs (1) through (4) of section 9503(b) of such Code which is related to appropriations or transfers to such Fund to have been extended through the end of the 24-month period referred to in section 9503(d)(1)(B) of such Code; and

"(2) with respect to each tax imposed under the sections referred to in section 9503(b)(1) of such Code, the rate of such tax during the 24-month period referred to in section 9503(d)(1)(B) of such Code to be the same as the rate of such tax as in effect on the date of the enactment of the Surface Transportation Extension Act of 2003."

—P.L. 108-310, Sec. 13(f), of this Act, reads as follows:

"(f) Apportionment of highway trust funds for fiscal year 2004. Section 9503(d)(3) of the Internal Revenue Code of 1986 shall not apply to any apportionment to the States of the amounts authorized to be appropriated from the Highway Trust Fund for the fiscal year ending September 30, 2004."

—P.L. 108-280, Sec. 10(a)(1)(A), substituted "October 1, 2004" for "August 1, 2004" in matter before subpara. (c)(1)(A) . . . Sec. 10(a)(1)(B), deleted "or" at the end of subpara. (c)(1)(H) . . . Sec. 10(a)(1)(C), substituted ", or" for the period at the end of subpara. (c)(1)(I) . . . Sec. 10(a)(1)(D), added subpara. (c)(1)(J) . . . Sec. 10(a)(1)(E), substituted "Surface Transportation Extension Act of 2004, Part IV" for "Surface Transportation Extension Act of 2004, Part III" in matter following subpara. (c)(1)(J) . . . Sec. 10(a)(2)(A), substituted "October 1, 2004" for "August 1, 2004" in matter before subpara. (e)(3)(A) . . . Sec. 10(a)(2)(B), deleted "or" at the end of subpara. (e)(3)(F) . . . Sec. 10(a)(2)(C), added "or" at the end of subpara. (e)(3)(G) . . . Sec. 10(a)(2)(D), added subpara. (e)(3)(H) . . . Sec. 10(a)(2)(E), substituted "Surface Transportation Extension Act of 2004, Part IV" for "Surface Transportation Extension Act of 2004, Part III" in matter after subpara. (e)(3)(H) . . . Sec. 10(a)(3), substituted "October 1, 2004" for "August 1, 2004" in subpara. (b)(5)(B), effective 7/30/2004.

—P.L. 108-280, Sec. 10(a)(4), of this Act, [prior to deletion by Sec. 13(a)(4) of P.L. 108-310, see above] reads as follows:

"(4) Special rule for core highway programs.

"(A) In general. In the case of a core highway program, subsections (b)(5) and (c)(1) of section 9503 of such Code shall be applied by substituting 'September 25, 2004' for 'October 1, 2004'.

"(B) Core highway program. For purposes of subparagraph (A), the term 'core highway program' means any program (other than any program carried out by the National Highway Traffic Safety Administration and any program carried out by the Federal Motor Carrier Administration) funded from the Highway Trust Fund (other than the Mass Transit Account)."

—P.L. 108-280, Sec. 10(d), of this Act, reads as follows:

"(d) Temporary rule regarding adjustments. During the period beginning on the date of the enactment of the Surface Transportation Extension Act of 2003 and ending on September 30, 2004, for purposes of making any estimate under section 9503(d) of the Internal Revenue Code of 1986 of receipts of the Highway Trust Fund, the Secretary of the Treasury shall treat—

"(1) each expiring provision of paragraphs (1) through (4) of section 9503(b) of such Code which is related to appropriations or transfers to such Fund to have been extended through the end of the 24-month period referred to in section 9503(d)(1)(B) of such Code, and

"(2) with respect to each tax imposed under the sections referred to in section 9503(b)(1) of such Code, the rate of such tax during the 24-month period referred to in section 9503(d)(1)(B) of such Code to be the same as the rate of such tax as in effect on the date of the enactment of the Surface Transportation Extension Act of 2003. "

—P.L. 108-263, Sec. 10(a)(1)(A), substituted "August 1, 2004" for "July 1, 2004" in matter before subpara. (c)(1)(A) . . . Sec. 10(a)(1)(B), deleted "or" at the end of subpara. (c)(1)(G) . . . Sec. 10(a)(1)(C), substituted ", or" for the period at

Establishment of trust funds Code Sec. 9503

the end of subpara. (c)(1)(H) . . . Sec. 10(a)(1)(D), added subpara. (c)(1)(I) . . . Sec. 10(a)(1)(E), substituted "Surface Transportation Extension Act of 2004, Part III" for "Surface Transportation Extension Act of 2004, Part II" in matter following subpara. (c)(1)(I) . . . Sec. 10(a)(2)(A), substituted "August 1, 2004" for "July 1, 2004" in matter before subpara. (e)(3)(A) . . . Sec. 10(a)(2)(B), deleted "or" at the end of subpara. (e)(3)(E) . . . Sec. 10(a)(2)(C), added ", or" at the end of subpara. (e)(3)(F) . . . Sec. 10(a)(2)(D), added subpara. (e)(3)(G) . . . Sec. 10(a)(2)(E), substituted "Surface Transportation Extension Act of 2004, Part III" for "Surface Transportation Extension Act of 2004, Part II" in matter after subpara. (e)(3)(G) . . . Sec. 10(a)(3), substituted "August 1, 2004" for "July 1, 2004" in subpara. (b)(5)(B), effective 6/30/2004.

—P.L. 108-263, Sec. 10(d), of this Act, reads as follows:

"(d) Temporary rule regarding adjustments. During the period beginning on the date of the enactment of the Surface Transportation Extension Act of 2003 and ending on July 31, 2004, for purposes of making any estimate under section 9503(d) of the Internal Revenue Code of 1986 of receipts of the Highway Trust Fund, the Secretary of the Treasury shall treat—

"(1) each expiring provision of paragraphs (1) through (4) of section 9503(b) of such Code which is related to appropriations or transfers to such Fund to have been extended through the end of the 24-month period referred to in section 9503(d)(1)(B) of such Code, and

"(2) with respect to each tax imposed under the sections referred to in section 9503(b)(1) of such Code, the rate of such tax during the 24-month period referred to in section 9503(d)(1)(B) of such Code to be the same as the rate of such tax as in effect on the date of the enactment of the Surface Transportation Extension Act of 2003."

—P.L. 108-224, Sec. 10(a)(1)(A), substituted "July 1, 2004" for "May 1, 2004" in matter before subpara. (c)(1)(A) . . . Sec. 10(a)(1)(B), deleted "or" at the end of subpara. (c)(1)(F) . . . Sec. 10(a)(1)(C), substituted ", or" for the period at the end of subpara. (c)(1)(G) . . . Sec. 10(a)(1)(D), added subpara. (c)(1)(H) . . . Sec. 10(a)(1)(E), substituted "Surface Transportation Extension Act of 2004, Part II" for "Surface Transportation Extension Act of 2004" in matter following subpara. (c)(1)(H) . . . Sec. 10(a)(2)(A), substituted "July 1, 2004" for "May 1, 2004" in matter before subpara. (e)(3)(A) . . . Sec. 10(a)(2)(B), deleted "or" at the end of subpara. (e)(3)(D) . . . Sec. 10(a)(2)(C), substituted "or" for the period at the end of subpara. (e)(3)(E) . . . Sec. 10(a)(2)(D), added subpara. (e)(3)(F) . . . Sec. 10(a)(2)(E), substituted "Surface Transportation Extension Act of 2004, Part II" for "Surface Transportation Extension Act of 2004" in matter after subpara. (e)(3)(F) . . . Sec. 10(a)(3), substituted "July 1, 2004" for "May 1, 2004" in subpara. (b)(5)(B), effective 4/30/2004.

—P.L. 108-224, Sec. 10(d), of this Act, reads as follows:

"(d) Temporary rule regarding adjustments. During the period beginning on the date of the enactment of the Surface Transportation Extension Act of 2003 and ending on June 30, 2004, for purposes of making any estimate under section 9503(d) of the Internal Revenue Code of 1986 of receipts of the Highway Trust Fund, the Secretary of the Treasury shall treat—

"(1) each expiring provision of paragraphs (1) through (4) of section 9503(b) of such Code which is related to appropriations or transfers to such Fund to have been extended through the end of the 24-month period referred to in section 9503(d)(1)(B) of such Code, and

"(2) with respect to each tax imposed under the sections referred to in section 9503(b)(1) of such Code, the rate of such tax during the 24-month period referred to in section 9503(d)(1)(B) of such Code to be the same as the rate of such tax as in effect on the date of the enactment of the Surface Transportation Extension Act of 2003."

—P.L. 108-202, Sec. 12(a)(1)(A), substituted "May 1, 2004" for "March 1, 2004" in matter before subpara. (c)(1)(A) . . . Sec. 12(a)(1)(B), deleted "or" at the end of subpara. (c)(1)(E) . . . Sec. 12(a)(1)(C), substituted ", or" for the period at the end of subpara. (c)(1)(F) . . . Sec. 12(a)(1)(D), added subpara. (c)(1)(G) . . . Sec. 12(a)(1)(E), substituted "Surface Transportation Extension Act of 2004" for "Surface Transportation Extension Act of 2003" in matter following subpara. (c)(1)(G) . . . Sec. 12(a)(2)(A), substituted "May 1, 2004" for "March 1, 2004" in matter before subpara. (e)(3)(A) . . . Sec. 12(a)(2)(B), deleted "or" at the end of subpara. (e)(3)(C) . . . Sec. 12(a)(2)(C), substituted "or" for the period at the end of subpara. (e)(3)(D) . . . Sec. 12(a)(2)(D), added subpara. (e)(3)(E) . . . Sec. 12(a)(2)(E), substituted "Surface Transportation Extension Act of 2004" for "Surface Transportation Extension Act of 2003" in matter after subpara. (e)(3)(E) . . . Sec. 12(a)(3), substituted "May 1, 2004" for "March 1, 2004" in subpara. (b)(5)(B), effective 2/29/2004.

—P.L. 108-202, Sec. 12(d), of this Act, reads as follows:

"(d) Temporary rule regarding adjustments. During the period beginning on the date of the enactment of the Surface Transportation Extension Act of 2003 and ending on April 30, 2004, for purposes of making any estimate under section 9503(d) of the Internal Revenue Code of 1986 of receipts of the Highway Trust Fund, the Secretary of the Treasury shall treat—

"(1) each expiring provision of paragraphs (1) through (4) of section 9503(b) of such Code which is related to appropriations or transfers to such Fund to have been extended through the end of the 24-month period referred to in section 9503(d)(1)(B) of such Code, and

"(2) with respect to each tax imposed under the sections referred to in section 9503(b)(1) of such Code, the rate of such tax during the 24-month period referred to in section 9503(d)(1)(B) of such Code to be the same as the rate of such tax as in effect on the date of the enactment of the Surface Transportation Extension Act of 2003."

In 2003, P.L. 108-88, Sec. 12(a)(1)(A), substituted "March 1, 2004" for "October 1, 2003" in matter before subpara. (c)(1)(A) . . . Sec. 12(a)(1)(B), deleted "or" at the end of subpara. (c)(1)(D) . . . Sec. 12(a)(1)(C), substituted ", or" for the period at the end of subpara. (c)(1)(E) . . . Sec. 12(a)(1)(D), added subpara. (c)(1)(F) . . . Sec. 12(a)(1)(E), substituted "Surface Transportation Extension Act of 2003" for "TEA 21 Restoration Act" in matter following subpara. (c)(1)(F) . . . Sec. 12(a)(2)(A), substituted "March 1, 2004" for "October 1, 2003" in matter before subpara. (e)(3)(A) . . . Sec. 12(a)(2)(B), deleted "or" at the end of subpara. (e)(3)(B) . . . Sec. 12(a)(2)(C), added "or" after "Century," at the end of subpara. (e)(3)(C) . . . Sec. 12(a)(2)(D), added subpara. (e)(3)(D) . . . Sec. 12(a)(2)(E), substituted "Surface Transportation Extension Act of 2003" for "TEA 21 Restoration Act" in matter after subpara. (e)(3)(D) . . . Sec. 12(a)(3), substituted "March 1, 2004" for "October 1, 2003" in subpara. (b)(5)(B), effective 9/30/2003.

—P.L. 108-88, Sec. 12(d), of this Act, reads as follows:

"(d) Temporary rule regarding adjustments. During the period beginning on the date of the enactment of this Act and ending on February 29, 2004, for purposes of making any estimate under section 9503(d) of the Internal Revenue Code of 1986 of receipts of the Highway Trust Fund, the Secretary of the Treasury shall treat—

"(1) each expiring provision of paragraphs (1) through (4) of section 9503(b) of such Code which is related to appropriations or transfers to such Fund to have been extended through the end of the 24-month period referred to in section 9503(d)(1)(B) of such Code, and

"(2) with respect to each tax imposed under the sections referred to in section 9503(b)(1) of such Code, the rate of such tax during the 24-month period referred to in section 9503(d)(1)(B) of such Code to be the same as the rate of such tax as in effect on the date of the enactment of this Act."

In 2000, P.L. 106-554, Sec. 1(a)(7), [which enacted into law Sec. 318(e)(1) of P.L. 106-554] deleted para. (b)(5) and redesignated para. (b)(6) as (b)(5), effective for taxes received in the Treasury after 12/21/2000.

Prior to deletion, para. (b)(5) read as follows:

"(5) General revenue deposits of certain taxes on alcohol mixtures. For purposes of this section, the amounts which would (but for this paragraph) be required to be appropriated under subparagraphs (A) and (E) of paragraph (1) shall be reduced by—

"(A) 0.6 cent per gallon in the case of taxes imposed on any mixture at least 10 percent of which is alcohol (as defined in section 4081(c)(3)) if any portion of such alcohol is ethanol, and

"(B) 0.67 cent per gallon in the case of gasoline, diesel fuel, or kerosene used in producing a mixture described in subparagraph (A)."

In 1998, P.L. 105-277, Sec. 4006(b)(1), amended para. (f)(2), effective 10/1/98.

Prior to amendment, para. (f)(2) read as follows:

"(2) no interest accruing after September 30, 1998, on any obligation held by such Fund shall be credited to such Fund."

—P.L. 105-206, Sec. 9015(a), added Sec. 9002(f)(1) and (2) of P.L. 105-178 [see below] effective 6/9/98.

—P.L. 105-178, Sec. 9002(c)(1)(A), substituted "2005" for "1999" each place it appeared in subsec. (b) and para. (c)(2) . . . Sec. 9002(c)(1)(B), substituted "2006" for "2000" each place it appeared in subsec. (b) and paras. (c)(2) and (3) . . . Sec. 9002(c)(2)(A), substituted "2005" for "1998" in clause (c)(4)(A)(i) and subpara. (c)(5)(A) . . . Sec. 9002(c)(3), amended the heading of para. (c)(3) . . . Sec. 9002(d)(1)(A), substituted "2003" for "1998" in para. (c)(1) . . . Sec. 9002(d)(1)(B)(i), deleted "or" at the end of subpara. (c)(1)(C) . . . Sec. 9002(d)(1)(B)(ii), substituted "1991, or

"(E) authorized to be paid out of the Highway Trust Fund under the Transportation Equity Act for the 21st Century.

In determining the authorizations under the Acts referred to in the preceding subparagraphs, such Acts shall be applied as in effect on the date of enactment of the Transportation Equity Act for the 21st Century.' for '1991.

In determining the authorizations under the Acts referred to in the preceding subparagraphs, such Acts shall be applied as in effect on the date of the enactment of this sentence.' in para. (c)(1) . . . Sec. 9002(d)(2)(A), substituted '2003' for '1998' in para. (e)(3) . . . Sec. 9002(d)(2)(B)(i), deleted 'or' at the end of subpara. (e)(3)(A) . . . Sec. 9002(d)(2)(B)(ii), added 'or' at the end of subpara. (e)(3)(B) . . . Sec. 9002(d)(2)(B)(iii), substituted '(C) the Transportation Equity Act for the 21st Century,

as such section and Acts are in effect on the date of enactment of the Transportation Equity Act for the 21st Century.' for

"as section 5338(a)(1) or (b)(1) and the Intermodal Surface Transportation Efficiency Act of 1991 were in effect on December 18, 1991." in para. (e)(3), effective 6/9/98.

Prior to amendment, the heading of para. (c)(3) read as follows:

"(3) 1999 floor stocks refunds."

—P.L. 105-178, Sec. 9002(e)(1), substituted "For purposes of the preceding sentence, the term 'mass transit portion' means, for any fuel with respect to which tax was imposed under section 4041 or 4081 and otherwise deposited into the Highway Trust Fund, the amount determined at the rate of—

"(A) except as otherwise provided in this sentence, 2.86 cents per gallon,

"(B) 1.43 cents per gallon in the case of any partially exempt methanol or ethanol fuel (as defined in section 4041(m)) none of the alcohol in which consists of ethanol,

"(C) 1.86 cents per gallon in the case of liquefied natural gas,

"(D) 2.13 cents per gallon in the case of liquefied petroleum gas, and

"(E) 9.71 cents per MCF (determined at standard temperature and pressure) in the case of compressed natural gas." for "For purposes of the preceding sentence, the term 'mass transit portion' means an amount determined at the rate of 2.85 cents for each gallon with respect to which tax was imposed under section 4041 or 4081." in para. (e)(2), effective for taxes received in the Treasury after 9/30/97.

—P.L. 105-178, Sec. 9002(f)(1), deleted subpara. (b)(1)(C), deleted "and tread rubber" after "tax on tires" in subpara. (b)(1)(D) and redesignated subparas.

Code Sec. 9503 — Establishment of trust funds

(b)(1)(D)-(F) as (b)(1)(C)-(E)... Sec. 9002(f)(2), added "and" at the end of subclause (c)(2)(A)(i)(II), deleted subclause (c)(2)(A)(i)(III), and redesignated subclause (c)(2)(A)(i)(IV) as (c)(2)(A)(i)(III)... Sec. 9002(f)(3), substituted "fuel" for "gasoline, special fuels, and lubricating oil" each place it appeared in clause (c)(2)(A)(ii)... Sec. 9002(f)(4), [as added by Sec. 9015(a) of P.L. 105-206, see above] substituted "the date of the enactment of the TEA 21 Restoration Act" for "the date of the enactment of the Transportation Equity Act for the 21st Century" in para. (c)(1) [as amended by Sec. 9002(d) of this Act, see above]... Sec. 9002(f)(5), [as added by Sec. 9015(a) of P.L. 105-206, see above] substituted "the date of the enactment of the TEA 21 Restoration Act" for "the date of enactment of the Transportation Equity Act for the 21st Century" in para. (e)(3) [as amended by Sec. 9002(d) of this Act, see above], effective 6/9/98.

Prior to deletion, subpara. (b)(1)(C) read as follows:

"(C) section 4061 (relating to tax on trucks and truck parts),"

Prior to deletion, subclause (c)(2)(A)(i)(III) read as follows:

"(III) section 6424 (relating to amounts paid in respect of lubricating oil used for certain nontaxable purposes), and"

—P.L. 105-178, Sec. 9004(a)(1), added subsec. (f), effective 10/1/98.
—P.L. 105-178, Sec. 9004(b)(1), deleted para. (c)(7), effective for taxes received in the Treasury after 9/30/97.

Prior to deletion, para. (c)(7) read as follows:

"(7) Limitation on expenditures. Notwithstanding any other provision of law, in calculating amounts under section 157(a) of title 23, United States Code, and sections 1013(c), 1015(a), and 1015(b) of the Intermodal Surface Transportation Efficiency Act of 1991 (P.L. 102-240; 105 Stat. 1914), deposits in the Highway Trust Fund resulting from the amendments made by the Taxpayer Relief Act of 1997 shall not be taken into account."

—P.L. 105-178, Sec. 9004(c), added para. (b)(6)... Sec. 9004(d), amended para. (e)(4), effective 6/9/98.

Prior to amendment, para. (e)(4) read as follows:

"(4) Limitation. Rules similar to the rules of subsection (d) shall apply to the Mass Transit Account except that subsection (d)(1) shall be applied by substituting '12-month' for '24-month'."

—P.L. 105-178, Sec. 9005(a)(1), substituted "exceeds—

"(i) 11.5 cents per gallon with respect to taxes imposed before October 1, 2001,
"(ii) 13 cents per gallon with respect to taxes imposed after September 30, 2001, and before October 1, 2003, and
"(iii) 13.5 cents per gallon with respect to taxes imposed after September 30, 2003, and before October 1, 2005," for "exceeds 11.5 cents per gallon," in para. (b)(4)(D) [as amended by Sec. 9011(b)(2) of this Act, see below]... Sec. 9005(a)(2), added a flush sentence at the end of clause (c)(4)(A)(ii), effective 6/9/98.

—P.L. 105-178, Sec. 9011(b)(1), deleted para. (c)(6)... Sec. 9011(b)(2), amended subpara. (b)(4)(D), effective 6/9/98.

Prior to amendment, subpara. (b)(4)(D) read as follows:

"(D) in the case of fuels used as described in paragraph (4)(D), (5)(B), or (6)(D) of subsection (c), section 4041 or 4081—
"(i) with respect to so much of the rate of tax on gasoline or special motor fuels as exceeds 11.5 cents per gallon, and
"(ii) with respect to so much of the rate of tax on diesel fuel or kerosene as exceeds 17.5 cents per gallon,"

Prior to deletion, para. (c)(6) read as follows:

"(6) Transfers from trust fund of certain recreational fuel taxes, etc.
"(A) In general. The Secretary shall pay from time to time from the Highway Trust Fund into the National Recreational Trails Trust Fund amounts (as determined by him) equivalent to 0.3 percent (as adjusted under subparagraph (C)) of the total Highway Trust Fund receipts for the period for which the payment is made.
"(B) Limitation. The amount paid into the National Recreational Trails Trust Fund under this paragraph during any fiscal year shall not exceed the amount obligated under section 1302 of the Intermodal Surface Transportation Efficiency Act of 1991 (as in effect on the date of the enactment of this paragraph) for such fiscal year to be expended from such Trust Fund.
"(C) Adjustment of percentage.
"(i) First year. Within 1 year after the date of the enactment of this paragraph, the Secretary shall adjust the percentage contained in subparagraph (A) so that it corresponds to the revenues received by the Highway Trust Fund from nonhighway recreational fuel taxes.
"(ii) Subsequent years. Not more frequently than once every 3 years, the Secretary may increase or decrease the percentage established under clause (i) to reflect, in the Secretary's estimation, changes in the amount of revenues received in the Highway Trust Fund from nonhighway recreational fuel taxes.
"(iii) Amount of adjustment. Any adjustment under clause (ii) shall be not more than 10 percent of the percentage in effect at the time the adjustment is made.
"(iv) Use of data. In making the adjustments under clauses (i) and (ii), the Secretary shall take into account data on off-highway recreational vehicle registrations and use.
"(D) Nonhighway recreational fuel taxes. For purposes of this paragraph, the term 'nonhighway recreational fuel taxes' means taxes under section 4041 and 4081 (to the extent deposited into the Highway Trust Fund) with respect to—
"(i) fuel used in vehicles on recreational trails or back country terrain (including vehicles registered for highway use when used on recreational trails, trail access roads not eligible for funding under title 23, United States Code, or back country terrain), and
"(ii) fuel used in campstoves and other nonengine uses in outdoor recreational equipment."

"Such term shall not include small-engine fuel taxes (as defined by paragraph (5)) and taxes which are credited or refunded.
"(E) Termination. No amount shall be paid under this paragraph after September 30, 1998."

In 1997, P.L. 105-130, Sec. 9(a)(1)(A)(i), substituted "1998" for "1997" in para. (c)(1)... Sec. 9(a)(1)(A)(ii), amended the last sentence of para. (c)(1)... Sec. 9(a)(1)(B), substituted "1998" for "1997" in clause (c)(4)(A)(i)... Sec. 9(a)(1)(C), substituted "1998" for "1997" in subpara. (c)(5)(A)... Sec. 9(a)(1)(D), substituted "1998" for "1997" in subpara. (c)(6)(E)... Sec. 9(a)(2)(A), substituted "1998" for "1997" in para. (e)(3)... Sec. 9(a)(2)(B), substituted "the last sentence of subsection (c)(1)." for "the Intermodal Surface Transportation Efficiency Act of 1991." at the end of para. (e)(3), effective 10/1/97.

Prior to amendment, the last sentence of para. (c)(1) read as follows:

"In determining the authorizations under the Acts referred to in the preceding subparagraphs, such Acts shall be applied as in effect on the date of the enactment of the Intermodal Surface Transportation Efficiency Act of 1991."

—P.L. 105-102, Sec. 1, substituted "section 5338(a)(1) or (b)(1) and the Intermodal Surface Transportation Efficiency Act of 1991 were in effect on December 18, 1991" for "such Acts are in effect on the date of the enactment of the Intermodal Surface Transportation Efficiency Act of 1991." in para. (e)(3), effective 11/20/97.

—P.L. 105-34, Sec. 901(a), amended para. (b)(4)... Sec. 901(b), substituted "2.85 cents" for "2 cents" in para. (e)(2)... Sec. 901(c), added para. (c)(7)... Sec. 901(d)(1), deleted subsec. (f)... Sec. 901(d)(2), substituted "by taking into account only the portion of the taxes which are deposited in to the Highway Trust Fund" for "by taking into account only the Highway Trust Fund financing rate applicable to any fuel" in subpara. (c)(2)(A)... Sec. 901(d)(3), substituted "deposited into the Highway Trust Fund" for "attributable to the Highway Trust Fund financing rate" in subparas. (c)(4)(D), (c)(5)(B) and (c)(6)(D), effective for taxes received in the Treasury after 9/30/97.

Prior to amendment, para. (b)(4) read as follows:

"(4) Certain additional taxes not transferred to highway trust fund. For purposes of paragraph (1) and (2)—
"(A) there shall not be taken into account the taxes imposed by section 4041(d), and
"(B) there shall be taken into account the taxes imposed by sections 4041 and 4081 only to the extent attributable to the Highway Trust Fund financing rate."

Prior to deletion, subsec. (f) read as follows:

"(f) Definition of Highway Trust Fund financing rate. For purposes of this section—
"(1) In general. Except as otherwise provided in this subsection, the Highway Trust Fund financing rate is—
"(A) in the case of gasoline and special motor fuels, 11.5 cents per gallon (14 cents per gallon after September 30, 1995), and
"(B) in the case of diesel fuel, 17.5 cents per gallon (20 cents per gallon after September 30, 1995).
"(2) Certain uses.
"(A) Trains. In the case of fuel used in a train, the Highway Trust Fund financing rate is zero.
"(B) Certain buses. In the case of diesel fuel used in a use described in section 6427(b)(1) (after the application of section 6427(b)(3)), the Highway Trust Fund financing rate is 3 cents per gallon.
"(C) Certain boats. In the case of diesel fuel used in a boat described in clause (iv) of section 6421(e)(2)(B), the Highway Trust Fund financing rate is zero.
"(D) Compressed natural gas. In the case of the tax imposed by section 4041(a)(3), the Highway Trust Fund financing rate is zero.
"(E) Certain other nonhighway uses. In the case of gasoline and special motor fuels used as described in paragraph (4)(D), (5)(B), or (6)(D) of subsection (c), the Highway Trust Fund financing rate is 11.5 cents per gallon; and, in the case of diesel fuel used as described in subsection (c)(6)(D), the Highway Trust Fund financing rate is 17.5 cents per gallon.
"(3) Alcohol fuels.
"(A) In general. If the rate of tax on any fuel is determined under section 4041(b)(2)(A), 4041(k), or 4081(c), the Highway Trust Fund financing rate is the excess (if any) of the rate so determined over—
"(i) 6.8 cents per gallon after September 30, 1993, and before October 1, 1999,
"(ii) 4.3 cents per gallon after September 30, 1999.
In the case of a rate of tax determined under section 4081(c), the preceding sentence shall be applied by increasing the rates specified in clauses (i) and (ii) by 0.1 cent.
"(B) Fuels used to produce mixtures. In the case of a rate of tax determined under section 4081(c)(2), subparagraph (A) shall be applied by substituting rates which are ¹⁰⁄₉ of the rates otherwise applicable under clauses (i) and (ii) of subparagraph (A).
"(C) Partially exempt methanol or ethanol fuel. In the case of a rate of tax determined under section 4041(m), the Highway Trust Fund financing rate is the excess (if any) of the rate so determined over—
"(i) 5.55 cents per gallon after September 30, 1993, and before October 1, 1995, and
"(ii) 4.3 cents per gallon after September 30, 1995.
"(4) Termination. Notwithstanding the preceding provisions of this subsection, the Highway Trust Fund financing rate is zero with respect to taxes received in the Treasury after June 30, 2000."

—P.L. 105-34, Sec. 1032(e)(13), substituted ", diesel fuel, and kerosene" for "and diesel fuel" in subpara. (b)(1)(E)... Sec. 1032(e)(14), substituted ", diesel fuel, or kerosene" for "or diesel fuel" in subpara. (b)(5)(B), effective 7/1/98.

—P.L. 105-34, Sec. 1601(f)(2)(A), deleted "(or with respect to qualified diesel-powered highway vehicles purchased before January 1, 1999)" after "October 1, 1999" in clause (c)(2)(A)(ii) . . . Sec. 1601(f)(2)(B), substituted a period for "; except that any such transfers to the extent attributable to section 6427(g) shall be borne only by the Highway Account." in subpara. (e)(5)(A), effective for vehicles purchased after 8/5/97.

In 1994, P.L. 103-429, Sec. 4, substituted "section 5338(a)(1) or (b)(1) of title 49" for "paragraph (1) or (3) of subsection (a), or paragraph (1) or (3) of subsection (b), of section 21 of the Federal Transit Act" in subpara. (e)(3)(A), effective 10/31/94.

In 1993, P.L. 103-66, Sec. 13242(d)(34)(A), substituted "gasoline and diesel fuel), and" for "gasoline)," in subpara. (b)(1)(E) . . . Sec. 13242(d)(34)(B), deleted subpara. (b)(1)(F) . . . Sec. 13242(d)(34)(C), redesignated subpara. (b)(1)(G) as subpara. (b)(1)(F) . . . Sec. 13242(d)(35)(A), substituted "and 4081" for ", 4081, and 4091" and substituted "rate" for "rates under such sections" in subpara. (b)(4)(B) . . . Sec. 13242(d)(35)(B), substituted "4081" for "4091" in subpara. (b)(4)(C) (as amended by subchapter A of this Act) [NOTE: amendment is invalid since no subpara. (b)(4)(C) was added by this Act] . . . Sec. 13242(d)(36), substituted "and (E)" for ", (E), and (F)" in para. (b)(5) . . . Sec. 13242(d)(37), substituted "and 4081" for ", 4081, and 4091" in subpara. (c)(6)(D) . . . Sec. 13242(d)(38), substituted "rate" for "rates under such sections" in subpara. (c)(4)(D) . . . Sec. 13242(d)(39), substituted "rate" for "rate under such section" in subpara. (c)(5)(B) . . . Sec. 13242(d)(40)(A), substituted "and 4081" for ", 4081, and 4091" in para. (e)(2) . . . Sec. 13242(d)(40)(B), substituted "or 4081" for ", 4081, or 4091" in para. (e)(2) . . . Sec. 13242(d)(41), added subsec. (f), effective 1/1/94.

Prior to deletion, subpara. (b)(1)(F) read as follows:

"(F) section 4091 (relating to tax on diesel fuel), and"

—P.L. 103-66, Sec. 13244(a), substituted "2 cents" for "1.5 cents" in para. (e)(2) [as amended by Sec. 13242(d)(40) of this Act, see above], effective for amounts attributable to taxes imposed on or after 10/1/95.

In 1991, P.L. 102-240, Sec. 8002(d)(1)(A), substituted "1999" for "1995" each place it appeared in subsec. (b) and paras. (c)(2) and (3) . . . Sec. 8002(d)(1)(B), substituted "2000" for "1996" each place it appeared in subsec. (b) and paras. (c)(2) and (3) . . . Sec. 8002(d)(2)(A), substituted "1997" for "1995" in clause (c)(4)(A)(i) and subpara. (c)(5)(A) . . . Sec. 8002(e)(1), substituted "1997" for "1993" in paras. (c)(1) and (e)(3) . . . Sec. 8002(e)(2), amended subpara. (c)(1)(D) and added the flush sentence to the end of para. (c)(1) . . . Sec. 8002(f)(1), inserted "or capital-related" after "capital" in para. (e)(3) . . . Sec. 8002(f)(2), substituted "in accordance with—

"(A) paragraph (1) or (3) of subsection (a), or paragraph (1) or (3) of subsection (b), of section 21 of the Federal Transit Act, or

"(B) the Intermodal Surface Transportation Efficiency Act of 1991,

as such Acts are in effect on the date of the enactment of the Intermodal Surface Transportation Efficiency Act of 1991 ' for 'in accordance with section 21(a)(2) of the Urban Mass Transportation Act of 1964' in para. (e)(3)."

. . . Sec. 8003(b), added para. (c)(6), effective 12/18/91.

—P.L. 102-240, Sec. 8002(g), and (h) of this Act provides:

"(g) Use of revenues for enforcement of Highway Trust Fund taxes. The Secretary of Transportation shall not impose any condition on the use of funds transferred under section 1040 of this Act to the Internal Revenue Service. The Secretary of the Treasury shall, at least 60 days before the beginning of each fiscal year (after fiscal year 1992) for which such funds are to be transferred, submit a report to the Committee on Ways and Means of the House of Representatives and the Committee on Finance of the Senate detailing the increased enforcement activities to be financed with such funds with respect to taxes referred to in section 9503(b)(1) of the Internal Revenue Code of 1986.

"(h) Tax evasion report. The Secretary of Transportation shall also submit each report prepared pursuant to section 1040(d) of this Act to the Committee on Ways and Means of the House of Representatives and the Committee on Finance of the Senate not later than the applicable date specified therein."

—P.L. 102-240, Sec. 8003(d), of this Act provides:

"(d) Report on nonhighway recreational fuel taxes. The Secretary of the Treasury shall, within a reasonable period after the close of each of fiscal years 1992 through 1996, submit a report to the Committee on Ways and Means of the House of Representatives and the Committee on Finance of the Senate specifying his estimate of the amount of nonhighway recreational fuel taxes (as defined in section 9503(c)(6) of the Internal Revenue Code of 1986, as added by this Act) received in the Treasury during such fiscal year."

Prior to amendment, subpara. (c)(1)(D) read as follows:

"(D) hereafter authorized by a law which does not authorize the expenditure out of the Highway Trust Fund of any amount for a general purpose not covered by subparagraph (A), (B), or (C) as in effect on the date of the enactment of the Surface Transportation and Uniform Relocation Assistance Act of 1987."

In 1990, P.L. 101-508, Sec. 11211(a)(5)(D), substituted "4041, 4081," for "4081" in subpara. (b)(4)(B) . . . Sec. 11211(a)(5)(E), added the last sentence to subpara. (c)(2)(A) . . . Sec. 11211(a)(5)(F), added para (b)(5), effective for gasoline removed (as defined in Code Sec. 4082) after 11/30/90.

—P.L. 101-508, Sec. 11211(b)(6)(H), deleted "(to the extent attributable to the Highway Trust Fund financing rate)" after "section 4081" in subpara. (c)(4)(D), and added ", but only to the extent such taxes are attributable to the Highway Trust Fund financing rates under such sections" before the period at the end of subpara. (c)(4)(D), effective 12/1/90.

—P.L. 101-508, Sec. 11211(g)(1)(A), substituted "1995" for "1993" each place it appeared in subsec. (b) and paras. (c)(2), (3) and (4) . . . Sec. 1121(g)(1)(B), substituted "1996" for "1994" each place it appeared in subsec. (b) and paras. (c)(2), (3) and (4) [sic , (b), (c)(2) and (3)], effective 11/5/90.

—P.L. 101-508, Sec. 11211(h)(1), substituted "1.5 cents" for "1 cent" in para. (e)(2), effective for amounts attributable to taxes imposed on or after 12/1/90.

—P.L. 101-508, Sec. 11211(i)(1), added para. (c)(5), effective 12/1/90.

In 1989, P.L. 101-239, Sec. 7822(b)(6), substituted "section 4041(d)" for "sections 4041(d)" in subpara. (b)(4)(A), effective for sales after 3/31/88.

In 1988, P.L. 100-448, Sec. 6(a)(1)(A), substituted "for each of fiscal years 1989 and 1990 and $70,000,000 for fiscal year thereafter" for "for Fiscal Year 1987 only and $45,000,000 for each Fiscal Year thereafter" in subclauses (c)(4)(A)(ii)(I) and (II) . . . Sec. 6(a)(1)(B), deleted the second sentence of subpara. (c)(4)(E) . . . Sec. 6(a)(3), deleted the quotation marks following "60,000,000" and deleted the semicolon before the period in subclauses (c)(4)(A)(ii)(I) and (II), effective 10/1/88.

Prior to deletion, the second sentence of of subpara. (c)(4)(E) read as follows:

"Further, a portion of the payments made by the Secretary from Fiscal Year 1987 motorfuel excise tax receipts shall be used to increase the funding for boating safety programs during Fiscal Year 1987 only."

In 1987, P.L. 100-203, Sec. 10502(d)(13), amended subpara. (b)(1)(F) . . . Sec. 10502(d)(14), amended para. (b)(4) . . . Sec. 10502(d)(15)(A), substituted "sections 4041, 4081, and 4091" for "sections 4041 and 4081" in para. (e)(2) . . . Sec. 10502(d)(15)(B), substituted "section 4041, 4081, or 4091" for "section 4041 or 4081" in para. (e)(2), effective for sales after 3/31/88.

Prior to amendment, subpara. (b)(1)(F) read as follows:

"(F) section 4091 (relating to tax on lubricating oil), and"

Prior to amendment, para. (b)(4) read as follows:

"(4) Certain additional taxes not transferred to highway trust fund. For purposes of paragraphs (1) and (2), there shall not be taken into account the taxes imposed by section 4041(d) and so much of the taxes imposed by section 4081 as is attributable to the Leaking Underground Storage Tank Trust Fund financing rate."

—P.L. 100-17, Sec. 503(a), substituted "1993" for "1988" and "1994" for "1989" each place it appeared in subsecs. (b), (c) and (e) . . . Sec. 503(b), deleted "or" at end of subpara. (c)(1)(B), deleted subpara. (c)(1)(C), and added new subparas. (c)(1)(C) and (D) . . . Sec. 504, added para. (e)(5), effective 4/2/87.

Prior to amendment, subpara. (c)(1)(C) read as follows:

"(C) hereafter authorized by a law which does not authorize the expenditure out of the Highway Trust Fund of any amount for a general purpose not covered by subparagraph (A) or (B) as in effect on December 31, 1982."

In 1986, P.L. 99-640, Sec. 7(a)(1), and (2), substituted "60,000,000 for Fiscal Year 1987 only and $45,000,000 for each fiscal year thereafter; " for "45,000,000" each place it appeared in subpara. (c)(4)(A) and added subpara. (c)(4)(E), effective 11/10/86.

—P.L. 99-499, Sec. 521(b)(1)(A), added para. (b)(4) . . . Sec. 521(b)(1)(B), substituted "section 4081 (to the extent attributable to the Highway Trust Fund financing rate)" for "section 4081" in subpara. (c)(4)(D), effective 1/1/87.

In 1984, P.L. 98-369, Sec. 474(r)(43), substituted "section 34" for "section 39" in clause (c)(2)(A)(ii), effective for tax. yrs. begin. after 12/31/83 and for carrybacks from tax. yrs. begin. after 12/31/83.

—P.L. 98-369, Sec. 911(d)(1)(A), amended para. (e)(2) . . . Sec. 911(d)(1)(B), added "(or with respect to qualified diesel-powered highway vehicles purchased before January 1, 1988)" after "used before October 1, 1988" in clause (c)(2)(A)(ii), effective 8/1/84.

Prior to amendment, para. (e)(2) read as follows:

"(2) Transfers to mass transit account. The Secretary of the Treasury shall transfer to the Mass Transit Account one-ninth of the amounts appropriated to the Highway Trust Fund under subsection (b) which are attributable to taxes under sections 4041 and 4081 imposed after March 31, 1983."

—P.L. 98-369, Sec. 1016(b)(1)(A), substituted "the Boat Safety Account in the Aquatic Resources Trust Fund" for "the National Recreational Boating Safety and Facilities Improvement Fund established by section 202 of the Recreational Boating Fund Act" in clause (c)(4)(A)(i) . . . Sec. 1016(b)(1)(B), substituted "the amount in the Boat Safety Account" for "the amount in the National Recreational Boating Safety and Facilities Improvement Fund" in clause (c)(4)(A)(ii) . . . Sec. 1016(b)(1)(C), substituted "boat safety account" for "national recreational boating safety and facilities improvement fund" in the heading of subpara. (c)(4)(A) . . . Sec. 1016(b)(2), redesignated subpara. (c)(4)(C) as subpara. (c)(4)(D), deleted subpara. (c)(4)(B) and added new subparas. (c)(4)(B) and (C), effective 10/1/84. Sec. 1016(e)(2) of this Act provides:

"(2) Boat safety account treated as continuation of National Recreational Boating Safety and Facilities Improvement Fund. The Boat Safety Account in the Aquatic Resources Trust Fund established by the amendments made by this section shall be treated for all purposes of law as the continuation of the National Recreational Boating Safety and Facilities Improvement Fund established by section 13107 of title 46, United States Code. Any reference in any law to the National Recreational Boating Safety and Facilities Improvement Fund established by such section shall be deemed to include (wherever appropriate) a reference to such Boat Safety Account."

Prior to deletion, subpara. (c)(4)(B) read as follows:

"(B) Excess funds transferred to land and water conservation fund. Any amount received in the Highway Trust Fund which is attributable to motorboat fuel taxes and which is not transferred from the Highway Trust Fund under subparagraph (A) shall be transferred by the Secretary from the Highway Trust Fund into the land and water conservation fund provided for in title I of the Land and Water Conservation Fund Act of 1965."

In 1983, P.L. 97-424, Sec. 531(a), added Code Sec. 9503, effective on 1/1/83. Sec. 531(e)(2) of this Act provides as follows:

"(2) New Highway Trust Fund treated as continuation of old. The Highway Trust Fund established by the amendments made by this section shall be treated for all purposes of law as the continuation of the Highway Trust Fund established by section 209 of the Highway Revenue Act of 1956. Any reference in any law to the Highway Trust Fund established by such section 209 shall be deemed to include (wherever appropriate) a reference to the Highway Trust Fund established by the amendments made by this section."

Sec. 9504. Sport Fish Restoration and Boating Trust Fund.

(a) Creation of trust fund.

There is hereby established in the Treasury of the United States a trust fund to be known as the "Sport Fish Restoration and Boating Trust Fund". Such Trust Fund shall consist of such amounts as may be appropriated, credited, or paid to it as provided in this section, section 9503(c)(3), section 9503(c)(4), or section 9602(b).

(b) Sport Fish Restoration and Boating Trust Fund.

(1) Transfer of certain taxes to Trust Fund. There is hereby appropriated to the Sport Fish Restoration and Boating Trust Fund amounts equivalent to the following amounts received in the Treasury on or after October 1, 1984—

(A) the taxes imposed by section 4161(a) (relating to sport fishing equipment), and

(B) the import duties imposed on fishing tackle under heading 9507 of the Harmonized Tariff Schedule of the United States (19 U.S.C. 1202) and on yachts and pleasure craft under chapter 89 of the Harmonized Tariff Schedule of the United States.

(2) Expenditures from Trust Fund. Amounts in the Sport Fish Restoration and Boating Trust Fund shall be available, as provided by appropriation Acts, for making expenditures—

(A) to carry out the purposes of the Dingell-Johnson Sport Fish Restoration Act (as in effect on the date of the enactment of the the Surface Transportation Extension Act of 2011),

(B) to carry out the purposes of section 7204(d) of the Transportation Equity Act for the 21st Century (as in effect on the date of the enactment of the Surface Transportation Extension Act of 2011),

(C) to carry out the purposes of the Coastal Wetlands Planning, Protection and Restoration Act (as in effect on the date of the enactment of the Surface Transportation Extension Act of 2010, Part II),

Amounts transferred to such account under section 9503(c)(4) may be used only for making expenditures described in subparagraph (C) of this paragraph.

(c) Expenditures from Boat Safety Account.

Amounts remaining in the Boat Safety Account on October 1, 2005, and amounts thereafter credited to the Account under section 9602(b), shall be available, without further appropriation, for making expenditures before October 1, 2010, to carry out the purposes of section 15 of the Dingell-Johnson Sport Fish Restoration Act (as in effect on the date of the enactment of the Safe, Accountable, Flexible, Efficient Transportation Equity Act: A Legacy for Users). For purposes of section 9602, the Boat Safety Account shall be treated as a Trust Fund established by this subchapter.

(d) Limitation on transfers to Trust Fund.

(1) In general. Except as provided in paragraph (2), no amount may be appropriated or paid to the Sport Fish Restoration and Boating Trust Fund on and after the date of any expenditure from such Trust Fund which is not permitted by this section. The determination of whether an expenditure is so permitted shall be made without regard to—

(A) any provision of law which is not contained or referenced in this title or in a revenue Act, and

(B) whether such provision of law is a subsequently enacted provision or directly or indirectly seeks to waive the application of this subsection.

(2) Exception for prior obligations. Paragraph (1) shall not apply to any expenditure to liquidate any contract entered into (or for any amount otherwise obligated) before October 1, 2011, in accordance with the provisions of this section.

(e) Cross reference.

For provision transferring motorboat fuels taxes to Sport Fish Restoration and Boating Trust Fund, see 9503(c)(3).

In 2011, P.L. 112-5, Sec. 401(b)(1), substituted "the Surface Transportation Extension Act of 2011" for "the Surface Transportation Extension Act of 2010, Part II" each place it appeared in para. (b)(2) ... Sec. 401(d)(2), substituted "October 1, 2011" for "March 5, 2011" in sbsec. (d)(2), effective 3/04/2011

In 2010, P.L. 111-322, Sec. 2401(b)(1), substituted "Surface Transportation Extension Act of 2010, Part II" for "Surface Transportation Extension Act of 2010" each place it appears in para. (b)(2) ... Sec. 2401(b)(2), substituted "March 5, 2011" for "January 1, 2011" in para. (d)(2), effective 12/31/2010

—P.L. 111-147, Sec. 444(b)(5), substituted "section 9503(c)(3), section 9503(c)(4)" for "section 9503(c)(4), section 9503(c)(5)" in subsec. (a) ... Sec. 444(b)(6), substituted "section 9503(c)(4)" for "section 9503(c)(5)" in para. (b)(2) ... Sec. 444(b)(7), substituted "9503(c)(3)" for "section 9503(c)(4)" in subsec. (e), effective for transfers relating to amounts paid and credits allowed after 3/18/2010.

—P.L. 111-147, Sec. 445(b)(1)(A), substituted "(as in effect on the date of the enactment of the Surface Transportation Extension Act of 2010)," for "(as in effect" and all that follows in subpara. (b)(2)(A) ... Sec. 445(b)(1)(B), substituted "(as in effect on the date of the enactment of the Surface Transportation Extension Act of 2010), and" for "(as in effect" and all that follows in subpara. (b)(2)(B) ... Sec. 445(b)(1)(C), substituted "(as in effect on the date of the enactment of the Surface Transportation Extension Act of 2010), and" for "(as in effect" and all that follows in subpara. (b)(2)(C) ... Sec. 445(b)(2), substituted "January 1, 2011" for "October 1, 2009" in para. (d)(2), effective 9/30/2009.

In 2008, P.L. 110-181, Sec. 121(c)(1), repealed the amendment made by section 16(c)(2) of P.L. 109-304, effective 1/28/2008. ... Sec. 121(c)(2), of this Act provides:

"(2) Intended effect. The provisions repealed by paragraph (1) shall be treated as if never enacted."

In 2006, P.L. 109-304, Sec. 16(c)(2), substituted "section 13107" for "section 13106" in subsec. (c) [Ed. Note: Amendment cannot be made as stated. It is our feeling that the Act will be corrected at a later date.], enacted 10/6/2006.

In 2005, P.L. 109-74, Sec. 301(a)(1), substituted "October 1, 2005" for "August 15, 2005" in subsec. (c) ... Sec. 301(a)(2), substituted "Sportfishing and Recreational Boating Safety Amendments Act of 2005" for "Surface Transportation Extension Act of 2005, Part VI" in subsec. (c), effective 9/29/2005.

—P.L. 109-59, Sec. 11101(d)(2)(A), substituted "Safe, Accountable, Flexible, Efficient Transportation Equity Act: A Legacy for Users" for "Surface Transportation Extension Act of 2005, Part V" each place it appeared in para. (b)(2) ... Sec. 11101(d)(2)(B), substituted "October 1, 2009" for "July 31, 2005" in para. (d)(2), effective 8/10/2005.

—P.L. 109-59, Sec. 11115(b)(1), amended subsec. (a) ... Sec. 11115(b)(2)(A)(i), substituted "and Boating Trust Fund" for "Account" in the heading of subsec. (b) ... Sec. 11115(b)(2)(A)(ii), substituted "and Boating Trust Fund" for "Account" each place it appeared in paras. (b)(1) and (2) ... Sec. 11115(b)(2)(A)(iii), substituted "trust fund" for "account" in the headings of paras. (b)(1) and (2) ... Sec. 11115(b)(2)(B)(i), deleted "Aquatic Resources" after "transfers to" in the heading of subsec. (d) ... Sec. 11115(b)(2)(B)(ii), substituted "the Sport Fish Restoration and Boating" for "any Account in the Aquatic Resources" in para. (d)(1) ... Sec. 11115(b)(2)(B)(iii), substituted "such Trust Fund" for "any such Account" in para. (d)(1) ... Sec. 11115(b)(2)(C), substituted "Sport Fish Restoration and Boating Trust Fund" for "Boat Safety Account and Sport Fish Restoration Account" in subsec. (e) ... Sec. 11115(b)(2)(D), substituted "Sport Fish Restoration and Boating" for "Aquatic Resources" in the heading of Code Sec. 9504 ... Sec. 11115(c), amended subsec. (c), effective 10/1/2005.

Prior to amendment, subsec. (a) read as follows:

"(a) Creation of trust fund.

"(1) In general. There is hereby established in the Treasury of the United States a trust fund to be known as the 'Aquatic Resources Trust Fund'.

"(2) Accounts in trust fund. The Aquatic Resources Trust Fund shall consist of

"(A) a Sport Fish Restoration Account, and

"(B) a Boat Safety Account.

Each such Account shall consist of such amounts as may be appropriated, credited, or paid to it as provided in this section, section 9503(c)(4), section 9503(c)(5), or section 9602(b)."

Prior to amendment, subsec. (c) read as follows:

"(c) Expenditures from boat safety account. Amounts in the Boat Safety Account shall be available, as provided by appropriation Acts, for making expenditures before August 15, 2005, to carry out the purposes of section 13106 of title 46, United States Code (as in effect on the date of enactment of the Surface Transportation Extension Act of 2005, Part VI)."

—P.L. 109-59, Sec. 11151(c), substituted "subparagraph (C)" for "subparagraph (B)" in para. (b)(2), effective 6/9/98, as if included in the Transportation Equity Act for the 21st Century.

—P.L. 109-59, Sec. 11151(e)(1), substituted "the Dingell-Johnson Sport Fish Restoration Act" for "the Act entitled 'An Act to provide that the United States shall aid the States in fish restoration and management projects, and for other purposes', approved August 9, 1950" in subpara. (b)(2)(A), effective 8/10/2005.

—P.L. 109-42, Sec. 7(b)(1), added "Subparagraphs (A), (B), and (C) shall each be applied by substituting 'Surface Transportation Extension Act of 2005, Part VI' for 'Surface Transportation Extension Act of 2005, Part V'." at the end of para. (b)(2) . . . Sec. 7(b)(2)(A), substituted "August 15, 2005" for "July 31, 2005" in subsec. (c) . . . Sec. 7(b)(2)(B), substituted "Surface Transportation Extension Act of 2005, Part VI" for "Surface Transportation Extension Act of 2005, Part V" in subsec. (c) . . . Sec. 7(b)(3), added "The preceding sentence shall be applied by substituting 'August 15, 2005' for the date therein." at the end of para. (d)(2), effective 7/30/2005.

—P.L. 109-42, Sec. 7(d)(2), deleted "Subparagraphs (A), (B), and (C) shall each be applied by substituting 'Surface Transportation Extension Act of 2005, Part VI' for 'Surface Transportation Extension Act of 2005, Part V'." at the end of para. (b)(2) . . . Sec. 7(d)(3), deleted "The preceding sentence shall be applied by substituting 'August 15, 2005' for the date therein." at the end of para. (d)(2), effective on the date of the enactment [8/10/2005] of the Safe, Accountable, Flexible, Efficient Transportation Equity Act: A Legacy for Users and shall be executed immediately before the amendments made by such Act.

—P.L. 109-40, Sec. 9(b)(1), substituted "Surface Transportation Extension Act of 2005, V" for "Surface Transportation Extension Act of 2005, Part IV" each place it appeared in para. (b)(2) . . . Sec. 9(b)(2)(A), substituted "July 31, 2005" for "July 28, 2005" in subsec. (c) . . . Sec. 9(b)(2)(B), substituted "Surface Transportation Extension Act of 2005, Part V" for "Surface Transportation Extension Act of 2005, Part IV" in subsec. (c) . . . Sec. 9(b)(3), substituted "July 31, 2005" for "July 28, 2005" in para. (d)(2), effective 7/28/2005.

—P.L. 109-37, Sec. 9(b)(1), substituted "Surface Transportation Extension Act of 2005, IV" for "Surface Transportation Extension Act of 2005, Part III" each place it appeared in para. (b)(2) . . . Sec. 9(b)(2)(A), substituted "July 28, 2005" for "July 22, 2005" in subsec. (c) . . . Sec. 9(b)(2)(B), substituted "Surface Transportation Extension Act of 2005, Part IV" for "Surface Transportation Extension Act of 2005, Part III" in subsec. (c) . . . Sec. 9(b)(3), substituted "July 28, 2005" for "July 22, 2005" in para. (d)(2), effective 7/22/2005.

—P.L. 109-35, Sec. 9(b)(1), substituted "Surface Transportation Extension Act of 2005, III" for "Surface Transportation Extension Act of 2005, Part II" each place it appeared in para. (b)(2) . . . Sec. 9(b)(2)(A), substituted "July 22, 2005" for "July 20, 2005" in subsec. (c) . . . Sec. 9(b)(2)(B), substituted "Surface Transportation Extension Act of 2005, Part III" for "Surface Transportation Extension Act of 2005, Part II" in subsec. (c) . . . Sec. 9(b)(3), substituted "July 22, 2005" for "July 20, 2005" in para. (d)(2), effective 7/20/2005.

—P.L. 109-20, Sec. 9(b)(1), substituted "Surface Transportation Extension Act of 2005, II" for "Surface Transportation Extension Act of 2005" each place it appeared in para. (b)(2) . . . Sec. 9(b)(2)(A), substituted "July 20, 2005" for "July 1, 2005" in subsec. (c) . . . Sec. 9(b)(2)(B), substituted "Surface Transportation Extension Act of 2005, Part II" for "Surface Transportation Extension Act of 2005" in subsec. (c) . . . Sec. 9(b)(3), substituted "July 20, 2005" for "July 1, 2005" in para. (d)(2), effective 7/1/2005.

—P.L. 109-14, Sec. 9(b)(1), substituted "Surface Transportation Extension Act of 2005" for "Surface Transportation Extension Act of 2004, Part V" each place it appeared in para. (b)(2) . . . Sec. 9(b)(2)(A), substituted "July 1, 2005" for "June 1, 2005" in subsec. (c) . . . Sec. 9(b)(2)(B), substituted "Surface Transportation Extension Act of 2005" for "Surface Transportation Extension Act of 2004, Part V" in subsec. (c) . . . Sec. 9(b)(3), substituted "July 1, 2005" for "June 1, 2005" in para. (d)(2), effective 5/31/2005.

In 2004, P.L. 108-310, Sec. 13(b)(1), substituted "Surface Transportation Extension Act of 2004, Part V" for "Surface Transportation Extension Act of 2004, Part IV" each place it appeared in para. (b)(2) . . . Sec. 13(b)(2)(A), substituted "June 1, 2005" for "October 1, 2004" in subsec. (c) . . . Sec. 13(b)(2)(B), substituted "Surface Transportation Extension Act of 2004, Part V" for "Surface Transportation Extension Act of 2004, Part IV" in subsec. (c) . . . Sec. 13(b)(3), substituted "June 1, 2005" for "October 1, 2004" in para. (d)(2), effective 9/30/2004.

—P.L. 108-280, Sec. 10(b)(1), substituted "Surface Transportation Extension Act of 2004, Part IV" for "Surface Transportation Extension Act of 2004, Part III" each place it appeared in para. (b)(2) . . . Sec. 10(b)(2)(A), substituted "October 1, 2004" for "August 1, 2004" in subsec. (c) . . . Sec. 10(b)(2)(B), substituted "Surface Transportation Extension Act of 2004, Part IV" for "Surface Transportation Extension Act of 2004, Part III" in subsec. (c) . . . Sec. 10(b)(3), substituted "October 1, 2004" for "August 1, 2004" in para. (d)(2), effective 7/30/2004.

—P.L. 108-263, Sec. 10(b)(1), substituted "Surface Transportation Extension Act of 2004, Part III" for "Surface Transportation Extension Act of 2004, Part II" each place it appeared in para. (b)(2) . . . Sec. 10(b)(2)(A), substituted "August 1, 2004" for "July 1, 2004" in subsec. (c) . . . Sec. 10(b)(2)(B), substituted "Surface Transportation Extension Act of 2004, Part III" for "Surface Transportation Extension Act of 2004, Part II" in subsec. (c) . . . Sec. 10(b)(3), substituted "August 1, 2004" for "July 1, 2004" in para. (d)(2), effective 6/30/2004.

—P.L. 108-224, Sec. 10(b)(1), substituted "Surface Transportation Extension Act of 2004, Part II" for "Surface Transportation Extension Act of 2004" each place it appeared in para. (b)(2) . . . Sec. 10(b)(2)(A), substituted "July 1, 2004" for "May 1, 2004" in subsec. (c) . . . Sec. 10(b)(2)(B), substituted "Surface Transportation Extension Act of 2004, Part II" for "Surface Transportation Extension Act of 2004" in subsec. (c) . . . Sec. 10(b)(3), substituted "July 1, 2004" for "May 1, 2004" in para. (d)(2), effective 4/30/2004.

—P.L. 108-202, Sec. 12(b)(1), substituted "Surface Transportation Extension Act of 2004" for "Surface Transportation Extension Act of 2003" each place it appeared in para. (b)(2) . . . Sec. 12(b)(2)(A), substituted "May 1, 2004" for "March 1, 2004" in subsec. (c) . . . Sec. 12(b)(2)(B), substituted "Surface Transportation Extension Act of 2004" for "Surface Transportation Extension Act of 2003" in subsec. (c) . . . Sec. 12(b)(3), substituted "May 1, 2004" for "March 1, 2004" in para. (d)(2), effective 2/29/2004.

In 2003, P.L. 108-88, Sec. 12(b)(1)(A), substituted "Surface Transportation Extension Act of 2003" for "Wildlife and Sport Fish Restoration Programs Improvement Act of 2000" in subpara. (b)(2)(A) . . . Sec. 12(b)(1)(B), substituted "Surface Transportation Extension Act of 2003" for "TEA 21 Restoration Act" in subparas. (b)(2)(B) and (C) . . . Sec. 12(b)(2)(A), substituted "March 1, 2004" for "October 1, 2003" in subsec. (c) . . . Sec. 12(b)(2)(B), substituted "Surface Transportation Extension Act of 2003" for "TEA 21 Restoration Act" in subsec. (c) . . . Sec. 12(b)(3), substituted "March 1, 2004" for "October 1, 2003" in para. (d)(2), effective 9/30/2003.

In 2000, P.L. 106-408, Sec. 126, substituted "(as in effect on the date of the enactment of the Wildlife and Sport Fish Restoration Programs Improvement Act of 2000)" for "(as in effect on the date of the enactment of the TEA 21 Restoration Act)" in subpara. (b)(2)(A), effective 11/1/2000.

In 1998, P.L. 105-206, Sec. 9015(b), added Sec. 9005(f) of P.L. 105-178 [see below], effective 6/9/98.

—P.L. 105-178, Sec. 9005(b)(1), substituted "the date of the enactment of the Transportation Equity Act for the 21st Century)," for "October 1, 1988), and" in subpara. (b)(2)(A) . . . Sec. 9005(b)(2), substituted "the date of the enactment of the Transportation Equity Act for the 21st Century" for "November 29, 1990" in subpara. (b)(2)(B) . . . Sec. 9005(b)(3), redesignated subpara. (b)(2)(B) as (C) and added subpara. (b)(2)(B) . . . Sec. 9005(c)(1), substituted "2003" for "1998" in subsec. (c) . . . Sec. 9005(c)(2), substituted "the date of enactment of the Transportation Equity Act for the 21st Century" for "October 1, 1988" in subsec. (c) . . . Sec. 9005(d), redesignated subsec. (d) as (e) and added subsec. (d) . . . Sec. 9005(f)(1), [as added by Sec. 9015(b) of P.L. 105-206, see above] substituted "the date of the enactment of the TEA 21 Restoration Act" for "the date of the enactment of the Transportation Equity Act for the 21st Century" in subpara. (b)(2)(A) [as amended by Sec. 9005(b)(1) of this Act, see above] . . . Sec. 9005(f)(2), [as added by Sec. 9015(b) of P.L. 105-206, see above] substituted "the TEA 21 Restoration Act" for "such Act" in subpara. (b)(2)(B) [as amended by Sec. 9005(b)(3) of this Act, see above] . . . Sec. 9005(f)(3), [as added by Sec. 9015(b) of P.L. 105-206, see above] substituted "the date of the enactment of the TEA 21 Restoration Act" for "the date of the enactment of the Transportation Equity Act for the 21st Century" in subpara. (b)(2)(C) [as amended by Sec. 9005(b)(2) of this Act, see above] . . . Sec. 9005(f)(4), [as added by Sec. 9015(b) of P.L. 105-206, see above] substituted "the date of the enactment of the TEA 21 Restoration Act" for "the date of enactment of the Transportation Equity Act for the 21st Century" in subpara. (c) [as amended by Sec. 9005(c)(2) of this Act, see above], effective 6/9/98.

In 1997, P.L. 105-130, Sec. 9(b), substituted "October 1, 1998" for "April 1, 1998" in subsec. (c), effective 10/1/97.

In 1991, P.L. 102-240, Sec. 8002(d)(2)(C), substituted "1998" for "1994" in subsec. (c) . . . Sec. 8002(i), amended subpara. (b)(2)(B), effective 12/18/91.

Prior to amendment, subpara. (b)(2)(B) read as follows:

"(B) to carry out the purposes of any law which is substantially identical to S. 3252 of the 101st Congress, as introduced."

In 1990, P.L. 101-508, Sec. 11211(i)(2), added "section 9503(c)(5)," after "section 9503(c)(4)" in para. (a)(2) . . . Sec. 11211(i)(3), amended para. (b)(2), effective 12/1/90.

Prior to amendment, para. (b)(2) read as follows:

"(2) Expenditures from account. Amounts in the Sport Fish Restoration Account shall be available, as provided by appropriation Acts, to carry out the purposes of the Act entitled 'An Act to provide that the United States shall aid the States in fish restoration and management projects, and for other purposes,' approved August 9, 1950 (as in effect on October 1, 1988)."

In 1988, P.L. 100-448, Sec. 6(a)(2)(A), and (B), substituted "before April 1, 1994" for "before April 1, 1989" and substituted "(as in effect on October 1, 1988)" for "(as in effect on June 1, 1984)" in subsec. (c) . . . Sec. 6(c)(3), substituted "(as in effect on October 1, 1988)" for "(as in effect on June 1, 1984)" in para. (b)(2), effective 10/1/88.

—P.L. 100-418, Sec. 1214(p)(2)(A), substituted "heading 9507 of the Harmonized Tariff Schedule of the United States" for "subpart B of part 5 of schedule 7 of the Tariff Schedules of the United States" in subpara. (b)(1)(B) . . . Sec. 1214(p)(2)(B), substituted "chapter 89 of the Harmonized Tariff Schedule of the United States" for "subpart D of part 6 of schedule 6 of such Schedules" in subpara. (b)(1)(B), effective 1/1/89, and applicable for articles entered on or after 1/1/89.

In 1984, P.L. 98-369, Sec. 1016(a), added Code Sec. 9504, effective after 9/30/84. Sec. 1016(e)(2) of the Act provides:

"(2) Boat safety account treated as continuation of national recreational boating safety and facilities improvement fund. The Boat Safety Account in the Aquatic Resources Trust Fund established by the amendments made by this section shall be treated for all purposes of law as the continuation of the National Recreational Boating Safety and Facilities Improvement Fund established by section 13107 of title 46, United States Code. Any reference in any law to the National Recreational Boating Safety and Facilities Improvement Fund established by such section shall be deemed to include (wherever appropriate) a reference to such Boat Safety Account."

Sec. 9505. Harbor Maintenance Trust Fund.
(a) Creation of trust fund.
There is hereby established in the Treasury of the United States a trust fund to be known as the "Harbor Maintenance Trust Fund", consisting of such amounts as may be—
   (1) appropriated to the Harbor Maintenance Trust Fund as provided in this section,
   (2) transferred to the Harbor Maintenance Trust Fund by the Saint Lawrence Seaway Development Corporation pursuant to section 13(a) of the Act of May 13, 1954, or
   (3) credited to the Harbor Maintenance Trust Fund as provided in section 9602(b).
(b) Transfer to Harbor Maintenance Trust Fund of amounts equivalent to certain taxes.
There are hereby appropriated to the Harbor Maintenance Trust Fund amounts equivalent to the taxes received in the Treasury under section 4461 (relating to harbor maintenance tax).
(c) Expenditures from Harbor Maintenance Trust Fund.
Amounts in the Harbor Maintenance Trust Fund shall be available, as provided by appropriation Acts, for making expenditures—
   (1) to carry out section 210 of the Water Resources Development Act of 1986 (as in effect on the date of the enactment of the Water Resources Development Act of 1996),
   (2) for payments of rebates of tolls or charges pursuant to section 13(b) of the Act of May 13, 1954 (as in effect on April 1, 1987), and
   (3) for the payment of all expenses of administration incurred by the Department of the Treasury, the Army Corps of Engineers, and the Department of Commerce related to the administration of subchapter A of chapter 36 (relating to harbor maintenance tax), but not in excess of $5,000,000 for any fiscal year.

In **1996**, P.L. 104-303, Sec. 601, amended para. (c)(1), enacted 10/12/1996. Prior to amendment, para. (c)(1) read as follows:
"(1) to carry out section 210(a) of the Water Resources Development Act of 1986 (as in effect on the date of enactment of this section)."
In **1993**, P.L. 103-182, Sec. 683(a), amended para. (c)(3), effective for fiscal yrs. begin. after 12/8/93.
Prior to amendment, para. (c)(3) read as follows:
"(3) for the payment of all expenses of administration incurred—
"(A) by the Department of the Treasury in administering subchapter A of chapter 36 (relating to harbor maintenance tax), but not in excess of $5,000,000 for any fiscal year, and
"(B) for periods during which no fee applies under paragraph (9) or (10) of section 13031(a) of the Consolidated Omnibus Budget Reconciliation Act of 1985."
In **1986**, P.L. 99-662, Sec. 1403(a), added Code Sec. 9505, effective 4/1/87.

Sec. 9506. Inland Waterways Trust Fund.
(a) Creation of trust fund.
There is hereby established in the Treasury of the United States a trust fund to be known as the "Inland Waterways Trust Fund", consisting of such amounts as may be appropriated or credited to such Trust Fund as provided in this section or section 9602(b).
(b) Transfer to trust fund of amounts equivalent to certain taxes.
There are hereby appropriated to the Inland Waterways Trust Fund amounts equivalent to the taxes received in the Treasury under section 4042 (relating to tax on fuel used in commercial transportation on inland waterways). The preceding sentence shall apply only to so much of such taxes as are attributable to the Inland Waterways Trust Fund financing rate under section 4042(b).
(c) Expenditures from trust fund.
   (1) In general. Except as provided in paragraph (2), amounts in the Inland Waterways Trust Fund shall be available, as provided by appropriation Acts, for making construction and rehabilitation expenditures for navigation on the inland and coastal waterways of the United States described in section 206 of the Inland Waterways Revenue Act of 1978, as in effect on the date of the enactment of this section.
   (2) Exception for certain projects. Not more than ½ of the cost of any construction to which section 102(a) of the Water Resources Development Act of 1986 applies (as in effect on the date of the enactment of this section) may be paid from the Inland Waterways Trust Fund.

In **1988**, P.L. 100-647, Sec. 1018(u)(18), corrected Sec. 521(b)(3) of P.L. 98-369 to add the last sentence to subsec. (b) instead of para. (b)(1), see below.
In **1986**, P.L. 99-662, Sec. 1405(a), added Code Sec. 9506, effective 1/1/87. Sec. 1405(d)(2) of this Act provides:
"(2) Inland waterways trust fund treated as continuation of old trust fund.— The Inland Waterways Trust Fund established by the amendments made by this section shall be treated for all purposes of law as a continuation of the Inland Waterways Trust Fund established by section 203 of the Inland Waterways Revenue Act of 1978. Any reference in any law to the Inland Waterways Trust Fund established by such section 203 shall be deemed to include (wherever appropriate) a reference to the Inland Waterways Trust Fund established by this section."
—P.L. 99-499, Sec. 521(b)(3), added the last sentence to subsec. (b) [see Sec. 1018(u)(18) of P.L. 100-647, above], effective on 1/1/87.

Sec. 9507. Hazardous Substance Superfund.
(a) Creation of trust fund.
There is established in the Treasury of the United States a trust fund to be known as the "Hazardous Substance Superfund" (hereinafter in this section referred to as the "Superfund"), consisting of such amounts as may be—
   (1) appropriated to the Superfund as provided in this section,
   (2) appropriated to the Superfund pursuant to section 517(b) of the Superfund Revenue Act of 1986, or
   (3) credited to the Superfund as provided in section 9602(b).
(b) Transfers to Superfund.
There are hereby appropriated to the Superfund amounts equivalent to—
   (1) the taxes received in the Treasury under section 59A, 4611, 4661, or 4671 (relating to environmental taxes),
   (2) amounts recovered on behalf of the Superfund under the Comprehensive Environmental Response, Compensation, and Liability Act of 1980 (hereinafter in this section referred to as "CERCLA"),
   (3) all moneys recovered or collected under section 311(b)(6)(B) of the Clean Water Act,
   (4) penalties assessed under title I of CERCLA, and
   (5) punitive damages under section 107(c)(3) of CERCLA.
In the case of the tax imposed by section 4611, paragraph (1) shall apply only to so much of such tax as is attributable to the Hazardous Substance Superfund financing rate under section 4611(c).
(c) Expenditures from Superfund
   (1) In general. Amounts in the Superfund shall be available, as provided in appropriation Acts, only for purposes of making expenditures—
      (A) to carry out the purposes of—
         (i) paragraphs (1), (2), (5), and (6) of section 111(a) of CERCLA as in effect on the date of the enactment of the Superfund Amendments and Reauthorization Act of 1986,
         (ii) section 111(c) of CERCLA (as so in effect), other than paragraphs (1) and (2) thereof, and
         (iii) section 111(m) of CERCLA (as so in effect), or
      (B) hereafter authorized by a law which does not authorize the expenditure out of the Superfund for a gen-

Establishment of trust funds — Code Sec. 9508(c)

eral purpose not covered by subparagraph (A) (as so in effect).

(2) Exception for certain transfers, etc., of hazardous substances. No amount in the Superfund or derived from the Superfund shall be available or used for the transfer or disposal of hazardous waste carried out pursuant to a cooperative agreement between the Administrator of the Environmental Protection Agency and a State if the following conditions apply—

(A) the transfer or disposal, if made on December 13, 1985, would not comply with a State or local requirement,

(B) the transfer is to a facility for which a final permit under section 3005(a) of the Solid Waste Disposal Act was issued after January 1, 1983, and before November 1, 1984, and

(C) the transfer is from a facility identified as the McColl Site in Fullerton, California.

(d) Authority to borrow.

(1) In general. There are authorized to be appropriated to the Superfund, as repayable advances, such sums as may be necessary to carry out the purposes of the Superfund.

(2) Limitation on aggregate advances. The maximum aggregate amount of repayable advances to the Superfund which is outstanding at any one time shall not exceed an amount equal to the amount which the Secretary estimates will be equal to the sum of the amounts appropriated to the Superfund under subsection (b)(1) during the following 24 months.

(3) Repayment of advances.

(A) In general. Advances made to the Superfund shall be repaid, and interest on such advances shall be paid, to the general fund of the Treasury when the Secretary determines that moneys are available for such purposes in the Superfund.

(B) Final repayment. No advance shall be made to the Superfund after December 31, 1995, and all advances to such Fund shall be repaid on or before such date.

(C) Rate of interest. Interest on advances made to the Superfund shall be at a rate determined by the Secretary of the Treasury (as of the close of the calendar month preceding the month in which the advance is made) to be equal to the current average market yield on outstanding marketable obligations of the United States with remaining periods to maturity comparable to the anticipated period during which the advance will be outstanding and shall be compounded annually.

(e) Liability of United States limited to amount in trust fund.

(1) General rule. Any claim filed against the Superfund may be paid only out of the Superfund.

(2) Coordination with other provisions. Nothing in CERCLA or the Superfund Amendments and Reauthorization Act of 1986 (or in any amendment made by either of such Acts) shall authorize the payment by the United States Government of any amount with respect to any such claim out of any source other than the Superfund.

(3) Order in which unpaid claims are to be paid. If at any time the Superfund has insufficient funds to pay all of the claims payable out of the Superfund at such time, such claims shall, to the extent permitted under paragraph (1), be paid in full in the order in which they were finally determined.

In **1996**, P.L. 104-188, Sec. 1704(t)(44), amended Sec. 11231(c) of P.L. 101-508, by substituting "comma" for "period" and substituted a comma for the period at the end of para. 517(b)(9), P.L. 99-499, as added by Sec. 11231(d) of P.L. 101-508.

In **1990**, P.L. 101-508, Sec. 11231(c), substituted "December 31, 1995" for "December 31, 1991" in subpara. (d)(3)(B), effective 11/5/90.

—P.L. 101-508, Sec. 11231(d), [as amended by Sec. 1704(t)(44) of P.L. 104-188, see above] deleted the "and" at the end of Sec. 517(b)(4), of P.L., 99-499 substituted ", and" for the comma at the end of Sec. 517(b)(5) of P.L. 99-499 and added Secs. 517(b)(6)-(9) [as amended by Sec. 1704(t)(44) of P.L. 104-188, see above] of P.L. 99-499, see below.

In **1986**, P.L. 99-509, Sec. 8032(c)(4), added the last sentence to subsec. (b), effective as provided in Sec. 8032(d) of this Act, which reads as follows:

"(d) Effective date.

"(1) In general.—Except as provided in paragraph (2), the amendments made by this section shall take effect on the commencement date (as defined in section 4611(f)(2) of the Internal Revenue Code of 1954, as added by this section).

"(2) Coordination with superfund reauthorization.—The amendments made by this section shall take effect only if the Superfund Amendments and Reauthorization Act of 1986 is enacted."

—P.L. 99-499, Sec. 517(a), added Code Sec. 9507, effective 1/1/87, except as provided in Sec. 517(e)(2) of this Act;

"(2) Superfund treated as continuation of old trust funds.—The Hazardous Substance Superfund established by the amendments made by this section shall be treated for all purposes of law as a continuation of the Hazardous Substance Response Trust Fund established by section 221 of the Hazardous Substance Response Revenue Act of 1980. Any reference in any law to the Hazardous Substance Response Trust Fund established by such section 221 shall be deemed to include (wherever appropriate) a reference to the Hazardous Substance Superfund established by the amendments made by this section."

—P.L. 99-499, Sec. 517(b), [as amended by Sec. 11231(d) of P.L. 101-508 and Sec. 1704(t)(44) of P.L. 104-188, see above] provides:

"(b) Authorization of appropriations.

"There is authorized to be appropriated, out of any money in the Treasury not otherwise appropriated, to the Hazardous Substance Superfund for fiscal year—

"(1) 1987, $250,000,000,

"(2) 1988, $250,000,000,

"(3) 1989, $250,000,000,

"(4) 1990, $250,000,000,

"(5) 1991, $250,000,000, and

"(6) 1992, $250,000,000,

"(7) 1993, $250,000,000,

"(8) 1994, $250,000,000, and

"(9) 1995, $250,000,000,

plus for each fiscal year an amount equal to so much of the aggregate amount authorized to be appropriated under this subsection (and paragraph (2) of section 221(b) of the Hazardous Substance Response Act of 1980, as in effect before its repeal) as has not been appropriated before the beginning of the fiscal year involved."

Sec. 9508. Leaking Underground Storage Tank Trust Fund.

(a) Creation of trust fund.

There is established in the Treasury of the United States a trust fund to be known as the "Leaking Underground Storage Tank Trust Fund", consisting of such amounts as may be appropriated or credited to such Trust Fund as provided in this section or section 9602(b).

(b) Transfers to trust fund.

There are hereby appropriated to the Leaking Underground Storage Tank Trust Fund amounts equivalent to—

(1) taxes received in the Treasury under section 4041(d) (relating to additional taxes on motor fuels),

(2) taxes received in the Treasury under section 4081 (relating to tax on gasoline, diesel fuel, and kerosene) to the extent attributable to the Leaking Underground Storage Tank Trust Fund financing rate under such section,

(3) taxes received in the Treasury under section 4042 (relating to tax on fuel used in commercial transportation on inland waterways) to the extent attributable to the Leaking Underground Storage Tank Trust Fund financing rate under such section, and

(4) amounts received in the Treasury and collected under section 9003(h)(6) of the Solid Waste Disposal Act.

For purposes of this subsection, there shall not be taken into account the taxes imposed by sections 4041 and 4081 on diesel fuel sold for use or used as fuel in a diesel-powered boat.

(c) Expenditures.

Amounts in the Leaking Underground Storage Tank Trust Fund shall be available, as provided in appropriation Acts,

4,013

only for purposes of making expenditures to carry out sections 9003(h), 9003(i), 9003(j), 9004(f), 9005(c), 9010, 9011, 9012, and 9013 of the Solid Waste Disposal Act as in effect on the date of the enactment of the Public Law 109-168.

(d) Liability of the United States limited to amount in trust fund.

   (1) General rule. Any claim filed against the Leaking Underground Storage Tank Trust Fund may be paid only out of such Trust Fund.

   (2) Coordination with other provisions. Nothing in the Comprehensive Environmental Response, Compensation, and Liability Act of 1980 or the Superfund amendments and Reauthorization Act of 1986 (or in any amendment made by either of such Acts) shall authorize the payment by the United States Government of any amount with respect to any such claim out of any source other than the Leaking Underground Storage Tank Trust Fund.

   (3) Order in which unpaid claims are to be paid. If at any time the Leaking Underground Storage Tank Trust Fund has insufficient funds to pay all of the claims out of such Trust Fund at such time, such claims shall, to the extent permitted under paragraph (1), be paid in full in the order in which they were finally determined.

(e) Limitation on transfers to Leaking Underground Storage Tank Trust Fund.

   (1) In general. Except as provided in paragraph (2), no amount may be appropriated to the Leaking Underground Storage Tank Trust Fund on and after the date of any expenditure from the Leaking Underground Storage Tank Trust Fund which is not permitted by this section. The determination of whether an expenditure is so permitted shall be made without regard to—

   (A) any provision of law which is not contained or referenced in this title or in a revenue Act, and

   (B) whether such provision of law is a subsequently enacted provision or directly or indirectly seeks to waive the application of this paragraph.

   (2) Exception for prior obligations. Paragraph (1) shall not apply to any expenditure to liquidate any contract entered into (or for any amount otherwise obligated) before October 1, 2011, in accordance with the provisions of this section.

In **2007**, P.L. 110-172, Sec. 11(a)(46), as relates to Sec. 1(a), P.L. 109-433, 12/20/2006 [see below] reads as follows:

"(46) The Internal Revenue Code of 1986 shall be applied and administered as if the amendments made by section 1(a) of Public Law 109-433 had never been enacted.

In **2006**, P.L. 109-433, Sec. 1(a)(1), and Sec. 1(b) make the same amendments, with the same effective date, as Sec. 210(a)(1) and (2) of P.L. 109-432, 12/20/2006, below. Sec. 11(a)(46), P.L. 110-172, 12/29/2007, instucts that Sec. 1(a), P.L. 109-433 shall be applied and administered as if it had never been enacted.

—P.L. 109-432, Sec. 210(a)(1), substituted 'sections 9003(h), 9003(i), 9003(j), 9004(f), 9005(c), 9010, 9011, 9012, and 9013' for 'section 9003(h)' in subsec. (c) . . . Sec. 210(a)(2), substituted 'P.L. 109-168' for 'Superfund Amendments and Reauthorization Act of 1986' in subsec. (c), effective 12/20/2006.

In **2005**, P.L. 109-59, Sec. 11147(a), added subsec. (e), effective 8/10/2005.

—P.L. 109-58, Sec. 1362(c), amended subsec. (c), effective 10/1/2005.

Prior to amendment, subsec. (c) read as follows:

"(c) Expenditures.

"(1) In general. Except as provided in paragraph (2), amounts in the Leaking Underground Storage Tank Trust Fund shall be available, as provided in appropriation Acts, only for purposes of making expenditures to carry out section 9003(h) of the Solid Waste Disposal Act as in effect on the date of the enactment of the Superfund Amendments and Reauthorization Act of 1986.

"(2) Transfers from trust fund for certain repayments and credits.

"(A) In general. The Secretary shall pay from time to time from the Leaking Underground Storage Tank Trust Fund into the general fund of the Treasury amounts equivalent to—

"(i) amounts paid under—

"(I) section 6420 (relating to amounts paid in respect of gasoline used on farms),

"(II) section 6421 (relating to amounts paid in respect of gasoline used for certain nonhighway purposes or by local transit systems), and

"(III) section 6427 (relating to fuels not used for taxable purposes), and

"(ii) credits allowed under section 34, with respect to the taxes imposed by section 4041(d) or by section 4081 (to the extent attributable to the Leaking Underground Storage Trust Fund financing rate under such sections).

"(B) Transfers based on estimates. Transfers under subparagraph (A) shall be made on the basis of estimates by the Secretary, and proper adjustments shall be made in amounts subsequently transferred to the extent prior estimates were in excess of or less than the amounts required to be transferred."

In **2004**, P.L. 108-357, Sec. 853(d)(2)(P), deleted para. (b)(3) and redesignated paras. (b)(4) and (5) as paras. (b)(3) and (4) . . . Sec. 853(d)(2)(Q), substituted "section 4081" for "sections 4081 and 4091" in clause (c)(2)(A)(ii), effective for aviation-grade kerosene removed, entered, or sold after 12/31/2004.

Prior to deletion, para. (b)(3) read as follows:

"(3) taxes received in the Treasury under section 4091 (relating to tax on aviation fuel) to the extent attributable to the Leaking Underground Storage Tank Trust Fund financing rate under such section,"

—P.L. 108-357, Sec. 853(f), of this Act, provides:

"(f) Floor stocks tax.

"(1) In general. There is hereby imposed on aviation-grade kerosene held on January 1, 2005, by any person a tax equal to—

"(A) the tax which would have been imposed before such date on such kerosene had the amendments made by this section been in effect at all times before such date, reduced by

"(B) the sum of—

"(i) the tax imposed before such date on such kerosene under section 4091 of the Internal Revenue Code of 1986, as in effect on such date, and

"(ii) in the case of kerosene held exclusively for such person's own use, the amount which such person would (but for this clause) reasonably expect (as of such date) to be paid as a refund under section 6427(l) of such Code with respect to such kerosene.

"(2) Exception for fuel held in aircraft fuel tank. Paragraph (1) shall not apply to kerosene held in the fuel tank of an aircraft on January 1, 2005.

"(3) Liability for tax and method of payment.

"(A) Liability for tax. The person holding the kerosene on January 1, 2005, to which the tax imposed by paragraph (1) applies shall be liable for such tax.

"(B) Method and time for payment. The tax imposed by paragraph (1) shall be paid at such time and in such manner as the Secretary of the Treasury (or the Secretary's delegate) shall prescribe, including the nonapplication of such tax on de minimis amounts of kerosene.

"(4) Transfer of floor stock tax revenues to trust funds. For purposes of determining the amount transferred to any trust fund, the tax imposed by this subsection shall be treated as imposed by section 4081 of the Internal Revenue Code of 1986—

"(A) in any case in which tax was not imposed by section 4091 of such Code, at the Leaking Underground Storage Tank Trust Fund financing rate under such section to the extent of 0.1 cents per gallon, and

"(B) at the rate under section 4081(a)(2)(A)(iv) of such Code to the extent of the remainder.

"(5) Held by a person. For purposes of this subsection, kerosene shall be considered as held by a person if title thereto has passed to such person (whether or not delivery to the person has been made).

"(6) Other laws applicable. All provisions of law, including penalties, applicable with respect to the tax imposed by section 4081 of such Code shall, insofar as applicable and not inconsistent with the provisions of this subsection, apply with respect to the floor stock tax imposed by paragraph (1) to the same extent as if such tax were imposed by such section."

In **1997**, P.L. 105-34, Sec. 1032(e)(13), substituted ", diesel fuel, and kerosene" for "and diesel fuel" in para. (b)(2), effective 7/1/98.

In **1993**, P.L. 103-66, Sec. 13163(c), added "For purposes of this subsection, there shall be not taken into account the taxes imposed by sections 4041 and 4081 on diesel fuel sold for use or used as fuel in a diesel-powered boat." at the end of subsec. (b), effective 1/1/94.

—P.L. 103-66, Sec. 13242(d)(42)(A), added "and diesel fuel" after "gasoline" in para. (b)(2) . . . Sec. 13242(d)(42)(B), deleted "diesel fuel" before "aviation fuel" in para. (b)(3) . . . Sec. 13242(d)(42)(C), substituted "4081" for "4091" [sic. "4081"] in the last sentence of subsec. (b) (as added by Sec. 13163(c) of this Act), effective 1/1/94.

In **1989**, P.L. 101-239, Sec. 7822(b)(7), substituted "Storage Tank Trust Fund" for "Storage Trust Fund" in para. (b)(3) and subpara. (c)(2)(A) [inoperative], effective for sales after 3/31/88.

In **1988**, P.L. 100-647, Sec. 2001(d)(1)(A), changed the effective date for amendments made by Sec. 10502(d)(17) of P.L. 100-203 from "sales after 3/31/88" to "12/31/86 except that [as provided in this section] the last sentence of paragraphs (2) and (3) of section 4041(d) of the Internal Revenue Code of 1986 (as amended by such subsection (b)(3) and the reference to section 4091 of such Code in section 9508(c)(2)(A) of such Code (as amended by such subsection (d)(1)) shall not apply to sales before April 1, 1988."

In **1987**, P.L. 100-203, Sec. 10502(d)(16), redesignated paras. (b)(3) and (4) as (b)(4) and (5) and added para. (b)(3), effective for sales after 3/31/88.

—P.L. 100-203, Sec. 10502(d)(17), amended clause (c)(2)(A)(ii), effective [as amended by Sec. 2001(d)(1)(A) of P.L. 100-647, above] 12/31/86 except that the reference to Code Sec. 4091 in clause (c)(2)(A)(ii) shall not apply to sales before 4/1/88.

Prior to amendment, clause (c)(2)(A)(ii) read as follows:

Establishment of trust funds   Code Sec. 9509(f)

"(ii) credits allowed under section 34, with respect to the taxes imposed by sections 4041(d) and 4081 (to the extent attributable to the Leaking Underground Storage Tank Trust Fund financing rate under section 4081)."

In 1986, P.L. 99-499, Sec. 522(a), added Code Sec. 9508, effective 1/1/87.

Sec. 9509. Oil Spill Liability Trust Fund.

(a) Creation of trust fund.

There is established in the Treasury of the United States a trust fund to be known as the "Oil Spill Liability Trust Fund", consisting of such amounts as may be appropriated or credited to such Trust Fund as provided in this section or section 9602(b).

(b) Transfers to trust fund.

There are hereby appropriated to the Oil Spill Liability Trust Fund amounts equivalent to—

(1) taxes received in the Treasury under section 4611 (relating to environmental tax on petroleum) to the extent attributable to the Oil Spill Liability Trust Fund financing rate under section 4611(c),

(2) amounts recovered under the Oil Pollution Act of 1990 for damages to natural resources which are required to be deposited in the Fund under section 1006(f) of such Act,

(3) amounts recovered by such Trust Fund under section 1015 of such Act,

(4) amounts required to be transferred by such Act from the revolving fund established under section 311(k) of the Federal Water Pollution Control Act,

(5) amounts required to be transferred by the Oil Pollution Act of 1990 from the Deepwater Port Liability Fund established under section 18(f) of the Deepwater Port Act of 1974,

(6) amounts required to be transferred by the Oil Pollution Act of 1990 from the Offshore Oil Pollution Compensation Fund established under section 302 of the Outer Continental Shelf Lands Act Amendments of 1978,

(7) amounts required to be transferred by the Oil Pollution Act of 1990 from the Trans-Alaska Pipeline Liability Fund established under section 204 of the Trans-Alaska Pipeline Authorization Act, and

(8) any penalty paid pursuant to section 311 of the Federal Water Pollution Control Act, section 309(c) of such Act (as a result of violations of such section 311), the Deepwater Port Act of 1974, or section 207 of the Trans-Alaska Pipeline Authorization Act.

(c) Expenditures.

(1) **Expenditure purposes.** Amounts in the Oil Spill Liability Trust Fund shall be available, as provided in appropriation Acts or section 6002(b) of the Oil Pollution Act of 1990, only for purposes of making expenditures—

(A) for the payment of removal costs and other costs, expenses, claims, and damages referred to in section 1012 of such Act,

(B) to carry out sections 5 and 7 of the Intervention on the High Seas Act relating to oil pollution or the substantial threat of oil pollution,

(C) for the payment of liabilities incurred by the revolving fund established by section 311(k) of the Federal Water Pollution Control Act,

(D) to carry out subsections (b), (c), (d), (j), and (l) of section 311 of the Federal Water Pollution Control Act with respect to prevention, removal, and enforcement related to oil discharges (as defined in such section),

(E) for the payment of liabilities incurred by the Deepwater Port Liability Fund, and

(F) for the payment of liabilities incurred by the Offshore Oil Pollution Compensation Fund.

(2) **Limitations on expenditures.**

(A) $1,000,000,000 per incident, etc. The maximum amount which may be paid from the Oil Spill Liability Trust Fund with respect to—

(i) any single incident shall not exceed $1,000,000,000, and

(ii) natural resource damage assessments and claims in connection with any single incident shall not exceed $500,000,000.

(B) $30,000,000 minimum balance. Except in the case of payments of removal costs, a payment may be made from such Trust Fund only if the amount in such Trust Fund after such payment will not be less than $30,000,000.

(d) Authority to borrow.

(1) **In general.** There are authorized to be appropriated to the Oil Spill Liability Trust Fund, as repayable advances, such sums as may be necessary to carry out the purposes of such Trust Fund.

(2) **Limitation on amount outstanding.** The maximum aggregate amount of repayable advances to the Oil Spill Liability Trust Fund which is outstanding at any one time shall not exceed $1,000,000,000.

(3) **Repayment of advances**

(A) In general. Advances made to the Oil Spill Liability Trust Fund shall be repaid, and interest on such advances shall be paid, to the general fund of the Treasury when the Secretary determines that moneys are available for such purposes in such Fund.

(B) Final repayment. No advance shall be made to the Oil Spill Liability Trust Fund after December 31, 1994, and all advances to such Fund shall be repaid on or before such date.

(C) Rate of interest. Interest on advances made pursuant to this subsection shall be—

(i) at a rate determined by the Secretary of the Treasury (as of the close of the calendar month preceding the month in which the advance is made) to be equal to the current average market yield on outstanding marketable obligations of the United States with remaining periods to maturity comparable to the anticipated period during which the advance will be outstanding, and

(ii) compounded annually.

(e) Liability of the United States limited to amount in trust fund.

(1) **General rule.** Any claim filed against the Oil Spill Liability Trust Fund may be paid only out of such Trust Fund.

(2) **Coordination with other provisions.** Nothing in the Oil Pollution Act of 1990 (or in any amendment made by such Act) shall authorize the payment by the United States Government of any amount with respect to any such claim out of any source other than the Oil Spill Liability Trust Fund.

(3) **Order in which unpaid claims are to be paid.** If at any time the Oil Spill Liability Trust Fund has insufficient funds (or is unable by reason of subsection (c)(2)) to pay all of the claims out of such Trust Fund at such time, such claims shall, to the extent permitted under paragraph (1) and such subsection, be paid in full in the order in which they were finally determined.

(f) References to Oil Pollution Act of 1990.

Any reference in this section to the Oil Pollution Act of 1990 or any other Act referred to in a subparagraph of subsection (c)(1) shall be treated as a reference to such Act as in effect on the date of the enactment of this subsection.

In 1990, P.L. 101-380, Sec. 9001(a), deleted all of subsec. (b) that followed para. (b)(1) and added paras. (b)(2)-(8)... Sec. 9001(b), amended para. (c)(1)... Sec. 9001(c)(1), substituted "$1,000,000,000" for "$500,000,000" each place it appeared in subpara. (c)(2)(A)... Sec. 9001(c)(2), substituted "$500,000,000" for "$250,000,000" in clause (c)(2)(A)(ii)... Sec. 9001(d)(1), substituted "$1,000,000,000" for "$500,000,000" in para. (d)(2)... Sec. 9001(d)(2), substituted "December 31, 1994" for "December 31, 1991" in subpara. (d)(3)(B)... Sec. 9001(e)(1), substituted "Oil Pollution Act of 1990" for "Comprehensive Oil Pollution Liability and Compensation Act" in para. (e)(2)... Sec. 9001(e)(2), substituted "of removal costs" for "described in paragraph (1)(A)(i)" in subpara. (c)(2)(B)... Sec. 9001(e)(3), amended subsec. (f), effective 8/18/90.

Prior to deletion, all of subsec. (b) that followed para. (b)(1) read as follows:

"(2) amounts recovered, collected, or received under subtitle A of the Comprehensive Oil Pollution Liability and Compensation Act,

"(3) amounts remaining (on January 1, 1990) in the Deepwater Port Liability Fund established by section 18(f) of the Deepwater Port Act of 1974.

"(4) amounts remaining (on such date) in the Offshore Oil Pollution Compensation Fund established under section 302 of the Outer Continental Shelf Lands Act Amendments of 1978, and

"(5) amounts credited to such trust fund under section 311(s) of the Federal Water Pollution Control Act.

In the case of the tax imposed by section 4611, paragraph (1) shall apply only to so much of such tax as is attributable to the Hazardous Substance Superfund financing rate under section 4611(c)."

Prior to amendment, para. (c)(1) read as follows:

"(1) General expenditure purposes.

"(A) In general. Amounts in the Oil Spill Liability Trust Fund shall be available, as provided in appropriation Acts, only for purposes of making expenditures for—

"(i) the payment of removal costs described in the Comprehensive Oil Pollution Liability and Compensation Act,

"(ii) the payment of claims under the Comprehensive Oil Pollution Liability and Compensation Act for damage which is not otherwise compensated,

"(iii) carrying out subsections (c), (d), (i), and (l) of section 311 of the Federal Water Pollution Control Act with respect to any discharge of oil (as defined in such section),

"(iv) carrying out section 5 of the Intervention on the High Seas Act relating to oil pollution or the substantial threat of oil pollution,

"(v) the payment of all expenses of administration incurred by the Federal Government under the Comprehensive Oil Pollution Liability and Compensation Act, and

"(vi) the payment of contributions to the International Fund under such Act.

"(B) Special rules.

"(i) Payments to governments only for removal costs and natural resource damage assessments and claims. Except in the case of payments described in subparagraph (A)(v), amounts shall be available under subparagraph (A) for payments to any government only for—

"(I) removal costs and natural resource damage assessments and claims, and

"(II) administrative expenses related to such costs, assessments, or claims.

"(ii) Restrictions on contributions to international fund. Under regulations prescribed by the Secretary, amounts shall be available under subparagraph (A) with respect to any contribution to the International Fund only in proportion to the portion of such fund used for a purpose for which amounts may be paid from the Oil Spill Liability Trust Fund."

Prior to amendment, subsec. (f) read as follows:

"(f) References to comprehensive Oil Pollution Liability and Compensation Act.

"For purposes of this section, references to the Comprehensive Oil Pollution Liability and Compensation Act shall be treated as references to any law enacted before December 31, 1990, which is substantially identical to subtitle E of title VI, or subtitle D of title VIII, of H.R. 5300 of the 99th Congress as passed by the House of Representatives."

In 1989, P.L. 101-239, Sec. 7505(d)(2)(A), added subsec. (f)... Sec. 7505(d)(2)(B), substituted "(on January 1, 1990)" for "(on the 1st day of the Oil Spill Liability Trust Fund financing rate under section 4611(c) applies)" in para. (b)(3)... Sec. 7505(d)(2)(C), deleted the last sentence of para. (c)(1), [sic subpara. (c)(1)(A)], effective 12/19/89.

Prior to deletion, the last sentence of para. (c)(1)[(A)] read as follows:

"For purposes of this subparagraph, references to the Comprehensive Oil Pollution Liability and Compensation Act shall be treated as references to qualified authorizing legislation (as defined in section 4611)."

—P.L. 101-239, Sec. 7505(d)(1), changed the effective date for changes made by Secs. 8032(d) and 8033(a) and (c) of P.L. 99-509, from effective on the commencement date as defined in Code Sec. 4611(f) to effective on the commencement date which is 1/1/90, see below.

—P.L. 101-239, Sec. 7811(m)(3), corrected Sec. 1018(u)(20) of P.L. 100-647, see below, so that it substituted "Deepwater" for "Deep Water" each place it appeared in Code Sec. 9509(b)(3) instead of Code Sec. 9507(b)(3).

In 1988, P.L. 100-647, Sec. 1018(u)(20), substituted "Deepwater" for "Deep Water" each place it appeared in para. (b)(3), effective as of the commencement date (as defined in section 4611(f)(2) of the Internal Revenue Code of 1954, as added by Sec. 8032(c)(4) of P.L. 99-509).

In 1986, P.L. 99-509, Sec. 8032(c)(4), added the last sentence to the end of subsec. (b) [as redesignated by Sec. 8033(c)92) of this Act], effective as of the commencement date which is 1/1/90 [see Sec. 7505(d)(1) of P.L. 101-239, see above]... Sec. 8032(d)(2) of this Act provides:

"(2) Coordination with superfund reauthorization.—The amendments made by this section shall take effect only if the Superfund Amendments and Reauthorization Act of 1986 is enacted."

—P.L. 99-509, Sec. 8033(a), added Code Sec. 9509, effective on the commencement date which is 1/1/90 [see Sec. 7505(d)(1) of P.L. 101-239, see above]

Sec. 9510. Vaccine Injury Compensation Trust Fund.
(a) Creation of trust fund.

There is established in the Treasury of the United States a trust fund to be known as the "Vaccine Injury Compensation Trust Fund", consisting of such amounts as may be appropriated or credited to such Trust Fund as provided in this section or section 9602(b).

(b) Transfers to trust fund.

(1) In general. There are hereby appropriated to the Vaccine Injury Compensation Trust Fund amounts equivalent to the net revenues received in the Treasury from the tax imposed by section 4131 (relating to tax on certain vaccines).

(2) Net revenues. For purposes of paragraph (1), the term "net revenues" means the amount estimated by the Secretary based on the excess of—

(A) the taxes received in the Treasury under section 4131 (relating to tax on certain vaccines), over

(B) the decrease in the tax imposed by chapter 1 resulting from the tax imposed by section 4131.

(3) Limitation on transfers to Vaccine Injury Compensation Trust Fund. No amount may be appropriated to the Vaccine Injury Compensation Trust Fund on and after the date of any expenditure from the Trust Fund which is not permitted by this section. The determination of whether an expenditure is so permitted shall be made without regard to—

(A) any provision of law which is not contained or referenced in this title or in a revenue Act, and

(B) whether such provision of law is a subsequently enacted provision or directly or indirectly seeks to waive the application of this paragraph.

(c) Expenditures from trust fund.

(1) In general. Amounts in the Vaccine Injury Compensation Trust Fund shall be available, as provided in appropriation Acts, only for—

(A) the payment of compensation under subtitle 2 of title XXI of the Public Health Service Act (as in effect on October 18, 2000) for vaccine-related injury or death with respect to any vaccine—

(i) which is administered after September 30, 1988, and

(ii) which is a taxable vaccine (as defined in section 4132(a)(1)) at the time compensation is paid under such subtitle 2, or

(B) the payment of all expenses of administration (but not in excess of $9,500,000 for any fiscal year) incurred by the Federal Government in administering such subtitle.

(2) Transfers for certain repayments.

(A) In general. The Secretary shall pay from time to time from the Vaccine Injury Compensation Trust Fund into the general fund of the Treasury amounts equivalent to amounts paid under section 4132(b) and section 6416 with respect to the taxes imposed by section 4131.

(B) Transfers based on estimates. Transfers under subparagraph (A) shall be made on the basis of estimates by the Secretary, and proper adjustments shall be made in the amounts subsequently transferred to the extent prior estimates were in excess of or less than the amounts required to be transferred.

Establishment of trust funds   Code Sec. 9511(d)(2)(C)(ii)

(d) Liability of United States limited to amount in trust fund.

(1) General rule. Any claim filed against the Vaccine Injury Compensation Trust Fund may be paid only out of such Trust Fund.

(2) Coordination with other provisions. Nothing in the National Childhood Vaccine Injury Act of 1986 (or in any amendment made by such Act) shall authorize the payment by the United States Government of any amount with respect to any such claim out of any source other than the Vaccine Injury Compensation Trust Fund.

(3) Order in which unpaid claims to be paid. If at any time the Vaccine Injury Compensation Trust Fund has insufficient funds to pay all of the claims out of such Trust Fund at such time, such claims shall, to the extent permitted under paragraph (1) be paid in full in the order in which they are finally determined.

In **2000**, P.L. 106-554, Sec. 1(a)(7), [which enacted into law Sec. 318(f) of P.L. 106-554] substituted "October 18, 2000" for "December 31, 1999" in subpara. (c)(1)(A), effective 12/21/2000.

In **1999**, P.L. 106-170, Sec. 523(b)(1), repealed Sec. 1504 of P.L. 105-277 [see below]... Sec. 523(b)(2), substituted "December 31, 1999" for "August 5, 1997" in subpara. (c)(1)(A), effective 8/6/97.

—P.L. 106-170, Sec. 523(c), of this Act, provides:

"(c) Report. Not later than January 31, 2000, the Comptroller General of the United States shall prepare and submit a report to the Committee on Ways and Means of the House of Representatives and the Committee on Finance of the Senate on the operation of the Vaccine Injury Compensation Trust Fund and on the adequacy of such Fund to meet future claims made under the Vaccine Injury Compensation Program."

In **1998**, P.L. 105-277, Sec. 1504, amended para. (c)(1) [duplication of Sec. 4003(d)(1) of this Act, see below, repealed by Sec. 523(b)(1) of P.L. 106-170, see above], effective 8/6/97.

Prior to amendment, para. (c)(1) read as follows:

"(1) In general. Amounts in the Vaccine Injury Compensation Trust Fund shall be available, as provided in appropriation Acts, only for the payment of compensation under subtitle 2 of title XXI of the Public Health Service Act (as in effect on the date of the enactment of this section) for vaccine-related injury or death with respect to vaccines administered after September 30, 1988, or for the payment of all expenses of administration (but not in excess of $6,000,000 for any fiscal year) incurred by the Federal Government in administering such subtitle."

—P.L. 105-277, Sec. 4003(d)(1), amended para. (c)(1)... Sec. 4003(d)(2), added para. (b)(3), effective 8/6/97.

Prior to amendment, para. (c)(1) read as follows:

"(1) In general. Amounts in the Vaccine Injury Compensation Trust Fund shall be available, as provided in appropriation Acts, only for the payment of compensation under subtitle 2 of title XXI of the Public Health Service Act (as in effect on the date of the enactment of this section) for vaccine-related injury or death with respect to vaccines administered after September 30, 1988, or for the payment of all expenses of administration (but not in excess of $6,000,000 for any fiscal year) incurred by the Federal Government in administering such subtitle."

In **1993**, P.L. 103-66, Sec. 13421(b), deleted "and before October 1, 1992," after "September 30, 1988," in para. (c)(1), effective 8/10/93.

In **1989**, P.L. 101-239, Sec. 7841(g)(1), added ", or for the payment of all expenses of administration (but not in excess of $6,000,000 for any fiscal year) incurred by the Federal Government in administering such subtitle" before the period at the end of para. (c)(1), effective for fiscal yrs. begin. after 9/30/89.

In **1988**, P.L. 100-647, Sec. 2006(b)(1), added "appropriated or" before "credited" in subsec. (a)... Sec. 2006(b)(2), added "this section or" before "section 9602(b)" in subsec. (a), effective 1/1/88.

In **1987**, P.L. 100-203, Sec. 9202(a), added Code Sec. 9510, effective 1/1/88.

Sec. 9511. Patient-centered outcomes research trust fund.

(a) Creation of trust fund.

There is established in the Treasury of the United States a trust fund to be known as the "Patient-Centered Outcomes Research Trust Fund" (hereafter in this section referred to as the "PCORTF"), consisting of such amounts as may be appropriated or credited to such Trust Fund as provided in this section and section 9602(b).

(a) Transfers to fund.

(1) Appropriation. There are hereby appropriated to the Trust Fund the following:

(A) For fiscal year 2010, $10,000,000.

(B) For fiscal year 2011, $50,000,000.

(C) For fiscal year 2012, $150,000,000.

(D) For fiscal year 2013—

(i) an amount equivalent to the net revenues received in the Treasury from the fees imposed under subchapter B of chapter 34 (relating to fees on health insurance and self-insured plans) for such fiscal year; and

(ii) $150,000,000.

(E) For each of fiscal years 2014, 2015, 2016, 2017, 2018, and 2019—

(i) an amount equivalent to the net revenues received in the Treasury from the fees imposed under subchapter B of chapter 34 (relating to fees on health insurance and self-insured plans) for such fiscal year; and

(ii) $150,000,000.

The amounts appropriated under subparagraphs (A), (B), (C), (D)(ii), and (E)(ii) shall be transferred from the general fund of the Treasury, from funds not otherwise appropriated.

(2) Trust fund transfers. In addition to the amounts appropriated under paragraph (1), there shall be credited to the PCORTF the amounts transferred under section 1183 of the Social Security Act.

(3) Limitation on transfers to PCORTF. No amount may be appropriated or transferred to the PCORTF on and after the date of any expenditure from the PCORTF which is not an expenditure permitted under this section. The determination of whether an expenditure is so permitted shall be made without regard to—

(A) any provision of law which is not contained or referenced in this chapter or in a revenue Act, and

(B) whether such provision of law is a subsequently enacted provision or directly or indirectly seeks to waive the application of this paragraph.

(c) Trustee.

The Secretary of the Treasury shall be a trustee of the PCORTF.

(d) Expenditures from fund.

(1) Amounts available to the Patient-Centered Outcomes Research Institute. Subject to paragraph (2), amounts in the PCORTF are available, without further appropriation, to the Patient-Centered Outcomes Research Institute established under section 1181(b) of the Social Security Act for carrying out part D of title XI of the Social Security Act (as in effect on the date of enactment of such Act).

(2) Transfer of funds.

(A) In general. The trustee of the PCORTF shall provide for the transfer from the PCORTF of 20 percent of the amounts appropriated or credited to the PCORTF for each of fiscal years 2011 through 2019 to the Secretary of Health and Human Services to carry out section 937 of the Public Health Service Act.

(B) Availability. Amounts transferred under subparagraph (A) shall remain available until expended.

(C) Requirements. Of the amounts transferred under subparagraph (A) with respect to a fiscal year, the Secretary of Health and Human Services shall distribute—

(i) 80 percent to the Office of Communication and Knowledge Transfer of the Agency for Healthcare Research and Quality (or any other relevant office designated by Agency for Healthcare Research and Quality) to carry out the activities described in section 937 of the Public Health Service Act; and

(ii) 20 percent to the Secretary to carry out the activities described in such section 937.

4,017

(e) Net revenues.

For purposes of this section, the term "net revenues" means the amount estimated by the Secretary of the Treasury based on the excess of—

(1) the fees received in the Treasury under subchapter B of chapter 34, over

(2) the decrease in the tax imposed by chapter 1 resulting from the fees imposed by such subchapter.

(f) Termination.

No amounts shall be available for expenditure from the PCORTF after September 30, 2019, and any amounts in such Trust Fund after such date shall be transferred to the general fund of the Treasury.

In 2010, P.L. 111-148, Sec. 6301(e)(1)(A), added Code Sec. 9511, enacted 3/23/2010.

Sec. 9511. Repealed.

In 1998, P.L. 105-178, Sec. 9011(a), repealed Code Sec. 9511, effective 6/9/98. Prior to repeal, Code Sec. 9511 read as follows:

"SEC. 9511. NATIONAL RECREATIONAL TRAILS TRUST FUND.

"(a) Creation of trust fund. There is established in the Treasury of the United States a trust fund to be known as the 'National Recreational Trails Trust Fund', consisting of such amounts as may be credited or paid to such Trust Fund as provided in this section, section 9503(c)(6), or section 9602(b).

"(b) Crediting of certain unexpended funds. There shall be credited to the National Recreational Trails Trust Fund amounts returned to such Trust Fund under section 1302(e)(8) of the Intermodal Surface Transportation Efficiency Act of 1991.

"(c) Expenditures from trust fund. Amounts in the National Recreational Trails Trust Fund shall be available, as provided in appropriation Acts, for making expenditures before October 1, 1998, to carry out the purposes of sections 1302 and 1303 of the Intermodal Surface Transportation Efficiency Act of 1991, as in effect on the date of the enactment of such Act."

In 1997, P.L. 105-130, Sec. 9(c), substituted "1998" for "1997" in subsec. (c), effective 10/1/97.

In 1991, P.L. 102-240, Sec. 8003(a), added Code Sec. 9511, effective 12/18/91.

Subchapter B.—General Provisions

Sec.
9601. Transfer of amounts.
9602. Management of Trust Funds.

Sec. 9601. Transfer of amounts.

The amounts appropriated by any section of subchapter A to any Trust Fund established by such subchapter shall be transferred at least monthly from the general fund of the Treasury to such Trust Fund on the basis of estimates made by the Secretary of the Treasury of the amounts referred to in such section. Proper adjustments shall be made in the amounts subsequently transferred to the extent prior estimates were in excess of or less than the amounts required to be transferred.

In 1981, P.L. 97-119, Sec. 103(a), added Sec. 9601, effective 1/1/82. Sec. 103(d)(2) of this Act provides:

"(2) Savings provisions.—The Black Lung Disability Trust Fund established by the amendments made by this section shall be treated for all purposes of law as the continuation of the Black Lung Disability Trust Fund established by section 3 of the Black Lung Benefits Revenue Act of 1977. Any reference in any law to the Black Lung Disability Trust Fund established by such section 3 shall be deemed to include a reference to the Black Lung Disability Trust Fund established by the amendments made by this section."

Sec. 9602. Management of trust funds.
(a) Report.

It shall be the duty of the Secretary of the Treasury to hold each Trust Fund established by subchapter A, and (after consultation with any other trustees of the Trust Fund) to report to the Congress each year on the financial condition and the results of the operations of each such Trust Fund during the preceding fiscal year and on its expected condition and operations during the next 5 fiscal years. Such report shall be printed as a House document of the session of the Congress to which the report is made.

(b) Investment.

(1) In general. It shall be the duty of the Secretary of the Treasury to invest such portion of any Trust Fund established by subchapter A as is not, in his judgment, required to meet current withdrawals. Such investments may be made only in interest-bearing obligations of the United States. For such purpose, such obligations may be acquired—

(A) on original issue at the issue price, or

(B) by purchase of outstanding obligations at the market price.

(2) Sale of obligations. Any obligation acquired by a Trust Fund established by subchapter A may be sold by the Secretary of the Treasury at the market price.

(3) Interest on certain proceeds. The interest on, and the proceeds from the sale or redemption of, any obligations held in a Trust Fund established by subchapter A shall be credited to and form a part of the Trust Fund.

In 2000, P.L. 106-554, Sec. 1(a)(7), [which enacted into law Sec. 301 of P.L. 106-554] of this Act, reads as follows:

"Section 3003(a)(1) of the Federal Reports Elimination and Sunset Act of 1995 (31 U.S.C. 1113 note) shall not apply to any report required to be submitted under any of the following provisions of law:"

* * * * * *

"15(E) Section 9602(a)"

In 1981, P.L. 97-119, Sec. 103(a), added Code Sec. 9602, effective 1/1/82. Sec. 103(d)(2) of this Act provides:

"(2) Savings provisions.—The Black Lung Disability Trust Fund established by the amendments made by this section shall be treated for all purposes of law as the continuation of the Black Lung Disability Trust Fund established by section 3 of the Black Lung Benefits Revenue Act of 1977. Any reference in any law to the Black Lung Disability Trust Fund established by such section 3 shall be deemed to include a reference to the Black Lung Disability Trust Fund established by the amendments made by this section."

Subtitle J.—Coal Industry Health Benefits

Chapter
99. Coal industry health benefits.

CHAPTER 99.—COAL INDUSTRY HEALTH BENEFITS

Subchapter
A. Definitions of general applicability.
B. Combined benefit fund.
C. Health benefits of certain miners.
D. Other provisions.

Subchapter A.—Definitions of General Applicability

Sec.
9701. Definitions of general applicability.

Sec. 9701. Definitions of general applicability.
(a) Plans and funds.

For purposes of this chapter—

(1) UMWA Benefit Plan.

(A) In general. The term "UMWA Benefit Plan" means a plan—

(i) which is described in section 404(c), or a continuation thereof; and

(ii) which provides health benefits to retirees and beneficiaries of the industry which maintained the 1950 UMWA Pension Plan.

(B) 1950 UMWA Benefit Plan. The term "1950 UMWA Benefit Plan" means a UMWA Benefit Plan, participation in which is substantially limited to individuals who retired before 1976.

Establishment of trust funds

Code Sec. 9701

(C) 1974 UMWA Benefit Plan. The term "1974 UMWA Benefit Plan" means a UMWA Benefit Plan, participation in which is substantially limited to individuals who retired on or after January 1, 1976.

(2) **1950 UMWA Pension Plan.** The term "1950 UMWA Pension Plan" means a pension plan described in section 404(c) (or a continuation thereof), participation in which is substantially limited to individuals who retired before 1976.

(3) **1974 UMWA Pension Plan.** The term "1974 UMWA Pension Plan" means a pension plan described in section 404(c) (or a continuation thereof), participation in which is substantially limited to individuals who retired in 1976 and thereafter.

(4) **1992 UMWA Benefit Plan.** The term "1992 UMWA Benefit Plan" means the plan referred to in section 9713A.

(5) **Combined Fund.** The term "Combined Fund" means the United Mine Workers of America Combined Benefit Fund established under section 9702.

(b) **Agreements.**

For purposes of this section—

(1) **Coal wage agreement.** The term "coal wage agreement" means—

(A) the National Bituminous Coal Wage Agreement, or

(B) any other agreement entered into between an employer in the coal industry and the United Mine Workers of America that required or requires one or both of the following:

(i) the provision of health benefits to retirees of such employer, eligibility for which is based on years of service credited under a plan established by the settlors and described in section 404(c) or a continuation of such plan; or

(ii) contributions to the 1950 UMWA Benefit Plan or the 1974 UMWA Benefit Plan, or any predecessor thereof.

(2) **Settlors.** The term "settlors" means the United Mine Workers of America and the Bituminous Coal Operators' Association, Inc. (referred to in this chapter as the "BCOA").

(3) **National Bituminous Coal Wage Agreement.** The term "National Bituminous Coal Wage Agreement" means a collective bargaining agreement negotiated by the BCOA and the United Mine Workers of America.

(c) **Terms relating to operators.**

For purposes of this section—

(1) **Signatory operator.** The term "signatory operator" means a person which is or was a signatory to a coal wage agreement.

(2) **Related persons.**

(A) In general. A person shall be considered to be a related person to a signatory operator if that person is—

(i) a member of the controlled group of corporations (within the meaning of section 52(a)) which includes such signatory operator;

(ii) a trade or business which is under common control (as determined under section 52(b)) with such signatory operator; or

(iii) any other person who is identified as having a partnership interest or joint venture with a signatory operator in a business within the coal industry, but only if such business employed eligible beneficiaries, except that this clause shall not apply to a person whose only interest is as a limited partner.

A related person shall also include a successor in interest of any person described in clause (i), (ii), or (iii).

(B) Time for determination. The relationships described in clauses (i), (ii), and (iii) of subparagraph (A) shall be determined as of July 20, 1992, except that if, on July 20, 1992, a signatory operator is no longer in business, the relationships shall be determined as of the time immediately before such operator ceased to be in business.

(3) **1988 agreement operator.** The term "1988 agreement operator" means—

(A) a signatory operator which was a signatory to the 1988 National Bituminous Coal Wage Agreement,

(B) an employer in the coal industry which was a signatory to an agreement containing pension and health care contribution and benefit provisions which are the same as those contained in the 1988 National Bituminous Coal Wage Agreement, or

(C) an employer from which contributions were actually received after 1987 and before July 20, 1992, by the 1950 UMWA Benefit Plan or the 1974 UMWA Benefit Plan in connection with employment in the coal industry during the period covered by the 1988 National Bituminous Coal Wage Agreement.

(4) **Last signatory operator.** The term "last signatory operator" means, with respect to a coal industry retiree, a signatory operator which was the most recent coal industry employer of such retiree.

(5) **Assigned operator.** The term "assigned operator" means, with respect to an eligible beneficiary defined in section 9703(f), the signatory operator to which liability under subchapter B with respect to the beneficiary is assigned under section 9706.

(6) **Operators of dependent beneficiaries.** For purposes of this chapter, the signatory operator, last signatory operator, or assigned operator of any eligible beneficiary under this chapter who is a coal industry retiree shall be considered to be the signatory operator, last signatory operator, or assigned operator with respect to any other individual who is an eligible beneficiary under this chapter by reason of a relationship to the retiree.

(7) **Business.** For purposes of this chapter, a person shall be considered to be in business if such person conducts or derives revenue from any business activity, whether or not in the coal industry.

(8) **Successor in interest.**

(A) Safe harbor. The term "successor in interest" shall not include any person who—

(i) is an unrelated person to an eligible seller described in subparagraph (C); and

(ii) purchases for fair market value assets, or all of the stock, of a related person to such seller, in a bona fide, arm's length sale.

(B) Unrelated person. The term "unrelated person" means a purchaser who does not bear a relationship to the eligible seller described in section 267(b).

(C) Eligible seller. For purposes of this paragraph, the term "eligible seller" means an assigned operator described in section 9704(j)(2) or a related person to such assigned operator.

(d) **Enactment date.**

For purposes of this chapter, the term "enactment date" means the date of the enactment of this chapter.

In **2006**, P.L. 109-432, Sec. 211(d), added para. (c)(8), effective for transactions after 12/20/2006.

In **1992**, P.L. 102-486, Sec. 19143(a), added Code Sec. 9701, effective 10/24/92.

4,019

Subchapter B.—Combined Benefit Fund

Part
I. Establishment and Benefits
II. Financing
III. Enforcement
IV. Other Provisions

PART I.—ESTABLISHMENT AND BENEFITS

Sec.
9702. Establishment of the United Mine Workers of America Combined Benefit Fund.
9703. Plan benefits.

Sec. 9702. Establishment of the United Mine Workers of America Combined Benefit Fund.

(a) Establishment.

(1) In general. As soon as practicable (but not later than 60 days) after the enactment date, the persons described in subsection (b) shall designate the individuals to serve as trustees. Such trustees shall create a new private plan to be known as the United Mine Workers of America Combined Benefit Fund.

(2) Merger of retiree benefit plans. As of February 1, 1993, the settlors of the 1950 UMWA Benefit Plan and the 1974 UMWA Benefit Plan shall cause such plans to be merged into the Combined Fund, and such merger shall not be treated as an employer withdrawal for purposes of any 1988 coal wage agreement.

(3) Treatment of plan. The Combined Fund shall be—
(A) a plan described in section 302(c)(5) of the Labor Management Relations Act, 1947 (29 U.S.C. 186(c)(5)),
(B) an employee welfare benefit plan within the meaning of section 3(1) of the Employee Retirement Income Security Act of 1974 (29 U.S.C. 1002(1)), and
(C) a multiemployer plan within the meaning of section 3(37) of such Act (29 U.S.C. 1002(37)).

(4) Tax treatment. For purposes of this title, the Combined Fund and any related trust shall be treated as an organization exempt from tax under section 501(a).

(b) Board of trustees.

(1) In general. For purposes of subsection (a), the board of trustees for the Combined Fund shall be appointed as follows:
(A) 2 individuals who represent employers in the coal mining industry shall be designated by the BCOA;
(B) 2 individuals designated by the United Mine Workers of America; and
(C) 3 individuals selected by the individuals appointed under subparagraphs (A) and (B).

(2) Successor trustees. Any successor trustee shall be appointed in the same manner as the trustee being succeeded. The plan establishing the Combined Fund shall provide for the removal of trustees.

(3) Special rule. If the BCOA ceases to exist, any trustee or successor under paragraph (1)(A) shall be designated by the 3 employers who were members of the BCOA on the enactment date and who have been assigned the greatest number of eligible beneficiaries under section 9706.

(c) Plan year.

The first plan year of the Combined Fund shall begin February 1, 1993, and end September 30, 1993. Each succeeding plan year shall begin on October 1 of each calendar year.

In 2006, P.L. 109-432, Sec. 213(a), amended subsec. (b), enacted 12/20/2006. Prior to amendment, subsec. (b) read as follows:
"(b) Board of trustees.
"(1) In general. For purposes of subsection (a), the board of trustees for the Combined Fund shall be appointed as follows:
"(A) one individual who represents employers in the coal mining industry shall be designated by the BCOA;
"(B) one individual shall be designated by the three employers, other than 1988 agreement operators, who have been assigned the greatest number of eligible beneficiaries under section 9706;
"(C) two individuals designated by the United Mine Workers of America; and
"(D) three persons selected by the persons appointed under subparagraphs (A), (B), and (C).
"(2) Successor trustees. Any successor trustee shall be appointed in the same manner as the trustee being succeeded. The plan establishing the Combined Fund shall provide for the removal of trustees.
"(3) Special rules.
"(A) BCOA. If the BCOA ceases to exist, any trustee or successor under paragraph (1)(A) shall be designated by the 3 employers who were members of the BCOA on the enactment date and who have been assigned the greatest number of eligible beneficiaries under section 9706.
"(B) Former signatories. The initial trustee under paragraph (1)(B) shall be designated by the 3 employers, other than 1988 agreement operators, which the records of the 1950 UMWA Benefit Plan and 1974 UMWA Benefit Plan indicate have the greatest number of eligible beneficiaries as of the enactment date, and such trustee and any successor shall serve until November 1, 1993."
In 1992, P.L. 102-486, Sec. 19143(a), added Code Sec. 9702, effective 10/24/92.

Sec. 9703. Plan benefits.

(a) In general.
Each eligible beneficiary of the Combined Fund shall receive—
(1) health benefits described in subsection (b), and
(2) in the case of an eligible beneficiary described in subsection (f)(1), death benefits coverage described in subsection (c).

(b) Health benefits.

(1) In general. The trustees of the Combined Fund shall provide health care benefits to each eligible beneficiary by enrolling the beneficiary in a health care services plan which undertakes to provide such benefits on a prepaid risk basis. The trustees shall utilize all available plan resources to ensure that, consistent with paragraph (2), coverage under the managed care system shall to the maximum extent feasible be substantially the same as (and subject to the same limitations of) coverage provided under the 1950 UMWA Benefit Plan and the 1974 UMWA Benefit Plan as of January 1, 1992.

(2) Plan payment rates.
(A) In general. The trustees of the Combined Fund shall negotiate payment rates with the health care services plans described in paragraph (1) for each plan year which are in amounts which—
(i) vary as necessary to ensure that beneficiaries in different geographic areas have access to a uniform level of health benefits; and
(ii) result in aggregate payments for such plan year from the Combined Fund which do not exceed the total premium payments required to be paid to the Combined Fund under section 9704(a) for the plan year, adjusted as provided in subparagraphs (B) and (C).
(B) Reductions. The amount determined under subparagraph (A)(ii) for any plan year shall be reduced—
(i) by the aggregate death benefit premiums determined under section 9704(c) for the plan year, and
(ii) by the amount reserved for plan administration under subsection (d).
(C) Increases. The amount determined under subparagraph (A)(ii) shall be increased—
(i) by any reduction in the total premium payments required to be paid under section 9704(a) by reason of transfers described in section 9705,
(ii) by any carryover to the plan year from any preceding plan year which—
(I) is derived from amounts described in section 9704(e)(3)(B)(i), and

Establishment of trust funds Code Sec. 9704(d)(1)(B)

(II) the trustees elect to use to pay benefits for the current plan year, and

(iii) any interest earned by the Combined Fund which the trustees elect to use to pay benefits for the current plan year.

(3) Qualified providers. The trustees of the Combined Fund shall not enter into an agreement under paragraph (1) with any provider of services which is of a type which is required to be certified by the Secretary of Health and Human Services when providing services under title XVIII of the Social Security Act unless the provider is so certified.

(4) Effective date. Benefits shall be provided under paragraph (1) on and after February 1, 1993.

(c) Death benefits coverage.

(1) In general. The trustees of the Combined Fund shall provide death benefits coverage to each eligible beneficiary described in subsection (f)(1) which is identical to the benefits provided under the 1950 UMWA Pension Plan or 1974 UMWA Pension Plan, whichever is applicable, on July 20, 1992. Such coverage shall be provided on and after February 1, 1993.

(2) Termination of coverage. The 1950 UMWA Pension Plan and the 1974 UMWA Pension Plan shall each be amended to provide that death benefits coverage shall not be provided to eligible beneficiaries on and after February 1, 1993. This paragraph shall not prohibit such plans from subsequently providing death benefits not described in paragraph (1).

(d) Reserves for administration.

The trustees of the Combined Fund may reserve for each plan year, for use in payment of the administrative costs of the Combined Fund, an amount not to exceed 5 percent of the premiums to be paid to the Combined Fund under section 9704(a) during the plan year.

(e) Limitation on enrollment.

The Combined Fund shall not enroll any individual who is not receiving benefits under the 1950 UMWA Benefit Plan or the 1974 UMWA Benefit Plan as of July 20, 1992.

(f) Eligible beneficiary.

For purposes of this subchapter, the term "eligible beneficiary" means an individual who—

(1) is a coal industry retiree who, on July 20, 1992, was eligible to receive, and receiving, benefits from the 1950 UMWA Benefit Plan or the 1974 UMWA Benefit Plan, or

(2) on such date was eligible to receive, and receiving, benefits in either such plan by reason of a relationship to such retiree.

In 1992, P.L. 102-486, Sec. 19143(a), added Code Sec. 9703, effective 10/24/92.

PART II.—FINANCING

Sec.
9704. Liability of assigned operators.
9705. Transfers.
9706. Assignment of eligible beneficiaries.

Sec. 9704. Liability of assigned operators.

(a) Annual premiums.

Each assigned operator shall pay to the Combined Fund for each plan year beginning on or after February 1, 1993, an annual premium equal to the sum of the following three premiums—

(1) the health benefit premium determined under subsection (b) for such plan year, plus

(2) the death benefit premium determined under subsection (c) for such plan year, plus

(3) the unassigned beneficiaries premium determined under subsection (d) for such plan year.

Any related person with respect to an assigned operator shall be jointly and severally liable for any premium required to be paid by such operator.

(b) Health benefit premium.

For purposes of this chapter—

(1) In general. The health benefit premium for any plan year for any assigned operator shall be an amount equal to the product of the per beneficiary premium for the plan year multiplied by the number of eligible beneficiaries assigned to such operator under section 9706.

(2) Per beneficiary premium. The Commissioner of Social Security shall calculate a per beneficiary premium for each plan year beginning on or after February 1, 1993, which is equal to the sum of—

(A) the amount determined by dividing—

(i) the aggregate amount of payments from the 1950 UMWA Benefit Plan and the 1974 UMWA Benefit Plan for health benefits (less reimbursements but including administrative costs) for the plan year beginning July 1, 1991, for all individuals covered under such plans for such plan year, by

(ii) the number of such individuals, plus

(B) the amount determined under subparagraph (A) multiplied by the percentage (if any) by which the medical component of the Consumer Price Index for the calendar year in which the plan year begins exceeds such component for 1992.

(3) Adjustments for Medicare reductions. If, by reason of a reduction in benefits under title XVIII of the Social Security Act, the level of health benefits under the Combined Fund would be reduced, the trustees of the Combined Fund shall increase the per beneficiary premium for the plan year in which the reduction occurs and each subsequent plan year by the amount necessary to maintain the level of health benefits which would have been provided without such reduction.

(c) Death benefit premium.

The death benefit premium for any plan year for any assigned operator shall be equal to the applicable percentage of the amount, actuarially determined, which the Combined Fund will be required to pay during the plan year for death benefits coverage described in section 9703(c).

(d) Unassigned beneficiaries premium.

(1) Plan years ending on or before September 30, 2006. For plan years ending on or before September 30, 2006, the unassigned beneficiaries premium for any assigned operator shall be equal to the applicable percentage of the product of the per beneficiary premium for the plan year multiplied by the number of eligible beneficiaries who are not assigned under section 9706 to any person for such plan year.

(2) Plan years beginning on or after October 1, 2006.

(A) In general. For plan years beginning on or after October 1, 2006, subject to subparagraph (B), there shall be no unassigned beneficiaries premium, and benefit costs with respect to eligible beneficiaries who are not assigned under section 9706 to any person for any such plan year shall be paid from amounts transferred under section 9705(b).

(B) Inadequate transfers. If, for any plan year beginning on or after October 1, 2006, the amounts transferred under section 9705(b) are less than the amounts required to be transferred to the Combined Fund under subsection (h)(2)(A) or (i) of section 402 of the Surface Mining Control and Reclamation Act of 1977 (30

4,021

U.S.C. 1232)), then the unassigned beneficiaries premium for any assigned operator shall be equal to the operator's applicable percentage of the amount required to be so transferred which was not so transferred.

(e) Premium accounts; adjustments.

(1) Accounts. The trustees of the Combined Fund shall establish and maintain 3 separate accounts for each of the premiums described in subsections (b), (c), and (d). Such accounts shall be credited with the premiums received and amounts transferred under section 9705(b) and debited with expenditures allocable to such premiums.

(2) Allocations.

(A) Administrative expenses. Administrative costs for any plan year shall be allocated to premium accounts under paragraph (1) on the basis of expenditures (other than administrative costs) from such accounts during the preceding plan year.

(B) Interest. Interest shall be allocated to the account established for health benefit premiums.

(3) Shortfalls and surpluses.

(A) In general. Except as provided in subparagraph (B), if, for any plan year, there is a shortfall or surplus in any premium account, the premium for the following plan year for each assigned operator shall be proportionately reduced or increased, whichever is applicable, by the amount of such shortfall or surplus. Amounts credited to an account from amounts transferred under section 9705(b) shall not be taken into account in determining whether there is a surplus in the account for purposes of this paragraph.

(B) Exception. Subparagraph (A) shall not apply to any surplus in the health benefit premium account or the unassigned beneficiaries premium account which is attributable to—

(i) the excess of the premiums credited to such account for a plan year over the benefits (and administrative costs) debited to such account for the plan year, but such excess shall only be available for purposes of the carryover described in section 9703(b)(2)(C)(ii) (relating to carryovers of premiums not used to provide benefits), or

(ii) interest credited under paragraph (2)(B) for the plan year or any preceding plan year.

(C) No authority for increased payments. Nothing in this paragraph shall be construed to allow expenditures for health care benefits for any plan year in excess of the limit under section 9703(b)(2).

(f) Applicable percentage.

For purposes of this section—

(1) In general. The term "applicable percentage" means, with respect to any assigned operator, the percentage determined by dividing the number of eligible beneficiaries assigned under section 9706 to such operator by the total number of beneficiaries assigned under section 9706 to all such operators (determined on the basis of assignments as of October 1, 1993).

(2) Annual adjustments. In the case of any plan year beginning on or after October 1, 1994, the applicable percentage for any assigned operator shall be redetermined under paragraph (1) by making the following changes to the assignments as of October 1, 1993:

(A) Such assignments shall be modified to reflect any changes during the period beginning October 1, 1993, and ending on the last day of the preceding plan year pursuant to the appeals process under section 9706(f).

(B) The total number of assigned eligible beneficiaries shall be reduced by the eligible beneficiaries of assigned operators which (and all related persons with respect to which) had ceased business (within the meaning of section 9701(c)(6)) during the period described in subparagraph (A).

(C) In the case of plan years beginning on or after October 1, 2007, the total number of assigned eligible beneficiaries shall be reduced by the eligible beneficiaries whose assignments have been revoked under section 9706(h).

(g) Payment of premiums.

(1) In general. The annual premium under subsection (a) for any plan year shall be payable in 12 equal monthly installments, due on the twenty-fifth day of each calendar month in the plan year. In the case of the plan year beginning February 1, 1993, the annual premium under subsection (a) shall be added to such premium for the plan year beginning October 1, 1993.

(2) Deductibility. Any premium required by this section shall be deductible without regard to any limitation on deductibility based on the prefunding of health benefits.

(h) Information. The trustees of the Combined Fund shall, not later than 60 days after the enactment date, furnish to the Commissioner of Social Security information as to the benefits and covered beneficiaries under the fund, and such other information as the Secretary may require to compute any premium under this section.

(i) Transition rules.

(1) 1988 agreement operators.

(A) 1st year costs. During the plan year of the Combined Fund beginning February 1, 1993, the 1988 agreement operators shall make contributions to the Combined Fund in amounts necessary to pay benefits and administrative costs of the Combined Fund incurred during such year, reduced by the amount transferred to the Combined Fund under section 9705(a) on February 1, 1993.

(B) Deficits from merged plans. During the period beginning February 1, 1993, and ending September 30, 1994, the 1988 agreement operators shall make contributions to the Combined Fund as are necessary to pay off the expenses accrued (and remaining unpaid) by the 1950 UMWA Benefit Plan and the 1974 UMWA Benefit Plan as of February 1, 1993, reduced by the assets of such plans as of such date.

(C) Failure. If any 1988 agreement operator fails to meet any obligation under this paragraph, any contributions of such operator to the Combined Fund or any other plan described in section 404(c) shall not be deductible under this title until such time as the failure is corrected.

(D) Premium reductions.

(i) 1st year payments. In the case of a 1988 agreement operator making contributions under subparagraph (A), the premium of such operator under subsection (a) shall be reduced by the amount paid under subparagraph (A) by such operator for the plan year beginning February 1, 1993.

(ii) Deficit payments. In the case a 1988 agreement operator making contributions under subparagraph (B), the premium of such operator under subsection (a) shall be reduced by the amounts which are paid to the Combined Fund by reason of claims arising in connection with the 1950 UMWA Benefit Plan and the 1974 UMWA Benefit Plan as of February 1, 1993, including claims based on the "evergreen clause" found in the language of the 1950 UMWA Benefit Plan and the 1974 UMWA Benefit Plan, and

Establishment of trust funds

Code Sec. 9704

which are allocated to such operator under subparagraph (E).

(iii) Limitation. Clause (ii) shall not apply to the extent the amounts paid exceed the contributions.

(iv) Plan years. Premiums under subsection (a) shall be reduced for the first plan year for which amounts described in clause (i) or (ii) are available and for any succeeding plan year until such amounts are exhausted.

(E) Allocations of contributions and refunds. Contributions under subparagraphs (A) and (B), and premium reductions under subparagraph (D)(ii), shall be made ratably on the basis of aggregate contributions made by such operators under the applicable 1988 coal wage agreements as of January 31, 1993.

(2) 1st plan year. In the case of the plan year of the Combined Fund beginning February 1, 1993—

(A) the premiums under subsections (a)(1) and (a)(3) shall be 67 percent of such premiums without regard to this paragraph, and

(B) the premiums under subsection (a) shall be paid as provided in subsection (g).

(3) Startup costs. The 1950 UMWA Benefit Plan and the 1974 UMWA Benefit Plan shall pay the costs of the Combined Fund incurred before February 1, 1993. For purposes of this section, such costs shall be treated as administrative expenses incurred for the plan year beginning February 1, 1993.

(j) Prepayment of premium liability.

(1) In general. If—

(A) a payment meeting the requirements of paragraph (3) is made to the Combined Fund by or on behalf of—

(i) any assigned operator to which this subsection applies, or

(ii) any related person to any assigned operator described in clause (i), and

(B) the common parent of the controlled group of corporations described in paragraph (2)(B) is jointly and severally liable for any premium under this section which (but for this subsection) would be required to be paid by the assigned operator or related person,

then such common parent (and no other person) shall be liable for such premium.

(2) Assigned operators to which subsection applies.

(A) In general. This subsection shall apply to any assigned operator if—

(i) the assigned operator (or a related person to the assigned operator)—

(I) made contributions to the 1950 UMWA Benefit Plan and the 1974 UMWA Benefit Plan for employment during the period covered by the 1988 agreement; and

(II) is not a 1988 agreement operator,

(ii) the assigned operator (and all related persons to the assigned operator) are not actively engaged in the production of coal as of July 1, 2005, and

(iii) the assigned operator was, as of July 20, 1992, a member of a controlled group of corporations described in subparagraph (B).

(B) Controlled group of corporations. A controlled group of corporations is described in this subparagraph if the common parent of such group is a corporation the shares of which are publicly traded on a United States exchange.

(C) Coordination with repeal of assignments. A person shall not fail to be treated as an assigned operator to which this subsection applies solely because the person ceases to be an assigned operator by reason of section 9706(h)(1) if the person otherwise meets the requirements of this subsection and is liable for the payment of premiums under section 9706(h)(3).

(D) Controlled group. For purposes of this subsection, the term "controlled group of corporations" has the meaning given such term by section 52(a).

(3) Requirements. A payment meets the requirements of this paragraph if—

(A) the amount of the payment is not less than the present value of the total premium liability under this chapter with respect to the Combined Fund of the assigned operators or related persons described in paragraph (1) or their assignees, as determined by the operator's or related person's enrolled actuary (as defined in section 7701(a)(35)) using actuarial methods and assumptions each of which is reasonable and which are reasonable in the aggregate, as determined by such enrolled actuary;

(B) such enrolled actuary files with the Secretary of Labor a signed actuarial report containing—

(i) the date of the actuarial valuation applicable to the report; and

(ii) a statement by the enrolled actuary signing the report that, to the best of the actuary's knowledge, the report is complete and accurate and that in the actuary's opinion the actuarial assumptions used are in the aggregate reasonably related to the experience of the operator and to reasonable expectations; and

(C) 90 calendar days have elapsed after the report required by subparagraph (B) is filed with the Secretary of Labor, and the Secretary of Labor has not notified the assigned operator in writing that the requirements of this paragraph have not been satisfied.

(4) Use of prepayment. The Combined Fund shall—

(A) establish and maintain an account for each assigned operator or related person by, or on whose behalf, a payment described in paragraph (3) was made,

(B) credit such account with such payment (and any earnings thereon), and

(C) use all amounts in such account exclusively to pay premiums that would (but for this subsection) be required to be paid by the assigned operator.

Upon termination of the obligations for the premium liability of any assigned operator or related person for which such account is maintained, all funds remaining in such account (and earnings thereon) shall be refunded to such person as may be designated by the common parent described in paragraph (1)(B).

In **2006**, P.L. 109-432, Sec. 211(a), added subsec. (j), effective 12/20/2006.
—P.L. 109-432, Sec. 212(a)(2)(A), amended subsec. (d) . . . Sec. 212(a)(2)(B)(i), added "and amounts transferred under section 9705(b)" after "premiums received" is para. (e)(1) . . . Sec. 212(a)(2)(B)(ii), added matter at the end of subpara. (e)(3)(A) . . . Sec. 212(a)(2)(B)(ii), added subpara. (f)(2)(C), effective for plan years of the Combined Fund beginning after 9/30/2006.
Prior to amendment, subsec. (d) read as follows:
"(d) Unassigned beneficiaries premium. The unassigned beneficiaries premium for any plan year for any assigned operator shall be equal to the applicable percentage of the product of the per beneficiary premium for the plan year multiplied by the number of eligible beneficiaries who are not assigned under section 9706 to any person for such plan year."
In **1994**, P.L. 103-296, Sec. 108(h)(9)(A), substituted "Commissioner of Social Security" for "Secretary of Health and Human Services" in para. (b)(2) and subsec. (h), effective 3/31/95.
In **1992**, P.L. 102-486, Sec. 19143(a), added Code Sec. 9704, effective 10/24/92.

Sec. 9705. Transfers.

(a) Transfer of assets from 1950 UMWA Pension Plan.
  (1) In general. From the funds reserved under paragraph (2), the board of trustees of the 1950 UMWA Pension Plan shall transfer to the Combined Fund—
    (A) $70,000,000 on February 1, 1993,
    (B) $70,000,000 on October 1, 1993, and
    (C) $70,000,000 on October 1, 1994.
  (2) Reservation. Immediately upon the enactment date, the board of trustees of the 1950 UMWA Pension Plan shall segregate $210,000,000 from the general assets of the plan. Such funds shall be held in the plan until disbursed pursuant to paragraph (1). Any interest on such funds shall be deposited into the general assets of the 1950 UMWA Pension Plan.
  (3) Use of funds. Amounts transferred to the Combined Fund under paragraph (1) shall—
    (A) in the case of the transfer on February 1, 1993, be used to proportionately reduce the premium of each assigned operator under section 9704(a) for the plan year of the Fund beginning February 1, 1993, and
    (B) in the case of any other such transfer, be used to proportionately reduce the unassigned beneficiary premium under section 9704(a)(3) and the death benefit premium under section 9704(a)(2) of each assigned operator for the plan year in which transferred and for any subsequent plan year in which such funds remain available.
  Such funds may not be used to pay any amounts required to be paid by the 1988 agreement operators under section 9704(i)(1)(B).
  (4) Tax treatment; Validity of transfer.
    (A) No deduction. No deduction shall be allowed under this title with respect to any transfer pursuant to paragraph (1), but such transfer shall not adversely affect the deductibility (under applicable provisions of this title) of contributions previously made by employers, or amounts hereafter contributed by employers, to the 1950 UMWA Pension Plan, the 1950 UMWA Benefit Plan, the 1974 UMWA Pension Plan, the 1974 UMWA Benefit Plan, the 1992 UMWA Benefit Plan, or the Combined Fund.
    (B) Other tax provisions. Any transfer pursuant to paragraph (1)—
      (i) shall not be treated as an employer reversion from a qualified plan for purposes of section 4980, and
      (ii) shall not be includible in the gross income of any employer maintaining the 1950 UMWA Pension Plan.
  (5) Treatment of transfer. Any transfer pursuant to paragraph (1) shall not be deemed to violate, or to be prohibited by, any provision of law, or to cause the settlors, joint board of trustees, employers or any related person to incur or be subject to liability, taxes, fines, or penalties of any kind whatsoever.

(b) Transfers .
  (1) In general. The Combined Fund shall include any amount transferred to the Fund under subsections (h) and (i) of section 402 of the Surface Mining Control and Reclamation Act of 1977 (30 U.S.C. 1232(h)).
  (2) Use of funds. Any amount transferred under paragraph (1) for any fiscal year shall be used to pay benefits and administrative costs of beneficiaries of the Combined Fund or for such other purposes as are specifically provided in the Acts described in paragraph (1).

In 2006, P.L. 109-432, Sec. 212(a)(1)(A), substituted "subsections (h) and (i) of section 402" for "section 402(h)" in para. (b)(1) . . . Sec. 212(a)(1)(B), amended para. (b)(2) . . . Sec. 212(a)(1)(C), amended the heading of subsec. (b), effective for plan yrs. of the Combined Fund begin. after 9/30/2006.
Prior to amendment, para. (b)(2) read as follows:
"(2) Use of funds. Any amount transferred under paragraph (1) for any fiscal year shall be used to proportionately reduce the unassigned beneficiary premium under section 9704(a)(3) of each assigned operator for the plan year in which transferred."
Prior to amendment, the heading to subsec. (b) read as follows:
"Transfers from Abandoned Mine Reclamation Fund."
In 1992, P.L. 102-486, Sec. 19143(a), added Code Sec. 9705, effective 10/24/92.

Sec. 9706. Assignment of eligible beneficiaries.
(a) In general.
For purposes of this chapter, the Commissioner of Social Security shall, before October 1, 1993, assign each coal industry retiree who is an eligible beneficiary to a signatory operator which (or any related person with respect to which) remains in business in the following order:
  (1) First, to the signatory operator which—
    (A) was a signatory to the 1978 coal wage agreement or any subsequent coal wage agreement, and
    (B) was the most recent signatory operator to employ the coal industry retiree in the coal industry for at least 2 years.
  (2) Second, if the retiree is not assigned under paragraph (1), to the signatory operator which—
    (A) was a signatory to the 1978 coal wage agreement or any subsequent coal wage agreement, and
    (B) was the most recent signatory operator to employ the coal industry retiree in the coal industry.
  (3) Third, if the retiree is not assigned under paragraph (1) or (2), to the signatory operator which employed the coal industry retiree in the coal industry for a longer period of time than any other signatory operator prior to the effective date of the 1978 coal wage agreement.

(b) Rules relating to employment and reassignment upon purchase.
For purposes of subsection (a)—
  (1) Aggregation rules.
    (A) Related person. Any employment of a coal industry retiree in the coal industry by a signatory operator shall be treated as employment by any related persons to such operator.
    (B) Certain employment disregarded. Employment with—
      (i) a person which is (and all related persons with respect to which are) no longer in business, or
      (ii) a person during a period during which such person was not a signatory to a coal wage agreement,
    shall not be taken into account.
  (2) Reassignment upon purchase. If a person becomes a successor of an assigned operator after the enactment date, the assigned operator may transfer the assignment of an eligible beneficiary under subsection (a) to such successor, and such successor shall be treated as the assigned operator with respect to such eligible beneficiary for purposes of this chapter. Notwithstanding the preceding sentence, the assigned operator transferring such assignment (and any related person) shall remain the guarantor of the benefits provided to the eligible beneficiary under this chapter. An assigned operator shall notify the trustees of the Combined Fund of any transfer described in this paragraph.

(c) Identification of eligible beneficiaries.
The 1950 UMWA Benefit Plan and the 1974 UMWA Benefit Plan shall, by the later of October 1, 1992, or the twentieth day after the enactment date, provide to the Com-

Establishment of trust funds

Code Sec. 9706(h)(3)(A)

missioner of Social Security a list of the names and social security account numbers of each eligible beneficiary, including each deceased eligible beneficiary if any other individual is an eligible beneficiary by reason of a relationship to such deceased eligible beneficiary. In addition, the plans shall provide, where ascertainable from plan records, the names of all persons described in subsection (a) with respect to any eligible beneficiary or deceased eligible beneficiary.

(d) Cooperation by other agencies and persons.

(1) Cooperation. The head of any department, agency, or instrumentality of the United States shall cooperate fully and promptly with the Commissioner of Social Security in providing information which will enable the Commissioner to carry out his responsibilities under this section.

(2) Providing of information.

(A) In general. Notwithstanding any other provision of law, including section 6103, the head of any other agency, department, or instrumentality shall, upon receiving a written request from the Commissioner of Social Security in connection with this section, cause a search to be made of the files and records maintained by such agency, department, or instrumentality with a view to determining whether the information requested is contained in such files or records. The Commissioner shall be advised whether the search disclosed the information requested, and, if so, such information shall be promptly transmitted to the Commissioner, except that if the disclosure of any requested information would contravene national policy or security interests of the United States, or the confidentiality of census data, the information shall not be transmitted and the Commissioner shall be so advised.

(B) Limitation. Any information provided under subparagraph (A) shall be limited to information necessary for the Commissioner to carry out his duties under this section.

(3) Trustees. The trustees of the Combined Fund, the 1950 UMWA Benefit Plan, the 1974 UMWA Benefit Plan, the 1950 UMWA Pension Plan, and the 1974 UMWA Pension Plan shall fully and promptly cooperate with the Commissioner in furnishing, or assisting the Commissioner to obtain, any information the Commissioner needs to carry out the Commissioner's responsibilities under this section.

(e) Notice by Commissioner.

(1) Notice to fund. The Commissioner of Social Security shall advise the trustees of the Combined Fund of the name of each person identified under this section as an assigned operator, and the names and social security account numbers of eligible beneficiaries with respect to whom he is identified.

(2) Other notice. The Commissioner of Social Security shall notify each assigned operator of the names and social security account numbers of eligible beneficiaries who have been assigned to such person under this section and a brief summary of the facts related to the basis for such assignments.

(f) Reconsideration by Commissioner.

(1) In general. Any assigned operator receiving a notice under subsection (e)(2) with respect to an eligible beneficiary may, within 30 days of receipt of such notice, request from the Commissioner of Social Security detailed information as to the work history of the beneficiary and the basis of the assignment.

(2) Review. An assigned operator may, within 30 days of receipt of the information under paragraph (1), request review of the assignment. The Commissioner of Social Security shall conduct such review if the Commissioner finds the operator provided evidence with the request constituting a prima facie case of error.

(3) Results of review.

(A) Error. If the Commissioner of Social Security determines under a review under paragraph (2) that an assignment was in error—

(i) the Commissioner shall notify the assigned operator and the trustees of the Combined Fund and the trustees shall reduce the premiums of the operator under section 9704 by (or if there are no such premiums, repay) all premiums paid under section 9704 with respect to the eligible beneficiary, and

(ii) the Commissioner shall review the beneficiary's record for reassignment under subsection (a).

(B) No error. If the Commissioner of Social Security determines under a review conducted under paragraph (2) that no error occurred, the Commissioner shall notify the assigned operator.

(4) Determinations. Any determination by the Commissioner of Social Security under paragraph (2) or (3) shall be final.

(5) Payment pending review. An assigned operator shall pay the premiums under section 9704 pending review by the Commissioner of Social Security or by a court under this subsection.

(6) Private actions. Nothing in this section shall preclude the right of any person to bring a separate civil action against another person for responsibility for assigned premiums, notwithstanding any prior decision by the Commissioner.

(g) Confidentiality of information.

Any person to which information is provided by the Commissioner of Social Security Services under this section shall not disclose such information except in any proceedings related to this section. Any civil or criminal penalty which is applicable to an unauthorized disclosure under section 6103 shall apply to any unauthorized disclosure under this section.

(h) Assignments as of October 1, 2007.

(1) In general. Subject to the premium obligation set forth in paragraph (3), the Commissioner of Social Security shall—

(A) revoke all assignments to persons other than 1988 agreement operators for purposes of assessing premiums for plan years beginning on and after October 1, 2007; and

(B) make no further assignments to persons other than 1988 agreement operators, except that no individual who becomes an unassigned beneficiary by reason of subparagraph (A) may be assigned to a 1988 agreement operator.

(2) Reassignment upon purchase. This subsection shall not be construed to prohibit the reassignment under subsection (b)(2) of an eligible beneficiary.

(3) Liability of persons during three fiscal years beginning on and after October 1, 2007. In the case of each of the fiscal years beginning on October 1, 2007, 2008, and 2009, each person other than a 1988 agreement operator shall pay to the Combined Fund the following percentage of the amount of annual premiums that such person would otherwise be required to pay under section 9704(a), determined on the basis of assignments in effect without regard to the revocation of assignments under paragraph (1)(A):

(A) For the fiscal year beginning on October 1, 2007, 55 percent.

(B) For the fiscal year beginning on October 1, 2008, 40 percent.
(C) For the fiscal year beginning on October 1, 2009, 15 percent.

In 2006, P.L. 109-432, Sec. 212(a)(3), added subsec. (h), effective for plan years of the Combined Fund beginning after 9/30/2006.
In 1994, P.L. 103-296, Sec. 108(h)(9)(B)(i), substituted "Commissioner of Social Security" for "Secretary of Health and Human Services" each place it appeared in Code Sec. 9706 ... Sec. 108(h)(9)(B)(ii), substituted "Commissioner" for "Secretary" each place it appeared in Code Sec. 9706, as amended by Sec. 108(h)(9)(B)(i) of this Act.... Sec. 108(h)(9)(B)(iii), substituted "Commissioner's" for "Secretary's" in para. (d)(3), effective 3/31/95.
In 1992, P.L. 102-486, Sec. 19143(a), added Code Sec. 9706, effective 10/24/92.

PART III.—ENFORCEMENT

Sec.
9707. Failure to pay premium.

Sec. 9707. Failure to pay premium.
(a) Failures to pay.
  (1) Premiums for eligible beneficiaries. There is hereby imposed a penalty on the failure of any assigned operator to pay any premum required to be paid under section 9704 with respect to any eligible beneficiary.
  (2) Contributions required under the mining laws. There is hereby imposed a penalty on the failure of any person to make a contribution required under section 402(h)(5)(B)(ii) of the Surface Mining Control and Reclamation Act of 1977 to a plan referred to in section 402(h)(2)(C) of such Act. For purposes of applying this section, each such required monthly contribution for the hours worked of any individual shall be treated as if it were a premium required to be paid under section 9704 with respect to an eligible beneficiary.
(b) Amount of penalty.
The amount of the penalty imposed by subsection (a) on any failure with respect to any eligible beneficiary shall be $100 per day in the noncompliance period with respect to any such failure.
(c) Noncompliance period.
For purposes of this section, the term "noncompliance period" means, with respect to any failure to pay any premium or installment thereof, the period—
  (1) beginning on the due date for such premium or installment, and
  (2) ending on the date of payment of such premium or installment.
(d) Limitations on amount of penalty.
  (1) In general. No penalty shall be imposed by subsection (a) on any failure during any period for which it is established to the satisfaction of the Secretary of the Treasury that none of the persons responsible for such failure knew, or exercising reasonable diligence would have known, that such failure existed.
  (2) Corrections. No penalty shall be imposed by subsection (a) on any failure if—
    (A) such failure was due to reasonable cause and not to willful neglect, and
    (B) such failure is corrected during the 30-day period beginning on the 1st date that any of the persons responsible for such failure knew, or exercising reasonable diligence would have known, that such failure existed.
  (3) Waiver. In the case of a failure that is due to reasonable cause and not to willful neglect, the Secretary of the Treasury may waive all or part of the penalty imposed by subsection (a) for failures to the extent that the Secretary determines, in his sole discretion, that the payment of such penalty would be excessive relative to the failure involved.
(e) Liability for penalty.
The person failing to meet the requirements of section 9704 shall be liable for the penalty imposed by subsection (a).
(f) Treatment.
For purposes of this title, the penalty imposed by this section shall be treated in the same manner as the tax imposed by section 4980B.

In 2006, P.L. 109-432, Sec. 213(b)(1), amended subsec. (a), enacted 12/20/2006. Prior to amendment, subsec. (a) read as follows:
"(a) General rule. There is hereby imposed a penalty on the failure of any assigned operator to pay any premium required to be paid under section 9704 with respect to any eligible beneficiary."
In 1996, P.L. 104-188, Sec. 1704(t)(65), substituted "diligence" for "diligence," in para. (d)(1), effective 8/20/96.
In 1992, P.L. 102-486, Sec. 19143(a), added Code Sec. 9707, effective 10/24/92.

PART IV.—OTHER PROVISIONS

Sec.
9708. Effect on pending claims or obligations.

Sec. 9708. Effect on pending claims or obligations.
All liability for contributions to the Combined Fund that arises on and after February 1, 1993, shall be determined exclusively under this chapter, including all liability for contributions to the 1950 UMWA Benefit Plan and the 1974 UMWA Benefit Plan for coal production on and after February 1, 1993. However, nothing in this chapter is intended to have any effect on any claims or obligations arising in connection with the 1950 UMWA Benefit Plan and the 1974 UMWA Benefit Plan as of February 1, 1993, including claims or obligations based on the "evergreen" clause found in the language of the 1950 UMWA Benefit Plan and the 1974 UMWA Benefit Plan. This chapter shall not be construed to affect any rights of subrogation of any 1988 agreement operator with respect to contributions due to the 1950 UMWA Benefit Plan or the 1974 UMWA Benefit Plan as of February 1, 1993.

In 1992, P.L. 102-486, Sec. 19143(a), added Code Sec. 9708, effective 10/24/92.

Subchapter C.—Health Benefits of Certain Miners

Part
  I. Individual employer plans
  II. 1992 UMWA benefit plan

PART I.—INDIVIDUAL EMPLOYER PLANS

Sec.
9711. Continued obligations of individual employer plans.

Sec. 9711. Continued obligations of individual employer plans.
(a) Coverage of current recipients.
The last signatory operator of any individual who, as of February 1, 1993, is receiving retiree health benefits from an individual employer plan maintained pursuant to a 1978 or subsequent coal wage agreement shall continue to provide health benefits coverage to such individual and the individual's eligible beneficiaries which is substantially the same as (and subject to all the limitations of) the coverage provided by such plan as of January 1, 1992. Such coverage shall continue to be provided for as long as the last signatory operator (and any related person) remains in business.
(b) Coverage of eligible recipients.
  (1) In general. The last signatory operator of any individual who, as of February 1, 1993, is not receiving retiree

Establishment of trust funds — Code Sec. 9712(a)(1)

health benefits under the individual employer plan maintained by the last signatory operator pursuant to a 1978 or subsequent coal wage agreement, but has met the age and service requirements for eligibility to receive benefits under such plan as of such date, shall, at such time as such individual becomes eligible to receive benefits under such plan, provide health benefits coverage to such individual and the individual's eligible beneficiaries which is described in paragraph (2). This paragraph shall not apply to any individual who retired from the coal industry after September 30, 1994, or any eligible beneficiary of such individual.

(2) Coverage. Subject to the provisions of subsection (d), health benefits coverage is described in this paragraph if it is substantially the same as (and subject to all the limitations of) the coverage provided by the individual employer plan as of January 1, 1992. Such coverage shall continue for as long as the last signatory operator (and any related person) remains in business.

(c) Joint and several liability of related persons.

(1) In general. Except as provided in paragraph (2), each related person of a last signatory operator to which subsection (a) or (b) applies shall be jointly and severally liable with the last signatory operator for the provision of health care coverage described in subsection (a) or (b).

(2) Liability limited if security provided. If—

(A) security meeting the requirements of paragraph (3) is provided by or on behalf of—

(i) any last signatory operator which is an assigned operator described in section 9704(j)(2), or

(ii) any related person to any last signatory operator described in clause (i), and

(B) the common parent of the controlled group of corporations described in section 9704(j)(2)(B) is jointly and severally liable for the provision of health care under this section which, but for this paragraph, would be required to be provided by the last signatory operator or related person,

then, as of the date the security is provided, such common parent (and no other person) shall be liable for the provision of health care under this section which the last signatory operator or related person would otherwise be required to provide. Security may be provided under this paragraph without regard to whether a payment was made under section 9704(j).

(3) Security. Security meets the requirements of this paragraph if—

(A) the security—

(i) is in the form of a bond, letter of credit, or cash escrow,

(ii) is provided to the trustees of the 1992 UMWA Benefit Plan solely for the purpose of paying premiums for beneficiaries who would be described in section 9712(b)(2)(B) if the requirements of this section were not met by the last signatory operator, and

(iii) is in an amount equal to 1 year of liability of the last signatory operator under this section, determined by using the average cost of such operator's liability during the prior 3 calendar years;

(B) the security is in addition to any other security required under any other provision of this title; and

(C) the security remains in place for 5 years.

(4) Refunds of security. The remaining amount of any security provided under this subsection (and earnings thereon) shall be refunded to the last signatory operator as of the earlier of—

(A) the termination of the obligations of the last signatory operator under this section, or

(B) the end of the 5-year period described in paragraph (4)(C).

(d) Managed care and cost containment.

The last signatory operator shall not be treated as failing to meet the requirements of subsection (a) or (b) if benefits are provided to eligible beneficiaries under managed care and cost containment rules and procedures described in section 9712(c) or agreed to by the last signatory operator and the United Mine Workers of America.

(e) Treatment of noncovered employees.

The existence, level, and duration of benefits provided to former employees of a last signatory operator (and their eligible beneficiaries) who are not otherwise covered by this chapter and who are (or were) covered by a coal wage agreement shall only be determined by, and shall be subject to, collective bargaining, lawful unilateral action, or other applicable law.

(f) Eligible beneficiary.

For purposes of this section, the term "eligible beneficiary" means any individual who is eligible for health benefits under a plan described in subsection (a) or (b) by reason of the individual's relationship with the retiree described in such subsection (or to an individual who, based on service and employment history at the time of death, would have been so described but for such death).

(g) Rules applicable to this part and part II.

For purposes of this part and part II—

(1) Successor. The term "last signatory operator" shall include a successor in interest of such operator.

(2) Reassignment upon purchase. If a person becomes a successor of a last signatory operator after the enactment date, the last signatory operator may transfer any liability of such operator under this chapter with respect to an eligible beneficiary to such successor, and such successor shall be treated as the last signatory operator with respect to such eligible beneficiary for purposes of this chapter. Notwithstanding the preceding sentence, the last signatory operator transferring such assignment (and any related person) shall remain the guarantor of the benefits provided to the eligible beneficiary under this chapter. A last signatory operator shall notify the trustees of the 1992 UMWA Benefit Plan of any transfer described in this paragraph.

In **2006**, P.L. 109-432, Sec. 211(b), amended subsec. (c), effective for transactions after 12/20/2006.

Prior to amendment, subsec. (c) read as follows:

"(c) Joint and several liability of related persons. Each related person of a last signatory operator to which subsection (a) or (b) applies shall be jointly and severally liable with the last signatory operator for the provision of health care coverage described in subsection (a) or (b)."

In **1992**, P.L. 102-486, Sec. 19143(a), added Code Sec. 9711, effective 10/24/92.

PART II.—1992 UMWA BENEFIT PLAN

Sec.

9712. Establishment and coverage of 1992 UMWA Benefit Plan.

Sec. 9712. Establishment and coverage of 1992 UMWA Benefit Plan.

(a) Creation of plan.

(1) In general. As soon as practicable after the enactment date, the settlors shall create a separate private plan which shall be known as the United Mine Workers of America 1992 Benefit Plan. For purposes of this title, the 1992 UMWA Benefit Plan shall be treated as an organization exempt from taxation under section 501(a). The settlors shall be responsible for designing the structure, administration and terms of the 1992 UMWA Benefit Plan, and for appointment and removal of the members of the board of trustees. The board of trustees shall initially consist of five members and shall thereafter be the number set by the settlors.

(2) Treatment of plan. The 1992 UMWA Benefit Plan shall be—

(A) a plan described in section 302(c)(5) of the Labor Management Relations Act, 1947 (29 U.S.C. 186(c)(5)),

(B) an employee welfare benefit plan within the meaning of section 3(1) of the Employee Retirement Income Security Act of 1974(29 U.S.C. 1002(1)), and

(C) a multiemployer plan within the meaning of section 3(37) of such Act (29 U.S.C. 1002(37)).

(3) Transfers under other federal statutes.

(A) In general. The 1992 UMWA Benefit Plan shall include any amount transferred to the plan under subsections (h) and (i) of section 402 of the Surface Mining Control and Reclamation Act of 1977 (30 U.S.C. 1232).

(B) Use of funds. Any amount transferred under subparagraph (A) for any fiscal year shall be used to provide the health benefits described in subsection (c) with respect to any beneficiary for whom no monthly per beneficiary premium is paid pursuant to paragraph (1)(A) or (3) of subsection (d).

(4) Special rule for 1993 plan.

(A) In general. The plan described in section 402(h)(2)(C) of the Surface Mining Control and Reclamation Act of 1977 (30 U.S.C. 1232(h)(2)(C)) shall include any amount transferred to the plan under subsections (h) and (i) of the Surface Mining Control and Reclamation Act of 1977 (30 U.S.C. 1232).

(B) Use of funds. Any amount transferred under subparagraph (A) for any fiscal year shall be used to provide the health benefits described in section 402(h)(2)(C)(i) of the Surface Mining Control and Reclamation Act of 1977 (30 U.S.C. 1232(h)(2)(C)(i)) to individuals described in section 402(h)(2)(C) of such Act (30 U.S.C. 1232(h)(2)(C)).

(b) Coverage requirement.

(1) In general. The 1992 UMWA Benefit Plan shall only provide health benefits coverage to any eligible beneficiary who is not eligible for benefits under the Combined Fund and shall not provide such coverage to any other individual.

(2) Eligible beneficiary. For purposes of this section, the term "eligible beneficiary" means an individual who—

(A) but for the enactment of this chapter, would be eligible to receive benefits from the 1950 UMWA Benefit Plan or the 1974 UMWA Benefit Plan, based upon age and service earned as of February 1, 1993; or

(B) with respect to whom coverage is required to be provided under section 9711, but who does not receive such coverage from the applicable last signatory operator or any related person,

and any individual who is eligible for benefits by reason of a relationship to an individual described in subparagraph (A) or (B). In no event shall the 1992 UMWA Benefit Plan provide health benefits coverage to any eligible beneficiary who is a coal industry retiree who retired from the coal industry after September 30, 1994, or any beneficiary of such individual.

(c) Health benefits.

(1) In general. The 1992 UMWA Benefit Plan shall provide health care benefits coverage to each eligible beneficiary which is substantially the same as (and subject to all the limitations of) coverage provided under the 1950 UMWA Benefit Plan and the 1974 UMWA Benefit Plan as of January 1, 1992.

(2) Managed care. The 1992 UMWA Benefit Plan shall develop managed care and cost containment rules which shall be applicable to the payment of benefits under this subsection. Application of such rules shall not cause the plan to be treated as failing to meet the requirements of this subsection. Such rules shall preserve freedom of choice while reinforcing managed care network use by allowing a point of service decision as to whether a network medical provider will be used. Major elements of such rules may include, but are not limited to, elements described in paragraph (3).

(3) Major elements of rules. Elements described in this paragraph are—

(A) implementing formulary for drugs and subjecting the prescription program to a rigorous review of appropriate use,

(B) obtaining a unit price discount in exchange for patient volume and preferred provider status with the amount of the potential discount varying by geographic region,

(C) limiting benefit payments to physicians to the allowable charge under title XVIII of the Social Security Act, while protecting beneficiaries from balance billing by providers,

(D) utilizing, in the claims payment function "appropriateness of service" protocols under title XVIII of the Social Security Act if more stringent,

(E) creating mandatory utilization review (UR) procedures, but placing the responsibility to follow such procedures on the physician or hospital, not the beneficiaries,

(F) selecting the most efficient physicians and state-of-the-art utilization management techniques, including ambulatory care techniques, for medical services delivered by the managed care network, and

(G) utilizing a managed care network provider system, as practiced in the health care industry, at the time medical services are needed (point-of-service) in order to receive maximum benefits available under this subsection.

(4) Last signatory operators. The board of trustees of the 1992 UMWA Benefit Plan shall permit any last signatory operator required to maintain an individual employer plan under section 9711 to utilize the managed care and cost containment rules and programs developed under this subsection if the operator elects to do so.

(5) Standards of quality. Any managed care system or cost containment adopted by the board of trustees of the 1992 UMWA Benefit Plan or by a last signatory operator may not be implemented unless it is approved by, and meets the standards of quality adopted by, a medical peer review panel, which has been established—

(A) by the settlors, or

(B) by the United Mine Workers of America and a last signatory operator or group of operators.

Standards of quality shall include accessibility to medical care, taking into account that accessibility requirements may differ depending on the nature of the medical need.

(d) Guarantee of benefits.

(1) In general. All 1988 last signatory operators shall be responsible for financing the benefits described in subsection (c) by meeting the following requirements in accordance with the contribution requirements established in the 1992 UMWA Benefit Plan:

(A) The payment of a monthly per beneficiary premium by each 1988 last signatory operator for each eligible beneficiary of such operator who is described in subsection (b)(2) and who is receiving benefits under the 1992 UMWA Benefit Plan.
(B) The provision of a security (in the form of a bond, letter of credit, or cash escrow) in an amount equal to a portion of the projected future cost to the 1992 UMWA Benefit Plan of providing health benefits for eligible and potentially eligible beneficiaries attributable to the 1988 last signatory operator.
(C) If the amounts transferred under subsection (a)(3) are less than the amounts required to be transferred to the 1992 UMWA Benefit Plan under subsections (h) and (i) of section 402 of the Surface Mining Control and Reclamation Act of 1977 (30 U.S.C. 1232), the payment of an additional backstop premium by each 1988 last signatory operator which is equal to such operator's share of the amounts required to be so transferred but which were not so transferred, determined on the basis of the number of eligible and potentially eligible beneficiaries attributable to the operator.

(2) **Adjustments.** The 1992 UMWA Benefit Plan shall provide for—
(A) annual adjustments of the per beneficiary premium to cover changes in the cost of providing benefits to eligible beneficiaries, and
(B) adjustments as necessary to the annual backstop premium to reflect changes in the cost of providing benefits to eligible beneficiaries for whom per beneficiary premiums are not paid.

(3) **Additional liability.** Any last signatory operator who is not a 1988 last signatory operator shall pay the monthly per beneficiary premium under paragraph (1)(A) for each eligible beneficiary described in such paragraph attributable to that operator.

(4) **Joint and several liability.** A 1988 last signatory operator or last signatory operator described in paragraph (3), and any related person to any such operator, shall be jointly and severally liable with such operator for any amount required to be paid by such operator under this section. The provisions of section 9711(c)(2) shall apply to any last signatory operator described in such section (without regard to whether security is provided under such section, a payment is made under section 9704(j), or both) and if security meeting the requirements of section 9711(c)(3) is provided, the common parent described in section 9711(c)(2)(B) shall be exclusively responsible for any liability for premiums under this section which, but for this sentence, would be required to be paid by the last signatory operator or any related person.

(5) **Deductibility.** Any premium required by this section shall be deductible without regard to any limitation on deductibility based on the prefunding of health benefits.

(6) **1988 last signatory operator.** For purposes of this section, the term "1988 last signatory operator" means a last signatory operator which is a 1988 agreement operator.

In 2006, P.L. 109-432, Sec. 211(c), added matter at the end of para. (d)(4), effective 12/20/2006.
—P.L. 109-432, Sec. 212(b)(1), amended paras. (a)(3) and (4) . . . Sec. 212(b)(2)(A), amended para. (d)(1) . . . Sec. 212(b)(2)(B)(i), substituted "backstop" for "prefunding" in subpara. (d)(2)(B) . . . Sec. 212(b)(2)(B)(ii), substituted "paragraph (1)(A)" for "paragraph (1)(B)" in para. (d)(3), effective for fiscal yrs. begin. on or after 10/1/2010.
Prior to amendment, para. (d)(1) read as follows:
"(1) In general. All 1988 last signatory operators shall be responsible for financing the benefits described in subsection (c), in accordance with contribution requirements established in the 1992 UMWA Benefit Plan. Such contribution requirements, which shall be applied uniformly to each 1988 last signatory operator, on the basis of the number of eligible and potentially eligible beneficiaries attributable to each operator, shall include:
"(A) the payment of an annual prefunding premium for all eligible and potentially eligible beneficiaries attributable to a 1988 last signatory operator,
"(B) the payment of a monthly per beneficiary premium by each 1988 last signatory operator for each eligible beneficiary of such operator who is described in subsection (b)(2) and who is receiving benefits under the 1992 UMWA Benefit Plan, and
"(C) the provision of security (in the form of a bond, letter of credit or cash escrow) in an amount equal to a portion of the projected future cost to the 1992 UMWA Benefit Plan of providing health benefits for eligible and potentially eligible beneficiaries attributable to the 1988 last signatory operator. If a 1988 last signatory operator is unable to provide the security required, the 1992 UMWA Benefit Plan shall require the operator to pay an annual prefunding premium that is greater than the premium otherwise applicable."
In 1992, P.L. 102-486, Sec. 19143(a), added Code Sec. 9712, effective 10/24/92.

Subchapter D.—Other Provisions

Sec.
9721. Civil enforcement.
9722. Sham transactions.

Sec. 9721. Civil enforcement.
The provisions of section 4301 of the Employee Retirement Income Security Act of 1974 shall apply, in the same manner as any claim arising out of an obligation to pay withdrawal liability under subtitle E of title IV of such Act, to any claim—
(1) arising out of an obligation to pay any amount required to be paid by this chapter; or
(2) arising out of an obligation to pay any amount required by section 402(h)(5)(B)(ii) of the Surface Mining Control and Reclamation Act of 1977 (30 U.S.C. 1232(h)(5)(B)(ii)).

In 2006, P.L. 109-432, Sec. 213(b)(2), amended Code Sec. 9721, enacted 12/20/2006.
Prior to amendment, Code Sec. 9721 read as follows:
"Sec. 9721 Civil enforcement.
"The provisions of section 4301 of the Employee Retirement Income Security Act of 1974 shall apply to any claim arising out of an obligation to pay any amount required to be paid by this chapter in the same manner as any claim arising out of an obligation to pay withdrawal liability under subtitle E of title IV of such Act. For purposes of the preceding sentence, a signatory operator and related persons shall be treated in the same manner as employers."
In 1992, P.L. 102-486, Sec. 19143(a), added Code Sec. 9721, effective 10/24/92.

Sec. 9722. Sham transactions.
If a principal purpose of any transaction is to evade or avoid liability under this chapter, this chapter shall be applied (and such liability shall be imposed) without regard to such transaction.

In 1992, P.L. 102-486, Sec. 19143(a), added Code Sec. 9722, effective 10/24/92.

Subtitle K.—Group Health Plan Requirements

Chapter
100. Group Health Plan Requirements.

In 1997, P.L. 105-34, Sec. 1531(a), amended table for Subtitle K.
Prior to amendment, table for subtitle K read has follows:
"Subtitle K. Group Health Plan Portability, Access, and Renewability Requirements
"Chapter 100. Group health plan portaiblity, access, and renewability requirements.
In 1996, P.L. 104-191, Sec. 401(a), added subtitle K.

CHAPTER 100.—GROUP HEALTH PLAN REQUIREMENTS

Subchapter
A. Requirements relating to portability, access, and renewability.

Chapter 100

B. Other requirements.
C. General provisions.

In 1997, P.L. 105-34, Sec. 1531(a)(1), amended chapter 100 of subtitle K.
Prior to amendment, chapter 100 read as follows.
 "Chapter 100. Group Health Plan Portability, Access, and Renewability Requirements.
 "Sec. 9801. Increased portability through limitation on pre-existing condition exclusions.
 "Sec. 9802. Prohibiting discrimination against individual participants and beneficiaries based on health status.
 "Sec. 9803. Guaranteed renewability in multiemployer plans and certain multiple employer welfare arrangements.
 "Sec. 9804. General exceptions.
 "Sec. 9805. Definitions.
 "Sec. 9806. Regulations."
In 1996, P.L. 104-191, Sec. 401(a), added chapter 100 of subtitle K.

Subchapter A.—Requirements Relating to Portability, Access, and Renewability

Sec.
9801. Increased portability through limitation on pre-existing condition exclusions.
9802. Prohibiting discrimination against individual participants and beneficiaries based on health status.
9803. Guaranteed renewability in multiemployer plans and certain multiple employer welfare arrangements.

In 1997, P.L. 105-34, Sec. 1531(a)(1), added subchapter A of chapter 100 of subtitle K.

Sec. 9801. Increased portability through limitation on preexisting condition exclusions.

(a) Limitation on preexisting condition exclusion period; crediting for periods of previous coverage.
Subject to subsection (d), a group health plan may, with respect to a participant or beneficiary, impose a preexisting condition exclusion only if—
(1) such exclusion relates to a condition (whether physical or mental), regardless of the cause of the condition, for which medical advice, diagnosis, care, or treatment was recommended or received within the 6-month period ending on the enrollment date;
(2) such exclusion extends for a period of not more than 12 months (or 18 months in the case of a late enrollee) after the enrollment date; and
(3) the period of any such preexisting condition exclusion is reduced by the length of the aggregate of the periods of creditable coverage (if any) applicable to the participant or beneficiary as of the enrollment date.

(b) Definitions.
For purposes of this section—
(1) Preexisting condition exclusion.
(A) In general. The term "preexisting condition exclusion" means, with respect to coverage, a limitation or exclusion of benefits relating to a condition based on the fact that the condition was present before the date of enrollment for such coverage, whether or not any medical advice, diagnosis, care, or treatment was recommended or received before such date.
(B) Treatment of genetic information. For purposes of this section, genetic information shall not be treated as a condition described in subsection (a)(1) in the absence of a diagnosis of the condition related to such information.
(2) Enrollment date. The term "enrollment date" means, with respect to an individual covered under a group health plan, the date of enrollment of the individual in the plan or, if earlier, the first day of the waiting period for such enrollment.
(3) Late enrollee. The term "late enrollee" means, with respect to coverage under a group health plan, a participant or beneficiary who enrolls under the plan other than during—
(A) the first period in which the individual is eligible to enroll under the plan, or
(B) a special enrollment period under subsection (f).
(4) Waiting period. The term "waiting period" means, with respect to a group health plan and an individual who is a potential participant or beneficiary in the plan, the period that must pass with respect to the individual before the individual is eligible to be covered for benefits under the terms of the plan.

(c) Rules relating to crediting previous coverage.
(1) Creditable coverage defined. For purposes of this part, the term "creditable coverage" means, with respect to an individual, coverage of the individual under any of the following:
(A) A group health plan.
(B) Health insurance coverage.
(C) Part A or part B of title XVIII of the Social Security Act.
(D) Title XIX of the Social Security Act, other than coverage consisting solely of benefits under section 1928.
(E) Chapter 55 of title 10, United States Code.
(F) A medical care program of the Indian Health Service or of a tribal organization.
(G) A State health benefits risk pool.
(H) A health plan offered under chapter 89 of title 5, United States Code.
(I) A public health plan (as defined in regulations).
(J) A health benefit plan under section 5(e) of the Peace Corps Act (22 U.S.C. 2504(e)).
Such term does not include coverage consisting solely of coverage of excepted benefits (as defined in section 9832(c)).
(2) Not counting periods before significant breaks in coverage.
(A) In general. A period of creditable coverage shall not be counted, with respect to enrollment of an individual under a group health plan, if, after such period and before the enrollment date, there was a 63-day period during all of which the individual was not covered under any creditable coverage.
(B) Waiting period not treated as a break in coverage. For purposes of subparagraph (A) and subsection (d)(4), any period that an individual is in a waiting period for any coverage under a group health plan or is in an affiliation period shall not be taken into account in determining the continuous period under subparagraph (A).
(C) Affiliation period.
 (i) In general. For purposes of this section, the term "affiliation period" means a period which, under the terms of the health insurance coverage offered by the health maintenance organization, must expire before the health insurance coverage becomes effective. During such an affiliation period, the organization is not required to provide health care services or benefits and no premium shall be charged to the participant or beneficiary.
 (ii) Beginning. Such period shall begin on the enrollment date.

Establishment of trust funds   Code Sec. 9801(f)(1)

(iii) Runs concurrently with waiting periods. Any such affiliation period shall run concurrently with any waiting period under the plan.

(D) TAA-eligible individuals. In the case of plan years beginning before February 13, 2011—

(i) TAA pre-certification period rule. In the case of a TAA-eligible individual, the period beginning on the date the individual has a TAA-related loss of coverage and ending on the date which is 7 days after the date of the issuance by the Secretary (or by any person or entity designated by the Secretary) of a qualified health insurance costs credit eligibility certificate for such individual for purposes of section 7527 shall not be taken into account in determining the continuous period under subparagraph (A).

(ii) Definitions. The terms "TAA-eligible individual" and "TAA-related loss of coverage" have the meanings given such terms in section 4980B(f)(5)(C)(iv).

(3) Method of crediting coverage.

(A) Standard method. Except as otherwise provided under subparagraph (B), for purposes of applying subsection (a)(3), a group health plan shall count a period of creditable coverage without regard to the specific benefits for which coverage is offered during the period.

(B) Election of alternative method. A group health plan may elect to apply subsection (a)(3) based on coverage of any benefits within each of several classes or categories of benefits specified in regulations rather than as provided under subparagraph (A). Such election shall be made on a uniform basis for all participants and beneficiaries. Under such election a group health plan shall count a period of creditable coverage with respect to any class or category of benefits if any level of benefits is covered within such class or category.

(C) Plan notice. In the case of an election with respect to a group health plan under subparagraph (B), the plan shall—

(i) prominently state in any disclosure statements concerning the plan, and state to each enrollee at the time of enrollment under the plan, that the plan has made such election, and

(ii) include in such statements a description of the effect of this election.

(4) Establishment of period. Periods of creditable coverage with respect to an individual shall be established through presentation of certifications described in subsection (e) or in such other manner as may be specified in regulations.

(d) Exceptions.

(1) Exclusions not applicable to certain newborns. Subject to paragraph (4), a group health plan may not impose any preexisting condition exclusion in the case of an individual who, as of the last day of the 30-day period beginning with the date of birth, is covered under creditable coverage.

(2) Exclusion not applicable to certain adopted children. Subject to paragraph (4), a group health plan may not impose any preexisting condition exclusion in the case of a child who is adopted or placed for adoption before attaining 18 years of age and who, as of the last day of the 30-day period beginning on the date of the adoption or placement for adoption, is covered under creditable coverage. The previous sentence shall not apply to coverage before the date of such adoption or placement for adoption.

(3) Exclusion not applicable to pregnancy. For purposes of this section, a group health plan may not impose any preexisting condition exclusion relating to pregnancy as a preexisting condition.

(4) Loss if break in coverage. Paragraphs (1) and (2) shall no longer apply to an individual after the end of the first 63-day period during all of which the individual was not covered under any creditable coverage.

(e) Certifications and disclosure of coverage.

(1) Requirement for certification of period of creditable coverage.

(A) In general. A group health plan shall provide the certification described in subparagraph (B)—

(i) at the time an individual ceases to be covered under the plan or otherwise becomes covered under a COBRA continuation provision,

(ii) in the case of an individual becoming covered under such a provision, at the time the individual ceases to be covered under such provision, and

(iii) on the request on behalf of an individual made not later than 24 months after the date of cessation of the coverage described in clause (i) or (ii), whichever is later.

The certification under clause (i) may be provided, to the extent practicable, at a time consistent with notices required under any applicable COBRA continuation provision.

(B) Certification. The certification described in this subparagraph is a written certification of—

(i) the period of creditable coverage of the individual under such plan and the coverage under such COBRA continuation provision, and

(ii) the waiting period (if any) (and affiliation period, if applicable) imposed with respect to the individual for any coverage under such plan.

(C) Issuer compliance. To the extent that medical care under a group health plan consists of health insurance coverage offered in connection with the plan, the plan is deemed to have satisfied the certification requirement under this paragraph if the issuer provides for such certification in accordance with this paragraph.

(2) Disclosure of information on previous benefits.

(A) In general. In the case of an election described in subsection (c)(3)(B) by a group health plan, if the plan enrolls an individual for coverage under the plan and the individual provides a certification of coverage of the individual under paragraph (1)—

(i) upon request of such plan, the entity which issued the certification provided by the individual shall promptly disclose to such requesting plan information on coverage of classes and categories of health benefits available under such entity's plan, and

(ii) such entity may charge the requesting plan or issuer for the reasonable cost of disclosing such information.

(3) Regulations. The Secretary shall establish rules to prevent an entity's failure to provide information under paragraph (1) or (2) with respect to previous coverage of an individual from adversely affecting any subsequent coverage of the individual under another group health plan or health insurance coverage.

(f) Special enrollment periods.

(1) Individuals losing other coverage. A group health plan shall permit an employee who is eligible, but not enrolled, for coverage under the terms of the plan (or a dependent of such employee if the dependent is eligible, but not enrolled, for coverage under such terms) to enroll

for coverage under the terms of the plan if each of the following conditions is met:

(A) The employee or dependent was covered under a group health plan or had health insurance coverage at the time coverage was previously offered to the employee or individual.

(B) The employee stated in writing at such time that coverage under a group health plan or health insurance coverage was the reason for declining enrollment, but only if the plan sponsor (or the health insurance issuer offering health insurance coverage in connection with the plan) required such a statement at such time and provided the employee with notice of such requirement (and the consequences of such requirement) at such time.

(C) The employee's or dependent's coverage described in subparagraph (A)—

(i) was under a COBRA continuation provision and the coverage under such provision was exhausted; or

(ii) was not under such a provision and either the coverage was terminated as a result of loss of eligibility for the coverage (including as a result of legal separation, divorce, death, termination of employment, or reduction in the number of hours of employment) or employer contributions towards such coverage were terminated.

(D) Under the terms of the plan, the employee requests such enrollment not later than 30 days after the date of exhaustion of coverage described in subparagraph (C)(i) or termination of coverage or employer contribution described in subparagraph (C)(ii).

(2) For dependent beneficiaries.

(A) In general. If—

(i) a group health plan makes coverage available with respect to a dependent of an individual,

(ii) the individual is a participant under the plan (or has met any waiting period applicable to becoming a participant under the plan and is eligible to be enrolled under the plan but for a failure to enroll during a previous enrollment period), and

(iii) a person becomes such a dependent of the individual through marriage, birth, or adoption or placement for adoption,

the group health plan shall provide for a dependent special enrollment period described in subparagraph (B) during which the person (or, if not otherwise enrolled, the individual) may be enrolled under the plan as a dependent of the individual, and in the case of the birth or adoption of a child, the spouse of the individual may be enrolled as a dependent of the individual if such spouse is otherwise eligible for coverage.

(B) Dependent special enrollment period. The dependent special enrollment period under this subparagraph shall be a period of not less than 30 days and shall begin on the later of—

(i) the date dependent coverage is made available, or

(ii) the date of the marriage, birth, or adoption or placement for adoption (as the case may be) described in subparagraph (A)(iii).

(C) No waiting period. If an individual seeks coverage of a dependent during the first 30 days of such a dependent special enrollment period, the coverage of the dependent shall become effective—

(i) in the case of marriage, not later than the first day of the first month beginning after the date the completed request for enrollment is received;

(ii) in the case of a dependent's birth, as of the date of such birth; or

(iii) in the case of a dependent's adoption or placement for adoption, the date of such adoption or placement for adoption.

(3) Special rules relating to Medicaid and CHIP.

(A) In general. A group health plan shall permit an employee who is eligible, but not enrolled, for coverage under the terms of the plan (or a dependent of such an employee if the dependent is eligible, but not enrolled, for coverage under such terms) to enroll for coverage under the terms of the plan if either of the following conditions is met:

(i) Termination of Medicaid or CHIP coverage. The employee or dependent is covered under a Medicaid plan under title XIX of the Social Security Act or under a State child health plan under title XXI of such Act and coverage of the employee or dependent under such a plan is terminated as a result of loss of eligibility for such coverage and the employee requests coverage under the group health plan not later than 60 days after the date of termination of such coverage.

(ii) Eligibility for employment assistance under Medicaid or CHIP. The employee or dependent becomes eligible for assistance, with respect to coverage under the group health plan under such Medicaid plan or State child health plan (including under any waiver or demonstration project conducted under or in relation to such a plan), if the employee requests coverage under the group health plan not later than 60 days after the date the employee or dependent is determined to be eligible for such assistance.

(B) Employee outreach and disclosure.

(i) Outreach to employees regarding availability of Medicaid and CHIP coverage.

(I) In general. Each employer that maintains a group health plan in a State that provides medical assistance under a State Medicaid plan under title XIX of the Social Security Act, or child health assistance under a State child health plan under title XXI of such Act, in the form of premium assistance for the purchase of coverage under a group health plan, shall provide to each employee a written notice informing the employee of potential opportunities then currently available in the State in which the employee resides for premium assistance under such plans for health coverage of the employee or the employee's dependents. For purposes of compliance with this clause, the employer may use any State-specific model notice developed in accordance with section 701(f)(3)(B)(i)(II) of the Employee Retirement Income Security Act of 1974 (29 U.S.C. 1181(f)(3)(B)(i)(II)).

(II) Option to provide concurrent with provision of plan materials to employee. An employer may provide the model notice applicable to the State in which an employee resides concurrent with the furnishing of materials notifying the employee of health plan eligibility, concurrent with materials provided to the employee in connection with an open season or election process conducted under the plan, or concurrent with the furnishing of the summary plan description as provided in section 104(b) of the Employee Retirement Income Security Act of 1974 (29 U.S.C. 1024).

Establishment of trust funds

Code Sec. 9802(a)(2)(A)

"(ii) Disclosure about group health plan benefits to States for Medicaid and CHIP eligible individuals. In the case of a participant or beneficiary of a group health plan who is covered under a Medicaid plan of a State under title XIX of the Social Security Act or under a State child health plan under title XXI of such Act, the plan administrator of the group health plan shall disclose to the State, upon request, information about the benefits available under the group health plan in sufficient specificity, as determined under regulations of the Secretary of Health and Human Services in consultation with the Secretary that require use of the model coverage coordination disclosure form developed under section 311(b)(1)(C) of the Children's Health Insurance Program Reauthorization Act of 2009, so as to permit the State to make a determination (under paragraph (2)(B), (3), or (10) of section 2105(c) of the Social Security Act or otherwise) concerning the cost-effectiveness of the State providing medical or child health assistance through premium assistance for the purchase of coverage under such group health plan and in order for the State to provide supplemental benefits required under paragraph (10)(E) of such section or other authority.

In 2010, P.L. 111-344, Sec. 114(a), substituted "February 13, 2011" for "January 1, 2011" in subpara. (c)(2)(D), effective for plan yrs. begin. after 12/31/2010.

In 2009, P.L. 111-5, Sec. 1899D(a), added subpara. (c)(2)(D), effective for plan years begin. after 2/17/2009.

—P.L. 111-3, Sec. 311(a), added para. (f)(3), effective as provided by Sec. 3 of this Act, which reads as follows:

"SEC. 3. GENERAL EFFECTIVE DATE; EXCEPTION FOR STATE LEGISLATION; CONTINGENT EFFECTIVE DATE; RELIANCE ON LAW.

"*(a) General effective date.* Unless otherwise provided in this Act, subject to subsections (b) through (d), this Act (and the amendments made by this Act) shall take effect on April 1, 2009, and shall apply to child health assistance and medical assistance provided on or after that date.

"*(b) Exception for state legislation.* In the case of a State plan under title XIX or State child health plan under XXI of the Social Security Act, which the Secretary of Health and Human Services determines requires State legislation in order for the respective plan to meet one or more additional requirements imposed by amendments made by this Act, the respective plan shall not be regarded as failing to comply with the requirements of such title solely on the basis of its failure to meet such an additional requirement before the first day of the first calendar quarter beginning after the close of the first regular session of the State legislature that begins after the date of enactment of this Act. For purposes of the previous sentence, in the case of a State that has a 2-year legislative session, each year of the session shall be considered to be a separate regular session of the State legislature.

"*(c) Coordination of CHIP Funding for fiscal year 2009.* Notwithstanding any other provision of law, insofar as funds have been appropriated under section 2104(a)(11), 2104(k), or 2104(l) of the Social Security Act, as amended by section 201 of Public Law 110-173, to provide allotments to States under CHIP for fiscal year 2009—

"(1) any amounts that are so appropriated that are not so allotted and obligated before April 1, 2009, are rescinded; and

"(2) any amount provided for CHIP allotments to a State under this Act (and the amendments made by this Act) for such fiscal year shall be reduced by the amount of such appropriations so allotted and obligated before such date.

"*(d) Reliance on law.* With respect to amendments made by this Act (other than title VII) that become effective as of a date—

"(1) such amendments are effective as of such date whether or not regulations implementing such amendments have been issued; and

"(2) Federal financial participation for medical assistance or child health assistance furnished under title XIX or XXI, respectively, of the Social Security Act on or after such date by a State in good faith reliance on such amendments before the date of promulgation of final regulations, if any, to carry out such amendments (or before the date of guidance, if any, regarding the implementation of such amendments) shall not be denied on the basis of the State's failure to comply with such regulations or guidance."

In 1997, P.L. 105-34, Sec. 1351(b)(1)(A), substituted "section 9832(c)" for "9805(c)" in para. (c)(1), effective for group health plans for plan yrs. begin. on or after 1/1/98.

In 1996, P.L. 104-191, Sec. 401(a), added Code Sec. 9801, effective for plan. yrs. begin. after 6/30/97. Sec. 401(c)(2)-(5) of this Act reads as follows:

"(2) Determination of creditable coverage.

"(A) Period of coverage.

"(i) In general. Subject to clause (ii), no period before July 1, 1996, shall be taken into account under chapter 100 of the Internal Revenue Code of 1986 (as added by this section) in determining creditable coverage.

"(ii) Special rule for certain periods. The Secretary of the Treasury, consistent with section 104, shall provide for a process whereby individuals who need to establish creditable coverage for periods before July 1, 1996, and who would have such coverage credited but for clause (i) may be given credit for creditable coverage for such periods through the presentation of documents or other means.

"(B) Certifications, etc.

"(i) In general. Subject to clauses (ii) and (iii), subsection (e) of section 9801 of the Internal Revenue Code of 1986 (as added by this section) shall apply to events occurring after June 30, 1996.

"(ii) No certification required to be provided before June 1, 1997. In no case is a certification required to be provided under such subsection before June 1, 1997.

"(iii) Certification only on written request for events occurring before October 1, 1996. In the case of an event occurring after June 30, 1996, and before October 1, 1996, a certification is not required to be provided under such subsection unless an individual (with respect to whom the certification is otherwise required to be made) requests such certification in writing.

"(C) Transitional rule. In the case of an individual who seeks to establish creditable coverage for any period for which certification is not required because it relates to an event occurring before June 30, 1996—

"(i) the individual may present other credible evidence of such coverage in order to establish the period of creditable coverage; and

"(ii) a group health plan and a health insurance issuer shall not be subject to any penalty or enforcement action with respect to the plan's or issuer's crediting (or not crediting) such coverage if the plan or issuer has sought to comply in good faith with the applicable requirements under the amendments made by this section.

"(3) Special rule for collective bargaining agreements. Except as provided in paragraph (2), in the case of a group health plan maintained pursuant to 1 or more collective bargaining agreements between employee representatives and one or more employers ratified before the date of the enactment of this Act, the amendments made by this section shall not apply to plan years beginning before the later of—

"(A) the date on which the last of the collective bargaining agreements relating to the plan terminates (determined without regard to any extension thereof agreed to after the date of the enactment of this Act), or

"(B) July 1, 1997.

For purposes of subparagraph (A), any plan amendment made pursuant to a collective bargaining agreement relating to the plan which amends the plan solely to conform to any requirement added by this section shall not be treated as a termination of such collective bargaining agreement.

"(4) Timely regulations. The Secretary of the Treasury, consistent with section 104, shall first issue by not later than April 1, 1997, such regulations as may be necessary to carry out the amendments made by this section.

"(5) Limitation on actions. No enforcement action shall be taken, pursuant to the amendments made by this section, against a group health plan or health insurance issuer with respect to a violation of a requirement imposed by such amendments before January 1, 1998, or, if later, the date of issuance of regulations referred to in paragraph (4), if the plan or issuer has sought to comply in good faith with such requirements."

Sec. 9802. Prohibiting discrimination against individual participants and beneficiaries based on health status.

(a) In eligibility to enroll.

(1) In general. Subject to paragraph (2), a group health plan may not establish rules for eligibility (including continued eligibility) of any individual to enroll under the terms of the plan based on any of the following factors in relation to the individual or a dependent of the individual:

(A) Health status.

(B) Medical condition (including both physical and mental illnesses).

(C) Claims experience.

(D) Receipt of health care.

(E) Medical history.

(F) Genetic information.

(G) Evidence of insurability (including conditions arising out of acts of domestic violence).

(H) Disability.

(2) No application to benefits or exclusions. To the extent consistent with section 9801, paragraph (1) shall not be construed—

(A) to require a group health plan to provide particular benefits (or benefits with respect to a specific procedure, treatment, or service) other than those provided under the terms of such plan; or

4,033

(B) to prevent such a plan from establishing limitations or restrictions on the amount, level, extent, or nature of the benefits or coverage for similarly situated individuals enrolled in the plan or coverage.

(3) **Construction.** For purposes of paragraph (1), rules for eligibility to enroll under a plan include rules defining any applicable waiting periods for such enrollment.

(b) In premium contributions.

(1) **In general.** A group health plan may not require any individual (as a condition of enrollment or continued enrollment under the plan) to pay a premium or contribution which is greater than such premium or contribution for a similarly situated individual enrolled in the plan on the basis of any factor described in subsection (a)(1) in relation to the individual or to an individual enrolled under the plan as a dependent of the individual.

(2) **Construction.** Nothing in paragraph (1) shall be construed—

(A) to restrict the amount that an employer may be charged for coverage under a group health plan except as provided in paragraph (3); or

(B) to prevent a group health plan from establishing premium discounts or rebates or modifying otherwise applicable copayments or deductibles in return for adherence to programs of health promotion and disease prevention.

(3) **No group-based discrimination on basis of genetic information.**

(A) In general. For purposes of this section, a group health plan may not adjust premium or contribution amounts for the group covered under such plan on the basis of genetic information.

(B) Rule of construction. Nothing in subparagraph (A) or in paragraphs (1) and (2) of subsection (d) shall be construed to limit the ability of a group health plan to increase the premium for an employer based on the manifestation of a disease or disorder of an individual who is enrolled in the plan. In such case, the manifestation of a disease or disorder in one individual cannot also be used as genetic information about other group members and to further increase the premium for the employer.

(c) Genetic testing.

(1) **Limitation on requesting or requiring genetic testing.** A group health plan may not request or require an individual or a family member of such individual to undergo a genetic test.

(2) **Rule of construction.** Paragraph (1) shall not be construed to limit the authority of a health care professional who is providing health care services to an individual to request that such individual undergo a genetic test.

(3) **Rule of construction regarding payment.**

(A) In general. Nothing in paragraph (1) shall be construed to preclude a group health plan from obtaining and using the results of a genetic test in making a determination regarding payment (as such term is defined for the purposes of applying the regulations promulgated by the Secretary of Health and Human Services under part C of title XI of the Social Security Act and section 264 of the Health Insurance Portability and Accountability Act of 1996, as may be revised from time to time) consistent with subsection (a).

(B) Limitation. For purposes of subparagraph (A), a group health plan may request only the minimum amount of information necessary to accomplish the intended purpose.

(4) **Research exception.** Notwithstanding paragraph (1), a group health plan may request, but not require, that a participant or beneficiary undergo a genetic test if each of the following conditions is met:

(A) The request is made pursuant to research that complies with part 46 of title 45, Code of Federal Regulations, or equivalent Federal regulations, and any applicable State or local law or regulations for the protection of human subjects in research.

(B) The plan clearly indicates to each participant or beneficiary, or in the case of a minor child, to the legal guardian of such beneficiary, to whom the request is made that—

(i) compliance with the request is voluntary; and

(ii) non-compliance will have no effect on enrollment status or premium or contribution amounts.

(C) No genetic information collected or acquired under this paragraph shall be used for underwriting purposes.

(D) The plan notifies the Secretary in writing that the plan is conducting activities pursuant to the exception provided for under this paragraph, including a description of the activities conducted.

(E) The plan complies with such other conditions as the Secretary may by regulation require for activities conducted under this paragraph.

(d) Prohibition on collection of genetic information.

(1) **In general.** A group health plan shall not request, require, or purchase genetic information for underwriting purposes (as defined in section 9832).

(2) **Prohibition on collection of genetic information prior to enrollment.** A group health plan shall not request, require, or purchase genetic information with respect to any individual prior to such individual's enrollment under the plan or in connection with such enrollment.

(3) **Incidental collection.** If a group health plan obtains genetic information incidental to the requesting, requiring, or purchasing of other information concerning any individual, such request, requirement, or purchase shall not be considered a violation of paragraph (2) if such request, requirement, or purchase is not in violation of paragraph (1).

(e) Application to all plans.

The provisions of subsections (a)(1)(F), (b)(3), (c), and (d) and subsection (b)(1) and section 9801 with respect to genetic information, shall apply to group health plans without regard to section 9831(a)(2).

(f) Special rules for church plans.

A church plan (as defined in section 414(e)) shall not be treated as failing to meet the requirements of this section solely because such plan requires evidence of good health for coverage of—

(1) both any employee of an employer of 10 or less employees (determined without regard to section 414(e)(3)(C)) and any self-employed individual, or

(2) any individual who enrolls after the first 90 days of initial eligibility under the plan.

This subsection shall apply to a plan for any year only if the plan included in the provisions described in the preceding sentence on July 15, 1997, and at all times thereafter before the beginning of such year.

(f sic[(g)]) Genetic information of a fetus or embryo.

Any reference in this chapter to genetic information concerning an individual or family member of an individual shall—

(1) with respect to such an individual or family member of an individual who is a pregnant woman, include genetic

Establishment of trust funds

Code Sec. 9803

information of any fetus carried by such pregnant woman; and

(2) with respect to an individual or family member utilizing an assisted reproductive technology, include genetic information of any embryo legally held by the individual or family member.

In 2008, P.L. 110-233, Sec. 103(a)(1), added matter in subpara. (b)(2)(A)... Sec. 103(a)(2), added para. (b)(3)... Sec. 103(b), redesignated subsec. (c) as subsec. (f) and added new subsecs. (c), (d) and (e)... Sec. 103(c), added subsec. (f) [sic (g)] effective for group health plans for plan yrs. begin. after the date that is 1 year after 5/21/2009.

Prior to amendment, subsec. (f) [as redesignated by this Act] read as follows:

"(c) Special rules for church plans. A church plan (as defined in section 414(e)) shall not be treated as failing to meet the requirements of this section solely because such plan requires evidence of good health for coverage of—

"(1) both any employee of an employer of 10 or less employees (determined without regard to section 414(e)(3)(C)) and any self-employed individual, or

"(2) any individual who enrolls after the first 90 days of initial eligibility under the plan.

"This subsection shall apply to a plan for any year only if the plan included in the provisions described in the preceding sentence on July 15, 1997, and at all times thereafter before the beginning of such year."

—P.L. 110-233, Sec. 103(f)(1), of this Act provides:

"(f) Regulations and effective date.

"(1) Regulations. The Secretary of the Treasury shall issue final regulations or other guidance not later than 12 months after the date of the enactment of this Act [5/21/2009] to carry out the amendments made by this section."

In 1997, P.L. 105-34, Sec. 1532(a), added subsec. (c), effective for plan yrs. begin. after 6/30/97.

In 1996, P.L. 104-191, Sec. 401(a), added Code Sec. 9802, effective for plan. yrs. begin. after 6/30/97. Sec. 401(c)(2)-(5) of this Act reads as follows:

"(2) Determination of creditable coverage.

"(A) Period of coverage.

"(i) In general. Subject to clause (ii), no period before July 1, 1996, shall be taken into account under chapter 100 of the Internal Revenue Code of 1986 (as added by this section) in determining creditable coverage.

"(ii) Special rule for certain periods. The Secretary of the Treasury, consistent with section 104, shall provide for a process whereby individuals who need to establish creditable coverage for periods before July 1, 1996, and who would have such coverage credited but for clause (i) may be given credit for creditable coverage for such periods through the presentation of documents or other means.

"(B) Certifications, etc.

"(i) In general. Subject to clauses (ii) and (iii), subsection (e) of section 9801 of the Internal Revenue Code of 1986 (as added by this section) shall apply to events occurring after June 30, 1996.

"(ii) No certification required to be provided before June 1, 1997. In no case is a certification required to be provided under such subsection before June 1, 1997.

"(iii) Certification only on written request for events occurring before October 1, 1996. In the case of an event occurring after June 30, 1996, and before October 1, 1996, a certification is not required to be provided under such subsection unless an individual (with respect to whom the certification is otherwise required to be made) requests such certification in writing.

"(C) Transitional rule. In the case of an individual who seeks to establish creditable coverage for any period for which certification is not required because it relates to an event occurring before June 30, 1996—

"(i) the individual may present other credible evidence of such coverage in order to establish the period of creditable coverage; and

"(ii) a group health plan and a health insurance issuer shall not be subject to any penalty or enforcement action with respect to the plan's or issuer's crediting (or not crediting) such coverage if the plan or issuer has sought to comply in good faith with the applicable requirements under the amendments made by this section.

"(3) Special rule for collective bargaining agreements. Except as provided in paragraph (2), in the case of a group health plan maintained pursuant to 1 or more collective bargaining agreements between employee representatives and one or more employers ratified before the date of the enactment of this Act, the amendments made by this section shall not apply to plan years beginning before the later of—

"(A) the date on which the last of the collective bargaining agreements relating to the plan terminates (determined without regard to any extension thereof agreed to after the date of the enactment of this Act), or

"(B) July 1, 1997.

For purposes of subparagraph (A), any plan amendment made pursuant to a collective bargaining agreement relating to the plan which amends the plan solely to conform to any requirement added by this section shall not be treated as a termination of such collective bargaining agreement.

"(4) Timely regulations. The Secretary of the Treasury, consistent with section 104, shall first issue by not later than April 1, 1997, such regulations as may be necessary to carry out the amendments made by this section.

"(5) Limitation on actions. No enforcement action shall be taken, pursuant to the amendments made by this section, against a group health plan or health insurance issuer with respect to a violation of a requirement imposed by such amendments before January 1, 1998, or, if later, the date of issuance of regulations referred to in paragraph (4), if the plan or issuer has sought to comply in good faith with such requirements."

Sec. 9803. Guaranteed renewability in multiemployer plans and certain multiple employer welfare arrangements.

(a) In general.

A group health plan which is a multiemployer plan (as defined in section 414(f)) or which is a multiple employer welfare arrangement may not deny an employer continued access to the same or different coverage under such plan, other than—

(1) for nonpayment of contributions.

(2) for fraud or other intentional misrepresentation of material fact by the employer;

(3) for noncompliance with material plan provisions;

(4) because the plan is ceasing to offer any coverage in a geographic area;

(5) in the case of a plan that offers benefits through a network plan, because there is no longer any individual enrolled through the employer who lives, resides, or works in the service area of the network plan and the plan applies this paragraph uniformly without regard to the claims experience of employers or a factor described in section 9802(a)(1) in relation to such individuals or their dependents; or

(6) for failure to meet the terms of an applicable collective bargaining agreement, to renew a collective bargaining or other agreement requiring or authorizing contributions to the plan, or to employ employees covered by such an agreement.

(b) Multiple employer welfare arrangement.

For purposes of subsection (a), the term "multiple employer welfare arrangement" has the meaning given such term by section 3(40) of the Employer Retirement Income Security Act of 1974, as in effect on the date of the enactment of this section.

In 1996, P.L. 104-191, Sec. 401(a), added Code Sec. 9803, effective for plan. yrs. begin. after 6/30/97. Sec. 401(c)(2)-(5) of this Act reads as follows:

"(2) Determination of creditable coverage.

"(A) Period of coverage.

"(i) In general. Subject to clause (ii), no period before July 1, 1996, shall be taken into account under chapter 100 of the Internal Revenue Code of 1986 (as added by this section) in determining creditable coverage.

"(ii) Special rule for certain periods. The Secretary of the Treasury, consistent with section 104, shall provide for a process whereby individuals who need to establish creditable coverage for periods before July 1, 1996, and who would have such coverage credited but for clause (i) may be given credit for creditable coverage for such periods through the presentation of documents or other means.

"(B) Certifications, etc.

"(i) In general. Subject to clauses (ii) and (iii), subsection (e) of section 9801 of the Internal Revenue Code of 1986 (as added by this section) shall apply to events occurring after June 30, 1996.

"(ii) No certification required to be provided before June 1, 1997. In no case is a certification required to be provided under such subsection before June 1, 1997.

"(iii) Certification only on written request for events occurring before October 1, 1996. In the case of an event occurring after June 30, 1996, and before October 1, 1996, a certification is not required to be provided under such subsection unless an individual (with respect to whom the certification is otherwise required to be made) requests such certification in writing.

"(C) Transitional rule. In the case of an individual who seeks to establish creditable coverage for any period for which certification is not required because it relates to an event occurring before June 30, 1996—

"(i) the individual may present other credible evidence of such coverage in order to establish the period of creditable coverage; and

"(ii) a group health plan and a health insurance issuer shall not be subject to any penalty or enforcement action with respect to the plan's or issuer's crediting (or not crediting) such coverage if the plan or issuer has sought to comply in good faith with the applicable requirements under the amendments made by this section.

"(3) Special rule for collective bargaining agreements. Except as provided in paragraph (2), in the case of a group health plan maintained pursuant to 1 or more collective bargaining agreements between employee representatives and one or more employers ratified before the date of the enactment of this Act, the amendments made by this section shall not apply to plan years beginning before the later of—

Code Sec. 9803 — Establishment of trust funds

"(A) the date on which the last of the collective bargaining agreements relating to the plan terminates (determined without regard to any extension thereof agreed to after the date of the enactment of this Act), or

"(B) July 1, 1997.

For purposes of subparagraph (A), any plan amendment made pursuant to a collective bargaining agreement relating to the plan which amends the plan solely to conform to any requirement added by this section shall not be treated as a termination of such collective bargaining agreement.

"(4) Timely regulations. The Secretary of the Treasury, consistent with section 104, shall first issue by not later than April 1, 1997, such regulations as may be necessary to carry out the amendments made by this section.

"(5) Limitation on actions. No enforcement action shall be taken, pursuant to the amendments made by this section, against a group health plan or health insurance issuer with respect to a violation of a requirement imposed by such amendments before January 1, 1998, or, if later, the date of issuance of regulations referred to in paragraph (4), if the plan or issuer has sought to comply in good faith with such requirements."

Subchapter B.—Other Requirements

Sec.
9811. Standards relating to benefits for mothers and newborns.
9812. Parity in the application of certain limits to mental health benefits.
9813. Coverage of dependent students on medically necessary leave of absence.
9815. Additional market reforms.

In 2010, P.L. 111-148, added item 9815
In 2008, P.L. 110-381, Sec. 2(c)(1), added item 9813.
In 1997, P.L. , Sec. 1531(a)(4), amended chapter 100 of Subtitle K by adding Subchapter B.

Sec. 9811. Standards relating to benefits for mothers and newborns.

(a) Requirements for minimum hospital stay following birth.

(1) In general. A group health plan may not—
  (A) except as provided in paragraph (2)—
    (i) restrict benefits for any hospital length of stay in connection with childbirth for the mother or newborn child, following a normal vaginal delivery, to less than 48 hours, or
    (ii) restrict benefits for any hospital length of stay in connection with childbirth for the mother or newborn child, following a caesarean section, to less than 96 hours; or
  (B) require that a provider obtain authorization from the plan or the issuer for prescribing any length of stay required under subparagraph (A) (without regard to paragraph (2)).

(2) Exception. Paragraph (1)(A) shall not apply in connection with any group health plan in any case in which the decision to discharge the mother or her newborn child prior to the expiration of the minimum length of stay otherwise required under paragraph (1)(A) is made by an attending provider in consultation with the mother.

(b) Prohibitions.

A group health plan may not—
(1) deny to the mother or her newborn child eligibility, or continued eligibility, to enroll or to renew coverage under the terms of the plan, solely for the purpose of avoiding the requirements of this section;
(2) provide monetary payments or rebates to mothers to encourage such mothers to accept less than the minimum protections available under this section;
(3) penalize or otherwise reduce or limit the reimbursement of an attending provider because such provider provided care to an individual participant or beneficiary in accordance with this section;
(4) provide incentives (monetary or otherwise) to an attending provider to induce such provider to provide care to an individual participant or beneficiary in a manner inconsistent with this section; or
(5) subject to subsection (c)(3), restrict benefits for any portion of a period within a hospital length of stay required under subsection (a) in a manner which is less favorable than the benefits provided for any preceding portion of such stay.

(c) Rules of construction.

(1) Nothing in this section shall be construed to require a mother who is a participant or beneficiary—
  (A) to give birth in a hospital; or
  (B) to stay in the hospital for a fixed period of time following the birth of her child.
(2) This section shall not apply with respect to any group health plan which does not provide benefits for hospital lengths of stay in connection with childbirth for a mother or her newborn child.
(3) Nothing in this section shall be construed as preventing a group health plan from imposing deductibles, coinsurance, or other cost-sharing in relation to benefits for hospital lengths of stay in connection with childbirth for a mother or newborn child under the plan, except that such coinsurance or other cost-sharing for any portion of a period within a hospital length of stay required under subsection (a) may not be greater than such coinsurance or cost-sharing for any preceding portion of such stay.

(d) Level and type of reimbursements.

Nothing in this section shall be construed to prevent a group health plan from negotiating the level and type of reimbursement with a provider for care provided in accordance with this section.

(e) Preemption; exception for health insurance coverage in certain states.

The requirements of this section shall not apply with respect to health insurance coverage if there is a State law (including a decision, rule, regulation, or other State action having the effect of law) for a State that regulates such coverage that is described in any of the following paragraphs:

(1) Such State law requires such coverage to provide for at least a 48-hour hospital length of stay following a normal vaginal delivery and at least a 96-hour hospital length of stay following a caesarean section.
(2) Such State law requires such coverage to provide for maternity and pediatric care in accordance with guidelines established by the American College of Obstetricians and Gynecologists, the American Academy of Pediatrics, or other established professional medical associations.
(3) Such State law requires, in connection with such coverage for maternity care, that the hospital length of stay for such care is left to the decision of (or required to be made by) the attending provider in consultation with the mother.

In 1998, P.L. 105-206, Sec. 6015(e), redesignated subsec. (f) as subsec. (e), effective for group health plans for plan yrs. begin. on or after 1/1/98.
In 1997, P.L. 105-34, Sec. 1531(a)(4), added Code Sec. 9811, effective for group health plans for plan yrs. begin. on or after 1/1/98.

Sec. 9812. Parity in mental health and substance use disorder benefits.

(a) In general.

(1) Aggregate lifetime limits. In the case of a group health plan that provides both medical and surgical benefits and mental health or substance use disorder benefits—
  (A) No lifetime limit. If the plan does not include an aggregate lifetime limit on substantially all medical and

Group Health Plans

Code Sec. 9812(c)(1)(B)

surgical benefits, the plan may not impose any aggregate lifetime limit on mental health or substance use disorder benefits.

(B) Lifetime limit. If the plan includes an aggregate lifetime limit on substantially all medical and surgical benefits (in this paragraph referred to as the "applicable lifetime limit"), the plan shall either—

(i) apply the applicable lifetime limit both to the medical and surgical benefits to which it otherwise would apply and to mental health and substance use disorder benefits and not distinguish in the application of such limit between such medical and surgical benefits and mental health and substance use disorder benefits; or

(ii) not include any aggregate lifetime limit on mental health or substance use disorder benefits that is less than the applicable lifetime limit.

(C) Rule in case of different limits. In the case of a plan that is not described in subparagraph (A) or (B) and that includes no or different aggregate lifetime limits on different categories of medical and surgical benefits, the Secretary shall establish rules under which subparagraph (B) is applied to such plan with respect to mental health and substance use disorder benefits by substituting for the applicable lifetime limit an average aggregate lifetime limit that is computed taking into account the weighted average of the aggregate lifetime limits applicable to such categories.

(2) **Annual limits.** In the case of a group health plan that provides both medical and surgical benefits and mental health or substance use disorder benefits—

(A) No annual limit. If the plan does not include an annual limit on substantially all medical and surgical benefits, the plan may not impose any annual limit on mental health or substance use disorder benefits.

(B) Annual limit. If the plan includes an annual limit on substantially all medical and surgical benefits (in this paragraph referred to as the "applicable annual limit"), the plan shall either—

(i) apply the applicable annual limit both to medical and surgical benefits to which it otherwise would apply and to mental health and substance use disorder benefits and not distinguish in the application of such limit between such medical and surgical benefits and mental health and substance use disorder benefits; or

(ii) not include any annual limit on mental health or substance use disorder benefits that is less than the applicable annual limit.

(C) Rule in case of different limits. In the case of a plan that is not described in subparagraph (A) or (B) and that includes no or different annual limits on different categories of medical and surgical benefits, the Secretary shall establish rules under which subparagraph (B) is applied to such plan with respect to mental health and substance use disorder benefits by substituting for the applicable annual limit an average annual limit that is computed taking into account the weighted average of the annual limits applicable to such categories.

(3) **Financial requirements and treatment limitations.**

(A) In general. In the case of a group health plan that provides both medical and surgical benefits and mental health or substance use disorder benefits, such plan shall ensure that—

(i) the financial requirements applicable to such mental health or substance use disorder benefits are no more restrictive than the predominant financial requirements applied to substantially all medical and surgical benefits covered by the plan, and there are no separate cost sharing requirements that are applicable only with respect to mental health or substance use disorder benefits; and

(ii) the treatment limitations applicable to such mental health or substance use disorder benefits are no more restrictive than the predominant treatment limitations applied to substantially all medical and surgical benefits covered by the plan and there are no separate treatment limitations that are applicable only with respect to mental health or substance use disorder benefits.

(B) Definitions. In this paragraph:

(i) Financial requirement. The term "financial requirement" includes deductibles, copayments, coinsurance, and out-of-pocket expenses, but excludes an aggregate lifetime limit and an annual limit subject to paragraphs (1) and (2),

(ii) Predominant. A financial requirement or treatment limit is considered to be predominant if it is the most common or frequent of such type of limit or requirement.

(iii) Treatment limitation. The term "treatment limitation" includes limits on the frequency of treatment, number of visits, days of coverage, or other similar limits on the scope or duration of treatment.

(4) **Availability of plan information.** The criteria for medical necessity determinations made under the plan with respect to mental health or substance use disorder benefits shall be made available by the plan administrator in accordance with regulations to any current or potential participant, beneficiary, or contracting provider upon request. The reason for any denial under the plan of reimbursement or payment for services with respect to mental health or substance use disorder benefits in the case of any participant or beneficiary shall, on request or as otherwise required, be made available by the plan administrator to the participant or beneficiary in accordance with regulations.

(5) **Out-of-network providers.** In the case of a plan that provides both medical and surgical benefits and mental health or substance use disorder benefits, if the plan provides coverage for medical or surgical benefits provided by out-of-network providers, the plan shall provide coverage for mental health or substance use disorder benefits provided by out-of-network providers in a manner that is consistent with the requirements of this section.

(b) **Construction.**

Nothing in this section shall be construed—

(1) as requiring a group health plan to provide any mental health or substance use disorder benefits; or

(2) in the case of a group health plan that provides mental health or substance use disorder benefits, as affecting the terms and conditions of the plan relating to such benefits under the plan, except as provided in subsection (a).

(c) **Exemptions.**

(1) **Small employer exemption.**

(A) In general. This section shall not apply to any group health plan for any plan year of a small employer.

(B) Small employer. For purposes of subparagraph (A), the term "small employer" means, with respect to a calendar year and a plan year, an employer who employed an average of at least 2 (or 1 in the case of an employer residing in a State that permits small groups to include a single individual) but not more than 50 employees on business days during the preceding calendar

4,037

year. For purposes of the preceding sentence, all persons treated as a single employer under subsection (b), (c), (m), or (o) of section 414 shall be treated as 1 employer and rules similar to rules of subparagraphs (B) and (C) of section 4980D(d)(2) shall apply.

(2) Cost exemption.

(A) In general. With respect to a group health plan, if the application of this section to such plan results in an increase for the plan year involved of the actual total costs of coverage with respect to medical and surgical benefits and mental health and substance use disorder benefits under the plan (as determined and certified under subparagraph (C)) by an amount that exceeds the applicable percentage described in subparagraph (B) of the actual total plan costs, the provisions of this section shall not apply to such plan during the following plan year, and such exemption shall apply to the plan for 1 plan year. An employer may elect to continue to apply mental health and substance use disorder parity pursuant to this section with respect to the group health plan involved regardless of any increase in total costs.

(B) Applicable percentage. With respect to a plan, the applicable percentage described in this subparagraph shall be—

(i) 2 percent in the case of the first plan year in which this section is applied; and

(ii) 1 percent in the case of each subsequent plan year.

(C) Determinations by actuaries. Determinations as to increases in actual costs under a plan for purposes of this section shall be made and certified by a qualified and licensed actuary who is a member in good standing of the American Academy of Actuaries. All such determinations shall be in a written report prepared by the actuary. The report, and all underlying documentation relied upon by the actuary, shall be maintained by the group health plan for a period of 6 years following the notification made under subparagraph (E).

(D) 6-month determinations. If a group health plan seeks an exemption under this paragraph, determinations under subparagraph (A) shall be made after such plan has complied with this section for the first 6 months of the plan year involved.

(E) Notification.

(i) In general. A group health plan that, based upon a certification described under subparagraph (C), qualifies for an exemption under this paragraph, and elects to implement the exemption, shall promptly notify the Secretary, the appropriate State agencies, and participants and beneficiaries in the plan of such election.

(ii) Requirement. A notification to the Secretary under clause (i) shall include—

(I) a description of the number of covered lives under the plan involved at the time of the notification, and as applicable, at the time of any prior election of the cost-exemption under this paragraph by such plan;

(II) for both the plan year upon which a cost exemption is sought and the year prior, a description of the actual total costs of coverage with respect to medical and surgical benefits and mental health and substance use disorder benefits under the plan; and

(III) for both the plan year upon which a cost exemption is sought and the year prior, the actual total costs of coverage with respect to mental health and substance use disorder benefits under the plan.

(iii) Confidentiality. A notification to the Secretary under clause (i) shall be confidential. The Secretary shall make available, upon request and on not more than an annual basis, an anonymous itemization of such notifications, that includes—

(I) a breakdown of States by the size and type of employers submitting such notification; and

(II) a summary of the data received under clause (ii).

(F) Audits by appropriate agencies. To determine compliance with this paragraph, the Secretary may audit the books and records of a group health plan relating to an exemption, including any actuarial reports prepared pursuant to subparagraph (C), during the 6 year period following the notification of such exemption under subparagraph (E). A State agency receiving a notification under subparagraph (E) may also conduct such an audit with respect to an exemption covered by such notification.

(d) Separate application to each option offered.

In the case of a group health plan that offers a participant or beneficiary two or more benefit package options under the plan, the requirements of this section shall be applied separately with respect to each such option.

(e) Definitions.

For purposes of this section:

(1) Aggregate lifetime limit. The term "aggregate lifetime limit" means, with respect to benefits under a group health plan, a dollar limitation on the total amount that may be paid with respect to such benefits under the plan with respect to an individual or other coverage unit.

(2) Annual limit. The term "annual limit" means, with respect to benefits under a group health plan, a dollar limitation on the total amount of benefits that may be paid with respect to such benefits in a 12-month period under the plan with respect to an individual or other coverage unit.

(3) Medical or surgical benefits. The term "medical or surgical benefits" means benefits with respect to medical or surgical services, as defined under the terms of the plan, but does not include mental health or substance use disorder benefits.

(4) Mental health or substance use disorder benefits. The term "mental health or substance use disorder benefits" means benefits with respect to services for mental health conditions, as defined under the terms of the plan and in accordance with applicable Federal and State law.

(5) Substance use disorder benefits. The term "substance use disorder benefits" means benefits with respect to services for substance use disorders, as defined under the terms of the plan and in accordance with applicable Federal and State law.

(f) Repealed.

In **2008**, P.L. 110-460, Sec. 1, substituted "January 1, 2010" for "January 1, 2009" in Sec. 512(e)(2)(B), P.L. 110-343, reproduced below. Sec. 512(e), P.L. 110-343, provides the effective dates for amendments made by Sec. 512, P.L. 110-343.

— P.L. 110-343, Sec. 512(c)(1)DivC, added paras. (a)(3)-(5) . . . Sec. 512(c)(2)DivC, amended para. (b)(2) . . . Sec. 512(c)(3)(A)DivC, amended para. (c)(1) . . . Sec. 512(c)(3)(B)DivC, amended para. (c)(2) . . . Sec. 512(c)(4)DivC, deleted para. (e)(4) and added paras. (e)(4)-(5) . . . Sec. 512(c)(5)DivC, deleted subsec. (f) . . . Sec. 512(c)(6)DivC, substituted "mental health and substance use disorder benefits" for "mental health benefits" each place it appeared in clause (a)(1)(B)(i), subpara. (a)(1)(C), clause (a)(2)(B)(i) and subpara. (a)(2)(C) . . . Sec. 512(c)(7)DivC, substituted "mental health or substance use disorder benefits" for "mental health benefits" each place it appeared in Code Sec. 9812, except for clause (a)(1)(B)(i), subpara. (a)(1)(C), clause (a)(2)(B)(i) and subpara. (a)(2)(C),

effective as provided in Sec. 512(e) Div C of this Act, [as amended by Sec. 1, P.L. 110-460, see above] which reads as follows:
"(e) *Effective date.*
"(1) In general. The amendments made by this section shall apply with respect to group health plans for plan years beginning after the date that is 1 year after the date of enactment of this Act, regardless of whether regulations have been issued to carry out such amendments by such effective date, except that the amendments made by subsections (a)(5), (b)(5), and (c)(5), relating to striking of certain sunset provisions, shall take effect on January 1, 2009.
"(2) Special rule for collective bargaining agreements. In the case of a group health plan maintained pursuant to one or more collective bargaining agreements between employee representatives and one or more employers ratified before the date of the enactment of this Act, the amendments made by this section shall not apply to plan years beginning before the later of—
"(A) the date on which the last of the collective bargaining agreements relating to the plan terminates (determined without regard to any extension thereof agreed to after the date of the enactment of this Act), or
"(B) January 1, 2010.
For purposes of subparagraph (A), any plan amendment made pursuant to a collective bargaining agreement relating to the plan which amends the plan solely to conform to any requirement added by this section shall not be treated as a termination of such collective bargaining agreement."
Prior to amendment, para. (b)(2) read as follows:
"(2) in the case of a group health plan that provides mental health benefits, as affecting the terms and conditions (including cost sharing, limits on numbers of visits or days of coverage, and requirements relating to medical necessity) relating to the amount, duration, or scope of mental health benefits under the plan, except as specifically provided in subsection (a) (in regard to parity in the imposition of aggregate lifetime limits and annual limits for mental health benefits)."
Prior to amendment, para. (c)(1) read as follows:
"(1) Small employer exemption. This section shall not apply to any group health plan for any plan year of a small employer (as defined in section 4980D(d)(2))."
Prior to amendment, para. (c)(2) read as follows:
"(2) Increased cost exemption. This section shall not apply with respect to a group health plan if the application of this section to such plan results in an increase in the cost under the plan of at least 1 percent."
Prior to deletion, para. (e)(4) read as follows:
"(4) Mental health benefits. The term 'mental health benefits' means benefits with respect to mental health services, as defined under the terms of the plan, but does not include benefits with respect to treatment of substance abuse or chemical dependency."
Prior to deletion, subsec. (f) read as follows:
"(f) *Application of section.* This section shall not apply to benefits for services furnished—
"(1) on or after September 30, 2001, and before January 10, 2002,
"(2) on or after January 1, 2004, and before the date of the enactment of the Working Families Tax Relief Act of 2004,
"(3) on or after January 1, 2008, and before the date of the enactment of the Heroes Earnings Assistance and Relief Tax Act of 2008, and
"(4) after December 31, 2008."
— P.L. 110-343, Sec. 512(d) Div C of this Act, reads as follows:
"(d) *Regulations.* Not later than 1 year after the date of enactment of this Act, the Secretaries of Labor, Health and Human Services, and the Treasury shall issue regulations to carry out the amendments made by subsections (a), (b), and (c), respectively."
— P.L. 110-343, Sec. 512(f)DivC, of this Act, reads as follows:
"(f) *Assuring coordination.* The Secretary of Health and Human Services, the Secretary of Labor, and the Secretary of the Treasury may ensure, through the execution or revision of an interagency memorandum of understanding among such Secretaries, that—
"(1) regulations, rulings, and interpretations issued by such Secretaries relating to the same matter over which two or more such Secretaries have responsibility under this section (and the amendments made by this section) are administered so as to have the same effect at all times; and
"(2) coordination of policies relating to enforcing the same requirements through such Secretaries in order to have a coordinated enforcement strategy that avoids duplication of enforcement efforts and assigns priorities in enforcement."
— P.L. 110-343, Sec. 512(g)(3)(A)DivC, amended the heading of Code Sec. 9812, effective as provided in Sec. 512(e) Div C of this Act [see above].
Prior to amendment, the heading of Code Sec. 9812 read as follows:
"SEC. 9812. PARITY IN THE APPLICATION OF CERTAIN LIMITS TO MENTAL HEALTH BENEFITS."
— P.L. 110-343, Sec. 512(h)DivC, of this Act, reads as follows:
"(h) *GAO study on coverage and exclusion of mental health and substance use disorder diagnoses.*
"(1) In general. The Comptroller General of the United States shall conduct a study that analyzes the specific rates, patterns, and trends in coverage and exclusion of specific mental health and substance use disorder diagnoses by health plans and health insurance. The study shall include an analysis of—
"(A) specific coverage rates for all mental health conditions and substance use disorders;
"(B) which diagnoses are most commonly covered or excluded;
"(C) whether implementation of this Act has affected trends in coverage or exclusion of such diagnoses; and

"(D) the impact of covering or excluding specific diagnoses on participants' and enrollees' health, their health care coverage, and the costs of delivering health care.
"(2) Reports. Not later than 3 years after the date of the enactment of this Act, and 2 years after the date of submission the first report under this paragraph, the Comptroller General shall submit to Congress a report on the results of the study con4 ducted under paragraph (1)."
— P.L. 110-245, Sec. 401(1), deleted "and" at the end of para. (f)(2)
— P.L. 110-245, Sec. 401(2), deleted para. (f)(3) and added paras. (f)(3) and (f)(4), effective 6/17/2008.
Prior to deletion, para. (f)(3) read as follows:
"(3) after December 31, 2007."
In 2006, P.L. 109-432, Sec. 115(a), substituted "2007" for "2006" in para. (f)(3), enacted 12/20/2006.
In 2005, P.L. 109-151, Sec. 1(a), substituted "December 31, 2006" for "December 31, 2005" in para. (f)(3), effective 12/30/2005.
In 2004, P.L. 108-311, Sec. 302(a)(1), deleted "and" at the end of para. (f)(1) . . . Sec. 302(a)(2), deleted para. (f)(2) and added paras. (f)(2) and (3), effective 10/4/2004.
Prior to deletion, para. (f)(2) read as follows:
"(2) after December 31, 2003."
In 2002, P.L. 107-147, Sec. 610(a), amended subsec. (f), effective for plan yrs. begin. after 12/31/2000.
Prior to amendment, subsec. (f) read as follows:
"(f) Sunset. This section shall not apply to benefits for services furnished on or after December 31, 2002."
— P.L. 107-116, Sec. 701(c), substituted "December 31, 2002" for "September 30, 2001" in subsec. (f), effective 1/10/2002.
In 1997, P.L. 105-34, Sec. 1531(a)(4), added Code Sec. 9812, effective for group health plans for plan yrs. begin. on or after 1/1/98.

Sec. 9813. Coverage of dependent students on medically necessary leave of absence.
(a) Medically Necessary Leave of Absence.
In this section, the term "medically necessary leave of absence" means, with respect to a dependent child described in subsection (b)(2) in connection with a group health plan, a leave of absence of such child from a postsecondary educational institution (including an institution of higher education as defined in section 102 of the Higher Education Act of 1965), or any other change in enrollment of such child at such an institution, that—
(1) commences while such child is suffering from a serious illness or injury;
(2) is medically necessary; and
(3) causes such child to lose student status for purposes of coverage under the terms of the plan or coverage.
(b) Requirement to Continue Coverage.
(1) In general. In the case of a dependent child described in paragraph (2), a group health plan shall not terminate coverage of such child under such plan due to a medically necessary leave of absence before the date that is the earlier of—
(A) the date that is 1 year after the first day of the medically necessary leave of absence; or
(B) the date on which such coverage would otherwise terminate under the terms of the plan.
(2) Dependent child described. A dependent child described in this paragraph is, with respect to a group health plan, a beneficiary under the plan who—
(A) is a dependent child, under the terms of the plan, of a participant or beneficiary under the plan; and
(B) was enrolled in the plan, on the basis of being a student at a postsecondary educational institution (as described in subsection (a)), immediately before the first day of the medically necessary leave of absence involved.
(3) Certification by physician. Paragraph (1) shall apply to a group health plan only if the plan, or the issuer of health insurance coverage offered in connection with the plan, has received written certification by a treating physician of the dependent child which states that the child is suffering from a serious illness or injury and that the leave

of absence (or other change of enrollment) described in subsection (a) is medically necessary.

(c) Notice.

A group health plan shall include, with any notice regarding a requirement for certification of student status for coverage under the plan, a description of the terms of this section for continued coverage during medically necessary leaves of absence. Such description shall be in language which is understandable to the typical plan participant.

(d) No Change in Benefits.

A dependent child whose benefits are continued under this section shall be entitled to the same benefits as if (during the medically necessary leave of absence) the child continued to be a covered student at the institution of higher education and was not on a medically necessary leave of absence.

(e) Continued Application in Case of Changed Coverage.

If—

(1) a dependent child of a participant or beneficiary is in a period of coverage under a group health plan, pursuant to a medically necessary leave of absence of the child described in subsection (b);

(2) the manner in which the participant or beneficiary is covered under the plan changes, whether through a change in health insurance coverage or health insurance issuer, a change between health insurance coverage and self-insured coverage, or otherwise; and

(3) the coverage as so changed continues to provide coverage of beneficiaries as dependent children,

this section shall apply to coverage of the child under the changed coverage for the remainder of the period of the medically necessary leave of absence of the dependent child under the plan in the same manner as it would have applied if the changed coverage had been the previous coverage.

In 2008, P.L. 110-381, Sec. 2(c)(1), added Code Sec. 9813, effective with respect to plan yrs. begin. on or after the date that is one year after 10/9/2008, and to medically necessary leaves of absence beginning during such plan years.

Sec. 9815. Additional market reforms.
(a) General rule.

Except as provided in subsection (b)—

(1) the provisions of part A of title XXVII of the Public Health Service Act (as amended by the Patient Protection and Affordable Care Act) shall apply to group health plans, and health insurance issuers providing health insurance coverage in connection with group health plans, as if included in this subchapter; and

(2) to the extent that any provision of this subchapter conflicts with a provision of such part A with respect to group health plans, or health insurance issuers providing health insurance coverage in connection with group health plans, the provisions of such part A shall apply.

(b) Exception.

Notwithstanding subsection (a), the provisions of sections 2716 and 2718 of title XXVII of the Public Health Service Act (as amended by the Patient Protection and Affordable Care Act) shall not apply with respect to self-insured group health plans, and the provisions of this subchapter shall continue to apply to such plans as if such sections of the Public Health Service Act (as so amended) had not been enacted.

In 2010, P.L. 111-148, Sec. 1562(f), added Code Sec. 9815, enacted 3/23/2010.

Subchapter C.—General Provisions

Sec.
9831. General exceptions.
9832. Definitions.
9833. Regulations.
9834. Enforcement.
9834. Enforcement.

In 2008, P.L. 110-233, Sec. 103(e)(2), added Code Sec. 9834, effective with respect to group health plans for plan yrs. begin. after the date that is 1 year after 5/21/2008.

In 1997, P.L. 105-34, Sec. 1531(a)(3), amended chapter 100 of Subtitle K by adding Subchapter C.

Sec. 9831. General exceptions.
(a) Exception for certain plans.

The requirements of this chapter shall not apply to—

(1) any governmental plan, and

(2) any group health plan for any plan year if, on the first day of such plan year, such plan has less than 2 participants who are current employees.

(b) Exception for certain benefits.

The requirements of this chapter shall not apply to any group health plan in relation to its provision of excepted benefits described in section 9832(c)(1).

(c) Exception for certain benefits if certain conditions met.

(1) **Limited, excepted benefits.** The requirements of this chapter shall not apply to any group health plan in relation to its provision of excepted benefits described in section 9832(c)(2) if the benefits—

(A) are provided under a separate policy, certificate, or contract of insurance; or

(B) are otherwise not an integral part of the plan.

(2) **Noncoordinated, excepted benefits.** The requirements of this chapter shall not apply to any group health plan in relation to its provision of excepted benefits described in section 9832(c)(3) if all of the following conditions are met:

(A) The benefits are provided under a separate policy, certificate, or contract of insurance.

(B) There is no coordination between the provision of such benefits and any exclusion of benefits under any group health plan maintained by the same plan sponsor.

(C) Such benefits are paid with respect to an event without regard to whether benefits are provided with respect to such an event under any group health plan maintained by the same plan sponsor.

(3) **Supplemental excepted benefits.** The requirements of this chapter shall not apply to any group health plan in relation to its provision of excepted benefits described in section 9832(c)(4) if the benefits are provided under a separate policy, certificate, or contract of insurance.

In 1997, P.L. 105-34, Sec. 1531(a)(2), redesignated Code Sec. 9804 as Code Sec. 9831 ... Sec. 1531(b)(1)(B), substituted "9832(c)(1)" for "9805(c)(1)" in subsec. (b) ... Sec. 1531(b)(1)(C), substituted "9832(c)(2)" for "9805(c)(2)" in para. (c)(1) ... Sec. 1531(b)(1)(D), substituted "9832(c)(3)" for "9805(c)(3)" in para. (c)(2) ... Sec. 1531(b)(1)(E), substituted "9832(c)(4)" for "9805(c)(4)" in para. (c)(3), effective for group health plans for plan yrs. begin. on or after 1/1/98.

In 1996, P.L. 104-191, Sec. 401(a), added Code Sec. 9804, effective for plan. yrs. begin. after 6/30/97. Sec. 401(c)(2)-(5) of this Act reads as follows:

"(2) Determination of creditable coverage.

"(A) Period of coverage.

"(i) In general. Subject to clause (ii), no period before July 1, 1996, shall be taken into account under chapter 100 of the Internal Revenue Code of 1986 (as added by this section) in determining creditable coverage.

"(ii) Special rule for certain periods. The Secretary of the Treasury, consistent with section 104, shall provide for a process whereby individuals who need to establish creditable coverage for periods before July 1, 1996, and who would have

Group Health Plans

such coverage credited but for clause (i) may be given credit for creditable coverage for such periods through the presentation of documents or other means.

"(B) Certifications, etc.

"(i) In general. Subject to clauses (ii) and (iii), subsection (e) of section 9801 of the Internal Revenue Code of 1986 (as added by this section) shall apply to events occurring after June 30, 1996.

"(ii) No certification required to be provided before June 1, 1997. In no case is a certification required to be provided under such subsection before June 1, 1997.

"(iii) Certification only on written request for events occurring before October 1, 1996. In the case of an event occurring after June 30, 1996, and before October 1, 1996, a certification is not required to be provided under such subsection unless an individual (with respect to whom the certification is otherwise required to be made) requests such certification in writing.

"(C) Transitional rule. In the case of an individual who seeks to establish creditable coverage for any period for which certification is not required because it relates to an event occurring before June 30, 1996—

"(i) the individual may present other credible evidence of such coverage in order to establish the period of creditable coverage; and

"(ii) a group health plan and a health insurance issuer shall not be subject to any penalty or enforcement action with respect to the plan's or issuer's crediting (or not crediting) such coverage if the plan or issuer has sought to comply in good faith with the applicable requirements under the amendments made by this section.

"(3) Special rule for collective bargaining agreements. Except as provided in paragraph (2), in the case of a group health plan maintained pursuant to 1 or more collective bargaining agreements between employee representatives and one or more employers ratified before the date of the enactment of this Act, the amendments made by this section shall not apply to plan years beginning before the later of—

"(A) the date on which the last of the collective bargaining agreements relating to the plan terminates (determined without regard to any extension thereof agreed to after the date of the enactment of this Act), or

"(B) July 1, 1997.

For purposes of subparagraph (A), any plan amendment made pursuant to a collective bargaining agreement relating to the plan which amends the plan solely to conform to any requirement added by this section shall not be treated as a termination of such collective bargaining agreement.

"(4) Timely regulations. The Secretary of the Treasury, consistent with section 104, shall first issue by not later than April 1, 1997, such regulations as may be necessary to carry out the amendments made by this section.

"(5) Limitation on actions. No enforcement action shall be taken, pursuant to the amendments made by this section, against a group health plan or health insurance issuer with respect to a violation of a requirement imposed by such amendments before January 1, 1998, or, if later, the date of issuance of regulations referred to in paragraph (4), if the plan or issuer has sought to comply in good faith with such requirements."

Sec. 9832. Definitions.

(a) Group health plan.

For purposes of this chapter, the term "group health plan" has the meaning given to such term by section 5000(b)(1).

(b) Definitions relating to health insurance.

For purposes of this chapter—

(1) Health insurance coverage.

(A) In general. Except as provided in subparagraph (B), the term "health insurance coverage" means benefits consisting of medical care (provided directly, through insurance or reimbursement, or otherwise) under any hospital or medical service policy or certificate, hospital or medical service plan contract, or health maintenance organization contract offered by a health insurance issuer.

(B) No application to certain excepted benefits. In applying subparagraph (A), excepted benefits described in subsection (c)(1) shall not be treated as benefits consisting of medical care.

(2) Health insurance issuer. The term "health insurance issuer" means an insurance company, insurance service, or insurance organization (including a health maintenance organization, as defined in paragraph (3)) which is licensed to engage in the business of insurance in a State and which is subject to State law which regulates insurance (within the meaning of section 514(b)(2) of the Employee Retirement Income Security Act of 1974, as in effect on the date of the enactment of this section). Such term does not include a group health plan.

(3) Health maintenance organization. The term "health maintenance organization" means—

(A) a Federally qualified health maintenance organization (as defined in section 1301(a) of the Public Health Service Act (42 U.S.C. 300e(a))).

(B) an organization recognized under State law as a health maintenance organization, or

(C) a similar organization regulated under State law for solvency in the same manner and to the same extent as such a health maintenance organization.

(c) Excepted benefits.

For purposes of this chapter, the term "excepted benefits" means benefits under one or more (or any combination thereof) of the following:

(1) Benefits not subject to requirements.

(A) Coverage only for accident, or disability income insurance, or any combination thereof.

(B) Coverage issued as a supplement to liability insurance.

(C) Liability insurance, including general liability insurance and automobile liability insurance.

(D) Workers' compensation or similar insurance.

(E) Automobile medical payment insurance.

(F) Credit-only insurance.

(G) Coverage for on-site medical clinics.

(H) Other similar insurance coverage, specified in regulations, under which benefits for medical care are secondary or incidental to other insurance benefits.

(2) Benefits not subject to requirements if offered separately.

(A) Limited scope dental or vision benefits.

(B) Benefits for long-term care, nursing home care, home health care, community-based care, or any combination thereof.

(C) Such other similar, limited benefits as are specified in regulations.

(3) Benefits not subject to requirements if offered as independent, noncoordinated benefits.

(A) Coverage only for a specified disease or illness.

(B) Hospital indemnity or other fixed indemnity insurance.

(4) Benefits not subject to requirements if offered as separate insurance policy. Medicare supplemental health insurance (as defined under section 1882(g)(1) of the Social Security Act), coverage supplemental to the coverage provided under chapter 55 of title 10, United States Code, and similar supplemental coverage provided to coverage under a group health plan.

(d) Other definitions.

For purposes of this chapter—

(1) COBRA continuation provision. The term "COBRA continuation provision" means any of the following:

(A) Section 4980B, other than subsection (f)(1) thereofinsofar as it relates to pediatric vaccines.

(B) Part 6 of subtitle B of title I of the Employee Retirement Income Security Act of 1974 (29 U.S.C. 1161 et seq.), other than section 609 of such Act.

(C) Title XXII of the Public Health Service Act.

(2) Governmental plan. The term "governmental plan" has the meaning given such term by section 414(d).

(3) Medical care. The term "medical care" has the meaning given such term by section 213(d) determined without regard to—

(A) paragraph (1)(C) thereof, and

(B) so much of paragraph (1)(D) thereof as relates to qualified long-term care insurance.

(4) Network plan. The term "network plan" means health insurance coverage of a health insurance issuer under which the financing and delivery of medical care are provided, in whole or in part, through a defined set of providers under contract with the issuer.

(5) Placed for adoption defined. The term "placement", or being "placed", for adoption, in connection with any placement for adoption of a child with any person, means the assumption and retention by such person of a legal obligation for total or partial support of such child in anticipation of adoption of such child. The child's placement with such person terminates upon the termination of such legal obligation.

(6) Family member. The term "family member" means, with respect to any individual—
  (A) a dependent (as such term is used for purposes of section 9801(f)(2)) of such individual, and
  (B) any other individual who is a first-degree, second-degree, third-degree, or fourth-degree relative of such individual or of an individual described in subparagraph (A).

(7) Genetic information.
  (A) In general. The term "genetic information" means, with respect to any individual, information about—
    (i) such individual's genetic tests,
    (ii) the genetic tests of family members of such individual, and
    (iii) the manifestation of a disease or disorder in family members of such individual.
  (B) Inclusion of genetic services and participation in genetic research. Such term includes, with respect to any individual, any request for, or receipt of, genetic services, or participation in clinical research which includes genetic services, by such individual or any family member of such individual.
  (C) Exclusions. The term "genetic information" shall not include information about the sex or age of any individual.

(8) Genetic test.
  (A) In general. The term "genetic test" means an analysis of human DNA, RNA, chromosomes, proteins, or metabolites, that detects genotypes, mutations, or chromosomal changes.
  (B) Exceptions. The term "genetic test" does not mean—
    (i) an analysis of proteins or metabolites that does not detect genotypes, mutations, or chromosomal changes, or
    (ii) an analysis of proteins or metabolites that is directly related to a manifested disease, disorder, or pathological condition that could reasonably be detected by a health care professional with appropriate training and expertise in the field of medicine involved.

(9) Genetic services. The term "genetic services" means—
  (A) a genetic test;
  (B) genetic counseling (including obtaining, interpreting, or assessing genetic information); or
  (C) genetic education.

(10) Underwriting purposes. The term "underwriting purposes" means, with respect to any group health plan, or health insurance coverage offered in connection with a group health plan—
  (A) rules for, or determination of, eligibility (including enrollment and continued eligibility) for benefits under the plan or coverage;
  (B) the computation of premium or contribution amounts under the plan or coverage;
  (C) the application of any pre-existing condition exclusion under the plan or coverage; and
  (D) other activities related to the creation, renewal, or replacement of a contract of health insurance or health benefits.

In **2008**, P.L. 110-233, Sec. 103(d), added paras. (d)(6)-(10), effective with respect to group health plans for plan yrs. begin. after 5/21/2009.
—P.L. 110-233, Sec. 103(f)(1), of this Act provides:
"(f) Regulations and effective date.
"(1) Regulations. The Secretary of the Treasury shall issue final regulations or other guidance not later than 12 months after the date of the enactment of this Act to carry out the amendments made by this section."

In **1997**, P.L. 105-34, Sec. 1531(a)(2), redesignated Code Sec. 9805 as Code Sec. 9832, effective for group health plans for plan yrs. begin. on or after 1/1/98.

In **1996**, P.L. 104-191, Sec. 401(a), added Code Sec. 9805, effective for plan. yrs. begin. after 6/30/97. Sec. 401(c)(2)-(5) of this Act reads as follows:
"(2) Determination of creditable coverage.
"(A) Period of coverage.
"(i) In general. Subject to clause (ii), no period before July 1, 1996, shall be taken into account under chapter 100 of the Internal Revenue Code of 1986 (as added by this section) in determining creditable coverage.
"(ii) Special rule for certain periods. The Secretary of the Treasury, consistent with section 104, shall provide for a process whereby individuals who need to establish creditable coverage for periods before July 1, 1996, and who would have such coverage credited but for clause (i) may be given credit for creditable coverage for such periods through the presentation of documents or other means.
"(B) Certifications, etc.
"(i) In general. Subject to clauses (ii) and (iii), subsection (e) of section 9801 of the Internal Revenue Code of 1986 (as added by this section) shall apply to events occurring after June 30, 1996.
"(ii) No certification required to be provided before June 1, 1997. In no case is a certification required to be provided under such subsection before June 1, 1997.
"(iii) Certification only on written request for events occurring before October 1, 1996. In the case of an event occurring after June 30, 1996, and before October 1, 1996, a certification is not required to be provided under such subsection unless an individual (with respect to whom the certification is otherwise required to be made) requests such certification in writing.
"(C) Transitional rule. In the case of an individual who seeks to establish creditable coverage for any period for which certification is not required because it relates to an event occurring before June 30, 1996—
"(i) the individual may present other credible evidence of such coverage in order to establish the period of creditable coverage; and
"(ii) a group health plan and a health insurance issuer shall not be subject to any penalty or enforcement action with respect to the plan's or issuer's crediting (or not crediting) such coverage if the plan or issuer has sought to comply in good faith with the applicable requirements under the amendments made by this section.
"(3) Special rule for collective bargaining agreements. Except as provided in paragraph (2), in the case of a group health plan maintained pursuant to 1 or more collective bargaining agreements between employee representatives and one or more employers ratified before the date of the enactment of this Act, the amendments made by this section shall not apply to plan years beginning before the later of—
"(A) the date on which the last of the collective bargaining agreements relating to the plan terminates (determined without regard to any extension thereof agreed to after the date of the enactment of this Act), or
"(B) July 1, 1997.
For purposes of subparagraph (A), any plan amendment made pursuant to a collective bargaining agreement relating to the plan which amends the plan solely to conform to any requirement added by this section shall not be treated as a termination of such collective bargaining agreement.
"(4) Timely regulations. The Secretary of the Treasury, consistent with section 104, shall first issue by not later than April 1, 1997, such regulations as may be necessary to carry out the amendments made by this section.
"(5) Limitation on actions. No enforcement action shall be taken, pursuant to the amendments made by this section, against a group health plan or health insurance issuer with respect to a violation of a requirement imposed by such amendments before January 1, 1998, or, if later, the date of issuance of regulations referred to in paragraph (4), if the plan or issuer has sought to comply in good faith with such requirements."

Sec. 9833. Regulations.

The Secretary, consistent with section 104 of the Health Care Portability and Accountability Act of 1996, may promulgate such regulations as may be necessary or appropriate to carry out the provisions of this chapter. The Secretary may promulgate any interim final rules as the Secretary determines are appropriate to carry out this chapter.

Group Health Plans

Code Sec. 9834

In 1997, P.L. 105-34, Sec. 1531(a)(2), redesignated Code Sec. 9806 as Code Sec. 9833, effective for group health plans for plan yrs. begin. on or after 1/1/98.

In 1996, P.L. 104-191, Sec. 401(a), added Code Sec. 9806, effective for plan. yrs. begin. after 6/30/97. Sec. 401(c)(2)-(5) of this Act reads as follows:

"(2) Determination of creditable coverage.

"(A) Period of coverage.

"(i) In general. Subject to clause (ii), no period before July 1, 1996, shall be taken into account under chapter 100 of the Internal Revenue Code of 1986 (as added by this section) in determining creditable coverage.

"(ii) Special rule for certain periods. The Secretary of the Treasury, consistent with section 104, shall provide for a process whereby individuals who need to establish creditable coverage for periods before July 1, 1996, and who would have such coverage credited but for clause (i) may be given credit for creditable coverage for such periods through the presentation of documents or other means.

"(B) Certifications, etc.

"(i) In general. Subject to clauses (ii) and (iii), subsection (e) of section 9801 of the Internal Revenue Code of 1986 (as added by this section) shall apply to events occurring after June 30, 1996.

"(ii) No certification required to be provided before June 1, 1997. In no case is a certification required to be provided under such subsection before June 1, 1997.

"(iii) Certification only on written request for events occurring before October 1, 1996. In the case of an event occurring after June 30, 1996, and before October 1, 1996, a certification is not required to be provided under such subsection unless an individual (with respect to whom the certification is otherwise required to be made) requests such certification in writing.

"(C) Transitional rule. In the case of an individual who seeks to establish creditable coverage for any period for which certification is not required because it relates to an event occurring before June 30, 1996—

"(i) the individual may present other credible evidence of such coverage in order to establish the period of creditable coverage; and

"(ii) a group health plan and a health insurance issuer shall not be subject to any penalty or enforcement action with respect to the plan's or issuer's crediting (or not crediting) such coverage if the plan or issuer has sought to comply in good faith with the applicable requirements under the amendments made by this section.

"(3) Special rule for collective bargaining agreements. Except as provided in paragraph (2), in the case of a group health plan maintained pursuant to 1 or more collective bargaining agreements between employee representatives and one or more employers ratified before the date of the enactment of this Act, the amendments made by this section shall not apply to plan years beginning before the later of—

"(A) the date on which the last of the collective bargaining agreements relating to the plan terminates (determined without regard to any extension thereof agreed to after the date of the enactment of this Act), or

"(B) July 1, 1997.

For purposes of subparagraph (A), any plan amendment made pursuant to a collective bargaining agreement relating to the plan which amends the plan solely to conform to any requirement added by this section shall not be treated as a termination of such collective bargaining agreement.

"(4) Timely regulations. The Secretary of the Treasury, consistent with section 104, shall first issue by not later than April 1, 1997, such regulations as may be necessary to carry out the amendments made by this section.

"(5) Limitation on actions. No enforcement action shall be taken, pursuant to the amendments made by this section, against a group health plan or health insurance issuer with respect to a violation of a requirement imposed by such amendments before January 1, 1998, or, if later, the date of issuance of regulations referred to in paragraph (4), if the plan or issuer has sought to comply in good faith with such requirements."

Sec. 9834. Enforcement.

For the imposition of tax on any failure of a group health plan to meet the requirements of this chapter, see section 4980D.

In 2008, P.L. 110-233, Sec. 103(e)(1), added Code Sec. 9834, effective with respect to group health plans for plan. yrs. begin. after 5/21/2009.

—P.L. 110-233, Sec. 103(f)(1), of this Act provides:

"(f) Regulations and effective date.

"(1) Regulations. The Secretary of the Treasury shall issue final regulations or other guidance not later than 12 months after the date of the enactment of this Act to carry out the amendments made by this section."